KU-150-164

CONTENTS

Introduction and Acknowledgements 5
Utilita – Welcome 6
Team of the Season 2020–21 – Jonathan Taylor 8
Jack Rollin 1932–2021 9
Football Awards 2020–21 10
Review of the Season 2020–21 – Jonathan Wilson 22
Cups and Ups and Downs Diary 26

THE FA PREMIER LEAGUE AND FOOTBALL LEAGUE: THE CLUBS
The English League Clubs 28
English League Players Directory 400
English League Players – Index 540

ENGLISH CLUBS STATISTICS
English League Tables, Leading Goalscorers and Results 2020–21 12
Football League Play-Offs 2020–21 20
The FA Community Shield Winners 1908–2020 27
The FA Community Shield 2020 27
National List of Referees and Assistants for Season 2020–21 548
Managers – In and Out 2020–21 550
Transfers 2020–21 552
The New Foreign Legion 2020–21 561
English League Honours 1888–2021 563
League Attendances since 1946–47 573

THE LEAGUE CUP AND EFL TROPHY
League Cup Finals 1961–2021 574
Carabao Cup 2020–21 575
League Cup Attendances 1960–2021 582
Football League Trophy Finals 1984–2021 583
Papa John's EFL Trophy Final 2019–20 583
Papa John's EFL Trophy 2020–21 584

THE FA CUP
FA Cup Finals 1872–2021 594
FA Cup Attendances 1969–2021 596
The Emirates FA Cup 2020–21 – Preliminary and Qualifying Rounds 597
The Emirates FA Cup 2020–21 – Competition Proper 602

NATIONAL LEAGUE
National League 2020–21 612
National League North 2020–21 614
National League South 2020–21 615
National League Clubs 616

SCOTTISH FOOTBALL
Scottish League Tables 2020–21 662
The Scottish Football League Clubs 664
Scottish League Honours 1890–2021 748
Scottish League Play-Offs 2020–21 754
Scottish League Cup Finals 1946–2021 756
Betfred Scottish League Cup 2020–21 757
Scottish Cup Finals 1874–2021 764
League Challenge Finals 1990–2020 765
William Hill Scottish Cup 2019–20 766
William Hill Scottish Cup 2020–21 766
Scottish Football Pyramid 2020–21 771

WOMEN'S FOOTBALL
FA Women's Super League 2020–21 772
FA Women's Championship 2020–21 772
Women's Continental Tyres League Cup 2020–21 773
FA Women's National League 2020–21 774
The Women's FA Cup 2019–20 776
The Vitality Women's FA Cup 2020–21 777
UEFA Women's Champions League 2020–21 779
UEFA Women's Euro 2022 – Qualifying 781
England Women's Internationals 2020–21 783
England Women's International Matches 1972–2021 784

WELSH AND NORTHERN IRISH FOOTBALL
Welsh Football 2020–21 ... 788
Northern Irish Football 2020–21 ... 791

EUROPEAN FOOTBALL
European Cup Finals 1956–1992 ... 795
UEFA Champions League Finals 1993–2021 ... 796
UEFA Champions League 2020–21 ... 797
UEFA Champions League 2021–22 – Participating Clubs ... 810
European Cup-Winners' Cup Finals 1961–99 ... 811
Inter-Cities Fairs Cup Finals 1958–71 ... 811
UEFA Cup Finals 1972–97 ... 812
UEFA Cup Finals 1998–2009 ... 812
UEFA Europa League Finals 2010–21 ... 812
UEFA Europa League 2020–21 ... 813
UEFA Europa League 2021–22 – Participating Clubs ... 839
UEFA Europa Conference League 2021–22 – Participating Clubs ... 839
British and Irish Clubs in Europe – Summary of Appearances ... 840
FIFA Club World Cup 2020 ... 842
World Club Championship ... 843
European Super Cup 2020 ... 843

INTERNATIONAL FOOTBALL
International Directory ... 844
Euro 2020 Play-offs ... 872
Euro 2020 Finals ... 873
European Football Championship 1960–2020 ... 877
FIFA World Cup 2022 Qualifying – Europe ... 878
UEFA Nations League 2020–21 ... 884
British and Irish International Results 1872–2021 ... 896
Other British and Irish International Matches 2020–21 – Friendlies ... 920
British and Irish International Appearances 1872–2021 ... 922
British and Irish International Goalscorers 1872–2021 ... 953
South America ... 958
Africa – Africa Cup of Nations 2021 – Qualifying ... 960
North America – Major League Soccer 2020 ... 961
UEFA Under-21 Championship 2019–21 – Qualifying ... 962
UEFA Under-21 Championship 2019–21 – Finals in Hungary and Slovenia ... 964
England Under-21 Results 1976–2021 ... 965
British and Irish Under-21 Teams 2020–21 ... 968
British Under-21 Appearances 1976–2021 ... 970
England Youth Games 2020–21 ... 985

NON-LEAGUE FOOTBALL
Non-League Tables 2020–21 – National League System Steps 3–4 ... 986
The Buildbase FA Trophy 2019–20 ... 990
The Buildbase FA Trophy 2020–21 ... 990
The FA Sunday Cup 2019–20 ... 992
The Buildbase FA Vase 2019–20 ... 993
The Buildbase FA Vase 2020–21 ... 993
The FA Youth Cup 2020–21 ... 998
Premier League 2 2020–21 ... 1002
Under-18 Professional Development League 2020–21 ... 1002
Central League 2020–21 ... 1002
Youth Alliance League 2020–21 ... 1003

INFORMATION AND RECORDS
Important Addresses ... 1004
Football Club Chaplaincy ... 1005
Obituaries ... 1006
The Football Records ... 1025
International Records ... 1036
The Premier League and Football League Fixtures 2021–22 ... 1037
National League Fixtures 2021–22 ... 1047
The Scottish Premier League and Scottish League Fixtures 2021–22 ... 1050
Stop Press: Euro 2020 Review – Jonathan Wilson ... 1054

INTRODUCTION

The 52nd edition of the *Football Yearbook* is sponsored for the first time by Utilita. In another season affected by the COVID-19 pandemic we have had curtailments, postponements, games behind closed doors and declarations of null-and-void competitions. Even so, the coverage in this edition is once again full and comprehensive.

Full coverage of the European Qualifying campaign for the FIFA World Cup 2020 and Euro 2020, delayed from last season, including match line-ups and league tables, is included. Other international football at various levels is well covered in this edition.

The concise feature entitled Cups and Ups and Downs Diary is included with dates of those events affecting cup finals, promotion and relegation issues. The Managers In and Out section is once again included, with a diary of the many managerial changes throughout the year.

At European level, the Champions League has its usual comprehensive details included, with results, goalscorers, attendances, full line-ups and formations from the preliminary rounds onwards and also includes all the league tables from the respective group stages. The Europa League includes full line-ups, formations and league tables from the preliminary rounds onwards.

The 2020–21 Premier League season saw Manchester City, after a slow start, reigning once more. Records again were made, with City setting a new mark for consecutive wins in all competitions at 21, stretching from mid-December until early May. Liverpool were top again at Christmas, but an unlikely run of home defeats saw them slip down the table. An end-of-season rally meant they finished third behind rivals Manchester United who were runners-up. Norwich City and Watford turned the pain of relegation into the joy of promotion, gaining the two automatic spots in the Championship. Unfortunately Bournemouth, although into the play-offs, couldn't make it a clean sweep as Brentford beat them in the Play-Off semi-final and went on to defeat Swansea City 2-0 in the final at Wembley. In League One, another relegated club, Hull City were promoted as champions, Peterborough United followed them into the Championship as runners-up. The League One Play-Off final saw Blackpool overcoming Lincoln City 2-1 after going behind in the first minute. League Two champions Cheltenham Town were joined in League One by Cambridge United and Bolton Wanderers with Morecambe defeating Newport County 1-0 after extra-time.

Manchester City new boy Ruben Dias won the Football Writers' Footballer of the Year award after an impressive first year at the Etihad Stadium. The PFA Player of the Year award was won by another City favourite, Phil Foden, after a brilliant season in which he made 28 league appearances and scored 9 times.

All of these statistics are reproduced in the pages devoted not only to the Premier League, but the three Football League competitions too, as well as all major allied cup competitions.

While women's football was affected by the COVID-19 pandemic and national lockdowns, coverage of the Women's Super League, Championship and National Leagues are included, together with the domestic cup competitions: Women's FA Cup and Continental Tyres League Cup. The UEFA Women's Champions League is also covered. England Women's Internationals since 1974 and all of the 2020–21 season's games are included. UEFA Women's Euro 2021 Qualifying is covered up-to-date, with the final competition coming next year.

In an age where transfer fees are frequently undisclosed and rarely given as official figures, this edition reflects those listed at the time.

In the club-by-club pages that contain the line-ups of all league matches, appearances are split into starting and substitute appearances. In the Players Directory the totals show figures combined.

The Players Directory and its accompanying A to Z index enable the reader to quickly find the club of any specific player.

Throughout the book players sent off are designated with ■; substitutes in the club pages are 12, 13 and 14. The Premier League voted to keep the number of substitutes at 3, whereas the Football League allowed 2 additional substitutes and these are shown as 15 and 16.

In addition to competitions already mentioned there is full coverage of Scottish Premiership, Scottish Football League and Scottish domestic cup competitions. There are also sections devoted to Welsh and Northern Irish football, Under-21s and various other UEFA youth levels, schools, reserve team, academies, referees and the leading non-league competitions as well as the work of club chaplains. The chief tournaments outside the UK at club and national level are not forgotten. The International Directory itself features Europe in some depth as well as every FIFA-affiliated country's international results for the year since July 2020; every reigning league and cup champion worldwide is listed.

Naturally there are international appearances and goals scored by players for England, Scotland, Northern Ireland, Wales and the Republic of Ireland. For easy reference, those players making appearances and scoring goals in the season covered are picked out in bold type.

The *Football Yearbook* would like to extend its appreciation to the publishers Headline for excellent support in the preparation of this edition, particularly Louise Rothwell for her continued help and Jonathan Taylor for the photographic selection throughout the book and his selection of the Team of the Season.

ACKNOWLEDGEMENTS

In addition the *Football Yearbook* is also keen to thank the following individuals and organisations for their co-operation. Special thanks to Jonathan Wilson for his Reviews of the Season and Euro 2020.

Thanks are also due to Ian Nannestad for the Obituaries and the Did You Know? and Fact File features in the club section. Many thanks also to John English for his conscientious proof reading and compilation of the International Directory.

The *Football Yearbook* is grateful to the Football Association, the Scottish Professional Football League, the Football League, Rev. Nigel Sands for his contribution to the Chaplain's page and Bob Bannister, Paul Anderson, Kenny Holmes and Martin Cooper for their help.

Sincere thanks to George Schley and Simon Dunnington for their excellent work on the database, and to Andy Cordiner, Robin Middlemiss and the staff at Paperghosts for their much appreciated efforts in the production of the book throughout the year.

WELCOME

Welcome to the 2021–22 edition of the *Football Yearbook*.

It has been a season like no other. Football, part of the very fabric of our society, has faced unprecedented challenges since March 2020. Part of that fabric is this weighty tome which, like every other aspect of the game – clubs, fans, players, communities – has felt the full impact of the global pandemic.

Sharing your love of 'the beautiful game', we at Utilita are delighted to secure a three-year partnership with the publishers, ensuring that this indispensable guide to British football survives into its fifty-second year and beyond. We consider it an honour to play a small part in this footballing institution.

Our national sport – our country's gift to the world – has survived and will, no doubt, thrive once more as empty seats are, again, filled with fans.

The past season has seen Pep Guardiola's outstanding Manchester City side deservedly reclaim their crown as Premier League champions but lose to Chelsea in a thrilling all-English Champions League final.

Leicester City – finally – won their first FA Cup at their fifth time of asking, while Brentford return to the top flight for the first time in seventy-four years.

In Scotland, Rangers, Steven Gerrard's 'Invincibles', won their first title in a decade, ending an extraordinary run of success for Glasgow rivals Celtic, while in Perth, St Johnstone achieved an unprecedented double domestic cup success in Callum Davidson's first year in management.

Emma Hayes' Chelsea side retained their FA Women's Super League crown but failed at the last hurdle in the Champions League final, losing 4-0 to Barcelona Femini, while north of the border Scott Booth's remarkable Glasgow City – despite heavy competition from the Old Firm – sealed their fourteenth successive title against the odds.

All of this was achieved against the backdrop of empty seats and silent stadiums.

As for Utilita, we entered the world of football as Presenting Partner to the Scottish League Cup back in 2015. Since then, we have partnered with around forty clubs across England, Scotland and Wales, engaging young fans on the need to reduce their energy consumption around the home as part of our 'Energy High 5' initiative – encouraging simple behavioural changes to save energy and reduce bills.

We have supported the next generation of footballers by partnering with a number of professional academies while also investing significantly in the burgeoning women's game, an investment that continues to grow each season.

During the pandemic we refocused our efforts to ensure we supported football clubs further down the pyramid, all the way down to grassroots. We have commissioned two high-profile reports – 'The State of Play' and 'The Final Whistle' – to examine the impact of the pandemic on Britain's 40,000 grassroots clubs.

And with the invaluable help of former England goalkeeper David James MBE, one of the country's leading champions of the grassroots game, we submitted our findings to the House of Lords Committee on a National Plan for Sport and Recreation.

We want our work in football to have a lasting impact, because football clubs – regardless of size, status and success – are at the centre of the communities we serve.

The pandemic has merely highlighted this.

Ultimately, we want 'the beautiful game' to be a force for good. That's why we have worked with Leeds United on better health and anti-bullying campaigns across 400 schools in West Yorkshire, why we set up employability programmes in the East End of Glasgow with Celtic FC, and why we continue to support Crystal Palace's Marathon March, which has raised hundreds of thousands of pounds for vulnerable families in south London.

And that's why in 2021 we launched football's biggest environment movement – 'Football Rebooted' – whereby we aim to collect a million pairs of used boots and recycle them so they can be used again by children and adults alike.

Whether you are playing or watching football, we hope you enjoy the new season with all its inevitable thrills, spills and heartache – but in the meantime, enjoy reading the fifty-second *Football Yearbook*.

Jem Maidment, Chief Marketing Officer, Utilita Energy

Brentford centre-back Ethan Pinnock had a fine season, ending with a place in the PFA Championship Team of the Year and with the Bees gaining promotion to the top flight. (Tom Dulat/Getty Images)

TEAM OF THE SEASON 2020–21

JONATHAN TAYLOR

Emiliano Martinez
(Aston Villa)

Joao Cancelo *(Manchester C)* | **Ruben Dias** *(Manchester C)* | **John Stones** *(Manchester C)* | **Luke Shaw** *(Manchester U)*

Kevin De Bruyne *(Manchester C)* | **Bruno Fernandes** *(Manchester U)* | **Ilkay Gundogan** *(Manchester C)*

Mohamed Salah *(Liverpool)* | **Harry Kane** *(Tottenham H)* | **Son Heung-min** *(Tottenham H)*

Manager: Pep Guardiola
(Manchester C)

Emiliano Martinez: Switched from Arsenal's number two to Villa's undoubted number 1 in September. Made a huge contribution to shoring up Villa's defence and enjoyed the highest save percentage in the top flight. No relegation worries this year at Villa Park, in part thanks to the ever-present Argentinian's assurance, shot-stopping and 15 clean sheets.

Joao Cancelo: Adaptable enough for his manager to play him in midfield at times, Cancelo had a breakthrough season, largely at full-back, and impressed with his intelligence and tactical sense.

Ruben Dias: Signed in September from Benfica for more than £61 million, the young Portuguese immediately showed himself to be a thoroughbred whose presence at the heart of City's defence proved to be a catalyst in turning around the patchy early season form of Pep's men and in driving them to the Premier League title and the Champions League final. A worthy winner of the FWA's Footballer of the Year award.

John Stones: Positively thrived with Dias alongside him, recapturing the form which had previously eluded him. Strong, calm, composed, and consequently rejuvenated and restored to the national side.

Luke Shaw: The difficult days under Mourinho seem a lifetime ago. Back to his best, both defensively and as an attacking threat. 46 appearances in all competitions tell their own story of a maturing talent.

Kevin De Bruyne: Is there a better attacking midfielder in world football? Another season of constant poetry in motion, exquisite vision, sublime passing and deadly set-piece delivery. His sixth season at the Etihad Stadium brought the Premier League title once more, plus the League Cup.

Bruno Fernandes: The latter half of the previous season was no fluke: Fernandes continued to make a huge impact for United. Scored 28 goals in all competitions and led the Premier League in chances created. As the key creative force at Old Trafford, United finished second in the Premier League and reached the Europa League final.

Ilkay Gundogan: From the middle of December, his influence drove City to crucial results: he scored 13 goals and ended up as City's top Premier League scorer of the title-winning campaign. With City often playing without a recognisable centre forward, Gundogan's contributions going forward proved vital. He won back-to-back Premier League Player of the Month prizes in January and February.

Mohamed Salah: The Reds may have fallen short of the extremely high bar they set last season, but the Egyptian was nevertheless frequently unstoppable. In all competitions he scored 31 goals; his pace, trickery and instinctive finishing continued to terrorise defences.

Harry Kane: Won the Golden Boot for a third time, scoring 23 Premier League goals (33 in all competitions) and contributing a remarkable 14 assists. Became the first player in 32 years to claim most goals and most assists in a single top-flight season.

Son Heung-min: The South Korean's partnership with Harry Kane was one of the few highlights of Spurs' season. His pace and directness on the counter-attack was a razor-sharp threat which regularly unpicked defences. He registered 17 goals and 10 assists in the Premier League.

Manager: Pep Guardiola: Despite a questionable tactical call in the Champions League final against Chelsea, the Spaniard's masterful orchestration of his Premier League side's performances was something to behold. After a relatively poor start to the campaign, his charges dominated the league season, finishing a full 12 points ahead of United and a massive 17 points in front of the previously all-conquering Liverpool in third. City's fluidity (83 goals), allied to a new-found defensive solidity (19 clean sheets), swept all before them. Guardiola skilfully marshalled the established stars at his disposal and masterminded the blossoming of young talents such as Dias, Cancelo and Phil Foden.

JACK ROLLIN 1932–2021

Jack Rollin was a soccer writer and statistician for more than 50 years, for much of the time being the pre-eminent figure in the world of the statistical record of British football.

He made his name writing for *Soccer Star* and *World Soccer*, becoming editor of *Soccer Star* in the early 1960s. The magazine was perhaps the most popular weekly football magazine in the country and the only reliable source for statistical information such as line-ups, goal scorers and attendances for all divisions of the Football and Scottish Leagues. The philosophy whereby the magazine gave good coverage to all levels of professional football as well as senior non-league clubs and the amateur game was one that transferred well to the new *Rothmans Football Yearbook*, as it then was, when it was launched in 1970.

Although best known for his work as editor of the *Rothmans Football Yearbook* and its successors, Jack wrote very widely on the game, his work ranging from a column for the *Sunday Telegraph* for many years, to contributions to the *Encyclopaedia Britannica*.

Jack was also author of numerous books on the game, many of which were statistical but others which covered subjects in which he had a personal interest. He was a long-standing supporter of Aldershot and wrote the first full history of the club, published in 1975, also contributing to the club programme for around 45 years. For several years he was a vice-president of Aldershot Town FC.

Aside from his work for the Rothmans Annuals, Jack is perhaps best known for his *Soccer at War* book, which remains the seminal work covering the history of English football in World War Two.

Jack's last book and one of his favourite works, *Tommy Lawton: Head and Shoulders Above the Rest*, was published by Pitch: https://www.pitchpublishing.co.uk/shop/tommy-lawton

Jack Rollin – A Tribute by Ian Marshall

For football fans of a certain age, the passing of Jack Rollin in January of this year marks the end of an era. And rightly so. He was the founding genius behind our national sport's statistical bible, the *Rothmans Football Yearbook*, which first appeared in the aftermath of the 1970 World Cup. Finally, football had its counterpart to cricket's *Wisden*, and Jack Rollin took on the challenge of ensuring his blue book matched the reputation for accuracy of the yellow one.

This was no easy feat. For *Wisden* employs a whole team to work on its pages; *Rothmans* was very much a one-man operation, though it expanded into a two-person job when daughter Glenda officially joined the team for the 1995–96 edition. In the pre-digital age, Jack would buy an enormous volume of newspapers and cross-check them to ensure he had accurate information on when and by whom goals were scored, when substitutes appeared, and so on. If discrepancies arose, he would check with the clubs concerned. In the early days of the Premier League, when they were trying to create a set of 'official' statistics, he was able to highlight a few errors of theirs, and so the official figures were corrected to match his.

Getting it right mattered to him, and his desire for accuracy was transmitted to fans and journalists alike; the *Football Yearbook* had all the answers. I remember the launch of the 1992–93 edition, when *Rothmans*' publishing home moved to Headline. Headline's production director of the time complained about an August publication of that size (1024pp) not being ready to go to print by the beginning of May; we explained that the season had not yet finished, and (by the way) that the European Championship final would need to be included, and that took place on 26 June. Impossible, we were told.

Finished copies duly arrived direct from the printer on the morning of the launch. Our production director came along to the party and what she saw amazed her. In most publishing parties with wine and food on offer, the guests focus on how much they can eat and drink. Here, she was astonished to see that people were more interested in getting their hands on the book; some guests left as soon as they had one. Afterwards, she commented on how unique this was. *Rothmans* was so important to them; and that was Jack Rollin's unique achievement.

Beyond his unrelenting quest for 100 per cent accuracy, Jack was generous and loyal: his house editor for more than 20 years, Lorraine Jerram, received an ever-expanding acknowledgement at the start of the book. He was also extremely principled. So it was that his beloved Aldershot received as many pages in the book as its alphabetical neighbour Arsenal; for statisticians of league football, they were equally important. In today's data-obsessed game, getting the facts right may not seem like such a big deal to achieve – most can be found at the press of a button, but Jack was there first. He may have been a traditionalist at heart, but Jack Rollin was also a pioneer for the modern game.

Ian Marshall, author of the *Playfair Cricket Annual*

FOOTBALL AWARDS 2020–21

THE FOOTBALL WRITERS' FOOTBALLER OF THE YEAR 2021

The Football Writers' Association Sir Stanley Matthews Trophy for the Footballer of the Year was awarded to Ruben Dias of Manchester C and Portugal. Harry Kane (Tottenham H and England) was runner-up and Kevin De Bruyne (Manchester C and Belgium) came third.

Past Winners
1947–48 Stanley Matthews (Blackpool), 1948–49 Johnny Carey (Manchester U), 1949–50 Joe Mercer (Arsenal), 1950–51 Harry Johnston (Blackpool), 1951–52 Billy Wright (Wolverhampton W), 1952–53 Nat Lofthouse (Bolton W), 1953–54 Tom Finney (Preston NE), 1954–55 Don Revie (Manchester C), 1955–56 Bert Trautmann (Manchester C), 1956–57 Tom Finney (Preston NE), 1957–58 Danny Blanchflower (Tottenham H), 1958–59 Syd Owen (Luton T), 1959–60 Bill Slater (Wolverhampton W), 1960–61 Danny Blanchflower (Tottenham H), 1961–62 Jimmy Adamson (Burnley), 1962–63 Stanley Matthews (Stoke C), 1963–64 Bobby Moore (West Ham U), 1964–65 Bobby Collins (Leeds U), 1965–66 Bobby Charlton (Manchester U), 1966–67 Jackie Charlton (Leeds U), 1967–68 George Best (Manchester U), 1968–69 Dave Mackay (Derby Co) shared with Tony Book (Manchester C), 1969–70 Billy Bremner (Leeds U), 1970–71 Frank McLintock (Arsenal), 1971–72 Gordon Banks (Stoke C), 1972–73 Pat Jennings (Tottenham H), 1973–74 Ian Callaghan (Liverpool), 1974–75 Alan Mullery (Fulham), 1975–76 Kevin Keegan (Liverpool), 1976–77 Emlyn Hughes (Liverpool), 1977–78 Kenny Burns (Nottingham F), 1978–79 Kenny Dalglish (Liverpool), 1979–80 Terry McDermott (Liverpool), 1980–81 Frans Thijssen (Ipswich T), 1981–82 Steve Perryman (Tottenham H), 1982–83 Kenny Dalglish (Liverpool), 1983–84 Ian Rush (Liverpool), 1984–85 Neville Southall (Everton), 1985–86 Gary Lineker (Everton), 1986–87 Clive Allen (Tottenham H), 1987–88 John Barnes (Liverpool), 1988–89 Steve Nicol (Liverpool), 1989–90 John Barnes (Liverpool), 1990–91 Gordon Strachan (Leeds U), 1991–92 Gary Lineker (Tottenham H), 1992–93 Chris Waddle (Sheffield W), 1993–94 Alan Shearer (Blackburn R), 1994–95 Jurgen Klinsmann (Tottenham H), 1995–96 Eric Cantona (Manchester U), 1996–97 Gianfranco Zola (Chelsea), 1997–98 Dennis Bergkamp (Arsenal), 1998–99 David Ginola (Tottenham H), 1999–2000 Roy Keane (Manchester U), 2000–01 Teddy Sheringham (Manchester U), 2001–02 Robert Pires (Arsenal), 2002–03 Thierry Henry (Arsenal), 2003–04 Thierry Henry (Arsenal), 2004–05 Frank Lampard (Chelsea), 2005–06 Thierry Henry (Arsenal), 2006–07 Cristiano Ronaldo (Manchester U), 2007–08 Cristiano Ronaldo (Manchester U), 2008–09 Ryan Giggs (Manchester U), 2009–10 Wayne Rooney (Manchester U), 2010–11 Scott Parker (West Ham U), 2011–12 Robin van Persie (Arsenal), 2012–13 Gareth Bale (Tottenham H), 2013–14 Luis Suárez (Liverpool), 2014–15 Eden Hazard (Chelsea), 2015–16 Jamie Vardy (Leicester C), 2016–17 N'Golo Kanté (Chelsea and France), 2017–18 Mohamed Salah (Liverpool and Egypt), 2018–19 Raheem Sterling (Manchester C and England), 2019–20 Jordan Henderson (Liverpool and England), 2020–21 Ruben Dias (Manchester C and Portugal).

THE FOOTBALL WRITERS' WOMEN'S FOOTBALLER OF THE YEAR 2021

Fran Kirby (Chelsea and England)

THE PFA AWARDS 2021

Player of the Year: Kevin De Bruyne (Manchester C and Belgium)
Young Player of the Year: Phil Foden (Manchester C and England)
Women's Player of the Year: Fran Kirby (Chelsea and England)
Women's Young Player of the Year: Lauren Hemp (Manchester C and England)
PFA Merit Award: Gordon Taylor OBE

PFA Premier League Team of the Year 2021
Ederson (Manchester C); Joao Cancelo (Manchester C), John Stones (Manchester C), Ruben Dias (Manchester C), Luke Shaw (Manchester U), Kevin De Bruyne (Manchester C), Ilkay Gundogan (Manchester C), Bruno Fernandes (Manchester U), Harry Kane (Tottenham H), Heung-Min Son (Tottenham H), Mo Salah (Liverpool).

PFA Championship Team of the Year 2021
Tim Krul (Norwich C); Max Aarons (Norwich C), Ethan Pinnock (Brentford), Grant Hanley (Norwich C), Rico Henry (Brentford), Emiliano Buendia (Norwich C), Michael Olise (Reading), Oliver Skipp (Norwich C, on loan from Tottenham H), Adam Armstrong (Blackburn R), Ivan Toney (Brentford), Teemu Pukki (Norwich C).

PFA League One Team of the Year 2021
Chris Maxwell (Blackpool); Callum Elder (Hull C), Lewis Coyle (Hull C), Lewis Montsma (Lincoln C), Robert Atkinson (Oxford U), Aiden McGeady (Sunderland), George Honeyman (Hull C), Jorge Grant (Lincoln C), Charlie Wyke (Sunderland), Jonson Clarke-Harris (Peterborough U), Mallik Wilks (Hull C).

PFA League Two Team of the Year 2021
Vaclav Hladky (Salford C); Ben Tozer (Cheltenham T), Kyle Knoyle (Cambridge U), Ricardo Santos (Bolton W), William Boyle (Cheltenham T), Josh Sheehan (Newport Co), Matt Jay (Exeter C), Wes Hoolahan (Cambridge U), Eoin Doyle (Bolton W), Paul Mullin (Cambridge U), James Vaughan (Tranmere R).

SCOTTISH AWARDS 2020–21

SCOTTISH PFA PLAYER OF THE YEAR AWARDS 2021

Player of the Year: James Tavernier (Rangers)
Young Player of the Year: David Turnbull (Celtic and Scotland U21)
Manager of the Year: Steven Gerrard (Rangers)
Championship Player of the Year: Liam Boyce (Hearts and Northern Ireland)
Special Merit Award: Scotland for reaching the Euro 2020 finals

Scottish PFA Premiership Team of the Year 2021
Allan McGregor (Rangers); James Tavernier (Rangers), Kristoffer Ajer (Celtic), Connor Goldson (Rangers), Borna Barisic (Rangers), Glen Kamara (Rangers), David Turnbull (Celtic), Steven Davis (Rangers), Odsonne Edouard (Celtic), Alfredo Morelos (Rangers), Ryan Kent (Rangers).

SCOTTISH FOOTBALL WRITERS' ASSOCIATION AWARDS 2021

Player of the Year: Steven Davis (Rangers and Northern Ireland)
Young Player of the Year: Josh Doig (Hibernian)
Manager of the Year: Steven Gerrard (Rangers)

PREMIER LEAGUE AWARDS 2020–21

PLAYER OF THE MONTH AWARDS 2020–21

September	Dominic Calvert-Lewin (Everton)
October	Son Heung-Min (Tottenham H)
November	Bruno Fernandes (Manchester U)
December	Bruno Fernandes (Manchester U)
January	Ilkay Gundogan (Manchester C)
February	Ilkay Gundogan (Manchester C)
March	Kelechi Iheanacho (Leicester C)
April	Jesse Lingard (West Ham U)

MANAGER OF THE MONTH AWARDS 2020–21

Carlo Ancelotti (Everton)
Nuno Espirito Santo (Wolverhampton W)
José Mourinho (Tottenham H)
Dean Smith (Aston Villa)
Pep Guardiola (Manchester C)
Pep Guardiola (Manchester C)
Thomas Tuchel (Chelsea)
Steve Bruce (Newcastle U)

SKY BET LEAGUE AWARDS 2020–21

SKY BET FOOTBALL LEAGUE PLAYER OF THE MONTH AWARDS 2020–21

	Championship	*League One*	*League Two*
September	Bradley Johnson (Blackburn R)	Madger Gomes (Doncaster R)	Ian Henderson (Salford C)
October	Ivan Toney (Brentford)	Ben Amos (Charlton Ath)	Paul Mullin (Cambridge U)
November	David Brooks (Bournemouth)	Callum Camps (Fleetwood T)	Jevani Brown (Colchester U)
December	Duncan Watmore (Middlesbrough)	Owen Dale (Crew Alex)	Max Watters (Crawley T)
January	Matt Crooks (Rotherham U)	Matthew Lund (Rochdale)	Wes Hoolahan (Cambridge U)
February	Teemu Pukki (Norwich C)	Jonson Clarke-Harris (Peterborough U)	Ricardo Santos (Bolton W)
March	Alex Mowatt (Barnsley)	Vadaine Oliver (Gillingham)	Matt Jay (Exeter C)
April	Amaut Danjuma (Bournemouth)	Josh Magennis (Hull C)	Ian Henderson (Salford C)
Player of the Season	Emi Buendia (Norwich C)	Jonson Clarke-Harris (Peterborough U)	Paul Mullin (Cambridge U)

SKY BET FOOTBALL LEAGUE MANAGER OF THE MONTH AWARDS 2020–21

	Championship	*League One*	*League Two*
September	Veljko Paunovic (Reading)	Paul Lambert (Ipswich T)	Mark Bonner (Cambridge U)
October	Neil Warnock (Middlesbrough)	Darren Ferguson (Peterborough U)	Michael Flynn (Newport Co)
November	Vladimir Ivic (Watford)	John Coleman (Accrington S)	Ian Evatt (Bolton W)
December	Thomas Frank (Brentford)	Steve Cotterill (Shrewbury T)	Derek Adamas (Morecambe)
January	Steve Cooper (Swansea C)	Grant McCann (Hull C)	Mark Bonner (Cambridge U)
February	Mick McCarthy (Cardiff C)	Darren Ferguson (Peterborough U)	Ian Evatt (Bolton W)
March	Xisco Munoz (Watford)	Steve Evans (Gillingham)	Ian Evatt (Bolton W)
April	Jonathan Woodgate (Bournemouth)	Grant McCann (Hull C)	Gary Bowyer (Salford C)
Manager of the Season	Daniel Farke (Norwich C)	Grant McCann (Hull C)	Michael Duff (Cheltenham T)

LEAGUE MANAGERS ASSOCIATION AWARDS 2020–21

SIR ALEX FERGUSON TROPHY FOR LMA MANAGER OF THE YEAR SPONSORED BY EVEREST
Pep Guardiola (Manchester C)

SKY BET FOOTBALL LEAGUE CHAMPIONSHIP MANAGER OF THE YEAR
Daniel Farke (Norwich C)

SKY BET FOOTBALL LEAGUE ONE MANAGER OF THE YEAR
Grant McCann (Hull C)

SKY BET FOOTBALL LEAGUE TWO MANAGER OF THE YEAR
Michael Duff (Cheltenham T)

BARCLAYS FA WOMEN'S SUPER LEAGUE MANAGER OF THE YEAR
Emma Hayes MBE (Chelsea)

FA WOMEN'S CHAMPIONSHIP MANAGER OF THE YEAR
Jonathan Morgan (Leicester C)

LMA SPECIAL ACHIEVEMENT AWARD SPONSORED BY PROSTATE CANCER UK
Steven Gerrard MBE (Rangers)

OTHER AWARDS

EUROPEAN FOOTBALLER OF THE YEAR 2020
Robert Lewandowski (Bayern Munich and Poland)

EUROPEAN WOMEN PLAYER OF THE YEAR 2020
Pernille Harder (Chelsea (formerly Wolfsburg) and Denmark)

FIFA BALLON D'OR PLAYER OF THE YEAR 2020
Robert Lewandowski (Bayern Munich and Poland)

FIFA BALLON D'OR WOMEN'S PLAYER OF THE YEAR 2020
Lucy Bronze (Manchester C (formerly Lyon) and England)

FIFA BEST GOALKEEPER OF THE YEAR 2020
Manuel Neuer (Bayern Munich and Germany)

FIFA BEST MEN'S COACH OF THE YEAR 2020
Jurgen Klopp (Liverpool)

FIFA BEST WOMEN'S COACH OF THE YEAR 2020
Sarina Wiegman (Netherlands)

FIFA PUSKAS AWARD GOAL OF THE YEAR 2019
Son Heung-min, Tottenham H v Burnley, Premier League, 7 December 2019

PREMIER LEAGUE 2020–21

(P) *Promoted into division at end of 2019–20 season.*

			Home					*Away*					*Total*						
		P	*W*	*D*	*L*	*F*	*A*	*W*	*D*	*L*	*F*	*A*	*W*	*D*	*L*	*F*	*A*	*GD*	*Pts*
1	Manchester C	38	13	2	4	43	17	14	3	2	40	15	27	5	6	83	32	51	86
2	Manchester U	38	9	4	6	38	28	12	7	0	35	16	21	11	6	73	44	29	74
3	Liverpool	38	10	3	6	29	20	10	6	3	39	22	20	9	9	68	42	26	69
4	Chelsea	38	9	6	4	31	18	10	4	5	27	18	19	10	9	58	36	22	67
5	Leicester C	38	9	1	9	34	30	11	5	3	34	20	20	6	12	68	50	18	66
6	West Ham U	38	10	4	5	32	22	9	4	6	30	25	19	8	11	62	47	15	65
7	Tottenham H	38	10	3	6	35	20	8	5	6	33	25	18	8	12	68	45	23	62
8	Arsenal	38	8	4	7	24	21	10	3	6	31	18	18	7	13	55	39	16	61
9	Leeds U (P)	38	8	5	6	28	21	10	0	9	34	33	18	5	15	62	54	8	59
10	Everton	38	6	4	9	24	28	11	4	4	23	20	17	8	13	47	48	–1	59
11	Aston Villa	38	7	4	8	29	27	9	3	7	26	19	16	7	15	55	46	9	55
12	Newcastle U	38	6	5	8	26	33	6	4	9	20	29	12	9	17	46	62	–16	45
13	Wolverhampton W	38	7	4	8	21	25	5	5	9	15	27	12	9	17	36	52	–16	45
14	Crystal Palace	38	6	5	8	20	32	6	3	10	21	34	12	8	18	41	66	–25	44
15	Southampton	38	8	3	8	28	25	4	4	11	19	43	12	7	19	47	68	–21	43
16	Brighton & HA	38	4	9	6	22	22	5	5	9	18	24	9	14	15	40	46	–6	41
17	Burnley	38	4	6	9	14	27	6	3	10	19	28	10	9	19	33	55	–22	39
18	Fulham (P)	38	2	4	13	9	28	3	9	7	18	25	5	13	20	27	53	–26	28
19	WBA (P)	38	3	6	10	15	39	2	5	12	20	37	5	11	22	35	76	–41	26
20	Sheffield U	38	5	1	13	12	27	2	1	16	8	36	7	2	29	20	63	–43	23

PREMIER LEAGUE LEADING GOALSCORERS 2020–21

Qualification 8 league goals	*League*	*FA Cup*	*EFL Cup*	*Other*	*Total*
Harry Kane *(Tottenham H)*	23	1	1	8	33
Mohamed Salah *(Liverpool)*	22	3	0	6	31
Bruno Fernandes *(Manchester U)*	18	1	0	9	28
Son Heung-min *(Tottenham H)*	17	0	1	4	22
Dominic Calvert-Lewin *(Everton)*	16	2	3	0	21
Marcus Rashford *(Manchester U)*	11	1	1	8	21
Kelechi Iheanacho *(Leicester C)*	12	4	0	3	19
Patrick Bamford *(Leeds U)*	17	0	0	0	17
Jamie Vardy *(Leicester C)*	15	0	0	2	17
Ilkay Gundogan *(Manchester C)*	13	1	0	3	17
Alexandre Lacazette *(Arsenal)*	13	0	1	3	17
Ollie Watkins *(Aston Villa)*	14	0	2	0	16
Gareth Bale *(Tottenham H)*	11	1	1	3	16
On loan from Real Madrid					
Edinson Cavani *(Manchester U)*	10	0	1	5	16
Nicolas Pepe *(Arsenal)*	10	0	0	6	16
Phil Foden *(Manchester C)*	9	2	2	3	16
Pierre-Emerick Aubameyang *(Arsenal)*	10	1	0	4	15
Sadio Mane *(Liverpool)*	11	0	0	3	14
Raheem Sterling *(Manchester C)*	10	1	2	1	14
Gabriel Jesus *(Manchester C)*	9	2	1	2	14
Riyad Mahrez *(Manchester C)*	9	0	1	4	14
Danny Ings *(Southampton)*	12	1	0		13
Harvey Barnes *(Leicester C)*	9	1	0	3	13
Diogo Jota *(Liverpool)*	9	0	0	4	13
Callum Wilson *(Newcastle U)*	12	0	0	0	12
Chris Wood *(Burnley)*	12	0	0	0	12
Matheus Pereira *(WBA)*	11	1	0	0	12
Wilfried Zaha *(Crystal Palace)*	11	0	0	0	11
Anwar El Ghazi *(Aston Villa)*	10	0	1	0	11
James Maddison *(Leicester C)*	8	1	0	2	11
Joe Willock *(Arsenal)*	8	0	0	3	11
Includes 8 Premier League goals on loan at Newcastle U.					
Michail Antonio *(West Ham U)*	10	0	0	0	10
Christian Benteke *(Crystal Palace)*	10	0	0	0	10
Tomas Soucek *(West Ham U)*	10	0	0	0	10
Che Adams *(Southampton)*	9	0	0	0	9
Roberto Firmino *(Liverpool)*	9	0	0	0	9
Jesse Lingard *(West Ham U)*	9	0	0	0	9
On loan from Manchester U					
David McGoldrick *(Sheffield U)*	8	0	1	0	9

Other matches consist of UEFA Champions League, UEFA Europa League, FIFA Club World Cup, European Super Cup, Community Shield, Football League Trophy.

PREMIER LEAGUE – RESULTS 2020–21

	Arsenal	Aston Villa	Brighton & HA	Burnley	Chelsea	Crystal Palace	Everton	Fulham	Leeds U	Leicester C	Liverpool	Manchester C	Manchester U	Newcastle U	Sheffield U	Southampton	Tottenham H	WBA	West Ham U	Wolverhampton W
Arsenal	—	0-3	2-0	0-1	3-1	0-0	0-1	1-1	4-2	0-1	0-3	0-1	0-0	3-0	2-1	1-1	2-1	3-1	2-1	1-2
Aston Villa	1-0	—	1-2	0-0	2-1	3-0	0-0	3-1	0-3	1-2	7-2	1-2	1-3	2-0	1-0	3-4	0-2	2-2	1-3	0-0
Brighton & HA	0-1	0-0	—	0-0	1-3	1-2	0-0	0-0	2-0	1-2	1-1	3-2	2-3	3-0	1-1	1-2	1-0	1-1	1-1	3-3
Burnley	1-1	3-2	1-1	—	0-3	1-0	1-1	1-1	0-4	1-1	0-3	0-2	0-1	1-2	1-0	0-1	0-1	0-0	1-2	2-1
Chelsea	0-1	1-1	0-0	2-0	—	4-0	2-0	2-0	3-1	2-1	0-2	1-3	0-0	2-0	4-1	3-3	0-0	2-5	3-0	0-0
Crystal Palace	1-3	3-2	1-1	0-3	1-4	—	1-2	0-0	4-1	1-1	0-7	0-2	0-0	0-2	2-0	1-0	1-1	1-0	2-3	1-0
Everton	2-1	1-2	4-2	1-2	1-0	1-1	—	0-2	0-1	1-1	2-2	1-3	1-3	0-2	0-1	1-0	2-2	5-2	0-1	1-0
Fulham	0-3	0-3	0-0	0-2	0-1	1-2	2-3	—	1-2	0-2	1-1	0-3	1-2	0-2	1-0	0-0	0-1	2-0	0-0	0-1
Leeds U	0-0	0-1	0-1	1-0	0-0	2-0	1-2	4-3	—	1-4	1-1	1-1	0-0	5-2	2-1	3-0	3-1	3-1	1-2	0-1
Leicester C	1-3	0-1	3-0	4-2	2-0	2-1	0-2	1-2	1-3	—	3-1	0-2	2-2	2-4	5-0	2-0	2-4	3-0	0-3	1-0
Liverpool	3-1	2-1	0-1	0-1	0-1	2-0	0-2	0-1	4-3	3-0	—	1-4	0-0	1-1	2-1	2-0	2-1	1-1	2-1	4-0
Manchester C	1-0	2-0	1-0	5-0	1-2	4-0	5-0	2-0	1-2	2-5	1-1	—	0-2	2-0	1-0	5-2	3-0	1-1	2-1	4-1
Manchester U	0-1	2-1	2-1	3-1	0-0	1-3	3-3	1-1	6-2	1-2	2-4	0-0	—	3-1	1-2	9-0	1-6	1-0	1-0	1-0
Newcastle U	0-2	1-1	0-3	3-1	0-2	1-2	2-1	1-1	1-2	1-2	0-0	3-4	1-4	—	1-0	3-2	2-2	2-1	3-2	1-1
Sheffield U	0-3	1-0	1-0	1-0	1-2	0-2	0-1	1-1	0-1	1-2	0-2	0-1	2-3	1-0	—	0-2	1-3	2-1	0-1	0-2
Southampton	1-3	0-1	1-2	3-2	1-1	3-1	2-0	3-1	0-2	1-1	1-0	0-1	2-3	2-0	3-0	—	2-5	2-0	0-0	1-2
Tottenham H	2-0	1-2	2-1	4-0	0-1	4-1	0-1	1-1	3-0	0-2	1-3	2-0	1-3	1-1	4-0	2-1	—	2-0	3-3	2-0
WBA	0-4	0-3	1-0	0-0	3-3	1-5	0-1	2-2	0-5	0-3	1-2	0-5	1-1	0-0	1-0	3-0	0-1	—	1-3	1-1
West Ham U	3-3	2-1	2-2	1-0	0-1	1-1	0-1	1-0	2-0	3-2	1-3	1-1	1-3	0-2	3-0	3-0	2-1	2-1	—	4-0
Wolverhampton W	2-1	0-1	2-1	0-4	2-1	2-0	1-2	1-0	1-0	0-0	0-1	1-3	1-2	1-1	1-0	1-1	1-1	2-3	2-3	—

SKY BET CHAMPIONSHIP 2020–21

(P) *Promoted into division at end of 2019–20 season.* (R) *Relegated into division at end of 2019–20 season.*

			Home					*Away*					*Total*						
		P	*W*	*D*	*L*	*F*	*A*	*W*	*D*	*L*	*F*	*A*	*W*	*D*	*L*	*F*	*A*	*GD*	*Pts*
1	Norwich C (R)	46	14	6	3	39	15	15	4	4	36	21	29	10	7	75	36	39	97
2	Watford (R)	46	19	2	2	44	12	8	8	7	19	18	27	10	9	63	30	33	91
3	Brentford¶	46	12	9	2	39	20	12	6	5	40	22	24	15	7	79	42	37	87
4	Swansea C	46	12	6	5	27	16	11	5	7	29	23	23	11	12	56	39	17	80
5	Barnsley	46	12	6	5	30	22	11	3	9	28	28	23	9	14	58	50	8	78
6	Bournemouth (R)	46	13	3	7	40	24	9	8	6	33	22	22	11	13	73	46	27	77
7	Reading	46	12	4	7	37	27	7	9	7	25	27	19	13	14	62	54	8	70
8	Cardiff C	46	8	6	9	37	26	10	8	5	29	23	18	14	14	66	49	17	68
9	QPR	46	11	4	8	32	27	8	7	8	25	28	19	11	16	57	55	2	68
10	Middlesbrough	46	11	4	8	30	25	7	6	10	25	28	18	10	18	55	53	2	64
11	Millwall	46	7	10	6	24	24	8	7	8	23	28	15	17	14	47	52	–5	62
12	Luton T	46	8	9	6	25	23	9	2	12	16	29	17	11	18	41	52	–11	62
13	Preston NE	46	7	5	11	21	24	11	2	10	28	32	18	7	21	49	56	–7	61
14	Stoke C	46	9	5	9	29	28	6	10	7	21	24	15	15	16	50	52	–2	60
15	Blackburn R	46	9	7	7	37	28	6	5	12	28	26	15	12	19	65	54	11	57
16	Coventry C (P)	46	10	7	6	30	22	4	6	13	19	39	14	13	19	49	61	–12	55
17	Nottingham F	46	6	8	9	21	24	6	8	9	16	21	12	16	18	37	45	–8	52
18	Birmingham C	46	6	4	13	18	37	7	9	7	19	24	13	13	20	37	61	–24	52
19	Bristol C	46	7	3	13	18	30	8	3	12	28	38	15	6	25	46	68	–22	51
20	Huddersfield T	46	8	7	8	28	23	4	6	13	22	48	12	13	21	50	71	–21	49
21	Derby Co	46	6	7	10	20	26	5	4	14	16	32	11	11	24	36	58	–22	44
22	Wycombe W (P)	46	7	5	11	17	28	4	5	14	22	41	11	10	25	39	69	–30	43
23	Rotherham U (P)	46	5	4	14	26	35	6	5	12	18	25	11	9	26	44	60	–16	42
24	Sheffield W*	46	8	8	7	22	17	4	3	16	18	44	12	11	23	40	61	–21	41

**Sheffield W deducted 6pts for breach of League rules.*
¶Brentford promoted via play-offs.

SKY BET CHAMPIONSHIP LEADING GOALSCORERS 2020–21

Qualification 8 League Goals	*League*	*FA Cup*	*EFL Cup*	*Play-Offs*	*Total*
Ivan Toney *(Brentford)*	31	0	0	2	33
Adam Armstrong *(Blackburn R)*	28	0	1	0	29
Teemu Pukki *(Norwich C)*	26	0	0	0	26
Lucas Joao *(Reading)*	19	0	3	0	22
Kieffer Moore *(Cardiff C)*	20	0	0	0	20
Andre Ayew *(Swansea C)*	16	0	0	1	17
Arnaut Groeneveld *(Bournemouth)*	15	0	0	2	17
Emiliano Buendia *(Norwich C)*	15	0	0	0	15
Dominic Solanke *(Bournemouth)*	15	0	0	0	15
Cauley Woodrow *(Barnsley)*	12	1	1	1	15
Lyndon Dykes *(QPR)*	14	0	0	0	14
Includes 2 Scottish Premiership goals for Livingston.					
Jamal Lowe *(Swansea C)*	14	0	0	0	14
Ismaila Sarr *(Watford)*	13	0	0	0	13
James Collins *(Luton T)*	10	0	3	0	13
Yakou Meite *(Reading)*	12	0	0	0	12
Nick Powell *(Stoke C)*	12	0	0	0	12
Jed Wallace *(Millwall)*	11	0	0	0	11
Junior Stanislas *(Bournemouth)*	10	1	0	0	11
Nakhi Wells *(Bristol C)*	10	1	0	0	11
Michael Smith *(Rotherham U)*	10	0	0	0	10
Josh Windass *(Sheffield W)*	9	0	1	0	10
Famara Diedhiou *(Bristol C)*	8	2	0	0	10
Daryl Dike *(Barnsley)*	9	0	0	0	9
On loan from Orlando C.					
Steven Fletcher *(Stoke C)*	9	0	0	0	9
Joao Pedro *(Watford)*	9	0	0	0	9
Freddie Ladapo *(Rotherham U)*	9	0	0	0	9
Sergi Canos *(Brentford)*	9	0	0	0	9
Scott Sinclair *(Preston NE)*	9	0	0	0	9
Duncan Watmore *(Middlesbrough)*	9	0	0	0	9
Callum Paterson *(Sheffield W)*	8	1	0	0	9
Charlie Austin *(QPR)*	8	0	0	0	8
On loan from WBA.					
Philip Billing *(Bournemouth)*	8	0	0	0	8
Ilias Chair *(QPR)*	8	0	0	0	8
Sam Gallagher *(Blackburn R)*	8	0	0	0	8
Lukas Jutkiewicz *(Birmingham C)*	8	0	0	0	8
Colin Kazim-Richards *(Derby Co)*	8	0	0	0	8
Josh Koroma *(Huddersfield T)*	8	0	0	0	8
Bryan Mbeumo *(Brentford)*	8	0	0	0	8
Alex Mowatt *(Barnsley)*	8	0	0	0	8

SKY BET CHAMPIONSHIP – RESULTS 2020–21

	Barnsley	Birmingham C	Blackburn R	Bournemouth	Brentford	Bristol C	Cardiff C	Coventry C	Derby Co	Huddersfield T	Luton T	Middlesbrough	Millwall	Norwich C	Nottingham F	Preston NE	QPR	Reading	Rotherham U	Sheffield W	Stoke C	Swansea C	Watford	Wycombe W
Barnsley	—	1-0	2-1	0-4	0-1	2-2	2-2	0-0	0-0	2-1	0-1	2-0	2-1	2-2	2-0	2-1	3-0	1-1	1-0	1-2	2-0	0-2	1-0	2-1
Birmingham C	1-2	—	0-2	1-3	1-0	0-3	0-4	1-1	0-4	2-1	0-1	1-4	0-0	1-3	1-1	0-1	2-1	2-1	1-1	0-1	2-0	1-0	0-1	1-2
Blackburn R	2-1	5-2	—	0-2	0-1	0-0	0-0	1-1	2-1	5-2	1-0	0-0	2-1	1-2	0-1	1-2	3-1	2-4	2-1	1-1	1-1	1-1	2-3	5-0
Bournemouth	2-3	3-2	3-2	—	0-1	1-0	1-2	4-1	1-1	5-0	0-1	3-1	1-1	1-0	2-0	2-3	0-0	4-2	1-0	1-2	0-2	3-0	1-0	1-0
Brentford	0-2	0-0	2-2	2-1	—	3-2	1-1	2-0	0-0	3-0	1-0	0-0	0-0	1-1	1-1	2-4	2-1	3-1	1-0	3-0	2-1	1-1	2-0	7-2
Bristol C	0-1	0-1	1-0	1-2	1-3	—	0-2	2-1	1-0	2-1	2-3	0-1	0-2	1-3	0-0	2-0	0-2	0-2	0-2	2-0	0-2	1-1	0-0	2-1
Cardiff C	3-0	3-2	2-2	1-1	2-3	0-1	—	3-1	4-0	3-0	4-0	1-1	1-1	1-2	0-1	4-0	0-1	1-2	1-1	0-2	0-0	0-2	1-2	2-1
Coventry C	2-0	0-0	0-4	1-3	2-0	3-1	1-0	—	1-0	0-0	0-0	1-2	6-1	0-2	1-2	0-1	3-2	3-2	3-1	2-0	0-0	1-1	0-0	0-0
Derby Co	0-2	1-2	0-4	1-0	2-2	1-0	1-1	1-1	—	2-0	2-0	2-1	0-1	0-1	1-1	0-1	0-1	0-2	0-1	3-3	0-0	2-0	0-1	1-1
Huddersfield T	0-1	1-1	2-1	1-2	1-1	1-2	0-0	1-1	1-0	—	1-1	3-2	0-1	0-1	1-0	1-2	2-0	1-2	0-0	2-0	1-1	4-1	2-0	2-3
Luton T	1-2	1-1	1-1	0-0	0-3	2-1	0-2	2-0	2-1	1-1	—	1-1	1-1	3-1	1-1	3-0	0-2	0-0	0-0	3-2	0-2	0-1	1-0	2-0
Middlesbrough	2-1	0-1	0-1	1-1	1-4	1-3	1-1	2-0	3-0	2-1	1-0	—	3-0	0-1	1-0	2-0	1-2	0-0	0-3	3-1	3-0	2-1	1-1	0-3
Millwall	1-1	2-0	0-2	1-4	1-1	4-1	1-1	1-2	0-1	0-3	2-0	1-0	—	0-0	1-1	2-1	1-1	1-1	1-0	4-1	0-0	0-3	0-0	0-0
Norwich C	1-0	1-0	1-1	1-3	1-0	2-0	2-0	1-1	0-1	7-0	3-0	0-0	0-0	—	2-1	2-2	1-1	4-1	1-0	2-1	4-1	1-0	0-1	2-1
Nottingham F	0-0	0-0	1-0	0-0	1-3	1-2	0-2	2-1	1-1	0-2	0-1	1-2	3-1	0-2	—	1-2	3-1	1-1	1-1	2-0	1-1	0-1	0-0	2-0
Preston NE	2-0	1-2	0-3	1-1	0-5	1-0	0-1	2-0	3-0	3-0	0-1	3-0	0-2	1-1	0-1	—	0-0	0-0	1-2	1-0	0-1	0-1	0-1	2-2
QPR	1-3	0-0	1-0	2-1	2-1	1-2	3-2	3-0	0-1	0-1	3-1	1-1	3-2	1-3	2-0	0-2	—	0-1	3-2	4-1	0-0	0-2	1-1	1-0
Reading	2-0	1-2	1-0	3-1	1-3	3-1	1-1	3-0	3-1	2-2	2-1	0-2	1-2	1-2	2-0	0-3	1-1	—	3-0	3-0	0-3	2-2	1-0	1-0
Rotherham U	1-2	0-1	1-1	2-2	0-2	2-0	1-2	0-1	3-0	1-1	0-1	1-2	0-1	1-2	0-1	2-1	3-1	0-1	—	3-0	3-3	1-3	1-4	0-3
Sheffield W	1-2	0-1	1-0	1-0	1-2	1-1	5-0	1-0	1-0	1-1	0-1	2-1	0-0	1-2	0-0	1-0	1-1	1-1	1-2	—	0-0	0-2	0-0	2-0
Stoke C	2-2	1-1	1-0	0-1	3-2	0-2	1-2	2-3	1-0	4-3	3-0	1-0	1-2	2-3	1-1	0-0	0-2	0-0	1-0	1-0	—	1-2	1-2	2-0
Swansea C	2-0	0-0	2-0	0-0	1-1	1-3	0-1	1-0	2-1	1-2	2-0	2-1	2-1	2-0	1-0	0-1	0-1	0-0	1-0	1-1	2-0	—	2-1	2-2
Watford	1-0	3-0	3-1	1-1	1-1	6-0	0-1	3-2	2-1	2-0	1-0	1-0	1-0	1-0	1-0	4-1	1-2	2-0	2-0	1-0	3-2	2-0	—	2-0
Wycombe W	1-3	0-0	1-0	1-0	0-0	2-1	2-1	1-2	1-2	0-0	1-3	1-3	1-2	0-2	0-3	1-0	1-1	1-0	0-1	1-0	0-1	0-2	1-1	—

SKY BET LEAGUE ONE 2020–21

(P) *Promoted into division at end of 2019–20 season.* (R) *Relegated into division at end of 2019–20 season.*

			Home					*Away*					*Total*						
		P	*W*	*D*	*L*	*F*	*A*	*W*	*D*	*L*	*F*	*A*	*W*	*D*	*L*	*F*	*A*	*GD*	*Pts*
1	Hull C (R)	46	14	4	5	32	14	13	4	6	48	24	27	8	11	80	38	42	89
2	Peterborough U	46	15	5	3	52	22	11	4	8	31	24	26	9	11	83	46	37	87
3	Blackpool¶	46	12	7	4	30	18	11	4	8	30	19	23	11	12	60	37	23	80
4	Sunderland	46	9	8	6	32	25	11	9	3	38	17	20	17	9	70	42	28	77
5	Lincoln C	46	9	5	9	35	30	13	6	4	34	20	22	11	13	69	50	19	77
6	Oxford U	46	13	4	6	39	21	9	4	10	38	35	22	8	16	77	56	21	74
7	Charlton Ath (R)	46	8	7	8	36	37	12	7	4	34	19	20	14	12	70	56	14	74
8	Portsmouth	46	9	5	9	29	24	12	4	7	36	27	21	9	16	65	51	14	72
9	Ipswich T	46	12	5	6	25	18	7	7	9	21	28	19	12	15	46	46	0	69
10	Gillingham	46	10	5	8	31	30	9	5	9	32	30	19	10	17	63	60	3	67
11	Accrington S	46	10	7	6	31	26	8	6	9	32	42	18	13	15	63	68	–5	67
12	Crewe Alex (P)	46	10	7	6	32	30	8	5	10	24	31	18	12	16	56	61	–5	66
13	Milton Keynes D	46	10	7	6	36	28	8	4	11	28	34	18	11	17	64	62	2	65
14	Doncaster R	46	11	4	8	34	32	8	3	12	29	35	19	7	20	63	67	–4	64
15	Fleetwood T	46	9	8	6	26	17	7	4	12	23	29	16	12	18	49	46	3	60
16	Burton Alb	46	7	4	12	32	42	8	8	7	29	31	15	12	19	61	73	–12	57
17	Shrewsbury T	46	5	8	10	28	31	8	7	8	22	26	13	15	18	50	57	–7	54
18	Plymouth Arg (P)	46	11	4	8	31	39	3	7	13	22	41	14	11	21	53	80	–27	53
19	AFC Wimbledon	46	7	5	11	32	39	5	10	8	22	31	12	15	19	54	70	–16	51
20	Wigan Ath (R)	46	5	6	12	26	42	8	3	12	28	35	13	9	24	54	77	–23	48
21	Rochdale	46	4	9	10	27	42	7	5	11	34	36	11	14	21	61	78	–17	47
22	Northampton T (P)	46	8	5	10	20	26	3	7	13	21	41	11	12	23	41	67	–26	45
23	Swindon T (P)	46	8	1	14	25	38	5	3	15	30	51	13	4	29	55	89	–34	43
24	Bristol R	46	7	2	14	23	32	3	6	14	17	38	10	8	28	40	70	–30	38

¶*Blackpool promoted via play-offs.*

SKY BET LEAGUE ONE LEADING GOALSCORERS 2020–21

Qualification 10 League Goals	*League*	*FA Cup*	*EFL Cup*	*EFL Trophy*	*Play-Offs*	*Total*
Jonson Clarke-Harris *(Peterborough U)*	31	0	0	2	0	33
Charlie Wyke *(Sunderland)*	25	0	0	5	1	31
Jerry Yates *(Blackpool)*	20	2	0	0	1	23
Joe Pigott *(AFC Wimbledon)*	20	1	0	1	0	22
Mallik Wilks *(Hull C)*	19	0	2	1	0	22
Dion Charles *(Accrington S)*	19	0	0	1	0	20
Vadaine Oliver *(Gillingham)*	17	2	0	1	0	20
Josh Magennis *(Hull C)*	18	1	0	0	0	19
Matty Taylor *(Oxford U)*	18	0	0	0	1	19
Luke Jephcott *(Plymouth Arg)*	16	2	0	0	0	18
John Marquis *(Portsmouth)*	16	0	1	1	0	18
Jorge Grant *(Lincoln C)*	13	2	0	2	0	17
Anthony Scully *(Lincoln C)*	11	2	1	3	0	17
Chuks Aneke *(Charlton Ath)*	15	0	1	0	0	16
Sammie Szmodics *(Peterborough U)*	15	0	0	1	0	16
Kane Hemmings *(Burton Alb)*	15	0	0	0	0	15
Cameron Jerome *(Milton Keynes D)*	13	2	0	0	0	15
Keane Lewis-Potter *(Hull C)*	13	0	0	2	0	15
Scott Fraser *(Milton Keynes D)*	14	0	0	0	0	14
Mikael Mandron *(Crewe Alex)*	11	1	0	2	0	14
Fejiri Okenabirhie *(Doncaster R)*	11	1	1	1	0	14
Ronan Curtis *(Portsmouth)*	10	1	1	2	0	14
Jordan Graham *(Gillingham)*	12	0	1	0	0	13
Siriki Dembele *(Peterborough U)*	11	1	0	1	0	13
Brennan Johnson *(Lincoln C)*	10	1	0	1	1	13
On loan from Nottingham F.						
Olamide Shodipo *(Oxford U)*	10	0	0	2	1	13
On loan from QPR.						
Callum Lang *(Wigan Ath)*	12	0	0	0	0	12
Includes 3 Scottish Premiership goals on loan at Motherwell.						
Owen Dale *(Crewe Alex)*	11	0	0	1	0	12
Stephen Humphrys *(Rochdale)*	11	0	0	1	0	12
Includes 1 EFL Trophy goal for Southend U.						
Matthew Lund *(Rochdale)*	11	1	0	0	0	12
Brett Pitman *(Swindon T)*	11	1	0	0	0	12
Colby Bishop *(Accrington)*	10	1	0	1	0	12
Conor Washington *(Charlton Ath)*	11	0	0	0	0	11
Will Keane *(Wigan Ath)*	10	0	0	1	0	11
Taylor Richards *(Doncaster R)*	10	1	0	0	0	11
On loan from Brighton & HA.						
Jimmy Keohane *(Rochdale)*	10	0	0	0	0	10

SKY BET LEAGUE ONE – RESULTS 2020–21

	Accrington S	AFC Wimbledon	Blackpool	Bristol R	Burton Alb	Charlton Ath	Crewe Alex	Doncaster R	Fleetwood T	Gillingham	Hull C	Ipswich T	Lincoln C	Milton Keynes D	Northampton T	Oxford U	Peterborough U	Plymouth Arg	Portsmouth	Rochdale	Shrewsbury T	Sunderland	Swindon T	Wigan Ath
Accrington S	—	1-5	0-0	6-1	0-0	1-1	1-0	2-1	1-0	0-1	2-0	1-2	0-0	2-1	0-0	1-4	2-0	0-1	3-3	2-1	1-1	0-2	2-1	3-1
AFC Wimbledon	1-2	—	1-0	2-4	0-1	2-2	1-2	2-2	0-1	1-0	0-3	3-0	1-2	0-2	1-0	2-1	2-1	4-4	1-3	3-3	0-1	0-3	4-1	1-1
Blackpool	0-0	1-1	—	1-0	1-1	0-1	1-1	2-0	0-0	4-1	3-2	1-4	2-3	1-0	2-0	0-0	3-1	2-2	1-0	1-0	0-1	1-0	2-0	1-0
Bristol R	4-1	0-0	2-1	—	1-1	0-1	0-1	2-1	1-4	0-2	1-3	0-2	0-1	0-2	2-0	0-2	0-2	3-0	3-1	1-2	2-1	0-1	0-1	1-2
Burton Alb	2-1	1-1	1-2	1-0	—	4-2	1-1	1-3	5-2	1-1	1-0	0-1	0-1	1-2	1-3	1-5	2-1	1-1	2-4	0-1	1-2	0-3	2-1	3-4
Charlton Ath	0-2	5-2	0-3	3-2	1-2	—	2-2	1-3	3-2	2-3	1-0	0-0	3-1	0-1	2-1	2-0	0-1	2-2	1-3	4-4	1-1	0-0	2-2	1-0
Crewe Alex	2-0	1-1	1-1	3-2	0-3	0-2	—	1-0	1-1	0-1	1-2	1-1	0-1	2-0	2-1	0-6	2-0	2-1	0-0	1-1	3-2	2-2	4-2	3-0
Doncaster R	0-1	2-0	3-2	4-1	0-3	0-1	1-2	—	0-1	2-1	3-3	4-1	1-0	1-1	0-0	3-2	1-4	2-1	2-1	1-0	0-1	1-1	2-1	1-4
Fleetwood T	1-1	0-1	0-1	0-0	2-1	1-1	0-2	3-1	—	1-0	4-1	2-0	0-0	1-1	0-0	2-0	0-1	5-1	0-1	1-0	1-0	1-1	0-2	1-1
Gillingham	0-2	2-1	2-0	2-0	0-1	1-1	4-1	2-2	0-2	—	0-2	3-1	0-3	3-2	2-2	3-1	1-3	1-0	0-2	2-2	0-0	0-2	2-0	1-0
Hull C	3-0	1-0	1-1	2-0	2-0	2-0	1-0	2-1	2-1	1-1	—	0-1	0-0	0-1	3-0	2-0	1-2	1-0	0-2	2-0	0-1	2-2	1-0	3-1
Ipswich T	2-0	0-0	2-0	2-1	2-1	0-2	1-0	2-1	3-1	1-0	0-3	—	1-1	0-0	0-0	0-0	0-1	1-0	0-2	2-0	2-1	0-1	2-3	2-0
Lincoln C	2-2	0-0	2-2	1-2	5-1	2-0	3-0	0-1	1-2	0-3	1-2	1-0	—	4-0	2-1	2-0	1-1	2-0	1-3	1-2	0-1	0-4	2-2	2-1
Milton Keynes D	3-2	1-1	0-1	2-0	1-1	0-1	0-2	1-0	3-1	2-0	1-3	1-1	1-2	—	4-3	1-1	1-1	2-1	1-0	0-3	2-2	2-2	5-0	2-0
Northampton T	0-1	2-2	0-3	1-1	0-2	0-2	0-1	0-2	1-0	3-1	0-2	3-0	0-4	0-0	—	1-0	0-2	2-0	4-1	0-0	1-0	0-0	2-1	0-1
Oxford U	1-2	2-0	0-2	2-0	4-0	0-0	0-2	3-0	1-0	3-2	1-1	0-0	2-1	3-2	4-0	—	0-0	3-1	0-1	3-1	4-1	0-2	1-2	2-1
Peterborough U	7-0	3-0	1-2	0-0	2-2	2-1	2-0	2-2	2-1	0-1	1-3	2-1	3-3	3-0	3-1	2-0	—	1-0	1-0	4-1	5-1	1-1	3-1	2-1
Plymouth Arg	2-2	1-0	1-0	2-0	2-0	0-6	1-1	2-1	1-0	1-0	0-3	1-2	4-3	1-0	2-1	2-3	0-3	—	2-2	0-4	1-1	1-3	4-2	0-2
Portsmouth	0-1	4-0	0-1	1-0	1-2	0-2	4-1	0-1	0-0	1-1	0-4	2-1	0-1	2-1	4-0	1-1	2-0	2-2	—	2-1	0-0	0-2	2-0	1-2
Rochdale	3-1	0-1	1-0	1-1	0-2	0-2	3-3	1-2	2-1	1-4	0-3	0-0	0-2	1-4	1-1	3-4	3-3	0-0	0-0	—	0-2	2-2	2-1	3-3
Shrewsbury T	2-2	1-1	1-0	0-1	1-1	1-1	0-1	0-2	0-2	1-1	1-1	0-0	0-1	4-2	1-2	2-3	2-0	3-0	1-2	1-2	—	2-1	3-3	1-2
Sunderland	3-3	1-1	0-1	1-1	1-1	1-2	1-0	4-1	2-0	2-2	1-1	2-1	1-1	1-2	1-1	3-1	1-0	1-2	1-3	2-0	1-0	—	1-0	0-1
Swindon T	0-3	0-1	0-2	1-0	4-2	2-2	2-1	1-2	0-1	1-3	2-1	1-2	0-1	1-4	2-1	1-2	0-3	0-2	3-1	3-1	0-1	0-2	—	1-0
Wigan Ath	4-3	2-3	0-5	0-0	1-1	0-1	2-0	1-0	0-0	2-3	0-5	0-0	1-2	3-0	2-3	1-2	0-1	1-1	0-1	0-5	1-1	2-1	3-4	—

SKY BET LEAGUE TWO 2020–21

(P) *Promoted into division at end of 2019–20 season.* (R) *Relegated into division at end of 2019–20 season.*

		Home						Away					Total						
		P	*W*	*D*	*L*	*F*	*A*	*W*	*D*	*L*	*F*	*A*	*W*	*D*	*L*	*F*	*A*	*GD*	*Pts*
1	Cheltenham T	46	13	5	5	37	21	11	5	7	24	18	24	10	12	61	39	22	82
2	Cambridge U	46	12	5	6	30	20	12	3	8	43	29	24	8	14	73	49	24	80
3	Bolton W (R)	46	11	5	7	27	23	12	5	6	32	27	23	10	13	59	50	9	79
4	Morecambe¶	46	13	5	5	38	27	10	4	9	31	31	23	9	14	69	58	11	78
5	Newport Co	46	13	5	5	27	17	7	8	8	30	25	20	13	13	57	42	15	73
6	Forest Green R	46	10	7	6	31	27	10	6	7	28	24	20	13	13	59	51	8	73
7	Tranmere R (R)	46	11	5	7	30	22	9	8	6	25	28	20	13	13	55	50	5	73
8	Salford C	46	11	11	1	36	15	8	3	12	18	19	19	14	13	54	34	20	71
9	Exeter C	46	11	7	5	38	20	7	9	7	33	30	18	16	12	71	50	21	70
10	Carlisle U	46	12	5	6	38	25	6	7	10	22	26	18	12	16	60	51	9	66
11	Leyton Orient	46	9	7	7	32	25	8	3	12	21	30	17	10	19	53	55	–2	61
12	Crawley T	46	10	6	7	30	27	6	7	10	26	35	16	13	17	56	62	–6	61
13	Port Vale	46	9	5	9	27	25	8	4	11	30	32	17	9	20	57	57	0	60
14	Stevenage	46	8	8	7	26	20	6	10	7	15	21	14	18	14	41	41	0	60
15	Bradford C	46	9	7	7	22	19	7	4	12	26	34	16	11	19	48	53	–5	59
16	Mansfield T	46	6	10	7	33	31	7	9	7	24	24	13	19	14	57	55	2	58
17	Harrogate T (P)	46	8	5	10	24	29	8	4	11	28	32	16	9	21	52	61	–9	57
18	Oldham Ath	46	6	2	15	31	42	9	7	7	41	39	15	9	22	72	81	–9	54
19	Walsall	46	7	6	10	20	27	4	14	5	25	26	11	20	15	45	53	–8	53
20	Colchester U	46	10	7	6	32	26	1	11	11	12	35	11	18	17	44	61	–17	51
21	Barrow (P)	46	7	8	8	32	32	6	3	14	21	27	13	11	22	53	59	–6	50
22	Scunthorpe U	46	7	6	10	22	28	6	3	14	19	36	13	9	24	41	64	–23	48
23	Southend U (R)	46	5	6	12	16	29	5	9	9	13	29	10	15	21	29	58	–29	45
24	Grimsby T	46	5	8	10	17	30	5	5	13	20	39	10	13	23	37	69	–32	43

¶Morecambe promoted via play-offs.

SKY BET LEAGUE TWO LEADING GOALSCORERS 2020–21

Qualification 9 League Goals	*League*	*FA Cup*	*EFL Cup*	*EFL EFL Trophy*	*Play-Offs*	*Total*
Paul Mullin *(Cambridge U)*	32	0	0	2	0	34
James Vaughan *(Tranmere R)*	18	0	2	1	1	22
Conor McAleny *(Oldham Ath)*	17	1	1	2	0	21
Matt Jay *(Exeter C)*	18	1	0	1	0	20
Danny Johnson *(Leyton Orient)*	17	0	2	1	0	20
Eoin Doyle *(Bolton W)*	19	0	0	0	0	19
Ian Henderson *(Salford C)*	17	0	1	0	0	18
Jamille Matt *(Forest Green R)*	16	0	0	0	1	17
Carlos Gomes *(Morecambe)*	15	0	0	0	1	16
Max Watters *(Crawley T)*	13	2	0	1	0	16
Jon Mellish *(Carlisle U)*	11	3	0	2	0	16
Elijah Adebayo *(Walsall)*	15	0	0	0	0	15
Includes 5 EFL Championship goals for Luton T.						
Jack Muldoon *(Harrogate T)*	15	0	0	0	0	15
Scott Quigley *(Barrow)*	15	0	0	0	0	15
Cole Stockton *(Morecambe)*	13	2	0	0	0	15
Conor Wilkinson *(Leyton Orient)*	12	0	1	2	0	15
Tom Nichols *(Crawley T)*	11	4	0	0	0	15
Ryan Bowman *(Exeter C)*	14	0	0	0	0	14
Joe Ironside *(Cambridge U)*	14	0	0	0	0	14
Alfie May *(Cheltenham T)*	9	4	0	0	0	13
Daniel Rowe *(Bradford C)*	9	2	0	2	0	13
Includes 4 EFL League Two goals, 2 FA Cup goals and 2 EFL Trophy goals for Oldham Ath.						
Devante Rodney *(Port Vale)*	11	0	0	1	0	12
Adam Phillips *(Morecambe)*	10	1	1	0	0	12
On loan from Burnley; includes 2 EFL League One goals for Accrington S on loan from Burnley.						
Andy Cook *(Mansfield T)*	11	0	0	0	0	11
Includes 8 EFL League Two goals on loan at Bradford C.						
Luke Norris *(Stevenage)*	11	0	0	0	0	11
Includes 4 EFL League Two goals for Colchester U.						
Aaron Collins *(Forest Green R)*	10	0	0	0	1	11
Davis Keillor-Dunn *(Bradford C)*	10	0	0	1	0	11
Elliott List *(Stevenage)*	9	1	1	0	0	11
Jordan Bowery *(Mansfield T)*	10	0	0	0	0	10
Tom Conlon *(Port Vale)*	10	0	0	0	0	10
Abobaker Eisa *(Scunthorpe U)*	9	0	0	0	0	9
Callum Harriott *(Colchester U)*	9	0	0	0	0	9

SKY BET LEAGUE TWO – RESULTS 2020–21

	Barrow	Bolton W	Bradford C	Cambridge U	Carlisle U	Cheltenham T	Colchester U	Crawley T	Exeter C	Forest Green R	Grimsby T	Harrogate T	Leyton Orient	Mansfield T	Morecambe	Newport Co	Oldham Ath	Port Vale	Salford C	Scunthorpe U	Southend U	Stevenage	Tranmere R	Walsall
Barrow	—	3-3	1-0	0-2	2-2	3-0	1-1	3-2	2-1	2-2	0-1	0-1	1-1	2-0	1-2	2-1	3-4	0-2	0-1	1-0	1-2	1-1	1-1	2-2
Bolton W	1-0	—	1-0	2-1	1-0	1-1	0-0	0-1	1-2	0-1	0-0	2-1	2-0	1-1	1-1	0-2	1-2	3-6	2-0	2-0	3-0	1-0	0-3	2-1
Bradford C	2-1	1-1	—	1-0	0-1	1-2	0-0	0-2	2-2	4-1	1-0	0-1	1-0	1-0	2-1	0-3	0-0	0-0	0-1	0-0	3-0	2-1	0-1	1-1
Cambridge U	1-1	1-1	0-0	—	3-0	0-1	2-1	3-1	1-4	1-0	3-0	2-1	2-1	0-1	2-1	2-1	1-2	3-1	2-1	0-1	0-0	0-1	0-0	1-0
Carlisle U	1-0	3-3	3-1	1-2	—	1-2	3-2	2-0	1-0	1-2	1-1	1-1	0-1	1-0	3-1	3-2	1-3	0-0	2-1	2-0	2-0	4-0	2-3	0-0
Cheltenham T	0-2	0-1	0-2	1-1	1-1	—	1-0	2-0	5-3	2-1	1-3	4-1	1-0	0-0	1-2	1-1	2-0	3-2	2-0	1-0	1-0	1-1	4-0	3-0
Colchester U	1-1	2-0	1-2	1-1	2-1	0-0	—	1-1	1-2	1-0	2-1	2-1	2-1	2-2	1-2	0-2	3-3	0-1	1-0	0-1	2-0	3-1	2-2	2-1
Crawley T	4-2	1-4	1-1	2-1	0-3	1-0	1-0	—	2-0	0-0	1-2	1-3	0-0	1-0	4-0	1-1	1-4	1-3	1-0	1-0	1-1	0-1	4-0	1-1
Exeter C	1-1	1-1	3-2	2-0	1-0	0-1	6-1	2-1	—	1-1	3-2	1-2	4-0	0-0	0-2	0-0	1-2	0-2	1-0	3-1	0-0	3-1	5-0	0-0
Forest Green R	0-2	0-1	2-2	2-0	1-0	0-0	3-0	1-2	0-0	—	1-0	2-1	2-1	1-2	2-2	1-1	4-3	1-1	0-2	3-2	1-3	1-0	2-1	1-1
Grimsby T	1-0	2-1	1-2	1-2	1-1	1-1	0-0	2-1	1-4	1-2	—	1-2	0-1	1-1	0-3	0-2	0-0	1-0	0-4	1-0	0-0	1-2	0-0	1-1
Harrogate T	1-0	1-2	2-1	5-4	1-0	0-1	3-0	1-1	0-0	0-1	1-0	—	2-2	1-0	0-1	2-1	0-3	0-2	0-1	2-5	0-1	0-0	0-1	2-2
Leyton Orient	2-0	4-0	1-0	2-4	2-3	0-2	0-0	1-2	1-1	0-1	2-3	3-0	—	2-2	2-0	2-1	2-1	1-1	1-0	1-1	2-0	0-0	1-3	0-0
Mansfield T	2-4	2-3	1-3	0-3	1-1	3-1	1-1	3-3	1-2	0-0	2-2	0-1	0-2	—	1-0	1-1	4-1	4-0	2-1	3-0	1-1	0-0	0-0	1-1
Morecambe	1-0	0-1	2-0	0-5	3-1	1-0	3-0	3-1	2-2	1-2	3-1	1-0	2-1	1-1	—	1-3	4-3	1-0	2-1	4-1	1-1	1-1	0-1	1-1
Newport Co	2-1	1-0	2-1	0-1	0-0	1-0	2-1	2-0	1-1	0-2	1-0	2-1	0-1	2-1	2-1	—	2-4	1-0	0-0	4-0	0-1	0-0	1-0	1-1
Oldham Ath	0-1	0-2	3-1	2-4	1-1	2-1	5-2	2-3	2-1	0-3	1-2	1-2	0-1	2-3	2-3	3-2	—	1-2	2-1	0-2	0-0	0-1	0-1	2-3
Port Vale	0-2	0-1	2-1	0-1	0-1	2-1	1-1	2-0	1-0	1-1	3-0	0-0	2-3	0-3	1-0	2-1	0-0	—	1-0	0-1	5-1	0-0	3-4	1-3
Salford C	1-0	0-1	3-0	4-1	1-1	0-0	0-0	1-1	2-2	0-0	1-1	2-2	3-0	2-0	2-1	1-1	2-0	1-0	—	1-1	3-0	2-1	2-2	2-0
Scunthorpe U	2-1	0-1	2-0	0-5	1-0	0-2	0-1	0-0	0-2	1-4	3-0	3-1	2-0	2-3	1-1	1-1	1-1	2-0	0-1	—	1-1	0-1	0-0	0-2
Southend U	1-0	0-1	1-3	1-2	0-2	0-2	2-0	0-0	2-2	0-1	3-1	0-4	2-1	0-1	1-2	1-1	1-2	0-2	0-0	1-0	—	0-0	0-2	0-0
Stevenage	2-1	1-2	1-1	1-0	3-1	0-1	0-0	3-3	0-1	3-0	0-0	1-0	0-2	0-1	2-2	0-1	3-0	2-1	0-1	3-1	0-0	—	0-0	1-1
Tranmere R	1-0	2-1	0-1	1-1	1-0	0-3	0-0	0-1	2-1	3-2	5-0	3-2	0-1	1-1	0-1	1-0	2-2	3-1	0-0	2-0	2-0	0-1	—	1-3
Walsall	0-1	2-1	1-2	0-2	0-2	1-2	1-1	1-0	0-0	2-1	1-0	0-0	2-1	1-1	0-2	0-1	1-1	4-3	0-2	1-2	0-1	1-1	1-0	—

FOOTBALL LEAGUE PLAY-OFFS 2020–21

▪ *Denotes player sent off.*

SKY BET CHAMPIONSHIP SEMI-FINALS FIRST LEG

Monday, 17 May 2021

Barnsley (0) 0

Swansea C (1) 1 *(Ayew 39)* 3787

Barnsley: (343) Collins; Helik, Andersen, Sibbick; Mowatt, Brittain, Styles, Palmer (Williams J 78); Woodrow, Frieser (Morris 46), Dike (Adeboyejo 88).
Swansea C: (433) Woodman; Naughton, Bidwell, Cabango, Guehi; Hourihane, Fulton, Grimes; Ayew, Lowe, Cullen (Routledge 69).
Referee: Geoff Eltringham.

Bournemouth (0) 1 *(Danjuma 55)*

Brentford (0) 0 2300

Bournemouth: (4231) Begovic; Smith, Carter-Vickers, Cook S (Mepham 45), Kelly; Lerma, Pearson (Stacey 72); Brooks (Wilshere 81), Billing, Danjuma; Solanke.
Brentford: (532) Raya; Roerslev (Henry 58), Jansson, Norgaard, Pinnock, Canos; Jensen (Ghoddos 86), Janelt (Dalsgaard 73), Fosu (Marcondes 59); Forss (Mbeumo 58), Toney.
Referee: Tim Robinson.

SKY BET CHAMPIONSHIP SEMI-FINALS SECOND LEG

Saturday, 22 May 2021

Brentford (1) 3 *(Toney 16 (pen), Janelt 50, Forss 81)*

Bournemouth (1) 1 *(Danjuma 5)* 3830

Brentford: (3412) Raya; Dalsgaard, Jansson, Pinnock; Roerslev (Forss 46), Jensen, Janelt (Ghoddos 64), Canos (Fosu 79); Marcondes; Toney, Mbeumo (Bidstrup 90).
Bournemouth: (4231) Begovic; Smith (Long 82), Carter-Vickers, Mepham▪, Kelly; Lerma, Pearson; Brooks (Rico 30), Billing, Danjuma; Solanke (Stacey 75).
Brentford won 3-2 on aggregate.
Referee: Jarred Gillett.

Swansea C (1) 1 *(Grimes 39)*

Barnsley (0) 1 *(Woodrow 71)* 3076

Swansea C: (433) Woodman; Naughton, Cabango, Guehi, Bidwell; Fulton, Grimes, Hourihane (Smith 74); Ayew, Routledge (Roberts 54), Lowe.
Barnsley: (3421) Collins; Sibbick (Kitching 89), Helik, Andersen; Brittain, Mowatt, Palmer (Williams J 46), Styles; Adeboyejo (Dike 46), Morris; Woodrow.
Swansea C won 2-1 on aggregate.
Referee: John Brooks.

SKY BET CHAMPIONSHIP FINAL

Wembley, Saturday, 29 May 2021

Brentford (2) 2 *(Toney 10 (pen), Marcondes 20)*

Swansea C (0) 0 11689

Brentford: (3412) Raya; Dalsgaard, Jansson (Reid 79), Pinnock; Roerslev, Jensen, Janelt (Ghoddos 74), Canos (Forss 74); Marcondes (Bidstrup 90); Toney, Mbeumo.
Swansea C: (3142) Woodman; Naughton (Cullen 60), Cabango, Guehi; Grimes; Roberts, Fulton▪, Hourihane (Dhanda 63), Bidwell (Manning 82); Ayew, Lowe.
Referee: Chris Kavanagh.

SKY BET LEAGUE ONE SEMI-FINALS FIRST LEG

Tuesday, 18 May 2021

Oxford U (0) 0

Blackpool (2) 3 *(Turton 23, Simms 26, 74)* 3204

Oxford U: (433) Stevens; Hanson (Forde 79), Moore, Atkinson, Ruffels; Henry, Brannagan, Sykes; Lee (Agyei 68), Taylor (Winnall 68 (Gorrin 86)), Barker (Shodipo 80).
Blackpool: (433) Maxwell; Turton, Ballard, Husband, Garbutt (Thorniley 53); Embleton (Lawrence-Gabriel 75), Stewart, Dougall; Yates (Madine 82), Simms, Anderson (Mitchell 75).
Referee: Robert Madley.

Wednesday, 19 May 2021

Lincoln C (0) 2 *(Hopper 51, Johnson 77)*

Sunderland (0) 0 3145

Lincoln C: (433) Bursik; Poole, Jackson (Montsma 15), Eyoma, Edun; Johnson (Anderson 90), Bridcutt, Grant; Scully (McGrandles 85), Hopper, Rogers.
Sunderland: (4231) Burge; O'Nien, Wright, Flanagan (Diamond 90), Hume (McFadzean 11); Power (Leadbitter 69), Scowen; Jones (Stewart 69), Gooch, McGeady; Wyke.
Referee: Craig Hicks.

Ivan Toney scores Brentford's opener from the penalty spot during the Championship Play-Off Final at Wembley Stadium on 29 May. A 2-0 victory over Swansea City ensured that the Bees became the fiftieth club to make it to the Premier League. (Mike Egerton/PA Wire/PA Images)

In the League One Play-Off Final, Blackpool defeated Lincoln City 2-1 at Wembley Stadium on 30 May. Blackpool's Kenneth Dougall scores their first goal. (Action Images/Lee Smith)

SKY BET LEAGUE ONE SEMI-FINALS SECOND LEG

Friday, 21 May 2021

Blackpool (2) 3 *(Embleton 11, Dougall 13, Yates 54)*

Oxford U (1) 3 *(Taylor 7, Atkinson 52, Shodipo 74)* 4000

Blackpool: (442) Maxwell; Turton, Ballard (Ekpiteta 46), Husband, Garbutt; Mitchell (Lawrence-Gabriel 73), Stewart, Dougall, Embleton (Anderson 72); Simms (Madine 73), Yates (Robson 90).

Oxford U: (433) Stevens; Forde, Moore, Atkinson, Ruffels; Henry, Brannagan, Sykes; Lee (Shodipo 69), Taylor, Barker (Agyei 68).

Blackpool won 6-3 on aggregate. Referee: Keith Stroud.

Saturday, 22 May 2021

Sunderland (2) 2 *(Stewart 13, Wyke 33)*

Lincoln C (0) 1 *(Hopper 56)* 10000

Sunderland: (4222) Burge; Gooch (Flanagan 90), Wright, O'Nien, McFadzean (Power 65); Scowen (Winchester 77), Leadbitter; Maguire (Diamond 65), McGeady; Stewart (O'Brien 78), Wyke.

Lincoln C: (433) Palmer; Poole, Montsma (Walsh 46), Eyoma, Edun; Johnson, Bridcutt, Grant; Scully (McGrandles 46), Hopper, Rogers.

Lincoln C won 3-2 on aggregate. Referee: Michael Salisbury.

SKY BET LEAGUE ONE FINAL

Wembley, Sunday, 30 May 2021

Blackpool (1) 2 *(Dougall 34, 54)*

Lincoln C (1) 1 *(Turton 1 (og))* 9751

Blackpool: (442) Maxwell; Turton, Ballard, Husband, Garbutt; Mitchell (Madine 69), Stewart, Dougall, Anderson (Ward 79); Embleton (Hamilton 79), Yates (Thorniley 90).

Lincoln C: (433) Palmer; Poole, Eyoma, Walsh (Montsma 88), Edun; Bridcutt, McGrandles, Grant (Scully 80); Johnson, Hopper (Morton 63), Rogers.

Referee: Tony Harrington.

SKY BET LEAGUE TWO SEMI-FINALS FIRST LEG

Tuesday, 18 May 2021

Newport Co (1) 2 *(Dolan 31, Collins 56)*

Forest Green R (0) 0 900

Newport Co: (352) King; Shephard, Bennett, Demetriou; Lewis A, Hartigan, Sheehan, Dolan (Farquharson 75), Haynes; Amond (Maynard 90), Collins (Taylor 61).

Forest Green R: (442) McGee; Wilson, Godwin-Malife, Stokes, Cargill; Richardson (Cadden 61), Bernard (Sweeney 62), Moore-Taylor, Bailey; Collins (Davison 84), Wagstaff (Matt 75).

Referee: Charles Breakspear.

Thursday, 20 May 2021

Tranmere R (1) 1 *(Clarke 19)*

Morecambe (2) 2 *(Knight-Percival 15, McAlinden 45)* 3000

Tranmere R: (41212) Murphy; O'Connor, Clarke, Monthe, Ridehalgh; Spearing; Morris, Khan (Lewis 71); Feeney (Lloyd 71); Vaughan (Nugent D 80), Blackett-Taylor (Woolery 71).

Morecambe: (4141) Letheren; Cooney, Lavelle, Knight-Percival, Hendrie (Gibson 54); Songo'o; McAlinden (Lyons 77), Wildig, Diagouraga, Mendes Gomes; Stockton.

Referee: Darren Drysdale.

SKY BET LEAGUE TWO SEMI-FINALS SECOND LEG

Sunday, 23 May 2021

Forest Green R (2) 4 *(Adams 7, Collins 8, Cadden 53, Matt 87)*

Newport Co (0) 3 *(Ellison 70, Labadie 76, Maynard 119)* 1100

Forest Green R: (3421) McGee; Bernard (Wagstaff 120), Godwin-Malife, Cargill; Wilson (Richardson 81), Sweeney, Moore-Taylor, Cadden (Bailey 81); Adams, Collins (Young 81); Matt (Davison 98).

Newport Co: (352) King; Shephard, Bennett (Farquharson 71), Demetriou; Lewis A (Ellison 62), Hartigan (Labadie 46), Sheehan, Dolan (Maynard 62), Haynes; Amond (Taylor 46), Collins.

aet; Newport Co won 5-4 on aggregate. Referee: Martin Coy.

Morecambe (1) 1 *(Wildig 9)*

Tranmere R (0) 1 *(Vaughan 53)* 1558

Morecambe: (4141) Letheren; Cooney, Lavelle, Knight-Percival, Gibson; Songo'o; McAlinden (Lyons 82), Wildig (Kenyon 88), Diagouraga, Mendes Gomes; Stockton.

Tranmere R: (41212) Murphy; O'Connor (Khan 46), Clarke, Monthe, Ridehalgh (MacDonald 64); Spearing; Morris (Nugent D 46), Lewis; Feeney; Vaughan, Blackett-Taylor (Woolery 64).

Morecambe won 3-2 on aggregate. Referee: Thomas Bramall.

SKY BET LEAGUE TWO FINAL

Wembley, Monday, 31 May 2021

Morecambe (0) 1 *(Mendes Gomes 107 (pen))*

Newport Co (0) 0 9083

Morecambe: (4141) Letheren; Cooney, Lavelle, Knight-Percival, Gibson (Mellor 106); Songo'o; McAlinden (Lyons 75), Wildig (O'Sullivan 91), Diagouraga, Mendes Gomes (Kenyon 114); Stockton.

Newport Co: (352) King; Shephard, Dolan (Hartigan 63), Demetriou; Lewis A (Taylor 62), Labadie, Sheehan, Bennett, Haynes (Farquharson 111); Amond (Maynard 80), Collins (Ellison 86).

aet. Referee: Robert Madley.

REVIEW OF THE SEASON 2020–21

It was a season, more than anything, about fans. Every truly memorable moment of 2020–21, it felt, involved fans.

There was the FA Cup final, in which, after months of empty stadiums, even a crowd of 21,000 fans – the lowest attendance for a Cup final, excluding the complete shut-out of the previous season, since 1890 – felt raucous and ebullient, a vital staging post on the road to recovery. Then there were the extraordinary scenes on the Fulham Road as word spread among demonstrating Chelsea fans that their club was withdrawing from the proposed European Super League. And there was also the opposition from some fans of their teams taking the knee, something that reached its grim culmination as the England national side were booed, even after Gareth Southgate had clearly laid out specifically what the gesture signified.

On the pitch, the season at Premier League level fell into three distinct periods. First there was the wildness of the opening, a series of unpredictable games played out in empty grounds that, before familiarity set in, still felt weird. With a truncated pre-season and a compressed calendar, the hard-pressing sides in particular found it hard to settle. Manchester City let in five against Leicester, Manchester United six against Tottenham and Liverpool seven against Aston Villa.

In mid-December, Tottenham went to Anfield needing a win to go top of the table. There was, fleetingly, a sense that in this oddest of seasons, when a lack of time for recovery or detailed planning meant the pressing teams were disadvantaged, the attritional approach of Jose Mourinho might be effective. But with the score at 1-1 and Spurs threatening regularly on the break, Mourinho withdrew Steven Bergwijn for Sergio Reguilon, adding a second left-back, presumably to deal with the attacking forays of Trent Alexander-Arnold from right-back. That diminished Tottenham's threat, Liverpool were able to apply pressure and they eventually found a winner from a corner.

Over-defensiveness cost Spurs repeatedly in the weeks that followed as promising positions were squandered, and Mourinho ended up being dismissed in April, a week before the EFL Cup final in which Tottenham were beaten by Manchester City, who lifted the trophy for a fourth successive year. That Harry Kane finished as top-scorer was little consolation either to him or Spurs fans.

The night before Spurs' defeat at Anfield, City had slipped to ninth in the table as they were held at home by West Bromwich Albion. There was a reasonable argument then that

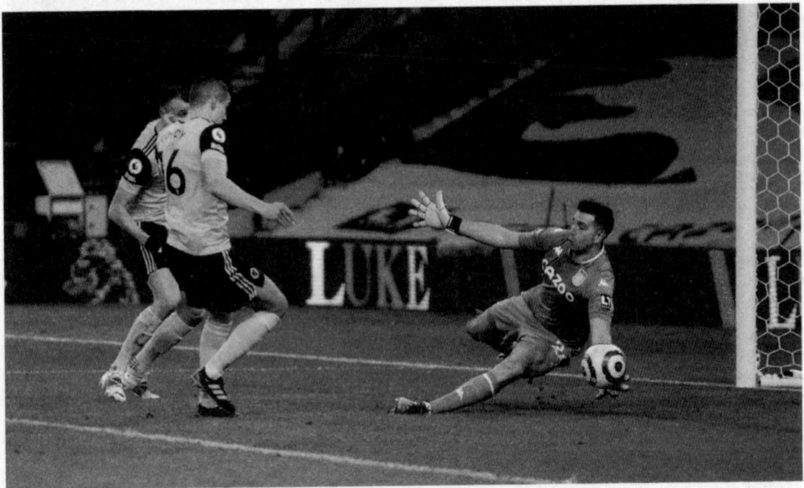

Aston Villa goalkeeper Emiliano Martinez makes a great save from Wolverhampton Wanderers' Conor Coady at Villa Park in March. (Pool via REUTERS/Peter Cziborra)

Ruben Dias was a revelation in the heart of Manchester City's defence. Here he is keeping PSG's Neymar quiet in the Champions League semi-final second leg at the Etihad Stadium in early May. (REUTERS/Phil Noble)

Pep Guardiola might be facing his worst-ever season in management. But that was when the season's second phase began in earnest.

After the chaos of the opening weeks, there was a general retrenchment. Teams began to curtail their press, to look for more balanced ways of playing, and at that nobody was as successful as Guardiola. City embarked on a run of 21 successive victories in all competitions and, by the time it, and the season's second phase, came to an end with a 2-0 defeat at home to Manchester United at the beginning of March, the title, a third in four years, was as good as won.

Guardiola spoke of this as one of his greatest achievements and in the sense that it showed a willingness and capacity to adapt, it probably was. In that 15-week period, City seemed unstoppable, maintaining possession as well as they ever had, opening teams up through the vision of Kevin De Bruyne, the PFA Player of the Year, and Phil Foden, the PFA Young Player of the Year, and the incisiveness of Riyad Mahrez and Ilkay Gundogan, but without looking vulnerable to any side who could play through their press.

That was partly down to a change in the way they pressed, with greater emphasis placed on slowing the pace of possession and, as far as possible, retaining five outfielders behind the ball. It was also down to the exceptional form of Ruben Dias, a defender with all the technical and tactical qualities Guardiola demands who is also adept at the more traditional arts of defending: heading, marking and tackling. He was named FWA Footballer of the Year.

Nowhere was that modification of approach more evident than in the Champions League, in which City defended with such a gleeful sense of urgency against Paris Saint-Germain in the semi-final that one block by Oleksandr Zinchenko on Neymar was celebrated almost like a goal. City, it seemed, had discovered a happy balance that allowed them to play something like their natural game but with a defensive solidity – a way for the more position-based game Guardiola had pioneered at Barcelona to strike back against the rise of the hard-pressing sides of the modern German school.

And then came the final against Chelsea. Having resisted the urge to tinker up to that point, Guardiola couldn't help himself against a side who had beaten City in the FA Cup semi-final. In those final weeks, that third phase, City suddenly didn't look quite so secure as the season became an exhausted scramble for the line. In Porto, for only the second time in the campaign, Guardiola picked neither Fernandinho nor Rodri, and City lost as Mason Mount played a pass through a holding-midfielder-shaped hole to Kai Havertz. As he had against Liverpool in 2018, as he had against Lyon in 2020, Guardiola in trying to combat a potential problem had been the architect of his own destruction.

But for Chelsea that was the glorious culmination of a very strange year. Frank Lampard, popular but never able to organise a defence, was sacked in January and the improvement under his replacement, Thomas Tuchel, was immediate. His success with a more possession-oriented pressing game – far more akin to Guardiola's model than any of the other managers of the German school – was best exemplified by the way they conceded only twice in seven Champions League knockout games. A lack of goals almost cost them fourth place in the league, but in knockout ties they were serene.

Liverpool, undone by a string of injuries at centre-back and never able to adapt to the amended calendar, collapsed in the New Year but did rally to take third behind Manchester United, whose defeat to Villarreal in the Europa League final was yet another example of their struggles under Ole Gunnar Solskjaer to break down massed defences.

The US owners of the two clubs were among the leaders of the proposed Super League. It may have fallen apart within hours of its announcement in April, but as the pandemic magnifies the concerns of the traditional elites about the rise of clubs whose wealth is not dependent upon football, the tensions that provoked the move remain. With fan protests at United, Spurs and Arsenal, who spent the season treading water, the sense is that football will have to find a new financial settlement.

Leicester's victory in the FA Cup final, thanks to a stunning goal from Youri Tielemans and two brilliant saves from Kasper Schmeichel, felt in the moment like a victory against the elites. But they too are funded by a billionaire, just one who seems to grasp that a football club has a community function and is not simply a vehicle for generating dividends. Finding a good billionaire isn't much of a model for football to follow. But for the second season running, Brendan Rodgers' side missed out on the Champions League as form declined in the final weeks of the season.

West Ham, inspired by David Moyes, a pair of Czech signings and Michail Antonio, took sixth, while Marcelo Bielsa's Leeds played some dazzling football in finishing ninth. Aston Villa and Everton both faltered after promising starts, although Villa, having narrowly avoided relegation the previous season, were happy enough with eleventh. Newcastle again rallied to finish in mid-table, leapfrogging a plummeting Southampton who lost a game 9-0 for the second season running, this time against Manchester United.

Manchester United's Bruno Fernandes (left) and Brighton & Hove Albion goalkeeper Robert Sanchez battle for the ball at Old Trafford in April. (Phil Noble/PA Wire/PA Images)

Tottenham Hotspur's Harry Kane scores their second goal in a 2-2 draw with Everton at Goodison Park. (Pool via REUTERS/Clive Brunskill)

Relegation, meanwhile, was settled relatively early. Sheffield United never recovered from an awful start, West Brom looked short of quality throughout and Fulham struggled to turn good performances into results.

Two of the three sides relegated the previous season returned immediately from the Championship. Norwich, having retained faith in Daniel Farke, were impressive throughout and amassed 97 points, while Watford, as is their way, sacked Vladimir Ivic in December and replaced him with Xisco Munoz. It was an appointment that meant every letter of the alphabet has featured in the names of their managers since October 2014 and, more significantly, carried them to second. Brentford, at last, came through in the play-offs to take the third promotion slot, returning to the top flight for the first time since 1948.

Wycombe, Rotherham and Sheffield Wednesday were all relegated, replaced by Hull, Peterborough and Blackpool. Sunderland lost in the play-offs again and so face a fourth season in League One, but at least ended a Wembley curse stretching back seven games to lift the Papa John's Trophy. Cheltenham, Cambridge and Bolton came up from League Two, along with the play-off winners Morecambe, who will be playing in the third tier for the first time in their history. Bristol Rovers, Swindon, Northampton and Rochdale slipped into League Two.

Financial issues underlay the relegations out of the league of Grimsby and Southend. They were replaced by Sutton United, who became a League club for the first time, and Hartlepool, who beat Torquay on penalties in the play-off final despite conceding a last-minute equaliser to their goalkeeper Lucas Covolad.

For many clubs, COVID became an existential threat and the full ramifications of that are yet to play out, particularly in the lower leagues where, once again, seasons were suspended or promotion and relegation cancelled. If fans are able to return next season, that should ease at least some of the pressure – although as the booing of the taking of the knee demonstrates, they present their own issues.

But after a year of empty stands and ghostly echoes, the hope must be that stadiums next season will be full again, and that this campaign will be remembered as the only year when COVID kept the fans out.

Jonathan Wilson

CUPS AND UPS AND DOWNS DIARY

AUGUST 2020
29 FA Community Shield: Arsenal 1 Liverpool 1 *(Arsenal won 5-4 on penalties).*

SEPTEMBER 2020
24 European Super Cup: Bayern Munich 2 Sevilla 1.

NOVEMBER 2020
1 The SSE Women's FA Cup Final 2019–20: Everton 1 Manchester C 3 *(aet.)*

DECEMBER 2020
20 Scottish FA Cup Final 2019–20 *(postponed from last season)*: Celtic 3 Hearts 3 *(Celtic won 4-3 on penalties).*
22 FIFA Club World Cup Final: Bayern Munich 1 Tigres UANL 0.

FEBRUARY 2021
28 Betfred Scottish League Cup Final: St Johnstone 1 Livingston 0.

MARCH 2021
7 Rangers champions of Scottish Premiership and qualify for Champions League Second Qualifying Round.
13 Papa John's EFL Trophy Final 2019–20 *(postponed from 5 April 2020)*: Portsmouth 0 Salford C 0 *(aet; Salford C won 4-2 on penalties).*
14 Women's Continental Tyres Cup Final: Chelsea 6 Bristol C 0.
14 Papa John's EFL Trophy Final 2020–21: Sunderland 1 Tranmere R 0.

APRIL 2021
10 Hearts champions of Scottish Championship and promoted to Scottish Premiership.
17 Sheffield U relegated from Premier League to EFL Championship; Norwich C promoted from EFL Championship to Premier League; Alloa Ath relegated from Scottish Championship to Scottish League One.
20 Queen's Park champions of Scottish League Two and promoted to Scottish League One.
24 Watford promoted from EFL Championship to Premier League; Hull C promoted from EFL League One to EFL Championship; Swindon T and Bristol R relegated from EFL League One to EFL League Two.
25 Carabao Cup Final: Manchester C 1 Tottenham H 0
27 Cheltenham T promoted from EFL League Two to EFL League One; Grimsby T relegated from EFL League Two to National League.
29 Partick Thistle promoted from Scottish League One to Scottish Championship.

MAY 2021
1 Norwich C champions of EFL Championship and promoted to Premier League; Hull C Champions of EFL League One; Peterborough U runners-up of EFL League One and promoted to EFL Championship; Rochdale and Northampton T relegated from EFL League One to EFL League Two; Southend U relegated from EFL League Two to National League; Forfar Ath relegated from Scottish League One to Scottish League Two.
3 The Buildbase FA Trophy Final 2019–20: Harrogate T 1 Concorde Rangers 0; The Buildbase FA Vase Final 2019–20: Hebburn T 3 Consett 2.
8 Sheffield W, Rotherham U and Wycombe W relegated from EFL Championship to EFL League One; Cheltenham T champions of EFL League Two; Cambridge U and Bolton W promoted from EFL League Two to EFL League One.
9 WBA relegated from Premier League to EFL Championship.
10 Fulham relegated from Premier League to EFL Championship.
11 Manchester C champions of Premier League.
15 The Emirates FA Cup Final: Leicester C 1 Chelsea 0.
16 Hamilton A relegated from Scottish Premiership to Scottish Championship; UEFA Women's Champions League Final: Barcelona 4 Chelsea 0; FA Sunday Cup Final 2019–20 *(postponed from last season)*: Campfield 1 St Joseph's (Luton) 0.
17 Scottish League One Play-Off Final First Leg: Edinburgh C 1 Dumbarton 3.
18 Scottish Championship Play-Off Final First Leg: Airdrieonians 0 Greenock Morton 1; Scottish League Two Play-Off Final First Leg: Kelty Hearts 2 Brechin C 1.
20 Scottish Premiership Play-Off Final First Leg: Dundee 2 Kilmarnock 1; Scottish League One Play-Off Final Second Leg: Dumbarton 0 Edinburgh C 1 *(Dumbarton won 3-2 on aggregate and remain in Scottish League One).*
21 Scottish Championship Play-Off Final Second Leg: Greenock Morton 3 Airdrieonians 0 *(Greenock Morton won 4-0 on aggregate and remain in the Scottish Championship)*; Sadler's Peaky Blinder Irish FA Cup Final: Linfield 2 Larne 1.
22 William Hill Scottish FA Cup Final: St Johnstone 1 Hibernian; The Buildbase FA Trophy Final 2020–21: Hornchurch 3 Hereford 1; The Buildbase FA Vase Final 2020–21: Warrington Rylands 3 Binfield 2.
23 Scottish League Two Play-Off Final Second Leg: Brechin C 0 Kelty Hearts 1 *(Kelty Hearts won 3-1 on aggregate and promoted to Scottish League Two*; Sutton U champions of National League and promoted to EFL League Two.
24 Scottish Premiership Play-Off Final Second Leg: Kilmarnock 1 Dundee 2 *(Dundee won 4-2 on aggregate and promoted from Scottish Championship to Scottish Premiership)*; FA Youth Cup Final: Aston Villa 2 Liverpool 1.
26 UEFA Europa League Final: Villareal 1 Manchester U 1 *(aet; Villareal won 11-10 on penalties).*
29 UEFA Champions League Final: Chelsea 1 Manchester C 0; EFL Championship Play-Off Final: Brentford 2 Swansea C 0 *(Brentford promoted to Premier League).*
30 EFL League One Play-Off Final: Blackpool 2 Lincoln C 1 *(Blackpool promoted to EFL Championship).*
31 EFL League Two Play-Off Final: Morecambe 1 Newport Co 0 *(aet; Morecambe promoted to EFL League One).*

JUNE 2021
20 National League Play-Off Final: Hartlepool U 1 Torquay U 1 *(aet; Hartlepool U won 5-4 on penalties and promoted to EFL Two).*

JULY 2021
10 Copa America Final: Argentina 1 Brazil 0.
11 Euro 2020 Final: Italy 1 England 1 *(aet; Italy won 3-2 on penalties).*

THE FA COMMUNITY SHIELD WINNERS 1908–2020

CHARITY SHIELD 1908–2001

1908	Manchester U v QPR	1-1
Replay	Manchester U v QPR	4-0
1909	Newcastle U v Northampton T	2-0
1910	Brighton v Aston Villa	1-0
1911	Manchester U v Swindon T	8-4
1912	Blackburn R v QPR	2-1
1913	Professionals v Amateurs	7-2
1920	WBA v Tottenham H	2-0
1921	Tottenham H v Burnley	2-0
1922	Huddersfield T v Liverpool	1-0
1923	Professionals v Amateurs	2-0
1924	Professionals v Amateurs	3-1
1925	Amateurs v Professionals	6-1
1926	Amateurs v Professionals	6-3
1927	Cardiff C v Corinthians	2-1
1928	Everton v Blackburn R	2-1
1929	Professionals v Amateurs	3-0
1930	Arsenal v Sheffield W	2-1
1931	Arsenal v WBA	1-0
1932	Everton v Newcastle U	5-3
1933	Arsenal v Everton	3-0
1934	Arsenal v Manchester C	4-0
1935	Sheffield W v Arsenal	1-0
1936	Sunderland v Arsenal	2-1
1937	Manchester C v Sunderland	2-0
1938	Arsenal v Preston NE	2-1
1948	Arsenal v Manchester U	4-3
1949	Portsmouth v Wolverhampton W	1-1*
1950	English World Cup XI v FA Canadian Touring Team	4-2
1951	Tottenham H v Newcastle U	2-1
1952	Manchester U v Newcastle U	4-2
1953	Arsenal v Blackpool	3-1
1954	Wolverhampton W v WBA	4-4*
1955	Chelsea v Newcastle U	3-0
1956	Manchester U v Manchester C	1-0
1957	Manchester U v Aston Villa	4-0
1958	Bolton W v Wolverhampton W	4-1
1959	Wolverhampton W v Nottingham F	3-1
1960	Burnley v Wolverhampton W	2-2*
1961	Tottenham H v FA XI	3-2
1962	Tottenham H v Ipswich T	5-1
1963	Everton v Manchester U	4-0
1964	Liverpool v West Ham U	2-2*
1965	Manchester U v Liverpool	2-2*
1966	Liverpool v Everton	1-0
1967	Manchester U v Tottenham H	3-3*
1968	Manchester C v WBA	6-1
1969	Leeds U v Manchester C	2-1
1970	Everton v Chelsea	2-1
1971	Leicester C v Liverpool	1-0
1972	Manchester C v Aston Villa	1-0
1973	Burnley v Manchester C	1-0
1974	Liverpool v Leeds U *Liverpool won 6-5 on penalties.*	1-1
1975	Derby Co v West Ham U	2-0
1976	Liverpool v Southampton	1-0
1977	Liverpool v Manchester U	0-0*
1978	Nottingham F v Ipswich T	5-0
1979	Liverpool v Arsenal	3-1
1980	Liverpool v West Ham U	1-0
1981	Aston Villa v Tottenham H	2-2*
1982	Liverpool v Tottenham H	1-0
1983	Manchester U v Liverpool	2-0
1984	Everton v Liverpool	1-0
1985	Everton v Manchester U	2-0
1986	Everton v Liverpool	1-1*
1987	Everton v Coventry C	1-0
1988	Liverpool v Wimbledon	2-1
1989	Liverpool v Arsenal	1-0
1990	Liverpool v Manchester U	1-1*
1991	Arsenal v Tottenham H	0-0*
1992	Leeds U v Liverpool	4-3
1993	Manchester U v Arsenal *Manchester U won 5-4 on penalties.*	1-1
1994	Manchester U v Blackburn R	2-0
1995	Everton v Blackburn R	1-0
1996	Manchester U v Newcastle U	4-0
1997	Manchester U v Chelsea *Manchester U won 4-2 on penalties.*	1-1
1998	Arsenal v Manchester U	3-0
1999	Arsenal v Manchester U	2-1
2000	Chelsea v Manchester U	2-0
2001	Liverpool v Manchester U	2-1

COMMUNITY SHIELD 2002–20

2002	Arsenal v Liverpool	1-0
2003	Manchester U v Arsenal *Manchester U won 4-3 on penalties.*	1-1
2004	Arsenal v Manchester U	3-1
2005	Chelsea v Arsenal	2-1
2006	Liverpool v Chelsea	2-1
2007	Manchester U v Chelsea *Manchester U won 3-0 on penalties.*	1-1
2008	Manchester U v Portsmouth *Manchester U won 3-1 on penalties.*	0-0
2009	Chelsea v Manchester U *Chelsea won 4-1 on penalties.*	2-2
2010	Manchester U v Chelsea	3-1
2011	Manchester U v Manchester C	3-2
2012	Manchester C v Chelsea	3-2
2013	Manchester U v Wigan Ath	2-0
2014	Arsenal v Manchester C	3-0
2015	Arsenal v Chelsea	1-0
2016	Manchester U v Leicester C	2-1
2017	Arsenal v Chelsea *Arsenal won 4-1 on penalties.*	1-1
2018	Manchester C v Chelsea	2-0
2019	Manchester C v Liverpool *Manchester C won 5-4 on penalties.*	1-1
2020	Arsenal v Liverpool *Arsenal won 5-4 on penalties.*	1-1

* *Each club retained shield for six months.* ■ *Denotes player sent off.*

THE FA COMMUNITY SHIELD 2020

Arsenal (1) 1 Liverpool (0) 1

at Wembley, Saturday 29 August 2020, behind closed doors

Arsenal: Martinez; Bellerin (Soares 58), Holding, Luiz, Tierney (Kolasinac 83), Elneny, Xhaka, Saka (Willock 82), Maitland-Niles, Nketiah (Nelson 82), Aubameyang.
Scorer: Aubameyang 12.

Liverpool: Alisson; Williams (Minamino 59), Gomez, van Dijk, Robertson, Milner (Keita 59), Fabinho (Jones 83), Wijnaldum (Brewster 90), Salah, Firmino, Mane.
Scorer: Minamino 73.

Arsenal won 5-4 on penalties.

Referee: Andre Mariner.

ACCRINGTON STANLEY

FOUNDATION

Accrington Football Club, founder members of the Football League in 1888, were not connected with Accrington Stanley. In fact both clubs ran concurrently between 1891 when Stanley were formed and 1895 when Accrington FC folded. Actually Stanley Villa was the original name, those responsible for forming the club living in Stanley Street and using the Stanley Arms as their meeting place. They became Accrington Stanley in 1893. In 1894–95 they joined the Accrington & District League, playing at Moorhead Park. Subsequently they played in the North-East Lancashire Combination and the Lancashire Combination before becoming founder members of the Third Division (North) in 1921, two years after moving to Peel Park. In 1962 they resigned from the Football League, were wound up, re-formed in 1963, disbanded in 1966 only to restart as Accrington Stanley (1968), returning to the Lancashire Combination in 1970.

Wham Stadium, Livingstone Road, Accrington, Lancashire BB5 5BX.

Telephone: (01254) 356 950.

Website: www.accringtonstanley.co.uk

Email: info@accringtonstanley.co.uk

Ground Capacity: 5,278.

Record Attendance: 13,181 v Hull C, Division 3 (N), 28 September 1948 (at Peel Park); 5,397 v Derby Co, FA Cup 4th rd, 26 January 2019.

Pitch Measurements: 102m × 66m (111.5yd × 72yd).

Chairman: Andy Holt. ***Managing Director:*** David Burgess.

Manager: John Coleman.

Assistant Manager: Jimmy Bell.

Colours: Red shirts with white trim, red shorts with white trim, red socks with white trim.

Year Formed: 1891, reformed 1968. ***Turned Professional:*** 1919.

Club Nickname: 'The Reds', 'Stanley'.

Previous Names: 1891, Stanley Villa; 1893, Accrington Stanley.

Grounds: 1891, Moorhead Park; 1897, Bell's Ground; 1919, Peel Park; 1970, Crown Ground (renamed Interlink Express Stadium, Fraser Eagle Stadium, Store First Stadium 2013, Wham Stadium 2015).

First Football League Game: 27 August 1921, Division 3 (N), v Rochdale (a) L 3–6 – Tattersall; Newton, Baines, Crawshaw, Popplewell, Burkinshaw, Oxley, Makin, Green (1), Hosker (2), Hartles.

Record League Victory: 8–0 v New Brighton, Division 3 (N), 17 March 1934 – Maidment; Armstrong (pen), Price, Dodds, Crawshaw, McCulloch, Wyper, Lennox (2), Cheetham (4), Leedham (1), Watson.

Record Cup Victory: 7–0 v Spennymoor U, FA Cup 2nd rd, 8 December 1938 – Tootill; Armstrong, Whittaker, Latham, Curran, Lee, Parry (2), Chadwick, Jepson (3), McLoughlin (2), Barclay; 7–0 v Leeds U U21, Football League Trophy, Northern Section Group G, 8 September 2020 – Savin; Sykes, Hughes, Burgess 1), Conneely, Allan, Sangare, Butcher (Sama), Uwakwe (3); Cassidy (2) (Scully), Charles (1) (Spinelli).

HONOURS

League Champions: FL 2 – 2017–18; Conference – 2005–06.
Runners-up: Division 3N – 1954–55, 1957–58.

FA Cup: 4th rd – 1927, 1937, 1959, 2010, 2017, 2019.

League Cup: 3rd rd – 2016–17.

FOOTBALL YEARBOOK FACT FILE

In 1992–93 Accrington Stanley played their FA Cup first round game against Gateshead at their Crown Ground, but the second round home tie with Crewe Alexandra was switched to Blackburn Rovers' Ewood Park stadium with a crowd of 10,801 watching as Stanley went down to a defeat. The following season Stanley, who at the time played in the Northern Premier League, were drawn at home to Scunthorpe United. This time the game was played at Burnley's Turf Moor ground.

Record Defeat: 1–9 v Lincoln C, Division 3 (N), 3 March 1951.

Most League Points (2 for a win): 61, Division 3 (N), 1954–55.

Most League Points (3 for a win): 93, FL 2, 2017–18.

Most League Goals: 96, Division 3 (N), 1954–55.

Highest League Scorer in Season: George Stewart, 35, Division 3 (N), 1955–56; George Hudson, 35, Division 4, 1960–61.

Most League Goals in Total Aggregate: George Stewart, 136, 1954–58.

Most League Goals in One Match: 5, Billy Harker v Gateshead, Division 3 (N), 16 November 1935; George Stewart v Gateshead, Division 3 (N), 27 November 1954.

Most Capped Player: Romuald Boco, 19 (51), Benin.

Most League Appearances: Sean McConville, 296, 2009–11; 2015–2021.

Youngest League Player: Ian Gibson, 15 years 358 days, v Norwich C, 23 March 1959.

Record Transfer Fee Received: £1,000,000 from Ipswich T for Kayden Jackson, August 2018.

Record Transfer Fee Paid: £85,000 (rising to £150,000) to Swansea C for Ian Craney, January 2008.

Football League Record: 1921 Original Member of Division 3 (N); 1958–60 Division 3; 1960–62 Division 4; 2006–18 FL 2; 2018– FL 1.

LATEST SEQUENCES

Longest Sequence of League Wins: 7, 24.2.2018 – 7.4.2018.

Longest Sequence of League Defeats: 9, 8.3.1930 – 21.4.1930.

Longest Sequence of League Draws: 4, 25.8.2018 – 15.9.2018.

Longest Sequence of Unbeaten League Matches: 15, 3.2.2018 – 21.4.2018.

Longest Sequence Without a League Win: 18, 17.9.1938 – 31.12.1938.

Successive Scoring Runs: 24 from 23.12.2017.

Successive Non-scoring Runs: 6 from 29.12.2018.

MANAGERS

William Cronshaw *c.*1894
John Haworth 1897–1910
Johnson Haworth *c.*1916
Sam Pilkingson 1919–24
(*Tommy Booth p-m 1923–24*)
Ernie Blackburn 1924–32
Amos Wade 1932–35
John Hacking 1935–49
Jimmy Porter 1949–51
Walter Crook 1951–53
Walter Galbraith 1953–58
George Eastham Snr 1958–59
Harold Bodle 1959–60
James Harrower 1960–61
Harold Mather 1962–63
Jimmy Hinksman 1963–64
Terry Neville 1964–65
Ian Bryson 1965
Danny Parker 1965–66
Jimmy Hinksman 1970–75
Don Bramley 1975–78
Dave Baron 1978–82
Mick Finn 1982
Dennis Cook 1982–83
Pat Lynch 1983–84
Gerry Keenan 1984–85
Frank O'Kane 1985–86
Eric Whalley 1986–88
Gary Pierce 1988–89
David Thornley 1989–90
Phil Staley 1990–93
Ken Wright 1993–94
Eric Whalley 1994–95
Stan Allan 1995–96
Tony Greenwood 1996–97
Leighton James 1997–98
Billy Rodaway 1998
Wayne Harrison 1998–99
John Coleman 1999–2012
Paul Cook 2012
Leam Richardson 2012–13
James Beattie 2013–14
John Coleman 2014–

TEN YEAR LEAGUE RECORD

		P	*W*	*D*	*L*	*F*	*A*	*Pts*	*Pos*
2011-12	FL 2	46	14	15	17	54	66	57	14
2012-13	FL 2	46	14	12	20	51	68	54	18
2013-14	FL 2	46	14	15	17	54	56	57	15
2014-15	FL 2	46	15	11	20	58	77	56	17
2015-16	FL 2	46	24	13	9	74	48	85	4
2016-17	FL 2	46	17	14	15	59	56	65	13
2017-18	FL 2	46	29	6	11	76	46	93	1
2018-19	FL 1	46	14	13	19	51	67	55	14
2019-20	FL 1	35	10	10	15	47	53	40	17§
2020-21	FL 1	46	18	13	15	63	68	67	11

§Decided on points-per-game (1.14)

DID YOU KNOW

Accrington Stanley were accepted into the Lancashire Combination for the 1970–71 season after giving the league an assurance that they had no connection with the club that folded back in 1962. Stanley began their career in their new league on 15 August 1970 with a 2-1 home win over Formby.

ACCRINGTON STANLEY – SKY BET LEAGUE ONE 2020–21 LEAGUE RECORD

Match No.	Date	Venue	Opponents	Result		H/T Score	Lg Pos.	Goalscorers	Attendance
1	Sept 12	H	Peterborough U	W	2-0	1-0	2	Charles [45], Uwakwe [85]	0
2	19	A	Burton Alb	L	1-2	0-0	8	Pritchard [83]	0
3	26	H	Oxford U	L	1-4	0-1	18	Cassidy (pen) [72]	0
4	Oct 3	A	AFC Wimbledon	W	2-1	2-1	9	Sykes [41], Butcher [45]	0
5	10	H	Rochdale	W	2-1	0-0	6	Pritchard [64], Russell [66]	0
6	17	A	Ipswich T	L	0-2	0-0	9		0
7	20	H	Fleetwood T	W	1-0	0-0	7	Charles [73]	0
8	Nov 14	A	Northampton T	W	1-0	1-0	11	Russell [2]	0
9	17	A	Swindon T	W	3-0	3-0	10	Fryer (og) [6], Bishop [25], Charles [38]	0
10	21	H	Lincoln C	D	0-0	0-0	9		0
11	24	H	Crewe Alex	W	1-0	0-0	9	Bishop [59]	0
12	Dec 2	A	Shrewsbury T	D	2-2	1-1	9	Pritchard [24], Cassidy [90]	0
13	5	H	Milton Keynes D	W	2-1	1-0	7	Charles 2 [8, 62]	0
14	12	A	Wigan Ath	L	3-4	0-3	10	Pritchard [61], Nottingham [65], Burgess [86]	0
15	15	A	Gillingham	W	2-0	1-0	8	Bishop [44], Charles [64]	0
16	19	H	Blackpool	D	0-0	0-0	8		0
17	Jan 8	A	Charlton Ath	W	2-0	1-0	5	Bishop 2 [36, 67]	0
18	16	H	Gillingham	L	0-1	0-1	9		0
19	19	A	Hull C	L	0-3	0-1	10		0
20	26	H	Hull C	W	2-0	0-0	8	Charles [50], Butcher [68]	0
21	30	A	Plymouth Arg	D	2-2	1-1	9	Pritchard [41], Charles [46]	0
22	Feb 2	H	Bristol R	W	6-1	4-1	7	Pritchard [8], Charles 3 [12, 17, 70], Bishop 2 [28, 48]	0
23	6	H	Northampton T	D	0-0	0-0	8		0
24	9	H	Plymouth Arg	L	0-1	0-0	8		0
25	14	A	Lincoln C	D	2-2	1-0	9	Charles 2 [6, 90]	0
26	17	A	Doncaster R	W	1-0	1-0	6	Smyth [42]	0
27	20	H	Shrewsbury T	D	1-1	0-0	7	Conneely [47]	0
28	23	A	Crewe Alex	L	0-2	0-1	7		0
29	27	A	Fleetwood T	D	1-1	1-1	7	Phillips [22]	0
30	Mar 2	H	Ipswich T	L	1-2	1-2	8	Charles [4]	0
31	6	H	Swindon T	W	2-1	2-1	7	Charles [11], Bishop [44]	0
32	9	A	Bristol R	L	1-4	0-2	10	Smyth [77]	0
33	13	A	Milton Keynes D	L	2-3	0-1	10	Charles [57], Surman (og) [62]	0
34	17	H	Sunderland	L	0-2	0-0	13		0
35	20	H	Wigan Ath	W	3-1	2-1	12	Burgess [3], Nottingham [15], Charles (pen) [61]	0
36	27	A	Peterborough U	L	0-7	0-3	13		0
37	Apr 2	H	Burton Alb	D	0-0	0-0	13		0
38	5	A	Oxford U	W	2-1	1-1	11	Smyth [16], Nottingham [70]	0
39	10	H	AFC Wimbledon	L	1-5	1-3	12	Nottingham [4]	0
40	13	A	Blackpool	D	0-0	0-0	11		0
41	17	A	Rochdale	L	1-3	1-1	13	Barclay [13]	0
42	20	H	Doncaster R	W	2-1	1-0	12	Charles 2 (2 pens) [41, 90]	0
43	24	A	Sunderland	D	3-3	0-2	12	Bishop [51], O'Nien (og) [68], McConville [85]	0
44	27	H	Portsmouth	D	3-3	2-0	11	Bishop [15], Burgess [43], Marquis (og) [90]	0
45	May 1	H	Charlton Ath	D	1-1	0-0	13	Pritchard [81]	0
46	9	A	Portsmouth	W	1-0	1-0	11	Phillips [23]	0

Final League Position: 11

GOALSCORERS

League (63): Charles 19 (3 pens), Bishop 10, Pritchard 7, Nottingham 4, Burgess 3, Smyth 3, Butcher 2, Cassidy 2 (1 pen), Phillips 2, Russell 2, Barclay 1, Conneely 1, McConville 1, Sykes 1, Uwakwe 1, own goals 4.
FA Cup (1): Bishop 1.
Carabao Cup (1): Burgess 1.
Papa John's Trophy (12): Uwakwe 3, Burgess 2, Cassidy 2, Pritchard 2, Bishop 1, Charles 1, Mansell 1.

Savin T 30 + 1	Sykes R 9	Hughes M 36	Burgess C 42 + 2	Pritchard J 25 + 3	Sangare M 1 + 1	Conneely S 37 + 1	Butcher M 39 + 3	Uwakwe T 12 + 3	Charles D 42	Cassidy R 5 + 6	Sama S 2 + 2	Bishop C 38 + 3	Barclay B 23 + 3	Allan T 1 + 3	Rodgers H 27 + 1	Scully T — + 3	Russell J 12 + 13	Nottingham M 41 + 1	McConville S 26 + 5	Mansell L — + 2	Baxter N 16	Roberts G — + 2	Fenlon R — + 2	Smyth P 15 + 6	Phillips A 13 + 9	Morgan D 9 + 7	Maguire J 5	Perritt H — + 2	Match No.
1	2	3	4	5	6^{3}	7^{1}	8	9	10	11^{2}	12	13	14																1
1	2	3	4	5		6	8	9	11	10^{1}	7^{2}	12		13															2
1	2	3	4	8^{3}		12	7		10▪	11	6^{1}	13		9^{2}	5	14													3
1	2	3	4	8		7	6	9		10^{1}		11^{2}		13	5		12												4
1	2	3	4	5		7	6	9^{1}		11^{2}		10		13			8	12											5
1	2	3	4	10		7^{1}	6	9		12		11					8	5											6
1	2	3	4	8			7	9^{1}	11			10	13				6^{2}	5	12										7
1		3	4	9		8	7		10			11			5		6	2											8
1		3	4	9		8	7		11			10^{1}			5		6	2		12									9
1		3	4	9		7	6		11			10			5		8^{1}	2	12▪										10
1		3	4	9	12	7	8		10	13		11			5^{2}		6^{1}	2											11
1		3	4	9		7	6		11	13		10	12		5^{2}		8^{1}	2											12
1		3	4	8		7	6	9	11			10			5			2											13
1		3	4	8		7^{3}	6	9^{1}	10	13		11			5^{2}		14	2	12										14
		3	4	9		7	6		10			11			5			2	8		1								15
		3	4	9		7	6		10			11			5			2	8		1								16
		3	4	9		7	6		10	12		11			5^{1}			2	8^{2}		1	13							17
	5^{2}	3	4	9		7	6^{1}		10	13		11					12	2	8		1								18
	2^{3}	3	4▪	9^{2}		7	6	16	10^{5}		14	11^{4}					15	5	8^{1}		1	13	12						19
		3		5		7	6	9	10			11	2					4	8		1								20
		3		5		7	6	9^{1}	10			11	2					4	8		1			12					21
		3	13	5^{4}		7	6^{1}	9^{2}	10			11	2		14	16	12	4^{3}	8^{5}		1			15					22
		3	12	5▪		7		9^{1}	10			11	2					4	8		1			13	6^{2}				23
		4	5			7	6		11			10	3					2			1			9	8				24
		4	5			7	6		9			10	3				13	2			1			11^{2}	8^{1}	12			25
		4	5			7	6		11			10	3					2			1			9	8				26
		4	5			7	6^{2}		10			11	3				13	2			1			9^{1}	8	12			27
		4	5			7^{3}	6	13	11			10			2▪		14	3	9^{2}		1				8^{1}	12			28
		3	4	9^{3}		7	8^{2}		11^{4}			10	2				15	5	12		1			13	6^{1}	14			29
12		3	4	8^{3}		7▪	6	15	10			11	2^{2}					5	14		1^{1}			9^{4}		13			30
1		4	5			7^{3}	6		10			11^{2}	3				13	2	8					9^{1}	14	12			31
1		3	4				6		10^{1}				2				11	5	8					9	12	7			32
1		4	5				7^{1}		11				6		2			3	9					10	12	8			33
1		4	5				12		11				6		2		13	3	10					9	8^{1}	7^{2}			34
1		3	4				8		10				6		5^{1}			2	11							7	9	12	35
1		3^{1}	4				8						6^{2}		5		12	2	11^{4}	15			14	10^{3}	13	7	9		36
1			4			6	7		11			10			2			3	8					9^{1}	12		5		37
1			4			6	7		10			11			2			3	8					9^{1}	12		5		38
1			4	13		6	7^{1}		10^{2}			11			2			3	8^{3}					9	14	12	5		39
1			4			7	13		9			10	2		5			3	8					11^{2}	12	6^{1}			40
1			4			7^{4}	13		9			10	2^{2}		5		15	3	8					11^{3}	12	6^{1}		14	41
1			5			6	7		11			10	4		2			3	8						9				42
1			5			7	9^{1}		11			10	3		2			4	8					12	6				43
1			5	12		6			10			11	3		2^{2}		9^{1}	4	8					13	7				44
1			5	12					11			10	3		2		9^{1}	4	8						6	7			45
1			5						11			10	3		2	12	9^{1}	4	8						7	6			46

FA Cup

First Round	Tranmere R	(a)	1-2

Carabao Cup

First Round	Burton Alb	(a)	1-1

(Burton Alb won 4-2 on penalties)

Papa John's Trophy

Group G (N)	Leeds U U21	(h)	7-0
Group G (N)	Blackpool	(h)	1-1
(Accrington Stanley won 4-3 on penalties)			
Group G (N)	Barrow	(a)	1-0
Second Round (N)	Manchester U U21	(h)	3-2
Third Round (N)	Lincoln C	(a)	0-4

AFC WIMBLEDON

FOUNDATION

While the history of AFC Wimbledon is straightforward since it was a new club formed in 2002, there were in effect two clubs operating for two years with Wimbledon connections. The other club was MK Dons, of course. In August 2001, the Football League had rejected the existing Wimbledon's application to move to Milton Keynes. In May 2002, they rejected local sites and were given permission to move by an independent commission set up by the Football League. AFC Wimbledon was founded in the summer of 2002 and held its first trials on Wimbledon Common. In subsequent years, there was considerable debate over the rightful home of the trophies obtained by the former Wimbledon football club. In October 2006, an agreement was reached between Milton Keynes Dons, its Supporters Association, the Wimbledon Independent Supporters Association and the Football Supporters Federation to transfer such trophies and honours to the London Borough of Merton.

Plough Lane Stadium, Plough Lane, London SW17 0NR.

Telephone: (0208) 547 3528.

Website: www.afcwimbledon.co.uk

Email: info@afcwimbledon.co.uk

Ground Capacity: 9,300.

Record Attendance: 4,870 v Accrington S, FL 2 Play-Offs, 14 May 2016.

Pitch Measurements: 104m × 66m (114yd × 72yd).

Chief Executive: Joe Palmer.

Head Coach: Mark Robinson.

Goalkeeping Coach: Ashley Bayes.

Club Nickname: 'The Dons'.

Colours: Blue shirts with yellow trim, blue shorts with yellow trim, blue socks with yellow trim.

Year Formed: 2002.

Turned Professional: 2002.

Grounds: 2002, Kingsmeadow (renamed The Cherry Red Records Stadium); 2020 Plough Lane.

First Football League Game: 6 August 2011, FL 2 v Bristol R (h) L 2–3 – Brown; Hatton, Gwillim (Bush), Porter (Minshull), Stuart (1), Johnson B, Moore L, Wellard, Jolley (Ademeno (1)), Midson, Yussuff.

HONOURS

League: *Runners-up:* FL 2 – (7th) 2015–16 *(promoted via play-offs)*; Conference – (2nd) 2010–11 *(promoted via play-offs)*.

FA Cup: 5th rd – 2019.

League Cup: 2nd rd 2019.

FOOTBALL YEARBOOK FACT FILE

AFC Wimbledon returned to Plough Lane on 3 November 2020 when their new ground was used for the first time for a League One game against Doncaster Rovers. The Dons initially ground-shared following their formation in 2002 but their aim was always to return to Plough Lane and the London Borough of Merton. That was finally achieved with the development of a former greyhound stadium 200 yards from the club's original home.

MANAGERS

Terry Eames 2002–04
Nicky English *(Caretaker)* 2004
Dave Anderson 2004–07
Terry Brown 2007–12
Neal Ardley 2012–18
Wally Downes 2018–19
Glyn Hodges 2019–21
Mark Robinson February 2021–

Record League Victory: 5–1 v Bury, FL 2, 19 November 2016 – Shea; Fuller, Robertson, Robinson (Taylor), Owens, Francomb (2 (1 pen)), Reeves, Parrett, Whelpdale (1), Elliott (1) (Nightingale), Poleon (1), (Barrett); 5–1 v Accrington S, FL 1, 10 April 2021 – Tzanev; O'Neill (Alexander), Heneghan', Nightingale, Guinness-Walker, Dobson (Oksanen), Woodyard, Rudoni, Assal (2) (Osew), Palmer (2) (McLoughlin), Pigott (1) (Longman).

Record Cup Victory: 5–0 v Bury, FA Cup 1st rd replay, 5 November 2016 – Shea; Fuller (Owens), Robertson, Robinson (1), Francomb. Parrett (1), Reeves, Bulman (Beere), Whelpdale, Barcham (Poleon (2)), Taylor (1).

Record Defeat: 0–5 v Oxford U, FL 2, 18 February 2020.

Most League Points (3 for a win): 75, FL 2, 2015–16.

Most League Goals: 64, FL 2, 2015–16.

Highest League Scorer in Season: Lyle Taylor, 20, 2015–16; Joe Pigott, 20, 2020–21.

Most League Goals in Total Aggregate: Kevin Cooper, 107, 2002–04.

Most League Goals in One Match: 3, Lyle Taylor v Rotherham U, FL 1, 17 October 2017; 3, Joe Pigott v Rochdale, FL 1, 19 February 2019; 3, Marcus Foss v Southend U, FL 1, 12 October 2019.

Most Capped Player: Shane Smeltz, 5 (58), New Zealand.

Most League Appearances: Barry Fuller, 205, 2013–18.

Youngest League Player: Jack Madelin, 17 years 186 days v Burton Alb, 22 October 2019.

Record Transfer Fee Received: £150,000 from Bradford C for Jake Reeves, July 2017.

Record Transfer Fee Paid: £25,000 (in excess of) to Stevenage for Byron Harrison, January 2012.

Football League Record: 2011 Promoted from Conference Premier; 2011–16 FL 2; 2016– FL 1.

LATEST SEQUENCES

Longest Sequence of League Wins: 5, 2.4.2016 – 23.4.2016.

Longest Sequence of League Defeats: 8, 2.10.2018 – 17.11.2018.

Longest Sequence of League Draws: 4, 6.4.2019 – 23.4.2019.

Longest Sequence of Unbeaten League Matches: 10, 7.4.2018 – 18.8.2018.

Longest Sequence Without a League Win: 12, 4.5.2019 – 28.9.2019.

Successive Scoring Runs: 11 from 24.10.2020.

Successive Non-scoring Runs: 6 from 1.4.2017.

TEN YEAR LEAGUE RECORD

		P	*W*	*D*	*L*	*F*	*A*	*Pts*	*Pos*
2011-12	FL 2	46	15	9	22	62	78	54	16
2012-13	FL 2	46	14	11	21	54	76	53	20
2013-14	FL 2	46	14	14	18	49	57	53*	20
2014-15	FL 2	46	14	16	16	54	60	58	15
2015-16	FL 2	46	21	12	13	64	50	75	7
2016-17	FL 1	46	13	18	15	52	55	57	15
2017-18	FL 1	46	13	14	19	47	58	53	18
2018-19	FL 1	46	13	11	22	42	63	50	20
2019-20	FL 1	35	8	11	16	39	52	35	20§
2020-21	FL 1	46	12	15	19	54	70	51	19

** 3 pts deducted. §Decided on points-per-game (1.00)*

DID YOU KNOW ?

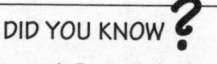

Team captain Danny Kedwell scored the decisive spot-kick when AFC Wimbledon defeated Luton Town on a penalty shoot-out to gain promotion to the Football League in May 2011. The game at Manchester City's stadium ended goalless after extra-time but Wimbledon triumphed 4-3 on penalties to secure promotion from the Conference.

AFC WIMBLEDON – SKY BET LEAGUE ONE 2020–21 LEAGUE RECORD

Match No.	Date	Venue	Opponents	Result		H/T Score	Lg Pos.	Goalscorers	Attendance
1	Sept 12	A	Northampton T	D	2-2	2-2	8	Chislett [1], Guinness-Walker [23]	0
2	19	H	Plymouth Arg	D	4-4	1-2	16	Pigott 2 [18, 60], McLoughlin [49], Longman [69]	0
3	26	A	Fleetwood T	W	1-0	1-0	8	Seddon [41]	0
4	Oct 3	H	Accrington S	L	1-2	1-2	12	Longman [18]	0
5	10	A	Swindon T	W	1-0	1-0	10	Pigott [28]	0
6	17	H	Shrewsbury T	L	0-1	0-0	11		0
7	20	A	Hull C	L	0-1	0-1	12		0
8	24	A	Burton Alb	D	1-1	0-0	15	Longman [65]	0
9	27	H	Blackpool	W	1-0	1-0	11	Reilly [13]	0
10	31	A	Milton Keynes D	D	1-1	1-1	11	Pigott [10]	0
11	Nov 3	H	Doncaster R	D	2-2	1-1	11	Pigott 2 [18, 82]	0
12	21	A	Rochdale	W	1-0	0-0	12	Chislett [90]	0
13	24	A	Gillingham	L	1-2	1-1	12	Heneghan [28]	0
14	Dec 2	H	Peterborough U	W	2-1	0-0	11	Longman [54], Pigott [60]	0
15	5	H	Bristol R	L	2-4	2-3	14	Pigott (pen) [5], Heneghan [30]	0
16	12	A	Charlton Ath	L	2-5	2-1	14	Pigott [42], Csoka [45]	0
17	15	A	Sunderland	D	1-1	1-0	14	Pigott (pen) [42]	0
18	19	H	Crewe Alex	L	1-2	0-0	15	Longman [90]	0
19	26	A	Oxford U	L	0-2	0-2	18		0
20	Jan 2	H	Lincoln C	L	1-2	1-1	19	Palmer [31]	0
21	16	H	Sunderland	L	0-3	0-1	20		0
22	19	A	Portsmouth	L	0-4	0-3	20		0
23	23	A	Crewe Alex	D	1-1	1-1	19	Pigott [2]	0
24	26	A	Doncaster R	L	0-2	0-2	20		0
25	30	H	Milton Keynes D	L	0-2	0-0	20		0
26	Feb 6	A	Wigan Ath	W	3-2	2-1	19	Rudoni [22], Pigott 2 (1 pen) [30, 76 (p)]	0
27	20	A	Peterborough U	L	0-3	0-0	20		0
28	23	H	Gillingham	W	1-0	0-0	20	Rudoni [89]	0
29	27	H	Hull C	L	0-3	0-2	21		0
30	Mar 2	A	Shrewsbury T	D	1-1	0-1	20	Assal [84]	0
31	6	A	Blackpool	D	1-1	0-0	21	Palmer [90]	0
32	9	H	Burton Alb	L	0-1	0-0	22		0
33	13	A	Bristol R	D	0-0	0-0	23		0
34	16	H	Wigan Ath	D	1-1	0-0	21	Dobson [79]	0
35	20	H	Charlton Ath	D	2-2	1-2	22	Longman 2 [15, 65]	0
36	27	H	Northampton T	W	1-0	0-0	21	Pigott [88]	0
37	Apr 2	A	Plymouth Arg	L	0-1	0-1	21		0
38	5	H	Fleetwood T	L	0-1	0-0	21		0
39	10	A	Accrington S	W	5-1	3-1	20	Palmer 2 [21, 42], Assal 2 [45, 64], Pigott [57]	0
40	13	H	Ipswich T	W	3-0	2-0	19	Nightingale [21], Rudoni [25], Longman [86]	0
41	17	H	Swindon T	W	4-1	3-0	19	Pigott 2 (1 pen) [20 (p), 53], Nightingale [26], Assal [44]	0
42	20	H	Oxford U	W	2-1	0-0	19	Pigott (pen) [62], Woodyard [64]	0
43	24	A	Ipswich T	D	0-0	0-0	19		0
44	27	H	Rochdale	D	3-3	0-1	19	Rudoni [61], Palmer [66], Pigott [90]	0
45	May 1	H	Portsmouth	L	1-3	1-3	19	Pigott [23]	0
46	9	A	Lincoln C	D	0-0	0-0	19		0

Final League Position: 19

GOALSCORERS

League (54): Pigott 20 (5 pens), Longman 8, Palmer 5, Assal 4, Rudoni 4, Chislett 2, Heneghan 2, Nightingale 2, Csoka 1, Dobson 1, Guinness-Walker 1, McLoughlin 1, Reilly 1, Seddon 1, Woodyard 1.
FA Cup (1): Pigott 1.
Carabao Cup (1): Own goal 1.
Papa John's Trophy (9): Roscrow 2 (1 pen), Chislett 1, Longman 1, Osew 1, Pigott 1, Robinson 1, Rudoni 1, Thomas 1.

Tzanev N 15	O'Neill L 24 + 4	Thomas T 17 + 2	Kalambayi P 10 + 4	McLoughlin S 23 + 15	Chislett E 12 + 15	Woodyard A 39 + 1	Reilly C 22 + 6	Guinness-Walker N 25 + 6	Pigott J 45	Longman R 35 + 9	Hartigan A 8 + 7	Roscrow A — + 6	Trueman C 19	Oksanen J 12 + 15	Seddon S 15 + 1	Csoka D 20	Rudoni J 33 + 6	Palmer O 10 + 13	Nightingale W 29 + 3	Alexander C 18 + 11	Heneghan B 20 + 3	Robinson Z — + 5	Walker S 12	Dobson G 22 + 2	Johnson D 11	Osew P — + 10	Harrison S — + 1	Assal A 10 + 4	*Match No.*
1	2	3	4	5	6^{1}	7	8	9	10	11^{2}	12	13																	1
	2	3	4	5	6^{1}	7	8	9	11	10^{2}	12	13	1																2
	2	3	4	5		6	8		10	11^{1}	13	12	1	7^{2}	9														3
	2	3^{2}	4	5	13	6	8		10	11	12		1	7^{1}	9														4
	2	3		5	8^{2}	6	13	12	11	10^{1}			1	7	9	4													5
	2	3		5	8	6			11	10^{1}		12	1	7	9	4													6
	2	3		5		6	8		11	13	12		1	7^{2}	9	4	10^{1}												7
	2	3		5	14	6	8		10	13	12		1	7^{1}	9	4^{3}	11^{2}												8
	2^{1}	3	12	5	8		6	14	11^{2}	10	7		1		9^{3}	4		13											9
		3	2	5	12	6	8		10		7		1		9	4	11^{1}												10
		4	2^{2}	5^{3}		6	8		11	10^{1}	7		1		9		13	12	3	14									11
		2^{2}		5	14	6^{4}	8^{1}		11	10^{3}	7		1		9	4	12	15	3		13								12
		12	2	5	15	6^{2}	8^{4}		11^{3}	10	7		1		9	4^{1}	14	13	16		3^{5}								13
		12			13	6	14	9	11	10^{2}	7		1			4^{1}	8^{3}		2	5	3								14
				13	12	6	15	9^{2}	11	10	7^{4}		1		14	4^{3}	8^{5}	16	2	5^{1}	3								15
		2^{3}		5	12	6	13		11	10	7^{1}		1		9	4^{4}	8^{2}	15	14		3								16
		3		2	12	8	9		11	7			1		6	5	10^{1}				4								17
		2^{3}		5	13	6^{4}	7		10^{1}	9	14		1		8	4	11^{2}	12	3	15									18
		3		14	10^{4}		8	6		7		16	1	13	2^{3}	5^{2}	9	11^{5}	12		4^{1}	15							19
		2	3^{2}	5	12	6			11^{1}			13	1	7		4	8	10		9									20
	12			2^{1}	10^{2}	6		5	11	8^{3}				7		4	9		3	13		14	1						21
	2^{1}		12			6	7	9	11	10^{2}						4	8		3	5		13	1						22
	2^{1}		12^{2}	14		6	7	9	11	10						4	8		3	5^{3}			1	13					23
				14	13	6^{2}	7^{1}	9	11	10				15		4	8^{3}		3	5^{4}			1	12	2				24
	2^{2}			5	13		6^{4}	9^{3}	11	10				15		4	8^{1}			16		12	1	7	3	14^{5}			25
	2				9	13	7^{1}	5	11	10^{2}							8^{3}		4	14			1	6	3	12			26
	2				9^{1}	6		5	11	10				16			8^{5}		4	13	14		1	7^{4}	3^{3}	15	12^{2}		27
				12	9^{1}	6		5	11	10^{2}							8		4		3		1	7	2	13			28
	15			12	9^{1}	6		5^{4}	11	10^{2}				16			8		4	14	3		1	7^{3}	2^{5}	13			29
	12			8^{4}		6	9^{3}		11	10				14			15		4	5	3		1	7^{2}	2^{1}			13	30
	2^{2}			9^{3}		6	13	12	11	8^{4}				16			10^{1}	14	4	5			1	7^{5}	3			15	31
				9^{1}		6	14	5	11	8^{3}				15			10^{2}	12		2	4		1	7^{4}	3			13	32
1				8^{1}		6^{3}	9	5	11	12				14			10	13	4	2				7^{2}	3				33
1	13						7^{1}	5	11	8				12			10^{2}	9	4	2^{3}	15			6	3^{4}	14			34
1	2^{2}					9		12	11	8				7			13		4	5	3			6				10^{1}	35
1	2			14	13	7			10	11^{1}				8			9^{2}	12	4	5	3			6^{3}					36
1	2				7^{2}			12	11^{3}	10				8			13	14	4	5^{1}	3			6				9	37
1					13			5	11^{1}	10^{2}				8			7	12	4	2	3	14		6				9^{3}	38
1	2^{2}			14		7		5	11^{1}	12				16			8	10^{3}	4	13	3			6^{5}		15		9^{4}	39
1	2^{4}		3	13		8		5^{5}	11	14				12			6^{2}	10^{3}	4	15				7		16		9^{1}	40
1	2		16	15		7		5^{3}	11^{2}	12				14			8^{4}	10	4^{5}		3			6^{1}		13		9	41
1				13		8		5	11	12							9^{2}	10^{3}	4	2	3			7		14		6^{1}	42
1	2^{2}			13		6		5	11	8							9		4	12	3			7				10^{1}	43
1	2^{2}			14		8		5	11	12							9^{3}	10	4	13	3			7				6^{1}	44
1				14		6		5	11	8				13			9^{3}	10^{1}	4	2	3			7^{2}				12	45
1	2^{3}		3	13		7		14	11	12				15			6^{2}	10^{1}	4	5				8^{4}				9	46

FA Cup

First Round	Barrow	(a)	0-0
(aet; AFC Wimbledon won 4-2 on penalties)			
Second Round	Crawley T	(h)	1-2

Carabao Cup

First Round	Oxford U	(a)	1-1
(Oxford U won 4-3 on penalties)			

Papa John's Trophy

Group G (S)	Charlton Ath	(h)	2-1
Group G (S)	Brighton & HA U21	(h)	2-0
Group G (S)	Leyton Orient	(a)	0-2
Second Round (S)	Arsenal U21	(h)	3-0
Third Round (S)	Bristol R	(a)	1-0
Quarter-Final	Oxford U	(a)	1-3

ARSENAL

FOUNDATION

Formed by workers at the Royal Arsenal, Woolwich in 1886, they began as Dial Square (name of one of the workshops), and included two former Nottingham Forest players, Fred Beardsley and Morris Bates. Beardsley wrote to his old club seeking help and they provided the new club with a full set of red jerseys and a ball. The club became known as the 'Woolwich Reds' although their official title soon after formation was Woolwich Arsenal.

Emirates Stadium, Highbury House, 75 Drayton Park, Islington, London N5 1BU.

Telephone: (020) 7619 5003.

Ticket Office: (020) 7619 5000.

Website: www.arsenal.com

Email: ask@arsenal.co.uk

Ground Capacity: 60,704.

Record Attendance: 73,295 v Sunderland, Div 1, 9 March 1935 (at Highbury); 73,707 v RC Lens, UEFA Champions League, 25 November 1998 (at Wembley); 60,383 v Wolverhampton W, Premier League, 2 November 2019 (at Emirates).

Pitch Measurements: 105m × 68m (115yd × 74.5yd).

Chief Executive: Vinai Venkatesham.

Manager: Mikel Arteta.

Assistant Coaches: Albert Stuiverberg, Steve Round.

Colours: Red shirts with white sleeves, white shorts with red trim, red socks with white trim.

Year Formed: 1886.

Turned Professional: 1891.

Previous Names: 1886, Dial Square; 1886, Royal Arsenal; 1891, Woolwich Arsenal; 1914, Arsenal.

Club Nickname: 'The Gunners'.

Grounds: 1886, Plumstead Common; 1887, Sportsman Ground; 1888, Manor Ground; 1890, Invicta Ground; 1893, Manor Ground; 1913, Highbury; 2006, Emirates Stadium.

HONOURS

League Champions: Premier League – 1997–98, 2001–02, 2003–04; Division 1 – 1930–31, 1932–33, 1933–34, 1934–35, 1937–38, 1947–48, 1952–53, 1970–71, 1988–89, 1990–91.
Runners-up: Premier League – 1998–99, 1999–2000, 2000–01, 2002–03, 2004–05, 2015–16; Division 1 – 1925–26, 1931–32, 1972–73; Division 2 – 1903–04.

FA Cup Winners: 1930, 1936, 1950, 1971, 1979, 1993, 1998, 2002, 2003, 2005, 2014, 2015, 2017, 2020.
Runners-up: 1927, 1932, 1952, 1972, 1978, 1980, 2001.

League Cup Winners: 1987, 1993.
Runners-up: 1968, 1969, 1988, 2007, 2011, 2018.

Double performed: 1970–71, 1997–98, 2001–02.

European Competitions
European Cup: 1971–72 *(qf)*, 1991–92.
UEFA Champions League: 1998–99, 1999–2000, 2000–01, 2001–02, 2002–03, 2003–04, 2004–05, 2005–06 *(runners-up)*, 2006–07, 2007–08 *(qf)*, 2008–09 *(sf)*, 2009–10 *(qf)*, 2010–11, 2011–12, 2012–13, 2013–14, 2014–15, 2015–16, 2016–17.
Fairs Cup: 1963–64, 1969–70 *(winners)*, 1970–71.
UEFA Cup: 1978–79, 1981–82, 1982–83, 1996–97, 1997–98, 1999–2000 *(runners-up)*.
Europa League: 2017–18 *(sf)*, 2018–19 *(runners-up)*, 2019–20, 2020–21 *(sf)*.
European Cup-Winners' Cup: 1979–80 *(runners-up)*, 1993–94 *(winners)*, 1994–95 *(runners-up)*.
Super Cup: 1994 *(runners-up)*.

FOOTBALL YEARBOOK FACT FILE

Arsenal became the first English professional club to host a team from Romania when they played the armed forces team CCA Bucharest at Highbury in October 1956. The game finished in a 1-1 draw with Cliff Holton netting an equaliser 12 minutes from time after the Gunners had earlier missed with a spot kick.

First Football League Game: 2 September 1893, Division 2, v Newcastle U (h) D 2–2 – Williams; Powell, Jeffrey; Devine, Buist, Howat; Gemmell, Henderson, Shaw (1), Elliott (1), Booth.

Record League Victory: 12–0 v Loughborough T, Division 2, 12 March 1900 – Orr; McNichol, Jackson; Moir, Dick (2), Anderson (1); Hunt, Cottrell (2), Main (2), Gaudie (3), Tennant (2).

Record Cup Victory: 11–1 v Darwen, FA Cup 3rd rd, 9 January 1932 – Moss; Parker, Hapgood; Jones, Roberts, John; Hulme (2), Jack (3), Lambert (2), James, Bastin (4).

Record Defeat: 0–8 v Loughborough T, Division 2, 12 December 1896.

Most League Points (2 for a win): 66, Division 1, 1930–31.

Most League Points (3 for a win): 90, Premier League, 2003–04.

Most League Goals: 127, Division 1, 1930–31.

Highest League Scorer in Season: Ted Drake, 42, 1934–35.

Most League Goals in Total Aggregate: Thierry Henry, 175, 1999–2007; 2011–12.

Most League Goals in One Match: 7, Ted Drake v Aston Villa, Division 1, 14 December 1935.

Most Capped Player: Thierry Henry, 81 (123), France.

Most League Appearances: David O'Leary, 558, 1975–93.

Youngest League Player: Jack Wilshere, 16 years 256 days v Blackburn R, 13 September 2008.

Record Transfer Fee Received: £40,000,000 from Liverpool for Alex Oxlade-Chamberlain, August 2017.

Record Transfer Fee Paid: £72,000,000 to Lille for Nicolas Pepe, August 2019.

Football League Record: 1893 Elected to Division 2; 1904–13 Division 1; 1913–19 Division 2; 1919–92 Division 1; 1992– Premier League.

MANAGERS

Sam Hollis 1894–97
Tom Mitchell 1897–98
George Elcoat 1898–99
Harry Bradshaw 1899–1904
Phil Kelso 1904–08
George Morrell 1908–15
Leslie Knighton 1919–25
Herbert Chapman 1925–34
George Allison 1934–47
Tom Whittaker 1947–56
Jack Crayston 1956–58
George Swindin 1958–62
Billy Wright 1962–66
Bertie Mee 1966–76
Terry Neill 1976–83
Don Howe 1984–86
George Graham 1986–95
Bruce Rioch 1995–96
Arsène Wenger 1996–2018
Unai Emery 2018–19
Mikel Arteta December 2019–

LATEST SEQUENCES

Longest Sequence of League Wins: 14, 10.2.2002 – 18.8.2002.

Longest Sequence of League Defeats: 7, 12.2.1977 – 12.3.1977.

Longest Sequence of League Draws: 6, 4.3.1961 – 1.4.1961.

Longest Sequence of Unbeaten League Matches: 49, 7.5.2003 – 24.10.2004.

Longest Sequence Without a League Win: 23, 28.9.1912 – 1.3.1913.

Successive Scoring Runs: 55 from 19.5.2001.

Successive Non-scoring Runs: 6 from 25.2.1987.

TEN YEAR LEAGUE RECORD

		P	*W*	*D*	*L*	*F*	*A*	*Pts*	*Pos*
2011-12	PR Lge	38	21	7	10	74	49	70	3
2012-13	PR Lge	38	21	10	7	72	37	73	4
2013-14	PR Lge	38	24	7	7	68	41	79	4
2014-15	PR Lge	38	22	9	7	71	36	75	3
2015-16	PR Lge	38	20	11	7	65	36	71	2
2016-17	PR Lge	38	23	6	9	77	44	75	5
2017-18	PR Lge	38	19	6	13	74	51	63	6
2018-19	PR Lge	38	21	7	10	73	51	70	5
2019-20	PR Lge	38	14	14	10	56	48	56	8
2020-21	PR Lge	38	18	7	13	55	39	61	8

DID YOU KNOW ?

The Arsenal team that defeated Liverpool to win the 1950 FA Cup final was one of the oldest on record. Eight of the players were over 30 years old and the average age of the team was 31 years and 54 days. Les Compton at 37 was the oldest player in the team and Peter Goring at 23 the youngest.

ARSENAL – PREMIER LEAGUE 2020–21 LEAGUE RECORD

Match No.	Date	Venue	Opponents	Result		H/T Score	Lg Pos.	Goalscorers	Attendance
1	Sept 12	A	Fulham	W	3-0	1-0	1	Lacazette [8], Gabriel [49], Aubameyang [57]	0
2	19	H	West Ham U	W	2-1	1-1	2	Lacazette [25], Nketiah [85]	0
3	28	A	Liverpool	L	1-3	1-2	5	Lacazette [25]	0
4	Oct 4	H	Sheffield U	W	2-1	0-0	4	Saka [61], Pepe [64]	0
5	17	A	Manchester C	L	0-1	0-1	5		0
6	25	H	Leicester C	L	0-1	0-0	10		0
7	Nov 1	A	Manchester U	W	1-0	0-0	9	Aubameyang (pen) [69]	0
8	8	H	Aston Villa	L	0-3	0-1	11		0
9	22	A	Leeds U	D	0-0	0-0	11		0
10	29	H	Wolverhampton W	L	1-2	1-2	14	Gabriel [30]	0
11	Dec 6	A	Tottenham H	L	0-2	0-2	15		2000
12	13	H	Burnley	L	0-1	0-0	15		0
13	16	H	Southampton	D	1-1	0-1	15	Aubameyang [52]	0
14	19	A	Everton	L	1-2	1-2	15	Pepe (pen) [35]	2000
15	26	H	Chelsea	W	3-1	2-0	14	Lacazette (pen) [35], Xhaka [44], Saka [56]	0
16	29	A	Brighton & HA	W	1-0	0-0	13	Lacazette [66]	0
17	Jan 2	A	WBA	W	4-0	2-0	11	Tierney [23], Saka [28], Lacazette 2 [60, 64]	0
18	14	H	Crystal Palace	D	0-0	0-0	11		0
19	18	H	Newcastle U	W	3-0	0-0	10	Aubameyang 2 [50, 77], Saka [60]	0
20	26	A	Southampton	W	3-1	2-1	8	Pepe [8], Saka [39], Lacazette [72]	0
21	30	H	Manchester U	D	0-0	0-0	9		0
22	Feb 2	A	Wolverhampton W	L	1-2	1-1	10	Pepe [32]	0
23	6	A	Aston Villa	L	0-1	0-1	10		0
24	14	H	Leeds U	W	4-2	3-0	10	Aubameyang 3 (1 pen) [13, 41 (p), 47], Bellerin [45]	0
25	21	H	Manchester C	L	0-1	0-1	10		0
26	28	A	Leicester C	W	3-1	2-1	10	Luiz [39], Lacazette (pen) [45], Pepe [52]	0
27	Mar 6	A	Burnley	D	1-1	1-1	10	Aubameyang [6]	0
28	14	H	Tottenham H	W	2-1	1-1	10	Odegaard [44], Lacazette (pen) [64]	0
29	21	A	West Ham U	D	3-3	1-3	9	Soucek (og) [38], Dawson (og) [61], Lacazette [82]	0
30	Apr 3	H	Liverpool	L	0-3	0-0	9		0
31	11	A	Sheffield U	W	3-0	1-0	9	Lacazette 2 [33, 85], Martinelli [71]	0
32	18	H	Fulham	D	1-1	0-0	9	Nketiah [90]	0
33	23	H	Everton	L	0-1	0-0	9		0
34	May 2	A	Newcastle U	W	2-0	1-0	9	Elneny [6], Aubameyang [66]	0
35	9	H	WBA	W	3-1	2-0	9	Smith-Rowe [29], Pepe [35], Willian [90]	0
36	12	A	Chelsea	W	1-0	1-0	8	Smith-Rowe [16]	0
37	19	A	Crystal Palace	W	3-1	1-0	9	Pepe 2 [35, 90], Martinelli [90]	6500
38	23	H	Brighton & HA	W	2-0	0-0	8	Pepe 2 [49, 60]	10,000

Final League Position: 8

GOALSCORERS

League (55): Lacazette 13 (3 pens), Aubameyang 10 (2 pens), Pepe 10 (1 pen), Saka 5, Gabriel 2, Martinelli 2, Nketiah 2, Smith-Rowe 2, Bellerin 1, Elneny 1, Luiz 1, Odegaard 1, Tierney 1, Willian 1, Xhaka 1, own goals 2.
FA Cup (2): Aubameyang 1, Smith-Rowe 1.
Carabao Cup (3): Lacazette 1, Nketiah 1, own goal 1.
UEFA Europa League (33): Pepe 6 (1 pen), Aubameyang 3, Lacazette 3 (1 pen), Nketiah 3, Willock 3, Balogun 2, Elneny 2, Saka 2, Gabriel 1, Luiz 1, Nelson 1, Odegaard 1, Pablo Mari 1, Smith-Rowe 1, Tierney 1, own goals 2.
Papa John's Trophy (5): Azeez 1, Balogun 1, Cirjan 1, Lewis 1, McEneff 1.

Leno B 35	Holding R 28 + 2	Gabriel M 22 + 1	Tierney K 26 + 1	Bellerin H 24 + 1	Elneny M 17 + 6	Xhaka G 29 + 2	Maitland-Niles A 5 + 6	Willian d 16 + 9	Lacazette A 22 + 9	Aubameyang P 26 + 3	Pepe N 16 + 13	Ceballos D 17 + 8	Nketiah E 4 + 13	Kolasinac S 1	Saka B 30 + 2	Luiz D 17 + 3	Thomas P 18 + 6	Mustafi S — + 3	Willock J 2 + 5	Nelson R — + 2	Cedric Soares R 8 + 2	Martinelli G 7 + 7	Pablo Mari V 10	Smith-Rowe E 18 + 2	Odegaard M 9 + 5	Runarsson R — + 1	Ryan M 3	Chambers C 8 + 2	*Match No.*
1	2	3	4	5	6	7^{2}	8	9^{1}	10^{3}	11	12	13	14																1
1	2	3		5		7		9^{1}	10^{2}	11	12	6	13	4	8^{3}	14													2
1	2		4	5	6	7^{1}	8	9^{2}	10^{3}	11	13	12	14			3													3
1		4	5	2	6	13	14	9		11	12	7^{2}	10^{1}		8^{3}	3													4
1		4	5	2		7^{2}		10^{1}	12	11	9^{3}	6	13		8	3	14												5
1		3	8^{3}	5		4			10	9	13	7	14		11^{2}	2^{1}	6	12											6
1	2	3	4	5	7		13	9^{2}	10^{1}	11^{3}			12		8		6	14											7
1	2	3	4	5	7			9^{3}	10^{2}	11	14	12	13		8		6^{1}												8
1	3	4	5	2		7	14	10^{1}		11	8■	6			13^{3}				9^{2}	12									9
1	12	4	5	2		7^{3}		8^{2}	14	11		6			10	3^{1}			9	13									10
1	3	4	5	2^{2}		8		6	10	11		12	13		9		7^{1}												11
1	3	4	5	2^{2}	6	7■	13	8^{3}	9^{1}	11		12	14		10														12
1	2	3■	4		6		5			11	9^{3}	7^{2}	10^{1}		8	12			13		14								13
1	2		4		7^{1}		5	11	14		9^{2}	6	10^{3}		8	3			12			13							14
1	3		5	2	6	7			11^{3}		13				8			14	12			10^{2}	4	9^{1}					15
1	3		5	2	6	7	14		12	11		13			8^{2}							10^{1}	4	9^{3}					16
1	3		5	2^{1}		7	12	13	11	10		6			8^{2}				14				4	9^{3}					17
1	3			2		7	5^{1}		11^{3}	10	12	6^{2}	14		8	4	13							9					18
1	3		5		12	7		13	11	10^{2}					8	4	6^{1}				2	14		9^{3}					19
1	3			2	13	7		12	11		10^{3}				8	4	6^{2}		14		5			9^{1}					20
1	3			2		7		12	11^{3}		8		14			4	6				5	10^{1}		9^{2}	13				21
1■	3	12		2		7			11^{1}	13	10^{2}				8	4■	6^{3}				5			9		14			22
	3	4		2		7		14	11^{1}	12	10				8		6^{3}				5^{2}			9	13		1		23
1	14	4		2	13	7		12		11		6^{3}			8	3					5			10^{1}	9^{2}				24
1	3^{3}		5	2	6^{4}	7			12	11	8^{1}	15			10	14							4	13	9^{2}				25
1			5		6^{2}	7		10	11^{3}	14	8					3	13				2		4	9^{1}	12				26
1			5			7		10^{2}	12	11	13	14			8	3	6^{3}						4		9^{1}			2	27
1		4	5		14	7		13	11^{3}		12				8^{1}	3	6				2			10^{2}	9				28
1			5			7^{1}			11	8^{3}	13				10^{2}	3	6					14	4	12	9			2	29
1	3	4	5^{1}		13				11	10^{3}	8	7^{2}					6				12	14			9			2	30
1	3				13	5		12	11^{3}		8	7	14		9^{1}		6					10^{2}	4					2	31
	3	4		2^{2}	6^{1}	5			11^{3}		13	7	14		8		12					10		9			1		32
1	3					5		14			10^{1}	7	11^{2}		8		6					12	4	9	13			2^{3}	33
		4		2	6	5		8		11^{2}	13	7				3^{1}	14					10			9^{3}		1	12	34
1	3	4	13		6			8	12		10	7^{3}			5		14					11^{1}		9^{2}				2	35
1	2	4	8	12^{3}	6				13	11^{2}					5^{1}		7						3	10	9			14	36
1	3	4	5^{2}		7	13				11	8				10^{1}		6^{3}					14		9	12			2	37
1	3	4	5			7			13	11^{2}	8				12		6					14		10^{1}	9^{3}			2	38

FA Cup

Third Round	Newcastle U	(h)	2-0
(aet)			
Fourth Round	Southampton	(a)	0-1

Carabao Cup

Third Round	Leicester C	(a)	2-0
Fourth Round	Liverpool	(a)	0-0
(Arsenal won 5-4 on penalties)			
Quarter-Final	Manchester C	(h)	1-4

Papa John's Trophy (Arsenal U21)

Group B (S)	Ipswich T	(a)	2-1
Group B (S)	Crawley T	(a)	2-1
Group B (S)	Gillingham	(a)	1-1
(Arsenal U21 won 4-2 on penalties)			
Second Round (S)	AFC Wimbledon	(a)	0-3

UEFA Europa League

Group B	Rapid Vienna	(a)	2-1
Group B	Dundalk	(h)	3-0
Group B	Molde	(h)	4-1
Group B	Molde	(a)	3-0
Group B	Rapid Vienna	(h)	4-1
Group B	Dundalk	(a)	4-2
Round of 32 1st leg	Benfica	(a)	1-1
Round of 32 2nd leg	Benfica	(h)	3-2
Round of 16 1st leg	Olympiacos	(a)	3-1
Round of 16 2nd leg	Olympiacos	(h)	0-1
Quarter-Final 1st leg	Slavia Prague	(h)	1-1
Quarter-Final 2nd leg	Slavia Prague	(a)	4-0
Semi-Final 1st leg	Villarreal	(a)	1-2
Semi-Final 2nd leg	Villarreal	(h)	0-0

ASTON VILLA

FOUNDATION

Cricketing enthusiasts of Villa Cross Wesleyan Chapel, Aston, Birmingham decided to form a football club during the winter of 1874–75. Football clubs were few and far between in the Birmingham area and in their first game against Aston Brook St Mary's rugby team they played one half rugby and the other soccer. In 1876 they were joined by Scottish soccer enthusiast George Ramsay who was immediately appointed captain and went on to lead Aston Villa from obscurity to one of the country's top clubs in a period of less than ten years.

Villa Park, Trinity Road, Birmingham B6 6HE.

Telephone: (0121) 327 2299.

Ticket Office: (0333) 323 1874.

Website: www.avfc.co.uk

Email: postmaster@avfc.co.uk

Ground Capacity: 42,749.

Record Attendance: 76,588 v Derby Co, FA Cup 6th rd, 2 March 1946.

Pitch Measurements: 105m × 68m (115yd × 74.5yd).

Executive Chairman: Nassef Sawiris.

Co-Chairman: Wes Edens.

Chief Executive: Christian Purslow.

Head Coach: Dean Smith.

Assistant Head Coaches: Richard O'Kelly, John Terry, Craig Shakespeare.

Colours: Claret shirts with sky blue sleeves, white shorts with sky blue trim, sky blue socks with claret trim.

Year Formed: 1874.

Turned Professional: 1885.

Club Nickname: 'The Villans'.

Grounds: 1874, Wilson Road and Aston Park (also used Aston Lower Grounds for some matches); 1876, Wellington Road, Perry Barr; 1897, Villa Park.

First Football League Game: 8 September 1888, Football League, v Wolverhampton W (a) D 1–1 – Warner; Cox, Coulton; Yates, Harry Devey, Dawson; Albert Brown, Green (1), Allen, Garvey, Hodgetts.

Record League Victory: 12–2 v Accrington S, Division 1, 12 March 1892 – Warner; Evans, Cox; Harry Devey, Jimmy Cowan, Baird; Athersmith (1), Dickson (2), John Devey (4), Lewis Campbell (4), Hodgetts (1).

HONOURS

League Champions: Division 1 – 1893–94, 1895–96, 1896–97, 1898–99, 1899–1900, 1909–10, 1980–81; Division 2 – 1937–38, 1959–60; Division 3 – 1971–72.
Runners-up: Premier League – 1992–93; Division 1 – 1902–03, 1907–08, 1910–11, 1912–13, 1913–14, 1930–31, 1932–33, 1989–90; Football League 1888–89; Division 2 – 1974–75, 1987–88.

FA Cup Winners: 1887, 1895, 1897, 1905, 1913, 1920, 1957.
Runners-up: 1892, 1924, 2000, 2015.

League Cup Winners: 1961, 1975, 1977, 1994, 1996.
Runners-up: 1963, 1971, 2010, 2020.

Double Performed: 1896–97.

European Competitions
European Cup: 1981–82 *(winners)*, 1982–83 *(qf)*.
UEFA Cup: 1975–76, 1977–78 *(qf)*, 1983–84, 1990–91, 1993–94, 1994–95, 1996–97, 1997–98 *(qf)*, 1998–99, 2001–02, 2008–09.
Europa League: 2009–10, 2010–11.
Intertoto Cup: 2000, 2001 *(winners)*, 2002 *(sf)*, 2008 *(qualified for UEFA Cup)*.
Super Cup: 1982 *(winners)*.
World Club Championship: 1982.

FOOTBALL YEARBOOK FACT FILE

Aston Villa began the 1925–26 campaign in tremendous fashion beating Burnley 10-0, equalling their biggest-ever winning margin in a Football League match. Centre forward Len Capewell, who had managed five League goals in 1924–25, matched that by scoring five on the day. The game was the first played following alterations to the offside law over the summer.

Record Cup Victory: 13–0 v Wednesbury Old Ath, FA Cup 1st rd, 30 October 1886 – Warner; Coulton, Simmonds; Yates, Robertson, Burton (2); Richard Davis (1), Albert Brown (3), Hunter (3), Loach (2), Hodgetts (2).

Record Defeat: 0–8 v Chelsea, Premier League, 23 December 2012.

Most League Points (2 for a win): 70, Division 3, 1971–72.

Most League Points (3 for a win): 83, FL C, 2017–18.

Most League Goals: 128, Division 1, 1930–31.

Highest League Scorer in Season: 'Pongo' Waring, 49, Division 1, 1930–31.

Most League Goals in Total Aggregate: Harry Hampton, 215, 1904–15.

Most League Goals in One Match: 5, Harry Hampton v Sheffield W, Division 1, 5 October 1912; 5, Harold Halse v Derby Co, Division 1, 19 October 1912; 5, Len Capewell v Burnley, Division 1, 29 August 1925; 5, George Brown v Leicester C, Division 1, 2 January 1932; 5, Gerry Hitchens v Charlton Ath, Division 2, 18 November 1959.

Most Capped Player: Steve Staunton, 64 (102), Republic of Ireland.

Most League Appearances: Charlie Aitken, 561, 1961–76.

Youngest League Player: Jimmy Brown, 15 years 349 days v Bolton W, 17 September 1969.

Record Transfer Fee Received: £32,500,000 from Liverpool for Christian Benteke, July 2015.

Record Transfer Fee Paid: £38,000,000 to Norwich C for Emiliano Buendia, June 2021.

Football League Record: 1888 Founder Member of the League; 1936–38 Division 2; 1938–59 Division 1; 1959–60 Division 2; 1960–67 Division 1; 1967–70 Division 2; 1970–72 Division 3; 1972–75 Division 2; 1975–87 Division 1; 1987–88 Division 2; 1988–92 Division 1; 1992–2016 Premier League; 2016–19 FL C; 2019– Premier League.

MANAGERS

George Ramsay 1884–1926 (*Secretary-Manager*)
W. J. Smith 1926–34 (*Secretary-Manager*)
Jimmy McMullan 1934–35
Jimmy Hogan 1936–44
Alex Massie 1945–50
George Martin 1950–53
Eric Houghton 1953–58
Joe Mercer 1958–64
Dick Taylor 1964–67
Tommy Cummings 1967–68
Tommy Docherty 1968–70
Vic Crowe 1970–74
Ron Saunders 1974–82
Tony Barton 1982–84
Graham Turner 1984–86
Billy McNeill 1986–87
Graham Taylor 1987–90
Dr Jozef Venglos 1990–91
Ron Atkinson 1991–94
Brian Little 1994–98
John Gregory 1998–2002
Graham Taylor OBE 2002–03
David O'Leary 2003–06
Martin O'Neill 2006–10
Gerard Houllier 2010–11
Alex McLeish 2011–12
Paul Lambert 2012–15
Tim Sherwood 2015
Remi Garde 2015–16
Roberto Di Matteo 2016
Steve Bruce 2016–18
Dean Smith October 2018–

LATEST SEQUENCES

Longest Sequence of League Wins: 10, 2.3.2019 – 22.4.2019.

Longest Sequence of League Defeats: 11, 14.2.2016 – 30.4.2016.

Longest Sequence of League Draws: 6, 12.9.1981 – 10.10.1981.

Longest Sequence of Unbeaten League Matches: 15, 12.3.1949 – 27.8.1949.

Longest Sequence Without a League Win: 19, 14.8.2015 – 2.1.2016.

Successive Scoring Runs: 35 from 10.11.1895.

Successive Non-scoring Runs: 6 from 26.12.2014.

TEN YEAR LEAGUE RECORD

		P	W	D	L	F	A	Pts	Pos
2011-12	PR Lge	38	7	17	14	37	53	38	16
2012-13	PR Lge	38	10	11	17	47	69	41	15
2013-14	PR Lge	38	10	8	20	39	61	38	15
2014-15	PR Lge	38	10	8	20	31	57	38	17
2015-16	PR Lge	38	3	8	27	27	76	17	20
2016-17	FL C	46	16	14	16	47	48	62	13
2017-18	FL C	46	24	11	11	72	42	83	4
2018-19	FL C	46	20	16	10	82	61	76	5
2019-20	PR Lge	38	9	8	21	41	67	35	17
2020-21	PR Lge	38	16	7	15	55	46	55	11

DID YOU KNOW ?

Aston Villa scored 86 home goals in the 1930–31 season, a record in English top-flight football. They netted in all 21 games and scored four or more on 15 occasions with their biggest win being 8-1 against Middlesbrough.

ASTON VILLA – PREMIER LEAGUE 2020–21 LEAGUE RECORD

Match No.	*Date*	*Venue*	*Opponents*	*Result*		*H/T Score*	*Lg Pos.*	*Goalscorers*	*Attendance*
1	Sept 21	H	Sheffield U	W	1-0	0-0	9	Konsa ^{63}	0
2	28	A	Fulham	W	3-0	2-0	4	Grealish ^{4}, Hourihane ^{15}, Mings ^{48}	0
3	Oct 4	H	Liverpool	W	7-2	4-1	2	Watkins 3 $^{4, 22, 39}$, McGinn ^{35}, Barkley ^{55}, Grealish 2 $^{66, 75}$	0
4	18	A	Leicester C	W	1-0	0-0	2	Barkley ^{90}	0
5	23	H	Leeds U	L	0-3	0-0	2		0
6	Nov 1	H	Southampton	L	3-4	0-3	7	Mings ^{62}, Grealish ^{90}, Watkins (pen) ^{90}	0
7	8	A	Arsenal	W	3-0	1-0	6	Saka (og) ^{25}, Watkins 2 $^{72, 75}$	0
8	21	H	Brighton & HA	L	1-2	0-1	6	Konsa ^{47}	0
9	30	A	West Ham U	L	1-2	1-1	10	Grealish ^{25}	0
10	Dec 12	A	Wolverhampton W	W	1-0	0-0	10	El Ghazi (pen) ^{90}	0
11	17	H	Burnley	D	0-0	0-0	11		0
12	20	A	WBA	W	3-0	1-0	9	El Ghazi 2 (1 pen) $^{5, 88 (p)}$, Traore ^{84}	0
13	26	H	Crystal Palace	W	3-0	1-0	6	Traore ^{5}, Hause ^{66}, El Ghazi ^{76}	0
14	28	A	Chelsea	D	1-1	0-1	5	El Ghazi ^{50}	0
15	Jan 1	A	Manchester U	L	1-2	0-1	6	Traore ^{58}	0
16	20	A	Manchester C	L	0-2	0-0	11		0
17	23	H	Newcastle U	W	2-0	2-0	8	Watkins ^{13}, Traore ^{42}	0
18	27	A	Burnley	L	2-3	1-0	10	Watkins ^{14}, Grealish ^{68}	0
19	30	A	Southampton	W	1-0	1-0	8	Barkley ^{41}	0
20	Feb 3	H	West Ham U	L	1-3	0-0	9	Watkins ^{81}	0
21	6	H	Arsenal	W	1-0	1-0	8	Watkins ^{2}	0
22	13	A	Brighton & HA	D	0-0	0-0	8		0
23	21	H	Leicester C	L	1-2	0-2	8	Traore ^{48}	0
24	27	A	Leeds U	W	1-0	1-0	8	El Ghazi ^{5}	0
25	Mar 3	A	Sheffield U	L	0-1	0-1	9		0
26	6	H	Wolverhampton W	D	0-0	0-0	9		0
27	12	A	Newcastle U	D	1-1	0-0	9	Clark (og) ^{86}	0
28	21	H	Tottenham H	L	0-2	0-1	10		0
29	Apr 4	H	Fulham	W	3-1	0-0	9	Trezeguet 2 $^{78, 81}$, Watkins ^{87}	0
30	10	A	Liverpool	L	1-2	1-0	10	Watkins ^{43}	0
31	21	H	Manchester C	L	1-2	1-2	11	McGinn ^{1}	0
32	25	H	WBA	D	2-2	1-1	11	El Ghazi (pen) ^{9}, Davis ^{90}	0
33	May 1	A	Everton	W	2-1	1-1	9	Watkins ^{13}, El Ghazi ^{80}	0
34	9	H	Manchester U	L	1-3	1-0	11	Traore ^{24}	0
35	13	H	Everton	D	0-0	0-0	11		0
36	16	A	Crystal Palace	L	2-3	2-1	11	McGinn ^{17}, El Ghazi ^{34}	0
37	19	A	Tottenham H	W	2-1	2-1	11	Reguilon (og) ^{20}, Watkins ^{39}	10,000
38	23	H	Chelsea	W	2-1	1-0	11	Traore ^{43}, El Ghazi (pen) ^{52}	10,000

Final League Position: 11

GOALSCORERS

League (55): Watkins 14 (1 pen), El Ghazi 10 (4 pens), Traore 7, Grealish 6, Barkley 3, McGinn 3, Konsa 2, Mings 2, Trezeguet 2, Davis 1, Hause 1, Hourihane 1, own goals 3.
FA Cup (1): Barry 1.
Carabao Cup (6): Watkins 2, Davis 1, El Ghazi 1, Grealish 1, Traore 1.
Papa John's Trophy (2): Sohna 1, Vassilev 1 (1 pen).

Martinez D 38	Cash M 28	Konsa E 35+1	Mings T 36	Targett M 38	Hourihane C 3+1	Douglas Luiz d 32+1	McGinn J 37	Trezeguet M 12+9	Watkins O 37	Grealish J 24+2	Davis K 1+14	Ramsey J 6+16	Traore B 29+7	Nakamba M 9+4	Barkley R 18+6	Elmohamady A 8+6	El Ghazi A 17+11	Hause K 7	Taylor N —+1	Sanson M 3+6	Wesley M —+3	Chukwuemeka C —+2	Philogene-Bidace J —+1	Match No.
1	2	3	4	5	6[1]	7	8	9	10	11	12													1
1	2	3	4	5	8[1]	7[3]	6	9[2]	10	11		12	13	14										2
1	2[2]	3	4	5		6[1]	7	8[3]	11	10			14	13	9	12								3
1	2	3	4	5		6	7	8[1]	11	10			12		9									4
1	2	3	4	5		7	6	8[1]	11	10			12		9									5
1	2[2]	3	4	5		7	6	12	11	10			8[1]		9	13								6
1	2	3	4	5		6	7	8[1]	11	10					9		12							7
1	2	3	4	5	14	6[3]	7	8	11	10			12[2]		9[1]		13							8
1	2[3]	3	4	5	8[2]	7	6	9[1]	10	11			13			14	12							9
1	2	3	4	5		7■	6		10	11		8[2]	9[1]	13			12							10
1			4	5			6		11	9	12		8[1]	7		2	10	3						11
1	2		4	5		6	7		11	9			8				10	3						12
1	2	12	4■	5		6[3]	7		11	9		14	8[1]			13	10[2]	3						13
1	2	3		5		6	7		11	9	13	12	8[2]				10[1]	4						14
1	2	3	4	5		6	7		11	9	13	12	8[1]				10[2]							15
1	2	3	4	5[3]		6	7		11	10		12	8[2]		9[1]		13		14					16
1	2	3	4	5		6		12	11	10[3]		14	8[2]	7	9[1]		13							17
1	2	3	4	5		6[3]	7	12	11	10	14		8[1]		9[2]		13							18
1	2	3	4	5		6	7		11	10			8	12	9[1]									19
1	2	3	4	5		7[3]	6	13	11	10			12		9[2]		8[1]			14				20
1	2	3	4	5			6	12	11	10		13	8[1]	7	9[2]									21
1	2[1]	3	4	5		6	7	13	11	10			8[2]		9[3]	12				14				22
1		3	4	5		6[3]	7	12	11			13	8		9[2]	2	10[1]			14				23
1		3	4	5			6	13	10			8[1]	9	7		2	11[2]			12				24
1		3	4	5			6		10		14	8[1]	9[3]	7[2]	13	2	11			12				25
1		3	4	5		7	6	11[2]	10		13	14	9[3]		12	2				8[1]				26
1		3	4	5		7	6	11[3]	10			8[2]	9[1]		14	2	12			13				27
1	2	3	4	5		7	8	11[3]	10		14		9[1]		13		12			6[2]				28
1	2	3	4	5		6[3]	7	12	11		13	14	8				10[1]			9[2]				29
1	2	3	4	5		6	9	10[3]	11			14	8[2]	7[1]	12		13							30
1	2■	3	4	5		9	8		11		12	10[1]	7[3]	6[2]	13		14							31
1		3	4	5		6[1]	7		11		13	12	8[3]		9[2]	2	10				14			32
1	2	3	4	5		6	7		11		13	12	8[1]		9		10[2]							33
1	2	3	4	5		7[1]	6		11■		13	12	8		9[2]		10[3]				14			34
1	2[1]	3	4	5		7	6			14	11	13	8[3]		9[2]	12	10							35
1		3		5		6	9		11	12	13	7[2]	8[1]			2	10[3]	4			14			36
1		2	4	5		12	6		11	9[1]			8[3]	7[2]			10	3				13	14	37
1		2	4	5			6		11	9		13	8[1]	7			10[2]	3				12		38

FA Cup

Third Round	Liverpool	(h)	1-4

Carabao Cup

Second Round	Burton Alb	(a)	3-1
Third Round	Bristol C	(a)	3-0
Fourth Round	Stoke C	(h)	0-1

Papa John's Trophy (Aston Villa U21)

Group A (N)	Sunderland	(a)	1-8
Group A (N)	Fleetwood T	(a)	0-3
Group A (N)	Carlisle U	(a)	1-3

BARNSLEY

FOUNDATION

Many clubs owe their inception to the Church and Barnsley are among them, for they were formed in 1887 by the Rev. T. T. Preedy, curate of Barnsley St Peter's, and went under that name until it was dropped in 1897 a year before being admitted to the Second Division of the Football League.

Oakwell Stadium, Grove Street, Barnsley, South Yorkshire S71 1ET.

Telephone: (01226) 211 211.

Ticket Office: (01226) 211 183.

Website: www.barnsleyfc.co.uk

Email: thereds@barnsleyfc.co.uk

Ground Capacity: 23,287.

Record Attendance: 40,255 v Stoke C, FA Cup 5th rd, 15 February 1936.

Pitch Measurements: 100.5m × 67m (110yd × 73.5yd).

Co-Chairmen: Chien Lee, Paul Conway.

Chief Executive: Dane Murphy.

Head Coach: Markus Schopp.

Assistant Coaches: Joseph Laumann, Tonda Eckert.

Colours: Red shirts with white trim, white shorts with red trim, red socks with white trim.

Year Formed: 1887.

Turned Professional: 1888.

Previous Name: 1887, Barnsley St Peter's; 1897, Barnsley.

Club Nickname: 'The Tykes', 'The Reds', 'The Colliers'.

Ground: 1887, Oakwell.

First Football League Game: 1 September 1898, Division 2, v Lincoln C (a) L 0–1 – Fawcett; McArtney, Nixon; King, Burleigh, Porteous; Davis, Lees, Murray, McCullough, McGee.

Record League Victory: 9–0 v Loughborough T, Division 2, 28 January 1899 – Greaves; McArtney, Nixon; Porteous, Burleigh, Howard; Davis (4), Hepworth (1), Lees (1), McCullough (1), Jones (2). 9–0 v Accrington S, Division 3 (N), 3 February 1934 – Ellis; Cookson, Shotton; Harper, Henderson, Whitworth; Spence (2), Smith (1), Blight (4), Andrews (1), Ashton (1).

Record Cup Victory: 6–0 v Blackpool, FA Cup 1st rd replay, 20 January 1910 – Mearns; Downs, Ness; Glendinning, Boyle (1), Utley; Bartrop, Gadsby (1), Lillycrop (2), Tufnell (2), Forman. 6–0 v Peterborough U, League Cup 1st rd 2nd leg, 15 September 1981 – Horn; Joyce, Chambers, Glavin (2), Banks, McCarthy, Evans, Parker (2), Aylott (1), McHale, Barrowclough (1).

Record Defeat: 0–9 v Notts Co, Division 2, 19 November 1927.

Most League Points (2 for a win): 67, Division 3 (N), 1938–39.

Most League Points (3 for a win): 91, FL 1, 2018–19.

HONOURS

League Champions: Division 3N – 1933–34, 1938–39, 1954–55.
Runners-up: First Division – 1996–97; FL 1 – 2018–19; Division 3 – 1980–81; Division 3N – 1953–54; Division 4 – 1967–68.

FA Cup Winners: 1912.
Runners-up: 1910.

League Cup: quarter-final – 1982.

League Trophy Winners: 2016.

FOOTBALL YEARBOOK FACT FILE

At the annual general meeting of Barnsley St Peter's, a proposal was made to change the name of the club to 'Barnsley Town Association Football Club'. This was defeated by 18 votes to 11 and it was not until 1897, when the previous Barnsley Football Club (a rugby club) had folded, that the present title was adopted.

Most League Goals: 118, Division 3 (N), 1933–34.

Highest League Scorer in Season: Cecil McCormack, 33, Division 2, 1950–51.

Most League Goals in Total Aggregate: Ernest Hine, 123, 1921–26 and 1934–38.

Most League Goals in One Match: 5, Frank Eaton v South Shields, Division 3 (N), 9 April 1927; 5, Peter Cunningham v Darlington, Division 3 (N), 4 February 1933; 5, Beau Asquith v Darlington, Division 3 (N), 12 November 1938; 5, Cecil McCormack v Luton T, Division 2, 9 September 1950.

Most Capped Player: Gerry Taggart, 35 (51), Northern Ireland.

Most League Appearances: Barry Murphy, 514, 1962–78.

Youngest League Player: Reuben Noble-Lazarus, 15 years 45 days v Ipswich T, 30 September 2008.

Record Transfer Fee Received: £3,000,000 (rising to £10,125,000) from Everton for John Stones, January 2013.

Record Transfer Fee Paid: £1,500,000 to Partizan Belgrade for Georgi Hristov, July 1997; £1,500,000 to QPR for Mike Sheron, January 1999.

Football League Record: 1898 Elected to Division 2; 1932–34 Division 3 (N); 1934–38 Division 2; 1938–39 Division 3 (N); 1946–53 Division 2; 1953–55 Division 3 (N); 1955–59 Division 2; 1959–65 Division 3; 1965–68 Division 4; 1968–72 Division 3; 1972–79 Division 4; 1979–81 Division 3; 1981–92 Division 2; 1992–97 Division 1; 1997–98 Premier League; 1998–2002 Division 1; 2002–04 Division 2; 2004–06 FL 1; 2006–14 FL C; 2014–16 FL 1; 2016–18 FL C; 2018–19 FL 1; 2019– FL C.

LATEST SEQUENCES

Longest Sequence of League Wins: 10, 5.3.1955 – 23.4.1955.

Longest Sequence of League Defeats: 9, 14.3.1953 – 25.4.1953.

Longest Sequence of League Draws: 7, 28.3.1911 – 22.4.1911.

Longest Sequence of Unbeaten League Matches: 21, 1.1.1934 – 5.5.1934.

Longest Sequence Without a League Win: 26, 13.12.1952 – 26.8.1953.

Successive Scoring Runs: 44 from 2.10.1926.

Successive Non-scoring Runs: 6 from 27.11.1971.

MANAGERS

Arthur Fairclough 1898–1901 (*Secretary-Manager*)
John McCartney 1901–04 (*Secretary-Manager*)
Arthur Fairclough 1904–12
John Hastie 1912–14
Percy Lewis 1914–19
Peter Sant 1919–26
John Commins 1926–29
Arthur Fairclough 1929–30
Brough Fletcher 1930–37
Angus Seed 1937–53
Tim Ward 1953–60
Johnny Steele 1960–71 (*continued as General Manager*)
John McSeveney 1971–72
Johnny Steele (*General Manager*) 1972–73
Jim Iley 1973–78
Allan Clarke 1978–80
Norman Hunter 1980–84
Bobby Collins 1984–85
Allan Clarke 1985–89
Mel Machin 1989–93
Viv Anderson 1993–94
Danny Wilson 1994–98
John Hendrie 1998–99
Dave Bassett 1999–2000
Nigel Spackman 2001
Steve Parkin 2001–02
Glyn Hodges 2002–03
Gudjon Thordarson 2003–04
Paul Hart 2004–05
Andy Ritchie 2005–06
Simon Davey 2007–09 (*Caretaker from November 2006*)
Mark Robins 2009–11
Keith Hill 2011–12
David Flitcroft 2012–13
Danny Wilson 2013–15
Lee Johnson 2015–16
Paul Heckingbottom 2016–18
Jose Morais 2018
Daniel Stendel 2018–19
Gerhard Struber 2019–20
Valerien Ismael 2020–21
Markus Schopp June 2021–

TEN YEAR LEAGUE RECORD

		P	*W*	*D*	*L*	*F*	*A*	*Pts*	*Pos*
2011-12	FL C	46	13	9	24	49	74	48	21
2012-13	FL C	46	14	13	19	56	70	55	21
2013-14	FL C	46	9	12	25	44	77	39	23
2014-15	FL 1	46	17	11	18	62	61	62	11
2015-16	FL 1	46	22	8	16	70	54	74	6
2016-17	FL C	46	15	13	18	64	67	58	14
2017-18	FL C	46	9	14	23	48	72	41	22
2018-19	FL 1	46	26	13	7	80	39	91	2
2019-20	FL C	46	12	13	21	49	69	49	21
2020-21	FL C	46	23	9	14	58	50	78	5

DID YOU KNOW?

Although Barnsley have played at Oakwell since the club was formed in 1887 it was not until 1907 that they were able to purchase the freehold of the ground. The club directors paid a sum of £1,376 for the five-acre plot, mostly funding the purchase from the sale of three players in the 1906–07 season.

BARNSLEY – SKY BET CHAMPIONSHIP 2020–21 LEAGUE RECORD

Match No.	Date	Venue	Opponents	Result	H/T Score	Lg Pos.	Goalscorers	Attendance
1	Sept 12	H	Luton T	L 0-1	0-0	15		0
2	19	A	Reading	L 0-2	0-0	20		0
3	26	H	Coventry C	D 0-0	0-0	20		0
4	Oct 3	A	Middlesbrough	L 1-2	0-1	21	Woodrow (pen) ^{89}	0
5	17	H	Bristol C	D 2-2	1-0	23	Helik ^{2}, Woodrow (pen) ^{90}	0
6	21	A	Stoke C	D 2-2	2-1	21	Simoes ^{18}, Frieser ^{45}	0
7	24	A	Millwall	D 1-1	1-1	21	Mowatt ^{44}	0
8	27	H	QPR	W 3-0	2-0	16	Woodrow (pen) ^{27}, Chaplin ^{37}, Barbet (og) ^{64}	0
9	31	H	Watford	W 1-0	1-0	15	Mowatt ^{6}	0
10	Nov 3	A	Cardiff C	L 0-3	0-2	17		0
11	7	A	Derby Co	W 2-0	1-0	16	Chaplin ^{30}, Adeboyejo ^{83}	0
12	21	H	Nottingham F	W 2-0	0-0	13	Styles ^{85}, Woodrow ^{88}	0
13	24	H	Brentford	L 0-1	0-0	14		0
14	28	A	Blackburn R	L 1-2	0-1	16	Palmer ^{90}	0
15	Dec 1	A	Birmingham C	W 2-1	0-0	13	Woodrow (pen) ^{71}, Styles ^{84}	0
16	4	H	Bournemouth	L 0-4	0-2	15		0
17	9	H	Wycombe W	W 2-1	1-0	16	Styles ^{30}, Woodrow (pen) ^{61}	0
18	12	A	Sheffield W	W 2-1	2-1	13	Woodrow ^{14}, Frieser ^{37}	0
19	15	H	Preston NE	W 2-1	0-1	9	Mowatt ^{54}, Adeboyejo ^{80}	0
20	19	A	Swansea C	L 0-2	0-1	13		0
21	26	H	Huddersfield T	W 2-1	1-1	10	Helik 2 $^{21, 90}$	0
22	29	A	Rotherham U	W 2-1	2-0	8	Woodrow ^{8}, Mowatt ^{15}	0
23	Jan 2	A	Norwich C	L 0-1	0-0	9		0
24	16	H	Swansea C	L 0-2	0-1	10		0
25	19	A	Watford	L 0-1	0-1	10		0
26	27	H	Cardiff C	D 2-2	1-0	12	Andersen ^{20}, Woodrow ^{52}	0
27	30	A	Nottingham F	D 0-0	0-0	12		0
28	Feb 14	A	Brentford	W 2-0	1-0	12	Chaplin ^{13}, Morris ^{47}	0
29	17	H	Blackburn R	W 2-1	0-0	10	Morris ^{72}, Mowatt ^{90}	0
30	20	A	Bristol C	W 1-0	0-0	10	Morris ^{67}	0
31	24	H	Stoke C	W 2-0	1-0	8	Styles ^{9}, Dike ^{90}	0
32	27	H	Millwall	W 2-1	1-1	7	Woodrow ^{2}, Helik ^{59}	0
33	Mar 3	A	QPR	W 3-1	2-1	7	Dike ^{23}, Mowatt ^{29}, Morris ^{57}	0
34	6	H	Birmingham C	W 1-0	0-0	6	Dike ^{49}	0
35	10	H	Derby Co	D 0-0	0-0	6		0
36	13	A	Bournemouth	W 3-2	1-2	6	Helik ^{16}, Frieser ^{60}, Morris ^{80}	0
37	17	A	Wycombe W	W 3-1	1-0	5	Woodrow (pen) ^{45}, Dike 2 $^{49, 81}$	0
38	20	H	Sheffield W	L 1-2	0-1	5	Morris ^{78}	0
39	Apr 2	H	Reading	D 1-1	0-1	5	Mowatt (pen) ^{61}	0
40	5	A	Luton T	W 2-1	1-0	5	Dike 2 $^{27, 59}$	0
41	10	H	Middlesbrough	W 2-0	0-0	5	Mowatt ^{62}, Dike ^{75}	0
42	18	A	Coventry C	L 0-2	0-1	6		0
43	21	A	Huddersfield T	W 1-0	0-0	6	Dike ^{65}	0
44	24	H	Rotherham U	W 1-0	1-0	5	Morris ^{2}	0
45	May 1	A	Preston NE	L 0-2	0-1	6		0
46	8	H	Norwich C	D 2-2	2-1	5	Woodrow ^{24}, Chaplin ^{43}	0

Final League Position: 5

GOALSCORERS

League (58): Woodrow 12 (6 pens), Dike 9, Mowatt 8 (1 pen), Morris 7, Helik 5, Chaplin 4, Styles 4, Frieser 3, Adeboyejo 2, Andersen 1, Palmer 1, Simoes 1, own goal 1.
FA Cup (3): Helik 1, Styles 1, Woodrow 1 (1 pen).
Carabao Cup (3): Schmidt 1, Williams J 1, Woodrow 1.
Championship Play-Offs (1): Woodrow 1.

Walton J 24	Sollbauer M 34 + 3	Andersen M 46	Williams J 7 + 14	Ludewig K 3 + 1	Mowatt A 44	Styles C 40 + 2	Ritzmaier M 3	Simoes E 4 + 4	Woodrow C 41 + 1	Chaplin C 31 + 3	Frieser D 26 + 16	Palmer R 22 + 12	Schmidt P 2 + 6	Helik M 43	Thomas L 7 + 12	Halme A 3 + 15	Collins B 22	Adeboyejo V 9 + 23	Odour C 5 + 6	Kane H 6 + 18	Brittain C 40	James M 13 + 2	Miller G — + 5	Moon J 1 + 2	Morris C 6 + 17	Sibbick T 11 + 10	Dike D 13 + 6	Kitching L — + 1	*Match No.*
1	2	3	4	5	6	7	8^2	9^1	10	11^3	12	13	14																1
1	2	4■	8	5	6	12	7			11^3	10^2		13	3■	9^1	14													2
1	2	4	8	5	7	6		13	10	11^3	12		14	3^1	9^2														3
	2	4	5	13	6	8	7^2	14	10		11^1			3	9^3		1	12											4
1	2	4	5		6			13	10	11^3	14	7^1		3	9				8^2	12									5
1		4	2		7			9^2	11		10	6^1	14	3	13				8	12	5^3								6
1	2	4			7^3			9^1		11	10	14		3	13				8	12	5	6^2							7
1	2	4			7	6		14	10^2	11	9^3		13	3					8^1		5	12							8
1	2	4			7	8				9	10		11^2	3					12	14	5^1	6^3	13						9
1	2	4			6	8		10^1		9	5		11^2	3		14		13	12			7^3							10
1	2	4			6	8			11^3	9	10^2			3		14		13		12	5	7^1							11
1	2	4	16		7^4	8			10	11^3	9^1			3	13			14	15	12	5^5	6^2							12
1	2	4			7^2	8			10	9^4	11^1			3	12			14	15	13	5	6^3							13
1	2	4			7^3	8^5			10^4	9^2	12	15		3	11^1			13	14	6	5		16						14
1	2	4			6^1	8			11^5	10^3	15	12		3	14	16		9^4		7^2	5	13							15
1	2	4			7	8^2			11	10^1	12	16		3^4	13	15		9^3	14	6^5	5								16
1	2	4			7^4	8			11	9^1	13	15			10^2	3		14		12	5	6^3							17
1	2	4			7^5	8			11^4	10^2	9^3	16			13	3		14		12	5	6^1	15						18
1	2	4			7	8			11	10^2	9^1			3	12			13		14	5	6^3							19
1	2	4			7^5				10^1	11^2	9^3	15		3	13			14	8	16	5	6^4	12						20
1	2	4			7^4	8			10^5	11^3	9^1	15		3	14			12		13	5	6^2	16						21
1	2	4			7^3	8			10		11^1	12		3	13			9			5	6^2		14					22
1	2	4				8			10		9^1	13	14	3	11^3			12		7	5	6^2							23
1	2^4	4			6	8			10	11^2		12		3	15			9^3		7^1	5				13	14			24
1	2	3			6	8^4			10	11^1	12	7^3		4				9^2		14	5				13	15			25
	14	4			7	8			10		9^1	6^2		3			1	11		13	5				12	2^3			26
	14	4	15		7	8			10	11^1	9^2			3			1	12		6^4	5				13	2^3			27
	2^4	4	16		7	8			12	11^1	13	6^5		3			1	14			5				10^3	15	9^2		28
		4	12		7	8^1			11^4	9^3	14	6^5		3			1	10^2		16	5				15	2	13		29
	2^4	4	14		7	8^2			11^3	9^1	16	6		3			1	12			5				13	15	10^5		30
	16	4			7	8			10^5	15	9^1	6^3		3		14	1	13			5				11^2	2^4	12		31
	2^1	4	15		7	8^4			9^5		16	6^2		3		13	1	14			5				11	12	10^3		32
		4	16		7	8^5			11^1	9^2	12	6^4		3		15	1	13			5				14	2	10^3		33
	2^4	4	13		7	8^1			10^5		9^2	6^3		3		14	1	16			5				12	15	11		34
		4	14		7	8^1			10^2	9^3		6^4		3			1	12		15	5				13	2	11		35
		4	8^1		7	14			10	11^2	9^4	6^3		3			1			12	5				13	2	15		36
	2^3	4	15		7■	8^4			10^5		9^2	6^1		3		12	1			16	5				14	13	11		37
	2^1	4			7	8			10^4	15	9^2	6^3		3		13	1				5				14	12	11		38
	2	4			7	8			11^2		9	6^3		3		14	1	10^1			5				13		12		39
		4			7	8			10^3		14	6^2		3		12	1	9^1			5				13	2	11		40
		4			6	8			10^2	14	9^1	7^3		3		13	1				5				12	2	11		41
		4			7	8			10^2	9^1	14	6^3		3		13	1				5				12	2	11		42
	2	4	13		7	8			11		9^1	6^2		3			1				5				10		12		43
	2^2	4	12		7	8^1			10					3		6	1	14			5				9^3	13	11		44
	2^3	4	16		7	8^5			11^4	9^2		6^1		3			1	15			5			14	13	12	10		45
		4	15			8			11^3	9^2	13	6		3			1	14			5			7^4	10^1	2^5	12	16	46

FA Cup

Third Round	Tranmere R	(h)	2-0
Fourth Round	Norwich C	(h)	1-0
Fifth Round	Chelsea	(h)	0-1

Carabao Cup

First Round	Nottingham F	(h)	1-0
Second Round	Middlesbrough	(a)	2-0
Third Round	Chelsea	(a)	0-6

Championship Play-Offs

Semi-Final 1st leg	Swansea C	(h)	0-1
Semi-Final 2nd leg	Swansea C	(a)	1-1

BARROW

FOUNDATION

Barrow was home to a number of junior soccer clubs at the start of the twentieth century before a public meeting was called to set up a senior team in the town. Almost 800 people attended the meeting held in the Drill Hall on the night of Tuesday 16 July 1901 which resulted in the formation of Barrow Association Football Club. A team was put together made up, in the main, of seasoned professionals, some of whom were described as "bordering the veteran stage" and £300 was spent on laying out the club's new ground. The newly formed Barrow AFC were elected to the Lancashire League for the 1901–02 season and after making a promising start they eventually finished 10th out of 14 clubs.

The Progression Solicitors Stadium, Wilkie Road, Barrow-in-Furness, Cumbria LA14 5UW.

Telephone: (01229) 666010.

Website: www.barrowafc.com

Email: office@barrowafc.com

Ground Capacity: 5,916.

Record Attendance: 16,854 v Swansea T, FA Cup 3rd rd, 9 January 1954.

Pitch Measurements: 101m × 68m (110.5yd × 74yd).

Chairman: Paul Hornby.

Directors: Tony Shearer, Kristian Wilkes.

Manager: Mark Cooper.

Assistant Manager: Richard Dryden.

Colours: Blue shirts with white trim, blue shorts with white trim, white socks with blue trim.

Year Formed: 1901.

Turned Professional: 1908.

Club Nickname: 'The Bluebirds'.

Grounds: 1901, The Strawberry Ground; 1904, Ainslie Street; 1905, Little Park, Roose; 1909, Holker Street (renamed The Progression Solicitors Stadium 2019).

First Football League Game (since 2020): 12 September 2020, FL, v Lincoln C (a) L 0–1 – Dixon; Barry, Jones J, Hird, Ntlhe, Brown (Wilson), Jones M, Hardcastle, Beadling (Biggins), Hindle (James), Angus (1 pen).

HONOURS

League Champions: National League – 2019–20; National League North – 2014–15. Lancashire Combination – 1920–21.
Runners-up: Lancashire Combination Division 2 – 1904–05.

FA Cup: Never past 3rd rd.

League Cup: Never past 2nd rd.

FA Trophy Winners: 1989–90, 2009–10.

Lancashire Senior Cup Winners: 1954–55.

FOOTBALL YEARBOOK FACT FILE

Barrow inside-forward Fred Laycock left the pitch during his team's game at Rotherham County in March 1925 and signed for rivals Nelson before returning to continue playing. The incident resulted in a complaint from Rotherham. Nelson were subsequently fined five guineas following a Football League management committee hearing over what was described as the 'unprecedented circumstances'.

Record League Victory: 12–1 v Gateshead, Division 3(N), 5 May 1934.

Record League Defeat: 1–10 v Hartlepools U, Division 4, 4 April 1966–67.

Most League Points (2 for a win): 59, Division 4, 1966–67.

Most League Points (3 for a win): 50, FL 2, 2020–21.

Most League Goals: 116, Division 3(N), 1933–34.

Highest League Scorer in Season: 39, Jimmy Shankly, Division 3(N), 1933–34.

Highest League Goals in One Match: 5, Jimmy Shankly v Gateshead, Division 3(N), 5 May 1934.

Most League Goals in Total Aggregate: Billy Gordon, 145, 1949–58.

Most Capped Player: Harry Panayiotou, 5 (29), Saint Kitts & Nevis.

Most League Appearances: Brian Arrowsmith, 378, 1952–71.

Youngest League Player (since 2020): Jayden Reid, 19 years 181 days v Bolton W, 20 October 2020.

Football League Record: 1921 Original Member of Division 3 (N); 1958–67 Division 4; 1967–70 Division 3; 1970–72 Division 4; 1972 Failed to gain re-election to Football League; 2020 Promoted from National League; 2020– FL 2.

LATEST SEQUENCES

Longest Sequence of League Wins: 4, 6.3.2021 – 20.3.2021.

Longest Sequence of League Defeats: 5, 24.11.2020 – 15.12.2020.

Longest Sequence of League Draws: 2, 5.4.2021 – 10.4.2021.

Longest Sequence of Unbeaten League Matches: 4, 2.4.2021 – 13.4.2021.

Longest Sequence Without a League Win: 8, 3.11.2020 – 15.12.2020.

Successive Scoring Runs: 5 from 27.3.2021.

Successive Non-scoring Runs: 3 from 17.4.2021.

MANAGERS

Jacob Fletcher 1901–04; **E. Freeland** 1904–05; **W. Smith** 1905–06; **Alec Craig** 1906–07; **Roger Charnley** 1907–08; **Jacob Fletcher** 1908–09; **Jas P. Phillips** 1909–13; **John Parker** 1913–20; **William Dickinson** 1920–22; **Jimmy Atkinson** 1922–23; **J. E. Moralee** 1923–26; **Robert Greenhalgh** 1926; **William Dickinson** 1926–27; **John S. Maconnachie** 1927–28; **Andrew Walker** 1929–30; **Thomas Miller** 1930; **John Commins** 1930–32; **Tommy Lowes** 1932–37; **James Y. Bissett** 1937; **Fred Pentland** 1938–40; **John Commins** 1945–47; **Andy Beattie** 1947–49; **Jack Hacking** 1949–55; **Joe Harvey** 1955–57; **Norman Dodgin** 1957–58; **Willie Brown** 1958–59; **Bill Rogers** 1959; **Ron Staniforth** 1959–64; **Don McEvoy** 1964–67; **Colin Appleton** 1967–69; **Fred Else** 1969; **Norman Bodell** 1969–70; **Don McEvoy** 1970–71; **Bill Rogers** 1971; **Jack Crompton** 1971–72; **Peter Kane** 1972–74; **Brian Arrowsmith** 1974–75; **Ron Yeats** 1975–77; **Alan Coglan and Billy McAdams** 1977; **David Hughes** 1977; **Brian McManus** 1977–79; **Micky Taylor** 1979–83; **Vic Halom** 1983–84; **Peter McDonnell** 1984; **Joe Wojciechowicz** 1984; **Brian Kidd** 1984–85; **John Cooke** 1985; **Bob Murphy** 1985; **Maurice Whittle** 1985; **David Johnson** 1985–86; **Glenn Skivington and Neil McDonald** 1986; **Ray Wilkie** 1986; **Neil McDonald** 1991; **John King** 1991–92; **Graham Heathcote** 1992; **Richard Dinnis** 1992–93; **Mick Cloudsdale** 1993–94; **Tony Hesketh** 1994–96; **Neil McDonald and Franny Ventre** 1996; **Mike Walsh** 1996; **Owen Brown** 1996–99; **Shane Westley** 1999; **Greg Challender** 1999; **Kenny Lowe** 1999–2003; **Lee Turnbull** 2003–05; **Darren Edmondson** 2005; **Phil Wilson** 2005–07; **Darren Sheridan and David Bayliss** 2007–12; **David Bayliss** 2012–13; **Alex Meechan** 2013; **Darren Edmondson** 2013–15; **Paul Cox** 2015–17; **Micky Moore** 2017; **Neill Hornby** 2017; **Ady Pennock** 2017–18; **Ian Evatt** 2018–20; **David Dunn** 2020; **Michael Jolly** 2020; **Mark Cooper** May 2021–

TEN YEAR LEAGUE RECORD

		P	W	D	L	F	A	Pts	Pos
2011-12	NL	46	17	9	20	62	76	60	13
2012-13	NL	46	11	13	22	45	83	46	22
2013-14	NLN	42	14	14	14	50	56	56	11
2014-15	NLN	42	26	9	7	81	43	87	1
2015-16	NL	46	17	14	15	64	71	65	11
2016-17	NL	46	20	15	11	72	53	75	7
2017-18	NL	46	11	16	19	51	63	49	20
2018-19	NL	46	17	13	16	52	51	64	11
2019-20	NL	37	21	7	9	68	39	70	1§
2020-21	FL 2	46	13	11	22	53	59	50	21

§Decided on points-per-game (1.89)

DID YOU KNOW ?

Bobby Knox became the first substitute to score when he netted for Barrow against Wrexham at Holker Street on the opening day of the 1965–66. Later in the season he became the first substitute to save a penalty when he came on as a direct replacement for injured keeper Lionel Duffin against Doncaster Rovers.

BARROW – SKY BET LEAGUE TWO 2020–21 LEAGUE RECORD

Match No.	Date	Venue	Opponents	Result	H/T Score	Lg Pos.	Goalscorers	Attendance
1	Sept 12	H	Stevenage	D 1-1	1-0	10	Angus (pen) [12]	0
2	19	A	Newport Co	L 1-2	1-1	17	Hardcastle [28]	0
3	26	H	Colchester U	D 1-1	0-1	19	Jones, M [54]	0
4	Oct 3	A	Carlisle U	L 0-1	0-1	21		0
5	10	H	Leyton Orient	D 1-1	1-0	21	Kay [16]	0
6	17	A	Harrogate T	L 0-1	0-1	22		0
7	20	H	Bolton W	D 3-3	3-2	21	Taylor, C [1], Jones, M [4], Angus [20]	0
8	24	H	Walsall	D 2-2	1-1	19	Angus (pen) [25], James [50]	0
9	27	A	Mansfield T	W 4-2	2-1	18	Barry [10], Brough [23], Kay [61], Biggins [79]	0
10	31	H	Bradford C	W 1-0	1-0	15	Brown [18]	0
11	Nov 3	A	Grimsby T	L 0-1	0-0	18		0
12	14	A	Cambridge U	D 1-1	0-0	18	Platt [90]	0
13	21	H	Forest Green R	D 2-2	0-0	18	James [73], Angus (pen) [83]	0
14	24	H	Oldham Ath	L 3-4	1-2	19	Quigley [16], Platt [79], Piergianni (og) [90]	0
15	Dec 1	A	Morecambe	L 0-1	0-1	20		0
16	5	H	Salford C	L 0-1	0-0	21		819
17	12	A	Crawley T	L 2-4	1-1	21	Kay [33], Hird [50]	0
18	15	A	Scunthorpe U	L 1-2	1-1	22	Quigley [16]	0
19	19	H	Cheltenham T	W 3-0	1-0	22	Quigley (pen) [43], James [52], Biggins [74]	1363
20	26	A	Port Vale	W 2-0	1-0	21	Quigley [23], Brough [50]	0
21	29	H	Tranmere R	D 1-1	0-1	20	Quigley (pen) [65]	1131
22	Jan 9	A	Southend U	L 0-1	0-1	21		0
23	16	H	Scunthorpe U	W 1-0	0-0	20	Kay [58]	0
24	30	A	Bradford C	L 1-2	1-1	22	Quigley (pen) [37]	0
25	Feb 6	H	Cambridge U	L 0-2	0-1	22		0
26	16	A	Salford C	L 0-1	0-1	23		0
27	20	H	Morecambe	L 1-2	0-1	23	Quigley [65]	0
28	23	A	Oldham Ath	W 1-0	0-0	22	Quigley [89]	0
29	27	A	Bolton W	L 0-1	0-0	23		0
30	Mar 2	H	Harrogate T	L 0-1	0-0	23		0
31	6	H	Mansfield T	W 2-0	0-0	22	Brough 2 [74, 77]	0
32	12	A	Walsall	W 1-0	0-0	22	Kay [87]	0
33	16	A	Cheltenham T	W 2-0	1-0	22	Jones, J [2], Long (og) [66]	0
34	20	H	Crawley T	W 3-2	2-1	21	Davies [9], Quigley 2 (1 pen) [36 (p), 90]	0
35	23	H	Grimsby T	L 0-1	0-0	22		0
36	27	A	Stevenage	L 1-2	0-0	22	Andrew [78]	0
37	Apr 2	H	Newport Co	W 2-1	0-1	21	Quigley [56], Devitt [84]	0
38	5	A	Colchester U	D 1-1	0-1	21	Beadling [88]	0
39	10	H	Carlisle U	D 2-2	2-1	21	Quigley [19], Brough [24]	0
40	13	H	Exeter C	W 2-1	1-0	20	Brough [45], Quigley [90]	0
41	17	A	Leyton Orient	L 0-2	0-0	21		0
42	20	H	Port Vale	L 0-2	0-1	22		0
43	24	A	Tranmere R	L 0-1	0-0	22		0
44	27	A	Forest Green R	W 2-0	2-0	20	Quigley (pen) [18], Thomas [25]	0
45	May 1	H	Southend U	L 1-2	1-1	21	Quigley [19]	0
46	8	A	Exeter C	D 1-1	0-1	21	Beadling [56]	0

Final League Position: 21

GOALSCORERS

League (53): Quigley 15 (5 pens), Brough 6, Kay 5, Angus 4 (3 pens), James 3, Beadling 2, Biggins 2, Jones, M 2, Platt 2, Andrew 1, Barry 1, Brown 1, Davies 1, Devitt 1, Hardcastle 1, Hird 1, Jones, J 1, Taylor, C 1, Thomas 1, own goals 2.
FA Cup (0).
Carabao Cup (0).
Papa John's Trophy (2): Angus 1, Taylor J 1.

Dixon J 46	Barry B 33	Jones J 18 + 3	Hird S 15	Ntlhe K 20 + 2	Brown C 15 + 4	Jones M 13	Hardcastle L 11 + 1	Beadling T 19 + 10	Hindle J 1 + 1	Angus D 12 + 10	James L 33 + 11	Biggins H 16 + 6	Wilson S 4 + 5	Gribbin C — + 1	Quigley S 37 + 1	Kay J 22 + 7	Brough P 39 + 4	Zouma Y 4	Taylor C 20 + 11	Platt M 24	Taylor J 28 + 6	Reid J 2 + 8	Sea D — + 8	Eardley N 17 + 2	Thomas B 18 + 3	Davies T 12	Banks O 15 + 5	Donohue D 3 + 1	Bramall D — + 3	Devitt J 7 + 10	Goodridge M — + 2	Ndjoli M — + 2	Andrew C 2 + 9	*Match No.*
1	2	3	4	5	6³	7	8	9²	10¹	11	12	13	14																					1
1	5	2	3²	4¹	9³	6	8	7	14	11	10		12	13																				2
1	2	3			5	6	9	8		11¹	12	7	4²		10	13																		3
1	5	2¹			9	8	7	3		11	13	6²			10	12	4																	4
1	5					8¹	7	3		10	11	12				9	4	2	6															5
1	5			9			7¹	8²		14	10	13				11	4	2³	6	3	12													6
1	5				14	8				7		12			10²	11³	4	2	6¹	3	9	13												7
1	5		2		12	7				10²	11	9³				8¹	4		14	3	6	13												8
1	5		2			7				11²	10	9				8	4		12	3	6¹	13												9
1	5		2		8	6				10¹	11	9²					4		13	3	7	12												10
1	5		2		8	7				10¹	11	9²					4		13	3	6³	12	14											11
1	5		2	13		6				10¹	11	9³			12	8	4²			3	7	14												12
1	5		2	8¹	12	7				13	10	9			11²		4			3	6													13
1	5²				8	6				14	11	9³			10	13	4	2	12	3	7¹													14
1	5		2■							14	11²	9³	12		10	8¹	4		6	3	7	13												15
1				5¹	2			6³		13	8	14	4		11	10	12		7	3		9²												16
1			2		5■			6		12	9²	13	4⁵		11	8³	16		14	3	7⁴	10¹	15											17
1			3					12		10²	13	8	5¹		11³	2	6		9	4	7	14												18
1			2		5			6		14	11	9²	12		10³	8¹	4		7	3	13													19
1			2		5			6			11	9¹	13		10	8²	4		7	3	12													20
1		13	2		5		7	6		14	11¹	9■			10³	8²	4			3	12													21
1		12	2¹		5²		8	6		13	11				10	9	4		7	3														22
1		3					8³	7		12	11¹	6²			10	9	5		14	4	13			2										23
1							7¹					9			11	10	8			4				5	2	3²	6³	12	13	14				24
1		16					14	12²			15				11⁵	9	5		6¹					2	3	4	7⁴	8	13	10³				25
1	6³						8¹				10				11	13	5							2	3	4	7	9²			12	14		26
1	6	3¹									13				11	9	5							2⁴	14	4³	7²	8	15	10	12			27
1	6	3		9¹							10				11		5				8			2		4	7			12				28
1	6	3		9¹							10				11	12	5				8			2	4		7²			13				29
1	6³	3		9¹							10				11		5		12		8			2	4		7²			13		14		30
1	5	2		4				12			13				11	10²	9		8¹		7					3				6				31
1	5¹	2²		4							11⁴				10	15	9		8		7			12	13	3	14			6³				32
1		2		4¹							14				10⁴	11³	9		8²		7		15	5	12	3	6			13				33
1	6¹	2						13			11²				10		9		12		7		14	5	4	3	8³							34
1	9	2⁴						12			11				10		14		8		7²			5³	4	3	6¹			13			15	35
1	5	2		4³				7¹			14				10⁴	11	9		8		6²				3		12			13			15	36
1	5	2		4				12			11				10		9				8				3		7			6¹				37
1	5	2		4⁵				13			10				11	12	9¹		14		8³			15	3		7⁴			6²			16	38
1	6	2		4				13			11				10		9		8²		12			5¹	3		7³						14	39
1	6			4				12			10²				11		9		8¹		7			5	2	3							13	40
1	5							12			10³				11		9		8¹		7²		14	2	4	3	6						13	41
1	6			4				8³			11				10		9			3	7²			5¹	2		12			14			13	42
1	5			4				7³			10¹				11²		9		8	3			14		2		6			13			12	43
1	6¹			14	5³			7			13				11		9			3	8			2	4					12			10²	44
1				4	5			7¹			11⁵				10³	9²	13		16	3	8		15		2		12			6⁴			14	45
1				4	14			7			12				11¹		9		8⁴	3	6		13	5	2³		15						10²	46

FA Cup
First Round AFC Wimbledon (h) 0-0
(aet; AFC Wimbledon won 4-2 on penalties)

Carabao Cup
First Round Derby Co (a) 0-0
(Derby Co won 3-2 on penalties)

Papa John's Trophy
Group G (N) Blackpool (a) 0-0
(Blackpool won 5-3 on penalties)
Group G (N) Leeds U U21 (h) 2-2
(Barrow won 4-3 on penalties)
Group G (N) Accrington S (h) 0-1

BIRMINGHAM CITY

FOUNDATION

In 1875, cricketing enthusiasts who were largely members of Trinity Church, Bordesley, determined to continue their sporting relationships throughout the year by forming a football club which they called Small Heath Alliance. For their earliest games played on waste land in Arthur Street, the team included three Edden brothers and two James brothers.

St Andrew's Trillion Trophy Stadium, Cattell Road, Birmingham B9 4RL.

Telephone: (0121) 772 0101.

Ticket Office: (0121) 772 0101 (option 2).

Website: www.bcfc.com

Email: reception@bcfc.com

Ground Capacity: 29,805.

Record Attendance: 66,844 v Everton, FA Cup 5th rd, 11 February 1939.

Pitch Measurements: 100m × 65m (109.5yd × 71yd).

Directors: Wenqing Zhao, Chun Kong Yiu, Gannan Zheng, Yao Wang, Xuandong Ren.

Head Coach: Lee Bowyer.

Assistant Head Coach: Craig Gardner.

Colours: Blue shirts with white sleeves, white shorts with blue trim, blue socks.

Year Formed: 1875.

Turned Professional: 1885.

Previous Names: 1875, Small Heath Alliance; 1888, dropped 'Alliance'; 1905, Birmingham; 1945, Birmingham City.

Club Nickname: 'Blues'.

Grounds: 1875, waste ground near Arthur St; 1877, Muntz St, Small Heath; 1906, St Andrew's (renamed St Andrew's Trillion Trophy Stadium 2018).

First Football League Game: 3 September 1892, Division 2, v Burslem Port Vale (h) W 5–1 – Charsley; Bayley, Speller; Ollis, Jenkyns, Devey; Hallam (1), Edwards (1), Short (1), Wheldon (2), Hands.

Record League Victory: 12–0 v Walsall T Swifts, Division 2, 17 December 1892 – Charsley; Bayley, Jones; Ollis, Jenkyns, Devey; Hallam (2), Walton (3), Mobley (3), Wheldon (2), Hands (2). 12–0 v Doncaster R, Division 2, 11 April 1903 – Dorrington; Goldie, Wassell; Beer, Dougherty (1), Howard; Athersmith, Leonard (4), McRoberts (1), Wilcox (4), Field (1), (1 og).

Record Cup Victory: 9–2 v Burton W, FA Cup 1st rd, 31 October 1885 – Hedges; Jones, Evetts (1); Fred James, Felton, Arthur James (1); Davenport (2), Stanley (4), Simms, Figures, Morris (1).

Record Defeat: 1–9 v Blackburn R, Division 1, 5 January 1895; 1–9 v Sheffield W, Division 1, 13 December 1930; 0–8 v Bournemouth, FLC, 25 October 2014.

HONOURS

League Champions: Division 2 – 1892–93, 1920–21, 1947–48, 1954–55; Second Division – 1994–95.
Runners-up: FL C – 2006–07, 2008–09; Division 2 – 1893–94, 1900–01, 1902–03; 1971–72, 1984–85; Division 3 – 1991–92.

FA Cup: *Runners-up:* 1931, 1956.

League Cup Winners: 1963, 2011.
Runners-up: 2001.

League Trophy Winners: 1991, 1995.

European Competitions
Fairs Cup: 1955–58, 1958–60 *(runners-up)*, 1960–61 *(runners-up)*, 1961–62.
Europa League: 2011–12.

FOOTBALL YEARBOOK FACT FILE

Centre-forward Bud Houghton, who made four appearances for Birmingham City after signing from Bradford Park Avenue in October 1957, is believed to have been the first Anglo Indian player to appear in the Football League. Houghton, who scored his only senior goal for the Blues at West Bromwich Albion, later played for Southend United, Oxford United and Lincoln City.

Most League Points (2 for a win): 59, Division 2, 1947–48.

Most League Points (3 for a win): 89, Division 2, 1994–95.

Most League Goals: 103, Division 2, 1893–94 (only 28 games).

Highest League Scorer in Season: Walter Abbott, 34, Division 2, 1898–99 (Small Heath); Joe Bradford, 29, Division 1, 1927–28 (Birmingham City).

Most League Goals in Total Aggregate: Joe Bradford, 249, 1920–35.

Most League Goals in One Match: 5, Walter Abbott v Darwen, Division 2, 26 November, 1898; 5, John McMillan v Blackpool, Division 2, 2 March 1901; 5, James Windridge v Glossop, Division 2, 23 January 1915.

Most Capped Player: Maik Taylor, 58 (including 8 on loan at Fulham) (88), Northern Ireland.

Most League Appearances: Frank Womack, 491, 1908–28.

Youngest League Player: Jude Bellingham, 16 years 57 days v Swansea C, 25 August 2019.

Record Transfer Fee Received: £20,000,000 from Borussia Dortmund for Jude Bellingham, July 2020.

Record Transfer Fee Paid: £7,000,000 to Dinamo Zagreb for Ivan Sunjic, July 2019.

Football League Record: 1892 Elected to Division 2; 1894–96 Division 1; 1896–1901 Division 2; 1901–02 Division 1; 1902–03 Division 2; 1903–08 Division 1; 1908–21 Division 2; 1921–39 Division 1; 1946–48 Division 2; 1948–50 Division 1; 1950–55 Division 2; 1955–65 Division 1; 1965–72 Division 2; 1972–79 Division 1; 1979–80 Division 2; 1980–84 Division 1; 1984–85 Division 2; 1985–86 Division 1; 1986–89 Division 2; 1989–92 Division 3; 1992–94 Division 1; 1994–95 Division 2; 1995–2002 Division 1; 2002–06 Premier League; 2006–07 FL C; 2007–08 Premier League; 2008–09 FL C; 2009–11 Premier League; 2011– FL C.

LATEST SEQUENCES

Longest Sequence of League Wins: 13, 17.12.1892 – 16.9.1893.

Longest Sequence of League Defeats: 8, 28.9.1985 – 23.11.1985.

Longest Sequence of League Draws: 8, 18.9.1990 – 23.10.1990.

Longest Sequence of Unbeaten League Matches: 20, 3.9.1994 – 2.1.1995.

Longest Sequence Without a League Win: 17, 28.9.1985 – 18.1.1986.

Successive Scoring Runs: 24 from 24.9.1892.

Successive Non-scoring Runs: 6 from 11.2.1989.

MANAGERS

Alfred Jones 1892–1908 (*Secretary-Manager*)
Alec Watson 1908–10
Bob McRoberts 1910–15
Frank Richards 1915–23
Billy Beer 1923–27
William Harvey 1927–28
Leslie Knighton 1928–33
George Liddell 1933–39
William Camkin and Ted Goodier 1939–45
Harry Storer 1945–48
Bob Brocklebank 1949–54
Arthur Turner 1954–58
Pat Beasley 1959–60
Gil Merrick 1960–64
Joe Mallett 1964–65
Stan Cullis 1965–70
Fred Goodwin 1970–75
Willie Bell 1975–77
Sir Alf Ramsay 1977–78
Jim Smith 1978–82
Ron Saunders 1982–86
John Bond 1986–87
Garry Pendrey 1987–89
Dave Mackay 1989–91
Lou Macari 1991
Terry Cooper 1991–93
Barry Fry 1993–96
Trevor Francis 1996–2001
Steve Bruce 2001–07
Alex McLeish 2007–11
Chris Hughton 2011–12
Lee Clark 2012–14
Gary Rowett 2014–16
Gianfranco Zola 2016–17
Harry Redknapp 2017
Steve Cotterill 2017–18
Garry Monk 2018–19
Pep Clotet 2019–20
Aitor Karanka 2020–21
Lee Bowyer March 2021–

TEN YEAR LEAGUE RECORD

		P	W	D	L	F	A	Pts	Pos
2011-12	FL C	46	20	16	10	78	51	76	4
2012-13	FL C	46	15	16	15	63	69	61	12
2013-14	FL C	46	11	11	24	58	74	44	21
2014-15	FL C	46	16	15	15	54	64	63	10
2015-16	FL C	46	16	15	15	53	49	63	10
2016-17	FL C	46	13	14	19	45	64	53	19
2017-18	FL C	46	13	7	26	38	68	46	19
2018-19	FL C	46	14	19	13	64	58	52*	17
2019-20	FL C	46	12	14	20	54	75	50	20
2020-21	FL C	46	13	13	20	37	61	52	18

** 9 pts deducted.*

DID YOU KNOW ?

Birmingham City inaugurated their floodlights with a friendly fixture against Borussia Dortmund on 31 October 1956. The Blues wore a new set of shirts with an extra satin sheen, which made them sparkle under the lights. The match ended in a 3-3 draw in front of a crowd of 45,000.

BIRMINGHAM CITY – SKY BET CHAMPIONSHIP 2020–21 LEAGUE RECORD

Match No.	Date	Venue	Opponents	Result		H/T Score	Lg Pos.	Goalscorers	Attendance
1	Sept 12	H	Brentford	W	1-0	1-0	5	Bela [37]	0
2	19	A	Swansea C	D	0-0	0-0	5		0
3	26	H	Rotherham U	D	1-1	0-0	7	Bela (pen) [90]	0
4	Oct 4	A	Stoke C	D	1-1	0-0	8	Dean [65]	0
5	17	H	Sheffield W	L	0-1	0-0	15		0
6	20	A	Norwich C	L	0-1	0-0	17		0
7	24	A	QPR	D	0-0	0-0	17		0
8	28	H	Huddersfield T	W	2-1	1-0	15	Gardner [27], Jutkiewicz [90]	0
9	31	A	Preston NE	W	2-1	1-1	11	McGree [2], Gardner [85]	0
10	Nov 4	H	Wycombe W	L	1-2	1-0	14	Roberts [40]	0
11	7	H	Bournemouth	L	1-3	0-2	17	Hogan [55]	0
12	20	A	Coventry C	D	0-0	0-0	14		0
13	24	A	Luton T	D	1-1	1-1	17	Jutkiewicz (pen) [23]	0
14	28	H	Millwall	D	0-0	0-0	17		0
15	Dec 1	H	Barnsley	L	1-2	0-0	18	Hogan [56]	0
16	5	A	Bristol C	W	1-0	0-0	16	Dean [80]	0
17	9	A	Reading	W	2-1	2-0	15	Toral 2 [29, 37]	0
18	12	H	Watford	L	0-1	0-0	16		0
19	16	A	Cardiff C	L	2-3	1-1	17	Roberts [31], Ivan Sanchez [57]	0
20	19	H	Middlesbrough	L	1-4	1-2	17	Colin [15]	0
21	26	A	Nottingham F	D	0-0	0-0	17		0
22	29	H	Derby Co	L	0-4	0-3	18		0
23	Jan 2	H	Blackburn R	L	0-2	0-1	18		0
24	16	A	Middlesbrough	W	1-0	1-0	18	Hogan [26]	0
25	20	H	Preston NE	L	0-1	0-0	19		0
26	30	H	Coventry C	D	1-1	1-1	20	Bela (pen) [18]	0
27	Feb 2	A	Wycombe W	D	0-0	0-0	21		0
28	6	A	Bournemouth	L	2-3	1-1	22	Hogan 2 [27, 68]	0
29	13	H	Luton T	L	0-1	0-1	23		0
30	17	A	Millwall	L	0-2	0-1	23		0
31	20	A	Sheffield W	W	1-0	0-0	21	Hogan [63]	0
32	23	H	Norwich C	L	1-3	1-1	21	Ivan Sanchez [38]	0
33	27	H	QPR	W	2-1	0-1	21	Pedersen [82], Halilovic [85]	0
34	Mar 2	A	Huddersfield T	D	1-1	0-0	21	Roberts [67]	0
35	6	A	Barnsley	L	0-1	0-0	21		0
36	13	H	Bristol C	L	0-3	0-1	21		0
37	17	H	Reading	W	2-1	1-1	21	Jutkiewicz [4], Dean [71]	0
38	20	A	Watford	L	0-3	0-1	21		0
39	Apr 2	H	Swansea C	W	1-0	0-0	20	Hogan (pen) [90]	0
40	6	A	Brentford	D	0-0	0-0	21		0
41	10	H	Stoke C	W	2-0	1-0	18	Jutkiewicz 2 [42, 53]	0
42	18	A	Rotherham U	W	1-0	0-0	19	Dean [88]	0
43	21	H	Nottingham F	D	1-1	0-0	19	Roberts [49]	0
44	24	A	Derby Co	W	2-1	0-1	16	Jutkiewicz 2 [62, 84]	0
45	May 1	H	Cardiff C	L	0-4	0-2	18		0
46	8	A	Blackburn R	L	2-5	1-2	18	Pedersen [22], Jutkiewicz [50]	0

Final League Position: 18

GOALSCORERS

League (37): Jutkiewicz 8 (1 pen), Hogan 7 (1 pen), Dean 4, Roberts 4, Bela 3 (2 pens), Gardner 2, Ivan Sanchez 2, Pedersen 2, Toral 2, Colin 1, Halilovic 1, McGree 1.
FA Cup (0).
Carabao Cup (0).

Jeacock Z 2	Colin M 39 + 3	Dean H 42 + 1	Friend G 21 + 5	Pedersen K 35	Sunjic I 38 + 5	Clayton A 10 + 4	Ivan Sanchez A 31 + 9	Toral J 10 + 6	Bela J 26 + 9	Jutkiewicz L 25 + 17	Crowley D 1 + 2	George A — + 1	Gardner G 25 + 12	Etheridge N 43	Hogan S 28 + 5	Roberts M 29 + 7	McGree R 8 + 7	Leko J 15 + 19	San Jose M 19 + 8	Dacres-Cogley J 5	Kieftenbeld M 8 + 2	Boyd-Munce C 1	Clarke-Salter J 9 + 1	Halilovic A 9 + 8	Harper R 11 + 7	Valery Y 2 + 5	Cosgrove S 2 + 10	Seddon S 6 + 1	Miller A 2 + 3	Stirk R 2	Gordon N 1 + 1	Trueman C 1	Simmonds K — + 1	*Match No.*
1	2	3	4	5	6	7	8^{2}	9^{1}	10	11^{3}	12	13	14																					1
	2	3	4	5	6	7	8	9^{1}	10	11			12	1																				2
	2	3	4	5	7^{2}	8	6	12	9	10			13	1	11^{1}																			3
	2	3	4	5	6	7	8	9^{1}	10^{2}	11^{3}	12			1	14	13																		4
	2	3	4	5		7	8		10^{2}		9^{1}		6^{3}	1	11	14	12	13																5
	2	4	5	6	9	8▮	7		12					1	11	3^{2}		10^{1}	13															6
	2	4	5	6	9		13			12			7	1	11^{2}	3		10^{1}	8															7
	2	4	5		9^{2}	13	6		10	12			7^{3}	1	11^{1}	3		14	8															8
	14	4		9	5		8		12	10			13	1		2	7^{2}	11^{1}	3	6^{3}														9
	2	4		5	8		7^{2}		10	11			9^{1}	1		3	12	13	6															10
	5	4							12	11			6	1	10^{2}	2	8^{1}	13	3		7	9												11
	2	4	5		6		8	12	10	11				1		3	9^{1}		7															12
	2	4	6		9		12		14	11			7^{1}	1	10^{2}	3	13		8				5^{3}											13
	5	3	4	8	11		6		12	10				1		2		9^{1}	7															14
	5	3	13	8^{1}	14		6	16	12	15				1	11^{4}	2	9^{3}	10^{5}	7				4^{2}											15
	2	4	5		7		8	9^{1}	10	13				1	11^{2}	3					6			12										16
	2	4▮		5	7		8^{1}	9^{3}		13			14	1	11^{2}	3		10	12		6													17
	14			9▮	8	12	15			10			6	1		2		11^{3}	3	5^{2}	7^{1}		4^{4}	13										18
	2	4			6		8	9^{1}	13	11				1		3		10^{2}			7		5	12										19
	2	4		5	13	6^{2}	8^{3}	9^{4}	10^{5}	14			16	1	11	3		15	7^{1}		12													20
	2	4	5		7	6	8		10	13			12	1	11^{2}	3								9^{1}										21
	2	3	4	5^{2}	9^{4}	6	7		10^{1}	12			8^{5}	1	11^{3}			15	13		16		14											22
	13		5		7^{4}	15	8	12		11^{3}				1	14		9^{1}	10	3	2^{2}	6		4											23
	2	4	5		7	14	8	9^{1}	10^{3}	13				1	11^{2}	12			3		6													24
	2	4	5		7		8^{4}	9^{2}	10^{3}	12			15	1	11^{1}			13	3		6			14										25
	2	4		5	7^{4}	6^{1}	8^{3}	9^{2}	10	16			12	1	11^{5}	13		14	3						15									26
	2	4	12	5	6		9^{1}		11	10			8	1		3▮			7															27
	2^{4}	3	4	5	9^{2}		7^{5}		10^{1}	14			8	1	11^{3}			13	6						12	15	16							28
		3	4	5	16		7^{2}		10^{4}	14			8^{3}	1	11^{5}			13	6					9^{1}	12	2	15							29
	5^{4}	2		9	7^{2}		13		14	10^{3}			6	1	11			15	3^{1}				4		8	12								30
	2	3		5	6^{1}		7^{3}		10^{2}				9	1	11^{4}	14		15	13				4	12	8									31
	2	3		5	9		7^{2}		10^{3}	14			8^{4}	1	11	15			12				4		6^{1}	13								32
	2	3		5	6		7^{5}		10^{3}	15			9^{1}	1	11^{4}	13		14					4^{2}	12	8	16								33
	2	4		5	9		7^{3}		10	11^{2}			13	1	12	3								8^{1}	6	14								34
		4	5^{1}	10	9		12		13	7^{2}			8	1	11^{4}	3		15							6^{3}	2	14							35
	2^{4}	4		5	7		8^{1}		10	13			15	1	11^{2}	3		12						9^{3}	6		14							36
	2	4		5	12				9^{2}	10^{3}			7^{1}	1	11	3		13						6^{4}	8		14	15						37
	2	4		5	16		13		9^{2}	10^{5}			7^{4}	1	11^{3}	3		12	14					6^{1}	8		15							38
	5	3	12	4	7			13		10^{3}			6^{5}	1	14	2		11^{4}						9^{2}	16		15	8^{1}						39
	5	2		4	7			12^{3}		11^{4}			6	1	10^{1}	3	8	13						9^{2}	14		15							40
	5	3	15	4	7					11^{4}			6	1		2	12	10^{2}						9^{1}			13	8^{3}	14					41
	5	3	16	4	7		12			11^{5}			6^{2}	1	14	2	9^{1}	10^{3}							13		15	8^{4}						42
	2	4		5	7		9^{2}		10^{3}	11			6^{4}	1	8^{1}	3	13	12							14				15					43
	5	3		4	6		12			11			9^{3}	1		2	7^{2}	10^{4}	13					14				8^{1}	15					44
1		16	4		8^{4}		12						15			3^{5}	14	11^{3}		2^{2}					7^{1}		10	5	9	6	13			45
				4						12			7				14	6^{1}	16	2				13	8^{3}		11^{2}	5	10^{4}	9^{5}	3	1	15	46

FA Cup
Third Round Manchester C (a) 0-3

Carabao Cup
First Round Cambridge U (h) 0-1

BLACKBURN ROVERS

FOUNDATION

It was in 1875 that some public school old boys called a meeting at which the Blackburn Rovers club was formed and the colours blue and white adopted. The leading light was John Lewis, later to become a founder of the Lancashire FA, a famous referee who was in charge of two FA Cup finals, and a vice-president of both the FA and the Football League.

Ewood Park, Blackburn, Lancashire BB2 4JF.

Telephone: (01254) 372 001.

Ticket Office: (01254) 372 000.

Website: www.rovers.co.uk

Email: enquiries@rovers.co.uk

Ground Capacity: 31,367.

Record Attendance: 62,522 v Bolton W, FA Cup 6th rd, 2 March 1929.

Pitch Measurements: 105m × 66m (115yd × 72yd).

Chief Executive: Steve Waggott.

Manager: Tony Mowbray.

Assistant Manager: Mark Venus.

Colours: Blue and white halved shirts with red trim, white shorts, blue socks with white and red trim.

Year Formed: 1875.

Turned Professional: 1880.

Club Nickname: 'Rovers'.

Grounds: 1875, all matches played away; 1876, Oozehead Ground; 1877, Pleasington Cricket Ground; 1878, Alexandra Meadows; 1881, Leamington Road; 1890, Ewood Park.

First Football League Game: 15 September 1888, Football League, v Accrington (h) D 5–5 – Arthur; Beverley, James Southworth; Douglas, Almond, Forrest; Beresford (1), Walton, John Southworth (1), Fecitt (1), Townley (2).

Record League Victory: 9–0 v Middlesbrough, Division 2, 6 November 1954 – Elvy; Suart, Eckersley; Clayton, Kelly, Bell; Mooney (3), Crossan (2), Briggs, Quigley (3), Langton (1).

Record Cup Victory: 11–0 v Rossendale, FA Cup 1st rd, 13 October 1884 – Arthur; Hopwood, McIntyre; Forrest, Blenkhorn, Lofthouse; Sowerbutts (2), Jimmy Brown (1), Fecitt (4), Barton (3), Birtwistle (1).

Record Defeat: 0–8 v Arsenal, Division 1, 25 February 1933; 0–8 v Lincoln C, Division 2, 29 August 1953.

HONOURS

League Champions: Premier League – 1994–95; Division 1 – 1911–12, 1913–14; Division 2 – 1938–39; Division 3 – 1974–75.
Runners-up: Premier League – 1993–94; FL 1 – 2017–18; First Division – 2000–01; Division 2 – 1957–58; Division 3 – 1979–80.

FA Cup Winners: 1884, 1885, 1886, 1890, 1891, 1928.
Runners-up: 1882, 1960.

League Cup Winners: 2002.

Full Members' Cup Winners: 1987.

European Competitions
European Cup: 1995–96.
UEFA Cup: 1994–95, 1998–99, 2002–03, 2003–04, 2006–07, 2007–08.
Intertoto Cup: 2007.

FOOTBALL YEARBOOK FACT FILE

Blackburn Rovers played a game under artificial lighting at Ewood Park on 31 October 1892. The occasion was a benefit match for Jack Southworth and a crowd of between seven and eight thousand turned out to see Rovers beat Darwen 2-0. The pitch was illuminated by Well's Lights, but the gathering evening mist prevented many spectators from getting a full view of the proceedings.

Most League Points (2 for a win): 60, Division 3, 1974–75.

Most League Points (3 for a win): 96, FL 1, 2017–18.

Most League Goals: 114, Division 2, 1954–55.

Highest League Scorer in Season: Ted Harper, 43, Division 1, 1925–26.

Most League Goals in Total Aggregate: Simon Garner, 168, 1978–92.

Most League Goals in One Match: 7, Tommy Briggs v Bristol R, Division 2, 5 February 1955.

Most Capped Player: Morten Gamst Pedersen, 70 (83), Norway.

Most League Appearances: Derek Fazackerley, 596, 1970–86.

Youngest League Player: Harry Dennison, 16 years 155 days v Bristol C, 8 April 1911.

Record Transfer Fee Received: £18,000,000 from Manchester C for Roque Santa Cruz, June 2009.

Record Transfer Fee Paid: £3,000,000 (rising to £10,000,000) to Arsenal for David Bentley, January 2006.

Football League Record: 1888 Founder Member of the League; 1936–39 Division 2; 1946–48 Division 1; 1948–58 Division 2; 1958–66 Division 1; 1966–71 Division 2; 1971–75 Division 3; 1975–79 Division 2; 1979–80 Division 3; 1980–92 Division 2; 1992–99 Premier League; 1999–2001 Division 1; 2001–12 Premier League; 2012–17 FL C; 2017–18 FL 1; 2018– FL C.

LATEST SEQUENCES

Longest Sequence of League Wins: 8, 1.3.1980 – 7.4.1980.

Longest Sequence of League Defeats: 7, 12.3.1966 – 16.4.1966.

Longest Sequence of League Draws: 5, 11.10.1975 – 1.11.1975.

Longest Sequence of Unbeaten League Matches: 23, 30.9.1987 – 27.2.1988.

Longest Sequence Without a League Win: 16, 11.11.1978 – 24.3.1979.

Successive Scoring Runs: 32 from 24.4.1954.

Successive Non-scoring Runs: 4 from 14.12.2015.

MANAGERS

Thomas Mitchell 1884–96
(*Secretary-Manager*)
J. Walmsley 1896–1903
(*Secretary-Manager*)
R. B. Middleton 1903–25
Jack Carr 1922–26
(*Team Manager under Middleton to 1925*)
Bob Crompton 1926–31
(*Hon. Team Manager*)
Arthur Barritt 1931–36
(*had been Secretary from 1927*)
Reg Taylor 1936–38
Bob Crompton 1938–41
Eddie Hapgood 1944–47
Will Scott 1947
Jack Bruton 1947–49
Jackie Bestall 1949–53
Johnny Carey 1953–58
Dally Duncan 1958–60
Jack Marshall 1960–67
Eddie Quigley 1967–70
Johnny Carey 1970–71
Ken Furphy 1971–73
Gordon Lee 1974–75
Jim Smith 1975–78
Jim Iley 1978
John Pickering 1978–79
Howard Kendall 1979–81
Bobby Saxton 1981–86
Don Mackay 1987–91
Kenny Dalglish 1991–95
Ray Harford 1995–96
Roy Hodgson 1997–98
Brian Kidd 1998–99
Graeme Souness 2000–04
Mark Hughes 2004–08
Paul Ince 2008
Sam Allardyce 2008–10
Steve Kean 2010–12
Henning Berg 2012
Michael Appleton 2013
Gary Bowyer 2013–15
Paul Lambert 2015–16
Owen Coyle 2016–17
Tony Mowbray February 2017–

TEN YEAR LEAGUE RECORD

		P	W	D	L	F	A	Pts	Pos
2011-12	PR Lge	38	8	7	23	48	78	31	19
2012-13	FL C	46	14	16	16	55	62	58	17
2013-14	FL C	46	18	16	12	70	62	70	8
2014-15	FL C	46	17	16	13	66	59	67	9
2015-16	FL C	46	13	16	17	46	46	55	15
2016-17	FL C	46	12	15	19	53	65	51	22
2017-18	FL 1	46	28	12	6	82	40	96	2
2018-19	FL C	46	16	12	18	64	69	60	15
2019-20	FL C	46	17	12	17	66	63	63	11
2020-21	FL C	46	15	12	19	65	54	57	15

DID YOU KNOW 

Red cards to indicate that a player had been sent off were first introduced to domestic English football on 2 October 1976. The first player to receive a red card in a Football League match was Dave Wagstaffe of Blackburn Rovers who was dismissed after 36 minutes for arguing in the club's game at Orient on the same day.

BLACKBURN ROVERS – SKY BET CHAMPIONSHIP 2020–21 LEAGUE RECORD

Match No.	*Date*	*Venue*	*Opponents*	*Result*		*H/T Score*	*Lg Pos.*	*Goalscorers*	*Attendance*
1	Sept 12	A	Bournemouth	L	2-3	1-1	13	Johnson [42], Armstrong [73]	0
2	19	H	Wycombe W	W	5-0	3-0	9	Armstrong 3 (1 pen) [16 (p), 33, 83], Dolan [20], Williams [67]	0
3	26	A	Derby Co	W	4-0	3-0	4	Dolan [11], Johnson 2 [12, 15], Armstrong [77]	0
4	Oct 3	H	Cardiff C	D	0-0	0-0	6		0
5	17	H	Nottingham F	L	0-1	0-0	9		0
6	21	A	Watford	L	1-3	1-2	14	Brereton [28]	0
7	24	A	Coventry C	W	4-0	1-0	10	Armstrong 2 (1 pen) [15 (p), 49], Elliott [62], Gallagher [88]	0
8	27	H	Reading	L	2-4	1-3	12	Armstrong 2 [3, 66]	0
9	31	A	Swansea C	L	0-2	0-1	14		0
10	Nov 3	H	Middlesbrough	D	0-0	0-0	15		0
11	7	H	QPR	W	3-1	0-0	12	Brereton [50], Armstrong 2 [73, 90]	0
12	21	A	Luton T	D	1-1	0-0	14	Gallagher [72]	0
13	24	A	Preston NE	W	3-0	1-0	10	Armstrong (pen) [45], Brereton [53], Dolan [76]	0
14	28	H	Barnsley	W	2-1	1-0	9	Armstrong [44], Gallagher [78]	0
15	Dec 2	H	Millwall	W	2-1	1-1	9	Elliott [25], Armstrong [90]	0
16	5	A	Brentford	D	2-2	1-1	9	Rothwell [18], Davenport [87]	2000
17	9	A	Bristol C	L	0-1	0-0	10		0
18	12	H	Norwich C	L	1-2	0-1	12	Elliott [59]	0
19	16	H	Rotherham U	W	2-1	0-0	11	Elliott [80], Armstrong [90]	0
20	19	A	Stoke C	L	0-1	0-1	11		0
21	26	H	Sheffield W	D	1-1	0-1	11	Rothwell [76]	0
22	29	A	Huddersfield T	L	1-2	0-0	14	Gallagher [86]	0
23	Jan 2	A	Birmingham C	W	2-0	1-0	11	Armstrong [10], Dack [90]	0
24	16	H	Stoke C	D	1-1	0-1	11	Buckley [76]	0
25	24	A	Middlesbrough	W	1-0	0-0	9	Rothwell [63]	0
26	30	H	Luton T	W	1-0	0-0	8	Armstrong [85]	0
27	Feb 6	A	QPR	L	0-1	0-0	8		0
28	12	H	Preston NE	L	1-2	1-2	8	Armstrong (pen) [45]	0
29	17	A	Barnsley	L	1-2	0-0	12	Armstrong [90]	0
30	20	A	Nottingham F	L	0-1	0-1	12		0
31	24	H	Watford	L	2-3	1-2	15	Elliott [43], Brereton [82]	0
32	27	H	Coventry C	D	1-1	1-0	15	Brereton [27]	0
33	Mar 2	A	Reading	L	0-1	0-1	15		0
34	6	A	Millwall	W	2-0	1-0	15	Dack [18], Gallagher [75]	0
35	9	H	Swansea C	D	1-1	1-1	14	Dack [37]	0
36	12	H	Brentford	L	0-1	0-1	14		0
37	17	H	Bristol C	D	0-0	0-0	15		0
38	20	A	Norwich C	D	1-1	0-0	15	Gallagher [77]	0
39	Apr 2	A	Wycombe W	L	0-1	0-0	15		0
40	5	H	Bournemouth	L	0-2	0-1	17		0
41	10	A	Cardiff C	D	2-2	1-1	17	Armstrong 2 [43, 90]	0
42	16	H	Derby Co	W	2-1	1-1	14	Gallagher [42], Elliott [66]	0
43	20	A	Sheffield W	L	0-1	0-1	16		0
44	24	H	Huddersfield T	W	5-2	2-1	15	Armstrong 3 [8, 54, 60], Brereton [22], Gallagher [57]	0
45	May 1	A	Rotherham U	D	1-1	1-0	15	Armstrong [17]	0
46	8	H	Birmingham C	W	5-2	2-1	15	Armstrong 3 (1 pen) [27 (p), 71, 85], Brereton [45], Elliott [83]	0

Final League Position: 15

GOALSCORERS

League (65): Armstrong 28 (5 pens), Gallagher 8, Brereton 7, Elliott 7, Dack 3, Dolan 3, Johnson 3, Rothwell 3, Buckley 1, Davenport 1, Williams 1.
FA Cup (0).
Carabao Cup (3): Armstrong 1 (1 pen), Holtby 1, Rankin-Costello 1.

Kaminski T 43	Nyambe R 33 + 5	Lenihan D 41	Williams D 10	Bell A 15 + 4	Travis L 16 + 3	Holtby L 20 + 7	Johnson B 25 + 5	Rankin-Costello J 14	Armstrong A 40	Brereton B 30 + 10	Dolan T 10 + 27	Rothwell J 29 + 10	Evans C 11 + 7	Chapman H — + 5	Buckley J 7 + 21	Davenport J 6 + 9	Bennett E 2 + 7	Ayala D 8 + 2	Gallagher S 24 + 15	Brennan L — + 1	Elliott H 31 + 10	Wharton S 5 + 2	Trybull T 18 + 7	Douglas B 29 + 1	Pears A 3	Downing S 2 + 16	Carter H — + 1	Butterworth D — + 1	Dack B 7 + 9	Branthwaite J 10	Harwood-Bellis T 17 + 2	*Match No.*
1	2	3	4	5	6^{3}	7	8	9^{1}	10	11^{2}	12	13	14																			1
1		3	4	5		6^{3}	7	2	10	11^{1}	9	8^{2}		12	13	14																2
1	12	3	4	5		6	7	2^{1}	10	11	9^{2}	8^{3}		13			14															3
1	2		4	5		6^{3}	7		10	11^{1}	9^{2}	8		14	13			3	12													4
1	2	4		5			7		10	11^{3}	9^{1}		8	13	6^{2}			3	12	14												5
1	2	3		5		6	8		10	11^{3}	14		7^{2}					4^{1}			9	12	13									6
1		3	4	12		6	8	2	10^{2}	11					14				13		9		7^{3}	5^{1}								7
		3	4			6^{3}		2	10	11^{2}	13		7^{1}		14				12		9		8	5	1							8
	2	3	4			8		5	10^{3}	11^{1}	12		7^{2}			14			13		9		6		1							9
	2	3	4^{3}			7		5		11	9^{1}	12	13						10		8	14	6^{2}		1							10
1	2	3					7	5	10	11^{2}	14	8	6^{1}		12				13		9^{3}	4										11
1	13	3					7	2^{2}	10	11		8							12		9	4	6^{1}	5								12
1	2	3				6^{3}			10^{4}	11	14	8^{2}			16	12			9		13^{5}	4	7^{1}	5		15						13
1	2	3		12		6	13		10	11		8							14		9^{2}	4^{4}	7^{3}	5^{1}			15					14
1	2	3		5		8^{4}	7		10^{5}	11^{1}	12	15			14			4	9^{2}		6^{3}		16			13						15
1	2	3		14			7		10^{4}		15	6^{5}			13	16		12	9		11	4^{1}	8^{2}	5^{3}								16
1	2		4			7^{1}	6		10		12	8^{2}			13	14		3	9^{3}		11			5								17
1	2	3	4			8^{2}	7^{3}		10			6^{1}			13	12			11		9			5		14						18
1	2	3		12		14	7^{3}		10		16	8^{2}			6^{4}			4	11^{5}		9		15	5^{1}		13						19
1	2^{4}	3				6^{1}	4		10		14	8^{5}		16	15				11^{3}		9		7^{2}	5		13		12				20
1	2	3				6^{3}	7^{2}		11	12		8						4	10^{1}		9			5		14			13			21
1	2^{4}	3		5		12	7		10	11		6^{2}			15			4^{5}	14		9^{3}		8^{1}			16			13			22
1		3		5	7^{3}		4		10^{4}	11^{2}	15	13				8			9		6^{1}		14	2					12			23
1	2	3			7^{4}	15	6^{1}		10	14		11^{2}			16	12			13^{3}		9			5					8^{5}	4		24
1	2	3			6		8^{1}		10	15		11^{2}			12^{3}	7^{5}			14		9^{4}		16	5					13	4		25
1	2	3			7	14			10	11^{4}	12	8^{2}							15		9^{3}			5		6^{1}			13	4		26
1	2^{2}	3		5	7	13^{5}			11	16	15	6^{1}				8^{3}			9^{4}		10								12	4	14	27
1	2^{3}	3			6^{5}				11	16	12	10^{2}				7^{1}			8^{4}		14			5		13			9	4	15	28
1		3			6^{4}				11	16	12	15	14				8^{1}		10^{5}		13			5		7^{3}			9^{2}	4	2	29
1	2^{5}			5	6^{3}				11	10^{2}	13	15			14	7^{4}	16		8^{1}		9								12	4	3	30
1	2				7^{1}				10	14	13	8^{3}	6								9			5		12			11^{2}	4	3	31
1	2	3			7^{1}				10	11	14	8^{3}	6^{2}								9		12	5					13	4		32
1	2	3		5^{5}					10	11	14	8^{2}	6^{1}		15						9^{3}		7^{4}	16		13			12		4	33
1	12	3					14	2^{1}		9^{2}	10	15	16		6^{3}				11		13		7^{5}	5					8^{4}		4	34
1	13	3			14			2^{2}		9	10	15			8				11^{1}		12		7^{4}	5					6^{3}		4	35
1	2	3			14^{4}		15			9^{2}	10	13			6^{5}		16		11^{1}		12		7^{3}	5					8		4	36
1		3				6	7^{4}	2	10^{3}	11^{1}	12	8^{5}	16		13				14		9^{2}		15	5							4	37
1		3				6^{5}	16	2^{4}		9^{2}	11	8	7^{3}		10^{1}		14		13		12			5		15					4	38
1	12	3				6^{2}	15	2^{1}		10^{3}	14	8			16				11		9^{4}		7^{5}	5		13					4	39
1	2^{4}	3				12	7		10		11^{2}	8^{1}			14		15		13		9^{5}		6^{3}	5		16					4	40
1	2	3			6^{4}	13	8^{3}		10	14	12					15			11^{1}		9^{2}		7^{5}	5		16					4	41
1	2				6	8^{1}	7		10^{4}	13		12	15				14		11^{3}		9^{2}			5						4	3	42
1		3			12				10	15	16	8^{5}	6^{3}		14		2		11^{2}		9^{1}		7^{4}	5		13					4	43
1	2^{4}	3		5	6^{1}				11^{3}	8	13	9^{5}	7		15	12	16		10^{2}		14										4	44
1	2	3		5	6		7		11	8	12	9^{2}							10^{1}		13										4	45
1	2	3		5	6				11	8^{4}	15		16		9^{5}	7^{3}		14	10^{2}		12					13					4^{1}	46

FA Cup
Third Round Doncaster R (h) 0-1

Carabao Cup
First Round Doncaster R (h) 3-2
Second Round Newcastle U (a) 0-1

BLACKPOOL

FOUNDATION

Old boys of St John's School, who had formed themselves into a football club, decided to establish a club bearing the name of their town and Blackpool FC came into being at a meeting at the Stanley Arms Hotel in the summer of 1887. In their first season playing at Raikes Hall Gardens, the club won both the Lancashire Junior Cup and the Fylde Cup.

Bloomfield Road, Seasiders Way, Blackpool, Lancashire FY1 6JJ.

Telephone: (01253) 599 344.

Ticket Office: (01253) 599 745.

Website: www.blackpoolfc.co.uk

Email: via website.

Ground Capacity: 16,616.

Record Attendance: 38,098 v Wolverhampton W, Division 1, 17 September 1955.

Pitch Measurements: 103m × 65m (112.5yd × 71yd).

Owner: Simon Sadler.

Chief Executive: Ben Mansford.

Head Coach: Neil Critchley.

Assistant Head Coach: Mike Garrity.

Colours: Tangerine shirts with white trim, white shorts with tangerine trim, tangerine socks with white trim.

Year Formed: 1887.

Turned Professional: 1887.

Previous Name: 'South Shore' combined with Blackpool in 1899, twelve years after the latter had been formed on the breaking up of the old 'Blackpool St John's' club.

Club Nickname: 'The Seasiders'.

Grounds: 1887, Raikes Hall Gardens; 1897, Athletic Grounds; 1899, Raikes Hall Gardens; 1899, Bloomfield Road.

First Football League Game: 5 September 1896, Division 2, v Lincoln C (a) L 1–3 – Douglas; Parr, Bowman; Stuart, Stirzaker, Norris; Clarkin, Donnelly, Robert Parkinson, Mount (1), Jack Parkinson.

Record League Victory: 7–0 v Reading, Division 2, 10 November 1928 – Mercer; Gibson, Hamilton, Watson, Wilson, Grant, Ritchie, Oxberry (2), Hampson (5), Tufnell, Neal. 7–0 v Preston NE (away), Division 1, 1 May 1948 – Robinson; Shimwell, Crosland; Buchan, Hayward, Kelly; Hobson, Munro (1), McIntosh (5), McCall, Rickett (1). 7–0 v Sunderland, Division 1, 5 October 1957 – Farm; Armfield, Garrett, Kelly J, Gratrix, Kelly H, Matthews, Taylor (2), Charnley (2), Durie (2), Perry (1).

Record Cup Victory: 7–1 v Charlton Ath, League Cup 2nd rd, 25 September 1963 – Harvey; Armfield, Martin; Crawford, Gratrix, Cranston; Lea, Ball (1), Charnley (4), Durie (1), Oates (1).

HONOURS

League Champions: Division 2 – 1929–30.
Runners-up: Division 1 – 1955–56; Division 2 – 1936–37, 1969–70; Division 4 – 1984–85.

FA Cup Winners: 1953.
Runners-up: 1948, 1951.

League Cup: semi-final – 1962.

League Trophy Winners: 2002, 2004.

Anglo-Italian Cup Winners: 1971.
Runners-up: 1972.

FOOTBALL YEARBOOK FACT FILE

Blackpool's Wembley victory over Lincoln City confirmed their position as the most successful team in the EFL play-offs. The 2-1 win earned the Tangerines promotion to the Championship and was the sixth occasion the club has been promoted via the play-offs. In contrast they last achieved automatic promotion back in 1984–85 when they finished runners-up in the old Fourth Division.

Record Defeat: 1–10 v Small Heath, Division 2, 2 March 1901 and v Huddersfield T, Division 1, 13 December 1930.

Most League Points (2 for a win): 58, Division 2, 1929–30 and Division 2, 1967–68.

Most League Points (3 for a win): 86, Division 4, 1984–85.

Most League Goals: 98, Division 2, 1929–30.

Highest League Scorer in Season: Jimmy Hampson, 45, Division 2, 1929–30.

Most League Goals in Total Aggregate: Jimmy Hampson, 248, 1927–38.

Most League Goals in One Match: 5, Jimmy Hampson v Reading, Division 2, 10 November 1928; 5, Jimmy McIntosh v Preston NE, Division 1, 1 May 1948.

Most Capped Player: Jimmy Armfield, 43, England.

Most League Appearances: Jimmy Armfield, 568, 1952–71.

Youngest League Player: Matty Kay, 16 years 32 days v Scunthorpe U, 13 November 2005.

Record Transfer Fee Received: £6,750,000 from Liverpool for Charlie Adam, July 2011.

Record Transfer Fee Paid: £1,250,000 to Leicester C for D.J. Campbell, August 2010.

Football League Record: 1896 Elected to Division 2; 1899 Failed re-election; 1900 Re-elected; 1900–30 Division 2; 1930–33 Division 1; 1933–37 Division 2; 1937–67 Division 1; 1967–70 Division 2; 1970–71 Division 1; 1971–78 Division 2; 1978–81 Division 3; 1981–85 Division 4; 1985–90 Division 3; 1990–92 Division 4; 1992–2000 Division 2; 2000–01 Division 3; 2001–04 Division 2; 2004–07 FL 1; 2007–10 FL C; 2010–11 Premier League; 2011–15 FL C; 2015–16 FL 1; 2016–17 FL 2; 2017–21 FL 1; 2021– FL C.

LATEST SEQUENCES

Longest Sequence of League Wins: 9, 21.11.1936 – 1.1.1937.

Longest Sequence of League Defeats: 8, 26.11.1898 – 7.1.1899.

Longest Sequence of League Draws: 5, 4.12.1976 – 1.1.1977.

Longest Sequence of Unbeaten League Matches: 17, 6.4.1968 – 21.9.1968.

Longest Sequence Without a League Win: 23, 7.2.2015 – 29.8.2015.

Successive Scoring Runs: 33 from 23.2.1929.

Successive Non-scoring Runs: 5 from 25.11.1989.

MANAGERS

Tom Barcroft 1903–33 (*Secretary-Manager*)
John Cox 1909–11
Bill Norman 1919–23
Maj. Frank Buckley 1923–27
Sid Beaumont 1927–28
Harry Evans 1928–33 (*Hon. Team Manager*)
Alex 'Sandy' Macfarlane 1933–35
Joe Smith 1935–58
Ronnie Suart 1958–67
Stan Mortensen 1967–69
Les Shannon 1969–70
Bob Stokoe 1970–72
Harry Potts 1972–76
Allan Brown 1976–78
Bob Stokoe 1978–79
Stan Ternent 1979–80
Alan Ball 1980–81
Allan Brown 1981–82
Sam Ellis 1982–89
Jimmy Mullen 1989–90
Graham Carr 1990
Bill Ayre 1990–94
Sam Allardyce 1994–96
Gary Megson 1996–97
Nigel Worthington 1997–99
Steve McMahon 2000–04
Colin Hendry 2004–05
Simon Grayson 2005–08
Ian Holloway 2009–12
Michael Appleton 2012–13
Paul Ince 2013–14
José Riga 2014
Lee Clark 2014–15
Neil McDonald 2015–16
Gary Bowyer 2016–18
Terry McPhillips 2018–19
Simon Grayson 2019–20
Neil Critchley March 2020–

TEN YEAR LEAGUE RECORD

		P	*W*	*D*	*L*	*F*	*A*	*Pts*	*Pos*
2011-12	FL C	46	20	15	11	79	59	75	5
2012-13	FL C	46	14	17	15	62	63	59	15
2013-14	FL C	46	11	13	22	38	66	46	20
2014-15	FL C	46	4	14	28	36	91	26	24
2015-16	FL 1	46	12	10	24	40	63	46	22
2016-17	FL 2	46	18	16	12	69	46	70	7
2017-18	FL 1	46	15	15	16	60	55	60	12
2018-19	FL 1	46	15	17	14	50	52	62	10
2019-20	FL 1	35	11	12	12	44	43	45	13§
2020-21	FL 1	46	23	11	12	60	37	80	3

§*Decided on points-per-game (1.29)*

DID YOU KNOW ?

Inside-left Alan Withers marked his Football League debut by scoring a first-half hat-trick for Blackpool against Huddersfield Town in November 1950. The 20-year-old scored all three of his team's goals in their 3-1 victory in the First Division match at Bloomfield Road.

BLACKPOOL – SKY BET LEAGUE ONE 2020–21 LEAGUE RECORD

Match No.	Date	Venue	Opponents	Result		H/T Score	Lg Pos.	Goalscorers	Atten-dance
1	Sept 12	A	Plymouth Arg	L	0-1	0-1	16		0
2	19	H	Swindon T	W	2-0	1-0	9	Hamilton 2 [41, 47]	0
3	26	A	Gillingham	L	0-2	0-1	14		0
4	Oct 3	H	Lincoln C	L	2-3	1-1	20	Hamilton [17], Mitchell [82]	0
5	10	H	Ipswich T	L	1-4	0-3	21	Madine [60]	0
6	17	A	Crewe Alex	D	1-1	0-0	19	Ward [71]	0
7	20	H	Charlton Ath	L	0-1	0-0	22		0
8	24	H	Milton Keynes D	W	1-0	0-0	16	KaiKai [66]	0
9	27	A	AFC Wimbledon	L	0-1	0-1	17		0
10	31	A	Burton Alb	W	2-1	1-0	15	Yates 2 (1 pen) [21, 75 (p)]	0
11	Nov 3	H	Wigan Ath	W	1-0	0-0	12	KaiKai [47]	0
12	21	A	Peterborough U	W	2-1	1-0	14	Yates [19], Madine [90]	0
13	24	A	Doncaster R	L	2-3	2-0	15	Yates (pen) [10], Hamilton [38]	0
14	Dec 1	H	Portsmouth	W	1-0	0-0	12	Anderson [64]	0
15	5	A	Fleetwood T	W	1-0	1-0	12	Madine [16]	0
16	12	H	Oxford U	D	0-0	0-0	13		0
17	15	H	Hull C	W	3-2	1-1	12	Yates [45], Anderson [66], Hamilton [90]	0
18	19	A	Accrington S	D	0-0	0-0	12		0
19	29	A	Shrewsbury T	L	0-1	0-1	12		0
20	Jan 2	A	Bristol R	L	1-2	1-2	13	Madine [8]	0
21	16	A	Hull C	D	1-1	0-0	14	Yates [81]	0
22	26	A	Wigan Ath	W	5-0	2-0	15	Ekpiteta [40], Yates [42], Virtue [53], Simms 2 [88, 90]	0
23	Feb 2	H	Northampton T	W	2-0	1-0	12	Ekpiteta [12], Yates [90]	0
24	6	A	Ipswich T	L	0-2	0-1	13		0
25	16	H	Rochdale	W	1-0	1-0	14	KaiKai [20]	0
26	20	A	Portsmouth	W	1-0	0-0	13	Yates [82]	0
27	27	A	Charlton Ath	W	3-0	2-0	13	Yates 2 (2 pens) [10, 52], Virtue [37]	0
28	Mar 2	H	Crewe Alex	D	1-1	1-0	13	Ballard [41]	0
29	6	H	AFC Wimbledon	D	1-1	0-0	12	Simms [59]	0
30	9	A	Milton Keynes D	W	1-0	1-0	11	Yates [33]	0
31	13	H	Fleetwood T	D	0-0	0-0	12		0
32	16	H	Burton Alb	D	1-1	0-1	12	Garbutt [64]	0
33	20	A	Oxford U	W	2-0	2-0	10	Dougall [16], Ballard [42]	0
34	23	H	Peterborough U	W	3-1	1-1	6	Yates 2 (1 pen) [1, 52 (p)], Garbutt [58]	0
35	27	H	Plymouth Arg	D	2-2	0-1	6	KaiKai [47], Yates (pen) [64]	0
36	Apr 2	A	Swindon T	W	2-0	1-0	6	Simms [44], Yates [61]	0
37	5	H	Gillingham	W	4-1	3-1	5	Yates 2 [5, 19], KaiKai [30], Embleton [61]	0
38	10	A	Lincoln C	D	2-2	1-0	4	Simms [37], KaiKai [48]	0
39	13	H	Accrington S	D	0-0	0-0	5		0
40	17	H	Sunderland	W	1-0	0-0	5	Garbutt [58]	0
41	20	A	Rochdale	L	0-1	0-0	5		0
42	24	H	Shrewsbury T	L	0-1	0-0	6		0
43	27	A	Sunderland	W	1-0	0-0	5	KaiKai [56]	0
44	May 1	A	Northampton T	W	3-0	1-0	5	Garbutt [19], Yates 2 [75, 86]	0
45	4	H	Doncaster R	W	2-0	1-0	3	Simms 2 [22, 80]	0
46	9	H	Bristol R	W	1-0	0-0	3	Simms [75]	0

Final League Position: 3

GOALSCORERS

League (60): Yates 20 (6 pens), Simms 8, KaiKai 7, Hamilton 5, Garbutt 4, Madine 4, Anderson 2, Ballard 2, Ekpiteta 2, Virtue 2, Dougall 1, Embleton 1, Mitchell 1, Ward 1.
FA Cup (10): Madine 4, Yates 2, Kemp 1, Lawrence-Gabriel 1, Ward 1, own goal 1.
Carabao Cup (0).
Papa John's Trophy (4): Anderson 1, Kemp 1, Robson 1, own goal 1.
League One Play-Offs (8): Dougall 3, Simms 2, Embleton 1, Turton 1, Yates 1.

Maxwell C 43	Turton O 33 + 4	Ekpiteta M 26 + 2	Nottingham M 3	Mitchell D 13 + 19	Ward G 29 + 7	Robson E 15 + 13	Anderson K 11 + 6	Hamilton C 19 + 3	Yates J 41 + 3	KaiKai S 33 + 3	Williams M 6 + 4	Kemp D 3 + 5	Lubula B 5 + 7	Madine G 15 + 6	Husband J 24 + 3	Garbutt L 25 + 6	Sarkic O 1 + 4	Lawrence-Gabriel J 18 + 9	Woodburn B 3 + 7	Ballard D 24 + 1	Gretarsson D 11 + 1	Dougall K 32 + 2	Virtue M 11 + 5	Walker S 2	Thorniley J 17 + 2	Simms E 17 + 4	Stewart K 10 + 3	Apter R — + 1	Embleton E 14 + 4	Shaw N — + 1	Holmes B 1 + 4	Moore S 1	*Match No.*
1	2	3	4	5^{1}	6	7	8^{3}	9	10	11^{2}	12	13	14																				1
1	2	3	4	5	6	7	8^{1}	9	10^{3}		12	13	11^{2}	14																			2
1	2	3	4^{1}	5	6	7	8^{3}	9	10	13			11^{2}	14	12																		3
1	2	3		5	7	6	8^{3}	11	10^{2}		14		9^{1}		4■	12	13																4
1	4	3			6	7	8^{1}	9	11		12			10		5		2															5
1	2	3		12	6	8		9	11		7			10	4	5^{1}																	6
1	2	3		5	8^{1}	6		9	13		7		14	10^{2}	4■				11^{3}	12													7
1	2	3		5	8			11	10^{3}	9^{2}	6	13		14			12		7^{1}	4													8
1	2	3		5	12	6■		14		11^{2}	7	9^{3}		10			8^{1}		13	4■													9
1	2	3			12			6	10^{2}	9^{1}	8			11	5		13				4	7											10
1		3			8			6	10^{1}	9^{2}		13	12	11	5			2			4	7											11
1	2	3			8^{1}	13	12	6^{4}	10^{3}	9^{2}				11	5			15	14		4	7											12
1	2^{2}	3		13	16	8^{5}	14	6	11^{1}	9^{3}				10	5^{4}			12	15		4	7											13
1	2	3				8	7^{1}	9	10^{2}	11				13	5				12	4		6											14
1	2	3			8		12	6	10^{1}	9^{2}				11	5	13					4	7											15
1		3			9^{4}		12	7	14	10^{2}		13		11^{3}	5			2	8^{1}		4	6	15										16
1	2	3				6^{2}	8	9	10^{3}	11^{1}				12		5			14		4	7	13										17
1	2	3			13		9	6	10^{1}				12	11		5				4		7	8^{2}										18
	13	3		12	15	6^{3}	7^{5}		14	11^{1}		9^{2}	16	10		5		2^{4}		4		8		1									19
	2	3		13	7^{5}	16	9^{1}		11^{3}			6^{2}	12	10	15	5^{4}			14	4		8		1									20
1	2^{3}	3			7	16			11	9^{1}			6^{2}	10	5^{5}	15		14	13	4		8^{4}	12										21
1		3				8^{1}			11^{2}	14	7^{5}		9^{3}	10	5		15	2					6^{4}		4	12	13	16					22
1	13	3		12					10	9					5			2				8^{1}	6		4	11^{2}	7						23
1		3		12	16				11	9^{2}			15		5^{3}	14		2				8^{5}	6^{1}		4	13	7		10^{4}				24
1		4^{1}			13				10	9					5	12		2				8^{2}	6		3	11	7						25
1				12	6^{3}				10	9^{2}					4	5		2		3		8	14			11^{1}	7		13				26
1				12	6^{3}	14			11^{2}	9^{1}						5		2		3			7		4	10^{4}	8		13	15			27
1				12	6			13	10	9^{1}						5		2		3			7		4	11^{2}	8						28
1	2			9^{2}				6^{1}	10	12					5	15				3		14	7^{4}		4	11^{3}	8		13				29
1	2			12	6			13	11	9^{1}					4	5				3		14	7^{3}				8		10^{2}				30
1	2			13				6^{2}	10	9					4	5				3		7	12			11	8^{1}						31
1	2			6					11	9					4	5				3		8	7			10^{1}			12				32
1	2			14	8	13			11^{3}	10^{4}						5		12		3		7	6^{1}		4	15			9^{2}				33
1	3			8	6	12			11	10						5		2				7			4				9^{1}				34
1	3			8	6	13			11	10						5		2			12	7			4^{1}				9^{2}				35
1	3			12	7	14			11	9^{3}						5		2			4^{2}	8			13	10^{1}			6				36
1	2			13	7	14			11^{2}	9^{3}						5		12		3		8			4	10			6^{1}				37
1	2				7	13			11	9						5		12		3	4	8				10^{2}			6^{1}				38
1					8				10	9						5		2		3	4	7				11			6				39
1	2			6^{2}	8	14			10	9^{4}					15	5		13		3	4^{1}	7			12	11^{3}							40
1	2			12	8^{4}	15			10	9^{2}						5		13		3		7			4	11^{1}			6^{3}		14		41
1	14			12	8	13			10	9						5		2^{3}		3		7^{4}			4	11^{1}			6^{2}		15		42
1	2			12	7^{2}	9			10	11^{1}					5	6				3		8			4		13						43
1	2	13		15		8^{1}	16		10^{3}						5^{2}	6		12		3		7			4	11^{5}			9^{4}		14		44
1	7	13		15			14		10^{4}						5^{3}	6		2^{1}		3		8			4	11^{5}	12^{2}		9		16		45
	13	3		8			10^{2}							14	5			2				6			4	12	7		9^{3}		11^{1}	1	46

FA Cup

First Round	Eastbourne Boro	(a)	3-0
Second Round	Harrogate T	(a)	4-0
Third Round	WBA	(h)	2-2
(aet; Blackpool won 3-2 on penalties)			
Fourth Round	Brighton & HA	(a)	1-2

Carabao Cup

First Round	Stoke C	(a)	0-0
(Stoke C won 5-4 on penalties)			

League One Play-Offs

Semi-Final 1st leg	Oxford U	(a)	3-0
Semi-Final 2nd leg	Oxford U	(h)	3-3
Final	Lincoln C	(Wembley)	2-1

Papa John's Trophy

Group G (N)	Barrow	(h)	0-0
(Blackpool won 5-3 on penalties)			
Group G (N)	Accrington S	(a)	1-1
(Accrington Stanley won 4-3 on penalties)			
Group G (N)	Leeds U U21	(h)	3-0
Second Round (N)	Fleetwood T	(a)	0-0
(Fleetwood T won 5-4 on penalties)			

BOLTON WANDERERS

FOUNDATION

In 1874 boys of Christ Church Sunday School, Blackburn Street, led by their master Thomas Ogden, established a football club which went under the name of the school and whose president was vicar of Christ Church. Membership was 6d (two and a half pence). When their president began to lay down too many rules about the use of church premises, the club broke away and formed Bolton Wanderers in 1877, holding their earliest meetings at the Gladstone Hotel.

University of Bolton Stadium, Burnden Way, Lostock, Bolton BL6 6JW.

Telephone: (01204) 673 673.

Ticket Office: (01204) 328 888.

Website: www.bwfc.co.uk

Email: reception@bwfc.co.uk (or via website).

Ground Capacity: 28,018.

Record Attendance: 69,912 v Manchester C, FA Cup 5th rd, 18 February 1933 (at Burnden Park); 28,353 v Leicester C, Premier League, 23 December 2003 (at The Reebok Stadium).

Pitch Measurements: 102m × 68m (111.5yd × 74.5yd).

Chairman: Sharon Brittan.

Directors: Michael James, Nick Luckcock.

Manager: Ian Evatt.

Assistant Manager: Peter Atherton.

Colours: White shirts with blue sleeves and blue and red trim, blue shorts with white and red trim, white socks with red and blue trim.

Year Formed: 1874.

Turned Professional: 1880.

Previous Name: 1874, Christ Church FC; 1877, Bolton Wanderers.

Club Nickname: 'The Trotters'.

Grounds: Park Recreation Ground and Cockle's Field before moving to Pike's Lane ground 1881; 1895, Burnden Park; 1997, Reebok Stadium (renamed Macron Stadium 2014; University of Bolton Stadium 2018).

First Football League Game: 8 September 1888, Football League, v Derby Co (h) L 3–6 – Harrison; Robinson, Mitchell; Roberts, Weir, Bullough, Davenport (2), Milne, Coupar, Barbour, Brogan (1).

Record League Victory: 8–0 v Barnsley, Division 2, 6 October 1934 – Jones; Smith, Finney; Goslin, Atkinson, George Taylor; George T. Taylor (2), Eastham, Milsom (1), Westwood (4), Cook, (1 og).

Record Cup Victory: 13–0 v Sheffield U, FA Cup 2nd rd, 1 February 1890 – Parkinson; Robinson (1), Jones; Bullough, Davenport, Roberts; Rushton, Brogan (3), Cassidy (5), McNee, Weir (4).

HONOURS

League Champions: First Division – 1996–97; Division 2 – 1908–09, 1977–78; Division 3 – 1972–73.
Runners-up: Division 2 – 1899–1900, 1904–05, 1910–11, 1934–35; Second Division – 1992–93; FL 1 – 2016–17.

FA Cup Winners: 1923, 1926, 1929, 1958.
Runners-up: 1894, 1904, 1953.

League Cup: *Runners-up:* 1995, 2004.

League Trophy Winners: 1989.
Runners-up: 1986.

European Competitions
UEFA Cup: 2005–06, 2007–08.

FOOTBALL YEARBOOK FACT FILE

Goalkeeper Jim McDonagh was an ever-present for Bolton Wanderers in the 1982–83 season when he also scored the only goal of his senior career. With 10 minutes remaining of the home game with Burnley he spotted the Clarets' keeper had wandered off his line and delivered a lengthy punt down the field. The ball bounced once and flew over the keeper and into the net to clinch a 3-0 victory.

Record Defeat: 1–9 v Preston NE, FA Cup 2nd rd, 5 November 1887.

Most League Points (2 for a win): 61, Division 3, 1972–73.

Most League Points (3 for a win): 98, Division 1, 1996–97.

Most League Goals: 100, Division 1, 1996–97.

Highest League Scorer in Season: Joe Smith, 38, Division 1, 1920–21.

Most League Goals in Total Aggregate: Nat Lofthouse, 255, 1946–61.

Most League Goals in One Match: 5, Tony Caldwell v Walsall, Division 3, 10 September 1983.

Most Capped Player: Ricardo Gardner, 72 (111), Jamaica.

Most League Appearances: Eddie Hopkinson, 519, 1956–70.

Youngest League Player: Ray Parry, 15 years 267 days v Wolverhampton W, 13 October 1951.

Record Transfer Fee Received: £15,000,000 from Chelsea for Nicolas Anelka, January 2008.

Record Transfer Fee Paid: £8,250,000 to Toulouse for Johan Elmander, June 2008.

Football League Record: 1888 Founder Member of the League; 1899–1900 Division 2; 1900–03 Division 1; 1903–05 Division 2; 1905–08 Division 1; 1908–09 Division 2; 1909–10 Division 1; 1910–11 Division 2; 1911–33 Division 1; 1933–35 Division 2; 1935–64 Division 1; 1964–71 Division 2; 1971–73 Division 3; 1973–78 Division 2; 1978–80 Division 1; 1980–83 Division 2; 1983–87 Division 3; 1987–88 Division 4; 1988–92 Division 3; 1992–93 Division 2; 1993–95 Division 1; 1995–96 Premier League; 1996–97 Division 1; 1997–98 Premier League; 1998–2001 Division 1; 2001–12 Premier League; 2012–16 FL C; 2016–17 FL 1; 2017–19 FL C; 2019–20 FL 1; 2020–21 FL 2; 2021– FL 1.

LATEST SEQUENCES

Longest Sequence of League Wins: 11, 5.11.1904 – 2.1.1905.

Longest Sequence of League Defeats: 11, 7.4.1902 – 18.10.1902.

Longest Sequence of League Draws: 6, 25.1.1913 – 8.3.1913.

Longest Sequence of Unbeaten League Matches: 23, 13.10.1990 – 9.3.1991.

Longest Sequence Without a League Win: 26, 7.4.1902 – 10.1.1903.

Successive Scoring Runs: 24 from 22.11.1996.

Successive Non-scoring Runs: 11 from 9.4.2019.

MANAGERS

Tom Rawthorne 1874–85 (*Secretary*)
J. J. Bentley 1885–86 (*Secretary*)
W. G. Struthers 1886–87 (*Secretary*)
Fitzroy Norris 1887 (*Secretary*)
J. J. Bentley 1887–95 (*Secretary*)
Harry Downs 1895–96 (*Secretary*)
Frank Brettell 1896–98 (*Secretary*)
John Somerville 1898–1910
Will Settle 1910–15
Tom Mather 1915–19
Charles Foweraker 1919–44
Walter Rowley 1944–50
Bill Ridding 1951–68
Nat Lofthouse 1968–70
Jimmy McIlroy 1970
Jimmy Meadows 1971
Nat Lofthouse 1971 (*then Admin. Manager to 1972*)
Jimmy Armfield 1971–74
Ian Greaves 1974–80
Stan Anderson 1980–81
George Mulhall 1981–82
John McGovern 1982–85
Charlie Wright 1985
Phil Neal 1985–92
Bruce Rioch 1992–95
Roy McFarland 1995–96
Colin Todd 1996–99
Roy McFarland and Colin Todd 1995–96
Sam Allardyce 1999–2007
Sammy Lee 2007
Gary Megson 2007–09
Owen Coyle 2010–12
Dougie Freedman 2012–14
Neil Lennon 2014–16
Phil Parkinson 2016–19
Keith Hill 2019–20
Ian Evatt July 2020–

TEN YEAR LEAGUE RECORD

		P	*W*	*D*	*L*	*F*	*A*	*Pts*	*Pos*
2011-12	PR Lge	38	10	6	22	46	77	36	18
2012-13	FL C	46	18	14	14	69	61	68	7
2013-14	FL C	46	14	17	15	59	60	59	14
2014-15	FL C	46	13	12	21	54	67	51	18
2015-16	FL C	46	5	15	26	41	81	30	24
2016-17	FL 1	46	25	11	10	68	36	86	2
2017-18	FL C	46	10	13	23	39	74	43	21
2018-19	FL C	46	8	8	30	29	78	32	23
2019-20	FL 1	34	5	11	18	27	66	14	23§
2020-21	FL 2	46	23	10	13	59	50	79	3

§Decided on points-per-game (0.41)

DID YOU KNOW ?

Bolton Wanderers' Divison 1 home game with Leeds United in February 1947 attracted an attendance of just 6,278 to Burnden Park. The Monday afternoon match was played in a blizzard with hard snow covering the pitch, but Wanderers managed to gain a 2-1 win.

BOLTON WANDERERS – SKY BET LEAGUE TWO 2020–21 LEAGUE RECORD

Match No.	*Date*	*Venue*	*Opponents*	*Result*		*H/T Score*	*Lg Pos.*	*Goalscorers*	*Attendance*
1	Sept 12	H	Forest Green R	L	0-1	0-0	19		0
2	19	A	Colchester U	L	0-2	0-1	21		0
3	26	H	Newport Co	L	0-2	0-0	22		0
4	Oct 3	A	Harrogate T	W	2-1	1-0	19	Doyle [11], Delfouneso [56]	0
5	10	H	Grimsby T	D	0-0	0-0	18		0
6	17	H	Oldham Ath	L	1-2	1-1	20	Delfouneso [32]	0
7	20	A	Barrow	D	3-3	2-3	20	Kioso [16], Doyle [41], Sarcevic [90]	0
8	24	A	Cambridge U	D	1-1	0-0	18	Sarcevic [82]	0
9	27	H	Bradford C	W	1-0	1-0	16	Delfouneso [13]	0
10	31	A	Leyton Orient	L	0-4	0-3	19		0
11	Nov 3	H	Mansfield T	D	1-1	0-0	20	Sarcevic [90]	0
12	13	H	Salford C	W	2-0	1-0	15	Doyle [23], Turnbull (og) [67]	0
13	21	A	Stevenage	W	2-1	2-1	16	Doyle [14], Crawford [36]	0
14	24	A	Scunthorpe U	W	1-0	0-0	13	Kioso [57]	0
15	28	H	Southend U	W	3-0	1-0	9	Delfouneso [45], Doyle 2 (1 pen) [65 (p), 81]	0
16	Dec 5	H	Port Vale	L	3-6	1-3	12	Jones [11], Doyle [66], Isgrove [78]	0
17	12	A	Walsall	L	1-2	1-1	16	Doyle [13]	0
18	15	A	Cheltenham T	W	1-0	0-0	12	Delaney [90]	1685
19	19	H	Tranmere R	L	0-3	0-1	15		0
20	26	A	Carlisle U	D	3-3	1-3	15	Thomason [43], Delfouneso [86], Kioso [88]	2000
21	Jan 2	H	Crawley T	L	0-1	0-0	15		0
22	12	A	Exeter C	D	1-1	0-0	16	Gnahoua [73]	0
23	16	H	Cheltenham T	D	1-1	0-0	17	Doyle [86]	0
24	23	A	Tranmere R	L	1-2	0-1	17	Sarcevic [66]	0
25	30	H	Leyton Orient	W	2-0	0-0	19	Brophy (og) [67], Doyle [69]	0
26	Feb 9	H	Morecambe	D	1-1	1-0	19	Doyle [43]	0
27	13	H	Stevenage	W	1-0	1-0	13	John [7]	0
28	17	A	Mansfield T	W	3-2	0-0	11	John [78], Benning (og) [85], Gnahoua [88]	0
29	20	A	Southend U	W	1-0	0-0	10	Miller [82]	0
30	23	H	Scunthorpe U	W	2-0	1-0	9	Doyle (pen) [37], Sarcevic [74]	0
31	27	H	Barrow	W	1-0	0-0	7	Miller [90]	0
32	Mar 2	A	Oldham Ath	W	2-0	2-0	6	Clarke (og) [19], Doyle [39]	0
33	6	A	Bradford C	D	1-1	0-0	7	Delfouneso [83]	0
34	9	H	Cambridge U	W	2-1	2-0	7	Doyle [38], Sarcevic [43]	0
35	13	A	Port Vale	W	1-0	0-0	6	Jones [63]	0
36	20	H	Walsall	W	2-1	0-1	5	Lee [67], Doyle (pen) [80]	0
37	27	A	Forest Green R	W	1-0	1-0	4	Doyle [39]	0
38	Apr 2	H	Colchester U	D	0-0	0-0	3		0
39	5	A	Newport Co	L	0-1	0-0	4		0
40	10	H	Harrogate T	W	2-1	0-1	3	Lee [53], Doyle [78]	0
41	13	A	Salford C	W	1-0	1-0	3	Isgrove [23]	0
42	17	A	Grimsby T	L	1-2	0-1	3	Miller [90]	0
43	20	H	Carlisle U	W	1-0	1-0	3	Doyle [28]	0
44	24	A	Morecambe	W	1-0	1-0	3	Jackson [45]	0
45	May 1	H	Exeter C	L	1-2	1-0	3	Jones [15]	0
46	8	A	Crawley T	W	4-1	2-0	3	Sarcevic [9], Afolayan [26], Doyle [48], Isgrove [77]	0

Final League Position: 3

GOALSCORERS

League (59): Doyle 19 (3 pens), Sarcevic 7, Delfouneso 6, Isgrove 3, Jones 3, Kioso 3, Miller 3, Gnahoua 2, John 2, Lee 2, Afolayan 1, Crawford 1, Delaney 1, Jackson 1, Thomason 1, own goals 4.
FA Cup (2): Delfouneso 2.
Carabao Cup (1): Sarcevic 1.
Papa John's Trophy (6): Delaney 1, Gnahoua 1, Hickman 1, Mascoll 1, Miller 1, Senior 1.

Crellin B 11	Santos R 46	Baptiste A 38+2	Greenidge R 3+2	Jones G 37+1	Comley B 5+5	White T 4+5	Gordon L 4+6	Sarcevic A 29+3	Delfouneso N 33+11	Doyle E 43	Crawford A 17+4	Amoateng B —+1	Tutte A 13+6	Hickman J 3+1	Hurford-Lockett F —+1	Mascoll J 2+5	Taft G 1	Gnahoua A 6+22	Isgrove L 21+11	Brockbank H 13+5	Delaney R 20	Kioso P 13	Darcy R 1+7	Miller S —+20	Gilks M 35	Thomason G 18+6	Lee K 20	Jackson B 5	Elbouzedi Z 2+12	John D 19+2	Williams M 21	Afolayan O 19+2	Maddison M 4+6	*Match No.*
1	2	3	4^3	5	6^1	7^2	8	9	10	11	12	13	14																					1
1	4	3		2	6	7	8		11^2	10	9			5^1	12	13																		2
1	4			2	6	7	8		11^1	10	9^3		12	5^2			3	13	14															3
1	3			5^1	14		13	6	10	11	9		7^3	12		8^2				2	4													4
1	3	12			13		14	7	11	10	9		6^2	5^1		8^3				2	4													5
1	3				7^1		8^3	6	11	10	9^2		12			14		13		2	4	5												6
1	3	2			7		12	6		10	9^2							11		8^1	4	5	13											7
1	3	2					13	6	11	10^1	9		7					12		8^2	4	5												8
1	3	2			13			6	11		9		7^2			12		10^3		8^1	4	5	14											9
1	3	2^2				13	14	6	11^1		9		7^3					10		8	4	5	12											10
1	3	2				7	12	6	11^3		9							13		8^1	4	5	10^2	14										11
	3	2		8		14		6	11^2	10^1	9^3		7						13		4	5		12	1									12
	3	2		8				6	11^1	10	9^2		7						13		4	5		12	1									13
	3	2		8				6	11^2	10^3	9^1		7						12		4	5	14	13	1									14
	3	2		8^3	16	12		6^4	11	10	9^2		7^1			14			13		4	5^5	15		1									15
	3	2^4	15	8	13	16		6^5	11	10	9^1								12		4^2	5	14		1	7^3								16
	3	2		8		14		7	10	11	9^1							12^2			4	5	13		1	6^3								17
	3	2	8^1	5				6	11	10						12			9		4				1	7								18
	3	2		5				6	11	10	12								9	8^1	4				1	7								19
	3	2^1	13	8				6	11	10^3			7						12	14	4^2	5■			1	9								20
	3		4■	8				9	11	10			7						5	2					1	6								21
	3			2				6	11^2	10	13		7					12	9	5	4				1		8^1							22
	3			2^3				8		10	15		12					13	9	14	4				1	7^4	6^1	5	11^2					23
	3	14		2				6	13	10	8^3		7					12	9^2		4■				1			5	11^1					24
	3	4							8	10								11	9^1	2					1	7	6	5^2	13	12				25
	3	4		14					9^5	11								8^2	10^1	2^3					1	7		5^4	16	15	6	12	13■	26
	3	4		2					9^1	11			14					12	13						1	6				5	7■	10^3	8^2	27
	3	4		2					12	11								13	10^3					14	1	15	7^4			5	6	9^2	8^1	28
	3	4		2				12	9^1	11^4								13	14					15	1		6			5	7	10^3	8^2	29
	3	4		2				12	10^2	11^3								14	8^4					13	1	7				5	6	9^1	15	30
	3	4		2				9	12	11^3								13	8^1					14	1		7			5	6	10^2		31
	3	4		2				9	10^2	11^4								15						14	1	12	6^1			5	7	8^3	13	32
	3	4		2				9^1	12	11^3								14	8^2					13	1		6			5	7	10		33
	3	4		2				9^1	8^2	11^4								15						14	1	13	7			5	6	10^3	12	34
	3	4		2				9^1	8	11^3								13	12						1		7		14	5	6	10^2		35
	3	4		2					9^4	11^3								12	8^2					15	1	14	7		13	5	6	10^1		36
	3	4		2					8^2	11^3			15					12	13					14	1	9^4	7			5	6	10^1		37
	3	4		2					9^1	11								8^2						14	1		7		13	5	6	10^3	12	38
	3	4		2					10^1	11									8^3						1	6	9		14	5	7^2	12	13	39
	3	4		2					13	11^4									8^3	16				15	1	12	7^5		14	5	6	10^2	9^1	40
	3	4		2					12	11^2									8^3					13	1	9	7		14	5	6	10^1		41
	3	4		2					12	11^5								16	8^1	15				14	1	7	9^3		13	5^4	6	10^2		42
	3	4		2					13	11									8^3	12					1	9	7		14	5^1	6	10^2		43
	3	4		2				13	12	11^3									8^4					14	1	7^2	9	5	15		6	10^1		44
	3	4		2				9^1	14	11								13	8^2					15	1	12	7^3			5	6	10^4		45
	3	4		2				9^1	12	11^4								15	8^3					14	1	7			13	5	6	10^2		46

FA Cup

First Round	Crewe Alex	(h)	2-3

Carabao Cup

First Round	Bradford C	(h)	1-2

Papa John's Trophy

Group C (N)	Crewe Alex	(h)	2-3
Group C (N)	Shrewsbury T	(a)	1-2
Group C (N)	Newcastle U U21	(h)	3-2

AFC BOURNEMOUTH

FOUNDATION

There was a Bournemouth FC as early as 1875, but the present club arose out of the remnants of the Boscombe St John's club (formed 1890). The meeting at which Boscombe FC came into being was held at a house in Gladstone Road in 1899. They began by playing in the Boscombe and District Junior League.

Vitality Stadium, Dean Court, Kings Park, Bournemouth, Dorset BH7 7AF.

Telephone: (01202) 726 300.

Ticket Office: (0344) 576 1910.

Website: www.afcb.co.uk

Email: enquiries@afcb.co.uk

Ground Capacity: 11,329.

Record Attendance: 28,799 v Manchester U, FA Cup 6th rd, 2 March 1957.

Pitch Measurements: 105m × 68m (115yd × 74.5yd).

Chairman: Jeff Mostyn.

Chief Executive: Neill Blake.

Manager: Scott Parker.

Assistant Manager: Matt Wells.

Colours: Red and black striped shirts, black shorts with red trim, black socks with red trim.

Year Formed: 1899.

Turned Professional: 1910.

Previous Names: 1890, Boscombe St John's; 1899, Boscombe FC; 1923, Bournemouth & Boscombe Ath FC; 1972, AFC Bournemouth.

Club Nickname: 'Cherries'.

Grounds: 1899, Castlemain Road, Pokesdown; 1910, Dean Court (renamed Fitness First Stadium 2001, Seward Stadium 2011, Goldsands Stadium 2012, Vitality Stadium 2015).

First Football League Game: 25 August 1923, Division 3 (S), v Swindon T (a) L 1–3 – Heron; Wingham, Lamb; Butt, Charles Smith, Voisey; Miller, Lister (1), Davey, Simpson, Robinson.

Record League Victory: 8–0 v Birmingham C, FL C, 25 October 2014 – Boruc; Francis, Elphick, Cook, Daniels; Ritchie (1), Arter (Gosling), Surman, Pugh (3); Pitman (1) (Rantie 2 (1 pen)), Wilson (1) (Fraser). 10–0 win v Northampton T at start of 1939–40 expunged from the records on outbreak of war.

Record Cup Victory: 11–0 v Margate, FA Cup 1st rd, 20 November 1971 – Davies; Machin (1), Kitchener, Benson, Jones, Powell, Cave (1), Boyer, MacDougall (9 incl. 1p), Miller, Scott (De Garis).

Record Defeat: 0–9 v Lincoln C, Division 3, 18 December 1982.

HONOURS

League Champions: FL C – 2014–15; Division 3 – 1986–87.
Runners-up: FL 1 – 2012–13; Division 3S – 1947–48; FL 2 – 2009–10; Division 4 – 1970–71.

FA Cup: 6th rd – 1957, 2021.

League Cup: quarter-final – 2015, 2018, 2019.

League Trophy Winners: 1984.
Runners-up: 1998.

FOOTBALL YEARBOOK FACT FILE

Although AFC Bournemouth, then known as Boscombe, employed a professional player during the 1911–12 season, it was not until 1913–14 that the club committee made a decision to embrace professionalism on a wider scale, and seven professionals were registered with the FA that season. It was initially decided that players would only be paid as compensation for loss of earnings when playing.

Most League Points (2 for a win): 62, Division 3, 1971–72.

Most League Points (3 for a win): 97, Division 3, 1986–87.

Most League Goals: 98, FL C, 2014–15.

Highest League Scorer in Season: Ted MacDougall, 42, 1970–71.

Most League Goals in Total Aggregate: Ron Eyre, 202, 1924–33.

Most League Goals in One Match: 4, Jack Russell v Clapton Orient, Division 3 (S), 7 January 1933; 4, Jack Russell v Bristol C, Division 3 (S), 28 January 1933; 4, Harry Mardon v Southend U, Division 3 (S), 1 January 1938; 4, Jack McDonald v Torquay U, Division 3 (S), 8 November 1947; 4, Ted MacDougall v Colchester U, 18 September 1970; 4, Brian Clark v Rotherham U, 10 October 1972; 4, Luther Blissett v Hull C, 29 November 1988; 4, James Hayter v Bury, Division 2, 21 October 2000.

Most Capped Player: Josh King, 34 (54), Norway.

Most League Appearances: Steve Fletcher, 628, 1992–2007; 2008–13.

Youngest League Player: Jimmy White, 15 years 321 days v Brentford, 30 April 1958.

Record Transfer Fee Received: £41,000,000 from Manchester C for Nathan Aké, August 2020.

Record Transfer Fee Paid: £25,200,000 to Levante for Jefferson Lerma, August 2018.

Football League Record: 1923 Elected to Division 3 (S) and remained a Third Division club for record number of years until 1970; 1970–71 Division 4; 1971–75 Division 3; 1975–82 Division 4; 1982–87 Division 3; 1987–90 Division 2; 1990–92 Division 3; 1992–2002 Division 2; 2002–03 Division 3; 2003–04 Division 2; 2004–08 FL 1; 2008–10 FL 2; 2010–13 FL 1; 2013–15 FL C; 2015–20 Premier League; 2020– FL C.

MANAGERS

Vincent Kitcher 1914–23 (*Secretary-Manager*)
Harry Kinghorn 1923–25
Leslie Knighton 1925–28
Frank Richards 1928–30
Billy Birrell 1930–35
Bob Crompton 1935–36
Charlie Bell 1936–39
Harry Kinghorn 1939–47
Harry Lowe 1947–50
Jack Bruton 1950–56
Fred Cox 1956–58
Don Welsh 1958–61
Bill McGarry 1961–63
Reg Flewin 1963–65
Fred Cox 1965–70
John Bond 1970–73
Trevor Hartley 1974–75
John Benson 1975–78
Alec Stock 1979–80
David Webb 1980–82
Don Megson 1983
Harry Redknapp 1983–92
Tony Pulis 1992–94
Mel Machin 1994–2000
Sean O'Driscoll 2000–06
Kevin Bond 2006–08
Jimmy Quinn 2008
Eddie Howe 2008–11
Lee Bradbury 2011–12
Paul Groves 2012
Eddie Howe 2012–20
Jason Tindall 2020–21
Jonathan Woodgate 2021
Scott Parker June 2021–

LATEST SEQUENCES

Longest Sequence of League Wins: 8, 12.3.2013 – 20.4.2013.

Longest Sequence of League Defeats: 7, 13.8.1994 – 13.9.1994.

Longest Sequence of League Draws: 5, 25.4.2000 – 19.8.2000.

Longest Sequence of Unbeaten League Matches: 18, 6.3.1982 – 28.8.1982.

Longest Sequence Without a League Win: 14, 6.3.1974 – 27.4.1974.

Successive Scoring Runs: 31 from 28.10.2000.

Successive Non-scoring Runs: 6 from 1.2.1975.

TEN YEAR LEAGUE RECORD

		P	W	D	L	F	A	Pts	Pos
2011-12	FL 1	46	15	13	18	48	52	58	11
2012-13	FL 1	46	24	11	11	76	53	83	2
2013-14	FL C	46	18	12	16	67	66	66	10
2014-15	FL C	46	26	12	8	98	45	90	1
2015-16	PR Lge	38	11	9	18	45	67	42	16
2016-17	PR Lge	38	12	10	16	55	67	46	9
2017-18	PR Lge	38	11	11	16	45	61	44	12
2018-19	PR Lge	38	13	6	19	56	70	45	14
2019-20	PR Lge	38	9	7	22	40	65	34	18
2020-21	FL C	46	22	11	13	73	46	77	6

DID YOU KNOW ?

AFC Bournemouth's nickname of 'The Cherries' dates back to the early 1900s when the club, under their previous name of Boscombe, wore red and white striped shirts. As a result they became known as 'The Cherry Stripes'. However, they switched colours during the 1920s and the nickname was shortened to 'The Cherries'.

AFC BOURNEMOUTH – SKY BET CHAMPIONSHIP 2020–21 LEAGUE RECORD

Match No.	Date	Venue	Opponents	Result		H/T Score	Lg Pos.	Goalscorers	Attendance
1	Sept 12	H	Blackburn R	W	3-2	1-1	3	Stacey[25], Lerma[53], Danjuma[84]	0
2	19	A	Middlesbrough	D	1-1	1-0	3	Solanke[38]	1000
3	27	H	Norwich C	W	1-0	1-0	4	Danjuma[35]	0
4	Oct 2	A	Coventry C	W	3-1	1-1	1	Lerma[7], Gosling 2[51, 60]	0
5	17	H	QPR	D	0-0	0-0	3		0
6	21	A	Cardiff C	D	1-1	1-0	4	Solanke[35]	0
7	24	A	Watford	D	1-1	0-1	4	Mepham[90]	0
8	28	H	Bristol C	W	1-0	0-0	2	Danjuma[81]	0
9	31	H	Derby Co	D	1-1	0-1	3	Riquelme[81]	0
10	Nov 3	A	Sheffield W	L	0-1	0-0	4		0
11	7	A	Birmingham C	W	3-1	2-0	4	Danjuma[9], Brooks 2[42, 50]	0
12	21	H	Reading	W	4-2	0-2	2	Solanke 2[56, 89], Danjuma[59], Cook, L[77]	0
13	24	H	Nottingham F	W	2-0	1-0	2	Stanislas 2 (1 pen)[3, 51 (p)]	0
14	28	A	Rotherham U	D	2-2	1-1	2	Stanislas (pen)[20], Solanke[63]	0
15	Dec 1	H	Preston NE	L	2-3	0-1	2	Stanislas[71], Surridge[86]	0
16	4	A	Barnsley	W	4-0	2-0	1	Billing[12], Solanke[45], Rico[52], Surridge[68]	0
17	8	A	Swansea C	D	0-0	0-0	1		0
18	12	H	Huddersfield T	W	5-0	3-0	2	Solanke 2[8, 13], Brooks[21], Stanislas[67], Surridge[70]	0
19	15	H	Wycombe W	W	1-0	0-0	1	Stanislas[68]	0
20	19	A	Luton T	D	0-0	0-0	2		0
21	30	A	Brentford	L	1-2	1-1	4	Solanke[25]	0
22	Jan 2	A	Stoke C	W	1-0	0-0	3	Stanislas[79]	0
23	12	H	Millwall	D	1-1	1-0	3	Solanke[45]	0
24	16	H	Luton T	L	0-1	0-0	3		0
25	19	A	Derby Co	L	0-1	0-1	5		0
26	29	A	Reading	L	1-3	0-3	6	Stanislas[85]	0
27	Feb 2	H	Sheffield W	L	1-2	0-1	6	Stanislas (pen)[66]	0
28	6	H	Birmingham C	W	3-2	1-1	6	Danjuma[36], Wilshere[61], Billing[77]	0
29	13	A	Nottingham F	D	0-0	0-0	6		0
30	17	H	Rotherham U	W	1-0	1-0	6	Billing[23]	0
31	20	A	QPR	L	1-2	0-0	6	Long[69]	0
32	24	H	Cardiff C	L	1-2	0-2	7	Long[67]	0
33	27	H	Watford	W	1-0	0-0	6	Danjuma[61]	0
34	Mar 3	A	Bristol C	W	2-1	1-1	6	Stanislas[45], Carter-Vickers[88]	0
35	6	A	Preston NE	D	1-1	1-0	7	Danjuma[37]	0
36	13	H	Barnsley	L	2-3	2-1	7	Danjuma[22], Solanke[45]	0
37	16	H	Swansea C	W	3-0	2-0	7	Billing[9], Latibeaudiere (og)[45], Danjuma[87]	0
38	Apr 2	H	Middlesbrough	W	3-1	1-0	7	Billing[14], Lerma[66], Solanke[83]	0
39	5	A	Blackburn R	W	2-0	1-0	7	Billing[29], Danjuma[75]	0
40	10	H	Coventry C	W	4-1	2-1	6	Danjuma 2[1, 28], Brooks[69], Solanke[90]	0
41	13	A	Huddersfield T	W	2-1	2-0	5	Billing[15], Solanke[45]	0
42	17	A	Norwich C	W	3-1	0-1	5	Surridge[50], Danjuma[57], Kelly[76]	0
43	21	A	Millwall	W	4-1	3-0	3	Billing[16], Danjuma[27], Brooks[44], Solanke[67]	0
44	24	H	Brentford	L	0-1	0-0	4		0
45	May 1	A	Wycombe W	L	0-1	0-1	5		0
46	8	H	Stoke C	L	0-2	0-1	6		0

Final League Position: 6

GOALSCORERS

League (73): Danjuma 15, Solanke 15, Stanislas 10 (3 pens), Billing 8, Brooks 5, Surridge 4, Lerma 3, Gosling 2, Long 2, Carter-Vickers 1, Cook, L 1, Kelly 1, Mepham 1, Rico 1, Riquelme 1, Stacey 1, Wilshere 1, own goal 1.
1, Riquelme 1, Stanislas 1 (1 pen), Surridge 1, Wilshere 1.
FA Cup (8): King 3, Brooks
Carabao Cup (1): Surridge 1.
Championship Play-Offs (2): Danjuma 2.

Travers M 1	Stacey J 18 + 12	Mepham C 20 + 4	Cook S 42	Kelly L 33 + 3	Smith A 38 + 3	Stanislas J 29 + 6	Cook L 30 + 1	Lerma J 40 + 2	Danjuma A 29 + 4	Solanke D 38 + 2	Gosling D 7 + 8	Brooks D 25 + 7	Billing P 23 + 11	Begovic A 45	Rico D 23 + 9	Surridge S 7 + 22	King J 5 + 7	Simpson J 6 + 3	Ofoborh N — + 3	Riquelme R 2 + 14	Anthony J — + 5	Kilkenny G — + 1	Burchall A — + 1	Zemura J — + 2	Carter-Vickers C 21	Wilshere J 9 + 5	Long S 4 + 7	Pearson B 11 + 5	*Match No.*
1	2	3^{2}	4	5	6	7^{3}	8	9^{1}	10	11	12	13	14																1
	5^{2}	2	3	4	8			6	11^{1}	10	7	9^{3}	13	1	12	14													2
	5	2	3		9		6	7	10^{3}	11^{1}	13		8^{2}	1	4	14	12												3
	2	3	4		6		8^{1}	7		11	9^{3}		12	1	5^{2}	10		13	14										4
	5	2	3		9	13	7	6^{2}	12	10	8			1	4	11^{1}													5
	5	2	3		8^{3}	9		6	11^{1}	10^{2}	7			1	4	13		14		12									6
	6	2	3	4		13	5	7^{1}	10^{2}	12			8	1	9^{3}		11			14									7
	5	2	3	4	8	9^{1}	6		12	10	7			1			11												8
	5^{2}	2	3		8	9^{1}	7		11	10		13	6^{3}	1	4		12			14									9
	14	2	3▮	4	5		13	6	11^{2}	12	7	9^{1}		1	8^{3}		10												10
	2	3		4		9	8^{1}	7	11	10	12	6		1	5														11
	2	12	3	4		8^{2}	7	6^{4}	11	10		9^{3}		1	5^{1}			14	15	13									12
		3	4	5	2	8	7	6^{2}	11^{3}	10	12	9^{1}		1	13					14									13
		3	4	5	2^{2}	11		6		10	8^{1}	9	7	1	12	13													14
		3	4	13	2	8^{4}	7^{3}	6		10		9	14	1	5^{2}	12				11^{1}	15								15
		2	3	4	5^{5}		7^{3}			10^{2}	13	8^{1}	6^{4}	1	9	11			15	14	12	16							16
		2	3	4	5	11	6	13		10		9^{1}	7^{2}	1	8	12													17
			2	4	6^{4}	9^{5}	5	7		11^{3}	13	10^{1}	8^{2}	1		12		3		14			15	16					18
			3	5	2	11	7^{4}	6		10^{2}	15	9^{3}	8^{1}	1	14	12	13	4											19
			3	5	2	11^{1}	7	6		10		9^{3}	8^{2}	1	12	13		4		14									20
			3	5	2	11	7^{1}	6^{3}		10	14	9^{2}	8	1		13	12	4											21
			3	5	2^{2}	8	7	9		10		12		1	6	11^{1}	13	4											22
	15		2	4	5	11^{1}	7	6^{3}		10		9^{2}	12	1	8^{4}		13	3		14									23
	5^{1}		2	12	8^{5}		7	6▮		10		9^{4}	13	1	4^{2}	14	11^{3}			15	16				3				24
	5	12	3	4	8^{2}		7	6	11^{3}	10		9^{4}		1		14	13								2^{1}	15			25
	2	3	4		14	15	7	6^{3}	11^{1}	10		13	8^{4}	1	5^{2}		9									12			26
	2^{3}	3	4	5	14	8^{4}	7	12	11	10^{2}		9		1		13				15						6^{1}			27
	13		4	5	2		6	7	11^{3}			9^{2}	12	1	14										3	8^{1}	10		28
			4^{1}	12	2	9		8	11			13	14	1	5	15									3	6^{2}	10^{4}	7^{3}	29
				4	2	9	7^{2}	6	11^{1}			12	8	1	5	10									3			13	30
		2		4	5	8	6^{2}	7	13				9	1		12									3	10^{1}	11		31
			3	4	5	10	6^{2}	7	13				9	1	8^{1}	11									2		12		32
			4	5	2	9^{1}	6	8	11	10^{2}			14	1											3	12▮	13	7^{3}	33
	14		4	5	2	9^{3}	6^{2}	8	11^{4}	10			12	1	15										3		13	7^{1}	34
			4	5	2	9^{2}	6^{1}	8	11	10				1											3	13	12	7	35
	12		4	5	2^{1}	8		7	10	9			13	1		14									3		11^{2}	6^{3}	36
	2	14	4			8^{1}		7	10^{3}	11			9	1	5					12					3	6^{2}		13	37
	12		4		2	8^{1}		7	10	11^{3}			9	1	5										3	6^{2}	14	13	38
	12		4	5	2			6	10^{3}	11^{2}		8^{1}	9	1	14	13									3			7	39
	16		4	5	2			7	10^{4}	11^{5}		8^{2}	9^{3}	1		14				13	15				3	6^{1}		12	40
	12		4	5	2	13		7	10^{2}	11^{3}		8^{1}	9	1		14									3			6	41
	14		4	5	2	13		7^{1}	10^{3}	11		8^{2}	9	1		12									3			6	42
	2		4	5^{1}	16	13		7	10^{2}	11^{3}		8^{4}	9	1	12	14									3	15		6^{5}	43
	13		4		2^{2}	8		7^{4}	10	11		12	9^{1}	1	5	14									3	6^{3}		15	44
	2	4				10^{1}						8^{2}		1	5^{3}	11				9	13			14	3	6	12	7	45
	15	13	4^{2}	5	2^{4}			6	10	11		8	9^{3}	1						12					3		14	7^{1}	46

FA Cup

Third Round	Oldham Ath	(a)	4-1
Fourth Round	Crawley T	(h)	2-1
Fifth Round	Burnley	(a)	2-0
Sixth Round	Southampton	(h)	0-3

Championship Play-Offs

Semi-Final 1st leg	Brentford	(h)	1-0
Semi-Final 2nd leg	Brentford	(a)	1-3

Carabao Cup

Second Round	Crystal Palace	(h)	0-0
(Bournemouth won 11-10 on penalties)			
Third Round	Manchester C	(a)	1-2

BRADFORD CITY

FOUNDATION

Bradford was a rugby stronghold around the turn of the 20th century but after Manningham RFC held an archery contest to help them out of financial difficulties in 1903, they were persuaded to give up the handling code and turn to soccer. So they formed Bradford City and continued at Valley Parade. Recognising this as an opportunity to spread the dribbling code in this part of Yorkshire, the Football League immediately accepted the new club's first application for membership of the Second Division.

The Utilita Energy Stadium, Valley Parade, Bradford, West Yorkshire BD8 7DY.

Telephone: (01274) 773 355.

Ticket Office: (01274) 770 012.

Website: www.bradfordcityafc.co.uk

Email: support@bradfordcityfc.co.uk

Ground Capacity: 24,433.

Record Attendance: 39,146 v Burnley, FA Cup 4th rd, 11 March 1911.

Pitch Measurements: 100m × 65m (109.5yd × 71yd).

Chairman: Stephan Rupp.

Director: Alan Biggin.

Manager: Derek Adams.

Recruitment Director: Lee Turnbull.

Colours: Claret shirts with amber stripes, black shorts with amber and claret trim, black socks with amber and claret trim.

Year Formed: 1903.

Turned Professional: 1903.

Club Nickname: 'The Bantams'.

Ground: 1903, Valley Parade (renamed Bradford & Bingley Stadium 1999, Intersonic Stadium 2007, Coral Windows Stadium 2007, Northern Commercials Stadium 2016, The Utilita Energy Stadium 2019).

First Football League Game: 1 September 1903, Division 2, v Grimsby T (a) L 0–2 – Seymour; Wilson, Halliday; Robinson, Millar, Farnall; Guy, Beckram, Forrest, McMillan, Graham.

Record League Victory: 11–1 v Rotherham U, Division 3 (N), 25 August 1928 – Sherlaw; Russell, Watson; Burkinshaw (1), Summers, Bauld; Harvey (2), Edmunds (3), White (3), Cairns, Scriven (2).

Record Cup Victory: 11–3 v Walker Celtic, FA Cup 1st rd (replay), 1 December 1937 – Parker; Rookes, McDermott; Murphy, Mackie, Moore; Bagley (1), Whittingham (1), Deakin (4 incl. 1p), Cooke (1), Bartholomew (4).

Record Defeat: 1–9 v Colchester U, Division 4, 30 December 1961.

HONOURS

League Champions: Division 2 – 1907–08; Division 3 – 1984–85; Division 3N – 1928–29.
Runners-up: First Division – 1998–99; Division 4 – 1981–82.

FA Cup Winners: 1911.

League Cup: *Runners-up:* 2013.

European Competitions
Intertoto Cup: 2000.

FOOTBALL YEARBOOK FACT FILE

Bradford City's FA Cup winning team of 1911 did not include a single Yorkshire-born player. Eight of the team, including match winner Jimmy Speirs, were born in Scotland, while Frank Thompson was born in Ireland, and Mark Mellors and George Robinson were born in Nottinghamshire.

Most League Points (2 for a win): 63, Division 3 (N), 1928–29.

Most League Points (3 for a win): 94, Division 3, 1984–85.

Most League Goals: 128, Division 3 (N), 1928–29.

Highest League Scorer in Season: David Layne, 34, Division 4, 1961–62.

Most League Goals in Total Aggregate: Bobby Campbell, 121, 1981–84, 1984–86.

Most League Goals in One Match: 7, Albert Whitehurst v Tranmere R, Division 3 (N), 6 March 1929.

Most Capped Player: Jamie Lawrence, 19 (24), Jamaica.

Most League Appearances: Cec Podd, 502, 1970–84.

Youngest League Player: Robert Cullingford, 16 years 141 days v Mansfield T, 22 April 1970.

Record Transfer Fee Received: £2,000,000 from Newcastle U for Des Hamilton, March 1997; £2,000,000 from Newcastle U for Andrew O'Brien, March 2001.

Record Transfer Fee Paid: £2,500,000 to Leeds U for David Hopkin, July 2000.

Football League Record: 1903 Elected to Division 2; 1908–22 Division 1; 1922–27 Division 2; 1927–29 Division 3 (N); 1929–37 Division 2; 1937–61 Division 3; 1961–69 Division 4; 1969–72 Division 3; 1972–77 Division 4; 1977–78 Division 3; 1978–82 Division 4; 1982–85 Division 3; 1985–90 Division 2; 1990–92 Division 3; 1992–96 Division 2; 1996–99 Division 1; 1999–2001 Premier League; 2001–04 Division 1; 2004–07 FL 1; 2007–13 FL 2; 2013–19 FL 1; 2019– FL 2.

LATEST SEQUENCES

Longest Sequence of League Wins: 10, 26.11.1983 – 3.2.1984.

Longest Sequence of League Defeats: 8, 21.1.1933 – 11.3.1933.

Longest Sequence of League Draws: 6, 30.1.1976 – 13.3.1976.

Longest Sequence of Unbeaten League Matches: 21, 11.1.1969 – 2.5.1969.

Longest Sequence Without a League Win: 16, 28.8.1948 – 20.11.1948.

Successive Scoring Runs: 30 from 26.12.1961.

Successive Non-scoring Runs: 7 from 18.4.1925.

MANAGERS

Robert Campbell 1903–05
Peter O'Rourke 1905–21
David Menzies 1921–26
Colin Veitch 1926–28
Peter O'Rourke 1928–30
Jack Peart 1930–35
Dick Ray 1935–37
Fred Westgarth 1938–43
Bob Sharp 1943–46
Jack Barker 1946–47
John Milburn 1947–48
David Steele 1948–52
Albert Harris 1952
Ivor Powell 1952–55
Peter Jackson 1955–61
Bob Brocklebank 1961–64
Bill Harris 1965–66
Willie Watson 1966–69
Grenville Hair 1967–68
Jimmy Wheeler 1968–71
Bryan Edwards 1971–75
Bobby Kennedy 1975–78
John Napier 1978
George Mulhall 1978–81
Roy McFarland 1981–82
Trevor Cherry 1982–87
Terry Dolan 1987–89
Terry Yorath 1989–90
John Docherty 1990–91
Frank Stapleton 1991–94
Lennie Lawrence 1994–95
Chris Kamara 1995–98
Paul Jewell 1998–2000
Chris Hutchings 2000
Jim Jefferies 2000–01
Nicky Law 2001–03
Bryan Robson 2003–04
Colin Todd 2004–07
Stuart McCall 2007–10
Peter Taylor 2010–11
Peter Jackson 2011
Phil Parkinson 2011–16
Stuart McCall 2016–18
Simon Grayson 2018
Michael Collins 2018
David Hopkin 2018–19
Gary Bowyer 2019–20
Stuart McCall 2020
Mark Trueman and Conor Sellars 2021
Derek Adams June 2021–

TEN YEAR LEAGUE RECORD

		P	W	D	L	F	A	Pts	Pos
2011-12	FL 2	46	12	14	20	54	59	50	18
2012-13	FL 2	46	18	15	13	63	52	69	7
2013-14	FL 1	46	14	17	15	57	54	59	11
2014-15	FL 1	46	17	14	15	55	55	65	7
2015-16	FL 1	46	23	11	12	55	40	80	5
2016-17	FL 1	46	20	19	7	62	43	79	5
2017-18	FL 1	46	18	9	19	57	67	63	11
2018-19	FL 1	46	11	8	27	49	77	41	24
2019-20	FL 2	37	14	12	11	44	40	54	9§
2020-21	FL 2	46	16	11	19	48	53	59	15

§Decided on points-per-game (1.46)

DID YOU KNOW ?

Bradford City's Jimmy Marshall became the first player to score a top-flight hat-trick after football resumed following the end of the First World War. Marshall netted after 35, 55 and 61 minutes of the Bantams' 5-1 win at Preston on 1 September 1919.

BRADFORD CITY – SKY BET LEAGUE TWO 2020–21 LEAGUE RECORD

Match No.	Date	Venue	Opponents	Result	H/T Score	Lg Pos.	Goalscorers	Attendance
1	Sept 12	H	Colchester U	D 0-0	0-0	14		0
2	19	A	Forest Green R	D 2-2	0-0	15	Novak 49, Watt 66	1000
3	26	H	Stevenage	W 2-1	0-1	9	Novak 2 61, 81	0
4	Oct 12	H	Harrogate T	L 0-1	0-0	16		0
5	17	A	Mansfield T	W 3-1	2-0	13	Stech (og) 8, Wood, Connor 14, Donaldson 69	0
6	20	H	Walsall	D 1-1	0-1	14	Clarke (pen) 76	0
7	24	H	Newport Co	L 0-3	0-2	15		0
8	27	A	Bolton W	L 0-1	0-1	15		0
9	31	A	Barrow	L 0-1	0-1	16		0
10	Nov 3	H	Southend U	W 3-0	3-0	15	Cooke 5, Watt 33, Pritchard 43	0
11	14	H	Exeter C	D 2-2	2-2	16	Clarke 10, Staunton 45	0
12	21	A	Salford C	L 0-3	0-3	19		0
13	24	A	Leyton Orient	L 0-1	0-0	20		0
14	Dec 1	H	Cheltenham T	L 1-2	1-1	21	Donaldson 23	0
15	5	H	Carlisle U	L 0-1	0-0	23		0
16	12	A	Oldham Ath	L 1-3	0-2	22	O'Connor, P 85	0
17	15	A	Crawley T	D 1-1	1-1	21	Novak 11	0
18	19	H	Cambridge U	W 1-0	1-0	21	Pritchard 42	0
19	22	A	Grimsby T	W 2-1	2-0	18	Novak 21, Sutton 45	0
20	26	A	Tranmere R	W 1-0	0-0	18	Novak 62	0
21	29	H	Port Vale	D 0-0	0-0	18		0
22	Jan 23	A	Cambridge U	D 0-0	0-0	20		0
23	26	A	Southend U	W 3-1	1-1	18	Evans 2 23, 74, Rowe 57	0
24	30	H	Barrow	W 2-1	1-1	17	Rowe 5, Cooke 49	0
25	Feb 6	A	Exeter C	L 2-3	2-1	19	Vernam 17, Crankshaw 45	0
26	16	H	Morecambe	W 2-1	1-1	16	O'Connor, A 27, Vernam 63	0
27	20	A	Cheltenham T	W 2-0	1-0	13	Cook 2 11, 51	0
28	23	H	Leyton Orient	W 1-0	0-0	11	Cooke (pen) 81	0
29	27	A	Walsall	W 2-1	1-0	11	Sutton 43, Cook 66	0
30	Mar 2	H	Mansfield T	W 1-0	1-0	10	Rowe 32	0
31	6	H	Bolton W	D 1-1	0-0	10	Rowe 90	0
32	9	A	Newport Co	L 1-2	0-0	12	Cook 46	0
33	13	A	Carlisle U	L 1-3	0-2	13	O'Connor, P 64	0
34	20	H	Oldham Ath	D 0-0	0-0	12		0
35	23	A	Scunthorpe U	L 0-2	0-1	14		0
36	27	A	Colchester U	W 2-1	1-1	12	Scales 10, Cook 58	0
37	Apr 2	H	Forest Green R	W 4-1	1-0	10	Watt 10, Cook 2 47, 76, Rowe 90	0
38	5	A	Stevenage	D 1-1	1-1	11	Donaldson 27	0
39	10	H	Grimsby T	W 1-0	1-0	11	O'Connor, A 42	0
40	13	H	Crawley T	L 0-2	0-1	12		0
41	17	A	Harrogate T	L 1-2	0-1	13	Cook 72	0
42	20	H	Tranmere R	L 0-1	0-1	13		0
43	24	A	Port Vale	L 1-2	1-2	14	Donaldson 14	0
44	27	H	Salford C	L 0-1	0-0	14		0
45	May 1	H	Scunthorpe U	D 0-0	0-0	14		0
46	8	A	Morecambe	L 0-2	0-1	15		0

Final League Position: 15

GOALSCORERS

League (48): Cook 8, Novak 6, Rowe 5, Donaldson 4, Cooke 3 (1 pen), Watt 3, Clarke 2 (1 pen), Evans 2, O'Connor, A 2, O'Connor, P 2, Pritchard 2, Sutton 2, Vernam 2, Crankshaw 1, Scales 1, Staunton 1, Wood, Connor 1, own goal 1.
FA Cup (8): Clarke 2, Donaldson 2 (1 pen), O'Connor A 1, Pritchard 1, Samuels 1, Wood, Connor 1.
Carabao Cup (2): Novak 1, Pritchard 1.
Papa John's Trophy (2): Donaldson 1, own goal 1.

O'Donnell R 28	O'Connor A 45	O'Connor P 41 + 1	Staunton R 8	Mottley-Henry D 4 + 7	Cooke C 30 + 4	Watt E 44 + 2	Wood Connor 46	Clarke B 20 + 9	Guthrie K 4 + 4	Novak L 15 + 2	Ismail Z 1 + 2	Donaldson C 19 + 16	Pritchard H 11 + 5	French T 7 + 7	Cousin-Dawson F 20 + 3	Richards-Everton B 9 + 1	Sutton L 30 + 4	Evans G 19 + 8	Longridge J — + 2	Samuels A 6 + 6	Hosannah B 8	Scales K 6 + 14	Hornby S 18	Rowe D 8 + 10	Stevens J 1 + 15	Burrell R — + 2	Cook A 16 + 5	Crankshaw O 11 + 8	Vernam C 15 + 6	Canavan N 15 + 1	Foulds M — + 3	Sikora J 1	Match No.
1	2	3	4	5^{1}	6^{3}	7	8	9	10^{2}	11	12	13	14																				1
1	2■	3■	4^{3}	12	13	6	8	7^{2}	11	10	9^{1}			5	14																		2
1			3		8^{1}	7	5	9^{2}	10	11				2		4	6	12	13														3
1	3		4		12	6	5	9^{2}	14	10		11^{3}		2			7	8^{1}		13													4
1	3			6^{1}	8	7	5			11		10^{2}	9^{3}	12		4			14	13	2												5
1	3			6	7	8	5	13	14	10		11^{3}	9^{2}	12		4					2^{1}												6
1	3	12		13	7	6	5	8	11^{3}	10		14		2^{1}		4				9^{2}													7
1	2	3			9	7	8	10^{2}				11	12		6^{1}	4				13	5												8
1	2	3	4	12	9	13	8					11			6^{2}		7■			10^{1}	5												9
1	2	3	4	12	6	7^{2}	8	11				10^{1}	9		13						5												10
1	2	3	4		7^{1}	5	9	10^{2}				11	8	6						12		13											11
1	2	3		13		5	9				15	11	7^{3}	6		4^{2}	14	8^{1}		10^{4}		12											12
1	2	3	4^{1}	14		7	8	9^{2}				11		5		12	6			10^{3}		13											13
1	2	3		11^{3}	8^{2}	7	5					10	13	12		4				14	9^{1}	6											14
1	2	3		13	6^{3}	7^{4}	5					11	8^{1}	14		4	15			10	9^{2}	12											15
1	2	3			6	7	9			10		11	8	12		4^{1}	13				5^{2}												16
1	4	3			9	7	5			11^{3}		14	10^{2}	13	2		6			8^{1}		12											17
1	4	3			9	6	5	7^{2}	14	11^{3}			10^{1}		2		8	12		13													18
1	4	3			9^{4}	7	5	8^{1}	12	11^{3}		14	10^{2}	15	2		6	13															19
1	4	3			13	7	5	8		9		11^{1}	12		2		6	10^{2}															20
	4	3			9	7	5	8		11			10^{1}		2		6	12					1										21
	4	3			9	7	5	8^{1}							2		6	10					1	11	12								22
	4	3			9^{1}	7	5	8^{2}				14			2		6	10^{4}				15	1	11^{3}	12	13							23
	4	3			9	7	5	8^{3}							2		6^{1}	10				14	1	11^{2}	12		13						24
	4	3			9	7	5					14	13		2^{1}		6^{2}					15	1		8^{3}	16		10^{5}	11^{4}	12			25
	2	3			9	7	5										6	10^{2}					1	12	14		11^{1}	13	8^{3}	4			26
	2	3			9^{3}	7	5										6^{4}	10				15	1	12	14		11^{1}	13	8^{2}	4			27
	2	3			9^{4}	7	5					15					6	10^{1}					1	11^{2}	14		13	12	8^{3}	4			28
	2	3			9^{2}	7	5	12				15					6						1	13	14		11^{1}	8^{4}	10^{3}	4			29
	2	3			9^{4}	7	5	12				14			15		6						1	11^{3}	13			10^{1}	8^{2}	4			30
	2	3			9^{1}	7	5	12				15					6						1	13	14		11^{3}	10^{4}	8^{2}	4			31
	2	3				7	5	8^{2}				15					6	13					1	9^{1}	14		11^{3}	10^{4}	12	4			32
	2	3				7^{2}	5	13									6^{4}	9				15	1	12	14		11	10^{1}	8^{3}	4			33
1	2	3				7	5										6	10				13		11^{1}			12	8	9^{2}	4			34
1	2	3				7^{2}	5					15					6	13				9^{3}		12	14		11	8^{4}	10^{1}	4			35
1	7	3				12	5					9^{3}			2^{1}		6	10				8^{4}		13	15		11^{2}			4	14		36
1	6	3				7	5	12				9^{2}			2			10^{1}				8^{4}		13			11^{3}	15	14	4			37
1	6	3				7	5	12				9^{4}			2			10^{1}				8^{2}		14			11^{3}	15	13	4			38
1	3	2				5^{4}	9	7^{1}				10^{3}			6			8				15		12			11^{2}	14	13	4			39
1	6	3				7	5	15				12			2		13	10^{4}				8^{2}		11^{3}			14	16	9^{5}	4^{1}			40
1	4	3				7^{2}	5	8^{3}				9			2		6	13				14					11	12	10^{1}				41
	4	3			13	7^{3}	5	8^{1}				14			2		6	9^{2}					1				11	10	12				42
	4	3			7	8	5			14		11^{3}					2	12					1				10	9^{1}	6^{2}		13		43
	4	3			9	7	5			12					2		6	10					1		13		11^{1}		8^{2}				44
	4	3			9	7	5			11^{3}		14			2^{1}		6	10^{2}				13	1				12		8				45
	2	4			9	8^{5}	5^{4}	14		11		13					7						1		12		10^{1}	6^{2}	16		15	3^{3}	46

FA Cup

First Round	Tonbridge Angels	(a)	7-0
Second Round	Oldham Ath	(h)	1-2

Carabao Cup

First Round	Bolton W	(a)	2-1
Second Round	Lincoln C	(h)	0-5

Papa John's Trophy

Group F (N) Doncaster R (a) 0-0
(Doncaster R won 4-1 on penalties)
Group F (N) Wolverhampton W U21 (h) 1-1
(Wolverhampton W U21 won 5-3 on penalties)
Group F (N) Oldham Ath (h) 1-3

BRENTFORD

FOUNDATION

Formed as a small amateur concern in 1889 they were very successful in local circles. They won the championship of the West London Alliance in 1893 and a year later the West Middlesex Junior Cup before carrying off the Senior Cup in 1895. After winning both the London Senior Amateur Cup and the Middlesex Senior Cup in 1898 they were admitted to the Second Division of the Southern League.

Brentford Community Stadium, 166 Lionel Road North, Brentford, Middlesex TW8 9QT.

Telephone: (0208) 847 2511 (option 0).

Ticket Office: (0208) 847 2511 (option 1).

Website: www.brentfordfc.com

Email: enquiries@brentfordfc.com

Ground Capacity: 17,250.

Record Attendance: 38,678 v Leicester C, FA Cup 6th rd, 26 February 1949 (at Griffin Park).

Pitch Measurements: 105m × 66m (115yd × 72yd).

Chairman: Cliff Crown.

Chief Executive: Jon Varney.

Head Coach: Thomas Frank.

Assistant Head Coach: Brian Riemer.

Colours: Red and white striped shirts with black trim, black shorts with red trim, black socks with red trim.

Year Formed: 1889.

Turned Professional: 1899.

Club Nickname: 'The Bees'.

Grounds: 1889, Clifden Road; 1891, Benns Fields, Little Ealing; 1895, Shotters Field; 1898, Cross Road, S. Ealing; 1900, Boston Park; 1904, Griffin Park; 2020, Brentford Community Stadium.

First Football League Game: 28 August 1920, Division 3, v Exeter C (a) L 0–3 – Young; Hodson, Rosier, Jimmy Elliott, Levitt, Amos, Smith, Thompson, Spreadbury, Morley, Henery.

Record League Victory: 9–0 v Wrexham, Division 3, 15 October 1963 – Cakebread; Coote, Jones; Slater, Scott, Higginson; Summers (1), Brooks (2), McAdams (2), Ward (2), Hales (1), (1 og).

Record Cup Victory: 7–0 v Windsor & Eton (away), FA Cup 1st rd, 20 November 1982 – Roche; Rowe, Harris (Booker), McNichol (1), Whitehead, Hurlock (2), Kamara, Joseph (1), Mahoney (3), Bowles, Roberts. *N.B.* 8–0 v Uxbridge: Frail, Jock Watson, Caie, Bellingham, Parsonage (1), Jay, Atherton, Leigh (1), Bell (2), Buchanan (2), Underwood (2), FA Cup, 3rd Qual rd, 31 October 1903.

Record Defeat: 0–7 v Swansea T, Division 3 (S), 8 November 1924; v Walsall, Division 3 (S), 19 January 1957; v Peterborough U, 24 November 2007.

HONOURS

League Champions: Division 2 – 1934–35; Division 3 – 1991–92; Division 3S – 1932–33; FL 2 – 2008–09; Third Division – 1998–99; Division 4 – 1962–63.
Runners-up: FL 1 – 2013–14; Second Division – 1994–95; Division 3S – 1929–30, 1957–58.

FA Cup: 6th rd – 1938, 1946, 1949, 1989.

League Cup: semi-final 2021.

League Trophy: *Runners-up:* 1985, 2001, 2011.

FOOTBALL YEARBOOK FACT FILE

Brentford FC was incorporated as a limited company on 7 August 1901 under the name Brentford Football and Sports Club. The initial share capital was £2,000 made up of 4,000 shares of 10s (50p) each, although by November 1901 only 1,275 of these had been taken up.

Most League Points (2 for a win): 62, Division 3 (S), 1932–33 and Division 4, 1962–63.

Most League Points (3 for a win): 94, FL 1, 2013–14.

Most League Goals: 98, Division 4, 1962–63.

Highest League Scorer in Season: Jack Holliday, 38, Division 3 (S), 1932–33.

Most League Goals in Total Aggregate: Jim Towers, 153, 1954–61.

Most League Goals in One Match: 5, Jack Holliday v Luton T, Division 3 (S), 28 January 1933; 5, Billy Scott v Barnsley, Division 2, 15 December 1934; 5, Peter McKennan v Bury, Division 2, 18 February 1949.

Most Capped Player: John Buttigieg, 22 (98), Malta; Henrik Dalsgaard, 22 (27), Denmark.

Most League Appearances: Ken Coote, 514, 1949–64.

Youngest League Player: Danis Salman, 15 years 248 days v Watford, 15 November 1975.

Record Transfer Fee Received: £28,000,000 from Aston Villa for Ollie Watkins, September 2020.

Record Transfer Fee Paid: £5,800,000 to Troyes for Bryan Mbeumo, July 2019.

Football League Record: 1920 Original Member of Division 3; 1921–33 Division 3 (S); 1933–35 Division 2; 1935–47 Division 1; 1947–54 Division 2; 1954–62 Division 3 (S); 1962–63 Division 4; 1963–66 Division 3; 1966–72 Division 4; 1972–73 Division 3; 1973–78 Division 4; 1978–92 Division 3; 1992–93 Division 1; 1993–98 Division 2; 1998–99 Division 3; 1999–2004 Division 2; 2004–07 FL 1; 2007–09 FL 2; 2009–14 FL 1; 2014–21 FL C; 2021– Premier League.

LATEST SEQUENCES

Longest Sequence of League Wins: 9, 30.4.1932 – 24.9.1932.

Longest Sequence of League Defeats: 9, 20.10.1928 – 25.12.1928.

Longest Sequence of League Draws: 5, 16.3.1957 – 6.4.1957.

Longest Sequence of Unbeaten League Matches: 26, 20.2.1999 – 16.10.1999.

Longest Sequence Without a League Win: 18, 9.9.2006 – 26.12.2006.

Successive Scoring Runs: 26 from 4.3.1963.

Successive Non-scoring Runs: 7 from 7.3.2000.

MANAGERS

Will Lewis 1900–03 (*Secretary-Manager*)
Dick Molyneux 1902–06
W. G. Brown 1906–08
Fred Halliday 1908–12, 1915–21, 1924–26 (*only Secretary to 1922*)
Ephraim Rhodes 1912–15
Archie Mitchell 1921–24
Harry Curtis 1926–49
Jackie Gibbons 1949–52
Jimmy Bain 1952–53
Tommy Lawton 1953
Bill Dodgin Snr 1953–57
Malcolm Macdonald 1957–65
Tommy Cavanagh 1965–66
Billy Gray 1966–67
Jimmy Sirrel 1967–69
Frank Blunstone 1969–73
Mike Everitt 1973–75
John Docherty 1975–76
Bill Dodgin Jnr 1976–80
Fred Callaghan 1980–84
Frank McLintock 1984–87
Steve Perryman 1987–90
Phil Holder 1990–93
David Webb 1993–97
Eddie May 1997
Micky Adams 1997–98
Ron Noades 1998–2000
Ray Lewington 2000–01
Steve Coppell 2001–02
Wally Downes 2002–04
Martin Allen 2004–06
Leroy Rosenior 2006
Scott Fitzgerald 2006–07
Terry Butcher 2007
Andy Scott 2007–11
Nicky Forster 2011
Uwe Rosler 2011–13
Mark Warburton 2013–15
Marinus Dijkhuizen 2015
Dean Smith 2015–18
Thomas Frank October 2018–

TEN YEAR LEAGUE RECORD

		P	W	D	L	F	A	Pts	Pos
2011-12	FL 1	46	18	13	15	63	52	67	9
2012-13	FL 1	46	21	16	9	62	47	79	3
2013-14	FL 1	46	28	10	8	72	43	94	2
2014-15	FL C	46	23	9	14	78	59	78	5
2015-16	FL C	46	19	8	19	72	67	65	9
2016-17	FL C	46	18	10	18	75	65	64	10
2017-18	FL C	46	18	15	13	62	52	69	9
2018-19	FL C	46	17	13	16	73	59	64	11
2019-20	FL C	46	24	9	13	80	38	81	3
2020-21	FL C	46	24	15	7	79	42	87	3

DID YOU KNOW 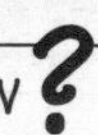

Brentford lifted their third trophy in three seasons when they won the West Middlesex Cup in 1894–95. The Bees defeated Hanwell, Yiewsley and Hounslow on their way to the final, where they beat local rivals the 8th Hussars (KRI) 4-2 in front of 4,000 fans at the White Hart Field, Southall.

BRENTFORD – SKY BET CHAMPIONSHIP 2020–21 LEAGUE RECORD

Match No.	Date	Venue	Opponents	Result		H/T Score	Lg Pos.	Goalscorers	Attendance
1	Sept 12	A	Birmingham C	L	0-1	0-1	15		0
2	19	H	Huddersfield T	W	3-0	0-0	10	Dasilva [57], Forss [86], Mbeumo [90]	0
3	26	A	Millwall	D	1-1	1-1	9	Toney (pen) [21]	0
4	Oct 4	H	Preston NE	L	2-4	2-0	14	Toney 2 [8, 43]	0
5	17	H	Coventry C	W	2-0	0-0	10	Toney 2 [46, 55]	0
6	21	A	Sheffield W	W	2-1	2-1	7	Toney 2 [7, 30]	0
7	24	A	Stoke C	L	2-3	0-2	11	Forss 2 [70, 90]	0
8	27	H	Norwich C	D	1-1	1-0	11	Toney [27]	0
9	31	A	Luton T	W	3-0	2-0	9	Henry [20], Toney [29], Forss [76]	0
10	Nov 3	H	Swansea C	D	1-1	1-0	8	Toney [36]	0
11	7	H	Middlesbrough	D	0-0	0-0	11		0
12	21	A	Wycombe W	D	0-0	0-0	11		0
13	24	A	Barnsley	W	1-0	0-0	8	Toney [66]	0
14	27	H	QPR	W	2-1	1-1	4	Janelt [14], Toney [64]	0
15	Dec 1	A	Rotherham U	W	2-0	0-0	4	Forss [57], Toney (pen) [82]	0
16	5	H	Blackburn R	D	2-2	1-1	6	Toney (pen) [37], Canos [61]	2000
17	9	H	Derby Co	D	0-0	0-0	7		2000
18	12	A	Nottingham F	W	3-1	1-0	6	Dalsgaard [15], Dasilva [83], Toney [88]	0
19	15	A	Watford	D	1-1	0-0	6	Toney (pen) [63]	0
20	19	H	Reading	W	3-1	3-0	4	Jensen [11], Mbeumo 2 [23, 29]	0
21	26	A	Cardiff C	W	3-2	0-1	4	Canos 3 [50, 65, 73]	0
22	30	H	Bournemouth	W	2-1	1-1	2	Dalsgaard [37], Fosu [79]	0
23	Jan 20	H	Luton T	W	1-0	1-0	3	Ghoddos [14]	0
24	27	A	Swansea C	D	1-1	0-0	4	Fosu [74]	0
25	30	H	Wycombe W	W	7-2	2-2	3	Pinnock [9], Toney 3 (1 pen) [41, 56 (p), 86], Fosu [50], Canos [81], Dasilva [89]	0
26	Feb 3	H	Bristol C	W	3-2	1-1	2	Canos [27], Toney [50], Ghoddos [65]	0
27	6	A	Middlesbrough	W	4-1	1-1	2	Toney 2 [38, 80], Janelt [58], Jensen [64]	0
28	10	A	Reading	W	3-1	1-1	1	Dasilva 2 [36, 86], Toney [88]	0
29	14	H	Barnsley	L	0-2	0-1	2		0
30	17	A	QPR	L	1-2	1-0	2	Toney [30]	0
31	20	A	Coventry C	L	0-2	0-1	2		0
32	24	H	Sheffield W	W	3-0	1-0	2	Mbeumo [23], Ghoddos [74], Sorensen [83]	0
33	27	H	Stoke C	W	2-1	0-1	2	Janelt [56], Toney [79]	0
34	Mar 3	A	Norwich C	L	0-1	0-1	2		0
35	12	A	Blackburn R	W	1-0	1-0	2	Toney (pen) [10]	0
36	16	A	Derby Co	D	2-2	2-0	4	Toney (pen) [8], Canos [23]	0
37	20	H	Nottingham F	D	1-1	1-0	4	Toney (pen) [12]	0
38	Apr 3	A	Huddersfield T	D	1-1	0-1	3	Sorensen [50]	0
39	6	H	Birmingham C	D	0-0	0-0	3		0
40	10	A	Preston NE	W	5-0	2-0	3	Mbeumo [9], Forss [26], Toney [75], Canos [82], Marcondes [90]	0
41	17	H	Millwall	D	0-0	0-0	4		0
42	20	H	Cardiff C	D	1-1	0-0	4	Fosu [63]	0
43	24	A	Bournemouth	W	1-0	0-0	3	Mbeumo [77]	0
44	27	H	Rotherham U	W	1-0	1-0	3	Mbeumo [26]	0
45	May 1	H	Watford	W	2-0	0-0	3	Forss [46], Toney (pen) [60]	0
46	8	A	Bristol C	W	3-1	0-0	3	Toney [57], Mbeumo [78], Canos [83]	0

Final League Position: 3

GOALSCORERS

League (79): Toney 31 (9 pens), Canos 9, Mbeumo 8, Forss 7, Dasilva 5, Fosu 4, Ghoddos 3, Janelt 3, Dalsgaard 2, Jensen 2, Sorensen 2, Henry 1, Marcondes 1, Pinnock 1.
FA Cup (3): Dervisoglu 1, Ghoddos 1, Sorensen 1.
Carabao Cup (9): Benrahma 2, Dasilva 2, Forss 2 (1 pen), Marcondes 1, Norgaard 1, Pinnock 1.
Championship Play-Offs (5): Toney 2 (2 pens), Forss 1, Janelt 1, Marcondes 1.

Daniels L 4	Dalsgaard H 34 + 1	Jansson P 23 + 1	Pinnock E 39	Henry R 30	Mbeumo B 37 + 7	Dasilva J 26 + 4	Norgaard C 15 + 2	Jensen M 35 + 10	Canos S 33 + 13	Toney I 44 + 1	Marcondes E 12 + 19	Forss M 9 + 30	Fosu T 19 + 20	Baptiste S — + 1	Thompson D 1 + 3	Benrahma S — + 2	Ghoddos S 16 + 24	Raya D 42	Janelt V 36 + 5	Sorensen M 29 + 3	Goode C 4 + 4	Pressley A — + 2	Haygarth M — + 1	Zamburek J — + 6	Roerslev Rasmussen M 10 + 7	Reid W 7 + 3	Bidstrup M 1 + 3	Stevens F — + 2	Match No.
1	2	3	4	5	6	7	8	9^{1}	10^{2}	11	12^{3}	13	14																1
1	2	3	4	5	9	6^{3}	7		11^{1}	10^{2}	8	13	12	14															2
1	2	3	4	5^{1}	9	6^{3}	7	14	11^{2}	10	8				12	13													3
1	2	3	4		9	8	7^{1}	12	11^{3}	10	6^{2}				5	13	14												4
	2	3	4	5	9	8^{3}		7	11	10^{1}	6^{2}	12					14	1	13										5
	2	3^{2}	4	5	9^{1}	8		6	12	10			14				11^{3}	1	7	13									6
	5		3	8	13	7		12	9	10		14					11^{1}	1	6^{3}	4^{2}	2								7
	2		3	5	9	8^{2}		7	12	10^{3}	6	14					11^{1}	1	13	4									8
	2		3	5	9^{3}	6		12	11	10^{2}	8^{1}	13	14					1	7	4									9
	2		4	5	9^{3}	8		7	12	10	6^{2}	14					11^{1}	1	13		3								10
	2		3	5	9^{1}	8		6	11^{2}	10		12	14				13	1	7^{3}	4									11
	2	3		5	9^{3}	8		7	11^{2}	10		12	13				6^{1}	1	14	4									12
	2	3	4	5	9^{2}	8^{1}		6	13	10^{4}	12	14	11^{3}				15	1	7										13
	2^{1}	13	3	5	9^{5}	6^{2}		12	14	10	8^{3}	15	11^{4}				16	1	7	4									14
		3	4	5	11^{1}	8^{2}		7	12	10^{3}	13	9^{4}	2				15	1	6			14							15
	2	3	4	5^{5}	13	8^{4}		6	9^{3}	10	12	11^{2}	14		15		16	1	7^{1}										16
	2	3		5	9^{2}	8		12	11^{3}	10	6^{1}	14	13				15	1	7^{4}	4									17
	2		3	5	9^{3}	13		8^{2}	12	10^{5}	6^{4}		11^{1}				14	1	7	4		15	16						18
	2		3■	5	9^{2}	6^{3}		8	11^{1}	10	14	13						1	7	4	12								19
				5^{1}	9^{3}	6^{2}		8	11^{4}	10	13	15	2		12		14	1	7	4	3								20
	2	3	4	5	9^{1}	13		8^{3}	11^{2}	10	6	14	12					1	7										21
	2	3	4	5	9^{3}	6^{2}		8	11^{1}	10	13		12				14	1	7										22
	2		3	5	9^{1}			8	11^{2}	10■		13	12				6^{3}	1	7	4				14					23
	2		3	5	9^{1}	6		8	11^{2}	10		13	12				14	1	7^{3}	4									24
	2		4	5^{4}		8		7^{1}	11	10		14	9^{2}				6^{3}	1	12	3				13	15				25
	2		3	5^{3}				8	11	10^{4}		13	9^{1}				6^{2}	1	7	4				12	15	14			26
	2		3	5	12			6	11^{1}	10^{4}		15	9^{2}				8^{3}	1	7	4				13		14			27
	2		3	5	9^{1}	6^{4}		8^{3}	12	10		15	11^{2}				13	1	7	4				14					28
	2^{3}		3	5	9^{1}	6^{4}		13	11	10		15	12				8^{2}	1	7	4					14				29
	2^{3}			5	12	6^{2}		8	11	10		15	9^{1}				13	1	7^{4}	4					14	3			30
	13		3	5^{4}	9^{2}	12		6	11			10	14				8^{3}	1	7	4					2^{1}	15			31
	2^{4}		4		10^{3}	13		6	11^{1}	12	15		9^{2}				8^{5}	1	7	5				14	16	3			32
	2		4		9	6^{2}	14	12	13	10	15		11^{1}				8^{4}	1	7^{3}	5						3			33
	2		4		9		12	6	11^{2}	10		15	13				8^{4}	1	7^{1}	5					14	3^{3}			34
	2		4		9^{4}		7^{3}	6^{2}	13	10	12	15	11^{1}				14	1	8	5						3			35
	2	3			9^{3}		7^{4}	6^{1}	11^{2}	10		15	12				13	1	8	5					14	4			36
	2	3			9^{2}		7	6^{4}	11^{3}	10	14	15	13				12	1	8^{1}	5						4			37
		3	4		9^{4}		7	12	11^{2}	10	13	15	14				6^{3}	1	8^{1}	5					2				38
		3	4		11^{3}		7	6^{2}	9^{4}	10	12	15	14				13	1	8^{1}	5					2				39
		2	4		8		3	7^{4}	12	10	15	9^{2}	6^{1}				13	1	11^{3}						5^{5}		14	16	40
		2	4		9		3	8^{2}	12	11	14	10	7^{3}				13	1	5						6^{1}				41
		2	4		8^{3}		3	7	12	11	14	10	9^{4}				13	1	6^{1}		15				5^{2}				42
		2■	4		14		3	6^{4}	8^{1}	11	15	10^{3}	9^{2}				16	1	7	13	12				5^{5}				43
			4		11^{2}			15	8^{1}	10	9	14	12				6^{3}	1	7^{4}	3	2				5		13		44
		2			12		3	6^{3}	8	10^{2}	14	11^{1}	9				13	1		4	15				5^{5}		7^{4}	16	45
		2	4^{1}		14		3	6	8	10^{3}	15	11^{2}	9^{4}				13	1	7^{5}	12					5		16		46

FA Cup

Third Round	Middlesbrough	(h)	2-1
Fourth Round	Leicester C	(h)	1-3

Championship Play-Offs

Semi-Final 1st leg	Bournemouth	(a)	0-1
Semi-Final 2nd leg	Bournemouth	(h)	3-1
Final	Swansea C	(Wembley)	2-0

Carabao Cup

First Round	Wycombe W	(h)	1-1
(Brentford won 4-2 on penalties)			
Second Round	Southampton	(a)	2-0
Third Round	WBA	(a)	2-2
(Brentford won 5-4 on penalties)			
Fourth Round	Fulham	(h)	3-0
Quarter-Final	Newcastle U	(h)	1-0
Semi-Final	Tottenham H	(a)	0-2

BRIGHTON & HOVE ALBION

FOUNDATION

A professional club Brighton United was formed in November 1897 at the Imperial Hotel, Queen's Road, but folded in March 1900 after less than two seasons in the Southern League at the County Ground. An amateur team Brighton & Hove Rangers was then formed by some prominent United supporters and after one season at Withdean, decided to turn semi-professional and play at the County Ground. Rangers were accepted into the Southern League but folded in June 1901. John Jackson, the former United manager, organised a meeting at the Seven Stars public house, Ship Street on 24 June 1901 at which a new third club Brighton & Hove United was formed. They took over Rangers' place in the Southern League and pitch at County Ground. The name was changed to Brighton & Hove Albion before a match was played because of objections by Hove FC.

American Express Community Stadium, Village Way, Falmer, Brighton BN1 9BL.

Telephone: (01273) 668 855.

Ticket Office: (0844) 327 1901.

Website: www.brightonandhovealbion.com

Email: supporter.services@bhafc.co.uk

Ground Capacity: 30,750.

Record Attendance: 36,747 v Fulham, Division 2, 27 December 1958 (at Goldstone Ground); 8,691 v Leeds U, FL 1, 20 October 2007 (at Withdean); 30,682 v Liverpool, Premier League, 12 January 2019 (at Amex).

Pitch Measurements: 105m × 68m (115yd × 74.5yd).

Chairman: Tony Bloom.

Chief Executive: Paul Barber.

Head Coach: Graham Potter.

Assistant Head Coach: Billy Reid.

Colours: Blue and white striped shirts with blue sleeves and white and orange trim, white shorts with orange trim, blue socks with black trim.

Year Formed: 1901.

Turned Professional: 1901.

Club Nickname: 'The Seagulls'.

Grounds: 1901, County Ground; 1902, Goldstone Ground; 1997, groundshare at Gillingham FC; 1999, Withdean Stadium; 2011, American Express Community Stadium.

First Football League Game: 28 August 1920, Division 3, v Southend U (a) L 0–2 – Hayes; Woodhouse, Little; Hall, Comber, Bentley; Longstaff, Ritchie, Doran, Rodgerson, March.

Record League Victory: 9–1 v Newport Co, Division 3 (S), 18 April 1951 – Ball; Tennant (1p), Mansell (1p); Willard, McCoy, Wilson; Reed, McNichol (4), Garbutt, Bennett (2), Keene (1). 9–1 v Southend U, Division 3, 27 November 1965 – Powney; Magill, Baxter; Leck, Gall, Turner; Gould (1), Collins (1), Livesey (2), Smith (3), Goodchild (2).

HONOURS

League Champions: FL 1 – 2010–11; Second Division – 2001–02; Division 3S – 1957–58; Third Division – 2000–01; Division 4 – 1964–65.
Runners-up: FL C – 2016–17; Division 2 – 1978–79; Division 3 – 1971–72, 1976–77, 1987–88; Division 3S – 1953–54, 1955–56.

FA Cup: *Runners-up:* 1983.

League Cup: 5th rd – 1979.

FOOTBALL YEARBOOK FACT FILE

Brighton & Hove Albion were members of the Southern League from 1901 to 1920 when the club was elected to the Football League. The Seagulls' reserve team continued to play in the competition for a further decade and were champions of the English Section of the competition in 1920–21. They then went on to defeat Welsh Section champions Barry in the play-off final for the overall championship.

Record Cup Victory: 10–1 v Wisbech, FA Cup 1st rd, 13 November 1965 – Powney; Magill, Baxter; Collins (1), Gall, Turner; Gould, Smith (2), Livesey (3), Cassidy (2), Goodchild (1), (1 og).

Record Defeat: 0–9 v Middlesbrough, Division 2, 23 August 1958.

Most League Points (2 for a win): 65, Division 3 (S), 1955–56 and Division 3, 1971–72.

Most League Points (3 for a win): 95, FL 1, 2010–11.

Most League Goals: 112, Division 3 (S), 1955–56.

Highest League Scorer in Season: Peter Ward, 32, Division 3, 1976–77.

Most League Goals in Total Aggregate: Tommy Cook, 114, 1922–29.

Most League Goals in One Match: 5, Jack Doran v Northampton T, Division 3 (S), 5 November 1921; 5, Adrian Thorne v Watford, Division 3 (S), 30 April 1958.

Most Capped Player: Shane Duffy, 38 (includes 11 on loan at Celtic) (44), Republic of Ireland.

Most League Appearances: Ernie 'Tug' Wilson, 509, 1922–36.

Youngest League Player: Ian Chapman, 16 years 259 days v Birmingham C, 14 February 1987.

Record Transfer Fee Received: £10,500,000 from Fulham for Anthony Knockaert, July 2020.

Record Transfer Fee Paid: £20,700,000 to RB Salzburg for Enoch Mwepu, July 2021.

Football League Record: 1920 Original Member of Division 3; 1921–58 Division 3 (S); 1958–62 Division 2; 1962–63 Division 3; 1963–65 Division 4; 1965–72 Division 3; 1972–73 Division 2; 1973–77 Division 3; 1977–79 Division 2; 1979–83 Division 1; 1983–87 Division 2; 1987–88 Division 3; 1988–96 Division 2; 1996–2001 Division 3; 2001–02 Division 2; 2002–03 Division 1; 2003–04 Division 2; 2004–06 FL C; 2006–11 FL 1; 2011–17 FL C; 2017– Premier League.

LATEST SEQUENCES

Longest Sequence of League Wins: 9, 2.10.1926 – 20.11.1926.

Longest Sequence of League Defeats: 12, 17.8.2002 – 26.10.2002.

Longest Sequence of League Draws: 6, 16.2.1980 – 15.3.1980.

Longest Sequence of Unbeaten League Matches: 22, 2.5.2015 – 15.12.2015.

Longest Sequence Without a League Win: 15, 21.10.1972 – 27.1.1973.

Successive Scoring Runs: 31 from 4.2.1956.

Successive Non-scoring Runs: 6 from 30.3.2019.

MANAGERS

John Jackson 1901–05
Frank Scott-Walford 1905–08
John Robson 1908–14
Charles Webb 1919–47
Tommy Cook 1947
Don Welsh 1947–51
Billy Lane 1951–61
George Curtis 1961–63
Archie Macaulay 1963–68
Fred Goodwin 1968–70
Pat Saward 1970–73
Brian Clough 1973–74
Peter Taylor 1974–76
Alan Mullery 1976–81
Mike Bailey 1981–82
Jimmy Melia 1982–83
Chris Cattlin 1983–86
Alan Mullery 1986–87
Barry Lloyd 1987–93
Liam Brady 1993–95
Jimmy Case 1995–96
Steve Gritt 1996–98
Brian Horton 1998–99
Jeff Wood 1999
Micky Adams 1999–2001
Peter Taylor 2001–02
Martin Hinshelwood 2002
Steve Coppell 2002–03
Mark McGhee 2003–06
Dean Wilkins 2006–08
Micky Adams 2008–09
Russell Slade 2009
Gus Poyet 2009–13
Óscar Garcia 2013–14
Sammi Hyypia 2014
Chris Hughton 2014–19
Graham Potter May 2019–

TEN YEAR LEAGUE RECORD

		P	W	D	L	F	A	Pts	Pos
2011-12	FL C	46	17	15	14	52	52	66	10
2012-13	FL C	46	19	18	9	69	43	75	4
2013-14	FL C	46	19	15	12	55	40	72	6
2014-15	FL C	46	10	17	19	44	54	47	20
2015-16	FL C	46	24	17	5	72	42	89	3
2016-17	FL C	46	28	9	9	74	40	93	2
2017-18	PR Lge	38	9	13	16	34	54	40	15
2018-19	PR Lge	38	9	9	20	35	60	36	17
2019-20	PR Lge	38	9	14	15	39	54	41	15
2020-21	PR Lge	38	9	14	15	40	46	41	16

DID YOU KNOW?

Brighton & Hove Albion formally opened their new ground, known as the Amex Stadium, with a friendly match against Tottenham Hotspur on 30 July 2011. Ashley Barnes had the distinction of scoring the first goal for the Seagulls at their new home when he found the net after 11 minutes, although Spurs went on to win the game 3-2.

BRIGHTON & HOVE ALBION – PREMIER LEAGUE 2020–21 LEAGUE RECORD

Match No.	Date	Venue	Opponents	Result		H/T Score	Lg Pos.	Goalscorers	Attendance
1	Sept 14	H	Chelsea	L	1-3	0-1	16	Trossard [54]	0
2	20	A	Newcastle U	W	3-0	2-0	8	Maupay 2 (1 pen) [4 (p), 7], Connolly [83]	0
3	26	H	Manchester U	L	2-3	1-1	11	Maupay (pen) [40], March [90]	0
4	Oct 3	A	Everton	L	2-4	1-2	14	Maupay [41], Bissouma [90]	0
5	18	A	Crystal Palace	D	1-1	0-1	16	Mac Allister [90]	0
6	26	H	WBA	D	1-1	1-0	16	Livermore (og) [40]	0
7	Nov 1	A	Tottenham H	L	1-2	0-1	16	Lamptey [56]	0
8	6	H	Burnley	D	0-0	0-0	16		0
9	21	A	Aston Villa	W	2-1	1-0	16	Welbeck [12], March [56]	0
10	28	H	Liverpool	D	1-1	0-0	16	Gross (pen) [90]	0
11	Dec 7	H	Southampton	L	1-2	1-1	16	Gross (pen) [26]	2000
12	13	A	Leicester C	L	0-3	0-3	16		0
13	16	A	Fulham	D	0-0	0-0	16		0
14	20	H	Sheffield U	D	1-1	0-0	16	Welbeck [87]	2000
15	27	A	West Ham U	D	2-2	1-0	16	Maupay [44], Dunk [70]	0
16	29	H	Arsenal	L	0-1	0-0	17		0
17	Jan 2	H	Wolverhampton W	D	3-3	1-3	17	Connolly [13], Maupay (pen) [46], Dunk [70]	0
18	13	A	Manchester C	L	0-1	0-1	17		0
19	16	A	Leeds U	W	1-0	1-0	16	Maupay [17]	0
20	27	H	Fulham	D	0-0	0-0	17		0
21	31	H	Tottenham H	W	1-0	1-0	17	Trossard [17]	0
22	Feb 3	A	Liverpool	W	1-0	0-0	15	Alzate [56]	0
23	6	A	Burnley	D	1-1	1-0	15	Dunk [36]	0
24	13	H	Aston Villa	D	0-0	0-0	15		0
25	22	H	Crystal Palace	L	1-2	0-1	16	Veltman [55]	0
26	27	A	WBA	L	0-1	0-1	16		0
27	Mar 6	H	Leicester C	L	1-2	1-0	16	Lallana [10]	0
28	14	A	Southampton	W	2-1	1-1	16	Dunk [16], Trossard [56]	0
29	20	H	Newcastle U	W	3-0	1-0	16	Trossard [45], Welbeck [51], Maupay [68]	0
30	Apr 4	A	Manchester U	L	1-2	1-0	16	Welbeck [13]	0
31	12	H	Everton	D	0-0	0-0	15		0
32	20	A	Chelsea	D	0-0	0-0	16		0
33	24	A	Sheffield U	L	0-1	0-1	16		0
34	May 1	H	Leeds U	W	2-0	1-0	14	Gross (pen) [14], Welbeck [79]	0
35	9	A	Wolverhampton W	L	1-2	1-0	15	Dunk [13]	0
36	15	H	West Ham U	D	1-1	0-0	17	Welbeck [84]	0
37	18	H	Manchester C	W	3-2	0-1	15	Trossard [50], Webster [72], Burn [76]	7945
38	23	A	Arsenal	L	0-2	0-0	16		10,000

Final League Position: 16

GOALSCORERS

League (40): Maupay 8 (3 pens), Welbeck 6, Dunk 5, Trossard 5, Gross 3 (3 pens), Connolly 2, March 2, Alzate 1, Bissouma 1, Burn 1, Lallana 1, Lamptey 1, Mac Allister 1, Veltman 1, Webster 1, own goal 1.
FA Cup (3): Alzate 1, Bissouma 1, March 1.
Carabao Cup (6): Jahanbakhsh 2, Mac Allister 2, Bernardo 1, Gyokeres 1.
Papa John's Trophy (3): Wilson 2, own goal 1.

Ryan M 11	White B 36	Dunk L 33	Webster A 29	Lamptey T 11	Lallana A 16 + 14	Bissouma Y 35 + 1	Alzate S 10 + 5	March S 19 + 2	Maupay N 29 + 4	Trossard L 30 + 5	Connolly A 9 + 8	Gross P 27 + 7	Jahanbakhsh A 6 + 15	Burn D 23 + 4	Veltman J 25 + 3	Mac Allister A 13 + 8	Sanchez R 27	Bernardo J 2 + 1	Welbeck D 17 + 7	Molumby J — + 1	Zeqiri A — + 9	Propper D 2 + 5	Tau P 1 + 2	Khadra R — + 1	Moder J 7 + 5	Izquierdo J — + 1	Match No.
1	2²	3	4	5	6¹	7	8³	9	10	11	12	13	14														1
1	2	3	4	5¹	13	6■	7	8²	10	9	11³		14	12													2
1	2	3	4	5	6¹		7	8	11	9	10²	12	13														3
1	2	3	4	5¹	13	6	7³	8	10	9	11²	14			12												4
1	6	3■	2	5	9¹	7		8	11	10²	12	14		4³		13											5
1	6		2	5	9¹	7	14	8²	11	10³		12		4	3	13											6
	7		2	5³	10	8		9¹		11²		6		4	3	14	1	12	13								7
1	4		5	2	9	8			11		13	7	12	6	3¹				10²								8
1	2	3	4	5■	9¹	6		8	11²			7³		13	12				10	14							9
1	2	3	4		13³	7		8	9¹	12	11²	6	14		5				10								10
1	6²	3	4	5		7		8	12	14	10¹	9	13		2				11³								11
1	3	4				7³	12	10	9		13	6	8¹	5	2	14			11²								12
	2	3	4	5¹	9³	6	7	8		10²		14	13		12		1		11								13
	2³	3	4		7	6		8	10²	9	11		12		5¹		1		13		14						14
	5	3	2		7¹	6	12	8	10³	9		13	14	4			1		11²								15
		4	3			7		13	12	14		8	10³	5	2	11¹	1	9				6²					16
	6	3	2		14	7¹		8	10	9	11²			4³	5		1				12	13					17
	7	3	2					13	12	10³				4	5	11	1	8				6²	9¹	14			18
	6	3	2			12		8	11³	9²		7		4	5	10¹	1					14	13				19
	2	3	4			7		9	10	11		6			5	8¹	1					12					20
	2	3	4		14	7		9	10³	11²	13	6		12	5¹	8	1										21
	2	3	4		12	6	7	5¹	11²	10³	13	9		8			1				14						22
	2	3	4³		14	7			11¹	13	10²	6		8	5	9	1		12								23
	2	3			12	7	8¹		11²	10		6		4	5	9	1		13								24
	2	3			13	7	8¹		11	9		6³	14	4	5	10²	1		12								25
	3³	4			12	6			11	8	10²	7		5	2	9¹	1		13						14		26
	3	4			10	7³	12		11²	9		6	14	5	2	8¹	1		13								27
	3	4			7	8			11	9³		6		5¹	2		1		10²		12	13			14		28
	2	3			6	7			10	9¹		5			4	12	1		11²		13	14			8³		29
	2	3			6³	7			10	9¹		5	14		4	12	1		11		13				8²		30
	2	3			6	7			11¹	9		5	12	13	4		1		10						8²		31
	2■	3	4		12	5			13	10¹		7		9	6	8²	1		11³						14		32
		3	2		6	7			10	9³	12	5¹	13		4		1		11						8²	14	33
	2	3	4			7³			10	9¹		6	12	8	5	14	1		11²						13		34
	2	4■	3			8			10■	9¹		7	6²	5		13	1		11³		14				12		35
	2		3		12	7	6¹			11³		5	9²	4			1		10		14		13		8		36
	2		3		13	7	8³			12		6	5²	4		10	1		11¹		14				9		37
	2	4	3		13	7	14			11²	12	6	9¹	5		10³	1								8		38

FA Cup

Third Round	Newport Co	(a)	1-1
(aet; Brighton & HA won 4-3 on penalties)			
Fourth Round	Blackpool	(h)	2-1
Fifth Round	Leicester C	(a)	0-1

Carabao Cup

Second Round	Portsmouth	(h)	4-0
Third Round	Preston NE	(a)	2-0
Fourth Round	Manchester U	(h)	0-3

Papa John's Trophy (Brighton & HA U21)

Group G (S)	Leyton Orient	(a)	2-3
Group G (S)	AFC Wimbledon	(a)	0-2
Group G (S)	Charlton Ath	(a)	1-1
(Charlton Ath won 4-1 on penalties)			

BRISTOL CITY

FOUNDATION

The name Bristol City came into being in 1897 when the Bristol South End club, formed three years earlier, decided to adopt professionalism and apply for admission to the Southern League after competing in the Western League. The historic meeting was held at the Albert Hall, Bedminster. Bristol City employed Sam Hollis from Woolwich Arsenal as manager and gave him £40 to buy players. In 1900 they merged with Bedminster, another leading Bristol club.

Ashton Gate Stadium, Ashton Road, Bristol BS3 2EJ.

Telephone: (0117) 963 0600.

Ticket Office: (0117) 963 0600 (option 1).

Website: www.bcfc.co.uk

Email: supporterservices@bristol-sport.co.uk

Ground Capacity: 26,459.

Record Attendance: 43,335 v Preston NE, FA Cup 5th rd, 16 February 1935.

Pitch Measurements: 105m × 67m (115yd × 73.5yd).

Chairman: Jon Lansdown.

Chief Executive Officer: Richard Gould.

Manager: Nigel Pearson.

Assistant Head Coaches: Keith Downing, Paul Simpson.

Colours: Red shirts with white trim, white shorts with red trim, red socks with white trim.

Year Formed: 1894.

Turned Professional: 1897.

Previous Name: 1894, Bristol South End; 1897, Bristol City.

Club Nickname: 'Robins'.

Grounds: 1894, St John's Lane; 1904, Ashton Gate.

First Football League Game: 7 September 1901, Division 2, v Blackpool (a) W 2–0 – Moles; Tuft, Davies; Jones, McLean, Chambers; Bradbury, Connor, Boucher, O'Brien (2), Flynn.

Record League Victory: 9–0 v Aldershot, Division 3 (S), 28 December 1946 – Eddols; Morgan, Fox; Peacock, Roberts, Jones (1); Chilcott, Thomas, Clark (4 incl. 1p), Cyril Williams (1), Hargreaves (3).

Record Cup Victory: 11–0 v Chichester C, FA Cup 1st rd, 5 November 1960 – Cook; Collinson, Thresher; Connor, Alan Williams, Etheridge; Tait (1), Bobby Williams (1), Atyeo (5), Adrian Williams (3), Derrick, (1 og).

Record Defeat: 0–9 v Coventry C, Division 3 (S), 28 April 1934.

Most League Points (2 for a win): 70, Division 3 (S), 1954–55.

HONOURS

League Champions: Division 2 – 1905–06; FL 1 – 2014–15; Division 3S – 1922–23, 1926–27, 1954–55.
Runners-up: Division 1 – 1906–07; Division 2 – 1975–76; FL 1 – 2006–07; Second Division – 1997–98; Division 3 – 1964–65, 1989–90; Division 3S – 1937–38.

FA Cup: *Runners-up:* 1909.

League Cup: semi-final – 1971, 1989, 2018.

League Trophy Winners: 1986, 2003, 2015.
Runners-up: 1987, 2000.

Welsh Cup Winners: 1934.

Anglo-Scottish Cup Winners: 1978.

FOOTBALL YEARBOOK FACT FILE

Alf Rowles made a sensational start to his first-team career with Bristol City, netting a hat-trick on his debut against Exeter City in January 1938 and going on to score in each of his first six Football League appearances. He finished the campaign as the Robins' leading scorer with 18 goals from 15 games but was then injured early on in the 1938–39 season and made little impact thereafter.

Most League Points (3 for a win): 99, FL 1, 2014–15.

Most League Goals: 104, Division 3 (S), 1926–27.

Highest League Scorer in Season: Don Clark, 36, Division 3 (S), 1946–47.

Most League Goals in Total Aggregate: John Atyeo, 314, 1951–66.

Most League Goals in One Match: 6, Tommy 'Tot' Walsh v Gillingham, Division 3 (S), 15 January 1927.

Most Capped Player: Billy Wedlock, 26, England.

Most League Appearances: John Atyeo, 596, 1951–66.

Youngest League Player: Marvin Brown, 16 years 105 days v Bristol R, 17 October 1999.

Record Transfer Fee Received: £20,000,000 from Brighton & HA for Adam Webster, August 2019.

Record Transfer Fee Paid: £8,000,000 to Chelsea for Tomas Kalas, July 2019.

Football League Record: 1901 Elected to Division 2; 1906–11 Division 1; 1911–22 Division 2; 1922–23 Division 3 (S); 1923–24 Division 2; 1924–27 Division 3 (S); 1927–32 Division 2; 1932–55 Division 3 (S); 1955–60 Division 2; 1960–65 Division 3; 1965–76 Division 2; 1976–80 Division 1; 1980–81 Division 2; 1981–82 Division 3; 1982–84 Division 4; 1984–90 Division 3; 1990–92 Division 2; 1992–95 Division 1; 1995–98 Division 2; 1998–99 Division 1; 1999–2004 Division 2; 2004–07 FL 1; 2007–13 FL C; 2013–15 FL 1; 2015– FL C.

LATEST SEQUENCES

Longest Sequence of League Wins: 14, 9.9.1905 – 2.12.1905.

Longest Sequence of League Defeats: 8, 10.12.2016 – 21.1.2017.

Longest Sequence of League Draws: 4, 6.11.1999 – 27.11.1999.

Longest Sequence of Unbeaten League Matches: 24, 9.9.1905 – 10.2.1906.

Longest Sequence Without a League Win: 21, 16.3.2013 – 22.10.2013.

Successive Scoring Runs: 25 from 26.12.1905.

Successive Non-scoring Runs: 6 from 20.12.1980.

MANAGERS

Sam Hollis 1897–99
Bob Campbell 1899–1901
Sam Hollis 1901–05
Harry Thickett 1905–10
Frank Bacon 1910–11
Sam Hollis 1911–13
George Hedley 1913–17
Jack Hamilton 1917–19
Joe Palmer 1919–21
Alex Raisbeck 1921–29
Joe Bradshaw 1929–32
Bob Hewison 1932–49
(*under suspension 1938–39*)
Bob Wright 1949–50
Pat Beasley 1950–58
Peter Doherty 1958–60
Fred Ford 1960–67
Alan Dicks 1967–80
Bobby Houghton 1980–82
Roy Hodgson 1982
Terry Cooper 1982–88
(*Director from 1983*)
Joe Jordan 1988–90
Jimmy Lumsden 1990–92
Denis Smith 1992–93
Russell Osman 1993–94
Joe Jordan 1994–97
John Ward 1997–98
Benny Lennartsson 1998–99
Tony Pulis 1999–2000
Tony Fawthrop 2000
Danny Wilson 2000–04
Brian Tinnion 2004–05
Gary Johnson 2005–10
Steve Coppell 2010
Keith Millen 2010–11
Derek McInnes 2011–13
Sean O'Driscoll 2013
Steve Cotterill 2013–16
Lee Johnson 2016–20
Dean Holden 2020–21
Nigel Pearson February 2021–

TEN YEAR LEAGUE RECORD

		P	*W*	*D*	*L*	*F*	*A*	*Pts*	*Pos*
2011-12	FL C	46	12	13	21	44	68	49	20
2012-13	FL C	46	11	8	27	59	84	41	24
2013-14	FL 1	46	13	19	14	70	67	58	12
2014-15	FL 1	46	29	12	5	96	38	99	1
2015-16	FL C	46	13	13	20	54	71	52	18
2016-17	FL C	46	15	9	22	60	66	54	17
2017-18	FL C	46	17	16	13	67	58	67	11
2018-19	FL C	46	19	13	14	59	53	70	8
2019-20	FL C	46	17	12	17	60	65	63	12
2020-21	FL C	46	15	6	25	46	68	51	19

DID YOU KNOW?

Following their change of name from Bristol South End in 1897, Bristol City played their first game under their new name against Southampton, who had also changed their name (from Southampton St Mary's) during the summer of that year. The Robins won 3-1 in front of an estimated crowd of 600, with Sandy Caie, Billy Higgins and Albert Carnelly scoring their goals.

BRISTOL CITY – SKY BET CHAMPIONSHIP 2020–21 LEAGUE RECORD

Match No.	Date	Venue	Opponents	Result	H/T Score	Lg Pos.	Goalscorers	Attendance
1	Sept 12	H	Coventry C	W 2-1	1-1	4	Paterson [1], Kalas [82]	0
2	20	A	Stoke C	W 2-0	1-0	2	Wells [45], Weimann [89]	0
3	27	H	Sheffield W	W 2-0	0-0	1	Rowe [59], Paterson [90]	0
4	Oct 3	A	Nottingham F	W 2-1	2-1	1	Weimann [12], Wells [22]	0
5	17	A	Barnsley	D 2-2	0-1	1	Hunt [47], Bakinson [51]	0
6	20	H	Middlesbrough	L 0-1	0-0	2		0
7	24	H	Swansea C	D 1-1	0-0	2	Wells (pen) [83]	0
8	28	A	Bournemouth	L 0-1	0-0	6		0
9	31	H	Norwich C	L 1-3	1-3	10	Hunt [15]	0
10	Nov 3	A	Huddersfield T	W 2-1	0-1	6	Dasilva [77], Paterson [83]	0
11	6	A	Cardiff C	W 1-0	1-0	2	Martin [2]	0
12	21	H	Derby Co	W 1-0	0-0	3	Diedhiou [78]	0
13	25	H	Watford	D 0-0	0-0	3		0
14	28	A	Reading	L 1-3	0-0	5	Wells [73]	0
15	Dec 1	A	QPR	W 2-1	1-1	3	Wells [40], Nagy [50]	0
16	5	H	Birmingham C	L 0-1	0-0	8		0
17	9	H	Blackburn R	W 1-0	0-0	6	Diedhiou [82]	0
18	12	A	Rotherham U	L 0-2	0-2	7		0
19	15	H	Millwall	L 0-2	0-1	8		0
20	18	A	Preston NE	L 0-1	0-1	9		0
21	26	H	Wycombe W	W 2-1	1-0	9	Martin [23], Diedhiou [87]	0
22	29	A	Luton T	L 1-2	0-1	10	Bradley (og) [61]	0
23	Jan 16	H	Preston NE	W 2-0	1-0	9	Diedhiou [8], Vyner [77]	0
24	20	A	Norwich C	L 0-2	0-1	9		0
25	26	H	Huddersfield T	W 2-1	2-0	8	Diedhiou 2 [23, 26]	0
26	30	A	Derby Co	L 0-1	0-1	9		0
27	Feb 3	A	Brentford	L 2-3	1-1	9	Vyner [3], Wells [90]	0
28	6	H	Cardiff C	L 0-2	0-2	10		0
29	13	A	Watford	L 0-6	0-4	12		0
30	16	H	Reading	L 0-2	0-2	13		0
31	20	H	Barnsley	L 0-1	0-0	15		0
32	23	A	Middlesbrough	W 3-1	3-0	12	Diedhiou 2 [21, 33], Wells [37]	0
33	27	A	Swansea C	W 3-1	0-0	11	Wells [66], Palmer [80], Semenyo [90]	0
34	Mar 3	H	Bournemouth	L 1-2	1-1	12	Bakinson [38]	0
35	6	H	QPR	L 0-2	0-2	12		0
36	13	A	Birmingham C	W 3-0	1-0	12	Palmer [35], Semenyo [62], O'Dowda [76]	0
37	17	A	Blackburn R	D 0-0	0-0	13		0
38	20	H	Rotherham U	L 0-2	0-1	14		0
39	Apr 2	H	Stoke C	L 0-2	0-1	14		0
40	5	A	Coventry C	L 1-3	0-1	14	Wells [79]	0
41	10	H	Nottingham F	D 0-0	0-0	14		0
42	17	A	Sheffield W	D 1-1	0-1	14	Bakinson [87]	0
43	21	A	Wycombe W	L 1-2	1-0	16	Bakinson [28]	0
44	25	H	Luton T	L 2-3	2-0	18	Wells [31], Nagy [38]	0
45	May 1	A	Millwall	L 1-4	1-2	19	Conway [16]	0
46	8	H	Brentford	L 1-3	0-0	19	Britton [87]	0

Final League Position: 19

GOALSCORERS

League (46): Wells 10 (1 pen), Diedhiou 8, Bakinson 4, Paterson 3, Hunt 2, Martin 2, Nagy 2, Palmer 2, Semenyo 2, Vyner 2, Weimann 2, Britton 1, Conway 1, Dasilva 1, Kalas 1, O'Dowda 1, Rowe 1, own goal 1.
FA Cup (5): Diedhiou 2 (1 pen), Martin 1, Semenyo 1, Wells 1.
Carabao Cup (6): Palmer 2, Semenyo 2, Martin 1, Paterson 1.

Bentley D 43	Vyner Z 38 + 5	Kalas T 38 + 2	Moore T 16 + 6	Massengo H 18 + 9	Hunt J 37 + 4	Weimann A 7	Paterson J 15 + 5	Rowe T 27 + 4	Diedhiou F 23 + 17	Wells N 36 + 10	Bakinson T 20 + 14	Martin C 20 + 6	Semenyo A 24 + 20	Mawson A 11	Brunt C 5 + 7	Sessegnon S 10 + 6	O'Leary M 3	O'Dowda C 14 + 5	Dasilva J 9 + 2	Nagy A 25 + 6	Edwards Opi — + 4	Mariappa A 19 + 6	Bell S 1 + 3	Adelakun H 2	Palmer K 16 + 7	Edwards Owura 1 + 2	Williams J 1	Lansbury H 12 + 4	Towler R 3	Pearson S 2 + 3	Walsh L 1 + 2	Watkins M — + 2	Britton L — + 1	Simpson D 3 + 1	Conway T 3 + 2	Janneh S — + 4	Scott A 1 + 2	Baker N 2 + 1	*Match No.*
1	2	3	4	5^2	6	7	8	9	10^1	11^3	12	13	14																										1
1	2		3		5	8	6^1	9	14	11^3	7	10^2	13	4	12																								2
1	2		3		5^3	8	6	9	13	11^1	7	10^2	12	4		14																							3
1	2		3		5	8	6^2	9	14	11^1	7	10^3	12	4	13																								4
	2	13	3		5	8	6^3	9		11^1	7	10^2	12	4			1	14																					5
1	2	12	3		5	6	8	9	13	11^3	7	10^2	14	4^1																									6
1	2	3	4^3			6^1	8		13	14		10	11		7	5^2		12	9																				7
1	2	3	4		5^3		6	9	10^2	14	7	13	11^1		12			8																					8
1	2	3	4^1		5		8		14	10^3	12	11	13		7^2			6	9																				9
1	2	3			5		13	4^1	12	10^2		11	14		8^3			6	9	7																			10
1	3	4	13		2		9^2	14		10^1		11	8		12			7	5^3	6																			11
1	3	4	14		2		6^4	15	12	11^3		10^2	9		13			8^1	5	7																			12
1	2		3		5		8	4	11^1	13		12	10^2					6	9	7																			13
1	2		3	15	5^4		6	4^1	11^2	13		12	10		14			8^5	9	7^3	16																		14
1	3	4	14					12	15	11^3	13	10^4	9^2		8			6	5^1	7		2																	15
1	3	4			13			5^4	14	9	12	10^2	11		7^1			8	15	6^5		2^3	16																16
1	3	4	13		2			5	12	11^2	8	10^3	9^1					6		7		14																	17
1	3^1	4		15	2^2			5	12	11	8^3	10	9^5		14			6		7^4	16	13																	18
1		3^3	2	8	5			9	12■	10	6	11^4	14					13		7^1	15	4^2																	19
1	2	3	4^2	6^1	5			9		10	12	11	13					8		7																			20
1	3^1	4			2			5	13	11^2	6	10	9					8^3		7	14	12																	21
1	3	4		9^1	2^2			5	12	11^3	7	10	6							8		13	14																22
1	7	3		12	2			5	10^2	13	14	11		4						8				6^3	9^1														23
1	7^3	3		14	2			5	10	13	15	11^4	12	4						8				6^1	9^2														24
1	7	3	15		12			5^1	10^2	11^3	8	13	6	4						14		2			9^4														25
1	7^3	3		16	2			5^1	10	11^4	13	14	6^2	4						8		12			9^5	15													26
1	8	3		9^1	2^4		13		11	14	15		6	4						7^2		5			12	10^3													27
1	15	3	13	6^1	2		14		10	9			11	4								5^3			12		7^2	8^4											28
1	2	3	4^1	8	5		6^3		10^5	16	14		11							13		12			15			7^4	9^2										29
1	5^1	3	4	15	9		6^2		10	11	14		13							8^4		2			12			7^3											30
1	6^3	3	4		5		13		11	14	12		10^2			9^4				15		2			8			7^1											31
1	2	4		15	5		14		10^1	11^4	7		12			13				8		3			6^2				9^3										32
1	2	4		14	5				10	11	7		13			12				8^3		3			6^2				9^1										33
1	6	4		14	2^1				11	10	8		13			5				9^3		3			7^2			12											34
1	6^3	4			2				11	10	8^1		12			5				9^2		3			7			13	14										35
1		4		6	2				11^3	10^1			8			5		12				3			9			7^2			13	14							36
	14	4		6	2				11	10^1			8^4			5	1	13		15		3			9^3			7^2			12								37
1	12	4^1		6^4	2^5				11^2	8			13			5		10				3	15		9^3			14		16	7								38
1	16	4		8	2			5^3	15	10^5	12		6									3	11^1		9^4			7^2				13		14					39
1	7	4		8				15	10^4	11			9^2			5^5				6^1		3^3			14			12		13				2	16				40
1	3	4		7	15			5	12	11^2	14		9												10			6^3		8^1				2^4	13				41
1	3	4		7^5	2^4			5	11^3	14	9		10^1			12				15					16			6■		8^2						13			42
1	3	4		9				5	11	10^1	7		13			2				8^2					14			6^3								12			43
1	3	4		10	12			5^2		11^1	6^5		13			2				8^3								7^4							9	16	14	15	44
		3		8	5^4			9^1		11^5			15			14	1		12	16		2			6			7^2							10^3		13	4	45
1	12			6						10^2	7					15			5			3^1			8^3	13							16	2^5	11^4	14	9	4	46

FA Cup

Third Round	Portsmouth	(h)	2-1
Fourth Round	Millwall	(a)	3-0
Fifth Round	Sheffield U	(a)	0-1

Carabao Cup

First Round	Exeter C	(h)	2-0
Second Round	Northampton T	(h)	4-0
Third Round	Aston Villa	(h)	0-3

BRISTOL ROVERS

FOUNDATION

Bristol Rovers were formed at a meeting in Stapleton Road, Eastville, in 1883. However, they first went under the name of the Black Arabs (wearing black shirts). Changing their name to Eastville Rovers in their second season in 1888–89, they won the Gloucestershire Senior Cup. Original members of the Bristol & District League in 1892, this eventually became the Western League and Eastville Rovers adopted professionalism in 1897.

The Memorial Stadium, Filton Avenue, Horfield, Bristol BS7 0BF.

Telephone: (0117) 909 6648.

Ticket Office: (0117) 909 8848.

Website: www.bristolrovers.co.uk

Email: admin@bristolrovers.co.uk

Ground Capacity: 11,796.

Record Attendance: 38,472 v Preston NE, FA Cup 4th rd, 30 January 1960 (at Eastville); 9,464 v Liverpool, FA Cup 4th rd, 8 February 1992 (at Twerton Park); 12,011 v WBA, FA Cup 6th rd, 9 March 2008 (at Memorial Stadium).

Pitch Measurements: 100m × 68m (109.5yd × 74.5yd).

Chief Executive: Martyn Starnes.

Manager: Joey Barton.

First-Team Coach: Clint Hill.

Colours: Blue and white quartered shirts, blue shorts with white trim, blue socks with white trim.

Year Formed: 1883.

Turned Professional: 1897.

Previous Names: 1883, Black Arabs; 1884, Eastville Rovers; 1897, Bristol Eastville Rovers; 1898, Bristol Rovers. ***Club Nicknames:*** 'The Pirates', 'The Gas'.

Grounds: 1883, Purdown; Three Acres, Ashley Hill; Rudgeway, Fishponds; 1897, Eastville; 1986, Twerton Park; 1996, The Memorial Stadium.

First Football League Game: 28 August 1920, Division 3, v Millwall (a) L 0–2 – Stansfield; Bethune, Panes; Boxley, Kenny, Steele; Chance, Bird, Sims, Bell, Palmer.

Record League Victory: 7–0 v Brighton & HA, Division 3 (S), 29 November 1952 – Hoyle; Bamford, Fox; Pitt, Warren, Sampson; McIlvenny, Roost (2), Lambden (1), Bradford (1), Petherbridge (2), (1 og). 7–0 v Swansea T, Division 2, 2 October 1954 – Radford; Bamford, Watkins; Pitt, Muir, Anderson; Petherbridge, Bradford (2), Meyer, Roost (1), Hooper (2), (2 og). 7–0 v Shrewsbury T, Division 3, 21 March 1964 – Hall; Hillard, Gwyn Jones; Oldfield, Stone (1), Mabbutt; Jarman (2), Brown (1), Biggs (1p), Hamilton, Bobby Jones (2).

Record Cup Victory: 7–1 v Dorchester, FA Cup 4th qualifying rd, 25 October 2014 – Midenhall; Locyer, Trotman (McChrystal), Parkes, Monkhouse (2), Clarke, Mansell (1) (Thomas), Brown, Gosling, Harrison (3), Taylor (1) (White).

Record Defeat: 0–12 v Luton T, Division 3 (S), 13 April 1936.

HONOURS

League Champions: Division 3 – 1989–90; Division 3S – 1952–53. *Runners-up:* Division 3 – 1973–74; Conference – (2nd) 2014–15 *(promoted via play-offs).*

FA Cup: 6th rd – 1951, 1958, 2008.

League Cup: 5th rd – 1971, 1972.

League Trophy: *Runners-up:* 1990, 2007.

FOOTBALL YEARBOOK FACT FILE

Bristol Rovers won the first-ever Football League Cup tie to be played. Rovers kicked off 15 minutes earlier than the only other game on the opening night of the competition and came from behind to defeat Fulham 2-1 at Eastville with goals from Harold Jarman and Geoff Bradford.

Most League Points (2 for a win): 64, Division 3 (S), 1952–53.

Most League Points (3 for a win): 93, Division 3, 1989–90.

Most League Goals: 92, Division 3 (S), 1952–53.

Highest League Scorer in Season: Geoff Bradford, 33, Division 3 (S), 1952–53.

Most League Goals in Total Aggregate: Geoff Bradford, 242, 1949–64.

Most League Goals in One Match: 4, Sidney Leigh v Exeter C, Division 3 (S), 2 May 1921; 4, Jonah Wilcox v Bournemouth, Division 3 (S), 12 December 1925; 4, Bill Culley v QPR, Division 3 (S), 5 March 1927; 4, Frank Curran v Swindon T, Division 3 (S), 25 March 1939; 4, Vic Lambden v Aldershot, Division 3 (S), 29 March 1947; 4, George Petherbridge v Torquay U, Division 3 (S), 1 December 1951; 4, Vic Lambden v Colchester U, Division 3 (S), 14 May 1952; 4, Geoff Bradford v Rotherham U, Division 2, 14 March 1959; 4, Robin Stubbs v Gillingham, Division 2, 10 October 1970; 4, Alan Warboys v Brighton & HA, Division 3, 1 December 1973; 4, Jamie Cureton v Reading, Division 2, 16 January 1999; 4, Ellis Harrison v Northampton T, FL 1, 7 January 2017.

Most Capped Player: Vitalijs Astafjevs, 31 (167), Latvia.

Most League Appearances: Stuart Taylor, 546, 1966–80.

Youngest League Player: Ronnie Dix, 15 years 173 days v Charlton Ath, 25 February 1928.

Record Transfer Fee Received: £2,000,000 from Fulham for Barry Hayles, November 1998; £2,000,000 from WBA for Jason Roberts, July 2000.

Record Transfer Fee Paid: £370,000 to QPR for Andy Tillson, November 1992.

Football League Record: 1920 Original Member of Division 3; 1921–53 Division 3 (S); 1953–62 Division 2; 1962–74 Division 3; 1974–81 Division 2; 1981–90 Division 3; 1990–92 Division 2. 1992–93 Division 1; 1993–2001 Division 2; 2001–04 Division 3; 2004–07 FL 2; 2007–11 FL 1; 2011–14 FL 2; 2014–15 Conference Premier; 2015–16 FL 2; 2016–21 FL 1; 2021– FL 2.

MANAGERS

Alfred Homer 1899–1920 (*continued as Secretary to 1928*)
Ben Hall 1920–21
Andy Wilson 1921–26
Joe Palmer 1926–29
Dave McLean 1929–30
Albert Prince-Cox 1930–36
Percy Smith 1936–37
Brough Fletcher 1938–49
Bert Tann 1950–68 (*continued as General Manager to 1972*)
Fred Ford 1968–69
Bill Dodgin Snr 1969–72
Don Megson 1972–77
Bobby Campbell 1978–79
Harold Jarman 1979–80
Terry Cooper 1980–81
Bobby Gould 1981–83
David Williams 1983–85
Bobby Gould 1985–87
Gerry Francis 1987–91
Martin Dobson 1991
Dennis Rofe 1992
Malcolm Allison 1992–93
John Ward 1993–96
Ian Holloway 1996–2001
Garry Thompson 2001
Gerry Francis 2001
Garry Thompson 2001–02
Ray Graydon 2002–04
Ian Atkins 2004–05
Paul Trollope 2005–10
Dave Penney 2011
Paul Buckle 2011–12
Mark McGhee 2012
John Ward 2012–14
Darrell Clarke 2014–18
Graham Coughlan 2018–19
Ben Garner 2019–20
Paul Tisdale 2020–21
Joey Barton February 2021–

LATEST SEQUENCES

Longest Sequence of League Wins: 12, 18.10.1952 – 17.1.1953.

Longest Sequence of League Defeats: 8, 26.10.2002 – 21.12.2002.

Longest Sequence of League Draws: 6, 4.2.2017 – 28.2.2017.

Longest Sequence of Unbeaten League Matches: 32, 7.4.1973 – 27.1.1974.

Longest Sequence Without a League Win: 20, 5.4.1980 – 1.11.1980.

Successive Scoring Runs: 26 from 26.3.1927.

Successive Non-scoring Runs: 6 from 14.10.1922.

TEN YEAR LEAGUE RECORD

		P	*W*	*D*	*L*	*F*	*A*	*Pts*	*Pos*
2011-12	FL 2	46	15	12	19	60	70	57	13
2012-13	FL 2	46	16	12	18	60	69	60	14
2013-14	FL 2	46	12	14	20	43	54	50	23
2014-15	Conf P	46	25	16	5	73	34	91	2
2015-16	FL 2	46	26	7	13	77	46	85	3
2016-17	FL 1	46	18	12	16	68	70	66	10
2017-18	FL 1	46	16	11	19	60	66	59	13
2018-19	FL 1	46	13	15	18	47	50	54	15
2019-20	FL 1	35	12	9	14	38	49	45	14§
2020-21	FL 1	46	10	8	28	40	70	38	24

§*Decided on points-per-game (1.29)*

DID YOU KNOW

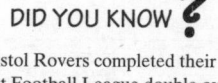

Bristol Rovers completed their first Football League double over Bristol City in 1933–34. Rovers won 3-0 at Ashton Gate on the opening day of the season and demolished the Robins 5-1 in their home Division Three South fixture. This is the Pirates' best-ever Football League win over their city rivals.

BRISTOL ROVERS – SKY BET LEAGUE ONE 2020–21 LEAGUE RECORD

Match No.	*Date*	*Venue*	*Opponents*	*Result*	*H/T Score*	*Lg Pos.*	*Goalscorers*	*Atten-dance*
1	Sept 12	A	Sunderland	D 1-1	1-0	22	Leahy (pen) [3]	0
2	19	H	Ipswich T	L 0-2	0-0	24		0
3	26	A	Doncaster R	L 1-4	1-2	24	Leahy [32]	0
4	Oct 3	H	Northampton T	W 2-0	0-0	24	Hanlan (pen) [55], Baldwin [79]	0
5	10	A	Lincoln C	W 2-1	0-0	24	Daly [48], Hanlan (pen) [58]	0
6	17	H	Burton Alb	D 1-1	0-0	24	Daly [52]	0
7	20	A	Shrewsbury T	W 1-0	1-0	24	Hanlan [15]	0
8	27	H	Hull C	L 1-3	1-0	24	Daly [2]	0
9	31	A	Rochdale	D 1-1	1-1	24	Nicholson [9]	0
10	Nov 3	H	Peterborough U	L 0-2	0-1	24		0
11	14	H	Fleetwood T	L 1-4	0-2	24	Grant [60]	0
12	21	A	Swindon T	L 0-1	0-0	24		0
13	24	A	Wigan Ath	D 0-0	0-0	24		0
14	Dec 2	H	Gillingham	L 0-2	0-1	24		0
15	5	A	AFC Wimbledon	W 4-2	3-2	24	Nicholson 2 [14, 64], Hanlan 2 [25, 45]	0
16	12	H	Plymouth Arg	W 3-0	2-0	24	Kilgour [7], McCormick [26], Westbrooke [85]	0
17	26	A	Milton Keynes D	L 0-2	0-1	24		0
18	Jan 2	H	Blackpool	W 2-1	2-1	24	Hanlan [34], Nicholson [36]	0
19	16	H	Charlton Ath	L 0-1	0-0	24		0
20	19	A	Crewe Alex	L 2-3	0-2	24	Ehmer [46], McCormick [51]	0
21	23	A	Oxford U	L 0-2	0-1	24		0
22	26	A	Peterborough U	D 0-0	0-0	24		0
23	30	H	Rochdale	L 1-2	1-1	24	Leahy [34]	0
24	Feb 2	A	Accrington S	L 1-6	1-4	24	Nicholson [11]	0
25	6	A	Fleetwood T	D 0-0	0-0	24		0
26	9	H	Oxford U	L 0-2	0-1	24		0
27	16	H	Portsmouth	W 3-1	2-1	24	Ayunga 2 [34, 44], Leahy (pen) [70]	0
28	20	A	Gillingham	L 0-2	0-0	24		0
29	23	H	Wigan Ath	L 1-2	0-0	24	McCormick [69]	0
30	27	H	Shrewsbury T	W 2-1	1-0	24	Leahy [45], Hanlan [60]	0
31	Mar 2	A	Burton Alb	L 0-1	0-0	24		0
32	6	A	Hull C	L 0-2	0-1	24		0
33	9	H	Accrington S	W 4-1	2-0	24	Leahy [14], Rodman [45], Nicholson [66], Westbrooke [68]	0
34	13	H	AFC Wimbledon	D 0-0	0-0	24		0
35	16	A	Charlton Ath	L 2-3	2-2	24	Leahy (pen) [18], Upson [32]	0
36	20	A	Plymouth Arg	L 0-2	0-2	24		0
37	23	H	Swindon T	L 0-1	0-0	24		0
38	27	H	Sunderland	L 0-1	0-1	24		0
39	Apr 2	A	Ipswich T	L 1-2	1-2	24	McCormick [18]	0
40	5	H	Doncaster R	W 2-1	1-1	24	McCormick 2 [37, 56]	0
41	10	A	Northampton T	D 1-1	1-0	24	Leahy [19]	0
42	17	H	Lincoln C	L 0-1	0-1	24		0
43	20	H	Milton Keynes D	L 0-2	0-1	24		0
44	24	A	Portsmouth	L 0-1	0-1	24		0
45	May 1	H	Crewe Alex	L 0-1	0-1	24		0
46	9	A	Blackpool	L 0-1	0-0	24		0

Final League Position: 24

GOALSCORERS

League (40): Leahy 8 (3 pens), Hanlan 7 (2 pens), McCormick 6, Nicholson 6, Daly 3, Ayunga 2, Westbrooke 2, Baldwin 1, Ehmer 1, Grant 1, Kilgour 1, Rodman 1, Upson 1.
FA Cup (10): Leahy 2 (2 pens), Baldwin 1, Daly 1, Ehmer 1, Hanlan 1, Hare 1, Kilgour 1, Nicholson 1, Oztumer 1.
Carabao Cup (0).
Papa John's Trophy (9): Mehew 2, Ayunga 1, Hanlan 1, Hare 1, Koiki 1, Nicholson 1, Westbrooke 1, own goal 1.

Jaakkola A 21	Harries C 26 + 2	Ehmer M 27 + 1	Kilgour A 33 + 2	Little M 2 + 3	Grant J 31 + 1	Westbrooke Z 33 + 9	Leahy L 37 + 1	Mitchell-Lawson J 3 + 2	Nicholson S 22 + 8	Hanlan B 40 + 4	Ayunga J 13 + 17	Hargreaves C 3 + 10	Tutonda D 10 + 10	Upson E 20 + 6	Daly J 13 + 15	McCormick L 36 + 3	Walker Z 4 + 7	Baldwin J 32 + 6	Hare J 14 + 5	Oztumer E 10 + 12	Koiki A 3 + 7	van Stappershoef J 6 + 2	Barrett J — + 9	Rodman A 11 + 5	Day J 18	Ogogo A 3	Williams G 25 + 1	Liddle B 1 + 2	Martinez P 8	Ward J 1	Mehew T — + 1	Match No.
1	2	3	4	5	6	7	8^{3}	9	10^{2}	11^{1}	12	13	14																			1
1	4	3	2	5	8	7	9^{3}	10^{2}		11^{1}	12		14	6	13																	2
1	4	3	2		6	7	5^{3}	9^{1}		10	12		14		11^{2}	8	13															3
1	4	2			7	8			12	11		13	9		10^{1}	6^{2}		3	5													4
1	2	4			8	6^{2}			12	11^{1}		14	9	13	10^{3}	7		3	5													5
1	4	2			7	6^{3}			13	11			9	12	10^{2}	8^{1}		3	5	14												6
1	4	2			6	8^{3}			13	10			9	14	11^{1}	7^{2}		3	5	12												7
1	4	2			7	8			13	10			9		11	6^{1}		3	5^{2}	12												8
1	4	2			6	8	12	13	7^{3}	11			9^{1}		10^{2}	14		3	5													9
1	4	3	2		6	8		14	7^{2}	11			9^{1}		10^{3}				5	13	12											10
	4	2			7	6			12	11			14		13	8^{1}		3	5^{2}	10	9^{3}	1										11
1	4^{1}	3	2		6	12			10	11			8^{2}	7		9^{3}		14	5		13											12
1		4	15		6	14	5		11					7		8^{3}	12	3	2^{4}	9^{2}	10^{1}		13									13
1		3	12		7	15	5^{3}		11	10				8^{4}		6^{1}	13	4	2^{2}	9	14											14
1		2	3		8	6	5		11	10				7				4		9												15
		2	3		8	6	5		11	10^{1}	12	13		7^{3}		9^{2}		4				1	14									16
		2	3				5		8	11^{3}	14	7^{1}		6		9		4			10^{2}	1	12	13								17
		2	3			6	5		11	10				7		8		4		9		1										18
	12		3		6^{3}	9	5			10	11			7		8^{2}		4	2^{1}				13	14	1							19
	4^{2}	5	3		6	10	9^{3}			11^{4}	15			8^{1}		7		2			14		12	13	1							20
	4	5	3		6	8^{4}	9			11	12	15				10^{2}		2^{3}					14		1	7^{1}	13					21
		2	3		6	13	8		11^{2}	10	12							4		9^{1}					1	7	5					22
	4	2	3		12	7^{4}	8		11	10^{3}	13					14				9^{2}			15		1	6^{1}	5					23
	16	3	4		6	7^{4}	5^{3}		11^{5}	10^{2}	12	15	14		13	8				9^{1}					1		2					24
		2	3		6		8		9	10^{3}	14				11^{2}	12		4						13	1		5	7^{1}				25
		2	3^{1}		6	12	8		13	14	15				10^{4}	7		4		9^{2}				11^{3}	1		5					26
	4		3		6		8		9	10	11^{2}			12	13	7^{1}		2							1		5					27
	4		3		6^{3}		8^{4}		12	10	11	15	14		9^{1}	7		2						13	1		5^{2}					28
	4		3		8	12	5		11^{3}	10^{5}	16			7^{1}	14	6^{4}				15	13			9^{2}	1		2					29
	4		3		6	9^{4}	8		10^{3}	11^{1}	12			14		7		15			13	16		5^{2}	1^{5}		2					30
	4^{3}	15	3		6	9	8		10^{2}	11^{1}	12				13	7■					14	1		5			2^{4}					31
	4^{4}	2^{2}	3		7^{1}	9	8		11^{5}	10^{3}	13			12	15		14	16						6	1		5					32
			3			9^{2}	8		10^{1}	12	11^{3}	13		6	14	7		4						5	1		2					33
			3			9	8		10	12	11^{2}			6	13	7		4						5^{1}	1		2					34
			3	13		8^{2}	5		9^{1}	11^{3}	10	12		7^{4}	14	6		4				15			1■		2					35
		2^{1}	3^{4}			9^{2}	8			10	11		15	6^{3}	14	7		4	12	13		1					5					36
			3		6^{4}	12	5			11	10		15	7^{1}	9^{2}	8		4^{3}	13	14					1		2					37
1			3^{4}		4	7^{1}	5			11	10^{2}		13			8	9^{3}	15		12			14				2		6			38
1						12	9			10	11^{4}		4^{1}	6^{3}		8	5^{2}	3	14	13			15				2		7			39
1	4					10	9			11	12			7		8	5^{1}	3									2		6			40
1	4					9^{1}	5			11^{2}	10			7	13	8		3	12								2		6			41
1	4		3			10^{2}	9			12	11			7■		8		14	5^{1}	13							2		6^{3}			42
1	4^{1}		3			13	8			9^{3}	10				15	7	11^{2}	14		12				5^{4}			2		6			43
1			3^{4}	15		9^{1}	8			10		14			11^{2}	7	13	4	16	12				5^{3}			2		6^{5}			44
			3			7^{4}	8			10^{3}		6	15		13		14	4	5^{1}	11^{2}				9	1		2	12				45
	4^{2}			13		8^{4}	5					7^{5}	10^{1}		12	9	16	3						11			2^{3}	15	6	1	14	46

FA Cup

First Round	Walsall	(a)	2-1
Second Round	Darlington	(h)	6-0
Third Round	Sheffield U	(h)	2-3

Carabao Cup

First Round	Ipswich T	(a)	0-3

Papa John's Trophy

Group D (S)	Walsall	(h)	2-2
(Walsall won 4-2 on penalties)			
Group D (S)	Oxford U	(a)	1-1
(Oxford U won 4-3 on penalties)			
Group D (S)	Chelsea U21	(h)	4-3
Second Round (S)	Leyton Orient	(a)	2-1
Third Round (S)	AFC Wimbledon	(h)	0-1

BURNLEY

FOUNDATION

On 18 May 1882 Burnley (Association) Football Club was still known as Burnley Rovers as members of that rugby club had decided on that date to play Association Football in the future. It was only a matter of days later that the members met again and decided to drop Rovers from the club's name.

Turf Moor, Harry Potts Way, Burnley, Lancashire BB10 4BX.

Telephone: (01282) 446 800.

Ticket Office: (0844) 807 1882.

Website: www.burnleyfc.com

Email: info@burnleyfc.com

Ground Capacity: 21,744.

Record Attendance: 54,775 v Huddersfield T, FA Cup 3rd rd, 23 February 1924.

Pitch Measurements: 105m × 68m (115yd × 74.5yd).

Chairman: Alan Pace.

Manager: Sean Dyche.

Assistant Manager: Ian Woan.

Colours: Claret shirts with sky blue sleeves, white shorts with claret trim, claret socks with sky blue trim.

Year Formed: 1882.

Turned Professional: 1883.

Previous Name: 1882, Burnley Rovers; 1882, Burnley.

Club Nickname: 'The Clarets'.

Grounds: 1882, Calder Vale; 1883, Turf Moor.

First Football League Game: 8 September 1888, Football League, v Preston NE (a) L 2–5 – Smith; Lang, Bury, Abrahams, Friel, Keenan, Brady, Tait, Poland (1), Gallocher (1), Yates.

Record League Victory: 9–0 v Darwen, Division 1, 9 January 1892 – Hillman; Walker, McFettridge, Lang, Matthews, Keenan, Nicol (3), Bowes, Espie (1), McLardie (3), Hill (2).

Record Cup Victory: 9–0 v Crystal Palace, FA Cup 2nd rd (replay), 10 February 1909 – Dawson; Barron, McLean; Cretney (2), Leake, Moffat; Morley, Ogden, Smith (3), Abbott (2), Smethams (1). 9–0 v New Brighton, FA Cup 4th rd, 26 January 1957 – Blacklaw; Angus, Winton; Seith, Adamson, Miller; Newlands (1), McIlroy (3), Lawson (3), Cheesebrough (1), Pilkington (1). 9–0 v Penrith, FA Cup 1st rd, 17 November 1984 – Hansbury; Miller, Hampton, Phelan, Overson (Kennedy), Hird (3 incl. 1p), Grewcock (1), Powell (2), Taylor (3), Biggins, Hutchison.

Record Defeat: 0–11 v Darwen, FA Cup 1st rd, 17 October 1885.

Most League Points (2 for a win): 62, Division 2, 1972–73.

Most League Points (3 for a win): 93, FL C, 2013–14; FL C, 2015–16.

HONOURS

League Champions: Division 1 – 1920–21, 1959–60; FL C – 2015–16; Division 2 – 1897–98, 1972–73; Division 3 – 1981–82; Division 4 – 1991–92.
Runners-up: Division 1 – 1919–20, 1961–62; FL C – 2013–14; Division 2 – 1912–13, 1946–47; Second Division – 1999–2000.

FA Cup Winners: 1914.
Runners-up: 1947, 1962.

League Cup: semi-final – 1961, 1969, 1983, 2009.

League Trophy: ***Runners-up:*** 1988.

Anglo-Scottish Cup Winners: 1979.

European Competitions
European Cup: 1960–61 *(qf)*.
Fairs Cup: 1966–67.
Europa League: 2018–19.

FOOTBALL YEARBOOK FACT FILE

After finishing as Division Two champions in 1897–98, Burnley were required to take part in the end-of-season test matches. In the final game they played at Stoke with both clubs needing a draw to ensure they achieved top-flight football the following season. The 0-0 result meant that both were successful but was widely criticised with the match described as a farce, and neither goalkeeper facing a meaningful shot.

Most League Goals: 102, Division 1, 1960–61.

Highest League Scorer in Season: George Beel, 35, Division 1, 1927–28.

Most League Goals in Total Aggregate: George Beel, 179, 1923–32.

Most League Goals in One Match: 6, Louis Page v Birmingham C, Division 1, 10 April 1926.

Most Capped Player: Jimmy McIlroy, 51 (55), Northern Ireland.

Most League Appearances: Jerry Dawson, 522, 1907–28.

Youngest League Player: Tommy Lawton, 16 years 174 days v Doncaster R, 28 March 1936.

Record Transfer Fee Received: £25,000,000 (rising to £30,000,000) from Everton for Michael Keane, July 2017.

Record Transfer Fee Paid: £15,000,000 to Leeds U for Chris Wood, August 2017; £15,000,000 to Middlesbrough for Ben Gibson, August 2018.

Football League Record: 1888 Original Member of the Football League; 1897–98 Division 2; 1898–1900 Division 1; 1900–13 Division 2; 1913–30 Division 1; 1930–47 Division 2; 1947–71 Division 1; 1971–73 Division 2; 1973–76 Division 1; 1976–80 Division 2; 1980–82 Division 3; 1982–83 Division 2; 1983–85 Division 3; 1985–92 Division 4; 1992–94 Division 2; 1994–95 Division 1; 1995–2000 Division 2; 2000–04 Division 1; 2004–09 FL C; 2009–10 Premier League; 2010–14 FL C; 2014–15 Premier League; 2015–16 FL C; 2016– Premier League.

LATEST SEQUENCES

Longest Sequence of League Wins: 10, 16.11.1912 – 18.1.1913.

Longest Sequence of League Defeats: 8, 2.1.1995 – 25.2.1995.

Longest Sequence of League Draws: 6, 21.2.1931 – 28.3.1931.

Longest Sequence of Unbeaten League Matches: 30, 6.9.1920 – 25.3.1921.

Longest Sequence Without a League Win: 24, 16.4.1979 – 17.11.1979.

Successive Scoring Runs: 27 from 13.2.1926.

Successive Non-scoring Runs: 6 from 21.3.2015.

MANAGERS

Harry Bradshaw 1894–99
(*Secretary-Manager from 1897*)
Club Directors 1899–1900
J. Ernest Mangnall 1900–03
(*Secretary-Manager*)
Spen Whittaker 1903–10
(*Secretary-Manager*)
John Haworth 1910–24
(*Secretary-Manager*)
Albert Pickles 1925–31
(*Secretary-Manager*)
Tom Bromilow 1932–35
Selection Committee 1935–45
Cliff Britton 1945–48
Frank Hill 1948–54
Alan Brown 1954–57
Billy Dougall 1957–58
Harry Potts 1958–70
(*General Manager to 1972*)
Jimmy Adamson 1970–76
Joe Brown 1976–77
Harry Potts 1977–79
Brian Miller 1979–83
John Bond 1983–84
John Benson 1984–85
Martin Buchan 1985
Tommy Cavanagh 1985–86
Brian Miller 1986–89
Frank Casper 1989–91
Jimmy Mullen 1991–96
Adrian Heath 1996–97
Chris Waddle 1997–98
Stan Ternent 1998–2004
Steve Cotterill 2004–07
Owen Coyle 2007–10
Brian Laws 2010
Eddie Howe 2011–12
Sean Dyche October 2012–

TEN YEAR LEAGUE RECORD

		P	W	D	L	F	A	Pts	Pos
2011-12	FL C	46	17	11	18	61	58	62	13
2012-13	FL C	46	16	13	17	62	60	61	11
2013-14	FL C	46	26	15	5	72	37	93	2
2014-15	PR Lge	38	7	12	19	28	53	33	19
2015-16	FL C	46	26	15	5	72	35	93	1
2016-17	PR Lge	38	11	7	20	39	55	40	16
2017-18	PR Lge	38	14	12	12	36	39	54	7
2018-19	PR Lge	38	11	7	20	45	68	40	15
2019-20	PR Lge	38	15	9	14	43	50	54	10
2020-21	PR Lge	38	10	9	19	33	55	39	17

DID YOU KNOW ?

Burnley were drawn away to Darlington in the first round of the FA Cup with the match scheduled for Saturday 14 March. The Feethams pitch was completely unplayable, and the rearranged game took place at Middlesbrough's Riverside Stadium the following Tuesday. Despite leading 2-0 with 10 minutes remaining the Clarets went down to a 3-2 defeat.

BURNLEY – PREMIER LEAGUE 2020–21 LEAGUE RECORD

Match No.	Date	Venue	Opponents	Result		H/T Score	Lg Pos.	Goalscorers	Attendance
1	Sept 20	A	Leicester C	L	2-4	1-1	14	Wood [10], Dunne [73]	0
2	26	H	Southampton	L	0-1	0-1	17		0
3	Oct 3	A	Newcastle U	L	1-3	0-1	19	Westwood [61]	0
4	19	A	WBA	D	0-0	0-0	18		0
5	26	H	Tottenham H	L	0-1	0-0	18		0
6	31	H	Chelsea	L	0-3	0-1	20		0
7	Nov 6	A	Brighton & HA	D	0-0	0-0	19		0
8	23	H	Crystal Palace	W	1-0	1-0	17	Wood [8]	0
9	28	A	Manchester C	L	0-5	0-3	18		0
10	Dec 5	H	Everton	D	1-1	1-1	19	Brady [3]	0
11	13	A	Arsenal	W	1-0	0-0	17	Aubameyang (og) [73]	0
12	17	A	Aston Villa	D	0-0	0-0	17		0
13	21	H	Wolverhampton W	W	2-1	1-0	16	Barnes [35], Wood [51]	0
14	27	A	Leeds U	L	0-1	0-1	17		0
15	29	H	Sheffield U	W	1-0	1-0	16	Mee [32]	0
16	Jan 12	H	Manchester U	L	0-1	0-0	16		0
17	16	A	West Ham U	L	0-1	0-1	17		0
18	21	A	Liverpool	W	1-0	0-0	16	Barnes (pen) [83]	0
19	27	H	Aston Villa	W	3-2	0-1	15	Mee [52], McNeil [76], Wood [79]	0
20	31	A	Chelsea	L	0-2	0-1	16		0
21	Feb 3	H	Manchester C	L	0-2	0-2	17		0
22	6	H	Brighton & HA	D	1-1	0-1	17	Gudmundsson [53]	0
23	13	A	Crystal Palace	W	3-0	2-0	16	Gudmundsson [5], Rodriguez [10], Lowton [47]	0
24	17	H	Fulham	D	1-1	0-0	15	Barnes [52]	0
25	20	H	WBA	D	0-0	0-0	15		0
26	28	A	Tottenham H	L	0-4	0-3	15		0
27	Mar 3	H	Leicester C	D	1-1	1-1	15	Vydra [4]	0
28	6	H	Arsenal	D	1-1	1-1	15	Wood [39]	0
29	13	A	Everton	W	2-1	2-1	15	Wood [13], McNeil [24]	0
30	Apr 4	A	Southampton	L	2-3	2-2	15	Wood (pen) [12], Vydra [28]	0
31	11	H	Newcastle U	L	1-2	1-0	15	Vydra [18]	0
32	18	A	Manchester U	L	1-3	0-0	17	Tarkowski [50]	0
33	25	A	Wolverhampton W	W	4-0	3-0	14	Wood 3 [15, 21, 44], Westwood [85]	0
34	May 3	H	West Ham U	L	1-2	1-2	16	Wood (pen) [19]	0
35	10	A	Fulham	W	2-0	2-0	14	Westwood [35], Wood [44]	0
36	15	H	Leeds U	L	0-4	0-1	15		0
37	19	H	Liverpool	L	0-3	0-1	17		3387
38	23	A	Sheffield U	L	0-1	0-1	17		5096

Final League Position: 17

GOALSCORERS

League (33): Wood 12 (2 pens), Barnes 3 (1 pen), Vydra 3, Westwood 3, Gudmundsson 2, McNeil 2, Mee 2, Brady 1, Dunne 1, Lowton 1, Rodriguez 1, Tarkowski 1, own goal 1.
FA Cup (4): Rodriguez 2 (1 pen), Long 1, Vydra 1.
Carabao Cup (3): Vydra 2, Brownhill 1.

Pope N 32	Bardsley P 3 + 1	Long K 7 + 1	Dunne J 3	Taylor C 28 + 1	Brady R 12 + 7	Westwood A 38	Brownhill J 32 + 1	McNeil D 34 + 2	Rodriguez J 12 + 19	Wood C 32 + 1	Pieters E 13 + 7	Vydra M 15 + 13	Stephens D 3 + 4	Tarkowski J 36	Barnes A 15 + 7	Gudmundsson J 16 + 6	Lowton M 34	Mee B 30	Peacock-Farrell B 4	Benson J 2 + 4	Cork J 15 + 1	Mumbongo J — + 4	Richardson L — + 2	Norris W 2	Match No.
1	2	3	4	5	6^{1}	7	8	9	10^{2}	11	12	13													1
1	2	3	4	5		7	6	9		10		11	8												2
1	2	3		5		7	6	9		11		13	8^{1}	4	10^{2}	12									3
1		3		5	12	7	8	9	13	11	2			4	10^{2}	6^{1}									4
1		3		5		7	8	9	12	11		13		4	10^{2}	6^{1}	2								5
1		3		5	13	7	6	9	12	10			8^{1}	4	11^{2}		2								6
1				5	6	7	8	9	12	10^{2}		13		3	11^{1}		2	4							7
1				5	12^{2}	7	8	9	11	10	13			3		6^{1}	2	4							8
				5		7		10	6	11^{1}	12	13		3	9^{2}		2	4	1	8					9
1				5	6^{2}	7	8	9	11^{1}	10				3	12		2	4		13					10
1				5	6	7	8	9	10^{1}	11^{2}		13		3	12		2	4							11
1				5	6^{3}	7	8	9	11^{1}	10^{2}	14	13		3	12		2	4							12
1				5	6^{1}	7	8	9^{3}	13	10	12			3	11^{2}		2	4		14					13
1				5		8	7		13	10	9^{2}		12	3	11		2	4		6^{1}					14
1				5^{1}	6	8	7			10	9		13	3	11^{2}		2	4		12					15
1					9^{1}	7	8	12	14	10^{2}	5	13		3	11^{3}	6	2	4							16
1					9	7	8	12	14	10^{3}	5	13		3	11^{2}	6^{1}	2	4							17
1				5^{1}	6^{2}	7	8	9		10	12			3	11	13	2	4							18
1					6^{2}	7	8^{1}	9	10^{3}	11	5	14		3		13	2	4			12				19
1					6^{3}	7		9	12	11^{2}	5	10^{1}		3		13	2	4			8	14			20
1						7^{3}		9	10^{2}		5	11	12	3		6	2	4		14	8^{1}	13			21
1						7		9			5	11		3	10	6	2	4			8				22
1	14	13			12	7		9	11		5^{3}			3	10	6^{1}	2	4^{2}			8				23
1		3		5	12^{2}	7	13	9	11					4	10	6^{1}	2				8				24
1				5		8	6	9	10^{1}			11		3			2	4			7	12			25
1				5		7	6	9	11^{3}	12		10^{1}	13	3			2	4			8^{2}		14		26
1				5		7	6	9	12	11		10^{1}		3			2	4			8				27
1				5^{1}	13	7	8	9	14	11	12	10^{3}		3		6^{2}	2	4							28
1					12	7	8	9	13	11	5	10^{2}		3		6^{1}	2	4							29
1				12		7	8	9	13	11	5^{1}	10^{2}		3		6^{3}	2	4					14		30
						7	8	9		11	5	10		3		6^{1}	2	4	1			12			31
				5		7	10^{1}	9	13	11		12		3		6^{2}	2	4	1		8				32
1				5		7	6	9	12	11		10^{1}		3			2	4			8				33
1				5		7	6	9^{2}	12	11^{3}		10^{1}		3	14	13	2	4			8				34
1				5		7	6	9	12	11^{2}		10^{1}		3	13		2	4			8				35
				5		7	6	9^{3}	13	11^{2}		10^{1}		3	12	14	2	4	1		8				36
				5		7	10	9		11		12		3		6	2	4			8^{1}			1	37
			4	5		7	10^{1}	9^{2}	13	11		12		3	14	6^{3}	2				8			1	38

FA Cup

Third Round	Milton Keynes D	(h)	1-1
(aet; Burnley won 4-3 on penalties)			
Fourth Round	Fulham	(a)	3-0
Fifth Round	Bournemouth	(h)	0-2

Carabao Cup

Second Round	Sheffield U	(h)	1-1
(Burnley won 5-4 on penalties)			
Third Round	Millwall	(a)	2-0
Fourth Round	Manchester C	(h)	0-3

BURTON ALBION

FOUNDATION

Once upon a time there were three Football League clubs bearing the name Burton. Then there were none. In reality it had been two. Originally Burton Swifts and Burton Wanderers competed in it until 1901 when they amalgamated to form Burton United. This club disbanded in 1910. There was no senior club representing the town until 1924 when Burton Town, formerly known as Burton All Saints, played in the Birmingham & District League, subsequently joining the Midland League in 1935–36. When the Second World War broke out the club fielded a team in a truncated version of the Birmingham & District League taking over from the club's reserves. But it was not revived in peacetime. So it was not until a further decade that a club bearing the name of Burton reappeared. Founded in 1950 Burton Albion made progress from the Birmingham & District League, too, then into the Southern League and because of its geographical situation later had spells in the Northern Premier League. In April 2009 Burton Albion restored the name of the town to the Football League competition as champions of the Blue Square Premier League.

Pirelli Stadium, Princess Way, Burton-on-Trent, Staffordshire DE13 0AR.

Telephone: (01283) 565 938.

Ticket Office: (01283) 565 938.

Website: www.burtonalbionfc.co.uk

Email: bafc@burtonalbionfc.co.uk

Ground Capactiy: 7,088.

Record Attendance: 5,806 v Weymouth, Southern League Cup final 2nd leg, 1964 (at Eton Park); 6,746 v Derby Co, FL C, 26 August 2016 (at Pirelli Stadium).

Pitch Measurements: 100m × 67m (109.5yd × 73.5yd).

Chairman: Ben Robinson.

Manager: Jimmy Floyd Hasselbaink.

Assistant Manager: Dino Maamria.

Colours: Yellow shirts with black trim, black shorts with yellow trim, yellow socks with black trim.

Year Formed: 1950.

Turned Professional: 1950.

Club Nickname: 'The Brewers'.

Grounds: 1950, Eton Park; 2005, Pirelli Stadium.

First Football League Game: 8 August 2009, FL 2, v Shrewsbury T (a) L 1–3 – Redmond; Edworthy, Boertien, Austin, Branston, McGrath, Maghoma, Penn, Phillips (Stride), Walker, Shroot (Pearson) (1).

HONOURS

League Champions: FL 2 – 2014–15; Conference – 2008–09.
Runners-up: FL 1 – 2015–16.

FA Cup: 4th rd – 2011.

League Cup: semi-final 2019.

FOOTBALL YEARBOOK FACT FILE

Burton Albion reached the third round of the FA Cup for the first time in 1955–56. They went down to a 7-0 defeat against Charlton Athletic at The Valley but later in the season the Addicks visited Burton to play a benefit match against the Brewers which raised almost £300 for Albion player Bert Hadfield.

Record League Victory: 6–1 v Aldershot T, FL 2, 12 December 2009 – Krysiak; James, Boertien, Stride, Webster, McGrath, Jackson, Penn, Kabba (2), Pearson (3) (Harrad) (1), Gilroy (Maghoma).

Record Cup Victory: 12–1 v Coalville T, Birmingham Senior Cup, 6 September 1954.

Record Defeat: 0–10 v Barnet, Southern League, 7 February 1970.

Most League Points (3 for a win): 94, FL 2, 2014–15.

Most League Goals: 71, FL 2, 2009–10; 2012–13.

Highest League Scorer in Season: Shaun Harrad, 21, 2009–10.

Most League Goals in Total Aggregate: Lucas Atkins, 62, 2014–21.

Most League Goals in One Match: 3, Greg Pearson v Aldershot T, FL 2, 12 December 2009; 3, Shaun Harrad v Rotherham U, FL 2, 11 September 2010; 3, Lucas Akins v Colchester U, FL 1, 23 April 2016; 3, Marcus Harness v Rochdale, FL 1, 5 January 2019; 3, Scott Fraser v Oxford U, FL 1, 20 August 2019; 3, Kane Hemmings v Crewe Alex, FL 1, 13 March 2021.

Most Capped Player: Liam Boyce, 11 (28), Northern Ireland.

Most League Appearances: Lucas Atkins, 285, 2014–21.

Youngest League Player: Sam Austin, 17 years 310 days v Stevenage, 25 October 2014.

Record Transfer Fee Received: £2,000,000 from Hull C for Jackson Irvine, August 2017.

Record Transfer Fee Paid: £500,000 to Ross Co for Liam Boyce, June 2017.

Football League Record: 2009 Promoted from Blue Square Premier; 2009–15 FL 2; 2015–16 FL 1; 2016–18 FL C; 2018– FL 1.

MANAGERS

Reg Weston 1953–57
Sammy Crooks 1957
Eddie Shimwell 1958
Bill Townsend 1959–62
Peter Taylor 1962–65
Alex Tait 1965–70
Richie Norman 1970–73
Ken Gutteridge 1973–74
Harold Bodle 1974–76
Ian Storey-Moore 1978–81
Neil Warnock 1981–86
Brian Fidler 1986–88
Vic Halom 1988
Bobby Hope 1988
Chris Wright 1988–89
Ken Blair 1989–90
Steve Powell 1990–91
Brian Fidler 1991–92
Brian Kenning 1992–94
John Barton 1994–98
Nigel Clough 1998–2009
Roy McFarland 2009
Paul Peschisolido 2009–12
Gary Rowett 2012–14
Jimmy Floyd Hasselbaink 2014–15
Nigel Clough 2015–20
Jake Buxton 2020
Jimmy Floyd Hasselbaink January 2021–

LATEST SEQUENCES

Longest Sequence of League Wins: 6, 23.2.2021 – 13.3.2021.

Longest Sequence of League Defeats: 8, 25.2.2012 – 24.3.2012.

Longest Sequence of League Draws: 6, 25.4.2011 – 16.8.2011.

Longest Sequence of Unbeaten League Matches: 13, 7.3.2015 – 8.8.2015.

Longest Sequence Without a League Win: 16, 31.12.2011 – 24.3.2012.

Successive Scoring Runs: 18 from 16.4.2011 – 8.10.2011.

Successive Non-scoring Runs: 5 from 23.9.2017.

TEN YEAR LEAGUE RECORD

		P	*W*	*D*	*L*	*F*	*A*	*Pts*	*Pos*
2011-12	FL 2	46	14	12	20	54	81	54	17
2012-13	FL 2	46	22	10	14	71	65	76	4
2013-14	FL 2	46	19	15	12	47	42	72	6
2014-15	FL 2	46	28	10	8	69	39	94	1
2015-16	FL 1	46	25	10	11	57	37	85	2
2016-17	FL C	46	13	13	20	49	63	52	20
2017-18	FL C	46	10	11	25	38	81	41	23
2018-19	FL 1	46	17	12	17	66	57	63	9
2019-20	FL 1	35	12	12	11	50	50	48	12§
2020-21	FL 1	46	15	12	19	61	73	57	16

§Decided on points-per-game (1.37)

DID YOU KNOW?

When Burton Albion were formed in 1950 it was the first time the town had had a senior football team for a decade. Albion are the fourth team from the town to play in the Football League following Burton Wanderers, Burton Swifts and Burton United.

BURTON ALBION – SKY BET LEAGUE ONE 2020–21 LEAGUE RECORD

Match No.	Date	Venue	Opponents	Result		H/T Score	Lg Pos.	Goalscorers	Attendance
1	Sept 12	A	Fleetwood T	L	1-2	0-1	15	Brayford [66]	0
2	19	H	Accrington S	W	2-1	0-0	10	Powell [72], Brayford [87]	0
3	26	A	Swindon T	L	2-4	1-3	16	Quinn [40], Akins [77]	0
4	Oct 3	H	Portsmouth	L	2-4	2-1	22	Akins [14], Naylor (og) [20]	0
5	10	A	Plymouth Arg	L	0-2	0-1	22		0
6	17	A	Bristol R	D	1-1	0-0	20	Hemmings [78]	0
7	20	H	Rochdale	L	0-1	0-0	23		0
8	24	H	AFC Wimbledon	D	1-1	0-0	23	Hemmings [66]	0
9	27	A	Peterborough U	D	2-2	1-1	23	Hemmings 2 [32, 60]	0
10	31	H	Blackpool	L	1-2	0-1	22	Gretarsson (og) [63]	0
11	Nov 3	A	Shrewsbury T	D	1-1	0-0	22	Hemmings [59]	0
12	14	A	Hull C	L	0-2	0-0	22		0
13	21	H	Northampton T	L	1-3	0-1	23	Akins (pen) [90]	0
14	24	H	Charlton Ath	W	4-2	2-1	21	Akins [9], Powell [39], Hughes [53], Vernam [76]	0
15	Dec 1	A	Sunderland	D	1-1	0-0	21	Vernam [60]	0
16	5	H	Crewe Alex	D	1-1	0-0	21	Hughes [76]	0
17	12	A	Milton Keynes D	D	1-1	1-0	23	Daniel [8]	0
18	15	A	Ipswich T	L	1-2	1-1	23	Powell [21]	0
19	19	H	Doncaster R	L	1-3	1-2	23	Akins (pen) [44]	0
20	26	A	Lincoln C	L	1-5	0-2	23	Hemmings [74]	0
21	29	H	Wigan Ath	L	3-4	2-2	23	O'Toole [13], Brayford [25], Hemmings [72]	0
22	Jan 2	H	Oxford U	L	1-5	1-3	23	Hemmings [40]	0
23	9	A	Gillingham	W	1-0	1-0	23	Carter [33]	0
24	16	H	Ipswich T	L	0-1	0-0	23		0
25	Feb 6	H	Hull C	W	1-0	0-0	23	Smith [90]	0
26	13	A	Northampton T	W	2-0	0-0	23	Bostwick [77], Edwards [90]	0
27	20	H	Sunderland	L	0-3	0-2	23		0
28	23	A	Charlton Ath	W	2-1	1-1	23	Fondop-Talom [25], Watson (og) [53]	0
29	27	A	Rochdale	W	2-0	0-0	20	Hemmings [65], Akins [86]	0
30	Mar 2	H	Bristol R	W	1-0	0-0	18	Smith [55]	0
31	6	H	Peterborough U	W	2-1	0-0	18	Hemmings [54], Carter [58]	0
32	9	A	AFC Wimbledon	W	1-0	0-0	18	Bostwick [59]	0
33	13	A	Crewe Alex	W	3-0	3-0	18	Hemmings 3 [9, 23, 34]	0
34	16	A	Blackpool	D	1-1	1-0	18	Carter [24]	0
35	20	H	Milton Keynes D	L	1-2	0-1	18	Akins (pen) [74]	0
36	23	H	Shrewsbury T	L	1-2	0-1	18	Clare [60]	0
37	Apr 2	A	Accrington S	D	0-0	0-0	18		0
38	5	H	Swindon T	W	2-1	1-1	18	Haymer [26], Brayford [83]	0
39	10	A	Portsmouth	W	2-1	1-0	18	Fondop-Talom [45], Powell [47]	0
40	13	A	Doncaster R	W	3-0	0-0	17	Akins [59], Haymer [72], Carter [78]	0
41	17	H	Plymouth Arg	D	1-1	0-0	17	Broom [90]	0
42	20	H	Lincoln C	L	0-1	0-1	17		0
43	24	A	Wigan Ath	D	1-1	1-1	17	Powell [16]	0
44	27	H	Fleetwood T	W	5-2	2-0	16	Akins [35], Powell [39], Haymer [72], Hemmings 2 [85, 90]	0
45	May 1	H	Gillingham	D	1-1	0-1	16	Broom [90]	0
46	9	A	Oxford U	L	0-4	0-2	16		0

Final League Position: 16

GOALSCORERS

League (61): Hemmings 15, Akins 9 (3 pens), Powell 6, Brayford 4, Carter 4, Haymer 3, Bostwick 2, Broom 2, Fondop-Talom 2, Hughes 2, Smith 2, Vernam 2, Clare 1, Daniel 1, Edwards 1, O'Toole 1, Quinn 1, own goals 3.
FA Cup (0).
Carabao Cup (2): Akins 1, Daniel 1.
Papa John's Trophy (6): Powell 3, Akins 1, Edwards 1, Lawless 1.

Garratt B 28	Eardley N 9+1	Brayford J 40+1	O'Toole J 12+4	Wallace K 9+3	Akins L 45	Powell J 23+16	Bostwick M 26+2	Quinn S 21+1	Lawless S 8+8	Hemmings K 26+10	Fox B 5+4	Daniel C 17+2	Edwards R 37+5	Vassilev I 8+4	Roles J —+2	Gilligan C 13+5	Vernam C 11+3	Hughes S 14	O'Hara K 17	Varney L —+4	Ennis N 6+3	Gallacher O 5+4	Hutchinson R —+1	Hewlett T —+1	Carter H 24	Clare S 19+1	Parker J 3+3	Haymer T 20+1	Earl J 7+1	Broom R 3+8	Smith J 13+3	Taylor T 6+10	Rowe D 8+7	Mancienne M 14+3	Fondop-Talom M 8+9	Barnes D 1	Match No.
1	2[1]	3	4■	5	6	7[3]	8	9	10[2]	11	12	13	14																								1
1		3		4	9	8		7	11[1]	10	2	5	6	12																							2
1		3		4	11	8		7[1]	9[2]	10	2	5	6[3]	13	12	14																					3
1		3	4		10	8[3]		7[2]	14	11	2	5	6	12	13		9[1]																				4
1	5	2[1]		12	9	8	3[2]	7	14	11		13	6	10[3]				4																			5
	2		4	5	9	12		8[1]		10	7			11[2]		6		3	1	13																	6
	2[2]		3	5	11	6[1]		8		10	7[3]			9		12		4	1	14	13																7
	2		3		9			7	8	10		5		11[1]		6		4	1		12																8
			4		2			7	8	10		5	12	11		6		3	1		9[1]																9
			3		2	14		7	8	10		5	12	11[1]		6[3]	13	4	1		9[2]																10
	2	3			9			7	8[1]	10		5	6				11	4	1	12																	11
1	2[3]	3	12				13	7[2]	11				8	9[1]		6		4■			10	5	14														12
1	2	3			10	14	4	7	12				8[2]	9[1]		6[4]	13				11	5[3]		15													13
		2			11	9[2]	4	6			13	5	8			7	10[1]	3	1			12															14
		2	14		11	9[1]	4	6[2]			13	5	8			7	10[3]	3	1			12															15
		2			11	9	4	6				5	8			7[1]	10	3	1		12																16
		2		13	11	9[1]	4	7[2]			12	5	8			6	10	3	1																		17
		2	4		11	8	6		12			5	7				9[1]	3	1		10																18
		2	12		10	6	4	7[2]	15	13		5	8[4]			14	11	3[1]	1		9[3]																19
	2	3		14	11	9	4	7	13	12		5[3]	8[1]			6	10[2]		1																		20
		2	3	7	9[2]	6	4	8	13	10		5[1]	12				11		1																		21
	14	2	3	4	5[4]	11[2]	7[3]	8[1]	15	10		9	12			6	13		1																		22
1		2	4	8	6	9[1]		12		11[2]		10	7							13		5			3												23
1		2	4[1]		6	9[3]	12			11			7	15		8	10[2]					5[4]			3	13	14										24
1		4			6	12				11[1]			7[3]												3	9	10	2	5	8[2]	13	14					25
1		2			11	12	4						7												3	9	6[3]		5	8[1]	10[2]		13	14			26
1		2			11[4]	12	4						7												3	6[1]	10[3]	13	5■	9[2]	8[5]	16	14		15		27
1		13		8[1]	10		4						7									5[2]			3	9		2			6		12	14	11[3]		28
1		2			10	12	4			13			7												3	6[3]		5		15	8[4]		9[1]	14	11[2]		29
1		2			10[3]	12	4			14			7												3	9		5			6	13		8[2]	11[1]		30
1		2			10[1]	13	4			11[3]			7									15			3		14	5			8[4]	12	9[2]	6			31
1		2			10		4			13			7												3			5			8	12	9[1]	6	11[2]		32
1		2	15		10	13				11[1]			9[2]												3	7		5		14	8[3]	6[4]		4	12		33
1		2			10	12				11			7												3	6		5			8		9[1]	4			34
1		2			10	12				11			9												3	7[1]		5			8	6[2]		4	13		35
1		2			8[3]	13	4			11			9												3	7[2]		5		12	10[1]			6	14		36
1		4			10					11[1]			9												3	7		2	5		8			6	12		37
1		2			10[3]	12	4			11			9												3	7[1]		5			8[2]	13		6	14		38
1		2			10	8[1]	4			12			9												3	7[3]		5				14	13	6	11[2]		39
1		2			10	8[3]	4			13			9[4]												3	7[1]		5		15		12	14	6	11[2]		40
1		2			10[4]	12	4			11			9[3]												3	7[2]		5		15		13	8[1]	6	14		41
1		2			10[3]	13	4			11			9[4]												3	7		5		14		12	8[2]	6[1]	15		42
1		2			10	8[3]	4[2]			14			9												3	7		5	12		15	6[1]	13		11[4]		43
		4			11	8[1]				12			9			14			1						3	7		2	5		13	6[3]	10[2]				44
		4			10	8[4]				11[2]			9[1]						1			12[3]			3	6		2	5	15		7	14		13		45
		4			10[4]	9[2]				12						14									3		15	2	5	13		7[3]	8	6	11[1]	1	46

FA Cup

First Round	Barnet	(a)	0-1

Carabao Cup

First Round	Accrington S	(h)	1-1
(Burton Alb won 4-2 on penalties)			
Second Round	Aston Villa	(h)	1-3

Papa John's Trophy

Group H (S)	Peterborough U	(a)	3-3
(Peterborough U won 5-4 on penalties)			
Group H (S)	Cambridge U	(h)	2-4
Group H (S)	Fulham U21	(h)	1-1
(Burton Alb won 4-1 on penalties)			

CAMBRIDGE UNITED

FOUNDATION

The football revival in Cambridge began soon after World War II when the Abbey United club (formed 1912) decided to turn professional in 1949. In 1951 they changed their name to Cambridge United. They were competing in the United Counties League before graduating to the Eastern Counties League in 1951 and the Southern League in 1958.

The Abbey Stadium, Newmarket Road, Cambridge CB5 8LN.

Telephone: (01223) 566 500.

Ticket Office: (01223) 566 500 (option 1).

Website: www.cambridge-united.co.uk

Email: info@cambridge-united.co.uk

Ground Capacity: 8,127.

Record Attendance: 14,000 v Chelsea, Friendly, 1 May 1970.

Pitch Measurements: 100.5m × 67.5m (110yd × 74yd).

Vice-Chairman: Eddie Clark.

Chief Executive: Ian Mather.

Head Coach: Mark Bonner.

Assistant Head Coach: Gary Waddock.

Colours: Amber and black striped shirts, black shorts with amber trim, black socks with amber trim.

Year Formed: 1912.

Turned Professional: 1949.

Ltd Co.: 1948.

Previous Name: 1919, Abbey United; 1951, Cambridge United.

Club Nickname: The 'U's'.

Grounds: 1932, Abbey Stadium (renamed R Costings Abbey Stadium 2009, Cambs Glass Stadium 2016, The Abbey Stadium 2017).

First Football League Game: 15 August 1970, Division 4, v Lincoln C (h) D 1–1 – Roberts; Thompson, Meldrum (1), Slack, Eades, Hardy, Leggett, Cassidy, Lindsey, McKinven, Harris.

Record League Victory: 7–0 v Morecambe, FL 2, 19 April 2016 – Norris; Roberts (1), Coulson, Clark, Dunne (Williams), Ismail (1), Berry (2 pens), Ledson (Spencer), Dunk (2), Williamson (1) (Simpson).

Record Cup Victory: 5–1 v Bristol C, FA Cup 5th rd second replay, 27 February 1990 – Vaughan; Fensome, Kimble, Bailie (O'Shea), Chapple, Daish, Cheetham (Robinson), Leadbitter (1), Dublin (2), Taylor (1), Philpott (1).

Record Defeat: 0–7 v Sunderland, League Cup 2nd rd, 1 October 2002; 0–7 v Luton T, FL 2, 18 November 2017.

HONOURS

League Champions: Division 3 – 1990–91; Division 4 – 1976–77.

Runners-up: FL 2 – 2020–21; Division 3 – 1977–78; Fourth Division – (6th) 1989–90 *(promoted via play-offs)*; Third Division – 1998–99; Conference – (2nd) 2013–14 *(promoted via play-offs)*.

FA Cup: 6th rd – 1990, 1991.

League Cup: quarter-final – 1993.

League Trophy: *Runners-up:* 2002.

FOOTBALL YEARBOOK FACT FILE

Cambridge United reached the second round of the FA Cup for the first time in 1953–54. Drawn at home to Bradford Park Avenue, they increased the capacity of the Abbey Stadium by installing a temporary stand made from steel scaffolding. The U's were rewarded with a new record attendance of 10,000 but went down to a 2-1 defeat.

Most League Points (2 for a win): 65, Division 4, 1976–77.

Most League Points (3 for a win): 86, Division 3, 1990–91.

Most League Goals: 87, Division 4, 1976–77.

Highest League Scorer in Season: Paul Mullin, 32, FL 2, 2020–21.

Most League Goals in Total Aggregate: John Taylor, 86, 1988–92; 1996–2001.

Most League Goals in One Match: 5, Steve Butler v Exeter C, Division 2, 4 April 1994.

Most Capped Player: Reggie Lambe, 12 (41), Bermuda.

Most League Appearances: Steve Spriggs, 416, 1975–87.

Youngest League Player: Andy Sinton, 16 years 228 days v Wolverhampton W, 2 November 1982.

Record Transfer Fee Received: £1,300,000 from Leicester C for Trevor Benjamin, July 2000.

Record Transfer Fee Paid: £190,000 to Luton T for Steve Claridge, November 1992.

Football League Record: 1970 Elected to Division 4; 1973–74 Division 3; 1974–77 Division 4; 1977–78 Division 3; 1978–84 Division 2; 1984–85 Division 3; 1985–90 Division 4; 1990–91 Division 3; 1991–92 Division 2; 1992–93 Division 1; 1993–95 Division 2; 1995–99 Division 3; 1999–2002 Division 2; 2002–04 Division 3; 2004–05 FL2; 2005–14 Conference Premier; 2014–21 FL 2; 2021– FL 1.

MANAGERS

Bill Whittaker 1949–55
Gerald Williams 1955
Bert Johnson 1955–59
Bill Craig 1959–60
Alan Moore 1960–63
Roy Kirk 1964–66
Bill Leivers 1967–74
Ron Atkinson 1974–78
John Docherty 1978–83
John Ryan 1984–85
Ken Shellito 1985
Chris Turner 1985–90
John Beck 1990–92
Ian Atkins 1992–93
Gary Johnson 1993–95
Tommy Taylor 1995–96
Roy McFarland 1996–2001
John Beck 2001
John Taylor 2001–04
Claude Le Roy 2004
Herve Renard 2004
Steve Thompson 2004–05
Rob Newman 2005–06
Jimmy Quinn 2006–08
Gary Brabin 2008–09
Martin Ling 2009–11
Jez George 2011–12
Richard Money 2012–15
Shaun Derry 2015–18
Joe Dunne 2018
Colin Calderwood 2018–20
Mark Bonner March 2020–

LATEST SEQUENCES

Longest Sequence of League Wins: 7, 19.2.1977 – 1.4.1977.

Longest Sequence of League Defeats: 7, 8.4.1985 – 30.4.1985.

Longest Sequence of League Draws: 6, 6.9.1986 – 30.9.1986.

Longest Sequence of Unbeaten League Matches: 14, 9.9.1972 – 10.11.1972.

Longest Sequence Without a League Win: 31, 8.10.1983 – 23.4.1984.

Successive Scoring Runs: 26 from 9.4.2002.

Successive Non-scoring Runs: 5 from 29.9.1973.

TEN YEAR LEAGUE RECORD

		P	W	D	L	F	A	Pts	Pos
2011-12	Conf P	46	19	14	13	57	41	71	9
2012-13	Conf P	46	15	14	17	68	69	59	14
2013-14	Conf P	46	23	13	10	72	35	82	2
2014-15	FL 2	46	13	12	21	61	66	51	19
2015-16	FL 2	46	18	14	14	66	55	68	9
2016-17	FL 2	46	19	9	18	58	50	66	11
2017-18	FL 2	46	17	13	16	56	60	64	12
2018-19	FL 2	46	12	11	23	40	66	47	21
2019-20	FL 2	37	12	9	16	40	48	45	16§
2020-21	FL 2	46	24	8	14	73	49	80	2

§Decided on points-per-game (1.22)

DID YOU KNOW?

Cambridge United's association with the song 'I've Got a Lovely Bunch of Coconuts' by the Billy Cotton Band dates back to the 1950s. The tune continues to be played at the Abbey Stadium after every victory by the U's.

CAMBRIDGE UNITED – SKY BET LEAGUE TWO 2020–21 LEAGUE RECORD

Match No.	*Date*	*Venue*	*Opponents*	*Result*	*H/T Score*	*Lg Pos.*	*Goalscorers*	*Attendance*
1	Sept 12	H	Carlisle U	W 3-0	2-0	2	Hannant ^{9}, Mullin ^{16}, Ironside ^{86}	0
2	19	A	Morecambe	W 5-0	3-0	1	Hoolahan ^{29}, Mullin 3 $^{34, 54, 64}$, May ^{37}	0
3	26	H	Tranmere R	D 0-0	0-0	1		0
4	Oct 3	A	Exeter C	L 0-2	0-2	4		0
5	10	H	Newport Co	W 2-1	1-0	2	Mullin 2 $^{38, 61}$	0
6	17	A	Scunthorpe U	W 5-0	2-0	1	Mullin 2 (2 pens) $^{35, 44}$, Hannant ^{51}, Ironside 2 $^{61, 83}$	0
7	20	H	Port Vale	W 3-1	1-1	1	Mullin 3 (1 pen) $^{3 (p), 51, 90}$	0
8	24	H	Bolton W	D 1-1	0-0	2	Crellin (og) ^{72}	0
9	27	A	Walsall	W 2-0	1-0	2	Mullin (pen) ^{9}, Ironside (pen) ^{80}	0
10	31	A	Crawley T	L 1-2	1-1	2	Ironside ^{3}	0
11	Nov 3	H	Salford C	W 2-1	1-1	2	Iredale ^{43}, Ironside (pen) ^{50}	0
12	14	H	Barrow	D 1-1	0-0	2	Ironside ^{56}	0
13	24	A	Cheltenham T	D 1-1	0-1	3	Mullin ^{90}	0
14	Dec 2	H	Mansfield T	L 0-1	0-0	6		1917
15	5	H	Oldham Ath	L 1-2	0-0	6	Mullin ^{90}	1970
16	12	A	Forest Green R	L 0-2	0-0	9		799
17	15	H	Colchester U	W 2-1	0-0	6	Mullin 2 $^{50, 65}$	1949
18	19	A	Bradford C	L 0-1	0-1	9		0
19	26	H	Leyton Orient	W 2-1	0-1	8	Hoolahan ^{55}, Mullin ^{57}	0
20	29	A	Stevenage	L 0-1	0-1	8		0
21	Jan 2	A	Grimsby T	W 2-1	2-0	5	May ^{4}, Mullin ^{36}	0
22	9	H	Harrogate T	W 2-1	0-1	3	Ironside ^{71}, Hoolahan ^{81}	0
23	16	A	Colchester U	D 1-1	1-1	3	Knibbs ^{12}	0
24	19	A	Southend U	W 2-1	0-1	1	Iredale ^{46}, Ironside ^{68}	0
25	23	H	Bradford C	D 0-0	0-0	1		0
26	30	H	Crawley T	W 3-1	2-1	1	Ironside ^{11}, Knoyle ^{45}, Hoolahan ^{85}	0
27	Feb 6	A	Barrow	W 2-0	1-0	1	Mullin ^{43}, Ironside ^{84}	0
28	9	A	Salford C	L 1-4	0-3	1	Mullin ^{71}	0
29	13	H	Southend U	D 0-0	0-0	1		0
30	20	A	Mansfield T	W 3-0	0-0	1	Mullin 2 $^{57, 65}$, Knibbs ^{90}	0
31	23	H	Cheltenham T	L 0-1	0-0	1		0
32	27	A	Port Vale	W 1-0	0-0	1	O'Neil ^{85}	0
33	Mar 2	H	Scunthorpe U	L 0-1	0-0	2		0
34	6	H	Walsall	W 1-0	0-0	2	Mullin ^{90}	0
35	9	A	Bolton W	L 1-2	0-2	2	Knoyle ^{80}	0
36	13	A	Oldham Ath	W 4-2	3-2	2	Mullin (pen) ^{25}, Iredale 2 $^{36, 45}$, Hannant ^{73}	0
37	20	H	Forest Green R	W 1-0	1-0	2	Hoolahan ^{38}	0
38	27	A	Carlisle U	W 2-1	1-0	1	Mullin ^{45}, May ^{90}	0
39	Apr 2	H	Morecambe	W 2-1	1-0	1	Mullin 2 (1 pen) $^{18, 81 (p)}$	0
40	5	A	Tranmere R	D 1-1	0-1	1	Mullin ^{60}	0
41	10	H	Exeter C	L 1-4	0-2	2	Ironside ^{55}	0
42	17	A	Newport Co	W 1-0	0-0	1	Drysdale ^{79}	0
43	20	A	Leyton Orient	W 4-2	1-1	1	Ironside 2 $^{19, 80}$, Tracey ^{64}, Mullin (pen) ^{69}	0
44	24	H	Stevenage	L 0-1	0-0	2		0
45	30	A	Harrogate T	L 4-5	2-4	2	Hoolahan ^{26}, Hannant ^{29}, Mullin 2 (1 pen) $^{58, 74 (p)}$	0
46	May 8	H	Grimsby T	W 3-0	1-0	2	O'Neil ^{25}, Hoolahan ^{57}, Mullin ^{80}	0

Final League Position: 2

GOALSCORERS

League (73): Mullin 32 (8 pens), Ironside 14 (2 pens), Hoolahan 7, Hannant 4, Iredale 4, May 3, Knibbs 2, Knoyle 2, O'Neil 2, Drysdale 1, Tracey 1, own goal 1.
FA Cup (0).
Carabao Cup (1): Cundy 1.
Papa John's Trophy (9): Hannant 3, Mullin 2 (1 pen), Darling 1, Knibbs 1, Knowles 1, Worman 1.

Mitov D 20	Knoyle K 46	Cundy R 14 + 3	Taylor G 46	Dunk H 33 + 8	Hoolahan W 30 + 4	O'Neil L 12 + 9	Digby P 34 + 1	Hannant L 38 + 5	Mullin P 45 + 1	Ironside J 33 + 11	May A 24 + 14	Iredale J 26 + 12	Knibbs H 7 + 16	Davies L 4 + 9	Dallas A — + 1	El Mizouni I 3 + 8	Darling H 15 + 1	Boateng H 20 + 5	Burton C 26 + 1	Okedina J 12 + 2	Tracey S 5 + 12	Drysdale D 12 + 1	Alese A 1 + 1	Match No.
1	2	3	4	5	6^{2}	7^{1}	8	9	10^{3}	11	12	13	14											1
1	2^{2}	3	4	5	6		7	9	11^{3}	10^{1}	8		12	13	14									2
1	2	3	4	5	6^{1}		7	9	11^{3}	10	8^{2}	13				12	14							3
1	2	3	4	5	9^{3}		7	6^{1}	11	10	8^{2}	14	12			13								4
1	2		3	10	9^{2}		6	8	11^{3}	13	7^{1}	5	14				4	12						5
1	2		4	9			8^{1}	6^{2}	10^{3}	11	7	5	14			13	3	12						6
1	2		4	9	10^{3}		7	6	11	14	13	5^{2}		12			3	8^{1}						7
1	2		4	9			7	6	11	12	13	5				10^{1}	3	8^{2}						8
1	2	4	3	5				9^{2}	11^{1}	10	8	12		6		13		7						9
1	2	3	4	9^{3}	12			7	10	11^{1}		5	14	6^{2}		13		8						10
1	2	4	8	5	10			6	12	11^{2}		9^{1}	13				3	7						11
1	2	14	4	5			8	6^{2}	10	11^{3}		12		13		9^{1}	3	7						12
1	2	4	3	9^{1}	10		8	6	11	12		5^{2}	13					7						13
1	2	4	3	5^{2}	9		8	6^{3}	10	11	12	13	14					7^{1}						14
1	2	4	3	5	12		7	6	10		8^{2}	9^{1}	11			13								15
	2	4	7^{2}	5	10^{3}		8	6^{4}	11		13	15	12	9^{1}		14	3		1					16
	2	4	8				7	6	11^{2}	13		5	10	12		9^{1}	3		1					17
	2	3^{2}	8	9	12		7	6^{4}	10	14	13	5^{1}	11^{3}	15			4		1					18
	2		4	14	9		8	6^{3}	10^{1}	11	7	5^{2}	12	13			3		1					19
	2		4	5			8	6	10	11^{1}	7^{3}	9^{2}	13	12		14	3		1					20
1	2	13	4	5	9^{3}		8	6	10	12	7	14	11^{1}				3^{2}							21
1	2		4	5	6^{2}		7	9	11	12	8		10^{1}	13			3							22
1	2	13	4	5	9	14	8	6^{1}	10	12	7^{3}		11				3^{2}							23
1	2		4	5		12	8		10^{1}	11	7	9		6			3							24
1^{1}	2	3	4	5^{3}	9		7	6^{2}	10	11	8	13	14						12					25
	2		3	5	6		8	9	10	11^{1}	7								1	4	12			26
	2		4	5	6^{3}	14		9^{1}	10^{2}	11	7^{4}	15	13						1	3	12	8		27
	2		4	5^{1}				9	10	13	7	12	11						1	3^{3}	6^{2}	8	14	28
	2		3		6^{2}	13		9	10	11	7^{1}	5							1	4	12	8		29
	2		3	5	6	8^{1}		9^{2}	11	10	7		13						1	4		12		30
	2		3	5		7^{2}		6^{3}	10	11	8	9^{1}	14					13	1	4	12			31
	2		3	5	9	12		10	11^{3}	13	6							7^{1}	1	14	8^{2}	4		32
	2		3	5		7^{1}			10	11	8	9^{2}		12				13	1		6	4		33
	2		4	5	9	6^{1}			10	11	7							8	1		12	3		34
	2		4	5^{1}		13	14	9	10	11	7^{2}	12						8^{3}	1		6	3		35
	2		4		6	8^{2}	7	13	10^{3}	11	14	9						12	1			3	5^{1}	36
	2		4		9	7^{1}	6	12	10	11^{3}	14	5						8^{2}	1	3	13			37
	2		4	15	9^{4}	7^{1}	6	12	11^{2}	10	14	5						8^{3}	1	3	13			38
	2		4	14	9^{3}	7^{1}	6	13	11^{2}	10		5						8	1	3	12			39
	2		4	14	13	9^{1}	6	8^{2}	10^{3}	11	12	5						7	1	3				40
	2		4		9	7^{1}	6	12	11	10		5						8^{2}	1	3	13			41
	2		4	13	9^{4}	14	7	6^{2}	10^{1}	11	15	5						8^{3}	1		12	3		42
	2		4	12		13	7	6	11^{3}	10	14	5						8^{2}	1		9^{1}	3		43
	2		4	14	9	13	6^{3}	7^{1}	10	11	15	5^{2}						8^{4}	1		12	3		44
	2		4	13	9		6^{4}	7	10	11	14	5^{1}						8^{3}	1	12	15	3^{2}		45
	2		4	5	9	8	6	7	10	11									1	3				46

FA Cup

First Round	Shrewsbury T	(h)	0-2

Carabao Cup

First Round	Birmingham C	(a)	1-0
Second Round	Newport Co	(a)	0-1

Papa John's Trophy

Group H (S)	Fulham U21	(h)	2-0
Group H (S)	Burton Alb	(a)	4-2
Group H (S)	Peterborough U	(h)	1-1
(Cambridge U won 3-1 on penalties)			
Second Round (S)	Gillingham	(h)	2-0
Third Round (S)	Oxford U	(a)	0-1

CARDIFF CITY

FOUNDATION

Credit for the establishment of a first class professional football club in such a rugby stronghold as Cardiff is due to members of the Riverside club formed in 1899 out of a cricket club of that name. Cardiff became a city in 1905 and in 1908 the South Wales and Monmouthshire FA granted Riverside permission to call themselves Cardiff City. The club turned professional under that name in 1910.

Cardiff City Stadium, Leckwith Road, Cardiff CF11 8AZ.

Telephone: (0845) 345 1400.

Ticket Office: (0333) 311 1920.

Website: www.cardiffcityfc.co.uk

Email: club@cardiffcityfc.co.uk

Ground Capacity: 33,280.

Record Attendance: 57,893 v Arsenal, Division 1, 22 April 1953 (at Ninian Park); 33,028 v Manchester U, Premier League, 22 December 2018 (at Cardiff City Stadium).

Ground Record Attendance: 62,634, Wales v England, 17 October 1959 (at Ninian Park); 33,280, Wales v Belgium, 12 June 2015 (at Cardiff City Stadium).

Pitch Measurements: 105m × 68m (115yd × 74.5yd).

Chairman: Mehmet Dalman.

Chief Executive: Ken Choo.

Manager: Mick McCarthy.

Assistant Manager: Terry Connor.

Colours: Blue shirts with white trim, white shorts with blue trim, blue socks with white trim.

Year Formed: 1899.

Turned Professional: 1910.

Previous Names: 1899, Riverside; 1902, Riverside Albion; 1908, Cardiff City.

Club Nickname: 'The Bluebirds'.

Grounds: Riverside, Sophia Gardens, Old Park and Fir Gardens; 1910, Ninian Park; 2009, Cardiff City Stadium.

First Football League Game: 28 August 1920, Division 2, v Stockport Co (a) W 5–2 – Kneeshaw; Brittan, Leyton; Keenor (1), Smith, Hardy; Grimshaw (1), Gill (2), Cashmore, West, Evans (1).

Record League Victory: 9–2 v Thames, Division 3 (S), 6 February 1932 – Farquharson; Eric Morris, Roberts; Galbraith, Harris, Ronan; Emmerson (1), Keating (1), Jones (1), McCambridge (1), Robbins (5).

Record Cup Victory: 8–0 v Enfield, FA Cup 1st rd, 28 November 1931 – Farquharson; Smith, Roberts; Harris (1), Galbraith, Ronan; Emmerson (2), Keating (3); O'Neill (2), Robbins, McCambridge.

HONOURS

League Champions: FL C – 2012–13; Division 3S – 1946–47; Third Division – 1992–93.
Runners-up: FL C – 2017–18; Division 1 – 1923–24; Division 2 – 1920–21, 1951–52, 1959–60; Division 3 – 1975–76, 1982–83; Third Division – 2000–01; Division 4 – 1987–88.

FA Cup Winners: 1927.
Runners-up: 1925, 2008.

League Cup: *Runners-up:* 2012.

Welsh Cup Winners: 22 times.

European Competitions
European Cup-Winners' Cup: 1964–65 *(qf)*, 1965–66, 1967–68 *(sf)*, 1968–69, 1969–70, 1970–71 *(qf)*, 1971–72, 1973–74, 1974–75, 1976–77, 1977–78, 1988–89, 1992–93, 1993–94.

FOOTBALL YEARBOOK FACT FILE

Although Cardiff City became a fully professional outfit from the 1910–11 season when they moved to Ninian Park, they had employed a number of professionals before this. Registered professionals with the FA of Wales for the 1909–10 season included goalkeeper Fred Simmonds, Lewis Nash and Frank Powell.

Record Defeat: 2–11 v Sheffield U, Division 1, 1 January 1926.

Most League Points (2 for a win): 66, Division 3 (S), 1946–47.

Most League Points (3 for a win): 90, FL C, 2017–18.

Most League Goals: 95, Division 3, 2000–01.

Highest League Scorer in Season: Robert Earnshaw, 31, Division 2, 2002–03.

Most League Goals in Total Aggregate: Len Davies, 128, 1920–31.

Most League Goals in One Match: 5, Hugh Ferguson v Burnley, Division 1, 1 September 1928; 5, Walter Robbins v Thames, Division 3 (S), 6 February 1932; 5, William Henderson v Northampton T, Division 3 (S), 22 April 1933.

Most Capped Player: Aron Gunnarsson, 59 (97), Iceland.

Most League Appearances: Phil Dwyer, 471, 1972–85.

Youngest League Player: Bob Adams, 15 years 355 days v Southend U, 18 February 1933.

Record Transfer Fee Received: £10,000,000 from Internazionale for Gary Medel, August 2014.

Record Transfer Fee Paid: £15,000,000 to Nantes for Emiliano Sala, January 2019.

Football League Record: 1920 Elected to Division 2; 1921–29 Division 1; 1929–31 Division 2; 1931–47 Division 3 (S); 1947–52 Division 2; 1952–57 Division 1; 1957–60 Division 2; 1960–62 Division 1; 1962–75 Division 2; 1975–76 Division 3; 1976–82 Division 2; 1982–83 Division 3; 1983–85 Division 2; 1985–86 Division 3; 1986–88 Division 4; 1988–90 Division 3; 1990–92 Division 4; 1992–93 Division 3; 1993–95 Division 2; 1995–99 Division 3; 1999–2000 Division 2; 2000–01 Division 3; 2001–03 Division 2; 2003–04 Division 1; 2004–13 FL C; 2013–14 Premier League; 2014–18 FL C; 2018–19 Premier League; 2019– FL C.

LATEST SEQUENCES

Longest Sequence of League Wins: 9, 26.10.1946 – 28.12.1946.

Longest Sequence of League Defeats: 7, 4.11.1933 – 25.12.1933.

Longest Sequence of League Draws: 6, 29.11.1980 – 17.1.1981.

Longest Sequence of Unbeaten League Matches: 21, 21.9.1946 – 1.3.1947.

Longest Sequence Without a League Win: 15, 21.11.1936 – 6.3.1937.

Successive Scoring Runs: 24 from 25.8.2012.

Successive Non-scoring Runs: 8 from 20.12.1952.

MANAGERS

Davy McDougall 1910–11
Fred Stewart 1911–33
Bartley Wilson 1933–34
B. Watts-Jones 1934–37
Bill Jennings 1937–39
Cyril Spiers 1939–46
Billy McCandless 1946–48
Cyril Spiers 1948–54
Trevor Morris 1954–58
Bill Jones 1958–62
George Swindin 1962–64
Jimmy Scoular 1964–73
Frank O'Farrell 1973–74
Jimmy Andrews 1974–78
Richie Morgan 1978–81
Graham Williams 1981–82
Len Ashurst 1982–84
Jimmy Goodfellow 1984
Alan Durban 1984–86
Frank Burrows 1986–89
Len Ashurst 1989–91
Eddie May 1991–94
Terry Yorath 1994–95
Eddie May 1995
Kenny Hibbitt (*Chief Coach*) 1995–96
Phil Neal 1996
Russell Osman 1996–97
Kenny Hibbitt 1997–98
Frank Burrows 1998–2000
Billy Ayre 2000
Bobby Gould 2000
Alan Cork 2000–02
Lennie Lawrence 2002–05
Dave Jones 2005–11
Malky Mackay 2011–13
Ole Gunnar Solskjaer 2014
Russell Slade 2014–16
Paul Trollope 2016
Neil Warnock 2016–19
Neil Harris 2019–21
Mick McCarthy January 2021–

TEN YEAR LEAGUE RECORD

		P	W	D	L	F	A	Pts	Pos
2011-12	FL C	46	19	18	9	66	53	75	6
2012-13	FL C	46	25	12	9	72	45	87	1
2013-14	PR Lge	38	7	9	22	32	74	30	20
2014-15	FL C	46	16	14	16	57	61	62	11
2015-16	FL C	46	17	17	12	56	51	68	8
2016-17	FL C	46	17	11	18	60	61	62	12
2017-18	FL C	46	27	9	10	69	39	90	2
2018-19	PR Lge	38	10	4	24	34	69	34	18
2019-20	FL C	46	19	16	11	68	58	73	5
2020-21	FL C	46	18	14	14	66	49	68	8

DID YOU KNOW ?

Cardiff City recorded their highest average attendance of 37,933 in the 1952–53 season following the club's promotion back to the First Division. The highest gate was 52,202 for the Boxing Day visit of Newcastle United, while the lowest figure was 19,830 for the game with Chelsea.

CARDIFF CITY – SKY BET CHAMPIONSHIP 2020–21 LEAGUE RECORD

Match No.	Date	Venue	Opponents	Result		H/T Score	Lg Pos.	Goalscorers	Attendance
1	Sept 12	H	Sheffield W	L	0-2	0-2	21		0
2	19	A	Nottingham F	W	2-0	2-0	14	Moore 2 3, 40	0
3	26	H	Reading	L	1-2	0-0	16	Tomlin 81	0
4	Oct 3	A	Blackburn R	D	0-0	0-0	15		0
5	18	A	Preston NE	W	1-0	0-0	12	Ojo 52	0
6	21	H	Bournemouth	D	1-1	0-1	13	Wilson 62	0
7	24	H	Middlesbrough	D	1-1	0-1	15	Ojo 70	0
8	28	A	Derby Co	D	1-1	0-1	14	Moore 77	0
9	31	A	QPR	L	2-3	0-2	17	Ralls 2 (1 pen) 49 (p), 85	0
10	Nov 3	H	Barnsley	W	3-0	2-0	11	Hoilett 4, Ralls (pen) 45, Wilson 77	0
11	6	H	Bristol C	L	0-1	0-1	13		0
12	21	A	Millwall	D	1-1	0-1	15	Moore 79	0
13	25	A	Coventry C	L	0-1	0-0	18		0
14	28	H	Luton T	W	4-0	2-0	14	Morrison 5, Harris 9, Moore 59, Ojo 82	0
15	Dec 1	H	Huddersfield T	W	3-0	1-0	11	Moore 2 35, 68, Glatzel 85	0
16	5	A	Watford	W	1-0	1-0	11	Moore 43	0
17	8	A	Stoke C	W	2-1	0-1	9	Morrison 76, Glatzel 66	0
18	12	H	Swansea C	L	0-2	0-1	10		0
19	16	H	Birmingham C	W	3-2	1-1	10	Glatzel 10, Wilson 77, Morrison 89	0
20	19	A	Norwich C	L	0-2	0-1	10		2000
21	26	H	Brentford	L	2-3	1-0	12	Vaulks 2 45, 76	0
22	29	A	Wycombe W	L	1-2	0-1	15	Hoilett 90	0
23	Jan 16	H	Norwich C	L	1-2	0-2	15	Ralls 65	0
24	20	H	QPR	L	0-1	0-0	15		0
25	27	A	Barnsley	D	2-2	0-1	15	Ojo 58, Moore 68	0
26	30	H	Millwall	D	1-1	0-1	15	Moore 71	0
27	Feb 6	A	Bristol C	W	2-0	2-0	14	Nelson 18, Moore 25	0
28	9	A	Rotherham U	W	2-1	1-0	11	Ojo 42, Bennett 85	0
29	13	H	Coventry C	W	3-1	2-0	7	Moore 2 31, 38, Murphy 46	0
30	16	A	Luton T	W	2-0	0-0	7	Wilson 53, Vaulks 57	0
31	20	H	Preston NE	W	4-0	1-0	7	Moore (pen) 2, Murphy 46, Pack 70, Harris 77	0
32	24	A	Bournemouth	W	2-1	2-0	6	Morrison 28, Moore (pen) 37	0
33	27	A	Middlesbrough	D	1-1	1-0	8	Morrison 37	0
34	Mar 2	H	Derby Co	W	4-0	1-0	6	Bacuna 2 22, 56, Moore 48, Vaulks 90	0
35	5	A	Huddersfield T	D	0-0	0-0	7		0
36	13	H	Watford	L	1-2	1-1	8	Sierralta (og) 13	0
37	16	H	Stoke C	D	0-0	0-0	9		0
38	20	A	Swansea C	W	1-0	1-0	8	Flint 8	0
39	Apr 2	H	Nottingham F	L	0-1	0-1	8		0
40	5	A	Sheffield W	L	0-5	0-3	8		0
41	10	H	Blackburn R	D	2-2	1-1	8	Vaulks 27, Ralls 70	0
42	16	A	Reading	D	1-1	0-0	8	Moore (pen) 87	0
43	20	A	Brentford	D	1-1	0-0	9	Moore (pen) 57	0
44	24	H	Wycombe W	W	2-1	1-1	8	Moore 2 22, 71	0
45	May 1	A	Birmingham C	W	4-0	2-0	8	Wilson 3 9, 40, 86, Harris 68	0
46	8	H	Rotherham U	D	1-1	0-1	8	Pack 88	0

Final League Position: 8

GOALSCORERS

League (66): Moore 20 (4 pens), Wilson 7, Morrison 5, Ojo 5, Ralls 5 (2 pens), Vaulks 5, Glatzel 3, Harris 3, Bacuna 2, Hoilett 2, Murphy 2, Pack 2, Bennett 1, Flint 1, Nelson 1, Tomlin 1, own goal 1.
FA Cup (0).
Carabao Cup (0).

Smithies A 31	Osei-Tutu J 6 + 2	Morrison S 37 + 1	Nelson C 44	Bennett J 28	Vaulks W 36 + 6	Bacuna L 32 + 10	Ojo S 25 + 16	Ralls J 34 + 5	Hoilett J 14 + 7	Moore K 40 + 2	Glatzel R 8 + 13	Murphy J 12 + 20	Tomlin L 1 + 4	Pack M 30 + 9	Bamba S — + 6	Cunningham G 3 + 2	Wilson H 33 + 4	Bagan J 5 + 2	Harris M 6 + 10	Whyte G 1 + 6	Benkovic F — + 1	Ng P 19	Watters M 1 + 2	Flint A 22	Phillips D 15 + 1	Colwill R 3 + 3	Williams J 1 + 8	Sang T 8 + 1	Brown C 11 + 1	*Match No.*
1	2	3	4	5	6	7	8^{3}	9^{1}	10^{2}	11	12	13	14																	1
1	2	3	4	5^{3}	12	6	8^{1}	9	10^{2}	11			13	7	14															2
1	2	3	4		6^{1}	9	8		10^{2}	11	13	14	12	7		5^{3}														3
1	2	3	4	5^{1}	14	6	8^{3}	13	10^{2}	11			9■	7		12														4
1	2^{2}	3	4		14	6	8^{3}	9	10	11				7	13	5^{1}	12													5
1		3	4		7	2	8^{3}	12	10	13	11^{2}	14		6^{1}			9	5												6
1	2^{2}	3	4		7	13	8^{3}	6	14	11	12	10^{1}					9	5												7
1		3	4	5	6^{1}	2	8	9	10	11	12			7																8
1		3	4	5	6^{1}	2^{3}	8	9	12	11		10^{2}	13	7					14											9
1		3	4	5	14	2	12	8^{3}	9	10	11^{1}			7			6^{2}			13										10
1		3	4	5		2	8^{1}	6	10^{2}	11	12	13		7			9													11
1		3	4	5		2	12	8	9^{1}	10	11^{2}	13		7			6													12
1		3	4	5	14	2	12	8^{4}	9^{1}	10	13	11^{2}		7^{3}			6		15											13
1		3	4	5	8	2	9^{5}	7^{2}	15	11^{1}	12	16		13			6^{4}		10^{3}	14										14
1		3	4	5	8	2	6^{4}	7^{3}	12	11^{2}	13	16		14			10^{5}		9^{1}	15										15
1		3	4	5	8	2	9^{2}	7^{3}	12	10^{4}	16			13	15		6^{5}		11^{1}	14										16
1		3	4	5	8	2	9	7^{2}		11^{4}	12			14	15		6^{1}		10^{3}	13										17
1		3	4	5	7^{3}	2	9	8■		11^{1}	12			13			6		10^{2}	14										18
1		3	4	5	6	2	10^{2}				11^{3}			7	14	13	9		12	8^{1}										19
1		3	4		8	2	9^{2}	11	12		10			7^{1}		5	6		13											20
1		3	4	5	6	2	8^{2}	7	10^{1}		11	13					9		12											21
1		3^{1}	4	5	8^{3}	2	9	7	13		11	14					6		10^{2}		12									22
1			3	4	6	2^{3}	13	8	11^{1}	12	10^{2}	14		7■			9	5												23
1		3	4	5	7^{2}	6	13	8		10	14	15					9^{4}		12			2^{3}	11^{1}							24
1		13	4		7	6^{2}	8^{3}	9	10^{1}	11		12		14				5				2		3						25
1		2	4	9	6	7^{2}	10^{1}	8		11^{3}	14	13					12					5		3						26
1^{1}		2	4	8	6	14	10^{3}	7		11				13			9^{2}					5		3	12					27
		2	4	8	6		11^{1}	7^{2}		10		12		13			9					5		3	1					28
		2	4	8	6	12				11		10^{1}		7			9^{2}					5		3	1	13				29
		2	4	8	6	13				11^{1}		10^{3}		7			9^{2}	14				5	12	3	1					30
		2	4	8	6	13	12			11^{3}		10^{1}		7			9^{2}		14			5		3	1					31
		2	4	8	6	13	12			11		10^{1}		7			9^{2}					5		3	1					32
		2	4	8	6^{2}	14	12	13		11		10^{1}		7			9^{3}					5		3	1					33
		2	4	8^{1}	6	10	9^{3}	14		11^{2}				7^{4}				12				5		3	1	13	15			34
		2	4		6		13	7		11		10^{2}		14			9^{3}	8^{1}						3	1			5	12	35
		2	4^{2}		6	14	13	7		10		11^{3}					9^{1}					5		3	1			12	8	36
		2			6	9^{2}	10^{1}			11				7			13					8		3	1		12	5	4	37
		2			6	9^{1}	13	8		10		12		7			11^{2}							3	1			5	4	38
			2		6^{4}	10^{2}	12	8^{1}		11^{5}		14		7			9^{3}		15					3	1	16	13	5	4	39
			2		7	9^{3}	14	8		11^{2}				6			12						13	3	1		10^{1}	5	4	40
1			2		6			12		11		10^{1}		7			9^{2}					8		3			13	5	4	41
1			2		7		13	10		11		12		6^{1}			9^{2}					8		3				5	4	42
1	15		2		6	12	13	10		11^{4}		14		7^{2}			9^{1}					8^{3}		3			16	5^{5}	4	43
1	12	2	4		15■	14		7^{4}		11		10^{3}		6								5^{1}		3		9^{2}	13		8	44
			4			6		7		11^{1}		13		2			10^{3}		12			5		3	1	9^{2}	14		8	45
			4			6^{3}	15	7		11^{2}		14^{5}		2	16		10^{4}		12			5		3	1	9^{1}	13		8	46

FA Cup
Third Round Nottingham F (a) 0-1

Carabao Cup
First Round Northampton T (a) 0-3

CARLISLE UNITED

FOUNDATION

Carlisle United came into being when members of Shaddongate United voted to change its name on 17 May 1904. The new club was admitted to the Second Division of the Lancashire Combination in 1905–06, winning promotion the following season. Devonshire Park was officially opened on 2 September 1905, when St Helens Town were the visitors. Despite defeat in a disappointing 3–2 start, a respectable mid-table position was achieved.

Brunton Park, Warwick Road, Carlisle, Cumbria CA1 1LL.

Telephone: (01228) 526 237.

Ticket Office: (0330) 094 5930 (option 1).

Website: www.carlisleunited.co.uk

Email: enquiries@carlisleunited.co.uk

Ground Capacity: 17,030.

Record Attendance: 27,500 v Birmingham C, FA Cup 3rd rd, 5 January 1957 and v Middlesbrough, FA Cup 5th rd, 7 February 1970.

Pitch Measurements: 102m × 68m (111.5yd × 74.5yd).

Chairman: Andrew Jenkins.

Chief Executive: Nigel Clibbens.

Head Coach: Chris Beech.

Assistant Head Coach: Gavin Skelton.

Colours: Blue shirts with dark blue sleeves and red trim, white shorts with dark blue trim, blue socks with dark blue and red trim.

Year Formed: 1904. ***Turned Professional:*** 1921.

Previous Name: 1904, Shaddongate United; 1904, Carlisle United.

Club Nicknames: 'The Cumbrians', 'The Blues'.

Grounds: 1904, Milholme Bank; 1905, Devonshire Park; 1909, Brunton Park.

First Football League Game: 25 August 1928, Division 3 (N), v Accrington S (a) W 3–2 – Prout; Coulthard, Cook; Harrison, Ross, Pigg; Agar (1), Hutchison, McConnell (1), Ward (1), Watson.

Record League Victory: 8–0 v Hartlepool U, Division 3 (N), 1 September 1928 – Prout; Smiles, Cook; Robinson (1) Ross, Pigg; Agar (1), Hutchison (1), McConnell (4), Ward (1), Watson. 8–0 v Scunthorpe U, Division 3 (N), 25 December 1952 – MacLaren; Hill, Scott; Stokoe, Twentyman, Waters; Harrison (1), Whitehouse (5), Ashman (2), Duffett, Bond.

Record Cup Victory: 6–0 v Shepshed Dynamo, FA Cup 1st rd, 16 November 1996 – Caig; Hopper, Archdeacon (pen), Walling, Robinson, Pounewatchy, Peacock (1), Conway (1) (Jansen), Smart (McAlindon (1)), Hayward, Aspinall (Thorpe), (2 og). 6–0 v Tipton T, FA Cup 1st rd, 6 November 2010 – Collin; Simek, Murphy, Chester, Cruise, Robson (McKenna), Berrett, Taiwo (Hurst), Marshall, Zoko (Curran) (2), Madine (4).

HONOURS

League Champions: Division 3 – 1964–65; FL 2 – 2005–06; Third Division – 1994–95.
Runners-up: Division 3 – 1981–82; Division 4 – 1963–64; Conference – (3rd) 2004–05 *(promoted via play-offs)*.

FA Cup: 6th rd – 1975.

League Cup: semi-final – 1970.

League Trophy Winners: 1997, 2011.
Runners-up: 1995, 2003, 2006, 2010.

FOOTBALL YEARBOOK FACT FILE

Carlisle United was first established as a limited company in 1906, but this company entered into voluntary liquidation in the summer of 1911 as a result of financial problems. The club continued to exist as a membership organisation with a committee until a new company, Carlisle United Football Club (1921) Ltd, was incorporated in June 1921.

Record Defeat: 1–11 v Hull C, Division 3 (N), 14 January 1939.

Most League Points (2 for a win): 62, Division 3 (N), 1950–51.

Most League Points (3 for a win): 91, Division 3, 1994–95.

Most League Goals: 113, Division 4, 1963–64.

Highest League Scorer in Season: Jimmy McConnell, 42, Division 3 (N), 1928–29.

Most League Goals in Total Aggregate: Jimmy McConnell, 124, 1928–32.

Most League Goals in One Match: 5, Hugh Mills v Halifax T, Division 3 (N), 11 September 1937; 5, Jim Whitehouse v Scunthorpe U, Division 3 (N), 25 December 1952.

Most Capped Player: Reggie Lambe, 6 (41), Bermuda; Hallam Hope, 6 (8) Barbados.

Most League Appearances: Allan Ross, 466, 1963–79.

Youngest League Player: John Slaven, 16 years 162 days v Scunthorpe U, 16 March 2002.

Record Transfer Fee Received: £1,000,000 from Crystal Palace for Matt Jansen, February 1998.

Record Transfer Fee Paid: £140,000 to Blackburn R for Joe Garner, August 2007.

Football League Record: 1928 Elected to Division 3 (N); 1958–62 Division 4; 1962–63 Division 3; 1963–64 Division 4; 1964–65 Division 3; 1965–74 Division 2; 1974–75 Division 1; 1975–77 Division 2; 1977–82 Division 3; 1982–86 Division 2; 1986–87 Division 3; 1987–92 Division 4; 1992–95 Division 3; 1995–96 Division 2; 1996–97 Division 3; 1997–98 Division 2; 1998–2004 Division 3; 2004–05 Conference; 2005–06 FL 2; 2006–14 FL 1; 2014– FL 2.

LATEST SEQUENCES

Longest Sequence of League Wins: 7, 18.2.2006 – 8.4.2006.

Longest Sequence of League Defeats: 12, 27.9.2003 – 13.12.2003.

Longest Sequence of League Draws: 6, 11.2.1978 – 11.3.1978.

Longest Sequence of Unbeaten League Matches: 19, 1.10.1994 – 11.2.1995.

Longest Sequence Without a League Win: 15, 12.4.2014 – 20.9.2014.

Successive Scoring Runs: 26 from 23.8.1947.

Successive Non-scoring Runs: 7 from 25.2.2017.

MANAGERS

Harry Kirkbride 1904–05 (*Secretary-Manager*)
McCumiskey 1905–06 (*Secretary-Manager*)
Jack Houston 1906–08 (*Secretary-Manager*)
Bert Stansfield 1908–10
Jack Houston 1910–12
Davie Graham 1912–13
George Bristow 1913–30
Billy Hampson 1930–33
Bill Clarke 1933–35
Robert Kelly 1935–36
Fred Westgarth 1936–38
David Taylor 1938–40
Howard Harkness 1940–45
Bill Clark 1945–46 (*Secretary-Manager*)
Ivor Broadis 1946–49
Bill Shankly 1949–51
Fred Emery 1951–58
Andy Beattie 1958–60
Ivor Powell 1960–63
Alan Ashman 1963–67
Tim Ward 1967–68
Bob Stokoe 1968–70
Ian MacFarlane 1970–72
Alan Ashman 1972–75
Dick Young 1975–76
Bobby Moncur 1976–80
Martin Harvey 1980
Bob Stokoe 1980–85
Bryan 'Pop' Robson 1985
Bob Stokoe 1985–86
Harry Gregg 1986–87
Cliff Middlemass 1987–91
Aidan McCaffery 1991–92
David McCreery 1992–93
Mick Wadsworth (*Director of Coaching*) 1993–96
Mervyn Day 1996–97
David Wilkes and John Halpin (*Directors of Coaching*), and **Michael Knighton** 1997–99
Nigel Pearson 1998–99
Keith Mincher 1999
Martin Wilkinson 1999–2000
Ian Atkins 2000–01
Roddy Collins 2001–02; 2002–03
Paul Simpson 2003–06
Neil McDonald 2006–07
John Ward 2007–08
Greg Abbott 2008–13
Graham Kavanagh 2013–14
Keith Curle 2014–18
John Sheridan 2018–19
Steven Pressley 2019
Chris Beech November 2019–

TEN YEAR LEAGUE RECORD

		P	W	D	L	F	A	Pts	Pos
2011-12	FL 1	46	18	15	13	65	66	69	8
2012-13	FL 1	46	14	13	19	56	77	55	17
2013-14	FL 1	46	11	12	23	43	76	45	22
2014-15	FL 2	46	14	8	24	56	74	50	20
2015-16	FL 2	46	17	16	13	67	62	67	10
2016-17	FL 2	46	18	17	11	69	68	71	6
2017-18	FL 2	46	17	16	13	62	54	67	10
2018-19	FL 2	46	20	8	18	67	62	68	11
2019-20	FL 2	37	10	12	15	39	56	42	18§
2020-21	FL 2	46	18	12	16	60	51	66	10

§Decided on points-per-game (1.14)

DID YOU KNOW ?

Ivor Broadis signed professional forms for Carlisle United in the summer of 1946 when he was appointed player-manager of the club. He took charge of the team for the visit to Oldham Athletic on 31 August 1946 at the age of 23 years and 256 days, making him the youngest manager in the history of the Football League.

CARLISLE UNITED – SKY BET LEAGUE TWO 2020–21 LEAGUE RECORD

Match No.	Date	Venue	Opponents	Result		H/T Score	Lg Pos.	Goalscorers	Attendance
1	Sept 12	A	Cambridge U	L	0-3	0-2	23		0
2	19	H	Southend U	W	2-0	2-0	12	Patrick 36, Kayode 39	1000
3	26	A	Scunthorpe U	L	0-1	0-1	17		0
4	Oct 3	H	Barrow	W	1-0	1-0	11	Mellish 24	0
5	10	A	Port Vale	W	1-0	0-0	7	Mellish 55	0
6	17	H	Colchester U	W	3-2	2-1	5	Alessandra 4, Mellish 29, Hayden 81	0
7	20	A	Oldham Ath	D	1-1	0-0	5	Hayden 54	0
8	24	A	Grimsby T	D	1-1	0-1	7	McKeown (og) 46	0
9	27	H	Morecambe	W	3-1	2-0	4	Songo'o (og) 1, Mellish 3, Tanner 86	0
10	31	A	Exeter C	L	0-1	0-0	8		0
11	Nov 3	H	Newport Co	W	3-2	1-0	5	Alessandra (pen) 15, Mellish 2 68, 81	0
12	14	H	Cheltenham T	L	1-2	1-2	6	Mellish 45	0
13	21	A	Crawley T	W	3-0	1-0	4	Bennett 43, Kayode 55, Hayden 62	0
14	24	A	Tranmere R	L	0-1	0-0	6		0
15	Dec 2	H	Salford C	W	2-1	1-0	5	Alessandra 33, Bennett 56	2000
16	5	A	Bradford C	W	1-0	0-0	4	Bennett 57	0
17	12	H	Stevenage	W	4-0	3-0	3	Anderton 10, Kayode 19, Alessandra 34, Riley 73	2000
18	15	H	Mansfield T	W	1-0	1-0	2	Patrick 39	0
19	19	A	Forest Green R	L	0-1	0-0	3		920
20	26	H	Bolton W	D	3-3	3-1	3	Hayden 5, Alessandra 7, Patrick 36	2000
21	Jan 2	A	Walsall	W	2-0	1-0	1	Patrick 26, Kayode 78	0
22	30	H	Exeter C	W	1-0	1-0	2	Alessandra 9	0
23	Feb 2	H	Forest Green R	L	1-2	0-0	3	Toure 72	0
24	16	A	Harrogate T	L	0-1	0-1	9		0
25	20	A	Salford C	D	1-1	1-0	9	Tanner 11	0
26	23	H	Tranmere R	L	2-3	2-2	10	Kayode 3, Anderton 27	0
27	27	H	Oldham Ath	L	1-3	1-0	10	Kayode 35	0
28	Mar 2	A	Colchester U	L	1-2	1-0	12	Mellish 29	0
29	6	A	Morecambe	L	1-3	0-2	13	Hayden 79	0
30	9	H	Grimsby T	D	1-1	0-1	13	Zanzala 90	0
31	13	H	Bradford C	W	3-1	2-0	12	Bennett 2 37, 39, Zanzala 56	0
32	16	A	Mansfield T	D	1-1	0-0	11	Zanzala 66	0
33	20	A	Stevenage	L	1-3	0-1	11	Dickenson 55	0
34	23	H	Leyton Orient	L	0-1	0-0	12		0
35	27	H	Cambridge U	L	1-2	0-1	14	Alessandra 78	0
36	30	H	Crawley T	W	2-0	2-0	11	Riley 17, Patrick 33	0
37	Apr 3	A	Southend U	W	2-0	1-0	10	Zanzala 17, Toure 79	0
38	6	H	Scunthorpe U	W	2-0	0-0	9	Mellish 2 60, 62	0
39	10	A	Barrow	D	2-2	1-2	10	Armer 3, Zanzala (pen) 79	0
40	13	A	Newport Co	D	0-0	0-0	9		0
41	17	H	Port Vale	D	0-0	0-0	10		0
42	20	A	Bolton W	L	0-1	0-1	11		0
43	24	H	Harrogate T	D	1-1	0-1	10	Kayode 75	0
44	27	A	Cheltenham T	D	1-1	1-0	10	Kayode 33	0
45	May 1	A	Leyton Orient	W	3-2	1-2	10	Mellish 42, Alessandra (pen) 54, Tanner 90	0
46	8	H	Walsall	D	0-0	0-0	10		0

Final League Position: 10

GOALSCORERS

League (60): Mellish 11, Alessandra 8 (2 pens), Kayode 8, Bennett 5, Hayden 5, Patrick 5, Zanzala 5 (1 pen), Tanner 3, Anderton 2, Riley 2, Toure 2, Armer 1, Dickenson 1, own goals 2.
FA Cup (3): Mellish 3.
Carabao Cup (0).
Papa John's Trophy (7): Mellish 2, Toure 2, Alessandra 1 (1 pen), Obiero 1, Reilly 1.

Farman P 42	Tanner G 36 + 1	Hayden A 42 + 2	McDonald R 28 + 1	Anderton N 33 + 7	Guy C 43	Mellish J 41 + 3	Kayode J 31 + 3	Alessandra L 37 + 8	Patrick O 27 + 10	Toure G 18 + 16	Walker E 3 + 13	Riley J 38 + 4	Armer J 22 + 2	Furman D 7 + 10	Reilly G 3 + 13	Devine D 5 + 6	Hunt M — + 2	Charters T 2 + 7	Malley C — + 3	Obiero M — + 4	Bennett R 22 + 2	Dixon J — + 2	Dickenson B 7 + 5	Bell L — + 1	Zanzala O 15 + 7	Scott C — + 7	Norman M 4	Match No.
1	2^{1}	3^{3}	4	5	6	7	8	9^{2}	10	11	12	13	14															1
1	2	3	4	5	6	8^{1}	10	12	11^{2}	9^{3}	13			7	14													2
1	2^{3}	3	4	5	6^{2}	8	10	9			11			7^{1}	12	13	14											3
1	2	3■	4	5	6	7	11	10^{2}		9^{3}	8^{1}				12	13		14										4
1	2	4	3	5	7	8		9		11		6^{2}			10^{1}	12			13									5
1	2	3	4	5	6	7	9	10^{3}		11^{1}		8^{2}		13	12				14									6
1	2	3	4	5	6^{2}	7	9	10		11^{1}		8^{3}		13	12				14									7
1	2	3	4	5	7	6	10	9		11		8^{1}			12													8
1	2	3	4	5	8	7	11	10^{3}		9^{1}		6^{2}		13	12					14								9
1	2	3^{1}	4	5	8	7^{3}	9	10	13	11■		6^{2}			14		12											10
1	2	3	4	5	6	7	9^{3}	11	12			8^{2}		13	10^{1}					14								11
1	2	3	4	5	6	7		11^{2}	9			8^{1}			10					12	13							12
1	2	3		5	6	7^{4}	9	10^{3}	12	11^{1}		8^{2}	13		14	15					4							13
1	2	3		5	7	8	10^{3}	9	12	11^{1}		6^{2}			13					14	4							14
1	2	3		5	8^{1}	6	10	9^{3}	11^{2}	13		14		12		7					4							15
1	2	3		5		8	10	9^{1}	11	12		13		6^{2}		7					4							16
1	2	3		5	6	8^{3}	9	10^{4}	11^{1}	12		13			15	7^{2}					4	14						17
1		3		5	6	8	9	10^{3}	11^{1}	12		7^{2}	2	13	14						4							18
1		3		5	6		11	9	8^{1}	10^{2}		7	2		12			13			4							19
1		2	4		6	8	10	9	11^{1}	12		7	5								3							20
1		2	4		7^{1}		9	10	11^{2}			6	5	12				8^{3}			3		13	14				21
1		3		5	7	8^{4}	13	9^{3}	11^{1}		14	6	2					15			4		12		10^{2}			22
1		3		5^{5}	6^{4}	8^{2}	9	10^{1}	11^{3}	13	15	7	2					16			4		14		12			23
1	2	3		5^{4}	6	15	9	10^{1}	14	13	11^{2}	7^{3}									4		8		12			24
1	2	3		5	6	8	9	13	11^{1}			7									4		10^{2}		12			25
1	2	4^{3}	14	5	7	8^{4}	10	12	11^{1}	9^{2}		6									3		15		13			26
1	2	4		5	6	8	10	14	9^{1}	11^{2}		7^{3}									3		12		13			27
1	2	3		5		6^{1}	10		12	9^{2}		8		7							4		11			13		28
1	2^{2}	3	4	5		6^{3}	10^{1}	9	11^{4}	12	15	8		7				14							13			29
1		3^{2}	5	13	6	15		10	9^{3}		14	7^{4}	2					8^{1}			4		11		12			30
1	2	13	4		7	8		10	14	12		6^{2}	5								3		11^{3}		9^{1}			31
	2		3		7	8		11^{1}			12	6	5								4		9		10		1	32
	2^{5}	12	4■	15	7	8^{2}		14	13	11^{1}		6^{3}	5^{4}					16			3		9		10		1	33
1		4		5	6	8		11		9			2	7							3				10			34
1	2	3	4	5	7	9^{2}		13	10	12		8		6^{1}											11^{3}	14		35
1	2	3	4		7	8		11^{2}	9^{1}	12	13	6^{4}	5	14											10^{3}	15		36
1	2	3	4	14	7	8^{3}		11	9^{1}	12	13	6	5												10^{2}			37
1	2	3	4		7	8		11^{3}	9^{4}	12	14	6^{2}	5	13											10^{1}	15		38
1	2^{2}	3	4	12	7	8		11	9	13		6^{1}	5^{3}			14									10			39
1		3	4	12	7	8^{1}	13	10	9			6	5			2									11^{2}			40
1	14	3	4	15	7	8	12	11	9^{2}	13		6	5^{4}			2^{3}									10^{1}			41
1	2	3	4^{1}	12	7	8	9	10	11^{3}	14		6^{2}	5	13														42
1	2	3		4	7	8	9	11^{1}	13		12	6^{3}	5^{2}								14				10^{4}	15		43
	5^{3}	2		4	7	8	11	14	15		13	6^{2}	9			12					3^{1}				10^{4}		1	44
	2	3		4	7	12	8	9	10^{2}		13^{3}	6	5												11^{1}	14	1	45
1	2		4	3	7	8^{4}	10	13	11^{3}	9^{2}		6^{1}	5					15				14				12		46

FA Cup

First Round	Hayes & Yeading U	(a)	2-2
(aet; Carlisle U won 4-3 on penalties)			
Second Round	Doncaster R	(h)	1-2

Carabao Cup

First Round	Oldham Ath	(a)	0-3

Papa John's Trophy

Group A (N)	Fleetwood T	(h)	1-3
Group A (N)	Sunderland	(a)	3-5
Group A (N)	Aston Villa U21	(h)	3-1

CHARLTON ATHLETIC

FOUNDATION

The club was formed on 9 June 1905, by a group of 14- and 15-year-old youths living in streets by the Thames in the area which now borders the Thames Barrier. The club's progress through local leagues was so rapid that after the First World War they joined the Kent League where they spent a season before turning professional and joining the Southern League in 1920. A year later they were elected to the Football League's Division 3 (South).

The Valley, Floyd Road, Charlton, London SE7 8BL.

Telephone: (020) 8333 4000.

Ticket Office: (03330) 144 444.

Website: www.cafc.co.uk

Email: info@cafc.co.uk

Ground Capacity: 27,111.

Record Attendance: 75,031 v Aston Villa, FA Cup 5th rd, 12 February 1938 (at The Valley).

Pitch Measurements: 102.5m × 67.5m (112yd × 74yd).

Owner, Chief Executive: Thomas Sandgaard.

Chief Operating Officer: Tony Keohane.

Manager: Nigel Adkins.

Assistant Manager: Johnnie Jackson.

Colours: Red shirts with white trim, white shorts with red trim, red socks with white trim.

Year Formed: 1905.

Turned Professional: 1920.

Club Nickname: 'The Addicks'.

Grounds: 1906, Siemen's Meadow; 1907, Woolwich Common; 1909, Pound Park; 1913, Horn Lane; 1920, The Valley; 1923, Catford (The Mount); 1924, The Valley; 1985, Selhurst Park; 1991, Upton Park; 1992, The Valley.

First Football League Game: 27 August 1921, Division 3 (S), v Exeter C (h) W 1–0 – Hughes; Johnny Mitchell, Goodman; Dowling (1), Hampson, Dunn; Castle, Bailey, Halse, Green, Wilson.

Record League Victory: 8–1 v Middlesbrough, Division 1, 12 September 1953 – Bartram; Campbell, Ellis; Fenton, Ufton, Hammond; Hurst (2), O'Linn (2), Leary (1), Firmani (3), Kiernan.

Record Cup Victory: 8–0 v Stevenage, FL Trophy, 9 October 2018 – Phillips; Marshall, Dijksteel, Sarr, Stevenson (3) (Reeves), Lapslie (1), Maloney, Ward (Morgan), Pratley (1), Vetokele (2), Ajose (1).

Record Defeat: 1–11 v Aston Villa, Division 2, 14 November 1959.

Most League Points (2 for a win): 61, Division 3 (S), 1934–35.

Most League Points (3 for a win): 101, FL 1, 2011–12.

HONOURS

League Champions: First Division – 1999–2000; FL 1 – 2011–12; Division 3S – 1928–29, 1934–35.
Runners-up: Division 1 – 1936–37; Division 2 – 1935–36, 1985–86.

FA Cup Winners: 1947.
Runners-up: 1946.

League Cup: quarter-final – 2007.

Full Members' Cup:
Runners-up 1987.

FOOTBALL YEARBOOK FACT FILE

Charlton Athletic goalkeeper Mike Rose was the first player to be substituted in a Football League match when he went off injured after just 11 minutes of the club's game at Bolton Wanderers on the opening day of the 1965–66 season. Substitute Keith Peacock replaced him with John Hewie going in goal. Bolton went on to win the game 4-2.

Most League Goals: 107, Division 2, 1957–58.

Highest League Scorer in Season: Ralph Allen, 32, Division 3 (S), 1934–35.

Most League Goals in Total Aggregate: Stuart Leary, 153, 1953–62.

Most League Goals in One Match: 5, Wilson Lennox v Exeter C, Division 3 (S), 2 February 1929; 5, Eddie Firmani v Aston Villa, Division 1, 5 February 1955; 5, John Summers v Huddersfield T, Division 2, 21 December 1957; 5, John Summers v Portsmouth, Division 2, 1 October 1960.

Most Capped Player: Jonatan Johansson, 42 (106), Finland.

Most League Appearances: Sam Bartram, 579, 1934–56.

Youngest League Player: Jonjo Shelvey, 16 years 59 days v Burnley, 26 April 2008.

Record Transfer Fee Received: £16,500,000 from Tottenham H for Darren Bent, June 2007.

Record Transfer Fee Paid: £4,750,000 to Wimbledon for Jason Euell, January 2001.

Football League Record: 1921 Elected to Division 3 (S); 1929–33 Division 2; 1933–35 Division 3 (S); 1935–36 Division 2; 1936–57 Division 1; 1957–72 Division 2; 1972–75 Division 3; 1975–80 Division 2; 1980–81 Division 3; 1981–86 Division 2; 1986–90 Division 1; 1990–92 Division 2; 1992–98 Division 1; 1998–99 Premier League; 1999–2000 Division 1; 2000–07 Premier League; 2007–09 FL C; 2009–12 FL 1; 2012–16 FL C; 2016–19 FL 1; 2019–20 FL C; 2020– FL 1.

LATEST SEQUENCES

Longest Sequence of League Wins: 12, 26.12.1999 – 7.3.2000.

Longest Sequence of League Defeats: 10, 11.4.1990 – 15.9.1990.

Longest Sequence of League Draws: 6, 13.12.1992 – 16.1.1993.

Longest Sequence of Unbeaten League Matches: 15, 4.10.1980 – 20.12.1980.

Longest Sequence Without a League Win: 18, 18.10.2008 – 17.1.2009.

Successive Scoring Runs: 25 from 26.12.1935.

Successive Non-scoring Runs: 5 from 17.10.2015.

MANAGERS

Walter Rayner 1920–25
Alex Macfarlane 1925–27
Albert Lindon 1928
Alex Macfarlane 1928–32
Albert Lindon 1932–33
Jimmy Seed 1933–56
Jimmy Trotter 1956–61
Frank Hill 1961–65
Bob Stokoe 1965–67
Eddie Firmani 1967–70
Theo Foley 1970–74
Andy Nelson 1974–79
Mike Bailey 1979–81
Alan Mullery 1981–82
Ken Craggs 1982
Lennie Lawrence 1982–91
Steve Gritt and Alan Curbishley 1991–95
Alan Curbishley 1995–2006
Iain Dowie 2006
Les Reed 2006
Alan Pardew 2006–08
Phil Parkinson 2008–11
Chris Powell 2011–14
José Riga 2014
Bob Peeters 2014–15
Guy Luzon 2015
Karel Fraeye 2015–16
José Riga 2016
Russell Slade 2016
Karl Robinson 2016–18
Lee Bowyer 2018–21
Nigel Adkins March 2021–

TEN YEAR LEAGUE RECORD

		P	W	D	L	F	A	Pts	Pos
2011-12	FL 1	46	30	11	5	82	36	101	1
2012-13	FL C	46	17	14	15	65	59	65	9
2013-14	FL C	46	13	12	21	41	61	51	18
2014-15	FL C	46	14	18	14	54	60	60	12
2015-16	FL C	46	9	13	24	40	80	40	22
2016-17	FL 1	46	14	18	14	60	53	60	13
2017-18	FL 1	46	20	11	15	58	51	71	6
2018-19	FL 1	46	26	10	10	73	40	88	3
2019-20	FL C	46	12	12	22	50	65	48	22
2020-21	FL 1	46	20	14	12	70	56	74	7

DID YOU KNOW ?

Striker Jim Melrose scored after just nine seconds from the start of Charlton Athletic's game at West Ham United on 25 October 1986 despite the Hammers kicking off. The goal is the quickest scored by a Charlton player with the Addicks going on to win 3-1.

CHARLTON ATHLETIC – SKY BET LEAGUE ONE 2020–21 LEAGUE RECORD

Match No.	Date	Venue	Opponents	Result		H/T Score	Lg Pos.	Goalscorers	Atten-dance
1	Sept 12	A	Crewe Alex	W	2-0	2-0	2	Doughty ^{24}, Washington ^{43}	0
2	19	H	Doncaster R	L	1-3	0-1	10	Washington ^{67}	1000
3	27	A	Lincoln C	L	0-2	0-1	18		0
4	Oct 3	H	Sunderland	D	0-0	0-0	14		0
5	17	H	Wigan Ath	W	1-0	0-0	14	Forster-Caskey ^{65}	0
6	20	A	Blackpool	W	1-0	0-0	10	Aneke ^{83}	0
7	24	A	Northampton T	W	2-0	0-0	8	Pratley ^{54}, Sowerby (og) ^{59}	0
8	27	H	Oxford U	W	2-0	2-0	6	Washington ^{32}, Shinnie ^{45}	0
9	31	A	Portsmouth	W	2-0	1-0	5	Williams ^{26}, Aneke ^{82}	0
10	Nov 3	H	Fleetwood T	W	3-2	2-2	3	Purrington ^{4}, Washington 2 (1 pen) $^{31, 50 (p)}$	0
11	21	A	Gillingham	D	1-1	0-0	5	Aneke ^{82}	0
12	24	A	Burton Alb	L	2-4	1-2	6	Smyth ^{41}, Aneke ^{67}	0
13	28	A	Ipswich T	W	2-0	1-0	3	Morgan ^{21}, Bogle ^{68}	0
14	Dec 2	H	Milton Keynes D	L	0-1	0-0	4		0
15	5	A	Shrewsbury T	D	1-1	0-0	6	Watson ^{71}	0
16	12	H	AFC Wimbledon	W	5-2	1-2	5	Washington ^{37}, Forster-Caskey ^{64}, Williams ^{65}, Aneke ^{85}, Purrington ^{90}	0
17	19	A	Swindon T	D	2-2	1-1	7	Bogle ^{37}, Aneke ^{61}	2000
18	26	H	Plymouth Arg	D	2-2	1-2	6	Gunter ^{32}, Maddison ^{67}	0
19	Jan 2	A	Hull C	L	0-2	0-1	6		0
20	8	H	Accrington S	L	0-2	0-1	7		0
21	12	H	Rochdale	D	4-4	2-4	7	Aneke 2 $^{22, 65}$, Forster-Caskey ^{37}, Schwartz ^{67}	0
22	16	A	Bristol R	W	1-0	0-0	6	Forster-Caskey ^{64}	0
23	19	A	Peterborough U	L	1-2	1-0	6	Washington (pen) ^{14}	0
24	23	H	Swindon T	D	2-2	0-2	6	Aneke ^{57}, Shinnie ^{90}	0
25	26	A	Milton Keynes D	W	1-0	1-0	6	Millar ^{18}	0
26	Feb 2	H	Portsmouth	L	1-3	0-1	8	Stockley ^{52}	0
27	6	A	Rochdale	W	2-0	2-0	6	Aneke ^{7}, Oshilaja ^{27}	0
28	13	H	Gillingham	L	2-3	1-2	7	Aneke ^{15}, Stockley ^{52}	0
29	20	A	Fleetwood T	D	1-1	1-1	9	Stockley ^{6}	0
30	23	H	Burton Alb	L	1-2	1-1	9	Stockley ^{9}	0
31	27	H	Blackpool	L	0-3	0-2	12		0
32	Mar 2	A	Wigan Ath	W	1-0	1-0	9	Aneke ^{19}	0
33	6	A	Oxford U	D	0-0	0-0	9		0
34	9	H	Northampton T	W	2-1	0-0	8	Washington 2 (1 pen) $^{65 (p), 84}$	0
35	13	H	Shrewsbury T	D	1-1	0-0	8	Washington ^{78}	0
36	16	H	Bristol R	W	3-2	2-2	6	Shinnie ^{33}, Forster-Caskey ^{42}, Washington ^{84}	0
37	20	A	AFC Wimbledon	D	2-2	2-1	6	Stockley ^{10}, Jaiyesimi ^{20}	0
38	Apr 2	A	Doncaster R	W	1-0	1-0	7	Maatsen ^{12}	0
39	10	A	Sunderland	W	2-1	1-0	7	Scowen (og) ^{31}, Gilbey ^{61}	0
40	17	H	Ipswich T	D	0-0	0-0	8		0
41	20	A	Plymouth Arg	W	6-0	2-0	6	Forster-Caskey ^{26}, Stockley ^{45}, Watts (og) ^{47}, Gilbey ^{49}, Millar ^{56}, Aneke ^{89}	0
42	24	H	Peterborough U	L	0-1	0-1	8		0
43	27	H	Crewe Alex	D	2-2	1-0	8	Stockley ^{10}, Gilbey ^{83}	0
44	May 1	A	Accrington S	D	1-1	0-0	8	Aneke ^{90}	0
45	4	H	Lincoln C	W	3-1	0-0	8	Stockley ^{47}, Inniss ^{65}, Aneke ^{67}	0
46	9	H	Hull C	W	1-0	0-0	7	Greaves (og) ^{75}	0

Final League Position: 7

GOALSCORERS

League (70): Aneke 15, Washington 11 (3 pens), Stockley 8, Forster-Caskey 6, Gilbey 3, Shinnie 3, Bogle 2, Millar 2, Purrington 2, Williams 2, Doughty 1, Gunter 1, Inniss 1, Jaiyesimi 1, Maatsen 1, Maddison 1, Morgan 1, Oshilaja 1, Pratley 1, Schwartz 1, Smyth 1, Watson 1, own goals 4.
FA Cup (0).
Carabao Cup (3): Aneke 1, Barker 1, Bonne 1.
Papa John's Trophy (5): Aouachira 1, Maddison 1, Mingi 1, Morgan 1, Oztumer 1.

Amos B 46	Barker C 3	Pratley D 33 + 6	Oshilaja A 16 + 1	Purrington B 19 + 9	Lapslie G 1 + 1	Forster-Caskey J 32 + 2	Gilbey A 18 + 5	Doughty A 7	Bonne M 3	Washington C 28 + 8	Williams J 7 + 11	Aneke C 11 + 27	Morgan A 14 + 14	Famewo A 20 + 2	Oztumer E 2	Levitt D 3	Watson B 24 + 5	Vennings J 1	Maddison M 4 + 4	Inniss R 12 + 1	Gunter C 31 + 5	Shinnie A 18 + 11	Smyth P 8 + 6	Bogle O 12 + 5	Maatsen I 31 + 3	Matthews A 22 + 5	Pearce J 24 + 2	Millar L 23 + 4	Schwartz R 3 + 13	Stockley J 20 + 2	Smith M 3 + 5	Jaiyesimi D 7 + 7	*Match No.*
1	2	3	4	5	6^1	7	8	9^3	10	11^2	12	13	14																				1
1	2^1	3	4	5	13	7	6	10	11	8	12		9^2																				2
1	2	7	3	5		14		9	10	11	13			4^1	6^2	8^3	12																3
1		3	2	4				7		11	12	13		5	9^1	8^3	6	10^2	14														4
1		4		13		8		9		14		11^1		2			7			3	5	6^2	10^3	12									5
1		7^1		5■				9		11^3		13		4			8			3	2	6	14	10^2	12								6
1		12				7		8^2		14	9^3			4		6^1				3	2	13	11	10	5								7
1		7		12		13				11^2				4			8			3■	2	6	9	10^1	5								8
1		8		14		6				11	7^2	12		4^3							2	9	13	10^1	5	3							9
1		4		5						10		13	6^1				7			3	2	8		11^2	9	12							10
1		4		15			14			9^2		12	6^4				7		11^3		3	8	13	10^1	5	2							11
1		4					9^4			14	15	12	13				7		6^3		3	8	10^2	11^1	5	2							12
1		4		14			12				9^1	10^3	6				7				3	8	11^2	13	5	2							13
1		4		5			9			11	14	13	6^2	15			7^4		12		3	8^1		10^3		2							14
1		8				7^2	9^1			11	13^4	10^3	12	3			6				2			14	5	15	4						15
1		4	15	14		8	9^1			11^4	13	12					7		6^3		2			10^2	5		3						16
1		3		13		8^2	7			11		12					6		9^3		2			10^1	5	14	4						17
1		3				8				11^4	9^2	10^3	12				7^1		13		6		15	14	5	2	4						18
1		3■				6	12			9	14		10^3				7^1				2		13	11^2	8	5	4						19
1			3	16		8	7			10^1	14	12	6^3						13^5		2		9^4		5		4	11^2	15				20
1			4			6	7^1			14	9^3	10	12								2		5^2		8	15	3■	11^4	13				21
1			4			8	15			9^3	7^2	10^1	6■								3		12^4	13	5	2		11	14				22
1		6	3			7^3	15			9^1	16	12									2	14	5^4	10^2	8		4	11^5	13				23
1		7^2	4			8				16	6^1	10^4	13								3	12			5^3	2	14	9	11^5	15			24
1		7	4	5		8				10^1		14	13								3	6^3				2	15	9^4	12	11^2			25
1		7^1	4			6						14	9^2				13				3	8^4			5	2		12	11^3	10	15		26
1		7	3	5		8^4						11^3	15								2^1	6^2				12	4	9	14	10		13	27
1		7^3	3	5^2		8^1						11■	14								2	6					4	9	13	10		12	28
1		7^3	3	15						13			12	4			14				2	9			5^4			6	11^1	10	8^2		29
1		2	4	8^3								12					7^4					6			14	5	3^2	11	13	10	15	9^1	30
1		6■	3	5^4						10^3		13■		4			14				2	9			15			8^1	16	11^5	12	7^2	31
1						8				11^4		10^3		3			7				14	13			5	2	4	9^1	15		6^2	12	32
1						8				11^3		10^2		3			7^5				12	16			5	2^1	4	9	14	13	6^4	15	33
1		3				8^2				11^4		12	9^3				7				2	13			5		4	6	15	10^1	14		34
1		8^1								11		13	6^4	3			7				2	14			5		4	9^3		10^2	12	15	35
1		14				6				10		13	7	3							2	9^3			5		4	8^1		11^2		12	36
1		14				8				11^1		13	6^3	3							2	7			5		4	9^2	15	10		12^4	37
1		7		5		8	6^3					13								3	15	14			9^4	2	4	12		10^2		11^1	38
1		7		5		8	6													3	13				9^1	2	4	12		10		11^2	39
1		7^1		5		8	6										12			3						2	4	11		10		9	40
1		16		5		8^5	6^3					15	13	3			7				12	14				2^1	4	11		10^4		9^2	41
1				5		8	6^2			15		13	12^4	14			7			3^3						2	4	11		10		9^1	42
1		15		5		8	6			12		13		3			7^4			14					9^1	2	4	11^2		10^3			43
1		7^3				6^4	8			11^1		12	14	4						2	5	15			9		3^2	13		10			44
1		14		5^2		8^1	6					13^3	12	4			7			3					9	2		11		10			45
1							6			10^1		12	8	4			7^2			3		13			5	2		9		11			46

FA Cup

First Round	Plymouth Arg	(h)	0-1

Carabao Cup

First Round	Swindon T	(a)	3-1
Second Round	West Ham U	(a)	0-3

Papa John's Trophy

Group G (S)	AFC Wimbledon	(a)	1-2
Group G (S)	Brighton & HA U21	(h)	1-1
(Charlton Ath won 4-1 on penalties)			
Group G (S)	Leyton Orient	(h)	3-1

CHELSEA

FOUNDATION

Chelsea may never have existed but for the fact that Fulham rejected an offer to rent the Stamford Bridge ground from Mr H. A. Mears who had owned it since 1904. Fortunately he was determined to develop it as a football stadium rather than sell it to the Great Western Railway and got together with Frederick Parker, who persuaded Mears of the financial advantages of developing a major sporting venue. Chelsea FC was formed in 1905 and applications made to join both the Southern League and Football League. The latter competition was decided upon because of its comparatively meagre representation in the south of England.

Stamford Bridge, Fulham Road, London SW6 1HS.

Telephone: (0371) 811 1955.

Ticket Office: (0371) 811 1905.

Website: www.chelseafc.com

Email: enquiries@chelseafc.com

Ground Capacity: 40,834.

Record Attendance: 82,905 v Arsenal, Division 1, 12 October 1935.

Pitch Measurements: 103m × 67.5m (112.5yd × 74yd).

Chairman: Bruce Buck.

Chief Executive: Guy Laurence.

Manager: Thomas Tuchel.

Assistant Managers: Arno Michels, Zsolt Low.

Colours: Rush blue shirts with black trim, rush blue shorts, white socks.

Year Formed: 1905. ***Turned Professional:*** 1905.

Club Nickname: 'The Blues'.

Ground: 1905, Stamford Bridge.

First Football League Game: 2 September 1905, Division 2, v Stockport Co (a) L 0–1 – Foulke; Mackie, McEwan; Key, Harris, Miller; Moran, Jack Robertson, Copeland, Windridge, Kirwan.

Record League Victory: 8–0 v Wigan Ath, Premier League, 9 May 2010 – Cech; Ivanovic (Belletti), Ashley Cole (1), Ballack (Matic), Terry, Alex, Kalou (1) (Joe Cole), Lampard (pen), Anelka (2), Drogba (3, 1 pen), Malouda; 8–0 v Aston Villa, Premier League, 23 December 2012 – Cech; Azpilicueta, Ivanovic (1), Cahill, Cole, Luiz (1), Lampard (1) (Ramirez (2)), Moses, Mata (Piazon), Hazard (1), Torres (1) (Oscar (1)).

HONOURS

League Champions: Premier League – 2004–05, 2005–06, 2009–10, 2014–15, 2016–17; Division 1 – 1954–55; Division 2 – 1983–84, 1988–89.
Runners-up: Premier League – 2003–04, 2006–07, 2007–08, 2010–11; Division 2 – 1906–07, 1911–12, 1929–30, 1962–63, 1976–77.

FA Cup Winners: 1970, 1997, 2000, 2007, 2009, 2010, 2012, 2018.
Runners-up: 1915, 1967, 1994, 2002, 2017, 2020, 2021.

League Cup Winners: 1965, 1998, 2005, 2007, 2015.
Runners-up: 1972, 2008, 2019.
Full Members' Cup Winners: 1986, 1990.

European Competitions
Champions League: 1999–2000, 2003–04 *(sf)*, 2004–05 *(sf)*, 2005–06, 2006–07 *(sf)*, 2007–08 *(runners-up)*, 2008–09 *(sf)*, 2009–10, 2010–11 *(qf)*, 2011–12 *(winners)*, 2012–13, 2013–14 *(sf)*, 2014–15, 2015–16, 2017–18, 2019–20, 2020–21 *(winners)*.
Fairs Cup: 1958–60, 1965–66, 1968–69.
UEFA Cup: 2000–01, 2001–02, 2002–03.
Europa League: 2012–13 *(winners)*, 2018–19 *(winners)*.
European Cup-Winners' Cup: 1970–71 *(winners)*, 1971–72, 1994–95 *(sf)*, 1997–98 *(winners)*, 1998–99 *(sf)*.
Super Cup: 1998 *(winners)*, 2012, 2013, 2019.
Club World Cup: 2012 *(runners-up)*.

FOOTBALL YEARBOOK FACT FILE

A total of 52 Chelsea players have gained full international honours for England in the period to 31 May 2021. The first player capped was George Hilsdon who made his debut on 16 February 1907 against Ireland. The landmark 50th capped player was Fikayo Tomori who came on as a substitute in the closing stages of the Euro 2020 qualifying round tie against Kosovo.

Record Cup Victory: 13–0 v Jeunesse Hautcharage, ECWC, 1st rd 2nd leg, 29 September 1971 – Bonetti; Boyle, Harris (1), Hollins (1p), Webb (1), Hinton, Cooke, Baldwin (3), Osgood (5), Hudson (1), Houseman (1).

Record Defeat: 1–8 v Wolverhampton W, Division 1, 26 September 1953; 0–7 v Nottingham F, Division 1, 20 April 1991.

Most League Points (2 for a win): 57, Division 2, 1906–07.

Most League Points (3 for a win): 99, Division 2, 1988–89.

Most League Goals: 103, Premier League, 2009–10.

Highest League Scorer in Season: Jimmy Greaves, 41, 1960–61.

Most League Goals in Total Aggregate: Bobby Tambling, 164, 1958–70.

Most League Goals in One Match: 5, George Hilsdon v Glossop, Division 2, 1 September 1906; 5, Jimmy Greaves v Wolverhampton W, Division 1, 30 August 1958; 5, Jimmy Greaves v Preston NE, Division 1, 19 December 1959; 5, Jimmy Greaves v WBA, Division 1, 3 December 1960; 5, Bobby Tambling v Aston Villa, Division 1, 17 September 1966; 5, Gordon Durie v Walsall, Division 2, 4 February 1989.

Most Capped Player: Frank Lampard, 104 (106), England.

Most League Appearances: Ron Harris, 655, 1962–80.

Youngest League Player: Ian Hamilton, 16 years 138 days v Tottenham H, 18 March 1967.

Record Transfer Fee Received: £88,500,000 from Real Madrid for Eden Hazard, June 2019.

Record Transfer Fee Paid: £72,000,000 to Bayer Leverkusen for Kai Havertz, September 2020.

Football League Record: 1905 Elected to Division 2; 1907–10 Division 1; 1910–12 Division 2; 1912–24 Division 1; 1924–30 Division 2; 1930–62 Division 1; 1962–63 Division 2; 1963–75 Division 1; 1975–77 Division 2; 1977–79 Division 1; 1979–84 Division 2; 1984–88 Division 1; 1988–89 Division 2; 1989–92 Division 1; 1992– Premier League.

MANAGERS

John Tait Robertson 1905–07
David Calderhead 1907–33
Leslie Knighton 1933–39
Billy Birrell 1939–52
Ted Drake 1952–61
Tommy Docherty 1961–67
Dave Sexton 1967–74
Ron Suart 1974–75
Eddie McCreadie 1975–77
Ken Shellito 1977–78
Danny Blanchflower 1978–79
Geoff Hurst 1979–81
John Neal 1981–85 (*Director to 1986*)
John Hollins 1985–88
Bobby Campbell 1988–91
Ian Porterfield 1991–93
David Webb 1993
Glenn Hoddle 1993–96
Ruud Gullit 1996–98
Gianluca Vialli 1998–2000
Claudio Ranieri 2000–04
Jose Mourinho 2004–07
Avram Grant 2007–08
Luiz Felipe Scolari 2008–09
Guus Hiddink 2009
Carlo Ancelotti 2009–11
Andre Villas-Boas 2011–12
Roberto Di Matteo 2012
Rafael Benitez 2012–13
Jose Mourinho 2013–15
Guus Hiddink 2015–16
Antonio Conte 2016–18
Maurizio Sarri 2018–19
Frank Lampard 2019–21
Thomas Tuchel January 2021–

LATEST SEQUENCES

Longest Sequence of League Wins: 13, 1.10.2016 – 31.12.2016.

Longest Sequence of League Defeats: 7, 1.11.1952 – 20.12.1952.

Longest Sequence of League Draws: 6, 20.8.1969 – 13.9.1969.

Longest Sequence of Unbeaten League Matches: 40, 23.10.2004 – 29.10.2005.

Longest Sequence Without a League Win: 21, 3.11.1987 – 2.4.1988.

Successive Scoring Runs: 27 from 29.10.1988.

Successive Non-scoring Runs: 9 from 14.3.1981.

TEN YEAR LEAGUE RECORD

		P	*W*	*D*	*L*	*F*	*A*	*Pts*	*Pos*
2011-12	PR Lge	38	18	10	10	65	46	64	6
2012-13	PR Lge	38	22	9	7	75	39	75	3
2013-14	PR Lge	38	25	7	6	71	27	82	3
2014-15	PR Lge	38	26	9	3	73	32	87	1
2015-16	PR Lge	38	12	14	12	59	53	50	10
2016-17	PR Lge	38	30	3	5	85	33	93	1
2017-18	PR Lge	38	21	7	10	62	38	70	5
2018-19	PR Lge	38	21	9	8	63	39	72	3
2019-20	PR Lge	38	20	6	12	69	54	66	4
2020-21	PR Lge	38	19	10	9	58	36	67	4

DID YOU KNOW ?

The two First Division fixtures between Chelsea and Preston North End in the 1959–60 season produced a total of 17 goals, with the teams drawing 4-4 at Stamford Bridge and the Blues winning the return match at Deepdale 5-4. Jimmy Greaves scored eight of his team's nine goals, with a hat-trick in the first match and all five in the second encounter.

CHELSEA – PREMIER LEAGUE 2020–21 LEAGUE RECORD

Match No.	*Date*	*Venue*	*Opponents*	*Result*	*H/T Score*	*Lg Pos.*	*Goalscorers*	*Attendance*
1	Sept 14	A	Brighton & HA	W 3-1	1-0	3	Jorginho (pen)[23], James[56], Zouma[66]	0
2	20	H	Liverpool	L 0-2	0-0	10		0
3	26	A	WBA	D 3-3	0-3	6	Mount[55], Hudson-Odoi[70], Abraham[90]	0
4	Oct 3	H	Crystal Palace	W 4-0	0-0	4	Chilwell[50], Zouma[66], Jorginho 2 (2 pens)[78, 82]	0
5	17	H	Southampton	D 3-3	2-1	6	Werner 2[15, 28], Havertz[59]	0
6	24	A	Manchester U	D 0-0	0-0	6		0
7	31	A	Burnley	W 3-0	1-0	4	Ziyech[26], Zouma[63], Werner[70]	0
8	Nov 7	H	Sheffield U	W 4-1	2-1	3	Abraham[23], Chilwell[34], Thiago Silva[77], Werner[80]	0
9	21	A	Newcastle U	W 2-0	1-0	2	Fernandez (og)[10], Abraham[65]	0
10	29	H	Tottenham H	D 0-0	0-0	3		0
11	Dec 5	H	Leeds U	W 3-1	1-1	1	Giroud[27], Zouma[61], Pulisic[90]	2000
12	12	A	Everton	L 0-1	0-1	3		2000
13	15	A	Wolverhampton W	L 1-2	0-0	5	Giroud[49]	0
14	21	H	West Ham U	W 3-0	1-0	5	Thiago Silva[10], Abraham 2[78, 80]	0
15	26	A	Arsenal	L 1-3	0-2	7	Abraham[85]	0
16	28	H	Aston Villa	D 1-1	1-0	6	Giroud[34]	0
17	Jan 3	H	Manchester C	L 1-3	0-3	8	Hudson-Odoi[90]	0
18	16	A	Fulham	W 1-0	0-0	7	Mount[78]	0
19	19	A	Leicester C	L 0-2	0-2	8		0
20	27	H	Wolverhampton W	D 0-0	0-0	8		0
21	31	H	Burnley	W 2-0	1-0	7	Azpilicueta[40], Alonso[84]	0
22	Feb 4	A	Tottenham H	W 1-0	1-0	6	Jorginho (pen)[24]	0
23	7	A	Sheffield U	W 2-1	1-0	5	Mount[43], Jorginho (pen)[58]	0
24	15	H	Newcastle U	W 2-0	2-0	4	Giroud[31], Werner[39]	0
25	20	A	Southampton	D 1-1	0-1	4	Mount (pen)[54]	0
26	28	H	Manchester U	D 0-0	0-0	5		0
27	Mar 4	A	Liverpool	W 1-0	1-0	4	Mount[42]	0
28	8	H	Everton	W 2-0	1-0	4	Godfrey (og)[31], Jorginho (pen)[65]	0
29	13	A	Leeds U	D 0-0	0-0	4		0
30	Apr 3	H	WBA	L 2-5	1-2	4	Pulisic[27], Mount[71]	0
31	10	A	Crystal Palace	W 4-1	3-0	4	Havertz[8], Pulisic 2[10, 78], Zouma[30]	0
32	20	H	Brighton & HA	D 0-0	0-0	4		0
33	24	A	West Ham U	W 1-0	1-0	4	Werner[43]	0
34	May 1	H	Fulham	W 2-0	1-0	4	Havertz 2[10, 49]	0
35	8	A	Manchester C	W 2-1	0-1	3	Ziyech[63], Alonso[90]	0
36	12	H	Arsenal	L 0-1	0-1	4		0
37	18	H	Leicester C	W 2-1	0-0	3	Rudiger[47], Jorginho (pen)[66]	7195
38	23	A	Aston Villa	L 1-2	0-1	4	Chilwell[70]	10,000

Final League Position: 4

GOALSCORERS

League (58): Jorginho 7 (7 pens), Abraham 6, Mount 6 (1 pen), Werner 6, Zouma 5, Giroud 4, Havertz 4, Pulisic 4, Chilwell 3, Alonso 2, Hudson-Odoi 2, Thiago Silva 2, Ziyech 2, Azpilicueta 1, James 1, Rudiger 1, own goals 2.
FA Cup (11): Abraham 4, Ziyech 2, Havertz 1, Hudson-Odoi 1, Mount 1, Werner 1, own goal 1.
Carabao Cup (7): Havertz 3, Abraham 1, Barkley 1, Giroud 1, Werner 1.
UEFA Champions League (23): Giroud 6 (1 pen), Werner 4 (3 pens), Hudson-Odoi 2, Mount 2, Pulisic 2, Ziyech 2, Abraham 1, Chilwell 1, Emerson Palmieri 1, Havertz 1, Jorginho 1 (1 pen).
Papa John's Trophy (5): Anjorin 2, Lewis 1, Russell 1, Simeu 1.

Arrizabalaga K 6 + 1	James R 25 + 7	Christensen A 15 + 2	Zouma K 22 + 2	Alonso M 11 + 2	Kante N 24 + 6	Jorginho F 23 + 5	Havertz K 18 + 9	Mount M 32 + 4	Loftus-Cheek R 1	Werner T 29 + 6	Barkley R — + 2	Hudson-Odoi C 10 + 13	Azpilicueta C 24 + 2	Kovacic M 21 + 6	Tomori F — + 1	Abraham T 12 + 10	Caballero W 1	Thiago Silva E 23	Giroud O 8 + 9	Mendy E 31	Chilwell B 27	Pulisic C 18 + 9	Ziyech H 15 + 8	Rudiger A 19	Emerson d — + 2	Gilmour B 3 + 2	Match No.
1	2	3	4	5	6	7[3]	8[2]	9	10[1]	11	12	13	14														1
1	2	3■	4	5	6	7[2]	10[1]	9		11	14			8[3]	12	13											2
	2	3		5[2]	6		9	8		10		12	13	7[1]		11	1	4[3]	14								3
			4		6[1]	7	9			10		8[2]	2	13		11		3		1	5	12					4
1	13	3	4		7	6	9	10[1]		11[3]			2			14					5	8[2]	12				5
	5		4		7	6	9[2]	13		11[1]			2			12		3		1	8	10[3]	14				6
	2		3		7	14	6[3]	8		11		12				10[2]		4	13	1	5		9[1]				7
	2		3		7	12		8		11[2]				6[1]		10		4	13	1	5		9				8
	2		3		7			8		11[1]		12		6		10			14	1	5[2]		9[3]	4	13		9
	2		3		7		14	8		11[1]				6		10[2]		4	13	1	5	12	9[3]				10
	2		3		7		6[2]	8		11				13		14		4	10[3]	1	5	12	9[1]				11
	2		3		7		9[1]	8		11				6[2]		12		4	10	1	5					13	12
	2		3		7		6[2]	8		9				13		12		4	10[1]	1	5	11					13
			3		6	7[2]	14	8		11			2	13		10		4		1	5[1]	9[3]			12		14
	2		3		7[3]	13	14	8		11[1]		12		6[2]		10		4		1	5	9					15
		3			6	7[1]	13	8		12		9	2						10[2]	1	5	11		4			16
			3		7[2]		14	8		10		12	2	6[3]				4		1	5	11	9[1]			13	17
						7[1]		8		14		13	2	6		12		3	10[2]	1	5	11	9[3]	4			18
	2						6[1]	8		13		9[2]		7		10		4		1	5	11	12	3			19
						6	10	14				8	2	7		13		3	11[2]	1	5[1]	12	9[3]	4			20
	13			8		6	14	9[3]		10		5[2]	2	7		11[1]		3		1		12		4			21
	5	12		8	14	6		10		11		9[2]	2	7[3]				3[1]		1		13		4			22
	5	3		13	14	6		9		11[3]		12	2	7					10[2]	1	8[1]			4			23
1	14	3		8	13	6		9[2]		10		5[3]	2	7		11[1]			12					4			24
	5		3	8	6	13		9		10		12[3]	2	7[2]		11[1]				1			14	4			25
	12	3			6			10		14		5[1]	2	7					11[2]	1	8	13	9[3]	4			26
	5	3			6	7	14	10[2]		11[3]			2	13						1	8	12	9[1]	4			27
	5	3	4	8	13	6	11	12		9[3]		10[1]	2	7[2]						1		14					28
	12	3			6	7	11	10[3]		13		14	2							1	5	8[1]	9[2]	4			29
	5	12	4	8		6[3]	14	13		11			2	7				3■		1		10[2]	9[1]				30
	13		3		12	6[1]	11	9				5[2]	2	7[3]						1	8	10	14	4			31
1	5	2	3	8[2]		6	10[1]	7		13		12							14			11	9[3]	4			32
	13	2			6	7		9		11[3]			5[2]			14		3		1	8	10[1]	12	4			33
	5	2	4	14	12		11	7[2]		10						13		3		1	8[3]		9[1]			6	34
	5	3[1]	12	8	7[2]	13				11		14	2							1		9	10[3]	4		6	35
1	5		4			7	11[2]	9				12	2[3]					3	13		8	10	14			6[1]	36
	2		13		6[1]	7		10		11[3]			5[2]	12				3	14	1	8	9		4			37
12	2					6[2]	14	9		11			5■	7[3]				3		1[1]	8	10	13	4			38

FA Cup

Third Round	Morecambe	(h)	4-0
Fourth Round	Luton T	(h)	3-1
Fifth Round	Barnsley	(a)	1-0
Sixth Round	Sheffield U	(h)	2-0
Semi-Final	Manchester C	(h)	1-0
Final	Leicester C	(Wembley)	0-1

Carabao Cup

Third Round	Barnsley	(h)	6-0
Fourth Round	Tottenham H	(a)	1-1

(Tottenham H won 5-4 on penalties)

Papa John's Trophy (Chelsea U21)

Group D (S)	Oxford U	(a)	1-2
Group D (S)	Walsall	(a)	1-1

(Chelsea U21 won 5-3 on penalties)

Group D (S)	Bristol R	(a)	3-4

UEFA Champions League

Group E	Sevilla	(h)	0-0
Group E	Krasnodar	(a)	4-0
Group E	Rennes	(h)	3-0
Group E	Rennes	(a)	2-1
Group E	Sevilla	(a)	4-0
Group E	Krasnodar	(h)	1-1
Round of 16 1st leg	Atletico Madrid	(a)	1-0
Round of 16 2nd leg	Atletico Madrid	(h)	2-0
Quarter-Final 1st leg	Porto	(a)	2-0
Quarter-Final 2nd leg	Porto	(h)	0-1
Semi-Final 1st leg	Real Madrid	(a)	1-1
Semi-Final 2nd leg	Real Madrid	(h)	2-0
Final	Manchester C	(Porto)	1-0

CHELTENHAM TOWN

FOUNDATION

The origins of Cheltenham Town date back to around 1887. A key figure in the development of football in the town was Albert Close White who had learnt the game whilst studying at St Mark's Teacher Training College in Chelsea. He returned to Cheltenham in 1884 and for the next 40 years he was a teacher at Cheltenham Parish Boys' School, where he introduced a range of sporting activities including association football. He later recalled the formation of the Cheltenham Town club: "The club was started somewhere between 1884–7, and its first matches were more or less practice or scratch games, and were played on the East Gloucestershire Cricket Ground." A fixture list from 1894–95 gave the club's ground as Eldorado Road, with team colours of chocolate and blue.

The Jonny-Rocks Stadium, Whaddon Road, Cheltenham, Gloucestershire GL52 5NA.

Telephone: (01242) 573 558.

Ticket Office: (01242) 573 558 (option 1).

Website: www.ctfc.com

Email: info@ctfc.com

Ground Capacity: 7,200.

Record Attendance: 10,389 v Blackpool, FA Cup 3rd rd, 13 January 1934 (at Cheltenham Athletic Ground); 8,326 v Reading, FA Cup 1st rd, 17 November 1956 (at Whaddon Road).

Pitch Measurements: 102m × 65m (111.5yd × 71yd).

Chairman: Andy Wilcox.

Vice-Chairman: David Bloxham.

Manager: Michael Duff.

Assistant Manager: Russell Milton.

Colours: Red shirts with thin white stripes and white sleeves and black trim, white shorts with red trim, red socks with white trim.

Year Formed: 1887.

Turned Professional: 1932.

Club Nickname: 'The Robins'.

Grounds: Pre-1932, Agg-Gardner's Recreation Ground; Whaddon Lane; Carter's Lane; 1932, Whaddon Road (renamed The Abbey Business Stadium 2009, World of Smile Stadium 2015, LCI Rail Stadium 2016, Jonny-Rocks Stadium 2019).

First Football League Game: 7 August 1999, Division 3, v Rochdale (h) L 0–2 – Book; Griffin, Victory, Banks, Freeman, Brough (Howarth), Howells, Bloomer (Devaney), Grayson, Watkins (McAuley), Yates.

Record League Victory: 5–0 v Mansfield T, FL 2, 6 May 2006 – Higgs; Gallinagh, Bell, McCann (1) (Connolly), Caines, Duff, Wilson, Bird (1p), Gillespie (1) (Spencer), Guinan (Odejayi (1)), Vincent (1).

Record Cup Victory: 12–0 v Chippenham R, FA Cup 3rd qual. rd, 2 November 1935 – Bowles; Whitehouse, Williams; Lang, Devonport (1), Partridge (2); Perkins, Hackett, Jones (4), Black (4), Griffiths (1).

HONOURS

League Champions: FL 2 – 2020–21; Conference – 1998–99, 2015–16.
Runners-up: Conference – 1997–98.

FA Cup: 5th rd – 2002.

League Cup: never past 2nd rd.

FOOTBALL YEARBOOK FACT FILE

Cheltenham Town stepped up the football ranks in the summer of 1932 when they joined the Birmingham Combination. Former Aston Villa and Cardiff City player George Blackburn was employed as a player-coach although the club expressed the wish to stay as an amateur organisation. However, soon after the start of the 1932–33 season they recruited a number of professionals and very quickly switched to semi-professional status.

Record Defeat: 1–8 v Crewe Alex, FL 2, 2 April 2011; 0–7 v Crystal Palace, League Cup 2nd rd, 2 October 2002.
N.B. 1–10 v Merthyr T, Southern League, 8 March 1952.

Most League Points (2 for a win): 60, Southern League Division 1, 1963–64.

Most League Points (3 for a win): 82, FL 2, 2020–21.

Most League Goals: 67, FL 2, 2017–18.

Highest League Scorer in Season: Mo Eisa, 23, FL 2, 2017–18.

Most League Goals in Total Aggregate: Julian Alsop, 39, 2000–03; 2009–10.

Most League Goals in One Match: 3, Martin Devaney v Plymouth Arg, Division 3, 23 September 2000; 3, Neil Grayson v Cardiff C, Division 3, 1 April 2001; 3, Damien Spencer v Hull C, Division 3, 23 August 2003; 3, Damien Spencer v Milton Keynes D, FL 1, 31 January 2009; 3, Michael Pook v Burton Alb, FL 2, 13 March 2010; 3, Mohamed Eisa v Port Vale, FL 2, 10 February 2018.

Most Capped Player: Grant McCann, 7 (40), Northern Ireland.

Most League Appearances: David Bird, 288, 2001–11.

Youngest League Player: Kyle Haynes, 17 years 85 days v Oldham Ath, 24 March 2009.

Record Transfer Fee Received: £1,400,000 from Bristol C for Mo Eisa, July 2018.

Record Transfer Fee Paid: £60,000 to Aldershot T for Jermaine McGlashan, January 2012.

Football League Record: 1999 Promoted to Division 3; 2002 Division 2; 2003–04 Division 3; 2004–06 FL 2; 2006–09 FL 1; 2009–15 FL 2; 2015–16 National League; 2016–21 FL 2; 2021– FL 1.

MANAGERS

George Blackburn 1932–34
George Carr 1934–37
Jimmy Brain 1937–48
Cyril Dean 1948–50
George Summerbee 1950–52
William Raeside 1952–53
Arch Anderson 1953–58
Ron Lewin 1958–60
Peter Donnelly 1960–61
Tommy Cavanagh 1961
Arch Anderson 1961–65
Harold Fletcher 1965–66
Bob Etheridge 1966–73
Willie Penman 1973–74
Dennis Allen 1974–79
Terry Paine 1979
Alan Grundy 1979–82
Alan Wood 1982–83
John Murphy 1983–88
Jim Barron 1988–90
John Murphy 1990
Dave Lewis 1990–91
Ally Robertson 1991–92
Lindsay Parsons 1992–95
Chris Robinson 1995–97
Steve Cotterill 1997–2002
Graham Allner 2002–03
Bobby Gould 2003
John Ward 2003–07
Keith Downing 2007–08
Martin Allen 2008–09
Mark Yates 2009–14
Paul Buckle 2014–15
Gary Johnson 2015–18
Michael Duff September 2018–

LATEST SEQUENCES

Longest Sequence of League Wins: 5, 11.2.2020 – 29.2.2020.

Longest Sequence of League Defeats: 7, 14.4.2018 – 18.8.2018.

Longest Sequence of League Draws: 5, 5.4.2003 – 21.4.2003.

Longest Sequence of Unbeaten League Matches: 16, 1.12.2001 – 12.3.2002.

Longest Sequence Without a League Win: 14, 20.12.2008 – 7.3.2009.

Successive Scoring Runs: 17 from 16.2.2008.

Successive Non-scoring Runs: 5 from 10.3.2012 – 30.3.2012.

TEN YEAR LEAGUE RECORD

		P	*W*	*D*	*L*	*F*	*A*	*Pts*	*Pos*
2011-12	FL 2	46	23	8	15	66	50	77	6
2012-13	FL 2	46	20	15	11	58	51	75	5
2013-14	FL 2	46	13	16	17	53	63	55	17
2014-15	FL 2	46	9	14	23	40	67	41	23
2015-16	NL	46	30	11	5	87	30	101	1
2016-17	FL 2	46	12	14	20	49	69	50	21
2017-18	FL 2	46	13	12	21	67	73	51	17
2018-19	FL 2	46	15	12	19	57	68	57	16
2019-20	FL 2	36	17	13	6	52	27	64	4§
2020-21	FL 2	46	24	10	12	61	39	82	1

§Decided on points-per-game (1.78)

DID YOU KNOW ?

Cheltenham Town gained their first significant success in the 1896–97 season when they won the Mid-Gloucestershire League. The Robins won 10 of their 12 games in the competition, scoring 38 and conceding 12. Among the club's players that season was Gilbert Jessop, better known as the Gloucestershire and England cricketer.

CHELTENHAM TOWN – SKY BET LEAGUE TWO 2020–21 LEAGUE RECORD

Match No.	*Date*	*Venue*	*Opponents*	*Result*	*H/T Score*	*Lg Pos.*	*Goalscorers*	*Attendance*
1	Sept 12	H	Morecambe	L 1-2	1-0	18	May [28]	0
2	19	A	Tranmere R	W 3-0	3-0	11	Raglan [6], Williams [20], Lewis (og) [39]	0
3	Oct 3	A	Leyton Orient	W 2-0	2-0	8	Ling (og) [16], Azaz [29]	0
4	10	H	Crawley T	W 2-0	1-0	4	Craig (og) [33], Williams [48]	0
5	13	H	Grimsby T	L 1-3	1-2	5	Williams [28]	0
6	17	A	Southend U	W 2-0	1-0	3	Sercombe (pen) [10], Lloyd [52]	0
7	20	H	Scunthorpe U	W 1-0	1-0	3	Reid (pen) [5]	0
8	24	H	Mansfield T	D 0-0	0-0	3		0
9	27	A	Port Vale	L 1-2	0-0	5	Williams [48]	0
10	31	H	Forest Green R	W 2-1	1-0	3	Boyle [11], Williams [57]	0
11	Nov 3	A	Oldham Ath	L 1-2	1-1	6	Reid [30]	0
12	14	A	Carlisle U	W 2-1	2-1	3	Boyle [15], Thomas (pen) [36]	0
13	21	H	Walsall	W 3-0	0-0	2	Scarr (og) [50], Blair [58], Tozer [88]	0
14	24	H	Cambridge U	D 1-1	1-0	2	Tozer [45]	0
15	Dec 1	A	Bradford C	W 2-1	1-1	2	May [45], Clements [76]	0
16	5	H	Exeter C	W 5-3	3-1	2	Sercombe 2 (1 pen) [7, 45 (p)], May [13], Williams [77], Boyle [90]	0
17	12	A	Salford C	D 0-0	0-0	2		0
18	15	H	Bolton W	L 0-1	0-0	3		1685
19	19	A	Barrow	L 0-3	0-1	4		1363
20	26	H	Stevenage	D 1-1	1-0	4	Sercombe [28]	0
21	29	A	Colchester U	D 0-0	0-0	4		0
22	Jan 16	A	Bolton W	D 1-1	0-0	6	May [54]	0
23	19	H	Newport Co	D 1-1	1-1	6	Blair [45]	0
24	26	H	Oldham Ath	W 2-0	0-0	4	Williams [54], May [83]	0
25	30	A	Forest Green R	D 0-0	0-0	4		0
26	Feb 9	A	Harrogate T	W 1-0	1-0	3	Boyle [43]	0
27	16	A	Walsall	W 2-1	2-1	3	Smith [35], Wright [43]	0
28	20	H	Bradford C	L 0-2	0-1	3		0
29	23	A	Cambridge U	W 1-0	0-0	3	Long [63]	0
30	27	A	Scunthorpe U	W 2-0	2-0	3	Smith [25], Wright [41]	0
31	Mar 2	H	Southend U	W 1-0	0-0	1	Thomas (pen) [53]	0
32	6	H	Port Vale	W 3-2	2-0	1	May 2 [14, 18], Sercombe [75]	0
33	9	A	Mansfield T	L 1-3	0-0	1	Smith [51]	0
34	13	A	Exeter C	W 1-0	0-0	1	Williams [90]	0
35	16	H	Barrow	L 0-2	0-1	1		0
36	20	H	Salford C	W 2-0	2-0	1	Long [3], Sercombe [41]	0
37	27	A	Morecambe	L 0-1	0-1	2		0
38	Apr 2	H	Tranmere R	W 4-0	3-0	2	Thomas [4], Boyle [14], May [42], Wright [57]	0
39	5	A	Grimsby T	D 1-1	1-1	2	Boyle [34]	0
40	10	H	Leyton Orient	W 1-0	1-0	1	Thomas (pen) [31]	0
41	16	A	Crawley T	L 0-1	0-0	1		0
42	20	A	Stevenage	W 1-0	1-0	2	Lloyd [43]	0
43	24	H	Colchester U	W 1-0	0-0	1	Thomas [82]	0
44	27	H	Carlisle U	D 1-1	0-1	1	Hussey [56]	0
45	May 1	A	Newport Co	L 0-1	0-1	1		0
46	8	H	Harrogate T	W 4-1	3-1	1	Sercombe [11], Smith [22], May [34], Wright [56]	0

Final League Position: 1

GOALSCORERS

League (61): May 9, Williams 8, Sercombe 7 (2 pens), Boyle 6, Thomas 5 (3 pens), Smith 4, Wright 4, Blair 2, Lloyd 2, Long 2, Reid 2 (1 pen), Tozer 2, Azaz 1, Clements 1, Hussey 1, Raglan 1, own goals 4.
FA Cup (8): May 4, Azaz 1, Boyle 1, Lloyd 1, Sercombe 1.
Carabao Cup (2): Azaz 1, Sercombe 1.
Papa John's Trophy (4): Reid 3, Lloyd 1.

Griffiths J 44	Raglan C 39 + 1	Tozer B 46	Boyle W 29	Thomas C 35 + 3	Sercombe L 35 + 3	Azaz F 27 + 10	Clements C 14 + 3	Hussey C 43	Williams A 20 + 25	May A 36 + 8	Addai A — + 10	Blair M 42 + 2	Reid R 4 + 8	Lloyd G 18 + 14	Bonds E 3 + 2	Freestone L 9 + 5	Sang T 3 + 7	Chapman E 9 + 12	Flinders S 2	Long S 18 + 4	Smith S 18 + 3	Vassilev I — + 12	Wright C 12 + 4	Horton G — + 1	Match No.
1	2	3	4	5	6	7	8^{2}	9	10^{3}	11^{1}	12	13	14												1
1	2	3	4	8	6	7^{1}		9	11			5		10^{2}	12	13									2
1	2^{3}	3	4	8	6	7^{2}	13	9	11	12		5		10^{1}	14										3
1	2	3	4	6	8	7^{1}		9	11	13		5		10^{2}			12								4
1	2^{2}	3	4	6	8			9	11^{1}	13	14	5	12	10^{3}	7										5
1	2^{3}	3	4	13	8		7	9	10	12		5		11^{1}	6^{2}	14									6
1	2	3	4		6		7	9	13		14	5	10^{2}	11^{3}	8^{1}		12								7
1	2	3	4	12	8		7	9	13	10^{2}	14	5^{1}	11				6^{3}								8
1	2	3	4	5	8		7^{2}	9	10	11	12		13				6^{1}								9
1	2	3	4	5	6		7	8	11	9^{2}	12		10^{1}					13							10
1	2	3	4	5	7		6^{1}	8	10	9	13	12	11^{2}												11
	2	3	4	6	8			9	11	10^{1}		5		12				7	1						12
1	2	3	4	6	8			9	11^{2}	10^{1}		5	13	12				7							13
1	2	3	4	7^{1}	8	12		9	11^{3}	10^{2}		5	14	13				6							14
1	2	3	4		6	7^{3}	12	9	13	10^{2}		5		11			14	8^{1}							15
1	2^{4}	3	4		6^{3}	7^{2}	8	9	13	10^{1}		5		11		15	12	14							16
1	2	3	4		6	7^{2}		9	12	10		5		11^{1}			13	8							17
1	2	3	4		6	7^{2}		9	12	11		5	14	10^{1}			13	8^{3}							18
1	2	3	4		8	14	7^{1}	9^{5}	11^{4}	10^{2}		5	15	12		16	6^{3}	13							19
1	2	3	4		6	8^{1}	7	9	11^{2}	10^{3}		5	14	13				12							20
1	2	3	4		8^{2}	6	7	9	14	11		5^{1}		10^{3}			12	13							21
1	2	3	4	7		6			11^{2}	10^{3}	14	5		13		9^{1}		8		12					22
1	2	3	4	7		6^{3}	12	9^{1}	14	10	13	5		11^{2}				8							23
1	2	3	4	7		6	8		11^{2}	10^{1}	13	5		12		9									24
1	2	3	4	6		8^{2}	7		11^{1}	10		5				9^{3}				14	12	13			25
1	2	3	4	6	13	8^{2}	7^{1}	9	11	10^{3}		5								12		14			26
1	2	3	4	6		8		9	14	11^{1}		5		12							10^{3}	13	7^{2}		27
1	2	3		6		8^{2}		9	15	11		5		13		4^{3}				12	10^{4}	14	7^{1}		28
1		3		6		7		8^{1}	13	11		5		9		4				2	10^{2}			12	29
1	2	3		7		8		9	14	11^{1}		5		12						4	10^{3}	13	6^{2}		30
1	2	3		7	13	8		9	12	11^{1}		5								4	10		6^{2}		31
1	2	3		7	12	8^{1}		9	13	11^{2}		5								4	10^{3}	14	6		32
1	2^{2}	3		7	8^{3}	12		9		10		5		14						4	11	13	6^{1}		33
1		3		7	8	6		9	13	12		5		11^{1}		4				2	10^{2}				34
1		3		7^{4}	6	8^{1}		9	12	10		5				4^{3}		14		2	11^{2}	13	15		35
1		3		7	6	14		9	13	11^{2}		5				4		12		2	10^{3}		8^{1}		36
		3		7	6	12		9	13	11^{4}		5^{1}				4^{3}		15	1	2	10	14	8^{2}		37
1	16	3	4	7^{1}	8	15		9	13	11^{3}		5^{5}						12		2	10^{2}	14	6^{4}		38
1		3	4	14	8	6^{3}		9	13	11^{1}		5		12				7^{4}		2	10^{2}		15		39
1	2	3		7	8	13		9	10^{1}	11^{3}		5		14						4	12		6^{2}		40
1	2	3		7^{3}	8	15		9	11^{4}	10^{2}		5						13		4	12	14	6^{1}		41
1	2	3		7	8	6^{2}		9	13	12		5		11^{1}				14		4	10^{3}				42
1	2	3		7	8	6^{3}		9	13	12		5		11^{2}						4	10^{1}		14		43
1	2	3		7	8^{4}	6^{2}		9	14	12		5		11^{1}		15		13		4	10^{3}				44
1	2^{1}	3		6	7	15		8	13	11^{2}		5		9^{4}						4	10^{3}	14	12		45
1	2	3		7	8	14		9	13	11^{1}		5		12						4	10^{2}		6^{3}		46

FA Cup

First Round	South Shields	(h)	3-1
Second Round *(aet)*	Crewe Alex	(h)	2-1
Third Round *(aet)*	Mansfield T	(h)	2-1
Fourth Round	Manchester C	(h)	1-3

Carabao Cup

First Round	Peterborough U	(a)	1-0
Second Round	Millwall	(a)	1-3

Papa John's Trophy

Group F (S)	Newport Co	(a)	1-0
Group F (S)	Plymouth Arg	(h)	2-0
Group F (S)	Norwich C U21	(h)	1-0
Second Round (S)	Portsmouth	(h)	0-3

COLCHESTER UNITED

FOUNDATION

Colchester United was formed in 1937 when a number of enthusiasts of the much older Colchester Town club decided to establish a professional concern as a limited liability company. The new club continued at Layer Road which had been the amateur club's home since 1909.

JobServe Community Stadium, United Way, Colchester, Essex CO4 5UP.

Telephone: (01206) 755 100.

Ticket Office: (01206) 755 161.

Website: www.cu-fc.com

Email: media@colchesterunited.net

Ground Capacity: 10,105.

Record Attendance: 19,072 v Reading, FA Cup 1st rd, 27 November 1948 (at Layer Road); 10,064 v Norwich C, FL 1, 16 January 2010 (at Community Stadium).

Pitch Measurements: 105m × 68m (115yd × 74.5yd).

Executive Chairman: Robbie Cowling.

Head Coach: Hayden Mullins.

First-Team Advisor: Paul Tisdale.

Colours: Royal blue shirts with white trim, royal blue shorts with white trim, white socks with royal blue trim.

Year Formed: 1937.

Turned Professional: 1937.

Club Nickname: 'The U's'.

Grounds: 1937, Layer Road; 2008, Weston Homes Community Stadium (renamed JobServe Community Stadium 2018).

First Football League Game: 19 August 1950, Division 3 (S), v Gillingham (a) D 0–0 – Wright; Kettle, Allen; Bearryman, Stewart, Elder; Jones, Curry, Turner, McKim, Church.

Record League Victory: 9–1 v Bradford C, Division 4, 30 December 1961 – Ames; Millar, Fowler; Harris, Abrey, Ron Hunt; Foster, Bobby Hunt (4), King (4), Hill (1), Wright.

Record Cup Victory: 9–1 v Leamington, FA Cup 1st rd, 5 November 2005 – Davison; Stockley (Garcia), Duguid, Brown (1), Chilvers, Watson (1), Halford (1), Izzet (Danns) (2), Iwelumo (1) (Williams), Cureton (2), Yeates (1).

HONOURS

League Champions: Conference – 1991–92.
Runners-up: FL 1 – 2005–06; Division 4 – 1961–62; Conference – 1990–91.

FA Cup: 6th rd – 1971.

League Cup: 5th rd – 1975.

League Trophy: *Runners-up:* 1997.

FOOTBALL YEARBOOK FACT FILE

Although Colchester United only won the Football Conference title in 1991–92 on goal difference from Wycombe Wanderers, they had led the table from mid-November onwards. They were almost unbeatable at Layer Road, recording 17 consecutive League and Cup wins in a run that extended from 21 December through to the end of the season.

Record Defeat: 0–8 v Leyton Orient, Division 4, 15 October 1988.

Most League Points (2 for a win): 60, Division 4, 1973–74.

Most League Points (3 for a win): 81, Division 4, 1982–83.

Most League Goals: 104, Division 4, 1961–62.

Highest League Scorer in Season: Bobby Hunt, 38, Division 4, 1961–62.

Most League Goals in Total Aggregate: Martyn King, 130, 1956–64.

Most League Goals in One Match: 4, Bobby Hunt v Bradford C, Division 4, 30 December 1961; 4, Martyn King v Bradford C, Division 4, 30 December 1961; 4, Bobby Hunt v Doncaster R, Division 4, 30 April 1962.

Most Capped Player: Luke Gambin 11 (includes 2 on loan at Newport Co) (30), Malta.

Most League Appearances: Micky Cook, 613, 1969–84.

Youngest League Player: Todd Miller, 16 years 166 days v Exeter C, 16 March 2019.

Record Transfer Fee Received: £2,500,000 from Reading for Greg Halford, January 2007.

Record Transfer Fee Paid: £400,000 to Cheltenham T for Steve Gillespie, July 2008.

Football League Record: 1950 Elected to Division 3 (S); 1958–61 Division 3; 1961–62 Division 4; 1962–65 Division 3; 1965–66 Division 4; 1966–68 Division 3; 1968–74 Division 4; 1974–76 Division 3, 1976–77 Division 4; 1977–81 Division 3; 1981–90 Division 4; 1990–92 Conference; 1992–98 Division 3; 1998–2004 Division 2; 2004–06 FL 1; 2006–08 FL C; 2008–16 FL 1; 2016– FL 2.

MANAGERS

Ted Fenton 1946–48
Jimmy Allen 1948–53
Jack Butler 1953–55
Benny Fenton 1955–63
Neil Franklin 1963–68
Dick Graham 1968–72
Jim Smith 1972–75
Bobby Roberts 1975–82
Allan Hunter 1982–83
Cyril Lea 1983–86
Mike Walker 1986–87
Roger Brown 1987–88
Jock Wallace 1989
Mick Mills 1990
Ian Atkins 1990–91
Roy McDonough 1991–94
George Burley 1994
Steve Wignall 1995–99
Mick Wadsworth 1999
Steve Whitton 1999–2003
Phil Parkinson 2003–06
Geraint Williams 2006–08
Paul Lambert 2008–09
Aidy Boothroyd 2009–10
John Ward 2010–12
Joe Dunne 2012–14
Tony Humes 2014–15
Kevin Keen 2015–16
John McGreal 2016–20
Steve Ball 2020–21
Hayden Mullins March 2021–

LATEST SEQUENCES

Longest Sequence of League Wins: 7, 31.12.2005 – 7.2.2006.

Longest Sequence of League Defeats: 9, 31.10.2015 – 28.12.2015.

Longest Sequence of League Draws: 6, 21.3.1977 – 11.4.1977.

Longest Sequence of Unbeaten League Matches: 20, 22.12.1956 – 19.4.1957.

Longest Sequence Without a League Win: 20, 2.3.1968 – 31.8.1968.

Successive Scoring Runs: 24 from 15.9.1962.

Successive Non-scoring Runs: 5 from 6.3.2021.

TEN YEAR LEAGUE RECORD

		P	W	D	L	F	A	Pts	Pos
2011-12	FL 1	46	13	20	13	61	66	59	10
2012-13	FL 1	46	14	9	23	47	68	51	20
2013-14	FL 1	46	13	14	19	53	61	53	16
2014-15	FL 1	46	14	10	22	58	77	52	19
2015-16	FL 1	46	9	13	24	57	99	40	23
2016-17	FL 2	46	19	12	15	67	57	69	8
2017-18	FL 2	46	16	14	16	53	52	62	13
2018-19	FL 2	46	20	10	16	65	53	70	8
2019-20	FL 2	37	15	13	9	52	37	58	6§
2020-21	FL 2	46	11	18	17	44	61	51	20

§Decided on points-per-game (1.57)

DID YOU KNOW ?

The first player to score for Colchester United in a competitive fixture was Reg Smith, who netted in the Southern League Midweek Section game against Bath City played on 2 September 1937. Smith went on to register a hat-trick and further goals from Arthur Pritchard (2) and Jack Hodge gave the U's a 6-1 victory.

COLCHESTER UNITED – SKY BET LEAGUE TWO 2020–21 LEAGUE RECORD

Match No.	*Date*	*Venue*	*Opponents*	*Result*		*H/T Score*	*Lg Pos.*	*Goalscorers*	*Attendance*
1	Sept 12	A	Bradford C	D	0-0	0-0	14		0
2	19	H	Bolton W	W	2-0	1-0	6	Eastman [44], Brown [71]	0
3	26	A	Barrow	D	1-1	1-0	8	Chilvers [34]	0
4	Oct 3	H	Oldham Ath	D	3-3	2-0	9	Stevenson [27], Harriott (pen) [37], Welch-Hayes [65]	0
5	10	A	Walsall	D	1-1	1-0	9	Harriott [24]	0
6	17	A	Carlisle U	L	2-3	1-2	14	Norris 2 (1 pen) [44, 52 (p)]	0
7	20	H	Forest Green R	W	1-0	1-0	11	Chilvers [2]	0
8	24	H	Harrogate T	W	2-1	0-0	9	Harriott [52], Stevenson [54]	0
9	27	A	Newport Co	L	1-2	0-0	11	Brown [89]	0
10	Nov 3	H	Stevenage	W	3-1	1-1	11	Brown 3 [11, 57, 81]	0
11	14	H	Leyton Orient	W	2-1	1-0	7	Brown 2 [10, 72]	0
12	20	A	Mansfield T	D	1-1	0-0	6	Norris [85]	0
13	24	A	Exeter C	L	1-6	0-1	10	Folivi [73]	0
14	Dec 1	H	Crawley T	D	1-1	1-1	12	Harriott [13]	0
15	5	H	Grimsby T	W	2-1	1-1	9	Smith [9], Harriott [56]	0
16	8	A	Scunthorpe U	W	1-0	1-0	6	Smith [26]	0
17	12	A	Port Vale	D	1-1	0-0	6	Norris [65]	0
18	15	A	Cambridge U	L	1-2	0-0	7	Folivi (pen) [68]	1949
19	19	H	Morecambe	L	1-2	1-1	10	Folivi [23]	1094
20	26	A	Southend U	L	0-2	0-2	11		0
21	29	H	Cheltenham T	D	0-0	0-0	12		0
22	Jan 16	H	Cambridge U	D	1-1	1-1	12	Taylor (og) [39]	0
23	23	A	Morecambe	L	0-3	0-1	15		0
24	26	A	Stevenage	D	0-0	0-0	14		0
25	29	H	Scunthorpe U	L	0-1	0-1	16		0
26	Feb 6	A	Leyton Orient	D	0-0	0-0	17		0
27	14	H	Mansfield T	D	2-2	1-1	17	Harriott [39], Nouble [89]	0
28	20	A	Crawley T	L	0-1	0-0	20		0
29	23	H	Exeter C	L	1-2	0-1	21	Oteh [66]	0
30	27	A	Forest Green R	L	0-3	0-2	21		0
31	Mar 2	H	Carlisle U	W	2-1	0-1	20	Harriott 2 (1 pen) [67 (p), 74]	0
32	6	H	Newport Co	L	0-2	0-1	20		0
33	9	A	Harrogate T	L	0-3	0-2	20		0
34	13	A	Grimsby T	D	0-0	0-0	20		0
35	16	A	Salford C	D	0-0	0-0	21		0
36	20	H	Port Vale	L	0-1	0-1	22		0
37	23	H	Tranmere R	D	2-2	1-0	21	Pell [30], Sarpeng-Wiredu [54]	0
38	27	H	Bradford C	L	1-2	1-1	21	Nouble [42]	0
39	Apr 2	A	Bolton W	D	0-0	0-0	22		0
40	5	H	Barrow	D	1-1	1-0	22	Harriott [33]	0
41	9	A	Oldham Ath	L	2-5	0-2	22	Nouble [64], Eastman [81]	0
42	17	H	Walsall	W	2-1	2-1	22	Folivi [37], Clampin [45]	0
43	20	H	Southend U	W	2-0	2-0	21	Folivi [30], Pell [37]	0
44	24	A	Cheltenham T	L	0-1	0-0	20		0
45	May 1	H	Salford C	W	1-0	0-0	20	Bohui [68]	0
46	8	A	Tranmere R	D	0-0	0-0	20		0

Final League Position: 20

GOALSCORERS

League (44): Harriott 9 (2 pens), Brown 7, Folivi 5 (1 pen), Norris 4 (1 pen), Nouble 3, Chilvers 2, Eastman 2, Pell 2, Smith 2, Stevenson 2, Bohui 1, Clampin 1, Oteh 1, Sarpeng-Wiredu 1, Welch-Hayes 1, own goal 1.
FA Cup (1): Pell 1.
Carabao Cup (1): Brown 1.
Papa John's Trophy (6): Brown 3 (1 pen), Chilvers 1, Folivi 1, Poku 1.

Gerken D 33	Welch-Hayes M 35 + 3	Eastman T 45	Smith T 45	Bramall C 23	Stevenson B 26 + 6	Pell H 24 + 1	Adubofour-Poku K 27 + 6	Chilvers N 36 + 8	Gambin L 6 + 5	Brown J 28 + 12	Senior C 23 + 12	Cowan-Hall P 2 + 11	Marshall M — + 1	Harriott C 33 + 3	McLeod S — + 1	Norris L 7 + 10	Scarlett M 2 + 1	Bohui J — + 13	Sowunmi O 8 + 7	Folivi M 12 + 15	Lapslie T 6 + 7	Tchamadeu J 8 + 3	Clampin R 17 + 4	Oteh A 4 + 9	George S 13 + 2	Doherty J 4 + 1	Sarpeng-Wiredu B 19 + 1	Nouble F 20	Sayer H — + 4	Cracknell B — + 1	Stagg T — + 1	*Match No.*
1	2	3	4	5	6	7	8^{2}	9^{3}	10^{1}	11	12	13	14																			1
1	2	3	4	5	7		8^{1}	6	9^{3}	11	10^{2}	13		12	14																	2
1	2	3	4	5	7		9^{3}	6	14	11	10^{1}	13		8^{2}		12																3
1	2	3	4	5	7		9	6^{3}	14	11	10^{1}	13		8^{2}		12																4
1		3	4	5	7		9^{2}	6		11	10^{1}	14		8^{3}		12	2	13														5
1	13	3	4	5		7	9^{3}	6		10^{2}	12			8		11	2^{1}	14														6
1	2	3	4	5		7	10^{1}	6	9^{3}	11^{2}				8		12		13	14													7
1	2	3	4	5	8	6	10^{3}	9^{1}		11^{2}	14			7		12			13													8
1	2	3	4	5	8	6^{1}	12	9		13	7			10^{3}		11^{2}		14														9
1	2	3	4	5	7	6	9^{2}	13		11^{3}	8			10^{1}				12		14												10
1	2	3	4	5		7	8	6		11^{2}	10^{3}	14				13		12		9^{1}												11
1	2^{4}	3	4	5	9^{3}	6	7^{1}	8		11	10^{2}			12		15		14		13												12
1	2^{1}	3	4	5	9	6	7^{2}	8^{3}		11^{5}	10^{4}			14		13	15	16		12												13
1	2	3		5	6^{3}		9^{1}	7		11^{2}	8			10		13			4	12	14											14
1		3	4	5			13	7	6	9^{1}	10^{2}			8		11^{3}			14	12		2										15
1	2	3	4	5			14	6	7	9^{2}	10^{3}			8^{1}		11^{4}			12	13			15									16
1	2	3	4	5	7		8^{1}	6^{3}	13	9^{2}	12			10^{4}		11			15	14												17
1	2^{4}	3	4	5^{5}	6		9	13	7^{1}	14	10^{3}			8		11^{2}				12		15	16									18
1	14	3	4	5	7		13	6^{4}	15	11^{1}	10			8^{3}		12				9		2^{2}										19
1		2	4		7^{2}		8^{1}	6	12	11	10							14	3	9^{3}	13		5									20
1	2		4		6		8^{2}	9^{3}			12	14				11		13	3	10^{1}	7		5									21
1		2	4	5	6	7	8^{1}	9		11	12			10^{2}				13	3													22
1	13	2	4	5	6	7■	8^{2}	9		11^{3}				10^{1}					3	14				12								23
1	2	3	4	5	7		9^{1}	6		11^{2}	8			10						12				13								24
1^{2}	2	3	4	5	7^{1}		9^{3}	6		11^{4}	8			10						15	12			14	13							25
	2	3	4		12		8^{2}	6^{1}			13			10							7		14		1	5^{3}	9	11				26
	2	3	4		12	7	9^{4}	14			10^{2}			8							6^{3}		13	15	1	5^{1}		11				27
1	2	4	5		8	7^{1}	6^{3}	14		13				9^{4}					3	15				11^{2}			12	10				28
1	2	3	4		6		15	9^{4}		13	14			8^{1}						10^{2}				12^{5}		5	7^{3}	11	16			29
1^{1}	2	3	4				9^{4}	6		15	13			10								8^{2}		14	12	5^{5}	7	11^{3}	16			30
	5^{1}	2	4					6		13				9					3	12		8		11^{2}	1		7	10^{3}		14		31
		3	4					8		13	12			7^{4}					14	11^{2}		2	5^{3}	9^{1}	1		6	10■	15			32
		2	4			12	15	6^{3}		13		14		9					3^{1}	11^{2}		5	8	10^{4}	1		7					33
	2	3	4			6		12		9		8^{1}		10									5	13	1		7	11^{2}				34
	2	3	4			6		12		9		8^{1}		10									5		1		7	11				35
	2^{2}	3	4		6^{3}	8		9^{1}		11	12											13	5	14	1		7	10				36
1		3	4		7	6				11	8^{2}	13								12		2	5				9	10^{1}				37
1		3	4		7^{2}	6		14		11^{4}	8	15									13	2	5^{1}			12	9^{3}	10				38
1	2	3	4		13	7		10^{3}		12	8	14									6^{2}		5				9	11^{1}				39
1	2	3	4			6				9^{1}	8^{2}			10							12	13	5				7	11				40
1	2	3	4		16	6		15		12	10^{2}			8^{1}					13	14	7^{5}		5				9^{3}	11^{4}				41
	2	3	4		12	7		6^{4}		14	13			9^{1}						11^{3}	15		5		1		8^{2}	10				42
	2	3	4			7		6		12				9						11^{1}			5		1		8	10				43
	2	3	4		13	7		6						9						11^{1}			5	12	1		8^{2}	10				44
	2	3	4		7		6	9^{1}										12		11	13		5		1		8^{2}	10				45
	2	3	4				6^{1}	9^{3}										12		10	7		5		1		8	11^{2}	14		13	46

FA Cup

First Round Marine (h) 1-1

(aet; Marine won 5-3 on penalties)

Carabao Cup

First Round Reading (a) 1-3

Papa John's Trophy

Group A (S)	Portsmouth	(a)	0-2
Group A (S)	West Ham U U21	(h)	0-1
Group A (S)	Southend U	(h)	6-1

COVENTRY CITY

FOUNDATION

Workers at Singers' cycle factory formed a club in 1883. The first success of Singers FC was to win the Birmingham Junior Cup in 1891 and this led in 1894 to their election to the Birmingham & District League. Four years later they changed their name to Coventry City and joined the Southern League in 1908 at which time they were playing in blue and white quarters.

The Ricoh Arena, Phoenix Way, Foleshill, Coventry CV6 6GE.

Postal Address: Sky Blue Lodge, Leamington Road, Coventry CV8 3FL.

Telephone: (02476) 991 987.

Ticket Office: (02476) 991 987.

Website: www.ccfc.co.uk

Email: info@ccfc.co.uk

Ground Capacity: 32,753.

Record Attendance: 51,455 v Wolverhampton W, Division 2, 29 April 1967 (at Highfield Road); 31,407 v Chelsea, FA Cup 6th rd, 7 March 2009 (at Ricoh Arena).

Pitch Measurements: 100m × 65m (109.5yd × 71yd).

Chairman: Tim Fisher.

Chief Executive: David Boddy.

Manager: Mark Robins.

Assistant Manager: Adi Viveash.

Colours: Sky blue shirts with black trim, sky blue shorts with black trim, sky blue socks with black trim.

Year Formed: 1883.

Turned Professional: 1893.

Previous Name: 1883, Singers FC; 1898, Coventry City.

Club Nickname: 'Sky Blues'.

Grounds: 1883, Binley Road; 1887, Stoke Road; 1899, Highfield Road; 2005, Ricoh Arena; 2013, Sixfields Stadium (groundshare with Northampton T); 2014, Ricoh Arena; 2019, St Andrew's Trillion Trophy Stadium (groundshare with Birmingham C); 2021, Ricoh Arena.

First Football League Game: 30 August 1919, Division 2, v Tottenham H (h) L 0–5 – Lindon; Roberts, Chaplin, Allan, Hawley, Clarke, Sheldon, Mercer, Sambrooke, Lowes, Gibson.

Record League Victory: 9–0 v Bristol C, Division 3 (S), 28 April 1934 – Pearson; Brown, Bisby; Perry, Davidson, Frith; White (2), Lauderdale, Bourton (5), Jones (2), Lake.

Record Cup Victory: 8–0 v Rushden & D, League Cup 2nd rd, 2 October 2002 – Debec; Caldwell, Quinn, Betts (1p), Konjic (Shaw), Davenport, Pipe, Safri (Stanford), Mills (2) (Bothroyd (2)), McSheffery (3), Partridge.

Record Defeat: 2–10 v Norwich C, Division 3 (S), 15 March 1930.

HONOURS

League Champions: Division 2 – 1966–67; FL 1 – 2019–20.
Division 3 – 1963–64; Division 3S – 1935–36.
Runners-up: Division 3S – 1933–34; Division 4 – 1958–59.

FA Cup Winners: 1987.

League Cup: semi-final – 1981, 1990.

League Trophy Winners: 2017.

European Competitions
Fairs Cup: 1970–71.

FOOTBALL YEARBOOK FACT FILE

There was a remarkable start to Coventry City's game at Cardiff City on 16 January 1935 with four goals scored in the first five minutes. Clarrie Bourton put the Sky Blues in front in the first minute, only for Cardiff to equalise almost immediately without an opposition player touching the ball. Les Jones regained the lead for the visitors only for Cardiff to level the score almost straight away. The game then calmed down, with Coventry ending up 4-2 winners.

Most League Points (2 for a win): 60, Division 4, 1958–59 and Division 3, 1963–64.

Most League Points (3 for a win): 75, FL 2, 2017–18.

Most League Goals: 108, Division 3 (S), 1931–32.

Highest League Scorer in Season: Clarrie Bourton, 49, Division 3 (S), 1931–32.

Most League Goals in Total Aggregate: Clarrie Bourton, 173, 1931–37.

Most League Goals in One Match: 5, Clarrie Bourton v Bournemouth, Division 3 (S), 17 October 1931; 5, Arthur Bacon v Gillingham, Division 3 (S), 30 December 1933.

Most Capped Player: Magnus Hedman, 44 (58), Sweden.

Most League Appearances: Steve Ogrizovic, 507, 1984–2000.

Youngest League Player: Ben Mackey, 16 years 167 days v Ipswich T, 12 April 2003.

Record Transfer Fee Received: £13,000,000 from Internazionale for Robbie Keane, July 2000.

Record Transfer Fee Paid: £6,500,000 to Norwich C for Craig Bellamy, August 2000.

Football League Record: 1919 Elected to Division 2; 1925–26 Division 3 (N); 1926–36 Division 3 (S); 1936–52 Division 2; 1952–58 Division 3 (S); 1958–59 Division 4; 1959–64 Division 3; 1964–67 Division 2; 1967–92 Division 1; 1992–2001 Premier League; 2001–04 Division 1; 2004–12 FL C; 2012–17 FL 1; 2017–18 FL 2; 2018–20 FL 1; 2020– FL C.

LATEST SEQUENCES

Longest Sequence of League Wins: 6, 25.4.1964 – 5.9.1964.

Longest Sequence of League Defeats: 9, 30.8.1919 – 11.10.1919.

Longest Sequence of League Draws: 6, 1.11.2003 – 29.11.2003.

Longest Sequence of Unbeaten League Matches: 25, 26.11.1966 – 13.5.1967.

Longest Sequence Without a League Win: 19, 30.8.1919 – 20.12.1919.

Successive Scoring Runs: 25 from 10.9.1966.

Successive Non-scoring Runs: 11 from 11.10.1919.

MANAGERS

H. R. Buckle 1909–10
Robert Wallace 1910–13
(Secretary-Manager)
Frank Scott-Walford 1913–15
William Clayton 1917–19
H. Pollitt 1919–20
Albert Evans 1920–24
Jimmy Kerr 1924–28
James McIntyre 1928–31
Harry Storer 1931–45
Dick Bayliss 1945–47
Billy Frith 1947–48
Harry Storer 1948–53
Jack Fairbrother 1953–54
Charlie Elliott 1954–55
Jesse Carver 1955–56
George Raynor 1956
Harry Warren 1956–57
Billy Frith 1957–61
Jimmy Hill 1961–67
Noel Cantwell 1967–72
Bob Dennison 1972
Joe Mercer 1972–75
Gordon Milne 1972–81
Dave Sexton 1981–83
Bobby Gould 1983–84
Don Mackay 1985–86
George Curtis 1986–87
(became Managing Director)
John Sillett 1987–90
Terry Butcher 1990–92
Don Howe 1992
Bobby Gould 1992–93
(with Don Howe, June 1992)
Phil Neal 1993–95
Ron Atkinson 1995–96
(became Director of Football)
Gordon Strachan 1996–2001
Roland Nilsson 2001–02
Gary McAllister 2002–04
Eric Black 2004
Peter Reid 2004–05
Micky Adams 2005–07
Iain Dowie 2007–08
Chris Coleman 2008–10
Aidy Boothroyd 2010–11
Andy Thorn 2011–12
Mark Robins 2012–13
Steven Pressley 2013–15
Tony Mowbray 2015–16
Russell Slade 2016–17
Mark Robins March 2017–

TEN YEAR LEAGUE RECORD

		P	W	D	L	F	A	Pts	Pos
2011-12	FL C	46	9	13	24	41	65	40	23
2012-13	FL 1	46	18	11	17	66	59	55*	15
2013-14	FL 1	46	16	13	17	74	77	51*	18
2014-15	FL 1	46	13	16	17	49	60	55	17
2015-16	FL 1	46	19	12	15	67	49	69	8
2016-17	FL 1	46	9	12	25	37	68	39	23
2017-18	FL 2	46	22	9	15	64	47	75	6
2018-19	FL 1	46	18	11	17	54	54	65	8
2019-20	FL 1	34	18	13	3	48	30	67	1§
2020-21	FL C	46	14	13	19	49	61	55	16

** 10 pts deducted. §Decided on points-per-game (1.97)*

DID YOU KNOW 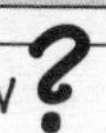

Reg Matthews was only the second player from the third division, and the only goalkeeper, to win a full cap for England. Matthews, who made his England debut against Scotland at Hampden in March 1956, made over 100 appearances for Coventry City before being transferred to Chelsea in November 1956 for £22,000, a British record fee for a goalkeeper at the time.

COVENTRY CITY – SKY BET CHAMPIONSHIP 2020–21 LEAGUE RECORD

Match No.	Date	Venue	Opponents	Result		H/T Score	Lg Pos.	Goalscorers	Attendance
1	Sept 12	A	Bristol C	L	1-2	1-1	14	Godden 33	0
2	18	H	QPR	W	3-2	1-1	11	Godden 44, O'Hare 50, McFadzean 84	0
3	26	A	Barnsley	D	0-0	0-0	13		0
4	Oct 2	H	Bournemouth	L	1-3	1-1	15	Godden (pen) 39	0
5	17	A	Brentford	L	0-2	0-0	19		0
6	20	H	Swansea C	D	1-1	1-1	18	Shipley 19	0
7	24	H	Blackburn R	L	0-4	0-1	20		0
8	27	A	Middlesbrough	L	0-2	0-0	21		0
9	30	H	Reading	W	3-2	1-0	18	Hamer 23, Godden 76, McCallum 85	0
10	Nov 4	A	Nottingham F	L	1-2	0-1	21	O'Hare 57	0
11	7	A	Watford	L	2-3	0-0	21	Hamer 63, Walker 64	0
12	20	H	Birmingham C	D	0-0	0-0	21		0
13	25	H	Cardiff C	W	1-0	0-0	21	Walker 54	0
14	28	A	Norwich C	D	1-1	0-1	20	Biamou 89	0
15	Dec 1	A	Derby Co	D	1-1	0-0	19	Hamer 90	0
16	5	H	Rotherham U	W	3-1	2-0	19	Biamou 5, Walker 12, Smith (og) 72	0
17	8	H	Luton T	D	0-0	0-0	19		0
18	12	A	Wycombe W	W	2-1	2-0	18	Kelly 2 34, 45	2000
19	16	H	Huddersfield T	D	0-0	0-0	18		0
20	19	A	Sheffield W	L	0-1	0-0	18		0
21	26	H	Stoke C	D	0-0	0-0	18		0
22	29	A	Preston NE	L	0-2	0-1	17		0
23	Jan 2	A	Millwall	W	2-1	2-0	16	Cooper (og) 20, Hamer 26	0
24	19	A	Reading	L	0-3	0-1	18		0
25	27	H	Sheffield W	W	2-0	0-0	17	Gyokeres 57, Allen 90	0
26	30	A	Birmingham C	D	1-1	1-1	17	Hamer 29	0
27	Feb 2	H	Nottingham F	L	1-2	1-1	18	Biamou 17	0
28	6	H	Watford	D	0-0	0-0	19		0
29	13	A	Cardiff C	L	1-3	0-2	20	Hyam 81	0
30	17	H	Norwich C	L	0-2	0-2	20		0
31	20	H	Brentford	W	2-0	1-0	20	Walker 2 (1 pen) 19 (p), 54	0
32	24	A	Swansea C	L	0-1	0-0	20		0
33	27	A	Blackburn R	D	1-1	0-1	20	James 50	0
34	Mar 2	H	Middlesbrough	L	1-2	1-1	20	Dijksteel (og) 11	0
35	6	H	Derby Co	W	1-0	1-0	20	Biamou 11	0
36	16	A	Luton T	L	0-2	0-2	20		0
37	20	H	Wycombe W	D	0-0	0-0	20		0
38	Apr 2	A	QPR	L	0-3	0-2	21		0
39	5	H	Bristol C	W	3-1	1-0	20	Ostigard 9, Godden (pen) 63, Gyokeres 87	0
40	10	A	Bournemouth	L	1-4	1-2	21	James 3	0
41	15	A	Rotherham U	W	1-0	0-0	18	Ostigard 70	0
42	18	H	Barnsley	W	2-0	1-0	18	Hyam 9, Godden 90	0
43	21	A	Stoke C	W	3-2	1-0	15	Walker 44, Biamou 68, Gyokeres 78	0
44	24	H	Preston NE	L	0-1	0-0	19		0
45	May 1	A	Huddersfield T	D	1-1	0-0	17	Shipley 69	0
46	8	H	Millwall	W	6-1	2-0	16	Shipley 16, McFadzean 45, Hyam 59, O'Hare 62, James 67, Walker 84	0

Final League Position: 16

GOALSCORERS

League (49): Walker 7 (1 pen), Godden 6 (2 pens), Biamou 5, Hamer 5, Gyokeres 3, Hyam 3, James 3, O'Hare 3, Shipley 3, Kelly 2, McFadzean 2, Ostigard 2, Allen 1, McCallum 1, own goals 3.
FA Cup (0).
Carabao Cup (2): Biamou 1, Walker 1.

Marosi M 20	Ostigard L 35 + 4	McFadzean K 37 + 1	Hyam D 43	Pask J 6 + 11	Hamer G 36 + 6	Kelly L 21 + 2	Giles R 15 + 4	O'Hare C 40 + 6	Allen J 16 + 6	Godden M 18 + 5	Shipley J 15 + 12	Sheaf B 21 + 9	Walker T 20 + 11	Dabo F 25 + 3	Rose M 15 + 2	McCallum S 37 + 4	Bakayoko A 2 + 12	Biamou M 20 + 14	Kastaneer G — + 2	Da Costa J 10 + 8	Wilson B 26 + 1	Jobello W — + 3	Bapaga W — + 2	James M 19 + 4	Gyokeres V 7 + 12	Thompson J — + 2	Eccles J 2 + 5	Burroughs J — + 2	Match No.
1	2	3	4	5	6^{2}	7^{1}	8	9	10^{3}	11	12	13	14																1
1	2	3	4		6		8	11	9	10	7^{1}	12		5															2
1	2	3	4		6		8	11	9^{2}	10	13	7^{1}	12	5															3
1	2^{2}	3	4		6■		8^{3}	9	12	11	10^{1}	7		5	13	14													4
1		4	5	2^{2}			6	9	7	11	12	8			3	13	10^{1}												5
1		3	4	13		12	8	10	9	11	6^{1}	7			2	5^{2}													6
1		3	4	13		6	8	10^{3}	9	11^{1}		7			2■	5^{2}		12	14										7
1	2	3	4		6		8^{1}	14	9^{3}	11	10^{2}	7	13	12		5													8
1	3		4		6^{1}		8	12	14	10	9^{3}	7		5^{2}	2	13		11											9
1	5	4			7		6^{2}	9		10^{1}		8	12		3	2		11		13									10
1	3		4		6^{1}		9	8	12			7	10		2	5^{2}		11		13									11
1	12	3	4		8	6	14	9			10^{1}	7^{2}	11	2^{3}		5		13											12
1^{3}	13	3	4		7^{1}	6	8	12			10^{2}	9	11	2		5					14								13
	3	4	5		12	8^{5}	6	7	10^{1}		13	9^{2}	14	2^{4}			11^{3}	16			1	15							14
	14	3	4		7	6	10	8^{4}			9^{1}		11^{2}	2		5^{3}	15	13			1	12							15
	2	3	4		6	7		11					9^{1}	5		8	12	10			1								16
	2	3	4		7	6		9^{1}			12		10^{2}	5		8	13	11			1								17
	2	3	4		12	6^{2}		9			10^{1}	7	11^{3}	5		8	13	14			1								18
	2	3	4		6		13	9^{2}	10			7	11^{1}	5^{3}		8		12		14	1								19
	2^{4}	3	4				14	9	6	15		7^{5}	11^{1}	5^{2}		8	12	10^{3}	16	13	1								20
	2	3	4		7			11^{3}	8	10^{1}	14	5^{2}		6		9	12	13			1								21
	2	3	4		6		9^{3}	10^{1}	8^{4}	11	12	7^{2}		5		14		13			1		15						22
	2	3	4		6		13	9		11^{1}	10^{2}	7		5		8		12			1								23
	2^{5}	3■	4		6			9			11^{4}	13		5^{2}		8		12		14	1		15	7^{3}	10^{1}	16			24
	3		4	12	7			9	15		13	6^{2}		2^{1}		5	14	10^{4}			1			8	11^{3}				25
	3		4	2	8			9			12	6^{1}				5		10			1			7	11				26
1	3		4	2^{1}	6			9				8^{2}			12	5	14^{4}	10		13		15		7	11^{3}				27
1	3		4	12	7^{2}			10^{3}	6		14				2	9		11		5^{1}				8	13				28
1	3^{1}	12	4		9^{2}			10	6		15		13		2	8^{3}		11^{4}		5				7	14				29
	12	3	4	14	10	16		9	6^{2}		8		11^{4}		2^{1}			13		5^{3}	1			7^{5}	15				30
	2	3	4	16	6^{3}	7^{1}		9				14	10^{4}			8	15	11^{2}		5^{5}	1			12	13				31
	2	3	4		6^{3}	7^{2}		9^{5}				14	10	12		8	16	11^{4}		5^{1}	1			13	15				32
	2■	3	4	13	14	6		12			7^{2}		10^{4}	5^{1}		8		11			1			9^{3}	15				33
		3	4		6	7^{1}		9					10	5	2	8		11			1			12					34
	2	3	4	13	6^{1}	7		10^{3}	12			14		5^{2}		9		11			1			8					35
	2	3■	4		6^{2}	7		10^{3}		14		12	15	5^{1}		9		11^{4}		13	1			8					36
	3		4	14	6	7^{2}		10^{4}		16		15	13	5^{1}	2^{3}	9		11^{5}		12	1			8					37
1	3		4	15	6^{5}			12	9^{3}	11^{2}	10^{1}		14		2^{4}	8				5				7	13		16		38
1	2	3		4	13	6^{2}		9		10^{1}			11			8								7	12		5		39
1	4	3		2^{1}	13	6^{2}		9^{4}	16	10^{3}			11^{5}			8	15							7	14	12	5		40
	2	3	4		14	6		9^{3}		10^{2}			11^{1}			8		13		5	1			7	12				41
	2	3	4		9^{2}	6		12		14			10^{1}			8		11^{3}		5	1			7	13				42
	2	3	4		7^{2}	6^{1}		9		11^{3}			10^{4}			8		15		5	1			12	14		13		43
		3	4		7^{1}			9^{4}		13			14	15	2	8	16	11^{3}		5^{5}	1			6	10^{2}		12		44
		3	4	15	6^{3}			9			12		11^{1}	5^{2}	2^{4}	8					1			7	10		14	13	45
1		3	2		7^{2}			9			10^{5}	15	16	5^{1}	4^{3}	8		14						6	11^{4}		12	13	46

FA Cup
Third Round Norwich C (a) 0-2

Carabao Cup
First Round Milton Keynes D (a) 1-0
Second Round Gillingham (a) 1-1
(Gillingham won 5-4 on penalties)

CRAWLEY TOWN

FOUNDATION

Formed in 1896, Crawley Town initially entered the West Sussex League before switching to the mid-Sussex League in 1901, winning the Second Division in its second season. The club remained at such level until 1951 when it became members of the Sussex County League and five years later moved to the Metropolitan League while remaining as an amateur club. It was not until 1962 that the club turned semi-professional and a year later, joined the Southern League. Many honours came the club's way, but the most successful run was achieved in 2010–11 when they reached the fifith round of the FA Cup and played before a crowd of 74,778 spectators at Old Trafford against Manchester United. Crawley Town spent 48 years at the Town Mead ground before a new site was occupied at Broadfield in 1997, ideally suited to access from the neighbouring motorway. History was also made on 9 April when the team won promotion to the Football League after beating Tamworth 3-0 to stretch their unbeaten League record to 26 games. They finished the season with a Conference record points total of 105 and at the same time, established another milestone for the longest unbeaten run, having extended it to 30 matches by the end of the season.

The People's Pension Stadium, Winfield Way, Crawley, West Sussex RH11 9RX.

Telephone: (01293) 410 000.

Ticket Office: (01293) 410 000.

Website: www.crawleytownfc.com

Email: feedback@crawleytownfc.com

Ground Capacity: 5,907.

Record Attendance: 5,880 v Reading, FA Cup 3rd rd, 5 January 2013.

Pitch Measurements: 103.5m × 66m (113yd × 72yd).

Chairman: Ziya Eren.

Managing Director: Selim Gaygusuz.

Head Coach: John Yems.

Assistant Head Coach: Lee Bradbury.

Colours: Red shirts with white trim, red shorts with white trim, red socks with white trim.

Year Formed: 1896. ***Turned Professional:*** 1962.

Club Nickname: 'The Red Devils'.

Grounds: Up to 1997, Town Mead; 1997 Broadfield Stadium (renamed Checkatrade.com Stadium 2013; The People's Pension Stadium 2018).

HONOURS

League Champions: Conference – 2010–11.
FL 2 – (3rd) 2011–12 *(promoted)*.

FA Cup: 5th rd – 2011, 2012.

League Cup: 3rd rd – 2013.

FOOTBALL YEARBOOK FACT FILE

Crawley Town's first-ever FA Cup tie took place on 6 September 1958 when Corinthian League side Horsham visited Town Mead for a preliminary qualifying round fixture. Crawley went down to a 1-0 defeat after conceding in the 38th minute, but 12 months later they gained their first win in the competition when they beat Southwick 6-1, also in the preliminary round.

First Football League Game: 6 August 2011, FL 2 v Port Vale (a) D 2–2 – Shearer; Hunt, Howell, Bulman, McFadzean (1), Dempster (Thomas), Simpson, Torres, Tubbs (Neilson), Barnett (1) (Wassmer), Smith.

Record League Victory: 5–1 v Barnsley, FL 1, 14 February 2015 – Price; Dickson, Bradley (1), Ward, Fowler (Smith); Young, Elliott (1), Edwards, Wordsworth (Morgan), Pogba (Tomlin); McLeod (3).

Record League Defeat: 6–0 v Morecambe, FL 2, 10 September 2011.

Most League Points (3 for a win): 84, FL 2, 2011–12.

Most League Goals: 76, FL 2, 2011–12.

Highest League Scorer in Season: James Collins, 20, FL 2, 2016–17.

Most League Goals in Total Aggregate: Ollie Palmer, 27, 2018–20.

Most League Goals in One Match: 3, Izale McLeod v Barnsley, FL 1, 14 February 2015; 3, Jimmy Smith v Colchester U, FL 2, 14 February 2017; 3, Max Watters v Barrow, FL 2, 12 December 2020.

Most Capped Player: Ricky German, 2, Grenada.

Most League Appearances: Dannie Bulman, 224, 2006–09; 2010–14; 2017–21.

MANAGERS

John Maggs 1978–90
Brian Sparrow 1990–92
Steve Wicks 1992–93
Ted Shepherd 1993–95
Colin Pates 1995–96
Billy Smith 1997–99
Cliff Cant 1999–2000
Billy Smith 2000–03
Francis Vines 2003–05
John Hollins 2005–06
David Woozley, Ben Judge and John Yems 2006–07
Steve Evans 2007–12
Sean O'Driscoll 2012
Richie Barker 2012–13
John Gregory 2013–14
Dean Saunders 2014–15
Mark Yates 2015–16
Dermot Drummy 2016–17
Harry Kewell 2017–18
Gabriele Cioffi 2018–19
John Yems December 2019–

Youngest League Player: Brian Galach, 17 years 353 days v Tranmere R, 4 May 2019.

Record Transfer Fee Received: £1,100,000 from Peterborough U for Tyrone Barnett, July 2012.

Record Transfer Fee Paid: £220,000 to York C for Richard Brodie, August 2010.

Football League Record: 2011 Promoted from Conference Premier; 2011–12 FL 2; 2012–15 FL 1; 2015– FL 2.

LATEST SEQUENCES

Longest Sequence of League Wins: 7, 17.9.2011 – 25.10.2011.

Longest Sequence of League Defeats: 8, 28.3.2016 – 7.5.2016.

Longest Sequence of League Draws: 5, 25.10.2014 – 29.11.2014.

Longest Sequence of Unbeaten League Matches: 13, 17.9.2011 – 17.12.2011.

Longest Sequence Without a League Win: 13, 25.10.2014 – 27.1.2015.

Successive Scoring Runs: 21 from 6.4.2019.

Successive Non-scoring Runs: 4 from 14.10.2017.

TEN YEAR LEAGUE RECORD

		P	*W*	*D*	*L*	*F*	*A*	*Pts*	*Pos*
2011-12	FL 2	46	23	15	8	76	54	84	3
2012-13	FL 1	46	18	14	14	59	58	68	10
2013-14	FL 1	46	14	15	17	48	54	57	14
2014-15	FL 1	46	13	11	22	53	79	50	22
2015-16	FL 2	46	13	8	25	45	78	47	20
2016-17	FL 2	46	13	12	21	53	71	51	19
2017-18	FL 2	46	16	11	19	58	66	59	14
2018-19	FL 2	46	15	8	23	51	68	53	19
2019-20	FL 2	37	11	15	11	51	47	48	13§
2020-21	FL 2	46	16	13	17	56	62	61	12

§*Decided on points-per-game (1.30)*

DID YOU KNOW ?

After defeating Cirencester Town in an FA Cup fourth qualifying round tie in 2003–04, Crawley Town failed to win a single match in the competition for seven years. They return to success in some style in 2010–11, however, defeating Swindon Town, Derby County and Torquay United before losing at Old Trafford in the fifth round.

CRAWLEY TOWN – SKY BET LEAGUE TWO 2020–21 LEAGUE RECORD

Match No.	*Date*	*Venue*	*Opponents*	*Result*		*H/T Score*	*Lg Pos.*	*Goalscorers*	*Attendance*
1	Sept 12	A	Port Vale	L	0-2	0-1	22		0
2	19	H	Scunthorpe U	W	1-0	1-0	13	Nichols [15]	0
3	26	A	Oldham Ath	W	3-2	2-1	4	Nadesan [31], Francomb [39], Nichols [69]	0
4	Oct 3	H	Southend U	D	1-1	1-0	7	Nadesan [21]	0
5	10	A	Cheltenham T	L	0-2	0-1	11		0
6	17	H	Morecambe	W	4-0	0-0	9	Francomb [52], Watters 2 [67, 71], Frost [77]	0
7	20	A	Exeter C	L	1-2	1-0	12	Watters [40]	0
8	24	A	Salford C	D	1-1	0-0	13	Francomb [72]	0
9	27	H	Tranmere R	W	4-0	3-0	9	Watters [13], Nichols [21], Tunnicliffe [24], Frost [77]	0
10	31	H	Cambridge U	W	2-1	1-1	7	Watters [44], Nichols [56]	0
11	Nov 3	A	Walsall	L	0-1	0-0	8		0
12	14	A	Harrogate T	D	1-1	1-0	9	Watters [27]	0
13	21	H	Carlisle U	L	0-3	0-1	12		0
14	24	H	Grimsby T	L	1-2	1-1	15	Watters [4]	0
15	Dec 1	A	Colchester U	D	1-1	1-1	13	Tunnicliffe [20]	0
16	5	A	Mansfield T	D	3-3	0-1	15	Watters 2 [49, 59], Dallison [54]	0
17	12	H	Barrow	W	4-2	1-1	13	Watters 3 [23, 58, 90], Nichols (pen) [81]	0
18	15	H	Bradford C	D	1-1	1-1	13	Pritchard (og) [25]	0
19	19	A	Leyton Orient	W	2-1	1-1	11	Matthews [14], Watters [82]	0
20	26	H	Newport Co	D	1-1	1-1	10	Demetriou (og) [32]	0
21	29	A	Forest Green R	W	2-1	1-0	9	Nichols 2 [16, 79]	0
22	Jan 2	A	Bolton W	W	1-0	0-0	6	Francomb [61]	0
23	30	A	Cambridge U	L	1-3	1-2	12	Hessenthaler [14]	0
24	Feb 2	H	Leyton Orient	D	0-0	0-0	11		0
25	6	H	Harrogate T	L	1-3	0-3	11	Dallison [53]	0
26	16	H	Stevenage	L	0-1	0-0	13		0
27	20	H	Colchester U	W	1-0	0-0	12	Tilley [90]	0
28	23	A	Grimsby T	L	1-2	1-1	14	Powell [30]	0
29	27	H	Exeter C	W	2-0	0-0	13	Nichols (pen) [62], Nadesan [83]	0
30	Mar 2	A	Morecambe	L	1-3	1-1	14	Nadesan [13]	0
31	6	A	Tranmere R	W	1-0	0-0	12	Nichols [58]	0
32	9	H	Salford C	W	1-0	1-0	11	Nichols [21]	0
33	13	H	Mansfield T	W	1-0	0-0	10	Tilley [90]	0
34	16	H	Walsall	D	1-1	0-0	10	Nichols (pen) [90]	0
35	20	A	Barrow	L	2-3	1-2	10	Francomb [31], Powell [84]	0
36	27	H	Port Vale	L	1-3	1-1	11	Nadesan [45]	0
37	30	A	Carlisle U	L	0-2	0-2	12		0
38	Apr 2	A	Scunthorpe U	D	0-0	0-0	13		0
39	5	H	Oldham Ath	L	1-4	0-2	14	Tilley [90]	0
40	10	A	Southend U	D	0-0	0-0	15		0
41	13	A	Bradford C	W	2-0	1-0	13	Tunnicliffe [20], McNerney [86]	0
42	16	H	Cheltenham T	W	1-0	0-0	10	Maguire-Drew [77]	0
43	20	A	Newport Co	L	0-2	0-0	12		0
44	24	H	Forest Green R	D	0-0	0-0	13		0
45	May 1	A	Stevenage	D	3-3	1-1	12	Francomb [24], Vancooten (og) [79], Powell [90]	0
46	8	H	Bolton W	L	1-4	0-2	12	Rodari [89]	0

Final League Position: 12

GOALSCORERS

League (56): Watters 13, Nichols 11 (3 pens), Francomb 6, Nadesan 5, Powell 3, Tilley 3, Tunnicliffe 3, Dallison 2, Frost 2, Hessenthaler 1, Maguire-Drew 1, Matthews 1, McNerney 1, Rodari 1, own goals 3.
FA Cup (12): Nichols 4 (1 pen), Nadesan 3, Tunnicliffe 2, Watters 2, Tsaroulla 1.
Carabao Cup (1): Ashford 1.
Papa John's Trophy (4): Galach 2, Ferguson 1, Watters 1.

Morris G 45	Davies A 18 + 16	Tunnicliffe J 39	Craig T 36 + 2	Doherty J 14 + 1	Ferguson N 4 + 5	Francomb G 32 + 1	Frost T 10 + 13	Powell J 40 + 4	Ashford S 2 + 6	Nadesan A 30 + 10	German R 1 + 3	Hessenthaler J 42 + 4	Nichols T 42 + 1	Matthews S 21 + 9	Bulman D 4 + 2	Allarakhia T 8 + 9	McNerney J 23 + 3	Watters M 12 + 3	Hesketh J 11 + 4	McGill T — + 1	Nelson S 1	Dallison T 12 + 2	Sesay D 5 + 8	Adebowale E 1	Tsaroulla N 14 + 3	Wright J 15 + 5	Maguire-Drew J 14 + 3	Tilley J 8 + 10	Rodari D 1 + 11	Wright M 1	*Match No.*
1	2	3	4	5	6	7	8^{3}	9^{1}	10^{2}	11	12	13	14																		1
1		3	4	5	8	2	9				11^{1}	13	10^{3}	6^{2}	7	12	14														2
1		3	4	5	7^{2}	2	6	13		10	14	12	11^{3}		8^{1}	9															3
1		3	4	5	8	2	6	12		11	13	7	10^{2}			9^{1}															4
1	14	3	4	5	13	2^{3}	10^{2}			8		6	11	12	7	9^{1}															5
1		3	4	5	14	2	6^{2}	8^{3}		10^{1}		7	11	9		13		12													6
1		3	4	5	13	2	9^{3}	7				8^{2}	11	6		14		10^{1}	12												7
1	13	3	4	5^{2}		2		8	12			7	11	6				10	9^{1}												8
1		3	4	5		2	12	8	13			7	11^{3}	6^{1}		14		10^{2}	9												9
1	13	3	4	5		2^{2}	14	7		12		8	10	6^{3}				11^{1}	9■												10
1^{1}	2	3	4	5			9^{2}	8	6^{3}	13		7	11			14		10		12											11
	2		4	5			12	7		11		8	9			6^{2}	3	10^{1}			1	13									12
1	2^{1}		4	5			14	7		10		8^{2}	11			6^{3}	3	13	9				12■								13
1			4	5			13	7	14	12		8	11^{3}	6^{1}			3	10	9^{2}					2							14
1		2	3				13	7	14	9		6	10^{2}	12				11^{3}				4	5		8^{1}						15
1		3	4				13	7		10^{2}		9	11^{4}	14	8^{3}		15	12				5	2		6^{1}						16
1	14	3	4		12		9^{2}	7		13		8	11	6^{1}				10				5^{3}	2								17
1	2	3	4		12			8	14	13		9	10^{3}	7^{2}				11				5^{1}			6						18
1	2^{1}	3	4					7		13		8	11	6^{2}	14	9^{3}		10				5	12								19
1	2^{3}	3	4			14		6		11^{2}		7	9	12		8■		10^{1}	13			5									20
1	12	3	4			7^{1}	14	8		13		9	11	10								5	2^{2}		6^{3}						21
1	2	4	3			7^{2}		6	13	10^{3}		8	11	9^{1}	12							5	14								22
1	15	4	3	14		2		6^{1}				7^{2}	10	9								5^{3}				8	11^{4}	12	13		23
1	12	3^{3}	4			2		7		11		6^{4}	10	9^{2}			14					5^{1}				8		13	15		24
1	15		3			2	16	8^{1}		10^{2}		9^{4}	11	6^{5}		13	4					12				7	14			5^{3}	25
1	12	3	4			2	10^{1}	9		13		8^{2}	11									5				7	6				26
1	12	3	4			2		7		10		8^{4}	11	14					9^{3}			5^{1}				15	6^{2}	13			27
1	12	3				2		8		10^{4}		6	11	5^{1}		14	4		13							7^{3}		9^{2}	15		28
1	13	3				2^{2}		7		9		6	10				4		12				15		8^{3}		5^{4}	14	11^{1}		29
1		2				4	14	7		10		6^{3}	11				3		9^{1}						8^{2}	12	5	13			30
1	2	4				5	12	8		11^{3}		7	10				3		9^{1}								6^{2}	13	14		31
1	2	3				5		8		10		7	11				4		9^{2}				13			12	6^{1}				32
1	2	3				5		8		10		7	11				4		9^{2}							12	6^{1}	13			33
1	2^{2}	3	13			5^{3}		8		10		7^{5}	11				4		9^{1}						15	14	6^{4}	12	16		34
1	7^{1}	3^{2}	5			2		11		12		6	10				4								13	8	14	9^{3}			35
1			4			2		7		10		8	11	13		12	3						5^{3}		14		6^{1}	9^{2}			36
1	13		4			2		8^{1}		10^{3}		6	11	12		9^{2}	3								5	7		14			37
1			4			2		7				9	11	12			3								5	8	6^{1}	10			38
1	14	3	4			5^{3}		6		12		7	11	10^{1}			2^{2}						15		9^{4}	8		13			39
1	2	3						13		10^{3}		7^{2}	11	12			4								5	8	6^{1}	9	14		40
1	2	3						7		10^{2}		12	11	6^{1}			4								5	8		9	13		41
1	2	3	13					7		10		8	11	6^{2}			4								5		12	9^{1}			42
1	2	3	5^{3}					13		10		7	11■	6^{1}			4						14			8		9^{2}	12		43
1	14	4	5			2^{3}		8		10		7		11		12	3									6^{1}	9^{2}		13		44
1	12	3	5			2	13	8		11		7					4^{3}								9^{1}	10	6^{2}		14		45
1	5^{2}	2	4			6■	14	9		11^{3}		7					3^{1}						13		8	10			12		46

FA Cup

First Round *(aet)*	Torquay U	(a)	6-5
Second Round	AFC Wimbledon	(a)	2-1
Third Round	Leeds U	(h)	3-0
Fourth Round	Bournemouth	(a)	1-2

Carabao Cup

First Round	Millwall	(h)	1-3

Papa John's Trophy

Group B (S)	Gillingham	(a)	1-2
Group B (S)	Arsenal U21	(h)	1-2
Group B (S)	Ipswich T	(h)	2-0

CREWE ALEXANDRA

FOUNDATION

The first match played at Crewe was on 1 December 1877 against Basford, the leading North Staffordshire team of that time. During the club's history they have also played in a number of other leagues including the Football Alliance, Football Combination, Lancashire League, Manchester League, Central League and Lancashire Combination. Two former players, Aaron Scragg in 1899 and Jackie Pearson in 1911, had the distinction of refereeing FA Cup finals. Pearson was also capped for England against Ireland in 1892.

The Alexandra Stadium, Gresty Road, Crewe, Cheshire CW2 6EB.

Telephone: (01270) 213 014.

Ticket Office: (01270) 252 610.

Website: www.crewealex.net

Email: info@crewealex.net

Ground Capacity: 10,109.

Record Attendance: 20,000 v Tottenham H, FA Cup 4th rd, 30 January 1960.

Pitch Measurements: 100.5m × 67m (110yd × 73.5yd).

Chairman: Charles Grant.

Manager: David Artell.

Assistant Manager: Kenny Lunt.

Colours: Red shirts with black trim, white shorts, red socks.

Year Formed: 1877. ***Turned Professional:*** 1893. ***Club Nickname:*** 'The Railwaymen'.

Ground: 1898, Gresty Road.

First Football League Game: 3 September 1892, Division 2, v Burton Swifts (a) L 1–7 – Hickton; Moore, Cope; Linnell, Johnson, Osborne; Bennett, Pearson (1), Bailey, Barnett, Roberts.

Record League Victory: 8–0 v Rotherham U, Division 3 (N), 1 October 1932 – Foster; Pringle, Dawson; Ward, Keenor (1), Turner (1); Gillespie, Swindells (1), McConnell (2), Deacon (2), Weale (1).

Record Cup Victory: 8–0 v Hartlepool U, Auto Windscreens Shield 1st rd, 17 October 1995 – Gayle; Collins (1), Booty, Westwood (Unsworth), Macauley (1), Whalley (1), Garvey (1), Murphy (1), Savage (1) (Rivers (1p)), Lennon, Edwards, (1 og). 8–0 v Doncaster R, LDV Vans Trophy 3rd rd, 10 November 2002 – Bankole; Wright, Walker, Foster, Tierney; Lunt (1), Brammer, Sorvel, Vaughan (1) (Bell); Ashton (3) (Miles), Jack (2) (Jones (1)).

Record Defeat: 2–13 v Tottenham H, FA Cup 4th rd replay, 3 February 1960.

HONOURS

League: *Runners-up:* Second Division – 2002–03; FL 2 – 2019–20.

FA Cup: semi-final – 1888.

League Cup: never past 3rd rd.

League Trophy Winners: 2013.

Welsh Cup Winners: 1936, 1937.

FOOTBALL YEARBOOK FACT FILE

Crewe Alexandra defeated Hartlepool 8-0 in an Auto Windscreens Shield group match in September 1995 with the goals coming from eight different players. Wayne Collins began the scoring spree, with the final goal coming from substitute Mark Rivers. Seven different Crewe players found the net with an own goal completing the scoring.

Most League Points (2 for a win): 59, Division 4, 1962–63.

Most League Points (3 for a win): 86, Division 2, 2002–03.

Most League Goals: 95, Division 3 (N), 1931–32.

Highest League Scorer in Season: Terry Harkin, 35, Division 4, 1964–65.

Most League Goals in Total Aggregate: Bert Swindells, 126, 1928–37.

Most League Goals in One Match: 5, Tony Naylor v Colchester U, Division 3, 24 April 1993.

Most Capped Player: Clayton Ince, 38 (79), Trinidad & Tobago.

Most League Appearances: Tommy Lowry, 436, 1966–78.

Youngest League Player: Steve Walters, 16 years 119 days v Peterborough U, 6 May 1988.

Record Transfer Fee Received: £3,000,000 (rising to £6,000,000) from Manchester U for Nick Powell, June 2012.

Record Transfer Fee Paid: £650,000 to Torquay U for Rodney Jack, July 1998.

Football League Record: 1892 Original Member of Division 2; 1896 Failed re-election; 1921 Re-entered Division (N); 1958–63 Division 4; 1963–64 Division 3; 1964–68 Division 4; 1968–69 Division 3; 1969–89 Division 4; 1989–91 Division 3; 1991–92 Division 4; 1992–94 Division 3; 1994–97 Division 2; 1997–2002 Division 1; 2002–03 Division 2; 2003–04 Division 1; 2004–06 FL C; 2006–09 FL 1; 2009–12 FL 2; 2012–16 FL 1; 2016–20 FL 2; 2020– FL 1.

LATEST SEQUENCES

Longest Sequence of League Wins: 7, 30.4.1994 – 3.9.1994.

Longest Sequence of League Defeats: 10, 16.4.1979 – 22.8.1979.

Longest Sequence of League Draws: 5, 18.9.2010 – 9.10.2010.

Longest Sequence of Unbeaten League Matches: 17, 25.3.1995 – 16.9.1995.

Longest Sequence Without a League Win: 30, 22.9.1956 – 6.4.1957.

Successive Scoring Runs: 26 from 7.4.1934.

Successive Non-scoring Runs: 9 from 6.11.1974.

MANAGERS

W. C. McNeill 1892–94 (*Secretary-Manager*)
J. G. Hall 1895–96 (*Secretary-Manager*)
R. Roberts (*1st team Secretary-Manager*) 1897
J. B. Blomerley 1898–1911 (*Secretary-Manager, continued as Hon. Secretary to 1925*)
Tom Bailey (*Secretary only*) 1925–38
George Lillycrop (*Trainer*) 1938–44
Frank Hill 1944–48
Arthur Turner 1948–51
Harry Catterick 1951–53
Ralph Ward 1953–55
Maurice Lindley 1956–57
Willie Cook 1957–58
Harry Ware 1958–60
Jimmy McGuigan 1960–64
Ernie Tagg 1964–71 (*continued as Secretary to 1972*)
Dennis Viollet 1971
Jimmy Melia 1972–74
Ernie Tagg 1974
Harry Gregg 1975–78
Warwick Rimmer 1978–79
Tony Waddington 1979–81
Arfon Griffiths 1981–82
Peter Morris 1982–83
Dario Gradi 1983–2007
Steve Holland 2007–08
Gudjon Thordarson 2008–09
Dario Gradi 2009–11
Steve Davis 2011–17
David Artell January 2017–

TEN YEAR LEAGUE RECORD

		P	W	D	L	F	A	Pts	Pos
2011-12	FL 2	46	20	12	14	67	59	72	7
2012-13	FL 1	46	18	10	18	54	62	64	13
2013-14	FL 1	46	13	12	21	54	80	51	19
2014-15	FL 1	46	14	10	22	43	75	52	20
2015-16	FL 1	46	7	13	26	46	83	34	24
2016-17	FL 2	46	14	13	19	58	67	55	17
2017-18	FL 2	46	17	5	24	62	75	56	15
2018-19	FL 2	46	19	8	19	60	59	65	12
2019-20	FL 2	37	20	9	8	67	43	69	2§
2020-21	FL 1	46	18	12	16	56	61	66	12

§*Decided on points-per-game (1.86)*

DID YOU KNOW?

Goalkeeper Bruce Grobbelaar scored for Crewe Alexandra when he netted from the penalty spot against York City in the final match of the 1979–80 season. Crewe won the game 2-0 to end the campaign with a six-match unbeaten run but still finished second to bottom of the Fourth Division.

CREWE ALEXANDRA – SKY BET LEAGUE ONE 2020–21 LEAGUE RECORD

Match No.	Date	Venue	Opponents	Result		H/T Score	Lg Pos.	Goalscorers	Attendance
1	Sept 12	H	Charlton Ath	L	0-2	0-2	18		0
2	19	A	Hull C	L	0-1	0-0	22		0
3	26	H	Milton Keynes D	W	2-0	2-0	14	Mandron [13], Finney [20]	0
4	Oct 10	H	Wigan Ath	W	3-0	2-0	12	Offord [27], Pickering [40], Mandron [59]	0
5	17	H	Blackpool	D	1-1	0-0	12	Mandron [54]	0
6	20	A	Sunderland	L	0-1	0-1	13		0
7	24	A	Doncaster R	W	2-1	1-1	12	Kirk [26], Pickering [70]	0
8	27	H	Lincoln C	L	0-1	0-1	14		0
9	31	A	Ipswich T	L	0-1	0-0	14		0
10	Nov 3	H	Gillingham	L	0-1	0-0	17		0
11	14	H	Peterborough U	W	2-0	2-0	13	Pickering [29], Kirk [41]	0
12	17	A	Oxford U	W	2-0	1-0	12	Mandron [28], Dale [90]	0
13	21	A	Portsmouth	L	1-4	0-2	13	Finney (pen) [90]	0
14	24	A	Accrington S	L	0-1	0-0	14		0
15	Dec 1	H	Swindon T	W	4-2	1-2	11	Powell [39], Ng [54], Lowery [62], Dale [66]	0
16	5	A	Burton Alb	D	1-1	0-0	13	Dale [88]	0
17	12	H	Northampton T	W	2-1	0-1	11	Dale [53], Wintle [90]	2000
18	15	H	Plymouth Arg	W	2-1	2-0	11	Kirk [22], Dale [43]	2000
19	19	A	AFC Wimbledon	W	2-1	0-0	9	Mandron [60], Finney [90]	0
20	26	H	Fleetwood T	D	1-1	0-0	9	Mandron [61]	0
21	Jan 9	A	Rochdale	D	3-3	3-0	9	Finney 2 [6, 35], Dale [23]	0
22	16	A	Plymouth Arg	D	1-1	0-1	10	Finney [64]	0
23	19	H	Bristol R	W	3-2	2-0	7	Kirk [4], Wintle [23], Lancashire [55]	0
24	23	H	AFC Wimbledon	D	1-1	1-1	8	Finney [31]	0
25	26	A	Gillingham	L	1-4	0-3	9	Porter [80]	0
26	30	H	Ipswich T	D	1-1	0-0	10	Kirk [59]	0
27	Feb 2	A	Shrewsbury T	W	1-0	1-0	9	Dale [27]	0
28	6	A	Peterborough U	L	0-2	0-2	9		0
29	20	A	Swindon T	L	1-2	1-1	14	Lowery [5]	0
30	23	H	Accrington S	W	2-0	1-0	11	Beckles [32], Porter [79]	0
31	27	H	Sunderland	D	2-2	2-0	11	Porter [30], Lowery [38]	0
32	Mar 2	A	Blackpool	D	1-1	0-1	11	Walker [86]	0
33	6	A	Lincoln C	L	0-3	0-1	13		0
34	9	H	Doncaster R	W	1-0	0-0	12	Mandron [56]	0
35	13	H	Burton Alb	L	0-3	0-3	13		0
36	20	A	Northampton T	W	1-0	0-0	14	Dale [74]	0
37	Apr 2	H	Hull C	L	1-2	0-0	15	Porter (pen) [66]	0
38	5	A	Milton Keynes D	W	2-0	2-0	14	Mandron 2 [15, 20]	0
39	10	H	Oxford U	L	0-6	0-3	15		0
40	13	H	Portsmouth	D	0-0	0-0	15		0
41	17	A	Wigan Ath	L	0-2	0-1	15		0
42	20	A	Fleetwood T	W	2-0	1-0	14	Dale [24], Porter (pen) [83]	0
43	24	H	Rochdale	D	1-1	0-0	15	Kirk [90]	0
44	27	A	Charlton Ath	D	2-2	0-1	14	Dale 2 [67, 90]	0
45	May 1	A	Bristol R	W	1-0	1-0	14	Ainley [18]	0
46	9	H	Shrewsbury T	W	3-2	2-2	12	Mandron 2 [10, 21], Porter [81]	0

Final League Position: 12

GOALSCORERS

League (56): Dale 11, Mandron 11, Finney 7 (1 pen), Kirk 6, Porter 6 (2 pens), Lowery 3, Pickering 3, Wintle 2, Ainley 1, Beckles 1, Lancashire 1, Ng 1, Offord 1, Powell 1, Walker 1.
FA Cup (4): Finney 1, Kirk 1, Mandron 1, Porter 1.
Carabao Cup (1): Sass-Davies 1.
Papa John's Trophy (7): Mandron 2 (1 pen), Powell 2, Dale 1, Pickering 1, Zanzala 1.

Jaaskelainen W 31	Ng P 15	Beckles O 37 + 4	Offord L 27 + 1	Pickering H 44	Murphy L 29 + 11	Wintle R 41 + 2	Finney O 19 + 7	Dale O 32 + 11	Mandron M 36 + 6	Kirk C 41 + 1	Ainley C 12 + 10	Lundstram J — + 4	Zanzala O 1 + 4	Richards D 15	Daniels D 11 + 4	Powell D 12 + 12	Lowery T 30 + 7	Porter C 14 + 21	Lancashire O 20 + 2	Griffiths R — + 2	Johnson T 6 + 1	Adebisi R 11 + 4	Jones B 3	Walker S 2 + 9	Evans A 6 + 8	Wood-Gordon N 11 + 1	Match No.
1	2	3	4	5	6^1	7	8^2	9^3	10	11	12	13	14														1
1	2	3	4	5	6^3	7	8^1	9^2	10	11	12	13	14														2
1	2	3	4	5	6	7	8^1	9^2	10	11	13	12															3
	2	12	4	5	6	7			10^3	11	8^2			1	3^1	9	13	14									4
1	2	3	4	5	6^2	7	12		10	11	8^1					9	13										5
1	2	3	4	5	6	7	8^2	12	10	11^3	13					9^1		14									6
1	2	3	4	5	13	7	14	12	10	11	8^3					9^1	6^2										7
1	2	3	4	5	6^1	7		9^3	10	11	8^2					14	12	13									8
1	2	3	4	5		7	14	9^1	10^2	11	8^3					13	6	12									9
1	2	3	4	5		7	13	12	10	11	6^2		14			9^1	8^3										10
1	2	3	4	5	13	7	6^2	12	10	11						9^1	8										11
1	2	3	4	5	13	7	8^1	14	10	11	12					9^3	6^2										12
1	2	3^1	4	5	14	7^4	8	13		11	15		10^5			9^2	6^3		12	16							13
1	2		4	5	15	7^3	8	9^2		11	12		14			13	6^1	10^4	3								14
1	2		4	5	6^2	7	12	9	13							11	8	10^1	3								15
1		3	4	5	8	7	12	9	10^3	13						11^2	6^1	14	15		2^4						16
1		4	2	5	13	7	8	9^1	10	11						12	6^2		3								17
1		3	2	5		7	8	9^1	10^2	11						12	6	13	4								18
1		4	2	5	6	7	8	9^2	10^1	11						13		12	3								19
1		4	3	5	6	7	8^2	9^1	10	11						13	12				2						20
1		4	3	5	6	7	8	9	10^1	11								12			2						21
		3	2	5	8^1	7	6	9	10^2	11				1			12	13	4								22
		4	2^1	5^2	15	7	8^4	9	14	11				1			6	10^3	3		12	13					23
		4			12	7	6	9		11				1			8^1	10^2	3			5	2	13			24
		4			13	7^3	6	9^1		11^4				1			8^2	10	3	15	2	5		12	14		25
		4		5	6^4	7	8^2	12	10	11^3				1		14		15	3				2	9^1	13		26
		4		5	6	7	8^2	11	10^3					1		9^1	13	14	3		2			12			27
		4		5	8	7		11	10^3					1		9^2	12	13	3				2	14	6^1		28
		4		5	6	7		9^1	10^2	11				1		12	8^3	13			2				14	3	29
		3		5	8	7			10	9				1	2		6	11								4	30
		4		5	8	7		12	10	9				1	2		6	11^1								3	31
		4		5		8		13	11^2	9^4				1	2^1	15	7	10				12		14	6^3	3	32
		4		5	6	7^4		14	12	11^3				1		13	8	10^1				2		9^2	15	3	33
		4		5	6	7		9	10^1	11^2				1		13	8	12				2				3	34
		4		5	8^2	7^3		9^4	10	11^1	12			1			6	13				2		15	14	3	35
1		4		5	8	12		9	13	11^3	6^1				2		7	10^2	3			14					36
1		4		5	12	7		9^4	13	11	8^1				2		6^3	10^2	3					14	15		37
1		4	2^5	5	6	7		9^1	10^4	11^2	14				15		8^3	16	3			13		12			38
1		4	14	5	6	7		9^5	10	11^4	8^1				2^3			12	3^2					16	15	13	39
1			4	5	8			10	13	9^2					12		7	11				2^1			6	3	40
1		4^1	2	5	8			9	10^1	11^2					12		7	13							6	3	41
1			5^1	6	8			9	10						12		7	11	4			2			13	3^2	42
1		15		4	7^1	12		13	9	11^4	14				2		6	10^3	3			8			5^2		43
1				5		7		9	10	11	8^1				4		6	12				2				3	44
1		12		5		7		9	10^2	11	8				4^1			13	3			2			6		45
1		12		5	13	7	15	9	10^5	11	8^2	14			4^1		6^4	16	3^3			2					46

FA Cup

First Round	Bolton W	(a)	3-2
Second Round	Cheltenham T	(a)	1-2
(aet)			

Carabao Cup

First Round	Lincoln C	(h)	1-2

Papa John's Trophy

Group C (N)	Bolton W	(a)	3-2
Group C (N)	Newcastle U U21	(h)	1-0
Group C (N)	Shrewsbury T	(h)	3-4
Second Round (N)	Hull C	(a)	0-0

(Hull C won 3-2 on penalties)

CRYSTAL PALACE

FOUNDATION

There was a Crystal Palace club as early as 1861 but the present organisation was born in 1905 after the formation of a club by the company that controlled the Crystal Palace (building) had been rejected by the FA, who did not like the idea of the Cup Final hosts running their own club. A separate company had to be formed and they had their home on the old Cup Final ground until 1915.

Selhurst Park Stadium, Whitehorse Lane, London SE25 6PU.

Telephone: (020) 8768 6000.

Ticket Office: (0871) 200 0071.

Website: www.cpfc.co.uk

Email: info@cpfc.co.uk

Ground Capacity: 25,486.

Record Attendance: 51,482 v Burnley, Division 2, 11 May 1979 (at Selhurst Park).

Pitch Measurements: 101m × 68m (110.5yd × 74.5yd).

Chairman: Steve Parish.

Chief Executive: Phil Alexander.

Manager: Patrick Vieira.

First-Team Coach: Kristian Wilson.

Colours: Red and blue striped shirts, blue shorts, blue socks with red trim.

Year Formed: 1905.

Turned Professional: 1905.

Club Nickname: 'The Eagles'.

Grounds: 1905, Crystal Palace; 1915, Herne Hill; 1918, The Nest; 1924, Selhurst Park.

First Football League Game: 28 August 1920, Division 3, v Merthyr T (a) L 1–2 – Alderson; Little, Rhodes; McCracken, Jones, Feebury; Bateman, Conner, Smith, Milligan (1), Whibley.

Record League Victory: 9–0 v Barrow, Division 4, 10 October 1959 – Rouse; Long, Noakes; Truett, Evans, McNichol; Gavin (1), Summersby (4 incl. 1p), Sexton, Byrne (2), Colfar (2).

Record Cup Victory: 8–0 v Southend U, Rumbelows League Cup 2nd rd (1st leg), 25 September 1990 – Martyn; Humphrey (Thompson (1)), Shaw, Pardew, Young, Thorn, McGoldrick, Thomas, Bright (3), Wright (3), Barber (Hodges (1)).

Record Defeat: 0–9 v Burnley, FA Cup 2nd rd replay, 10 February 1909; 0–9 v Liverpool, Division 1, 12 September 1990.

HONOURS

League Champions: First Division – 1993–94; Division 2 – 1978–79; Division 3S – 1920–21.
Runners-up: Division 2 – 1968–69; Division 3 – 1963–64; Division 3S – 1928–29, 1930–31, 1938–39; Division 4 – 1960–61.

FA Cup: *Runners-up:* 1990, 2016.

League Cup: semi-final – 1993, 1995, 2001, 2012.

Full Members' Cup Winners: 1991.

European Competition
Intertoto Cup: 1998.

FOOTBALL YEARBOOK FACT FILE

Bill Bark signed as an inside forward for Crystal Palace in January 1939 and appeared in the first team both before and after the Second World War. While out of the team through injury in October 1946 he changed his surname to Naylor and reappeared after a month's absence under the name Bill Naylor, a name he used for the remainder of his career.

Most League Points (2 for a win): 64, Division 4, 1960–61.

Most League Points (3 for a win): 90, Division 1, 1993–94.

Most League Goals: 110, Division 4, 1960–61.

Highest League Scorer in Season: Peter Simpson, 46, Division 3 (S), 1930–31.

Most League Goals in Total Aggregate: Peter Simpson, 153, 1930–36.

Most League Goals in One Match: 6, Peter Simpson v Exeter C, Division 3 (S), 4 October 1930.

Most Capped Player: Wayne Hennessey, 55 (96), Wales.

Most League Appearances: Jim Cannon, 571, 1973–88.

Youngest League Player: John Bostock, 15 years 287 days v Watford, 29 October 2007.

Record Transfer Fee Received: £45,000,000 from Manchester U for Aaron Wan-Bissaka, July 2019.

Record Transfer Fee Paid: £27,000,000 to Liverpool for Christian Benteke, August 2016.

Football League Record: 1920 Original Members of Division 3; 1921–25 Division 2; 1925–58 Division 3 (S); 1958–61 Division 4; 1961–64 Division 3; 1964–69 Division 2; 1969–73 Division 1; 1973–74 Division 2; 1974–77 Division 3; 1977–79 Division 2; 1979–81 Division 1; 1981–89 Division 2; 1989–92 Division 1; 1992–93 Premier League; 1993–94 Division 1; 1994–95 Premier League; 1995–97 Division 1; 1997–98 Premier League; 1998–2004 Division 1; 2004–05 Premier League; 2005–13 FL C; 2013– Premier League.

LATEST SEQUENCES

Longest Sequence of League Wins: 8, 21.5.2017 – 30.9.2017.

Longest Sequence of League Defeats: 8, 10.1.1998 – 14.3.1998.

Longest Sequence of League Draws: 5, 21.9.2002 – 19.10.2002.

Longest Sequence of Unbeaten League Matches: 18, 22.2.1969 – 13.8.1969.

Longest Sequence Without a League Win: 20, 3.3.1962 – 8.9.1962.

Successive Scoring Runs: 24 from 27.4.1929.

Successive Non-scoring Runs: 9 from 19.11.1994.

MANAGERS

John T. Robson 1905–07
Edmund Goodman 1907–25 (*Secretary 1905–33*)
Alex Maley 1925–27
Fred Mavin 1927–30
Jack Tresadern 1930–35
Tom Bromilow 1935–36
R. S. Moyes 1936
Tom Bromilow 1936–39
George Irwin 1939–47
Jack Butler 1947–49
Ronnie Rooke 1949–50
Charlie Slade and Fred Dawes (*Joint Managers*) 1950–51
Laurie Scott 1951–54
Cyril Spiers 1954–58
George Smith 1958–60
Arthur Rowe 1960–62
Dick Graham 1962–66
Bert Head 1966–72 (*continued as General Manager to 1973*)
Malcolm Allison 1973–76
Terry Venables 1976–80
Ernie Walley 1980
Malcolm Allison 1980–81
Dario Gradi 1981
Steve Kember 1981–82
Alan Mullery 1982–84
Steve Coppell 1984–93
Alan Smith 1993–95
Steve Coppell (*Technical Director*) 1995–96
Dave Bassett 1996–97
Steve Coppell 1997–98
Attilio Lombardo 1998
Terry Venables (*Head Coach*) 1998–99
Steve Coppell 1999–2000
Alan Smith 2000–01
Steve Bruce 2001
Trevor Francis 2001–03
Steve Kember 2003
Iain Dowie 2003–06
Peter Taylor 2006–07
Neil Warnock 2007–10
Paul Hart 2010
George Burley 2010–11
Dougie Freedman 2011–12
Ian Holloway 2012–13
Tony Pulis 2013–14
Neil Warnock 2014
Alan Pardew 2015–16
Sam Allardyce 2016–17
Frank de Boer 2017
Roy Hodgson 2017–21
Patrick Vieira July 2021–

TEN YEAR LEAGUE RECORD

		P	*W*	*D*	*L*	*F*	*A*	*Pts*	*Pos*
2011-12	FL C	46	13	17	16	46	51	56	17
2012-13	FL C	46	19	15	12	73	62	72	5
2013-14	PR Lge	38	13	6	19	33	48	45	11
2014-15	PR Lge	38	13	9	16	47	51	48	10
2015-16	PR Lge	38	11	9	18	39	51	42	15
2016-17	PR Lge	38	12	5	21	50	63	41	14
2017-18	PR Lge	38	11	11	16	45	55	44	11
2018-19	PR Lge	38	14	7	17	51	53	49	12
2019-20	PR Lge	38	11	10	17	31	50	43	14
2020-21	PR Lge	38	12	8	18	41	66	44	14

DID YOU KNOW ?

Crystal Palace had the distinction of winning a title in both their first season as Southern League members and their first season as Football League members. Palace won the Southern League Second Division in 1905–06 and the inaugural Third Division of the Football League in 1920–21.

CRYSTAL PALACE – PREMIER LEAGUE 2020–21 LEAGUE RECORD

Match No.	Date	Venue	Opponents	Result	H/T Score	Lg Pos.	Goalscorers	Attendance
1	Sept 12	H	Southampton	W 1-0	1-0	4	Zaha ^{13}	0
2	19	A	Manchester U	W 3-1	1-0	3	Townsend ^{7}, Zaha 2 (1 pen) $^{74 (p), 85}$	0
3	26	H	Everton	L 1-2	1-2	5	Kouyate ^{26}	0
4	Oct 3	A	Chelsea	L 0-4	0-0	9		0
5	18	H	Brighton & HA	D 1-1	1-0	13	Zaha (pen) ^{19}	0
6	24	A	Fulham	W 2-1	1-0	5	Riedewald ^{8}, Zaha ^{64}	0
7	30	A	Wolverhampton W	L 0-2	0-2	9		0
8	Nov 7	H	Leeds U	W 4-1	3-1	7	Dann ^{12}, Eze ^{22}, Helder Costa (og) ^{42}, Ayew ^{70}	0
9	23	A	Burnley	L 0-1	0-1	11		0
10	27	H	Newcastle U	L 0-2	0-0	13		0
11	Dec 6	A	WBA	W 5-1	1-1	11	Furlong (og) ^{8}, Zaha 2 $^{55, 68}$, Benteke 2 $^{59, 82}$	0
12	13	H	Tottenham H	D 1-1	0-1	11	Schlupp ^{81}	2000
13	16	A	West Ham U	D 1-1	1-0	12	Benteke ^{34}	0
14	19	H	Liverpool	L 0-7	0-3	13		0
15	26	A	Aston Villa	L 0-3	0-1	13		0
16	28	H	Leicester C	D 1-1	0-0	13	Zaha ^{58}	0
17	Jan 2	H	Sheffield U	W 2-0	2-0	14	Schlupp ^{4}, Eze ^{45}	0
18	14	A	Arsenal	D 0-0	0-0	13		0
19	17	A	Manchester C	L 0-4	0-1	13		0
20	26	H	West Ham U	L 2-3	1-2	13	Zaha ^{3}, Batshuayi ^{90}	0
21	30	H	Wolverhampton W	W 1-0	0-0	13	Eze ^{60}	0
22	Feb 2	A	Newcastle U	W 2-1	2-1	13	Riedewald ^{21}, Cahill ^{25}	0
23	8	A	Leeds U	L 0-2	0-1	13		0
24	13	H	Burnley	L 0-3	0-2	13		0
25	22	A	Brighton & HA	W 2-1	1-0	13	Mateta ^{28}, Benteke ^{90}	0
26	28	H	Fulham	D 0-0	0-0	13		0
27	Mar 3	H	Manchester U	D 0-0	0-0	13		0
28	7	A	Tottenham H	L 1-4	1-1	13	Benteke ^{45}	0
29	13	H	WBA	W 1-0	1-0	11	Milivojevic (pen) ^{37}	0
30	Apr 5	A	Everton	D 1-1	0-0	12	Batshuayi ^{86}	0
31	10	H	Chelsea	L 1-4	0-3	13	Benteke ^{63}	0
32	26	A	Leicester C	L 1-2	1-0	13	Zaha ^{12}	0
33	May 1	H	Manchester C	L 0-2	0-0	13		0
34	8	A	Sheffield U	W 2-0	1-0	13	Benteke ^{2}, Eze ^{88}	0
35	11	A	Southampton	L 1-3	1-1	13	Benteke ^{2}	0
36	16	H	Aston Villa	W 3-2	1-2	13	Benteke ^{32}, Zaha ^{76}, Mitchell ^{84}	0
37	19	H	Arsenal	L 1-3	0-1	13	Benteke ^{62}	6500
38	23	A	Liverpool	L 0-2	0-1	14		9901

Final League Position: 14

GOALSCORERS

League (41): Zaha 11 (2 pens), Benteke 10, Eze 4, Batshuayi 2, Riedewald 2, Schlupp 2, Ayew 1, Cahill 1, Dann 1, Kouyate 1, Mateta 1, Milivojevic 1 (1 pen), Mitchell 1, Townsend 1, own goals 2.
FA Cup (0).
Carabao Cup (0).

Guaita V 37	Ward J 25 + 1	Kouyate C 35 + 1	Dann S 15	Mitchell T 19	Townsend A 25 + 9	McArthur J 17 + 1	McCarthy J 10 + 6	Schlupp J 15 + 12	Zaha W 29 + 1	Ayew J 23 + 10	Milivojevic L 27 + 4	Eze E 29 + 5	Sakho M 3 + 1	Batshuayi M 7 + 11	Benteke C 21 + 9	Riedewald J 19 + 14	Cahill G 20	Clyne N 13	Van Aanholt P 20 + 2	Tomkins J 6 + 2	Mateta J 2 + 5	Butland J 1	Kelly M — + 1	Match No.
1	2	3	4	5	6	7	8[1]	9[2]	10	11	12	13												1
1	2	3		5	6	7	8[3]	9[1]	11	10[2]	14	12	4	13										2
1	2	3		5	6	8[3]	7		11	10[2]		9[1]	4	12	13	14								3
1	2	3		5	6	7[2]	8[1]		10	11	12	9	4			13								4
1	2	3		5	6	8		9[2]	11		12			10[1]	13	7	4							5
1		3	4	5	6			9[2]	11		7	13	14	10		8[3]		2[1]	12					6
1		3	4		6[2]			9[1]	11	13	8■	12		10[3]	14	7		2	5					7
1		3	4		6[1]	8	13	12	11	10[3]		9			14	7[2]		2	5					8
1		3	4		6	8		12		11[2]		9		10	13	7[1]		2	5					9
1		6	3		8[2]	7[3]		9		11[1]		10		14	12	13	4	2	5					10
1		3				8[1]		6[2]	11[3]	13	7	9		14	10	12	4	2	5					11
1		3			13	8		6	11		7[1]	9[2]			10	12	4	2	5					12
1	2	3	4		6[2]	8		13	11	12	7	9[1]			10■				5					13
1		3[1]				8[3]		6	10	11	7	9[2]		13		14	4	2	5	12				14
1	2	3	4		14	8[2]		6[3]	10		7[1]	9		13	11	12			5					15
1		4		5	6	12		9[2]	11	13	7				10	8[1]		2		3				16
1	2	4		5	6	7		9[1]	11	13	8[3]	12			10[2]	14				3				17
1	2	4		5	6	7	13		11	12	8[2]	9			10[1]					3				18
1	2			5	7[2]	9	8			11	6[1]	10		13		12	4			3				19
1	2	3		5	6[1]	7			11	13	8[3]	9		12	10[2]	14	4							20
1	14	3	4		13		6[1]		10	8	7	9		11[2]		12		2[3]	5					21
1		14	3		12				10[1]	8	7	9		11[2]	13	6[3]	4	2	5					22
1			3	5	12					11[3]	7	6		13	14	8	4	2	9[1]		10[2]			23
1		3	4		12					6	7	9		11[1]	10[2]	8		2	5		13			24
1	2	3		5	11		13			9	7	8[2]			12	6	4				10[1]			25
1	2	3			11		12			9	7	8[1]			10	6	4		5					26
1	2	3			6		7[1]	13		10	8	9[2]			11	12	4		5					27
1	2	3			6[2]			13	12	11	7	9[1]			10[3]	8	4		5		14			28
1	2	3			13			12	11	6[2]	7	9[1]			10	8	4		5					29
1	2	3						12	11	6[3]	7	9		14	10[2]	8[1]	4		5		13			30
1	2	3			14		12	13	11	6[3]	7	9[2]			10	8[1]	4		5					31
1	2	3	4		12		13	14	11	9[1]	7[2]	8			10	6[3]			5					32
1	2	3	4	5	9[3]			12	11	14	7	8			10[2]	6[1]					13			33
1	2	3		5	9[2]			8[1]	11	13	7	6			10	12	4							34
1	2	3	4	5				12	11	9[2]	7[1]	6		13	10[3]	8					14			35
	2	3		5	9		7[1]	8	11			6			10		4			12		1		36
1	2	6		5	9		7[2]	8	11	12					10[1]	13	4			3				37
1	2	6[3]		5	9		7[2]	12	10	11						8	4		13	3[1]			14	38

FA Cup
Third Round Wolverhampton W (a) 0-1

Carabao Cup
Second Round Bournemouth (a) 0-0
(Bournemouth won 11-10 on penalties)

DERBY COUNTY

FOUNDATION

Derby County was formed by members of the Derbyshire County Cricket Club in 1884, when football was booming in the area and the cricketers thought that a football club would help boost finances for the summer game. To begin with, they sported the cricket club's colours of amber, chocolate and pale blue, and went into the game at the top immediately entering the FA Cup.

Pride Park Stadium, Pride Park, Derby DE24 8XL.

Telephone: (0871) 472 1884.

Ticket Office: (0871) 472 1884 (option 1).

Website: www.dcfc.co.uk

Email: derby.county@dcfc.co.uk

Ground Capacity: 32,956.

Record Attendance: 41,826 v Tottenham H, Division 1, 20 September 1969 (at Baseball Ground); 33,378 v Liverpool, Premier League, 18 March 2000 (at Pride Park).

Stadium Record Attendance: 33,597, England v Mexico, 25 May 2001 (at Pride Park).

Pitch Measurements: 105m × 68m (115yd × 74.5yd).

Executive Chairman: Mel Morris CBE.

Chief Executive Officer: Stephen Pearce.

Manager: Wayne Rooney.

Assistant Manager: Liam Rosenior.

Colours: White shirts with black trim, black shorts with white trim, white socks with black trim.

Year Formed: 1884.

Turned Professional: 1884.

Club Nickname: 'The Rams'.

Grounds: 1884, Racecourse Ground; 1895, Baseball Ground; 1997, Pride Park (renamed The iPro Stadium 2013; Pride Park Stadium 2016).

First Football League Game: 8 September 1888, Football League, v Bolton W (a) W 6–3 – Marshall; Latham, Ferguson, Williamson; Monks, Walter Roulstone; Bakewell (2), Cooper (2), Higgins, Harry Plackett, Lol Plackett (2).

Record League Victory: 9–0 v Wolverhampton W, Division 1, 10 January 1891 – Bunyan; Archie Goodall, Roberts; Walker, Chalmers, Walter Roulstone (1); Bakewell, McLachlan, Johnny Goodall (1), Holmes (2), McMillan (5). 9–0 v Sheffield W, Division 1, 21 January 1899 – Fryer; Methven, Staley; Cox, Archie Goodall, May; Oakden (1), Bloomer (6), Boag, McDonald (1), Allen, (1 og).

Record Cup Victory: 12–0 v Finn Harps, UEFA Cup 1st rd 1st leg, 15 September 1976 – Moseley; Thomas, Nish, Rioch (1), McFarland, Todd (King), Macken, Gemmill, Hector (5), George (3), James (3).

HONOURS

League Champions: Division 1 – 1971–72, 1974–75; Division 2 – 1911–12, 1914–15, 1968–69, 1986–87; Division 3N – 1956–57.
Runners-up: Division 1 – 1895–96, 1929–30, 1935–36; First Division – 1995–96; Division 2 – 1925–26; Division 3N – 1955–56.

FA Cup Winners: 1946.
Runners-up: 1898, 1899, 1903.

League Cup: semi-final – 1968, 2009.

Texaco Cup Winners: 1972.

Anglo-Italian Cup: *Runners-up:* 1993–94, 1994–95.

European Competitions
European Cup: 1972–73 *(sf)*, 1975–76.
UEFA Cup: 1974–75, 1976–77.

FOOTBALL YEARBOOK FACT FILE

Llewellyn Gwynne, who appeared as an amateur for Derby County in their FA Cup fifth round tie at Crewe Alexandra in January 1888, was also curate of St Chad's Church in Derby at the time. He went on to enjoy a successful career in the Anglican Church and served as Bishop of Egypt and Sudan from 1920 to 1946.

Record Defeat: 2–11 v Everton, FA Cup 1st rd, 1889–90.

Most League Points (2 for a win): 63, Division 2, 1968–69 and Division 3 (N), 1955–56 and 1956–57.

Most League Points (3 for a win): 85, FL C, 2013–14.

Most League Goals: 111, Division 3 (N), 1956–57.

Highest League Scorer in Season: Jack Bowers, 37, Division 1, 1930–31; Ray Straw, 37 Division 3 (N), 1956–57.

Most League Goals in Total Aggregate: Steve Bloomer, 292, 1892–1906 and 1910–14.

Most League Goals in One Match: 6, Steve Bloomer v Sheffield W, Division 1, 2 January 1899.

Most Capped Player: Deon Burton, 42 (61), Jamaica.

Most League Appearances: Kevin Hector, 486, 1966–78 and 1980–82.

Youngest League Player: Mason Bennett, 15 years 99 days v Middlesbrough 22 October 2011.

Record Transfer Fee Received: £8,500,000 (rising to £11,000,000) from Huddersfield T for Tom Ince, July 2017.

Record Transfer Fee Paid: £7,500,000 (rising to £10,000,000) to Arsenal for Krystian Bielik, August 2019.

Football League Record: 1888 Founder Member of the Football League; 1907–12 Division 2; 1912–14 Division 1; 1914–15 Division 2; 1915–21 Division 1; 1921–26 Division 2; 1926–53 Division 1; 1953–55 Division 2; 1955–57 Division 3 (N); 1957–69 Division 2; 1969–80 Division 1; 1980–84 Division 2; 1984–86 Division 3; 1986–87 Division 2; 1987–91 Division 1; 1991–92 Division 2; 1992–96 Division 1; 1996–2002 Premier League; 2002–04 Division 1; 2004–07 FL C; 2007–08 Premier League; 2008– FL C.

MANAGERS

W. D. Clark 1896–1900
Harry Newbould 1900–06
Jimmy Methven 1906–22
Cecil Potter 1922–25
George Jobey 1925–41
Ted Magner 1944–46
Stuart McMillan 1946–53
Jack Barker 1953–55
Harry Storer 1955–62
Tim Ward 1962–67
Brian Clough 1967–73
Dave Mackay 1973–76
Colin Murphy 1977
Tommy Docherty 1977–79
Colin Addison 1979–82
Johnny Newman 1982
Peter Taylor 1982–84
Roy McFarland 1984
Arthur Cox 1984–93
Roy McFarland 1993–95
Jim Smith 1995–2001
Colin Todd 2001–02
John Gregory 2002–03
George Burley 2003–05
Phil Brown 2005–06
Billy Davies 2006–07
Paul Jewell 2007–08
Nigel Clough 2009–13
Steve McClaren 2013–15
Paul Clement 2015–16
Darren Wassall 2016
Nigel Pearson 2016
Steve McClaren 2016–17
Gary Rowett 2017–18
Frank Lampard 2018–19
Phillip Cocu 2019–20
Wayne Rooney November 2020–

LATEST SEQUENCES

Longest Sequence of League Wins: 9, 15.3.1969 – 19.4.1969.

Longest Sequence of League Defeats: 8, 12.12.1987 – 10.2.1988.

Longest Sequence of League Draws: 6, 26.3.1927 – 18.4.1927.

Longest Sequence of Unbeaten League Matches: 22, 8.3.1969 – 20.9.1969.

Longest Sequence Without a League Win: 36, 22.9.2007 – 30.8.2008.

Successive Scoring Runs: 29 from 3.12.1960.

Successive Non-scoring Runs: 8 from 30.10.1920.

TEN YEAR LEAGUE RECORD

		P	*W*	*D*	*L*	*F*	*A*	*Pts*	*Pos*
2011-12	FL C	46	18	10	18	50	58	64	12
2012-13	FL C	46	16	13	17	65	62	61	10
2013-14	FL C	46	25	10	11	84	52	85	3
2014-15	FL C	46	21	14	11	85	56	77	8
2015-16	FL C	46	21	15	10	66	43	78	5
2016-17	FL C	46	18	13	15	54	50	67	9
2017-18	FL C	46	20	15	11	70	48	75	6
2018-19	FL C	46	20	14	12	69	54	74	6
2019-20	FL C	46	17	13	16	62	64	64	10
2020-21	FL C	46	11	11	24	36	58	44	21

DID YOU KNOW ?

Derby County got off to a somewhat difficult start, losing their first-ever FA Cup match at home to Walsall Town on 8 November 1884 by 7-0. The Rams were unable to field a full-strength side but nevertheless trailed by a single goal at half-time, only to concede six more after the break.

DERBY COUNTY – SKY BET CHAMPIONSHIP 2020–21 LEAGUE RECORD

Match No.	Date	Venue	Opponents	Result		H/T Score	Lg Pos.	Goalscorers	Attendance
1	Sept 12	H	Reading	L	0-2	0-2	21		0
2	19	A	Luton T	L	1-2	0-1	19	Marriott 52	0
3	26	H	Blackburn R	L	0-4	0-3	22		0
4	Oct 3	A	Norwich C	W	1-0	0-0	19	Rooney 87	0
5	16	H	Watford	L	0-1	0-0	20		0
6	20	A	Huddersfield T	L	0-1	0-0	21		0
7	23	A	Nottingham F	D	1-1	1-0	21	Waghorn 30	0
8	28	H	Cardiff C	D	1-1	1-0	21	Waghorn 24	0
9	31	A	Bournemouth	D	1-1	1-0	22	Shinnie 13	0
10	Nov 4	H	QPR	L	0-1	0-0	23		0
11	7	H	Barnsley	L	0-2	0-1	24		0
12	21	A	Bristol C	L	0-1	0-0	24		0
13	25	A	Middlesbrough	L	0-3	0-1	24		0
14	28	H	Wycombe W	D	1-1	1-0	24	Holmes 36	0
15	Dec 1	H	Coventry C	D	1-1	0-0	24	Kazim-Richards 83	0
16	5	A	Millwall	W	1-0	0-0	23	Knight 69	2000
17	9	A	Brentford	D	0-0	0-0	22		2000
18	12	H	Stoke C	D	0-0	0-0	22		0
19	16	H	Swansea C	W	2-0	2-0	22	Kazim-Richards 4, Jozwiak 37	0
20	26	H	Preston NE	L	0-1	0-0	22		0
21	29	A	Birmingham C	W	4-0	3-0	20	Bielik 15, Shinnie (pen) 17, Kazim-Richards 25, Knight 77	0
22	Jan 1	A	Sheffield W	L	0-1	0-0	21		0
23	16	H	Rotherham U	L	0-1	0-0	23		0
24	19	H	Bournemouth	W	1-0	1-0	21	Bielik 32	0
25	23	A	QPR	W	1-0	0-0	21	Kazim-Richards 56	0
26	30	H	Bristol C	W	1-0	1-0	18	Kazim-Richards 4	0
27	Feb 3	A	Rotherham U	L	0-3	0-0	20		0
28	13	H	Middlesbrough	W	2-1	2-1	19	Gregory 15, Kazim-Richards 32	0
29	16	A	Wycombe W	W	2-1	1-0	16	Ikpeazu (og) 16, Wisdom 90	0
30	19	A	Watford	L	1-2	0-2	17	Troost-Ekong (og) 77	0
31	23	H	Huddersfield T	W	2-0	1-0	18	Edmundson 22, Waghorn 66	0
32	26	H	Nottingham F	D	1-1	0-1	17	Kazim-Richards 84	0
33	Mar 2	A	Cardiff C	L	0-4	0-1	18		0
34	6	A	Coventry C	L	0-1	0-1	19		0
35	10	A	Barnsley	D	0-0	0-0	18		0
36	13	H	Millwall	L	0-1	0-1	19		0
37	16	H	Brentford	D	2-2	0-2	19	Gregory 47, Sibley 87	0
38	20	A	Stoke C	L	0-1	0-0	19		0
39	Apr 2	H	Luton T	W	2-0	1-0	18	Gregory 7, Shinnie (pen) 49	0
40	5	A	Reading	L	1-3	0-1	19	Lawrence 79	0
41	10	H	Norwich C	L	0-1	0-1	20		0
42	16	A	Blackburn R	L	1-2	1-1	21	Lawrence 22	0
43	20	A	Preston NE	L	0-3	0-1	21		0
44	24	H	Birmingham C	L	1-2	1-0	21	Kazim-Richards 36	0
45	May 1	A	Swansea C	L	1-2	0-0	21	Lawrence 48	0
46	8	H	Sheffield W	D	3-3	0-1	21	Waghorn 2 (1 pen) 49, 78 (p), Roberts 52	0

Final League Position: 21

GOALSCORERS

League (36): Kazim-Richards 8, Waghorn 5 (1 pen), Gregory 3, Lawrence 3, Shinnie 3 (2 pens), Bielik 2, Knight 2, Edmundson 1, Holmes 1, Jozwiak 1, Marriott 1, Roberts 1, Rooney 1, Sibley 1, Wisdom 1, own goals 2.
FA Cup (0).
Carabao Cup (1): Knight 1.

Marshall D 33	Wisdom A 36 + 2	te Wierik M 3 + 1	Clarke M 42	Forsyth C 19 + 1	Shinnie G 41	Bird M 21 + 12	Whittaker M 1 + 8	Sibley L 10 + 20	Knight J 41 + 2	Marriott J 3 + 1	Byrne N 39 + 2	Rooney W 9 + 1	Jozwiak K 30 + 11	Hector-Ingram J — + 7	Buchanan L 28 + 7	Evans G 5 + 1	Holmes D 7 + 7	Davies C 11 + 2	Lawrence T 19 + 4	Waghorn M 21 + 11	Kazim-Richards C 30 + 8	Roos K 13 + 1	Bielik K 13	Stretton J — + 4	McDonald K 1 + 6	Ibe J — + 1	Watson L 1 + 8	Gordon K — + 1	Mitchell-Lawson J — + 1	Gregory L 6 + 5	Roberts P 7 + 8	Baningime B 1 + 1	Mengi T 7 + 2	Edmundson S 8 + 2	Cresswell C — + 1	Ebosele F — + 3	*Match No.*
1	2^{1}	3	4	5	6^{2}	7	8	9	10	11	12	13																									1
1	3		4	5	7^{1}	6	14	12	10	11^{2}	2	9	8^{3}	13																							2
1	4	3				7^{2}	14	9^{3}	8	11^{1}	2	6	10		5	12	13																				3
1			5		9	13	12		8	14	2	11^{3}	10^{2}		6	3	7^{1}	4																			4
1			5		9^{2}	8	14		10		2	11		13	6^{3}	3	7^{1}	4	12																		5
1	2		4		7^{2}	6			9		5		10		8^{3}		12	3	11^{1}	13	14																6
1	2		4		7			14	6		5^{1}		9		8		12	3	11^{2}	10^{3}	13																7
	2	13	4	12	7				6		5^{1}		9		8^{2}			3	11^{3}	10	14	1															8
1	13	2^{2}	4		7			14	6		5	11^{1}			8		12	3	10	9^{3}																	9
1			4	5	7			14	6^{1}		2	9^{3}	8				13	3	10	11^{2}	12																10
1			4^{1}		7^{2}			13	6		5	10	12		8			3	11^{3}	9	14		2														11
1	3		4			7^{2}	12	13	8		2^{3}	6		14	5		9^{1}		10	11																	12
1	3		4			6	15	12	9		2	7	10^{2}		5^{3}		14		8^{4}	11^{1}	13																13
1	2		4	5	7			9^{3}	12				14			6^{4}	8^{1}	3	10	13	11^{2}			15													14
1	3		4			7			8		2^{3}		13		5		9^{1}	14	10^{2}		11		6	12													15
1	15		4	5	7^{1}	12			9		2		10^{4}		14		8^{2}	3		13	11^{3}		6														16
1	2		4	5	7		15		9				10^{4}				8^{1}	3^{2}	12	14	11^{3}		6		13												17
1	3		4			7^{2}	12^{3}	13	10		2		8^{4}		5				9^{1}	14	11		6			15											18
1	3		4		8			14	6		2		11^{2}		5		12			9^{1}	10^{3}		7	13													19
1	3		4		8			12	6		2		11^{1}	13	5					9^{1}	10^{2}		7														20
1	3		4	5	8^{4}	12		9^{1}	6^{3}		2		11	13							10^{2}		7				14	15									21
1	3		4	5^{1}	8^{2}	13		11^{3}	6		2		9	14	12						10		7														22
	3		4		7^{2}	12		13	9		2		10		5					8	11	1	6^{1}														23
	3		4		6				11^{2}		5		9^{1}		8	2					10	1	7		12				13								24
	3		4		7	12			11		5		9^{3}		8	2^{1}				13	10^{2}	1	6		14												25
1	3		4		7	9			10		2		8^{2}	14	5					12	11^{3}		6^{1}		13												26
1	3		4		7^{3}	6		15	9		2		10^{1}		5					8^{2}	11^{4}									12	13	14					27
1	3		4		8	12			7		2		9^{2}		5					6	10									11^{1}			13				28
1	3		4^{1}	5^{4}	8	13			7		16		9^{3}		15					6	10									11^{2}	14		2^{5}	12			29
1	3				8^{1}	7		14	11		2		12		5					9^{3}	10									13	6^{2}			4			30
1	4		5		8	7			9^{3}		2		12		6					13	11						14			10^{1}				3^{2}			31
1^{1}	3		4		7^{3}	6		14	9		2		10^{2}		5					8^{4}	11	12								13	15						32
	2^{4}		4		9^{2}	13		10^{1}					7^{3}		5					14		1			15		12			11		8	3	6			33
	3		4		8^{3}	7			9		2		12		5					10^{1}	11	1					14			13	6^{2}						34
	5		4	8	7			12	6				10^{2}							13	9	1								11^{1}			3	2			35
			4	8	7			14	6^{2}		5		9^{3}							10	11	1					12				13		3	2^{1}			36
	3^{5}		4		7	6^{2}		14	9		2		8^{1}		5				15		11^{4}	1					10^{3}			12	16		13				37
	2^{4}		4		7^{5}	13		11^{1}	6		5		14		8				12		10^{2}	1					16				9^{3}		3		15		38
1	2		3	4	7	6		9^{3}	14		5		13		15				10^{4}	11^{1}	12									8^{2}							39
1	3			5	6	9		7^{3}	8^{2}		2^{1}		14						10		11			13^{4}	12						15		4				40
1	3			5	8	7		12					9^{1}						11^{3}		10				2^{2}		13				6		4			14	41
1	3		4	5^{2}	7	6		11^{1}			2		10^{3}		13				9^{4}		12						14				8					15	42
1	3^{1}		4	5^{2}	7^{4}	6			10^{3}		2				13				9	14	11										8			12		15	43
			3	4	7^{3}	13		12	6^{4}		5		15		8^{2}				9	10	11^{1}	1									14			2			44
			4	5	8			13	7		2		6^{1}						11	10^{2}	9	1									12			3			45
			4	5^{2}	7^{3}	12			6^{1}		2		13		14			15	10	8^{4}	11	1									9			3			46

FA Cup
Third Round Chorley (a) 0-2

Carabao Cup
First Round Barrow (h) 0-0
(Derby Co won 3-2 on penalties)
Second Round Preston NE (h) 1-2

DONCASTER ROVERS

FOUNDATION

In 1879, Mr Albert Jenkins assembled a team to play a match against the Yorkshire Institution for the Deaf. The players remained together as Doncaster Rovers, joining the Midland Alliance in 1889 and the Midland Counties League in 1891.

Keepmoat Stadium, Stadium Way, Lakeside, Doncaster, South Yorkshire DN4 5JW.

Telephone: (01302) 764 664.

Ticket Office: (01302) 762 576.

Website: www.doncasterroversfc.co.uk

Email: info@clubdoncaster.co.uk

Ground Capacity: 15,148.

Record Attendance: 37,149 v Hull C, Division 3 (N), 2 October 1948 (at Belle Vue); 15,001 v Leeds U, FL 1, 1 April 2008 (at Keepmoat Stadium).

Pitch Measurements: 100m × 66m (109.5yd × 72yd).

Chairman: David Blunt.

Chief Executive: Gavin Baldwin.

Manager: Richie Wellens.

Assistant Manager: Noel Hunt.

Colours: Red and white hooped shirts with red sleeves and black trim, red shorts with black trim, red socks with black and white trim.

Year Formed: 1879.

Turned Professional: 1885.

Club Nickname: 'Rovers', 'Donny'.

Grounds: 1880–1916, Intake Ground; 1920, Benetthorpe Ground; 1922, Low Pasture, Belle Vue; 2007, Keepmoat Stadium.

First Football League Game: 7 September 1901, Division 2, v Burslem Port Vale (h) D 3–3 – Eggett; Simpson, Layton; Longden, Jones, Wright, Langham, Murphy, Price, Goodson (2), Bailey (1).

Record League Victory: 10–0 v Darlington, Division 4, 25 January 1964 – Potter; Raine, Meadows, Windross (1), White, Ripley (2), Robinson, Booth (2), Hale (4), Jeffrey, Broadbent (1).

Record Cup Victory: 7–0 v Blyth Spartans, FA Cup 1st rd, 27 November 1937 – Imrie; Shaw, Rodgers, McFarlane, Bycroft, Cyril Smith, Burton (1), Killourhy (4), Morgan (2), Malam, Dutton; 7–0 v Chorley, FA Cup 1st rd replay, 20 November 2018 – Lawlor; Mason, Butler, Anderson T■, Andrew, Whiteman (Rowe), Coppinger (Taylor), Kane (1) (Crawford), May (4), Marquis (1), Blair (1).

Record Defeat: 0–12 v Small Heath, Division 2, 11 April 1903.

HONOURS

League Champions: FL 1 – 2012–13; Division 3N – 1934–35, 1946–47, 1949–50; Third Division – 2003–04; Division 4 – 1965–66, 1968–69.
Runners-up: Division 3N – 1937–38, 1938–39; Division 4 – 1983–84; Conference – (3rd) 2002–03 *(promoted via play-offs (and golden goal)).*

FA Cup: 5th rd – 1952, 1954, 1955, 1956, 2019.

League Cup: 5th rd – 1976, 2006.

League Trophy Winners: 2007.

FOOTBALL YEARBOOK FACT FILE

Chris Balderstone appeared for Doncaster Rovers against Brentford on 15 September 1975 after earlier in the day hitting a half century for Leicestershire against Derbyshire in the cricket County Championship. Leicestershire's bonus points from the game clinched the title for them but Balderstone missed out on the celebrations as immediately after the close of play he drove up the M1 to Doncaster where he played in Rovers' 1-1 draw with the Bees at Belle Vue.

Most League Points (2 for a win): 72, Division 3 (N), 1946–47.

Most League Points (3 for a win): 92, Division 3, 2003–04.

Most League Goals: 123, Division 3 (N), 1946–47.

Highest League Scorer in Season: Clarrie Jordan, 42, Division 3 (N), 1946–47.

Most League Goals in Total Aggregate: Tom Keetley, 180, 1923–29.

Most League Goals in One Match: 6, Tom Keetley v Ashington, Division 3 (N), 16 February 1929.

Most Capped Player: Len Graham, 14, Northern Ireland.

Most League Appearances: James Coppinger, 614, 2004–21.

Youngest League Player: Alick Jeffrey, 15 years 229 days v Fulham, 15 September 1954.

Record Transfer Fee Received: £2,000,000 from Reading for Matthew Mills, July 2009.

Record Transfer Fee Paid: £1,150,000 to Sheffield U for Billy Sharp, August 2010.

Football League Record: 1901 Elected to Division 2; 1903 Failed re-election; 1904 Re-elected; 1905 Failed re-election; 1923 Re-elected to Division 3 (N); 1935–37 Division 2; 1937–47 Division 3 (N); 1947–48 Division 2; 1948–50 Division 3 (N); 1950–58 Division 2; 1958–59 Division 3; 1959–66 Division 4; 1966–67 Division 3; 1967–69 Division 4; 1969–71 Division 3; 1971–81 Division 4; 1981–83 Division 3; 1983–84 Division 4; 1984–88 Division 3; 1988–92 Division 4; 1992–98 Division 3; 1998–2003 Conference; 2003–04 Division 3; 2004–08 FL 1; 2008–12 FL C; 2012–13 FL 1; 2013–14 FL C; 2014–16 FL 1; 2016–17 FL 2; 2017– FL 1.

LATEST SEQUENCES

Longest Sequence of League Wins: 10, 22.1.1947 – 4.4.1947.

Longest Sequence of League Defeats: 9, 14.1.1905 – 1.4.1905.

Longest Sequence of League Draws: 4, 1.1.2018 – 23.1.2018.

Longest Sequence of Unbeaten League Matches: 20, 26.12.1968 – 12.4.1969.

Longest Sequence Without a League Win: 20, 9.8.1997 – 29.11.1997.

Successive Scoring Runs: 27 from 10.11.1934.

Successive Non-scoring Runs: 7 from 27.9.1947.

MANAGERS

Arthur Porter 1920–21
Harry Tufnell 1921–22
Arthur Porter 1922–23
Dick Ray 1923–27
David Menzies 1928–36
Fred Emery 1936–40
Bill Marsden 1944–46
Jackie Bestall 1946–49
Peter Doherty 1949–58
Jack Hodgson and Sid Bycroft (*Joint Managers*) 1958
Jack Crayston 1958–59 (*continued as Secretary-Manager to 1961*)
Jackie Bestall 1959–60
Norman Curtis 1960–61
Danny Malloy 1961–62
Oscar Hold 1962–64
Bill Leivers 1964–66
Keith Kettleborough 1966–67
George Raynor 1967–68
Lawrie McMenemy 1968–71
Maurice Setters 1971–74
Stan Anderson 1975–78
Billy Bremner 1978–85
Dave Cusack 1985–87
Dave Mackay 1987–89
Billy Bremner 1989–91
Steve Beaglehole 1991–93
Ian Atkins 1994
Sammy Chung 1994–96
Kerry Dixon (*Player-Manager*) 1996–97
Dave Cowling 1997
Mark Weaver 1997–98
Ian Snodin 1998–99
Steve Wignall 1999–2001
Dave Penney 2002–06
Sean O'Driscoll 2006–11
Dean Saunders 2011–13
Brian Flynn 2013
Paul Dickov 2013–15
Darren Ferguson 2015–18
Grant McCann 2018–19
Darren Moore 2019–21
Andy Butler 2021
Richie Wellens May 2021–

TEN YEAR LEAGUE RECORD

		P	W	D	L	F	A	Pts	Pos
2011-12	FL C	46	8	12	26	43	80	36	24
2012-13	FL 1	46	25	9	12	62	44	84	1
2013-14	FL C	46	11	11	24	39	70	44	22
2014-15	FL 1	46	16	13	17	58	62	61	13
2015-16	FL 1	46	11	13	22	48	64	46	21
2016-17	FL 2	46	25	10	11	85	55	85	3
2017-18	FL 1	46	13	17	16	52	52	56	15
2018-19	FL 1	46	20	13	13	76	58	73	6
2019-20	FL 1	34	15	9	10	51	33	54	9§
2020-21	FL 1	46	19	7	20	63	67	64	14

§Decided on points-per-game (1.59)

DID YOU KNOW ?

Doncaster Rovers led the Second Division table in September 1953 for the first time in their history after a 4-1 win at Brentford put them two points clear of second-placed Everton. Rovers won six out of their first seven games and drew the other but were unable to maintain their run and finished the season in a mid-table position.

DONCASTER ROVERS – SKY BET LEAGUE ONE 2020–21 LEAGUE RECORD

Match No.	*Date*	*Venue*	*Opponents*	*Result*		*H/T Score*	*Lg Pos.*	*Goalscorers*	*Attendance*
1	Sept 12	H	Milton Keynes D	D	1-1	0-0	10	Gomes [53]	0
2	19	A	Charlton Ath	W	3-1	1-0	4	Gomes [25], Barker (og) [49], John-Jules [63]	1000
3	26	H	Bristol R	W	4-1	2-1	3	Wright [23], Gomes [30], Richards [57], Taylor [62]	0
4	Oct 3	A	Wigan Ath	L	0-1	0-0	5		0
5	17	A	Portsmouth	W	1-0	0-0	7	James [79]	0
6	20	H	Ipswich T	W	4-1	2-1	6	John [28], Whiteman 2 (1 pen) [37, 62 (p)], Okenabirhie [63]	0
7	24	H	Crewe Alex	L	1-2	1-1	7	Sims [27]	0
8	27	A	Plymouth Arg	L	1-2	0-1	9	Okenabirhie [73]	0
9	31	H	Lincoln C	W	1-0	1-0	8	Whiteman [43]	0
10	Nov 3	A	AFC Wimbledon	D	2-2	1-1	9	Smith [24], Coppinger [90]	0
11	21	H	Sunderland	D	1-1	0-1	11	Okenabirhie [90]	0
12	24	H	Blackpool	W	3-2	0-2	10	John [48], James [52], Whiteman (pen) [76]	0
13	Dec 2	A	Hull C	L	1-2	0-1	10	John-Jules [81]	0
14	5	A	Northampton T	W	2-0	1-0	8	John-Jules [36], Wright [57]	1164
15	12	H	Gillingham	W	2-1	1-0	7	James [29], Halliday [53]	0
16	15	H	Swindon T	W	2-1	0-0	6	James 2 [47, 72]	0
17	19	A	Burton Alb	W	3-1	2-1	4	Okenabirhie [8], Whiteman (pen) [45], Richards [59]	0
18	22	H	Shrewsbury T	L	0-1	0-0	4		0
19	Jan 16	A	Swindon T	W	2-1	2-0	4	Okenabirhie 2 [5, 45]	0
20	19	H	Rochdale	W	1-0	1-0	5	Taylor [31]	0
21	26	H	AFC Wimbledon	W	2-0	2-0	4	Okenabirhie [10], Richards [37]	0
22	30	A	Lincoln C	W	1-0	1-0	3	Richards [15]	0
23	Feb 6	H	Oxford U	W	3-2	1-1	2	Taylor [31], Okenabirhie [47], Richards [51]	0
24	9	A	Fleetwood T	L	1-3	1-0	5	Lokilo [8]	0
25	13	A	Sunderland	L	1-4	0-3	5	Burge (og) [53]	0
26	17	H	Accrington S	L	0-1	0-1	5		0
27	20	H	Hull C	D	3-3	1-3	4	James [33], Bogle (pen) [68], Coppinger [90]	0
28	27	A	Ipswich T	L	1-2	0-1	6	Taylor [73]	0
29	Mar 2	H	Portsmouth	W	2-1	1-0	6	James [12], Okenabirhie [70]	0
30	6	H	Plymouth Arg	W	2-1	1-0	5	Anderson [7], Bogle [47]	0
31	9	A	Crewe Alex	L	0-1	0-0	5		0
32	13	H	Northampton T	D	0-0	0-0	5		0
33	16	A	Oxford U	L	0-3	0-3	5		0
34	20	A	Gillingham	D	2-2	2-2	5	Anderson [19], Coppinger [23]	0
35	27	A	Milton Keynes D	L	0-1	0-0	7		0
36	Apr 2	H	Charlton Ath	L	0-1	0-1	10		0
37	5	A	Bristol R	L	1-2	1-1	10	Coppinger [13]	0
38	10	H	Wigan Ath	L	1-4	1-3	11	Richards [45]	0
39	13	H	Burton Alb	L	0-3	0-0	12		0
40	17	A	Shrewsbury T	W	2-0	1-0	10	Okenabirhie [15], Richards [80]	0
41	20	A	Accrington S	L	1-2	0-1	13	John-Jules [76]	0
42	24	H	Fleetwood T	L	0-1	0-0	13		0
43	27	A	Peterborough U	D	2-2	1-2	13	Okenabirhie [37], Richards [59]	0
44	May 1	A	Rochdale	W	2-1	1-0	12	Richards 2 [30, 56]	0
45	4	A	Blackpool	L	0-2	0-1	12		0
46	9	H	Peterborough U	L	1-4	0-4	14	John-Jules [90]	0

Final League Position: 14

GOALSCORERS

League (63): Okenabirhie 11, Richards 10, James 7, John-Jules 5, Whiteman 5 (3 pens), Coppinger 4, Taylor 4, Gomes 3, Anderson 2, Bogle 2 (1 pen), John 2, Wright 2, Halliday 1, Lokilo 1, Sims 1, Smith 1, own goals 2.
FA Cup (8): Whiteman 3, Sims 2, Coppinger 1, Okenabirhie 1, Richards 1.
Carabao Cup (2): Gomes 1, Okenabirhie 1 (1 pen).
Papa John's Trophy (1): Okenabirhie 1 (1 pen).

Bursik J 10	Halliday B 34 + 3	Wright J 36 + 4	Anderson T 44	James R 42 + 1	Whiteman B 18	Gomes M 11 + 11	Taylor J 19 + 6	Richards T 28 + 13	Tulloch R 2	John-Jules T 13 + 5	Lokilo J 13 + 19	Okenabirhie F 30 + 9	Williams E — + 11	John C 21 + 10	Coppinger J 17 + 15	Sims J 20 + 8	Smith M 37 + 3	Amos D 4 + 4	Lumley J 8	Butler A 20	Hasani L — + 2	Balcombe E 15	Simoes E 7 + 1	Greaves A 4 + 6	Robertson S 6 + 9	Bostock J 11 + 7	Bogle O 14 + 3	Jones L 13	Horton B 9 + 2	Blythe B — + 1	*Match No.*
1	2	3	4	5	6	7	8^3	9	10^1	11^2	12	13	14																		1
1	2	3	4	5^2	7	6	8	9^3	10^1	11	12			13	14																2
1	2	4	3	5	6	7	10^3	9^2		11	8^1	14		13	12																3
1	2	4	3	5^1	7	6	8	9^3		11		13	14	12	10^2																4
1	2	3	4	10	7	6	8^1	13				11^3		5	9^2	12	14														5
1	2	3	4	12	6	7	8	13				11^2	14	5		10^1	9^3														6
1	2	4	3	5	7	6^3	8^1				12	11		14	13	10	9^2														7
1	2^2	3	4	10	6		8					11	14	5	9^3	12	7^1	13													8
1	12	2	3	7	6		8^1				13	11		4		10^2	9	5													9
1	12	2^1	3	7	6		8^3				14	11		4	13	10	9	5^2													10
	2	3	4	6^2	7			12			8^1	11		5	13	10	9		1												11
	2	3	4	7	6			12				11		5	8^1	10	9		1												12
	2	3	4	7	6			8^1		13		11		5	12	10	9^2		1												13
	8^2	2	3	7	6			9^4		11^3		13	16	5^1	14	10^5	12		1	4	15										14
	2		3	10	7		12	9^1		11^2		13		5	14	8	6^3		1	4											15
	2		3	10	7		12	13		11^4		15		14	9^1	8^2	6^3	5	1	4											16
	2		3	10	7		8^2	9^1		13	12	11		5			6^3		1	4	14										17
	2		3	5	6		8^1	9^2		11	12	10			13		7		1	4											18
	2		3	7			14	6^2		11^4	10^3	8		5			12	15		4		1	9^1	13							19
	2	15	3				8^1	9^2			12	11^4	13	5			6	14		4		1	10^3	7							20
	2	14	3	7			8^1	9^2				11	12	5			6			4		1	10^3	13							21
	8	2	3	7		13	14	9^1			12	11^3		5			6			4		1	10^2								22
	2	14	3	10		7^2	8^3	9^1			13	11^4		5			6			4		1			12	15					23
	2	12	3^1	10		14	16	13			8^5	11		5			6^4			4		1			9^3	7^2	15				24
	2	3		10		7^1	8^3	9^4			14			5^2		13	6			4		1			15	12	11				25
	2	3		5		14	8^1	9^2						13		12				4		1	10		6^3	7	11				26
	2	3	4	5		7^1	8^4	9			13				14	10^2	6^3					1			15	12	11				27
	2	3	4	5			12	9^3			15	8^4			14	10^1	6^2					1			13	7	11				28
	2	3	4	5			8^1	15			13	12			9^4	10^2	6								14	7^3	11	1			29
	2	3	4	5		15		8^4			13			14	9^2	10	6^3								12	7^1	11	1			30
	2	3	4	5^3		11^2		8			10			14	9	13	6								12	7^1		1			31
	2	3	4	10		14		12			8	11		5^2	13		7^3						9		6^1			1			32
	2	3	4			14		9			12	11	15		10^4		6	5^2					8^1	7^3				1	13		33
	2	3	4	7		14		12			13	10^3			9^1	8^2	6										11	1	5		34
	2	3^4	4	7		14		9			8	12		15	10^1										13	6^3	11	1	5^2		35
	2	3^2	4	5				12			14	9^3		13	11		7^4							15	8^1	6	10	1			36
			3	5		15		8^1			10	7		4	9^2		6^3					1	12	14		13	11		2^4		37
		2	3	8^3		15		12			9	16		4		11^5	7^4	14				1			6^1	13	10		5^2		38
		3	4					12				10			9	8	6					1		2		7^1	11		5		39
		2	4	5				9^3		12	13	11	14		8^1	10^2	7			3		1				6					40
		2	4	5				9		12	10^1	11	14		8^3		7			3		1			13	6^2					41
		2	3	5				9		11^2		10			13	8^3	6			4					7^1	12		1	14		42
		2	3	8				12		13	9	11				6^1	7			4							10^2	1	5		43
		2	3	8				9^3		10^2	6^1	11^4			13	14	7^5			4				16		15	12	1	5		44
		2	3	8^2				9		10^4	6^3	11^1			14	15	7			4				13			12	1	5		45
	12	2^1	3	10		15				8			16		9^5	13	6			4^3				7^2			11^4	1	5	14	46

FA Cup

First Round	FC U Manchester	(a)	5-1
Second Round	Carlisle U	(a)	2-1
Third Round	Blackburn R	(a)	1-0
Fourth Round	West Ham U	(a)	0-4

Carabao Cup

First Round	Blackburn R	(a)	2-3

Papa John's Trophy

Group F (N)	Bradford C	(h)	0-0
(Doncaster R won 4-1 on penalties)			
Group F (N)	Oldham Ath	(a)	0-2
Group F (N)	Wolverhampton W U21	(h)	1-2

EVERTON

FOUNDATION

St Domingo Church Sunday School formed a football club in 1878 which played at Stanley Park. Enthusiasm was so great that in November 1879 they decided to expand membership and changed the name to Everton, playing in black shirts with a scarlet sash and nicknamed the 'Black Watch'. After wearing several other colours, royal blue was adopted in 1901.

Goodison Park, Goodison Road, Liverpool L4 4EL.

Telephone: (0151) 556 1878.

Ticket Office: (0151) 556 1878.

Website: www.evertonfc.com

Email: everton@evertonfc.com

Ground Capacity: 39,414.

Record Attendance: 78,299 v Liverpool, Division 1, 18 September 1948.

Pitch Measurements: 100.48m × 68m (110yd × 74.5yd).

Chairman: Bill Kenwright CBE.

Chief Executive: Dr Denise Barrett-Baxendale MBE.

Manager: Rafael Benitez.

Assistant Manager: Duncan Ferguson.

Colours: Blue shirts with white trim, white shorts with blue trim, white socks with blue trim.

Year Formed: 1878.

Turned Professional: 1885.

Previous Name: 1878, St Domingo FC; 1879, Everton.

Club Nickname: 'The Toffees'.

Grounds: 1878, Stanley Park; 1882, Priory Road; 1884, Anfield Road; 1892, Goodison Park.

First Football League Game: 8 September 1888, Football League, v Accrington (h) W 2–1 – Smalley; Dick, Ross; Holt, Jones, Dobson; Fleming (2), Waugh, Lewis, Edgar Chadwick, Farmer.

Record League Victory: 9–1 v Manchester C, Division 1, 3 September 1906 – Scott; Balmer, Crelley; Booth, Taylor (1), Abbott (1); Sharp, Bolton (1), Young (4), Settle (2), George Wilson; 9–1 v Plymouth Arg, Division 2, 27 December 1930 – Coggins; Williams, Cresswell; McPherson, Griffiths, Thomson; Critchley, Dunn, Dean (4), Johnson (1), Stein (4).

HONOURS

League Champions: Division 1 – 1914–15, 1927–28, 1931–32, 1938–39, 1962–63, 1969–70, 1984–85, 1986–87; Football League 1890–91; Division 2 – 1930–31.
Runners-up: Division 1 – 1894–95, 1901–02, 1904–05, 1908–09, 1911–12, 1985–86; Football League 1889–90; Division 2 – 1953–54.

FA Cup Winners: 1906, 1933, 1966, 1984, 1995.
Runners-up: 1893, 1897, 1907, 1968, 1985, 1986, 1989, 2009.

League Cup: *Runners-up:* 1977, 1984.

League Super Cup: *Runners-up:* 1986.

Full Members' Cup: *Runners-up:* 1989, 1991.

European Competitions
European Cup: 1963–64, 1970–71 *(qf)*.
Champions League: 2005–06.
Fairs Cup: 1962–63, 1964–65, 1965–66.
UEFA Cup: 1975–76, 1978–79, 1979–80, 2005–06, 2007–08, 2008–09.
Europa League: 2009–10, 2014–15, 2017–18.
European Cup-Winners' Cup: 1966–67, 1984–85 *(winners)*, 1995–96.

FOOTBALL YEARBOOK FACT FILE

Everton's team at Leeds United or the First Division game played on 16 April 1966, a week before their FA Cup semi-final against Manchester United, included six teenagers, with three players making their Football League debuts. The average age was just 20 years and 333 days, making it the youngest to feature in a Football League match for the club. The Toffees were later fined for fielding a weakened line-up.

Record Cup Victory: 11–2 v Derby Co, FA Cup 1st rd, 18 January 1890 – Smalley; Hannah, Doyle (1); Kirkwood, Holt (1), Parry; Latta, Brady (3), Geary (3), Edgar Chadwick, Millward (3).

Record Defeat: 4–10 v Tottenham H, Division 1, 11 October 1958.

Most League Points (2 for a win): 66, Division 1, 1969–70.

Most League Points (3 for a win): 90, Division 1, 1984–85.

Most League Goals: 121, Division 2, 1930–31.

Highest League Scorer in Season: William Ralph 'Dixie' Dean, 60, Division 1, 1927–28 (All-time League record).

Most League Goals in Total Aggregate: William Ralph 'Dixie' Dean, 349, 1925–37.

Most League Goals in One Match: 6, Jack Southworth v WBA, Division 1, 30 December 1893.

Most Capped Player: Tim Howard, 93 (121), USA.

Most League Appearances: Neville Southall, 578, 1981–98.

Youngest League Player: Jose Baxter, 16 years 191 days v Blackburn R, 16 August 2008.

Record Transfer Fee Received: £75,000,000 from Manchester U for Romelu Lukaku, July 2017.

Record Transfer Fee Paid: £40,000,000 (rising to £45,000,000) to Swansea C for Gylfi Sigurdsson, August 2017.

Football League Record: 1888 Founder Member of the Football League; 1930–31 Division 2; 1931–51 Division 1; 1951–54 Division 2; 1954–92 Division 1; 1992– Premier League.

MANAGERS

W. E. Barclay 1888–89
(Secretary-Manager)
Dick Molyneux 1889–1901
(Secretary-Manager)
William C. Cuff 1901–18
(Secretary-Manager)
W. J. Sawyer 1918–19
(Secretary-Manager)
Thomas H. McIntosh 1919–35
(Secretary-Manager)
Theo Kelly 1936–48
Cliff Britton 1948–56
Ian Buchan 1956–58
Johnny Carey 1958–61
Harry Catterick 1961–73
Billy Bingham 1973–77
Gordon Lee 1977–81
Howard Kendall 1981–87
Colin Harvey 1987–90
Howard Kendall 1990–93
Mike Walker 1994
Joe Royle 1994–97
Howard Kendall 1997–98
Walter Smith 1998–2002
David Moyes 2002–13
Roberto Martinez 2013–16
Ronald Koeman 2016–17
Sam Allardyce 2017–18
Marco Silva 2018–19
Carlo Ancelotti 2019–21
Rafael Benitez June 2021–

LATEST SEQUENCES

Longest Sequence of League Wins: 12, 24.3.1894 – 13.10.1894.

Longest Sequence of League Defeats: 6, 27.8.2005– 15.10.2005.

Longest Sequence of League Draws: 5, 4.5.1977 – 16.5.1977.

Longest Sequence of Unbeaten League Matches: 20, 29.4.1978 – 16.12.1978.

Longest Sequence Without a League Win: 14, 6.3.1937 – 4.9.1937.

Successive Scoring Runs: 40 from 15.3.1930.

Successive Non-scoring Runs: 6 from 27.8.2005.

TEN YEAR LEAGUE RECORD

		P	*W*	*D*	*L*	*F*	*A*	*Pts*	*Pos*
2011-12	PR Lge	38	15	11	12	50	40	56	7
2012-13	PR Lge	38	16	15	7	55	40	63	6
2013-14	PR Lge	38	21	9	8	61	39	72	5
2014-15	PR Lge	38	12	11	15	48	50	47	11
2015-16	PR Lge	38	11	14	13	59	55	47	11
2016-17	PR Lge	38	17	10	11	62	44	61	7
2017-18	PR Lge	38	13	10	15	44	58	49	8
2018-19	PR Lge	38	15	9	14	54	46	54	8
2019-20	PR Lge	38	13	10	15	44	56	49	12
2020-21	PR Lge	38	17	8	13	47	48	59	10

DID YOU KNOW 

Leighton Baines holds the career record for penalties scored for Everton, having been successful on 25 occasions from 28 attempts between 2009 and 2017. His tally in Premier League fixtures is 19 from 21 attempts, also a club record. Roy Vernon with 18 successes from 19 attempts has a higher percentage record.

EVERTON – PREMIER LEAGUE 2020–21 LEAGUE RECORD

Match No.	Date	Venue	Opponents	Result	H/T Score	Lg Pos.	Goalscorers	Attendance
1	Sept 13	A	Tottenham H	W 1-0	0-0	5	Calvert-Lewin [55]	0
2	19	H	WBA	W 5-2	2-1	1	Calvert-Lewin 3 [31, 62, 66], Rodriguez [45], Keane [54]	0
3	26	A	Crystal Palace	W 2-1	2-1	1	Calvert-Lewin [10], Richarlison (pen) [40]	0
4	Oct 3	H	Brighton & HA	W 4-2	2-1	1	Calvert-Lewin [16], Mina [45], Rodriguez 2 [52, 70]	0
5	17	H	Liverpool	D 2-2	1-1	1	Keane [19], Calvert-Lewin [81]	0
6	25	A	Southampton	L 0-2	0-2	1		0
7	Nov 1	A	Newcastle U	L 1-2	0-0	3	Calvert-Lewin [90]	0
8	7	H	Manchester U	L 1-3	1-2	6	Bernard [19]	0
9	22	A	Fulham	W 3-2	3-1	6	Calvert-Lewin 2 [1, 29], Doucoure [35]	0
10	28	H	Leeds U	L 0-1	0-0	6		0
11	Dec 5	A	Burnley	D 1-1	1-1	9	Calvert-Lewin [45]	0
12	12	H	Chelsea	W 1-0	1-0	7	Sigurdsson (pen) [22]	2000
13	16	A	Leicester C	W 2-0	1-0	5	Richarlison [21], Holgate [72]	0
14	19	H	Arsenal	W 2-1	2-1	2	Holding (og) [22], Mina [45]	2000
15	26	A	Sheffield U	W 1-0	0-0	2	Sigurdsson [80]	0
16	Jan 1	H	West Ham U	L 0-1	0-0	4		0
17	12	A	Wolverhampton W	W 2-1	1-1	4	Iwobi [6], Keane [77]	0
18	27	H	Leicester C	D 1-1	1-0	7	Rodriguez [30]	0
19	30	H	Newcastle U	L 0-2	0-0	7		0
20	Feb 3	A	Leeds U	W 2-1	2-0	6	Sigurdsson [9], Calvert-Lewin [41]	0
21	6	A	Manchester U	D 3-3	0-2	6	Doucoure [49], Rodriguez [52], Calvert-Lewin [90]	0
22	14	H	Fulham	L 0-2	0-0	7		0
23	17	H	Manchester C	L 1-3	1-1	7	Richarlison [37]	0
24	20	A	Liverpool	W 2-0	1-0	7	Richarlison [3], Sigurdsson (pen) [83]	0
25	Mar 1	H	Southampton	W 1-0	1-0	7	Richarlison [9]	0
26	4	A	WBA	W 1-0	0-0	5	Richarlison [65]	0
27	8	A	Chelsea	L 0-2	0-1	6		0
28	13	H	Burnley	L 1-2	1-2	6	Calvert-Lewin [32]	0
29	Apr 5	H	Crystal Palace	D 1-1	0-0	8	Rodriguez [56]	0
30	12	A	Brighton & HA	D 0-0	0-0	8		0
31	16	H	Tottenham H	D 2-2	1-1	8	Sigurdsson 2 (1 pen) [31 (p), 62]	0
32	23	A	Arsenal	W 1-0	0-0	8	Leno (og) [76]	0
33	May 1	H	Aston Villa	L 1-2	1-1	8	Calvert-Lewin [19]	0
34	9	A	West Ham U	W 1-0	1-0	8	Calvert-Lewin [24]	0
35	13	A	Aston Villa	D 0-0	0-0	8		0
36	16	H	Sheffield U	L 0-1	0-1	8		0
37	19	H	Wolverhampton W	W 1-0	0-0	8	Richarlison [48]	6068
38	23	A	Manchester C	L 0-5	0-2	10		10,000

Final League Position: 10

GOALSCORERS

League (47): Calvert-Lewin 16, Richarlison 7 (1 pen), Rodriguez 6, Sigurdsson 6 (3 pens), Keane 3, Doucoure 2, Mina 2, Bernard 1, Holgate 1, Iwobi 1, own goals 2.
FA Cup (10): Richarlison 3, Calvert-Lewin 2, Bernard 1, Doucoure 1, Mina 1, Sigurdsson 1 (1 pen), Tosun 1.
Carabao Cup (12): Calvert-Lewin 3, Richarlison 3, Kean 2 (1 pen), Bernard 1, Iwobi 1, Keane 1, Sigurdsson 1.

Pickford J 31	Coleman S 18 + 7	Mina Y 23 + 1	Keane M 33 + 2	Digne L 30	Doucoure A 29	Allan M 23 + 1	Andre Gomes F 17 + 11	Rodriguez J 21 + 2	Calvert-Lewin D 32 + 1	Richarlison d 33 + 1	Sigurdsson G 24 + 12	Kean M — + 2	Davies T 17 + 8	Iwobi A 17 + 13	Delph F 2 + 6	Walcott T — + 1	Godfrey B 29 + 2	Bernard C 3 + 9	Gordon A 1 + 2	Olsen R 7	Kenny J 1 + 3	Nkounkou N 1 + 1	Tosun C — + 5	Holgate M 26 + 2	King J — + 11	Virginia J — + 1	Gbamin J — + 1	Broadhead N — + 1	*Match No.*
1	2	3	4	5	6	7	8^{1}	9^{3}	10^{2}	11	12	13	14																1
1	2	3	4	5	6^{1}	7	8	9^{3}	10^{2}	11	12	14		13															2
1	2	3	4	5	6	7	8^{1}	9^{2}	10	11^{3}	12		14	13															3
1	2^{2}	3	4	5	6			9^{3}	10	11^{1}	8		7	12	13	14													4
1	2^{1}	3	4	5	6^{3}	7	8^{2}	9	10	11■	13			14			12												5
1		3	4	5■	6^{2}	7		9	10		8^{3}			11^{1}	14		2	12	13										6
		3	4		6	7	10^{1}		11		9			14	8			12		1	2^{3}	5^{2}	13						7
1	2		3	5	6	7		9^{2}	10		8^{1}			12				11					13	4					8
1		3	4	8	6	7		9^{1}	10	11^{2}	13		12	5			2												9
1			3		6	7	13	9	10	11			5^{1}	8^{2}	12		2	14						4^{3}					10
1		3	4		6^{2}	7^{3}	12	9	10	11	13			5	8^{1}		2						14						11
1		3	4		8	7	12		10	11^{3}	6^{1}		13	9^{2}			5				14			2					12
		3	4		8	7^{1}	12		10^{2}	11	6			9^{3}			5		14	1	13			2					13
1	12	3	4		6				11^{2}	10^{3}	9		7	8^{1}			5				13		14	2					14
1	13	3	4^{2}		6		14		11		9		7^{3}	8			5	12	10^{1}					2					15
1	2	3			6		13	12	11^{3}	10	9^{2}		7				5	8^{1}					14	4					16
1	14	3	4	9	7		12	10^{3}		13	11^{2}		8^{1}	6			5							2					17
1	14	3	4	9			8	10^{2}	11^{3}	6	13		7	12			5							2^{1}					18
1	2	3	4	5	6		12	9	11	10	7			8^{1}															19
		3	12	5	6		7		11	10^{1}	9^{3}		14	8^{2}			4			1				2	13				20
			3	5	6^{3}		8	9^{1}	10	11	12		7^{2}	13			4			1				2	14				21
	2^{1}		13	5	6		8	9^{3}		11	10		7^{2}				3	14		1				4	12				22
1	12	3^{1}	4	9	7			14		11	10		8^{2}	6^{3}			5							2	13				23
1	2		4	6	7		9^{1}	10^{2}	13	11^{3}	12		8	14			5							3					24
1			3	5	6	7	8^{1}		10	11^{2}	9			12			4							2	13				25
1			3	8	6^{2}	12	7		10	11	13			5^{1}			4	9^{3}						2	14				26
1			3	8		7	6^{3}		10	11	9^{2}		12	5^{1}			4	14						2	13				27
1^{1}	14		3	5		6	8		10	11			7^{2}	9			4							2^{3}	13	12			28
	5^{2}	3	2	8			7^{1}	9^{3}	10	11	12		6				13			1				4			14		29
	2	4^{1}	5	6				10		11	9		7^{2}	12			3			1				8				13	30
1	12		3	9		6		10		11	8		7^{2}	5^{1}			2							4	13				31
1	2	14		5		7	8^{1}	6^{2}	10	9^{3}	11		13		12		3							4					32
1	2			5		6	7^{1}		11	10	9^{3}			8^{2}	12		3	13						4	14				33
1	2	4^{1}	5	6		7			10	11^{2}	9^{3}		8		14		3							12	13				34
1	6^{2}		3	5	7	8	12		11	10	9^{1}			13			4							2					35
1	5		3	8	6^{2}	7	13	9^{3}	10	11	12						4	14						2^{1}					36
1	6^{1}	4	2	3	8^{3}	9	13		10	11	7^{2}		12				5							14					37
1			3	5	6^{1}	7			10	11^{3}	9^{2}		8	12			4	13				14		2					38

FA Cup

Third Round *(aet)*	Rotherham U	(h)	2-1
Fourth Round	Sheffield W	(h)	3-0
Fifth Round *(aet)*	Tottenham H	(h)	5-4
Sixth Round	Manchester C	(h)	0-2

Carabao Cup

Second Round	Salford C	(h)	3-0
Third Round	Fleetwood T	(a)	5-2
Fourth Round	West Ham U	(h)	4-1
Quarter-Final	Manchester U	(h)	0-2

EXETER CITY

FOUNDATION

Exeter City was formed in 1904 by the amalgamation of St Sidwell's United and Exeter United. The club first played in the East Devon League and then the Plymouth & District League. After an exhibition match between West Bromwich Albion and Woolwich Arsenal, which was held to test interest as Exeter was then a rugby stronghold, it was decided to form Exeter City. At a meeting at the Red Lion Hotel in 1908, the club turned professional.

St James Park, Stadium Way, Exeter, Devon EX4 6PX.

Telephone: (01392) 411 243.

Ticket Office: (01392) 413 952.

Website: www.exetercityfc.co.uk

Email: reception@ecfc.co.uk

Ground Capacity: 8,541.

Record Attendance: 20,984 v Sunderland, FA Cup 6th rd (replay), 4 March 1931.

Pitch Measurements: 103m × 64m (112.5yd × 70yd).

Chairman: Julian Tagg.

Chief Operating Officer: Justin Quick.

Manager: Matt Taylor.

Assistant Manager: Wayne Carlisle.

Colours: Red and white striped shirts with white sleeves and black trim, black shorts with white trim, white socks with black hoops.

Year Formed: 1904.

Turned Professional: 1908.

Club Nickname: 'The Grecians'.

Ground: 1904, St James Park.

First Football League Game: 28 August 1920, Division 3, v Brentford (h) W 3–0 – Pym; Coleburne, Feebury (1p); Crawshaw, Carrick, Mitton; Appleton, Makin, Wright (1), Vowles (1), Dockray.

Record League Victory: 8–1 v Coventry C, Division 3 (S), 4 December 1926 – Bailey; Pollard, Charlton; Pullen, Pool, Garrett; Purcell (2), McDevitt, Blackmore (2), Dent (2), Compton (2). 8–1 v Aldershot, Division 3 (S), 4 May 1935 – Chesters; Gray, Miller; Risdon, Webb, Angus; Jack Scott (1), Wrightson (1), Poulter (3), McArthur (1), Dryden (1), (1 og).

Record Cup Victory: 14–0 v Weymouth, FA Cup 1st qual rd, 3 October 1908 – Fletcher; Craig, Bulcock; Ambler, Chadwick, Wake; Parnell (1), Watson (1), McGuigan (4), Bell (6), Copestake (2).

Record Defeat: 0–9 v Notts Co, Division 3 (S), 16 October 1948. 0–9 v Northampton T, Division 3 (S), 12 April 1958.

HONOURS

League Champions: Division 4 – 1989–90.
Runners-up: Division 3S – 1932–33; FL 2 – 2008–09; Division 4 – 1976–77; Conference – (4th) 2007–08 *(promoted via play-offs).*

FA Cup: 6th rd replay – 1931; 6th rd – 1981.

League Cup: never past 4th rd.

FOOTBALL YEARBOOK FACT FILE

Exeter City's nickname of the Grecians derives from a name given to residents of St Sidwell's parish, and this was a name used for the club's predecessors, St Sidwell's United. A 1908 newspaper report noted that players of the newly professional Exeter City club 'have been popularly named "the Grecians", the ancient name of St Sidwellians'.

Most League Points (2 for a win): 62, Division 4, 1976–77.

Most League Points (3 for a win): 89, Division 4, 1989–90.

Most League Goals: 88, Division 3 (S), 1932–33.

Highest League Scorer in Season: Fred Whitlow, 33, Division 3 (S), 1932–33.

Most League Goals in Total Aggregate: Tony Kellow, 129, 1976–78, 1980–83, 1985–88.

Most League Goals in One Match: 4, Harold 'Jazzo' Kirk v Portsmouth, Division 3 (S), 3 March 1923; 4, Fred Dent v Bristol R, Division 3 (S), 5 November 1927; 4, Fred Whitlow v Watford, Division 3 (S), 29 October 1932.

Most Capped Player: Joel Grant, 2 (14), Jamaica.

Most League Appearances: Arnold Mitchell, 495, 1952–66.

Youngest League Player: Ethan Ampadu, 15 years 337 days v Crawley T, 16 August 2016.

Record Transfer Fee Received: £1,800,000 from Brentford for Ollie Watkins, July 2017.

Record Transfer Fee Paid: £100,000 to Aberdeen for Jayden Stockley, August 2017.

Football League Record: 1920 Elected to Division 3; 1921–58 Division 3 (S); 1958–64 Division 4; 1964–66 Division 3; 1966–77 Division 4; 1977–84 Division 3; 1984–90 Division 4; 1990–92 Division 3; 1992–94 Division 2; 1994–2003 Division 3; 2003–08 Conference; 2008–09 FL 2; 2009–12 FL 1; 2012– FL 2.

MANAGERS

Arthur Chadwick 1910–22
Fred Mavin 1923–27
Dave Wilson 1928–29
Billy McDevitt 1929–35
Jack English 1935–39
George Roughton 1945–52
Norman Kirkman 1952–53
Norman Dodgin 1953–57
Bill Thompson 1957–58
Frank Broome 1958–60
Glen Wilson 1960–62
Cyril Spiers 1962–63
Jack Edwards 1963–65
Ellis Stuttard 1965–66
Jock Basford 1966–67
Frank Broome 1967–69
Johnny Newman 1969–76
Bobby Saxton 1977–79
Brian Godfrey 1979–83
Gerry Francis 1983–84
Jim Iley 1984–85
Colin Appleton 1985–87
Terry Cooper 1988–91
Alan Ball 1991–94
Terry Cooper 1994–95
Peter Fox 1995–2000
Noel Blake 2000–01
John Cornforth 2001–02
Neil McNab 2002–03
Gary Peters 2003
Eamonn Dolan 2003–04
Alex Inglethorpe 2004–06
Paul Tisdale 2006–18
Matt Taylor June 2018–

LATEST SEQUENCES

Longest Sequence of League Wins: 7, 31.12.2016 – 4.2.2017.

Longest Sequence of League Defeats: 7, 14.1.1984 – 25.2.1984.

Longest Sequence of League Draws: 6, 13.9.1986 – 4.10.1986.

Longest Sequence of Unbeaten League Matches: 13, 22.4.2019 – 21.9.2019.

Longest Sequence Without a League Win: 18, 21.2.1995 – 19.8.1995.

Successive Scoring Runs: 22 from 15.9.1958.

Successive Non-scoring Runs: 6 from 17.1.1986.

TEN YEAR LEAGUE RECORD

		P	W	D	L	F	A	Pts	Pos
2011-12	FL 1	46	10	12	24	46	75	42	23
2012-13	FL 2	46	18	10	18	63	62	64	10
2013-14	FL 2	46	14	13	19	54	57	55	16
2014-15	FL 2	46	17	13	16	61	65	64	10
2015-16	FL 2	46	17	13	16	63	65	64	14
2016-17	FL 2	46	21	8	17	75	56	71	5
2017-18	FL 2	46	24	8	14	64	54	80	4
2018-19	FL 2	46	19	13	14	60	49	70	9
2019-20	FL 2	37	18	11	8	53	43	65	5§
2020-21	FL 2	46	18	16	12	71	50	70	9

§Decided on points-per-game (1.76)

DID YOU KNOW ?

The first competitive game played by Exeter City under their current name took place at St James Park on 10 September 1904. City faced a team from the 110th Royal Field Artillery in an East Devon Senior League fixture and ran out 2-1 winners. The Grecians went on to clinch the title with 11 wins from their 14 games.

EXETER CITY – SKY BET LEAGUE TWO 2020–21 LEAGUE RECORD

Match No.	Date	Venue	Opponents	Result		H/T Score	Lg Pos.	Goalscorers	Attendance
1	Sept 12	A	Salford C	D	2-2	2-1	8	Jay [22], Randall [34]	0
2	19	H	Port Vale	L	0-2	0-1	19		0
3	26	A	Mansfield T	W	2-1	1-1	15	Rawson (og) [40], Key [76]	0
4	Oct 3	H	Cambridge U	W	2-0	2-0	6	Jay (pen) [16], Randall [34]	0
5	10	A	Southend U	D	2-2	1-1	8	Randall [40], Fisher [90]	0
6	17	A	Walsall	D	0-0	0-0	12		0
7	20	H	Crawley T	W	2-1	0-1	9	Taylor [77], Bowman [84]	0
8	24	H	Scunthorpe U	W	3-1	2-0	5	Randall [36], Jay [39], Taylor [90]	0
9	27	A	Leyton Orient	D	1-1	0-1	6	Taylor [47]	0
10	31	H	Carlisle U	W	1-0	0-0	4	Parkes [48]	0
11	Nov 3	A	Morecambe	D	2-2	1-2	4	Randall [33], Taylor [72]	0
12	14	A	Bradford C	D	2-2	2-2	4	Jay [20], Bowman [27]	0
13	21	H	Oldham Ath	L	1-2	1-2	6	Williams [12]	0
14	24	H	Colchester U	W	6-1	1-0	5	Jay 2 [20, 90], Randall [53], Bowman 3 [57, 71, 90]	0
15	Dec 1	A	Grimsby T	W	4-1	3-1	3	Bowman [19], Williams 2 [40, 44], Jay [68]	0
16	5	A	Cheltenham T	L	3-5	1-3	5	Collins [4], Jay [56], Law [88]	0
17	12	H	Tranmere R	W	5-0	3-0	5	Bowman 3 [8, 27, 77], Jay (pen) [18], Taylor [73]	1630
18	15	H	Harrogate T	L	1-2	0-1	5	Taylor [46]	1559
19	26	H	Forest Green R	D	1-1	1-1	7	Collins [37]	1767
20	Jan 12	H	Bolton W	D	1-1	0-0	10	Santos (og) [62]	0
21	19	A	Harrogate T	D	0-0	0-0	10		0
22	23	H	Stevenage	W	3-1	1-0	8	Collins [10], Jay [79], Bowman [85]	0
23	26	H	Morecambe	L	0-2	0-1	9		0
24	30	A	Carlisle U	L	0-1	0-1	9		0
25	Feb 2	A	Stevenage	W	1-0	1-0	8	McArdle [28]	0
26	6	H	Bradford C	W	3-2	1-2	5	Sweeney [41], Bowman [61], Jay (pen) [79]	0
27	16	A	Newport Co	D	1-1	1-0	7	Bowman [22]	0
28	23	A	Colchester U	W	2-1	1-0	6	Willmott [27], Seymour [64]	0
29	27	A	Crawley T	L	0-2	0-0	8		0
30	Mar 2	H	Walsall	D	0-0	0-0	9		0
31	6	H	Leyton Orient	W	4-0	3-0	8	Randall [11], Jay 3 (1 pen) [13, 42, 50 (p)]	0
32	9	A	Scunthorpe U	W	2-0	1-0	8	Jay [11], Sparkes [89]	0
33	13	H	Cheltenham T	L	0-1	0-0	8		0
34	20	A	Tranmere R	L	1-2	1-1	8	Randall [20]	0
35	23	A	Oldham Ath	L	1-2	0-1	8	Sparkes [67]	0
36	27	H	Salford C	W	1-0	1-0	8	Jay [34]	0
37	Apr 2	A	Port Vale	L	0-1	0-1	8		0
38	5	H	Mansfield T	D	0-0	0-0	8		0
39	10	A	Cambridge U	W	4-1	2-0	8	Bowman [3], Sparkes [15], Collins [67], Jay [80]	0
40	13	A	Barrow	L	1-2	0-1	8	Sweeney [90]	0
41	17	H	Southend U	D	0-0	0-0	8		0
42	20	A	Forest Green R	D	0-0	0-0	8		0
43	24	H	Newport Co	D	0-0	0-0	9		0
44	27	H	Grimsby T	W	3-2	1-1	9	Waterfall (og) [33], Fisher [83], Bowman [88]	0
45	May 1	A	Bolton W	W	2-1	0-1	8	Williams [49], Sweeney [90]	0
46	8	H	Barrow	D	1-1	1-0	9	Jay [25]	0

Final League Position: 9

GOALSCORERS

League (71): Jay 18 (4 pens), Bowman 14, Randall 8, Taylor 6, Collins 4, Williams 4, Sparkes 3, Sweeney 3, Fisher 2, Key 1, Law 1, McArdle 1, Parkes 1, Seymour 1, Willmott 1, own goals 3.
FA Cup (5): Randall 2, Hartridge 1, Jay 1, Law 1.
Carabao Cup (0).
Papa John's Trophy (12): Atangana 2, Kite 2, Seymour 2 (1 pen), Ajose 1, Hartridge 1, Jay 1, Key 1, Law 1, Sparkes 1.

Ward L 8	Key J 36 + 7	McArdle R 18 + 3	Dean W 2	Page L 26 + 6	Taylor J 40 + 4	Atangana N 11 + 17	Collins A 46	Randall J 26 + 4	Jay M 43 + 1	Bowman R 39 + 3	Law N 4 + 14	Sweeney P 32 + 6	Williams R 24 + 5	Seymour B 8 + 25	Parkes T 28 + 3	Caprice J 13 + 21	Sparkes J 27 + 15	Fisher A 3 + 15	Kite H 1 + 3	Andersson J 29	Hartridge A 20 + 9	Ajose N — + 4	Maxted J 9	Willmott R 13 + 4	Dyer J — + 1	*Match No.*
1	2	3	4	5	6^{2}	7	8	9	10^{1}	11	12	13														1
1	2^{3}	3	4	5	6	7^{1}	8	9	10^{2}	11	13		12	14												2
1	2	4		5	7		6	10^{2}	9^{1}	11	12		8^{3}		3	13	14									3
1	2	3		5	7		8	9^{1}	11^{2}	10	12		6		4		13									4
1	2	3^{3}		5	7		8	9	10^{1}	11^{2}			6	13	4	12		14								5
1	2			5	8		7	9^{1}	10		13	3	6	12	4			11^{2}								6
1	14				8		7	9		13	10^{2}	3	6	12	4	2^{3}	5	11^{1}								7
1	2			5^{1}	13		7	9	11	10		3	6^{3}		4	14	12		8^{2}							8
	6				7		8	12	11^{1}	10		3	9		4	2	5			1						9
	2				7		8	9		11	10	3	6		4		5			1						10
	2				7^{2}		8	9	10^{1}	11	12	3	6^{3}	13	4	14	5			1						11
	2^{3}	12			7		8	9	10^{2}	11	13	3	6		4^{1}	14	5			1						12
		3			7^{3}		8	9^{2}	11^{4}	10	13	4	6			2^{1}	5	15		1	12	14				13
	2				7	13	8^{2}	9^{1}	11	10		3	6^{3}		4		5			1	12	14				14
	2				7^{4}	13	8	9^{2}	10^{5}	11^{3}	16	3	6^{1}		4		5	14			12	15	1			15
	2				7^{1}		8	9^{3}	10	11	13	3	6^{2}	14	4		5				12		1			16
	2^{4}				7	12	8^{1}	9	11^{3}	10^{2}		3	6		4^{5}	16	5	14			15	13	1			17
	2				7^{3}	14	8	9^{2}	11^{4}	10	13	3	6^{1}			12	5	15			4		1			18
					7		8	9	11	10		2^{1}	6		4	12	5				3		1			19
	6			5^{2}	7^{1}	12	8	9^{6}	11^{3}	10	15	3		16	4	2^{4}	13				14		1			20
	6^{1}			5^{3}		8^{2}	7	9^{4}	11	10	14	3		15	4	2	12				13		1			21
	12			13		8^{3}	7		11	10^{4}	6	2		15	3	5^{1}	9		14		4^{2}		1			22
	5^{3}			8	15	7^{4}	6		9	10	12	2		11^{1}	3	13	14				4^{2}		1			23
	2^{3}			5^{4}	12	8^{1}	7		10^{2}	11	9	3		14	4	13	6	15		1						24
		3^{3}		12	7		6		9	10		2^{1}		11^{2}	14	5	8			1	4			13		25
	2^{2}			5^{1}	7		8	13	11^{3}	10		3		14	4	12	9			1	15			6^{4}		26
	12				6^{4}	15	7	13	9^{2}	$10^{\blacksquare}$		2		11^{1}	3	5^{3}	8		14	1	$4^{\blacksquare}$					27
	2^{1}			5	7	13	8	9^{4}	10^{2}			3		11	4	12	14	15		1				6^{3}		28
	14	13		16	7^{4}	12	6	15	9^{2}			2^{3}		11^{1}	$3^{\blacksquare}$	5	8^{5}	10		1	4					29
	2	3		5	8^{1}	12	7	9^{2}	11					10			13	14		1	4			6^{3}		30
	2^{5}	3		5^{2}	7	13	8^{1}	9^{4}	11	10^{3}				14		16	12			1	4			6	15	31
	2^{3}	3		5^{2}	7	16	8	9^{4}	10^{5}	11		12		15		14	13			1	4			6^{1}		32
	2	3		13	6		7	11^{4}	9^{3}	10				14		5^{1}	8^{2}	15		1	4			12		33
	2	3^{3}		5	7^{4}	15	8	9^{1}	10^{2}	11				13		14	12			1	4			6		34
	12	3^{3}		13	6^{5}	8^{2}	7		11	10^{4}		2		15		5^{1}	9	16		1	4			14		35
	2	3		5	7^{1}	12	8		10	13		14	15	11^{2}			9^{3}			1	4			6^{4}		36
	2	3^{4}		5^{1}	14	8^{3}	7		10^{5}	11		12	16	15	13		9			1	4^{2}			6		37
	2^{2}			5	7		8		11	10		3	12	14	4	13	9^{1}			1				6^{3}		38
	2^{3}	12		5^{2}	7^{5}	13	8		10	11^{4}		3	6^{1}	15	4	14	9		16	1						39
	2			13	6	7^{4}	8		9^{2}	11		3	10^{1}	12	4^{3}	14	5	15		1						40
	13	3		5^{1}	7^{5}	16	8		11^{4}	10		14	6^{2}	15		2	9^{3}			1	4			12		41
	2	3^{1}		5^{4}	7		8		11	10		12	6^{5}	14	15	16	13			1	4^{2}			9^{3}		42
	12	3^{4}			9^{3}	7^{2}	6		11	10		2	14	13		5^{1}	8	15		1	4					43
	2			5^{4}	9	8^{1}	7		12	13		3	6	11^{2}	4^{5}		16	14		1	15			10^{3}		44
	2^{4}			5^{2}	7^{3}	12	8		11	10		3	6^{5}	14		16	13	15		1	4			9^{1}		45
	2^{4}			5^{1}	7^{5}	16	8		11	10		3	6^{2}	12		15	13	14		1	4			9^{3}		46

FA Cup

First Round	AFC Fylde	(h)	2-1
Second Round	Gillingham	(a)	3-2
Third Round	Sheffield W	(h)	0-2

Carabao Cup

First Round	Bristol C	(a)	0-2

Papa John's Trophy

Group E (S)	Forest Green R	(h)	3-2
Group E (S)	Swindon T	(a)	4-3
Group E (S)	WBA U21	(h)	4-0
Second Round (S)	Northampton T	(h)	1-2

FLEETWOOD TOWN

FOUNDATION

Originally formed in 1908 as Fleetwood FC, it was liquidated in 1976. Re-formed as Fleetwood Town in 1977, it folded again in 1996. Once again, it was re-formed a year later as Fleetwood Wanderers, but a sponsorship deal saw the club's name immediately changed to Fleetwood Freeport through the local retail outlet centre. This sponsorship ended in 2002, but since then local energy businessman Andy Pilley took charge and the club has risen through the non-league pyramid until finally achieving Football League status in 2012 as Fleetwood Town.

Highbury Stadium, Park Avenue, Fleetwood, Lancashire FY7 6TX.

Telephone: (01253) 775 080.

Ticket Office: (01253) 775 080.

Website: www.fleetwoodtownfc.com

Email: info@fleetwoodtownfc.com

HONOURS

League Champions: Conference – 2011–12.

FA Cup: 3rd rd – 2012, 2017, 2018, 2019, 2020.

League Cup: 3rd rd – 2021.

League Trophy: 3rd rd – 2020.

Ground Capacity: 5,103.

Record Attendance: (Before 1997) 6,150 v Rochdale, FA Cup 1st rd, 13 November 1965; (Since 1997) 5,194 v York C, FL 2 Play-Off semi-final 2nd leg, 16 May 2014.

Pitch Measurements: 100.5m × 65m (110yd × 71yd).

Chairman: Andy Pilley.

Chief Executive: Steve Curwood.

Head Coach: Simon Grayson.

Assistant Head Coach: David Dunn.

Colours: Red shirts with white sleeves and red and black trim, white shorts with red and black trim, red socks with white and black trim.

Year Formed: 1908 (re-formed 1997).

Previous Names: 1908, Fleetwood FC; 1977, Fleetwood Town; 1997, Fleetwood Wanderers; 2002 Fleetwood Town.

Club Nicknames: 'The Trawlermen', 'The Cod Army'.

Grounds: 1908, North Euston Hotel; 1934, Memorial Park (now Highbury Stadium).

First Football League Game: 18 August 2012, FL 2, v Torquay U (h) D 0–0 – Davies; Beeley, Mawene, McNulty, Howell, Nicolson, Johnson, McGuire, Ball, Parkin, Mangan.

FOOTBALL YEARBOOK FACT FILE

Jamie Milligan scored a spectacular goal from his own half for Fleetwood Town in their 2-0 home win over Farsley Celtic in January 2010 only for his effort to later be removed from the record books because Farsley failed to finish the season. Farsley's results were expunged but Fleetwood still went on to clinch promotion from Conference North.

MANAGERS

Alan Tinsley 1997
Mark Hughes 1998
Brian Wilson 1998–99
Mick Hoyle 1999–2001
Les Attwood 2001
Mark Hughes 2001
Alan Tinsley 2001–02
Mick Hoyle 2002–03
Tony Greenwood 2003–08
Micky Mellon 2008–12
Graham Alexander 2012–15
Steven Pressley 2015–16
Uwe Rosler 2016–18
John Sheridan 2018
Joey Barton 2018–21
Simon Grayson January 2021–

Record League Victory: 13–0 v Oldham T, North West Counties Div 2, 5 December 1998.

Record Defeat: 0–7 v Billingham T, FA Cup 1st qual rd, 15 September 2001.

Most League Points (3 for a win): 82, FL 1, 2016–17.

Most League Goals: 66, FL 2, 2013–14.

Highest League Scorer in Season: Ched Evans, 17, FL 1, 2018–19.

Most League Goals in Total Aggregate: David Ball, 41, 2012–17.

Most League Goals in One Match: 3, Steven Schumacher v Newport Co, FL 2, 2 November 2013; 3, Paddy Madden v Burton Alb, FL 1, 19 October 2019.

Most Capped Player: Conor McLaughlin, 25 (43), Northern Ireland.

Most League Appearances: Ashley Hunter, 181, 2015–20.

Youngest League Player: Barry Baggley, 17 years 26 days v Walsall, 9 March 2019.

Record Transfer Fee Received: £1,000,000 (rising to £1,700,000) from Leicester C for Jamie Vardy, May 2012.

Record Transfer Fee Paid: £300,000 to Kidderminster H for Jamille Matt, January 2013; £300,000 to Huddersfield T for Kyle Dempsey, May 2017.

Football League Record: 2012 Promoted from Conference Premier; 2012–14 FL 2; 2014– FL 1.

LATEST SEQUENCES

Longest Sequence of League Wins: 5, 1.2.2020 – 22.2.2020.

Longest Sequence of League Defeats: 6, 20.1.2018 – 20.2.2018.

Longest Sequence of League Draws: 3, 15.12.2020 – 26.12.2020.

Longest Sequence of Unbeaten League Matches: 18, 19.11.2016 – 4.3.2017.

Longest Sequence Without a League Win: 9, 15.12.2020 – 6.2.2021.

Successive Scoring Runs: 24 from 2.5.2016.

Successive Non-scoring Runs: 4 from 23.1.2021.

TEN YEAR LEAGUE RECORD

		P	*W*	*D*	*L*	*F*	*A*	*Pts*	*Pos*
2011-12	Conf P	46	31	10	5	102	48	103	1
2012-13	FL 2	46	15	15	16	55	57	60	13
2013-14	FL 2	46	22	10	14	66	52	76	4
2014-15	FL 1	46	17	12	17	49	52	63	10
2015-16	FL 1	46	12	15	19	52	56	51	19
2016-17	FL 1	46	23	13	10	64	43	82	4
2017-18	FL 1	46	16	9	21	59	68	57	14
2018-19	FL 1	46	16	13	17	58	52	61	11
2019-20	FL 1	35	16	12	7	51	38	60	6§
2020-21	FL 1	46	16	12	18	49	46	60	15

§Decided on points-per-game (1.71)

DID YOU KNOW ?

Fleetwood Town's training ground at Poolfoot Farm was opened in April 2016 by Sir Alex Ferguson. The £7 million complex at Thornton Cleveleys on the Fylde Coast is used by all of Fleetwood's teams from the Academy through to the first team.

FLEETWOOD TOWN – SKY BET LEAGUE ONE 2020–21 LEAGUE RECORD

Match No.	Date	Venue	Opponents	Result		H/T Score	Lg Pos.	Goalscorers	Attendance
1	Sept 12	H	Burton Alb	W	2-1	1-0	6	Camps [17], Madden [79]	0
2	19	A	Peterborough U	L	1-2	0-0	10	Camps [55]	0
3	26	H	AFC Wimbledon	L	0-1	0-1	13		0
4	Oct 3	A	Rochdale	L	1-2	0-1	20	Saunders [77]	0
5	9	H	Hull C	W	4-1	1-1	7	Saunders 2 [17, 67], Camps [47], Stubbs [73]	0
6	17	H	Lincoln C	D	0-0	0-0	13		0
7	20	A	Accrington S	L	0-1	0-0	14		0
8	24	A	Gillingham	W	2-0	0-0	11	Madden [66], Evans [90]	0
9	27	H	Shrewsbury T	W	1-0	1-0	10	Evans [25]	0
10	31	H	Oxford U	W	2-0	1-0	9	Camps [1], Madden [76]	0
11	Nov 3	A	Charlton Ath	L	2-3	2-2	10	Evans 2 [33, 34]	0
12	14	A	Bristol R	W	4-1	2-0	8	Camps 2 [30, 82], Madden [39], Evans (pen) [86]	0
13	21	H	Plymouth Arg	W	5-1	3-0	7	Finley [4], Camps 2 [7, 67], Burns [38], Mulgrew [55]	0
14	27	H	Sunderland	D	1-1	0-0	6	Connolly [73]	0
15	Dec 1	A	Northampton T	L	0-1	0-0	8		0
16	5	H	Blackpool	L	0-1	0-1	10		0
17	12	A	Swindon T	W	1-0	1-0	9	Madden [29]	2000
18	15	A	Portsmouth	D	0-0	0-0	10		2000
19	19	H	Wigan Ath	D	1-1	1-0	10	Andrew [28]	0
20	26	A	Crewe Alex	D	1-1	0-0	10	Burns [49]	0
21	Jan 16	H	Portsmouth	L	0-1	0-1	11		0
22	19	A	Milton Keynes D	L	1-3	0-3	12	Finley [83]	0
23	23	A	Wigan Ath	D	0-0	0-0	12		0
24	26	H	Northampton T	D	0-0	0-0	14		0
25	30	A	Oxford U	L	0-1	0-1	14		0
26	Feb 6	H	Bristol R	D	0-0	0-0	15		0
27	9	H	Doncaster R	W	3-1	0-1	13	Vassell [60], Madden [66], Andrew [88]	0
28	13	A	Plymouth Arg	L	0-1	0-1	15		0
29	20	H	Charlton Ath	D	1-1	1-1	16	Madden [41]	0
30	23	A	Sunderland	L	0-2	0-0	17		0
31	27	H	Accrington S	D	1-1	1-1	16	Burns [24]	0
32	Mar 2	A	Lincoln C	W	2-1	1-0	16	Garner [43], Camps [53]	0
33	6	A	Shrewsbury T	W	2-0	1-0	15	Burns [45], Vassell [70]	0
34	9	H	Gillingham	W	1-0	1-0	14	Vassell (pen) [2]	0
35	13	A	Blackpool	D	0-0	0-0	14		0
36	16	H	Ipswich T	W	2-0	1-0	11	Connolly [9], Garner [57]	0
37	20	H	Swindon T	L	0-2	0-1	15		0
38	Apr 2	H	Peterborough U	L	0-1	0-0	16		0
39	5	A	AFC Wimbledon	W	1-0	0-0	15	McKay [88]	0
40	10	H	Rochdale	W	1-0	0-0	13	O'Connell (og) [52]	0
41	17	A	Hull C	L	1-2	1-0	14	Vassell [22]	0
42	20	H	Crewe Alex	L	0-2	0-1	15		0
43	24	A	Doncaster R	W	1-0	0-0	14	McKay [51]	0
44	27	A	Burton Alb	L	2-5	0-2	15	Finley [62], Rossiter [90]	0
45	May 1	H	Milton Keynes D	D	1-1	0-0	15	Garner [61]	0
46	9	A	Ipswich T	L	1-3	0-3	15	Burns [72]	0

Final League Position: 15

GOALSCORERS

League (49): Camps 9, Madden 7, Burns 5, Evans 5 (1 pen), Vassell 4 (1 pen), Finley 3, Garner 3, Saunders 3, Andrew 2, Connolly 2, McKay 2, Mulgrew 1, Rossiter 1, Stubbs 1, own goal 1.
FA Cup (0).
Carabao Cup (7): Evans 2, Morris J 2, Camps 1, Duffy 1, Madden 1.
Papa John's Trophy (10): Saunders 5, Burns 1, Camps 1, Duffy 1, Madden 1, McKay 1.

Cairns A 28	Burns W 29 + 4	Stubbs S 5	Hill J 24 + 4	Andrew D 45	Whelan G 14 + 9	Madden P 24 + 8	Coutts P 13 + 7	Morris J 14 + 10	Evans C 11 + 6	Camps C 36 + 6	Duffy M 8 + 16	Matete J 3 + 4	Holgate H 13 + 5	Saunders H 6 + 15	Boyes M 2	McKay B 15 + 11	Leutwiler J 16	Mulgrew C 22 + 1	Connolly C 40	Edwards T 10 + 1	Finley S 19 + 10	Rossiter J 30 + 5	Hilton J 2	Rydel R 4 + 3	Vassell K 24 + 2	Morris S 1 + 4	Donacien J 16 + 3	Garner G 11 + 6	Batty D 17	Biggins H 4 + 6	Baggley B — + 2	Sheron N — + 1	*Match No.*
1	2	3	4	5	6	7^3	8	9^1	10	11^2	12	13	14																				1
1	2	4	3	5	7	12	6^2	8	11^3	9	10^1	13		14																			2
1		2^3	5	9	4		8^1	6	11	7	10^2	13		14	3	12																	3
1	2		3^2	5	7	8^3	12		11	9	13	6^1		14	4	10																	4
	2	3	12	5	6	11	7^1		10^3	8	14	13	4	9^2			1																5
	2	4^1		5	7	10^3	6	14	11	9			3	8^2		13	1	12															6
	5^3			8	7	10		9^2	12	6			3^1			11	1	4	2	13	14												7
				5	7	10	14		12	9^3	13	6		11^1			1	3	4	2	8^2												8
	8^3			5	13	10	6	14	11	12	9^2	7^1					1	4	3	2													9
	8			5	7	12	13		11	9^3	14					10^2	1	3	4	2	6^1												10
	8			5	7^2	12	6		11	13	9^3					10^1	1	3	4	2	14												11
	8		12	5		11	6	10^3	14	9							1	3	4	2^1	7^2	13											12
	8^3			5	13	11^2	14	10^5	12	9	15					16	1	4	3	2	6^4	7^1											13
	5^3			8	16	10^2	14	11^1	12	9	15					13	1	4	3	2	7^5	6^4											14
	13			5	7	11	6^1	15	10	9^3	14					12	1	4	3^5	2^2	8^4	16											15
	8^1			5	12	13		14	11	9	15					10^4	1	4	3	2	6^3	7^2											16
	2			5	14	11	7^3	8^4	12	9^2	15					10^1	1	3	4		6	13											17
	2		12	5		11	13	10^3		9	14					8^1	1	3	4		6^2	7											18
	2		13	5	12	11	7^3	8^2		9	14					10^1	1	3	4			6											19
	8^1			5	7	11^3	12	10^2		9	13			14			1	4	3	2		6											20
			3		6^1	10	7	11^2		8								4	2			12	1	5	9	13							21
			3^2	5^4	6^5	11	8^1	9^3		7			13					4	2		12	16	1	15	10	14							22
1				5	12^3	10		13		9	14			15				4	3		6	7^1			11^4	8^2	2						23
1				5		11		15		9^3	8^2		12	10		13		4^1	3		6^4	7			14		2						24
1				5		11				7	8^2		12	9^1		13		4■	3			6			10^3		2	14					25
1				5		9		11^3		8^1	12		3	13		14			4			7			10^2		2		6^4	15			26
1				9		10				7			2	13				4	3		12	8^1			11^2		5		6				27
1				8^3		11				9^4			2^2	13		15		4	3		12	7^1		14	10		5		6				28
1	12		2	9		10				13	6^2		4						3			7			11		5^1		8				29
1	12		2	9						15	8^2		4^3	10^1					3			7			11	14	5		6^4	13			30
1	5		2	9				12		6				13				4^1	3			7			10^2			11	8				31
1	5		2	4		14				6				13					3			7		9^1	11^3		12	10^2	8				32
1	5^5		2	4		13				6			16	12					3		15	7		9^1	10^3		14	11^2	8^4				33
1			2	9		12				8^2			4						3		13	7			11		5	10^1	6^3	14			34
1	9		2	4		12													3		7	8			11		5	10^1	6				35
1	5		2	9				13					4	14					3		8^2	7^1			11			10^3	6	12			36
1	5		2	9						13			4^1						3		8^2	7			11	12		10	6				37
1	5		2	9						13			4	12		14			3		8^1	7^3			11			10^2	6				38
1	5		2	9						6			4^3			13			3		12	7			11		14	10^2	8^1				39
1	9^4		3	5						6				14		11^3			4			7		15	10^2		2	12	8^1	13			40
1	5^4		2	9						6^5	16			14		10^2			3		12	7^3			11^1		4	13	8	15			41
1			2	4						8						10			3		12	7^2		9^1	11		5	13	6^3		14		42
1			3	5						9						11			4		8	7			10^1		2	12		6			43
1	12		3	5						9^1						11			4		6	7			10		2	13		8^2			44
1	8		3	5	14			12								10^2			4		6^3	7			13		2	11^1		9			45
1	2		3	5^2	15			13								11^3			4		8^4	7			10^1			9		6	14	12	46

FA Cup

First Round	Hull C	(a)	0-2

Carabao Cup

First Round	Wigan Ath	(h)	3-2
Second Round	Port Vale	(h)	2-1
Third Round	Everton	(h)	2-5

Papa John's Trophy

Group A (N)	Carlisle U	(a)	3-1
Group A (N)	Aston Villa U21	(h)	3-0
Group A (N)	Sunderland	(h)	2-1
Second Round (N)	Blackpool	(h)	0-0
(Fleetwood T won 5-4 on penalties)			
Third Round (N)	Hull C	(a)	2-3

FOREST GREEN ROVERS

FOUNDATION

A football club was recorded at Forest Green as early as October 1889, established by Rev Edward Peach, a local Congregationalist minister. This club joined the Mid-Gloucestershire League for 1894–95 but disappeared around 1896 and was reformed as Forest Green Rovers in 1898. Rovers affiliated to the Gloucestershire county FA from 1899–1900 and competed in local leagues, mostly the Stroud & District and Dursley & District Leagues before joining the Gloucestershire Senior League North in 1937, where they remained until 1968. They became founder members of the Gloucestershire County League in 1968 and progressed to the Hellenic League in 1975. Success over Rainworth MW in the 1982 FA Vase final at Wembley was the start of the club's rise up the pyramid, firstly to the Southern League for the 1982–83 season and then the Football Conference from 1998–99. Rovers reached the play-offs in 2014–15 and 2015–16, losing to Bristol Rovers and Grimsby Town respectively, before finally achieving their goal of a place in the Football League with their 3-1 Play-Off victory over Tranmere Rovers on 14 May 2017.

The innocent New Lawn Stadium, Another Way, Nailsworth, GL6 0FG.

Telephone: (0333) 123 1889.

Ticket Office: (0333) 123 1889.

Website: fgr.co.uk

Email: reception@fgr.co.uk

Ground Capacity: 5,009.

Record Attendance: 4,836 v Derby Co, FA Cup 3rd rd, 3 January 2009.

Pitch Measurements: 100m × 66m (109.5yd × 72yd).

Chairman: Dale Vince.

Chief Executive: Henry Staelens.

Head Coach: Rob Edwards.

Assistant Head Coach: Richie Kyle.

Colours: Green and black patterned shirts, green shorts with black trim, green and black hooped socks.

Year Formed: 1889.

Previous Names: 1889, Forest Green; 1898, Forest Green Rovers; 1911, Nailsworth & Forest Green United; 1919 Forest Green Rovers; 1989, Stroud; 1992, Forest Green Rovers.

Club Nicknames: Rovers, The Green, FGR, The Little Club on the Hill, Green Army, The Green Devils.

HONOURS

League Champions: Southern League – 1997–98.

FA Cup: 3rd rd – 2009, 2010.

League Cup: never past 2nd rd.

FA Trophy: *Runners-up:* 1998–99, 2000–01.

FA Vase: *Winners:* 1981–82.

FOOTBALL YEARBOOK FACT FILE

Forest Green Rovers won their first league title in 1902–03 when they were declared champions of the Dursley and District League in unusual circumstances. Rovers were unable to complete two of their fixtures and the league management committee awarded them full points bringing them level with Stonehouse. The two played off for the league title and Forest Green ran out 2-1 winners.

Grounds: 1890, The Lawn Ground; 2006, The New Lawn (renamed The innocent New Lawn, 2020).

First Football League Game: 5 August 2017, FL 2 v Barnet (h) D 2-2 – Collins B; Bennett, Collins L, Monthe, Evans (Bugiel), Laird, Traore (Mullings), Noble, Cooper, Brown (Marsh-Brown), Doidge (2).

Record Victory: 8–0 v Fareham T, Southern League Southern Division, 1996–97; 8–0 v Hyde U, Football Conference, 10 August 2013.

Record Defeat: 0–10 v Gloucester, Mid-Gloucestershire League, 13 January 1900.

Most League Points (3 for a win): 74, FL 2, 2018–19.

Most League Goals: 68, FL 2, 2018–19.

Highest League Scorer in Season: Christian Doidge, 20, FL 2, 2017–18.

Most League Goals in Total Aggregate: Christian Doidge, 34, 2017–19.

Most League Goals in One Match: 3, George Williams v Newport Co, FL 2, 26 December 2018; 3, Jamille Matt v Scunthorpe U, FL 2, 10 October 2020.

Most Capped Player: Omar Bugiel, 1 (7), Lebanon.

Most League Appearances: Carl Winchester, 98, 2018–21.

Youngest League Player: Vaughan Covil, 16 years 159 days v Exeter C, 1 January 2020.

Record Transfer Fee Received: £500,000 from Barnsley for Ethan Pinnock, June 2017.

Record Transfer Fee Paid: £25,000 to Bury for Adrian Randall, August 1999.

Football League Record: 2017 Promoted from National League; 2017– FL 2.

MANAGERS

Bill Thomas 1955–56
Eddie Cowley 1957–58
Don Cowley 1958–60
Jimmy Sewell 1966–67
Alan Morris 1967–68
Peter Goring 1968–79
Tony Morris 1979–80
Bob Mursell 1980–82
Roy Hillman 1982
Steve Millard 1983–87
John Evans 1987–90
Jeff Evans 1990
Bobby Jones 1990–91
Tim Harris 1991–92
Pat Casey 1992–94
Frank Gregan 1994–2000
Nigel Spink and David Norton 2000–01
Nigel Spink 2001–02
Colin Addison 2002–03
Tim Harris 2003–04
Alan Lewer 2004–05
Gary Owers 2005–06
Jim Harvey 2006–09
Dave Hockaday 2009–13
Adrian Pennock 2013–16
Mark Cooper 2016–21
Rob Edwards May 2021–

LATEST SEQUENCES

Longest Sequence of League Wins: 4, 6.4.2019 – 22.4.2019.

Longest Sequence of League Defeats: 5, 9.12.2017 – 1.1.2018.

Longest Sequence of League Draws: 4, 11.8.2018 – 25.8.2018.

Longest Sequence of Unbeaten League Matches: 12, 4.8.2018 – 6.10.2018.

Longest Sequence Without a League Win: 10, 26.8.2017 – 14.10.2017.

Successive Scoring Runs: 17 from 24.10.2020.

Successive Non-scoring Runs: 3 from 20.4.2021.

TEN YEAR LEAGUE RECORD

		P	*W*	*D*	*L*	*F*	*A*	*Pts*	*Pos*
2011-12	Conf	46	19	13	14	66	45	70	10
2012-13	Conf	46	18	11	17	63	49	65	10
2013-14	Conf	46	19	10	17	80	66	67	10
2014-15	Conf	46	22	16	8	80	54	79*	5
2015-16	NL	46	26	11	9	69	42	89	2
2016-17	NL	46	25	11	10	88	56	86	3
2017-18	FL 2	46	13	8	25	54	77	47	21
2018-19	FL 2	46	20	14	12	68	47	74	5
2019-20	FL 2	36	13	10	13	43	40	49	10§
2020-21	FL 2	46	20	13	13	59	51	73	6

**3 pts deducted. §Decided on points-per-game (1.36)*

DID YOU KNOW ?

Forest Green Rovers reached the first round proper of the FA Cup for the first time in their history in 1999–2000 when they were drawn at home to Northern Premier League club Guiseley. Rovers won 6-0 in front of a crowd of 1,047 with Paul Hunt scoring a hat-trick.

FOREST GREEN ROVERS – SKY BET LEAGUE TWO 2020–21 LEAGUE RECORD

Match No.	Date	Venue	Opponents	Result		H/T Score	Lg Pos.	Goalscorers	Attendance
1	Sept 12	A	Bolton W	W	1-0	0-0	5	Winchester [50]	0
2	19	H	Bradford C	D	2-2	0-0	7	Winchester [60], Collins [90]	1000
3	26	A	Salford C	D	0-0	0-0	10		0
4	Oct 3	H	Walsall	D	1-1	0-1	10	Matt [61]	0
5	10	A	Scunthorpe U	W	4-1	2-1	6	Matt 3 [24, 32, 83], Stevens [90]	0
6	17	H	Stevenage	W	1-0	1-0	4	Young [23]	0
7	20	A	Colchester U	L	0-1	0-1	8		0
8	24	A	Morecambe	W	2-1	0-1	4	Young [79], Matt [83]	0
9	27	H	Grimsby T	W	1-0	1-0	3	Young [24]	0
10	31	A	Cheltenham T	L	1-2	0-1	6	Collins (pen) [73]	0
11	Nov 3	H	Leyton Orient	W	2-1	1-1	3	Bailey [30], Stevens [82]	0
12	14	H	Mansfield T	L	1-2	0-2	5	Bailey [84]	0
13	21	A	Barrow	D	2-2	0-0	5	Whitehouse [52], Cadden [90]	0
14	24	A	Southend U	W	1-0	0-0	4	Young [63]	0
15	Dec 1	H	Newport Co	D	1-1	0-1	4	Matt [76]	0
16	5	A	Harrogate T	W	1-0	0-0	3	Matt [57]	410
17	12	H	Cambridge U	W	2-0	0-0	4	Collins [58], Matt (pen) [65]	799
18	15	A	Port Vale	D	1-1	1-1	4	Collins [41]	0
19	19	H	Carlisle U	W	1-0	0-0	2	Matt [76]	920
20	26	A	Exeter C	D	1-1	1-1	2	Collins [16]	1767
21	29	H	Crawley T	L	1-2	0-1	2	Young [50]	0
22	Jan 16	H	Port Vale	D	1-1	1-0	4	Cadden [20]	0
23	19	A	Tranmere R	L	2-3	0-1	4	Whitehouse [65], Wagstaff [90]	0
24	23	A	Leyton Orient	W	1-0	1-0	2	Cadden [22]	0
25	30	H	Cheltenham T	D	0-0	0-0	3		0
26	Feb 2	A	Carlisle U	W	2-1	0-0	2	Collins (pen) [60], Bailey [75]	0
27	16	H	Oldham Ath	W	4-3	2-1	2	Cargill 2 [12, 35], Matt [60], Davison [67]	0
28	21	A	Newport Co	W	2-0	1-0	2	Davison [43], Matt (pen) [63]	0
29	24	H	Southend U	L	1-3	0-1	2	Matt [86]	0
30	27	H	Colchester U	W	3-0	2-0	2	Matt 2 [25, 31], Sarpeng-Wiredu (og) [67]	0
31	Mar 2	A	Stevenage	L	0-3	0-2	3		0
32	6	A	Grimsby T	W	2-1	1-1	3	Matt (pen) [19], Adams [66]	0
33	9	H	Morecambe	D	2-2	1-1	3	Collins [10], Matt [79]	0
34	13	H	Harrogate T	W	2-1	1-0	3	Stokes [22], Wilson [50]	0
35	20	A	Cambridge U	L	0-1	0-1	3		0
36	23	A	Mansfield T	D	0-0	0-0	3		0
37	27	H	Bolton W	L	0-1	0-1	5		0
38	Apr 2	A	Bradford C	L	1-4	0-1	5	Young [90]	0
39	5	H	Salford C	L	0-2	0-1	5		0
40	10	A	Walsall	L	1-2	0-1	6	Moore-Taylor [72]	0
41	17	H	Scunthorpe U	W	3-2	1-1	6	Moore-Taylor [21], Adams [71], Stokes [80]	0
42	20	H	Exeter C	D	0-0	0-0	6		0
43	24	A	Crawley T	D	0-0	0-0	6		0
44	27	H	Barrow	L	0-2	0-2	8		0
45	May 1	H	Tranmere R	W	2-1	0-0	7	Davison [50], Collins (pen) [81]	0
46	8	A	Oldham Ath	W	3-0	0-0	6	Collins 2 (1 pen) [63 (p), 80], Bailey [65]	0

Final League Position: 6

GOALSCORERS

League (59): Matt 16 (3 pens), Collins 10 (4 pens), Young 6, Bailey 4, Cadden 3, Davison 3, Adams 2, Cargill 2, Moore-Taylor 2, Stevens 2, Stokes 2, Whitehouse 2, Winchester 2, Wagstaff 1, Wilson 1, own goal 1.
FA Cup (2): Whitehouse 1, Young 1.
Carabao Cup (1): Own goal 1.
Papa John's Trophy (6): Stevens 3, Bailey 1, Stokes 1, Young 1.
League Two Play-Offs (4): Adams 1, Cadden 1, Collins 1, Matt 1.

McGee L 33	Godwin-Malife U 43 + 1	Moore-Taylor J 28 + 1	Kitching L 15	Wilson K 19 + 6	Winchester C 16 + 2	Adams E 36 + 1	Sweeney D 16 + 5	Cadden N 33	Collins A 36 + 8	Matt J 33 + 3	Wagstaff S 21 + 12	McCoulsky S — + 2	Bernard D 23 + 2	Stevens M — + 10	Young J 10 + 19	Richardson J 15 + 17	Whitehouse E 18 + 9	Stokes C 34	March J 1 + 3	Bailey O 24 + 10	Cargill B 23	Hutchinson I 3 + 7	Thomas L 13	Davison J 11 + 9	Hallett L — + 1	Allen T 2 + 3	Evans J — + 2	Match No.
1	2	3	4	5	6	7	8	9	10^{1}	11^{2}	12	13																1
1	2	3	4^{3}		6	9	7^{2}	8	10	11	12		5^{1}	13	14													2
1	2	3	4		6	9	7^{2}	8	10	11^{3}	12	14		13		5^{1}												3
1	2	3	4		6	9	7	8	10	11	12					5^{1}												4
1	2	3	4		6	9	7	8	10^{1}	11^{2}	5			13			12											5
1	2		4			9			11	10	8		12		6^{2}	5^{1}	7	3	13									6
1	5		4		7	6			13	11	9^{3}		2^{1}		14		8^{2}	3	12	10								7
1	2		4		6	7^{3}			10^{2}	11	13				12	5	14	3	8^{1}	9								8
1	2		4		7		12	9^{2}		10	5				11^{1}	13	6	3	14	8^{3}								9
1	2	8	4	14	7	9	6^{1}		12	11	5				10^{2}			3^{3}		13								10
1	2	3	4	5^{3}	6	7	14		11^{2}	10	8^{1}			12	13					9								11
1	2	3^{3}	4	5^{1}	7	6		8	12	10^{2}				14	11	13				9								12
1	3	12	4		7	6		5	13	10				14	11	2^{3}	8^{2}			9^{1}								13
1	2	4		5^{3}	6^{4}	10	7^{2}	8	13	11					12	14	15	3		9^{1}								14
1	3	6	5		8^{2}	7		9^{1}	11	10				13		2		4		12								15
1	2	5	4		8^{2}	7	12	9	11^{1}	10	13					6		3										16
1	2					6	7	8	11^{3}	10^{2}	13		4	12		5	14	3		9^{1}								17
1	2					7	6	8^{3}	11	10^{1}	14		4	12	13	5		3		9^{2}								18
1	2				13	7	6	8	11^{2}	10			4			5	12	3		9^{1}								19
1	2				12	7	6	8	10^{3}	11			4		14	5^{2}	13	3		9^{1}								20
1	2				6^{4}	7	3	8	11^{3}	10	13			15	12	5	14	4^{1}		9^{2}								21
1	2	5^{1}				8	7^{3}	9	11	10	6^{2}				14	12		3		13	4							22
1	2	3				7	5^{1}	9	11^{2}	12	15				13	6^{4}	14			10	4	8^{3}						23
	2	5		13		7	14	9	11^{1}	10	6^{2}						8^{3}	3			4		1	12				24
	2	4				7■	14	9	12	10^{4}	6^{2}				11^{1}		8	3		13^{3}	5		1	15				25
	2	4		12			8	9	10								7	3		6^{1}	5		1	11				26
	2			14		8	4^{2}	9	11^{1}	12			15				7	3		6^{4}	5	13	1	10^{3}				27
	2	4				7		10		11^{2}			5		13	12	6	3			8		1	9^{1}				28
	2	4				7		11	13	12	15				16	14	8^{4}	3^{2}		9^{5}	5	6^{1}	1	10^{3}				29
	3			2		8■		6^{1}	11^{4}	10^{3}	9		4			13	12			7^{2}	5	15	1	14				30
	2			5		12			11	10^{5}	7^{4}		3		13	8^{2}	6^{1}			9	4^{3}	15	1	16	14			31
1	2			5		6^{1}			9	11	8		4			12	7	3						10				32
1	8			2					11	10	7^{1}		6			12	5	3		13	4			9^{2}				33
	2			5				8^{2}	9^{3}	10	13		7			14	6■	3		12	4		1	11^{1}				34
	2^{5}			5^{2}				8^{3}	9	10	7^{4}		6		14	13		3		12	4	15	1	11^{1}		16		35
				5				8^{2}	9	11			2		13		7	3		10^{1}	4		1	12		6		36
	14	4		9					11	10^{1}			2		13		7	3		6^{2}	5		1	12		8^{3}		37
		7		5				9^{2}	11				2		10		6	3		13	4	8^{1}	1			12		38
1	2	4		5^{3}		7^{2}		9	12				8		11	13	6	3		14				10^{1}				39
1	3	6		2^{1}		8		5^{2}	11		7				10	12				9	4			13				40
1	2	7		5		10		8	11^{1}		9^{2}		6			12		3			4			13				41
1	3	8		6^{1}		7		10^{2}	11^{4}		9^{3}		2		15	12		4		13	5	14						42
1	2	6		12		7			11		10^{2}		5		13	9^{1}		3		8	4							43
1	4	7		12		8^{1}			11		6^{4}		2		9^{3}			3^{2}		10	5	14		15			13	44
1	3	7		6		8■			9		11		2			12		4			5			10^{1}				45
1	3	8		6^{5}					9^{3}		11^{2}		2		14	12		4		7^{4}	5	16		10^{1}		13	15	46

FA Cup

First Round	Lincoln C	(a)	2-6

Carabao Cup

First Round	Leyton Orient	(h)	1-2

League Two Play-Offs

Semi-Final 1st leg	Newport Co	(a)	0-2
Semi-Final 2nd leg	Newport Co	(h)	4-3

(aet)

Papa John's Trophy

Group E (S)	Exeter C	(a)	2-3
Group E (S)	WBA U21	(h)	3-0
Group E (S)	Swindon T	(h)	0-1
Second Round (S)	Oxford U	(a)	1-1

(Oxford U won 4-1 on penalties)

FULHAM

FOUNDATION

Churchgoers were responsible for the foundation of Fulham, which first saw the light of day as Fulham St Andrew's Church Sunday School FC in 1879. They won the West London Amateur Cup in 1887 and the championship of the West London League in its initial season of 1892–93. The name Fulham had been adopted in 1888.

Craven Cottage, Stevenage Road, London SW6 6HH.

Telephone: (0843) 208 1222.

Ticket Office: (0203) 871 0810.

Website: www.fulhamfc.com

Email: enquiries@fulhamfc.com

Ground Capacity: Temporarily 19,359.

Record Attendance: 49,335 v Millwall, Division 2, 8 October 1938.

Pitch Measurements: 100m × 65m (109.5yd × 71yd).

Chairman: Shahid Khan.

Chief Executive: Alistair Mackintosh.

Head Coach: Marco Silva.

Assistant Head Coach: Luis Boa Morte.

Colours: White shirts with black trim, black shorts with white trim, white socks with black trim.

Year Formed: 1879.

Turned Professional: 1898.

Reformed: 1987.

Previous Name: 1879, Fulham St Andrew's; 1888, Fulham.

Club Nickname: 'The Cottagers'.

Grounds: 1879, Star Road, Fulham; c.1883, Eel Brook Common, 1884, Lillie Road; 1885, Putney Lower Common; 1886, Ranelagh House, Fulham; 1888, Barn Elms, Castelnau; 1889, Purser's Cross (Roskell's Field), Parsons Green Lane; 1891, Eel Brook Common; 1891, Half Moon, Putney; 1895, Captain James Field, West Brompton; 1896, Craven Cottage.

First Football League Game: 3 September 1907, Division 2, v Hull C (h) L 0–1 – Skene; Ross, Lindsay; Collins, Morrison, Goldie; Dalrymple, Freeman, Bevan, Hubbard, Threlfall.

Record League Victory: 10–1 v Ipswich T, Division 1, 26 December 1963 – Macedo; Cohen, Langley; Mullery (1), Keetch, Robson (1); Key, Cook (1), Leggat (4), Haynes, Howfield (3).

Record Cup Victory: 7–0 v Swansea C, FA Cup 1st rd, 11 November 1995 – Lange; Jupp (1), Herrera, Barkus (Brooker (1)), Moore, Angus, Thomas (1), Morgan, Brazil (Hamill), Conroy (3) (Bolt), Cusack (1).

Record Defeat: 0–10 v Liverpool, League Cup 2nd rd 1st leg, 23 September 1986.

HONOURS

League Champions: First Division – 2000–01; Division 2 – 1948–49; Second Division – 1998–99; Division 3S – 1931–32.
Runners-up: Division 2 – 1958–59; Division 3 – 1970–71; Third Division – 1996–97.

FA Cup: *Runners-up:* 1975.

League Cup: quarter-final – 1968, 1971, 2000, 2005.

European Competitions
UEFA Cup: 2002–03.
Europa League: 2009–10 *(runners-up)*, 2011–12.
Intertoto Cup: 2002 *(winners)*.

FOOTBALL YEARBOOK FACT FILE

Maurice Cook scored the first-ever goal in the Football League Cup competition when he found the net from Johnny Key's cross after just nine minutes of Fulham's first round tie with Bristol Rovers on 26 September 1960. However, it was not enough to give the Cottagers victory as they went down to a 2-1 defeat in front of a crowd of 20,051.

Most League Points (2 for a win): 60, Division 2, 1958–59 and Division 3, 1970–71.

Most League Points (3 for a win): 101, Division 2, 1998–99. 101, Division 1, 2000–01.

Most League Goals: 111, Division 3 (S), 1931–32.

Highest League Scorer in Season: Frank Newton, 43, Division 3 (S), 1931–32.

Most League Goals in Total Aggregate: Gordon Davies, 159, 1978–84, 1986–91.

Most League Goals in One Match: 5, Fred Harrison v Stockport Co, Division 2, 5 September 1908; 5, Bedford Jezzard v Hull C, Division 2, 8 October 1955; 5, Jimmy Hill v Doncaster R, Division 2, 15 March 1958; 5, Steve Earle v Halifax T, Division 3, 16 September 1969.

Most Capped Player: Johnny Haynes, 56, England.

Most League Appearances: Johnny Haynes, 594, 1952–70.

Youngest League Player: Harvey Elliott, 16 years 30 days v Wolverhampton W, 4 May 2019.

Record Transfer Fee Received: £25,000,000 from Tottenham H for Ryan Sessegnon, August 2019.

Record Transfer Fee Paid: £22,800,000 to Marseille for André-Frank Zambo Anguissa, August 2018.

Football League Record: 1907 Elected to Division 2; 1928–32 Division 3 (S); 1932–49 Division 2; 1949–52 Division 1; 1952–59 Division 2; 1959–68 Division 1; 1968–69 Division 2; 1969–71 Division 3; 1971–80 Division 2; 1980–82 Division 3; 1982–86 Division 2; 1986–92 Division 3; 1992–94 Division 2; 1994–97 Division 3; 1997–99 Division 2; 1999–2001 Division 1; 2001–14 Premier League; 2014–18 FL C; 2018–19 Premier League; 2019–20 FL C; 2020–21 Premier League; 2021– FL C.

LATEST SEQUENCES

Longest Sequence of League Wins: 12, 7.5.2000 – 18.10.2000.

Longest Sequence of League Defeats: 11, 2.12.1961 – 24.2.1962.

Longest Sequence of League Draws: 6, 23.12.2006 – 20.1.2007.

Longest Sequence of Unbeaten League Matches: 23, 23.12.2017 – 27.4.2018.

Longest Sequence Without a League Win: 15, 25.2.1950 – 23.8.1950.

Successive Scoring Runs: 26 from 28.3.1931.

Successive Non-scoring Runs: 6 from 21.8.1971.

MANAGERS

Harry Bradshaw 1904–09
Phil Kelso 1909–24
Andy Ducat 1924–26
Joe Bradshaw 1926–29
Ned Liddell 1929–31
Jim McIntyre 1931–34
Jimmy Hogan 1934–35
Jack Peart 1935–48
Frank Osborne 1948–64
(was Secretary-Manager or General Manager for most of this period and Team Manager 1953–56)
Bill Dodgin Snr 1949–53
Duggie Livingstone 1956–58
Bedford Jezzard 1958–64
(General Manager for last two months)
Vic Buckingham 1965–68
Bobby Robson 1968
Bill Dodgin Jnr 1968–72
Alec Stock 1972–76
Bobby Campbell 1976–80
Malcolm Macdonald 1980–84
Ray Harford 1984–96
Ray Lewington 1986–90
Alan Dicks 1990–91
Don Mackay 1991–94
Ian Branfoot 1994–96
(continued as General Manager)
Micky Adams 1996–97
Ray Wilkins 1997–98
Kevin Keegan 1998–99
(Chief Operating Officer)
Paul Bracewell 1999–2000
Jean Tigana 2000–03
Chris Coleman 2003–07
Lawrie Sanchez 2007
Roy Hodgson 2007–10
Mark Hughes 2010–11
Martin Jol 2011–13
Rene Muelenstein 2013–14
Felix Magath 2014
Kit Symons 2014–15
Slavisa Jokanovic 2015–18
Claudio Ranieri 2018–19
Scott Parker 2019–21
Marco Silva July 2021–

TEN YEAR LEAGUE RECORD

		P	W	D	L	F	A	Pts	Pos
2011-12	PR Lge	38	14	10	14	48	51	52	9
2012-13	PR Lge	38	11	10	17	50	60	43	12
2013-14	PR Lge	38	9	5	24	40	85	32	19
2014-15	FL C	46	14	10	22	62	83	52	17
2015-16	FL C	46	12	15	19	66	79	51	20
2016-17	FL C	46	22	14	10	85	57	80	6
2017-18	FL C	46	25	13	8	79	46	88	3
2018-19	PR Lge	38	7	5	26	34	81	26	19
2019-20	FL C	46	23	12	11	64	48	81	4
2020-21	PR Lge	38	5	13	20	27	53	28	18

DID YOU KNOW ?

Fulham appeared doomed to relegation from the First Division in 1965–66 and after losing at Tottenham Hotspur on 19 February they were five points adrift from safety. The Cottagers went on to win nine of their next 11 games and comfortably avoided the drop.

FULHAM – PREMIER LEAGUE 2020–21 LEAGUE RECORD

Match No.	Date	Venue	Opponents	Result		H/T Score	Lg Pos.	Goalscorers	Attendance
1	Sept 12	H	Arsenal	L	0-3	0-1	20		0
2	19	A	Leeds U	L	3-4	1-2	19	Mitrovic 2 (1 pen) 34 (p), 67, Decordova-Reid 62	0
3	28	H	Aston Villa	L	0-3	0-2	20		0
4	Oct 4	A	Wolverhampton W	L	0-1	0-0	20		0
5	18	A	Sheffield U	D	1-1	0-0	19	Lookman 77	0
6	24	H	Crystal Palace	L	1-2	0-1	20	Cairney 90	0
7	Nov 2	H	WBA	W	2-0	2-0	17	Decordova-Reid 26, Aina 30	0
8	7	A	West Ham U	L	0-1	0-0	17		0
9	22	H	Everton	L	2-3	1-3	17	Decordova-Reid 15, Loftus-Cheek 70	0
10	30	A	Leicester C	W	2-1	2-0	17	Lookman 30, Ivan Cavaleiro (pen) 38	0
11	Dec 5	A	Manchester C	L	0-2	0-2	17		0
12	13	H	Liverpool	D	1-1	1-0	18	Decordova-Reid 25	2000
13	16	H	Brighton & HA	D	0-0	0-0	17		0
14	19	A	Newcastle U	D	1-1	1-0	17	Ritchie (og) 42	0
15	26	H	Southampton	D	0-0	0-0	18		0
16	Jan 13	A	Tottenham H	D	1-1	0-1	18	Ivan Cavaleiro 74	0
17	16	H	Chelsea	L	0-1	0-0	18		0
18	20	H	Manchester U	L	1-2	1-1	18	Lookman 5	0
19	27	A	Brighton & HA	D	0-0	0-0	18		0
20	30	A	WBA	D	2-2	1-0	18	Decordova-Reid 10, Ivan Cavaleiro 76	0
21	Feb 3	H	Leicester C	L	0-2	0-2	18		0
22	6	H	West Ham U	D	0-0	0-0	18		0
23	14	A	Everton	W	2-0	0-0	18	Maja 2 48, 65	0
24	17	A	Burnley	D	1-1	0-0	18	Aina 49	0
25	20	H	Sheffield U	W	1-0	0-0	18	Lookman 61	0
26	28	A	Crystal Palace	D	0-0	0-0	18		0
27	Mar 4	H	Tottenham H	L	0-1	0-1	18		0
28	7	A	Liverpool	W	1-0	1-0	18	Lemina 45	0
29	13	H	Manchester C	L	0-3	0-0	18		0
30	19	H	Leeds U	L	1-2	1-1	18	Andersen 38	0
31	Apr 4	A	Aston Villa	L	1-3	0-0	18	Mitrovic 61	0
32	9	H	Wolverhampton W	L	0-1	0-0	18		0
33	18	A	Arsenal	D	1-1	0-0	18	Maja (pen) 59	0
34	May 1	A	Chelsea	L	0-2	0-1	18		0
35	10	H	Burnley	L	0-2	0-2	18		0
36	15	A	Southampton	L	1-3	0-1	18	Carvalho 75	0
37	18	A	Manchester U	D	1-1	0-1	18	Bryan 76	10,000
38	23	H	Newcastle U	L	0-2	0-1	18		2000

Final League Position: 18

GOALSCORERS

League (27): Decordova-Reid 5, Lookman 4, Ivan Cavaleiro 3 (1 pen), Maja 3 (1 pen), Mitrovic 3 (1 pen), Aina 2, Andersen 1, Bryan 1, Cairney 1, Carvalho 1, Lemina 1, Loftus-Cheek 1, own goal 1.
FA Cup (2): Decordova-Reid 1, Kebano 1.
Carabao Cup (3): Decordova-Reid 1, Kamara 1, Mitrovic 1.
Papa John's Trophy (3): Harris 1, Tiehi 1, own goal 1.

Rodak M 2	Odoi D 3	Hector M 3 + 1	Ream T 7	Bryan J 7 + 9	Reed H 26 + 5	Cairney T 9 + 1	Kebano N 1 + 4	Onomah J 4 + 7	Ivan Cavaleiro R 27 + 9	Kamara A 2 + 9	Zambo A 29 + 7	Mitrovic A 13 + 14	Decordova-Reid B 28 + 5	Areola A 36	Tete K 18 + 4	Lemina M 19 + 9	Le Marchand M 1 + 1	Aina O 31	Robinson A 24 + 4	Lookman A 31 + 3	Adarabioyo T 33	Loftus-Cheek R 21 + 9	Andersen J 30 + 1	Maja J 9 + 6	Kongolo T 1	Carvalho F 3 + 1	Francois T — + 1	*Match No.*
1	2	3	4	5	6	7	8^1	9^3	10	11^2	12	13	14															1
	4	3		5	7^3		13	9^1	10	8^2	6	11	12	1	2	14												2
	2	3^2	4	8		7	14		11	12	6	10	9^3	1	5^1		13											3
			3	10^2		6	14		8^1	13	7	11	9^3	1			4	2	5	12								4
			4			6			8		7	11		1		12		2	5	10	3	9^1						5
			4		14	8				12■	6^1	10	13	1		7^3		2	5	11	3	9^2						6
				14	12	9			13		6	11	8^2	1		7^1		2	5	10^3	4		3					7
					7	9			13		6^2	11	8^1	1				2	5	10	4	12	3					8
					6	9^2			11		14	13	8^1	1		7^3		2	5	10	4	12	3					9
				14	8				11^2		9	13	2	1		12		3	6	10^3	5	7^1	4					10
					7^1	14			11	13	6		5^2	1		12		2	8	10	4	9^3	3					11
				14	13				11	12	6		5	1		7^2		2	8	10^3	4	9^1	3					12
					7^2				11	12	6	14	5^1	1		13		2	8	10	4	9^3	3					13
		12		14		9^1					6	11^2	8	1		7		2	5	10^3	4	13	3■					14
					7		13		10		8	12	5^1	1				2	9	11^2	4	6	3					15
					6			14	11^2	13	7		9	1	5^1			2	8	12	4	10^3	3					16
				14	7			12	10^1	13	8		6^3	1	5			2^2	9■	11	4		3					17
				8	7				10^1	12	6^2	14		1	5	13		2^3		11	4	9	3					18
				13	7^1				10^2		6	14	8	1	5^3	12		2		11	4	9	3					19
					13				12		7	10	5^2	1	14	6^1		2^3	8	11	4	9	3					20
					6				13		7^1	10	14	1	5^2	12		2	8	11	4	9^3	3					21
					6				11		14	13	8^3	1	2	7^2			5^1	10	4	9	3	12				22
					7			14	12		13		11	1	2	8^3		5		9^2	4	6	3	10^1				23
					7				13		12		10^2	1	2^3	8^1		5	14	9	4	6	3	11				24
					7				8^1		6		14	1	12	13		2	5	10^3	4	9	3	11^2				25
					6				13		7^3	14	8^2	1	2			5^1	12	10	4	9	3	11				26
				14	7				8^2		12	13		1		6		2	5^3	10	4	9^1	3	11				27
					8				10^3			14	6	1	2	7		5	13	9^2	4	12	3	11^1				28
					7			13	11^3		6	12		1	2	8^2		5	14	9	4	10^1	3					29
					6^2				8		9	12		1	14	7		2^3	5	10	4	13	3	11^1				30
					6			13	12			11	8	1	2	7^2		5		10^1	4	9^3	3	14				31
					6^2				14		12	11	10	1	5	7		2^3	8			9^1	3	13	4			32
				14	12				11^3		7		6	1		8		2	5	9^1	4	13	3	10^2				33
								13	8^2		6	14	9	1		7^1		2	5	10	4		3	11^3		12		34
								13	8		6	11	9^2	1	2^1	7			5	10	4^3	14	3	12				35
				12	6			9^3	5		10^2		8	1	2			7^1		13	4		3	14		11		36
			2	6	7^1				9		8		5	1	14	3				10^3	4	13	12			11^2		37
1			4	8^3				7	11		6^1		5		2					10^2	3	12		13		9	14	38

FA Cup

Third Round	QPR	(a)	2-0
(aet)			
Fourth Round	Burnley	(h)	0-3

Carabao Cup

Second Round	Ipswich T	(a)	1-0
Third Round	Sheffield W	(h)	2-0
Fourth Round	Brentford	(a)	0-3

Papa John's Trophy (Fulham U21)

Group H (S)	Cambridge U	(a)	0-2
Group H (S)	Peterborough U	(a)	2-4
Group H (S)	Burton Alb	(a)	1-1

(Burton Alb won 4-1 on penalties)

GILLINGHAM

FOUNDATION

The success of the pioneering Royal Engineers of Chatham excited the interest of the residents of the Medway Towns and led to the formation of many clubs including Excelsior. After winning the Kent Junior Cup and the Chatham District League in 1893, Excelsior decided to go for bigger things and it was at a meeting in the Napier Arms, Brompton, in 1893 that New Brompton FC came into being, buying and developing the ground which is now Priestfield Stadium. They changed their name to Gillingham in 1913, when they also changed their strip from black and white stripes to predominantly blue.

MEMS Priestfield Stadium, Redfern Avenue, Gillingham, Kent ME7 4DD.

Telephone: (01634) 300 000.

Ticket Office: (01634) 300 000 (option 1).

Website: www.gillinghamfootballclub.com

Email: enquries@priestfield.com

Ground Capacity: 10,500.

Record Attendance: 23,002 v QPR, FA Cup 3rd rd, 10 January 1948.

Pitch Measurements: 100.5m × 64m (110yd × 70yd).

Chairman: Paul Scally.

Manager: Steve Evans.

Assistant Manager: Paul Raynor.

Colours: Blue shirts with white trim, blue shorts with white trim, blue socks with white trim.

Year Formed: 1893.

Turned Professional: 1894.

Previous Name: 1893, New Brompton; 1913, Gillingham.

Club Nickname: 'The Gills'.

Ground: 1893, Priestfield Stadium (renamed KRBS Priestfield Stadium 2009, MEMS Priestfield Stadium 2011).

First Football League Game: 28 August 1920, Division 3, v Southampton (h) D 1–1 – Branfield; Robertson, Sissons; Battiste, Baxter, Wigmore; Holt, Hall, Gilbey (1), Roe, Gore.

Record League Victory: 10–0 v Chesterfield, Division 3, 5 September 1987 – Kite; Haylock, Pearce, Shipley (2) (Lillis), West, Greenall (1), Pritchard (2), Shearer (2), Lovell, Elsey (2), David Smith (1).

Record Cup Victory: 10–1 v Gorleston, FA Cup 1st rd, 16 November 1957 – Brodie; Parry, Hannaway; Riggs, Boswell, Laing; Payne, Fletcher (2), Saunders (5), Morgan (1), Clark (2).

Record Defeat: 2–9 v Nottingham F, Division 3 (S), 18 November 1950.

HONOURS

League Champions: FL 2 – 2012–13; Division 4 – 1963–64.
Runners-up: Third Division – 1995–96; Division 4 – 1973–74.

FA Cup: 6th rd – 2000.

League Cup: 4th rd – 1964, 1997.

FOOTBALL YEARBOOK FACT FILE

In March 1961 Gillingham played their Fourth Division home fixture against Wrexham at Gravesend and Northfleet's Stonebridge Road ground after Priestfield Stadium was closed for 14 days by the Football Association due to 'spectator misconduct'. The Gills lost the game 3-0 in front of a crowd of 3,934.

Most League Points (2 for a win): 62, Division 4, 1973–74.

Most League Points (3 for a win): 85, Division 2, 1999–2000.

Most League Goals: 90, Division 4, 1973–74.

Highest League Scorer in Season: Ernie Morgan, 31, Division 3 (S), 1954–55; Brian Yeo, 31, Division 4, 1973–74.

Most League Goals in Total Aggregate: Brian Yeo, 135, 1963–75.

Most League Goals in One Match: 6, Fred Cheesmur v Merthyr T, Division 3 (S), 26 April 1930.

Most Capped Player: Andrew Crofts, 13 (includes 1 on loan from Brighton & HA) (29), Wales.

Most League Appearances: John Simpson, 571, 1957–72.

Youngest League Player: Luke Freeman, 15 years 247 days v Hartlepool U, 24 November 2007.

Record Transfer Fee Received: £1,500,000 from Manchester C for Robert Taylor, November 1999.

Record Transfer Fee Paid: £600,000 to Reading for Carl Asaba, August 1998.

Football League Record: 1920 Original Member of Division 3; 1921 Division 3 (S); 1938 Failed re-election; Southern League 1938–44; Kent League 1944–46; Southern League 1946–50; 1950 Re-elected to Division 3 (S); 1958–64 Division 4; 1964–71 Division 3; 1971–74 Division 4; 1974–89 Division 3; 1989–92 Division 4; 1992–96; Division 3; 1996–2000 Division 2; 2000–04 Division 1; 2004–05 FL C; 2005–08 FL 1; 2008–09 FL 2; 2009–10 FL 1; 2010–13 FL 2; 2013– FL 1.

LATEST SEQUENCES

Longest Sequence of League Wins: 7, 18.12.1954 – 29.1.1955.

Longest Sequence of League Defeats: 10, 20.9.1988 – 5.11.1988.

Longest Sequence of League Draws: 5, 21.1.2017 – 14.2.2017.

Longest Sequence of Unbeaten League Matches: 20, 13.10.1973 – 10.2.1974.

Longest Sequence Without a League Win: 15, 1.4.1972 – 2.9.1972.

Successive Scoring Runs: 20 from 31.10.1959.

Successive Non-scoring Runs: 6 from 11.2.1961.

MANAGERS

W. Ironside Groombridge 1896–1906 *(Secretary-Manager) (previously Financial Secretary)*
Steve Smith 1906–08
W. I. Groombridge 1908–19 *(Secretary-Manager)*
George Collins 1919–20
John McMillan 1920–23
Harry Curtis 1923–26
Albert Hoskins 1926–29
Dick Hendrie 1929–31
Fred Mavin 1932–37
Alan Ure 1937–38
Bill Harvey 1938–39
Archie Clark 1939–58
Harry Barratt 1958–62
Freddie Cox 1962–65
Basil Hayward 1966–71
Andy Nelson 1971–74
Len Ashurst 1974–75
Gerry Summers 1975–81
Keith Peacock 1981–87
Paul Taylor 1988
Keith Burkinshaw 1988–89
Damien Richardson 1989–92
Glenn Roeder 1992–93
Mike Flanagan 1993–95
Neil Smillie 1995
Tony Pulis 1995–99
Peter Taylor 1999–2000
Andy Hessenthaler 2000–04
Stan Ternent 2004–05
Neale Cooper 2005
Ronnie Jepson 2005–07
Mark Stimson 2007–10
Andy Hessenthaler 2010–12
Martin Allen 2012–13
Peter Taylor 2013–14
Justin Edinburgh 2015–17
Adrian Pennock 2017
Steve Lovell 2017–19
Steve Evans May 2019–

TEN YEAR LEAGUE RECORD

		P	W	D	L	F	A	Pts	Pos
2011-12	FL 2	46	20	10	16	79	62	70	8
2012-13	FL 2	46	23	14	9	66	39	83	1
2013-14	FL 1	46	15	8	23	60	79	53	17
2014-15	FL 1	46	16	14	16	65	66	62	12
2015-16	FL 1	46	19	12	15	71	56	69	9
2016-17	FL 1	46	12	14	20	59	79	50	20
2017-18	FL 1	46	13	17	16	50	55	56	17
2018-19	FL 1	46	15	10	21	61	72	55	13
2019-20	FL 1	35	12	15	8	42	34	51	10§
2020-21	FL 1	46	19	10	17	63	60	67	10

§Decided on points-per-game (1.46)

DID YOU KNOW ?

In his first season with Gillingham goalkeeper Jim Stannard set a new club record when he kept 29 clean sheets during the 1995–96 campaign. Jim, who signed from Fulham, played in all 46 Third Division games, conceding just 20 goals over the season. The Gills won promotion finishing second in the table.

GILLINGHAM – SKY BET LEAGUE ONE 2020–21 LEAGUE RECORD

Match No.	Date	Venue	Opponents	Result		H/T Score	Lg Pos.	Goalscorers	Attendance
1	Sept 12	H	Hull C	L	0-2	0-1	18		0
2	19	A	Wigan Ath	W	3-2	2-1	14	Graham 2 [22, 30], Coyle [62]	0
3	26	H	Blackpool	W	2-0	1-0	7	Samuel 2 [3, 49]	0
4	Oct 3	A	Shrewsbury T	D	1-1	0-1	6	Graham [90]	0
5	10	H	Oxford U	W	3-1	2-0	4	Oliver [18], Mellis [22], Graham [70]	0
6	17	A	Milton Keynes D	L	0-2	0-1	8		0
7	20	H	Portsmouth	L	0-2	0-2	11		0
8	24	H	Fleetwood T	L	0-2	0-0	13		0
9	27	A	Ipswich T	L	0-1	0-0	15		0
10	31	H	Sunderland	L	0-2	0-0	16		0
11	Nov 3	A	Crewe Alex	W	1-0	0-0	13	Akinde [58]	0
12	21	H	Charlton Ath	D	1-1	0-0	15	Graham (pen) [73]	0
13	24	H	AFC Wimbledon	W	2-1	1-1	13	Dempsey [3], Samuel [57]	0
14	Dec 2	A	Bristol R	W	2-0	1-0	12	Oliver 2 [26, 74]	0
15	5	H	Swindon T	W	2-0	1-0	11	Oliver [17], Coyle [80]	0
16	12	A	Doncaster R	L	1-2	0-1	12	Dempsey [51]	0
17	15	H	Accrington S	L	0-2	0-1	13		0
18	19	A	Rochdale	W	4-1	3-0	13	McKenzie [9], Akinde 2 (1 pen) [21, 47 (p)], Ogilvie [45]	0
19	29	A	Northampton T	L	1-3	1-2	13	Dempsey [45]	0
20	Jan 2	A	Plymouth Arg	L	0-1	0-1	14		0
21	9	H	Burton Alb	L	0-1	0-1	14		0
22	16	A	Accrington S	W	1-0	1-0	12	Dempsey [45]	0
23	23	H	Rochdale	D	2-2	1-0	13	Oliver [43], Akinde [90]	0
24	26	H	Crewe Alex	W	4-1	3-0	12	Graham (pen) [11], Lee 2 [38, 62], Dempsey [45]	0
25	30	A	Sunderland	D	2-2	1-2	12	MacDonald [28], Graham [90]	0
26	Feb 5	H	Lincoln C	L	0-3	0-1	13		0
27	13	A	Charlton Ath	W	3-2	2-1	14	Lee [1], Ogilvie [37], Dempsey [86]	0
28	16	H	Peterborough U	L	1-3	1-0	15	Akinde (pen) [31]	0
29	20	H	Bristol R	W	2-0	0-0	15	Akinde 2 [67, 90]	0
30	23	A	AFC Wimbledon	L	0-1	0-0	15		0
31	27	A	Portsmouth	D	1-1	1-1	15	Oliver [40]	0
32	Mar 2	H	Milton Keynes D	W	3-2	2-2	14	Graham (pen) [28], Oliver [44], Ogilvie [74]	0
33	6	H	Ipswich T	W	3-1	1-0	11	Tucker [7], Oliver 2 [73, 80]	0
34	9	A	Fleetwood T	L	0-1	0-1	13		0
35	13	A	Swindon T	W	3-1	0-1	11	Oliver 2 [59, 63], Dempsey [68]	0
36	16	A	Lincoln C	W	3-0	2-0	9	Oliver [10], Dempsey [20], Graham (pen) [87]	0
37	20	H	Doncaster R	D	2-2	2-2	8	Graham [2], Oliver [4]	0
38	27	A	Hull C	D	1-1	0-1	10	Lee [67]	0
39	31	H	Wigan Ath	W	1-0	0-0	6	Oliver [76]	0
40	Apr 5	A	Blackpool	L	1-4	1-3	9	Graham [14]	0
41	10	H	Shrewsbury T	D	0-0	0-0	10		0
42	17	A	Oxford U	L	2-3	1-0	11	Oliver [39], Cundy [72]	0
43	20	A	Peterborough U	W	1-0	1-0	9	Ogilvie [15]	0
44	24	H	Northampton T	D	2-2	1-0	10	Oliver [11], Lee [68]	0
45	May 1	A	Burton Alb	D	1-1	1-0	11	Graham [37]	0
46	9	H	Plymouth Arg	W	1-0	1-0	10	Oliver [28]	0

Final League Position: 10

GOALSCORERS

League (63): Oliver 17, Graham 12 (4 pens), Dempsey 8, Akinde 7 (2 pens), Lee 5, Ogilvie 4, Samuel 3, Coyle 2, Cundy 1, MacDonald 1, McKenzie 1, Mellis 1, Tucker 1.
FA Cup (5): Samuel 3, Oliver 2.
Carabao Cup (2): Graham 1 (1 pen), Ogilvie 1.
Papa John's Trophy (3): Coyle 2, Oliver 1.

Bonham J 44	McKenzie R 17 + 16	Maghoma C 4	Medley Z 11 + 1	Ogilvie C 45	O'Keefe S 18 + 6	Mellis J 7 + 1	Dempsey K 40	Graham J 36 + 3	Akinde J 19 + 25	Coyle T 3 + 10	Robertson S 11 + 4	Oliver V 39 + 4	Willock M — + 11	Jackson R 43	Tucker J 42 + 1	Eccles J 10 + 2	Samuel D 15 + 7	MacDonald A 22 + 15	O'Connor T 27 + 7	Drysdale D 6 + 4	Woods H — + 4	Walsh J — + 1	Lumley J 2	Johnson T 1 + 6	Slattery C 7	Lee O 19 + 6	Cundy R 18	Morton J — + 1	Sithole G — + 1	*Match No.*
1	2	3	4	5	6	7[1]	8[3]	9	10	11[2]	12	13	14																	1
1		3		5		8[1]		9	13	11	7	10[2]	12	2	4	6														2
1	12		4	5		7		11	13		8[1]	10[2]		2	3	6	9[3]	14												3
1			4	5		6[1]		11	14	13		10		2	3	7	9[3]		8[2]	12										4
1			4	5		8[1]		11	14			10[2]		2	3	6	9[3]	12		7	13									5
1			4	5			6	11	12	14	8[3]	10		2	3	13	9[2]			7[1]										6
1		3		5		7		11	12			10[2]		2		6	9[1]	13	8	4										7
1			5	4▮				6	11	14	7[2]		13	2	3	8	10[3]	12	9[1]											8
1[1]	7	3	5				8[3]	6	10		13	14		2[2]	4		11	9				12								9
	7		5	4			8	6[3]	13	14	12	11[2]		2	3		10[1]	9▮					1							10
	8		5	4			7	6	12	10[1]		11[2]	14	2	3		13		9[3]				1							11
1	6		4	5			7	9	12	13	8[1]	10[2]		2	3		11													12
1	7		4	5			8	6	14	12		10[3]		2	3		11[2]	9[1]			13									13
1	7			4			6		11[1]	13	8[3]	10[2]		2	3		9	12	5	14										14
1	6			4			7		11[1]	12	8	10[3]		2	3		9[2]	13	5	14										15
1	8		12	4		13[4]	7		10[2]	14		11		2	3	15	6	9[1]	5[3]											16
1	7[3]			5		9[2]	6		12		15	11[4]		2	4	8	10[1]	14	13	3										17
1	7			4			9		11		8[1]		13	2	3	6[2]		10	5	12										18
1	7			4			9		11	14	8[1]	12	13	2	3	6[2]		10[3]	5											19
1	9[3]			4			10	8	13		7[2]	11	14	2		6[1]		12	5	3										20
1	7[4]			4			6	9	13		8[2]	10[3]	15	2	12			14	5	3[1]				11						21
1				4	13		7	8[2]	12			11[1]		2	3			10	5						6	9				22
1				4			6	8	13			11[1]	14	2	3			10[2]	5					12	7[3]	9				23
1				5	14		6	8[2]	12			11[1]		2	3			13	10						7	9[3]	4			24
1				5	12		6[1]	8	13			11		2	4			10[2]						14	7[3]	9	3			25
1				5	14		7[3]	8	13			11		2	4			10[1]	12						6[4]	9[2]	3	15		26
1	12			5	7[1]		6		10			11[2]		2	4			13	9							8	3			27
1	15			5			7	12	10			11[1]		2	4			14	8[2]					13	6[4]	9[3]	3			28
1	13			5	15		6	8[4]	11[5]			14	16	2	4			10[2]	12						7[1]	9[3]	3			29
1	6[1]			5	12		7	13	11			10		2	3				8[3]					14		9[2]	4			30
1				5	6		7	8	12			11		2	4				10							9[1]	3			31
1	12			5	7		6	8	13			11[2]		2	4				10							9[1]	3			32
1	14			5	6		7	8[3]	12			11		2	4			13	10[2]							9[1]	3			33
1	12			5	6		7	8[4]	13			11	14	2[1]	4			15	10[2]							9[3]	3			34
1	15			5	7[4]		6	8[3]	13			11		2	4			12	10[1]		14					9[2]	3			35
1	12			5	8		7	6[3]	10[2]			11[4]		2	4			9[1]	13					14		15	3			36
1	14			5	8[2]		7	6	10[1]			11		2	4			9[3]	13							12	3			37
1	13			4	8		7	6[3]	11[1]			10		2	3		14	9[2]	5							12				38
1	14			4	8		7	6[3]	10[1]			11[2]		2	3		12	9	5							13				39
1				4	8		7	6	11[2]			10		2	3		13	9[1]	5							12				40
1	13			5	8[2]		7	6	10[1]			11		2	4		12	9[3]								14	3			41
1	12			5	8		7	6[2]				11		2	4			9	13							10[1]	3			42
1	14			5	8		7	6[3]	11					2	3		12	9[2]	13							10[1]	4			43
1	14			5	7		6	13				11		2[3]	4		10[2]	8								9[1]	3		12	44
1	2			5	7		6	8	13			11[2]			3		12	10	4							9[1]				45
1	2			5	7[2]		8	6	12			11[1]			3			9[3]	4		13			14		10				46

FA Cup

First Round	Woking	(h)	3-2
Second Round	Exeter C	(h)	2-3

Carabao Cup

First Round	Southend U	(h)	1-0
Second Round	Coventry C	(h)	1-1
(Gillingham won 5-4 on penalties)			
Third Round	Stoke C	(a)	0-1

Papa John's Trophy

Group B (S)	Crawley T	(h)	2-1
Group B (S)	Ipswich T	(a)	0-2
Group B (S)	Arsenal U21	(h)	1-1
(Arsenal U21 won 4-2 on penalties)			
Second Round (S)	Cambridge U	(a)	0-2

GRIMSBY TOWN

FOUNDATION

Grimsby Pelham FC, as they were first known, came into being at a meeting held at the Wellington Arms in September 1878. Pelham is the family name of big landowners in the area, the Earls of Yarborough. The receipts for their first game amounted to 6s. 9d. (equivalent to approx. £25 today). After a year, the club name was changed to Grimsby Town.

Blundell Park, Cleethorpes, North East Lincolnshire DN35 7PY.

Telephone: (01472) 605 050.

Ticket Office: (01472) 605 050 (option 4).

Website: www.grimsby-townfc.co.uk

Email: enquiries@gtfc.co.uk

Ground Capacity: 8,916.

Record Attendance: 31,651 v Wolverhampton W, FA Cup 5th rd, 20 February 1937.

Pitch Measurements: 101.5m × 68.5m (111yd × 75yd).

Chairman: Jason Stockwood.

Chief Executive: Debbie Cook.

Manager: Paul Hurst.

Assistant Manager: Chris Doig.

Colours: Black and white striped shirts with red and white trim, black shorts with red and white trim, black socks with red and white trim.

Year Formed. 1878. ***Turned Professional:*** 1890. ***Ltd Co.:*** 1890.

Previous Name: 1878, Grimsby Pelham; 1879, Grimsby Town.

Club Nickname: 'The Mariners'.

Grounds: 1880, Clee Park; 1889, Abbey Park; 1899, Blundell Park.

First Football League Game: 3 September 1892, Division 2, v Northwich Victoria (h) W 2–1 – Whitehouse; Lundie, T. Frith; C. Frith, Walker, Murrell; Higgins, Henderson, Brayshaw, Riddoch (2), Ackroyd.

Record League Victory: 9–2 v Darwen, Division 2, 15 April 1899 – Bagshaw; Lockie, Nidd; Griffiths, Bell (1), Nelmes; Jenkinson (3), Richards (1), Cockshutt (3), Robinson, Chadburn (1).

Record Cup Victory: 8–0 v Darlington, FA Cup 2nd rd, 21 November 1885 – G. Atkinson; J. H. Taylor, H. Taylor; Hall, Kimpson, Hopewell; H. Atkinson (1), Garnham, Seal (3), Sharman, Monument (4).

Record Defeat: 1–9 v Arsenal, Division 1, 28 January 1931.

Most League Points (2 for a win): 68, Division 3 (N), 1955–56.

Most League Points (3 for a win): 83, Division 3, 1990–91.

HONOURS

League Champions: Division 2 – 1900–01, 1933–34; Division 3 – 1979–80; Division 3N – 1925–26, 1955–56; Division 4 – 1971–72.
Runners-up: Division 2 – 1928–29; Division 3 – 1961–62; Division 3N – 1951–52; Division 4 – 1978–79, 1989–90. Conference – (4th) 2015–16 *(promoted via play-offs)*.

FA Cup: semi-final – 1936, 1939.

League Cup: 5th rd – 1980, 1985.

League Trophy Winners: 1998.
Runners-up: 2008.

FOOTBALL YEARBOOK FACT FILE

Grimsby Town were one of eight teams that took part in the inaugural *Daily Express* Five-a-Side Championships held at Wembley Pool in May 1968. The Mariners defeated Lincoln City 1-0 in the first round with a goal from Doug Collins but then went out to Charlton Athletic in the semi-finals by a 5-4 margin, this time Bobby Smith (2), Graham Taylor and Dave Worthington found the net.

Most League Goals: 103, Division 2, 1933–34.

Highest League Scorer in Season: Pat Glover, 42, Division 2, 1933–34.

Most League Goals in Total Aggregate: Pat Glover, 180, 1930–39.

Most League Goals in One Match: 6, Tommy McCairns v Leicester Fosse, Division 2, 11 April 1896.

Most Capped Player: Pat Glover, 7, Wales.

Most League Appearances: John McDermott, 647, 1987–2007.

Youngest League Player: Louis Boyd, 15 years 326 days v Walsall, 12 September 2020.

Record Transfer Fee Received: £1,500,000 from Everton for John Oster, July 1997.

Record Transfer Fee Paid: £500,000 to Preston NE for Lee Ashcroft, August 1998.

Football League Record: 1892 Original Member of Division 2; 1901–03 Division 1; 1903 Division 2; 1910 Failed re-election; 1911 re-elected Division 2; 1920–21 Division 3; 1921–26 Division 3 (N); 1926–29 Division 2; 1929–32 Division 1; 1932–34 Division 2; 1934–48 Division 1; 1948–51 Division 2; 1951–56 Division 3 (N); 1956–59 Division 2; 1959–62 Division 3; 1962–64 Division 2; 1964–68 Division 3; 1968–72 Division 4; 1972–77 Division 3; 1977–79 Division 4; 1979–80 Division 3; 1980–87 Division 2; 1987–88 Division 3; 1988–90 Division 4; 1990–91 Division 3; 1991–92 Division 2; 1992–97 Division 1; 1997–98 Division 2; 1998–2003 Division 1; 2003–04 Division 2; 2004–10 FL 2; 2010–16 Conference National League; 2016–21 FL 2; 2021– National League.

LATEST SEQUENCES

Longest Sequence of League Wins: 11, 19.1.1952 – 29.3.1952.

Longest Sequence of League Defeats: 9, 30.11.1907 – 18.1.1908.

Longest Sequence of League Draws: 5, 6.2.1965 – 6.3.1965.

Longest Sequence of Unbeaten League Matches: 19, 16.2.1980 – 30.8.1980.

Longest Sequence Without a League Win: 22, 24.3.2008 – 1.11.2008.

Successive Scoring Runs: 33 from 6.10.1928.

Successive Non-scoring Runs: 7 from 19.10.2019.

MANAGERS

H. N. Hickson 1902–20 *(Secretary-Manager)*
Haydn Price 1920
George Fraser 1921–24
Wilf Gillow 1924–32
Frank Womack 1932–36
Charles Spencer 1937–51
Bill Shankly 1951–53
Billy Walsh 1954–55
Allenby Chilton 1955–59
Tim Ward 1960–62
Tom Johnston 1962–64
Jimmy McGuigan 1964–67
Don McEvoy 1967–68
Bill Harvey 1968–69
Bobby Kennedy 1969–71
Lawrie McMenemy 1971–73
Ron Ashman 1973–75
Tom Casey 1975–76
Johnny Newman 1976–79
George Kerr 1979–82
David Booth 1982–85
Mike Lyons 1985–87
Bobby Roberts 1987–88
Alan Buckley 1988–94
Brian Laws 1994–96
Kenny Swain 1997
Alan Buckley 1997–2000
Lennie Lawrence 2000–01
Paul Groves 2001–04
Nicky Law 2004
Russell Slade 2004–06
Graham Rodger 2006
Alan Buckley 2006–08
Mike Newell 2008–09
Neil Woods 2009–11
Rob Scott and Paul Hurst 2011–13
Paul Hurst 2013–16
Marcus Bignot 2016–17
Russell Slade 2017–18
Michael Jolley 2018–19
Ian Holloway 2019–20
Paul Hurst December 2020–

TEN YEAR LEAGUE RECORD

		P	W	D	L	F	A	Pts	Pos
2011-12	Conf	46	19	13	14	79	60	70	11
2012-13	Conf	46	23	14	9	70	38	83	4
2013-14	Conf	46	22	12	12	65	46	78	4
2014-15	Conf	46	25	11	10	74	40	86	3
2015-16	NL	46	22	14	10	82	45	80	4
2016-17	FL 2	46	17	11	18	59	63	62	14
2017-18	FL 2	46	13	12	21	42	66	51	18
2018-19	FL 2	46	16	8	22	45	56	56	17
2019-20	FL 2	37	12	11	14	45	51	47	15§
2020-21	FL 2	46	10	13	23	37	69	43	24

§*Decided on points-per-game (1.27)*

DID YOU KNOW

Ray Lancaster was the first substitute to be used for Grimsby Town when he came off the bench to replace the injured Matt Tees in the Mariners' game at York City on 27 August 1965. The 1-1 draw briefly pushed the club into second place in the Division Three table, the highest they would reach all season.

GRIMSBY TOWN – SKY BET LEAGUE TWO 2020–21 LEAGUE RECORD

Match No.	Date	Venue	Opponents	Result	H/T Score	Lg Pos.	Goalscorers	Attendance
1	Sept 12	A	Walsall	L 0-1	0-0	19		0
2	19	H	Salford C	L 0-4	0-1	23		0
3	Oct 10	A	Bolton W	D 0-0	0-0	23		0
4	13	A	Cheltenham T	W 3-1	2-1	18	Edwards [23], Tilley [39], Windsor [90]	0
5	17	A	Leyton Orient	W 3-2	2-1	15	Waterfall [22], Williams [32], Gibson (pen) [90]	0
6	20	H	Harrogate T	L 1-2	1-2	16	Tilley [26]	0
7	24	H	Carlisle U	D 1-1	1-0	17	Pollock [24]	0
8	27	A	Forest Green R	L 0-1	0-1	19		0
9	31	A	Stevenage	D 0-0	0-0	17		0
10	Nov 3	H	Barrow	W 1-0	0-0	16	Gibson [60]	0
11	21	A	Tranmere R	L 0-5	0-4	20		0
12	24	A	Crawley T	W 2-1	1-1	18	Green [35], Wright [51]	0
13	Dec 1	H	Exeter C	L 1-4	1-3	18	Hendrie [31]	0
14	5	A	Colchester U	L 1-2	1-1	20	Hendrie [23]	0
15	8	H	Newport Co	L 0-2	0-2	20		0
16	12	H	Mansfield T	D 1-1	0-0	20	Jackson [63]	0
17	15	A	Southend U	L 1-3	1-1	20	Jackson [45]	2000
18	19	H	Scunthorpe U	W 1-0	1-0	19	Pollock [21]	0
19	22	H	Bradford C	L 1-2	0-2	20	Clifton [49]	0
20	26	A	Morecambe	L 1-3	1-0	22	Pollock [21]	0
21	29	H	Oldham Ath	D 0-0	0-0	22		0
22	Jan 2	H	Cambridge U	L 1-2	0-2	23	Hewitt [72]	0
23	9	A	Port Vale	L 0-3	0-2	23		0
24	16	H	Southend U	D 0-0	0-0	23		0
25	23	A	Scunthorpe U	L 0-3	0-2	23		0
26	30	H	Stevenage	L 1-2	0-1	23	Payne [90]	0
27	Feb 6	A	Newport Co	L 0-1	0-0	23		0
28	23	H	Crawley T	W 2-1	1-1	23	Morais [21], Adams [79]	0
29	27	A	Harrogate T	L 0-1	0-0	24		0
30	Mar 2	H	Leyton Orient	L 0-1	0-1	24		0
31	6	H	Forest Green R	L 1-2	1-1	24	Hanson [38]	0
32	9	A	Carlisle U	D 1-1	1-0	24	John-Lewis [16]	0
33	13	H	Colchester U	D 0-0	0-0	24		0
34	17	H	Tranmere R	D 0-0	0-0	24		0
35	20	A	Mansfield T	D 2-2	0-1	24	John-Lewis [63], Williams [90]	0
36	23	A	Barrow	W 1-0	0-0	24	Spokes [71]	0
37	27	H	Walsall	D 1-1	1-1	24	Hanson [9]	0
38	Apr 2	A	Salford C	D 1-1	1-0	24	Clifton [2]	0
39	5	H	Cheltenham T	D 1-1	1-1	24	John-Lewis [8]	0
40	10	A	Bradford C	L 0-1	0-1	24		0
41	17	H	Bolton W	W 2-1	1-0	24	Matete [1], Jackson [86]	0
42	20	H	Morecambe	L 0-3	0-2	24		0
43	24	A	Oldham Ath	W 2-1	1-1	24	Green [36], Matete [80]	0
44	27	A	Exeter C	L 2-3	1-1	24	John-Lewis (pen) [41], Matete [58]	0
45	May 1	H	Port Vale	W 1-0	1-0	24	Green [32]	0
46	8	A	Cambridge U	L 0-3	0-1	24		0

Final League Position: 24

GOALSCORERS

League (37): John-Lewis 4 (1 pen), Green 3, Jackson 3, Matete 3, Pollock 3, Clifton 2, Gibson 2 (1 pen), Hanson 2, Hendrie 2, Tilley 2, Williams 2, Adams 1, Edwards 1, Hewitt 1, Morais 1, Payne 1, Spokes 1, Waterfall 1, Windsor 1, Wright 1.
FA Cup (1): Windsor 1 (1 pen).
Carabao Cup (1): Green 1.
Papa John's Trophy (3): Boyd 1, Gibson 1 (1 pen), Pollock 1.

McKeown J 34+1	Hewitt E 36+1	Ohman L 3 / Bunney J 3+2	Idehen D 5+1	Preston D 22+3 / Adams J 3+3	Taylor T 11+2	Rose D 19+3	Williams G 10+9	Edwards O 11+6 / Lamy J 6+3	Green M 17+11	Scannell S 5+6	Gibson M 7+12	Boyd L —+1 / John-Lewis L 14+6	Tilley J 7+7	Clifton H 30+5	Mohsni B —+1	Starbuck J —+6 / Coke G 14+3	Hendrie L 37+1	Waterfall L 30+3	Pollock M 23+2	Windsor O 10+2 / Khouri E 6	Morton J 4+3	Hanson J 16+7	Spokes L 10+7	Bennett K 10+3	Gomis V —+5	Wright M 4+2	Adlard L —+3	Russell S 5	Jackson I 7+13	Morais F 13+3	Sisay A —+1	Habergham S 10+3	Menayese R 21	Matete J 20	El Mizouni I 6	Payne S 10+3	Eastwood J 7	Match No.
1	2	3	4	5	6	7^2	8^3	9	10^1	11	12	13	14																									1
1	2	3▮	4	5	6		10^3	9	11^2		12		8^1	7	13	14																							2
1				6	7	8	9^1	12	11^2	14	13			2			3	4	5	10^3																	3
1		2^2	13	8				11			10^1		9^3	6			5	3	4	12	7	14															4
1				6	7	8^1	9^3	13	11^2		14			2			3	4	5	10	12																5
1				6				11^1			10		7	2			3	4	5		9	14	8^3	12^2	13												6
1				5	6		10^3		14				9^1	8^2		13	2	3	4	11	7	12															7
1			4^1	8	7				14		12		5				2	3	6	9^3	11	10^2			13												8
1				9	7	8			10^2		14		5^1				2	3	4	11		13		6^3	12												9
1				14	6^2	8	12				10			5			2	3	4	9	13			7^3		11^1											10
1	13			12	7^3	8^5	9^1	6	14	16	10^2			5			2	3	4	11^4						15											11
1	6		4^1	5		7		11^2	10^3	9^4				12		15	2	3							13	8	14										12
1	8^5		4^1	5	16	7		11^4	10^3	9				6^2			2	3	12					13	14		15										13
1	7			5	14	6	12	8		9^1	13						2	3	4^3	11				10^2													14
	8				6^4	7^1	13	9^2			10^3			5		14	2	3	4	12	15			11				1									15
	6			5	8^2	7	11^3	12			13		16	2				3	4^5	10^4				9^1				1	14	15								16
	8			5		7^1		9^5			14		13	6^2			2	3▮	4	10^3				16				1	11^4	12	15							17
1	3			5				12	13		10^1		14	7		15	2		4				8	9^2					11^3	6^4								18
1	4			5^4		16		13	12		10^1		14	7		15	2	3					8	9^3					11^2	6^5								19
1	8			5			15	13	10^3		12		14	7			2	3	4					9^2					11^1	6^4								20
	7			5		8	10^1	9^3	11				12	13			2	3	4									1	14	6^2								21
	7			5		8^2	15		11^4		12		10^1	13			2	3	4					9^3				1	14	6								22
1	7			5^1		8	13		11^3		14			9^2			2	4	3					10		15				6^4		12						23
1	7			9			10^1		11^2	14							2	3	4			12	8			6^3			13			5						24
1	7^2			9^3		14	12		10^5	15							2		4			11^4	13			6^1			16			5	3	8				25
1				13		8											2	4	5			11	14						10^1			6^2	3^3	7	9	12		26
	2	5		6^1				12				13		8				4				10^2											3	7	9	11	1	27
	2	5▮		10^3		7^1						13				14	15	3				12								6^4			4	8	9	11^2	1	28
	2			14								12				8	6	4	3^3			11								13			5	7^2	9	10^1	1	29
	2	5		9^3		7^2		14				12						3				13								6			4	8	10	11^1	1	30
	3	12							13			11^2				8	2					10								6^3		5	4	7	9^1	14	1	31
	3	12						9^2	14			10^3		13		8	2	15				11								6^4		5^1	4	7			1	32
1	3			13				9^2				11^1		5		8	2					10							14	6^3			4	7		12		33
1	3							9				11		5		8	2					10							12	6^1			4	7				34
1	4			15			13	6^1	14			10		5		8^2	2	3					12						9^3					7^4		11		35
1	3					6^1			13			9		5		12	2					10	8										4	7		11^2		36
1	4					12	13					9^3		5		6	2					10	8^2						14				3	7^1		11		37
1	3							8^3	13			11		5		7	2					10^2	14									12	4	6		9^1		38
1	2								13			9^1		7		12	5	3				10										8	4	6		11^2		39
1	3						9^2	16				12		14		7^4	2	13				11	15							8^1		5^3	4	6^5		10▮		40
1	3											10		6		7	2^2			9^1		11	12						13			5	4	8				41
1	3							6^2				11		2				13		9^1		10	8						12			5	4	7				42
1	2								11^1			10		5		7		3		9			8						12				4	6				43
1	2								11^1	14		10		5		7		3^3		9			8^2						13			12	4	6▮				44
13	3								11^1	6^4		12		7		8	2		14	9			15						10			5^3	4				1^2	45
1	3								11^3	12		10		7		8	2		4^2	6			9^1				13		14				5					46

FA Cup
First Round Dagenham & R (a) 1-3

Carabao Cup
First Round Morecambe (h) 1-1
(Morecambe won 4-3 on penalties)

Papa John's Trophy
Group H (N) Harrogate T (h) 2-2
(Grimsby T won 5-4 on penalties)
Group H (N) Leicester C U21 (h) 1-3
Group H (N) Hull C (a) 0-3

HARROGATE TOWN

FOUNDATION

An earlier club, Harrogate AFC, was formed in 1914, but did not start the 1914–15 season and was reformed in 1919. They competed in the Midland, Yorkshire and Northern Leagues before folding in 1932. The current club was established in the summer of 1935 as Harrogate Hotspurs, several of the players having previously played for Harrogate YMCA. Harry Lunn, the club's first secretary, had previously been secretary of the YMCA team. Hotspurs began life in the Harrogate & District League in 1935–36 when they finished in fourth position, gaining their first trophy when they won the Harrogate Charity Cup. By 1948 they had reached the West Yorkshire League and they changed their name to Harrogate Town to reflect their status as the town's leading club.

The EnviroVent Stadium, Wetherby Road, Harrogate HG2 7SA.

Telephone: (01423) 210 600.

Ticket Office: (01423) 210 600.

Website: harrogatetownafc.com

Email: enquiries@harrogatetownafc.com

Ground Capacity: 5,000.

Record Attendance: 4,280 v Harrogate Railway, Whitworth Cup Final, May 1950.

Pitch Measurements: 100m × 66m (109.5yd × 72yd).

Chairman: Irving Weaver.

Vice-Chairman: Howard Matthews.

Managing Director: Garry Plant.

Manager: Simon Weaver.

Assistant Manager: Paul Thirlwell.

Colours: Yellow shirts with black trim, black shorts, black socks.

Year Formed: 1914. ***Turned Professional:*** 2017.

Previous Names: 1914, Harrogate AFC; 1935, Harrogate Hotspurs; 1948, Harrogate Town.

Club Nickname: 'Town', 'Sulphurites'.

Grounds: 1919, Starbeck Lane; 1920, Wetherby Lane; 1935, Christ Church Stray; 1937, Old Showground; 1946, Wetherby Road (renamed The EnviroVent Stadium, 2020).

First League Game: (As Harrogate AFC) 30 August 1919, West Riding League v Horsforth (h) (at Starbeck Lane) W 1–0 – Middleton; Deans, Bell, Goodall, Carroll, Jenkinson, H (Capt), Day, O'Rourke, Priestley, Craven (1), Codd.

First Football League Game: 12 September 2020, FL 2 v Southend U (a) W 4–0 – Cracknell; Fallowfield, Falkingham, Smith, Burrell, Thomson, Beck (Stead 58), Martin (1) (Walker 75), Kerry (1), Muldoon (2), Hall.

HONOURS

League Champions: Northern Premier League Division One – 2001–02.
Yorkshire League Division One – 1926–27.
Yorkshire League Division Two – 1981–82.

FA Cup: 2nd rd – 2012–13, 2020–21.

FA Trophy Winners: 2019–20 (final played in 2021).

FA Vase: 4th rd – 1989–90.

Northern Premier League Division One Cup Winners: 1989–90.

West Riding County Challenge Cup Winners: 1924–25, 1926–27.

West Riding County Cup Winners: 1962–63, 1972–73, 1985–86, 2001–02, 2002–03, 2007–08.

Whitworth Cup Winners: 1919–20, 1924–25, 1931–32, 1946–47, 1947–48, 1950–51, 1954–55, 1959–60, 1961–62, 1972–73, 1977–78, 1983–84, 1995–96.

FOOTBALL YEARBOOK FACT FILE

Harrogate Town made the significant step up from the West Yorkshire League to Division Two of the Yorkshire League for the 1957–58 campaign. They found life much more challenging and in their first season managed just four wins from 26 games, two of which came against Goole Town Reserves.

Record League Victory: 4–0 v Southend U, FL 2, 12 September 2020 (a) – Cracknell; Fallowfield, Falkingham, Smith, Burrell, Thomson, Beck (Stead 58), Martin (1) (Walker 75), Kerry (1), Muldoon (2), Hall.

Record Cup Victory: 11–2 v Yeadon Celtic, West Riding County Challenge Cup, 5 November 1938 – McLaren; Hebblethwaite, Keogan, Atha, Harker, Clelland, Annakin (4), Sibson, Stanley (7), Everitt C, Richardson.

Record Defeat: 1–10, v Methley U (h), West Yorkshire League Division One, 20 August 1956.

Most League Points in a Season (3 for a win): 57, FL 2, 2020–21.

Most League Goals in a Season: 52, FL 2, 2020–21.

Highest League Scorer in Season: Jack Muldoon, 15, FL 2, 2020–21.

Most League Goals in Total Aggregate: Jack Muldoon, 15, 2020–21.

Most League Goals in One Match: 3, Brendan Kiernan v Cambridge U, FL 2, 30 April 2021.

Most League Appearances: George Thomson, 46, 2020–21.

Youngest League Player: Josh Andrews, 19 years 113 days v Crawley T, 6 February 2021.

Football League Record: 2020 Promoted from National League; 2020– FL 2.

LATEST SEQUENCES

Longest Sequence of League Wins: 3, 23.2.2021 – 2.3.2021

Longest Sequence of League Defeats: 3, 13.3.2021 – 27.3.2021.

Longest Sequence of League Draws: 2, 19.1.2021 – 22.1.2021.

Longest Sequence of Unbeaten League Matches: 3, 23.2.2021 – 2.3.2021.

Longest Sequence Without a League Win: 7. 13.3.2021 – 13.4.2021.

Successive Scoring Runs: 5 from 16.2.2021.

Successive Non-scoring Runs: 4 from 20.3.2021.

MANAGERS

Tommy Codd 1919–20
J. C. Field 1920–21
Jimmy Dyer 1921–23
Mr Gill 1923–24
Mr Sixton 1924–29
C. Edwards 1929–30
Selection Committee 1930–31
Tom Bell 1931–32
Eddie Smith 1935–46
Selection Committee 1946–50
Walter Cook 1950–53
Bernard Cross 1953–55
Jack (Boss) Townrow 1955–67
Selection Committee 1967–69
Stan Hall 1969–70
Thomas (Chick) Farr 1970–71
Peter Gunby 1971–77
Alan Milburn 1977–78
Reg Taylor 1978–79
Alan Smith 1979–88
Denis Metcalf 1988–89
Alan Smith 1989–90
John Reed 1990–91
Alan Smith 1991–93
Mick Doig and John Deacey 1993
Frank Gray 1994
John Deacey then Alan Smith 1994–96
Mick Doig 1996–97
Paul Marshall 1997–98
Gavin Liddle 1998–99
Alan Smith (caretaker) 1999
Paul Ward 1999
Dave Fell 1999–2000
Mick Hennigan 2000–01
John Reed 2001–05
Neil Aspin 2005–09
Simon Weaver 2009–

TEN YEAR LEAGUE RECORD

		P	W	D	L	F	A	Pts	Pos
2011-12	NLN	42	14	10	18	59	69	52	15
2012-13	NLN	42	20	9	13	72	50	69	6
2013-14	NLN	42	19	9	14	75	59	63*	9
2014-15	NLN	42	14	10	18	50	62	52	15
2015-16	NLN	42	21	9	12	73	46	72	4
2016-17	NLN	42	16	11	15	71	63	59	11
2017-18	NLN	42	26	7	9	100	49	85	2
2018-19	NL	46	21	11	14	78	57	74	6
2019-20	NL	37	19	9	9	61	44	66	2§
2020-21	FL 2	46	16	9	21	52	61	57	17

**3 pts deducted. §Decided on points-per-game (1.78).*

DID YOU KNOW ?

Harrogate Town first entered the FA Amateur Cup in 1950–51 when they reached the third qualifying round stage where they went out to Guiseley in a replay. They subsequently entered the competition on a further 18 occasions without improving on that performance.

HARROGATE TOWN – SKY BET LEAGUE TWO 2020–21 LEAGUE RECORD

Match No.	*Date*	*Venue*	*Opponents*	*Result*		*H/T Score*	*Lg Pos.*	*Goalscorers*	*Attendance*
1	Sept 12	A	Southend U	W	4-0	2-0	1	Muldoon 2 $^{25, 69}$, Kerry ^{44}, Martin ^{60}	0
2	19	H	Walsall	D	2-2	2-1	3	Martin ^{32}, Muldoon ^{42}	0
3	26	A	Port Vale	D	0-0	0-0	6		0
4	Oct 3	H	Bolton W	L	1-2	0-1	12	Thomson ^{61}	0
5	12	A	Bradford C	W	1-0	0-0	8	Kerry ^{74}	0
6	17	H	Barrow	W	1-0	1-0	7	Muldoon ^{22}	0
7	20	A	Grimsby T	W	2-1	2-1	4	Muldoon 2 $^{25, 43}$	0
8	24	A	Colchester U	L	1-2	0-0	6	Stead ^{61}	0
9	27	H	Stevenage	D	0-0	0-0	8		0
10	31	A	Newport Co	L	1-2	1-1	12	Smith ^{43}	0
11	Nov 3	H	Tranmere R	L	0-1	0-0	14		0
12	14	H	Crawley T	D	1-1	0-1	12	Muldoon ^{85}	0
13	21	A	Leyton Orient	L	0-3	0-2	14		0
14	24	A	Mansfield T	W	1-0	1-0	12	Miller ^{27}	0
15	Dec 1	H	Scunthorpe U	L	2-5	1-2	15	Muldoon ^{35}, Hall ^{90}	0
16	5	H	Forest Green R	L	0-1	0-0	17		410
17	12	A	Morecambe	L	0-1	0-0	17		0
18	15	A	Exeter C	W	2-1	1-0	17	Kiernan ^{31}, Muldoon ^{75}	1559
19	19	H	Salford C	L	0-1	0-1	17		495
20	26	A	Oldham Ath	W	2-1	1-1	16	Thomson 2 $^{30, 71}$	0
21	Jan 9	A	Cambridge U	L	1-2	1-0	18	Muldoon ^{10}	0
22	19	H	Exeter C	D	0-0	0-0	18		0
23	22	A	Salford C	D	2-2	1-1	18	Muldoon ^{37}, Francis ^{90}	0
24	26	A	Tranmere R	L	2-3	1-1	20	McPake ^{25}, March ^{72}	0
25	30	H	Newport Co	W	2-1	1-1	20	March ^{34}, Martin ^{66}	0
26	Feb 6	A	Crawley T	W	3-1	3-0	14	Martin ^{13}, March (pen) ^{30}, Power ^{45}	0
27	9	H	Cheltenham T	L	0-1	0-1	15		0
28	16	H	Carlisle U	W	1-0	1-0	12	March (pen) ^{28}	0
29	20	A	Scunthorpe U	L	1-3	1-2	15	March (pen) ^{27}	0
30	23	H	Mansfield T	W	1-0	0-0	13	Martin ^{46}	0
31	27	H	Grimsby T	W	1-0	0-0	12	Beck ^{77}	0
32	Mar 2	A	Barrow	W	1-0	0-0	11	Muldoon ^{84}	0
33	6	A	Stevenage	L	0-1	0-0	11		0
34	9	H	Colchester U	W	3-0	2-0	10	Beck ^{1}, Smith ^{45}, McPake ^{56}	0
35	13	A	Forest Green R	L	1-2	0-1	11	Williams ^{90}	0
36	20	H	Morecambe	L	0-1	0-1	13		0
37	27	H	Southend U	L	0-1	0-0	15		0
38	Apr 2	A	Walsall	D	0-0	0-0	15		0
39	5	H	Port Vale	L	0-2	0-0	16		0
40	10	A	Bolton W	L	1-2	1-0	17	Beck ^{13}	0
41	13	H	Leyton Orient	D	2-2	0-0	17	Jones ^{58}, McPake ^{74}	0
42	17	H	Bradford C	W	2-1	1-0	16	Muldoon ^{22}, McPake ^{89}	0
43	20	H	Oldham Ath	L	0-3	0-1	17		0
44	24	A	Carlisle U	D	1-1	1-0	17	Muldoon ^{11}	0
45	30	H	Cambridge U	W	5-4	4-2	15	Kiernan 3 (1 pen) $^{9, 20 (p), 32}$, Beck ^{13}, Lokko ^{84}	0
46	May 8	A	Cheltenham T	L	1-4	1-3	17	Muldoon ^{7}	0

Final League Position: 17

GOALSCORERS

League (52): Muldoon 15, March 5 (3 pens), Martin 5, Beck 4, Kiernan 4 (1 pen), McPake 4, Thomson 3, Kerry 2, Smith 2, Francis 1, Hall 1, Jones 1, Lokko 1, Miller 1, Power 1, Stead 1, Williams 1.
FA Cup (4): Beck 1, Lawlor 1, Martin 1, Miller 1.
Carabao Cup (1): Kerry 1.
Papa John's Trophy (5): Kiernan 2, Jones 1, Lokko 1, Stead 1.

Cracknell J 8	Fallowfield R 26 + 5	Smith W 32	Hall C 39 + 2	Burrell W 39 + 4	Thomson G 46	Falkingham J 37 + 6	Kerry L 23 + 8	Muldoon J 34 + 8	Beck M 14 + 12	Martin A 27 + 9	Stead J 8 + 11	Walker T 1 + 6	Kiernan B 15 + 15	Kirby C 10 + 6	Belshaw J 38	Jones D 18 + 3	Miller C 8 + 2	Lokko K 2 + 1	Lawlor J 14 + 3	Francis E 15 + 5	Roberts M 4	McPake J 22 + 1	March J 10 + 4	Williams J 3 + 4	Hondermarck W 2 + 1	Power S 11 + 2	Andrews J — + 3	Match No.
1	2	3	4	5	6	7	8	9	10^{1}	11^{2}	12	13																1
1	2	3	4	5	6	7	8	9	10^{1}	11	12																	2
1	2	3	4	5	6	7	8^{2}		10^{1}	11	12	14	9^{3}	13														3
	2	3	4		6	7			10^{3}	11^{1}	14	13	12	8	1	5	9^{2}											4
	2	3	4	5	6	7	8	11^{2}		12	10^{1}		13		1		9											5
	2	3	4	5	6	8	7	10		13	11^{2}		12		1		9^{1}											6
	2	3	4	5	6	7	8^{2}	10		11^{3}	14		13	12	1		9^{1}											7
	2	3	4	5^{3}	6	7	8	10		11^{1}	12		13		1	14	9^{2}											8
	2	3	4	5	6^{3}	7		11	13		10^{2}	14	12	8	1		9^{1}											9
		3	4	2	6	7■	8	11	13	10^{2}			9^{1}	12	1	5												10
		3^{3}	4	2	6		7	10		11^{2}	13	12	9^{1}	8	1	5		14										11
	2		4	5^{2}	6	8	7^{3}	10		12		9^{1}	11	14	1	13			3									12
	2		4	12	6	7	8^{2}	11		10^{3}	13	15	9^{4}	14	1	5			3^{1}									13
	2^{3}		4	3	6	7	8	11^{2}	10	13			12		1	5	9^{1}		14									14
			4	5	6	8	7^{2}	10	11	13			12	2^{1}	1		9		3									15
	2		4	5	8	7		9	12	10			11	6^{1}	1				3									16
	2		4	5	8	7		9		10^{1}	12		11	6	1				3									17
	2		4	5	6	7^{1}		11		10			9^{2}	8	1		13		3	12								18
	2		4	5	6^{1}		12	11		10			9	8	1		13		3	7^{2}								19
	2		4	5	6	12	13	11		10			9	8^{1}	1				3	7^{2}								20
			4	2	7	13	14■	10			16			8^{2}	1				3	6^{3}	5^{1}	9^{4}	11^{5}	12	15			21
	12		4	5■	6	8		10^{3}		11			9^{2}	13	1				3	7			14	2^{1}				22
			4		7	8		11^{1}		10			6^{2}		1				3	5		9	13	2		12		23
			4■	2	8	7		11^{1}		10			6^{2}		1				3	5		9	13			12		24
		4		2	7	8		12		11					1				3	5		9	10^{1}			6		25
		3■	4	2	7	8	13	14		11^{4}					1				12	5		9^{1}	10^{3}			6^{2}	15	26
	12		4	2^{1}	7	8		13		10					1				3^{3}	5		9^{2}	11			6	14	27
		3	4	2	7	8^{3}	14		12	10					1				13	5^{2}		9	11^{1}			6		28
		3	4	2	7	8		13	12	10^{1}					1					5		9	11			6^{2}		29
		3	4	2	7	8	12	14	15	11^{4}					1	13				5^{2}		9	10^{3}			6^{1}		30
	2	3	4	12	7	15	8^{4}	13	14	11^{2}					1	5^{3}						9	10^{1}			6		31
	2	3		4	7	13	8^{3}	14	11^{1}	12					1	5						9	10^{2}			6		32
	2	3		4	7	12	8^{1}	10	11^{2}						1	5						9	13			6		33
	2	3		4	6	8	7^{3}	12	11^{4}	15			13		1	5				14		9^{2}	10^{1}					34
	2	3	14	4^{2}	6	8^{4}		11	10^{3}	13			12		1	5				7^{1}		9		15				35
	2	3	4		7	8		10	12	11^{1}			13		1	5						9^{2}				6		36
		3	4	2	7	8		10	13	11^{2}			12		1	5				14		9^{3}				6^{1}		37
	2	3	4	8^{1}	6	7	12	9	10	11^{2}					1	5						13						38
		3	4	2	6^{1}	8	7	10^{2}	11	12			13		1	5						9						39
	15	3	4	2^{4}	6	8	7^{2}	10	11^{1}		12		13		1	5				14		9^{3}						40
		3	4	2	6	7	8	11			10				1	5						9						41
1	12	3	4	2	6	8	7	10	13^{3}		11^{2}					5^{1}						9		14				42
1	13	3	4	2^{2}	6^{4}	8^{5}	7^{3}	10	12		11^{1}		16							14	5	9		15				43
1		3	4	2	6	8	7	10	12		11^{1}					5						9						44
1	2	3		12	6				11				10					4		8	5^{1}			7	9			45
1	2	3	15	12	6	14	13	9			11^{5}		10					4^{4}		8^{2}	5^{1}				7^{3}		16	46

FA Cup

First Round	Skelmersdale U	(h)	4-1
Second Round	Blackpool	(h)	0-4

Carabao Cup

First Round	Tranmere R	(a)	1-1
(Harrogate T won 8-7 on penalties)			
Second Round	WBA	(a)	0-3

Papa John's Trophy

Group H (N)	Grimsby T	(a)	2-2
(Grimsby T won 5-4 on penalties)			
Group H (N)	Leicester C U21	(h)	3-1
Group H (N)	Hull C	(h)	0-2

HARTLEPOOL UNITED

FOUNDATION

The inspiration for the launching of Hartlepool United was the West Hartlepool club which won the FA Amateur Cup in 1904–05. They had been in existence since 1881 and their cup success led in 1908 to the formation of the new professional concern which first joined the North-Eastern League. In those days they were Hartlepools United and won the Durham Senior Cup in their first two seasons.

Victoria Park, Clarence Road, Hartlepool TS24 8BZ.

Telephone: (01429) 272 584.

Ticket Office: (01429) 272 584 (option 2).

Website: www.hartlepoolunited.co.uk

Email: enquires@hartlepoolunited.co.uk

Ground Capacity: 7,865.

Record Attendance: 17,426 v Manchester U, FA Cup 3rd rd, 5 January 1957.

Pitch Measurements: 100.5m × 67.5m (110yd × 74yd).

Chairman: Raj Singh.

Honorary President: Jeff Stelling.

Manager: Dave Challinor.

Assistant Manager: Joe Parkinson.

Colours: Blue shirts with white trim, blue shorts with white trim, blue socks.

Year Formed: 1908.

Turned Professional: 1908.

Previous Names: 1908, Hartlepools United; 1968, Hartlepool; 1977, Hartlepool United.

Club Nickname: 'The Pool', 'Monkey Hangers'.

Ground: 1908, Victoria Park; 2016, renamed The Northern Gas & Power Stadium; 2018 renamed The Super Six Stadium; 2019 renamed Victoria Park.

First Football League Game: 27 August 1921, Division 3 (N), v Wrexham (a) W 2–0 – Gill; Thomas, Crilly; Dougherty, Hopkins, Short; Kessler, Mulholland (1), Lister (1), Robertson, Donald.

Record League Victory: 10–1 v Barrow, Division 4, 4 April 1959 – Oakley; Cameron, Waugh; Johnson, Moore, Anderson; Scott (1), Langland (1), Smith (3), Clark (2), Luke (2), (1 og).

Record Cup Victory: 6–0 v North Shields, FA Cup 1st rd, 30 November 1946 – Heywood; Brown, Gregory; Spelman, Lambert, Jones; Price, Scott (2), Sloan (4), Moses, McMahon; 6–0 v Gainsborough Trinity (a), FA Cup 1st rd, 10 November 2007 – Budtz; McCunnie, Humphreys, Liddle (1) (Antwi), Nelson, Clark, Moore (1), Sweeney, Barker (2) (Monkhouse), Mackay (Porter 1), Brown (1).

Record Defeat: 1–10 v Wrexham, Division 4, 3 March 1962.

Most League Points (2 for a win): 60, Division 4, 1967–68.

HONOURS

League: *Runners-up:* Division 3N – 1956–57; FL 2 – 2006–07; Third Division – 2002–03.

FA Cup: 4th rd – 1955, 1978, 1989, 1993, 2005, 2009.

League Cup: 4th rd – 1975.

FOOTBALL YEARBOOK FACT FILE

Hartlepool United played their first-ever FA Cup match on 3 October 1908 when they faced local rivals West Hartlepool at the Victoria Ground in a first qualifying round tie. The two clubs shared the ground, with United technically the away team. They won 2-1 in front of an estimated 7,000 attendance, with the goals coming from Tommy Brown and Christopher Smith.

Most League Points (3 for a win): 88, FL 2, 2006–07.

Most League Goals: 90, Division 3 (N), 1956–57.

Highest League Scorer in Season: William Robinson, 28, Division 3 (N), 1927–28; Joe Allon, 28, Division 4, 1990–91.

Most League Goals in Total Aggregate: Ken Johnson, 98, 1949–64.

Most League Goals in One Match: 5, Harry Simmons v Wigan Borough, Division 3 (N), 1 January 1931; 5, Bobby Folland v Oldham Ath, Division 3 (N), 15 April 1961.

Most Capped Player: Ambrose Fogarty, 1 (11), Republic of Ireland; David Edgar, 1 (42), Canada; Zaine Francis-Angol 1 (23), Antigua and Barbuda.

Most League Appearances: Richie Humphreys, 481, 2001–13.

Youngest League Player: David Foley, 16 years 105 days v Port Vale, 25 August 2003.

Record Transfer Fee Received: £750,000 from Ipswich T for Tommy Miller, July 2001.

Record Transfer Fee Paid: £80,000 to Mansfield T for Darrell Clarke, July 2001.

Football League Record: 1921 Original Member of Division 3 (N); 1958–68 Division 4; 1968–69 Division 3; 1969–91 Division 4; 1991–92 Division 3; 1992–94 Division 2; 1994–2003 Division 3; 2003–04 Division 2; 2004–06 FL 1; 2006–07 FL 2; 2007–13 FL 1; 2013–17 FL 2; 2017–21 National League; 2021– FL 2.

LATEST SEQUENCES

Longest Sequence of League Wins: 9, 18.11.2006 – 1.1.2007.

Longest Sequence of League Defeats: 8, 27.1.1993 – 27.2.1993.

Longest Sequence of League Draws: 6, 30.4.2011 – 20.8.2011.

Longest Sequence of Unbeaten League Matches: 23, 18.11.2006 – 30.3.2007.

Longest Sequence Without a League Win: 20, 8.9.2012 – 26.12.2012.

Successive Scoring Runs: 27 from 18.11.2006.

Successive Non-scoring Runs: 11 from 9.1.1993.

MANAGERS

Alfred Priest 1908–12
Percy Humphreys 1912–13
Jack Manners 1913–20
Cecil Potter 1920–22
David Gordon 1922–24
Jack Manners 1924–27
Bill Norman 1927–31
Jack Carr 1932–35
(had been Player-Coach from 1931)
Jimmy Hamilton 1935–43
Fred Westgarth 1943–57
Ray Middleton 1957–59
Bill Robinson 1959–62
Allenby Chilton 1962–63
Bob Gurney 1963–64
Alvan Williams 1964–65
Geoff Twentyman 1965
Brian Clough 1965–67
Angus McLean 1967–70
John Simpson 1970–71
Len Ashurst 1971–74
Ken Hale 1974–76
Billy Horner 1976–83
Johnny Duncan 1983
Mike Docherty 1983
Billy Horner 1984–86
John Bird 1986–88
Bobby Moncur 1988–89
Cyril Knowles 1989–91
Alan Murray 1991–93
Viv Busby 1993
John MacPhail 1993–94
David McCreery 1994–95
Keith Houchen 1995–96
Mick Tait 1996–99
Chris Turner 1999–2002
Mike Newell 2002–03
Neale Cooper 2003–05
Martin Scott 2005–06
Danny Wilson 2006–08
Chris Turner 2008–10
Mick Wadsworth 2010–11
Neale Cooper 2011–12
John Hughes 2012–13
Colin Cooper 2013–14
Paul Murray 2014
Ronnie Moore 2014–16
Craig Hignett 2016–17
Dave Jones 2017
Craig Harrison 2017–18
Matthew Bates 2018
Richard Money 2018–19
Craig Hignett 2019
Dave Challinor November 2019–

TEN YEAR LEAGUE RECORD

		P	W	D	L	F	A	Pts	Pos
2011-12	FL 1	46	14	14	18	50	55	56	13
2012-13	FL 1	46	9	14	23	39	67	41	23
2013-14	FL 2	46	14	11	21	50	56	53	19
2014-15	FL 2	46	12	9	25	39	70	45	22
2015-16	FL 2	46	15	6	25	49	72	51	16
2016-17	FL 2	46	11	13	22	54	75	46	23
2017-18	NL	46	14	14	18	53	63	56	15
2018-19	NL	46	15	14	17	56	62	59	16
2019-20	NL	39	14	13	12	56	50	55	12§
2020-21	NL	42	22	10	10	66	43	76	4

§Decided on points-per-game (1.41)

DID YOU KNOW 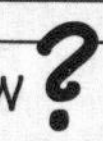

Hartlepool United's League One fixture against Notts County on 2 November 2010 lasted just three minutes before the game was called off. With rain falling heavily and the surface already waterlogged, Referee Carl Boyesen decided a pitch inspection was necessary and called the proceedings to a halt shortly after kick-off.

HUDDERSFIELD TOWN

FOUNDATION

A meeting, attended largely by members of the Huddersfield & District FA, was held at the Imperial Hotel in 1906 to discuss the feasibility of establishing a football club in this rugby stronghold. However, it was not until a man with both the enthusiasm and the money to back the scheme came on the scene that real progress was made. This benefactor was Mr Hilton Crowther and it was at a meeting at the Albert Hotel in 1908 that the club formally came into existence with an investment of £2,000 and joined the North-Eastern League.

The John Smith's Stadium, Stadium Way, Leeds Road, Huddersfield, West Yorkshire HD1 6PX.

Telephone: (01484) 960 600.

Ticket Office: (01484) 960 606.

Website: www.htafc.com

Email: info@htafc.com

Ground Capacity: 24,169.

Record Attendance: 67,037 v Arsenal, FA Cup 6th rd, 27 February 1932 (at Leeds Road); 24,169 v Tottenham H, Premier League, 30 September 2017; 24,169 v Manchester U, Premier League, 21 October 2017; 24,169 v WBA, Premier League, 4 November 2017; 24,169 v Chelsea, Premier League, 12 December 2017 (at John Smith's Stadium).

Pitch Measurements: 106m × 68m (116yd × 74.5yd).

Chairman: Paul Hodgkinson.

Chief Executive: Mark Devlin.

Head Coach: Carlos Corberán.

Assistant Head Coaches: Jorge Alarcón, Narcís Pèlach, Danny Schofield.

Colours: Blue and white striped shirts, white shorts with blue trim, white socks with blue trim.

Year Formed: 1908.

Turned Professional: 1908.

Club Nickname: 'The Terriers'.

Grounds: 1908, Leeds Road; 1994, The Alfred McAlpine Stadium (renamed the Galpharm Stadium 2004, John Smith's Stadium 2012).

First Football League Game: 3 September 1910, Division 2, v Bradford PA (a) W 1–0 – Mutch; Taylor, Morris; Beaton, Hall, Bartlett; Blackburn, Wood, Hamilton (1), McCubbin, Jee.

Record League Victory: 10–1 v Blackpool, Division 1, 13 December 1930 – Turner; Goodall, Spencer; Redfern, Wilson, Campbell; Bob Kelly (1), McLean (4), Robson (3), Davies (1), Smailes (1).

Record Cup Victory: 7–0 v Lincoln U, FA Cup 1st rd, 16 November 1991 – Clarke; Trevitt, Charlton, Donovan (2), Mitchell, Doherty, O'Regan (1), Stapleton (1) (Wright), Roberts (2), Onuora (1), Barnett (Ireland). *N.B.* 11–0 v Heckmondwike (a), FA Cup pr rd, 18 September 1909 – Doggart; Roberts, Ewing; Hooton, Stevenson, Randall; Kenworthy (2), McCreadie (1), Foster (4), Stacey (4), Jee.

Record Defeat: 1–10 v Manchester C, Division 2, 7 November 1987.

HONOURS

League Champions: Division 1 – 1923–24, 1924–25, 1925–26; Division 2 – 1969–70; Division 4 – 1979–80.
Runners-up: Division 1 – 1926–27, 1927–28, 1933–34; Division 2 – 1919–20, 1952–53.

FA Cup Winners: 1922.
Runners-up: 1920, 1928, 1930, 1938.

League Cup: semi-final – 1968.

League Trophy: *Runners-up:* 1994.

FOOTBALL YEARBOOK FACT FILE

Huddersfield Town were members of League Two in the 2002–03 season and progressed to the Premier League for 2017–18 by three promotions. On each occasion they went up through the play-off system and each time the play-off final finished goalless. The Terriers defeated, in order, Mansfield Town, Sheffield United and Reading on penalty kicks to reach the top flight of English football.

Most League Points (2 for a win): 66, Division 4, 1979–80.

Most League Points (3 for a win): 87, FL 1, 2010–11.

Most League Goals: 101, Division 4, 1979–80.

Highest League Scorer in Season: Sam Taylor, 35, Division 2, 1919–20; George Brown, 35, Division 1, 1925–26; Jordan Rhodes, 35, 2011–12.

Most League Goals in Total Aggregate: George Brown, 142, 1921–29; Jimmy Glazzard, 142, 1946–56.

Most League Goals in One Match: 5, Dave Mangnall v Derby Co, Division 1, 21 November 1931; 5, Alf Lythgoe v Blackburn R, Division 1, 13 April 1935; 5, Jordan Rhodes v Wycombe W, FL 1, 6 January 2012.

Most Capped Player: Jimmy Nicholson, 31 (41), Northern Ireland.

Most League Appearances: Billy Smith, 521, 1914–34.

Youngest League Player: Denis Law, 16 years 303 days v Notts Co, 24 December 1956.

Record Transfer Fee Received: £15,000,000 from AFC Bournemouth for Philip Billing, July 2019.

Record Transfer Fee Paid: £17,500,000 to Monaco for Terence Kongolo, June 2018.

Football League Record: 1910 Elected to Division 2; 1920–52 Division 1; 1952–53 Division 2; 1953–56 Division 1; 1956–70 Division 2; 1970–72 Division 1; 1972–73 Division 2; 1973–75 Division 3; 1975–80 Division 4; 1980–83 Division 3; 1983–88 Division 2; 1988–92 Division 3; 1992–95 Division 2; 1995–2001 Division 1; 2001–03 Division 2; 2003–04 Division 3; 2004–12 FL 1; 2012–17 FL C; 2017–19 Premier League; 2019– FL C.

LATEST SEQUENCES

Longest Sequence of League Wins: 11, 5.4.1920 – 4.9.1920.

Longest Sequence of League Defeats: 8, 2.3.2019 – 26.4.2019.

Longest Sequence of League Draws: 6, 3.3.1987 – 3.4.1987.

Longest Sequence of Unbeaten League Matches: 43, 1.1.2011 – 19.11.2011.

Longest Sequence Without a League Win: 22, 4.12.1971 – 29.4.1972.

Successive Scoring Runs: 27 from 12.3.2005.

Successive Non-scoring Runs: 7 from 14.10.2000.

MANAGERS

Fred Walker 1908–10
Richard Pudan 1910–12
Arthur Fairclough 1912–19
Ambrose Langley 1919–21
Herbert Chapman 1921–25
Cecil Potter 1925–26
Jack Chaplin 1926–29
Clem Stephenson 1929–42
Ted Magner 1942–43
David Steele 1943–47
George Stephenson 1947–52
Andy Beattie 1952–56
Bill Shankly 1956–59
Eddie Boot 1960–64
Tom Johnston 1964–68
Ian Greaves 1968–74
Bobby Collins 1974
Tom Johnston 1975–78
(had been General Manager since 1975)
Mike Buxton 1978–86
Steve Smith 1986–87
Malcolm Macdonald 1987–88
Eoin Hand 1988–92
Ian Ross 1992–93
Neil Warnock 1993–95
Brian Horton 1995–97
Peter Jackson 1997–99
Steve Bruce 1999–2000
Lou Macari 2000–02
Mick Wadsworth 2002–03
Peter Jackson 2003–07
Andy Ritchie 2007–08
Stan Ternent 2008
Lee Clark 2008–12
Simon Grayson 2012–13
Mark Robins 2013–14
Chris Powell 2014–15
David Wagner 2015–19
Jan Siewert 2019
Danny Cowley 2019–20
Carlos Corberán July 2020–

TEN YEAR LEAGUE RECORD

		P	W	D	L	F	A	Pts	Pos
2011-12	FL 1	46	21	18	7	79	47	81	4
2012-13	FL C	46	15	13	18	53	73	58	19
2013-14	FL C	46	14	11	21	58	65	53	17
2014-15	FL C	46	13	16	17	58	75	55	16
2015-16	FL C	46	13	12	21	59	70	51	19
2016-17	FL C	46	25	6	15	56	58	81	5
2017-18	PR Lge	38	9	10	19	28	58	37	16
2018-19	PR Lge	38	3	7	28	22	76	16	20
2019-20	FL C	46	13	12	21	52	70	51	18
2020-21	FL C	46	12	13	21	50	71	49	20

DID YOU KNOW ?

Huddersfield Town were elected as members of the Football League at the Annual General Meeting held at the Imperial Hotel in London on Monday 13 June 1910. They were one of four prospective members seeking election along with the bottom two clubs from 1909–10. Huddersfield finished second in the poll with 26 votes, 14 ahead of Grimsby Town, the club that they replaced.

HUDDERSFIELD TOWN – SKY BET CHAMPIONSHIP 2020–21 LEAGUE RECORD

Match No.	Date	Venue	Opponents	Result		H/T Score	Lg Pos.	Goalscorers	Attendance
1	Sept 12	H	Norwich C	L	0-1	0-0	15		0
2	19	A	Brentford	L	0-3	0-0	21		0
3	25	H	Nottingham F	W	1-0	0-0	16	Campbell [54]	0
4	Oct 3	A	Rotherham U	D	1-1	0-1	18	MacDonald, A (og) [90]	0
5	17	A	Swansea C	W	2-1	1-1	12	Toffolo [23], Koroma [67]	0
6	20	H	Derby Co	W	1-0	0-0	8	Bacuna [53]	0
7	24	H	Preston NE	L	1-2	1-0	14	Campbell [8]	0
8	28	A	Birmingham C	L	1-2	0-1	16	Mbenza [85]	0
9	31	A	Millwall	W	3-0	1-0	12	Koroma [18], Pipa [89], O'Brien [90]	0
10	Nov 3	H	Bristol C	L	1-2	1-0	13	Koroma [43]	0
11	7	H	Luton T	D	1-1	0-1	13	Eiting [60]	0
12	21	A	Stoke C	L	3-4	2-3	16	Eiting [24], Mbenza [40], Sarr [60]	0
13	24	A	Wycombe W	D	0-0	0-0	16		0
14	28	H	Middlesbrough	W	3-2	2-1	13	Eiting [37], Campbell [45], Koroma [85]	0
15	Dec 1	A	Cardiff C	L	0-3	0-1	16		0
16	5	H	QPR	W	2-0	2-0	13	Koroma [3], Toffolo [39]	0
17	8	H	Sheffield W	W	2-0	2-0	12	Koroma [11], Mbenza [24]	0
18	12	A	Bournemouth	L	0-5	0-3	14		0
19	16	A	Coventry C	D	0-0	0-0	14		0
20	19	H	Watford	W	2-0	2-0	12	Campbell [9], Capoue (og) [32]	0
21	26	A	Barnsley	L	1-2	1-1	14	Edmonds-Green [13]	0
22	29	H	Blackburn R	W	2-1	0-0	12	Sarr 2 [53, 90]	0
23	Jan 2	H	Reading	L	1-2	1-0	13	Campbell [6]	0
24	16	A	Watford	L	0-2	0-0	14		0
25	20	H	Millwall	L	0-1	0-1	14		0
26	26	A	Bristol C	L	1-2	0-2	14	Bacuna [59]	0
27	30	H	Stoke C	D	1-1	1-1	14	Pipa [5]	0
28	Feb 6	A	Luton T	D	1-1	0-1	17	Sarr [74]	0
29	13	H	Wycombe W	L	2-3	2-1	18	Bacuna [18], Mbenza [41]	0
30	16	A	Middlesbrough	L	1-2	1-2	19	Mbenza [9]	0
31	20	H	Swansea C	W	4-1	1-1	18	Campbell [22], O'Brien [49], Holmes 2 [52, 55]	0
32	23	A	Derby Co	L	0-2	0-1	19		0
33	27	A	Preston NE	L	0-3	0-1	19		0
34	Mar 2	H	Birmingham C	D	1-1	0-0	19	Campbell [63]	0
35	5	H	Cardiff C	D	0-0	0-0	18		0
36	13	A	QPR	W	1-0	0-0	18	Bacuna [55]	0
37	17	A	Sheffield W	D	1-1	0-1	17	Paterson (og) [72]	0
38	Apr 3	H	Brentford	D	1-1	1-0	18	O'Brien [7]	0
39	6	A	Norwich C	L	0-7	0-5	19		0
40	10	H	Rotherham U	D	0-0	0-0	19		0
41	13	H	Bournemouth	L	1-2	0-2	19	Hogg [76]	0
42	17	A	Nottingham F	W	2-0	1-0	18	Rowe [45], Bacuna [61]	0
43	21	H	Barnsley	L	0-1	0-0	20		0
44	24	A	Blackburn R	L	2-5	1-2	20	Nyambe (og) [45], Koroma [82]	0
45	May 1	H	Coventry C	D	1-1	0-0	20	Ward [79]	0
46	8	A	Reading	D	2-2	1-2	20	Koroma [15], Edmonds-Green [90]	0

Final League Position: 20

GOALSCORERS

League (50): Koroma 8, Campbell 7, Bacuna 5, Mbenza 5, Sarr 4, Eiting 3, O'Brien 3, Edmonds-Green 2, Holmes 2, Pipa 2, Toffolo 2, Hogg 1, Rowe 1, Ward 1, own goals 4.
FA Cup (2): Crichlow-Noble 1, Rowe 1.
Carabao Cup (0).

Hamer B 15	Pipa G 35 + 2	Schindler C 10 + 2	Stearman R 14 + 7	Toffolo H 31	Pritchard A 6 + 12	Hogg J 37	Jackson B 1	Bacuna J 37 + 6	Koroma J 19 + 1	Diakhaby A 7 + 9	Mbenza I 28 + 8	Brown J 1 + 12	Campbell F 35 + 5	Crichlow-Noble R 2 + 2	Eiting C 17 + 6	Sarr N 41	Daly M 1 + 4	O'Brien L 39 + 3	Duhaney D 7 + 6	Ward D 6 + 13	Castro J 2	Schofield R 29 + 1	Edmonds-Green R 16 + 8	Rowe A 10 + 10	Vallejo A 12 + 4	Diarra B — + 1	Phillips K — + 10	Aarons R 5 + 5	Jones P — + 2	High S 1 + 13	Keogh R 21	Holmes D 16 + 3	Thomas S — + 7	Sanogo Y 5 + 4	Match No.
1	2	3	4^{3}	5	6	7	8^{1}	9	10	11^{2}	12	13	14																						1
1	2	3^{2}	4	5^{1}	6	7		8	11	9^{3}	10	12	14	13																					2
1	2		3	5	9	7^{1}		6	10	13	8^{2}	14	11^{3}	4	12																				3
1	2		3	5		7		9^{1}	10	13	8^{2}		11		6	4	12																		4
1	5	3	2	9		7		6^{2}	11		10^{1}		12		8^{3}	4		13	14																5
1	2^{3}	12	3	5		7		6	9		11^{1}		10		8^{2}	4		13	14																6
1	5	3^{1}	2	9		7		6	14	13	11^{3}		10		12	4■		8^{2}																	7
1	5	2	4	9	12	3^{2}		6^{1}	8	10^{3}	14		11		7			13																	8
1	13	3		5	6^{1}	7		12	10	9^{2}	11^{3}		14			4		8	2																9
1	5	3^{3}	2	8		6			11^{1}	13	9^{2}		10		12	4	14	7																	10
1	2^{3}	12	3	5		7			11^{2}	9^{1}			10		6	4		8	14	13															11
			3	5		7^{4}		12	11^{2}	15	9^{3}		10		6	4	14	8	2^{1}	13	1														12
		3^{1}	12	5		7		2		11^{2}	9		10		6	4		8		13		1													13
			3^{1}	5		7		2^{3}	11^{4}		9^{5}	16	10^{2}		6	4		8	13	14		1	12	15											14
1		3^{3}		5^{4}		7^{2}			11	16	12	15	13		8	4	9^{1}	6	2^{5}	10			14												15
1	2^{1}	3^{3}		5		7		12	11		9^{4}		10^{2}		6	4		8	15	13			14												16
1	2			5		7^{1}		12	11^{2}		9^{4}	13	10^{3}		6	4		8		15			3		14										17
1^{1}				5^{5}	6			8		9	14	11^{2}		16		4		7^{4}		10^{3}		12	3	2	15	13									18
	2			5	12	7		10^{1}		13	9^{2}		11		6	4		8				1	3												19
	2			5	12	7		11^{3}		14	9^{2}		10		6^{1}	4		8				1	3	13											20
	2			5	12	7		11		13	9^{2}		10		6^{1}	4		8				1	3												21
	2			5	13	7		11^{2}			6^{1}	14	10		8^{3}	4		9				1	3	12											22
	2			5	12	6		9			8		11		7^{1}	4		10				1	3^{2}				13								23
	5			8				6					10	4				7		14		1	2	9^{2}	3^{3}			11^{1}	12	13					24
	5			8	15			6^{4}			12		10			4		7		9^{1}		1			3		14	11^{2}	13		2^{3}				25
	2			5	12			6			9		10			4		8				1			7^{1}		13	11^{2}			3				26
	2			5	14			6			9^{3}		10			4		8				1			7		13	11^{1}			3^{2}	12			27
	2^{2}			5■	13^{4}	7		6			9^{1}		10			4		8				1			15			12		14	3	11^{3}			28
	2				12	6		9			10^{3}		11			4		5				1			7^{1}					13	3	8^{2}	14		29
	2				6^{2}	7		8			11^{1}		10			4	15	5				1		13	12		14				3^{4}	9^{3}			30
	5		14		16	7^{4}		6^{2}				15	10^{1}			4		8				1		9^{5}	2		12			13	3	11^{3}			31
	5^{5}							6^{2}			13	15■	10^{1}			4		8	2			1		9^{4}	7		12			14	3	11^{3}	16		32
	8		16					5			9^{3}		10^{5}			4		7				1	2^{1}	12	6		13			14	3^{4}	11^{2}		15	33
	5		3					6			11^{1}		10^{3}			4		8				1	2	12	7^{2}					13		9		14	34
	5		13					7					11			4		9				1	2	6^{2}	8		12				3			10^{1}	35
	5		15			7		8^{4}			11^{2}		10^{3}			4		6	12			1	2	9^{1}							3	13		14	36
	8		14			7		9			12		11^{4}			4		6	5^{3}			1	2^{1}	15							3	10^{2}		13	37
	5^{3}		14			7		12					9^{4}			4		10	2	15		1		13	6^{1}						3	8^{2}		11	38
			2^{1}			5^{3}		7			10	16				4^{4}		9^{5}	6	11	1		15	13						12	3	8^{2}	14		39
	9^{1}					7		6^{3}			15		10^{2}			4		8		13		1	2							14	3	5^{4}	12	11	40
						5		7^{4}			6^{1}	16	10^{3}			4		8		14		1	2^{2}	9				12		15	3	11^{5}	13		41
	2^{4}			5^{2}		7		6				15	11^{1}			4		9		12		1	13	10						14	3	8^{3}			42
						5		7^{4}	10^{3}						15	4		8		14		1	2^{2}	6^{1}				16		12	3	9^{5}	13	11	43
	2^{1}			5		7^{5}		10^{2}	8						6^{3}	4		9		11		1	15	12				13		16	3^{4}	14			44
	12			5		7		6^{4}	11						15	4		8		14		1	16	2^{1}				13			3^{5}	9^{2}		10^{3}	45
						6		16	9						12	4^{5}		7		11^{3}		1	15		2		14	5^{1}		8^{4}	3	10^{2}	13		46

FA Cup
Third Round Plymouth Arg (h) 2-3

Carabao Cup
First Round Rochdale (h) 0-1

HULL CITY

FOUNDATION

The enthusiasts who formed Hull City in 1904 were brave men indeed. More than that, they were audacious for they immediately put the club on the map in this Rugby League fortress by obtaining a three-year agreement with the Hull Rugby League club to rent their ground! They had obtained quite a number of conversions to the dribbling code, before the Rugby League forbade the use of any of their club grounds by Association Football clubs. By that time, Hull City were well away, having entered the FA Cup in their initial season and the Football League, Second Division after only a year.

The KCOM Stadium, West Park, Hull, East Yorkshire HU3 6HU.

Telephone: (01482) 504 600.

Ticket Office: (01482) 505 600.

Website: www.hullcitytigers.com

Email: info@hulltigers.com

Ground Capacity: 24,983.

Record Attendance: 55,019 v Manchester U, FA Cup 6th rd, 26 February 1949 (at Boothferry Park); 25,512 v Sunderland, FL C, 28 October 2007 (at KC Stadium).

Pitch Measurements: 105m × 68m (115yd × 74.5yd).

Chairman: Dr Assem Allam.

Vice-Chairman: Ehab Allam.

Manager: Grant McCann.

Assistant Manager: Cliff Byrne.

Colours: Amber shirts with black stripes, black shorts with amber trim, amber socks with black trim.

Year Formed: 1904.

Turned Professional: 1905.

Club Nickname: 'The Tigers'.

Grounds: 1904, Boulevard Ground (Hull RFC); 1905, Anlaby Road (Hull CC); 1944, Boulevard Ground; 1946, Boothferry Park; 2002, Kingston Communications Stadium; 2016, renamed KCOM Stadium.

First Football League Game: 2 September 1905, Division 2, v Barnsley (h) W 4–1 – Spendiff; Langley, Jones; Martin, Robinson, Gordon (2); Rushton, Spence (1), Wilson (1), Howe, Raisbeck.

Record League Victory: 11–1 v Carlisle U, Division 3 (N), 14 January 1939 – Ellis; Woodhead, Dowen; Robinson (1), Blyth, Hardy; Hubbard (2), Richardson (2), Dickinson (2), Davies (2), Cunliffe (2).

Record Cup Victory: 8–2 v Stalybridge Celtic (a), FA Cup 1st rd, 26 November 1932 – Maddison; Goldsmith, Woodhead; Gardner, Hill (1), Denby; Forward (1), Duncan, McNaughton (1), Wainscoat (4), Sargeant (1).

Record Defeat: 0–8 v Wolverhampton W, Division 2, 4 November 1911; 0–8 v Wigan Ath, FL C, 14 July 2020.

HONOURS

League Champions: FL 1 2020–21; Division 3 – 1965–66; Division 3N – 1932–33, 1948–49.
Runners-up: FL C – 2012–13; FL 1 – 2004–05; Division 3 – 1958–59; Third Division – 2003–04; Division 4 – 1982–83.

FA Cup: *Runners-up:* 2014.

League Cup: semi-final – 2017.

League Trophy: *Runners-up:* 1984.

European Competitions
Europa League: 2014–15.

FOOTBALL YEARBOOK FACT FILE

Hull City attracted a Division Three North record gate for their top of the table clash with Rotherham United on Christmas Day 1948. A crowd of 54,652 watched the game and saw Hull lead 3-0 only to concede twice in the final five minutes. Rotherham remained in first position, but the Tigers had two games in hand and finished champions at the end of the season.

Most League Points (2 for a win): 69, Division 3, 1965–66.

Most League Points (3 for a win): 90, Division 4, 1982–83.

Most League Goals: 109, Division 3, 1965–66.

Highest League Scorer in Season: Bill McNaughton, 39, Division 3 (N), 1932–33.

Most League Goals in Total Aggregate: Chris Chilton, 193, 1960–71.

Most League Goals in One Match: 5, Ken McDonald v Bristol C, Division 2, 17 November 1928; 5, Simon 'Slim' Raleigh v Halifax T, Division 3 (N), 26 December 1930.

Most Capped Player: Theo Whitmore, 28 (119), Jamaica.

Most League Appearances: Andy Davidson, 520, 1952–67.

Youngest League Player: Matthew Edeson, 16 years 63 days v Fulham, 10 October 1992.

Record Transfer Fee Received: £22,000,000 from West Ham U for Jarrod Bowen, January 2020.

Record Transfer Fee Paid: £13,000,000 to Tottenham H for Ryan Mason, August 2016.

Football League Record: 1905 Elected to Division 2; 1930–33 Division 3 (N); 1933–36 Division 2; 1936–49 Division 3 (N); 1949–56 Division 2; 1956–58 Division 3 (N); 1958–59 Division 3; 1959–60 Division 2; 1960–66 Division 3; 1966–78 Division 2; 1978–81 Division 3; 1981–83 Division 4; 1983–85 Division 3; 1985–91 Division 2; 1991–92 Division 3; 1992–96 Division 2; 1996–2004 Division 3; 2004–05 FL 1; 2005–08 FL C; 2008–10 Premier League; 2010–13 FL C; 2013–15 Premier League; 2015–16 FL C; 2016–17 Premier League; 2017–20 FL C; 2020–21 FL 1; 2021– FL C.

LATEST SEQUENCES

Longest Sequence of League Wins: 10, 23.2.1966 – 20.4.1966.

Longest Sequence of League Defeats: 8, 7.4.1934 – 8.9.1934.

Longest Sequence of League Draws: 5, 14.2.2012 – 10.3.2012.

Longest Sequence of Unbeaten League Matches: 19, 13.3.2001 – 22.9.2001.

Longest Sequence Without a League Win: 27, 27.3.1989 – 4.11.1989.

Successive Scoring Runs: 26 from 10.4.1990.

Successive Non-scoring Runs: 6 from 13.11.1920.

MANAGERS

James Ramster 1904–05 *(Secretary-Manager)*
Ambrose Langley 1905–13
Harry Chapman 1913–14
Fred Stringer 1914–16
David Menzies 1916–21
Percy Lewis 1921–23
Bill McCracken 1923–31
Haydn Green 1931–34
John Hill 1934–36
David Menzies 1936
Ernest Blackburn 1936–46
Major Frank Buckley 1946–48
Raich Carter 1948–51
Bob Jackson 1952–55
Bob Brocklebank 1955–61
Cliff Britton 1961–70 *(continued as General Manager to 1971)*
Terry Neill 1970–74
John Kaye 1974–77
Bobby Collins 1977–78
Ken Houghton 1978–79
Mike Smith 1979–82
Bobby Brown 1982
Colin Appleton 1982–84
Brian Horton 1984–88
Eddie Gray 1988–89
Colin Appleton 1989
Stan Ternent 1989–91
Terry Dolan 1991–97
Mark Hateley 1997–98
Warren Joyce 1998–2000
Brian Little 2000–02
Jan Molby 2002
Peter Taylor 2002–06
Phil Parkinson 2006
Phil Brown *(after caretaker role December 2006)* 2007–10
Ian Dowie *(consultant)* 2010
Nigel Pearson 2010–11
Nick Barmby 2011–12
Steve Bruce 2012–16
Mike Phelan 2016–17
Marco Silva 2017
Leonid Slutsky 2017
Nigel Adkins 2017–19
Grant McCann June 2019–

TEN YEAR LEAGUE RECORD

		P	W	D	L	F	A	Pts	Pos
2011-12	FL C	46	19	11	16	47	44	68	8
2012-13	FL C	46	24	7	15	61	52	79	2
2013-14	PR Lge	38	10	7	21	38	53	37	16
2014-15	PR Lge	38	8	11	19	33	51	35	18
2015-16	FL C	46	24	11	11	69	35	83	4
2016-17	PR Lge	38	9	7	22	37	80	34	18
2017-18	FL C	46	11	16	19	70	70	49	18
2018-19	FL C	46	17	11	18	66	68	62	13
2019-20	FL C	46	12	9	25	57	87	45	24
2020-21	FL 1	46	27	8	11	80	38	89	1

DID YOU KNOW ?

In 1909–10 Hull City missed out on promotion to the First Division after losing 3-0 to Oldham Athletic on the final day of the season. The result put the Latics level on points with Hull but the Lancashire club were promoted because their goal average was 0.29 better than the Tigers. It was another 100 years before the Tigers eventually reached the top division.

HULL CITY – SKY BET LEAGUE ONE 2020–21 LEAGUE RECORD

Match No.	Date	Venue	Opponents	Result		H/T Score	Lg Pos.	Goalscorers	Attendance
1	Sept 12	A	Gillingham	W	2-0	1-0	2	Lewis-Potter ^{3}, Magennis ^{82}	0
2	19	H	Crewe Alex	W	1-0	0-0	3	Wilks ^{81}	0
3	26	A	Northampton T	W	2-0	2-0	2	Lewis-Potter ^{34}, Honeyman ^{44}	0
4	Oct 3	H	Plymouth Arg	W	1-0	1-0	2	Adelakun ^{10}	0
5	9	A	Fleetwood T	L	1-4	1-1	2	Honeyman ^{21}	0
6	17	A	Rochdale	W	3-0	1-0	2	Wilks 2 $^{20, 73}$, Magennis ^{75}	0
7	20	H	AFC Wimbledon	W	1-0	1-0	1	Lewis-Potter ^{45}	0
8	24	H	Peterborough U	L	1-2	1-0	2	Wilks ^{36}	0
9	27	A	Bristol R	W	3-1	0-1	2	Lewis-Potter ^{63}, Slater ^{75}, Eaves ^{90}	0
10	31	A	Swindon T	L	1-2	1-1	4	Lewis-Potter ^{16}	0
11	Nov 14	H	Burton Alb	W	2-0	0-0	2	Wilks ^{62}, Adelakun ^{88}	0
12	21	A	Milton Keynes D	W	3-1	2-1	1	Magennis 2 $^{8, 12}$, Scott ^{76}	0
13	24	A	Ipswich T	W	3-0	2-0	1	Wilks ^{2}, Magennis ^{45}, Eaves ^{77}	0
14	Dec 2	H	Doncaster R	W	2-1	1-0	1	Magennis ^{26}, Eaves ^{87}	0
15	5	A	Oxford U	D	1-1	0-1	1	Docherty ^{68}	0
16	12	H	Shrewsbury T	L	0-1	0-1	1		0
17	15	A	Blackpool	L	2-3	1-1	1	Wilks ^{38}, Burke ^{89}	0
18	18	H	Portsmouth	L	0-2	0-1	2		0
19	Jan 2	H	Charlton Ath	W	2-0	1-0	2	Adelakun ^{18}, Docherty ^{75}	0
20	9	A	Sunderland	D	1-1	1-1	2	Burke ^{13}	0
21	16	H	Blackpool	D	1-1	0-0	2	Wilks ^{51}	0
22	19	H	Accrington S	W	3-0	1-0	1	Wilks ^{37}, Whyte ^{55}, Magennis (pen) ^{67}	0
23	23	A	Portsmouth	W	4-0	1-0	1	Whatmough0 (2 ogs) $^{23, 63}$, Honeyman ^{61}, Magennis ^{90}	0
24	26	A	Accrington S	L	0-2	0-0	2		0
25	30	H	Swindon T	W	1-0	1-0	1	Docherty ^{5}	0
26	Feb 6	A	Burton Alb	L	0-1	0-0	2		0
27	9	H	Lincoln C	D	0-0	0-0	2		0
28	13	H	Milton Keynes D	L	0-1	0-0	2		0
29	17	A	Wigan Ath	W	5-0	2-0	2	Wilks 3 $^{27, 32, 64}$, Lewis-Potter ^{48}, Magennis ^{53}	0
30	20	A	Doncaster R	D	3-3	3-1	3	Wilks 2 $^{19, 24}$, Magennis ^{38}	0
31	23	H	Ipswich T	L	0-1	0-1	3		0
32	27	A	AFC Wimbledon	W	3-0	2-0	3	Magennis (pen) ^{24}, Burke ^{43}, Wilks (pen) ^{64}	0
33	Mar 2	H	Rochdale	W	2-0	1-0	2	Wilks ^{24}, Osho (og) ^{69}	0
34	6	H	Bristol R	W	2-0	1-0	1	Whyte 2 $^{32, 60}$	0
35	9	A	Peterborough U	W	3-1	1-1	1	Burke ^{21}, Lewis-Potter ^{49}, Wilks (pen) ^{60}	0
36	13	H	Oxford U	W	2-0	1-0	1	Lewis-Potter 2 $^{22, 71}$	0
37	20	A	Shrewsbury T	D	1-1	0-0	1	Docherty ^{62}	0
38	27	H	Gillingham	D	1-1	1-0	1	Eaves ^{9}	0
39	Apr 2	A	Crewe Alex	W	2-1	0-0	1	Magennis (pen) ^{71}, Wilks ^{90}	0
40	5	H	Northampton T	W	3-0	2-0	1	Elder ^{30}, Lewis-Potter ^{44}, Whyte ^{90}	0
41	10	A	Plymouth Arg	W	3-0	1-0	1	Lewis-Potter ^{11}, Magennis ^{58}, Docherty ^{74}	0
42	17	H	Fleetwood T	W	2-1	0-1	1	Magennis ^{61}, Lewis-Potter ^{70}	0
43	20	H	Sunderland	D	2-2	1-2	1	Magennis 2 $^{28, 64}$	0
44	24	A	Lincoln C	W	2-1	1-0	1	Magennis ^{4}, Wilks (pen) ^{83}	0
45	May 1	H	Wigan Ath	W	3-1	2-1	1	Lewis-Potter ^{17}, Honeyman ^{22}, Magennis ^{66}	0
46	9	A	Charlton Ath	L	0-1	0-0	1		0

Final League Position: 1

GOALSCORERS

League (80): Wilks 19 (3 pens), Magennis 18 (3 pens), Lewis-Potter 13, Docherty 5, Burke 4, Eaves 4, Honeyman 4, Whyte 4, Adelakun 3, Elder 1, Scott 1, Slater 1, own goals 3.
FA Cup (3): Burke 1, Eaves 1 (1 pen), Magennis 1.
Carabao Cup (2): Wilks 2.
Papa John's Trophy (10): Lewis-Potter 2, Samuelsen 2, Scott 2, Coyle 1, Docherty 1, Jones C 1 (1 pen), Wilks 1.

Ingram M 38	Emmanuel J 21 + 7	Burke R 31 + 3	De Wijs J 7	Fleming B 3	Smallwood R 23 + 4	Docherty G 44	Wilks M 42 + 2	Honeyman G 42	Lewis-Potter K 33 + 10	Magennis J 29 + 11	Scott J 3 + 15	Batty D 2 + 4	Jones C — + 1	Elder C 43 + 1	Mayer T 1 + 5	Jones A 27 + 4	Adelakun H 11 + 3	Slater R 11 + 16	Samuelsen M — + 5	Greaves J 39	Eaves T 6 + 20	Coyle L 26 + 2	Long G 8	Whyte G 10 + 10	Crowley D 6 + 16	Flores J — + 3	Chadwick B — + 3	McLoughlin S — + 3	Wood H — + 1	Match No.
1	2	3	4	5	6	7^3	8	9^1	10	11^2	12	13	14																	1
1	2	3	4		8	6	9	7	11^1	10^2	13			5	12															2
1	2	3	4			8		7	11^2	10	12	13		5		6	9^1													3
1	2	3	4			6		7	11^3	10		8^2		5	12		9^1	13	14											4
1	2	3	4			8	10^3	6	11			7^1		5	12		9^2	13	14											5
1	2	3			8^3	6^1	9	7	11	10^2				5		14		12		4	13									6
1	12	3			8	6	13	7	11	10^3				5			9^2			4	14	2^1								7
1	2	3			8	6	9	7	11^1	10^2				5			12			4	13									8
1	2	3	4		8	6^3	9	7	12	10^2				5			11^1	13			14									9
1	2	3	4		8	6^3	9^2	7	11	12	13			5	14						10^1									10
1	2	3			8	6^3	10	7			11^2			5	9^1		12		14	4	13									11
1	2	4			8^3		11^5	7^4		10^2	12	15		5		6	9^1	14	16	3	13									12
1	2	4			8		9^5	7^4		10^3	12			5		13	11^2	6^1	15	3	14	16								13
1	2				7	6	9^2	8	12	10^3	13			5		3	11^1			4	14									14
1	2	13			7	8	9	6	12	10^3				5		3^2	11^1			4	14									15
1	2^3	3			6^1	8	9	7	12	10				5			11^2			4	13	14								16
1		3			7	8	9		12	13	11^1			5			14	6^3		4	10^2	2								17
1	2	3			7	8	9		12	10	11^1			5				6^2		4	13									18
	2			5	6^4	8	9	7^3	12			15			13	3	11^2	14		4	10^1		1							19
	2	3		5^3	6	9	10	8	13	12				14		7^2				4	11^1		1							20
	2	3			8	6	11	7	12	10^1				5		13				4			1	9^2						21
	16				8^4	6^5	11	7^3	10^1	12				5		3		14		4		2	1	9^2	13	15				22
					6	8^3	11^2	7	10^4	12				5		3		14		4		2	1	9^1	13		15			23
		14			7^2	8	11	6^3	9	10^1				5		3				4		2	1	13	12					24
		3			12	8	9^4	6	10^3	13	14			5		7^1				4		2	1		11^2		15			25
		3			7^1	8	11^3	6	10	13	14			5				12		4		2	1		9^2					26
1	9	3				7	12	6	11	10				5				13		4		2^1			8^2					27
1		3				8	9	6	11	10				5						4		2			7^1		12			28
1	16	3				7^1	8^4	9^5	10	11^3	15			5		6^2		13		4		2			14	12				29
1	14	3				8^1	9^3	6	11	10^2				5		7		12		4		2		13						30
1	2	3				7	10^3	6	11	12	14			5		13				4				9^2	8^1					31
1		3				6	8^2	9^4	10^3	11^1				5		7^5		15		4	13	2		12	14			16		32
1		3				7^4	8	9	11^3		13			5		6^2		14		4	12	2		10^1	15					33
1		3				7	8	9^1	12	11^2				5		6^4		15		4	13	2		10^3	14					34
1		3				7	8	9	11^2		13			5		6				4	12	2		10^1						35
1	14	3				6	11	9	10^1	12				5		7				4		2^3		8^2	13					36
1		3				7	11^3	9	10^2	12				5		6				4	14	2		8^1	13					37
1						7	8	9	10		12			5		3^2		6		4	11^1	2						13		38
1						7	8	9^2	10^3	12				5		3		6		4	11^1	2		14	13					39
1						7	8^1	9^4	10^3	11^2				5		3		6		4^5	13	2		12	14	15		16		40
1	14					7	8	9^1	10^3	11^4				5		3		6		4	15	2^2		13	12					41
1					13	7	8^2		10	11				5		3		6		4		2		12	9^1					42
1					12	7	8	9^2	10^3	11				5		3		6^1		4		2		13	14					43
1		12				7	8	9^1	10^2	11^4				5		3		6^3		4	15	2		13	14					44
1					6^1	7	8^3	9^4	10	11^2				5		3		12		4	14	2		13	15					45
1	12				15	7^4	8		10^2	11^3	14			5^1		3		6^5		4		2		9	13				16	46

FA Cup

First Round	Fleetwood T	(h)	2-0
Second Round	Stevenage	(a)	1-1

(aet; Stevenage won 6-5 on penalties)

Carabao Cup

First Round	Sunderland	(a)	0-0

(Hull C won 5-4 on penalties)

Second Round	Leeds U	(a)	1-1

(Hull C won 9-8 on penalties)

Third Round	West Ham U	(a)	1-5

Papa John's Trophy

Group H (N)	Leicester C U21	(h)	1-2
Group H (N)	Harrogate T	(a)	2-0
Group H (N)	Grimsby T	(h)	3-0
Second Round (N)	Crewe Alex	(h)	0-0

(Hull C won 3-2 on penalties)

Third Round (N)	Fleetwood T	(h)	3-2
Quarter-Final	Lincoln C	(h)	1-1

(Lincoln C won 4-3 on penalties)

IPSWICH TOWN

FOUNDATION

Considering that Ipswich Town only reached the Football League in 1938, many people outside of East Anglia may be surprised to learn that this club was formed at a meeting held in the Town Hall as far back as 1878 when Mr T. C. Cobbold, MP, was voted president. Originally it was the Ipswich Association FC to distinguish it from the older Ipswich Football Club which played rugby. These two amalgamated in 1888 and the handling game was dropped in 1893.

Portman Road, Ipswich, Suffolk IP1 2DA.

Telephone: (01473) 400 500.

Ticket Office: (03330) 050 503.

Website: www.itfc.co.uk

Email: enquiries@itfc.co.uk

Ground Capacity: 30,311.

Record Attendance: 38,010 v Leeds U, FA Cup 6th rd, 8 March 1975.

Pitch Measurements: 102.5m × 66m (112yd × 72yd).

Chairman: Mike O'Leary.

Director: Mark Ashton.

Manager: Paul Cook.

First-Team Coaches: Gary Roberts, Franny Jeffers.

Colours: Blue shirts with white trim, blue shorts with white trim, blue socks with white trim.

Year Formed: 1878.

Turned Professional: 1936.

Previous Name: 1878, Ipswich Association FC; 1888, Ipswich Town.

Club Nicknames: 'The Blues', 'Town', 'The Tractor Boys'.

Grounds: 1878, Broom Hill and Brook's Hall; 1884, Portman Road.

First Football League Game: 27 August 1938, Division 3 (S), v Southend U (h) W 4–2 – Burns; Dale, Parry; Perrett, Fillingham, McLuckie; Williams, Davies (1), Jones (2), Alsop (1), Little.

Record League Victory: 7–0 v Portsmouth, Division 2, 7 November 1964 – Thorburn; Smith, McNeil; Baxter, Bolton, Thompson; Broadfoot (1), Hegan (2), Baker (1), Leadbetter, Brogan (3). 7–0 v Southampton, Division 1, 2 February 1974 – Sivell; Burley, Mills (1), Morris, Hunter, Beattie (1), Hamilton (2), Viljoen, Johnson, Whymark (2), Lambert (1) (Woods). 7–0 v WBA, Division 1, 6 November 1976 – Sivell; Burley, Mills, Talbot, Hunter, Beattie (1), Osborne, Wark (1), Mariner (1) (Bertschin), Whymark (4), Woods.

HONOURS

League Champions: Division 1 – 1961–62; Division 2 – 1960–61, 1967–68, 1991–92; Division 3S – 1953–54, 1956–57.
Runners-up: Division 1 – 1980–81, 1981–82.

FA Cup Winners: 1978.

League Cup: semi-final – 1982, 1985, 2001, 2011.

Texaco Cup Winners: 1973.

European Competitions
European Cup: 1962–63.
UEFA Cup: 1973–74, 1974–75, 1975–76, 1977–78, 1979–80, 1980–81 *(winners)*, 1981–82, 1982–83, 2001–02, 2002–03.
European Cup-Winners' Cup: 1978–79 *(qf)*.

FOOTBALL YEARBOOK FACT FILE

Ipswich Town have an excellent home record in European competitions having not lost at Portman Road in any of their 31 matches. The run began in September 1962 with a 10-0 victory over the Maltese club Floriana in the European Cup and continued through to their most recent home game in October 2002 when they defeated the Czech side Slovan Liberec in the UEFA Cup.

Record Cup Victory: 10–0 v Floriana, European Cup prel. rd, 25 September 1962 – Bailey; Malcolm, Compton; Baxter, Laurel, Elsworthy (1); Stephenson, Moran (2), Crawford (5), Phillips (2), Blackwood.

Record Defeat: 1–10 v Fulham, Division 1, 26 December 1963.

Most League Points (2 for a win): 64, Division 3 (S), 1953–54 and 1955–56.

Most League Points (3 for a win): 87, Division 1, 1999–2000.

Most League Goals: 106, Division 3 (S), 1955–56.

Highest League Scorer in Season: Ted Phillips, 41, Division 3 (S), 1956–57.

Most League Goals in Total Aggregate: Ray Crawford, 204, 1958–63 and 1966–69.

Most League Goals in One Match: 5, Alan Brazil v Southampton, Division 1, 16 February 1981.

Most Capped Player: Allan Hunter, 47 (53), Northern Ireland.

Most League Appearances: Mick Mills, 591, 1966–82.

Youngest League Player: Connor Wickham, 16 years 11 days, v Doncaster R, 11 April 2009.

Record Transfer Fee Received: £8,000,000 (rising to £12,000,000) from Sunderland for Connor Wickham, June 2011.

Record Transfer Fee Paid: £4,800,000 to Sampdoria for Matteo Sereni, August 2001.

Football League Record: 1938 Elected to Division 3 (S); 1954–55 Division 2; 1955–57 Division 3 (S); 1957–61 Division 2; 1961–64 Division 1; 1964–68 Division 2; 1968–86 Division 1; 1986–92 Division 2; 1992–95 Premier League; 1995–2000 Division 1; 2000–02 Premier League; 2002–04 Division 1; 2004–19 FL C; 2019– FL 1.

MANAGERS

Mick O'Brien 1936–37
Scott Duncan 1937–55
(continued as Secretary)
Alf Ramsey 1955–63
Jackie Milburn 1963–64
Bill McGarry 1964–68
Bobby Robson 1969–82
Bobby Ferguson 1982–87
Johnny Duncan 1987–90
John Lyall 1990–94
George Burley 1994–2002
Joe Royle 2002–06
Jim Magilton 2006–09
Roy Keane 2009–11
Paul Jewell 2011–12
Mick McCarthy 2012–18
Paul Hurst 2018
Paul Lambert 2018–21
Paul Cook March 2021–

LATEST SEQUENCES

Longest Sequence of League Wins: 8, 23.9.1953 – 31.10.1953.

Longest Sequence of League Defeats: 10, 4.9.1954 – 16.10.1954.

Longest Sequence of League Draws: 7, 10.11.1990 – 21.12.1990.

Longest Sequence of Unbeaten League Matches: 23, 8.12.1979 – 26.4.1980.

Longest Sequence Without a League Win: 21, 28.8.1963 – 14.12.1963.

Successive Scoring Runs: 31 from 7.3.2004.

Successive Non-scoring Runs: 7 from 28.2.1995.

TEN YEAR LEAGUE RECORD

		P	*W*	*D*	*L*	*F*	*A*	*Pts*	*Pos*
2011-12	FL C	46	17	10	19	69	77	61	15
2012-13	FL C	46	16	12	18	48	61	60	14
2013-14	FL C	46	18	14	14	60	54	68	9
2014-15	FL C	46	22	12	12	72	54	78	6
2015-16	FL C	46	18	15	13	53	51	69	7
2016-17	FL C	46	13	16	17	48	58	55	16
2017-18	FL C	46	17	9	20	57	60	60	12
2018-19	FL C	46	5	16	25	36	77	31	24
2019-20	FL 1	36	14	10	12	46	36	52	11§
2020-21	FL 1	46	19	12	15	46	46	69	9

§Decided on points-per-game (1.44)

DID YOU KNOW ?

Ipswich Town were twice champions of the Southern Amateur League in their last three seasons in the competition before leaving to join the Eastern Counties League for 1935–36. After finishing sixth they switched to the Southern League and were champions in 1936–37 before being elected to the Football League in 1938.

IPSWICH TOWN – SKY BET LEAGUE ONE 2020–21 LEAGUE RECORD

Match No.	Date	Venue	Opponents	Result		H/T Score	Lg Pos.	Goalscorers	Attendance
1	Sept 13	H	Wigan Ath	W	2-0	1-0	2	Bishop [11], Edwards [80]	0
2	19	A	Bristol R	W	2-0	0-0	1	Ehmer (og) [80], Nolan [89]	0
3	26	H	Rochdale	W	2-0	0-0	1	Bishop [53], Edwards [59]	0
4	Oct 3	A	Milton Keynes D	D	1-1	1-0	3	Nolan [7]	0
5	10	A	Blackpool	W	4-1	3-0	1	Chambers [16], Edwards 2 [36, 80], Bishop [45]	0
6	17	H	Accrington S	W	2-0	0-0	1	Edwards [54], Sears [71]	0
7	20	A	Doncaster R	L	1-4	1-2	2	Wright (og) [15]	0
8	24	A	Lincoln C	L	0-1	0-0	4		0
9	27	H	Gillingham	W	1-0	0-0	3	Bishop [86]	0
10	31	H	Crewe Alex	W	1-0	0-0	2	Hawkins [62]	0
11	Nov 3	A	Sunderland	L	1-2	1-1	2	Lankester [38]	0
12	21	H	Shrewsbury T	W	2-1	0-1	3	Ebanks-Landell (og) [75], Lankester [90]	0
13	24	H	Hull C	L	0-3	0-2	5		0
14	28	H	Charlton Ath	L	0-2	0-1	6		0
15	Dec 1	A	Oxford U	D	0-0	0-0	5		0
16	5	A	Plymouth Arg	W	2-1	0-1	3	Nolan [73], Jackson [74]	1808
17	12	H	Portsmouth	L	0-2	0-2	6		2000
18	15	H	Burton Alb	W	2-1	1-1	5	Bennetts [4], Huws [80]	0
19	Jan 9	H	Swindon T	L	2-3	0-1	8	Norwood [62], Judge [87]	0
20	16	A	Burton Alb	W	1-0	0-0	7	McGuinness [72]	0
21	23	H	Peterborough U	L	0-1	0-0	9		0
22	26	H	Sunderland	L	0-1	0-1	10		0
23	30	A	Crewe Alex	D	1-1	0-0	11	Drinan [75]	0
24	Feb 6	H	Blackpool	W	2-0	1-0	10	Judge [43], Woolfenden [49]	0
25	9	A	Peterborough U	L	1-2	1-1	11	Norwood [6]	0
26	16	H	Northampton T	D	0-0	0-0	11		0
27	20	H	Oxford U	D	0-0	0-0	12		0
28	23	A	Hull C	W	1-0	1-0	10	Norwood [15]	0
29	27	H	Doncaster R	W	2-1	1-0	8	Judge [24], Norwood [54]	0
30	Mar 2	A	Accrington S	W	2-1	2-1	7	Wilson [40], Norwood [45]	0
31	6	A	Gillingham	L	1-3	0-1	8	Chambers [65]	0
32	9	H	Lincoln C	D	1-1	0-1	7	Wilson [72]	0
33	13	H	Plymouth Arg	W	1-0	1-0	6	Parrott [4]	0
34	16	A	Fleetwood T	L	0-2	0-1	7		0
35	20	A	Portsmouth	L	1-2	1-1	9	Norwood [32]	0
36	27	A	Wigan Ath	D	0-0	0-0	11		0
37	Apr 2	H	Bristol R	W	2-1	2-1	9	Leahy (og) [1], Judge [11]	0
38	5	A	Rochdale	D	0-0	0-0	8		0
39	10	H	Milton Keynes D	D	0-0	0-0	8		0
40	13	A	AFC Wimbledon	L	0-3	0-2	9		0
41	17	A	Charlton Ath	D	0-0	0-0	9		0
42	20	A	Northampton T	L	0-3	0-2	11		0
43	24	H	AFC Wimbledon	D	0-0	0-0	11		0
44	May 1	A	Swindon T	W	2-1	1-0	10	Norwood 2 (1 pen) [44 (p), 57]	0
45	4	A	Shrewsbury T	D	0-0	0-0	9		0
46	9	H	Fleetwood T	W	3-1	3-0	9	Norwood [3], Edwards [9], Parrott [29]	0

Final League Position: 9

GOALSCORERS

League (46): Norwood 9 (1 pen), Edwards 6, Bishop 4, Judge 4, Nolan 3, Chambers 2, Lankester 2, Parrott 2, Wilson 2, Bennetts 1, Drinan 1, Hawkins 1, Huws 1, Jackson 1, McGuinness 1, Sears 1, Woolfenden 1, own goals 4.
FA Cup (2): Nolan 1, Norwood 1.
Carabao Cup (3): Sears 2, Chambers 1.
Papa John's Trophy (3): Dobra 1, Folami 1, Nolan 1.

Holy T 36	Chambers L 39	Nsiala A 27	Wilson J 17	Ward S 29 + 1	Bishop T 28 + 8	Dozzell A 42 + 1	Nolan J 11 + 2	Judge A 29 + 5	Drinan A 6 + 16	Sears F 15 + 11	Norwood J 19 + 7	Edwards G 29 + 7	Huws E 6 + 3	Lankester J 7 + 10	Hawkins O 8 + 12	Downes F 17 + 7	Kenlock M 17 + 4	Jackson K 12 + 13	Bennetts K 13 + 15	Simpson T — + 1	Woolfenden L 24 + 1	McGuinness M 23 + 1	Dobra A 8 + 9	McGavin B 4 + 1	Cornell D 10	Gibbs L 1	Thomas L 4 + 1	Matheson L 2	Parrott T 13 + 5	Harrop J 3 + 12	Skuse C 1 + 3	Vincent-Young K 6 + 1	Nydam T — + 1	*Match No.*
1	2	3	4	5	6^{3}	7	8	9	10^{1}	11^{2}	12	13	14																					1
1	2	3	4	5	8^{2}	7	6			11^{1}	10^{3}	9		12	13	14																		2
1	2	3	4	5	6^{1}	7	8			11^{2}	13	9		14	10^{3}	12																		3
1	2	3	4	5^{1}	6^{3}	7	8	13		11^{2}		9			10	14	12																	4
1	2	3	4		6^{2}	7		11				9	8		10^{1}		5	12	13															5
1	2	3	4		6	7	12	10^{2}		11^{3}		9	8^{1}				5		13	14														6
1	2	3	4		12	7	8	9		10^{2}		11^{3}	6^{1}		13		5		14															7
1	2	3	4	5	6	7	8▮					11		9^{1}	10				12															8
1	2			5	6^{3}	8				11^{1}		9	13	7^{2}	10				14		3	4	12											9
1	2			5	6^{2}	7		8		11^{3}		9		13	10^{1}			12	14		3	4												10
1	2	3		5	6	7▮		9				8		11^{2}	12			10^{1}	13			4												11
1	2	3		5	6^{2}		8^{1}	9		11^{3}	15		13	12				10^{4}	14			4		7										12
1	2			5				6		11^{1}	10^{3}		8	12	13			14	9^{2}		3	4		7										13
	2	3^{4}		5		8		9	12		10^{1}			14				13	11		4	15		7^{3}	1	6^{2}								14
	2			5		7	8	14	10^{2}					6^{1}	13			12	11		3	4	9^{3}		1									15
	2			5			6	11						9^{2}	13			10	12		3	4	8	7^{1}	1									16
	2			5		6	7^{1}	9^{2}	14					10^{4}	15			11^{3}	13		3	4	8	12	1									17
	2			5		7		9	13				6		11			8^{2}	10^{1}		3	4	12		1									18
	2			5		7		9	11^{1}		12		6^{2}	14		13		8			3	4	10^{3}		1									19
1	2	3		5	9^{2}	6		8	12	14	11^{1}	10^{3}			13	7						4												20
1	2	3		5	9^{3}	7	12	8^{2}	11^{1}	13		10				6						4					14							21
1	2			5^{3}	13	7	8^{1}		12	14		10^{4}				6	15	11▮			3	4					9^{2}							22
1	2				13▮	8		6	14	10^{1}	12	11^{3}				7	5				3	4					9^{2}							23
1						8^{2}		7		11	14	12				6	5				3	4					9^{1}	2	10^{3}	13				24
1	2			5	9^{3}	8		7^{2}		14	10^{1}	12				6					3	4							11	13				25
1					14	8^{4}		13		11^{3}	15			12		6▮	5				3	4					9^{1}	2	10	7^{2}				26
1	2	3	4		6^{1}	7		10	13	14	11^{2}						5		8^{3}										9	12				27
1	2	3	4		6	7		10^{1}	13		11^{2}	12					5		8										9^{3}	14				28
1	2	3	4		6	7^{1}		10^{2}	16	15	11^{5}	13				12	5		8^{3}										9^{4}	14				29
1	2	3	4		6^{1}	7^{3}		10	16	15	11^{4}	13				12	5		8^{2}										9^{5}	14				30
1	2	3	4		6	7^{4}				12	11	14				13	5	15	8^{1}										9^{2}	10^{3}				31
1	2	3	4		9^{2}	7		13			11^{4}	8^{1}		10^{3}		6	5	15	12										14					32
1	2	3	4		12	7		10^{4}	13			8^{5}		15		6^{1}	5	11^{3}	16										9^{2}		14			33
1	2	3	4	13	16	7		10	14			8^{1}		15			5^{2}	11^{4}											9^{3}	12	6^{5}			34
1	2	3	4^{2}	5	6^{4}	7		9^{3}			11	8						14	10^{1}				12						15			13		35
1	4	3		5	7	6		9^{2}		10^{3}	11	8^{4}						14			12		15							13		2^{1}		36
1	4	3		8	6^{3}	7		9^{4}	12		10^{1}	5						11^{2}			2		15						13	14				37
1	4	3		8	7^{5}	6		9^{1}	15			5^{3}			13		16	10^{4}			2		14						11^{2}	12				38
1	4	3		9	6^{3}	8^{2}		14	10^{5}	12		5^{4}			16	7					2		11^{1}						15				13	39
1	4	3		9^{4}	15	13		8^{2}	11^{3}	12	10^{5}	5^{1}				7		16	14		2									6▮				40
1				5^{4}	9^{3}	6				14	11^{1}	10				7	15	12	8^{2}		3	4	13									2		41
1				5		7			13	11^{2}		9			14	8		10^{3}	6^{1}		3	4	12									2		42
				5	9^{2}	7^{4}			14			10			11^{3}	6		15	8^{1}		3	4	12		1						13	2		43
					9^{1}	7					11	10^{3}				6	5		13		3	4	8^{2}		1				12	14		2		44
						7					11	10			12	6	5				3	4	8		1				9			2^{1}		45
	2				13	7					11^{2}	10^{1}				6	5	16	12^{3}		3	4	8^{4}		1				9^{5}	15	14			46

FA Cup

First Round *(aet)*	Portsmouth	(h)	2-3

Carabao Cup

First Round	Bristol R	(h)	3-0
Second Round	Fulham	(h)	0-1

Papa John's Trophy

Group B (S)	Arsenal U21	(h)	1-2
Group B (S)	Gillingham	(h)	2-0
Group B (S)	Crawley T	(a)	0-2

LEEDS UNITED

FOUNDATION

Immediately the Leeds City club (founded in 1904) was wound up by the FA in October 1919, following allegations of illegal payments to players, a meeting was called by a Leeds solicitor, Mr Alf Masser, at which Leeds United was formed. They joined the Midland League, playing their first game in that competition in November 1919. It was in this same month that the new club had discussions with the directors of a virtually bankrupt Huddersfield Town who wanted to move to Leeds in an amalgamation. But Huddersfield survived even that crisis.

Elland Road Stadium, Elland Road, Leeds, West Yorkshire LS11 0ES.

Telephone: (0871) 334 1919.

Ticket Office: (0371) 334 1992.

Website: www.leedsunited.com

Email: reception@leedsunited.com

Ground Capacity: 37,792.

Record Attendance: 57,892 v Sunderland, FA Cup 5th rd (replay), 15 March 1967.

Pitch Measurements: 105m × 68m (115yd × 74.5yd).

Chairman: Andrea Radrizzani.

Chief Executive: Angus Kinnear.

Head Coach: Marcelo Bielsa.

Assistant Head Coaches: Pablo Quiroga, Diego Flores, Diego Reyes.

Colours: White shirts with blue trim, white shorts with blue trim, white socks with blue trim.

Year Formed: 1919, as Leeds United after disbandment (by FA order) of Leeds City (formed in 1904).

Turned Professional: 1920.

Club Nickname: 'The Whites'.

Ground: 1919, Elland Road.

First Football League Game: 28 August 1920, Division 2, v Port Vale (a) L 0–2 – Down; Duffield, Tillotson; Musgrove, Baker, Walton; Mason, Goldthorpe, Thompson, Lyon, Best.

Record League Victory: 8–0 v Leicester C, Division 1, 7 April 1934 – Moore; George Milburn, Jack Milburn; Edwards, Hart, Copping; Mahon (2), Firth (2), Duggan (2), Furness (2), Cochrane.

HONOURS

League Champions: Division 1 – 1968–69, 1973–74, 1991–92; FL C – 2019–20. Division 2 – 1923–24, 1963–64, 1989–90.
Runners-up: Division 1 – 1964–65, 1965–66, 1969–70, 1970–71, 1971–72; Division 2 – 1927–28, 1931–32, 1955–56; FL 1 – 2009–10.

FA Cup Winners: 1972.
Runners-up: 1965, 1970, 1973.

League Cup Winners: 1968.
Runners-up: 1996.

European Competitions
European Cup: 1969–70 *(sf)*, 1974–75 *(runners-up)*.
Champions League: 1992–93, 2000–01 *(sf)*.
Fairs Cup: 1965–66 *(sf)*, 1966–67 *(runners-up)*, 1967–68 *(winners)*, 1968–69 *(qf)*, 1970–71 *(winners)*.
UEFA Cup: 1971–72, 1973–74, 1979–80, 1995–96, 1998–99, 1999–2000 *(sf)*, 2001–02, 2002–03.
European Cup-Winners' Cup: 1972–73 *(runners-up)*.

FOOTBALL YEARBOOK FACT FILE

Faced with an injury crisis and a backlog of fixtures in the closing stages of the 1969–70, Leeds United fielded an inexperienced team for their visit to Derby County on Easter Monday. Three of the side were making their Football League debuts and the defence had previously made a combined total of just 18 League starts. The Elland Road club were subsequently fined a record £5,000 for fielding a weakened line-up.

Record Cup Victory: 10–0 v Lyn (Oslo), European Cup 1st rd 1st leg, 17 September 1969 – Sprake; Reaney, Cooper, Bremner (2), Charlton, Hunter, Madeley, Clarke (2), Jones (3), Giles (2) (Bates), O'Grady (1).

Record Defeat: 1–8 v Stoke C, Division 1, 27 August 1934.

Most League Points (2 for a win): 67, Division 1, 1968–69.

Most League Points (3 for a win): 93, FL C, 2019–20.

Most League Goals: 98, Division 2, 1927–28.

Highest League Scorer in Season: John Charles, 42, Division 2, 1953–54.

Most League Goals in Total Aggregate: Peter Lorimer, 168, 1965–79 and 1983–86.

Most League Goals in One Match: 5, Gordon Hodgson v Leicester C, Division 1, 1 October 1938.

Most Capped Player: Lucas Radebe, 58 (70), South Africa.

Most League Appearances: Jack Charlton, 629, 1953–73.

Youngest League Player: Peter Lorimer, 15 years 289 days v Southampton, 29 September 1962.

Record Transfer Fee Received: £30,800,000 from Manchester U for Rio Ferdinand, July 2002.

Record Transfer Fee Paid: £30,000,000 to Valencia for Rodrigo, August 2020.

Football League Record: 1920 Elected to Division 2; 1924–27 Division 1; 1927–28 Division 2; 1928–31 Division 1; 1931–32 Division 2; 1932–47 Division 1; 1947–56 Division 2; 1956–60 Division 1; 1960–64 Division 2; 1964–82 Division 1; 1982–90 Division 2; 1990–92 Division 1; 1992–2004 Premier League; 2004–07 FL C; 2007–10 FL 1; 2010–20 FL C; 2020– Premier League.

MANAGERS

Dick Ray 1919–20
Arthur Fairclough 1920–27
Dick Ray 1927–35
Bill Hampson 1935–47
Willis Edwards 1947–48
Major Frank Buckley 1948–53
Raich Carter 1953–58
Bill Lambton 1958–59
Jack Taylor 1959–61
Don Revie OBE 1961–74
Brian Clough 1974
Jimmy Armfield 1974–78
Jock Stein CBE 1978
Jimmy Adamson 1978–80
Allan Clarke 1980–82
Eddie Gray MBE 1982–85
Billy Bremner 1985–88
Howard Wilkinson 1988–96
George Graham 1996–98
David O'Leary 1998–2002
Terry Venables 2002–03
Peter Reid 2003
Eddie Gray *(Caretaker)* 2003–04
Kevin Blackwell 2004–06
Dennis Wise 2006–08
Gary McAllister 2008
Simon Grayson 2008–12
Neil Warnock 2012–13
Brian McDermott 2013–14
Dave Hockaday 2014
Darko Milanic 2014
Neil Redfearn 2014–15
Uwe Rosler 2015
Steve Evans 2015–16
Garry Monk 2016–17
Thomas Christiansen 2017–18
Paul Heckingbottom 2018
Marcelo Bielsa June 2018–

LATEST SEQUENCES

Longest Sequence of League Wins: 9, 18.4.2009 – 5.9.2009.

Longest Sequence of League Defeats: 6, 28.12.2003 – 7.2.2004.

Longest Sequence of League Draws: 5, 2.5.2015 – 22.8.2015.

Longest Sequence of Unbeaten League Matches: 34, 26.10.1968 – 26.8.1969.

Longest Sequence Without a League Win: 17, 1.2.1947 – 26.5.1947.

Successive Scoring Runs: 30 from 27.8.1927.

Successive Non-scoring Runs: 6 from 30.1.1982.

TEN YEAR LEAGUE RECORD

		P	W	D	L	F	A	Pts	Pos
2011-12	FL C	46	17	10	19	65	68	61	14
2012-13	FL C	46	17	10	19	57	66	61	13
2013-14	FL C	46	16	9	21	59	67	57	15
2014-15	FL C	46	15	11	20	50	61	56	15
2015-16	FL C	46	14	17	15	50	58	59	13
2016-17	FL C	46	22	9	15	61	47	75	7
2017-18	FL C	46	17	9	20	59	64	60	13
2018-19	FL C	46	25	8	13	73	50	83	3
2019-20	FL C	46	28	9	9	77	35	93	1
2020-21	PR Lge	38	18	5	15	62	54	59	9

DID YOU KNOW ?

Although the main stand at Elland Road was destroyed by fire in the early hours of 18 September 1956, Leeds United continued to play home matches there, albeit with a reduced capacity. The players changed at a nearby sports centre and travelled to the ground by coach until temporary accommodation was provided. The fire was so fierce that it damaged a section of the pitch.

LEEDS UNITED – PREMIER LEAGUE 2020–21 LEAGUE RECORD

Match No.	Date	Venue	Opponents	Result		H/T Score	Lg Pos.	Goalscorers	Attendance
1	Sept 12	A	Liverpool	L	3-4	2-3	17	Harrison [12], Bamford [30], Klich [66]	0
2	19	H	Fulham	W	4-3	2-1	9	Helder Costa 2 [5, 57], Klich (pen) [41], Bamford [50]	0
3	27	A	Sheffield U	W	1-0	0-0	6	Bamford [88]	0
4	Oct 3	H	Manchester C	D	1-1	0-1	5	Rodrigo [59]	0
5	19	H	Wolverhampton W	L	0-1	0-0	10		0
6	23	A	Aston Villa	W	3-0	0-0	3	Bamford 3 [55, 67, 74]	0
7	Nov 2	H	Leicester C	L	1-4	0-2	12	Dallas [48]	0
8	7	A	Crystal Palace	L	1-4	1-3	15	Bamford [27]	0
9	22	H	Arsenal	D	0-0	0-0	14		0
10	28	A	Everton	W	1-0	0-0	11	Raphinha [79]	0
11	Dec 5	A	Chelsea	L	1-3	1-1	13	Bamford [4]	2000
12	11	H	West Ham U	L	1-2	1-1	14	Klich (pen) [6]	0
13	16	H	Newcastle U	W	5-2	1-1	13	Bamford [35], Rodrigo [61], Dallas [77], Alioski [85], Harrison [88]	0
14	20	A	Manchester U	L	2-6	1-4	14	Cooper [42], Dallas [73]	0
15	27	H	Burnley	W	1-0	1-0	12	Bamford (pen) [5]	0
16	29	A	WBA	W	5-0	4-0	11	Sawyers (og) [9], Alioski [31], Harrison [36], Rodrigo [40], Raphinha [72]	0
17	Jan 2	A	Tottenham H	L	0-3	0-2	12		0
18	16	H	Brighton & HA	L	0-1	0-1	12		0
19	26	A	Newcastle U	W	2-1	1-0	12	Raphinha [17], Harrison [61]	0
20	31	A	Leicester C	W	3-1	1-1	12	Dallas [15], Bamford [70], Harrison [84]	0
21	Feb 3	H	Everton	L	1-2	0-2	11	Raphinha [48]	0
22	8	H	Crystal Palace	W	2-0	1-0	10	Harrison [3], Bamford [52]	0
23	14	A	Arsenal	L	2-4	0-3	11	Struijk [58], Helder Costa [69]	0
24	19	A	Wolverhampton W	L	0-1	0-0	12		0
25	23	H	Southampton	W	3-0	0-0	10	Bamford [47], Dallas [78], Raphinha [84]	0
26	27	H	Aston Villa	L	0-1	0-1	10		0
27	Mar 8	A	West Ham U	L	0-2	0-2	11		0
28	13	H	Chelsea	D	0-0	0-0	12		0
29	19	A	Fulham	W	2-1	1-1	11	Bamford [29], Raphinha [58]	0
30	Apr 3	H	Sheffield U	W	2-1	1-1	10	Harrison [12], Jagielka (og) [49]	0
31	10	A	Manchester C	W	2-1	1-0	9	Dallas 2 [42, 90]	0
32	19	H	Liverpool	D	1-1	0-1	10	Llorente [87]	0
33	25	H	Manchester U	D	0-0	0-0	9		0
34	May 1	A	Brighton & HA	L	0-2	0-1	10		0
35	8	H	Tottenham H	W	3-1	2-1	9	Dallas [13], Bamford [42], Rodrigo [84]	0
36	15	A	Burnley	W	4-0	1-0	10	Klich [44], Harrison [59], Rodrigo 2 [77, 79]	0
37	18	A	Southampton	W	2-0	0-0	8	Bamford [73], Roberts [90]	7291
38	23	H	WBA	W	3-1	2-0	9	Rodrigo [17], Phillips [42], Bamford (pen) [79]	8000

Final League Position: 9

GOALSCORERS

League (62): Bamford 17 (2 pens), Dallas 8, Harrison 8, Rodrigo 7, Raphinha 6, Klich 4 (2 pens), Helder Costa 3, Alioski 2, Cooper 1, Llorente 1, Phillips 1, Roberts 1, Struijk 1, own goals 2.
FA Cup (0).
Carabao Cup (1): Alioski 1.
Papa John's Trophy (2): Dean 2.

Meslier I 35	Ayling L 38	Koch R 13 + 4	Struijk P 22 + 5	Dallas S 38	Phillips K 28 + 1	Helder Costa W 13 + 9	Hernandez P 3 + 13	Klich M 28 + 7	Harrison J 34 + 2	Bamford P 37 + 1	Roberts T 14 + 13	Rodrigo M 14 + 12	Shackleton J 3 + 10	Cooper L 25	Alioski E 29 + 7	Poveda-Ocampo I — + 14	Davis L — + 2	Raphinha R 26 + 4	Llorente D 14 + 1	Casilla F 3	Huggins N — + 1	Berardi G 1 + 1	Match No.
1	2	3	4	5	6	7	8^{1}	9^{3}	10	11^{2}	12	13	14										1
1	2	3		5	6	7		9	10	11^{2}	12	8^{1}		4	13								2
1	2	3		8	5	6^{2}		7	9	10	11^{1}	12^{3}		4	14	13							3
1	2	3		5	6	7		9^{3}		11	8^{2}	13		4	10^{1}	12	14						4
1	2	3	4^{2}	5	6	7^{1}	13	8	10^{3}	11		9				12		14					5
1	4	3	7^{1}	2		6^{3}	13	8	9	11		10^{2}	12		5			14					6
1	2	3		5^{3}		7	8^{2}	6	10	11	13		9^{1}	4	14	12							7
1	2	3	6^{2}	5		8^{1}		9	10	11	13			4	7			12					8
1	2^{1}	3		9	6			8	10^{2}	11		12		4	5	13		7					9
1	2	3		5	6	13		8	9^{2}	11^{3}		14		4	10	12		7^{1}					10
1	2	3^{1}		7	8			10	9^{2}	11		14		4	5^{3}	13		6	12				11
1	3			2	6	12		9	10^{1}	11^{3}	14	8	13	4	5^{2}			7					12
1	3			2	6		12	9^{3}	10	11^{2}	13	8^{1}	14	4	5			7					13
1	3		12	2	6^{1}			9^{2}	10	11		8	13	4^{3}	5		14	7					14
1	3		4	2	6		12	8^{2}	10	11		9^{1}	13		5	14		7^{3}					15
1	3		4	2	6	14	13	9^{1}	10	11		8^{2}	12		5			7^{3}					16
1	3		4	2	6		14	9	10^{1}	11		8^{3}	13		5^{2}	12		7					17
	3		6	2			13	9	7	11	12	8^{1}		4	5^{2}	14		10^{3}		1			18
1	2		12	8	6			13	10	11^{3}	14	9		4	5^{2}			7	3^{1}				19
1	2		3	9	6	13		12	10	11		8^{1}		4	5			7^{2}					20
1	2		3	9	6	14	13	8^{1}	10^{3}	11	12			4	5^{2}			7					21
1	2		3	8	6^{1}			9	10	11			12	4	5			7					22
1	3		6	8		12		9^{2}	10^{1}	11	13		2	4	5^{3}			7			14		23
1	2		3	5		13	12	8^{2}	9^{3}	11	10		7^{1}	4	14			6					24
1	5		4	7		12	14	6^{2}	8^{1}	11	9^{3}			3	13			10	2				25
1	2		6^{1}	5		7^{2}	14	9	13	11	8^{3}			4	12			10	3				26
1	2			5	6	7^{1}		9^{2}	12	11	8^{3}	14		4	13			10	3				27
1	2		4	8	6	13		14	10^{2}	11^{1}	9	12^{3}			5			7	3				28
1	2	13	4	8	6			12	10	11^{1}	9^{2}				5			7	3				29
1	2	14		8^{3}	6			13	10	11^{1}	9^{2}	12		4	5			7	3				30
1	2	13	12	8	6	10				11^{1}	9^{2}		14	4■	5			7^{3}	3				31
1	2		4	8	6	7^{1}	14	13	10	11	9^{3}				5^{2}	12			3				32
1	2	14	4	8	6	7^{2}		13	10^{1}	11	9^{3}				5	12			3				33
1	2	6	4	7			14	8	10	11^{2}	9	13			5^{1}	12			3^{3}				34
1	2	6	4	7	14			9^{3}	10	11^{2}	8^{1}	13			5			12	3				35
1	2		4	8	6			9^{2}	10	11^{1}	13	12			5	14		7^{3}	3				36
	2		12	5	6^{1}				10	11	14	9^{3}		4	7			8	3^{2}	1		13	37
	3		13	5	6		9^{3}		10	12	14	11^{1}		4	7			8		1		2^{2}	38

FA Cup
Third Round Crawley T (a) 0-3

Carabao Cup
Second Round Hull C (h) 1-1
(Hull C won 9-8 on penalties)

Papa John's Trophy (Leeds U U21)
Group G (N) Accrington S (a) 0-7
Group G (N) Barrow (a) 2-2
(Barrow won 4-3 on penalties)
Group G (N) Blackpool (a) 0-3

LEICESTER CITY

FOUNDATION

In 1884 a number of young footballers, who were mostly old boys of Wyggeston School, held a meeting at a house on the Roman Fosse Way and formed Leicester Fosse FC. They collected 9d (less than 4p) towards the cost of a ball, plus the same amount for membership. Their first professional, Harry Webb from Stafford Rangers, was signed in 1888 for 2s 6d (12p) per week, plus travelling expenses.

King Power Stadium, Filbert Way, Leicester LE2 7FL.

Telephone: (0344) 815 5000.

Ticket Office: (0344) 815 5000 (option 1).

Website: www.lcfc.com

Email: lcfchelp@lcfc.co.uk

Ground Capacity: 32,261.

Record Attendance: 47,298 v Tottenham H, FA Cup 5th rd, 18 February 1928 (at Filbert Street); 32,242 v Sunderland, Premier League, 8 August 2015 (at King Power Stadium).

Pitch Measurements: 105m × 68m (115yd × 74.5yd).

Chairman: Aiyawatt 'Top' Srivaddhanaprabha.

Chief Executive: Susan Whelan.

Manager: Brendan Rodgers.

Assistant Manager: Chris Davies.

Colours: Blue shirts with white trim, blue shorts with white trim, blue socks with white trim.

Year Formed: 1884.

Turned Professional: 1888.

Previous Name: 1884, Leicester Fosse; 1919, Leicester City.

Club Nickname: 'The Foxes'.

Grounds: 1884, Victoria Park; 1887, Belgrave Road; 1888, Victoria Park; 1891, Filbert Street; 2002, Walkers Stadium (now known as King Power Stadium from 2011).

First Football League Game: 1 September 1894, Division 2, v Grimsby T (a) L 3–4 – Thraves; Smith, Bailey; Seymour, Brown, Henrys; Hill, Hughes, McArthur (1), Skea (2), Priestman.

Record League Victory: 10–0 v Portsmouth, Division 1, 20 October 1928 – McLaren; Black, Brown; Findlay, Carr, Watson; Adcock, Hine (3), Chandler (6), Lochhead, Barry (1).

Record Cup Victory: 8–1 v Coventry C (a), League Cup 5th rd, 1 December 1964 – Banks; Sjoberg, Norman (2); Roberts, King, McDerment; Hodgson (2), Cross, Goodfellow, Gibson (1), Stringfellow (2), (1 og).

Record Defeat: 0–12 (as Leicester Fosse) v Nottingham F, Division 1, 21 April 1909.

HONOURS

League Champions: Premier League – 2015–16; FL C – 2013–14; Division 2 – 1924–25, 1936–37, 1953–54, 1956–57, 1970–71, 1979–80; FL 1 – 2008–09.
Runners-up: Division 1 – 1928–29; First Division – 2002–03; Division 2 – 1907–08.

FA Cup Winners: 2021.
Runners-up: 1949, 1961, 1963, 1969.

League Cup Winners: 1964, 1997, 2000.
Runners-up: 1965, 1999.

European Competitions
UEFA Champions League: 2016–17 (*qf*).
UEFA Cup: 1997–98, 2000–01.
Europa League: 2020–21.
European Cup-Winners' Cup: 1961–62.

FOOTBALL YEARBOOK FACT FILE

David Skea had the distinction of scoring the first-ever Football League goal for Leicester Fosse in the opening match of the 1894–95 season at Grimsby Town. The following Saturday he achieved another first, registering the club's first hat-trick in the competition, while he finished the season as the club's first-ever leading scorer.

Most League Points (2 for a win): 61, Division 2, 1956–57.

Most League Points (3 for a win): 102, FL C, 2013–14.

Most League Goals: 109, Division 2, 1956–57.

Highest League Scorer in Season: Arthur Rowley, 44, Division 2, 1956–57.

Most League Goals in Total Aggregate: Arthur Chandler, 259, 1923–35.

Most League Goals in One Match: 6, John Duncan v Port Vale, Division 2, 25 December 1924; 6, Arthur Chandler v Portsmouth, Division 1, 20 October 1928.

Most Capped Player: Kasper Schmeichel, 71, Denmark.

Most League Appearances: Adam Black, 528, 1920–35.

Youngest League Player: Dave Buchanan, 16 years 192 days v Oldham Ath, 1 January 1979.

Record Transfer Fee Received: £80,000,000 from Manchester U for Harry Maguire, August 2019.

Record Transfer Fee Paid: £40,000,000 to Monaco for Youri Tielemans, July 2019.

Football League Record: 1894 Elected to Division 2; 1908–09 Division 1; 1909–25 Division 2; 1925–35 Division 1; 1935–37 Division 2; 1937–39 Division 1; 1946–54 Division 2; 1954–55 Division 1; 1955–57 Division 2; 1957–69 Division 1; 1969–71 Division 2; 1971–78 Division 1; 1978–80 Division 2; 1980–81 Division 1; 1981–83 Division 2; 1983–87 Division 1; 1987–92 Division 2; 1992–94 Division 1; 1994–95 Premier League; 1995–96 Division 1; 1996–2002 Premier League; 2002–03 Division 1; 2003–04 Premier League; 2004–08 FL C; 2008–09 FL 1; 2009–14 FL C; 2014– Premier League.

LATEST SEQUENCES

Longest Sequence of League Wins: 9, 21.12.2013 – 1.2.2014.

Longest Sequence of League Defeats: 8, 17.3.2001 – 28.4.2001.

Longest Sequence of League Draws: 6, 2.10.2004 – 2.11.2004.

Longest Sequence of Unbeaten League Matches: 23, 1.11.2008 – 7.3.2009.

Longest Sequence Without a League Win: 18, 12.4.1975 – 1.11.1975.

Successive Scoring Runs: 32 from 23.11.2013.

Successive Non-scoring Runs: 7 from 21.11.1987.

MANAGERS

Frank Gardner 1884–92
Ernest Marson 1892–94
J. Lee 1894–95
Henry Jackson 1895–97
William Clark 1897–98
George Johnson 1898–1912
Jack Bartlett 1912–14
Louis Ford 1914–15
Harry Linney 1915–19
Peter Hodge 1919–26
Willie Orr 1926–32
Peter Hodge 1932–34
Arthur Lochhead 1934–36
Frank Womack 1936–39
Tom Bromilow 1939–45
Tom Mather 1945–46
John Duncan 1946–49
Norman Bullock 1949–55
David Halliday 1955–58
Matt Gillies 1958–68
Frank O'Farrell 1968–71
Jimmy Bloomfield 1971–77
Frank McLintock 1977–78
Jock Wallace 1978–82
Gordon Milne 1982–86
Bryan Hamilton 1986–87
David Pleat 1987–91
Gordon Lee 1991
Brian Little 1991–94
Mark McGhee 1994–95
Martin O'Neill 1995–2000
Peter Taylor 2000–01
Dave Bassett 2001–02
Micky Adams 2002–04
Craig Levein 2004–06
Robert Kelly 2006–07
Martin Allen 2007
Gary Megson 2007
Ian Holloway 2007–08
Nigel Pearson 2008–10
Paulo Sousa 2010
Sven-Göran Eriksson 2010–11
Nigel Pearson 2011–15
Claudio Ranieri 2015–17
Craig Shakespeare 2017
Claude Puel 2017–19
Brendan Rodgers February 2019–

TEN YEAR LEAGUE RECORD

		P	W	D	L	F	A	Pts	Pos
2011-12	FL C	46	18	12	16	66	55	66	9
2012-13	FL C	46	19	11	16	71	48	68	6
2013-14	FL C	46	31	9	6	83	43	102	1
2014-15	PR Lge	38	11	8	19	46	55	41	14
2015-16	PR Lge	38	23	12	3	68	36	81	1
2016-17	PR Lge	38	12	8	18	48	63	44	12
2017-18	PR Lge	38	12	11	15	56	60	47	9
2018-19	PR Lge	38	15	7	16	51	48	52	9
2019-20	PR Lge	38	18	8	12	67	41	62	5
2020-21	PR Lge	38	20	6	12	68	50	66	5

DID YOU KNOW ?

Inside-forward Tom Sweenie became the first substitute to score a Football League goal for Leicester City when he found the net after 47 minutes of the home game with Blackburn Rovers on 12 April 1966. Sweenie had earlier replaced broken-nose victim Mike Stringfellow midway through the first half of the match.

LEICESTER CITY – PREMIER LEAGUE 2020–21 LEAGUE RECORD

Match No.	*Date*	*Venue*	*Opponents*	*Result*	*H/T Score*	*Lg Pos.*	*Goalscorers*	*Attendance*
1	Sept 13	A	WBA	W 3-0	0-0	1	Castagne [56], Vardy 2 (2 pens) [74, 84]	0
2	20	H	Burnley	W 4-2	1-1	1	Barnes [20], Pieters (og) [50], Justin [61], Praet [79]	0
3	27	A	Manchester C	W 5-2	1-1	1	Vardy 3 (2 pens) [37 (p), 53, 58 (p)], Maddison [77], Tielemans (pen) [88]	0
4	Oct 4	H	West Ham U	L 0-3	0-2	3		0
5	18	H	Aston Villa	L 0-1	0-0	4		0
6	25	A	Arsenal	W 1-0	0-0	4	Vardy [80]	0
7	Nov 2	A	Leeds U	W 4-1	2-0	2	Barnes [3], Tielemans 2 (1 pen) [21, 90 (p)], Vardy [76]	0
8	8	H	Wolverhampton W	W 1-0	1-0	1	Vardy (pen) [15]	0
9	22	A	Liverpool	L 0-3	0-2	4		0
10	30	H	Fulham	L 1-2	0-2	4	Barnes [86]	0
11	Dec 6	A	Sheffield U	W 2-1	1-1	4	Perez [24], Vardy [90]	0
12	13	H	Brighton & HA	W 3-0	3-0	3	Maddison 2 [27, 44], Vardy [41]	0
13	16	H	Everton	L 0-2	0-1	4		0
14	20	A	Tottenham H	W 2-0	1-0	2	Vardy (pen) [45], Alderweireld (og) [59]	0
15	26	H	Manchester U	D 2-2	1-1	3	Barnes [31], Tuanzebe (og) [85]	0
16	28	A	Crystal Palace	D 1-1	0-0	2	Barnes [83]	0
17	Jan 3	A	Newcastle U	W 2-1	0-0	3	Maddison [55], Tielemans [72]	0
18	16	H	Southampton	W 2-0	1-0	2	Maddison [37], Barnes [90]	0
19	19	H	Chelsea	W 2-0	2-0	1	Ndidi [6], Maddison [41]	0
20	27	A	Everton	D 1-1	0-1	3	Tielemans [67]	0
21	31	H	Leeds U	L 1-3	1-1	4	Barnes [13]	0
22	Feb 3	A	Fulham	W 2-0	2-0	3	Iheanacho [17], Justin [44]	0
23	7	A	Wolverhampton W	D 0-0	0-0	3		0
24	13	H	Liverpool	W 3-1	0-0	2	Maddison [78], Vardy [81], Barnes [85]	0
25	21	A	Aston Villa	W 2-1	2-0	3	Maddison [19], Barnes [23]	0
26	28	H	Arsenal	L 1-3	1-2	3	Tielemans [6]	0
27	Mar 3	A	Burnley	D 1-1	1-1	3	Iheanacho [34]	0
28	6	A	Brighton & HA	W 2-1	0-1	2	Iheanacho [62], Amartey [87]	0
29	14	H	Sheffield U	W 5-0	1-0	3	Iheanacho 3 [39, 69, 78], Perez [64], Ampadu (og) [80]	0
30	Apr 3	H	Manchester C	L 0-2	0-0	3		0
31	11	A	West Ham U	L 2-3	0-2	3	Iheanacho 2 [70, 90]	0
32	22	H	WBA	W 3-0	3-0	3	Vardy [23], Evans [26], Iheanacho [36]	0
33	26	H	Crystal Palace	W 2-1	0-1	3	Castagne [50], Iheanacho [80]	0
34	30	A	Southampton	D 1-1	0-0	3	Evans [68]	0
35	May 7	H	Newcastle U	L 2-4	0-2	3	Albrighton [80], Iheanacho [87]	0
36	11	A	Manchester U	W 2-1	1-1	3	Thomas [10], Soyuncu [66]	0
37	18	A	Chelsea	L 1-2	0-0	4	Iheanacho [76]	7195
38	23	H	Tottenham H	L 2-4	1-1	5	Vardy 2 (2 pens) [18, 52]	8000

Final League Position: 5

GOALSCORERS

League (68): Vardy 15 (8 pens), Iheanacho 12, Barnes 9, Maddison 8, Tielemans 6 (2 pens), Castagne 2, Evans 2, Justin 2, Perez 2, Albrighton 1, Amartey 1, Ndidi 1, Praet 1, Soyuncu 1, Thomas 1, own goals 4.
FA Cup (13): Iheanacho 4, Tielemans 3 (1 pen), Albrighton 1, Barnes 1, Justin 1, Maddison 1, Perez 1, Under 1.
Carabao Cup (0).
UEFA Europa League (14): Barnes 3, Iheanacho 3, Maddison 2, Vardy 2 (1 pen), Choudhury 1, Praet 1, Thomas 1, Under 1.
Papa John's Trophy (11): Muskwe 3, Suengchitthawon 2, Wright 2, Flynn 1, Hirst 1 (1 pen), Tavares 1, Wakeling 1.

Schmeichel K 38	Castagne T 27	Ndidi O 25 + 1	Soyuncu C 19 + 4	Justin J 23	Mendy N 15 + 8	Perez A 15 + 10	Tielemans Y 37 + 1	Praet D 10 + 5	Barnes H 22 + 3	Vardy J 31 + 3	Albrighton M 17 + 14	Maddison J 24 + 7	Morgan W — + 3	Amartey D 8 + 4	Evans J 28	Fuchs C 8 + 1	Iheanacho K 16 + 9	Under C 1 + 8	Choudhury H 4 + 6	Fofana W 27 + 1	Slimani I — + 1	Thomas L 12 + 2	Gray D — + 1	Ricardo Pereira D 10 + 5	Tavares S 1 + 1	Leshabela T — + 1	*Match No.*
1	2	3	4	5	6	7^1	8	9^2	10	11	12	13															1
1	2	3	4	5	6	7^1	8	9^2	10^3	11	13	12	14														2
1	2		5	6	9		8	7^1	10	11^3		12		3	4^2	13	14										3
1	5		4	8	7^3	9^2	6		11	10				2^1	3		13	12	14								4
1	2			5	6^3	7	8	9^1	10			12			4		11^2		14	3	13						5
1	5			8	7		6	9^1	11^2	12	14	10^3			3	4		13		2							6
1				2	7		6	9^1	10^2	11^3	5	12	14			4		13		3		8					7
1				5	7		6	9^3	13	11	12	10^2	14		3	4				2		8^1					8
1				8	7		6	13	10^1	11	5	9			3	4^2		12		2							9
1				5	7^3		6	9^2	13	11		10			3	4	14	12		2		8^1					10
1		13		8	7^2	9^1	6	14		11	5	10^3			3	4	12			2							11
1		6^3		8	14	9^1	7	13	12	11	5	10^2			3	4				2							12
1		4		2	7^2	12	6		10	11		9				5	13	8^1		3							13
1	5^1	6		2			7	13	10^2	11^3	8	9		12	4		14			3							14
1	5	6		2		12	7		10	11	8^1	9			4					3							15
1				2	7	8	12	9^2	10	13				3	4		11^3		6^1			5	14				16
1	5	6	12	2			7		10	11	8	9^1			4					3							17
1	2	6	12	5		13	7		10	11^3	8	9^2			4		14			3^1							18
1	2	6		5		12	8		10	11^3	7^1	9^2			4		14			3				13			19
1	2	6^1	14	5	12	11	7		10		8^2	9			4^3			13		3							20
1	2^1		13	5	7	11	6		10		8^2	9			4			14		3^3				12			21
1			4	5	12	8^1	6		10^3		13	9		14	3		11		7^2					2			22
1			4	5		8^2	6		10	12	13	9			3		11^1		7					2			23
1		6	4		14	12^3	7^2		10	11	8^1	9		2	3				13					5			24
1	2	7	4		12		6^3		10	11		9^1		13	3				14			5		8^2			25
1	2	7	4				8		9^2	11	12			14	3^3		10	13				5^1		6			26
1	9	3	4		5^1		8			11	13			2			10^2		7^3	12				6	14		27
1	9	5	4				8			11	12			2			10^2		13	3				6	7^1		28
1	8	6	4			9^2	7			11	12				3		10			2				5^1		13	29
1	8	6^3			14	9	7			11	5^1	13		2	3		10^2			4				12			30
1	8	7					6	9^2		11	13			2^1	3		10			4		12		5			31
1	5	6	4			13	7	14		11^3	12	9^2			3		10			2^1		8					32
1	5	6	4			12	7			11	13	9^1			3		10			2		8^2					33
1	5	6	4			12	7			11	13	9			3		10			2^1		8^2					34
1	2	7^1	4		14	12	6			11	8	9^3					10			3		13		5^2			35
1	2	8	4			9^1	7			11^2	6	12					10		13	3		5					36
1	2	7	4			9	6			11	5^2	10^1					12			3		8		13			37
1	2	7	4		12	14	6			11	5^3	9^2					10			3^1		8		13			38

FA Cup

Third Round	Stoke C	(a)	4-0
Fourth Round	Brentford	(a)	3-1
Fifth Round	Brighton & HA	(h)	1-0
Sixth Round	Manchester U	(h)	3-1
Semi-Final	Southampton	(h)	1-0
Final	Chelsea	(Wembley)	1-0

Carabao Cup

Third Round	Arsenal	(h)	0-2

Papa John's Trophy (Leicester C U21)

Group H (N)	Hull C	(a)	2-1
Group H (N)	Harrogate T	(a)	1-3
Group H (N)	Grimsby T	(a)	3-1
Second Round (N)	Salford C	(a)	3-3
(Leicester C U21 won 6-5 on penalties)			
Third Round (N)	Tranmere R	(a)	2-4

UEFA Europa League

Group G	Zorya Luhansk	(h)	3-0
Group G	AEK Athens	(a)	2-1
Group G	Braga	(h)	4-0
Group G	Braga	(a)	3-3
Group G	Zorya Luhansk	(a)	0-1
Group G	AEK Athens	(h)	2-0
Round of 32 1st leg	Slavia Prague	(a)	0-0
Round of 32 2nd leg	Slavia Prague	(h)	0-2

LEYTON ORIENT

FOUNDATION

There is some doubt about the foundation of Leyton Orient, and, indeed, some confusion with clubs like Leyton and Clapton over their early history. As regards the foundation, the most favoured version is that Leyton Orient was formed originally by members of Homerton Theological College who established Glyn Cricket Club in 1881 and then carried on through the following winter playing football. Eventually many employees of the Orient Shipping Line became involved and so the name Orient was chosen in 1888.

The Breyer Group Stadium, Brisbane Road, Leyton, London E10 5NF.

Telephone: (0208) 926 1111.

Ticket Office: (0208) 926 1010.

Website: www.leytonorient.com

Email: info@leytonorient.net

Ground Capacity: 9,241.

Record Attendance: 34,345 v West Ham U, FA Cup 4th rd, 25 January 1964.

Pitch Measurements: 100m × 67m (109.5yd × 73.5yd).

Chairman: Nigel Travis.

Chief Executive: Danny Macklin.

Director of Football: Martin Ling.

Head Coach: Kenny Jackett.

Assistant Head Coach: Danny Senda.

Colours: Red shirts with white trim, red shorts, red socks.

Year Formed: 1881. ***Turned Professional:*** 1903.

Previous Names: 1881, Glyn Cricket and Football Club; 1886, Eagle Football Club; 1888, Orient Football Club; 1898, Clapton Orient; 1946, Leyton Orient; 1966, Orient; 1987, Leyton Orient.

Club Nickname: 'The O's'.

Grounds: 1884, Glyn Road; 1896, Whittles Athletic Ground; 1900, Millfields Road; 1930, Lea Bridge Road; 1937, Brisbane Road (renamed Matchroom Stadium; 2018, The Breyer Group Stadium).

First Football League Game: 2 September 1905, Division 2, v Leicester Fosse (a) L 1–2 – Butler; Holmes, Codling; Lamberton, Boden, Boyle; Kingaby (1), Wootten, Leigh, Evenson, Bourne.

Record League Victory: 8–0 v Crystal Palace, Division 3 (S), 12 November 1955 – Welton; Lee, Earl; Blizzard, Aldous, McKnight; White (1), Facey (3), Burgess (2), Heckman, Hartburn (2). 8–0 v Rochdale, Division 4, 20 October 1987 – Wells; Howard, Dickenson (1), Smalley (1), Day, Hull, Hales (2), Castle (Sussex), Shinners (2), Godfrey (Harvey), Comfort (2). 8–0 v Colchester U, Division 4, 15 October 1988 – Wells; Howard, Dickenson, Hales (1p), Day (1), Sitton (1), Baker (1), Ward, Hull (3), Juryeff, Comfort (1). 8–0 v Doncaster R, Division 3, 28 December 1997 – Hyde; Channing, Naylor, Smith (1p), Hicks, Clark, Ling, Roger Joseph, Griffiths (3) (Harris), Richards (2) (Baker (1)), Inglethorpe (1) (Simpson).

HONOURS

League Champions: Division 3 – 1969–70; Division 3S – 1955–56.
Runners-up: Division 2 – 1961–62; Division 3S – 1954–55.

FA Cup: semi-final – 1978.

League Cup: 5th rd – 1963.

FOOTBALL YEARBOOK FACT FILE

Clapton Orient, as the club were then known, turned professional in November 1903 after being expelled from membership by the Middlesex and London FAs. They immediately signed two professionals, George Seeley and James Wallace, and in their first game under their new status defeated Shepherd's Bush 11-0 on 14 November.

Record Cup Victory: 9–2 v Chester, League Cup 3rd rd, 15 October 1962 – Robertson; Charlton, Taylor; Gibbs, Bishop, Lea; Deeley (1), Waites (3), Dunmore (2), Graham (3), Wedge.

Record Defeat: 0–8 v Aston Villa, FA Cup 4th rd, 30 January 1929.

Most League Points (2 for a win): 66, Division 3 (S), 1955–56.

Most League Points (3 for a win): 86, FL 1, 2013–14.

Most League Goals: 106, Division 3 (S), 1955–56.

Highest League Scorer in Season: Tom Johnston, 35, Division 2, 1957–58.

Most League Goals in Total Aggregate: Tom Johnston, 121, 1956–58, 1959–61.

Most League Goals in One Match: 4, Wally Leigh v Bradford C, Division 2, 13 April 1906; 4, Albert Pape v Oldham Ath, Division 2, 1 September 1924; 4, Peter Kitchen v Millwall, Division 3, 21 April 1984.

Most Capped Player: Jobi McAnuff, 22 (32), Jamaica.

Most League Appearances: Peter Allen, 432, 1965–78.

Youngest League Player: Paul Went, 15 years 327 days v Preston NE, 4 September 1965.

Record Transfer Fee Received: £1,000,000 (rising to £1,500,000) from Fulham for Gabriel Zakuani, July 2006.

Record Transfer Fee Paid: £200,000 to Oldham Ath for Liam Kelly, July 2016.

Football League Record: 1905 Elected to Division 2; 1929–56 Division 3 (S); 1956–62 Division 2; 1962–63 Division 1; 1963–66 Division 2; 1966–70 Division 3; 1970–82 Division 2; 1982–85 Division 3; 1985–89 Division 4; 1989–92 Division 3; 1992–95 Division 2; 1995–2004 Division 3; 2004–06 FL 2; 2006–15 FL 1; 2015–17 FL 2; 2017–19 National League; 2019– FL 2.

LATEST SEQUENCES

Longest Sequence of League Wins: 10, 21.1.1956 – 30.3.1956.

Longest Sequence of League Defeats: 9, 1.4.1995 – 6.5.1995.

Longest Sequence of League Draws: 6, 30.11.1974 – 28.12.1974.

Longest Sequence of Unbeaten League Matches: 15, 13.4.2013 – 19.10.2013.

Longest Sequence Without a League Win: 23, 6.10.1962 – 13.4.1963.

Successive Scoring Runs: 22 from 12.3.1927.

Successive Non-scoring Runs: 8 from 19.11.1994.

MANAGERS

Sam Omerod 1905–06
Ike Ivenson 1906
Billy Holmes 1907–22
Peter Proudfoot 1922–29
Arthur Grimsdell 1929–30
Peter Proudfoot 1930–31
Jimmy Seed 1931–33
David Pratt 1933–34
Peter Proudfoot 1935–39
Tom Halsey 1939
Bill Wright 1939–45
Willie Hall 1945
Bill Wright 1945–46
Charlie Hewitt 1946–48
Neil McBain 1948–49
Alec Stock 1949–59
Les Gore 1959–61
Johnny Carey 1961–63
Benny Fenton 1963–64
Dave Sexton 1965
Dick Graham 1966–68
Jimmy Bloomfield 1968–71
George Petchey 1971–77
Jimmy Bloomfield 1977–81
Paul Went 1981
Ken Knighton 1981–83
Frank Clark 1983–91 *(Managing Director)*
Peter Eustace 1991–94
Chris Turner and John Sitton 1994–95
Pat Holland 1995–96
Tommy Taylor 1996–2001
Paul Brush 2001–03
Martin Ling 2003–09
Geraint Williams 2009–10
Russell Slade 2010–14
Kevin Nugent 2014
Mauro Milanese 2014
Fabio Liverani 2014–15
Ian Hendon 2015–16
Kevin Nolan 2016
Andy Hessenthaler 2016
Alberto Cavasin 2016
Andy Edwards 2016–17
Danny Webb 2017
Martin Ling 2017
Omer Riza 2017
Steve Davis 2017
Justin Edinburgh 2017–19
Carl Fletcher 2019
Ross Embleton 2019–21
Kenny Jackett May 2021–

TEN YEAR LEAGUE RECORD

		P	W	D	L	F	A	Pts	Pos
2011-12	FL 1	46	13	11	22	48	75	50	20
2012-13	FL 1	46	21	8	17	55	48	71	7
2013-14	FL 1	46	25	11	10	85	45	86	3
2014-15	FL 1	46	12	13	21	59	69	49	23
2015-16	FL 2	46	19	12	15	60	61	69	8
2016-17	FL 2	46	10	6	30	47	87	36	24
2017-18	NL	46	16	12	18	58	56	60	13
2018-19	NL	46	25	14	7	73	35	89	1
2019-20	FL 2	36	10	12	14	47	55	42	17§
2020-21	FL 2	46	17	10	19	53	55	61	11

§Decided on points-per-game (1.17)

DID YOU KNOW ?

Leyton Orient had considered moving to Mitcham Stadium in the 1930s before choosing Brisbane Road as their new home. Mitcham Stadium was eventually sold to a property developer in 1955 and Orient subsequently purchased the main stand, which reappeared shortly afterwards as the East Stand at Brisbane Road.

LEYTON ORIENT – SKY BET LEAGUE TWO 2020–21 LEAGUE RECORD

Match No.	Date	Venue	Opponents	Result		H/T Score	Lg Pos.	Goalscorers	Attendance
1	Sept 12	A	Oldham Ath	W	1-0	0-0	5	Johnson 89	0
2	19	H	Mansfield T	D	2-2	0-0	7	Johnson 82, Sotiriou 90	0
3	Oct 3	H	Cheltenham T	L	0-2	0-2	17		0
4	10	A	Barrow	D	1-1	0-1	17	Johnson 50	0
5	13	A	Walsall	L	1-2	1-1	17	Johnson 15	0
6	17	H	Grimsby T	L	2-3	1-2	18	Wilkinson 5, Maguire-Drew 74	0
7	20	A	Tranmere R	W	1-0	0-0	15	Johnson 71	0
8	24	A	Stevenage	W	2-0	0-0	14	Maguire-Drew 62, Wilkinson 66	0
9	27	H	Exeter C	D	1-1	1-0	13	Wilkinson 4	0
10	31	H	Bolton W	W	4-0	3-0	11	Johnson 8, McAnuff 41, Wilkinson 44, Clay 57	0
11	Nov 3	A	Forest Green R	L	1-2	1-1	13	Wright 40	0
12	14	A	Colchester U	L	1-2	0-1	14	Wilkinson 88	0
13	21	H	Harrogate T	W	3-0	2-0	11	Johnson 3 18, 31, 73	0
14	24	H	Bradford C	W	1-0	0-0	8	Happe 64	0
15	28	A	Port Vale	W	3-2	2-1	6	Johnson 11, Wilkinson 31, Brophy 85	0
16	Dec 5	A	Scunthorpe U	L	0-2	0-1	8		0
17	12	H	Newport Co	W	2-1	0-1	7	Johnson 62, Brophy 70	1734
18	15	A	Morecambe	L	1-2	1-0	10	Johnson 18	0
19	19	H	Crawley T	L	1-2	1-1	12	Dallison (og) 41	0
20	26	A	Cambridge U	L	1-2	1-0	12	Johnson 23	0
21	29	H	Southend U	W	2-0	0-0	10	McAnuff 53, Wilkinson 78	0
22	Jan 2	H	Salford C	W	1-0	1-0	9	Johnson 31	0
23	16	H	Morecambe	W	2-0	0-0	7	Knight-Percival (og) 88, Angol 90	0
24	23	H	Forest Green R	L	0-1	0-1	9		0
25	30	A	Bolton W	L	0-2	0-0	10		0
26	Feb 2	A	Crawley T	D	0-0	0-0	10		0
27	6	H	Colchester U	D	0-0	0-0	10		0
28	20	H	Port Vale	D	1-1	0-0	11	Kemp 63	0
29	23	A	Bradford C	L	0-1	0-0	12		0
30	27	H	Tranmere R	L	1-3	0-1	14	Turley 67	0
31	Mar 2	A	Grimsby T	W	1-0	1-0	13	Happe 20	0
32	6	A	Exeter C	L	0-4	0-3	14		0
33	9	H	Stevenage	D	0-0	0-0	14		0
34	13	H	Scunthorpe U	D	1-1	1-1	14	Cisse 34	0
35	20	A	Newport Co	W	1-0	0-0	14	Wilkinson 61	0
36	23	A	Carlisle U	W	1-0	0-0	11	Wilkinson 88	0
37	27	H	Oldham Ath	W	2-1	2-0	9	Wilkinson 8, Kemp 43	0
38	Apr 2	A	Mansfield T	W	2-0	1-0	9	Johnson 2 4, 77	0
39	5	H	Walsall	D	0-0	0-0	9		0
40	10	A	Cheltenham T	L	0-1	0-1	12		0
41	13	A	Harrogate T	D	2-2	0-0	11	Wilkinson 46, Johnson 63	0
42	17	H	Barrow	W	2-0	0-0	9	Happe 52, Kemp 63	0
43	20	H	Cambridge U	L	2-4	1-1	10	Kemp 45, Taylor (og) 73	0
44	24	A	Southend U	L	1-2	1-1	11	Dennis 45	0
45	May 1	H	Carlisle U	L	2-3	2-1	11	Wilkinson 3, Kemp 45	0
46	8	A	Salford C	L	0-3	0-1	11		0

Final League Position: 11

GOALSCORERS

League (53): Johnson 17, Wilkinson 12, Kemp 5, Happe 3, Brophy 2, Maguire-Drew 2, McAnuff 2, Angol 1, Cisse 1, Clay 1, Dennis 1, Sotiriou 1, Turley 1, Wright 1, own goals 3.
FA Cup (1): Kyprianou 1.
Carabao Cup (5): Johnson 2, Dennis 1, McAnuff 1, Wilkinson 1.
Papa John's Trophy (7): Wilkinson 2, Angol 1 (1 pen), Dennis 1, Johnson 1, Ling 1, own goal 1.

Vigouroux L 46	Ling S 27 + 3	Coulson J 19 + 1	Happe D 38 + 2	Brophy J 44	Dayton J 4 + 8	Clay C 32 + 7	Cisse O 40 + 2	Angol L 7 + 5	Wilkinson C 40 + 2	Johnson D 36 + 6	McAnuff J 26 + 14	Sotiriou R 8 + 14	Turley J 15 + 3	Maguire-Drew J 3 + 10	Dennis L 11 + 13	Widdowson J 21 + 5	Wright J 4 + 5	Akinola T 31 + 2	Thomas J 1	Kyprianou H 12 + 10	Kemp D 22 + 2	Freeman N 10 + 5	Thompson A 6	Abrahams T 3 + 11	Young M — + 1	Sweeney J — + 1	*Match No.*
1	2	3	4^{3}	5	6^{1}	7	8	9	10^{2}	11	12	13	14														1
1	2	3	4	5	8	6^{1}	7^{3}	14		10	12	9		11^{2}	13												2
1	2	3		5			7	12	9^{1}	10	6	14		13	11^{3}	4	8^{2}										3
1	2^{3}	3	4■	5	8^{1}	6	7		9	10	14				11^{2}	12		13									4
1		3		5	11^{1}	13	7^{3}		9	10	8		14	12		4	6^{2}	2									5
1			4	5		8	7		9^{1}	10	13	11	3^{2}	12			6	2									6
1		3	4	5^{3}	14	8	7		12	10	6	11^{2}		9^{1}		13		2									7
1		3	4	5		8	7		9^{3}	10	6^{2}	11^{1}		12	13		14	2									8
1		3	4	5^{1}	14	8	7		9^{2}	10	6^{3}			11	13	12		2									9
1		3	4	11^{2}		8	7		9^{3}	10	6^{1}			14	13	5	12	2									10
1			4	11		6	7		9^{3}	10^{1}	13	12	3		14	5	8^{2}	2									11
1	14	3	4	9			7		10	12	6			13	11			2^{1}	5^{3}	8^{2}							12
1	2	3	4	11^{2}	12		7		9^{3}	10	6^{1}			14	13	5	15			8^{4}							13
1	2	3	4	10^{4}			6		8^{1}	11	13			12	9^{3}	5	14	15		7^{2}							14
1	2	3	4	10			6^{3}		7^{1}	11	8	12			9^{2}	5	14			13							15
1	2	3	4	10		12	6	13	7^{2}	11	8	14			9^{1}	5^{3}											16
1	2	3	4	11^{2}		6	7	12	9^{1}	10	8	13				5											17
1	2	3	4	5	15	8^{3}	7^{4}	11^{1}	9	10	12	13			14					6^{2}							18
1	2	3	4	11		6	7^{2}	9^{1}		10	8	14		12		5^{3}				13							19
1	2	3	4	11		6^{4}	7^{1}	12	9^{3}	10	8	14		15	13	5^{2}											20
1	2		4	5	13	6^{2}	7	11	9	10^{3}	8^{1}	14						3		12							21
1	2		4	5		6	7	11	9	10^{1}	8	12						3									22
1	2		4	5		8	7^{1}	10	9		6	11^{2}						3		12	13						23
1	2	15	4■	5		8^{4}	7^{2}	10^{1}	9		6	11^{3}			14			3			12	13					24
1	2	4		5	14	8^{3}			11		6	10				12		3		7^{2}	9^{1}	13					25
1	2^{3}			5		8			9		13	10^{1}				14		3		7■	11^{2}	6	4	12			26
1	2^{2}		13	5		8^{1}	7		9	14	12							3			11^{3}	6	4	10			27
1			4	5			7		9	10	8							2			11^{1}	6	3	12			28
1			4	5	13		7^{2}		9	10	8							2			11^{1}	6	3	12			29
1			4	5		14	7^{2}		11	10	6		15					2		12	9^{4}	8^{3}	3^{1}	13			30
1			12	11		6^{2}	7			10^{3}			3			5		2		13	9	8	4^{1}	14			31
1	13		4	11		6	7		12	10			3			5^{1}		2^{2}			9^{3}	8		14			32
1	2		4	5	12	6	7		8	13			3								9	10^{1}		11^{2}			33
1	2		4	5		6	7^{2}		8	12			3							13	9	10		11^{1}			34
1			4			6	7^{1}		8	11	10		3			5		2		12	9						35
1			4			6	7		8	11	9^{1}		3		12	5		2			10						36
1			4	10		6	7^{1}		8^{2}	11^{3}	12		3		13	5		2			9			14			37
1	2			10		6	7			11	9^{1}		4			5		3		12	8						38
1	2			10		6^{3}	7^{1}		8	11	14		4		13	5^{2}		3		12	9						39
1	2		4	10		6^{2}			8	11			3			5^{1}				7	9	13		12			40
1	2		4	5		6			8^{2}	11	9^{1}				13			3		7^{3}	10	12		14			41
1			4	5		7^{1}	14		8	11^{4}	12		3		10^{2}			2		6	9^{3}	13		15			42
1			4	5		12	7^{3}		8	11	14	13	3		10^{2}			2		6^{1}	9						43
1	2		4	5		13	12		8	11^{3}	15	14			10^{4}			3^{5}		6^{1}	9	7^{2}		16			44
1	12		4	10		14	7		11	13	6^{3}		3^{1}		8^{2}	5		2			9						45
1	2		4	10		14	7^{3}		11^{5}	12		13			8^{1}	5^{2}		3		6^{4}	9				15	16	46

FA Cup

First Round	Newport Co	(h)	1-2

Carabao Cup

First Round	Forest Green R	(a)	2-1
Second Round	Plymouth Arg	(h)	3-2

Papa John's Trophy

Group G (S)	Brighton & HA U21	(h)	3-2
Group G (S)	AFC Wimbledon	(h)	2-0
Group G (S)	Charlton Ath	(a)	1-3
Second Round (S)	Bristol R	(h)	1-2

LINCOLN CITY

FOUNDATION

The original Lincoln Football Club was established in the early 1860s and was one of the first provisional clubs to affiliate to the Football Association. In their early years, they regularly played matches against the famous Sheffield Football Club and later became known as Lincoln Lindum. The present organisation was formed at a public meeting held in the Monson Arms Hotel in June 1884 and won the Lincolnshire Cup in only their third season. They were founder members of the Midland League in 1889 and that competition's first champions.

LNER Stadium, Sincil Bank, Lincoln LN5 8LD.

Telephone: (01522) 880 011.

Ticket Office: (01522) 880 011.

Website: www.weareimps.com

Email: admin@theredimps.com

Ground Capacity: 10,653.

Record Attendance: 23,196 v Derby Co, League Cup 4th rd, 15 November 1967.

Pitch Measurements: 100m × 65m (109.5yd × 71yd).

Chairman: Clive Nates.

Chief Executive Officer: Liam Scully.

Manager: Michael Appleton.

Assistant Manager: David Kerslake.

Colours: Red shirts with thin white stripes and black trim, black shorts with red trim, red socks with black and white trim.

Year Formed: 1884.

Turned Professional: 1885.

Ltd Co.: 1895.

Club Nickname: 'The Red Imps'.

Grounds: 1884, John O'Gaunt's; 1894, Sincil Bank (renamed LNER Stadium 2019).

First Football League Game: 3 September 1892, Division 2, v Sheffield U (a) L 2–4 – William Gresham; Coulton, Neill; Shaw, Mettam, Moore; Smallman, Irving (1), Cameron (1), Kelly, James Gresham.

Record League Victory: 11–1 v Crewe Alex, Division 3 (N), 29 September 1951 – Jones; Green (1p), Varney; Wright, Emery, Grummett (1); Troops (1), Garvey, Graver (6), Whittle (1), Johnson (1).

Record Cup Victory: 13-0 v Peterborough, FA Cup 1st qual rd, 12 October 1895 – Shaw, McFarlane, Eyre, Richardson, Neaves (1), Burke (2), Frettingham (2), Smith (1), Gillespie W (2), Gillespie M (3), Hulme (2).

Record Defeat: 3–11 v Manchester C, Division 2, 23 March 1895.

Most League Points (2 for a win): 74, Division 4, 1975–76.

Most League Points (3 for a win): 85, FL 2, 2018–19.

Most League Goals: 121, Division 3 (N), 1951–52.

HONOURS

League Champions: Division 3 (N) – 1931–32, 1947–48, 1951–52; FL 2 – 2018–19; Division 4 – 1975–76; National League – 1987–88, 2016–17.
Runners-up: Division 3 (N) – 1927–28, 1930–31, 1936–37; Division 4 – 1980–81.

FA Cup: quarter-final – 2017.

League Cup: 4th rd – 1968.

League Trophy Winners: 2018.

FOOTBALL YEARBOOK FACT FILE

Yorkshire and England cricketer Fred Trueman signed amateur forms for Lincoln City in November 1952 and scored four goals on his debut for the club's Lincolnshire League team. He was promoted to the reserves the following week and played in a 0-0 draw against Peterborough United at Sincil Bank. The game attracted a record reserve crowd for Lincoln of 7,328. Shortly afterwards he ended his connection with the club and concentrated on cricket.

Highest League Scorer in Season: Allan Hall, 41, Division 3 (N), 1931–32.

Most League Goals in Total Aggregate: Andy Graver, 143, 1950–55 and 1958–61.

Most League Goals in One Match: 6, Frank Keetley v Halifax T, Division 3 (N), 16 January 1932; 6, Andy Graver v Crewe Alex, Division 3 (N), 29 September 1951.

Most Capped Player: Delroy Facey, 8 (15) Grenada.

Most League Appearances: Grant Brown, 407, 1989–2002.

Youngest League Player: Jack Hobbs, 16 years 150 days v Bristol R, 15 January 2005.

Record Transfer Fee Received: £750,000 from Liverpool for Jack Hobbs, August 2005.

Record Transfer Fee Paid: £100,000 to Barnet for John Akinde, July 2018.

Football League Record: 1892 Founder member of Division 2. Remained in Division 2 until 1920 when they failed re-election but also missed seasons 1908–09 and 1911–12 when not re-elected. 1921–32 Division 3 (N); 1932–34 Division 2; 1934–48 Division 3 (N); 1948–49 Division 2; 1949–52 Division 3 (N); 1952–61 Division 2; 1961–62 Division 3; 1962–76 Division 4; 1976–79 Division 3; 1979–81 Division 4; 1981–86 Division 3; 1986–87 Division 4; 1987–88 GM Vauxhall Conference; 1988–92 Division 4; 1992–98 Division 3; 1998–99 Division 2; 1999–2004 Division 3; 2004–11 FL 2; 2011–17 Conference National League; 2017–19 FL 2; 2019– FL 1.

LATEST SEQUENCES

Longest Sequence of League Wins: 10, 1.9.1930 – 18.10.1930.

Longest Sequence of League Defeats: 12, 21.9.1896 – 9.1.1897.

Longest Sequence of League Draws: 5, 21.2.1981 – 7.3.1981.

Longest Sequence of Unbeaten League Matches: 19, 29.12.2018 – 13.4.2019.

Longest Sequence Without a League Win: 19, 22.8.1978 – 23.12.1978.

Successive Scoring Runs: 37 from 1.3.1930.

Successive Non-scoring Runs: 5 from 15.11.1913.

MANAGERS

Jack Strawson 1884–96 *(hon. secretary)*
Alf Martin 1896–97 *(sec.-manager)*
James West 1897–1900 *(hon. secretary)*
David Calderhead, snr 1900–07 *(sec.-manager)*
Jack Strawson 1907–08 *(managing director & secretary)*
Jack Strawson 1908–19 *(secretary)*
Clem Jackson 1919–20 *(player-manager)*
George Fraser 1919–21 *(sec.-manager)*
David Calderhead, jnr 1921–24 *(sec.-manager)*
Horace Henshall 1924–27 *(sec.-manager)*
Harry Parkes 1927–36 *(sec.-manager)*
Joe McClelland 1936–47 *(sec.-manager)*
Bill Anderson 1947–65
Con Moulson 1965–65
Roy Chapman 1965–66
Ron Gray 1966–70
Bert Loxley 1970–71
David Herd 1971–72
Graham Taylor 1972–77
George Kerr 1977
Willie Bell 1977–78
Colin Murphy 1978–85
John Pickering 1985
George Kerr 1985–87
Peter Daniel 1987 *(caretaker)*
Colin Murphy 1987–90
Allan Clarke 1990
Steve Thompson 1990–93
Keith Alexander 1993–94
Sam Ellis 1994–95
Steve Wicks 1995 *(head coach)*
John Beck 1995–98
Shane Westley 1998
John Reames 1998–2000 *(chairman-manager)*
Phil Stant 2000–01
Alan Buckley 2001–02
Keith Alexander 2002–06
John Schofield 2006–07
Peter Jackson 2007–09
Chris Sutton 2009–10
Steve Tilson 2010–11
David Holdsworth 2011–13
Gary Simpson 2013–14
Chris Moyses 2014–16
Danny Cowley 2016–19
Michael Appleton Sept 2019–

TEN YEAR LEAGUE RECORD

		P	W	D	L	F	A	Pts	Pos
2011-12	Conf	46	13	10	23	56	66	49	17
2012-13	Conf	46	15	11	20	72	86	54	16
2013-14	Conf	46	17	14	15	60	59	65	14
2014-15	Conf	46	16	10	20	62	71	58	15
2015-16	NL	46	16	13	17	69	68	61	13
2016-17	NL	46	30	9	7	83	40	99	1
2017-18	FL 2	46	20	15	11	64	48	75	7
2018-19	FL 2	46	23	16	7	73	43	85	1
2019-20	FL 1	35	12	6	17	44	46	42	16§
2020-21	FL 1	46	22	11	13	69	50	77	5

§Decided on points-per-game (1.20)

DID YOU KNOW ?

On the three occasions Lincoln City have reached the play-off finals they have lost to clubs from seaside towns. City were beaten by both AFC Bournemouth and Southend United at the Millennium Stadium and in May lost 2-1 to Blackpool at Wembley.

LINCOLN CITY – SKY BET LEAGUE ONE 2020–21 LEAGUE RECORD

Match No.	Date	Venue	Opponents	Result	H/T Score	Lg Pos.	Goalscorers	Attendance
1	Sept 12	H	Oxford U	W 2-0	1-0	2	Scully [7], Jackson [74]	0
2	19	A	Milton Keynes D	W 2-1	1-0	2	Grant (pen) [11], Hopper [78]	0
3	27	H	Charlton Ath	W 2-0	1-0	2	Grant [45], Montsma [88]	0
4	Oct 3	A	Blackpool	W 3-2	1-1	1	Grant 2 (2 pens) [25, 85], Montsma [88]	0
5	10	H	Bristol R	L 1-2	0-0	2	Montsma [46]	0
6	17	A	Fleetwood T	D 0-0	0-0	3		0
7	20	H	Plymouth Arg	W 2-0	0-0	3	Grant (pen) [50], Johnson [72]	0
8	24	H	Ipswich T	W 1-0	0-0	1	Grant (pen) [77]	0
9	27	A	Crewe Alex	W 1-0	1-0	1	Anderson [39]	0
10	31	A	Doncaster R	L 0-1	0-1	3		0
11	Nov 3	H	Portsmouth	L 1-3	0-1	4	Hopper [73]	0
12	21	A	Accrington S	D 0-0	0-0	6		0
13	24	A	Swindon T	W 1-0	0-0	3	Montsma [74]	0
14	Dec 1	H	Wigan Ath	W 2-1	0-0	2	Grant [69], Hopper [83]	0
15	5	A	Rochdale	W 2-0	1-0	2	Jones [38], Montsma [68]	0
16	12	H	Sunderland	L 0-4	0-3	2		0
17	15	H	Shrewsbury T	L 0-1	0-1	4		0
18	19	A	Northampton T	W 4-0	2-0	2	Scully [2], Hopper [42], Johnson 2 [83, 90]	2000
19	26	H	Burton Alb	W 5-1	2-0	1	Howarth [4], Johnson 2 [7, 63], Scully [56], Anderson [81]	0
20	Jan 2	A	AFC Wimbledon	W 2-1	1-1	1	Edun [8], Hopper [83]	0
21	9	H	Peterborough U	D 1-1	0-1	1	Scully [49]	0
22	23	H	Northampton T	W 2-1	0-0	2	McGrandles [75], Scully [84]	0
23	26	A	Portsmouth	W 1-0	0-0	1	Rogers [79]	0
24	30	H	Doncaster R	L 0-1	0-1	2		0
25	Feb 5	A	Gillingham	W 3-0	1-0	1	McGrandles [14], Grant (pen) [59], Hopper [64]	0
26	9	A	Hull C	D 0-0	0-0	1		0
27	14	H	Accrington S	D 2-2	0-1	1	Rogers [53], Hopper [84]	0
28	20	A	Wigan Ath	W 2-1	1-1	1	Scully [34], Hopper [73]	0
29	23	H	Swindon T	D 2-2	1-2	2	Grant (pen) [26], Rogers [59]	0
30	27	A	Plymouth Arg	L 3-4	1-2	2	McGrandles [22], Grant 2 (2 pens) [59, 62]	0
31	Mar 2	H	Fleetwood T	L 1-2	0-1	3	Morton [71]	0
32	6	H	Crewe Alex	W 3-0	1-0	3	Rogers [21], McGrandles [52], Johnson [80]	0
33	9	A	Ipswich T	D 1-1	1-0	3	Rogers [29]	0
34	13	H	Rochdale	L 1-2	0-1	3	Rogers [60]	0
35	16	H	Gillingham	L 0-3	0-2	3		0
36	20	A	Sunderland	D 1-1	0-1	4	Morton [63]	0
37	26	A	Oxford U	L 1-2	1-1	4	Scully [4]	0
38	Apr 10	H	Blackpool	D 2-2	0-1	6	Scully [75], Johnson [84]	0
39	13	H	Milton Keynes D	W 4-0	0-0	4	Johnson 3 (1 pen) [48, 53, 59 (p)], Fisher (og) [73]	0
40	17	A	Bristol R	W 1-0	1-0	4	Scully [16]	0
41	20	A	Burton Alb	W 1-0	1-0	4	Eyoma [27]	0
42	24	H	Hull C	L 1-2	0-1	4	Montsma [65]	0
43	27	A	Shrewsbury T	W 1-0	1-0	3	Grant [11]	0
44	May 1	A	Peterborough U	D 3-3	2-0	4	Scully 2 [31, 53], Grant (pen) [45]	0
45	4	A	Charlton Ath	L 1-3	0-0	5	Anderson [89]	0
46	9	H	AFC Wimbledon	D 0-0	0-0	5		0

Final League Position: 5

GOALSCORERS

League (69): Grant 13 (10 pens), Scully 11, Johnson 10 (1 pen), Hopper 8, Montsma 6, Rogers 6, McGrandles 4, Anderson 3, Morton 2, Edun 1, Eyoma 1, Howarth 1, Jackson 1, Jones 1, own goal 1.
FA Cup (6): Grant 2 (1 pen), Scully 2, Johnson 1, Jones 1.
Carabao Cup (9): Montsma 3, Edun 1, Hopper 1, Jones 1, Morton 1, Scully 1, own goal 1.
Papa John's Trophy (15): Anderson 3, Scully 3, Elbouzedi 2, Grant 2 (1 pen), Archibald 1, Gotts 1, Howarth 1, Johnson 1, Soule 1.
League One Play-Offs (4): Hopper 2, Johnson 1, own goal 1.

Palmer A 46	Eyoma T 34 + 5	Montsma L 38 + 2	Jackson A 27 + 1	Roughan S 6	McGrandles C 35 + 4	Grant J 35 + 1	Jones J 28 + 8	Anderson H 14 + 15	Hopper T 33 + 6	Scully A 22 + 18	Morton C 11 + 6	Melbourne M 1 + 7	Bridcutt L 22 + 1	Archibald T — + 7	Johnson B 38 + 2	Edun T 36 + 5	Howarth R 4 + 7	Walsh J 18 + 3	Soule J — + 1	Gotts R 4 + 3	Elbouzedi Z — + 2	Rogers M 23 + 2	Poole R 18 + 4	Bramall C 12 + 5	Sanders M 1 + 4	Match No.
1	2	3	4	5^{2}	6	7	8	9	10	11^{1}	12	13														1
1	2	3	4	5^{1}	7	11	8	9^{3}	10		12	13	6^{2}	14												2
1	2	3	4	5	8^{1}	11	6	9^{2}	10	13			7		12											3
1	2	3	4	5^{1}	8^{2}	11	6	13	10				7		9	12										4
1	2^{1}	3	4■		8^{3}	11	6	9	10^{2}	13			7	14		5	12									5
1	2	3			13	11^{2}	6	9	10^{1}	12			7		8	5		4								6
1	2	3		5	8^{1}	11	6	12	10^{2}	13			7	14	9^{3}			4								7
1	2	3			8	11	6	9	12				7		10^{1}	5		4								8
1	2	3			8	7	6	9	10						11	5		4								9
1	2	3	4		8^{2}	7	6	9^{1}	10^{3}	13				12	11	5			14							10
1	3		4	5	8	7	6^{2}	12	10	9				13	11					2^{1}						11
1	2^{3}	4	3		11^{2}	8	6	9^{1}	10	13		5^{4}	7		12	14				15						12
1	13	3	4		12	8	6		10	9^{1}			7		11	5				2^{2}						13
1		3	4^{1}		8^{2}	7	6	13	10	9				14	11^{3}	5		12		2						14
1	2	3			8	7	6	9	10	12		13			11^{1}	5^{2}		4								15
1	2^{1}	3				7	8	9	10	12					11^{2}	5	13	4		6						16
1	2^{1}	3				8	6	12	10	9					11	5	7	4								17
1	2	3				8	6	12	10	9^{2}					11^{3}	5	7^{1}	4		13	14					18
1	2^{2}	3				7	6	12	10	9^{4}		14			11	5^{3}	8^{1}	4		13	15					19
1	2	3				6	8		10	9		13	7		11^{1}	5^{2}	12	4								20
1	2	3	4			8	6			9			7		10	5	11^{1}					12				21
1	2		3		12	6		13	11	8^{3}		14	7		9	5^{2}		4				10^{1}				22
1	2		3		6	8		14	10	9^{1}		13	7		11^{3}	5^{2}		4				12				23
1	2		3		6^{1}	8			10	12			7		9	5		4				11				24
1	2^{1}		3		6	8		13	10				7		9^{2}	5		4				11	12			25
1	2^{3}		3		6	8	12		10				7^{1}		9	5^{2}		4				11	13	14		26
1	14	3			8	7	6^{2}		10	13					9	12		4				11	2^{3}	5^{1}		27
1		3	4		8	7			10	9^{1}					6	5^{2}	14					11^{3}	2	12	13	28
1	2^{3}	3	4		8^{2}	7	13		10	9					6	12						11	14	5^{1}		29
1		3	4		8	7^{1}	12		10	9					6	5						11	2			30
1	14	3	4		8		7^{4}		10	9^{2}	12				6	5^{1}						11	2^{3}	13	15	31
1		3	4		8		6		12	14	10^{1}			13	9^{2}	7						11^{3}	2	5		32
1	2^{3}	3	4		8		6		10^{1}	13	12				9	7^{2}						11	14	5		33
1		3	4		8		6		13	12	10				9	7						11^{2}	2	5^{1}		34
1		3	4		7				10^{2}	13	11		8^{1}		6	5						9	2	12		35
1		3	4		7					12	11		8		10^{1}	6						9	2	5		36
1	4	3			6		12	9^{2}		10			8^{1}			7	13					11	2	5		37
1	14	3^{1}	4^{5}		6		16	12		15	10				9	8^{3}		13				11^{4}	2	5	7^{2}	38
1	12	14	3^{1}		7		15	13		9	10				6^{2}	8		4^{3}				11	2	5^{4}		39
1	4	3			6		12	14		8^{2}	11				9^{3}	7^{1}						10	2	5	13	40
1	4	3			7	12	6^{1}	13		8	11				9^{3}	5	14					10^{2}	2			41
1	4	3			7^{2}	6^{1}	14		15	8^{4}	11		13		9	5^{3}						10	2	12		42
1	4	3			8	7		14	13	12	10^{3}		6^{2}		9^{1}	5						11	2			43
1	4	3			12	9		6^{3}	11^{2}	10	13		7^{1}			14						8	2	5		44
1	4^{4}	3				6^{3}	8	7	14	10^{1}	11					9	12	15					2	5^{2}	13	45
1	3^{1}	12	13		6^{3}	8			10^{4}	14	15		7		9	5		4^{2}				11	2			46

FA Cup First Round	Forest Green R	(h)	6-2
Second Round	Plymouth Arg	(a)	0-2

Carabao Cup First Round	Crewe Alex	(a)	2-1
Second Round	Bradford C	(a)	5-0
Third Round	Liverpool	(h)	2-7

League One Play-Offs

Semi-Final 1st leg	Sunderland	(h)	2-0
Semi-Final 2nd leg	Sunderland	(a)	1-2
Final	Blackpool	(Wembley)	1-2

Papa John's Trophy

Group E (N)	Scunthorpe U	(h)	1-1
(Lincoln C won 4-2 on penalties)			
Group E (N)	Mansfield T	(a)	3-1
Group E (N)	Manchester C U21	(h)	1-1
(Lincoln C won 4-3 on penalties)			
Second Round (N)	Shrewsbury T	(a)	4-1
Third Round (N)	Accrington S	(h)	4-0
Quarter-Final	Hull C	(a)	1-1
(Lincoln C won 4-3 on penalties)			
Semi-Final	Sunderland	(a)	1-1
(Sunderland won 5-3 on penalties)			

LIVERPOOL

FOUNDATION

But for a dispute between Everton FC and their landlord at Anfield in 1892, there may never have been a Liverpool club. This dispute persuaded the majority of Evertonians to quit Anfield for Goodison Park, leaving the landlord, Mr John Houlding, to form a new club. He originally tried to retain the name 'Everton' but when this failed, he founded Liverpool Association FC on 15 March 1892.

Anfield Stadium, Anfield Road, Anfield, Liverpool L4 0TH.

Telephone: (0151) 263 2361.

Ticket Office: (0843) 170 5555.

Website: www.liverpoolfc.com

Email: customerservices@liverpoolfc.com

Ground Capacity: 53,394.

Record Attendance: 61,905 v Wolverhampton W, FA Cup 4th rd, 2 February 1952.

Pitch Measurements: 101m × 68m (110.5yd × 74.5yd).

Chairman: Tom Werner.

Chief Executive: Billy Hogan.

Manager: Jürgen Klopp.

Assistant Managers: Peter Krawietz, Pepijn Lijnders.

Colours: Red shirts with white and teal trim, red shorts with white trim, red socks with white and teal trim.

Year Formed: 1892.

Turned Professional: 1892.

Club Nicknames: 'The Reds', 'Pool'.

Ground: 1892, Anfield.

First Football League Game: 2 September 1893, Division 2, v Middlesbrough Ironopolis (a) W 2–0 – McOwen; Hannah, McLean; Henderson, McQue (1), McBride; Gordon, McVean (1), Matt McQueen, Stott, Hugh McQueen.

HONOURS

League Champions: Premier League – 2019–20; Division 1 – 1900–01, 1905–06, 1921–22, 1922–23, 1946–47, 1963–64, 1965–66, 1972–73, 1975–76, 1976–77, 1978–79, 1979–80, 1981–82, 1982–83, 1983–84, 1985–86, 1987–88, 1989–90; Division 2 – 1893–94, 1895–96, 1904–05, 1961–62.
Runners-up: Premier League – 2001–02, 2008–09, 2013–14, 2018–19; Division 1 – 1898–99, 1909–10, 1968–69, 1973–74, 1974–75, 1977–78, 1984–85, 1986–87, 1988–89, 1990–91.

FA Cup Winners: 1965, 1974, 1986, 1989, 1992, 2001, 2006.
Runners-up: 1914, 1950, 1971, 1977, 1988, 1996, 2012.

League Cup Winners: 1981, 1982, 1983, 1984, 1995, 2001, 2003, 2012.
Runners-up: 1978, 1987, 2005, 2016.

League Super Cup Winners: 1986.

European Competitions

European Cup: 1964–65 *(sf)*, 1966–67, 1973–74, 1976–77 *(winners)*, 1977–78 *(winners)*, 1978–79, 1979–80, 1980–81 *(winners)*, 1981–82 *(qf)*, 1982–83 *(qf)*, 1983–84 *(winners)*, 1984–85 *(runners-up)*.
Champions League: 2001–02 *(qf)*, 2002–03, 2004–05 *(winners)*, 2005–06, 2006–07 *(runners-up)*, 2007–08 *(sf)*, 2008–09 *(qf)*, 2009–10, 2014–15, 2017–18 *(runners-up)*, 2018–19 *(winners)*, 2019–20, 2020–21*(qf)*.
Fairs Cup: 1967–68, 1968–69, 1969–70, 1970–71 *(sf)*.
UEFA Cup: 1972–73 *(winners)*, 1975–76 *(winners)*, 1991–92 *(qf)*, 1995–96, 1997–98, 1998–99, 2000–01 *(winners)*, 2002–03 *(qf)*, 2003–04.
Europa League: 2009–10 *(sf)*, 2010–11, 2012–13, 2014–15, 2015–16 *(runners-up)*.
European Cup-Winners' Cup: 1965–66 *(runners-up)*, 1971–72, 1974–75, 1992–93, 1996–97 *(sf)*.
Super Cup: 1977 *(winners)*, 1978, 1984, 2001 *(winners)*, 2005 *(winners)*, 2019 *(winners)*.
World Club Championship: 1981, 1984.
FIFA Club World Cup: 2005, 2019 *(winners)*.

FOOTBALL YEARBOOK FACT FILE

Liverpool's Jan Molby scored a hat-trick of penalties in the League Cup tie with Coventry City on 26 November 1986, each goal coming with a right-foot shot to the goalkeeper's left. Four days later he scored again from the spot, once more against Coventry City, although in a League game. On this occasion he placed the ball to the goalkeeper's right.

Record League Victory: 10–1 v Rotherham T, Division 2, 18 February 1896 – Storer; Goldie, Wilkie; McCartney, McQue, Holmes; McVean (3), Ross (2), Allan (4), Becton (1), Bradshaw.

Record Cup Victory: 11–0 v Stromsgodset Drammen, ECWC 1st rd 1st leg, 17 September 1974 – Clemence; Smith (1), Lindsay (1p), Thompson (2), Cormack (1), Hughes (1), Boersma (2), Hall, Heighway (1), Kennedy (1), Callaghan (1).

Record Defeat: 1–9 v Birmingham C, Division 2, 11 December 1954.

Most League Points (2 for a win): 68, Division 1, 1978–79.

Most League Points (3 for a win): 99, Premier League, 2019–20.

Most League Goals: 106, Division 2, 1895–96.

Highest League Scorer in Season: Roger Hunt, 41, Division 2, 1961–62.

Most League Goals in Total Aggregate: Roger Hunt, 245, 1959–69.

Most League Goals in One Match: 5, Andy McGuigan v Stoke C, Division 1, 4 January 1902; 5, John Evans v Bristol R, Division 2, 15 September 1954; 5, Ian Rush v Luton T, Division 1, 29 October 1983.

Most Capped Player: Steven Gerrard, 114, England.

Most League Appearances: Ian Callaghan, 640, 1960–78.

Youngest League Player: Jack Robinson, 16 years 250 days v Hull C, 9 May 2010.

Record Transfer Fee Received: £142,000,000 from Barcelona for Philippe Coutinho, January 2018.

Record Transfer Fee Paid: £75,000,000 to Southampton for Virgil van Dijk, January 2018.

Football League Record: 1893 Elected to Division 2; 1894–95 Division 1; 1895–96 Division 2; 1896–1904 Division 1; 1904–05 Division 2; 1905–54 Division 1; 1954–62 Division 2; 1962–92 Division 1; 1992– Premier League.

MANAGERS

W. E. Barclay 1892–96
Tom Watson 1896–1915
David Ashworth 1920–23
Matt McQueen 1923–28
George Patterson 1928–36
(continued as Secretary)
George Kay 1936–51
Don Welsh 1951–56
Phil Taylor 1956–59
Bill Shankly 1959–74
Bob Paisley 1974–83
Joe Fagan 1983–85
Kenny Dalglish 1985–91
Graeme Souness 1991–94
Roy Evans 1994–98
(then Joint Manager)
Gerard Houllier 1998–2004
Rafael Benitez 2004–10
Roy Hodgson 2010–11
Kenny Dalglish 2011–12
Brendan Rodgers 2012–15
Jürgen Klopp October 2015–

LATEST SEQUENCES

Longest Sequence of League Wins: 18, 27.10.2019 – 24.2.2020.

Longest Sequence of League Defeats: 9, 29.4.1899 – 14.10.1899.

Longest Sequence of League Draws: 6, 19.2.1975 – 19.3.1975.

Longest Sequence of Unbeaten League Matches: 44, 12.1.2019 – 24.2.2020.

Longest Sequence Without a League Win: 14, 12.12.1953 – 20.3.1954.

Successive Scoring Runs: 36 from 10.3.2019.

Successive Non-scoring Runs: 5 from 21.4.2000.

TEN YEAR LEAGUE RECORD

		P	W	D	L	F	A	Pts	Pos
2011-12	PR Lge	38	14	10	14	47	40	52	8
2012-13	PR Lge	38	16	13	9	71	43	61	7
2013-14	PR Lge	38	26	6	6	101	50	84	2
2014-15	PR Lge	38	18	8	12	52	48	62	6
2015-16	PR Lge	38	16	12	10	63	50	60	8
2016-17	PR Lge	38	22	10	6	78	42	76	4
2017-18	PR Lge	38	21	12	5	84	38	75	4
2018-19	PR Lge	38	30	7	1	89	22	97	2
2019-20	PR Lge	38	32	3	3	85	33	99	1
2020-21	PR Lge	38	20	9	9	68	42	69	3

DID YOU KNOW?

Midfielder Gary McAllister signed for Liverpool in the summer of 2000 and spent two years on the books at Anfield. He made his debut for the Reds as a substitute in the home game with Bradford City on 19 August 2000 at the age of 35 years and 237 days, making him the club's oldest outfield debutant.

LIVERPOOL – PREMIER LEAGUE 2020–21 LEAGUE RECORD

Match No.	*Date*	*Venue*	*Opponents*	*Result*		*H/T Score*	*Lg Pos.*	*Goalscorers*	*Attendance*
1	Sept 12	H	Leeds U	W	4-3	3-2	3	Salah 3 (2 pens) [4 (p), 33, 88 (p)], van Dijk [20]	0
2	20	A	Chelsea	W	2-0	0-0	4	Mane 2 [50, 54]	0
3	28	H	Arsenal	W	3-1	2-1	2	Mane [28], Robertson [34], Jota [88]	0
4	Oct 4	A	Aston Villa	L	2-7	1-4	5	Salah 2 [33, 60]	0
5	17	A	Everton	D	2-2	1-1	2	Mane [3], Salah [72]	0
6	24	H	Sheffield U	W	2-1	1-1	2	Firmino [41], Jota [64]	0
7	31	H	West Ham U	W	2-1	1-1	1	Salah (pen) [42], Jota [85]	0
8	Nov 8	A	Manchester C	D	1-1	1-1	3	Salah (pen) [13]	0
9	22	H	Leicester C	W	3-0	2-0	2	Evans (og) [21], Jota [41], Firmino [86]	0
10	28	A	Brighton & HA	D	1-1	0-0	1	Jota [60]	0
11	Dec 6	H	Wolverhampton W	W	4-0	1-0	2	Salah [24], Wijnaldum [58], Matip [67], Nelson Semedo (og) [78]	2000
12	13	A	Fulham	D	1-1	0-1	2	Salah (pen) [79]	2000
13	16	H	Tottenham H	W	2-1	1-1	1	Salah [26], Firmino [90]	2000
14	19	A	Crystal Palace	W	7-0	3-0	1	Minamino [3], Mane [35], Firmino 2 [44, 68], Henderson [52], Salah 2 [81, 84]	0
15	27	H	WBA	D	1-1	1-0	1	Mane [12]	2000
16	30	A	Newcastle U	D	0-0	0-0	1		0
17	Jan 4	A	Southampton	L	0-1	0-1	1		0
18	17	H	Manchester U	D	0-0	0-0	4		0
19	21	H	Burnley	L	0-1	0-0	4		0
20	28	A	Tottenham H	W	3-1	1-0	4	Firmino [45], Alexander-Arnold [47], Mane [65]	0
21	31	A	West Ham U	W	3-1	0-0	3	Salah 2 [57, 68], Wijnaldum [84]	0
22	Feb 3	H	Brighton & HA	L	0-1	0-0	4		0
23	7	H	Manchester C	L	1-4	0-0	4	Salah (pen) [63]	0
24	13	A	Leicester C	L	1-3	0-0	4	Salah [67]	0
25	20	H	Everton	L	0-2	0-1	6		0
26	28	A	Sheffield U	W	2-0	0-0	6	Jones [48], Bryan (og) [65]	0
27	Mar 4	H	Chelsea	L	0-1	0-1	7		0
28	7	H	Fulham	L	0-1	0-1	8		0
29	15	A	Wolverhampton W	W	1-0	1-0	6	Jota [45]	0
30	Apr 3	A	Arsenal	W	3-0	0-0	5	Jota 2 [64, 82], Salah [68]	0
31	10	H	Aston Villa	W	2-1	0-1	5	Salah [57], Alexander-Arnold [90]	0
32	19	A	Leeds U	D	1-1	1-0	6	Mane [31]	0
33	24	H	Newcastle U	D	1-1	1-0	6	Salah [3]	0
34	May 8	H	Southampton	W	2-0	1-0	6	Mane [31], Thiago [90]	0
35	13	A	Manchester U	W	4-2	2-1	5	Jota [34], Firmino 2 [45, 47], Salah [90]	0
36	16	A	WBA	W	2-1	1-1	5	Salah [33], Alisson [90]	0
37	19	A	Burnley	W	3-0	1-0	4	Firmino [43], Phillips [52], Oxlade-Chamberlain [88]	3387
38	23	H	Crystal Palace	W	2-0	1-0	3	Mane 2 [36, 74]	9901

Final League Position: 3

GOALSCORERS

League (68): Salah 22 (6 pens), Mane 11, Firmino 9, Jota 9, Alexander-Arnold 2, Wijnaldum 2, Alisson 1, Henderson 1, Jones 1, Matip 1, Minamino 1, Oxlade-Chamberlain 1, Phillips 1, Robertson 1, Thiago 1, van Dijk 1, own goals 3.
FA Cup (6): Salah 3, Mane 2, Wijnaldum 1.
Carabao Cup (7): Jones 2, Minamino 2, Grujic 1, Origi 1, Shaqiri 1.
UEFA Champions League (15): Salah 6 (1 pen), Jota 4, Mane 3, Jones 1, own goal 1.
Papa John's Trophy (5): Millar 2, Cain 1, Clarkson 1, Longstaff 1.

Alisson R 33	Alexander-Arnold T 34 + 2	Gomez J 6 + 1	van Dijk V 5	Robertson A 38	Keita N 7 + 3	Henderson J 20 + 1	Wijnaldum G 34 + 4	Salah M 34 + 3	Firmino R 33 + 3	Mane S 31 + 4	Fabinho H 28 + 2	Jones C 13 + 11	Matip J 9 + 1	Thiago A 20 + 4	Milner J 11 + 15	Minamino T 2 + 7	Jota D 12 + 7	Adrian 3	Phillips N 15 + 2	Shaqiri X 5 + 9	Williams N 3 + 3	Origi D 2 + 7	Kelleher C 2	Williams R 7 + 2	Oxlade-Chamberlain A 2 + 11	Tsimikas K — + 2	Kabak O 9	Match No.
1	2^{3}	3	4	5	6^{1}	7^{2}	8	9	10	11	12	13	14															1
1	2		4	5	6^{2}	7^{1}	8	9	10^{3}	11	3			12	13	14												2
1	2	3	4	5	6^{1}		8	9	10^{3}	11^{2}	7				12	14	13											3
	2	3^{2}	4	5	6^{1}		8	9	10^{3}		7	13			14	12	11	1										4
	2	12	4^{1}	5		6	14	9	10^{2}	11	7^{3}		3	8			13	1										5
1	2	4		5		6	7	11	9^{2}	10	3				13	12	8^{1}											6
1	2	4		5		7	8	9^{3}	10^{1}	11		6^{2}			14		12		3	13								7
1	2^{2}	4		5		6	7	11	9^{1}	10			3		13		8			12								8
1				5	8^{1}		7		10	11^{3}	4	6	3		2	14	9^{2}				12	13						9
1				5		12	7	9^{2}	10	13	4	14			8^{3}	6	11		3		2^{1}							10
	12			5	14	7^{3}	8	9	10^{2}	11	4	6	3				13				2^{1}		1					11
1	2^{2}			5		7	8	9^{3}	10	11	4	6	3^{1}			12					13	14						12
1	2			5		7	8	9	10	11	4	6												3				13
1	2			5	6	7	8^{2}	12	10^{3}	9^{1}	4	13	3			11									14			14
1	2			5		7	8	9	10^{3}	11	4	6^{2}	3^{1}									14		12	13			15
1	2			5		7	12	9^{3}	10	11	4	6^{1}		13	8^{2}				3	14								16
1	2^{2}			5		3	8	9	10	11	4			7	13					12					6^{1}			17
1	2			5		4	8^{3}	9	10^{2}	11	3	12		7	14					6^{1}		13						18
1	2			5			8	12	13	11	4		3	7		14				6^{3}		10^{1}			9^{2}			19
1	2			5		4	7	9	10^{3}	11		13	3^{1}	5^{2}	8				12			14						20
1	2			5		4	7	10	13			12		6	8^{1}				3	9^{2}		11^{3}			14			21
	2			5		4	7^{1}	9	10^{3}			14		6	8				3	11^{2}		12	1		13			22
1	2			5^{3}		4	7	9	10	11	3	8^{1}		6^{2}	13					12						14		23
1	2			5		4	7^{3}	9	10	11		8^{2}		12	6^{1}					14					13		3	24
1	2			5		4^{1}	7	9	10	11		6^{2}		8^{3}					12	13		14					3	25
	2			5	13		7	9	10	11		8^{2}		6^{1}	12			1	3								4	26
1	2			5			7	9^{2}	10	11	3	8^{1}		6^{3}	14		12								13		4	27
1	13			5	8		7^{1}	10		12	14				6^{3}		11		3	9	2^{2}			4				28
1	2			5	12		8^{2}	9		11	7			6^{1}	13		10^{3}		3						14		4	29
1	2			5^{1}			13	9	10^{2}	11	7			6	8		12		3					14			4^{3}	30
1	2			5			6^{1}	9	10^{2}	13	7			12	8		11		3	14							4^{3}	31
1	2			5			7	12	10	11^{1}	3			6	8		9^{2}								13		4	32
1	2			5			7	6	10	9	3	13		8^{2}	12		11^{1}										4	33
1	2			5			8	9^{2}	12	11^{3}	7	14		6			10^{1}		3					4	13			34
1	2			5			8^{1}	9^{3}	10	12	7	13		6			11^{2}		3		14			4				35
1	2			5			13	9	10	11	7	8^{1}		6					3	12				4^{2}				36
1	2			5			8^{2}	9	10^{1}	11^{3}	7			6	13				3					4	12	14		37
1	2			5^{2}			8^{1}	9	10^{3}	11	7			6	12		13		3					4	14			38

FA Cup

Third Round	Aston Villa	(a)	4-1
Fourth Round	Manchester U	(a)	2-3

Carabao Cup

Third Round	Lincoln C	(a)	7-2
Fourth Round	Arsenal	(h)	0-0

(Arsenal won 5-4 on penalties)

Papa John's Trophy (Liverpool U21)

Group D (N)	Wigan Ath	(a)	1-6
Group D (N)	Tranmere R	(a)	2-3
Group D (N)	Port Vale	(a)	2-4

UEFA Champions League

Group D	Ajax	(a)	1-0
Group D	FC Midtjylland	(h)	2-0
Group D	Atalanta	(a)	5-0
Group D	Atalanta	(h)	0-2
Group D	Ajax	(h)	1-0
Group D	FC Midtjylland	(a)	1-1
Round of 16 1st leg	RB Leipzig	(a)	2-0
Round of 16 2nd leg	RB Leipzig	(h)	2-0
Quarter-Final 1st leg	Real Madrid	(a)	1-3
Quarter-Final 2nd leg	Real Madrid	(h)	0-0

LUTON TOWN

FOUNDATION

Formed by an amalgamation of two leading local clubs, Wanderers and Excelsior a works team, at a meeting in Luton Town Hall in April 1885. The Wanderers had three months earlier changed their name to Luton Town Wanderers and did not take too kindly to the formation of another Town club but were talked around at this meeting. Wanderers had already appeared in the FA Cup and the new club entered in its inaugural season.

Kenilworth Road Stadium, 1 Maple Road, Luton, Bedfordshire LU4 8AW.

Telephone: (01582) 411 622.

Ticket Office: (01582) 416 976.

Website: www.lutontown.co.uk

Email: info@lutontown.co.uk

Ground Capacity: 10,265.

Record Attendance: 30,069 v Blackpool, FA Cup 6th rd replay, 4 March 1959.

Pitch Measurements: 101m × 66m (110.5yd × 72yd).

Chairman: David Wilkinson.

Chief Executive: Gary Sweet.

Manager: Nathan Jones.

Assistant Manager: Mick Harford.

Colours: Orange shirts with navy blue and white trim, navy blue shorts, orange socks with navy blue trim.

Year Formed: 1885.

Turned Professional: 1890.

Ltd Co.: 1897.

Club Nickname: 'The Hatters'.

Grounds: 1885, Excelsior, Dallow Lane; 1897, Dunstable Road; 1905, Kenilworth Road.

First Football League Game: 4 September 1897, Division 2, v Leicester Fosse (a) D 1–1 – Williams; McCartney, McEwen; Davies, Stewart, Docherty; Gallacher, Coupar, Birch, McInnes, Ekins (1).

Record League Victory: 12–0 v Bristol R, Division 3 (S), 13 April 1936 – Dolman; Mackey, Smith; Finlayson, Nelson, Godfrey; Rich, Martin (1), Payne (10), Roberts (1), Stephenson.

Record Cup Victory: 9–0 v Clapton, FA Cup 1st rd (replay after abandoned game), 30 November 1927 – Abbott; Kingham, Graham; Black, Rennie, Fraser; Pointon, Yardley (4), Reid (2), Woods (1), Dennis (2).

Record Defeat: 0–9 v Small Heath, Division 2, 12 November 1898.

HONOURS

League Champions: Division 2 – 1981–82; FL 1 – 2004–05, 2018–19; Division 3S – 1936–37; Division 4 – 1967–68; Conference – 2013–14.
Runners-up: FL 2 – 2017–18; Division 2 – 1954–55, 1973–74; Division 3 – 1969–70; Division 3S – 1935–36; Third Division – 2001–02.

FA Cup: *Runners-up:* 1959.

League Cup Winners: 1988.
Runners-up: 1989.

League Trophy Winners: 2009.

Full Members' Cup: *Runners-up:* 1988.

FOOTBALL YEARBOOK FACT FILE

Arthur Pembleton joined the Luton Town groundstaff as assistant trainer in 1931 and was promoted to the post of trainer for the 1938–39 season. In November 1940 he turned out for the Hatters in their wartime game against Millwall at the age of 45 years and 289 days, more than a decade since he had turned out for Norwich City in the Football League.

Most League Points (2 for a win): 66, Division 4, 1967–68.

Most League Points (3 for a win): 98, FL 1 2004–05.

Most League Goals: 103, Division 3 (S), 1936–37.

Highest League Scorer in Season: Joe Payne, 55, Division 3 (S), 1936–37.

Most League Goals in Total Aggregate: Gordon Turner, 243, 1949–64.

Most League Goals in One Match: 10, Joe Payne v Bristol R, Division 3 (S), 13 April 1936.

Most Capped Player: Mal Donaghy, 58 (91), Northern Ireland.

Most League Appearances: Bob Morton, 495, 1948–64.

Youngest League Player: Mike O'Hara, 16 years 32 days v Stoke C, 1 October 1960.

Record Transfer Fee Received: £6,000,000 from Leicester C for James Justin, June 2019.

Record Transfer Fee Paid: £1,340,000 to HNK Rijeka for Simon Sluga, July 2019.

Football League Record: 1897 Elected to Division 2; 1900 Failed re-election; 1920 Division 3; 1921–37 Division 3 (S); 1937–55 Division 2; 1955–60 Division 1; 1960–63 Division 2; 1963–65 Division 3; 1965–68 Division 4; 1968–70 Division 3; 1970–74 Division 2; 1974–75 Division 1; 1975–82 Division 2; 1982–96 Division 1; 1996–2001 Division 2; 2001–02 Division 3; 2002–04 Division 2; 2004–05 FL 1; 2005–07 FL C; 2007–08 FL 1; 2008–09 FL 2; 2009–14 Conference Premier; 2014–18 FL 2; 2018–19 FL 1; 2019– FL C.

LATEST SEQUENCES

Longest Sequence of League Wins: 12, 19.2.2002 – 6.4.2002.

Longest Sequence of League Defeats: 8, 11.11.1899 – 6.1.1900.

Longest Sequence of League Draws: 5, 28.8.1971 – 18.9.1971.

Longest Sequence of Unbeaten League Matches: 28, 20.10.2018 – 6.4.2019.

Longest Sequence Without a League Win: 16, 9.9.1964 – 6.11.1964.

Successive Scoring Runs: 25 from 24.10.1931.

Successive Non-scoring Runs: 5 from 10.4.1973.

MANAGERS

Charlie Green 1901–28 *(Secretary-Manager)*
George Thomson 1925
John McCartney 1927–29
George Kay 1929–31
Harold Wightman 1931–35
Ted Liddell 1936–38
Neil McBain 1938–39
George Martin 1939–47
Dally Duncan 1947–58
Syd Owen 1959–60
Sam Bartram 1960–62
Bill Harvey 1962–64
George Martin 1965–66
Allan Brown 1966–68
Alec Stock 1968–72
Harry Haslam 1972–78
David Pleat 1978–86
John Moore 1986–87
Ray Harford 1987–89
Jim Ryan 1990–91
David Pleat 1991–95
Terry Westley 1995
Lennie Lawrence 1995–2000
Ricky Hill 2000
Lil Fuccillo 2000
Joe Kinnear 2001–03
Mike Newell 2003–07
Kevin Blackwell 2007–08
Mick Harford 2008–09
Richard Money 2009–11
Gary Brabin 2011–12
Paul Buckle 2012–13
John Still 2013–15
Nathan Jones 2016–19
Mick Harford 2019 *(caretaker)*
Graeme Jones 2019–20
Nathan Jones May 2020–

TEN YEAR LEAGUE RECORD

		P	*W*	*D*	*L*	*F*	*A*	*Pts*	*Pos*
2011-12	Conf P	46	22	15	9	78	42	81	5
2012-13	Conf P	46	18	13	15	70	62	67	7
2013-14	Conf P	46	30	11	5	102	35	101	1
2014-15	FL 2	46	19	11	16	54	44	68	8
2015-16	FL 2	46	19	9	18	63	61	66	11
2016-17	FL 2	46	20	17	9	70	43	77	4
2017-18	FL 2	46	25	13	8	94	46	88	2
2018-19	FL 1	46	27	13	6	90	42	94	1
2019-20	FL C	46	14	9	23	54	82	51	19
2020-21	FL C	46	17	11	18	41	52	62	12

DID YOU KNOW ?

Luton Town became the first English professional club to visit Romania with two fixtures included as part of the itinerary for their five-match tour of Eastern Europe in the summer of 1956. The Hatters beat Dinamo 2-1 but lost to the armed forces team CCA by a 5-1 margin, both games being played in front of attendances estimated at over 100,000.

LUTON TOWN – SKY BET CHAMPIONSHIP 2020–21 LEAGUE RECORD

Match No.	Date	Venue	Opponents	Result	H/T Score	Lg Pos.	Goalscorers	Attendance
1	Sept 12	A	Barnsley	W 1-0	0-0	5	Collins 71	0
2	19	H	Derby Co	W 2-1	1-0	2	Berry 34, Clark 87	0
3	26	A	Watford	L 0-1	0-1	6		0
4	Oct 3	H	Wycombe W	W 2-0	0-0	5	Ruddock 59, Lee 89	0
5	17	H	Stoke C	L 0-2	0-0	6		0
6	20	A	Millwall	L 0-2	0-1	10		0
7	24	A	Sheffield W	W 1-0	0-0	9	Ruddock 74	0
8	28	H	Nottingham F	D 1-1	1-0	9	Rea 22	0
9	31	H	Brentford	L 0-3	0-2	13		0
10	Nov 4	A	Rotherham U	W 1-0	0-0	9	Collins 70	0
11	7	A	Huddersfield T	D 1-1	1-0	10	Moncur 21	0
12	21	H	Blackburn R	D 1-1	0-0	10	Berry 69	0
13	24	H	Birmingham C	D 1-1	1-1	9	Pearson 37	0
14	28	A	Cardiff C	L 0-4	0-2	12		0
15	Dec 2	H	Norwich C	W 3-1	2-1	11	Moncur 15, Pearson 22, Collins (pen) 47	0
16	5	A	Swansea C	L 0-2	0-1	12		0
17	8	A	Coventry C	D 0-0	0-0	13		0
18	12	H	Preston NE	W 3-0	2-0	11	Collins 3 20, 29, 66	2000
19	16	A	Middlesbrough	L 0-1	0-0	13		0
20	19	H	Bournemouth	D 0-0	0-0	14		0
21	26	A	Reading	L 1-2	0-2	15	LuaLua 90	0
22	29	H	Bristol C	W 2-1	1-0	13	Rea 17, Dewsbury-Hall 68	0
23	Jan 12	H	QPR	L 0-2	0-1	14		0
24	16	A	Bournemouth	W 1-0	0-0	12	Dewsbury-Hall 67	0
25	20	A	Brentford	L 0-1	0-1	13		0
26	30	A	Blackburn R	L 0-1	0-0	13		0
27	Feb 6	H	Huddersfield T	D 1-1	1-0	15	Collins 11	0
28	13	A	Birmingham C	W 1-0	1-0	14	Potts 31	0
29	16	H	Cardiff C	L 0-2	0-0	15		0
30	20	A	Stoke C	L 0-3	0-1	16		0
31	23	H	Millwall	D 1-1	0-0	17	Adebayo 55	0
32	27	H	Sheffield W	W 3-2	0-2	14	Naismith 50, Tunnicliffe 58, Adebayo 86	0
33	Mar 2	A	Nottingham F	W 1-0	0-0	13	Tunnicliffe 64	0
34	6	A	Norwich C	L 0-3	0-2	14		0
35	13	H	Swansea C	L 0-1	0-1	16		0
36	16	H	Coventry C	W 2-0	2-0	13	Bree 23, Adebayo (pen) 42	0
37	20	A	Preston NE	W 1-0	0-0	13	Iversen (og) 83	0
38	Apr 2	A	Derby Co	L 0-2	0-1	13		0
39	5	H	Barnsley	L 1-2	0-1	13	Collins 83	0
40	10	A	Wycombe W	W 3-1	0-1	13	Moncur 80, LuaLua 85, Adebayo 88	0
41	17	H	Watford	W 1-0	0-0	13	Collins (pen) 78	0
42	21	H	Reading	D 0-0	0-0	12		0
43	25	A	Bristol C	W 3-2	0-2	11	Collins 59, Adebayo 68, Cornick 74	0
44	May 1	H	Middlesbrough	D 1-1	1-1	12	Rea 19	0
45	4	H	Rotherham U	D 0-0	0-0	12		0
46	8	A	QPR	L 1-3	1-1	12	Dewsbury-Hall 43	0

Final League Position: 12

GOALSCORERS

League (41): Collins 10 (2 pens), Adebayo 5 (1 pen), Dewsbury-Hall 3, Moncur 3, Rea 3, Berry 2, LuaLua 2, Pearson 2, Ruddock 2, Tunnicliffe 2, Bree 1, Clark 1, Cornick 1, Lee 1, Naismith 1, Potts 1, own goal 1.
FA Cup (2): Clark 1, Moncur 1.
Carabao Cup (4): Collins 3 (1 pen), Clark 1.

Sluga S 39	Cranie M 20 + 3	Pearson M 38 + 2	Bradley S 36 + 1	Norrington-Davies R 16 + 2	Berry L 22 + 9	Ruddock P 38 + 6	Rea G 33 + 7	Cornick H 28 + 12	Collins J 29 + 13	Lee E 8 + 4	LuaLua K 5 + 18	Bree J 16 + 8	Hylton D 6 + 10	Moncur G 10 + 11	Clark J 23 + 11	Tunnicliffe R 17 + 7	Morrell J 5 + 5	Lockyer T 18 + 2	Dewsbury-Hall K 36 + 3	Nombe S 1 + 10	Shea J 7	Potts D 20 + 4	Naismith K 17 + 5	Ince T 3 + 4	Adebayo E 15 + 3	Pereira D — + 1	Match No.
1	2	3	4	5	6	7	8	9^{2}	10^{3}	11^{1}	12	13	14														1
1	2	3	4	5	6	8	7^{1}	9^{2}	10	11^{3}		12		13	14												2
1	2	3	4	5	8	6		7	11^{2}	10^{1}	14		13		12	9^{3}											3
1	2	3	4	5	8	9	6	7^{2}	11^{3}	13	12		14		10^{1}												4
1	2^{2}	3	4	5	8^{3}	6	7	9		11^{1}			10	14	13		12										5
1	2	3^{3}	4	5	8^{1}	9	6			13	10		11^{2}	14	7		12										6
1	5	3	4	9		10				8^{1}	12		11			13	6^{2}	2	7								7
1	2	4	5	6		9	7		11	10^{1}	12			14	13			3^{2}	8^{3}								8
1	5	3^{1}	4	8^{2}	13	6	7		14		12		11		10^{3}			2	9								9
1	5	2	4		9	12	3	8^{2}	11		13			10^{3}		7	6^{1}	14									10
1	5	2	4		9^{3}	7	3	8^{2}	11		13	12		10^{1}		14			6								11
1	2^{5}	3	4	5	9^{4}	15	6	11^{2}	13	8^{1}	14	12		10^{3}		16			7								12
1		2	4	5	7	6	3	9^{2}	10	11^{1}				12	13				8								13
1		2	4	5	11^{2}	8^{1}	3	9^{3}	10	14		13				6^{5}	15	16	7^{4}	12							14
	2^{1}	4		5	8		6		11			12		10^{2}	7		13	3	9^{3}		1	14					15
		4■			8^{3}		6	12	11	13	14	2		10^{2}	7			3	9^{1}		1	5					16
			5		8^{1}	9	4	10^{2}	11						2		7	3	12	13	1	6					17
		2	4	12	15	8^{4}	7	9^{2}	10^{5}					11^{1}	13	14		3	6^{3}	16	1	5					18
		2	4	10^{2}	12	9^{4}	7^{5}	8^{3}	11				16	14	15	13		3	6^{1}		1	5					19
	2	14	4	6	9	7		12	11^{2}				10^{1}					3	8	13	1	5^{3}					20
	2^{3}		4	13	8	9^{4}	6^{2}	16	11		15		14	10^{1}	7			3	12		1	5^{5}					21
1		2	4	5		10^{2}	6	7^{3}	11		13				14	8^{1}		3	9			12					22
1			4		13	6^{4}	7	9	10^{2}		11^{3}	2	15	14				3	8	12		5^{1}					23
1		14	5		7	8	4	10^{2}	11^{3}			2^{4}	15		13			3^{1}	9			6	12				24
1			4		8^{2}	6		7	11^{3}		14	2	16	10^{1}	12	13		3■	9^{5}			5^{4}	15				25
1	13	2^{2}	4			8	6^{4}	7	11^{1}				12		10^{3}			3	9	15		5	14				26
1		2	4		7^{1}	6	12	9^{2}	10						11^{3}			3	8			5	14	13			27
1		2	4			9	6	7	11						10^{1}			3	8			5	12				28
1	12	2^{2}	4		13	8	6	14	11^{5}				7^{3}					3^{1}	9			5	10^{4}	15	16		29
1	3^{3}		4			6^{2}	7	9^{5}	10^{4}			2^{1}	16	14	11	13	12		8			5			15		30
1	2		3		14	13	12	16	15						5	6^{3}	7^{1}		8^{4}			4	9	10^{2}	11^{5}		31
1	3^{3}	2				12	14	13							5	6	7^{2}		8			4	9	10^{1}	11		32
1		3				9	6	10^{2}	12			13			2	7			8			5	4		11^{1}		33
1	2	3			10^{1}	13		14	11^{3}			16		9^{4}	12	7			8^{5}			5	4	6^{2}	15		34
1	12	2^{3}				6		10^{2}	13		14	5			9	7			8			4^{1}	3		11		35
1		2				6	3	10^{2}	13			5			9	7			8	12			4		11^{1}		36
1		3				7	6	10^{3}	14			2			5	9^{1}			8	13			4	12	11^{2}		37
1		3			15	6	7^{1}	10^{3}	14			2			5	9			8^{4}	13			4	12	11^{2}		38
1	5^{4}	3	13		16	9	7^{2}	12	14		15				2	6^{5}			8	10^{1}			4		11^{3}		39
1		3^{4}	4		9^{2}	6	16	13	11^{5}		14	2^{3}		15	8	7^{1}			12				5		10		40
1		3	4		9^{2}	7	13		12		10	2			8				6			14	5^{3}		11^{1}		41
1		3	4			7	14	12	15		10^{1}	2		13	8^{2}	6^{3}			9				5		11^{4}		42
1		3	4			6	15	12	13		10^{1}	2			8^{3}	9^{2}			7			14	5		11^{4}		43
1		3	4			6	7	8^{1}	11^{2}			2		12					9	13			5		10		44
1		2	3			13	7	12	11^{2}		14	5				6^{3}			8			9^{1}	4		10		45
1		3	4		12	8	7^{3}	9^{2}	13		14	2^{4}		11^{1}					6				5		10	15	46

FA Cup

Third Round	Reading	(h)	1-0
Fourth Round	Chelsea	(a)	1-3

Carabao Cup

First Round	Norwich C	(h)	3-1
Second Round	Reading	(a)	1-0
Third Round	Manchester U	(h)	0-3

MANCHESTER CITY

FOUNDATION

Manchester City was formed as a limited company in 1894 after their predecessors Ardwick had been forced into bankruptcy. However, many historians like to trace the club's lineage as far back as 1880 when St Mark's Church, West Gorton added a football section to their cricket club. They amalgamated with Belle Vue for one season before splitting again under the name Gorton Association FC in 1884–85. In 1887 Gorton AFC turned professional and moved ground to Hyde Road under the new name Ardwick AFC.

Etihad Stadium, Etihad Campus, Manchester M11 3FF.

Telephone: (0161) 444 1894.

Ticket Office: (0161) 444 1894.

Website: www.mancity.com

Email: mancity@mancity.com

Ground Capacity: 55,017.

Record Attendance: 84,569 v Stoke C, FA Cup 6th rd, 3 March 1934 (at Maine Road; British record for any game outside London or Glasgow); 54,693 v Leicester C, Premier League, 6 February 2016 (at Etihad Stadium).

Pitch Measurements: 105m × 68m (115yd × 74.5yd).

Chairman: Khaldoon Al Mubarak.

Chief Executive: Ferran Soriano.

Manager: Pep Guardiola.

Assistant Managers: Juan Manuel Lillo, Rodolfo Borrell, Lorenzo Buenaventura, Manel Estiarte, Xabier Manisidor, Carles Planchart.

Colours: Light blue shirts with white trim, white shorts, light blue socks.

Year Formed: 1887 as Ardwick FC; 1894 as Manchester City.

Turned Professional: 1887 as Ardwick FC.

Previous Names: 1880, St Mark's Church, West Gorton; 1884, Gorton; 1887, Ardwick; 1894, Manchester City.

Club Nicknames: 'The Blues', 'The Citizens'.

Grounds: 1880, Clowes Street; 1881, Kirkmanshulme Cricket Ground; 1882, Queens Road; 1884, Pink Bank Lane; 1887, Hyde Road (1894–1923 as City); 1923, Maine Road; 2003, City of Manchester Stadium (renamed Etihad Stadium 2011).

First Football League Game: 3 September 1892, Division 2, v Bootle (h) W 7–0 – Douglas; McVickers, Robson; Middleton, Russell, Hopkins; Davies (3), Morris (2), Angus (1), Weir (1), Milarvie.

Record League Victory: 10–1 v Huddersfield T, Division 2, 7 November 1987 – Nixon; Gidman, Hinchcliffe, Clements, Lake, Redmond, White (3), Stewart (3), Adcock (3), McNab (1), Simpson.

Record Cup Victory: 10–1 v Swindon T, FA Cup 4th rd, 29 January 1930 – Barber; Felton, McCloy; Barrass, Cowan, Heinemann; Toseland, Marshall (5), Tait (3), Johnson (1), Brook (1).

HONOURS

League Champions: Premier League – 2011–12, 2013–14, 2017–18, 2018–19, 2020–21; Division 1 – 1936–37, 1967–68; First Division – 2001–02; Division 2 – 1898–99, 1902–03, 1909–10, 1927–28, 1946–47, 1965–66.
Runners-up: Premier League – 2012–13, 2014–15, 2019–20; Division 1 – 1903–04, 1920–21, 1976–77; First Division – 1999–2000; Division 2 – 1895–96, 1950–51, 1988–89.

FA Cup Winners: 1904, 1934, 1956, 1969, 2011, 2019.
Runners-up: 1926, 1933, 1955, 1981, 2013.

League Cup Winners: 1970, 1976, 2014, 2016, 2018, 2019, 2020, 2021.
Runners-up: 1974.

Full Members Cup: *Runners-up:* 1986.

European Competitions
European Cup: 1968–69.
Champions League: 2011–12, 2012–13, 2013–14, 2014–15, 2015–16 *(sf)*, 2016–17, 2017–18 *(qf)*, 2018–19 *(sf)*, 2019–20 *(qf)*, 2020–21 *(runners-up)*.
UEFA Cup: 1972–73, 1976–77, 1977–78, 1978–79 *(qf)*, 2003–04, 2008–09 *(qf)*.
Europa League: 2010–11, 2011–12.
European Cup-Winners' Cup: 1969–70 *(winners)*, 1970–71 *(sf)*.

FOOTBALL YEARBOOK FACT FILE

Peter Dobing achieved the rare feat of scoring a hat-trick for Manchester City in both the home and away Football League fixtures against West Ham United in the 1961–62 season. He scored three in the game at Maine Road in November and a further triple in the return match the following March.

Record Defeat: 1–9 v Everton, Division 1, 3 September 1906.

Most League Points (2 for a win): 62, Division 2, 1946–47.

Most League Points (3 for a win): 100, Premier League, 2017–18.

Most League Goals: 108, Division 2, 1926–27, 108, Division 1, 2001–02.

Highest League Scorer in Season: Tommy Johnson, 38, Division 1, 1928–29.

Most League Goals in Total Aggregate: Sergio Aguero, 180, 2011–20.

Most League Goals in One Match: 5, Fred Williams v Darwen, Division 2, 18 February 1899; 5, Tom Browell v Burnley, Division 2, 24 October 1925; 5, Tom Johnson v Everton, Division 1, 15 September 1928; 5, George Smith v Newport Co, Division 2, 14 June 1947; 5, Sergio Aguero v Newcastle U, Premier League, 3 October 2015.

Most Capped Player: David Silva, 87 (125), Spain.

Most League Appearances: Alan Oakes, 564, 1959–76.

Youngest League Player: Glyn Pardoe, 15 years 314 days v Birmingham C, 11 April 1962.

Record Transfer Fee Received: £44,700,000 from Bayern Munich for Leroy Sane, July 2020.

Record Transfer Fee Paid: £65,000,000 to Benfica for Ruben Dias, September 2020.

Football League Record: 1892 Ardwick elected founder member of Division 2; 1894 Newly-formed Manchester C elected to Division 2; Division 1 1899–1902, 1903–09, 1910–26, 1928–38, 1947–50, 1951–63, 1966–83, 1985–87, 1989–92; Division 2 1902–03, 1909–10, 1926–28, 1938–47, 1950–51, 1963–66, 1983–85, 1987–89; 1992–96 Premier League; 1996–98 Division 1; 1998–99 Division 2; 1999–2000 Division 1; 2000–01 Premier League; 2001–02 Division 1; 2002– Premier League.

LATEST SEQUENCES

Longest Sequence of League Wins: 18, 26.8.2017 – 27.12.2017.

Longest Sequence of League Defeats: 8, 23.8.1995 – 14.10.1995.

Longest Sequence of League Draws: 7, 5.10.2009 – 28.11.2009.

Longest Sequence of Unbeaten League Matches: 30, 8.4.2017 – 2.1.2018.

Longest Sequence Without a League Win: 17, 26.12.1979 – 7.4.1980.

Successive Scoring Runs: 44 from 3.10.1936.

Successive Non-scoring Runs: 6 from 30.1.1971.

MANAGERS

Joshua Parlby 1893–95
(Secretary-Manager)
Sam Omerod 1895–1902
Tom Maley 1902–06
Harry Newbould 1906–12
Ernest Magnall 1912–24
David Ashworth 1924–25
Peter Hodge 1926–32
Wilf Wild 1932–46
(continued as Secretary to 1950)
Sam Cowan 1946–47
John 'Jock' Thomson 1947–50
Leslie McDowall 1950–63
George Poyser 1963–65
Joe Mercer 1965–71
(continued as General Manager to 1972)
Malcolm Allison 1972–73
Johnny Hart 1973
Ron Saunders 1973–74
Tony Book 1974–79
Malcolm Allison 1979–80
John Bond 1980–83
John Benson 1983
Billy McNeill 1983–86
Jimmy Frizzell 1986–87
(continued as General Manager)
Mel Machin 1987–89
Howard Kendall 1989–90
Peter Reid 1990–93
Brian Horton 1993–95
Alan Ball 1995–96
Steve Coppell 1996
Frank Clark 1996–98
Joe Royle 1998–2001
Kevin Keegan 2001–05
Stuart Pearce 2005–07
Sven-Göran Eriksson 2007–08
Mark Hughes 2008–09
Roberto Mancini 2009–13
Manuel Pellegrini 2013–16
Pep Guardiola June 2016–

TEN YEAR LEAGUE RECORD

		P	W	D	L	F	A	Pts	Pos
2011-12	PR Lge	38	28	5	5	93	29	89	1
2012-13	PR Lge	38	23	9	6	66	34	78	2
2013-14	PR Lge	38	27	5	6	102	37	86	1
2014-15	PR Lge	38	24	7	7	83	38	79	2
2015-16	PR Lge	38	19	9	10	71	41	66	4
2016-17	PR Lge	38	23	9	6	80	39	78	3
2017-18	PR Lge	38	32	4	2	106	27	100	1
2018-19	PR Lge	38	32	2	4	95	23	98	1
2019-20	PR Lge	38	26	3	9	102	35	81	2
2020-21	PR Lge	38	27	5	6	83	32	86	1

Manchester City wing-half Ken Barnes scored a hat-trick of penalties in the 6-2 home win over Everton on 7 December 1957. Barnes achieved the remarkable feat with goals after 15, 17 and 48 minutes of the game thus giving him a record of eight successes from nine kicks in the season to date.

MANCHESTER CITY – PREMIER LEAGUE 2020–21 LEAGUE RECORD

Match No.	Date	Venue	Opponents	Result	H/T Score	Lg Pos.	Goalscorers	Attendance
1	Sept 21	A	Wolverhampton W	W 3-1	2-0	7	De Bruyne (pen) [20], Foden [32], Gabriel Jesus [90]	0
2	27	H	Leicester C	L 2-5	1-1	13	Mahrez [4], Ake [84]	0
3	Oct 3	A	Leeds U	D 1-1	1-0	11	Sterling [17]	0
4	17	H	Arsenal	W 1-0	1-0	9	Sterling [23]	0
5	24	A	West Ham U	D 1-1	0-1	12	Foden [51]	0
6	31	A	Sheffield U	W 1-0	1-0	8	Walker [28]	0
7	Nov 8	H	Liverpool	D 1-1	1-1	10	Gabriel Jesus [31]	0
8	21	A	Tottenham H	L 0-2	0-1	11		0
9	28	H	Burnley	W 5-0	3-0	8	Mahrez 3 [6, 22, 69], Mendy [41], Torres [66]	0
10	Dec 5	H	Fulham	W 2-0	2-0	5	Sterling [5], De Bruyne (pen) [26]	0
11	12	A	Manchester U	D 0-0	0-0	9		0
12	15	H	WBA	D 1-1	1-1	6	Gundogan [30]	0
13	19	A	Southampton	W 1-0	1-0	6	Sterling [16]	2000
14	26	H	Newcastle U	W 2-0	1-0	5	Gundogan [14], Torres [55]	0
15	Jan 3	A	Chelsea	W 3-1	3-0	5	Gundogan [18], Foden [21], De Bruyne [34]	0
16	13	H	Brighton & HA	W 1-0	1-0	3	Foden [44]	0
17	17	H	Crystal Palace	W 4-0	1-0	2	Stones 2 [26, 68], Gundogan [56], Sterling [88]	0
18	20	H	Aston Villa	W 2-0	0-0	2	Bernardo Silva [79], Gundogan (pen) [90]	0
19	26	A	WBA	W 5-0	4-0	1	Gundogan 2 [6, 30], Joao Cancelo [20], Mahrez [45], Sterling [57]	0
20	30	H	Sheffield U	W 1-0	1-0	1	Gabriel Jesus [9]	0
21	Feb 3	A	Burnley	W 2-0	2-0	1	Gabriel Jesus [3], Sterling [38]	0
22	7	A	Liverpool	W 4-1	0-0	1	Gundogan 2 [49, 73], Sterling [76], Foden [83]	0
23	13	H	Tottenham H	W 3-0	1-0	1	Rodri (pen) [23], Gundogan 2 [50, 66]	0
24	17	A	Everton	W 3-1	1-1	1	Foden [32], Mahrez [63], Bernardo Silva [77]	0
25	21	A	Arsenal	W 1-0	1-0	1	Sterling [2]	0
26	27	H	West Ham U	W 2-1	1-1	1	Dias [30], Stones [68]	0
27	Mar 2	H	Wolverhampton W	W 4-1	1-0	1	Dendoncker (og) [15], Gabriel Jesus 2 [80, 90], Mahrez [90]	0
28	7	H	Manchester U	L 0-2	0-1	1		0
29	10	H	Southampton	W 5-2	3-1	1	De Bruyne 2 [15, 59], Mahrez 2 [40, 55], Gundogan [45]	0
30	13	A	Fulham	W 3-0	0-0	1	Stones [47], Gabriel Jesus [56], Aguero (pen) [60]	0
31	Apr 3	A	Leicester C	W 2-0	0-0	1	Mendy [58], Gabriel Jesus [74]	0
32	10	H	Leeds U	L 1-2	0-1	1	Torres [76]	0
33	21	A	Aston Villa	W 2-1	2-1	1	Foden [22], Rodri [40]	0
34	May 1	A	Crystal Palace	W 2-0	0-0	1	Aguero [57], Torres [59]	0
35	8	H	Chelsea	L 1-2	1-0	1	Sterling [44]	0
36	14	A	Newcastle U	W 4-3	2-2	1	Joao Cancelo [39], Torres 3 [42, 64, 66]	0
37	18	A	Brighton & HA	L 2-3	1-0	1	Gundogan [2], Foden [48]	7945
38	23	H	Everton	W 5-0	2-0	1	De Bruyne [11], Gabriel Jesus [14], Foden [53], Aguero 2 [71, 76]	10,000

Final League Position: 1

GOALSCORERS

League (83): Gundogan 13 (1 pen), Sterling 10, Foden 9, Gabriel Jesus 9, Mahrez 9, Torres 7, De Bruyne 6 (2 pens), Aguero 4 (1 pen), Stones 4, Bernardo Silva 2, Joao Cancelo 2, Mendy 2, Rodri 2 (1 pen), Ake 1, Dias 1, Walker 1, own goal 1.
FA Cup (11): Bernardo Silva 2, Foden 2, Gabriel Jesus 2, De Bruyne 1, Gundogan 1, Sterling 1, Torres 1, Walker 1.
Carabao Cup (12): Foden 2, Laporte 2, Sterling 2, Delap 1, Fernandinho 1, Gabriel Jesus 1, Mahrez 1, Stones 1, Torres 1.
UEFA Champions League (25): Mahrez 4 (1 pen), Torres 4, De Bruyne 3, Foden 3, Gundogan 3, Aguero 2 (1 pen), Gabriel Jesus 2, Bernardo Silva 1, Joao Cancelo 1, Sterling 1, own goal 1.
Papa John's Trophy (9): Delap 3, Edozie 2, Knight 2, Bernabe 1, Simmonds 1.

Ederson d 36	Walker K 22 + 2	Stones J 22	Ake N 9 + 1	Mendy B 11 + 2	Fernandinho L 12 + 9	Rodri R 31 + 3	Foden P 17 + 11	De Bruyne K 23 + 2	Sterling R 28 + 3	Gabriel Jesus F 22 + 7	Torres F 15 + 9	Garcia E 3 + 3	Mahrez R 23 + 4	Delap L — + 1	Dias R 32	Laporte A 14 + 2	Bernardo Silva M 24 + 2	Joao Cancelo C 27 + 1	Aguero S 7 + 5	Gundogan I 23 + 5	Zinchenko A 15 + 5	Steffen Z 1	Carson S 1	Match No.
1	2	3	4	5	6	7	8	9	10^1	11	12													1
1	2		4	5	6^1	7	10^2	9	11		13	3	8	12										2
1	2		13	5^2	14	7	8	6	11		9^1		10^3		3	4	12							3
1	2		4		13	5	9^2		10				6		3		8	7	11^1	12				4
1	2^3					7	12	13	11			4	9		3		6^2	5	10^1	8	14			5
1	2					7	12	6	11		10^1		9^2		3	4	8	5		13				6
1	2					6		9	10	11	8^1				3	4	12	5		7				7
1	2					7	13	6	12	10	11		9^1		3	4	8^2	5						8
1	2	3		5	12	6^1	13	9		11	10^2	14	8		4^3					7				9
1		3		5		6		9	10	11			8		4			2		7				10
1	2	3			7	6		9	10	11	12		8^1		4			5						11
1	12		4	5^1		6	10^2	9	8	11					3			2	13	7				12
1	2	3				7		9	10		11^1		12		4		8	5		6				13
1		2	4		12	6^1	14	7	9		10^2				3		11	5	13	8^3				14
		3			12	7	10^2	9^3	11				14		4		8	2	13	6^1	5	1		15
1		3				7	11^2	6	13	12			9^1		4		10	2		8	5			16
1	2	3			7		12	6^3	11	10	13				4		9^1	14		8^2	5			17
1	2^1	3				7	11	6^2	9^3	13			14		4		10	5		8	12			18
1		3				7	11^1		9	14	12		10		4	13	6^3	2		8^2	5			19
1	2				7	12	11			10	9^1				3	4	6			8	5			20
1		3				7			11	10			9		4	5	6	2^1		8	12			21
1		3				7	10		11	12			9^1		4		6	2		8	5			22
1		3				7	9		11	10^2	12		13			4	6	2		8^1	5			23
1	2				13	7^2	8	12	11^1	10			9		3	4	6	5						24
1		3			7			6^1	11	12			9		4		10	2		8	5			25
1	2	3			7	14	13	6		12	11^2		9		4				10^1	8^3	5			26
1	2					7		8	11	10			9		3	4	6^1	5		12				27
1	12	3				7	13	6	11	10^2			9		4			2^1		8	5			28
1	2			14	7		11	6^2			12		9^1		3	4	10		13	8	5^3			29
1		2		8	12	7				11	9	13			3^2	4	6^1	5	10					30
1	2			5	6	7	14	9^3	12	10	13		8^2		3	4			11^1					31
1		3	4^1	5^2	7		13		11	10	9						6	2		12	8			32
1	2	3■			13	7	11			10^1			9^2		4	12	6			8	5			33
1			3	5	7^1	8			9	11	6					4		2	10		12			34
1			4	9^3		5	12		8	10	7^2				2	3		6	11^1	13	14			35
	2		4	12		7			11	10	9	3					6	5^1		8			1	36
1		3			13	7	11			14	10^1	12	9		4		6^3	2■		8^2	5			37
1	2	3			7	12	8^1	6	11	10^3	14		9^2		4				13		5			38

FA Cup

Third Round	Birmingham C	(h)	3-0
Fourth Round	Cheltenham T	(a)	3-1
Fifth Round	Swansea C	(a)	3-1
Sixth Round	Everton	(a)	2-0
Semi-Final	Chelsea	(a)	0-1

Carabao Cup

Third Round	Bournemouth	(h)	2-1
Fourth Round	Burnley	(a)	3-0
Quarter-Final	Arsenal	(a)	4-1
Semi-Final	Manchester U	(a)	2-0
Final	Tottenham H	(Wembley)	1-0

Papa John's Trophy (Manchester C U21)

Group E (N)	Mansfield T	(a)	3-0
Group E (N)	Scunthorpe U	(a)	4-0
Group E (N)	Lincoln C	(a)	1-1

(Lincoln C won 4-3 on penalties)

Second Round (N)	Tranmere R	(a)	1-2

UEFA Champions League

Group C	Porto	(h)	3-1
Group C	Marseille	(a)	3-0
Group C	Olympiacos	(h)	3-0
Group C	Olympiacos	(a)	1-0
Group C	Porto	(a)	0-0
Group C	Marseille	(h)	3-0
Round of 16 1st leg	Borussia M'Gladbach	(a)	2-0
Round of 16 2nd leg	Borussia M'Gladbach	(h)	2-0
Quarter-Final 1st leg	Borussia Dortmund	(h)	2-1
Quarter-Final 2nd leg	Borussia Dortmund	(a)	2-1
Semi-Final 1st leg	Paris Saint-Germain	(a)	2-1
Semi-Final 2nd leg	Paris Saint-Germain	(h)	2-0
Final	Chelsea	(Porto)	0-1

MANCHESTER UNITED

FOUNDATION

Manchester United was formed as comparatively recently as 1902 after their predecessors, Newton Heath, went bankrupt. However, it is usual to give the date of the club's foundation as 1878 when the dining room committee of the carriage and waggon works of the Lancashire and Yorkshire Railway Company formed Newton Heath L and YR Cricket and Football Club. They won the Manchester Cup in 1886 and as Newton Heath FC were admitted to the Second Division in 1892.

Old Trafford, Sir Matt Busby Way, Manchester M16 0RA.

Telephone: (0161) 868 8000.

Ticket Office: (0161) 868 8000 (option 1).

Website: www.manutd.co.uk

Email: enquiries@manutd.co.uk

Ground Capacity: 74,140.

Record Attendance: 76,098 v Blackburn R, Premier League, 31 March 2007. 83,260 v Arsenal, First Division, 17 January 1948 (at Maine Road – United shared City's ground after Old Trafford suffered World War II bomb damage).

Ground Record Attendance: 76,962 Wolverhampton W v Grimsby T, FA Cup semi-final, 25 March 1939.

Pitch Measurements: 105m × 68m (115yd × 74.5yd).

Co-Chairmen: Joel Glazer, Avram Glazer.

Chief Executive: Edward Woodward.

Manager: Ole Gunnar Solskjaer.

Assistant Managers: Mike Phelan, Martyn Pert.

Colours: Red shirts with white trim, white shorts with red trim, black socks with white trim.

Year Formed: 1878 as Newton Heath LYR; 1902, Manchester United.

Turned Professional: 1885.

Previous Name: 1880, Newton Heath; 1902, Manchester United.

Club Nickname: 'Red Devils'.

Grounds: 1880, North Road, Monsall Road; 1893, Bank Street; 1910, Old Trafford (played at Maine Road 1941–49).

HONOURS

League Champions: Premier League – 1992–93, 1993–94, 1995–96, 1996–97, 1998–99, 1999–2000, 2000–01, 2002–03, 2006–07, 2007–08, 2008–09, 2010–11, 2012–13; Division 1 – 1907–08, 1910–11, 1951–52, 1955–56, 1956–57, 1964–65, 1966–67; Division 2 – 1935–36, 1974–75.
Runners-up: Premier League – 1994–95, 1997–98, 2005–06, 2009–10, 2011–12, 2017–18, 2020–21; Division 1 – 1946–47, 1947–48, 1948–49, 1950–51, 1958–59, 1963–64, 1967–68, 1979–80, 1987–88, 1991–92; Division 2 – 1896–97, 1905–06, 1924–25, 1937–38.

FA Cup Winners: 1909, 1948, 1963, 1977, 1983, 1985, 1990, 1994, 1996, 1999, 2004, 2016.
Runners-up: 1957, 1958, 1976, 1979, 1995, 2005, 2007, 2018.

League Cup Winners: 1992, 2006, 2009, 2010, 2017.
Runners-up: 1983, 1991, 1994, 2003.

European Competitions
European Cup: 1956–57 *(sf)*, 1957–58 *(sf)*, 1965–66 *(sf)*, 1967–68 *(winners)*, 1968–69 *(sf)*.
Champions League: 1993–94, 1994–95, 1996–97 *(sf)*, 1997–98 *(qf)*, 1998–99 *(winners)*, 1999–2000 *(qf)*, 2000–01 *(qf)*, 2001–02 *(sf)*, 2002–03 *(qf)*, 2003–04, 2004–05, 2005–06, 2006–07 *(sf)*, 2007–08 *(winners)*, 2008–09 *(runners-up)*, 2009–10 *(qf)*, 2010–11 *(runners-up)*, 2011–12, 2012–13, 2013–14 *(qf)*, 2015–16, 2017–18, 2018–19, 2020–21.
Fairs Cup: 1964–65.
UEFA Cup: 1976–77, 1980–81, 1982–83, 1984–85 *(qf)*, 1992–93, 1995–96.
Europa League: 2011–12, 2015–16, 2016–17 *(winners)*, 2019–20, 2020–21 *(runners-up)*.
European Cup-Winners' Cup: 1963–64 *(qf)*, 1977–78, 1983–84 *(sf)*, 1990–91 *(winners)*. 1991–92.
Super Cup: 1991 *(winners)*, 1999, 2008.
World Club Championship: 1968, 1999 *(winners)*, 2000.
FIFA Club World Cup: 2008 *(winners)*.
NB: In 1958–59 FA refused permission to compete in European Cup.

FOOTBALL YEARBOOK FACT FILE

The first player to sign for Manchester United as a professional following their change of name from Newton Heath was centre-forward Dick Pegg. Pegg, whose contract was registered with the FA on 3 June 1902, went on to stay at the club for two seasons, scoring 20 goals from 51 appearances before moving on to play for Fulham.

First Football League Game: 3 September 1892, Division 1, v Blackburn R (a) L 3–4 – Warner; Clements, Brown; Perrins, Stewart, Erentz; Farman (1), Coupar (1), Donaldson (1), Carson, Mathieson.

Record League Victory (as Newton Heath): 10–1 v Wolverhampton W, Division 1, 15 October 1892 – Warner; Mitchell, Clements; Perrins, Stewart (3), Erentz; Farman (1), Hood (1), Donaldson (3), Carson (1), Hendry (1).

Record League Victory (as Manchester U): 9–0 v Ipswich T, Premier League, 4 March 1995 – Schmeichel; Keane (1) (Sharpe), Irwin, Bruce (Butt), Kanchelskis, Pallister, Cole (5), Ince (1), McClair, Hughes (2), Giggs; 9–0 v Southampton, Premier League, 2 February 2021 – De Gea, Wan Bissaka (1), Lindelof, Maguire, Shaw (Martial (2)), McTominay (1), Fred, Rashford (1) (James (1)), Bruno Fernandes (1 pen), Greenwood, Cavani (1) (van der Beek), 1 own goal.

Record Cup Victory: 10–0 v RSC Anderlecht, European Cup prel. rd 2nd leg, 26 September 1956 – Wood; Foulkes, Byrne; Colman, Jones, Edwards; Berry (1), Whelan (2), Taylor (3), Viollet (4), Pegg.

Record Defeat: 0–7 v Blackburn R, Division 1, 10 April 1926; 0–7 v Aston Villa, Division 1, 27 December 1930; 0–7 v Wolverhampton W, Division 2, 26 December 1931.

Most League Points (2 for a win): 64, Division 1, 1956–57.

Most League Points (3 for a win): 92, Premier League, 1993–94.

Most League Goals: 103, Division 1, 1956–57 and 1958–59.

Highest League Scorer in Season: Dennis Viollet, 32, 1959–60.

Most League Goals in Total Aggregate: Bobby Charlton, 199, 1956–73.

Most League Goals in One Match: 5, Andrew Cole v Ipswich T, Premier League, 3 March 1995; 5, Dimitar Berbatov v Blackburn R, Premier League, 27 November 2010.

Most Capped Player: Bobby Charlton, 106, England.

Most League Appearances: Ryan Giggs, 672, 1991–2014.

Youngest League Player: Jeff Whitefoot, 16 years 105 days v Portsmouth, 15 April 1950.

Record Transfer Fee Received: £80,000,000 from Real Madrid for Cristiano Ronaldo, July 2009.

Record Transfer Fee Paid: £89,300,000 to Juventus for Paul Pogba, August 2016.

Football League Record: 1892 Newton Heath elected to Division 1; 1894–1906 Division 2; 1906–22 Division 1; 1922–25 Division 2; 1925–31 Division 1; 1931–36 Division 2; 1936–37 Division 1; 1937–38 Division 2; 1938–74 Division 1; 1974–75 Division 2; 1975–92 Division 1; 1992– Premier League.

MANAGERS

J. Ernest Mangnall 1903–12
John Bentley 1912–14
John Robson 1914–21
(Secretary-Manager from 1916)
John Chapman 1921–26
Clarence Hilditch 1926–27
Herbert Bamlett 1927–31
Walter Crickmer 1931–32
Scott Duncan 1932–37
Walter Crickmer 1937–45
(Secretary-Manager)
Matt Busby 1945–69
(continued as General Manager then Director)
Wilf McGuinness 1969–70
Sir Matt Busby 1970–71
Frank O'Farrell 1971–72
Tommy Docherty 1972–77
Dave Sexton 1977–81
Ron Atkinson 1981–86
Sir Alex Ferguson 1986–2013
David Moyes 2013–14
Louis van Gaal 2014–16
Jose Mourinho 2016–18
Ole Gunnar Solskjaer December 2018–

LATEST SEQUENCES

Longest Sequence of League Wins: 14, 15.10.1904 – 3.1.1905.

Longest Sequence of League Defeats: 14, 26.4.1930 – 25.10.1930.

Longest Sequence of League Draws: 6, 30.10.1988 – 27.11.1988.

Longest Sequence of Unbeaten League Matches: 29, 11.4.2010 – 1.2.2011.

Longest Sequence Without a League Win: 16, 19.4.1930 – 25.10.1930.

Successive Scoring Runs: 36 from 3.12.2007.

Successive Non-scoring Runs: 5 from 7.2.1981.

TEN YEAR LEAGUE RECORD

		P	W	D	L	F	A	Pts	Pos
2011-12	PR Lge	38	28	5	5	89	33	89	2
2012-13	PR Lge	38	28	5	5	86	43	89	1
2013-14	PR Lge	38	19	7	12	64	43	64	7
2014-15	PR Lge	38	20	10	8	62	37	70	4
2015-16	PR Lge	38	19	9	10	49	35	66	5
2016-17	PR Lge	38	18	15	5	54	29	69	6
2017-18	PR Lge	38	25	6	7	68	28	81	2
2018-19	PR Lge	38	19	9	10	65	54	66	6
2019-20	PR Lge	38	18	12	8	66	36	66	3
2020-21	PR Lge	38	21	11	6	73	44	74	2

DID YOU KNOW ?

Dennis Viollet scored hat-tricks for Manchester United in both the home and away fixtures against Burnley in the 1960–61 campaign. Viollet, who missed much of the season through injury and loss of form, netted his trebles in a 5-3 defeat at Turf Moor in October, and a 6-0 win at Old Trafford in April.

MANCHESTER UNITED – PREMIER LEAGUE 2020–21 LEAGUE RECORD

Match No.	*Date*	*Venue*	*Opponents*	*Result*		*H/T Score*	*Lg Pos.*	*Goalscorers*	*Attendance*
1	Sept 19	H	Crystal Palace	L	1-3	0-1	15	van de Beek [80]	0
2	26	A	Brighton & HA	W	3-2	1-1	13	Dunk (og) [43], Rashford [55], Bruno Fernandes (pen) [90]	0
3	Oct 4	H	Tottenham H	L	1-6	1-4	16	Bruno Fernandes (pen) [2]	0
4	17	A	Newcastle U	W	4-1	1-1	14	Maguire [23], Bruno Fernandes [86], Wan Bissaka [90], Rashford [90]	0
5	24	H	Chelsea	D	0-0	0-0	15		0
6	Nov 1	H	Arsenal	L	0-1	0-0	15		0
7	7	A	Everton	W	3-1	2-1	14	Bruno Fernandes 2 [25, 32], Cavani [90]	0
8	21	H	WBA	W	1-0	0-0	9	Bruno Fernandes (pen) [56]	0
9	29	A	Southampton	W	3-2	0-2	8	Bruno Fernandes [60], Cavani 2 [74, 90]	0
10	Dec 5	A	West Ham U	W	3-1	0-1	4	Pogba [65], Greenwood [68], Rashford [78]	2000
11	12	H	Manchester C	D	0-0	0-0	8		0
12	17	A	Sheffield U	W	3-2	2-1	6	Rashford 2 [26, 51], Martial [33]	0
13	20	H	Leeds U	W	6-2	4-1	3	McTominay 2 [2, 3], Bruno Fernandes 2 (1 pen) [20, 70 (p)], Lindelof [37], James [66]	0
14	26	A	Leicester C	D	2-2	1-1	4	Rashford [23], Bruno Fernandes [79]	0
15	29	H	Wolverhampton W	W	1-0	0-0	2	Rashford [90]	0
16	Jan 1	H	Aston Villa	W	2-1	1-0	2	Martial [40], Bruno Fernandes (pen) [61]	0
17	12	A	Burnley	W	1-0	0-0	1	Pogba [71]	0
18	17	A	Liverpool	D	0-0	0-0	1		0
19	20	A	Fulham	W	2-1	1-1	1	Cavani [21], Pogba [65]	0
20	27	H	Sheffield U	L	1-2	0-1	2	Maguire [64]	0
21	30	A	Arsenal	D	0-0	0-0	2		0
22	Feb 2	H	Southampton	W	9-0	4-0	2	Wan Bissaka [18], Rashford [25], Bednarek (og) [34], Cavani [39], Martial 2 [69, 90], McTominay [71], Bruno Fernandes (pen) [87], James [90]	0
23	6	H	Everton	D	3-3	2-0	2	Cavani [24], Bruno Fernandes [45], McTominay [70]	0
24	14	A	WBA	D	1-1	1-1	2	Bruno Fernandes [44]	0
25	21	H	Newcastle U	W	3-1	1-1	2	Rashford [30], James [57], Bruno Fernandes (pen) [75]	0
26	28	A	Chelsea	D	0-0	0-0	2		0
27	Mar 3	A	Crystal Palace	D	0-0	0-0	2		0
28	7	A	Manchester C	W	2-0	1-0	2	Bruno Fernandes (pen) [2], Shaw [50]	0
29	14	H	West Ham U	W	1-0	0-0	2	Dawson (og) [53]	0
30	Apr 4	H	Brighton & HA	W	2-1	0-1	2	Rashford [62], Greenwood [83]	0
31	11	A	Tottenham H	W	3-1	0-1	2	Fred [57], Cavani [79], Greenwood [90]	0
32	18	H	Burnley	W	3-1	0-0	2	Greenwood 2 [48, 84], Cavani [90]	0
33	25	A	Leeds U	D	0-0	0-0	2		0
34	May 9	A	Aston Villa	W	3-1	0-1	2	Bruno Fernandes (pen) [52], Greenwood [56], Cavani [87]	0
35	11	H	Leicester C	L	1-2	1-1	2	Greenwood [15]	0
36	13	H	Liverpool	L	2-4	1-2	2	Bruno Fernandes [10], Rashford [68]	0
37	18	H	Fulham	D	1-1	1-0	2	Cavani [15]	10,000
38	23	A	Wolverhampton W	W	2-1	2-1	2	Elanga [13], Mata (pen) [45]	4500

Final League Position: 2

GOALSCORERS

League (73): Bruno Fernandes 18 (9 pens), Rashford 11, Cavani 10, Greenwood 7, Martial 4, McTominay 4, James 3, Pogba 3, Maguire 2, Wan Bissaka 2, Elanga 1, Fred 1, Lindelof 1, Mata 1 (1 pen), Shaw 1, van de Beek 1, own goals 3.
FA Cup (6): Greenwood 2, McTominay 2, Bruno Fernandes 1, Rashford 1.
Carabao Cup (8): Mata 2 (1 pen), Cavani 1, Greenwood 1, Martial 1, McTominay 1, Pogba 1, Rashford 1.
UEFA Champions League (15): Rashford 6 (1 pen), Bruno Fernandes 4 (2 pens), Martial 2 (1 pen), Greenwood 1, James 1, own goal 1.
UEFA Europa League (19): Cavani 6, Bruno Fernandes 5 (2 pens), Pogba 2, Rashford 2, Diallo 1, Greenwood 1, James 1, own goal 1.
Papa John's Trophy (8): Elanga 2, Helm 2, McCann 1, Mejbri 1, Pellistri 1, Puigmal 1.

De Gea D 26	Fosu-Mensah T 1	Lindelof V 29	Maguire H 34	Shaw L 30 + 2	Pogba P 21 + 5	McTominay S 24 + 8	James D 11 + 4	Bruno Fernandes M 35 + 2	Rashford M 33 + 4	Martial A 17 + 5	Greenwood M 21 + 10	van de Beek D 4 + 15	Ighalo O — + 1	Wan Bissaka A 34	Matic N 12 + 8	Fred F 27 + 3	Bailly E 10 + 2	Mata J 6 + 3	Cavani E 13 + 13	Tuanzebe A 4 + 5	Alex Telles N 8 + 1	Henderson D 12 + 1	Williams B 2 + 2	Shoretire S — + 2	Diallo A 2 + 1	Elanga A 2	Mejbri H — + 1	Fish W — + 1	*Match No.*
1	2^{3}	3	4	5	6^{2}	7	8^{1}	9	10	11	12	13	14																1
1		3	4	5	6^{1}			9	10	11^{3}	8^{2}	14		2	7	12	13												2
1			4	5	7	12		9^{1}	10	11■	8^{3}	14		2	6^{2}	13	3												3
1		3	4	5	12	6	10^{2}	9	11			13		2	14	7^{1}		8^{3}											4
1		3	4	5	12	6^{3}	10^{1}	9	11		14			2		7		8^{2}	13										5
1		3	4	5	8	7		9^{3}	11		10^{2}	13		2	12	6^{1}			14										6
1		3	4	5^{1}	13	6		9	10	11^{3}				2		7		8^{2}	14	12									7
1		3	4			14		9	10^{2}	11		13		2	6	7^{3}		8^{1}	12		5								8
1^{2}		3	4					9	11		10^{1}	8		2	7	6			12		5^{3}	13	14						9
		3	4		7	6		13	12	10^{3}	8	9^{1}		2				14	11^{2}		5	1							10
1		3	4	5	8	7		9	11	12	10^{1}			2		6													11
		3	4		7	14		9^{2}	10	11^{3}	8^{1}	13		2	6			12			5	1							12
1		3	4	5^{1}		6	8	9^{3}	10^{2}	11		13		2		7			14		12								13
1		2^{2}	4	5	12	6	8^{1}	9	10	11^{3}						7	3		14	13									14
1			4	12	6	14		9^{3}	10	13	8^{2}			2	7		3		11		5^{1}								15
1			4	5	10	6^{1}	13	9^{2}	8	11				2	12	7^{3}	3			14									16
1			4	5	6	13		9^{2}	8^{1}	10^{3}	12			2	7		3		11	14									17
1		3	4	5	8	6		9^{2}	11	10^{1}	13			2		7			12										18
1			4	5	6	12		9^{3}	13	10^{2}	8^{1}			2	14	7	3		11										19
1			4	14	6			9	10	11	8^{1}	13		2	7				12	3^{3}	5^{2}								20
1		3	4	5	10	6^{1}		9	8^{2}	12	13			2		7			11										21
1		3	4	5^{2}		6	14	9	8^{3}	13	10	12		2		7			11^{1}										22
1		3	4	5	7^{1}	6		9	10		8^{2}			2		12			11	13									23
1		3	4	5		6		9	8	10^{1}	12	13		2		7^{2}			11										24
1		3	4	5			8^{2}	9	10^{3}	11^{1}	12			2	7	6		13						14					25
1		3	4	5		6	8	9	10	12	11^{1}			2		7													26
			4	5		12	13	9	10		8			2	7	6^{1}	3		11^{2}			1							27
		3	4	5		6	8	9^{3}	10^{1}	11^{2}	12			2	13	7						1	14						28
		3	4	5		6	8	9	10		11			2		7						1							29
		3	4	5	6^{3}	14	12	9	10^{1}		8	13		2		7			11^{2}			1							30
		3	4	5	10	6		9^{2}	8^{1}		12			2	13	7			11			1							31
		3	4	5	10	6		9	11^{2}		8	13		2		7^{1}			12			1							32
		3	4	5	12	6	8^{1}	9	10^{2}		11	14		2		7^{3}			13			1							33
		3	4^{2}	5	10	6		9^{3}	11		8^{1}			2	14	7	13		12			1							34
1								14	12		11^{1}	6			7		3	9	13	4	5		2		8^{3}	10^{2}			35
		4		5	10	6		9	8		12			2	13	7^{1}	3^{2}		11			1							36
1		2		3	6	9^{1}		8	12		10^{2}	14		5		7			11^{3}	4					13				37
							10^{3}					6			7		3	9^{1}		4	5	1	2	12	8^{2}	11	13	14	38

FA Cup

Third Round	Watford	(h)	1-0
Fourth Round	Liverpool	(h)	3-2
Fifth Round	West Ham U	(h)	1-0
(aet)			
Sixth Round	Leicester C	(a)	1-3

Carabao Cup

Third Round	Luton T	(a)	3-0
Fourth Round	Brighton & HA	(a)	3-0
Quarter-Final	Everton	(a)	2-0
Semi-Final	Manchester C	(h)	0-2

Papa John's Trophy (Manchester U U21)

Group B (N)	Salford C	(a)	6-0
Group B (N)	Rochdale	(a)	0-0
(Manchester U U21 won 5-4 on penalties)			
Group B (N)	Morecambe	(a)	0-4
Second Round (N)	Accrington S	(a)	2-3

UEFA Champions League

Group H	Paris Saint-Germain	(a)	2-1
Group H	RB Leipzig	(h)	5-0
Group H	Istanbul Basaksehir	(a)	1-2
Group H	Istanbul Basaksehir	(h)	4-1
Group H	Paris Saint-Germain	(h)	1-3
Group H	RB Leipzig	(a)	2-3

UEFA Europa League

Round of 32 1st leg	Real Sociedad	(a)	4-0
Round of 32 2nd leg	Real Sociedad	(h)	0-0
Round of 16 1st leg	AC Milan	(h)	1-1
Round of 16 2nd leg	AC Milan	(a)	1-0
Quarter-Final 1st leg	Granada	(a)	2-0
Quarter-Final 2nd leg	Granada	(h)	2-0
Semi-Final 1st leg	Roma	(h)	6-2
Semi-Final 2nd leg	Roma	(a)	2-3
Final	Villarreal	(Gdansk)	1-1
(aet; Villarreal won 11-10 on penalties)			

MANSFIELD TOWN

FOUNDATION

The club was formed as Mansfield Wesleyans in 1897, and changed their name to Mansfield Wesley in 1906 and Mansfield Town in 1910. This was after the Mansfield Wesleyan Chapel trustees had requested that the club change its name as 'it has no longer had any connection with either the chapel or school'. The new club participated in the Notts and Derby District League, but in the following season 1911–12 joined the Central Alliance.

One Call Stadium, Quarry Lane, Mansfield, Nottinghamshire NG18 5DA.

Telephone: (01623) 482 482.

Ticket Office: (01623) 482 482 (option 1).

Website: www.mansfieldtown.net

Email: info@mansfieldtown.net

Ground Capacity: 9,376.

Record Attendance: 24,467 v Nottingham F, FA Cup 3rd rd, 10 January 1953.

Pitch Measurements: 100.5m × 64m (110yd × 70yd).

Chairman: John Radford.

Co-chairwoman: Carolyn Radford.

Chief Executive: David Sharpe.

Manager: Nigel Clough.

Assistant Manager: Gary Crosby.

Colours: Yellow shirts with blue trim, blue shorts with yellow trim, yellow socks with blue trim.

Year Formed: 1897.

Turned Professional: 1906.

Ltd Co.: 1922.

Previous Name: 1897, Mansfield Wesleyans; 1906, Mansfield Wesley; 1910, Mansfield Town.

Grounds: 1897–99, Westfield Lane; 1899–1901, Ratcliffe Gate; 1901–12, Newgate Lane; 1912–16, Ratcliffe Gate; 1916, Field Mill (renamed One Call Stadium 2012).

Club Nickname: 'The Stags'.

First Football League Game: 29 August 1931, Division 3 (S), v Swindon T (h) W 3–2 – Wilson; Clifford, England; Wake, Davis, Blackburn; Gilhespy, Readman (1), Johnson, Broom (2), Baxter.

Record League Victory: 9–2 v Rotherham U, Division 3 (N), 27 December 1932 – Wilson; Anthony, England; Davies, S. Robinson, Slack; Prior, Broom, Readman (3), Hoyland (3), Bowater (3).

Record Cup Victory: 8–0 v Scarborough (a), FA Cup 1st rd, 22 November 1952 – Bramley; Chessell, Bradley; Field, Plummer, Lewis; Scott, Fox (3), Marron (2), Sid Watson (1), Adam (2).

Record Defeat: 1–8 v Walsall, Division 3 (N), 19 January 1933.

Most League Points (2 for a win): 68, Division 4, 1974–75.

HONOURS

League Champions: Division 3 – 1976–77; Division 4 – 1974–75; Conference – 2012–13.
Runners-up: Division 3N – 1950–51, Third Division – (3rd) 2001–02 *(promoted to Second Division).*

FA Cup: 6th rd – 1969.

League Cup: 5th rd – 1976.

League Trophy Winners: 1987.

FOOTBALL YEARBOOK FACT FILE

The first Mansfield Town game to be screened live on television was also the first FA Cup tie to be shown live on a Saturday evening, with a 7.30 kick-off. The match, a first round tie at home to Preston North End in November 1991, was shown on the Sky channel. It was abandoned due to fog after 62 minutes with the teams level at 1-1.

Most League Points (3 for a win): 81, Division 4, 1985–86.

Most League Goals: 108, Division 4, 1962–63.

Highest League Scorer in Season: Ted Harston, 55, Division 3 (N), 1936–37.

Most League Goals in Total Aggregate: Harry Johnson, 104, 1931–36.

Most League Goals in One Match: 7, Ted Harston v Hartlepools U, Division 3N, 23 January 1937.

Most Capped Player: John McClelland, 6 (53), Northern Ireland; Reggie Lambe, 6 (41), Bermuda; Omari Sterling-James, 6 (13), Saint Kitts & Nevis.

Most League Appearances: Rod Arnold, 440, 1970–83.

Youngest League Player: Cyril Poole, 15 years 351 days v New Brighton, 27 February 1937.

Record Transfer Fee Received: £30,000 (rising to £655,000) from Swindon T for Colin Calderwood, July 1985.

Record Transfer Fee Paid: £150,000 to Peterborough U for Lee Angol, May 2017.

Football League Record: 1931 Elected to Division 3 (S); 1932–37 Division 3 (N); 1937–47 Division 3 (S); 1947–58 Division 3 (N); 1958–60 Division 3; 1960–63 Division 4; 1963–72 Division 3; 1972–75 Division 4; 1975–77 Division 3; 1977–78 Division 2; 1978–80 Division 3; 1980–86 Division 4; 1986–91 Division 3; 1991–92 Division 4; 1992–93 Division 2; 1993–2002 Division 3; 2002–03 Division 2; 2003–04 Division 3; 2004–08 FL 2; 2008–13 Conference Premier; 2013– FL 2.

LATEST SEQUENCES

Longest Sequence of League Wins: 7, 13.9.1991 – 26.10.1991.

Longest Sequence of League Defeats: 7, 18.1.1947 – 15.3.1947.

Longest Sequence of League Draws: 5, 18.10.1986 – 22.11.1986.

Longest Sequence of Unbeaten League Matches: 20, 14.2.1976 – 21.8.1976.

Longest Sequence Without a League Win: 14, 25.3.2000 – 2.9.2000.

Successive Scoring Runs: 27 from 1.10.1962.

Successive Non-scoring Runs: 8 from 25.3.2000.

MANAGERS

John Baynes 1922–25
Ted Davison 1926–28
Jack Hickling 1928–33
Henry Martin 1933–35
Charlie Bell 1935
Harold Wightman 1936
Harold Parkes 1936–38
Jack Poole 1938–44
Lloyd Barke 1944–45
Roy Goodall 1945–49
Freddie Steele 1949–51
George Jobey 1952–53
Stan Mercer 1953–55
Charlie Mitten 1956–58
Sam Weaver 1958–60
Raich Carter 1960–63
Tommy Cummings 1963–67
Tommy Eggleston 1967–70
Jock Basford 1970–71
Danny Williams 1971–74
Dave Smith 1974–76
Peter Morris 1976–78
Billy Bingham 1978–79
Mick Jones 1979–81
Stuart Boam 1981–83
Ian Greaves 1983–89
George Foster 1989–93
Andy King 1993–96
Steve Parkin 1996–99
Billy Dearden 1999–2002
Stuart Watkiss 2002
Keith Curle 2002–04
Carlton Palmer 2004–05
Peter Shirtliff 2005–06
Billy Dearden 2006–08
Paul Holland 2008
Billy McEwan 2008
David Holdsworth 2008–10
Duncan Russell 2010–11
Paul Cox 2011–14
Adam Murray 2014–16
Steve Evans 2016–18
David Flitcroft 2018–19
John Dempster 2019
Graham Coughlan 2019–20
Nigel Clough November 2020–

TEN YEAR LEAGUE RECORD

		P	*W*	*D*	*L*	*F*	*A*	*Pts*	*Pos*
2011-12	Conf P	46	25	14	7	87	48	89	3
2012-13	Conf P	46	30	5	11	92	52	95	1
2013-14	FL 2	46	15	15	16	49	58	60	11
2014-15	FL 2	46	13	9	24	38	62	48	21
2015-16	FL 2	46	17	13	16	61	53	64	12
2016-17	FL 2	46	17	15	14	54	50	66	12
2017-18	FL 2	46	18	18	10	67	52	72	8
2018-19	FL 2	46	20	16	10	69	41	76	4
2019-20	FL 2	36	9	11	16	48	55	38	21§
2020-21	FL 2	46	13	19	14	57	55	58	16

§Decided on points-per-game (1.06)

DID YOU KNOW ?

Ted Harston scored a hat-trick on his debut for Mansfield Town at Southport in October 1935 and went on to score 85 goals in 75 League and Cup games for the Stags. His tally included a club record of 11 career hat-tricks out of which just one goal was scored from the penalty spot.

MANSFIELD TOWN – SKY BET LEAGUE TWO 2020–21 LEAGUE RECORD

Match No.	Date	Venue	Opponents	Result		H/T Score	Lg Pos.	Goalscorers	Attendance
1	Sept 12	H	Tranmere R	D	0-0	0-0	14		0
2	19	A	Leyton Orient	D	2-2	0-0	15	Bowery (pen) 52, Cook 72	0
3	26	H	Exeter C	L	1-2	1-1	18	Menayese 20	0
4	Oct 3	A	Newport Co	L	1-2	0-0	20	McLaughlin 69	0
5	10	H	Stevenage	D	0-0	0-0	20		0
6	17	H	Bradford C	L	1-3	0-2	23	Cook 85	0
7	20	A	Morecambe	D	1-1	1-1	22	Charsley 26	0
8	24	A	Cheltenham T	D	0-0	0-0	21		0
9	27	H	Barrow	L	2-4	1-2	22	Perch 35, Charsley 89	0
10	31	H	Walsall	D	1-1	1-0	22	Maynard 33	0
11	Nov 3	A	Bolton W	D	1-1	0-0	22	Lapslie 56	0
12	14	A	Forest Green R	W	2-1	2-0	21	Lapslie 5, Charsley 35	0
13	20	H	Colchester U	D	1-1	0-0	20	Maynard 67	0
14	24	H	Harrogate T	L	0-1	0-1	22		0
15	Dec 2	A	Cambridge U	W	1-0	0-0	19	Reid 64	1917
16	5	H	Crawley T	D	3-3	1-0	19	Sweeney 4, Lapslie 72, Cook 90	0
17	12	A	Grimsby T	D	1-1	0-0	19	Maynard (pen) 69	0
18	15	A	Carlisle U	L	0-1	0-1	19		0
19	19	H	Southend U	D	1-1	0-1	20	Bowery 79	0
20	26	A	Scunthorpe U	W	3-2	2-1	19	Lapslie 16, Onariase (og) 29, Bowery 60	0
21	Jan 2	H	Port Vale	W	4-0	2-0	19	Clarke, O 1, Bowery 3 (1 pen) 32, 77 (p), 80	0
22	5	H	Salford C	W	2-1	2-0	15	Lapslie 15, Bowery 30	0
23	13	A	Oldham Ath	W	3-2	2-1	12	Charsley 36, Sweeney 38, Reid 49	0
24	23	A	Southend U	W	1-0	0-0	13	Reid 64	0
25	Feb 9	A	Walsall	D	1-1	1-1	14	Clarke, O 31	0
26	14	A	Colchester U	D	2-2	1-1	14	Smith (og) 4, Perch 81	0
27	17	H	Bolton W	L	2-3	0-0	15	Clarke, O 65, Reid 72	0
28	20	H	Cambridge U	L	0-3	0-0	18		0
29	23	A	Harrogate T	L	0-1	0-0	19		0
30	27	H	Morecambe	W	1-0	1-0	16	Bowery 41	0
31	Mar 2	A	Bradford C	L	0-1	0-1	19		0
32	6	A	Barrow	L	0-2	0-0	19		0
33	9	H	Cheltenham T	W	3-1	0-0	16	Bowery 2 55, 65, Reid 63	0
34	13	A	Crawley T	L	0-1	0-0	16		0
35	16	H	Carlisle U	D	1-1	0-0	16	McLaughlin 80	0
36	20	H	Grimsby T	D	2-2	1-0	16	Maris 20, Law 67	0
37	23	H	Forest Green R	D	0-0	0-0	18		0
38	27	A	Tranmere R	D	1-1	0-1	19	Quinn 76	0
39	Apr 2	H	Leyton Orient	L	0-2	0-1	19		0
40	5	A	Exeter C	D	0-0	0-0	19		0
41	9	H	Newport Co	D	1-1	0-0	18	Sinclair 84	0
42	17	A	Stevenage	W	1-0	1-0	18	Sweeney 24	0
43	20	H	Scunthorpe U	W	3-0	1-0	18	Lapslie 19, Perch 80, Sinclair 83	0
44	24	A	Salford C	L	0-2	0-1	18		0
45	May 1	H	Oldham Ath	W	4-1	2-0	17	Sinclair 12, Lapslie 2 38, 80, Reid 88	0
46	8	A	Port Vale	W	3-0	2-0	16	McLaughlin 2 10, 63, Quinn 30	0

Final League Position: 16

GOALSCORERS

League (57): Bowery 10 (2 pens), Lapslie 8, Reid 6, Charsley 4, McLaughlin 4, Clarke, O 3, Cook 3, Maynard 3 (1 pen), Perch 3, Sinclair 3, Sweeney 3, Quinn 2, Law 1, Maris 1, Menayese 1, own goals 2.
FA Cup (4): Charsley 1, Lapslie 1, Maynard 1, McLaughlin 1.
Carabao Cup (0).
Papa John's Trophy (3): Menayese 1, Reid 1, Sweeney 1.

Stech M 23 + 1	Menayese R 10	Rawson F 43	Sweeney R 33 + 3	O'Keeffe C 7 + 6	Maris G 39 + 1	Clarke O 27 + 6	Benning M 25 + 7	Charsley H 32 + 11	Bowery J 38 + 5	Cook A 8 + 12	Maynard N 9 + 8	Sinclair T 7 + 12	Gordon K 28 + 4	McLaughlin S 29 + 7	Stone A 22	Perch J 31 + 1	Reid J 31 + 8	Smith A — + 1	Lapslie G 27 + 2	O'Driscoll A 1 + 2	Quinn S 21 + 2	Sarkic O — + 4	Law J 12 + 5	Ward K 1 + 6	Wright J — + 2	Pardington J 1 + 1	Clarke J 1 + 1	Charles J — + 2	Match No.
1	2	3	4	5	6	7	8	9^2	10^1	11	12	13																	1
1	4	3	2	5	6	7	8	9	10	11^1	12																		2
1	3	4	5	2	9	8	6^2	7^3	10^1	11	12		13	14															3
	2	3	4	5^3	7	6^2			12	14	10^1			9	1	8	11	13											4
1	2	3	4	5	8		12	7		13	10^2			9^1		6	11												5
1	3	4^1	5	2	7^3		13	12	11	14	10^2			6		8			9▮										6
1	3	4	5	2	7			10	13	9^2		12	11	6^1		8													7
1	2	3	4		8^2			10		11^1	13		5	9		6	12		7										8
1	2	3			13			8		11	10^2		6	9		5^1	12		7	4▮									9
1		3			8			6	12	11^1	10		2	5		4	9		7										10
1		3		12	8^3		5^1	6	9		10^2		2	11		4	13		7	14									11
1		3		13	8^1	12	5	7	9		10^2		2	11		4			6										12
1		3		12		7^1	5	6	11		10		2	9		4			8										13
1		3				8	5	6^2	11	12	10^1	14	2	9^3		4	13		7										14
1	3		4	13	9^2	8	5	6^3	10	14	12		2				11^1		7										15
1		3	4		9^2	7	5	6	11	13	12		2				10^1		8										16
1		3	4		8^1	6	5	9	11^2	14	13		2	12			10^3		7										17
1		3	4		8^1	6	5	9	11	12		13	2				10^2		7										18
1		3	4	14	9^1	7	5	6	11	12			2^3	13			10^2		8										19
1		3	4		8	6	5	9	11	12			2				10^1		7										20
1		3	4	16	9	8^5	5^1	6^3	11^4	13		15		12		2	10^2		7	14									21
1		3	4		6	8	5	7	11							2	10		9										22
		3	4		7		12	6	11^1	10^2	13		2	5	1		9		8										23
		3	4		7		13	9	11	12			2	5^2	1		10		8		6^1								24
		3	4		7	12		9	11				2	5	1		10		8^1		6^2	13							25
		3	4		7	8	12	9	11					5	1	2	10				6^1								26
		3	4		7	8	12	9	11					5	1	2	10				6^1								27
		3	4		9	7		6^2	11^3			13		5	1	2	10				8^1	14	12						28
		3	4		7^4	8	12	6^2	11			15	13	5^1	1	2	10				14		9^3						29
		3	4		7	6	5	12	11				2		1		10				8		9^1						30
		3	4		9^1	6▮	5	12	11			13	2		1		10				8^2		7						31
13		3	4▮			7	5	9^1	11^3			14	2^4		1^2	12	10				8^5		6	15	16				32
1		3				7^1	5	13	11				2	6		4	10		12		8^2		9						33
1		3				6^1	5	14	11			13	2	7		4	10^2				8		9^3	12					34
		3				13	5	6	11				2	7	1	4	10				8^1	12	9^2						35
		3	15		6^3		5	7	10				2	8^1	1	4	11^2				12	13^5	9^4	14	16				36
		3			6		5	7	11				2	12	1	4	10				8^1		9						37
		3	15		6^2	14	5	7^3	10^1			16	2	12	1	4	11		13		8^4		9^5						38
		3	16		6	12	5	14	11			15	2^5	13	1	4	10^3		7^1		8^4		9^2						39
		3	4		6	7			11			10^1		5	1	2	12		9		8								40
		3	4		6	7^1			11			10		5	1	2	12		9		8								41
		3	4		6	12		14	11			9^3		5	1	2	10		7^2		8^1		13						42
		3	4		6	7^3		13	12			10	15	5	1	2^5	11^1		9^2		8^4		14	16					43
		3	4		6^2			15	11			10	13	5	1^4	2	12		7^1		8^5		9^3	16		14			44
			4		6			16	12			10^3	2^2	5	1	3	11		9^5		8^4		15	7^1			13	14	45
			4		6^4	7^2		13	10^3			11		5^5		3	14		9		8^1		12	16		1	2	15	46

FA Cup

First Round	Sunderland	(a)	1-0
Second Round *(aet)*	Dagenham & R	(h)	2-1
Third Round *(aet)*	Cheltenham T	(a)	1-2

Carabao Cup

First Round	Preston NE	(a)	0-4

Papa John's Trophy

Group E (N)	Manchester C U21	(h)	0-3
Group E (N)	Lincoln C	(h)	1-3
Group E (N)	Scunthorpe U	(a)	2-1

MIDDLESBROUGH

FOUNDATION

A previous belief that Middlesbrough Football Club was founded at a tripe supper at the Corporation Hotel has proved to be erroneous. In fact, members of Middlesbrough Cricket Club were responsible for forming it at a meeting in the gymnasium of the Albert Park Hotel in 1875.

Riverside Stadium, Middlehaven Way, Middlesbrough TS3 6RS.

Telephone: (01642) 929 420.

Ticket Office: (01642) 929 421.

Website: www.mfc.co.uk

Email: enquiries@mfc.co.uk

Ground Capacity: 34,742.

Record Attendance: 53,802 v Newcastle U, Division 1, 27 December 1949 (at Ayresome Park); 34,814 v Newcastle U, Premier League, 5 March 2003 (at Riverside Stadium); 35,000, England v Slovakia, Euro 2004 qualifier, 11 June 2003.

Pitch Measurements: 105m × 68m (115yd × 74.5yd).

Chairman: Steve Gibson.

Chief Executive: Neil Bausor.

Manager: Neil Warnock.

Assistant Manager: Kevin Blackwell.

Colours: Red shirts with white trim, white shorts with red trim, white socks with red trim.

Year Formed: 1876; re-formed 1986.

Turned Professional: 1889; became amateur 1892, and professional again, 1899.

Club Nickname: 'Boro'.

Grounds: 1877, Old Archery Ground, Albert Park; 1879, Breckon Hill; 1882, Linthorpe Road Ground; 1903, Ayresome Park; 1995, Riverside Stadium.

First Football League Game: 2 September 1899, Division 2, v Lincoln C (a) L 0–3 – Smith; Shaw, Ramsey; Allport, McNally, McCracken; Wanless, Longstaffe, Gettins, Page, Pugh.

Record League Victory: 9–0 v Brighton & HA, Division 2, 23 August 1958 – Taylor; Bilcliff, Robinson; Harris (2p), Phillips, Walley; Day, McLean, Clough (5), Peacock (2), Holliday.

Record Cup Victory: 7–0 v Hereford U, Coca-Cola Cup 2nd rd, 1st leg, 18 September 1996 – Miller; Fleming (1), Branco (1), Whyte, Vickers, Whelan, Emerson (1), Mustoe, Stamp, Juninho, Ravanelli (4).

Record Defeat: 0–9 v Blackburn R, Division 2, 6 November 1954.

HONOURS

League Champions: First Division – 1994–95; Division 2 – 1926–27, 1928–29, 1973–74.
Runners-up: FL C – 2015–16; First Division – 1997–98; Division 2 – 1901–02, 1991–92; Division 3 – 1966–67, 1986–87.

FA Cup: *Runners-up:* 1997.

League Cup Winners: 2004.
Runners-up: 1997, 1998.

Amateur Cup Winners: 1895, 1898.

Anglo-Scottish Cup Winners: 1976.

Full Members' Cup: *Runners-up:* 1990.

European Competitions
UEFA Cup: 2004–05, 2005–06 *(runners-up)*.

FOOTBALL YEARBOOK FACT FILE

Middlesbrough's line-up for the Football League Cup tie at Preston North End on 25 September 2018 included two players with an age difference of more than 23 years. Goalkeeper Dimi Konstantopoulos was 39 years and 300 days old, while Nathan Wood was just 16 years and 143 days old.

Most League Points (2 for a win): 65, Division 2, 1973–74.

Most League Points (3 for a win): 94, Division 3, 1986–87.

Most League Goals: 122, Division 2, 1926–27.

Highest League Scorer in Season: George Camsell, 59, Division 2, 1926–27 (Second Division record).

Most League Goals in Total Aggregate: George Camsell, 325, 1925–39.

Most League Goals in One Match: 5, John Wilkie v Gainsborough T, Division 2, 2 March 1901; 5, Andy Wilson v Nottingham F, Division 1, 6 October 1923; 5, George Camsell v Manchester C, Division 2, 25 December 1926; 5, George Camsell v Aston Villa, Division 1, 9 September 1935; 5, Brian Clough v Brighton & HA, Division 2, 22 August 1958.

Most Capped Player: Mark Schwarzer, 52 (109), Australia.

Most League Appearances: Tim Williamson, 563, 1902–23.

Youngest League Player: Luke Williams, 16 years 200 days v Barnsley, 18 December 2009.

Record Transfer Fee Received: £18,000,000 from Wolverhampton W for Adama Traore, August 2019.

Record Transfer Fee Paid: £15,000,000 to Nottingham F for Britt Assombalonga, July 2017.

Football League Record: 1899 Elected to Division 2; 1902–24 Division 1; 1924–27 Division 2; 1927–28 Division 1; 1928–29 Division 2; 1929–54 Division 1; 1954–66 Division 2; 1966–67 Division 3; 1967–74 Division 2; 1974–82 Division 1; 1982–86 Division 2; 1986–87 Division 3; 1987–88 Division 2; 1988–89 Division 1; 1989–92 Division 2; 1992–93 Premier League; 1993–95 Division 1; 1995–97 Premier League; 1997–98 Division 1; 1998–2009 Premier League; 2009–16 FL C; 2016–17 Premier League; 2017– FL C.

MANAGERS

John Robson 1899–1905
Alex Mackie 1905–06
Andy Aitken 1906–09
J. Gunter 1908–10
(Secretary-Manager)
Andy Walker 1910–11
Tom McIntosh 1911–19
Jimmy Howie 1920–23
Herbert Bamlett 1923–26
Peter McWilliam 1927–34
Wilf Gillow 1934–44
David Jack 1944–52
Walter Rowley 1952–54
Bob Dennison 1954–63
Raich Carter 1963–66
Stan Anderson 1966–73
Jack Charlton 1973–77
John Neal 1977–81
Bobby Murdoch 1981–82
Malcolm Allison 1982–84
Willie Maddren 1984–86
Bruce Rioch 1986–90
Colin Todd 1990–91
Lennie Lawrence 1991–94
Bryan Robson 1994–2001
Steve McClaren 2001–06
Gareth Southgate 2006–09
Gordon Strachan 2009–10
Tony Mowbray 2010–13
Aitor Karanka 2013–17
Garry Monk 2017
Tony Pulis 2017–19
Jonathan Woodgate 2019–20
Neil Warnock June 2020–

LATEST SEQUENCES

Longest Sequence of League Wins: 9, 16.2.1974 – 6.4.1974.

Longest Sequence of League Defeats: 8, 26.12.1995 – 17.2.1996.

Longest Sequence of League Draws: 8, 3.4.1971 – 1.5.1971.

Longest Sequence of Unbeaten League Matches: 24, 8.9.1973 – 19.1.1974.

Longest Sequence Without a League Win: 19, 3.10.1981 – 6.3.1982.

Successive Scoring Runs: 26 from 21.9.1946.

Successive Non-scoring Runs: 7, 25.1.2014 – 1.3.2014.

TEN YEAR LEAGUE RECORD

		P	*W*	*D*	*L*	*F*	*A*	*Pts*	*Pos*
2011-12	FL C	46	18	16	12	52	51	70	7
2012-13	FL C	46	18	5	23	61	70	59	16
2013-14	FL C	46	16	16	14	62	50	64	12
2014-15	FL C	46	25	10	11	68	37	85	4
2015-16	FL C	46	26	11	9	63	31	89	2
2016-17	PR Lge	38	5	13	20	27	53	28	19
2017-18	FL C	46	22	10	14	67	45	76	5
2018-19	FL C	46	20	13	13	49	41	73	7
2019-20	FL C	46	13	14	19	48	61	53	17
2020-21	FL C	46	18	10	18	55	53	64	10

DID YOU KNOW ?

In the early 1900s it was fashionable for clubs to have live animals as mascots. The mascot chosen by Middlesbrough was a pigeon which accompanied the team to home and away games. Sadly, it died early in 1909 and was buried next to the Ayresome Park pitch.

MIDDLESBROUGH – SKY BET CHAMPIONSHIP 2020–21 LEAGUE RECORD

Match No.	Date	Venue	Opponents	Result		H/T Score	Lg Pos.	Goalscorers	Attendance
1	Sept 11	A	Watford	L	0-1	0-1	23		0
2	19	H	Bournemouth	D	1-1	0-1	18	Browne 81	1000
3	26	A	QPR	D	1-1	1-1	18	Akpom 19	0
4	Oct 3	H	Barnsley	W	2-1	1-0	10	Howson 45, Akpom 48	0
5	17	H	Reading	D	0-0	0-0	14		0
6	20	A	Bristol C	W	1-0	0-0	9	Saville 73	0
7	24	A	Cardiff C	D	1-1	1-0	13	Saville 36	0
8	27	H	Coventry C	W	2-0	0-0	7	Assombalonga 81, Spence 90	0
9	31	H	Nottingham F	W	1-0	0-0	5	Johnson 81	0
10	Nov 3	A	Blackburn R	D	0-0	0-0	5		0
11	7	A	Brentford	D	0-0	0-0	7		0
12	21	H	Norwich C	L	0-1	0-0	8		0
13	25	H	Derby Co	W	3-0	1-0	7	Assombalonga 33, Clarke (og) 71, Johnson 83	0
14	28	A	Huddersfield T	L	2-3	1-2	10	Johnson 14, Assombalonga (pen) 83	0
15	Dec 2	H	Swansea C	W	2-1	1-0	10	Watmore 2 26, 67	0
16	5	A	Stoke C	L	0-1	0-1	10		0
17	9	A	Preston NE	L	0-3	0-0	11		0
18	12	H	Millwall	W	3-0	3-0	9	Watmore 2 13, 20, Tavernier 15	0
19	16	H	Luton T	W	1-0	0-0	7	Akpom 52	0
20	19	A	Birmingham C	W	4-1	2-1	6	Assombalonga 27, Saville 31, Wing 2 56, 82	0
21	29	A	Sheffield W	L	1-2	0-2	9	Watmore 49	0
22	Jan 2	A	Wycombe W	W	3-1	2-1	7	Browne 30, Tavernier 36, Akpom 81	0
23	16	H	Birmingham C	L	0-1	0-1	7		0
24	20	A	Nottingham F	W	2-1	1-0	7	Assombalonga 14, Saville 50	0
25	24	H	Blackburn R	L	0-1	0-0	7		0
26	27	H	Rotherham U	L	0-3	0-1	7		0
27	30	A	Norwich C	D	0-0	0-0	7		0
28	Feb 6	H	Brentford	L	1-4	1-1	7	Raya (og) 3	0
29	13	A	Derby Co	L	1-2	1-2	8	Kebano 38	0
30	16	H	Huddersfield T	W	2-1	2-1	8	Watmore 31, Fletcher, A (pen) 45	0
31	20	A	Reading	W	2-0	2-0	8	Fletcher, A 22, Bola 29	0
32	23	H	Bristol C	L	1-3	0-3	8	Fry 80	0
33	27	H	Cardiff C	D	1-1	0-1	9	McNair 82	0
34	Mar 2	A	Coventry C	W	2-1	1-1	9	Hall 41, Saville 87	0
35	6	A	Swansea C	L	1-2	0-1	9	Morsy 90	0
36	13	H	Stoke C	W	3-0	2-0	9	Hall 21, McNair 40, Mendez-Laing 88	0
37	16	H	Preston NE	W	2-0	1-0	8	Storey (og) 22, Tavernier 51	0
38	20	A	Millwall	L	0-1	0-1	9		0
39	Apr 2	A	Bournemouth	L	1-3	0-1	9	Watmore 63	0
40	5	H	Watford	D	1-1	0-1	10	Bolasie 78	0
41	10	A	Barnsley	L	0-2	0-0	10		0
42	17	H	QPR	L	1-2	1-2	11	Bolasie 28	0
43	21	A	Rotherham U	W	2-1	1-1	10	Saville 33, Akpom 55	0
44	24	H	Sheffield W	W	3-1	1-1	9	Bolasie 20, Coburn 73, Watmore 81	0
45	May 1	A	Luton T	D	1-1	1-1	10	Watmore 21	0
46	8	H	Wycombe W	L	0-3	0-2	10		0

Final League Position: 10

GOALSCORERS

League (55): Watmore 9, Saville 6, Akpom 5, Assombalonga 5 (1 pen), Bolasie 3, Johnson 3, Tavernier 3, Browne 2, Fletcher, A 2 (1 pen), Hall 2, McNair 2, Wing 2, Bola 1, Coburn 1, Fry 1, Howson 1, Kebano 1, Mendez-Laing 1, Morsy 1, Spence 1, own goals 3.
FA Cup (1): Folarin 1.
Carabao Cup (4): Fletcher A 2, Johnson 1, Tavernier 1.

Bettinelli M 41	Dijksteel A 29	Hall G 18 + 1	McNair P 46	Spence D 22 + 16	Howson J 40 + 1	Saville G 35 + 7	Tavernier M 25 + 4	Johnson M 22 + 20	Fletcher A 5 + 7	Assombalonga B 19 + 12	Wing L 4 + 8	Browne M 1 + 4	Fry D 30 + 2	Morsy S 29 + 2	Akpom C 20 + 18	Bola M 41	Coulson H 5 + 12	Roberts P 4 + 5	Wood-Gordon N 2 + 2	Folarin S — + 2	Watmore D 23 + 7	Fisher D 11 + 1	Bolasie Y 12 + 3	Kebano N 15 + 3	Mendez-Laing N 2 + 7	Archer J 5	Malley C — + 3	Coburn J — + 4	Hackney H — + 1	Robinson J — + 1	*Match No.*
1	2	3	4	5	6	7^{1}	8	9	10	11	12																				1
1	2	3	4	5^{2}	6	7	8^{3}	9	10^{1}	11		12	13	14																	2
1	2	3^{1}	4	6^{2}	5	8	7	9		10			12	13	11																3
1	2		4		5	8	6			10			3	7	11^{1}	9	12														4
1	2		4	13	5	8	6^{2}	12		10^{1}			3	7	11	9															5
1	2		4	6^{1}	5	8	12	9				13	3	7	11^{3}			10^{2}	14												6
1	2		4	13	5	8	6	11^{2}		12			3	7	10^{1}	9															7
1	2		4	6	5	8	9^{1}			11		13	3	7			12	10^{2}													8
1	2		4	12	6	8	9	14		10^{2}				7^{1}	13	5	11^{3}		3												9
1	2		4	9	7	8	6	12		10^{2}			3		13	5	11^{1}														10
1	2		4	8	6		7	12		13	9		3		11^{2}	5	10^{1}														11
1	2		4	8^{2}	6	7	9^{4}	10^{1}		14			3		11^{3}	5	12	15		13											12
1	2		4	13	6	7	8^{4}	12		11^{3}	15		3		14	5		9^{2}			10^{1}										13
1	2^{2}		4	8	6	7^{3}	9^{1}	10		11	14		3		12	5					13										14
1			2	5	8	12	6	9^{2}			13		3	7^{3}	11	4	14				10^{1}										15
1			4	2	6	9^{4}	7^{5}	10^{1}		14	15		3	8^{2}	11^{3}	5		13		16	12										16
1			4	2	6^{1}	9^{3}	12	10		11			3	8	13	5		14			7^{2}										17
1	2^{5}		4	12		7	9^{4}	10^{3}		13	15		3	6	11^{1}	5	14	16			8^{2}										18
1	2		4	13		7	8	10^{2}		14	12		3	6■	11^{3}	5					9^{1}										19
1	2		4	12		9	8	10^{1}		11^{2}	7		3	6	13	5															20
1	2^{4}		4	15		9	13	10^{3}		11^{1}	7^{2}	14	3	6	12	5					8										21
1	2		4	12		7	9	10		13		8^{1}	3	6	11^{2}	5															22
1	2		4	13	12	8	9^{5}	11^{4}		14	6^{3}		3	7^{1}	10^{2}	5	16				15										23
1	2		4	13	7	8	9^{2}	12		10			3	6		5					11^{1}										24
1			4	2	7	8	9^{4}	14	13	10			3^{1}	6^{3}		5		15	12		11^{2}										25
1			4	2^{2}	6	8		16	15	11^{3}	12			7	14	5^{5}	13	9^{1}	3		10^{4}										26
1			4	6	7	9		10					3^{3}	8	12	5	13				14	2^{2}	11^{1}								27
1	3		4	12	6	9				11^{2}				7	13	5					14	2	10^{3}	8^{1}							28
1	3	12	4		7	9^{2}		16	15	11^{1}				6^{4}	13	5					10^{3}	2		8^{5}	14						29
1	2	3	4■	13	7	12		14	10^{4}					5	15	9					11^{3}	6^{2}		8^{1}							30
1	2		4		7	13		12	10				3	5		9					11^{1}	6^{3}		8^{2}	14						31
1	2		4		6	14		16	10^{1}	15			3	7	12	8^{5}					11^{3}	5^{2}		9^{4}	13						32
1	2	3	7	14	8		6	12		11^{4}			4		15	5^{2}					10^{3}			13	9^{1}						33
1	2	3	7	5	8	15	6^{4}	14					4		10^{2}	9^{3}					12		13	11^{1}							34
1	6^{1}	3	4	12^{5}	8	7		15					2	5	13	9^{4}					11^{2}		10^{3}	14	16						35
1		3	4	5^{4}	6			12		14			2	7	11^{3}	8						13	10^{2}	9^{1}	15						36
1		4	6^{2}		7	13	12	14	15				3	8^{1}	10^{4}	5						2	9^{3}	11^{5}	16						37
1		2	7^{5}	5^{4}	6	12	9^{1}	8	14				3		10^{3}	4					13		11^{2}	16	15						38
1		3	4		8			14	13					7	15	5	12				11^{3}	2	9^{2}	10^{4}	6^{1}						39
1		3	4	8	6	9								7^{1}	14	5	12				11^{2}	2	13	10^{3}							40
1		3	4	8^{4}	6	7		16	14	13					11^{3}	5^{5}	15				9^{1}	2	12	10^{2}							41
		3	4	5^{2}	7	6		12		14						8	13				11	2^{1}	10^{3}	9		1					42
		3^{1}	2		7	6		8							10	4					9		11^{2}	5		1	12	13			43
		3	2	13	6	7		8							10^{1}	4					11		9^{3}	5^{2}		1	14	12			44
		2	4		5	7		9								3	8				11		10^{1}	6		1		12			45
		3	2	5^{2}	6	7^{5}		8^{1}							13	4	9^{3}				10		11^{4}			1	12	14	15	16	46

FA Cup

Third Round	Brentford	(a)	1-2

Carabao Cup

First Round	Shrewsbury T	(h)	4-3
Second Round	Barnsley	(h)	0-2

MILLWALL

FOUNDATION

Formed in 1885 as Millwall Rovers by employees of Morton & Co, a jam and marmalade factory in West Ferry Road. The founders were predominantly Scotsmen. Their first headquarters was The Islanders pub in Tooke Street, Millwall. Their first trophy was the East End Cup in 1887.

The Den, Zampa Road, Bermondsey, London SE16 3LN.

Telephone: (020) 7232 1222.

Ticket Office: (0844) 826 2004.

Website: www.millwallfc.co.uk

Email: jnewman@millwallplc.com

Ground Capacity: 19,734.

Record Attendance: 48,672 v Derby Co, FA Cup 5th rd, 20 February 1937 (at The Den, Cold Blow Lane); 20,093 v Arsenal, FA Cup 3rd rd, 10 January 1994 (at The Den, Bermondsey).

Pitch Measurements: 106m × 68m (116yd × 74.5yd).

Chairman: John Berylson.

Chief Executive: Steve Kavanagh.

Manager: Gary Rowett.

Assistant Manager: Adam Barrett.

Colours: Blue shirts with white trim, white shorts with blue trim, blue socks with white trim.

Year Formed: 1885.

Turned Professional: 1893.

Previous Names: 1885, Millwall Rovers; 1889, Millwall Athletic; 1899, Millwall; 1985, Millwall Football & Athletic Company.

Club Nickname: 'The Lions'.

Grounds: 1885, Glengall Road, Millwall; 1886, Back of 'Lord Nelson'; 1890, East Ferry Road; 1901, North Greenwich; 1910, The Den, Cold Blow Lane; 1993, The Den, Bermondsey.

First Football League Game: 28 August 1920, Division 3, v Bristol R (h) W 2–0 – Lansdale; Fort, Hodge; Voisey (1), Riddell, McAlpine; Waterall, Travers, Broad (1), Sutherland, Dempsey.

Record League Victory: 9–1 v Torquay U, Division 3 (S), 29 August 1927 – Lansdale, Tilling, Hill, Amos, Bryant (3), Graham, Chance, Hawkins (3), Landells (1), Phillips (2), Black. 9–1 v Coventry C, Division 3 (S), 19 November 1927 – Lansdale, Fort, Hill, Amos, Collins (1), Graham, Chance, Landells (4), Cock (2), Phillips (2), Black.

Record Cup Victory: 7–0 v Gateshead, FA Cup 2nd rd, 12 December 1936 – Yuill; Ted Smith, Inns; Brolly, Hancock, Forsyth; Thomas (1), Mangnall (1), Ken Burditt (2), McCartney (2), Thorogood (1).

Record Defeat: 1–9 v Aston Villa, FA Cup 4th rd, 28 January 1946.

Most League Points (2 for a win): 65, Division 3 (S), 1927–28 and Division 3, 1965–66.

HONOURS

League Champions: Division 2 – 1987–88; Second Division – 2000–01; Division 3S – 1927–28, 1937–38; Division 4 – 1961–62.
Runners-up: Division 3 – 1965–66, 1984–85; Division 3S – 1952–53; Division 4 – 1964–65.

FA Cup: *Runners-up:* 2004.

League Cup: 5th rd – 1974, 1977, 1995.

League Trophy: *Runners-up:* 1999.

European Competitions
UEFA Cup: 2004–05.

FOOTBALL YEARBOOK FACT FILE

After failing to win their first six matches of the 1947–48 campaign, Millwall travelled to the Netherlands for a midweek friendly match against VV Zwaluwen. The Lions crashed to a 9-3 defeat but bounced back the following Saturday with a 2-0 home win over Nottingham Forest to register their first win of the campaign.

Most League Points (3 for a win): 93, Division 2, 2000–01.

Most League Goals: 127, Division 3 (S), 1927–28.

Highest League Scorer in Season: Richard Parker, 37, Division 3 (S), 1926–27.

Most League Goals in Total Aggregate: Neil Harris, 124, 1995–2004; 2006–11.

Most League Goals in One Match: 5, Richard Parker v Norwich C, Division 3 (S), 28 August 1926.

Most Capped Player: Shane Ferguson, 31 (including 4 whilst on loan from Newcastle U) (49), Northern Ireland.

Most League Appearances: Barry Kitchener, 523, 1967–82.

Youngest League Player: Moses Ashikodi, 15 years 240 days v Brighton & HA, 22 February 2003.

Record Transfer Fee Received: £8,000,000 from Middlesbrough for George Saville, January 2019.

Record Transfer Fee Paid: £1,000,000 (rising to £1,500,000) to Sheffield U for Ryan Leonard, August 2018.

Football League Record: 1920 Original Members of Division 3; 1921 Division 3 (S); 1928–34 Division 2; 1934–38 Division 3 (S); 1938–48 Division 2; 1948–58 Division 3 (S); 1958–62 Division 4; 1962–64 Division 3; 1964–65 Division 4; 1965–66 Division 3; 1966–75 Division 2; 1975–76 Division 3; 1976–79 Division 2; 1979–85 Division 3; 1985–88 Division 2; 1988–90 Division 1; 1990–92 Division 2; 1992–96 Division 1; 1996–2001 Division 2; 2001–04 Division 1; 2004–06 FL C; 2006–10 FL 1; 2010–15 FL C; 2015–17 FL 1; 2017– FL C.

LATEST SEQUENCES

Longest Sequence of League Wins: 10, 10.3.1928 – 25.4.1928.

Longest Sequence of League Defeats: 11, 10.4.1929 – 16.9.1929.

Longest Sequence of League Draws: 5, 3.11.2020 – 28.11.2020.

Longest Sequence of Unbeaten League Matches: 19, 22.8.1959 – 31.10.1959.

Longest Sequence Without a League Win: 20, 26.12.1989 – 5.5.1990.

Successive Scoring Runs: 22 from 27.11.1954.

Successive Non-scoring Runs: 6 from 27.4.2013.

MANAGERS

F. B. Kidd 1894–99
(Hon. Treasurer/Manager)
E. R. Stopher 1899–1900
(Hon. Treasurer/Manager)
George Saunders 1900–11
(Hon. Treasurer/Manager)
Herbert Lipsham 1911–19
Robert Hunter 1919–33
Bill McCracken 1933–36
Charlie Hewitt 1936–40
Bill Voisey 1940–44
Jack Cock 1944–48
Charlie Hewitt 1948–56
Ron Gray 1956–57
Jimmy Seed 1958–59
Reg Smith 1959–61
Ron Gray 1961–63
Billy Gray 1963–66
Benny Fenton 1966–74
Gordon Jago 1974–77
George Petchey 1978–80
Peter Anderson 1980–82
George Graham 1982–86
John Docherty 1986–90
Bob Pearson 1990
Bruce Rioch 1990–92
Mick McCarthy 1992–96
Jimmy Nicholl 1996–97
John Docherty 1997
Billy Bonds 1997–98
Keith Stevens 1998–2000
(then Joint Manager)
(*plus* **Alan McLeary** 1999–2000)
Mark McGhee 2000–03
Dennis Wise 2003–05
Steve Claridge 2005
Colin Lee 2005
David Tuttle 2005–06
Nigel Spackman 2006
Willie Donachie 2006–07
Kenny Jackett 2007–13
Steve Lomas 2013
Ian Holloway 2014–15
Neil Harris 2015–19
Gary Rowett October 2019–

TEN YEAR LEAGUE RECORD

		P	W	D	L	F	A	Pts	Pos
2011-12	FL C	46	15	12	19	55	57	57	16
2012-13	FL C	46	15	11	20	51	62	56	20
2013-14	FL C	46	11	15	20	46	74	48	19
2014-15	FL C	46	9	14	23	42	76	41	22
2015-16	FL 1	46	24	9	13	73	49	81	4
2016-17	FL 1	46	20	13	13	66	57	73	6
2017-18	FL C	46	19	15	12	56	45	72	8
2018-19	FL C	46	10	14	22	48	64	44	21
2019-20	FL C	46	17	17	12	57	51	68	8
2020-21	FL C	46	15	17	14	47	52	62	11

DID YOU KNOW ?

Millwall's ground at the Den was opened in October 1910 and shortly afterwards the club was rewarded for its enterprise by being chosen to host a full England match for what proved to be the only time in its history. On 13 March 1911 England comfortably defeated Wales 3-0 in a match watched by an estimated 21,400 spectators.

MILLWALL – SKY BET CHAMPIONSHIP 2020–21 LEAGUE RECORD

Match No.	*Date*	*Venue*	*Opponents*	*Result*		*H/T Score*	*Lg Pos.*	*Goalscorers*	*Attendance*
1	Sept 12	H	Stoke C	D	0-0	0-0	11		0
2	19	A	Rotherham U	W	1-0	0-0	5	Wallace, J [50]	0
3	26	H	Brentford	D	1-1	1-1	7	Wallace, J [4]	0
4	Oct 3	A	Swansea C	L	1-2	0-0	11	Bradshaw [51]	0
5	17	A	Wycombe W	W	2-1	0-1	7	Wallace, J (pen) [48], Leonard [63]	0
6	20	H	Luton T	W	2-0	1-0	4	Cranie (og) [45], Mahoney [79]	0
7	24	H	Barnsley	D	1-1	1-1	6	Cooper [45]	0
8	28	A	Preston NE	W	2-0	0-0	3	Zohore [54], Wallace, J (pen) [84]	0
9	31	H	Huddersfield T	L	0-3	0-1	7		0
10	Nov 3	A	Norwich C	D	0-0	0-0	7		0
11	7	A	Sheffield W	D	0-0	0-0	9		0
12	21	H	Cardiff C	D	1-1	1-0	9	Smith [35]	0
13	25	H	Reading	D	1-1	1-0	10	Wallace, J [45]	0
14	28	A	Birmingham C	D	0-0	0-0	11		0
15	Dec 2	A	Blackburn R	L	1-2	1-1	13	Malone [34]	0
16	5	H	Derby Co	L	0-1	0-0	14		2000
17	8	H	QPR	D	1-1	0-0	14	Bodvarsson [70]	2000
18	12	A	Middlesbrough	L	0-3	0-3	17		0
19	15	A	Bristol C	W	2-0	1-0	14	Bradshaw [17], Bennett [68]	0
20	19	H	Nottingham F	D	1-1	0-0	16	Bradshaw [47]	0
21	Jan 2	H	Coventry C	L	1-2	0-2	17	Wallace, J (pen) [74]	0
22	12	A	Bournemouth	D	1-1	0-1	16	Smith [79]	0
23	16	A	Nottingham F	L	1-3	0-1	16	Thompson [89]	0
24	20	A	Huddersfield T	W	1-0	1-0	16	Malone [4]	0
25	26	H	Watford	D	0-0	0-0	15		0
26	30	A	Cardiff C	D	1-1	1-0	16	Flint (og) [9]	0
27	Feb 2	H	Norwich C	D	0-0	0-0	14		0
28	6	H	Sheffield W	W	4-1	1-1	13	Zohore (pen) [39], Malone [68], Thompson [69], Romeo [90]	0
29	13	A	Reading	W	2-1	0-1	13	Smith [76], Bennett [85]	0
30	17	H	Birmingham C	W	2-0	1-0	11	Wallace, J [2], Thompson [75]	0
31	20	H	Wycombe W	D	0-0	0-0	11		0
32	23	A	Luton T	D	1-1	0-0	11	Evans [90]	0
33	27	A	Barnsley	L	1-2	1-1	12	Bennett [6]	0
34	Mar 2	H	Preston NE	W	2-1	1-1	10	Malone [39], Bennett [86]	0
35	6	H	Blackburn R	L	0-2	0-1	11		0
36	13	A	Derby Co	W	1-0	1-0	10	Hutchinson [45]	0
37	17	A	QPR	L	2-3	2-0	10	Wallace, J [6], Bennett [39]	0
38	20	H	Middlesbrough	W	1-0	1-0	10	Hall (og) [31]	0
39	Apr 2	H	Rotherham U	W	1-0	0-0	10	Wallace, J [64]	0
40	5	A	Stoke C	W	2-1	1-1	9	Wallace, M [35], Bennett [71]	0
41	10	H	Swansea C	L	0-3	0-1	9		0
42	17	A	Brentford	D	0-0	0-0	9		0
43	21	H	Bournemouth	L	1-4	0-3	11	Wallace, J [49]	0
44	24	A	Watford	L	0-1	0-1	11		0
45	May 1	H	Bristol C	W	4-1	2-1	11	Wallace, J [5], Malone [31], Mitchell [52], Bradshaw [58]	0
46	8	A	Coventry C	L	1-6	0-2	11	McFadzean (og) [54]	0

Final League Position: 11

GOALSCORERS

League (47): Wallace, J 11 (3 pens), Bennett 6, Malone 5, Bradshaw 4, Smith 3, Thompson 3, Zohore 2 (1 pen), Bodvarsson 1, Cooper 1, Evans 1, Hutchinson 1, Leonard 1, Mahoney 1, Mitchell 1, Romeo 1, Wallace, M 1, own goals 4.
FA Cup (2): Hutchinson 1, Zohore 1.
Carabao Cup (6): Smith 2, Leonard 1, Mahoney 1, Malone 1, own goal 1.

Bialkowski B 46	Hutchinson S 39	Pearce A 20 + 4	Cooper J 42	Leonard R 24 + 2	Williams S 12 + 15	Thompson B 16 + 14	Malone S 37 + 4	Bennett M 29 + 8	Bodvarsson J 13 + 25	Wallace J 44 + 1	Smith M 7 + 22	Mahoney C 4 + 10	Wallace M 20 + 3	Romeo M 30 + 5	Woods R 39 + 2	Bradshaw T 12 + 17	Ferguson S 2 + 11	Zohore K 10 + 7	Parrott T 7 + 4	Skalak J 1 + 2	Burey T — + 13	McNamara D 15 + 1	Kieftenbeld M 8 + 3	Evans G 19	Mitchell B 10 + 6	Muller H — + 2	*Match No.*
1	2	3	4	5	6	7	8^3	9^2	10^1	11	12	13	14														1
1	2	3	4	6	13		8^1	11^3		9	14		12	5^2	7	10											2
1	2	3	4	6			8^3	10^2	12	9		13	14	5	7	11^1											3
1	2	3^3	4	6			8	10^1	14	9	13	12		5	7	11^2											4
1	3	13	4	7		12				6	11^3	9^2	5	2	8	10^1	14										5
1	3		4	7		14	12	10^2		6	11^1	9^3	5	2	8			13									6
1	2	3	4	6	7^2	14	8	11^3		9		10^1		5	13			12									7
1	2		3	6			8	10^1	12	9^3			4	5	7	13	14	11^2									8
1	2		3	6			8^2	13	14	10	12	9^3	4	5	7	11^1											9
1	2		4		13	6^2	8	12	10^3	9	14		3	5	7		11^1										10
1	2		4	7			8	11^2	13	9^1	10^3	12	3	5	6	14											11
1	3		4	2	7	9^2	12	10^1	13	8	11^3		5		6				14								12
1	3		4	2	7	9^2	10^3		12	8	13		5		6		14		11^1								13
1	2	3	4	6		13			10^2	9^3	12		8		7	14			11^1	5							14
1	2	3		14	6^3	12	8		10^2	9	16		4	5^5	7^4	13			11^1	15							15
1	3		4	6^4	15	9^1			14	8	11^2		5	2	7		10^3		12		13						16
1	2	3^1	4	12	7^3		8	10^2	14	9^5	13			5	6	15			11^4		16						17
1	2	3^1	4	6		14	8	10^3	12	9^5	13			5^4	7		16		11^2		15						18
1	3		4	7	6^2	13	12	10^1	11^4	8	15		5	2	14	9^3											19
1	3		4	6	7^4	15		10^1	11^3	8^5	12		5	2		9^2			13	14	16						20
1	3		4		7^4		13	10^2	11^1	8	15		5■	2^5	6	9^3		14	12		16						21
1	2	3^1	4	6		15	8	12	14	9^4	13				7			10^2	11^3			5					22
1	2	3^1	4	6		14	8	12	16	9^5	13				7^3	15		10^2	11^4			5					23
1	3		4	2	7^2	9	8		11^4	10^1				13	6	14	12	15				5^3					24
1	3		4	2	14	9^1	8	12	13	10^3					6			11^2				5	7				25
1	3		4	2		11^1	8		12	9					7			10				5	6				26
1	3		4	2		8^1	9	12		11	15			14	7^2		13	10^4				5^3	6				27
1	3		4	7^2	13	12	9		11^4		15			5	8	14		10^3					6^1	2			28
1	3		4		7^2	9^3	8	12	11^1	13	14			5	6^5	15		10^4						2	16		29
1	3	12	4^1			6^4	8	11^2	13	9^5	10^3			5	7	16	15							2	14		30
1	2	3				7^3	8	11^1	15	9^4	10^2			5	6	13	14							4	12		31
1	2	3			14	7^2	8	12	10^3	9	13			5	6^4	11^1					15			4			32
1	2	3^2			11^3	7^1	8	10^4	13	9^5	12			5	6	16	15				14			4			33
1	3		4			13	8	11^2	10^1	9	12			5	6									2	7		34
1	3		4		16		8	11^4	10	9^2	12			5^3	7^5		14				13	15		2	6^1		35
1	2	3	4		16	8^2		11^3	15	10^5			9^1	5	7	14	12							6^4	13		36
1	2	3^5	4		13	8^2	9	11^1	14	10				5	6^3	16					15			7^4	12		37
1	2	15	4		13		9^4	11^1	12	10^3			3	16	7^2	14						5^5		6	8		38
1	2^1	12	4				9	11^3	14	10^4		15	3		7^5			13				5	16	6	8^2		39
1		3	4				9	11^2	13	7^4			2	14		15		10^1				5^3	12	6	8		40
1		3^3	4		15		9	11^4	16	10		14	2	13				12				5^2	6^1	8	7^5		41
1		3	4				9	11^1	13	10^3			2		7						14	5	6	8^2	12		42
1		3^1	4		13		9			11^3		12			7^4	15		10^2			14	5	6	2	8		43
1			4		13		9^4	8^5		10		15		2		11^2		12			16	5^3	6	3	7^1	14	44
1			4		12	16	9	8	14	10^1		13		2	7^4	11^3						5^5		3	6^2	15	45
1			4		13	16	9	8^1		10		14		2	6^5	11^4					15	5^2	12	3	7^3		46

FA Cup
Third Round	Boreham Wood	(a)	2-0
Fourth Round	Bristol C	(h)	0-3

Carabao Cup
First Round	Crawley T	(a)	3-1
Second Round	Cheltenham T	(h)	3-1
Third Round	Burnley	(h)	0-2

MILTON KEYNES DONS

FOUNDATION

In July 2004 Wimbledon became MK Dons and relocated to Milton Keynes. In 2007 it recognised itself as a new club with no connection to the old Wimbledon FC. In August of that year the replica trophies and other Wimbledon FC memorabilia were returned to the London Borough of Merton.

Stadium MK, Stadium Way West, Milton Keynes, Buckinghamshire MK1 1ST.

Telephone: (01908) 622 922.

Ticket Office: (01908) 622 933.

Website: www.mkdons.com

Email: info@mkdons.com

Ground Capacity: 30,303.

Record Attendance: 28,521 v Liverpool, EFL Cup 3rd rd, 25 September 2019.

Pitch Measurements: 105m × 68m (115yd × 74.5yd).

Chairman: Pete Winkelman.

Manager: Russell Martin.

Assistant Manager: Luke Williams.

Colours: White shirts with gold and black trim, white shorts with gold and black trim, white socks with gold and black trim.

Year Formed: 2004.

Turned Professional: 2004.

Club Nickname: 'The Dons'.

Grounds: 2004, The National Hockey Stadium; 2007, Stadium MK.

First Football League Game: 7 August 2004, FL 1, v Barnsley (h) D 1–1 – Rachubka; Palmer, Lewington, Harding, Williams, Oyedele, Kamara, Smith, Smart (Herve), McLeod (1) (Hornuss), Small.

Record League Victory: 7–0 v Oldham Ath, FL 1, 20 December 2014 – Martin; Spence, McFadzean, Kay (Baldock), Lewington; Potter (1), Alli (1); Baker C (1), Carruthers (Green), Bowditch (1) (Afobe (1)); Grigg (2).

HONOURS

League Champions: FL 2 – 2007–08.
Runners-up: FL 1 – 2014–15.

FA Cup: 5th rd – 2013.

League Cup: 4th rd – 2015.

League Trophy Winners: 2008.

FOOTBALL YEARBOOK FACT FILE

Milton Keynes Dons' first-ever Football League Cup tie ended in a 3-0 victory over Peterborough United at London Road on 24 August 2004. After a goalless first half Dons took the lead through Izale McLeod and added two more in the final 10 minutes.

Record Cup Victory: 6–0 v Nantwich T, FA Cup 1st rd, 12 November 2011 – Martin; Chicksen, Baldock G, Doumbe (1), Flanagan, Williams S, Powell (1) (O'Shea (1), Chadwick (Galloway), Bowditch (2), MacDonald (Williams G (1)), Balanta; 6–0 v Norwich C U21, EFL Trophy Southern Section 2nd rd, 8 December 2020 – Nicholls; Poole (2), Williams (Davies), Cargill, Harvie; Sorensen (1), Kasumu (Surman), Freeman (Johnson), Sorinola; Walker S (1), Agard (2).

Record Defeat: 0–6 v Southampton, Capital One Cup 3rd rd, 23 September 2015.

Most League Points (3 for a win): 97, FL 2, 2007–08.

Most League Goals: 101, FL 1, 2014–15.

Highest League Scorer in Season: Izale McLeod, 21, 2006–07.

Most League Goals in Total Aggregate: Izale McLeod, 62, 2004–07; 2012–14.

Most Capped Player: Lee Hodson, 7 (24), Northern Ireland.

Most League Goals in One Match: 4, Will Grigg v Swindon T, FL 1, 24 April 2021.

Most League Appearances: Dean Lewington, 695, 2004–21.

Youngest League Player: Brendon Galloway, 16 years 42 days v Rochdale, 28 April 2012.

Record Transfer Fee Received: £5,000,000 from Tottenham H for Dele Alli, February 2015.

Record Transfer Fee Paid: £400,000 to Bristol C for Kieran Agard, August 2016.

Football League Record: 2004–06 FL 1; 2006–08 FL 2; 2008–15 FL 1; 2015–16 FL C; 2016–18 FL 1; 2018–19 FL 2; 2019– FL 1.

MANAGERS

Stuart Murdock 2004
Danny Wilson 2004–06
Martin Allen 2006–07
Paul Ince 2007–08
Roberto Di Matteo 2008–09
Paul Ince 2009–10
Karl Robinson 2010–16
Robbie Neilson 2016–18
Dan Micciche 2018
Paul Tisdale 2018–19
Russell Martin November 2019–

LATEST SEQUENCES

Longest Sequence of League Wins: 8, 7.9.2007 – 20.10.2007.

Longest Sequence of League Defeats: 6, 2.4.2018 – 28.4.2018.

Longest Sequence of League Draws: 4, 12.2.2013 – 2.3.2013.

Longest Sequence of Unbeaten League Matches: 18, 29.1.2008 – 3.5.2008.

Longest Sequence Without a League Win: 12, 17.9.2019 – 7.12.2019.

Successive Scoring Runs: 18 from 21.8.2018.

Successive Non-scoring Runs: 5 from 5.10.2019.

TEN YEAR LEAGUE RECORD

		P	W	D	L	F	A	Pts	Pos
2011-12	FL 1	46	22	14	10	84	47	80	5
2012-13	FL 1	46	19	13	14	62	45	70	8
2013-14	FL 1	46	17	9	20	63	65	60	10
2014-15	FL 1	46	27	10	9	101	44	91	2
2015-16	FL C	46	9	12	25	39	69	39	23
2016-17	FL 1	46	16	13	17	60	58	61	12
2017-18	FL 1	46	11	12	23	43	69	45	23
2018-19	FL 2	46	23	10	13	71	49	79	3
2019-20	FL 1	35	10	7	18	36	47	37	19§
2020-21	FL 1	46	18	11	17	64	62	65	13

§Decided on points-per-game (1.06)

DID YOU KNOW ?

In 2007–08 Milton Keynes Dons won 18 of their 23 away games on their way to clinching the League Two title. After losing at Rochdale on 1 September Dons lost only one more away game and ended the season five points clear of their nearest rivals.

MILTON KEYNES DONS FC – SKY BET LEAGUE ONE 2020–21 LEAGUE RECORD

Match No.	Date	Venue	Opponents	Result	H/T Score	Lg Pos.	Goalscorers	Attendance
1	Sept 12	A	Doncaster R	D 1-1	0-0	10	Cargill [88]	0
2	19	H	Lincoln C	L 1-2	0-1	18	Mason [59]	0
3	26	A	Crewe Alex	L 0-2	0-2	22		0
4	Oct 3	H	Ipswich T	D 1-1	0-1	23	Harvie [54]	0
5	10	A	Portsmouth	L 1-2	1-2	23	Fraser (pen) [12]	0
6	17	H	Gillingham	W 2-0	1-0	18	Jerome [19], Morris [47]	0
7	20	A	Oxford U	L 2-3	1-1	21	Jerome [11], Gladwin [90]	0
8	24	A	Blackpool	L 0-1	0-0	22		0
9	27	H	Wigan Ath	W 2-0	0-0	16	Fraser (pen) [48], Walker, S [52]	0
10	31	H	AFC Wimbledon	D 1-1	1-1	18	Fraser [13]	0
11	Nov 3	A	Northampton T	D 0-0	0-0	18		0
12	14	A	Sunderland	W 2-1	1-1	14	Jerome [16], Fraser (pen) [47]	0
13	21	H	Hull C	L 1-3	1-2	17	Walker, S [11]	0
14	24	H	Shrewsbury T	D 2-2	0-1	17	Morris [54], Jerome [70]	0
15	Dec 2	A	Charlton Ath	W 1-0	0-0	17	Fraser [75]	0
16	5	A	Accrington S	L 1-2	0-1	17	Morris [53]	0
17	12	H	Burton Alb	D 1-1	0-1	16	Fraser (pen) [73]	0
18	15	H	Peterborough U	D 1-1	0-1	15	Jerome [78]	0
19	19	A	Plymouth Arg	L 0-1	0-0	16		2000
20	26	H	Bristol R	W 2-0	1-0	15	Gladwin [45], Fraser [62]	0
21	29	A	Swindon T	W 4-1	3-1	14	Jerome 2 [4, 40], Harvie [28], Poole [77]	0
22	Jan 16	A	Peterborough U	L 0-3	0-2	16		0
23	19	H	Fleetwood T	W 3-1	3-0	15	Mason 3 [4, 21, 28]	0
24	26	H	Charlton Ath	L 0-1	0-1	16		0
25	30	A	AFC Wimbledon	W 2-0	0-0	16	O'Riley [60], Sorinola [62]	0
26	Feb 6	H	Sunderland	D 2-2	2-1	16	Mason [9], Jerome [19]	0
27	9	A	Rochdale	W 4-1	1-1	14	O'Riley [5], Jules [55], Fraser [58], Jerome [62]	0
28	13	A	Hull C	W 1-0	0-0	13	Fraser (pen) [80]	0
29	20	H	Northampton T	W 4-3	2-1	11	Surman [13], Grigg [34], Jerome [83], Brown [88]	0
30	23	A	Shrewsbury T	L 2-4	1-3	13	Grigg [22], Brown [82]	0
31	27	H	Oxford U	D 1-1	1-0	14	Surman [13]	0
32	Mar 2	A	Gillingham	L 2-3	2-2	15	Grigg [4], O'Hora [45]	0
33	6	A	Wigan Ath	L 0-3	0-1	16		0
34	9	H	Blackpool	L 0-1	0-1	16		0
35	13	H	Accrington S	W 3-2	1-0	15	Jerome 2 [6, 55], O'Riley [90]	0
36	16	H	Plymouth Arg	W 2-1	1-0	14	Jerome [22], Fraser (pen) [89]	0
37	20	A	Burton Alb	W 2-1	1-0	13	Fraser (pen) [15], O'Hora [61]	0
38	27	H	Doncaster R	W 1-0	0-0	12	Harvie [76]	0
39	Apr 5	H	Crewe Alex	L 0-2	0-2	13		0
40	10	A	Ipswich T	D 0-0	0-0	14		0
41	13	A	Lincoln C	L 0-4	0-0	14		0
42	17	H	Portsmouth	W 1-0	1-0	12	Fraser (pen) [41]	0
43	20	A	Bristol R	W 2-0	1-0	10	Fraser [17], Grigg [60]	0
44	24	H	Swindon T	W 5-0	3-0	9	Grigg 4 [16, 45, 46, 49], Fraser (pen) [26]	0
45	May 1	A	Fleetwood T	D 1-1	0-0	9	Brown [83]	0
46	9	H	Rochdale	L 0-3	0-0	13		0

Final League Position: 13

GOALSCORERS

League (64): Fraser 14 (9 pens), Jerome 13, Grigg 8, Mason 5, Brown 3, Harvie 3, Morris 3, O'Riley 3, Gladwin 2, O'Hora 2, Surman 2, Walker, S 2, Cargill 1, Jules 1, Poole 1, Sorinola 1.
FA Cup (2): Jerome 2.
Carabao Cup (0).
Papa John's Trophy (15): Poole 3, Walker S 3 (1 pen), Agard 2, Bird 2, Sorinola 2, Morris 1, Nombe 1, Sorensen 1.

Nicholls L 7	Poole R 14 + 6	O'Hora W 31	Lewington D 43	Cargill B 7 + 4	Houghton J 9 + 10	Sorenson L 12 + 12	Harvie D 18 + 13	Kasumu D 20 + 4	Morris C 14 + 4	Nombe S 2 + 2	Mason J 12 + 12	Brittain C 3 + 1	Sorinola M 23 + 11	Gladwin B 12 + 14	Fraser S 41 + 3	Keogh R 17 + 1	Williams G 8	Thompson L 7 + 10	Jerome C 28 + 6	Fisher A 39	Walker S 5 + 7	Freeman J — + 4	Surman A 25 + 6	Johnson L — + 4	Laird E 23 + 1	Brown C 1 + 19	Davies J — + 1	Darling H 23	O'Riley M 22 + 1	Jules Z 15 + 5	Grigg W 14 + 6	McEachran J 11 + 3	Bird J — + 2	Ilunga B — + 1	Match No.
1	2	3	4	5	6	7^1	8^3	9	10	11^2	12	13	14																							1
1	5^3	2	3	4	7		9^1	8^2	11		10	6	12	13	14																					2
1		2	3	4	7	6^1			11	13	10^2	5	9^3	8	12	14																				3
1	12		4			8^1	9	6	11^2	13	10	5			7	3	2																			4
1			4	9	12	14		7	11	10^1			5^3		8	3	2	6^2	13																	5
1	5		4		13		9	7	11		12			14	8^2	3	2	6^3	10^1																	6
1	5		4	3	7		9^3	6^2	11		12			14	8		2	13	10^1																	7
	5		4				9	7	10^2		11^3			12	8	3	2	6^1	13	1	14															8
	5	2	4		7	6^3					12		9	13	8^2	3			10	1	11^1	14														9
	5	2	4		7	6^2	14		12				9^3	13	8	3			11	1	10^1															10
	5	2	4		7		9	6^2	10					13	8^1	3		12	11^3	1	14															11
		2	4	13		14		6	12				5	9^2	8	3		7^3	11	1	10^1															12
	13	2	4^4	16	7^1	15		6^3	14				5	9^2	8	3			11^5	1	10		12												13
	5	2		4		6^1	15	12	13				9^4	14	8	3			11	1	10^2		7^3												14
	13	2	4			12		6	10				5	9^2	8	3			11^3	1	14		7^1												15
	12	2	4			14	13	6	10				8^2	5^1	9	3			11^4	1	15		7^3												16
		2	4			13	12	7	10					9^1	8	3	5		11^3	1	14		6^2												17
	13	2	4			6	12	7^3	10				9^1		8	3	5^2		11^4	1	14		15												18
	5^2		4	15		6^1		7	10		14		9^4	13	8	3	2^5		11^3	1	16		12												19
	2	3^1	5	12		7	10				14			8^3	9	4			11^2	1		15	6^4	13											20
	5^3		4	2		8	9				12			6^1	10	3			11	1		14	7^2	13											21
	3		4			6^2	10^4				12		5	8	9				11^3	1			7^1	13	2	14	15								22
	2	3	4			6^3	9				11^2		12	7	8				10^4	1		15		13	5^1	14									23
	14	2	4				9^3				11		13	7^4	8			12	10	1					5^2	15		3	6^1						24
		2	4			14	9^2				11^4		13	12	8			6^1	10	1					5	15		3	7^3						25
		2	4				13				10^3				9			6^1	11	1			12		5	14		3	7	8^2					26
		2	4			16	15				12		13		9				11^1	1			7^5		5^4	14		3	6	8^2	10^3				27
		2	4				13				10^3		12	14	9					1			7		5^2			3	6	8^1	11				28
		2	4				16				11^1		14	13	9				12	1			7		5^4	15		3	6^2	8^5	10^3				29
		2	4		13	16	12				14			7^1					10^4	1			8		5^5	15		3	6	9^3	11^2				30
		2	4		13		8^1				10^3			16	9^5				15	1			7^4		5	11^2		3	6	12	14				31
		2	4^5		13						14		15		9				11^2	1			7^1		5	16		3	6	8^4	10^3	12			32
		2	4		7^1		8^2				11^3				9				14	1			12		5			3	6	13	10^4	15			33
		2	4									9		10^3			13	11	1			7^1		5	14		3	6		12	8^2			34
		2	4								14		9^4		10			13	11^2	1			7^3		5			3	6	15	12	8^1			35
		2	4				13						9^5	15	10			12	11^3	1			7^2		5^4			3	6	16	14	8^1			36
		2	4				13						9^4		10			12	11^2	1			8^5		5^3	16		3	6	15	14	7^1			37
		2					5						9^2		10^1			12	14	1			7^3		13	15		3	6	4	11^4	8			38
		2					9	14					15		13			6^2	11^1	1			7^5		5^4	16		3	10	4	12	8^3			39
			2				9^1	13					12		10					1			7		5	14		3	6	4	11^2	8^3			40
			2		15		12	13					9		10					1			7^4		5^1	14		3	6	4	11^3	8^2			41
			2		14			7^1					9		10^2					1			8^3		5	12		3	6	4	11	13			42
			2		14	15		7^1					9		10^4					1			12		5	13		3	6	4	11^2	8^3			43
			2		12	14		7^2					9		10					1			8^3		5	13		3	6	4	11^1				44
			2		14	12		7^2					9		10			13		1			8^4			15		3	5^1	4	11^5	6^3	16		45
			2					7					9		10			12		1			6^2		5^1			3	13^4	4	11	8^3	14	15	46

FA Cup

First Round	Eastleigh	(a)	0-0
(aet; Milton Keynes D won 4-3 on penalties)			
Second Round	Barnet	(a)	1-0
Third Round	Burnley	(a)	1-1
(aet; Burnley won 4-3 on penalties)			

Carabao Cup

First Round	Coventry C	(h)	0-1

Papa John's Trophy

Group C (S)	Northampton T	(h)	3-1
Group C (S)	Stevenage	(a)	3-2
Group C (S)	Southampton U21	(h)	1-2
Second Round (S)	Norwich C U21	(h)	6-0
Third Round (S)	Northampton T	(a)	2-0
Quarter-Final	Sunderland	(h)	0-3

MORECAMBE

FOUNDATION

Several attempts to start a senior football club in a rugby stronghold finally succeeded on 7 May 1920 at the West View Hotel, Morecambe and a team competed in the Lancashire Combination for 1920–21. The club shared with a local cricket club at Woodhill Lane for the first season and a crowd of 3,000 watched the first game. The club moved to Roseberry Park, the name of which was changed to Christie Park after J.B. Christie who as President had purchased the ground.

Mazuma Stadium, Christie Way, Westgate, Morecambe, Lancashire LA4 4TB.

Telephone: (01524) 411 797.

Ticket Office: (01524) 411 797.

Website: www.morecambefc.com

Email: office@morecambefc.com

Ground Capacity: 6,241.

Record Attendance: 9,383 v Weymouth, FA Cup 3rd rd, 6 January 1962 (at Christie Park); 5,375 v Newcastle U, League Cup, 28 August 2013 (at Globe Arena).

Pitch Measurements: 103m × 71m (112.5yd × 77.5yd).

Co-Chairmen: Graham Howse, Rod Taylor.

Manager: Stephen Robinson.

Assistant Manager: John McMahon.

Colours: Red shirts with white trim, white shorts with red trim, black socks with red trim.

Year Formed: 1920.

Turned Professional: 1920.

Club Nickname: 'The Shrimps'.

Grounds: 1920, Woodhill Lane; 1921, Christie Park; 2010, Globe Arena (renamed Mazuma Stadium 2020).

First Football League game: 11 August 2007, FL 2, v Barnet (h) D 0–0 – Lewis; Yates, Adams, Artell, Bentley, Stanley, Baker (Burns), Sorvel, Twiss (Newby), Curtis, Hunter (Thompson).

HONOURS

League: *Runners-up:* Conference – (3rd) 2006–07 *(promoted via play-offs).*

FA Cup: 3rd rd – 1962, 2001, 2003, 2020.

League Cup: 3rd rd – 2008, 2021.

FOOTBALL YEARBOOK FACT FILE

Morecambe have never won automatic promotion and have never been relegated since the club was formed. Their two promotions to date, from the Football Conference in 2006–07 and from EFL League Two in 2020–21, were both achieved in play-off finals at Wembley Stadium.

Record League Victory: 6–0 v Crawley T, FL 2, 10 September 2011 – Roche; Reid, Wilson (pen), McCready, Haining (Parrish), Fenton (1), Drummond, McDonald, Price (Jevons), Carlton (3) (Alessandra), Ellison (1).

Record Cup Victory: 6–2 v Nelson (a), Lancashire Trophy, 27 January 2004.

Record Defeat: 0–7 v Cambridge U, FL 2, 19 April 2016; 0–7 v Newcastle U, League Cup 3rd rd, 23 September 2020.

Most League Points (3 for a win): 73, FL 2, 2009–10.

Most League Goals: 73, FL 2, 2009–10.

Highest League Scorer in Season: Phil Jevons, 18, 2009–10.

Most League Goals in Total Aggregate: Kevin Ellison, 81, 2011–20.

Most League Goals in One Match: 3, Jon Newby v Rotherham U, FL 2, 29 March 2008.

Most League Appearances: Barry Roche, 436, 2008–20.

Youngest League Player: Aaron McGowan, 16 years 263 days, 20 April 2013.

Record Transfer Fee Received: £225,000 from Stockport Co for Carl Baker, July 2008.

Record Transfer Fee Paid: £50,000 to Southport for Carl Baker, July 2007.

Football League Record: 2006–07 Promoted from Conference; 2007–21 FL 2; 2021– FL 1.

MANAGERS

Jimmy Milne 1947–48
Albert Dainty 1955–56
Ken Horton 1956–61
Joe Dunn 1961–64
Geoff Twentyman 1964–65
Ken Waterhouse 1965–69
Ronnie Clayton 1969–70
Gerry Irving and Ronnie Mitchell 1970
Ken Waterhouse 1970–72
Dave Roberts 1972–75
Alan Spavin 1975–76
Johnny Johnson 1976–77
Tommy Ferber 1977–78
Mick Hogarth 1978–79
Don Curbage 1979–81
Jim Thompson 1981
Les Rigby 1981–84
Sean Gallagher 1984–85
Joe Wojciechowicz 1985–88
Eric Whalley 1988
Billy Wright 1988–89
Lawrie Milligan 1989
Bryan Griffiths 1989–93
Leighton James 1994
Jim Harvey 1994–2006
Sammy McIlroy 2006–11
Jim Bentley 2011–19
Derek Adams 2019–21
Stephen Robinson June 2021

LATEST SEQUENCES

Longest Sequence of League Wins: 7, 31.10.2009 – 12.12.2009.

Longest Sequence of League Defeats: 7, 4.3.2017 – 1.4.2017.

Longest Sequence of League Draws: 5, 3.1.2015 – 31.1.2015.

Longest Sequence of Unbeaten League Matches: 12, 31.1.2009 – 21.3.2009.

Longest Sequence Without a League Win: 13, 20.3.2018 – 18.8.2018.

Successive Scoring Runs: 17 from 13.8.2011.

Successive Non-scoring Runs: 7 from 21.4.2018.

TEN YEAR LEAGUE RECORD

		P	*W*	*D*	*L*	*F*	*A*	*Pts*	*Pos*
2011-12	FL 2	46	14	14	18	63	57	56	15
2012-13	FL 2	46	15	13	18	55	61	58	16
2013-14	FL 2	46	13	15	18	52	64	54	18
2014-15	FL 2	46	17	12	17	53	52	63	11
2015-16	FL 2	46	12	10	24	69	91	46	21
2016-17	FL 2	46	14	10	22	53	73	52	18
2017-18	FL 2	46	9	19	18	41	56	46	22
2018-19	FL 2	46	14	12	20	54	70	54	18
2019-20	FL 2	37	7	11	19	35	60	32	22§
2020-21	FL 2	46	23	9	14	69	58	78	4

§*Decided on points-per-game (0.86)*

DID YOU KNOW ?

Morecambe played their first-ever FA Cup tie at home to Breightmet United in a preliminary qualifying round tie on 25 September 1920. The teams drew 1-1, but the Shrimps lost the replay, also played at Morecambe by agreement, 2-0.

MORECAMBE – SKY BET LEAGUE TWO 2020–21 LEAGUE RECORD

Match No.	*Date*	*Venue*	*Opponents*	*Result*		*H/T Score*	*Lg Pos.*	*Goalscorers*	*Attendance*
1	Sept 12	A	Cheltenham T	W	2-1	0-1	4	Phillips (pen) [78], Mendes Gomes [90]	0
2	19	H	Cambridge U	L	0-5	0-3	14		0
3	26	A	Southend U	W	2-1	0-1	5	Wildig [55], Phillips [73]	0
4	Oct 3	H	Port Vale	W	1-0	0-0	2	Phillips (pen) [76]	0
5	10	A	Oldham Ath	W	3-2	1-0	1	Wildig [42], Kenyon [59], Stockton [66]	0
6	17	A	Crawley T	L	0-4	0-0	6		0
7	20	H	Mansfield T	D	1-1	1-1	6	Phillips [3]	0
8	24	H	Forest Green R	L	1-2	1-0	11	Leitch-Smith [19]	0
9	27	A	Carlisle U	L	1-3	0-2	12	Songo'o [79]	0
10	31	A	Tranmere R	W	1-0	0-0	10	Phillips (pen) [57]	0
11	Nov 3	H	Exeter C	D	2-2	2-1	9	Mendes Gomes [41], Hendrie [45]	0
12	14	H	Stevenage	D	1-1	0-1	10	Slew [80]	0
13	21	A	Scunthorpe U	D	1-1	0-0	10	Wildig [90]	0
14	24	A	Salford C	L	1-2	0-2	14	Stockton [54]	0
15	Dec 1	H	Barrow	W	1-0	1-0	11	Mendes Gomes [12]	0
16	5	A	Newport Co	L	1-2	1-1	13	Mendes Gomes [32]	0
17	12	H	Harrogate T	W	1-0	0-0	10	Wildig [56]	0
18	15	H	Leyton Orient	W	2-1	0-1	8	Lavelle [56], Mendes Gomes [73]	0
19	19	A	Colchester U	W	2-1	1-1	5	O'Sullivan [8], Songo'o [61]	1094
20	26	H	Grimsby T	W	3-1	0-1	5	Mendes Gomes 2 [57, 71], Phillips [90]	0
21	Jan 16	A	Leyton Orient	L	0-2	0-0	9		0
22	19	H	Walsall	D	1-1	0-1	8	Mendes Gomes [80]	0
23	23	H	Colchester U	W	3-0	1-0	6	Phillips [45], Diagouraga [58], O'Sullivan [80]	0
24	26	A	Exeter C	W	2-0	1-0	3	Phillips (pen) [9], Stockton [66]	0
25	30	H	Tranmere R	L	0-1	0-0	6		0
26	Feb 6	A	Stevenage	D	2-2	2-1	7	Diagouraga [28], Stockton [32]	0
27	9	A	Bolton W	D	1-1	0-1	6	Lyons [83]	0
28	16	A	Bradford C	L	1-2	1-1	8	O'Sullivan [9]	0
29	20	A	Barrow	W	2-1	1-0	4	Wildig [24], Mellor [66]	0
30	23	H	Salford C	W	2-1	0-1	4	Wildig [90], Mendes Gomes [90]	0
31	27	A	Mansfield T	L	0-1	0-1	5		0
32	Mar 2	H	Crawley T	W	3-1	1-1	5	Stockton [5], Mendes Gomes 2 [59, 88]	0
33	6	H	Carlisle U	W	3-1	2-0	4	Wildig [32], Diagouraga [37], Stockton [53]	0
34	9	A	Forest Green R	D	2-2	1-1	5	Stockton [22], Mendes Gomes [90]	0
35	13	H	Newport Co	L	1-3	1-2	7	Songo'o [20]	0
36	20	A	Harrogate T	W	1-0	1-0	6	O'Sullivan [1]	0
37	27	H	Cheltenham T	W	1-0	1-0	6	McAlinden [20]	0
38	Apr 2	A	Cambridge U	L	1-2	0-1	6	Price [88]	0
39	6	H	Southend U	D	1-1	0-1	5	Stockton [56]	0
40	10	A	Port Vale	L	0-1	0-1	5		0
41	13	H	Scunthorpe U	W	4-1	2-0	4	Stockton [25], Mendes Gomes [37], Bedeau (og) [49], Songo'o [60]	0
42	17	H	Oldham Ath	W	4-3	3-1	4	Mendes Gomes 2 [5, 53], Wildig [42], Stockton [45]	0
43	20	A	Grimsby T	W	3-0	2-0	4	Stockton [22], Songo'o [28], Waterfall (og) [81]	0
44	24	H	Bolton W	L	0-1	0-1	4		0
45	May 1	A	Walsall	W	2-0	1-0	4	Stockton [45], Songo'o [77]	0
46	8	H	Bradford C	W	2-0	1-0	4	McAlinden [28], Stockton [57]	0

Final League Position: 4

GOALSCORERS

League (69): Mendes Gomes 15, Stockton 13, Phillips 8 (4 pens), Wildig 8, Songo'o 6, O'Sullivan 4, Diagouraga 3, McAlinden 2, Hendrie 1, Kenyon 1, Lavelle 1, Leitch-Smith 1, Lyons 1, Mellor 1, Price 1, Slew 1, own goals 2.
FA Cup (5): Stockton 2, O'Sullivan 1, Phillips 1 (1 pen), own goal 1.
Carabao Cup (2): Phillips 1, Wildig 1.
Papa John's Trophy (5): Cooney 2, Davis 1, Lavelle 1, Price 1.
League Two Play-Offs (4): Knight-Percival 1, McAlinden 1, Mendes Gomes 1 (1 pen), Wildig 1.

Turner J 14	Lavelle S 44 + 1	Davis H 22 + 5	Knight-Percival N 29 + 2	Mellor K 29 + 3	Phillips A 24 + 1	Diagouraga T 28 + 8	Pringle B 4 + 7	Hendrie S 22 + 14	Stockton C 38 + 2	Mendes Gomes C 43	McAlinden L 4 + 24	Kenyon A 10 + 8	O'Sullivan J 32 + 6	Wildig A 37	Cooney R 20 + 16	Gibson L 21 + 2	Songo'o Y 34 + 4	Slew J 10 + 7	Leitch-Smith A 1 + 4	Price F 2 + 9	Halstead M 9	Lyons B 5 + 9	Andersson J 2	Letheren K 21	Denny A 1 + 5	Match No.
1	2	3	4	5	6^3	7	8^2	9	10^1	11	12	13	14													1
1	13	4	3	2^1	8^3	6	10	5^2		9	11		12	7	14											2
1	3	4		12	8				11^3	9	14	7^2	6	10	2	5^1	13									3
1	3	4		14	9^2				11	10^1	12	7	8	6	2	5^3	13									4
1	3	4	14		9^1				11^2	10^3	13	7	8	6	2	5	12									5
1	3	4	14		9				11^3	10^2	13	7^1	8	6	2	5	12									6
1	3		4	12	8^2	7		14	11				10	9	2^3	5^1	6	13								7
1	3		4	2	9^2	7	13	5			12		8	10			6		11^1							8
1	3		4	2	12	6^3		5		10^1	14		8^2	9			7	11		13						9
1	3		5	2	7^2		13	6		11^1		8	12	9			4	10								10
1	3		4	2	10	13	8^1	5		9	14	7^2	12				6	11^3								11
1	3		4	2	8^2	7		5	13	10				9			6^1	11		12						12
1	3	16	4^5	2	8	6^1		5^3	12	10^4			15	9	13		7^2	11		14						13
1	3	4		5	6				10	9				8	2		7	11								14
	2	3	4^1	5	6	14		8^2	10^3	11			9		13		7		12		1					15
	2	3	4^3	5	9^1			8■		11	13	7			12		6	10^2	14		1					16
	3	4		2	6^1				11	10		12	8	9	5		7				1					17
	3	4		2	7				11^1	10		13	8^2	9	5		6		12		1					18
	3	4			9^1	12		5	11	10		14	8^3	6^2	2	13	7				1					19
	3	4			9	12		5	11	10				6	2		7	8^1			1					20
	3		4		9^3	13		5	11^2	10^4	14		8^1	6	2		7	15			1	12				21
	3		4		9			5	11	10	12		8^1	6	2		7				1					22
	3		4		6	12		5	11^2	9	13		8^3		2		7	10^1		14			1			23
	3		4		9^3	7	14	5	11	10^1	13		8^2		2		6	12					1			24
	3^3	12	4		9	7		5	11	10^1	14		8^2		2		6■					13		1		25
	3	12	4			7		5	11	10		6^1	8^2	9	2							13		1		26
	3		4	2^2		6		14	11^4	10	12		8	9^5	13	5^3		16				15		1	7^1	27
	3		4	2^2		7		14	11	10	15		8^4	9^1	12	5^3	6^5	16				13		1		28
	4		3	2		6		13	11^1	10			8	9		5^2	7	12						1		29
	2		4^1	5^2		7		12	10	11			9	6	13	8	3							1		30
	3	4		2		9^2		12	11	10	15		7^3	8		5^1	6^4		14			13		1		31
	3	4				13		5^3	11	10			12	9^2	2	14	7	8			1	6^1				32
	3	4		2		9			11	10^1			7	8^2		5	6	12						1	13	33
	3	4^2		2^3		9		12	11	10	13		7	8	14	5^1	6							1		34
	3■	4		2		9^5	16	13	11^1	10	12		7^2	8^4	14	5^3	6							1	15	35
		3	4■	2		9			11^1	10^2	13	6	7	8	12	5								1		36
	3	4^2		2		6	14	13	11	9	10^1		7^3	8	12	5								1		37
	3	4		2^2		6^4	8^1	13	11^3	10^5	14		7	9	12	5■				16				1	15	38
	3	4		2		9		5	11	10		6	7	8										1		39
	3		4^4			13		14	11	10	12		7	9	2^3	5	6^2			15		8^1		1		40
	3		4	2		9			11	10^2			7	8^1	14	5	6^3			13		12		1		41
	3		4	2		9		14	11^3	10			7^1	8^2	12	5	6					13		1		42
	3		4	2		9^5		13	11^3	10	14	16		8^2	12	5	6^4			7^1		15		1		43
	3		4^4	2■		9		12	11	10	15	16		8^3	13	5^1	6^5			14		7^2		1		44
	3	15	4^4			7	12	5	11		8^2	14			2		6^3			10^1		9		1	13	45
	3	12	4^1			7^5	16	5	11^2	10^4	8	15			2		6^3			14		9		1	13	46

FA Cup

First Round	Maldon & Tiptree	(a)	1-0
Second Round	Solihull Moors	(h)	4-2
(aet)			
Third Round	Chelsea	(a)	0-4

Carabao Cup

First Round	Grimsby T	(a)	1-1
(Morecambe won 4-3 on penalties)			
Second Round	Oldham Ath	(h)	1-0
Third Round	Newcastle U	(h)	0-7

Papa John's Trophy

Group B (N)	Rochdale	(h)	1-2
Group B (N)	Salford C	(a)	0-2
Group B (N)	Manchester U U21	(h)	4-0

League Two Play-Offs

Semi-Final 1st leg	Tranmere R	(a)	2-1
Semi-Final 2nd leg	Tranmere R	(h)	1-1
Final	Newport Co	(Wembley)	1-0
(aet)			

NEWCASTLE UNITED

FOUNDATION

In October 1882 a club called Stanley, which had been formed in 1881, changed its name to Newcastle East End to avoid confusion with two other local clubs, Stanley Nops and Stanley Albion. Shortly afterwards another club, Rosewood, merged with them. Newcastle West End had been formed in August 1882 and they played on a pitch which was part of the Town Moor. They moved to Brandling Park in 1885 and St James' Park 1886 (home of Newcastle Rangers). West End went out of existence after a bad run and the remaining committee men invited East End to move to St James' Park. They accepted and, at a meeting in Bath Lane Hall in 1892, changed their name to Newcastle United.

St James' Park, Newcastle-upon-Tyne NE1 4ST.

Telephone: (0344) 372 1892.

Ticket Office: (0344) 372 1892 (option 1).

Website: www.nufc.co.uk

Email: admin@nufc.com

Ground Capacity: 52,305.

Record Attendance: 68,386 v Chelsea, Division 1, 3 September 1930.

Pitch Measurements: 105m × 68m (115yd × 74.5yd).

Managing Director: Lee Charnley.

Head Coach: Steve Bruce.

First-Team Coaches: Steve Agnew, Stephen Clemence, Graeme Jones.

Colours: Black and white striped shirts, black shorts, black socks with white trim.

Year Formed: 1881.

Turned Professional: 1889.

Previous Names: 1881, Stanley; 1882, Newcastle East End; 1892, Newcastle United.

Club Nickname: 'The Magpies', 'The Toon'.

Grounds: 1881, South Byker; 1886, Chillingham Road, Heaton; 1892, St James' Park.

First Football League Game: 2 September 1893, Division 2, v Royal Arsenal (a) D 2–2 – Ramsay; Jeffery, Miller; Crielly, Graham, McKane; Bowman, Crate (1), Thompson, Sorley (1), Wallace. Graham not Crate scored according to some reports.

Record League Victory: 13–0 v Newport Co, Division 2, 5 October 1946 – Garbutt; Cowell, Graham; Harvey, Brennan, Wright; Milburn (2), Bentley (1), Wayman (4), Shackleton (6), Pearson.

HONOURS

League Champions: Division 1 – 1904–05, 1906–07, 1908–09, 1926–27; FL C – 2009–10, 2016–17; First Division – 1992–93; Division 2 – 1964–65.
Runners-up: Premier League – 1995–96, 1996–97; Division 2 – 1897–98, 1947–48.

FA Cup Winners: 1910, 1924, 1932, 1951, 1952, 1955.
Runners-up: 1905, 1906, 1908, 1911, 1974, 1998, 1999.

League Cup: *Runners-up:* 1976.

Texaco Cup Winners: 1974, 1975.
Anglo-Italian Cup Winners: 1972–73.

European Competitions
Champions League: 1997–98, 2002–03, 2003–04.
Fairs Cup: 1968–69 *(winners)*, 1969–70 *(qf)*, 1970–71.
UEFA Cup: 1977–78, 1994–95, 1996–97 *(qf)*, 1999–2000, 2003–04 *(sf)*, 2004–05 *(qf)*, 2006–07.
Europa League: 2012–13 *(qf)*.
European Cup Winners' Cup: 1998–99.
Intertoto Cup: 2001 *(runners-up)*, 2005, 2006 *(winners)*.

FOOTBALL YEARBOOK FACT FILE

Stan Seymour, often described as 'Mr Newcastle United', served the Magpies in different roles for around 50 years. He made over 250 first-team appearances as a player between 1920 and 1929 and then served as a director (1938 to 1976) and vice president (1976–78). During his time on the board he also had two spells as honorary manager and one as chairman.

Record Cup Victory: 9–0 v Southport (at Hillsborough), FA Cup 4th rd, 1 February 1932 – McInroy; Nelson, Fairhurst; McKenzie, Davidson, Weaver (1); Boyd (1), Jimmy Richardson (3), Cape (2), McMenemy (1), Lang (1).

Record Defeat: 0–9 v Burton Wanderers, Division 2, 15 April 1895.

Most League Points (2 for a win): 57, Division 2, 1964–65.

Most League Points (3 for a win): 102, FL C, 2009–10.

Most League Goals: 98, Division 1, 1951–52.

Highest League Scorer in Season: Hughie Gallacher, 36, Division 1, 1926–27.

Most League Goals in Total Aggregate: Jackie Milburn, 177, 1946–57.

Most League Goals in One Match: 6, Len Shackleton v Newport Co, Division 2, 5 October 1946.

Most Capped Player: Shay Given, 82 (134), Republic of Ireland.

Most League Appearances: Jim Lawrence, 432, 1904–22.

Youngest League Player: Steve Watson, 16 years 223 days v Wolverhampton W, 10 November 1990.

Record Transfer Fee Received: £35,000,000 from Liverpool for Andy Carroll, January 2011.

Record Transfer Fee Paid: £40,000,000 to TSG 1899 Hoffenheim for Joelinton, July 2019.

Football League Record: 1893 Elected to Division 2; 1898–1934 Division 1; 1934–48 Division 2; 1948–61 Division 1; 1961–65 Division 2; 1965–78 Division 1; 1978–84 Division 2; 1984–89 Division 1; 1989–92 Division 2; 1992–93 Division 1; 1993–2009 Premier League; 2009–10 FL C; 2010–16 Premier League; 2016–17 FL C; 2017– Premier League.

MANAGERS

Frank Watt 1895–32 *(Secretary-Manager)*
Andy Cunningham 1930–35
Tom Mather 1935–39
Stan Seymour 1939–47 *(Hon. Manager)*
George Martin 1947–50
Stan Seymour 1950–54 *(Hon. Manager)*
Duggie Livingstone 1954–56
Stan Seymour 1956–58 *(Hon. Manager)*
Charlie Mitten 1958–61
Norman Smith 1961–62
Joe Harvey 1962–75
Gordon Lee 1975–77
Richard Dinnis 1977
Bill McGarry 1977–80
Arthur Cox 1980–84
Jack Charlton 1984
Willie McFaul 1985–88
Jim Smith 1988–91
Ossie Ardiles 1991–92
Kevin Keegan 1992–97
Kenny Dalglish 1997–98
Ruud Gullit 1998–99
Sir Bobby Robson 1999–2004
Graeme Souness 2004–06
Glenn Roeder 2006–07
Sam Allardyce 2007–08
Kevin Keegan 2008
Joe Kinnear 2008–09
Alan Shearer 2009
Chris Hughton 2009–10
Alan Pardew 2010–15
John Carver 2015
Steve McClaren 2015–16
Rafael Benitez 2016–19
Steve Bruce July 2019–

LATEST SEQUENCES

Longest Sequence of League Wins: 13, 25.4.1992 – 18.10.1992.

Longest Sequence of League Defeats: 10, 23.8.1977 – 15.10.1977.

Longest Sequence of League Draws: 4, 15.11.2008 – 6.12.2008.

Longest Sequence of Unbeaten League Matches: 17, 13.2.2010 – 2.5.2010.

Longest Sequence Without a League Win: 21, 14.1.1978 – 23.8.1978.

Successive Scoring Runs: 25 from 15.4.1939.

Successive Non-scoring Runs: 6 from 29.10.1988.

TEN YEAR LEAGUE RECORD

		P	W	D	L	F	A	Pts	Pos
2011-12	PR Lge	38	19	8	11	56	51	65	5
2012-13	PR Lge	38	11	8	19	45	68	41	16
2013-14	PR Lge	38	15	4	19	43	59	49	10
2014-15	PR Lge	38	10	9	19	40	63	39	15
2015-16	PR Lge	38	9	10	19	44	65	37	18
2016-17	FL C	46	29	7	10	85	40	94	1
2017-18	PR Lge	38	12	8	18	39	47	44	10
2018-19	PR Lge	38	12	9	17	42	48	45	13
2019-20	PR Lge	38	11	11	16	38	58	44	13
2020-21	PR Lge	38	12	9	17	46	62	45	12

DID YOU KNOW ?

Newcastle United have worn black and white shirts as their first-choice colours since the 1894–95 season, although it was not until after the First World War that they changed the colour of their shorts from blue to black. In their first two seasons as a Football League club United had worn red shirts with white shorts.

NEWCASTLE UNITED – PREMIER LEAGUE 2020–21 LEAGUE RECORD

Match No.	*Date*	*Venue*	*Opponents*	*Result*	*H/T Score*	*Lg Pos.*	*Goalscorers*	*Attendance*
1	Sept 12	A	West Ham U	W 2-0	0-0	2	Wilson ^{56}, Hendrick ^{87}	0
2	20	H	Brighton & HA	L 0-3	0-2	11		0
3	27	A	Tottenham H	D 1-1	0-1	9	Wilson (pen) ^{90}	0
4	Oct 3	H	Burnley	W 3-1	1-0	6	Saint-Maximin ^{14}, Wilson 2 (1 pen) $^{65, 77 (p)}$	0
5	17	H	Manchester U	L 1-4	1-1	11	Shaw (og) ^{2}	0
6	25	A	Wolverhampton W	D 1-1	0-0	14	Murphy ^{89}	0
7	Nov 1	H	Everton	W 2-1	0-0	11	Wilson 2 (1 pen) $^{56 (p), 84}$	0
8	6	A	Southampton	L 0-2	0-1	11		0
9	21	H	Chelsea	L 0-2	0-1	14		0
10	27	A	Crystal Palace	W 2-0	0-0	10	Wilson ^{88}, Joelinton ^{90}	0
11	Dec 12	H	WBA	W 2-1	1-0	11	Almiron ^{1}, Gayle ^{82}	0
12	16	A	Leeds U	L 2-5	1-1	14	Hendrick ^{26}, Clark ^{65}	0
13	19	H	Fulham	D 1-1	0-1	12	Wilson (pen) ^{64}	0
14	26	A	Manchester C	L 0-2	0-1	12		0
15	30	H	Liverpool	D 0-0	0-0	14		0
16	Jan 3	H	Leicester C	L 1-2	0-0	15	Carroll ^{82}	0
17	12	A	Sheffield U	L 0-1	0-0	15		0
18	18	A	Arsenal	L 0-3	0-0	15		0
19	23	A	Aston Villa	L 0-2	0-2	16		0
20	26	H	Leeds U	L 1-2	0-1	16	Almiron ^{57}	0
21	30	A	Everton	W 2-0	0-0	16	Wilson 2 $^{73, 90}$	0
22	Feb 2	H	Crystal Palace	L 1-2	1-2	16	Shelvey ^{2}	0
23	6	H	Southampton	W 3-2	3-1	16	Willock ^{16}, Almiron 2 $^{26, 45}$	0
24	15	A	Chelsea	L 0-2	0-2	17		0
25	21	A	Manchester U	L 1-3	1-1	17	Saint-Maximin ^{36}	0
26	27	H	Wolverhampton W	D 1-1	0-0	17	Lascelles ^{52}	0
27	Mar 7	A	WBA	D 0-0	0-0	16		0
28	12	H	Aston Villa	D 1-1	0-0	16	Lascelles ^{90}	0
29	20	A	Brighton & HA	L 0-3	0-1	17		0
30	Apr 4	H	Tottenham H	D 2-2	1-2	17	Joelinton ^{28}, Willock ^{85}	0
31	11	A	Burnley	W 2-1	0-1	17	Murphy ^{59}, Saint-Maximin ^{64}	0
32	17	H	West Ham U	W 3-2	2-0	15	Diop (og) ^{36}, Joelinton ^{41}, Willock ^{82}	0
33	24	A	Liverpool	D 1-1	0-1	15	Willock ^{90}	0
34	May 2	H	Arsenal	L 0-2	0-1	17		0
35	7	A	Leicester C	W 4-2	2-0	13	Willock ^{22}, Dummett ^{34}, Wilson 2 $^{64, 73}$	0
36	14	H	Manchester C	L 3-4	2-2	16	Krafth ^{25}, Joelinton (pen) ^{45}, Willock ^{62}	0
37	19	H	Sheffield U	W 1-0	1-0	15	Willock ^{45}	10,000
38	23	A	Fulham	W 2-0	1-0	12	Willock ^{23}, Schar (pen) ^{88}	2000

Final League Position: 12

GOALSCORERS

League (46): Wilson 12 (4 pens), Willock 8, Almiron 4, Joelinton 4 (1 pen), Saint-Maximin 3, Hendrick 2, Lascelles 2, Murphy 2, Carroll 1, Clark 1, Dummett 1, Gayle 1, Krafth 1, Schar 1 (1 pen), Shelvey 1, own goals 2.
FA Cup (0).
Carabao Cup (9): Joelinton 2, Almiron 1, Fraser 1, Hayden 1, Lascelles 1, Murphy 1, Shelvey 1, own goal 1.
Papa John's Trophy (2): Anderson 2.

Darlow K 25	Manquillo J 10 + 3	Lascelles J 19	Fernandez F 24	Lewis J 20 + 4	Saint-Maximin A 19 + 6	Shelvey J 29 + 1	Hayden I 22 + 2	Hendrick J 17 + 5	Wilson C 23 + 3	Carroll A 4 + 14	Joelinton d 23 + 8	Almiron M 28 + 6	Longstaff S 15 + 7	Fraser R 9 + 9	Ritchie M 15 + 3	Murphy J 17 + 9	Krafth E 14 + 2	Schar F 13 + 5	Longstaff M 4 + 1	Clark C 21 + 1	Gayle D 4 + 14	Yedlin D 5 + 1	Dummett P 14 + 1	Anderson E — + 1	Willock J 11 + 3	Dubravka M 13	*Match No.*
1	2	3	4	5	6^1	7	8	9	10^2	11^3	12	13	14														1
1	2	3	4	5	9^1	7^3	8	6	11	10^2	14	13		12													2
1	2	4	5	12		8	3	9^2	11	14	10	7^3			6^1	13											3
1	12		4	5	9^2	7	8	6	11		10^3		14	13			2	3^1									4
1		3	4	5	10	8	6^1	9^3	11		7^2	14		13			2	12									5
1		4^3	5	6	11^2			8	10	14	12	9	13	7^1		2		3									6
1		4	5	6	11^1		13	8	10^3	14		9^2	7	12		2		3									7
1		4	5	6	11			8^1	10^2	13	14	9	7			2^3		3	12								8
1	2^2	4^1	3	6	10^3		9			14	11	13	8			7		12		5							9
1	2		3	5		8		6	10		11^2	9^1	7		12			13		4							10
1				5^1		8	3		10		11	6^3	7		9	13	2^2			4	12	14					11
1			3	5			8	6^1	10		11^2	14	7	9^3		2	12			4	13						12
1			3^1			7	12		10		11^2	9	8	14	6					4	13	2	5^3				13
1			3	12			8			13	11^2	10^3			6^1	7		4	9	5	14	2					14
1			3	13			8		11		10	12			6^2	7^1		4	9	5		2					15
1			3			13			11	14	10^2	7^1	8		6	12		4	9	5		2^3					16
1			3^2				8	9	11	13			7	10■	12	14		4		5		2^3	6^1				17
1		3		5		8		13	10	11^1	9	6^3				12	2		7^2	4				14			18
1	2^1	4		6	12	7	3	8	11	10^2		9^3		13				5			14						19
1		3		5	12	7	2	8	11			9		10^2		6^1		4			13						20
1	2	3^1		5	13	8	7	6	10			9		11^2				4		12							21
1	2^2			5	12	8	7	6^1	10	14		9		11				3		4^3	13						22
1	2^1			5	10^3	7	3	6■	11^2		13	9					12	4					14		8		23
1		3		5	11^2	8	7			14	12	10		13			2			4	9^1				6^3		24
1		3		5	11^2	8	7				10^1	9^3		12		13	2			4	14				6		25
		3		5	11^2	7	8				9	10^1		12	14	13	2^3			4					6	1	26
		3				7	8	6^1		13	10			11^2			2			4	12		5		9	1	27
	13	3				7	8^3			14	9			10^1		12	2^2			4	11		5		6	1	28
	2	3				7	8^1	12			9	10^3	14	11		13				4			5		6^2	1	29
	14	4			12	8					10	7	9		6	2^3	3^2				11^1		5		13	1	30
			3		12	8		14	13		10^2	7^3	9		6	2				4	11^1		5			1	31
			3		10^1	8			12	14	11^3	9	7^2		6	2				4			5		13	1	32
			3		10	9			12		11^1	7^3	8		6	2				4^2	14		5		13	1	33
			3^1		11	8			10		13	9^2	7		6	2		12■		4^3	14		5			1	34
			4		11^2	8		14	10		13	9^3	12		6	2	3						5		7^1	1	35
			4^3	13	10	8					11^1	9	12		6^2	2	3				14		5		7	1	36
			3		10^2	8				14	11^1	7	13		2	5	6				12		4		9^3	1	37
			4		11^1	8		14				10^3	9		6	2	3^2	13			12		5		7	1	38

FA Cup

Third Round	Arsenal	(a)	0-2
(aet)			

Carabao Cup

Second Round	Blackburn R	(h)	1-0
Third Round	Morecambe	(a)	7-0
Fourth Round	Newport Co	(a)	1-1
(Newcastle U won 5-4 on penalties)			
Quarter-Final	Brentford	(a)	0-1

Papa John's Trophy (Newcastle U U21)

Group C (N)	Shrewsbury T	(a)	0-3
Group C (N)	Crewe Alex	(a)	0-1
Group C (N)	Bolton W	(a)	2-3

NEWPORT COUNTY

FOUNDATION

In 1912 Newport County were formed following a meeting at The Tredegar Arms Hotel. A professional football club had existed in the town called Newport FC, but they ceased to exist in 1907. The first season as Newport County was in the second division of the Southern League. They started life playing at Somerton Park where they remained through their League years. They were elected to the Football League for the beginning of the 1920–21 season as founder members of Division 3. At the end of the 1987–88 season, they were relegated from the Football League and replaced by Lincoln City. On February 27 1989, Newport County went out of business and from the ashes Newport AFC was born. Starting down the pyramid in the Hellenic League, they eventally gained promotion to the Conference in 2011 and were promoted to the Football League after a play-off with Wrexham in 2013.

Rodney Parade, Rodney Road, Newport, South Wales NP19 0UU.

Telephone: (01633) 302 012.

Ticket Office: (01633) 264 572.

Website: www.newport-county.co.uk

Email: office@newport-county.co.uk

Ground Capacity: 8,700.

Record Attendance: 24,268 v Cardiff C, Division 3 (S), 16 October 1937 (Somerton Park); 4,660 v Swansea C, FA Cup 1st rd, 11 November 2006 (Newport Stadium); 9,836 v Tottenham H, FA Cup 4th rd, 27 January 2018 (Rodney Parade).

Pitch Measurements: 100m × 68m (109.5yd × 74.5yd).

Chairman: Gavin Foxall.

Manager: Michael Flynn.

Assistant Manager: Wayne Hatswell.

Colours: Amber shirts with black sleeves and white trim, black shorts with amber trim, amber socks with black trim.

Year Formed: 1912.

Turned Professional: 1912.

Previous Names: Newport County, 1912; Newport AFC, 1989; Newport County, 1999.

Club Nicknames: 'The Exiles', 'The Ironsides', 'The Port', 'The County'.

Grounds: 1912–89, 1990–92, Somerton Park; 1992–94, Meadow Park Stadium; 1994, Newport Stadium; 2012, Rodney Parade.

First Football League Game: 28 August 1920, Division 3, v Reading (h) L 0–1.

HONOURS

League Champions: Division 3S – 1938–39.
Runners-up: Conference – (3rd) 2012–13 *(promoted via play-offs)*.

FA Cup: 5th rd – 1949, 2019.

League Cup: 4th rd – 2021.

Welsh Cup Winners: 1980.
Runners-up: 1963, 1987.

European Competitions
European Cup Winners' Cup: 1980–81 *(qf)*.

FOOTBALL YEARBOOK FACT FILE

Newport County were rock bottom of League One at the beginning of March 2017, and with the team 11 points from safety they seemed certain to lose their place in the EFL. The club appointed Mike Flynn as manager and he led them to seven wins from the final 12 games, with a last gasp win over Notts County in the final game of the season keeping them from relegation.

Record League Victory: 10–0 v Merthyr T, Division 3(S), 10 April 1930 – Martin (5), Gittins (2), Thomas (1), Bagley (1), Lawson (1).

Record Cup Victory: 7–0 v Working, FA Cup 1st rd, 24 November 1928 – Young (3), Pugh (2) Gittins (1), Reid (1).

Record Defeat: 0–13 v Newcastle U, Division 2, 5 October 1946.

Most League Points (2 for a win): 61, Division 4, 1979–80.

Most League Points (3 for a win): 78, Division 3, 1982–83.

Most League Goals: 85, Division 4, 1964–65.

Highest League Scorer in Season: Tudor Martin, 34, Division 3 (S), 1929–30.

Most League Goals in Total Aggregate: Reg Parker, 99, 1948–54.

Most League Goals in One Match: 5, Tudor Martin v Merthyr T, Dvision 3 (S), 10 April 1930.

Most Capped Player: Keanu Marsh Brown, 10, Guyana.

Most League Appearances: Len Weare, 527, 1955–70.

Youngest League Player: Regan Poole, 16 years 94 days v Shrewsbury T, 20 September 2014.

Record Transfer Fee Received: £500,000 (rising to £1,000,000) from Peterborough U for Conor Washington, January 2014.

Record Transfer Fee Paid: £80,000 to Swansea C for Alan Waddle, January 1981.

Football League Record: 1920 Original member of Division 3; 1921–31 Division 3 (S) – dropped out of Football League; 1932 Re-elected to Division 3 (S); 1932–39 Division 3 (S); 1946–47 Division 2; 1947–58 Division 3 (S); 1958–62 Division 3; 1962–80 Division 4; 1980–87 Division 3; 1987–88 Division 4 (relegated from Football League); 2011 Promoted to Conference; 2011–13 Conference Premier; 2013– FL 2.

LATEST SEQUENCES

Longest Sequence of League Wins: 5, 17.10.2020 – 31.10.2020.

Longest Sequence of League Defeats: 8, 22.11.2016 – 7.1.2017.

Longest Sequence of League Draws: 4, 31.10.2015 – 24.11.2015.

Longest Sequence of Unbeaten League Matches: 17, 15.3.2019 – 7.9.2019.

Longest Sequence Without a League Win: 12, 15.3.2016 – 6.8.2017.

Successive Scoring Runs: 20 from 12.9.2020.

Successive Non-scoring Runs: 4 from 1.2.2020.

MANAGERS

Davy McDougle 1912–13 *(Player-Manager)*
Sam Hollis 1913–17
Harry Parkes 1919–22
Jimmy Hindmarsh 1922–35
Louis Page 1935–36
Tom Bromilow 1936–37
Billy McCandless 1937–45
Tom Bromilow 1945–50
Fred Stansfield 1950–53
Billy Lucas 1953–61
Bobby Evans 1961–62
Billy Lucas 1962–67
Leslie Graham 1967–69
Bobby Ferguson 1969–70 *(Player-Manager)*
Billy Lucas 1970–74
Brian Harris 1974–75
Dave Elliott 1975–76 *(Player-Manager)*
Jimmy Scoular 1976–77
Colin Addison 1977–78
Len Ashurst 1978–82
Colin Addison 1982–85
Bobby Smith 1985–86
John Relish 1986
Jimmy Mullen 1986–87
John Lewis 1987
Brian Eastick 1987–88
David Williams 1988
Eddie May 1988
John Mahoney 1988–89
John Relish 1989–93
Graham Rogers 1993–96
Chris Price 1997
Tim Harris 1997–2002
Peter Nicholas 2002–04
John Cornforth 2004–05
Peter Beadle 2005–08
Dean Holdsworth 2008–11
Anthony Hudson 2011
Justin Edinburgh 2011–15
Jimmy Dack 2015
Terry Butcher 2015
John Sheridan 2015–16
Warren Feeney 2016
Graham Westley 2016–17
Michael Flynn May 2017–

TEN YEAR LEAGUE RECORD

		P	W	D	L	F	A	Pts	Pos
2011-12	Conf P	46	11	14	21	53	65	47	19
2012-13	Conf P	46	25	10	11	85	60	85	3
2013-14	FL 2	46	14	16	16	56	59	58	14
2014-15	FL 2	46	18	11	17	51	54	65	9
2015-16	FL 2	46	10	13	23	43	64	43	22
2016-17	FL 2	46	12	12	22	51	73	48	22
2017-18	FL 2	46	16	16	14	56	58	64	11
2018-19	FL 2	46	20	11	15	59	59	71	7
2019-20	FL 2	36	12	10	14	32	39	46	14§
2020-21	FL 2	46	20	13	13	57	42	73	5

§Decided on points-per-game (1.28)

DID YOU KNOW ?

Newport County won the Conference South title in 2009–10 in record breaking style. Their points total of 103 has yet to be beaten, while they also established records for most wins, fewest defeats, fewest goals conceded and most clean sheets. They won 18 and drew three of their home games, conceding just eight goals.

NEWPORT COUNTY – SKY BET LEAGUE TWO 2020–21 LEAGUE RECORD

Match No.	Date	Venue	Opponents	Result	H/T Score	Lg Pos.	Goalscorers	Attendance
1	Sept 12	A	Scunthorpe U	D 1-1	1-0	10	Taylor [31]	0
2	19	H	Barrow	W 2-1	1-1	7	Shephard [19], Taylor [48]	0
3	26	A	Bolton W	W 2-0	0-0	3	Abrahams 2 [54, 63]	0
4	Oct 3	H	Mansfield T	W 2-1	0-0	1	Twine [78], Dolan (pen) [88]	0
5	10	A	Cambridge U	L 1-2	0-1	3	Twine [67]	0
6	17	H	Tranmere R	W 1-0	1-0	2	Janneh [25]	0
7	20	A	Stevenage	W 1-0	1-0	2	Abrahams (pen) [8]	0
8	24	A	Bradford C	W 3-0	2-0	1	Demetriou [1], Amond [44], Dolan (pen) [90]	0
9	27	H	Colchester U	W 2-1	0-0	1	Twine [51], Amond [90]	0
10	31	H	Harrogate T	W 2-1	1-1	1	Amond [30], Cooper [88]	0
11	Nov 3	A	Carlisle U	L 2-3	0-1	1	Devitt [84], Sheehan [90]	0
12	21	H	Port Vale	W 1-0	0-0	1	Ellison [90]	0
13	24	H	Walsall	D 1-1	1-1	1	Twine [23]	0
14	Dec 1	A	Forest Green R	D 1-1	1-0	1	Abrahams (pen) [45]	0
15	5	H	Morecambe	W 2-1	1-1	1	Amond [11], Dolan (pen) [83]	0
16	8	A	Grimsby T	W 2-0	2-0	1	Twine [25], Amond (pen) [45]	0
17	12	A	Leyton Orient	L 1-2	1-0	1	Proctor [20]	1734
18	15	A	Salford C	D 1-1	0-1	1	Sheehan (pen) [90]	0
19	19	H	Oldham Ath	L 2-4	2-1	1	Twine [8], Bennett [41]	0
20	26	A	Crawley T	D 1-1	1-1	1	Haynes [5]	0
21	Jan 16	H	Salford C	D 0-0	0-0	2		0
22	19	A	Cheltenham T	D 1-1	1-1	2	King [12]	0
23	23	A	Oldham Ath	L 2-3	2-2	3	Scrimshaw [3], Gambin [40]	0
24	30	A	Harrogate T	L 1-2	1-1	7	Scrimshaw [17]	0
25	Feb 6	H	Grimsby T	W 1-0	0-0	4	Maynard [51]	0
26	9	H	Southend U	L 0-1	0-0	5		0
27	16	H	Exeter C	D 1-1	0-1	5	Telford [88]	0
28	21	H	Forest Green R	L 0-2	0-1	7		0
29	24	A	Walsall	W 1-0	0-0	6	Labadie [70]	0
30	27	H	Stevenage	D 0-0	0-0	6		0
31	Mar 2	A	Tranmere R	L 0-1	0-1	8		0
32	6	A	Colchester U	W 2-0	1-0	6	Labadie [30], Amond [78]	0
33	9	H	Bradford C	W 2-1	0-0	6	Dolan 2 (1 pen) [77, 90 (p)]	0
34	13	A	Morecambe	W 3-1	2-1	4	Dolan (pen) [8], Sheehan [45], Ellison [79]	0
35	16	A	Port Vale	L 1-2	0-1	4	Scrimshaw [55]	0
36	20	H	Leyton Orient	L 0-1	0-0	7		0
37	Apr 2	A	Barrow	L 1-2	1-0	7	Bennett [24]	0
38	5	H	Bolton W	W 1-0	0-0	7	Maynard [63]	0
39	9	A	Mansfield T	D 1-1	0-0	7	Labadie [75]	0
40	13	H	Carlisle U	D 0-0	0-0	6		0
41	17	H	Cambridge U	L 0-1	0-0	7		0
42	20	H	Crawley T	W 2-0	0-0	7	Shephard [52], Lewis, A [90]	0
43	24	A	Exeter C	D 0-0	0-0	7		0
44	27	H	Scunthorpe U	W 4-0	3-0	6	Taft (og) [29], Demetriou 2 [34, 85], Collins [39]	0
45	May 1	H	Cheltenham T	W 1-0	1-0	5	Labadie [4]	0
46	8	A	Southend U	D 1-1	0-1	5	Demetriou [56]	0

Final League Position: 5

GOALSCORERS

League (57): Amond 6 (1 pen), Dolan 6 (5 pens), Twine 6, Abrahams 4 (2 pens), Demetriou 4, Labadie 4, Scrimshaw 3, Sheehan 3 (1 pen), Bennett 2, Ellison 2, Maynard 2, Shephard 2, Taylor 2, Collins 1, Cooper 1, Devitt 1, Gambin 1, Haynes 1, Janneh 1, King 1, Lewis, A 1, Proctor 1, Telford 1, own goal 1.
FA Cup (6): Amond 1 (1 pen), Baker 1, Devitt 1, Janneh 1, Proctor 1, own goal 1.
Carabao Cup (7): Abrahams 4 (1 pen), Amond 1, Labadie 1, Twine 1.
Papa John's Trophy (1): Amond 1.
League Two Play-Offs (5): Collins 1, Dolan 1, Ellison 1, Labadie 1, Maynard 1.

Townsend N 38	Shephard L 42	Howkins K 2	Demetriou M 45	Haynes R 37	Dolan M 35 + 3	Labadie J 35 + 3	Sheehan J 43	Twine S 18 + 1	Taylor R 15 + 10	Abrahams T 15 + 8	Cooper B 18 + 1	Janneh S 4 + 4	Willmott R 5 + 14	Baker A 1 + 3	Bennett S 32 + 6	Amond P 23 + 18	Ellison K 2 + 21	Proctor J 5 + 5	Devitt J 1 + 7	Longe-King D 8 + 3	Lewis A 15 + 5	Collins L 8 + 8	King T 8 + 1	Scrimshaw J 6 + 10	Windsor O — + 1	Gambin L 5 + 6	Hartigan A 9 + 2	Telford D 5 + 10	Maynard N 12 + 7	Farquharson P 12 + 1	Evans J — + 1	Ledley J 2 + 2	Match No.
1	2	3	4	5	6^{1}	7	8	9^{3}	10^{2}	11	12	13	14																				1
1	5^{3}	2	4	9		13	7	8^{2}	11^{1}	12	3	10	6	14																			2
1	5		4	9	3	6^{2}	7	8^{1}	11^{3}	10	2		12		13	14																	3
1	5		4	9	3	6	7	8^{3}	11^{1}	10^{2}	2	12			14	13																	4
1	5^{3}		4	9	3	6	7	8		10		13	14		2^{2}	11^{1}	12																5
1	5		4	9	3	6	7	8		11	2	10^{1}				12																	6
1	5		4	9	3	8	7	6^{2}		10^{1}	2	11^{3}	14		13	12																	7
1	5		4	8	3	6^{2}	7	9		10^{3}	2	11^{1}			13	12		14															8
1	5		4	9	3	6^{1}	7	8		11^{2}	2		13		12	10^{3}	14																9
1	5^{1}		4	9		7	6	8		11^{2}	2		12		3^{3}	10		13	14														10
1			4	9^{3}	3	7^{1}	6			11^{2}	2		5		8	10	14	13	12														11
1	5^{3}		4	8^{4}	3	12	6	7		11	2		14			13	15	10^{1}	9^{2}														12
1	5^{3}		4	9^{2}	3	6	7	8		12	2		14			10^{4}	15	11^{1}	13														13
1	5		4	9	3	8^{3}	6	14		11^{2}	2	13			7	12		10^{1}															14
1	5		4	9^{1}	3		6	7		11^{2}	2		12		8^{3}	10^{4}	14	13		15													15
1	2		4	5^{1}	12	6^{3}	7	9		14	3		8		13	11^{4}	10^{2}		15														16
1	5^{4}		4		3	12	6	7^{5}		13	2		14		8^{1}	10^{2}	16	11	15		9^{3}												17
1	5		4	9^{5}	3^{1}		6	7^{2}		11^{3}	2		12		8	10^{4}	15		13	16		14											18
1	2		4	5^{4}			7	10		15	3		8^{3}		6	12	14	11^{1}	13			9^{2}											19
1^{1}	5		4	8	3		7	10		11^{2}	2		14		6^{4}	15		13				9^{3}	12										20
	5		4	9^{1}	3	6	7▪		10^{2}	13				12	8	15	14^{4}			2			1	11^{3}									21
	5		4	9	3	7			12	13			6^{3}		8	11^{1}				2			1	10^{2}	14								22
	2^{4}		4	5^{5}	7	8▪			10^{2}	13			15	12	6	14				3		16	1	11^{3}		9^{1}							23
1	5▪		4	8	3^{1}				11				13		6	14				2		15		10^{2}		9^{3}	7^{4}	12					24
1			4	9	3		7							5^{1}	6▪	15				2	14			13		8^{4}		10^{2}	11^{3}	12			25
1			4	5^{5}	8^{1}		7		13							11^{2}				3	16			14		9^{3}	6^{4}	15	10	2	12		26
1			4	5	8^{1}	7	6		11^{3}							15				3^{2}	12	14		16		9^{4}		13	10	2^{5}			27
1	2		4	5		7	6		12							13	14				15			11^{3}			8^{4}	9^{1}	10^{2}	3			28
1	5		4	9	3	6^{3}	7		13						8	12											14	11^{1}	10^{2}	2			29
1	5		4	9^{4}	3^{5}		7		14						6	12	16							13		15	8^{3}	10^{2}	11^{1}	2			30
1	5		4	9^{3}	3^{5}	7	8		12						6^{4}	10^{2}	15							13		16		14	11^{1}	2			31
1	5^{3}		4	9	3	6^{2}	8		12						7	11^{4}					15			14			13		10^{1}	2			32
1	5		4		3	6	8		12						7^{2}	11^{3}	15				9^{4}			14				13	10^{1}	2			33
1	5		4		3	6	8		11^{4}						7^{2}	10^{1}	13			14	9							15	12	2^{3}			34
1	5		4		3^{4}	6	8		11^{3}						7^{2}	10^{1}	15				9			13		12		14		2			35
1	5		4		3^{2}	6	8		12						7^{3}		16				9^{5}			10^{1}		14		15	11^{4}	2		13	36
1	5		4▪		3	6	8		11^{2}						7^{4}	10^{1}	15				9	13		14					12			2^{3}	37
1	5				3	6	7		11						8		14			4^{1}	9	12							10^{3}	2^{2}		13	38
1	5		4		3	6	7		10						2						9	13		12				11^{1}				8^{2}	39
1	5		4		3^{2}	8	7		11						2	12	13				9	6							10^{1}				40
1	2		4	5		7	8		11^{1}						3	10^{3}	9^{2}				6^{4}	13				14		15	12				41
	5		3	4		6	7								2	11					9	10^{1}	1				8		12				42
	2		4	9		6	7								3	11					5	10^{1}	1				8		12				43
	2		4	9^{2}	14	6^{4}	7^{3}								3	11^{1}	15				5	10^{5}	1			13	8	16	12				44
	2		4	9		6	7								3	10					5	11^{1}	1				8		12				45
	2		4	9	12	6^{1}	7		13						3	10^{2}					5	11	1				8						46

FA Cup

First Round	Leyton Orient	(a)	2-1
Second Round	Salford C	(h)	3-0
Third Round	Brighton & HA	(h)	1-1

(aet; Brighton & HA won 4-3 on penalties)

Carabao Cup

First Round	Swansea C	(h)	2-0
Second Round	Cambridge U	(h)	1-0
Third Round	Watford	(h)	3-1
Fourth Round	Newcastle U	(h)	1-1

(Newcastle U won 5-4 on penalties)

Papa John's Trophy

Group F (S)	Cheltenham T	(h)	0-1
Group F (S)	Norwich C U21	(h)	0-5
Group F (S)	Plymouth Arg	(a)	1-3

League Two Play-Offs

Semi-Final 1st leg	Forest Green R	(h)	2-0
Semi-Final 2nd leg	Forest Green R	(a)	3-4
(aet)			
Final	Morecambe	(Wembley)	0-1
(aet)			

NORTHAMPTON TOWN

FOUNDATION

Formed in 1897 by schoolteachers connected with the Northampton & District Elementary Schools' Association, they survived a financial crisis at the end of their first year when they were £675 in the red and became members of the Midland League – a fast move indeed for a new club. They achieved Southern League membership in 1901.

PTS Academy Stadium, Upton Way, Northampton NN5 5QA.

Telephone: (01604) 683 700.

Ticket Office: (01604) 683 777.

Website: www.ntfc.co.uk

Email: wendy.lambell@ntfc.co.uk

Ground Capacity: 7,798.

Record Attendance: 24,523 v Fulham, Division 1, 23 April 1966 (at County Ground); 7,798 v Manchester U, EFL Cup 3rd rd, 21 September 2016; 7,798 v Derby Co, FA Cup 4th rd, 24 January 2019 (at Sixfields Stadium).

Pitch Measurements: 106m × 64m (116yd × 70yd).

Chairman: Kelvin Thomas.

Chief Executive: James Whiting.

Manager: Jon Brady.

Assistant Manager: Colin Calderwood.

Colours: Claret shirts with white sleeves, white shorts with claret trim, claret socks with white trim.

Year Formed: 1897.

Turned Professional: 1901.

Grounds: 1897, County Ground; 1994, Sixfields Stadium (renamed PTS Academy Stadium 2018).

Club Nickname: 'The Cobblers'.

First Football League Game: 28 August 1920, Division 3, v Grimsby T (a) L 0–2 – Thorpe; Sproston, Hewison; Jobey, Tomkins, Pease; Whitworth, Lockett, Thomas, Freeman, MacKechnie.

Record League Victory: 10–0 v Walsall, Division 3 (S), 5 November 1927 – Hammond; Watson, Jeffs; Allen, Brett, Odell; Daley, Smith (3), Loasby (3), Hoten (1), Wells (3).

Record Cup Victory: 10–0 v Sutton T, FA Cup prel rd, 7 December 1907 – Cooch; Drennan, Lloyd Davies, Tirrell (1), McCartney, Hickleton, Badenock (3), Platt (3), Lowe (1), Chapman (2), McDiarmid.

Record Defeat: 0–11 v Southampton, Southern League, 28 December 1901.

Most League Points (2 for a win): 68, Division 4, 1975–76.

Most League Points (3 for a win): 99, Division 4, 1986–87; FL 2, 2015–16.

HONOURS

League Champions: Division 3 – 1962–63; FL 2 – 2015–16; Division 4 – 1986–87.
Runners-up: Division 2 – 1964–65; Division 3S – 1927–28, 1949–50; FL 2 – 2005–06; Division 4 – 1975–76.

FA Cup: 5th rd – 1934, 1950, 1970.

League Cup: 5th rd – 1965, 1967.

FOOTBALL YEARBOOK FACT FILE

Goalkeeper Alan Starling scored for the Cobblers from the penalty spot in Town's 5-2 home win over Hartlepool in April 1976. His goal meant that every regular player for Town scored during the season when the club won promotion from the Fourth Division. It was the only goal he scored in over 350 Football League appearances during his 11-year career.

Most League Goals: 109, Division 3, 1962–63 and Division 3 (S), 1952–53.

Highest League Scorer in Season: Cliff Holton, 36, Division 3, 1961–62.

Most League Goals in Total Aggregate: Jack English, 135, 1947–60.

Most League Goals in One Match: 5, Ralph Hoten v Crystal Palace, Division 3 (S), 27 October 1928.

Most Capped Player: Edwin Lloyd Davies, 12 (16), Wales.

Most League Appearances: Tommy Fowler, 521, 1946–61.

Youngest League Player: Adrian Mann, 16 years 297 days v Bury, 5 May 1984.

Record Transfer Fee Received: £1,000,000 (rising to £1,500,000) from Brentford for Charlie Goode, August 2020.

Record Transfer Fee Paid: £165,000 to Oldham Ath for Josh Low, July 2003.

Football League Record: 1920 Original Member of Division 3; 1921 Division 3 (S); 1958–61 Division 4; 1961–63 Division 3; 1963–65 Division 2; 1965–66 Division 1; 1966–67 Division 2; 1967–69 Division 3; 1969–76 Division 4; 1976–77 Division 3; 1977–87 Division 4; 1987–90 Division 3; 1990–92 Division 4; 1992–97 Division 3; 1997–99 Division 2; 1999–2000 Division 3; 2000–03 Division 2; 2003–04 Division 3; 2004–06 FL 2; 2006–09 FL 1; 2009–16 FL 2; 2016–18 FL 1; 2018–20 FL 2; 2020–21 FL 1; 2021– FL 2.

LATEST SEQUENCES

Longest Sequence of League Wins: 10, 28.12.2015 – 23.2.2016.

Longest Sequence of League Defeats: 8, 26.10.1935 – 21.12.1935.

Longest Sequence of League Draws: 6, 5.2.2011 – 26.2.2011.

Longest Sequence of Unbeaten League Matches: 31, 28.12.2015 – 10.9.2016.

Longest Sequence Without a League Win: 18, 5.2.2011 – 25.4.2011.

Successive Scoring Runs: 28 from 29.8.2015.

Successive Non-scoring Runs: 7 from 7.4.1939.

MANAGERS

Arthur Jones 1897–1907
(Secretary-Manager)
Herbert Chapman 1907–12
Walter Bull 1912–13
Fred Lessons 1913–19
Bob Hewison 1920–25
Jack Tresadern 1925–30
Jack English 1931–35
Syd Puddefoot 1935–37
Warney Cresswell 1937–39
Tom Smith 1939–49
Bob Dennison 1949–54
Dave Smith 1954–59
David Bowen 1959–67
Tony Marchi 1967–68
Ron Flowers 1968–69
Dave Bowen 1969–72
(continued as General Manager and Secretary 1972–85 when joined the board)
Billy Baxter 1972–73
Bill Dodgin Jnr 1973–76
Pat Crerand 1976–77
By committee 1977
Bill Dodgin Jnr 1977
John Petts 1977–78
Mike Keen 1978–79
Clive Walker 1979–80
Bill Dodgin Jnr 1980–82
Clive Walker 1982–84
Tony Barton 1984–85
Graham Carr 1985–90
Theo Foley 1990–92
Phil Chard 1992–93
John Barnwell 1993–94
Ian Atkins 1995–99
Kevin Wilson 1999–2001
Kevan Broadhurst 2001–03
Terry Fenwick 2003
Martin Wilkinson 2003
Colin Calderwood 2003–06
John Gorman 2006
Stuart Gray 2007–09
Ian Sampson 2009–11
Gary Johnson 2011
Aidy Boothroyd 2011–13
Chris Wilder 2014–16
Rob Page 2016–17
Justin Edinburgh 2017
Jimmy Floyd Hasselbaink 2017–18
Dean Austin 2018
Keith Curle 2018–21
Jon Brady February 2021–

TEN YEAR LEAGUE RECORD

		P	W	D	L	F	A	Pts	Pos
2011-12	FL 2	46	12	12	22	56	79	48	20
2012-13	FL 2	46	21	10	15	64	55	73	6
2013-14	FL 2	46	13	14	19	42	57	53	21
2014-15	FL 2	46	18	7	21	67	62	61	12
2015-16	FL 2	46	29	12	5	82	46	99	1
2016-17	FL 1	46	14	11	21	60	73	53	16
2017-18	FL 1	46	12	11	23	43	77	47	22
2018-19	FL 2	46	14	19	13	64	63	61	15
2019-20	FL 2	37	17	7	13	54	40	58	7§
2020-21	FL 1	46	11	12	23	41	67	45	22

§*Decided on points-per-game (1.57)*

DID YOU KNOW ?

Northampton Town forward Barry Lines became the first player to score in all four divisions for the same club when he netted for the Cobblers in a First Division game against West Bromwich Albion in September 1965. Town lost the game 4-3 and their only season in top-flight football ended in relegation.

NORTHAMPTON TOWN – SKY BET LEAGUE ONE 2020–21 LEAGUE RECORD

Match No.	Date	Venue	Opponents	Result		H/T Score	Lg Pos.	Goalscorers	Attendance
1	Sept 12	H	AFC Wimbledon	D	2-2	2-2	8	Warburton[19], Korboa[31]	0
2	19	A	Shrewsbury T	W	2-1	1-0	7	Marshall[12], Hoskins[65]	0
3	26	H	Hull C	L	0-2	0-2	10		0
4	Oct 3	A	Bristol R	L	0-2	0-0	15		0
5	10	H	Peterborough U	L	0-2	0-1	18		0
6	17	A	Plymouth Arg	L	1-2	0-1	21	Korboa[62]	0
7	20	H	Swindon T	W	2-1	2-0	15	Missilou[7], Rose[28]	0
8	24	H	Charlton Ath	L	0-2	0-0	18		0
9	27	A	Portsmouth	L	0-4	0-1	19		0
10	31	A	Wigan Ath	W	3-2	2-0	17	Rose[13], Hoskins[21], Chukwuemeka[66]	0
11	Nov 3	H	Milton Keynes D	D	0-0	0-0	16		0
12	14	H	Accrington S	L	0-1	0-1	18		0
13	21	A	Burton Alb	W	3-1	1-0	16	Smith 2[2, 67], Lines[81]	0
14	24	A	Rochdale	D	1-1	1-0	16	Smith[19]	0
15	Dec 1	H	Fleetwood T	W	1-0	0-0	14	Bolger[47]	0
16	5	H	Doncaster R	L	0-2	0-1	16		1164
17	12	A	Crewe Alex	L	1-2	1-0	17	Holmes[3]	2000
18	15	A	Oxford U	L	0-4	0-0	19		2000
19	19	H	Lincoln C	L	0-4	0-2	19		2000
20	29	H	Gillingham	W	3-1	2-1	19	Hoskins (pen)[31], Rose[35], Sheehan[47]	0
21	Jan 2	H	Sunderland	D	0-0	0-0	18		0
22	23	A	Lincoln C	L	1-2	0-0	20	Rose[90]	0
23	26	A	Fleetwood T	D	0-0	0-0	19		0
24	Feb 2	A	Blackpool	L	0-2	0-1	20		0
25	6	A	Accrington S	D	0-0	0-0	21		0
26	9	H	Wigan Ath	L	0-1	0-0	22		0
27	13	H	Burton Alb	L	0-2	0-0	22		0
28	16	A	Ipswich T	D	0-0	0-0	20		0
29	20	A	Milton Keynes D	L	3-4	1-2	21	Horsfall[2], Watson[46], Kioso[78]	0
30	23	H	Rochdale	D	0-0	0-0	22		0
31	27	A	Swindon T	L	1-2	1-1	23	Watson[26]	0
32	Mar 2	H	Plymouth Arg	W	2-0	1-0	21	Watson 2[40, 65]	0
33	6	H	Portsmouth	W	4-1	4-0	19	Watson 2[20, 23], Horsfall[32], Edmondson[43]	0
34	9	A	Charlton Ath	L	1-2	0-0	20	Jones, A[90]	0
35	13	A	Doncaster R	D	0-0	0-0	19		0
36	20	H	Crewe Alex	L	0-1	0-0	21		0
37	23	H	Oxford U	W	1-0	0-0	20	Hoskins[55]	0
38	27	A	AFC Wimbledon	L	0-1	0-0	20		0
39	Apr 2	H	Shrewsbury T	W	1-0	1-0	19	Watson[27]	0
40	5	A	Hull C	L	0-3	0-2	19		0
41	10	H	Bristol R	D	1-1	0-1	19	Hoskins (pen)[78]	0
42	16	A	Peterborough U	L	1-3	1-1	21	Hoskins (pen)[43]	0
43	20	H	Ipswich T	W	3-0	2-0	21	Kioso 2[8, 32], Watson[84]	0
44	24	A	Gillingham	D	2-2	0-1	21	Edmondson[79], Horsfall[83]	0
45	May 1	H	Blackpool	L	0-3	0-1	22		0
46	9	A	Sunderland	D	1-1	0-0	22	Hoskins[84]	0

Final League Position: 22

GOALSCORERS

League (41): Watson 8, Hoskins 7 (3 pens), Rose 4, Horsfall 3, Kioso 3, Smith 3, Edmondson 2, Korboa 2, Bolger 1, Chukwuemeka 1, Holmes 1, Jones, A 1, Lines 1, Marshall 1, Missilou 1, Sheehan 1, Warburton 1.
FA Cup (1): Hoskins 1.
Carabao Cup (3): Smith 1 (1 pen), Warburton 1, Watson 1.
Papa John's Trophy (8): Ashley-Seal 3, Mills 2, Chukwuemeka 1, Marshall 1, Rose 1.

Arnold S 11	Racic L 4 + 2	Bolger C 26	Horsfall F 37 + 3	Harriman M 22 + 8	Watson R 32 + 7	Missilou C 11 + 4	Marshall M 18 + 11	Warburton M 4	Ashley-Seal B 7 + 16	Korboa R 5 + 11	Hoskins S 44 + 2	Chukwuemeka C 2 + 20	Martin J 5 + 1	Mills J 27	Lines C 1 + 3	Roberts M — + 2	Smith H 13 + 3	Nuttall J — + 1	Adams N 10 + 4	Sowerby J 26 + 2	Rose D 23 + 16	McWilliams S 30 + 2	Mitchell J 35	Sheehan A 12 + 2	Holmes R 5 + 4	Dyche M 1 + 1	Jones L 27	Morris B 19 + 3	Edmondson R 13 + 8	Miller M 11 + 1	Kioso P 21	Jones A 4 + 5	Cross L — + 1	Match No.
1	2	3	4	5	6	7	8	9^{2}	10^{1}	11	12	13																						1
1		3		2	6	7	5^{3}	9^{2}	11^{1}		10	12	4	8	13	14																		2
1	2^{3}	3			6	7	5^{2}	9^{1}			11	13	4	8			10	12	14															3
1	2	3		5^{2}	6	7^{3}		11^{1}	13	12	9		4▮	8			10			14														4
1		3	4	2	12	6^{1}			13	14	9			8^{3}			10^{2}		5	7	11													5
1	12	3	2	5	8				13	10^{3}	9	14	4							7	11^{2}	6^{1}												6
		3	4	2	13	7	14		10^{1}	9	5						12		8^{3}	6	11^{2}		1											7
	2^{3}	3	4	5		7	14		12	9^{2}	10	13							8^{1}	6	11		1											8
		2	4	8	9	7^{1}				11^{2}	5	13	14				10			6	12		1	3^{3}										9
	14	2	3	5	7		13				9	12					10^{3}		8^{2}	6	11^{1}		1	4										10
		3	2	5	7^{1}		8^{2}		14		9						10		12	6	11^{3}		1	4	13									11
		2	3	5^{1}	6				13		9						10		8	7	11^{2}		1	4	12									12
		2	3	13		15	8		14		5	11^{2}			12		10^{4}			7		6^{3}	1	4	9^{1}									13
		2	3	5		13	8				11				12		10			7		6^{1}	1	4	9^{2}									14
1		2	3	5		13	12		11^{1}		9						10^{3}		8^{2}	7	14	6		4										15
1		3^{3}	4	2		7	9^{2}		12		5	15					11^{4}		14	6	13	8▮			10^{1}									16
1		3	4	2	13	7^{3}			15		11	12	5▮				10^{4}		6^{1}	8					9^{2}	14								17
1			3	2	7	14					5	12			8^{2}		10		13	6^{3}	11^{1}				9	4								18
1		3	4	2^{3}	7	6^{2}	8^{1}		9	12	10						13		5		11				14									19
		3	14	13	9				11^{4}		8	12							5^{2}	7	10^{1}	6	1	4^{3}	15		2							20
		3	12	14	8				10		5						13		9^{3}	7	11^{2}	6	1	4^{1}			2							21
		4		2					13	12	9			5						8^{2}	14	6	1				3	7	10^{3}	11^{1}				22
		3	2		13				14	12	8			9^{1}							10^{3}	6	1				4	7	11^{2}		5			23
		2	4^{3}		9^{1}					14	11^{2}	12		8						6^{4}	15	13	1				3	7	10		5			24
		3	4				14			13	9^{3}			8^{1}						7	10	6	1				2	12	11^{2}		5			25
		3^{5}	4		13				14	15	9	16		8^{4}						7^{2}	10	6^{1}	1				2	12	11^{3}		5			26
		3		12	6		10				9			5							11^{2}	7^{1}	1				4	8	13		2			27
			3		13		11^{2}		12		9			5						7^{3}	10^{1}	6	1				4	8	14		2			28
			3		13		11^{5}				9^{4}	16		5						8^{2}	10^{1}	6^{3}	1	15			4	7	12	14	2			29
					8^{2}		9^{3}				12			5						13	14	6	1	4			3	7	10	11^{1}	2			30
			12		7		9^{3}				8	13		5							14	15	1	4^{1}			3	6^{4}	10^{2}	11	2			31
			4		8					13	9			5						6	12	7	1				3		10^{2}	11^{1}	2			32
			4	12	8						9			5^{1}						6	13	7^{2}	1				3		10	11	2			33
			4	5	8		12				9^{2}									6	13	7^{1}	1				3		10^{3}	11	2	14		34
			3		9		14				8			5						7	13	6^{1}	1				4	12	11^{2}	10^{3}	2			35
			4		8		9^{1}				10			5							12	7^{3}	1				3	6	13	11^{2}	2	14		36
			4		8		9^{1}		13	12	11			5							10^{2}	7	1				3	6			2			37
			4		8^{3}		9^{1}		12		11			5							10^{2}	7	1				3	6	14		2	13		38
			4		8						9			5							10	7	1	12			3	6	11^{1}		2			39
			5	12	9						10			6							11^{2}	8	1	4^{3}			3	7	13		2^{1}	14		40
			4	2	8		14				9	13		5							11^{2}	7	1				3	6^{3}	10^{1}			12		41
			4	2	8		11^{1}			14	9	12		5							13	7^{2}	1				3	6				10^{3}		42
			4	14	8		12				9	11^{1}		5							13	7	1				3	6			2^{3}	10^{2}		43
			4		8^{4}		14				9	15		5							12	6^{2}	1				3	7	13	11^{3}	2	10^{1}		44
			4	12	8^{4}		16				9	15		5^{1}							13	7^{2}	1				3	6	14	11^{5}	2	10^{3}		45
			4	5	8^{4}		9^{2}		14		2	12				15					10^{3}	6	1				3	7		11^{1}			13	46

FA Cup

First Round	Oxford C	(a)	1-2

Carabao Cup

First Round	Cardiff C	(h)	3-0
Second Round	Bristol C	(a)	0-4

Papa John's Trophy

Group C (S)	Milton Keynes D	(a)	1-3
Group C (S)	Southampton U21	(h)	5-0
Group C (S)	Stevenage	(h)	0-0
(Northampton T won 4-2 on penalties)			
Second Round (S)	Exeter C	(a)	2-1
Third Round (S)	Milton Keynes D	(h)	0-2

NORWICH CITY

FOUNDATION

Formed in 1902, largely through the initiative of two local schoolmasters who called a meeting at the Criterion Cafe, they were shocked by an FA Commission which in 1904 declared the club professional and ejected them from the FA Amateur Cup. However, this only served to strengthen their determination. New officials were appointed and a professional club established at a meeting in the Agricultural Hall in March 1905.

Carrow Road, Norwich, Norfolk NR1 1JE.

Telephone: (01603) 760 760.

Ticket Office: (01603) 721 902 (option 1).

Website: www.canaries.co.uk

Email: reception@canaries.co.uk

Ground Capacity: 27,329.

Record Attendance: 25,037 v Sheffield W, FA Cup 5th rd, 16 February 1935 (at The Nest); 43,984 v Leicester C, FA Cup 6th rd, 30 March 1963 (at Carrow Road).

Pitch Measurements: 105m × 68m (115yd × 74.5yd).

Joint Majority Shareholders: Delia Smith, Michael Wynn-Jones.

Chief Operating Officer: Ben Kensell.

Head Coach: Daniel Farke.

Assistant Head Coach: Edmund Riemer.

HONOURS

League Champions: FL C – 2018–19, 2020–21; First Division – 2003–04; Division 2 – 1971–72, 1985–86; FL 1 – 2009–10; Division 3S – 1933–34.
Runners-up: FL C – 2010–11; Division 3 – 1959–60; Division 3S – 1950–51.

FA Cup: semi-final – 1959, 1989, 1992.

League Cup Winners: 1962, 1985.
Runners-up: 1973, 1975.

European Competitions
UEFA Cup: 1993–94.

Colours: Yellow shirts with green trim, green shorts with yellow trim, yellow socks with green trim.

Year Formed: 1902.

Turned Professional: 1905.

Club Nickname: 'The Canaries'.

Grounds: 1902, Newmarket Road; 1908, The Nest, Rosary Road; 1935, Carrow Road.

First Football League Game: 28 August 1920, Division 3, v Plymouth Arg (a) D 1–1 – Skermer; Gray, Gadsden; Wilkinson, Addy, Martin; Laxton, Kidger, Parker, Whitham (1), Dobson.

Record League Victory: 10–2 v Coventry C, Division 3 (S), 15 March 1930 – Jarvie; Hannah, Graham; Brown, O'Brien, Lochhead (1); Porter (1), Anderson, Hunt (5), Scott (2), Slicer (1).

Record Cup Victory: 8–0 v Sutton U, FA Cup 4th rd, 28 January 1989 – Gunn; Culverhouse, Bowen, Butterworth, Linighan, Townsend (Crook), Gordon, Fleck (3), Allen (4), Phelan, Putney (1).

Record Defeat: 2–10 v Swindon T, Southern League, 5 September 1908.

Most League Points (2 for a win): 64, Division 3 (S), 1950–51.

Most League Points (3 for a win): 97, FL C, 2020–21.

Most League Goals: 99, Division 3 (S), 1952–53.

Highest League Scorer in Season: Ralph Hunt, 31, Division 3 (S), 1955–56.

FOOTBALL YEARBOOK FACT FILE

The Football Association decided that Norwich City should play their FA Cup third round second replay against Bradford City in March 1915 at Sincil Bank, Lincoln, behind closed doors to ensure munitions workers from the local factories stayed away. However, contemporary reports state that several hundred were present at the start including the largest number of newspaper reporters ever seen at the ground!

Most League Goals in Total Aggregate: Johnny Gavin, 122, 1945–54, 1955–58.

Most League Goals in One Match: 5, Tommy Hunt v Coventry C, Division 3 (S), 15 March 1930; 5, Roy Hollis v Walsall, Division 3 (S), 29 December 1951.

Most Capped Player: Wes Hoolahan, 42 (43), Republic of Ireland.

Most League Appearances: Ron Ashman, 592, 1947–64.

Youngest League Player: Ryan Jarvis, 16 years 282 days v Walsall, 19 April 2003.

Record Transfer Fee Received: £38,000,000 from Aston Villa for Emiliano Buendia, June 2021.

Record Transfer Fee Paid: £9,400,000 to Werden Bremen for Milot Rashica, June 2021.

Football League Record: 1920 Original Member of Division 3; 1921 Division 3 (S); 1934–39 Division 2; 1946–58 Division 3 (S); 1958–60 Division 3; 1960–72 Division 2; 1972–74 Division 1; 1974–75 Division 2; 1975–81 Division 1; 1981–82 Division 2; 1982–85 Division 1; 1985–86 Division 2; 1986–92 Division 1; 1992–95 Premier League; 1995–2004 Division 1; 2004–05 Premier League; 2005–09 FL C; 2009–10 FL 1; 2010–11 FL C; 2011–14 Premier League; 2014–15 FL C; 2015–16 Premier League; 2016–19 FL C; 2019–20 Premier League; 2020–21 FL C; 2021– Premier League.

LATEST SEQUENCES

Longest Sequence of League Wins: 10, 23.11.1985 – 25.1.1986.

Longest Sequence of League Defeats: 10, 7.3.2020 – 26.7.2020.

Longest Sequence of League Draws: 7, 15.1.1994 – 26.2.1994.

Longest Sequence of Unbeaten League Matches: 20, 31.8.1950 – 30.12.1950.

Longest Sequence Without a League Win: 25, 22.9.1956 – 23.2.1957.

Successive Scoring Runs: 30 from 1.12.2018.

Successive Non-scoring Runs: 5 from 7.3.2020.

MANAGERS

John Bowman 1905–07
James McEwen 1907–08
Arthur Turner 1909–10
Bert Stansfield 1910–15
Major Frank Buckley 1919–20
Charles O'Hagan 1920–21
Albert Gosnell 1921–26
Bert Stansfield 1926
Cecil Potter 1926–29
James Kerr 1929–33
Tom Parker 1933–37
Bob Young 1937–39
Jimmy Jewell 1939
Bob Young 1939–45
Duggie Lochhead 1945–46
Cyril Spiers 1946–47
Duggie Lochhead 1947–50
Norman Low 1950–55
Tom Parker 1955–57
Archie Macaulay 1957–61
Willie Reid 1961–62
George Swindin 1962
Ron Ashman 1962–66
Lol Morgan 1966–69
Ron Saunders 1969–73
John Bond 1973–80
Ken Brown 1980–87
Dave Stringer 1987–92
Mike Walker 1992–94
John Deehan 1994–95
Martin O'Neill 1995
Gary Megson 1995–96
Mike Walker 1996–98
Bruce Rioch 1998–2000
Bryan Hamilton 2000
Nigel Worthington 2000–06
Peter Grant 2006–07
Glenn Roeder 2007–09
Bryan Gunn 2009
Paul Lambert 2009–12
Chris Hughton 2012–14
Neil Adams 2014–15
Alex Neil 2015–17
Daniel Farke May 2017–

TEN YEAR LEAGUE RECORD

		P	W	D	L	F	A	Pts	Pos
2011-12	PR Lge	38	12	11	15	52	66	47	12
2012-13	PR Lge	38	10	14	14	41	58	44	11
2013-14	PR Lge	38	8	9	21	28	62	33	18
2014-15	FL C	46	25	11	10	88	48	86	3
2015-16	PR Lge	38	9	7	22	39	67	34	19
2016-17	FL C	46	20	10	16	85	69	70	8
2017-18	FL C	46	15	15	16	49	60	60	14
2018-19	FL C	46	27	13	6	93	57	94	1
2019-20	PR Lge	38	5	6	27	26	75	21	20
2020-21	FL C	46	29	10	7	75	36	97	1

DID YOU KNOW ?

Norwich City inside-forward Cyril Dunning won five England Amateur international caps in the 1908–09 season. He scored in each of his appearances, netting 12 goals altogether including hat-tricks against Germany and Belgium. In August 1909 he signed professional forms for the Canaries and remained with the club a further two seasons.

NORWICH CITY – SKY BET CHAMPIONSHIP 2020–21 LEAGUE RECORD

Match No.	Date	Venue	Opponents	Result		H/T Score	Lg Pos.	Goalscorers	Attendance
1	Sept 12	A	Huddersfield T	W	1-0	0-0	5	Idah [80]	0
2	19	H	Preston NE	D	2-2	1-2	4	Pukki [31], Placheta [85]	0
3	27	A	Bournemouth	L	0-1	0-1	13		0
4	Oct 3	H	Derby Co	L	0-1	0-0	14		0
5	17	A	Rotherham U	W	2-1	0-1	11	Ihiekwe (og) [68], Hugill (pen) [90]	0
6	20	H	Birmingham C	W	1-0	0-0	7	Vrancic [87]	0
7	24	H	Wycombe W	W	2-1	1-1	5	Pukki [3], Vrancic [90]	0
8	27	A	Brentford	D	1-1	0-1	5	McLean [87]	0
9	31	A	Bristol C	W	3-1	3-1	4	Pukki 2 [6, 14], Emi [45]	0
10	Nov 3	H	Millwall	D	0-0	0-0	3		0
11	7	H	Swansea C	W	1-0	0-0	3	Stiepermann [84]	0
12	21	A	Middlesbrough	W	1-0	0-0	1	Pukki (pen) [72]	0
13	24	A	Stoke C	W	3-2	2-0	1	Emi [18], Pukki 2 [27, 57]	0
14	28	H	Coventry C	D	1-1	1-0	1	Vrancic (pen) [27]	0
15	Dec 2	A	Luton T	L	1-3	1-2	1	Emi (pen) [19]	0
16	5	H	Sheffield W	W	2-1	0-0	1	Martin [81], Aarons [84]	2000
17	9	H	Nottingham F	W	2-1	1-0	1	Sorensen [45], Emi [77]	2000
18	12	A	Blackburn R	W	2-1	1-0	1	Pukki 2 [22, 65]	0
19	16	A	Reading	W	2-1	1-1	1	Emi [11], Pukki (pen) [55]	0
20	19	H	Cardiff C	W	2-0	1-0	1	Emi [27], Cantwell [70]	2000
21	26	A	Watford	L	0-1	0-1	1		0
22	29	H	QPR	D	1-1	0-0	1	Pukki (pen) [75]	0
23	Jan 2	H	Barnsley	W	1-0	0-0	1	Emi [62]	0
24	16	A	Cardiff C	W	2-1	2-0	1	Hanley [3], Cantwell [22]	0
25	20	H	Bristol C	W	2-0	1-0	1	Hugill 2 [36, 76]	0
26	30	H	Middlesbrough	D	0-0	0-0	1		0
27	Feb 2	A	Millwall	D	0-0	0-0	1		0
28	5	A	Swansea C	L	0-2	0-1	1		0
29	13	H	Stoke C	W	4-1	2-0	1	Cantwell [15], Pukki 2 (1 pen) [44, 80 (p)], Emi [64]	0
30	17	A	Coventry C	W	2-0	2-0	1	Pukki [28], Emi [45]	0
31	20	H	Rotherham U	W	1-0	1-0	1	Pukki [17]	0
32	23	A	Birmingham C	W	3-1	1-1	1	Pukki 2 [26, 76], Skipp [90]	0
33	28	A	Wycombe W	W	2-0	0-0	1	Pukki [51], Idah [87]	0
34	Mar 3	H	Brentford	W	1-0	1-0	1	Emi [26]	0
35	6	H	Luton T	W	3-0	2-0	1	Pukki 2 [12, 43], Cantwell [73]	0
36	14	A	Sheffield W	W	2-1	0-1	1	Pukki [61], Cantwell [77]	0
37	17	A	Nottingham F	W	2-0	2-0	1	Pukki [9], Dowell [13]	0
38	20	H	Blackburn R	D	1-1	0-0	1	McLean [53]	0
39	Apr 2	A	Preston NE	D	1-1	1-0	1	Emi [17]	0
40	6	H	Huddersfield T	W	7-0	5-0	1	Pukki 3 (1 pen) [8, 20, 61 (p)], Emi [24], Cantwell [29], Dowell [42], Hugill [78]	0
41	10	A	Derby Co	W	1-0	1-0	1	Dowell [21]	0
42	17	H	Bournemouth	L	1-3	1-0	1	Emi [5]	0
43	20	H	Watford	L	0-1	0-0	1		0
44	24	A	QPR	W	3-1	1-0	1	Quintilla [32], Aarons [57], Emi [82]	0
45	May 1	H	Reading	W	4-1	1-1	1	Dowell 2 [30, 64], Quintilla [78], Pukki [85]	0
46	8	A	Barnsley	D	2-2	1-2	1	Emi [26], Idah [53]	0

Final League Position: 1

GOALSCORERS

League (75): Pukki 26 (5 pens), Emi 15 (1 pen), Cantwell 6, Dowell 5, Hugill 4 (1 pen), Idah 3, Vrancic 3 (1 pen), Aarons 2, McLean 2, Quintilla 2, Hanley 1, Martin 1, Placheta 1, Skipp 1, Sorensen 1, Stiepermann 1, own goal 1.
FA Cup (2): Hugill 1, McLean 1.
Carabao Cup (1): Dowell 1.
Papa John's Trophy (8): Omotoye 4, Dennis 2, Hondermarck 1, Martin 1 (1 pen).

Krul T 36	Aarons M 45	Zimmermann C 13 + 9	Godfrey B 3	Quintilla X 11	Skipp O 44 + 1	McLean K 30 + 8	Cantwell T 30 + 3	Dowell K 12 + 12	Hernandez O 6 + 15	Pukki T 39 + 2	Idah A 1 + 16	Placheta P 10 + 16	Rupp L 15 + 8	Hugill J 7 + 24	Vrancic M 19 + 13	Gibson B 26 + 1	Emi B 39	Stiepermann M 12 + 6	Hanley G 42	Sorensen J 20 + 12	Mumba B 1 + 3	Martin J 6 + 3	Tettey A 5 + 14	McGovern M 9 + 1	McAlear R — + 1	Omotoye T — + 3	Barden D 1 + 1	Omobamidele A 8 + 1	Giannoulis D 16	*Match No.*
1	2	3	4	5	6	7	8^{3}	9^{1}	10^{2}	11	12	13	14																	1
1	2	3	4	5	6	7	8^{3}	9^{1}	10^{2}	11	13	12		14																2
1	2	3	4	5	6	9^{1}			7^{2}	11	13	10	8^{3}	14	12															3
1	2	3		5	7				10^{1}	11	12		6	14	13	4	8^{3}	9^{2}												4
1	2			5	6^{2}	14				13	10		7	11	12	4	8^{3}	9^{1}	3											5
1	2			5	6^{2}		10			11^{3}	12	14	7	9^{1}	13	4	8		3											6
1	2			5	6^{2}		10			9	12■	14	7^{3}	11^{1}	13	4	8		3											7
1	2				6^{3}	13	10^{1}			11		12	7^{2}	14	9	4	8		3	5										8
1	2				6	12				11^{2}		10^{3}	7	13		4	8	9^{1}	3	5	14									9
1	2				7	13				11		10^{1}	6^{2}	12	14	4	8	9^{3}	3	5										10
1	2	3			6	7				11		10^{2}					8^{3}	9	4	5^{1}	13	12	14							11
1	2	16			7	13				12		10^{5}	6	11^{1}	14	4	8^{2}	9^{4}	3	5^{3}			15							12
1^{1}	2	15			7					11^{4}		14			13	4	8■	9^{2}	3	5		10^{3}	6	12						13
	2^{2}	12			7							10			9	4		11	3	5		8^{1}	6	1	13					14
	2	13			7							11			12	4	8^{2}	9	3	5		10^{3}	6^{1}	1		14				15
	2				6					11		10^{2}			7^{3}	4	8	9^{1}	3	5		12	13	1		14				16
	2	3			6	14	13			11^{4}					7		8^{3}	9^{2}	4	5		10^{1}	12	1		15				17
	2	3			7	12	13			11^{3}				14	9^{1}		8^{4}	15	4	5		10^{2}	6	1						18
	2	3			6	7	12	13^{4}		11^{3}				14			8	9^{1}	4	5		10^{2}	15	1						19
	2^{4}	3			6	7	10	13		11^{3}				14	9^{1}		8^{2}	12	4	5			15	1						20
	2	3^{4}			7	6^{5}	10^{1}	9^{2}		11			15	12	14	13	8		4	5^{3}		16		1						21
	2	3			6	7	10^{3}	14		11				13	9		8		4	5^{2}				1^{1}			12			22
1	2				6	7	10^{3}	12		11^{4}		15		14	9^{1}	4	8^{2}		3	5			13							23
	2				6	7	10^{2}					12		11	9^{1}	4	8^{3}		3	5			14				1	13		24
1	2				6	7	10^{3}	14	13			12		11^{2}	9^{1}	4	8		3	5										25
1	2				6		10^{2}		13	11^{3}	14	12	7		9^{1}	4	8■		3										5	26
1	2				7	13	10^{4}	12	14	11	15	8^{3}	6^{2}		9^{1}	4			3										5	27
1	2				7^{1}	6	8^{4}	15	14	11	12	10^{2}	9^{3}		13	4			3	5										28
1	2				6^{2}	7	10^{3}	16	14	11^{4}	15		12		9^{1}	4	8^{5}		3	13									5	29
1	2	14			6^{4}	7	10^{2}	12		11^{5}	15		13		9^{1}	4	8^{3}		3				16						5	30
1	2	3			6	7	10^{2}			11^{3}	12		13		9^{1}		8		4				14						5	31
1	2	3			6	7	10^{2}		12^{4}	11^{3}	14		13	15	9^{1}		8^{5}		4	16									5	32
1	2	14			6^{4}	7			10^{2}	11^{3}	13	16	12		9^{1}	4	8^{5}		3	15									5	33
1	2				6	7			10^{2}	11^{3}			12	14	9^{1}	4	8		3	13									5	34
1	2				6	7^{5}	10^{2}	15	13	11^{4}	16		9^{1}	14		4	8^{3}		3	12									5	35
1	2	15			6	7	10^{2}	12		11^{4}			9^{1}	14		4	8^{3}		3	13									5	36
1	2	16			6^{4}	7	10^{5}	8^{2}	14	11^{3}			9^{1}	13		4			3	12			15						5	37
1	2	14			6	7	10	9^{2}		11						4^{3}	8	13	3	12									5^{1}	38
1				5	13	7	10^{3}	9^{1}	15	11^{4}				14			8^{2}	12	4	6	2							3		39
1	2				6	7^{1}	10^{5}	9^{2}	16	11^{4}		15		14			8^{3}	13	4	12								3	5	40
1	2				6	7	10^{4}	9^{1}		11^{3}		13		14			8^{2}	12	4				15					3	5	41
1	2				6	7	10^{4}	9^{1}	15	11^{2}		13		14			8^{3}		4	12								3	5■	42
1	2			5^{2}	6	7	10^{4}	9^{1}	13	11		14		12	15		8		4									3^{3}		43
1	2			5^{4}	6	7	10^{3}	9^{1}	14	11^{2}		16		13			8^{5}		4	12			15					3		44
1	2^{5}			5^{4}	6	7	10^{3}	9^{2}	14	11				15	13		8^{1}		4		16		12					3		45
1	2					7^{1}	10^{4}	13	15		12			11^{2}	9		8		4	14			6^{3}					3	5	46

FA Cup

Third Round	Coventry C	(h)	2-0
Fourth Round	Barnsley	(a)	0-1

Carabao Cup

First Round	Luton T	(a)	1-3

Papa John's Trophy (Norwich C U21)

Group F (S)	Plymouth Arg	(a)	3-2
Group F (S)	Newport Co	(a)	5-0
Group F (S)	Cheltenham T	(a)	0-1
Second Round (S)	Milton Keynes D	(a)	0-6

NOTTINGHAM FOREST

FOUNDATION

One of the oldest football clubs in the world, Nottingham Forest was formed at a meeting in the Clinton Arms in 1865. Known originally as the Forest Football Club, the game which first drew the founders together was 'shinney', a form of hockey. When they determined to change to football in 1865, one of their first moves was to buy a set of red caps to wear on the field.

The City Ground, Pavilion Road, Nottingham NG2 5FJ.
Telephone: (0115) 982 4444.
Ticket Office: (0115) 982 4388.
Website: www.nottinghamforest.co.uk
Email: enquiries@nottinghamforest.co.uk
Ground Capacity: 30,332.
Record Attendance: 49,946 v Manchester U, Division 1, 28 October 1967.
Pitch Measurements: 102.5m × 67.5m (112yd × 74yd).
Chairman: Nicholas Randall QC.
Chief Executive: Ioannis Vrentzos.
Manager: Chris Hughton.
Assistant Manager: Paul Trollope.
Colours: Red shirts with white trim, white shorts with red trim, red socks.
Year Formed: 1865.
Turned Professional: 1889.
Previous Name: Forest Football Club.
Club Nickname: 'The Reds'.
Grounds: 1865, Forest Racecourse; 1879, The Meadows; 1880, Trent Bridge Cricket Ground; 1882, Parkside, Lenton; 1885, Gregory, Lenton; 1890, Town Ground; 1898, City Ground.
First Football League Game: 3 September 1892, Division 1, v Everton (a) D 2–2 – Brown; Earp, Scott; Hamilton, Albert Smith, McCracken; McCallum, 'Tich' Smith, Higgins (2), Pike, McInnes.
Record League Victory: 12–0 v Leicester Fosse, Division 1, 12 April 1909 – Iremonger; Dudley, Maltby; Hughes (1), Needham, Armstrong; Hooper (3), Marrison, West (3), Morris (2), Spouncer (3 incl. 1p).
Record Cup Victory: 14–0 v Clapton (away), FA Cup 1st rd, 17 January 1891 – Brown; Earp, Scott; Albert Smith, Russell, Jeacock; McCallum (2), 'Tich' Smith (1), Higgins (5), Lindley (4), Shaw (2).
Record Defeat: 1–9 v Blackburn R, Division 2, 10 April 1937.
Most League Points (2 for a win): 70, Division 3 (S), 1950–51.
Most League Points (3 for a win): 94, Division 1, 1997–98.
Most League Goals: 110, Division 3 (S), 1950–51.
Highest League Scorer in Season: Wally Ardron, 36, Division 3 (S), 1950–51.

HONOURS

League Champions: Division 1 – 1977–78; First Division – 1997–98; Division 2 – 1906–07, 1921–22; Division 3S – 1950–51.
Runners-up: Division 1 – 1966–67, 1978–79; First Division – 1993–94; Division 2 – 1956–57; FL 1 – 2007–08.
FA Cup Winners: 1898, 1959.
Runners-up: 1991.
League Cup Winners: 1978, 1979, 1989, 1990.
Runners-up: 1980, 1992.
Anglo-Scottish Cup Winners: 1977.
Full Members' Cup Winners: 1989, 1992.

European Competitions
European Cup: 1978–79 *(winners)*, 1979–80 *(winners)*, 1980–81.
Fairs Cup: 1961–62, 1967–68.
UEFA Cup: 1983–84 *(sf)*, 1984–85, 1995–96 *(qf)*.
Super Cup: 1979 *(winners)*, 1980.
World Club Championship: 1980.

FOOTBALL YEARBOOK FACT FILE

Goalkeeper Chris Woods never made a Football League appearance for Nottingham Forest but was the club's regular keeper for their League Cup fixtures in the 1977–78 season. He played in seven games in the competition altogether, keeping clean sheets in both the final and the replay, as Forest defeated Liverpool to lift the trophy and so earning Woods a winners' medal.

Most League Goals in Total Aggregate: Grenville Morris, 199, 1898–1913.

Most League Goals in One Match: 4, Enoch West v Sunderland, Division 1, 9 November 1907; 4, Tommy Gibson v Burnley, Division 2, 25 January 1913; 4, Tom Peacock v Port Vale, Division 2, 23 December 1933; 4, Tom Peacock v Barnsley, Division 2, 9 November 1935; 4, Tom Peacock v Port Vale, Division 2, 23 November 1935; 4, Tom Peacock v Doncaster R, Division 2, 26 December 1935; 4, Tommy Capel v Gillingham, Division 3 (S), 18 November 1950; 4, Wally Ardron v Hull C, Division 2, 26 December 1952; 4, Tommy Wilson v Barnsley, Division 2, 9 February 1957; 4, Peter Withe v Ipswich T, Division 1, 4 October 1977; 4, Marlon Harewood v Stoke C, Division 1, 22 February 2003; Gareth McCleary v Leeds U, FL C, 20 March 2012.

Most Capped Player: Stuart Pearce, 76 (78), England.

Most League Appearances: Bob McKinlay, 614, 1951–70.

Youngest League Player: Craig Westcarr, 16 years 257 days v Burnley, 13 October 2001.

Record Transfer Fee Received: £15,000,000 from Middlesbrough for Britt Assombalonga, July 2017.

Record Transfer Fee Paid: £13,200,000 to Benfica for João Carvalho, June 2018.

Football League Record: 1892 Elected to Division 1; 1906–07 Division 2; 1907–11 Division 1; 1911–22 Division 2; 1922–25 Division 1; 1925–49 Division 2; 1949–51 Division 3 (S); 1951–57 Division 2; 1957–72 Division 1; 1972–77 Division 2; 1977–92 Division 1; 1992–93 Premier League; 1993–94 Division 1; 1994–97 Premier League; 1997–98 Division 1; 1998–99 Premier League; 1999–2004 Division 1; 2004–05 FL C; 2005–08 FL 1; 2008– FL C.

LATEST SEQUENCES

Longest Sequence of League Wins: 7, 9.5.1979 – 1.9.1979.

Longest Sequence of League Defeats: 14, 21.3.1913 – 27.9.1913.

Longest Sequence of League Draws: 7, 29.4.1978 – 2.9.1978.

Longest Sequence of Unbeaten League Matches: 42, 26.11.1977 – 25.11.1978.

Longest Sequence Without a League Win: 19, 8.9.1998 – 16.1.1999.

Successive Scoring Runs: 22 from 28.3.1931.

Successive Non-scoring Runs: 7 from 26.11.2011.

MANAGERS

Harry Radford 1889–97
(Secretary-Manager)
Harry Haslam 1897–1909
(Secretary-Manager)
Fred Earp 1909–12
Bob Masters 1912–25
John Baynes 1925–29
Stan Hardy 1930–31
Noel Watson 1931–36
Harold Wightman 1936–39
Billy Walker 1939–60
Andy Beattie 1960–63
Johnny Carey 1963–68
Matt Gillies 1969–72
Dave Mackay 1972
Allan Brown 1973–75
Brian Clough 1975–93
Frank Clark 1993–96
Stuart Pearce 1996–97
Dave Bassett 1997–99
(previously General Manager)
Ron Atkinson 1999
David Platt 1999–2001
Paul Hart 2001–04
Joe Kinnear 2004
Gary Megson 2005–06
Colin Calderwood 2006–08
Billy Davies 2009–11
Steve McClaren 2011
Steve Cotterill 2011–12
Sean O'Driscoll 2012
Alex McLeish 2012–13
Billy Davies 2013–14
Stuart Pearce 2014–15
Dougie Freedman 2015–16
Philippe Montanier 2016–17
Mark Warburton 2017
Aitor Karanka 2018–19
Martin O'Neill 2019
Sabri Lamouchi 2019–20
Chris Hughton October 2020–

TEN YEAR LEAGUE RECORD

		P	W	D	L	F	A	Pts	Pos
2011-12	FL C	46	14	8	24	48	63	50	19
2012-13	FL C	46	17	16	13	63	59	67	8
2013-14	FL C	46	16	17	13	67	64	65	11
2014-15	FL C	46	15	14	17	71	69	59	14
2015-16	FL C	46	13	16	17	43	47	55	16
2016-17	FL C	46	14	9	23	62	72	51	21
2017-18	FL C	46	15	8	23	51	65	53	17
2018-19	FL C	46	17	15	14	61	54	66	9
2019-20	FL C	46	18	16	12	58	50	70	7
2020-21	FL C	46	12	16	18	37	45	52	17

DID YOU KNOW ?

Nottingham Forest played their first game under artificial lighting at their Gregory Ground in Lenton on 25 March 1889. The pitch was illuminated by 14 portable Well's Lights and a whitewashed ball was used to aid visibility. The game attracted an attendance of around 5,000 but Forest went down to a 2-0 defeat to local rivals Notts Rangers.

NOTTINGHAM FOREST – SKY BET CHAMPIONSHIP 2020–21 LEAGUE RECORD

Match No.	Date	Venue	Opponents	Result		H/T Score	Lg Pos.	Goalscorers	Attendance
1	Sept 12	A	QPR	L	0-2	0-0	21		0
2	19	H	Cardiff C	L	0-2	0-2	21		0
3	25	A	Huddersfield T	L	0-1	0-0	22		0
4	Oct 3	H	Bristol C	L	1-2	1-2	22	Freeman 35	0
5	17	A	Blackburn R	W	1-0	0-0	20	Lolley 90	0
6	20	H	Rotherham U	D	1-1	0-0	20	Ameobi 79	0
7	23	H	Derby Co	D	1-1	0-1	20	Taylor 64	0
8	28	A	Luton T	D	1-1	0-1	20	Rea (og) 64	0
9	31	A	Middlesbrough	L	0-1	0-0	21		0
10	Nov 4	H	Coventry C	W	2-1	1-0	20	McKenna 30, Taylor (pen) 90	0
11	7	H	Wycombe W	W	2-0	1-0	20	Taylor 2 28, 74	0
12	21	A	Barnsley	L	0-2	0-0	20		0
13	24	A	Bournemouth	L	0-2	0-1	20		0
14	29	H	Swansea C	L	0-1	0-1	21		0
15	Dec 2	H	Watford	D	0-0	0-0	21		0
16	5	A	Reading	L	0-2	0-1	21		2000
17	9	A	Norwich C	L	1-2	0-1	21	Knockaert 73	2000
18	12	H	Brentford	L	1-3	0-1	21	Worrall 90	0
19	15	H	Sheffield W	W	2-0	1-0	21	Yuri Ribeiro 4, Grabban 87	0
20	19	A	Millwall	D	1-1	0-0	20	Mighten 49	0
21	26	H	Birmingham C	D	0-0	0-0	20		0
22	29	A	Stoke C	D	1-1	0-1	21	Chester (og) 65	0
23	Jan 2	A	Preston NE	W	1-0	0-0	19	Grabban (pen) 70	0
24	16	H	Millwall	W	3-1	1-0	19	Ameobi 2 34, 70, Yates 83	0
25	20	H	Middlesbrough	L	1-2	0-1	20	Mbe Soh 90	0
26	30	H	Barnsley	D	0-0	0-0	21		0
27	Feb 2	A	Coventry C	W	2-1	1-1	19	Grabban 22, Rose (og) 53	0
28	6	A	Wycombe W	W	3-0	1-0	18	Murray 2 (1 pen) 7, 54 (p), Knockaert 72	0
29	13	H	Bournemouth	D	0-0	0-0	16		0
30	17	A	Swansea C	L	0-1	0-0	18		0
31	20	H	Blackburn R	W	1-0	1-0	17	Mighten 25	0
32	23	A	Rotherham U	W	1-0	0-0	15	Yates 67	0
33	26	A	Derby Co	D	1-1	1-0	14	Garner 33	0
34	Mar 2	H	Luton T	L	0-1	0-0	17		0
35	6	A	Watford	L	0-1	0-1	17		0
36	13	H	Reading	D	1-1	0-0	17	Holmes (og) 49	0
37	17	H	Norwich C	L	0-2	0-2	18		0
38	20	A	Brentford	D	1-1	0-1	17	Krovinovic 63	0
39	Apr 2	A	Cardiff C	W	1-0	1-0	16	Garner 29	0
40	5	H	QPR	W	3-1	1-0	15	Mighten 44, Grabban 63, Garner 69	0
41	10	A	Bristol C	D	0-0	0-0	15		0
42	17	H	Huddersfield T	L	0-2	0-1	16		0
43	21	A	Birmingham C	D	1-1	0-0	18	Grabban (pen) 90	0
44	24	H	Stoke C	D	1-1	0-1	17	Grabban 50	0
45	May 1	A	Sheffield W	D	0-0	0-0	16		0
46	8	H	Preston NE	L	1-2	1-0	17	Garner 17	0

Final League Position: 17

GOALSCORERS

League (37): Grabban 6 (2 pens), Garner 4, Taylor 4 (1 pen), Ameobi 3, Mighten 3, Knockaert 2, Murray 2 (1 pen), Yates 2, Freeman 1, Krovinovic 1, Lolley 1, Mbe Soh 1, McKenna 1, Worrall 1, Yuri Ribeiro 1, own goals 4.
FA Cup (2): Knockaert 1, Taylor 1.
Carabao Cup (0).

Samba B 45	Lawrence-Gabriel J 1	Tobias Figueiredo P 31 + 1	Worrall J 31	Blackett T 9 + 5	Yates R 31 + 3	Colback J 13 + 4	Lolley J 16 + 12	Freeman L 16 + 7	Nuno Da Costa J 1 + 1	Grabban L 24 + 4	Ameobi S 27 + 5	Taylor L 15 + 24	Mighten A 13 + 11	Jenkinson C 1 + 2	Yuri Ribeiro O 24 + 1	Guerrero M 4 + 5	Christie C 44	Mbe Soh L 5 + 2	McKenna S 24	Sow S 12 + 3	Arter H 8 + 5	Ioannou N 5	Knockaert A 24 + 10	Bong G 9 + 1	Cafu D 26 + 5	Swan W — + 2	Krovinovic F 19	Bachirou F — + 1	Garner J 19 + 1	Murray G 8 + 8	Smith J 1	Match No.
1	2	3	4	5	6	7	8^{1}	9^{3}	10^{2}	11	12	13	14																			1
1		4	3		6	7	8^{1}	9		11^{2}	10	12	14	2^{3}	5	13																2
1				5		7	14	9^{3}		13	11	10^{2}	12				2	3	4	6^{1}	8											3
1				4		7		9	12	11	10^{1}	13	8^{3}				2	3		14	6^{2}	5										4
1		3			6	7^{1}	8^{3}	9		11^{2}	10	13					2		4	14	12	5										5
1		3			6	7^{2}	8	9^{1}		11	10	12					2		4		13	5										6
1		3			8		6			10^{1}	9	11					2		4		7	5	12									7
1		3			6	7	9				10^{1}	11		12			2		4			5■	8									8
1		3			6	7	12	9^{2}			10^{1}	14				11^{3}	2		4				8	5	13							9
1		3			12	7	10	9^{1}			13	11			5	14	2		4	6^{2}			8^{3}									10
1		3			12	8	13				9^{2}	11			5	10^{3}	2		4	7^{1}	14		6									11
1		3			7	8	9	12				11			5	10^{1}	2		4				6									12
1		3			7	8	9^{1}				6	10			5	13	2		4		11^{2}		12									13
1		3			6	7^{1}	13				10^{3}	11			5	9^{2}	2		4		12		8			14						14
1		3	4		7		9^{1}				12	10			5		2				6		11		8							15
1		12	3		7■		9				13	10^{4}			5		2		4^{1}	14	8^{3}		11^{2}		6	15						16
1		3	4				8				10	11^{1}	14	15	5	12	2^{3}			6^{4}	9^{2}		13		7							17
1		3	4		6		7^{1}				10	11			5	12	2				9^{2}		13■		8							18
1			4		7		13			12	8	11^{1}	10^{2}		5		2	3		6					9							19
1			4		7					11^{1}	8	12	10^{2}		5		2	3		6			13		9							20
1		3	4		6		14			11	8^{2}	12	10^{3}		5		2			7^{1}			13		9							21
1		3	4		6		12			11^{2}	10^{1}	13			5		2			7			8		9							22
1		3	4		6		12			11^{3}	10^{1}	14			5		2			7	13		8		9^{2}							23
1			3		6					11	8	12	10^{2}		5		2		4	7^{1}				13	9							24
1			3		6^{4}		14			11	8^{3}	12	10^{2}		5■		2	15	4	7^{1}			13		9							25
1		3^{3}	4							11	10		13				2	14		7^{1}			8^{2}	5	6		9	12				26
1		3	4	15		13		12		11^{3}	10^{1}						2						8	5	6^{2}		9^{4}		7	14		27
1		3	4			14	12	10^{1}				13					2						8	5	6^{3}		9		7	11^{2}		28
1		3	4					9									2						8	5	7		10		6	11		29
1		3	4				10			11^{1}		13	14		5		2						8^{3}		7		9^{2}		6	12		30
1		3	4	15	13			14				12	10^{3}		5		2						8^{4}		6^{2}		9		7	11^{1}		31
1		3	4	14	6		12	10^{1}				13					2						8^{3}	5	7		9^{4}		15	11^{2}		32
1		3	4	13				10^{2}				12			5		2						8		7		9		6	11^{1}		33
1		3	4				10^{2}				12	13	14		5		2						8^{3}		7		9^{1}		6	11		34
1		3	4	15	7^{2}		13	10^{1}				14					2						8	5^{4}	12		9^{3}		6	11		35
1		3					10^{1}	14		13	8						2		4				12	5	7		9^{3}		6	11^{2}		36
		3		5	7^{3}			10^{2}		11^{1}	8	12	13				2		4						9				6	14	1	37
1		3								11^{2}	8		10		12		2		4					5^{1}	6		9		7	13		38
1			3	5	6	13				11^{1}	8	12	10				2		4						9^{2}				7			39
1			3	5	6^{3}	14		13		11^{2}	8^{1}		10				2		4								9		7	12		40
1			3	5	6			14		11^{1}		12	10^{3}				2		4				8		13		9^{2}		7			41
1			3	5	6^{1}			15		11^{4}		13	10				2		4				8^{3}		12		9^{2}		7	14		42
1			3	5	6			8^{2}		13		11^{1}	10				2		4				14		15		9^{3}		7^{4}	12		43
1			3		6			8^{1}		11			13		5		2		4				12		9^{2}		10		7			44
1			3		7					11^{2}		13	12		5		2		4				8		9^{1}		10		6			45
1			4		6					9^{2}		11	12		5		2	3					8				10^{1}		7	13		46

FA Cup

Third Round	Cardiff C	(h)	1-0
Fourth Round	Swansea C	(a)	1-5

Carabao Cup

First Round	Barnsley	(a)	0-1

OLDHAM ATHLETIC

FOUNDATION

It was in 1895 that John Garland, the landlord of the Featherstall and Junction Hotel, decided to form a football club. As Pine Villa they played in the Oldham Junior League. In 1899 the local professional club, Oldham County, went out of existence and one of the liquidators persuaded Pine Villa to take over their ground at Sheepfoot Lane and change their name to Oldham Athletic.

Boundary Park, Furtherwood Road, Oldham, Lancashire OL1 2PB.

Telephone: (0161) 624 4972.

Ticket Office: (0161) 785 5150.

Website: www.oldhamathletic.co.uk

Email: enquiries@oldhamathletic.co.uk

Ground Capacity: 13,513.

Record Attendance: 47,671 v Sheffield W, FA Cup 4th rd, 25 January 1930.

Pitch Measurements: 100m × 68m (109.5yd × 74.5yd).

Chairman: Abdallah Lemsagam.

Chief Executive: Karl Evans.

Head Coach: Keith Curle.

Assistant Head Coach: Paul Butler.

Colours: Blue shirts with black and white trim, white shorts with blue and gold trim, blue socks with white trim.

Year Formed: 1895.

Turned Professional: 1899.

Previous Name: 1895, Pine Villa; 1899, Oldham Athletic.

Club Nickname: 'The Latics'.

Grounds: 1895, Sheepfoot Lane; 1900, Hudson Field; 1906, Sheepfoot Lane; 1907, Boundary Park (renamed SportsDirect.com Park 2014, Boundary Park 2018).

First Football League Game: 9 September 1907, Division 2, v Stoke (a) W 3–1 – Hewitson; Hodson, Hamilton; Fay, Walders, Wilson; Ward, Billy Dodds (1), Newton (1), Hancock, Swarbrick (1).

Record League Victory: 11–0 v Southport, Division 4, 26 December 1962 – Bollands; Branagan, Marshall; McCall, Williams, Scott; Ledger (1), Johnstone, Lister (6), Colquhoun (1), Whitaker (3).

Record Cup Victory: 10–1 v Lytham, FA Cup 1st rd, 28 November 1925 – Gray; Wynne, Grundy; Adlam, Heaton, Naylor (1), Douglas, Pynegar (2), Ormston (2), Barnes (3), Watson (2).

Record Defeat: 4–13 v Tranmere R, Division 3 (N), 26 December 1935.

HONOURS

League Champions: Division 2 – 1990–91; Division 3 – 1973–74; Division 3N – 1952–53.
Runners-up: Division 1 – 1914–15; Division 2 – 1909–10; Division 4 – 1962–63.

FA Cup: semi-final – 1913, 1990, 1994.

League Cup: *Runners-up:* 1990.

FOOTBALL YEARBOOK FACT FILE

Oldham Athletic's Division Two fixture at Middlesbrough on 3 April 1915 came to an abrupt conclusion after the referee abandoned the game after around 60 minutes. The Latics' full-back Billy Cook had been sent off but refused to leave the field of play, leaving the official with little option but to end the match. The points were awarded to Middlesbrough and Cook was suspended from the game for 12 months.

Most League Points (2 for a win): 62, Division 3, 1973–74.

Most League Points (3 for a win): 88, Division 2, 1990–91.

Most League Goals: 95, Division 4, 1962–63.

Highest League Scorer in Season: Tom Davis, 33, Division 3 (N), 1936–37.

Most League Goals in Total Aggregate: Roger Palmer, 141, 1980–94.

Most League Goals in One Match: 7, Eric Gemmell v Chester, Division 3 (N), 19 January 1952.

Most Capped Player: Gunnar Halle, 24 (64), Norway.

Most League Appearances: Ian Wood, 525, 1966–80.

Youngest League Player: Wayne Harrison, 16 years 347 days v Notts Co, 27 October 1984.

Record Transfer Fee Received: £1,700,000 from Aston Villa for Earl Barrett, February 1992.

Record Transfer Fee Paid: £750,000 to Aston Villa for Ian Olney, June 1992.

Football League Record: 1907 Elected to Division 2; 1910–23 Division 1; 1923–35 Division 2; 1935–53 Division 3 (N); 1953–54 Division 2; 1954–58 Division 3 (N); 1958–63 Division 4; 1963–69 Division 3; 1969–71 Division 4; 1971–74 Division 3; 1974–91 Division 2; 1991–92 Division 1; 1992–94 Premier League; 1994–97 Division 1; 1997–2004 Division 2; 2004–18 FL 1; 2018– FL 2.

LATEST SEQUENCES

Longest Sequence of League Wins: 10, 12.1.1974 – 12.3.1974.

Longest Sequence of League Defeats: 8, 15.12.1934 – 2.2.1935.

Longest Sequence of League Draws: 5, 7.4.2018 – 21.4.2018.

Longest Sequence of Unbeaten League Matches: 20, 1.5.1990 – 10.11.1990.

Longest Sequence Without a League Win: 17, 4.9.1920 – 18.12.1920.

Successive Scoring Runs: 25 from 25.8.1962.

Successive Non-scoring Runs: 6 from 12.2.2011.

MANAGERS

David Ashworth 1906–14
Herbert Bamlett 1914–21
Charlie Roberts 1921–22
David Ashworth 1923–24
Bob Mellor 1924–27
Andy Wilson 1927–32
Bob Mellor 1932–33
Jimmy McMullan 1933–34
Bob Mellor 1934–45
(continued as Secretary to 1953)
Frank Womack 1945–47
Billy Wootton 1947–50
George Hardwick 1950–56
Ted Goodier 1956–58
Norman Dodgin 1958–60
Danny McLennan 1960
Jack Rowley 1960–63
Les McDowall 1963–65
Gordon Hurst 1965–66
Jimmy McIlroy 1966–68
Jack Rowley 1968–69
Jimmy Frizzell 1970–82
Joe Royle 1982–94
Graeme Sharp 1994–97
Neil Warnock 1997–98
Andy Ritchie 1998–2001
Mick Wadsworth 2001–02
Iain Dowie 2002–03
Brian Talbot 2004–05
Ronnie Moore 2005–06
John Sheridan 2006–09
Joe Royle 2009
Dave Penney 2009–10
Paul Dickov 2010–13
Lee Johnson 2013–15
Dean Holden 2015
Darren Kelly 2015
David Dunn 2015–16
John Sheridan 2016
Stephen Robinson 2016–17
John Sheridan 2017
Richie Wellens 2017–18
Frankie Bunn 2018
Paul Scholes 2019
Laurent Banide 2019
Dino Maamria 2019–20
Harry Kewell 2020–21
Keith Curle March 2021–

TEN YEAR LEAGUE RECORD

		P	W	D	L	F	A	Pts	Pos
2011-12	FL 1	46	14	12	20	50	66	54	16
2012-13	FL 1	46	14	9	23	46	59	51	19
2013-14	FL 1	46	14	14	18	50	59	56	15
2014-15	FL 1	46	14	15	17	54	67	57	15
2015-16	FL 1	46	12	18	16	44	58	54	17
2016-17	FL 1	46	12	17	17	31	44	53	17
2017-18	FL 1	46	11	17	18	58	75	50	21
2018-19	FL 2	46	16	14	16	67	60	62	14
2019-20	FL 2	37	9	14	14	44	57	41	19§
2020-21	FL 2	46	15	9	22	72	81	54	18

§*Decided on points-per-game (1.11)*

DID YOU KNOW

When Earl Barrett lined up against New Zealand in June 1991, he became the first Oldham Athletic player to appear for England for over 60 years. The previous Latics player to win international honours for England was Jack Hacking back in April 1929.

OLDHAM ATHLETIC – SKY BET LEAGUE TWO 2020–21 LEAGUE RECORD

Match No.	*Date*	*Venue*	*Opponents*	*Result*	*H/T Score*	*Lg Pos.*	*Goalscorers*	*Attendance*
1	Sept 12	H	Leyton Orient	L 0-1	0-0	19		0
2	19	A	Stevenage	L 0-3	0-0	22		0
3	26	H	Crawley T	L 2-3	1-2	21	Rowe [30], McAleny [79]	0
4	Oct 3	A	Colchester U	D 3-3	0-2	22	McAleny 2 (1 pen) [52 (p), 89], Piergianni [53]	0
5	10	H	Morecambe	L 2-3	0-1	24	McAleny 2 [52, 90]	0
6	17	A	Bolton W	W 2-1	1-1	19	Garrity [27], Dearnley [90]	0
7	20	H	Carlisle U	D 1-1	0-0	19	Dearnley [80]	0
8	24	H	Port Vale	L 1-2	0-2	22	Dearnley [49]	0
9	27	A	Southend U	W 2-1	0-0	20	Grant [49], Dearnley [89]	0
10	31	A	Salford C	L 0-2	0-1	20		0
11	Nov 3	H	Cheltenham T	W 2-1	1-1	19	Blackwood [34], Clarke [85]	0
12	14	H	Scunthorpe U	L 0-2	0-0	20		0
13	21	A	Exeter C	W 2-1	2-1	17	Blackwood [21], Rowe [32]	0
14	24	A	Barrow	W 4-3	2-1	17	Garrity [39], Rowe 2 (1 pen) [45, 82 (p)], McAleny [90]	0
15	Dec 1	H	Tranmere R	L 0-1	0-1	17		0
16	5	A	Cambridge U	W 2-1	0-0	16	McAleny [57], McCalmont [60]	1970
17	12	H	Bradford C	W 3-1	2-0	15	Bahamboula [10], Piergianni [26], Keillor-Dunn [74]	0
18	15	H	Walsall	L 2-3	0-1	16	Piergianni [68], Fage [55]	0
19	19	A	Newport Co	W 4-2	1-2	14	Keillor-Dunn [14], McAleny [57], McCalmont [85], Dearnley [90]	0
20	26	H	Harrogate T	L 1-2	1-1	14	McAleny (pen) [19]	0
21	29	A	Grimsby T	D 0-0	0-0	14		0
22	Jan 13	H	Mansfield T	L 2-3	1-2	16	McCalmont [6], McAleny [84]	0
23	16	A	Walsall	D 1-1	0-1	16	Keillor-Dunn [75]	0
24	23	H	Newport Co	W 3-2	2-2	14	Keillor-Dunn [8], Grant [29], Demetriou (og) [74]	0
25	26	A	Cheltenham T	L 0-2	0-0	15		0
26	30	H	Salford C	W 2-1	0-1	13	Bahamboula [75], Keillor-Dunn [90]	0
27	Feb 16	A	Forest Green R	L 3-4	1-2	17	Grant [40], McAleny 2 [54, 63]	0
28	20	A	Tranmere R	D 2-2	1-1	17	Keillor-Dunn [2], Bahamboula [78]	0
29	23	H	Barrow	L 0-1	0-0	17		0
30	27	A	Carlisle U	W 3-1	0-1	15	Hilssner (pen) [71], Bahamboula [78], Piergianni [86]	0
31	Mar 2	H	Bolton W	L 0-2	0-2	17		0
32	6	H	Southend U	D 0-0	0-0	16		0
33	9	A	Port Vale	D 0-0	0-0	17		0
34	13	H	Cambridge U	L 2-4	2-3	17	Keillor-Dunn 2 [3, 11]	0
35	16	A	Scunthorpe U	D 1-1	0-0	17	McCalmont [48]	0
36	20	A	Bradford C	D 0-0	0-0	17		0
37	23	H	Exeter C	W 2-1	1-0	17	Jameson [35], McCalmont [55]	0
38	27	A	Leyton Orient	L 1-2	0-2	17	McCalmont [61]	0
39	Apr 2	H	Stevenage	L 0-1	0-1	18		0
40	5	A	Crawley T	W 4-1	2-0	17	McAleny 2 [40, 47], Borthwick-Jackson [42], Bahamboula [90]	0
41	9	H	Colchester U	W 5-2	2-0	15	McAleny (pen) [37], McCalmont [42], Piergianni [56], Keillor-Dunn 2 [90, 90]	0
42	17	A	Morecambe	L 3-4	1-3	17	McAleny [39], Borthwick-Jackson [78], Jameson [88]	0
43	20	A	Harrogate T	W 3-0	1-0	15	McCalmont [7], Bahamboula [46], Blackwood [75]	0
44	24	H	Grimsby T	L 1-2	1-1	16	McAleny [30]	0
45	May 1	A	Mansfield T	L 1-4	0-2	18	Dearnley [51]	0
46	8	H	Forest Green R	L 0-3	0-0	18		0

Final League Position: 18

GOALSCORERS

League (72): McAleny 17 (3 pens), Keillor-Dunn 10, McCalmont 8, Bahamboula 6, Dearnley 6, Piergianni 5, Rowe 4 (1 pen), Blackwood 3, Grant 3, Borthwick-Jackson 2, Garrity 2, Jameson 2, Clarke 1, Fage 1, Hilssner 1 (1 pen), own goal 1.
FA Cup (6): Rowe 2, Bahamboula 1 (1 pen), Garrity 1, Grant 1, McAleny 1.
Carabao Cup (3): Garrity 1, Grant 1, McAleny 1.
Papa John's Trophy (10): Grant 2, McAleny 2, McCalmont 2, Rowe 2, Dearnley 1, Keillor-Dunn 1.

Lawlor I 30	Haymer T 11 + 1	Jombati S 16 + 3	Piergianni C 36 + 2	Borthwick-Jackson C 25 + 6	Garrity B 21 + 8	Whelan C 23 + 8	Grant B 18 + 5	Fage D 22 + 12	Keillor-Dunn D 34 + 7	McAleny C 37 + 3	Rowe D 9 + 6	Dearnley Z 6 + 9	Badan A 11 + 7	McCalmont A 31 + 4	Blackwood G 6 + 7	Barnett J 7 + 10	Bahamboula D 27 + 11	Chapman M — + 1	Bilboe L 3	Ntambwe B 19 + 5	Jameson K 20 + 5	Clarke H 30 + 2	Diarra R 10 + 6	Luamba J 1 + 1	Hilssner M 15 + 5	Adams N 20 + 3	Barnes M 1 + 6	Tasdemir S 4 + 3	Vaughan H — + 6	Walker L 13	Sutton W — + 1	*Match No.*
1	2	3	4	5	6	7	8^2	9^1	10	11	12	13																				1
1	2	3	4	5^1	7	8	6		9	11	10		12																			2
1	2	3	4			7	8^2	13	10^1	9	11^3		5	6	12	14																3
1	3	2	4	12^3	8	7^2		6		10			5^1	9	11	14	13															4
1^1	2	3^3	4		6	7		5		11	14	10^2			9	8	13	12														5
	5	3^1	4		6	7^2				11	10	14		13		8	9^3		1	2	12											6
1	5		3		6		10^2			11	13	9		7		8	12			2^1	4^3	14										7
1	2^2		4	12		7^3		13	14	9	11	10		6		5^1	8					3										8
1			3	8		6	9	5^2	10^1	11		12					13			7	4	2										9
1			3	8		6	9^3	5	11		14	13			10^2		12			7	4^1	2										10
1	5			4	14	6^3			11		13	10^1			9^2	8	12			7	3	2										11
1	2^2			5	8		13	12	9		11				7^1		10			6	4	3										12
1		14	4	5	8^4	15	13	2	9		11				10^1	12	7^2			6			3^3									13
1		6	4	5	8		10^3	2	9^1	12	11				14	13	7^2						3									14
1			4	5	8	13		2^3	7^1	10	11			9		14				6^2		12	3									15
1		2		5	9	13	11	7^3		10^2				8^1		14	12			6		4	3									16
1			4	5^2	8		11^3	2	12	10		14		9		13	7^1			6		3										17
1			4	5	8		11	2	12	10^2		13		9^3		14	7			6^1		3										18
1	15	2	4	5^1	8		11^2		9	10^3		13		14		12	7^4			6		3										19
1		2^2	4	5	12	15	11■	13	9^4	10^1		14		8^5		16	7^3			6		3										20
1			4	5	7			2	12			10				9	6			8		3		11^1								21
1			4	12	6	7^3		14	9^4	11	15	13^5	16	8		5^1	10					3	2^2									22
1	2^1	3		5	14			8	13	10	11			6^2			12			7^3	15	4			9^4							23
		3		5^1	8		10^3		6^2	11^4			12				9		1	14	15	4			7	2	13					24
		5			7		12		9^3	10			13	14			11		1	6^1	4^2	3			8	2						25
1		3	13	5			10		12	11				8			9^2			7^1		4			6	2						26
1		3	4				10^2		8	11			5	9			6^1								7	2	13	12				27
1		3■				15			9	11^2			5^5	8^3	14		7				12	4	13		6^4	2	16	10^1				28
1						13			9	11			5^1	8	14		7^2				4	3	12		6^4	2	15^5	10^3	16			29
1			13	5^3			11	15	9	10^2				6	12		8				14	4	3^1		7^4	2						30
1			4			14	11^1	13	9					6^3			8			12	5■	3^4	7			2		10^2	15			31
1			4				11	2	9	12				7			8^2			13			3		6	5		10^1				32
1		14	3			13		12	9	10			4	7			11			6^2			2^3		8^1	5						33
			3				12	8	10^3	11^2			4	6			13			7			2		9^1	5		14		1		34
			3			7^3	12	8	11	10			4	6^2						14	2		13		9^1	5				1		35
			3			6		5	11	10			13	7			12				4	2			9^1	8^2				1		36
			3	13		6		5^4	11^1	10			4	7							2		15	14	9^2	8^3		12		1		37
			3	14		6		13	11	10			8^2	7							4	2	12		9^1	5^3				1		38
			3	14	9^1	6		13	10	11			8^2	7							4^3	2			12	5				1		39
			3	8	12	7^1		5	11^2	10				6^4			9			15	4	2^3			13	14				1		40
			3	8	13	7		5^4	11	10^2				6			9^3				4^1	2	14		15	12				1		41
			3	8	14	7		5^3	11^5	10				6^1	13		9^2				4	2^4			15	12			16	1		42
			3	4	14	7			11^5	10^3			16	6^2	13		9^1				2	5				8^4	12		15	1		43
			3	4	14	6^3		15	11^1	10				7^5			9^2				2^4	5			13	8	12		16	1		44
			3	4	6	7		15	12	10^1		11^2		14			13				2	5				8^4	9^3			1		45
		16	3		8	7		9^2	11	12			15	6			10^1				4^3	2^5				5^4			14	1	13	46

FA Cup

First Round	Hampton & R	(a)	3-2
Second Round	Bradford C	(a)	2-1
Third Round	Bournemouth	(h)	1-4

Carabao Cup

First Round	Carlisle U	(h)	3-0
Second Round	Morecambe	(a)	0-1

Papa John's Trophy

Group F (N)	Wolverhampton W U21	(h)	4-0
Group F (N)	Doncaster R	(h)	2-0
Group F (N)	Bradford C	(a)	3-1
Second Round (N)	Sunderland	(h)	1-2

OXFORD UNITED

FOUNDATION

There had been an Oxford United club around the time of World War I but only in the Oxfordshire Thursday League and there is no connection with the modern club which began as Headington in 1893, adding 'United' a year later. Playing first on Quarry Fields and subsequently Wootten's Fields, they owe much to a Dr Hitchings for their early development.

The Kassam Stadium, Grenoble Road, Oxford OX4 4XP.

Telephone: (01865) 337 500.

Ticket Office: (01865) 337 533.

Website: www.oufc.co.uk

Email: gm@oufc.co.uk

Ground Capacity: 12,537.

Record Attendance: 22,750 v Preston NE, FA Cup 6th rd, 29 February 1964 (at Manor Ground); 12,243 v Leyton Orient, FL 2, 6 May 2006 (at The Kassam Stadium).

Pitch Measurements: 100.5m × 67m (110yd × 73.5yd).

Chairman: Sumrith 'Tiger' Thanakarnjanasuth.

Head Coach: Karl Robinson.

Assistant Manager: Craig Short.

HONOURS

League Champions: Division 2 – 1984–85; Division 3 – 1967–68, 1983–84.
Runners-up: Second Division – 1995–96; FL 2 – 2015–16; Conference – (3rd) 2009–10 *(promoted via play-offs)*.

FA Cup: 6th rd – 1964.

League Cup Winners: 1986.

League Trophy: *Runners-up:* 2016, 2017.

Colours: Yellow shirts with blue trim, blue shorts with yellow trim, yellow socks with blue trim.

Year Formed: 1893.

Turned Professional: 1949.

Previous Names: 1893, Headington; 1894, Headington United; 1960, Oxford United.

Club Nickname: 'The U's'.

Grounds: 1893, Headington Quarry; 1894, Wootten's Fields; 1898, Sandy Lane Ground; 1902, Britannia Field; 1909, Sandy Lane; 1910, Quarry Recreation Ground; 1914, Sandy Lane; 1922, The Paddock Manor Road; 1925, Manor Ground; 2001, The Kassam Stadium.

First Football League Game: 18 August 1962, Division 4, v Barrow (a) L 2–3 – Medlock; Beavon, Quartermain; Ron Atkinson, Kyle, Jones; Knight, Graham Atkinson (1), Houghton (1), Cornwell, Colfar.

Record League Victory: 7–0 v Barrow, Division 4, 19 December 1964 – Fearnley; Beavon, Quartermain; Ron Atkinson (1), Kyle, Jones; Morris, Booth (3), Willey (1), Graham Atkinson (1), Harrington (1).

Record Cup Victory: 9–1 v Dorchester T, FA Cup 1st rd, 11 November 1995 – Whitehead; Wood (2), Mike Ford (1), Smith, Elliott, Gilchrist, Rush (1), Massey (Murphy), Moody (3), Bobby Ford (1), Angel (Beauchamp (1)).

Record Defeat: 0–7 v Sunderland, Division 1, 19 September 1998; 0–7 v Wigan Ath, FL 1, 23 December 2017.

Most League Points (2 for a win): 61, Division 4, 1964–65.

FOOTBALL YEARBOOK FACT FILE

Oxford United's first win in the Football League Cup came in September 1964 when they defeated Walsall 6-1 in a first round replay at the Manor Ground with centre-forward Bill Calder netting four goals. United went out of the competition in the next round, losing 2-0 at Fulham.

Most League Points (3 for a win): 95, Division 3, 1983–84.

Most League Goals: 91, Division 3, 1983–84.

Highest League Scorer in Season: John Aldridge, 30, Division 2, 1984–85.

Most League Goals in Total Aggregate: Graham Atkinson, 77, 1962–73.

Most League Goals in One Match: 4, Tony Jones v Newport Co, Division 4, 22 September 1962; 4, Arthur Longbottom v Darlington, Division 4, 26 October 1963; 4, Richard Hill v Walsall, Division 2, 26 December 1988; 4, John Durnin v Luton T, 14 November 1992; 4, Tom Craddock v Accrington S, FL 2, 20 October 2011.

Most Capped Player: Jim Magilton, 18 (52), Northern Ireland.

Most League Appearances: John Shuker, 478, 1962–77.

Youngest League Player: Jason Seacole, 16 years 149 days v Mansfield T, 7 September 1976.

Record Transfer Fee Received: £3,000,000 from Leeds U for Kemar Roofe, July 2016.

Record Transfer Fee Paid: £470,000 to Aberdeen for Dean Windass, July 1998.

Football League Record: 1962 Elected to Division 4; 1965–68 Division 3; 1968–76 Division 2; 1976–84 Division 3; 1984–85 Division 2; 1985–88 Division 1; 1988–92 Division 2; 1992–94 Division 1; 1994–96 Division 2; 1996–99 Division 1; 1999–2001 Division 2; 2001–04 Division 3; 2004–06 FL 2; 2006–10 Conference; 2010–16 FL 2; 2016– FL 1.

MANAGERS

Harry Thompson 1949–58
(Player-Manager) 1949-51
Arthur Turner 1959–69
(continued as General Manager to 1972)
Ron Saunders 1969
Gerry Summers 1969–75
Mick Brown 1975–79
Bill Asprey 1979–80
Ian Greaves 1980–82
Jim Smith 1982–85
Maurice Evans 1985–88
Mark Lawrenson 1988
Brian Horton 1988–93
Denis Smith 1993–97
Malcolm Crosby 1997–98
Malcolm Shotton 1998–99
Micky Lewis 1999–2000
Denis Smith 2000
David Kemp 2000–01
Mark Wright 2001
Ian Atkins 2001–04
Graham Rix 2004
Ramon Diaz 2004–05
Brian Talbot 2005–06
Darren Patterson 2006
Jim Smith 2006–07
Darren Patterson 2007–08
Chris Wilder 2008–14
Gary Waddock 2014
Michael Appleton 2014–17
Pep Clotet 2017–18
Karl Robinson March 2018–

LATEST SEQUENCES

Longest Sequence of League Wins: 7, 15.12.2020 – 30.1.2021.

Longest Sequence of League Defeats: 8, 18.4.2014 – 23.8.2014.

Longest Sequence of League Draws: 5, 7.10.1978 – 28.10.1978.

Longest Sequence of Unbeaten League Matches: 20, 17.3.1984 – 29.9.1984.

Longest Sequence Without a League Win: 27, 14.11.1987 – 27.8.1988.

Successive Scoring Runs: 17 from 22.4.2006.

Successive Non-scoring Runs: 6 from 26.3.1988.

TEN YEAR LEAGUE RECORD

		P	*W*	*D*	*L*	*F*	*A*	*Pts*	*Pos*
2011-12	FL 2	46	17	17	12	59	48	68	9
2012-13	FL 2	46	19	8	19	60	61	65	9
2013-14	FL 2	46	16	14	16	53	50	62	8
2014-15	FL 2	46	15	16	15	50	49	61	13
2015-16	FL 2	46	24	14	8	84	41	86	2
2016-17	FL 1	46	20	9	17	65	52	69	8
2017-18	FL 1	46	15	11	20	61	66	56	16
2018-19	FL 1	46	15	15	16	58	64	60	12
2019-20	FL 1	35	17	9	9	61	37	60	4§
2020-21	FL 1	46	22	8	16	77	56	74	6

§Decided on points-per-game (1.71)

DID YOU KNOW ?

Oxford United marked their 1,000th Football League game with a 5-0 victory over Crystal Palace at the Manor Ground in December 1984. United went on to finish the season as champions of Division Two, earning promotion to top-flight football for the 1985–86 season.

OXFORD UNITED – SKY BET LEAGUE ONE 2020–21 LEAGUE RECORD

Match No.	Date	Venue	Opponents	Result	H/T Score	Lg Pos.	Goalscorers	Attendance
1	Sept 12	A	Lincoln C	L 0-2	0-1	18		0
2	19	H	Sunderland	L 0-2	0-0	23		0
3	26	A	Accrington S	W 4-1	1-0	12	Henry [45], Pritchard (og) [73], Taylor 2 [85, 87]	0
4	Oct 10	A	Gillingham	L 1-3	0-2	20	Agyei [48]	0
5	17	A	Peterborough U	L 0-2	0-1	23		0
6	20	H	Milton Keynes D	W 3-2	1-1	19	Taylor [6], Long [57], Shodipo [88]	0
7	27	A	Charlton Ath	L 0-2	0-2	22		0
8	31	A	Fleetwood T	L 0-2	0-1	23		0
9	Nov 3	H	Rochdale	W 3-1	1-1	20	Moore 2 [35, 82], Shodipo [58]	0
10	17	H	Crewe Alex	L 0-2	0-1	20		0
11	21	A	Wigan Ath	W 2-1	0-0	19	Taylor [61], Henry [86]	0
12	24	A	Portsmouth	D 1-1	0-1	18	Gorrin (pen) [69]	0
13	28	H	Swindon T	L 1-2	1-0	19	Taylor [15]	0
14	Dec 1	H	Ipswich T	D 0-0	0-0	20		0
15	5	H	Hull C	D 1-1	1-0	20	Henry [10]	0
16	12	A	Blackpool	D 0-0	0-0	18		0
17	15	H	Northampton T	W 4-0	0-0	17	Taylor 2 [49, 89], Shodipo [65], Agyei [90]	2000
18	26	H	AFC Wimbledon	W 2-0	2-0	16	Obita [13], Taylor [22]	0
19	29	A	Plymouth Arg	W 3-2	1-1	15	Ruffels [37], Long [74], Shodipo (pen) [82]	2000
20	Jan 2	A	Burton Alb	W 5-1	3-1	12	Taylor [9], Shodipo 2 [18, 31], Ruffels 2 [56, 63]	0
21	23	H	Bristol R	W 2-0	1-0	11	Taylor 2 [32, 73]	0
22	26	A	Rochdale	W 4-3	1-2	11	Agyei [12], Moore [49], Henry [62], Shodipo [90]	0
23	30	H	Fleetwood T	W 1-0	1-0	8	Ruffels [28]	0
24	Feb 6	A	Doncaster R	L 2-3	1-1	11	Long [41], Shodipo [70]	0
25	9	A	Bristol R	W 2-0	1-0	9	Lee [29], Barker [90]	0
26	14	H	Wigan Ath	W 2-1	0-0	7	Winnall [72], Moore [83]	0
27	20	A	Ipswich T	D 0-0	0-0	8		0
28	23	H	Portsmouth	L 0-1	0-0	8		0
29	27	A	Milton Keynes D	D 1-1	0-1	9	Lee [90]	0
30	Mar 2	H	Peterborough U	D 0-0	0-0	10		0
31	6	H	Charlton Ath	D 0-0	0-0	10		0
32	9	A	Swindon T	W 2-1	1-0	9	Barker [3], Agyei [82]	0
33	13	A	Hull C	L 0-2	0-1	9		0
34	16	H	Doncaster R	W 3-0	3-0	8	Taylor 2 [19, 41], Shodipo [44]	0
35	20	H	Blackpool	L 0-2	0-2	11		0
36	23	A	Northampton T	L 0-1	0-0	11		0
37	26	H	Lincoln C	W 2-1	1-1	7	Forde [29], Taylor [57]	0
38	Apr 2	A	Sunderland	L 1-3	1-1	11	Henry [21]	0
39	5	H	Accrington S	L 1-2	1-1	12	Lee [25]	0
40	10	A	Crewe Alex	W 6-0	3-0	9	Ruffels [36], Henry [40], Moore [45], Barker [47], Brannagan [50], Winnall [84]	0
41	13	H	Shrewsbury T	W 4-1	2-0	7	Atkinson [13], Lee [36], Taylor [66], Long [77]	0
42	17	H	Gillingham	W 3-2	0-1	6	Winnall [74], Long 2 [84, 90]	0
43	20	A	AFC Wimbledon	L 1-2	0-0	7	Ruffels [52]	0
44	24	H	Plymouth Arg	W 3-1	1-0	5	Edwards (og) [29], Taylor 2 [69, 80]	0
45	May 1	A	Shrewsbury T	W 3-2	1-2	7	Lee [3], Henry [68], Agyei [85]	0
46	9	H	Burton Alb	W 4-0	2-0	6	Shodipo [10], Taylor [28], Lee [57], Winnall [90]	0

Final League Position: 6

GOALSCORERS

League (77): Taylor 18, Shodipo 10 (1 pen), Henry 7, Lee 6, Long 6, Ruffels 6, Agyei 5, Moore 5, Winnall 4, Barker 3, Atkinson 1, Brannagan 1, Forde 1, Gorrin 1 (1 pen), Obita 1, own goals 2.
FA Cup (1): Ruffels 1.
Carabao Cup (2): Brannagan 1, Hall 1.
Papa John's Trophy (9): Osei Yaw 3, Shodipo 2, Winnall 2, Agyei 1, Hall 1.
League One Play-Offs (3): Atkinson 1, Shodipo 1, Taylor 1.

Eastwood S 13	Long S 35 + 1	Moore E 46	Atkinson R 39	Ruffels J 42	Brannagan C 28 + 3	Kelly L 21 + 5	McGuane M 13 + 2	Sykes M 21 + 11	Taylor M 39 + 7	Henry J 34 + 3	Clare S 10 + 7	Cooper J — + 4	Agyei D 11 + 28	Osei Yaw D 1 + 2	Hall R 1 + 8	Forde A 18 + 17	Winnall S 3 + 21	Gorrin A 28 + 7	Shodipo O 24 + 15	Mousinho J 1 + 6	Obita J 6 + 6	Stephens J 33	Hanson J 9 + 15	Lee E 15 + 3	Barker B 14 + 5	Grayson J 1 + 3	Chambers L — + 3	Match No.
1	2	3	4■	5^{1}	6	7^{3}	8^{2}	9	10	11	12	13	14															1
1	5	3	4		8	7^{2}		6^{3}	11	9	2	13	12	10^{1}	14													2
1	5	3	4		12	7			10^{3}	8	2	13	11^{2}	14	9^{1}	6												3
1	4	3		5	8	7^{2}			10	9	2		11^{1}		13	6	12											4
1	4	3		5		7^{2}		6^{3}	10	9	2		11^{1}	12		8	14	13										5
1	12	3	4^{1}	5			11	6	10^{3}	9	2		13			8^{2}		7	14									6
1	4	3		5		12		8	10	9	2		13		14	6^{3}		7^{2}	11^{1}									7
1	4	3		5		6^{2}			10	9	2	13	12		14	7^{3}		8	11^{1}									8
1	4	3		5			11^{2}	13	10	6	2		9^{1}			8		7^{3}	12	14								9
1	4	3		5			14	8^{1}	10^{2}	9	2					6^{3}	13	7	11		12							10
1	2	3	4	5		6^{2}	8^{1}	12	10^{5}	9^{4}	14		16					7	13	15	11^{3}							11
1	2	3	4	5			13	14	15	6^{3}	9^{5}		10^{4}			8^{2}		7	11^{1}	16	12							12
1	2	3	4	5		6	8^{2}	12	10	9^{1}			14					7	13		11^{3}							13
	2	3	4	5		6^{4}	8		10^{3}	9^{2}	13		14					7	11^{1}	15	12	1						14
	2	3	4	5		6^{4}	8^{2}		10^{3}	9	12		15			14		7^{1}		13	11	1						15
	2	3	4^{1}	5		6^{2}	8^{4}		10	9^{5}			14		16			7	15	12	11^{3}	1	13					16
	2	3		5		8^{2}	6^{4}		10	9^{5}	12		14		16			7	11^{3}	4^{1}	15	1	13					17
	2	3	4	5		6^{1}	8^{2}		10^{4}	9	15		12					7	14		11^{3}	1	13					18
	2	3	4	5		8^{2}	6	14	15	9^{1}	13		10			12			11^{4}			1	7^{3}					19
	2	3	4	5	15		6^{3}		11^{2}	9^{5}					16	8^{1}	12	7	10^{4}		14	1	13					20
	2	3	4	5	12	8^{4}	6^{1}		10^{3}	9^{2}			16			15	14	7	11^{5}		13	1						21
	2	3	4	5	9				11^{4}	12			8^{3}			13	15	6	14		10^{2}	1	7^{1}					22
	2	3	4	5	6	8^{1}			10^{4}	9			13			15	14	7^{2}	11^{3}			1	12					23
	2	3	4	5	8	13		14	10^{2}	6							15	7^{4}	12			1		9^{3}	11^{1}			24
	2^{1}	3	4	5	8	15		16	10^{4}	6^{3}						12	14	7	11^{2}			1		9^{5}	13			25
		3	4	5	8	6^{2}		9^{4}	14							2	10^{3}	7^{1}	12			1	16	13	11^{5}	15		26
		3	4	5	8	15		6	10^{3}	13						2	14	7^{1}	12			1		9^{2}	11^{4}			27
	2	3	4^{4}	5	7			8^{2}	14	6^{3}						15	10	12	11			1		9^{1}	13			28
	2	3	4	5	6			15	11^{2}	14			13			16	12^{4}	7^{5}	8^{3}			1		9	10^{1}			29
	2^{2}	3	4	5	8			11	10^{3}				14			12		7	15			1	13	6^{1}	9^{4}			30
		3	4	5	8	6^{1}		14	13				10^{2}			9^{3}		7	11			1	2^{4}		12		15	31
		3	4	5	8	6^{2}		9^{1}	10^{4}				15			2		7	13			1	12		11^{3}		14	32
		3	4	5	8			9^{1}	13				10			2			11			1	7	6^{2}	12			33
		3	4	5	8^{3}	6^{4}		15	10^{2}				14		16			7	9^{5}			1	2	12	11^{1}	13		34
		3	4	5	8	6^{2}		9^{3}	10^{4}				14			12	15	7^{1}	13			1	2		11			35
		3	4	5	9			13	15				8			2	11^{3}	7^{2}	10^{4}			1	12		14	6^{1}		36
		3	4	5^{1}	7			8	10^{3}	6^{2}			14			12	15		9^{4}			1	2		11		13	37
		3	4		7^{4}	12		8■	10^{3}	6^{1}			14			2^{5}	16		9^{2}			1	5	13	11	15		38
	2^{3}	3	4		7				10	6^{1}			14			13	12		9^{2}			1	5	8	11			39
	2^{2}	3	4	5	7			8	10^{1}	6^{5}			15			16	12		13			1	14	9^{4}	11^{3}			40
	2^{4}	3	4	5	7			8	10^{2}	6^{3}			14			15	13		12			1	16	9^{5}	11^{1}			41
	2	3	4	5	7				10^{3}	6			12			8^{1}	13	15	11^{2}			1	14	9^{4}				42
	2	3	4	5	7^{5}			8^{4}	10^{1}	6■			13			14	12	16	11^{2}			1	15	9^{3}				43
	2	3	4	5	7			8	10				9^{2}			12		13	11			1		6^{1}				44
	2	3	4	5	7			8	10^{3}	6^{4}			12				13	15				1	14	9^{1}	11^{2}			45
	2^{2}	3	4	5	7			8	10^{4}	6^{3}			13			14	15	16	11^{1}			1	12	9^{5}				46

FA Cup
First Round | Peterborough U | (h) | 1-2

Carabao Cup
First Round | AFC Wimbledon | (h) | 1-1
(Oxford U won 4-3 on penalties)
Second Round | Watford | (h) | 1-1
(Watford won 3-0 on penalties)

League One Play-Offs
Semi-Final 1st leg | Blackpool | (h) | 0-3
Semi-Final 2nd leg | Blackpool | (a) | 3-3

Papa John's Trophy
Group D (S) | Chelsea U21 | (h) | 2-1
Group D (S) | Bristol R | (h) | 1-1
(Oxford U won 4-3 on penalties)
Group D (S) | Walsall | (a) | 1-0
Second Round (S) | Forest Green R | (h) | 1-1
(Oxford U won 4-1 on penalties)
Third Round (S) | Cambridge U | (h) | 1-0
Quarter-Final | AFC Wimbledon | (h) | 3-1
Semi-Final | Tranmere R | (h) | 0-2

PETERBOROUGH UNITED

FOUNDATION

The old Peterborough & Fletton club, founded in 1923, was suspended by the FA during season 1932–33 and disbanded. Local enthusiasts determined to carry on and in 1934 a new professional club, Peterborough United, was formed and entered the Midland League the following year. Peterborough's first success came in 1939–40, but from 1955–56 to 1959–60 they won five successive titles. During the 1958–59 season they were undefeated in the Midland League. They reached the third round of the FA Cup, won the Northamptonshire Senior Cup, the Maunsell Cup and were runners-up in the East Anglian Cup.

Weston Homes Stadium, London Road, Peterborough PE2 8AL.

Telephone: (01733) 563 947.

Ticket Office: (0844) 847 1934.

Website: www.theposh.com

Email: info@theposh.com

Ground Capacity: 15,314.

Record Attendance: 30,096 v Swansea T, FA Cup 5th rd, 20 February 1965.

Pitch Measurements: 102.5m × 64m (112yd × 70yd).

Chairman: Darragh MacAnthony.

Chief Executive: Bob Symns.

Manager: Darren Ferguson.

Assistant Manager: Mark Robson.

Colours: Blue shirts with white sleeves, white shorts with blue trim, blue socks with white trim.

Year Formed: 1934.

Turned Professional: 1934.

Club Nickname: 'The Posh'.

Ground: 1934, London Road Stadium (renamed ABAX Stadium 2014; Weston Homes Stadium 2019).

First Football League Game: 20 August 1960, Division 4, v Wrexham (h) W 3–0 – Walls; Stafford, Walker; Rayner, Rigby, Norris; Hails, Emery (1), Bly (1), Smith, McNamee (1).

Record League Victory: 9–1 v Barnet (a) Division 3, 5 September 1998 – Griemink; Hooper (1), Drury (Farell), Gill, Bodley, Edwards, Davies, Payne, Grazioli (5), Quinn (2) (Rowe), Houghton (Etherington) (1).

Record Cup Victory: 9–1 v Rushden T, FA Cup 1st qual rd, 6 October 1945 – Hilliard; Bryan, Parrott, Warner, Hobbs, Woods, Polhill (1), Fairchild, Laxton (6), Tasker (1), Rodgers (1); 9–1 v Kingstonian, FA Cup 1st rd, 25 November 1992. Match ordered to be replayed by FA. Peterborough won replay 1–0.

HONOURS

League Champions: Division 4 – 1960–61, 1973–74.
Runners-up: FL 1 – 2008–09, 2020–21; FL 2 – 2007–08.

FA Cup: 6th rd – 1965.

League Cup: semi-final – 1966.

League Trophy Winners: 2014.

FOOTBALL YEARBOOK FACT FILE

Before entering the Football League in 1960 Peterborough United had one of the best FA Cup records among non-league clubs. But their first entry into the competition in 1935–36 resulted in a 3-0 home defeat to Rushden Town in a first qualifying round tie. The following season Posh won their way through four qualifying rounds to reach the first round proper.

Record Defeat: 1–8 v Northampton T, FA Cup 2nd rd (2nd replay), 18 December 1946.

Most League Points (2 for a win): 66, Division 4, 1960–61.

Most League Points (3 for a win): 92, FL 2, 2007–08.

Most League Goals: 134, Division 4, 1960–61.

Highest League Scorer in Season: Terry Bly, 52, Division 4, 1960–61.

Most League Goals in Total Aggregate: Jim Hall, 122, 1967–75.

Most League Goals in One Match: 5, Guiliano Grazioli v Barnet, Division 3, 5 September 1998.

Most Capped Player: Gabriel Zakuani, 17 (29), DR Congo.

Most League Appearances: Tommy Robson, 482, 1968–81.

Youngest League Player: Matthew Etherington, 15 years 262 days v Brentford, 3 May 1997.

Record Transfer Fee Received: £5,500,000 from Nottingham F for Britt Assombalonga, August 2014.

Record Transfer Fee Paid: £1,250,000 (in excess of) to Bristol C for Mo Eisa, June 2019.

Football League Record: 1960 Elected to Division 4; 1961–68 Division 3, when they were demoted for financial irregularities; 1968–74 Division 4; 1974–79 Division 3; 1979–91 Division 4; 1991–92 Division 3; 1992–94 Division 1; 1994–97 Division 2; 1997–2000 Division 3; 2000–04 Division 2; 2004–05 FL 1; 2005–08 FL 2; 2008–09 FL 1; 2009–10 FL C; 2010–11 FL 1; 2011–13 FL C; 2013–21 FL 1; 2021– FL C.

LATEST SEQUENCES

Longest Sequence of League Wins: 9, 1.2.1992 – 14.3.1992.

Longest Sequence of League Defeats: 8, 16.12.2006 – 27.1.2007.

Longest Sequence of League Draws: 8, 18.12.1971 – 12.2.1972.

Longest Sequence of Unbeaten League Matches: 17, 15.1.2008 – 5.4.2008.

Longest Sequence Without a League Win: 17, 23.9.1978 – 30.12.1978.

Successive Scoring Runs: 33 from 20.9.1960.

Successive Non-scoring Runs: 6 from 13.8.2002.

MANAGERS

Jock Porter 1934–36
Fred Taylor 1936–37
Vic Poulter 1937–38
Sam Haden 1938–48
Jack Blood 1948–50
Bob Gurney 1950–52
Jack Fairbrother 1952–54
George Swindin 1954–58
Jimmy Hagan 1958–62
Jack Fairbrother 1962–64
Gordon Clark 1964–67
Norman Rigby 1967–69
Jim Iley 1969–72
Noel Cantwell 1972–77
John Barnwell 1977–78
Billy Hails 1978–79
Peter Morris 1979–82
Martin Wilkinson 1982–83
John Wile 1983–86
Noel Cantwell 1986–88 *(continued as General Manager)*
Mick Jones 1988–89
Mark Lawrenson 1989–90
Dave Booth 1990–91
Chris Turner 1991–92
Lil Fuccillo 1992–93
Chris Turner 1993–94
John Still 1994–95
Mick Halsall 1995–96
Barry Fry 1996–2005
Mark Wright 2005–06
Steve Bleasdale 2006
Keith Alexander 2006–07
Darren Ferguson 2007–09
Mark Cooper 2009–10
Jim Gannon 2010
Gary Johnson 2010–11
Darren Ferguson 2011–15
Dave Robertson 2015
Graham Westley 2015–16
Grant McCann 2016–18
Steve Evans 2018–19
Darren Ferguson January 2019–

TEN YEAR LEAGUE RECORD

		P	*W*	*D*	*L*	*F*	*A*	*Pts*	*Pos*
2011-12	FL C	46	13	11	22	67	77	50	18
2012-13	FL C	46	15	9	22	66	75	54	22
2013-14	FL 1	46	23	5	18	72	58	74	6
2014-15	FL 1	46	18	9	19	53	56	63	9
2015-16	FL 1	46	19	6	21	82	73	63	13
2016-17	FL 1	46	17	11	18	62	62	62	11
2017-18	FL 1	46	17	13	16	68	60	64	9
2018-19	FL 1	46	20	12	14	71	62	72	7
2019-20	FL 1	35	17	8	10	68	40	59	7§
2020-21	FL 1	46	26	9	11	83	46	87	2

§*Decided on points-per-game (1.69)*

DID YOU KNOW ?

Peterborough United won the Midland League championship in 1958–59 without losing a game. Posh won 32 of their 36 games finishing the season with a run of 11 straight victories, leaving them eight points ahead of second-placed Ashington.

PETERBOROUGH UNITED – SKY BET LEAGUE ONE 2020–21 LEAGUE RECORD

Match No.	Date	Venue	Opponents	Result	H/T Score	Lg Pos.	Goalscorers	Attendance
1	Sept 12	A	Accrington S	L 0-2	0-1	18		0
2	19	H	Fleetwood T	W 2-1	0-0	15	Taylor [90], Szmidics [90]	0
3	26	A	Sunderland	L 0-1	0-0	19		0
4	Oct 3	H	Swindon T	W 3-1	0-1	8	Clarke-Harris 2 (1 pen) [48, 69 (p)], Broom [78]	0
5	10	A	Northampton T	W 2-0	1-0	5	Thompson [33], Brown [80]	0
6	17	H	Oxford U	W 2-0	1-0	4	Ward [43], Dembele [65]	0
7	20	A	Wigan Ath	W 1-0	1-0	4	Clarke-Harris [28]	0
8	24	A	Hull C	W 2-1	0-1	3	Clarke-Harris [63], Dembele [75]	0
9	27	H	Burton Alb	D 2-2	1-1	4	Clarke-Harris [10], Ward [48]	0
10	31	H	Shrewsbury T	W 5-1	2-1	1	Clarke-Harris (pen) [16], Dembele 3 [42, 69, 80], Taylor [88]	0
11	Nov 3	A	Bristol R	W 2-0	1-0	1	Taylor [42], Butler [64]	0
12	14	A	Crewe Alex	L 0-2	0-2	1		0
13	21	H	Blackpool	L 1-2	0-1	2	Kent [84]	0
14	24	H	Plymouth Arg	W 1-0	1-0	2	Clarke-Harris [41]	0
15	Dec 2	A	AFC Wimbledon	L 1-2	0-0	3	Clarke-Harris [71]	0
16	5	A	Portsmouth	L 0-2	0-0	5		2000
17	12	H	Rochdale	W 4-1	4-1	4	Clarke-Harris 3 (1 pen) [5 (p), 10, 22], Thompson [40]	0
18	15	A	Milton Keynes D	D 1-1	1-0	3	Clarke-Harris [25]	0
19	Jan 9	A	Lincoln C	D 1-1	1-0	5	Eyoma (og) [10]	0
20	16	H	Milton Keynes D	W 3-0	2-0	5	Clarke-Harris [7], Szmidics 2 [30, 65]	0
21	19	H	Charlton Ath	W 2-1	0-1	4	Szmidics 2 [66, 79]	0
22	23	A	Ipswich T	W 1-0	0-0	3	McGuinness (og) [69]	0
23	26	H	Bristol R	D 0-0	0-0	3		0
24	30	A	Shrewsbury T	L 0-2	0-0	4		0
25	Feb 6	H	Crewe Alex	W 2-0	2-0	4	Szmidics [25], Clarke-Harris [31]	0
26	9	H	Ipswich T	W 2-1	1-1	3	Clarke-Harris [38], Ward [50]	0
27	16	A	Gillingham	W 3-1	0-1	2	Clarke-Harris 2 [47, 67], Dembele [52]	0
28	20	H	AFC Wimbledon	W 3-0	0-0	2	Szmidics 2 [49, 52], Clarke-Harris [90]	0
29	23	A	Plymouth Arg	W 3-0	0-0	1	Szmidics [46], Clarke-Harris [63], Taylor [84]	0
30	27	H	Wigan Ath	W 2-1	0-0	1	Clarke-Harris 2 (1 pen) [82, 85 (p)]	0
31	Mar 2	A	Oxford U	D 0-0	0-0	1		0
32	6	A	Burton Alb	L 1-2	0-0	2	Burrows [90]	0
33	9	H	Hull C	L 1-3	1-1	2	Brown [8]	0
34	16	H	Portsmouth	W 1-0	1-0	2	Nicolaisen (og) [32]	0
35	20	A	Rochdale	D 3-3	2-0	2	Dembele [5], Szmidics [45], Clarke-Harris (pen) [90]	0
36	23	A	Blackpool	L 1-3	1-1	2	Ward [45]	0
37	27	H	Accrington S	W 7-0	3-0	2	Clarke-Harris 3 [3, 9, 65], Szmidics 2 [23, 48], Eisa [77], Kanu [82]	0
38	Apr 2	A	Fleetwood T	W 1-0	0-0	2	Clarke-Harris [89]	0
39	5	H	Sunderland	D 1-1	0-0	2	Dembele [66]	0
40	10	A	Swindon T	W 3-0	2-0	2	Dembele 2 [17, 23], Clarke-Harris [90]	0
41	16	H	Northampton T	W 3-1	1-1	2	Szmidics 2 [33, 48], Clarke-Harris (pen) [67]	0
42	20	H	Gillingham	L 0-1	0-1	2		0
43	24	A	Charlton Ath	W 1-0	1-0	2	Clarke-Harris [9]	0
44	27	H	Doncaster R	D 2-2	2-1	2	Ward [10], Szmidics [23]	0
45	May 1	H	Lincoln C	D 3-3	0-2	2	Dembele [65], Clarke-Harris 2 (1 pen) [75, 90 (p)]	0
46	9	A	Doncaster R	W 4-1	4-0	2	Eisa [6], Mason [8], Kanu [16], Jade-Jones [39]	0

Final League Position: 2

GOALSCORERS

League (83): Clarke-Harris 31 (7 pens), Szmidics 15, Dembele 11, Ward 5, Taylor 4, Brown 2, Eisa 2, Kanu 2, Thompson 2, Broom 1, Burrows 1, Butler 1, Jade-Jones 1, Kent 1, Mason 1, own goals 3.
FA Cup (3): Taylor 2, Dembele 1.
Carabao Cup (0).
Papa John's Trophy (17): Clarke 3, Eisa 3, Clarke-Harris 2 (1 pen), Boyd 1, Dembele 1, Hamilton 1, Kent 1, Mason 1, Reed 1, Szmodics 1, Tasdemir 1, Taylor 1.

Pym C 40	Thompson N 39	Beevers M 45	Kent F 45	Ward J 35 + 2	Taylor J 35 + 1	Hamilton E 13 + 21	Butler D 40 + 2	Szmidics S 40 + 2	Clarke-Harris J 45	Eisa M 6 + 21	Clarke F 2 + 2	Broom R 5 + 10	Mason N 6 + 20	Reed L 12 + 5	Dembele S 38 + 4	Jade-Jones R 1 + 14	Brown R 33 + 5	Kanu I 7 + 10	Blake-Tracy F 3 + 6	Burrows H 8 + 13	Edwards R 2	Bursik J 6	Nascimento A — + 1	Barker K — + 1	Blackmore W — + 1	O'Connell C — + 1	*Match No.*
1	2^{3}	3	4	5^{1}	6	7^{2}	8	9	10	11	12	13	14														1
1	2^{3}	3	4	13	6		8	9	10	11^{1}		5^{2}	14	7	12												2
1	2	3	4	12	6		8	9^{2}	11			5^{1}		7	10	13											3
1	2	3	4	5	7		8	9^{2}	11			13		6^{1}	10		12										4
1	2	3	4	5		6	8	9^{1}	11			12			10		7										5
1	2	4	3	5	7	13	8	9^{1}	10			12			11^{2}		6										6
1	2	4	3	8	6		5^{1}	9	11			13	12		10^{2}		7										7
1	2^{2}	4	3	5	6		8		10		12	9^{1}	13		11		7										8
1	2^{2}	4	3	8	7		5	9^{1}	11			12	13		10		6										9
1		3	2	5^{3}	7		8	9	10^{2}	13			4	12	11		6^{1}	14									10
1	2	4	3	5	7		8	9	10						11		6										11
1		4	3	5		13	8	9^{3}	10	14			2^{1}	6^{2}	11		7		12								12
1		4	3	5^{1}	7	15	8	9^{3}	10	14		12	2^{2}		11		6^{4}		13								13
1		3	2		6	12	8	9^{4}	10^{3}	14		5^{2}	13	15	11		7^{1}		4								14
1	2^{2}	3	4		6	12		9	11			8^{1}		7	10			13	5								15
1	2^{3}	3	4		6	8^{2}		9^{4}	11	15		13	14	7	10			12	5^{1}								16
1	3	4^{5}	2		7			13	10^{3}	12	9^{2}	15	16	14	11^{1}		6^{4}	5		8							17
1		4	2		7	15	14	13	10	12	9^{2}		16		11^{1}		6^{5}	5^{3}		8^{4}	3						18
1	3▮	4	2		6	15	13	9^{2}	11			16	14		10^{3}	12	7^{5}	5^{4}		8^{1}							19
1		4	2	5^{1}	7	6	8^{4}	10^{3}	11^{2}	16			3		9^{5}	12	14	13	15								20
1	3	4	2		7	6^{2}	8	10	11						9		13	5^{1}		12							21
1	3	4	2		6	12	8	9^{2}	11				14		10^{3}	13	7^{1}	5									22
1	3	4	2		6	12	8^{2}	9	11						10		7^{1}	5		13							23
1	3	4		5	6^{1}	7	8^{2}	9^{4}	11^{5}	14			2^{3}		10	15	12	16	13								24
1	3	4	2^{3}	5^{2}	6	12	8	9	11	15			13		10^{4}		7^{1}	14									25
1	3	4	2	5^{2}	7	12	8	9	11	10^{1}						14	6^{3}	13									26
1	3	4	2	5	6		8	9	11	10^{1}					12		7										27
1	3^{2}	4	2	5^{5}	7	12	8	9^{3}	11^{4}	14			13		10	16	6^{1}			15							28
1	2^{4}	4	3	8^{5}	6	12	5	9	11^{2}	13			15		10^{3}	16	7^{1}			14							29
1	2	4^{2}	3	5	6	13	8	9^{1}	11	12					10^{4}	15	7^{3}			14							30
1	2	4	3	8		6	5	9^{2}	11	13				12	10		7^{1}										31
1	2	4	3	8		7	5^{2}	9	11^{1}	12					10		6			13							32
1	3	4	2	5^{2}		7▮	8	10^{1}	11^{3}				12		9	14	6			13							33
1	3	4	2	5			8		11	12			13	6^{2}	10^{1}		7		14	9^{3}							34
1	3	4	2	5^{1}		6	8	10^{2}	11	13					9		7	12									35
1	3	4	2	5		7^{2}	8^{1}	9^{4}	11	15			13		10^{3}	14	6			12							36
1	2^{2}	4	3	8^{3}		15	5	9	11^{1}	12			13	7		16	6^{4}	14		10^{5}							37
1	2	4	3	8	12	14	5	9	11					7^{3}	13		6^{2}			10^{1}							38
1	2	4	3	8	6		5^{3}	9^{4}	11	15			14	7^{1}	13		12			10^{2}							39
	2	4	3	6	8	13	5		11	10^{1}					9^{3}	15	7^{2}	14		12^{4}		1					40
	2	4	3	8	6	13	5	9	11^{2}						10^{1}	14	7^{3}			12		1					41
	3	4^{2}	2	5	7	12	8	9	11						10		6^{1}			13		1					42
	2^{2}	4	3	8	7	6^{1}	5	9	11				13	12	10^{3}					14		1					43
	2	4	3	8	7	12	5^{2}	9	11					6^{1}	10					13		1					44
	3	4	2	5	6^{1}	12	8	9	11	13					10		7^{2}					1					45
1^{4}			2^{2}	5^{1}		7				10			4	6^{3}		11^{5}		9	12	8	3		13	14	15	16	46

FA Cup

First Round	Oxford U	(a)	2-1
Second Round	Chorley	(h)	1-2

Carabao Cup

First Round	Cheltenham T	(h)	0-1

Papa John's Trophy

Group H (S)	Burton Alb	(h)	3-3
(Peterborough U won 5-4 on penalties)			
Group H (S)	Fulham U21	(h)	4-2
Group H (S)	Cambridge U	(a)	1-1
(Cambridge U won 3-1 on penalties)			
Second Round (S)	West Ham U U21	(h)	3-0
Third Round (S)	Portsmouth	(h)	5-1
Quarter-Final	Tranmere R	(a)	1-2

PLYMOUTH ARGYLE

FOUNDATION

The club was formed in September 1886 as the Argyle Athletic Club by former public and private school pupils who wanted to continue playing the game. The meeting was held in a room above the Borough Arms (a coffee house), Bedford Street, Plymouth. It was common then to choose a local street/terrace as a club name and Argyle or Argyll was a fashionable name throughout the land due to Queen Victoria's great interest in Scotland.

Home Park, Plymouth, Devon PL2 3DQ.

Telephone: (01752) 562 561.

Ticket Office: (01752) 907 700.

Website: www.pafc.co.uk

Email: argyle@pafc.co.uk

Ground Capacity: 18,050.

Record Attendance: 43,596 v Aston Villa, Division 2, 10 October 1936.

Pitch Measurements: 103m × 66m (112.5yd × 72yd).

Chairman: Simon Hallett.

Chief Executive: Andrew Parkinson.

Manager: Ryan Lowe.

Assistant Manager: Steven Schumacher.

Colours: Dark green shirts with black trim, black shorts, white socks with dark green trim.

Year Formed: 1886.

Turned Professional: 1903.

Previous Name: 1886, Argyle Athletic Club; 1903, Plymouth Argyle.

Club Nickname: 'The Pilgrims'.

Ground: 1886, Home Park.

First Football League Game: 28 August 1920, Division 3, v Norwich C (h) D 1–1 – Craig; Russell, Atterbury; Logan, Dickinson, Forbes; Kirkpatrick, Jack, Bowler, Heeps (1), Dixon.

Record League Victory: 8–1 v Millwall, Division 2, 16 January 1932 – Harper; Roberts, Titmuss; Mackay, Pullan, Reed; Grozier, Bowden (2), Vidler (3), Leslie (1), Black (1), (1 og). 8–1 v Hartlepool U (a), Division 2, 7 May 1994 – Nicholls; Patterson (Naylor), Hill, Burrows, Comyn, McCall (1), Barlow, Castle (1), Landon (3), Marshall (1), Dalton (2).

Record Cup Victory: 6–0 v Corby T, FA Cup 3rd rd, 22 January 1966 – Leiper; Book, Baird; Williams, Nelson, Newman; Jones (1), Jackson (1), Bickle (3), Piper (1), Jennings.

Record Defeat: 0–9 v Stoke C, Division 2, 17 December 1960.

Most League Points (2 for a win): 68, Division 3 (S), 1929–30.

HONOURS

League Champions: Second Division – 2003–04; Division 3 – 1958–59; Division 3S – 1929–30, 1951–52; Third Division – 2001–02.
Runners-up: FL 2 – 2016–17; Division 3 – 1974–75, 1985–86; Division 3S – 1921–22, 1922–23, 1923–24, 1924–25, 1925–26, 1926–27.

FA Cup: semi-final – 1984.

League Cup: semi-final – 1965, 1974.

FOOTBALL YEARBOOK FACT FILE

Plymouth Argyle's Home Park ground hosted rugby union in January 1958 when a South West Counties XV met the Australian Tourists. A crowd of 15,000 saw a hard-fought game which ended in a 3-3 draw with the tourists scoring an equalising try in the final minutes.

Most League Points (3 for a win): 102, Division 3, 2001–02.

Most League Goals: 107, Division 3 (S), 1925–26 and 1951–52.

Highest League Scorer in Season: Jack Cock, 32, Division 3 (S), 1926–27.

Most League Goals in Total Aggregate: Sammy Black, 174, 1924–38.

Most League Goals in One Match: 5, Wilf Carter v Charlton Ath, Division 2, 27 December 1960.

Most Capped Player: Moses Russell, 20 (23), Wales.

Most League Appearances: Kevin Hodges, 530, 1978–92.

Youngest League Player: Lee Phillips, 16 years 43 days v Gillingham, 29 October 1996.

Record Transfer Fee Received: £2,000,000 from Hull C for Peter Halmosi, July 2008.

Record Transfer Fee Paid: £500,000 to Cardiff C for Steve MacLean, January 2008.

Football League Record: 1920 Original Member of Division 3; 1921–30 Division 3 (S); 1930–50 Division 2; 1950–52 Division 3 (S); 1952–56 Division 2; 1956–58 Division 3 (S); 1958–59 Division 3; 1959–68 Division 2; 1968–75 Division 3; 1975–77 Division 2; 1977–86 Division 3; 1986–95 Division 2; 1995–96 Division 3; 1996–98 Division 2; 1998–2002 Division 3; 2002–04 Division 2; 2004–10 FL C; 2010–11 FL 1; 2011–17 FL 2; 2017–19 FL 1; 2019–20 FL 2; 2020– FL 1.

LATEST SEQUENCES

Longest Sequence of League Wins: 9, 8.3.1986 – 12.4.1986.

Longest Sequence of League Defeats: 9, 12.10.1963 – 7.12.1963.

Longest Sequence of League Draws: 5, 26.2.2000 – 14.3.2000.

Longest Sequence of Unbeaten League Matches: 22, 20.4.1929 – 21.12.1929.

Longest Sequence Without a League Win: 13, 1.5.2018 – 2.10.2018.

Successive Scoring Runs: 39 from 15.4.1939.

Successive Non-scoring Runs: 5 from 21.11.2009.

MANAGERS

Frank Brettell 1903–05
Bob Jack 1905–06
Bill Fullerton 1906–07
Bob Jack 1910–38
Jack Tresadern 1938–47
Jimmy Rae 1948–55
Jack Rowley 1955–60
Neil Dougall 1961
Ellis Stuttard 1961–63
Andy Beattie 1963–64
Malcolm Allison 1964–65
Derek Ufton 1965–68
Billy Bingham 1968–70
Ellis Stuttard 1970–72
Tony Waiters 1972–77
Mike Kelly 1977–78
Malcolm Allison 1978–79
Bobby Saxton 1979–81
Bobby Moncur 1981–83
Johnny Hore 1983–84
Dave Smith 1984–88
Ken Brown 1988–90
David Kemp 1990–92
Peter Shilton 1992–95
Steve McCall 1995
Neil Warnock 1995–97
Mick Jones 1997–98
Kevin Hodges 1998–2000
Paul Sturrock 2000–04
Bobby Williamson 2004–05
Tony Pulis 2005–06
Ian Holloway 2006–07
Paul Sturrock 2007–09
Paul Mariner 2009–10
Peter Reid 2010–11
Carl Fletcher 2011–13
John Sheridan 2013–15
Derek Adams 2015–19
Ryan Lowe June 2019–

TEN YEAR LEAGUE RECORD

		P	*W*	*D*	*L*	*F*	*A*	*Pts*	*Pos*
2011-12	FL 2	46	10	16	20	47	64	46	21
2012-13	FL 2	46	13	13	20	46	55	52	21
2013-14	FL 2	46	16	12	18	51	58	60	10
2014-15	FL 2	46	20	11	15	55	37	71	7
2015-16	FL 2	46	24	9	13	72	46	81	5
2016-17	FL 2	46	26	9	11	71	46	87	2
2017-18	FL 1	46	19	11	16	58	59	68	7
2018-19	FL 1	46	13	11	22	56	80	50	21
2019-20	FL 2	37	20	8	9	61	39	68	3§
2020-21	FL 1	46	14	11	21	53	80	53	18

§*Decided on points-per-game (1.84)*

DID YOU KNOW ?

Teenager John Hore was the first substitute to be used by Plymouth Argyle when he replaced Frank Lord in a Second Division game at Charlton Athletic on 31 August 1965. He went on to make over 400 first-team appearances during a 12-year career with the club.

PLYMOUTH ARGYLE – SKY BET LEAGUE ONE 2020–21 LEAGUE RECORD

Match No.	*Date*	*Venue*	*Opponents*	*Result*		*H/T Score*	*Lg Pos.*	*Goalscorers*	*Attendance*
1	Sept 12	H	Blackpool	W	1-0	1-0	7	Jephcott [3]	0
2	19	A	AFC Wimbledon	D	4-4	2-1	6	Cooper, G [16], Grant, C [45], Canavan [76], Telford [78]	0
3	26	H	Shrewsbury T	D	1-1	1-1	9	Grant, C [29]	0
4	Oct 3	A	Hull C	L	0-1	0-1	13		0
5	10	H	Burton Alb	W	2-0	1-0	8	Jephcott [25], Moore, B [47]	0
6	17	H	Northampton T	W	2-1	1-0	6	Nouble [41], Watts [86]	0
7	20	A	Lincoln C	L	0-2	0-0	9		0
8	24	A	Wigan Ath	D	1-1	1-0	9	Hardie [34]	0
9	27	H	Doncaster R	W	2-1	1-0	8	Jephcott [34], Edwards [68]	0
10	Nov 3	H	Swindon T	W	4-2	3-2	8	Jephcott 2 [6, 25], Edwards [7], Grant, C [89]	0
11	16	H	Portsmouth	D	2-2	1-0	9	Raggett (og) [11], Opoku [78]	0
12	21	A	Fleetwood T	L	1-5	0-3	10	Jephcott [84]	0
13	24	A	Peterborough U	L	0-1	0-1	11		0
14	Dec 1	H	Rochdale	L	0-4	0-3	13		0
15	5	H	Ipswich T	L	1-2	1-0	15	Jephcott [13]	1808
16	12	A	Bristol R	L	0-3	0-2	15		0
17	15	A	Crewe Alex	L	1-2	0-2	18	Jephcott [85]	2000
18	19	H	Milton Keynes D	W	1-0	0-0	14	Hardie [68]	2000
19	26	A	Charlton Ath	D	2-2	2-1	14	Jephcott 2 [5, 36]	0
20	29	H	Oxford U	L	2-3	1-1	17	Camara [12], Jephcott (pen) [84]	2000
21	Jan 2	H	Gillingham	W	1-0	1-0	15	Jephcott [33]	0
22	16	H	Crewe Alex	D	1-1	1-0	15	Jephcott (pen) [11]	0
23	19	A	Sunderland	W	2-1	1-0	11	Lewis [11], Edwards [56]	0
24	26	A	Swindon T	W	2-0	1-0	13	Camara [36], Hardie [67]	0
25	30	H	Accrington S	D	2-2	1-1	13	Jephcott [43], Ennis [78]	0
26	Feb 6	A	Portsmouth	D	2-2	0-0	12	Jephcott 2 [71, 82]	0
27	9	A	Accrington S	W	1-0	0-0	12	Ennis [51]	0
28	13	H	Fleetwood T	W	1-0	1-0	9	Holgate (og) [11]	0
29	20	A	Rochdale	D	0-0	0-0	10		0
30	23	H	Peterborough U	L	0-3	0-0	12		0
31	27	H	Lincoln C	W	4-3	2-1	10	Watts [3], Mayor [13], Edwards 2 [77, 90]	0
32	Mar 2	A	Northampton T	L	0-2	0-1	12		0
33	6	A	Doncaster R	L	1-2	0-1	14	Ennis [49]	0
34	9	H	Wigan Ath	L	0-2	0-2	15		0
35	13	A	Ipswich T	L	0-1	0-1	16		0
36	16	A	Milton Keynes D	L	1-2	0-1	16	Grant, C [61]	0
37	20	H	Bristol R	W	2-0	2-0	16	Ennis 2 [7, 45]	0
38	27	A	Blackpool	D	2-2	1-0	16	Hardie [12], Edwards [90]	0
39	Apr 2	H	AFC Wimbledon	W	1-0	1-0	14	Woods [11]	0
40	5	A	Shrewsbury T	L	0-3	0-0	16		0
41	10	H	Hull C	L	0-3	0-1	16		0
42	17	A	Burton Alb	D	1-1	0-0	16	Hardie [69]	0
43	20	H	Charlton Ath	L	0-6	0-2	16		0
44	24	A	Oxford U	L	1-3	0-1	18	Ennis [65]	0
45	May 1	H	Sunderland	L	1-3	0-1	18	Edwards [62]	0
46	9	A	Gillingham	L	0-1	0-1	18		0

Final League Position: 18

GOALSCORERS

League (53): Jephcott 16 (2 pens), Edwards 7, Ennis 6, Hardie 5, Grant, C 4, Camara 2, Watts 2, Canavan 1, Cooper, G 1, Lewis 1, Mayor 1, Moore, B 1, Nouble 1, Opoku 1, Telford 1, Woods 1, own goals 2.
FA Cup (7): Camara 2, Jephcott 2, Edwards 1, Hardie 1, Reeves 1.
Carabao Cup (5): Camara 1, Edwards 1, Mayor 1, Nouble 1, Watts 1.
Papa John's Trophy (5): Cooper, G 1, Lolos 1 (1 pen), Reeves 1, Telford 1, own goal 1.

Cooper M 46	Aimson W 39 + 1	Wootton S 7 + 3	Watts K 42 + 2	Edwards J 35 + 5	Mayor D 44	Macleod L 10 + 5	Grant C 34 + 4	Cooper G 10 + 2	Jephcott L 31 + 10	Nouble F 12 + 12	Camara P 35 + 6	Telford D 2 + 14	Moore B 16 + 22	Hardie R 26 + 17	Canavan N 10 + 2	Opoku J 30 + 3	Reeves B 5 + 23	Fornah T 34 + 5	Abraham T 1 + 2	Lewis A 9 + 11	Ennis N 18 + 6	Woods S 5 + 4	Lolos K — + 8	Law R 4	Tomlinson O 1 + 1	McCormick L — + 2	Craske F — + 1	*Match No.*
1	2	3	4	5	6	7	8^{1}	9^{3}	10^{2}	11	12	13	14															1
1	2	3^{2}	4	5^{1}	8	7	6	9		10		14	12	11^{3}	13													2
1		2	4		9	6^{1}	7	8		10	12	11^{2}	5	13	3													3
1		2	4		8		7^{2}	12		10	6	13	5	11^{3}	3	9^{1}	14											4
1	2		4	12	8		6^{2}	9^{1}	11^{3}	10		14	5		3		13	7										5
1	2		4		8		6^{1}	9^{3}	11^{2}	10			5		3	14	12	7	13									6
1	2		3		8			9	12	10^{2}	6^{3}		5	13		4	14	7	11^{1}									7
1	2		3	5	8				10^{1}	12	14	13	9	11^{2}		4	6^{3}	7										8
1	2		4	5	8				10^{1}	12	6		9	11^{2}		3		7	13									9
1	2		4	5	8		12		10^{2}	13	6	14	9	11^{3}		3		7^{1}										10
1	2		4	5	8		13	9		10	6^{3}	12		11^{1}		3	14	7^{2}										11
1	2^{2}	13	4	5	8		7^{5}		15	10	6^{1}	11^{3}	9	16	14■	3^{4}		12										12
1		2	4	5^{3}	8		7^{2}	9	10^{4}	12		15	13	11^{1}		3	14	6										13
1	15	2^{3}	4^{5}	5^{2}			6	9^{1}	11	10	16		12	14	3^{4}	13	8	7										14
1	4		2	5^{3}	8■		9		11^{1}	10^{2}	6	15	13	12		3	14	7^{4}										15
1	2		4	5^{1}		16	9^{5}	12	11^{3}	15	6	14	13	10		3	8^{2}	7^{4}										16
1	5	2	4^{1}	16	9^{5}	12	15	10	13	11^{3}	7		6^{4}	14	3			8^{2}										17
1	2		4	5	8	7^{4}	9		11^{3}	13	6^{1}	14		10^{2}	3		15	12										18
1	2		4	5	8	7^{1}	9		10^{3}	13	6		14	11^{2}	3			12										19
1	2		4	5^{3}	8	7^{4}	9^{1}		11	13	6	14	12	10^{2}	3			15										20
1	2		4	5	8	7^{1}	9^{2}		11^{4}	14	6	15		10^{3}	3	13		12										21
1	2		4	5	8^{2}		9		10^{3}	12	6■	14		11^{1}		3		7		13								22
1	2	15	4	5	8		6		10^{2}	14				11^{4}		3	12	7^{3}		9^{1}	13							23
1	2	16	4	5	8^{5}		9^{2}		11^{1}	15	6		13	10^{4}		3	14	7^{3}			12							24
1	2		4	5	8		9^{1}		11^{2}		6			10		3	14	7^{3}		12	13							25
1	2		4		8		9		10^{2}		6^{3}		5	11^{1}		3		7		14	12	13						26
1	2		4		8		9		10^{2}		6^{1}		5	13		3		7		12	11							27
1	2		4	14	8		9		11^{1}		6^{2}		5^{3}	12		3		7		13	10							28
1	2		4	14	8		9		11^{4}		6^{1}		5^{3}	15		3	12	7^{2}		13	10							29
1	2		4^{3}	14	8		9^{1}		11		6^{5}		5^{4}	12		3^{2}	16	7		15	10	13						30
1	2		4	5	8		6		14		12			11^{4}		3^{2}	16	7^{1}		9^{5}	10^{3}	13	15					31
1	2		4	5^{3}	8		12		10		6^{4}		14	11^{1}			15	7^{5}		9^{2}	13	3■	16					32
1	2		4	5^{4}	8	13	9^{2}		10^{5}		14		15	16		3	6^{3}	7^{1}		12	11							33
1	2^{3}		4	5	8	7^{4}	9^{2}		10^{1}		6		14	12		3	15			13	11							34
1	2		4	5	10	6^{3}	7^{4}		12		9		14	13		3	15			8^{2}	11^{1}							35
1	2		4^{3}	5	8		9		11^{1}		6		14	12		3		7^{2}		13	10^{4}	15						36
1	3			2	9		8		10^{2}		6		13	12		4		7		5	11^{1}							37
1	4			2	9		8		13		6^{1}		12	10^{3}				7		5^{2}	11	3	14					38
1	4		13	2	9		8		12		6		15	10^{1}			14	7		5^{2}	11^{4}	3^{3}						39
1	2		4	5^{5}	8		9		13		6^{4}		14	11^{2}		3	16	7^{3}		15	10^{1}		12					40
1	2		4^{1}	5	8	16			10^{3}		6^{2}		12	14		3	13	7^{5}		9	11^{4}		15					41
1	2		4	5	8	14			12		6		13	10^{2}		3		7^{3}		9	11^{1}							42
1	2^{1}		4	5	8	7^{3}			10		6		12	11^{2}			13				14	3		9				43
1			14	2	9				10^{1}		7		6^{2}	12		4	15	8^{4}			11	3^{3}	13	5				44
1^{3}			3	2	9		8				6^{4}			10^{1}		4■	14	7			11^{2}		12	5	13	15		45
1^{5}			4^{1}	2	9^{4}				14		6		12^{3}	10			8	7			11^{2}		13	5	3	15	16	46

FA Cup

First Round	Charlton Ath	(a)	1-0
Second Round	Lincoln C	(h)	2-0
Third Round	Huddersfield T	(a)	3-2
Fourth Round	Sheffield U	(a)	1-2

Carabao Cup

First Round	QPR	(h)	3-2
Second Round	Leyton Orient	(a)	2-3

Papa John's Trophy

Group F (S)	Norwich C U21	(h)	2-3
Group F (S)	Cheltenham T	(a)	0-2
Group F (S)	Newport Co	(h)	3-1

PORT VALE

FOUNDATION

Port Vale Football Club was formed in 1876 and took its name from the venue of the inaugural meeting at 'Port Vale House' situated in a suburb of Stoke-on-Trent. Upon moving to Burslem in 1884 the club changed its name to 'Burslem Port Vale' and after several seasons in the Midland League became founder members of the Football League Division Two in 1892. The prefix 'Burslem' was dropped from the name as a new ground several miles away was acquired.

Vale Park, Hamil Road, Burslem, Stoke-on-Trent, Staffordshire ST6 1AW.

Telephone: (01782) 655 800.

Ticket Office: (01782) 655 821.

Website: www.port-vale.co.uk

Email: enquiries@port-vale.co.uk

Ground Capacity: 19,052.

Record Attendance: 22,993 v Stoke C, Division 2, 6 March 1920 (at Recreation Ground); 49,768 v Aston Villa, FA Cup 5th rd, 20 February 1960 (at Vale Park).

Pitch Measurements: 105m × 70m (115yd × 76.5yd).

Co-Chair: Kevin Shanahan, Carol Shanahan.

Chief Executive: Colin Garlick.

Manager: Darrell Clarke.

Assistant Manager: Andy Crosby.

Colours: White shirts with black features and yellow trim, black shorts with white trim, white socks with black trim.

Year Formed: 1876.

Turned Professional: 1885.

Previous Names: 1876, Port Vale; 1884, Burslem Port Vale; 1909, Port Vale.

Club Nickname: 'Valiants'.

Grounds: 1876, Limekin Lane, Longport; 1881, Westport; 1884, Moorland Road, Burslem; 1886, Athletic Ground, Cobridge; 1913, Recreation Ground, Hanley; 1950, Vale Park.

First Football League Game: 3 September 1892, Division 2, v Small Heath (a) L 1–5 – Frail; Clutton, Elson; Farrington, McCrindle, Delves; Walker, Scarratt, Bliss (1), Jones. (Only 10 men).

Record League Victory: 9–1 v Chesterfield, Division 2, 24 September 1932 – Leckie; Shenton, Poyser; Sherlock, Round, Jones; McGrath, Mills, Littlewood (6), Kirkham (2), Morton (1).

Record Cup Victory: 7–1 v Irthlingborough, FA Cup 1st rd, 12 January 1907 – Matthews; Dunn, Hamilton; Eardley, Baddeley, Holyhead; Carter, Dodds (2), Beats, Mountford (2), Coxon (3).

Record Defeat: 0–10 v Sheffield U, Division 2, 10 December 1892. 0–10 v Notts Co, Division 2, 26 February 1895.

HONOURS

League Champions: Division 3N – 1929–30, 1953–54; Division 4 – 1958–59.
Runners-up: Second Division – 1993–94; Division 3N – 1952–53.

FA Cup: semi-final – 1954.

League Cup: 4th rd – 2007.

League Trophy Winners: 1993, 2001.

Anglo-Italian Cup: *Runners-up:* 1996.

FOOTBALL YEARBOOK FACT FILE

The Sproson family had a near unbroken connection with Port Vale for more than 50 years. Defender Jess Sproson played from the 1938–39 season through to 1945–46. His younger brother Roy, who holds the record for appearances for the club, played from 1949–50 until 1971–72, then stayed on with the backroom staff and later as manager until 1978. Jess's son Phil was already on the books as a player by this time and remained until the summer of 1989.

Most League Points (2 for a win): 69, Division 3 (N), 1953–54.

Most League Points (3 for a win): 89, Division 2, 1992–93.

Most League Goals: 110, Division 4, 1958–59.

Highest League Scorer in Season: Wilf Kirkham 38, Division 2, 1926–27.

Most League Goals in Total Aggregate: Wilf Kirkham, 153, 1923–29, 1931–33.

Most League Goals in One Match: 6, Stewart Littlewood v Chesterfield, Division 2, 24 September 1922.

Most Capped Player: Chris Birchall, 27 (44), Trinidad & Tobago.

Most League Appearances: Roy Sproson, 760, 1950–72.

Youngest League Player: Malcolm McKenzie, 15 years 347 days v Newport Co, 12 April 1966.

Record Transfer Fee Received: £2,000,000 from Wimbledon for Gareth Ainsworth, October 1998.

Record Transfer Fee Paid: £500,000 to Lincoln C for Gareth Ainsworth, September 1997.

Football League Record: 1892 Original Member of Division 2. Failed re-election in 1896; Re-elected 1898; Resigned 1907; Returned in Oct, 1919, when they took over the fixtures of Leeds City; 1929–30 Division 3 (N); 1930–36 Division 2; 1936–38 Division 3 (N); 1938–52 Division 3 (S); 1952–54 Division 3 (N); 1954–57 Division 2; 1957–58 Division 3 (S); 1958–59 Division 4; 1959–65 Division 3; 1965–70 Division 4; 1970–78 Division 3; 1978–83 Division 4; 1983–84 Division 3; 1984–86 Division 4; 1986–89 Division 3; 1989–94 Division 2; 1994–2000 Division 1; 2000–04 Division 2; 2004–08 FL 1; 2008–13 FL 2; 2013–17 FL 1; 2017– FL 2.

LATEST SEQUENCES

Longest Sequence of League Wins: 8, 8.4.1893 – 30.9.1893.

Longest Sequence of League Defeats: 9, 9.3.1957 – 20.4.1957.

Longest Sequence of League Draws: 6, 26.4.1981 – 12.9.1981.

Longest Sequence of Unbeaten League Matches: 19, 5.5.1969 – 8.11.1969.

Longest Sequence Without a League Win: 17, 7.12.1991 – 21.3.1992.

Successive Scoring Runs: 22 from 12.9.1992.

Successive Non-scoring Runs: 5 from 19.8.2017.

MANAGERS

Sam Gleaves 1896–1905
(Secretary-Manager)
Tom Clare 1905–11
A. S. Walker 1911–12
H. Myatt 1912–14
Tom Holford 1919–24
(continued as Trainer)
Joe Schofield 1924–30
Tom Morgan 1930–32
Tom Holford 1932–35
Warney Cresswell 1936–37
Tom Morgan 1937–38
Billy Frith 1945–46
Gordon Hodgson 1946–51
Ivor Powell 1951
Freddie Steele 1951–57
Norman Low 1957–62
Freddie Steele 1962–65
Jackie Mudie 1965–67
Sir Stanley Matthews
(General Manager) 1965–68
Gordon Lee 1968–74
Roy Sproson 1974–77
Colin Harper 1977
Bobby Smith 1977–78
Dennis Butler 1978–79
Alan Bloor 1979
John McGrath 1980–83
John Rudge 1983–99
Brian Horton 1999–2004
Martin Foyle 2004–07
Lee Sinnott 2007–08
Dean Glover 2008–09
Micky Adams 2009–10
Jim Gannon 2011
Micky Adams 2011–14
Robert Page 2014–16
Bruno Ribeiro 2016
Michael Brown 2017
Neil Aspin 2017–19
John Askey 2019–21
Darrell Clarke February 2021–

TEN YEAR LEAGUE RECORD

		P	W	D	L	F	A	Pts	Pos
2011-12	FL 2	46	20	9	17	68	60	59*	12
2012-13	FL 2	46	21	15	10	87	52	78	3
2013-14	FL 1	46	18	7	21	59	73	61	9
2014-15	FL 1	46	15	9	22	55	65	54	18
2015-16	FL 1	46	18	11	17	56	58	65	12
2016-17	FL 1	46	12	13	21	45	70	49	21
2017-18	FL 2	46	11	14	21	49	67	47	20
2018-19	FL 2	46	12	13	21	39	55	49	20
2019-20	FL 2	37	14	15	8	50	44	57	8§
2020-21	FL 2	46	17	9	20	57	57	60	13

**10 pts deducted. §Decided on points-per-game (1.54)*

DID YOU KNOW ?

Although Port Vale have generally had black and white as the main team colours this has not always been the case and they are one of the few senior clubs to have worn a wide range of colours. At various times in the past they have worn claret and blue, red and white, and black and gold in addition to their 'traditional' strip of white shirts with black shorts.

PORT VALE – SKY BET LEAGUE TWO 2020–21 LEAGUE RECORD

Match No.	*Date*	*Venue*	*Opponents*	*Result*		*H/T Score*	*Lg Pos.*	*Goalscorers*	*Attendance*
1	Sept 12	H	Crawley T	W	2-0	1-0	3	Cullen 2 [39, 66]	0
2	19	A	Exeter C	W	2-0	1-0	2	Conlon [21], Rodney [71]	0
3	26	H	Harrogate T	D	0-0	0-0	2		0
4	Oct 3	A	Morecambe	L	0-1	0-0	5		0
5	10	H	Carlisle U	L	0-1	0-0	10		0
6	17	H	Salford C	W	1-0	0-0	8	Montano [86]	0
7	20	A	Cambridge U	L	1-3	1-1	13	Robinson (pen) [18]	0
8	24	A	Oldham Ath	W	2-1	2-0	10	Smith [11], Clark [39]	0
9	27	H	Cheltenham T	W	2-1	0-0	7	Legge [52], Worrall [68]	0
10	31	A	Southend U	W	2-0	0-0	5	Pope 2 [48, 64]	0
11	Nov 14	H	Tranmere R	L	3-4	2-0	8	Conlon (pen) [16], Amoo [24], Rodney [75]	0
12	17	H	Scunthorpe U	L	0-1	0-1	8		0
13	21	A	Newport Co	L	0-1	0-0	9		0
14	24	A	Stevenage	L	1-2	0-1	11	Rodney [80]	0
15	28	H	Leyton Orient	L	2-3	1-2	13	Legge [8], Montano [76]	0
16	Dec 5	A	Bolton W	W	6-3	3-1	11	Oyeleke [6], Legge [9], Conlon (pen) [42], Montano [46], Worrall [50], Smith [62]	0
17	12	H	Colchester U	D	1-1	0-0	14	Rodney [58]	0
18	15	H	Forest Green R	D	1-1	1-1	14	Stokes (og) [34]	0
19	19	A	Walsall	L	3-4	2-0	16	Pope [37], Conlon [44], Rodney [75]	0
20	26	H	Barrow	L	0-2	0-1	17		0
21	29	A	Bradford C	D	0-0	0-0	16		0
22	Jan 2	A	Mansfield T	L	0-4	0-2	17		0
23	9	H	Grimsby T	W	3-0	2-0	13	Brisley [8], Rodney [15], Waterfall (og) [60]	0
24	16	A	Forest Green R	D	1-1	0-1	14	Rodney [76]	0
25	23	H	Walsall	L	1-3	1-1	16	Conlon [33]	0
26	26	A	Scunthorpe U	L	0-2	0-2	16		0
27	30	H	Southend U	W	5-1	4-0	15	Rodney 2 [1, 45], Cordner (og) [20], Crookes [27], Oyeleke [89]	0
28	Feb 6	A	Tranmere R	L	1-3	1-2	16	Taylor [41]	0
29	20	A	Leyton Orient	D	1-1	0-0	19	Worrall [46]	0
30	23	H	Stevenage	D	0-0	0-0	18		0
31	27	H	Cambridge U	L	0-1	0-0	20		0
32	Mar 2	A	Salford C	L	0-1	0-1	21		0
33	6	A	Cheltenham T	L	2-3	0-2	21	Swan [83], Hurst [85]	0
34	9	H	Oldham Ath	D	0-0	0-0	21		0
35	13	H	Bolton W	L	0-1	0-0	21		0
36	16	H	Newport Co	W	2-1	1-0	20	Conlon [12], Rodney [75]	0
37	20	A	Colchester U	W	1-0	1-0	19	Rodney [19]	0
38	27	A	Crawley T	W	3-1	1-1	18	Conlon [12], Smith [65], Worrall [76]	0
39	Apr 2	H	Exeter C	W	1-0	1-0	16	Robinson [2]	0
40	5	A	Harrogate T	W	2-0	0-0	15	Worrall [48], Guthrie [90]	0
41	10	H	Morecambe	W	1-0	1-0	13	Smith [34]	0
42	17	A	Carlisle U	D	0-0	0-0	14		0
43	20	A	Barrow	W	2-0	1-0	14	Conlon 2 [30, 76]	0
44	24	H	Bradford C	W	2-1	2-1	12	Robinson [16], Conlon (pen) [32]	0
45	May 1	A	Grimsby T	L	0-1	0-1	13		0
46	8	H	Mansfield T	L	0-3	0-2	13		0

Final League Position: 13

GOALSCORERS

League (57): Rodney 11, Conlon 10 (3 pens), Worrall 5, Smith 4, Legge 3, Montano 3, Pope 3, Robinson 3 (1 pen), Cullen 2, Oyeleke 2, Amoo 1, Brisley 1, Clark 1, Crookes 1, Guthrie 1, Hurst 1, Swan 1, Taylor 1, own goals 3.
FA Cup (0).
Carabao Cup (3): Mills 1, Robinson 1, Whitehead 1.
Papa John's Trophy (9): McKirdy 2, Robinson 2, Cullen 1, Hurst 1, Mills 1, Montano 1, Rodney 1.

Brown S 46	Mills Z 18 + 3	Legge L 36 + 1	Smith N 44	Fitzpatrick D 18 + 4	Conlon T 41 + 1	Joyce L 40 + 1	Burgess S 18 + 6	Worrall D 35 + 2	Cullen M 8 + 10	Rodney D 35 + 5	Montano C 22 + 7	Robinson T 15 + 14	Oyeleke E 14 + 6	Whitehead D 9 + 6	Brisley S 19 + 5	McKirdy H 2 + 6	Gibbons J 8 + 3	Amoo D 10 + 16	Clark M 11	Crookes A 13 + 3	Pope T 8 + 11	Hurst A 13 + 7	Taylor J 8 + 4	Guthrie K 9 + 8	Swan W 4 + 6	Olagunju M 2 + 4	Match No.
1	2	3	4	5	6	7	8	9	10^{2}	11^{1}	12	13															1
1	2	3	4	5	6	7		9	10^{2}	11^{3}	13	14	8^{1}	12													2
1	2^{1}	3	4	5	6	7^{3}		9	10^{2}	11		14	8		12	13											3
1		4		5	8	7	6^{2}	9	10^{1}	11^{3}		12		13	3		2	14									4
1		4			12		8^{1}	6		9	5	10		7		13			2	3	11^{2}						5
1		4	3	5	8	7		9		10^{1}	11	12		6^{2}	13				2								6
1		4	3	5	8	7		9		12	11^{2}	10		6^{1}					2		13						7
1		3	4	12	8	7	6	11		14	5^{3}	10^{2}						9^{1}	2		13						8
1		3	4	12	8	7	6	9			5^{1}	10^{2}		14				11^{3}	2		13						9
1	12	3	4		6	7	8	11										9^{1}	2	5	10						10
1		3	4		6	7■	8	11		12			13					9^{2}	2	5	10^{1}						11
1		3	4		6		8^{2}	11	10	14	12		7			13		9^{3}	2	5^{1}							12
1		3■	4	12	8^{1}		6	9	10^{3}	11^{2}	5^{4}	13	7		14				2	15							13
1			3	5			6	9	12	13	11^{2}	10	7		4	8^{1}			2								14
1		3	4	5^{3}	8	7^{2}		9	13	10	12		6					11^{1}	2		14						15
1	2	3	4	5	8	7	13	9		10	11^{1}		6^{2}									12					16
1	2	3	4	5	8	7^{2}		9^{1}		10			6			12					13	11					17
1	2	3	4	5	8	7	6			9								12			10	11^{1}					18
1	2	3	4^{2}	5	8	7^{3}	6			9		14						12		13	10^{1}	11					19
1	2		4	5		7	6			9		13		8^{1}				12		3	10	11^{2}					20
1		3	2	5		7	6			10				8	4			9			12	11^{1}					21
1	15	3■	2	5^{1}		7	6	14		10	13			8^{3}	4			9^{4}			12	11^{2}					22
1	2		3		8	7	12	6^{3}		10^{1}	5	14		15	4			13			11^{4}	9^{2}					23
1	2		3	5	6	7	13			10					4			9				11^{1}	8^{2}	12			24
1	2^{3}		4	5	8	7^{2}	15	11	13						3		14	9^{1}				12	6^{4}	10			25
1	2^{2}		3	5	7	13		6	10^{1}				15		4		14	12				9^{4}	8^{3}	11			26
1	13		4	15	8	7		11^{4}		9	5^{5}		14		3^{1}		2^{2}			12		16	6^{3}	10			27
1	2		3		8	7		9^{1}		11	5									4		12	6^{2}	10	13		28
1		13	4		8	7		6^{1}		10	14		12				2			5		9^{3}		11		3^{2}	29
1		4	3		7	8^{1}	12		13	11^{3}	6						2			5			9	14	10^{2}		30
1	2	4^{4}	3		8		7		14	11^{3}	6^{1}	13								5		12	9	10^{2}	15		31
1		4	3		7	9^{4}			15	11	6^{1}	10^{5}		8^{3}	13		2^{2}			5		12	14	16			32
1	2	3	4		8	7				9		12								5		11	6^{2}	10^{1}	13		33
1	2	3	4		8	7^{3}		6		9^{1}		13	14					12		5		15		10^{2}	11^{4}		34
1	2^{4}	3	4		8	7^{5}		6	15	10^{3}		12	14					13		5		9^{2}	16		11^{1}		35
1	2	3	4		8	7		9		11	5	10^{2}	6^{1}		13			12									36
1		3	2		8	7		9		11^{2}	5^{3}	10^{1}	6		4			12						13		14	37
1		3	2		8^{3}	7		9		11	5^{2}	10^{1}	6		4			14						12		13	38
1		3	2		8	7		9	13	11^{2}	5	10^{1}	6		4									12			39
1		3	2		8	7		9	14	11^{2}	5^{4}	10^{3}	6^{1}		4								12	13		15	40
1		3	2		8	7^{3}		9		11		10^{2}	6^{1}		4		5^{4}	14					13	12		15	41
1		3	5		6	7		9^{4}	14	11^{3}	8^{1}	10^{2}			4	13	2	12			15						42
1		3	2		8	7	6^{2}	9	10^{1}		5^{4}			13	4		15				12			11^{3}	14		43
1		4	3		9	8	13	2^{3}			14	11^{4}		7^{2}	5		6	12			15				10^{1}		44
1		3^{2}	2		8	7^{4}		5		11	9■	10^{3}		6^{1}	4	12		14			13				15		45
1			2		8	7^{3}	6	14		11		15		12	3	5^{5}		13			10^{4}	9^{2}			16	4^{1}	46

FA Cup

First Round	King's Lynn T	(h)	0-1

Carabao Cup

First Round	Scunthorpe U	(a)	2-1
Second Round	Fleetwood T	(a)	1-2

Papa John's Trophy

Group D (N)	Tranmere R	(h)	0-0
(Port Vale won 4-3 on penalties)			
Group D (N)	Wigan Ath	(a)	3-1
Group D (N)	Liverpool U21	(h)	4-2
Second Round (N)	Wolverhampton W U21	(h)	2-1
Third Round (N)	Sunderland	(a)	0-2

PORTSMOUTH

FOUNDATION

At a meeting held in his High Street, Portsmouth offices in 1898, solicitor Alderman J. E. Pink and five other business and professional men agreed to buy some ground close to Goldsmith Avenue for £4,950 which they developed into Fratton Park in record breaking time. A team of professionals was signed up by manager Frank Brettell and entry to the Southern League obtained for the new club's September 1899 kick-off.

Fratton Park, Frogmore Road, Portsmouth, Hampshire PO4 8RA.

Telephone: (0345) 646 1898.

Ticket Office: (0345) 646 1898.

Website: www.portsmouthfc.co.uk

Email: info@pompeyfc.co.uk

Ground Capacity: 18,948.

Record Attendance: 51,385 v Derby Co, FA Cup 6th rd, 26 February 1949.

Pitch Measurements: 100m × 66m (109.5yd × 72yd).

Chairman: Michael Eisner.

Chief Executive: Andrew Cullen.

Head Coach: Danny Cowley.

Assistant Head Coach: Nicky Cowley.

Colours: Blue shirts with white and red trim, white shorts with blue trim, red socks.

Year Formed: 1898.

Turned Professional: 1898.

Club Nickname: 'Pompey'.

Ground: 1898, Fratton Park.

First Football League Game: 28 August 1920, Division 3, v Swansea T (h) W 3–0 – Robson; Probert, Potts; Abbott, Harwood, Turner; Thompson, Stringfellow (1), Reid (1), James (1), Beedie.

Record League Victory: 9–1 v Notts Co, Division 2, 9 April 1927 – McPhail; Clifford, Ted Smith; Reg Davies (1), Foxall, Moffat; Forward (1), Mackie (2), Haines (3), Watson, Cook (2).

Record Cup Victory: 7–0 v Stockport Co, FA Cup 3rd rd, 8 January 1949 – Butler; Rookes, Ferrier; Scoular, Flewin, Dickinson; Harris (3), Barlow, Clarke (2), Phillips (2), Froggatt.

Record Defeat: 0–10 v Leicester C, Division 1, 20 October 1928.

Most League Points (2 for a win): 65, Division 3, 1961–62.

HONOURS

League Champions: Division 1 – 1948–49, 1949–50; First Division – 2002–03; Division 3 – 1961–62, 1982–83; Division 3S – 1923–24; FL 2 – 2016–17.
Runners-up: Division 2 – 1926–27, 1986–87.

FA Cup Winners: 1939, 2008.
Runners-up: 1929, 1934, 2010.

League Cup: 5th rd – 1961, 1986, 1994, 2005, 2010.

League Trophy Winners: 2019.
Finalists: 2020.

European Competitions
UEFA Cup: 2008–09.

FOOTBALL YEARBOOK FACT FILE

Portsmouth's home Second Division game against Middlesbrough on 16 December 1972 attracted a then club record low attendance to Fratton Park. The crowd was just 4,688 for a game which ended in a goalless draw, leaving Pompey second to bottom of the table.

Most League Points (3 for a win): 98, Division 1, 2002–03.

Most League Goals: 97, Division 1, 2002–03.

Highest League Scorer in Season: Guy Whittingham, 42, Division 1, 1992–93.

Most League Goals in Total Aggregate: Peter Harris, 194, 1946–60.

Most League Goals in One Match: 5, Alf Strange v Gillingham, Division 3, 27 January 1923; 5, Peter Harris v Aston Villa, Division 1, 3 September 1958.

Most Capped Player: Jimmy Dickinson, 48, England.

Most League Appearances: Jimmy Dickinson, 764, 1946–65.

Youngest League Player: Clive Green, 16 years 259 days v Wrexham, 21 August 1976.

Record Transfer Fee Received: £18,800,000 from Real Madrid for Lassana Diarra, January 2009.

Record Transfer Fee Paid: £9,000,000 (rising to £11,000,000) to Liverpool for Peter Crouch, July 2008.

Football League Record: 1920 Original Member of Division 3; 1921 Division 3 (S); 1924–27 Division 2; 1927–59 Division 1; 1959–61 Division 2; 1961–62 Division 3; 1962–76 Division 2; 1976–78 Division 3; 1978–80 Division 4; 1980–83 Division 3; 1983–87 Division 2; 1987–88 Division 1; 1988–92 Division 2; 1992–2003 Division 1; 2003–10 Premier League; 2010–12 FL C; 2012–13 FL 1; 2013–17 FL 2; 2017– FL 1.

LATEST SEQUENCES

Longest Sequence of League Wins: 7, 12.3.2019 – 22.4.2019.

Longest Sequence of League Defeats: 9, 26.12.2012 – 9.2.2013.

Longest Sequence of League Draws: 5, 2.2.2019 – 23.2.2019.

Longest Sequence of Unbeaten League Matches: 15, 18.4.1924 – 18.10.1924.

Longest Sequence Without a League Win: 25, 29.11.1958 – 22.8.1959.

Successive Scoring Runs: 23 from 30.8.1930.

Successive Non-scoring Runs: 6 from 27.12.1993.

MANAGERS

Frank Brettell 1898–1901
Bob Blyth 1901–04
Richard Bonney 1905–08
Bob Brown 1911–20
John McCartney 1920–27
Jack Tinn 1927–47
Bob Jackson 1947–52
Eddie Lever 1952–58
Freddie Cox 1958–61
George Smith 1961–70
Ron Tindall 1970–73
(General Manager to 1974)
John Mortimore 1973–74
Ian St John 1974–77
Jimmy Dickinson 1977–79
Frank Burrows 1979–82
Bobby Campbell 1982–84
Alan Ball 1984–89
John Gregory 1989–90
Frank Burrows 1990–91
Jim Smith 1991–95
Terry Fenwick 1995–98
Alan Ball 1998–99
Tony Pulis 2000
Steve Claridge 2000–01
Graham Rix 2001–02
Harry Redknapp 2002–04
Velimir Zajec 2004–05
Alain Perrin 2005
Harry Redknapp 2005–08
Tony Adams 2008–09
Paul Hart 2009
Avram Grant 2009–10
Steve Cotterill 2010–11
Michael Appleton 2011–12
Guy Whittingham 2012–13
Richie Barker 2013–14
Andy Awford 2014–15
Paul Cook 2015–17
Kenny Jackett 2017–21
Danny Cowley March 2021–

TEN YEAR LEAGUE RECORD

		P	W	D	L	F	A	Pts	Pos
2011-12	FL C	46	13	11	22	50	59	40*	22
2012-13	FL 1	46	10	12	24	51	69	32*	24
2013-14	FL 2	46	14	17	15	56	66	59	13
2014-15	FL 2	46	14	15	17	52	54	57	16
2015-16	FL 2	46	21	15	10	75	44	78	6
2016-17	FL 2	46	26	9	11	79	40	87	1
2017-18	FL 1	46	20	6	20	57	56	66	8
2018-19	FL 1	46	25	13	8	83	51	88	4
2019-20	FL 1	35	17	9	9	53	36	60	5§
2020-21	FL 1	46	21	9	16	65	51	72	8

** 10 pts deducted. §Decided on points-per-game (1.71)*

DID YOU KNOW ?

Portsmouth were one of 41 clubs given a first-round bye in the inaugural Football League Cup competition played in 1960–61. Pompey went on to defeat Coventry City, Manchester City and Chelsea before losing to Rotherham United in the quarter-finals.

PORTSMOUTH – SKY BET LEAGUE ONE 2020–21 LEAGUE RECORD

Match No.	Date	Venue	Opponents	Result		H/T Score	Lg Pos.	Goalscorers	Attendance
1	Sept 12	H	Shrewsbury T	D	0-0	0-0	13		0
2	20	A	Rochdale	D	0-0	0-0	17		0
3	26	H	Wigan Ath	L	1-2	0-1	21	Harrison [89]	0
4	Oct 3	A	Burton Alb	W	4-2	1-2	11	Harness 3 [2, 47, 73], Whatmough [60]	0
5	10	H	Milton Keynes D	W	2-1	2-1	9	Naylor [2], Harrison (pen) [23]	0
6	17	H	Doncaster R	L	0-1	0-0	10		0
7	20	A	Gillingham	W	2-0	2-0	8	Marquis [14], Jacobs [17]	0
8	24	A	Sunderland	W	3-1	2-1	5	Harness [7], Marquis 2 (1 pen) [25, 85 (p)]	0
9	27	H	Northampton T	W	4-0	1-0	5	Marquis 2 [39, 47], Curtis [50], Harness [83]	0
10	31	H	Charlton Ath	L	0-2	0-1	7		0
11	Nov 3	A	Lincoln C	W	3-1	1-0	7	Marquis 2 [5, 50], Curtis [61]	0
12	16	A	Plymouth Arg	D	2-2	0-1	6	Marquis (pen) [63], Naylor [65]	0
13	21	H	Crewe Alex	W	4-1	2-0	4	Curtis 2 [15, 40], Naylor [50], Marquis [56]	0
14	24	H	Oxford U	D	1-1	1-0	4	Raggett [19]	0
15	Dec 1	A	Blackpool	L	0-1	0-0	6		0
16	5	H	Peterborough U	W	2-0	0-0	4	Whatmough [61], Naylor [75]	2000
17	12	A	Ipswich T	W	2-0	2-0	3	Williams 2 [29, 44]	2000
18	15	H	Fleetwood T	D	0-0	0-0	2		2000
19	18	A	Hull C	W	2-0	1-0	1	Greaves (og) [6], Magennis (og) [55]	0
20	Jan 16	A	Fleetwood T	W	1-0	1-0	3	Marquis [16]	0
21	19	H	AFC Wimbledon	W	4-0	3-0	3	Marquis [28], Williams [36], Raggett [44], Close [89]	0
22	23	H	Hull C	L	0-4	0-1	4		0
23	26	H	Lincoln C	L	0-1	0-0	5		0
24	Feb 2	A	Charlton Ath	W	3-1	1-0	4	Jacobs [39], Naylor [55], Cannon [61]	0
25	6	H	Plymouth Arg	D	2-2	0-0	5	Curtis [86], Bolton [87]	0
26	9	H	Swindon T	W	2-0	1-0	4	Curtis [8], Harrison (pen) [64]	0
27	16	A	Bristol R	L	1-3	1-2	4	Marquis [26]	0
28	20	H	Blackpool	L	0-1	0-0	5		0
29	23	A	Oxford U	W	1-0	0-0	4	White [48]	0
30	27	H	Gillingham	D	1-1	1-1	4	Raggett [32]	0
31	Mar 2	A	Doncaster R	L	1-2	0-1	5	Marquis [90]	0
32	6	A	Northampton T	L	1-4	0-4	6	Harrison (pen) [73]	0
33	9	H	Sunderland	L	0-2	0-1	6		0
34	16	A	Peterborough U	L	0-1	0-1	10		0
35	20	H	Ipswich T	W	2-1	1-1	7	Naylor [41], Harness [72]	0
36	27	A	Shrewsbury T	W	2-1	2-0	5	Harness [25], Marquis [36]	0
37	Apr 2	H	Rochdale	W	2-1	2-0	5	Williams [5], Curtis [37]	0
38	5	A	Wigan Ath	W	1-0	0-0	4	Cannon [46]	0
39	10	H	Burton Alb	L	1-2	0-1	5	Daniels [88]	0
40	13	A	Crewe Alex	D	0-0	0-0	6		0
41	17	A	Milton Keynes D	L	0-1	0-1	7		0
42	20	A	Swindon T	L	1-3	0-1	8	Curtis [82]	0
43	24	H	Bristol R	W	1-0	1-0	7	Curtis [27]	0
44	27	A	Accrington S	D	3-3	0-2	6	Marquis 2 [49, 90], Williams [54]	0
45	May 1	A	AFC Wimbledon	W	3-1	3-1	6	Curtis [24], Brown 2 [45, 45]	0
46	9	H	Accrington S	L	0-1	0-1	8		0

Final League Position: 8

GOALSCORERS

League (65): Marquis 16 (2 pens), Curtis 10, Harness 7, Naylor 6, Williams 5, Harrison 4 (3 pens), Raggett 3, Brown 2, Cannon 2, Jacobs 2, Whatmough 2, Bolton 1, Close 1, Daniels 1, White 1, own goals 2.
FA Cup (10): Naylor 2, Raggett 2, Curtis 1, Harness 1, Harrison 1 (1 pen), Hiwula 1, Johnson 1, Nicolaisen 1.
Carabao Cup (3): Curtis 1, Evans 1 (1 pen), Marquis 1.
Papa John's Trophy (9): Curtis 2, Harness 2, Hiwula 2, Harrison 1, Marquis 1 (1 pen), Mnoga 1.

MacGillivray C 46	Johnson C 39 + 1	Whatmough J 32 + 2	Raggett S 45	Brown L 28 + 4	Naylor T 46	Morris B 5 + 4	Harness M 42 + 4	Evans G 1	Curtis R 36 + 6	Marquis J 35 + 6	Cannon A 31 + 12	Williams R 33 + 8	Close B 13 + 9	Jacobs M 12 + 8	Harrison E 11 + 14	Pring C 6 + 3	Nicolaisen R 12 + 9	Hiwula J 1 + 8	Mnoga H 3 + 2	White H 5 + 16	Daniels C 10 + 7	Byers G 4 + 10	Bolton J 8 + 5	Downing P 2 + 1	Match No.
1	2	3	4	5	6	7^{3}	8^{2}	9^{1}	10	11	12	13	14												1
1	2	3	4	5	6	7	8		10^{2}	11	9^{1}			12	13										2
1	2	3	4		6	7^{3}	8^{1}		10	11	13	14		9^{2}	12	5									3
1	2	3	4	5	6	7	8^{3}		12	13	14	10^{1}		9	11^{2}										4
1	2	3	4	5	6	7	9^{2}		8^{1}	13		14		10^{3}	11		12								5
1	2	3	4	5	6		8		10^{1}	13	9	14	7^{3}	12	11^{2}										6
1	2	3	4	5	6		8^{1}		13	11	9^{2}	7	12	10^{3}		14									7
1	2	3	4	5	7		10^{2}		12	11	8	6		9^{1}			13								8
1	2	3	4	5	7	12	11		9	10	8^{1}	6^{2}	13												9
1	2^{3}	3^{1}	4	5	7		11^{2}		9	10	8	6			13		12	14							10
1	2		3		8^{2}	13	6^{3}		9^{1}	10	7	11	12			5	4		14						11
1	2	13	3		8		6			10	9	11^{3}	7^{1}		12	5	4^{2}		14						12
1	13	3	4	12	7	14	6^{3}		9	11	8				10^{4}	5^{2}		15	2^{1}						13
1	2	3	4	5	7	12	6^{2}		9	11	8^{1}	13			10										14
1	2	3	4	5	7		10		9^{1}	11	8^{2}	6^{3}	13		12	14									15
1	2	3	4	5	7		6		9	10^{1}	8	11			12										16
1	2	3	4	5^{1}	7		6		9^{2}	10	8	11		13		12									17
1	2	3	4		7		10		9^{2}	11	8	6^{1}		13	12	5									18
1	2		3		7		6^{2}		9	11	8	10^{1}	12	13		5	4								19
1	2	3	4	5	6		8			11	7	10		9											20
1	2	3	4	5	6		8		12	11^{2}	7^{3}	10^{4}	15	9^{1}	14					13					21
1	2	3	4	5	7		6		9^{3}	11	8^{1}	10^{2}	13		14					12					22
1	2	3■	4	5^{5}	7		6^{1}		9	11^{2}	8^{4}	10^{3}		14	13		12				15	16			23
1	2		4		7		12			10^{2}	8	6^{1}		9^{3}	11					14	5	13	3		24
1	2		4		7		6		12	10	8			9^{1}	11^{2}					13	5		3		25
1	2		4	14	7		6^{1}		9	11^{2}	8^{4}	10			12					15	5^{3}	13	3		26
1	2		4	13	7		12		11^{3}	10	8^{4}	9^{5}			15		14			16	5^{1}	6	3^{2}		27
1	2		3		7		9^{1}		6	11^{2}	8	10^{3}			14		4	13			5	12			28
1	2		3	5	7		6^{1}		10^{2}	13	8	12			11^{3}		4	14		9					29
1		14	3	5	8		6		10^{2}	12	7	13			11^{1}		4		2^{3}	9					30
1		2	3	14	6		9		11^{2}	13	12				10^{4}		4	15	5^{1}	7	8^{3}				31
1		2	3	5	6		8		10^{4}	11^{1}	7				12		4^{3}	14		15		9^{2}	13		32
1		3	4		7		14		12	11	8^{3}	6		13	10^{2}					9^{1}	5		2		33
1		2	3^{2}	9	7		12		11		8^{1}	10^{3}	6				4	13		14			5		34
1		3	4	5	7		6		9		8^{1}	10	12	13				11^{2}					2		35
1	2	3	4	5	6		8			11■	12	9^{3}	7^{2}	10^{1}			14				13				36
1	2	3	4	5	7		6^{2}		11		13	10	8^{3}	9^{1}						12	14				37
1	2	3	4^{3}	5	6		8^{4}		11		12	9	7^{2}	10^{1}			14			13			15		38
1	2^{5}	3	4^{2}	5^{1}	6^{4}		8		11		9^{3}	10	7				14			15	12	13	16		39
1	2	3	4		6		8		10	11		9^{2}	7^{1}							12	5	13			40
1	2	3■	4^{3}		6		8		10	11	14	9^{1}					12			7^{2}	5	13			41
1	2		3^{2}		8		6		9	11	14	10	7^{3}				4				5^{1}	12	13		42
1	2		3		7		5^{4}		10	11	12	9^{3}	6^{1}				4			13	14	8^{2}	15		43
1	5^{3}		3		6		9^{5}		10	11	12	13	7^{2}				4			16	15	8^{4}	2^{1}	14	44
1	2		3	5	6		8^{2}		10^{1}	11	14	9	7^{3}							12		13		4	45
1	2^{1}	4		5	6		8		10	11		9^{4}	7^{3}					12		13	15	14		3^{2}	46

FA Cup

First Round	Ipswich T	(a)	3-2
(aet)			
Second Round	King's Lynn T	(h)	6-1
Third Round	Bristol C	(a)	1-2

Carabao Cup

First Round	Stevenage	(a)	3-3
(Portsmouth won 3-1 on penalties)			
Second Round	Brighton & HA	(a)	0-4

Papa John's Trophy 2019–20 (postponed from last year)

Final	Salford C	(Wembley)	0-0
(aet; Salford C won 4-2 on penalties)			

Papa John's Trophy

Group A (S)	Colchester U	(h)	2-0
Group A (S)	Southend U	(a)	3-0
Group A (S)	West Ham U U21	(h)	0-1
Second Round (S)	Cheltenham T	(a)	3-0
Third Round (S)	Peterborough U	(a)	1-5

PRESTON NORTH END

FOUNDATION

North End Cricket and Rugby Club, which was formed in 1863, indulged in most sports before taking up soccer in about 1879. In 1881 they decided to stick to football to the exclusion of other sports and even a 16–0 drubbing by Blackburn Rovers in an invitation game at Deepdale, a few weeks after taking this decision, did not deter them for they immediately became affiliated to the Lancashire FA.

Deepdale Stadium, Sir Tom Finney Way, Deepdale, Preston, Lancashire PR1 6RU.

Telephone: (0344) 856 1964.

Ticket Office: (0344) 856 1966.

Website: www.pnefc.net

Email: enquiries@pne.co.uk

Ground Capacity: 23,404.

Record Attendance: 42,684 v Arsenal, Division 1, 23 April 1938.

Pitch Measurements: 100m × 68m (109.5yd × 74.5yd).

Chairman: Craig Hemmings.

Manager: Frankie McAvoy.

First-Team Coach: Steve Thompson.

Colours: White shirts with blue sleeves, blue shorts with white trim, white socks with blue trim.

Year Formed: 1880.

Turned Professional: 1885.

Club Nicknames: 'The Lilywhites', 'North End'.

Ground: 1881, Deepdale.

First Football League Game: 8 September 1888, Football League, v Burnley (h) W 5–2 – Trainer; Howarth, Holmes; Robertson, William Graham, Johnny Graham; Gordon (1), Jimmy Ross (2), Goodall, Dewhurst (2), Drummond.

Record League Victory: 10–0 v Stoke, Division 1, 14 September 1889 – Trainer; Howarth, Holmes; Kelso, Russell (1), Johnny Graham; Gordon, Jimmy Ross (2), Nick Ross (3), Thomson (2), Drummond (2).

Record Cup Victory: 26–0 v Hyde, FA Cup 1st rd, 15 October 1887 – Addision; Howarth, Nick Ross; Russell (1), Thomson (5), Johnny Graham (1); Gordon (5), Jimmy Ross (8), John Goodall (1), Dewhurst (3), Drummond (2).

Record Defeat: 0–7 v Nottingham F, Division 2, 9 April 1927; 0–7 v Blackpool, Division 1, 1 May 1948.

Most League Points (2 for a win): 61, Division 3, 1970–71.

Most League Points (3 for a win): 95, Division 2, 1999–2000.

Most League Goals: 100, Division 2, 1927–28 and Division 1, 1957–58.

Highest League Scorer in Season: Ted Harper, 37, Division 2, 1932–33.

HONOURS

League Champions: Football League 1888–89, 1889–90; Division 2 – 1903–04, 1912–13, 1950–51; Second Division – 1999–2000; Division 3 – 1970–71; Third Division – 1995–96.
Runners-up: Football League 1890–91, 1891–92; Division 1 – 1892–93, 1905–06, 1952–53, 1957–58; Division 2 – 1914–15, 1933–34; Division 4 – 1986–87.

FA Cup Winners: 1889, 1938.
Runners-up: 1888, 1922, 1937, 1954, 1964.

League Cup: 4th rd – 1963, 1966, 1972, 1981, 2003, 2017.

Double Performed: 1888–89.

FOOTBALL YEARBOOK FACT FILE

Preston North End replaced their 'plastic' pitch with a grass surface during the summer of 1994. The new pitch cost £170,000 to install and was not in use until the beginning of September. As a result, North End played their first four League games away from home, while the home leg of their League Cup tie with Stockport County was switched to Bury's Gigg Lane ground.

Most League Goals in Total Aggregate: Tom Finney, 187, 1946–60.

Most League Goals in One Match: 4, Jimmy Ross v Stoke, Division 1, 6 October 1888; 4, Nick Ross v Derby Co, Division 1, 11 January 1890; 4, George Drummond v Notts Co, Division 1, 12 December 1891; 4, Frank Becton v Notts Co, Division 1, 31 March 1893; 4, George Harrison v Grimsby T, Division 2, 3 November 1928; 4, Alex Reid v Port Vale, Division 2, 23 February 1929; 4, James McClelland v Reading, Division 2, 6 September 1930; 4, Dick Rowley v Notts Co, Division 2, 16 April 1932; 4, Ted Harper v Burnley, Division 2, 29 August 1932; 4, Ted Harper v Lincoln C, Division 2, 11 March 1933; 4, Charlie Wayman v QPR, Division 2, 25 December 1950; 4, Alex Bruce v Colchester U, Division 3, 28 February 1978; 4, Joe Garner v Crewe Alex, FL 1, 14 March 2015.

Most Capped Player: Tom Finney, 76, England.

Most League Appearances: Alan Kelly, 447, 1961–75.

Youngest League Player: Ethan Walker, 16 years 154 days v Aston Villa, 29 December 2018.

Record Transfer Fee Received: £10,000,000 from West Ham U for Jordan Hugill, January 2018.

Record Transfer Fee Paid: £1,550,000 to Doncaster R for Ben Whiteman, January 2021.

Football League Record: 1888 Founder Member of League; 1901–04 Division 2; 1904–12 Division 1; 1912–13 Division 2; 1913–14 Division 1; 1914–15 Division 2; 1919–25 Division 1; 1925–34 Division 2; 1934–49 Division 1; 1949–51 Division 2; 1951–61 Division 1; 1961–70 Division 2; 1970–71 Division 3; 1971–74 Division 2; 1974–78 Division 3; 1978–81 Division 2; 1981–85 Division 3; 1985–87 Division 4; 1987–92 Division 3; 1992–93 Division 2; 1993–96 Division 3; 1996–2000 Division 2; 2000–04 Division 1; 2004–11 FL C; 2011–15 FL 1; 2015– FL C.

LATEST SEQUENCES

Longest Sequence of League Wins: 14, 25.12.1950 – 27.3.1951.

Longest Sequence of League Defeats: 8, 22.9.1984 – 27.10.1984.

Longest Sequence of League Draws: 6, 24.2.1979 – 20.3.1979.

Longest Sequence of Unbeaten League Matches: 23, 8.9.1888 – 14.9.1889.

Longest Sequence Without a League Win: 15, 14.4.1923 – 20.10.1923.

Successive Scoring Runs: 30 from 15.11.1952.

Successive Non-scoring Runs: 6 from 19.11.1960.

MANAGERS

Charlie Parker 1906–15
Vincent Hayes 1919–23
Jim Lawrence 1923–25
Frank Richards 1925–27
Alex Gibson 1927–31
Lincoln Hayes 1931–32
Run by committee 1932–36
Tommy Muirhead 1936–37
Run by committee 1937–49
Will Scott 1949–53
Scot Symon 1953–54
Frank Hill 1954–56
Cliff Britton 1956–61
Jimmy Milne 1961–68
Bobby Seith 1968–70
Alan Ball Snr 1970–73
Bobby Charlton 1973–75
Harry Catterick 1975–77
Nobby Stiles 1977–81
Tommy Docherty 1981
Gordon Lee 1981–83
Alan Kelly 1983–85
Tommy Booth 1985–86
Brian Kidd 1986
John McGrath 1986–90
Les Chapman 1990–92
Sam Allardyce 1992 (*Caretaker*)
John Beck 1992–94
Gary Peters 1994–98
David Moyes 1998–2002
Kelham O'Hanlon 2002 (*Caretaker*)
Craig Brown 2002–04
Billy Davies 2004–06
Paul Simpson 2006–07
Alan Irvine 2007–09
Darren Ferguson 2010
Phil Brown 2011
Graham Westley 2012–13
Simon Grayson 2013–17
Alex Neil 2017–21
Frankie McAvoy March 2021–

TEN YEAR LEAGUE RECORD

		P	W	D	L	F	A	Pts	Pos
2011-12	FL 1	46	13	15	18	54	68	54	15
2012-13	FL 1	46	14	17	15	54	49	59	14
2013-14	FL 1	46	23	16	7	72	46	85	5
2014-15	FL 1	46	25	14	7	79	40	89	3
2015-16	FL C	46	15	17	14	45	45	62	11
2016-17	FL C	46	16	14	16	64	63	62	11
2017-18	FL C	46	19	16	11	57	46	73	7
2018-19	FL C	46	16	13	17	67	67	61	14
2019-20	FL C	46	18	12	16	59	54	66	9
2020-21	FL C	46	18	7	21	49	56	61	13

DID YOU KNOW ?

Preston North End struggled badly in the 1929–30 season and came very close to being relegated to Division Three North. They were bottom of the table for four weeks in the autumn and only escaped the drop thanks to a run of three successive wins in the closing stages of the campaign.

PRESTON NORTH END – SKY BET CHAMPIONSHIP 2020–21 LEAGUE RECORD

Match No.	Date	Venue	Opponents	Result	H/T Score	Lg Pos.	Goalscorers	Attendance
1	Sept 12	H	Swansea C	L 0-1	0-0	15		0
2	19	A	Norwich C	D 2-2	2-1	17	Sinclair (pen) 14, Fisher 42	0
3	26	H	Stoke C	L 0-1	0-1	19		0
4	Oct 4	A	Brentford	W 4-2	0-2	14	Sinclair 2 52, 60, Potts 63, Maguire 70	0
5	18	H	Cardiff C	L 0-1	0-0	18		0
6	21	A	QPR	W 2-0	1-0	15	Johnson (pen) 24, Sinclair (pen) 60	0
7	24	A	Huddersfield T	W 2-1	0-1	12	Browne 2 51, 53	0
8	28	H	Millwall	L 0-2	0-0	13		0
9	31	H	Birmingham C	L 1-2	1-1	16	Stockley 24	0
10	Nov 4	A	Reading	W 3-0	0-0	12	Sinclair 64, Jakobsen 68, Potts 90	0
11	7	A	Rotherham U	L 1-2	0-0	14	Ledson 80	0
12	21	H	Sheffield W	W 1-0	0-0	12	Barkhuizen 48	0
13	24	H	Blackburn R	L 0-3	0-1	15		0
14	28	A	Watford	L 1-4	0-1	18	Barkhuizen 55	0
15	Dec 1	A	Bournemouth	W 3-2	1-0	14	Barkhuizen 16, Sinclair 49, Bauer 68	0
16	5	H	Wycombe W	D 2-2	1-0	15	Barkhuizen 14, McCarthy (og) 87	0
17	9	H	Middlesbrough	W 3-0	0-0	13	Potts 62, Sinclair 81, Jakobsen 83	0
18	12	A	Luton T	L 0-3	0-2	15		2000
19	15	A	Barnsley	L 1-2	1-0	16	Maguire 2	0
20	18	H	Bristol C	W 1-0	1-0	13	Johnson (pen) 21	0
21	26	A	Derby Co	W 1-0	0-0	13	Browne 90	0
22	29	H	Coventry C	W 2-0	1-0	11	Johnson 18, Maguire 53	0
23	Jan 2	H	Nottingham F	L 0-1	0-0	12		0
24	16	A	Bristol C	L 0-2	0-1	13		0
25	20	A	Birmingham C	W 1-0	0-0	10	Sinclair 61	0
26	24	H	Reading	D 0-0	0-0	11		0
27	30	A	Sheffield W	L 0-1	0-1	11		0
28	Feb 6	H	Rotherham U	L 1-2	0-1	11	Evans 65	0
29	12	A	Blackburn R	W 2-1	2-1	10	Cunningham 19, Lindsay 43	0
30	16	H	Watford	L 0-1	0-0	12		0
31	20	A	Cardiff C	L 0-4	0-1	14		0
32	24	H	QPR	D 0-0	0-0	14		0
33	27	H	Huddersfield T	W 3-0	1-0	13	Potts 23, Evans 67, Sinclair 80	0
34	Mar 2	A	Millwall	L 1-2	1-1	14	Evans 12	0
35	6	H	Bournemouth	D 1-1	0-1	13	Johnson 71	0
36	13	A	Wycombe W	L 0-1	0-1	15		0
37	16	A	Middlesbrough	L 0-2	0-1	16		0
38	20	H	Luton T	L 0-1	0-0	16		0
39	Apr 2	H	Norwich C	D 1-1	0-1	17	Potts 90	0
40	5	A	Swansea C	W 1-0	0-0	16	Grimes (og) 90	0
41	10	H	Brentford	L 0-5	0-2	16		0
42	17	A	Stoke C	D 0-0	0-0	17		0
43	20	H	Derby Co	W 3-0	1-0	14	Whiteman 18, Evans 73, Ledson 87	0
44	24	A	Coventry C	W 1-0	0-0	14	Browne (pen) 67	0
45	May 1	H	Barnsley	W 2-0	1-0	13	Storey 38, Evans 49	0
46	8	A	Nottingham F	W 2-1	0-1	13	Bayliss 53, Lindsay 67	0

Final League Position: 13

GOALSCORERS

League (49): Sinclair 9 (2 pens), Evans 5, Potts 5, Barkhuizen 4, Browne 4 (1 pen), Johnson 4 (2 pens), Maguire 3, Jakobsen 2, Ledson 2, Lindsay 2, Bauer 1, Bayliss 1, Cunningham 1, Fisher 1, Stockley 1, Storey 1, Whiteman 1, own goals 2.
FA Cup (1): Jakobsen 1 (1 pen).
Carabao Cup (6): Barkhuizen 2, Bauer 1, Harrop 1, Johnson 1 (1 pen), Maguire 1.

Ripley C 1	Browne A 37 + 1	Storey J 27 + 3	Davies B 19	Hughes A 32 + 2	Pearson B 8 + 1	Ledson R 31 + 5	Bodin B 1 + 3	Potts B 22 + 20	Sinclair S 33 + 4	Barkhuizen T 29 + 16	Stockley J 4 + 12	Maguire S 15 + 14	Gallagher P 6 + 7	Rudd D 22	Fisher D 14	Bauer P 12	Rafferty J 15 + 7	Jakobsen E 17 + 21	Johnson D 24 + 9	Harrop J 1 + 4	Huntington P 18 + 3	Bayliss T 2 + 9	Earl J 4 + 1	Iversen D 23	Whiteman B 20 + 3	Evans C 19 + 2	Molumby J 7 + 8	Cunningham G 10 + 1	Lindsay L 13	Gordon A 5 + 6	van den Berg S 15 + 1	Match No.
1	2	3	4	5	6	7[3]	8[1]	9	10[2]	11	12	13	14																			1
	9[2]	14	4[1]	13	7	6		12	8	10		11		1	2	3	5[3]															2
	7	2[1]	4	12	6	8[3]		13	9[2]	5■	11	10		1		3	14															3
	9		4	5	7	6		8	10			11[1]		1		3	2	12														4
	9		4	5	6	7[3]		8[1]	10	12	14	11[2]		1		3	2	13														5
	6	4		5		7		10	8[3]	12	14	13		1		3	2	11[2]	9[1]													6
	5	2		4		7[3]		6	10[1]	12		13		1		3	8	11	9[2]	14												7
	6	4		5		7[3]		10[2]	8	14				1		3[1]	2	11	9	13	12											8
	9	4		5		12				8	11[3]		6[1]	1	2[2]	3	13	14	7	10												9
	6	4				7		10	8[1]	12				1	2		5	11	9		3											10
	9	4				6		8	10[1]	13	12		14	1	2[3]		5	11[2]	7		3											11
					15	6[4]		9[1]	10	8	12	14	13	1	2	3	5[2]	11[3]	7		4											12
	6	13				7		12	10[1]	8	15	14		1	2[2]	3	5■	11[3]	9[4]		4											13
		2	4[4]		5[1]	12		7	6	9	14	11		1		3		10[2]	8[3]		15	13										14
	2		4		6	7		12	10	8[1]		11[3]		1		3[4]	5	14	9[2]		15	13										15
	2		4		7[1]	6		14	10	8	15	11[2]		1			5[3]	13	9[4]	12	3											16
	6[3]		4	5[1]		7		9	10	8[2]	11[4]	12		1	2			15			3	14	13									17
	6	13	4	5		7[2]		9[5]	10	8[4]	11[3]	15		1	2			14	12		3[1]	16										18
	6		3	4					12	8[3]	14	11[2]	7[4]	1	2		13	10[1]	9			15	5									19
	7		4						10	8	15	11[1]	6[3]	1	2[2]		13	12	9[4]		3	14	5									20
	6		4			15			10[4]	8[5]	12	11[2]	7[3]	1	2[1]			13	9	16	3	14	5									21
	6[1]		3	4		13		12		10		11	7[2]	1	5			14	9		2		8[3]									22
			4	5		7		8[2]		10	14	11[3]	13	1	2			12	9		3	6[1]										23
	6		4	5		16		12	10	8[2]		11[4]			2[5]			15	9[1]		3			1	7[3]	13	14					24
	2		4	5		7		10	8[1]	12								11	13		3			1	6		9[2]					25
	2		4			6		10	8[3]	12							5	11[1]	13		3			1	7	14	9[2]					26
	2		4	5[5]		6[2]	16	10[1]	8	13							15	11[4]	12		3			1	7		9[3]	14				27
				5		7[2]		12	14	8		16					2[5]		13		3[4]			1	6	11	9[3]		4	10[1]	15	28
	5	2		4		6		12		10[1]								13	9[2]					1	7	11[3]	14	8	3			29
	2	3		5				14	8[2]	10[1]								13	9[3]					1	6	11	7		4	12		30
	5[5]	2		4				15		12			14				16	10[1]	9[2]					1	7[3]	11	6[4]	8	3	13		31
	6	3		4				9[3]	8	12								13	14					1	7	11[2]		5		10[1]	2	32
	7[3]	3		4				9	8[2]	12									14					1	6	11	13	5		10[1]	2	33
		3		4				9[3]	8[2]	12								14	13					1	7	11	6	5		10[1]	2	34
	6	4						14	10[2]	8[1]		13							9[3]		3			1	7	11		5		12	2	35
	6	4		5				12	8[3]	14		10[4]	13					16	9[1]		3			1	7[2]	11				15	2[5]	36
	6■	3		5				9	10[1]	8[3]			7[2]				16	14	13					1	15	11[4]	12		4[5]		2	37
		3				7[5]	14	15	8[2]	13		12	16				5		9[3]					1	6	11[4]			4	10[1]	2	38
		3		5		6		13	7[1]	8[5]		15						10[4]	9[2]					1	16	11[3]	12		4	14	2	39
		3		5		7		9[2]	12	8								11[1]						1	6	10	13		4		2	40
	13	2		4		7	16	8[2]	14	9								10[1]						1	6[4]	11[5]	15		3[3]	12	5	41
	9	3		4		7		12		5		13						11[2]						1	6	10[1]		8			2	42
	7	2		4		6[4]		12		10[2]		15						13						1	8[1]	11[3]	14	9	3		5	43
	6	2		4		8		13		9		11[1]						12				14		1	7[2]	10[3]			3		5	44
	9	2		4		6		13		11[1]								12				14		1	7[2]	10[3]		8	3		5	45
	9	2		4		6[1]		14	11[3]	13		15										7[2]		1	12	10[4]		8	3		5	46

FA Cup

Third Round	Wycombe W	(a)	1-4

Carabao Cup

First Round	Mansfield T	(h)	4-0
Second Round	Derby Co	(a)	2-1
Third Round	Brighton & HA	(h)	0-2

QUEENS PARK RANGERS

FOUNDATION

There is an element of doubt about the date of the foundation of this club, but it is believed that in either 1885 or 1886 it was formed through the amalgamation of Christchurch Rangers and St Jude's Institute FC. The leading light was George Wodehouse, whose family maintained a connection with the club until comparatively recent times. Most of the players came from the Queen's Park district so this name was adopted after a year as St Jude's Institute.

The Kiyan Prince Foundation Stadium, South Africa Road, Shepherds Bush, London W12 7PJ.

Telephone: (020) 8743 0262.

Ticket Office: (08444) 777 007.

Website: www.qpr.co.uk

Email: boxoffice@qpr.co.uk

Ground Capacity: 18,181.

Record Attendance: 41,097 v Leeds U, FA Cup 3rd rd, 9 January 1932 (at White City); 35,353 v Leeds U, Division 1, 27 April 1974 (at Loftus Road).

Pitch Measurements: 100m × 66m (109.5yd × 72yd).

Chairman: Amit Bhatia.

Chief Executive: Lee Hoos.

Manager: Mark Warburton.

Assistant Manager: John Eustace.

HONOURS

League Champions: FL C – 2010–11; Division 2 – 1982–83; Division 3 – 1966–67; Division 3S – 1947–48.
Runners-up: Division 1 – 1975–76; Division 2 – 1967–68, 1972–73; Second Division – 2003–04; Division 3S – 1946–47.

FA Cup: *Runners-up:* 1982.

League Cup Winners: 1967.
Runners-up: 1986.

European Competitions
UEFA Cup: 1976–77 *(qf)*, 1984–85.

Colours: Blue and white hooped shirts with red trim, white shorts with blue trim, white socks with blue trim.

Year Formed: 1885* (*see Foundation*).

Turned Professional: 1898.

Previous Name: 1885, St Jude's; 1887, Queens Park Rangers. ***Club Nicknames:*** 'Rangers', 'The Hoops', 'R's'.

Grounds: 1885* (*see Foundation*), Welford's Fields; 1888–99, London Scottish Ground, Brondesbury, Home Farm, Kensal Rise Green, Gun Club Wormwood Scrubs, Kilburn Cricket Ground; 1899, Kensal Rise Athletic Ground; 1901, Latimer Road, Notting Hill; 1904, Agricultural Society, Park Royal; 1907, Park Royal Ground; 1917, Loftus Road; 1931, White City; 1933, Loftus Road; 1962, White City; 1963, Loftus Road (renamed The Kiyan Prince Foundation Stadium 2019).

First Football League Game: 28 August 1920, Division 3, v Watford (h) L 1–2 – Price; Blackman, Wingrove; McGovern, Grant, O'Brien; Faulkner, Birch (1), Smith, Gregory, Middlemiss.

Record League Victory: 9–2 v Tranmere R, Division 3, 3 December 1960 – Drinkwater; Woods, Ingham; Keen, Rutter, Angell; Lazarus (2), Bedford (2), Evans (2), Andrews (1), Clark (2).

Record Cup Victory: 8–1 v Bristol R (a), FA Cup 1st rd, 27 November 1937 – Gilfillan; Smith, Jefferson; Lowe, James, March; Cape, Mallett, Cheetham (3), Fitzgerald (3) Bott (2). 8–1 v Crewe Alex, Milk Cup 1st rd, 3 October 1983 – Hucker; Neill, Dawes, Waddock (1), McDonald (1), Fenwick, Micklewhite (1), Stewart (1), Allen (1), Stainrod (3), Gregory.

FOOTBALL YEARBOOK FACT FILE

Joe Cini became the first Maltese player to appear in the Football League when he made his debut for Queens Park Rangers against Swindon Town on 22 August 1959. Cini, who scored one goal in seven appearances for Rangers, remained an amateur during his season at Loftus Road enabling him to play for Malta in their Olympic Games qualifying matches.

Record Defeat: 1–8 v Mansfield T, Division 3, 15 March 1965. 1–8 v Manchester U, Division 1, 19 March 1969.

Most League Points (2 for a win): 67, Division 3, 1966–67.

Most League Points (3 for a win): 88, FL C, 2010–11.

Most League Goals: 111, Division 3, 1961–62.

Highest League Scorer in Season: George Goddard, 37, Division 3 (S), 1929–30.

Most League Goals in Total Aggregate: George Goddard, 174, 1926–34.

Most League Goals in One Match: 4, George Goddard v Merthyr T, Division 3 (S), 9 March 1929; 4, George Goddard v Swindon T, Division 3 (S), 12 April 1930; 4, George Goddard v Exeter C, Division 3 (S), 20 December 1930; 4, George Goddard v Watford, Division 3 (S), 19 September 1931; 4, Tom Cheetham v Aldershot, Division 3 (S), 14 September 1935; 4, Tom Cheetham v Aldershot, Division 3 (S), 12 November 1938.

Most Capped Player: Alan McDonald, 52, Northern Ireland.

Most League Appearances: Tony Ingham, 514, 1950–63.

Youngest League Player: Frank Sibley, 16 years 97 days v Bristol C, 10 March 1964.

Record Transfer Fee Received: £19,500,000 from Crystal Palace for Eberechi Eze, August 2020.

Record Transfer Fee Paid: £12,500,000 to Anzhi Makhachkala for Chris Samba, January 2013.

Football League Record: 1920 Original Members of Division 3; 1921–48 Division 3 (S); 1948–52 Division 2; 1952–58 Division 3 (S); 1958–67 Division 3; 1967–68 Division 2; 1968–69 Division 1; 1969–73 Division 2; 1973–79 Division 1; 1979–83 Division 2; 1983–92 Division 1; 1992–96 Premier League; 1996–2001 Division 1; 2001–04 Division 2; 2004–11 FL C; 2011–13 Premier League; 2013–14 FL C; 2014–15 Premier League; 2015– FL C.

LATEST SEQUENCES

Longest Sequence of League Wins: 8, 7.11.1931 – 28.12.1931.

Longest Sequence of League Defeats: 9, 25.2.1969 – 5.4.1969.

Longest Sequence of League Draws: 6, 29.1.2000 – 5.3.2000.

Longest Sequence of Unbeaten League Matches: 20, 11.3.1972 – 23.9.1972.

Longest Sequence Without a League Win: 20, 7.12.1968 – 7.4.1969.

Successive Scoring Runs: 33 from 9.12.1961.

Successive Non-scoring Runs: 6 from 18.3.1939.

MANAGERS

James Cowan 1906–13
Jimmy Howie 1913–20
Ned Liddell 1920–24
Will Wood 1924–25
(had been Secretary since 1903)
Bob Hewison 1925–31
John Bowman 1931
Archie Mitchell 1931–33
Mick O'Brien 1933–35
Billy Birrell 1935–39
Ted Vizard 1939–44
Dave Mangnall 1944–52
Jack Taylor 1952–59
Alec Stock 1959–65
(General Manager to 1968)
Bill Dodgin Jnr 1968
Tommy Docherty 1968
Les Allen 1968–71
Gordon Jago 1971–74
Dave Sexton 1974–77
Frank Sibley 1977–78
Steve Burtenshaw 1978–79
Tommy Docherty 1979–80
Terry Venables 1980–84
Gordon Jago 1984
Alan Mullery 1984
Frank Sibley 1984–85
Jim Smith 1985–88
Trevor Francis 1988–89
Don Howe 1989–91
Gerry Francis 1991–94
Ray Wilkins 1994–96
Stewart Houston 1996–97
Ray Harford 1997–98
Gerry Francis 1998–2001
Ian Holloway 2001–06
Gary Waddock 2006
John Gregory 2006–07
Luigi Di Canio 2007–08
Iain Dowie 2008
Paulo Sousa 2008–09
Jim Magilton 2009
Paul Hart 2009–10
Neil Warnock 2010–12
Mark Hughes 2012
Harry Redknapp 2012–15
Chris Ramsey 2015
Jimmy Floyd Hasselbaink 2015–16
Ian Holloway 2016–18
Steve McClaren 2018–19
Mark Warburton May 2019–

TEN YEAR LEAGUE RECORD

		P	W	D	L	F	A	Pts	Pos
2011-12	PR Lge	38	10	7	21	43	66	37	17
2012-13	PR Lge	38	4	13	21	30	60	25	20
2013-14	FL C	46	23	11	12	60	44	80	4
2014-15	PR Lge	38	8	6	24	42	73	30	20
2015-16	FL C	46	14	18	14	54	54	60	12
2016-17	FL C	46	15	8	23	52	66	53	18
2017-18	FL C	46	15	11	20	58	70	56	16
2018-19	FL C	46	14	9	23	53	71	51	19
2019-20	FL C	46	16	10	20	67	76	58	13
2020-21	FL C	46	19	11	16	57	55	68	9

DID YOU KNOW ?

Queens Park Rangers were drawn away to Aylesbury United in the third round of the FA Cup in 1994–95 but the tie was switched to Loftus Road as the Isthmian League club's ground was unable to host the fixture. Rangers had to use the away changing rooms and dug-outs but recorded a comfortable 4-0 victory in front of a crowd of 15,417.

QUEENS PARK RANGERS – SKY BET CHAMPIONSHIP 2020–21 LEAGUE RECORD

Match No.	Date	Venue	Opponents	Result	H/T Score	Lg Pos.	Goalscorers	Attendance
1	Sept 12	H	Nottingham F	W 2-0	0-0	1	Dykes (pen) 54, Chair 90	0
2	18	A	Coventry C	L 2-3	1-1	2	Dykes (pen) 41, Barbet 75	0
3	26	H	Middlesbrough	D 1-1	1-1	10	Samuel 28	0
4	Oct 3	A	Sheffield W	D 1-1	0-0	8	Bonne 90	0
5	17	A	Bournemouth	D 0-0	0-0	13		0
6	21	H	Preston NE	L 0-2	0-1	16		0
7	24	H	Birmingham C	D 0-0	0-0	16		0
8	27	A	Barnsley	L 0-3	0-2	18		0
9	31	H	Cardiff C	W 3-2	2-0	18	Chair 15, Kane 27, Ball 90	0
10	Nov 4	A	Derby Co	W 1-0	0-0	16	Bonne 88	0
11	7	A	Blackburn R	L 1-3	0-0	18	Dykes (pen) 61	0
12	21	H	Watford	D 1-1	0-1	18	Chair 77	0
13	24	H	Rotherham U	W 3-2	3-1	13	Chair 20, Samuel 45, Dykes (pen) 45	0
14	27	A	Brentford	L 1-2	1-1	13	Dykes 26	0
15	Dec 1	H	Bristol C	L 1-2	1-1	17	Dickie 12	0
16	5	A	Huddersfield T	L 0-2	0-2	18		0
17	8	A	Millwall	D 1-1	0-0	18	Chair 53	2000
18	12	H	Reading	L 0-1	0-0	19		2000
19	15	H	Stoke C	D 0-0	0-0	19		0
20	19	A	Wycombe W	D 1-1	1-0	19	McCarthy (og) 28	0
21	26	H	Swansea C	L 0-2	0-1	19		0
22	29	A	Norwich C	D 1-1	0-0	19	Samuel (pen) 84	0
23	Jan 12	A	Luton T	W 2-0	1-0	18	Austin 39, Bonne 89	0
24	20	A	Cardiff C	W 1-0	0-0	17	Willock 71	0
25	23	H	Derby Co	L 0-1	0-0	17		0
26	Feb 1	A	Watford	W 2-1	0-0	17	Austin 73, Adomah 90	0
27	6	H	Blackburn R	W 1-0	0-0	16	Barbet 54	0
28	17	H	Brentford	W 2-1	0-1	16	Field 72, Austin 76	0
29	20	H	Bournemouth	W 2-1	0-0	13	Johansen 58, Kane 83	0
30	24	A	Preston NE	D 0-0	0-0	13		0
31	27	A	Birmingham C	L 1-2	1-0	17	Austin 44	0
32	Mar 3	H	Barnsley	L 1-3	1-2	17	Austin 26	0
33	6	A	Bristol C	W 2-0	2-0	16	Chair 11, Dickie 22	0
34	9	H	Wycombe W	W 1-0	1-0	12	Chair 23	0
35	13	H	Huddersfield T	L 0-1	0-0	13		0
36	17	H	Millwall	W 3-2	0-2	12	Austin 51, Johansen 67, De Wijs 86	0
37	20	A	Reading	D 1-1	1-0	12	Dykes 45	0
38	Apr 2	H	Coventry C	W 3-0	2-0	12	Willock 2, Rose (og) 22, Chair 68	0
39	5	A	Nottingham F	L 1-3	0-1	12	Dykes 90	0
40	10	H	Sheffield W	W 4-1	1-1	11	Dykes 2 27, 60, Johansen 50, Willock 90	0
41	13	A	Rotherham U	L 1-3	0-0	11	Dykes 52	0
42	17	A	Middlesbrough	W 2-1	2-1	10	Dickie 15, Wallace 18	0
43	20	A	Swansea C	W 1-0	0-0	8	Dykes 89	0
44	24	H	Norwich C	L 1-3	0-1	10	Dykes 71	0
45	May 1	A	Stoke C	W 2-0	1-0	9	Austin 17, Kakay 70	0
46	8	H	Luton T	W 3-1	1-1	9	Austin 20, Johansen 60, Adomah 90	0

Final League Position: 9

GOALSCORERS

League (57): Dykes 12 (4 pens), Austin 8, Chair 8, Johansen 4, Bonne 3, Dickie 3, Samuel 3 (1 pen), Willock 3, Adomah 2, Barbet 2, Kane 2, Ball 1, De Wijs 1, Field 1, Kakay 1, Wallace 1, own goals 2.
FA Cup (0).
Carabao Cup (2): Kakay 1, Manning 1.

Lumley J 4 + 1	Kakay O 23 + 5	Dickie R 43	Barbet Y 46	Wallace L 27	Cameron G 31 + 3	Carroll T 19 + 3	Samuel B 20 + 1	Amos L 5	Chair I 43 + 2	Dykes L 36 + 6	Thomas G 5 + 12	Ball D 24 + 15	Smyth P — + 3	Dieng T 42	Bonne M 8 + 26	Adomah A 7 + 27	Willock C 20 + 18	Hamalainen N 18 + 4	Masterson C 3 + 1	Kane T 24 + 4	Kelman C 1 + 10	Austin C 19 + 2	Bettache F — + 6	Johansen S 21	Field S 8 + 11	De Wijs J 9	Duke-Mckenna S — + 1	Match No.
1	2	3	4	5	6	7^{1}	8^{3}	9^{2}	10	11	12	13	14															1
1	2	3	4	5	7	6^{1}	8	9^{3}	10^{2}	11	14	13	12															2
	2	3	4	5	7	12	10	6	9^{2}	11	8^{1}		13	1														3
	2	3	4	5	7	10^{1}	8	6^{2}	9	11		13		1	12													4
	2	3	4	5	7	13	8^{1}	9^{2}	10^{3}			6		1	11	12	14											5
	2	3	4	5	7	10	8		9^{2}			6^{1}		1	11	12	13											6
	2	3	4	5^{1}	6		9		8	10^{2}		13		1	11	7^{3}	14	12										7
	2	3■	4			7			10^{1}	11		6		1	9^{3}	8^{2}	14	5	12	13								8
			4		6	7	10^{3}		9^{2}	11		13		1	14	8^{1}	12	5	3	2								9
		3	4		7	6	10^{3}		9	11^{2}		12		1	13	8^{1}	14	5		2								10
	12	3	4		7	9			10	11^{3}		6^{2}		1	14	8^{1}	13	5		2								11
			4	5^{1}	6	7	8^{4}		10	14		9^{3}		1	11^{2}	15	13	12	3	2								12
	2		4		7^{2}	13	8^{3}		9	11		6		1	12	14	10^{1}	5	3									13
		3	4			7	8		9	11	12	6^{2}		1	14	13	10^{1}	5^{3}		2■								14
	2	3	4	5^{3}		7	8		9	11^{1}		6^{2}		1	12	13	10^{4}	14			15							15
		3	4		6^{3}	7	8^{5}		9^{4}	11^{1}	13	14		1	12	15	10^{2}	5		2	16							16
	2	3	4		7	8^{1}	9		11^{2}	10	13	6		1	12			5										17
	2^{2}	3	4		6	7	8^{3}		9	11				1	14	12	10^{1}	5		13								18
		3	4		6	7^{1}	10		9	11^{3}		12		1	14	8^{2}	13	5		2								19
		3	4		6	9^{1}	8		10^{2}	11		7		1	13		12	5		2								20
		2	4		3	6^{3}	12		10	9		7		1	11^{1}	14	15	8^{2}		5^{4}	13							21
		3	5		4	9	11		7^{2}	10^{1}		8		1	12	13		6		2								22
		3	5		4	9	6		8^{2}	10^{3}		7		1	12	13				2	14	11^{1}						23
	13	3	5		4				8	10		7		1	12		9^{2}	6		2		11^{1}						24
		2	4		3				7	10^{2}		6		1	13	14	8^{1}	9^{4}		5	15	11^{3}	12					25
		2	4	9	3				7^{2}		15	8		1	10^{4}	13	12			5	14	11^{3}		6^{1}				26
		2	4	8	3				9	11^{3}		6		1	12	14				5		10^{2}	13	7^{1}				27
	14	2	4	8^{3}	3				9	11^{2}		6^{1}		1			13			5		10		7	12			28
		2	4	8^{3}	3				9^{5}	11^{4}		7		1	15	16	14	13		5		10^{2}		6^{1}	12			29
		2	4	8	3				9	11^{1}		6		1	13		12			5		10^{3}		7^{2}	14			30
		2	4		3					13		6		1	10^{3}	14	9^{1}	8		5	15	11^{2}		7^{4}	12			31
		2	4	8	3				9^{5}	11^{1}		6^{2}		1	15	13	14			5^{3}	16	10^{4}		7	12			32
	12	2	4	8					10^{4}		15	13		1	14	16	9^{5}			5		11^{2}		6	7^{3}	3^{1}		33
	14	2	4	8	12				9^{1}	13				1		15	10^{4}			5		11^{2}		6	7	3^{3}		34
	2	3	4	8					10^{2}	13	15			1	14	12	9			5^{1}		11^{3}		7	6^{4}			35
		2	4	8	7^{2}				13	9^{5}		16		1	15	14	10^{1}			5^{3}		11^{4}		6	12	3		36
	5	2	4	8	12				9^{2}	10		13^{4}		1			14			15		11^{3}		6	7	3^{1}		37
1	5	2	4	8^{5}	3				10^{3}	12	13	15				14	9^{2}				16	11^{1}		7^{4}	6			38
	5	2	4	8					10	12		6^{1}		1		13	9^{2}				14	11^{4}	15	7	3^{3}			39
	5	2	4	8					10^{2}	11	13	14		1		12	9						15	6^{3}	7^{4}	3^{1}		40
	5	2	4						15	11	9^{4}			1	13		14	8		12	10^{2}			7	6^{3}	3^{1}		41
12	2	3	4	9					8^{4}	10	7^{1}	13		1■		6^{2}	11^{3}							5	14		15	42
1	5^{2}	2	4						9^{3}	11	6^{1}	3				13	10	8				12		7	14			43
	5^{2}	2	4	8					10^{3}	11	7^{1}	15		1		14	9					13	16	6^{5}	12	3^{4}		44
	5	2	4	8					6^{2}	10	13			1	14		9^{3}					11^{1}	15	7^{4}	12	3		45
	5^{3}	2	4	8	16				6^{4}	10^{1}	15			1	13	14	9					11^{2}		7^{5}	12	3		46

FA Cup
Third Round Fulham (h) 0-2
(aet)

Carabao Cup
First Round Plymouth Arg (a) 2-3

READING

FOUNDATION

Reading was formed as far back as 1871 at a public meeting held at the Bridge Street Rooms. They first entered the FA Cup as early as 1877 when they amalgamated with the Reading Hornets. The club was further strengthened in 1889 when Earley FC joined them. They were the first winners of the Berks & Bucks Cup in 1878–79.

Madejski Stadium, Junction 11, M4, Reading, Berkshire RG2 0FL.

Telephone: (0118) 968 1100.

Ticket Office: (0118) 968 1313.

Website: www.readingfc.co.uk

Email: supporterservice@readingfc.co.uk

Ground Capacity: 24,162.

Record Attendance: 33,042 v Brentford, FA Cup 5th rd, 19 February 1927 (at Elm Park); 24,184 v Everton, Premier League, 17 November 2012 (at Madejski Stadium).

Pitch Measurements: 103m × 68m (112.5yd × 74.5yd).

Vice-Chairman: Sir John Madejski.

Chief Executive: Nigel Howe.

Manager: Veljko Paunović.

Assistant Managers: Eddie Niedzwiecki, Marko Mitrovic.

Colours: Blue and white hooped shirts with red trim, white shorts with blue and red trim, white socks with blue and red trim.

Year Formed: 1871.

Turned Professional: 1895.

Club Nickname: 'The Royals'.

Grounds: 1871, Reading Recreation; Reading Cricket Ground; 1882, Coley Park; 1889, Caversham Cricket Ground; 1896, Elm Park; 1998, Madejski Stadium.

First Football League Game: 28 August 1920, Division 3, v Newport Co (a) W 1–0 – Crawford; Smith, Horler; Christie, Mavin, Getgood; Spence, Weston, Yarnell, Bailey (1), Andrews.

Record League Victory: 10–2 v Crystal Palace, Division 3 (S), 4 September 1946 – Groves; Glidden, Gulliver; McKenna, Ratcliffe, Young; Chitty, Maurice Edelston (3), McPhee (4), Barney (1), Deverell (2).

Record Cup Victory: 6–0 v Leyton, FA Cup 2nd rd, 12 December 1925 – Duckworth; Eggo, McConnell; Wilson, Messer, Evans; Smith (2), Braithwaite (1), Davey (1), Tinsley, Robson (2).

Record Defeat: 0–18 v Preston NE, FA Cup 1st rd, 1893–94.

Most League Points (2 for a win): 65, Division 4, 1978–79.

HONOURS

League Champions: FL C – 2005–06, 2011–12; Second Division – 1993–94; Division 3 – 1985–86; Division 3S – 1925–26; Division 4 – 1978–79.
Runners-up: First Division – 1994–95; Second Division – 2001–02; Division 3S – 1931–32, 1934–35, 1948–49, 1951–52.

FA Cup: semi-final – 1927, 2015.

League Cup: 5th rd – 1996, 1998.

Full Members' Cup Winners: 1988.

FOOTBALL YEARBOOK FACT FILE

Reading were founder members of the Southern League in 1894–95 and retained membership through until 1920 when they joined the new Third Division of the Football League. Their only success in that period came in 1910–11 when they held off Stoke on goal average to win the Second Division title and promotion back to the top division.

Most League Points (3 for a win): 106, Championship, 2005–06 (Football League Record).

Most League Goals: 112, Division 3 (S), 1951–52.

Highest League Scorer in Season: Ronnie Blackman, 39, Division 3 (S), 1951–52.

Most League Goals in Total Aggregate: Ronnie Blackman, 158, 1947–54.

Most League Goals in One Match: 6, Arthur Bacon v Stoke C, Division 2, 3 April 1931.

Most Capped Player: Chris Gunter, 59 (102), Wales.

Most League Appearances: Martin Hicks, 500, 1978–91.

Youngest League Player: Peter Castle, 16 years 49 days v Watford, 30 April 2003.

Record Transfer Fee Received: £8,000,000 from Crystal Palace for Michael Olise, July 2021.

Record Transfer Fee Paid: £7,500,000 to Internazionale for George Puscas, August 2019.

Football League Record: 1920 Original Member of Division 3; 1921–26 Division 3 (S); 1926–31 Division 2; 1931–58 Division 3 (S); 1958–71 Division 3; 1971–76 Division 4; 1976–77 Division 3; 1977–79 Division 4; 1979–83 Division 3; 1983–84 Division 4; 1984–86 Division 3; 1986–88 Division 2; 1988–92 Division 3; 1992–94 Division 2; 1994–98 Division 1; 1998–2002 Division 2; 2002–04 Division 1; 2004–06 FL C; 2006–08 Premier League; 2008–12 FL C; 2012–13 Premier League; 2013– FL C.

LATEST SEQUENCES

Longest Sequence of League Wins: 13, 17.8.1985 – 19.10.1985.

Longest Sequence of League Defeats: 8, 29.12.2007 – 24.2.2008.

Longest Sequence of League Draws: 6, 23.3.2002 – 20.4.2002.

Longest Sequence of Unbeaten League Matches: 33, 9.8.2005 – 14.2.2006.

Longest Sequence Without a League Win: 14, 30.4.1927 – 29.10.1927.

Successive Scoring Runs: 32 from 1.10.1932.

Successive Non-scoring Runs: 6 from 29.3.2008.

MANAGERS

Thomas Sefton 1897–1901 *(Secretary-Manager)*
James Sharp 1901–02
Harry Matthews 1902–20
Harry Marshall 1920–22
Arthur Chadwick 1923–25
H. S. Bray 1925–26 *(Secretary only since 1922 and 1926–35)*
Andrew Wylie 1926–31
Joe Smith 1931–35
Billy Butler 1935–39
John Cochrane 1939
Joe Edelston 1939–47
Ted Drake 1947–52
Jack Smith 1952–55
Harry Johnston 1955–63
Roy Bentley 1963–69
Jack Mansell 1969–71
Charlie Hurley 1972–77
Maurice Evans 1977–84
Ian Branfoot 1984–89
Ian Porterfield 1989–91
Mark McGhee 1991–94
Jimmy Quinn and Mick Gooding 1994–97
Terry Bullivant 1997–98
Tommy Burns 1998–99
Alan Pardew 1999–2003
Steve Coppell 2003–09
Brendan Rodgers 2009
Brian McDermott 2009–13
Nigel Adkins 2013–14
Steve Clarke 2014–15
Brian McDermott 2015–16
Jaap Stam 2016–18
Paul Clement 2018
José Gomes 2018–19
Mark Bowen 2019–20
Veljko Paunović August 2020–

TEN YEAR LEAGUE RECORD

		P	*W*	*D*	*L*	*F*	*A*	*Pts*	*Pos*
2011-12	FL C	46	27	8	11	69	41	89	1
2012-13	PR Lge	38	6	10	22	43	73	28	19
2013-14	FL C	46	19	14	13	70	56	71	7
2014-15	FL C	46	13	11	22	48	69	50	19
2015-16	FL C	46	13	13	20	52	59	52	17
2016-17	FL C	46	26	7	13	68	64	85	3
2017-18	FL C	46	10	14	22	48	70	44	20
2018-19	FL C	46	10	17	19	49	66	47	20
2019-20	FL C	46	15	11	20	59	58	56	14
2020-21	FL C	46	19	13	14	62	54	70	7

DID YOU KNOW ?

Reading were drawn to play away at Norwich City in the FA Cup first round in 1908–09 but the match was switched to Stamford Bridge because the Canaries' new home at The Nest was deemed to fail to meet the required pitch dimensions for the competition. The match ended in a 0-0 draw with 15,372 spectators turning out.

READING – SKY BET CHAMPIONSHIP 2020–21 LEAGUE RECORD

Match No.	Date	Venue	Opponents	Result		H/T Score	Lg Pos.	Goalscorers	Attendance
1	Sept 12	A	Derby Co	W	2-0	2-0	1	Lucas Joao [40], Ejaria [45]	0
2	19	H	Barnsley	W	2-0	0-0	1	Meite [67], Olise [76]	0
3	26	A	Cardiff C	W	2-1	0-0	1	Morrison [47], Lucas Joao [66]	0
4	Oct 3	H	Watford	W	1-0	1-0	2	Puscas [41]	0
5	17	A	Middlesbrough	D	0-0	0-0	2		0
6	20	H	Wycombe W	W	1-0	0-0	1	Lucas Joao [63]	0
7	24	H	Rotherham U	W	3-0	1-0	1	Meite 2 [41, 79], Lucas Joao (pen) [90]	0
8	27	A	Blackburn R	W	4-2	3-1	1	Meite [1], Olise [15], Laurent [18], Lucas Joao [82]	0
9	30	A	Coventry C	L	2-3	0-1	1	Lucas Joao [66], Puscas [90]	0
10	Nov 4	H	Preston NE	L	0-3	0-0	1		0
11	7	H	Stoke C	L	0-3	0-2	1		0
12	21	A	Bournemouth	L	2-4	2-0	6	Lucas Joao (pen) [4], Aluko [43]	0
13	25	A	Millwall	D	1-1	0-1	6	Lucas Joao [53]	0
14	28	H	Bristol C	W	3-1	0-0	4	Ejaria [54], Meite [76], Lucas Joao [90]	0
15	Dec 2	A	Sheffield W	D	1-1	1-1	4	Lucas Joao [44]	0
16	5	H	Nottingham F	W	2-0	1-0	3	Lucas Joao (pen) [16], Morrison [53]	2000
17	9	H	Birmingham C	L	1-2	0-2	5	Meite [61]	0
18	12	A	QPR	W	1-0	0-0	5	Olise [89]	2000
19	16	H	Norwich C	L	1-2	1-1	5	Olise [14]	0
20	19	A	Brentford	L	1-3	0-3	8	Aluko [64]	0
21	26	H	Luton T	W	2-1	2-0	6	McIntyre [9], Semedo [41]	0
22	30	A	Swansea C	D	0-0	0-0	6		0
23	Jan 2	A	Huddersfield T	W	2-1	0-1	5	Lucas Joao 2 [52, 65]	0
24	19	H	Coventry C	W	3-0	1-0	4	Lucas Joao [16], Rinomhota [46], Swift [72]	0
25	24	A	Preston NE	D	0-0	0-0	5		0
26	29	H	Bournemouth	W	3-1	3-0	4	Laurent [24], McIntyre [31], Lucas Joao [43]	0
27	Feb 6	A	Stoke C	D	0-0	0-0	4		0
28	10	H	Brentford	L	1-3	1-1	5	Lucas Joao (pen) [24]	0
29	13	H	Millwall	L	1-2	1-0	5	Semedo [17]	0
30	16	A	Bristol C	W	2-0	2-0	5	Lucas Joao [42], Morrison [45]	0
31	20	H	Middlesbrough	L	0-2	0-2	5		0
32	23	A	Wycombe W	L	0-1	0-0	5		0
33	27	A	Rotherham U	W	1-0	1-0	5	Morrison [26]	0
34	Mar 2	H	Blackburn R	W	1-0	1-0	5	Puscas [24]	0
35	6	H	Sheffield W	W	3-0	1-0	5	Olise (pen) [30], Lucas Joao [65], Yiadom [88]	0
36	13	A	Nottingham F	D	1-1	0-0	5	Meite [81]	0
37	17	A	Birmingham C	L	1-2	1-1	6	Meite [35]	0
38	20	H	QPR	D	1-1	0-1	6	Meite [57]	0
39	Apr 2	A	Barnsley	D	1-1	1-0	6	Ejaria [34]	0
40	5	H	Derby Co	W	3-1	1-0	6	Olise [45], Puscas [57], Lucas Joao [84]	0
41	9	A	Watford	L	0-2	0-2	6		0
42	16	H	Cardiff C	D	1-1	0-0	7	Meite [90]	0
43	21	A	Luton T	D	0-0	0-0	7		0
44	25	H	Swansea C	D	2-2	1-0	7	Meite [31], Tomas Esteves [90]	0
45	May 1	A	Norwich C	L	1-4	1-1	7	Laurent [12]	0
46	8	H	Huddersfield T	D	2-2	2-1	7	Olise (pen) [18], Meite [26]	0

Final League Position: 7

GOALSCORERS

League (62): Lucas Joao 19 (4 pens), Meite 12, Olise 7 (2 pens), Morrison 4, Puscas 4, Ejaria 3, Laurent 3, Aluko 2, McIntyre 2, Semedo 2, Rinomhota 1, Swift 1, Tomas Esteves 1, Yiadom 1.
FA Cup (0).
Carabao Cup (3): Lucas Joao 3.

Rafael Cabral B 45	Yiadom A 18 + 3	Morrison M 35	Moore L 31 + 1	Richards O 38 + 3	Rinomhota A 41 + 1	Laurent J 45	Olise M 37 + 7	Swift J 10 + 4	Ejaria O 37 + 1	Lucas Joao E 35 + 4	Aluko S 9 + 24	Baldock S 4 + 16	Holmes T 30 + 9	Felipe Araruna H 2	Meite Y 19 + 6	Puscas G 9 + 12	McIntyre T 16 + 10	Tetek D 1 + 6	Semedo A 24 + 15	Tomas Esteves L 12 + 17	Gibson L 7 + 6	Onen J — + 1	Watson T — + 1	Azeez F — + 1	Camara M — + 1	Southwood L 1	Match No.
1	2	3	4	5	6	7	8^{3}	9^{2}	10^{1}	11	12	13	14														1
1		3	4	5	6	7^{1}	8	9^{3}	10	11^{2}	14			2	12	13											2
1		3	4	5	6	7	10		9	11^{3}			12	2^{1}	8^{2}	14	13										3
1		3	4	5	6	7	10^{1}				9^{2}		2		8	11	12	13									4
1		3	4	5	6	7	9^{3}		10	11^{1}	14		2		8^{2}	13			12								5
1		3	4	5	6	7	9^{3}		10	11			2^{1}		8^{2}		14		13	12							6
1		3	4	5	6	7	12		10^{2}	13					8	11^{1}	14		9^{3}	2							7
1		3	4	5	6	7	10			11^{2}	12				8^{1}		13		9	2							8
1		3	4^{2}	5	7	6	9^{1}			11	10					12	13		8	2							9
1	14	3		5	6	7	8^{2}			11	10^{1}	13				12	4		9	2^{3}							10
1	2^{3}	3		5	7	8	12			11	14	13				10^{2}			9	6^{1}	4						11
1		4	3	5	6	7	12		10^{3}	11	8^{2}	15	13		14				9^{4}	2^{1}							12
1		3	4	5	7	6	12		10	11		13	2		8^{2}				9^{1}								13
1		3	4	5	6	7	9^{1}		10^{3}	11	14		2		8^{2}				12	13							14
1		3	4	5	6^{1}	7	9^{3}		10	11	13	14	2^{2}						8	12							15
1		3	4	5^{5}	6	7	9^{2}		10^{3}	11^{4}	14	16	2		8^{1}				12	13	15						16
1		3	4	5	6	7	9^{1}		10^{3}	11	14		2^{2}		8				12	13							17
1		3	4	5^{1}	6	7	13		10		8^{2}	11^{4}	14				15		9	2^{3}	12						18
1		3	4		6^{4}	7	9		10		8^{1}	12	2^{3}				15		11^{2}	13	5	14					19
1		3	4		7	6	10		11		12	9	2						8^{1}	5							20
1		4			6	7		12	10		8^{2}	11	3				5		9^{1}	2			13				21
1		4		14	6	7	8	13	10^{3}		12	11^{2}	3				5		9^{1}	2							22
1		3		5	6	7	12	9^{1}	10^{3}	11^{2}	8^{4}	14	2				4		13	15							23
1		3		5	6^{5}	7	8^{2}	9^{3}	10^{4}	11	13	16	2^{1}				4	15	14	12							24
1		3		5	6	7		9	10	11	8^{1}		2				4		12								25
1	14	3		5	6	7	8^{5}	9^{1}	10^{2}	11^{4}	13		2^{3}		16		4		12	15							26
1		3		5	6	7	8^{2}	9^{1}	10	11	13		2		12		4										27
1	2	3		5	6	7	8		10^{2}	11	12		13				4		9^{1}								28
1	12	3		13	9	7^{3}	8		10	11		14	2^{1}				4		6		5^{2}						29
1	2	3		5	6		9^{4}		10^{3}	11^{2}			12			13	4	15	7	8^{1}	14						30
1	2	3		5^{2}	6	7	8^{4}		10^{3}	11	15					14	4		9^{1}	12	13						31
1		3	4		6	7	8^{1}		10^{2}	11	13	14	2^{3}			12	5		9								32
1	2	3	4	5	8^{2}	7	9^{3}		10^{1}	11			14				12		6	13							33
1	2	3^{1}	4	5		6	9^{3}		8	11^{2}			12			10	13		7	14							34
1	2^{5}		4	5		8^{4}	9^{3}			11^{1}	12	14	3			10^{2}	6	13	7	15				16			35
1	2		4	5		8	9			11	13		3		12	10^{2}	6		7^{1}								36
1	2		4	5	14	8^{2}	9		13	11			3		10^{1}	12	7		6^{3}								37
1			3	5	6	7	9^{1}		10	11^{2}			2^{3}		8	12			13	14	4						38
1	2	3^{1}	4		6	7	9^{2}		10	11			12		8				13		5						39
1	2		4	5^{1}	6	7	9^{2}		10^{5}	14	16		3		8^{4}	11^{3}			13	15	12						40
1	2		4	12	6^{3}	7	9		10^{4}	13	14	15	3		8	11^{2}					5^{1}						41
1	2^{5}		4	5^{4}	6^{2}	7	9^{3}	13	10	11^{1}	15	16	3		8	12		14									42
1	2		4^{5}	5^{3}	6	7	9^{2}	12	10^{4}		15	13	3		8	11^{1}			14		16						43
1	2^{3}		4	5^{5}	6	7	12	9^{2}	10^{4}	11	16		3		8^{1}	15			13	14							44
1	2			5		7	8^{2}	9^{1}	10	11^{4}			3		12			6^{3}	14	13	4				15		45
	3		14	5	8	7	10^{3}	9^{1}		13			4		11^{2}			12	6	2						1	46

FA Cup

Third Round	Luton T	(a)	0-1

Carabao Cup

First Round	Colchester U	(h)	3-1
Second Round	Luton T	(h)	0-1

ROCHDALE

FOUNDATION

Considering the love of rugby in their area, it is not surprising that Rochdale had difficulty in establishing an Association Football club. The earlier Rochdale Town club formed in 1900 went out of existence in 1907 when the present club was immediately established and joined the Manchester League, before graduating to the Lancashire Combination in 1908.

Crown Oil Arena, Sandy Lane, Rochdale, Lancashire OL11 5DR.

Telephone: (01706) 644 648.

Ticket Office: (01706) 644 648 (option 8).

Website: www.rochdaleafc.co.uk

Email: office@rochdaleafc.co.uk

Ground Capacity: 9,507.

Record Attendance: 24,231 v Notts Co, FA Cup 2nd rd, 10 December 1949.

Pitch Measurements: 104m × 69.5m (114yd × 76yd).

Interim Chairman: Andrew Kelly.

Chief Executive: David Bottomley.

Manager: Robbie Stockdale.

Assistant Manager: Jimmy Shan.

Colours: Blue shirts with black stripes and black sleeves, black shorts with blue trim, blue socks.

Year Formed: 1907.

Turned Professional: 1907.

Club Nickname: 'The Dale'.

Ground: 1907, St Clements Playing Fields (renamed Spotland, 1921; renamed Crown Oil Arena, 2016).

First Football League Game: 27 August 1921, Division 3 (N), v Accrington Stanley (h) W 6–3 – Crabtree; Nuttall, Sheehan; Hill, Farrer, Yarwood; Hoad, Sandiford, Dennison (2), Owens (3), Carney (1).

Record League Victory: 8–1 v Chesterfield, Division 3 (N), 18 December 1926 – Hill; Brown, Ward; Hillhouse, Parkes, Braidwood; Hughes, Bertram, Whitehurst (5), Schofield (2), Martin (1).

Record Cup Victory: 8–2 v Crook T, FA Cup 1st rd, 26 November 1927 – Moody; Hopkins, Ward; Braidwood, Parkes, Barker; Tompkinson, Clennell (3) Whitehurst (4), Hall, Martin (1).

Record Defeat: 1–9 v Tranmere R, Division 3 (N), 25 December 1931.

HONOURS

League: *Runners-up:* Division 3N – 1923–24, 1926–27.

FA Cup: 5th rd – 1990, 2003, 2018.

League Cup: *Runners-up:* 1962.

FOOTBALL YEARBOOK FACT FILE

Rochdale included a local GP in their team during their first season in the Football League in 1921–22. Dr Samuel Wilson McGhee, who had previously played for Queen's Park, signed amateur forms for the club shortly before the start of the campaign. He was an outside-left who mainly played for Dale's reserve team but made two first-team appearances in Division Three North.

Most League Points (2 for a win): 62, Division 3 (N), 1923–24.

Most League Points (3 for a win): 82, FL 2, 2009–10.

Most League Goals: 105, Division 3 (N), 1926–27.

Highest League Scorer in Season: Albert Whitehurst, 44, Division 3 (N), 1926–27.

Most League Goals in Total Aggregate: Reg Jenkins, 119, 1964–73.

Most League Goals in One Match: 6, Tommy Tippett v Hartlepools U, Division 3 (N), 21 April 1930.

Most Capped Player: Leo Bertos, 6 (56), New Zealand.

Most League Appearances: Gary Jones, 470, 1998–2001; 2003–12.

Youngest League Player: Zac Hughes, 16 years 105 days v Exeter C, 19 September 1987.

Record Transfer Fee Received: £1,000,000 from Wolverhampton W for Luke Matheson, January 2020.

Record Transfer Fee Paid: £150,000 to Stoke C for Paul Connor, March 2001.

Football League Record: 1921 Elected to Division 3 (N); 1958–59 Division 3; 1959–69 Division 4; 1969–74 Division 3; 1974–92 Division 4; 1992–2004 Division 3; 2004–10 FL 2; 2010–12 FL 1; 2012–14 FL 2; 2014–21 FL 1; 2021– FL 2.

LATEST SEQUENCES

Longest Sequence of League Wins: 8, 29.9.1969 – 3.11.1969.

Longest Sequence of League Defeats: 17, 14.11.1931 – 12.3.1932.

Longest Sequence of League Draws: 6, 17.8.1968 – 14.9.1968.

Longest Sequence of Unbeaten League Matches: 20, 15.9.1923 – 19.1.1924.

Longest Sequence Without a League Win: 28, 14.11.1931 – 29.8.1932.

Successive Scoring Runs: 29 from 10.10.2008.

Successive Non-scoring Runs: 9 from 14.3.1980.

MANAGERS

Billy Bradshaw 1920
Run by committee 1920–22
Tom Wilson 1922–23
Jack Peart 1923–30
Will Cameron 1930–31
Herbert Hopkinson 1932–34
Billy Smith 1934–35
Ernest Nixon 1935–37
Sam Jennings 1937–38
Ted Goodier 1938–52
Jack Warner 1952–53
Harry Catterick 1953–58
Jack Marshall 1958–60
Tony Collins 1960–68
Bob Stokoe 1967–68
Len Richley 1968–70
Dick Conner 1970–73
Walter Joyce 1973–76
Brian Green 1976–77
Mike Ferguson 1977–78
Doug Collins 1979
Bob Stokoe 1979–80
Peter Madden 1980–83
Jimmy Greenhoff 1983–84
Vic Halom 1984–86
Eddie Gray 1986–88
Danny Bergara 1988–89
Terry Dolan 1989–91
Dave Sutton 1991–94
Mick Docherty 1994–96
Graham Barrow 1996–99
Steve Parkin 1999–2001
John Hollins 2001–02
Paul Simpson 2002–03
Alan Buckley 2003
Steve Parkin 2003–06
Keith Hill 2007–11
(Caretaker from December 2006)
Steve Eyre 2011
John Coleman 2012–13
Keith Hill 2013–19
Brian Barry-Murphy 2019–21
Robbie Stockdale July 2021–

TEN YEAR LEAGUE RECORD

		P	*W*	*D*	*L*	*F*	*A*	*Pts*	*Pos*
2011-12	FL 1	46	8	14	24	47	81	38	24
2012-13	FL 2	46	16	13	17	68	70	61	12
2013-14	FL 2	46	24	9	13	69	48	81	3
2014-15	FL 1	46	19	6	21	72	66	63	8
2015-16	FL 1	46	19	12	15	68	61	69	10
2016-17	FL 1	46	19	12	15	71	62	69	9
2017-18	FL 1	46	11	18	17	49	57	51	20
2018-19	FL 1	46	15	9	22	54	87	54	16
2019-20	FL 1	34	10	6	18	39	57	36	18§
2020-21	FL 1	46	11	14	21	61	78	47	21

§Decided on points-per-game (1.06)

DID YOU KNOW ?

When Rochdale won promotion to League One in 2009–10 it ended a 41-year run of playing in the bottom division of the Football League. Dale won just one of their final nine games but still clinched the final automatic promotion place, finishing nine points clear of fourth-placed Morecambe.

ROCHDALE – SKY BET LEAGUE ONE 2020–21 LEAGUE RECORD

Match No.	Date	Venue	Opponents	Result		H/T Score	Lg Pos.	Goalscorers	Attendance
1	Sept 12	A	Swindon T	L	1-3	0-3	17	Keohane [90]	0
2	20	H	Portsmouth	D	0-0	0-0	20		0
3	26	A	Ipswich T	L	0-2	0-0	23		0
4	Oct 3	H	Fleetwood T	W	2-1	1-0	16	Lund [13], Tavares [90]	0
5	10	A	Accrington S	L	1-2	0-0	17	Keohane [54]	0
6	17	H	Hull C	L	0-3	0-1	22		0
7	20	A	Burton Alb	W	1-0	0-0	16	Lund [49]	0
8	24	A	Shrewsbury T	W	2-1	2-1	14	Rathbone [22], Newby [36]	0
9	27	H	Sunderland	D	2-2	2-2	13	Lund 2 [25, 44]	0
10	31	H	Bristol R	D	1-1	1-1	13	Newby [25]	0
11	Nov 3	A	Oxford U	L	1-3	1-1	15	Lund (pen) [42]	0
12	21	H	AFC Wimbledon	L	0-1	0-0	20		0
13	24	H	Northampton T	D	1-1	0-1	20	Humphrys [85]	0
14	Dec 1	A	Plymouth Arg	W	4-0	3-0	17	Beesley [3], Morley [23], Keohane [45], Humphrys [72]	0
15	5	H	Lincoln C	L	0-2	0-1	18		0
16	12	A	Peterborough U	L	1-4	1-4	19	Humphrys [9]	0
17	15	A	Wigan Ath	W	5-0	2-0	16	Baah [4], Lund [18], Dooley [58], Newby 2 (1 pen) [64 (p), 90]	0
18	19	H	Gillingham	L	1-4	0-3	18	O'Connell [90]	0
19	Jan 9	H	Crewe Alex	D	3-3	0-3	20	Humphrys [46], Lund 2 [60, 84]	0
20	12	A	Charlton Ath	D	4-4	4-2	19	Lund [12], Baah 2 [21, 30], Humphrys [42]	0
21	16	H	Wigan Ath	D	3-3	1-2	18	Humphrys 2 [7, 90], Beesley [58]	0
22	19	A	Doncaster R	L	0-1	0-1	18		0
23	23	A	Gillingham	D	2-2	0-1	18	Keohane 2 [69, 75]	0
24	26	H	Oxford U	L	3-4	2-1	18	Done [22], Humphrys [30], Lund [64]	0
25	30	A	Bristol R	W	2-1	1-1	18	Newby 2 [16, 64]	0
26	Feb 6	H	Charlton Ath	L	0-2	0-2	18		0
27	9	H	Milton Keynes D	L	1-4	1-1	18	Lund [39]	0
28	16	A	Blackpool	L	0-1	0-1	18		0
29	20	H	Plymouth Arg	D	0-0	0-0	18		0
30	23	A	Northampton T	D	0-0	0-0	18		0
31	27	H	Burton Alb	L	0-2	0-0	19		0
32	Mar 2	A	Hull C	L	0-2	0-1	22		0
33	6	A	Sunderland	L	0-2	0-2	23		0
34	9	H	Shrewsbury T	L	0-2	0-0	23		0
35	13	A	Lincoln C	W	2-1	1-0	21	Rathbone [36], Humphrys [74]	0
36	20	H	Peterborough U	D	3-3	0-2	23	Humphrys (pen) [55], Beesley [87], Keohane [90]	0
37	Apr 2	A	Portsmouth	L	1-2	0-2	23	Beesley [90]	0
38	5	H	Ipswich T	D	0-0	0-0	23		0
39	10	A	Fleetwood T	L	0-1	0-0	23		0
40	13	H	Swindon T	W	2-1	1-0	23	Keohane [11], Grant [64]	0
41	17	H	Accrington S	W	3-1	1-1	22	Keohane [10], Beesley [66], Shaughnessy [90]	0
42	20	H	Blackpool	W	1-0	0-0	22	Rathbone [69]	0
43	24	A	Crewe Alex	D	1-1	0-0	22	Done [90]	0
44	27	A	AFC Wimbledon	D	3-3	1-0	21	Beesley [41], Osho [57], Keohane [73]	0
45	May 1	H	Doncaster R	L	1-2	0-1	21	Done [83]	0
46	9	A	Milton Keynes D	W	3-0	0-0	21	Morley [46], Keohane [50], Humphrys [85]	0

Final League Position: 21

GOALSCORERS

League (61): Humphrys 11 (1 pen), Lund 11 (1 pen), Keohane 10, Beesley 6, Newby 6 (1 pen), Baah 3, Done 3, Rathbone 3, Morley 2, Dooley 1, Grant 1, O'Connell 1, Osho 1, Shaughnessy 1, Tavares 1.
FA Cup (1): Lund 1.
Carabao Cup (1): O'Connell 1.
Papa John's Trophy (3): Beesley 1, Newby 1, Tavares 1.

Bazunu G 29	McLaughlin R 23 + 11	O'Connell E 39	McShane P 18 + 1	Keohane J 40 + 4	Morley A 39 + 5	Lund M 28 + 4	Rathbone O 40	Dooley S 16 + 15	Done M 20 + 17	Newby A 27 + 11	Tavares F — + 12	Baah K 13 + 17	Ryan J 11 + 3	Humphrys S 24 + 5	McNulty J 9 + 8	Beesley J 27	Brierley E 1 + 4	Lynch J 17	Bola T 9 + 2	Roberts H 24 + 2	Osho G 22	Hopper H — + 1	Grant C 16 + 4	Vale J — + 3	Shaughnessy C 14 + 4	Odoh A — + 2	Match No.
1	2	3	4	5	6^1	7	8	9^2	10	11	12	13															1
1	2	3^3	4	5	8	6	9	13	12	10^2			7	11^1	14												2
1		4	3	2	8^3	7	10	12	5	6	14		9^1			11^2	13										3
1		3	4	2	8	7	9	10	5	6^1	12					11											4
	13	4	3^1	2^3	8	9	7	10^2	5	6	14				12	11		1									5
1	12	3	4^1	2	8	7^3	10	13	14	6			9^2			11			5								6
1	13			2	8	7	10			6^1	12		9		4^2	11			5	3							7
1	12	4		2	8	9	10		14	6^1			7^3		13	11^2			5	3							8
1	2	3			8	9	10		12	6^2			7^1		13	11			5	4							9
1	2^3	3		14	8^2	9	10	12		6	13		7^1			11			5	4							10
1	12	3		2^1	8	9	10		14	6	13		7^2			11			5^3	4							11
		3		2	8	9	10^3	15	13	6^4		14	7^1	12		11^2		1	5	4							12
	12	3		2	8^2	7	9			6		13		10		11		1	5^1	4							13
	2	3		5	8^3	7	9	12	13	6^2	15		14	10^4		11^1		1		4							14
	2	3		5	7	8	9^1	6^2	14	11^3	15	12	13	10^4				1		4							15
		3		2	8^3	10		9^5	13	6^2	16	14	7	11^4	12		15	1	5^1	4							16
		3		2	7	10^5		12	13	6	15	9^2	8^1	11^4	4		16	1	14	5^3							17
		3		2	7			6	13	10^3	14	9^2		11	4		8^1	1	12	5							18
1	15	3^1	12	2^4	7	8	9^3	13	5	6^2		14		10		11				4							19
1	2			5	7	10	8	12				9^1		11	3	6				4							20
1	12			2	7^3	10^2	8	13	5	14		9^1		11	3■	6				4							21
1	2			5	3	7	8	6		12		9		11		10^1				4							22
1	2			5	7	10	8	9		11		6^1								4	3	12					23
1				2	7	11	8	9	5	12		6^1		10						4	3						24
1				2	8	10	7	9	5	6^2		12		11^1	13					4	3						25
1	2^3	4		15	7	11	8^4	6^1	13	12		9		10						5^2	3^5		14	16			26
1	14	4^1		12	7^2	10	9		5^4	6^3		13		11^5						3	2		16	15	8		27
1	13	3		14	8	10	9		5^2	6		12		11	4						2^3				7^1		28
1	12	3	4	5	8	13^3	9		14	6		11^4		10							2^1		15		7^2		29
1	2	3		5	7		9			6		12		10	4								11^1		8		30
1	2	3	4		8^1		7■		5	6		9^3		11						12			13		10^2	14	31
1	2	8	4^1	5^3	9				14	6^2		12		11	13						3		10		7■		32
1	2^2	8	4	5	9				13	12		6		11							3^1		10		7		33
1	5^2	7	3^1	9	13				11	14		12		10						4	2^3		8		6		34
1	5	2	3	9	12		7	13	11^2					10							4		8^1		6		35
1		2	3	5	13		7		9			12		11^1		10					4		8^2		6		36
1		2	3^1	5^4	13		7	14	9	15		11				10				12	4		8^2		6^3		37
		3		5			7	12	9	13		11^1				10		1		4	2		6^2		8		38
	5	3		9	14		7	13	11^1			12				10		1		4^4	2		8^2	15	6^3		39
	2^1	3	4	10	8		9	6							12	11		1			5		7^2		13		40
	5	2	3	9	7^3	14	10	6^1		12						11		1			4		8^2		13		41
	5	2	3	9	7^3	13	10	6^2	12							11		1			4		8^1		14		42
	5	2	3^3	9	7		10^4	6^1	13			14		12		11		1			4		8^2		15		43
	5	2		9		12	7		10^2			14		13	3^3	11		1			4		8^1		6		44
	5^3	3		9	2^4	6^2	7	12	11	15		13		14		10		1			4		8^1				45
		2		5	7^5		10^1	6^4	9	12			16	14	3	11^3	15	1			4		8^2			13	46

FA Cup

First Round	Stockport Co	(h)	1-2

Carabao Cup

First Round	Huddersfield T	(a)	1-0
Second Round	Sheffield W	(h)	0-2

Papa John's Trophy

Group B (N)	Morecambe	(a)	2-1
Group B (N)	Manchester U U21	(h)	0-0
(Manchester U U21 won 5-4 on penalties)			
Group B (N)	Salford C	(h)	1-2

ROTHERHAM UNITED

FOUNDATION

Rotherham were formed in 1870 before becoming Town in the late 1880s. Thornhill United were founded in 1877 and changed their name to Rotherham County in 1905. The Town amalgamated with Rotherham County to form Rotherham United in 1925.

The AESSEAL New York Stadium, New York Way, Rotherham, South Yorkshire S60 1AH.

Telephone: (0170) 9827 760.

Ticket Office: (0170) 9827 768.

Website: www.themillers.co.uk

Email: office@rotherhamunited.net

Ground Capacity: 12,088.

Record Attendance: 25,170 v Sheffield U, Division 2, 13 December 1952 (at Millmoor); 7,082 v Aldershot T, FL 2 Play-offs semi-final 2nd leg, 19 May 2010 (at Don Valley); 11,758 v Sheffield U, FL 1, 7 September 2013 (at New York Stadium).

Pitch Measurements: 102m × 64m (111.5yd × 70yd).

Chairman: Tony Stewart OBE.

Chief Operating Officer: Paul Douglas.

Manager: Paul Warne.

Assistant Manager: Richie Barker.

Colours: Red shirts with white sleeves, white shorts with red trim, red socks with white trim.

Year Formed: 1870. ***Turned Professional:*** 1905. ***Club Nickname:*** 'The Millers'.

Previous Names: 1877, Thornhill United; 1905, Rotherham County; 1925, amalgamated with Rotherham Town under Rotherham United.

Grounds: 1870, Red House Ground; 1907, Millmoor; 2008, Don Valley Stadium; 2012, New York Stadium (renamed The AESSEAL New York Stadium, 2014).

First Football League Game: 2 September 1893, Division 2, Rotherham T v Lincoln C (a) D 1–1 – McKay; Thickett, Watson; Barr, Brown, Broadhead; Longden, Cutts, Leatherbarrow, McCormick, Pickering, (1 og). 30 August 1919, Division 2, Rotherham Co v Nottingham F (h) W 2–0 – Branston; Alton, Baines; Bailey, Coe, Stanton; Lee (1), Cawley (1), Glennon, Lees, Lamb.

Record League Victory: 8–0 v Oldham Ath, Division 3 (N), 26 May 1947 – Warnes; Selkirk, Ibbotson; Edwards, Horace Williams, Danny Williams; Wilson (2), Shaw (1), Ardron (3), Guest (1), Hainsworth (1).

Record Cup Victory: 6–0 v Spennymoor U, FA Cup 2nd rd, 17 December 1977 – McAlister; Forrest, Breckin, Womble, Stancliffe, Green, Finney, Phillips (3), Gwyther (2) (Smith), Goodfellow, Crawford (1). 6–0 v Wolverhampton W, FA Cup 1st rd, 16 November 1985 – O'Hanlon; Forrest, Dungworth, Gooding (1), Smith (1), Pickering, Birch (2), Emerson, Tynan (1), Simmons (1), Pugh. 6–0 v King's Lynn, FA Cup 2nd rd, 6 December 1997 – Mimms; Clark, Hurst (Goodwin), Garner (1) (Hudson) (1), Warner (Bass), Richardson (1), Berry (1), Thompson, Druce (1), Glover (1), Roscoe.

Record Defeat: 1–11 v Bradford C, Division 3 (N), 25 August 1928.

HONOURS

League Champions: Division 3 – 1980–81; Division 3N – 1950–51; Division 4 – 1988–89.
Runners-up: Second Division – 2000–01; FL 1 – 2019–20; Division 3N – 1946–47, 1947–48, 1948–49; FL 2 – 2012–13; Third Division – 1999–2000; Division 4 – 1991–92.

FA Cup: 5th rd – 1953, 1968.

League Cup: *Runners-up:* 1961.

League Trophy Winners: 1996.

FOOTBALL YEARBOOK FACT FILE

The closest Rotherham United have come to top-flight football was in 1954–55 when they missed out on goal difference. The Millers finished the campaign with a 6-1 thrashing of Liverpool, leaving them in second place. However, Birmingham City had a match remaining and although the Blues were drawing 1-1 at half-time at Doncaster Rovers, they went on to win 5-1, pushing Rotherham back into third place.

Most League Points (2 for a win): 71, Division 3 (N), 1950–51.

Most League Points (3 for a win): 91, Division 2, 2000–01.

Most League Goals: 114, Division 3 (N), 1946–47.

Highest League Scorer in Season: Wally Ardron, 38, Division 3 (N), 1946–47.

Most League Goals in Total Aggregate: Gladstone Guest, 130, 1946–56.

Most League Goals in One Match: 4, Roland Bastow v York C, Division 3 (N), 9 November 1935; 4, Roland Bastow v Rochdale, Division 3 (N), 7 March 1936; 4, Wally Ardron v Crewe Alex, Division 3 (N), 5 October 1946; 4, Wally Ardron v Carlisle U, Division 3 (N), 13 September 1947; 4, Wally Ardron v Hartlepools U, Division 3 (N), 13 October 1948; 4, Ian Wilson v Liverpool, Division 2, 2 May 1955; 4, Carl Gilbert v Swansea C, Division 3, 28 September 1971; 4, Carl Airey v Chester, Division 3, 31 August 1987; 4, Shaun Goater v Hartlepool U, Division 3, 9 April 1994; 4, Lee Glover v Hull C, Division 3, 28 December 1997; 4, Darren Byfield v Millwall, Division 1, 10 August 2002; 4, Adam Le Fondre v Cheltenham T, FL 2, 21 August 2010.

Most Capped Player: Kari Arnason, 20 (89), Iceland.

Most League Appearances: Danny Williams, 461, 1946–62.

Youngest League Player: Kevin Eley, 16 years 72 days v Scunthorpe U, 15 May 1984.

Record Transfer Fee Received: £2,100,000 (rising to £3,500,000) from Cardiff C for Will Vaulks, June 2019.

Record Transfer Fee Paid: £500,000 (in excess of) to Plymouth Arg for Freddie Ladapo, June 2019.

Football League Record: 1893 Rotherham Town elected to Division 2; 1896 Failed re-election; 1919 Rotherham County elected to Division 2; 1923–51 Division 3 (N); 1951–68 Division 2; 1968–73 Division 3; 1973–75 Division 4; 1975–81 Division 3; 1981–83 Division 2; 1983–88 Division 3; 1988–89 Division 4; 1989–91 Division 3; 1991–92 Division 4; 1992–97 Division 2; 1997–2000 Division 3; 2000–01 Division 2; 2001–04 Division 1; 2004–05 FL C; 2005–07 FL 1; 2007–13 FL 2; 2013–14 FL 1; 2014–17 FL C; 2017–18 FL 1; 2018–19 FL C; 2019–20 FL 1; 2020–21 FL C; 2021– FL 1.

MANAGERS

Billy Heald 1925–29 *(Secretary only for several years)*
Stanley Davies 1929–30
Billy Heald 1930–33
Reg Freeman 1934–52
Andy Smailes 1952–58
Tom Johnston 1958–62
Danny Williams 1962–65
Jack Mansell 1965–67
Tommy Docherty 1967–68
Jimmy McAnearney 1968–73
Jimmy McGuigan 1973–79
Ian Porterfield 1979–81
Emlyn Hughes 1981–83
George Kerr 1983–85
Norman Hunter 1985–87
Dave Cusack 1987–88
Billy McEwan 1988–91
Phil Henson 1991–94
Archie Gemmill and John McGovern 1994–96
Danny Bergara 1996–97
Ronnie Moore 1997–2005
Mick Harford 2005
Alan Knill 2005–07
Mark Robins 2007–09
Ronnie Moore 2009–11
Andy Scott 2011–12
Steve Evans 2012–15
Neil Redfearn 2015–16
Neil Warnock 2016
Alan Stubbs 2016
Kenny Jackett 2016
Paul Warne November 2016–

LATEST SEQUENCES

Longest Sequence of League Wins: 9, 2.2.1982 – 6.3.1982.

Longest Sequence of League Defeats: 10, 14.2.2017 – 8.4.2017.

Longest Sequence of League Draws: 6, 13.10.1969 – 22.11.1969.

Longest Sequence of Unbeaten League Matches: 18, 13.10.1969 – 7.2.1970.

Longest Sequence Without a League Win: 21, 9.5.2004 – 20.11.2004.

Successive Scoring Runs: 30 from 3.4.1954.

Successive Non-scoring Runs: 6 from 21.8.2004.

TEN YEAR LEAGUE RECORD

		P	*W*	*D*	*L*	*F*	*A*	*Pts*	*Pos*
2011-12	FL 2	46	18	13	15	67	63	67	10
2012-13	FL 2	46	24	7	15	74	59	79	2
2013-14	FL 1	46	24	14	8	86	58	86	4
2014-15	FL C	46	11	16	19	46	67	46*	21
2015-16	FL C	46	13	10	23	53	71	49	21
2016-17	FL C	46	5	8	33	40	98	23	24
2017-18	FL 1	46	24	7	15	73	53	79	4
2018-19	FL C	46	8	16	22	52	83	40	22
2019-20	FL 1	35	18	8	9	61	38	62	2§
2020-21	FL C	46	11	9	26	44	60	42	23

**3 pts deducted. §Decided on points-per-game (1.77)*

DID YOU KNOW ?

Rotherham United were one of a number of clubs badly affected by the Asian flu pandemic which swept the country at the start of the 1957–58 season. The Millers had two games postponed during September, away to Liverpool and at home to Grimsby Town, due to a lack of available players.

ROTHERHAM UNITED – SKY BET CHAMPIONSHIP 2020–21 LEAGUE RECORD

Match No.	Date	Venue	Opponents	Result		H/T Score	Lg Pos.	Goalscorers	Attendance
1	Sept 12	A	Wycombe W	W	1-0	0-0	5	Ihiekwe 90	0
2	19	H	Millwall	L	0-1	0-0	15		0
3	26	A	Birmingham C	D	1-1	0-0	14	Sadlier (pen) 87	0
4	Oct 3	H	Huddersfield T	D	1-1	1-0	12	Wiles 33	0
5	17	H	Norwich C	L	1-2	1-0	16	Ladapo 3	0
6	20	A	Nottingham F	D	1-1	0-0	16	Barlaser (pen) 51	0
7	24	A	Reading	L	0-3	0-1	18		0
8	28	H	Sheffield W	W	3-0	3-0	17	Lindsay 2 5, 45, Barlaser (pen) 40	0
9	31	A	Stoke C	L	0-1	0-1	19		0
10	Nov 4	H	Luton T	L	0-1	0-0	19		0
11	7	H	Preston NE	W	2-1	0-0	19	Wood 53, Crooks 86	0
12	21	A	Swansea C	L	0-1	0-1	19		0
13	24	A	QPR	L	2-3	1-3	19	Smith 38, Ladapo 84	0
14	28	H	Bournemouth	D	2-2	1-1	19	Ladapo 2 37, 50	0
15	Dec 1	H	Brentford	L	0-2	0-0	20		0
16	5	A	Coventry C	L	1-3	0-2	20	Barlaser (pen) 85	0
17	8	A	Watford	L	0-2	0-2	20		1976
18	12	H	Bristol C	W	2-0	2-0	20	Crooks 4, Smith 41	0
19	16	A	Blackburn R	L	1-2	0-0	20	Smith 61	0
20	29	H	Barnsley	L	1-2	0-2	23	Smith 57	0
21	Jan 16	A	Derby Co	W	1-0	0-0	22	Lindsay 86	0
22	19	H	Stoke C	D	3-3	1-1	22	Crooks 2 31, 67, Smith 51	0
23	27	A	Middlesbrough	W	3-0	1-0	22	Crooks 43, Smith (pen) 79, Giles 90	0
24	30	H	Swansea C	L	1-3	0-2	22	Ladapo 65	0
25	Feb 3	H	Derby Co	W	3-0	0-0	22	Ihiekwe 76, Smith 81, Giles 88	0
26	6	A	Preston NE	W	2-1	1-0	20	Rafferty (og) 1, Wiles 55	0
27	9	H	Cardiff C	L	1-2	0-1	20	Crooks 61	0
28	17	A	Bournemouth	L	0-1	0-1	21		0
29	20	A	Norwich C	L	0-1	0-1	22		0
30	23	H	Nottingham F	L	0-1	0-0	22		0
31	27	H	Reading	L	0-1	0-1	22		0
32	Mar 3	A	Sheffield W	W	2-1	1-0	22	Smith 17, Ladapo 90	0
33	16	H	Watford	L	1-4	0-3	22	Ladapo 68	0
34	20	A	Bristol C	W	2-0	1-0	22	Smith 44, Wood 74	0
35	Apr 2	A	Millwall	L	0-1	0-0	22		0
36	5	H	Wycombe W	L	0-3	0-2	22		0
37	10	A	Huddersfield T	D	0-0	0-0	22		0
38	13	H	QPR	W	3-1	0-0	22	Ladapo 2 64, 66, Smith 90	0
39	15	H	Coventry C	L	0-1	0-0	22		0
40	18	H	Birmingham C	L	0-1	0-0	22		0
41	21	H	Middlesbrough	L	1-2	1-1	22	MacDonald, A 3	0
42	24	A	Barnsley	L	0-1	0-1	22		0
43	27	A	Brentford	L	0-1	0-1	22		0
44	May 1	H	Blackburn R	D	1-1	0-1	22	Wing 86	0
45	4	A	Luton T	D	0-0	0-0	22		0
46	8	A	Cardiff C	D	1-1	1-0	23	Wing 8	0

Final League Position: 23

GOALSCORERS

League (44): Smith 10 (1 pen), Ladapo 9, Crooks 6, Barlaser 3 (3 pens), Lindsay 3, Giles 2, Ihiekwe 2, Wiles 2, Wing 2, Wood 2, MacDonald, A 1, Sadlier 1 (1 pen), own goal 1.
FA Cup (1): Olosunde 1.
Carabao Cup (1): Crooks 1.

Blackman J 25 + 1	Harding W 41 + 5	Ihiekwe M 42	Robertson C 11 + 5	Mattock J 12 + 2	Ogbene C 6 + 5	MacDonald S 15 + 4	Lindsay J 28 + 7	Sadlier K 5 + 10	Crooks M 34 + 6	Ladapo F 23 + 19	Smith M 34 + 10	Wiles B 36 + 8	Vassell K 6 + 6	MacDonald A 36 + 3	Hirst G 4 + 27	Jones B 3 + 2	Miller M 6 + 3	Barlaser D 29 + 4	Jozefzoon F 9 + 15	Wood R 27 + 3	Olosunde M 22 + 10	Johansson V 21	Clarke T 1 + 8	Giles R 12 + 11	Wing L 18 + 2	Match No.
1	2	3	4	5	6	7	8	9^{2}	10^{1}	11^{3}	12	13	14													1
1	2	3		5	6	7	8^{3}	9^{2}	14	10^{1}	11	12		4	13											2
1	2	3			6	7		13	10		12	8		4	11^{1}	5	9^{2}									3
1	2	3		5		8^{3}	14	9	7	11^{2}	12	6	13	4	10^{1}											4
1	2	3	5			7^{2}			6	10^{3}	14	9		4■			11^{1}	8	12	13						5
1	2	3				12	6^{1}	14	7	10		9				5^{3}	11^{2}	8		4	13					6
1	2^{3}	3		5		6	8^{1}			14	11	10			12			9	7^{2}	4	13					7
1	2	3		5		14	8			10^{2}	12	6			13		11^{3}	7^{1}	9	4						8
1	2	3		5		7^{2}	8^{1}		12	11^{3}	13			4	14		10	9	6							9
1	2	3		5^{1}			9		12	14	11^{2}	8		4	13		10	6	7^{3}							10
	5	3					6	9^{1}	13	10		8	11^{2}	14				7	12	4	2^{3}	1				11
1	5	3					6^{2}		8		14	11	15	4	10^{3}		12	7	9^{4}		2^{1}		13			12
1	2^{5}	3		5			12		13	15	11	7	10^{4}	4	16			8^{1}	6^{3}		14		9^{2}			13
1	2	3		9			6		8	10^{2}	11	7	13	4							5^{1}		12			14
1	2			9^{1}			6^{3}		8	11^{4}	10	7	15	4	14		13■		12	3	5^{2}					15
1	6	2		9^{1}			7^{4}		8	10^{3}	11^{5}	5	15	4	14			13	16	3^{2}	12					16
1	3	4					7^{1}		9	16	11^{5}	6	10^{4}	5		2^{2}	15	8^{3}	13		12		14			17
	13	2					7^{3}		8	12	10^{4}	9	11^{1}	4	15	14		6		3	5^{2}	1				18
	13	2					7		8	14	11^{1}	9^{3}	10^{2}	4	12	15		6^{4}		3	5	1				19
	3	5					9			11	12	6	10^{2}		13			8	7^{1}	4^{3}	2	1	14			20
1	6^{2}	3	13				7		11	12	10^{1}	9		5				8		4	2					21
1	9	2	12				6		10	13	11^{3}	8		4^{1}	14			7^{2}		3	5					22
1	9	2	13			5^{1}	7^{3}		11^{2}		10	8		4	12					3	6			14		23
1	9	2	14			7^{2}	6		10^{5}	13	11^{4}	8		4	15				16	3^{3}	5^{1}			12		24
	9	2	4			16	6^{4}		10	15	11^{3}	8^{5}		14				7^{1}		3	5^{2}	1		13	12	25
	5	2	4				8^{1}		15	10^{3}	13	12		3	11^{4}			7^{5}		16	14	1		9^{2}	6	26
	9	2	4						10	13	11	8			14			7^{2}		3^{3}	5^{1}	1		12	6	27
	9^{5}	2	4						10	15	11^{4}	8		16	14			7^{1}	12	3	5^{2}	1		13	6^{3}	28
	5^{5}	3	4					15	11^{4}	14	10^{2}	6		2^{1}	13			7^{3}	16		12	1		9	8	29
	9	2	4					14	10	12	11	6^{3}		3				7^{2}			5^{1}	1		13	8	30
	2		4^{1}			7^{3}		14	8	10^{5}	11	12		3	15				16		5	1	13	9^{2}	6^{4}	31
	3							14	9	12	11■	5		4				6^{3}	7^{1}		2	1	13	10^{2}	8	32
1	12	2				7^{3}		14	8	11^{4}	10^{5}	9^{1}		4	16			6	15	3	5^{2}			13		33
	5	2				14			8	10^{2}	11^{3}			4	15			7^{4}	13	3	12	1	16	9^{1}	6^{5}	34
	6	2					13		8^{3}	11^{2}	10	12		4	15			5^{5}	14	3■		1	16	9^{1}	7^{4}	35
	2	3			13		7^{3}		8	11^{4}	10	9^{1}		4	15			5^{2}	12			1		14	6	36
	9	2					6^{2}		11		10	8		4				13		3	5^{1}	1		12	7	37
	2		4			7^{3}	14	16	10^{4}	11^{5}	15	8^{2}		3				6		12	5^{1}	1		9	13	38
	9^{4}	2^{5}	14		15		6^{3}	16	10	13	11	8^{1}		4						3	5^{2}	1		12	7	39
	5	2	9^{3}			7^{2}	13		6	11^{1}	10	12		4	14					3		1			8	40
	2^{4}	3		5^{2}	14		12	6^{3}	8■	10	11^{5}	9		4	16			7^{1}			13	1		15		41
12	15	2			9	7^{4}	5^{3}			11^{2}	10	16		4	13				14	3^{5}		1^{1}		8	6	42
1	5^{2}	2			10^{4}		9^{3}	16		12	11	7^{5}		4	13			15		3^{1}	14			8	6	43
1	12	2			5^{3}	7^{2}	6^{5}			11	10^{4}	13		4^{1}	15			16	14	3				9	8	44
1	4	2		14	13				9	12	11^{2}	10						7^{3}		3	5^{1}			8	6	45
1	5	2^{4}		13	15		12		10	14	11	7^{2}		4					9^{1}	3				8	6^{3}	46

FA Cup
Third Round Everton (a) 1-2
(aet)

Carabao Cup
First Round Salford C (a) 1-1
(Salford C won 4-2 on penalties)

SALFORD CITY

FOUNDATION

The club was formed as Salford Central Mission in 1940 and in 1947 changed its name to Salford Central. The club competed in local junior leagues including the Eccles and District League until 1963 when the name was changed to Salford Amateurs and they entered the Manchester League. In 1980 this club merged with another local club, Anson Villa, and adopted the name Salford. They were members of the Cheshire County League and then the North West Counties League. In 1990 Salford became Salford City and after gaining promotion to the Northern Premier League for 2008–09 they made rapid progress and went on to achieve Football League status.

The Peninsula Stadium, Moor Lane, Salford, Greater Manchester M7 3PZ.

Telephone: (0161) 241 9772.

Ticket Office: (0845) 847 2252.

Website: salfordcityfc.co.uk

Email: enquiries@salfordcityfc.co.uk

Ground Capacity: 5,032.

Record Attendance: 4,518 v Leeds U, EFL Cup 1st rd, 13 August 2019.

Pitch Measurements: 101m × 64m (110.5yd × 70yd).

Chairman: Karen Baird.

President: Dave Russell.

Manager: Gary Bowyer.

Assistant Manager: Warren Joyce.

Colours: Red shirts with white trim, white shorts, white socks.

Year Formed: 1940.

Turned Professional: 2017.

Previous Names: 1940, Salford Central; 1963, Salford Amateurs; 1989, Salford City.

Club Nickname: 'The Ammies'.

Grounds: 1979, Moor Lane (renamed The Peninsula Stadium 2017).

First Football League Game: 3 August 2019, FL 2, v AFC Wimbledon (a) W 2–1 – Neal; Maynard, Pond, Piergianni, Wiseman, Towell (Armstrong), Smith, Shelton, Touray, Rooney (Beesley), Dieseruwe (2) (Threlkeld).

HONOURS

League Champions: National League North – 2017–18; Northern Premier League Division One North – 2014–15.
Runners-up: North West Counties League Premier Division – 2007–08.
Play-Off Winners: National League – 2018–19 (*promoted to FL 2*); Northern Premier League Premier Division – 2015–16 (*promoted to National League North*).

FA Cup: 2nd rd – 2015–16.

League Cup: never past 2nd rd.

League Trophy: *Winners:* 2020 (final played in 2021).

Manchester Premier Cup Winners: 1977–78, 1978–79.
Runners-up: 1989–90, 2001–02, 2012–13.

North West Counties League Challenge Cup Winners: 2005–06.

Lancashire Amateur Cup Winners: 1973, 1975, 1977.

FOOTBALL YEARBOOK FACT FILE

Salford City first entered the FA Cup in the 1990–91 season and over the next 10 seasons they only once progressed beyond the first qualifying round. On that occasion, in 1998–99, they lost their first qualifying round tie to Glasshoughton Welfare 3-1, but their opponents were subsequently removed from the competition for fielding an ineligible player and City were allowed to go forward to the next round.

Record League Victory: 4–0 v Cambridge U (a), FL 2, 28 January 2020 – Letheren; Wiseman, Pond (Towell), Burgess, Touray (1), Andrade, O'Connor (Armstrong), Baldwin, Hunter (1), Thomas-Asante (Hogan), Rooney (2); 4–0 v Grimsby T, FL 2, 19 September 2020 – Hladky, Threlkeld, Eastham, Turnbull, Touray, Towell (1 pen), Lowe, Hunter (Andrade), Thomas-Asante, Elliott, Henderson (3 (2 pens)) (Smith).

Record Cup Victory: 5–0 v Kennek Ryhope, FA Cup Preliminary rd, 2000–01; 5–0 v Atherton Laburnum R, FA Cup 1st Qualifying rd, 2008–09; 5–0 v Whitby T, FA Cup 1st Qualifying rd, 2015–16.

Record Cup Defeat: 1–7 v St Helen's T, FA Cup prel rd, 2001–02.

Most League Points (3 for a win): 71, FL 2, 2020–21.

Most League Goals: 54, FL 2, 2020–21.

Highest League Scorer in Season: Ian Henderson, 17, FL 2, 2020–21.

Most League Goals in Total Aggregate: Ian Henderson, 17, 2020–21.

Most League Goals in One Match: 3, Ian Henderson v Grimsby T, FL 2, 19 September 2020.

Most Capped Player: Nathan Pond, 4, Montserrat.

Most League Appearances: Ibou Touray, 81, 2019–21.

Youngest League Player: Di'shon Bernard, 20 years 10 days v Crawley T, 24 October 2020.

Football League Record: 2019 Promoted from National League; 2019– FL 2.

MANAGERS

John Torkington 1983–84
David Entwhistle 1984–87
Alf Murphy 1987–89
Steve Canaghan 1989–92
Billy Garton 1992–93
Syd White 1993–96
Alan Lord 1996–99
Tom Foster and Matt Wardrop 1999–2001
Andy Brown 2001–03
Chris Willcock 2003–04
Mark Molyneaux 2004–05
Darren Lyons 2005
John Foster 2005
Gary Fellows 2005–08
Ashley Berry 2008
Paul Wright 2009–10
Rhodri Giggs 2010–12
Darren Sheridan 2012–13
Andy Heald 2013
Barry Massey and Phil Power 2013
Phil Power 2013–15
Anthony Johnson and Bernard Morley 2015–18
Graham Alexander 2018–20
Richie Wellens 2020–21
Gary Bowyer March 2021–

LATEST SEQUENCES

Longest Sequence of League Wins: 3, 20.4.2021 – 27.4.2021.

Longest Sequence of League Defeats: 3, 1.1.2020 – 11.1.2020.

Longest Sequence of League Draws: 5, 17.8.2019 – 7.9.2019.

Longest Sequence of Unbeaten League Matches: 7, 29.2.2020 – 10.10.2020

Longest Sequence Without a League Win: 7, 10.8.2019 – 14.9.2019.

Successive Scoring Runs: 7 from 11.2.2020.

Successive Non-scoring Runs: 4 from 9.3.2021.

TEN YEAR LEAGUE RECORD

		P	*W*	*D*	*L*	*F*	*A*	*Pts*	*Pos*
2011–12	NPL1N	42	14	10	18	69	71	52	13
2012–13	NPL1N	42	11	13	18	65	79	46	16
2013–14	NPL1N	42	15	7	20	68	80	52	12
2014–15	NPL1N	42	30	5	7	92	42	95	1
2015–16	NPLP	46	27	9	10	94	48	90	3
2016–17	NLN	42	22	11	9	79	44	77	4
2017–18	NLN	42	28	7	7	80	45	91	1
2018–19	NL	46	25	10	11	77	45	85	3
2019-20	FL 2	37	13	11	13	49	46	50	11§
2020-21	FL 2	46	19	14	13	54	34	71	8

§*Decided on points-per-game (1.35)*

DID YOU KNOW ?

Salford City attendances have risen dramatically in recent seasons. In 2012–13 their average attendance playing in Division One North of the Northern Premier League was just 117, but by 2019–20 this had risen to 2,997, an increase of more than 2,400 per cent.

SALFORD CITY – SKY BET LEAGUE TWO 2020–21 LEAGUE RECORD

Match No.	Date	Venue	Opponents	Result		H/T Score	Lg Pos.	Goalscorers	Attendance
1	Sept 12	H	Exeter C	D	2-2	1-2	8	Henderson [2], Hunter [69]	0
2	19	A	Grimsby T	W	4-0	1-0	3	Henderson 3 (2 pens) [32 (p), 63 (p), 76], Towell (pen) [90]	0
3	26	H	Forest Green R	D	0-0	0-0	6		0
4	Oct 3	A	Stevenage	W	1-0	1-0	3	Hunter [2]	0
5	10	H	Tranmere R	D	2-2	2-0	5	Towell [2], Wilson [20]	0
6	17	A	Port Vale	L	0-1	0-0	11		0
7	20	H	Southend U	W	3-0	1-0	7	Lennon (og) [26], Wilson [58], Demetriou (og) [63]	0
8	24	H	Crawley T	D	1-1	0-0	8	Wilson [57]	0
9	31	H	Oldham Ath	W	2-0	1-0	9	Wilson [24], Hunter [73]	0
10	Nov 3	A	Cambridge U	L	1-2	1-1	10	Eastham [30]	0
11	13	A	Bolton W	L	0-2	0-1	10		0
12	21	H	Bradford C	W	3-0	3-0	8	Burgess 2 [8, 45], Henderson [21]	0
13	24	H	Morecambe	W	2-1	2-0	7	Hunter 2 [41, 44]	0
14	Dec 2	A	Carlisle U	L	1-2	0-1	9	Bernard [90]	2000
15	5	A	Barrow	W	1-0	0-0	7	Hunter [49]	819
16	12	H	Cheltenham T	D	0-0	0-0	8		0
17	15	H	Newport Co	D	1-1	1-0	9	Clarke [44]	0
18	19	A	Harrogate T	W	1-0	1-0	7	Wilson [17]	495
19	26	H	Walsall	W	2-0	1-0	6	Wilson [16], Burgess [87]	0
20	Jan 2	A	Leyton Orient	L	0-1	0-1	8		0
21	5	A	Mansfield T	L	1-2	0-2	8	Bernard [90]	0
22	12	A	Scunthorpe U	W	1-0	0-0	5	Henderson [89]	0
23	16	A	Newport Co	D	0-0	0-0	5		0
24	22	H	Harrogate T	D	2-2	1-1	4	Gotts [21], Thomas-Asante [70]	0
25	30	A	Oldham Ath	L	1-2	1-0	8	Henderson [9]	0
26	Feb 9	H	Cambridge U	W	4-1	3-0	9	Henderson 2 [19, 69], Towell [33], Gotts [42]	0
27	16	H	Barrow	W	1-0	1-0	4	Henderson [29]	0
28	20	H	Carlisle U	D	1-1	0-1	5	Wilson [79]	0
29	23	A	Morecambe	L	1-2	1-0	7	Thomas-Asante [45]	0
30	27	A	Southend U	D	0-0	0-0	9		0
31	Mar 2	H	Port Vale	W	1-0	1-0	7	Henderson [45]	0
32	6	H	Scunthorpe U	D	1-1	1-1	9	Clarke [33]	0
33	9	A	Crawley T	L	0-1	0-1	9		0
34	16	H	Colchester U	D	0-0	0-0	9		0
35	20	A	Cheltenham T	L	0-2	0-2	9		0
36	27	A	Exeter C	L	0-1	0-1	10		0
37	Apr 2	H	Grimsby T	D	1-1	0-1	11	Touray, I [88]	0
38	5	A	Forest Green R	W	2-0	1-0	10	Henderson 2 [38, 77]	0
39	10	H	Stevenage	W	2-1	0-0	9	Thomas-Asante [52], Henderson [76]	0
40	13	H	Bolton W	L	0-1	0-1	10		0
41	17	A	Tranmere R	D	0-0	0-0	11		0
42	20	A	Walsall	W	2-0	1-0	9	Henderson [19], Turnbull [57]	0
43	24	H	Mansfield T	W	2-0	1-0	8	Hunter [5], Henderson [62]	0
44	27	A	Bradford C	W	1-0	0-0	7	Henderson [90]	0
45	May 1	A	Colchester U	L	0-1	0-0	9		0
46	8	H	Leyton Orient	W	3-0	1-0	8	Gotts [42], Thomas-Asante 2 [50, 66]	0

Final League Position: 8

GOALSCORERS

League (54): Henderson 17 (2 pens), Hunter 7, Wilson 7, Thomas-Asante 5, Burgess 3, Gotts 3, Towell 3 (1 pen), Bernard 2, Clarke 2, Eastham 1, Touray, I 1, Turnbull 1, own goals 2.
FA Cup (2): Andrade 1, Dieseruvwe 1.
Carabao Cup (1): Henderson 1 (1 pen).
Papa John's Trophy (7): Dieseruvwe 3 (1 pen), Andrade 1, Hunter 1, Thomas-Asante 1, Wilson 1.

Hladky V 46	Threlkeld O 29 + 6	Eastham A 38 + 1	Clarke T 27 + 5	Touray I 45 + 1	Lowe J 44 + 1	Gibson D 4 + 1	Hunter A 37 + 4	Armstrong L 1 + 3	Henderson I 45 + 1	Andrade B 8 + 11	Elliott T 3 + 11	Towell R 16 + 8	Thomas-Asante B 27 + 15	Turnbull J 35 + 7	Smith M 1 + 3	Golden T 6 + 1	Wilson J 17 + 7	Dieseruvwe E 1 + 13	Denny A 4 + 5	Bernard D 27 + 3	Jones J — + 1	Boyd G 2 + 9	Burgess L 7 + 10	Gotts R 20 + 3	James T 2 + 2	Coutts P 14 + 5	*Match No.*
1	2^{3}	3	4	5	6	7	8	9^{1}	10	11^{2}	12	13	14														1
1	2	3		5	7		8^{1}		11^{2}	12	10	6	9	4	13												2
1		3		5	6		8		9	7^{1}	11		10	4		2	12										3
1		3	14	5	8	7	11		10^{3}			6	12	4		2^{1}	9^{2}	13									4
1		3		5	8	7^{3}	11		10		14	6^{1}		4		2	9^{2}	13	12								5
1		3		5	7	8^{2}	9		11^{3}	6^{1}	14		12	4		2	10		13								6
1	7	3	2	5	6		10^{3}	12	9	13			8^{2}	4	14		11^{1}										7
1	7^{1}	3	2	5	6		8^{2}		9				10	4		13	11			12							8
1	7	3	2	5	8		9	12	10^{2}				6	4			11^{1}				13						9
1	7^{3}	3	2	5	8		9		10^{2}	13			6^{1}	4			11					12	14				10
1	7		3	5	8		9^{3}		10	12			11^{2}	4				14		2		6^{1}	13				11
1	12	3	2	5	7^{1}		10^{3}		11	9^{2}			13	15					6	4		14	8^{4}				12
1	12	3	2	5			10		11	9^{4}	13		14	15	6^{1}				7^{3}	4			8^{2}				13
1		3	2	5	7		10^{3}	12	11^{1}	9				6^{2}				14	13	4			8				14
1		3	2	5	7		10^{1}		11	9^{3}	14	12^{4}		13	15				6	4			8^{2}				15
1	13	3	2	5	7		10		11^{4}	9^{3}	14			15			12		6^{2}	4			8^{1}				16
1	6	3	2	5	7		10^{2}		11^{4}	12	14		8^{3}	13			9^{1}		15	4							17
1	6	3	2	5	7		10		11	12			8^{1}				9^{2}	13		4							18
1	7	3	2	5	6		10^{4}		11^{3}	15			8^{1}	12			9^{2}	14		4			13				19
1	6	3	2^{3}	5	7				11	12	13		10^{2}				9		14	4			8^{1}				20
1	6	3	2^{1}	5	7		10		11	14	12		8^{2}	13			9^{3}			4							21
1	6		3	5	7		10^{3}		11		13		8^{1}	4		2	9^{2}					14	12				22
1	7		2	5	6		8		9		11^{1}		13	3			12			4				10^{2}			23
1	6^{3}		12	5	7		10^{2}		11			13	15	4						3			8^{4}	9	2^{1}	14	24
1	7^{2}	3	2	8^{3}	12		15		11	14		9^{1}	13	4										10	5^{4}	6	25
1		12	2^{1}	8	6		5		11^{2}			10^{3}	13	4						3				9	14	7	26
1	14	3		8	6		5		11^{2}			9^{1}	13	4			12			2				10^{3}		7	27
1		3		8^{2}	6		5		11			9^{1}	12	4			13			2				10		7	28
1	14	3		8	6		5^{3}		11^{2}			12	9	4			13			2				10^{1}		7	29
1		3		12	6		8		11			13	10^{3}	4			9^{2}	14		2				5^{1}		7	30
1			2	8	6		5^{2}		11			9	10^{1}	4				13		3				12		7	31
1	13		2	8	6		5^{4}		11	15		9^{1}	12	4				14		3				10^{3}		7^{2}	32
1	6		3^{1}	5	2		10^{3}		11			8^{2}	9	4			13			12				14		7	33
1	6	3		8	5		13		12			14	9^{4}	4			11^{3}			2			15	10^{1}		7^{2}	34
1	7	3		8	6		5		11				13	4			9^{3}	12		2^{1}				10^{2}	14		35
1	8	3	2	5	7		9^{2}		11			12	6	4			10^{1}	13									36
1	8	3	2^{3}	5	7		6^{2}		10			12	9	4				11^{1}						13		14	37
1	7	3	14	5	2				8			9^{2}	6^{3}	4				13				12		11^{1}		10	38
1	8^{1}	3	12	5	2				11			6^{3}	10	4								13	14	9^{2}		7	39
1		3	2^{2}	5	8		13		11			6^{3}	10	4						12			14	9		7^{1}	40
1	8^{3}	3		5	7				11			6^{2}	10^{1}	4				14		2		12	13	9^{4}		15	41
1	7	3		5	6		10^{2}		11			9^{1}	13	4						2		12		8			42
1	7^{4}	3		5	6		10^{1}		11^{2}			9■	13	4						2		12	15	8^{3}		14	43
1	7	3		5	6		10^{1}		11				8	4						2				9		12	44
1	8	3	12	5	6		14■		10				11^{2}	4						2■		13		9^{3}		7^{1}	45
1	7^{2}	3	4	5	8	13			11		14		10^{3}			2						9^{1}	12	6			46

FA Cup

First Round	Hartlepool U	(h)	2-0
(aet)			
Second Round	Newport Co	(a)	0-3

Carabao Cup

First Round	Rotherham U	(h)	1-1
(Salford C won 4-2 on penalties)			
Second Round	Everton	(a)	0-3

Papa John's Trophy 2019–20 (postponed from last year)

Final	Portsmouth	(Wembley)	0-0
(aet; Salford C won 4-2 on penalties)			

Papa John's Trophy

Group B (N)	Manchester U U21	(h)	0-6
Group B (N)	Morecambe	(h)	2-0
Group B (N)	Rochdale	(a)	2-1
Second Round (N)	Leicester C U21	(h)	3-3
(Leicester C U21 won 6-5 on penalties)			

SCUNTHORPE UNITED

FOUNDATION

The year of foundation for Scunthorpe United has often been quoted as 1910, but the club can trace its history back to 1899 when Brumby Hall FC, who played on the Old Showground, consolidated their position by amalgamating with some other clubs and changing their name to Scunthorpe United. The year 1910 was when that club amalgamated with North Lindsey United as Scunthorpe and Lindsey United. The link is Mr W. T. Lockwood whose chairmanship covers both years.

The Sands Venue Stadium, Glandford Park, Jack Brownsword Way, Scunthorpe, North Lincolnshire DN15 8TD.

Telephone: (01724) 840 139.

Ticket Office: (01724) 747 670.

Website: www.scunthorpe-united.co.uk

Email: admin@scunthorpe-united.co.uk

Ground Capacity: 9,088.

Record Attendance: 23,935 v Portsmouth, FA Cup 4th rd, 30 January 1954 (at Old Showground); 9,077 v Manchester U, League Cup 3rd rd, 22 September 2010 (at Glanford Park).

Pitch Measurements: 102.5m × 66m (112yd × 72yd).

Chairman: Peter Swann.

President: Sir Ian Botham.

Chief Executive: Leanne Mayo.

Manager: Neil Cox.

Assistant Manager: Mark Lillis.

Colours: Claret shirts with light blue trim and sleeves, claret shorts with light blue trim, light blue socks with claret trim.

Year Formed: 1899.

Turned Professional: 1912.

Previous Names: Amalgamated first with Brumby Hall then North Lindsey United to become Scunthorpe and Lindsey United, 1910; 1958, Scunthorpe United.

Club Nickname: 'The Iron'.

Grounds: 1899, Old Showground; 1988, Glanford Park (renamed The Sands Venue Stadium 2019).

First Football League Game: 19 August 1950, Division 3 (N), v Shrewsbury T (h) D 0–0 – Thompson; Barker, Brownsword; Allen, Taylor, McCormick; Mosby, Payne, Gorin, Rees, Boyes.

Record League Victory: 8–1 v Luton T (h), Division 3, 24 April 1965 – Sidebottom; Horstead, Hemstead; Smith, Neale, Lindsey; Bramley (1), Scott, Thomas (5), Mahy (1), Wilson (1). 8–1 v Torquay U (a), Division 3, 28 October 1995 – Samways; Housham, Wilson, Ford (1), Knill (1), Hope (Nicholson), Thornber, Bullimore (Walsh), McFarlane (4) (Young), Eyre (2), Paterson.

HONOURS

League Champions: FL 1 – 2006–07; Division 3N – 1957–58.
Runners-up: FL 2 – 2004–05, 2013–14.

FA Cup: 5th rd – 1958, 1970.

League Cup: 4th rd – 2010.

League Trophy: *Runners-up:* 2009.

FOOTBALL YEARBOOK FACT FILE

Scunthorpe United first wore a sponsor's name on their shirts during the 1983–84 season. The name that appeared on the shirts was 'Scunthorpe EZ' which stood for Scunthorpe Enterprise Zone, a recently launched scheme aimed at developing economic growth and run by Scunthorpe Borough Council.

Record Cup Victory: 9–0 v Boston U, FA Cup 1st rd, 21 November 1953 – Malan; Hubbard, Brownsword; Sharpe, White, Bushby; Mosby (1), Haigh (3), Whitfield (2), Gregory (1), Mervyn Jones (2).

Record Defeat: 0–8 v Carlisle U, Division 3 (N), 25 December 1952.

Most League Points (2 for a win): 66, Division 3 (N), 1956–57, 1957–58.

Most League Points (3 for a win): 91, FL 1, 2006–07.

Most League Goals: 88, Division 3 (N), 1957–58.

Highest League Scorer in Season: Barrie Thomas, 31, Division 2, 1961–62.

Most League Goals in Total Aggregate: Steve Cammack, 110, 1979–81, 1981–86.

Most League Goals in One Match: 5, Barrie Thomas v Luton T, Division 3, 24 April 1965.

Most Capped Player: Grant McCann, 12 (40), Northern Ireland.

Most League Appearances: Jack Brownsword, 597, 1950–65.

Youngest League Player: Hakeeb Adelakun, 16 years 201 days v Tranmere R, 29 December 2012.

Record Transfer Fee Received: £2,400,000 from Celtic for Gary Hooper, July 2010.

Record Transfer Fee Paid: £700,000 to Hibernian for Rob Jones, July 2009.

Football League Record: 1950 Elected to Division 3 (N); 1958–64 Division 2; 1964–68 Division 3; 1968–72 Division 4; 1972–73 Division 3; 1973–83 Division 4; 1983–84 Division 3; 1984–92 Division 4; 1992–99 Division 3; 1999–2000 Division 2; 2000–04 Division 3; 2004–05 FL 2; 2005–07 FL 1; 2007–08 FL C; 2008–09 FL 1; 2009–11 FL C; 2011–13 FL 1; 2013–14 FL 2; 2014–19 FL 1; 2019– FL 2.

MANAGERS

Harry Allcock 1915–53
(Secretary-Manager)
Tom Crilly 1936–37
Bernard Harper 1946–48
Leslie Jones 1950–51
Bill Corkhill 1952–56
Ron Suart 1956–58
Tony McShane 1959
Bill Lambton 1959
Frank Soo 1959–60
Dick Duckworth 1960–64
Fred Goodwin 1964–66
Ron Ashman 1967–73
Ron Bradley 1973–74
Dick Rooks 1974–76
Ron Ashman 1976–81
John Duncan 1981–83
Allan Clarke 1983–84
Frank Barlow 1984–87
Mick Buxton 1987–91
Bill Green 1991–93
Richard Money 1993–94
David Moore 1994–96
Mick Buxton 1996–97
Brian Laws 1997–2004; 2004–06
Nigel Adkins 2006–10
Ian Baraclough 2010–11
Alan Knill 2011–12
Brian Laws 2012–13
Russ Wilcox 2013–14
Mark Robins 2014–16
Nick Daws 2016
Graham Alexander 2016–18
Nick Daws 2018
Stuart McCall 2018–19
Paul Hurst 2019–20
Neil Cox August 2020–

LATEST SEQUENCES

Longest Sequence of League Wins: 7, 9.4.2016 – 6.8.2017.

Longest Sequence of League Defeats: 8, 29.11.1997 – 20.1.1998.

Longest Sequence of League Draws: 6, 2.1.1984 – 25.2.1984.

Longest Sequence of Unbeaten League Matches: 28, 23.11.2013 – 21.4.2014.

Longest Sequence Without a League Win: 16, 16.3.2019 – 7.9.2019.

Successive Scoring Runs: 24 from 13.1.2007.

Successive Non-scoring Runs: 7 from 19.4.1975.

TEN YEAR LEAGUE RECORD

		P	*W*	*D*	*L*	*F*	*A*	*Pts*	*Pos*
2011-12	FL 1	46	10	22	14	55	59	52	18
2012-13	FL 1	46	13	9	24	49	73	48	21
2013-14	FL 2	46	20	21	5	68	44	81	2
2014-15	FL 1	46	14	14	18	62	75	56	16
2015-16	FL 1	46	21	11	14	60	47	74	7
2016-17	FL 1	46	24	10	12	80	54	82	3
2017-18	FL 1	46	19	17	10	65	50	74	5
2018-19	FL 1	46	12	10	24	53	83	46	23
2019-20	FL 2	37	10	10	17	44	56	40	20§
2020-21	FL 2	46	13	9	24	41	64	48	22

§Decided on points-per-game (1.08)

DID YOU KNOW ?

Scunthorpe United played in the local North Lindsey League for their first two seasons before making the step up to the Midland League for the 1912–13 term. They lost the first six games in the new competition, including defeats of 7-1 and 9-1 before eventually recovering to finish the campaign in 15th position.

SCUNTHORPE UNITED – SKY BET LEAGUE TWO 2020–21 LEAGUE RECORD

Match No.	Date	Venue	Opponents	Result		H/T Score	Lg Pos.	Goalscorers	Attendance
1	Sept 12	H	Newport Co	D	1-1	0-1	10	Loft [58]	0
2	19	A	Crawley T	L	0-1	0-1	18		0
3	26	H	Carlisle U	W	1-0	1-0	14	Hallam [35]	0
4	Oct 3	A	Tranmere R	L	0-2	0-1	18		0
5	10	H	Forest Green R	L	1-4	1-2	19	Jarvis [9]	0
6	17	H	Cambridge U	L	0-5	0-2	21		0
7	20	A	Cheltenham T	L	0-1	0-1	23		0
8	24	A	Exeter C	L	1-3	0-2	23	Rowe [49]	0
9	Nov 14	A	Oldham Ath	W	2-0	0-0	23	Bedeau [60], van Veen [78]	0
10	17	A	Port Vale	W	1-0	1-0	22	Eisa [28]	0
11	21	H	Morecambe	D	1-1	0-0	22	Onariase [80]	0
12	24	H	Bolton W	L	0-1	0-0	23		0
13	Dec 1	A	Harrogate T	W	5-2	2-1	19	Onariase [16], Eisa 2 (1 pen) [41, 63 (p)], Loft [74], Jarvis [89]	0
14	5	H	Leyton Orient	W	2-0	1-0	18	Loft [28], Beestin [78]	0
15	8	H	Colchester U	L	0-1	0-1	18		0
16	12	A	Southend U	L	0-1	0-0	18		2000
17	15	H	Barrow	W	2-1	1-1	18	Eisa [13], Clarke [90]	0
18	19	A	Grimsby T	L	0-1	0-1	18		0
19	26	H	Mansfield T	L	2-3	1-2	20	Rawson (og) [37], McAtee [70]	0
20	29	A	Walsall	W	2-1	1-0	19	Hippolyte [27], Gilliead [69]	0
21	Jan 2	A	Stevenage	L	1-3	1-2	20	Green [5]	0
22	12	H	Salford C	L	0-1	0-0	20		0
23	16	A	Barrow	L	0-1	0-0	21		0
24	23	H	Grimsby T	W	3-0	2-0	19	Eisa 2 [14, 65], Loft [38]	0
25	26	H	Port Vale	W	2-0	2-0	17	Loft 2 [26, 32]	0
26	29	A	Colchester U	W	1-0	1-0	14	Beestin [5]	0
27	Feb 20	H	Harrogate T	W	3-1	2-1	16	Green [4], Loft [45], Spence [90]	0
28	23	A	Bolton W	L	0-2	0-1	16		0
29	27	H	Cheltenham T	L	0-2	0-2	19		0
30	Mar 2	A	Cambridge U	W	1-0	0-0	18	Beestin [78]	0
31	6	A	Salford C	D	1-1	1-1	17	Eisa (pen) [43]	0
32	9	H	Exeter C	L	0-2	0-1	18		0
33	13	A	Leyton Orient	D	1-1	1-1	18	Loft [12]	0
34	16	H	Oldham Ath	D	1-1	0-0	18	Hallam [90]	0
35	20	H	Southend U	D	1-1	0-0	18	Beestin [90]	0
36	23	H	Bradford C	W	2-0	1-0	16	Eisa [5], Green [59]	0
37	Apr 2	H	Crawley T	D	0-0	0-0	17		0
38	6	A	Carlisle U	L	0-2	0-0	18		0
39	10	H	Tranmere R	D	0-0	0-0	18		0
40	13	A	Morecambe	L	1-4	0-2	19	Beestin [83]	0
41	17	A	Forest Green R	L	2-3	1-1	20	McGahey [45], Eisa [52]	0
42	20	A	Mansfield T	L	0-3	0-1	20		0
43	24	H	Walsall	L	0-2	0-2	21		0
44	27	A	Newport Co	L	0-4	0-3	22		0
45	May 1	A	Bradford C	D	0-0	0-0	22		0
46	8	H	Stevenage	L	0-1	0-0	22		0

Final League Position: 22

GOALSCORERS

League (41): Eisa 9 (2 pens), Loft 8, Beestin 5, Green 3, Hallam 2, Jarvis 2, Onariase 2, Bedeau 1, Clarke 1, Gilliead 1, Hippolyte 1, McAtee 1, McGahey 1, Rowe 1, Spence 1, van Veen 1, own goal 1.
FA Cup (2): McAtee 1, van Veen 1.
Carabao Cup (1): Loft 1.
Papa John's Trophy (2): Cordner 1, Olomola 1.

Watson R 12	Hornshaw G 7 + 1	McGahey H 14 + 2	Cordner T 10 + 2	Bedeau J 28 + 6	Gilliead A 43 + 1	Vincent F 5 + 1	Spence L 30 + 11	Hippolyte M 15 + 11	Eisa A 28 + 11	Loft R 35 + 6	Green D 23 + 13	Jarvis A 6 + 7	Dunnwald K 1 + 4	O'Malley M 27 + 2	Hallam J 3 + 10	Onariase M 23 + 3	Beestin A 32 + 8	Butroid L — + 1	Taylor J 8 + 5	McAtee J 12 + 18	Howard M 34	Rowe J 15 + 10	Clarke J 22 + 2	Brown J 14	van Veen K 14 + 5	Olomola O — + 5	Taft G 16	Karacan J 22 + 2	Howe T 7 + 5	Jessop H — + 3	Pugh T — + 1	Match No.
1	2	3	4	5	6	7¹	8	9	10	11²	12	13																				1
1	2	3¹	4	5	6	7	8	9³	13	10²			11	12	14																	2
1	2³		3	4	6	7²	8	9		11				5¹	10	12	13	14														3
1	2³		3	4	6	7¹	9	10²	13	11	14		12	5					8													4
1	2		3	4	6	7¹	8³		9	13		11²		5			14		10	12												5
1			2	4	5	13	6	8▮	12	10¹		11				3			7	9²												6
1	2¹		5	4	9		7²		11	14	12	10³		6		3			8	13												7
	2							9²		12	6	10	13	5		4	7		8	11¹	1	3										8
				4	6		7	13	9²	11						3	8			12	1	14	2³	5	10¹							9
		3		14	6		8		9³	11²	13					4	7			12	1	2		5	10¹							10
		3			6		8³	15	9⁴	11	13				12²	4	7			14	1	2		5	10¹							11
		2		4	5		7	12	11	10²	9³				15	3	6⁴			14	1			8¹		13						12
		4			6		8		9	11¹		12		5		3	7		13	10²	1	14	2³									13
		3			6		8		9³	11²	14	12		5		4	7		13	10¹	1		2									14
		4¹		12	6		8		14	13	9³	11		5		3	7		10²		1	15	2⁴									15
				4	6¹		7⁴		9	10³	12	13		5	15	3	8		14	11²	1	2										16
			14	4	6		8³	5	9	11²		13			12	3	7			10¹	1		2									17
				4	6		8	5	9	11		12				3	7²		13	10¹	1		2									18
			12	4	6		8²		9	13	15	11³		5		3¹	7⁴		14	10	1		2									19
	15		4	3	8			9	13	11¹	6³	12²		5			7		10⁴	14	1		2									20
			3	4	7		13		9	11	6²		14	5			8¹		10³	12	1		2									21
			3		6		9		10	11²			13				7			12	1		2	5			4	8¹				22
		3¹			6		9	10⁴	13	11²	15					12	7³			14	1		2	5▮			4	8				23
					6		13		10	11⁴	9²			5	15	3	8			14	1	12	2¹				4	7³				24
				13	6		8	14	10	11³	9²			5		3	12				1	2					4	7¹				25
					6		12	14	10	11³	9²					3	8			13	1	2		5			4	7¹				26
				14	6		13		10	11⁴	9¹				15	3²	8				1		2	5	12		4	7³				27
		13		3²	6		15		10	11	9³			16			7				1	2¹	12	5⁵	14		4	8⁴				28
		3			6		7		13	11²	9			5	15	12	14				1		2		10⁴		4¹	8³				29
		3		4²	6		12	14	9		10³						8				1	13	2	5	11¹			7				30
		3¹		4	9		6	8⁴	7		15			5	11³		14				1	2	12		10²			13				31
				4	13		14	10²	9	11¹	6⁴			5	15		8				1	2⁵	3		12			7³	16			32
				4	6		12		13	11³	14				9¹		8				1	2	3	5	10²			7				33
				4	6		8³			10	9				14		12			13	1	2⁴	3	5	11²			7¹	15			34
				4	6			15	12	11¹	9⁴						8			13	1	2³	3▮	5	10²			7	14			35
				4	6		8	12	9	10³	11²						13			15	1	16	3	5¹		14		7⁴	2⁵			36
				3	6		12		10	11³	9			5		4	8¹			13	1					14		7²	2			37
1				4	8		9		12	11²	10¹			5			7³			14			3			13		6	2			38
1				3	6			9						5			8			10¹		13			11	12	4	7	2²			39
1		15		4⁴	6		8	9²			13			5			14			10		12			11⁵		3	7³	2¹	16		40
1		3		12	6		14	15	10		5²			9⁴						8⁵		13	2¹		11		4	7³		16		41
1					6		12	15	9	11³	10			5		3⁴	7					2¹			14		4	8²	13			42
					6¹		7			10	9			5		3	8³			12	1	2²			11		4	14	13			43
				2	6				10¹	11²	12			9		3	8				1				13		4	7	5			44
					6		8	14	12	13	9¹			5		3	10				1	2			11³		4	7²				45
		3²		12			6	8		11⁴	10			5			7			9³	1	13					4¹		2	15	14	46

FA Cup
First Round — Solihull Moors — (h) — 2-3

Carabao Cup
First Round — Port Vale — (h) — 1-2

Papa John's Trophy
Group E (N) — Lincoln C — (a) — 1-1
(Lincoln C won 4-2 on penalties)
Group E (N) — Manchester C U21 — (h) — 0-4
Group E (N) — Mansfield T — (h) — 1-2

SHEFFIELD UNITED

FOUNDATION

In March 1889, Yorkshire County Cricket Club formed Sheffield United six days after an FA Cup semi-final between Preston North End and West Bromwich Albion had finally convinced Charles Stokes, a member of the cricket club, that the formation of a professional football club would prove successful at Bramall Lane. The United's first secretary, Mr J. B. Wostinholm, was also secretary of the cricket club.

Bramall Lane Ground, Cherry Street, Bramall Lane, Sheffield, South Yorkshire S2 4SU.

Telephone: (01142) 537 200.

Ticket Office: (01142) 537 200 (option 1).

Website: www.sufc.co.uk

Email: info@sufc.co.uk

Ground Capacity: 32,050.

Record Attendance: 68,287 v Leeds U, FA Cup 5th rd, 15 February 1936.

Pitch Measurements: 101m × 68m (110.5yd × 74.5yd).

Chairman: H.H. Prince Musa'ad bin Khalid Al Saud.

Chief Executive Officer: Stephen Bettis.

Manager: Slavisa Jokanovic.

Assistant Manager: Chema Sanz.

Colours: Red and white striped shirts with black trim, black shorts with white trim, red socks with white trim.

Year Formed: 1889.

Turned Professional: 1889.

Club Nickname: 'The Blades'.

Ground: 1889, Bramall Lane.

First Football League Game: 3 September 1892, Division 2, v Lincoln C (h) W 4–2 – Lilley; Witham, Cain; Howell, Hendry, Needham (1); Wallace, Dobson, Hammond (3), Davies, Drummond.

Record League Victory: 10–0 v Burslem Port Vale (a), Division 2, 10 December 1892 – Howlett; Witham, Lilley; Howell, Hendry, Needham; Drummond (1), Wallace (1), Hammond (4), Davies (2), Watson (2). 10–0 v Burnley, Division 1 (h), 19 January 1929.

Record Cup Victory: 6–0 v Leyton Orient (h), FA Cup 1st rd, 6 November 2016 – Ramsdale; Basham (1), O'Connell, Wright, Freeman (1), Coutts (Whiteman), Duffy (Brooks), Fleck, Lafferty, Scougall (1) (Lavery), Chapman (3).

Record Defeat: 0–13 v Bolton W, FA Cup 2nd rd, 1 February 1890.

Most League Points (2 for a win): 60, Division 2, 1952–53.

HONOURS

League Champions: Division 1 – 1897–98; Division 2 – 1952–53; FL 1 – 2016–17; Division 4 – 1981–82.
Runners-up: Division 1 – 1896–97, 1899–1900; FL C – 2005–06, 2018–19; Division 2 – 1892–93, 1938–39, 1960–61, 1970–71, 1989–90; Division 3 – 1988–89.

FA Cup Winners: 1899, 1902, 1915, 1925.
Runners-up: 1901, 1936.

League Cup: semi-final – 2003, 2015.

FOOTBALL YEARBOOK FACT FILE

Keith Edwards was the first player to come off the bench to score a hat-trick for Sheffield United in a competitive match. He achieved this in the second round second leg Football League Cup game against Grimsby Town on 26 October 1982. The Blades won 5-1 on the night and 8-4 on aggregate.

Most League Points (3 for a win): 100, FL 1, 2016–17.

Most League Goals: 102, Division 1, 1925–26.

Highest League Scorer in Season: Jimmy Dunne, 41, Division 1, 1930–31.

Most League Goals in Total Aggregate: Harry Johnson, 201, 1919–30.

Most League Goals in One Match: 5, Harry Hammond v Bootle, Division 2, 26 November 1892; 5, Harry Johnson v West Ham U, Division 1, 26 December 1927.

Most Capped Player: Billy Gillespie, 25, Northern Ireland.

Most League Appearances: Joe Shaw, 632, 1948–66.

Youngest League Player: Louis Reed, 16 years 257 days v Rotherham U, 8 April 2014.

Record Transfer Fee Received: £12,000,000 from Bournemouth for David Brooks, July 2018.

Record Transfer Fee Paid: £23,500,000 to Liverpool for Rhian Brewster, October 2020.

Football League Record: 1892 Elected to Division 2; 1893–1934 Division 1; 1934–39 Division 2; 1946–49 Division 1; 1949–53 Division 2; 1953–56 Division 1; 1956–61 Division 2; 1961–68 Division 1; 1968–71 Division 2; 1971–76 Division 1; 1976–79 Division 2; 1979–81 Division 3; 1981–82 Division 4; 1982–84 Division 3; 1984–88 Division 2; 1988–89 Division 3; 1989–90 Division 2; 1990–92 Division 1; 1992–94 Premier League; 1994–2004 Division 1; 2004–06 FL C; 2006–07 Premier League; 2007–11 FL C; 2011–17 FL 1; 2017–19 FL C; 2019–21 Premier League; 2021– FL C.

MANAGERS

J. B. Wostinholm 1889–99 *(Secretary-Manager)*
John Nicholson 1899–1932
Ted Davison 1932–52
Reg Freeman 1952–55
Joe Mercer 1955–58
Johnny Harris 1959–68 *(continued as General Manager to 1970)*
Arthur Rowley 1968–69
Johnny Harris *(General Manager resumed Team Manager duties)* 1969–73
Ken Furphy 1973–75
Jimmy Sirrel 1975–77
Harry Haslam 1978–81
Martin Peters 1981
Ian Porterfield 1981–86
Billy McEwan 1986–88
Dave Bassett 1988–95
Howard Kendall 1995–97
Nigel Spackman 1997–98
Steve Bruce 1998–99
Adrian Heath 1999
Neil Warnock 1999–2007
Bryan Robson 2007–08
Kevin Blackwell 2008–10
Gary Speed 2010
Micky Adams 2010–11
Danny Wilson 2011–13
David Weir 2013
Nigel Clough 2013–15
Nigel Adkins 2015–16
Chris Wilder 2016–21
Paul Heckingbottom 2021
Slavisa Jokanovic May 2021–

LATEST SEQUENCES

Longest Sequence of League Wins: 8, 28.3.2017 – 5.8.2017.

Longest Sequence of League Defeats: 8, 24.10.2020 – 17.12.2020.

Longest Sequence of League Draws: 6, 6.5.2001 – 8.9.2001.

Longest Sequence of Unbeaten League Matches: 22, 2.9.1899 – 13.1.1900.

Longest Sequence Without a League Win: 20, 16.7.2020 – 2.1.2021.

Successive Scoring Runs: 34 from 30.3.1956.

Successive Non-scoring Runs: 6 from 4.12.1993.

TEN YEAR LEAGUE RECORD

		P	W	D	L	F	A	Pts	Pos
2011-12	FL 1	46	27	9	10	92	51	90	3
2012-13	FL 1	46	19	18	9	56	42	75	5
2013-14	FL 1	46	18	13	15	48	46	67	7
2014-15	FL 1	46	19	14	13	66	53	71	5
2015-16	FL 1	46	18	12	16	64	59	66	11
2016-17	FL 1	46	30	10	6	92	47	100	1
2017-18	FL C	46	20	9	17	62	55	69	10
2018-19	FL C	46	26	11	9	78	41	89	2
2019-20	PR Lge	38	14	12	12	39	39	54	9
2020-21	PR Lge	38	7	2	29	20	63	23	20

DID YOU KNOW ?

In the opening game of the 1923–24 season away to Manchester City, Sheffield United goalkeeper Harold Hough suffered an injury to his left hand and had to leave the field with 20 minutes remaining. Wing-half Harry Pantling took over in goal and promptly saved a penalty from Frank Roberts.

SHEFFIELD UNITED – PREMIER LEAGUE 2020–21 LEAGUE RECORD

Match No.	*Date*	*Venue*	*Opponents*	*Result*		*H/T Score*	*Lg Pos.*	*Goalscorers*	*Attendance*
1	Sept 14	H	Wolverhampton W	L	0-2	0-2	17		0
2	21	A	Aston Villa	L	0-1	0-0	17		0
3	27	H	Leeds U	L	0-1	0-0	20		0
4	Oct 4	A	Arsenal	L	1-2	0-0	19	McGoldrick [84]	0
5	18	H	Fulham	D	1-1	0-0	17	Sharp (pen) [85]	0
6	24	A	Liverpool	L	1-2	1-1	19	Berge (pen) [13]	0
7	31	H	Manchester C	L	0-1	0-1	18		0
8	Nov 7	A	Chelsea	L	1-4	1-2	20	McGoldrick [9]	0
9	22	H	West Ham U	L	0-1	0-0	20		0
10	28	A	WBA	L	0-1	0-1	20		0
11	Dec 6	H	Leicester C	L	1-2	1-1	20	McBurnie [26]	0
12	13	A	Southampton	L	0-3	0-1	20		2000
13	17	H	Manchester U	L	2-3	1-2	20	McGoldrick 2 [5, 87]	0
14	20	A	Brighton & HA	D	1-1	0-0	20	Bogle [63]	2000
15	26	H	Everton	L	0-1	0-0	20		0
16	29	A	Burnley	L	0-1	0-1	20		0
17	Jan 2	A	Crystal Palace	L	0-2	0-2	20		0
18	12	H	Newcastle U	W	1-0	0-0	20	Sharp (pen) [73]	0
19	17	H	Tottenham H	L	1-3	0-2	20	McGoldrick [59]	0
20	27	A	Manchester U	W	2-1	1-0	20	Bryan [23], Burke [74]	0
21	30	A	Manchester C	L	0-1	0-1	20		0
22	Feb 2	H	WBA	W	2-1	0-1	20	Bogle [56], Sharp [73]	0
23	7	H	Chelsea	L	1-2	0-1	20	Rudiger (og) [55]	0
24	15	A	West Ham U	L	0-3	0-1	20		0
25	20	A	Fulham	L	0-1	0-0	20		0
26	28	H	Liverpool	L	0-2	0-0	20		0
27	Mar 3	H	Aston Villa	W	1-0	1-0	20	McGoldrick [30]	0
28	6	H	Southampton	L	0-2	0-1	20		0
29	14	A	Leicester C	L	0-5	0-1	20		0
30	Apr 3	A	Leeds U	L	1-2	1-1	20	Osborn [45]	0
31	11	H	Arsenal	L	0-3	0-1	20		0
32	17	A	Wolverhampton W	L	0-1	0-0	20		0
33	24	H	Brighton & HA	W	1-0	1-0	20	McGoldrick [19]	0
34	May 2	A	Tottenham H	L	0-4	0-1	20		0
35	8	H	Crystal Palace	L	0-2	0-1	20		0
36	16	A	Everton	W	1-0	1-0	20	Jebbison [7]	0
37	19	A	Newcastle U	L	0-1	0-1	20		10,000
38	23	H	Burnley	W	1-0	1-0	20	McGoldrick [24]	5096

Final League Position: 20

GOALSCORERS

League (20): McGoldrick 8, Sharp 3 (2 pens), Bogle 2, Berge 1 (1 pen), Bryan 1, Burke 1, Jebbison 1, McBurnie 1, Osborn 1, own goal 1.
FA Cup (6): Sharp 2 (1 pen), Basham 1, Bogle 1, Burke 1, own goal 1.
Carabao Cup (1): McGoldrick 1.

Ramsdale A 38	Basham C 31	Egan J 30 + 1	O'Connell J 2	Baldock G 32	Lundstram J 23 + 5	Norwood O 26 + 6	Fleck J 29 + 2	Stevens E 30	McBurnie O 12 + 11	Sharp B 7 + 9	McGoldrick D 28 + 7	Berge S 13 + 2	Burke O 14 + 11	Ampadu E 23 + 2	Osborn B 17 + 7	Robinson J 9 + 2	Lowe M 7 + 1	Brewster R 12 + 15	Bryan K 12 + 1	Mousset L 2 + 9	Jagielka P 6 + 4	Bogle J 12 + 4	Hackford A — + 1	Ndiaye I — + 1	Jebbison D 3 + 1	Seriki F — + 1	Match No.
1	2^{1}	3	4	5	6	7^{2}	8	9	10	11	12	13															1
1	2^{3}	3■	4	5	6		8^{2}	9	14		11^{1}	7	10	12	13												2
1	2			5	6^{1}	12		9	14	13	10^{2}	7	11^{3}	3	8	4											3
1	2^{3}	3		5	6		13	9	12	14	11	7	10^{1}		8^{2}	4											4
1	2^{3}	3		5	8	7		4	10	14	11^{2}	6				12	9^{1}	13									5
1	2	3		5	8^{2}			4	10		13	6	12	7	9			11^{1}									6
1	3	4		2	12	13		5	10		14	7		8^{2}	9^{1}		6^{3}	11									7
1	2	3		5	8	7^{1}		4	13		11	6			12		9	10^{2}									8
1	2^{3}	3		5	14	7^{2}	8		10		11	6		4^{1}		12	9	13									9
1	2	3		5	13	7^{1}	8		10			6	11^{3}				9	12	4^{2}	14							10
1	3	4		2	7^{2}	13	9		11			8	10^{3}		12		6^{1}	14	5								11
1	3^{3}	4		2			9	6	10^{1}	11^{2}	12	7		8				13		14	5						12
1	3	4		2			9	6			11	7^{1}	10^{3}	8		5		14		13	12^{2}						13
1	3	4		2	7■		9^{1}	6			11^{3}		12	8	14	5		10^{2}				13					14
1	2	3		5		13		8	12		9^{2}		11^{1}	6	7	4		10^{3}		14							15
1	2	3		5		14	12	8			9		13	6^{3}	7	4^{1}		11		10^{2}							16
1	6	3				7	8	4			10			2	9^{2}			12		11^{1}		5	13				17
1	2^{1}	3			6	7	8			13	10^{3}		11^{2}	4	9			12			14	5					18
1	2^{3}	3			6	7^{1}	8	9		14	10		11^{2}	4				13	12			5					19
1	2			5	6	7	8			11^{2}	10^{3}		13	4				14	9^{1}		3	12					20
1	3^{3}	4		2	7	8	9		14	13	12		10^{2}	5				11^{1}				6					21
1	2	3		5^{1}	6	7^{2}	8		13	11^{3}	10		14	4			12					9					22
1	2	3			6	7^{3}	8		11	13	12		10^{1}				9	14	4^{2}			5					23
1	2	3^{2}			6	7^{1}		9	12	11	10			4	8						13	5					24
1	6^{1}			5	7^{2}	12	8	9	10	11	13			2					4		3^{3}	14					25
1				5	6	7	8^{3}	9	11	14	10^{2}		12	2	13				4		3^{1}						26
1				5	6	7	8	9	14		10^{2}		12^{3}	2	13			11^{1}	4		3■						27
1				2	6	7^{1}	8	9	12	14	11^{2}			3				10^{3}	4	13		5					28
1	2			5	6	7^{2}	8	9		11			10^{1}	3					4	12				13			29
1		15		2^{1}	6	7^{2}	8	4	11^{4}		10		13	12	9			14			3	5^{3}					30
1		3		5	6	7	8	4	13^{3}		11^{2}		10^{1}	2	9			12		14							31
1		3		5		7	8	9			11		13	2^{3}	6^{1}			10^{2}	4	12		14					32
1		3		2	13	6	7	8			11		12		9^{2}			10^{1}	4			5					33
1	4	3		2		6	7	8			10^{3}	13	12		9			11^{2}		14		5^{1}					34
1	2	3		5	14	7	8	9			11	6^{1}	10^{2}		12				4^{3}						13		35
1	2	3		5		6	7	8			9				11	4									10		36
1	2	3				6	5	7			9				10^{1}	4		12				8^{2}			11	13	37
1	2	3		5		6	7	8			9				10^{2}	4		12			13				11^{1}		38

FA Cup

Third Round	Bristol R	(a)	3-2
Fourth Round	Plymouth Arg	(h)	2-1
Fifth Round	Bristol C	(h)	1-0
Sixth Round	Chelsea	(a)	0-2

Carabao Cup

Second Round	Burnley	(a)	1-1

(Burnley won 5-4 on penalties)

SHEFFIELD WEDNESDAY

FOUNDATION

Sheffield being one of the principal centres of early Association Football, this club was formed as long ago as 1867 by the Sheffield Wednesday Cricket Club (formed 1825) and their colours from the start were blue and white. The inaugural meeting was held at the Adelphi Hotel and the original committee included Charles Stokes who was subsequently a founder member of Sheffield United.

Hillsborough Stadium, Hillsborough, Sheffield, South Yorkshire S6 1SW.

Telephone: (0370) 020 1867.

Ticket Office: (0370) 020 1867 (option 1).

Website: www.swfc.co.uk

Email: footballenquiries@swfc.co.uk

Ground Capacity: 39,732.

Record Attendance: 72,841 v Manchester C, FA Cup 5th rd, 17 February 1934.

Pitch Measurements: 105m × 64m (115yd × 70yd).

Chairman: Dejphon Chansiri.

Manager: Darren Moore.

Assistant Manager: Jamie Smith.

Colours: Blue and white striped shirts with black trim, black shorts with blue and white trim, black socks with blue trim.

Year Formed: 1867 (fifth oldest League club).

Turned Professional: 1887.

Previous Name: The Wednesday until 1929.

Club Nickname: 'The Owls'.

Grounds: 1867, Highfield; 1869, Myrtle Road; 1877, Sheaf House; 1887, Olive Grove; 1899, Owlerton (since 1912 known as Hillsborough). Some games were played at Endcliffe in the 1880s. Until 1895 Bramall Lane was used for some games.

First Football League Game: 3 September 1892, Division 1, v Notts Co (a) W 1–0 – Allan; Tom Brandon (1), Mumford; Hall, Betts, Harry Brandon; Spiksley, Brady, Davis, Bob Brown, Dunlop.

Record League Victory: 9–1 v Birmingham, Division 1, 13 December 1930 – Brown; Walker, Blenkinsop; Strange, Leach, Wilson; Hooper (3), Seed (2), Ball (2), Burgess (1), Rimmer (1).

Record Cup Victory: 12–0 v Halliwell, FA Cup 1st rd, 17 January 1891 – Smith; Thompson, Brayshaw; Harry Brandon (1), Betts, Cawley (2); Winterbottom, Mumford (2), Bob Brandon (1), Woolhouse (5), Ingram (1).

Record Defeat: 0–10 v Aston Villa, Division 1, 5 October 1912.

Most League Points (2 for a win): 62, Division 2, 1958–59.

HONOURS

League Champions: Division 1 – 1902–03, 1903–04, 1928–29, 1929–30; Division 2 – 1899–1900, 1925–26, 1951–52, 1955–56, 1958–59.
Runners-up: Division 1 – 1960–61; Division 2 – 1949–50, 1983–84; FL 1 – 2011–12.

FA Cup Winners: 1896, 1907, 1935.
Runners-up: 1890, 1966, 1993.

League Cup Winners: 1991.
Runners-up: 1993.

European Competitions
Fairs Cup: 1961–62 *(qf)*, 1963–64.
UEFA Cup: 1992–93.
Intertoto Cup: 1995.

FOOTBALL YEARBOOK FACT FILE

Sheffield Wednesday were one of the clubs worst affected by the Asian flu pandemic in the late 1950s and at one point had 15 players on the sick list. Consequently the club's first two games of the 1957–58 season, away to Manchester City and at home to Newcastle United, both had to be postponed. This was the first occasion that the Football League had authorised the postponement of games due to non-availability of players.

Most League Points (3 for a win): 93, FL 1, 2011–12.

Most League Goals: 106, Division 2, 1958–59.

Highest League Scorer in Season: Derek Dooley, 46, Division 2, 1951–52.

Most League Goals in Total Aggregate: Andrew Wilson, 199, 1900–20.

Most League Goals in One Match: 6, Doug Hunt v Norwich C, Division 2, 19 November 1938.

Most Capped Player: Nigel Worthington, 50 (66), Northern Ireland.

Most League Appearances: Andrew Wilson, 501, 1900–20.

Youngest League Player: Peter Fox, 15 years 269 days v Orient, 31 March 1973.

Record Transfer Fee Received: £5,000,000 from Reading for Lucas Joao, August 2019.

Record Transfer Fee Paid: £10,000,000 to Middlesbrough for Jordan Rhodes, July 2017.

Football League Record: 1892 Elected to Division 1; 1899–1900 Division 2; 1900–20 Division 1; 1920–26 Division 2; 1926–37 Division 1; 1937–50 Division 2; 1950–51 Division 1; 1951–52 Division 2; 1952–55 Division 1; 1955–56 Division 2; 1956–58 Division 1; 1958–59 Division 2; 1959–70 Division 1; 1970–75 Division 2; 1975–80 Division 3; 1980–84 Division 2; 1984–90 Division 1; 1990–91 Division 2; 1991–92 Division 1; 1992–2000 Premier League; 2000–03 Division 1; 2003–04 Division 2; 2004–05 FL 1; 2005–10 FL C; 2010–12 FL 1; 2012–21 FL C; 2021– FL 1.

LATEST SEQUENCES

Longest Sequence of League Wins: 9, 23.4.1904 – 15.10.1904.

Longest Sequence of League Defeats: 8, 9.9.2000 – 17.10.2000.

Longest Sequence of League Draws: 7, 15.3.2008 – 14.4.2008.

Longest Sequence of Unbeaten League Matches: 19, 10.12.1960 – 8.4.1961.

Longest Sequence Without a League Win: 20, 11.1.1975 – 30.8.1975.

Successive Scoring Runs: 40 from 14.11.1959.

Successive Non-scoring Runs: 8 from 8.3.1975.

MANAGERS

Arthur Dickinson 1891–1920
(Secretary-Manager)
Robert Brown 1920–33
Billy Walker 1933–37
Jimmy McMullan 1937–42
Eric Taylor 1942–58
(continued as General Manager to 1974)
Harry Catterick 1958–61
Vic Buckingham 1961–64
Alan Brown 1964–68
Jack Marshall 1968–69
Danny Williams 1969–71
Derek Dooley 1971–73
Steve Burtenshaw 1974–75
Len Ashurst 1975–77
Jackie Charlton 1977–83
Howard Wilkinson 1983–88
Peter Eustace 1988–89
Ron Atkinson 1989–91
Trevor Francis 1991–95
David Pleat 1995–97
Ron Atkinson 1997–98
Danny Wilson 1998–2000
Peter Shreeves *(Acting)* 2000
Paul Jewell 2000–01
Peter Shreeves 2001
Terry Yorath 2001–02
Chris Turner 2002–04
Paul Sturrock 2004–06
Brian Laws 2006–09
Alan Irvine 2010–11
Gary Megson 2011–12
Dave Jones 2012–13
Stuart Gray 2013–15
Carlos Carvalhal 2015–18
Jos Luhukay 2018
Steve Bruce 2019
Garry Monk 2019–20
Tony Pulis 2020
Darren Moore March 2021–

TEN YEAR LEAGUE RECORD

		P	*W*	*D*	*L*	*F*	*A*	*Pts*	*Pos*
2011-12	FL 1	46	28	9	9	81	48	93	2
2012-13	FL C	46	16	10	20	53	61	58	18
2013-14	FL C	46	13	14	19	63	65	53	16
2014-15	FL C	46	14	18	14	43	49	60	13
2015-16	FL C	46	19	17	10	66	45	74	6
2016-17	FL C	46	24	9	13	60	45	81	4
2017-18	FL C	46	14	15	17	59	60	57	15
2018-19	FL C	46	16	16	14	60	62	64	12
2019-20	FL C	46	15	11	20	58	66	56	16
2020-21	FL C	46	12	11	23	40	61	41*	24

**6 pts deducted.*

DID YOU KNOW ?

Sheffield Wednesday struggled in their first season as Football League members in 1892–93 and seemed certainties to finish in the bottom three of the First Division, which would have left them needing to take part in the test matches to decide their fate. After gaining just one point from the previous eight games they defeated Notts County with a late goal from Harry Brandon in their final match to keep their place in the top flight.

SHEFFIELD WEDNESDAY – SKY BET CHAMPIONSHIP 2020–21 LEAGUE RECORD

Match No.	Date	Venue	Opponents	Result		H/T Score	Lg Pos.	Goalscorers	Attendance
1	Sept 12	A	Cardiff C	W	2-0	2-0	24	Windass [4], Rhodes [44]	0
2	19	H	Watford	D	0-0	0-0	24		0
3	27	A	Bristol C	L	0-2	0-0	24		0
4	Oct 3	H	QPR	D	1-1	0-0	24	Barbet (og) [54]	0
5	17	A	Birmingham C	W	1-0	0-0	22	Bannan (pen) [49]	0
6	21	H	Brentford	L	1-2	1-2	23	Paterson [25]	0
7	24	H	Luton T	L	0-1	0-0	23		0
8	28	A	Rotherham U	L	0-3	0-3	23		0
9	31	A	Wycombe W	L	0-1	0-1	24		0
10	Nov 3	H	Bournemouth	W	1-0	0-0	23	Bannan (pen) [71]	0
11	7	H	Millwall	D	0-0	0-0	23		0
12	21	A	Preston NE	L	0-1	0-0	23		0
13	25	A	Swansea C	D	1-1	1-0	23	Reach [27]	0
14	28	H	Stoke C	D	0-0	0-0	23		0
15	Dec 2	H	Reading	D	1-1	1-1	23	Paterson [12]	0
16	5	A	Norwich C	L	1-2	0-0	24	Windass [60]	2000
17	8	A	Huddersfield T	L	0-2	0-2	24		0
18	12	H	Barnsley	L	1-2	1-2	24	Windass [4]	0
19	15	A	Nottingham F	L	0-2	0-1	24		0
20	19	H	Coventry C	W	1-0	0-0	23	Lees [67]	0
21	26	A	Blackburn R	D	1-1	1-0	23	Reach [41]	0
22	29	H	Middlesbrough	W	2-1	2-0	22	Paterson [30], Shaw [40]	0
23	Jan 1	H	Derby Co	W	1-0	0-0	20	Paterson [61]	0
24	27	A	Coventry C	L	0-2	0-0	23		0
25	30	H	Preston NE	W	1-0	1-0	23	Palmer [45]	0
26	Feb 2	A	Bournemouth	W	2-1	1-0	22	Paterson [44], Rhodes [90]	0
27	6	A	Millwall	L	1-4	1-1	23	Paterson [10]	0
28	9	H	Wycombe W	W	2-0	1-0	21	Rhodes [34], Reach [76]	0
29	16	A	Stoke C	L	0-1	0-0	22		0
30	20	H	Birmingham C	L	0-1	0-0	23		0
31	24	A	Brentford	L	0-3	0-1	23		0
32	27	A	Luton T	L	2-3	2-0	23	Windass 2 [6, 42]	0
33	Mar 3	H	Rotherham U	L	1-2	0-1	23	Olosunde (og) [82]	0
34	6	A	Reading	L	0-3	0-1	23		0
35	14	H	Norwich C	L	1-2	1-0	23	Rhodes [7]	0
36	17	H	Huddersfield T	D	1-1	1-0	23	Windass [36]	0
37	20	A	Barnsley	W	2-1	1-0	23	Rhodes 2 [38, 53]	0
38	Apr 2	A	Watford	L	0-1	0-1	23		0
39	5	H	Cardiff C	W	5-0	3-0	23	Borner [4], Paterson [20], Reach 2 [23, 69], Rhodes [65]	0
40	10	A	QPR	L	1-4	1-1	23	Windass [30]	0
41	13	H	Swansea C	L	0-2	0-1	23		0
42	17	H	Bristol C	D	1-1	1-0	23	Borner [4]	0
43	20	H	Blackburn R	W	1-0	1-0	23	Windass [37]	0
44	24	A	Middlesbrough	L	1-3	1-1	23	Windass (pen) [39]	0
45	May 1	H	Nottingham F	D	0-0	0-0	23		0
46	8	A	Derby Co	D	3-3	1-0	24	Hutchinson [45], Paterson [62], Borner [69]	0

Final League Position: 24 (deducted 6 points from start of season)

GOALSCORERS

League (40): Windass 9 (1 pen), Paterson 8, Rhodes 7, Reach 5, Borner 3, Bannan 2 (2 pens), Hutchinson 1, Lees 1, Palmer 1, Shaw 1, own goals 2.
FA Cup (2): Paterson 1, Reach 1.
Carabao Cup (2): Kachunga 1, Windass 1.

Dawson C 8	Iorfa D 9 + 1	Lees T 38	van Aken J 16 + 1	Harris K 30 + 8	Luongo M 10 + 2	Bannan B 46	Penney M 10 + 2	Brown I 4 + 15	Rhodes J 15 + 21	Windass J 35 + 6	Reach A 38 + 6	Kachunga E 9 + 18	Palmer L 31 + 8	Dele-Bashiru F 2 + 6	Shaw L 13 + 6	Paterson C 34 + 9	Odubajo M 15 + 3	Pelupessy J 24 + 15	Flint A 4	Marriott J 4 + 8	Hunt A 1 + 2	Borner J 25 + 1	Wildsmith J 18 + 1	Westwood K 20	Dunkley C 10 + 2	Hutchinson S 22	Green A 3 + 8	Urhoghide O 12 + 4	*Match No.*
1	2	3	4	5	6	7	8^{3}	9	10^{1}	11^{2}	12	13	14																1
1	2	3	4	5	6	7	9^{1}	8	10^{2}	11^{3}	14	13	12																2
1	2	3	4	8	6	7		9^{1}	14	10	13	11^{2}	5^{3}	12															3
1		3	4	5	6	7				10	8		12^{2}	9^{3}	2^{1}	11	13	14											4
1			4	5	8	7				10^{1}	6	9^{2}		13		11^{3}	2	14	3	12									5
1			4	5		7			14	9^{2}	8			13		10	2	12	3	11^{3}	6^{1}								6
1			4■	5		7			14	12	8	11				10^{1}	2	6^{3}	3	9^{2}		13							7
1		3■		9		8				13	14		12	6		10^{2}	5	7	2^{1}	11^{3}		4							8
	3			5^{1}		7		12	14	8	9	13	2			10		6^{2}		11^{3}		4	1						9
	3			8■		7		13		10^{3}	11^{2}	9^{1}	2			12	5	6		14		4	1						10
	3		2^{3}			7		12		11	10	9^{2}	5			13	8	6^{1}		14		4	1						11
		3	5		8^{1}	9		14	13	11■	10		2			7^{3}	6^{2}	12				4		1					12
		3	5^{3}		9^{4}	8			11^{2}		10	13	2		14	7	6	15				4	12	1^{1}					13
		3	5	9^{2}	7	8		14	12^{3}		11		2		6^{1}	10	13					4	1						14
	14	3	5^{2}	6^{4}	7	9^{1}					10	15	2^{3}		8■	11	13	12				4	1						15
	9^{1}	3	5	7^{3}		10		15		11^{2}	6	14	13			8	2^{4}	12				4	1						16
	2	3		6	8^{2}	9^{5}		16	15	11^{4}	10	14	12			7^{3}	5	13				4^{1}	1						17
	7^{3}	3	5^{1}	8		6		15	14	11	10		13			9^{4}	2	12					1		4^{2}				18
		3	5^{4}	7^{1}		10		14	15	11^{2}	6				9^{3}	12	2	8			13		1		4				19
		2	13	5		7^{2}			12	11^{3}	9	14	4		8^{1}	10		6						1	3				20
		3	5^{1}	13		10		14		11^{3}	7^{2}		2		12	9	6	8						1	4				21
		2		9		8	13	12		11^{2}			4		7	10^{1}	5	6						1	3				22
		3		9		8			13	11^{1}	6	12	5		4	10^{2}	2	7					1						23
		3		13		9	5	16		11^{3}	6		2^{5}	12		14		7^{1}		15		4		1		8^{4}	10^{2}		24
		3			13	8	9		14	12	6^{2}	10^{1}	2			11^{3}		7						1		4		5	25
		3		14	15	7	9		12	13	6	11^{2}	2^{5}			10^{1}		8^{4}						1	16	4		5^{3}	26
		3		12		8	6^{1}		13	16	7	11^{3}	2^{2}		14	10^{5}		9						1	4	5^{4}		15	27
		3		2		9^{2}			11^{1}		6	12			7	10		13						1	4	8		5	28
		2		5		8			11^{1}	14	9	13			6	10		12						1	3^{2}	7		4^{3}	29
		4		6		9	5		14	11^{3}	12	13	2^{4}	15	7■	10^{2}								1	3^{1}	8			30
		3		5		7	8	14	10		9^{1}	11^{2}	2	12^{3}		13		15					1			6^{4}		4	31
		3		5		8	9^{1}	7	12	11^{3}	13					10^{2}				14		4^{4}	1		15	6		2	32
		3		13		10^{5}	5	14	15	9^{1}	6^{2}	12	2^{4}		8	11				16		4	1			7^{3}			33
		3		6^{3}		10^{1}	12		14	9^{4}			5		8	11^{2}		15		13		4■	1			7		2	34
		2		5		6			11^{1}	9^{2}	10		8			13		7		12				1		3		4	35
		2		9^{3}		7			10^{1}	11^{4}	8	15	5		13	14		6				4		1		3^{2}		12	36
		3				7			11	10^{1}	8		5			9		6				4	1				12	2	37
		3^{3}				9			10	11	8		12		14	5^{2}		6^{1}				4	1			7	13	2	38
		3				7^{4}			11^{2}	9^{1}	8	12	5		15	10		13				4	1			6^{3}	14	2	39
		3		13		7			11^{3}	9	8	12	5			10^{1}		15				4	1			6^{4}	14	2^{2}	40
		3				7		13	10^{1}	11	8		5		9^{2}	12		6				4^{3}		1		2	14		41
		3		9^{1}		7			12	10	8	14	5			11^{2}		6				4		1		2^{3}	13		42
		3		9^{1}		7			11^{2}	10	8		5			13		6				4^{3}		1		2	12	14	43
		3^{1}		15		7			13	9	8		5			10^{2}		6			14	4^{4}		1		2	11^{3}	12	44
				10		9			12	11	6		3			2		8				5		1		4	7^{1}		45
				13		7			11^{1}	10	8	12	5			9		6^{3}				4		1	3^{2}	2	14		46

FA Cup

Third Round	Exeter C	(a)	2-0
Fourth Round	Everton	(a)	0-3

Carabao Cup

First Round	Walsall	(a)	0-0
(Sheffield W won 4-2 on penalties)			
Second Round	Rochdale	(a)	2-0
Third Round	Fulham	(a)	0-2

SHREWSBURY TOWN

FOUNDATION

Shrewsbury School having provided a number of the early England and Wales international players it is not surprising that there was a Town club as early as 1876 which won the Birmingham Senior Cup in 1879. However, the present Shrewsbury Town club was formed in 1886 and won the Welsh FA Cup as early as 1891.

Montgomery Waters Meadow, Oteley Road, Shrewsbury, Shropshire SY2 6ST.

Telephone: (01743) 289 177.

Ticket Office: (01743) 273 943.

Website: www.shrewsburytown.com

Email: info@shrewsburytown.co.uk

Ground Capacity: 9,875.

Record Attendance: 18,917 v Walsall, Division 3, 26 April 1961 (at Gay Meadow); 10,210 v Chelsea, League Cup 4th rd, 28 October 2014 (at New Meadow).

Pitch Measurements: 100m × 67m (109.5yd × 73.5yd).

Chairman: Roland Wycherley.

Chief Executive: Brian Caldwell.

Manager: Steve Cotterill.

Assistant Manager: Aaron Wilbraham.

Colours: Blue and yellow striped shirts, blue shorts with yellow trim, blue socks with yellow trim.

Year Formed: 1886.

Turned Professional: 1896.

Club Nicknames: 'Town', 'Blues', 'Salop'. The name 'Salop' is a colloquialism for the county of Shropshire. Since Shrewsbury is the only club in Shropshire, cries of 'Come on Salop' are frequently used!

Grounds: 1886, Old Racecourse Ground; 1889, Ambler's Field; 1893, Sutton Lane; 1895, Barracks Ground; 1910, Gay Meadow; 2007, New Meadow (renamed ProStar Stadium 2008; Greenhous Meadow 2010; Montgomery Waters Meadow 2017).

First Football League Game: 19 August 1950, Division 3 (N), v Scunthorpe U (a) D 0–0 – Egglestone; Fisher, Lewis; Wheatley, Depear, Robinson; Griffin, Hope, Jackson, Brown, Barker.

Record League Victory: 7–0 v Swindon T, Division 3 (S), 6 May 1955 – McBride; Bannister, Skeech; Wallace, Maloney, Candlin; Price, O'Donnell (1), Weigh (4), Russell, McCue (2); 7–0 v Gillingham, FL 2, 13 September 2008 – Daniels; Herd, Tierney, Davies (2), Jackson (1) (Langmead), Coughlan (1), Cansdell-Sherriff (1), Thornton, Hibbert (1) (Hindmarch), Holt (pen), McIntyre (Ashton).

Record Cup Victory: 11–2 v Marine, FA Cup 1st rd, 11 November 1995 – Edwards; Seabury (Dempsey (1)), Withe (1), Evans (1), Whiston (2), Scott (1), Woods, Stevens (1), Spink (3) (Anthrobus), Walton, Berkley, (1 og).

HONOURS

League Champions: Division 3 – 1978–79; Third Division – 1993–94.
Runners-up: FL 2 – 2011–12, 2014–15; Division 4 – 1974–75; Conference – (3rd) 2003–04 *(promoted via play-offs)*.

FA Cup: 6th rd – 1979, 1982.

League Cup: semi-final – 1961.

League Trophy: *Runners-up:* 1996, 2018.

Welsh Cup Winners: 1891, 1938, 1977, 1979, 1984, 1985.
Runners-up: 1931, 1948, 1980.

FOOTBALL YEARBOOK FACT FILE

In 1894–95 Shrewsbury Town were drawn away to Mold Alyn Stars in the first round of the Welsh Cup but persuaded their opponents to switch the game to Town's ground with the promise of a guaranteed income from the gate. Shrewsbury, who at the time were top of the Shropshire and District League, led 9-0 at half time and added a further 12 goals in the second half to complete a club record 21-0 victory. Centre-forward Alfred Ellis scored seven goals in the game.

Record Defeat: 1–8 v Norwich C, Division 3 (S), 13 September 1952; 1–8 v Coventry C, Division 3, 22 October 1963.

Most League Points (2 for a win): 62, Division 4, 1974–75.

Most League Points (3 for a win): 89, FL 2, 2014–15.

Most League Goals: 101, Division 4, 1958–59.

Highest League Scorer in Season: Arthur Rowley, 38, Division 4, 1958–59.

Most League Goals in Total Aggregate: Arthur Rowley, 152, 1958–65 (thus completing his League record of 434 goals).

Most League Goals in One Match: 5, Alf Wood v Blackburn R, Division 3, 2 October 1971.

Most Capped Player: Aaron Pierre, 7 (12), Grenada.

Most League Appearances: Mickey Brown, 418, 1986–91; 1992–94; 1996–2001.

Youngest League Player: Graham French, 16 years 177 days v Reading, 30 September 1961.

Record Transfer Fee Received: £600,000 (rising to £1,500,000) from Manchester C for Joe Hart, May 2006.

Record Transfer Fee Paid: £200,000 to Tranmere R for Oliver Norburn, August 2018.

Football League Record: 1950 Elected to Division 3 (N); 1951–58 Division 3 (S); 1958–59 Division 4; 1959–74 Division 3; 1974–75 Division 4; 1975–79 Division 3; 1979–89 Division 2; 1989–94 Division 3; 1994–97 Division 2; 1997–2003 Division 3; 2003–04 Conference; 2004–12 FL 2; 2012–14 FL 1; 2014–15 FL 2; 2015– FL 1.

MANAGERS

W. Adams 1905–12
(Secretary-Manager)
A. Weston 1912–34
(Secretary-Manager)
Jack Roscamp 1934–35
Sam Ramsey 1935–36
Ted Bousted 1936–40
Leslie Knighton 1945–49
Harry Chapman 1949–50
Sammy Crooks 1950–54
Walter Rowley 1955–57
Harry Potts 1957–58
Johnny Spuhler 1958
Arthur Rowley 1958–68
Harry Gregg 1968–72
Maurice Evans 1972–73
Alan Durban 1974–78
Richie Barker 1978
Graham Turner 1978–84
Chic Bates 1984–87
Ian McNeill 1987–90
Asa Hartford 1990–91
John Bond 1991–93
Fred Davies 1994–97
(previously Caretaker-Manager 1993–94)
Jake King 1997–99
Kevin Ratcliffe 1999–2003
Jimmy Quinn 2003–04
Gary Peters 2004–08
Paul Simpson 2008–10
Graham Turner 2010–14
Mike Jackson 2014
Micky Mellon 2014–16
Paul Hurst 2016–18
John Askey 2018
Sam Ricketts 2018–20
Steve Cotterill November 2020–

LATEST SEQUENCES

Longest Sequence of League Wins: 7, 28.10.1995 – 16.12.1995.

Longest Sequence of League Defeats: 11, 9.4.2003 – 14.8.2004. (Spread over 2 periods in Football League. 2003–04 season in Conference.)

Longest Sequence of League Draws: 6, 30.10.1963 – 14.12.1963.

Longest Sequence of Unbeaten League Matches: 16, 30.10.1993 – 26.2.1994.

Longest Sequence Without a League Win: 18, 8.3.2003 – 14.8.2004.

Successive Scoring Runs: 28 from 7.9.1960.

Successive Non-scoring Runs: 6 from 1.1.1991.

TEN YEAR LEAGUE RECORD

		P	*W*	*D*	*L*	*F*	*A*	*Pts*	*Pos*
2011-12	FL 2	46	26	10	10	66	41	88	2
2012-13	FL 1	46	13	16	17	54	60	55	16
2013-14	FL 1	46	9	15	22	44	65	42	23
2014-15	FL 2	46	27	8	11	67	31	89	2
2015-16	FL 1	46	13	11	22	58	79	50	20
2016-17	FL 1	46	13	12	21	46	63	51	18
2017-18	FL 1	46	25	12	9	60	39	87	3
2018-19	FL 1	46	12	16	18	51	59	52	18
2019-20	FL 1	34	10	11	13	31	42	41	15§
2020-21	FL 1	46	13	15	18	50	57	54	17

§Decided on points-per-game (1.21)

DID YOU KNOW ?

Shrewsbury Town have reached Wembley on five occasions but have yet to win. The Shrews have been beaten in three play-off finals and have twice reached the final of the EFL Trophy, losing 2-1 to Rotherham United in 1996 and 1-0 to Lincoln City in 2018.

SHREWSBURY TOWN – SKY BET LEAGUE ONE 2020–21 LEAGUE RECORD

Match No.	Date	Venue	Opponents	Result		H/T Score	Lg Pos.	Goalscorers	Attendance
1	Sept 12	A	Portsmouth	D	0-0	0-0	13		0
2	19	H	Northampton T	L	1-2	0-1	19	Whalley [54]	0
3	26	A	Plymouth Arg	D	1-1	1-1	20	Vela [14]	0
4	Oct 3	H	Gillingham	D	1-1	1-0	18	Walker [12]	0
5	17	A	AFC Wimbledon	W	1-0	0-0	15	Clarke [90]	0
6	20	H	Bristol R	L	0-1	0-1	17		0
7	24	H	Rochdale	L	1-2	1-2	19	Pierre [45]	0
8	27	A	Fleetwood T	L	0-1	0-1	20		0
9	31	A	Peterborough U	L	1-5	1-2	21	Daniels, J [18]	0
10	Nov 3	H	Burton Alb	D	1-1	0-0	21	Udoh [90]	0
11	14	H	Swindon T	D	3-3	2-1	21	Pierre [11], Millar [16], Edwards [56]	0
12	21	A	Ipswich T	L	1-2	1-0	21	Norburn (pen) [4]	0
13	24	A	Milton Keynes D	D	2-2	1-0	22	Whalley [1], Pugh [49]	0
14	Dec 2	H	Accrington S	D	2-2	1-1	22	Pierre [26], Whalley [86]	0
15	5	H	Charlton Ath	D	1-1	0-0	22	Norburn (pen) [90]	0
16	12	A	Hull C	W	1-0	1-0	21	Daniels, C [27]	0
17	15	A	Lincoln C	W	1-0	1-0	20	Whalley [38]	0
18	22	A	Doncaster R	W	1-0	0-0	16	Pierre [53]	0
19	26	A	Wigan Ath	D	1-1	0-0	17	Whalley [66]	0
20	29	H	Blackpool	W	1-0	1-0	16	Udoh [38]	0
21	Jan 23	A	Sunderland	L	0-1	0-1	17		0
22	30	H	Peterborough U	W	2-0	0-0	17	Chapman 2 [51, 86]	0
23	Feb 2	H	Crewe Alex	L	0-1	0-1	17		0
24	6	A	Swindon T	W	1-0	1-0	17	Chapman [34]	0
25	9	H	Sunderland	W	2-1	0-1	17	Ebanks-Landell [52], Chapman [67]	0
26	20	A	Accrington S	D	1-1	0-0	17	Whalley [77]	0
27	23	H	Milton Keynes D	W	4-2	3-1	16	Goss 2 [4, 57], Norburn (pen) [8], Main (pen) [20]	0
28	27	A	Bristol R	L	1-2	0-1	17	Udoh [90]	0
29	Mar 2	H	AFC Wimbledon	D	1-1	1-0	17	Chapman [35]	0
30	6	H	Fleetwood T	L	0-2	0-1	17		0
31	9	A	Rochdale	W	2-0	0-0	17	Daniels, J [55], Vela [64]	0
32	13	A	Charlton Ath	D	1-1	0-0	17	Goss [56]	0
33	20	H	Hull C	D	1-1	0-0	17	Ingram (og) [53]	0
34	23	A	Burton Alb	W	2-1	1-0	17	Main [6], Chapman [56]	0
35	27	H	Portsmouth	L	1-2	0-2	17	Ogbeta [52]	0
36	Apr 2	A	Northampton T	L	0-1	0-1	17		0
37	5	H	Plymouth Arg	W	3-0	0-0	17	Whalley 2 [52, 77], Ogbeta [81]	0
38	10	A	Gillingham	D	0-0	0-0	17		0
39	13	A	Oxford U	L	1-4	0-2	18	Chapman [51]	0
40	17	H	Doncaster R	L	0-2	0-1	18		0
41	20	H	Wigan Ath	L	1-2	0-2	18	Norburn [66]	0
42	24	A	Blackpool	W	1-0	0-0	16	Pennington [53]	0
43	27	H	Lincoln C	L	0-1	0-1	17		0
44	May 1	H	Oxford U	L	2-3	2-1	17	Pennington [16], Vela [25]	0
45	4	H	Ipswich T	D	0-0	0-0	17		0
46	9	A	Crewe Alex	L	2-3	2-2	17	Whalley [34], Udoh [42]	0

Final League Position: 17

GOALSCORERS

League (50): Whalley 9, Chapman 7, Norburn 4 (3 pens), Pierre 4, Udoh 4, Goss 3, Vela 3, Daniels, J 2, Main 2 (1 pen), Ogbeta 2, Pennington 2, Clarke 1, Daniels, C 1, Ebanks-Landell 1, Edwards 1, Millar 1, Pugh 1, Walker 1, own goal 1.
FA Cup (3): Daniels C 1, Udoh 1, Walker 1.
Carabao Cup (3): Cummings 1, High 1, Pyke 1.
Papa John's Trophy (10): Tracey 4, Barnett 2, Cummings 2, High 1, Millar 1.

Sarkic M 26	Williams R 39+1	Ebanks-Landell E 41	Pierre A 25+1	Golbourne S 6+4	Vela J 43+1	High S 8+4	Walker B 15+8	Whalley S 32+6	Pyke R 2+10	Cummings J 7+4	Fossey M 6+1	Norburn O 37+2	Barnett R 3+4	Daniels J 8+11	Udoh D 23+16	Love D 12+2	Burgoyne H 17+1	Clarke L 6+4	Iliev D 3	Zamburek J 4+2	Tracey S 2+6	Daniels C 14	Pugh M 6+2	Millar M 9	Edwards D 5+26	Goss S 15+5	Pennington M 18+1	Chapman H 16+7	Sears R 2+3	Ogbeta N 25	Davis D 14+7	Main C 14+6	Caton C 1+2	Bloxham T 2+2	Match No.
1	2[1]	3	4▮	5	6[2]	7	8	9	10	11[3]	12	13	14																						1
1	4	3[1]		5	6	7	8	11	10[2]	9	2[3]			12	13	14																			2
1[1]	4		3	5	8	6[2]	7	11		9	2	13			10[3]		12	14																	3
		3	4	5	6	13	7	11[1]			2	8	9[2]	12			1	10																	4
	2	3	4	5	8	14	12			11[2]		7	9[3]		13			10	1	6[1]															5
		3	4	5[1]	6	2	7[3]			9		8		14	11[2]			10	1	12	13														6
	3		4		6[2]	8[1]	13			11	2[3]	7	12		9		1	10		14		5													7
	4	3	14		6		7[3]				2	8	9[2]	13	10		1	12				5	11[1]												8
	2	3	4		6▮	7				12		8		9	10[2]		1				13	5	11[1]												9
	3	4	5			7[3]	12			11	2[1]	8		13	10		1			9[2]		6	14												10
	2	3	4			14	12	11[3]				7			13		1				10[2]	8	9	5[1]	6										11
	2	3	4		12		15	9[3]				6[1]	13		14		1				11[2]	8	10[4]	5	7										12
	2		4		11	6	3	9[3]		12			14	13					1			8	10[1]	5	7[2]										13
1	3		2	14	6	12	4[2]	11				7			10[3]							9		5	13	8[1]									14
1	2	3	4		7			10		13		6		14	11[2]							8	9[1]	5[3]	12										15
1	2	3	4		8			10[1]				6			11[3]						14	9	12	5	13	7[2]									16
1	2	3	4		8			10[3]		14		6		13	11[2]							9		5	12	7[1]									17
1	2	3	4	14	6			10				7			11[2]			13			12[3]	9		5	8[1]										18
1	2	3	4		7			10				6			12			11[1]		9[2]	13	8		5											19
1	2	3	4	14	7			10[3]				6		5[1]	11[4]			15		9[2]	12	8			13										20
1	5[1]	3	4		6			10				7			14	8[3]		11[2]								13	2	9	12						21
1	2	3	4		8			10	14			6			11[3]	5[1]									13			7[2]	12	9					22
1	3[3]	4	5		9			10	14			7		12	11[2]													8	2[1]	6	13				23
1	3	4			6			11[3]	13			8			15	2									14	7[1]		9[2]		5	12	10[4]			24
1	4	3			6			11				8		12	14	2									13	7[2]		9[1]		5		10[3]			25
1	4	3			6			11				8[2]			12	2									13	7[3]		9		5	14	10[1]			26
1	4	3		14	8			9[4]	13			6		12	16	2[1]									15	7[3]		11[5]		5		10[2]			27
1	4	3			8[3]			9	15			6			12										13	7[2]	2	11[1]		5	14	10[4]			28
1	5	4			7			13				9[1]		2[2]	11										14		3	12		6	8[3]	10			29
1	4	3			6		13	11	14					5[1]	16										15	12	2[2]	9[4]		8	7[5]	10[3]			30
	4	3			8		2[1]	11[3]	15					5	10[4]		1								13	7	12			9	6[2]	14			31
	4	3			8		6[4]	15						5	13		1								12	7[3]	2	11[1]		9	14	10[2]			32
1	4	3			7		6[1]	10[4]				8[3]		5	11[2]										15		2	14		9	12	13			33
	4	3			8									5[1]			1								13	7	2	10[2]	12	9	6	11			34
	4	3			7			13	15						11[2]		1								14	9[3]	2[4]	12	5[1]	8	6	10			35
1	2[3]	3	4		6			13	12			7[4]				5									15	14		11[2]		9	8	10[1]			36
1	4	3			6			10[4]	15			8			11[1]	5[2]									14	7[3]	2			9	13	12			37
1	4	3			6			10[1]				8			11[2]	5									14	7[3]	2	12		9		13			38
1	4[3]	3			6[1]		14					8[4]			12	5									15	13	2	10		9	7	11[2]			39
1	4[1]	3			8		12	9				7			11[2]												2	10		5	6		13		40
	4[1]	3			7		8[2]	11[4]				6			10[3]		1								14		2	12		9	5	13	15		41
		4			8			12				6				13	1								7		3	10[2]		5	2	11	9[1]		42
		3			8		4	10[3]				6[1]				5	1								14		2	12		9	7	11[2]		13	43
	14	3	4		6		8[3]	12				7			15		1										2	10[1]		9[4]	5	13		11[2]	44
			4		7		3	10[4]				6			13	5[1]	1								12	14	2	15		9[3]	8			11[2]	45
		3	4		6			10				7			11		1								12	8[1]	2			9[2]	5			13	46

FA Cup

First Round	Cambridge U	(a)	2-0
Second Round (aet)	Oxford C	(h)	1-0
Third Round	Southampton	(a)	0-2

Carabao Cup

First Round	Middlesbrough	(a)	3-4

Papa John's Trophy

Group C (N)	Newcastle U U21	(h)	3-0
Group C (N)	Bolton W	(h)	2-1
Group C (N)	Crewe Alex	(a)	4-3
Second Round (N)	Lincoln C	(h)	1-4

SOUTHAMPTON

FOUNDATION

The club was formed by members of the St Mary's Church of England Young Men's Association at a meeting of the Y.M.A. in November 1885 and it was named as such. For the sake of brevity this was usually shortened to St Mary's Y.M.A. The rector Canon Albert Basil Orme Wilberforce was elected president. The name was changed to plain St Mary's during 1887–88 and did not become Southampton St Mary's until 1894, the inaugural season in the Southern League.

St Mary's Stadium, Britannia Road, Southampton, Hampshire SO14 5FP.

Telephone: (0845) 688 9448.

Ticket Office: (0845) 688 9288.

Website: www.southamptonfc.com

Email: sfc@southamptonfc.com

Ground Capacity: 32,384.

Record Attendance: 31,044 v Manchester U, Division 1, 8 October 1969 (at The Dell); 32,363 v Coventry C, FL C, 28 April 2012 (at St Mary's).

Pitch Measurements: 105m × 68m (115yd × 74.5yd).

Chairman: Gao Jisheng.

Managing Director: Toby Steele.

Manager: Ralph Hasenhüttl.

First-Team Assistant Coaches: Richard Kitzbichler, Dave Watson, Craig Fleming, Kelvin Davis.

Colours: Red shirt with white diagonal sash and black trim, black shorts, red socks with white hoop.

Year Formed: 1885. ***Turned Professional:*** 1894.

Previous Names: 1885, St Mary's Young Men's Association; 1887–88, St Mary's; 1894–95, Southampton St Mary's; 1897, Southampton.

Club Nickname: 'Saints'.

Grounds: 1885, 'The Common' (from 1887 also used the County Cricket Ground and Antelope Cricket Ground); 1889, Antelope Cricket Ground; 1896, The County Cricket Ground; 1898, The Dell; 2001, St Mary's.

First Football League Game: 28 August 1920, Division 3, v Gillingham (a) D 1–1 – Allen; Parker, Titmuss; Shelley, Campbell, Turner; Barratt, Dominy (1), Rawlings, Moore, Foxall.

Record League Victory: 8–0 v Sunderland, Premier League, 18 October 2014 – Forster; Clyne, Fonte, Alderweireld, Bertrand; Davis S (Mané), Schneiderlin, Cork (1); Long (Wanyama (1)), Pelle (2) (Mayuka), Tadic (1) (plus 3 Sunderland own goals).

Record Cup Victory: 7–1 v Ipswich T, FA Cup 3rd rd, 7 January 1961 – Reynolds; Davies, Traynor, Conner, Page, Huxford, Paine (1), O'Brien (3 incl. 1p), Reeves, Mulgrew (2), Penk (1).

HONOURS

League Champions: Division 3 – 1959–60; Division 3S – 1921–22.
Runners-up: Division 1 – 1983–84; FL C – 2011–12; Division 2 – 1965–66, 1977–78; FL 1 – 2010–11; Division 3 – 1920–21.

FA Cup Winners: 1976.
Runners-up: 1900, 1902, 2003.

League Cup: *Runners-up:* 1979, 2017.

League Trophy Winners: 2010.

Full Members' Cup: *Runners-up:* 1992.

European Competitions
Fairs Cup: 1969–70.
UEFA Cup: 1971–72, 1981–82, 1982–83, 1984–85, 2003–04.
Europa League: 2015–16, 2016–17.
European Cup-Winners' Cup: 1976–77 *(qf)*.

FOOTBALL YEARBOOK FACT FILE

Southampton and Norwich City were both promoted from the Third Division in 1959–60 and after the season concluded played each other in home and away charity matches. The game at The Dell, which was to help raise funds for the World Refugee Appeal, ended in a 1-1 draw with Saints' goalscorer being Tommy Traynor.

Record Defeat: 0–9 v Leicester C, Premier League, 25 October 2019; 0–9 v Manchester U, Premier League, 25 October 2020.

Most League Points (2 for a win): 61, Division 3 (S), 1921–22 and Division 3, 1959–60.

Most League Points (3 for a win): 92, FL 1, 2010–11.

Most League Goals: 112, Division 3 (S), 1957–58.

Highest League Scorer in Season: Derek Reeves, 39, Division 3, 1959–60.

Most League Goals in Total Aggregate: Mike Channon, 185, 1966–77, 1979–82.

Most League Goals in One Match: 5, Charlie Wayman v Leicester C, Division 2, 23 October 1948.

Most Capped Player: Maya Yoshida, 83 (107), Japan.

Most League Appearances: Terry Paine, 713, 1956–74.

Youngest League Player: Theo Walcott, 16 years 143 days v Wolverhampton W, 6 August 2005.

Record Transfer Fee Received: £75,000,000 from Liverpool for Virgil van Dijk, January 2018.

Record Transfer Fee Paid: £20,000,000 to Liverpool for Danny Ings, July 2019.

Football League Record: 1920 Original Member of Division 3; 1921–22 Division 3 (S); 1922–53 Division 2; 1953–58 Division 3 (S); 1958–60 Division 3; 1960–66 Division 2; 1966–74 Division 1; 1974–78 Division 2; 1978–92 Division 1; 1992–2005 Premier League; 2005–09 FL C; 2009–11 FL 1; 2011–12 FL C; 2012– Premier League.

LATEST SEQUENCES

Longest Sequence of League Wins: 10, 16.4.2011 – 20.8.2011.

Longest Sequence of League Defeats: 6, 16.1.2021 – 14.2.2021.

Longest Sequence of League Draws: 8, 29.8.2005 – 15.10.2005.

Longest Sequence of Unbeaten League Matches: 19, 5.9.1921 – 31.12.1921.

Longest Sequence Without a League Win: 20, 30.8.1969 – 27.12.1969.

Successive Scoring Runs: 28 from 10.2.2008.

Successive Non-scoring Runs: 5 from 22.9.2018.

MANAGERS

Cecil Knight 1894–95
(Secretary-Manager)
Charles Robson 1895–97
Ernest Arnfield 1897–1911
(Secretary-Manager)
(continued as Secretary)
George Swift 1911–12
Ernest Arnfield 1912–19
Jimmy McIntyre 1919–24
Arthur Chadwick 1925–31
George Kay 1931–36
George Gross 1936–37
Tom Parker 1937–43
J. R. Sarjantson stepped down from the board to act as Secretary-Manager 1943–47 with the next two listed being Team Managers during this period
Arthur Dominy 1943–46
Bill Dodgin Snr 1946–49
Sid Cann 1949–51
George Roughton 1952–55
Ted Bates 1955–73
Lawrie McMenemy 1973–85
Chris Nicholl 1985–91
Ian Branfoot 1991–94
Alan Ball 1994–95
Dave Merrington 1995–96
Graeme Souness 1996–97
Dave Jones 1997–2000
Glenn Hoddle 2000–01
Stuart Gray 2001
Gordon Strachan 2001–04
Paul Sturrock 2004
Steve Wigley 2004
Harry Redknapp 2004–05
George Burley 2005–08
Nigel Pearson 2008
Jan Poortvliet 2008–09
Mark Wotte 2009
Alan Pardew 2009–10
Nigel Adkins 2010–13
Mauricio Pochettino 2013–14
Ronald Koeman 2014–16
Claude Puel 2016–17
Mauricio Pellegrino 2017–18
Mark Hughes 2018
Ralph Hasenhüttl December 2018–

TEN YEAR LEAGUE RECORD

		P	W	D	L	F	A	Pts	Pos
2011-12	FL C	46	26	10	10	85	46	88	2
2012-13	PR Lge	38	9	14	15	49	60	41	14
2013-14	PR Lge	38	15	11	12	54	46	56	8
2014-15	PR Lge	38	18	6	14	54	33	60	7
2015-16	PR Lge	38	18	9	11	59	41	63	6
2016-17	PR Lge	38	12	10	16	41	48	46	8
2017-18	PR Lge	38	7	15	16	37	56	36	17
2018-19	PR Lge	38	9	12	17	45	65	39	16
2019-20	PR Lge	38	15	7	16	51	60	52	11
2020-21	PR Lge	38	12	7	19	47	68	43	15

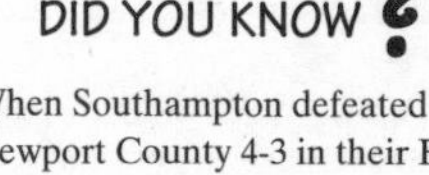

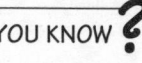

When Southampton defeated Newport County 4-3 in their FA Cup third round first leg tie in January 1946 it was their first home win in the competition since 1927. Saints had trailed 2-0 after 10 minutes of the match but fought back to win with goals from Jack Bradley, Don Roper, Ted Bates and Doug McGibbon.

SOUTHAMPTON – PREMIER LEAGUE 2020–21 LEAGUE RECORD

Match No.	*Date*	*Venue*	*Opponents*	*Result*	*H/T Score*	*Lg Pos.*	*Goalscorers*	*Attendance*
1	Sept 12	A	Crystal Palace	L 0-1	0-1	18		0
2	20	H	Tottenham H	L 2-5	1-1	19	Ings 2 (1 pen) $^{32, 90 (p)}$	0
3	26	A	Burnley	W 1-0	1-0	15	Ings ^{5}	0
4	Oct 4	H	WBA	W 2-0	1-0	11	Djenepo ^{41}, Romeu ^{69}	0
5	17	A	Chelsea	D 3-3	1-2	10	Ings ^{43}, Adams ^{57}, Vestergaard ^{90}	0
6	25	H	Everton	W 2-0	2-0	6	Ward-Prowse ^{27}, Adams ^{35}	0
7	Nov 1	A	Aston Villa	W 4-3	3-0	4	Vestergaard ^{20}, Ward-Prowse 2 $^{33, 45}$, Ings ^{58}	0
8	6	H	Newcastle U	W 2-0	1-0	1	Adams ^{7}, Armstrong ^{82}	0
9	23	A	Wolverhampton W	D 1-1	0-0	5	Walcott ^{58}	0
10	29	H	Manchester U	L 2-3	2-0	5	Bednarek ^{23}, Ward-Prowse ^{33}	0
11	Dec 7	A	Brighton & HA	W 2-1	1-1	5	Vestergaard ^{45}, Ings (pen) ^{81}	2000
12	13	H	Sheffield U	W 3-0	1-0	4	Adams ^{34}, Armstrong ^{62}, Redmond ^{83}	2000
13	16	A	Arsenal	D 1-1	1-0	3	Walcott ^{18}	0
14	19	H	Manchester C	L 0-1	0-1	5		2000
15	26	A	Fulham	D 0-0	0-0	9		0
16	29	H	West Ham U	D 0-0	0-0	9		0
17	Jan 4	H	Liverpool	W 1-0	1-0	6	Ings ^{2}	0
18	16	A	Leicester C	L 0-2	0-1	8		0
19	26	H	Arsenal	L 1-3	1-2	11	Armstrong ^{3}	0
20	30	H	Aston Villa	L 0-1	0-1	11		0
21	Feb 2	A	Manchester U	L 0-9	0-4	12		0
22	6	A	Newcastle U	L 2-3	1-3	12	Minamino ^{30}, Ward-Prowse ^{48}	0
23	14	H	Wolverhampton W	L 1-2	1-0	13	Ings ^{25}	0
24	20	H	Chelsea	D 1-1	1-0	13	Minamino ^{33}	0
25	23	A	Leeds U	L 0-3	0-0	14		0
26	Mar 1	A	Everton	L 0-1	0-1	14		0
27	6	A	Sheffield U	W 2-0	1-0	14	Ward-Prowse (pen) ^{32}, Adams ^{49}	0
28	10	A	Manchester C	L 2-5	1-3	14	Ward-Prowse (pen) ^{25}, Adams ^{56}	0
29	14	H	Brighton & HA	L 1-2	1-1	14	Adams ^{27}	0
30	Apr 4	H	Burnley	W 3-2	2-2	13	Armstrong ^{31}, Ings ^{42}, Redmond ^{66}	0
31	12	A	WBA	L 0-3	0-2	14		0
32	21	A	Tottenham H	L 1-2	1-0	14	Ings ^{30}	0
33	30	H	Leicester C	D 1-1	0-0	14	Ward-Prowse (pen) ^{61}	0
34	May 8	A	Liverpool	L 0-2	0-1	16		0
35	11	H	Crystal Palace	W 3-1	1-1	14	Ings 2 $^{19, 75}$, Adams ^{48}	0
36	15	H	Fulham	W 3-1	1-0	13	Adams ^{27}, Tella ^{60}, Walcott ^{82}	0
37	18	H	Leeds U	L 0-2	0-0	14		7291
38	23	A	West Ham U	L 0-3	0-2	15		10,000

Final League Position: 15

GOALSCORERS

League (47): Ings 12 (2 pens), Adams 9, Ward-Prowse 8 (3 pens), Armstrong 4, Vestergaard 3, Walcott 3, Minamino 2, Redmond 2, Bednarek 1, Djenepo 1, Romeu 1, Tella 1.
FA Cup (8): Redmond 2, Armstrong 1, Djenepo 1, Ings 1, N'Lundulu 1, Ward-Prowse 1, own goal 1.
Carabao Cup (0).
Papa John's Trophy (3): Bellis 1, Olaigbe 1, Slattery 1.

McCarthy A 30	Walker-Peters K 30	Stephens J 17 + 1	Bednarek J 36	Bertrand R 29	Smallbone W 2 + 1	Ward-Prowse J 38	Romeu O 20 + 1	Redmond N 17 + 12	Adams C 30 + 6	Ings D 26 + 3	Vestergaard J 29 + 1	Djenepo M 15 + 12	Long S 1 + 10	Armstrong S 32 + 1	Tella N 7 + 11	Obafemi M — + 4	Walcott T 20 + 1	Diallo I 10 + 12	N'Lundulu D — + 13	Forster F 8	Valery Y 1 + 2	Vokins J 1	Watts C — + 3	Jankewitz A 1 + 1	Ramsey K 1	Tchaptchet A — + 1	Minamino T 9 + 1	Salisu M 8 + 4	*Match No.*
1	2	3	4^1	5	6^2	7	8	9	10^3	11	12	13	14																1
1	2	3	4	5	12	7	8^1		10^3	11		9	14	6^2	13														2
1	2		3	5		7	8		10^2	11	4	9^1		6	13	12													3
1	2		3	5		7	8	12	10^2	11	4	9^1	13	6															4
1	2		3	5		7	8^3	9^1	10^2	11	4		13		12		6	14											5
1	2		3	5		7	8	9	11^2	10	4			6^1				12	13										6
1	2	12	3^1	5^2		8	7		11	10^3	4		14	6			9	13											7
1	2	5	3			8	7	12	10		4	9^1	13	6			11^2												8
1	2		3	5		7	8		11		4	9^1	12	6^2			10	13											9
1	2^2		3	5		7	8		11		4	9^1	12	6^3			10	14	13										10
1	2		3	5		7	8	13	11	12	4	9^1		6			10^2												11
1	2		3	5		7	8^3	12	11^2	10	4			6			9^1	14	13										12
1	2		3	5		7	8	12	11	10	4	13		6^2			9^1												13
1	2		3	5		7	8	13	11^3	10^1	4	9^2			12		6		14										14
1	2	4	3	5		7			10			13	11^1	6^2			9	8	12										15
1	2	4	3	5		7	8		11^1	10		9^2	12	13			6												16
	2	4	3	5		8				10^2		9^1		6	12		11^3	7	13	1	14								17
1	2	4	3	5	9^1	8			11^2				13	6			10	7^3	12		14								18
1		4	3			8		12	10	11^3				9			6^2	7	13		2	5^1	14						19
1		4	3	5		2	7^3	11	13	10		12		9			6^2	8^1						14					20
1		4	3■	5		7		12	10	11^1		6^2		9										8■	2	13			21
1		2^1	3	5		7	8	6	10	11	4								12								9		22
1	2^3		3	5		7	8	11	13	10	4	12		6^2													9^1	14	23
1			2	5		7	8	11^3	13	10^2	4	6			12				14								9^1	3	24
1			2	5		7	8^3	11^2	10	13	3	14		6	9^1												12	4	25
			2	5		7		9^3	10^2	11	3	6		8	12				13	1			14					4^1	26
	2		3	5		8		13	12	10^1	4	14		6	11^2			7		1							9^3		27
1		7^2	3	2		6		8	11		4	10^1		9^3	12			13					14					5	28
	2		3	5		7		12	9		4	13		6^3	10^2			8	14	1							11^1		29
	2		3	5		7		11	13	10^2	4	14		6^1			9^3	8		1								12	30
	2^2		3	5		7		11	12	10^3	4	14		9	13		6^1	8		1									31
1	2		3			7		14	10	11^1	4	13		8	9^3		6^2	12										5	32
1	2	5	3			7		11	10^3		4■			8	9^1			13	14								6^2	12	33
	2	5	3			7		9	10^3		4	14		8	11^1	12	6^2	13		1									34
	2	5	3^1			7		9	10	11^2	4			8		13				1							6	12	35
1	2	3				7		9	11	10^1	4			8^3	12		13	14									6^2	5	36
1	2	3				7		13	10^1	12	4	9		8	11^2		6^3	14										5	37
1	2^1		3			7	12	9		10^3	4			6	13	14		8									11^2	5	38

FA Cup

Third Round	Shrewsbury T	(h)	2-0
Fourth Round	Arsenal	(h)	1-0
Fifth Round	Wolverhampton W	(a)	2-0
Sixth Round	Bournemouth	(a)	3-0
Semi-Final	Leicester C	(a)	0-1

Carabao Cup

Second Round	Brentford	(h)	0-2

Papa John's Trophy (Southampton U21)

Group C (S)	Stevenage	(a)	1-2
Group C (S)	Northampton T	(a)	0-5
Group C (S)	Milton Keynes D	(a)	2-1

SOUTHEND UNITED

FOUNDATION

The leading club in Southend around the turn of the 20th century was Southend Athletic, but they were an amateur concern. Southend United was a more ambitious professional club when they were founded in 1906, employing Bob Jack as secretary-manager and immediately joining the Second Division of the Southern League.

Roots Hall Stadium, Victoria Avenue, Southend-on-Sea, Essex SS2 6NQ.

Telephone: (01702) 304 050.

Ticket Office: (08444) 770 077.

Website: www.southendunited.co.uk

Email: info@southend-united.co.uk

Ground Capacity: 12,055.

Record Attendance: 22,862 v Tottenham H, FA Cup 3rd rd replay, 11 January 1936 (at Southend Stadium); 31,090 v Liverpool, FA Cup 3rd rd, 10 January 1979 (at Roots Hall).

Pitch Measurements: 100.5m × 67.5m (110yd × 74yd).

Chairman: Ron Martin.

Chief Executive: Tom Lawrence.

Manager: Phil Brown.

Assistant Manager: Ricky Duncan.

Colours: Navy blue shirts with white trim, navy blue shorts, white socks.

Year Formed: 1906.

Turned Professional: 1906.

Club Nicknames: 'The Blues', 'The Shrimpers'.

Grounds: 1906, Roots Hall, Prittlewell; 1920, Kursaal; 1934, Southend Stadium; 1955, Roots Hall Football Ground.

First Football League Game: 28 August 1920, Division 3, v Brighton & HA (a) W 2–0 – Capper; Reid, Newton; Wileman, Henderson, Martin; Nicholls, Nuttall, Fairclough (2), Myers, Dorsett.

Record League Victory: 9–2 v Newport Co, Division 3 (S), 5 September 1936 – McKenzie; Nelson, Everest (1); Deacon, Turner, Carr; Bolan, Lane (1), Goddard (4), Dickinson (2), Oswald (1).

Record Cup Victory: 10–1 v Golders Green, FA Cup 1st rd, 24 November 1934 – Moore; Morfitt, Kelly; Mackay, Joe Wilson, Carr (1); Lane (1), Johnson (5), Cheesmuir (2), Deacon (1), Oswald. 10–1 v Brentwood, FA Cup 2nd rd, 7 December 1968 – Roberts; Bentley, Birks; McMillan (1) Beesley, Kurila; Clayton, Chisnall, Moore (4), Best (5), Hamilton. 10–1 v Aldershot, Leyland DAF Cup prel rd, 6 November 1990 – Sansome; Austin, Powell, Cornwell, Prior (1), Tilson (3), Cawley, Butler, Ansah (1), Benjamin (1), Angell (4).

Record Defeat: 1–9 v Brighton & HA, Division 3, 27 November 1965; 0–8 v Crystal Palace, League Cup 2nd rd (1st leg), 25 September 1990.

HONOURS

League Champions: FL 1 – 2005–06; Division 4 – 1980–81.
Runners-up: Division 3 – 1990–91; Division 4 – 1971–72, 1977–78.

FA Cup: 3rd rd – 1921; 5th rd – 1926, 1952, 1976, 1993.

League Cup: quarter-final – 2007.

League Trophy: *Runners-up:* 2004, 2005, 2013.

FOOTBALL YEARBOOK FACT FILE

Southend United were originally formed as Prittlewell United at a meeting in April 1906 but changed their name to their current title the following month without playing a game. The new club played its first-ever game at home to Swindon Town Reserves in a Southern League Division Two match. United went down to a 1-0 defeat with the visitors scoring a second-half winner.

Most League Points (2 for a win): 67, Division 4, 1980–81.

Most League Points (3 for a win): 85, Division 3, 1990–91.

Most League Goals: 92, Division 3 (S), 1950–51.

Highest League Scorer in Season: Jim Shankly, 31, 1928–29; Sammy McCrory, 1957–58, both in Division 3 (S).

Most League Goals in Total Aggregate: Roy Hollis, 122, 1953–60.

Most League Goals in One Match: 5, Jim Shankly v Merthyr T, Division 3 (S), 1 March 1930.

Most Capped Player: Jason Demetriou, 20 (51), Cyprus.

Most League Appearances: Sandy Anderson, 452, 1950–63.

Youngest League Player: Phil O'Connor, 16 years 76 days v Lincoln C, 26 December 1969.

Record Transfer Fee Received: £2,000,000 (rising to £2,750,000) from Nottingham F for Stan Collymore, June 1993.

Record Transfer Fee Paid: £500,000 to Galatasaray for Mike Marsh, September 1995.

Football League Record: 1920 Original Member of Division 3; 1921–58 Division 3 (S); 1958–66 Division 3; 1966–72 Division 4; 1972–76 Division 3; 1976–78 Division 4; 1978–80 Division 3; 1980–81 Division 4; 1981–84 Division 3; 1984–87 Division 4; 1987–89 Division 3; 1989–90 Division 4; 1990–91 Division 3; 1991–92 Division 2; 1992–97 Division 1; 1997–98 Division 2; 1998–2004 Division 3; 2004–05 FL 2; 2005–06 FL 1; 2006–07 FL C; 2007–10 FL 1; 2010–15 FL 2; 2015–20 FL 1; 2020–21 FL 2; 2021– National League.

LATEST SEQUENCES

Longest Sequence of League Wins: 8, 29.8.2005 – 9.10.2005.

Longest Sequence of League Defeats: 7, 16.4.2016 – 13.8.2016.

Longest Sequence of League Draws: 6, 30.1.1982 – 19.2.1982.

Longest Sequence of Unbeaten League Matches: 16, 20.2.1932 – 29.8.1932.

Longest Sequence Without a League Win: 17, 26.8.2006 – 2.12.2006.

Successive Scoring Runs: 24 from 23.3.1929.

Successive Non-scoring Runs: 6 from 6.4.1979.

MANAGERS

Bob Jack 1906–10
George Molyneux 1910–11
O. M. Howard 1911–12
Joe Bradshaw 1912–19
Ned Liddell 1919–20
Tom Mather 1920–21
Ted Birnie 1921–34
David Jack 1934–40
Harry Warren 1946–56
Eddie Perry 1956–60
Frank Broome 1960
Ted Fenton 1961–65
Alvan Williams 1965–67
Ernie Shepherd 1967–69
Geoff Hudson 1969–70
Arthur Rowley 1970–76
Dave Smith 1976–83
Peter Morris 1983–84
Bobby Moore 1984–86
Dave Webb 1986–87
Dick Bate 1987
Paul Clark 1987–88
Dave Webb *(General Manager)* 1988–92
Colin Murphy 1992–93
Barry Fry 1993
Peter Taylor 1993–95
Steve Thompson 1995
Ronnie Whelan 1995–97
Alvin Martin 1997–99
Alan Little 1999–2000
David Webb 2000–01
Rob Newman 2001–03
Steve Wignall 2003
Steve Tilson 2003–10
Paul Sturrock 2010–13
Phil Brown 2013–18
Chris Powell 2018–19
Kevin Bond 2019
Sol Campbell 2019–20
Mark Molesley 2020–21
Phil Brown April 2021–

TEN YEAR LEAGUE RECORD

		P	*W*	*D*	*L*	*F*	*A*	*Pts*	*Pos*
2011-12	FL 2	46	25	8	13	77	48	83	4
2012-13	FL 2	46	16	13	17	61	55	61	11
2013-14	FL 2	46	19	15	12	56	39	72	5
2014-15	FL 2	46	24	12	10	54	38	84	5
2015-16	FL 1	46	16	11	19	58	64	59	14
2016-17	FL 1	46	20	12	14	70	53	72	7
2017-18	FL 1	46	17	12	17	58	62	63	10
2018-19	FL 1	46	14	8	24	55	68	50	19
2019-20	FL 1	35	4	7	24	39	85	19	22§
2020-21	FL 2	46	10	15	21	29	58	45	23

§Decided on points-per-game (0.54)

DID YOU KNOW ?

Southend United did not progress beyond the first round of the Football League Cup in any season between 1999–2000 and 2005–06, a run of seven seasons. During that time they played a total of nine matches, scoring just three goals and conceding a total of 23.

SOUTHEND UNITED – SKY BET LEAGUE TWO 2020–21 LEAGUE RECORD

Match No.	Date	Venue	Opponents	Result		H/T Score	Lg Pos.	Goalscorers	Attendance
1	Sept 12	H	Harrogate T	L	0-4	0-2	24		0
2	19	A	Carlisle U	L	0-2	0-2	24		1000
3	26	H	Morecambe	L	1-2	1-0	24	Acquah [5]	0
4	Oct 3	A	Crawley T	D	1-1	0-1	23	Ralph [84]	0
5	10	H	Exeter C	D	2-2	1-1	22	Goodship [26], Demetriou (pen) [65]	0
6	17	H	Cheltenham T	L	0-2	0-1	24		0
7	20	A	Salford C	L	0-3	0-1	24		0
8	24	A	Tranmere R	L	0-2	0-1	24		0
9	27	H	Oldham Ath	L	1-2	0-0	24	Clifford [76]	0
10	31	H	Port Vale	L	0-2	0-0	24		0
11	Nov 3	A	Bradford C	L	0-3	0-3	24		0
12	14	A	Walsall	W	1-0	0-0	24	Acquah [88]	0
13	24	H	Forest Green R	L	0-1	0-0	24		0
14	28	A	Bolton W	L	0-3	0-1	24		0
15	Dec 5	A	Stevenage	D	0-0	0-0	24		0
16	12	H	Scunthorpe U	W	1-0	0-0	24	Olayinka [80]	2000
17	15	H	Grimsby T	W	3-1	1-1	24	Taylor, K [1], Clifford [57], Halford [75]	2000
18	19	A	Mansfield T	D	1-1	1-0	24	Olayinka [27]	0
19	26	H	Colchester U	W	2-0	2-0	23	Akinola [10], Dieng [22]	0
20	29	A	Leyton Orient	L	0-2	0-0	24		0
21	Jan 9	H	Barrow	W	1-0	1-0	24	Hackett-Fairchild [3]	0
22	16	A	Grimsby T	D	0-0	0-0	24		0
23	19	H	Cambridge U	L	1-2	1-0	24	Akinola [27]	0
24	23	H	Mansfield T	L	0-1	0-0	24		0
25	26	H	Bradford C	L	1-3	1-1	24	Bwomono [31]	0
26	30	A	Port Vale	L	1-5	0-4	24	Ferguson [85]	0
27	Feb 9	A	Newport Co	W	1-0	0-0	23	Clifford [74]	0
28	13	A	Cambridge U	D	0-0	0-0	22		0
29	20	H	Bolton W	L	0-1	0-0	22		0
30	24	A	Forest Green R	W	3-1	1-0	22	Hobson [20], Dieng [55], Ferguson [70]	0
31	27	H	Salford C	D	0-0	0-0	22		0
32	Mar 2	A	Cheltenham T	L	0-1	0-0	22		0
33	6	A	Oldham Ath	D	0-0	0-0	23		0
34	9	H	Tranmere R	L	0-2	0-2	23		0
35	13	H	Stevenage	D	0-0	0-0	23		0
36	20	A	Scunthorpe U	D	1-1	0-0	23	Nathaniel-George (pen) [80]	0
37	23	H	Walsall	D	0-0	0-0	23		0
38	27	A	Harrogate T	W	1-0	0-0	23	Nathaniel-George [69]	0
39	Apr 3	H	Carlisle U	L	0-2	0-1	23		0
40	6	A	Morecambe	D	1-1	1-0	23	Dieng [18]	0
41	10	H	Crawley T	D	0-0	0-0	23		0
42	17	A	Exeter C	D	0-0	0-0	23		0
43	20	A	Colchester U	L	0-2	0-2	23		0
44	24	H	Leyton Orient	W	2-1	1-1	23	Cordner [42], Rush [76]	0
45	May 1	A	Barrow	W	2-1	1-1	23	White [30], Egbri [52]	0
46	8	H	Newport Co	D	1-1	1-0	23	Hobson [11]	0

Final League Position: 23

GOALSCORERS

League (29): Clifford 3, Dieng 3, Acquah 2, Akinola 2, Ferguson 2, Hobson 2, Nathaniel-George 2 (1 pen), Olayinka 2, Bwomono 1, Cordner 1, Demetriou 1 (1 pen), Egbri 1, Goodship 1, Hackett-Fairchild 1, Halford 1, Ralph 1, Rush 1, Taylor, K 1, White 1.
FA Cup (3): Egbri 1, Goodship 1, Olayinka 1.
Carabao Cup (0).
Papa John's Trophy (2): Humphrys 1, Sterling 1.

Oxley M 41	Bwomono E 38 + 3	Hobson S 41 + 3	Taylor R 4 + 8	Ralph N 7 / Seaden H — + 1	Gard L 1 + 2	Hutchinson I 2 / Ranger N — + 1	Egbri T 18 + 7	Goodship B 15 + 14	Green J 3	Kelman C 2 + 1 / Montgomery J 4	Kyprianou H 2 + 3	Kinali E — + 2 / Mellis J — + 3	Phillips H — + 1	McCormack A 12 + 8	Clifford T 22 + 6	Demetriou J 34 + 4	Taylor K 21 + 10	Acquah E 20 + 11	Rush M 2 + 5	Lennon H 9 / Coker O — + 1	Dieng T 35 + 1	Sterling K 5 + 5	Nathaniel-George A 16 + 13	Coker K — + 2	Olayinka J 17 + 3	White J 28	Akinola S 20 + 4	Hart S 18 + 3	Halford G 9 + 7	Klass M — + 2	Howard R — + 2	Walsh L 2 + 3	Hackett-Fairchild R 21 + 4	Cordner T 11 + 3	Ferguson N 17 + 2	Holmes R 8 + 6	Bass A 1	*Match No.*
1	2	3	4	5^{1}	6^{3}	7	8^{2}	9	10	11	12	13	14																									1
1	2	3	4	5	12	7	8	9^{3}	10	11^{2}		14		6^{1}	13																							2
1	2	4	3	5			6^{3}	11	9^{1}	12					13	7	8	10^{2}	14																			3
1	2	4	12	10	14		8	9^{3}							5^{1}	7	6	11		3^{2}	13																	4
1		2		5			10	9^{1}								6	7	11		3	4	8	12															5
1	5	2		8			12	9^{3}								7	6^{2}	10^{1}		4	3	11	13	14														6
1	2	14	12	5^{1}			8	9^{2}								7	10			4^{3}	3	11	13		6													7
1	2						6^{3}	13							5	8	9	11^{1}	14	4	3	12	10		7^{2}													8
1	2	14					8	13							5	6	7	11^{1}		4^{2}	3	12	10		9^{3}													9
1	2	3					6^{2}	10^{3}							5	13	9^{1}	14		4	8	11	12		7													10
1	2	3					12	10^{2}							6	8		11^{3}	13	5	4	14	7^{1}		9													11
1		2					6^{2}	11							5	7		12		4	8	13	9		10	3^{1}												12
1	2	3					9	11			5			13		6^{2}			10^{1}		7			12	8	4												13
1	2	4	13				10^{4}	11^{2}			5^{3}			7^{1}	14	9		15			8	12			6	3												14
1	2	4	6^{2}				13	10			12			7	5^{1}	8		11			3				9													15
1	2	4	14				13	15						6	5	7	12	11^{3}			3				8^{4}		9^{1}	10^{2}										16
1	2	4					12							14	5	6	7^{3}	11^{1}			3	9^{2}			8^{5}		13	10^{4}	15	16								17
1	2	3	15				8							6^{5}	5^{1}		7	11^{3}			4				9^{2}		10^{4}	12	16	13	14							18
1	2	4					6									8	9^{2}	12			7		10^{3}			3	11^{1}	5	13		14							19
1	2	3	12				8									7					6		10^{2}		9^{3}	4^{1}	11	5	14			13						20
1	5	4	13											12		6					7		14		11^{2}	2	10^{3}	8	3■				9^{1}					21
1	2	3												12		6					7		10		9^{1}	4	11	5					8					22
1	5	4												6^{4}	15	8^{2}	13	11^{1}			7		14			3	10	9	2^{3}				12					23
1	2^{1}	4												7^{2}	12		8	14			6■		13			3	11	5	10^{3}				9					24
1	2	3	12													8^{2}	9	13					7			4^{1}	11	6					10	5				25
1	2^{3}	3													13	8^{5}	9	15			7		12			4^{1}	11	6^{2}				16	10^{4}	5	14			26
1	5	2													9	7					6		11			3	12		4^{1}				10^{2}	13	8			27
1	2	4						13							5		6^{1}	10			7		9			3	11^{2}						12		8			28
1	2	3													5^{3}	6^{4}	15	14			7		10			4	11	13					8^{1}		9^{2}	12		29
1	2	3						16						12	5	15	6^{1}	10^{2}			7		13			4	11^{4}						9^{3}		8^{5}	14		30
	2	3		12		15^{5}								13	5	16	6^{2}	11^{4}			7		14			4	10^{3}						8		9		1^{1}	31
		2						16		1					5	7^{2}	15	11^{1}			8		6^{5}			3	13		9^{4}				12	4	14	10^{3}		32
	13	2^{3}								1					5	15	6^{2}	11^{1}			7		12			4	10^{4}		14				8	3	9			33
	2							13		1				16	5^{2}	6^{4}	14	11^{1}			7		15			4		12					8	3	9^{5}	10^{3}		34
	2	3						14		1		13		7^{1}		6^{2}					11					4	10	5					9^{3}		8	12		35
1		4						14				15		7^{2}		2	12				10		13			3	11^{3}	5					9^{4}		8	6^{1}		36
1		3						9^{1}						7^{2}		2					11		10		13	4	12	5■					8		6			37
1	15	3												8^{3}	5	2	14	10					6^{4}		9^{2}	4^{1}	11							12	7	13		38
1	15	3						14				16		7^{1}	5	2^{4}	12	10^{2}					9				11^{3}						6	4	8^{5}	13		39
1	2	3													5	7^{3}	14	13			10		6^{1}						11^{2}				9	4	8	12		40
1	2	3					14	12							5	7		13			10^{1}				15				11^{2}				9^{3}	4	8	6^{4}		41
1	2	4						12						14		6									13	3	11^{1}	5				8^{3}	10		7	9^{2}		42
1	2^{4}	4					14	11^{2}								6■	12	16								3		5	13			8^{1}	10^{3}	15	7	9^{5}		43
1	2	14					8										7		13		11^{1}					3		5	12			15	10^{3}	4	6^{4}	9^{2}		44
1	2	4					8	13									7		12							3		5	11				10^{2}	6		9^{1}		45
1	2	4					6^{4}	14			12						8		10^{2}	15					9^{3}	3		5^{1}	11				13	7				46

FA Cup			
First Round	Boreham Wood	(a)	3-3
(aet; Boreham Wood won 4-3 on penalties)			

Carabao Cup			
First Round	Gillingham	(a)	0-1

Papa John's Trophy			
Group A (S)	West Ham U U21	(h)	1-3
Group A (S)	Portsmouth	(h)	0-3
Group A (S)	Colchester U	(a)	1-6

STEVENAGE

FOUNDATION

There have been several clubs associated with the town of Stevenage. Stevenage Town was formed in 1884. They absorbed Stevenage Rangers in 1955 and later played at Broadhall Way. The club went into liquidation in 1968 and Stevenage Athletic was formed, but they, too, followed a similar path in 1976. Then Stevenage Borough was founded. The Broadhall Way pitch was dug up and remained unused for three years. Thus the new club started its life in the modest surrounds of the King George V playing fields with a roped-off ground in the Chiltern League. A change of competition followed to the Wallspan Southern Combination and by 1980 the club returned to the council-owned Broadhall Way when "Borough" was added to the name. Entry into the United Counties League was so successful the league and cup were won in the first season. On to the Isthmian League Division Two and the climb up the pyramid continued. In 1995–96 Stevenage Borough won the Conference but was denied a place in the Football League as the ground did not measure up to the competition's standards. Subsequent improvements changed this and the 7,100 capacity venue became one of the best appointed grounds in non-league football. After winning elevation to the Football League the club dropped Borough from its title.

Lamex Stadium, Broadhall Way, Stevenage, Hertfordshire SG2 8RH.

Telephone: (01438) 223 223.

Ticket Office: (01438) 223 223.

Website: stevenagefc.com

Email: info@stevenagefc.com

Ground Capacity: 7,800.

Record Attendance: 8,040 v Newcastle U, FA Cup 4th rd, 25 January 1998.

Pitch Measurements: 104m × 64m (114yd × 70yd).

Chairman: Phil Wallace.

Chief Executive Officer: Alex Tunbridge.

Manager: Alex Revell.

Assistant Manager: Dean Wilkins.

Colours: Red and white striped shirts, red shorts with white trim, red socks.

Year Formed: 1976.

Turned Professional: 1976.

Nickname: 'The Boro'.

Previous Name: 1976, Stevenage Borough; 2010, Stevenage.

HONOURS

League Champions: Conference – 1995–96, 2009–10.

FA Cup: 5th rd – 2012.

League Cup: 2nd rd – 2012, 2017.

FOOTBALL YEARBOOK FACT FILE

When Stevenage Borough, as the club was then known, won the Isthmian League Division Two North in 1985–86 they enjoyed the best start possible, winning their first nine league matches. They scored 21 goals and conceded just three during this run, winning the first six games without letting in a goal.

Grounds: 1976, King George V playing fields; 1980, Broadhall Way (renamed Lamex Stadium 2009).

First Football League Game: 7 August 2010, FL 2, v Macclesfield T (h) D 2–2 – Day; Henry, Laird, Bostwick, Roberts, Foster, Wilson (Sinclair), Byrom, Griffin (1), Winn (Odubade), Vincenti (1) (Beardsley).

Record League Victory: 6–0 v Yeovil T, FL 2, 14 April 2012 – Day; Lascelles (1), Laird, Roberts (1), Ashton (1), Shroot (Mousinho), Wilson (Myrie-Williams), Long, Agyemang (1), Reid (Slew), Freeman (2).

Record Victory: 11–1 v British Timken Ath 1980–81.

Record Defeat: 0–8 v Charlton Ath, FL Trophy, 9 October 2018.

Most League Points (3 for a win): 73, FL 1, 2011–12.

Most League Goals: 69, FL 1, 2011–12.

Highest League Scorer in Season: Matthew Godden, 20, FL 2, 2016–17.

Most League Goals in Total Aggregate: Matthew Godden, 30, 2016–18.

Most League Goals in One Match: 3, Chris Holroyd v Hereford U, FL 2, 28 September 2010; 3, Dani Lopez v Sheffield U, FL 1, 16 March 2013; 3, Chris Whelpdale v Morecambe, FL 2, 28 November 2015; 3, Matthew Godden v Newport Co, FL 2, 7 January 2017; 3, Alex Revell v Exeter C, FL 2, 28 April 2018.

Most Capped Player: Terence Vancooten, 15, Guyana.

Most League Appearances: Ronnie Henry, 230, 2014–19.

Youngest League Player: Liam Smyth, 17 years 47 days v Port Vale, 23 October 2018.

Record Transfer Fee Received: £1,500,000 from Watford for Ben Wilmot, May 2018.

Record Transfer Fee Paid: £125,000 to Exeter C for James Dunne, May 2012.

Football League Record: 2010 Promoted from Conference Premier; 2010–11 FL 2; 2011–14 FL 1; 2014– FL 2.

MANAGERS

Derek Montgomery 1976–83
Frank Cornwell 1983–87
John Bailey 1987–88
Brian Wilcox 1988–90
Paul Fairclough 1990–98
Richard Hill 1998–2000
Steve Wignall 2000
Paul Fairclough 2000–02
Wayne Turner 2002–03
Graham Westley 2003–06
Mark Stimson 2006–07
Peter Taylor 2007–08
Graham Westley 2008–12
Gary Smith 2012–13
Graham Westley 2013–15
Teddy Sheringham 2015–16
Darren Sarll 2016–18
Dino Maamria 2018–19
Graham Westley 2019–20
Alex Revell February 2020–

LATEST SEQUENCES

Longest Sequence of League Wins: 6, 12.3.2011 – 2.4.2011.

Longest Sequence of League Defeats: 8, 25.1.2020 – 7.3.2020.

Longest Sequence of League Draws: 5, 17.3.2012 – 31.3.2012.

Longest Sequence of Unbeaten League Matches: 17, 9.4.2012 – 5.10.2012.

Longest Sequence Without a League Win: 12, 3.8.2019 – 5.10.2019.

Successive Scoring Runs: 17 from 9.4.2012.

Successive Non-scoring Runs: 7 from 3.10.2020.

TEN YEAR LEAGUE RECORD

		P	*W*	*D*	*L*	*F*	*A*	*Pts*	*Pos*
2011-12	FL 1	46	18	19	9	69	44	73	6
2012-13	FL 1	46	15	9	22	47	64	54	18
2013-14	FL 1	46	11	9	26	46	72	42	24
2014-15	FL 2	46	20	12	14	62	54	72	6
2015-16	FL 2	46	11	15	20	52	67	48	18
2016-17	FL 2	46	20	7	19	67	63	67	10
2017-18	FL 2	46	14	13	19	60	65	55	16
2018-19	FL 2	46	20	10	16	59	55	70	10
2019-20	FL 2	36	3	13	20	24	50	22	23§
2020-21	FL 2	46	14	18	14	41	41	60	14

§Decided on points-per-game (0.61)

DID YOU KNOW ?

The all-time record goalscorer for Stevenage is Martin Gittings, who netted 217 goals in all competitions for the club. Gittings enjoyed four separate spells with the Boro between 1981 and 1994 and was the club's leading scorer on five occasions.

STEVENAGE – SKY BET LEAGUE TWO 2020–21 LEAGUE RECORD

Match No.	Date	Venue	Opponents	Result		H/T Score	Lg Pos.	Goalscorers	Attendance
1	Sept 12	A	Barrow	D	1-1	0-1	10	Effiong (pen) [85]	0
2	19	H	Oldham Ath	W	3-0	0-0	5	Osborne [61], Wildin [65], Prosser [82]	0
3	26	A	Bradford C	L	1-2	1-0	11	List [37]	0
4	Oct 3	H	Salford C	L	0-1	0-1	16		0
5	10	A	Mansfield T	D	0-0	0-0	15		0
6	17	A	Forest Green R	L	0-1	0-1	17		0
7	20	H	Newport Co	L	0-1	0-1	18		0
8	24	H	Leyton Orient	L	0-2	0-0	20		0
9	27	A	Harrogate T	D	0-0	0-0	21		0
10	31	H	Grimsby T	D	0-0	0-0	21		0
11	Nov 3	A	Colchester U	L	1-3	1-1	21	Dinanga [15]	0
12	14	A	Morecambe	D	1-1	1-0	22	Oteh (pen) [27]	0
13	21	H	Bolton W	L	1-2	1-2	23	Pett [44]	0
14	24	H	Port Vale	W	2-1	1-0	21	Oteh [10], Newton [53]	0
15	Dec 2	A	Walsall	D	1-1	0-0	23	Oteh (pen) [50]	0
16	5	H	Southend U	D	0-0	0-0	22		0
17	12	A	Carlisle U	L	0-4	0-3	23		2000
18	26	A	Cheltenham T	D	1-1	0-1	24	Aitchison [80]	0
19	29	H	Cambridge U	W	1-0	1-0	23	Carter [22]	0
20	Jan 2	H	Scunthorpe U	W	3-1	2-1	22	Carter 2 [11, 22], Oteh [90]	0
21	16	H	Tranmere R	D	0-0	0-0	22		0
22	23	A	Exeter C	L	1-3	0-1	22	List [81]	0
23	26	H	Colchester U	D	0-0	0-0	22		0
24	30	A	Grimsby T	W	2-1	1-0	21	List [42], Stevens [90]	0
25	Feb 2	H	Exeter C	L	0-1	0-1	21		0
26	6	H	Morecambe	D	2-2	1-2	21	List [8], Norris [81]	0
27	9	A	Tranmere R	W	1-0	0-0	21	Newton [82]	0
28	13	A	Bolton W	L	0-1	0-1	21		0
29	16	A	Crawley T	W	1-0	0-0	21	Osborne [83]	0
30	20	H	Walsall	D	1-1	0-1	21	List [70]	0
31	23	A	Port Vale	D	0-0	0-0	20		0
32	27	A	Newport Co	D	0-0	0-0	18		0
33	Mar 2	H	Forest Green R	W	3-0	2-0	16	Newton 2 [30, 37], List [64]	0
34	6	H	Harrogate T	W	1-0	0-0	15	List [52]	0
35	9	A	Leyton Orient	D	0-0	0-0	15		0
36	13	A	Southend U	D	0-0	0-0	15		0
37	20	H	Carlisle U	W	3-1	1-0	15	Pett [23], Norris [60], Read [71]	0
38	27	H	Barrow	W	2-1	0-0	13	List [53], Norris (pen) [87]	0
39	Apr 2	A	Oldham Ath	W	1-0	1-0	12	Cuthbert [24]	0
40	5	H	Bradford C	D	1-1	1-1	13	Norris [15]	0
41	10	A	Salford C	L	1-2	0-0	14	Wildin [56]	0
42	17	H	Mansfield T	L	0-1	0-1	15		0
43	20	H	Cheltenham T	L	0-1	0-1	16		0
44	24	A	Cambridge U	W	1-0	0-0	15	Norris [63]	0
45	May 1	H	Crawley T	D	3-3	1-1	15	Norris 2 (1 pen) [21 (p), 74], Read [81]	0
46	8	A	Scunthorpe U	W	1-0	0-0	14	List [59]	0

Final League Position: 14

GOALSCORERS

League (41): List 9, Norris 7 (2 pens), Newton 4, Oteh 4 (2 pens), Carter 3, Osborne 2, Pett 2, Read 2, Wildin 2, Aitchison 1, Cuthbert 1, Dinanga 1, Effiong 1 (1 pen), Prosser 1, Stevens 1.
FA Cup (3): Coker 1, List 1, Newton 1.
Carabao Cup (3): Carter 1, Cuthbert 1, List 1.
Papa John's Trophy (4): Dinanga 1, Effiong 1 (1 pen), Marsh 1, own goal 1.

Cumming J 41	Wildin L 36 + 3	Cuthbert S 31 + 2	Prosser L 27 + 3	Hutton R 20 + 6	Smith J 17 + 8	Vincelot R 14 + 12	Osborne E 20 + 6	List E 36 + 8	Newton D 21 + 14	Marsh T 4 + 6	Read A 26 + 6	Effiong I 3 + 6	Marshall R 10 + 5	Dinanga M 5 + 1	Akinwande F 3 + 4	Aitchison J 17 + 9	Oteh A 7 + 6	Coker B 32 + 6	Vancooten T 29	Carter C 16 + 2	Pett T 29 + 2	Iontton A 1 + 1	Fernandez L 1	Lines C 20	Norris L 21 + 2	Stevens M 4 + 14	Martin J 9 + 5	Stockdale D 5	Roles J 1 + 1	Hector-Ingram J — + 1	Williams A — + 1	Match No.
1	2	3	4	5	6	7[1]	8	9	10	11[2]	12	13																				1
1	2	3	4	5	8[3]	12	6	9	11	13	7[1]	10[2]	14																			2
1	2	3	4[2]	5	6		8	9	10		7[1]		12	11	13																	3
1	2[3]	3	4	5	13		6[2]	9	10		8[1]	12	7	11	14																	4
1	5	3	4	8	6[2]	13		9[1]	12		7	10	2			11																5
1	5	3[2]	4	8[1]	6[3]			9	14		7	10	2			11	12	13														6
1	2	3	4	5[3]		6[1]	7		9	13	12	14				10	11[2]	8														7
1	2	3		5			6	10[2]	11[1]	12	7	13	4			9	14	8[3]														8
1		3	4			8	9	6[2]	14		7		13	11	10[3]			5	2[1]	12												9
1	2	3	4			8		6	12		9			11[2]	10[1]		13	5		7												10
1	2	3	4		13	8[2]		6[1]	14		9	12		10[3]	11			5		7												11
1		3		2		6		12	11		8		4	13			10[1]	5		7	9[2]											12
1		3		2	7[1]			15	12	13	8[3]		4		14		10	5[4]		9[2]	11	6										13
1	2	3	4	5	7[3]	6		14	10[2]			15	12				11[4]			8[1]	9	13										14
1	2	3	4	5	6	8		12	10								11[1]	13		7[2]	9											15
1			4	2		6		12	10	8	13						11	5	3	7[1]	9[2]											16
1	2		4▪	10[1]	15	7[2]		13		8[4]			12		14		11[3]	5	3	6	9											17
1	2	4			6	7[1]		9[2]	10		8					12	13		3	11			5									18
1	13	4		2	7				10		8					6[1]	12	5[2]	3	11	9											19
1	12	4	16	2[1]	7	15		14	11[5]		8					6[3]	13	5	3	10[2]	9[4]											20
1	2	4			14			10[1]	13	9[4]	8[3]					15		5	3	6				7	11[2]	12						21
1	2[2]	4		13	7[4]			14	11[1]	15	8							5	3	9	6[3]				10	12						22
1	2				14	7[3]	15	9[1]	13	12	8		4					5	3	6[4]					10	11[2]						23
1	2			16	14	7		11[2]	13		8[3]		4			9[4]		5[5]	3	6					10[1]	12	15					24
	14			2[5]	8[1]	7[2]	15	6	16		12		4[3]			9		5	3		13				11	10[4]		1				25
	2							6[1]	13		8[4]		4[3]			9		15	3	12	14			7	11	10[2]	5	1				26
	2		4					6	14							9		12	3	10[2]	8			7	11[3]	13	5[1]	1				27
	2[2]		4	13				6	10[1]							9[3]		5	3		7			8	11	12		1	14			28
	2	14	4				12	6[4]			13							5	3		7			8	11[3]	10[2]	15	1	9[1]			29
1	2		4[2]					6	11[3]	12						9		5	3		7			8	10[1]	14	13					30
1		4		2[1]		14	6	11	10[3]							9[2]		12	3		7			8		13	5					31
1	2	4				13	7[2]	11[1]	10									6	3		8			9		12	5					32
1	2	3		12		13	6[1]	11	10[3]									9[2]	4		7			8			5			14		33
1	2	4	5			13	7	11[3]	10[1]							14		6	3		9			8[2]	12							34
1	2	4		14			6[2]	9[1]	11		8					12		5	3		7				10[3]	13						35
1	2	4[1]	12			14	6	11	10[2]							9[3]		5	3		7			8	13							36
1	2		4				6[1]	10			9					12		5	3		7			8	11							37
1	2	3	4		14	16	6[3]	11[2]			9[1]					13		5			7			8[5]	10[4]	12	15					38
1	2	3	4	14			6[1]	11[2]			9[3]							5			7			8	10	13	12					39
1	2	3	4[1]				12	11			6[3]					14		9			7			8	10[2]	13	5					40
1	2	4	13				6[2]	11[1]			9					12		5	3		7			8	10							41
1	2		4		12		6[1]	10								9		13	3		7			8	11		5[2]					42
1			4	2	6[2]		13	10								12		9	3		7			8	11		5[1]					43
1	2		4		6[3]	14	12	10								9[1]		5	3		7			8	11[2]	13						44
1	2	13	4[2]		8	15	6[1]	10[3]			12					9[4]		5	3		7				11	14						45
1		4		2	6[2]	12		10[1]	13		9[3]								3		7			8	11		5				14	46

FA Cup

First Round	Concord R	(h)	2-2
(aet; Stevenage won 5-4 on penalties)			
Second Round	Hull C	(h)	1-1
(aet; Stevenage won 6-5 on penalties)			
Third Round	Swansea C	(h)	0-2

Carabao Cup

First Round	Portsmouth	(h)	3-3
(Portsmouth won 3-1 on penalties)			

Papa John's Trophy

Group C (S)	Southampton U21	(h)	2-1
Group C (S)	Milton Keynes D	(h)	2-3
Group C (S)	Northampton T	(a)	0-0
(Northampton T won 4-2 on penalties)			

STOKE CITY

FOUNDATION

The date of the formation of this club has long been in doubt. The year 1863 was claimed, but more recent research by local club historian Wade Martin has uncovered nothing earlier than 1868, when a couple of Old Carthusians, who were apprentices at the local works of the old North Staffordshire Railway Company, met with some others from that works, to form Stoke Ramblers. It should also be noted that the old Stoke club went bankrupt in 1908 when a new club was formed.

bet365 Stadium, Stanley Matthews Way, Stoke-on-Trent, Staffordshire ST4 4EG.

Telephone: (01782) 367 598 or (01782) 592 233.

Ticket Office: (01782) 367 599.

Website: www.stokecityfc.com

Email: info@stokecityfc.com

Ground Capacity: 30,089.

Record Attendance: 51,380 v Arsenal, Division 1, 29 March 1937 (at Victoria Ground); 30,022 v Everton, Premier League, 17 March 2018 (at bet365 Stadium).

Pitch Measurements: 105m × 68m (115yd × 74.5yd).

Joint Chairmen: John Coates, Peter Coates.

Chief Executive: Tony Scholes.

Manager: Michael O'Neill MBE.

Assistant Manager: Dean Holden.

Colours: Red and white striped shirts, white shorts with red trim, white socks with red trim.

Year Formed: 1863* (*see Foundation*).

Turned Professional: 1885.

Previous Names: 1868, Stoke Ramblers; 1870, Stoke; 1925, Stoke City.

Club Nickname: 'The Potters'.

Grounds: 1875, Sweeting's Field; 1878, Victoria Ground (previously known as the Athletic Club Ground); 1997, Britannia Stadium (renamed bet365 Stadium, 2016).

First Football League Game: 8 September 1888, Football League, v WBA (h) L 0–2 – Rowley; Clare, Underwood; Ramsey, Shutt, Smith; Sayer, McSkimming, Staton, Edge, Tunnicliffe.

Record League Victory: 10–3 v WBA, Division 1, 4 February 1937 – Doug Westland; Brigham, Harbot; Tutin, Turner (1p), Kirton; Matthews, Antonio (2), Freddie Steele (5), Jimmy Westland, Johnson (2).

Record Cup Victory: 7–1 v Burnley, FA Cup 2nd rd (replay), 20 February 1896 – Clawley; Clare, Eccles; Turner, Grewe, Robertson; Willie Maxwell, Dickson, Alan Maxwell (3), Hyslop (4), Schofield.

Record Defeat: 0–10 v Preston NE, Division 1, 14 September 1889.

Most League Points (2 for a win): 63, Division 3 (N), 1926–27.

Most League Points (3 for a win): 93, Division 2, 1992–93.

HONOURS

League Champions: Division 2 – 1932–33, 1962–63; Second Division – 1992–93; Division 3N – 1926–27.
Runners-up: FL C – 2007–08; Division 2 – 1921–22.

FA Cup: *Runners-up:* 2011.

League Cup Winners: 1972.
Runners-up: 1964.

League Trophy Winners: 1992, 2000.

European Competitions
UEFA Cup: 1972–73, 1974–75.
Europa League: 2011–12.

FOOTBALL YEARBOOK FACT FILE

The closest Stoke City have come to winning the Football League championship was in the 1946–47 season. Going into their final match of the season on 14 June they needed to win away to Sheffield United to take the title on goal average from Liverpool. The Potters conceded a goal after two minutes and although they fought back to equalise, they struggled on the heavy pitch and eventually went down to a 2-1 defeat.

Most League Goals: 92, Division 3 (N), 1926–27.

Highest League Scorer in Season: Freddie Steele, 33, Division 1, 1936–37.

Most League Goals in Total Aggregate: Freddie Steele, 142, 1934–49.

Most League Goals in One Match: 7, Neville Coleman v Lincoln C, Division 2, 23 February 1957.

Most Capped Player: Glenn Whelan, 81 (91), Republic of Ireland.

Most League Appearances: Eric Skeels, 507, 1958–76.

Youngest League Player: Peter Bullock, 16 years 163 days v Swansea C, 19 April 1958.

Record Transfer Fee Received: £20,000,000 (rising to £25,000,000) from West Ham U for Marko Arnautovic, July 2017.

Record Transfer Fee Paid: £18,300,000 to Porto for Giannelli Imbula, February 2016.

Football League Record: 1888 Founder Member of Football League; 1890 Not re-elected; 1891 Re-elected; relegated in 1907, and after one year in Division 2, resigned for financial reasons; 1919 re-elected to Division 2; 1922–23 Division 1; 1923–26 Division 2; 1926–27 Division 3 (N); 1927–33 Division 2; 1933–53 Division 1; 1953–63 Division 2; 1963–77 Division 1; 1977–79 Division 2; 1979–85 Division 1; 1985–90 Division 2; 1990–92 Division 3; 1992–93 Division 2; 1993–98 Division 1; 1998–2002 Division 2; 2002–04 Division 1; 2004–08 FL C; 2008–18 Premier League; 2018– FL C.

LATEST SEQUENCES

Longest Sequence of League Wins: 8, 30.3.1895 – 21.9.1895.

Longest Sequence of League Defeats: 11, 6.4.1985 – 17.8.1985.

Longest Sequence of League Draws: 5, 13.5.2012 – 15.9.2012.

Longest Sequence of Unbeaten League Matches: 25, 5.9.1992 – 20.2.1993.

Longest Sequence Without a League Win: 17, 22.4.1989 – 14.10.1989.

Successive Scoring Runs: 21 from 24.12.1921.

Successive Non-scoring Runs: 8 from 29.12.1984.

MANAGERS

Tom Slaney 1874–83
(Secretary-Manager)
Walter Cox 1883–84
(Secretary-Manager)
Harry Lockett 1884–90
Joseph Bradshaw 1890–92
Arthur Reeves 1892–95
William Rowley 1895–97
H. D. Austerberry 1897–1908
A. J. Barker 1908–14
Peter Hodge 1914–15
Joe Schofield 1915–19
Arthur Shallcross 1919–23
John 'Jock' Rutherford 1923
Tom Mather 1923–35
Bob McGrory 1935–52
Frank Taylor 1952–60
Tony Waddington 1960–77
George Eastham 1977–78
Alan A'Court 1978
Alan Durban 1978–81
Richie Barker 1981–83
Bill Asprey 1984–85
Mick Mills 1985–89
Alan Ball 1989–91
Lou Macari 1991–93
Joe Jordan 1993–94
Lou Macari 1994–97
Chic Bates 1997–98
Chris Kamara 1998
Brian Little 1998–99
Gary Megson 1999
Gudjon Thordarson 1999–2002
Steve Cotterill 2002
Tony Pulis 2002–05
Johan Boskamp 2005–06
Tony Pulis 2006–13
Mark Hughes 2013–18
Paul Lambert 2018
Gary Rowett 2018–19
Nathan Jones 2019
Michael O'Neill November 2019–

TEN YEAR LEAGUE RECORD

		P	W	D	L	F	A	Pts	Pos
2011-12	PR Lge	38	11	12	15	36	53	45	14
2012-13	PR Lge	38	9	15	14	34	45	42	13
2013-14	PR Lge	38	13	11	14	45	52	50	9
2014-15	PR Lge	38	15	9	14	48	45	54	9
2015-16	PR Lge	38	14	9	15	41	55	51	9
2016-17	PR Lge	38	11	11	16	41	56	44	13
2017-18	PR Lge	38	7	12	19	35	68	33	19
2018-19	FL C	46	11	22	13	45	52	55	16
2019-20	FL C	46	16	8	22	62	68	56	15
2020-21	FL C	46	15	15	16	50	52	60	14

DID YOU KNOW ?

Stoke City hosted three full England matches at their former home, the Victoria Ground. The most recent of these took place against Northern Ireland on Wednesday 18 November 1936. Despite the game being played on a midweek afternoon when many fans would have been at work, a huge crowd of 47,886 turned out to see England win 3-1.

STOKE CITY – SKY BET CHAMPIONSHIP 2020–21 LEAGUE RECORD

Match No.	Date	Venue	Opponents	Result		H/T Score	Lg Pos.	Goalscorers	Attendance
1	Sept 12	A	Millwall	D	0-0	0-0	11		0
2	20	H	Bristol C	L	0-2	0-1	18		0
3	26	A	Preston NE	W	1-0	1-0	15	Gregory [39]	0
4	Oct 4	H	Birmingham C	D	1-1	0-0	13	Powell [86]	0
5	17	A	Luton T	W	2-0	0-0	8	Fletcher [46], Powell [55]	0
6	21	H	Barnsley	D	2-2	1-2	10	Campbell [44], Smith [48]	0
7	24	H	Brentford	W	3-2	2-0	8	Fletcher [9], McClean [35], Campbell [59]	0
8	27	A	Swansea C	L	0-2	0-1	9		0
9	31	H	Rotherham U	W	1-0	1-0	8	McClean [27]	0
10	Nov 4	A	Watford	L	2-3	1-1	11	Fletcher [2], Powell [81]	0
11	7	A	Reading	W	3-0	2-0	8	Campbell [23], Fletcher [35], Brown [90]	0
12	21	H	Huddersfield T	W	4-3	3-2	7	Campbell 2 [31, 33], Stearman (og) [45], Clucas [57]	0
13	24	H	Norwich C	L	2-3	0-2	7	Campbell [69], Collins [79]	0
14	28	A	Sheffield W	D	0-0	0-0	8		0
15	Dec 2	A	Wycombe W	W	1-0	0-0	8	Powell [72]	0
16	5	H	Middlesbrough	W	1-0	1-0	5	Collins [19]	0
17	8	H	Cardiff C	L	1-2	1-0	6	Morrison (og) [25]	0
18	12	A	Derby Co	D	0-0	0-0	8		0
19	15	A	QPR	D	0-0	0-0	7		0
20	19	H	Blackburn R	W	1-0	1-0	7	Powell [7]	0
21	26	A	Coventry C	D	0-0	0-0	7		0
22	29	H	Nottingham F	D	1-1	1-0	7	Thompson [18]	0
23	Jan 2	H	Bournemouth	L	0-1	0-0	8		0
24	16	A	Blackburn R	D	1-1	1-0	8	Powell [38]	0
25	19	A	Rotherham U	D	3-3	1-1	7	MacDonald, A (og) [14], Batth [62], Powell [75]	0
26	22	H	Watford	L	1-2	0-0	8	Fletcher [83]	0
27	30	A	Huddersfield T	D	1-1	1-1	10	Fletcher (pen) [24]	0
28	Feb 6	H	Reading	D	0-0	0-0	9		0
29	13	A	Norwich C	L	1-4	0-2	10	Powell [61]	0
30	16	H	Sheffield W	W	1-0	0-0	9	Fletcher [83]	0
31	20	H	Luton T	W	3-0	1-0	9	Powell 2 [20, 63], Fletcher [78]	0
32	24	A	Barnsley	L	0-2	0-1	10		0
33	27	A	Brentford	L	1-2	1-0	10	Brown [1]	0
34	Mar 3	H	Swansea C	L	1-2	1-1	11	Powell [6]	0
35	6	H	Wycombe W	W	2-0	0-0	10	Norrington-Davies [64], Soutar [69]	0
36	13	A	Middlesbrough	L	0-3	0-2	11		0
37	16	A	Cardiff C	D	0-0	0-0	11		0
38	20	H	Derby Co	W	1-0	0-0	11	Brown [74]	0
39	Apr 2	A	Bristol C	W	2-0	1-0	11	Powell [25], Fletcher [62]	0
40	5	H	Millwall	L	1-2	1-1	11	Brown [41]	0
41	10	A	Birmingham C	L	0-2	0-1	12		0
42	17	H	Preston NE	D	0-0	0-0	12		0
43	21	H	Coventry C	L	2-3	0-1	13	Brown [58], Clucas [70]	0
44	24	A	Nottingham F	D	1-1	1-0	12	Matondo [27]	0
45	May 1	H	QPR	L	0-2	0-1	14		0
46	8	A	Bournemouth	W	2-0	1-0	14	Forrester [36], Smith [52]	0

Final League Position: 14

GOALSCORERS

League (50): Powell 12, Fletcher 9 (1 pen), Campbell 6, Brown 5, Clucas 2, Collins 2, McClean 2, Smith 2, Batth 1, Forrester 1, Gregory 1, Matondo 1, Norrington-Davies 1, Soutar 1, Thompson 1, own goals 3.
FA Cup (0).
Carabao Cup (4): Brown 1, Campbell 1, Thompson 1, Vokes 1.

Davies A 17	Chester J 32	Batth D 27 + 2	Martins Indi B 2	Smith T 34 + 1	Powell N 38 + 1	Mikel J 35 + 4	Clucas S 18 + 6	Fox M 20	Vokes S 5 + 25	Campbell T 13 + 3	Fletcher S 30 + 7	Brown J 27 + 14	Thompson J 24 + 10	Tymon J 16 + 10	Soutar H 38	McClean J 17 + 7	Oakley-Boothe T 3 + 13	Gregory L 3 + 3	Collins N 19 + 3	Ince T 2 + 5	Gunn A 14 + 1	Cousins J 8 + 11	Bursik J 15	Shawcross R — + 2	Verlinden T — + 1	Allen J 15 + 3	Matondo R 5 + 5	Norrington-Davies R 20	Clarke J 6 + 8	Norton C 2 + 4	Taylor C — + 1	Forrester W 1	*Match No.*
1	2	3	4	5	6^{3}	7	8	9	10^{2}	11^{1}	12	13	14																				1
1	2	3	4^{3}	5	9	6	7	8	11^{1}	13	12	10^{2}		14																			2
1	2			5		6	7	4			11^{2}	13	14	12	3	8^{1}	9^{3}	10															3
1	2			5	13	6	7	4		12	11			8^{3}	3	14	9^{2}	10^{1}															4
1		3		5	11^{2}	6	7			9^{1}	10^{3}	12	13	8	2			14	4														5
1	4			5	9^{2}	6				11^{3}	10^{1}	12	7	8	3		13		2▪	14													6
1	4			5		6			13	11^{1}	10^{2}	9^{3}	7	12	3	8	14		2														7
1^{1}	3			2		8		5^{3}	11	13	14	10		9^{2}	4	6	7				12												8
		3		5	10^{3}	6		4		9^{1}	11	13	7^{2}		2	8	14				1	12											9
		4		2^{2}	11^{3}	7		5	13	6	10^{1}	12	8		3	9					1	14											10
		4		2	11^{1}	7		5		6^{3}	10^{2}	14	8		3	9	12		13		1												11
		4		2	9^{4}	6	7	5	14	10^{3}	11^{2}	8^{1}			3			15	12			13	1										12
		3^{4}		5^{2}	9	6	7	4	15	11	10^{1}			8^{3}	2			12	13	14			1										13
	3	4			9	6^{2}	7	5	12	8		14				10^{3}		11^{1}	2			13	1										14
	3	4		14	9^{2}		7	5	11^{3}	10		8^{1}				12	13		2			6	1										15
	3	4^{2}			9^{3}		7^{1}	5		8		11		12		10	14		2			6	1	13									16
	4			2^{4}	9			5	12	8^{1}		11^{2}		7^{3}		10	14		3	15		6	1	13									17
	4				9			5			11^{2}	8	7^{1}	10	3		13		2	12		6	1										18
	4				6^{4}			5			12	11^{1}	13	9^{2}	3	10^{3}	15		2	8		7	1		14								19
	4				9^{1}			5	14		11^{3}	8^{2}	15	7	3	13	12		2	10^{4}		6	1										20
	4			5	6						11	10	8^{1}		3	9			2			7	1			12							21
	4			5	7^{3}	13	12		11			10^{4}	6^{2}		3	9	15		2	14			1			8^{1}							22
	4			5^{3}	10	7	13		14		11^{1}	12	8^{2}	15	3	9^{4}			2				1			6							23
	4▪	13			11^{1}	7						10	8		3				2			14	1			6^{2}	5^{3}	9	12				24
		4			11	7					12	10^{2}	8^{3}		3	14			2			6^{1}	1			13	5^{4}	9	15				25
	4				10	7	8^{1}		14		12				3	11			2				1			6	13	5^{2}	9^{3}				26
	4					7					10^{1}	12	8		3	11			2		1	13				6		5▪	9^{2}				27
		4				7	8	5	14		10^{3}	12			3	11			2		1	13				6^{2}			9^{1}				28
	4				10	7^{2}	9^{4}	5	14		11^{3}		15		3	13			2		1	16				6^{5}	12		8^{1}				29
		4		2	9	15	13	5^{1}			11^{4}	8	7^{3}	12	3	10^{2}					1	16				6^{5}			14				30
		4		2	9^{1}	13	12		16		11^{5}	8^{3}	7^{2}	10^{4}	3	15					1					6		5	14				31
		4		2^{4}	9	6			12		11^{2}	8^{5}	7^{1}	10^{3}	3		16				1	15				13		5	14				32
	4^{3}	3		5	11	7			15			10^{4}	8^{1}	12	2						1	13				6		9^{2}	14				33
	2	4^{1}		5	10^{2}	7					11	9	13		3						1					6		8	12				34
	4			2	9^{2}	6					11	8^{1}	13		3		12				1					7		5	10				35
	4			2	9	6			14		11	8^{1}		12	3						1					7	13	5^{3}	10^{2}				36
1	2	4		5	10^{2}	7			12		11^{1}		8		3											6		9		13			37
1	2	4		5	10^{2}	7			12			11^{3}	8	14	3											6^{1}		9	13				38
1	2	4		5	6^{2}	7			12		11^{1}	10^{3}	8	13	3													9		14			39
1	2	4^{2}		5^{4}	9	6	12		15		11	10^{1}	7^{3}		3	14											13	8					40
1	2	4		5^{1}	9	6	14		13		11^{2}	10	7^{3}		3													8		12			41
1	3	15		2	9	7	6^{2}		14		10^{3}	12	13	8^{4}	4▪													5		11^{1}			42
	2^{1}	3		5	9	14	6^{4}		15		13	10^{5}	7^{2}	8							1						16	4		11^{3}	12		43
1		3		2		6	8		13		11^{1}	12	9	10	4												7^{2}	5					44
1		3		2^{3}	9^{1}	6	8		14		11^{2}	13	12	10	4												7	5					45
1		4		2		7	6		13			10^{2}	8	11													9^{1}	5		12		3	46

FA Cup

Third Round	Leicester C	(h)	0-4

Carabao Cup

First Round	Blackpool	(h)	0-0
(Stoke C won 5-4 on penalties)			
Second Round	Wolverhampton W	(a)	1-0
Third Round	Gillingham	(h)	1-0
Fourth Round	Aston Villa	(a)	1-0
Quarter-Final	Tottenham H	(h)	1-3

SUNDERLAND

FOUNDATION

A Scottish schoolmaster named James Allan, working at Hendon Board School, took the initiative in the foundation of Sunderland in 1879 when they were formed as The Sunderland and District Teachers' Association FC at a meeting in the Adults School, Norfolk Street. Due to financial difficulties, they quickly allowed members from outside the teaching profession and so became Sunderland AFC in October 1880.

Stadium of Light, Sunderland, Tyne and Wear SR5 1SU.

Telephone: (0371) 911 1200.

Ticket Office: (0371) 911 1973.

Website: www.safc.com

Email: enquiries@safc.com

Ground Capacity: 48,095.

Record Attendance: 75,118 v Derby Co, FA Cup 6th rd replay, 8 March 1933 (at Roker Park); 48,335 v Liverpool, Premier League, 13 April 2002 (at Stadium of Light).

Pitch Measurements: 105m × 68m (115yd × 74.5yd).

Chairman: Kyril Louis-Dreyfus.

Sporting Director: Kristjaan Speakman.

Head Coach: Lee Johnson.

Assistant Head Coach: Jamie McAllister.

Colours: Red and white striped shirts with red sleeves, black shorts with white trim, red socks.

Year Formed: 1879.

Turned Professional: 1886.

Previous Names: 1879, Sunderland and District Teachers AFC; 1880, Sunderland.

Club Nickname: 'The Black Cats'.

Grounds: 1879, Blue House Field, Hendon; 1882, Groves Field, Ashbrooke; 1883, Horatio Street; 1884, Abbs Field, Fulwell; 1886, Newcastle Road; 1898, Roker Park; 1997, Stadium of Light.

First Football League Game: 13 September 1890, Football League, v Burnley (h) L 2–3 – Kirtley; Porteous, Oliver; Wilson, Auld, Gibson; Spence (1), Miller, Campbell (1), Scott, Davy Hannah.

Record League Victory: 9–1 v Newcastle U (a), Division 1, 5 December 1908 – Roose; Forster, Melton; Daykin, Thomson, Low; Mordue (1), Hogg (3), Brown, Holley (3), Bridgett (2).

Record Cup Victory: 11–1 v Fairfield, FA Cup 1st rd, 2 February 1895 – Doig; McNeill, Johnston; Dunlop, McCreadie (1), Wilson; Gillespie (1), Millar (5), Campbell, Jimmy Hannah (3), Scott (1).

HONOURS

League Champions: Division 1 – 1892–93, 1894–95, 1901–02, 1912–13, 1935–36; Football League 1891–92; FL C – 2004–05, 2006–07; First Division – 1995–96, 1998–99; Division 2 – 1975–76; Division 3 – 1987–88.
Runners-up: Division 1 – 1893–94, 1897–98, 1900–01, 1922–23, 1934–35; Division 2 – 1963–64, 1979–80.

FA Cup Winners: 1937, 1973.
Runners-up: 1913, 1992.

League Cup: *Runners-up:* 1985, 2014.

League Trophy Winners: 2021.
Runners-up: 2019.

European Competitions
European Cup-Winners' Cup: 1973–74.

FOOTBALL YEARBOOK FACT FILE

Derek Forster became the youngest goalkeeper to appear in the Football League when he was called into the Sunderland first team at the age of 15 years and 185 days to replace the injured Jim Montgomery on the opening day of the 1964–65 season. The First Division game against Leicester City at Roker Park ended in a 3-3 draw in front of an attendance of 45,465.

Record Defeat: 0–8 v Sheff Wed, Division 1, 26 December 1911; 0–8 v West Ham U, Division 1, 19 October 1968; 0–8 v Watford, Division 1, 25 September 1982; 0–8 v Southampton, Premier League, 18 October 2014.

Most League Points (2 for a win): 61, Division 2, 1963–64.

Most League Points (3 for a win): 105, Division 1, 1998–99.

Most League Goals: 109, Division 1, 1935–36.

Highest League Scorer in Season: Dave Halliday, 43, Division 1, 1928–29.

Most League Goals in Total Aggregate: Charlie Buchan, 209, 1911–25.

Most League Goals in One Match: 5, Charlie Buchan v Liverpool, Division 1, 7 December 1919; 5, Bobby Gurney v Bolton W, Division 1, 7 December 1935; 5, Dominic Sharkey v Norwich C, Division 2, 20 February 1962.

Most Capped Player: Seb Larsson, 59 (133), Sweden.

Most League Appearances: Jim Montgomery, 537, 1962–77.

Youngest League Player: Derek Forster, 15 years 184 days v Leicester C, 22 August 1964.

Record Transfer Fee Received: £25,000,000 (rising to £30,000,000) from Everton for Jordan Pickford, June 2017.

Record Transfer Fee Paid: £13,800,000 (rising to £17,100,000) to FC Lorient for Didier Ndong, August 2016.

Football League Record: 1890 Elected to Division 1; 1958–64 Division 2; 1964–70 Division 1; 1970–76 Division 2; 1976–77 Division 1; 1977–80 Division 2; 1980–85 Division 1; 1985–87 Division 2; 1987–88 Division 3; 1988–90 Division 2; 1990–91 Division 1; 1991–92 Division 2; 1992–96 Division 1; 1996–97 Premier League; 1997–99 Division 1; 1999–2003 Premier League; 2003–04 Division 1; 2004–05 FL C; 2005–06 Premier League; 2006–07 FL C; 2007–17 Premier League; 2017–18 FL C: 2018– FL 1.

MANAGERS

Tom Watson 1888–96
Bob Campbell 1896–99
Alex Mackie 1899–1905
Bob Kyle 1905–28
Johnny Cochrane 1928–39
Bill Murray 1939–57
Alan Brown 1957–64
George Hardwick 1964–65
Ian McColl 1965–68
Alan Brown 1968–72
Bob Stokoe 1972–76
Jimmy Adamson 1976–78
Ken Knighton 1979–81
Alan Durban 1981–84
Len Ashurst 1984–85
Lawrie McMenemy 1985–87
Denis Smith 1987–91
Malcolm Crosby 1991–93
Terry Butcher 1993
Mick Buxton 1993–95
Peter Reid 1995–2002
Howard Wilkinson 2002–03
Mick McCarthy 2003–06
Niall Quinn 2006
Roy Keane 2006–08
Ricky Sbragia 2008–09
Steve Bruce 2009–11
Martin O'Neill 2011–13
Paolo Di Canio 2013
Gus Poyet 2013–15
Dick Advocaat 2015
Sam Allardyce 2015–16
David Moyes 2016–17
Simon Grayson 2017
Chris Coleman 2017–18
Jack Ross 2018–19
Phil Parkinson 2019–20
Lee Johnson December 2020–

LATEST SEQUENCES

Longest Sequence of League Wins: 13, 14.11.1891 – 2.4.1892.

Longest Sequence of League Defeats: 17, 18.1.2003 – 16.8.2003.

Longest Sequence of League Draws: 6, 26.3.1949 – 19.4.1949.

Longest Sequence of Unbeaten League Matches: 19, 26.12.2018 – 9.4.2019

Longest Sequence Without a League Win: 22, 21.12.2002 – 16.8.2003.

Successive Scoring Runs: 43 from 30.3.2018.

Successive Non-scoring Runs: 10 from 27.11.1976.

TEN YEAR LEAGUE RECORD

		P	W	D	L	F	A	Pts	Pos
2011-12	PR Lge	38	11	12	15	45	46	45	13
2012-13	PR Lge	38	9	12	17	41	54	39	17
2013-14	PR Lge	38	10	8	20	41	60	38	14
2014-15	PR Lge	38	7	17	14	31	53	38	16
2015-16	PR Lge	38	9	12	17	48	62	39	17
2016-17	PR Lge	38	6	6	26	29	69	24	20
2017-18	FL C	46	7	16	23	52	80	37	24
2018-19	FL 1	46	22	19	5	80	47	85	5
2019-20	FL 1	36	16	11	9	48	32	59	8§
2020-21	FL 1	46	20	17	9	70	42	77	4

§Decided on points-per-game (1.64)

In 1973 Sunderland were awarded the BBC Sports Personality Team of the Year Award for their achievement in defeating Leeds United to win the FA Cup final. Sunderland, who finished sixth in the Second Division table that season, remain the only club outside of top-flight football to win the award.

SUNDERLAND – SKY BET LEAGUE ONE 2020–21 LEAGUE RECORD

Match No.	Date	Venue	Opponents	Result	H/T Score	Lg Pos.	Goalscorers	Attendance
1	Sept 12	H	Bristol R	D 1-1	0-1	10	Maguire [82]	0
2	19	A	Oxford U	W 2-0	0-0	5	O'Nien [46], Gooch [82]	0
3	26	H	Peterborough U	W 1-0	0-0	4	Leadbitter (pen) [81]	0
4	Oct 3	A	Charlton Ath	D 0-0	0-0	4		0
5	17	A	Swindon T	W 2-0	1-0	5	Wyke [37], Maguire (pen) [57]	0
6	20	H	Crewe Alex	W 1-0	1-0	5	Offord (og) [45]	0
7	24	H	Portsmouth	L 1-3	1-2	6	Wyke [10]	0
8	27	A	Rochdale	D 2-2	2-2	7	Wyke [15], Wright [40]	0
9	31	A	Gillingham	W 2-0	0-0	6	Maguire (pen) [84], Gooch [90]	0
10	Nov 3	H	Ipswich T	W 2-1	1-1	6	Wyke [8], Leadbitter (pen) [84]	0
11	14	H	Milton Keynes D	L 1-2	1-1	6	Power [12]	0
12	21	A	Doncaster R	D 1-1	1-0	8	Leadbitter [43]	0
13	27	A	Fleetwood T	D 1-1	0-0	7	Wyke [59]	0
14	Dec 1	H	Burton Alb	D 1-1	0-0	7	Power [85]	0
15	5	H	Wigan Ath	L 0-1	0-1	9		0
16	12	A	Lincoln C	W 4-0	3-0	8	Leadbitter (pen) [16], Wyke 2 [25, 72], Diamond [42]	0
17	15	H	AFC Wimbledon	D 1-1	0-1	9	Wright [62]	0
18	Jan 2	A	Northampton T	D 0-0	0-0	11		0
19	9	H	Hull C	D 1-1	1-1	10	McGeady [21]	0
20	16	A	AFC Wimbledon	W 3-0	1-0	8	Wyke 3 [7, 87, 90]	0
21	19	H	Plymouth Arg	L 1-2	0-1	9	O'Brien [51]	0
22	23	H	Shrewsbury T	W 1-0	1-0	7	Wyke [18]	0
23	26	A	Ipswich T	W 1-0	1-0	7	Wyke [45]	0
24	30	H	Gillingham	D 2-2	2-1	6	McGeady [6], Leadbitter [43]	0
25	Feb 6	A	Milton Keynes D	D 2-2	1-2	7	Wyke [5], O'Nien [56]	0
26	9	A	Shrewsbury T	L 1-2	1-0	7	O'Brien [21]	0
27	13	H	Doncaster R	W 4-1	3-0	6	Wyke 4 [7, 12, 31, 54]	0
28	20	A	Burton Alb	W 3-0	2-0	6	Leadbitter [6], Gooch [32], Wyke [76]	0
29	23	H	Fleetwood T	W 2-0	0-0	5	O'Brien [61], Power [82]	0
30	27	A	Crewe Alex	D 2-2	0-2	5	Jones [76], Maguire [90]	0
31	Mar 2	H	Swindon T	W 1-0	0-0	4	Wyke [70]	0
32	6	H	Rochdale	W 2-0	2-0	4	Sanderson [7], Wyke [35]	0
33	9	A	Portsmouth	W 2-0	1-0	4	Wyke [13], Jones [58]	0
34	17	A	Accrington S	W 2-0	0-0	3	Stewart [62], Wyke [86]	0
35	20	H	Lincoln C	D 1-1	1-0	3	McFadzean [40]	0
36	27	A	Bristol R	W 1-0	1-0	3	O'Brien [39]	0
37	Apr 2	H	Oxford U	W 3-1	1-1	3	Gooch [45], McGeady [81], Power [90]	0
38	5	A	Peterborough U	D 1-1	0-0	3	McGeady [81]	0
39	10	H	Charlton Ath	L 1-2	0-1	3	Scowen [77]	0
40	13	A	Wigan Ath	L 1-2	1-1	3	Wyke [32]	0
41	17	A	Blackpool	L 0-1	0-0	3		0
42	20	A	Hull C	D 2-2	2-1	3	Jones [10], Leadbitter (pen) [34]	0
43	24	H	Accrington S	D 3-3	2-0	3	Wyke 2 [6, 11], Power [83]	0
44	27	H	Blackpool	L 0-1	0-0	4		0
45	May 1	A	Plymouth Arg	W 3-1	1-0	3	Stewart [21], Maguire (pen) [84], Hume [90]	0
46	9	H	Northampton T	D 1-1	0-0	4	Winchester [87]	0

Final League Position: 4

GOALSCORERS

League (70): Wyke 25, Leadbitter 7 (4 pens), Maguire 5 (3 pens), Power 5, Gooch 4, McGeady 4, O'Brien 4, Jones 3, O'Nien 2, Stewart 2, Wright 2, Diamond 1, Hume 1, McFadzean 1, Sanderson 1, Scowen 1, Winchester 1, own goal 1.
FA Cup (0).
Carabao Cup (0).
Papa John's Trophy (23): Wyke 5, Maguire 3, McGeady 2 (1 pen), O'Brien 2, Scowen 2, Diamond 1, Dobson 1, Feeney 1, Gooch 1, Graham 1, Hume 1, McFadzean 1, Power 1, own goal 1.
League One Play-Offs (2): Stewart 1, Wyke 1.

Burge L 41	Willis J 14 + 1	Wright B 33	Flanagan T 14 + 2	O'Nien L 34 + 4	Dobson G 3 + 2	Power M 38 + 4	Hume D 19 + 4	Maguire C 11 + 22	Grigg W 4 + 5	O'Brien A 22 + 10	Graham D 3 + 11	Wyke C 40 + 3	Gooch L 26 + 12	Leadbitter G 30 + 10	Scowen J 35 + 8	McLaughlin C 22 + 3	Diamond J 11 + 13	Sanderson D 19 + 7	Matthews R 5 + 1	Embleton E 3 + 6	McFadzean C 21 + 4	McGeady A 28 + 1	Curry M — + 1	Winchester C 12 + 8	Vokins J 4	Jones J 11 + 8	Neill D — + 2	Younger O 1	Stewart R 2 + 9	Match No.
1	2	3^{3}	4	5	6■	7	8	9	10^{1}	11^{2}	12	13	14																	1
1	2	3	4	5		7^{1}	8	9		11^{3}	10^{2}	13	14	6	12															2
1	2	3	4	5			8	9^{1}		12	13	10^{2}	11^{3}	7	6	14														3
1	2	3	4■	5			8		13	9^{2}	10^{1}	12	11	7	6															4
1	2^{1}	3		4		8		10^{2}		13		11	9	7	6	5	12													5
1		3	14	4	13	6	9	10^{1}		12		11	5^{3}	7	8^{2}	2														6
1	2	3		4■		8	9	10	12		13	11	5	7^{2}	6^{1}															7
1		3	4		7	6	8	9^{1}			13	10^{2}	11		12	5		2												8
1		3	4	5			9	13		10^{1}	12	11	8	7	6^{2}	2														9
1		3	4	5		12	9	10^{2}			13	11	8^{3}	7	6^{1}	2		14												10
	2^{3}	3		4		8^{1}	9	12	11^{2}		13	10	5	7	6		14		1											11
		3	4	5		13	8	9^{1}				10	11^{2}	6	7	2			1	12										12
		3	4	5		14	9^{2}	7^{3}	12		11^{1}	10		8	6	2			1		13									13
		3	4^{3}	5^{4}		6	9	14	13		12	10^{1}		7	8	2		15	1	11^{2}										14
1		3	4			8^{3}	5^{1}	9	10^{2}	13				7	6	2	15			14	12	11^{4}								15
1		3	4		13	6		12	16			10^{5}		7	8^{2}	2^{4}	9^{1}	15		14	5	11^{3}								16
1	14	4			6^{1}				10^{2}	11			12	7		2	9	3		8	5^{3}		13							17
1		3	4			6^{2}		13		14	15	10^{4}	12	7	8	2	9^{1}	5				11^{3}								18
1^{2}		3				8		15			14	10^{5}	12	7	6	2^{1}	9^{4}	4	13	16	5	11^{3}								19
1	4	3				2		14		10^{3}		11		6	7		13			8^{1}	5	9^{2}		12						20
1	3^{1}	4				12		13		10		11		15	7		8	2		14	5^{3}	9^{2}		6^{4}						21
1	3	4		14		2		12		11		10		7	6^{3}		8^{1}				5	9^{2}		13						22
1	3	4^{2}		15		2				9^{4}		10	14	7	8			13		12	5	11^{3}		6^{1}						23
1	3		4	14		2				10		11^{2}	12	6^{3}	7		8^{1}	13			5	9								24
1	4	3		7^{2}		2		15		10^{3}		11	6^{1}	8	13			14				9			5^{4}	12				25
	3^{1}	4		15		2^{3}				10		11	13	6	7		14	12	1			9			5^{4}	8^{2}				26
1		4		8^{3}		7				14		10	9^{2}	12	6	2^{1}	13	3			5	11^{4}				15				27
1				4		6^{5}		16		9		10^{4}	5	7^{2}	12	2	15	3				11^{1}		13	8^{3}	14				28
1				4		7		14		10^{3}		11	6^{2}	8		2		3			5	9^{1}		13		12				29
1				4		6		13		9^{4}		10	5^{1}	15^{5}	7	2	12	3			8^{3}	11^{2}		16		14				30
1				4		2		12		13		11	8^{1}		6^{3}		14	3			5	9^{4}		7		10^{2}	15			31
1				4		7		13		11		10			12		14	3			5	9^{4}		8^{2}		6^{3}	15	2^{1}		32
1			12	4		2		13		10^{1}		11	14		6			3			5	9^{3}		7		8^{2}				33
1				4		7		16				11^{5}	6^{3}	14	13	2	10^{1}	3			15	9^{2}		8	5^{4}				12	34
1				4		6		14				10	9^{3}	8^{2}	12	2		3			5	11		7^{1}					13	35
1				4		2				10^{1}		11	8^{2}	13	6			3			5	9		7					12	36
1				4		6		13				11	10	14	7	2^{1}		3			5	9^{3}				8^{2}			12	37
1				4		2	12			15		10	13	6^{1}	16	14		3			5^{2}	9		7^{5}		8^{4}			11^{3}	38
1				4		2	14			9^{2}		10	5^{4}		6	12		3			8^{3}	11		7^{1}		13			15	39
1		4		2		6^{3}	5^{1}					11	13	12	7		10^{4}	3			15	9				8^{2}			14	40
1		3		4		2	12			9^{2}		11	15	6	7^{4}		14				5^{1}	10				8^{3}			13	41
1		3		4		2	14	15		13		11	8	7^{1}	9		12				5^{3}			6^{2}		10^{4}				42
1		3		4		2	5			11^{3}		10	8^{1}	12	7		13					9^{4}		6^{2}		14			15	43
1		3		4		2	5			10^{1}		11	8	7^{3}	6^{2}							9		14		13			12	44
1		3		4		6	5	13		15			11	14	7^{3}	2^{1}	8^{2}							12		9			10^{4}	45
1		3		4		6^{3}	5	13		16		11^{4}	10	14	7^{5}	2^{2}	8^{1}					12		15		9				46

FA Cup

First Round	Mansfield T	(h)	0-1

Carabao Cup

First Round	Hull C	(h)	0-0

(Hull C won 5-4 on penalties)

League One Play-Offs

Semi-Final 1st leg	Lincoln C	(a)	0-2
Semi-Final 2nd leg	Lincoln C	(h)	2-1

Papa John's Trophy

Group A (N)	Aston Villa U21	(h)	8-1
Group A (N)	Carlisle U	(h)	5-3
Group A (N)	Fleetwood T	(a)	1-2
Second Round (N)	Oldham Ath	(a)	2-1
Third Round (N)	Port Vale	(h)	2-0
Quarter-Final	Milton Keynes D	(a)	3-0
Semi-Final	Lincoln C	(h)	1-1

(Sunderland won 5-3 on penalties)

Final	Tranmere R	(Wembley)	1-0

SUTTON UNITED

FOUNDATION

The club was formed at a meeting held on 5 March 1898, when two local clubs who were both members of the Surrey Herald League, Sutton Guild Rovers and Sutton Association, agreed on a merger. The amber and chocolate colours of Sutton Association were chosen for the new organisation. Sutton United were members of the Surrey Junior League (1898–1905), and then the Southern Suburban League (1905–1921) before joining the Athenian League. In 1909–10 they reached the final of the Surrey Junior Cup and the divisional final of the London Junior Cup, and the following season became a senior club. They remained an amateur organisation until 1974 when the FA abolished amateur status.

The Borough Sports Ground, Gander Green Lane, Sutton, Surrey SM1 2EY.

Telephone: (0208) 644 4440.

Ticket Office: (0208) 644 4440.

Website: www.suttonunited.net

Email: info@suttonunited.net

Ground Capacity: 7,032.

Record Attendance: 14,000 v Leeds U, FA Cup 4th rd, 24 January 1970.

Chairman: Bruce Elliott.

Commercial Manager: Graham Baker.

Manager: Matt Gray.

Assistant Managers: Micky Stephens, Jason Goodliffe.

Colours: Amber shirts with chocolate trim, amber sorts with chocolate trim, amber socks with chocolate trim.

HONOURS

League Champions: National League South – 2015–16.
Isthmian League – 1966–67, 1984–85, 1985–86, 1998–99, 2010–11.
Athenian League – 1927–28, 1945–46, 1957–58.
Runners-up: Conference South – 2013–14;
Isthmian League – 1967–68, 1970–71, 1981–82, 2003–04;
Athenian League – 1946–47.

FA Cup: 5th rd – 2017.

FA Trophy: runners-up – 1980–81.

FA Amateur Cup: runners-up – 1962–63, 1968–69.

Isthmian League Cup Winners: 1982–83, 1983–84, 1985–86, 1997–98.

Full Members' Cup Winners: 1991–92, 1995–96.

Athenian League Challenge Cup: Winners – 1945–46, 1955–56, 1961–62, 1962–63.

Anglo-Italian Cup Winners: 1978–79.
Runners-up: 1979–80, 1981–82.

Bob Lord Trophy Winners: 1990–91.

London Senior Cup Winners: 1957–58, 1982–83.

Surrey Senior Cup Winners: 1945–46, 1964–65, 1967–68, 1969–70, 1979–80, 1982–83, 1983–84, 1984–85, 1985–86, 1986–87, 1987–88, 1992–93, 1994–95, 1998–99, 2002–03.

FOOTBALL YEARBOOK FACT FILE

In September 1934 Sutton United defeated a full-strength Queens Park Rangers team in a match at Gander Green Lane to mark the award of Municipal Borough status to Sutton and Cheam. Sutton, then members of the Athenian League, led 2-1 at half-time and went on to win 4-2 against their opponents who played in Division Three South.

Year Formed: 1898.

Previous Names: Sutton Guild Rovers, Sutton Association.

Grounds: Western Road, Manor Lane, London Road, The Find, Gander Green Lane (renamed The Knights Community Stadium, 2017; renamed The Borough Sports Ground, 2020).

Club Nickname: 'The U's'.

Record Victory: 11–1 v Clapton, Isthmian League 1966; 11–1 v Leatherhead, 1983.

Record Defeat: 0–13 v Barking, Athenian League, 1925–26.

Most League Goals: 115, Isthmian Premier League, 1984–85.

Most League Points: 95, Isthmian Premier League, 1985–86.

Most Goals: 279, Paul McKinnon.

Most Appearances: Larry Pritchard, 786, 1965–84.

Record Transfer Fee Received: £100,000 from Bournemouth for Efan Ekoku, May 1990.

Record Transfer Fee Paid: Undisclosed to Malmo FF for Paul McKinnon, 1983.

Football League Record: 2021 Promoted to FL 2.

MANAGERS

Paul Doswell 2011–2019
Ian Baird 2019
Matt Gray May 2019–

TEN YEAR LEAGUE RECORD

		P	W	D	L	F	A	Pts	Pos
2011–12	CONFS	42	20	14	8	68	53	74	4
2012–13	CONFS	42	20	10	12	66	49	70	6
2013–14	CONFS	42	23	12	7	77	39	81	2
2014–15	CONFS	40	13	11	16	50	54	50	15
2015–16	NLS	42	26	12	4	83	32	90	1
2016–17	NL	46	15	13	18	61	63	58	12
2017–18	NL	46	23	10	13	67	53	79	3
2018–19	NL	46	17	14	15	55	60	65	10
2019–20	NL	38	12	14	12	47	42	50	15
2020–21	NL	42	25	9	8	72	36	84	1

DID YOU KNOW?

Sutton United were one of two teams from the National League to compete in the 2018–19 Scottish League Challenge Cup. United defeated Airdrieonians in their opening game but in the next round lost 4-3 in a penalty shoot-out to League of Ireland club Bohemians after the teams drew 0-0.

SWANSEA CITY

FOUNDATION

The earliest Association Football in Wales was played in the northern part of the country and no international took place in the south until 1894, when a local paper still thought it necessary to publish an outline of the rules and an illustration of the pitch markings. There had been an earlier Swansea club, but this has no connection with Swansea Town (now City) formed at a public meeting in June 1912.

Liberty Stadium, Morfa, Landore, Swansea SA1 2FA.

Telephone: (01792) 616 400.

Ticket Office: (01792) 616 400.

Website: www.swanseacity.com

Email: support@swanseacity.com

Ground Capacity: 20,520.

Record Attendance: 32,796 v Arsenal, FA Cup 4th rd, 17 February 1968 (at Vetch Field); 20,972 v Liverpool, Premier League, 1 May 2016 (at Liberty Stadium).

Pitch Measurements: 105m × 68m (115yd × 74.5yd).

Chief Executive: Julian Winter.

Head Coach: Steve Cooper.

Assistant First-Team Coach: Mike Marsh.

Colours: White shirts with black trim, black shorts with white trim, white socks with black trim.

Year Formed: 1912.

Turned Professional: 1912.

Previous Name: 1912, Swansea Town; 1970, Swansea City.

Club Nicknames: 'The Swans', 'The Jacks'.

Grounds: 1912, Vetch Field; 2005, Liberty Stadium.

First Football League Game: 28 August 1920, Division 3, v Portsmouth (a) L 0–3 – Crumley; Robson, Evans; Smith, Holdsworth, Williams; Hole, Ivor Jones, Edmundson, Rigsby, Spottiswood.

Record League Victory: 8–0 v Hartlepool U, Division 4, 1 April 1978 – Barber; Evans, Bartley, Lally (1) (Morris), May, Bruton, Kevin Moore, Robbie James (3 incl. 1p), Curtis (3), Toshack (1), Chappell.

Record Cup Victory: 12–0 v Sliema W (Malta), ECWC 1st rd 1st leg, 15 September 1982 – Davies; Marustik, Hadziabdic (1), Irwin (1), Kennedy, Rajkovic (1), Loveridge (2) (Leighton James), Robbie James, Charles (2), Stevenson (1), Latchford (1) (Walsh (3)).

Record Defeat: 0–8 v Liverpool, FA Cup 3rd rd, 9 January 1990; 0–8 v Monaco, ECWC, 1st rd 2nd leg, 1 October 1991.

Most League Points (2 for a win): 62, Division 3 (S), 1948–49.

Most League Points (3 for a win): 92, FL 1, 2007–08.

Most League Goals: 90, Division 2, 1956–57.

HONOURS

League Champions: FL 1 – 2007–08; Division 3S – 1924–25, 1948–49; Third Division – 1999–2000.

FA Cup: semi-final – 1926, 1964.

League Cup Winners: 2013.

League Trophy Winners: 1994, 2006.

Welsh Cup Winners: 11 times; *Runners-up:* 8 times.

European Competitions
Europa League: 2013–14.
European Cup-Winners' Cup: 1961–62, 1966–67, 1981–82, 1982–83, 1983–84, 1989–90, 1991–92.

FOOTBALL YEARBOOK FACT FILE

Jonjo Shelvey is the only Swansea City player to win full international honours for England while on the club's books. He won five caps during the 2015–16 season, having previously made his international debut while a Liverpool player. Tammy Abraham was also capped for England during his loan period with the Swans from Chelsea.

Highest League Scorer in Season: Cyril Pearce, 35, Division 2, 1931–32.

Most League Goals in Total Aggregate: Ivor Allchurch, 166, 1949–58, 1965–68.

Most League Goals in One Match: 5, Jack Fowler v Charlton Ath, Division 3S, 27 December 1924.

Most Capped Player: Ashley Williams, 64 (86), Wales.

Most League Appearances: Wilfred Milne, 587, 1919–37.

Youngest League Player: Nigel Dalling, 15 years 289 days v Southport, 6 December 1974.

Record Transfer Fee Received: £40,000,000 (rising to £45,000,000) from Everton for Gylfi Sigurdsson, August 2017.

Record Transfer Fee Paid: £18,000,000 to West Ham U for André Ayew, January 2018.

Football League Record: 1920 Original Member of Division 3; 1921–25 Division 3 (S); 1925–47 Division 2; 1947–49 Division 3 (S); 1949–65 Division 2; 1965–67 Division 3; 1967–70 Division 4; 1970–73 Division 3; 1973–78 Division 4; 1978–79 Division 3; 1979–81 Division 2; 1981–83 Division 1; 1983–84 Division 2; 1984–86 Division 3; 1986–88 Division 4; 1988–92 Division 3; 1992–96 Division 2; 1996–2000 Division 3; 2000–01 Division 2; 2001–04 Division 3; 2004–05 FL 2; 2005–08 FL 1; 2008–11 FL C; 2011–18 Premier League; 2018– FL C.

LATEST SEQUENCES

Longest Sequence of League Wins: 9, 27.11.1999 – 22.1.2000.

Longest Sequence of League Defeats: 9, 26.1.1991 – 19.3.1991.

Longest Sequence of League Draws: 8, 25.11.2008 – 28.12.2008.

Longest Sequence of Unbeaten League Matches: 19, 19.10.1970 – 9.3.1971.

Longest Sequence Without a League Win: 15, 25.3.1989 – 2.9.1989.

Successive Scoring Runs: 27 from 28.8.1947.

Successive Non-scoring Runs: 6 from 6.2.1996.

MANAGERS

Walter Whittaker 1912–14
William Bartlett 1914–15
Joe Bradshaw 1919–26
Jimmy Thomson 1927–31
Neil Harris 1934–39
Haydn Green 1939–47
Bill McCandless 1947–55
Ron Burgess 1955–58
Trevor Morris 1958–65
Glyn Davies 1965–66
Billy Lucas 1967–69
Roy Bentley 1969–72
Harry Gregg 1972–75
Harry Griffiths 1975–77
John Toshack 1978–83
(resigned October re-appointed in December) 1983–84
Colin Appleton 1984
John Bond 1984–85
Tommy Hutchison 1985–86
Terry Yorath 1986–89
Ian Evans 1989–90
Terry Yorath 1990–91
Frank Burrows 1991–95
Bobby Smith 1995
Kevin Cullis 1996
Jan Molby 1996–97
Micky Adams 1997
Alan Cork 1997–98
John Hollins 1998–2001
Colin Addison 2001–02
Nick Cusack 2002
Brian Flynn 2002–04
Kenny Jackett 2004–07
Roberto Martinez 2007–09
Paulo Sousa 2009–10
Brendan Rodgers 2010–12
Michael Laudrup 2012–14
Garry Monk 2014–15
Francesco Guidolin 2016
Bob Bradley 2016
Paul Clement 2017
Carlos Carvalhal 2017–18
Graham Potter 2018–19
Steve Cooper June 2019–

TEN YEAR LEAGUE RECORD

		P	W	D	L	F	A	Pts	Pos
2011-12	PR Lge	38	12	11	15	44	51	47	11
2012-13	PR Lge	38	11	13	14	47	51	46	9
2013-14	PR Lge	38	11	9	18	54	54	42	12
2014-15	PR Lge	38	16	8	14	46	49	56	8
2015-16	PR Lge	38	12	11	15	42	52	47	12
2016-17	PR Lge	38	12	5	21	45	70	41	15
2017-18	PR Lge	38	8	9	21	28	56	33	18
2018-19	FL C	46	18	11	17	65	62	65	10
2019-20	FL C	46	18	16	12	62	53	70	6
2020-21	FL C	46	23	11	12	56	39	80	4

DID YOU KNOW ?

Swansea Town supporters were renowned for their singing at important matches throughout the 1920s. One of the great favourites of the Vetch Field crowd was 'I'm Forever Blowing Bubbles', which was often sung while thousands of fans waved white handkerchiefs in the air.

SWANSEA CITY – SKY BET CHAMPIONSHIP 2020–21 LEAGUE RECORD

Match No.	Date	Venue	Opponents	Result		H/T Score	Lg Pos.	Goalscorers	Attendance
1	Sept 12	A	Preston NE	W	1-0	0-0	5	White ^{53}	0
2	19	H	Birmingham C	D	0-0	0-0	5		0
3	26	A	Wycombe W	W	2-0	2-0	2	Ayew ^{13}, Lowe ^{23}	0
4	Oct 3	H	Millwall	W	2-1	0-0	4	Bidwell ^{46}, Cabango ^{68}	0
5	17	H	Huddersfield T	L	1-2	1-1	4	Ayew (pen) ^{33}	0
6	20	A	Coventry C	D	1-1	1-1	5	Ayew ^{41}	0
7	24	A	Bristol C	D	1-1	0-0	7	Lowe ^{51}	0
8	27	H	Stoke C	W	2-0	1-0	2	Fulton ^{30}, Palmer ^{87}	0
9	31	H	Blackburn R	W	2-0	1-0	2	Cabango ^{25}, Ayew ^{61}	0
10	Nov 3	A	Brentford	D	1-1	0-1	2	Ayew ^{77}	0
11	7	A	Norwich C	L	0-1	0-0	6		0
12	21	H	Rotherham U	W	1-0	1-0	4	Grimes ^{28}	0
13	25	H	Sheffield W	D	1-1	0-1	4	Ayew ^{60}	0
14	29	A	Nottingham F	W	1-0	1-0	4	Roberts ^{43}	0
15	Dec 2	A	Middlesbrough	L	1-2	0-1	7	Dhanda ^{78}	0
16	5	H	Luton T	W	2-0	1-0	4	Roberts ^{2}, Ayew ^{89}	0
17	8	H	Bournemouth	D	0-0	0-0	4		0
18	12	A	Cardiff C	W	2-0	1-0	3	Lowe 2 $^{6, 72}$	0
19	16	A	Derby Co	L	0-2	0-2	4		0
20	19	H	Barnsley	W	2-0	1-0	3	Lowe ^{2}, Adeboyejo (og) ^{66}	0
21	26	A	QPR	W	2-0	1-0	2	Ayew ^{44}, Lowe ^{54}	0
22	30	H	Reading	D	0-0	0-0	3		0
23	Jan 2	H	Watford	W	2-1	1-1	2	Lowe 2 $^{43, 67}$	0
24	16	A	Barnsley	W	2-0	1-0	2	Cabango ^{45}, Lowe ^{55}	0
25	27	H	Brentford	D	1-1	0-0	2	Hourihane ^{78}	0
26	30	A	Rotherham U	W	3-1	2-0	2	Hourihane ^{28}, Grimes ^{38}, Fulton ^{74}	0
27	Feb 5	H	Norwich C	W	2-0	1-0	2	Ayew ^{42}, Hourihane ^{48}	0
28	17	H	Nottingham F	W	1-0	0-0	3	Roberts ^{87}	0
29	20	A	Huddersfield T	L	1-4	1-1	4	Hourihane ^{45}	0
30	24	H	Coventry C	W	1-0	0-0	4	Cabango ^{54}	0
31	27	H	Bristol C	L	1-3	0-0	4	Ayew (pen) ^{55}	0
32	Mar 3	A	Stoke C	W	2-1	1-1	4	Roberts ^{19}, Ayew (pen) ^{90}	0
33	6	H	Middlesbrough	W	2-1	1-0	3	Ayew 2 (1 pen) $^{40, 90 (p)}$	0
34	9	A	Blackburn R	D	1-1	1-1	3	Ayew (pen) ^{41}	0
35	13	A	Luton T	W	1-0	1-0	3	Hourihane ^{3}	0
36	16	A	Bournemouth	L	0-3	0-2	3		0
37	20	H	Cardiff C	L	0-1	0-1	3		0
38	Apr 2	A	Birmingham C	L	0-1	0-0	3		0
39	5	H	Preston NE	L	0-1	0-0	4		0
40	10	A	Millwall	W	3-0	1-0	4	Ayew ^{45}, Lowe 2 $^{76, 85}$	0
41	13	A	Sheffield W	W	2-0	1-0	3	Lowe ^{31}, Fulton ^{73}	0
42	17	H	Wycombe W	D	2-2	0-0	3	Lowe (pen) ^{80}, Cullen ^{82}	0
43	20	H	QPR	L	0-1	0-0	3		0
44	25	A	Reading	D	2-2	0-1	5	Lowe ^{67}, Ayew ^{83}	0
45	May 1	H	Derby Co	W	2-1	0-0	4	Whittaker ^{63}, Roberts ^{66}	0
46	8	A	Watford	L	0-2	0-0	4		0

Final League Position: 4

GOALSCORERS

League (56): Ayew 16 (5 pens), Lowe 14 (1 pen), Hourihane 5, Roberts 5, Cabango 4, Fulton 3, Grimes 2, Bidwell 1, Cullen 1, Dhanda 1, Palmer 1, White 1, Whittaker 1, own goal 1.
FA Cup (8): Cullen 2, Grimes 2 (1 pen), Cooper 1, Gyokeres 1, Routledge 1, Whittaker 1.
Carabao Cup (0).
Championship Play-Offs (2): Ayew 1, Grimes 1.

Woodman F 45	Cabango B 28 + 2	Rodon J 4	Guehi M 40	Roberts C 43 + 3	Smith K 27 + 10	Grimes M 42 + 3	Bidwell J 36 + 3	White M 4 + 1	Lowe J 42 + 4	Ayew A 41 + 2	Fulton J 31 + 9	Routledge W 4 + 12	Cullen L 6 + 7	Benda S 1	Gyokeres V 2 + 9	Naughton K 30	Palmer K 2 + 10	Garrick J — + 3	Bennett R 28	Manning R 11 + 6	Dhanda Y 14 + 12	Latibeaudiere J 4 + 4	Hourihane C 18 + 1	Morris J — + 4	Arriola P — + 2	Whittaker M 3 + 9	Cooper O — + 3	Cooper B — + 1	*Match No.*
1	2	3	4	5	6	7	8	9^{1}	10^{2}	11	12	13																	1
1	2	3	4	5	6	7	8	9	10^{1}	11			12																2
1	2	3	4	5	6	7	8	10^{1}	9^{2}	11	13		12																3
	2	3	4	5	6	7	8	9^{2}	11^{1}	10	13			1	12														4
1	3		4	5	6	7	8		11^{3}	9			13		10^{1}	2^{2}	12	14											5
1	2		4	5	6	7	8		11^{2}	9	12		13		10^{1}				3										6
1	2		4	5	6	8	9		11^{1}	10	7				12				3										7
1	12		4	5		7	13		11	10	6					2	14		3^{2}	8^{3}	9^{1}								8
1	3		4	5	7		8		11^{1}	10	6				12	2	13				9^{2}								9
1			4	5	7	12	8		11^{3}	10	6^{1}				14	2	13		3		9^{2}								10
1			4	5	7	12	8		11	10	6^{3}				13	2^{1}	9^{2}		3		14								11
1	3			2	14	7	8		11^{3}		6	12	10^{1}			5	13		4		9^{2}								12
1	2			5	6	7	8^{4}		10^{3}	12		15	11^{1}			4^{2}	13		3	14	9								13
1			4	5	6	9	8		10^{1}	11	7	12				2			3										14
1	2^{2}		4	5	7^{5}	12			11^{1}	10	6^{3}	13			14		9^{4}	16	3	8	15								15
1	3		4^{3}	5	6	7	8		12	10^{4}			11^{1}		15	2	13				9^{2}	14							16
1	3			5	6	7	8		11^{1}	10					12	2	13				9^{2}	4							17
1			4	5	6	8	9		11^{1}	10	7	12				2			3										18
1			4	5	6^{5}	8	9^{1}		10^{4}	11	7^{2}		16			2^{3}	13	15	3	14	12								19
1	2		4	5		7	8		11	10	6								3		9								20
1	2		4	5	12	7	8		11	10	6								3		9^{1}								21
1	2		4	5	9^{2}	7	8		11^{3}	10	6				14		13		3^{1}			12							22
1	3		2	5	9	7	4	12	11	10	6									8^{1}									23
1	3		4	5	9	6	8		11	10	7					2													24
1	3		4	6		5	9		10^{1}	11	7					2				12			8						25
1	2		4	6		5	9		10^{2}	11	12								3		7^{1}		8	13					26
1			4	5		7	8		11^{1}	10	6					2			3				9	12					27
1			4	5	14	7	8		10^{2}	11	6					2^{1}			3				9^{3}	12	13				28
1	12		4	6		5	9^{4}		11^{1}	10	7^{3}					2^{5}			3^{2}	14	16		8	13		15			29
1	3		4	5	13	6	8		11	10	12					2^{3}					9^{2}	14	7^{1}						30
1	3		4	5		6	8		11	10	12										9^{1}	2^{3}	7^{2}		13	14			31
1	3		4	5	6	7			11^{1}	10	8					2				9			12						32
1	3		4	5	9^{1}	7	13		12	11	6					2				8^{2}			10						33
1	3		4^{1}	5	14	7	8		10^{4}	11	6^{3}	15				2					13	12	9^{2}						34
1				5	6	7			12	11	13					2			3	8	10^{2}	4	9^{1}						35
1				5	6^{2}	7			11	10		14				2			3	8	13	4^{1}	9^{3}			12			36
1			4	5	12	7	8^{2}		13	10	6^{4}					2^{3}			3	14	15		9^{1}			11			37
1			4	5	6^{1}	7	8		11^{2}	10	9	13				2^{3}			3		12					14			38
1	3		4	2		7			11	10	6	13								5	12		8^{2}			9^{1}			39
1			4	12		7			11^{3}	9^{2}	6	10^{1}				2			3	5			8			13	14		40
1			4	12	14	7	13		11	9	6	10^{1}				2			3	5^{2}			8^{3}						41
1			4	5	13	6			11	10^{1}	7^{4}	12^{5}	16			2^{3}			3	8	15		9^{2}			14			42
1			4	5	6	8	9		11^{3}		7^{2}	10^{1}	12			2			3		13					14			43
1	3		4	14	15	6	5		11	13	7	9^{2}	10^{1}			2^{3}							8^{4}			12			44
1	3			2	6	8	5^{1}		11^{4}		14		10						4	13	7^{3}					9^{2}	12	15	45
1			4	2	13	7^{3}	5		11^{4}	9^{1}	6	15	10^{2}						3		14		8^{5}			16	12		46

FA Cup

Third Round	Stevenage	(a)	2-0
Fourth Round	Nottingham F	(h)	5-1
Fifth Round	Manchester C	(h)	1-3

Carabao Cup

First Round	Newport Co	(a)	0-2

Championship Play-Offs

Semi-Final 1st leg	Barnsley	(a)	1-0
Semi-Final 2nd leg	Barnsley	(h)	1-1
Final	Brentford	(Wembley)	0-2

SWINDON TOWN

FOUNDATION

It is generally accepted that Swindon Town came into being in 1881, although there is no firm evidence that the club's founder, Rev. William Pitt, captain of the Spartans (an offshoot of a cricket club), changed his club's name to Swindon Town before 1883, when the Spartans amalgamated with St Mark's Young Men's Friendly Society.

The Energy Check County Ground, County Road, Swindon, Wiltshire SN1 2ED.

Telephone: (0330) 002 1879.

Ticket Office: (0330) 002 1879.

Website: www.swindontownfc.co.uk

Email: enquiries@swindontownfc.co.uk

Ground Capacity: 15,547.

Record Attendance: 32,000 v Arsenal, FA Cup 3rd rd, 15 January 1972.

Pitch Measurements: 100m × 68m (109.5yd × 74.5yd).

Chairman: Lee Power.

Chief Executive: Steve Anderson.

Director of Football: Paul Jewell.

Manager: TBC.

First-Team Coach: TBC.

Colours: Red shirts with white trim, white shorts with red trim, red socks with white trim.

Year Formed: 1881* (*see Foundation*).

Turned Professional: 1894.

Club Nickname: 'The Robins'.

Grounds: 1881, The Croft; 1896, County Ground (renamed The Energy Check County Ground 2017).

First Football League Game: 28 August 1920, Division 3, v Luton T (h) W 9–1 – Nash; Kay, Macconachie; Langford, Hawley, Wareing; Jefferson (1), Fleming (4), Rogers, Batty (2), Davies (1), (1 og).

Record League Victory: 9–1 v Luton T, Division 3 (S), 28 August 1920 – Nash; Kay, Macconachie; Langford, Hawley, Wareing; Jefferson (1), Fleming (4), Rogers, Batty (2), Davies (1), (1 og).

Record Cup Victory: 10–1 v Farnham U Breweries (a), FA Cup 1st rd (replay), 28 November 1925 – Nash; Dickenson, Weston, Archer, Bew, Adey; Denyer (2), Wall (1), Richardson (4), Johnson (3), Davies.

Record Defeat: 1–10 v Manchester C, FA Cup 4th rd (replay), 25 January 1930.

Most League Points (2 for a win): 64, Division 3, 1968–69.

HONOURS

League Champions: Second Division – 1995–96; FL 2 – 2011–12, 2019–20; Division 4 – 1985–86.
Runners-up: Division 3 – 1962–63, 1968–69.

FA Cup: semi-final – 1910, 1912.

League Cup Winners: 1969.

League Trophy: *Runners-up:* 2012.

Anglo-Italian Cup Winners: 1970.

FOOTBALL YEARBOOK FACT FILE

In 1993–94 Swindon Town became the first top-flight team in 30 years to concede 100 goals in a season. The Robins won just five games in what was to prove their only season in the Premier League, with a 5-0 defeat at home to Leeds United on the final day bringing up the unwanted achievement.

Most League Points (3 for a win): 102, Division 4, 1985–86.

Most League Goals: 100, Division 3 (S), 1926–27.

Highest League Scorer in Season: Harry Morris, 47, Division 3 (S), 1926–27.

Most League Goals in Total Aggregate: Harry Morris, 216, 1926–33.

Most League Goals in One Match: 5, Harry Morris v QPR, Division 3 (S), 18 December 1926; 5, Harry Morris v Norwich C, Division 3 (S), 26 April 1930; 5, Keith East v Mansfield T, Division 3, 20 November 1965.

Most Capped Player: Rod Thomas, 30 (50), Wales.

Most League Appearances: John Trollope, 770, 1960–80.

Youngest League Player: Paul Rideout, 16 years 107 days v Hull C, 29 November 1980.

Record Transfer Fee Received: A combined £4,000,000 from QPR for Ben Gladwin and Massimo Luongo, May 2015.

Record Transfer Fee Paid: £800,000 to West Ham U for Joey Beauchamp, August 1994.

Football League Record: 1920 Original Member of Division 3; 1921–58 Division 3 (S); 1958–63 Division 3; 1963–65 Division 2; 1965–69 Division 3; 1969–74 Division 2; 1974–82 Division 3; 1982–86 Division 4; 1986–87 Division 3; 1987–92 Division 2; 1992–93 Division 1; 1993–94 Premier League; 1994–95 Division 1; 1995–96 Division 2; 1996–2000 Division 1; 2000–04 Division 2; 2004–06 FL 1; 2006–07 FL 2; 2007–11 FL 1; 2011–12 FL 2; 2012–17 FL 1; 2017–20 FL 2; 2020–21 FL 1; 2021– FL 2.

MANAGERS

Sam Allen 1902–33
Ted Vizard 1933–39
Neil Harris 1939–41
Louis Page 1945–53
Maurice Lindley 1953–55
Bert Head 1956–65
Danny Williams 1965–69
Fred Ford 1969–71
Dave Mackay 1971–72
Les Allen 1972–74
Danny Williams 1974–78
Bobby Smith 1978–80
John Trollope 1980–83
Ken Beamish 1983–84
Lou Macari 1984–89
Ossie Ardiles 1989–91
Glenn Hoddle 1991–93
John Gorman 1993–94
Steve McMahon 1994–98
Jimmy Quinn 1998–2000
Colin Todd 2000
Andy King 2000–01
Roy Evans 2001
Andy King 2001–05
Iffy Onuora 2005–06
Dennis Wise 2006
Paul Sturrock 2006–07
Maurice Malpas 2008
Danny Wilson 2008–11
Paul Hart 2011
Paolo Di Canio 2011–13
Kevin MacDonald 2013
Mark Cooper 2013–15
Martin Ling 2015
Luke Williams 2015–17
David Flitcroft 2017–18
Phil Brown 2018
Richie Wellens 2018–20
John Sheridan 2020–21
John McGreal 2021

LATEST SEQUENCES

Longest Sequence of League Wins: 10, 31.12.2011 – 28.2.2012.

Longest Sequence of League Defeats: 8, 29.8.2005 – 8.10.2005.

Longest Sequence of League Draws: 6, 22.11.1991 – 28.12.1991.

Longest Sequence of Unbeaten League Matches: 22, 12.1.1986 – 23.8.1986.

Longest Sequence Without a League Win: 19, 30.10.1999 – 4.3.2000.

Successive Scoring Runs: 31 from 17.4.1926.

Successive Non-scoring Runs: 5 from 5.4.1997.

TEN YEAR LEAGUE RECORD

		P	W	D	L	F	A	Pts	Pos
2011-12	FL 2	46	29	6	11	75	32	93	1
2012-13	FL 1	46	20	14	12	72	39	74	6
2013-14	FL 1	46	19	9	18	63	59	66	8
2014-15	FL 1	46	23	10	13	76	57	79	4
2015-16	FL 1	46	16	11	19	64	71	59	15
2016-17	FL 1	46	11	11	24	44	66	44	22
2017-18	FL 2	46	20	8	18	67	65	68	9
2018-19	FL 2	46	16	16	14	59	56	64	13
2019-20	FL 2	36	21	6	9	62	39	69	1§
2020-21	FL 1	46	13	4	29	55	89	43	23

§*Decided on points-per-game (1.92)*

DID YOU KNOW ?

Swindon Town's Trevor Anderson achieved the rare feat of scoring a hat-trick of penalties in the club's Third Division game against Walsall at the County Ground on 24 April 1976. Town won 5-1 with the victory helping them narrowly avoid relegation.

SWINDON TOWN – SKY BET LEAGUE ONE 2020–21 LEAGUE RECORD

Match No.	*Date*	*Venue*	*Opponents*	*Result*		*H/T Score*	*Lg Pos.*	*Goalscorers*	*Atten-dance*
1	Sept 12	H	Rochdale	W	3-1	3-0	1	Smith, T [4], Grant, A [33], Smith, M [41]	0
2	19	A	Blackpool	L	0-2	0-1	10		0
3	26	H	Burton Alb	W	4-2	3-1	6	Stevens [7], Pitman [31], Baudry [35], Smith, J [60]	0
4	Oct 3	A	Peterborough U	L	1-3	1-0	7	Payne [6]	0
5	10	H	AFC Wimbledon	L	0-1	0-1	14		0
6	17	H	Sunderland	L	0-2	0-1	16		0
7	20	A	Northampton T	L	1-2	0-2	18	Smith, T (pen) [76]	0
8	31	H	Hull C	W	2-1	1-1	19	Caddis [31], Grant, J [54]	0
9	Nov 3	A	Plymouth Arg	L	2-4	2-3	19	Hope [10], Grant, A [23]	0
10	14	A	Shrewsbury T	D	3-3	1-2	19	Grant, J [43], Hope [61], Smith, M [90]	0
11	17	H	Accrington S	L	0-3	0-3	19		0
12	21	H	Bristol R	W	1-0	0-0	18	Pitman [75]	0
13	24	H	Lincoln C	L	0-1	0-0	19		0
14	28	A	Oxford U	W	2-1	0-1	16	Broadbent [84], Smith, T [90]	0
15	Dec 1	A	Crewe Alex	L	2-4	2-1	18	Grant, A [20], Smith, T [37]	0
16	5	A	Gillingham	L	0-2	0-1	19		0
17	12	H	Fleetwood T	L	0-1	0-1	20		2000
18	15	A	Doncaster R	L	1-2	0-0	21	Jaiyesimi (pen) [90]	0
19	19	H	Charlton Ath	D	2-2	1-1	21	Jaiyesimi [26], Pitman [90]	2000
20	29	H	Milton Keynes D	L	1-4	1-3	22	Payne [38]	0
21	Jan 9	A	Ipswich T	W	3-2	1-0	21	Jaiyesimi 2 [16, 74], Twine [67]	0
22	16	H	Doncaster R	L	1-2	0-2	22	Hope [73]	0
23	23	A	Charlton Ath	D	2-2	2-0	22	Hope [5], Palmer [39]	0
24	26	H	Plymouth Arg	L	0-2	0-1	21		0
25	30	A	Hull C	L	0-1	0-1	21		0
26	Feb 2	H	Wigan Ath	W	1-0	1-0	19	Pitman [17]	0
27	6	H	Shrewsbury T	L	0-1	0-1	20		0
28	9	A	Portsmouth	L	0-2	0-1	21		0
29	20	H	Crewe Alex	W	2-1	1-1	19	Johnson (og) [10], Twine [90]	0
30	23	A	Lincoln C	D	2-2	2-1	19	Garrick [2], Pitman [44]	0
31	27	H	Northampton T	W	2-1	1-1	18	Twine [45], Pitman [69]	0
32	Mar 2	A	Sunderland	L	0-1	0-0	19		0
33	6	A	Accrington S	L	1-2	1-2	20	Pitman [30]	0
34	9	H	Oxford U	L	1-2	0-1	21	Curran [90]	0
35	13	H	Gillingham	L	1-3	1-0	22	Pitman [41]	0
36	20	A	Fleetwood T	W	2-0	1-0	19	Twine 2 [5, 60]	0
37	23	A	Bristol R	W	1-0	0-0	19	Payne [71]	0
38	Apr 2	H	Blackpool	L	0-2	0-1	20		0
39	5	A	Burton Alb	L	1-2	1-1	20	Payne [35]	0
40	10	H	Peterborough U	L	0-3	0-2	22		0
41	13	A	Rochdale	L	1-2	0-1	22	Garrick [88]	0
42	17	A	AFC Wimbledon	L	1-4	0-3	23	Smith, T [79]	0
43	20	H	Portsmouth	W	3-1	1-0	23	Pitman 2 (1 pen) [17, 61 (p)], Smith, T [90]	0
44	24	A	Milton Keynes D	L	0-5	0-3	23		0
45	May 1	H	Ipswich T	L	1-2	0-1	23	Pitman [71]	0
46	9	A	Wigan Ath	W	4-3	0-1	23	Twine 2 [59, 90], Hope [77], Smith, T [90]	0

Final League Position: 23

GOALSCORERS

League (55): Pitman 11 (1 pen), Smith, T 7 (1 pen), Twine 7, Hope 5, Jaiyesimi 4 (1 pen), Payne 4, Grant, A 3, Garrick 2, Grant, J 2, Smith, M 2, Baudry 1, Broadbent 1, Caddis 1, Curran 1, Palmer 1, Smith, J 1, Stevens 1, own goal 1.
FA Cup (1): Pitman 1.
Carabao Cup (1): Smith J 1.
Papa John's Trophy (6): Smith T 3, Broadbent 1, Caddis 1, Palmer 1.

Kovar M 18	Caddis P 24 + 2	Odimayo A 25 + 5	Fryers Z 9 + 1	Hunt R 13 + 6	Grant A 31 + 2	Smith M 22 + 2	Jaiyesimi D 15 + 3	Payne J 36 + 7	Smith J 13 + 3	Smith T 15 + 8	Pitman B 27 + 11	Hope H 18 + 14	Curran T 3 + 8	Baudry M 15 + 1	Grant J 9 + 11	Stevens J 6 + 7	Donohue D 9 + 1	Grounds J 27 + 4	Iandolo E 5 + 3	Fryer J 2	Broadbent T 11 + 7	Parsons H — + 2	Conroy D 18 + 1	Lyden J 11 + 3	Travers M 8	Thompson D 23 + 2	Palmer M 24	Twine S 22 + 3	Freeman K 2	Masterson C 5	Omotoye T 1 + 6	Garrick J 13 + 6	Missilou C 8 + 3	Wollacott J 2	Matthews A 1	Trueman C 4	Camp L 11	*Match No.*
1	2	3	4	5	6	7	8^2	9^3	10	11^1	12	13	14																									1
1	2		4	5	6	7	10	9^3	8^1	11^2	13	14		3	12																							2
1	2		4	5	6	7		9^2	10^1		11	13		3^3		8	12	14																				3
1	2		4^1	5	6	7	13	9	10^2	14	11			3		8^3		12																				4
1		12			6	7	8	9^2	10	13	11^1			3	14	2^3	5	4																				5
1		4		2^1	8	9	10^2	7	13	11^3		14		3		12	6	5																				6
1	2	4			6	7	12	9^1	10	14		11^3		3	13	8^2		5																				7
1	2	3			6	7		9	8^2		13	11			10^1		5	4	12																			8
1	2	3			6	7		8^1	9■		13	11^3			10^2	12	5	4	14																			9
	2	3		5	7	6		9^1	8		12	11			10			4		1																		10
	2^2	4		5^1	7	8			9		10	11		12	6	13		3		1																		11
1		2			7	6		9^2	8^1		11^3	10		3	13	12	5	4			14																	12
1	2	3			8^1	9		12				11		4	10	7	6				5																	13
1	2^3	3		12	8	9	14	13		11				4^1	10^2	7^4	6	5			15																	14
1	2	3			7	8	9^2	6		10^1			13			12	5	4			11^3	14																15
1		5			6^2	7	11	8		10^3			2	3			9^1	4				14	12	13														16
1		2	12		7	6	11	8	13	10^2		9		3				5					4^1															17
1		2	4			6	10	8	9	13		11^1		3		12		5					7^2															18
1		2	4	14	6^3	8	9	12	11^1	10^2	13			3				5					7															19
1	15	2^2	4	12■	7^1	10	8	9		11^3	14			3^5		13		5^4					6	16														20
	2		4		12	9^1	10				11												3	7	1	5	6	8										21
	2		4^1			6^2	11		14		10^3	13	12										3	7	1	5	9	8										22
		14				13	11	12			15	10^4			8^1								4	7	1	5	6	9^2	2^3	3								23
				2		12	9	15			14	10^1	13										4	8^4	1	5	7	6^2		3	11^3							24
							9	13		10^1	12	6^3											4	8	1	5	7	11^2	2	3	14							25
		2		12				6		10^1	11	9											4■	7	1	5	8			3								26
		3		2				6			11	9^3	12											7^2	1	5	8	13		4^1	14	10^4	15					27
	12	3		2^2				6^3			11	9^1											4		1	5	8	14			13	10	7					28
	2^3	14						9			11	13						3			4		6			5	7	12				10^2	8^1	1				29
		5		12				8			11							4			3		2^1			9	6	7				10		1				30
	5							8			11	12						4			3		2			9^1	6	7				10			1			31
				5				6			11^2	12						4			3		2			9^1	8^3	7			13	10	14			1		32
		5		14				7			10	11^2						3^1	8^4		4		2	6^3				9			13	12	15			1		33
	2	15			12			9			11	13	14								4^4		3^3	8^1		5	6^2	7				10				1		34
	2	13			6^5			14		16	11		15		10^2				12		4^4		3^3	7		5^1		9				8				1		35
	5	2			3			9			11								4					12^2		8	7	10				13	6^1				1	36
	5	2			3			6			11				9^1				4							8	7	10				12					1	37
	5^2	2			3			7		12	11^4	15			13			14	4							8^1	6	10^3				9					1	38
	5^2	2			3			9		13	11				14			12	4^1							8^3	6	10					7				1	39
					3			10^1			12	11	2		14			4			13					9^2	6	8				5	7^3				1	40
	5				3			8			10^2	9^4	2^3		12			4			13					14	6	11				15	7^1				1	41
	2^1				4			8		11	10^5	15			14			5			3^3			6^2		13	7^4	9			16	12					1	42
					3			6		11	10^2	12						4			13					5	7	9				2	8^1				1	43
					3			9		11	10^2	13		2^1	14			4			12					5^3	7	8				6					1	44
				2	3			6^2		10	11		14		15			4^1			12					5	8	9^4				13	7^3				1	45
				2	8			9^2		13	10	12						3			4					5	7	11				6^1					1	46

FA Cup

First Round	Darlington	(h)	1-2

Carabao Cup

First Round	Charlton Ath	(h)	1-3

Papa John's Trophy

Group E (S)	WBA U21	(h)	2-3
Group E (S)	Exeter C	(h)	3-4
Group E (S)	Forest Green R	(a)	1-0

TOTTENHAM HOTSPUR

FOUNDATION

The Hotspur Football Club was formed from an older cricket club in 1882. Most of the founders were old boys of St John's Presbyterian School and Tottenham Grammar School. The Casey brothers were well to the fore as the family provided the club's first goalposts (painted blue and white) and their first ball. They soon adopted the local YMCA as their meeting place, but after a couple of moves settled at the Red House.

Tottenham Hotspur Stadium, Lilywhite House, 782 High Road, Tottenham, London N17 0BX.

Telephone: (0344) 499 5000.

Ticket Office: (0344) 844 0102.

Website: www.tottenhamhotspur.com

Email: supporterservices@tottenhamhotspur.com

Ground Capacity: 62,303.

Record Attendance: 75,038 v Sunderland, FA Cup 6th rd, 5 March 1938 (at White Hart Lane); 85,512 v Bayer Leverkusen, UEFA Champions League Group E, 2 November 2016 (at Wembley); 61,104 v Chelsea, Premier League, 22 December 2019 (at Tottenham Hotspur Stadium).

Pitch Measurements: 105m × 68m (115yd × 74.5yd).

Executive Chairman: Daniel Levy.

Head Coach: Nuno Espirito Santo.

Assistant Head Coach: Ian Cathro.

Colours: White shirts with navy blue and yellow trim, navy blue shorts with yellow trim, white socks with navy blue and yellow trim.

Year Formed: 1882. ***Turned Professional:*** 1895.

Previous Names: 1882, Hotspur Football Club; 1884, Tottenham Hotspur.

Club Nickname: 'Spurs'.

Grounds: 1882, Tottenham Marshes; 1888, Northumberland Park; 1899, White Hart Lane; 2018, Tottenham Hotspur Stadium.

First Football League Game: 1 September 1908, Division 2, v Wolverhampton W (h) W 3–0 – Hewitson; Coquet, Burton; Morris (1), Danny Steel, Darnell; Walton, Woodward (2), Macfarlane, Bobby Steel, Middlemiss.

Record League Victory: 9–0 v Bristol R, Division 2, 22 October 1977 – Daines; Naylor, Holmes, Hoddle (1), McAllister, Perryman, Pratt, McNab, Moores (3), Lee (4), Taylor (1).

HONOURS

League Champions: Division 1 – 1950–51, 1960–61; Division 2 – 1919–20, 1949–50.
Runners-up: Premier League – 2016–17; Division 1 – 1921–22, 1951–52, 1956–57, 1962–63; Division 2 – 1908–09, 1932–33.

FA Cup Winners: 1901 (as non-league club), 1921, 1961, 1962, 1967, 1981, 1982, 1991.
Runners-up: 1987.

League Cup Winners: 1971, 1973, 1999, 2008.
Runners-up: 1982, 2002, 2009, 2015, 2021.

European Competitions
European Cup: 1961–62 *(sf)*.
Champions League: 2010–11 *(qf)*, 2016–17, 2017–18, 2018–19 *(runners-up)*, 2019–20.
UEFA Cup: 1971–72 *(winners)*, 1972–73 *(sf)*, 1973–74 *(runners-up)*, 1983–84 *(winners)*, 1984–85 *(qf)*, 1999–2000, 2006–07 *(qf)*, 2007–08, 2008–09.
Europa League: 2011–12, 2012–13 *(qf)*, 2013–14, 2014–15, 2015–16, 2016–17, 2020–21.
European Cup-Winners' Cup: 1962–63 *(winners)*, 1963–64, 1967–68, 1981–82 *(sf)*, 1982–83, 1991–92 *(qf)*.
Intertoto Cup: 1995.

FOOTBALL YEARBOOK FACT FILE

Tottenham Hotspur have had 78 individual players capped by England up to the end of May 2021, more than any other club. Their first capped player was Vivian Woodward who made his debut against Ireland in February 1903, while their most recent international was Harry Winks, who won his first cap against Lithuania in October 2017.

Record Cup Victory: 13–2 v Crewe Alex, FA Cup 4th rd (replay), 3 February 1960 – Brown; Hills, Henry; Blanchflower, Norman, Mackay; White, Harmer (1), Smith (4), Allen (5), Jones (3 incl. 1p).

Record Defeat: 0–8 v Cologne, UEFA Intertoto Cup, 22 July 1995.

Most League Points (2 for a win): 70, Division 2, 1919–20.

Most League Points (3 for a win): 86, Premier League, 2016–17.

Most League Goals: 115, Division 1, 1960–61.

Highest League Scorer in Season: Jimmy Greaves, 37, Division 1, 1962–63.

Most League Goals in Total Aggregate: Jimmy Greaves, 220, 1961–70.

Most League Goals in One Match: 5, Ted Harper v Reading, Division 2, 30 August 1930; 5, Alf Stokes v Birmingham C, Division 1, 18 September 1957; 5, Bobby Smith v Aston Villa, Division 1, 29 March 1958; 5, Jermain Defoe v Wigan Ath, Premier League, 22 November 2009.

Most Capped Player: Hugo Lloris, 91 (129), France.

Most League Appearances: Steve Perryman, 655, 1969–86.

Youngest League Player: Ally Dick, 16 years 301 days v Manchester C, 20 February 1982.

Record Transfer Fee Received: £85,300,000 from Real Madrid for Gareth Bale, September 2013.

Record Transfer Fee Paid: £55,500,000 (rising to £63,000,000) to Lyon for Tanguy Ndombele, July 2019.

Football League Record: 1908 Elected to Division 2; 1909–15 Division 1; 1919–20 Division 2; 1920–28 Division 1; 1928–33 Division 2; 1933–35 Division 1; 1935–50 Division 2; 1950–77 Division 1; 1977–78 Division 2; 1978–92 Division 1; 1992– Premier League.

MANAGERS

Frank Brettell 1898–99
John Cameron 1899–1906
Fred Kirkham 1907–08
Peter McWilliam 1912–27
Billy Minter 1927–29
Percy Smith 1930–35
Jack Tresadern 1935–38
Peter McWilliam 1938–42
Arthur Turner 1942–46
Joe Hulme 1946–49
Arthur Rowe 1949–55
Jimmy Anderson 1955–58
Bill Nicholson 1958–74
Terry Neill 1974–76
Keith Burkinshaw 1976–84
Peter Shreeves 1984–86
David Pleat 1986–87
Terry Venables 1987–91
Peter Shreeves 1991–92
Doug Livermore 1992–93
Ossie Ardiles 1993–94
Gerry Francis 1994–97
Christian Gross *(Head Coach)* 1997–98
George Graham 1998–2001
Glenn Hoddle 2001–03
David Pleat (*Caretaker*) 2003–04
Jacques Santini 2004
Martin Jol 2004–07
Juande Ramos 2007–08
Harry Redknapp 2008–12
Andre Villas-Boas 2012–13
Tim Sherwood 2013–14
Mauricio Pochettino 2014–19
Jose Mourinho 2019–21
Nuno Espirito Santo June 2021–

LATEST SEQUENCES

Longest Sequence of League Wins: 13, 23.4.1960 – 1.10.1960.

Longest Sequence of League Defeats: 7, 1.1.1994 – 27.2.1994.

Longest Sequence of League Draws: 6, 9.1.1999 – 27.2.1999.

Longest Sequence of Unbeaten League Matches: 22, 31.8.1949 – 31.12.1949.

Longest Sequence Without a League Win: 16, 29.12.1934 – 13.4.1935.

Successive Scoring Runs: 32 from 24.2.1962.

Successive Non-scoring Runs: 6 from 28.12.1985.

TEN YEAR LEAGUE RECORD

		P	*W*	*D*	*L*	*F*	*A*	*Pts*	*Pos*
2011-12	PR Lge	38	20	9	9	66	41	69	4
2012-13	PR Lge	38	21	9	8	66	46	72	5
2013-14	PR Lge	38	21	6	11	55	51	69	6
2014-15	PR Lge	38	19	7	12	58	53	64	5
2015-16	PR Lge	38	19	13	6	69	35	70	3
2016-17	PR Lge	38	26	8	4	86	26	86	2
2017-18	PR Lge	38	23	8	7	74	36	77	3
2018-19	PR Lge	38	23	2	13	67	39	71	4
2019-20	PR Lg	38	16	11	11	61	47	59	6
2020-21	PR Lge	38	18	8	12	68	45	62	7

DID YOU KNOW ?

Charlie Wilson stepped in to replace first-choice centre-forward Len Cantrell at South Shields on 20 September 1919 and scored a hat-trick on what was his Football League debut. He was one of only half-a-dozen players to perform this feat in the period between the two World Wars.

TOTTENHAM HOTSPUR – PREMIER LEAGUE 2020–21 LEAGUE RECORD

Match No.	*Date*	*Venue*	*Opponents*	*Result*		*H/T Score*	*Lg Pos.*	*Goalscorers*	*Attendance*
1	Sept 13	H	Everton	L	0-1	0-0	16		0
2	20	A	Southampton	W	5-2	1-1	6	Son 4 [45, 47, 64, 73], Kane [82]	0
3	27	H	Newcastle U	D	1-1	1-0	7	Lucas Moura [25]	0
4	Oct 4	A	Manchester U	W	6-1	4-1	6	Ndombele [4], Son 2 [7, 37], Kane 2 (1 pen) [30, 79 (p)], Aurier [51]	0
5	18	H	West Ham U	D	3-3	3-0	6	Son [1], Kane 2 [8, 16]	0
6	26	A	Burnley	W	1-0	0-0	5	Son [76]	0
7	Nov 1	H	Brighton & HA	W	2-1	1-0	2	Kane (pen) [13], Bale [73]	0
8	8	A	WBA	W	1-0	0-0	2	Kane [88]	0
9	21	H	Manchester C	W	2-0	1-0	1	Son [5], Lo Celso [65]	0
10	29	A	Chelsea	D	0-0	0-0	1		0
11	Dec 6	H	Arsenal	W	2-0	2-0	1	Son [13], Kane [45]	2000
12	13	A	Crystal Palace	D	1-1	1-0	1	Kane [23]	2000
13	16	A	Liverpool	L	1-2	1-1	2	Son [33]	2000
14	20	H	Leicester C	L	0-2	0-1	5		0
15	27	A	Wolverhampton W	D	1-1	1-0	5	Ndombele [1]	0
16	Jan 2	H	Leeds U	W	3-0	2-0	3	Kane (pen) [29], Son [43], Alderweireld [50]	0
17	13	H	Fulham	D	1-1	1-0	6	Kane [25]	0
18	17	A	Sheffield U	W	3-1	2-0	5	Aurier [5], Kane [40], Ndombele [62]	0
19	28	H	Liverpool	L	1-3	0-1	6	Hojbjerg [49]	0
20	31	A	Brighton & HA	L	0-1	0-1	6		0
21	Feb 4	H	Chelsea	L	0-1	0-1	8		0
22	7	H	WBA	W	2-0	0-0	8	Kane [54], Son [58]	0
23	13	A	Manchester C	L	0-3	0-1	9		0
24	21	A	West Ham U	L	1-2	0-1	9	Lucas Moura [64]	0
25	28	H	Burnley	W	4-0	3-0	8	Bale 2 [2, 55], Kane [15], Lucas Moura [31]	0
26	Mar 4	A	Fulham	W	1-0	1-0	8	Adarabioyo (og) [19]	0
27	7	H	Crystal Palace	W	4-1	1-1	6	Bale 2 [25, 49], Kane 2 [52, 76]	0
28	14	A	Arsenal	L	1-2	1-1	7	Lamela [33]	0
29	21	A	Aston Villa	W	2-0	1-0	6	Vinicius [29], Kane (pen) [68]	0
30	Apr 4	A	Newcastle U	D	2-2	2-1	5	Kane 2 [30, 34]	0
31	11	H	Manchester U	L	1-3	1-0	7	Son [40]	0
32	16	A	Everton	D	2-2	1-1	7	Kane 2 [27, 68]	0
33	21	H	Southampton	W	2-1	0-1	6	Bale [60], Son (pen) [90]	0
34	May 2	H	Sheffield U	W	4-0	1-0	5	Bale 3 [36, 61, 69], Son [77]	0
35	8	A	Leeds U	L	1-3	1-2	7	Son [25]	0
36	16	H	Wolverhampton W	W	2-0	1-0	6	Kane [45], Hojbjerg [62]	0
37	19	H	Aston Villa	L	1-2	1-2	7	Bergwijn [8]	10,000
38	23	A	Leicester C	W	4-2	1-1	7	Kane [41], Schmeichel (og) [76], Bale 2 [87, 90]	8000

Final League Position: 7

GOALSCORERS

League (68): Kane 23 (4 pens), Son 17 (1 pen), Bale 11, Lucas Moura 3, Ndombele 3, Aurier 2, Hojbjerg 2, Alderweireld 1, Bergwijn 1, Lamela 1, Lo Celso 1, Vinicius 1, own goals 2.
FA Cup (13): Vinicius 3, Ndombele 2, Sanchez 2, Bale 1, Devine 1, Kane 1, Lamela 1, Lucas Moura 1, Winks 1.
Carabao Cup (6): Bale 1, Davies 1, Kane 1, Lamela 1, Sissoko 1, Son 1.
UEFA Europa League (37): Kane 8 (2 pens), Vinicius 6, Lucas Moura 5, Lo Celso 4, Son 4, Alli 3 (2 pens), Bale 3 (1 pen), Lamela 1, Ndombele 1, Winks 1, own goal 1.

Lloris H 38	Doherty M 13 + 4	Alderweireld T 25	Dier E 28	Davies B 14 + 6	Hojbjerg P 38	Winks H 9 + 6	Lucas Moura R 14 + 16	Alli B 7 + 8	Son H 36 + 1	Kane H 35	Sissoko M 15 + 10	Bergwijn S 13 + 8	Ndombele T 28 + 5	Sanchez D 17 + 1	Lo Celso G 11 + 7	Lamela E 5 + 18	Aurier S 19	Reguilon S 26 + 1	Bale G 10 + 10	Rodon J 8 + 4	Vinicius C 3 + 6	Scarlett D — + 1	Tanganga J 6	Match No.
1	2^{3}	3	4	5	6	7^{2}	8	9^{1}	10	11	12	13	14											1
1	2		4	5	6	7	9^{2}		11	10^{3}		14	8^{1}	3	12	13								2
1	2		4	5	6	7	8^{3}		10^{1}	11		12	13	3	9^{2}	14								3
1			4	14	7		12	13	11^{3}	10	6		8^{2}	3		9^{1}	2	5						4
1		3			7	13	14		10^{3}	11	6	8^{1}	9^{2}	4			2	5	12					5
1	2	3	4	5	7		8^{1}		10^{3}	11	6		9^{2}		13	12				14				6
1	2	3	4	14	7				10^{3}	11	6		9^{1}		12	8^{2}		5	13					7
1	2	3	4		7		14		10	11	6^{2}		9^{1}		12			5	8^{3}		13			8
1		3^{3}	4		7		13		8	11	6	10^{2}	9^{1}		12		2	5		14				9
1			4	13	7		14		8^{3}	11	6	10^{2}	9^{1}		12		2	5		3				10
1		3	4	12	7		13		10^{2}	11	6	8^{3}			9^{1}		2	5		14				11
1		3	4	13	7			14	10	11	6	8^{3}	9^{1}		12		2	5^{2}						12
1		3	4	5	7		12	14	11^{3}	10	6	9^{2}			8^{1}		2	13						13
1		3	4		7	14	13		10	11	6		9^{1}		8^{2}		2^{3}	5	12					14
1	5		3	4	7	6			11^{3}	10	13	12	9^{2}	2		14		8^{1}						15
1	2■	3	4	5	7	6^{1}	13		10	11^{3}	12	8	9^{2}								14			16
1			4		6	7^{1}			10	11	8		9^{2}	3		12	2	5			13			17
1			3	4	7		12		11^{3}	10		9^{1}	6	14			5	8^{2}		2	13			18
1	8		3	4	6	12			11	10^{1}		9^{3}	7			13	5^{2}		14	2				19
1		3		8	7		13		10		5	11	6^{3}	2^{1}		14			9^{2}	4	12			20
1		3	4	5	7		13		10		6	8^{1}	9^{2}			12	2				11			21
1	12	4		5	7		9		10^{3}	11		13	6	3		8^{2}	2^{1}					14		22
1			4	5	7		9^{1}	13	10	11	12		6^{2}	3		8^{3}			14				2	23
1	13		4		7		8	14	10	11			6	3		9^{2}		5^{3}	12				2^{1}	24
1	14	4			7		9^{1}	12	10	11			6	3		13	2^{3}	5	8^{2}					25
1	2	4		5	7		13	9^{1}	10	11	12		6^{3}	3		14			8^{2}					26
1	2	4			7	6^{2}	9		10	11^{3}	13			3		12		5	8^{1}		14			27
1	2	4			6		9	14	10^{1}	11	13		7^{3}	3		12■		5	8^{2}					28
1				12	8		9			11	14	13	7^{3}	3	6^{2}			5^{1}		4	10		2	29
1					8		9^{2}		12	11			7	3	6^{3}	13		5	14	4	10^{1}		2	30
1			3		7		9^{3}		11	10	12		8^{2}		6^{1}	13	2	5	14	4				31
1		2	4		7		13	14	10	11^{3}	6		9^{1}			12	5	8^{2}		3				32
1		3	4		7	12	11		10			14	6^{1}		9^{2}	13	2	5	8^{3}					33
1		3	4		7	12		9^{3}	10	11		13			6^{1}	14	2	5	8^{2}					34
1		3	4		7		13	9^{1}	10	11			14		6^{3}	12	2	5	8^{2}					35
1		3	4		7	12		9^{2}	10	11	14		13		6^{1}			5	8^{3}				2	36
1	14	3	4		7	6^{2}		9	10	11		8^{1}	13					5	12				2^{3}	37
1	2	4			6	7	13	9^{1}	10^{3}	11		8^{2}		3				5	12	14				38

FA Cup

Third Round	Marine	(a)	5-0
Fourth Round	Wycombe W	(a)	4-1
Fifth Round	Everton	(a)	4-5

(aet)

Carabao Cup

Fourth Round	Chelsea	(h)	1-1

(Tottenham H won 5-4 on penalties)

Quarter-Final	Stoke C	(a)	3-1
Semi-Final	Brentford	(h)	2-0
Final	Manchester C	(Wembley)	0-1

UEFA Europa League

2nd Qualifying Round	Lokomotiv Plovdiv	(a)	2-1
3rd Qualifying Round	Shkendija	(a)	3-1
Play-Offs	Maccabi Haifa	(h)	7-2
Group J	LASK	(h)	3-0
Group J	Antwerp	(a)	0-1
Group J	Ludogorets Razgrad	(a)	3-1
Group J	Ludogorets Razgrad	(h)	4-0
Group J	LASK	(a)	3-3
Group J	Antwerp	(h)	2-0
Round of 32 1st leg	Wolfsberg	(a)	4-1
Round of 32 2nd leg	Wolfsberg	(h)	4-0
Round of 16 1st leg	Dinamo Zagreb	(h)	2-0
Round of 16 2nd leg	Dinamo Zagreb	(a)	0-3

(aet)

TRANMERE ROVERS

FOUNDATION

Formed in 1884 as Belmont they adopted their present title the following year and eventually joined their first league, the West Lancashire League, in 1889–90, the same year as their first success in the Wirral Challenge Cup. The club almost folded in 1899–1900 when all the players left en bloc to join a rival club, but they survived the crisis and went from strength to strength, winning the 'Combination' title in 1907–08 and the Lancashire Combination in 1913–14. They joined the Football League in 1921 from the Central League.

Prenton Park, Prenton Road West, Birkenhead, Merseyside CH42 9PY.

Telephone: (0333) 014 4452.

Ticket Office: (0333) 014 4452 (Option 2).

Website: www.tranmererovers.co.uk

Email: via website.

Ground Capacity: 15,012.

Record Attendance: 24,424 v Stoke C, FA Cup 4th rd, 5 February 1972.

Pitch Measurements: 100m × 64m (109.5yd × 70yd).

Chairman: Mark Palios.

Vice-Chairman: Nicola Palios.

Manager: Micky Mellon.

Assistant Manager: Ian Dawes.

HONOURS

League Champions: Division 3 (N) – 1937–38.
Runners-up: Division 4 – 1988–89.

FA Cup: quarter-final – 2000, 2001, 2004.

League Cup: *Runners-up:* 2000.

Welsh Cup Winners: 1935.
Runners-up: 1934.

League Trophy Winners: 1990.
Runners-up: 1991, 2021.

Colours: White shirts with blue trim, white shorts with blue trim, white socks with blue trim.

Year Formed: 1884.

Turned Professional: 1912.

Previous Name: 1884, Belmont AFC; 1885, Tranmere Rovers.

Club Nickname: 'Rovers'.

Grounds: 1884, Steeles Field; 1887, Ravenshaws Field/Old Prenton Park; 1912, Prenton Park.

First Football League Game: 27 August 1921, Division 3 (N), v Crewe Alex (h) W 4–1 – Bradshaw; Grainger, Stuart (1); Campbell, Milnes (1), Heslop; Moreton, Groves (1), Hyam, Ford (1), Hughes.

Record League Victory: 13–4 v Oldham Ath, Division 3 (N), 26 December 1935 – Gray; Platt, Fairhurst; McLaren, Newton, Spencer; Eden, MacDonald (1), Bell (9), Woodward (2), Urmson (1).

Record Cup Victory: 13–0 v Oswestry U, FA Cup 2nd prel rd, 10 October 1914 – Ashcroft; Stevenson, Bullough, Hancock, Taylor, Holden (1), Moreton (1), Cunningham (2), Smith (5), Leck (3), Gould (1).

FOOTBALL YEARBOOK FACT FILE

Tranmere Rovers signed Norman Sutton on amateur forms in September 1928 and he scored a hat-trick for the reserves on his debut. He featured regularly for the club's second string and once for the first team in a Cheshire Senior Medals tie before moving on. Sutton had recently reached the semi-final of the English Amateur Golf Championship and went on to become one of the country's leading professional golfers, sharing sixth place at the 1951 Open Championship.

Record Defeat: 1–9 v Tottenham H, FA Cup 3rd rd (replay), 14 January 1953.

Most League Points (2 for a win): 60, Division 4, 1964–65.

Most League Points (3 for a win): 80, Division 4, 1988–89; Division 3, 1989–90; Division 2, 2002–03.

Most League Goals: 111, Division 3 (N), 1930–31.

Highest League Scorer in Season: Bunny Bell, 35, Division 3 (N), 1933–34.

Most League Goals in Total Aggregate: Ian Muir, 142, 1985–95.

Most League Goals in One Match: 9, Bunny Bell v Oldham Ath, Division 3 (N), 26 December 1935.

Most Capped Player: John Aldridge, 30 (69), Republic of Ireland.

Most League Appearances: Harold Bell, 595, 1946–64 (incl. League record 401 consecutive appearances).

Youngest League Player: Iain Hume, 16 years 167 days v Swindon T, 15 April 2000.

Record Transfer Fee Received: £2,250,000 from WBA for Jason Koumas, August 2002.

Record Transfer Fee Paid: £450,000 to Aston Villa for Shaun Teale, August 1995.

Football League Record: 1921 Original Member of Division 3 (N): 1938–39 Division 2; 1946–58 Division 3 (N); 1958–61 Division 3; 1961–67 Division 4; 1967–75 Division 3; 1975–76 Division 4; 1976–79 Division 3; 1979–89 Division 4; 1989–91 Division 3; 1991–92 Division 2; 1992–2001 Division 1; 2001–04 Division 2; 2004–14 FL 1; 2014–15 FL 2; 2015–18 National League; 2018–19 FL 2; 2019–20 FL 1; 2020– FL 2.

MANAGERS

Bert Cooke 1912–35
Jackie Carr 1935–36
Jim Knowles 1936–39
Bill Ridding 1939–45
Ernie Blackburn 1946–55
Noel Kelly 1955–57
Peter Farrell 1957–60
Walter Galbraith 1961
Dave Russell 1961–69
Jackie Wright 1969–72
Ron Yeats 1972–75
John King 1975–80
Bryan Hamilton 1980–85
Frank Worthington 1985–87
Ronnie Moore 1987
John King 1987–96
John Aldridge 1996–2001
Dave Watson 2001–02
Ray Mathias 2002–03
Brian Little 2003–06
Ronnie Moore 2006–09
John Barnes 2009
Les Parry 2009–12
Ronnie Moore 2012–14
Robert Edwards 2014
Micky Adams 2014–15
Gary Brabin 2015–16
Paul Cardin 2016
Micky Mellon 2016–20
Mike Jackson 2020
Keith Hill 2020–21
Micky Mellon May 2021–

LATEST SEQUENCES

Longest Sequence of League Wins: 9, 9.2.1990 – 19.3.1990.

Longest Sequence of League Defeats: 8, 29.10.1938 – 17.12.1938.

Longest Sequence of League Draws: 5, 26.12.1997 – 31.1.1998.

Longest Sequence of Unbeaten League Matches: 18, 16.3.1970 – 4.9.1970.

Longest Sequence Without a League Win: 16, 8.11.1969 – 14.3.1970.

Successive Scoring Runs: 32 from 24.2.1934.

Successive Non-scoring Runs: 7 from 20.12.1997.

TEN YEAR LEAGUE RECORD

		P	*W*	*D*	*L*	*F*	*A*	*Pts*	*Pos*
2011-12	FL 1	46	14	14	18	49	53	56	12
2012-13	FL 1	46	19	10	17	58	48	67	11
2013-14	FL 1	46	12	11	23	52	79	47	21
2014-15	FL 2	46	9	12	25	45	67	39	24
2015-16	NL	46	22	12	12	61	44	78	6
2016-17	NL	46	29	8	9	79	39	95	2
2017-18	NL	46	24	10	12	78	46	82	2
2018-19	FL 2	46	20	13	13	63	50	73	6
2019-20	FL 1	34	8	8	18	36	60	32	21§
2020-21	FL 2	46	20	13	13	55	50	73	7

§Decided on points-per-game (0.94)

DID YOU KNOW ?

Tranmere Rovers were the best supported club in Division Three North in 1935–36 with an average attendance of 8,872. Rovers led the division for most of the season but fell away badly in the closing stages, having once been five points clear at the top of the table. They eventually finished in third place.

TRANMERE ROVERS – SKY BET LEAGUE TWO 2020–21 LEAGUE RECORD

Match No.	Date	Venue	Opponents	Result	H/T Score	Lg Pos.	Goalscorers	Attendance
1	Sept 12	A	Mansfield T	D 0-0	0-0	14		0
2	19	H	Cheltenham T	L 0-3	0-3	20		0
3	26	A	Cambridge U	D 0-0	0-0	20		0
4	Oct 3	H	Scunthorpe U	W 2-0	1-0	15	Vaughan 2 $^{41, 66}$	0
5	10	A	Salford C	D 2-2	0-2	13	Morris ^{86}, Lewis ^{90}	0
6	17	A	Newport Co	L 0-1	0-1	16		0
7	20	H	Leyton Orient	L 0-1	0-0	17		0
8	24	H	Southend U	W 2-0	1-0	16	Clarke ^{31}, Vaughan ^{52}	0
9	27	A	Crawley T	L 0-4	0-3	17		0
10	31	H	Morecambe	L 0-1	0-0	18		0
11	Nov 3	A	Harrogate T	W 1-0	0-0	17	Khan ^{79}	0
12	14	A	Port Vale	W 4-3	0-2	15	Vaughan 2 (1 pen) $^{58, 71 (p)}$, Morris ^{90}, Woolery ^{90}	0
13	21	H	Grimsby T	W 5-0	4-0	13	Vaughan 2 (1 pen) $^{10, 29 (p)}$, Clarke ^{27}, Khan ^{33}, Lewis ^{86}	0
14	24	H	Carlisle U	W 1-0	0-0	9	Taylor ^{51}	0
15	Dec 1	A	Oldham Ath	W 1-0	1-0	7	Vaughan ^{27}	0
16	5	H	Walsall	L 1-3	1-1	10	Feeney ^{31}	2000
17	12	A	Exeter C	L 0-5	0-3	12		1630
18	19	A	Bolton W	W 3-0	1-0	13	Clarke ^{28}, Morris ^{68}, Vaughan (pen) ^{75}	0
19	26	H	Bradford C	L 0-1	0-0	13		0
20	29	A	Barrow	D 1-1	1-0	13	Vaughan ^{23}	1131
21	Jan 16	A	Stevenage	D 0-0	0-0	15		0
22	19	H	Forest Green R	W 3-2	1-0	11	Lewis ^{12}, Vaughan ^{47}, Feeney ^{76}	0
23	23	H	Bolton W	W 2-1	1-0	10	Lloyd ^{4}, Vaughan (pen) ^{56}	0
24	26	H	Harrogate T	W 3-2	1-1	8	Vaughan 2 (1 pen) $^{36 (p), 53}$, Woolery ^{51}	0
25	30	A	Morecambe	W 1-0	0-0	5	Woolery ^{74}	0
26	Feb 6	H	Port Vale	W 3-1	2-1	3	Woolery ^{17}, Vaughan 2 $^{30, 59}$	0
27	9	H	Stevenage	L 0-1	0-0	4		0
28	20	H	Oldham Ath	D 2-2	1-1	6	MacDonald ^{42}, Woolery ^{51}	0
29	23	A	Carlisle U	W 3-2	2-2	5	Woolery ^{21}, Vaughan 2 $^{43, 88}$	0
30	27	A	Leyton Orient	W 3-1	1-0	4	Lewis ^{24}, Woolery ^{56}, Morris ^{63}	0
31	Mar 2	H	Newport Co	W 1-0	1-0	4	Feeney ^{6}	0
32	6	H	Crawley T	L 0-1	0-0	5		0
33	9	A	Southend U	W 2-0	2-0	4	Lewis ^{8}, Ray ^{24}	0
34	17	A	Grimsby T	D 0-0	0-0	4		0
35	20	H	Exeter C	W 2-1	1-1	4	Nugent, D (pen) ^{18}, Lloyd (pen) ^{68}	0
36	23	A	Colchester U	D 2-2	0-1	4	Lloyd (pen) ^{62}, Spearing ^{67}	0
37	27	H	Mansfield T	D 1-1	1-0	3	Woolery ^{45}	0
38	Apr 2	A	Cheltenham T	L 0-4	0-3	4		0
39	5	H	Cambridge U	D 1-1	1-0	3	Lewis ^{11}	0
40	10	A	Scunthorpe U	D 0-0	0-0	4		0
41	13	A	Walsall	L 0-1	0-0	5		0
42	17	H	Salford C	D 0-0	0-0	5		0
43	20	A	Bradford C	W 1-0	1-0	5	O'Connor, P (og) ^{45}	0
44	24	H	Barrow	W 1-0	0-0	5	Nugent, D ^{66}	0
45	May 1	A	Forest Green R	L 1-2	0-0	6	Morris ^{90}	0
46	8	H	Colchester U	D 0-0	0-0	7		0

Final League Position: 7

GOALSCORERS

League (55): Vaughan 18 (5 pens), Woolery 8, Lewis 6, Morris 5, Clarke 3, Feeney 3, Lloyd 3 (2 pens), Khan 2, Nugent, D 2 (1 pen), MacDonald 1, Ray 1, Spearing 1, Taylor 1, own goal 1.
FA Cup (3): Blackett-Taylor 1, Clarke 1, Woolery 1.
Carabao Cup (1): Vaughan 1.
Papa John's Trophy (15): Lloyd 4, Morris 2, Vaughan 2, Woolery 2, Banks 1 (1 pen), Blackett-Taylor 1, Ferrier 1, Lewis 1, Payne 1.
League Two Play-Offs (2): Clarke 1, Vaughan 1.

Davies S 34	O'Connor L 28 + 5	Clarke P 46	Monthe E 30 + 4	Ridehalgh L 15 + 9	Morris K 29 + 13	Spearing J 43	Banks O 7 + 5	MacDonald C 37 + 2	Khan O 29 + 6	Vaughan J 26 + 3	Ellis M 5 + 1	Payne S 1 + 3	Lewis P 33 + 7	Feeney L 37 + 4	Woolery K 30 + 10	Murphy J 12 + 1	Nelson S 6 + 3	Burton J 1 + 1	Walker-Rice D — + 1	Young J 4 + 1	Smith S 2 + 3	Taylor C 9 + 11	Lloyd D 17 + 14	Ferrier M 2 + 8	Kirby N 2 + 4	Ray G 10 + 1	Crawford A 4 + 5	Jolley C — + 2	Nugent D 7 + 11	Match No.
1	2	3	4	5	6	7	8	9^{1}	10	11^{2}	12	13																		1
1	5	3	4	8	9	6^{2}	13		11^{3}	10	2^{1}	14	7	12																2
1	2	3	4	5	6^{2}	9	8		10^{1}	11			13	7	12															3
1	2	3	4	5	6	7	8	13	9^{2}	10		11^{1}	12																	4
		4	5		8	7			9		3		6		11	1	2	10^{1}	12											5
	2	3	4	5	6	7^{3}	9^{1}		10^{2}				8▪	12	11	1		14		13										6
	2^{1}	3		5	8	7	9^{2}		13		4			10	6	1	12				11									7
1	2^{1}	4		5	9	6^{3}	14	13	10^{2}	11	3			8						7	12									8
1	12	2		4^{1}	6	8^{3}		9		11	3^{2}			5			13			7	10	14								9
1	2	3	4		9^{3}		7	5	10^{1}	11			6	12	8^{2}						14	13								10
1	2	3	4	5	9^{1}	6			12	11			7	8	13							10^{2}								11
1		3	4		7	6		5	8	10					13		2^{3}				14	11^{2}	9^{1}	12						12
1	2	3	4		9	6		5	8^{4}	11^{3}			13	7^{2}	12							10^{1}	15	14						13
1	2	3	4		9	6		5	7^{2}	11^{4}			12	8^{1}	13		15					10^{3}	14							14
1	2	3	4		9	6		5	13	11			7	8^{2}	10^{1}								12							15
1	2	3	4		7^{4}	6		5	15	11^{1}			9^{2}	8	12							10^{3}	14	13						16
1	2	3	4	14	9^{3}	6	12	5^{1}	8^{2}				13	7	10^{5}							16	11^{4}	15						17
1	14	4		5	6^{3}	7^{1}	12	2		10^{4}				9^{5}	15		3			8		11^{2}	16	13						18
1		3		5	13	6		2^{4}		10			15	9	14		4			8^{3}		11^{2}	7^{1}	12						19
1		4		5	8^{2}	6	13	2		11			7	9	12		3							10^{1}						20
1		3	4			7	6^{2}	5	2	10			8	12	9^{1}							14	13	11^{3}						21
1		3	4		12	7		5	2	10^{3}		14	6	11	9^{1}								8^{2}	13						22
1		3	4		13	7		5	2	10			6	8	11^{1}								9^{2}		12					23
1		3	4	13	12	6		5	2	11^{4}			8	9^{3}	7^{1}								10^{2}	14		15				24
1		4	3	13		6		5	2	11			9	10	7^{2}								12		8^{1}					25
1	13	3	4		12	7		5	2	10			6	8^{2}	9								11^{1}							26
1		3	4		12	7		5	2	10			6		9^{2}								11^{1}		13		8^{3}	14		27
1	2	3	4		6^{2}	7		5		10^{1}			8	9	11							13							12	28
1	12	3			13	7		5		10			6	8	9^{3}		2^{1}						11^{2}			4			14	29
1	2	4		13	12	7		5		10^{3}			6	8	11^{2}								9^{1}			3			14	30
1	2	3		12	9^{2}	7		5					6	8	11								13			4			10^{1}	31
1	2^{3}	3	13			6		5					8	9	11							14	12		7^{1}	4^{2}	15		10^{4}	32
1	2	3		13	10^{1}	7		5^{3}					6	8	9							14	11^{2}			4			12	33
1		3	15	2	13	7		5					6^{2}	8^{4}	9							11^{1}	12			4	14		10^{3}	34
1	6	3	12	15	8^{3}	7		5	2				13	9	10^{4}								14			4^{1}			11^{2}	35
1		3	4	5^{2}	8^{1}	7		11	2				10	6									9^{3}		14		13		12	36
1^{1}		3			7^{2}	6		5	2				11	9	10	12									13	4	8^{3}		14	37
	6^{1}	3		14	8^{2}	7		5	2				10	9^{4}	11	1							13			4^{3}	15		12	38
	6	3	4		12	8^{1}		5	2				11	7	10^{2}	1						14	9^{3}						13	39
	6	3	4		14			5	2				7	9^{3}	10	1						13	11^{1}				8^{2}		12	40
	12	3	4		15	6▪		5	2	14			9	7^{4}	10^{2}	1							13				8^{1}		11^{3}	41
	6	3	4		11^{3}			5	2	12			8	9	7^{2}	1						14	10^{1}						13	42
	2	3	4	13	11	6		5	12				9	7^{2}	8	1							10^{1}							43
	2	3	4		8^{2}	7		5	12				6	9	11	1							10^{1}						13	44
	3	4	5		12	8		6^{3}	2^{4}				9^{1}	7	10^{2}	1						13	14					15	11	45
	2	3	14	9		7			5	13			8	6^{4}	12	1						10^{1}				4^{3}	15		11^{2}	46

FA Cup

First Round	Accrington S	(h)	2-1
Second Round	Brackley T	(h)	1-0
Third Round	Barnsley	(a)	0-2

Carabao Cup

First Round	Harrogate T	(h)	1-1

(Harrogate T won 8-7 on penalties)

League Two Play-Offs

Semi-Final 1st leg	Morecambe	(h)	1-2
Semi-Final 2nd leg	Morecambe	(a)	1-1

Papa John's Trophy

Group D (N)	Port Vale	(a)	0-0
(Port Vale won 4-3 on penalties)			
Group D (N)	Liverpool U21	(h)	3-2
Group D (N)	Wigan Ath	(h)	2-2
(Tranmere R won 3-1 on penalties)			
Second Round (N)	Manchester C U21	(h)	2-1
Third Round (N)	Leicester C U21	(h)	4-2
Quarter-Final	Peterborough U	(h)	2-1
Semi-Final	Oxford U	(a)	2-0
Final	Sunderland	(Wembley)	0-1

WALSALL

FOUNDATION

Two of the leading clubs around Walsall in the 1880s were Walsall Swifts (formed 1877) and Walsall Town (formed 1879). The Swifts were winners of the Birmingham Senior Cup in 1881, while the Town reached the 4th round (5th round modern equivalent) of the FA Cup in 1883. These clubs amalgamated as Walsall Town Swifts in 1888, becoming simply Walsall in 1895.

Banks's Stadium, Bescot Crescent, Walsall WS1 4SA.
Telephone: (01922) 622 791.
Ticket Office: (01922) 651 414/416.
Website: www.saddlers.co.uk
Email: info@walsallfc.co.uk
Ground Capacity: 10,862.
Record Attendance: 25,453 v Newcastle U, Division 2, 29 August 1961 (at Fellows Park); 11,049 v Rotherham U, Division 1, 9 May 2004 (at Bescot Stadium).
Pitch Measurements: 100.5m × 67m (110yd × 73.5yd).
Chairman: Lee Pomlett.
Chief Executive: Stefan Gamble.
Manager: Matthew Taylor.
First-Team Coach: Neil McDonald.
Colours: Red shirts with white and green trim, white shorts with red and green trim, green socks with red trim.
Year Formed: 1888.
Turned Professional: 1888.
Previous Names: Walsall Swifts (founded 1877) and Walsall Town (founded 1879) amalgamated in 1888 as Walsall Town Swifts; 1895, Walsall.
Club Nickname: 'The Saddlers'.
Grounds: 1888, Fellows Park; 1990, Bescot Stadium (renamed Banks's Stadium 2007).
First Football League Game: 3 September 1892, Division 2, v Darwen (h) L 1–2 – Hawkins; Withington, Pinches; Robinson, Whitrick, Forsyth; Marshall, Holmes, Turner, Gray (1), Pangbourn.
Record League Victory: 10–0 v Darwen, Division 2, 4 March 1899 – Tennent; Ted Peers (1), Davies; Hickinbotham, Jenkyns, Taggart; Dean (3), Vail (2), Aston (4), Martin, Griffin.
Record Cup Victory: 7–0 v Macclesfield T (a), FA Cup 2nd rd, 6 December 1997 – Walker; Evans, Marsh, Viveash (1), Ryder, Peron, Boli (2 incl. 1p) (Ricketts), Porter (2), Keates, Watson (Platt), Hodge (2 incl. 1p).
Record Defeat: 0–12 v Small Heath, 17 December 1892; 0–12 v Darwen, 26 December 1896, both Division 2.
Most League Points (2 for a win): 65, Division 4, 1959–60.
Most League Points (3 for a win): 89, FL 2, 2006–07.
Most League Goals: 102, Division 4, 1959–60.

HONOURS

League Champions: FL 2 – 2006–07; Division 4 – 1959–60.
Runners-up: Second Division – 1998–99; Division 3 – 1960–61; Third Division – 1994–95; Division 4 – 1979–80.
FA Cup: last 16 – 1889; 5th rd – 1939, 1975, 1978, 1987, 2002, 2003.
League Cup: semi-final – 1984.
League Trophy: *Runners-up:* 2015.

FOOTBALL YEARBOOK FACT FILE

The first-ever game played by Walsall Town Swifts was against Aston Villa in the Mayor of Birmingham's Charity Cup on 9 April 1888. The match was abandoned in extra time due to poor light with no goals scored and the Saddlers subsequently withdrew from the competition after being told the replay must take place in Birmingham.

Highest League Scorer in Season: Gilbert Alsop, 40, Division 3 (N), 1933–34 and 1934–35.

Most League Goals in Total Aggregate: Tony Richards, 184, 1954–63; Colin Taylor, 184, 1958–63, 1964–68, 1969–73.

Most League Goals in One Match: 5, Gilbert Alsop v Carlisle U, Division 3 (N), 2 February 1935; 5, Bill Evans v Mansfield T, Division 3 (N), 5 October 1935; 5, Johnny Devlin v Torquay U, Division 3 (S), 1 September 1949.

Most Capped Player: Mick Kearns, 15 (18), Republic of Ireland.

Most League Appearances: Colin Harrison, 473, 1964–82.

Youngest League Player: Geoff Morris, 16 years 218 days v Scunthorpe U, 14 September 1965.

Record Transfer Fee Received: £1,500,000 (rising to £5,000,000) from Brentford for Rico Henry, August 2016.

Record Transfer Fee Paid: £300,000 to Anorthosis Famagusta for Andreas Makris, August 2016.

Football League Record: 1892 Elected to Division 2; 1895 Failed re-election; 1896–1901 Division 2; 1901 Failed re-election; 1921 Original Member of Division 3 (N); 1927–31 Division 3 (S); 1931–36 Division 3 (N); 1936–58 Division 3 (S); 1958–60 Division 4; 1960–61 Division 3; 1961–63 Division 2; 1963–79 Division 3; 1979–80 Division 4; 1980–88 Division 3; 1988–89 Division 2; 1989–90 Division 3; 1990–92 Division 4; 1992–95 Division 3; 1995–99 Division 2; 1999–2000 Division 1; 2000–01 Division 2; 2001–04 Division 1; 2004–06 FL 1; 2006–07 FL 2; 2007–19 FL 1; 2019– FL 2.

LATEST SEQUENCES

Longest Sequence of League Wins: 7, 9.4.2005 – 9.8.2005.

Longest Sequence of League Defeats: 15, 29.10.1988 – 4.2.1989.

Longest Sequence of League Draws: 5, 7.5.1988 – 17.9.1988.

Longest Sequence of Unbeaten League Matches: 21, 6.11.1979 – 22.3.1980.

Longest Sequence Without a League Win: 18, 15.10.1988 – 4.2.1989.

Successive Scoring Runs: 27 from 6.11.1979.

Successive Non-scoring Runs: 5 from 10.4.2004.

MANAGERS

H. Smallwood 1888–91 *(Secretary-Manager)*
A. G. Burton 1891–93
J. H. Robinson 1893–95
C. H. Ailso 1895–96 *(Secretary-Manager)*
A. E. Parsloe 1896–97 *(Secretary-Manager)*
L. Ford 1897–98 *(Secretary-Manager)*
G. Hughes 1898–99 *(Secretary-Manager)*
L. Ford 1899–1901 *(Secretary-Manager)*
J. E. Shutt 1908–13 *(Secretary-Manager)*
Haydn Price 1914–20
Joe Burchell 1920–26
David Ashworth 1926–27
Jack Torrance 1927–28
James Kerr 1928–29
Sid Scholey 1929–30
Peter O'Rourke 1930–32
Bill Slade 1932–34
Andy Wilson 1934–37
Tommy Lowes 1937–44
Harry Hibbs 1944–51
Tony McPhee 1951
Brough Fletcher 1952–53
Major Frank Buckley 1953–55
John Love 1955–57
Billy Moore 1957–64
Alf Wood 1964
Reg Shaw 1964–68
Dick Graham 1968
Ron Lewin 1968–69
Billy Moore 1969–72
John Smith 1972–73
Ronnie Allen 1973
Doug Fraser 1973–77
Dave Mackay 1977–78
Alan Ashman 1978
Frank Sibley 1979
Alan Buckley 1979–86
Neil Martin *(Joint Manager with Buckley)* 1981–82
Tommy Coakley 1986–88
John Barnwell 1989–90
Kenny Hibbitt 1990–94
Chris Nicholl 1994–97
Jan Sorensen 1997–98
Ray Graydon 1998–2002
Colin Lee 2002–04
Paul Merson 2004–06
Kevin Broadhurst 2006
Richard Money 2006–08
Jimmy Mullen 2008–09
Chris Hutchings 2009–11
Dean Smith 2011–15
Sean O'Driscoll 2015–16
Jon Whitney 2016–18
Dean Keates 2018–19
Martin O'Connor 2019
Darrell Clarke 2019–21
Brian Dutton 2021
Matthew Taylor May 2021–

TEN YEAR LEAGUE RECORD

		P	W	D	L	F	A	Pts	Pos
2011-12	FL 1	46	10	20	16	51	57	50	19
2012-13	FL 1	46	17	17	12	65	58	68	9
2013-14	FL 1	46	14	16	16	49	49	58	13
2014-15	FL 1	46	14	17	15	50	54	59	14
2015-16	FL 1	46	24	12	10	71	49	84	3
2016-17	FL 1	46	14	16	16	51	58	58	14
2017-18	FL 1	46	13	13	20	53	66	52	19
2018-19	FL 1	46	12	11	23	49	71	47	22
2019-20	FL 2	36	13	8	15	40	49	47	12§
2020-21	FL 2	46	11	20	15	45	53	53	19

§Decided on points-per-game (1.31)

DID YOU KNOW ?

Walsall were one of a number of clubs that experimented with live music to entertain fans before matches during the 1960s. In the 1964–65 season popular local beat band The Jaguars, managed by a Saddlers season ticket holder, Ron Hawkins, played at Fellows Park.

WALSALL – SKY BET LEAGUE TWO 2020–21 LEAGUE RECORD

Match No.	Date	Venue	Opponents	Result		H/T Score	Lg Pos.	Goalscorers	Attendance
1	Sept 12	H	Grimsby T	W	1-0	0-0	5	Adebayo[60]	0
2	19	A	Harrogate T	D	2-2	1-2	7	Holden[4], Gordon[81]	0
3	Oct 3	A	Forest Green R	D	1-1	1-0	13	Lavery[14]	0
4	10	H	Colchester U	D	1-1	0-1	12	Adebayo[53]	0
5	13	H	Leyton Orient	W	2-1	1-1	7	Holden[25], Adebayo[61]	0
6	17	H	Exeter C	D	0-0	0-0	10		0
7	20	A	Bradford C	D	1-1	1-0	10	Nurse[23]	0
8	24	A	Barrow	D	2-2	1-1	12	Lavery 2 (1 pen)[45, 58 (p)]	0
9	27	H	Cambridge U	L	0-2	0-1	14		0
10	31	A	Mansfield T	D	1-1	0-1	14	Adebayo[49]	0
11	Nov 3	H	Crawley T	W	1-0	0-0	12	Sadler[74]	0
12	14	H	Southend U	L	0-1	0-0	13		0
13	21	A	Cheltenham T	L	0-3	0-0	15		0
14	24	A	Newport Co	D	1-1	1-1	16	Adebayo[21]	0
15	Dec 2	H	Stevenage	D	1-1	0-0	16	Gordon (pen)[90]	0
16	5	A	Tranmere R	W	3-1	1-1	14	Adebayo[19], McDonald[48], Scarr[66]	2000
17	12	H	Bolton W	W	2-1	1-1	11	Adebayo[44], Holden[57]	0
18	15	A	Oldham Ath	W	3-2	1-0	11	Gordon (pen)[23], Piergianni (og)[52], Adebayo[73]	0
19	19	H	Port Vale	W	4-3	0-2	8	Scrimshaw 2[52, 80], Scarr 2[56, 82]	0
20	26	A	Salford C	L	0-2	0-1	9		0
21	29	H	Scunthorpe U	L	1-2	0-1	11	McDonald[55]	0
22	Jan 2	H	Carlisle U	L	0-2	0-1	11		0
23	16	H	Oldham Ath	D	1-1	1-0	11	Jules[45]	0
24	19	A	Morecambe	D	1-1	1-0	12	Gordon[37]	0
25	23	A	Port Vale	W	3-1	1-1	11	Adebayo 2[6, 55], Fitzpatrick (og)[68]	0
26	Feb 9	H	Mansfield T	D	1-1	1-1	11	Melbourne[23]	0
27	16	H	Cheltenham T	L	1-2	1-2	11	Lavery[3]	0
28	20	A	Stevenage	D	1-1	1-0	14	Lavery[1]	0
29	24	H	Newport Co	L	0-1	0-0	15		0
30	27	H	Bradford C	L	1-2	0-1	17	Scarr[77]	0
31	Mar 2	A	Exeter C	D	0-0	0-0	15		0
32	6	A	Cambridge U	L	0-1	0-0	18		0
33	12	H	Barrow	L	0-1	0-0	19		0
34	16	A	Crawley T	D	1-1	0-0	19	Osaoabe (pen)[55]	0
35	20	A	Bolton W	L	1-2	1-0	20	Perry[28]	0
36	23	A	Southend U	D	0-0	0-0	20		0
37	27	A	Grimsby T	D	1-1	1-1	20	Lavery[45]	0
38	Apr 2	H	Harrogate T	D	0-0	0-0	20		0
39	5	A	Leyton Orient	D	0-0	0-0	20		0
40	10	H	Forest Green R	W	2-1	1-0	20	Holden[6], Clarke[65]	0
41	13	H	Tranmere R	W	1-0	0-0	18	Osaoabe[70]	0
42	17	A	Colchester U	L	1-2	1-2	19	Clarke[20]	0
43	20	H	Salford C	L	0-2	0-1	19		0
44	24	A	Scunthorpe U	W	2-0	2-0	19	Osaoabe[13], Gordon[23]	0
45	May 1	H	Morecambe	L	0-2	0-1	19		0
46	8	A	Carlisle U	D	0-0	0-0	19		0

Final League Position: 19

GOALSCORERS

League (45): Adebayo 10, Lavery 6 (1 pen), Gordon 5 (2 pens), Holden 4, Scarr 4, Osaoabe 3 (1 pen), Clarke 2, McDonald 2, Scrimshaw 2, Jules 1, Melbourne 1, Nurse 1, Perry 1, Sadler 1, own goals 2.
FA Cup (1): Lavery 1.
Carabao Cup (0).
Papa John's Trophy (3): Gordon 1, Jules 1, McDonald 1.

Roberts L 31 + 1	Norman C 27 + 8	Scarr D 34 + 1	Clarke J 30 + 1	Cockerill-Mollett C 5 + 6	Gordon J 31 + 5	Kinsella L 42 + 1	Bates A 21 + 15	McDonald W 27 + 14	Holden R 19 + 2	Adebayo E 24 + 1	Osaoabe E 26 + 12	Lavery C 22 + 19	Sinclair S 9 + 8	Jules Z 16 + 1	Guthrie D 7 + 7	White H 26 + 2	Nurse G 9 + 1	Scrimshaw J 4 + 10	Sadler M 23 + 3	Nolan J 2 + 7	Rose J 15	Wright T 13 + 3	Vincent F 3 + 5	Melbourne M 20	Osei Yaw D 1 + 10	Perry S 14 + 2	Reid J 1	Leak T 4 + 2	Willis J — + 2	*Match No.*
1	2	3	4	5	6	7	8^{3}	9	10^{2}	11^{1}	12	13	14																	1
1	2	3	4		8	6	7^{1}	10	9^{3}	11^{2}	14	13		5	12■															2
1		3	2		11	7	12	13	9	14		10^{3}	6^{2}	4		5	8^{1}													3
1	2	3	4		6^{1}	7	13	9^{3}	10	11	14	12			8^{2}		5													4
1	2	3	4			8		9^{3}	6	11	13	10^{2}	12	14	7^{1}		5													5
1	2	3	4			8^{3}	14	9	6	11	10^{2}	13	7^{1}		12		5													6
1		3	4			8	12	9^{3}	6	11	14	10^{2}			7^{1}	2	5	13												7
1	5	3	2^{1}			6	7^{2}	12		11^{3}	8	10		4	13		9	14												8
1		3				7^{1}	12	9	10	11^{3}	13	6		4	8	2	5^{2}	14												9
1	13	3				12		10	9	11	8	14	6^{3}	4	7^{1}	2^{2}	5													10
1	2	3		14		7	8^{2}	9^{3}	6	11	13	10^{1}		5				12	4											11
1	2	3		5^{2}		7^{3}	8■	9	6	11	14	10^{1}		4				12	13											12
1	2	3	13	5^{1}		8		12	7	11^{3}	9^{4}	14	15	4	6^{2}			10^{5}		16										13
1	2	3	4			7	8	12	6	11^{2}	9^{3}	13		5				10^{1}		14										14
	2	3	4		15	7	8^{4}	9		11^{2}	10^{1}	14		5	13			6^{3}		12	1									15
	2	3	4		12	7	8	9^{3}	6	11^{1}	10^{2}		13	5				14			1									16
	2	3	4		12	8	6	10^{2}	7	11^{3}	9^{1}	14		5		13					1									17
	2	3	4		7^{2}	9	6	10^{3}	8	11^{4}		15	13	5^{1}		12		14			1									18
	2^{2}	3	4		8^{1}	7	6^{3}	10^{5}	9	11^{4}	16	13			12	5		15	14		1									19
	5	3	4		7	8	6^{2}	10		11^{4}	9^{1}	14			13	2^{3}		12		15	1									20
12	2	3	4		6^{4}	7		9		10	13	15			8		5^{3}	11^{2}	14		1^{1}									21
1	2^{4}	4	3		9	7	8^{2}	11		10	15		6^{3}		14		13	12	5^{1}											22
1		3		14	10^{2}	7	8	9		11	12	13		5^{3}		2			4	6^{1}										23
1	12	3			10	6		9		11			7	5		2			4	8^{1}										24
1	14	3			9	7	6^{1}	10		11^{2}		13	12	5		2^{4}			4			8^{3}	15							25
1		3			11	8	7^{3}	9				10^{2}				2			4	12		6^{1}	13	5	14					26
1	7	3			9	8	13	11^{3}				10^{1}				2			4	12			6^{2}	5	14					27
1	5	3		14	12	6■	13	11^{1}			9^{3}	10^{2}				2			4				7	8						28
1	5	3			9		6	12			11^{1}	10	13			2^{3}			4				7^{2}	8	14					29
1	14	3		5^{3}	11		8	9				12				2			4			6	13		10^{1}	7^{2}				30
1	5			4^{1}	13		7					10	6^{3}			2			3			9	12	8		14	11^{2}			31
1	5^{1}	3			11	6	13	14			9	10^{3}				2			4			12		8		7^{2}				32
1	12	3^{1}			10^{3}	8	7	13			11^{2}					2			4			9		5	14	6				33
1	5		3		9^{2}	6	12				11^{1}	10^{3}	7			2			4			13		8	14					34
1	5		3	12	9^{1}	6	14	13			11^{2}	10^{4}				2■			4^{3}					8	15	7				35
1	5^{5}		3	14	9^{3}	6		12			11	10^{1}	7^{4}						4				16	8^{2}	13	15		2		36
1			3	12	9	6					11	10	7						4					5^{1}		8		2		37
1			3		10	2	8^{1}	12	13		9	11							4			6^{2}		5		7				38
			3		11^{2}	7			12		9	10^{1}				2			4		1	6		5	13	8				39
	14		3		10	6			11^{2}		8					2^{1}			4		1	9^{3}		5	13	7		12		40
	12		3		11^{3}	6	15	13	9^{2}		10	14							4		1	8^{4}		5		7		2^{1}		41
			3		11	6^{1}	13	12			8^{3}	10				2			4		1	9^{2}		5	14	7				42
	5	15	3		9	7	12	14			11^{4}	10				2^{1}			4^{2}		1	13		8		6^{3}				43
		3^{2}	4		10^{1}	6^{4}	13	11			8^{3}	12				2					1	9		5		7		15	14	44
		3	4		10^{1}	8^{2}	13	11			7	12				2					1	9		5		6				45
	14		4		10^{1}	8^{4}		12			9^{5}	11	15			2^{3}				13	1	6^{2}		5		7		3	16	46

FA Cup

First Round	Bristol R	(h)	1-2

Carabao Cup

First Round	Sheffield W	(h)	0-0

(Sheffield W won 4-2 on penalties)

Papa John's Trophy

Group D (S)	Bristol R	(a)	2-2
(Walsall won 4-2 on penalties)			
Group D (S)	Chelsea U21	(h)	1-1
(Chelsea U21 won 5-3 on penalties)			
Group D (S)	Oxford U	(h)	0-1

WATFORD

FOUNDATION

The club was formed as Watford Rovers in 1881. The name was changed to West Herts in 1893 and then the name Watford was adopted after rival club Watford St Mary's was absorbed in 1898.

Vicarage Road Stadium, Vicarage Road, Watford, Hertfordshire WD18 0ER.

Telephone: (01923) 496 000.

Ticket Office: (01923) 223 023.

Website: www.watfordfc.com

Email: yourvoice@watfordfc.com

Ground Capacity: 22,200.

Record Attendance: 34,099 v Manchester U, FA Cup 4th rd (replay), 3 February 1969.

Pitch Measurements: 105m × 68m (115yd × 74.5yd).

Chairman and Chief Executive: Scott Duxbury.

Head Coach: Xisco Muñoz.

Assistant Head Coach: Roberto Cuesta.

Colours: Yellow and black shirts, black shorts, black socks.

Year Formed: 1881.

Turned Professional: 1897.

Previous Names: 1881, Watford Rovers; 1893, West Herts; 1898, Watford.

Club Nickname: 'The Hornets'.

Grounds: 1883, Vicarage Meadow, Rose and Crown Meadow; 1889, Colney Butts; 1890, Cassio Road; 1922, Vicarage Road.

First Football League Game: 28 August 1920, Division 3, v QPR (a) W 2–1 – Williams; Horseman, Fred Gregory; Bacon, Toone, Wilkinson; Bassett, Ronald (1), Hoddinott, White (1), Waterall.

Record League Victory: 8–0 v Sunderland, Division 1, 25 September 1982 – Sherwood; Rice, Rostron, Taylor, Terry, Bolton, Callaghan (2), Blissett (4), Jenkins (2), Jackett, Barnes.

Record Cup Victory: 10–1 v Lowestoft T, FA Cup 1st rd, 27 November 1926 – Yates; Prior, Fletcher (1); Frank Smith, Bert Smith, Strain; Stephenson, Warner (3), Edmonds (3), Swan (1), Daniels (1), (1 og).

Record Defeat: 0–10 v Wolverhampton W, FA Cup 1st rd (replay), 24 January 1912.

Most League Points (2 for a win): 71, Division 4, 1977–78.

Most League Points (3 for a win): 91, FL C, 2020–21.

Most League Goals: 92, Division 4, 1959–60.

HONOURS

League Champions: Second Division – 1997–98; Division 3 – 1968–69; Division 4 – 1977–78.
Runners-up: Division 1 – 1982–83; FL C – 2014–15, 2020–21; Division 2 – 1981–82; Division 3 – 1978–79.

FA Cup: *Runners-up:* 1984, 2019.

League Cup: semi-final – 1979, 2005.

European Competitions
UEFA Cup: 1983–84.

FOOTBALL YEARBOOK FACT FILE

Watford goalkeeper Billy Biggar both saved and scored a penalty kick in the same match. Playing for the Hornets at home to Coventry City in a Southern League fixture on 20 February 1909 he performed both feats in the first half of the game, which Watford went on to win 3-1.

Highest League Scorer in Season: Cliff Holton, 42, Division 4, 1959–60.

Most League Goals in Total Aggregate: Luther Blissett, 148, 1976–83, 1984–88, 1991–92.

Most League Goals in One Match: 5, Eddie Mummery v Newport Co, Division 3 (S), 5 January 1924.

Most Capped Player: Craig Cathcart, 43 (61), Northern Ireland.

Most League Appearances: Luther Blissett, 415, 1976–83, 1984–88, 1991–92.

Youngest League Player: Keith Mercer, 16 years 125 days v Tranmere R, 16 February 1973.

Record Transfer Fee Received: £35,000,000 from Everton for Richarlison, July 2018.

Record Transfer Fee Paid: £30,000,000 to Rennes for Ismaila Sarr, August 2019.

Football League Record: 1920 Original Member of Division 3; 1921–58 Division 3 (S); 1958–60 Division 4; 1960–69 Division 3; 1969–72 Division 2; 1972–75 Division 3; 1975–78 Division 4; 1978–79 Division 3; 1979–82 Division 2; 1982–88 Division 1; 1988–92 Division 2; 1992–96 Division 1; 1996–98 Division 2; 1998–99 Division 1; 1999–2000 Premier League; 2000–04 Division 1; 2004–06 FL C; 2006–07 Premier League; 2007–15 FL C; 2015–20 Premier League; 2020–21 FL C; 2021– Premier League.

LATEST SEQUENCES

Longest Sequence of League Wins: 7, 28.8.2000 – 14.10.2000.

Longest Sequence of League Defeats: 9, 26.12.1972 – 27.2.1973.

Longest Sequence of League Draws: 7, 16.2.2008 – 22.3.2008.

Longest Sequence of Unbeaten League Matches: 22, 1.10.1996 – 1.3.1997.

Longest Sequence Without a League Win: 19, 27.11.1971 – 8.4.1972.

Successive Scoring Runs: 22 from 20.8.1985.

Successive Non-scoring Runs: 7 from 18.12.1971.

MANAGERS

John Goodall 1903–10
Harry Kent 1910–26
Fred Pagnam 1926–29
Neil McBain 1929–37
Bill Findlay 1938–47
Jack Bray 1947–48
Eddie Hapgood 1948–50
Ron Gray 1950–51
Haydn Green 1951–52
Len Goulden 1952–55
(General Manager to 1956)
Johnny Paton 1955–56
Neil McBain 1956–59
Ron Burgess 1959–63
Bill McGarry 1963–64
Ken Furphy 1964–71
George Kirby 1971–73
Mike Keen 1973–77
Graham Taylor 1977–87
Dave Bassett 1987–88
Steve Harrison 1988–90
Colin Lee 1990
Steve Perryman 1990–93
Glenn Roeder 1993–96
Graham Taylor 1996
Kenny Jackett 1996–97
Graham Taylor 1997–2001
Gianluca Vialli 2001–02
Ray Lewington 2002–05
Adrian Boothroyd 2005–08
Brendan Rodgers 2008–09
Malky Mackay 2009–11
Sean Dyche 2011–12
Gianfranco Zola 2012–13
Beppe Sannino 2013–14
Oscar Garcia 2014
Billy McKinlay 2014
Slavisa Jokanovic 2014–15
Quique Sanchez Flores 2015–16
Walter Mazzarri 2016–17
Marco Silva 2017–18
Javi Gracia 2018–19
Quique Sanchez Flores 2019
Nigel Pearson 2019–20
Vladimir Ivić 2020
Xisco Muñoz December 2020–

TEN YEAR LEAGUE RECORD

		P	*W*	*D*	*L*	*F*	*A*	*Pts*	*Pos*
2011-12	FL C	46	16	16	14	56	64	64	11
2012-13	FL C	46	23	8	15	85	58	77	3
2013-14	FL C	46	15	15	16	74	64	60	13
2014-15	FL C	46	27	8	11	91	50	89	2
2015-16	PR Lge	38	12	9	17	40	50	45	13
2016-17	PR Lge	38	11	7	20	40	68	40	17
2017-18	PR Lge	38	11	8	19	44	64	41	14
2018-19	PR Lge	38	14	8	16	52	59	50	11
2019-20	PR Lge	38	8	10	20	36	64	34	19
2020-21	FL C	46	27	10	9	63	30	91	2

DID YOU KNOW ?

Since losing at Oxford in September 1970, Watford have played the U's away from home on 15 occasions in competitive matches and not suffered a single defeat. The Hornets have won five of the games with the remaining 10 being drawn.

WATFORD – SKY BET CHAMPIONSHIP 2020–21 LEAGUE RECORD

Match No.	Date	Venue	Opponents	Result	H/T Score	Lg Pos.	Goalscorers	Attendance
1	Sept 11	H	Middlesbrough	W 1-0	1-0	1	Cathcart [11]	0
2	19	A	Sheffield W	D 0-0	0-0	5		0
3	26	H	Luton T	W 1-0	1-0	3	Joao Pedro [35]	0
4	Oct 3	A	Reading	L 0-1	0-1	7		0
5	16	A	Derby Co	W 1-0	0-0	5	Joao Pedro [76]	0
6	21	H	Blackburn R	W 3-1	2-1	3	Joao Pedro [13], Cleverley [17], Lenihan (og) [49]	0
7	24	H	Bournemouth	D 1-1	1-0	3	Perica [12]	0
8	27	A	Wycombe W	D 1-1	0-0	3	Sarr [52]	0
9	31	A	Barnsley	L 0-1	0-1	6		0
10	Nov 4	H	Stoke C	W 3-2	1-1	4	Cleverley [28], Joao Pedro (pen) [61], Sarr [90]	0
11	7	H	Coventry C	W 3-2	0-0	2	Gray [53], Troost-Ekong [66], Sarr (pen) [83]	0
12	21	A	QPR	D 1-1	1-0	5	Wilmot [3]	0
13	25	A	Bristol C	D 0-0	0-0	5		0
14	28	H	Preston NE	W 4-1	1-0	3	Quina [9], Deeney (pen) [52], Chalobah [58], Joao Pedro [74]	0
15	Dec 2	A	Nottingham F	D 0-0	0-0	3		0
16	5	H	Cardiff C	L 0-1	0-1	7		0
17	8	H	Rotherham U	W 2-0	2-0	3	Kabasele [4], Deeney [15]	1976
18	12	A	Birmingham C	W 1-0	0-0	4	Deeney (pen) [85]	0
19	15	H	Brentford	D 1-1	0-0	3	Deeney (pen) [60]	0
20	19	A	Huddersfield T	L 0-2	0-2	5		0
21	26	H	Norwich C	W 1-0	1-0	5	Sarr [39]	0
22	Jan 2	A	Swansea C	L 1-2	1-1	6	Cleverley [20]	0
23	16	H	Huddersfield T	W 2-0	0-0	5	Cleverley [54], Joao Pedro [64]	0
24	19	H	Barnsley	W 1-0	1-0	3	Deeney (pen) [27]	0
25	22	A	Stoke C	W 2-1	0-0	3	Deeney (pen) [64], Sarr [68]	0
26	26	A	Millwall	D 0-0	0-0	2		0
27	Feb 1	H	QPR	L 1-2	0-0	5	Deeney (pen) [52]	0
28	6	A	Coventry C	D 0-0	0-0	5		0
29	13	H	Bristol C	W 6-0	4-0	4	Sema 2 [2, 35], Sarr 2 [15, 55], Hughes [30], Zinckernagel [90]	0
30	16	A	Preston NE	W 1-0	0-0	3	Joao Pedro (pen) [51]	0
31	19	H	Derby Co	W 2-1	2-0	3	Joao Pedro [19], Hughes [21]	0
32	24	A	Blackburn R	W 3-2	2-1	3	Joao Pedro [25], Sarr [38], Sema [61]	0
33	27	A	Bournemouth	L 0-1	0-0	3		0
34	Mar 3	H	Wycombe W	W 2-0	1-0	3	Gray 2 [14, 57]	0
35	6	H	Nottingham F	W 1-0	1-0	2	Masina [17]	0
36	13	A	Cardiff C	W 2-1	1-1	2	Chalobah [15], Masina [90]	0
37	16	A	Rotherham U	W 4-1	3-0	2	Sierralta [9], Sarr [26], Sema [39], Gosling [69]	0
38	20	H	Birmingham C	W 3-0	1-0	2	Sema [4], Chalobah [55], Gray [80]	0
39	Apr 2	H	Sheffield W	W 1-0	1-0	2	Lees (og) [7]	0
40	5	A	Middlesbrough	D 1-1	1-0	2	Sarr [32]	0
41	9	H	Reading	W 2-0	2-0	2	Sarr 2 [12, 14]	0
42	17	A	Luton T	L 0-1	0-0	2		0
43	20	A	Norwich C	W 1-0	0-0	2	Gosling [57]	0
44	24	H	Millwall	W 1-0	1-0	2	Sarr (pen) [11]	0
45	May 1	A	Brentford	L 0-2	0-0	2		0
46	8	H	Swansea C	W 2-0	0-0	2	Gray [56], Success [87]	0

Final League Position: 2

GOALSCORERS

League (63): Sarr 13 (2 pens), Joao Pedro 9 (2 pens), Deeney 7 (6 pens), Gray 5, Sema 5, Cleverley 4, Chalobah 3, Gosling 2, Hughes 2, Masina 2, Cathcart 1, Kabasele 1, Perica 1, Quina 1, Sierralta 1, Success 1, Troost-Ekong 1, Wilmot 1, Zinckernagel 1, own goals 2.
FA Cup (0).
Carabao Cup (2): Penaranda 1 (1 pen), Sema 1.

Foster B 23	Ngakia J 18 + 7	Cathcart C 20 + 5	Kabasele C 19 + 1	Wilmot B 14 + 11	Femenia K 36 + 1	Quina D 8 + 6	Cleverley T 32 + 2	Chalobah N 32 + 6	Sema K 38 + 3	Joao Pedro d 31 + 7	Murray G 1 + 4	Navarro M 2 + 4	Philips D — + 2	Perica S 2 + 14	Garner J 12 + 8	Pussetto I — + 1	Sarr I 39	Dele-Bashiru A 1 + 1	Deeney T 14 + 5	Troost-Ekong W 31 + 1	Capoue E 7 + 4	Gray A 14 + 16	Hughes W 21 + 9	Sierralta F 24 + 2	Masina A 21 + 4	Bachmann D 23	Zinckernagel P 9 + 11	Gosling D 6 + 7	Lazaar A 2 + 3	Hungbo J 1 + 4	Sanchez C 2 + 7	Success I 3 + 7	Pochettino M — + 1	Match No.
1	2	3	4	5	6^{2}	7^{3}	8	9	10^{1}	11	12	13	14																					1
1	2	3	4	5		7^{2}	8	9	6	10^{3}	11^{1}			12	13	14																		2
1	2	3	4	5		14	8	9^{1}	6	11^{2}					7		10^{3}	12	13															3
1	5	2	3	4	9^{2}		13	7	12	11	14				6		10^{3}	8^{1}																4
1	5	12	2	4	9	8^{3}	6	7	11	10^{2}	13				14					3^{1}														5
1	13	2	3	4	5^{2}	14	8^{1}	7	9	11					6		10^{3}				12													6
1	5	4	2			13	8^{2}	7	9	14				11^{3}	6^{1}		10			3	12													7
1		5	3^{2}		2	10^{1}	8^{3}	13	6	11	12				14		7			4	9													8
1		3		5	2		8^{3}	7^{1}	6	11					12		10			4^{2}	9	13	14											9
1		2	3	4	5		8^{1}	6^{3}	9	10^{2}					13		11				7	12	14											10
1	12	4	2		5^{1}		8	14	9						6^{3}		10		13	3	7	11^{2}												11
1		4		2	5	13		8	9	10^{1}							6		12	3	7	11^{2}												12
1	2^{2}	4	3		5	9		7		11^{3}				14	8		6		12	13		10^{1}												13
1	2	4^{5}	3	14	5^{3}	9		7		12			15	13	8^{4}		6		11^{2}			10^{1}		16										14
1	2	4^{2}	3	13	5	9^{1}		7		10				12	8		6		11															15
1	2^{1}		3	5^{4}	12	14	7^{3}		9^{2}	11				15	8		6		10	4			13											16
1	2		4	15	5^{4}	16	7^{1}	8	9^{3}	13				10	14		6^{5}		11^{2}	3			12											17
1	2			4	5	7^{1}	9	6	10					12	8^{2}				11	3	13													18
1	2^{3}		4		5		7	6^{1}	10					13	9^{2}		8		11	3	12	14												19
1	6^{3}		2	4^{4}			8		9			14		13	7		10			3^{1}	5^{2}	11		12	15									20
1	5^{1}			4	2^{4}		7^{2}	16	9			15		14			6		11		8^{5}	10^{3}	13	3	12									21
1	5^{1}			4	2		7^{3}	8^{2}	9						13		6		11			10	14	3	12									22
					2^{5}		7^{4}	8^{1}	9^{3}	10		16			14		6		11^{2}	3		12	13	4	5	1	15							23
	15	16			2		7^{3}	14	9^{2}	12							6		10^{1}	3^{4}		11^{5}	8	4	5	1	13							24
	13	14		16	2^{3}		6^{5}	8		11^{4}							9		10	3		15	7^{1}	4^{2}	5	1	12							25
					2		7^{2}	8		12							6		10	3		11^{1}	9	4	5	1	13							26
	5^{4}			15			7	8^{3}	13	11^{1}		2					6		10	3		12	9^{2}	4		1	14							27
	2^{3}						7	6^{2}	10	12				14			8		9	3		11^{1}	13	4	5	1								28
				15	2^{5}		6^{3}	8^{1}	11^{2}	10							9			3		13	7	4	5^{4}	1	14	12	16					29
		3			2		6	8^{1}	11^{3}	10^{2}				13			9						7	4	5	1	14	12						30
		4		14	2		8	6^{1}	11^{3}	10							9			3			7^{2}		5	1	13	12						31
				14	2		6		11^{2}	10^{3}							9			3		13	7	4	5	1	12	8^{1}						32
		3			2		6	8^{1}	11^{3}	10■				14			9						7	4	5^{2}	1		12	13					33
	12			15	2^{1}		7^{4}		11^{2}					14			9			3		10^{3}	6	4	5	1	8			13				34
					2				10	8^{3}							7			3		11^{1}	6	4	5	1	9^{2}			13	12	14		35
					2			6^{2}	11^{1}	10							9			3		13	7	4	5	1	8^{3}				14	12		36
	13				2^{2}			6^{3}	11	10							9^{1}			3		12	7^{5}	4	5	1	8^{4}	14			15	16		37
	16				2			6	11^{5}	9^{4}										3		15	7	4	5^{3}	1		8^{1}	14	13	12	10^{2}		38
					2			6^{4}	14	11^{3}							9			3		13	7	4	5	1	8^{1}	12			15	10^{2}		39
					2			6	11^{2}	10							9			3			7	4	5	1	8^{1}	12				13		40
		13			2			6^{1}	11^{3}	10^{4}							9			3^{2}		14	7	4	5	1	8				12	15		41
					2■		13		11^{3}	10							9			3		15	7	4		1	8^{1}		5^{4}	14	6^{2}	12		42
		2^{4}	15				6^{3}	13	11	10^{2}							9			3		12	7	4	5	1	14	8^{1}						43
		12			2^{1}		6^{4}	14	11	10^{3}							9			3		13	7	4	5	1		8^{2}			15			44
		2	4	16			6^{2}		11					15								10^{5}	7^{4}	3	5	1	12	8^{3}		9^{1}		13	14	45
1		4	3	16					11^{4}	13		2							14			10^{3}	12		15		6^{1}	8^{5}	5		7^{2}	9		46

FA Cup

Third Round	Manchester U	(a)	0-1

Carabao Cup

Second Round	Oxford U	(a)	1-1
(Watford won 3-0 on penalties)			
Third Round	Newport Co	(a)	1-3

WEST BROMWICH ALBION

FOUNDATION

There is a well known story that when employees of Salter's Spring Works in West Bromwich decided to form a football club, they had to send someone to the nearby Association Football stronghold of Wednesbury to purchase a football. A weekly subscription of 2d (less than 1p) was imposed and the name of the new club was West Bromwich Strollers.

The Hawthorns, West Bromwich, West Midlands B71 4LF.

Telephone: (0871) 271 1100.

Ticket Office: (0121) 227 2227.

Website: www.wba.co.uk

Email: enquiries@wbafc.co.uk

Ground Capacity: 26,688.

Record Attendance: 64,815 v Arsenal, FA Cup 6th rd, 6 March 1937.

Pitch Measurements: 105m × 68m (115yd × 74.5yd).

Chairman: Li Piyue.

Chief Executive: Xu Ke.

Head Coach: Valerien Ismael.

Assistant Coach: James Morrison.

Colours: Navy blue and white striped shirts, white shorts with navy blue trim, navy blue socks with white trim.

Year Formed: 1878.

Turned Professional: 1885.

Previous Name: 1878, West Bromwich Strollers; 1881, West Bromwich Albion.

Club Nicknames: 'The Throstles', 'The Baggies', 'Albion'.

Grounds: 1878, Coopers Hill; 1879, Dartmouth Park; 1881, Bunns Field, Walsall Street; 1882, Four Acres (Dartmouth Cricket Club); 1885, Stoney Lane; 1900, The Hawthorns.

First Football League Game: 8 September 1888, Football League, v Stoke (a) W 2–0 – Roberts; Jack Horton, Green; Ezra Horton, Perry, Bayliss; Bassett, Woodhall (1), Hendry, Pearson, Wilson (1).

Record League Victory: 12–0 v Darwen, Division 1, 4 April 1892 – Reader; Jack Horton, McCulloch; Reynolds (2), Perry, Groves; Bassett (3), McLeod, Nicholls (1), Pearson (4), Geddes (1), (1 og).

Record Cup Victory: 10–1 v Chatham (away), FA Cup 3rd rd, 2 March 1889 – Roberts; Jack Horton, Green; Timmins (1), Charles Perry, Ezra Horton; Bassett (2), Walter Perry (1), Bayliss (2), Pearson, Wilson (3), (1 og).

Record Defeat: 3–10 v Stoke C, Division 1, 4 February 1937.

League Champions: Division 1 – 1919–20; FL C – 2007–08; Division 2 – 1901–02, 1910–11.
Runners-up: Division 1 – 1924–25, 1953–54; FL C – 2009–10, 2019–20; First Division – 2001–02, 2003–04; Division 2 – 1930–31, 1948–49.

FA Cup Winners: 1888, 1892, 1931, 1954, 1968.
Runners-up: 1886, 1887, 1895, 1912, 1935.

League Cup Winners: 1966.
Runners-up: 1967, 1970.

European Competitions
Fairs Cup: 1966–67.
UEFA Cup: 1978–79 *(qf)*, 1979–80, 1981–82.
European Cup-Winners' Cup: 1968–69 *(qf)*.

FOOTBALL YEARBOOK FACT FILE

West Bromwich Albion played seven competitive games in a period of 10 days in the closing stages of the 1911–12 season and did not win a single one of them. After losing the Cup final replay against Barnsley after extra time on 24 April, they played on each of the next three days with the results including a 5-1 home defeat to Sheffield Wednesday.

Most League Points (2 for a win): 60, Division 1, 1919–20.

Most League Points (3 for a win): 91, FL C, 2009–10.

Most League Goals: 105, Division 2, 1929–30.

Highest League Scorer in Season: William 'Ginger' Richardson, 39, Division 1, 1935–36.

Most League Goals in Total Aggregate: Tony Brown, 218, 1963–79.

Most League Goals in One Match: 6, Jimmy Cookson v Blackpool, Division 2, 17 September 1927.

Most Capped Player: James Morrison, 46, Scotland.

Most League Appearances: Tony Brown, 574, 1963–80.

Youngest League Player: Charlie Wilson, 16 years 73 days v Oldham Ath, 1 October 1921.

Record Transfer Fee Received: £16,500,000 from Dalian Yifang for Salomon Rondon, July 2019.

Record Transfer Fee Paid: £18,000,000 to West Ham U for Grady Diangana, September 2020.

Football League Record: 1888 Founder Member of Football League; 1901–02 Division 2; 1902–04 Division 1; 1904–11 Division 2; 1911–27 Division 1; 1927–31 Division 2; 1931–38 Division 1; 1938–49 Division 2; 1949–73 Division 1; 1973–76 Division 2; 1976–86 Division 1; 1986–91 Division 2; 1991–92 Division 3; 1992–93 Division 2; 1993–2002 Division 1; 2002–03 Premier League; 2003–04 Division 1; 2004–06 Premier League; 2006–08 FL C; 2008–09 Premier League; 2009–10 FL C; 2010–18 Premier League; 2018–20 FL C; 2020–21 Premier League; 2021– FL C.

LATEST SEQUENCES

Longest Sequence of League Wins: 11, 5.4.1930 – 8.9.1930.

Longest Sequence of League Defeats: 11, 28.10.1995 – 26.12.1995.

Longest Sequence of League Draws: 5, 30.8.1999 – 3.10.1999.

Longest Sequence of Unbeaten League Matches: 17, 7.9.1957 – 7.12.1957.

Longest Sequence Without a League Win: 20, 27.8.2017 – 2.1.2018.

Successive Scoring Runs: 36 from 26.4.1958.

Successive Non-scoring Runs: 5 from 1.4.2017.

MANAGERS

Louis Ford 1890–92
(Secretary-Manager)
Henry Jackson 1892–94
(Secretary-Manager)
Edward Stephenson 1894–95
(Secretary-Manager)
Clement Keys 1895–96
(Secretary-Manager)
Frank Heaven 1896–1902
(Secretary-Manager)
Fred Everiss 1902–48
Jack Smith 1948–52
Jesse Carver 1952
Vic Buckingham 1953–59
Gordon Clark 1959–61
Archie Macaulay 1961–63
Jimmy Hagan 1963–67
Alan Ashman 1967–71
Don Howe 1971–75
Johnny Giles 1975–77
Ronnie Allen 1977
Ron Atkinson 1978–81
Ronnie Allen 1981–82
Ron Wylie 1982–84
Johnny Giles 1984–85
Nobby Stiles 1985–86
Ron Saunders 1986–87
Ron Atkinson 1987–88
Brian Talbot 1988–91
Bobby Gould 1991–92
Ossie Ardiles 1992–93
Keith Burkinshaw 1993–94
Alan Buckley 1994–97
Ray Harford 1997
Denis Smith 1997–1999
Brian Little 1999–2000
Gary Megson 2000–04
Bryan Robson 2004–06
Tony Mowbray 2006–09
Roberto Di Matteo 2009–11
Roy Hodgson 2011–12
Steve Clarke 2012–13
Pepe Mel 2014
Alan Irvine 2014
Tony Pulis 2015–17
Alan Pardew 2017–18
Darren Moore 2018–19
Slaven Bilic 2019–20
Sam Allardyce 2020–21
Valerien Ismael June 2021–

TEN YEAR LEAGUE RECORD

		P	W	D	L	F	A	Pts	Pos
2011-12	PR Lge	38	13	8	17	45	52	47	10
2012-13	PR Lge	38	14	7	17	53	57	49	8
2013-14	PR Lge	38	7	15	16	43	59	36	17
2014-15	PR Lge	38	11	11	16	38	51	44	13
2015-16	PR Lge	38	10	13	15	34	48	43	14
2016-17	PR Lge	38	12	9	17	43	51	45	10
2017-18	PR Lge	38	6	13	19	31	56	31	20
2018-19	FL C	46	23	11	12	87	62	80	4
2019-20	FL C	46	22	17	7	77	45	83	2
2020-21	PR Lge	38	5	11	22	35	76	26	19

DID YOU KNOW 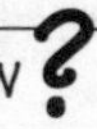

Dennis Clarke became the first substitute to be used in an FA Cup final when he came on for West Bromwich Albion against Everton in the 1968 final. Clarke, who replaced the injured John Kaye during the period between full time and extra time, was also the first substitute to gain a Cup winners' medal.

WEST BROMWICH ALBION – PREMIER LEAGUE 2020–21 LEAGUE RECORD

Match No.	*Date*	*Venue*	*Opponents*	*Result*		*H/T Score*	*Lg Pos.*	*Goalscorers*	*Atten-dance*
1	Sept 13	H	Leicester C	L	0-3	0-0	19		0
2	19	A	Everton	L	2-5	1-2	20	Diangana [10], Matheus Pereira [47]	0
3	26	H	Chelsea	D	3-3	3-0	16	Robinson 2 [4, 25], Bartley [27]	0
4	Oct 4	A	Southampton	L	0-2	0-1	17		0
5	19	H	Burnley	D	0-0	0-0	17		0
6	26	A	Brighton & HA	D	1-1	0-1	17	Ahearne-Grant [83]	0
7	Nov 2	A	Fulham	L	0-2	0-2	18		0
8	8	H	Tottenham H	L	0-1	0-0	18		0
9	21	A	Manchester U	L	0-1	0-0	18		0
10	28	H	Sheffield U	W	1-0	1-0	17	Gallagher [13]	0
11	Dec 6	H	Crystal Palace	L	1-5	1-1	19	Gallagher [30]	0
12	12	A	Newcastle U	L	1-2	0-1	19	Furlong [50]	0
13	15	A	Manchester C	D	1-1	1-1	19	Dias (og) [43]	0
14	20	H	Aston Villa	L	0-3	0-1	19		0
15	27	A	Liverpool	D	1-1	0-1	19	Ajayi [82]	2000
16	29	H	Leeds U	L	0-5	0-4	19		0
17	Jan 2	H	Arsenal	L	0-4	0-2	19		0
18	16	A	Wolverhampton W	W	3-2	1-2	19	Matheus Pereira 2 (2 pens) [8, 56], Ajayi [52]	0
19	19	A	West Ham U	L	1-2	0-1	19	Matheus Pereira [51]	0
20	26	H	Manchester C	L	0-5	0-4	19		0
21	30	H	Fulham	D	2-2	0-1	19	Bartley [47], Matheus Pereira [66]	0
22	Feb 2	A	Sheffield U	L	1-2	1-0	19	Phillips [41]	0
23	7	A	Tottenham H	L	0-2	0-0	19		0
24	14	H	Manchester U	D	1-1	1-1	19	Diagne [2]	0
25	20	A	Burnley	D	0-0	0-0	19		0
26	27	H	Brighton & HA	W	1-0	1-0	19	Bartley [11]	0
27	Mar 4	H	Everton	L	0-1	0-0	19		0
28	7	H	Newcastle U	D	0-0	0-0	19		0
29	13	A	Crystal Palace	L	0-1	0-1	19		0
30	Apr 3	A	Chelsea	W	5-2	2-1	19	Matheus Pereira 2 [45, 45], Robinson 2 [63, 90], Diagne [68]	0
31	12	H	Southampton	W	3-0	2-0	19	Matheus Pereira (pen) [32], Phillips [35], Robinson [69]	0
32	22	A	Leicester C	L	0-3	0-3	19		0
33	25	A	Aston Villa	D	2-2	1-1	19	Matheus Pereira (pen) [23], Mings (og) [47]	0
34	May 3	H	Wolverhampton W	D	1-1	0-1	19	Diagne [62]	0
35	9	A	Arsenal	L	1-3	0-2	19	Matheus Pereira [67]	0
36	16	H	Liverpool	L	1-2	1-1	19	Robson-Kanu [15]	0
37	19	H	West Ham U	L	1-3	1-1	19	Matheus Pereira [27]	5371
38	23	A	Leeds U	L	1-3	0-2	19	Robson-Kanu [90]	8000

Final League Position: 19

GOALSCORERS

League (35): Matheus Pereira 11 (4 pens), Robinson 5, Bartley 3, Diagne 3, Ajayi 2, Gallagher 2, Phillips 2, Robson-Kanu 2, Ahearne-Grant 1, Diangana 1, Furlong 1, own goals 2.
FA Cup (2): Ajayi 1, Matheus Pereira 1 (1 pen).
Carabao Cup (5): Robson-Kanu 3 (2 pens), Harper 1, Robinson 1.
Papa John's Trophy (3): Dyce 1, Gardner-Hickman 1, Windsor 1.

Johnstone S 37	Furlong D 32 + 3	Ajayi S 31 + 2	Bartley K 28 + 2	O'Shea D 25 + 3	Gibbs K 9 + 1	Matheus Pereira F 30 + 3	Livermore J 15 + 3	Sawyers R 17 + 2	Diangana G 15 + 5	Robinson C 20 + 8	Robson-Kanu H 2 + 17	Edwards K 1 + 4	Harper R — + 2	Phillips M 20 + 13	Field S — + 3	Townsend C 25	Krovinovic F 5 + 6	Ivanovic B 8 + 5	Hegazi A 1	Gallagher C 28 + 2	Ahearne-Grant K 14 + 7	Austin C — + 5	Grosicki K 2 + 1	Peltier L 3 + 1	Button D 1	Snodgrass R 6 + 2	Diagne M 14 + 2	Maitland-Niles A 14 + 1	Yokuslu O 15 + 1	Match No.
1	2^3	3	4	5	6	7	8	9^2	10	11^1	12	13	14																	1
1	2	3	4	5	6■	7^2	8	9^3	10^1	11		13		12	14															2
1	2	3	4	5		7^3	8	9	10^2	11^1	12			13	14	6														3
1		3	4	2		9	6	7^3	10	11^2	13	8^1			12	5	14													4
1	2					7^3	6	13	10	12				14		5	9^2	3	4	8	11^1									5
1	2	4				7	6^1		10^2	12		13		14		5	9	3		8	11^3									6
1	2	4				7^1	8^2	12	10	13				14		5	6^3	3		9	11									7
1	2	3	4	5			8^3		12	10^1		14		13		6	9			7	11^2									8
1	2	3	5			7		8	10^1	12	13					6	14	4^3		9	11^2									9
1	5	2	4			9		7		11^1	12			14		8^2	13	3		6	10^3									10
1	5	2	4	14		9■		6^3	10^1	13				8			12	3		7	11^2									11
1	5	2		4	13			7		10^2				8			9	3		6^3	11^1	12	14							12
1	2	3		4	5		8^2	6	10					7^3			13			9	11^1	12		14						13
1	2	3		4	5		8■	6	10^2	14				7^1				13		9	11^3	12								14
1	2	3		4	5	12		8	10	6^1				7				14		9^3	11^2	13								15
1	2	3		4		13		6	10^3	7				8^1			14	12		9	11^2			5						16
1	2	3	13	5		10		7	9^1	11			14	6^3				4^2		8		12								17
	13	3	4	2	5	9^2	6	7		11	12												10^1		1	8				18
1	12	3	4	2	5	10	7^2	8		11	13									6			9^1							19
1	2	3	12	4	5	10	7	8		11^1	14			13							9^3					6^2				20
1	5	2	3	4^1	8	9	6^3			11^2				14						7	12					10	13			21
1		3	4	2		9	7			10^2	13			6^3		5				14	12					8	11^1			22
1		3	4			14		6^2						12		5				9	10^1			2		7^3	11	8	13	23
1	12	3	4			10	13							14		5				9				2^1		7^3	11	8	6^2	24
1	2	3■	4	12		7								10^1		5				8							11	9	6	25
1	2		4	3		7^2			12		14			10^1		5		13		8							11^3	9	6	26
1	2		4	3		7					13			10^1		5				8^2						12	11	9	6	27
1	2		4	3		7					13			10^1		5				8	12						11^2	9	6	28
1	2		4	3		10^1					12			7^2		5				8						13	11	9	6	29
1	2	5	4	3^1		10	14			13				7^3		6		12^2									11	9	8	30
1	2	14	4^3	3		10				9^1	13			6		5				12							11^2	8	7	31
1	2	12	4	3		10^3				9^1	13			6		5					14						11^2	8	7	32
1	2	3	4	13		7				10^1				12		5				8							11	9^2	6	33
1	5	2	3	4^1		10				13				12		9				6							11	8^2	7	34
1	2	3	4			9			13	6^2	12			8		5				10							11^1		7	35
1	2	3	4			10	13		9^1		11^3			6		5				7	14							12	8^2	36
1	2	3	4			10			12		11^3			6		5				7	13						14	9^1	8^2	37
1	2	3	4	5^1					13	11^2	12			7		6				8	14							10^3	9	38

FA Cup

Third Round	Blackpool	(a)	2-2

(aet; Blackpool won 3-2 on penalties)

Carabao Cup

Second Round	Harrogate T	(h)	3-0
Third Round	Brentford	(h)	2-2

(Brentford won 5-4 on penalties)

Papa John's Trophy (WBA U21)

Group E (S)	Swindon T	(a)	3-2
Group E (S)	Forest Green R	(a)	0-3
Group E (S)	Exeter C	(a)	0-4

WEST HAM UNITED

FOUNDATION

Thames Ironworks FC was formed by employees of this famous shipbuilding company in 1895 and entered the FA Cup in their initial season at Chatham and the London League in their second. The committee wanted to introduce professional players, so Thames Ironworks was wound up in June 1900 and relaunched a month later as West Ham United.

London Stadium, Queen Elizabeth Olympic Park, London E20 2ST.

Telephone: (020) 8548 2748.

Ticket Office: (0333) 030 1966.

Website: www.whufc.com

Email: supporterservices@westhamunited.co.uk

Ground Capacity: 60,000.

Record Attendance: 42,322 v Tottenham H, Division 1, 17 October 1970 (at Boleyn Ground); 59,988 v Everton, Premier League, 30 March 2019 (at London Stadium).

Pitch Measurements: 105m × 68m (115yd × 74.5yd).

Joint Chairmen: David Sullivan and David Gold.

Vice-Chairman: Baroness Karren Brady CBE.

Manager: David Moyes.

First-Team Coaches: Stuart Pearce, Kevin Nolan.

Colours: Claret shirts with sky blue sleeves, white shorts with claret and sky blue trim, white socks with claret and sky blue trim.

Year Formed: 1895.

Turned Professional: 1900.

Previous Name: 1895, Thames Ironworks FC; 1900, West Ham United.

Club Nicknames: 'The Hammers', 'The Irons'.

Grounds: 1895, Memorial Recreation Ground, Canning Town; 1904, Boleyn Ground; 2016, London Stadium.

First Football League Game: 30 August 1919, Division 2, v Lincoln C (h) D 1–1 – Hufton; Cope, Lee; Lane, Fenwick, McCrae; David Smith, Moyes (1), Puddefoot, Morris, Bradshaw.

Record League Victory: 8–0 v Rotherham U, Division 2, 8 March 1958 – Gregory; Bond, Wright; Malcolm, Brown, Lansdowne; Grice, Smith (2), Keeble (2), Dick (4), Musgrove. 8–0 v Sunderland, Division 1, 19 October 1968 – Ferguson; Bonds, Charles; Peters, Stephenson, Moore (1); Redknapp, Boyce, Brooking (1), Hurst (6), Sissons.

Record Cup Victory: 10–0 v Bury, League Cup 2nd rd (2nd leg), 25 October 1983 – Parkes; Stewart (1), Walford, Bonds (Orr), Martin (1), Devonshire (2), Allen, Cottee (4), Swindlehurst, Brooking (2), Pike.

HONOURS

League Champions: Division 2 – 1957–58, 1980–81.
Runners-up: First Division – 1992–93; Division 2 – 1922–23, 1990–91.

FA Cup Winners: 1964, 1975, 1980.
Runners-up: 1923, 2006.

League Cup: *Runners-up:* 1966, 1981.

European Competitions
UEFA Cup: 1999–2000; 2006–07.
Europa League: 2015–16, 2016–17.
European Cup-Winners' Cup: 1964–65 *(winners)*, 1965–66 *(sf)*, 1975–76 *(runners-up)*, 1980–81 *(qf)*.
Intertoto Cup: 1999 *(winners)*.

FOOTBALL YEARBOOK FACT FILE

Jimmy Marshall who made over 50 appearances for West Ham United in the late 1930s was also a qualified medical practitioner who was often referred to as 'Doc Marshall' in the media. During his time with the Hammers, he qualified as a Medical Officer of Health and after spells in an assistant role in Bermondsey and Kent County, he served as Medical Officer of Health for Ashford, Kent, for many years.

Record Defeat: 2–8 v Blackburn R, Division 1, 26 December 1963; 0–6 v Oldham Ath, League Cup semi-final (1st leg), 14 February 1990.

Most League Points (2 for a win): 66, Division 2, 1980–81.

Most League Points (3 for a win): 88, Division 1, 1992–93.

Most League Goals: 101, Division 2, 1957–58.

Highest League Scorer in Season: Vic Watson, 42, Division 1, 1929–30.

Most League Goals in Total Aggregate: Vic Watson, 298, 1920–35.

Most League Goals in One Match: 6, Vic Watson v Leeds U, Division 1, 9 February 1929; 6, Geoff Hurst v Sunderland, Division 1, 19 October 1968.

Most Capped Player: Bobby Moore, 108, England.

Most League Appearances: Billy Bonds, 663, 1967–88.

Youngest League Player: Billy Williams, 16 years 221 days v Blackpool, 6 May 1922.

Record Transfer Fee Received: £25,000,000 from Marseille for Dmitri Payet, January 2017.

Record Transfer Fee Paid: £45,000,000 to Eintracht Frankfurt for Sebastien Haller, July 2019.

Football League Record: 1919 Elected to Division 2; 1923–32 Division 1; 1932–58 Division 2; 1958–78 Division 1; 1978–81 Division 2; 1981–89 Division 1; 1989–91 Division 2; 1991–93 Division 1; 1993–2003 Premier League; 2003–04 Division 1; 2004–05 FL C; 2005–11 Premier League; 2011–12 FL C; 2012– Premier League.

MANAGERS

Syd King 1902–32
Charlie Paynter 1932–50
Ted Fenton 1950–61
Ron Greenwood 1961–74
(continued as General Manager to 1977)
John Lyall 1974–89
Lou Macari 1989–90
Billy Bonds 1990–94
Harry Redknapp 1994–2001
Glenn Roeder 2001–03
Alan Pardew 2003–06
Alan Curbishley 2006–08
Gianfranco Zola 2008–10
Avram Grant 2010–11
Sam Allardyce 2011–15
Slaven Bilic 2015–17
David Moyes 2017–18
Manuel Pellegrini 2018–19
David Moyes December 2019–

LATEST SEQUENCES

Longest Sequence of League Wins: 9, 19.10.1985 – 14.12.1985.

Longest Sequence of League Defeats: 9, 28.3.1932 – 29.8.1932.

Longest Sequence of League Draws: 5, 29.11.2015 – 26.12.2015.

Longest Sequence of Unbeaten League Matches: 27, 27.12.1980 – 10.10.1981.

Longest Sequence Without a League Win: 17, 31.1.1976 – 21.8.1976.

Successive Scoring Runs: 27 from 5.10.1957.

Successive Non-scoring Runs: 5 from 17.9.2006.

TEN YEAR LEAGUE RECORD

		P	W	D	L	F	A	Pts	Pos
2011-12	FL C	46	24	14	8	81	48	86	3
2012-13	PR Lge	38	12	10	16	45	53	46	10
2013-14	PR Lge	38	11	7	20	40	51	40	13
2014-15	PR Lge	38	12	11	15	44	47	47	12
2015-16	PR Lge	38	16	14	8	65	51	62	7
2016-17	PR Lge	38	12	9	17	47	64	45	11
2017-18	PR Lge	38	10	12	16	48	68	42	13
2018-19	PR Lge	38	15	7	16	52	55	52	10
2019-20	PR Lge	38	10	9	19	49	62	39	16
2020-21	PR Lge	38	19	8	11	62	47	65	6

DID YOU KNOW ?

Arnold Hills, who was managing director of the Thames Ironworks Company and a key figure in the formation of the club that later became West Ham United, was a vegetarian activist and teetotaller. The Hammers were sometimes given the nickname 'the water drinkers' in the early days as the players were required to be teetotal.

WEST HAM UNITED – PREMIER LEAGUE 2020–21 LEAGUE RECORD

Match No.	*Date*	*Venue*	*Opponents*	*Result*		*H/T Score*	*Lg Pos.*	*Goalscorers*	*Attendance*
1	Sept 12	H	Newcastle U	L	0-2	0-0	19		0
2	19	A	Arsenal	L	1-2	1-1	18	Antonio 45	0
3	27	H	Wolverhampton W	W	4-0	1-0	10	Bowen 2 17, 57, Jimenez (og) 66, Haller 90	0
4	Oct 4	A	Leicester C	W	3-0	2-0	10	Antonio 14, Fornals 34, Bowen 83	0
5	18	A	Tottenham H	D	3-3	0-3	8	Balbuena 82, Sanchez (og) 85, Lanzini 90	0
6	24	H	Manchester C	D	1-1	1-0	11	Antonio 18	0
7	31	A	Liverpool	L	1-2	1-1	13	Fornals 10	0
8	Nov 7	H	Fulham	W	1-0	0-0	11	Soucek 90	0
9	22	A	Sheffield U	W	1-0	0-0	8	Haller 56	0
10	30	H	Aston Villa	W	2-1	1-1	5	Ogbonna 2, Bowen 46	0
11	Dec 5	H	Manchester U	L	1-3	1-0	7	Soucek 38	2000
12	11	A	Leeds U	W	2-1	1-1	5	Soucek 25, Ogbonna 80	0
13	16	H	Crystal Palace	D	1-1	0-1	7	Haller 55	0
14	21	A	Chelsea	L	0-3	0-1	10		0
15	27	H	Brighton & HA	D	2-2	0-1	10	Johnson 60, Soucek 82	0
16	29	A	Southampton	D	0-0	0-0	10		0
17	Jan 1	A	Everton	W	1-0	0-0	10	Soucek 86	0
18	16	H	Burnley	W	1-0	1-0	9	Antonio 9	0
19	19	H	WBA	W	2-1	1-0	7	Bowen 45, Antonio 66	0
20	26	A	Crystal Palace	W	3-2	2-1	4	Soucek 2 9, 25, Dawson 65	0
21	31	H	Liverpool	L	1-3	0-0	5	Dawson 87	0
22	Feb 3	A	Aston Villa	W	3-1	0-0	5	Soucek 51, Lingard 2 56, 83	0
23	6	A	Fulham	D	0-0	0-0	5		0
24	15	H	Sheffield U	W	3-0	1-0	5	Rice (pen) 41, Diop 58, Fredericks 90	0
25	21	H	Tottenham H	W	2-1	1-0	4	Antonio 5, Lingard 47	0
26	27	A	Manchester C	L	1-2	1-1	4	Antonio 43	0
27	Mar 8	H	Leeds U	W	2-0	2-0	5	Lingard 21, Dawson 28	0
28	14	A	Manchester U	L	0-1	0-0	5		0
29	21	H	Arsenal	D	3-3	3-1	5	Lingard 15, Bowen 17, Soucek 32	0
30	Apr 5	A	Wolverhampton W	W	3-2	3-1	4	Lingard 6, Fornals 14, Bowen 38	0
31	11	H	Leicester C	W	3-2	2-0	4	Lingard 2 29, 44, Bowen 48	0
32	17	A	Newcastle U	L	2-3	0-2	4	Diop 73, Lingard (pen) 80	0
33	24	H	Chelsea	L	0-1	0-1	5		0
34	May 3	A	Burnley	W	2-1	2-1	5	Antonio 2 21, 29	0
35	9	H	Everton	L	0-1	0-1	5		0
36	15	A	Brighton & HA	D	1-1	0-0	6	Benrahma 87	0
37	19	A	WBA	W	3-1	1-1	6	Soucek 45, Ogbonna 82, Antonio 88	5371
38	23	H	Southampton	W	3-0	2-0	6	Fornals 2 30, 33, Rice 86	10,000

Final League Position: 6

GOALSCORERS

League (62): Antonio 10, Soucek 10, Lingard 9 (1 pen), Bowen 8, Fornals 5, Dawson 3, Haller 3, Ogbonna 3, Diop 2, Rice 2 (1 pen), Balbuena 1, Benrahma 1, Fredericks 1, Johnson 1, Lanzini 1, own goals 2.
FA Cup (5): Afolayan 1, Dawson 1, Fornals 1, Yarmolenko 1, own goal 1.
Carabao Cup (9): Haller 4, Snodgrass 2, Yarmolenko 2 (1 pen), Felipe Anderson 1.
Papa John's Trophy (5): Coventry 2, Odubeko 2, Corbett 1.

Fabianski L 35	Fredericks R 6 + 8	Diop I 15 + 3	Ogbonna A 28	Cresswell A 36	Soucek T 38	Rice D 32	Bowen J 30 + 8	Noble M 8 + 13	Fornals P 31 + 2	Antonio M 24 + 2	Haller S 10 + 6	Yarmolenko A 1 + 14	Felipe Anderson G — + 2	Masuaku A 12	Balbuena F 13 + 1	Johnson B 5 + 9	Coufal V 34	Lanzini M 5 + 12	Snodgrass R — + 3	Benrahma S 14 + 16	Dawson C 22	Randolph D 3	Lingard J 16	Match No.
1	2	3	4	5	6	7	8^3	9^1	10^2	11	12	13	14											1
1	2	3	4	5	8	9	7^1		10^2	11	13	12	14	6^3										2
1	2^1		4	5	8	9	7^3	14	10	11^2	13			6	3	12								3
1			4	5	8	9	7^1	13	10	11^2	12			6	3		2							4
1			4	5	8	9	7		10^2	11^1		13		6^3	3		2	12	14					5
1			4	5	8	9	7^2		10	11^1	13	12		6	3		2							6
1			4	5	8	9	7^3		10		11^1	12		6^2	3		2	13		14				7
1		12	3^1	4	7	6	9^3		11^2		10			8	2		5	14		13				8
1			3	4	7	6	9^2	13	11^1		10			8	2		5	12						9
1			3	4	7	6	9^3	14	10	11^1	13			8^2	2		5			12				10
1			3	4	7	6	9^2		10^1		11			8	2	14	5^3	13		12				11
1			4	5	7	6	8^2	12	10^3		11				3	13	2		14	9^1				12
1		3	4	5	7	6	8^2		10^1		11	13					2	12	14	9^3				13
1	13		4	5	6	7	8^2	9	10^1		11				3		2			12				14
1			3	4	6	7	10^1	9^2			11	13			2	8	5	12						15
1	2		4	5	9	6	13		10	14	11^3	7^2						8^1		12	3			16
			4	5	7	6	8^2		10^3	12	11^1	14					2	13		9	3	1		17
1			4	5	6	7	8^2		10	11		13					2	12		9^1	3			18
1			4	5	6	7	8	14	12	11^3		13					2	9^2		10^1	3			19
1	12		4	5	6	7	8^1	14	10	11^2		13					2			9^3	3			20
1	14		4	5	6	7	8^3	13	10^1	11^2		12					2			9	3			21
1	8^1		4	5	6	7	14		12	11						13	2			10^2	3		9^3	22
1	14		4	5	6■	7	8^2	13		11^3		12					2			10^1	3		9	23
1	14	2		4	6	7	11	12								8^3	5	9^1		13	3		10^2	24
1		4		5	7	6	8^1	14	10^2	11						13	2			12	3		9^3	25
		2		4	6	7	13		9	11^2						8^1	5			12	3	1	10	26
1		4		5	6	7	12		8	11						13	2			10^1	3		9^2	27
1		2		4	8	5	10	7^1		11						9^2	6	13		12	3			28
1	13	4		5	6	7	8^1	12		11							2			10^2	3		9	29
1		4		5	6		12	7	8^3	11^1				10^2		13	2			14	3		9	30
1		3		5^1	7		11^3	6^2	8					10	12	13	2			14	4		9	31
1	14	2	4		7		10	6^1	9							8^3	5	13		12	3■		11^2	32
1	8^3	4	3		7		10	6^1	9^2						2■	14	5	13		12			11	33
1		4		5	6		12		8	11							2	7		10^1	3		9	34
1	13	4		5^2	6		12		8	11		14					2	7^1		10^3	3		9	35
1			4	5	6	7	8^1		10	11							2			12	3		9	36
		13	4	5	6	7	12		8^2	11							2			10^1	3	1	9	37
1		14	4	5	6	7^3	8^2	13	10	11^1							2			12	3		9	38

FA Cup

Third Round	Stockport Co	(a)	1-0
Fourth Round	Doncaster R	(h)	4-0
Fifth Round	Manchester U	(a)	0-1
(aet)			

Carabao Cup

Second Round	Charlton Ath	(h)	3-0
Third Round	Hull C	(h)	5-1
Fourth Round	Everton	(a)	1-4

Papa John's Trophy (West Ham U U21)

Group A (S)	Southend U	(a)	3-1
Group A (S)	Colchester U	(a)	1-0
Group A (S)	Portsmouth	(a)	1-0
Second Round (S)	Peterborough U	(a)	0-3

WIGAN ATHLETIC

FOUNDATION

Following the demise of Wigan Borough and their resignation from the Football League in 1931, a public meeting was called in Wigan at the Queen's Hall in May 1932 at which a new club, Wigan Athletic, was founded in the hope of carrying on in the Football League. With this in mind, they bought Springfield Park for £2,250, but failed to gain admission to the Football League until 46 years later.

DW Stadium, Loire Drive, Newtown, Wigan, Lancashire WN5 0UZ.

Telephone: (01942) 774 000.

Ticket Office: (01942) 311 111.

Website: www.wiganathletic.com

Email: feedback@wiganathletic.com

Ground Capacity: 25,113.

Record Attendance: 27,526 v Hereford U, 12 December 1953 (at Springfield Park); 25,133 v Manchester U, Premier League, 11 May 2008 (at DW Stadium).

Pitch Measurements: 105m × 68m (115yd × 74.5yd).

Chairman: Talal Al-Hammad.

Chief Executive: Mal Brannigan.

Manager: Leam Richardson.

Assistant Manager: Gregor Rioch.

Colours: Blue and white striped shirts with blue sleeves, blue shorts with white trim, blue socks with white trim.

Year Formed: 1932.

Turned Professional: 1932.

Club Nickname: 'The Latics'.

Grounds: 1932, Springfield Park; 1999, JJB Stadium (renamed DW Stadium, 2009).

First Football League Game: 19 August 1978, Division 4, v Hereford U (a) D 0–0 – Brown; Hinnigan, Gore, Gillibrand, Ward, Davids, Corrigan, Purdie, Houghton, Wilkie, Wright.

Record League Victory: 8–0 v Hull C, FL C, 14 July 2020 – Marshall; Byrne, Kipre, Balogun (Dobre), Robinson (Evans), Williams (1) (Massey), Morsy, Naismith (1), Dowell (3) (Roberts), Lowe (1), Moore (2) (Pearce).

Record Cup Victory: 6–0 v Carlisle U (a), FA Cup 1st rd, 24 November 1934 – Caunce; Robinson, Talbot; Paterson, Watson, Tufnell; Armes (2), Robson (1), Roberts (2), Felton, Scott (1).

HONOURS

League Champions: FL 1 – 2015–16, 2017–18; Second Division – 2002–03; Third Division – 1996–97.
Runners-up: FL C – 2004–05.

FA Cup Winners: 2013.

League Cup: *Runners-up:* 2006.

League Trophy Winners: 1985, 1999.

European Competitions
Europa League: 2013–14.

FOOTBALL YEARBOOK FACT FILE

Wigan Athletic completed the double winning both the Cheshire League championship and the League Cup in 1964–65 as well as reaching the final of both the Lancashire Junior Cup and the Liverpool Non-League Cup. The Latics had a 28-match unbeaten run during the season and finished the campaign five points clear of second-placed Macclesfield Town after clinching the title over Easter.

Record Defeat: 1–9 v Tottenham H, Premier League, 22 November 2009; 0–8 v Chelsea, Premier League, 9 May 2010.

Most League Points (2 for a win): 55, Division 4, 1978–79 and 1979–80.

Most League Points (3 for a win): 100, Division 2, 2002–03.

Most League Goals: 89, FL 1, 2017–18.

Highest League Scorer in Season: Graeme Jones, 31, Division 3, 1996–97.

Most League Goals in Total Aggregate: Andy Liddell, 70, 1998–2004.

Most League Goals in One Match: Not more than three goals by one player.

Most Capped Players: Kevin Kilbane, 22 (110), Republic of Ireland; Henri Camara, 22 (99), Senegal.

Most League Appearances: Kevin Langley, 317, 1981–86, 1990–94.

Youngest League Player: Steve Nugent, 16 years 132 days v Leyton Orient, 16 September 1989.

Record Transfer Fee Received: £15,250,000 from Manchester U for Antonio Valencia, June 2009.

Record Transfer Fee Paid: £7,000,000 to Newcastle U for Charles N'Zogbia, January 2009.

Football League Record: 1978 Elected to Division 4; 1982–92 Division 3; 1992–93 Division 2; 1993–97 Division 3; 1997–2003 Division 2; 2003–04 Division 1; 2004–05 FL C; 2005–13 Premier League; 2013–15 FL C; 2015–16 FL 1; 2016–17 FL C; 2017–18 FL 1; 2018–20 FL C; 2020– FL 1.

LATEST SEQUENCES

Longest Sequence of League Wins: 11, 2.11.2002 – 18.1.2003.

Longest Sequence of League Defeats: 8, 10.9.2011 – 6.11.2011.

Longest Sequence of League Draws: 6, 11.12.2001 – 5.1.2002.

Longest Sequence of Unbeaten League Matches: 25, 8.5.1999 – 3.1.2000.

Longest Sequence Without a League Win: 14, 9.5.1989 – 17.10.1989.

Successive Scoring Runs: 24 from 27.4.1996.

Successive Non-scoring Runs: 4 from 8.12.2018.

MANAGERS

Charlie Spencer 1932–37
Jimmy Milne 1946–47
Bob Pryde 1949–52
Ted Goodier 1952–54
Walter Crook 1954–55
Ron Suart 1955–56
Billy Cooke 1956
Sam Barkas 1957
Trevor Hitchen 1957–58
Malcolm Barrass 1958–59
Jimmy Shirley 1959
Pat Murphy 1959–60
Allenby Chilton 1960
Johnny Ball 1961–63
Allan Brown 1963–66
Alf Craig 1966–67
Harry Leyland 1967–68
Alan Saunders 1968
Ian McNeill 1968–70
Gordon Milne 1970–72
Les Rigby 1972–74
Brian Tiler 1974–76
Ian McNeill 1976–81
Larry Lloyd 1981–83
Harry McNally 1983–85
Bryan Hamilton 1985–86
Ray Mathias 1986–89
Bryan Hamilton 1989–93
Dave Philpotts 1993
Kenny Swain 1993–94
Graham Barrow 1994–95
John Deehan 1995–98
Ray Mathias 1998–99
John Benson 1999–2000
Bruce Rioch 2000–01
Steve Bruce 2001
Paul Jewell 2001–07
Chris Hutchings 2007
Steve Bruce 2007–09
Roberto Martinez 2009–13
Owen Coyle 2013
Uwe Rosler 2013–14
Malky Mackay 2014–15
Gary Caldwell 2015–16
Warren Joyce 2016–17
Paul Cook 2017–20
John Sheridan 2020
Leam Richardson April 2021–

TEN YEAR LEAGUE RECORD

		P	*W*	*D*	*L*	*F*	*A*	*Pts*	*Pos*
2011-12	PR Lge	38	11	10	17	42	62	43	15
2012-13	PR Lge	38	9	9	20	47	73	36	18
2013-14	FL C	46	21	10	15	61	48	73	5
2014-15	FL C	46	9	12	25	39	64	39	23
2015-16	FL 1	46	24	15	7	82	45	87	1
2016-17	FL C	46	10	12	24	40	57	42	23
2017-18	FL 1	46	29	11	6	89	29	98	1
2018-19	FL C	46	13	13	20	51	64	52	18
2019-20	FL C	46	15	14	17	57	56	47	23*
2020-21	FL 1	46	13	9	24	54	77	48	20

** 12 pts deducted.*

DID YOU KNOW ?

Wigan Athletic were elected to the Football League in 1978 despite only finishing in second place in the Northern Premier League. Champions Boston United were ruled out of moving up because their ground did not meet the League's criteria. Wigan tied with Southport on a first ballot but on a second vote the Latics were elected by 29 votes to 20.

WIGAN ATHLETIC – SKY BET LEAGUE ONE 2020–21 LEAGUE RECORD

Match No.	Date	Venue	Opponents	Result		H/T Score	Lg Pos.	Goalscorers	Attendance
1	Sept 13	A	Ipswich T	L	0-2	0-1	19		0
2	19	H	Gillingham	L	2-3	1-2	21	Garner [21], Naismith [64]	0
3	26	A	Portsmouth	W	2-1	1-0	17	Evans, L [39], James [59]	0
4	Oct 3	H	Doncaster R	W	1-0	0-0	10	Garner [59]	0
5	10	A	Crewe Alex	L	0-3	0-2	15		0
6	17	A	Charlton Ath	L	0-1	0-0	17		0
7	20	H	Peterborough U	L	0-1	0-1	20		0
8	24	H	Plymouth Arg	D	1-1	0-1	17	Keane [69]	0
9	27	A	Milton Keynes D	L	0-2	0-0	18		0
10	31	H	Northampton T	L	2-3	0-2	20	Garner (pen) [63], James [75]	0
11	Nov 3	A	Blackpool	L	0-1	0-0	23		0
12	21	H	Oxford U	L	1-2	0-0	22	Aasgaard [88]	0
13	24	H	Bristol R	D	0-0	0-0	23		0
14	Dec 1	A	Lincoln C	L	1-2	0-0	23	Naismith [52]	0
15	5	A	Sunderland	W	1-0	1-0	23	Joseph [16]	0
16	12	H	Accrington S	W	4-3	3-0	22	James [14], Gardner [19], Keane (pen) [32], Hughes (og) [83]	0
17	15	H	Rochdale	L	0-5	0-2	22		0
18	19	A	Fleetwood T	D	1-1	0-1	22	Crankshaw [90]	0
19	26	H	Shrewsbury T	D	1-1	0-0	22	Keane (pen) [47]	0
20	29	A	Burton Alb	W	4-3	2-2	21	Joseph 3 [18, 28, 73], Keane [83]	0
21	Jan 16	A	Rochdale	D	3-3	2-1	21	Joseph [9], Lang [16], Keane [77]	0
22	23	H	Fleetwood T	D	0-0	0-0	21		0
23	26	H	Blackpool	L	0-5	0-2	22		0
24	Feb 2	A	Swindon T	L	0-1	0-1	22		0
25	6	H	AFC Wimbledon	L	2-3	1-2	22	Tilt [45], Proctor [68]	0
26	9	A	Northampton T	W	1-0	0-0	20	Lang [81]	0
27	14	A	Oxford U	L	1-2	0-0	21	Lang [57]	0
28	17	H	Hull C	L	0-5	0-2	22		0
29	20	H	Lincoln C	L	1-2	1-1	22	Lang [33]	0
30	23	A	Bristol R	W	2-1	0-0	21	Lang [51], Wootton [90]	0
31	27	A	Peterborough U	L	1-2	0-0	22	Aasgaard [72]	0
32	Mar 2	H	Charlton Ath	L	0-1	0-1	23		0
33	6	H	Milton Keynes D	W	3-0	1-0	22	Johnston [23], Lang [64], Dodoo [70]	0
34	9	A	Plymouth Arg	W	2-0	2-0	19	Solomon-Otabor [13], Tilt [32]	0
35	16	A	AFC Wimbledon	D	1-1	0-0	19	Proctor [58]	0
36	20	A	Accrington S	L	1-3	1-2	20	Lang [1]	0
37	27	H	Ipswich T	D	0-0	0-0	22		0
38	31	A	Gillingham	L	0-1	0-0	22		0
39	Apr 5	H	Portsmouth	L	0-1	0-0	22		0
40	10	A	Doncaster R	W	4-1	3-1	21	Dodoo [3], Aasgaard [15], Solomon-Otabor [33], Keane [81]	0
41	13	H	Sunderland	W	2-1	1-1	20	Keane [42], Lang [58]	0
42	17	H	Crewe Alex	W	2-0	1-0	20	Dodoo [15], Evans, L (pen) [72]	0
43	20	A	Shrewsbury T	W	2-1	2-0	20	Keane [26], Lang [45]	0
44	24	H	Burton Alb	D	1-1	1-1	20	Keane [37]	0
45	May 1	A	Hull C	L	1-3	1-2	20	Dodoo [19]	0
46	9	H	Swindon T	L	3-4	1-0	20	Tilt [17], Keane [56], Clough [60]	0

Final League Position: 20

GOALSCORERS

League (54): Keane 10 (2 pens), Lang 9, Joseph 5, Dodoo 4, Aasgaard 3, Garner 3 (1 pen), James 3, Tilt 3, Evans, L 2 (1 pen), Naismith 2, Proctor 2, Solomon-Otabor 2, Clough 1, Crankshaw 1, Gardner 1, Johnston 1, Wootton 1, own goal 1.
FA Cup (2): Garner 1, James 1.
Carabao Cup (2): Garner 2 (1 pen).
Papa John's Trophy (9): Crankshaw 2, Jolley 2, Garner 1 (1 pen), Keane 1, McHugh 1, Naismith 1, Pearce 1.

Jones J 45	Obi C 3 + 1	Naismith K 12	Long A 10 + 3	Pearce T 23	Evans L 21	Merrie C 24 + 2	Solomon-Otabor V 25 + 3	Roberts G 2	Gardner D 20 + 16	Garner J 11	Perry A 17 + 4	Crankshaw O 2 + 17	James T 20	Cameron N 2	Fox D 2	Massey G 13 + 3	Johnson D 10	Keane W 25 + 7	Jolley C — + 2	Tilt C 36	Palmer M 10	Aasgaard T 13 + 20	Joseph K 12 + 6	McHugh H — + 1	Robinson L 20 + 5	Evans O 1	Darikwa T 26	Lang C 22 + 1	Whelan C 2 + 6	Johnston G 19 + 3	Clough Z 4 + 9	Wootton S 12 + 1	Ojo F 23	Proctor J 7 + 8	Dodoo J 12 + 8	Match No.
1	2	3	4	5	6	7^{2}	8	9	10^{1}	11	12	13																								1
1		10		5	6		8	9^{1}		11	7	12	2	3	4																					2
1		8		5^{1}	9	7^{3}	10^{2}		12	11	6	14	2	3	4	13																				3
1		4		5	9	6	8			11^{1}	7	12	2			10	3																			4
1		4		5	9	7^{2}	8		13		6^{1}	12	2			10	3	11^{3}	14																	5
1		6			8		9		7	10			5			2	3	11		4																6
1		6			8	12	9			10^{2}		13	5			2	3	11^{1}		4	7^{3}	14														7
1		9	13	5	6		10^{1}			11			2			8	3^{2}	12		4	7															8
1			4	9		7			8	11	14	12	3			5^{2}		10^{1}		2^{3}	6	13														9
1	12		4	5		7			10	11	6	2^{1}	3								8	9^{2}	13													10
1	3		4	5		8^{1}			9	11	7	13	2								6	12	10^{2}													11
1	3			5		7			9^{2}	10	12	13	2			6^{3}				4	8^{1}	14	11													12
1			4	5		7^{1}					8	13	2			6				3	9	10^{2}	11	12												13
1		9	4	5		7			8^{1}		6		2							3	10	12	11													14
1		9^{1}	4	5	7	13			10^{3}		6^{2}	12	2							3		8	11		14											15
1			3^{1}	9		8			6^{2}		11	12	5				2	10	13	4			7													16
1			4	9^{2}		8			6^{3}		7	14	5				2	10^{1}		3		12	11		13											17
1		8		5		7			10^{2}		6	12	2				3	9		4			11^{1}		13											18
1		10^{2}	12	5		7			9^{3}		8		2				3	11		4	6^{1}	14	13													19
1			13	5		7			12			8^{2}	2				3	9		4	6	10^{1}	11													20
			4^{2}	5		6			8^{1}		7	14	3					11				12	10		13	1	2	9^{3}								21
1				5		8			9		7	13										12	11				2	6^{2}	3	4	10^{1}					22
1				5		7			12		6	13						9^{3}				14	11^{2}				2	8	3	4	10^{1}					23
1				5		7^{2}			10									9		4		12					2	11		13	8^{1}	3	6			24
1				5		8^{3}	12		9^{1}									10^{2}		4		13					2	6			14	3	7	11		25
1						9	12											7^{2}		4		10^{1}			6		2	11^{3}	14	5		3	8		13	26
1						9	15		13									7^{4}		4		10^{2}			6		2	11^{1}		5^{3}	14	3	8		12	27
1						7	8^{3}		10^{4}									9^{2}		4					13		2	15	12	5	16	3^{1}	6	11^{5}	14	28
1						7^{1}	8^{2}									12		13		4		9			5		2	10				3	6	11		29
1							7^{2}									13		11^{1}		4		9			5		2	8		12		3	6		10	30
1							8^{3}		7^{1}							10^{2}		14		4		12			5		2	9		13		3	6		11	31
1							8		13		7^{1}					10^{2}				4		9			5		2				12	3	6		11	32
1							10^{2}		14		16					8^{5}				4		13			5		2	9^{3}		7	15	3	6^{4}	12	11^{1}	33
1					7^{3}		10^{5}		16							8^{4}		13		3		15			5		2	9^{1}	14	4			6	11^{2}	12	34
1					8		10		12							6^{1}				4					5		2			9		3	7	11^{2}	13	35
1					9				10^{1}									13		4					6		2	11		5		3	8	12	7^{2}	36
1					7		10^{2}		12									11^{3}		3		9^{1}			5		2	8		4	13		6		14	37
1					7		9^{3}		14									13		3		8^{2}			5		2	10		4			6	11^{1}	12	38
1					7		10^{2}		13									12		3		9^{1}			5		2	8^{3}		4			6	11	14	39
1					6		8^{1}		12									11^{2}		3		9^{3}			5		2		15	4	13		7	14	10^{4}	40
1					7		10^{1}											9^{2}		3		13			5		2	8	12	4			6	14	11^{3}	41
1					7		10^{1}		13									9^{2}		3		12	15		5		2	8^{5}		4	16		6^{4}	14	11^{3}	42
1					7		10^{1}		12									9^{2}		3		13			5		2	8		4			6		11	43
1					7		10^{1}											9		3			13		5		2	8		4			6	12	11^{2}	44
1					6		10^{1}		14									9^{3}		3		13	12		5		2	8^{2}		4	15		7^{5}	16	11^{4}	45
1									7^{1}									9^{2}		3■		14	13		5		2	8^{5}	16	4	10^{3}	12	6	15	11^{4}	46

FA Cup

First Round	Chorley	(h)	2-3
(aet)			

Carabao Cup

First Round	Fleetwood T	(a)	2-3

Papa John's Trophy

Group D (N)	Liverpool U21	(h)	6-1
Group D (N)	Port Vale	(h)	1-3
Group D (N)	Tranmere R	(a)	2-2

(Tranmere R won 3-1 on penalties)

WOLVERHAMPTON WANDERERS

FOUNDATION

Enthusiasts of the game at St Luke's School, Blakenhall formed a club in 1877. In the same neighbourhood a cricket club called Blakenhall Wanderers had a football section. Several St Luke's footballers played cricket for them and shortly before the start of the 1879–80 season the two amalgamated and Wolverhampton Wanderers FC was brought into being.

Molineux Stadium, Waterloo Road, Wolverhampton, West Midlands WV1 4QR.

Telephone: (0371) 222 2220.

Ticket Office: (0371) 222 1877.

Website: wolves.co.uk

Email: info@wolves.co.uk

Ground Capacity: 32,050.

Record Attendance: 61,315 v Liverpool, FA Cup 5th rd, 11 February 1939.

Pitch Measurements: 105m × 68m (115yd × 74.5yd).

Executive Chairman: Jeff Shi.

Head Coach: Bruno Lage.

Assistant Head Coach: Alex Silva.

Colours: Gold shirts with black trim, black shorts with gold trim, gold socks.

Year Formed: 1877* (*see Foundation*).

Turned Professional: 1888.

Previous Names: 1879, St Luke's combined with Wanderers Cricket Club to become Wolverhampton Wanderers (1923) Ltd. New limited companies followed in 1982 and 1986 (current).

Club Nickname: 'Wolves'.

Grounds: 1877, Windmill Field; 1879, John Harper's Field; 1881, Dudley Road; 1889, Molineux.

First Football League Game: 8 September 1888, Football League, v Aston Villa (h) D 1–1 – Baynton; Baugh, Mason; Fletcher, Allen, Lowder; Hunter, Cooper, Anderson, White, Cannon, (1 og).

Record League Victory: 10–1 v Leicester C, Division 1, 15 April 1938 – Sidlow; Morris, Dowen; Galley, Cullis, Gardiner; Maguire (1), Horace Wright, Westcott (4), Jones (1), Dorsett (4).

Record Cup Victory: 14–0 v Crosswell's Brewery, FA Cup 2nd rd, 13 November 1886 – Ike Griffiths; Baugh, Mason; Pearson, Allen (1), Lowder; Hunter (4), Knight (2), Brodie (4), Bernie Griffiths (2), Wood. Plus one goal 'scrambled through'.

Record Defeat: 1–10 v Newton Heath, Division 1, 15 October 1892.

Most League Points (2 for a win): 64, Division 1, 1957–58.

HONOURS

League Champions: Division 1 – 1953–54, 1957–58, 1958–59; FL C – 2008–09, 2017–18; Division 2 – 1931–32, 1976–77; FL 1 – 2013–14; Division 3 – 1988–89; Division 3N – 1923–24; Division 4 – 1987–88.
Runners-up: Division 1 – 1937–38, 1938–39, 1949–50, 1954–55, 1959–60; Division 2 – 1966–67, 1982–83.

FA Cup Winners: 1893, 1908, 1949, 1960.
Runners-up: 1889, 1896, 1921, 1939.

League Cup Winners: 1974, 1980.

League Trophy Winners: 1988.

Texaco Cup Winners: 1971.

European Competitions
European Cup: 1958–59, 1959–60 *(qf)*.
UEFA Cup: 1971–72 (*runners-up*), 1973–74, 1974–75, 1980–81.
Europa League: 2019–20.
European Cup-Winners' Cup: 1960–61 *(sf)*.

FOOTBALL YEARBOOK FACT FILE

Wolverhampton Wanderers centre-forward Roy Swinbourne was in fine form at the start of the 1955–56 season, scoring 17 goals from his first 12 games including three hat-tricks. However, he was injured in his 13th appearance at Luton Town, when he pulled up sharply to avoid the youngsters sat around the sides of the pitch, and then suffered a bad knee injury in his comeback game at Preston North End which effectively ended his career.

Most League Points (3 for a win): 103, FL 1, 2013–14.

Most League Goals: 115, Division 2, 1931–32.

Highest League Scorer in Season: Dennis Westcott, 38, Division 1, 1946–47.

Most League Goals in Total Aggregate: Steve Bull, 250, 1986–99.

Most League Goals in One Match: 5, Joe Butcher v Accrington, Division 1, 19 November 1892; 5, Tom Phillipson v Barnsley, Division 2, 26 April 1926; 5, Tom Phillipson v Bradford C, Division 2, 25 December 1926; 5, Billy Hartill v Notts Co, Division 2, 12 October 1929; 5, Billy Hartill v Aston Villa, Division 1, 3 September 1934.

Most Capped Player: Billy Wright, 105, England (70 consecutive).

Most League Appearances: Derek Parkin, 501, 1967–82.

Youngest League Player: Jimmy Mullen, 16 years 43 days v Leeds U, 18 February 1939.

Record Transfer Fee Received: £41,000,000 from Liverpool for Diogo Jota, September 2020.

Record Transfer Fee Paid: £35,600,000 to Porto for Fabio Silva, September 2020.

Football League Record: 1888 Founder Member of Football League: 1906–23 Division 2; 1923–24 Division 3 (N); 1924–32 Division 2; 1932–65 Division 1; 1965–67 Division 2; 1967–76 Division 1; 1976–77 Division 2; 1977–82 Division 1; 1982–83 Division 2; 1983–84 Division 1; 1984–85 Division 2; 1985–86 Division 3; 1986–88 Division 4; 1988–89 Division 3; 1989–92 Division 2; 1992–2003 Division 1; 2003–04 Premier League; 2004–09 FL C; 2009–12 Premier League; 2012–13 FL C; 2013–14 FL 1; 2014–18 FL C; 2018– Premier League.

MANAGERS

George Worrall 1877–85
(Secretary-Manager)
John Addenbrooke 1885–1922
George Jobey 1922–24
Albert Hoskins 1924–26
(had been Secretary since 1922)
Fred Scotchbrook 1926–27
Major Frank Buckley 1927–44
Ted Vizard 1944–48
Stan Cullis 1948–64
Andy Beattie 1964–65
Ronnie Allen 1966–68
Bill McGarry 1968–76
Sammy Chung 1976–78
John Barnwell 1978–81
Ian Greaves 1982
Graham Hawkins 1982–84
Tommy Docherty 1984–85
Bill McGarry 1985
Sammy Chapman 1985–86
Brian Little 1986
Graham Turner 1986–94
Graham Taylor 1994–95
Mark McGhee 1995–98
Colin Lee 1998–2000
Dave Jones 2001–04
Glenn Hoddle 2004–06
Mick McCarthy 2006–12
Stale Solbakken 2012–13
Dean Saunders 2013
Kenny Jackett 2013–16
Walter Zenga 2016
Paul Lambert 2016–17
Nuno Espirito Santo 2017–21
Bruno Lage June 2021–

LATEST SEQUENCES

Longest Sequence of League Wins: 9, 11.1.2014 – 11.3.2014.

Longest Sequence of League Defeats: 8, 5.12.1981 – 13.2.1982.

Longest Sequence of League Draws: 6, 22.4.1995 – 20.8.1995.

Longest Sequence of Unbeaten League Matches: 21, 15.1.2005 – 13.8.2005.

Longest Sequence Without a League Win: 19, 1.12.1984 – 6.4.1985.

Successive Scoring Runs: 41 from 20.12.1958.

Successive Non-scoring Runs: 7 from 2.2.1985.

TEN YEAR LEAGUE RECORD

		P	W	D	L	F	A	Pts	Pos
2011-12	PR Lge	38	5	10	23	40	82	25	20
2012-13	FL C	46	14	9	23	55	69	51	23
2013-14	FL 1	46	31	10	5	89	31	103	1
2014-15	FL C	46	22	12	12	70	56	78	7
2015-16	FL C	46	14	16	16	53	58	58	14
2016-17	FL C	46	16	10	20	54	58	58	15
2017-18	FL C	46	30	9	7	82	39	99	1
2018-19	PR Lge	38	16	9	13	47	46	57	7
2019-20	PR Lge	38	15	14	9	51	40	59	7
2020-21	PR Lge	38	12	9	17	36	52	45	13

DID YOU KNOW ?

Wolverhampton Wanderers defeated their local rivals West Bromwich Albion 3-1 at The Hawthorns in a Coronation charities match played on 4 May 1953. Ron Flowers, Roy Swinbourne and Dennis Wilshaw scored the Wolves goals in front of a disappointing attendance of just 5,300.

WOLVERHAMPTON WANDERERS – PREMIER LEAGUE 2020–21 LEAGUE RECORD

Match No.	*Date*	*Venue*	*Opponents*	*Result*	*H/T Score*	*Lg Pos.*	*Goalscorers*	*Atten-dance*
1	Sept 14	A	Sheffield U	W 2-0	2-0	4	Jimenez [3], Saiss [6]	0
2	21	H	Manchester C	L 1-3	0-2	11	Jimenez [78]	0
3	27	A	West Ham U	L 0-4	0-1	16		0
4	Oct 4	H	Fulham	W 1-0	0-0	13	Pedro Neto [56]	0
5	19	A	Leeds U	W 1-0	0-0	6	Jimenez [70]	0
6	25	H	Newcastle U	D 1-1	0-0	8	Jimenez [80]	0
7	30	H	Crystal Palace	W 2-0	2-0	3	Ait Nouri [18], Daniel Podence [27]	0
8	Nov 8	A	Leicester C	L 0-1	0-1	9		0
9	23	H	Southampton	D 1-1	0-0	9	Pedro Neto [75]	0
10	29	A	Arsenal	W 2-1	2-1	6	Pedro Neto [27], Daniel Podence [42]	0
11	Dec 6	A	Liverpool	L 0-4	0-1	10		2000
12	12	H	Aston Villa	L 0-1	0-0	12		0
13	15	H	Chelsea	W 2-1	0-0	10	Daniel Podence [66], Pedro Neto [90]	0
14	21	A	Burnley	L 1-2	0-1	11	Silva (pen) [89]	0
15	27	H	Tottenham H	D 1-1	0-1	11	Saiss [86]	0
16	29	A	Manchester U	L 0-1	0-0	12		0
17	Jan 2	A	Brighton & HA	D 3-3	3-1	13	Saiss [19], Burn (og) [34], Neves (pen) [44]	0
18	12	H	Everton	L 1-2	1-1	14	Neves [14]	0
19	16	H	WBA	L 2-3	2-1	14	Silva [38], Boly [43]	0
20	27	A	Chelsea	D 0-0	0-0	13		0
21	30	A	Crystal Palace	L 0-1	0-0	14		0
22	Feb 2	H	Arsenal	W 2-1	1-1	14	Neves (pen) [45], Joao Moutinho [49]	0
23	7	H	Leicester C	D 0-0	0-0	14		0
24	14	A	Southampton	W 2-1	0-1	12	Neves (pen) [53], Pedro Neto [66]	0
25	19	H	Leeds U	W 1-0	0-0	11	Meslier (og) [64]	0
26	27	A	Newcastle U	D 1-1	0-0	12	Neves [73]	0
27	Mar 2	A	Manchester C	L 1-4	0-1	12	Coady [61]	0
28	6	A	Aston Villa	D 0-0	0-0	12		0
29	15	H	Liverpool	L 0-1	0-1	13		0
30	Apr 5	H	West Ham U	L 2-3	1-3	14	Dendoncker [44], Silva [68]	0
31	9	A	Fulham	W 1-0	0-0	12	Traore [90]	0
32	17	H	Sheffield U	W 1-0	0-0	12	Willian Jose [60]	0
33	25	H	Burnley	L 0-4	0-3	12		0
34	May 3	A	WBA	D 1-1	1-0	12	Silva [45]	0
35	9	H	Brighton & HA	W 2-1	0-1	12	Traore [76], White [90]	0
36	16	A	Tottenham H	L 0-2	0-1	12		0
37	19	A	Everton	L 0-1	0-0	12		6068
38	23	H	Manchester U	L 1-2	1-2	13	Nelson Semedo [39]	4500

Final League Position: 13

GOALSCORERS

League (36): Neves 5 (3 pens), Pedro Neto 5, Jimenez 4, Silva 4 (1 pen), Daniel Podence 3, Saiss 3, Traore 2, Ait Nouri 1, Boly 1, Coady 1, Dendoncker 1, Joao Moutinho 1, Nelson Semedo 1, White 1, Willian Jose 1, own goals 2.
FA Cup (2): Traore 1, Vitinha 1.
Carabao Cup (0).
Papa John's Trophy (4): Silva 2, Perry 1, Samuels 1.

Rui Patricio P 37	Boly W 21	Coady C 37	Saiss R 27	Traore A 28 + 9	Dendoncker L 28 + 5	Joao Moutinho F 28 + 5	Marcal F 7 + 6	Jimenez R 10	Daniel Podence C 22 + 2	Pedro Neto L 30 + 1	Buur O — + 1	Neves R 31 + 5	Vitinha F 5 + 14	Ruben Vinagre G 1 + 1	Silva F 11 + 21	Nelson Semedo C 34	Hoever K 5 + 7	Kilman M 14 + 4	Ait Nouri R 16 + 5	Otasowie O 2 + 4	White M 4 + 7	Cutrone P — + 2	Willian Jose d 12 + 5	Jonny C 7	Ruddy J 1 + 1	Corbeanu T — + 1	Match No.
1	2	3	4	5	6	7^{3}	8	9	10^{2}	11^{1}	12	13	14														1
1	3	4	5	2	13	7^{3}	6^{1}	10	11	9^{2}		8		12	14												2
1	2	3	4	9^{1}		7^{3}		10		11		6	13	8	12	5^{2}	14										3
1	2	3	9	14	6	12		10	11^{1}	8^{3}		7				5^{2}	13	4									4
1	2	3	9	12	6	7^{2}	14	10	11^{1}	8^{3}		13				5		4									5
1	2	3	8^{2}	12	6	14	13	10	11^{1}	9		7^{3}				5		4									6
1	2	3		13	6	12		11^{3}	10^{2}	9^{1}		7			14	5		4	8								7
1	2	3		12	6		13	11	10^{1}	9^{3}		7			14	5		4	8^{2}								8
1	4			9	6	8		10	11^{2}	12		7^{1}	13			2		3	5								9
1	3	4		8	6	7	5	11^{1}	9^{2}	10		13			12^{3}	2		14									10
1	3	4		9	6	7	5		10^{2}	11^{3}		8^{1}	14		12	2			13								11
1		3	4	8	6^{1}	7■	5		9	10		12			11	2											12
1	2	3	4	13	6^{1}		8		9^{3}	11		7	14		10^{2}	5				12							13
1		3	4	13		7			11	10		6^{3}	14		12	5		2	8^{2}	9^{1}							14
1		3	4	8		7^{2}	5^{1}		9^{3}	10		6	14		11	2			12	13							15
1		2	3	10		8			12	11^{2}		6	7^{1}		13		5	4	9								16
1		3	4	8		6				10		7	9^{1}		11^{2}	2		12	5	13							17
1		3	4		6	8^{3}				9		7	14		11^{2}	2	12		5		10^{1}	13					18
1	3	4^{2}	5	9	6	8^{3}				11		7^{1}			10	2			13		12	14					19
1	2	3		10^{3}	6	14			9^{2}	11		7				5	12	4	8^{1}				13				20
1	2	3		12	6	7^{3}			10^{2}	9			13		14	8	5^{1}	4					11				21
1	4	3		8	13	7			9^{1}	10		6^{2}	12		14	2		5					11^{3}				22
1		3		9	2	7				11^{3}		6			13	5	12	4			14		10^{2}	8^{1}			23
1		3	4	9	2	7	12			11^{3}		6			13	5		14					10^{2}	8^{1}			24
1		3	4	11	2	7	12^{2}			9		6			14	5			13				10^{3}	8^{1}			25
1		3	4	10	2	7				9		6			12	5^{2}	13		14				11^{1}	8^{3}			26
1		3	4	11	2	7				10		6^{2}			12	9	5			13				8^{1}			27
1		3	4	11	2	7				9		6			12	5							10^{1}	8			28
1^{4}	4	3	2	9	13	7				10		6^{2}			12	5^{3}					14		11^{1}	8	15		29
1		3	4	10	6				9^{1}	8		7	13		12	2	14		5^{3}				11^{2}				30
1		3	4	10	6	12			9^{2}	8^{1}		7			14	2			5		13		11^{3}				31
1	4	3	2	9	6	7			10^{1}				12		13	5			8				11^{2}				32
1	4	3	2	10	7				9^{2}			6^{3}	13		12	5^{1}			8		14		11				33
1		3	4	10	6				12			7	9^{2}		11	2		14	5^{3}	8^{1}	13						34
1		3		12	14	6			10^{2}			7^{1}	9^{3}		11		2	4	5		8		13				35
1		3	4	8	7	6						13	9^{1}		11^{3}	5	2				10^{2}		12			14	36
	2^{2}	3		9	13	5^{3}						6	14		11	7		4	8		10^{1}		12		1		37
1	4	3	2	10^{1}	6^{2}	8	14					7			11	5			9^{3}		13		12				38

FA Cup

Third Round	Crystal Palace	(h)	1-0
Fourth Round	Chorley	(a)	1-0
Fifth Round	Southampton	(h)	0-2

Carabao Cup

Second Round	Stoke C	(h)	0-1

Papa John's Trophy (Wolverhampton W U21)

Group F (N)	Oldham Ath	(a)	0-4
Group F (N)	Bradford C	(a)	1-1
(Wolverhampton W U21 won 5-3 on penalties)			
Group F (N)	Doncaster R	(a)	2-1
Second Round (N)	Port Vale	(a)	1-2

WYCOMBE WANDERERS

FOUNDATION

In 1887 a group of young furniture trade workers called a meeting at the Steam Engine public house with the aim of forming a football club and entering junior football. It is thought that they were named after the famous FA Cup winners, The Wanderers, who had visited the town in 1877 for a tie with the original High Wycombe club. It is also possible that they played informally before their formation, although there is no proof of this.

Adams Park, Hillbottom Road, High Wycombe, Buckinghamshire HP12 4HJ.

Telephone: (01494) 472 100.

Ticket Office: (01494) 441 118.

Website: www.wycombewanderers.co.uk

Email: wwfc@wwfc.com

Ground Capacity: 9,558.

Record Attendance: 15,850 v St Albans C, FA Amateur Cup 4th rd, 25 February 1950 (at Loakes Park); 9,921 v Fulham, FA Cup 3rd rd, 9 January 2002 (at Adams Park).

Pitch Measurements: 100m × 64m (109.5yd × 70yd).

Chairman: Rob Couhig.

Manager: Gareth Ainsworth.

Assistant Manager: Richard Dobson.

Colours: Light blue and dark blue quartered shirts, dark blue shorts with light blue trim, dark blue socks.

Year Formed: 1887. ***Turned Professional:*** 1974.

Club Nicknames: 'The Chairboys' (after High Wycombe's tradition of furniture making), 'The Blues'.

Grounds: 1887, The Rye; 1893, Spring Meadow; 1895, Loakes Park; 1899, Daws Hill Park; 1901, Loakes Park; 1990, Adams Park.

First Football League Game: 14 August 1993, Division 3 v Carlisle U (a) D 2–2: Hyde; Cousins, Horton (Langford), Kerr, Crossley, Ryan, Carroll, Stapleton, Thompson, Scott, Guppy (1) (Hutchinson), (1 og).

Record League Victory: 5–0 v Burnley, Division 2, 15 April 1997 – Parkin; Cousins, Bell, Kavanagh, McCarthy, Forsyth, Carroll (2p) (Simpson), Scott (Farrell), Stallard (1), McGavin (1) (Read (1)), Brown.
5–0 v Northampton T, Division 2, 4 January 2003 – Talia; Senda, Ryan, Thomson, McCarthy, Johnson, Bulman, Simpson (1), Faulconbridge (Harris), Dixon (1) (Roberts 3), Brown (Currie).
5–0 v Hartlepool U, FL 1, 25 February 2012 – Bull; McCoy, Basey, Eastmond (Bloomfield), Laing, Doherty (1), Hackett, Lewis, Bevon (2) (Strevons), Hayes (2) (McClure), McNamee.

Record Cup Victory: 5–0 v Hitchin T (a), FA Cup 2nd rd, 3 December 1994 – Hyde; Cousins, Brown, Crossley, Evans, Ryan (1), Carroll, Bell (1), Thompson, Garner (3) (Hemmings), Stapleton (Langford).
5–0 v Chesterfield (a), FA Cup 2nd rd, 3 December 2017 – Blackman; Harriman, Stewart (1), Pierre, Jacobson, Bloomfield (Wood), O'Nien, Gape (Bean), Kashket (3) (Cowan-Hall), Hayes (1), Akinfenwa.

Record Defeat: 0–7 v Shrewsbury T, Johnstone's Paint Trophy, 7 October 2008.

HONOURS

League Champions: Conference – 1992–93.
Runners-up: FL 2 – (3rd) 2008–09, 2010–11 *(promoted to FL 1)*; Conference – 1991–92.

FA Cup: semi-final – 2001.

League Cup: semi-final – 2007.

FA Amateur Cup Winners: 1931.

FOOTBALL YEARBOOK FACT FILE

Wycombe Wanderers were members of the Southern League from 1896 to 1908, competing in the Second Division of the competition. However, the Chairboys had a disastrous season in 1907–08, finishing bottom of the table with just three points from 16 games. By now the only amateur club in the league, they resigned their membership and switched to the Great Western Suburban League.

Most League Points (3 for a win): 84, FL 2, 2014–15; 84, FL 2, 2017–18.

Most League Goals: 79, FL 2, 2017–18.

Highest League Scorer in Season: Scott McGleish, 25, 2007–08.

Most League Goals in Total Aggregate: Nathan Tyson, 51, 2004–06, 2017–19.

Most League Goals in One Match: 3, Miquel Desouza v Bradford C, Division 2, 2 September 1995; 3, John Williams v Stockport Co, Division 2, 24 February 1996; 3, Mark Stallard v Walsall, Division 2, 21 October 1997; 3, Sean Devine v Reading, Division 2, 2 October 1999; 3, Sean Divine v Bury, Division 2, 26 February 2000; 3, Stuart Roberts v Northampton T, Division 2, 4 January 2003; 3, Nathan Tyson v Lincoln C, FL 2, 5 March 2005; 3, Nathan Tyson v Kidderminster H, FL 2, 2 April 2005; 3, Nathan Tyson v Stockport Co, FL 2, 10 September 2005; 3, Kevin Betsy v Mansfield T, FL 2, 24 September 2005; 3, Scott McGleish v Mansfield T, FL 2, 8 January 2008; 3, Stuart Beavon v Bury, FL 1, 17 March 2012; 3, Craig Mackail-Smith v Crawley T, FL 2, 18 November 2017; 3, Joe Jacobson v Lincoln C, FL 1, 7 September 2019.

Most Capped Player: Daryl Horgan, 8 (14), Republic of Ireland.

Most League Appearances: Matt Bloomfield, 486, 2003–21.

Youngest League Player: Jordon Ibe, 15 years 311 days v Hartlepool U, 15 October 2011.

Record Transfer Fee Received: £750,000 (rising to £1,000,000) from Middlesbrough for Uche Ikpeazu, July 2021.

Record Transfer Fee Paid: £200,000 to Barnet for Sean Devine, April 1999; £200,000 to Barnet for Darren Currie, July 2001.

Football League Record: 1993 Promoted to Division 3 from Conference; 1993–94 Division 3; 1994–2004 Division 2; 2004–09 FL 2; 2009–10 FL 1; 2010–11 FL 2; 2011–12 FL 1; 2012–18 FL 2; 2018–20 FL 1; 2020–21 FL C; 2021– FL 1.

MANAGERS

First coach appointed 1951.

Prior to Brian Lee's appointment in 1969 the team was selected by a Match Committee which met every Monday evening.

James McCormack 1951–52
Sid Cann 1952–61
Graham Adams 1961–62
Don Welsh 1962–64
Barry Darvill 1964–68
Brian Lee 1969–76
Ted Powell 1976–77
John Reardon 1977–78
Andy Williams 1978–80
Mike Keen 1980–84
Paul Bence 1984–86
Alan Gane 1986–87
Peter Suddaby 1987–88
Jim Kelman 1988–90
Martin O'Neill 1990–95
Alan Smith 1995–96
John Gregory 1996–98
Neil Smillie 1998–99
Lawrie Sanchez 1999–2003
Tony Adams 2003–04
John Gorman 2004–06
Paul Lambert 2006–08
Peter Taylor 2008–09
Gary Waddock 2009–12
Gareth Ainsworth November 2012–

LATEST SEQUENCES

Longest Sequence of League Wins: 6, 12.11.2016 – 17.12.2016.

Longest Sequence of League Defeats: 8, 29.2.2020 – 24.10.2020.

Longest Sequence of League Draws: 5, 24.1.2004 – 21.2.2004.

Longest Sequence of Unbeaten League Matches: 21, 6.8.2005 – 10.12.2005.

Longest Sequence Without a League Win: 13, 10.1.2004 – 20.3.2004.

Successive Scoring Runs: 16 from 13.9.2014.

Successive Non-scoring Runs: 5 from 15.10.1996.

TEN YEAR LEAGUE RECORD

		P	*W*	*D*	*L*	*F*	*A*	*Pts*	*Pos*
2011-12	FL 1	46	11	10	25	65	88	43	21
2012-13	FL 2	46	17	9	20	50	60	60	15
2013-14	FL 2	46	12	14	20	46	54	50	22
2014-15	FL 2	46	23	15	8	67	45	84	4
2015-16	FL 2	46	17	13	16	45	44	64	13
2016-17	FL 2	46	19	12	15	58	53	69	9
2017-18	FL 2	46	24	12	10	79	60	84	3
2018-19	FL 1	46	14	11	21	55	67	53	17
2019-20	FL 1	34	17	8	9	45	40	59	3§
2020-21	FL C	46	11	10	25	39	69	43	22

§Decided on points-per-game (1.74)

DID YOU KNOW ?

Goalkeeper Paul Hyde played in the Chairboys' first 93 Football League games following their promotion from the Football Conference in 1993. Hyde, who did not make his League debut until he was 30, played in the club's first 119 fixtures as a senior club.

WYCOMBE WANDERERS – SKY BET CHAMPIONSHIP 2020–21 LEAGUE RECORD

Match No.	Date	Venue	Opponents	Result	H/T Score	Lg Pos.	Goalscorers	Attendance
1	Sept 12	H	Rotherham U	L 0-1	0-0	15		0
2	19	A	Blackburn R	L 0-5	0-3	23		0
3	26	H	Swansea C	L 0-2	0-2	23		0
4	Oct 3	A	Luton T	L 0-2	0-0	23		0
5	17	H	Millwall	L 1-2	1-0	24	Kashket 9	0
6	20	A	Reading	L 0-1	0-0	24		0
7	24	A	Norwich C	L 1-2	1-1	24	Kashket 12	0
8	27	H	Watford	D 1-1	0-0	24	Stewart 66	0
9	31	H	Sheffield W	W 1-0	1-0	23	Wheeler 45	0
10	Nov 4	A	Birmingham C	W 2-1	0-1	22	Kashket 75, Pedersen (og) 90	0
11	7	A	Nottingham F	L 0-2	0-1	22		0
12	21	H	Brentford	D 0-0	0-0	22		0
13	24	H	Huddersfield T	D 0-0	0-0	22		0
14	28	A	Derby Co	D 1-1	0-1	22	Bloomfield 81	0
15	Dec 2	H	Stoke C	L 0-1	0-0	22		0
16	5	A	Preston NE	D 2-2	0-1	22	McCleary 48, Kashket 75	0
17	9	A	Barnsley	L 1-2	0-1	23	Jacobson (pen) 49	0
18	12	H	Coventry C	L 1-2	0-2	23	Jacobson (pen) 61	2000
19	15	A	Bournemouth	L 0-1	0-0	23		0
20	19	H	QPR	D 1-1	0-1	24	Mehmeti 88	0
21	26	A	Bristol C	L 1-2	0-1	24	McCleary 68	0
22	29	H	Cardiff C	W 2-1	1-0	24	Tafazolli 33, Wheeler 63	0
23	Jan 2	H	Middlesbrough	L 1-3	1-2	24	Ikpeazu 3	0
24	30	A	Brentford	L 2-7	2-2	24	Ikpeazu 14, Muskwe 43	0
25	Feb 2	H	Birmingham C	D 0-0	0-0	24		0
26	6	H	Nottingham F	L 0-3	0-1	24		0
27	9	A	Sheffield W	L 0-2	0-1	24		0
28	13	A	Huddersfield T	W 3-2	1-2	24	Mehmeti 45, Jacobson (pen) 63, Knight 87	0
29	16	H	Derby Co	L 1-2	0-1	24	Ikpeazu (pen) 48	0
30	20	A	Millwall	D 0-0	0-0	24		0
31	23	H	Reading	W 1-0	0-0	24	Onyedinma 49	0
32	28	H	Norwich C	L 0-2	0-0	24		0
33	Mar 3	A	Watford	L 0-2	0-1	24		0
34	6	A	Stoke C	L 0-2	0-0	24		0
35	9	A	QPR	L 0-1	0-1	24		0
36	13	H	Preston NE	W 1-0	1-0	24	Tafazolli 27	0
37	17	H	Barnsley	L 1-3	0-1	24	Ikpeazu 85	0
38	20	A	Coventry C	D 0-0	0-0	24		0
39	Apr 2	H	Blackburn R	W 1-0	0-0	24	Onyedinma 47	0
40	5	A	Rotherham U	W 3-0	2-0	24	Muskwe 2, McCarthy 24, Wheeler 83	0
41	10	H	Luton T	L 1-3	1-0	24	Mehmeti (pen) 37	0
42	17	A	Swansea C	D 2-2	0-0	24	Muskwe 46, McCleary 51	0
43	21	H	Bristol C	W 2-1	0-1	24	Ikpeazu 65, Akinfenwa (pen) 90	0
44	24	A	Cardiff C	L 1-2	1-1	24	Jacobson (pen) 43	0
45	May 1	H	Bournemouth	W 1-0	1-0	24	Ikpeazu 4	0
46	8	A	Middlesbrough	W 3-0	2-0	22	Onyedinma 14, McCleary 33, McCarthy 56	0

Final League Position: 22

GOALSCORERS

League (39): Ikpeazu 6 (1 pen), Jacobson 4 (4 pens), Kashket 4, McCleary 4, Mehmeti 3 (1 pen), Muskwe 3, Onyedinma 3, Wheeler 3, McCarthy 2, Tafazolli 2, Akinfenwa 1 (1 pen), Bloomfield 1, Knight 1, Stewart 1, own goal 1.
FA Cup (5): Onyedinma 2, Jacobson 1 (1 pen), Knight 1, Samuel 1.
Carabao Cup (1): Horgan 1.

Allsop R 29	Grimmer J 39 + 1	Stewart A 31 + 1	Charles D 5	Jacobson J 36 + 1	Bloomfield M 8 + 8	Pattison A 4 + 2	Wheeler D 27 + 11	Horgan D 28 + 12	Onyedinma F 26 + 17	Kashket S 18 + 11	Freeman N 3 + 4	McCarthy J 22 + 2	Parker J — + 3	Tafazolli R 17 + 3	Ikpeazu U 23 + 8	Adeniran D 18 + 3	Samuel A 7 + 14	Thompson C 28 + 5	Knight J 36 + 1	Akinfenwa A 11 + 22	Mehmeti A 18 + 11	McCleary G 20 + 12	Gape D 12 + 2	Muskwe A 13 + 4	Obita J 7 + 2	Ofoborh N 3 + 5	Stockdale D 17	Match No.
1	2	3	4	5	6^{1}	7^{2}	8	9	10	11^{3}	12	13	14															1
1	2	3	4■	5	7^{2}	6	8	9	10^{3}	11^{1}	14			12	13													2
1	2	3			10^{2}		6^{3}	12	9^{1}	14	8	5	13	4		7	11											3
1	2	3	4	5			6^{1}	9^{3}	12	13	7		14			8	11^{2}	10										4
1	2	4		5			9	13	6^{2}	10						8^{3}	11^{1}	7	3	12	14							5
1	2	4		5	6^{3}			9	12	10^{1}						8	11^{2}	7	3	13	14							6
1	2	4		5	13		11^{3}	6^{2}	9	10^{1}					12	8		7	3	14								7
1	2	4		5			10	9^{2}	13	8^{3}					12	7	14	6	3	11^{1}								8
1	2	3		5	12		7^{2}	9	13	10					14	6^{1}		8	4	11^{3}								9
1	2	4		5			6^{1}	10	12	9						8^{2}		7	3	11	13							10
1	2	4		5			11^{2}	10	6	9^{1}							14	7	3	12	8^{3}	13						11
1	2	4		5			6^{2}	10	14	9^{1}							12	8	3	11		13	7^{3}					12
1	2	4		5			12	13	9^{4}	11^{2}						6^{3}	15	8	3	10		14	7^{1}					13
1	2	4		5	14	12	16	11^{5}	15	9^{2}						8^{4}		7^{1}	3	13	6^{3}	10						14
1	2	4		5	8^{3}		11	7	9	13		6^{1}					10^{2}		3	12		14						15
1	2	4^{1}		5	14		12	7^{2}	11^{3}	9	13	6					15		3	10^{4}		8						16
1	4			5	15		9^{3}	8^{2}	12	11^{1}		2					14		3	10^{4}	13	7	6					17
1	2			5	7^{3}	8^{4}	13	9^{1}	11	15		4					10^{2}		3	12		14	6					18
1	2			5		8■	7	14	13	11^{2}	12	4			15				3	10^{4}		9^{3}	6^{1}					19
1	2			5			7	9	12	11^{3}	8^{2}	4			14				3	10	13	6^{1}						20
1	2		4	5				8	9^{1}	10						13		6^{2}	3	11	12	7						21
1	2			5	15		6	9^{1}	12					4	10^{2}		14	7	3	13	8^{4}	11^{3}						22
1	2			5			6	9^{4}	15	12				4	10^{3}	13		7^{2}	3	14	8^{1}	11						23
1	2		4		14		7^{2}		9^{5}			5			10^{3}	8	15	6^{4}	3	13	16	12		11^{1}				24
1	2				8^{3}		14		9	13				4	10^{2}			7	3	12				11^{1}	5	6		25
1	2				8^{2}		6	9^{4}	11^{1}					4	10^{5}		16	14	3	15	13	12			5	7^{3}		26
1		3						11^{4}	14	9^{3}		2		4	12			7		10^{1}	6^{2}	15		13	5	8		27
1	2	3		5^{1}			6	11	13					4	10				7		8	9^{2}			12			28
1	2	3					6	9	12					4	10				7		8^{2}	11^{1}	13		5			29
	2	3					8	10^{1}	7					4	11^{2}				6		9	12		13	5		1	30
	2	3					6		11^{2}			13		4■	10^{4}			12	7		8^{1}	9^{3}	14	15	5		1	31
	2	4		12			8^{5}	13	9	16					11			14	3		10^{2}	6^{3}	7^{4}		5^{1}	15	1	32
	2	4		5			8	9^{5}	10^{2}	16				3	11^{4}			12	6^{3}	15		14	7^{1}			13	1	33
		3		5			8^{2}	12	13	15		2		4	11^{4}				6^{5}	14	9	10^{1}		7^{3}		16	1	34
				5				10		15		2		4	13		8^{4}	6^{2}	3	12	9		7^{3}	11^{1}		14	1	35
	14			5				10				2		4	11^{3}			7	3		9	8^{2}	6^{1}	13		12	1	36
				5				10^{2}		12		2^{3}		4	11		14	7	3	13	9^{1}	8	6				1	37
		3		5			7^{1}	14	13			2		4	11^{5}			12	8^{4}	15	10^{2}	16	6	9^{3}			1	38
	3			5				13	6			2			11^{4}	12	15	9	4	14	10^{2}		8^{1}	7^{3}			1	39
	3	12		5^{1}			13	16	6			2			11^{3}	8		9^{4}	4	14	7^{2}	15		10^{5}			1	40
	2	3					12		9			5			11^{2}	7	13	8	4■	14	6^{1}			10^{3}			1	41
	2	3		4				12	8			5			11^{2}	6		7		13		9^{1}		10			1	42
	2	3		4		15	12	14	8^{3}			5			11	6^{1}		7^{5}		16	13	9^{2}		10^{4}			1	43
	2^{2}	3		4			12		8			5		13	11	6^{3}	15	7			14	9^{4}		10^{1}			1	44
	2^{2}	3		4			13		8			5		14	10	6^{1}		7^{3}	12^{4}			9		11	15		1	45
		2		4	16		12	13	8			5		3	10^{4}	7^{1}	15	6^{5}			14	9^{2}		11^{3}			1	46

FA Cup

Third Round	Preston NE	(h)	4-1
Fourth Round	Tottenham H	(h)	1-4

Carabao Cup

First Round	Brentford	(a)	1-1

(Brentford won 4-2 on penalties)

ENGLISH LEAGUE PLAYERS DIRECTORY

Players listed represent those with their clubs during the 2020–21 season.

Club names in *italic* indicate loans.

Players are listed alphabetically on pages 540–547 where the number alongside each player corresponds to the team number heading. (Aarons, Maximillian 59 = team 59 (Norwich C)).

ACCRINGTON S (1)

BARCLAY, Ben (D) **47 2**
b. 7-10-96

2018–19	Brighton & HA	0	0		
2018–19	*Notts Co*	13	1	**13**	**1**
2019–20	Accrington S	8	0		
2020–21	Accrington S	26	1	**34**	**1**

BISHOP, Colby (M) **72 20**
H: 5 11 W: 11 05 b. 14-11-94

2013–14	Notts Co	0	0		
2014–15	Notts Co	3	0		
2015–16	Notts Co	1	0	**4**	**0**
From Worcester C, Boston U, Leamington.					
2019–20	Accrington S	27	10		
2020–21	Accrington S	41	10	**68**	**20**

BOLTON, Jack (D) **0 0**

2019–20	Accrington S	0	0		
2020–21	Accrington S	0	0		

BUCKLEY, Jack (G) **0 0**

2020–21	Accrington S	0	0		

BURGESS, Cameron (D) **179 9**
H: 6 4 W: 12 11 b.Aberdeen 21-10-95
Internationals: Scotland U18, U19. Australia U20, U23.

2014–15	Fulham	4	0		
2014–15	*Ross Co*	0	0		
2015–16	Fulham	0	0		
2016–17	Fulham	0	0	**4**	**0**
2016–17	*Oldham Ath*	23	1	**23**	**1**
2016–17	*Bury*	18	0	**18**	**0**
2017–18	Scunthorpe U	25	2		
2018–19	Scunthorpe U	36	1		
2019–20	Scunthorpe U	0	0	**61**	**3**
2019–20	*Salford C*	29	2	**29**	**2**
2020–21	Accrington S	44	3	**44**	**3**

BUTCHER, Matt (M) **82 4**
H: 6 2 W: 12 13 b.Portsmouth 14-5-97
From Poole T.

2015–16	Bournemouth	0	0		
2016–17	Bournemouth	0	0		
2016–17	*Yeovil T*	34	2	**34**	**2**
2017–18	Bournemouth	0	0		
2018–19	Bournemouth	0	0		
2019–20	Bournemouth	0	0		
2019–20	*St Johnstone*	6	0	**6**	**0**
2020–21	Accrington S	42	2	**42**	**2**

CHARLES, Dion (M) **75 27**
H: 5 10 W: 10 08 b.Preston 7-10-95
Internationals: Northern Ireland U21.

2013–14	Blackpool	0	0		
From AFC Fylde.					
2016–17	Fleetwood T	0	0		
From Southport.					
2019–20	Accrington S	33	8		
2020–21	Accrington S	42	19	**75**	**27**

CONNEELY, Seamus (D) **374 17**
H: 5 9 W: 10 10 b.Galway 9-7-88
Internationals: Republic of Ireland U21, U23.

2008	Galway U	20	0		
2009	Galway U	34	2		
2010	Galway U	32	0	**86**	**2**
2010–11	Sheffield U	0	0		
2011–12	Sheffield U	0	0		
2012	Sligo R	13	1		
2013	Sligo R	21	1		
2014	Sligo R	25	1	**59**	**3**
2014–15	Accrington S	16	3		
2015–16	Accrington S	46	3		
2016–17	Accrington S	38	1		
2017–18	Accrington S	33	2		
2018–19	Accrington S	27	1		
2019–20	Accrington S	31	1		
2020–21	Accrington S	38	1	**229**	**12**

FENLON, Rhys-James (M) **2 0**
b. 2-11-01
From Burnley.

2020–21	Accrington S	2	0	**2**	**0**

HUGHES, Mark (D) **524 27**
H: 6 1 W: 13 03 b.Liverpool 9-12-86

2004–05	Everton	0	0		
2005–06	Everton	0	0		
2005–06	*Stockport Co*	3	0	**3**	**0**
2006–07	Everton	1	0	**1**	**0**
2006–07	Northampton T	17	2		
2007–08	Northampton T	35	1		
2008–09	Northampton T	41	1	**93**	**4**
2009–10	Walsall	26	1	**26**	**1**
2010–11	N Queensland Fury	30	4	**30**	**4**
2011–12	Bury	25	0		
2012–13	Bury	27	0	**52**	**0**
2012–13	*Accrington S*	5	0		
2013–14	Morecambe	44	5		
2014–15	Morecambe	40	3	**84**	**8**
2015–16	Stevenage	20	1	**20**	**1**
2015–16	Accrington S	15	1		
2016–17	Accrington S	36	2		
2017–18	Accrington S	46	4		
2018–19	Accrington S	46	1		
2019–20	Accrington S	31	1		
2020–21	Accrington S	36	0	**215**	**9**

ISHERWOOD, Liam (G) **0 0**

2020–21	Accrington S	0	0		

MAGUIRE, Joe (D) **48 1**
H: 5 10 W: 11 00 b.Manchester 18-1-96

2015–16	Liverpool	0	0		
2015–16	*Leyton Orient*	0	0		
2016–17	Liverpool	0	0		
2016–17	Fleetwood T	3	0		
2017–18	Fleetwood T	2	0		
2018–19	Fleetwood T	0	0	**5**	**0**
2018–19	*Crawley T*	27	1	**27**	**1**
2019–20	Accrington S	11	0		
2020–21	Accrington S	5	0	**16**	**0**

MANSELL, Lewis (F) **23 2**
H: 6 2 W: 11 11 b.Burnley 20-9-97

2017–18	Blackburn R	0	0		
2018–19	Blackburn R	0	0		
2018–19	*Partick Thistle*	8	1		
2019–20	Partick Thistle	13	1	**21**	**2**
2020–21	Accrington S	2	0	**2**	**0**

MARTIN, Dan (M) **0 0**

2019–20	Accrington S	0	0		
2020–21	Accrington S	0	0		

McCONVILLE, Sean (M) **300 57**
H: 5 8 W: 11 07 b.Liverpool 6-3-89

2008–09	Accrington S	5	0		
2009–10	Accrington S	28	1		
2010–11	Accrington S	43	13		
2011–12	Rochdale	4	0	**4**	**0**
From Barrow, Stalybridge Celtic, Chester.					
2015–16	Accrington S	42	5		
2016–17	Accrington S	41	5		
2017–18	Accrington S	43	12		
2018–19	Accrington S	45	15		
2019–20	Accrington S	18	5		
2020–21	Accrington S	31	1	**296**	**57**

MOHAMMED, Zehn (D) **0 0**
b. 28-2-00

2017–18	Accrington S	0	0		
2018–19	Accrington S	0	0		
2019–20	Accrington S	0	0		
2020–21	Accrington S	0	0		

MORGAN, David (M) **17 0**
b.Northern Ireland 4-7-94

2011–12	Nottingham F	0	0		
2012–13	Nottingham F	0	0		
2012–13	*Dundee*	1	0	**1**	**0**
2013–14	Nottingham F	0	0		
From Ilkeston, Nuneaton T, AFC Fylde, Harrogate T, Southport.					
2020–21	Accrington S	16	0	**16**	**0**

NOTTINGHAM, Michael (D) **89 7**
b.Birmingham 14-4-89
Internationals: Saint Kitts and Nevis Full caps.
From Gresley, Solihull Moors, Salford C.

2018–19	Blackpool	29	2		
2019–20	Blackpool	3	0		
2019–20	*Crewe Alex*	12	1	**12**	**1**
2020–21	Blackpool	3	0	**35**	**2**
2020–21	Accrington S	42	4	**42**	**4**

OGLE, Reagan (D) **4 0**
H: 5 8 W: 10 06 b. 29-3-99

2016–17	Accrington S	1	0		
2017–18	Accrington S	3	0		
2018–19	Accrington S	0	0		
2019–20	Accrington S	0	0		
2020–21	Accrington S	0	0	**4**	**0**

PERRITT, Harry (M) **2 0**
b. 16-2-01

2018–19	Accrington S	0	0		
2019–20	Accrington S	0	0		
2020–21	Accrington S	2	0	**2**	**0**

PRITCHARD, Joe (M) **62 9**
H: 5 8 W: 10 06 b.Watford 10-9-96
From Tottenham H.

2018–19	Bolton W	4	0	**4**	**0**
2019–20	Accrington S	30	2		
2020–21	Accrington S	28	7	**58**	**9**

ROBERTS, Gary (F) **477 84**
H: 5 10 W: 11 09 b.Chester 18-3-84
Internationals: England C.
From Welshpool T.

2006–07	Accrington S	14	8		
2006–07	Ipswich T	33	3		
2007–08	Ipswich T	21	1	**54**	**4**
2007–08	*Crewe Alex*	4	0	**4**	**0**
2008–09	Huddersfield T	43	9		
2009–10	Huddersfield T	43	7		
2010–11	Huddersfield T	37	9		
2011–12	Huddersfield T	39	6	**162**	**31**
2012–13	Swindon T	39	4	**39**	**4**
2013–14	Chesterfield	40	11		
2014–15	Chesterfield	34	6	**74**	**17**
2015–16	Portsmouth	33	7		
2016–17	Portsmouth	41	10		
2017–18	Portsmouth	0	0	**74**	**17**
2017–18	Wigan Ath	27	1		
2018–19	Wigan Ath	16	2		
2019–20	Wigan Ath	9	0		
2020–21	Wigan Ath	2	0	**54**	**3**
2020–21	Accrington S	2	0	**16**	**8**

RODGERS, Harvey (M) **64 1**
H: 5 10 W: 12 06 b.York 20-10-96

2016–17	Hull C	0	0		
2016–17	*Accrington S*	19	1		
2017–18	Fleetwood T	0	0		
2017–18	Accrington S	5	0		
2018–19	Accrington S	6	0		
2019–20	Accrington S	6	0		
2020–21	Accrington S	28	0	**64**	**1**

SAMA, Stephen (D) **29 0**
H: 6 2 W: 13 01 b.Cameroon 5-3-93
Internationals: Germany U17, U18, U19, U20.

2009–10	Liverpool	0	0		
2010–11	Liverpool	0	0		
2011–12	Liverpool	0	0		
2012–13	Liverpool	0	0		
2013–14	Liverpool	0	0		
2014–15	Liverpool	0	0		
2015–16	Stuttgart	0	0		
2016–17	Greuther Furth	4	0		
2017–18	Greuther Furth	0	0	**4**	**0**
2017–18	*Osnabruck*	13	0	**13**	**0**
2018–19	Heracles	8	0		
2019–20	Heracles	0	0	**8**	**0**
2020–21	Accrington S	4	0	**4**	**0**

SAVIN, Toby (G) **31 0**
b. 4-5-01

2017–18	Accrington S	0	0		
2018–19	Accrington S	0	0		
2019–20	Accrington S	0	0		
2020–21	Accrington S	31	0	**31**	**0**

SCULLY, Thomas (M) **3 0**
b. 1-10-99

2019–20	Norwich C	0	0		
2020–21	Accrington S	3	0	**3**	**0**

SPINELLI, Kevin (F) **0 0**

2020–21	Accrington S	0	0		

STOWE, Luke (M) **0 0**

2020–21	Accrington S	0	0		

SYKES, Ross (D) 62 5
H: 6 5 W: 11 07 b.Burnley 26-3-99
2016–17 Accrington S 0 0
2017–18 Accrington S 2 0
2018–19 Accrington S 20 3
2019–20 Accrington S 31 1
2020–21 Accrington S 9 1 62 5

Scholars
Adekoya, Leslie Toluwani Adetokunbo; Akukwe, Vandis Chima; Buckley, Jack Joseph; Doherty, Jack Edward; Evans, Jack Robert Matthew; Eze, George Emenaike; Graham, Ryan Richard; Hood, Louis Owen; Kardacz, Mateusz; Madzura, Rigobert; McKinlay, Jak Thomas; Muldoon, Ryan Paul; O'Brien, Connor David; Spinelli, Lorenzo Kevin; Stowe, Luke Dean; Sung, Warren James.

AFC WIMBLEDON (2)

ALEXANDER, Cheye (D) 29 0
b. 24-5-95
2013–14 Port Vale 0 0
From Concorde Rangers, Bishop's Stortford, Aldershot T, Barnet.
2020–21 AFC Wimbledon 29 0 29 0

ANDREWS, Corie (F) 0 0
b.Lambeth 20-9-97
From Kingstonian.
2020–21 AFC Wimbledon 0 0

ASSAL, Ayoub (M) 14 4
b. 21-1-02
2019–20 AFC Wimbledon 0 0
2020–21 AFC Wimbledon 14 4 14 4

BILER, Huseyin (D) 0 0
2019–20 AFC Wimbledon 0 0
2020–21 AFC Wimbledon 0 0

BOLTON, Elliott (M) 0 0
b.Kingston upon Thames 18-10-01
2020–21 AFC Wimbledon 0 0

CHISLETT, Ethan (M) 27 2
b. 22-2-00
From Metropolitan Police, Aldershot T.
2020–21 AFC Wimbledon 27 2 27 2

COX, Matthew (G) 0 0
b.Sutton 2-5-03
2020–21 AFC Wimbledon 0 0

CSOKA, Daniel (D) 21 1
b.Zalaegerszeg 4-4-00
2017–18 Wolverhampton W 0 0
2018–19 Wolverhampton W 0 0
2018–19 *DAC* 0 0
2019–20 Wolverhampton W 0 0
2019–20 *Samorin* 1 0 1 0
2020–21 AFC Wimbledon 20 1 20 1

CURRIE, Jack (D) 0 0
b.Kingston upon Thames 16-12-01
2020–21 AFC Wimbledon 0 0

GUINNESS-WALKER, Nesta (D) 54 2
b.Hounslow 30-11-99
From Metropolitan Police.
2019–20 AFC Wimbledon 23 1
2020–21 AFC Wimbledon 31 1 54 2

HARRISON, Shayon (F) 70 13
H: 6 0 W: 10 10 b.Hornsey 13-7-97
2016–17 Tottenham H 0 0
2016–17 *Yeovil T* 14 1 14 1
2017–18 Tottenham H 0 0
2017–18 *Southend U* 13 0 13 0
2018–19 Tottenham H 0 0
2018–19 *Melbourne C* 10 4 10 4
2019–20 Almere C 21 7
2020–21 Almere C 11 1 32 8
2020–21 AFC Wimbledon 1 0 1 0

HARTIGAN, Anthony (M) 95 0
H: 5 10 W: 10 10 b.Kingston upon Thames 27-1-00
2017–18 AFC Wimbledon 11 0
2018–19 AFC Wimbledon 31 0
2019–20 AFC Wimbledon 27 0
2020–21 AFC Wimbledon 15 0 84 0
2020–21 *Newport Co* 11 0 11 0

HENEGHAN, Ben (D) 132 6
b.Bolton 19-9-93
Internationals: England C.
From Everton, Stoke C, Chester.
2016–17 Motherwell 37 0
2017–18 Motherwell 4 1 41 1
2017–18 Sheffield U 0 0
2018–19 Sheffield U 0 0
2018–19 *Blackpool* 42 1
2019–20 Sheffield U 0 0
2019–20 *Blackpool* 26 2 68 3
2020–21 AFC Wimbledon 23 2 23 2

KALAMBAYI, Paul (D) 47 0
b. 28-7-99
2015–16 AFC Wimbledon 0 0
2016–17 AFC Wimbledon 0 0
2017–18 AFC Wimbledon 0 0
2018–19 AFC Wimbledon 17 0
2019–20 AFC Wimbledon 16 0
2020–21 AFC Wimbledon 14 0 47 0

McLOUGHLIN, Shane (D) 72 3
b.Castleisland 1-3-97
Internationals: Republic of Ireland U16, U18.
2014–15 Ipswich T 0 0
2015–16 Ipswich T 0 0
2016–17 Ipswich T 0 0
2017–18 Ipswich T 1 0
2018–19 Ipswich T 0 0 1 0
2018–19 AFC Wimbledon 10 1
2019–20 AFC Wimbledon 23 1
2020–21 AFC Wimbledon 38 1 71 3

NIGHTINGALE, Will (M) 118 3
H: 6 1 W: 13 03 b.Wandsworth 2-7-95
2013–14 AFC Wimbledon 0 0
2014–15 AFC Wimbledon 4 0
2015–16 AFC Wimbledon 4 0
2016–17 AFC Wimbledon 12 0
2017–18 AFC Wimbledon 18 1
2018–19 AFC Wimbledon 39 0
2019–20 AFC Wimbledon 9 0
2020–21 AFC Wimbledon 32 2 118 3

O'NEILL, Luke (D) 209 7
H: 6 0 W: 11 04 b.Slough 20-8-91
Internationals: England U17.
2009–10 Leicester C 1 0 1 0
2009–10 *Tranmere R* 4 0 4 0
From Kettering T, Mansfield T
2012–13 Burnley 1 0
2013–14 Burnley 0 0
2013–14 *York C* 15 1 15 1
2013–14 *Southend U* 1 0
2014–15 Burnley 0 0 1 0
2014–15 *Scunthorpe U* 13 0 13 0
2014–15 *Leyton Orient* 8 0 8 0
2015–16 Southend U 14 0
2016–17 Southend U 17 1 32 1
2017–18 Gillingham 38 1
2018–19 Gillingham 38 3 76 4
2019–20 AFC Wimbledon 31 1
2020–21 AFC Wimbledon 28 0 59 1

OSEW, Paul (D) 28 1
b. 25-11-00
From Brentford.
2019–20 AFC Wimbledon 18 1
2020–21 AFC Wimbledon 10 0 28 1

PALMER, Oliver (F) 272 60
b.London 21-1-92
From Woking, Havant & Waterlooville.
2013–14 Mansfield T 38 4
2014–15 Mansfield T 16 1 54 5
2015–16 Leyton Orient 45 7
2016–17 Leyton Orient 20 5 65 12
2016–17 *Luton T* 17 3 17 3
2017–18 Lincoln C 45 8 45 8
2018–19 Crawley T 40 14
2019–20 Crawley T 28 13
2020–21 Crawley T 0 0 68 27
2020–21 AFC Wimbledon 23 5 23 5

PIGOTT, Joe (F) 234 64
H: 6 0 W: 9 05 b.London 24-11-93
2012–13 Charlton Ath 0 0
2013–14 Charlton Ath 11 0
2013–14 *Gillingham* 7 1 7 1
2014–15 Charlton Ath 1 0
2014–15 *Newport Co* 10 3 10 3
2014–15 *Southend U* 20 6
2015–16 Charlton Ath 0 0 12 0
2015–16 *Southend U* 23 3 43 9
2015–16 *Luton T* 15 4 15 4
2016–17 Cambridge U 10 0 10 0
From Maidstone U.
2017–18 AFC Wimbledon 18 5
2018–19 AFC Wimbledon 40 15
2019–20 AFC Wimbledon 34 7
2020–21 AFC Wimbledon 45 20 137 47

PROCTER, Archie (D) 0 0
b. 13-11-01
2019–20 AFC Wimbledon 0 0
2020–21 AFC Wimbledon 0 0

REILLY, Callum (M) 210 12
H: 6 1 W: 12 03 b.Warrington 3-10-93
Internationals: Republic of Ireland U21.
2012–13 Birmingham C 18 1
2013–14 Birmingham C 25 0
2014–15 Birmingham C 17 1 60 2
2014–15 *Burton Alb* 2 0
2015–16 Burton Alb 14 0
2016–17 Burton Alb 0 0 16 0
2016–17 *Coventry C* 18 0 18 0
2017–18 Bury 18 0 18 0
2017–18 *Gillingham* 15 0
2018–19 Gillingham 25 5 40 5
2019–20 AFC Wimbledon 30 4
2020–21 AFC Wimbledon 28 1 58 5

ROBINSON, Zach (F) 5 0
b. 11-6-02
2019–20 AFC Wimbledon 0 0
2020–21 AFC Wimbledon 5 0 5 0

ROSCROW, Adam (F) 16 0
b. 17-2-95
Internationals: Wales C.
From Cardiff Metropolitan University.
2019–20 AFC Wimbledon 10 0
2020–21 AFC Wimbledon 6 0 16 0

RUDONI, Jack (M) 50 4
b. 26-5-01
2018–19 AFC Wimbledon 0 0
2019–20 AFC Wimbledon 11 0
2020–21 AFC Wimbledon 39 4 50 4

SUTCLIFFE, Ethan (D) 0 0
2020–21 AFC Wimbledon 0 0

THOMAS, Terell (D) 76 1
H: 6 0 b. 13-10-97
From Arsenal.
2014–15 Charlton Ath 0 0
2015–16 Charlton Ath 0 0
2016–17 Charlton Ath 0 0
2017–18 Wigan Ath 3 0 3 0
2018–19 AFC Wimbledon 23 0
2019–20 AFC Wimbledon 31 1
2020–21 AFC Wimbledon 19 0 73 1

TZANEV, Nikola (G) 17 0
b. 23-12-96
Internationals: New Zealand U20, Full caps.
From Brentford.
2016–17 AFC Wimbledon 0 0
2017–18 AFC Wimbledon 0 0
2018–19 AFC Wimbledon 0 0
2019–20 AFC Wimbledon 2 0
2020–21 AFC Wimbledon 15 0 17 0

WOODYARD, Alex (M) 162 4
H: 5 9 W: 10 00 b.Gravesend 3-5-93
Internationals: England C.
From Charlton Ath.
2010–11 Southend U 3 0
2011–12 Southend U 0 0
2012–13 Southend U 5 0
2013–14 Southend U 0 0 8 0
From Dartford, Concord Rangers, Braintree T.
2017–18 Lincoln C 46 2 46 2
2018–19 Peterborough U 43 0
2019–20 Peterborough U 14 0 57 0
2019–20 *Tranmere R* 11 1 11 1
2020–21 AFC Wimbledon 40 1 40 1

Scholars
Adjei-Hersey, Dylan Francis; Bartley, Quaine Asani; Campbell, Marcel Simon; Chiabi, Muumbe Troy Makowani; Frimpong, Kwaku Amponsah; Hallard, Josh Robert; Jenkins, Luke; Jones, Aaron Michael; Mason, Benjamin Nicholas; Ogundere, Isaac Ifeoluwa Foloronso; Olaniyan, Isaac Humayun Kola; Sarmiento-Ramirez, Julian Andres; Shiekh Ali, Abdkariim Abdulkadir; Sutcliffe, Ethan Jack; Yeboah, Obed Kwabena.

ARSENAL (3)

AKINOLA, Tim (M) 0 0
H: 5 11 b. 8-5-01
From Lincoln C, Huddersfield T.
2020–21 Arsenal 0 0

ALEBIOSU, Ryan (D) 0 0
b.Islington 17-12-01
2020–21 Arsenal 0 0

AUBAMEYANG, Pierre-Emerick (F) 412 211
H: 6 2 W: 11 09 b.Bitam 18-6-89
Internationals: France U21. Gabon U23, Full caps.
2008–09 AC Milan 0 0
2008–09 *Dijon* 34 8 34 8
2009–10 AC Milan 0 0
2009–10 *Lille* 14 2 14 2
2010–11 AC Milan 0 0
2010–11 *Monaco* 19 2 19 2

2010–11	*Saint-Etienne*	14	2		
2011–12	Saint-Etienne	36	16		
2012–13	Saint-Etienne	37	19	**87**	**37**
2013–14	Borussia Dortmund	32	13		
2014–15	Borussia Dortmund	33	16		
2015–16	Borussia Dortmund	31	25		
2016–17	Borussia Dortmund	32	31		
2017–18	Borussia Dortmund	16	13	**144**	**98**
2017–18	Arsenal	13	10		
2018–19	Arsenal	36	22		
2019–20	Arsenal	36	22		
2020–21	Arsenal	29	10	**114**	**64**

AWE, Zacharia (D) **0 0**
b. 9-1-04

2020–21	Arsenal	0	0

AZEEZ, Miguel (M) **0 0**
b. 20-9-02
Internationals: England U16, U17, U18.

2019–20	Arsenal	0	0
2020–21	Arsenal	0	0

BALLARD, Daniel (D) **26 2**
b. 22-9-99
Internationals: Northern Ireland U18, U21.

2019–20	Arsenal	0	0		
2019–20	*Swindon T*	1	0	**1**	**0**
2020–21	Arsenal	0	0		
2020–21	*Blackpool*	25	2	**25**	**2**

BALOGUN, Folarin (M) **0 0**
b. 3-7-01
Internationals: England U17, U18. USA U18.

2019–20	Arsenal	0	0
2020–21	Arsenal	0	0

BELLERIN, Hector (D) **191 8**
H: 5 10 W: 11 09 b.Barcelona 19-3-95
Internationals: Spain U16, U17, U19, U21, Full caps.
From Barcelona.

2012–13	Arsenal	0	0		
2013–14	Arsenal	0	0		
2013–14	*Watford*	8	0	**8**	**0**
2014–15	Arsenal	20	2		
2015–16	Arsenal	36	1		
2016–17	Arsenal	33	1		
2017–18	Arsenal	35	2		
2018–19	Arsenal	19	0		
2019–20	Arsenal	15	1		
2020–21	Arsenal	25	1	**183**	**8**

BOLA, Tolaji (D) **11 0**
b. 4-1-99
Internationals: England U16, U17, U18.

2019–20	Arsenal	0	0		
2020–21	Arsenal	0	0		
2020–21	*Rochdale*	11	0	**11**	**0**

CEBALLOS, Dani (M) **182 12**
b.Seville 7-8-96
Internationals: Spain U19, U21, Full caps.

2013–14	Real Betis	1	0		
2014–15	Real Betis	33	5		
2015–16	Real Betis	34	0		
2016–17	Real Betis	30	2	**98**	**7**
2017–18	Real Madrid	12	2		
2018–19	Real Madrid	23	3		
2019–20	Real Madrid	0	0		
2019–20	*Arsenal*	24	0		
2020–21	Real Madrid	0	0	**35**	**5**

On loan from Real Madrid.

2020–21	Arsenal	25	0	**49**	**0**

CEDRIC SOARES, Ricardo (D) **230 4**
H: 5 8 W: 10 08 b.Gelsenkirchen, Germany 31-8-91
Internationals: Portugal U16, U17, U18, U19, U20, U21, Full caps.

2010–11	Sporting Lisbon	2	0		
2011–12	Sporting Lisbon	0	0		
2011–12	*Academica*	24	0	**24**	**0**
2012–13	Sporting Lisbon	13	1		
2013–14	Sporting Lisbon	28	1		
2014–15	Sporting Lisbon	24	0	**67**	**2**
2015–16	Southampton	24	0		
2016–17	Southampton	30	0		
2017–18	Southampton	32	0		
2018–19	Southampton	18	1		
2018–19	*Inter Milan*	4	0	**4**	**0**
2019–20	Southampton	16	0	**120**	**1**
2019–20	Arsenal	5	1		
2020–21	Arsenal	10	0	**15**	**1**

CHAMBERS, Calum (M) **149 6**
H: 6 0 W: 10 05 b.Petersfield 20-1-95
Internationals: England U17, U19, U21, Full caps.

2011–12	Southampton	0	0		
2012–13	Southampton	0	0		
2013–14	Southampton	22	0	**22**	**0**
2014–15	Arsenal	23	1		
2015–16	Arsenal	12	0		
2016–17	Arsenal	1	1		
2016–17	*Middlesbrough*	24	1	**24**	**1**
2017–18	Arsenal	12	0		
2018–19	Arsenal	0	0		
2018–19	*Fulham*	31	2	**31**	**2**
2019–20	Arsenal	14	1		
2020–21	Arsenal	10	0	**72**	**3**

CIRJAN, Catalin (M) **0 0**
b. 1-12-02
Internationals: Romania U16, U19.
From Viitorul Domnesti.

2020–21	Arsenal	0	0

CLARKE, Harrison (D) **32 1**
b.Ipswich 2-3-01
Internationals: England U17.

2019–20	Arsenal	0	0		
2020–21	Arsenal	0	0		
2020–21	*Oldham Ath*	32	1	**32**	**1**

COTTRELL, Ben (M) **0 0**
b. 31-10-01

2020–21	Arsenal	0	0

COYLE, Trae (F) **13 2**
b. 11-1-01
Internationals: England U16, U17.

2019–20	Arsenal	0	0		
2020–21	Arsenal	0	0		
2020–21	*Gillingham*	13	2	**13**	**2**

DINZEYI, Jonathan (D) **0 0**
H: 5 10 W: 13 01 b.Islington 13-10-99
Internationals: England U18.
From Tottenham H.

2020–21	Arsenal	0	0

ELNENY, Mohamed (M) **222 9**
H: 5 11 W: 11 00 b.Al-Mahalla Al-Kubra 11-7-92
Internationals: Egypt U20, U23, Full caps.

2010–11	Al Mokawloon	21	2		
2011–12	Al Mokawloon	14	0	**35**	**2**
2012–13	Basel	15	0		
2013–14	Basel	32	1		
2014–15	Basel	28	2	**75**	**3**
2015–16	Basel	16	2	**16**	**2**
2015–16	Arsenal	11	0		
2016–17	Arsenal	14	0		
2017–18	Arsenal	13	0		
2018–19	Arsenal	8	0		
2019–20	Arsenal	0	0		
2019–20	*Besiktas*	27	1	**27**	**1**
2020–21	Arsenal	23	1	**69**	**1**

FLORES, Marcelo (M) **0 0**
b. 1-10-03
Internationals: Mexico U16.
From Ipswich T.

2020–21	Arsenal	0	0

GABRIEL, Magalhaes (D) **85 5**
b.Sao Paulo 19-12-97

2016	Avai	21	1	**21**	**1**
2016–17	Lille	1	0		
2017–18	Lille	0	0		
2017–18	*Troyes*	1	0	**1**	**0**
2017–18	*Dinamo Zagreb*	1	0	**1**	**0**
2018–19	Lille	14	1		
2019–20	Lille	24	1		
2020–21	Lille	0	0	**39**	**2**
2020–21	Arsenal	23	2	**23**	**2**

GIRAUD-HUTCHINSON, Omari (M) **0 0**
H: 5 9 b. 29-10-03

2020–21	Arsenal	0	0

GRACZYK, Hubert (G) **0 0**
H: 6 4 b.Skwierzyna 28-2-03
Internationals: England U16, U18.

2020–21	Arsenal	0	0

HEIN, Karl Jakob (G) **0 0**
b. 13-4-02
Internationals: Estonia U16, U17, U19, U21.
From Nomme U.

2019–20	Arsenal	0	0
2020–21	Arsenal	0	0

HILLSON, James (G) **0 0**
b. 14-1-01
From Reading.

2019–20	Arsenal	0	0
2020–21	Arsenal	0	0

HOLDING, Rob (D) **96 1**
b.Tameside 20-9-95
Internationals: England U21.

2014–15	Bolton W	0	0		
2014–15	*Bury*	1	0	**1**	**0**
2015–16	Bolton W	26	1	**26**	**1**
2016–17	Arsenal	9	0		
2017–18	Arsenal	12	0		
2018–19	Arsenal	10	0		
2019–20	Arsenal	8	0		
2020–21	Arsenal	30	0	**69**	**0**

IDEHO, Joel (F) **0 0**
b. 17-7-03
From Willem II.

2020–21	Arsenal	0	0

ILIEV, Dejan (G) **25 0**
H: 6 5 b.Strumica 25-2-95
Internationals: Macedonia U17, U19, U21.

2012–13	Arsenal	0	0		
2013–14	Arsenal	0	0		
2014–15	Arsenal	0	0		
2015–16	Arsenal	0	0		
2016–17	Arsenal	0	0		
2017–18	Arsenal	0	0		
2018–19	Arsenal	0	0		
2019–20	Arsenal	0	0		
2019–20	*Clinic Sered*	18	0	**18**	**0**
2019–20	*Jagiellonia*	4	0	**4**	**0**
2020–21	Arsenal	0	0		
2020–21	*Shrewsbury T*	3	0	**3**	**0**

JOHN-JULES, Tyreece (F) **25 6**
H: 6 0 b. 14-2-01
Internationals: England U16, U17, U18, U19.

2018–19	Arsenal	0	0		
2019–20	Arsenal	0	0		
2019–20	*Lincoln C*	7	1	**7**	**1**
2020–21	Arsenal	0	0		
2020–21	*Doncaster R*	18	5	**18**	**5**

KIRK, Alex (D) **0 0**
b. 27-10-02

2020–21	Arsenal	0	0

KOLASINAC, Sead (D) **189 7**
H: 6 0 W: 12 13 b.Karlsruhe 20-6-93
Internationals: Germany U18, U19, U20. Bosnia and Herzegovina Full caps.

2012–13	Schalke 04	16	0		
2013–14	Schalke 04	24	0		
2014–15	Schalke 04	6	0		
2015–16	Schalke 04	23	1		
2016–17	Schalke 04	25	3		
2017–18	Arsenal	27	2		
2018–19	Arsenal	24	0		
2019–20	Arsenal	26	0		
2020–21	Arsenal	1	0	**78**	**2**
2020–21	*Schalke 04*	17	1	**111**	**5**

LACAZETTE, Alexandre (F) **331 150**
H: 5 9 W: 10 12 b.Lyon 28-5-91
Internationals: France U16, U17, U18, U19, U20, U21, Full caps.

2009–10	Lyon	1	0		
2010–11	Lyon	9	1		
2011–12	Lyon	29	5		
2012–13	Lyon	31	3		
2013–14	Lyon	36	15		
2014–15	Lyon	33	27		
2015–16	Lyon	34	21		
2016–17	Lyon	30	28	**203**	**100**
2017–18	Arsenal	32	14		
2018–19	Arsenal	35	13		
2019–20	Arsenal	30	10		
2020–21	Arsenal	31	13	**128**	**50**

LENO, Bernd (G) **330 0**
H: 6 3 W: 12 06 b.Bietigheim-Bissingen 4-3-92
Internationals: Germany, U17, U18, U19, U21, Full caps.
From Stuttgart.

2011–12	Bayer Leverkusen	33	0		
2012–13	Bayer Leverkusen	32	0		
2013–14	Bayer Leverkusen	34	0		
2014–15	Bayer Leverkusen	34	0		
2015–16	Bayer Leverkusen	33	0		
2016–17	Bayer Leverkusen	34	0		
2017–18	Bayer Leverkusen	33	0	**233**	**0**
2018–19	Arsenal	32	0		
2019–20	Arsenal	30	0		
2020–21	Arsenal	35	0	**97**	**0**

LEWIS, George (F) **0 0**
H: 5 7 b.Kigali 16-6-00
From Fram Larvik.

2020–21	Arsenal	0	0

LOPEZ, Joel (D) **0 0**

2020–21	Arsenal	0	0

LUIZ, David (D) **377 22**
H: 6 2 W: 13 03 b.Sao Paulo 22-4-87
Internationals: Brazil U20, Full caps.

2005	Vitoria	0	0		
2006	Vitoria	26	1	**26**	**1**
2006–07	Benfica	10	0		
2007–08	Benfica	8	0		
2008–09	Benfica	19	2		
2009–10	Benfica	29	2		
2010–11	Benfica	16	0	**82**	**4**
2010–11	Chelsea	12	2		
2011–12	Chelsea	20	2		

2012–13 Chelsea 30 2
2013–14 Chelsea 19 0
2014–15 Paris Saint-Germain 28 2
2015–16 Paris Saint-Germain 25 1
2016–17 Paris Saint-Germain 3 0 **56 3**
2016–17 Chelsea 33 1
2017–18 Chelsea 10 1
2018–19 Chelsea 36 3
2019–20 Chelsea 0 0 **160 11**
2019–20 Arsenal 33 2
2020–21 Arsenal 20 1 **53 3**

MACEY, Matt (G) 49 0
H: 6 6 W: 14 05 b.Bristol 9-9-94
2011–12 Bristol R 0 0
2012–13 Bristol R 0 0
2013–14 Arsenal 0 0
2014–15 Arsenal 0 0
2014–15 *Accrington S* 4 0 **4 0**
2015–16 Arsenal 0 0
2016–17 Arsenal 0 0
2016–17 *Luton T* 11 0 **11 0**
2017–18 Arsenal 0 0
2018–19 Arsenal 0 0
2018–19 *Plymouth Arg* 34 0 **34 0**
2019–20 Arsenal 0 0
2020–21 Arsenal 0 0
Transferred to Hibernian January 2021.

MAITLAND-NILES, Ainsley (F) 109 2
H: 5 10 W: 11 05 b.Goodmayes 29-8-97
Internationals: England U17, U18, U19, U20, U21.
2014–15 Arsenal 1 0
2015–16 Arsenal 0 0
2015–16 *Ipswich T* 30 1 **30 1**
2016–17 Arsenal 1 0
2017–18 Arsenal 15 0
2018–19 Arsenal 16 1
2019–20 Arsenal 20 0
2020–21 Arsenal 11 0 **64 1**
2020–21 *WBA* 15 0 **15 0**

MARTINELLI, Gabriel (F) 28 5
b.Guarulhos 18-6-01
Internationals: Brazil U23.
From Ituano.
2019–20 Arsenal 14 3
2020–21 Arsenal 14 2 **28 5**

McGUINNESS, Mark (D) 24 1
b. 5-1-01
2019–20 Arsenal 0 0
2020–21 Arsenal 0 0
2020–21 *Ipswich T* 24 1 **24 1**

MEDLEY, Zechariah (D) 20 1
b. 7-7-00
Internationals: England U16.
2018–19 Arsenal 0 0
2019–20 Arsenal 0 0
2020–21 Arsenal 0 0
2020–21 *Gillingham* 12 0 **12 0**
2020–21 *Kilmarnock* 8 1 **8 1**

MOLLER, Nikolaj (F) 0 0
H: 6 3 W: 11 05 b.Helsingborg 20-7-02
From Bologna, Malmo.
2020–21 Arsenal 0 0

MONLOUIS, Zane (D) 0 0
b.Lewisham 16-10-03
Internationals: England U17.
2020–21 Arsenal 0 0

MUSTAFI, Shkodran (D) 216 14
H: 6 0 W: 11 07 b.Bad Hersfeld 17-4-92
Internationals: Germany U16, U17, U18, U19, U20, U21, Full caps.
2009–10 Everton 0 0
2010–11 Everton 0 0
2011–12 Everton 0 0
2011–12 Sampdoria 1 0
2012–13 Sampdoria 17 0
2013–14 Sampdoria 33 1 **51 1**
2014–15 Valencia 33 4
2015–16 Valencia 30 2 **63 6**
2016–17 Arsenal 26 2
2017–18 Arsenal 27 3
2018–19 Arsenal 31 2
2019–20 Arsenal 15 0
2020–21 Arsenal 3 0 **102 7**
Transferred to Schalke 04 February 2021.

NELSON, Reiss (F) 45 8
H: 5 9 W: 11 00 b.London 10-12-99
Internationals: England U16, U17, U18, U19, U20, U21.
From Lewisham Bor.
2017–18 Arsenal 3 0
2018–19 Arsenal 0 0
2018–19 *Hoffenheim* 23 7 **23 7**
2019–20 Arsenal 17 1
2020–21 Arsenal 2 0 **22 1**

NKETIAH, Eddie (F) 55 8
b.Lewisham 30-5-99
Internationals: England U18, U19, U20, U21.
From Chelsea.
2017–18 Arsenal 3 0
2018–19 Arsenal 5 1
2019–20 Arsenal 13 2
2019–20 *Leeds U* 17 3 **17 3**
2020–21 Arsenal 17 2 **38 5**

NORTON-CUFFY, Brooke (D) 0 0
b.Hammersmith 12-1-04
From Chelsea.
2020–21 Arsenal 0 0

ODEGAARD, Martin (M) 145 21
b.Drammen 17-12-98
2014 Stromsgodset 23 5 **23 5**
2014–15 Real Madrid 1 0
2015–16 Real Madrid 0 0
2016–17 Real Madrid 0 0
2016–17 *Heerenveen* 14 1
2017–18 Real Madrid 0 0
2017–18 *Heerenveen* 24 2 **38 3**
2018–19 Real Madrid 0 0
2018–19 Vitesse 31 8 **31 8**
2019–20 Real Madrid 0 0
2019–20 *Real Sociedad* 31 4 **31 4**
2020–21 Real Madrid 7 0 **8 0**
On loan from Real Madrid.
2020–21 Arsenal 14 1 **14 1**

OKONKWO, Arthur (G) 0 0
b. 9-9-01
Internationals: England U16, U17, U18.
2019–20 Arsenal 0 0
2020–21 Arsenal 0 0

OLAYINKA, James (M) 21 2
b. 5-10-00
2019–20 Arsenal 0 0
2019–20 *Northampton T* 1 0 **1 0**
2020–21 Arsenal 0 0
2020–21 *Southend U* 20 2 **20 2**

OSEI-TUTU, Jordi (D) 29 5
b.Slough 2-10-98
2017–18 Arsenal 0 0
2018–19 Arsenal 0 0
2019–20 Arsenal 0 0
2019–20 *Bochum* 21 5 **21 5**
2020–21 Arsenal 0 0
2020–21 *Cardiff C* 8 0 **8 0**

OULAD M'HAND, Salah (M) 0 0
H: 5 10 b. 20-8-03
Internationals: Netherlands U17.
From Feyenoord.
2020–21 Arsenal 0 0

PABLO MARI, Villar (M) 193 11
b.Almussafes 31-8-93
2011–12 Real Mallorca 2 0
2012–13 Real Mallorca 0 0 **2 0**
2013–14 Gimnastic 29 2
2014–15 Gimnastic 37 3
2015–16 Gimnastic 25 1 **91 6**
2016–17 Manchester C 0 0
2016–17 *Girona* 8 0 **8 0**
2017–18 Manchester C 0 0
2017–18 NAC Breda 20 1 **20 1**
2018–19 Manchester C 0 0
2018–19 *Deportivo La Coruna* 38 2 **38 2**
2019 Flamengo 22 2 **22 2**
2019–20 *Arsenal* 2 0
2020–21 Arsenal 10 0 **12 0**

PAPASTATHOPOULOS, Sokratis (D) 338 15
H: 6 1 W: 12 13 b.Kalamata 9-6-88
Internationals: Greece U17, U19, U21, Full caps.
2005–06 AEK Athens 0 0
2005–06 *Niki Volou* 11 0 **11 0**
2006–07 AEK Athens 14 0
2007–08 AEK Athens 24 1 **38 1**
2008–09 Genoa 21 2
2009–10 Genoa 30 0 **51 2**
2010–11 AC Milan 5 0
2010–11 AC Milan 0 0
2011–12 AC Milan 0 0 **5 0**
2012–13 *Werder Bremen* 30 1
2012–13 Werder Bremen 29 1 **59 2**
2013–14 Borussia Dortmund 28 1
2014–15 Borussia Dortmund 21 1
2015–16 Borussia Dortmund 25 1
2016–17 Borussia Dortmund 26 2
2017–18 Borussia Dortmund 30 2 **130 7**
2018–19 Arsenal 25 1
2019–20 Arsenal 19 2
2020–21 Arsenal 0 0 **44 3**
Transferred to Olympiacos January 2021.

PATINO, Charlie (M) 0 0
H: 6 0 b.Watford 17-10-03
Internationals: England U16, U17.
2020–21 Arsenal 0 0

PEPE, Nicolas (M) 203 60
b.Mantes la Jolie 29-5-95
Internationals: Ivory Coast Full caps.
From Poitiers.
2014–15 Angers 7 0
2015–16 Angers 0 0
2015–16 *Orleans* 29 7 **29 7**
2016–17 Angers 33 3 **40 3**
2017–18 Lille 36 13
2018–19 Lille 38 22 **74 35**
2019–20 Arsenal 31 5
2020–21 Arsenal 29 10 **60 15**

REKIK, Omar (D) 0 0
H: 6 1 W: 12 08 b.Den Haag 20-12-01
Internationals: Netherlands U18. Tunisia U21, Full caps.
From Hertha Berlin.
2020–21 Arsenal 0 0

RUNARSSON, Runar (G) 100 0
b.Reykjavik 18-2-95
2013 Reykjavik 3 0 **3 0**
2013–14 Nordsjaelland 0 0
2014–15 Nordsjaelland 1 0
2015–16 Nordsjaelland 3 0
2016–17 Nordsjaelland 20 0
2017–18 Nordsjaelland 36 0 **60 0**
2018–19 Dijon 25 0
2019–20 Dijon 11 0
2020–21 Dijon 0 0 **36 0**
2020–21 Arsenal 1 0 **1 0**

SAKA, Bukayo (M) 59 6
H: 5 10 b.London 5-9-01
Internationals: England U16, U17, U18, U19.
2018–19 Arsenal 1 0
2019–20 Arsenal 26 1
2020–21 Arsenal 32 5 **59 6**

SALIBA, William Alain Andre Gabriel (D) 48 1
b.Bondy 24-3-01
Internationals: France U16, U17, U18, U19, U20.
2018–19 Saint Etienne 16 0
2019–20 Arsenal 0 0
2019–20 *Saint Etienne* 12 0 **28 0**
2020–21 Arsenal 0 0
2020–21 *Nice* 20 1 **20 1**

SHEAF, Ben (M) 72 1
H: 5 10 W: 10 01 b.Dartford 5-2-98
Internationals: England U16, U18.
2015–16 Arsenal 0 0
2016–17 Arsenal 0 0
2017–18 Arsenal 0 0
2017–18 *Stevenage* 10 0 **10 0**
2018–19 Arsenal 0 0
2019–20 Arsenal 0 0
2019–20 *Doncaster R* 32 1 **32 1**
2020–21 Arsenal 0 0
2020–21 *Coventry C* 30 0 **30 0**

SMITH, Matthew (D) 32 2
b. 5-10-00
2019–20 Arsenal 0 0
2020–21 Swindon T 24 2 **24 2**
2020–21 Arsenal 0 0
2020–21 *Charlton Ath* 8 0 **8 0**

SMITH-ROWE, Emile (M) 44 4
H: 6 0 W: 11 07 b.London 28-6-00
Internationals: England U16, U17, U18, U19, U20.
2017–18 Arsenal 0 0
2018–19 Arsenal 0 0
2018–19 *RB Leipzig* 3 0 **3 0**
2019–20 Arsenal 2 0
2019–20 *Huddersfield T* 19 2 **19 2**
2020–21 Arsenal 20 2 **22 2**

THOMAS, Partey (M) 221 21
b.Odumase Krobo 13-6-93
2011–12 Atletico Madrid 0 0
2012–13 Atletico Madrid 0 0
2013–14 Atletico Madrid 0 0
2013–14 *Mallorca* 37 5 **37 5**
2014–15 Atletico Madrid 0 0
2014–15 *Almeria* 31 4 **31 4**
2015–16 Atletico Madrid 13 2
2016–17 Atletico Madrid 16 1
2017–18 Atletico Madrid 33 3
2018–19 Atletico Madrid 32 3
2019–20 Atletico Madrid 35 3
2020–21 Atletico Madrid 0 0 **129 12**
2020–21 Arsenal 24 0 **24 0**

TIERNEY, Kieran (D) 144 7
b.Douglas 5-6-97
Internationals: Scotland U18, U19, Full caps.

2014–15	Celtic	2	0		
2015–16	Celtic	23	1		
2016–17	Celtic	24	1		
2017–18	Celtic	32	3		
2018–19	Celtic	21	0	**102**	**5**
2019–20	Arsenal	15	1		
2020–21	Arsenal	27	1	**42**	**2**

TORREIRA, Lucas (M) 187 12
H: 5 5 W: 9 06 b.Fray Bentos 11-2-96
Internationals: Uruguay Full caps.

2014–15	Pescara	5	0		
2015–16	Sampdoria	0	0		
2015–16	*Pescara*	29	4	**34**	**4**
2016–17	Sampdoria	35	0		
2017–18	Sampdoria	36	4	**71**	**4**
2018–19	Arsenal	34	2		
2019–20	Arsenal	29	1		
2020–21	Arsenal	0	0	**63**	**3**
2020–21	*Atletico Madrid*	19	1	**19**	**1**

WILLIAN, da Silva (M) 430 61
H: 5 9 W: 11 10 b.Ribeirao 9-8-88
Internationals: Brazil U20, Full caps.

2006	Corinthians	5	0		
2007	Corinthians	15	2	**20**	**2**
2007–08	Shakhtar Donetsk	20	0		
2008–09	Shakhtar Donetsk	29	5		
2009–10	Shakhtar Donetsk	22	5		
2010–11	Shakhtar Donetsk	28	3		
2011–12	Shakhtar Donetsk	27	5		
2012–13	Shakhtar Donetsk	14	2	**140**	**20**
2012–13	Anzhi Makhachkala	7	1		
2013–14	Anzhi Makhachkala	4	0	**11**	**1**
2013–14	Chelsea	25	4		
2014–15	Chelsea	36	2		
2015–16	Chelsea	35	5		
2016–17	Chelsea	34	8		
2017–18	Chelsea	36	6		
2018–19	Chelsea	32	3		
2019–20	Chelsea	36	9	**234**	**37**
2020–21	Arsenal	25	1	**25**	**1**

WILLOCK, Joe (M) 54 9
b.Waltham Forest 20-8-99
Internationals: England U16, U19, U20, U21.

2017–18	Arsenal	2	0		
2018–19	Arsenal	2	0		
2019–20	Arsenal	29	1		
2020–21	Arsenal	7	0	**40**	**1**
2020–21	*Newcastle U*	14	8	**14**	**8**

XHAKA, Granit (M) 311 16
H: 6 0 W: 11 00 b.Gnjilane 27-9-92
Internationals: Switzerland U17, U18, U19, U21, Full caps.

2010–11	Basel	19	1		
2011–12	Basel	23	0	**42**	**1**
2012–13	Borussia M'gladbach	22	1		
2013–14	Borussia M'gladbach	28	0		
2014–15	Borussia M'gladbach	30	2		
2015–16	Borussia M'gladbach	28	3	**108**	**6**
2016–17	Arsenal	32	2		
2017–18	Arsenal	38	1		
2018–19	Arsenal	29	4		
2019–20	Arsenal	31	1		
2020–21	Arsenal	31	1	**161**	**9**

Scholars
Adamo Gaspar, Luigi; Butler-Oyedeji, Nathan Jerome Chatoyer; Edwards, Khayon; Ejeheri, Ovie Prince; Foran, Taylor; Gomes Bandeira, Mauro; Henry-Francis, Jack; Jeffcott, Henry; Lannin-Sweet, James; Mitchell, Remy; Ogungbo, Mazeed; Oyegoke, Daniel Oladele Akinbiyi; Plange, Luke Elliot; Sagoe Jr, Charles Kwame; Sraha, Jason Robert Osei; Taylor-Hart, Kido; Vigar, Billy Joseph.

ASTON VILLA (4)

ABLDEEN-GOODRIDGE, Tristan (F) 0 0
H: 5 5 b. 28-11-02
From AFC Wimbledon.

2020–21	Aston Villa	0	0

APPIAH, Paul (D) 0 0
H: 6 0 W: 11 00 b.Enfield 13-10-02
From Chelsea.

2020–21	Aston Villa	0	0

BARRY, Louie (F) 0 0
b.Aston 21-6-03
From WBA, Barcelona.

2020–21	Aston Villa	0	0

BOGARDE, Lamar (M) 0 0
b. 5-1-04
From Feyenoord.

2020–21	Aston Villa	0	0

BRIDGE, Mungo (D) 0 0

2020–21	Aston Villa	0	0

CAMPTON-STURRIDGE, DJ (F) 0 0
H: 5 9 b. 17-10-02

2020–21	Aston Villa	0	0

CASH, Matty (M) 169 14
H: 6 2 W: 10 01 b.Slough 7-8-97

2015–16	Nottingham F	0	0		
2015–16	*Dagenham & R*	12	3	**12**	**3**
2016–17	Nottingham F	28	0		
2017–18	Nottingham F	23	2		
2018–19	Nottingham F	36	6		
2019–20	Nottingham F	42	3		
2020–21	Nottingham F	0	0	**129**	**11**
2020–21	Aston Villa	28	0	**28**	**0**

CHRISENE, Benjamin (M) 1 0
b. 12-1-04
Internationals: England U16.

2019–20	Exeter C	1	0	**1**	**0**
2020–21	Aston Villa	0	0		

CHUKWUEMEKA, Carney (M) 2 0
b.Northampton 20-10-03

2020–21	Aston Villa	2	0	**2**	**0**

DAVIS, Keinan (M) 72 3
H: 5 6 W: 10 10 b.Stevenage 13-2-98
Internationals: England U20.
From Stevenage, Biggleswade T.

2015–16	Aston Villa	0	0		
2016–17	Aston Villa	6	0		
2017–18	Aston Villa	28	2		
2018–19	Aston Villa	5	0		
2019–20	Aston Villa	18	0		
2020–21	Aston Villa	15	1	**72**	**3**

DOUGLAS LUIZ, de Paulo (M) 132 6
b.Rio 9-5-98
Internationals: Brazil U20, U23, Full caps.

2016	Vasco da Gama	14	2		
2017	Vasco da Gama	11	1	**25**	**3**
2017–18	Manchester C	0	0		
2017–18	*Girona*	15	0		
2018–19	Manchester C	0	0		
2018–19	*Girona*	23	0	**38**	**0**
2019–20	Aston Villa	36	3		
2020–21	Aston Villa	33	0	**69**	**3**

EALING, Frankie (D) 0 0

2020–21	Aston Villa	0	0

EL GHAZI, Anwar (F) 202 44
H: 6 2 W: 12 00 b.Barendrecht 3-5-95
Internationals: Netherlands U17, U18, U21, Full caps.

2014–15	Ajax	31	9		
2015–16	Ajax	27	11		
2016–17	Ajax	12	0	**70**	**20**
2016–17	Lille	12	1		
2017–18	Lille	27	4	**39**	**5**
2018–19	*Aston Villa*	31	5		
2019–20	Aston Villa	34	4		
2020–21	Aston Villa	28	10	**93**	**19**

ELMOHAMADY, Ahmed (M) 449 30
H: 5 11 W: 12 10 b.El Mahalla El-Kubra 9-9-87
Internationals: Egypt Full caps.

2003–04	Ghazi Al-Mehalla	0	0		
2004–05	Ghazi Al-Mehalla	14	4		
2005–06	Ghazi Al-Mehalla	3	0	**17**	**4**
2006–07	ENPPI	12	2		
2007–08	ENPPI	6	1		
2008–09	ENPPI	28	6		
2009–10	ENPPI	26	3	**72**	**12**
2010–11	Sunderland	36	0		
2011–12	Sunderland	18	1		
2012–13	Sunderland	2	0	**56**	**1**
2012–13	*Hull C*	41	3		
2013–14	Hull C	38	2		
2014–15	Hull C	38	2		
2015–16	Hull C	41	3		
2016–17	Hull C	33	0	**191**	**10**
2017–18	Aston Villa	43	0		
2018–19	Aston Villa	38	2		
2019–20	Aston Villa	18	1		
2020–21	Aston Villa	14	0	**113**	**3**

ENGELS, Bjorn (D) 124 16
b.Kaprijke 15-9-94
Internationals: Belgium U17, U18, U19, U21.

2012–13	Club Brugge	0	0		
2013–14	Club Brugge	23	4		
2014–15	Club Brugge	7	3		
2015–16	Club Brugge	10	2		
2016–17	Club Brugge	15	2		
2017–18	Club Brugge	2	0	**57**	**11**
2017–18	Olympiacos	17	3	**17**	**3**
2018–19	Reims	33	1	**33**	**1**
2019–20	Aston Villa	17	1		
2020–21	Aston Villa	0	0	**17**	**1**

GREALISH, Jack (M) 222 34
H: 5 9 W: 10 10 b.Birmingham 10-9-95
Internationals: Republic of Ireland U17, U18, U21. England U21.

2012–13	Aston Villa	0	0		
2013–14	Aston Villa	1	0		
2013–14	*Notts Co*	37	5	**37**	**5**
2014–15	Aston Villa	17	0		
2015–16	Aston Villa	16	1		
2016–17	Aston Villa	31	5		
2017–18	Aston Villa	27	3		
2018–19	Aston Villa	31	6		
2019–20	Aston Villa	36	8		
2020–21	Aston Villa	26	6	**185**	**29**

GUILBERT, Frederic (D) 195 3
b.Valognes 24-12-94
Internationals: France U21.

2011–12	Caen	0	0		
2012–13	Caen	0	0		
2013–14	Cherbourg	28	0	**28**	**0**
2014–15	Bordeaux	3	0		
2015–16	Bordeaux	30	0		
2016–17	Bordeaux	3	0	**36**	**0**
2016–17	*Caen*	23	0		
2017–18	Caen	36	1		
2018–19	Caen	34	1	**93**	**2**
2019–20	Aston Villa	25	0		
2020–21	Aston Villa	0	0	**25**	**0**
2020–21	*Strasbourg*	13	1	**13**	**1**

HAUSE, Kortney (D) 140 8
H: 6 2 W: 13 03 b.Goodmayes 16-7-95
Internationals: England U20, U21.

2012–13	Wycombe W	9	1		
2013–14	Wycombe W	14	1	**23**	**2**
2013–14	Wolverhampton W	0	0		
2014–15	Wolverhampton W	17	0		
2014–15	*Gillingham*	14	1	**14**	**1**
2015–16	Wolverhampton W	25	0		
2016–17	Wolverhampton W	24	2		
2017–18	Wolverhampton W	1	0		
2018–19	Wolverhampton W	0	0	**67**	**2**
2018–19	*Aston Villa*	11	1		
2019–20	Aston Villa	18	1		
2020–21	Aston Villa	7	1	**36**	**3**

HAYDEN, Kaine (D) 0 0

2019–20	Aston Villa	0	0
2020–21	Aston Villa	0	0

HEATON, Tom (G) 343 0
H: 6 1 W: 13 12 b.Chester 15-4-86
Internationals: England U16, U17, U18, U19, U21, Full caps.

2003–04	Manchester U	0	0		
2004–05	Manchester U	0	0		
2005–06	Manchester U	0	0		
2005–06	*Swindon T*	14	0	**14**	**0**
2006–07	Manchester U	0	0		
2007–08	Manchester U	0	0		
2008–09	Manchester U	0	0		
2008–09	*Cardiff C*	21	0		
2009–10	Manchester U	0	0		
2009–10	*Rochdale*	12	0	**12**	**0**
2009–10	*Wycombe W*	16	0	**16**	**0**
2010–11	Cardiff C	27	0		
2011–12	Cardiff C	2	0	**50**	**0**
2012–13	Bristol C	43	0	**43**	**0**
2013–14	Burnley	46	0		
2014–15	Burnley	38	0		
2015–16	Burnley	46	0		
2016–17	Burnley	35	0		
2017–18	Burnley	4	0		
2018–19	Burnley	19	0	**188**	**0**
2019–20	Aston Villa	20	0		
2020–21	Aston Villa	0	0	**20**	**0**

HOURIHANE, Conor (M) 388 72
H: 5 11 W: 9 11 b.Cork 2-2-91
Internationals: Republic of Ireland U19, U21, Full caps.

2008–09	Sunderland	0	0		
2009–10	Sunderland	0	0		
2010–11	Ipswich T	0	0		
2011–12	Plymouth Arg	38	2		
2012–13	Plymouth Arg	42	5		
2013–14	Plymouth Arg	45	8	**125**	**15**
2014–15	Barnsley	46	13		
2015–16	Barnsley	41	10		
2016–17	Barnsley	25	6	**112**	**29**
2016–17	Aston Villa	17	1		
2017–18	Aston Villa	41	11		
2018–19	Aston Villa	43	7		
2019–20	Aston Villa	27	3		
2020–21	Aston Villa	4	1	**132**	**23**
2020–21	*Swansea C*	19	5	**19**	**5**

JAY-HART, Taylor (M) **0** **0**

2020–21	Aston Villa	0	0		

JOTA, Ramallo (M) **211** **42**
H: 5 11 W: 10 08 b. La Coruna 16-6-91

2010–11	Celta Vigo	4	0		
2011–12	Celta Vigo	0	0		
2012–13	Celta Vigo	0	0		
2013–14	Celta Vigo	0	0	**4**	**0**
2013–14	*Eibar*	35	11		
2014–15	Brentford	42	11		
2015–16	Brentford	5	0		
2015–16	*Eibar*	13	0		
2016–17	Brentford	21	12		
2016–17	*Eibar*	5	0	**53**	**11**
2017–18	Brentford	4	0	**72**	**23**
2017–18	Birmingham C	32	5		
2018–19	Birmingham C	40	3	**72**	**8**
2019–20	Aston Villa	10	0		
2020–21	Aston Villa	0	0	**10**	**0**

Transferred to Alaves October 2020.

KALINIC, Lovre (G) **240** **0**
H: 6 7 W: 12 06 b.Split 3-4-90
Internationals: Croatia U16, U17, U21, Full caps.

2008–09	Hadjuk Split	0	0		
2008–09	*Junak Sinj*	4	0	**4**	**0**
2009–10	Hadjuk Split	0	0		
2009–10	*Novalja*	23	0	**23**	**0**
2010–11	Hadjuk Split	1	0		
2011–12	Hadjuk Split	1	0		
2011–12	*Karlovac*	11	0	**11**	**0**
2012–13	Hadjuk Split	4	0		
2013–14	Hadjuk Split	24	0		
2014–15	Hadjuk Split	28	0		
2015–16	Hadjuk Split	31	0		
2016–17	Hadjuk Split	13	0	**102**	**0**
2016–17	Gent	19	0		
2017–18	Gent	35	0		
2018–19	Gent	14	0	**68**	**0**
2018–19	Aston Villa	7	0		
2019–20	Aston Villa	0	0		
2019–20	*Toulouse*	4	0	**4**	**0**
2020–21	Aston Villa	0	0	**7**	**0**
2020–21	*Hajduk Split*	21	0	**21**	**0**

KONSA, Ezri (D) **174** **4**
H: 6 0 W: 12 02 b. 23-10-97
Internationals: England U20, U21.

2015–16	Charlton Ath	0	0		
2016–17	Charlton Ath	32	0		
2017–18	Charlton Ath	39	0	**71**	**0**
2018–19	Brentford	42	1	**42**	**1**
2019–20	Aston Villa	25	1		
2020–21	Aston Villa	36	2	**61**	**3**

LINDLEY, Hayden (M) **0** **0**
b. 2-9-02
From Manchester C.

2020–21	Aston Villa	0	0		

MARTINEZ, Damian (G) **109** **0**
H: 6 3 W: 13 05 b.Mar del Plata 2-9-92
Internationals: Argentina U17, U20.
From Independiente.

2010–11	Arsenal	0	0		
2011–12	Arsenal	0	0		
2011–12	*Oxford U*	1	0	**1**	**0**
2012–13	Arsenal	0	0		
2013–14	Arsenal	0	0		
2013–14	*Sheffield W*	11	0	**11**	**0**
2014–15	Arsenal	4	0		
2014–15	*Rotherham U*	8	0	**8**	**0**
2015–16	Arsenal	0	0		
2015–16	*Wolverhampton W*	13	0	**13**	**0**
2016–17	Arsenal	2	0		
2017–18	Arsenal	0	0		
2017–18	*Getafe*	5	0	**5**	**0**
2018–19	Arsenal	0	0		
2018–19	*Reading*	18	0		
2019–20	Arsenal	9	0		
2019–20	*Reading*	0	0	**18**	**0**
2020–21	Arsenal	0	0	**15**	**0**
2020–21	Aston Villa	38	0	**38**	**0**

McGINN, John (M) **293** **28**
H: 5 8 W: 10 08 b.Glasgow 18-10-94
Internationals: Scotland U19, U21, Full caps.

2012–13	St Mirren	22	1		
2013–14	St Mirren	35	3		
2014–15	St Mirren	30	0	**87**	**4**
2015–16	Hibernian	36	3		
2016–17	Hibernian	29	4		
2017–18	Hibernian	35	5		
2018–19	Hibernian	1	0	**101**	**12**
2018–19	Aston Villa	40	6		
2019–20	Aston Villa	28	3		
2020–21	Aston Villa	37	3	**105**	**12**

MINGS, Tyrone (D) **158** **7**
H: 6 3 W: 12 00 b.Bath 19-3-93
Internationals: England Full caps.
From Southampton.

2012–13	Ipswich T	1	0		
2013–14	Ipswich T	16	0		
2014–15	Ipswich T	40	1	**57**	**1**
2015–16	Bournemouth	1	0		
2016–17	Bournemouth	7	0		
2017–18	Bournemouth	4	0		
2018–19	Bournemouth	5	0	**17**	**0**
2018–19	*Aston Villa*	15	2		
2019–20	Aston Villa	33	2		
2020–21	Aston Villa	36	2	**84**	**6**

NAKAMBA, Marvelous (M) **164** **2**
b.Hwange 19-1-94
Internationals: Zimbabwe U20, Full caps.

2012–13	Nancy	0	0		
2013–14	Nancy	2	0	**2**	**0**
2014–15	Vitesse	6	0		
2015–16	Vitesse	30	1		
2016–17	Vitesse	31	1	**67**	**2**
2017–18	Club Brugge	35	0		
2018–19	Club Brugge	18	0	**53**	**0**
2019–20	Aston Villa	29	0		
2020–21	Aston Villa	13	0	**42**	**0**

ONODI, Akos (G) **0** **0**
From Gyor.

2020–21	Aston Villa	0	0		

PHILOGENE-BIDACE, Jayden (F) **1** **0**
b. 18-5-02

2020–21	Aston Villa	1	0	**1**	**0**

RAIKHY, Arjan (M) **0** **0**

2020–21	Aston Villa	0	0		

RAMSEY, Aaron (M) **0** **0**
b.Birmingham 21-1-03
Internationals: England U16, U17, U18.

2020–21	Aston Villa	0	0		

RAMSEY, Jacob (M) **30** **3**
b. 28-5-01
Internationals: England U18, U19.

2018–19	Aston Villa	1	0		
2019–20	Aston Villa	0	0		
2019–20	*Doncaster R*	7	3	**7**	**3**
2020–21	Aston Villa	22	0	**23**	**0**

REVAN, Dominic (D) **0** **0**
b. 19-9-00

2018–19	Aston Villa	0	0		
2020–21	Aston Villa	0	0		

ROWE, Callum (D) **0** **0**
b. 2-9-91

2020–21	Aston Villa	0	0		

ROWE, Edward (M) **0** **0**
b. 17-10-03

2020–21	Aston Villa	0	0		

SAMATTA, Mbwana (F) **308** **112**
b.Salaam 23-12-92
Internationals: Tanzania Full caps.

2010–11	Simba	25	13	**25**	**13**
2011	TP Mazembe	8	2		
2012	TP Mazembe	29	3		
2013	TP Mazembe	37	20		
2013–14	TP Mazembe	29	15		
2014–15	TP Mazembe	0	0		
2015–16	TP Mazembe	0	0	**103**	**40**
2015–16	Genk	16	4		
2016–17	Genk	35	12		
2017–18	Genk	30	7		
2018–19	Genk	38	23		
2019–20	Genk	20	7	**139**	**53**
2019–20	Aston Villa	14	1		
2020–21	Aston Villa	0	0	**14**	**1**
2020–21	*Fenerbahce*	27	5	**27**	**5**

SANSON, Morgan (M) **244** **36**
b.Saint-Doulchard 18-8-94

2012–13	Le Mans	27	3	**27**	**3**
2013–14	Montpellier	32	1		
2014–15	Montpellier	32	6		
2015–16	Montpellier	14	3		
2016–17	Montpellier	20	3	**98**	**13**
2016–17	Marseille	17	1		
2017–18	Marseille	33	9		
2018–19	Marseille	33	5		
2019–20	Marseille	27	5		
2020–21	Marseille	0	0	**110**	**20**
2020–21	Aston Villa	9	0	**9**	**0**

SHAKPOKE, Ruben (F) **0** **0**
b. 23-4-04
From Norwich C.

2020–21	Aston Villa	0	0		

SINISALO, Viljami (G) **22** **0**
H: 6 5 W: 12 04 b.Espoo 11-10-01
Internationals: Finland U17, U19, U21.
From Espoo.

2020–21	Aston Villa	0	0		
2020–21	*Ayr U*	22	0	**22**	**0**

SOHNA, Harrison (M) **0** **0**
b. 1-7-02

2020–21	Aston Villa	0	0		

STEER, Jed (G) **112** **0**
H: 6 2 W: 14 00 b.Norwich 23-9-92
Internationals: England U16, U17, U19.

2009–10	Norwich C	0	0		
2010–11	Norwich C	0	0		
2011–12	Norwich C	0	0		
2011–12	*Yeovil T*	12	0		
2012–13	Cambridge U	0	0		
2012–13	Norwich C	0	0		
2013–14	Aston Villa	0	0		
2014–15	Aston Villa	1	0		
2014–15	*Doncaster R*	13	0	**13**	**0**
2014–15	*Yeovil T*	12	0	**24**	**0**
2015–16	Aston Villa	0	0		
2015–16	*Huddersfield T*	38	0	**38**	**0**
2016–17	Aston Villa	0	0		
2017–18	Aston Villa	0	0		
2018–19	Aston Villa	16	0		
2018–19	*Charlton Ath*	19	0	**19**	**0**
2019–20	Aston Villa	1	0		
2020–21	Aston Villa	0	0	**18**	**0**

SWINKELS, Sil (D) **0** **0**
b. 6-1-04
From Vitesse.

2020–21	Aston Villa	0	0		

SYLLA, Mamadou (M) **0** **0**
b. 12-8-02

2020–21	Aston Villa	0	0		

TAIT, Michael (F) **0** **0**

2019–20	Aston Villa	0	0		
2020–21	Aston Villa	0	0		

TARGETT, Matt (D) **127** **3**
H: 6 0 W: 12 11 b.Edinburgh 18-9-95
Internationals: Scotland U19, England U19, U20, U21.

2013–14	Southampton	0	0		
2014–15	Southampton	6	0		
2015–16	Southampton	14	0		
2016–17	Southampton	5	0		
2017–18	Southampton	2	0		
2017–18	*Fulham*	18	1	**18**	**1**
2018–19	Southampton	16	1	**43**	**1**
2019–20	Aston Villa	28	1		
2020–21	Aston Villa	38	0	**66**	**1**

TAYLOR, Neil (D) **275** **0**
H: 5 9 W: 10 02 b.Ruthin 7-2-89
Internationals: Wales U17, U19, U21, C, Full caps. Great Britain.

2007–08	Wrexham	26	0	**26**	**0**

From Wrexham.

2010–11	Swansea C	29	0		
2011–12	Swansea C	36	0		
2012–13	Swansea C	6	0		
2013–14	Swansea C	10	0		
2014–15	Swansea C	34	0		
2015–16	Swansea C	34	0		
2016–17	Swansea C	11	0	**160**	**0**
2016–17	Aston Villa	14	0		
2017–18	Aston Villa	29	0		
2018–19	Aston Villa	31	0		
2019–20	Aston Villa	14	0		
2020–21	Aston Villa	1	0	**89**	**0**

TRAORE, Bertrand (M) **199** **55**
H: 5 10 W: 12 00 b.Bob-Dioulasso 6-9-95
Internationals: Burkina Faso U17, Full caps
From Auxerre.

2013–14	Chelsea	0	0		
2013–14	*Vitesse*	13	3		
2014–15	Chelsea	0	0		
2014–15	*Vitesse*	29	13	**42**	**16**
2015–16	Chelsea	10	2		
2016–17	Chelsea	0	0	**10**	**2**
2016–17	*Ajax*	24	9	**24**	**9**
2017–18	Lyon	31	13		
2018–19	Lyon	33	7		
2019–20	Lyon	23	1	**87**	**21**
2020–21	Aston Villa	36	7	**36**	**7**

TREZEGUET, Mahmoud (M) **206** **41**
b.Kafr el-Sheikh 1-10-94
Internationals: Egypt U20, U23, Full caps.

2012–13	Al Ahly	7	0		
2013–14	Al Ahly	20	2		
2014–15	Al Ahly	31	5		
2015–16	Al Ahly	0	0	**58**	**7**
2015–16	*Anderlecht*	7	0		

2016–17 Anderlecht 1 0
2016–17 *Royal Excel Mouscron* 20 4 **20 4**
2017–18 Anderlecht 0 0 **8 0**
2017–18 *Kasimpasa* 31 13
2018–19 Kasimpasa 34 9 **65 22**
2019–20 Aston Villa 34 6
2020–21 Aston Villa 21 2 **55 8**

VASSILEV, Indiana (M) 28 0
b.Georgia 16-2-01
Internationals: USA U17, U18, U20.
2019–20 Aston Villa 4 0
2020–21 Aston Villa 0 0 **4 0**
2020–21 *Burton Alb* 12 0 **12 0**
2020–21 *Cheltenham T* 12 0 **12 0**

WALKER, Jake (D) 0 0
2020–21 Aston Villa 0 0

WATKINS, Ollie (F) 237 80
H: 5 10 W: 11 00 b.Torbay 30-12-95
2013–14 Exeter C 1 0
2014–15 Exeter C 2 0
2015–16 Exeter C 20 8
2016–17 Exeter C 45 13 **68 21**
2017–18 Brentford 45 10
2018–19 Brentford 41 10
2019–20 Brentford 46 25
2020–21 Brentford 0 0 **132 45**
2020–21 Aston Villa 37 14 **37 14**

WESLEY, Moraes (F) 149 43
b.Juiz de Fora 26-11-96
Internationals: Brazil Full caps.
2015–16 Trencin 18 6 **18 6**
2015–16 Club Brugge 6 2
2016–17 Club Brugge 25 6
2017–18 Club Brugge 38 11
2018–19 Club Brugge 38 13 **107 32**
2019–20 Aston Villa 21 5
2020–21 Aston Villa 3 0 **24 5**

WRIGHT, Tyreik (F) 16 0
b. 22-9-01
2020–21 Aston Villa 0 0
2020–21 *Walsall* 16 0 **16 0**

YOUNG, Brad (F) 0 0
2020–21 Aston Villa 0 0

ZYCH, Oliwier (G) 0 0
b. 28-6-04
From Lubin.
2020–21 Aston Villa 0 0

Scholars
Afoka, Chisom Kenneth; Ealing, Frankie; Hart, Taylor-Jay Phillip; Lane, Jos hua Thomas; Lindley, Hayden Taylor; Marschall, Filip; McBride, Caolan James; O'Reilly, Aaron Christopher; O'Reilly, Tommi Dylan; Raikhy, Arjan Singh; Reddin, Kahrel Azariah; Rowe, Edward James; Sewell, Dewain Leon; Swinkels, Sil Laurentius; Sylla Diallo, Mamadou; Young, Bradley Jamie Ethan; Zito, Patrick Tchuako; Zych, Oliwier.

BARNSLEY (5)

ADDAI, Corey (G) 0 0
b. 10-10-97
2015–16 Coventry C 0 0
2016–17 Coventry C 0 0
2017–18 Coventry C 0 0
2018–19 Coventry C 0 0
2019–20 Coventry C 0 0
2020–21 Barnsley 0 0

ADEBOYEJO, Victor (F) 98 6
b. 12-1-98
From Arsenal, AFC Wimbledon, Charlton Ath.
2014–15 Leyton Orient 1 0
2015–16 Leyton Orient 1 0
2016–17 Leyton Orient 13 1 **15 1**
2017–18 Barnsley 0 0
2018–19 Barnsley 25 2
2019–20 *Bristol R* 18 1 **18 1**
2019–20 *Cambridge U* 8 0 **8 0**
2020–21 Barnsley 32 2 **57 4**

AITCHISON, Jack (F) 71 8
b.Fauldhouse 5-3-00
Internationals: Scotland U16, U17, U19.
2015–16 Celtic 1 1
2016–17 Celtic 2 0
2017–18 Celtic 0 0
2018–19 Celtic 0 0
2018–19 *Dumbarton* 4 0 **4 0**
2018–19 *Alloa Ath* 10 1 **10 1**
2019–20 Celtic 0 0 **3 1**
2019–20 *Forest Green R* 28 5 **28 5**
2020–21 Barnsley 0 0
2020–21 *Stevenage* 26 1 **26 1**

ANDERSEN, Mads (D) 137 7
b. 27-12-97
Internationals: Denmark U19.
2016–17 Brondy 0 0
2016–17 *Koge* 25 2 **25 2**
2017–18 Horsens 8 1
2018–19 Horsens 20 3 **28 4**
2019–20 Barnsley 38 0
2020–21 Barnsley 46 1 **84 1**

BRAMALL, Daniel (D) 3 0
b.Sheffield 3-9-98
From Matlock T, Buxton.
2020–21 Barnsley 0 0
2020–21 *Barrow* 3 0 **3 0**

BRITTAIN, Callum (F) 147 4
H: 5 10 W: 10 10 b.Bedford 12-3-98
Internationals: England U20.
2015–16 Milton Keynes D 0 0
2016 *Protur Reykjavik* 6 0 **6 0**
2016–17 Milton Keynes D 6 0
2017–18 Milton Keynes D 29 2
2018–19 Milton Keynes D 31 1
2019–20 Milton Keynes D 31 1
2020–21 Milton Keynes D 4 0 **101 4**
2020–21 Barnsley 40 0 **40 0**

CHAPLIN, Conor (M) 213 45
H: 5 10 W: 10 12 b.Worthing 16-2-97
2014–15 Portsmouth 9 1
2015–16 Portsmouth 30 8
2016–17 Portsmouth 39 8
2017–18 Portsmouth 26 5 **104 22**
2018–19 Coventry C 31 8 **31 8**
2019–20 Barnsley 44 11
2020–21 Barnsley 34 4 **78 15**

CHRISTIE-DAVIES, Isaac (M) 0 0
b.Brighton 18-9-97
Internationals: England U16, U17. Wales U21.
From Chelsea.
2018–19 Liverpool 0 0
2019–20 Liverpool 0 0
2019–20 *Cercle Brugge* 0 0
2020–21 Barnsley 0 0

COLLINS, Bradley (G) 111 0
H: 6 0 W: 10 12 b. 18-2-97
2017–18 Chelsea 0 0
2017–18 *Forest Green R* 39 0 **39 0**
2018–19 Chelsea 0 0
2018–19 *Burton Alb* 31 0 **31 0**
2019–20 Barnsley 19 0
2020–21 Barnsley 22 0 **41 0**

DIKE, Daryl (F) 36 17
b.Edmond 3-6-00
From OKC Energy.
2020 Orlando C 17 8 **17 8**
On loan from Orlando C.
2020–21 Barnsley 19 9 **19 9**

FRIESER, Dominik (M) 245 30
b.Graz 9-9-93
2013–14 Hartberg 7 0
2013–14 *Kalsdorf* 14 1 **14 1**
2014–15 Hartberg 30 1 **37 1**
2015–16 Kapfenberger 35 5
2016–17 Kapfenberger 34 2 **69 7**
2017–18 Wolfsberger 22 4 **22 4**
2018–19 LASK Linz 31 6
2019–20 LASK Linz 30 8 **61 14**
2020–21 LASK 0 0
2020–21 Barnsley 42 3 **42 3**

GREEN, Jordan (F) 92 8
H: 5 6 W: 10 03 b.London 22-2-95
2015–16 Bournemouth 0 0
2016–17 Bournemouth 0 0
2016–17 *Newport Co* 10 0
2017–18 Yeovil T 37 2
2018–19 Yeovil T 19 4 **56 6**
2018–19 Barnsley 10 1
2019–20 Barnsley 2 0
2019–20 *Newport Co* 11 1 **21 1**
2020–21 Barnsley 0 0 **12 1**
2020–21 *Southend U* 3 0 **3 0**

HALME, Aapo (D) 99 5
b.Helsinki 22-5-98
Internationals: Finland U16, U17, U18, U19, U21.
2014 Honka 1 0 **1 0**
2015 Klubi 04 15 1 **15 1**
2015 HJK Helsinki 2 0
2016 HJK Helsinki 14 0
2017 HJK Helsinki 13 0 **29 0**
2018–19 Leeds U 4 0 **4 0**
2019–20 Barnsley 32 4
2020–21 Barnsley 18 0 **50 4**

HELIK, Michal (D) 176 15
b. 9-9-95
2013–14 Ruch Chorzow 8 0
2014–15 Ruch Chorzow 18 1
2015–16 Ruch Chorzow 0 0
2016–17 Ruch Chorzow 20 0 **46 1**
2017–18 Cracovia 32 8
2018–19 Cracovia 32 0
2019–20 Cracovia 23 1
2020–21 Cracovia 0 0 **87 9**
2020–21 Barnsley 43 5 **43 5**

KANE, Herbie (M) 69 6
H: 5 9 W: 10 08 b.Bristol 23-11-98
Internationals: England U16, U17, U18.
From Bristol C.
2018–19 Liverpool 0 0
2018–19 *Doncaster R* 38 4 **38 4**
2019–20 Liverpool 0 0
2019–20 *Hull C* 7 2 **7 2**
2020–21 Barnsley 24 0 **24 0**

KENDRICK, Henry (G) 0 0
H: 6 3 b.Barnsley 3-12-00
2018–19 Barnsley 0 0
2019–20 Barnsley 0 0
2020–21 Barnsley 0 0

KITCHING, Liam (D) 45 0
b. 1-10-99
2017–18 Leeds U 0 0
2018–19 Leeds U 0 0
2019–20 Forest Green R 29 0
2020–21 Forest Green R 15 0 **44 0**
2020–21 Barnsley 1 0 **1 0**

LANCASTER, Will (M) 0 0
H: 6 0 W: 10 12 b.Sheffield 3-8-02
2020–21 Barnsley 0 0

LUDEWIG, Kilian (D) 40 1
b. 5-3-00
Internationals: Germany U16, U17, U18.
2018–19 Liefering 18 1 **18 1**
2019–20 Red Bull Salzburg 0 0
On loan from Red Bull Salzburg.
2019–20 Barnsley 18 0
2020–21 Red Bull Salzburg 0 0
On loan from Red Bull Salzburg.
2020–21 Barnsley 4 0 **22 0**

MARSH, Aiden (F) 0 0
H: 5 8 W: 9 06 b.Barnsley 5-5-03
2020–21 Barnsley 0 0

MILLER, George (F) 108 19
H: 5 10 W: 10 01 b.Bolton 11-8-98
2015–16 Bury 1 0
2016–17 Bury 28 7
2017–18 Middlesbrough 0 0
2017–18 *Bury* 19 8 **48 15**
2018–19 Middlesbrough 0 0
2018–19 *Bradford C* 39 3 **39 3**
2018–19 Barnsley 0 0
2019–20 Barnsley 1 0
2019–20 *Scunthorpe U* 15 1 **15 1**
2020–21 Barnsley 5 0 **6 0**

MOON, Jasper (M) 3 0
H: 6 1 b.Coventry 24-11-00
From Leicester C.
2018–19 Barnsley 0 0
2019–20 Barnsley 0 0
2020–21 Barnsley 3 0 **3 0**

MORRIS, Carlton (F) 170 29
H: 6 1 W: 13 05 b.Cambridge 16-12-95
Internationals: England U19.
2014–15 Norwich C 1 0
2014–15 *Oxford U* 7 0 **7 0**
2014–15 *York C* 8 0 **8 0**
2015–16 Norwich C 0 0
2015–16 *Hamilton A* 32 8 **32 8**
2016–17 Norwich C 0 0
2016–17 *Rotherham U* 8 0
2017–18 Norwich C 0 0
2017–18 *Shrewsbury T* 42 6 **42 6**
2018–19 Norwich C 0 0
2019–20 Norwich C 0 0
2019–20 *Rotherham U* 21 3 **29 3**
2019–20 *Milton Keynes D* 10 2
2020–21 Norwich C 0 0 **1 0**
2020–21 *Milton Keynes D* 18 3 **28 5**
2020–21 Barnsley 23 7 **23 7**

MOWATT, Alex (D) 292 34
H: 5 10 W: 11 03 b.Doncaster 13-2-95
Internationals: England U19, U20.
2013–14 Leeds U 29 1
2014–15 Leeds U 38 9
2015–16 Leeds U 34 2
2016–17 Leeds U 15 0 **116 12**
2016–17 Barnsley 11 1
2017–18 Barnsley 1 0

2017–18 *Oxford U* 30 2 **30 2**
2018–19 Barnsley 46 8
2019–20 Barnsley 44 3
2020–21 Barnsley 44 8 **146 20**

ODOUR, Clarke (F) 27 1
b. 25-6-99
2018–19 Leeds U 0 0
2019–20 Leeds U 0 0
2019–20 Barnsley 16 1
2020–21 Barnsley 11 0 **27 1**

OMAR, Ali (D) 0 0
b. 14-9-99
2018–19 QPR 0 0
2019–20 Barnsley 0 0
2020–21 Barnsley 0 0

PACHE, Rudi (D) 0 0
H: 6 0 W: 10 12 b.Slough 20-7-02
2020–21 Barnsley 0 0

PALMER, Romal (M) 37 1
b. 30-9-99
From Manchester C.
2019–20 Barnsley 3 0
2020–21 Barnsley 34 1 **37 1**

RITZMAIER, Marcel (M) 178 11
b.Knittelfeld 22-4-93
Internationals: Austria U16, U17, U18, U19, U21.
2009–10 Austria Karnten 1 0 **1 0**
2010–11 PSV Eindhoven 0 0
2011–12 PSV Eindhoven 0 0
2012–13 PSV Eindhoven 4 0
2013–14 PSV Eindhoven 0 0
2013–14 *Cambuur* 31 3 **31 3**
2014–15 PSV Eindhoven 5 0
2015–16 PSV Eindhoven 0 0
2015–16 *NEC* 20 1 **20 1**
2016–17 PSV Eindhoven 0 0
2016–17 *Go Ahead Eagles* 28 2 **28 2**
2017–18 PSV Eindhoven 0 0 **9 0**
2018–19 Wolfsberger 29 1
2019–20 Wolfsberger 18 2 **47 3**
2019–20 Barnsley 15 0
2020–21 Barnsley 3 0 **18 0**
2020–21 *Rapid Vienna* 24 2 **24 2**

SCHMIDT, Patrick (F) 111 19
b.Eisenstadt 22-7-98
Internationals: Austria U16, U17, U18, U19, U21.
2016–17 Admira Wacker 15 1
2017–18 Admira Wacker 20 6
2018–19 Admira Wacker 27 8
2019–20 Admira Wacker 2 0 **64 15**
2019–20 Barnsley 29 3
2020–21 Barnsley 8 0 **37 3**
2020–21 *SV Ried* 10 1 **10 1**

SIBBICK, Toby (D) 67 0
H: 6 0 W: 10 12 b.Isleworth 23-5-99
2016–17 AFC Wimbledon 2 0
2017–18 AFC Wimbledon 1 0
2018–19 AFC Wimbledon 23 0 **26 0**
2019–20 Barnsley 18 0
2019–20 *Hearts* 2 0 **2 0**
2020–21 Barnsley 21 0 **39 0**
2020–21 *KV Oostende* 0 0

SIMOES, Elliot (F) 33 3
b. 20-12-99
From FC United of Manchester.
2019–20 Barnsley 17 2
2020–21 Barnsley 8 1 **25 3**
2020–21 *Doncaster R* 8 0 **8 0**

SIMPSON, Steven (F) 0 0
b. 5-4-00
2020–21 Barnsley 0 0

SOLLBAUER , Michael (D) 352 7
b. 15-5-90
2009–10 Austria Karnten 18 0 **18 0**
2010–11 Wolfsberger 29 1
2011–12 Wolfsberger 31 3
2012–13 Wolfsberger 34 0
2013–14 Wolfsberger 34 0
2014–15 Wolfsberger 32 0
2015–16 Wolfsberger 25 0
2016–17 Wolfsberger 23 1
2017–18 Wolfsberger 24 1
2018–19 Wolfsberger 30 1
2019–20 Wolfsberger 18 0 **280 7**
2019–20 Barnsley 17 0
2020–21 Barnsley 37 0 **54 0**

STYLES, Callum (F) 107 5
b. 28-3-00
From Burnley.
2015–16 Bury 1 0
2016–17 Bury 13 0
2017–18 Bury 11 0
2018–19 Bury 16 0 **41 0**
2018–19 Barnsley 7 0
2019–20 Barnsley 17 1
2020–21 Barnsley 42 4 **66 5**

THOMAS, Luke (F) 108 5
H: 5 7 W: 10 08 b. 19-2-99
Internationals: England U20.
From Cheltenham T.
2015–16 Derby Co 0 0
2016–17 Derby Co 0 0
2017–18 Derby Co 2 0
2018–19 Derby Co 0 0 **2 0**
2018–19 *Coventry C* 43 4 **43 4**
2019–20 Barnsley 39 1
2020–21 Barnsley 19 0 **58 1**
2020–21 *Ipswich T* 5 0 **5 0**

THOMPSON, Cameron (F) 0 0
b.London 21-2-00
From Fulham.
2020–21 Barnsley 0 0

WALTON, Jack (G) 39 0
H: 6 0 W: 12 02 b.Bury 23-4-98
From Bolton W.
2014–15 Barnsley 0 0
2015–16 Barnsley 0 0
2016–17 Barnsley 0 0
2017–18 Barnsley 3 0
2018–19 Barnsley 3 0
2019–20 Barnsley 9 0
2020–21 Barnsley 24 0 **39 0**

WILLIAMS, Jordan (D) 71 0
b. 22-10-99
Internationals: England U17, U18.
2017–18 Huddersfield T 0 0
2017–18 *Bury* 9 0 **9 0**
2018–19 Barnsley 11 0
2019–20 Barnsley 30 0
2020–21 Barnsley 21 0 **62 0**

WINFIELD, Charlie (D) 0 0
H: 5 7 W: 9 02 b.Barnsley 8-5-02
2020–21 Barnsley 0 0

WOODROW, Cauley (F) 214 59
H: 6 0 W: 12 04 b.Hemel Hempstead 2-12-94
Internationals: England U17, U20, U21.
From Luton T.
2011–12 Fulham 0 0
2012–13 Fulham 0 0
2013–14 Fulham 6 1
2013–14 *Southend U* 19 2 **19 2**
2014–15 Fulham 29 3
2015–16 Fulham 14 4
2016–17 Fulham 5 0
2016–17 *Burton Alb* 14 5 **14 5**
2017–18 Fulham 0 0 **54 8**
2017–18 *Bristol C* 14 2 **14 2**
2018–19 Barnsley 31 16
2019–20 Barnsley 40 14
2020–21 Barnsley 42 12 **113 42**

Scholars
Ackroyd, Joe; Ariely, Amir Moshe; Benson, Daniel Richard; Birks, Jack; Brown, Archie Myles; Calligan, William Marcus; Chapman, Angus Charles; Flavell, Kieren James; Goucher, Blake Callum; Hall, Ben Lawson; Hartley, Keegan James; Hassan-Smith, Kareem David; Hassell, Bayley Robert John; Hodgson, Connor James; Nejman, Harrison Luke; Nicholson, Sam Oliver; Sherlock, Jack Edward; Sila-Conde, Newton; Smith, Lloyd Dion; Widdop, Harry Jacob.

BARROW (6)

ANDREW, Calvin (F) 397 37
H: 6 0 W: 12 11 b.Luton 19-12-86
2004–05 Luton T 8 0
2005–06 Luton T 1 1
2005–06 *Grimsby T* 8 1 **8 1**
2005–06 *Bristol C* 3 0 **3 0**
2006–07 Luton T 7 1
2007–08 Luton T 39 2 **55 4**
2008–09 Crystal Palace 7 0
2008–09 *Brighton & HA* 9 2 **9 2**
2009–10 Crystal Palace 27 1
2010–11 Crystal Palace 13 0
2010–11 *Millwall* 3 0 **3 0**
2010–11 *Swindon T* 10 1 **10 1**
2011–12 Crystal Palace 6 0 **53 1**
2011–12 *Leyton Orient* 10 0 **10 0**
2012–13 Port Vale 22 1
2013–14 Port Vale 0 0 **22 1**
2013–14 Mansfield T 15 1 **15 1**
2013–14 York C 8 1 **8 1**
2014–15 Rochdale 32 5
2015–16 Rochdale 30 6
2016–17 Rochdale 39 7
2017–18 Rochdale 31 3
2018–19 Rochdale 38 3
2019–20 Rochdale 20 0 **190 24**
2020–21 Barrow 11 1 **11 1**

ANGUS, Dior (F) 25 5
H: 6 0 W: 12 00 b. 18-1-94
From Solihull Moors, Kidderminster H, Daventry T, Stratford T, Redditch U.
2017–18 Port Vale 3 1
2018–19 Port Vale 0 0 **3 1**
2020–21 Barrow 22 4 **22 4**

BANKS, Oliver (D) 218 21
H: 6 3 W: 11 11 b.Rotherham 21-9-92
2010–11 Rotherham U 1 1
2011–12 Rotherham U 0 0 **1 1**
2013–14 Chesterfield 25 7
2014–15 Chesterfield 24 0
2014–15 *Northampton T* 3 0 **3 0**
2015–16 Chesterfield 32 2 **81 9**
2016–17 Oldham Ath 33 2
2017–18 Oldham Ath 7 0 **40 2**
2017–18 *Swindon T* 17 3 **17 3**
2018–19 Tranmere R 33 3
2019–20 Tranmere R 11 3
2020–21 Tranmere R 12 0 **56 6**
2020–21 Barrow 20 0 **20 0**

BARRY, Bradley (D) 120 2
H: 6 0 W: 12 00 b.Hastings 13-12-95
2013–14 Brighton & HA 0 0
2014–15 Brighton & HA 0 0
2015–16 Swindon T 35 0
2016–17 Swindon T 23 1 **58 1**
2016–17 Chesterfield 0 0
2017–18 Chesterfield 29 0 **29 0**
2020–21 Barrow 33 1 **33 1**

BEADLING, Tom (D) 82 6
H: 6 1 W: 12 08 b.Barrow-in-Furness 16-1-96
2014–15 Sunderland 0 0
2015–16 Sunderland 0 0
2016–17 Sunderland 0 0
2016–17 *Bury* 2 0 **2 0**
2017–18 Sunderland 0 0
2017–18 *Dunfermline Ath* 11 1
2018–19 Dunfermline Ath 19 3
2019–20 Dunfermline Ath 21 0 **51 4**
2020–21 Barrow 29 2 **29 2**

BROUGH, Patrick (M) 119 6
H: 5 8 b.Carlisle 20-2-96
2013–14 Carlisle U 3 0
2014–15 Carlisle U 29 0
2015–16 Carlisle U 7 0
2016–17 Carlisle U 1 0 **40 0**
2017–18 Morecambe 20 0 **20 0**
2018–19 Falkirk 16 0 **16 0**
2020–21 Barrow 43 6 **43 6**

BROWN, Connor (D) 116 2
H: 5 8 W: 10 12 b.Sheffield 2-10-91
2010–11 Sheffield U 0 0
2011–12 Sheffield U 0 0
2012–13 Oldham Ath 25 0
2013–14 Oldham Ath 27 1
2014–15 Oldham Ath 24 0
2014–15 *Carlisle U* 8 0 **8 0**
2015–16 Oldham Ath 13 0 **89 1**
2020–21 Barrow 19 1 **19 1**

BURNS, Bobby (D) 70 6
H: 5 8 W: 11 05 b.Belfast 7-10-99
Internationals: Northern Ireland U17, U19, U21.
2015–16 Glenavon 1 0
2016–17 Glenavon 1 0
2017–18 Glenavon 37 5 **39 5**
2018–19 Hearts 4 1
2018–19 *Livingston* 8 0 **8 0**
2019–20 Hearts 0 0 **4 1**
2019–20 *Newcastle Jets* 16 0 **16 0**
2020–21 Barrow 0 0
2020–21 *Glentoran* 3 0 **3 0**

DEVITT, Jamie (F) 306 45
H: 5 10 W: 10 05 b.Dublin 6-7-90
Internationals: Republic of Ireland U21.
2007–08 Hull C 0 0
2008–09 Hull C 0 0
2009–10 Hull C 0 0
2009–10 *Darlington* 6 1 **6 1**
2009–10 *Shrewsbury T* 9 2 **9 2**
2009–10 *Grimsby T* 15 5 **15 5**
2010–11 Hull C 16 0
2011–12 Hull C 0 0
2011–12 *Bradford C* 7 1
2011–12 *Accrington S* 16 2 **16 2**
2012–13 Hull C 0 0 **16 0**

2012–13	*Rotherham U*	1	0	**1**	**0**
2013–14	Chesterfield	7	0	**7**	**0**
2013–14	*Morecambe*	14	2		
2014–15	Morecambe	36	3		
2015–16	Morecambe	39	6	**89**	**11**
2016–17	Carlisle U	35	0		
2017–18	Carlisle U	40	10		
2018–19	Carlisle U	35	11	**110**	**21**
2019–20	Blackpool	0	0		
2019–20	*Bradford C*	5	0	**12**	**1**
2020–21	Blackpool	0	0		
2020–21	*Newport Co*	8	1	**8**	**1**
2020–21	Barrow	17	1	**17**	**1**

DIXON, Joel (G)				**46**	**0**
b.Middlesbrough 30-11-92					
2012–13	Sunderland	0	0		
2013–14	Sunderland	0	0		
2020–21	Barrow	46	0	**46**	**0**

DONOHUE, Dion (M)				**117**	**1**
H: 5 11 W: 10 06 b.Bodedern 26-8-93					
From Holyhead H, Caernarfon T, Sutton Coldfield T.					
2015–16	Chesterfield	17	0		
2016–17	Chesterfield	37	1		
2017–18	Chesterfield	2	0	**56**	**1**
2017–18	Portsmouth	32	0		
2018–19	Portsmouth	10	0	**42**	**0**
2019–20	Mansfield T	0	0		
2019–20	Swindon T	5	0		
2020–21	Swindon T	10	0	**15**	**0**
2020–21	Barrow	4	0	**4**	**0**

GRIBBIN, Callum (M)				**1**	**0**
b.Salford 18-12-98					
From Manchester U, Sheffield U.					
2020–21	Barrow	1	0	**1**	**0**

HARDCASTLE, Lewis (M)				**18**	**1**
H: 5 9 W: 12 00 b.Bolton 4-7-98					
2017–18	Blackburn R	0	0		
2018–19	Blackburn R	0	0		
2018–19	*Port Vale*	6	0	**6**	**0**
2020–21	Barrow	12	1	**12**	**1**

HINDLE, Jack (F)				**2**	**0**
b. 29-10-93					
From Radcliffe Bor, 1874 Northwich, Colwyn Bay.					
2020–21	Barrow	2	0	**2**	**0**

HIRD, Samuel (D)				**380**	**12**
H: 5 7 W: 10 12 b.Askern 7-9-87					
2005–06	Leeds U	0	0		
2006–07	Leeds U	0	0		
2006–07	*Doncaster R*	5	0		
2007–08	Doncaster R	4	0		
2007–08	*Grimsby T*	17	0	**17**	**0**
2008–09	Doncaster R	37	1		
2009–10	Doncaster R	36	0		
2010–11	Doncaster R	32	0		
2011–12	Doncaster R	31	0	**145**	**1**
2012–13	Chesterfield	41	2		
2013–14	Chesterfield	35	2		
2014–15	Chesterfield	28	3		
2015–16	Chesterfield	40	2		
2016–17	Chesterfield	35	1		
2017–18	Chesterfield	24	0	**203**	**10**
From Alfreton T.					
2020–21	Barrow	15	1	**15**	**1**

JAMES, Luke (M)				**234**	**24**
H: 6 0 W: 12 08 b.Amble 4-11-94					
2011–12	Hartlepool U	19	3		
2012–13	Hartlepool U	26	3		
2013–14	Hartlepool U	42	13		
2014–15	Hartlepool U	4	0		
2014–15	Peterborough U	32	1		
2015–16	Peterborough U	0	0		
2015–16	*Bradford C*	9	0	**9**	**0**
2015–16	*Hartlepool U*	20	1	**111**	**20**
2016–17	Peterborough U	0	0	**32**	**1**
2016–17	*Bristol R*	24	0	**24**	**0**
2017–18	Forest Green R	14	0	**14**	**0**
From Hartlepool U.					
2020–21	Barrow	44	3	**44**	**3**

JONES, James (D)				**21**	**1**
b.Wrexham 13-3-97					
From The New Saints, Altrincham.					
2020–21	Barrow	21	1	**21**	**1**

JONES, Mike (M)				**493**	**38**
H: 5 11 W: 12 04 b.Birkenhead 15-8-87					
2005–06	Tranmere R	1	0		
2006–07	Tranmere R	0	0		
2006–07	*Shrewsbury T*	13	1	**13**	**1**
2007–08	Tranmere R	9	1	**10**	**1**
2008–09	Bury	46	4		
2009–10	Bury	41	5		
2010–11	Bury	42	8		
2011–12	Bury	24	3	**153**	**20**
2011–12	Sheffield W	10	0		
2012–13	Sheffield W	0	0	**10**	**0**
2012–13	Crawley T	40	1		
2013–14	Crawley T	42	3	**82**	**4**
2014–15	Oldham Ath	45	6		
2015–16	Oldham Ath	35	3	**80**	**9**
2016–17	Carlisle U	28	0		
2017–18	Carlisle U	43	0		
2018–19	Carlisle U	24	1		
2019–20	Carlisle U	37	0	**132**	**1**
2020–21	Barrow	13	2	**13**	**2**

KAY, Josh (M)				**41**	**5**
H: 5 5 W: 10 01 b.Blackpool 28-10-96					
From AFC Fylde.					
2015–16	Barnsley	0	0		
2016–17	Barnsley	1	0		
2017–18	Barnsley	0	0	**1**	**0**
2017–18	*Chesterfield*	11	0	**11**	**0**
2020–21	Barrow	29	5	**29**	**5**

LILLIS, Josh (G)				**299**	**0**
H: 6 0 W: 12 08 b.Derby 24-6-87					
2006–07	Scunthorpe U	1	0		
2007–08	Scunthorpe U	3	0		
2008–09	Scunthorpe U	5	0		
2008–09	*Notts Co*	5	0	**5**	**0**
2009–10	Scunthorpe U	8	0		
2009–10	*Grimsby T*	4	0	**4**	**0**
2009–10	*Rochdale*	1	0		
2010–11	Scunthorpe U	15	0		
2010–11	*Rochdale*	23	0		
2011–12	Scunthorpe U	6	0	**38**	**0**
2012–13	Rochdale	46	0		
2013–14	Rochdale	45	0		
2014–15	Rochdale	16	0		
2015–16	Rochdale	40	0		
2016–17	Rochdale	14	0		
2017–18	Rochdale	40	0		
2018–19	Rochdale	27	0		
2019–20	Rochdale	0	0	**252**	**0**
2020–21	Barrow	0	0		

MALONEY, Scott (G)				**0**	**0**
2017–18	Bury	0	0		
2018–19	Bury	0	0		
2020–21	Barrow	0	0		

NDJOLI, Mikael (F)				**39**	**4**
b. 16-12-98					
From Millwall.					
2017–18	Bournemouth	0	0		
2018–19	Bournemouth	0	0		
2018–19	*Kilmarnock*	24	2	**24**	**2**
2019–20	Bournemouth	0	0		
2019–20	*Gillingham*	12	2	**12**	**2**
2019–20	*Motherwell*	1	0	**1**	**0**
2020–21	Barrow	2	0	**2**	**0**

NTLHE, Kgosietsile (D)				**177**	**8**
H: 5 9 W: 10 05 b.Pretoria 21-2-94					
Internationals: South Africa U20, Full caps.					
2010–11	Peterborough U	0	0		
2011–12	Peterborough U	2	0		
2012–13	Peterborough U	12	1		
2013–14	Peterborough U	27	2		
2014–15	Peterborough U	28	1		
2015–16	Peterborough U	7	0		
2016–17	Peterborough U	0	0	**76**	**4**
2016–17	Stevenage	22	0	**22**	**0**
2017–18	Rochdale	20	0		
2018–19	Rochdale	19	3	**39**	**3**
2019–20	Scunthorpe U	18	1	**18**	**1**
2020–21	Barrow	22	0	**22**	**0**

PENFOLD, Morgan (F)				**0**	**0**
2016–17	Peterborough U	0	0		
2017–18	Peterborough U	0	0		
2018–19	Peterborough U	0	0		
2020–21	Barrow	0	0		

PLATT, Matt (D)				**24**	**2**
b. 3-10-97					
2016–17	Blackburn R	0	0		
2017–18	Blackburn R	0	0		
2018–19	Blackburn R	0	0		
2018–19	*Accrington S*	0	0		
2019–20	Blackburn R	0	0		
2020–21	Barrow	24	2	**24**	**2**

QUIGLEY, Scott (F)				**58**	**15**
H: 6 4 W: 14 02 b. 2-9-92					
From The New Saints.					
2017–18	Blackpool	9	0		
2018–19	Blackpool	0	0	**9**	**0**
2018–19	*Port Vale*	11	0	**11**	**0**
2020–21	Barrow	38	15	**38**	**15**

SEA, Dimitri (F)				**8**	**0**
b.Paris 2-5-01					
2019–20	Aston Villa	0	0		
2020–21	Barrow	8	0	**8**	**0**

TAYLOR, Chris (M)				**437**	**42**
H: 5 11 W: 11 00 b.Oldham 20-12-86					
2005–06	Oldham Ath	14	0		
2006–07	Oldham Ath	44	4		
2007–08	Oldham Ath	42	5		
2008–09	Oldham Ath	42	10		
2009–10	Oldham Ath	32	1		
2010–11	Oldham Ath	42	11		
2011–12	Oldham Ath	38	2		
2012–13	Millwall	22	3		
2013–14	Blackburn R	34	0		
2014–15	Blackburn R	16	1		
2015–16	Blackburn R	12	0	**62**	**1**
2015–16	*Millwall*	10	3	**32**	**6**
2016–17	Bolton W	16	0		
2016–17	*Oldham Ath*	16	0	**270**	**33**
2017–18	Bolton W	0	0	**16**	**0**
2018–19	Blackpool	12	1	**12**	**1**
2019–20	Bradford C	14	0	**14**	**0**
2020–21	Barrow	31	1	**31**	**1**

TAYLOR, Jason (M)				**395**	**20**
H: 6 1 W: 11 03 b.Ashton-under-Lyne 28-1-87					
2005–06	Oldham Ath	0	0		
2005–06	*Stockport Co*	9	0		
2006–07	Stockport Co	45	1		
2007–08	Stockport Co	42	4		
2008–09	Stockport Co	8	1	**104**	**6**
2008–09	Rotherham U	15	1		
2009–10	Rotherham U	2	0		
2009–10	*Rochdale*	23	1	**23**	**1**
2010–11	Rotherham U	42	5		
2011–12	Rotherham U	39	2		
2012–13	Rotherham U	20	2	**118**	**10**
2012–13	Cheltenham T	16	0		
2013–14	Cheltenham T	33	2		
2014–15	Cheltenham T	16	0	**65**	**2**
2014–15	Northampton T	21	0		
2015–16	Northampton T	30	1	**51**	**1**
From Eastleigh, AFC Fylde.					
2020–21	Barrow	34	0	**34**	**0**

WILSON, Scott (D)				**9**	**0**
b.Burnley 10-1-00					
2018–19	Burnley	0	0		
2019–20	Burnley	0	0		
From Burnley.					
2020–21	Barrow	9	0	**9**	**0**

ZOUMA, Yoan (D)				**21**	**0**
b. 6-5-98					
2017–18	Angers	0	0		
2018–19	Angers	0	0		
2019–20	Bolton W	17	0		
2020–21	Bolton W	0	0	**17**	**0**
2020–21	Barrow	4	0	**4**	**0**

BIRMINGHAM C (7)

ANDRES, Prieto (G)				**4**	**0**
b.Alicante 17-10-93					
2012–13	Real Madrid	0	0		
2013–14	Real Madrid	0	0		
2014–15	Espanyol	0	0		
2015–16	Espanyol	0	0		
2016–17	Espanyol	0	0		
2017–18	Malaga	4	0		
2018–19	Malaga	0	0	**4**	**0**
2018–19	Leganes	0	0		
2019–20	Espanyol	0	0		
2020–21	Espanyol	0	0		
2020–21	Birmingham C	0	0		

ANDREWS, Josh (F)				**3**	**0**
b. 16-10-01					
2020–21	Birmingham C	0	0		
2020–21	*Harrogate T*	3	0	**3**	**0**

BAILEY, Odin (M)				**45**	**6**
b. 8-12-99					
Internationals: England U16.					
2017–18	Birmingham C	0	0		
2018–19	Birmingham C	0	0		
2019–20	Birmingham C	6	1		
2019–20	*Forest Green R*	5	1		
2020–21	Birmingham C	0	0	**6**	**1**
2020–21	*Forest Green R*	34	4	**39**	**5**

BELA, Jeremie (M)				**223**	**32**
b.Melun 8-4-93					
Internationals: France U16.					
2010–11	Lens	0	0		
2011–12	Lens	0	0		
2012–13	Lens	16	1		
2013–14	Lens	1	0	**17**	**1**
2013–14	Dijon	4	0		
2014–15	Dijon	33	6		
2015–16	Dijon	23	4		
2016–17	Dijon	14	0	**74**	**10**
2017–18	Albacete	33	5		

2018–19 Albacete 34 11
2019–20 Albacete 0 0 **67 16**
2019–20 Birmingham C 30 2
2020–21 Birmingham C 35 3 **65 5**

BOYD-MUNCE, Caolan (M) 7 0
b.Belfast 26-1-00
Internationals: Northern Ireland U16, U17, U19, U21.
From Glentoran.
2018–19 Birmingham C 0 0
2019–20 Birmingham C 6 0
2020–21 Birmingham C 1 0 **7 0**

CAMPBELL, Tate (M) 0 0
b.Birmingham 27-6-02
2020–21 Birmingham C 0 0

CLAYTON, Adam (M) 400 20
H: 5 9 W: 11 11 b.Manchester 14-1-89
Internationals: England U20.
2007–08 Manchester C 0 0
2008–09 Manchester C 0 0
2009–10 Manchester C 0 0
2009–10 *Carlisle U* 28 1 **28 1**
2010–11 Leeds U 4 0
2010–11 *Peterborough U* 7 0 **7 0**
2010–11 *Milton Keynes D* 6 1 **6 1**
2011–12 Leeds U 43 6 **47 6**
2012–13 Huddersfield T 43 4
2013–14 Huddersfield T 42 7 **85 11**
2014–15 Middlesbrough 41 0
2015–16 Middlesbrough 43 1
2016–17 Middlesbrough 34 0
2017–18 Middlesbrough 32 0
2018–19 Middlesbrough 36 0
2019–20 Middlesbrough 27 0
2020–21 Middlesbrough 0 0 **213 1**
2020–21 Birmingham C 14 0 **14 0**

COLIN, Maxime (D) 352 9
H: 5 11 W: 12 00 b.Arras 15-11-91
Internationals: France U20.
2010–11 Boulogne 26 0
2011–12 Boulogne 23 0
2012–13 Boulogne 4 0 **53 0**
2012–13 Troyes 18 0
2013–14 Troyes 35 0
2014–15 Troyes 2 0 **55 0**
2014–15 Anderlecht 17 1
2015–16 Anderlecht 1 0 **18 1**
2015–16 Brentford 21 0
2016–17 Brentford 38 4
2017–18 Brentford 3 0 **62 4**
2017–18 Birmingham C 35 2
2018–19 Birmingham C 43 0
2019–20 Birmingham C 44 1
2020–21 Birmingham C 42 1 **164 4**

COSGROVE, Sam (F) 99 32
b.Beverley 2-12-96
2014–15 Wigan Ath 0 0
2015–16 Wigan Ath 0 0
2016–17 Wigan Ath 0 0
2017–18 Carlisle U 8 1 **8 1**
2017–18 Aberdeen 5 0
2018–19 Aberdeen 35 17
2019–20 Aberdeen 25 11
2020–21 Aberdeen 14 3 **79 31**
2020–21 Birmingham C 12 0 **12 0**

CROWLEY, Daniel (M) 140 10
H: 5 9 W: 10 10 b.Coventry 3-8-97
Internationals: Republic of Ireland U16, U17. England U16, U17, U19.
From Aston Villa.
2015–16 Arsenal 0 0
2015–16 *Barnsley* 11 0 **11 0**
2016–17 Arsenal 0 0
2016–17 *Oxford U* 6 2 **6 2**
2016–17 *Go Ahead Eagles* 16 2 **16 2**
2017–18 Willem II 10 0
2018–19 Willem II 34 5 **44 5**
2019–20 Birmingham C 38 1
2020–21 Birmingham C 3 0 **41 1**
2020–21 *Hull C* 22 0 **22 0**

DACRES-COGLEY, Josh (D) 39 0
H: 5 9 W: 10 10 b.Coventry 12-3-96
2016–17 Birmingham C 14 0
2017–18 Birmingham C 3 0
2018–19 Birmingham C 1 0
2019–20 Birmingham C 0 0
2019–20 *Crawley T* 16 0 **16 0**
2020–21 Birmingham C 5 0 **23 0**

DEAN, Harlee (M) 385 15
H: 6 0 W: 11 10 b.Basingstoke 26-7-91
2008–09 Dagenham & R 0 0
2009–10 Dagenham & R 1 0 **1 0**
2010–11 Southampton 0 0
2011–12 Southampton 0 0
2011–12 *Brentford* 26 1
2012–13 Brentford 44 3
2013–14 Brentford 32 0
2014–15 Brentford 35 1
2015–16 Brentford 42 0
2016–17 Brentford 42 3
2017–18 Brentford 3 0 **224 8**
2017–18 Birmingham C 34 1
2018–19 Birmingham C 44 1
2019–20 Birmingham C 39 1
2020–21 Birmingham C 43 4 **160 7**

ETHERIDGE, Neil (G) 243 0
H: 6 3 W: 14 00 b.Enfield 7-2-90
Internationals: England U16. Philippines Full caps.
From Chelsea.
2008–09 Fulham 0 0
2009–10 Fulham 0 0
2010–11 Fulham 0 0
2011–12 Fulham 0 0
2012–13 Fulham 0 0
2012–13 *Bristol R* 12 0 **12 0**
2013–14 Fulham 0 0
2013–14 *Crewe Alex* 4 0 **4 0**
2014–15 Oldham Ath 0 0
2014–15 Charlton Ath 4 0 **4 0**
2015–16 Walsall 40 0
2016–17 Walsall 41 0 **81 0**
2017–18 Cardiff C 45 0
2018–19 Cardiff C 38 0
2019–20 Cardiff C 16 0
2020–21 Cardiff C 0 0 **99 0**
2020–21 Birmingham C 43 0 **43 0**

FRIEND, George (D) 391 12
H: 6 2 W: 13 01 b.Barnstaple 19-10-87
2008–09 Exeter C 4 0
2008–09 Wolverhampton W 6 0
2009–10 Wolverhampton W 1 0 **7 0**
2009–10 *Millwall* 6 0 **6 0**
2009–10 *Southend U* 6 1 **6 1**
2009–10 *Scunthorpe U* 4 0 **4 0**
2009–10 *Exeter C* 13 1 **17 1**
2010–11 Doncaster R 32 1
2011–12 Doncaster R 27 0
2012–13 Doncaster R 0 0 **59 1**
2012–13 Middlesbrough 34 0
2013–14 Middlesbrough 41 3
2014–15 Middlesbrough 42 1
2015–16 Middlesbrough 40 1
2016–17 Middlesbrough 24 0
2017–18 Middlesbrough 33 2
2018–19 Middlesbrough 38 2
2019–20 Middlesbrough 14 0
2020–21 Middlesbrough 0 0 **266 9**
2020–21 Birmingham C 26 0 **26 0**

GARDNER, Gary (M) 245 20
H: 6 2 W: 12 13 b.Solihull 29-6-92
Internationals: England U17, U19, U20, U21.
2009–10 Aston Villa 0 0
2010–11 Aston Villa 0 0
2011–12 Aston Villa 14 0
2011–12 *Coventry C* 4 1 **4 1**
2012–13 Aston Villa 2 0
2013–14 Aston Villa 0 0
2013–14 *Sheffield W* 3 0 **3 0**
2014–15 Aston Villa 0 0
2014–15 *Brighton & HA* 17 2 **17 2**
2014–15 Nottingham F 18 4
2015–16 Aston Villa 0 0
2015–16 *Nottingham F* 20 2 **38 6**
2016–17 Aston Villa 26 1
2017–18 Aston Villa 0 0
2017–18 *Barnsley* 29 2 **29 2**
2018–19 Aston Villa 0 0 **42 1**
2018–19 *Birmingham C* 40 2
2019–20 Birmingham C 35 4
2020–21 Birmingham C 37 2 **112 8**

GEORGE, Adan (F) 1 0
b. 30-7-02
From WBA.
2020–21 Birmingham C 1 0 **1 0**
2020–21 *Walsall* 0 0

GORDON, Nico (D) 4 0
b. 28-4-02
2019–20 Birmingham C 2 0
2020–21 Birmingham C 2 0 **4 0**

HALILOVIC, Alen (M) 172 14
b.Dubrovnik 18-6-96
2012–13 Dinamo Zagreb 18 2
2013–14 Dinamo Zagreb 26 5 **44 7**
2014–15 Barcelona 0 0
2015–16 Barcelona 0 0
2015–16 *Sporting Gijon* 36 3 **36 3**
2016–17 Hamburg 6 0
2016–17 *Las Palmas* 18 0
2017–18 Hamburg 0 0 **6 0**
2017–18 *Las Palmas* 20 2 **38 2**
2018–19 AC Milan 0 0
2018–19 *Standard Liege* 14 0 **14 0**
2019–20 AC Milan 0 0
2019–20 *Heerenveen* 17 1 **17 1**
2020–21 AC Milan 0 0
2020–21 Birmingham C 17 1 **17 1**

HOGAN, Scott (F) 193 64
H: 5 11 W: 10 01 b.Salford 13-4-92
Internationals: Republic of Ireland Full caps.
2009–10 Rochdale 0 0
From FC Halifax T, Stocksbridge PS, Ashton U, Hyde U.
2013–14 Rochdale 33 17 **33 17**
2014–15 Brentford 1 0
2015–16 Brentford 7 7
2016–17 Brentford 25 14 **33 21**
2016–17 Aston Villa 13 1
2017–18 Aston Villa 37 6
2018–19 Aston Villa 6 0
2018–19 *Sheffield U* 8 2 **8 2**
2019–20 Aston Villa 0 0
2019–20 *Stoke C* 13 3 **13 3**
2019–20 *Birmingham C* 17 7
2020–21 Aston Villa 0 0 **56 7**
2020–21 Birmingham C 33 7 **50 14**

HURST, Kyle (M) 0 0
b.Milton Keynes 20-1-02
2020–21 Birmingham C 0 0

HUTTON, Remeao (D) 26 0
b. 28-9-98
From Hednesford T.
2017–18 Birmingham C 0 0
2018–19 Birmingham C 0 0
2019–20 Birmingham C 0 0
2020–21 Birmingham C 0 0
2020–21 *Stevenage* 26 0 **26 0**

IVAN SANCHEZ, Aguayo (M) 189 12
b. 23-9-92
2014–15 Almeria 0 0
2015–16 Almeria 24 0
2016–17 Almeria 9 0 **33 0**
2016–17 *Albacete* 14 1
2017–18 Albacete 0 0 **14 1**
2017–18 *Elche* 29 1
2018–19 Elche 36 7
2019–20 Elche 37 1
2020–21 Elche 0 0 **102 9**
2020–21 Birmingham C 40 2 **40 2**

JEACOCK, Zach (G) 2 0
b.Birmingham 8-5-01
2020–21 Birmingham C 2 0 **2 0**

JUTKIEWICZ, Lucas (F) 473 106
H: 6 1 W: 12 11 b.Southampton 20-3-89
2005–06 Swindon T 5 0
2006–07 Swindon T 33 5 **38 5**
2006–07 Everton 0 0
2007–08 Everton 0 0
2007–08 *Plymouth Arg* 3 0 **3 0**
2008–09 Everton 1 0
2008–09 *Huddersfield T* 7 0 **7 0**
2009–10 Everton 0 0 **1 0**
2009–10 *Motherwell* 33 12 **33 12**
2010–11 Coventry C 42 9
2011–12 Coventry C 25 9 **67 18**
2011–12 Middlesbrough 19 2
2012–13 Middlesbrough 24 8
2013–14 Middlesbrough 22 1 **65 11**
2013–14 *Bolton W* 20 7 **20 7**
2014–15 Burnley 25 0
2015–16 Burnley 5 0
2016–17 Burnley 2 0 **32 0**
2016–17 Birmingham C 38 11
2017–18 Birmingham C 35 5
2018–19 Birmingham C 46 14
2019–20 Birmingham C 46 15
2020–21 Birmingham C 42 8 **207 53**

LAKIN, Charlie (M) 49 5
b.Solihull 8-5-99
2017–18 Birmingham C 0 0
2018–19 Birmingham C 10 0
2019–20 Birmingham C 0 0
2019–20 *Stevenage* 20 2 **20 2**
2020–21 Birmingham C 0 0 **10 0**
2020–21 *Ross Co* 19 3 **19 3**

LEKO, Jonathan (M) 82 5
H: 6 0 W: 11 11 b.Kinshasa 24-4-99
Internationals: England U16, U17, U18, U19, U20.
2015–16 WBA 5 0
2016–17 WBA 9 0
2017–18 Bristol C 11 0 **11 0**
2017–18 WBA 0 0
2018–19 WBA 2 0
2019–20 WBA 0 0 **16 0**
2019–20 *Charlton Ath* 21 5 **21 5**
2020–21 Birmingham C 34 0 **34 0**

McGREE, Riley (M) **94 24**
b.Gawler 2-11-98
2015–16 Adelaide U 1 0
2016–17 Adelaide U 16 1
2017–18 Club Brugge 0 0
2017–18 *Newcastle Jets* 12 5 **12 5**
2018–19 Club Brugge 0 0
2018–19 *Melbourne C* 27 7 **27 7**
2019–20 Adelaide U 23 10 **40 11**
2020–21 Charlotte 0 0
On loan from Charlotte.
2020–21 Birmingham C 15 1 **15 1**

MEDINA, Agus (M) **134 16**
b.Barbera del Valles 8-9-94
2014–15 Sabadell 7 0
2015–16 Sabadell 30 3 **37 3**
2016–17 Celta Vigo 0 0
2017–18 Celta Vigo 0 0
2018–19 Cornella 35 3
2019–20 Birmingham C 1 0
2019–20 *Cornella* 35 3
2020–21 Birmingham C 0 0 **1 0**
2020–21 *Cornella* 26 7 **96 13**

MILLER, Amari (M) **5 0**
b. 4-11-02
2020–21 Birmingham C 5 0 **5 0**

PEDERSEN, Kristian (D) **237 10**
H: 6 2 W: 13 01 b.Ringsted 4-8-94
Internationals: Denmark U21.
2014–15 HB Koge 28 1
2015–16 HB Koge 30 1 **58 2**
2016–17 Union Berlin 29 0
2017–18 Union Berlin 32 1 **61 1**
2018–19 Birmingham C 39 1
2019–20 Birmingham C 44 4
2020–21 Birmingham C 35 2 **118 7**

PRIETO, Andres (G) **4 0**
H: 6 4 W: 14 07 b.Alicante 17-10-93
2012–13 Real Madrid 0 0
2013–14 Real Madrid 0 0
2014–15 Espanyol 0 0
2015–16 Espanyol 0 0
2016–17 Espanyol 0 0
2017–18 Malaga 4 0
2018–19 Malaga 0 0 **4 0**
2018–19 Leganes 0 0
2019–20 Espanyol 0 0
2020–21 Birmingham C 0 0

REID, Jayden (F) **15 0**
b. 22-4-01
From Swansea C.
2019–20 Birmingham C 4 0
2020–21 Birmingham C 0 0 **4 0**
2020–21 *Barrow* 10 0 **10 0**
2020–21 *Walsall* 1 0 **1 0**

ROBERTS, Marc (D) **180 10**
H: 6 0 W: 12 11 b.Wakefield 26-7-90
Internationals: England C.
From FC Halifax T.
2014–15 Barnsley 0 0
2015–16 Barnsley 32 1
2016–17 Barnsley 40 4 **72 5**
2017–18 Birmingham C 30 1
2018–19 Birmingham C 8 0
2019–20 Birmingham C 34 0
2020–21 Birmingham C 36 4 **108 5**

ROBERTS, Mitchell (D) **4 0**
b. 16-9-00
2020–21 Birmingham C 0 0
2020–21 *Harrogate T* 4 0 **4 0**

SAN JOSE, Mikel (D) **331 27**
b.Bilbao 30-5-89
2007–08 Liverpool 0 0
2008–09 Liverpool 0 0
2009–10 *Athletic Bilbao* 25 1
2010–11 Athletic Bilbao 31 2
2011–12 Athletic Bilbao 24 2
2012–13 Athletic Bilbao 34 5
2013–14 Athletic Bilbao 25 5
2014–15 Athletic Bilbao 28 5
2015–16 Athletic Bilbao 34 2
2016–17 Athletic Bilbao 35 4
2017–18 Athletic Bilbao 26 1
2018–19 Athletic Bilbao 33 0
2019–20 Athletic Bilbao 9 0
2020–21 Athletic Bilbao 0 0 **304 27**
2020–21 Birmingham C 27 0 **27 0**

SEDDON, Steve (D) **80 8**
b.Reading 25-12-97
2017–18 Birmingham C 0 0
2018–19 Birmingham C 0 0
2018–19 *Stevenage* 23 3 **23 3**
2018–19 *AFC Wimbledon* 18 3
2019–20 Birmingham C 4 0
2019–20 *Portsmouth* 12 1 **12 1**
2020–21 Birmingham C 7 0 **11 0**
2020–21 *AFC Wimbledon* 16 1 **34 4**

SIMMONDS, Keyendrah (F) **1 0**
b. 31-5-01
2020–21 Birmingham C 1 0 **1 0**

SOLDEVILA, Oriol (M) **0 0**
H: 6 1 b.Barcelona 26-3-01
Internationals: Spain U16, U18.
From Barcelona.
2020–21 Birmingham C 0 0

STIRK, Ryan (M) **2 0**
b. 25-9-00
Internationals: Wales U17, U19.
2019–20 Birmingham C 0 0
2020–21 Birmingham C 2 0 **2 0**

SUNJIC, Ivan (M) **170 10**
b.Zenica 9-10-96
Internationals: Croatia U16, U17, U18, U19, U21, Full caps.
2013–14 Dinamo Zagreb 1 0
2014–15 Dinamo Zagreb 0 0
2015–16 Dinamo Zagreb 0 0
2015–16 Lokomativa 10 0
2016–17 Lokomativa 23 1
2017–18 Lokomativa 29 6 **62 7**
2018–19 Dinamo Zagreb 24 0 **25 0**
2019–20 Birmingham C 40 3
2020–21 Birmingham C 43 0 **83 3**

THOMPSON-SOMMERS, Kane (M) **0 0**
b.London 1-12-00
From Tottenham H.
2020–21 Birmingham C 0 0

TORAL, Jon (M) **152 19**
H: 6 0 W: 12 07 b.Reus 5-2-95
From Barcelona.
2013–14 Arsenal 0 0
2014–15 Arsenal 0 0
2014–15 *Brentford* 34 6 **34 6**
2015–16 Arsenal 0 0
2015–16 *Birmingham C* 36 8
2016–17 Arsenal 0 0
2016–17 *Granada* 5 0 **5 0**
2016–17 *Rangers* 12 2 **12 2**
2017–18 Hull C 27 1
2018–19 Hull C 8 0
2019–20 Hull C 14 0 **49 1**
2020–21 Birmingham C 16 2 **52 10**

TRUEMAN, Connal (G) **36 0**
H: 6 1 W: 11 10 b.Birmingham 26-3-96
2014–15 Birmingham C 0 0
2014–15 *Oldham Ath* 0 0
2015–16 Birmingham C 0 0
2016–17 Birmingham C 0 0
2017–18 Birmingham C 0 0
2018–19 Birmingham C 2 0
2019–20 Birmingham C 10 0
2020–21 Birmingham C 1 0 **13 0**
2020–21 *AFC Wimbledon* 19 0 **19 0**
2020–21 *Swindon T* 4 0 **4 0**

Scholars
Barratt, Connor James; Brooks, Alfie Joe; Browne, Rico Franklin; Chang, Alfie James; Clayton, Aaron Edwin Thomas; Craig, Kade Elliott James; Djurovic, Daniel Ray; Dugmore, Joshua Wayne; Fogarty, Tommy Patrick; Hall, George Cardinal Joseph; Hamilton, Harley Farrell; James, Jordan Anthony; Manton, Harry James; Miller, Amari Miquel; Nguepissi, Cianole Nguepissi; Noakes, Charlie Andrew John; Oakley, Marcel Errol Emmanuel; Patterson, Rico Amani; Rouse, Elias James; Sullivan, Callum John; Wakefield, Kieran Lee; Walker, Remi Ian; Williams, Joshua Aaron; Zohore, Yoane.

BLACKBURN R (8)

ANNESLEY, Louie (D) **0 0**
b.St Helier 3-5-00
Internationals: Gibraltar U16, U17, U19, U21, Full caps.
From Lincoln Red Imps.
2020–21 Blackburn R 0 0

ARMSTRONG, Adam (F) **262 85**
H: 5 8 W: 10 12 b.Newcastle upon Tyne 10-2-97
Internationals: England U16, U17, U18, U19, U20, U21.
2013–14 Newcastle U 4 0
2014–15 Newcastle U 11 0
2015–16 Newcastle U 0 0
2015–16 *Coventry C* 40 20 **40 20**
2016–17 Newcastle U 2 0
2016–17 *Barnsley* 34 6 **34 6**
2017–18 Newcastle U 0 0 **17 0**
2017–18 *Bolton W* 20 1 **20 1**
2017–18 *Blackburn R* 21 9
2018–19 Blackburn R 44 5
2019–20 Blackburn R 46 16
2020–21 Blackburn R 40 28 **151 58**

AYALA, Daniel (M) **252 23**
H: 6 3 W: 13 03 b.Sevilla 7-11-90
Internationals: Spain U21.
From Sevilla.
2007–08 Liverpool 0 0
2008–09 Liverpool 0 0
2009–10 Liverpool 5 0
2010–11 Liverpool 0 0 **5 0**
2010–11 *Hull C* 12 1 **12 1**
2010–11 *Derby Co* 17 0 **17 0**
2011–12 Norwich C 7 0
2012–13 Norwich C 0 0
2012–13 *Nottingham F* 12 1 **12 1**
2013–14 Norwich C 0 0 **7 0**
2013–14 Middlesbrough 19 3
2014–15 Middlesbrough 30 4
2015–16 Middlesbrough 35 3
2016–17 Middlesbrough 14 1
2017–18 Middlesbrough 33 7
2018–19 Middlesbrough 33 1
2019–20 Middlesbrough 25 2 **189 21**
2020–21 Blackburn R 10 0 **10 0**

BARNES, Samuel (D) **0 0**
b.Blackburn 10-3-01
2020–21 Blackburn R 0 0

BELL, Amari (D) **223 9**
H: 5 11 W: 12 00 b.Burton-upon-Trent 5-5-94
2012–13 Birmingham C 0 0
2013–14 Birmingham C 1 0
2014–15 Birmingham C 0 0 **1 0**
2014–15 *Swindon T* 10 0 **10 0**
2014–15 *Gillingham* 7 0 **7 0**
2015–16 Fleetwood T 44 0
2016–17 Fleetwood T 44 2
2017–18 Fleetwood T 27 4 **115 6**
2017–18 Blackburn R 12 0
2018–19 Blackburn R 38 3
2019–20 Blackburn R 21 0
2020–21 Blackburn R 19 0 **90 3**

BENNETT, Elliott (M) **430 28**
H: 5 9 W: 10 11 b.Telford 18-12-88
2006–07 Wolverhampton W 0 0
2007–08 Wolverhampton W 0 0
2007–08 *Crewe Alex* 9 1 **9 1**
2007–08 *Bury* 19 1
2008–09 Wolverhampton W 0 0
2008–09 *Bury* 46 3 **65 4**
2009–10 Wolverhampton W 0 0
2009–10 *Brighton & HA* 43 7
2010–11 Brighton & HA 46 6
2011–12 Norwich C 33 1
2012–13 Norwich C 24 1
2013–14 Norwich C 2 0
2014–15 Norwich C 9 0
2014–15 *Brighton & HA* 7 0 **96 13**
2015–16 Norwich C 0 0 **68 2**
2015–16 *Bristol C* 15 0 **15 0**
2015–16 Blackburn R 21 2
2016–17 Blackburn R 25 3
2017–18 Blackburn R 41 2
2018–19 Blackburn R 40 1
2019–20 Blackburn R 41 0
2020–21 Blackburn R 9 0 **177 8**

BRENNAN, Luke (M) **1 0**
b. 19-10-01
2020–21 Blackburn R 1 0 **1 0**

BRERETON, Ben (F) **133 17**
b.Stoke-on-Trent 18-4-99
Internationals: England U19, U20.
From Stoke C.
2016–17 Nottingham F 18 3
2017–18 Nottingham F 35 5 **53 8**
2018–19 Blackburn R 25 1
2019–20 Blackburn R 15 1
2020–21 Blackburn R 40 7 **80 9**

BUCKLEY, John (M) **50 3**
b. 13-10-99
2018–19 Blackburn R 2 0
2019–20 Blackburn R 20 2
2020–21 Blackburn R 28 1 **50 3**

BURNS, Samuel (F) **0 0**
b. 9-8-02
2020–21 Blackburn R 0 0

BUTTERWORTH, Daniel (F) **2 0**
H: 5 11 W: 10 12 b.Manchester 14-9-94
From Manchester U.
2017–18 Blackburn R 0 0

2018–19 Blackburn R 1 0
2019–20 Blackburn R 0 0
2020–21 Blackburn R 1 0 2 0

CARTER, Hayden (D) 27 4
b. 17-12-99
From Manchester C.
2019–20 Blackburn R 2 0
2020–21 Blackburn R 1 0 3 0
2020–21 *Burton Alb* 24 4 24 4

CHAPMAN, Harry (M) 70 10
H: 5 10 W: 11 00 b.Hartlepool 5-11-97
Internationals: England U18, U20.
2015–16 Middlesbrough 0 0
2015–16 *Barnsley* 11 1 11 1
2016–17 Middlesbrough 0 0
2016–17 *Sheffield U* 12 1 12 1
2017–18 Middlesbrough 0 0
2017–18 *Blackburn R* 12 1
2018–19 Middlesbrough 0 0
2018–19 *Blackburn R* 2 0
2019–20 Blackburn R 5 0
2020–21 Blackburn R 5 0 24 1
2020–21 *Shrewsbury T* 23 7 23 7

DACK, Bradley (M) 282 76
H: 5 9 b.Greenwich 31-12-93
2012–13 Gillingham 16 1
2013–14 Gillingham 28 3
2014–15 Gillingham 42 9
2015–16 Gillingham 40 13
2016–17 Gillingham 34 5 160 31
2017–18 Blackburn R 42 18
2018–19 Blackburn R 42 15
2019–20 Blackburn R 22 9
2020–21 Blackburn R 16 3 122 45

DAVENPORT, Jacob (M) 42 2
b.Manchester 28-12-98
2017–18 Manchester C 0 0
2017–18 *Burton Alb* 17 1 17 1
2018–19 Blackburn R 1 0
2019–20 Blackburn R 9 0
2020–21 Blackburn R 15 1 25 1

DOLAN, Tyrhys (M) 37 3
b.Manchester 21-12-98
2020–21 Blackburn R 37 3 37 3

DOWNING, Stewart (M) 597 50
H: 5 11 W: 10 04 b.Middlesbrough 22-7-84
Internationals: England U21, B, Full caps.
2001–02 Middlesbrough 3 0
2002–03 Middlesbrough 2 0
2003–04 Middlesbrough 20 0
2003–04 *Sunderland* 7 3 7 3
2004–05 Middlesbrough 35 5
2005–06 Middlesbrough 12 1
2006–07 Middlesbrough 34 2
2007–08 Middlesbrough 38 9
2008–09 Middlesbrough 37 0
2009–10 Aston Villa 25 2
2010–11 Aston Villa 38 7 63 9
2011–12 Liverpool 36 0
2012–13 Liverpool 29 3
2013–14 Liverpool 0 0 65 3
2013–14 West Ham U 32 1
2014–15 West Ham U 37 6 69 7
2015–16 Middlesbrough 45 3
2016–17 Middlesbrough 30 1
2017–18 Middlesbrough 40 3
2018–19 Middlesbrough 38 2 334 26
2019–20 Blackburn R 41 2
2020–21 Blackburn R 18 0 59 2

EASTHAM, Jordan (G) 0 0
b. 8-9-01
2019–20 Blackburn R 0 0
2020–21 Blackburn R 0 0

EVANS, Corry (M) 300 10
H: 5 8 W: 10 12 b.Belfast 30-7-90
Internationals: Northern Ireland U16, U17, U19, U21, B, Full caps.
2007–08 Manchester U 0 0
2008–09 Manchester U 0 0
2009–10 Manchester U 0 0
2010–11 Manchester U 0 0
2010–11 *Carlisle U* 1 0 1 0
2010–11 *Hull C* 18 3
2011–12 Hull C 43 2
2012–13 Hull C 32 1
2013–14 Hull C 0 0 93 6
2013–14 Blackburn R 21 1
2014–15 Blackburn R 38 1
2015–16 Blackburn R 30 1
2016–17 Blackburn R 19 0
2017–18 Blackburn R 32 0
2018–19 Blackburn R 35 0
2019–20 Blackburn R 13 1
2020–21 Blackburn R 18 0 206 4

GALLAGHER, Sam (F) 192 32
H: 6 4 W: 11 11 b.Crediton 15-9-95
Internationals: Scotland U19, England U19, U20.
From Plymouth Arg.
2013–14 Southampton 18 1
2014–15 Southampton 0 0
2015–16 Southampton 0 0
2015–16 *Milton Keynes D* 13 0 13 0
2016–17 Southampton 0 0
2016–17 *Blackburn R* 43 11
2017–18 Southampton 0 0
2017–18 *Birmingham C* 33 6 33 6
2018–19 Southampton 4 0 22 1
2019–20 Blackburn R 42 6
2020–21 Blackburn R 39 8 124 25

GARRETT, Jake (D) 0 0
b. 10-3-03
Internationals: England U16.
2020–21 Blackburn R 0 0

GRAYSON, Joe (M) 12 2
H: 5 10 W: 11 09 b. 26-3-99
2018–19 Blackburn R 0 0
2018–19 *Grimsby T* 8 2 8 2
2019–20 Blackburn R 0 0
2020–21 Blackburn R 0 0
2020–21 *Oxford U* 4 0 4 0

HILTON, Joe (G) 2 0
b. 11-10-99
From Manchester C.
2018–19 Everton 0 0
2019–20 Blackburn R 0 0
2020–21 Blackburn R 0 0
2020–21 *Fleetwood T* 2 0 2 0
2020–21 *Ross Co* 0 0

HOLTBY, Lewis (M) 351 43
H: 5 8 W: 10 04 b.Erkelenz 18-9-90
Internationals: Germany U18, U19, U20, U21, Full caps.
2007–08 Alemania Aachen 2 0
2008–09 Alemania Aachen 31 8 33 8
2009–10 Schalke 04 9 0
2009–10 *VfL Bochum* 14 2 14 2
2010–11 *Mainz* 30 4 30 4
2011–12 Schalke 04 27 6
2012–13 Schalke 04 19 4 55 10
2012–13 Tottenham H 11 0
2013–14 Tottenham H 13 1
2013–14 *Fulham* 13 1 13 1
2014–15 Tottenham H 1 0 25 1
2014–15 *Hamburg* 22 0
2015–16 Hamburg 34 3
2016–17 Hamburg 29 1
2017–18 Hamburg 16 6
2018–19 Hamburg 26 4 127 14
2019–20 Blackburn R 27 3
2020–21 Blackburn R 27 0 54 3

JOHNSON, Bradley (M) 512 68
H: 6 0 W: 12 10 b.Hackney 28-4-87
2004–05 Cambridge U 1 0 1 0
2005–06 Northampton T 3 0
2006–07 Northampton T 27 5
2007–08 Northampton T 23 2 53 7
2007–08 Leeds U 21 3
2008–09 Leeds U 15 1
2008–09 *Brighton & HA* 10 4 10 4
2009–10 Leeds U 36 7
2010–11 Leeds U 45 5 117 16
2011–12 Norwich C 28 2
2012–13 Norwich C 37 1
2013–14 Norwich C 32 3
2014–15 Norwich C 41 15
2015–16 Norwich C 4 0 142 21
2015–16 Derby Co 31 5
2016–17 Derby Co 33 3
2017–18 Derby Co 33 4
2018–19 Derby Co 28 2 125 14
2019–20 Blackburn R 34 3
2020–21 Blackburn R 30 3 64 6

KAMINSKI, Thomas (G) 283 0
b.Dendermonde 23-10-92
2008–09 Beerschot 2 0
2009–10 Beerschot 4 0
2010–11 Beerschot 30 0
2011–12 Beerschot 2 0 38 0
2011–12 OH Leuven 25 0 25 0
2012–13 Anderlecht 1 0
2013–14 Anderlecht 10 0
2014–15 Anderlecht 2 0
2014–15 *Anorthosis Famagusta* 30 0 30 0
2015–16 Anderlecht 0 0 13 0
2015–16 *FC Copenhagen* 2 0 2 0
2016–17 Kortrijk 32 0
2017–18 Kortrijk 34 0
2018–19 Kortrijk 18 0 84 0
2018–19 Gent 19 0
2019–20 Gent 29 0
2020–21 Gent 0 0 48 0
2020–21 Blackburn R 43 0 43 0

LENIHAN, Darragh (M) 209 7
H: 5 10 W: 12 00 b.Dublin 16-3-94
Internationals: Republic of Ireland U17, U19, U21, Full caps.
2011–12 Blackburn R 0 0
2012–13 Blackburn R 0 0
2013–14 Blackburn R 0 0
2014–15 Blackburn R 3 0
2014–15 *Burton Alb* 17 1 17 1
2015–16 Blackburn R 23 0
2016–17 Blackburn R 40 0
2017–18 Blackburn R 14 1
2018–19 Blackburn R 34 2
2019–20 Blackburn R 37 3
2020–21 Blackburn R 41 0 192 6

LYONS, Brad (F) 29 2
b. 26-5-97
From Coleraine.
2018–19 Blackburn R 0 0
2018–19 *St Mirren* 15 1 15 1
2019–20 Blackburn R 0 0
2020–21 Blackburn R 0 0
2020–21 *Morecambe* 14 1 14 1

MAGLIORE, Tyler (D) 14 0
b. 21-12-98
2018–19 Blackburn R 2 0
2019–20 Blackburn R 0 0
2019–20 *Rochdale* 2 0 2 0
2020–21 Blackburn R 0 0 2 0
2020–21 *Motherwell* 10 0 10 0

McBRIDE, Connor (F) 0 0
b.Falkirk 20-3-01
From Falkirk, Celtic.
2020–21 Blackburn R 0 0

MULGREW, Charlie (D) 378 60
H: 6 3 W: 13 01 b.Glasgow 6-3-86
Internationals: Scotland U21, Full caps.
2002–03 Celtic 0 0
2003–04 Celtic 0 0
2004–05 Celtic 0 0
2005–06 Celtic 0 0
2005–06 *Dundee U* 13 2 13 2
2006–07 Wolverhampton W 6 0
2007–08 Wolverhampton W 0 0 6 0
2007–08 *Southend U* 18 1 18 1
2008–09 Aberdeen 35 5
2009–10 Aberdeen 37 4 72 9
2010–11 Celtic 23 0
2011–12 Celtic 30 8
2012–13 Celtic 30 5
2013–14 Celtic 28 6
2014–15 Celtic 10 0
2015–16 Celtic 13 1 134 20
2016–17 Blackburn R 28 3
2017–18 Blackburn R 41 14
2018–19 Blackburn R 29 10
2019–20 Blackburn R 2 0
2019–20 *Wigan Ath* 12 0 12 0
2020–21 Blackburn R 0 0 100 27
2020–21 *Fleetwood T* 23 1 23 1

NOLAN, Joseph (M) 0 0
b. 25-3-02
2020–21 Blackburn R 0 0

NYAMBE, Ryan (D) 152 0
H: 6 0 W: 12 00 b.Katima Mulilo 4-12-97
Internationals: Namibia Full caps.
2014–15 Blackburn R 0 0
2015–16 Blackburn R 0 0
2016–17 Blackburn R 25 0
2017–18 Blackburn R 29 0
2018–19 Blackburn R 29 0
2019–20 Blackburn R 31 0
2020–21 Blackburn R 38 0 152 0

PEARS, Aynsley (G) 27 0
b. 23-4-98
Internationals: England U19.
2017–18 Middlesbrough 0 0
2018–19 Middlesbrough 0 0
2019–20 Middlesbrough 24 0 24 0
2020–21 Blackburn R 3 0 3 0

PICKERING, Harry (M) 146 9
H: 6 1 W: 12 04 b. 29-12-98
2017–18 Crewe Alex 35 3
2018–19 Crewe Alex 32 0
2019–20 Crewe Alex 35 3
2020–21 Blackburn R 0 0
2020–21 *Crewe Alex* 44 3 146 9

PIKE, Dan (D) 0 0
b. 9-1-02
2020–21 Blackburn R 0 0

RANKIN-COSTELLO, Joe (M) 25 0
H: 5 10 W: 11 00 b.Stockport 26-7-99
From Manchester U.
2017–18 Blackburn R 0 0
2018–19 Blackburn R 0 0
2019–20 Blackburn R 11 0
2020–21 Blackburn R 14 0 **25 0**

ROTHWELL, Joe (M) 184 13
H: 6 1 W: 12 02 b.Manchester 11-1-95
Internationals: England U16, U17, U19, U20.
2014–15 Manchester U 0 0
2014–15 *Blackpool* 3 0 **3 0**
2015–16 Manchester U 0 0
2015–16 *Barnsley* 4 0 **4 0**
2016–17 Oxford U 33 1
2017–18 Oxford U 36 5 **69 6**
2018–19 Blackburn R 33 2
2019–20 Blackburn R 36 2
2020–21 Blackburn R 39 3 **108 7**

SAADI, Jalil (M) 0 0
H: 6 3 b. 3-11-01
From Toulouse.
2020–21 Blackburn R 0 0

STERGIAKIS, Antonios (G) 61 0
b. 16-3-99
From Thyella Filota.
2015–16 Slavia Sofia 0 0
2016–17 Slavia Sofia 8 0
2017–18 Slavia Sofia 22 0
2018–19 Slavia Sofia 17 0
2019–20 Slavia Sofia 14 0
2020–21 Slavia Sofia 0 0 **61 0**
2020–21 Blackburn R 0 0

TRAVIS, Lewis (D) 93 3
b. 16-10-97
2016–17 Blackburn R 0 0
2017–18 Blackburn R 5 0
2018–19 Blackburn R 26 1
2019–20 Blackburn R 43 2
2020–21 Blackburn R 19 0 **93 3**

VALE, Jack (F) 4 0
b. 3-3-01
Internationals: Wales U17, U19, U21.
From The New Saints.
2019–20 Blackburn R 1 0
2020–21 Blackburn R 0 0 **1 0**
2020–21 *Rochdale* 3 0 **3 0**

WHARTON, Scott (D) 90 9
b.Blackburn 3-10-97
2015–16 Blackburn R 0 0
2016–17 Blackburn R 2 0
2016–17 *Cambridge U* 9 1 **9 1**
2017–18 Blackburn R 0 0
2017–18 *Lincoln C* 14 2
2018–19 Blackburn R 0 0
2018–19 *Lincoln C* 11 1 **25 3**
2018–19 *Bury* 15 2 **15 2**
2019–20 Blackburn R 0 0
2019–20 *Northampton T* 32 3 **32 3**
2020–21 Blackburn R 7 0 **9 0**

WHITE, Tom (M) 9 0
b. 9-5-97
From Gateshead.
2020–21 Blackburn R 0 0
2020–21 *Bolton W* 9 0 **9 0**

WHITEHALL, Isaac (M) 0 0
b. 29-3-02
2020–21 Blackburn R 0 0

WILLIAMS, Derrick (D) 250 10
H: 5 11 W: 11 11 b.Waterford 17-1-93
Internationals: Republic of Ireland U19, U21, Full caps.
2009–10 Aston Villa 0 0
2010–11 Aston Villa 0 0
2011–12 Aston Villa 0 0
2012–13 Aston Villa 1 0 **1 0**
2013–14 Bristol C 43 1
2014–15 Bristol C 44 2
2015–16 Bristol C 24 1 **111 4**
2016–17 Blackburn R 39 1
2017–18 Blackburn R 45 1
2018–19 Blackburn R 27 0
2019–20 Blackburn R 17 3
2020–21 Blackburn R 10 1 **138 6**
Transferred to LA Galaxy March 2021.

Scholars
Baker, Alexander John William; Cirino, Lenni Rae Rowan; Connolly, James Alfred; Cunningham, Evan William; Dowling, Aidan Paul Harvey; Ferguson, Joseph Martua; Fyles, Ben William; Gamble, Patrick; Gent, Georgie Simon; Gilsenan, Zak Thomas; Goddard, Felix Benjamin; Haddow, Jay; Harlock, Jared Alan; Leonard, Harry Paul; Lonsdale, Brandon Lee James; Montgomery, Kristi Julian; Pleavin, Ben Spencer; Pratt, George Christopher John; Weston, Charlie Daniel; Wharton, Adam James; Wood, Harrison Jack; Wyatt, George Ray.

BLACKPOOL (9)

ANDERSON, Keshi (F) 146 24
H: 5 9 W: 10 10 b.Luton 15-11-95
2014–15 Crystal Palace 0 0
2015–16 Crystal Palace 0 0
2015–16 *Doncaster R* 7 3 **7 3**
2016–17 Crystal Palace 0 0
2016–17 *Bolton W* 8 1 **8 1**
2016–17 *Northampton T* 14 3 **14 3**
2017–18 Swindon T 37 5
2018–19 Swindon T 43 4
2019–20 Swindon T 20 6 **100 15**
2020–21 Blackpool 17 2 **17 2**

ANTWI, Cameron (M) 0 0
b. 7-10-01
From Fulham.
2020–21 Blackpool 0 0

APTER, Robert (M) 1 0
b. 16-1-03
2020–21 Blackpool 1 0 **1 0**

BANGE, Ewan (M) 0 0
2019–20 Blackpool 0 0
2020–21 Blackpool 0 0

DOUGALL, Kenneth (M) 217 14
H: 6 0 W: 12 06 b.Brisbane 7-5-93
Internationals: Australia U23.
2013–14 Brisbane C 34 10 **34 10**
2014–15 Telstar 29 1 **29 1**
2015–16 Sparta Rotterdam 32 0
2016–17 Sparta Rotterdam 20 1
2017–18 Sparta Rotterdam 29 1 **81 2**
2018–19 Barnsley 27 0
2019–20 Barnsley 12 0 **39 0**
2020–21 Blackpool 34 1 **34 1**

EKPITETA, Marvin (D) 55 2
b. 26-8-95
Internationals: Nigeria U20. England C.
From Chelmsford C, Concord Rangers, East Thurrock U.
2019–20 Leyton Orient 27 0 **27 0**
2020–21 Blackpool 28 2 **28 2**

FEENEY, Liam (M) 440 30
H: 5 10 W: 12 02 b.Hammersmith 21-1-87
From Hayes, Salisbury C.
2008–09 Southend U 1 0 **1 0**
2008–09 Bournemouth 14 3
2009–10 Bournemouth 44 5
2010–11 Bournemouth 46 4
2011–12 Bournemouth 5 0 **109 12**
2011–12 Millwall 34 4
2012–13 Millwall 22 1
2013–14 Millwall 17 0 **73 5**
2013–14 *Bolton W* 4 0
2013–14 *Blackburn R* 6 0
2014–15 Bolton W 41 3
2015–16 Bolton W 37 5 **82 8**
2015–16 *Ipswich T* 9 1 **9 1**
2016–17 Blackburn R 34 0
2017–18 Blackburn R 1 0 **41 0**
2017–18 *Cardiff C* 15 0 **15 0**
2018–19 Blackpool 34 0
2019–20 Blackpool 35 1
2020–21 Blackpool 0 0 **69 1**
2020–21 *Tranmere R* 41 3 **41 3**

FOJTICEK, Alex (G) 0 0
b.Presov 3-3-00
From Tatran Presov, Manchester U.
2020–21 Blackpool 0 0

GARBUTT, Luke (D) 175 18
H: 5 10 W: 11 07 b.Harrogate 21-5-93
Internationals: England U16, U17, U18, U19, U20, U21.
From Leeds U.
2010–11 Everton 0 0
2011–12 Everton 0 0
2011–12 *Cheltenham T* 34 2 **34 2**
2012–13 Everton 0 0
2013–14 Everton 1 0
2013–14 *Colchester U* 19 2 **19 2**
2014–15 Everton 4 0
2015–16 Everton 0 0
2015–16 *Fulham* 25 1 **25 1**
2016–17 Everton 0 0
2016–17 *Wigan Ath* 8 0 **8 0**
2017–18 Everton 0 0
2018–19 Everton 0 0
2018–19 *Oxford U* 25 4 **25 4**
2019–20 Everton 0 0 **5 0**
2019–20 *Ipswich T* 28 5 **28 5**
2020–21 Blackpool 31 4 **31 4**

GARRITY, Ben (M) 29 2
b. 21-2-97
From Warrington T.
2019–20 Blackpool 0 0
2020–21 Blackpool 0 0
2020–21 *Oldham Ath* 29 2 **29 2**

GRETARSSON, Daniel (D) 166 10
b. 2-10-95
2012 Grindavik 6 1
2013 Grindavik 21 3
2014 Grindavik 22 1 **49 5**
2015 Aalesund 8 0
2016 Aalesund 12 0
2017 Aalesund 27 1
2018 Aalesund 15 1
2019 Aalesund 29 3
2020 Aalesund 14 0
2020–21 Aalesund 0 0 **105 5**
2020–21 Blackpool 12 0 **12 0**

HAMILTON, CJ (M) 164 20
H: 5 7 W: 11 09 b.Harrow 23-3-95
2015–16 Sheffield U 0 0
2016–17 Mansfield T 29 0
2017–18 Mansfield T 33 2
2018–19 Mansfield T 46 11
2019–20 Mansfield T 34 2 **142 15**
2019–20 Blackpool 0 0
2020–21 Blackpool 22 5 **22 5**

HILL, Cameron (D) 0 0
b. 30-11-02
From Salford C.
2020–21 Blackpool 0 0

HOLMES, Bradley (M) 5 0
b. 16-12-02
From Bolton W.
2020–21 Blackpool 5 0 **5 0**

HOWE, Teddy (D) 13 0
b. 9-10-98
2018–19 Reading 1 0
2019–20 Reading 0 0 **1 0**
2019–20 Blackpool 0 0
2020–21 Blackpool 0 0
2020–21 *Scunthorpe U* 12 0 **12 0**

HUSBAND, James (D) 203 5
H: 5 10 W: 10 00 b.Leeds 3-1-94
2011–12 Doncaster R 3 0
2012–13 Doncaster R 33 3
2013–14 Doncaster R 28 1 **64 4**
2014–15 Middlesbrough 3 0
2014–15 *Fulham* 5 0
2015–16 Middlesbrough 0 0
2015–16 *Fulham* 12 0 **17 0**
2015–16 *Huddersfield T* 11 0 **11 0**
2016–17 Middlesbrough 1 0 **4 0**
2017–18 Norwich C 18 0
2018–19 Norwich C 1 0 **19 0**
2018–19 *Fleetwood T* 33 1 **33 1**
2019–20 Blackpool 28 0
2020–21 Blackpool 27 0 **55 0**

KAIKAI, Sullay (F) 155 31
H: 6 0 W: 11 07 b.London 26-8-95
2013–14 Crystal Palace 0 0
2013–14 *Crawley T* 5 0 **5 0**
2014–15 Crystal Palace 0 0
2014–15 *Cambridge U* 25 5 **25 5**
2015–16 Crystal Palace 1 0
2015–16 *Shrewsbury T* 26 12 **26 12**
2016–17 Brentford 18 3 **18 3**
2016–17 Crystal Palace 1 0
2017–18 Crystal Palace 1 0
2017–18 *Charlton Ath* 14 0 **14 0**
2018–19 Crystal Palace 0 0 **3 0**
2018–19 NAC Breda 6 0 **6 0**
2019–20 Blackpool 22 4
2020–21 Blackpool 36 7 **58 11**

LUBULA, Beryly (F) 50 12
b. 8-1-98
2017–18 Birmingham C 1 0
2018–19 Birmingham C 3 0 **4 0**
2019–20 Crawley T 34 12 **34 12**
2020–21 Blackpool 12 0 **12 0**

MADINE, Gary (F) 383 80
H: 6 1 W: 12 00 b.Gateshead 24-8-90
2007–08 Carlisle U 11 0
2008–09 Carlisle U 14 1
2008–09 *Rochdale* 3 0 **3 0**
2009–10 Carlisle U 20 4
2009–10 *Coventry C* 9 0
2009–10 *Chesterfield* 4 0 **4 0**
2010–11 Carlisle U 21 8
2010–11 Sheffield W 22 5

2011–12 Sheffield W 38 18
2012–13 Sheffield W 30 3
2013–14 Sheffield W 1 0
2013–14 *Carlisle U* 5 2 **71 15**
2014–15 Sheffield W 10 0 **101 26**
2014–15 *Coventry C* 11 3 **20 3**
2014–15 *Blackpool* 15 3
2015–16 Bolton W 32 5
2016–17 Bolton W 36 9
2017–18 Bolton W 28 10 **96 24**
2017–18 Cardiff C 13 0
2018–19 Cardiff C 5 0
2018–19 *Sheffield U* 16 3 **16 3**
2019–20 Cardiff C 8 0 **26 0**
2019–20 Blackpool 10 2
2020–21 Blackpool 21 4 **46 9**

MARIETTE, Luke (F) **0 0**
2020–21 Blackpool 0 0

MAXWELL, Chris (G) **250 0**
H: 6 0 W: 11 07 b.Wrexham 30-7-90
Internationals: Wales U17, U19, U21, U23.
From Wrexham.
2012–13 Fleetwood T 0 0
2013–14 Fleetwood T 18 0
2014–15 Fleetwood T 46 0
2015–16 Fleetwood T 46 0 **110 0**
2016–17 Preston NE 38 0
2017–18 Preston NE 30 0
2018–19 Preston NE 8 0
2018–19 *Charlton Ath* 0 0
2019–20 Preston NE 0 0 **76 0**
2019–20 *Hibernian* 12 0 **12 0**
2019–20 Blackpool 9 0
2020–21 Blackpool 43 0 **52 0**

MITCHELL, Demetri (D) **62 1**
H: 5 9 W: 11 11 b.Manchester 11-1-97
Internationals: England U16, U17, U18, U20.
2016–17 Manchester U 1 0
2017–18 Manchester U 0 0
2017–18 *Hearts* 9 0
2018–19 Manchester U 0 0
2018–19 *Hearts* 20 0 **29 0**
2019–20 Manchester U 0 0 **1 0**
2020–21 Blackpool 32 1 **32 1**

MONKS, Charles (G) **0 0**
b. 10-1-03
2020–21 Blackpool 0 0

MOORE, Stuart (G) **29 0**
H: 6 2 W: 11 05 b.Sandown 8-9-94
2013–14 Reading 0 0
2014–15 Reading 0 0
2015–16 Reading 0 0
2015–16 *Peterborough U* 4 0 **4 0**
2016–17 Reading 0 0
2016–17 *Luton T* 8 0 **8 0**
2017–18 Swindon T 10 0 **10 0**
2018–19 Milton Keynes D 6 0
2019–20 Milton Keynes D 0 0 **6 0**
2020–21 Blackpool 1 0 **1 0**

NUTTALL, Joe (F) **69 8**
H: 6 0 W: 11 05 b.Bury 27-1-97
From Manchester C.
2015–16 Aberdeen 2 0
2016–17 Aberdeen 0 0 **2 0**
2016–17 *Stranraer* 9 2 **9 2**
2016–17 *Dumbarton* 2 0 **2 0**
2017–18 Blackburn R 13 2
2018–19 Blackburn R 15 2 **28 4**
2019–20 Blackpool 27 2
2020–21 Blackpool 0 0 **27 2**
2020–21 *Northampton T* 1 0 **1 0**

ROBSON, Ethan (M) **66 5**
H: 5 8 W: 10 12 b. 25-10-96
2016–17 Sunderland 0 0
2017–18 Sunderland 9 0
2018–19 Sunderland 0 0
2018–19 *Dundee* 13 2 **13 2**
2019–20 Sunderland 0 0 **9 0**
2019–20 *Grimsby T* 16 3 **16 3**
2020–21 Blackpool 28 0 **28 0**

SARKIC, Oliver (F) **67 6**
b. 23-7-97
From Anderlecht.
2014–15 Benfica 0 0
2015–16 Benfica 0 0
2016–17 Benfica 0 0
2016–17 *Fafe* 18 2 **18 2**
2017–18 Benfica 0 0
2018–19 Leeds U 0 0
2018–19 *Barakaldo* 12 1 **12 1**
2019–20 Burton Alb 28 3 **28 3**
2019–20 Blackpool 0 0
2020–21 Blackpool 5 0 **5 0**
2020–21 *Mansfield T* 4 0 **4 0**

SHAW, Nathan (M) **1 0**
b. 22-11-00
2018–19 Blackpool 0 0
2019–20 Blackpool 0 0
2020–21 Blackpool 1 0 **1 0**

SIMS, Jack (G) **1 0**
H: 6 2 W: 11 07 b.Southend-on-Sea 10-3-00
2018–19 Blackpool 0 0
2019–20 Blackpool 1 0
2020–21 Blackpool 0 0 **1 0**

SINCLAIR, Sky (D) **0 0**
b.Westminster 16-10-02
2020–21 Blackpool 0 0

STEWART, Kevin (D) **115 6**
H: 5 7 W: 11 06 b.Enfield 7-9-93
2012–13 Tottenham H 0 0
2012–13 *Crewe Alex* 4 0
2013–14 Crewe Alex 0 0 **4 0**
2014–15 Liverpool 0 0
2014–15 *Cheltenham T* 4 1 **4 1**
2014–15 *Burton Alb* 7 2 **7 2**
2015–16 Liverpool 7 0
2015–16 *Swindon T* 5 0 **5 0**
2016–17 Liverpool 4 0 **11 0**
2017–18 Hull C 17 0
2018–19 Hull C 27 0
2019–20 Hull C 27 3 **71 3**
2020–21 Blackpool 13 0 **13 0**

THORNILEY, Jordan (D) **66 0**
b.Warrington 24-11-96
From Everton.
2016–17 Sheffield W 0 0
2017–18 Sheffield W 11 0
2017–18 *Accrington S* 14 0 **14 0**
2018–19 Sheffield W 20 0
2019–20 Sheffield W 0 0 **31 0**
2019–20 Blackpool 2 0
2020–21 Blackpool 19 0 **21 0**

TURTON, Oliver (D) **310 6**
H: 5 11 W: 11 11 b.Manchester 6-12-92
2010–11 Crewe Alex 1 0
2011–12 Crewe Alex 2 0
2012–13 Crewe Alex 20 0
2013–14 Crewe Alex 12 1
2014–15 Crewe Alex 44 1
2015–16 Crewe Alex 46 1
2016–17 Crewe Alex 45 1 **170 4**
2017–18 Blackpool 41 1
2018–19 Blackpool 32 1
2019–20 Blackpool 30 0
2020–21 Blackpool 37 0 **140 2**

VIRTUE, Matthew (M) **66 7**
b.Epsom 2-5-97
2017–18 Liverpool 0 0
2017–18 *Notts Co* 13 0 **13 0**
2018–19 Blackpool 13 3
2019–20 Blackpool 24 2
2020–21 Blackpool 16 2 **53 7**

WARD, Grant (M) **209 12**
H: 5 10 W: 11 07 b.Lewisham 5-12-94
2013–14 Tottenham H 0 0
2014 *Chicago Fire* 23 1 **23 1**
2014–15 Tottenham H 0 0
2014–15 *Coventry C* 11 0 **11 0**
2015–16 Tottenham H 0 0
2015–16 *Rotherham U* 40 2 **40 2**
2016–17 Ipswich T 43 6
2017–18 Ipswich T 37 2
2018–19 Ipswich T 14 0 **94 8**
2019–20 Blackpool 5 0
2020–21 Blackpool 36 1 **41 1**

YATES, Jerry (M) **145 41**
H: 5 9 W: 10 10 b.Doncaster 10-11-96
2014–15 Rotherham U 1 0
2015–16 Rotherham U 0 0
2016–17 Rotherham U 21 1
2017–18 Rotherham U 17 1
2018–19 Carlisle U 23 6 **23 6**
2018–19 Rotherham U 7 0
2019–20 Rotherham U 1 0 **47 2**
2019–20 *Swindon T* 31 13 **31 13**
2020–21 Blackpool 44 20 **44 20**

Scholars
Fitzgerald, Michael Stephen; Goumou, Perez Julius Oluwaseyi; Harrison, James; Liptrott, Matthew Benjamin; Matshazi, Arnold Tawanda; McLachlan, Alexander James Chree; Moore, Jack Lewis; Rogers, Max; Squires, William Joseph; Strawn, Joseph Michael; Trusty, Tayt-Lemar; Turner, Aaron Harry; Wilson, Ellis; Wood, Jak Daniel; Wyllie, Sebastian Merlin; Yelegon, Prince Junior.

BOLTON W (10)

AFOLAYAN, Oladapo (F) **37 2**
H: 5 11 b. 1-1-97
Internationals: England C.
From Solihull Moors.
2018–19 West Ham U 0 0
2018–19 *Oldham Ath* 10 0 **10 0**
2019–20 West Ham U 0 0
2019–20 *Mansfield T* 6 1 **6 1**
2020–21 West Ham U 0 0
2020–21 Bolton W 21 1 **21 1**

ALEXANDER, Matthew (G) **1 0**
2019–20 Bolton W 1 0
2020–21 Bolton W 0 0 **1 0**

AMOATENG, Bright (F) **1 0**
b. 22-11-02
2020–21 Bolton W 1 0 **1 0**

ASSARSSON, Markus (D) **0 0**
2020–21 Bolton W 0 0

BAPTISTE, Alex (D) **524 24**
H: 6 0 W: 11 11 b.Sutton-in-Ashfield 31-1-86
2002–03 Mansfield T 4 0
2003–04 Mansfield T 17 0
2004–05 Mansfield T 41 1
2005–06 Mansfield T 41 1
2006–07 Mansfield T 46 3
2007–08 Mansfield T 25 0 **174 5**
2008–09 Blackpool 21 1
2009–10 Blackpool 42 3
2010–11 Blackpool 21 2
2011–12 Blackpool 43 1
2012–13 Blackpool 43 1 **170 8**
2013–14 Bolton W 39 4
2014–15 Bolton W 0 0
2014–15 *Blackburn R* 32 3 **32 3**
2015–16 Middlesbrough 0 0
2015–16 *Sheffield U* 11 1 **11 1**
2016–17 Middlesbrough 0 0
2016–17 *Preston NE* 24 3 **24 3**
2017–18 QPR 26 0
2018–19 QPR 4 0 **30 0**
2018–19 *Luton T* 2 0 **2 0**
2019–20 Doncaster R 2 0 **2 0**
2020–21 Bolton W 40 0 **79 4**

BROCKBANK, Harry (F) **27 0**
H: 5 11 W: 12 08 b.Bolton 26-9-98
2017–18 Bolton W 0 0
2018–19 Bolton W 3 0
2019–20 Bolton W 6 0
2020–21 Bolton W 18 0 **27 0**

COMLEY, Brandon (M) **132 2**
H: 5 11 W: 11 05 b.Islington 18-11-95
Internationals: Montserrat Full caps.
2014–15 QPR 1 0
2015–16 QPR 0 0
2015–16 *Carlisle U* 12 0 **12 0**
2016–17 QPR 1 0 **2 0**
2016–17 *Grimsby T* 33 0
2017–18 Grimsby T 0 0 **33 0**
2017–18 Colchester U 38 1
2018–19 Colchester U 13 0
2019–20 Colchester U 24 1 **75 2**
2020–21 Bolton W 10 0 **10 0**

CONWAY, Max (M) **0 0**
2020–21 Bolton W 0 0

CRAWFORD, Ali (M) **305 35**
H: 5 7 W: 9 09 b.Lanark 30-7-91
2009–10 Hamilton A 7 0
2010–11 Hamilton A 14 0
2011–12 Hamilton A 19 2
2012–13 Hamilton A 33 3
2013–14 Hamilton A 36 2
2014–15 Hamilton A 38 10
2015–16 Hamilton A 33 5
2016–17 Hamilton A 33 8
2017–18 Hamilton A 14 1 **227 31**
2018–19 Doncaster R 35 3
2019–20 Doncaster R 1 0 **36 3**
2019–20 Bolton W 12 0
2020–21 *Tranmere R* 9 0 **9 0**
2020–21 Bolton W 21 1 **33 1**

DARCY, Ronan (M) **28 1**
b. 20-8-00
2018–19 Bolton W 1 0
2019–20 Bolton W 19 1
2020–21 Bolton W 8 0 **28 1**

DELANEY, Ryan (D) **116 12**
H: 6 0 W: 11 05 b.Wexford 6-9-96
Internationals: Republic of Ireland U21.
From Wexford.
2016–17 Burton Alb 0 0

2017	*Cork C*	30	6	**30**	**6**
2017–18	Rochdale	18	2		
2018–19	Rochdale	30	1		
2019–20	*AFC Wimbledon*	14	1	**14**	**1**
2019–20	Rochdale	0	0	**48**	**3**
2019–20	Bolton W	4	1		
2020–21	Bolton W	20	1	**24**	**2**

DELFOUNESO, Nathan (F) **355 47**
H: 6 1 W: 12 04 b.Birmingham 2-2-91
Internationals: England U16, U17, U19, U21.

2007–08	Aston Villa	0	0		
2008–09	Aston Villa	4	0		
2009–10	Aston Villa	9	1		
2010–11	Aston Villa	11	1		
2010–11	*Burnley*	11	1	**11**	**1**
2011–12	Aston Villa	6	0		
2011–12	*Leicester C*	4	0	**4**	**0**
2012–13	Aston Villa	1	0		
2012–13	*Blackpool*	40	6		
2013–14	Aston Villa	0	0	**31**	**2**
2013–14	*Blackpool*	11	0		
2013–14	*Coventry C*	14	3	**14**	**3**
2014–15	Blackpool	38	3		
2015–16	Blackburn R	15	1	**15**	**1**
2015–16	*Bury*	4	0	**4**	**0**
2016–17	Swindon T	18	1	**18**	**1**
2016–17	Blackpool	18	5		
2017–18	Blackpool	40	9		
2018–19	Blackpool	39	7		
2019–20	Blackpool	28	3		
2020–21	Blackpool	0	0	**214**	**33**
2020–21	Bolton W	44	6	**44**	**6**

DOYLE, Eoin (F) **452 158**
H: 6 0 W: 11 07 b.Tallaght 12-3-88

2008	Shamrock R	30	5		
2009	Shamrock R	2	0	**32**	**5**
2009	Sligo	15	3		
2010	Sligo	35	6		
2011	Sligo	34	20	**84**	**29**
2011–12	Hibernian	13	1		
2012–13	Hibernian	36	10	**49**	**11**
2013–14	Chesterfield	43	11		
2014–15	Chesterfield	26	21	**69**	**32**
2014–15	Cardiff C	16	5		
2015–16	Cardiff C	0	0	**16**	**5**
2015–16	*Preston NE*	28	4		
2016–17	Preston NE	11	1		
2016–17	*Portsmouth*	12	2	**12**	**2**
2017–18	Preston NE	0	0	**39**	**5**
2017–18	*Oldham Ath*	30	14	**30**	**14**
2018–19	Bradford C	44	11		
2019–20	Bradford C	6	0	**50**	**11**
2019–20	Swindon T	28	25	**28**	**25**
2020–21	Bolton W	43	19	**43**	**19**

GILKS, Matthew (G) **470 0**
H: 6 3 W: 13 12 b.Rochdale 4-6-82
Internationals: Scotland Full caps.

2000–01	Rochdale	3	0		
2001–02	Rochdale	19	0		
2002–03	Rochdale	20	0		
2003–04	Rochdale	12	0		
2004–05	Rochdale	30	0		
2005–06	Rochdale	46	0		
2006–07	Rochdale	46	0	**176**	**0**
2007–08	Norwich C	0	0		
2008–09	Blackpool	5	0		
2008–09	*Shrewsbury T*	4	0	**4**	**0**
2009–10	Blackpool	26	0		
2010–11	Blackpool	18	0		
2011–12	Blackpool	42	0		
2012–13	Blackpool	45	0		
2013–14	Blackpool	46	0	**182**	**0**
2014–15	Burnley	0	0		
2015–16	Burnley	0	0		
2016–17	Rangers	0	0		
2016–17	Wigan Ath	14	0	**14**	**0**
2017–18	Scunthorpe U	42	0		
2018–19	Scunthorpe U	0	0	**42**	**0**
2018–19	Lincoln C	12	0	**12**	**0**
2019–20	Fleetwood T	5	0	**5**	**0**
2020–21	Bolton W	35	0	**35**	**0**

GNAHOUA, Arthur (F) **70 7**
H: 6 2 W: 12 08 b.London 5-4-92
From Stalybridge Celtic, Macclesfield T, Kidderminster H.

2017–18	Shrewsbury T	11	1		
2018–19	Shrewsbury T	1	0	**12**	**1**
2018–19	Carlisle U	1	0	**1**	**0**
2019–20	Macclesfield T	29	4	**29**	**4**
2020–21	Bolton W	28	2	**28**	**2**

GORDON, Liam (D) **10 0**
b.Croyden 15-5-99
From Dagenham & R.

2020–21	Bolton W	10	0	**10**	**0**

GREENIDGE, Reiss (D) **43 2**
b. 10-8-96

2014–15	WBA	0	0		
2014–15	*Port Vale*	0	0		

From Ebbsfleet U.

2017	Sogndal	10	1		
2018	Sogndal	9	0		
2019	Sogndal	0	0		
2019	*Arendal*	19	1	**19**	**1**
2020	Sogndal	0	0	**19**	**1**
2020	*Arandal*	0	0		
2020–21	Bolton W	5	0	**5**	**0**

HENRY, Mitchell (F) **0 0**
b.Salford 2-9-03

2020–21	Bolton W	0	0		

HICKMAN, Jak (F) **4 0**
b. 11-9-98

2017–18	Coventry C	0	0		
2018–19	Coventry C	0	0		
2019–20	Coventry C	0	0		
2020–21	Bolton W	4	0	**4**	**0**

HURFORD-LOCKETT, Finlay (M) **3 0**
b. 10-4-03

2019–20	Bolton W	2	0		
2020–21	Bolton W	1	0	**3**	**0**

ISGROVE, Lloyd (M) **123 5**
H: 5 10 W: 11 05 b.Yeovil 12-1-93
Internationals: Wales U21, Full caps.

2011–12	Southampton	0	0		
2012–13	Southampton	0	0		
2013–14	Southampton	0	0		
2013–14	*Peterborough U*	8	1	**8**	**1**
2014–15	Southampton	1	0		
2014–15	*Sheffield W*	8	0	**8**	**0**
2015–16	Southampton	0	0		
2015–16	*Barnsley*	27	0		
2016–17	Southampton	0	0	**1**	**0**
2017–18	Barnsley	16	1		
2018–19	Barnsley	2	0	**45**	**1**
2018–19	*Portsmouth*	0	0		
2019–20	Swindon T	29	0		
2020–21	Swindon T	0	0	**29**	**0**
2020–21	Bolton W	32	3	**32**	**3**

JONES, Gethin (D) **119 3**
H: 5 10 W: 11 09 b.Perth 13-10-95
Internationals: Wales U17, U19, U21.

2014–15	Everton	0	0		
2014–15	*Plymouth Arg*	6	0	**6**	**0**
2015–16	Everton	0	0		
2016–17	Everton	0	0		
2016–17	*Barnsley*	17	0	**17**	**0**
2017–18	Fleetwood T	10	0		
2018–19	Fleetwood T	3	0	**13**	**0**
2018–19	*Mansfield T*	15	0	**15**	**0**
2019–20	Carlisle U	30	0		
2020–21	Carlisle U	0	0	**30**	**0**
2020–21	Bolton W	38	3	**38**	**3**

LE FONDRE, Kian (M) **0 0**

2020–21	Bolton W	0	0		

LEE, Kieran (D) **341 27**
H: 6 1 W: 12 00 b.Stalybridge 22-6-88

2006–07	Manchester U	1	0		
2007–08	Manchester U	0	0	**1**	**0**
2007–08	*QPR*	7	0	**7**	**0**
2008–09	Oldham Ath	7	0		
2009–10	Oldham Ath	24	1		
2010–11	Oldham Ath	43	2		
2011–12	Oldham Ath	43	2	**117**	**5**
2012–13	Sheffield W	23	0		
2013–14	Sheffield W	26	1		
2014–15	Sheffield W	33	6		
2015–16	Sheffield W	43	5		
2016–17	Sheffield W	26	5		
2017–18	Sheffield W	15	3		
2018–19	Sheffield W	2	0		
2019–20	Sheffield W	28	0		
2020–21	Sheffield W	0	0	**196**	**20**
2020–21	Bolton W	20	2	**20**	**2**

MASCOLL, Jamie (M) **24 1**
b. 15-3-97
From Dulwich Hamlet.

2017–18	Charlton Ath	0	0		
2018–19	Charlton Ath	0	0		
2019–20	Wycombe W	4	0		
2020–21	Wycombe W	0	0	**4**	**0**
2020–21	Bolton W	7	0	**7**	**0**
2020–21	*Waterford*	13	1	**13**	**1**

MILLER, Shaun (F) **394 82**
H: 5 10 W: 11 08 b.Alsager 25-9-87

2006–07	Crewe Alex	7	3		
2007–08	Crewe Alex	15	1		
2008–09	Crewe Alex	33	4		
2009–10	Crewe Alex	33	7		
2010–11	Crewe Alex	42	18		
2011–12	Crewe Alex	33	5		
2012–13	Sheffield U	15	4		
2013–14	Sheffield U	13	0	**28**	**4**
2013–14	*Shrewsbury T*	8	3	**8**	**3**
2014–15	Coventry C	12	1	**12**	**1**
2014–15	*Crawley T*	5	0	**5**	**0**
2014–15	*York C*	6	0	**6**	**0**
2015–16	Morecambe	37	15		
2016–17	Carlisle U	30	4		
2017–18	Carlisle U	23	3	**53**	**7**
2017–18	*Crewe Alex*	15	6		
2018–19	Crewe Alex	29	3		
2019–20	Crewe Alex	0	0	**207**	**47**
2019–20	*Morecambe*	18	2	**55**	**17**
2020–21	Bolton W	20	3	**20**	**3**

SANTOS, Ricardo (D) **166 6**
H: 6 5 W: 12 02 b.Almada 18-6-95

2012–13	Dagenham & R	0	0		
2013–14	Dagenham & R	0	0		
2013–14	Peterborough U	1	0		
2014–15	Peterborough U	24	0		
2015–16	Peterborough U	37	1		
2016–17	Peterborough U	1	0	**63**	**1**
2016–17	Barnet	15	2		
2017–18	Barnet	42	3	**57**	**5**
2020–21	Bolton W	46	0	**46**	**0**

SARCEVIC, Antoni (M) **290 44**
H: 5 10 W: 11 00 b.Manchester 13-3-92
Internationals: England C.

2009–10	Crewe Alex	0	0		
2010–11	Crewe Alex	6	1		
2011–12	Crewe Alex	6	0	**12**	**1**

From Chester.

2013–14	Fleetwood T	42	13		
2014–15	Fleetwood T	37	2		
2015–16	Fleetwood T	39	3	**118**	**18**
2016–17	Shrewsbury T	12	0	**12**	**0**
2016–17	Plymouth Arg	17	2		
2017–18	Plymouth Arg	30	3		
2018–19	Plymouth Arg	37	3		
2019–20	Plymouth Arg	32	10	**116**	**18**
2020–21	Bolton W	32	7	**32**	**7**

SENIOR, Adam (D) **2 0**

2019–20	Bolton W	2	0		
2020–21	Bolton W	0	0	**2**	**0**

THOMASON, George (M) **24 1**
b. 12-1-01
From Longridge T.

2019–20	Bolton W	0	0		
2020–21	Bolton W	24	1	**24**	**1**

TUTTE, Andrew (M) **277 23**
H: 5 9 W: 10 10 b.Huyton 21-9-90
Internationals: England U19, U20.

2007–08	Manchester C	0	0		
2008–09	Manchester C	0	0		
2009–10	Manchester C	0	0		
2010–11	Manchester C	0	0		
2010–11	*Rochdale*	7	0		
2010–11	*Shrewsbury T*	2	0	**2**	**0**
2010–11	*Yeovil T*	15	2	**15**	**2**
2011–12	Rochdale	40	1		
2012–13	Rochdale	37	7		
2013–14	Rochdale	11	2	**95**	**10**
2013–14	Bury	19	1		
2014–15	Bury	42	3		
2015–16	Bury	22	4		
2016–17	Bury	17	1		
2017–18	Bury	16	0	**116**	**9**
2018–19	Morecambe	18	2		
2019–20	Morecambe	12	0	**30**	**2**
2020–21	Bolton W	19	0	**19**	**0**

TWEEDLEY, Matthew (M) **0 0**

2020–21	Bolton W	0	0		

WILLIAMS, M Jordan (M) **116 0**
H: 6 0 W: 12 02 b.Bangor 6-11-95
Internationals: Wales U17, U21.

2014–15	Liverpool	0	0		
2014–15	*Notts Co*	8	0	**8**	**0**
2015–16	Liverpool	0	0		
2015–16	*Swindon T*	9	0		
2016–17	Liverpool	0	0		
2016–17	*Swindon T*	0	0	**9**	**0**
2017–18	Liverpool	0	0		
2017–18	*Rochdale*	12	0		
2018–19	Rochdale	28	0		
2019–20	Rochdale	28	0	**68**	**0**
2020–21	Blackpool	10	0	**10**	**0**
2020–21	Bolton W	21	0	**21**	**0**

Scholars
Amoateng, Bright; Assarsson, Markus Daniel Bernard; Brown, Joseph Christopher; Colvin, Ryan Taylor Thomas Lee; Conway, Maxwell John; Fitzmartin, Jay Leon; Henry, Mitchell Devon; Hurford-Lockett, Finlay; Hutchinson, Luke; Litherland-Riding, Ellis James;

Pettifer, Arran James; Thompson, Jack William Nicholas; Toure, Lamine Cheriff; Tweedley, Matthew James; Whalley, Nathan Mark; Wilcox, Max Keith.

BOURNEMOUTH (11)

ANTHONY, Jaidon (F) 5 0
b. 1-12-99
From Arsenal.

2019–20	Bournemouth	0	0		
2020–21	Bournemouth	5	0	**5**	**0**

BEGOVIC, Asmir (G) 344 1
H: 6 5 W: 13 01 b.Trebinje 20-6-87
Internationals: Canada U20. Bosnia & Herzogovina Full caps.

2005–06	Portsmouth	0	0		
2005–06	*La Louviere*	2	0	**2**	**0**
2006–07	Portsmouth	0	0		
2006–07	*Macclesfield T*	3	0	**3**	**0**
2007–08	Portsmouth	0	0		
2007–08	*Bournemouth*	8	0		
2007–08	*Yeovil T*	2	0		
2008–09	Portsmouth	2	0		
2008–09	*Yeovil T*	14	0	**16**	**0**
2009–10	Portsmouth	9	0	**11**	**0**
2009–10	*Ipswich T*	6	0	**6**	**0**
2009–10	Stoke C	4	0		
2010–11	Stoke C	28	0		
2011–12	Stoke C	23	0		
2012–13	Stoke C	38	0		
2013–14	Stoke C	32	1		
2014–15	Stoke C	35	0	**160**	**1**
2015–16	Chelsea	17	0		
2016–17	Chelsea	2	0	**19**	**0**
2017–18	Bournemouth	38	0		
2018–19	Bournemouth	24	0		
2019–20	Bournemouth	0	0		
2019–20	*Qarabag*	10	0	**10**	**0**
2019–20	*AC Milan*	2	0	**2**	**0**
2020–21	Bournemouth	45	0	**115**	**0**

BILLING, Phillip (M) 149 14
H: 6 4 W: 12 08 b. 11-6-96
Internationals: Denmark U19, U21.
From Esbjerg.

2013–14	Huddersfield T	1	0		
2014–15	Huddersfield T	0	0		
2015–16	Huddersfield T	13	1		
2016–17	Huddersfield T	24	2		
2017–18	Huddersfield T	16	0		
2018–19	Huddersfield T	27	2	**81**	**5**
2019–20	Bournemouth	34	1		
2020–21	Bournemouth	34	8	**68**	**9**

BROOKS, David (M) 101 16
b. 8-7-98
Internationals: England U20. Wales U21, Full caps.
From Manchester C.

2015–16	Sheffield U	0	0		
2016–17	Sheffield U	0	0		
2017–18	Sheffield U	30	3	**30**	**3**
2018–19	Bournemouth	30	7		
2019–20	Bournemouth	9	1		
2020–21	Bournemouth	32	5	**71**	**13**

BURCHALL, Ajani (M) 1 0
b. 5-11-04

2020–21	Bournemouth	1	0	**1**	**0**

COOK, Lewis (M) 186 2
H: 5 9 W: 11 03 b.York 3-2-97
Internationals: England U16, U17, U18, U19, U20, U21, Full caps.

2014–15	Leeds U	37	0		
2015–16	Leeds U	43	1	**80**	**1**
2016–17	Bournemouth	6	0		
2017–18	Bournemouth	29	0		
2018–19	Bournemouth	13	0		
2019–20	Bournemouth	27	0		
2020–21	Bournemouth	31	1	**106**	**1**

COOK, Steve (D) 356 19
H: 6 1 W: 12 13 b.Hastings 19-4-91

2008–09	Brighton & HA	2	0		
2009–10	Brighton & HA	0	0		
2010–11	Brighton & HA	0	0		
2011–12	Brighton & HA	1	0	**3**	**0**
2011–12	Bournemouth	26	0		
2012–13	Bournemouth	33	1		
2013–14	Bournemouth	38	3		
2014–15	Bournemouth	46	5		
2015–16	Bournemouth	36	4		
2016–17	Bournemouth	38	2		
2017–18	Bournemouth	34	2		
2018–19	Bournemouth	31	1		
2019–20	Bournemouth	29	1		
2020–21	Bournemouth	42	0	**353**	**19**

CORDNER, Tyler (D) 26 1
b.Southampton 4-12-98

2018–19	Bournemouth	0	0		
2019–20	Bournemouth	0	0		
2020–21	Scunthorpe U	12	0	**12**	**0**
2020–21	Bournemouth	0	0		
2020–21	*Southend U*	14	1	**14**	**1**

DANJUMA, Arnaut (F) 108 32
b.Oss 31-1-97
Internationals: Netherlands U21, Full caps.

2015–16	PSV Eindhoven	0	0		
2016–17	NEC Nijmegen	12	1		
2017–18	NEC Nijmegen	28	11	**40**	**12**
2018–19	Club Brugge	20	5		
2019–20	Club Brugge	1	0	**21**	**5**
2019–20	Bournemouth	14	0		
2020–21	Bournemouth	33	15	**47**	**15**

DENNIS, William (G) 0 0
b.Watford 10-7-00
From Watford.

2019–20	Bournemouth	0	0		
2020–21	Bournemouth	0	0		

GLOVER, Ryan (M) 0 0
b. 9-11-00

2020–21	Bournemouth	0	0		

IBSEN ROSSI, Zeno (D) 14 0
H: 6 4 b.Streatham 28-10-00

2020–21	Bournemouth	0	0		
2020–21	*Kilmarnock*	14	0	**14**	**0**

KELLY, Lloyd (D) 87 3
H: 5 10 W: 11 00 b. 1-10-98
Internationals: England U20, U21.

2016–17	Bristol C	0	0		
2017–18	Bristol C	11	1		
2018–19	Bristol C	32	1	**43**	**2**
2019–20	Bournemouth	8	0		
2020–21	Bournemouth	36	1	**44**	**1**

KILKENNY, Gavin (M) 1 0
b.Dublin 1-2-00
Internationals: Republic of Ireland U21.

2019–20	Bournemouth	0	0		
2020–21	Bournemouth	1	0	**1**	**0**

LERMA, Jefferson (M) 278 15
H: 5 10 W: 11 00 b.El Cerrito 25-10-94
Internationals: Colombia Full caps.

2013	Atletico Huila	24	0		
2014	Atletico Huila	37	4		
2015	Atletico Huila	23	2	**84**	**6**
2015–16	*Levante*	33	1		
2016–17	Levante	30	2		
2017–18	Levante	26	0	**89**	**3**
2018–19	Bournemouth	30	2		
2019–20	Bournemouth	33	1		
2020–21	Bournemouth	42	3	**105**	**6**

MEPHAM, Chris (D) 92 3
H: 6 3 W: 11 11 b. 5-11-97
Internationals: Wales U20, U21, Full caps.

2016–17	Brentford	0	0		
2017–18	Brentford	21	1		
2018–19	Brentford	22	0	**43**	**1**
2018–19	Bournemouth	13	0		
2019–20	Bournemouth	12	1		
2020–21	Bournemouth	24	1	**49**	**2**

MORIAH-WELSH, Nathan (M) 0 0
From Reading.

2020–21	Bournemouth	0	0		

NIPPARD, Luke (M) 0 0
b. 29-12-00

2020–21	Bournemouth	0	0		

OFOBORH, Nnamdi (F) 29 0
H: 6 0 W: 12 02 b.Southwark 7-11-99
Internationals: Nigeria U20.

2018–19	Bournemouth	0	0		
2019–20	Bournemouth	0	0		
2019–20	*Wycombe W*	18	0		
2020–21	Bournemouth	3	0	**3**	**0**
2020–21	*Wycombe W*	8	0	**26**	**0**

PEARSON, Ben (M) 219 4
H: 5 5 W: 11 03 b.Oldham 4-1-95
Internationals: England U16, U17, U18, U19, U21, Full caps.

2013–14	Manchester U	0	0		
2014–15	Manchester U	0	0		
2014–15	*Barnsley*	22	1		
2015–16	Manchester U	0	0		
2015–16	*Barnsley*	23	1	**45**	**2**
2015–16	Preston NE	15	0		
2016–17	Preston NE	31	1		
2017–18	Preston NE	35	0		
2018–19	Preston NE	30	0		
2019–20	Preston NE	38	1		
2020–21	Preston NE	9	0	**158**	**2**
2020–21	Bournemouth	16	0	**16**	**0**

RICO, Diego (D) 228 9
H: 5 11 W: 11 11 b.Burgos 26-4-93

2011–12	Zaragoza	0	0		
2012–13	Zaragoza	0	0		
2013–14	Zaragoza	30	2		
2014–15	Zaragoza	37	2		
2015–16	Zaragoza	39	1	**106**	**5**
2016–17	Leganes	25	1		
2017–18	Leganes	26	2	**51**	**3**
2018–19	Bournemouth	12	0		
2019–20	Bournemouth	27	0		
2020–21	Bournemouth	32	1	**71**	**1**

RIQUELME, Rodrigo (M) 17 1
b.Madrid 2-4-00

2018–19	Atletico Madrid	0	0		
2019–20	Atletico Madrid	1	0		
2020–21	Atletico Madrid	0	0	**1**	**0**

On loan from Atletico Madrid.

2020–21	Bournemouth	16	1	**16**	**1**

SAYDEE, Christian (F) 0 0
b.Hillingdon 10-5-02

2019–20	Bournemouth	0	0		
2020–21	Bournemouth	0	0		

SCRIMSHAW, Jake (F) 30 5
b. 13-9-00

2018–19	Bournemouth	0	0		
2019–20	Bournemouth	0	0		
2020–21	Bournemouth	0	0		
2020–21	*Walsall*	14	2	**14**	**2**
2020–21	*Newport Co*	16	3	**16**	**3**

SHERRING, Sam (D) 0 0
H: 6 2 b.Dorchester 8-5-00

2020–21	Bournemouth	0	0		

SIMPSON, Jack (D) 20 0
H: 5 10 W: 13 01 b. 8-1-97
Internationals: England U21.

2015–16	Bournemouth	0	0		
2016–17	Bournemouth	0	0		
2017–18	Bournemouth	1	0		
2018–19	Bournemouth	6	0		
2019–20	Bournemouth	4	0		
2020–21	Bournemouth	9	0	**20**	**0**

Transferred to Rangers February 2021.

SMITH, Adam (D) 329 9
H: 5 8 W: 10 07 b.Leytonstone 29-4-91
Internationals: England U16, U17, U19, U20, U21.

2007–08	Tottenham H	0	0		
2008–09	Tottenham H	0	0		
2009–10	Tottenham H	0	0		
2009–10	*Wycombe W*	3	0	**3**	**0**
2009–10	*Torquay U*	16	0	**16**	**0**
2010–11	Tottenham H	0	0		
2010–11	*Bournemouth*	38	1		
2011–12	Tottenham H	1	0		
2011–12	*Milton Keynes D*	17	2	**17**	**2**
2011–12	*Leeds U*	3	0	**3**	**0**
2012–13	Tottenham H	0	0		
2012–13	*Millwall*	25	1	**25**	**1**
2013–14	Tottenham H	0	0	**1**	**0**
2013–14	*Derby Co*	8	0	**8**	**0**
2013–14	Bournemouth	5	0		
2014–15	Bournemouth	29	0		
2015–16	Bournemouth	31	2		
2016–17	Bournemouth	36	1		
2017–18	Bournemouth	27	1		
2018–19	Bournemouth	25	1		
2019–20	Bournemouth	24	0		
2020–21	Bournemouth	41	0	**256**	**6**

SOLANKE, Dominic (F) 128 26
H: 6 1 W: 11 11 b.Reading 14-9-97
Internationals: England U16, U17, U18, U19, U20, U21, Full caps.

2014–15	Chelsea	0	0		
2015–16	Chelsea	0	0		
2015–16	*Vitesse*	25	7	**25**	**7**
2016–17	Chelsea	0	0		
2017–18	Liverpool	21	1		
2018–19	Liverpool	0	0	**21**	**1**
2018–19	Bournemouth	10	0		
2019–20	Bournemouth	32	3		
2020–21	Bournemouth	40	15	**82**	**18**

STACEY, Jack (M) 186 8
H: 6 4 W: 13 05 b.Bracknell 6-4-96

2014–15	Reading	6	0		
2015–16	Reading	0	0		
2015–16	*Barnet*	2	0	**2**	**0**
2015–16	*Carlisle U*	9	2	**9**	**2**
2016–17	Reading	0	0	**6**	**0**
2016–17	*Exeter C*	34	0	**34**	**0**
2017–18	Luton T	41	1		
2018–19	Luton T	45	4	**86**	**5**
2019–20	Bournemouth	19	0		
2020–21	Bournemouth	30	1	**49**	**1**

STANISLAS, Junior (M) **288** **45**
H: 6 0 W: 12 00 b.Kidbrooke 26-11-89
Internationals: England U20, U21.

2007–08	West Ham U	0	0		
2008–09	West Ham U	9	2		
2008–09	*Southend U*	6	1	**6**	**1**
2009–10	West Ham U	26	3		
2010–11	West Ham U	6	1		
2011–12	West Ham U	1	0	**42**	**6**
2011–12	Burnley	31	0		
2012–13	Burnley	35	5		
2013–14	Burnley	27	2	**93**	**7**
2014–15	Bournemouth	13	1		
2015–16	Bournemouth	21	3		
2016–17	Bournemouth	21	7		
2017–18	Bournemouth	19	5		
2018–19	Bournemouth	23	2		
2019–20	Bournemouth	15	3		
2020–21	Bournemouth	35	10	**147**	**31**

SURRIDGE, Sam (F) **111** **24**
b.Wimborne 28-7-98
Internationals: England U21.

2015–16	Bournemouth	0	0		
2016–17	Bournemouth	0	0		
2017–18	Bournemouth	0	0		
2017–18	*Yeovil T*	41	8	**41**	**8**
2018–19	Bournemouth	2	0		
2018–19	*Oldham Ath*	15	8	**15**	**8**
2019–20	Bournemouth	4	0		
2019–20	*Swansea C*	20	4	**20**	**4**
2020–21	Bournemouth	29	4	**35**	**4**

TAYLOR, Kyle (M) **36** **1**
b. 28-8-99

2017–18	Bournemouth	0	0		
2018–19	Bournemouth	0	0		
2019–20	Bournemouth	0	0		
2019–20	*Forest Green R*	5	0	**5**	**0**
2020–21	Bournemouth	0	0		
2020–21	*Southend U*	31	1	**31**	**1**

TRAVERS, Mark (G) **12** **0**
H: 6 3 W: 12 13 b. 18-5-99
Internationals: Republic of Ireland U16, U17, U18, U19, U21.
From Shamrock R.

2018–19	Bournemouth	2	0		
2019–20	Bournemouth	1	0		
2020–21	Bournemouth	1	0	**4**	**0**
2020–21	*Swindon T*	8	0	**8**	**0**

VINCENT, Frankie (M) **14** **0**
b. 23-4-99

2018–19	Bournemouth	0	0		
2019–20	Bournemouth	0	0		
2020–21	Bournemouth	0	0		
2020–21	*Scunthorpe U*	6	0	**6**	**0**
2020–21	*Walsall*	8	0	**8**	**0**

WILSHERE, Jack (M) **196** **9**
H: 5 7 W: 11 03 b.Stevenage 1-1-92
Internationals: England U16, U17, U19, U21, Full caps.

2008–09	Arsenal	1	0		
2009–10	Arsenal	1	0		
2009–10	*Bolton W*	14	1	**14**	**1**
2010–11	Arsenal	35	1		
2011–12	Arsenal	0	0		
2012–13	Arsenal	25	0		
2013–14	Arsenal	24	3		
2014–15	Arsenal	14	2		
2015–16	Arsenal	3	0		
2016–17	Arsenal	2	0		
2016–17	*Bournemouth*	27	0		
2017–18	Arsenal	20	1	**125**	**7**
2018–19	West Ham U	8	0		
2019–20	West Ham U	8	0	**16**	**0**
2020–21	Bournemouth	14	1	**41**	**1**

ZEMURA, Jordan (D) **2** **0**
b. 14-11-99

2018–19	Charlton Ath	0	0		
2019–20	Bournemouth	0	0		
2020–21	Bournemouth	2	0	**2**	**0**

Scholars
Adams, Jake; Besant, Joe Matthew; Bevan, Owen Lucas; Boutin, Noa; Burgess, Matthew Richard; Channell, Brandon Antony Emmanuel; Clarke, Josh Samuel; Daws, Marcus James; Ferguson, Joshua; Genesini, Brooklyn David Anthony; Gidaree, Tarik Andre Calvin; Greenwood, Benjamin Sean; Kurran-Browne, Connor Chadney; Mohamed, Abdirahman Adan; Moriah-Welsh, Nathan Daniel; Okoh, Osanebi Ferdinand; Palmer, Owen; Plain, Cameron Christopher; Pollock, Euan George; Roberts, Aaron Joseph; Rolls, Thomas Alexander; Saydee, Christian; Seddon, Jack; Terrell, Billy Edwards James; Wadham, Jack.

BRADFORD C (12)

CANAVAN, Niall (D) **290** **23**
H: 6 3 W: 12 00 b.Guiseley 11-4-91
Internationals: Republic of Ireland U21.

2009–10	Scunthorpe U	7	1		
2010–11	Scunthorpe U	8	0		
2010–11	*Shrewsbury T*	3	0	**3**	**0**
2011–12	Scunthorpe U	12	1		
2012–13	Scunthorpe U	40	6		
2013–14	Scunthorpe U	45	4		
2014–15	Scunthorpe U	32	3		
2015–16	Scunthorpe U	10	0	**154**	**15**
2015–16	*Rochdale*	11	1		
2016–17	Rochdale	25	2		
2017–18	Rochdale	3	0	**39**	**3**
2018–19	Plymouth Arg	33	2		
2019–20	Plymouth Arg	33	2		
2020–21	Plymouth Arg	12	1	**78**	**5**
2020–21	Bradford C	16	0	**16**	**0**

CLARKE, Billy (F) **390** **73**
H: 5 7 W: 10 01 b.Cork 13-12-87
Internationals: Republic of Ireland U17, U19, U21.

2004–05	Ipswich T	0	0		
2005–06	Ipswich T	2	0		
2005–06	*Colchester U*	6	0	**6**	**0**
2006–07	Ipswich T	27	3		
2007–08	Ipswich T	20	0		
2007–08	*Falkirk*	8	1	**8**	**1**
2008–09	Ipswich T	0	0	**49**	**3**
2008–09	*Darlington*	20	8	**20**	**8**
2008–09	*Northampton T*	5	3	**5**	**3**
2008–09	*Brentford*	8	6	**8**	**6**
2009–10	Blackpool	18	1		
2010–11	Blackpool	0	0		
2011–12	Blackpool	9	0	**27**	**1**
2011–12	*Sheffield U*	5	1	**5**	**1**
2011–12	Crawley T	17	3		
2012–13	Crawley T	36	10		
2013–14	Crawley T	29	7	**82**	**20**
2014–15	Bradford C	36	13		
2015–16	Bradford C	29	4		
2016–17	Bradford C	33	7		
2017–18	Charlton Ath	17	1		
2018–19	Charlton Ath	0	0	**17**	**1**
2018–19	Bradford C	14	1		
2019–20	Plymouth Arg	9	0	**9**	**0**
2019–20	Grimsby T	13	2	**13**	**2**
2020–21	Bradford C	29	2	**141**	**27**

COOKE, Callum (F) **120** **10**
H: 5 8 W: 11 05 b.Peterlee 21-2-97
Internationals: England U16, U17, U18.

2016–17	Middlesbrough	0	0		
2016–17	*Crewe Alex*	18	4	**18**	**4**
2017–18	Middlesbrough	0	0		
2017–18	*Blackpool*	30	2	**30**	**2**
2018–19	Peterborough U	13	1		
2019–20	Peterborough U	0	0	**13**	**1**
2019–20	*Bradford C*	25	0		
2020–21	Bradford C	34	3	**59**	**3**

COUSIN-DAWSON, Finn (D) **23** **0**
b. 10-5-01

2019–20	Bradford C	0	0		
2020–21	Bradford C	23	0	**23**	**0**

CRANKSHAW, Oliver (M) **38** **2**
b.Preston 12-8-98

2020–21	Wigan Ath	19	1	**19**	**1**
2020–21	Bradford C	19	1	**19**	**1**

DONALDSON, Clayton (F) **498** **144**
H: 6 1 W: 11 07 b.Bradford 7-2-84
Internationals: England C. Jamaica Full caps.

2002–03	Hull C	2	0		
2003–04	Hull C	0	0		
2004–05	Hull C	0	0	**2**	**0**
From York C					
2007–08	Hibernian	18	5	**18**	**5**
2008–09	Crewe Alex	37	6		
2009–10	Crewe Alex	37	13		
2010–11	Crewe Alex	43	28	**117**	**47**
2011–12	Brentford	46	11		
2012–13	Brentford	44	18		
2013–14	Brentford	46	17	**136**	**46**
2014–15	Birmingham C	46	15		
2015–16	Birmingham C	40	11		
2016–17	Birmingham C	23	6		
2017–18	Birmingham C	4	0	**113**	**32**
2017–18	Sheffield U	26	5	**26**	**5**
2018–19	Bolton W	31	1	**31**	**1**
2019–20	Bradford C	20	4		
2020–21	Bradford C	35	4	**55**	**8**

EVANS, Gary (F) **499** **86**
H: 6 0 W: 12 08 b.Stockport 26-4-88

2006–07	Crewe Alex	0	0		
2007–08	Macclesfield T	42	7		
2008–09	Macclesfield T	40	12	**82**	**19**
2009–10	Bradford C	43	11		
2010–11	Bradford C	36	3		
2011–12	Rotherham U	32	7		
2012–13	Rotherham U	13	2	**45**	**9**
2012–13	Fleetwood T	16	1		
2013–14	Fleetwood T	34	6		
2014–15	Fleetwood T	43	3	**93**	**10**
2015–16	Portsmouth	40	10		
2016–17	Portsmouth	41	5		
2017–18	Portsmouth	32	2		
2018–19	Portsmouth	42	10		
2019–20	Portsmouth	17	5		
2020–21	Portsmouth	1	0	**173**	**32**
2020–21	Bradford C	27	2	**106**	**16**

FOULDS, Matthew (D) **6** **0**
b.Bradford 1-2-98

2015–16	Bury	0	0		
2015–16	Everton	0	0		
2016–17	Everton	0	0		
2017–18	Everon	0	0		
2018–19	Everton	0	0		
2019–20	Everton	0	0		
2020–21	Como	3	0	**3**	**0**
2020–21	Bradford C	3	0	**3**	**0**

FRENCH, Tyler (D) **16** **0**
b.Bury St Edmunds 12-2-99
From Long Melford, Hadleigh U, AFC Sudbury.

2019–20	Bradford C	2	0		
2020–21	Bradford C	14	0	**16**	**0**

HORNBY, Sam (G) **29** **0**
b. 14-2-95
From Hednesford T, Redditch U.

2015–16	Burton Alb	0	0		
2016–17	Burton Alb	0	0		
2017–18	Port Vale	11	0		
2018–19	Port Vale	0	0	**11**	**0**
2019–20	Bradford C	0	0		
2020–21	Bradford C	18	0	**18**	**0**

HUFFER, Will (G) **1** **0**
b.London 30-10-98
Internationals: England U17, U18.

2018–19	Leeds U	1	0		
2019–20	Leeds U	0	0	**1**	**0**
2020–21	Bradford C	0	0		

ISMAIL, Zeli (M) **163** **16**
H: 5 8 W: 11 12 b.Kukes 12-12-93
Internationals: England U16, U17.

2010–11	Wolverhampton W	0	0		
2011–12	Wolverhampton W	0	0		
2012–13	Wolverhampton W	0	0		
2012–13	*Milton Keynes D*	7	0	**7**	**0**
2013–14	Wolverhampton W	9	0		
2013–14	*Burton Alb*	15	3		
2014–15	Wolverhampton W	0	0		
2014–15	*Notts Co*	14	4	**14**	**4**
2015–16	Wolverhampton W	0	0	**9**	**0**
2015–16	*Burton Alb*	3	0	**18**	**3**
2015–16	*Oxford U*	5	0	**5**	**0**
2015–16	*Cambridge U*	11	1	**11**	**1**
2016–17	Bury	16	3		
2017–18	Bury	21	0	**37**	**3**
2017–18	*Walsall*	16	1		
2018–19	Walsall	32	3	**48**	**4**
2019–20	Bradford C	11	1		
2020–21	Bradford C	3	0	**14**	**1**

LONGRIDGE, Jackson (D) **170** **12**
b.Glasgow 12-4-95

2011–12	Ayr U	2	0		
2012–13	Ayr U	3	0		
2013–14	Ayr U	4	0	**9**	**0**
2014–15	Stranraer	34	1	**34**	**1**
2015–16	Livingston	30	1		
2016–17	Livingston	30	3		
2017–18	Livingston	31	3	**91**	**7**
2018–19	Dunfermline Ath	33	4	**33**	**4**
2019–20	Bradford C	1	0		
2020–21	Bradford C	2	0	**3**	**0**

Transferred to Livingston January 2021.

MOTTLEY-HENRY, Dylan (F) **33** **0**
b. 2-8-97

2014–15	Bradford C	1	0		
2015–16	Bradford C	1	0		
From Altrincham, Bradford PA, Tranmere R.					
2017–18	Barnsley	1	0		
2018–19	Barnsley	0	0		
2018–19	*Tranmere R*	12	0	**12**	**0**
2019–20	Barnsley	0	0	**1**	**0**
2019–20	Bradford C	7	0		
2020–21	Bradford C	11	0	**20**	**0**

Transferred to Larne February 2021.

NOVAK, Lee (F) **386** **91**
H: 6 0 W: 12 04 b.Newcastle upon Tyne 28-9-88
From Gretna, Gateshead, Newcastle Blue Star.

2008–09	Huddersfield T	0	0		
2009–10	Huddersfield T	37	12		
2010–11	Huddersfield T	31	5		
2011–12	Huddersfield T	41	13		
2012–13	Huddersfield T	35	4	**144**	**34**
2013–14	Birmingham C	38	9		
2014–15	Birmingham C	21	1		
2015–16	Birmingham C	0	0	**59**	**10**
2015–16	*Chesterfield*	35	14	**35**	**14**
2016–17	Charlton Ath	29	2		
2017–18	Charlton Ath	2	0	**31**	**2**
2017–18	Scunthorpe U	32	6		
2018–19	Scunthorpe U	43	12		
2019–20	Scunthorpe U	19	5	**94**	**23**
2019–20	Bradford C	6	2		
2020–21	Bradford C	17	6	**23**	**8**

O'CONNOR, Anthony (D) **331** **17**
H: 6 2 W: 12 06 b.Cork 25-10-92
Internationals: Republic of Ireland U17, U19, U21.

2010–11	Blackburn R	0	0		
2011–12	Blackburn R	0	0		
2012–13	Blackburn R	0	0		
2012–13	*Burton Alb*	46	0		
2013–14	Blackburn R	0	0		
2013–14	*Torquay U*	31	0	**31**	**0**
2014–15	Plymouth Arg	40	3	**40**	**3**
2015–16	Burton Alb	21	1	**67**	**1**
2016–17	Aberdeen	32	3		
2017–18	Aberdeen	38	2	**70**	**5**
2018–19	Bradford C	42	6		
2019–20	Bradford C	36	0		
2020–21	Bradford C	45	2	**123**	**8**

O'CONNOR, Paudie (D) **84** **4**
b.Limerick 14-7-97
From Limerick.

2017–18	Leeds U	4	0		
2018–19	Leeds U	0	0	**4**	**0**
2018–19	*Blackpool*	10	0	**10**	**0**
2018–19	*Bradford C*	9	0		
2019–20	Bradford C	19	2		
2020–21	Bradford C	42	2	**70**	**4**

O'DONNELL, Richard (G) **317** **0**
H: 6 2 W: 13 05 b.Sheffield 12-9-88

2007–08	Sheffield W	0	0		
2007–08	*Rotherham U*	0	0		
2007–08	*Oldham Ath*	4	0	**4**	**0**
2008–09	Sheffield W	0	0		
2009–10	Sheffield W	0	0		
2010–11	Sheffield W	9	0		
2011–12	Sheffield W	6	0	**15**	**0**
2011–12	*Macclesfield T*	11	0	**11**	**0**
2012–13	Chesterfield	14	0	**14**	**0**
2013–14	Walsall	46	0		
2014–15	Walsall	44	0	**90**	**0**
2015–16	Wigan Ath	10	0	**10**	**0**
2015–16	Bristol C	21	0		
2016–17	Bristol C	8	0	**29**	**0**
2016–17	Rotherham U	12	0		
2017–18	Rotherham U	10	0	**22**	**0**
2017–18	Northampton T	19	0	**19**	**0**
2018–19	Bradford C	42	0		
2019–20	Bradford C	33	0		
2020–21	Bradford C	28	0	**103**	**0**

PRITCHARD, Harry (M) **76** **8**
b.High Wycombe 14-9-92
From Flackwell Heath, Burnham, Maidenhead U.

2018–19	Blackpool	37	3		
2019–20	Blackpool	2	0	**39**	**3**
2019–20	Bradford C	21	3		
2020–21	Bradford C	16	2	**37**	**5**

RICHARDS-EVERTON, Ben (D) **141** **5**
H: 6 2 W: 14 00 b.Birmingham 17-10-92
Internationals: England C.
From Hinckley U, Tamworth.

2014–15	Partick Thistle	2	0	**2**	**0**
2014–15	*Airdrieonians*	18	0	**18**	**0**
2015–16	Dunfermline Ath	34	2		
2016–17	Dunfermline Ath	6	0	**40**	**2**
2017–18	Accrington S	22	1		
2018–19	Accrington S	17	0	**39**	**1**
2018–19	Bradford C	0	0		
2019–20	Bradford C	32	2		
2020–21	Bradford C	10	0	**42**	**2**

Transferred to Barnet January 2021.

ROWE, Danny (F) **43** **12**
H: 6 1 W: 13 02 b.Blackpool 29-1-90

2012–13	Fleetwood T	0	0		

From Lincoln C, AFC Fylde.

2019–20	Oldham Ath	10	3		
2020–21	Oldham Ath	15	4	**25**	**7**
2020–21	Bradford C	18	5	**18**	**5**

Transferred to Chesterfield April 2021.

SCALES, Kian (M) **20** **1**
b.Leeds 1-12-02

2020–21	Bradford C	20	1	**20**	**1**

SHANKS, Connor (M) **0** **0**
b.Halifax 11-4-02

2020–21	Bradford C	0	0		

SIKORA, Jorge (D) **1** **0**
b. 29-3-02

2019–20	Bradford C	0	0		
2020–21	Bradford C	1	0	**1**	**0**

STAUNTON, Reece (D) **9** **1**
b. 10-12-01
Internationals: Republic of Ireland U18.

2017–18	Bradford C	1	0		
2018–19	Bradford C	0	0		
2019–20	Bradford C	0	0		
2020–21	Bradford C	8	1	**9**	**1**

SUKLENICKI, Oliver (M) **0** **0**
b.Czestochowa --

2020–21	Bradford C	0	0		

SUTTON, Levi (M) **92** **3**
b. 24-3-96

2014–15	Scunthorpe U	0	0		
2015–16	Scunthorpe U	1	0		
2016–17	Scunthorpe U	8	0		
2017–18	Scunthorpe U	15	0		
2018–19	Scunthorpe U	18	1		
2019–20	Scunthorpe U	16	0	**58**	**1**
2019–20	Bradford C	0	0		
2020–21	Bradford C	34	2	**34**	**2**

VERNAM, Charles (F) **119** **16**
b. 8-10-96
From Scunthorpe U.

2013–14	Derby Co	0	0		
2014–15	Derby Co	0	0		
2015–16	Derby Co	0	0		
2016	*Vestmannaeyjar*	9	1	**9**	**1**
2016–17	Derby Co	0	0		
2016–17	*Coventry C*	4	0	**4**	**0**
2017–18	Derby Co	0	0		
2017–18	*Grimsby T*	9	1		
2018–19	Grimsby T	35	3		
2019–20	Grimsby T	27	7	**71**	**11**
2020–21	Burton Alb	14	2	**14**	**2**
2020–21	Bradford C	21	2	**21**	**2**

WATT, Elliot (M) **58** **4**
b.Preston 11-3-18
Internationals: Scotland U17, U19, U21.
From Preston NE.

2018–19	Wolverhampton W	0	0		
2019–20	Wolverhampton W	0	0		
2019–20	*Carlisle U*	12	1	**12**	**1**
2020–21	Bradford C	46	3	**46**	**3**

WOOD, Charlie (F) **0** **0**

2020–21	Bradford C	0	0		

WOOD, Connor (D) **103** **2**
b.Harlow 17-7-96
From Soham Town Rangers, Chesham U.

2016–17	Leicester C	0	0		
2017–18	Leicester C	0	0		
2018–19	Bradford C	22	1		
2019–20	Bradford C	35	0		
2020–21	Bradford C	46	1	**103**	**2**

Scholars
Ajibode, Oluwagbemileke Immanuel; Harrop, Luke; Maumbe, Tanaka Christian; Monthe Youmbi, Rooney Dylan; Morris, Connor Alan; Norman, Oliver Max; Ormerod, Harvey Steven; Pointon, Bobby; Roberts, Cole; Rowe, Harvey Oliver; Sukiennicki, Olivier Mariusz; Thewlis, George Gary; Tunkara Saho, Yahaya; White, Jonathan Paul; Wilson, Jack Lewis; Wood, Charles Hamilton.

BRENTFORD (13)

ADAMS, Joe (M) **9** **1**
b. 13-2-01
Internationals: Wales U17, U19.

2017–18	Bury	2	0		
2018–19	Bury	1	0	**3**	**0**
2019–20	Brentford	0	0		
2020–21	Brentford	0	0		
2020–21	*Grimsby T*	6	1	**6**	**1**

BALCOMBE, Ellery (G) **23** **0**
b. 15-10-99
Internationals: England U18, U19, U20.

2016–17	Brentford	0	0		
2017–18	Brentford	0	0		
2018–19	Brentford	0	0		
2019–20	Brentford	0	0		
2019–20	*Viborg*	8	0	**8**	**0**
2020–21	Brentford	0	0		
2020–21	*Doncaster R*	15	0	**15**	**0**

BAPTISTE, Shandon (M) **39** **1**
b. 8-4-98
Internationals: Grenada Full caps.

2017–18	Oxford U	0	0		
2018–19	Oxford U	9	0		
2019–20	Oxford U	17	1	**26**	**1**
2019–20	Brentford	12	0		
2020–21	Brentford	1	0	**13**	**0**

BIDSTRUP, Mads (M) **4** **0**
b.Koge 25-2-01
From RB Leipzig.

2020–21	Brentford	4	0	**4**	**0**

BROOK, Lachlan (F) **8** **1**
H: 5 10 b.Gawler 8-2-01
Internationals: Australia U17, U20, U23.

2016–17	Adelaide U	0	0		
2017–18	Adelaide U	1	0		
2018–19	Adelaide U	0	0		
2019–20	Adelaide U	7	1	**8**	**1**
2020–21	Brentford	0	0		

CANOS, Sergi (M) **193** **30**
H: 5 8 W: 11 11 b.Nules 2-2-97
Internationals: Spain U16, U17, U19, U20.
From Barcelona.

2015–16	Liverpool	1	0	**1**	**0**
2015–16	*Brentford*	38	7		
2016–17	Norwich C	3	0	**3**	**0**
2016–17	Brentford	18	4		
2017–18	Brentford	30	3		
2018–19	Brentford	44	7		
2019–20	Brentford	13	0		
2020–21	Brentford	46	9	**189**	**30**

CRAMA, Tristan (D) **0** **0**
H: 6 4 b.Beziers 8-11-01
From Beziers.

2020–21	Brentford	0	0		

DA SILVA, Josh (M) **89** **16**
b. 23-10-98
Internationals: England U19, U20.

2016–17	Arsenal	0	0		
2017–18	Arsenal	0	0		
2018–19	Brentford	17	1		
2019–20	Brentford	42	10		
2020–21	Brentford	30	5	**89**	**16**

DALSGAARD, Henrik (F) **348** **24**
H: 6 4 W: 12 11 b.Viborg 27-7-89
Internationals: Denmark U20, U21, Full caps.

2008–09	Aalborg	4	1		
2009–10	Aalborg	25	0		
2010–11	Aalborg	15	1		
2011–12	Aalborg	30	2		
2012–13	Aalborg	31	2		
2013–14	Aalborg	18	2		
2014–15	Aalborg	26	1		
2015–16	Aalborg	17	0	**166**	**9**
2015–16	Zulte Waregem	19	3		
2016–17	Zulte Waregem	16	6	**35**	**9**
2017–18	Brentford	29	1		
2018–19	Brentford	40	2		
2019–20	Brentford	43	1		
2020–21	Brentford	35	2	**147**	**6**

DANIELS, Luke (G) **215** **0**
H: 6 1 W: 12 10 b.Bolton 5-1-88
Internationals: England U18, U19.

2006–07	WBA	0	0		
2007–08	*Motherwell*	2	0	**2**	**0**
2007–08	WBA	0	0		
2008–09	WBA	0	0		
2008–09	*Shrewsbury T*	38	0	**38**	**0**
2009–10	WBA	0	0		
2009–10	*Tranmere R*	37	0	**37**	**0**
2010–11	WBA	0	0		
2010–11	*Charlton Ath*	0	0		
2010–11	*Rochdale*	1	0	**1**	**0**
2010–11	*Bristol R*	9	0	**9**	**0**
2011–12	WBA	0	0		
2011–12	*Southend U*	9	0	**9**	**0**
2012–13	WBA	0	0		
2013–14	WBA	1	0		
2014–15	WBA	0	0	**1**	**0**
2014–15	Scunthorpe U	23	0		
2015–16	Scunthorpe U	39	0		
2016–17	Scunthorpe U	39	0	**101**	**0**
2016–17	Brentford	0	0		
2017–18	Brentford	1	0		
2018–19	Brentford	12	0		
2019–20	Brentford	0	0		
2020–21	Brentford	4	0	**17**	**0**

DERVISOGLU, Halil (F)				**76**	**18**
Internationals: Turkey U19, U21.					
2017–18	Sparta Rotterdam	0	0		
2018–19	Sparta Rotterdam	34	10		
2019–20	Sparta Rotterdam	17	5	**51**	**15**
2019–20	Brentford	4	0		
2020–21	Brentford	0	0	**4**	**0**
2020–21	*FC Twente*	9	0	**9**	**0**
2020–21	*Galatasaray*	12	3	**12**	**3**

FORSS, Marcus (F)				**65**	**19**
H: 6 1 b. 18-6-99					
Internationals: Finland U17, U18, U19, U21.					
From WBA.					
2018–19	Brentford	6	1		
2019–20	Brentford	2	0		
2019–20	*AFC Wimbledon*	18	11	**18**	**11**
2020–21	Brentford	39	7	**47**	**8**

FOSU, Tarique (M)				**179**	**33**
H: 5 7 W: 10 08 b. 5-11-95					
Internationals: England U18.					
2013–14	Reading	0	0		
2014–15	Reading	1	0		
2015–16	Reading	0	0		
2015–16	*Fleetwood T*	6	1	**6**	**1**
2015–16	*Accrington S*	8	3	**8**	**3**
2016–17	Reading	0	0	**1**	**0**
2016–17	*Colchester U*	33	5	**33**	**5**
2017–18	Charlton Ath	30	9		
2018–19	Charlton Ath	27	2	**57**	**11**
2019–20	Oxford U	25	8	**25**	**8**
2019–20	Brentford	10	1		
2020–21	Brentford	39	4	**49**	**5**

GHODDOS, Saman (F)				**252**	**54**
b.Malmo 6-9-93					
2011	Limhamn Bunkeflo	17	0		
2012	Limhamn Bunkeflo	24	4	**41**	**4**
2013	Trelleborg	18	1	**18**	**1**
2014	Syrianska	29	6		
2015	Syrianska	25	8	**54**	**14**
2016	Ostersund	27	10		
2017	Ostersund	23	8		
2018	Ostersund	15	9	**65**	**27**
2018–19	Amiens	27	4		
2019–20	Amiens	5	1		
2020–21	Amiens	2	0	**34**	**5**
2020–21	Brentford	40	3	**40**	**3**

GILBERT, Alex (F)				**0**	**0**
b. 28-12-01					
From WBA.					
2020–21	Brentford	0	0		

GOODE, Charlie (D)				**125**	**8**
b. 3-8-95					
Internationals: England C.					
From Hadley, AFC Hayes, Hendon.					
2015–16	Scunthorpe U	10	1		
2016–17	Scunthorpe U	20	0		
2017–18	Scunthorpe U	13	1		
2018–19	Scunthorpe U	21	3	**64**	**5**
2018–19	*Northampton T*	17	0		
2019–20	Northampton T	36	3	**53**	**3**
2020–21	Brentford	8	0	**8**	**0**

GORDON, Lewis (D)				**0**	**0**
b. 12-2-01					
2018–19	Watford	0	0		
2019–20	Watford	0	0		
2020–21	Brentford	0	0		

HAMMAR, Fredrik (M)				**13**	**4**
b. 26-2-01					
Internationals: Sweden U17, U19.					
2017	Brommapojkarna	1	0		
2018	Brommapojkarna	0	0		
2018	Akropolis	12	4	**12**	**4**
2019–20	Brommapojkarna	0	0	**1**	**0**
2019–20	Brentford	0	0		
2020–21	Brentford	0	0		
Transferred to Akropolis January 2021.					

HAYGARTH, Max (M)				**1**	**0**
b. 21-1-02					
2019–20	Manchester U	0	0		
2020–21	Manchester U	0	0		
2020–21	Brentford	1	0	**1**	**0**

HENRY, Rico (D)				**156**	**4**
H: 5 7 W: 10 06 b.Birmingham 8-7-97					
Internationals: England U19, U20.					
2014–15	Walsall	9	0		
2015–16	Walsall	35	2		
2016–17	Walsall	2	0	**46**	**2**
2016–17	Brentford	12	0		
2017–18	Brentford	8	0		
2018–19	Brentford	14	1		
2019–20	Brentford	46	0		
2020–21	Brentford	30	1	**110**	**2**

HERCULES, Wraynel (F)				**0**	**0**
b. 19-1-02					
From Barnet.					
2020–21	Brentford	0	0		

HOCKENHULL, Ben (D)				**0**	**0**
H: 6 1 b. 3-9-01					
From Manchester U.					
2020–21	Brentford	0	0		

JANELT, Vitaly (M)				**94**	**5**
b.Hamburg 10-5-98					
2016–17	RB Leipzig	0	0		
2016–17	*VfL Bochum*	7	0		
2017–18	RB Leipzig	0	0		
2017–18	*VfL Bochum*	13	0		
2018–19	VfL Bochum	9	1		
2019–20	VfL Bochum	24	1		
2020–21	VfL Bochum	0	0	**53**	**2**
2020–21	Brentford	41	3	**41**	**3**

JANSSON, Pontus (D)				**296**	**20**
H: 6 3 W: 13 08 b.Arlov 13-2-91					
Internationals: Sweden U17, U19, U21, Full caps.					
2009	Malmo	2	0		
2009	*IFK Malmo*	9	4	**9**	**4**
2010	Malmo	18	1		
2011	Malmo	15	2		
2012	Malmo	30	1		
2013	Malmo	24	1		
2014	Malmo	9	1	**98**	**6**
2014–15	Torino	9	0		
2015–16	Torino	7	1		
2015–16	Torino	0	0	**16**	**1**
2016–17	*Leeds U*	34	3		
2017–18	Leeds U	42	3		
2018–19	Leeds U	39	3	**115**	**9**
2019–20	Brentford	34	0		
2020–21	Brentford	24	0	**58**	**0**

JEANVIER, Julian (D)				**163**	**10**
H: 6 0 W: 12 04 b.Clichy 31-3-92					
Internationals: Guinea Full caps.					
2012–13	Nancy	6	0	**6**	**0**
2013–14	Lille	0	0		
2014–15	Lille	0	0		
2014–15	*Mouscron-Peruwelz*	17	0	**17**	**0**
2015–16	Lille	0	0		
2015–16	*Red Star*	24	2	**24**	**2**
2016–17	Reims	29	3		
2017–18	Reims	33	2	**62**	**5**
2018–19	Brentford	24	2		
2019–20	Brentford	26	1		
2020–21	Brentford	0	0	**50**	**3**
2020–21	*Kasimpasa*	4	0	**4**	**0**

JENSEN, Mathias (M)				**153**	**18**
b. 1-1-96					
Internationals: Denmark U18, U19, U20, U21.					
2015–16	Nordsjaelland	5	1		
2016–17	Nordsjaelland	22	2		
2017–18	Nordsjaelland	35	12		
2018–19	Nordsjaelland	1	0	**63**	**15**
2018–19	Celta Vigo	6	0	**6**	**0**
2019–20	Brentford	39	1		
2020–21	Brentford	45	2	**84**	**3**

MAGHOMA, Edmond-Paris (M)				**0**	**0**
b.Enfield 8-5-01					
From Tottenham H.					
2020–21	Brentford	0	0		

MARCONDES, Emiliano (M)				**205**	**42**
H: 6 0 W: 11 11 b.Hvidovre 9-3-95					
Internationals: Denmark U17, U18, U19, U20, U21.					
2012–13	Nordsjaelland	3	0		
2013–14	Nordsjaelland	11	1		
2014–15	Nordsjaelland	24	5		
2015–16	Nordsjaelland	30	2		
2016–17	Nordsjaelland	25	12		
2017–18	Nordsjaelland	19	17	**112**	**37**
2017–18	Brentford	12	0		
2018–19	Brentford	13	0		
2019–20	Brentford	25	2		
2019–20	*Midtjylland*	12	2	**12**	**2**
2020–21	Brentford	31	1	**81**	**3**

MBEUMO, Bryan (M)				**127**	**34**
b.Avallon 7-8-99					
Internationals: France U17, U20, U21.					
2016–17	Troyes	0	0		
2017–18	Troyes	4	0		
2018–19	Troyes	35	10		
2019–20	Troyes	2	1	**41**	**11**
2019–20	Brentford	42	15		
2020–21	Brentford	44	8	**86**	**23**

NORGAARD, Christian (M)				**182**	**8**
b.Copenhagen 10-3-94					
Internationals: Denmark U16, U17, U19, U20, U21.					
2011–12	Lyngby	1	0	**1**	**0**
2012–13	Hamburg	0	0		
2013–14	Brondby	13	0		
2014–15	Brondby	21	3		
2015–16	Brondby	16	0		
2016–17	Brondby	31	4		
2017–18	Brondby	34	1		
2018–19	Brondby	1	0	**116**	**8**
2018–19	Fiorentina	6	0	**6**	**0**
2019–20	Brentford	42	0		
2020–21	Brentford	17	0	**59**	**0**

O'CONNER, Kane (D)				**0**	**0**
b. 17-1-01					
2019–20	Hibernian	0	0		
2020–21	Hibernian	0	0		
2020–21	Brentford	0	0		

OKSANEN, Jaako (D)				**53**	**2**
H: 6 0 W: 11 05 b.Helsinki 7-11-00					
Internationals: Finland U16, U17, U18, U19, U21.					
From HJK Helsinki.					
2016	Klubi 04	1	0		
2017	Klubi 04	22	2	**23**	**2**
2017	HJK Helsinki	1	0	**1**	**0**
2018–19	Brentford	1	0		
2019–20	Brentford	1	0		
2020–21	Brentford	0	0	**2**	**0**
2020–21	*AFC Wimbledon*	27	0	**27**	**0**

PINNOCK, Ethan (D)				**133**	**6**
H: 6 4 W: 12 06 b.Lambeth 29-5-93					
Internationals: England C.					
From Dulwich Hamlet.					
2017–18	Barnsley	12	2		
2018–19	Barnsley	46	1	**58**	**3**
2019–20	Brentford	36	2		
2020–21	Brentford	39	1	**75**	**3**

PRESSLEY, Aaron (F)				**2**	**0**
b.Edinburgh 7-11-01					
From Hearts.					
2019–20	Aston Villa	0	0		
2020–21	Aston Villa	0	0		
2020–21	Brentford	2	0	**2**	**0**

RACIC, Luka (D)				**12**	**1**
b.Greve 8-5-99					
Internationals: Denmark U16, U17, U18, U19, U20, U21.					
From Copenhagen.					
2018–19	Brentford	2	0		
2019–20	Brentford	4	1		
2020–21	Brentford	0	0	**6**	**1**
2020–21	*Northampton T*	6	0	**6**	**0**

RAYA, David (G)				**186**	**0**
H: 6 0 W: 12 08 b.Barcelona 15-9-95					
2013–14	Blackburn R	0	0		
2014–15	Blackburn R	2	0		
2015–16	Blackburn R	5	0		
2016–17	Blackburn R	5	0		
2017–18	Blackburn R	45	0		
2018–19	Blackburn R	41	0	**98**	**0**
2019–20	Brentford	46	0		
2020–21	Brentford	42	0	**88**	**0**

READ, Arthur (M)				**32**	**2**
H: 5 10 W: 10 01 b.Leighton Buzzard 3-11-99					
2018–19	Luton T	0	0		
2019–20	Brentford	0	0		
2020–21	Brentford	0	0		
2020–21	*Stevenage*	32	2	**32**	**2**

ROERSLEV RASMUSSEN, Mads (D)				**38**	**0**
b. 24-6-99					
Internationals: Denmark U17, U18, U19, U20, U21.					
2016–17	FC Copenhagen	3	0		
2016–17	*Halmstads*	1	0	**1**	**0**
2017–18	FC Copenhagen	2	0		
2018–19	FC Copenhagen	0	0	**5**	**0**
2018–19	*Vendsyssel*	4	0	**4**	**0**
2019–20	Brentford	11	0		
2020–21	Brentford	17	0	**28**	**0**

SHEPPERD, Nathan (G)				**0**	**0**
b. 10-9-00					
2020–21	Brentford	0	0		

SORENSEN, Mads (D)				**70**	**3**
H: 6 1 W: 11 07 b. 7-1-99					
Internationals: Denmark U18, U19, U21.					
2014–15	Horsens	6	0		
2015–16	Horsens	5	0		
2016–17	Horsens	6	0		
2017–18	Horsens	3	1	**20**	**1**
2017–18	Brentford	0	0		

2018–19 Brentford 8 0
2019–20 Brentford 1 0
2019–20 *AFC Wimbledon* 9 0 **9 0**
2020–21 Brentford 32 2 **41 2**

STEVENS, Fin (D) 2 0
b.Brighton 10-4-01
From Arsenal, Worthing.
2020–21 Brentford 2 0 **2 0**

THOMPSON, Dominic (M) 31 0
b.Barnet 26-7-00
2018–19 Arsenal 0 0
2019–20 Brentford 2 0
2020–21 Brentford 4 0 **6 0**
2020–21 *Swindon T* 25 0 **25 0**

TONEY, Ivan (F) 265 107
H: 5 10 W: 12 00 b.Northampton 16-3-96
2012–13 Northampton T 0 0
2013–14 Northampton T 13 3
2014–15 Northampton T 40 8 **53 11**
2015–16 Newcastle U 2 0
2015–16 *Barnsley* 15 1 **15 1**
2016–17 Newcastle U 0 0
2016–17 *Shrewsbury T* 19 6 **19 6**
2016–17 *Scunthorpe U* 15 6
2017–18 Newcastle U 0 0 **2 0**
2017–18 *Wigan Ath* 24 4 **24 4**
2017–18 *Scunthorpe U* 16 8 **31 14**
2018–19 Peterborough U 44 16
2019–20 Peterborough U 32 24 **76 40**
2020–21 Brentford 45 31 **45 31**

TREVITT, Ryan (M) 0 0
b. 12-3-03
2020–21 Brentford 0 0

VALENCIA, Joel (F) 163 12
b.Esmeraldas 16-11-94
Internationals: Spain U17. Ecuador U17.
2011–12 Zaragoza 1 0
2012–13 Zaragoza 0 0
2013–14 Zaragoza 0 0 **1 0**
2014–15 Logrones 33 1
2015–16 Logrones 17 0 **50 1**
2015–16 Koper 13 1
2016–17 Koper 13 0 **26 1**
2017–18 Piast Gliwice 25 3
2018–19 Piast Gliwice 33 6
2019–20 Piast Gliwice 1 0 **59 9**
2019–20 Brentford 19 1
2020–21 Brentford 0 0 **19 1**
2020–21 *Legia Warsaw* 8 0 **8 0**

ZAMBUREK, Jan (M) 29 0
H: 6 0 b. 13-2-01
Internationals: Czech Republic U16, U17, U18, U19.
From Slavia Prague.
2018–19 Brentford 1 0
2019–20 Brentford 16 0
2020–21 Brentford 6 0 **23 0**
2020–21 *Shrewsbury T* 6 0 **6 0**

BRIGHTON & HA (14)

ALZATE, Steve (M) 68 4
H: 5 10 W: 10 03 b.Camden Town 1-9-98
Internationals: Colombia Full caps.
2016–17 Leyton Orient 12 1 **12 1**
2017–18 Brighton & HA 0 0
2018–18 Brighton & HA 0 0
2018–19 *Swindon T* 22 2 **22 2**
2019–20 Brighton & HA 19 0
2020–21 Brighton & HA 15 1 **34 1**

ANDONE, Florin (F) 191 63
H: 6 0 W: 11 07 b.Botosani 5-1-94
Internationals: Romania U19, Full caps.
2012–13 Villarreal 0 0
2013–14 Villarreal 0 0
2013–14 *Atletico Baleares* 34 12 **34 12**
2014–15 Cordoba 20 5
2015–16 Cordoba 36 21 **56 26**
2016–17 Deportivo La Coruna 37 12
2017–18 Deportivo La Coruna 29 7 **66 19**
2018–19 Brighton & HA 23 3
2019–20 Brighton & HA 3 1
2019–20 *Galatasaray* 9 2 **9 2**
2020–21 Brighton & HA 0 0 **26 4**

BALUTA, Tudor (M) 58 2
b.Craiova 27-3-99
Internationals: Romania U19, U21, Full caps.
2015–16 Viitorul Constanta 2 0
2016–17 Viitorul Constanta 0 0
2017–18 Viitorul Constanta 24 0
2018–19 Viitorul Constanta 27 2 **53 2**
2019–20 Brighton & HA 0 0
2019–20 *Den Haag* 4 0 **4 0**
2020–21 Brighton & HA 0 0
2020–21 *Dynamo Kyiv* 1 0 **1 0**

BERNARDO, Junior (D) 113 3
H: 6 1 W: 12 00 b.S„o Paulo 14-5-95
2014 Red Bull Brasil 0 0
2015 Red Bull Brasil 3 0 **3 0**
2015 *Ponte Preta* 0 0
2015–16 Liefering 1 0 **1 0**
2015–16 Red Bull Salzburg 13 0
2016–17 Red Bull Salzburg 3 1
2016–17 RB Leipzig 22 0
2017–18 RB Leipzig 18 1 **40 1**
2018–19 Brighton & HA 22 0
2019–20 Brighton & HA 14 0
2020–21 Brighton & HA 3 0 **39 0**
2020–21 *Red Bull Salzburg* 14 1 **30 2**

BISSOUMA, Yves (M) 133 5
H: 5 9 W: 12 04 b.Issia 30-8-96
Internationals: Mali Full caps.
From Real Bamako.
2016–17 Lille 23 1
2017–18 Lille 24 2 **47 3**
2018–19 Brighton & HA 28 0
2019–20 Brighton & HA 22 1
2020–21 Brighton & HA 36 1 **86 2**

BURN, Dan (D) 285 10
H: 6 6 W: 13 00 b.Blyth 1-5-92
2009–10 Darlington 4 0 **4 0**
2010–11 Fulham 0 0
2011–12 Fulham 0 0
2012–13 Fulham 0 0
2012–13 *Yeovil T* 34 2 **34 2**
2013–14 Fulham 9 0
2013–14 *Birmingham C* 24 0 **24 0**
2014–15 Fulham 20 1
2015–16 Fulham 32 0 **61 1**
2016–17 Wigan Ath 42 1
2017–18 Wigan Ath 45 5
2018–19 Brighton & HA 0 0
2018–19 *Wigan Ath* 14 0 **101 6**
2019–20 Brighton & HA 34 0
2020–21 Brighton & HA 27 1 **61 1**

CAICEDO, Moises (M) 25 4
b.Santo Domingo 2-11-01
2019 Independiente del Valle 3 0
2020 Independiente del Valle 22 4
2020–21 Independiente del Valle 0 0 **25 4**
2020–21 Brighton & HA 0 0

CLARKE, Matthew (M) 231 8
H: 5 11 W: 11 00 b.Ipswich 22-9-96
2013–14 Ipswich T 0 0
2014–15 Ipswich T 4 0
2015–16 Ipswich T 0 0 **4 0**
2015–16 *Portsmouth* 29 1
2016–17 Portsmouth 33 1
2017–18 Portsmouth 42 2
2018–19 Portsmouth 46 3 **150 7**
2019–20 Brighton & HA 0 0
2019–20 *Derby Co* 35 1
2020–21 Brighton & HA 0 0
2020–21 *Derby Co* 42 0 **77 1**

COCHRANE, Alex (M) 7 0
b. 21-4-00
Internationals: England U16, U20.
2019–20 Brighton & HA 0 0
2020–21 Brighton & HA 0 0
2020–21 *US Gilloise* 7 0 **7 0**

COLLYER, Toby (M) 0 0
b.Worthing 3-1-04
Internationals: England U16.
2020–21 Brighton & HA 0 0

CONNOLLY, Aaron (F) 43 5
b. 28-1-00
Internationals: Republic of Ireland U17, U19, U21, Full caps.
2017–18 Brighton & HA 0 0
2018–19 Brighton & HA 0 0
2018–19 *Luton T* 2 0 **2 0**
2019–20 Brighton & HA 24 3
2020–21 Brighton & HA 17 2 **41 5**

DENDONCKER, Lars (D) 0 0
b.Passandale 3-4-01
From Club Brugge.
2020–21 Brighton & HA 0 0

DESBOIS, Adam (G) 0 0
b.Reading 5-1-01
2020–21 Brighton & HA 0 0

DUNK, Lewis (D) 315 21
H: 6 3 W: 12 02 b.Brighton 1-12-91
Internationals: England Full caps.
2009–10 Brighton & HA 1 0
2010–11 Brighton & HA 5 0
2011–12 Brighton & HA 31 0
2012–13 Brighton & HA 8 0
2013–14 Brighton & HA 6 0
2013–14 *Bristol C* 2 0 **2 0**
2014–15 Brighton & HA 38 5
2015–16 Brighton & HA 38 3
2016–17 Brighton & HA 43 2
2017–18 Brighton & HA 38 1
2018–19 Brighton & HA 36 2
2019–20 Brighton & HA 36 3
2020–21 Brighton & HA 33 5 **313 21**

ENEME ELLA, Ulrick (F) 0 0
H: 6 0 W: 11 11 b.Sens 22-5-01
Internationals: France U16, U17, U18.
From Amiens.
2020–21 Brighton & HA 0 0

FURLONG, James (D) 0 0
H: 5 10 W: 11 03 b.Dublin 7-6-02
2020–21 Brighton & HA 0 0

GROSS, Pascal (M) 314 35
H: 5 7 W: 10 06 b.Bad Salzungen 15-6-91
Internationals: Germany U18, U19.
2008–09 1899 Hoffenheim 4 0
2009–10 1899 Hoffenheim 1 0
2010–11 1899 Hoffenheim 0 0 **5 0**
2010–11 Karlsruher 3 1
2011–12 Karlsruher 22 2 **25 3**
2012–13 Ingolstadt 04 30 2
2013–14 Ingolstadt 04 29 2
2014–15 Ingolstadt 04 34 7
2015–16 Ingolstadt 04 32 1
2016–17 Ingolstadt 04 33 5 **158 17**
2017–18 Brighton & HA 38 7
2018–19 Brighton & HA 25 3
2019–20 Brighton & HA 29 2
2020–21 Brighton & HA 34 3 **126 15**

GWARGIS, Peter (M) 35 4
b.Sidney 4-9-00
Internationals: Sweden U17, U19.
2017 Husqvarna 19 1 **19 1**
2018 Jonkopings 16 3 **16 3**
2019–20 Brighton & HA 0 0
2020–21 Brighton & HA 0 0

GYOKERES, Viktor (F) 112 30
H: 6 2 W: 13 08 b.Brommapoijkarna 4-6-98
Internationals: Sweden U19, U21, Full caps.
2015 Brommapojkarna 8 0
2016 Brommapojkarna 19 7
2017 Brommapojkarna 29 13 **56 20**
2017–18 Brighton & HA 0 0
2018–19 Brighton & HA 0 0
2019–20 Brighton & HA 0 0
2019–20 *St Pauli* 26 7 **26 7**
2020–21 Brighton & HA 0 0
2020–21 *Swansea C* 11 0 **11 0**
2020–21 *Coventry C* 19 3 **19 3**

IZQUIERDO, Jose (D) 241 65
H: 5 7 W: 11 07 b.Pereira 7-7-92
Internationals: Colombia Full caps.
2010 Deportivo Pereira 9 1
2011 Deportivo Pereira 21 1
2012 Deportivo Pereira 24 10
2013 Deportivo Pereira 15 2 **69 14**
2013 Once Caldas 16 3
2014 Once Caldas 24 9 **40 12**
2014–15 Club Brugge 32 13
2015–16 Club Brugge 24 7
2016–17 Club Brugge 28 14 **84 34**
2017–18 Brighton & HA 32 5
2018–19 Brighton & HA 15 0
2019–20 Brighton & HA 0 0
2020–21 Brighton & HA 1 0 **48 5**

JAHANBAKHSH, Alireza (M) 246 63
H: 5 11 W: 12 02 b.Jirandeh 11-8-93
Internationals: Iran U20, U23, Full caps.
2010–11 Damash Tehran 12 0 **12 0**
2011–12 Damash Gilan 16 2
2012–13 Damash Gilan 28 8 **44 10**
2013–14 NEC Nijmegen 27 5
2014–15 NEC Nijmegen 28 12 **55 17**
2015–16 AZ Alkmaar 23 3
2016–17 AZ Alkmaar 29 10
2017–18 AZ Alkmaar 33 21 **85 34**
2018–19 Brighton & HA 19 0
2019–20 Brighton & HA 10 2
2020–21 Brighton & HA 21 0 **50 2**

JENKS, Teddy (M) 0 0
b. 12-3-02
Internationals: England U16, U17.
2019–20 Brighton & HA 0 0
2020–21 Brighton & HA 0 0

KARBOWNIK, Michal (D) 36 0
b.Radom 13-3-01
2017–18 Legia Warsaw 0 0
2018–19 Legia Warsaw 0 0
2019–20 Legia Warzaw 28 0 **28 0**

2020–21 Brighton & HA 0 0
2020–21 *Legia Warsaw* 8 0 **8 0**

KHADRA, Reda (M) 1 0
b.Berlin 4-7-01
From Borussia Dortmund.
2020–21 Brighton & HA 1 0 **1 0**

LALLANA, Adam (M) 396 67
H: 5 8 W: 11 06 b.St Albans 10-5-88
Internationals: England U18, U19, U21, Full caps.
2005–06 Southampton 0 0
2006–07 Southampton 1 0
2007–08 Southampton 5 1
2007–08 *Bournemouth* 3 0 **3 0**
2008–09 Southampton 40 1
2009–10 Southampton 44 15
2010–11 Southampton 36 8
2011–12 Southampton 41 11
2012–13 Southampton 30 3
2013–14 Southampton 38 9 **235 48**
2014–15 Liverpool 27 5
2015–16 Liverpool 30 4
2016–17 Liverpool 31 8
2017–18 Liverpool 12 0
2018–19 Liverpool 13 0
2019–20 Liverpool 15 1 **128 18**
2020–21 Brighton & HA 30 1 **30 1**

LAMPTEY, Tariq (M) 20 1
b.Hillingdon 30-9-00
Internationals: England U18, U19, U20.
2019–20 Chelsea 1 0 **1 0**
2019–20 Brighton & HA 8 0
2020–21 Brighton & HA 11 1 **19 1**

LEONARD, Marc (M) 0 0
b.Glasgow 19-12-01
Internationals: Scotland U17, U19.
From Hearts.
2020–21 Brighton & HA 0 0

LONGMAN, Ryan (M) 44 8
b. 6-11-00
2019–20 Brighton & HA 0 0
2020–21 Brighton & HA 0 0
2020–21 *AFC Wimbledon* 44 8 **44 8**

MAC ALLISTER, Alexis (M) 109 12
b. 24-12-98
Internationals: Argentina U23, Full caps.
2016–17 Argentinos Juniors 23 3
2017–18 Argentinos Juniors 24 2
2018–19 Argentinos Juniors 19 5 **66 10**
2019–20 Brighton & HA 9 0
2019–20 *Boca Juniors* 13 1 **13 1**
2020–21 Brighton & HA 21 1 **30 1**

MARCH, Solly (M) 186 11
H: 6 1 W: 12 02 b.Lewes 26-7-94
Internationals: England U20, U21.
From Lewes.
2012–13 Brighton & HA 0 0
2013–14 Brighton & HA 23 0
2014–15 Brighton & HA 11 1
2015–16 Brighton & HA 16 3
2016–17 Brighton & HA 25 3
2017–18 Brighton & HA 36 1
2018–19 Brighton & HA 35 1
2019–20 Brighton & HA 19 0
2020–21 Brighton & HA 21 2 **186 11**

MAUPAY, Neal (F) 242 73
H: 5 7 W: 10 12 b.Versailles 14-8-96
Internationals: France U16, U17, U19, U21.
2012–13 Nice 15 3
2013–14 Nice 16 2
2014–15 Nice 13 1 **44 6**
2015–16 Saint-Etienne 15 1
2016–17 Saint-Etienne 0 0 **15 1**
2016–17 *Brest* 28 11 **28 11**
2017–18 Brentford 42 12
2018–19 Brentford 43 25 **85 37**
2019–20 Brighton & HA 37 10
2020–21 Brighton & HA 33 8 **70 18**

McGILL, Thomas (G) 1 0
b. 25-3-00
Internationals: England U16, U17, U19, U20.
2019–20 Brighton & HA 0 0
2019–20 *Crawley T* 0 0
2020–21 Brighton & HA 0 0
2020–21 *Crawley T* 1 0 **1 0**

MLAKAR, Jan (F) 81 30
b.Ljubljana 23-10-98
Internationals: Slovenia U17, U19, U21, B.
2016–17 Fiorentina 1 0
2017–18 Fiorentina 0 0 **1 0**
2017–18 *Venezia* 3 0 **3 0**
2017–18 Maribor 12 3
2018–19 Maribor 26 13
2019–20 Brighton & HA 0 0
2019–20 *QPR* 6 0 **6 0**
2019–20 *Wigan Ath* 1 0 **1 0**
2020–21 Brighton & HA 0 0
2020–21 *Maribor* 32 14 **70 30**
Transferred to Hajduk Split July 2021.

MODER, Jakub (M) 70 9
b.Szczecinek 7-4-99
2016–17 Lech Poznan 0 0
2017–18 Lech Poznan 1 0
2018–19 Lech Poznan 0 0
2018–19 *Odra Opole* 31 4 **31 4**
2019–20 Lech Poznan 26 5
2020–21 Lech Poznan 0 0 **27 5**
2020–21 Brighton & HA 12 0 **12 0**

MOLUMBY, Jayson (M) 52 1
b. 6-8-99
Internationals: Republic of Ireland U16, U17, U19, U21.
2017–18 Brighton & HA 0 0
2018–19 Brighton & HA 0 0
2019–20 Brighton & HA 0 0
2019–20 *Millwall* 36 1 **36 1**
2020–21 Brighton & HA 1 0 **1 0**
2020–21 *Preston NE* 15 0 **15 0**

OFFIAH, Odel (D) 0 0
b.Camden 26-10-02
2020–21 Brighton & HA 0 0

OSTIGARD, Leo (D) 85 3
b. 28-11-99
Internationals: Norway U16, U17, U18, U19, U20, U21, U23.
2017 Molde 7 0
2018 Molde 0 0 **7 0**
2018 *Viking* 11 0 **11 0**
2018–19 Brighton & HA 0 0
2019–20 Brighton & HA 0 0
2019–20 *St Pauli* 28 1 **28 1**
2020–21 Brighton & HA 0 0
2020–21 *Coventry C* 39 2 **39 2**

PACKHAM, Sam (M) 0 0
b.Redhill 8-11-01
2020–21 Brighton & HA 0 0

PEUPION, Cameron (M) 0 0
H: 5 9 b.Sydney 23-9-02
From Sydney FC.
2020–21 Brighton & HA 0 0

PROPPER, Davy (M) 316 36
H: 6 1 W: 11 05 b.Arnhem 2-9-91
Internationals: Netherlands U19, U21, Full caps.
2009–10 Vitesse 11 0
2010–11 Vitesse 29 3
2011–12 Vitesse 19 1
2012–13 Vitesse 14 0
2013–14 Vitesse 35 7
2014–15 Vitesse 34 7 **142 18**
2015–16 PSV Eindhoven 33 10
2016–17 PSV Eindhoven 34 6 **67 16**
2017–18 Brighton & HA 35 0
2018–19 Brighton & HA 30 1
2019–20 Brighton & HA 35 1
2020–21 Brighton & HA 7 0 **107 2**

RICHARDS, Taylor (M) 41 10
b.London 4-12-00
Internationals: England U17.
2018–19 Manchester C 0 0
2019–20 Brighton & HA 0 0
2020–21 Brighton & HA 0 0
2020–21 *Doncaster R* 41 10 **41 10**

ROBERTS, Haydon (D) 26 0
b. 10-5-02
Internationals: England U17, U18.
2019–20 Brighton & HA 0 0
2020–21 Brighton & HA 0 0
2020–21 *Rochdale* 26 0 **26 0**

RUSHWORTH, Carl (G) 0 0
b.Halifax 2-7-01
2020–21 Brighton & HA 0 0

RYAN, Mathew (G) 319 0
H: 6 0 W: 12 13 b.Plumpton 8-4-82
Internationals: Australia U23, Full caps.
2009 Blacktown C 0 0
2010 Blacktown C 11 0 **11 0**
2010–11 Central Coast Mariners 31 0
2011–12 Central Coast Mariners 24 0
2012–13 Central Coast Mariners 25 0 **80 0**
2013–14 Club Brugge 40 0
2014–15 Club Brugge 37 0 **77 0**
2015–16 Valencia 8 0
2016–17 Valencia 2 0 **10 0**
2016–17 *Genk* 17 0 **17 0**
2017–18 Brighton & HA 38 0
2018–19 Brighton & HA 34 0
2019–20 Brighton & HA 38 0
2020–21 Brighton & HA 11 0 **121 0**
2020–21 *Arsenal* 3 0 **3 0**

SANCHEZ, Robert (G) 70 0
b. 18-11-97
From Levante.
2018–19 Brighton & HA 0 0
2018–19 *Forest Green R* 17 0 **17 0**
2019–20 Brighton & HA 0 0
2019–20 *Rochdale* 26 0 **26 0**
2020–21 Brighton & HA 27 0 **27 0**

STEELE, Jason (G) 272 0
H: 6 2 W: 12 07 b.Newton Aycliffe 18-8-90
Internationals: England U16, U17, U19, U21. Great Britain.
2007–08 Middlesbrough 0 0
2008–09 Middlesbrough 0 0
2009–10 Middlesbrough 0 0
2009–10 *Northampton T* 13 0 **13 0**
2010–11 Middlesbrough 35 0
2011–12 Middlesbrough 34 0
2012–13 Middlesbrough 46 0
2013–14 Middlesbrough 16 0
2014–15 Middlesbrough 0 0 **131 0**
2014–15 *Blackburn R* 31 0
2015–16 Blackburn R 41 0
2016–17 Blackburn R 41 0 **113 0**
2017–18 Sunderland 15 0 **15 0**
2018–19 Brighton & HA 0 0
2019–20 Brighton & HA 0 0
2020–21 Brighton & HA 0 0

TALLEY, Fynn (G) 0 0
b.Bexley 14-9-02
From Arsenal.
2020–21 Brighton & HA 0 0

TANIMOWO, Ayo (D) 0 0
b.Redbridge 9-11-01
From Norwich C.
2020–21 Brighton & HA 0 0

TAU, Percy (F) 134 34
b.Witbank 13-5-94
Internationals: South Africa Full caps.
2013–14 Mamelodi Sundowns 1 0
2014–15 Mamelodi Sundowns 5 0
2015–16 Mamelodi Sundowns 0 0
2015–16 *Witbank Spurs* 11 3 **11 3**
2016–17 Mamelodi Sundowns 29 7
2017–18 Mamelodi Sundowns 30 11 **65 18**
2018–19 Brighton & HA 0 0
2018–19 *Union* 23 6 **23 6**
2019–20 Brighton & HA 0 0
2019–20 *Club Brugge* 18 3 **18 3**
2020–21 Brighton & HA 3 0 **3 0**
2020–21 *Anderlecht* 14 4 **14 4**

TOLAJ, Lorent (F) 0 0
b.Aigle 23-10-01
Internationals: Switzerland U17, U18, U19.
From Sion.
2020–21 Brighton & HA 0 0

TROSSARD, Leandro (M) 238 71
b.Waterschei 4-12-94
Internationals: Belgium U16, U17, U18, U19, U21.
2011–12 Genk 1 0
2012–13 Genk 0 0
2012–13 *Lommel U* 12 7
2013–14 Genk 0 0
2013–14 *Westerlo* 17 3 **17 3**
2014–15 Genk 0 0
2014–15 *Lommel U* 30 16 **42 23**
2015–16 Genk 0 0
2015–16 *OH Leuven* 30 8 **30 8**
2016–17 Genk 31 6
2017–18 Genk 17 7
2018–19 Genk 34 14 **83 27**
2019–20 Brighton & HA 31 5
2020–21 Brighton & HA 35 5 **66 10**

TSOUNGUI, Antef (D) 0 0
H: 6 1 b.Brussels 30-12-02
Internationals: Belgium U17, U18.
From Chelsea.
2020–21 Brighton & HA 0 0

VAN HECKE, Jan (D) 11 3
H: 6 2 b.Amemuiden 8-6-00
2019–20 NAC Breda 11 3 **11 3**
2020–21 Brighton & HA 0 0

VELTMAN, Joel (D) 207 11
b.Velsen 15-1-92
2011–12 Ajax 0 0
2012–13 Ajax 7 0
2013–14 Ajax 25 2
2014–15 Ajax 25 4
2015–16 Ajax 34 2
2016–17 Ajax 30 0

2017–18	Ajax	30	1		
2018–19	Ajax	9	1		
2019–20	Ajax	19	0	**179**	**10**
2020–21	Brighton & HA	28	1	**28**	**1**

WALTON, Christian (G) 156 0
H: 6 0 W: 11 11 b.Wadebridge 9-11-95
Internationals: England U19, U20, U21.

2011–12	Plymouth Arg	0	0		
2012–13	Plymouth Arg	0	0		
2013–14	Brighton & HA	0	0		
2014–15	Brighton & HA	3	0		
2015–16	Brighton & HA	0	0		
2015–16	*Bury*	4	0	**4**	**0**
2015–16	*Plymouth Arg*	4	0	**4**	**0**
2016–17	Brighton & HA	0	0		
2016–17	*Luton T*	27	0	**27**	**0**
2016–17	*Southend U*	7	0	**7**	**0**
2017–18	Brighton & HA	0	0		
2017–18	*Wigan Ath*	31	0		
2018–19	Brighton & HA	0	0		
2018–19	*Wigan Ath*	34	0	**65**	**0**
2019–20	Brighton & HA	0	0		
2019–20	*Blackburn R*	46	0	**46**	**0**
2020–21	Brighton & HA	0	0	**3**	**0**

WEBSTER, Adam (D) 222 13
H: 6 1 W: 11 11 b.West Wittering 4-1-95
Internationals: England U18, U19.

2011–12	Portsmouth	3	0		
2012–13	Portsmouth	18	0		
2013–14	Portsmouth	4	2		
2014–15	Portsmouth	15	1		
2015–16	Portsmouth	27	2	**67**	**5**
2016–17	Ipswich T	23	1		
2017–18	Ipswich T	28	0	**51**	**1**
2018–19	Bristol C	44	3		
2019–20	Bristol C	0	0	**44**	**3**
2019–20	Brighton & HA	31	3		
2020–21	Brighton & HA	29	1	**60**	**4**

WEIR, Jensen (M) 1 0
b.Warrington 31-1-02
Internationals: Scotland U16, U17. England U17, U18.

2017–18	Wigan Ath	0	0		
2018–19	Wigan Ath	1	0		
2019–20	Wigan Ath	0	0	**1**	**0**
2020–21	Brighton & HA	0	0		

WELBECK, Danny (F) 256 52
H: 6 1 W: 11 07 b.Manchester 26-11-90
Internationals: England U17, U18, U19, U21, Full caps.

2007–08	Manchester U	0	0		
2008–09	Manchester U	3	1		
2009–10	Manchester U	5	0		
2009–10	*Preston NE*	8	2	**8**	**2**
2010–11	Manchester U	0	0		
2010–11	*Sunderland*	26	6	**26**	**6**
2011–12	Manchester U	30	9		
2012–13	Manchester U	27	1		
2013–14	Manchester U	25	9		
2014–15	Manchester U	2	0	**92**	**20**
2014–15	Arsenal	25	4		
2015–16	Arsenal	11	4		
2016–17	Arsenal	16	2		
2017–18	Arsenal	28	5		
2018–19	Arsenal	8	1	**88**	**16**
2019–20	Watford	18	2		
2020–21	Watford	0	0	**18**	**2**
2020–21	Brighton & HA	24	6	**24**	**6**

WHITE, Ben (D) 139 3
b.Poole 8-11-97

2016–17	Brighton & HA	0	0		
2017–18	Brighton & HA	0	0		
2017–18	*Newport Co*	42	1	**42**	**1**
2018–19	Brighton & HA	0	0		
2018–19	*Peterborough U*	15	1	**15**	**1**
2019–20	Brighton & HA	0	0		
2019–20	*Leeds U*	46	1	**46**	**1**
2020–21	Brighton & HA	36	0	**36**	**0**

YAPI, Romaric (D) 0 0
b.Evry 13-7-00

2017–18	Paris Saint-Germain	0	0		
2018–19	Paris Saint-Germain	0	0		
2019–20	Brighton & HA	0	0		
2020–21	Brighton & HA	0	0		

ZEQIRI, Andi (F) 102 28
b.Lausanne 22-6-99

2014–15	Lausanne	3	0		
2015–16	Lausanne	14	2		
2016–17	Lausanne	0	0		
2017–18	Lausanne	19	2		
2018–19	Lausanne	24	7		
2019–20	Lausanne	33	17	**93**	**28**
2020–21	Lahti	0	0		
2020–21	Lausanne Sports	0	0		
2020–21	Brighton & HA	9	0	**9**	**0**

Scholars
Bull, Toby Graham; Chouchane, Samy Olivier; Dackers, Marcus Matthias; Emmerson, Zak Ben; Everitt, Matthew; Jackson, Benjamin Harvey; Jenkins, Nathan Euan; Kavanagh, Leigh Robert; Leahy, Jack; Lucero, John Albert Luis; Moran, Andrew; Qureshi, Jaami Muhammad; Sturge, Zak Norton; Turns, Edward James.

BRISTOL C (15)

ADELAKUN, Hakeeb (F) 169 19
H: 6 3 W: 11 11 b.Hackney 11-6-96

2012–13	Scunthorpe U	2	0		
2013–14	Scunthorpe U	28	2		
2014–15	Scunthorpe U	32	6		
2015–16	Scunthorpe U	21	2		
2016–17	Scunthorpe U	17	2		
2017–18	Scunthorpe U	39	4	**139**	**16**
2018–19	Bristol C	5	0		
2019–20	Bristol C	0	0		
2019–20	*Rotherham U*	9	0	**9**	**0**
2020–21	Bristol C	2	0	**7**	**0**
2020–21	*Hull C*	14	3	**14**	**3**

BAKER, Nathan (D) 258 3
H: 6 2 W: 11 11 b.Worcester 23-4-91
Internationals: England U19, U20, U21.

2008–09	Aston Villa	0	0		
2009–10	Aston Villa	0	0		
2009–10	*Lincoln C*	18	0	**18**	**0**
2010–11	Aston Villa	4	0		
2011–12	Aston Villa	8	0		
2011–12	*Millwall*	6	0	**6**	**0**
2012–13	Aston Villa	26	0		
2013–14	Aston Villa	30	0		
2014–15	Aston Villa	11	0		
2015–16	Aston Villa	0	0		
2015–16	*Bristol C*	36	1		
2016–17	Aston Villa	32	1	**111**	**1**
2017–18	Bristol C	34	0		
2018–19	Bristol C	16	0		
2019–20	Bristol C	34	1		
2020–21	Bristol C	3	0	**123**	**2**

BAKINSON, Tyreeq (M) 79 7
H: 6 1 W: 11 00 b.Camden 8-1-98

2015–16	Luton T	1	0		
2016–17	Luton T	0	0		
2017–18	Luton T	0	0	**1**	**0**
2017–18	Bristol C	0	0		
2018–19	Bristol C	0	0		
2018–19	*Newport Co*	30	1	**30**	**1**
2019–20	Bristol C	0	0		
2019–20	*Plymouth Arg*	14	2	**14**	**2**
2020–21	Bristol C	34	4	**34**	**4**

BELL, Sam (F) 4 0
b.Bristol 23-5-02

2018–19	Bristol C	0	0		
2019–20	Bristol C	0	0		
2020–21	Bristol C	4	0	**4**	**0**

BENAROUS, Ayman (M) 0 0
b.Bristol 27-7-03

2020–21	Bristol C	0	0		

BENTLEY, Daniel (G) 350 0
H: 6 2 W: 11 05 b.Wickford 13-7-93

2011–12	Southend U	1	0		
2012–13	Southend U	9	0		
2013–14	Southend U	46	0		
2014–15	Southend U	42	0		
2015–16	Southend U	43	0	**141**	**0**
2016–17	Brentford	45	0		
2017–18	Brentford	45	0		
2018–19	Brentford	33	0	**123**	**0**
2019–20	Bristol C	43	0		
2020–21	Bristol C	43	0	**86**	**0**

BRITTON, Louis (F) 1 1
b. 17-3-01

2020–21	Bristol C	1	1	**1**	**1**

BRUNT, Chris (M) 534 67
H: 6 1 W: 13 04 b.Belfast 14-12-84
Internationals: Northern Ireland U19, U21, U23, Full caps.

2002–03	Middlesbrough	0	0		
2003–04	Middlesbrough	0	0		
2003–04	Sheffield W	9	2		
2004–05	Sheffield W	42	4		
2005–06	Sheffield W	44	7		
2006–07	Sheffield W	44	11		
2007–08	Sheffield W	1	0	**140**	**24**
2007–08	WBA	34	4		
2008–09	WBA	34	8		
2009–10	WBA	40	13		
2010–11	WBA	34	4		
2011–12	WBA	29	2		
2012–13	WBA	31	2		
2013–14	WBA	28	3		
2014–15	WBA	34	2		
2015–16	WBA	22	0		
2016–17	WBA	31	3		
2017–18	WBA	26	0		
2018–19	WBA	32	2		
2019–20	WBA	7	0	**382**	**43**
2020–21	Bristol C	12	0	**12**	**0**

BUSE, William (G) 0 0

2020–21	Bristol C	0	0		

CONWAY, Tommy (F) 5 1
b. 6-8-02

2020–21	Bristol C	5	1	**5**	**1**

CUNDY, Robbie (D) 35 1
b. 30-5-97

2014–15	Oxford U	0	0		
2015–16	Oxford U	0	0		
2016–17	Oxford U	0	0		

From Gloucester C.

2019–20	Bristol C	0	0		
2020–21	Bristol C	0	0		
2020–21	*Cambridge U*	17	0	**17**	**0**
2020–21	*Gillingham*	18	1	**18**	**1**

DASILVA, Jay (D) 111 1
b. 22-4-98
Internationals: England U16, U17, U18, U19, U20, U21.

2016–17	Chelsea	0	0		
2016–17	*Charlton Ath*	10	0		
2017–18	Chelsea	0	0		
2017–18	*Charlton Ath*	38	0	**48**	**0**
2018–19	Chelsea	0	0		
2018–19	*Bristol C*	28	0		
2019–20	Bristol C	24	0		
2020–21	Bristol C	11	1	**63**	**1**

DIEDHIOU, Famara (F) 322 106
H: 6 4 W: 12 08 b.Saint-Louis 15-12-92
Internationals: Senegal Full caps.

2011–12	Belfort	11	3	**11**	**3**
2012–13	Epinal	30	12	**30**	**12**
2013–14	Gazelec Ajaccio	33	13	**33**	**13**
2014–15	Sochaux	13	1		
2014–15	*Clermont*	14	2		
2015–16	Sochaux	0	0	**13**	**1**
2015–16	*Clermont*	36	21	**50**	**23**
2016–17	Angers	31	8	**31**	**8**
2017–18	Bristol C	32	13		
2018–19	Bristol C	41	13		
2019–20	Bristol C	41	12		
2020–21	Bristol C	40	8	**154**	**46**

EDWARDS, Opi (M) 4 0
b.Bristol 30-4-99

2017–18	Bristol C	0	0		
2018–19	Bristol C	0	0		
2019–20	Bristol C	0	0		
2020–21	Bristol C	4	0	**4**	**0**

EDWARDS, Owura (F) 20 1
b. 10-4-01

2020–21	Grimsby T	17	1	**17**	**1**
2020–21	Bristol C	3	0	**3**	**0**

ELIASSON, Niclas (M) 173 11
H: 5 9 W: 10 06 b.Varberg 7-12-95
Internationals: Sweden U17, U19, U21.

2012	Falkenberg	0	0		
2013	Falkenberg	29	1	**29**	**1**
2014	AIK Solna	16	1		
2015	AIK Solna	10	0		
2016	AIK Solna	5	0	**31**	**1**
2016	*Norrkoping*	13	1		
2017	Norrkoping	17	3	**30**	**4**
2017–18	IFK Norrkoping	0	0		
2017–18	Bristol C	13	0		
2018–19	Bristol C	33	2		
2019–20	Bristol C	37	3		
2020–21	Bristol C	0	0	**83**	**5**

Transferred to Nimes October 2020.

FRANCOIS, Marlee (F) 0 0
H: 5 11 b.Sydney 29-12-02
From Fulham.

2020–21	Bristol C	0	0		

HUNT, Jack (D) 372 5
H: 5 9 W: 11 02 b.Rothwell 6-12-90

2009–10	Huddersfield T	0	0		
2010–11	Huddersfield T	19	1		
2010–11	*Chesterfield*	20	0	**20**	**0**
2011–12	Huddersfield T	43	1		
2012–13	Huddersfield T	40	0		
2013–14	Huddersfield T	2	0	**104**	**2**
2013–14	Crystal Palace	0	0		
2013–14	*Barnsley*	11	0	**11**	**0**
2014–15	Crystal Palace	0	0		
2014–15	*Nottingham F*	17	0	**17**	**0**
2014–15	*Rotherham U*	16	0	**16**	**0**
2015–16	Sheffield W	34	0		

2016–17 Sheffield W 32 0
2017–18 Sheffield W 29 0 **95 0**
2018–19 Bristol C 33 1
2019–20 Bristol C 35 0
2020–21 Bristol C 41 2 **109 3**

JANNEH, Saikou (F) 12 1
b. 11-1-00
From Bath C, Clevedon T.
2018–19 Bristol C 0 0
2019–20 Bristol C 0 0
2020–21 Bristol C 4 0 **4 0**
2020–21 *Newport Co* 8 1 **8 1**

KALAS, Tomas (D) 254 3
H: 6 0 W: 12 00 b.Olomouc 15-5-93
Internationals: Czech Republic U17, U18, U19, U21, Full caps.
2009–10 Sigma Olomouc 1 0
2010–11 Chelsea 0 0
2010–11 *Sigma Olomouc* 4 0 **5 0**
2011–12 Chelsea 0 0
2012–13 Chelsea 0 0
2012–13 *Vitesse* 34 1 **34 1**
2013–14 Chelsea 2 0
2014–15 Chelsea 0 0
2014–15 *Cologne* 0 0
2014–15 *Middlesbrough* 17 0
2015–16 Chelsea 0 0
2015–16 *Middlesbrough* 26 0 **43 0**
2016–17 Chelsea 0 0
2016–17 *Fulham* 36 1
2017–18 Chelsea 0 0
2017–18 *Fulham* 33 0 **69 1**
2018–19 Chelsea 0 0 **2 0**
2018–19 *Bristol C* 38 0
2019–20 Bristol C 23 0
2020–21 Bristol C 40 1 **101 1**

LANSBURY, Henri (M) 303 48
H: 6 0 W: 13 06 b.Enfield 12-10-90
Internationals: England U16, U17, U19, U21.
2007–08 Arsenal 0 0
2008–09 Arsenal 0 0
2008–09 *Scunthorpe U* 16 4 **16 4**
2009–10 Arsenal 1 0
2009–10 *Watford* 37 5 **37 5**
2010–11 Arsenal 0 0
2010–11 *Norwich C* 23 4 **23 4**
2011–12 Arsenal 2 0
2011–12 *West Ham U* 22 1 **22 1**
2012–13 Arsenal 0 0 **3 0**
2012–13 Nottingham F 32 5
2013–14 Nottingham F 29 7
2014–15 Nottingham F 39 10
2015–16 Nottingham F 28 4
2016–17 Nottingham F 17 6 **145 32**
2016–17 Aston Villa 18 0
2017–18 Aston Villa 10 2
2018–19 Aston Villa 3 0
2019–20 Aston Villa 10 0
2020–21 Aston Villa 0 0 **41 2**
2020–21 Bristol C 16 0 **16 0**

LOW, Joseph (D) 0 0
b. 20-2-02
Internationals: Wales U17.
2020–21 Bristol C 0 0

MARIAPPA, Adrian (D) 390 6
H: 5 10 W: 11 12 b.Harrow 3-10-86
Internationals: Jamaica Full caps.
2005–06 Watford 3 0
2006–07 Watford 19 0
2007–08 Watford 25 0
2008–09 Watford 39 1
2009–10 Watford 46 1
2010–11 Watford 45 1
2011–12 Watford 39 1
2012–13 Reading 29 1
2013–14 Reading 0 0 **29 1**
2013–14 Crystal Palace 24 1
2014–15 Crystal Palace 12 0
2015–16 Crystal Palace 3 0 **39 1**
2016–17 Watford 7 0
2017–18 Watford 28 0
2018–19 Watford 26 0
2019–20 Watford 20 0 **297 4**
2020–21 Bristol C 25 0 **25 0**

MARTIN, Chris (F) 477 126
H: 6 2 W: 12 06 b.Beccles 4-11-88
Internationals: England U19. Scotland Full caps.
2006–07 Norwich C 18 4
2007–08 Norwich C 7 0
2008–09 Norwich C 0 0
2008–09 *Luton T* 40 11 **40 11**
2009–10 Norwich C 42 17
2010–11 Norwich C 30 4
2011–12 Norwich C 4 0
2011–12 *Crystal Palace* 26 7 **26 7**
2012–13 Norwich C 1 0 **102 25**
2012–13 *Swindon T* 12 1 **12 1**
2012–13 *Derby Co* 13 2
2013–14 Derby Co 44 20
2014–15 Derby Co 35 18
2015–16 Derby Co 45 15
2016–17 Derby Co 5 0
2016–17 *Fulham* 31 10 **31 10**
2017–18 Derby Co 23 1
2017–18 *Reading* 10 1 **10 1**
2018–19 Derby Co 0 0
2018–19 *Hull C* 30 2 **30 2**
2019–20 Derby Co 35 11 **200 67**
2020–21 Bristol C 26 2 **26 2**

MASSENGO, Han-Noah (M) 55 0
b.Villepinte 7-7-01
Internationals: France U17, U18.
2018–19 Monaco 3 0 **3 0**
2019–20 Bristol C 25 0
2020–21 Bristol C 27 0 **52 0**

MOORE, Taylor (D) 154 2
H: 6 0 W: 12 08 b.Walthamstow 12-5-97
Internationals: England U17, U18, U19, U20.
From West Ham U.
2014–15 Lens 4 0
2015–16 Lens 5 0 **9 0**
2016–17 Bristol C 5 0
2016–17 *Bury* 19 0 **19 0**
2017–18 Bristol C 0 0
2017–18 *Cheltenham T* 36 0 **36 0**
2018–19 Bristol C 0 0
2018–19 *Southend U* 34 1 **34 1**
2019–20 Bristol C 21 1
2019–20 *Blackpool* 8 0 **8 0**
2020–21 Bristol C 22 0 **48 1**

MORTON, James (M) 20 0
b. 22-4-99
2017–18 Bristol C 0 0
2018–19 Bristol C 0 0
2019–20 Bristol C 0 0
2019–20 *Forest Green R* 12 0 **12 0**
2020–21 Bristol C 0 0
2020–21 *Grimsby T* 7 0 **7 0**
2020–21 *Gillingham* 1 0 **1 0**

NAGY, Adam (F) 131 4
b.Budapest 17-6-95
Internationals: Hungary U20, U21, Full caps.
2013–14 Ferencvaros 0 0
2014–15 Ferencvaros 1 0
2015–16 Ferencvaros 25 0 **26 0**
2016–17 Bologna 25 0
2017–18 Bologna 12 1
2018–19 Bologna 14 0 **51 1**
2019–20 Bristol C 23 1
2020–21 Bristol C 31 2 **54 3**

NURSE, George (M) 27 2
b. 30-4-99
2019–20 Bristol C 0 0
2019–20 *Newport Co* 17 1 **17 1**
2020–21 Bristol C 0 0
2020–21 *Walsall* 10 1 **10 1**

O'DOWDA, Callum (M) 227 19
H: 5 11 W: 11 11 b.Oxford 23-4-95
Internationals: Republic of Ireland U21, Full caps.
2012–13 Oxford U 0 0
2013–14 Oxford U 10 0
2014–15 Oxford U 39 4
2015–16 Oxford U 38 8 **87 12**
2016–17 Bristol C 34 0
2017–18 Bristol C 24 1
2018–19 Bristol C 31 4
2019–20 Bristol C 32 1
2020–21 Bristol C 19 1 **140 7**

O'LEARY, Max (G) 48 0
H: 6 1 W: 12 03 b.Bath 10-10-96
2013–14 Bristol C 0 0
2014–15 Bristol C 0 0
2015–16 Bristol C 0 0
2016–17 Bristol C 0 0
2017–18 Bristol C 0 0
2018–19 Bristol C 15 0
2019–20 Bristol C 0 0
2019–20 *Shrewsbury T* 30 0 **30 0**
2020–21 Bristol C 3 0 **18 0**

OWERS, Josh (M) 0 0
H: 6 1 b.Bristol 16-3-02
2020–21 Bristol C 0 0

PALMER, Kasey (M) 132 13
H: 5 11 W: 10 10 b.London 9-11-96
Internationals: England U17, U18, U20, U21.
From Charlton Ath.
2015–16 Chelsea 0 0
2016–17 Chelsea 0 0
2016–17 *Huddersfield T* 24 4
2017–18 Chelsea 0 0
2017–18 *Huddersfield T* 4 0 **28 4**
2017–18 *Derby Co* 15 2 **15 2**
2018–19 Chelsea 0 0
2018–19 *Blackburn R* 14 1 **14 1**
2018–19 *Bristol C* 15 2
2019–20 Bristol C 25 1
2020–21 Bristol C 23 2 **63 5**
2020–21 *Swansea C* 12 1 **12 1**

PATERSON, Jamie (F) 336 54
H: 5 9 W: 10 07 b.Coventry 20-12-91
2010–11 Walsall 14 0
2011–12 Walsall 34 3
2012–13 Walsall 46 12 **94 15**
2013–14 Nottingham F 32 8
2014–15 Nottingham F 21 1
2015–16 Nottingham F 1 0 **54 9**
2015–16 *Huddersfield T* 34 6 **34 6**
2016–17 Bristol C 22 4
2017–18 Bristol C 41 5
2018–19 Bristol C 40 5
2019–20 Bristol C 21 6
2019–20 *Derby Co* 10 1 **10 1**
2020–21 Bristol C 20 3 **144 23**

PEARSON, Sam (M) 5 0
b. 26-10-01
Internationals: Wales U19.
2018–19 Bristol C 0 0
2019–20 Bristol C 0 0
2020–21 Bristol C 5 0 **5 0**

PRING, Cameron (D) 45 1
b. 22-1-98
2018–19 Bristol C 0 0
2018–19 *Newport Co* 7 1 **7 1**
2018–19 *Cheltenham T* 8 0 **8 0**
2019–20 Bristol C 0 0
2019–20 *Walsall* 21 0 **21 0**
2020–21 Bristol C 0 0
2020–21 *Portsmouth* 9 0 **9 0**

ROWE, Tommy (M) 466 65
H: 5 11 W: 12 11 b.Manchester 1-5-89
2006–07 Stockport Co 4 0
2007–08 Stockport Co 24 6
2008–09 Stockport Co 44 7 **72 13**
2008–09 Peterborough U 0 0
2009–10 Peterborough U 32 2
2010–11 Peterborough U 35 5
2011–12 Peterborough U 43 4
2012–13 Peterborough U 31 5
2013–14 Peterborough U 34 7 **175 23**
2014–15 Wolverhampton W 14 0
2015–16 Wolverhampton W 3 0 **17 0**
2015–16 *Scunthorpe U* 14 1 **14 1**
2015–16 *Doncaster R* 10 3
2016–17 Doncaster R 46 13
2017–18 Doncaster R 40 4
2018–19 Doncaster R 32 5 **128 25**
2019–20 Bristol C 29 2
2020–21 Bristol C 31 1 **60 3**

SCOTT, Alex (M) 3 0
b. 21-8-03
From Guernsey.
2020–21 Bristol C 3 0 **3 0**

SEMENYO, Antoine (F) 86 5
b. 7-1-00
2017–18 Bristol C 1 0
2018–19 Bristol C 4 0
2018–19 *Newport Co* 21 3 **21 3**
2019–20 Bristol C 9 0
2019–20 *Sunderland* 7 0 **7 0**
2020–21 Bristol C 44 2 **58 2**

SIMPSON, Danny (D) 335 1
H: 5 9 W: 11 05 b.Eccles 4-1-87
2005–06 Manchester U 0 0
2006–07 Manchester U 0 0
2006–07 *Sunderland* 14 0 **14 0**
2007–08 Manchester U 3 0
2007–08 *Ipswich T* 8 0 **8 0**
2008–09 Manchester U 0 0
2008–09 *Blackburn R* 12 0 **12 0**
2009–10 Manchester U 0 0 **3 0**
2009–10 Newcastle U 39 1
2010–11 Newcastle U 30 0
2011–12 Newcastle U 35 0
2012–13 Newcastle U 19 0 **123 1**
2013–14 QPR 33 0
2014–15 QPR 1 0 **34 0**
2014–15 Leicester C 14 0
2015–16 Leicester C 30 0
2016–17 Leicester C 35 0
2017–18 Leicester C 28 0
2018–19 Leicester C 6 0 **113 0**
2019–20 Huddersfield T 24 0 **24 0**
2020–21 Bristol C 4 0 **4 0**

SMITH, Zachary (M) 0 0
b.Bristol 15-9-00
2020–21 Bristol C 0 0

TAYLOR, James (D) 0 0
2020–21 Bristol C 0 0

TOWLER, Ryley (M) 3 0
b.Bristol 2-5-01
2020–21 Bristol C 3 0 **3 0**

VYNER, Zak (D) 139 4
H: 5 10 W: 10 10 b.Bath 14-5-97
2015–16 Bristol C 4 0
2016–17 Bristol C 3 0
2016–17 *Accrington S* 16 0 **16 0**
2017–18 Bristol C 1 0
2017–18 *Plymouth Arg* 17 1 **17 1**
2018–19 Bristol C 0 0
2018–19 *Rotherham U* 31 0 **31 0**
2019–20 Bristol C 8 0
2019–20 *Aberdeen* 16 1 **16 1**
2020–21 Bristol C 43 2 **59 2**

WALSH, Liam (M) 62 4
b. 15-9-97
Internationals: England U16, U18.
2015–16 Everton 0 0
2015–16 *Yeovil T* 15 1 **15 1**
2016–17 Everton 0 0
2017–18 Everton 0 0
2017–18 *Birmingham C* 3 0 **3 0**
2017–18 Bristol C 6 0
2018–19 Bristol C 9 0
2019–20 Bristol C 0 0
2019–20 *Coventry C* 26 3 **26 3**
2020–21 Bristol C 3 0 **18 0**

WATKINS, Marley (M) 221 29
H: 5 10 W: 10 03 b.London 17-10-90
Internationals: Wales Full caps.
From Swansea C.
2008–09 Cheltenham T 12 0
2009–10 Cheltenham T 13 1
2010–11 Cheltenham T 1 0 **26 1**
From Bath C, Hereford U
2013–14 Inverness CT 26 1
2014–15 Inverness CT 33 7 **59 8**
2015–16 Barnsley 34 5
2016–17 Barnsley 42 10 **76 15**
2017–18 Norwich C 24 0 **24 0**
2018–19 Bristol C 16 2
2019–20 Bristol C 9 1
2020–21 Bristol C 2 0 **27 3**
2020–21 *Aberdeen* 9 2 **9 2**

WEBB, Bradley (D) 0 0
b. 9-6-01
2019–20 Bristol C 0 0
2020–21 Bristol C 0 0
2020–21 *Newport Co* 0 0

WEIMANN, Andreas (F) 330 53
H: 5 9 W: 11 09 b.Vienna 5-8-91
Internationals: Austria U17, U19, U20, U21, Full caps.
From Rapid Vienna.
2008–09 Aston Villa 0 0
2009–10 Aston Villa 0 0
2010–11 Aston Villa 1 0
2010–11 *Watford* 18 4
2011–12 Aston Villa 14 2
2011–12 *Watford* 3 0 **21 4**
2012–13 Aston Villa 30 7
2013–14 Aston Villa 37 5
2014–15 Aston Villa 31 3 **113 17**
2015–16 Derby Co 30 4
2016–17 Derby Co 11 0
2016–17 *Wolverhampton W* 19 2 **19 2**
2017–18 Derby Co 40 5 **81 9**
2018–19 Bristol C 44 10
2019–20 Bristol C 45 9
2020–21 Bristol C 7 2 **96 21**

WELLS, Nahki (F) 376 122
H: 5 7 W: 11 00 b.Bermuda 1-6-90
Internationals: Bermuda Full caps.
2010–11 Carlisle U 3 0 **3 0**
2011–12 Bradford C 33 10
2012–13 Bradford C 39 18
2013–14 Bradford C 19 14 **91 42**
2013–14 Huddersfield T 22 7
2014–15 Huddersfield T 35 11
2015–16 Huddersfield T 44 17
2016–17 Huddersfield T 43 10
2017–18 Huddersfield T 0 0 **144 45**
2017–18 Burnley 9 0
2018–19 Burnley 0 0
2018–19 *QPR* 40 7
2019–20 Burnley 0 0 **9 0**
2019–20 *QPR* 26 13 **66 20**
2019–20 Bristol C 17 5
2020–21 Bristol C 46 10 **63 15**

WILES-RICHARDS, Harvey (G) 0 0
2020–21 Bristol C 0 0

WILLIAMS, Joe (M) 103 2
H: 5 10 W: 10 06 b.Liverpool 8-12-96
Internationals: England U20.
2014–15 Everton 0 0
2015–16 Everton 0 0
2016–17 Everton 0 0
2017–18 Everton 0 0
2017–18 *Barnsley* 34 1 **34 1**
2018–19 Everton 0 0
2018–19 *Bolton W* 30 0 **30 0**
2019–20 Wigan Ath 38 1 **38 1**
2020–21 Bristol C 1 0 **1 0**

WOLLACOTT, Jojo (G) 12 0
b. 8-9-96
2015–16 Bristol C 0 0
2016–17 Bristol C 0 0
2017–18 Bristol C 0 0
2018–19 Bristol C 0 0
2019–20 Bristol C 0 0
2019–20 *Forest Green R* 10 0 **10 0**
2020–21 Bristol C 0 0
2020–21 *Swindon T* 2 0 **2 0**

Scholars
Allen, Khari Jarell Marlon; Backwell, Tommy George; Bell, Zachary Caleb; Cray, Samuel David; Henry, Prince; Kadji, Dylan Wesley Nkongape; Leeson, Harry Richard; Lewis, Dylan Maxwell; Morris, Matthew Thomas; Nelson, Rohan Eugene; Palmer Houlden, Sebastian Alexander; Porton, Joseph John; Sage, William Mark; Salmon, Cameron James; Smith, Luca Alexander Mark; South Thomas, Jemar D'Andre; Swaby, Thierry John Paul; Taylor-Clarke, Omar Rivaldo; Thuo, Mark Williams; Walker, James Dylan; Williams, Nathaniel James.

BRISTOL R (16)

ANDRE, Alexis (G) 1 0
b. 31-5-97
2017–18 Bristol R 1 0
2018–19 Bristol R 0 0
2019–20 Bristol R 0 0
2020–21 Bristol R 0 0 **1 0**

ARMSTRONG, Liam (G) 0 0
2020–21 Bristol R 0 0

AYUNGA, Jonah (F) 30 2
b. 24-5-97
From Sutton U, Havant & Waterlooville.
2020–21 Bristol R 30 2 **30 2**

BALDWIN, Jack (D) 262 13
H: 6 1 W: 11 00 b.Barking 30-6-93
2011–12 Hartlepool U 17 0
2012–13 Hartlepool U 32 2
2013–14 Hartlepool U 28 2 **77 4**
2013–14 Peterborough U 11 0
2014–15 Peterborough U 11 0
2015–16 Peterborough U 18 1
2016–17 Peterborough U 27 1
2017–18 Peterborough U 33 2 **100 4**
2018–19 Sunderland 34 3
2019–20 Sunderland 0 0 **34 3**
2019–20 *Salford C* 13 1 **13 1**
2020–21 Bristol R 38 1 **38 1**

BARRETT, Josh (F) 32 0
b. 21-6-98
Internationals: Republic of Ireland U17, U19, U21.
2015–16 Reading 3 0
2016–17 Reading 0 0
2017–18 Reading 0 0
2017–18 *Coventry C* 6 0 **6 0**
2018–19 Reading 2 0
2019–20 Reading 5 0 **10 0**
2019–20 Bristol R 7 0
2020–21 Bristol R 9 0 **16 0**

BENNETT, Kyle (F) 345 37
H: 5 5 W: 9 08 b.Telford 9-9-90
Internationals: England U18.
2007–08 Wolverhampton W 0 0
2008–09 Wolverhampton W 0 0
2009–10 Wolverhampton W 0 0
2010–11 Bury 32 2 **32 2**
2011–12 Doncaster R 36 4
2012–13 Doncaster R 35 3
2013–14 Doncaster R 3 0
2013–14 *Crawley T* 4 0 **4 0**
2013–14 *Bradford C* 18 1 **18 1**
2014–15 Doncaster R 42 8 **116 15**
2015–16 Portsmouth 42 6
2016–17 Portsmouth 39 6
2017–18 Portsmouth 18 0 **99 12**
2017–18 Bristol R 17 3
2018–19 Bristol R 19 0
2018–19 *Swindon T* 15 4 **15 4**
2019–20 Bristol R 12 0
2020–21 Bristol R 0 0 **48 3**
2020–21 *Grimsby T* 13 0 **13 0**

DALY, James (F) 31 3
b. 12-1-00
2017–18 Crystal Palace 0 0
2018–19 Crystal Palace 0 0
2019–20 Crystal Palace 0 0
2019–20 Bristol R 3 0
2020–21 Bristol R 28 3 **31 3**

DAVIES, Tom (D) 119 3
H: 5 11 W: 11 00 b.Warrington 18-4-92
From FC United of Manchester.
2014–15 Fleetwood T 0 0
2015–16 Accrington S 32 1 **32 1**
2016–17 Portsmouth 12 0
2017–18 Portsmouth 0 0 **12 0**
2017–18 Coventry C 21 0
2018–19 Coventry C 23 0 **44 0**
2019–20 Bristol R 19 1
2020–21 Bristol R 0 0 **19 1**
2020–21 *Barrow* 12 1 **12 1**

EHMER, Max (M) 326 14
H: 6 2 W: 11 00 b.Frankfurt 3-2-92
2009–10 QPR 0 0
2010–11 QPR 0 0
2010–11 *Yeovil T* 27 0
2011–12 QPR 0 0
2011–12 *Yeovil T* 24 0 **51 0**
2011–12 *Preston NE* 9 0 **9 0**
2012–13 QPR 0 0
2012–13 *Stevenage* 6 1 **6 1**
2013–14 QPR 1 0
2013–14 *Carlisle U* 12 1 **12 1**
2014–15 QPR 0 0 **1 0**
2014–15 *Gillingham* 27 1
2015–16 Gillingham 30 0
2016–17 Gillingham 45 6
2017–18 Gillingham 42 2
2018–19 Gillingham 40 1
2019–20 Gillingham 35 1 **219 11**
2020–21 Bristol R 28 1 **28 1**

GRANT, Josh (D) 62 1
b. 11-10-98
Internationals: England U18, U20.
2018–19 Chelsea 0 0
2018–19 *Yeovil T* 8 0 **8 0**
2019–20 Chelsea 0 0
2019–20 *Plymouth Arg* 22 0 **22 0**
2020–21 Bristol R 32 1 **32 1**

HANLAN, Brandon (F) 145 22
H: 6 0 W: 11 07 b.Chelsea 31-5-97
2016–17 Charlton Ath 9 0
2017–18 *Colchester U* 18 2 **18 2**
2017–18 Charlton Ath 0 0 **9 0**
2018–19 Gillingham 39 9
2019–20 Gillingham 35 4 **74 13**
2020–21 Bristol R 44 7 **44 7**

HARE, Josh (D) 31 0
H: 6 0 W: 12 04 b.Cantebury 12-8-94
2012–13 Gillingham 0 0
2013–14 Gillingham 0 0
2014–15 Gillingham 2 0
2015–16 Gillingham 0 0 **2 0**
From Eastbourne Bor, Maidstone U, Eastleigh.
2019–20 Bristol R 10 0
2020–21 Bristol R 19 0 **29 0**

HARGREAVES, Cameron (D) 19 0
b. 1-12-98
From Exeter C.
2017–18 Bristol R 0 0
2018–19 Bristol R 0 0
2019–20 Bristol R 6 0
2020–21 Bristol R 13 0 **19 0**

HARRIES, Cian (D) 50 1
H: 6 1 W: 12 02 b. 1-4-97
Internationals: Wales U17, U19, U20, U21.
2015–16 Coventry C 1 0
2016–17 Coventry C 8 0 **9 0**
2017–18 Swansea C 0 0
2018–19 Swansea C 2 0
2019–20 Swansea C 0 0 **2 0**
2019–20 *Fortuna Sittard* 8 1 **8 1**
2019–20 Bristol R 3 0
2020–21 Bristol R 28 0 **31 0**

HEAL, Sam (D) 0 0
2020–21 Bristol R 0 0

HULBERT, Ollie (F) 0 0
H: 5 11 b.Bristol 25-2-03

2020–21	Bristol R	0	0		

JAAKKOLA, Anssi (G) 180 0
H: 6 4 W: 13 12 b.Kemi 13-3-87
Internationals: Finland U21, Full caps.

2005	TP-47	3	0		
2006	TP-47	14	0	**17**	**0**
2006–07	Siena	0	0		
2007–08	Siena	1	0		
2008–09	Siena	0	0		
2008–09	*Colligiana*	7	0	**7**	**0**
2009–10	Siena	0	0	**1**	**0**
2010–11	Slavia Prague	2	0	**2**	**0**
2010–11	Kilmarnock	8	0		
2011–12	Kilmarnock	5	0		
2012–13	Kilmarnock	0	0	**13**	**0**
2013–14	Ajax Cape Town	24	0		
2014–15	Ajax Cape Town	28	0		
2015–16	Ajax Cape Town	26	0	**78**	**0**
2016–17	Reading	0	0		
2017–18	Reading	5	0		
2018–19	Reading	15	0	**20**	**0**
2019–20	Bristol R	21	0		
2020–21	Bristol R	21	0	**42**	**0**

JONES, Ryan (M) 0 0

2020–21	Bristol R	0	0		

KELLY, Michael (D) 27 0
H: 5 11 b.Kilmarnock 3-11-97
Internationals: Scotland U16, U17.

2017–18	Bristol R	1	0		
2018–19	Bristol R	21	0		
2019–20	Bristol R	5	0		
2020–21	Bristol R	0	0	**27**	**0**

KILGOUR, Alfie (D) 72 3
b. 18-5-98

2015–16	Bristol R	0	0		
2016–17	Bristol R	0	0		
2017–18	Bristol R	0	0		
2018–19	Bristol R	4	0		
2019–20	Bristol R	33	2		
2020–21	Bristol R	35	1	**72**	**3**

KOIKI, Ali (D) 25 0
b. 22-8-99

2018–19	Burnley	0	0		
2018–19	*Swindon T*	15	0	**15**	**0**
2019–20	Burnley	0	0		
2020–21	Burnley	0	0		
2020–21	Bristol R	10	0	**10**	**0**

LEAHY, Luke (M) 287 24
H: 5 10 W: 11 07 b.Coventry 19-11-92
From Rugby T.

2012–13	Falkirk	8	1		
2013–14	Falkirk	19	1		
2014–15	Falkirk	33	3		
2015–16	Falkirk	36	3		
2016–17	Falkirk	31	3	**127**	**11**
2017–18	Walsall	46	2		
2018–19	Walsall	44	3	**90**	**5**
2019–20	Bristol R	32	0		
2020–21	Bristol R	38	8	**70**	**8**

LIDDLE, Ben (M) 10 0
b.Durham 21-9-98

2018–19	Middlesbrough	0	0		
2018–19	*Forest Green R*	2	0	**2**	**0**
2019–20	Middlesbrough	1	0	**1**	**0**
2019–20	*Scunthorpe U*	4	0	**4**	**0**
2020–21	Bristol R	3	0	**3**	**0**

LITTLE, Mark (D) 356 5
H: 6 1 W: 12 10 b.Worcester 20-8-88
Internationals: England U19.

2005–06	Wolverhampton W	0	0		
2006–07	Wolverhampton W	26	0		
2007–08	Wolverhampton W	1	0		
2007–08	*Northampton T*	17	0		
2008–09	Wolverhampton W	0	0		
2008–09	*Northampton T*	9	0	**26**	**0**
2009–10	Wolverhampton W	0	0	**27**	**0**
2009–10	*Chesterfield*	12	0	**12**	**0**
2009–10	*Peterborough U*	9	0		
2010–11	Peterborough U	35	0		
2011–12	Peterborough U	35	1		
2012–13	Peterborough U	40	1		
2013–14	Peterborough U	38	1	**157**	**3**
2014–15	Bristol C	37	1		
2015–16	Bristol C	23	0		
2016–17	Bristol C	28	0	**88**	**1**
2017–18	Bolton W	28	1		
2018–19	Bolton W	2	0	**30**	**1**
2019–20	Bristol R	11	0		
2020–21	Bristol R	5	0	**16**	**0**

MARTINEZ, Pablo (D) 8 0
b.Oxford 11-10-00
From Reading, WBA.

2020–21	Bristol R	8	0	**8**	**0**

MEHEW, Tom (M) 1 0
b. 26-5-01

2020–21	Bristol R	1	0	**1**	**0**

NICHOLSON, Sam (M) 207 25
b.Edinburgh 20-1-95

2013–14	Hearts	25	2		
2014–15	Hearts	29	5		
2015–16	Hearts	36	3		
2016–17	Hearts	19	3	**109**	**13**
2017	Minnesota U	12	1		
2018	Minnesota U	8	1	**20**	**2**
2018	Colorado Rapids	19	2		
2019	Colorado Rapids	27	2		
2020	Colorado Rapids	2	0	**48**	**4**
2020–21	Bristol R	30	6	**30**	**6**

OGOGO, Abu (D) 393 25
H: 5 8 W: 10 02 b.Epsom 3-11-89

2007–08	Arsenal	0	0		
2008–09	Arsenal	0	0		
2008–09	*Barnet*	9	1	**9**	**1**
2009–10	Dagenham & R	30	2		
2010–11	Dagenham & R	33	1		
2011–12	Dagenham & R	40	1		
2012–13	Dagenham & R	46	1		
2013–14	Dagenham & R	44	8		
2014–15	Dagenham & R	32	4	**225**	**17**
2015–16	Shrewsbury T	42	2		
2016–17	Shrewsbury T	26	0		
2017–18	Shrewsbury T	35	2	**103**	**4**
2018–19	Coventry C	10	0	**10**	**0**
2018–19	Bristol R	16	0		
2019–20	Bristol R	27	3		
2020–21	Bristol R	3	0	**46**	**3**

PHILLIPS, Kieran (F) 0 0

2019–20	Bristol R	0	0		
2020–21	Bristol R	0	0		

RODMAN, Alex (F) 239 27
H: 6 2 W: 12 08 b.Sutton Coldfield 15-2-87
Internationals: England C.

2010–11	Aldershot T	14	5		
2011–12	Aldershot T	18	1		
2012–13	Aldershot T	11	1	**43**	**7**
2012–13	*York C*	18	1	**18**	**1**

From Grimsby T, Gateshead.

2015–16	Newport Co	29	4	**29**	**4**
2016–17	Notts Co	16	1	**16**	**1**
2016–17	Shrewsbury T	20	1		
2017–18	Shrewsbury T	41	5	**61**	**6**
2018–19	Bristol R	27	5		
2019–20	Bristol R	29	2		
2020–21	Bristol R	16	1	**72**	**8**

TUTONDA, David (D) 92 3
H: 5 11 W: 11 00 b.Kinshasa 11-10-95

2014–15	Cardiff C	0	0		
2014–15	*Newport Co*	12	2	**12**	**2**
2015–16	Cardiff C	0	0		
2015–16	*York C*	12	0	**12**	**0**
2016–17	Cardiff C	0	0		
2016–17	Barnet	7	1		
2017–18	Barnet	41	0	**48**	**1**

From Barnet.

2020–21	Bristol R	20	0	**20**	**0**

UPSON, Edward (M) 379 22
H: 5 10 W: 11 07 b.Bury St Edmunds 21-11-89
Internationals: England U17, U19.

2006–07	Ipswich T	0	0		
2007–08	Ipswich T	0	0		
2008–09	Ipswich T	0	0		
2009–10	Ipswich T	0	0		
2009–10	*Barnet*	9	1	**9**	**1**
2010–11	Yeovil T	23	0		
2011–12	Yeovil T	41	3		
2012–13	Yeovil T	41	2		
2013–14	Yeovil T	24	4	**129**	**9**
2013–14	Millwall	10	0		
2014–15	Millwall	26	2		
2015–16	Millwall	32	0	**68**	**2**
2016–17	Milton Keynes D	42	3		
2017–18	Milton Keynes D	37	3	**79**	**6**
2018–19	Bristol R	35	1		
2019–20	Bristol R	33	2		
2020–21	Bristol R	26	1	**94**	**4**

VAN STAPPERSHOEF, Jordi (G) 36 0
b. 10-3-96

2014–15	Volendam	1	0		
2015–16	Volendam	0	0		
2016–17	Volendam	2	0		
2017–18	Volendam	0	0		
2018–19	Volendam	20	0	**23**	**0**
2019–20	Bristol R	5	0		
2020–21	Bristol R	8	0	**13**	**0**

WALKER, Zain (M) 11 0
b. 8-1-02
From Fulham.

2018–19	Bristol R	0	0		
2020–21	Bristol R	11	0	**11**	**0**

WARD, Jed (G) 1 0
b. 20-5-03

2020–21	Bristol R	1	0	**1**	**0**

WESTBROOKE, Zain (M) 75 6
b. 28-10-96
From Chelsea.

2016–17	Brentford	1	0		
2017–18	Brentford	0	0	**1**	**0**
2017–18	Coventry C	0	0		
2018–19	Coventry C	7	0		
2019–20	Coventry C	25	4	**32**	**4**
2020–21	Bristol R	42	2	**42**	**2**

WILLIAMS, George B (D) 193 5
H: 5 9 W: 11 00 b.Hillingdon 14-4-93

2011–12	Milton Keynes D	2	0		

From Worcester C.

2014–15	Barnsley	4	0		
2015–16	Barnsley	19	1	**23**	**1**
2016–17	Milton Keynes D	33	2		
2017–18	Milton Keynes D	43	1		
2018–19	Milton Keynes D	30	0		
2019–20	Milton Keynes D	28	1		
2020–21	Milton Keynes D	8	0	**144**	**4**
2020–21	Bristol R	26	0	**26**	**0**

Scholars
Biss, Adam David; Brain, Owen Barry James; Budd, Joseph William; Egan, Jamie; Ford, Zak Terence Samuel; Gorman, James Cameron; Greenslade, Harvey Thomas; Heal, Samuel William; Jenkins, Joshua Robert; Lovelock, Niall Christopher; Mbuenimo, Tyron Thomson; Murray, Kinsly Lile; Njonjo, Henry Gichanga; Reed, Matthew James; Smolka, Andreas Jonas; Vilinauskas, Airidas.

BURNLEY (17)

BARDSLEY, Phillip (D) 336 8
H: 5 11 W: 11 13 b.Salford 28-6-85
Internationals: Scotland Full caps.

2003–04	Manchester U	0	0		
2003–04	*Royal Antwerp*	6	0	**6**	**0**
2004–05	Manchester U	0	0		
2005–06	Manchester U	8	0		
2005–06	*Burnley*	6	0		
2006–07	Manchester U	0	0		
2006–07	*Rangers*	5	1	**5**	**1**
2006–07	*Aston Villa*	13	0	**13**	**0**
2007–08	Manchester U	0	0	**8**	**0**
2007–08	*Sheffield U*	16	0	**16**	**0**
2007–08	Sunderland	11	0		
2008–09	Sunderland	28	0		
2009–10	Sunderland	26	0		
2010–11	Sunderland	34	3		
2011–12	Sunderland	31	1		
2012–13	Sunderland	18	1		
2013–14	Sunderland	26	2	**174**	**7**
2014–15	Stoke C	25	0		
2015–16	Stoke C	11	0		
2016–17	Stoke C	15	0	**51**	**0**
2017–18	Burnley	13	0		
2018–19	Burnley	19	0		
2019–20	Burnley	21	0		
2020–21	Burnley	4	0	**63**	**0**

BARNES, Ashley (F) 383 92
H: 6 0 W: 12 00 b.Bath 30-10-89
Internationals: Austria U20.
From Paulton R.

2006–07	Plymouth Arg	0	0		
2007–08	Plymouth Arg	0	0		
2008–09	Plymouth Arg	15	1		
2009–10	Plymouth Arg	7	1	**22**	**2**
2009–10	*Torquay U*	6	0	**6**	**0**
2009–10	*Brighton & HA*	8	4		
2010–11	Brighton & HA	42	18		
2011–12	Brighton & HA	43	11		
2012–13	Brighton & HA	34	8		
2013–14	Brighton & HA	22	5	**149**	**46**
2013–14	Burnley	21	3		
2014–15	Burnley	35	5		
2015–16	Burnley	8	0		
2016–17	Burnley	28	6		
2017–18	Burnley	36	9		
2018–19	Burnley	37	12		
2019–20	Burnley	19	6		
2020–21	Burnley	22	3	**206**	**44**

BENSON, Josh (M) **17 2**
H: 5 9 W: 11 03 b. 5-12-99
From Arsenal.

2018–19	Burnley	0	0		
2019–20	Burnley	0	0		
2019–20	*Grimsby T*	11	2	**11**	**2**
2020–21	Burnley	6	0	**6**	**0**

BRADY, Robert (F) **254 21**
H: 5 9 W: 10 12 b.Belfast 14-1-92
Internationals: Republic of Ireland Youth, U21, Full caps.

2008–09	Manchester U	0	0		
2009–10	Manchester U	0	0		
2010–11	Manchester U	0	0		
2011–12	Manchester U	0	0		
2011–12	*Hull C*	39	3		
2012–13	Manchester U	0	0		
2012–13	Hull C	32	4		
2013–14	Hull C	16	3		
2014–15	Hull C	27	0	**114**	**10**
2015–16	Norwich C	36	3		
2016–17	Norwich C	23	4	**59**	**7**
2016–17	Burnley	14	1		
2017–18	Burnley	15	1		
2018–19	Burnley	16	0		
2019–20	Burnley	17	1		
2020–21	Burnley	19	1	**81**	**4**

BROWNHILL, Josh (M) **255 23**
H: 5 10 W: 10 12 b.Warrington 19-12-95

2013–14	Preston NE	24	3		
2014–15	Preston NE	18	2		
2015–16	Preston NE	3	0	**45**	**5**
2015–16	*Barnsley*	22	2	**22**	**2**
2016–17	Bristol C	27	1		
2017–18	Bristol C	45	5		
2018–19	Bristol C	45	5		
2019–20	Bristol C	28	5	**145**	**16**
2019–20	Burnley	10	0		
2020–21	Burnley	33	0	**43**	**0**

COONEY, Ryan (M) **68 0**
b. 26-2-00

2016–17	Bury	0	0		
2017–18	Bury	12	0		
2018–19	Bury	9	0	**21**	**0**
2019–20	Burnley	0	0		
2019–20	*Morecambe*	11	0		
2020–21	Burnley	0	0		
2020–21	*Morecambe*	36	0	**47**	**0**

CORK, Jack (D) **470 13**
H: 6 0 W: 10 12 b.Carshalton 25-6-89
Internationals: England U16, U17, U18, U19, U20, U21, Full caps. Great Britain.

2006–07	Chelsea	0	0		
2006–07	*Bournemouth*	7	0	**7**	**0**
2007–08	Chelsea	0	0		
2007–08	*Scunthorpe U*	34	2	**34**	**2**
2008–09	Chelsea	0	0		
2008–09	*Southampton*	23	0		
2008–09	*Watford*	19	0	**19**	**0**
2009–10	Chelsea	0	0		
2009–10	*Coventry C*	21	0	**21**	**0**
2009–10	*Burnley*	11	1		
2010–11	Chelsea	0	0		
2010–11	*Burnley*	40	3		
2011–12	Southampton	46	0		
2012–13	Southampton	28	0		
2013–14	Southampton	28	0		
2014–15	Southampton	12	2	**137**	**2**
2014–15	Swansea C	15	1		
2015–16	Swansea C	35	1		
2016–17	Swansea C	30	0	**80**	**2**
2017–18	Burnley	38	2		
2018–19	Burnley	37	1		
2019–20	Burnley	30	0		
2020–21	Burnley	16	0	**172**	**7**

COSTELLO, Dara (F) **0 0**
b.Limerick 11-12-02
From Galway.

2020–21	Burnley	0	0		

DRISCOLL-GLENNON, Anthony (D) **12 1**
b.Bootle 26-11-99
From Liverpool.

2018–19	Burnley	0	0		
2019–20	Burnley	0	0		
2019–20	*Grimsby T*	12	1	**12**	**1**
2020–21	Burnley	0	0		

DUNNE, Jimmy (D) **56 5**
b.Drogheda 19-10-97
Internationals: Republic of Ireland U21.
From Manchester U.

2017–18	Burnley	0	0		
2017–18	*Accrington S*	20	0	**20**	**0**
2018–19	Burnley	0	0		
2018–19	*Hearts*	12	2	**12**	**2**
2018–19	*Sunderland*	12	1	**12**	**1**
2019–20	Burnley	0	0		
2019–20	*Fleetwood T*	9	1	**9**	**1**
2020–21	Burnley	3	1	**3**	**1**

GIBSON, Ben (D) **254 6**
H: 6 1 W: 12 04 b.Nunthorpe 15-1-93
Internationals: England U17, U18, U20, U21.

2010–11	Middlesbrough	1	0		
2011–12	Middlesbrough	0	0		
2011–12	*Plymouth Arg*	13	0	**13**	**0**
2012–13	Middlesbrough	1	0		
2012–13	*Tranmere R*	28	1	**28**	**1**
2013–14	Middlesbrough	31	1		
2014–15	Middlesbrough	36	0		
2015–16	Middlesbrough	33	1		
2016–17	Middlesbrough	38	1		
2017–18	Middlesbrough	45	1	**185**	**4**
2018–19	Burnley	1	1		
2019–20	Burnley	0	0		
2020–21	Burnley	0	0	**1**	**1**
2020–21	*Norwich C*	27	0	**27**	**0**

GOODRIDGE, Mace (M) **2 0**
b. 13-9-99
From Newcastle U.

2019–20	Burnley	0	0		
2020–21	Burnley	0	0		
2020–21	*Barrow*	2	0	**2**	**0**

GUDMUNDSSON, Johann Berg (M) **318 34**
H: 6 1 W: 12 06 b.Reykjavik 27-10-90
Internationals: Iceland U19, U21, Full caps.

2009–10	AZ Alkmaar	0	0		
2010–11	AZ Alkmaar	23	1		
2011–12	AZ Alkmaar	30	3		
2012–13	AZ Alkmaar	31	2		
2013–14	AZ Alkmaar	35	3	**119**	**9**
2014–15	Charlton Ath	41	10		
2015–16	Charlton Ath	40	6	**81**	**16**
2016–17	Burnley	20	1		
2017–18	Burnley	35	2		
2018–19	Burnley	29	3		
2019–20	Burnley	12	1		
2020–21	Burnley	22	2	**118**	**9**

JENSEN, Lukas (G) **12 0**
b. 8-10-94

2017–18	Helsingor	1	0		
2018–19	Helsingor	0	0	**1**	**0**
2018–19	HIK	6	0	**6**	**0**
2019–20	Burnley	0	0		
2020–21	Burnley	0	0		
2020–21	*Bolton W*	0	0		
2020–21	*Kordrengir*	5	0	**5**	**0**

LONG, Kevin (D) **152 8**
H: 6 3 W: 13 01 b.Cork 18-8-90
Internationals: Republic of Ireland Full caps.

2009	Cork C	16	1	**16**	**1**
2009–10	Burnley	0	0		
2010–11	Burnley	0	0		
2010–11	*Accrington S*	15	0		
2011–12	Burnley	0	0		
2011–12	*Accrington S*	24	4	**39**	**4**
2011–12	*Rochdale*	16	0	**16**	**0**
2012–13	Burnley	14	0		
2012–13	*Portsmouth*	5	0	**5**	**0**
2013–14	Burnley	7	0		
2014–15	Burnley	1	0		
2015–16	Burnley	0	0		
2015–16	*Barnsley*	11	2	**11**	**2**
2015–16	*Milton Keynes D*	2	0	**2**	**0**
2016–17	Burnley	3	0		
2017–18	Burnley	16	1		
2018–19	Burnley	6	0		
2019–20	Burnley	8	0		
2020–21	Burnley	8	0	**63**	**1**

LOWTON, Matt (M) **316 14**
H: 5 11 W: 12 04 b.Chesterfield 9-6-89

2008–09	Sheffield U	0	0		
2009–10	Sheffield U	2	0		
2009–10	*Ferencvaros*	5	0	**5**	**0**
2010–11	Sheffield U	32	4		
2011–12	Sheffield U	44	6	**78**	**10**
2012–13	Aston Villa	37	2		
2013–14	Aston Villa	23	0		
2014–15	Aston Villa	12	0	**72**	**2**
2015–16	Burnley	27	1		
2016–17	Burnley	36	0		
2017–18	Burnley	26	0		
2018–19	Burnley	21	0		
2019–20	Burnley	17	0		
2020–21	Burnley	34	1	**161**	**2**

MANCINI, Anthony (M) **0 0**
b.Saint Priest 6-4-01
From Tours.

2018–19	Angers	0	0		
2019–20	Angers	0	0		
2020–21	Angers	0	0		

On loan from Angers.

2020–21	Burnley	0	0		

McNEIL, Dwight (F) **96 7**
b. 22-11-99
Internationals: England U20, U21.
From Manchester U.

2017–18	Burnley	1	0		
2018–19	Burnley	21	3		
2019–20	Burnley	38	2		
2020–21	Burnley	36	2	**96**	**7**

MEE, Ben (D) **345 9**
H: 5 11 W: 11 09 b.Sale 21-9-89
Internationals: England U19, U20, U21.

2007–08	Manchester C	0	0		
2008–09	Manchester C	0	0		
2009–10	Manchester C	0	0		
2010–11	Manchester C	0	0		
2010–11	*Leicester C*	15	0	**15**	**0**
2011–12	Manchester C	0	0		
2011–12	Burnley	31	0		
2012–13	Burnley	19	1		
2013–14	Burnley	38	0		
2014–15	Burnley	33	2		
2015–16	Burnley	46	2		
2016–17	Burnley	34	1		
2017–18	Burnley	29	0		
2018–19	Burnley	38	0		
2019–20	Burnley	32	1		
2020–21	Burnley	30	2	**330**	**9**

MUMBONGO, Joel (F) **19 7**
b. 9-1-99
Internationals: Sweden U17, U18, U19.

2017	Hacken	0	0		
2018	Utsiktens	15	7	**15**	**7**
2018–19	Verona	0	0		
2019–20	Burnley	0	0		
2020–21	Burnley	4	0	**4**	**0**

NARTEY, Richard (D) **25 0**
b.London 6-9-98

2019–20	Chelsea	0	0		
2019–20	*Burton Alb*	25	0	**25**	**0**
2020–21	Burnley	0	0		

NORRIS, Will (G) **88 0**
H: 6 5 W: 11 09 b.Royston 12-7-93
From Hatfield T, Royston T.

2014–15	Cambridge U	3	0		
2015–16	Cambridge U	21	0		
2016–17	Cambridge U	45	0	**69**	**0**
2017–18	Wolverhampton W	1	0		
2018–19	Wolverhampton W	1	0		
2019–20	Wolverhampton W	0	0	**2**	**0**
2019–20	*Ipswich T*	15	0	**15**	**0**
2020–21	Burnley	2	0	**2**	**0**

PEACOCK-FARRELL, Bailey (G) **44 0**
H: 6 2 W: 11 07 b.Darlington 29-10-96
Internationals: Northern Ireland U21, Full caps.
From Middlesbrough.

2015–16	Leeds U	1	0		
2016–17	Leeds U	0	0		
2017–18	Leeds U	11	0		
2018–19	Leeds U	28	0		
2019–20	Leeds U	0	0	**40**	**0**
2019–20	Burnley	0	0		
2020–21	Burnley	4	0	**4**	**0**

PHILLIPS, Adam (M) **62 14**
b.Garstang 15-1-98
Internationals: England U16, U17.

2014–15	Liverpool	0	0		
2015–16	Liverpool	0	0		
2016–17	Liverpool	0	0		
2017–18	Norwich C	0	0		
2017–18	*Cambridge U*	4	0	**4**	**0**
2018–19	Norwich C	0	0		
2018–19	*Hamilton A*	0	0		
2019–20	Burnley	0	0		
2019–20	*Morecambe*	11	4		
2020–21	Burnley	0	0		
2020–21	*Morecambe*	25	8	**36**	**12**
2020–21	*Accrington S*	22	2	**22**	**2**

PIETERS, Erik (D) **393 6**
H: 6 0 W: 13 00 b.Tiel 7-8-88
Internationals: Netherlands U17, U19, U21, Full caps.

2006–07	Utrecht	20	0		
2007–08	Utrecht	31	2	**51**	**2**
2008–09	PSV Eindhoven	17	0		
2009–10	PSV Eindhoven	27	0		
2010–11	PSV Eindhoven	31	0		
2011–12	PSV Eindhoven	16	0		
2012–13	PSV Eindhoven	2	0	**93**	**0**
2013–14	Stoke C	36	1		
2014–15	Stoke C	31	0		
2015–16	Stoke C	35	0		
2016–17	Stoke C	36	0		
2017–18	Stoke C	31	0		
2018–19	Stoke C	21	2	**190**	**3**
2018–19	*Amiens*	15	1	**15**	**1**

2019–20 Burnley 24 0
2020–21 Burnley 20 0 **44 0**

POPE, Nick (G) 182 0
H: 6 3 W: 11 13 b.Cambridge 19-4-92
Internationals: England Full caps.
From Bury T.
2011–12 Charlton Ath 0 0
2012–13 Charlton Ath 1 0
2013–14 Charlton Ath 0 0
2013–14 *York C* 22 0 **22 0**
2014–15 Charlton Ath 8 0
2014–15 *Bury* 22 0 **22 0**
2015–16 Charlton Ath 24 0 **33 0**
2016–17 Burnley 0 0
2017–18 Burnley 35 0
2018–19 Burnley 0 0
2019–20 Burnley 38 0
2020–21 Burnley 32 0 **105 0**

RICHARDSON, Lewis (F) 2 0
b. 7-2-03
Internationals: England U16, U17.
2019–20 Burnley 0 0
2020–21 Burnley 2 0 **2 0**

RICHTER, Marc (G) 0 0
H: 6 6 b. 31-12-99
From Augsburg.
2020–21 Burnley 0 0

RODRIGUEZ, Jay (F) 375 99
H: 6 0 W: 12 00 b.Burnley 29-7-89
Internationals: England U21, Full caps.
2007–08 Burnley 1 0
2007–08 *Stirling Alb* 11 3 **11 3**
2008–09 Burnley 25 2
2009–10 Burnley 0 0
2009–10 *Barnsley* 6 1 **6 1**
2010–11 Burnley 42 14
2011–12 Burnley 37 15
2012–13 Southampton 35 6
2013–14 Southampton 33 15
2014–15 Southampton 0 0
2015–16 Southampton 12 0
2016–17 Southampton 24 5 **104 26**
2017–18 WBA 37 7
2018–19 WBA 45 22 **82 29**
2019–20 Burnley 36 8
2020–21 Burnley 31 1 **172 40**

STEPHENS, Dale (M) 385 37
H: 5 7 W: 11 04 b.Bolton 12-6-89
2006–07 Bury 3 0
2007–08 Bury 6 1 **9 1**
2008–09 Oldham Ath 0 0
2009–10 Oldham Ath 26 2
2009–10 *Rochdale* 6 1 **6 1**
2010–11 Oldham Ath 34 9 **60 11**
2010–11 *Southampton* 6 0 **6 0**
2011–12 Charlton Ath 30 5
2012–13 Charlton Ath 28 2
2013–14 Charlton Ath 26 3 **84 10**
2013–14 Brighton & HA 14 2
2014–15 Brighton & HA 16 2
2015–16 Brighton & HA 45 7
2016–17 Brighton & HA 39 2
2017–18 Brighton & HA 36 0
2018–19 Brighton & HA 30 1
2019–20 Brighton & HA 33 0
2020–21 Brighton & HA 0 0 **213 14**
2020–21 Burnley 7 0 **7 0**

TARKOWSKI, James (D) 305 15
H: 6 1 W: 12 10 b.Manchester 19-11-92
Internationals: England Full caps.
2010–11 Oldham Ath 9 0
2011–12 Oldham Ath 16 1
2012–13 Oldham Ath 21 2
2013–14 Oldham Ath 26 2 **72 5**
2013–14 Brentford 13 2
2014–15 Brentford 34 1
2015–16 Brentford 23 1 **70 4**
2015–16 Burnley 4 0
2016–17 Burnley 19 0
2017–18 Burnley 31 0
2018–19 Burnley 35 3
2019–20 Burnley 38 2
2020–21 Burnley 36 1 **163 6**

TAYLOR, Charlie (D) 241 3
H: 5 9 W: 11 00 b.York 18-9-93
Internationals: England U19.
2011–12 Leeds U 2 0
2011–12 *Bradford C* 3 0 **3 0**
2012–13 Leeds U 0 0
2012–13 *York C* 4 0 **4 0**
2012–13 *Inverness CT* 7 0 **7 0**
2013–14 Leeds U 0 0
2013–14 *Fleetwood T* 32 0 **32 0**
2014–15 Leeds U 23 2
2015–16 Leeds U 39 1
2016–17 Leeds U 29 0 **93 3**
2017–18 Burnley 11 0
2018–19 Burnley 38 0
2019–20 Burnley 24 0
2020–21 Burnley 29 0 **102 0**

THOMAS, Bobby (D) 21 1
b. 30-1-01
2019–20 Burnley 0 0
2020–21 Burnley 0 0
2020–21 *Barrow* 21 1 **21 1**

THOMPSON, Max (F) 1 0
b. 9-2-02
From Everton.
2019–20 Burnley 1 0
2020–21 Burnley 0 0 **1 0**

VYDRA, Matej (F) 315 83
H: 5 10 W: 11 09 b.Chotebor 1-5-92
Internationals: Czech Republic U16, U17, U18, U19, U21, Full caps.
2008–09 Vysocina Jihlava 12 2
2009–10 Vysocina Jihlava 15 3 **27 5**
2009–10 Banik Ostrava 14 4 **14 4**
2010–11 Udinese 2 0
2011–12 Udinese 0 0
2011–12 *Club Brugge* 1 0 **1 0**
2012–13 Udinese 0 0
2012–13 *Watford* 41 20
2013–14 Udinese 0 0
2013–14 *WBA* 23 3 **23 3**
2014–15 Udinese 0 0 **2 0**
2014–15 *Watford* 42 16
2015–16 Watford 0 0
2015–16 *Reading* 31 3 **31 3**
2016–17 Watford 1 0 **84 36**
2016–17 Derby Co 33 5
2017–18 Derby Co 40 21 **73 26**
2018–19 Burnley 13 1
2019–20 Burnley 19 2
2020–21 Burnley 28 3 **60 6**

WESTWOOD, Ashley (M) 410 26
H: 5 10 W: 11 00 b.Nantwich 1-4-90
2008–09 Crewe Alex 2 0
2009–10 Crewe Alex 36 6
2010–11 Crewe Alex 46 5
2011–12 Crewe Alex 41 3
2012–13 Crewe Alex 3 0 **128 14**
2012–13 Aston Villa 30 0
2013–14 Aston Villa 35 3
2014–15 Aston Villa 27 0
2015–16 Aston Villa 32 2
2016–17 Aston Villa 23 0 **147 5**
2016–17 Burnley 9 0
2017–18 Burnley 19 0
2018–19 Burnley 34 2
2019–20 Burnley 35 2
2020–21 Burnley 38 3 **135 7**

WOOD, Chris (F) 389 133
H: 6 3 W: 12 10 b.Auckland 7-12-91
Internationals: New Zealand U17, U23, Full caps.
From Waikato.
2008–09 WBA 2 0
2009–10 WBA 18 1
2010–11 WBA 1 0
2010–11 *Barnsley* 7 0 **7 0**
2010–11 *Brighton & HA* 29 8 **29 8**
2011–12 WBA 0 0
2011–12 *Birmingham C* 23 9 **23 9**
2011–12 *Bristol C* 19 3 **19 3**
2012–13 WBA 0 0 **21 1**
2012–13 *Millwall* 19 11 **19 11**
2012–13 Leicester C 20 9
2013–14 Leicester C 26 4
2014–15 Leicester C 7 1 **53 14**
2014–15 *Ipswich T* 8 0 **8 0**
2015–16 Leeds U 36 13
2016–17 Leeds U 44 27
2017–18 Leeds U 3 1 **83 41**
2017–18 Burnley 24 10
2018–19 Burnley 38 10
2019–20 Burnley 32 14
2020–21 Burnley 33 12 **127 46**

Scholars
Allen, Harry George; Armstrong, Finlay Patric; Behan, Ruairi; Brennan, Corey Carl; Carson, Matthew Alan; Connolly, Joel Alexander George; Coppack, Jacson David; Couch, William Antony; Dodgson, Owen Joel; Eastmond, Tremaine Leroy Winston; Etaluku, Sean Kesena Temitope; Gallagher-Allison, Calen; Hamilton, Jacob Luke; Hugill, William James; Leckie, Jack James; McCullough, Dane Neil; McGlynn, Joseph Peter; Mellon, Michael Jordan Donald; Moonan, Dylan; Rain, Matthew; Ratchford, Kade; Rooney, Jake Richard; Sassi, Daniel; Smyth-Ferguson, Joseph Ian; Thomas, Lewis Luka; Thompson, Max; Tucker, Ne'Jai; Unwin, Samual Connor; Waller, Sam William John; Walters, Steven Tomos George; Ward, Benn David; Williams, Keelan Ellis; Woods, Benjamin Jack.

BURTON ALB (18)

AKINS, Lucas (F) 464 83
H: 5 10 W: 11 07 b.Huddersfield 25-2-89
2006–07 Huddersfield T 2 0
2007–08 Huddersfield T 3 0 **5 0**
2008–09 Hamilton A 11 0
2008–09 *Partick Thistle* 9 1 **9 1**
2009–10 Hamilton A 0 0 **11 0**
2010–11 Tranmere R 33 2
2011–12 Tranmere R 44 5 **77 7**
2012–13 Stevenage 46 10
2013–14 Stevenage 31 3 **77 13**
2014–15 Burton Alb 35 9
2015–16 Burton Alb 44 12
2016–17 Burton Alb 38 5
2017–18 Burton Alb 42 5
2018–19 Burton Alb 46 13
2019–20 Burton Alb 35 9
2020–21 Burton Alb 45 9 **285 62**

ANDERSON, Jevan (D) 1 0
b. 3-3-00
From Aberdeen, Formartine U.
2019–20 Burton Alb 1 0
2020–21 Burton Alb 0 0 **1 0**

ARMITAGE, Tom (D) 0 0
b. 21-6-03
2020–21 Burton Alb 0 0

BOSTWICK, Michael (D) 413 43
H: 6 4 W: 14 00 b.Eltham 17-5-88
Internationals: England C.
2006–07 Millwall 0 0
From Rushden & D, Ebbsfleet U
2010–11 Stevenage 41 2
2011–12 Stevenage 43 7 **84 9**
2012–13 Peterborough U 39 5
2013–14 Peterborough U 42 4
2014–15 Peterborough U 38 7
2015–16 Peterborough U 36 4
2016–17 Peterborough U 39 3 **194 23**
2017–18 Lincoln C 44 6
2018–19 Lincoln C 45 2
2019–20 Lincoln C 18 1 **107 9**
2020–21 Burton Alb 28 2 **28 2**

BRAYFORD, John (D) 450 16
H: 5 8 W: 11 02 b.Stoke 29-12-87
Internationals: England C.
From Burton Alb.
2008–09 Crewe Alex 36 2
2009–10 Crewe Alex 45 0 **81 2**
2010–11 Derby Co 46 1
2011–12 Derby Co 23 0
2012–13 Derby Co 40 1 **109 2**
2013–14 Cardiff C 0 0
2013–14 *Sheffield U* 15 1
2014–15 Cardiff C 26 0 **26 0**
2014–15 Sheffield U 22 1
2015–16 Sheffield U 19 1
2016–17 Sheffield U 3 0
2016–17 *Burton Alb* 33 0
2017–18 Sheffield U 0 0 **59 3**
2017–18 Burton Alb 28 0
2018–19 Burton Alb 41 3
2019–20 Burton Alb 32 2
2020–21 Burton Alb 41 4 **175 9**

DANIEL, Colin (M) 382 33
H: 5 11 W: 11 06 b.Eastwood 15-2-88
From Eastwood T.
2006–07 Crewe Alex 0 0
2007–08 Crewe Alex 1 0
2008–09 Crewe Alex 13 1 **14 1**
2008–09 *Macclesfield T* 8 0
2009–10 Macclesfield T 38 3
2010–11 Macclesfield T 43 8
2011–12 Macclesfield T 36 2 **125 13**
2013–14 Mansfield T 28 2
2014–15 Port Vale 28 4
2015–16 Port Vale 20 2 **48 6**
2015–16 *Mansfield T* 9 2 **37 4**
2016–17 Blackpool 34 4
2017–18 Blackpool 44 4 **78 8**
2018–19 Peterborough U 20 0 **20 0**
2018–19 Burton Alb 17 0
2019–20 Burton Alb 24 0
2020–21 Burton Alb 19 1 **60 1**

EARDLEY, Neal (M) 395 15
H: 5 11 W: 11 10 b.Llandudno 6-11-88
Internationals: Wales U17, U19, U21, Full caps.
2005–06 Oldham Ath 1 0

2006–07 Oldham Ath 36 2
2007–08 Oldham Ath 42 6
2008–09 Oldham Ath 34 2
2009–10 Oldham Ath 0 0 **113 10**
2009–10 Blackpool 24 0
2010–11 Blackpool 31 1
2011–12 Blackpool 26 1
2012–13 Blackpool 23 0 **104 2**
2013–14 Birmingham C 5 0
2014–15 Birmingham C 4 0
2014–15 *Leyton Orient* 1 0 **1 0**
2015–16 Birmingham C 5 0 **14 0**
2016–17 Hibernian 2 0 **2 0**
2016–17 Northampton T 10 0 **10 0**
2017–18 Lincoln C 44 1
2018–19 Lincoln C 43 2
2019–20 Lincoln C 35 0 **122 3**
2020–21 Burton Alb 10 0 **10 0**
2020–21 *Barrow* 19 0 **19 0**

EDWARDS, Ryan (M) 206 13
H: 5 7 W: 11 07 b.Sydney 17-11-93
Internationals: Australia U20, U23.
2011–12 Reading 0 0
2012–13 Reading 0 0
2012–13 *Rochdale* 0 0
2013–14 Reading 0 0
2013–14 *Perth Glory* 15 0 **15 0**
2014–15 Reading 7 0 **7 0**
2015–16 Partick Thistle 17 2
2016–17 Partick Thistle 38 1
2017–18 Partick Thistle 36 4 **91 7**
2018–19 Hearts 4 0 **4 0**
2018–19 *St Mirren* 14 0 **14 0**
2019–20 Burton Alb 33 5
2020–21 Burton Alb 42 1 **75 6**

FONDOP-TALOM, Mike (F) 17 2
b.Yaounde 27-11-93
2020–21 Burton Alb 17 2 **17 2**

FOX, Ben (M) 37 1
H: 5 11 W: 12 00 b.Burton upon Trent 1-2-98
2016–17 Burton Alb 1 0
2017–18 Burton Alb 0 0
2018–19 Burton Alb 27 1
2019–20 Burton Alb 0 0
2020–21 Burton Alb 9 0 **37 1**

GALLACHER, Owen (M) 9 0
b. 6-4-99
From Newcastle U, Nottingham F.
2020–21 Burton Alb 9 0 **9 0**

GARRATT, Ben (G) 254 0
H: 6 1 W: 10 06 b.Market Drayton 25-4-94
Internationals: England U17, U18, U19.
2011–12 Crewe Alex 0 0
2012–13 Crewe Alex 1 0
2013–14 Crewe Alex 26 0
2014–15 Crewe Alex 30 0
2015–16 Crewe Alex 46 0
2016–17 Crewe Alex 46 0
2017–18 Crewe Alex 36 0
2018–19 Crewe Alex 38 0 **223 0**
2019–20 Burton Alb 3 0
2020–21 Burton Alb 28 0 **31 0**

GILLIGAN, Ciaran (M) 18 0
b. 5-2-02
2020–21 Burton Alb 18 0 **18 0**

HART, Ben (D) 3 0
2018–19 Burton Alb 0 0
2019–20 Burton Alb 3 0
2020–21 Burton Alb 0 0 **3 0**

HAWKINS, Callum (G) 0 0
b.Rotherham 12-12-99
2018–19 Burton Alb 0 0
2019–20 Burton Alb 0 0
2020–21 Burton Alb 0 0

HAYMER, Tom (D) 105 9
b. 16-11-99
2017–18 Oldham Ath 7 1
2018–19 Oldham Ath 28 2
2019–20 Oldham Ath 37 3
2020–21 Oldham Ath 12 0 **84 6**
2020–21 Burton Alb 21 3 **21 3**

HEMMINGS, Kane (F) 281 107
b.Burton 8-4-92
From Tamworth.
2010–11 Rangers 0 0
2011–12 Rangers 4 0
2012–13 Rangers 5 1 **9 1**
2012–13 *Cowdenbeath* 7 4
2013–14 Cowdenbeath 31 18 **38 22**
2014–15 Barnsley 23 3 **23 3**
2015–16 Dundee 37 21
2016–17 Oxford U 40 6
2017–18 Oxford U 0 0 **40 6**
2017–18 *Mansfield T* 37 15 **37 15**
2018–19 Notts Co 36 14 **36 14**
2019–20 Dundee 25 10 **62 31**
2020–21 Burton Alb 36 15 **36 15**

HEWLETT, Tom (F) 1 0
2020–21 Rushall Olympic 0 0
2020–21 Burton Alb 1 0 **1 0**

HUTCHINSON, Reece (D) 43 0
b. 14-4-00
2017–18 Burton Alb 0 0
2018–19 Burton Alb 25 0
2019–20 Burton Alb 17 0
2020–21 Burton Alb 1 0 **43 0**

LATTY-FAIRWEATHER, Thierry (D) 0 0
2020–21 Burton Alb 0 0

LAWLESS, Steven (F) 306 45
b.Glasgow 12-4-91
2010–11 Motherwell 0 0
2010–11 *Annan Ath* 0 0
2010–11 *Albion R* 25 3
2011–12 Motherwell 0 0
2011–12 *Albion R* 10 3 **35 6**
2012–13 Partick Thistle 35 13
2013–14 Partick Thistle 28 4
2014–15 Partick Thistle 33 3
2015–16 Partick Thistle 37 5
2016–17 Partick Thistle 30 2
2017–18 Partick Thistle 27 1 **190 28**
2018–19 Livingston 35 3
2019–20 Livingston 30 8 **65 11**
2020–21 Burton Alb 16 0 **16 0**
Transferred to Motherwell January 2021.

MANCIENNE, Michael (D) 341 1
H: 6 0 W: 11 09 b.Isleworth 8-1-88
Internationals: England U16, U17, U18, U19, U21.
2005–06 Chelsea 0 0
2006–07 Chelsea 0 0
2006–07 *QPR* 28 0
2007–08 Chelsea 0 0
2007–08 *QPR* 30 0 **58 0**
2008–09 Chelsea 4 0
2008–09 *Wolverhampton W* 10 0
2009–10 Chelsea 0 0
2009–10 *Wolverhampton W* 30 0
2010–11 Chelsea 0 0 **4 0**
2010–11 *Wolverhampton W* 16 0 **56 0**
2011–12 Hamburg 16 0
2012–13 Hamburg 21 0
2013–14 Hamburg 12 0 **49 0**
2014–15 Nottingham F 36 0
2015–16 Nottingham F 31 0
2016–17 Nottingham F 28 0
2017–18 Nottingham F 29 0 **124 0**
2018 New England Revolution 10 0
2019 New England Revolution 16 1
2020 New England Revolution 7 0 **33 1**
2020–21 Burton Alb 17 0 **17 0**

NIEMcZYK, Jakub (M) 0 0
2020–21 Burton Alb 0 0

O'HARA, Kieran (G) 92 0
b. 22-4-96
Internationals: Republic of Ireland U21, Full caps.
2015–16 Manchester U 0 0
2015–16 *Morecambe* 5 0
2016–17 Morecambe 0 0 **5 0**
2016–17 Manchester U 0 0
2017–18 Manchester U 0 0
2018–19 Manchester U 0 0
2018–19 *Macclesfield T* 37 0 **37 0**
2019–20 Manchester U 0 0
2019–20 *Burton Alb* 33 0
2020–21 Burton Alb 17 0 **50 0**

O'TOOLE, John (M) 413 63
H: 6 2 W: 13 07 b.Harrow 30-9-88
Internationals: Republic of Ireland U21.
2007–08 Watford 35 3
2008–09 Watford 22 7
2008–09 *Sheffield U* 9 1 **9 1**
2009–10 Watford 0 0 **57 10**
2009–10 Colchester U 31 2
2010–11 Colchester U 11 0
2011–12 Colchester U 15 0
2012–13 Colchester U 15 0 **72 2**
2012–13 *Bristol R* 18 3
2013–14 Bristol R 41 13 **59 16**
2014–15 Northampton T 35 2
2014–15 *Southend U* 2 0 **2 0**
2015–16 Northampton T 38 12
2016–17 Northampton T 40 10
2017–18 Northampton T 29 6
2018–19 Northampton T 31 3 **173 33**
2019–20 Burton Alb 25 0
2020–21 Burton Alb 16 1 **41 1**

PARKER, Josh (F) 217 34
H: 5 11 W: 12 00 b.Slough 1-12-90
Internationals: Antigua and Barbuda Full caps.
2009–10 QPR 4 0
2010–11 QPR 1 0 **5 0**
2010–11 *Northampton T* 3 0 **3 0**
2010–11 *Wycombe W* 1 0
2011–12 Oldham Ath 13 0 **13 0**
2011–12 *Dagenham & R* 8 0 **8 0**
2012–13 Oxford U 15 0 **15 0**
2013–14 Domzale 25 11
2014–15 Domzale 17 3 **42 14**
2014–15 Red Star Belgrade 9 2
2015–16 Red Star Belgrade 3 2 **12 4**
2015–16 *Aberdeen* 7 0 **7 0**
2016–17 Gillingham 16 2
2017–18 Gillingham 42 10
2018–19 Gillingham 21 4 **79 16**
2018–19 Charlton Ath 10 0 **10 0**
2019–20 Wycombe W 13 0
2020–21 Wycombe W 3 0 **17 0**
2020–21 Burton Alb 6 0 **6 0**

POWELL, Joe (F) 59 11
b. 30-10-98
2018–19 West Ham U 0 0
2018–19 *Northampton T* 10 2 **10 2**
2019–20 West Ham U 0 0
2019–20 Burton Alb 10 3
2020–21 Burton Alb 39 6 **49 9**

QUINN, Stephen (M) 473 29
H: 5 6 W: 9 08 b.Dublin 4-4-86
Internationals: Republic of Ireland U21, Full caps.
2004 St Patrick's Ath 1 0
2005 St Patrick's Ath 0 0 **1 0**
2005–06 Sheffield U 0 0
2005–06 *Milton Keynes D* 15 0 **15 0**
2005–06 *Rotherham U* 16 0 **16 0**
2006–07 Sheffield U 15 2
2007–08 Sheffield U 19 2
2008–09 Sheffield U 43 7
2009–10 Sheffield U 44 4
2010–11 Sheffield U 37 1
2011–12 Sheffield U 45 4
2012–13 Sheffield U 3 0 **206 20**
2012–13 Hull C 42 3
2013–14 Hull C 15 0
2014–15 Hull C 28 1 **85 4**
2015–16 Reading 27 1
2016–17 Reading 7 0
2017–18 Reading 0 0 **34 1**
2018–19 Burton Alb 42 1
2019–20 Burton Alb 29 0
2020–21 Burton Alb 22 1 **93 2**
2020–21 *Mansfield T* 23 2 **23 2**

ROWE, Danny (M) 91 7
H: 6 0 b.Wythenshawe 9-3-92
2008–09 Stockport Co 3 0
2009–10 Stockport Co 4 0
2010–11 Stockport Co 17 1 **24 1**
From Stockport Co, Barrow, Macclesfield T.
2016–17 Ipswich T 4 0
2017–18 Ipswich T 2 0
2017–18 *Lincoln C* 12 1
2018–19 Ipswich T 3 0
2018–19 *Lincoln C* 17 4 **29 5**
2019–20 Ipswich T 14 1 **23 1**
2020–21 Burton Alb 15 0 **15 0**

SMITH, Jonny (F) 60 12
b. 28-7-97
From Wrexham.
2019–20 Bristol C 0 0
2019–20 *Oldham Ath* 28 9 **28 9**
2020–21 Burton Alb 16 2 **16 2**
2020–21 *Swindon T* 16 1 **16 1**

TAYLOR, Terry (M) 29 0
b. 29-6-01
Internationals: Wales U21.
From Aberdeen.
2019–20 Wolverhampton W 0 0
2020–21 Wolverhampton W 0 0
2020–21 *Grimsby T* 13 0 **13 0**
2020–21 Burton Alb 16 0 **16 0**

VARNEY, Luke (F) 471 93
H: 5 11 W: 11 00 b.Leicester 28-9-82
From Quorn.
2002–03 Crewe Alex 0 0
2003–04 Crewe Alex 8 1
2004–05 Crewe Alex 26 4
2005–06 Crewe Alex 27 5
2006–07 Crewe Alex 34 17 **95 27**
2007–08 Charlton Ath 39 8
2008–09 Charlton Ath 18 2 **57 10**
2008–09 *Sheffield W* 4 2
2008–09 Derby Co 10 1

2009–10 Derby Co 1 0
2009–10 *Sheffield W* 39 9 **43 11**
2010–11 Derby Co 1 0 **12 1**
2010–11 *Blackpool* 30 5 **30 5**
2011–12 Portsmouth 30 6 **30 6**
2012–13 Leeds U 34 4
2013–14 Leeds U 11 2 **45 6**
2013–14 *Blackburn R* 12 0
2014–15 Blackburn R 11 0 **23 0**
2014–15 *Ipswich T* 10 1
2015–16 Ipswich T 18 1
2016–17 Ipswich T 15 3 **43 5**
2016–17 Burton Alb 15 1
2017–18 Burton Alb 18 0
2018–19 Cheltenham T 35 14
2019–20 Cheltenham T 21 7
2020–21 Cheltenham T 0 0 **56 21**
2020–21 Burton Alb 4 0 **37 1**

WALLACE, Kieran (M) 75 2
H: 6 1 W: 11 11 b.Nottingham 26-1-95
Internationals: England U16, U17.
2013–14 Nottingham F 0 0
From Ilkeston.
2014–15 Sheffield U 4 0
2015–16 Sheffield U 11 0
2016–17 Sheffield U 0 0 **15 0**
2016–17 *Fleetwood T* 0 0
From Matlock T.
2018–19 Burton Alb 22 1
2019–20 Burton Alb 26 1
2020–21 Burton Alb 12 0 **60 2**

WILLIAMS, Charlie (M) 0 0
2020–21 Burton Alb 0 0

Scholars
Emery, Huw Alexander; Hill, Tommy; Idouarab, Said Yussuf; Lewis, Gregory Alexander Leslie; Matthews, James Keith; McLean, Ben Angus; Niemczyk, Jakub Michal; Niven, Callum Marcus; Noon-Brandy, Braeden Harold; Nyirenda, Yewo; Power, John Joseph; Radcliffe, William Benjamin Callister; Raine, Max Robert; Redfern, Luke Harry Michael; Richardson, Matthew James; Williams, Charlie Jack.

CAMBRIDGE U (19)

BURTON, Callum (G) 38 0
H: 6 2 W: 12 00 b.Newport, Shropshire 15-8-96
Internationals: England U16, U17, U18.
2013–14 Shrewsbury T 0 0
2014–15 Shrewsbury T 0 0
2015–16 Shrewsbury T 1 0
2016–17 Shrewsbury T 0 0 **1 0**
2017–18 Hull C 0 0
2018–19 Cambridge U 0 0
2019–20 Cambridge U 10 0
2020–21 Cambridge U 27 0 **37 0**

CHADWICK, Louis (G) 0 0
2020–21 Cambridge U 0 0

DALLAS, Andrew (F) 41 5
b. 22-7-99
2017–18 Rangers 0 0
2017–18 *Stenhousemuir* 6 3 **6 3**
2018–19 Rangers 0 0
2018–19 *Greenock Morton* 12 0 **12 0**
2019–20 Cambridge U 22 2
2020–21 Cambridge U 1 0 **23 2**

DAVIES, Leon (D) 44 0
b. 21-11-99
2015–16 Cambridge U 0 0
2016–17 Cambridge U 5 0
2017–18 Cambridge U 4 0
2018–19 Cambridge U 6 0
2019–20 Cambridge U 16 0
2020–21 Cambridge U 13 0 **44 0**

DIGBY, Paul (M) 133 1
H: 5 9 W: 10 00 b.Sheffield 2-2-95
Internationals: England U19, U20.
2011–12 Barnsley 4 0
2012–13 Barnsley 0 0
2013–14 Barnsley 5 0
2014–15 Barnsley 11 0
2015–16 Barnsley 1 0 **21 0**
2015–16 *Ipswich T* 4 0
2016–17 Ipswich T 4 0 **8 0**
2016–17 Mansfield T 0 0
2017–18 Mansfield T 15 0 **15 0**
2018–19 Forest Green R 37 1 **37 1**
2019–20 Stevenage 17 0 **17 0**
2020–21 Cambridge U 35 0 **35 0**

DUNK, Harrison (M) 248 10
H: 6 0 W: 11 07 b. 25-10-90
From Bromley.
2014–15 Cambridge U 32 2
2015–16 Cambridge U 45 4
2016–17 Cambridge U 38 2
2017–18 Cambridge U 37 2
2018–19 Cambridge U 26 0
2019–20 Cambridge U 29 0
2020–21 Cambridge U 41 0 **248 10**

HANNANT, Luke (M) 133 9
b. 4-11-93
From Dereham T, Team Northumbria, Gateshead.
2017–18 Port Vale 18 1
2018–19 Port Vale 45 3 **63 4**
2019–20 Cambridge U 27 1
2020–21 Cambridge U 43 4 **70 5**

HOOLAHAN, Wes (M) 571 76
H: 5 6 W: 10 03 b.Dublin 10-8-83
Internationals: Republic of Ireland U21, B, Full caps.
2001–02 Shelbourne 20 3
2002–03 Shelbourne 23 0
2004 Shelbourne 31 2
2005 Shelbourne 29 4 **103 9**
2005–06 Livingston 16 0 **16 0**
2006–07 Blackpool 42 8
2007–08 Blackpool 45 5 **87 13**
2008–09 Norwich C 32 2
2009–10 Norwich C 37 11
2010–11 Norwich C 41 10
2011–12 Norwich C 33 4
2012–13 Norwich C 33 3
2013–14 Norwich C 16 1
2014–15 Norwich C 36 4
2015–16 Norwich C 30 4
2016–17 Norwich C 33 7
2017–18 Norwich C 29 1 **320 47**
2018–19 WBA 6 0 **6 0**
2019–20 Newcastle Jets 5 0 **5 0**
2020–21 Cambridge U 34 7 **34 7**

IREDALE, Jack (D) 133 13
b.Greenock 2-5-96
Internationals: Australia U17.
2016–17 Perth Glory 23 2 **23 2**
2017 ECU Joondalup 4 1 **4 1**
2017–18 Greenock Morton 9 2
2017–18 *Queen's Park* 14 1 **14 1**
2018–19 Greenock Morton 23 1 **32 3**
2019–20 Carlisle U 22 2 **22 2**
2020–21 Cambridge U 38 4 **38 4**

IRONSIDE, Joe (F) 97 21
H: 5 11 W: 11 11 b.Middlesbrough 16-10-93
Internationals: England C.
2012–13 Sheffield U 12 0
2013–14 Sheffield U 4 0
2014–15 Sheffield U 0 0 **16 0**
2014–15 *Hartlepool U* 4 1 **4 1**
From Alfreton T, Nuneaton T, Kidderminster H.
2019–20 Macclesfield T 33 6 **33 6**
2020–21 Cambridge U 44 14 **44 14**

KNIBBS, Harvey (F) 47 9
b.Bristol 26-4-99
2017–18 Aston Villa 0 0
2018–19 Aston Villa 0 0
2019–20 Cambridge U 24 7
2020–21 Cambridge U 23 2 **47 9**

KNOWLES, Tom (M) 4 1
b. 27-9-98
2017–18 Cambridge U 1 0
2018–19 Cambridge U 3 1
2019–20 Cambridge U 0 0
2020–21 Cambridge U 0 0 **4 1**
Transferred to Yeovil T November 2020.

KNOYLE, Kyle (D) 142 3
H: 5 10 W: 9 13 b.Newham 24-9-96
Internationals: England U18.
2015–16 West Ham U 0 0
2015–16 *Dundee U* 9 0 **9 0**
2016–17 West Ham U 0 0
2016–17 *Wigan Ath* 1 0 **1 0**
2017–18 Swindon T 18 0
2018–19 Swindon T 42 0 **60 0**
2019–20 Cambridge U 26 1
2020–21 Cambridge U 46 2 **72 3**

MAY, Adam (M) 62 3
b. 6-12-97
2014–15 Portsmouth 1 0
2015–16 Portsmouth 1 0
2016–17 Portsmouth 0 0
2017–18 Portsmouth 13 0
2018–19 Portsmouth 0 0
2019–20 Portsmouth 0 0 **15 0**
2019–20 *Swindon T* 9 0 **9 0**
2020–21 Cambridge U 38 3 **38 3**

McKENZIE-LYLE, Kai (G) 1 0
H: 6 5 W: 13 08 b. 30-11-97
Internationals: Guyana Full caps.
2015–16 Barnet 1 0
2016–17 Barnet 0 0
2017–18 Barnet 0 0 **1 0**
2018–19 Liverpool 0 0
2019–20 Liverpool 0 0
2020–21 Cambridge U 0 0

MITOV, Dimitar (G) 71 0
H: 6 2 W: 12 00 b. 22-1-97
Internationals: Bulgaria U16, U17, U19, U21.
2014–15 Charlton Ath 0 0
2015–16 Charlton Ath 0 0
2016–17 Charlton Ath 0 0
2017–18 Cambridge U 3 0
2018–19 Cambridge U 21 0
2019–20 Cambridge U 27 0
2020–21 Cambridge U 20 0 **71 0**

MULLIN, Paul (F) 256 73
H: 5 10 W: 11 01 b. 6-11-94
2013–14 Huddersfield T 0 0
2014–15 Morecambe 42 8
2015–16 Morecambe 40 9
2016–17 Morecambe 40 8 **122 25**
2017–18 Swindon T 40 6 **40 6**
2018–19 Tranmere R 22 5
2019–20 Tranmere R 20 3 **42 8**
2019–20 *Cambridge U* 6 2
2020–21 Cambridge U 46 32 **52 34**

NEAL, Joe (F) 0 0
2018–19 Cambridge U 0 0
2019–20 Cambridge U 0 0
2020–21 Cambridge U 0 0

O'NEIL, Liam (D) 193 9
H: 6 0 W: 12 06 b.Cambridge 31-7-93
2011–12 WBA 0 0
2011–12 *VPS* 18 1 **18 1**
2012–13 WBA 0 0
2013–14 WBA 3 0
2014–15 WBA 0 0 **3 0**
2014–15 *Scunthorpe U* 22 2 **22 2**
2015–16 Chesterfield 26 0
2016–17 Chesterfield 17 2 **43 2**
2016–17 Cambridge U 13 1
2017–18 Cambridge U 26 0
2018–19 Cambridge U 19 0
2019–20 Cambridge U 28 1
2020–21 Cambridge U 21 2 **107 4**

SIMPER, Lewis (D) 0 0
b. 7-4-01
2019–20 Cambridge U 0 0
2020–21 Cambridge U 0 0

TAYLOR, Greg (D) 253 6
H: 6 1 W: 12 02 b.Bedford 15-1-90
Internationals: England C.
2008–09 Northampton T 0 0
From Kettering T, Darlington, Luton T.
2014–15 Cambridge U 43 0
2015–16 Cambridge U 16 0
2016–17 Cambridge U 36 2
2017–18 Cambridge U 43 1
2018–19 Cambridge U 39 2
2019–20 Cambridge U 30 1
2020–21 Cambridge U 46 0 **253 6**

WORMAN, Ben (M) 1 0
b. 30-8-01
2017–18 Cambridge U 0 0
2018–19 Cambridge U 1 0
2019–20 Cambridge U 0 0
2020–21 Cambridge U 0 0 **1 0**

YEARN, Kai (M) 0 0
b.Cambridge --
2020–21 Cambridge U 0 0

Scholars
Akanbi, Saleem Abdul; Beckett, Harvey Robertson; Brathwaite, Nathan; Brown, Nathaniel Gary; Brumby, Adam William; Chadwick, Louis; Chipps, Jordan; Cowling, Myles Alex Eddie; Gill, Jonah James; Mansaray, Mustapha Alex; Maragh, Geneiro Dicaprio; Miller, Diego Lewis; Nzeh, Chibuikem; Richard-Noel, Nehemiah Constantine; Rider, Joseph Anthony; Tarpey, Joe Robert.

CARDIFF C (20)

BACUNA, Leandro (M) 378 28
H: 6 2 W: 12 00 b.Groningen 21-8-91
Internationals: Netherlands U19, U21. Curacao Full caps.

2009–10	Groningen	20	2		
2010–11	Groningen	24	0		
2011–12	Groningen	32	7		
2012–13	Groningen	33	5	**109**	**14**
2013–14	Aston Villa	35	5		
2014–15	Aston Villa	19	0		
2015–16	Aston Villa	31	1		
2016–17	Aston Villa	30	1		
2017–18	Aston Villa	1	0	**116**	**7**
2017–18	Reading	33	1		
2018–19	Reading	26	3	**59**	**4**
2018–19	Cardiff C	11	0		
2019–20	Cardiff C	41	1		
2020–21	Cardiff C	42	2	**94**	**3**

BAGAN, Joel (D) 7 0
b. 3-9-01
From Southampton.

2019–20	Cardiff C	0	0		
2020–21	Cardiff C	7	0	**7**	**0**

BAMBA, Souleymane (D) 358 22
H: 6 3 W: 14 02 b.Ivry-sur-Seine 13-1-85
Internationals: Ivory Coast Full caps.

2004–05	Paris Saint-Germain	1	0		
2005–06	Paris Saint-Germain	0	0	**1**	**0**
2006–07	Dunfermline Ath	23	0		
2007–08	Dunfermline Ath	15	0		
2008–09	Dunfermline Ath	1	0	**39**	**0**
2008–09	Hibernian	29	0		
2009–10	Hibernian	30	2		
2010–11	Hibernian	16	2	**75**	**4**
2010–11	Leicester C	16	2		
2011–12	Leicester C	36	1	**52**	**3**
2012–13	Trabzonspor	18	0		
2013–14	Trabzonspor	9	0	**27**	**0**
2014–15	Palermo	1	0	**1**	**0**
2014–15	*Leeds U*	19	1		
2015–16	Leeds U	30	4		
2016–17	Leeds U	2	0	**51**	**5**
2016–17	Cardiff C	26	2		
2017–18	Cardiff C	46	4		
2018–19	Cardiff C	28	4		
2019–20	Cardiff C	6	0		
2020–21	Cardiff C	6	0	**112**	**10**

BENNETT, Joe (D) 323 7
H: 5 10 W: 10 04 b.Rochdale 28-3-90
Internationals: England U19, U20, U21.

2008–09	Middlesbrough	1	0		
2009–10	Middlesbrough	12	0		
2010–11	Middlesbrough	31	0		
2011–12	Middlesbrough	41	1		
2012–13	Middlesbrough	0	0	**85**	**1**
2012–13	Aston Villa	25	0		
2013–14	Aston Villa	5	0		
2014–15	Aston Villa	0	0		
2014–15	*Brighton & HA*	41	1	**41**	**1**
2015–16	Aston Villa	0	0		
2015–16	*Bournemouth*	0	0		
2015–16	*Sheffield W*	3	0	**3**	**0**
2016–17	Aston Villa	0	0	**30**	**0**
2016–17	Cardiff C	24	3		
2017–18	Cardiff C	38	1		
2018–19	Cardiff C	30	0		
2019–20	Cardiff C	44	0		
2020–21	Cardiff C	28	1	**164**	**5**

BOWEN, Sam (M) 0 0
Internationals: Wales U19.

2019–20	Cardiff C	0	0		
2020–21	Cardiff C	0	0		

BROWN, Ciaron (D) 43 1
b. 1-1-01
Internationals: Northern Ireland U21, Full caps.
From Bedfont Sports, Wealdstone.

2018–19	Cardiff C	0	0		
2018–19	*Livingston*	6	0		
2019–20	Cardiff C	0	0		
2019–20	*Livingston*	9	0		
2020–21	Cardiff C	12	0	**12**	**0**
2020–21	*Livingston*	16	1	**31**	**1**

COLWILL, Rubin (M) 6 0
b. 27-4-02

2020–21	Cardiff C	6	0	**6**	**0**

D'ALMEIDA, Tavio (D) 0 0
b. 11-12-00
From Auxerre.

2019–20	Cardiff C	0	0		
2020–21	Cardiff C	0	0		

DAVIES, Isaak (F) 0 0
b. 25-9-01

2020–21	Cardiff C	0	0		

DAY, Joe (G) 243 0
H: 6 1 W: 12 00 b.Brighton 13-8-90
From Rushden & D.

2011–12	Peterborough U	0	0		
2012–13	Peterborough U	0	0		
2013–14	Peterborough U	4	0		
2014–15	Peterborough U	0	0	**4**	**0**
2014–15	*Newport Co*	36	0		
2015–16	Newport Co	41	0		
2016–17	Newport Co	45	0		
2017–18	Newport Co	46	0		
2018–19	Newport Co	43	0	**211**	**0**
2019–20	Cardiff C	1	0		
2019–20	*AFC Wimbledon*	9	0	**9**	**0**
2020–21	Cardiff C	0	0	**1**	**0**
2020–21	*Bristol R*	18	0	**18**	**0**

EVANS, Kieron (M) 0 0
b.Caerphilly 19-12-01

2020–21	Cardiff C	0	0		

FLINT, Aiden (D) 364 45
H: 6 2 W: 12 00 b.Pinxton 11-7-89
Internationals: England C.
From Alfreton T.

2010–11	Swindon T	3	0		
2011–12	Swindon T	32	2		
2012–13	Swindon T	29	2	**64**	**4**
2013–14	Bristol C	34	3		
2014–15	Bristol C	46	14		
2015–16	Bristol C	44	6		
2016–17	Bristol C	46	5		
2017–18	Bristol C	39	8	**209**	**36**
2018–19	Middlesbrough	39	1	**39**	**1**
2019–20	Cardiff C	26	3		
2020–21	Cardiff C	22	1	**48**	**4**
2020–21	*Sheffield W*	4	0	**4**	**0**

GLATZEL, Robert (F) 206 54
b.Munich 8-1-94

2012–13	1860 Munich	0	0		
2012–13	Heimstetten	4	1	**4**	**1**
2013–14	Wacker Burghasen	4	0	**4**	**0**
2014–15	1860 Munich	30	5	**30**	**5**
2015–16	Kaiserslautern	30	15		
2016–17	Kaiserslautern	19	4	**49**	**19**
2017–18	Heidenheim	29	4		
2018–19	Heidenheim	26	13	**55**	**17**
2019–20	Cardiff C	30	7		
2020–21	Cardiff C	21	3	**51**	**10**
2020–21	*Mainz*	13	2	**13**	**2**

HARRIS, Mark (M) 40 5
b. 29-12-98
Internationals: Wales U17, U19, U20, U21.

2016–17	Cardiff C	2	0		
2017–18	Cardiff C	0	0		
2018–19	Cardiff C	0	0		
2018–19	*Newport Co*	16	2	**16**	**2**
2018–19	*Port Vale*	6	0	**6**	**0**
2019–20	Cardiff C	0	0		
2020–21	Cardiff C	16	3	**18**	**3**

HOILETT, Junior (M) 399 53
H: 5 8 W: 11 00 b.Ottawa 5-6-90
Internationals: Canada Full caps.

2007–08	Blackburn R	0	0		
2007–08	*Paderborn*	12	1	**12**	**1**
2008–09	Blackburn R	0	0		
2008–09	*St Pauli*	21	6	**21**	**6**
2009–10	Blackburn R	23	0		
2010–11	Blackburn R	24	5		
2011–12	Blackburn R	34	7	**81**	**12**
2012–13	QPR	26	1		
2013–14	QPR	35	4		
2014–15	QPR	22	0		
2015–16	QPR	29	6		
2016–17	QPR	0	0	**112**	**11**
2016–17	Cardiff C	33	2		
2017–18	Cardiff C	46	9		
2018–19	Cardiff C	32	3		
2019–20	Cardiff C	41	7		
2020–21	Cardiff C	21	2	**173**	**23**

HUGHES, Caleb (M) 0 0

2020–21	Cardiff C	0	0		

MOORE, Kieffer (F) 221 71
H: 6 5 W: 13 01 b.Torquay 8-8-92
Internationals: England C. Wales Full caps.
From Truro C, Dorchester T.

2013–14	Yeovil T	20	4		
2014–15	Yeovil T	30	3	**50**	**7**
2015	Viking	9	0	**9**	**0**

From Forest Green R.

2016–17	Ipswich T	11	0		
2017–18	Ipswich T	0	0	**11**	**0**
2017–18	*Rotherham U*	22	13	**22**	**13**
2017–18	Barnsley	20	4		
2018–19	Barnsley	31	17		
2019–20	Barnsley	0	0	**51**	**21**
2019–20	Wigan Ath	36	10	**36**	**10**
2020–21	Cardiff C	42	20	**42**	**20**

MORRISON, Sean (D) 377 41
H: 6 4 W: 14 00 b.Plymouth 8-1-91

2007–08	Swindon T	2	0		
2008–09	Swindon T	20	1		
2009–10	Swindon T	9	1		
2009–10	*Southend U*	8	0	**8**	**0**
2010–11	Swindon T	19	4	**50**	**6**
2010–11	Reading	0	0		
2010–11	*Huddersfield T*	0	0		
2011–12	Reading	0	0		
2011–12	*Huddersfield T*	19	1	**19**	**1**
2012–13	Reading	16	2		
2013–14	Reading	21	1		
2014–15	Reading	1	1	**38**	**4**
2014–15	Cardiff C	41	6		
2015–16	Cardiff C	30	3		
2016–17	Cardiff C	44	4		
2017–18	Cardiff C	39	7		
2018–19	Cardiff C	34	1		
2019–20	Cardiff C	36	4		
2020–21	Cardiff C	38	5	**262**	**30**

MURPHY, Josh (F) 225 27
H: 5 8 W: 10 07 b.Wembley 24-2-95
Internationals: England U18, U19, U20.

2012–13	Norwich C	0	0		
2013–14	Norwich C	9	0		
2014–15	Norwich C	13	1		
2014–15	*Wigan Ath*	5	0	**5**	**0**
2015–16	Norwich C	0	0		
2015–16	*Milton Keynes D*	42	5	**42**	**5**
2016–17	Norwich C	27	4		
2017–18	Norwich C	41	7	**90**	**12**
2018–19	Cardiff C	29	3		
2019–20	Cardiff C	27	5		
2020–21	Cardiff C	32	2	**88**	**10**

NELSON, Curtis (D) 387 17
H: 6 0 W: 11 07 b.Newcastle-under-Lyme 21-5-93
Internationals: England U18.
From Stoke C.

2010–11	Plymouth Arg	35	0		
2011–12	Plymouth Arg	17	0		
2012–13	Plymouth Arg	27	3		
2013–14	Plymouth Arg	44	1		
2014–15	Plymouth Arg	42	1		
2015–16	Plymouth Arg	46	3	**211**	**8**
2016–17	Oxford U	33	2		
2017–18	Oxford U	20	1		
2018–19	Oxford U	46	4	**99**	**7**
2019–20	Cardiff C	33	1		
2020–21	Cardiff C	44	1	**77**	**2**

NG, Perry (D) 174 7
H: 5 11 W: 12 02 b.Liverpool 24-6-94

2014–15	Crewe Alex	0	0		
2015–16	Crewe Alex	6	0		
2016–17	Crewe Alex	16	0		
2017–18	Crewe Alex	38	4		
2018–19	Crewe Alex	44	0		
2019–20	Crewe Alex	36	2		
2020–21	Crewe Alex	15	1	**155**	**7**
2020–21	Cardiff C	19	0	**19**	**0**

PACK, Marlon (M) 470 30
H: 6 2 W: 11 09 b.Portsmouth 25-3-91

2008–09	Portsmouth	0	0		
2009–10	Portsmouth	0	0		
2009–10	*Wycombe W*	8	0	**8**	**0**
2009–10	*Dagenham & R*	17	1	**17**	**1**
2010–11	Portsmouth	1	0	**1**	**0**
2010–11	*Cheltenham T*	38	2		
2011–12	Cheltenham T	43	5		
2012–13	Cheltenham T	43	7		
2013–14	Cheltenham T	0	0	**124**	**14**
2013–14	Bristol C	43	0		
2014–15	Bristol C	34	3		
2015–16	Bristol C	45	1		
2016–17	Bristol C	33	2		
2017–18	Bristol C	42	3		
2018–19	Bristol C	46	2		
2019–20	Bristol C	1	0	**244**	**11**
2019–20	Cardiff C	37	2		
2020–21	Cardiff C	39	2	**76**	**4**

PATTEN, Keenan (M) 0 0
b. 7-4-01

2020–21	Penybont	0	0		
2020–21	Cardiff C	0	0		

PHILLIPS, Dillon (M) 97 0
H: 6 2 W: 11 11 b. 11-6-95

2012–13	Charlton Ath	0	0		
2013–14	Charlton Ath	0	0		
2014–15	Charlton Ath	0	0		
2015–16	Charlton Ath	0	0		
2016–17	Charlton Ath	8	0		

2017–18 Charlton Ath 0 0
2018–19 Charlton Ath 27 0
2019–20 Charlton Ath 46 0 **81 0**
2020–21 Cardiff C 16 0 **16 0**

RALLS, Joe (M) 295 32
H: 5 10 W: 11 00 b.Farnborough 13-10-93
Internationals: England U19.
From Aldershot T, Farnborough.
2011–12 Cardiff C 10 1
2012–13 Cardiff C 4 0
2013–14 Cardiff C 0 0
2013–14 *Yeovil T* 37 3 **37 3**
2014–15 Cardiff C 28 2
2015–16 Cardiff C 43 1
2016–17 Cardiff C 42 6
2017–18 Cardiff C 37 7
2018–19 Cardiff C 28 0
2019–20 Cardiff C 27 7
2020–21 Cardiff C 39 5 **258 29**

RATCLIFFE, George (G) 0 0
2020–21 Cardiff C 0 0

SANG, Tom (M) 19 0
b. 29-6-99
From Bolton W, Manchester U.
2019–20 Cardiff C 0 0
2020–21 Cardiff C 9 0 **9 0**
2020–21 *Cheltenham T* 10 0 **10 0**

SMITHIES, Alex (G) 415 0
H: 6 1 W: 10 01 b.Huddersfield 25-3-90
Internationals: England U16, U17, U18, U19.
2006–07 Huddersfield T 0 0
2007–08 Huddersfield T 2 0
2008–09 Huddersfield T 27 0
2009–10 Huddersfield T 46 0
2010–11 Huddersfield T 22 0
2011–12 Huddersfield T 13 0
2012–13 Huddersfield T 46 0
2013–14 Huddersfield T 46 0
2014–15 Huddersfield T 44 0
2015–16 Huddersfield T 1 0 **247 0**
2015–16 QPR 18 0
2016–17 QPR 46 0
2017–18 QPR 43 0 **107 0**
2018–19 Cardiff C 0 0
2019–20 Cardiff C 30 0
2020–21 Cardiff C 31 0 **61 0**

TOMLIN, Lee (F) 338 71
H: 5 11 W: 11 09 b.Leicester 12-1-89
Internationals: England C.
From Rushden & D.
2010–11 Peterborough U 37 8
2011–12 Peterborough U 37 8
2012–13 Peterborough U 42 11
2013–14 Peterborough U 19 5
2013–14 Middlesbrough 14 4
2014–15 Middlesbrough 42 7 **56 11**
2015–16 Bournemouth 6 0 **6 0**
2015–16 *Bristol C* 18 6
2016–17 Bristol C 38 6 **56 12**
2017–18 Cardiff C 13 1
2017–18 *Nottingham F* 15 4 **15 4**
2018–19 Cardiff C 0 0
2018–19 *Peterborough U* 19 2 **154 34**
2019–20 Cardiff C 33 8
2020–21 Cardiff C 5 1 **51 10**

VAULKS, Will (D) 302 32
H: 5 11 b.Birkenhead 13-9-93
Internationals: Wales Full caps.
2012–13 Tranmere R 0 0
2012–13 Falkirk 6 0
2013–14 Falkirk 33 1
2014–15 Falkirk 34 3
2015–16 Falkirk 35 6 **108 10**
2016–17 Rotherham U 40 1
2017–18 Rotherham U 44 5
2018–19 Rotherham U 41 7 **125 13**
2019–20 Cardiff C 27 4
2020–21 Cardiff C 42 5 **69 9**

WATTERS, Max (D) 23 13
b. 23-3-99
From Thurrock, Barking, Ashford U.
2019–20 Doncaster R 5 0 **5 0**
2020–21 Crawley T 15 13 **15 13**
2020–21 Cardiff C 3 0 **3 0**

WHYTE, Gavin (F) 219 54
b.Belfast 31-1-96
Internationals: Northern Ireland U21, Full caps.
2013–14 Crusaders 1 0
2014–15 Crusaders 34 9
2015–16 Crusaders 27 3
2016–17 Crusaders 34 10
2017–18 Crusaders 36 21 **132 43**
2018–19 Oxford U 36 7 **36 7**
2019–20 Cardiff C 24 0
2020–21 Cardiff C 7 0 **31 0**
2020–21 *Hull C* 20 4 **20 4**

WILLIAMS, Jon (M) 187 5
H: 5 6 W: 10 00 b.Tunbridge Wells 9-10-93
Internationals: Wales U17, U19, U21, Full caps.
2010–11 Crystal Palace 0 0
2011–12 Crystal Palace 14 0
2012–13 Crystal Palace 29 0
2013–14 Crystal Palace 9 0
2013–14 *Ipswich T* 13 1
2014–15 Crystal Palace 2 0
2014–15 *Ipswich T* 7 1
2015–16 Crystal Palace 1 0
2015–16 *Nottingham F* 10 0 **10 0**
2015–16 *Milton Keynes D* 13 0 **13 0**
2016–17 Crystal Palace 0 0
2016–17 *Ipswich T* 8 0 **28 2**
2017–18 Crystal Palace 0 0
2017–18 *Sunderland* 12 1 **12 1**
2018–19 Crystal Palace 0 0 **55 0**
2018–19 Charlton Ath 16 0
2019–20 Charlton Ath 26 0
2020–21 Charlton Ath 18 2 **60 2**
2020–21 Cardiff C 9 0 **9 0**

ZIMBA, Chanka (F) 0 0
b. 29-12-01
From Blackburn R.
2020–21 Cardiff C 0 0

Scholars
Chiabi, Mweembe Thomas Dimba; Clay, Jac Rhys; Cogman, Jaimie Michael; Coley, Benjamin William; Crole, James William Thomas; Davies, Thomas Alfred; Jones, Taylor Kian; Kavanagh, Ryan William; King, Eli Josef; Ligendza, Siyabonga Wes-Lee; MacNamara, Aidan; Masrani, Jack Michael; Pritchard, Owen Robert; Rippon, Joshua Marshall; Schwank, Rhys Morgan; Stewart, Bradley Luke; Thomas, Frazer Lee; Vaughan, Ethan Rhys; Yanko, Nativ.

CARLISLE U (21)

ALESSANDRA, Lewis (F) 442 68
H: 5 9 W: 11 07 b.Heywood 8-2-89
2007–08 Oldham Ath 15 2
2008–09 Oldham Ath 32 5
2009–10 Oldham Ath 1 0
2010–11 Oldham Ath 19 1 **67 8**
2011–12 Morecambe 42 4
2012–13 Morecambe 40 3
2013–14 Plymouth Arg 42 7
2014–15 Plymouth Arg 44 11 **86 18**
2015–16 Rochdale 8 1 **8 1**
2015–16 *York C* 11 2 **11 2**
2016–17 Hartlepool U 46 9 **46 9**
2017–18 Notts Co 39 7
2018–19 Notts Co 26 2 **65 9**
2019–20 Morecambe 22 5 **104 12**
2019–20 Carlisle U 10 1
2020–21 Carlisle U 45 8 **55 9**

ANDERTON, Nick (D) 88 4
H: 6 2 W: 12 06 b. 22-4-96
2014–15 Preston NE 0 0
2015–16 Preston NE 0 0
From Barrow.
2017–18 Blackpool 4 0
2018–19 Accrington S 22 0 **22 0**
2018–19 Blackpool 10 0
2019–20 Blackpool 2 0 **16 0**
2019–20 Carlisle U 10 2
2020–21 Carlisle U 40 2 **50 4**

ARMER, Jack (D) 24 1
b. 16-4-01
Internationals: Scotland U17.
2019–20 Preston NE 0 0
2020–21 Carlisle U 24 1 **24 1**

ARMSTRONG, Jamie (M) 0 0
b. 5-10-01
2020–21 Carlisle U 0 0

BARNETT, Josh (M) 0 0
b.Sunderland 6-9-03
2020–21 Carlisle U 0 0

BELL, Lewis (M) 1 0
b.Carlisle 29-9-02
2020–21 Carlisle U 1 0 **1 0**

BENNETT, Rhys (D) 287 19
H: 6 3 W: 12 00 b.Manchester 1-9-91
2011–12 Bolton W 0 0
2011–12 *Falkirk* 19 0 **19 0**
2012–13 Rochdale 33 2
2013–14 Rochdale 22 0
2014–15 Rochdale 39 2
2015–16 Rochdale 16 2 **110 6**
2016–17 Mansfield T 46 2
2017–18 Mansfield T 38 2 **84 4**
2018–19 Peterborough U 37 4
2019–20 Peterborough U 13 0 **50 4**
2020–21 Carlisle U 24 5 **24 5**

BIRCH, Charlie (M) 1 0
2018–19 Carlisle U 0 0
2019–20 Carlisle U 1 0
2020–21 Carlisle U 0 0 **1 0**

BREEZE, Gabriel (G) 0 0
2020–21 Carlisle U 0 0

CHARTERS, Taylor (M) 16 0
b.Whitehaven 2-10-01
2019–20 Carlisle U 7 0
2020–21 Carlisle U 9 0 **16 0**

DEVINE, Daniel (M) 41 1
H: 5 11 W: 12 00 b.Bradford 4-9-97
2015–16 Bradford C 0 0
2016–17 Bradford C 11 0
2017–18 Bradford C 3 0
2018–19 Bradford C 3 0
2019–20 Bradford C 13 1 **30 1**
2020–21 Carlisle U 11 0 **11 0**

DICKENSON, Brennan (F) 212 24
H: 6 0 W: 12 07 b.Ferndown 26-2-93
From Dorchester T.
2012–13 Brighton & HA 0 0
2012–13 *Chesterfield* 11 1 **11 1**
2012–13 *AFC Wimbledon* 7 2 **7 2**
2013–14 Brighton & HA 0 0
2013–14 *Northampton T* 13 1 **13 1**
2014–15 Gillingham 34 1
2015–16 Gillingham 33 1 **67 2**
2016–17 Colchester U 36 12
2017–18 Colchester U 7 0
2018–19 Colchester U 42 3 **85 15**
2019–20 Milton Keynes D 7 0 **7 0**
2019–20 Exeter C 10 2 **10 2**
2020–21 Carlisle U 12 1 **12 1**

DIXON, Josh (M) 2 0
b.Carlisle 7-2-01
2020–21 Carlisle U 2 0 **2 0**

FARMAN, Paul (G) 123 0
H: 6 5 W: 14 07 b.North Shields 2-11-89
Internationals: England C.
From Blyth Spartans, Gateshead.
2017–18 Lincoln C 13 0 **13 0**
2018–19 Stevenage 33 0
2019–20 Stevenage 35 0 **68 0**
2020–21 Carlisle U 42 0 **42 0**

FEENEY, Morgan (D) 1 0
H: 6 3 W: 12 02 b.Bootle 6-2-98
Internationals: England U17, U18, U19.
2017–18 Everton 0 0
2018–19 Everton 0 0
2019–20 Everton 0 0
2019–20 *Tranmere R* 1 0 **1 0**
2020–21 Sunderland 0 0
2020–21 Carlisle U 0 0

FISHBURN, Sam (F) 0 0
b.Gateshead 26-11-03
2020–21 Carlisle U 0 0

FURMAN, Dean (M) 374 20
H: 6 0 W: 11 08 b.Cape Town 22-6-88
Internationals: South Africa Full caps.
From Chelsea.
2007–08 Rangers 1 0 **1 0**
2008–09 *Bradford C* 32 4 **32 4**
2009–10 Oldham Ath 38 0
2010–11 Oldham Ath 42 5
2011–12 Oldham Ath 23 1
2012–13 Oldham Ath 28 2 **131 8**
2012–13 *Doncaster R* 8 0
2013–14 Doncaster R 32 1
2014–15 Doncaster R 34 2 **74 3**
2015–16 SuperSport U 24 1
2016–17 SuperSport U 27 1
2017–18 SuperSport U 27 1
2018–19 SuperSport U 19 0
2019–20 SuperSport U 22 2 **119 5**
2020–21 Carlisle U 17 0 **17 0**

GUY, Callum (M) 104 0
b. 25-11-96
2015–16 Derby Co 0 0
2016–17 Derby Co 0 0
2016–17 *Port Vale* 11 0 **11 0**
2017–18 Derby Co 0 0
2017–18 *Bradford C* 17 0 **17 0**
2018–19 Blackpool 15 0
2019–20 Blackpool 15 0 **30 0**
2019–20 Carlisle U 3 0
2020–21 Carlisle U 43 0 **46 0**

HAYDEN, Aaron (D) **67 7**
b. 16-1-97
From Chelsea.
2015–16 Wolverhampton W 0 0
2015–16 *Newport Co* 5 0 **5 0**
2016–17 Wolverhampton W 0 0
2017–18 Wolverhampton W 0 0
2018–19 Wolverhampton W 0 0
2019–20 Carlisle U 18 2
2020–21 Carlisle U 44 5 **62 7**

HUNT, Max (D) **6 0**
b. 1-5-99
2017–18 Derby Co 0 0
2018–19 Derby Co 0 0
2019–20 Derby Co 0 0
2019–20 Carlisle U 4 0
2020–21 Carlisle U 2 0 **6 0**

KILSBY, Max (D) **0 0**
b.North Shields 4-10-03
2020–21 Carlisle U 0 0

McDONALD, Rod (D) **134 3**
H: 6 3 W: 12 13 b.Crewe 11-4-92
2009–10 Stoke C 0 0
2010–11 Oldham Ath 0 0
From Colwyn Bay, Hereford U, AFC Telford U.
2015–16 Northampton T 23 3
2016–17 Northampton T 7 0 **30 3**
2016–17 Coventry C 0 0
2017–18 Coventry C 37 0 **37 0**
2018–19 AFC Wimbledon 23 0
2019–20 AFC Wimbledon 15 0 **38 0**
2020–21 Carlisle U 29 0 **29 0**

MELLISH, Jon (D) **59 11**
b.South Shields 19-9-19
From Gateshead.
2019–20 Carlisle U 15 0
2020–21 Carlisle U 44 11 **59 11**

NORMAN, Magnus (G) **11 0**
H: 6 3 W: 12 13 b.Kingston Upon Thames 19-1-97
Internationals: England U16, U18.
2017–18 Fulham 0 0
2018–19 Fulham 0 0
2018–19 *Rochdale* 7 0 **7 0**
2019–20 Fulham 0 0
2020–21 Carlisle U 4 0 **4 0**

PATRICK, Omari (F) **56 8**
b. 26-5-96
From Kidderminster H.
2018–19 Bradford C 1 0
2018–19 *Yeovil T* 9 1 **9 1**
2019–20 Bradford C 2 0 **3 0**
2019–20 Carlisle U 7 2
2020–21 Carlisle U 37 5 **44 7**

REILLY, Gavin (F) **267 63**
H: 5 9 W: 10 05 b.Dumfries 10-5-93
2010–11 Queen of the South 1 0
2011–12 Queen of the South 14 2
2012–13 Queen of the South 30 12
2013–14 Queen of the South 34 12
2014–15 Queen of the South 32 13 **111 39**
2015–16 Hearts 28 4
2016–17 Hearts 0 0 **28 4**
2016–17 *Dunfermline Ath* 22 1 **22 1**
2017–18 St Mirren 35 11 **35 11**
2018–19 Bristol R 30 4
2019–20 *Cheltenham T* 21 4 **21 4**
2019–20 Bristol R 4 0 **34 4**
2020–21 Carlisle U 16 0 **16 0**
Transferred to Livingston January 2021.

RILEY, Joe (D) **50 2**
H: 6 0 W: 11 03 b.Blackpool 6-12-96
2016–17 Manchester U 0 0
2016–17 *Sheffield U* 2 0 **2 0**
2017–18 Manchester u 0 0
2018–19 Bradford C 6 0
2019–20 Bradford C 0 0 **6 0**
2020–21 Carlisle U 42 2 **42 2**

SCOTT, Cedwyn (F) **21 3**
b.Hexham 6-12-97
2017–18 Dundee 3 0
2018–19 Dundee 0 0 **3 0**
2018–19 *Berwick Rangers* 7 3 **7 3**
2018–19 *Forfar Ath* 4 0 **4 0**
From Dunston UTS, Hebburn T.
2020–21 Carlisle U 7 0 **7 0**

TANNER, George (D) **60 3**
b. 16-11-99
2019–20 Manchester U 0 0
2019–20 *Morecambe* 23 0 **23 0**
2019–20 *Salford C* 0 0
2020–21 Carlisle U 37 3 **37 3**

TOURE, Gime (F) **34 2**
b. 7-5-94
2020–21 Carlisle U 34 2 **34 2**

WILSON, Tom (D) **0 0**
b.Carlisle 8-12-01
2020–21 Carlisle U 0 0

ZANZALA, Offrande (F) **86 16**
b. 13-12-97
2015–16 Derby Co 0 0
2015–16 *Stevenage* 2 0 **2 0**
2016–17 Derby Co 0 0
2017–18 Derby Co 0 0
2017–18 *Accrington S* 6 1
2018–19 Accrington S 27 4
2019–20 Accrington S 24 6 **57 11**
2020–21 Crewe Alex 5 0 **5 0**
2020–21 Carlisle U 22 5 **22 5**

Scholars
Barnett, Joshua Kenneth; Bell, Lewis James; Breeze, Gabriel Hendrix; Day, Elliott; Ellis, Jack Ethan James; Fishburn, Sam; Garvey, Dylan Paul; Kilsby, Max Robert; Leslie, Keelan James; Robinson, Isaac John; Rooks, Lewis Jack; Simons, Scott James; Steele, Roan Oliver; Swailes, Ryan Lee; Taylor, Dj; Walton, Adam Jack; Watt, Charles Neal; Wilson, Thomas Jackson.

CHARLTON ATH (22)

AIDOO, Kasim (D) **0 0**
b. 3-1-01
2020–21 Charlton Ath 0 0

AMOS, Ben (G) **221 0**
H: 6 1 W: 13 00 b.Macclesfield 10-4-90
Internationals: England U16, U17, U18, U19, U20, U21.
2007–08 Manchester U 0 0
2008–09 Manchester U 0 0
2009–10 Manchester U 0 0
2009–10 *Peterborough U* 1 0 **1 0**
2010 *Molde* 8 0 **8 0**
2010–11 Manchester U 0 0
2010–11 *Oldham Ath* 16 0 **16 0**
2011–12 Manchester U 1 0
2012–13 Manchester U 0 0
2012–13 *Hull C* 17 0 **17 0**
2013–14 Manchester U 0 0
2013–14 *Carlisle U* 9 0 **9 0**
2014–15 Manchester U 0 0 **1 0**
2014–15 *Bolton W* 9 0
2015–16 Bolton W 40 0
2016–17 Bolton W 0 0
2016–17 *Cardiff C* 16 0 **16 0**
2017–18 Bolton W 0 0
2017–18 *Charlton Ath* 46 0
2018–19 Bolton W 0 0 **49 0**
2018–19 *Millwall* 12 0 **12 0**
2019–20 Charlton Ath 0 0
2020–21 Charlton Ath 46 0 **92 0**

ANEKE, Chuks (M) **266 72**
H: 6 3 W: 13 01 b.Newham 3-7-93
Internationals: England U16, U17, U18, U19.
2010–11 Arsenal 0 0
2011–12 Arsenal 0 0
2011–12 *Stevenage* 6 0 **6 0**
2011–12 *Preston NE* 7 1 **7 1**
2012–13 Arsenal 0 0
2012–13 *Crewe Alex* 30 6
2013–14 Arsenal 0 0
2013–14 *Crewe Alex* 40 15 **70 21**
2014–15 Arsenal 0 0
2014–15 Zulte-Waregem 30 2
2015–16 Zulte-Waregem 11 2 **41 4**
2016–17 Milton Keynes D 15 4
2017–18 Milton Keynes D 31 9
2018–19 Milton Keynes D 38 17 **84 30**
2019–20 Charlton Ath 20 1
2020–21 Charlton Ath 38 15 **58 16**

AOUACHIRA, Wassim (F) **0 0**
b. 12-3-00
From Marseille.
2020–21 Charlton Ath 0 0

BARKER, Charlie (D) **3 0**
b. 12-2-03
2020–21 Charlton Ath 3 0 **3 0**

CLAYDEN, Charles (F) **0 0**
b. 16-11-00
From Leyton Orient.
2019–20 Charlton Ath 0 0
2020–21 Charlton Ath 0 0

DAVISON, Joshua (F) **29 4**
b. 16-9-99
From Peterborough U, Enfield T.
2019–20 Charlton Ath 9 1
2020–21 Charlton Ath 0 0 **9 1**
2020–21 *Forest Green R* 20 3 **20 3**

DEMPSEY, Ben (M) **4 0**
b. 25-11-99
2018–19 Charlton Ath 0 0
2019–20 Charlton Ath 4 0
2020–21 Charlton Ath 0 0 **4 0**

FORSTER-CASKEY, Jake (M) **211 22**
H: 5 10 W: 10 00 b.Southend 25-4-94
Internationals: England U16, U17, U18, U20, U21.
2009–10 Brighton & HA 1 0
2010–11 Brighton & HA 0 0
2011–12 Brighton & HA 4 1
2012–13 Brighton & HA 3 0
2012–13 *Oxford U* 16 3 **16 3**
2013–14 Brighton & HA 28 3
2014–15 Brighton & HA 29 1
2015–16 Brighton & HA 2 0 **67 5**
2015–16 *Milton Keynes D* 20 1 **20 1**
2016–17 Charlton Ath 15 2
2016–17 *Rotherham U* 6 0 **6 0**
2017–18 Charlton Ath 41 5
2018–19 Charlton Ath 1 0
2019–20 Charlton Ath 11 0
2020–21 Charlton Ath 34 6 **102 13**

FRENCH, Billy (D) **0 0**
b. 27-11-02
2020–21 Charlton Ath 0 0

GAVIN, Dylan (F) **0 0**
2020–21 Charlton Ath 0 0

GHANDOUR, Hady (F) **0 0**
From Tooting & Mitcham U.
2020–21 Charlton Ath 0 0

GILBEY, Alex (M) **242 23**
H: 6 0 W: 11 07 b.Dagenham 9-12-94
2011–12 Colchester U 0 0
2012–13 Colchester U 3 0
2013–14 Colchester U 36 1
2014–15 Colchester U 34 1
2015–16 Colchester U 37 5 **110 7**
2016–17 Wigan Ath 15 2
2017–18 Wigan Ath 2 0 **17 2**
2017–18 Milton Keynes D 23 3
2018–19 Milton Keynes D 39 3
2019–20 Milton Keynes D 30 5 **92 11**
2020–21 Charlton Ath 23 3 **23 3**

GUNTER, Chris (D) **490 5**
H: 5 11 W: 11 02 b.Newport 21-7-89
Internationals: Wales U17, U19, U21, Full caps.
2006–07 Cardiff C 15 0
2007–08 Cardiff C 13 0 **28 0**
2007–08 Tottenham H 2 0
2008–09 Tottenham H 3 0 **5 0**
2008–09 *Nottingham F* 8 0
2009–10 Nottingham F 44 1
2010–11 Nottingham F 43 0
2011–12 Nottingham F 46 1 **141 2**
2012–13 Reading 20 0
2013–14 Reading 44 0
2014–15 Reading 38 0
2015–16 Reading 44 0
2016–17 Reading 46 1
2017–18 Reading 46 1
2018–19 Reading 22 0
2019–20 Reading 20 0 **280 2**
2020–21 Charlton Ath 36 1 **36 1**

HARNESS, Nathan (G) **0 0**
b. 19-1-00
From Stevenage, Dunstable.
2019–20 Charlton Ath 0 0
2020–21 Charlton Ath 0 0

HARVEY, Nathan (G) **0 0**
H: 6 1 b.London 8-6-02
From West Ham U.
2020–21 Charlton Ath 0 0

HENRY, Aaron (M) **0 0**
b. 31-8-03
Internationals: England U16.
2019–20 Charlton Ath 0 0
2020–21 Charlton Ath 0 0

INNISS, Ryan (D) **105 2**
H: 6 5 W: 13 02 b.Kent 5-6-95
Internationals: England U16, U17.
2012–13 Crystal Palace 0 0
2013–14 Crystal Palace 0 0
2013–14 *Cheltenham T* 2 0 **2 0**
2013–14 *Gillingham* 3 0 **3 0**
2014–15 Crystal Palace 0 0
2014–15 *Yeovil T* 6 0 **6 0**
2014–15 *Port Vale* 5 0
2015–16 Crystal Palace 0 0

2015–16	*Port Vale*	15	0	20	0
2016–17	Crystal Palace	0	0		
2016–17	*Southend U*	10	0	10	0
2017–18	Crystal Palace	0	0		
2017–18	*Colchester U*	18	0	18	0
2018–19	Crystal Palace	0	0		
2018–19	*Dundee*	11	0	11	0
2019–20	Crystal Palace	0	0		
2019–20	*Newport Co*	22	1	22	1
2020–21	Charlton Ath	13	1	13	1

JAIYESIMI, Diallang (M) 92 12
b.Southwark 18-3-99
From Dulwich Hamlet.

2017–18	Norwich C	0	0		
2017–18	*Grimsby T*	30	0	30	0
2018–19	Norwich C	0	0		
2018–19	*Yeovil T*	9	2	9	2
2019–20	Norwich C	0	0		
2019–20	*Swindon T*	21	5		
2020–21	Swindon T	18	4	39	9
2020–21	Charlton Ath	14	1	14	1

MADDISON, Marcus (M) 237 54
H: 5 9 W: 11 03 b.Sedgefield 26-9-93
Internationals: England C.

2013–14	Newcastle U	0	0		
2014–15	Peterborough U	29	7		
2015–16	Peterborough U	39	11		
2016–17	Peterborough U	41	9		
2017–18	Peterborough U	41	8		
2018–19	Peterborough U	40	8		
2019–20	Peterborough U	22	9	212	52
2019–20	*Hull C*	7	1	7	1
2020–21	Charlton Ath	8	1	8	1
2020–21	*Bolton W*	10	0	10	0

MATTHEWS, Adam (D) 276 7
H: 5 10 W: 11 02 b.Swansea 13-1-92
Internationals: Wales U17, U19, U21, Full caps.

2008–09	Cardiff C	0	0		
2009–10	Cardiff C	32	1		
2010–11	Cardiff C	8	0	40	1
2011–12	Celtic	27	0		
2012–13	Celtic	22	2		
2013–14	Celtic	23	1		
2014–15	Celtic	29	1	101	4
2015–16	Sunderland	1	0		
2015–16	*Bristol C*	9	0		
2016–17	Sunderland	0	0		
2016–17	*Bristol C*	12	0	21	0
2017–18	Sunderland	34	1		
2018–19	Sunderland	23	1	58	2
2019–20	Charlton Ath	29	0		
2020–21	Charlton Ath	27	0	56	0

MAYNARD-BREWER, Ashley (G) 0 0
b. 25-6-99
Internationals: Australia U23.

2017–18	Charlton Ath	0	0		
2018–19	Charlton Ath	0	0		
2019–20	Charlton Ath	0	0		
2020–21	Charlton Ath	0	0		

MINGI, Jade (M) 0 0
b. 22-10-00
From West Ham U.

2020–21	Charlton Ath	0	0		

MORGAN, Albie (M) 57 1
b.Portsmouth 2-2-00

2018–19	Charlton Ath	8	0		
2019–20	Charlton Ath	21	0		
2020–21	Charlton Ath	28	1	57	1

NESS, Lukas (D) 0 0

2020–21	Charlton Ath	0	0		

OSAGHAE, Joseph (G) 0 0
b. 20-2-01

2018–19	Charlton Ath	0	0		
2019–20	Charlton Ath	0	0		
2020–21	Charlton Ath	0	0		

OSHILAJA, Adedeji (D) 197 10
H: 5 11 W: 11 10 b.Bermondsey 16-7-93

2012–13	Cardiff C	0	0		
2013–14	Cardiff C	0	0		
2013–14	*Newport Co*	8	0	8	0
2013–14	*Sheffield W*	2	0	2	0
2014–15	Cardiff C	0	0		
2014–15	*AFC Wimbledon*	23	1		
2015–16	Cardiff C	0	0		
2015–16	*Gillingham*	22	3		
2016–17	Cardiff C	0	0		
2016–17	*Gillingham*	33	2	55	5
2017–18	AFC Wimbledon	42	2		
2018–19	AFC Wimbledon	25	1	90	4
2019–20	Charlton Ath	25	0		
2020–21	Charlton Ath	17	1	42	1

OZTUMER, Erhun (M) 192 37
b.Greenwich 29-5-91
From Dulwich Hamlet.

2014–15	Peterborough U	20	1		
2015–16	Peterborough U	30	6	50	7
2016–17	Walsall	41	15		
2017–18	Walsall	45	15	86	30
2018–19	Bolton W	17	0		
2019–20	Bolton W	1	0	18	0
2019–20	Charlton Ath	14	0		
2020–21	Charlton Ath	2	0	16	0
2020–21	*Bristol R*	22	0	22	0

PEARCE, Jason (D) 490 21
H: 5 11 W: 12 00 b.Hillingdon 6-12-87

2006–07	Portsmouth	0	0		
2007–08	Bournemouth	33	1		
2008–09	Bournemouth	44	2		
2009–10	Bournemouth	39	1		
2010–11	Bournemouth	46	3	162	7
2011–12	Portsmouth	43	2	43	2
2011–12	Leeds U	0	0		
2012–13	Leeds U	33	0		
2013–14	Leeds U	45	2		
2014–15	Leeds U	21	0	99	2
2014–15	Wigan Ath	16	2		
2015–16	Wigan Ath	31	2	47	4
2016–17	Charlton Ath	23	1		
2017–18	Charlton Ath	25	2		
2018–19	Charlton Ath	26	2		
2019–20	Charlton Ath	39	1		
2020–21	Charlton Ath	26	0	139	6

POWELL, Johl (D) 0 0

2019–20	Charlton Ath	0	0		
2020–21	Charlton Ath	0	0		

PRATLEY, Darren (M) 505 48
H: 6 1 W: 10 12 b.Barking 22-4-85

2001–02	Fulham	0	0		
2002–03	Fulham	0	0		
2003–04	Fulham	1	0		
2004–05	Fulham	0	0		
2004–05	*Brentford*	14	1		
2005–06	Fulham	0	0	1	0
2005–06	*Brentford*	32	4	46	5
2006–07	Swansea C	28	1		
2007–08	Swansea C	42	5		
2008–09	Swansea C	37	4		
2009–10	Swansea C	36	7		
2010–11	Swansea C	34	9	177	26
2011–12	Bolton W	25	1		
2012–13	Bolton W	31	2		
2013–14	Bolton W	20	2		
2014–15	Bolton W	22	4		
2015–16	Bolton W	36	1		
2016–17	Bolton W	12	0		
2017–18	Bolton W	32	2	178	12
2018–19	Charlton Ath	28	2		
2019–20	Charlton Ath	36	2		
2020–21	Charlton Ath	39	1	103	5

PURRINGTON, Ben (D) 175 4
H: 5 9 W: 11 07 b.Exeter 5-5-96

2013–14	Plymouth Arg	12	0		
2014–15	Plymouth Arg	8	0		
2015–16	Plymouth Arg	13	0		
2016–17	Plymouth Arg	19	0	52	0
2016–17	Rotherham U	10	0		
2017–18	Rotherham U	10	0		
2018–19	Rotherham U	0	0	20	0
2018–19	*AFC Wimbledon*	26	0	26	0
2018–19	*Charlton Ath*	18	0		
2019–20	Charlton Ath	31	2		
2020–21	Charlton Ath	28	2	77	4

QUITIRNA, Junior (M) 0 0
b. 1-1-01

2019–20	Charlton Ath	0	0		
2020–21	Charlton Ath	0	0		

SCHWARTZ, Ronnie (F) 272 106
b.Ulsted 29-8-89

2007–08	Aalborg	3	0		
2008–09	Aalborg	6	0		
2009–10	Aalborg	22	5		
2010–11	Aalborg	15	4	46	9
2011–12	Randers	22	8		
2012–13	Randers	31	14		
2013–14	Randers	26	15	79	37
2014–15	Guingamp	14	2		
2015–16	Guingamp	0	0	14	2
2015–16	*Brondby*	16	4	16	4
2015–16	*Esbjerg*	12	4	12	4
2016–17	Waasland-Beveren	12	1		
2017–18	Waasland-Beveren	0	0	12	1
2018	Sarpsborg 08	15	5	15	5
2018–19	Silkeborg	27	25		
2019–20	Silkeborg	20	12	47	37
2019–20	Midtjylland	15	6	15	6
2020–21	FC Midtjylland	0	0		
2020–21	Charlton Ath	16	1	16	1

SHINNIE, Andrew (M) 307 34
H: 5 11 W: 10 13 b.Aberdeen 17-7-89
Internationals: Scotland U19, U21, Full caps.

2005–06	Rangers	0	0		
2006–07	Rangers	2	0		
2007–08	Rangers	0	0		
2008–09	Rangers	0	0		
2008–09	*Dundee*	20	1		
2009–10	Rangers	0	0		
2009–10	*Dundee*	12	0	32	1
2010–11	Rangers	0	0	2	0
2011–12	Inverness CT	19	7		
2012–13	Inverness CT	38	12	57	19
2013–14	Birmingham C	26	2		
2014–15	Birmingham C	27	2		
2015–16	Birmingham C	14	0		
2015–16	*Rotherham U*	3	0	3	0
2016–17	Birmingham C	0	0	67	4
2016–17	*Hibernian*	27	1	27	1
2017–18	Luton T	28	1		
2018–19	Luton T	41	4		
2019–20	Luton T	21	1		
2020–21	Luton T	0	0	90	6
2020–21	Charlton Ath	29	3	29	3

VEGA, Luca (D) 0 0
b. 30-12-00

2020–21	Charlton Ath	0	0		

VENNINGS, James (M) 4 0
b. 24-5-00

2019–20	Charlton Ath	3	0		
2020–21	Charlton Ath	1	0	4	0

WASHINGTON, Conor (F) 264 58
H: 5 10 W: 11 09 b.Chatham 18-5-92
Internationals: Northern Ireland Full caps.
From St Ives T.

2013–14	Newport Co	24	4	24	4
2013–14	Peterborough U	17	4		
2014–15	Peterborough U	40	13		
2015–16	Peterborough U	25	10	82	27
2015–16	QPR	15	0		
2016–17	QPR	40	7		
2017–18	QPR	33	6		
2018–19	QPR	4	0	92	13
2018–19	Sheffield U	15	0	15	0
2019–20	Hearts	15	3	15	3
2020–21	Charlton Ath	36	11	36	11

WATSON, Ben (M) 475 40
H: 5 10 W: 10 11 b.Camberwell 9-7-85
Internationals: England U21.

2002–03	Crystal Palace	5	0		
2003–04	Crystal Palace	16	1		
2004–05	Crystal Palace	21	0		
2005–06	Crystal Palace	42	4		
2006–07	Crystal Palace	25	3		
2007–08	Crystal Palace	42	5		
2008–09	Crystal Palace	18	5	169	18
2008–09	Wigan Ath	10	2		
2009–10	Wigan Ath	5	1		
2009–10	*QPR*	16	2	16	2
2009–10	*WBA*	7	1	7	1
2010–11	Wigan Ath	29	3		
2011–12	Wigan Ath	21	3		
2012–13	Wigan Ath	12	1		
2013–14	Wigan Ath	25	2		
2014–15	Wigan Ath	9	1	111	13
2014–15	Watford	20	0		
2015–16	Watford	35	2		
2016–17	Watford	4	0		
2017–18	Watford	8	0	67	2
2017–18	Nottingham F	14	0		
2018–19	Nottingham F	17	0		
2019–20	Nottingham F	45	3	76	3
2020–21	Charlton Ath	29	1	29	1

WILLIAMS, Euan (M) 0 0
b. 15-1-03

2020–21	Charlton Ath	0	0		

Scholars
Adigun, Jason David Abiodun Dayo; Agyemang, Terrell Nana Obeng; Appiah, Jimmy Akumi; Bakrin, Nazir Oladayo Temitope; Beadle, James Giles; Burstow, Mason Paul James; Campbell, Tyreece Anthony Tupac; Dench, Matthew Robert; Elerewe, Ayodeji Joshua Oluwapelumi; Garande, Kai Tapiwa Ocean; Gavin, Dylan John; Ladapo, Joseph Toluwadara; Leaburn, Miles Lester; Reilly, Mack Kevin David; Santos Hurtado, Jeremy Andres; Thompson-Fearon, Andre Anthony; Toure, Seydil Moukhtar; Watkins, Joe Christopher; Whitling, Harry James.

CHELSEA (23)

ABRAHAM, Tammy (F) 167 74
H: 6 3 W: 12 13 b.London 2-10-97
Internationals: England U18, U19, U21, Full caps.
2015–16 Chelsea 2 0
2016–17 Chelsea 0 0
2016–17 *Bristol C* 41 23 **41 23**
2017–18 Chelsea 0 0
2017–18 *Swansea C* 31 5 **31 5**
2018–19 Chelsea 0 0
2018–19 *Aston Villa* 37 25 **37 25**
2019–20 Chelsea 34 15
2020–21 Chelsea 22 6 **58 21**

ABU, Derrick (D) 0 0
b.Regensburg 18-12-03
2020–21 Chelsea 0 0

ADEGOKE, Prince (G) 0 0
b.Farnborough 3-11-03
2020–21 Chelsea 0 0

ALONSO, Marcus (D) 236 30
H: 6 2 W: 13 05 b.Madrid 28-12-90
Internationals: Spain U19, Full caps.
2008–09 Real Madrid 0 0
2009–10 Real Madrid 0 0
2009–10 Real Madrid 1 0 **1 0**
2010–11 Bolton W 4 0
2011–12 Bolton W 5 1
2012–13 Bolton W 26 4 **35 5**
2013–14 Fiorentina 3 0
2013–14 *Sunderland* 16 0 **16 0**
2014–15 Fiorentina 22 1
2015–16 Fiorentina 31 3
2016–17 Fiorentina 2 0 **58 4**
2016–17 Chelsea 31 6
2017–18 Chelsea 33 7
2018–19 Chelsea 31 2
2019–20 Chelsea 18 4
2020–21 Chelsea 13 2 **126 21**

AMPADU, Ethan (M) 37 0
b.Exeter 14-9-00
Internationals: England U16, Wales U17, U19, Full caps.
2016–17 Exeter C 8 0 **8 0**
2017–18 Chelsea 1 0
2018–19 Chelsea 0 0
2019–20 Chelsea 0 0
2019–20 *RB Leipzig* 3 0 **3 0**
2020–21 Chelsea 0 0 **1 0**
2020–21 *Sheffield U* 25 0 **25 0**

ANDERSSON, Edwin (F) 0 0
b.Domkyrko 7-11-03
Internationals: Sweden U16, U17.
From Gothenburg.
2020–21 Chelsea 0 0

ANJORIN, Faustino (M) 1 0
b.Poole 23-11-01
Internationals: England U17, U18, U19.
2019–20 Chelsea 1 0
2020–21 Chelsea 0 0 **1 0**

ARRIZABALAGA, Kepa (G) 269 0
H: 6 1 W: 12 11 b.Ondorroa 3-10-94
Internationals: Spain U18, U19, U21, Full caps.
2011–12 Basconia 12 0
2012–13 Basconia 19 0 **31 0**
2012–13 Athletic Bilbao 7 0
2013–14 Athletic Bilbao 26 0
2014–15 Athletic Bilbao 17 0
2014–15 *Ponferradina* 20 0 **20 0**
2015–16 Athletic Bilbao 0 0
2015–16 *Vallodolid* 39 0 **39 0**
2016–17 Athletic Bilbao 23 0
2017–18 Athletic Bilbao 30 0 **103 0**
2018–19 Chelsea 36 0
2019–20 Chelsea 33 0
2020–21 Chelsea 7 0 **76 0**

AZPILICUETA, Cesar (D) 443 10
H: 5 10 W: 10 13 b.Pamplona 28-8-89
Internationals: Spain U16, U17, U19, U20, U21, U23, Full caps.
2006–07 Osasuna 1 0
2007–08 Osasuna 29 0
2008–09 Osasuna 36 0
2009–10 Osasuna 33 0 **99 0**
2010–11 Marseille 15 0
2011–12 Marseille 30 1
2012–13 Marseille 2 0 **47 1**
2012–13 Chelsea 27 0
2013–14 Chelsea 29 0
2014–15 Chelsea 29 0
2015–16 Chelsea 37 2
2016–17 Chelsea 38 1
2017–18 Chelsea 37 2
2018–19 Chelsea 38 1
2019–20 Chelsea 36 2
2020–21 Chelsea 26 1 **297 9**

BALLO, Thierno (M) 0 0
H: 5 8 W: 9 06 b.Abidjan 2-1-02
Internationals: Austria U16, U17, U18, U19, U21.
2020–21 Chelsea 0 0

BARKLEY, Ross (M) 243 32
H: 6 2 W: 12 00 b.Liverpool 5-12-93
Internationals: England U16, U17, U19, U20, U21, Full caps.
2010–11 Everton 0 0
2011–12 Everton 6 0
2012–13 Everton 7 0
2012–13 *Sheffield W* 13 4 **13 4**
2012–13 *Leeds U* 4 0 **4 0**
2013–14 Everton 34 6
2014–15 Everton 29 2
2015–16 Everton 38 8
2016–17 Everton 36 5
2017–18 Everton 0 0 **150 21**
2017–18 Chelsea 2 0
2018–19 Chelsea 27 3
2019–20 Chelsea 21 1
2020–21 Chelsea 2 0 **52 4**
2020–21 *Aston Villa* 24 3 **24 3**

BATE, Lewis (M) 0 0
b.London 29-10-02
Internationals: England U17, U18.
2019–20 Chelsea 0 0
2020–21 Chelsea 0 0

BATSHUAYI, Michy (F) 261 88
H: 5 11 W: 12 04 b.Brussels 2-10-93
Internationals: Belgium U21, Full caps.
2010–11 Standard Liege 2 0
2011–12 Standard Liege 23 6
2012–13 Standard Liege 34 12
2013–14 Standard Liege 38 21 **97 39**
2014–15 Marseille 26 9
2015–16 Marseille 36 17 **62 26**
2016–17 Chelsea 20 5
2017–18 Chelsea 12 2
2017–18 *Borussia Dortmund* 10 7 **10 7**
2018–19 Chelsea 0 0
2018–19 *Valencia* 15 1 **15 1**
2018–19 *Crystal Palace* 11 5
2019–20 Chelsea 16 1
2020–21 Chelsea 0 0 **48 8**
2020–21 *Crystal Palace* 18 2 **29 7**

BAXTER, Nathan (G) 63 0
b.London 8-11-98
2018–19 Chelsea 0 0
2018–19 *Yeovil T* 34 0 **34 0**
2019–20 Chelsea 0 0
2019–20 *Ross Co* 13 0 **13 0**
2020–21 Chelsea 0 0
2020–21 *Accrington S* 16 0 **16 0**

BERGSTROM, Lucas (G) 0 0
H: 6 9 W: 12 13 b.Paragas 5-9-02
Internationals: Finland U16, U17.
2020–21 Chelsea 0 0

BLACKMAN, Jamal (G) 121 0
H: 6 6 W: 14 09 b.Croydon 27-10-93
Internationals: England U16, U17, U18, U19.
2011–12 Chelsea 0 0
2012–13 Chelsea 0 0
2013–14 Chelsea 0 0
2014–15 Chelsea 0 0
2014–15 *Middlesbrough* 0 0
2015–16 Chelsea 0 0
2015–16 *Ostersunds FK* 12 0 **12 0**
2016–17 Chelsea 0 0
2016–17 *Wycombe W* 42 0 **42 0**
2017–18 Chelsea 0 0
2017–18 *Sheffield U* 31 0 **31 0**
2018–19 Chelsea 0 0
2018–19 *Leeds U* 0 0
2019–20 Chelsea 0 0
2019–20 *Vitesse* 0 0
2019–20 *Bristol R* 10 0 **10 0**
2020–21 Chelsea 0 0
2020–21 *Rotherham U* 26 0 **26 0**

BRADLEY-MORGAN, Luke (D) 0 0
b.London 22-10-03
2020–21 Chelsea 0 0

BROJA, Armando (F) 31 10
b.Slough 10-9-01
Internationals: Albania U19, U21.
2019–20 Chelsea 1 0
2020–21 Chelsea 0 0 **1 0**
2020–21 *Vitesse* 30 10 **30 10**

BROOKING, Josh (D) 0 0
b.Reading 1-9-02
Internationals: England U16.
From Reading.
2020–21 Chelsea 0 0

BROWN, Isaiah (M) 117 9
H: 6 0 W: 10 13 b.Peterborough 7-1-97
Internationals: England U16, U17, U19, U20.
2012–13 WBA 1 0 **1 0**
2013–14 Chelsea 0 0
2014–15 Chelsea 1 0
2015–16 Chelsea 0 0
2015–16 *Vitesse* 22 1 **22 1**
2016–17 Chelsea 0 0
2016–17 *Rotherham U* 20 3 **20 3**
2016–17 *Huddersfield T* 15 4 **15 4**
2017–18 Chelsea 0 0
2017–18 *Brighton & HA* 13 0 **13 0**
2018–19 Chelsea 0 0
2018–19 *Leeds U* 1 0 **1 0**
2019–20 Chelsea 0 0
2019–20 *Luton T* 25 1 **25 1**
2020–21 Chelsea 0 0 **1 0**
2020–21 *Sheffield W* 19 0 **19 0**

CABALLERO, Willy (G) 365 0
H: 6 1 W: 12 08 b.Santa Elena 28-9-81
Internationals: Argentina U21, Full caps.
2001–02 Boca Juniors 4 0
2002–03 Boca Juniors 4 0
2003–04 Boca Juniors 1 0
2004–05 Boca Juniors 6 0 **15 0**
2005–06 Elche 10 0
2006–07 Elche 39 0
2006–07 *Arsenal Sarandi* 13 0 **13 0**
2007–08 Elche 38 0
2008–09 Elche 38 0
2009–10 Elche 39 0
2010–11 Elche 22 0 **186 0**
2010–11 Malaga 15 0
2011–12 Malaga 28 0
2012–13 Malaga 36 0
2013–14 Malaga 38 0 **117 0**
2014–15 Manchester C 2 0
2015–16 Manchester C 4 0
2016–17 Manchester C 17 0 **23 0**
2017–18 Chelsea 3 0
2018–19 Chelsea 2 0
2019–20 Chelsea 5 0
2020–21 Chelsea 1 0 **11 0**

CASTILLO, Juan (M) 0 0
H: 5 11 W: 12 02 b.Amsterdam 13-1-00
Internationals: Netherlands U16, U17, U18, U19, U20.
2020–21 Chelsea 0 0

CHILWELL, Ben (D) 134 7
H: 5 10 W: 11 03 b.Milton Keynes 21-12-96
Internationals: England U18, U19, U20, U21, Full caps.
2015–16 Leicester C 0 0
2015–16 *Huddersfield T* 8 0 **8 0**
2016–17 Leicester C 12 1
2017–18 Leicester C 24 0
2018–19 Leicester C 36 0
2019–20 Leicester C 27 3 **99 4**
2020–21 Chelsea 27 3 **27 3**

CHRISTENSEN, Andreas (D) 136 5
H: 6 2 W: 11 09 b.Allerod 10-4-96
Internationals: Denmark U16, U17, U19, U21, Full caps.
From Bondby.
2012–13 Chelsea 0 0
2013–14 Chelsea 0 0
2014–15 Chelsea 1 0
2015–16 Chelsea 0 0
2015–16 *Borussia M'gladbach* 31 3
2016–17 Chelsea 0 0
2016–17 *Borussia M'gladbach* 31 2 **62 5**
2017–18 Chelsea 27 0
2018–19 Chelsea 8 0
2019–20 Chelsea 21 0
2020–21 Chelsea 17 0 **74 0**

CLARKE-SALTER, Jake (D) 81 3
H: 6 2 W: 11 00 b.Carshalton 22-9-97
Internationals: England U18, U19, U20, U21.
2015–16 Chelsea 1 0
2016–17 Chelsea 0 0
2016–17 *Bristol R* 12 1 **12 1**
2017–18 Chelsea 0 0
2017–18 *Sunderland* 11 0 **11 0**
2018–19 Chelsea 0 0
2018–19 *Vitesse* 28 1 **28 1**
2019–20 Chelsea 0 0
2019–20 *Birmingham C* 19 1
2020–21 Chelsea 0 0 **1 0**
2020–21 *Birmingham C* 10 0 **29 1**

COLWILL, Levi (D) 0 0
H: 6 2 W: 11 11 b.Southampton 26-2-03
Internationals: England U16, U17.
2020–21 Chelsea 0 0

CUMMING, Jamie (G) 41 0
b.Winchester 4-9-99
Internationals: England U17, U19.
2018–19 Chelsea 0 0
2019–20 Chelsea 0 0
2020–21 Chelsea 0 0
2020–21 *Stevenage* 41 0 **41 0**

EKWAH, Pierre (D) 0 0
H: 6 2 b.Massy 15-1-02
Internationals: France U16.
From Nantes.
2020–21 Chelsea 0 0

EMERSON, dos Santos (D) 93 2
H: 5 9 W: 9 13 b.Santos 13-3-94
Internationals: Brazil U17. Italy Full caps.
2011 Santos 0 0
2012 Santos 1 0
2013 Santos 14 1
2014 Santos 3 0 **18 1**
2014–15 *Palermo* 9 0 **9 0**
2015–16 Roma 8 1
2016–17 Roma 25 0
2017–18 Roma 1 0 **34 1**
2017–18 Chelsea 5 0
2018–19 Chelsea 10 0
2019–20 Chelsea 15 0
2020–21 Chelsea 2 0 **32 0**

FIABEMA, Bryan (F) 1 0
H: 6 0 b.Tromso 16-2-03
Internationals: Norway U16, U17, U18.
2019 Tromso 1 0 **1 0**
2020–21 Chelsea 0 0

GALLAGHER, Conor (M) 75 8
b.Epsom 6-2-00
Internationals: England U17, U18, U19, U20, U21.
2019–20 Chelsea 0 0
2019–20 *Charlton Ath* 26 6 **26 6**
2019–20 *Swansea C* 19 0 **19 0**
2020–21 Chelsea 0 0
2020–21 *WBA* 30 2 **30 2**

GILMOUR, Billy (M) 11 0
b.Glasgow 11-6-01
Internationals: Scotland U16, U17, U19, U21.
From Rangers.
2019–20 Chelsea 6 0
2020–21 Chelsea 5 0 **11 0**

GIROUD, Olivier (F) 445 169
H: 6 3 W: 13 11 b.Chambery 30-9-86
Internationals: France Full caps.
2005–06 Grenoble 6 0
2006–07 Grenoble 17 2
2007–08 Grenoble 0 0 **23 2**
2007–08 *Istres* 33 14 **33 14**
2008–09 Tours 23 9
2009–10 Tours 38 21 **61 30**
2010–11 Montpellier 37 12
2011–12 Montpellier 36 21 **73 33**
2012–13 Arsenal 34 11
2013–14 Arsenal 36 16
2014–15 Arsenal 27 14
2015–16 Arsenal 38 16
2016–17 Arsenal 29 12
2017–18 Arsenal 16 4 **180 73**
2017–18 Chelsea 13 3
2018–19 Chelsea 27 2
2019–20 Chelsea 18 8
2020–21 Chelsea 17 4 **75 17**

GUEHI, Marc (D) 52 0
b. 13-7-00
Internationals: England U16, U17, U18, U19, U20, U21.
2018–19 Chelsea 0 0
2019–20 Chelsea 0 0
2019–20 *Swansea C* 12 0
2020–21 Chelsea 0 0
2020–21 *Swansea C* 40 0 **52 0**

HAIGH, Joe (M) 0 0
b.Tooting 16-3-03
2020–21 Chelsea 0 0

HAVERTZ, Kai (M) 145 40
b.Aachen 11-6-99
2016–17 Bayer Leverkusen 24 4
2017–18 Bayer Leverkusen 30 3
2018–19 Bayer Leverkusen 34 17
2019–20 Bayer Leverkusen 30 12
2020–21 Bayer Leverkusen 0 0 **118 36**
2020–21 Chelsea 27 4 **27 4**

HUDSON-ODOI, Callum (M) 57 3
H: 6 0 b.Wandsworth 7-11-00
Internationals: England U16, U17, U18, U19, Full caps.
2017–18 Chelsea 2 0
2018–19 Chelsea 10 0
2019–20 Chelsea 22 1
2020–21 Chelsea 23 2 **57 3**

HUMPHREYS, Bashir (D) 0 0
b.Exeter 15-3-03
Internationals: England U16.
2020–21 Chelsea 0 0

JAMES, Reece (D) 101 4
b.London 8-12-99
Internationals: England U18, U19, U20, U21.
2018–19 Chelsea 0 0
2018–19 *Wigan Ath* 45 3 **45 3**
2019–20 Chelsea 24 0
2020–21 Chelsea 32 1 **56 1**

JORGINHO, Filho Jorge (M) 349 27
H: 5 11 W: 11 03 b.Imbituba 20-12-91
Internationals: Italy Full caps.
2010–11 Verona 0 0
2010–11 *Sambonifacese* 31 1 **31 1**
2011–12 Verona 30 2
2012–13 Verona 41 2
2013–14 Verona 18 7 **89 11**
2013–14 Napoli 15 0
2014–15 Napoli 23 0
2015–16 Napoli 35 0
2016–17 Napoli 27 0
2017–18 Napoli 33 2 **133 2**
2018–19 Chelsea 37 2
2019–20 Chelsea 31 4
2020–21 Chelsea 28 7 **96 13**

KANTE, Ngolo (M) 307 17
H: 5 7 W: 11 00 b.Paris 29-3-91
Internationals: France Full caps.
2011–12 Boulogne 1 0
2012–13 Boulogne 37 3 **38 3**
2013–14 Caen 38 2
2014–15 Caen 37 2 **75 4**
2015–16 Leicester C 37 1 **37 1**
2016–17 Chelsea 35 1
2017–18 Chelsea 34 1
2018–19 Chelsea 36 4
2019–20 Chelsea 22 3
2020–21 Chelsea 30 0 **157 9**

KOVACIC, Mateo (M) 286 13
H: 5 11 W: 11 07 b.Linz 6-5-94
Internationals: Croatia U17, U19, U21, Full caps.
2010–11 Dinamo Zagreb 7 1
2011–12 Dinamo Zagreb 25 4
2012–13 Dinamo Zagreb 11 1 **43 6**
2012–13 InterMilan 13 0
2013–14 InterMilan 32 0
2014–15 InterMilan 35 5 **80 5**
2015–16 Real Madrid 25 0
2016–17 Real Madrid 27 1
2017–18 Real Madrid 21 0
2018–19 Real Madrid 0 0 **73 1**
2018–19 *Chelsea* 32 0
2019–20 Chelsea 31 1
2020–21 Chelsea 27 0 **90 1**

LAWRENCE, Henry (D) 0 0
2020–21 Chelsea 0 0

LEWIS, Marcel (M) 0 0
b.Cambridge 30-9-01
2020–21 Chelsea 0 0

LIVRAMENTO, Valentino (D) 0 0
b.London 12-11-02
2020–21 Chelsea 0 0

LOFTUS-CHEEK, Ruben (M) 108 10
H: 6 4 W: 11 03 b.Lewisham 23-1-96
Internationals: England U16, U17, U19, U21, Full caps.
2012–13 Chelsea 0 0
2013–14 Chelsea 0 0
2014–15 Chelsea 3 0
2015–16 Chelsea 13 1
2016–17 Chelsea 6 0
2017–18 Chelsea 0 0
2017–18 *Crystal Palace* 24 2 **24 2**
2018–19 Chelsea 24 6
2019–20 Chelsea 7 0
2020–21 Chelsea 1 0 **54 7**
2020–21 *Fulham* 30 1 **30 1**

MAATSEN, Ian (D) 34 1
b.Vlaardingen 10-3-02
Internationals: Netherlands U16, U17, U18.
From PSV Eindhoven.
2019–20 Chelsea 0 0
2020–21 Chelsea 0 0
2020–21 *Charlton Ath* 34 1 **34 1**

MBUYAMBA, Xavier (D) 0 0
H: 6 5 b.Maastricht 31-12-01
Internationals: Netherlands U19
2020–21 Chelsea 0 0

McCLELLAND, Sam (D) 0 0
H: 6 3 b.Coleraine 4-1-02
Internationals: Northern Ireland U17, U19, Full caps.
From Coleraine.
2020–21 Chelsea 0 0

McCORMICK, Luke (M) 44 6
b. 21-1-99
2019–20 Chelsea 0 0
2019–20 *Shrewsbury T* 5 0 **5 0**
2020–21 Chelsea 0 0
2020–21 *Bristol R* 39 6 **39 6**

MENDY, Edouard (G) 161 0
b.Montivilliers 1-3-92
2011–12 Cherbourg 5 0
2012–13 Cherbourg 3 0
2013–14 Cherbourg 18 0 **26 0**
2014–15 Marseille 0 0
2015–16 Marseille 0 0
2016–17 Reims 8 0
2017–18 Reims 34 0
2018–19 Reims 38 0 **80 0**
2019–20 Rennes 24 0
2020–21 Rennes 0 0 **24 0**
2020–21 Chelsea 31 0 **31 0**

MOSES, Victor (M) 323 39
H: 5 10 W: 11 07 b.Lagos 12-12-90
Internationals: England U16, U17, U19, U21. Nigeria Full caps.
2007–08 Crystal Palace 13 3
2008–09 Crystal Palace 27 2
2009–10 Crystal Palace 18 6 **58 11**
2009–10 Wigan Ath 14 1
2010–11 Wigan Ath 21 1
2011–12 Wigan Ath 38 6
2012–13 Wigan Ath 1 0 **74 8**
2012–13 Chelsea 23 1
2013–14 Chelsea 0 0
2013–14 *Liverpool* 19 1 **19 1**
2014–15 Chelsea 0 0
2014–15 *Stoke C* 19 3 **19 3**
2015–16 Chelsea 0 0
2015–16 *West Ham U* 21 1 **21 1**
2016–17 Chelsea 34 3
2017–18 Chelsea 28 3
2018–19 Chelsea 2 0
2018–19 *Fenerbahce* 14 4 **14 4**
2019–20 Chelsea 0 0
2019–20 *Inter Milan* 12 0 **12 0**
2020–21 Chelsea 0 0 **87 7**
2020–21 *Spartak Moscow* 19 4 **19 4**
Transferred to Spartak Moscow July 2021.

MOTHERSILLE, Malik (F) 0 0
b.London 23-10-03
From Leyton Orient.
2020–21 Chelsea 0 0

MOUNT, Mason (M) 137 30
H: 5 10 b.Portsmouth 10-1-99
Internationals: England U16, U17, U18, U19, U21, Full caps.
2017–18 Chelsea 0 0
2017–18 *Vitesse* 29 9 **29 9**
2018–19 Chelsea 0 0
2018–19 *Derby Co* 35 8 **35 8**
2019–20 Chelsea 37 7
2020–21 Chelsea 36 6 **73 13**

NUNN, George (F) 0 0
b.Crewe 23-11-01
From Crewe Alex.
2020–21 Chelsea 0 0

PULISIC, Christian (M) 142 26
b.Hershey 18-9-98
Internationals: USA U17, Full caps.
2015–16 Borussia Dortmund 9 2
2016–17 Borussia Dortmund 29 3
2017–18 Borussia Dortmund 32 4
2018–19 Borussia Dortmund 20 4 **90 13**
2019–20 Chelsea 25 9
2020–21 Chelsea 27 4 **52 13**

RANKINE, Dion (M) 0 0
b.Barnet 15-10-02
2020–21 Chelsea 0 0

RUDIGER, Antonio (D) 221 10
H: 6 3 W: 13 05 b.Berlin 3-3-93
Internationals: Germany U18, U19, U20, U21, Full caps.
2011–12 Stuttgart 1 0
2012–13 Stuttgart 16 0

2013–14 Stuttgart 30 2
2014–15 Stuttgart 19 0 **66 2**
2015–16 *Roma* 30 2
2016–17 Roma 26 0 **56 2**
2017–18 Chelsea 27 2
2018–19 Chelsea 33 1
2019–20 Chelsea 20 2
2020–21 Chelsea 19 1 **99 6**

RUSSELL, Jonathan (M) 25 2
b. 9-10-00
2020–21 Chelsea 0 0
2020–21 *Accrington S* 25 2 **25 2**

SARR, Malang (D) 110 3
2016–17 Nice 27 1
2017–18 Nice 21 0
2018–19 Nice 35 1
2019–20 Nice 19 1 **102 3**
2020–21 Chelsea 0 0
2020–21 *Porto* 8 0 **8 0**

SHARMAN-LOWE, Teddy (G) 0 0
2019–20 Burton Alb 0 0
2020–21 Chelsea 0 0
2020–21 *Burton Alb* 0 0

SIMEU, Dynel (D) 0 0
b. 13-3-02
2020–21 Chelsea 0 0

SIMONS, Xavier (M) 0 0
b.Hammersmith 20-2-03
Internationals: England U16, U17.
2020–21 Chelsea 0 0

SOONSUP-BELL, Jude (F) 0 0
b.Chippenham 10-1-04
Internationals: England U16.
2020–21 Chelsea 0 0

TAURIAINEN, Jimi (F) 0 0
b.Helsinki 8-3-04
Internationals: Finland U16.
From Helsinki.
2020–21 Chelsea 0 0

THIAGO SILVA, Emiliano (D) 429 25
b.Rio De Janeiro 22-9-84
2002 RS Futebol 0 0
2003 RS Futebol 0 0
2004 Juventude 28 3 **28 3**
2004–05 Porto 0 0
2005 Dynamo Moscow 0 0
2006 Fluminense 31 0
2007 Fluminense 30 5
2008 Fluminense 20 1 **81 6**
2009–10 AC Milan 33 2
2010–11 AC Milan 33 1
2011–12 AC Milan 27 2 **93 5**
2012–13 Paris Saint-Germain 22 0
2013–14 Paris Saint-Germain 28 3
2014–15 Paris Saint-Germain 26 1
2015–16 Paris Saint-Germain 30 1
2016–17 Paris Saint-Germain 27 3
2017–18 Paris Saint-Germain 25 1
2018–19 Paris Saint-Germain 25 0
2019–20 Paris Saint-Germain 21 0 **204 9**
2020–21 Chelsea 23 2 **23 2**

TOMORI, Fikayo (D) 112 3
H: 6 0 W: 11 11 b.Calgary 19-12-97
Internationals: Canada U20. England U19, U20, U21, Full caps.
2015–16 Chelsea 1 0
2016–17 Chelsea 0 0
2016–17 *Brighton & HA* 9 0 **9 0**
2017–18 Chelsea 0 0
2017–18 *Hull C* 25 0 **25 0**
2018–19 Chelsea 0 0
2018–19 *Derby Co* 44 1 **44 1**
2019–20 Chelsea 15 1
2020–21 Chelsea 1 0 **17 1**
2020–21 *AC Milan* 17 1 **17 1**

UWAKWE , Tariq (M) 15 1
b. 19-11-99
2020–21 Chelsea 0 0
2020–21 *Accrington S* 15 1 **15 1**

VALE, Harvey (M) 0 0
b.Hawyards Heath 11-9-03
2020–21 Chelsea 0 0

WADY, Ethan (G) 0 0
b.San Jose 25-1-02
2020–21 Chelsea 0 0

WAREHAM, Jayden (F) 0 0
b.Windsor 30-5-03
From QPR.
2020–21 Chelsea 0 0

WEBSTER, Charlie (M) 0 0
b.Kingston upon Thames 31-10-04
Internationals: England U16.
2020–21 Chelsea 0 0

WERNER, Timo (F) 257 97
b.Stuttgart 6-3-96
2013–14 VfB Stuttgart 30 4
2014–15 VfB Stuttgart 32 3
2015–16 VfB Stuttgart 33 6
2016–17 VfB Stuttgart 31 21
2017–18 VfB Stuttgart 32 13
2018–19 VfB Stuttgart 30 16
2019–20 VfB Stuttgart 34 28 **222 91**
2020–21 Chelsea 35 6 **35 6**

WIGGETT, Charlie (D) 0 0
b.Reading 2-11-02
2020–21 Chelsea 0 0

ZIGER, Karlo (G) 0 0
b.Zagreb 11-5-01
From NK Zegreb.
2020–21 Chelsea 0 0

ZIYECH, Hakim (M) 239 81
b.Dronten 19-3-93
2012–13 Heerenveen 3 0
2013–14 Heerenveen 31 9
2014–15 Heerenveen 2 2 **36 11**
2014–15 FC Twente 31 11
2015–16 FC Twente 33 17
2016–17 FC Twente 4 2 **68 30**
2016–17 Ajax 28 7
2017–18 Ajax 34 9
2018–19 Ajax 29 16
2019–20 Ajax 21 6 **112 38**
2020–21 Chelsea 23 2 **23 2**

ZOUMA, Kurt (D) 227 12
H: 6 2 W: 13 04 b.Lyon 27-10-94
Internationals: France U16, U17, U19, U20, U21, Full caps.
2010–11 Saint-Etienne 0 0
2011–12 Saint-Etienne 20 1
2012–13 Saint-Etienne 18 2
2013–14 Chelsea 0 0
2013–14 *Saint-Etienne* 24 0 **62 3**
2014–15 Chelsea 15 0
2015–16 Chelsea 23 1
2016–17 Chelsea 9 0
2017–18 Chelsea 0 0
2017–18 *Stoke C* 34 1 **34 1**
2018–19 Chelsea 0 0
2018–19 *Everton* 32 2 **32 2**
2019–20 Chelsea 28 0
2020–21 Chelsea 24 5 **99 6**

Scholars
Heino, Aleksi Peter; Thomas, Silko Amari Otieno; Tlemcani, Sami; Tobin, Joshua Louis.

CHELTENHAM T (24)

ADDAI, Alex (M) 56 4
b.Stepney 20-12-93
2011–12 Blackpool 0 0
2012–13 Blackpool 0 0
2013–14 Blackpool 0 0
From Carshalton Ath, Whitehawk, Crawley Down Gatwick, Kingstonian, Grays Ath, Wingate & Finchley, Merstham.
2018–19 Cheltenham T 21 0
2019–20 Cheltenham T 25 4
2020–21 Cheltenham T 10 0 **56 4**

BLAIR, Matty (M) 299 22
H: 5 10 W: 11 09 b.Coventry 30-11-87
Internationals: England C.
From Stratford T, Bedworth U, Redditch U, AFC Telford U, Kidderminster Harriers.
2012–13 York C 44 6 **44 6**
2013–14 Fleetwood T 24 3
2013–14 *Northampton T* 3 1 **3 1**
2014–15 Fleetwood T 8 0 **32 3**
2014–15 *Cambridge U* 2 0 **2 0**
2014–15 Mansfield T 3 0
2015–16 Mansfield T 32 2 **35 2**
2016–17 Doncaster R 45 3
2017–18 Doncaster R 40 2
2018–19 Doncaster R 42 3
2019–20 Doncaster R 12 0 **139 8**
2020–21 Cheltenham T 44 2 **44 2**

BOWRY, Dan (D) 1 0
b.Croydon 29-4-98
Internationals: Antigua and Barbuda Full caps.
2016–17 Charlton Ath 0 0
2017–18 Charlton Ath 0 0
2018–19 Charlton Ath 0 0
2019–20 Cheltenham T 1 0
2020–21 Cheltenham T 0 0 **1 0**

BOYLE, William (D) 160 19
H: 6 2 W: 11 00 b.Garforth 1-9-95
2014–15 Huddersfield T 1 0
2015–16 Huddersfield T 1 0
2015–16 *York C* 12 0 **12 0**
2016–17 Huddersfield T 0 0 **2 0**
2016–17 *Kilmarnock* 11 0 **11 0**
2016–17 Cheltenham T 21 2
2017–18 Cheltenham T 34 5
2018–19 Cheltenham T 38 4
2019–20 Cheltenham T 13 2
2020–21 Cheltenham T 29 6 **135 19**

CAMPBELL, Tahvon (F) 95 7
b. 10-1-97
2015–16 WBA 0 0
2015–16 *Yeovil T* 17 1
2016–17 WBA 0 0
2016–17 *Yeovil T* 19 1 **36 2**
2016–17 *Notts Co* 11 0 **11 0**
2017–18 WBA 0 0
2017–18 *Forest Green R* 14 2
2018–19 Forest Green R 18 3 **32 5**
2018–19 *Gillingham* 5 0 **5 0**
2019–20 Cheltenham T 11 0
2020–21 Cheltenham T 0 0 **11 0**

CHAMBERLAIN, Tom (M) 0 0
2019–20 Cheltenham T 0 0
2020–21 Cheltenham T 0 0

CHAPMAN, Ellis (M) 37 0
b.Lincoln 8-1-01
From Leicester C.
2017–18 Lincoln C 0 0
2018–19 Lincoln C 5 0
2019–20 Lincoln C 11 0 **16 0**
2020–21 Cheltenham T 21 0 **21 0**

CLEMENTS, Chris (M) 229 19
H: 5 9 W: 10 04 b.Birmingham 6-2-90
2008–09 Crewe Alex 0 0
2009 *IBV* 15 1 **15 1**
2009–10 Crewe Alex 0 0
2010–11 Crewe Alex 0 0
From Hednesford T.
2013–14 Mansfield T 23 1
2014–15 Mansfield T 34 1
2015–16 Mansfield T 38 5
2016–17 Mansfield T 20 3 **115 10**
2016–17 Grimsby T 16 4
2017–18 Grimsby T 0 0 **16 4**
2017–18 *Forest Green R* 14 1 **14 1**
2018–19 Cheltenham T 30 2
2019–20 Cheltenham T 22 0
2020–21 Cheltenham T 17 1 **69 3**

EBANKS, Callum (F) 0 0
2019–20 Cheltenham T 0 0
2020–21 Cheltenham T 0 0

FLINDERS, Scott (G) 461 1
H: 6 4 W: 13 00 b.Rotherham 12-6-86
Internationals: England U20.
2004–05 Barnsley 11 0
2005–06 Barnsley 3 0 **14 0**
2006–07 Crystal Palace 8 0
2006–07 *Gillingham* 9 0 **9 0**
2006–07 *Brighton & HA* 12 0 **12 0**
2007–08 Crystal Palace 0 0
2007–08 *Yeovil T* 9 0 **9 0**
2008–09 Crystal Palace 0 0 **8 0**
2009–10 Hartlepool U 46 0
2010–11 Hartlepool U 26 1
2011–12 Hartlepool U 45 0
2012–13 Hartlepool U 46 0
2013–14 Hartlepool U 43 0
2014–15 Hartlepool U 46 0 **252 1**
2015–16 York C 43 0 **43 0**
From Macclesfield T.
2017–18 Cheltenham T 41 0
2018–19 Cheltenham T 46 0
2019–20 Cheltenham T 25 0
2020–21 Cheltenham T 2 0 **114 0**

FREESTONE, Lewis (D) 22 0
b.King's Lynn 26-10-99
2016–17 Peterborough U 4 0
2017–18 Peterborough U 4 0
2018–19 Peterborough U 0 0 **8 0**
2019–20 Brighton & HA 0 0
2020–21 Cheltenham T 14 0 **14 0**

HARRIS, Max (G) 0 0
b.Gloucester 14-9-99
2018–19 Oxford U 0 0
2019–20 Oxford U 0 0
2020–21 Cheltenham T 0 0

HORTON, Grant (D) **2 0**
b.Colchester 13-9-01
2019–20 Cheltenham T 1 0
2020–21 Cheltenham T 1 0 **2 0**

HUSSEY, Chris (D) **329 9**
H: 5 10 W: 10 03 b.Hammersmith 2-1-89
From AFC Wimbledon.
2009–10 Coventry C 8 0
2010–11 Coventry C 11 0
2010–11 *Crewe Alex* 0 0
2011–12 Coventry C 29 0
2012–13 Coventry C 10 0 **58 0**
2012–13 AFC Wimbledon 19 0
2013–14 AFC Wimbledon 0 0 **19 0**
2013–14 Burton Alb 27 1 **27 1**
2013–14 *Bury* 11 2
2014–15 Bury 38 0
2015–16 Bury 41 1 **90 3**
2016–17 Sheffield U 7 0
2017–18 Sheffield U 0 0 **7 0**
2017–18 *Swindon T* 18 1 **18 1**
2018–19 Cheltenham T 34 1
2019–20 Cheltenham T 33 2
2020–21 Cheltenham T 43 1 **110 4**

JAKEWAYS, Connor (D) **0 0**
2020–21 Cheltenham T 0 0

LLOYD, George (M) **59 5**
H: 5 8 W: 9 13 b. 11-2-00
2017–18 Cheltenham T 7 2
2018–19 Cheltenham T 7 1
2019–20 Cheltenham T 13 0
2020–21 Cheltenham T 32 2 **59 5**

LONG, Sean (D) **94 3**
H: 5 10 W: 11 00 b.Dublin 2-5-95
Internationals: Republic of Ireland U16, U17, U18, U19, U21.
2013–14 Reading 0 0
2014–15 Reading 0 0
2015–16 Reading 0 0
2015–16 *Luton T* 9 0 **9 0**
2016–17 Reading 0 0
2016–17 *Cambridge U* 7 0 **7 0**
2017–18 Lincoln C 17 0 **17 0**
2018–19 Cheltenham T 5 0
2019–20 Cheltenham T 34 1
2020–21 Cheltenham T 22 2 **61 3**

MAY, Alfie (F) **148 25**
H: 5 9 W: 11 05 b. 2-7-93
From Billericay T, Chatham T, VCD Ath, Erith & Belvedere, Farnborough, Hythe T.
2016–17 Doncaster R 16 3
2017–18 Doncaster R 27 4
2018–19 Doncaster R 34 2
2019–20 Doncaster R 15 1 **92 10**
2019–20 Cheltenham T 12 6
2020–21 Cheltenham T 44 9 **56 15**

MILES, Felix (M) **0 0**
2020–21 Cheltenham T 0 0

RAGLAN, Charlie (D) **167 5**
H: 6 0 W: 11 13 b.Wythenshawe 28-4-93
2011–12 Port Vale 0 0
2012–13 Port Vale 0 0
2013–14 Port Vale 0 0
2014–15 Chesterfield 18 1
2015–16 Chesterfield 27 0
2016–17 Chesterfield 1 0 **46 1**
2016–17 *Oxford U* 16 0
2017–18 Oxford U 0 0
2017–18 *Port Vale* 10 0 **10 0**
2018–19 Oxford U 1 0 **17 0**
2018–19 *Cheltenham T* 19 2
2019–20 Cheltenham T 35 1
2020–21 Cheltenham T 40 1 **94 4**

REID, Reuben (F) **434 118**
H: 6 0 W: 12 02 b.Bristol 26-7-88
2005–06 Plymouth Arg 1 0
2006–07 Plymouth Arg 6 0
2006–07 *Rochdale* 2 0 **2 0**
2006–07 *Torquay U* 7 2 **7 2**
2007–08 Plymouth Arg 0 0
2007–08 *Wycombe W* 11 1 **11 1**
2007–08 Brentford 10 1 **10 1**
2008–09 Rotherham U 41 18 **41 18**
2009–10 WBA 4 0
2009–10 *Peterborough U* 13 0 **13 0**
2010–11 WBA 0 0 **4 0**
2010–11 *Walsall* 18 3 **18 3**
2010–11 Oldham Ath 19 2
2011–12 Oldham Ath 20 5 **39 7**
2012–13 Yeovil T 19 4 **19 4**
2012–13 *Plymouth Arg* 18 2
2013–14 Plymouth Arg 46 17
2014–15 Plymouth Arg 42 18
2015–16 Plymouth Arg 29 7
2016–17 Plymouth Arg 0 0 **142 44**
2016–17 Exeter C 36 13
2017–18 Exeter C 21 7 **57 20**
2017–18 Forest Green R 21 6
2018–19 Forest Green R 29 7 **50 13**
2019–20 Cheltenham T 9 3
2020–21 Cheltenham T 12 2 **21 5**
Transferred to Yeovil T January 2021.

SERCOMBE, Liam (M) **452 60**
H: 5 10 W: 10 10 b.Exeter 25-4-90
2008–09 Exeter C 29 2
2009–10 Exeter C 28 1
2010–11 Exeter C 42 3
2011–12 Exeter C 33 7
2012–13 Exeter C 20 1
2013–14 Exeter C 44 5
2014–15 Exeter C 40 4 **236 23**
2015–16 Oxford U 45 14
2016–17 Oxford U 30 3 **75 17**
2017–18 Bristol R 42 8
2018–19 Bristol R 39 4
2019–20 Bristol R 22 1 **103 13**
2020–21 Cheltenham T 38 7 **38 7**

SKUREK, Harvey (D) **0 0**
b.Bristol --
2020–21 Cheltenham T 0 0

THOMAS, Conor (M) **231 19**
H: 6 1 W: 11 05 b.Coventry 29-10-93
Internationals: England U17, U18.
2010–11 Coventry C 0 0
2010–11 *Liverpool* 0 0
2011–12 Coventry C 27 1
2012–13 Coventry C 11 0
2013–14 Coventry C 43 0
2014–15 Coventry C 16 0
2015–16 Coventry C 3 0 **100 1**
2016–17 Swindon T 33 1
2017–18 Swindon T 2 0 **35 1**
2018–19 Cheltenham T 32 6
2019–20 Cheltenham T 26 6
2020–21 Cheltenham T 38 5 **96 17**

TOZER, Ben (D) **382 16**
H: 6 1 W: 12 11 b.Plymouth 1-3-90
From Plymouth Arg.
2007–08 Swindon T 2 0 **2 0**
2007–08 Newcastle U 0 0
2008–09 Newcastle U 0 0
2009–10 Newcastle U 1 0
2010–11 Newcastle U 0 0 **1 0**
2010–11 *Northampton T* 31 3
2011–12 Northampton T 45 3
2012–13 Northampton T 46 0
2013–14 Northampton T 29 0
2013–14 *Colchester U* 1 0 **1 0**
2014–15 Northampton T 22 0 **173 6**
2015–16 Yeovil T 26 0 **26 0**
2016–17 Newport Co 23 1
2017–18 Newport Co 39 3 **62 4**
2017–18 Cheltenham T 0 0
2018–19 Cheltenham T 37 1
2019–20 Cheltenham T 34 3
2020–21 Cheltenham T 46 2 **117 6**

WILLIAMS, Andy (F) **533 123**
H: 5 11 W: 11 09 b.Hereford 14-8-86
2006–07 Hereford U 41 8
2007–08 Bristol R 41 4
2008–09 Bristol R 4 1
2008–09 *Hereford U* 26 2 **67 10**
2009–10 Bristol R 43 3 **88 8**
2010–11 Yeovil T 37 6
2011–12 Yeovil T 35 16
2012–13 Swindon T 40 11
2013–14 Swindon T 3 0
2013–14 *Yeovil T* 9 0 **81 22**
2014–15 Swindon T 46 21 **89 32**
2015–16 Doncaster R 46 12
2016–17 Doncaster R 37 11
2017–18 Doncaster R 9 0 **92 23**
2018–19 Northampton T 39 12
2019–20 Northampton T 32 8 **71 20**
2020–21 Cheltenham T 45 8 **45 8**

Scholars
Aldridge, Joshua Francis; Atwell, Liam Alfie; Clark, George Ian Hartley; Dashfield, Charlie Thomas; Davis, Felix William; Denness-Barrett, Brennan H'Onre; Guinan, Zachary Josiah; Hunt, Joseph Daniel; Jakeways, Connor John; Lawrence, Toby Paul; Miles, Felix William; Parsisson, Jake William; Paterson, Charlie Jack; Skurek, Harvey Scott; Stevens, Daniel Lloyd; Taylor, William Alexander; Woodall, Archie Joe.

COLCHESTER U (25)

ADUBOFOUR-POKU, Kwame (M) **62 5**
b. 11-8-01
From Cray W, Worthing.
2019–20 Colchester U 29 5
2020–21 Colchester U 33 0 **62 5**

BOHUI, Joshua (M) **17 1**
b.London 3-3-99
2019–20 NAC Breda 4 0 **4 0**
2020–21 NAC 0 0
2020–21 Colchester U 13 1 **13 1**

BROWN, Jevani (M) **140 20**
b. 16-10-94
Internationals: Jamaica U17.
2013–14 Peterborough U 0 0
2014–15 Peterborough U 0 0
From Barton R, Arlesey T, Kettering T, Stamford, St Neots T.
2017–18 Cambridge U 41 6
2018–19 Cambridge U 43 7 **84 13**
2019–20 Colchester U 11 0
2019–20 *Forest Green R* 5 0 **5 0**
2020–21 Colchester U 40 7 **51 7**

CHILVERS, Noah (M) **46 2**
b. 22-2-01
2018–19 Colchester U 2 0
2019–20 Colchester U 0 0
2020–21 Colchester U 44 2 **46 2**

CLAMPIN, Ryan (M) **34 1**
b. 29-1-99
2018–19 Colchester U 0 0
2019–20 Colchester U 13 0
2020–21 Colchester U 21 1 **34 1**

CORNISH, Sam (M) **0 0**
2020–21 Colchester U 0 0

COULTER, Callum (G) **0 0**
2019–20 Colchester U 0 0
2020–21 Colchester U 0 0

COWAN-HALL, Paris (F) **218 30**
H: 5 8 W: 11 08 b.Portsmouth 5-10-90
From Rushden & D.
2008–09 Portsmouth 0 0
2009–10 Portsmouth 0 0
2009–10 *Grimsby T* 3 0 **3 0**
2010–11 Portsmouth 0 0
2010–11 Scunthorpe U 1 0 **1 0**
From Woking.
2012–13 Plymouth Arg 40 3 **40 3**
2013–14 Wycombe W 25 4
2014–15 Wycombe W 20 6
2014–15 Millwall 5 0
2015–16 Millwall 3 0 **8 0**
2015–16 *Bristol R* 3 0 **3 0**
2015–16 *Wycombe W* 5 1
2016–17 Wycombe W 28 4
2017–18 Wycombe W 34 8
2018–19 Wycombe W 33 4 **145 27**
2019–20 Colchester U 5 0
2020–21 Colchester U 13 0 **18 0**

CRACKNELL, Billy (D) **1 0**
b.Brentwood 19-1-02
2020–21 Colchester U 1 0 **1 0**

EASTMAN, Tom (D) **384 21**
H: 6 3 W: 13 12 b.Clacton 21-10-91
2009–10 Ipswich T 1 0
2010–11 Ipswich T 9 0 **10 0**
2011–12 Colchester U 25 3
2011–12 *Crawley T* 6 0 **6 0**
2012–13 Colchester U 29 2
2013–14 Colchester U 36 0
2014–15 Colchester U 46 1
2015–16 Colchester U 43 2
2016–17 Colchester U 35 3
2017–18 Colchester U 42 3
2018–19 Colchester U 31 3
2019–20 Colchester U 36 2
2020–21 Colchester U 45 2 **368 21**

FOLIVI, Michael (F) **49 7**
H: 5 11 W: 12 06 b.Brent 25-2-98
2016–17 Watford 1 0
2016–17 *Coventry C* 1 0 **1 0**
2017–18 Watford 0 0
2018–19 Watford 0 0
2018–19 *AFC Wimbledon* 10 2
2019–20 Watford 0 0 **1 0**
2019–20 *AFC Wimbledon* 10 0 **20 2**
2020–21 Colchester U 27 5 **27 5**

FREITAS GOUVEIA, Diogo (M) **0 0**
b. 16-6-01
2020–21 Colchester U 0 0

GAMBIN, Luke (M) 179 17
H: 5 6 W: 11 00 b.Surrey 16-3-93
Internationals: Malta Full caps.
2011–12 Barnet 1 0
2012–13 Barnet 10 2
2015–16 Barnet 44 4
2016–17 Barnet 19 4 **74 10**
2016–17 Luton T 16 1
2017–18 Luton T 13 1
2018–19 Luton T 0 0 **29 2**
2018–19 *Crawley T* 26 3 **26 3**
2019–20 Colchester U 28 1
2020–21 Colchester U 11 0 **39 1**
2020–21 *Newport Co* 11 1 **11 1**

GEORGE, Shamal (G) 19 0
b.Wirral 6-1-98
2017–18 Liverpool 0 0
2017–18 *Carlisle U* 4 0 **4 0**
2018–19 Liverpool 0 0
2018–19 *Tranmere R* 0 0
2019–20 Liverpool 0 0
2020–21 Colchester U 15 0 **15 0**

GERKEN, Dean (G) 342 0
H: 6 3 W: 12 08 b.Southend 22-5-85
2003–04 Colchester U 1 0
2004–05 Colchester U 13 0
2005–06 Colchester U 7 0
2006–07 Colchester U 27 0
2007–08 Colchester U 40 0
2008–09 Colchester U 21 0
2008–09 *Darlington* 7 0 **7 0**
2009–10 Bristol C 39 0
2010–11 Bristol C 1 0
2011–12 Bristol C 10 0
2012–13 Bristol C 3 0 **53 0**
2013–14 Ipswich T 41 0
2014–15 Ipswich T 16 0
2015–16 Ipswich T 26 0
2016–17 Ipswich T 2 0
2017–18 Ipswich T 1 0
2018–19 Ipswich T 18 0 **104 0**
2019–20 Colchester U 36 0
2020–21 Colchester U 33 0 **178 0**

HARRIOTT, Callum (M) 188 30
H: 5 5 W: 10 05 b.Norbury 4-3-94
Internationals: England U19. Guyana Full caps.
2010–11 Charlton Ath 3 0
2011–12 Charlton Ath 0 0
2012–13 Charlton Ath 14 2
2013–14 Charlton Ath 28 5
2014–15 Charlton Ath 21 1
2015–16 Charlton Ath 20 3 **86 11**
2015–16 *Colchester U* 20 5
2016–17 Reading 12 1
2017–18 Reading 0 0
2018–19 Reading 12 1 **24 2**
2019–20 Colchester U 22 3
2020–21 Colchester U 36 9 **78 17**

HUTCHINSON, Jake (F) 0 0
b.Colchester 8-4-01
2020–21 Colchester U 0 0

KAZEEM, Al-Amin (D) 0 0
H: 5 9 W: 10 06 b. 6-4-02
2020–21 Colchester U 0 0

KENSDALE, Ollie (D) 3 0
b. 20-4-00
2017–18 Colchester U 0 0
2018–19 Colchester U 2 0
2019–20 Colchester U 1 0
2020–21 Colchester U 0 0 **3 0**
Transferred to Concord Rangers February 2021.

LAPSLIE, Tom (M) 152 3
H: 5 6 W: 10 12 b.Waltham Forest 5-5-95
2013–14 Colchester U 0 0
2014–15 Colchester U 11 1
2015–16 Colchester U 10 1
2016–17 Colchester U 37 0
2017–18 Colchester U 29 0
2018–19 Colchester U 35 1
2019–20 Colchester U 17 0
2020–21 Colchester U 13 0 **152 3**

MARSHALL, Marley (M) 1 0
b. 22-10-02
2020–21 Colchester U 1 0 **1 0**

McLEOD, Sammie (M) 1 0
b. 23-4-00
From Maldon & Tiptree.
2019–20 Colchester U 0 0
2020–21 Colchester U 1 0 **1 0**

PELL, Harry (M) 263 32
H: 6 4 W: 13 05 b.Tilbury 21-10-91
2009–10 Charlton Ath 0 0
2010–11 Bristol R 10 0 **10 0**
2010–11 *Hereford U* 7 0
2011–12 Hereford U 30 3 **37 3**
2012–13 AFC Wimbledon 17 2
2013–14 AFC Wimbledon 33 4
2014–15 AFC Wimbledon 9 0 **59 6**
2016–17 Cheltenham T 42 7
2017–18 Cheltenham T 37 5 **79 12**
2018–19 Colchester U 31 6
2019–20 Colchester U 22 3
2020–21 Colchester U 25 2 **78 11**

SARPENG-WIREDU, Brendan (M) 27 1
b. 7-11-99
2018–19 Charlton Ath 0 0
2019–20 Charlton Ath 0 0
2019–20 *Colchester U* 7 0
2020–21 Charlton Ath 0 0
2020–21 Colchester U 20 1 **27 1**

SAYER, Harvey (D) 4 0
b.Great Yarmouth 6-1-03
2020–21 Colchester U 4 0 **4 0**

SCARLETT, Miquel (D) 3 0
b. 27-9-00
2017–18 Gillingham 0 0
2018–19 Gillingham 0 0
2019–20 Colchester U 0 0
2020–21 Colchester U 3 0 **3 0**

SENIOR, Courtney (F) 125 12
b. 30-6-97
2014–15 Brentford 0 0
2014–15 *Wycombe W* 1 0 **1 0**
2015–16 Brentford 0 0
2016–17 Colchester U 0 0
2017–18 Colchester U 18 4
2018–19 Colchester U 42 6
2019–20 Colchester U 29 2
2020–21 Colchester U 35 0 **124 12**

SMITH, Tommy (D) 366 30
H: 6 2 W: 12 02 b.Macclesfield 31-3-90
Internationals: England U17, U18. New Zealand Full caps.
2007–08 Ipswich T 0 0
2008–09 Ipswich T 2 0
2009–10 Ipswich T 14 0
2009–10 *Brentford* 8 0 **8 0**
2010–11 Ipswich T 22 3
2010–11 *Colchester U* 6 0
2011–12 Ipswich T 26 3
2012–13 Ipswich T 38 3
2013–14 Ipswich T 45 6
2014–15 Ipswich T 42 4
2015–16 Ipswich T 45 2
2016–17 Ipswich T 10 0
2017–18 Ipswich T 3 0 **247 21**
2018 Colorado Rapids 33 4
2019 Colorado Rapids 27 3 **60 7**
2019–20 Sunderland 0 0
2020–21 Colchester U 45 2 **51 2**

SOWUNMI, Omar (D) 91 3
H: 6 6 W: 14 09 b.Colchester 7-11-95
2014–15 Ipswich T 0 0
2015–16 Yeovil T 5 1
2016–17 Yeovil T 11 0
2017–18 Yeovil T 36 2
2018–19 Yeovil T 17 0 **69 3**
2019–20 Colchester U 7 0
2020–21 Colchester U 15 0 **22 0**

STAGG, Thomas (F) 1 0
b. 9-9-02
2020–21 Colchester U 1 0 **1 0**

STEVENSON, Ben (M) 120 8
H: 6 0 W: 10 08 b.Leicester 23-3-97
2015–16 Coventry C 0 0
2016–17 Coventry C 28 2
2017–18 Coventry C 5 0 **33 2**
2017–18 Wolverhampton W 0 0
2017–18 *Colchester U* 13 2
2018–19 Wolverhampton W 0 0
2018–19 Colchester U 14 0
2019–20 Colchester U 28 2
2020–21 Colchester U 32 2 **87 6**

TCHAMADEU, Junior (D) 11 0
b. 22-12-03
2020–21 Colchester U 11 0 **11 0**

TOVIDE, Samson (F) 0 0
2020–21 Colchester U 0 0

WELCH-HAYES, Miles (D) 86 2
b.Oxford 25-10-96
2016–17 Oxford U 1 0 **1 0**
From Bath C.
2018–19 Macclesfield T 23 0
2019–20 Macclesfield T 24 1 **47 1**
2019–20 Colchester U 0 0
2020–21 Colchester U 38 1 **38 1**

Scholars
Akolbire, Lordon; Asare-Williams, Darnell Nana Kwame; Brown, Aaron Ellis John; Collins, Ted Jamie; Cornish, Sam David; Cracknell, William David; Fouche, Joshua Alexander; Johnson, Endurance Izogie Isokpan; Kane, Namory Olorunleke Ahmed; Kennedy, Gene John; Lowe, Ryan Michael; Parish, Kacy Ray; Redgrave, Kai Christopher Ray; Stagg, Thomas Jack; Sullivan, Ellis Daniel; Tchamadeu, Junior Baptiste; Terry, Frankie Edward; Thomas, Donell Tyrell Arnold; Tovide, Samson Jolaoluwa Gbolahan; Tricker, Matthew James Elliot.

COVENTRY C (26)

ALLEN, Jamie (M) 237 21
H: 5 11 W: 11 05 b.Rochdale 29-1-95
2012–13 Rochdale 0 0
2013–14 Rochdale 25 6
2014–15 Rochdale 35 0
2015–16 Rochdale 38 3
2016–17 Rochdale 31 2
2017–18 Rochdale 4 0 **133 11**
2017–18 Burton Alb 29 1
2018–19 Burton Alb 42 7 **71 8**
2019–20 Coventry C 11 1
2020–21 Coventry C 22 1 **33 2**

BAKAYOKO, Amadou (F) 161 20
H: 6 4 W: 13 05 b. 1-1-96
2013–14 Walsall 6 0
2014–15 Walsall 7 0
2015–16 Walsall 0 0
2016–17 Walsall 39 4
2017–18 Walsall 41 5 **93 9**
2018–19 Coventry C 31 7
2019–20 Coventry C 23 4
2020–21 Coventry C 14 0 **68 11**

BAPAGA, Will (F) 3 0
b. 11-2-03
2019–20 Coventry C 1 0
2020–21 Coventry C 2 0 **3 0**

BIAMOU, Maxime (F) 140 23
b. 13-11-90
2014–15 Villemomble Sports 15 3 **15 3**
2015–16 Yzeure 30 6 **30 6**
From Sutton U.
2017–18 Coventry C 39 5
2018–19 Coventry C 4 0
2019–20 Coventry C 18 4
2020–21 Coventry C 34 5 **95 14**

BILSON, Tom (G) 0 0
b.Shrewsbury --
2017–18 Coventry C 0 0
2018–19 Coventry C 0 0
2019–20 Coventry C 0 0
2020–21 Coventry C 0 0

BURROUGHS, Jack (M) 2 0
b. 21-3-01
Internationals: Scotland U19.
2018–19 Coventry C 0 0
2019–20 Coventry C 0 0
2020–21 Coventry C 2 0 **2 0**

DA COSTA, Julien (D) 93 0
b.Marseille 29-5-96
2015–16 Marseille 0 0
2016–17 Marseille 0 0
2017–18 Chamois Niortas 26 0
2018–19 Chamois Niortas 27 0
2019–20 Chamois Niortas 22 0 **75 0**
2020–21 Coventry C 18 0 **18 0**

DABO, Fankaty (D) 122 1
H: 5 11 W: 12 02 b.Southwark 11-10-95
Internationals: England U16, U17, U20.
2016–17 Chelsea 0 0
2016–17 *Swindon T* 15 1 **15 1**
2017–18 Chelsea 0 0
2017–18 *Vitesse* 26 0 **26 0**
2018–19 Chelsea 0 0
2018–19 *Sparta Rotterdam* 21 0 **21 0**
2019–20 Coventry C 32 0
2020–21 Coventry C 28 0 **60 0**

DRYSDALE, Declan (D) 24 1
b. 14-11-99
2018–19 Tranmere R 0 0
2018–19 Coventry C 0 0
2019–20 Coventry C 1 0
2020–21 Coventry C 0 0 **1 0**
2020–21 *Gillingham* 10 0 **10 0**
2020–21 *Cambridge U* 13 1 **13 1**

ECCLES, Josh (D) 22 0
b. 6-4-00
2018–19 Coventry C 0 0

2019–20	Coventry C	3	0		
2020–21	Coventry C	7	0	**10**	**0**
2020–21	*Gillingham*	12	0	**12**	**0**

FINNEGAN, Aidan (M) **0 0**
b.Solihull 18-2-03
From Birmingham C.

2020–21	Coventry C	0	0		

GODDEN, Matthew (F) **181 64**
H: 6 1 W: 12 03 b.Canterbury 29-7-91

2009–10	Scunthorpe U	0	0		
2010–11	Scunthorpe U	5	0		
2011–12	Scunthorpe U	1	0		
2012–13	Scunthorpe U	8	0		
2013–14	Scunthorpe U	4	0		
2014–15	Scunthorpe U	0	0	**18**	**0**
From Ebbsfleet U.					
2016–17	Stevenage	38	20		
2017–18	Stevenage	38	10	**76**	**30**
2018–19	Peterborough U	38	14		
2019–20	Peterborough U	0	0	**38**	**14**
2019–20	Coventry C	26	14		
2020–21	Coventry C	23	6	**49**	**20**

HAMER, Gustavo (M) **126 12**
b.Itajai 24-6-97

2016–17	Feyenoord	2	0		
2017–18	Feyenoord	0	0	**2**	**0**
2017–18	*Dordrecht*	34	3	**34**	**3**
2018–19	PEC Zwolle	23	0		
2019–20	PEC Zwolle	25	4	**48**	**4**
2020–21	Coventry C	42	5	**42**	**5**

HILSSNER, Marcel (M) **82 9**
b. 30-1-95

2013–14	Werder Bremen	0	0		
2014–15	Werder Bremen	0	0		
2015–16	Werder Bremen	1	0	**1**	**0**
2016–17	Dynamo Dresden	8	0		
2017–18	Dynamo Dresden	0	0	**8**	**0**
2017–18	Hansa Rostock	18	4		
2018–19	Hansa Rostock	21	2	**39**	**6**
2019–20	Paderborn 07	0	0		
2019–20	*Hallescher*	14	2	**14**	**2**
2020–21	Coventry C	0	0		
2020–21	*Oldham Ath*	20	1	**20**	**1**

HOWLEY, Ryan (M) **0 0**

2020–21	Coventry C	0	0		

HYAM, Dominic (D) **140 6**
H: 6 2 W: 11 00 b.Leuchars 20-12-95
Internationals: Scotland U19, U21.

2014–15	Reading	0	0		
2015–16	Reading	0	0		
2015–16	*Dagenham & R*	16	0	**16**	**0**
2016–17	Reading	0	0		
2016–17	*Portsmouth*	0	0		
2017–18	Coventry C	14	0		
2018–19	Coventry C	38	1		
2019–20	Coventry C	29	2		
2020–21	Coventry C	43	3	**124**	**6**

JOBELLO, Wesley (M) **128 8**
b.Gennevilliers 23-1-94
Internationals: France U18. Martinique Full caps.

2011–12	Marseille	1	0		
2012–13	Marseille	0	0		
2013–14	Marseille	0	0		
2014–15	Marseille	0	0	**1**	**0**
2015–16	Clermont Foot	26	0		
2016–17	Clermont Foot	27	3	**53**	**3**
2017–18	Gazelec Ajaccio	24	2		
2018–19	Gazelec Ajaccio	37	2	**61**	**4**
2019–20	Coventry C	10	1		
2020–21	Coventry C	3	0	**13**	**1**

KASTANEER, Gervane (F) **93 13**
b.Rotterdam 9-6-96
Internationals: Netherlands U19, U20, U21. Curacao Full caps.

2012–13	Dordrecht	3	0	**3**	**0**
2013–14	ADO Den Haag	0	0		
2014–15	ADO Den Haag	8	1		
2015–16	ADO Den Haag	5	0		
2015–16	*FC Eindhoven*	14	4	**14**	**4**
2016–17	ADO Den Haag	14	4	**27**	**5**
2017–18	Kaiserslautern	10	1	**10**	**1**
2018–19	NAC Breda	21	2	**21**	**2**
2019–20	Coventry C	10	1		
2020–21	Coventry C	2	0	**12**	**1**
2020–21	*Hearts*	6	0	**6**	**0**

KELLY, Liam (M) **333 29**
H: 6 2 W: 13 11 b.Milton Keynes 10-2-90
Internationals: Scotland U18, U21, Full caps.

2009–10	Kilmarnock	15	1		
2010–11	Kilmarnock	32	7		
2011–12	Kilmarnock	34	1		
2012–13	Kilmarnock	19	6	**100**	**15**
2012–13	Bristol C	19	0		
2013–14	Bristol C	2	0	**21**	**0**
2014–15	Oldham Ath	37	1		
2015–16	Oldham Ath	41	6	**78**	**7**
2016–17	Leyton Orient	21	4	**21**	**4**
2017–18	Coventry C	33	1		
2018–19	Coventry C	30	0		
2019–20	Coventry C	27	0		
2020–21	Coventry C	23	2	**113**	**3**

LAFFERTY, Dan (M) **0 0**
b. 22-12-01

2020–21	Coventry C	0	0		

MAROSI, Marko (G) **132 0**
H: 6 3 W: 12 08 b. 23-10-93
Internationals: Slovakia U21.
From Barnoldswick T.

2013–14	Wigan Ath	0	0		
2014–15	Doncaster R	3	0		
2015–16	Doncaster R	1	0		
2016–17	Doncaster R	25	0		
2017–18	Doncaster R	13	0		
2018–19	Doncaster R	36	0	**78**	**0**
2019–20	Coventry C	34	0		
2020–21	Coventry C	20	0	**54**	**0**

MASON, Brandon (M) **46 0**
H: 5 9 W: 11 00 b.Westminster 30-9-97

2016–17	Watford	2	0		
2017–18	Watford	0	0	**2**	**0**
2017–18	*Dundee U*	1	0	**1**	**0**
2018–19	Coventry C	25	0		
2019–20	Coventry C	11	0		
2020–21	Coventry C	0	0	**36**	**0**
2020–21	*St Mirren*	7	0	**7**	**0**

McFADZEAN, Kyle (D) **352 16**
H: 6 1 W: 13 04 b.Sheffield 20-2-87
Internationals: England C.

2004–05	Sheffield U	0	0		
2005–06	Sheffield U	0	0		
2006–07	Sheffield U	0	0		
From Alfreton T.					
2011–12	Crawley T	37	2		
2012–13	Crawley T	17	3		
2013–14	Crawley T	42	1	**96**	**6**
2014–15	Milton Keynes D	41	3		
2015–16	Milton Keynes D	39	0	**80**	**3**
2016–17	Burton Alb	31	1		
2017–18	Burton Alb	42	0		
2018–19	Burton Alb	35	4	**108**	**5**
2018–19	Coventry C	0	0		
2019–20	Coventry C	30	0		
2020–21	Coventry C	38	2	**68**	**2**

McGRATH, Jay (D) **0 0**

2020–21	Coventry C	0	0		

O'HARE, Callum (F) **95 9**
b.Solihull 1-5-98
Internationals: England U20.

2016–17	Aston Villa	0	0		
2017–18	Aston Villa	4	0		
2018–19	Aston Villa	0	0		
2018–19	*Carlisle U*	16	3	**16**	**3**
2019–20	Aston Villa	0	0	**4**	**0**
2019–20	*Coventry C*	29	3		
2020–21	Coventry C	46	3	**75**	**6**

PASK, Josh (D) **34 0**
b. 1-11-97

2015–16	West Ham U	0	0		
2015–16	*Dagenham & R*	5	0	**5**	**0**
2016–17	West Ham U	0	0		
2016–17	*Gillingham*	10	0	**10**	**0**
2017–18	West Ham U	0	0		
2018–19	West Ham U	0	0		
2019–20	Coventry C	2	0		
2020–21	Coventry C	17	0	**19**	**0**

REID, Josh (D) **20 0**
H: 5 11 W: 10 08 b.Dingwall 3-5-02

2019–20	Ross Co	20	0	**20**	**0**
2020–21	Coventry C	0	0		

ROSE, Michael (D) **144 7**
b.Aberdeen 11-10-95

2015–16	Aberdeen	1	0	**1**	**0**
2015–16	*Forfar Ath*	7	0	**7**	**0**
2016–17	Ayr U	20	1		
2017–18	Ayr U	34	2		
2018–19	Ayr U	34	2	**88**	**5**
2019–20	Coventry C	31	2		
2020–21	Coventry C	17	0	**48**	**2**

ROWE, Blaine (D) **0 0**

2019–20	Coventry C	0	0		
2020–21	Coventry C	0	0		

SHIPLEY, Jordan (M) **122 15**
b. 26-6-97
Internationals: Republic of Ireland U21.

2016–17	Coventry C	1	0		
2017–18	Coventry C	30	4		
2018–19	Coventry C	33	3		
2019–20	Coventry C	31	5		
2020–21	Coventry C	27	3	**122**	**15**

TAVARES, Fabio (F) **26 2**
b. 22-1-01

2018–19	Rochdale	0	0		
2019–20	Rochdale	14	1		
2020–21	Rochdale	12	1	**26**	**2**
2020–21	Coventry C	0	0		

THOMPSON, Jordan (D) **6 0**
b. 8-4-99

2016–17	Coventry C	0	0		
2017–18	Coventry C	0	0		
2018–19	Coventry C	4	0		
2019–20	Coventry C	0	0		
2020–21	Coventry C	2	0	**6**	**0**

TYLER, Cian (G) **0 0**
b. 22-3-02
Internationals: Wales U17.

2019–20	Coventry C	0	0		
2020–21	Coventry C	0	0		

WALKER, Tyler (F) **169 54**
H: 5 10 W: 9 13 b. 17-10-96
Internationals: England U20.

2013–14	Nottingham F	0	0		
2014–15	Nottingham F	7	1		
2015–16	Nottingham F	14	0		
2015–16	*Burton Alb*	6	1	**6**	**1**
2016–17	Nottingham F	0	0		
2016–17	*Stevenage*	8	3	**8**	**3**
2016–17	*Port Vale*	6	2	**6**	**2**
2017–18	Nottingham F	12	3		
2017–18	*Bolton W*	5	0	**5**	**0**
2018–19	Nottingham F	0	0		
2018–19	*Mansfield T*	44	22	**44**	**22**
2019–20	*Lincoln C*	29	14	**29**	**14**
2019–20	Nottingham F	7	1	**40**	**5**
2020–21	Coventry C	31	7	**31**	**7**

WILLIAMS, Morgan (D) **1 0**
b. 30-8-99
From Mickleover Sports.

2018–19	Coventry C	1	0		
2019–20	Coventry C	0	0		
2020–21	Coventry C	0	0	**1**	**0**

WILSON, Ben (G) **55 0**
H: 6 1 W: 11 09 b.Stanley 9-8-92

2010–11	Sunderland	0	0		
2011–12	Sunderland	0	0		
2012–13	Sunderland	0	0		
2013–14	Accrington S	0	0		
2013–14	Cardiff C	0	0		
2014–15	Cardiff C	0	0		
2015–16	Cardiff C	0	0		
2015–16	*AFC Wimbledon*	8	0	**8**	**0**
2016–17	Cardiff C	3	0		
2016–17	*Rochdale*	8	0	**8**	**0**
2017–18	Cardiff C	0	0	**3**	**0**
2017–18	*Oldham Ath*	5	0	**5**	**0**
2018–19	Bradford C	4	0	**4**	**0**
2019–20	Coventry C	0	0		
2020–21	Coventry C	27	0	**27**	**0**

Scholars
Bell, Luke Stephen; Burroughs, George Gilbert; Costa, Alexander; Fallows, Keelan Brian; Forsyth, Kai Joseph William; Harland, Matthew; Hewitt, Craig; Lafferty, Daniel Paul; Massey, Reece Peter; Nee, Harrison; Nightingale, Joseph; O'Brien, Fionn Eamonn; Pitts-Eckersall, Samuel; Purves, Hayden James; Reeve, Malakai Sean Alexander; Rodber, Samuel Leslie; Rus, Marco-Alin; Taylor, Adam Simon.

CRAWLEY T (27)

ADEBOWALE, Emmanuel (D) **2 0**
b. 19-9-97
From Sheffield U, Hayes & Yeading U, Bishop's Stortford, Dover Ath, Eastbourne Bor.

2019–20	Crawley T	1	0		
2020–21	Crawley T	1	0	**2**	**0**

AL-HUSSAINI, Zaid (M) **0 0**
b.London --

2020–21	Crawley T	0	0		

ALLARAKHIA, Tarryn (M) **41 0**
b. 17-10-97
From Leyton Orient, Aveley, Maldon and Tiptree.

2017–18	Colchester U	0	0		
2018–19	Crawley T	5	0		
2019–20	Crawley T	19	0		
2020–21	Crawley T	17	0	**41**	**0**

ASHFORD, Sam (F)				**8**	**0**
b.Chelmsford 21-12-95					
From Maldon & Tiptree, Heybridge Swifts, Stansted, Witham T, Brightlingsea Regent, East Thurrock U, Concorde R, Hemel Hempstead T.					
2020–21	Crawley T	8	0	**8**	**0**

BULMAN, Dannie (M)				**552**	**25**
H: 5 9 W: 11 12 b.Ashford 24-1-79					
From Ashford T.					
1998–99	Wycombe W	11	1		
1999–2000	Wycombe W	29	1		
2000–01	Wycombe W	36	4		
2001–02	Wycombe W	46	5		
2002–03	Wycombe W	42	3		
2003–04	Wycombe W	38	0	**202**	**14**
From Stevenage, Crawley T.					
2010–11	Oxford U	5	0	**5**	**0**
2011–12	Crawley T	41	3		
2012–13	Crawley T	36	1		
2013–14	Crawley T	39	0		
2014–15	AFC Wimbledon	41	1		
2015–16	AFC Wimbledon	42	3		
2016–17	AFC Wimbledon	38	0	**121**	**4**
2017–18	Crawley T	37	0		
2018–19	Crawley T	36	3		
2019–20	Crawley T	29	0		
2020–21	Crawley T	6	0	**224**	**7**

BURNETT, Henry (M)				**0**	**0**
From Dagenham & R.					
2019–20	Southend U	0	0		
2020–21	Crawley T	0	0		

CRAIG, Tony (D)				**547**	**14**
H: 6 0 W: 10 03 b.Greenwich 20-4-85					
2002–03	Millwall	2	1		
2003–04	Millwall	9	0		
2004–05	Millwall	10	0		
2004–05	*Wycombe W*	14	0	**14**	**0**
2005–06	Millwall	28	0		
2006–07	Millwall	30	1		
2007–08	Crystal Palace	13	0	**13**	**0**
2007–08	*Millwall*	5	1		
2008–09	Millwall	44	2		
2009–10	Millwall	30	2		
2010–11	Millwall	24	0		
2011–12	Millwall	23	0		
2011–12	*Leyton Orient*	4	0	**4**	**0**
2012–13	Brentford	44	0		
2013–14	Brentford	44	0		
2014–15	Brentford	23	0	**111**	**0**
2015–16	Millwall	18	1		
2016–17	Millwall	43	1		
2017–18	Millwall	4	0	**270**	**9**
2017–18	Bristol R	17	1		
2018–19	Bristol R	46	2		
2019–20	Bristol R	34	2	**97**	**5**
2020–21	Crawley T	38	0	**38**	**0**

DALLISON, Tom (M)				**74**	**2**
H: 5 10 W: 14 01 b. 2-2-96					
2012–13	Arsenal	0	0		
2013–14	Brighton & HA	0	0		
2014–15	Brighton & HA	0	0		
2015–16	Brighton & HA	0	0		
2015–16	*Crawley T*	1	0		
2016–17	Brighton & HA	0	0		
2016–17	*Cambridge U*	5	0	**5**	**0**
2017–18	Brighton & HA	0	0		
2017–18	*Accrington S*	2	0	**2**	**0**
2018–19	Falkirk	12	0	**12**	**0**
2018–19	Crawley T	19	0		
2019–20	Crawley T	21	0		
2020–21	Crawley T	14	2	**55**	**2**

DAVIES, Archie (M)				**34**	**0**
b. 7-10-98					
2019–20	Brighton & HA	0	0		
2020–21	Brighton & HA	0	0		
2020–21	Crawley T	34	0	**34**	**0**

DOHERTY, Josh (M)				**85**	**0**
H: 5 10 W: 11 00 b.Newtownards 15-3-96					
Internationals: Northern Ireland U17, U19, U21.					
2013–14	Watford	1	0		
2014–15	Watford	0	0		
2015–16	Watford	0	0	**1**	**0**
From Leyton Orient, Ards.					
2017–18	Crawley T	15	0		
2018–19	Crawley T	18	0		
2019–20	Crawley T	31	0		
2020–21	Crawley T	15	0	**79**	**0**
2020–21	*Colchester U*	5	0	**5**	**0**

FRANCOMB, George (D)				**314**	**17**
H: 5 11 W: 11 07 b.Hackney 8-9-91					
2009–10	Norwich C	2	0		
2010–11	Norwich C	0	0		
2010–11	*Barnet*	13	0	**13**	**0**
2011–12	Norwich C	0	0		
2011–12	*Hibernian*	14	0	**14**	**0**
2012–13	Norwich C	0	0	**2**	**0**
2012–13	*AFC Wimbledon*	15	0		
2013–14	AFC Wimbledon	33	3		
2014–15	AFC Wimbledon	37	3		
2015–16	AFC Wimbledon	40	3		
2016–17	AFC Wimbledon	34	2		
2017–18	AFC Wimbledon	37	0	**196**	**11**
2018–19	Crawley T	41	0		
2019–20	Crawley T	15	0		
2020–21	Crawley T	33	6	**89**	**6**

FROST, Tyler (M)				**23**	**2**
b. 7-7-99					
2017–18	Reading	0	0		
2018–19	Reading	0	0		
2019–20	Reading	0	0		
2020–21	Crawley T	23	2	**23**	**2**

GALACH, Brian (F)				**1**	**0**
H: 5 9 W: 10 03 b.Waltham Forest 16-5-01					
From Leyton Orient, Aldershot T.					
2018–19	Crawley T	1	0		
2019–20	Crawley T	0	0		
2020–21	Crawley T	0	0	**1**	**0**
Transferred to Wisla Plock February 2021.					

GERMAN, Ricky (F)				**25**	**1**
H: 6 2 W: 12 08 b.Brent 13-1-99					
2016–17	Chesterfield	7	0		
2017–18	Chesterfield	2	0	**9**	**0**
2018–19	Crawley T	4	0		
2019–20	Crawley T	8	1		
2020–21	Crawley T	4	0	**16**	**1**

HESSENTHALER, Jake (M)				**277**	**9**
b.Gravesend 20-4-94					
2012–13	Gillingham	0	0		
2013–14	Gillingham	19	1		
2014–15	Gillingham	37	1		
2015–16	Gillingham	38	4		
2016–17	Gillingham	28	1		
2017–18	Gillingham	37	0	**159**	**7**
2018–19	Grimsby T	44	0		
2019–20	Grimsby T	28	1	**72**	**1**
2020–21	Crawley T	46	1	**46**	**1**

HUSSEIN, Mustafa (F)				**0**	**0**
b. 8-6-99					
From Tampere U.					
2020–21	Crawley T	0	0		

JONES, Alfie (G)				**0**	**0**
2017–18	Milton Keynes D	0	0		
2018–19	Crawley T	0	0		
2019–20	Crawley T	0	0		
2020–21	Crawley T	0	0		

KHALEEL, Rafiq (M)				**0**	**0**
b.Camden 24-2-03					
2020–21	Crawley T	0	0		

KOWALCZYK, Szymon (M)				**0**	**0**
b. 20-8-03					
2020–21	Crawley T	0	0		

MATTHEWS, Sam (M)				**46**	**1**
b. 1-3-97					
2013–14	Bournemouth	0	0		
2014–15	Bournemouth	0	0		
2015–16	Bournemouth	0	0		
2016–17	Bournemouth	0	0		
2017–18	Bournemouth	0	0		
From Braintree T, Eastleigh.					
2018–19	Bristol R	16	0		
2019–20	Bristol R	0	0	**16**	**0**
2020–21	Crawley T	30	1	**30**	**1**

McNERNEY, Joe (D)				**122**	**7**
H: 6 4 W: 13 03 b. 24-1-89					
From Woking.					
2015–16	Crawley T	11	1		
2016–17	Crawley T	34	3		
2017–18	Crawley T	16	1		
2018–19	Crawley T	29	1		
2019–20	Crawley T	6	0		
2020–21	Crawley T	26	1	**122**	**7**

MORRIS, Glenn (G)				**404**	**0**
H: 6 0 W: 12 03 b.Woolwich 20-12-83					
2001–02	Leyton Orient	2	0		
2002–03	Leyton Orient	23	0		
2003–04	Leyton Orient	27	0		
2004–05	Leyton Orient	12	0		
2005–06	Leyton Orient	4	0		
2006–07	Leyton Orient	3	0		
2007–08	Leyton Orient	16	0		
2008–09	Leyton Orient	26	0		
2009–10	Leyton Orient	11	0	**124**	**0**
2010–11	Southend U	33	0		
2011–12	Southend U	24	0		
2012–13	Southend U	0	0	**57**	**0**
2012–13	Aldershot T	2	0	**2**	**0**
From Woking, Eastleigh.					
2014–15	Gillingham	10	0		
2015–16	Gillingham	0	0	**10**	**0**
2016–17	Crawley T	39	0		
2017–18	Crawley T	44	0		
2018–19	Crawley T	46	0		
2019–20	Crawley T	37	0		
2020–21	Crawley T	45	0	**211**	**0**

NADESAN, Ashley (F)				**126**	**23**
H: 6 2 W: 11 11 b. 9-9-94					
2015–16	Fleetwood T	0	0		
2016–17	Fleetwood T	0	0		
2017–18	Fleetwood T	1	0		
2017–18	*Carlisle U*	15	4		
2018–19	Fleetwood T	20	1	**21**	**1**
2018–19	*Carlisle U*	25	8	**40**	**12**
2019–20	Crawley T	25	5		
2020–21	Crawley T	40	5	**65**	**10**

NELSON, Stuart (G)				**441**	**0**
H: 6 1 W: 12 12 b.Stroud 17-9-81					
From Doncaster R, Hucknall T.					
2003–04	Brentford	9	0		
2004–05	Brentford	43	0		
2005–06	Brentford	45	0		
2006–07	Brentford	19	0	**116**	**0**
2007–08	Leyton Orient	30	0	**30**	**0**
2008–09	Norwich C	0	0		
2009–10	Aberdeen	3	0	**3**	**0**
2010–11	Notts Co	33	0		
2011–12	Notts Co	46	0	**79**	**0**
2012–13	Gillingham	45	0		
2013–14	Gillingham	46	0		
2014–15	Gillingham	24	0		
2015–16	Gillingham	46	0		
2016–17	Gillingham	34	0		
2017–18	Gillingham	0	0	**195**	**0**
2017–18	Yeovil T	5	0		
2018–19	Yeovil T	12	0	**17**	**0**
2020–21	Crawley T	1	0	**1**	**0**

NICHOLS, Tom (F)				**290**	**58**
H: 5 10 W: 10 10 b.Wellington 1-9-93					
2010–11	Exeter C	1	0		
2011–12	Exeter C	7	1		
2012–13	Exeter C	3	0		
2013–14	Exeter C	28	6		
2014–15	Exeter C	36	15		
2015–16	Exeter C	23	10	**98**	**32**
2015–16	Peterborough U	7	1		
2016–17	Peterborough U	43	10	**50**	**11**
2017–18	Bristol R	39	1		
2018–19	Bristol R	36	1		
2019–20	Bristol R	19	2	**94**	**4**
2019–20	*Cheltenham T*	5	0	**5**	**0**
2020–21	Crawley T	43	11	**43**	**11**

POWELL, Jack (M)				**56**	**3**
b. 29-1-94					
Internationals: England C.					
2013–14	Millwall	0	0		
2014–15	Millwall	5	0		
2015–16	Millwall	1	0	**6**	**0**
From Ebbsfleet U, Maidstone U.					
2019–20	Crawley T	6	0		
2020–21	Crawley T	44	3	**50**	**3**

RODARI, Davide (F)				**12**	**1**
b. 23-6-99					
2020–21	Crawley T	12	1	**12**	**1**

SESAY, David (D)				**56**	**0**
b. 18-9-98					
From Watford.					
2018–19	Crawley T	18	0		
2019–20	Crawley T	25	0		
2020–21	Crawley T	13	0	**56**	**0**

TILLEY, James (F)				**62**	**5**
H: 5 6 W: 9 04 b.Billingshurt 13-6-98					
2014–15	Brighton & HA	1	0		
2015–16	Brighton & HA	0	0		
2016–17	Brighton & HA	0	0		
2017–18	Brighton & HA	0	0		
2018–19	Brighton & HA	0	0		
2019	*Cork C*	19	0	**19**	**0**
2019–20	Brighton & HA	0	0	**1**	**0**
2019–20	Grimsby T	10	0		
2020–21	Grimsby T	14	2	**24**	**2**
2020–21	Crawley T	18	3	**18**	**3**

TSAROULLA, Nicholas (D)				**17**	**0**
b.Bristol 29-3-99					
2020–21	Crawley T	17	0	**17**	**0**

TUNNICLIFFE, Jordan (D)				**76**	**4**
b.Nuneaton 13-10-93					
From WBA.					
2013–14	Barnsley	0	0		
2014–15	Barnsley	0	0		
2014–15	Kidderminster H	0	0		
From Kidderminster H, AFC Fylde.					
2019–20	Crawley T	37	1		
2020–21	Crawley T	39	3	**76**	**4**

WRIGHT, Josh (M) **386 28**
H: 6 1 W: 11 07 b.Bethnal Green 6-11-89
Internationals: England U16, U17, U18, U19.

2007–08	Charlton Ath	0	0		
2007–08	*Barnet*	32	1	**32**	**1**
2008–09	Charlton Ath	2	0	**2**	**0**
2008–09	*Brentford*	5	0	**5**	**0**
2008–09	*Gillingham*	5	0		
2009–10	Scunthorpe U	35	0		
2010–11	Scunthorpe U	36	0	**71**	**0**
2011–12	Millwall	18	1		
2012–13	Millwall	24	0		
2013–14	Millwall	3	0		
2013–14	*Leyton Orient*	2	0		
2014–15	Millwall	1	0	**46**	**1**
2014–15	*Crawley T*	4	0		
2014–15	Leyton Orient	29	2		
2015–16	Gillingham	41	1		
2016–17	Gillingham	41	13		
2017–18	Gillingham	3	0	**90**	**14**
2017–18	Southend U	23	1	**23**	**1**
2018–19	Bradford C	18	0	**18**	**0**
2019–20	Leyton Orient	35	8		
2020–21	Leyton Orient	9	1	**75**	**11**
2020–21	Crawley T	20	0	**24**	**0**

WRIGHT, Mark (D) **1 0**
b.Essex 29-1-87

2020–21	Crawley T	1	0	**1**	**0**

CREWE ALEX (28)

ADEBISI, Rio (D) **17 0**
b.Croydon 27-9-00

2019–20	Crewe Alex	2	0		
2020–21	Crewe Alex	15	0	**17**	**0**

AINLEY, Callum (M) **178 15**
H: 5 8 W: 10 01 b.Middlewich 2-11-97

2015–16	Crewe Alex	16	1		
2016–17	Crewe Alex	27	1		
2017–18	Crewe Alex	45	4		
2018–19	Crewe Alex	43	6		
2019–20	Crewe Alex	25	2		
2020–21	Crewe Alex	22	1	**178**	**15**

BECKLES, Omar (D) **181 11**
H: 6 2 W: 12 04 b.Kettering 25-10-91
Internationals: Grenada Full caps.
From Jerez Industrial, Boreham Wood, Kettering T, Billericay T, Histon, St Albans C, Aldershot T.

2016–17	Accrington S	41	2		
2017–18	Accrington S	2	1	**43**	**3**
2017–18	Shrewsbury T	33	3		
2018–19	Shrewsbury T	36	1		
2019–20	Shrewsbury T	28	3	**97**	**7**
2020–21	Crewe Alex	41	1	**41**	**1**

BOOTH, Sam (G) **0 0**
b. 6-12-00

2019–20	Crewe Alex	0	0		
2020–21	Crewe Alex	0	0		

DALE, Owen (F) **90 12**
H: 5 9 W: 10 03 b.Warrington 1-11-98

2016–17	Crewe Alex	0	0		
2017–18	Crewe Alex	4	0		
2018–19	Crewe Alex	16	1		
2019–20	Crewe Alex	27	0		
2020–21	Crewe Alex	43	11	**90**	**12**

DANIELS, Donervon (D) **155 7**
H: 6 1 W: 14 05 b.Montserrat 24-11-93
Internationals: England U20.

2011–12	WBA	0	0		
2012–13	WBA	0	0		
2012–13	*Tranmere R*	13	1	**13**	**1**
2013–14	WBA	0	0		
2013–14	*Gillingham*	3	1	**3**	**1**
2014–15	WBA	0	0		
2014–15	*Blackpool*	19	1		
2014–15	*Aberdeen*	9	0	**9**	**0**
2015–16	Wigan Ath	42	3		
2016–17	Wigan Ath	1	0		
2017–18	Wigan Ath	1	0	**44**	**3**
2017–18	*Rochdale*	15	0	**15**	**0**
2018–19	Blackpool	24	0	**43**	**1**
2019–20	Luton T	3	1	**3**	**1**
2019–20	*Doncaster R*	10	0	**10**	**0**
2020–21	Crewe Alex	15	0	**15**	**0**

EVANS, Antony (M) **46 2**
b.Fazakerley 23-9-98

2016–17	Everton	0	0		
2016–17	*Morecambe*	14	2	**14**	**2**
2017–18	Everton	0	0		
2018–19	Everton	0	0		
2018–19	*Blackpool*	12	0	**12**	**0**
2019–20	Paderborn	6	0		
2020–21	Paderborn	0	0	**6**	**0**

On loan from Paderborn.

2020–21	Crewe Alex	14	0	**14**	**0**

FINNEY, Oliver (M) **63 12**
b.Stoke-on-Trent 15-12-97

2015–16	Crewe Alex	0	0		
2016–17	Crewe Alex	1	0		
2017–18	Crewe Alex	1	0		
2018–19	Crewe Alex	17	0		
2019–20	Crewe Alex	18	5		
2020–21	Crewe Alex	26	7	**63**	**12**

GRIFFITHS, Regan (M) **2 0**
b. 1-5-00

2019–20	Crewe Alex	0	0		
2020–21	Crewe Alex	2	0	**2**	**0**

JAASKELAINEN, William (G) **70 0**
b. 25-7-98
Internationals: Finland U19.

2015–16	Bolton W	0	0		
2016–17	Bolton W	0	0		
2017–18	Bolton W	0	0		
2017–18	Crewe Alex	0	0		
2018–19	Crewe Alex	4	0		
2019–20	Crewe Alex	35	0		
2020–21	Crewe Alex	31	0	**70**	**0**

JOHNSON, Travis (D) **8 0**
b. 28-8-00

2018–19	Crewe Alex	0	0		
2019–20	Crewe Alex	1	0		
2020–21	Crewe Alex	7	0	**8**	**0**

KIRK, Charlie (M) **181 29**
H: 5 7 W: 11 00 b.Winsford 24-12-97

2015–16	Crewe Alex	14	0		
2016–17	Crewe Alex	22	0		
2017–18	Crewe Alex	25	5		
2018–19	Crewe Alex	42	11		
2019–20	Crewe Alex	36	7		
2020–21	Crewe Alex	42	6	**181**	**29**

LANCASHIRE, Oliver (D) **294 7**
H: 6 1 W: 11 10 b.Basingstoke 13-12-88

2006–07	Southampton	0	0		
2007–08	Southampton	0	0		
2008–09	Southampton	11	0		
2009–10	Southampton	2	0	**13**	**0**
2009–10	*Grimsby T*	25	1	**25**	**1**
2010–11	Walsall	29	0		
2011–12	Walsall	20	1	**49**	**1**
2012–13	Aldershot T	12	0	**12**	**0**
2013–14	Rochdale	38	0		
2014–15	Rochdale	21	0		
2015–16	Rochdale	34	2	**93**	**2**
2016–17	Shrewsbury T	16	1	**16**	**1**
2017–18	Swindon T	35	1		
2018–19	Swindon T	20	0	**55**	**1**
2019–20	Crewe Alex	9	0		
2020–21	Crewe Alex	22	1	**31**	**1**

LOWERY, Tom (M) **119 9**
b.Holmes Chapel 31-12-97

2016–17	Crewe Alex	7	0		
2017–18	Crewe Alex	31	0		
2018–19	Crewe Alex	15	1		
2019–20	Crewe Alex	29	5		
2020–21	Crewe Alex	37	3	**119**	**9**

LUNDSTRAM, Josh (M) **4 0**
b. 19-9-99

2017–18	Crewe Alex	0	0		
2018–19	Crewe Alex	0	0		
2019–20	Crewe Alex	0	0		
2020–21	Crewe Alex	4	0	**4**	**0**

MANDRON, Mikael (F) **175 29**
H: 6 3 W: 12 13 b.Boulogne 11-10-94
Internationals: Scotland U20.

2011–12	Sunderland	0	0		
2012–13	Sunderland	2	0		
2013–14	Sunderland	0	0		
2013–14	*Fleetwood T*	11	1	**11**	**1**
2014–15	Sunderland	1	0		
2014–15	*Shrewsbury T*	3	0	**3**	**0**
2015–16	Sunderland	0	0	**3**	**0**
2015–16	*Hartlepool U*	5	0	**5**	**0**
2016–17	Wigan Ath	3	0	**3**	**0**
2017–18	Colchester U	44	10		
2018–19	Colchester U	41	2	**85**	**12**
2019–20	Gillingham	23	5	**23**	**5**
2020–21	Crewe Alex	42	11	**42**	**11**

MURPHY, Luke (M) **401 32**
H: 6 1 W: 11 05 b.Alsager 21-10-89

2008–09	Crewe Alex	9	1		
2009–10	Crewe Alex	32	3		
2010–11	Crewe Alex	39	3		
2011–12	Crewe Alex	42	8		
2012–13	Crewe Alex	39	6		
2013–14	Leeds U	37	3		
2014–15	Leeds U	30	3		
2015–16	Leeds U	36	1		
2016–17	Leeds U	0	0		
2016–17	*Burton Alb*	19	1		
2017–18	Leeds U	0	0		
2017–18	*Burton Alb*	38	1	**57**	**2**
2018–19	Leeds U	0	0	**103**	**7**
2018–19	Bolton W	11	0		
2019–20	Bolton W	29	2	**40**	**2**
2020–21	Crewe Alex	40	0	**201**	**21**

NOLAN, Eddie (D) **303 7**
H: 6 0 W: 13 05 b.Waterford 5-8-88
Internationals: Republic of Ireland U21, B, Full caps.

2005–06	Blackburn R	0	0		
2006–07	Blackburn R	0	0		
2006–07	*Stockport Co*	4	0	**4**	**0**
2007–08	Blackburn R	0	0		
2007–08	*Hartlepool U*	11	0	**11**	**0**
2008–09	Blackburn R	0	0		
2008–09	Preston NE	21	0		
2009–10	Preston NE	19	0		
2009–10	*Sheffield W*	14	1	**14**	**1**
2010–11	Preston NE	0	0	**40**	**0**
2010–11	Scunthorpe U	35	0		
2011–12	Scunthorpe U	30	1		
2012–13	Scunthorpe U	12	0		
2013–14	Scunthorpe U	39	0		
2014–15	Scunthorpe U	6	0	**122**	**1**
2015–16	York C	15	1	**15**	**1**
2016–17	Blackpool	3	0	**3**	**0**
2017–18	Crewe Alex	42	0		
2018–19	Crewe Alex	33	1		
2019–20	Crewe Alex	19	3		
2020–21	Crewe Alex	0	0	**94**	**4**
2020–21	*Motherwell*	0	0		

OFFORD, Luke (M) **37 1**
b.Chichester 19-11-99

2017–18	Crewe Alex	0	0		
2018–19	Crewe Alex	0	0		
2019–20	Crewe Alex	9	0		
2020–21	Crewe Alex	28	1	**37**	**1**

ONYEKA, Tyreece (F) **0 0**
b. 1-2-01

2020–21	Crewe Alex	0	0		

PORTER, Chris (F) **559 164**
H: 6 1 W: 12 09 b.Wigan 12-12-83

2002–03	Bury	2	0		
2003–04	Bury	37	9		
2004–05	Bury	32	9	**71**	**18**
2005–06	Oldham Ath	31	7		
2006–07	Oldham Ath	35	21	**66**	**28**
2007–08	Motherwell	37	14		
2008–09	Motherwell	22	9	**59**	**23**
2008–09	Derby Co	5	3		
2009–10	Derby Co	21	4		
2010–11	Derby Co	18	2	**44**	**9**
2011–12	Sheffield U	34	5		
2012–13	Sheffield U	21	3		
2012–13	*Shrewsbury T*	5	1	**5**	**1**
2013–14	Sheffield U	32	7		
2013–14	*Chesterfield*	3	0	**3**	**0**
2014–15	Sheffield U	1	0	**88**	**15**
2014–15	Colchester U	21	7		
2015–16	Colchester U	32	7		
2016–17	Colchester U	38	16	**91**	**30**
2017–18	Crewe Alex	31	9		
2018–19	Crewe Alex	40	13		
2019–20	Crewe Alex	26	12		
2020–21	Crewe Alex	35	6	**132**	**40**

POWELL, Daniel (F) **349 55**
H: 5 11 W: 13 03 b.Luton 12-3-91

2008–09	Milton Keynes D	7	1		
2009–10	Milton Keynes D	2	1		
2010–11	Milton Keynes D	29	9		
2011–12	Milton Keynes D	43	6		
2012–13	Milton Keynes D	34	7		
2013–14	Milton Keynes D	32	1		
2014–15	Milton Keynes D	42	8		
2015–16	Milton Keynes D	22	2		
2016–17	Milton Keynes D	20	2	**231**	**37**
2017–18	Northampton T	29	2		
2018–19	Northampton T	35	6	**64**	**8**
2019–20	Crewe Alex	30	9		
2020–21	Crewe Alex	24	1	**54**	**10**

RICHARDS, Dave (G) **32 0**
H: 5 11 W: 11 11 b.Abergavenny 31-12-93

2013–14	Cardiff C	0	0		
2013–14	Bristol C	0	0		
2014–15	Bristol C	0	0		
2015–16	Crewe Alex	0	0		
2016–17	Crewe Alex	0	0		
2017–18	Crewe Alex	11	0		
2018–19	Crewe Alex	4	0		
2019–20	Crewe Alex	2	0		
2020–21	Crewe Alex	15	0	**32**	**0**

ROBBINS, Joe (M) 0 0
b. 20-2-02
2020–21 Crewe Alex 0 0

SASS-DAVIES, Billy (D) 2 0
b.Manchester 17-2-00
Internationals: Wales U19.
2017–18 Crewe Alex 0 0
2018–19 Crewe Alex 2 0
2019–20 Crewe Alex 0 0
2020–21 Crewe Alex 0 0 **2 0**

WILLIAMS, Zac (D) 0 0
b. 27-3-04
2020–21 Crewe Alex 0 0

WINTLE, Ryan (M) 164 9
H: 5 5 W: 10 01 b.Newcastle-under-Lyme 13-6-97
2015–16 Crewe Alex 3 0
2016–17 Crewe Alex 17 1
2017–18 Crewe Alex 18 2
2018–19 Crewe Alex 46 1
2019–20 Crewe Alex 37 3
2020–21 Crewe Alex 43 2 **164 9**

WOODTHORPE, Nathan (D) 0 0
b. 6-12-01
2020–21 Crewe Alex 0 0

Scholars
Akpo, Jerry Le Grand; Bebbington, Harrison Thomas; Billington, Lewis Carl; Booth, Thomas Luke; Finney, Charlie Joe; Green, Fenton Lloyd; Higgins, Alex Kieran; Kennington, Liam Dean Kevin; Lawton, Sean Paul; Levey, Joseph Paul Michael; Marrow, Jack Robert David; Marsden, Bailey; McDonald, Matthew David; O'Riordan, Connor Patrick; Salisbury, Connor Paul; Stubbs, Kyle; Tabiner, Joel William; Williams, Michael Isaac; Wood, Ben Christopher.

CRYSTAL PALACE (29)

ADARAMOLA, Omotayo (D) 0 0
b. 14-11-03
2020–21 Crystal Palace 0 0

AKROBAR-BOATENG, David (D) 0 0
H: 5 9 b. 8-5-01
2020–21 Crystal Palace 0 0

AYEW, Jordan (F) 350 59
H: 6 0 W: 12 11 b.Marseille 11-9-91
Internationals: Ghana U20, Full caps.
2009–10 Marseille 4 1
2010–11 Marseille 22 2
2011–12 Marseille 34 3
2012–13 Marseille 35 7
2013–14 Marseille 16 1 **111 14**
2013–14 *Sochaux* 17 5 **17 5**
2014–15 Lorient 31 12 **31 12**
2015–16 Aston Villa 30 7
2016–17 Aston Villa 21 2 **51 9**
2016–17 Swansea C 14 1
2017–18 Swansea C 36 7
2018–19 Swansea C 0 0 **50 8**
2018–19 *Crystal Palace* 20 1
2019–20 Crystal Palace 37 9
2020–21 Crystal Palace 33 1 **90 11**

BANKS, Scott (M) 29 1
2018–19 Dundee U 0 0
2018–19 *Clyde* 12 1 **12 1**
2019–20 Dundee U 2 0 **2 0**
2019–20 Crystal Palace 0 0
2019–20 *Alloa Ath* 4 0 **4 0**
2020–21 Crystal Palace 0 0
2020–21 *Dunfermline Ath* 11 0 **11 0**

BENTEKE, Christian (F) 372 125
H: 6 3 W: 13 00 b.Kinshasa 3-12-90
Internationals: Belgium U17, U18, U19, U21, Full caps.
2007–08 Genk 7 1
2008–09 Genk 3 0
2008–09 Standard Liege 9 3
2009–10 *KV Kortrijk* 34 14 **34 14**
2010–11 Standard Liege 5 0
2010–11 *KV Mechelen* 18 6 **18 6**
2011–12 Standard Liege 4 0 **18 3**
2011–12 Genk 32 16
2012–13 Genk 5 3 **47 20**
2012–13 Aston Villa 34 19
2013–14 Aston Villa 26 10
2014–15 Aston Villa 29 13 **89 42**
2015–16 Liverpool 29 9 **29 9**
2016–17 Crystal Palace 36 15
2017–18 Crystal Palace 31 3
2018–19 Crystal Palace 16 1
2019–20 Crystal Palace 24 2
2020–21 Crystal Palace 30 10 **137 31**

BOATENG, Malachi (M) 0 0
H: 6 0 b. 5-7-02
2020–21 Crystal Palace 0 0

BUTLAND, Jack (G) 263 0
H: 6 4 W: 12 00 b.Clevedon 10-3-93
Internationals: England U16, U17, U19, U20, U21, Full caps.
2009–10 Birmingham C 0 0
2010–11 Birmingham C 0 0
2011–12 Birmingham C 0 0
2011–12 *Cheltenham T* 24 0 **24 0**
2012–13 Birmingham C 46 0 **46 0**
2012–13 Stoke C 0 0
2013–14 Stoke C 3 0
2013–14 *Barnsley* 13 0 **13 0**
2013–14 *Leeds U* 16 0 **16 0**
2014–15 Stoke C 3 0
2014–15 *Derby Co* 6 0 **6 0**
2015–16 Stoke C 31 0
2016–17 Stoke C 5 0
2017–18 Stoke C 35 0
2018–19 Stoke C 45 0
2019–20 Stoke C 35 0
2020–21 Stoke C 0 0 **157 0**
2020–21 Crystal Palace 1 0 **1 0**

CAHILL, Gary (D) 437 31
H: 6 2 W: 12 06 b.Dronfield 19-12-85
Internationals: England U20, U21, Full caps.
2003–04 Aston Villa 0 0
2004–05 Aston Villa 0 0
2004–05 *Burnley* 27 1 **27 1**
2005–06 Aston Villa 7 1
2006–07 Aston Villa 20 0
2007–08 Aston Villa 1 0 **28 1**
2007–08 *Sheffield U* 16 2 **16 2**
2007–08 Bolton W 13 0
2008–09 Bolton W 33 3
2009–10 Bolton W 29 5
2010–11 Bolton W 36 3
2011–12 Bolton W 19 2 **130 13**
2011–12 Chelsea 10 1
2012–13 Chelsea 26 2
2013–14 Chelsea 30 1
2014–15 Chelsea 36 1
2015–16 Chelsea 23 2
2016–17 Chelsea 37 6
2017–18 Chelsea 27 0
2018–19 Chelsea 2 0
2019–20 Chelsea 0 0 **191 13**
2019–20 Crystal Palace 25 0
2020–21 Crystal Palace 20 1 **45 1**

CLYNE, Nathaniel (D) 320 5
H: 5 9 W: 10 07 b.Stockwell 5-4-91
Internationals: England U19, U21, Full caps.
2008–09 Crystal Palace 26 0
2009–10 Crystal Palace 22 1
2010–11 Crystal Palace 46 0
2011–12 Crystal Palace 28 0
2012–13 Southampton 34 1
2013–14 Southampton 25 0
2014–15 Southampton 35 2 **94 3**
2015–16 Liverpool 33 1
2016–17 Liverpool 37 0
2017–18 Liverpool 3 0
2018–19 Liverpool 4 0
2018–19 *Bournemouth* 14 0 **14 0**
2019–20 Liverpool 0 0 **77 1**
2020–21 Crystal Palace 13 0 **135 1**

DANN, Scott (D) 418 30
H: 6 2 W: 12 00 b.Liverpool 14-2-87
Internationals: England U21.
2004–05 Walsall 1 0
2005–06 Walsall 0 0
2006–07 Walsall 30 4
2007–08 Walsall 28 3 **59 7**
2007–08 Coventry C 16 0
2008–09 Coventry C 31 3 **47 3**
2009–10 Birmingham C 30 0
2010–11 Birmingham C 20 2
2011–12 Birmingham C 0 0 **50 2**
2011–12 Blackburn R 27 1
2012–13 Blackburn R 46 4
2013–14 Blackburn R 25 0 **98 5**
2013–14 Crystal Palace 14 1
2014–15 Crystal Palace 34 2
2015–16 Crystal Palace 35 5
2016–17 Crystal Palace 23 3
2017–18 Crystal Palace 17 1
2018–19 Crystal Palace 10 0
2019–20 Crystal Palace 16 0
2020–21 Crystal Palace 15 1 **164 13**

EZE, Eberechi (M) 158 29
H: 5 8 W: 10 08 b. 29-6-98
Internationals: England U20, U21.
From Millwall.
2016–17 QPR 0 0
2017–18 *Wycombe W* 20 5 **20 5**
2017–18 QPR 16 2
2018–19 QPR 42 4
2019–20 QPR 46 14 **104 20**
2020–21 Crystal Palace 34 4 **34 4**

GIDDINGS, Jake (M) 0 0
b.London 7-11-01
From West Ham U.
2020–21 Crystal Palace 0 0

GUAITA, Vicente (G) 306 0
H: 6 3 W: 12 08 b.Valencia 18-2-87
2006–07 Valencia 0 0
2007–08 Valencia 0 0
2008–09 Valencia 2 0
2009–10 Valencia 0 0
2009–10 *Recreativo* 30 0 **30 0**
2010–11 Valencia 21 0
2011–12 Valencia 26 0
2012–13 Valencia 14 0
2013–14 Valencia 13 0 **76 0**
2014–15 Getafe 29 0
2015–16 Getafe 38 0
2016–17 Getafe 8 0
2017–18 Getafe 33 0 **108 0**
2018–19 Crystal Palace 20 0
2019–20 Crystal Palace 35 0
2020–21 Crystal Palace 37 0 **92 0**

HANNAM, Reece (D) 0 0
From West Ham U.
2020–21 Crystal Palace 0 0

HENDERSON, Stephen (G) 166 0
H: 6 3 W: 11 00 b.Dublin 2-5-88
Internationals: Republic of Ireland U16, U17, U19, U21.
2005–06 Aston Villa 0 0
2006–07 Aston Villa 0 0
2007–08 Bristol C 1 0
2008–09 Bristol C 1 0
2009–10 Bristol C 3 0
2009–10 *Aldershot T* 8 0 **8 0**
2010–11 Bristol C 0 0 **5 0**
2010–11 *Yeovil T* 33 0 **33 0**
2011–12 Portsmouth 25 0
2011–12 *West Ham U* 0 0
2012–13 West Ham U 0 0
2012–13 *Ipswich T* 24 0 **24 0**
2013–14 West Ham U 0 0
2013–14 *Bournemouth* 2 0 **2 0**
2014–15 Charlton Ath 31 0
2015–16 Charlton Ath 22 0 **53 0**
2016–17 Nottingham F 12 0
2017–18 Nottingham F 0 0
2017–18 *Portsmouth* 1 0 **26 0**
2018–19 Nottingham F 0 0 **12 0**
2018–19 *Wycombe W* 3 0 **3 0**
2019–20 Crystal Palace 0 0
2020–21 Crystal Palace 0 0

HENNESSEY, Wayne (G) 289 0
H: 6 0 W: 11 06 b.Anglesey 24-1-87
Internationals: Wales U17, U19, U21, Full caps.
2004–05 Wolverhampton W 0 0
2005–06 Wolverhampton W 0 0
2006–07 Wolverhampton W 0 0
2006–07 *Bristol C* 0 0
2006–07 *Stockport Co* 15 0 **15 0**
2007–08 Wolverhampton W 46 0
2008–09 Wolverhampton W 35 0
2009–10 Wolverhampton W 13 0
2010–11 Wolverhampton W 24 0
2011–12 Wolverhampton W 34 0
2012–13 Wolverhampton W 0 0
2013–14 Wolverhampton W 0 0 **152 0**
2013–14 *Yeovil T* 12 0 **12 0**
2013–14 Crystal Palace 1 0
2014–15 Crystal Palace 3 0
2015–16 Crystal Palace 29 0
2016–17 Crystal Palace 29 0
2017–18 Crystal Palace 27 0
2018–19 Crystal Palace 18 0
2019–20 Crystal Palace 3 0
2020–21 Crystal Palace 0 0 **110 0**

IMRAY, Daniel (D) 0 0
H: 5 10 b.Harold Wood 27-7-03
From Chelmsford.
2020–21 Crystal Palace 0 0

JACH, Jaroslaw (D) 112 4
H: 6 3 W: 12 11 b.Bielawa 17-2-94
Internationals: Poland U21, Full caps.
2013–14 Zagkebie Lubin 2 0
2014–15 Zagkebie Lubin 13 0

2015–16 Zagkebie Lubin 13 2
2016–17 Zagkebie Lubin 23 1 **51 3**
2017–18 Zaglebie Lubin 17 1 **17 1**
2017–18 Crystal Palace 0 0
2018–19 Crystal Palace 0 0
2018–19 *Caykur Rizesport* 5 0 **5 0**
2018–19 *Sheriff Tiraspol* 14 0 **14 0**
2019–20 Crystal Palace 0 0
2019–20 *Rakow Czestochowa* 12 0
2020–21 Crystal Palace 0 0
2020–21 *Fortuna Sittard* 3 0 **3 0**
2020–21 *Rakow Czestochowa* 10 0 **22 0**

KELLY, Martin (D) 161 1
H: 6 3 W: 12 02 b.Bolton 27-4-90
Internationals: England U19, U20, U21, Full caps.
2007–08 Liverpool 0 0
2008–09 Liverpool 0 0
2008–09 *Huddersfield T* 7 1 **7 1**
2009–10 Liverpool 1 0
2010–11 Liverpool 11 0
2011–12 Liverpool 12 0
2012–13 Liverpool 4 0
2013–14 Liverpool 5 0 **33 0**
2014–15 Crystal Palace 31 0
2015–16 Crystal Palace 13 0
2016–17 Crystal Palace 29 0
2017–18 Crystal Palace 15 0
2018–19 Crystal Palace 13 0
2019–20 Crystal Palace 19 0
2020–21 Crystal Palace 1 0 **121 0**

KIRBY, Nya (M) 17 1
H: 5 9 W: 10 06 b.Islington 31-1-00
Internationals: England U16, U17, U18, U19.
From Tottenham H.
2017–18 Crystal Palace 0 0
2018–19 Crystal Palace 0 0
2018–19 *Blackpool* 11 1 **11 1**
2019–20 Crystal Palace 0 0
2020–21 Crystal Palace 0 0
2020–21 *Tranmere R* 6 0 **6 0**

KOUYATE, Cheikhou (M) 420 21
H: 6 3 W: 11 11 b.Dakar 21-12-89
Internationals: Senegal U20, Full caps.
2007–08 Brussels 10 0 **10 0**
2008–09 Anderlecht 0 0
2008–09 *Kortrijk* 26 3 **26 3**
2009–10 Anderlecht 21 1
2010–11 Anderlecht 23 1
2011–12 Anderlecht 38 0
2012–13 Anderlecht 33 1
2013–14 Anderlecht 38 1 **153 4**
2014–15 West Ham U 31 4
2015–16 West Ham U 34 5
2016–17 West Ham U 31 1
2017–18 West Ham U 33 2 **129 12**
2018–19 Crystal Palace 31 0
2019–20 Crystal Palace 35 1
2020–21 Crystal Palace 36 1 **102 2**

MATETA, Jean-Philippe (F) 139 57
b. 28-6-97
2015–16 Chateauroux 22 11
2016–17 Chateauroux 4 2 **26 13**
2016–17 Lyon 2 0
2017–18 Lyon 0 0 **2 0**
2017–18 *Le Havre* 37 19 **37 19**
2018–19 Mainz 05 34 14
2019–20 Mainz 05 18 3
2020–21 Mainz 05 15 7 **67 24**
On loan from Mainz 05.
2020–21 Crystal Palace 7 1 **7 1**

McARTHUR, James (M) 512 37
H: 5 6 W: 9 13 b.Glasgow 7-10-87
Internationals: Scotland U21, Full caps.
2004–05 Hamilton A 6 0
2005–06 Hamilton A 20 1
2006–07 Hamilton A 36 1
2007–08 Hamilton A 34 4
2008–09 Hamilton A 37 2
2009–10 Hamilton A 35 1 **168 9**
2010–11 Wigan Ath 18 0
2011–12 Wigan Ath 31 3
2012–13 Wigan Ath 34 3
2013–14 Wigan Ath 41 4
2014–15 Wigan Ath 5 1 **129 11**
2014–15 Crystal Palace 32 2
2015–16 Crystal Palace 28 2
2016–17 Crystal Palace 29 5
2017–18 Crystal Palace 33 5
2018–19 Crystal Palace 38 3
2019–20 Crystal Palace 37 0
2020–21 Crystal Palace 18 0 **215 17**

McCARTHY, James (M) 372 27
H: 5 11 W: 11 05 b.Glasgow 12-11-90
Internationals: Republic of Ireland U17, U18, U19, U21, Full caps.
2006–07 Hamilton A 23 1
2007–08 Hamilton A 35 7
2008–09 Hamilton A 37 6 **95 14**
2009–10 Wigan Ath 20 1
2010–11 Wigan Ath 24 3
2011–12 Wigan Ath 33 0
2012–13 Wigan Ath 38 3
2013–14 Wigan Ath 5 0 **120 7**
2013–14 Everton 34 1
2014–15 Everton 28 2
2015–16 Everton 29 2
2016–17 Everton 12 1
2017–18 Everton 4 0
2018–19 Everton 1 0
2019–20 Everton 0 0 **108 6**
2019–20 Crystal Palace 33 0
2020–21 Crystal Palace 16 0 **49 0**

MEYER, Max (M) 192 18
H: 5 7 W: 10 03 b.Oberhausen 18-9-95
Internationals: Germany U16, U17, U19, U21, U23, Full caps.
2012–13 Schalke 04 5 0
2013–14 Schalke 04 30 6
2014–15 Schalke 04 28 5
2015–16 Schalke 04 32 5
2016–17 Schalke 04 27 1
2017–18 Schalke 04 24 0 **146 17**
2018–19 Crystal Palace 29 1
2019–20 Crystal Palace 17 0
2020–21 Crystal Palace 0 0 **46 1**
Transferred to Cologne January 2021.

MILIVOJEVIC, Luka (M) 321 50
H: 6 0 b.Kragujevac 7-4-91
Internationals: Serbia U21, Full caps.
2007–08 Radnicki Kraguejevac 5 1 **5 1**
2008–09 Rad Belgrade 1 0
2009–10 Rad Belgrade 9 0
2010–11 Rad Belgrade 26 0
2011–12 Rad Belgrade 13 3 **49 3**
2011–12 Red Star Belgrade 11 1
2012–13 Red Star Belgrade 25 6 **36 7**
2013–14 Anderlecht 16 0
2014–15 Anderlecht 3 0 **19 0**
2014–15 Olympiacos 23 2
2015–16 Olympiacos 22 3
2016–17 Olympiacos 17 6 **62 11**
2016–17 Crystal Palace 14 2
2017–18 Crystal Palace 36 10
2018–19 Crystal Palace 38 12
2019–20 Crystal Palace 31 3
2020–21 Crystal Palace 31 1 **150 28**

MITCHELL, Tyrick (D) 23 1
b. 1-9-99
From Brentford.
2019–20 Crystal Palace 4 0
2020–21 Crystal Palace 19 1 **23 1**

MOONEY, Fionn (M) 0 0
b. 12-10-03
2020–21 Crystal Palace 0 0

OMILABU, David (F) 0 0
b. 27-9-02
2020–21 Crystal Palace 0 0

PIERRICK, Brandon (M) 5 0
b. 10-12-01
2019–20 Crystal Palace 2 0
2020–21 Crystal Palace 0 0 **2 0**
2020–21 *Kilmarnock* 3 0 **3 0**

RAK-SAKYI, Jesurun (M) 0 0
b. 5-10-02
2020–21 Crystal Palace 0 0

RAYMOND, Jadan (M) 0 0
b.London 15-10-03
Internationals: England U16, U17.
2020–21 Crystal Palace 0 0

RICH-BAGHUELOU, Jay (D) 0 0
H: 6 5 b. 22-10-99
2020–21 Crystal Palace 0 0

RIEDEWALD, Jairo (D) 125 4
H: 6 0 W: 12 06 b.Amsterdam 9-9-96
Internationals: Netherlands U16, U17, U19, U21, Full caps.
2013–14 Ajax 5 2
2014–15 Ajax 19 0
2015–16 Ajax 23 0
2016–17 Ajax 16 0 **63 2**
2017–18 Crystal Palace 12 0
2018–19 Crystal Palace 0 0
2019–20 Crystal Palace 17 0
2020–21 Crystal Palace 33 2 **62 2**

ROBERTSON, Sean (M) 0 0
b. 6-6-01
2020–21 Crystal Palace 0 0

SAKHO, Mamadou (D) 279 10
H: 6 2 W: 12 07 b.Paris 13-2-90
Internationals: France U16, U17, U18, U19, U21, Full caps.
2006–07 Paris Saint-Germain 0 0
2007–08 Paris Saint-Germain 12 0
2008–09 Paris Saint-Germain 23 1
2009–10 Paris Saint-Germain 32 0
2010–11 Paris Saint-Germain 35 4
2011–12 Paris Saint-Germain 22 0
2012–13 Paris Saint-Germain 27 2 **151 7**
2013–14 Liverpool 18 1
2014–15 Liverpool 16 0
2015–16 Liverpool 22 1
2016–17 Liverpool 0 0
2016–17 *Crystal Palace* 8 0
2017–18 Liverpool 0 0 **56 2**
2017–18 Crystal Palace 19 1
2018–19 Crystal Palace 27 0
2019–20 Crystal Palace 14 0
2020–21 Crystal Palace 4 0 **72 1**

SCHLUPP, Jeffrey (M) 248 25
H: 5 8 W: 11 00 b.Hamburg 23-12-92
Internationals: Ghana Full caps.
2010–11 Leicester C 0 0
2010–11 *Brentford* 9 6 **9 6**
2011–12 Leicester C 21 2
2012–13 Leicester C 19 3
2013–14 Leicester C 26 1
2014–15 Leicester C 32 3
2015–16 Leicester C 24 1
2016–17 Leicester C 4 0 **126 10**
2016–17 Crystal Palace 15 0
2017–18 Crystal Palace 24 0
2018–19 Crystal Palace 30 4
2019–20 Crystal Palace 17 3
2020–21 Crystal Palace 27 2 **113 9**

SPENCE, Sion (M) 0 0
b. 2-10-00
Internationals: Wales U19, U21.
2020–21 Crystal Palace 0 0

STREET, Robert (F) 0 0
H: 6 1 b. 26-9-01
2020–21 Crystal Palace 0 0

TAYLOR, James (M) 0 0
b.Hereford 20-1-02
From Bristol C.
2020–21 Crystal Palace 0 0

TOMKINS, James (D) 322 16
H: 6 3 W: 11 10 b.Basildon 29-3-89
Internationals: England U16, U17, U18, U19, U20, U21. Great Britain.
2005–06 West Ham U 0 0
2006–07 West Ham U 0 0
2007–08 West Ham U 6 0
2008–09 West Ham U 12 1
2008–09 *Derby Co* 7 0 **7 0**
2009–10 West Ham U 23 0
2010–11 West Ham U 19 1
2011–12 West Ham U 44 4
2012–13 West Ham U 26 1
2013–14 West Ham U 31 0
2014–15 West Ham U 22 1
2015–16 West Ham U 25 0 **208 8**
2016–17 Crystal Palace 24 3
2017–18 Crystal Palace 28 3
2018–19 Crystal Palace 29 1
2019–20 Crystal Palace 18 1
2020–21 Crystal Palace 8 0 **107 8**

TOWNSEND, Andros (M) 332 31
H: 6 0 W: 12 00 b.Chingford 16-7-91
Internationals: England U16, U17, U19, U21, Full caps.
2008–09 Tottenham H 0 0
2008–09 *Yeovil T* 10 1 **10 1**
2009–10 Tottenham H 0 0
2009–10 *Leyton Orient* 22 2 **22 2**
2009–10 *Milton Keynes D* 9 2 **9 2**
2010–11 Tottenham H 0 0
2010–11 *Ipswich T* 13 1 **13 1**
2010–11 *Watford* 3 0 **3 0**
2010–11 *Millwall* 11 2 **11 2**
2011–12 Tottenham H 0 0
2011–12 *Leeds U* 6 1 **6 1**
2011–12 *Birmingham C* 15 0 **15 0**
2012–13 Tottenham H 5 0
2012–13 *QPR* 12 2 **12 2**
2013–14 Tottenham H 25 1
2014–15 Tottenham H 17 2
2015–16 Tottenham H 3 0 **50 3**
2015–16 Newcastle U 13 4 **13 4**
2016–17 Crystal Palace 36 3
2017–18 Crystal Palace 36 2

2018–19 Crystal Palace 38 6
2019–20 Crystal Palace 24 1
2020–21 Crystal Palace 34 1 **168 13**

VAN AANHOLT, Patrick (D) 319 26
H: 5 9 W: 10 08 b.Den Bosch 3-7-88
Internationals: Netherlands U16, U17, U18, U19, U20, U21, Full caps.
2007–08 Chelsea 0 0
2008–09 Chelsea 0 0
2009–10 Chelsea 2 0
2009–10 *Coventry C* 20 0 **20 0**
2009–10 *Newcastle U* 7 0 **7 0**
2010–11 Chelsea 0 0
2010–11 *Leicester C* 12 1 **12 1**
2011–12 Chelsea 0 0
2011–12 *Wigan Ath* 3 0 **3 0**
2011–12 *Vitesse* 9 0
2012–13 Chelsea 0 0
2012–13 *Vitesse* 31 1
2013–14 Chelsea 0 0 **2 0**
2013–14 *Vitesse* 27 4 **67 5**
2014–15 Sunderland 28 0
2015–16 Sunderland 33 4
2016–17 Sunderland 21 3 **82 7**
2016–17 Crystal Palace 11 2
2017–18 Crystal Palace 28 5
2018–19 Crystal Palace 36 3
2019–20 Crystal Palace 29 3
2020–21 Crystal Palace 22 0 **126 13**

WARD, Joel (D) 357 11
H: 6 2 W: 11 13 b.Emsworth 29-10-89
2008–09 Portsmouth 0 0
2008–09 *Bournemouth* 21 1 **21 1**
2009–10 Portsmouth 3 0
2010–11 Portsmouth 42 3
2011–12 Portsmouth 44 3 **89 6**
2012–13 Crystal Palace 25 0
2013–14 Crystal Palace 36 0
2014–15 Crystal Palace 37 1
2015–16 Crystal Palace 30 2
2016–17 Crystal Palace 38 0
2017–18 Crystal Palace 19 0
2018–19 Crystal Palace 7 1
2019–20 Crystal Palace 29 0
2020–21 Crystal Palace 26 0 **247 4**

WEBBER, Oliver (G) 0 0
b.Portsmouth 26-6-00
Internationals: Northern Ireland U19.
From Glentoran.
2020–21 Crystal Palace 0 0

WICKHAM, Connor (F) 220 43
H: 6 0 W: 14 01 b.Hereford 31-3-93
Internationals: England U16, U17, U19, U21.
2008–09 Ipswich T 2 0
2009–10 Ipswich T 26 4
2010–11 Ipswich T 37 9 **65 13**
2011–12 Sunderland 16 1
2012–13 Sunderland 12 0
2012–13 *Sheffield W* 6 1
2013–14 Sunderland 15 5
2013–14 *Sheffield W* 11 8
2013–14 *Leeds U* 5 0 **5 0**
2014–15 Sunderland 36 5 **79 11**
2015–16 Crystal Palace 21 5
2016–17 Crystal Palace 8 2
2017–18 Crystal Palace 0 0
2018–19 Crystal Palace 6 0
2019–20 Crystal Palace 6 1
2019–20 *Sheffield W* 13 2 **30 11**
2020–21 Crystal Palace 0 0 **41 8**

WOODS, Sam (D) 12 2
b.Bromley 11-9-98
2018–19 Crystal Palace 0 0
2019–20 Crystal Palace 0 0
2019–20 *Hamilton A* 3 1 **3 1**
2020–21 Crystal Palace 0 0
2020–21 *Plymouth Arg* 9 1 **9 1**

ZAHA, Wilfried (F) 371 60
H: 5 11 W: 10 05 b.Ivory Coast 10-11-92
Internationals: England U19, U21, Full caps. Ivory Coast Full caps.
2009–10 Crystal Palace 1 0
2010–11 Crystal Palace 41 1
2011–12 Crystal Palace 41 6
2012–13 Crystal Palace 43 6
2012–13 Manchester U 0 0
2013–14 Manchester U 2 0 **2 0**
2013–14 *Cardiff C* 12 0 **12 0**
2014–15 Crystal Palace 31 4
2015–16 Crystal Palace 34 2
2016–17 Crystal Palace 35 7
2017–18 Crystal Palace 29 9
2018–19 Crystal Palace 34 10
2019–20 Crystal Palace 38 4
2020–21 Crystal Palace 30 11 **357 60**

Scholars
Akinwale, Victor Tolulope Oluwatosin; Bartley, Ryan Christopher; Bello, Lion; Cadogan, Maliq Anthony; Goodman, Owen Olamidayo; Henderson, Kyran Kayode Gavin Tidoye; Jessup, Cameron Lewis; Jobson, Kanye Claudio; Lewis, Cameron Jorrell Garrington; Ling, Joseph Edward; Ola-Adebomi, Ademola Oladipupo; Quick, Daniel James; Sheridan, Joe; Siddik, Cardo; Smith, Rowan Darren; Steele, Aidan Daniel; Thiselton, Dylan; Vigor, Matthew; Watson, Noah Christopher; Wells Morrison, Jack Campbell; Whitworth, Joseph Charles; Wright, Ellison Paul.

DERBY CO (30)

AGHATISE, Osazee (M) 0 0
From Manchester C.
2020–21 Derby Co 0 0

BARDWELL, Max (D) 0 0
From Manchester C.
2020–21 Derby Co 0 0

BATEMAN, Joe (D) 0 0
b. 6-12-98
2020–21 Derby Co 0 0

BIELIK, Krystian (M) 79 5
H: 5 10 W: 11 00 b.Vrinnevi 4-1-98
Internationals: Poland U16, U17, U18, U19, U21, Full caps.
2014–15 Legia Warsaw 5 0 **5 0**
2014–15 Arsenal 0 0
2015–16 Arsenal 0 0
2016–17 Arsenal 0 0
2016–17 *Birmingham C* 10 0 **10 0**
2017–18 Arsenal 0 0
2017–18 *Walsall* 0 0
2018–19 Arsenal 0 0
2018–19 *Charlton Ath* 31 3 **31 3**
2019–20 Derby Co 20 0
2020–21 Derby Co 13 2 **33 2**

BIRD, Max (M) 59 0
H: 6 0 W: 10 10 b.Burton 18-9-00
2017–18 Derby Co 0 0
2018–19 Derby Co 4 0
2019–20 Derby Co 22 0
2020–21 Derby Co 33 0 **59 0**

BROWN, Archie (D) 0 0
H: 6 3 b. 28-5-02
2020–21 Derby Co 0 0

BROWN, Jordan (D) 1 0
b. 21-6-01
2019–20 Derby Co 1 0
2020–21 Derby Co 0 0 **1 0**

BUCHANAN, Lee (D) 40 0
b. 7-3-01
Internationals: England U19.
2018–19 Derby Co 0 0
2019–20 Derby Co 5 0
2020–21 Derby Co 35 0 **40 0**

BYRNE, Nathan (D) 331 16
H: 5 10 W: 10 10 b.St Albans 5-6-92
2010–11 Tottenham H 0 0
2010–11 *Brentford* 11 0 **11 0**
2011–12 Tottenham H 0 0
2011–12 *Bournemouth* 9 0 **9 0**
2012–13 Tottenham H 0 0
2012–13 *Crawley T* 12 1 **12 1**
2012–13 *Swindon T* 7 0
2013–14 Swindon T 36 4
2014–15 Swindon T 42 3
2015–16 Swindon T 5 3 **90 10**
2015–16 Wolverhampton W 24 2
2016–17 Wolverhampton W 0 0 **24 2**
2016–17 Wigan Ath 14 0
2016–17 *Charlton Ath* 17 1 **17 1**
2017–18 Wigan Ath 44 0
2018–19 Wigan Ath 30 1
2019–20 Wigan Ath 39 1 **127 2**
2020–21 Derby Co 41 0 **41 0**

CARSON, Scott (G) 469 0
H: 6 0 W: 13 06 b.Whitehaven 3-9-85
Internationals: England U18, U21, B, Full caps.
2002–03 Leeds U 0 0
2003–04 Leeds U 3 0
2004–05 Leeds U 0 0 **3 0**
2004–05 Liverpool 4 0
2005–06 Liverpool 0 0
2005–06 *Sheffield W* 9 0 **9 0**
2006–07 Liverpool 0 0
2006–07 *Charlton Ath* 36 0 **36 0**
2007–08 Liverpool 0 0 **4 0**
2007–08 *Aston Villa* 35 0 **35 0**
2008–09 WBA 35 0
2009–10 WBA 43 0
2010–11 WBA 32 0 **110 0**
2011–12 Bursaspor 34 0
2012–13 Bursaspor 29 0 **63 0**
2013–14 Wigan Ath 16 0
2014–15 Wigan Ath 34 0 **50 0**
2015–16 Derby Co 36 0
2016–17 Derby Co 46 0
2017–18 Derby Co 46 0
2018–19 Derby Co 30 0
2019–20 Derby Co 0 0
2019–20 *Manchester C* 0 0
2020–21 Derby Co 0 0 **158 0**
2020–21 *Manchester C* 1 0 **1 0**

CASHIN, Eiran (D) 0 0
b. 9-11-01
2020–21 Derby Co 0 0

CHRISTIE, Eli (D) 0 0
2020–21 Derby Co 0 0

CLARKE, Courtney (M) 0 0
From Whytleafe
2020–21 Derby Co 0 0

CRESSWELL, Cameron (M) 1 0
b. 12-9-99
2020–21 Derby Co 1 0 **1 0**

CYBULSKI, Bartosz (F) 0 0
2020–21 Derby Co 0 0

DAVIES, Curtis (D) 490 23
H: 6 2 W: 11 13 b.Waltham Forest 15-3-85
Internationals: England U21.
2003–04 Luton T 6 0
2004–05 Luton T 44 1
2005–06 Luton T 6 1 **56 2**
2005–06 WBA 33 2
2006–07 WBA 32 0
2007–08 WBA 0 0 **65 2**
2007–08 *Aston Villa* 12 1
2008–09 Aston Villa 35 1
2009–10 Aston Villa 2 1
2010–11 Aston Villa 0 0 **49 3**
2010–11 *Leicester C* 12 0 **12 0**
2010–11 Birmingham C 6 0
2011–12 Birmingham C 42 5
2012–13 Birmingham C 41 6 **89 11**
2013–14 Hull C 37 2
2014–15 Hull C 21 0
2015–16 Hull C 39 2
2016–17 Hull C 26 0 **123 4**
2017–18 Derby Co 46 1
2018–19 Derby Co 5 0
2019–20 Derby Co 32 0
2020–21 Derby Co 13 0 **96 1**

DIXON, Connor (M) 0 0
b. 20-9-00
2020–21 Derby Co 0 0

DUNCAN, Bobby (F) 0 0
b. 26-1-01
From Wigan Ath, Manchester C, Liverpool.
2020–21 Fiorentina 0 0
2020–21 Derby Co 0 0

EBOSELE , Festy (D) 3 0
b.Wexford 2-8-02
From Bray W.
2020–21 Derby Co 3 0 **3 0**

EDMUNDSON, Sam (D) 83 5
H: 6 1 W: 11 11 b.Timperley 15-8-97
2015–16 Oldham Ath 2 0
2016–17 Oldham Ath 3 0
2017–18 Oldham Ath 15 1
2018–19 Oldham Ath 45 2 **65 3**
2019–20 Rangers 7 1
2020–21 Rangers 1 0 **8 1**
On loan from Rangers.
2020–21 Derby Co 10 1 **10 1**

FORSYTH, Craig (M) 324 19
H: 6 0 W: 12 00 b.Carnoustie 24-2-89
Internationals: Scotland Full caps.
2006–07 Dundee 1 0
2007–08 Dundee 0 0
2007–08 *Montrose* 9 0 **9 0**
2008–09 Dundee 1 0
2008–09 *Arbroath* 26 2 **26 2**
2009–10 Dundee 24 2
2010–11 Dundee 33 8 **59 10**
2011–12 Watford 20 3
2012–13 Watford 2 0 **22 3**
2012–13 *Bradford C* 7 0 **7 0**
2012–13 *Derby Co* 10 0
2013–14 Derby Co 46 2
2014–15 Derby Co 44 1
2015–16 Derby Co 12 0
2016–17 Derby Co 3 1

2017–18 Derby Co 31 0
2018–19 Derby Co 13 0
2019–20 Derby Co 22 0
2020–21 Derby Co 20 0 **201 4**

FOSTER, Bradley (G) 0 0
b. 5-10-01
From Stoke C.
2020–21 Derby Co 0 0

HECTOR-INGRAM, Jahmal (F) 9 0
b. 11-11-98
Internationals: England U16, U17.
From West Ham U.
2019–20 Derby Co 1 0
2020–21 Derby Co 7 0 **8 0**
2020–21 *Stevenage* 1 0 **1 0**

HUTCHINSON, Isaac (M) 42 1
b.Eastbourne 10-4-00
From Brighton & HA.
2018–19 Southend U 8 0
2019–20 Southend U 22 1
2020–21 Southend U 2 0 **32 1**
2020–21 Derby Co 0 0
2020–21 *Forest Green R* 10 0 **10 0**

IBE, Jordan (F) 158 11
H: 5 9 W: 11 00 b.Southwark 8-12-95
Internationals: England U18, U19, U20, U21.
2011–12 Wycombe W 7 1 **7 1**
2011–12 Liverpool 0 0
2012–13 Liverpool 1 0
2013–14 Liverpool 1 0
2013–14 *Birmingham C* 11 1 **11 1**
2014–15 Liverpool 12 0
2014–15 *Derby Co* 20 5
2015–16 Liverpool 27 1 **41 1**
2016–17 Bournemouth 25 0
2017–18 Bournemouth 32 2
2018–19 Bournemouth 19 1
2019–20 Bournemouth 2 0 **78 3**
2020–21 Derby Co 1 0 **21 5**

IBRAHIM, Ola (M) 0 0
b. 23-9-03
From Manchester U.
2020–21 Derby Co 0 0

IDEM, Manny (G) 0 0
2018–19 Aston Villa 0 0
2018–19 Macclesfield T 0 0
From Canvey Island.
2020–21 Derby Co 0 0

JINKINSON, Hugo (D) 0 0
2020–21 Derby Co 0 0

JOZEFZOON, Florian (F) 222 22
H: 5 8 W: 11 00 b.Amsterdam 9-2-91
Internationals: Netherlands U19, U21.
2010–11 Ajax 4 0
2011–12 Ajax 0 0 **4 0**
2011–12 *NAC Breda* 16 0 **16 0**
2012–13 RKC Waalwijk 34 7 **34 7**
2013–14 PSV Eindhoven 16 2
2014–15 PSV Eindhoven 15 2
2015–16 PSV Eindhoven 9 1
2016–17 PSV Eindhoven 5 0 **45 5**
2016–17 Brentford 19 1
2017–18 Brentford 39 7 **58 8**
2018–19 Derby Co 27 2
2019–20 Derby Co 14 0
2020–21 Derby Co 0 0 **41 2**
2020–21 *Rotherham U* 24 0 **24 0**

JOZWIAK, Kamil (F) 143 16
b.Miedzyrzecz 22-4-98
2015–16 Lech Poznan 10 1
2016–17 Lech Poznan 6 0
2017–18 Lech Poznan 20 3
2018–19 Lech Poznan 31 3
2019–20 Lech Poznan 35 8
2020–21 Lech Poznan 0 0 **102 15**
2020–21 Derby Co 41 1 **41 1**

KAZIM-RICHARDS, Colin (F) 434 65
H: 6 1 W: 10 09 b.Leyton 26-8-86
Internationals: Turkey U21, Full caps.
2004–05 Bury 30 3 **30 3**
2005–06 Brighton & HA 42 6
2006–07 Brighton & HA 1 0 **43 6**
2006–07 Sheffield U 27 1 **27 1**
2007–08 Fenerbahce 28 0
2008–09 Fenerbahce 22 2
2009–10 Fenerbahce 11 3
2009–10 *Toulouse* 15 2 **15 2**
2010–11 Fenerbahce 5 0 **66 5**
2010–11 Galatasaray 13 3
2011–12 Galatasaray 18 2 **31 5**
2011–12 *Olympiacos* 9 1 **9 1**
2012–13 *Blackburn R* 28 3 **28 3**
2013–14 Bursaspor 16 0
2014–15 Bursaspor 0 0 **16 0**
2014–15 *Feyenoord* 27 11
2015–16 Feyenoord 11 1 **38 12**
2015–16 Celtic 11 1 **11 1**
2016 Coritiba 21 3 **21 3**
2017 Corinthians 14 1
2018 Corinthians 1 0 **15 1**
2018–19 *Lobos BUAP* 10 3 **10 3**
2018–19 Veracruz 15 4
2019–20 Veracruz 8 4 **23 8**
2019–20 Pachuca 9 2
2020–21 Pachuca 4 1 **13 3**
2020–21 Derby Co 38 8 **38 8**

KNIGHT, Jason (M) 74 8
b. 13-2-01
Internationals: Republic of Ireland U17, U18, U19, U21.
2018–19 Derby Co 0 0
2019–20 Derby Co 31 6
2020–21 Derby Co 43 2 **74 8**

LAWRENCE, Tom (F) 239 42
H: 5 9 W: 11 11 b.Wrexham 13-1-94
Internationals: Wales U17, U19, U21, Full caps.
2012–13 Manchester U 0 0
2013–14 Manchester U 1 0 **1 0**
2013–14 *Carlisle U* 9 3 **9 3**
2013–14 *Yeovil T* 19 2 **19 2**
2014–15 Leicester C 3 0
2014–15 *Rotherham U* 6 1 **6 1**
2015–16 Leicester C 0 0
2015–16 *Blackburn R* 21 2 **21 2**
2015–16 *Cardiff C* 14 0 **14 0**
2016–17 Leicester C 0 0 **3 0**
2016–17 *Ipswich T* 34 9 **34 9**
2017–18 Derby Co 39 6
2018–19 Derby Co 33 6
2019–20 Derby Co 37 10
2020–21 Derby Co 23 3 **132 25**

MALONE, Scott (D) 344 28
H: 6 2 W: 11 11 b.Rowley Regis 25-3-91
Internationals: England U19.
2008–09 Wolverhampton W 0 0
2008–09 *Ujpest* 7 1 **7 1**
2009–10 Wolverhampton W 0 0
2009–10 *Southend U* 17 0 **17 0**
2010–11 Wolverhampton W 0 0
2010–11 *Burton Alb* 22 1 **22 1**
2011–12 Wolverhampton W 0 0
2011–12 Bournemouth 32 5 **32 5**
2012–13 Millwall 15 1
2013–14 Millwall 33 3
2014–15 Millwall 20 1
2014–15 Cardiff C 13 0
2015–16 Cardiff C 41 2 **54 2**
2016–17 Fulham 36 6 **36 6**
2017–18 Huddersfield T 22 0 **22 0**
2018–19 Derby Co 27 2
2019–20 Derby Co 18 1
2020–21 Derby Co 0 0 **45 3**
2020–21 *Millwall* 41 5 **109 10**

MARRIOTT, Jack (F) 216 60
H: 5 8 W: 11 03 b.Beverley 9-9-94
2012–13 Ipswich T 1 0
2013–14 Ipswich T 1 0
2013–14 *Gillingham* 1 0 **1 0**
2014–15 Ipswich T 0 0 **2 0**
2014–15 *Carlisle U* 4 0 **4 0**
2014–15 *Colchester U* 5 1 **5 1**
2015–16 Luton T 40 14
2016–17 Luton T 39 8 **79 22**
2017–18 Peterborough U 44 27 **44 27**
2018–19 Derby Co 33 7
2019–20 Derby Co 32 2
2020–21 Derby Co 4 1 **69 10**
2020–21 *Sheffield W* 12 0 **12 0**

MARSHALL, David (G) 526 0
H: 6 3 W: 13 04 b.Glasgow 5-3-85
Internationals: Scotland Youth, U21, B, Full caps.
2003–04 Celtic 11 0
2004–05 Celtic 18 0
2005–06 Celtic 4 0
2006–07 Celtic 2 0 **35 0**
2006–07 Norwich C 2 0
2007–08 Norwich C 46 0
2008–09 Norwich C 46 0 **94 0**
2008–09 Cardiff C 0 0
2009–10 Cardiff C 43 0
2010–11 Cardiff C 11 0
2011–12 Cardiff C 45 0
2012–13 Cardiff C 46 0
2013–14 Cardiff C 37 0
2014–15 Cardiff C 38 0
2015–16 Cardiff C 40 0
2016–17 Cardiff C 4 0 **264 0**
2016–17 Hull C 16 0
2017–18 Hull C 2 0
2018–19 Hull C 43 0 **61 0**
2019–20 Wigan Ath 39 0 **39 0**
2020–21 Derby Co 33 0 **33 0**

McDONALD, Kornell (D) 7 0
b.Nottingham 1-10-01
2020–21 Derby Co 7 0 **7 0**

MITCHELL, Jonathan (G) 70 0
H: 5 11 W: 13 08 b.Hartlepool 24-11-94
Internationals: England U21.
2012–13 Newcastle U 0 0
2013–14 Newcastle U 0 0
2014–15 Derby Co 0 0
2015–16 Derby Co 0 0
2015–16 *Luton T* 5 0 **5 0**
2016–17 Derby Co 0 0
2017–18 Derby Co 0 0
2018–19 Derby Co 0 0
2018–19 *Oxford U* 10 0 **10 0**
2018–19 *Shrewsbury T* 9 0 **9 0**
2019–20 Derby Co 0 0
2019–20 *Macclesfield T* 11 0 **11 0**
2020–21 Derby Co 0 0
2020–21 *Northampton T* 35 0 **35 0**

MITCHELL-LAWSON, Jayden (M) 17 2
b. 17-9-99
From Swindon T.
2018–19 Derby Co 1 0
2019–20 Derby Co 0 0
2019–20 *Bristol R* 10 2
2020–21 Derby Co 1 0 **2 0**
2020–21 *Bristol R* 5 0 **15 2**

RAVAS, Henrich (G) 0 0
From Boston U.
2018–19 Derby Co 0 0
2019–20 Derby Co 0 0
2020–21 Derby Co 0 0

ROGERS, Jack (M) 0 0
2020–21 Derby Co 0 0

ROONEY, Wayne (F) 569 237
H: 5 10 W: 12 13 b.Liverpool 24-10-85
Internationals: England U15, U16, U19, Full caps.
2002–03 Everton 33 6
2003–04 Everton 34 9
2004–05 Manchester U 29 11
2005–06 Manchester U 36 16
2006–07 Manchester U 35 14
2007–08 Manchester U 27 12
2008–09 Manchester U 30 12
2009–10 Manchester U 32 26
2010–11 Manchester U 28 11
2011–12 Manchester U 34 27
2012–13 Manchester U 27 12
2013–14 Manchester U 29 17
2014–15 Manchester U 33 12
2015–16 Manchester U 28 8
2016–17 Manchester U 25 5 **393 183**
2017–18 Everton 31 10 **98 25**
2018 DC United 20 12
2019 DC United 28 11 **48 23**
2019–20 Derby Co 20 5
2020–21 Derby Co 10 1 **30 6**

ROOS, Kelle (G) 101 0
H: 6 4 W: 14 02 b.Rijkevoort 31-5-92
From PSV Eindhoven, Willem II, NEC Nijmegen, Nuneaton T.
2013–14 Derby Co 0 0
2014–15 Derby Co 0 0
2015–16 Derby Co 0 0
2015–16 *Rotherham U* 4 0 **4 0**
2015–16 *AFC Wimbledon* 17 0 **17 0**
2016–17 Derby Co 0 0
2016–17 *Bristol R* 16 0 **16 0**
2017–18 Derby Co 0 0
2017–18 *Port Vale* 8 0 **8 0**
2017–18 *Plymouth Arg* 4 0 **4 0**
2018–19 Derby Co 16 0
2019–20 Derby Co 22 0
2020–21 Derby Co 14 0 **52 0**

RUTT, Charlie (D) 0 0
2020–21 Derby Co 0 0

SHINNIE, Graeme (D) 364 19
b.Aberdeen 4-8-91
Internationals: Scotland U21, Full caps.
2009–10 Inverness CT 1 0
2010–11 Inverness CT 19 0
2011–12 Inverness CT 26 1
2012–13 Inverness CT 37 0
2013–14 Inverness CT 36 3
2014–15 Inverness CT 37 2 **156 6**
2015–16 Aberdeen 37 1
2016–17 Aberdeen 36 2
2017–18 Aberdeen 35 2
2018–19 Aberdeen 36 3 **144 8**

2019–20 Derby Co 23 2
2020–21 Derby Co 41 3 **64 5**

SHONIBARE, Josh (M) 0 0
b.Bromley 29-5-98
From Greenwich Bor.
2020–21 Derby Co 0 0

SIBLEY, Louie (M) 41 6
b. 1-9-01
Internationals: England U17, U18, U19.
2019–20 Derby Co 11 5
2020–21 Derby Co 30 1 **41 6**

SOLOMON, Harrison (D) 0 0
b.Burton 1-11-02
2020–21 Derby Co 0 0

STRETTON, Jack (F) 4 0
b. 6-9-01
From Nottingham F.
2020–21 Derby Co 4 0 **4 0**

SYKES-KENWORTHY, George (G) 0 0
2017–18 Bradford C 0 0
2018–19 Bradford C 0 0
2019–20 Bradford C 0 0
2020–21 Derby Co 0 0

TE WIERIK, Mike (D) 237 8
b.Hengevelde 8-6-92
2010–11 Heracles 4 0
2011–12 Heracles 9 0
2012–13 Heracles 18 3
2013–14 Heracles 28 2
2014–15 Heracles 24 0
2015–16 Heracles 32 0
2016–17 Heracles 29 1 **144 6**
2017–18 Groningen 33 1
2018–19 Groningen 33 0
2019–20 Groningen 23 1 **89 2**
2020–21 Derby Co 4 0 **4 0**
Transferred to Groningen January 2021.

THOMPSON, Liam (M) 0 0
2020–21 Derby Co 0 0

THOMPSON, Seb (F) 0 0
From Leicester C.
2020–21 Derby Co 0 0

WAGHORN, Martyn (F) 385 102
H: 5 9 W: 13 01 b.South Shields 23-1-90
Internationals: England U19, U21.
2007–08 Sunderland 3 0
2008–09 Sunderland 1 0
2008–09 *Charlton Ath* 7 1 **7 1**
2009–10 Sunderland 0 0
2009–10 *Leicester C* 43 12
2010–11 Sunderland 2 0 **6 0**
2010–11 Leicester C 30 4
2011–12 Leicester C 4 1
2011–12 *Hull C* 5 1 **5 1**
2012–13 Leicester C 24 3
2013–14 Leicester C 2 0 **103 20**
2013–14 *Millwall* 14 3 **14 3**
2013–14 Wigan Ath 15 5
2014–15 Wigan Ath 23 3 **38 8**
2015–16 Rangers 25 20
2016–17 Rangers 32 7 **57 27**
2017–18 Ipswich T 44 16 **44 16**
2018–19 Derby Co 36 9
2019–20 Derby Co 43 12
2020–21 Derby Co 32 5 **111 26**

WATSON, Louis (M) 9 0
b.London 7-6-01
From West Ham U.
2020–21 Derby Co 9 0 **9 0**

WILLIAMS, Dylan (D) 0 0
2020–21 Derby Co 0 0

WILSON, Tyree (M) 0 0
2018–19 Derby Co 0 0
2019–20 Derby Co 0 0
2020–21 Derby Co 0 0

WISDOM, Andre (D) 195 1
H: 6 1 W: 12 04 b.Leeds 9-5-93
Internationals: England U16, U17, U19, U21.
2009–10 Liverpool 0 0
2010–11 Liverpool 0 0
2011–12 Liverpool 0 0
2012–13 Liverpool 12 0
2013–14 Liverpool 2 0
2013–14 *Derby Co* 34 0
2014–15 Liverpool 0 0
2014–15 *WBA* 24 0 **24 0**
2015–16 Liverpool 0 0
2015–16 *Norwich C* 10 0 **10 0**
2016–17 Liverpool 0 0 **14 0**
2016–17 *Red Bull Salzburg* 16 0 **16 0**
2017–18 Derby Co 30 0
2018–19 Derby Co 11 0

2019–20 Derby Co 18 0
2020–21 Derby Co 38 1 **131 1**

YATES, Matthew (G) 0 0
Internationals: England U17.
2017–18 Derby Co 0 0
2018–19 Derby Co 0 0
2019–20 Derby Co 0 0
2020–21 Derby Co 0 0

Scholars
Borkovic, Marko; Brailsford, Rhys Ellis; Christie, Eli James; Cybulski, Bartosz Marcin; Grewal-Pollard, William Michael; Jinkinson, Hugo Raymond Junior; Kelly Caprani, Cian Mark; Matthews, Alexander Niall; Perez De Gracia, Andres Alvaro; Randle, Harvey; Roberts, Alfie James; Rogers, Jack Aaron; Rutt, Charlie Owen; Solomon, Harrison James; Thompson, Sebastian Blake; Williams, Dylan Riley.

DONCASTER R (31)

AMOS, Danny (D) 14 0
H: 5 11 W: 10 10 b.Sheffield 22-12-99
Internationals: Northern Ireland U19, U21.
2016–17 Doncaster R 0 0
2017–18 Doncaster R 3 0
2018–19 Doncaster R 1 0
2019–20 Doncaster R 2 0
2020–21 Doncaster R 8 0 **14 0**

ANDERSON, Thomas (M) 187 8
H: 6 4 W: 13 01 b.Burnley 2-9-93
2012–13 Burnley 0 0
2013–14 Burnley 0 0
2014–15 Burnley 0 0
2014–15 *Carlisle U* 8 0 **8 0**
2015–16 Burnley 0 0
2015–16 *Chesterfield* 18 0
2016–17 Burnley 0 0
2016–17 *Chesterfield* 35 2 **53 2**
2017–18 Burnley 0 0
2017–18 *Port Vale* 20 0 **20 0**
2017–18 *Doncaster R* 7 2
2018–19 Doncaster R 23 1
2019–20 Doncaster R 32 1
2020–21 Doncaster R 44 2 **106 6**

BLYTHE, Ben (D) 1 0
b. 13-1-02
2020–21 Doncaster R 1 0 **1 0**

BOGLE, Omar (F) 137 37
H: 6 3 W: 12 08 b.Birmingham 26-7-92
Internationals: England C.
From Celtic, Hinckley U, Solihull Moors.
2016–17 Grimsby T 27 19 **27 19**
2016–17 Wigan Ath 14 3 **14 3**
2017–18 Cardiff C 10 3
2017–18 *Peterborough U* 9 1 **9 1**
2018–19 Cardiff C 0 0
2018–19 *Birmingham C* 15 1 **15 1**
2018–19 *Portsmouth* 12 4 **12 4**
2019–20 Cardiff C 11 1 **21 4**
2019–20 *ADO Den Haag* 5 1 **5 1**
2020–21 Charlton Ath 17 2 **17 2**
2020–21 Doncaster R 17 2 **17 2**

BOSTOCK, John (M) 219 28
b.Lambeth 15-1-92
Internationals: England U16, U17, U19.
2007–08 Crystal Palace 4 0 **4 0**
2008–09 Tottenham H 0 0
2009–10 Tottenham H 0 0
2009–10 *Brentford* 9 2 **9 2**
2010–11 Tottenham H 0 0
2010–11 *Hull C* 11 2 **11 2**
2011–12 Tottenham H 0 0
2011–12 *Sheffield W* 4 0 **4 0**
2011–12 *Swindon T* 3 0
2012–13 Tottenham H 0 0
2012–13 *Swindon T* 8 0 **11 0**
2013 *Toronto* 7 0 **7 0**
2013–14 Royal Antwerp 29 1
2014–15 Royal Antwerp 2 0 **31 1**
2014–15 OH Leuven 26 11
2015–16 OH Leuven 25 7 **51 18**
2016–17 Lens 31 5
2017–18 Lens 11 0 **42 5**
2017–18 Bursaspor 8 0 **8 0**
2018–19 Toulouse 16 0
2019–20 Toulouse 0 0 **16 0**
2019–20 *Nottingham F* 7 0 **7 0**
2020–21 Doncaster R 18 0 **18 0**

BOTTOMLEY, Ben (G) 0 0
2020–21 Doncaster R 0 0

BUTLER, Andy (D) 596 49
H: 6 0 W: 13 00 b.Doncaster 4-11-83
2003–04 Scunthorpe U 35 2
2004–05 Scunthorpe U 37 10
2005–06 Scunthorpe U 16 1
2006–07 Scunthorpe U 11 1
2006–07 *Grimsby T* 4 0 **4 0**
2007–08 Scunthorpe U 36 2
2008–09 Huddersfield T 42 4
2009–10 Huddersfield T 11 0 **53 4**
2009–10 *Blackpool* 7 0 **7 0**
2010–11 Walsall 31 4
2011–12 Walsall 42 5
2012–13 Walsall 41 3
2013–14 Walsall 45 2
2014–15 Sheffield U 0 0
2014–15 *Walsall* 7 0 **166 14**
2014–15 Doncaster R 33 3
2015–16 Doncaster R 40 4
2016–17 Doncaster R 44 3
2017–18 Doncaster R 36 4
2018–19 Doncaster R 40 1
2019–20 Scunthorpe U 18 0 **153 16**
2020–21 Doncaster R 20 0 **213 15**

COPPINGER, James (F) 688 77
H: 5 7 W: 10 03 b.Middlesbrough 10-1-81
Internationals: England U16.
1997–98 Newcastle U 0 0
1998–99 Newcastle U 0 0
1999–2000 Newcastle U 0 0
1999–2000 *Hartlepool U* 10 3
2000–01 Newcastle U 1 0
2001–02 Newcastle U 0 0 **1 0**
2001–02 *Hartlepool U* 14 2 **24 5**
2002–03 Exeter C 43 5 **43 5**
2004–05 Doncaster R 31 0
2005–06 Doncaster R 36 5
2006–07 Doncaster R 39 4
2007–08 Doncaster R 39 3
2008–09 Doncaster R 32 5
2009–10 Doncaster R 39 4
2010–11 Doncaster R 40 7
2011–12 Doncaster R 38 2
2012–13 Doncaster R 25 2
2012–13 *Nottingham F* 6 0 **6 0**
2013–14 Doncaster R 41 4
2014–15 Doncaster R 34 4
2015–16 Doncaster R 39 3
2016–17 Doncaster R 39 10
2017–18 Doncaster R 38 3
2018–19 Doncaster R 43 4
2019–20 Doncaster R 29 3
2020–21 Doncaster R 32 4 **614 67**

GOMES, Madger (M) 50 3
b.Alicante 1-2-97
Internationals: Spain U17, U18.
From Villareal, Liverpool.
2017–18 Leeds U 0 0
2018–19 Istra 1961 5 0 **5 0**
2019–20 Doncaster R 23 0
2020–21 Doncaster R 22 3 **45 3**

GREAVES, Anthony (M) 10 0
b. 17-11-00
2018–19 Doncaster R 0 0
2019–20 Doncaster R 0 0
2020–21 Doncaster R 10 0 **10 0**

HALLIDAY, Bradley (M) 244 4
H: 5 11 W: 10 10 b.Redcar 10-7-95
2013–14 Middlesbrough 0 0
2014–15 Middlesbrough 0 0
2014–15 *York C* 24 1 **24 1**
2015–16 Middlesbrough 0 0
2015–16 *Hartlepool U* 6 0 **6 0**
2015–16 *Accrington S* 32 0 **32 0**
2016–17 Middlesbrough 0 0
2016–17 Cambridge U 30 1
2017–18 Cambridge U 43 1
2018–19 Cambridge U 38 0 **111 2**
2019–20 Doncaster R 34 0
2020–21 Doncaster R 37 1 **71 1**

HASANI, Lirak (M) 4 0
b.Doncaster 25-6-02
2018–19 Doncaster R 2 0
2019–20 Doncaster R 0 0
2020–21 Doncaster R 2 0 **4 0**

HORTON, Branden (D) 11 0
b. 9-9-00
2017–18 Doncaster R 0 0
2018–19 Doncaster R 0 0
2019–20 Doncaster R 0 0
2020–21 Doncaster R 11 0 **11 0**

JAMES, Reece (D) 159 11
H: 5 6 W: 11 03 b.Bacup 7-11-93
2012–13 Manchester U 0 0
2013–14 Manchester U 0 0
2013–14 *Carlisle U* 1 0 **1 0**
2014–15 Manchester U 0 0
2014–15 *Rotherham U* 7 0 **7 0**
2014–15 *Huddersfield T* 6 1 **6 1**
2015–16 Wigan Ath 26 1
2016–17 Wigan Ath 0 0
2017–18 Wigan Ath 22 0 **48 1**
2018–19 Sunderland 27 0 **27 0**
2019–20 Doncaster R 27 2
2020–21 Doncaster R 43 7 **70 9**

JOHN, Cameron (D) 49 4
b. 24-8-99
From Southend U.
2018–19 Wolverhampton W 0 0
2019–20 Wolverhampton W 0 0
2019–20 *Doncaster R* 18 2
2020–21 Doncaster R 31 2 **49 4**

JONES, Louis (G) 13 0
b. 12-10-98
2015–16 Doncaster R 0 0
2016–17 Doncaster R 0 0
2017–18 Doncaster R 0 0
2018–19 Doncaster R 0 0
2019–20 Doncaster R 0 0
2020–21 Doncaster R 13 0 **13 0**

LAWLOR, Ian (G) 121 0
H: 6 4 W: 12 08 b.Dublin 27-10-94
Internationals: Republic of Ireland U17, U19, U21.
2011–12 Manchester C 0 0
2012–13 Manchester C 0 0
2013–14 Manchester C 0 0
2014–15 Manchester C 0 0
2015–16 Manchester C 0 0
2015–16 *Barnet* 5 0 **5 0**
2015–16 *Bury* 12 0 **12 0**
2016–17 Doncaster R 19 0
2017–18 Doncaster R 34 0
2018–19 Doncaster R 10 0
2019–20 Doncaster R 7 0
2019–20 *Scunthorpe U* 4 0 **4 0**
2020–21 Doncaster R 0 0 **70 0**
2020–21 *Oldham Ath* 30 0 **30 0**

LOKILO, Jason (M) 37 1
H: 5 9 b.Brussel 17-9-98
Internationals: DR Congo U20.
2014–15 Anderlecht 0 0
2015–16 Crystal Palace 0 0
2016–17 Crystal Palace 0 0
2017–18 Crystal Palace 0 0
2018–19 Crystal Palace 0 0
2018–19 *Lorient* 4 0 **4 0**
2019–20 Crystal Palace 0 0
2019–20 *Doncaster R* 1 0
2020–21 Doncaster R 32 1 **33 1**

OKENABIRHIE, Fejiri (F) 102 25
H: 5 10 W: 11 09 b. 25-2-96
Internationals: England C.
2013–14 Stevenage 3 0
2014–15 Stevenage 0 0
2015–16 Stevenage 0 0 **3 0**
From Harrow Bor, Dagenham & R.
2018–19 Shrewsbury T 38 10
2019–20 Shrewsbury T 17 2 **55 12**
2019–20 Doncaster R 5 2
2020–21 Doncaster R 39 11 **44 13**

RAVENHILL, Liam (M) 0 0
2020–21 Doncaster R 0 0

ROBERTSON, Scott (M) 30 0
b.Dundee 27-7-01
2019–20 Celtic 0 0
2019–20 Celtic 0 0
2020–21 Celtic 0 0
On loan from Celtic.
2020–21 Gillingham 15 0 **15 0**
On loan from Celtic.
2020–21 Doncaster R 15 0 **15 0**

SEAMAN, Charlie (D) 18 0
H: 5 8 b. 30-9-99
2017–18 Bournemouth 0 0
2018–19 Bournemouth 0 0
2018–19 *Dundee U* 18 0 **18 0**
2019–20 Bournemouth 0 0
From Bournemouth.
2020–21 Doncaster R 0 0

TAYLOR, Jon (M) 362 58
H: 5 11 W: 12 04 b.Liverpool 23-12-89
2009–10 Shrewsbury T 2 0
2010–11 Shrewsbury T 20 6
2011–12 Shrewsbury T 33 0
2012–13 Shrewsbury T 37 7
2013–14 Shrewsbury T 41 9 **133 22**
2014–15 Peterborough U 24 3
2015–16 Peterborough U 44 11 **68 14**
2016–17 Rotherham U 42 4
2017–18 Rotherham U 25 4
2018–19 Rotherham U 41 4
2019–20 Rotherham U 0 0 **108 12**
2019–20 Doncaster R 28 6
2020–21 Doncaster R 25 4 **53 10**

WILLIAMS, Ed (M) 11 0
b. 20-7-95
2012–13 Cheltenham T 0 0
2013–14 Cheltenham T 0 0
From Kidderminster H.
2020–21 Doncaster R 11 0 **11 0**

WRIGHT, Joe (D) 149 4
H: 6 4 W: 12 06 b. 26-2-95
Internationals: Wales U21.
2013–14 Huddersfield T 0 0
2014–15 Huddersfield T 0 0
2015–16 Huddersfield T 0 0
2015–16 *Accrington S* 20 0 **20 0**
2016–17 Doncaster R 22 0
2017–18 Doncaster R 33 0
2018–19 Doncaster R 14 2
2019–20 Doncaster R 20 0
2020–21 Doncaster R 40 2 **129 4**

Scholars
Bell, Charlie John; Bojang, Ethan; Bottomley, Benjamin Phillip; Chadwick, Luke William; Clemitson, Joshua Daniel; Cole, Corie Matthew; Cunningham, Lewis Thomas; Derrett, Owan Mackenzie; Henson, Thomas Owen; Hollings, William John Wing Houng; Jemson, Maxwell; Kuleya, Tavonga Daniel; Nelson, Luca David; Nesbitt, Michael Robert; Ravenhill, Liam; Wilds, Daniel Peter; Wolny, Aleksander Jan.

EVERTON (32)

ADENIRAN, Dennis (M) 22 0
H: 5 11 b.London 2-1-99
Internationals: England U17, U18, U19.
2016–17 Fulham 1 0 **1 0**
2017–18 Everton 0 0
2018–19 Everton 0 0
2019–20 Everton 0 0
2020–21 Everton 0 0
2020–21 *Wycombe W* 21 0 **21 0**

ALLAN, Marques (M) 337 12
b.Rio de Janeiro 8-1-91
2009 Vasco da Gama 13 0
2010 Vasco da Gama 15 0
2011 Vasco da Gama 19 0
2012 Vasco da Gama 4 0 **51 0**
2012–13 Udinese 36 0
2013–14 Udinese 33 0
2014–15 Udinese 35 1 **104 1**
2015–16 Napoli 35 3
2016–17 Napoli 29 1
2017–18 Napoli 38 4
2018–19 Napoli 33 1
2019–20 Napoli 23 2
2020–21 Napoli 0 0 **158 11**
2020–21 Everton 24 0 **24 0**

ANDRE GOMES, Filipe (M) 197 13
H: 6 2 W: 13 01 b.Porto 30-7-93
Internationals: Portugal U17, U28, U19, U20, U21, Full caps.
2012–13 Benfica 7 1
2013–14 Benfica 7 1
2014–15 Benfica 0 0 **14 2**
2014–15 *Valencia* 33 4
2015–16 Valencia 30 3 **63 7**
2016–17 Barcelona 30 3
2017–18 Barcelona 16 0
2018–19 Barcelona 0 0 **46 3**
2018–19 *Everton* 27 1
2019–20 Everton 19 0
2020–21 Everton 28 0 **74 1**

ASTLEY, Ryan (D) 0 0
b. 4-10-01
2020–21 Everton 0 0

BANINGIME, Beni (M) 11 0
H: 5 10 W: 11 00 b.Kinshasa 9-9-98
2017–18 Everton 8 0
2018–19 Everton 0 0
2018–19 *Wigan Ath* 1 0 **1 0**
2019–20 Everton 0 0
2020–21 Everton 0 0 **8 0**
2020–21 *Derby Co* 2 0 **2 0**

BARRETT, Jack (G) 0 0
b. 4-6-02
2020–21 Everton 0 0

BERNARD, Caldeira (M) 231 31
H: 5 4 W: 8 11 b.Belo Horizonte 8-9-92
Internationals: Brazil Full caps.
2011 Atletico Mineiro 23 0
2012 Atletico Mineiro 36 11
2013 Atletico Mineiro 3 1 **62 12**
2013–14 Shaktar Donetsk 18 2
2014–15 Shaktar Donetsk 14 0
2015–16 Shaktar Donetsk 21 2
2016–17 Shaktar Donetsk 24 4
2017–18 Shaktar Donetsk 19 6 **96 14**
2018–19 Everton 34 1
2019–20 Everton 27 3
2020–21 Everton 12 1 **73 5**

BOLASIE, Yannick (M) 369 44
H: 6 2 W: 13 02 b.DR Congo 24-5-89
Internationals: DR Congo Full caps.
From Rushden & D, Hillingdon Bor.
2007–08 Floriana 24 4 **24 4**
2008–09 Plymouth Arg 0 0
2008–09 *Barnet* 20 3
2009–10 Plymouth Arg 16 1
2009–10 *Barnet* 22 2 **42 5**
2010–11 Plymouth Arg 35 7 **51 8**
2011–12 Bristol C 23 1
2012–13 Bristol C 0 0 **23 1**
2012–13 Crystal Palace 43 3
2013–14 Crystal Palace 29 0
2014–15 Crystal Palace 34 4
2015–16 Crystal Palace 26 5
2016–17 Crystal Palace 1 0 **133 12**
2016–17 Everton 13 1
2017–18 Everton 16 1
2018–19 Everton 0 0
2018–19 *Aston Villa* 21 2 **21 2**
2018–19 *Anderlecht* 17 6 **17 6**
2019–20 Everton 0 0
2019–20 *Sporting Lisbon* 14 1 **14 1**
2020–21 Everton 0 0 **29 2**
2020–21 *Middlesbrough* 15 3 **15 3**

BRANTHWAITE, Jarrad (M) 23 0
b. 27-6-02
2018–19 Carlisle U 0 0
2019–20 Carlisle U 9 0 **9 0**
2019–20 Everton 4 0
2020–21 Everton 0 0 **4 0**
2020–21 *Blackburn R* 10 0 **10 0**

BROADHEAD, Nathan (F) 20 2
H: 5 10 W: 11 07 b.Bangor 5-4-98
Internationals: Wales U17, U19, U20, U21.
2017–18 Everton 0 0
2018–19 Everton 0 0
2019–20 Everton 0 0
2019–20 *Burton Alb* 19 2 **19 2**
2020–21 Everton 1 0 **1 0**

BUTTERFIELD, Luke (M) 0 0
H: 5 9 b. 29-9-03
Internationals: Scotland U16.
2020–21 Everton 0 0

CALVERT-LEWIN, Dominic (M) 178 45
b. 16-3-97
Internationals: England U20, U21.
2013–14 Sheffield U 0 0
2014–15 Sheffield U 2 0
2015–16 Sheffield U 9 0
2015–16 *Northampton T* 20 5 **20 5**
2016–17 Sheffield U 0 0 **11 0**
2016–17 Everton 11 1
2017–18 Everton 32 4
2018–19 Everton 35 6
2019–20 Everton 36 13
2020–21 Everton 33 16 **147 40**

CANNON, Thomas (F) 0 0
b.Aintree 28-11-02
Internationals: Republic of Ireland U19.
2020–21 Everton 0 0

COLEMAN, Seamus (D) 364 22
H: 6 4 W: 10 07 b.Donegal 11-10-88
Internationals: Republic of Ireland U21, U23, Full caps.
2006 Sligo R 4 0
2007 Sligo R 26 0
2008 Sligo R 26 1 **56 1**
2008–09 Everton 0 0
2009–10 Everton 3 0
2009–10 *Blackpool* 9 1 **9 1**
2010–11 Everton 34 4
2011–12 Everton 18 0
2012–13 Everton 26 0
2013–14 Everton 36 6
2014–15 Everton 35 3

2015–16 Everton 28 1
2016–17 Everton 26 4
2017–18 Everton 12 0
2018–19 Everton 29 2
2019–20 Everton 27 0
2020–21 Everton 25 0 **299 20**

CONNOLLY, Callum (D) 152 13
b.Liverpool 23-9-97
Internationals: England U17, U18, U19, U20, U21.
2015–16 Everton 1 0
2015–16 *Barnsley* 3 0 **3 0**
2016–17 Everton 0 0
2016–17 *Wigan Ath* 17 2
2017–18 Everton 0 0
2017–18 *Ipswich T* 34 4 **34 4**
2018–19 Everton 0 0
2018–19 *Wigan Ath* 17 1 **34 3**
2018–19 *Bolton W* 16 2 **16 2**
2019–20 Everton 0 0
2019–20 *Lincoln C* 11 0 **11 0**
2019–20 *Fleetwood T* 13 2
2020–21 Everton 0 0 **1 0**
2020–21 *Fleetwood T* 40 2 **53 4**

DAVIES, Tom (M) 130 5
b.Liverpool 30-6-98
Internationals: England U16, U17, U18, U19, U21.
2015–16 Everton 2 0
2016–17 Everton 24 2
2017–18 Everton 33 2
2018–19 Everton 16 0
2019–20 Everton 30 1
2020–21 Everton 25 0 **130 5**

DELPH, Fabian (D) 242 13
H: 5 8 W: 11 00 b.Bradford 21-11-89
Internationals: England U19, U21, Full caps.
2006–07 Leeds U 1 0
2007–08 Leeds U 1 0
2008–09 Leeds U 42 6
2009–10 Aston Villa 8 0
2010–11 Aston Villa 7 0
2011–12 Aston Villa 11 0
2011–12 *Leeds U* 5 0 **49 6**
2012–13 Aston Villa 24 0
2013–14 Aston Villa 34 3
2014–15 Aston Villa 28 0 **112 3**
2015–16 Manchester C 17 2
2016–17 Manchester C 7 1
2017–18 Manchester C 22 1
2018–19 Manchester C 11 0 **57 4**
2019–20 Everton 16 0
2020–21 Everton 8 0 **24 0**

DIGNE, Lucas (D) 241 9
H: 5 10 W: 11 11 b.Meaux 20-7-93
Internationals: France U16, U17, U18, U19, U21, Full caps.
2011–12 Lille 16 0
2012–13 Lille 33 2 **49 2**
2013–14 Paris Saint-Germain 15 0
2014–15 Paris Saint-Germain 15 0
2014–15 Paris Saint-Germain 0 0
2015–16 Paris Saint-Germain 0 0 **30 0**
2015–16 *Roma* 33 3 **33 3**
2016–17 Barcelona 17 0
2017–18 Barcelona 12 0 **29 0**
2018–19 Everton 35 4
2019–20 Everton 35 0
2020–21 Everton 30 0 **100 4**

DOBBIN, Lewis (F) 0 0
b.Stoke 3-1-03
Internationals: England U16.
2020–21 Everton 0 0

DOBBIN, Lewis (F) 0 0
H: 5 9 b.Stoke 3-1-03
Internationals: England U16, U17
2020–21 Everton 0 0

DOUCOURE, Abdoulaye (M) 248 31
b.Meulan-en-Yvelines 1-1-93
Internationals: France U17, U18, U19, U20, U21.
2012–13 Rennes 4 1
2013–14 Rennes 20 6
2014–15 Rennes 35 3
2015–16 Rennes 16 2 **75 12**
2015–16 Watford 0 0
2015–16 *Granada* 15 0 **15 0**
2016–17 Watford 20 1
2017–18 Watford 37 7
2018–19 Watford 35 5
2019–20 Watford 37 4 **129 17**
2020–21 Everton 29 2 **29 2**

GARCIA FERREIRA, Rafael (F) 0 0
H: 5 9 b.London 7-10-02
Internationals: England U16.
From Fulham.
2020–21 Everton 0 0

GBAMIN, Jean-Philippe (M) 180 5
b.San Pedro 25-5-95
Internationals: France U18, U19, U20, U21. Ivory Coast Full caps.
2012–13 Lens 2 0
2013–14 Lens 30 2
2014–15 Lens 33 0
2015–16 Lens 26 1 **91 3**
2016–17 Mainz 05 25 0
2017–18 Mainz 05 30 1
2018–19 Mainz 05 31 1 **86 2**
2019–20 Everton 2 0
2020–21 Everton 1 0 **3 0**

GIBSON, Lewis (D) 22 0
b. 19-7-00
Internationals: England U17, U18, U20.
From Newcastle U.
2019–20 Everton 0 0
2019–20 *Fleetwood T* 9 0 **9 0**
2020–21 Everton 0 0
2020–21 *Reading* 13 0 **13 0**

GODFREY, Ben (M) 149 6
H: 6 0 W: 11 09 b.York 15-1-98
Internationals: England U20, U21.
2014–15 York C 0 0
2015–16 York C 12 1 **12 1**
2015–16 Norwich C 0 0
2016–17 Norwich C 2 0
2017–18 Norwich C 0 0
2017–18 *Shrewsbury T* 40 1
2018–19 Norwich C 31 4
2019–20 Norwich C 30 0
2019–20 *Shrewsbury T* 0 0 **40 1**
2020–21 Norwich C 3 0 **66 4**
2020–21 Everton 31 0 **31 0**

GORDON, Anthony (M) 25 0
b. 24-2-01
Internationals: England U18, U19.
2017–18 Everton 0 0
2018–19 Everton 0 0
2019–20 Everton 11 0
2020–21 Everton 3 0 **14 0**
2020–21 *Preston NE* 11 0 **11 0**

HAGAN, Harry (D) 0 0
b.Liverpool 24-4-03
Internationals: England U16.
2020–21 Everton 0 0

HOLGATE, Mason (D) 132 3
H: 5 11 W: 11 11 b.Doncaster 22-10-96
Internationals: England U20, U21.
2014–15 Barnsley 20 1 **20 1**
2015–16 Everton 0 0
2016–17 Everton 18 0
2017–18 Everton 15 0
2018–19 Everton 5 0
2018–19 *WBA* 19 1 **19 1**
2019–20 Everton 27 0
2020–21 Everton 28 1 **93 1**

HUGHES, Rhys (M) 0 0
b.Wrexham 21-9-01
Internationals: Wales U17.
2020–21 Everton 0 0

HUNT, MacKenzie (M) 0 0
b. 14-11-01
2020–21 Everton 0 0

IVERSEN, Einar (M) 0 0
b.Stord 6-6-01
Internationals: Norway U17, U18, U21.
2020–21 Everton 0 0

IWOBI, Alex (M) 155 13
H: 5 11 W: 11 11 b.Lagos 3-5-96
Internationals: England U16, U17, U18. Nigeria Full caps.
2012–13 Arsenal 0 0
2013–14 Arsenal 0 0
2014–15 Arsenal 0 0
2015–16 Arsenal 13 2
2016–17 Arsenal 26 3
2017–18 Arsenal 26 3
2018–19 Arsenal 35 3
2019–20 Arsenal 0 0 **100 11**
2019–20 Everton 25 1
2020–21 Everton 30 1 **55 2**

JAGNE, Seedy (M) 0 0
H: 6 0 b.Gambia 1-10-03
Internationals: Sweden U17.
From Hacken.
2020–21 Everton 0 0

JOHN, Kyle (D) 0 0
b. 13-2-01
2020–21 Everton 0 0

KEAN, Moise (F) 92 26
b.Vercelli 28-2-00
Internationals: Italy U16, U17, U19, U20, U21, Full caps.
2016–17 Juventus 3 1
2017–18 Juventus 0 0
2017–18 *Verona* 19 4 **19 4**
2018–19 Juventus 13 6 **16 7**
2019–20 Everton 29 2
2020–21 Everton 2 0 **31 2**
2020–21 *Paris Saint-Germain* 26 13 **26 13**

KEANE, Michael (D) 272 18
H: 5 7 W: 12 13 b.Stockport 11-1-93
Internationals: Republic of Ireland U17, U19. England U19, U20, U21, Full caps.
2011–12 Manchester U 0 0
2012–13 Manchester U 0 0
2012–13 *Leicester C* 22 2 **22 2**
2013–14 Manchester U 0 0
2013–14 *Derby Co* 7 0 **7 0**
2013–14 *Blackburn R* 13 3 **13 3**
2014–15 Manchester U 1 0 **1 0**
2014–15 Burnley 21 0
2015–16 Burnley 44 5
2016–17 Burnley 35 2 **100 7**
2017–18 Everton 30 0
2018–19 Everton 33 1
2019–20 Everton 31 2
2020–21 Everton 35 3 **129 6**

KENNY, Jonjoe (D) 104 2
H: 5 9 W: 10 08 b.Kirkdale 15-3-97
Internationals: England U16, U17, U18, U19, U20, U21.
2014–15 Everton 0 0
2015–16 Everton 1 0
2015–16 *Wigan Ath* 7 0 **7 0**
2015–16 *Oxford U* 17 0 **17 0**
2016–17 Everton 1 0
2017–18 Everton 19 0
2018–19 Everton 10 0
2019–20 Everton 0 0
2019–20 *Schalke 04* 31 2 **31 2**
2020–21 Everton 4 0 **35 0**
2020–21 *Celtic* 14 0 **14 0**

KING, Josh (F) 276 54
H: 5 11 W: 11 09 b.Oslo 15-1-92
Internationals: Norway U15, U16, U18, U19, U21, Full caps.
2008–09 Manchester U 0 0
2009–10 Manchester U 0 0
2010–11 Manchester U 0 0
2010–11 *Preston NE* 8 0 **8 0**
2011–12 Manchester U 0 0
2011–12 *Borussia M'gladbach* 2 0 **2 0**
2011–12 *Hull C* 18 1 **18 1**
2012–13 Manchester U 0 0
2012–13 Blackburn R 16 2
2013–14 Blackburn R 32 2
2014–15 Blackburn R 16 1 **64 5**
2015–16 Bournemouth 31 6
2016–17 Bournemouth 36 16
2017–18 Bournemouth 33 8
2018–19 Bournemouth 35 12
2019–20 Bournemouth 26 6
2020–21 Bournemouth 12 0 **173 48**
2020–21 Everton 11 0 **11 0**

KRISTENSEN, Sebastian (D) 0 0
b. 4-2-03
From Lyngby.
2020–21 Everton 0 0

LEBAN, Zan-Luk (G) 0 0
b. 15-12-02
From Escola.
2020–21 Everton 0 0

LOSSL, Jonas (G) 305 0
H: 6 5 W: 14 00 b.Kolding 1-2-89
Internationals: Denmark U17, U18, U19, U20, U21, Full caps.
2009–10 Midtjylland 12 0
2010–11 Midtjylland 30 0
2011–12 Midtjylland 25 0
2012–13 Midtjylland 27 0
2013–14 Midtjylland 33 0 **127 0**
2014–15 Guingamp 30 0
2015–16 Guingamp 37 0 **67 0**
2016–17 Mainz 27 0
2017–18 Mainz 0 0 **27 0**
2017–18 *Huddersfield T* 38 0
2018–19 Huddersfield T 31 0
2019–20 Everton 0 0
2019–20 *Huddersfield T* 15 0 **84 0**
2020–21 Everton 0 0
Transferred to Midtjylland February 2021.

MARKELO, Nathangelo (M) 0 0
H: 6 0 b.Groningen 7-1-99
Internationals: Netherlands U18, U19, U20, U21.
From Volendam.
2020–21 Everton 0 0

McALLISTER, Sean (M) 0 0
H: 5 10 b.Randalstown 1-1-03
From Dungannon.
2020–21 Everton 0 0

MINA, Yerry (D) 180 19
H: 6 5 W: 11 11 b.Guachene 23-9-94
Internationals: Colombia U23, Full caps.
2013 Deportivo Pasto 14 1 **14 1**
2014 Santa Fe 34 3
2015 Santa Fe 23 2
2016 Santa Fe 10 2 **67 7**
2016 Palmeiras 13 4
2017 Palmeiras 15 2 **28 6**
2017–18 Barcelona 5 0 **5 0**
2018–19 Everton 13 1
2019–20 Everton 29 2
2020–21 Everton 24 2 **66 5**

NKOUNKOU, Niels (D) 2 0
b.Pontoise 1-11-00
2017–18 Marseille 0 0
2018–19 Marseille 0 0
2019–20 Marseille 0 0
2020–21 Everton 2 0 **2 0**

OLSEN, Robin (G) 231 0
b.Malmo 8-1-90
2007 Limhamn Bunkeflo 0 0
2008 Limhamn Bunkeflo 0 0
2009 Limhamn Bunkeflo 8 0 **8 0**
2010 Bunkeflo 18 0 **18 0**
2011 Klagshamn 19 0 **19 0**
2012 Malmo 1 0
2013 Malmo 10 0
2014 Malmo 29 0
2015 Malmo 13 0 **53 0**
2015–16 PAOK 11 0 **11 0**
2015–16 *Copenhagen* 14 0
2016–17 Copenhagen 33 0
2017–18 Copenhagen 24 0 **71 0**
2018–19 Roma 27 0
2019–20 Roma 0 0
2019–20 *Cagliari* 17 0 **17 0**
2020–21 Roma 0 0 **27 0**
On loan from Roma.
2020–21 Everton 7 0 **7 0**

ONYANGO, Tyler (M) 0 0
b.Luton 4-3-03
2019–20 Everton 0 0
2020–21 Everton 0 0

PENNINGTON, Matthew (D) 140 6
H: 6 1 W: 12 02 b.Warrington 6-10-94
Internationals: England U19.
2013–14 Everton 0 0
2013–14 *Tranmere R* 17 2 **17 2**
2014–15 Everton 0 0
2014–15 *Coventry C* 24 0 **24 0**
2015–16 Everton 4 0
2015–16 *Walsall* 5 0 **5 0**
2016–17 Everton 3 1
2017–18 Everton 0 0
2017–18 *Leeds U* 24 0 **24 0**
2018–19 Everton 0 0
2018–19 *Ipswich T* 30 1 **30 1**
2019–20 Everton 0 0
2019–20 *Hull C* 14 0 **14 0**
2020–21 Everton 0 0 **7 1**
2020–21 *Shrewsbury T* 19 2 **19 2**

PICKFORD, Jordan (G) 263 0
H: 6 1 b.Washington 7-3-94
Internationals: England U16, U17, U18, U19, U20, U21, Full caps.
2010–11 Sunderland 0 0
2011–12 Sunderland 0 0
2012–13 Sunderland 0 0
2013–14 Sunderland 0 0
2013–14 *Burton Alb* 12 0 **12 0**
2013–14 *Carlisle U* 18 0 **18 0**
2014–15 Sunderland 0 0
2014–15 *Bradford C* 33 0 **33 0**
2015–16 Sunderland 2 0
2015–16 *Preston NE* 24 0 **24 0**
2016–17 Sunderland 29 0 **31 0**
2017–18 Everton 38 0
2018–19 Everton 38 0
2019–20 Everton 38 0
2020–21 Everton 31 0 **145 0**

PRICE, Isaac (M) 0 0
b. 26-9-03
2020–21 Everton 0 0

QUIRK, Sebastian (M) 0 0
b.Liverpool 5-12-01
2020–21 Everton 0 0

RICHARLISON, de Andrade (F) 209 56
H: 5 10 W: 11 03 b.Nova Venecia 10-5-97
Internationals: Brazil U20, Full caps.
2015 America Mineiro 24 9 **24 9**
2016 Fluminense 28 4
2017 Fluminense 14 5 **42 9**
2017–18 Watford 38 5 **38 5**
2018–19 Everton 35 13
2019–20 Everton 36 13
2020–21 Everton 34 7 **105 33**

RODRIGUEZ, James (M) 321 97
b.Cucuta 12-7-91
2007 Envigado 8 0
2008 Envigado 22 9 **30 9**
2008–09 Banfield 11 1
2009–10 Banfield 30 4 **41 5**
2010–11 Porto 15 2
2011–12 Porto 26 13
2012–13 Porto 24 10 **65 25**
2013–14 Monaco 34 9 **34 9**
2014–15 Real Madrid 29 13
2015–16 Real Madrid 26 7
2016–17 Real Madrid 22 8
2017–18 Real Madrid 0 0
2017–18 *Bayern Munich* 23 7
2018–19 Real Madrid 0 0
2018–19 *Bayern Munich* 20 7 **43 14**
2019–20 Real Madrid 8 1
2020–21 Real Madrid 0 0 **85 29**
2020–21 Everton 23 6 **23 6**

SIGURDSSON, Gylfi (M) 416 98
H: 6 1 W: 12 02 b.Reykjavik 9-9-89
Internationals: Iceland U17, U18, U19, U21, Full caps.
From Breidablik.
2007–08 Reading 0 0
2008–09 Reading 0 0
2008–09 *Shrewsbury T* 5 1 **5 1**
2008–09 *Crewe Alex* 15 3 **15 3**
2009–10 Reading 38 16
2010–11 Reading 4 2 **42 18**
2010–11 Hoffenheim 29 9
2011–12 Hoffenheim 7 0 **36 9**
2011–12 *Swansea C* 18 7
2012–13 Tottenham H 33 3
2013–14 Tottenham H 25 5 **58 8**
2014–15 Swansea C 32 7
2015–16 Swansea C 36 11
2016–17 Swansea C 38 9 **124 34**
2017–18 Everton 27 4
2018–19 Everton 38 13
2019–20 Everton 35 2
2020–21 Everton 36 6 **136 25**

SIMMS, Ellis (F) 21 8
b.Oldham 5-1-01
From Manchester C.
2019–20 Everton 0 0
2020–21 Everton 0 0
2020–21 *Blackpool* 21 8 **21 8**

SMALL, Thierry (D) 0 0
b.Solihull 1-8-04
From WBA.
2020–21 Everton 0 0

TOSUN, Cenk (M) 263 93
H: 6 0 W: 12 04 b.Wetzlar 7-6-91
Internationals: Germany U16, U18, U19, U21. Turkey U21, Full caps.
2009–10 Eintracht Frankfurt 1 0 **1 0**
2010–11 Gaziantepspor 14 10
2011–12 Gaziantepspor 32 6
2012–13 Gaziantepspor 32 10
2013–14 Gaziantepspor 31 13 **109 39**
2014–15 Besiktas 18 5
2015–16 Besiktas 29 8
2016–17 Besiktas 33 20
2017–18 Besiktas 16 8
2017–18 Everton 14 5
2018–19 Everton 25 3
2019–20 Everton 5 1
2019–20 *Crystal Palace* 5 1 **5 1**
2020–21 Everton 5 0 **49 9**
2020–21 *Besiktas* 3 3 **99 44**

TYRER, Harry (G) 0 0
2020–21 Everton 0 0

VIRGINIA, Joao (G) 3 0
H: 6 3 W: 13 01 b.Faro 10-10-99
Internationals: Portugal U16, U17, U18, U19, U20, U21.
From Benfica, Arsenal.
2018–19 Everton 0 0
2019–20 *Reading* 2 0 **2 0**
2019–20 Everton 0 0
2020–21 Everton 1 0 **1 0**

WALCOTT, Theo (F) 389 82
H: 5 9 W: 11 01 b.Stanmore 16-3-89
Internationals: England U16, U17, U19, U21, Full caps.
2005–06 Southampton 21 4
2005–06 Arsenal 0 0
2006–07 Arsenal 16 0
2007–08 Arsenal 25 4
2008–09 Arsenal 22 2
2009–10 Arsenal 23 3
2010–11 Arsenal 28 9
2011–12 Arsenal 35 8
2012–13 Arsenal 32 14
2013–14 Arsenal 13 5
2014–15 Arsenal 14 5
2015–16 Arsenal 28 5
2016–17 Arsenal 28 10
2017–18 Arsenal 6 0 **270 65**
2017–18 Everton 14 3
2018–19 Everton 37 5
2019–20 Everton 25 2
2020–21 Everton 1 0 **77 10**
2020–21 *Southampton* 21 3 **42 7**

WARRINGTON, Lewis (M) 0 0
H: 6 0 b.Birkenhead 10-10-02
2020–21 Everton 0 0

WELCH, Reece (D) 0 0
b.Huddersfield 19-9-03
2020–21 Everton 0 0

WHITAKER, Charlie (M) 0 0
b. 16-9-03
2020–21 Everton 0 0

Scholars
Campbell, Elijah Xavier; Davidson, Joel; Higgins, Liam Thomas; Lowey, Daniel Harry; Mallon, Mathew John; McIntyre, Jack Cameron; Mills, Stanley; Small, Thierry; Stewart, Jak Oliver; Thompson, Dylan Isaac.

EXETER C (33)

AJOSE, Nicholas (F) 286 83
H: 5 8 W: 11 00 b.Bury 7-10-91
Internationals: England U16, U17.
2009–10 Manchester U 0 0
2010–11 Manchester U 0 0
2010–11 *Bury* 28 13
2011–12 Peterborough U 2 0
2011–12 *Scunthorpe U* 7 0 **7 0**
2011–12 *Chesterfield* 12 1 **12 1**
2012–13 *Crawley T* 19 2 **19 2**
2012–13 Peterborough U 0 0
2012–13 *Bury* 19 4
2013–14 Peterborough U 22 7 **24 7**
2013–14 *Swindon T* 16 6
2014–15 Leeds U 3 0
2014–15 *Crewe Alex* 27 8 **27 8**
2015–16 Leeds U 0 0 **3 0**
2015–16 Swindon T 38 24
2016–17 Charlton Ath 21 6
2016–17 *Swindon T* 15 5 **69 35**
2017–18 Charlton Ath 12 1
2017–18 *Bury* 9 1 **56 18**
2018–19 Charlton Ath 9 1 **42 8**
2018–19 *Mansfield T* 10 2 **10 2**
2019–20 Exeter C 13 2
2020–21 Exeter C 4 0 **17 2**

ATANGANA, Nigel (M) 196 5
H: 6 2 W: 11 05 b.Corbeil-Essonnes 9-9-89
From Havant & Waterlooville.
2014–15 Portsmouth 30 1
2015–16 Portsmouth 13 0 **43 1**
2015–16 Leyton Orient 16 0
2016–17 Leyton Orient 29 0 **45 0**
2017–18 Cheltenham T 32 1
2018–19 Cheltenham T 26 2 **58 3**
2019–20 Exeter C 22 1
2020–21 Exeter C 28 0 **50 1**

BOWMAN, Ryan (F) 215 50
H: 6 2 W: 11 12 b.Carlisle 30-11-91
2009–10 Carlisle U 6 0
2010–11 Carlisle U 3 0 **9 0**
From Darlington, Hereford U
2013–14 York C 37 8 **37 8**
From York C, Gateshead.
2016–17 Motherwell 24 2
2017–18 Motherwell 32 7
2018–19 Motherwell 16 1 **72 10**
2018–19 Exeter C 18 5
2019–20 Exeter C 37 13
2020–21 Exeter C 42 14 **97 32**

CAPRICE, Jake (M)				**109**	**0**
H: 5 10 W: 11 07 b.Lambeth 11-11-92					
2011–12	Crystal Palace	0	0		
2012–13	Blackpool	0	0		
2012–13	*Dagenham & R*	8	0	**8**	**0**
2013–14	Blackpool	0	0		
2013–14	*St Mirren*	6	0	**6**	**0**
From Lincoln C, Woking, Leyton Orient.					
2018–19	Tranmere R	41	0		
2019–20	Tranmere R	20	0	**61**	**0**
2020–21	Exeter C	34	0	**34**	**0**

COLLINS, Archie (M)				**108**	**6**
b. 31-8-99					
2016–17	Exeter C	0	0		
2017–18	Exeter C	0	0		
2018–19	Exeter C	26	1		
2019–20	Exeter C	36	1		
2020–21	Exeter C	46	4	**108**	**6**

COX, Sonny (M)				**0**	**0**
2020–21	Exeter C	0	0		

DEAN, Will (M)				**2**	**0**
b. 7-8-00					
2017–18	Exeter C	0	0		
2018–19	Exeter C	0	0		
2019–20	Exeter C	0	0		
2020–21	Exeter C	2	0	**2**	**0**

DIABATE, Cheick (D)				**0**	**0**
2019–20	Exeter C	0	0		
2020–21	Exeter C	0	0		

DYER, Jordan (D)				**1**	**0**
b. 29-5-00					
2018–19	Exeter C	0	0		
2019–20	Exeter C	0	0		
2020–21	Exeter C	1	0	**1**	**0**

FISHER, Alex (F)				**222**	**48**
H: 6 2 W: 12 00 b. 30-6-90					
2006–07	Oxford U	0	0		
2007–08	Oxford U	10	1		
2008–09	Oxford U	3	1	**13**	**2**
2009–10	Jerez Industrial	0	0		
2010–11	Jerez Industrial	21	11	**21**	**11**
2011–12	Tienen	7	1	**7**	**1**
2012–13	Racing Mechelen	27	7	**27**	**7**
2013–14	Heist	2	0	**2**	**0**
2013–14	Monza	14	2	**14**	**2**
2014–15	Mansfield T	14	1	**14**	**1**
From Torquay U.					
2015–16	Inverness CT	1	0		
2016–17	Inverness CT	21	8	**22**	**8**
2017–18	Motherwell	11	0	**11**	**0**
2017–18	Yeovil T	17	6		
2018–19	Yeovil T	40	7	**57**	**13**
2019–20	Exeter C	16	1		
2020–21	Exeter C	18	2	**34**	**3**

HARTRIDGE, Alex (D)				**32**	**0**
b. 9-3-99					
2017–18	Exeter C	0	0		
2018–19	Exeter C	3	0		
2019–20	Exeter C	0	0		
2020–21	Exeter C	29	0	**32**	**0**

ISEGUAN, Nelson (M)				**0**	**0**
b. 11-12-02					
2020–21	Exeter C	0	0		

JAY, Matt (D)				**100**	**27**
H: 5 10 W: 10 12 b.Torbay 27-2-96					
2013–14	Exeter C	2	0		
2014–15	Exeter C	3	0		
2015–16	Exeter C	0	0		
2016–17	Exeter C	2	0		
2017–18	Exeter C	17	1		
2018–19	Exeter C	18	4		
2019–20	Exeter C	14	4		
2020–21	Exeter C	44	18	**100**	**27**

KEY, Josh (M)				**43**	**1**
b. 1-11-99					
2017–18	Exeter C	0	0		
2018–19	Exeter C	0	0		
2019–20	Exeter C	0	0		
2020–21	Exeter C	43	1	**43**	**1**

KITE, Harry (M)				**4**	**0**
b.Exeter 29-6-00					
2017–18	Exeter C	0	0		
2018–19	Exeter C	0	0		
2019–20	Exeter C	0	0		
2020–21	Exeter C	4	0	**4**	**0**

LAW, Nicky (M)				**473**	**62**
H: 5 10 W: 11 07 b.Nottingham 29-3-88					
2005–06	Sheffield U	0	0		
2006–07	Sheffield U	4	0		
2006–07	*Yeovil T*	6	0	**6**	**0**
2007–08	Sheffield U	1	0		
2007–08	*Bradford C*	10	2		
2008–09	Sheffield U	0	0	**5**	**0**
2008–09	*Bradford C*	33	0		
2009–10	Rotherham U	42	4		
2010–11	Rotherham U	44	4	**86**	**8**
2011–12	Motherwell	38	4		
2012–13	Motherwell	38	6	**76**	**10**
2013–14	Rangers	32	9		
2014–15	Rangers	36	10		
2015–16	Rangers	18	1	**86**	**20**
2016–17	Bradford C	40	4		
2017–18	Bradford C	38	0	**121**	**6**
2018–19	Exeter C	43	10		
2019–20	Exeter C	32	7		
2020–21	Exeter C	18	1	**93**	**18**
Transferred to Indy Eleven January 2021.					

LEE, Harry (G)				**0**	**0**
2020–21	Exeter C	0	0		

MAXTED, Jonathan (G)				**46**	**0**
H: 6 0 W: 11 03 b. 26-10-93					
2012–13	Doncaster R	0	0		
2013–14	Doncaster R	0	0		
2014–15	Hartlepool U	0	0		
2017–18	Accrington S	1	0		
2018–19	Accrington S	19	0	**20**	**0**
2019–20	Exeter C	17	0		
2020–21	Exeter C	9	0	**26**	**0**

McARDLE, Rory (D)				**506**	**25**
H: 6 1 W: 11 04 b.Doncaster 1-5-87					
Internationals: Northern Ireland U21, Full caps.					
2005–06	Sheffield W	0	0		
2005–06	*Rochdale*	19	1		
2006–07	Sheffield W	1	0	**1**	**0**
2006–07	Rochdale	25	0		
2007–08	Rochdale	43	3		
2008–09	Rochdale	41	2		
2009–10	Rochdale	20	0	**148**	**6**
2010–11	Aberdeen	28	2		
2011–12	Aberdeen	25	0	**53**	**2**
2012–13	Bradford C	40	2		
2013–14	Bradford C	41	3		
2014–15	Bradford C	43	3		
2015–16	Bradford C	35	3		
2016–17	Bradford C	24	1	**183**	**12**
2017–18	Scunthorpe U	36	1		
2018–19	Scunthorpe U	38	0		
2019–20	Scunthorpe U	26	3	**100**	**4**
2020–21	Exeter C	21	1	**21**	**1**

MORISON, Louis (M)				**0**	**0**
2019–20	Exeter C	0	0		
2020–21	Exeter C	0	0		

PAGE, Lewis (D)				**87**	**1**
b.London 20-5-96					
2014–15	West Ham U	0	0		
2015–16	West Ham U	0	0		
2015–16	*Cambridge U*	6	0	**6**	**0**
2016–17	West Ham U	0	0		
2016–17	*Coventry C*	22	0	**22**	**0**
2016–17	Charlton Ath	8	0		
2017–18	Charlton Ath	8	1		
2018–19	Charlton Ath	11	0		
2019–20	Charlton Ath	0	0	**27**	**1**
2020–21	Exeter C	32	0	**32**	**0**

PARKES, Tom (D)				**340**	**9**
H: 6 3 W: 12 05 b.Sutton-in-Ashfield 15-1-92					
Internationals: England U17. England C.					
2008–09	Leicester C	0	0		
2009–10	Leicester C	0	0		
2009–10	*Burton Alb*	22	1		
2010–11	Leicester C	0	0		
2010–11	*Yeovil T*	1	0	**1**	**0**
2010–11	*Burton Alb*	5	0		
2011–12	Leicester C	0	0		
2011–12	*Burton Alb*	4	0	**31**	**1**
2011–12	*Bristol R*	14	0		
2012–13	Leicester C	0	0		
2012–13	Bristol R	40	1		
2013–14	Bristol R	44	1		
2015–16	Bristol R	31	0	**129**	**2**
2016–17	Leyton Orient	41	1	**41**	**1**
2017–18	Carlisle U	37	1		
2018–19	Carlisle U	39	1	**76**	**2**
2019–20	Exeter C	31	2		
2020–21	Exeter C	31	1	**62**	**3**

POND, Alfie (D)				**0**	**0**
2020–21	Exeter C	0	0		

RANDALL, Joel (M)				**32**	**8**
b.Salisbury 29-10-99					
2017–18	Exeter C	0	0		
2018–19	Exeter C	0	0		
2019–20	Exeter C	2	0		
2020–21	Exeter C	30	8	**32**	**8**

SEYMOUR, Ben (F)				**44**	**1**
b.Watford 16-4-99					
2019–20	Exeter C	11	0		
2020–21	Exeter C	33	1	**44**	**1**

SMERDON, Noah (M)				**0**	**0**
2019–20	Exeter C	0	0		
2020–21	Exeter C	0	0		

SPARKES, Jack (M)				**62**	**3**
b.Exeter 29-9-00					
2017–18	Exeter C	3	0		
2018–19	Exeter C	0	0		
2019–20	Exeter C	17	0		
2020–21	Exeter C	42	3	**62**	**3**

STUBBS, Sam (D)				**49**	**1**
b. 20-11-98					
From Everton.					
2016–17	Wigan Ath	0	0		
2017–18	Wigan Ath	0	0		
2017–18	*Crewe Alex*	5	0	**5**	**0**
2018–19	Middlesbrough	0	0		
2018–19	*Notts Co*	17	0	**17**	**0**
2019–20	Middlesbrough	0	0		
2019–20	*Hamilton A*	19	0		
2019–20	*ADO Den Haag*	3	0	**3**	**0**
2020–21	Hamilton A	0	0	**19**	**0**
2020–21	Middlesbrough	0	0		
2020–21	Fleetwood T	5	1	**5**	**1**
2020–21	Exeter C	0	0		

SWEENEY, Pierce (D)				**198**	**17**
H: 5 10 W: 12 07 b.Dublin 11-9-94					
Internationals: Republic of Ireland U17, U19, U21.					
2012	Bray W	12	0	**12**	**0**
2012–13	Reading	0	0		
2013–14	Reading	0	0		
2014–15	Reading	0	0		
2015–16	Reading	0	0		
2016–17	Exeter C	29	0		
2017–18	Exeter C	40	8		
2018–19	Exeter C	43	4		
2019–20	Exeter C	36	2		
2020–21	Exeter C	38	3	**186**	**17**

TAYLOR, Jake (M)				**312**	**33**
H: 5 10 W: 12 01 b.Ascot 1-12-91					
Internationals: Wales U17, U19, U21, Full caps.					
2010–11	Reading	1	0		
2011–12	Reading	0	0		
2011–12	*Aldershot T*	3	0	**3**	**0**
2011–12	*Exeter C*	30	3		
2012–13	Reading	0	0		
2012–13	*Cheltenham T*	8	1	**8**	**1**
2012–13	*Crawley T*	4	0	**4**	**0**
2013–14	Reading	8	0		
2014–15	Reading	22	2		
2014–15	*Leyton Orient*	3	0	**3**	**0**
2015–16	Reading	0	0	**31**	**2**
2015–16	*Motherwell*	7	0	**7**	**0**
2015–16	Exeter C	16	4		
2016–17	Exeter C	43	4		
2017–18	Exeter C	44	8		
2018–19	Exeter C	46	3		
2019–20	Exeter C	33	2		
2020–21	Exeter C	44	6	**256**	**30**

VEALE, Jack (M)				**0**	**0**
2020–21	Exeter C	0	0		

WARD, Lewis (G)				**40**	**0**
b. 5-3-97					
Internationals: England U16.					
2014–15	Reading	0	0		
2015–16	Reading	0	0		
2016–17	Reading	0	0		
2017–18	Reading	0	0		
2018–19	Reading	0	0		
2018–19	*Northampton T*	0	0		
2018–19	*Forest Green R*	12	0	**12**	**0**
2019–20	Exeter C	20	0		
2020–21	Exeter C	8	0	**28**	**0**
2020–21	*Portsmouth*	0	0		

WILLIAMS, Randell (F)				**102**	**12**
H: 6 3 b.London 30-12-96					
From Tower Hamlets.					
2016–17	Crystal Palace	0	0		
2017–18	Watford	0	0		
2017–18	*Wycombe W*	6	1		
2018–19	Watford	0	0		
2018–19	*Wycombe W*	20	2	**26**	**3**
2018–19	Exeter C	10	0		
2019–20	Exeter C	37	5		
2020–21	Exeter C	29	4	**76**	**9**

WILSON, Lewis (F)				**0**	**0**
2020–21	Exeter C	0	0		

Scholars
Arthur, Jack Jamie; Clark, Max Harry; Collins, Eli; Collins, Zeph; Ford, Harry Joseph; Hanson, Charles Harry; Johnson, Ellis Oren; Lilley, Michael; Lovett, Frank Eli; Nevile, Toby John Sandford; Nicholson, Jamie Keletea; Veale, Jack Lewis; Wragg, Joseph.

FLEETWOOD T (34)

ANDREW, Danny (D) 258 12
H: 5 11 W: 11 06 b.Holbeach 23-12-90
2009–10 Peterborough U 2 0 **2 0**
2009–10 *Cheltenham T* 10 0
2010–11 Cheltenham T 43 4
2011–12 Cheltenham T 10 0
2012–13 Cheltenham T 1 0 **64 4**
From Gloucester C, Macclesfield T.
2014–15 Fleetwood T 7 0
2015–16 Fleetwood T 9 0
2016–17 Grimsby T 46 0 **46 0**
2017–18 Doncaster R 4 0
2018–19 Doncaster R 46 4 **50 4**
2019–20 Fleetwood T 35 2
2020–21 Fleetwood T 45 2 **96 4**

BAGGLEY, Barry (M) 5 0
b.Belfast 11-2-02
Internationals: Northern Ireland U17.
2018–19 Fleetwood T 3 0
2019–20 Fleetwood T 0 0
2020–21 Fleetwood T 2 0 **5 0**

BARRETT, Sam (D) 0 0
2020–21 Fleetwood T 0 0

BATCH, Billy (D) 0 0
2020–21 Fleetwood T 0 0

BATTY, Daniel (D) 81 1
b.Featherstone 10-12-97
2016–17 Hull C 0 0
2017–18 Hull C 1 0
2018–19 Hull C 27 0
2019–20 Hull C 30 1
2020–21 Hull C 6 0 **64 1**
2020–21 Fleetwood T 17 0 **17 0**

BIGGINS, Harrison (M) 72 3
b. 15-3-96
From Stocksbridge Park Steels.
2017–18 Fleetwood T 7 0
2018–19 Fleetwood T 23 1
2019–20 Fleetwood T 10 0
2020–21 Fleetwood T 10 0 **50 1**
2020–21 *Barrow* 22 2 **22 2**

BIRD, Samuel (D) 0 0
b. 12-3-03
2020–21 Fleetwood T 0 0

BORWICK, Johnathon (G) 0 0
2020–21 Fleetwood T 0 0

BOYLE, Dylan (M) 0 0
Internationals: Northern Ireland U17.
2018–19 Fleetwood T 0 0
2019–20 Fleetwood T 0 0
2020–21 Fleetwood T 0 0

BURNS, Wes (F) 237 29
H: 5 8 W: 10 10 b.Cardiff 28-12-95
Internationals: Wales U21.
2012–13 Bristol C 6 0
2013–14 Bristol C 20 1
2014–15 Bristol C 3 1
2014–15 *Oxford U* 9 1 **9 1**
2014–15 *Cheltenham T* 14 4 **14 4**
2015–16 Bristol C 14 1 **43 3**
2015–16 *Fleetwood T* 14 5
2016–17 Fleetwood T 10 0
2016–17 *Aberdeen* 13 0 **13 0**
2017–18 Fleetwood T 28 2
2018–19 Fleetwood T 39 7
2019–20 Fleetwood T 34 2
2020–21 Fleetwood T 33 5 **158 21**

CAIRNS, Alex (G) 168 0
H: 6 0 W: 11 05 b.Doncaster 4-1-93
2011–12 Leeds U 1 0
2012–13 Leeds U 0 0
2013–14 Leeds U 0 0
2014–15 Leeds U 0 0 **1 0**
2015–16 Chesterfield 0 0
2015–16 Rotherham U 0 0
2016–17 Fleetwood T 30 0
2017–18 Fleetwood T 38 0
2018–19 Fleetwood T 46 0
2019–20 Fleetwood T 25 0
2020–21 Fleetwood T 28 0 **167 0**

CAMPS, Callum (M) 243 34
b.Stockport 30-11-95
Internationals: Northern Ireland U18, U21.
2012–13 Rochdale 2 0
2013–14 Rochdale 0 0
2014–15 Rochdale 12 1
2015–16 Rochdale 32 5
2016–17 Rochdale 44 8
2017–18 Rochdale 42 2
2018–19 Rochdale 41 3
2019–20 Rochdale 28 6 **201 25**
2020–21 Fleetwood T 42 9 **42 9**

COLEMAN, Joel (G) 68 0
H: 6 6 W: 12 13 b.Bolton 26-9-95
2013–14 Oldham Ath 0 0
2014–15 Oldham Ath 11 0
2015–16 Oldham Ath 32 0 **43 0**
2016–17 Huddersfield T 5 0
2017–18 Huddersfield T 0 0
2018–19 Huddersfield T 1 0
2018–19 *Shrewsbury T* 16 0 **16 0**
2019–20 Huddersfield T 3 0 **9 0**
2020–21 Fleetwood T 0 0

COUTTS, Paul (M) 384 10
H: 5 9 W: 11 11 b.Aberdeen 22-7-88
Internationals: Scotland U21.
From Aberdeen.
2008–09 Peterborough U 37 0
2009–10 Peterborough U 16 0 **53 0**
2009–10 Preston NE 13 1
2010–11 Preston NE 23 1
2011–12 Preston NE 41 2 **77 4**
2012–13 Derby Co 44 3
2013–14 Derby Co 8 0
2014–15 Derby Co 7 0 **59 3**
2014–15 Sheffield U 20 0
2015–16 Sheffield U 32 0
2016–17 Sheffield U 43 2
2017–18 Sheffield U 16 1
2018–19 Sheffield U 13 0 **124 3**
2019–20 Fleetwood T 32 0
2020–21 Fleetwood T 20 0 **52 0**
2020–21 *Salford C* 19 0 **19 0**

CRELLIN, Billy (G) 16 0
b. 30-1-00
Internationals: England U17, U18, U19, U20.
2017–18 Fleetwood T 0 0
2018–19 Fleetwood T 0 0
2019–20 Fleetwood T 5 0
2020–21 Fleetwood T 0 0 **5 0**
2020–21 *Bolton W* 11 0 **11 0**

DONAGHY, Thomas (G) 0 0
From Bradford C.
2020–21 Fleetwood T 0 0

DUFFY, Mark (M) 402 38
H: 5 9 W: 11 05 b.Liverpool 7-10-85
From Vauxhall Motor, Prescott Cables, Southport.
2008–09 Morecambe 9 1
2009–10 Morecambe 35 4
2010–11 Morecambe 22 0 **66 5**
2010–11 Scunthorpe U 22 1
2011–12 Scunthorpe U 37 2
2012–13 Scunthorpe U 43 5 **102 8**
2013–14 Doncaster R 36 2 **36 2**
2014–15 Birmingham C 4 0
2014–15 *Chesterfield* 3 0 **3 0**
2015–16 Birmingham C 0 0 **4 0**
2015–16 *Burton Alb* 45 8 **45 8**
2016–17 Sheffield U 39 6
2017–18 Sheffield U 36 3
2018–19 Sheffield U 36 6
2019–20 Sheffield U 0 0 **111 15**
2019–20 *Stoke C* 6 0 **6 0**
2019–20 *ADO Den Haag* 5 0 **5 0**
2020–21 Fleetwood T 24 0 **24 0**

EDWARDS, Danny (M) 0 0
2020–21 Fleetwood T 0 0

FEENEY, Josh (D) 0 0
2020–21 Fleetwood T 0 0

FINLEY, Sam (M) 97 6
H: 5 7 W: 10 10 b.Liverpool 4-8-92
From Southport, Warrington T, The New Saints, AFC Fylde.
2018–19 Accrington S 37 1
2019–20 Accrington S 31 2 **68 3**
2020–21 Fleetwood T 29 3 **29 3**

GARNER, Gerard (F) 18 3
b.Liverpool 2-11-98
2017–18 Fleetwood 0 0
2018–19 Fleetwood T 1 0
2019–20 Fleetwood T 0 0
2020–21 Fleetwood T 17 3 **18 3**

HAYES, Cian (F) 0 0
2019–20 Fleetwood T 0 0
2020–21 Fleetwood T 0 0

HILL, James (D) 30 0
b. 10-1-02
2018–19 Fleetwood T 2 0
2019–20 Fleetwood T 0 0
2020–21 Fleetwood T 28 0 **30 0**

HOLGATE, Harrison (D) 18 0
b. 5-10-00
2018–19 Fleetwood T 0 0
2019–20 Fleetwood T 0 0
2020–21 Fleetwood T 18 0 **18 0**

JOHNSTON, Carl (M) 0 0
b. 29-5-02
Internationals: Northern Ireland U17, U19.
From Linfield.
2019–20 Fleetwood T 0 0
2020–21 Fleetwood T 0 0

MADDEN, Patrick (F) 441 139
H: 6 0 W: 11 13 b.Dublin 4-3-90
Internationals: Republic of Ireland U19, U21, U23, Full caps.
2008 Bohemians 18 4
2009 Bohemians 2 0
2009 Shelbourne 13 6 **13 6**
2010 Bohemians 34 10 **54 14**
2010–11 Carlisle U 13 0
2011–12 Carlisle U 18 1
2012–13 Carlisle U 1 1 **32 2**
2012–13 *Yeovil T* 35 22
2013–14 Yeovil T 9 0 **44 22**
2013–14 Scunthorpe U 21 5
2014–15 Scunthorpe U 46 14
2015–16 Scunthorpe U 46 20
2016–17 Scunthorpe U 34 11
2017–18 Scunthorpe U 20 2 **167 52**
2017–18 Fleetwood T 20 6
2018–19 Fleetwood T 44 15
2019–20 Fleetwood T 35 15
2020–21 Fleetwood T 32 7 **131 43**
Transferred to Stockport Co March 2021.

MATETE, Jay (M) 27 3
b. 11-2-01
From Reading.
2019–20 Fleetwood T 0 0
2020–21 Fleetwood T 7 0 **7 0**
2020–21 *Grimsby T* 20 3 **20 3**

McMILLAN, Max (F) 0 0
H: 6 0 b.York 3-10-02
From Leeds U.
2020–21 Fleetwood T 0 0

MORRIS, Josh (M) 272 53
H: 5 9 W: 10 00 b.Preston 30-9-91
Internationals: England U20.
2010–11 Blackburn R 4 0
2011–12 Blackburn R 2 0
2011–12 *Yeovil T* 5 0 **5 0**
2012–13 Blackburn R 10 0
2012–13 *Rotherham U* 5 0 **5 0**
2013–14 Blackburn R 4 0
2013–14 *Carlisle U* 6 0 **6 0**
2013–14 *Fleetwood T* 14 2
2014–15 Blackburn R 0 0 **20 0**
2014–15 *Fleetwood T* 45 8
2015–16 Bradford C 13 1 **13 1**
2016–17 Scunthorpe U 44 19
2017–18 Scunthorpe U 44 11
2018–19 Scunthorpe U 19 5 **107 35**
2019–20 Fleetwood T 33 7
2020–21 Fleetwood T 24 0 **116 17**

MORRIS, Shayden (M) 5 0
b. 3-11-01
From Southend U.
2019–20 Fleetwood T 0 0
2020–21 Fleetwood T 5 0 **5 0**

RAFFIE, Akiel (M) 0 0
2020–21 Fleetwood T 0 0

ROSSITER, Jordan (M) 77 3
H: 5 8 W: 10 10 b.Liverpool 24-3-97
Internationals: England U16, U17, U18, U19.
2013–14 Liverpool 0 0
2014–15 Liverpool 0 0
2015–16 Liverpool 1 0 **1 0**
2016–17 Rangers 4 0
2017–18 Rangers 2 1
2018–19 Rangers 4 0
2018–19 *Bury* 16 1 **16 1**
2019–20 Rangers 0 0 **10 1**
2019–20 *Fleetwood T* 15 0
2020–21 Fleetwood T 35 1 **50 1**

RYDEL, Ryan (D)				**12**	**0**
b. 9-2-01					
2018–19	Fleetwood T	5	0		
2019–20	Fleetwood T	0	0		
2020–21	Fleetwood T	7	0	**12**	**0**

Transferred to Stockport Co April 2021.

SAUNDERS, Harvey (M)				**27**	**3**

b. 20-7-97
From Darlington Railway Ath, Bishop Auckland, Durham C, Darlington.

2018–19	Fleetwood T	0	0		
2019–20	Fleetwood T	6	0		
2020–21	Fleetwood T	21	3	**27**	**3**

SHERON, Nathan (D)				**41**	**0**
b.Whiston 4-10-97					
2017–18	Fleetwood T	0	0		
2018–19	Fleetwood T	26	0		
2019–20	Fleetwood T	0	0		
2019–20	*Walsall*	7	0	**7**	**0**
2020–21	Fleetwood T	1	0	**27**	**0**
2020–21	*St Mirren*	7	0	**7**	**0**

SMITH, Lawrence (M)				**0**	**0**
2018–19	Fleetwood T	0	0		
2019–20	Fleetwood T	0	0		
2020–21	Fleetwood T	0	0		

TAKPE, Enoch (F)				**0**	**0**
2020–21	Fleetwood T	0	0		

TEALE, Connor (D)				**0**	**0**
b. 8-10-02					
From Leeds U.					
2020–21	Fleetwood T	0	0		

THOMPSON, Ben (M)				**0**	**0**
2020–21	Fleetwood T	0	0		

WHELAN, Glenn (M)				**563**	**19**

H: 5 11 W: 12 07 b.Dublin 13-1-84
Internationals: Republic of Ireland U16, U21, B, Full caps.

2000–01	Manchester C	0	0		
2001–02	Manchester C	0	0		
2002–03	Manchester C	0	0		
2003–04	Manchester C	0	0		
2003–04	*Bury*	13	0	**13**	**0**
2004–05	Sheffield W	36	2		
2005–06	Sheffield W	43	1		
2006–07	Sheffield W	38	7		
2007–08	Sheffield W	25	2	**142**	**12**
2007–08	Stoke C	14	1		
2008–09	Stoke C	26	1		
2009–10	Stoke C	33	2		
2010–11	Stoke C	29	0		
2011–12	Stoke C	30	1		
2012–13	Stoke C	32	0		
2013–14	Stoke C	32	0		
2014–15	Stoke C	28	0		
2015–16	Stoke C	37	0		
2016–17	Stoke C	30	0	**291**	**5**
2017–18	Aston Villa	33	1		
2018–19	Aston Villa	35	1	**68**	**2**
2019–20	Hearts	15	0	**15**	**0**
2019–20	Fleetwood T	11	0		
2020–21	Fleetwood T	23	0	**34**	**0**

Scholars

Barratt, Samuel Anthony William; Borwick, Johnathon Robert; Collins, Joseph Francis; Eastham, Connor Jake; Fenton, Matthew James; Hoyle, Thomas Joseph; Patterson, Lewis Thomas; Sithole, Shaun Thabo; Smith, Covy-Leigh Mark; Takpe, Enoch Oluwakayode; Thompson-Prempeh, Donte; Wallace, Jake David; Wilson, Harry Oliver Haslett.

FOREST GREEN R (35)

ADAMS, Ebou (M)				**76**	**6**

b. 15-1-96
Internationals: Gambia Full caps.
From Dartford.

2017–18	Norwich C	0	0		
2017–18	*Shrewsbury T*	5	0	**5**	**0**

From Ebbsfleet U.

2019–20	Forest Green R	34	4		
2020–21	Forest Green R	37	2	**71**	**6**

ALLEN, Taylor (F)				**10**	**1**
b. 16-6-00					
From Romulus, Nuneaton Bor.					
2019–20	Forest Green R	5	1		
2020–21	Forest Green R	5	0	**10**	**1**

BELL, Finn (M)				**0**	**0**
2020–21	Forest Green R	0	0		

BERNARD, Dominic (D)				**53**	**0**

b.Gloucester 29-3-97
Internationals: Republic of Ireland U17, U18.

2018–19	Birmingham C	0	0		
2019–20	Forest Green R	28	0		
2020–21	Forest Green R	25	0	**53**	**0**

BUNKER, Harvey (M)				**0**	**0**
2019–20	Forest Green R	0	0		
2020–21	Forest Green R	0	0		

CADDEN, Nicky (M)				**177**	**18**
b.Bellshill 19-9-96					
2013–14	Airdrieonians	12	0		
2014–15	Airdrieonians	4	0		
2015–16	Airdrieonians	24	3	**40**	**3**
2016–17	Livingston	34	6		
2017–18	Livingston	26	1		
2018–19	Livingston	12	0	**72**	**7**
2018–19	*Ayr U*	10	0	**10**	**0**
2019–20	Greenock Morton	22	5	**22**	**5**
2020–21	Forest Green R	33	3	**33**	**3**

CARGILL, Baily (D)				**122**	**5**

H: 6 2 W: 13 10 b.Winchester 13-10-95
Internationals: England U20.

2012–13	Bournemouth	0	0		
2013–14	Bournemouth	0	0		
2013–14	*Torquay U*	5	0	**5**	**0**
2014–15	Bournemouth	0	0		
2015–16	Bournemouth	0	0		
2015–16	*Coventry C*	5	1	**5**	**1**
2016–17	Bournemouth	1	0		
2016–17	*Gillingham*	9	1	**9**	**1**
2017–18	Bournemouth	0	0	**1**	**0**
2017–18	*Fleetwood T*	11	0	**11**	**0**
2017–18	*Partick Thistle*	16	0	**16**	**0**
2018–19	Milton Keynes D	29	0		
2019–20	Milton Keynes D	12	0		
2020–21	Milton Keynes D	11	1	**52**	**1**
2020–21	Forest Green R	23	2	**23**	**2**

CARTER, Jack (M)				**0**	**0**
2020–21	Forest Green R	0	0		

COLLINS, Aaron (F)				**142**	**26**

b. 27-5-97
Internationals: Wales U19.

2014–15	Newport Co	2	0		
2015–16	Newport Co	18	2		
2015–16	Wolverhampton W	0	0		
2016–17	Wolverhampton W	0	0		
2016–17	*Notts Co*	18	2	**18**	**2**
2017–18	Wolverhampton W	0	0		
2017–18	*Newport Co*	10	0	**30**	**2**
2018–19	Wolverhampton W	0	0		
2018–19	*Colchester U*	7	0	**7**	**0**
2018–19	Morecambe	15	8	**15**	**8**
2019–20	Forest Green R	28	4		
2020–21	Forest Green R	44	10	**72**	**14**

COVIL, Vaughn (M)				**2**	**0**

b. 26-7-03
Internationals: USA U16.
From Southampton.

2019–20	Forest Green R	2	0		
2020–21	Forest Green R	0	0	**2**	**0**

EVANS, Jack (D)				**2**	**0**
b. 10-8-00					
2019–20	Blackburn R	0	0		
2020–21	Forest Green R	2	0	**2**	**0**

GODWIN-MALIFE, Udoka (D)				**61**	**0**
b. 9-5-00					
From Oxford C.					
2018–19	Forest Green R	5	0		
2019–20	Forest Green R	12	0		
2020–21	Forest Green R	44	0	**61**	**0**

HALLETT, Luke (F)				**1**	**0**
b. 9-10-02					
2020–21	Forest Green R	1	0	**1**	**0**

MARCH, Josh (M)				**28**	**7**
b. 18-3-97					
2019–20	Forest Green R	10	2		
2020–21	Forest Green R	4	0	**14**	**2**
2020–21	*Harrogate T*	14	5	**14**	**5**

MATT, Jamille (F)				**253**	**63**

H: 6 1 W: 11 11 b.Walsall 20-10-89
From Sutton Coldfield T, Kidderminster H.

2012–13	Fleetwood T	14	3		
2013–14	Fleetwood T	25	8		
2014–15	Fleetwood T	0	0		
2015–16	Fleetwood T	17	3	**56**	**14**
2015–16	*Stevenage*	8	1	**8**	**1**
2015–16	*Plymouth Arg*	11	5	**11**	**5**
2016–17	Blackpool	32	3		
2017–18	Blackpool	0	0	**32**	**3**
2017–18	*Grimsby T*	34	4	**34**	**4**
2018–19	Newport Co	43	14		
2019–20	Newport Co	33	6	**76**	**20**
2020–21	Forest Green R	36	16	**36**	**16**

McCOULSKY, Shawn (F)				**63**	**6**
b.Lewisham 6-1-97					
From Dulwich Hamlet.					
2017–18	Bristol C	0	0		
2017–18	*Newport Co*	27	6	**27**	**6**
2018–19	Bristol C	0	0		
2018–19	*Southend U*	15	0	**15**	**0**
2018–19	Forest Green R	13	0		
2019–20	Forest Green R	6	0		
2020–21	Forest Green R	2	0	**21**	**0**

McGEE, Luke (G)				**120**	**0**

H: 6 2 W: 12 08 b.Edgware 9-2-95
Internationals: England U17.

2014–15	Tottenham H	0	0		
2015–16	Tottenham H	0	0		
2016–17	Tottenham H	0	0		
2016–17	*Peterborough U*	39	0	**39**	**0**
2017–18	Portsmouth	44	0		
2018–19	Portsmouth	0	0		
2019–20	Portsmouth	0	0	**44**	**0**
2019–20	*Bradford C*	4	0	**4**	**0**
2020–21	Forest Green R	33	0	**33**	**0**

MOORE-TAYLOR, Jordan (D)				**226**	**13**
H: 5 10 W: 13 01 b.Exeter 21-1-94					
2012–13	Exeter C	7	0		
2013–14	Exeter C	29	1		
2014–15	Exeter C	26	2		
2015–16	Exeter C	32	0		
2016–17	Exeter C	42	5		
2017–18	Exeter C	24	2	**160**	**10**
2018–19	Milton Keynes D	23	1		
2019–20	Milton Keynes D	14	0	**37**	**1**
2020–21	Forest Green R	29	2	**29**	**2**

STEVENS, Mathew (F)				**71**	**8**
H: 5 11 W: 11 09 b. 12-2-98					
2015–16	Barnet	10	1	**10**	**1**
2016–17	Peterborough U	1	0		
2017–18	Peterborough U	0	0		
2018–19	Peterborough U	3	0	**4**	**0**
2019–20	Forest Green R	29	4		
2020–21	Forest Green R	10	2	**39**	**6**
2020–21	*Stevenage*	18	1	**18**	**1**

STOKES, Chris (M)				**191**	**9**

H: 5 7 W: 10 04 b.Trowbridge 8-3-91
Internationals: England U17, C.

2009–10	Bolton W	0	0		
2009–10	*Crewe Alex*	2	0	**2**	**0**

From Swindon Supermarine, Forest Green R.

2014–15	Coventry C	16	1		
2015–16	Coventry C	36	2		
2016–17	Coventry C	7	0		
2017–18	Coventry C	29	0	**88**	**3**
2018–19	Bury	37	4	**37**	**4**
2019–20	Stevenage	25	0	**25**	**0**
2019–20	Forest Green R	5	0		
2020–21	Forest Green R	34	2	**39**	**2**

SWEENEY, Dan (M)				**46**	**0**

H: 6 3 W: 11 11 b.Kingston upon Thames 25-4-94
Internationals: England C.
From AFC Wimbledon, Kingstonian, Dulwich Hamlet, Maidstone U.

2016–17	Barnet	4	0		
2017–18	Barnet	21	0	**25**	**0**
2020–21	Forest Green R	21	0	**21**	**0**

THOMAS, Lewis (G)				**28**	**0**

b. 20-9-97
Internationals: Wales U17.
From Swansea C.

2018–19	Forest Green R	0	0		
2019–20	Forest Green R	15	0		
2020–21	Forest Green R	13	0	**28**	**0**

WAGSTAFF, Scott (M)				**352**	**30**
H: 5 10 W: 10 03 b.Maidstone 31-3-90					
2007–08	Charlton Ath	2	0		
2008–09	Charlton Ath	2	0		
2008–09	*Bournemouth*	5	0	**5**	**0**
2009–10	Charlton Ath	30	4		
2010–11	Charlton Ath	40	8		
2011–12	Charlton Ath	34	4		
2012–13	Charlton Ath	9	1	**117**	**17**
2012–13	*Leyton Orient*	7	0	**7**	**0**
2013–14	Bristol C	37	5		
2014–15	Bristol C	26	2		
2015–16	Bristol C	9	1	**72**	**8**
2016–17	Gillingham	26	1		
2017–18	Gillingham	31	0	**57**	**1**
2018–19	AFC Wimbledon	35	2		
2019–20	AFC Wimbledon	26	1	**61**	**3**
2020–21	Forest Green R	33	1	**33**	**1**

WHITEHOUSE, Elliott (M) 117 8
H: 5 11 W: 12 08 b.Worksop 27-10-93
Internationals: England C.
2012–13 Sheffield U 3 0
2013–14 Sheffield U 0 0 **3 0**
2013–14 *York C* 15 0 **15 0**
2014–15 Notts Co 7 1 **7 1**
2017–18 Lincoln C 32 2 **32 2**
2019–20 Grimsby T 33 3 **33 3**
2020–21 Forest Green R 27 2 **27 2**

WILSON, Kane (D) 88 2
H: 5 10 W: 11 03 b. 11-3-00
Internationals: England U16, U17.
2016–17 WBA 0 0
2017–18 WBA 0 0
2017–18 *Exeter C* 19 1
2018–19 WBA 0 0
2018–19 *Walsall* 14 0 **14 0**
2018–19 *Exeter C* 17 0 **36 1**
2019–20 WBA 0 0
2019–20 *Tranmere R* 13 0 **13 0**
2020–21 Forest Green R 25 1 **25 1**

YOUNG , Jake (F) 29 6
b.Huddersfield 22-7-01
2020–21 Forest Green R 29 6 **29 6**

Scholars
Baxter, Benjamin David; Clapp, Thomas Patrick; Hallett, Luke James; Jenkins, Joshua Paul; Jeremiah, Joseph Kenneth; Joseph, Shawn Franklyn; McIntosh, Marcel Philip; Morgan, Dylan James; Olawale Oyebamiji, Jireh Joshua; Pierpoint, Alessandro; Rees, Luc William; Thayer, Archie David; Thompson-Roberts, Jago; Yang, Seung Woo.

FULHAM (36)

ABLADE, Terry (F) 0 0
b.Accra 12-10-01
Internationals: Finland U16, U17, U18, U19.
From Jazz.
2020–21 Fulham 0 0

ABRAHAM, Timmy (F) 14 0
b. 28-12-00
From Charlton Ath.
2019–20 Fulham 0 0
2019–20 *Bristol R* 4 0 **4 0**
2020–21 Fulham 0 0
2020–21 *Plymouth Arg* 3 0 **3 0**
2020–21 *Raith R* 7 0 **7 0**

ADARABIOYO, Tosin (D) 96 3
H: 6 3 b. 24-9-97
Internationals: England U16, U17, U18, U19.
2014–15 Manchester C 0 0
2015–16 Manchester C 0 0
2016–17 Manchester C 0 0
2017–18 Manchester C 0 0
2018–19 Manchester C 0 0
2018–19 *WBA* 29 0 **29 0**
2019–20 Manchester C 0 0
2019–20 *Blackburn R* 34 3 **34 3**
2020–21 Fulham 33 0 **33 0**

AINA, Ola (D) 140 3
H: 5 9 W: 10 03 b.London 8-10-96
Internationals: England U16, U17, U18, U19, U20. Nigeria Full caps.
2015–16 Chelsea 0 0
2016–17 Chelsea 3 0
2017–18 Chelsea 0 0
2017–18 *Hull C* 44 0 **44 0**
2018–19 Chelsea 0 0 **3 0**
2018–19 *Torino* 30 1
2019–20 Torino 32 0
2020–21 Torino 0 0 **62 1**
On loan from Torino.
2020–21 Fulham 31 2 **31 2**

AMEYAW, Eric (D) 0 0
b. 17-6-02
2020–21 Fulham 0 0

ANDERSEN, Joachim (D) 140 6
b.Frederiksberg 31-5-96
2014–15 FC Twente 7 1
2015–16 FC Twente 18 1
2016–17 FC Twente 22 2
2017–18 FC Twente 2 0 **49 4**
2017–18 Sampdoria 7 0
2018–19 Sampdoria 32 0 **39 0**
2019–20 Lyon 18 1
2020–21 Lyon 3 0 **21 1**
On loan from Lyon.
2020–21 Fulham 31 1 **31 1**

AREOLA, Alphonse (G) 217 0
b.Paris 27-2-93
2012–13 Paris Saint-Germain 2 0
2013–14 Paris Saint-Germain 0 0
2013–14 *Lens* 35 0 **35 0**
2014–15 Paris Saint-Germain 0 0
2014–15 *Bastia* 35 0 **35 0**
2015–16 Paris Saint-Germain 0 0
2015–16 *Villarreal* 32 0 **32 0**
2016–17 Paris Saint-Germain 15 0
2017–18 Paris Saint-Germain 34 0
2018–19 Paris Saint-Germain 21 0
2019–20 Paris Saint-Germain 3 0
2019–20 *Real Madrid* 4 0 **4 0**
2020–21 Paris Saint-Germain 0 0 **75 0**
On loan from Paris Saint-Germain.
2020–21 Fulham 36 0 **36 0**

ASHBY-HAMMOND, Taye (G) 0 0
b.London 21-3-99
Internationals: England U16, U17.
2020–21 Fulham 0 0

BETTINELLI, Marcus (G) 183 0
H: 6 4 W: 12 13 b.Camberwell 24-5-92
Internationals: England U21.
2010–11 Fulham 0 0
2011–12 Fulham 0 0
2012–13 Fulham 0 0
2013–14 Fulham 0 0
2013–14 *Accrington S* 39 0 **39 0**
2014–15 Fulham 39 0
2015–16 Fulham 11 0
2016–17 Fulham 6 0
2017–18 Fulham 26 0
2018–19 Fulham 7 0
2019–20 Fulham 14 0
2020–21 Fulham 0 0 **103 0**
2020–21 *Middlesbrough* 41 0 **41 0**

BRYAN, Joe (D) 300 19
H: 5 7 W: 11 05 b.Bristol 17-9-93
2011–12 Bristol C 1 0
2012–13 Bristol C 13 0
2012–13 *Plymouth Arg* 10 1 **10 1**
2013–14 Bristol C 21 2
2014–15 Bristol C 41 6
2015–16 Bristol C 39 2
2016–17 Bristol C 44 1
2017–18 Bristol C 43 5
2018–19 Bristol C 1 0 **203 16**
2018–19 Fulham 28 0
2019–20 Fulham 43 1
2020–21 Fulham 16 1 **87 2**

CAIRNEY, Tom (M) 344 45
H: 6 0 W: 11 05 b.Nottingham 20-1-91
Internationals: Scotland U19, U21, Full caps.
From Leeds U.
2009–10 Hull C 11 1
2010–11 Hull C 22 1
2011–12 Hull C 27 0
2012–13 Hull C 10 0
2013–14 Hull C 0 0 **70 2**
2013–14 Blackburn R 37 5
2014–15 Blackburn R 39 3 **76 8**
2015–16 Fulham 39 8
2016–17 Fulham 45 12
2017–18 Fulham 34 5
2018–19 Fulham 31 1
2019–20 Fulham 39 8
2020–21 Fulham 10 1 **198 35**

CARVALHO, Fabio (M) 4 1
b.Lisbon 30-8-02
2020–21 Oliveirense 0 0
2020–21 Fulham 4 1 **4 1**

CHRISTIE, Cyrus (D) 335 6
H: 6 2 W: 12 03 b.Coventry 30-9-92
Internationals: Republic of Ireland Full caps.
2011–12 Coventry C 37 0
2012–13 Coventry C 31 2
2013–14 Coventry C 34 0 **102 2**
2014–15 Derby Co 38 0
2015–16 Derby Co 42 1
2016–17 Derby Co 27 1
2017–18 Derby Co 0 0 **107 2**
2017–18 Middlesbrough 25 1 **25 1**
2017–18 Fulham 5 0
2018–19 Fulham 28 0
2019–20 Fulham 24 1
2020–21 Fulham 0 0 **57 1**
2020–21 *Nottingham F* 44 0 **44 0**

DECORDOVA-REID, Bobby (M) 278 45
H: 5 7 W: 10 10 b.Bristol 1-3-93
Internationals: Jamaica Full caps.
2010–11 Bristol C 1 0
2011–12 Bristol C 0 0
2011–12 *Cheltenham T* 1 0 **1 0**
2012–13 Bristol C 4 1
2012–13 *Oldham Ath* 7 0 **7 0**
2013–14 Bristol C 24 1
2014–15 Bristol C 2 0
2014–15 *Plymouth Arg* 33 3 **33 3**
2015–16 Bristol C 28 2
2016–17 Bristol C 30 3
2017–18 Bristol C 46 19 **135 26**
2018–19 Cardiff C 27 5
2019–20 Cardiff C 1 0 **28 5**
2019–20 Fulham 41 6
2020–21 Fulham 33 5 **74 11**

FOSSEY, Marlon (D) 7 0
b. 9-9-98
2019–20 Fulham 0 0
2020–21 Fulham 0 0
2020–21 *Shrewsbury T* 7 0 **7 0**

FRANCOIS, Tyrese (M) 1 0
b.Campbelltown 16-7-00
2019–20 Fulham 0 0
2020–21 Fulham 1 0 **1 0**

HECTOR, Michael (D) 291 15
H: 6 4 W: 12 13 b.Newham 19-7-92
Internationals: Jamaica Full caps.
2009–10 Reading 0 0
2010–11 Reading 0 0
2011 *Dundalk* 11 2 **11 2**
2011–12 Reading 0 0
2011–12 *Barnet* 27 2 **27 2**
2012–13 Reading 0 0
2012–13 *Shrewsbury T* 8 0 **8 0**
2012–13 *Aldershot T* 8 1 **8 1**
2012–13 *Cheltenham T* 18 1 **18 1**
2013–14 Reading 9 0
2013–14 *Aberdeen* 20 1 **20 1**
2014–15 Reading 41 3
2015–16 Chelsea 0 0
2015–16 *Reading* 30 1 **80 4**
2016–17 Chelsea 0 0
2016–17 *Eintracht Frankfurt* 22 1 **22 1**
2017–18 Chelsea 0 0
2017–18 *Hull C* 36 1 **36 1**
2018–19 Chelsea 0 0
2018–19 *Sheffield W* 37 2 **37 2**
2019–20 Fulham 20 0
2020–21 Fulham 4 0 **24 0**

HILTON, Sonny (M) 0 0
H: 5 5 W: 9 00 b.Liverpool 30-1-01
Internationals: England U16, U17, U19.
2020–21 Fulham 0 0

IVAN CAVALEIRO, Ricardo (M) 231 30
H: 5 9 W: 11 07 b.Vialonga 18-10-93
Internationals: Portugal U17, U18, U19, U20, U21, Full caps.
2012–13 Benfica 0 0
2013–14 Benfica 8 0
2014–15 Benfica 0 0 **8 0**
2014–15 *Deportivo La Coruna* 34 3 **34 3**
2015–16 Monaco 12 1
2016–17 Monaco 2 0 **14 1**
2016–17 Wolverhampton W 31 5
2017–18 Wolverhampton W 42 9
2018–19 Wolverhampton W 23 3 **96 17**
2019–20 Fulham 43 6
2020–21 Fulham 36 3 **79 9**

JASPER, Sylvester (M) 2 0
2019–20 Fulham 2 0
2020–21 Fulham 0 0 **2 0**

JOHANSEN, Stefan (F) 328 45
H: 6 0 W: 12 04 b.Vardo 8-1-91
Internationals: Norway U16, U17, U18, U19, U21, U23, Full caps.
2007 Bodo/Glimt 4 0
2008 Bodo/Glimt 1 0
2009 Bodo/Glimt 4 0
2010 Bodo/Glimt 20 0 **29 0**
2011 Stromsgodset 13 1
2012 Stromsgodset 27 3
2013 Stromsgodset 27 4 **67 8**
2013–14 Celtic 16 2
2014–15 Celtic 34 9
2015–16 Celtic 23 1 **73 12**
2016–17 Fulham 36 11
2017–18 Fulham 45 8
2018–19 Fulham 12 0
2018–19 *WBA* 12 2 **12 2**
2019–20 Fulham 33 0
2020–21 Fulham 0 0 **126 19**
2020–21 *QPR* 21 4 **21 4**

KAMARA, Aboubakar (F) 158 31
H: 5 10 W: 12 08 b.Gonesse 7-3-95
2013–14 Monaco 0 0
2014–15 Monaco 2 0 **2 0**
2015–16 Kortrijk 12 0 **12 0**
2015–16 Amiens 16 5
2016–17 Amiens 29 10 **45 15**
2017–18 Fulham 30 7
2018–19 Fulham 13 3
2018–19 *Yeni Malatyaspor* 10 1 **10 1**
2019–20 Fulham 25 4

2020–21	Fulham	11	0	**79**	**14**
2020–21	*Dijon*	10	1	**10**	**1**

KEBANO, Neeskens (M) **216** **38**
H: 5 11 W: 11 11 b.Montereau 10-3-92
Internationals: France U17, U18, U19, U20. DR Congo Full caps.

2010–11	Paris Saint-Germain	3	0		
2011–12	Paris Saint-Germain	0	0		
2012–13	Paris Saint-Germain	0	0	**3**	**0**
2012–13	*Caen*	12	1	**12**	**1**
2013–14	Charleroi	26	5		
2014–15	Charleroi	33	12		
2015–16	Charleroi	5	1	**64**	**18**
2015–16	Genk	34	6		
2016–17	Genk	3	0	**37**	**6**
2016–17	Fulham	28	6		
2017–18	Fulham	26	3		
2018–19	Fulham	7	0		
2019–20	Fulham	16	3		
2020–21	Fulham	5	0	**82**	**12**
2020–21	*Middlesbrough*	18	1	**18**	**1**

KNOCKAERT, Anthony (M) **350** **58**
H: 5 8 W: 10 11 b.Lille 20-11-91
Internationals: France U20, U21.

2011–12	Guingamp	34	10	**34**	**10**
2012–13	Leicester C	42	8		
2013–14	Leicester C	42	5		
2014–15	Leicester C	9	0	**93**	**13**
2015–16	Standard Liege	20	5	**20**	**5**
2015–16	Brighton & HA	19	5		
2016–17	Brighton & HA	45	15		
2017–18	Brighton & HA	33	3		
2018–19	Brighton & HA	30	2	**127**	**25**
2019–20	Fulham	42	3		
2020–21	Fulham	0	0	**42**	**3**
2020–21	*Nottingham F*	34	2	**34**	**2**

KONGOLO, Terence (D) **167** **2**
H: 6 0 W: 11 00 b.Rotterdam 14-2-94
Internationals: Netherlands U16, U17, U18, U19, U20, U21, Full caps.

2011–12	Feyenoord	1	0		
2012–13	Feyenoord	5	0		
2013–14	Feyenoord	17	0		
2014–15	Feyenoord	31	0		
2015–16	Feyenoord	29	0		
2016–17	Feyenoord	23	1	**106**	**1**
2017–18	Monaco	3	0	**3**	**0**
2017–18	*Huddersfield T*	13	0		
2018–19	Huddersfield T	32	1		
2019–20	Huddersfield T	11	0	**56**	**1**
2019–20	*Fulham*	1	0		
2020–21	Fulham	1	0	**2**	**0**

LARKECHE, Ziyad (D) **0** **0**
H: 6 0 W: 10 08 b.Paris 19-9-02
From Paris Saint-Germain.

2020–21	Fulham	0	0		

LAS, Damian (G) **0** **0**
H: 6 1 W: 11 05 b.Des Plaines 11-4-02
Internationals: USA U17.
From North Carolina.

2020–21	Fulham	0	0		

LE MARCHAND, Maxime (M) **279** **9**
H: 5 11 W: 10 10 b.Saint Melo 10-11-89

2009–10	Rennes	0	0		
2009–10	*Le Havre*	27	1		
2010–11	Le Havre	22	0		
2011–12	Le Havre	20	1		
2012–13	Le Havre	28	0		
2013–14	Le Havre	31	2		
2014–15	Le Havre	33	1	**161**	**5**
2015–16	Nice	26	1		
2016–17	Nice	10	0		
2017–18	Nice	29	0	**65**	**1**
2018–19	Fulham	26	0		
2019–20	Fulham	12	0		
2020–21	Fulham	2	0	**40**	**0**
2020–21	*Antwerp*	13	3	**13**	**3**

LOOKMAN, Ademola (F) **137** **20**
H: 5 9 b.Wandsworth 18-7-98
Internationals: England U19, U20, U21.

2015–16	Charlton Ath	24	5		
2016–17	Charlton Ath	21	5	**45**	**10**
2016–17	Everton	8	1		
2017–18	Everton	7	0		
2017–18	*RB Leipzig*	11	5		
2018–19	Everton	21	0	**36**	**1**
2019–20	RB Leipzig	11	0		
2020–21	RB Leipzig	0	0	**22**	**5**

On loan from RB Leipzig.

2020–21	Fulham	34	4	**34**	**4**

MAJA, Josh (F) **101** **28**
H: 5 11 W: 11 09 b. 27-12-98
From Fulham.

2016–17	Sunderland	0	0		
2017–18	Sunderland	17	1		
2018–19	Sunderland	24	15	**41**	**16**
2018–19	Bordeaux	7	1		
2019–20	Bordeaux	21	6		
2020–21	Bordeaux	17	2	**45**	**9**

On loan from Bordeaux.

2020–21	Fulham	15	3	**15**	**3**

AWSON, Alfie (D) **212** **20**
H: 5 8 W: 12 11 b.Hillingdon 19-1-94
Internationals: England U21.

2012–13	Brentford	0	0		
2013–14	Brentford	0	0		
2014–15	Brentford	0	0		
2014–15	*Wycombe W*	45	6	**45**	**6**
2015–16	Barnsley	45	6		
2016–17	Barnsley	4	2	**49**	**8**
2016–17	Swansea C	27	4		
2017–18	Swansea C	38	2	**65**	**6**
2018–19	Fulham	15	0		
2019–20	Fulham	27	0		
2020–21	Fulham	0	0	**42**	**0**
2020–21	*Bristol C*	11	0	**11**	**0**

McAVOY, Connor (D) **0** **0**
b.Chertsey 16-2-02
Internationals: Scotland U17, U19.

2020–21	Fulham	0	0		

McDONALD, Kevin (M) **470** **36**
H: 6 2 W: 13 03 b.Carnoustie 4-11-88
Internationals: Scotland U19, U21, Full caps.

2005–06	Dundee	26	3		
2006–07	Dundee	30	2		
2007–08	Dundee	34	9	**90**	**14**
2008–09	Burnley	25	1		
2009–10	Burnley	26	1		
2010–11	Burnley	0	0	**51**	**2**
2010–11	*Scunthorpe U*	5	1	**5**	**1**
2010–11	*Notts Co*	11	0	**11**	**0**
2011–12	Sheffield U	31	3		
2012–13	Sheffield U	45	1		
2013–14	Sheffield U	1	1	**77**	**5**
2013–14	Wolverhampton W	41	5		
2014–15	Wolverhampton W	46	0		
2015–16	Wolverhampton W	33	3	**120**	**8**
2016–17	Fulham	43	3		
2017–18	Fulham	42	3		
2018–19	Fulham	15	0		
2019–20	Fulham	16	0		
2020–21	Fulham	0	0	**116**	**6**

MITROVIC, Aleksandar (F) **308** **122**
H: 6 2 W: 13 10 b.Smederevo 16-9-94
Internationals: Serbia U19, U21, Full caps.

2011–12	Teleoptik	25	7	**25**	**7**
2012–13	Partizan Belgrade	25	10		
2013–14	Partizan Belgrade	3	3	**28**	**13**
2013–14	Anderlecht	32	16		
2014–15	Anderlecht	37	20	**69**	**36**
2015–16	Newcastle U	34	9		
2016–17	Newcastle U	25	4		
2017–18	Newcastle U	6	1	**65**	**14**
2017–18	*Fulham*	17	12		
2018–19	Fulham	37	11		
2019–20	Fulham	40	26		
2020–21	Fulham	27	3	**121**	**52**

O'NEILL, Ollie (M) **0** **0**
b.Hammersmith 8-1-03
Internationals: Republic of Ireland U19.

2020–21	Fulham	0	0		

ODOI, Denis (D) **392** **11**
H: 5 10 W: 11 09 b.Leuven 27-5-88
Internationals: Belgium U20, U21, Full caps.

2006–07	Oud-Heverlee Leuven	3	0		
2007–08	Oud-Heverlee Leuven	21	0		
2008–09	Oud-Heverlee Leuven	33	3	**57**	**3**
2009–10	Sint-Truiden	26	1		
2010–11	Sint-Truiden	33	2	**59**	**3**
2011–12	Anderlecht	19	0		
2012–13	Anderlecht	14	0	**33**	**0**
2013–14	Lokeren	37	1		
2014–15	Lokeren	35	0		
2015–16	Lokeren	35	1	**107**	**2**
2016–17	Fulham	30	2		
2017–18	Fulham	38	1		
2018–19	Fulham	31	0		
2019–20	Fulham	34	0		
2020–21	Fulham	3	0	**136**	**3**

ONOMAH, Joshua (M) **103** **7**
H: 5 11 W: 10 01 b.Enfield 27-4-97
Internationals: England U16, U17, U18, U19, U20, U21.

2013–14	Tottenham H	0	0		
2014–15	Tottenham H	0	0		
2015–16	Tottenham H	8	0		
2016–17	Tottenham H	5	0		
2017–18	Tottenham H	0	0		
2017–18	*Aston Villa*	33	4	**33**	**4**
2018–19	Tottenham H	0	0	**13**	**0**
2018–19	*Sheffield W*	15	0	**15**	**0**
2019–20	Fulham	31	3		
2020–21	Fulham	11	0	**42**	**3**

OPOKU, Jerome (D) **54** **1**
b.London 14-10-98

2019–20	Fulham	0	0		
2019–20	*Accrington S*	21	0	**21**	**0**
2020–21	Fulham	0	0		
2020–21	*Plymouth Arg*	33	1	**33**	**1**

PAGE, Jonathon (M) **0** **0**
b.Chertsey 6-9-01

2020–21	Fulham	0	0		

PAJAZITI, Adrion (M) **0** **0**
H: 5 11 b.Camden 16-11-02
Internationals: Kosovo U21.

2020–21	Fulham	0	0		

RAMIREZ, Fabricio (G) **170** **0**
H: 6 1 W: 12 02 b.Las Palmas 31-12-87
Internationals: Spain U20.

2006–07	Deportivo La Coruna	0	0		
2007–08	Deportivo La Coruna	6	0		
2008–09	Deportivo La Coruna	0	0		
2009–10	Valladolid	1	0		
2010–11	Valladolid	0	0	**1**	**0**
2010–11	*Recreativo*	40	0	**40**	**0**
2011–12	Real Betis	15	0		
2012–13	Real Betis	2	0	**17**	**0**
2013–14	Deportivo La Coruna	6	0		
2014–15	Deportivo La Coruna	31	0		
2015–16	Deportivo La Coruna	0	0	**43**	**0**
2016–17	Besiktas	32	0		
2017–18	Besiktas	34	0	**66**	**0**
2018–19	Fulham	2	0		
2019–20	Fulham	0	0		
2019–20	*Mallorca*	1	0	**1**	**0**
2020–21	Fulham	0	0	**2**	**0**

REAM, Tim (D) **457** **9**
H: 6 1 W: 11 05 b.St Louis 5-10-87
Internationals: USA Full caps.

2006	St Louis Billikens	19	0		
2007	St Louis Billikens	19	0		
2008	St Louis Billikens	22	0		
2008	Chicago Fire	12	0		
2009	Chicago Fire	7	0	**19**	**0**
2009	St Louis Billikens	22	6	**82**	**6**
2010	New York RB	30	1		
2011	New York RB	28	0	**58**	**1**
2011–12	Bolton W	13	0		
2012–13	Bolton W	15	0		
2013–14	Bolton W	42	0		
2014–15	Bolton W	44	0	**114**	**0**
2015–16	Fulham	29	0		
2016–17	Fulham	34	1		
2017–18	Fulham	44	1		
2018–19	Fulham	26	0		
2019–20	Fulham	44	0		
2020–21	Fulham	7	0	**184**	**2**

REED, Harrison (M) **145** **4**
H: 5 9 W: 11 09 b.Worthing 27-1-95
Internationals: England U19, U20.

2011–12	Southampton	0	0		
2012–13	Southampton	0	0		
2013–14	Southampton	4	0		
2014–15	Southampton	9	0		
2015–16	Southampton	1	0		
2016–17	Southampton	3	0		
2017–18	Southampton	0	0		
2017–18	*Norwich C*	39	1	**39**	**1**
2018–19	Southampton	0	0		
2018–19	*Blackburn R*	33	3	**33**	**3**
2019–20	Southampton	0	0	**17**	**0**
2019–20	*Fulham*	25	0		
2020–21	Fulham	31	0	**56**	**0**

ROBINSON, Antonee (D) **122** **1**
H: 6 0 W: 11 07 b.Milton Keynes 8-8-97
Internationals: USA U18, Full caps.

2015–16	Everton	0	0		
2016–17	Everton	0	0		
2017–18	Everton	0	0		
2017–18	*Bolton W*	30	0	**30**	**0**
2018–19	Everton	0	0		
2018–19	*Wigan Ath*	26	0		
2019–20	Wigan Ath	38	1	**64**	**1**
2020–21	Fulham	28	0	**28**	**0**

RODAK, Marek (G) **135** **0**
H: 6 2 W: 10 12 b. 13-12-96
Internationals: Slovakia U17, U19, U21.

2014–15	Fulham	0	0		
2015–16	Fulham	0	0		
2016–17	Fulham	0	0		
2016–17	*Accrington S*	20	0	**20**	**0**
2017–18	Fulham	0	0		
2017–18	*Rotherham U*	35	0		
2018–19	Fulham	0	0		
2018–19	*Rotherham U*	45	0	**80**	**0**

2019–20	Fulham	33	0		
2020–21	Fulham	2	0	**35**	**0**

SERI, Jean (M) 228 17
H: 5 5 W: 10 08 b.Grand-Bereby 19-7-91
Internationals: Ivory Coast U23, Full caps.

2013–14	Pacos de Ferreira	21	1		
2014–15	Pacos de Ferreira	33	1	**54**	**2**
2015–16	Nice	38	3		
2016–17	Nice	34	7		
2017–18	Nice	31	2	**103**	**12**
2018–19	Fulham	32	1		
2019–20	Fulham	0	0		
2019–20	*Galatasaray*	27	2	**27**	**2**
2020–21	Fulham	0	0	**32**	**1**
2020–21	*Bordeaux*	12	0	**12**	**0**

SESSEGNON, Steven (D) 30 0
H: 5 8 W: 10 06 b.Roehampton 18-5-00
Internationals: England U16, U17, U18, U19, U20, U21.

2017–18	Fulham	0	0		
2018–19	Fulham	0	0		
2019–20	Fulham	14	0		
2020–21	Fulham	0	0	**14**	**0**
2020–21	*Bristol C*	16	0	**16**	**0**

TAYLOR-CROSSDALE, Martell (F) 0 0
b.London 26-12-99
Internationals: England U16, U17, U18, U20.
From Chelsea.

2019–20	Fulham	0	0		
2020–21	Fulham	0	0		
2020–21	*Colchester U*	0	0		

TETE, Kenny (D) 106 1
b.Amsterdam 9-10-95

2013–14	Ajax	0	0		
2014–15	Ajax	5	0		
2015–16	Ajax	21	0		
2016–17	Ajax	5	0	**31**	**0**
2017–18	Lyon	22	1		
2018–19	Lyon	13	0		
2019–20	Lyon	18	0		
2020–21	Lyon	0	0	**53**	**1**
2020–21	Fulham	22	0	**22**	**0**

TIEHI, Jean-Pierre (F) 0 0
b.Paris 24-1-02
From Le Havre.

2020–21	Fulham	0	0		

WICKENS, George (G) 0 0
b.Petersfield 8-11-01
Internationals: England U18.

2020–21	Fulham	0	0		

ZAMBO, Andre-Franck (M) 173 2
H: 6 0 W: 11 09 b.Yaounde 16-11-95
Internationals: Cameroon Full caps.
From Reims.

2015–16	Marseille	9	0		
2016–17	Marseille	33	0		
2017–18	Marseille	37	0	**79**	**0**
2018–19	Fulham	22	0		
2019–20	Fulham	0	0		
2019–20	*Villarreal*	36	2	**36**	**2**
2020–21	Fulham	36	0	**58**	**0**

Scholars
Antonsson, Thorsteinn Aron; Benjamin, Xavier Deandrae; Biereth, Mika Miles; Bowat, Ibane; Caton, Tyler Lewis; D'Auria-Henry, Luciano Paul; Dibley-Dias, Matthew Max; Lanquedoc, Imani Jamal; Odutayo, Idris Adewale Olarewaju; Okkas, Georgios; Olakigbe, Michael Oluwakorede; Parkes, Stefan Charles Earl; Sanderson, Oliver; Tanton Pedraza, Devan Austin; Wildbore, Jaylan Sebastian.

GILLINGHAM (37)

AKINDE, John (F) 347 96
H: 6 2 W: 10 01 b.Camberwell 8-7-89

2008–09	Bristol C	7	1		
2008–09	*Wycombe W*	11	7		
2009–10	Bristol C	7	0		
2009–10	*Wycombe W*	6	1	**17**	**8**
2009–10	*Brentford*	2	0	**2**	**0**
2010–11	Bristol C	2	0	**16**	**1**
2010–11	*Bristol R*	14	0	**14**	**0**
2010–11	*Dagenham & R*	9	2		
2011–12	Crawley T	25	1		
2011–12	*Dagenham & R*	5	0	**14**	**2**
2012–13	Crawley T	6	0	**31**	**1**
2012–13	Portsmouth	11	0		
2013–14	Portsmouth	0	0	**11**	**0**

From Alfreton T.

2015–16	Barnet	43	23		
2016–17	Barnet	46	26		
2017–18	Barnet	32	7	**121**	**56**
2018–19	Lincoln C	45	15		
2019–20	Lincoln C	23	5	**68**	**20**
2019–20	Gillingham	9	1		
2020–21	Gillingham	44	7	**53**	**8**

BASTIEN, Sacha (G) 15 0
b. 22-1-95

2013–14	Reims	0	0		
2014–15	Reims	1	0	**1**	**0**
2017–18	Bastia-Borgo	3	0	**3**	**0**
2018–19	US Granville	10	0	**10**	**0**
2019–20	Stevenage	1	0	**1**	**0**
2020–21	Gillingham	0	0		

BONHAM, Jack (G) 164 0
H: 6 4 W: 14 13 b.Stevenage 14-9-93
Internationals: Republic of Ireland U17.

2010–11	Watford	0	0		
2011–12	Watford	0	0		
2012–13	Watford	1	0	**1**	**0**
2013–14	Brentford	1	0		
2014–15	Brentford	0	0		
2015–16	Brentford	0	0		
2016–17	Brentford	1	0		
2017–18	Brentford	0	0		
2017–18	*Carlisle U*	42	0	**42**	**0**
2018–19	Brentford	0	0	**2**	**0**
2018–19	*Bristol R*	40	0	**40**	**0**
2019–20	Gillingham	35	0		
2020–21	Gillingham	44	0	**79**	**0**

DEMPSEY, Kyle (M) 237 24
b.Whitehaven 17-9-95

2013–14	Carlisle U	4	0		
2014–15	Carlisle U	43	10	**47**	**10**
2015–16	Huddersfield T	21	1		
2016–17	Huddersfield T	0	0	**21**	**1**
2016–17	*Fleetwood T*	38	2		
2017–18	Fleetwood T	45	1		
2018–19	Fleetwood T	14	0		
2018–19	*Peterborough U*	11	0	**11**	**0**
2019–20	Fleetwood T	21	2	**118**	**5**
2020–21	Gillingham	40	8	**40**	**8**

GRAHAM, Jordan (M) 91 14
H: 6 0 W: 10 10 b.Coventry 5-3-95
Internationals: England U16, U17.

2011–12	Aston Villa	0	0		
2012–13	Aston Villa	0	0		
2013–14	Aston Villa	0	0		
2013–14	*Ipswich T*	2	0		
2013–14	*Bradford C*	1	0	**1**	**0**
2014–15	Wolverhampton W	0	0		
2015–16	Wolverhampton W	11	1		
2015–16	*Oxford U*	5	0		
2016–17	Wolverhampton W	2	0		
2017–18	Wolverhampton W	1	0		
2017–18	*Fulham*	3	0	**3**	**0**
2018–19	Wolverhampton W	0	0		
2018–19	*Ipswich T*	4	0	**6**	**0**
2018–19	*Oxford U*	16	1	**21**	**1**
2019–20	Wolverhampton W	0	0	**14**	**1**
2019–20	*Gillingham*	7	0		
2020–21	Gillingham	39	12	**46**	**12**

JACKSON, Ryan (M) 306 9
H: 5 9 W: 10 03 b.Streatham 31-7-90
Internationals: England C.

2011–12	AFC Wimbledon	7	0	**7**	**0**
2013–14	Newport Co	29	0		
2014–15	Newport Co	34	0	**63**	**0**
2015–16	Gillingham	37	2		
2016–17	Gillingham	34	1		
2017–18	Colchester U	42	2		
2018–19	Colchester U	46	2		
2019–20	Colchester U	34	2	**122**	**6**
2020–21	Gillingham	43	0	**114**	**3**

JOHNSON, Tyreke (M) 8 0
b.Swindon 3-11-98
From Watford, Swindon T.

2018–19	Southampton	1	0		
2019–20	Southampton	0	0		
2020–21	Southampton	0	0	**1**	**0**
2020–21	Gillingham	7	0	**7**	**0**

LEE, Oliver (M) 270 29
H: 5 11 W: 12 07 b.Hornchurch 11-7-91

2009–10	West Ham U	0	0		
2010–11	West Ham U	0	0		
2010–11	*Dagenham & R*	5	0		
2011–12	West Ham U	0	0		
2011–12	*Dagenham & R*	16	3	**21**	**3**
2011–12	*Gillingham*	8	0		
2012–13	Barnet	11	0	**11**	**0**
2012–13	Birmingham C	0	0		
2013–14	Birmingham C	16	1		
2014–15	Birmingham C	0	0	**16**	**1**
2014–15	*Plymouth Arg*	15	2	**15**	**2**
2015–16	Luton T	34	3		
2016–17	Luton T	33	1		
2017–18	Luton T	38	6	**105**	**10**
2018–19	Hearts	31	3		

On loan from Hearts.

2019–20	Gillingham	28	4		
2020–21	Hearts	10	1	**41**	**4**

On loan from Hearts.

2020–21	Gillingham	25	5	**61**	**9**

LINTOTT, Harvey (M) 0 0

2020–21	Gillingham	0	0		

MACDONALD, Alex (F) 360 29
H: 5 7 W: 11 04 b.Warrington 14-4-90
Internationals: Scotland U19, U21.

2007–08	Burnley	2	0		
2008–09	Burnley	3	0		
2009–10	Burnley	0	0		
2009–10	*Falkirk*	11	0	**11**	**0**
2010–11	Burnley	0	0		
2010–11	*Inverness CT*	10	1	**10**	**1**
2011–12	Burnley	5	0		
2011–12	*Plymouth Arg*	18	4		
2012–13	Burnley	1	0	**11**	**0**
2012–13	*Plymouth Arg*	16	1	**34**	**5**
2012–13	*Burton Alb*	15	1		
2013–14	Burton Alb	35	0		
2014–15	Burton Alb	21	6	**71**	**7**
2014–15	Oxford U	15	3		
2015–16	Oxford U	40	5		
2016–17	Oxford U	22	1	**77**	**9**
2016–17	Mansfield T	18	1		
2017–18	Mansfield T	41	3		
2018–19	Mansfield T	21	1		
2019–20	Mansfield T	29	1	**109**	**6**
2020–21	Gillingham	37	1	**37**	**1**

MAGHOMA, Christian (D) 39 0
b. 8-11-97

2015–16	Tottenham H	0	0		
2015–16	*Yeovil T*	0	0		
2016–17	Tottenham H	0	0		
2017–18	Tottenham H	0	0		
2018–19	Arka Gdynia	15	0		
2019–20	Arka Gdynia	20	0	**35**	**0**
2020–21	Gillingham	4	0	**4**	**0**

McKENZIE, Robbie (M) 59 1
b.Kingston upon Hull 25-9-98

2017–18	Hull C	0	0		
2018–19	Hull C	18	0		
2019–20	Hull C	8	0	**26**	**0**
2020–21	Gillingham	33	1	**33**	**1**

O'KEEFE, Stuart (M) 192 10
H: 5 8 W: 10 00 b.Eye 4-3-91

2008–09	Southend U	3	0		
2009–10	Southend U	7	0		
2010–11	Southend U	0	0	**10**	**0**
2010–11	Crystal Palace	4	0		
2011–12	Crystal Palace	13	0		
2012–13	Crystal Palace	5	0		
2013–14	Crystal Palace	12	1		
2014–15	Crystal Palace	2	0	**36**	**1**
2014–15	*Blackpool*	4	0	**4**	**0**
2014–15	Cardiff C	6	0		
2015–16	Cardiff C	24	2		
2016–17	Cardiff C	8	0		
2016–17	*Milton Keynes D*	18	4	**18**	**4**
2017–18	Cardiff C	0	0		
2017–18	*Portsmouth*	21	0	**21**	**0**
2018–19	Cardiff C	0	0	**38**	**2**
2018–19	*Plymouth Arg*	11	0	**11**	**0**
2019–20	Gillingham	30	3		
2020–21	Gillingham	24	0	**54**	**3**

OGILVIE, Connor (D) 185 10
H: 6 0 W: 12 08 b.Harlow 14-2-96
Internationals: England U16, U17.

2013–14	Tottenham H	0	0		
2014–15	Tottenham H	0	0		
2015–16	Tottenham H	0	0		
2015–16	*Stevenage*	21	1		
2016–17	Tottenham H	0	0		
2016–17	*Stevenage*	18	0	**39**	**1**
2017–18	Tottenham H	0	0		
2017–18	*Gillingham*	37	1		
2018–19	Tottenham H	0	0		
2018–19	*Gillingham*	31	0		
2019–20	Gillingham	33	4		
2020–21	Gillingham	45	4	**146**	**9**

OLIVER, Vadaine (F) 257 46
H: 6 2 W: 12 04 b.Sheffield 21-10-91

2010–11	Sheffield W	0	0		
2011–12	Sheffield W	0	0		

From Lincoln C.

2013–14	Crewe Alex	25	2		
2014–15	Crewe Alex	9	1	**34**	**3**
2014–15	*Mansfield T*	30	7	**30**	**7**
2015–16	York C	37	7	**37**	**7**
2016–17	Notts Co	19	1	**19**	**1**
2017–18	Morecambe	34	3		
2018–19	Morecambe	30	4	**64**	**7**
2019–20	Northampton T	30	4	**30**	**4**
2020–21	Gillingham	43	17	**43**	**17**

SAMUEL, Dominic (F) **133** **25**
H: 6 0 W: 14 00 b.Southwark 1-4-94
Internationals: England U19.

2011–12	Reading	0	0		
2012–13	Reading	1	0		
2012–13	*Colchester U*	2	0	**2**	**0**
2013–14	Reading	0	0		
2013–14	*Dagenham & R*	1	0	**1**	**0**
2014–15	Reading	0	0		
2014–15	*Coventry C*	13	6	**13**	**6**
2015–16	Reading	1	0		
2015–16	*Gillingham*	25	7		
2016–17	Reading	9	2	**11**	**2**
2016–17	*Ipswich T*	6	0	**6**	**0**
2017–18	Blackburn R	36	5		
2018–19	Blackburn R	2	0		
2019–20	Blackburn R	15	2	**53**	**7**
2020–21	Gillingham	22	3	**47**	**10**

SITHOLE, Gerald (M) **1** **0**
b. 28-12-02

2020–21	Gillingham	1	0	**1**	**0**

TUCKER, Jack (D) **72** **1**
b. 13-11-99

2017–18	Gillingham	1	0		
2018–19	Gillingham	0	0		
2019–20	Gillingham	28	0		
2020–21	Gillingham	43	1	**72**	**1**

WILLOCK, Matthew (M) **55** **1**
b. 20-8-96

2016–17	Manchester U	0	0		
2017–18	Manchester U	0	0		
2017–18	*Utrecht*	3	0	**3**	**0**
2017–18	*St Johnstone*	11	1	**11**	**1**
2018–19	Manchester U	0	0		
2018–19	*St Mirren*	12	0	**12**	**0**
2018–19	*Crawley T*	11	0	**11**	**0**
2019–20	Gillingham	7	0		
2020–21	Gillingham	11	0	**18**	**0**

WOODS, Henry (M) **4** **0**
b. 7-9-99

2018–19	Gillingham	0	0		
2019–20	Gillingham	0	0		
2020–21	Gillingham	4	0	**4**	**0**

Scholars
Akehurst, Bailey Roy; Baker, Matthew; Baker-Moran, George Henry David Kevin; Bancroft, Toby William Day; Britton, Oliver Joseph; Chambers, Joshua James; Crump, Thomas James Frederick; Leach, Joshua Leslie; Lintott, Harvey Daniel; Maher, Harry; Medhurst, Vinnie Regan; Nelson, Ronny Alex Scott Hall; Smith, Ethan Michael; Walker, Charlie Jack.

GRIMSBY T (38)

ADLARD, Luis (F) **3** **0**
b. 13-10-02

2019–20	Grimsby T	0	0		
2020–21	Grimsby T	3	0	**3**	**0**

BATTERSBY, Ollie (G) **0** **0**

2018–19	Grimsby T	0	0		
2019–20	Grimsby T	0	0		
2020–21	Grimsby T	0	0		

BOYD, Louis (F) **1** **0**
b. 22-10-04

2020–21	Grimsby T	1	0	**1**	**0**

BUNNEY, Joe (F) **166** **16**
H: 6 1 W: 11 00 b.Manchester 26-9-93
From Lancaster C, Kendal T, Stockport Co.

2012–13	Rochdale	1	1		
2013–14	Rochdale	21	3		
2014–15	Rochdale	19	2		
2015–16	Rochdale	32	9		
2016–17	Rochdale	29	1		
2017–18	Rochdale	20	0		
2017–18	Northampton T	12	0		
2018–19	Northampton T	0	0		
2018–19	*Blackpool*	5	0	**5**	**0**
2018–19	*Rochdale*	16	0	**138**	**16**
2019–20	Northampton T	4	0	**16**	**0**
2019–20	Bolton W	2	0	**2**	**0**
2020–21	Grimsby T	5	0	**5**	**0**

CLIFTON, Harry (M) **109** **4**
H: 5 11 W: 13 12 b. 12-6-98
Internationals: Wales U21.

2016–17	Grimsby T	0	0		
2017–18	Grimsby T	10	0		
2018–19	Grimsby T	39	2		
2019–20	Grimsby T	25	0		
2020–21	Grimsby T	35	2	**109**	**4**

COKE, Giles (M) **309** **26**
H: 6 0 W: 11 11 b.Westminster 3-6-86
From Kingstonian.

2004–05	Mansfield T	9	0		
2005–06	Mansfield T	40	4		
2006–07	Mansfield T	21	1	**70**	**5**
2007–08	Northampton T	20	5		
2008–09	Northampton T	32	2	**52**	**7**
2009–10	Motherwell	32	2	**32**	**2**
2010–11	Sheffield W	27	4		
2011–12	Sheffield W	0	0		
2011–12	*Bury*	30	6	**30**	**6**
2012–13	Sheffield W	16	0		
2012–13	*Swindon T*	4	0	**4**	**0**
2013–14	Sheffield W	28	1		
2014–15	Sheffield W	13	1	**84**	**6**
2014–15	*Bolton W*	4	0	**4**	**0**
2015–16	Ipswich T	10	0		
2016–17	Ipswich T	0	0	**10**	**0**
2017–18	Chesterfield	2	0	**2**	**0**
2018–19	Oldham Ath	4	0		
2019–20	Oldham Ath	0	0	**4**	**0**
2020–21	Grimsby T	17	0	**17**	**0**

GIBSON, Montel (F) **24** **2**
b.Birmingham 15-12-97

2015–16	Notts Co	4	0		
2016–17	Notts Co	1	0	**5**	**0**

From Ilkeston T, Redditch U, Bedworth U, Halesowen T.

2020–21	Grimsby T	19	2	**19**	**2**

GREEN, Matt (F) **263** **47**
H: 6 0 W: 12 09 b.Bath 2-1-87
Internationals: England C.

2006–07	Cardiff C	6	0		
2007–08	Cardiff C	0	0	**6**	**0**
2007–08	*Darlington*	4	0	**4**	**0**

From Torquay U.

2010–11	Oxford U	17	0	**17**	**0**
2010–11	*Cheltenham T*	19	0	**19**	**0**

From Mansfield T.

2013–14	Birmingham C	10	1		
2014–15	Birmingham C	0	0	**10**	**1**
2015–16	Mansfield T	44	16		
2016–17	Mansfield T	42	10	**86**	**26**
2017–18	Lincoln C	45	13		
2018–19	Lincoln C	19	2	**64**	**15**
2019–20	Grimsby T	29	2		
2020–21	Grimsby T	28	3	**57**	**5**

GRIST, Ben (D) **0** **0**

2020–21	Grimsby T	0	0		

HABERGHAM, Sam (D) **46** **0**
H: 6 0 W: 11 07 b.Rotherham 20-2-92
Internationals: England C, U17.
From Norwich C, Tamworth, Braintree T.

2017–18	Lincoln C	33	0		
2018–19	Lincoln C	0	0	**33**	**0**
2020–21	Grimsby T	13	0	**13**	**0**

HANSON, James (F) **395** **94**
H: 6 4 W: 12 04 b.Bradford 9-11-87

2009–10	Bradford C	34	12		
2010–11	Bradford C	36	6		
2011–12	Bradford C	39	13		
2012–13	Bradford C	43	10		
2013–14	Bradford C	35	12		
2014–15	Bradford C	38	9		
2015–16	Bradford C	41	11		
2016–17	Bradford C	17	4	**283**	**77**
2016–17	Sheffield U	13	1		
2017–18	Sheffield U	1	0	**14**	**1**
2017–18	*Bury*	17	0	**17**	**0**
2018–19	AFC Wimbledon	29	5	**29**	**5**
2019–20	Grimsby T	29	9		
2020–21	Grimsby T	23	2	**52**	**11**

HENDRIE, Luke (M) **187** **5**
b. 27-8-94
Internationals: England U16, U17.

2012–13	Manchester U	0	0		
2013–14	Derby Co	0	0		
2014–15	Derby Co	0	0		
2015–16	Burnley	0	0		
2015–16	*Hartlepool U*	3	0	**3**	**0**
2015–16	*York C*	18	0	**18**	**0**
2016–17	Burnley	0	0		
2016–17	*Kilmarnock*	32	0	**32**	**0**
2017–18	Burnley	0	0		
2017–18	*Bradford C*	13	0	**13**	**0**
2017–18	Shrewsbury T	10	0	**10**	**0**
2018–19	Grimsby T	41	2		
2019–20	Grimsby T	32	1		
2020–21	Grimsby T	38	2	**111**	**5**

HOPE, Joseph (D) **0** **0**

2019–20	Grimsby T	0	0		
2020–21	Grimsby T	0	0		

IDEHEN, Duncan (M) **6** **0**
b. 3-7-02

2018–19	Lincoln C	0	0		
2019–20	Grimsby T	0	0		
2020–21	Grimsby T	6	0	**6**	**0**

JACKSON, Ira (F) **20** **3**
b. 28-1-97

2020–21	Grimsby T	20	3	**20**	**3**

JOHN-LEWIS, Lenell (M) **258** **27**
H: 5 10 W: 11 10 b.Hammersmith 17-5-89

2006–07	Lincoln C	0	0		
2007–08	Lincoln C	21	3		
2008–09	Lincoln C	27	4		
2009–10	Lincoln C	24	1	**72**	**8**
2010–11	Bury	39	2		
2011–12	Bury	28	5		
2012–13	Bury	16	2	**83**	**9**

From Grimsby T.

2015–16	Newport Co	28	3		
2016–17	Newport Co	2	0	**30**	**3**
2017–18	Shrewsbury T	34	2		
2018–19	Shrewsbury T	17	1		
2019–20	Shrewsbury T	2	0	**53**	**3**
2020–21	Grimsby T	20	4	**20**	**4**

KHOURI, Evan (M) **6** **0**
b. 21-1-03
From West Ham U.

2019–20	Grimsby T	0	0		
2020–21	Grimsby T	6	0	**6**	**0**

LAMY, Julien (F) **30** **1**
b.Paris 6-11-99

2016–17	Brest	0	0		
2017–18	Plabennec	16	1	**16**	**1**
2018–19	WBA	0	0		
2019–20	Rotherham U	3	0	**3**	**0**
2019–20	*AFC Wimbledon*	2	0	**2**	**0**
2020–21	Grimsby T	9	0	**9**	**0**

McKEOWN, James (G) **196** **0**
H: 6 1 W: 14 00 b.Birmingham 24-7-89
Internationals: Republic of Ireland U19.

2005–06	Walsall	0	0		
2006–07	Walsall	0	0		
2007–08	Peterborough U	1	0		
2008–09	Peterborough U	1	0		
2009–10	Peterborough U	4	0	**6**	**0**
2016–17	Grimsby T	39	0		
2017–18	Grimsby T	37	0		
2018–19	Grimsby T	43	0		
2019–20	Grimsby T	36	0		
2020–21	Grimsby T	35	0	**190**	**0**

MOHSNI, Bilel (D) **145** **32**
H: 6 3 W: 11 11 b.Tunisia 21-7-87

2010–11	Southend U	23	5		
2011–12	Southend U	31	13		
2012–13	Southend U	8	0	**62**	**18**
2012–13	*Ipswich T*	5	0	**5**	**0**
2013–14	Rangers	28	10		
2014–15	Rangers	15	1	**43**	**11**
2015–16	Angers	4	0	**4**	**0**
2015–16	Paris FC	14	0	**14**	**0**
2016–17	Etiole du Sahel	1	0	**1**	**0**
2017–18	Dundee U	10	3	**10**	**3**
2018–19	Panachaiki	5	0		
2019–20	Panachaiki	0	0	**5**	**0**
2020–21	Grimsby T	1	0	**1**	**0**

Transferred to Barnet December 2020.

MORAIS, Filipe (M) **401** **42**
H: 5 9 W: 11 10 b.Lisbon 21-11-85
Internationals: Portugal U21.

2003–04	Chelsea	0	0		
2004–05	Chelsea	0	0		
2005–06	Chelsea	0	0		
2005–06	*Milton Keynes D*	13	0	**13**	**0**
2006–07	Millwall	12	1	**12**	**1**
2006–07	*St Johnstone*	13	1		
2007–08	Hibernian	28	1		
2008–09	Hibernian	2	0	**30**	**1**
2008–09	Inverness CT	12	3	**12**	**3**
2009–10	St Johnstone	30	2	**43**	**3**
2010–11	Oldham Ath	23	3		
2011–12	Oldham Ath	36	5		
2012–13	Oldham Ath	0	0		
2012–13	Stevenage	28	3		
2013–14	Stevenage	27	4	**55**	**7**
2014–15	Bradford C	30	3		
2015–16	Bradford C	7	1		
2016–17	Bradford C	17	1	**54**	**5**
2016–17	Bolton W	19	2		
2017–18	Bolton W	33	1	**52**	**3**
2018–19	Crawley T	34	8		
2019–20	*Oldham Ath*	16	2	**75**	**10**
2019–20	Crawley T	5	0	**39**	**8**
2020–21	Grimsby T	16	1	**16**	**1**

OHMAN, Ludvig (D) **145 3**
H: 6 2 W: 12 08 b.Umea 9-10-91
Internationals: Sweden U17, U19.
2010 Kalmar 1 0
2011 Kalmar 0 0
2012 Kalmar 16 0
2013 Kalmar 15 0
2014 Kalmar 6 0
2015 Kalmar 19 0 **57 0**
2016 Nagoya Grampus 9 0 **9 0**
2017 Eskilstuna 26 2 **26 2**
2018 Brommapojkarna 22 0 **22 0**
2018–19 Grimsby T 13 0
2019–20 Grimsby T 15 1
2020–21 Grimsby T 3 0 **31 1**

PAYNE, Stefan (F) **146 21**
H: 5 10 W: 11 07 b.Lambeth 10-8-91
Internationals: England C.
From Croydon, Sutton U.
2009–10 Fulham 0 0
2010–11 Gillingham 16 0
2011–12 Gillingham 12 1 **28 1**
2011–12 *Aldershot T* 1 0 **1 0**
From Sutton U, Macclesfield T, Ebbsfleet U, AFC Hornchurch, Dover Ath.
2015–16 Barnsley 0 0
2016–17 Barnsley 7 0
2016–17 *Shrewsbury T* 12 2
2017–18 Barnsley 2 0 **9 0**
2017–18 Shrewsbury T 38 11
2018–19 Bristol R 20 2 **20 2**
2018–19 *Shrewsbury T* 6 0 **56 13**
2019–20 Tranmere R 15 4
2020–21 Tranmere R 4 0 **19 4**
2020–21 Grimsby T 13 1 **13 1**

POLLOCK, Matthew (D) **46 3**
b. 28-9-01
2018–19 Grimsby T 2 0
2019–20 Grimsby T 19 0
2020–21 Grimsby T 25 3 **46 3**

ROSE, Danny (M) **236 15**
H: 5 7 W: 10 04 b.Bristol 21-2-88
Internationals: England C.
2006–07 Manchester U 0 0
2007–08 Manchester U 0 0
From Oxford U, Newport Co
2012–13 Fleetwood T 0 0
2012–13 *Aldershot T* 34 2 **34 2**
2013–14 Oxford U 40 4
2014–15 Oxford U 29 2
2015–16 Oxford U 13 0 **82 6**
2015–16 Northampton T 15 1 **15 1**
2016–17 Portsmouth 38 5
2017–18 Portsmouth 15 0
2018–19 Portsmouth 1 0 **54 5**
2018–19 Swindon T 10 0
2019–20 Swindon T 19 1 **29 1**
2020–21 Grimsby T 22 0 **22 0**

RUSSELL, Sam (G) **172 0**
H: 6 0 W: 10 12 b.Middlesbrough 4-10-82
2001–02 Middlesbrough 0 0
2002–03 Middlesbrough 0 0
2002–03 *Darlington* 1 0
2003–04 Middlesbrough 0 0
2003–04 *Scunthorpe U* 10 0 **10 0**
2004–05 Darlington 46 0
2005–06 Darlington 30 0
2006–07 Darlington 31 0 **108 0**
2007–08 Rochdale 15 0
2008–09 Rochdale 23 0 **38 0**
From Wrexham, Darlington, Forest Green R.
2017–18 Forest Green R 5 0 **5 0**
2018–19 Grimsby T 5 0
2019–20 Grimsby T 1 0
2020–21 Grimsby T 5 0 **11 0**

SCANNELL, Sean (F) **346 22**
H: 5 9 W: 11 07 b.Croydon 19-9-90
Internationals: Republic of Ireland U17, U18, U19, U21, B.
2007–08 Crystal Palace 23 2
2008–09 Crystal Palace 25 2
2009–10 Crystal Palace 26 2
2010–11 Crystal Palace 19 2
2011–12 Crystal Palace 37 4 **130 12**
2012–13 Huddersfield T 34 2
2013–14 Huddersfield T 38 1
2014–15 Huddersfield T 42 4
2015–16 Huddersfield T 29 1
2016–17 Huddersfield T 15 0
2017–18 Huddersfield T 0 0 **158 8**
2017–18 *Burton Alb* 18 0 **18 0**
2018–19 Bradford C 16 0
2019–20 Bradford C 5 1 **21 1**
2019–20 Blackpool 8 1 **8 1**
2020–21 Grimsby T 11 0 **11 0**

SISAY, Alhagi (F) **1 0**
2020–21 Grimsby T 1 0 **1 0**

SPOKES, Luke (M) **17 1**
b. 6-8-00
2020–21 Grimsby T 17 1 **17 1**

STARBUCK, Joseph (M) **6 0**
b. 3-8-02
2019–20 Grimsby T 0 0
2020–21 Grimsby T 6 0 **6 0**

TOMLINSON, Harvey (F) **0 0**
2020–21 Grimsby T 0 0

WATERFALL, Luke (D) **152 11**
H: 6 2 W: 13 02 b.Sheffield 30-7-90
2008–09 Tranmere R 0 0
From Ilkeston, Gainsborough T
2013–14 Scunthorpe U 9 1
2014–15 Scunthorpe U 0 0 **9 1**
2014–15 *Mansfield T* 5 0 **5 0**
From Wrexham, Lincoln C.
2017–18 Lincoln C 30 2
2018–19 Lincoln C 1 0 **31 2**
2018–19 Shrewsbury T 44 5
2019–20 Shrewsbury T 0 0 **44 5**
2019–20 Grimsby T 30 2
2020–21 Grimsby T 33 1 **63 3**

WILLIAMS, George C (F) **114 10**
H: 5 10 W: 12 04 b.Milton Keynes 7-9-95
Internationals: Wales U17, U19, U21, Full caps.
2011–12 Milton Keynes D 2 0
2012–13 Fulham 0 0
2013–14 Fulham 0 0
2014–15 Fulham 14 0
2014–15 *Milton Keynes D* 4 0
2015–16 Fulham 1 0
2015–16 *Gillingham* 10 0 **10 0**
2016–17 Fulham 0 0
2016–17 *Milton Keynes D* 11 0 **17 0**
2017–18 Fulham 0 0 **15 0**
2017–18 *St Johnstone* 11 0 **11 0**
2018–19 Forest Green R 38 7
2019–20 Forest Green R 4 1 **42 8**
2020–21 Grimsby T 19 2 **19 2**

WRIGHT, Max (M) **33 3**
b.Grimsby 6-4-98
2016–17 Grimsby T 0 0
2017–18 Grimsby T 0 0
2018–19 Grimsby T 2 0
2019–20 Grimsby T 25 2
2020–21 Grimsby T 6 1 **33 3**

Scholars
Adlard, Luis Samuel; Antoine, Dominic Davis; Blakeley, Adam Thomas; Boyes, Patrick William; Braithwaite, Aaron David; Bramwell, Jamie; Davey, Owen Jay; Drinkell, Harvey John; Essel, Edwin; Goundry, Jaz Leo; Jacobs, Tom Charlie; Khouri, Evan Marley; Potts, Jamie; Scott, Ethan Joseph; Smaller, Joshua James; Stratton, Callum Robert; Tomlinson, Harvey Joseph; Walker, Aidan James.

HARROGATE T (39)

AGNEW, Liam (M) **0 0**
H: 5 10 W: 11 05 b.Sunderland 9-12-93
2013–14 Sunderland 0 0
2014–15 Sunderland 0 0
2015–16 Sunderland 0 0
From Boston U, Harrogate T.
2020–21 Harrogate T 0 0

BECK, Mark (F) **115 16**
H: 6 5 W: 12 08 b.Sunderland 2-2-94
Internationals: Scotland U19.
2011–12 Carlisle U 2 0
2012–13 Carlisle U 27 4
2013–14 Carlisle U 10 0
2013–14 *Falkirk* 15 5 **15 5**
2014–15 Carlisle U 27 3 **66 7**
2015–16 Yeovil T 8 0 **8 0**
From Darlington, Harrogate T.
2020–21 Harrogate T 26 4 **26 4**

BELSHAW, James (G) **38 0**
b.Nottingham 12-10-90
2020–21 Harrogate T 38 0 **38 0**

BURRELL, Warren (M) **43 0**
b.Sheffield 3-6-90
2020–21 Harrogate T 43 0 **43 0**

CRACKNELL, Joe (G) **8 0**
H: 6 0 W: 11 02 b.Hull 5-6-94
2012–13 Hull C 0 0
2013–14 Hull C 0 0
2015–16 Bradford C 0 0
2016–17 Bradford C 0 0
From Bradford Park Avenue, Harrogate T.
2020–21 Harrogate T 8 0 **8 0**

EMMETT, Jack (M) **0 0**
b.Harrogate 22-10-93
2020–21 Harrogate T 0 0

FALKINGHAM, Joshua (M) **234 31**
b.Leeds 25-8-90
2009–10 St Johnstone 1 0 **1 0**
2010–11 Arbroath 35 9
2011–12 Arbroath 35 8 **70 17**
2012–13 Dunfermline Ath 30 3
2013–14 Dunfermline Ath 30 5
2014–15 Dunfermline Ath 32 3
2015–16 Dunfermline Ath 28 3 **120 14**
From Darlington.
2020–21 Harrogate T 43 0 **43 0**

FALLOWFIELD, Ryan (M) **31 0**
b.Kingston upon Hull 3-1-96
2020–21 Harrogate T 31 0 **31 0**

FRANCIS, Edward (D) **21 1**
b. 11-9-91
2017–18 Manchester C 0 0
2018–19 Manchester C 0 0
2018–19 *Almere C* 1 0 **1 0**
2019–20 Wolverhampton W 0 0
2019–20 *Grasshopper* 0 0
2020–21 Wolverhampton W 0 0
2020–21 Harrogate T 20 1 **20 1**

HALL, Connor (D) **41 1**
b. 23-5-93
2020–21 Harrogate T 41 1 **41 1**

KERRY, Lloyd (M) **31 2**
b.Chesterfield 22-7-88
2020–21 Harrogate T 31 2 **31 2**

KIERNAN, Brendan (M) **45 4**
H: 5 9 W: 11 11 b.Lambeth 10-11-92
2011–12 AFC Wimbledon 9 0
2012–13 AFC Wimbledon 6 0
2013–14 AFC Wimbledon 0 0 **15 0**
From Bromley, Staines T, Ebbsfleet U, Lingfield, Hayes & Yeading U, Bromley, Hampton & Richmond Bor, Welling U.
2020–21 Harrogate T 30 4 **30 4**

KIRBY, Connor (M) **52 1**
b. 10-9-98
2017–18 Sheffield W 1 0
2018–19 Sheffield W 1 0
2019–20 Sheffield W 0 0 **2 0**
2019–20 *Macclesfield T* 34 1 **34 1**
2020–21 Harrogate T 16 0 **16 0**

LAWLOR, Jake (M) **17 0**
b. 8-4-91
2020–21 Harrogate T 17 0 **17 0**

LOKKO, Kevin (D) **5 1**
b.Whitechapel 3-11-95
Internationals: England C.
From Colchester U, Welling U, Maidstone U, Stevenage.
2017–18 Stevenage 2 0 **2 0**
From Dover Ath.
2020–21 Harrogate T 3 1 **3 1**

MARTIN, Aaron (F) **36 5**
b. 5-7-91
2020–21 Harrogate T 36 5 **36 5**

McPAKE, Joshua (M) **36 4**
b.Coatbridge 31-8-01
2018–19 Rangers 0 0
2019–20 Rangers 0 0
2019–20 *Dundee* 7 0 **7 0**
2020–21 Rangers 0 0
2020–21 *Greenock Morton* 6 0 **6 0**
On loan from Rangers
2020–21 Harrogate T 23 4 **23 4**

MILLER, Calvin (D) **43 3**
b.Glasgow 9-1-98
2016–17 Celtic 1 0
2017–18 Celtic 3 0
2018–19 Celtic 0 0
2018–19 *Dundee* 16 1 **16 1**
2018–19 *Ayr U* 13 1 **13 1**
2019–20 Celtic 0 0 **4 0**
2020–21 Harrogate T 10 1 **10 1**

MINTER, Melvin (G) **0 0**
2020–21 Harrogate T 0 0

MULDOON, Jack (F) **45 15**
b.Scunthorpe 19-5-89
2014–15 Rochdale 3 0 **3 0**
From Brigg T, Sheffield, Glapwell, Alfreton T, Stocksbridge Park Steels, Brigg T, North Ferriby U, Worksop T.
2020–21 Harrogate T 42 15 **42 15**

POWER, Simon (M) **24 2**
b.Greystones 13-5-98
2018–19 Norwich C 0 0
2018–19 *Dordrecht* 10 1 **10 1**
2019–20 Norwich C 0 0
2019–20 *Ross Co* 1 0 **1 0**
2020–21 Harrogate T 13 1 **13 1**

SMITH, Will (D) **32 2**
b. 4-11-98
2016–17 Barnsley 0 0
2017–18 Barnsley 0 0
2018–19 Barnsley 0 0
From Lincoln C, AFC Fylde, Harrogate T.
2020–21 Harrogate T 32 2 **32 2**

STEAD, Jon (F) **599 136**
H: 6 3 W: 13 03 b.Huddersfield 7-4-83
Internationals: England U21.
2001–02 Huddersfield T 0 0
2002–03 Huddersfield T 42 6
2003–04 Huddersfield T 26 16
2003–04 Blackburn R 13 6
2004–05 Blackburn R 29 2 **42 8**
2005–06 Sunderland 30 1
2006–07 Sunderland 5 1 **35 2**
2006–07 *Derby Co* 17 3 **17 3**
2006–07 Sheffield U 14 5
2007–08 Sheffield U 24 3
2008–09 Sheffield U 1 0 **39 8**
2008–09 Ipswich T 39 12
2009–10 Ipswich T 22 6
2009–10 *Coventry C* 10 2 **10 2**
2010–11 Ipswich T 3 1 **64 19**
2010–11 Bristol C 27 9
2011–12 Bristol C 24 6
2012–13 Bristol C 28 5 **79 20**
2013–14 Huddersfield T 12 1
2013–14 *Oldham Ath* 5 0 **5 0**
2013–14 *Bradford C* 8 1
2014–15 Huddersfield T 7 1 **87 24**
2014–15 *Bradford C* 32 6 **40 7**
2015–16 Notts Co 43 11
2016–17 Notts Co 38 14
2017–18 Notts Co 43 9
2018–19 Notts Co 38 8 **162 42**
From Harrogate T.
2020–21 Harrogate T 19 1 **19 1**

THOMSON, George (M) **46 3**
b.Melton Mowbray 19-5-92
2020–21 Harrogate T 46 3 **46 3**

WALKER, Tom (M) **40 1**
H: 6 0 b.Salford 12-12-95
Internationals: England C.
2014–15 Bolton W 11 1
2015–16 Bolton W 7 0
2016–17 Bolton W 0 0 **18 1**
2016–17 *Bury* 11 0 **11 0**
From Stockport C, FC United of Manchester.
2019–20 Salford C 4 0 **4 0**
2020–21 Harrogate T 7 0 **7 0**

WILLIAMS, Jay (D) **17 1**
b. 4-10-00
2018–19 Northampton T 10 0
2019–20 Northampton T 0 0 **10 0**
2020–21 Harrogate T 7 1 **7 1**

HUDDERSFIELD T (40)

AARONS, Rolando (M) **80 4**
H: 5 9 W: 10 08 b.Kingston 16-11-95
Internationals: England U20.
From Bristol C.
2014–15 Newcastle U 4 1
2015–16 Newcastle U 10 1
2016–17 Newcastle U 4 0
2017–18 Newcastle U 4 0
2017–18 *Verona* 11 0 **11 0**
2018–19 Newcastle U 0 0
2018–19 *Liberec* 12 0 **12 0**
2018–19 *Sheffield W* 9 1 **9 1**
2019–20 Newcastle U 0 0
2019–20 *Wycombe W* 10 1 **10 1**
2019–20 *Motherwell* 6 0 **6 0**
2020–21 Newcastle U 0 0 **22 2**
2020–21 Huddersfield T 10 0 **10 0**

AUSTERFIELD, Joshua (M) **0 0**
b. 2-11-01
2019–20 Huddersfield T 0 0
2020–21 Huddersfield T 0 0

AYINA, Loick (D) **0 0**
b.Brazzaville 20-4-03
From Sarcelles.
2020–21 Huddersfield T 0 0

BACUNA, Juninho (F) **184 14**
H: 6 1 W: 12 04 b.Groningen 7-8-97
Internationals: Netherlands U18, U20, U21. Curacao Full caps.
2014–15 Groningen 11 0
2015–16 Groningen 14 0
2016–17 Groningen 24 1
2017–18 Groningen 33 1 **82 2**
2018–19 Huddersfield T 21 1
2019–20 Huddersfield T 38 6
2020–21 Huddersfield T 43 5 **102 12**

BELLAGAMBI, Giosue (G) **0 0**
H: 6 2 W: 12 02 b.Croydon 8-11-01
2020–21 Huddersfield T 0 0

BILOKAPIC, Nicholas (G) **0 0**
H: 6 5 b. 8-9-02
Internationals: Australia U17.
From Sydney U.
2020–21 Huddersfield T 0 0

BRIGHT, Myles (M) **0 0**
b.London 18-10-02
2020–21 Huddersfield T 0 0

BROWN, Jaden (D) **28 0**
b. 24-1-99
Internationals: England U16, U17, U18, U19.
From Tottenham H.
2018–19 Huddersfield T 0 0
2018–19 *Exeter C* 0 0
2019–20 Huddersfield T 15 0
2020–21 Huddersfield T 13 0 **28 0**

BROWN, Reece (M) **147 15**
H: 5 9 W: 12 04 b.Dudley 3-3-96
Internationals: England U16, U17, U18, U20.
2013–14 Birmingham C 6 0
2014–15 Birmingham C 1 0
2014–15 *Notts Co* 3 0 **3 0**
2015–16 Birmingham C 1 0
2016–17 Birmingham C 8 0 **16 0**
2016–17 *Chesterfield* 2 0 **2 0**
2017–18 Forest Green R 33 2
2018–19 Forest Green R 45 11 **78 13**
2019–20 Huddersfield T 0 0
2019–20 *Peterborough U* 10 0
2020–21 Huddersfield T 0 0
2020–21 *Peterborough U* 38 2 **48 2**

CAMARA, Etienne (D) **0 0**
b. 30-3-03
From Angers.
2020–21 Huddersfield T 0 0

CAMPBELL, Frazier (F) **375 88**
H: 5 11 W: 12 04 b.Huddersfield 13-9-87
Internationals: England U16, U17, U18, U21, Full caps.
2005–06 Manchester U 0 0
2006–07 Manchester U 0 0
2006–07 *Antwerp* 31 20 **31 20**
2007–08 Manchester U 1 0
2007–08 *Hull C* 34 15
2008–09 Manchester U 1 0
2008–09 *Tottenham H* 10 1 **10 1**
2009–10 Manchester U 0 0 **2 0**
2009–10 Sunderland 31 4
2010–11 Sunderland 3 0
2011–12 Sunderland 12 1
2012–13 Sunderland 12 1 **58 6**
2012–13 Cardiff C 12 7
2013–14 Cardiff C 37 6 **49 13**
2014–15 Crystal Palace 20 4
2015–16 Crystal Palace 11 0
2016–17 Crystal Palace 12 1 **43 5**
2017–18 Hull C 36 6
2018–19 Hull C 39 12 **109 33**
2019–20 Huddersfield T 33 3
2020–21 Huddersfield T 40 7 **73 10**

CRICHLOW-NOBLE, Romoney (D) **4 0**
b.Luton 3-6-99
From Enfield Bor.
2017–18 Huddersfield T 0 0
2018–19 Huddersfield T 0 0
2019–20 Huddersfield T 0 0
2020–21 Huddersfield T 4 0 **4 0**

DALEY, Luke (D) **0 0**
b. 30-1-03
From Port Vale.
2020–21 Huddersfield T 0 0

DALY, Matty (M) **11 1**
H: 5 9 b. 10-3-01
Internationals: England U17, U18.
2018–19 Huddersfield T 2 0
2019–20 Huddersfield T 4 1
2020–21 Huddersfield T 5 0 **11 1**

DIAKHABY, Adama (F) **107 6**
H: 6 0 W: 10 03 b.Ajaccio 5-7-95
Internationals: France U21.
From Caen.
2015–16 Rennes 0 0
2016–17 Rennes 25 4 **25 4**
2017–18 Monaco 22 2 **22 2**
2018–19 Huddersfield T 12 0
2019–20 Huddersfield T 18 0
2019–20 *Nottingham F* 14 0 **14 0**
2020–21 Huddersfield T 16 0 **46 0**
Transferred to Amiens February 2021.

DIARRA, Brahima (M) **1 0**
b.Paris 5-7-03
2020–21 Huddersfield T 1 0 **1 0**

DUHANEY, Demeaco (D) **20 0**
H: 5 11 W: 11 00 b.Manchester 13-10-98
Internationals: England U18, U20.
2017–18 Manchester C 0 0
2018–19 Huddersfield T 1 0
2019–20 Huddersfield T 6 0
2020–21 Huddersfield T 13 0 **20 0**

EDMONDS-GREEN, Rarmani (D) **35 3**
b.London 14-1-99
2019–20 Huddersfield T 2 0
2019–20 *Swindon T* 9 1 **9 1**
2020–21 Huddersfield T 24 2 **26 2**

EITING, Carel (M) **40 3**
b.Amsterdam 11-2-98
2016–17 Ajax 0 0
2017–18 Ajax 4 0
2018–19 Ajax 7 0
2019–20 Ajax 6 0
2020–21 Ajax 0 0 **17 0**
On loan from Ajax.
2020–21 Huddersfield T 23 3 **23 3**

ELLIOTT, Kit (F) **0 0**
b. 22-3-01
2020–21 Cork C 0 0
2020–21 Huddersfield T 0 0

ELPHICK, Tommy (M) **360 14**
H: 5 11 W: 11 07 b.Brighton 7-9-87
2005–06 Brighton & HA 1 0
2006–07 Brighton & HA 3 0
2007–08 Brighton & HA 39 2
2008–09 Brighton & HA 39 1
2009–10 Brighton & HA 44 3
2010–11 Brighton & HA 27 1
2011–12 Brighton & HA 0 0
2012–13 Brighton & HA 0 0 **153 7**
2012–13 Bournemouth 34 2
2013–14 Bournemouth 38 1
2014–15 Bournemouth 46 1
2015–16 Bournemouth 12 1 **130 5**
2016–17 Aston Villa 26 0
2017–18 Aston Villa 4 0
2017–18 *Reading* 4 0 **4 0**
2018–19 Aston Villa 11 1 **41 1**
2018–19 *Hull C* 18 1 **18 1**
2019–20 Huddersfield T 14 0
2020–21 Huddersfield T 0 0 **14 0**

GRANT, Daniel (F) **0 0**
H: 5 8 W: 11 00 b.Dublin 23-10-00
Internationals: Republic of Ireland U21.
From Bohemians.
2020–21 Huddersfield T 0 0

HARRATT, Kian (F) **1 0**
b. 21-6-02
From Barnsley, Leeds U.
2019–20 Huddersfield T 1 0
2020–21 Huddersfield T 0 0 **1 0**

HEADLEY, Jaheim (D) **0 0**
b.London 24-9-01
2020–21 Huddersfield T 0 0

HIGH, Scott (M) **27 0**
b.Dewsbury 15-2-01
2019–20 Huddersfield T 1 0
2020–21 Huddersfield T 14 0 **15 0**
2020–21 *Shrewsbury T* 12 0 **12 0**

HOGG, Jonathan (M) **359 3**
H: 5 7 W: 10 05 b.Middlesbrough 6-12-88
2007–08 Aston Villa 0 0
2008–09 Aston Villa 0 0
2009–10 Aston Villa 0 0
2009–10 *Darlington* 5 1 **5 1**
2010–11 Aston Villa 5 0
2010–11 *Portsmouth* 19 0 **19 0**
2011–12 Aston Villa 0 0 **5 0**
2011–12 Watford 40 0
2012–13 Watford 38 0 **78 0**
2013–14 Huddersfield T 34 0
2014–15 Huddersfield T 26 0
2015–16 Huddersfield T 22 0

2016–17 Huddersfield T 37 1
2017–18 Huddersfield T 30 0
2018–19 Huddersfield T 29 0
2019–20 Huddersfield T 37 0
2020–21 Huddersfield T 37 1 **252 2**

HOLMES, Duane (M) 202 18
H: 5 8 W: 10 03 b.Wakefield 6-11-94
Internationals: USA Full caps.
2012–13 Huddersfield T 0 0
2013–14 Huddersfield T 16 0
2013–14 *Yeovil T* 5 0 **5 0**
2014–15 Huddersfield T 0 0
2014–15 *Bury* 6 0 **6 0**
2015–16 Huddersfield T 6 1
2016–17 Scunthorpe U 32 3
2017–18 Scunthorpe U 45 7
2018–19 Scunthorpe U 1 0 **78 10**
2018–19 Derby Co 25 2
2019–20 Derby Co 33 2
2020–21 Derby Co 14 1 **72 5**
2020–21 Huddersfield T 19 2 **41 3**

JACKSON, Ben (M) 6 1
b. 22-2-01
2019–20 Huddersfield T 0 0
2020–21 Huddersfield T 1 0 **1 0**
2020–21 *Bolton W* 5 1 **5 1**

JONES, Patrick (F) 2 0
b. 9-6-03
From Wrexham.
2020–21 Huddersfield T 2 0 **2 0**

KEOGH, Richard (D) 588 19
H: 6 0 W: 11 02 b.Harlow 11-8-86
Internationals: Republic of Ireland U21, Full caps.
2004–05 Stoke C 0 0
2005–06 Bristol C 9 1
2005–06 *Wycombe W* 3 0 **3 0**
2006–07 Bristol C 31 2
2007–08 Bristol C 0 0 **40 3**
2007–08 *Huddersfield T* 9 1
2007–08 *Carlisle U* 7 0
2007–08 *Cheltenham T* 10 0 **10 0**
2008–09 Carlisle U 32 1
2009–10 Carlisle U 41 3 **80 4**
2010–11 Coventry C 46 1
2011–12 Coventry C 45 0 **91 1**
2012–13 Derby Co 46 4
2013–14 Derby Co 41 1
2014–15 Derby Co 45 0
2015–16 Derby Co 46 1
2016–17 Derby Co 42 0
2017–18 Derby Co 42 1
2018–19 Derby Co 46 3
2019–20 Derby Co 8 0 **316 10**
2020–21 Milton Keynes D 18 0 **18 0**
2020–21 Huddersfield T 21 0 **30 1**

KHERBOUCHE, Nasim (D) 0 0
H: 6 4 b.London 9-1-02
2020–21 Huddersfield T 0 0

KOROMA, Josh (F) 57 11
H: 5 10 W: 10 06 b. 8-11-98
Internationals: England C.
2015–16 Leyton Orient 3 0
2016–17 Leyton Orient 22 3 **25 3**
From Leyton Orient.
2019–20 Huddersfield T 7 0
2019–20 *Rotherham U* 5 0 **5 0**
2020–21 Huddersfield T 20 8 **27 8**

LEUTWILER, Jayson (G) 143 0
H: 6 3 W: 12 07 b.Basel 25-4-89
Internationals: Switzerland U16, U17, U18, U19, U20, U21. Canada Full caps.
From Basel.
2012–13 Middlesbrough 0 0
2013–14 Middlesbrough 3 0 **3 0**
2014–15 Shrewsbury T 46 0
2015–16 Shrewsbury T 29 0
2016–17 Shrewsbury T 43 0 **118 0**
2017–18 Blackburn R 1 0
2018–19 Blackburn R 5 0
2019–20 Blackburn R 0 0 **6 0**
2020–21 Fleetwood T 16 0 **16 0**
2020–21 Huddersfield T 0 0

MBENZA, Isaac (F) 189 25
H: 6 2 W: 12 02 b.Saint-Denis 8-3-96
Internationals: Belgium U17, U19, U21.
2014–15 Valenciennes 13 1
2015–16 Valenciennes 35 6 **48 7**
2016–17 Standard Liege 21 1 **21 1**
2016–17 Montpellier 16 3
2017–18 Montpellier 38 8
2018–19 Montpellier 0 0 **54 11**
2018–19 *Huddersfield T* 22 1
2019–20 Huddersfield T 5 0
2019–20 *Amiens* 3 0 **3 0**
2020–21 Huddersfield T 36 5 **63 6**

O'BRIEN, Lewis (M) 120 9
H: 5 8 W: 9 13 b.Colchester 14-10-98
2017–18 Huddersfield T 0 0
2018–19 Huddersfield T 0 0
2018–19 *Bradford C* 40 4 **40 4**
2019–20 Huddersfield T 38 2
2020–21 Huddersfield T 42 3 **80 5**

OBIERO, Micah (F) 4 0
b. 22-2-01
2018–19 Huddersfield T 0 0
2019–20 Huddersfield T 0 0
2020–21 Huddersfield T 0 0
2020–21 *Carlisle U* 4 0 **4 0**

OLAGUNJU, Mustapha (D) 6 0
b. 1-1-02
2020–21 Huddersfield T 0 0
2020–21 *Port Vale* 6 0 **6 0**

PHILLIPS, Kieran (F) 10 0
b. 18-2-00
From Everton.
2020–21 Huddersfield T 10 0 **10 0**

PIPA, Gonzalo (D) 62 2
b.Esparraguera 26-1-98
2015–16 Espanyol 0 0
2016–17 Espanyol 0 0
2017–18 Espanyol 0 0
2018–19 Espanyol 0 0
2019–20 Espanyol 7 0
2019–20 *Gimnastic* 18 0 **18 0**
2020–21 Espanyol 0 0 **7 0**
2020–21 Huddersfield T 37 2 **37 2**

PRITCHARD, Alex (M) 209 28
H: 5 7 W: 9 11 b.Grays 3-5-93
Internationals: England U20, U21.
2011–12 Tottenham H 0 0
2012–13 Tottenham H 0 0
2012–13 *Peterborough U* 6 0 **6 0**
2013–14 Tottenham H 1 0
2013–14 *Swindon T* 36 6 **36 6**
2014–15 Tottenham H 0 0
2014–15 *Brentford* 45 12 **45 12**
2015–16 Tottenham H 1 0 **2 0**
2015–16 *WBA* 2 0 **2 0**
2016–17 Norwich C 30 6
2017–18 Norwich C 8 1 **38 7**
2017–18 Huddersfield T 14 1
2018–19 Huddersfield T 30 2
2019–20 Huddersfield T 18 0
2020–21 Huddersfield T 18 0 **80 3**

ROWE, Aaron (M) 23 1
b. 7-9-00
From Leyton Orient.
2018–19 Huddersfield T 2 0
2019–20 Huddersfield T 1 0
2020–21 Huddersfield T 20 1 **23 1**

SANOGO, Yaya (F) 124 25
H: 6 3 W: 11 08 b.Massy 27-1-93
Internationals: France U16, U17, U19, U20, U21.
2009–10 Auxerre 0 0
2010–11 Auxerre 0 0
2011–12 Auxerre 7 1
2012–13 Auxerre 13 9 **20 10**
2013–14 Arsenal 8 0
2014–15 Arsenal 3 0
2014–15 *Crystal Palace* 10 0 **10 0**
2015–16 Arsenal 0 0
2015–16 *Ajax* 3 0 **3 0**
2015–16 *Charlton Ath* 8 3 **8 3**
2016–17 Arsenal 0 0 **11 0**
2017–18 Toulouse 27 6
2018–19 Toulouse 21 3
2019–20 Toulouse 15 3 **63 12**
2020–21 Huddersfield T 9 0 **9 0**

SARR, Naby (D) 168 12
H: 6 5 W: 14 11 b.Marseille 13-8-93
Internationals: France U20, U21.
2012–13 Lyon 0 0
2013–14 Lyon 2 0 **2 0**
2014–15 Sporting Lisbon 8 0 **8 0**
2015–16 Charlton Ath 12 1
2016–17 Charlton Ath 0 0
2016–17 *Red Star* 22 2 **22 2**
2017–18 Charlton Ath 18 0
2018–19 Charlton Ath 36 2
2019–20 Charlton Ath 29 3 **95 6**
2020–21 Huddersfield T 41 4 **41 4**

SCHINDLER, Christopher (D) 327 9
H: 6 2 W: 12 02 b.Munich 29-4-90
Internationals: Germany U21.
2009–10 1860 Munich 0 0
2010–11 1860 Munich 16 1
2011–12 1860 Munich 30 1
2012–13 1860 Munich 18 0
2013–14 1860 Munich 26 0
2014–15 1860 Munich 29 1
2015–16 1860 Munich 33 1 **152 4**
2016–17 Huddersfield T 44 2
2017–18 Huddersfield T 37 0
2018–19 Huddersfield T 37 1
2019–20 Huddersfield T 45 2
2020–21 Huddersfield T 12 0 **175 5**

SCHOFIELD, Ryan (G) 49 0
H: 6 3 W: 11 00 b.Huddersfield 11-12-99
Internationals: England U18, U19, U20.
2018–19 Huddersfield T 0 0
2018–19 *Notts Co* 17 0 **17 0**
2019–20 Huddersfield T 1 0
2019–20 *Livingston* 1 0 **1 0**
2020–21 Huddersfield T 30 0 **31 0**

SHARROCK-PEPLOW, Sam (D) 0 0
b.Leigh 14-7-02
2020–21 Huddersfield T 0 0

STEARMAN, Richard (D) 472 15
H: 6 2 W: 10 08 b.Wolverhampton 19-8-87
Internationals: England U16, U17, U19, U21.
2004–05 Leicester C 8 1
2005–06 Leicester C 34 3
2006–07 Leicester C 35 1
2007–08 Leicester C 39 2 **116 7**
2008–09 Wolverhampton W 37 1
2009–10 Wolverhampton W 16 1
2010–11 Wolverhampton W 31 0
2011–12 Wolverhampton W 30 0
2012–13 Wolverhampton W 12 1
2012–13 *Ipswich T* 15 0 **15 0**
2013–14 Wolverhampton W 40 2
2014–15 Wolverhampton W 42 0
2015–16 Wolverhampton W 4 0
2015–16 Fulham 29 0
2016–17 Fulham 0 0 **29 0**
2016–17 *Wolverhampton W* 18 0 **230 5**
2017–18 Sheffield U 28 2
2018–19 Sheffield U 16 1
2019–20 Sheffield U 0 0 **44 3**
2019–20 Huddersfield T 17 0
2020–21 Huddersfield T 21 0 **38 0**

THOMAS, Sorba (F) 7 0
b. 22-8-99
From Boreham Wood.
2020–21 Huddersfield T 7 0 **7 0**

TOFFOLO, Harry (D) 199 10
H: 6 0 W: 11 03 b. 19-8-95
Internationals: England U18, U19, U20.
2014–15 Norwich C 0 0
2014–15 *Swindon T* 28 1 **28 1**
2015–16 Norwich C 0 0
2015–16 *Rotherham U* 7 0 **7 0**
2015–16 *Peterborough U* 7 0 **7 0**
2016–17 Norwich C 0 0
2016–17 *Scunthorpe U* 22 2 **22 2**
2017–18 Norwich C 0 0
2017–18 *Doncaster R* 13 0 **13 0**
2017–18 Millwall 0 0
2018–19 Lincoln C 46 3
2019–20 Lincoln C 26 1 **72 4**
2019–20 Huddersfield T 19 1
2020–21 Huddersfield T 31 2 **50 3**

VALLEJO, Alex (M) 103 1
b.Vitoria-Gasteiz 16-1-92
2011–12 Alaves 1 0 **1 0**
2011–12 *Sestao* 7 0 **7 0**
2012–13 Mallorca 0 0
2013–14 Mallorca 6 0
2014–15 Mallorca 4 1
2015–16 Mallorca 0 0
2016–17 Mallorca 13 0 **23 1**
2017–18 Cordoba 18 0
2018–19 Cordoba 28 0 **46 0**
2019–20 Fuenlabrada 10 0
2020–21 Fuenlabrada 0 0 **10 0**
2020–21 Huddersfield T 16 0 **16 0**

WARD, Danny (M) 329 56
H: 5 11 W: 12 05 b.Bradford 11-12-91
From Leeds U.
2008–09 Bolton W 0 0
2009–10 Bolton W 2 0
2009–10 *Swindon T* 28 7 **28 7**
2010–11 Bolton W 0 0 **2 0**
2010–11 *Coventry C* 5 0 **5 0**
2010–11 *Huddersfield T* 7 3
2011–12 Huddersfield T 39 4
2012–13 Huddersfield T 28 2
2013–14 Huddersfield T 38 10
2014–15 Huddersfield T 12 0
2014–15 *Rotherham U* 16 3
2015–16 Rotherham U 34 4

2016–17 Rotherham U 41 10 **91** **17**
2017–18 Cardiff C 18 4
2018–19 Cardiff C 14 1
2019–20 Cardiff C 28 7 **60** **12**
2020–21 Huddersfield T 19 1 **143** **20**

Scholars
Adewoju, David Oluwafemi Ayomikun; Baxter-Alleyne, Darnel Darren; Billam, Luke Andrew; Bright, Myles Iain Christian; Eccleston, Neo Arlee Ifny; Edionhon, Andre Egbe Silveria; Falls, Conor Niall; Gilmore, Brodie; Grubb, Evander Marvin; Krasniqi, Ernaldo; Maroodza, Shane Takudzwa; Midgley, Benjamin James; Nduwuisi Ondo, Charles; O'Brien-Brady, Donay Kaylin; Okpolokpo, Joshua Melive Oghenrukewe; Roxburgh, Michael David; Shipley, Robson Leslie; Stewart, Jeremy Robert; Whittingham, Sonny; Zunda, Gulutte.

HULL C (41)

ARTHUR, Festus (D) 0 0
b.Hamburg 27-2-00
From Stockport Co.
2020–21 Hull C 0 0

BECKETT, Louis (M) 0 0
b.Scarborough 8-10-02
2020–21 Hull C 0 0

BERRY, James (F) 1 0
b.Wigan 10-2-00
From Liverpool.
2017–18 Wigan Ath 0 0
2018–19 Wigan Ath 0 0
2019–20 Hull C 1 0
2020–21 Hull C 0 0 **1** **0**

BONDS, Elliott (M) 5 0
b.London 23-3-00
Internationals: Guyana Full caps.
From Dagenham & R.
2019–20 Hull C 0 0
2020–21 Hull C 0 0
2020–21 *Cheltenham T* 5 0 **5** **0**

BURKE, Reece (D) 178 8
H: 6 2 W: 12 11 b.London 2-9-96
Internationals: England U18, U19, U20.
2013–14 West Ham U 0 0
2014–15 West Ham U 5 0
2015–16 West Ham U 0 0
2015–16 *Bradford C* 34 2 **34** **2**
2016–17 West Ham U 0 0
2016–17 *Wigan Ath* 10 1 **10** **1**
2017–18 West Ham U 0 0 **5** **0**
2017–18 *Bolton W* 25 1 **25** **1**
2018–19 Hull C 34 0
2019–20 Hull C 36 0
2020–21 Hull C 34 4 **104** **4**

CARTWRIGHT, Harvey (G) 0 0
b.Grimsby 9-5-02
2020–21 Hull C 0 0

CHADWICK, Billy (M) 3 0
b.Hull 19-1-00
2020–21 Hull C 3 0 **3** **0**

CLARK, Max (D) 109 3
H: 5 11 W: 11 07 b.Hull 19-1-96
Internationals: England U16, U17.
2015–16 Hull C 0 0
2015–16 *Cambridge U* 9 0
2016–17 Hull C 0 0
2016–17 *Cambridge U* 27 1 **36** **1**
2017–18 Hull C 27 0
2018–19 Vitesse 23 1
2019–20 Vitesse 23 1
2020–21 Vitesse 0 0 **46** **2**
2020–21 Hull C 0 0 **27** **0**

COYLE, Lewie (M) 160 1
H: 5 8 W: 10 08 b.Hull 15-10-95
2015–16 Leeds U 11 0
2016–17 Leeds U 4 0
2017–18 Leeds U 0 0
2017–18 *Fleetwood T* 42 0
2018–19 Leeds U 0 0 **15** **0**
2018–19 *Fleetwood T* 41 0
2019–20 Fleetwood T 34 1
2020–21 Fleetwood T 0 0 **117** **1**
2020–21 Hull C 28 0 **28** **0**

DOCHERTY, Greg (M) 196 18
H: 5 10 W: 11 05 b.Glasgow 10-9-96
Internationals: Scotland U17, U21.
2013–14 Hamilton A 3 0
2014–15 Hamilton A 7 1
2015–16 Hamilton A 34 1
2016–17 Hamilton A 29 1
2017–18 Hamilton A 21 3 **94** **6**
2017–18 Rangers 11 0
2018–19 Rangers 0 0
2018–19 *Shrewsbury T* 41 7 **41** **7**
2019–20 Rangers 0 0 **11** **0**
2019–20 *Hibernian* 6 0 **6** **0**
2020–21 Hull C 44 5 **44** **5**

EAVES, Tom (M) 282 67
H: 6 3 W: 13 07 b.Liverpool 14-1-92
2009–10 Oldham Ath 15 0
2010–11 Bolton W 0 0
2010–11 *Oldham Ath* 0 0 **15** **0**
2011–12 Bolton W 0 0
2012–13 Bolton W 3 0
2012–13 *Bristol R* 16 7 **16** **7**
2012–13 *Shrewsbury T* 10 6
2013–14 Bolton W 0 0
2013–14 *Rotherham U* 8 0 **8** **0**
2013–14 *Shrewsbury T* 25 2 **35** **8**
2014–15 Bolton W 1 0
2014–15 *Yeovil T* 5 0
2014–15 *Bury* 9 1 **9** **1**
2015–16 Bolton W 0 0 **4** **0**
2016–17 Yeovil T 40 4 **45** **4**
2017–18 Gillingham 41 17
2018–19 Gillingham 43 21 **84** **38**
2019–20 Hull C 40 5
2020–21 Hull C 26 4 **66** **9**

ELDER, Callum (D) 155 2
H: 5 11 W: 10 08 b.Sydney 27-1-95
Internationals: Australia U20.
2013–14 Leicester C 0 0
2014–15 Leicester C 0 0
2014–15 *Mansfield T* 21 0 **21** **0**
2015–16 Leicester C 0 0
2015–16 *Peterborough U* 18 1 **18** **1**
2016–17 Leicester C 0 0
2016–17 *Brentford* 6 0 **6** **0**
2016–17 *Barnsley* 5 0 **5** **0**
2017–18 Leicester C 0 0
2017–18 *Wigan Ath* 27 0 **27** **0**
2018–19 Leicester C 0 0
2018–19 *Ipswich T* 4 0
2019–20 Ipswich T 0 0 **4** **0**
2019–20 Hull C 30 0
2020–21 Hull C 44 1 **74** **1**

EMMANUEL, Josh (D) 125 0
H: 5 11 W: 11 00 b.London 18-8-97
From West Ham U.
2015–16 Ipswich T 4 0
2015–16 *Crawley T* 2 0 **2** **0**
2016–17 Ipswich T 15 0
2017–18 Ipswich T 0 0
2017–18 *Rotherham U* 31 0 **31** **0**
2018–19 Ipswich T 4 0
2018–19 *Shrewsbury T* 14 0 **14** **0**
2019–20 Ipswich T 0 0 **23** **0**
2019–20 Bolton W 27 0 **27** **0**
2020–21 Hull C 28 0 **28** **0**

FLEMING, Brandon (D) 21 0
b.Dewsbury 3-12-99
2017–18 Hull C 0 0
2018–19 Hull C 4 0
2019–20 Hull C 4 0
2019–20 *Bolton W* 10 0 **10** **0**
2020–21 Hull C 3 0 **11** **0**

FLORES, Jordan (F) 70 9
H: 5 9 W: 10 08 b.Wigan 4-10-95
2014–15 Wigan Ath 1 0
2015–16 Wigan Ath 3 1
2016–17 Wigan Ath 2 0
2016–17 *Blackpool* 19 3 **19** **3**
2017–18 Wigan Ath 0 0
2017–18 *Chesterfield* 13 1 **13** **1**
2018–19 Wigan Ath 0 0 **6** **1**
2018–19 *Ostersund* 0 0
2019 Dundalk 16 1
2020 Dundalk 13 3 **29** **4**
2020–21 Hull C 3 0 **3** **0**

GREAVES, Jacob (D) 68 0
b.Cottingham 12-9-00
2019–20 Hull C 0 0
2019–20 *Cheltenham T* 29 0 **29** **0**
2020–21 Hull C 39 0 **39** **0**

HANSON, Ryan (M) 0 0
b. 6-12-00
2020–21 Hull C 0 0

HICKEY, Jordan (M) 0 0
b.Sunderland 4-10-99
From Sunderland.
2020–21 Hull C 0 0

HINDS, Anthony (M) 0 0
b.Essex 29-3-03
From West Ham U.
2020–21 Hull C 0 0

HONEYMAN, George (M) 167 17
H: 5 8 W: 11 05 b.Prudhoe 8-9-94
2014–15 Sunderland 0 0
2015–16 Sunderland 1 0
2016–17 Sunderland 5 0
2017–18 Sunderland 42 6
2018–19 Sunderland 35 6
2019–20 Sunderland 0 0 **83** **12**
2019–20 Hull C 42 1
2020–21 Hull C 42 4 **84** **5**

INGRAM, Matt (G) 194 0
H: 6 3 W: 12 13 b.Croydon 18-12-93
2011–12 Wycombe W 0 0
2012–13 Wycombe W 8 0
2013–14 Wycombe W 46 0
2014–15 Wycombe W 46 0
2015–16 Wycombe W 24 0
2015–16 QPR 4 0
2016–17 QPR 0 0
2017–18 Northampton T 20 0 **20** **0**
2017–18 QPR 2 0
2018–19 Wycombe W 1 0 **125** **0**
2018–19 QPR 4 0 **10** **0**
2019–20 Hull C 1 0
2020–21 Hull C 38 0 **39** **0**

JACOB, Matty (D) 0 0
b.Barnsley 3-6-01
2020–21 Hull C 0 0

JARVIS, Will (F) 0 0
b.York 17-12-02
2020–21 Hull C 0 0

JONES, Alfie (D) 75 3
b. 7-10-97
2018–19 Southampton 0 0
2018–19 *St Mirren* 14 1 **14** **1**
2019–20 Southampton 0 0
2019–20 *Gillingham* 30 2 **30** **2**
2020–21 Hull C 31 0 **31** **0**

JONES, Callum (M) 1 0
b. 5-4-01
From The New Saints, Owestry T, Bury.
2019–20 Hull C 0 0
2020–21 Hull C 1 0 **1** **0**

LEAKE, Jake (D) 0 0
b.Hull 20-2-03
2020–21 Hull C 0 0

LEWIS-POTTER, Keane (F) 64 15
b. 22-2-01
2018–19 Hull C 0 0
2019–20 Hull C 21 2
2020–21 Hull C 43 13 **64** **15**

LONG, George (G) 225 0
H: 6 0 W: 12 05 b.Sheffield 5-11-93
Internationals: England U18, U20.
2010–11 Sheffield U 1 0
2011–12 Sheffield U 2 0
2012–13 Sheffield U 36 0
2013–14 Sheffield U 27 0
2014–15 Sheffield U 0 0
2014–15 *Oxford U* 10 0 **10** **0**
2014–15 *Motherwell* 13 0 **13** **0**
2015–16 Sheffield U 31 0
2016–17 Sheffield U 3 0
2017–18 Sheffield U 0 0 **100** **0**
2017–18 *AFC Wimbledon* 45 0 **45** **0**
2018–19 Hull C 4 0
2019–20 Hull C 45 0
2020–21 Hull C 8 0 **57** **0**

LOVICK, Harry (M) 0 0
b.Cottingham 20-12-02
2020–21 Hull C 0 0

MAGENNIS, Josh (F) 393 74
H: 6 2 W: 14 07 b.Bangor 15-8-90
Internationals: Northern Ireland U17, U19, U21, Full caps.
2009–10 Cardiff C 9 0 **9** **0**
2009–10 *Grimsby T* 2 0 **2** **0**
2010–11 Aberdeen 29 3
2011–12 Aberdeen 23 1
2012–13 Aberdeen 35 5
2013–14 Aberdeen 18 1 **105** **10**
2013–14 *St Mirren* 13 0 **13** **0**
2014–15 Kilmarnock 38 8
2015–16 Kilmarnock 34 10 **72** **18**
2016–17 Charlton Ath 39 10
2017–18 Charlton Ath 42 10 **81** **20**
2018–19 Bolton W 42 4
2019–20 Bolton W 0 0 **42** **4**
2019–20 Hull C 29 4
2020–21 Hull C 40 18 **69** **22**

MAYER, Thomas (M) 129 17
b.Linz 23-8-95
2012–13 Rapid Vienna 0 0

2013–14	Pasching	11	0		
2014–15	Liefering	0	0		
2014–15	*Pasching*	0	0		
2015–16	Liefering	0	0		
2015–16	*Pasching*	0	0	**11**	**0**
2015–16	*LASK Linz*	4	0		
2016–17	Liefering	6	1		
2016–17	*LASK Linz*	26	2	**30**	**2**
2017–18	Liefering	0	0		
2017–18	*Ried*	25	5		
2018–19	Liefering	0	0	**6**	**1**
2018–19	*Ried*	22	3	**47**	**8**
2019–20	Austria Lustenau	29	6	**29**	**6**
2020–21	Hull C	6	0	**6**	**0**

McLOUGHLIN, Sean (D) 79 6
b.Cork 13-11-96
Internationals: Republic of Ireland U21.

2017	Cork C	1	0		
2018	Cork C	27	3		
2019	Cork C	20	2	**48**	**5**
2019–20	Hull C	7	0		
2019–20	*St Mirren*	21	1	**21**	**1**
2020–21	Hull C	3	0	**10**	**0**

ROBSON, David (G) 0 0
b.North Allerton 22-1-02

2020–21	Hull C	0	0		

SALAM, Ahmed (M) 0 0
b.Hull 30-12-00

2020–21	Hull C	0	0		

SAMUELSEN, Martin (F) 104 8
H: 6 2 W: 11 05 b.Haugesund 17-4-97
Internationals: Norway U16, U17, U18, U21, Full caps.
From Manchester C.

2015–16	West Ham U	0	0		
2015–16	*Peterborough U*	17	1		
2016–17	West Ham U	0	0		
2016–17	*Blackburn R*	3	0	**3**	**0**
2016–17	*Peterborough U*	11	1		
2017–18	Peterborough U	0	0	**28**	**2**
2017–18	West Ham U	0	0		
2017–18	*Burton Alb*	9	0	**9**	**0**
2018–19	West Ham U	0	0		
2018–19	*VVV Venlo*	10	0	**10**	**0**
2019	*Haugesund*	28	6	**28**	**6**
2019–20	Hull C	7	0		
2020–21	Hull C	5	0	**12**	**0**
2020–21	*Aalborg*	14	0	**14**	**0**

SCOTT, James (F) 61 6
b. 30-8-00
Internationals: Scotland U21.

2016–17	Motherwell	0	0		
2017–18	Motherwell	2	0		
2018–19	Motherwell	12	1		
2019–20	Motherwell	22	3	**36**	**4**
2019–20	Hull C	7	1		
2020–21	Hull C	18	1	**25**	**2**

SHEAF, Max (M) 20 2
b.Gravesend 10-3-00

2018–19	Hull C	1	0		
2019–20	Hull C	0	0		
2019–20	*Cheltenham T*	19	2	**19**	**2**
2020–21	Hull C	0	0	**1**	**0**

SMALLWOOD, Richard (M) 309 9
H: 5 11 W: 11 05 b.Redcar 29-12-90
Internationals: England U18.

2008–09	Middlesbrough	0	0		
2009–10	Middlesbrough	0	0		
2010–11	Middlesbrough	13	1		
2011–12	Middlesbrough	13	0		
2012–13	Middlesbrough	22	2		
2013–14	Middlesbrough	13	0		
2013–14	*Rotherham U*	18	0		
2014–15	Middlesbrough	0	0	**61**	**3**
2014–15	*Rotherham U*	41	1		
2015–16	Rotherham U	43	1		
2016–17	Scunthorpe U	16	1	**16**	**1**
2016–17	Rotherham U	25	1	**127**	**3**
2017–18	Blackburn R	46	2		
2018–19	Blackburn R	32	0		
2019–20	Blackburn R	0	0	**78**	**2**
2020–21	Hull C	27	0	**27**	**0**

SMITH, Andy (D) 0 0
b. 11-9-01

2019–20	Hull C	0	0		
2020–21	Hull C	0	0		

SNELGROVE, McCauley (M) 0 0
b. 9-9-02

2020–21	Hull C	0	0		

WILKS, Mallik (F) 148 42
b.Leeds 15-12-98

2016–17	Leeds U	0	0		
2017–18	Leeds U	0	0		
2017–18	*Accrington S*	19	3	**19**	**3**
2017–18	*Grimsby T*	6	0	**6**	**0**
2018–19	Leeds U	0	0		
2018–19	*Doncaster R*	46	14	**46**	**14**
2019–20	Barnsley	15	1	**15**	**1**
2019–20	*Hull C*	18	5		
2020–21	Hull C	44	19	**62**	**24**

WOOD, Harry (F) 1 0
b.Leeds 2-8-02

2020–21	Hull C	1	0	**1**	**0**

Scholars
Carew, Harvey James; Curtis, Henry James Martland; Deacon, Samuel Joseph; Dyer, Rio Laurence; Leach, Billy Ben; MacAuley, Thomas John Edward; Mills, Jevon John; Power, McCauley Thomas; Rees, Luke James; Taylor, Alfie James; Wallis, Harry Owen; Ward, Joshua Andrew.

IPSWICH T (42)

ANDOH, Levi (D) 0 0
b.Amsterdam 12-3-00
From Worcester C, Solihull U.

2020–21	Ipswich T	0	0		

ARMIN, Albie (D) 0 0

2020–21	Ipswich T	0	0		

BAGGOTT, Elkan (D) 0 0
b.Bangkok 23-10-02

2020–21	Ipswich T	0	0		

BENNETTS, Keanan (M) 31 1
b.London 9-3-99

2017–18	Tottenham H	0	0		
2018–19	Borussia M'gladbach	0	0		
2019–20	Borussia M'gladbach	1	0		
2020–21	Borussia M'gladbach	2	0	**3**	**0**

On loan from Borussia M'gladbach.

2020–21	Ipswich T	28	1	**28**	**1**

BISHOP, Teddy (M) 123 5
H: 5 11 W: 10 03 b.Cambridge 15-7-96

2013–14	Ipswich T	0	0		
2014–15	Ipswich T	33	1		
2015–16	Ipswich T	4	0		
2016–17	Ipswich T	19	0		
2017–18	Ipswich T	4	0		
2018–19	Ipswich T	18	0		
2019–20	Ipswich T	9	0		
2020–21	Ipswich T	36	4	**123**	**5**

BROWN, Zak (F) 0 0
b.Felixstowe 1-1-01

2020–21	Ipswich T	0	0		

CHAMBERS, Luke (D) 705 36
H: 6 1 W: 11 13 b.Kettering 29-8-85

2002–03	Northampton T	1	0		
2003–04	Northampton T	24	0		
2004–05	Northampton T	27	0		
2005–06	Northampton T	43	0		
2006–07	Northampton T	29	1	**124**	**1**
2006–07	Nottingham F	14	0		
2007–08	Nottingham F	42	6		
2008–09	Nottingham F	39	2		
2009–10	Nottingham F	23	3		
2010–11	Nottingham F	44	6		
2011–12	Nottingham F	43	0	**205**	**17**
2012–13	Ipswich T	44	3		
2013–14	Ipswich T	46	3		
2014–15	Ipswich T	45	1		
2015–16	Ipswich T	45	3		
2016–17	Ipswich T	46	4		
2017–18	Ipswich T	37	1		
2018–19	Ipswich T	43	0		
2019–20	Ipswich T	31	1		
2020–21	Ipswich T	39	2	**376**	**18**

CHIREWA, Tawanda (M) 0 0

2019–20	Ipswich T	0	0		
2020–21	Ipswich T	0	0		

CORNELL, David (G) 146 0
H: 5 11 W: 11 07 b.Gorseinon 28-3-91
Internationals: Wales U17, U19, U21.

2009–10	Swansea C	0	0		
2010–11	Swansea C	0	0		
2011–12	Swansea C	0	0		
2011–12	*Hereford U*	25	0	**25**	**0**
2012–13	Swansea C	0	0		
2013–14	Swansea C	0	0		
2013–14	*St Mirren*	5	0	**5**	**0**
2014–15	Swansea C	0	0		
2014–15	*Portsmouth*	0	0		
2015–16	Oldham Ath	14	0	**14**	**0**
2016–17	Northampton T	6	0		
2017–18	Northampton T	6	0		
2018–19	Northampton T	46	0		
2019–20	Northampton T	34	0	**92**	**0**
2020–21	Ipswich T	10	0	**10**	**0**

CRANE, Ross (M) 0 0
From AFC Sudbury, Bury T.

2020–21	Ipswich T	0	0		

CROWE, Dylan (M) 0 0
b. 13-4-01

2020–21	Ipswich T	0	0		

DOBRA, Armando (M) 20 0
b. 14-4-01
Internationals: Albania U19.

2019–20	Ipswich T	3	0		
2020–21	Ipswich T	17	0	**20**	**0**

DONACIEN, Janoi (D) 203 1
H: 6 0 W: 11 11 b.St Lucia 3-11-93
Internationals: St Lucia Full caps.

2011–12	Aston Villa	0	0		
2012–13	Aston Villa	0	0		
2013–14	Aston Villa	0	0		
2014–15	Aston Villa	0	0		
2014–15	*Tranmere R*	31	0	**31**	**0**
2015–16	Aston Villa	0	0		
2015–16	*Wycombe W*	2	0	**2**	**0**
2015–16	*Newport Co*	29	0	**29**	**0**
2016–17	Accrington S	35	1		
2017–18	Accrington S	45	0		
2018–19	Ipswich T	10	0		
2018–19	*Accrington S*	19	0	**99**	**1**
2019–20	Ipswich T	13	0		
2020–21	Ipswich T	0	0	**23**	**0**
2020–21	*Fleetwood T*	19	0	**19**	**0**

DOWNES, Flynn (M) 102 3
H: 5 8 W: 11 00 b. 20-1-99
Internationals: England U19, U20.

2016–17	Ipswich T	0	0		
2017–18	Ipswich T	10	0		
2017–18	*Luton T*	10	0	**10**	**0**
2018–19	Ipswich T	29	1		
2019–20	Ipswich T	29	2		
2020–21	Ipswich T	24	0	**92**	**3**

DOZZELL, Andre (M) 81 2
b.Ipswich 2-5-99
Internationals: England U16, U17, U18, U19, U20.

2015–16	Ipswich T	2	1		
2016–17	Ipswich T	6	0		
2017–18	Ipswich T	1	0		
2018–19	Ipswich T	19	1		
2019–20	Ipswich T	10	0		
2020–21	Ipswich T	43	0	**81**	**2**

DRINAN, Aaron (F) 27 2
b.Cork 6-5-98
From Cork C.

2017	Waterford	5	1	**5**	**1**
2017–18	Ipswich T	0	0		
2018–19	Ipswich T	0	0		
2019–20	Ipswich T	0	0		
2020–21	Ipswich T	22	1	**22**	**1**

EDWARDS, Gwion (M) 259 39
H: 5 9 W: 12 00 b.Carmarthen 1-3-93
Internationals: Wales U19, U21.

2011–12	Swansea C	0	0		
2012–13	Swansea C	0	0		
2012–13	*St Johnstone*	6	0		
2013–14	Swansea C	0	0		
2013–14	*St Johnstone*	13	0	**19**	**0**
2013–14	*Crawley T*	6	2		
2014–15	Crawley T	37	4		
2015–16	Crawley T	42	8	**85**	**14**
2016–17	Peterborough U	33	7		
2017–18	Peterborough U	26	4	**59**	**11**
2018–19	Ipswich T	33	6		
2019–20	Ipswich T	27	2		
2020–21	Ipswich T	36	6	**96**	**14**

EL MIZOUNI, Idris (M) 31 1
b. 26-9-00
Internationals: Tunisia U23, Tunisia Full caps.

2018–19	Ipswich T	4	0		
2019–20	Ipswich T	3	0		
2019–20	*Cambridge U*	7	1		
2020–21	Ipswich T	0	0	**7**	**0**
2020–21	*Cambridge U*	11	0	**18**	**1**
2020–21	*Grimsby T*	6	0	**6**	**0**

FOLAMI, Ben (F) 23 3
b.Sydney 8-6-99

2017–18	Ipswich T	4	0		
2018–19	Ipswich T	0	0		
2019–20	Ipswich T	0	0		
2019–20	*Stevenage*	2	0	**2**	**0**
2020–21	Ipswich T	0	0	**4**	**0**
2020–21	*Melbourne Victory*	17	3	**17**	**3**

GIBBS, Liam (M) 1 0
b. 16-12-02

2019–20	Ipswich T	0	0		
2020–21	Ipswich T	1	0	**1**	**0**

HAWKINS, Oliver (F) 115 16
b. 8-4-92
From North Greenford U, Hillingdon Bor, Northwood, Hemel Hempstead T.
2015–16 Dagenham & R 18 1 **18 1**
From Dagenham & R.
2017–18 Portsmouth 31 7
2018–19 Portsmouth 39 7
2019–20 Portsmouth 7 0 **77 14**
2020–21 Ipswich T 20 1 **20 1**

HEALY, Matthew (M) 0 0
b. 12-4-02
From Corinthians.
2020–21 Ipswich T 0 0

HOLY, Tomas (G) 224 0
H: 6 9 W: 16 05 b.Rychnov nad Kneznou 10-12-91
Internationals: Czech Republic U16, U17, U18.
2010–11 Sparta Prague 0 0
2011–12 Sparta Prague 0 0
2012–13 Sparta Prague 0 0
2013–14 Sparta Prague 0 0
2013–14 *Vlasim* 9 0 **9 0**
2013–14 *Viktoria Zizkov* 14 0
2014–15 Sparta Prague 0 0
2014–15 *Viktoria Zizkov* 27 0 **41 0**
2015–16 Sparta Prague 0 0
2015–16 *Fastav Zlin* 20 0 **20 0**
2016–17 Sparta Prague 0 0
2016–17 *Fastav Zlin* 0 0
2016–17 Gillingham 6 0
2017–18 Gillingham 45 0
2018–19 Gillingham 46 0 **97 0**
2019–20 Ipswich T 21 0
2020–21 Ipswich T 36 0 **57 0**

HUWS, Emyr (M) 120 11
H: 5 10 W: 11 07 b.Llanelli 30-9-93
Internationals: Wales U17, U19, U21, Full caps.
2010–11 Manchester C 0 0
2011–12 Manchester C 0 0
2012–13 Manchester C 0 0
2012–13 *Northampton T* 10 0 **10 0**
2013–14 Manchester C 0 0
2013–14 *Birmingham C* 17 2 **17 2**
2014–15 Wigan Ath 16 0
2015–16 Wigan Ath 0 0 **16 0**
2015–16 *Huddersfield T* 30 5 **30 5**
2016–17 Cardiff C 3 0
2016–17 *Ipswich T* 13 3
2017–18 Cardiff C 0 0 **3 0**
2017–18 Ipswich T 5 0
2018–19 Ipswich T 0 0
2019–20 Ipswich T 17 0
2020–21 Ipswich T 9 1 **44 4**

JACKSON, Kayden (F) 158 32
H: 5 11 W: 11 07 b.Bradford 22-2-94
Internationals: England C.
2013–14 Swindon T 0 0
2014–15 Swindon T 0 0
From Oxford C, Tamworth, Wrexham.
2016–17 Barnsley 0 0
2016–17 *Grimsby T* 20 1 **20 1**
2017–18 Accrington S 44 16
2018–19 Accrington S 1 0 **45 16**
2018–19 Ipswich T 36 3
2019–20 Ipswich T 32 11
2020–21 Ipswich T 25 1 **93 15**

JUDGE, Alan (F) 379 55
H: 5 6 W: 11 03 b.Dublin 11-11-88
Internationals: Republic of Ireland U17, U8, U19, U21, U23, Full caps.
2006–07 Blackburn R 0 0
2007–08 Blackburn R 0 0
2008–09 Blackburn R 0 0
2008–09 *Plymouth Arg* 17 2
2009–10 Blackburn R 0 0
2009–10 *Plymouth Arg* 37 5 **54 7**
2010–11 Blackburn R 0 0
2010–11 Notts Co 19 1
2011–12 Notts Co 43 7
2012–13 Notts Co 39 8 **101 16**
2013–14 Blackburn R 11 0 **11 0**
2013–14 Brentford 22 7
2014–15 Brentford 37 3
2015–16 Brentford 38 14
2016–17 Brentford 0 0
2017–18 Brentford 13 0
2018–19 Brentford 20 1 **130 25**
2018–19 Ipswich T 19 0
2019–20 Ipswich T 30 3
2020–21 Ipswich T 34 4 **83 7**

KENLOCK, Myles (D) 85 0
H: 6 1 W: 10 08 b.Croydon 29-11-96
2015–16 Ipswich T 2 0
2016–17 Ipswich T 18 0
2017–18 Ipswich T 16 0
2018–19 Ipswich T 19 0
2019–20 Ipswich T 9 0
2020–21 Ipswich T 21 0 **85 0**

LANKESTER, Jack (F) 28 3
b.Ipswich 19-1-00
2018–19 Ipswich T 11 1
2019–20 Ipswich T 0 0
2020–21 Ipswich T 17 2 **28 3**

MANLY, Jack (M) 0 0
b. 19-10-04
2020–21 Ipswich T 0 0

McGAVIN, Brett (M) 7 0
b.Bury St Edmunds 21-12-99
2019–20 Ipswich T 1 0
2020–21 Ipswich T 5 0 **6 0**
2020–21 *Ayr U* 1 0 **1 0**

NDABA, Corrie (D) 13 0
Internationals: Republic of Ireland U18.
2018–19 Ipswich T 0 0
2019–20 Ipswich T 0 0
2020–21 Ipswich T 0 0
2020–21 *Ayr U* 13 0 **13 0**

NOLAN, Jon (M) 134 18
H: 5 11 W: 11 05 b.Huyton 22-4-92
Internationals: England C.
From Everton, Stockport Co, Lindoln C, Grimsby T.
2016–17 Chesterfield 30 1 **30 1**
2017–18 Shrewsbury T 43 9 **43 9**
2018–19 Ipswich T 26 3
2019–20 Ipswich T 22 2
2020–21 Ipswich T 13 3 **61 8**

NORWOOD, James (F) 103 49
H: 6 0 W: 12 13 b.Eastbourne 5-9-90
Internationals: England U18, C.
From Eastbourne T.
2009–10 Exeter C 3 0
2010–11 Exeter C 1 0 **4 0**
From Forest Green R.
2018–19 Tranmere R 45 29 **45 29**
2019–20 Ipswich T 28 11
2020–21 Ipswich T 26 9 **54 20**

NSIALA, Aristote (D) 196 6
H: 6 4 W: 14 09 b.DR Congo 25-3-92
Internationals: DR Congo Full caps.
2009–10 Everton 0 0
2010–11 Everton 0 0
2010–11 *Macclesfield T* 10 0 **10 0**
2011–12 Everton 0 0
2011–12 *Accrington S* 19 0
2012–13 Accrington S 17 0
2013–14 Accrington S 0 0 **36 0**
From Southport, Grimsby T.
2016–17 Hartlepool U 21 1 **21 1**
2016–17 Shrewsbury T 21 1
2017–18 Shrewsbury T 44 3 **65 4**
2018–19 Ipswich T 22 1
2019–20 Ipswich T 3 0
2019–20 *Bolton W* 12 0 **12 0**
2020–21 Ipswich T 27 0 **52 1**

NYDAM, Tristan (M) 25 0
H: 5 7 W: 9 06 b. 6-11-99
Internationals: England U18, U19.
2016–17 Ipswich T 0 0
2017–18 Ipswich T 18 0
2018–19 Ipswich T 1 0
2018–19 *St Johnstone* 5 0 **5 0**
2019–20 Ipswich T 0 0
2020–21 Ipswich T 1 0 **20 0**

SEARS, Freddie (F) 388 65
H: 5 8 W: 10 01 b.Hornchurch 27-11-89
Internationals: England U19, U20, U21.
2007–08 West Ham U 7 1
2008–09 West Ham U 17 0
2009–10 West Ham U 1 0
2009–10 *Crystal Palace* 18 0 **18 0**
2009–10 *Coventry C* 10 0 **10 0**
2010–11 West Ham U 11 1
2010–11 *Scunthorpe U* 9 0 **9 0**
2011–12 West Ham U 10 0 **46 2**
2011–12 *Colchester U* 11 2
2012–13 Colchester U 35 7
2013–14 Colchester U 32 12
2014–15 Colchester U 24 10 **102 31**
2014–15 Ipswich T 21 9
2015–16 Ipswich T 45 6
2016–17 Ipswich T 40 7
2017–18 Ipswich T 36 2
2018–19 Ipswich T 24 6
2019–20 Ipswich T 11 1
2020–21 Ipswich T 26 1 **203 32**

SIMPSON, Tyreece (F) 4 0
b. 7-2-02
2019–20 Ipswich T 3 0
2020–21 Ipswich T 1 0 **4 0**

SIZIBA, Zanda (M) 0 0
b. 19-7-03
From Dagenham & R, Tottenham H.
2020–21 Ipswich T 0 0

SKUSE, Cole (M) 547 11
H: 6 1 W: 11 05 b.Bristol 29-3-86
2004–05 Bristol C 7 0
2005–06 Bristol C 38 2
2006–07 Bristol C 42 0
2007–08 Bristol C 25 0
2008–09 Bristol C 33 2
2009–10 Bristol C 43 2
2010–11 Bristol C 30 1
2011–12 Bristol C 36 2
2012–13 Bristol C 25 0 **279 9**
2013–14 Ipswich T 43 0
2014–15 Ipswich T 40 1
2015–16 Ipswich T 39 0
2016–17 Ipswich T 40 0
2017–18 Ipswich T 39 1
2018–19 Ipswich T 34 0
2019–20 Ipswich T 29 0
2020–21 Ipswich T 4 0 **268 2**

SMITH, Tommy (D) 0 0
b. 18-11-01
2019–20 Ipswich T 0 0
2020–21 Ipswich T 0 0

VINCENT-YOUNG, Kane (D) 128 6
H: 5 11 W: 11 00 b.Camden Town 15-3-96
From Tottenham H, Banbury U.
2014–15 Colchester U 0 0
2015–16 Colchester U 14 0
2016–17 Colchester U 18 0
2017–18 Colchester U 38 1
2018–19 Colchester U 40 3
2019–20 Colchester U 2 0 **112 4**
2019–20 Ipswich T 9 2
2020–21 Ipswich T 7 0 **16 2**

VIRAL, Allan (M) 0 0
b.Paris 3-12-01
2020–21 Ipswich T 0 0

WARD, Stephen (D) 486 27
H: 5 11 W: 12 02 b.Dublin 20-8-85
Internationals: Republic of Ireland U20, U21, B, Full caps.
2003 Bohemians 6 0
2004 Bohemians 16 2
2005 Bohemians 29 7
2006 Bohemians 23 2 **74 11**
2006–07 Wolverhampton W 18 3
2007–08 Wolverhampton W 29 0
2008–09 Wolverhampton W 42 0
2009–10 Wolverhampton W 22 0
2010–11 Wolverhampton W 34 1
2011–12 Wolverhampton W 38 3
2012–13 Wolverhampton W 39 2
2013–14 Wolverhampton W 0 0 **222 9**
2013–14 *Brighton & HA* 44 4 **44 4**
2014–15 Burnley 9 0
2015–16 Burnley 24 1
2016–17 Burnley 37 1
2017–18 Burnley 28 1
2018–19 Burnley 3 0 **101 3**
2019–20 Stoke C 15 0 **15 0**
2020–21 Ipswich T 30 0 **30 0**

WHITE, Albert (G) 0 0
b. 29-10-01
From AFC Wimbledon.
2020–21 Ipswich T 0 0

WOOLFENDEN, Luke (D) 91 4
b.Ipswich 21-10-98
2017–18 Ipswich T 2 0
2018–19 Ipswich T 1 0
2018–19 *Swindon T* 32 2 **32 2**
2019–20 Ipswich T 31 1
2020–21 Ipswich T 25 1 **59 2**

Scholars
Agbaje, Edwin Olamide; Alexander, Fraser; Armin, Albie; Bareck, Michael Oluwasegun; Bello, Samson Olaoluwa; Bort, Antoni Krzysztof; Bradshaw, Zak Dominic; Curtis, Harley William; Cutbush, Alfie; Healy, Matthew James; Hoque, Mohammed Yousuf; Humphreys, Cameron; Kabongolo, Brooklyn Lukongola; Knock, Harry John; Nwabueze, Jesse Chizoba; O'Reilly, Connor Anthony; Oppong, Colin; Osbourne, Tyrese Lamar; Ridd, Lewis Paul Joseph; Siziba, Zandazenkosi Dumisle; Stephenson, Sean; Stewart, Cameron Jack; Viral, Allan Miloud Bernard; Wyss, Benjamin Robert.

LEEDS U (43)

ALIOSKI, Ezgjan (M) **298 44**
b.Prilep 12-2-92
Internationals: Macedonia U19, U21, Full caps.

2012–13	Young Boys	0	0		
2012–13	Schaffhausen	10	0		
2013–14	Schaffhausen	26	2		
2014–15	Schaffhausen	35	2		
2015–16	Schaffhausen	16	0	**87**	**4**
2015–16	Lugano	16	3		
2016–17	Lugano	34	16	**50**	**19**
2017–18	Leeds U	42	7		
2018–19	Leeds U	44	7		
2019–20	Leeds U	39	5		
2020–21	Leeds U	36	2	**161**	**21**

ALLEN, Charlie (F) **4 0**
b.Belfast 22-11-03
Internationals: Northern Ireland U17.

2018–19	Linfield	1	0		
2019–20	Linfield	3	0	**4**	**0**
2020–21	Leeds U	0	0		

AYLING, Luke (D) **428 12**
H: 5 11 W: 10 08 b.Lambeth 25-8-91

2009–10	Arsenal	0	0		
2009–10	*Yeovil T*	4	0		
2010–11	Yeovil T	37	0		
2011–12	Yeovil T	44	0		
2012–13	Yeovil T	39	0		
2013–14	Yeovil T	42	2	**166**	**2**
2014–15	Bristol C	46	4		
2015–16	Bristol C	33	0		
2016–17	Bristol C	1	0	**80**	**4**
2016–17	Leeds U	42	0		
2017–18	Leeds U	27	0		
2018–19	Leeds U	38	2		
2019–20	Leeds U	37	4		
2020–21	Leeds U	38	0	**182**	**6**

BAMFORD, Patrick (F) **269 97**
H: 6 1 W: 11 02 b.Newark 5-9-93
Internationals: Republic of Ireland U18. England U18, U19, U21.

2010–11	Nottingham F	0	0		
2011–12	Nottingham F	2	0	**2**	**0**
2011–12	Chelsea	0	0		
2012–13	Chelsea	0	0		
2012–13	*Milton Keynes D*	14	4		
2013–14	Chelsea	0	0		
2013–14	*Milton Keynes D*	23	14	**37**	**18**
2013–14	*Derby Co*	21	8	**21**	**8**
2014–15	Chelsea	0	0		
2014–15	*Middlesbrough*	38	17		
2015–16	Chelsea	0	0		
2015–16	*Crystal Palace*	6	0	**6**	**0**
2015–16	*Norwich C*	7	0	**7**	**0**
2016–17	Chelsea	0	0		
2016–17	*Burnley*	6	0	**6**	**0**
2016–17	*Middlesbrough*	8	1		
2017–18	Middlesbrough	39	11	**85**	**29**
2018–19	Leeds U	22	9		
2019–20	Leeds U	45	16		
2020–21	Leeds U	38	17	**105**	**42**

BERARDI, Gaetano (D) **284 0**
H: 5 10 W: 11 00 b.Sorengo 21-8-88
Internationals: Switzerland U20, U21, Full caps.

2006–07	Brescia	1	0		
2007–08	Brescia	9	0		
2008–09	Brescia	26	0		
2009–10	Brescia	29	0		
2010–11	Brescia	27	0		
2011–12	Brescia	13	0	**105**	**0**
2011–12	Sampdoria	9	0		
2012–13	Sampdoria	21	0		
2013–14	Sampdoria	5	0	**35**	**0**
2014–15	Leeds U	22	0		
2015–16	Leeds U	28	0		
2016–17	Leeds U	26	0		
2017–18	Leeds U	31	0		
2018–19	Leeds U	13	0		
2019–20	Leeds U	22	0		
2020–21	Leeds U	2	0	**144**	**0**

BOGUSZ, Mateusz (M) **24 1**
H: 5 9 b.Ruda Slalka 22-8-01
Internationals: Poland U16, U17, U19, U20, U21.

2018–19	Leeds U	0	0		
2019–20	Leeds U	1	0		
2020–21	Leeds U	0	0	**1**	**0**
2020–21	*Logrones*	23	1	**23**	**1**

CAPRILE, Elia (G) **0 0**
b.Verona 25-8-01
Internationals: Italy U18.
From Verona.

2019–20	Leeds U	0	0		
2020–21	Leeds U	0	0		

CASEY, Oliver (D) **1 0**
b. 14-10-00

2019–20	Leeds U	1	0		
2020–21	Leeds U	0	0	**1**	**0**

CASILLA, Francisco (G) **297 0**
H: 6 4 W: 13 01 b.Alcocer 2-10-86
Internationals: Spain U19, U21, Full caps.

2004–05	Real Madrid	0	0		
2005–06	Real Madrid	0	0		
2006–07	Real Madrid	0	0		
2007–08	Espanyol	4	0		
2008–09	Espanyol	0	0		
2008–09	*Cadiz*	35	0		
2009–10	Espanyol	0	0		
2009–10	*Cadiz*	31	0	**66**	**0**
2010–11	Espanyol	0	0		
2010–11	*Cartagena*	35	0	**35**	**0**
2011–12	Espanyol	16	0		
2012–13	Espanyol	21	0		
2013–14	Espanyol	37	0		
2014–15	Espanyol	37	0	**115**	**0**
2015–16	Real Madrid	4	0		
2016–17	Real Madrid	11	0		
2017–18	Real Madrid	10	0	**25**	**0**
2018–19	Leeds U	17	0		
2019–20	Leeds U	36	0		
2020–21	Leeds U	3	0	**56**	**0**

COOPER, Liam (D) **300 15**
H: 6 2 W: 13 07 b.Hull 30-8-91
Internationals: Scotland U17, U19, Full caps.

2008–09	Hull C	0	0		
2009–10	Hull C	2	0		
2010–11	Hull C	2	0		
2010–11	*Carlisle U*	6	1	**6**	**1**
2011–12	Hull C	7	0		
2011–12	*Huddersfield T*	4	0	**4**	**0**
2012–13	Hull C	0	0	**11**	**0**
2012–13	Chesterfield	29	2		
2013–14	Chesterfield	41	3		
2014–15	Chesterfield	1	0	**71**	**5**
2014–15	Leeds U	29	1		
2015–16	Leeds U	39	1		
2016–17	Leeds U	11	0		
2017–18	Leeds U	30	1		
2018–19	Leeds U	36	3		
2019–20	Leeds U	38	2		
2020–21	Leeds U	25	1	**208**	**9**

CRESSWELL, Charlie (D) **0 0**
b.Preston 7-12-00

2020–21	Leeds U	0	0		

DALLAS, Stuart (M) **310 59**
H: 6 0 W: 12 09 b.Cookstown 19-4-91
Internationals: Northern Ireland U21, U23, Full caps.

2010–11	Crusaders	13	16		
2011–12	Crusaders	8	8	**21**	**24**
2012–13	Brentford	7	0		
2013–14	Brentford	18	2		
2013–14	*Northampton T*	12	3	**12**	**3**
2014–15	Brentford	38	6	**63**	**8**
2015–16	Leeds U	45	5		
2016–17	Leeds U	31	2		
2017–18	Leeds U	29	2		
2018–19	Leeds U	26	2		
2019–20	Leeds U	45	5		
2020–21	Leeds U	38	8	**214**	**24**

DAVIS, Leif (D) **9 0**
b.Newcastle upon Tyne 12-1-00
From Morecambe.

2018–19	Leeds U	4	0		
2019–20	Leeds U	3	0		
2020–21	Leeds U	2	0	**9**	**0**

DEAN, Max (F) **0 0**
H: 5 10 b.Ormskirk 21-2-04

2020–21	Leeds U	0	0		

DOUGLAS, Barry (D) **329 22**
H: 5 9 W: 10 00 b.Glasgow 4-9-89
Internationals: Scotland Full caps.

2008–09	Queen's Park	30	2		
2009–10	Queen's Park	35	8	**65**	**10**
2010–11	Dundee U	23	2		
2011–12	Dundee U	10	1		
2012–13	Dundee U	28	1	**61**	**4**
2013–14	Lech Poznan	18	0		
2014–15	Lech Poznan	27	3		
2015–16	Lech Poznan	13	0	**58**	**3**
2015–16	Konyaspor	12	0		
2016–17	Konyaspor	22	0	**34**	**0**
2017–18	Wolverhampton W	39	5	**39**	**5**
2018–19	Leeds U	27	0		
2019–20	Leeds U	15	0		
2020–21	Leeds U	0	0	**42**	**0**
2020–21	*Blackburn R*	30	0	**30**	**0**

DRAMEH, Cody (D) **0 0**
b.London 8-12-01
From Fulham.

2020–21	Leeds U	0	0		

EDMONDSON, Ryan (F) **37 4**
b. 20-5-01
Internationals: England U19.
From York C.

2017–18	Leeds U	1	0		
2018–19	Leeds U	1	0		
2019–20	Leeds U	0	0		
2020–21	Leeds U	0	0	**2**	**0**
2020–21	*Aberdeen*	14	2	**14**	**2**
2020–21	*Northampton T*	21	2	**21**	**2**

GELHARDT, Joe (F) **19 1**
b.Liverpool 4-5-02
Internationals: England U16, U17, U18.

2018–19	Wigan Ath	1	0		
2019–20	Wigan Ath	18	1	**19**	**1**
2020–21	Leeds U	0	0		

GOTTS, Robbie (D) **31 3**
b.Harrogate 9-11-99

2018–19	Leeds U	0	0		
2019–20	Leeds U	1	0		
2020–21	Leeds U	0	0	**1**	**0**
2020–21	*Lincoln C*	7	0	**7**	**0**
2020–21	*Salford C*	23	3	**23**	**3**

GREENWOOD, Sam (F) **0 0**
b.Sunderland 26-1-02
Internationals: England U16, U17, U18.

2019–20	Arsenal	0	0		
2020–21	Leeds U	0	0		

HELDER COSTA, Wander (M) **192 26**
H: 5 10 W: 11 07 b.Luanda 12-1-94
Internationals: Portugal U16, U17, U18, U19, U20, U21, U23, Full caps.

2013–14	Benfica	0	0		
2014–15	Benfica	0	0		
2014–15	*Deportivo La Coruna*	6	0	**6**	**0**
2015–16	Benfica	0	0		
2015–16	*Monaco*	25	3	**25**	**3**
2016–17	Benfica	0	0		
2016–17	*Wolverhampton W*	35	10		
2017–18	Wolverhampton W	36	5		
2018–19	Wolverhampton W	25	1		
2019–20	Wolverhampton W	0	0	**96**	**16**
2019–20	*Leeds U*	43	4		
2020–21	Leeds U	22	3	**65**	**7**

HERNANDEZ, Pablo (M) **430 75**
H: 5 8 W: 10 00 b.Castellon 11-4-85
Internationals: Spain Full caps.

2005–06	Valencia	1	0		
2006–07	Valencia	0	0		
2006–07	*Cadiz*	14	4	**14**	**4**
2007–08	Getafe	28	3	**28**	**3**
2008–09	Valencia	21	4		
2009–10	Valencia	33	5		
2010–11	Valencia	27	5		
2011–12	Valencia	30	3	**112**	**17**
2012–13	Swansea C	30	3		
2013–14	Swansea C	27	2	**57**	**5**
2014–15	Al Arabi	13	6		
2014–15	*Al-Nasr*	12	3	**12**	**3**
2015–16	Al Arabi	0	0		
2015–16	*Rayo Vallecano*	27	3	**27**	**3**
2016–17	Al Arabi	0	0	**13**	**6**
2016–17	*Leeds U*	35	6		
2017–18	Leeds U	41	7		
2018–19	Leeds U	39	12		
2019–20	Leeds U	36	9		
2020–21	Leeds U	16	0	**167**	**34**

HOSANNAH, Bryce (D) **8 0**
b. 8-4-99
From Crystal Palace.

2019–20	Leeds U	0	0		
2020–21	Leeds U	0	0		
2020–21	*Bradford C*	8	0	**8**	**0**

HUGGINS, Niall (M) **1 0**
b.York 18-12-00

2020–21	Leeds U	1	0	**1**	**0**

JENKINS, Jack (M) **0 0**
b. 23-3-02

2020–21	Leeds U	0	0		

KAMWA, Bobby (M) **0 0**
H: 6 0 W: 12 02 b.Yaounde 18-3-00

2020–21	Leeds U	0	0		

KENNEH, Nohan (M) **0 0**
H: 6 3 W: 12 06 b.Monrovia 10-1-03
Internationals: England U16, U17.

2020–21	Leeds U	0	0		

KLICH, Mateusz (M) **290** **42**
H: 6 0 W: 10 10 b.Tarnow 13-6-90
Internationals: Poland U18, U19, U20, U21, Full caps.

2008–09	Cracovia	5	0		
2009–10	Cracovia	21	1		
2010–11	Cracovia	27	4	**53**	**5**
2011–12	Wolfsburg	0	0		
2012–13	Wolfsburg	0	0		
2012–13	*Zwolle*	13	2		
2013–14	Zwolle	30	4	**43**	**6**
2014–15	Wolfsburg	0	0		
2014–15	Kaiserslautern	5	1		
2015–16	Kaiserslautern	16	3	**21**	**4**
2016–17	FC Twente	29	6	**29**	**6**
2017–18	Leeds U	4	0		
2017–18	*Utrecht*	14	1	**14**	**1**
2018–19	Leeds U	46	10		
2019–20	Leeds U	45	6		
2020–21	Leeds U	35	4	**130**	**20**

KOCH, Robin (D) **126** **4**
b.Kaiserslaurten 17-7-96

2015–16	Kaiserslautern	0	0		
2016–17	Kaiserslautern	24	0		
2017–18	Kaiserslautern	3	0	**27**	**0**
2017–18	Freiburg	26	2		
2018–19	Freiburg	24	1		
2019–20	Freiburg	32	1		
2020–21	Freiburg	0	0	**82**	**4**
2020–21	Leeds U	17	0	**17**	**0**

LLORENTE, Diego (D) **152** **9**
b.Madrid 16-8-93

2012–13	Real Madrid	1	0		
2013–14	Real Madrid	1	0		
2014–15	Real Madrid	0	0		
2015–16	Real Madrid	0	0		
2015–16	*Vallecano*	33	2	**33**	**2**
2016–17	Real Madrid	0	0	**2**	**0**
2016–17	*Malaga*	25	2	**25**	**2**
2017–18	Real Sociedad	27	3		
2018–19	Real Sociedad	21	0		
2019–20	Real Sociedad	29	1		
2020–21	Real Sociedad	0	0	**77**	**4**
2020–21	Leeds U	15	1	**15**	**1**

McCALMONT, Alfie (M) **35** **8**
b.Thirsk 25-3-00
Internationals: Northern Ireland U17, U19, U21, Full caps.

2019–20	Leeds U	0	0		
2020–21	Leeds U	0	0		
2020–21	*Oldham Ath*	35	8	**35**	**8**

McKINSTRY, Stuart (M) **0** **0**
H: 5 10 W: 10 10 b.Wishaw 18-9-02
Internationals: Scotland U17.
From Motherwell.

2020–21	Leeds U	0	0		

MESLIER, Illan (G) **73** **0**
b.Lorient 2-3-00
Internationals: France U18, U19, U20.

2016–17	Lorient	0	0		
2017–18	Lorient	0	0		
2018–19	Lorient	28	0		
2019–20	Lorient	0	0	**28**	**0**
2019–20	*Leeds U*	10	0		
2020–21	Leeds U	35	0	**45**	**0**

PHILLIPS, Kalvin (M) **194** **13**
H: 5 10 W: 11 05 b.Leeds 2-12-95

2014–15	Leeds U	2	1		
2015–16	Leeds U	10	0		
2016–17	Leeds U	33	1		
2017–18	Leeds U	41	7		
2018–19	Leeds U	42	1		
2019–20	Leeds U	37	2		
2020–21	Leeds U	29	1	**194**	**13**

POVEDA-OCAMPO, Ian (M) **18** **0**
b.London 9-2-00
Internationals: England U16, U17, U18, U19, U20.
From Chelsea, Arsenal, Barcelona, Brentford.

2018–19	Manchester C	0	0		
2019–20	Manchester C	0	0		
2019–20	Leeds U	4	0		
2020–21	Leeds U	14	0	**18**	**0**

RAPHINHA, Raphael (F) **145** **36**
b.Porto Alegre 14-2-96

2014–15	Avai	0	0		
2015–16	Vitoria Guimaraes	1	0		
2016–17	Vitoria Guimaraes	32	4		
2017–18	Vitoria Guimaraes	32	15	**65**	**19**
2018–19	Sporting Lisbon	24	4		
2019–20	Sporting Lisbon	4	2	**28**	**6**
2019–20	Rennes	22	5		
2020–21	Rennes	0	0	**22**	**5**
2020–21	Leeds U	30	6	**30**	**6**

ROBERTS, Tyler (F) **123** **17**
H: 5 11 W: 11 11 b.Gloucester 12-1-98
Internationals: Wales U16, U17, U19, U20, U21, Full caps.

2014–15	WBA	0	0		
2015–16	WBA	1	0		
2016–17	WBA	0	0	**1**	**0**
2016–17	*Oxford U*	14	0	**14**	**0**
2016–17	*Shrewsbury T*	13	4	**13**	**4**
2017–18	Leeds U	0	0		
2017–18	*Walsall*	17	5	**17**	**5**
2018–19	Leeds U	28	3		
2019–20	Leeds U	23	4		
2020–21	Leeds U	27	1	**78**	**8**

RODRIGO, Moreno (F) **283** **73**
b.Rio de Janeiro 6-3-91

2009–10	Real Madrid	0	0		
2010–11	Real Madrid	0	0		
2010–11	*Bolton W*	17	1	**17**	**1**
2011–12	Benfica	22	9		
2012–13	Benfica	20	7		
2013–14	Benfica	26	11	**68**	**27**
2014–15	Valencia	31	3		
2015–16	Valencia	25	2		
2016–17	Valencia	19	5		
2017–18	Valencia	37	16		
2018–19	Valencia	33	8		
2019–20	Valencia	27	4		
2020–21	Valencia	0	0	**172**	**38**
2020–21	Leeds U	26	7	**26**	**7**

SHACKLETON, Jamie (M) **54** **2**
b.Leeds 8-10-99
Internationals: England U20.

2018–19	Leeds U	19	0		
2019–20	Leeds U	22	2		
2020–21	Leeds U	13	0	**54**	**2**

SPENCER, Morten (M) **0** **0**
b.Darlington 14-3-04
From Sunderland.

2020–21	Leeds U	0	0		

STEVENS, Jordan (M) **43** **1**
b. 25-3-00

2017–18	Forest Green R	9	0	**9**	**0**
2017–18	Leeds U	0	0		
2018–19	Leeds U	1	0		
2019–20	Leeds U	4	0		
2020–21	Leeds U	0	0	**5**	**0**
2020–21	*Swindon T*	13	1	**13**	**1**
2020–21	*Bradford C*	16	0	**16**	**0**

STRUIJK, Pascal (D) **32** **1**
b. 11-8-99
Internationals: Netherlands U17.
From Ajax.

2017–18	Leeds U	0	0		
2018–19	Leeds U	0	0		
2019–20	Leeds U	5	0		
2020–21	Leeds U	27	1	**32**	**1**

SUMMERVILLE, Crysencio (M) **39** **7**
b.Rotterdam 30-10-01

2018–19	Feyenoord	0	0		
2018–19	*Dordrecht*	18	5	**18**	**5**
2019–20	Feyenoord	0	0		
2019–20	*ADO Den Haag*	21	2	**21**	**2**
2020–21	Leeds U	0	0		

VAN DEN HEUVEL, Dani (G) **0** **0**
H: 6 0 W: 11 07 b.Delft 28-5-03
Internationals: Netherlands U16, U17.
From Ajax.

2020–21	Leeds U	0	0		

Scholars
Amissah, Emmanuel Agyekum; Bradbury, Lui Oliver; Bray, Owen Anthony; Brook, William Michael; Carole, Keenan Nino; Chikukwa, Jimiel Takunda; Chilokoa Mullen, Jeremiah Chukwuedo; Christy, Harry Thomas; Fewster, William Charles Storm; Hughes, Alfie Thomas; Kachosa, Ethan Takudzwa; Leverett, Samuel George; Littlewood, Joe Wilson; Moore, Kristan Richard; Picksley, Mitchell James; Pilkington, Aaron Jon; Ragan, Taylor Peter; Rigby, Maximus Marlon William; Skerry, Cooper Mark; Snowdon, Joseph Leonard; Sutcliffe, Harvey Frederick.

LEICESTER C (44)

ALBRIGHTON, Marc (M) **291** **18**
H: 6 2 W: 12 06 b.Tamworth 18-11-89
Internationals: England U20, U21.

2008–09	Aston Villa	0	0		
2009–10	Aston Villa	3	0		
2010–11	Aston Villa	29	5		
2011–12	Aston Villa	26	2		
2012–13	Aston Villa	9	0		
2013–14	Aston Villa	19	0	**86**	**7**
2013–14	*Wigan Ath*	4	0	**4**	**0**
2014–15	Leicester C	18	2		
2015–16	Leicester C	38	2		
2016–17	Leicester C	33	2		
2017–18	Leicester C	34	2		
2018–19	Leicester C	27	2		
2019–20	Leicester C	20	0		
2020–21	Leicester C	31	1	**201**	**11**

AMARTEY, Daniel (M) **136** **5**
H: 6 0 W: 12 04 b.Accra 1-12-94
Internationals: Ghana U20, Full caps.

2013	Djurgardens	23	0		
2014	Djurgardens	11	0	**34**	**0**
2014–15	Copenhagen	29	3		
2015–16	Copenhagen	15	0	**44**	**3**
2015–16	Leicester C	5	0		
2016–17	Leicester C	24	1		
2017–18	Leicester C	8	0		
2018–19	Leicester C	9	0		
2019–20	Leicester C	0	0		
2020–21	Leicester C	12	1	**58**	**2**

BARNES, Harvey (M) **150** **36**
b. 8-12-97
Internationals: England U18, U20, U21.

2016–17	Leicester C	0	0		
2016–17	*Milton Keynes D*	21	6	**21**	**6**
2017–18	Leicester C	3	0		
2017–18	*Barnsley*	23	5	**23**	**5**
2018–19	Leicester C	16	1		
2018–19	*WBA*	26	9	**26**	**9**
2019–20	Leicester C	36	6		
2020–21	Leicester C	25	9	**80**	**16**

BENKOVIC, Filip (D) **88** **10**
H: 6 4 W: 14 05 b.Zagreb 13-7-97
Internationals: Croatia U17, U19, U21, Full caps.

2015–16	Dinamo Zagreb	13	0		
2016–17	Dinamo Zagreb	18	2		
2017–18	Dinamo Zagreb	25	4	**56**	**6**
2018–19	Leicester C	0	0		
2018–19	*Celtic*	20	2	**20**	**2**
2019–20	Leicester C	0	0		
2019–20	*Bristol C*	10	2	**10**	**2**
2020–21	Leicester C	0	0		
2020–21	*Cardiff C*	1	0	**1**	**0**
2020–21	*OH Leuven*	1	0	**1**	**0**

CASTAGNE, Timothy (D) **182** **8**
b.Arlon 5-12-95

2013–14	Genk	0	0		
2014–15	Genk	27	1		
2015–16	Genk	21	0		
2016–17	Genk	32	0	**80**	**1**
2017–18	Atalanta	20	0		
2018–19	Atalanta	28	4		
2019–20	Atalanta	27	1		
2020–21	Atalanta	0	0	**75**	**5**
2020–21	Leicester C	27	2	**27**	**2**

CHOUDHURY, Hamza (M) **73** **1**
H: 5 10 W: 10 01 b.Loughborough 1-10-97
Internationals: England U21.

2015–16	Leicester C	0	0		
2015–16	*Burton Alb*	13	0		
2016–17	Leicester C	0	0		
2016–17	*Burton Alb*	13	0	**26**	**0**
2017–18	Leicester C	8	0		
2018–19	Leicester C	9	0		
2019–20	Leicester C	20	1		
2020–21	Leicester C	10	0	**47**	**1**

CLARK, Mitchell (D) **55** **1**
b.Nuneaton 13-3-99
Internationals: Wales U17, U19.

2017–18	Aston Villa	0	0		
2018–19	Aston Villa	0	0		
2018–19	*Port Vale*	40	0		
2019–20	Leicester C	0	0		
2019–20	*Port Vale*	4	0		
2020–21	Leicester C	0	0		
2020–21	*Port Vale*	11	1	**55**	**1**

DALEY-CAMPBELL, Vontae (D) **0** **0**
b. 2-4-01
From Arsenal.

2020–21	Leicester C	0	0		

DEWSBURY-HALL, Kiernan (M) **49** **7**
b. 6-9-98

2019–20	Leicester C	0	0		
2019–20	*Blackpool*	10	4	**10**	**4**
2020–21	Leicester C	0	0		
2020–21	*Luton T*	39	3	**39**	**3**

EVANS, Jonny (D) **354** **16**
H: 6 2 W: 12 02 b.Belfast 3-1-88
Internationals: Northern Ireland U16, U17, U21, Full caps.

2004–05	Manchester U	0	0		

2005–06 Manchester U 0 0
2006–07 Manchester U 0 0
2006–07 *Antwerp* 11 2 **11 2**
2006–07 *Sunderland* 18 1
2007–08 Manchester U 0 0
2007–08 *Sunderland* 15 0 **33 1**
2008–09 Manchester U 17 0
2009–10 Manchester U 18 0
2010–11 Manchester U 13 0
2011–12 Manchester U 29 1
2012–13 Manchester U 23 3
2013–14 Manchester U 17 0
2014–15 Manchester U 14 0
2015–16 Manchester U 0 0 **131 4**
2015–16 WBA 30 1
2016–17 WBA 31 2
2017–18 WBA 28 2 **89 5**
2018–19 Leicester C 24 1
2019–20 Leicester C 38 1
2020–21 Leicester C 28 2 **90 4**

FITZHUGH, Ethan (M) 0 0
b. 27-11-02
2020–21 Leicester C 0 0

FLYNN, Shane (M) 0 0
b.Dublin 14-10-01
From St Joseph's, Bray W.
2020–21 Leicester C 0 0

FOFANA, Wesley (D) 44 1
b.Marseille 17-12-00
2018–19 Saint-Etienne 2 0
2019–20 Saint-Etienne 14 1 **16 1**
2020–21 St Etienne 0 0
2020–21 Leicester C 28 0 **28 0**

FUCHS, Christian (D) 452 23
H: 6 1 W: 12 08 b.Pitten 7-4-86
Internationals: Austria U17, U19, U21, Full caps.
2002–03 Wiener Neustadt 12 0 **12 0**
2003–04 Mattersburg 13 0
2004–05 Mattersburg 25 2
2005–06 Mattersburg 35 1
2006–07 Mattersburg 35 6
2007–08 Mattersburg 33 2 **141 11**
2008–09 Bochum 22 2
2009–10 Bochum 31 4
2010–11 Bochum 0 0 **53 6**
2010–11 *Mainz 05* 31 0 **31 0**
2011–12 Schalke 29 2
2012–13 Schalke 29 0
2013–14 Schalke 16 0
2014–15 Schalke 25 2 **99 4**
2015–16 Leicester C 32 0
2016–17 Leicester C 36 2
2017–18 Leicester C 25 0
2018–19 Leicester C 3 0
2019–20 Leicester C 11 0
2020–21 Leicester C 9 0 **116 2**

GRAY, Demarai (M) 205 18
H: 5 10 W: 10 04 b.Birmingham 28-6-96
Internationals: England U18, U19, U20, U21.
2013–14 Birmingham C 7 1
2014–15 Birmingham C 41 6
2015–16 Birmingham C 24 1 **72 8**
2015–16 Leicester C 12 0
2016–17 Leicester C 30 1
2017–18 Leicester C 35 3
2018–19 Leicester C 34 4
2019–20 Leicester C 21 2
2020–21 Leicester C 1 0 **133 10**
Transferred to Bayer Leverkusen January 2021.

HIRST, George (F) 56 3
b.Sheffield 15-2-99
Internationals: England U17, U18, U20.
2016–17 Sheffield W 1 0
2017–18 Sheffield W 0 0 **1 0**
2018–19 Oh Leuven 22 3 **22 3**
2019–20 Leicester C 2 0
2020–21 Leicester C 0 0 **2 0**
2020–21 *Rotherham U* 31 0 **31 0**

HUGHES, Sam (M) 22 2
b.West Kirby 15-4-97
From Chester.
2017–18 Leicester C 0 0
2018–19 Leicester C 0 0
2019–20 Leicester C 0 0
2019–20 *Salford C* 8 0 **8 0**
2020–21 Leicester C 0 0
2020–21 *Burton Alb* 14 2 **14 2**

IHEANACHO, Kelechi (M) 142 33
H: 6 2 W: 13 08 b.Imo 3-10-96
Internationals: Nigeria U17, U20, Full caps.
2014–15 Manchester C 0 0
2015–16 Manchester C 26 8
2016–17 Manchester C 20 4 **46 12**
2017–18 Leicester C 21 3
2018–19 Leicester C 30 1
2019–20 Leicester C 20 5
2020–21 Leicester C 25 12 **96 21**

IVERSEN, Daniel (G) 104 0
b. 19-7-97
Internationals: Denmark U16, U17, U18, U19, U20, U21.
2014–15 Esbjerg 0 0
2015–16 Esbjerg 0 0
2015–16 Leicester C 0 0
2016–17 Leicester C 0 0
2017–18 Leicester C 0 0
2018–19 Leicester C 0 0
2018–19 *Oldham Ath* 42 0 **42 0**
2019–20 Leicester C 0 0
2019–20 *Rotherham U* 34 0 **34 0**
2020–21 Leicester C 0 0
2020–21 *OH Leuven* 5 0 **5 0**
2020–21 *Preston NE* 23 0 **23 0**

JAKUPOVIC, Eldin (G) 189 1
H: 6 3 W: 13 00 b.Kozarac 2-10-84
Internationals: Bosnia & Herzegovina U21, Switzerland U21, Full caps.
2004–05 Grasshoppers 8 0
2005–06 FC Thun 22 0 **22 0**
2006–07 Lokomotiv Moscow 20 0
2007–08 Lokomotiv Moscow 0 0
2007–08 *Grasshoppers* 23 1
2008–09 Lokomotiv Moscow 0 0 **20 0**
2008–09 *Grasshoppers* 34 0 **65 1**
2010–11 Olympiacos Volou 33 0 **33 0**
2011–12 Aris Salonika 1 0 **1 0**
2012–13 Hull C 5 0
2013–14 Hull C 1 0
2013–14 *Leyton Orient* 13 0 **13 0**
2014–15 Hull C 3 0
2015–16 Hull C 2 0
2016–17 Hull C 22 0 **33 0**
2017–18 Leicester C 2 0
2018–19 Leicester C 0 0
2019–20 Leicester C 0 0
2020–21 Leicester C 0 0 **2 0**

JAMES, Matthew (M) 185 10
H: 6 0 W: 11 12 b.Bacup 22-7-91
Internationals: England U16, U17, U19, U20.
2007–08 Manchester U 0 0
2008–09 Manchester U 0 0
2009–10 Manchester U 0 0
2009–10 *Preston NE* 18 2
2010–11 Manchester U 0 0
2010–11 *Preston NE* 10 0 **28 2**
2011–12 Manchester U 0 0
2012–13 Leicester C 24 3
2013–14 Leicester C 35 1
2014–15 Leicester C 27 0
2015–16 Leicester C 0 0
2016–17 Leicester C 1 0
2016–17 *Barnsley* 18 1
2017–18 Leicester C 13 0
2018–19 Leicester C 0 0
2019–20 Leicester C 1 0
2020–21 Leicester C 0 0 **101 4**
2020–21 *Barnsley* 15 0 **33 1**
2020–21 *Coventry C* 23 3 **23 3**

JOHNSON, Darnell (D) 22 0
b. 3-9-98
Internationals: England U16, U17, U18, U19, U20.
2019–20 Leicester C 0 0
2019–20 *Hibernian* 1 0 **1 0**
2020–21 Leicester C 0 0
2020–21 *Wigan Ath* 10 0 **10 0**
2020–21 *AFC Wimbledon* 11 0 **11 0**

JUSTIN, James (F) 126 8
H: 6 0 W: 11 03 b.Luton 11-7-97
Internationals: England U20, U21.
2015–16 Luton T 1 0
2016–17 Luton T 29 1
2017–18 Luton T 17 2
2018–19 Luton T 43 3 **90 6**
2019–20 Leicester C 13 0
2020–21 Leicester C 23 2 **36 2**

KNIGHT, Josh (D) 69 4
b.Leicester 7-9-97
2017–18 Leicester C 0 0
2018–19 Leicester C 0 0
2018–19 *Peterborough U* 8 0
2019–20 Leicester C 0 0
2019–20 *Peterborough U* 24 3 **32 3**
2020–21 Leicester C 0 0
2020–21 *Wycombe W* 37 1 **37 1**

LESHABELA, Thakgalo (M) 1 0
b. 18-9-99
Internationals: South Africa U20.
2018–19 Leicester C 0 0
2019–20 Leicester C 0 0
2020–21 Leicester C 1 0 **1 0**

MADDISON, James (M) 194 43
H: 5 10 W: 11 07 b.Coventry 23-11-96
Internationals: England U21, Full caps.
2013–14 Coventry C 0 0
2014–15 Coventry C 12 2
2015–16 Norwich C 0 0
2015–16 *Coventry C* 23 3 **35 5**
2016–17 Norwich C 3 1
2016–17 *Aberdeen* 14 2 **14 2**
2017–18 Norwich C 44 14 **47 15**
2018–19 Leicester C 36 7
2019–20 Leicester C 31 6
2020–21 Leicester C 31 8 **98 21**

MASWANHISE, Tawanda (M) 0 0
2020–21 Leicester C 0 0

MENDY, Nampalys (D) 263 1
H: 5 6 W: 10 10 b.La Seyne-sur-Mer 9-6-92
Internationals: France U18, U19, U20, U21.
2010–11 Monaco 14 0
2011–12 Monaco 28 0
2012–13 Monaco 32 0 **74 0**
2013–14 Nice 36 0
2014–15 Nice 36 0
2015–16 Nice 38 1
2016–17 Leicester C 4 0
2017–18 Leicester C 0 0
2017–18 *Nice* 14 0 **124 1**
2018–19 Leicester C 31 0
2019–20 Leicester C 7 0
2020–21 Leicester C 23 0 **65 0**

MORGAN, Wes (D) 634 24
H: 6 2 W: 14 00 b.Nottingham 21-1-84
Internationals: Jamaica Full caps.
2002–03 Nottingham F 0 0
2002–03 *Kidderminster H* 5 1 **5 1**
2003–04 Nottingham F 32 2
2004–05 Nottingham F 43 1
2005–06 Nottingham F 43 2
2006–07 Nottingham F 38 0
2007–08 Nottingham F 42 1
2008–09 Nottingham F 42 1
2009–10 Nottingham F 44 3
2010–11 Nottingham F 46 1
2011–12 Nottingham F 22 1 **352 12**
2011–12 Leicester C 17 0
2012–13 Leicester C 45 1
2013–14 Leicester C 45 2
2014–15 Leicester C 37 2
2015–16 Leicester C 38 2
2016–17 Leicester C 27 1
2017–18 Leicester C 32 0
2018–19 Leicester C 22 3
2019–20 Leicester C 11 0
2020–21 Leicester C 3 0 **277 11**

MUSKWE, Admiral (F) 22 3
b. 21-8-98
Internationals: England U17. Zimbabwe Full caps.
2019–20 Leicester C 0 0
2019–20 *Swindon T* 5 0 **5 0**
2020–21 Leicester C 0 0
2020–21 *Wycombe W* 17 3 **17 3**

NDIDI, Onyinye (D) 209 11
b. 16-12-96
Internationals: Nigeria U20, Full caps.
2014–15 Genk 6 0
2015–16 Genk 38 4
2016–17 Genk 19 0 **63 4**
2016–17 Leicester C 17 2
2017–18 Leicester C 33 0
2018–19 Leicester C 38 2
2019–20 Leicester C 32 2
2020–21 Leicester C 26 1 **146 7**

NELSON, Ben (D) 0 0
b.Northampton 18-3-04
2020–21 Leicester C 0 0

ODUNZE, Chituru (G) 0 0
H: 6 7 W: 12 06 b.Raleigh 14-10-02
Internationals: USA U17, U20.
From Vancouver Whitecaps.
2020–21 Leicester C 0 0

PENNANT, Terell (F) 0 0
b.Leicester 14-9-02
Internationals: England U16.
2020–21 Leicester C 0 0

PEREZ, Ayoze (F) 287 69
H: 5 10 W: 10 06 b.Santa Cruz de Tenerife 23-7-93
Internationals: Spain U21.
2012–13 Tenerife 16 1
2013–14 Tenerife 34 16 **50 17**
2014–15 Newcastle U 36 7

2015–16 Newcastle U 34 6
2016–17 Newcastle U 36 9
2017–18 Newcastle U 36 8
2018–19 Newcastle U 37 12 **179 42**
2019–20 Leicester C 33 8
2020–21 Leicester C 25 2 **58 10**

PRAET, Dennis (M) 279 26
b.Leuven 14-5-94
Internationals: Belgium U16, U17, U18, U19, U21, Full caps.
2011–12 Anderlecht 7 0
2012–13 Anderlecht 27 2
2013–14 Anderlecht 37 5
2014–15 Anderlecht 30 7
2015–16 Anderlecht 37 6
2016–17 Anderlecht 1 0 **139 20**
2016–17 Sampdoria 32 1
2017–18 Sampdoria 32 1
2018–19 Sampdoria 34 2 **98 4**
2019–20 Leicester C 27 1
2020–21 Leicester C 15 1 **42 2**
Transferred to Lyon January 2021.

REGHBA, Ali (F) 12 2
H: 5 11 W: 11 05 b.Essen 14-1-00
Internationals: Republic of Ireland U19.
2018 Bohemians 1 2
2019 Bohemians 11 0 **12 2**
2020–21 Leicester C 0 0

RICARDO PEREIRA, Domingos (D) 204 11
H: 5 9 W: 11 00 b.Lisbon 6-10-93
Internationals: Portugal U19, U20, U21, Full caps.
2011–12 Vitoria Guimaraes 3 0
2012–13 Vitoria Guimaraes 27 0 **30 0**
2013–14 Porto 14 2
2014–15 Porto 5 0
2015–16 Porto 0 0
2015–16 *Nice* 26 0
2016–17 Porto 0 0
2016–17 *Nice* 24 2 **50 2**
2017–18 Porto 27 2 **46 4**
2018–19 Leicester C 35 2
2019–20 Leicester C 28 3
2020–21 Leicester C 15 0 **78 5**

SCHMEICHEL, Kasper (G) 536 0
H: 6 1 W: 13 00 b.Copenhagen 5-11-86
Internationals: Denmark U19, U20, U21, Full caps.
2003–04 Manchester C 0 0
2004–05 Manchester C 0 0
2005–06 Manchester C 0 0
2005–06 *Darlington* 4 0 **4 0**
2005–06 *Bury* 15 0
2006–07 Manchester C 0 0
2006–07 *Falkirk* 15 0 **15 0**
2006–07 *Bury* 14 0 **29 0**
2007–08 Manchester C 7 0
2007–08 *Cardiff C* 14 0 **14 0**
2007–08 *Coventry C* 9 0 **9 0**
2008–09 Manchester C 1 0
2009–10 Manchester C 0 0 **8 0**
2009–10 Notts Co 43 0 **43 0**
2010–11 Leeds U 37 0 **37 0**
2011–12 Leicester C 46 0
2012–13 Leicester C 46 0
2013–14 Leicester C 46 0
2014–15 Leicester C 24 0
2015–16 Leicester C 38 0
2016–17 Leicester C 30 0
2017–18 Leicester C 33 0
2018–19 Leicester C 38 0
2019–20 Leicester C 38 0
2020–21 Leicester C 38 0 **377 0**

SHADE, Tyrese (M) 0 0
H: 6 0 W: 12 04 b.Birmingham 9-6-00
Internationals: St Kitts and Nevis U20.
From Solihull Moors.
2020–21 Leicester C 0 0

SLIMANI, Islam (F) 273 116
H: 6 2 W: 12 06 b.Algiers 18-6-88
Internationals: Algeria Full caps.
2008–09 JSM Cheraga 20 18 **20 18**
2009–10 CR Belouizdad 30 8
2010–11 CR Belouizdad 27 10
2011–12 CR Belouizdad 26 10
2012–13 CR Belouizdad 15 4 **98 32**
2013–14 Sporting Lisbon 26 8
2014–15 Sporting Lisbon 21 12
2015–16 Sporting Lisbon 33 27
2016–17 Sporting Lisbon 2 1 **82 48**
2016–17 Leicester C 23 7
2017–18 Leicester C 12 1
2017–18 *Newcastle U* 4 0 **4 0**
2018–19 Leicester C 0 0
2018–19 *Fenerbahce* 15 1 **15 1**
2019–20 Leicester C 0 0
2019–20 *Monaco* 18 9 **18 9**
2020–21 Leicester C 1 0 **36 8**
Transferred to Lyon February 2021.

SOWAH, Kamal (M) 27 3
H: 5 10 b.Accra 9-1-00
2017–18 Leicester C 0 0
2017–18 *Leuven* 0 0
2018–19 Leicester C 0 0
2018–19 *Leuven* 2 0
2019–20 Leicester C 0 0
2019–20 *Leuven* 25 3 **27 3**
2020–21 Leicester C 0 0

SOYUNCU, Caglar (D) 147 5
H: 6 2 W: 12 08 b.Izmir 23-5-96
Internationals: Turkey U18, U19, U20, U21, Full caps.
2014–15 Altinordu 4 0
2015–16 Altinordu 30 2 **34 2**
2016–17 Freiburg 24 0
2017–18 Freiburg 26 1 **50 1**
2018–19 Leicester C 6 0
2019–20 Leicester C 34 1
2020–21 Leicester C 23 1 **63 2**

STOLARCZYK, Jakub (G) 0 0
b. 19-12-00
2020–21 Leicester C 0 0

SUENGCHITTHAWON, Thanawat (M) 0 0
b. 8-1-00
From Nancy.
2020–21 Leicester C 0 0

TAVARES, Sidnei (M) 2 0
b. 29-9-01
2020–21 Leicester C 2 0 **2 0**

THOMAS, Luke (M) 17 1
b. 10-6-01
Internationals: England U18, U19.
2019–20 Leicester C 3 0
2020–21 Leicester C 14 1 **17 1**

TIELEMANS, Youri (M) 274 43
H: 5 9 W: 10 08 b.Sint-Pieters-Leeuw 7-5-97
Internationals: Belgium U16, U21, Full caps.
2013–14 Anderlecht 29 1
2014–15 Anderlecht 39 6
2015–16 Anderlecht 34 6
2016–17 Anderlecht 37 13 **139 26**
2017–18 Monaco 27 0
2018–19 Monaco 20 5 **47 5**
2018–19 *Leicester C* 13 3
2019–20 Leicester C 37 3
2020–21 Leicester C 38 6 **88 12**

UNDER, Cengiz (M) 162 31
b.Sindirgi 14-7-97
2014–15 Altinordu 20 5
2015–16 Altinordu 31 6 **51 11**
2016–17 Basaksehir 32 7 **32 7**
2017–18 Roma 26 7
2018–19 Roma 26 3
2019–20 Roma 18 3
2020–21 Roma 0 0 **70 13**
On loan from Roma.
2020–21 Leicester C 9 0 **9 0**

VARDY, Jamie (F) 308 138
H: 5 10 W: 11 12 b.Sheffield 11-1-87
Internationals: England Full caps.
From Stocksbridge Park Steels, FC Halifax T, Fleetwood T.
2012–13 Leicester C 26 4
2013–14 Leicester C 37 16
2014–15 Leicester C 34 5
2015–16 Leicester C 36 24
2016–17 Leicester C 35 13
2017–18 Leicester C 37 20
2018–19 Leicester C 34 18
2019–20 Leicester C 35 23
2020–21 Leicester C 34 15 **308 138**

WAKELING, Jacob (F) 0 0
b.Redditch 15-9-01
From WBA, Alevechurch.
2020–21 Leicester C 0 0

WARD, Danny (G) 71 0
H: 5 11 W: 13 12 b.Wrexham 22-6-93
Internationals: Wales U17, U19, U21, Full caps.
From Wrexham.
2011–12 Liverpool 0 0
2012–13 Liverpool 0 0
2013–14 Liverpool 0 0
2014–15 Liverpool 0 0
2014–15 *Morecambe* 5 0 **5 0**
2015–16 Liverpool 2 0
2015–16 *Aberdeen* 21 0 **21 0**
2016–17 Liverpool 0 0
2016–17 *Huddersfield T* 43 0 **43 0**
2017–18 Liverpool 0 0 **2 0**
2018–19 Leicester C 0 0
2019–20 Leicester C 0 0
2020–21 Leicester C 0 0

WRIGHT, Callum (M) 16 4
b.Liverpool 2-5-00
2020–21 Leicester C 0 0
2020–21 *Cheltenham T* 16 4 **16 4**

Scholars
Aisthorpe, Bailey Trafford; Booth, Chadwick Zachary; Braybrooke, Samuel Charles; Butterfill, Jack James Harry; Cover, Brandon Ashley; Dawkins, Kartell Sabie; Doherty, Arlo Ricky Hugh; Fitzhugh, Ethan Michael; Godsmark-Ford, Harvey George; Gyamfi, Johnson Adu; Kutshienza, Jesper; Leathers, Adam James; Marcal-Madivadua, Wanya; Maswanhise, Tawanda Jethro; Nelson, Benjamin Harvey; Obi, Daniel Iheukwu; Pennant, Kian Darnell Leroy; Read, Cody Lewis; Russ, Brian William James; Wormleighton, Joseph Oliver; Yfeko, Johnly Levi.

LEYTON ORIENT (45)

ANGOL, Lee (M) 135 29
H: 5 10 W: 11 04 b. 4-8-94
2012–13 Wycombe W 3 0
2013–14 Wycombe W 0 0 **3 0**
2014–15 Luton T 0 0
2015–16 Peterborough U 33 11
2016–17 Peterborough U 13 1 **46 12**
2017–18 Mansfield T 29 9 **29 9**
2018–19 *Lincoln C* 2 0 **2 0**
2018–19 Shrewsbury T 17 3 **17 3**
2019–20 Leyton Orient 26 4
2020–21 Leyton Orient 12 1 **38 5**

BROPHY, James (D) 142 4
b. 25-7-94
From Harrow Bor, Woodlands U, Broadfields U.
2015–16 Swindon T 28 0
2016–17 Swindon T 30 0
2017–18 Swindon T 6 0 **64 0**
2018–19 Leyton Orient 0 0
2019–20 Leyton Orient 34 2
2020–21 Leyton Orient 44 2 **78 4**

CISSE, Ousseynou (D) 280 12
H: 6 5 W: 13 05 b.Dakar 6-4-91
Internationals: Mali Full caps.
2009–10 Amiens 9 0
2010–11 Amiens 8 0
2011–12 Amiens 19 0 **36 0**
2012–13 Dijon 24 0
2013–14 Dijon 36 4
2014–15 Dijon 35 1 **95 5**
2015–16 Rayo Vallecano 0 0
2015–16 *Waasland-Beveren* 12 1 **12 1**
2016–17 Tours 25 1 **25 1**
2017–18 Milton Keynes D 32 0
2018–19 Milton Keynes D 26 2 **58 2**
2019–20 Gillingham 2 1 **2 1**
2019–20 *Leyton Orient* 10 1
2020–21 Leyton Orient 42 1 **52 2**

CLAY, Craig (M) 144 3
H: 5 11 W: 11 07 b.Nottingham 5-5-92
Internationals: England C.
2010–11 Chesterfield 3 1
2011–12 Chesterfield 5 0
2012–13 Chesterfield 19 0 **27 1**
2013–14 York C 8 0 **8 0**
From Grimsby T.
2016–17 Motherwell 35 1
2017–18 Motherwell 0 0 **35 1**
2019–20 Leyton Orient 35 0
2020–21 Leyton Orient 39 1 **74 1**

COULSON, Josh (D) 124 3
H: 6 3 W: 11 11 b.Cambridge 28-1-89
2014–15 Cambridge U 46 1
2015–16 Cambridge U 23 1
2016–17 Cambridge U 7 0
2017–18 Cambridge U 0 0 **76 2**
2019–20 Leyton Orient 28 1
2020–21 Leyton Orient 20 0 **48 1**

DAYTON, James (M) 182 15
H: 5 8 W: 10 00 b.Enfield 12-12-88
2007–08 Crystal Palace 0 0
2008–09 Crystal Palace 0 0
2008–09 *Yeovil T* 2 0 **2 0**
From Bishop's Stortford, Bromley.
2010–11 Kilmarnock 10 2
2011–12 Kilmarnock 28 3
2012–13 Kilmarnock 27 1 **65 6**
2013–14 Oldham Ath 34 3

2014–15 Oldham Ath 17 1 **51 4**
2014–15 *St Mirren* 13 1 **13 1**
2015–16 Swindon T 0 0
2016–17 Cheltenham T 28 3 **28 3**
2019–20 Leyton Orient 11 1
2020–21 Leyton Orient 12 0 **23 1**

DENNIS, Louis (F) 49 2
H: 6 1 W: 10 12 b.Hendon 9-10-92
2011–12 Dagenham & R 0 0
2012–13 Dagenham & R 6 0
2013–14 Dagenham & R 2 0 **8 0**
From Bromley.
2018–19 Portsmouth 1 0 **1 0**
2019–20 Leyton Orient 16 1
2020–21 Leyton Orient 24 1 **40 2**

HAPPE, Daniel (D) 74 4
b.Tower Hamlets 28-9-98
Internationals: England C.
2016–17 Leyton Orient 2 0
2019–20 Leyton Orient 32 1
2020–21 Leyton Orient 40 3 **74 4**

JOHNSON, Danny (F) 97 30
b. 28-2-93
From Harrogate T, Billingham Synthonia, Guisborough T.
2014–15 Cardiff C 0 0
2014–15 *Tranmere R* 4 0 **4 0**
2014–15 *Stevenage* 4 0 **4 0**
From Gateshead.
2018–19 Motherwell 22 6 **22 6**
2019–20 Dundee 19 5 **19 5**
2019–20 Leyton Orient 6 2
2020–21 Leyton Orient 42 17 **48 19**

JUDD, Myles (D) 29 0
H: 5 10 W: 10 08 b.Redbridge 26-8-99
2015–16 Leyton Orient 0 0
2016–17 Leyton Orient 20 0
2019–20 Leyton Orient 9 0
2020–21 Leyton Orient 0 0 **29 0**

KEMP, Daniel (M) 38 6
b. 11-1-99
Internationals: England U19, U20.
From Chelsea.
2016–17 West Ham U 0 0
2017–18 West Ham U 0 0
2018–19 West Ham U 0 0
2019–20 West Ham U 0 0
2019–20 *Stevenage* 6 1 **6 1**
2020–21 West Ham U 0 0
2020–21 *Blackpool* 8 0 **8 0**
2020–21 Leyton Orient 24 5 **24 5**

KYPRIANOU, Hector (M) 28 0
b. 27-5-01
Internationals: Cyprus U19.
2019–20 Leyton Orient 6 0
2020–21 Leyton Orient 22 0 **28 0**

LING, Sam (D) 45 0
b. 17-12-96
2013–14 Leyton Orient 0 0
2014–15 Leyton Orient 0 0
2015–16 Leyton Orient 0 0
From Dagenham & R.
2019–20 Leyton Orient 15 0
2020–21 Leyton Orient 30 0 **45 0**

MAGUIRE-DREW, Jordan (M) 77 10
b. 15-9-97
2017–18 Brighton & HA 0 0
2017–18 *Lincoln C* 11 0 **11 0**
2017–18 *Coventry C* 3 0 **3 0**
2018–19 Brighton & HA 0 0
2019–20 Leyton Orient 33 7
2020–21 Leyton Orient 13 2 **46 9**
2020–21 *Crawley T* 17 1 **17 1**

McANUFF, Jobi (M) 621 60
H: 5 11 W: 11 05 b.Edmonton 9-11-81
Internationals: Jamaica Full caps.
2000–01 Wimbledon 0 0
2001–02 Wimbledon 38 4
2002–03 Wimbledon 31 4
2003–04 Wimbledon 27 5 **96 13**
2003–04 West Ham U 12 1
2004–05 West Ham U 1 0 **13 1**
2004–05 Cardiff C 43 2 **43 2**
2005–06 Crystal Palace 41 8
2006–07 Crystal Palace 34 5 **75 13**
2007–08 Watford 39 2
2008–09 Watford 40 3
2009–10 Watford 3 0 **82 5**
2009–10 Reading 36 3
2010–11 Reading 40 4
2011–12 Reading 40 5
2012–13 Reading 38 0
2013–14 Reading 35 2 **189 14**
2014–15 Leyton Orient 34 3
2015–16 Leyton Orient 17 3
2016–17 Stevenage 31 4 **31 4**
2019–20 Leyton Orient 1 0
2020–21 Leyton Orient 40 2 **92 8**

OGIE, Shadrach (D) 0 0
b.Limerick 26-8-01
Internationals: Republic of Ireland U18, U19.
From Hornchurch.
2019–20 Leyton Orient 0 0
2020–21 Leyton Orient 0 0

SARGEANT, Sam (G) 28 0
H: 6 0 W: 10 08 b. 23-9-97
2014–15 Leyton Orient 0 0
2015–16 Leyton Orient 1 0
2016–17 Leyton Orient 15 0
2019–20 Leyton Orient 12 0
2020–21 Leyton Orient 0 0 **28 0**

SHABANI, Brendon (M) 0 0
2019–20 Leyton Orient 0 0
2020–21 Leyton Orient 0 0

SOTIRIOU, Ruel (F) 32 6
b. 24-8-00
Internationals: Cyprus U19, U21.
2019–20 Leyton Orient 10 5
2020–21 Leyton Orient 22 1 **32 6**

SWEENEY, Jayden (D) 1 0
b. 4-12-01
2019–20 Leyton Orient 0 0
2020–21 Leyton Orient 1 0 **1 0**

THOMPSON, Adam (D) 230 5
H: 6 2 W: 12 10 b.Harlow 28-9-92
Internationals: Northern Ireland U17, U19, U21, Full caps.
2010–11 Watford 10 1
2011–12 Watford 0 0
2011–12 *Brentford* 20 0 **20 0**
2012–13 Watford 4 0
2012–13 *Wycombe W* 2 0 **2 0**
2012–13 *Barnet* 1 0 **1 0**
2013–14 Watford 0 0 **14 1**
2013–14 Southend U 16 0
2014–15 Southend U 28 0
2015–16 Southend U 25 2
2016–17 Southend U 40 1 **109 3**
2017–18 Bury 15 0
2017–18 *Bradford C* 9 0 **9 0**
2018–19 Bury 44 1 **59 1**
2019–20 Rotherham U 10 0
2020–21 Rotherham U 0 0 **10 0**
2020–21 Leyton Orient 6 0 **6 0**

TURLEY, Jamie (D) 50 3
H: 6 1 W: 12 13 b.Reading 7-4-90
Internationals: England C.
From Salisbury C, Forest Green R, Eastleigh.
2015–16 Newport Co 0 0
2016–17 Newport Co 6 1 **6 1**
2018–19 Notts Co 18 0 **18 0**
2019–20 Leyton Orient 8 1
2020–21 Leyton Orient 18 1 **26 2**

VIGOUROUX, Lawrence (G) 171 0
b.London 19-11-93
Internationals: Chile U20.
2012–13 Tottenham H 0 0
2013–14 Tottenham H 0 0
2014–15 Liverpool 0 0
2015–16 Liverpool 0 0
2015–16 *Swindon T* 33 0
2016–17 Swindon T 43 0
2017–18 Swindon T 14 0
2018–19 Swindon T 29 0 **119 0**
2019–20 Leyton Orient 6 0
2020–21 Leyton Orient 46 0 **52 0**

WIDDOWSON, Joe (D) 294 2
H: 6 0 W: 12 00 b.Forest Gate 28-3-89
2007–08 West Ham U 0 0
2007–08 *Rotherham U* 3 0 **3 0**
2008–09 West Ham U 0 0
2008–09 *Grimsby T* 20 1
2009–10 Grimsby T 38 0 **58 1**
2010–11 Rochdale 34 0
2011–12 Rochdale 32 0 **66 0**
2012–13 Northampton T 39 0
2013–14 Northampton T 25 0 **64 0**
2014–15 Bury 1 0 **1 0**
2014–15 *Morecambe* 8 0 **8 0**
2014–15 Dagenham & R 21 0
2015–16 Dagenham & R 31 0 **52 0**
2019–20 Leyton Orient 16 1
2020–21 Leyton Orient 26 0 **42 1**

WILKINSON, Conor (F) 175 29
H: 6 1 W: 12 02 b.Croydon 23-1-95
Internationals: Republic of Ireland U17, U19, U21.
2012–13 Millwall 0 0
2013–14 Bolton W 0 0
2013–14 *Torquay U* 3 0 **3 0**
2014–15 Bolton W 4 0
2014–15 *Oldham Ath* 17 3 **17 3**
2015–16 Bolton W 0 0
2015–16 *Barnsley* 8 1 **8 1**
2015–16 *Newport Co* 12 1 **12 1**
2015–16 *Portsmouth* 1 0 **1 0**
2016–17 Bolton W 9 0 **13 0**
2016–17 *Chesterfield* 12 4 **12 4**
2017–18 Gillingham 34 3
2018–19 Gillingham 7 0 **41 3**
2019–20 Leyton Orient 26 5
2020–21 Leyton Orient 42 12 **68 17**

YOUNG, Matt (M) 1 0
b. 9-12-02
2020–21 Leyton Orient 1 0 **1 0**

Scholars
Apat, Mert; Byrne, Rhys John Howard; Campbell, Sean Kehinde Temitope; Dunbar-Bonnie, Deago Michael-David; Eaton, Shimron Clan; Francois-Vernal, Tristan Dion; Frempong, Kevin Asante-Atta; Ifeanyi, Sharon; Lovatt, Finlay Dean; Marfo, Wynford Domfeh; Mirza, Ahmad Reshad; Nkrumah, Daniel Kwaku Amankwah; Palmer, Kyrell Lee; Papadopoulos, Antony; Pegrum, Reggie John; Sanders, William James; Sodje, Harrison Okiemute; Solomon, Alexander; Staerck, Benjamin Laurie; Tanga, Jephte Matuba; Young, Jayden.

LINCOLN C (46)

ANDERSON, Harry (F) 158 19
H: 5 6 W: 9 11 b. 9-1-97
From Crawley T.
2014–15 Peterborough U 10 0
2015–16 Peterborough U 5 0
2016–17 Peterborough U 1 0 **16 0**
2017–18 Lincoln C 40 6
2018–19 Lincoln C 43 5
2019–20 Lincoln C 30 5
2020–21 Lincoln C 29 3 **142 19**

ARCHIBALD, Theo (M) 65 5
H: 5 11 W: 9 06 b.Glasgow 5-3-98
Internationals: Scotland U16, U19, U21.
2016–17 Celtic 0 0
2016–17 *Albion R* 14 0 **14 0**
2017–18 Brentford 2 0
2018–19 Brentford 0 0 **2 0**
2018–19 *Forest Green R* 14 1 **14 1**
2018–19 Brentford 0 0
2019–20 Macclesfield T 28 4 **28 4**
2020–21 Lincoln C 7 0 **7 0**

BRADLEY, Alex (M) 7 1
b.Worcester 27-1-99
Internationals: Finland U17, U19.
2018–19 WBA 0 0
2018–19 *Burton Alb* 7 1 **7 1**
2019–20 Lincoln C 0 0
2020–21 Lincoln C 0 0
Transferred to Yeovil T January 2021.

BRAMALL, Cohen (D) 69 1
H: 5 9 W: 11 00 b.Crewe 2-4-95
From Hednesford T.
2017–18 Arsenal 0 0
2017–18 *Birmingham C* 5 0 **5 0**
2018–19 Arsenal 0 0
2019–20 Colchester U 24 1
2020–21 Colchester U 23 0 **47 1**
2020–21 Lincoln C 17 0 **17 0**

BRIDCUTT, Liam (M) 308 4
H: 5 9 W: 11 07 b.Reading 8-5-89
Internationals: Scotland Full caps.
2007–08 Chelsea 0 0
2007–08 *Yeovil T* 9 0 **9 0**
2008–09 Chelsea 0 0
2008–09 *Watford* 6 0 **6 0**
2009–10 Chelsea 0 0
2009–10 *Stockport Co* 15 0 **15 0**
2010–11 Chelsea 0 0
2010–11 Brighton & HA 37 2
2011–12 Brighton & HA 43 0
2012–13 Brighton & HA 41 0
2013–14 Brighton & HA 11 0 **132 2**
2013–14 Sunderland 12 0
2014–15 Sunderland 18 0
2015–16 Sunderland 0 0 **30 0**
2015–16 *Leeds U* 24 0
2016–17 Leeds U 25 0 **49 0**
2017–18 Nottingham F 27 1
2018–19 Nottingham F 1 0
2019–20 Nottingham F 0 0
2019–20 *Bolton W* 11 0 **11 0**
2019–20 *Lincoln C* 5 1

2020–21 Nottingham F 0 0 28 1
2020–21 Lincoln C 23 0 28 1

CANN, Hayden (D) 0 0
2020–21 Lincoln C 0 0

DRAPER, Freddie (F) 0 0
2020–21 Lincoln C 0 0

EDUN, Tayo (D) 55 2
H: 5 9 b.London 14-5-98
Internationals: England U17, U18, U19, U20.
2016–17 Fulham 0 0
2017–18 Fulham 2 0
2018–19 Fulham 0 0
2018–19 *Ipswich T* 6 1 6 1
2019–20 Fulham 0 0 2 0
2019–20 Lincoln C 6 0
2020–21 Lincoln C 41 1 47 1

ELBOUZEDI, Zak (M) 55 6
b. 5-4-98
Internationals: Republic of Ireland U16, U17, U18, U19, U21.
2016–17 WBA 0 0
2017–18 Inverness CT 4 0
2017–18 *Elgin C* 3 0 3 0
2018–19 Inverness CT 0 0 4 0
2019 Waterford 27 6 27 6
2019–20 Lincoln C 5 0
2020–21 Lincoln C 2 0 7 0
2020–21 *Bolton W* 14 0 14 0

GRANT, Jorge (M) 181 42
H: 5 9 W: 11 07 b.Oxford 26-9-94
2013–14 Nottingham F 0 0
2014–15 Nottingham F 1 0
2015–16 Nottingham F 10 0
2016–17 Nottingham F 6 0
2016–17 *Notts Co* 17 6
2017–18 Nottingham F 0 0
2017–18 *Notts Co* 45 15 62 21
2018–19 Nottingham F 0 0 17 0
2018–19 *Luton T* 17 2 17 2
2018–19 *Mansfield T* 17 4 17 4
2019–20 Lincoln C 32 2
2020–21 Lincoln C 36 13 68 15

HOPPER, Tom (F) 212 46
H: 6 1 W: 12 00 b.Boston 14-12-93
Internationals: England U18.
From Boston U.
2011–12 Leicester C 0 0
2012–13 Leicester C 0 0
2012–13 *Bury* 22 3 22 3
2013–14 Leicester C 0 0
2014–15 Leicester C 0 0
2014–15 *Scunthorpe U* 12 4
2015–16 Scunthorpe U 34 8
2016–17 Scunthorpe U 31 5
2017–18 Scunthorpe U 38 7 115 24
2018–19 Southend U 14 7
2019–20 Southend U 14 2 28 9
2019–20 Lincoln C 8 2
2020–21 Lincoln C 39 8 47 10

HOWARTH, Ramirez (F) 11 1
b. 14-9-97
From Ashton U, West Didsbury & Chorlton, Cefn Druids.
2020–21 Lincoln C 11 1 11 1

JACKSON, Adam (D) 109 8
H: 6 2 W: 12 04 b.Darlington 18-5-94
Internationals: England U16, U17, U18, U19.
2011–12 Middlesbrough 0 0
2012–13 Middlesbrough 0 0
2013–14 Middlesbrough 0 0
2014–15 Middlesbrough 0 0
2015–16 Middlesbrough 0 0
2015–16 *Coventry C* 0 0
2015–16 *Hartlepool U* 29 3 29 3
2016–17 Barnsley 10 0
2017–18 Barnsley 22 1
2018–19 Barnsley 6 0 38 1
2019–20 Hibernian 14 3 14 3
2020–21 Lincoln C 28 1 28 1

JONES, James (M) 203 20
H: 5 9 W: 10 10 b.Winsford 1-2-96
Internationals: Scotland U19, U21.
2014–15 Crewe Alex 24 1
2015–16 Crewe Alex 31 0
2016–17 Crewe Alex 45 10
2017–18 Crewe Alex 6 1
2018–19 Crewe Alex 38 5
2019–20 Crewe Alex 23 2 167 19
2019–20 Lincoln C 0 0
2020–21 Lincoln C 36 1 36 1

LONG, Sam (G) 0 0
b. 12-11-02
2020–21 Lincoln C 0 0

MAKAMA, Jovon (F) 0 0
2020–21 Lincoln C 0 0

McGRANDLES, Conor (M) 185 13
H: 6 0 W: 10 00 b.Falkirk 24-9-95
2012–13 Falkirk 26 2
2013–14 Falkirk 36 5
2014–15 Falkirk 3 0
2014–15 Norwich C 1 0
2015–16 Norwich C 0 0
2015–16 *Falkirk* 5 0 70 7
2016–17 Norwich C 0 0 1 0
2017–18 Milton Keynes D 19 0
2018–19 Milton Keynes D 25 1
2019–20 Milton Keynes D 31 1 75 2
2020–21 Lincoln C 39 4 39 4

MELBOURNE, Max (D) 42 1
b.Solihull 24-10-98
2017–18 WBA 0 0
2017–18 *Ross Co* 3 0 3 0
2018–19 WBA 0 0
2018–19 *Partick Thistle* 3 0 3 0
2019–20 Lincoln C 8 0
2020–21 Lincoln C 8 0 16 0
2020–21 *Walsall* 20 1 20 1

MONTSMA, Lewis (D) 86 7
b. 25-4-98
2018–19 Dordrecht 23 1
2019–20 Dordrecht 23 0 46 1
2020–21 Lincoln C 40 6 40 6

POOLE, Regan (D) 118 1
b.Cardiff 18-6-98
Internationals: Wales U17, U19, U20, U21.
2014–15 Newport Co 11 0
2015–16 Newport Co 4 0
2015–16 Manchester U 0 0
2016–17 Manchester U 0 0
2017–18 Manchester U 0 0
2017–18 *Northampton T* 22 0 22 0
2018–19 Manchester U 0 0
2018–19 *Newport Co* 20 0 35 0
2019–20 Milton Keynes D 19 0
2020–21 Milton Keynes D 20 1 39 1
2020–21 Lincoln C 22 0 22 0

ROSS, Ethan (G) 4 0
b. 6-3-97
From WBA.
2018–19 Colchester U 3 0
2019–20 Colchester U 1 0 4 0
2020–21 Lincoln C 0 0

ROUGHAN, Sean (D) 6 0
b. 31-8-03
2020–21 Lincoln C 6 0 6 0

SANDERS, Max (M) 25 1
b. 4-1-99
Internationals: England U19.
2017–18 Brighton & HA 0 0
2018–19 Brighton & HA 0 0
2019–20 Brighton & HA 0 0
2019–20 *AFC Wimbledon* 20 1 20 1
2020–21 Brighton & HA 0 0
2020–21 Lincoln C 5 0 5 0

SCULLY, Anthony (M) 45 13
b. 3-12-99
2018–19 West Ham U 0 0
2019–20 Lincoln C 5 2
2020–21 Lincoln C 40 11 45 13

WALSH, Joe (D) 241 12
H: 5 11 W: 11 00 b.Cardiff 15-5-92
Internationals: Wales U17, U19, U21.
2010–11 Swansea C 0 0
2011–12 Swansea C 0 0
2012–13 Crawley T 30 2
2013–14 Crawley T 39 5
2014–15 Crawley T 28 1 97 8
2014–15 *Milton Keynes D* 2 0
2015–16 Milton Keynes D 18 1
2016–17 Milton Keynes D 39 1
2017–18 Milton Keynes D 10 0
2018–19 Milton Keynes D 30 2
2019–20 Milton Keynes D 24 0 123 4
2020–21 Lincoln C 21 0 21 0

Scholars
Al-Oyouni, Ziyad; Angol, Mekhi Hayden; Boylan, Matthew Edward; Brooks, Billy; Deane, Robert Louis; Draper, Frederick Charles; Gruszczynski, Kacper Daniel; Hilton, Ethan James; Odokonyero, Nathan Atoro; Sault, Ben Jack; Scott, Cameo Ferrell Chino; Simpson, Joshua Luke; Tear, Haydn Matthew; Tetlow, Jasper Michael Brian.

LIVERPOOL (47)

ADRIAN (G) 171 0
H: 6 2 W: 12 00 b.Seville 3-1-87
2008–09 Real Betis 0 0
2009–10 Real Betis 0 0
2010–11 Real Betis 0 0
2011–12 Real Betis 0 0
2012–13 Real Betis 32 0 32 0
2013–14 West Ham U 20 0
2014–15 West Ham U 38 0
2015–16 West Ham U 32 0
2016–17 West Ham U 16 0
2017–18 West Ham U 19 0
2018–19 West Ham U 0 0 125 0
2019–20 Liverpool 11 0
2020–21 Liverpool 3 0 14 0

ALEXANDER-ARNOLD, Trent (M) 129 8
b. 7-10-98
Internationals: England U16, U17, U18, U19, U21, Full caps.
2016–17 Liverpool 7 0
2017–18 Liverpool 19 1
2018–19 Liverpool 29 1
2019–20 Liverpool 38 4
2020–21 Liverpool 36 2 129 8

ALISSON, Ramses (G) 181 1
H: 6 4 W: 14 05 b.Novo Hamburgo 2-10-92
Internationals: Brazil U17, U21, Full caps.
2013 Internacional 6 0
2014 Internacional 11 0
2015 Internacional 26 0
2016 Internacional 1 0 44 0
2016–17 Roma 0 0
2017–18 Roma 37 0 37 0
2018–19 Liverpool 38 0
2019–20 Liverpool 29 0
2020–21 Liverpool 33 1 100 1

ARROYO, Anderson (D) 40 0
H: 5 9 b.Quibdo 27-9-99
Internationals: Colombia U17, U20, U23.
2015 Fortaleza 2 0
2016 Fortaleza 8 0
2017 Fortaleza 4 0 14 0
2018–19 Liverpool 0 0
2018–19 *Mallorca* 0 0
2018–19 *Gent* 0 0
2019–20 Liverpool 0 0
2019–20 *Mlada Boleslav* 5 0 5 0
2020–21 Liverpool 0 0
2020–21 *Salamanca* 21 0 21 0

AWONIYI, Taiwo (F) 116 23
H: 6 0 b.Ilorin 12-8-97
Internationals: Nigeria U17, U20, U23.
2015–16 Liverpool 0 0
2015–16 *Frankfurt* 13 1 13 1
2016–17 Liverpool 0 0
2016–17 *NEC Nijmegen* 18 2 18 2
2017–18 Liverpool 0 0
2017–18 *Mouscron* 27 7
2018–19 Liverpool 0 0
2018–19 *Gent* 16 0 16 0
2018–19 *Mouscron* 9 7 36 14
2019–20 Liverpool 0 0
2019–20 *Mainz 05* 12 1 12 1
2020–21 Liverpool 0 0
2020–21 *Union Berlin* 21 5 21 5

BALAGIZI, James (M) 0 0
b.Manchester 20-9-03
Internationals: England U16, U17, U18.
2020–21 Liverpool 0 0

BECK, Owen (D) 0 0
b.Wrexham 9-8-02
Internationals: Wales U17, U21.
2020–21 Liverpool 0 0

BLAIR, Harvey (F) 0 0
b.Huddersfield 14-9-03
2020–21 Liverpool 0 0

BOYES, Morgan (D) 2 0
b. 22-4-01
Internationals: Wales U19.
2019–20 Liverpool 0 0
2020–21 Liverpool 0 0
2020–21 *Fleetwood T* 2 0 2 0

BRADLEY, Conor (M) 0 0
H: 5 11 b.Tyrone 9-7-03
Internationals: Northern Ireland U16, U17, Full caps.
From Dungannon Swifts.
2020–21 Liverpool 0 0

CAIN, Jake (M) 0 0
2019–20 Liverpool 0 0
2020–21 Liverpool 0 0

CLARKSON, Leighton (M) **0 0**
2019–20 Liverpool 0 0
2020–21 Liverpool 0 0

CORNESS, Dominic (M) **0 0**
b.Liverpool 5-5-03
2020–21 Liverpool 0 0

DAVIES, Ben (D) **224 3**
H: 6 1 W: 11 09 b.Barrow 11-8-95
2012–13 Preston NE 3 0
2013–14 Preston NE 0 0
2013–14 *York C* 44 0 **44 0**
2014–15 Preston NE 4 0
2014–15 *Tranmere R* 3 0 **3 0**
2015–16 Preston NE 0 0
2015–16 *Newport Co* 19 0 **19 0**
2016–17 Preston NE 0 0
2016–17 *Fleetwood T* 22 1 **22 1**
2017–18 Preston NE 34 1
2018–19 Preston NE 40 1
2019–20 Preston NE 36 0
2020–21 Preston NE 19 0 **136 2**
2020–21 Liverpool 0 0

DAVIES, Harvey (G) **0 0**
b.Liverpool 3-9-03
2020–21 Liverpool 0 0

ELLIOTT, Harvey (M) **45 7**
b.Esbjerg 4-4-03
Internationals: England U16, U17.
2018–19 Fulham 2 0 **2 0**
2019–20 Liverpool 2 0
2020–21 Liverpool 0 0 **2 0**
2020–21 *Blackburn R* 41 7 **41 7**

FABINHO, Henrique (M) **254 26**
H: 6 2 W: 12 04 b.Campinas 23-10-93
Internationals: Brazil Full caps.
From Fluminese.
2012–13 Rio Ave 0 0
2012–13 *Real Madrid* 1 0 **1 0**
2013–14 Rio Ave 0 0
2013–14 *Monaco* 26 0
2014–15 Rio Ave 0 0
2014–15 *Monaco* 36 1
2015–16 Monaco 34 6
2016–17 Monaco 37 9
2017–18 Monaco 34 7 **167 23**
2018–19 Liverpool 28 1
2019–20 Liverpool 28 2
2020–21 Liverpool 30 0 **86 3**

FIRMINO, Roberto (M) **389 112**
H: 5 11 W: 12 00 b.Maceio 2-10-91
Internationals: Brazil Full caps.
2009 Figueirense 2 0
2010 Figueirense 36 8 **38 8**
2010–11 Hoffenheim 11 3
2011–12 Hoffenheim 30 7
2012–13 Hoffenheim 33 5
2013–14 Hoffenheim 33 16
2014–15 Hoffenheim 33 7 **140 38**
2015–16 Liverpool 31 10
2016–17 Liverpool 35 11
2017–18 Liverpool 37 15
2018–19 Liverpool 34 12
2019–20 Liverpool 38 9
2020–21 Liverpool 36 9 **211 66**

GLATZEL, Paul (F) **0 0**
b.Liverpool 20-2-01
Internationals: England U16. Germany U18.
2020–21 Liverpool 0 0

GOMEZ, Joseph (D) **100 0**
H: 6 2 W: 14 00 b.Catford 23-5-97
Internationals: England U16, U17, U19, U21, Full caps.
2014–15 Charlton Ath 21 0 **21 0**
2015–16 Liverpool 5 0
2016–17 Liverpool 0 0
2017–18 Liverpool 23 0
2018–19 Liverpool 16 0
2019–20 Liverpool 28 0
2020–21 Liverpool 7 0 **79 0**

GORDON, Kaide (M) **1 0**
b. 5-10-04
2020–21 Derby Co 1 0 **1 0**
2020–21 Liverpool 0 0

GRABARA, Kamil (G) **73 0**
H: 6 3 W: 11 11 b.Ruda Slaska 8-1-99
Internationals: Poland U17, U18, U21.
From Ruch Chorzow.
2016–17 Liverpool 0 0
2017–18 Liverpool 0 0
2018–19 Liverpool 0 0
2018–19 *AGF Aarhus* 16 0
2019–20 Liverpool 0 0
2019–20 *Huddersfield T* 28 0 **28 0**
2020–21 Liverpool 0 0
2020–21 *AGF Aarhus* 29 0 **45 0**
Transferred to Copenhagen July 2021.

GRUJIC, Marko (M) **139 20**
b. 13-4-96
Internationals: Serbia U16, U17, U19, U20, U21, Full caps.
2012–13 Red Star Belgrade 1 0
2013–14 Red Star Belgrade 0 0
2014–15 Red Star Belgrade 9 0
2014–15 *Kolubara* 5 2 **5 2**
2015–16 Red Star Belgrade 29 6 **39 6**
2016–17 Liverpool 5 0
2017–18 Liverpool 3 0
2017–18 *Cardiff C* 13 1 **13 1**
2018–19 Liverpool 0 0
2018–19 *Hertha Berlin* 22 5
2019–20 Liverpool 0 0
2019–20 *Hertha Berlin* 29 4 **51 9**
2020–21 Liverpool 0 0 **8 0**
2020–21 *Porto* 23 2 **23 2**

HENDERSON, Jordan (M) **371 32**
H: 6 0 W: 10 07 b.Sunderland 17-6-90
Internationals: England U19, U20, U21, Full caps.
2008–09 Sunderland 1 0
2008–09 *Coventry C* 10 1 **10 1**
2009–10 Sunderland 33 1
2010–11 Sunderland 37 3 **71 4**
2011–12 Liverpool 37 2
2012–13 Liverpool 30 5
2013–14 Liverpool 35 4
2014–15 Liverpool 37 6
2015–16 Liverpool 17 2
2016–17 Liverpool 24 1
2017–18 Liverpool 27 1
2018–19 Liverpool 32 1
2019–20 Liverpool 30 4
2020–21 Liverpool 21 1 **290 27**

HUGHES, Liam (G) **0 0**
From Portadown, Dungannon Swifts, Celtic.
2020–21 Liverpool 0 0

JAROS, Vitezslav (G) **0 0**
b.Pribram 23-7-01
From Slavia Prague.
2020–21 Liverpool 0 0

JOHNSTON, George (D) **26 1**
b.Manchester 1-9-98
2019–20 Feyenoord 0 0
2020–21 Feyenoord 4 0 **4 0**
2020–21 Liverpool 0 0
2020–21 *Wigan Ath* 22 1 **22 1**

JONES, Curtis (M) **30 2**
b. 30-1-01
Internationals: England U16, U17, U18, U19.
2017–18 Liverpool 0 0
2018–19 Liverpool 0 0
2019–20 Liverpool 6 1
2020–21 Liverpool 24 1 **30 2**

JOTA, Diogo (F) **198 64**
H: 5 10 W: 11 00 b.Massarelos 4-12-96
Internationals: Portugal U19, U21, U23, Full caps.
2014–15 Pacos Ferreira 10 2
2015–16 Pacos Ferreira 31 12 **41 14**
2016–17 Atletico Madrid 0 0
2016–17 *Porto* 27 8 **27 8**
2017–18 Atletico Madrid 0 0
2017–18 *Wolverhampton W* 44 17
2018–19 Wolverhampton W 33 9
2019–20 Wolverhampton W 34 7 **111 33**
2020–21 Liverpool 19 9 **19 9**

KABAK, Ozan (D) **78 6**
b.Ankara 25-3-00
2017–18 Galatasaray 1 0
2018–19 Galatasaray 13 0 **14 0**
2018–19 VfB Stuttgart 15 3 **15 3**
2019–20 Schalke 04 26 3
2020–21 Schalke 04 14 0 **40 3**
On loan from Schalke 04.
2020–21 Liverpool 9 0 **9 0**

KEITA, Naby (M) **193 39**
H: 5 8 W: 10 01 b.Conakry 10-2-95
Internationals: Guinea Full caps.
2013–14 Istres 23 4 **23 4**
2014–15 Red Bull Salzburg 30 5
2015–16 Red Bull Salzburg 29 12 **59 17**
2016–17 RB Leipzig 31 8
2017–18 RB Leipzig 27 6 **58 14**
2018–19 Liverpool 25 2
2019–20 Liverpool 18 2
2020–21 Liverpool 10 0 **53 4**

KELLEHER, Caoimhin (G) **2 0**
H: 5 11 b.Cork 23-11-98
Internationals: Republic of Ireland U17, U19, U21.
2018–19 Liverpool 0 0
2019–20 Liverpool 0 0
2020–21 Liverpool 2 0 **2 0**

KOURMETIO, Billy (D) **0 0**
b. 14-11-02
From Lyon, Orleans.
2019–20 Liverpool 0 0
2020–21 Liverpool 0 0

LAROUCI, Yasser (D) **0 0**
H: 5 9 W: 10 12 b.El Oued 1-1-01
From Le Havre.
2020–21 Liverpool 0 0

LEWIS, Adam (D) **29 1**
b.Liverpool 8-11-99
Internationals: England U16, U17, U19, U20.
2019–20 Liverpool 0 0
2020–21 Liverpool 0 0
2020–21 *Amiens* 9 0 **9 0**
2020–21 *Plymouth Arg* 20 1 **20 1**

MANE, Sadio (F) **314 128**
H: 5 9 W: 12 00 b.Sedhiou 10-4-92
Internationals: Senegal U23, Full caps.
2011–12 Metz 19 1
2012–13 Metz 3 1 **22 2**
2012–13 Red Bull Salzburg 26 16
2013–14 Red Bull Salzburg 33 13
2014–15 Red Bull Salzburg 4 2 **63 31**
2014–15 Southampton 30 10
2015–16 Southampton 37 11 **67 21**
2016–17 Liverpool 27 13
2017–18 Liverpool 29 10
2018–19 Liverpool 36 22
2019–20 Liverpool 35 18
2020–21 Liverpool 35 11 **162 74**

MARCELO (G) **0 0**
H: 6 3 b.Niteroi 20-12-02
Internationals: Brazil U17.
From Fluminese.
2020–21 Liverpool 0 0

MATIP, Joel (M) **289 19**
H: 6 4 W: 13 01 b.Bochum 8-8-91
Internationals: Cameroon Full caps.
2009–10 Schalke 04 20 3
2010–11 Schalke 04 26 0
2011–12 Schalke 04 30 3
2012–13 Schalke 04 32 0
2013–14 Schalke 04 31 3
2014–15 Schalke 04 21 2
2015–16 Schalke 04 34 3 **194 14**
2016–17 Liverpool 29 1
2017–18 Liverpool 25 1
2018–19 Liverpool 22 1
2019–20 Liverpool 9 1
2020–21 Liverpool 10 1 **95 5**

MILLAR, Liam (F) **60 4**
b. 27-9-99
Internationals: Canada U20, U23, Full caps.
2018–19 Liverpool 0 0
2018–19 *Kilmarnock* 13 1
2019–20 Liverpool 0 0
2019–20 *Kilmarnock* 20 1 **33 2**
2020–21 Liverpool 0 0
2020–21 *Charlton Ath* 27 2 **27 2**

MILNER, James (M) **570 57**
H: 5 9 W: 11 00 b.Leeds 4-1-86
Internationals: England U16, U17, U19, U20, U21, Full caps.
2002–03 Leeds U 18 2
2003–04 Leeds U 30 3 **48 5**
2003–04 *Swindon T* 6 2 **6 2**
2004–05 Newcastle U 25 1
2005–06 Newcastle U 3 0
2005–06 *Aston Villa* 27 1
2006–07 Newcastle U 35 3
2007–08 Newcastle U 29 2
2008–09 Newcastle U 2 0 **94 6**
2008–09 Aston Villa 36 3
2009–10 Aston Villa 36 7
2010–11 Aston Villa 1 1 **100 12**
2010–11 Manchester C 32 0
2011–12 Manchester C 26 3
2012–13 Manchester C 26 4
2013–14 Manchester C 31 1
2014–15 Manchester C 32 5 **147 13**
2015–16 Liverpool 28 5
2016–17 Liverpool 36 7
2017–18 Liverpool 32 0
2018–19 Liverpool 31 5
2019–20 Liverpool 22 2
2020–21 Liverpool 26 0 **175 19**

MINAMINO, Takumi (F) 227 52
b. 16-1-95
Internationals: Japan U17, U20, U23, Full caps.
2012 Cerezo Osaka 3 0
2013 Cerezo Osaka 29 5
2014 Cerezo Osaka 30 2 **62 7**
2014–15 Red Bull Salzburg 14 3
2015–16 Red Bull Salzburg 32 10
2016–17 Red Bull Salzburg 21 11
2017–18 Red Bull Salzburg 28 7
2018–19 Red Bull Salzburg 27 6
2019–20 Red Bull Salzburg 14 5 **136 42**
2019–20 Liverpool 10 0
2020–21 Liverpool 9 1 **19 1**
2020–21 *Southampton* 10 2 **10 2**

MORTON, Tyler (M) 0 0
H: 5 10 b.Wirral 31-10-02
2020–21 Liverpool 0 0

O'ROURKE, Fidel (F) 0 0
b.Liverpool 5-2-02
Internationals: England U16.
2020–21 Liverpool 0 0

OJO, Sheyi (M) 133 12
H: 5 10 W: 10 01 b.Hemel Hempstead 19-6-97
Internationals: England U16, U17, U18, U19, U20, U21.
2014–15 Liverpool 0 0
2014–15 *Wigan Ath* 11 0 **11 0**
2015–16 Liverpool 8 0
2015–16 *Wolverhampton W* 17 2 **17 2**
2016–17 Liverpool 0 0
2017–18 Liverpool 0 0
2017–18 *Fulham* 22 4 **22 4**
2018–19 Liverpool 0 0
2018–19 *Reims* 15 0 **15 0**
2019–20 Liverpool 0 0
2019–20 *Rangers* 19 1 **19 1**
2020–21 Liverpool 0 0 **8 0**
2020–21 *Cardiff C* 41 5 **41 5**

OJRZYNSKI, Jakub (G) 0 0
b. 19-2-03
From Korona, Legia Warsaw.
2020–21 Liverpool 0 0

ORIGI, Divock (F) 204 39
H: 6 1 W: 11 11 b.Oostende 18-4-95
Internationals: Belgium U16, U17, U19, U21, Full caps.
From Genk.
2012–13 Lille 10 1
2013–14 Lille 30 5
2014–15 Lille 33 8 **73 14**
2015–16 Liverpool 16 5
2016–17 Liverpool 34 7
2017–18 Liverpool 1 0
2017–18 *Wolfsburg* 31 6 **31 6**
2018–19 Liverpool 12 3
2019–20 Liverpool 28 4
2020–21 Liverpool 9 0 **100 19**

OXLADE-CHAMBERLAIN, Alex (M) 245 26
H: 5 11 W: 11 00 b.Portsmouth 15-8-93
Internationals: England U18, U19, U21, Full caps.
2009–10 Southampton 2 0
2010–11 Southampton 34 9 **36 9**
2011–12 Arsenal 16 2
2012–13 Arsenal 25 1
2013–14 Arsenal 14 2
2014–15 Arsenal 23 1
2015–16 Arsenal 22 1
2016–17 Arsenal 29 2
2017–18 Arsenal 3 0 **132 9**
2017–18 Liverpool 32 3
2018–19 Liverpool 2 0
2019–20 Liverpool 30 4
2020–21 Liverpool 13 1 **77 8**

PHILLIPS, Nathaniel (D) 36 1
b.Bolton 21-3-97
2019–20 Liverpool 0 0
2019–20 *Stuttgart* 19 0 **19 0**
2020–21 Liverpool 17 1 **17 1**

QUANSAH, Jarell (D) 0 0
b.Warrington 29-1-03
Internationals: England U16, U17, U18.
2020–21 Liverpool 0 0

RITACCIO, Matteo (M) 0 0
b.Westbury, New York 4-10-01
Internationals: USA U20.
2020–21 Liverpool 0 0

ROBERTSON, Andrew (D) 301 12
H: 5 10 W: 10 00 b.Glasgow 11-3-94
Internationals: Scotland U21, Full caps.
2012–13 Queen's Park 34 2 **34 2**
2013–14 Dundee U 36 3 **36 3**
2014–15 Hull C 24 0
2015–16 Hull C 42 2
2016–17 Hull C 33 1 **99 3**
2017–18 Liverpool 22 1
2018–19 Liverpool 36 0
2019–20 Liverpool 36 2
2020–21 Liverpool 38 1 **132 4**

SALAH, Mohamed (M) 324 152
H: 5 9 W: 11 04 b.Basion 15-6-92
Internationals: Egypt U20, U23, Full caps.
2009–10 Al-Mokawloon 3 0
2010–11 Al-Mokawloon 20 4
2011–12 Al-Mokawloon 15 7 **38 11**
2012–13 Basel 29 5
2013–14 Basel 18 4 **47 9**
2013–14 Chelsea 10 2
2014–15 Chelsea 3 0
2014–15 *Fiorentina* 16 6 **16 6**
2015–16 Chelsea 0 0 **13 2**
2015–16 *Roma* 34 14
2016–17 Roma 31 15 **65 29**
2017–18 Liverpool 36 32
2018–19 Liverpool 38 22
2019–20 Liverpool 34 19
2020–21 Liverpool 37 22 **145 95**

SAVAGE, Remi (D) 0 0
b.Liverpool 26-10-01
2020–21 Liverpool 0 0

SHAQIRI, Xherdan (M) 288 52
H: 5 7 W: 11 05 b.Gnjilane 10-10-91
Internationals: Switzerland U17, U18, U19, U21, Full caps.
2009–10 Basel 32 4
2010–11 Basel 29 5
2011–12 Basel 31 9 **92 18**
2012–13 Bayern Munich 26 4
2013–14 Bayern Munich 17 6
2014–15 Bayern Munich 9 1 **52 11**
2014–15 Inter Milan 15 1 **15 1**
2015–16 Stoke C 27 3
2016–17 Stoke C 21 4
2017–18 Stoke C 36 8 **84 15**
2018–19 Liverpool 24 6
2019–20 Liverpool 7 1
2020–21 Liverpool 14 0 **45 7**

THIAGO, Alcantara (M) 242 25
b.San Pietro Vernotico, Italy 11-4-91
2007–08 Barcelona 0 0
2008–09 Barcelona 1 0
2009–10 Barcelona 1 1
2010–11 Barcelona 12 2
2011–12 Barcelona 27 2
2012–13 Barcelona 27 2 **68 7**
2013–14 Bayern Munich 16 2
2014–15 Bayern Munich 7 0
2015–16 Bayern Munich 27 2
2016–17 Bayern Munich 27 6
2017–18 Bayern Munich 19 2
2018–19 Bayern Munich 30 2
2019–20 Bayern Munich 24 3
2020–21 Bayern Munich 0 0 **150 17**
2020–21 Liverpool 24 1 **24 1**

TSIMIKAS, Konstantinos (D) 57 2
b.Thessaloniki 12-5-96
2015–16 Olympiacos 3 0
2016–17 Olympiacos 1 0
2016–17 *Esbjerg* 9 2 **9 2**
2017–18 Olympiacos 0 0
2017–18 *Willem* 0 0
2018–19 Olympiacos 15 0
2019–20 Olympiacos 27 0
2020–21 Olympiacos 0 0 **46 0**
2020–21 Liverpool 2 0 **2 0**

VAN DEN BERG, Sepp (D) 38 0
b.Zwolle 20-12-01
Internationals: Netherlands U19.
2017–18 PEC Zwolle 7 0
2018–19 PEC Zwolle 15 0 **22 0**
2019–20 Liverpool 0 0
2020–21 Liverpool 0 0
2020–21 *Preston NE* 16 0 **16 0**

VAN DIJK, Virgil (D) 300 30
H: 6 4 W: 14 07 b.Breda 8-7-91
Internationals: Netherlands U19, U21, Full caps.
From Willem II.
2010–11 Groningen 5 2
2011–12 Groningen 23 3
2012–13 Groningen 34 2 **62 7**
2013–14 Celtic 36 5
2014–15 Celtic 35 4
2015–16 Celtic 5 0 **76 9**
2015–16 Southampton 34 3
2016–17 Southampton 21 1
2017–18 Southampton 12 0 **67 4**
2017–18 Liverpool 14 0
2018–19 Liverpool 38 4
2019–20 Liverpool 38 5
2020–21 Liverpool 5 1 **95 10**

WIJNALDUM, Georginio (M) 437 91
H: 5 8 W: 10 10 b.Rotterdam 11-11-90
Internationals: Netherlands U17, U19, U21, Full caps.
2006–07 Feyenoord 3 0
2007–08 Feyenoord 10 1
2008–09 Feyenoord 33 4
2009–10 Feyenoord 31 4
2010–11 Feyenoord 34 14 **111 23**
2011–12 PSV Eindhoven 32 9
2012–13 PSV Eindhoven 33 14
2013–14 PSV Eindhoven 11 4
2014–15 PSV Eindhoven 33 14 **109 41**
2015–16 Newcastle U 38 11 **38 11**
2016–17 Liverpool 36 6
2017–18 Liverpool 33 1
2018–19 Liverpool 35 3
2019–20 Liverpool 37 4
2020–21 Liverpool 38 2 **179 16**

WILLIAMS, Neco (D) 12 0
b. 13-4-01
Internationals: Wales U19.
2019–20 Liverpool 6 0
2020–21 Liverpool 6 0 **12 0**

WILLIAMS, Rhys (D) 9 0
b.Preston 3-2-01
2019–20 Liverpool 0 0
2020–21 Liverpool 9 0 **9 0**

WILSON, Harry (M) 128 36
H: 5 8 W: 11 00 b.Wrexham 22-3-97
Internationals: Wales U17, U19, U21, Full caps.
2015–16 Liverpool 0 0
2015–16 *Crewe Alex* 7 0 **7 0**
2016–17 Liverpool 0 0
2017–18 Liverpool 0 0
2017–18 *Hull C* 13 7 **13 7**
2018–19 Liverpool 0 0
2018–19 *Derby Co* 40 15 **40 15**
2019–20 Liverpool 0 0
2019–20 *Bournemouth* 31 7 **31 7**
2020–21 Liverpool 0 0
2020–21 *Cardiff C* 37 7 **37 7**

WOLTMAN, Max (F) 0 0
b. 20-8-03
2020–21 Liverpool 0 0

WOODBURN, Ben (F) 34 1
H: 5 9 W: 11 05 b.Chester 16-11-99
Internationals: Wales U16, U17, U19, Full caps.
2016–17 Liverpool 5 0
2017–18 Liverpool 1 0
2018–19 Liverpool 0 0
2018–19 *Sheffield U* 7 0 **7 0**
2019–20 Liverpool 0 0
2019–20 *Oxford U* 11 1 **11 1**
2020–21 Liverpool 0 0 **6 0**
2020–21 *Blackpool* 10 0 **10 0**

Scholars
Cannonier, Oakley William; Chambers, Luke; Davies, Harvey; Frauendorf, Melkamu Benjamin Daniel; Jonas, Lee; Kelly, Oscar George; Mrozek, Fabian; Musialowski, Mateusz Konrad.

LUTON T (48)

ADDY, TQ (F) 0 0
b.London 1-2-02
2020–21 Luton T 0 0

ADEBAYO, Elijah (D) 107 30
b.Brent 7-1-98
2017–18 Fulham 0 0
2017–18 *Cheltenham T* 7 2 **7 2**
2018–19 Fulham 0 0
2018–19 *Swindon T* 25 5 **25 5**
2018–19 *Stevenage* 2 0 **2 0**
2019–20 Walsall 30 8
2020–21 Walsall 25 10 **55 18**
2020–21 Luton T 18 5 **18 5**

BECKWITH, Sam (M) 0 0
2020–21 Luton T 0 0

BERRY, Luke (D) 232 43
H: 5 10 W: 11 05 b.Bassingbourn 12-7-92
From Cambridge U.
2014–15 Barnsley 31 1 **31 1**
2015–16 Cambridge U 46 12
2016–17 Cambridge U 45 17
2017–18 Cambridge U 3 0 **94 29**

2017–18 Luton T 34 7
2018–19 Luton T 21 3
2019–20 Luton T 21 1
2020–21 Luton T 31 2 **107 13**

BRADLEY, Sonny (D) 369 19
H: 6 0 W: 11 05 b.Hedon 14-6-92
2011–12 Hull C 2 0
2011–12 *Aldershot T* 14 0
2012–13 Hull C 0 0 **2 0**
2012–13 *Aldershot T* 42 1 **56 1**
2013–14 Portsmouth 33 2 **33 2**
2014–15 Crawley T 26 1
2015–16 Crawley T 46 1 **72 2**
2016–17 Plymouth Arg 44 7
2017–18 Plymouth Arg 40 4 **84 11**
2018–19 Luton T 45 0
2019–20 Luton T 40 3
2020–21 Luton T 37 0 **122 3**

BREE, James (D) 148 1
H: 5 10 W: 11 09 b.Wakefield 11-10-97
2013–14 Barnsley 1 0
2014–15 Barnsley 11 0
2015–16 Barnsley 19 0
2016–17 Barnsley 19 0 **50 0**
2016–17 Aston Villa 7 0
2017–18 Aston Villa 6 0
2018–19 Aston Villa 8 0
2018–19 *Ipswich T* 14 0 **14 0**
2019–20 Aston Villa 0 0 **21 0**
2019–20 *Luton T* 39 0
2020–21 Luton T 24 1 **63 1**

CLARK, Jordan (F) 252 26
H: 6 0 W: 11 07 b.Barnsley 22-9-93
2010–11 Barnsley 4 0
2011–12 Barnsley 2 0
2012–13 Barnsley 0 0
2012–13 *Chesterfield* 2 0 **2 0**
2013–14 Barnsley 0 0 **6 0**
2013–14 *Scunthorpe U* 1 0 **1 0**
2014–15 Shrewsbury T 27 3
2015–16 Shrewsbury T 20 2 **47 5**
2016–17 Accrington S 42 1
2017–18 Accrington S 43 8
2018–19 Accrington S 43 5
2019–20 Accrington S 34 6 **162 20**
2020–21 Luton T 34 1 **34 1**

COLLINS, James S (F) 472 165
H: 6 2 W: 13 08 b.Coventry 1-12-90
Internationals: Republic of Ireland U19, U21, Full caps.
2008–09 Aston Villa 0 0
2009–10 Aston Villa 0 0
2009–10 *Darlington* 7 2 **7 2**
2010–11 Aston Villa 0 0
2010–11 *Burton Alb* 10 4 **10 4**
2010–11 Shrewsbury T 24 8
2011–12 Shrewsbury T 42 14
2012–13 Swindon T 45 15 **45 15**
2013–14 Hibernian 36 6 **36 6**
2014–15 Shrewsbury T 45 15
2015–16 Shrewsbury T 23 5 **134 42**
2015–16 *Northampton T* 21 8 **21 8**
2016–17 Crawley T 45 20 **45 20**
2017–18 Luton T 42 19
2018–19 Luton T 44 25
2019–20 Luton T 46 14
2020–21 Luton T 42 10 **174 68**

CORNICK, Harry (F) 207 29
H: 5 11 W: 13 03 b.Poole 6-3-95
From Christchurch.
2013–14 Bournemouth 0 0
2014–15 Bournemouth 0 0
2015–16 Bournemouth 0 0
2015–16 *Yeovil T* 36 7 **36 7**
2016–17 Bournemouth 0 0
2016–17 *Leyton Orient* 11 1 **11 1**
2016–17 *Gillingham* 6 0 **6 0**
2017–18 Luton T 37 5
2018–19 Luton T 32 6
2019–20 Luton T 45 9
2020–21 Luton T 40 1 **154 21**

CRANIE, Martin (D) 407 4
H: 6 1 W: 12 09 b.Yeovil 23-9-86
Internationals: England U17, U18, U19, U20, U21.
2003–04 Southampton 1 0
2004–05 Southampton 3 0
2004–05 *Bournemouth* 3 0 **3 0**
2005–06 Southampton 11 0
2006–07 Southampton 1 0 **16 0**
2006–07 *Yeovil T* 12 0 **12 0**
2007–08 Portsmouth 2 0
2007–08 *QPR* 6 0 **6 0**
2008–09 Portsmouth 0 0
2008–09 *Charlton Ath* 19 0 **19 0**
2009–10 Portsmouth 0 0 **2 0**
2009–10 Coventry C 40 1
2010–11 Coventry C 36 0
2011–12 Coventry C 38 0 **114 1**
2012–13 Barnsley 36 0
2013–14 Barnsley 35 0
2014–15 Barnsley 39 1 **110 1**
2015–16 Huddersfield T 37 0
2016–17 Huddersfield T 14 0
2017–18 Huddersfield T 3 0 **54 0**
2017–18 Middlesbrough 9 0
2018–19 Middlesbrough 0 0 **9 0**
2018–19 Sheffield U 15 0 **15 0**
2019–20 Luton T 24 2
2020–21 Luton T 23 0 **47 2**

GALLOWAY, Brendon (M) 40 0
H: 6 2 W: 13 10 b.Zimbabwe 17-3-96
Internationals: England U17, U18, U19, U21.
2011–12 Milton Keynes D 1 0
2012–13 Milton Keynes D 1 0
2013–14 Milton Keynes D 8 0 **10 0**
2014–15 Everton 2 0
2015–16 Everton 15 0
2016–17 Everton 0 0
2016–17 *WBA* 3 0 **3 0**
2017–18 Everton 0 0
2017–18 *Sunderland* 7 0 **7 0**
2018–19 Everton 0 0 **17 0**
2019–20 Luton T 3 0
2020–21 Shrewsbury T 0 0
2020–21 Luton T 0 0 **3 0**

HYLTON, Danny (F) 394 111
H: 6 0 W: 11 13 b.Camden 25-2-89
2008–09 Aldershot T 29 5
2009–10 Aldershot T 21 3
2010–11 Aldershot T 33 5
2011–12 Aldershot T 44 13
2012–13 Aldershot T 27 4 **154 30**
2013–14 Rotherham U 1 0 **1 0**
2013–14 *Bury* 7 2 **7 2**
2013–14 *AFC Wimbledon* 17 3 **17 3**
2014–15 Oxford U 44 14
2015–16 Oxford U 41 12 **85 26**
2016–17 Luton T 39 21
2017–18 Luton T 39 21
2018–19 Luton T 25 8
2019–20 Luton T 11 0
2020–21 Luton T 16 0 **130 50**

ISTED, Harry (G) 0 0
b. 5-3-97
From Southampton, Stoke C.
2017–18 Luton T 0 0
2018–19 Luton T 0 0
2019–20 Luton T 0 0
2020–21 Luton T 0 0

JONES, Avan (D) 0 0
b.Luton 2-11-01
2020–21 Luton T 0 0

KIOSO, Peter (D) 35 6
b.Swords 15-8-99
From Milton Keynes D, Dunstable T, Hartlepool U.
2019–20 Luton T 1 0
2020–21 Bolton W 13 3 **13 3**
2020–21 Luton T 0 0 **1 0**
2020–21 *Northampton T* 21 3 **21 3**

LEE, Elliot (F) 153 36
H: 5 11 W: 11 05 b.Co. Durham 16-12-94
2011–12 West Ham U 0 0
2012–13 West Ham U 0 0
2013–14 West Ham U 1 0
2013–14 *Colchester U* 4 1
2014–15 West Ham U 1 0
2014–15 *Southend U* 0 0
2014–15 *Luton T* 11 3
2015–16 West Ham U 0 0 **2 0**
2015–16 *Blackpool* 4 0 **4 0**
2015–16 *Colchester U* 15 2 **19 3**
2016–17 Barnsley 6 0 **6 0**
2017–18 Luton T 32 10
2018–19 Luton T 38 12
2019–20 Luton T 11 1
2020–21 Luton T 12 1 **104 27**
2020–21 *Oxford U* 18 6 **18 6**

LOCKYER, Tom (D) 274 6
H: 6 0 W: 11 05 b.Bristol 30-12-94
Internationals: Wales U21, Full caps.
2012–13 Bristol R 4 0
2013–14 Bristol R 41 1
2015–16 Bristol R 43 0
2016–17 Bristol R 46 0
2017–18 Bristol R 37 1
2018–19 Bristol R 40 3 **211 5**
2019–20 Charlton Ath 43 1 **43 1**
2020–21 Luton T 20 0 **20 0**

LUALUA, Kazenga (F) 269 25
H: 5 11 W: 12 00 b.Kinshasa 10-12-90
2007–08 Newcastle U 2 0
2008–09 Newcastle U 3 0
2008–09 *Doncaster R* 4 0 **4 0**
2009–10 Newcastle U 1 0
2009–10 *Brighton & HA* 11 0
2010–11 Newcastle U 2 0
2010–11 *Brighton & HA* 11 4
2011–12 Newcastle U 0 0 **8 0**
2011–12 Brighton & HA 27 1
2012–13 Brighton & HA 22 5
2013–14 Brighton & HA 32 1
2014–15 Brighton & HA 34 3
2015–16 Brighton & HA 18 3
2016–17 Brighton & HA 3 0
2016–17 *QPR* 11 1
2017–18 Brighton & HA 0 0 **158 17**
2017–18 *QPR* 8 0 **19 1**
2017–18 Sunderland 6 0 **6 0**
2018–19 Luton T 22 2
2019–20 Luton T 29 3
2020–21 Luton T 23 2 **74 7**

McJANNET, Edward (F) 0 0
2020–21 Luton T 0 0

MONCUR, George (M) 240 40
H: 5 9 W: 10 00 b.Swindon 18-8-93
Internationals: England U18.
2010–11 West Ham U 0 0
2011–12 West Ham U 0 0
2011–12 *AFC Wimbledon* 20 2 **20 2**
2012–13 West Ham U 0 0
2013–14 West Ham U 0 0
2013–14 *Partick Thistle* 2 1 **2 1**
2014–15 Colchester U 41 8
2015–16 Colchester U 45 12 **86 20**
2016–17 Peterborough U 13 2 **13 2**
2016–17 Barnsley 12 2
2017–18 Barnsley 34 2
2018–19 Barnsley 21 1 **67 5**
2018–19 Luton T 14 6
2019–20 Luton T 17 1
2020–21 Luton T 21 3 **52 10**

MORRELL, Joe (M) 78 3
H: 5 3 W: 11 04 b.Ipswich 3-1-97
Internationals: Wales U17, U19, U21, Full caps.
2013–14 Bristol C 0 0
2014–15 Bristol C 0 0
2015–16 Bristol C 0 0
2016–17 Bristol C 0 0
2017–18 Bristol C 0 0
2017–18 *Cheltenham T* 38 3 **38 3**
2018–19 Bristol C 1 0
2019–20 Bristol C 0 0 **1 0**
2019–20 *Lincoln C* 29 0 **29 0**
2020–21 Luton T 10 0 **10 0**

NAISMITH, Kal (F) 294 42
H: 5 7 W: 13 02 b.Glasgow 18-2-92
Internationals: Scotland U16, U17.
2011–12 Rangers 0 0
2011–12 *Cowdenbeath* 9 2 **9 2**
2011–12 *Partick Thistle* 8 0 **8 0**
2012–13 Rangers 17 1 **17 1**
2013–14 Accrington S 38 10
2014–15 Accrington S 35 4 **73 14**
2015–16 Portsmouth 19 3
2015–16 *Hartlepool U* 4 0 **4 0**
2016–17 Portsmouth 37 13
2017–18 Portsmouth 26 2 **82 18**
2018–19 Wigan Ath 30 1
2019–20 Wigan Ath 37 3
2020–21 Wigan Ath 12 2 **79 6**
2020–21 Luton T 22 1 **22 1**

OSHO, Gabriel (D) 29 1
b.Reading 14-8-98
2018–19 Reading 2 0
2019–20 Reading 5 0 **7 0**
2020–21 Luton T 0 0
2020–21 *Rochdale* 22 1 **22 1**

PEARSON, Matthew (D) 243 21
H: 6 3 W: 11 05 b.Keighley 3-8-93
Internationals: England U18, C.
2011–12 Blackburn R 0 0
2012–13 Rochdale 9 0
2013–14 Rochdale 0 0 **9 0**
From FC Halifax T.
2015–16 Accrington S 46 3
2016–17 Accrington S 43 8 **89 11**
2017–18 Barnsley 17 0 **17 0**
2018–19 Luton T 46 6
2019–20 Luton T 42 2
2020–21 Luton T 40 2 **128 10**

PEREIRA, Dion (M) 21 0
b.Watford 25-3-99
2016–17 Watford 2 0

2017–18 Watford 0 0
2018–19 Watford 0 0 **2 0**
2019 Atalanta U 18 0 **18 0**
2020–21 Luton T 1 0 **1 0**

POTTS, Danny (D) 175 9
H: 5 8 W: 11 00 b.Barking 13-4-94
Internationals: USA U20. England U18, U19, U20.
2011–12 West Ham U 3 0
2012–13 West Ham U 2 0
2012–13 *Colchester U* 5 0 **5 0**
2013–14 West Ham U 0 0
2013–14 *Portsmouth* 5 0 **5 0**
2014–15 West Ham U 0 0 **5 0**
2015–16 Luton T 14 0
2016–17 Luton T 23 0
2017–18 Luton T 42 6
2018–19 Luton T 24 1
2019–20 Luton T 33 1
2020–21 Luton T 24 1 **160 9**

REA, Glen (D) 186 7
H: 6 0 W: 11 07 b.Brighton 3-9-94
Internationals: Republic of Ireland U21.
2013–14 Brighton & HA 0 0
2014–15 Brighton & HA 0 0
2015–16 Brighton & HA 0 0
2015–16 *Southend U* 14 0 **14 0**
2015–16 *Luton T* 10 0
2016–17 Luton T 39 2
2017–18 Luton T 46 1
2018–19 Luton T 22 1
2019–20 Luton T 15 0
2020–21 Luton T 40 3 **172 7**

RUDDOCK, Pelly (M) 241 17
H: 5 9 W: 9 13 b.Hendon 17-7-93
2011–12 West Ham U 0 0
2012–13 West Ham U 0 0
2013–14 West Ham U 0 0
2014–15 Luton T 16 1
2015–16 Luton T 21 2
2016–17 Luton T 42 2
2017–18 Luton T 28 2
2018–19 Luton T 46 5
2019–20 Luton T 44 3
2020–21 Luton T 44 2 **241 17**

SHEA, James (G) 165 0
H: 5 11 W: 12 00 b.Islington 16-6-91
2009–10 Arsenal 0 0
2010–11 Arsenal 0 0
2011–12 Arsenal 0 0
2011–12 *Dagenham & R* 1 0 **1 0**
2012–13 Arsenal 0 0
2013–14 Arsenal 0 0
2014–15 AFC Wimbledon 38 0
2015–16 AFC Wimbledon 21 0
2016–17 AFC Wimbledon 36 0 **95 0**
2017–18 Luton T 8 0
2018–19 Luton T 41 0
2019–20 Luton T 13 0
2020–21 Luton T 7 0 **69 0**

SLUGA, Simon (G) 193 0
b. 17-3-93
2013–14 Rijeka 0 0
2013–14 *Pomorac* 31 0 **31 0**
2014–15 Rijeka 0 0
2014–15 *Lokomotiva* 26 0 **26 0**
2015–16 Rijeka 2 0
2015–16 *Spezia* 0 0
2016–17 Rijeka 0 0
2017–18 Rijeka 27 0
2018–19 Rijeka 35 0 **64 0**
2019–20 Luton T 33 0
2020–21 Luton T 39 0 **72 0**

TUNNICLIFFE, Ryan (M) 260 11
H: 6 0 W: 14 02 b.Bury 30-12-92
Internationals: England U16, U17.
2009–10 Manchester U 0 0
2010–11 Manchester U 0 0
2011–12 Manchester U 0 0
2011–12 *Peterborough U* 27 0 **27 0**
2012–13 Manchester U 0 0
2012–13 *Barnsley* 2 0 **2 0**
2013–14 Manchester U 0 0
2013–14 *Ipswich T* 27 0 **27 0**
2013–14 Fulham 3 0
2013–14 *Wigan Ath* 5 0
2014–15 Fulham 22 0
2014–15 *Blackburn R* 17 1 **17 1**
2015–16 Fulham 27 2
2016–17 Fulham 7 0 **59 2**
2016–17 *Wigan Ath* 9 1 **14 1**
2017–18 Millwall 24 1
2018–19 Millwall 26 3 **50 4**
2019–20 Luton T 40 1
2020–21 Luton T 24 2 **64 3**

Scholars
Allen, Joshua Richard Charles; Corbit, Edward Leigh; Cowler, Jacob Mackenzie; Francis-Clarke, Aidan; Halsey, Joseph Zak Jake; Horlick, Jameson Edward Alexander; Lucas, Tra; Moloney, Matthew Thomas; Newton, Tyrelle Benjamin; Nicolson, Callum Andrew; Pettit, Casey Anthony; Stevens, Ben Charles; Swan, Joshua Leigh; Tompkins, Ben Joseph; Wedd, Adam John; Wilson, Coree Jason.

MANCHESTER C (49)

AGUERO, Sergio (F) 504 281
H: 5 8 W: 11 09 b.Buenos Aires 2-6-88
Internationals: Argentina U17, U20, U23, Full caps.
2002–03 Independiente 1 0
2003–04 Independiente 5 0
2004–05 Independiente 12 5
2005–06 Independiente 36 18 **54 23**
2006–07 Atletico Madrid 38 6
2007–08 Atletico Madrid 37 19
2008–09 Atletico Madrid 37 17
2009–10 Atletico Madrid 31 12
2010–11 Atletico Madrid 32 20 **175 74**
2011–12 Manchester C 34 23
2012–13 Manchester C 30 12
2013–14 Manchester C 23 17
2014–15 Manchester C 33 26
2015–16 Manchester C 30 24
2016–17 Manchester C 31 20
2017–18 Manchester C 25 21
2018–19 Manchester C 33 21
2019–20 Manchester C 24 16
2020–21 Manchester C 12 4 **275 184**
Transferred to Barcelona July 2021.

AKE, Nathan (M) 161 13
H: 5 11 W: 11 01 b.Den Haag 18-2-95
Internationals: Netherlands U15, U16, U17, U19, U21, Full caps.
From Feyenoord.
2012–13 Chelsea 3 0
2013–14 Chelsea 1 0
2014–15 Chelsea 1 0
2014–15 *Reading* 5 0 **5 0**
2015–16 Chelsea 0 0
2015–16 *Watford* 24 1 **24 1**
2016–17 Chelsea 2 0 **7 0**
2016–17 *Bournemouth* 10 3
2017–18 Bournemouth 38 2
2018–19 Bournemouth 38 4
2019–20 Bournemouth 29 2 **115 11**
2020–21 Manchester C 10 1 **10 1**

AMANKWAH, Yeboah (D) 0 0
b.London 19-10-20
2019–20 Manchester C 0 0
2020–21 Manchester C 0 0
2020–21 *Rochdale* 0 0

AMINU, Mohammed (F) 0 0
H: 5 9 b. 10-8-00
Internationals: Ghana U17.
2020–21 Manchester C 0 0

BAZUNU, Gavin (G) 29 0
b.Dublin 20-2-02
From Shamrock R.
2019–20 Manchester C 0 0
2020–21 Manchester C 0 0
2020–21 *Rochdale* 29 0 **29 0**

BERNABE, Adrian (M) 0 0
b. 26-5-01
Internationals: Spain U17.
From Espanyol, Barcelona.
2018–19 Manchester C 0 0
2019–20 Manchester C 0 0
2020–21 Manchester C 0 0

BERNARDO SILVA, Mota (M) 233 45
H: 5 8 W: 9 11 b.Lisbon 10-8-94
Internationals: Portugal U19, U21, Full caps.
2013–14 Benfica 1 0 **1 0**
2014–15 Monaco 32 9
2015–16 Monaco 32 7
2016–17 Monaco 37 8 **101 24**
2017–18 Manchester C 35 6
2018–19 Manchester C 36 7
2019–20 Manchester C 34 6
2020–21 Manchester C 26 2 **131 21**

BOBB, Oscar (M) 0 0
b.Oslo 12-7-03
Internationals: Norway U16, U17, U18.
From Valerenga.
2020–21 Manchester C 0 0

BRAAF, Jayden (F) 4 1
H: 5 10 W: 10 03 b.Amsterdam 31-8-02
Internationals: Netherlands U17, U18.
2020–21 Manchester C 0 0
2020–21 *Udinese* 4 1 **4 1**

BRAVO, Claudio (G) 421 2
H: 6 0 W: 11 00 b.Viluco 13-4-83
Internationals: Chile U23, Full caps.
2003 Colo Colo 25 1
2004 Colo Colo 18 0
2005 Colo Colo 36 0
2006 Colo Colo 14 0 **93 1**
2006–07 Real Sociedad 29 0
2007–08 Real Sociedad 0 0
2008–09 Real Sociedad 32 0
2009–10 Real Sociedad 25 1
2010–11 Real Sociedad 38 0
2011–12 Real Sociedad 37 0
2012–13 Real Sociedad 31 0
2013–14 Real Sociedad 37 0 **229 1**
2014–15 Barcelona 37 0
2015–16 Barcelona 32 0
2016–17 Barcelona 1 0 **70 0**
2016–17 Manchester C 22 0
2017–18 Manchester C 3 0
2018–19 Manchester C 0 0
2019–20 Manchester C 4 0
2020–21 Manchester C 0 0 **29 0**
Transferred to Real Betis August 2020.

BURNS, Finley (D) 0 0
b.Southwark 17-6-03
Internationals: England U16, U17.
2020–21 Manchester C 0 0

COUTO, Yan (D) 23 2
H: 5 6 b.Curitiba 3-6-02
Internationals: Brazil U17.
2020–21 Manchester C 0 0
2020–21 *Girona* 23 2 **23 2**

DE BRUYNE, Kevin (M) 362 81
H: 5 11 W: 12 00 b.Ghent 28-6-91
Internationals: Belgium U18, U19, U21, Full caps.
2008–09 Genk 2 0
2009–10 Genk 35 3
2010–11 Genk 32 5
2011–12 Genk 28 8 **97 16**
2011–12 Chelsea 0 0
2012–13 Chelsea 0 0
2012–13 *Werder Bremen* 33 10 **33 10**
2013–14 Chelsea 3 0 **3 0**
2013–14 Wolfsburg 16 3
2014–15 Wolfsburg 34 10
2015–16 Wolfsburg 2 0 **52 13**
2015–16 Manchester C 25 7
2016–17 Manchester C 36 6
2017–18 Manchester C 37 8
2018–19 Manchester C 19 2
2019–20 Manchester C 35 13
2020–21 Manchester C 25 6 **177 42**

DELAP, Liam (F) 1 0
b.Winchester 8-2-03
From Derby Co.
2020–21 Manchester C 1 0 **1 0**

DIAS, Ruben (D) 121 9
b.Amadora 14-5-97
2015–16 Benfica 0 0
2016–17 Benfica 0 0
2017–18 Benfica 24 3
2018–19 Benfica 32 3
2019–20 Benfica 33 2
2020–21 Benfica 0 0 **89 8**
2020–21 Manchester C 32 1 **32 1**

DIONKOU, Alpha (D) 0 0
H: 6 0 W: 11 00 b.Sindone 10-10-01
Internationals: Spain U17. Senegal U20.
From Real Mallorca.
2020–21 Manchester C 0 0

DOYLE, Tommy (M) 1 0
b. 17-10-01
Internationals: England U16, U17, U18, U19.
2019–20 Manchester C 1 0
2020–21 Manchester C 0 0 **1 0**

EDERSON, de Moraes (G) 248 0
H: 6 2 W: 13 08 b.Osasco 17-8-93
Internationals: Brazil U23, Full caps.
2011–12 Ribeirao 29 0 **29 0**
2012–13 Rio Ave 2 0
2013–14 Rio Ave 18 0
2014–15 Rio Ave 17 0 **37 0**
2015–16 Benfica 10 0
2016–17 Benfica 27 0 **37 0**
2017–18 Manchester C 36 0
2018–19 Manchester C 38 0

2019–20	Manchester C	35	0		
2020–21	Manchester C	36	0	**145**	**0**

EDOZIE, Samuel (F) **0 0**
H: 5 6 b.Lewisham 28-1-03
Internationals: England U18.
From Millwall.

2020–21	Manchester C	0	0

EGAN-RILEY, CJ (D) **0 0**
H: 6 0 W: 11 00 b.Manchester 2-1-03
Internationals: Republic of Ireland U16. England U16, U17, U18.

2020–21	Manchester C	0	0

FERNANDINHO, Luis (M) **500 63**
H: 5 10 W: 10 09 b.Londrina 4-5-85
Internationals: Brazil Full caps.

2003	Paranaense	29	5		
2004	Paranaense	41	9		
2005	Paranaense	2	0	**72**	**14**
2005–06	Shakhtar Donetsk	22	1		
2006–07	Shakhtar Donetsk	25	1		
2007–08	Shakhtar Donetsk	29	11		
2008–09	Shakhtar Donetsk	21	5		
2009–10	Shakhtar Donetsk	24	4		
2010–11	Shakhtar Donetsk	15	3		
2011–12	Shakhtar Donetsk	24	4		
2012–13	Shakhtar Donetsk	23	2	**183**	**31**
2013–14	Manchester C	33	5		
2014–15	Manchester C	33	3		
2015–16	Manchester C	33	2		
2016–17	Manchester C	32	2		
2017–18	Manchester C	34	5		
2018–19	Manchester C	29	1		
2019–20	Manchester C	30	0		
2020–21	Manchester C	21	0	**245**	**18**

FIORINI, Lewis (M) **32 5**
H: 5 10 b.Manchester 17-5-02
Internationals: Scotland U16, U17, U19.

2020–21	Manchester C	0	0		
2020–21	*NAC Breda*	32	5	**32**	**5**

FODEN, Phil (M) **69 15**
H: 5 7 W: 11 00 b. 28-5-00
Internationals: England U16, U17, U18, U19, U21.

2016–17	Manchester C	0	0		
2017–18	Manchester C	5	0		
2018–19	Manchester C	13	1		
2019–20	Manchester C	23	5		
2020–21	Manchester C	28	9	**69**	**15**

GABRIEL JESUS, Fernando (F) **178 66**
b. 3-4-97
Internationals: Brazil U20, U23, Full caps.

2015	Palmeiras	20	4		
2016	Palmeiras	27	12	**47**	**16**
2016–17	Manchester C	10	7		
2017–18	Manchester C	29	13		
2018–19	Manchester C	29	7		
2019–20	Manchester C	34	14		
2020–21	Manchester C	29	9	**131**	**50**

GARCIA, Eric (D) **19 0**
H: 6 0 b.Barcelona 9-1-01
Internationals: Spain U17, U19, U21.
From Barcelona.

2018–19	Manchester C	0	0		
2019–20	Manchester C	13	0		
2020–21	Manchester C	6	0	**19**	**0**

Transferred to Barcelona July 2021.

GBADEBO, Camron (D) **0 0**
b.Lambeth 1-7-02
From Leicester C.

2020–21	Manchester C	0	0

GOMES, Claudio (M) **0 0**
H: 5 11 W: 11 00 b.Argenteuil 23-7-00
Internationals: France U16, U17, U18, U19, U20.

2017–18	Paris Saint-Germain	0	0
2018–19	Manchester C	0	0
2019–20	Manchester C	0	0
2019–20	*PSV Eindhoven*	0	0
2020–21	Manchester C	0	0

GUNDOGAN, Ilkay (M) **283 44**
H: 5 11 W: 11 00 b.Gelsenkirchen 24-10-90
Internationals: Germany U18, U19, U20, U21, Full caps.

2008–09	Bochum	0	0		
2008–09	Nuremburg	1	0		
2009–10	Nuremburg	22	1		
2010–11	Nuremburg	25	5	**48**	**6**
2011–12	Borussia Dortmund	28	3		
2012–13	Borussia Dortmund	28	3		
2013–14	Borussia Dortmund	1	0		
2014–15	Borussia Dortmund	23	3		
2015–16	Borussia Dortmund	25	1	**105**	**10**
2016–17	Manchester C	10	3		
2017–18	Manchester C	30	4		
2018–19	Manchester C	31	6		
2019–20	Manchester C	31	2		
2020–21	Manchester C	28	13	**130**	**28**

HARRISON, Jack (M) **178 32**
b.Stoke-on-Trent 20-11-96
Internationals: England U21.

2016	New York C	21	4		
2017	New York C	34	10	**55**	**14**
2017–18	Manchester C	0	0		
2017–18	*Middlesbrough*	4	0	**4**	**0**
2018–19	Manchester C	0	0		
2018–19	*Leeds U*	37	4		
2019–20	Manchester C	0	0		
2019–20	*Leeds U*	46	6		
2020–21	Manchester C	0	0		
2020–21	*Leeds U*	36	8	**119**	**18**

HARWOOD-BELLIS, Taylor (D) **19 0**
b.Stockport 30-1-02
Internationals: England U16, U17, U19.

2019–20	Manchester C	0	0		
2020–21	Manchester C	0	0		
2020–21	*Blackburn R*	19	0	**19**	**0**

HERRERA, Yangel (M) **167 18**
H: 6 0 b.La Guaira 7-1-98
Internationals: Venezuela U17, U20, Full caps.

2014	Monagas	19	4		
2015	Monagas	16	5	**35**	**9**
2016	Atletico Venezuela	32	3	**32**	**3**
2017	*New York C*	20	1		
2017–18	Manchester C	0	0		
2018	*New York C*	18	0	**38**	**1**
2018–19	Manchester C	0	0		
2019–20	Manchester C	0	0		
2019–20	*Granada*	30	2		
2020–21	Manchester C	0	0		
2020–21	*Granada*	32	3	**62**	**5**

HODGE, Joseph (M) **0 0**
b. 14-9-02
Internationals: Republic of Ireland U16, U17, U19. England U16, U17.

2020–21	Manchester C	0	0

ITAKURA, Ko (D) **88 4**
H: 6 1 b.Yokohama 27-1-97
Internationals: Japan U16, U18, U19, U20, U21, U23, Full caps.

2015	Kawasaki Frontale	0	0		
2016	Kawasaki Frontale	2	0		
2017	Kawasaki Frontale	5	0		
2018	Kawasaki Frontale	0	0	**7**	**0**
2018	*Vegallta Sendai*	24	3	**24**	**3**
2018–19	Manchester C	0	0		
2018–19	*Groningen*	0	0		
2019–20	Manchester C	0	0		
2019–20	*Groningen*	22	0		
2020–21	Manchester C	0	0		
2020–21	*Groningen*	35	1	**57**	**1**

JOAO CANCELO, Cavaco (D) **171 6**
b.Barreiro 27-5-94
Internationals: Portugal U16, U17, U18, U19, U20, U21, Full caps.

2012–13	Benfica	0	0		
2013–14	Benfica	1	0		
2014–15	Benfica	0	0	**1**	**0**
2014–15	*Valencia*	10	0		
2015–16	Valencia	28	1		
2016–17	Valencia	35	1		
2017–18	Valencia	1	0	**74**	**2**
2017–18	*Inter Milan*	26	1	**26**	**1**
2018–19	Juventus	25	1		
2019–20	Juventus	0	0	**25**	**1**
2019–20	Manchester C	17	0		
2020–21	Manchester C	28	2	**45**	**2**

KABORE, Issa (D) **32 0**
b.Ouagadougou 12-5-01
Internationals: Burkina Faso U20, Full caps.

2019–20	Mechelen	5	0		
2019–20	Manchester C	0	0		
2020–21	Manchester C	0	0		
2020–21	*Mechelen*	27	0	**32**	**0**

KNIGHT, Ben (M) **0 0**
b.Cambridge 14-6-02
Internationals: England U16, U17, U18.
From Ipswich T.

2020–21	Manchester C	0	0

KNIGHT, Benjamin (F) **0 0**
b.Cambridge 14-6-02
Internationals: England U16, U17, U18.
From Ipswich T.

2020–21	Manchester C	0	0

LAPORTE, Aymeric (D) **269 13**
H: 6 2 W: 13 05 b.Agen 27-5-94
Internationals: France U17, U18, U19, U21.

2011–12	Basconia	33	2	**33**	**2**
2012–13	Athletic Bilbao	15	0		
2013–14	Athletic Bilbao	35	2		
2014–15	Athletic Bilbao	33	0		
2015–16	Athletic Bilbao	26	3		
2016–17	Athletic Bilbao	33	2		
2017–18	Athletic Bilbao	19	0	**161**	**7**
2017–18	Manchester C	9	0		
2018–19	Manchester C	35	3		
2019–20	Manchester C	15	1		
2020–21	Manchester C	16	0	**75**	**4**

MAHREZ, Riyad (M) **305 75**
H: 5 10 W: 9 10 b.Sarcelles 21-2-91
Internationals: Algeria Full caps.
From Quimper.

2011–12	Le Havre	9	0		
2012–13	Le Havre	34	4		
2013–14	Le Havre	17	2	**60**	**6**
2013–14	Leicester C	19	3		
2014–15	Leicester C	30	4		
2015–16	Leicester C	37	17		
2016–17	Leicester C	36	6		
2017–18	Leicester C	36	12	**158**	**42**
2018–19	Manchester C	27	7		
2019–20	Manchester C	33	11		
2020–21	Manchester C	27	9	**87**	**27**

MBETE-TABU, Luke (D) **0 0**
b.London 18-9-03

2020–21	Manchester C	0	0

McATEE, James (M) **0 0**
H: 6 2 b.Salford 18-10-02
Internationals: England U18.

2020–21	Manchester C	0	0

McDONALD, Rowan (D) **0 0**
H: 5 11 b.Oldham 20-10-01
Internationals: England U18.

2020–21	Manchester C	0	0

MENDY, Benjamin (D) **212 4**
H: 5 11 W: 11 05 b.Longjumeau 17-7-94
Internationals: France U16, U17, U18, U19, U21, Full caps.

2011–12	Le Havre	29	0		
2012–13	Le Havre	28	0	**57**	**0**
2013–14	Marseille	24	1		
2014–15	Marseille	33	0		
2015–16	Marseille	24	1	**81**	**2**
2016–17	Monaco	25	0	**25**	**0**
2017–18	Manchester C	7	0		
2018–19	Manchester C	10	0		
2019–20	Manchester C	19	0		
2020–21	Manchester C	13	2	**49**	**2**

MESHINO, Ryotaro (F) **56 9**
H: 5 7 b.Osaka 18-6-98
Internationals: Japan U23.

2017	Gamba Osaka	0	0		
2018	Gamba Osaka	11	0		
2019	Gamba Osaka	12	3	**23**	**3**
2019–20	Manchester C	0	0		
2019–20	*Hearts*	20	3	**20**	**3**
2020–21	Manchester C	0	0		
2020–21	*Rio Ave*	13	3	**13**	**3**

MORENO, Marlos (F) **119 12**
H: 5 7 b.Medellin 20-9-96
Internationals: Colombia U17, Full caps.

2014	Atletico Nacional	1	0		
2015	Atletico Nacional	17	5		
2016	Atletico Nacional	9	0	**27**	**5**
2016–17	Manchester C	0	0		
2016–17	*Deportivo La Coruna*	19	0	**19**	**0**
2017–18	Manchester C	0	0		
2017–18	*Girona*	2	0	**2**	**0**
2018–19	Manchester C	0	0		
2018–19	*Flamengo*	21	1	**21**	**1**
2018–19	*Santa Laguna*	11	1	**11**	**1**
2019–20	Manchester C	0	0		
2019–20	*Portimonense*	16	0	**16**	**0**
2020–21	Manchester C	0	0		
2020–21	*Lommel*	23	5	**23**	**5**

MORENO , Pablo (F) **0 0**
H: 5 11 b.Granada 3-5-02
Internationals: Spain U16, U17, U18.
From Juventus.

2020–21	Manchester C	0	0

NMECHA, Felix (M) **0 0**
b.Hamburg 10-10-00
Internationals: England U16, U18, U19. Germany U18

2018–19	Manchester C	0	0
2019–20	Manchester C	0	0
2020–21	Manchester C	0	0

OTAMENDI, Nicolas (D) **293 22**
H: 5 10 W: 11 09 b.Buenos Aires 12-2-88
Internationals: Argentina Full caps.

2007–08	Velez Sarsfield	1	0
2008–09	Velez Sarsfield	18	0

2009–10	Velez Sarsfield	19	1		
2010–11	Velez Sarsfield	2	0	**40**	**1**
2010–11	Porto	15	5		
2011–12	Porto	20	1		
2012–13	Porto	29	1		
2013–14	Porto	13	0	**77**	**7**
2013–14	*Atletico Mineiro*	5	0	**5**	**0**
2014–15	Valencia	35	6	**35**	**6**
2015–16	Manchester C	30	1		
2016–17	Manchester C	30	1		
2017–18	Manchester C	34	4		
2018–19	Manchester C	18	0		
2019–20	Manchester C	24	2		
2020–21	Manchester C	0	0	**136**	**8**

Transferred to Benfica October 2020.

PALAVERSA, Ante (M) 44 4
H: 6 2 b.Split 6-4-00
Internationals: Croatia U16, U17, U18, U19, U20.

2017–18	Hajduk Split	0	0		
2018–19	Hajduk Split	14	2	**14**	**2**
2019–20	Manchester C	0	0		
2019–20	*Oostende*	19	0	**19**	**0**
2020–21	Manchester C	0	0		
2020–21	*Getafe*	2	0	**2**	**0**
2020–21	*Kortrijk*	9	2	**9**	**2**

PALMER, Cole (M) 0 0
b. 6-5-02
Internationals: England U16, U17, U18.

2019–20	Manchester C	0	0		
2020–21	Manchester C	0	0		

PALMER-BROWN, Erik (D) 99 3
H: 6 1 b.Ohio 24-4-97
Internationals: USA U17, U18, U20, Full caps.

2013	Sporting Kansas C	0	0		
2014	Sporting Kansas C	3	0		
2015	Sporting Kansas C	7	0		
2016	Sporting Kansas C	0	0		
2017	Sporting Kansas C	10	0	**20**	**0**
2017–18	Manchester C	0	0		
2017–18	*Kortrijk*	9	0	**9**	**0**
2018–19	Manchester C	0	0		
2018–19	*NAC Breda*	18	1	**18**	**1**
2019–20	Manchester C	0	0		
2019–20	*Austria Vienna*	25	2		
2020–21	Manchester C	0	0		
2020–21	*Austria Vienna*	27	0	**52**	**2**

PORRO, Pedro (D) 85 9
H: 5 9 b.Don Benito 13-9-99
Internationals: Spain U21, Full caps.

2017–18	Peralada	5	3	**5**	**3**
2017–18	Girona	5	3		
2018–19	Girona	32	0	**37**	**3**
2019–20	Manchester C	0	0		
2019–20	*Real Valladolid*	13	0	**13**	**0**
2020–21	Manchester C	0	0		
2020–21	*Sporting Lisbon*	30	3	**30**	**3**

POZO, Iker (M) 28 3
H: 5 8 b.Fuengirola 6-8-00

2020–21	Manchester C	0	0		
2020–21	*PSV Eindhoven*	28	3	**28**	**3**

ROBERTS, Patrick (M) 131 17
H: 5 6 W: 10 06 b.Kingston upon Thames 5-2-97
Internationals: England U16, U17, U18, U19, U20.

2013–14	Fulham	2	0		
2014–15	Fulham	17	0	**19**	**0**
2015–16	Manchester C	1	0		
2015–16	*Celtic*	11	6		
2016–17	Manchester C	0	0		
2016–17	*Celtic*	32	9		
2017–18	Manchester C	0	0		
2017–18	*Celtic*	12	0	**55**	**15**
2018–19	Manchester C	0	0		
2018–19	*Girona*	19	0	**19**	**0**
2019–20	Manchester C	0	0		
2019–20	*Norwich C*	3	0	**3**	**0**
2019–20	*Middlesbrough*	10	1		
2020–21	Manchester C	0	0	**1**	**0**
2020–21	*Middlesbrough*	9	0	**19**	**1**
2020–21	*Derby Co*	15	1	**15**	**1**

ROBINSON, Sammy (D) 0 0
b.Cheltenham 9-1-02
Internationals: England U16, U17.

2020–21	Manchester C	0	0		

RODRI, Rodrigo Hernandez (M) 166 9
b.Madrid 22-6-96
Internationals: Spain U16, U19, U21, Full caps.

2014–15	Villareal	0	0		
2015–16	Villareal	3	0		
2016–17	Villareal	23	0		
2017–18	Villareal	37	1	**63**	**1**
2018–19	Atletico Madrid	34	3	**34**	**3**
2019–20	Manchester C	35	3		
2020–21	Manchester C	34	2	**69**	**5**

ROGERS, Morgan (M) 25 6
b.Halesowen 26-7-02
Internationals: England U16, U17, U18.

2018–19	WBA	0	0		
2019–20	Manchester C	0	0		
2020–21	Manchester C	0	0		
2020–21	*Lincoln C*	25	6	**25**	**6**

SLICKER, Cieran (G) 0 0
b.Oldham 15-9-02
Internationals: Scotland U17, U18, U21.

2020–21	Manchester C	0	0		

SMITH, Matthew (M) 84 3
b.Redditch 22-11-99
Internationals: Wales U17, U19, U21, Full caps.

2018–19	Manchester C	0	0		
2018–19	*FC Twente*	34	2	**34**	**2**
2019–20	Manchester C	0	0		
2019–20	*QPR*	8	0	**8**	**0**
2019–20	*Charlton Ath*	2	0	**2**	**0**
2020–21	Manchester C	0	0		
2020–21	*Doncaster R*	40	1	**40**	**1**

STEFFEN, Zackary (G) 103 0
b.Coatesville 2-4-95

2014–15	Frieburg	0	0		
2015–16	Frieburg	0	0		
2016	Columbus Crew	0	0		
2016	*Pittsburg Riverhounds*	9	0	**9**	**0**
2017	Columbus Crew	34	0		
2018	Columbus Crew	29	0		
2019	Columbus Crew	13	0	**76**	**0**
2019–20	Manchester C	0	0		
2019–20	*Fortuna Dusseldorf*	17	0	**17**	**0**
2020–21	Manchester C	1	0	**1**	**0**

STERLING, Raheem (F) 290 96
H: 5 7 W: 10 00 b.Kingston 8-12-94
Internationals: England U16, U17, U19, U21, Full caps.
From QPR.

2011–12	Liverpool	3	0		
2012–13	Liverpool	24	2		
2013–14	Liverpool	33	9		
2014–15	Liverpool	35	7	**95**	**18**
2015–16	Manchester C	31	6		
2016–17	Manchester C	33	7		
2017–18	Manchester C	33	18		
2018–19	Manchester C	34	17		
2019–20	Manchester C	33	20		
2020–21	Manchester C	31	10	**195**	**78**

STEVANOVIC, Filip (F) 56 11
H: 5 9 b.Arilje 25-9-02
Internationals: Serbia U16, U19, U21.

2018–19	Partizan Belgrade	4	0		
2019–20	Partizan Belgrade	25	7		
2020–21	Partizan Belgrade	27	4	**56**	**11**
2020–21	Manchester C	0	0		

STONES, John (D) 208 5
H: 6 2 W: 11 00 b.Barnsley 28-5-94
Internationals: England U19, U20, U21, Full caps.

2010–11	Barnsley	0	0		
2011–12	Barnsley	2	0		
2012–13	Barnsley	22	0	**24**	**0**
2012–13	Everton	0	0		
2013–14	Everton	21	0		
2014–15	Everton	23	1		
2015–16	Everton	33	0	**77**	**1**
2016–17	Manchester C	27	0		
2017–18	Manchester C	18	0		
2018–19	Manchester C	24	0		
2019–20	Manchester C	16	0		
2020–21	Manchester C	22	4	**107**	**4**

TARENSI, Oscar (D) 0 0
b. 10-1-03
From Espanyol.

2020–21	Manchester C	0	0		

TEDIC, Slobodan (F) 0 0
H: 6 3 b.Podorica 13-4-00
Internationals: Serbia, U17, U19, U21.
From Cukaricki.

2020–21	Manchester C	0	0		

TORRES, Ferran (M) 95 13
b.Foios 29-2-00

2016–17	Valencia	0	0		
2017–18	Valencia	13	0		
2018–19	Valencia	24	2		
2019–20	Valencia	34	4		
2020–21	Valencia	0	0	**71**	**6**
2020–21	Manchester C	24	7	**24**	**7**

TRAFFORD, James (G) 0 0
b. 10-10-02

2020–21	Manchester C	0	0		

WALKER, Kyle (D) 373 8
H: 5 10 W: 11 07 b.Sheffield 28-5-90
Internationals: England U19, U21, Full caps.

2008–09	Sheffield U	2	0		
2008–09	*Northampton T*	9	0	**9**	**0**
2009–10	Tottenham H	2	0		
2009–10	*Sheffield U*	26	0	**28**	**0**
2010–11	Tottenham H	1	0		
2010–11	*QPR*	20	0	**20**	**0**
2010–11	*Aston Villa*	15	1	**15**	**1**
2011–12	Tottenham H	37	2		
2012–13	Tottenham H	36	0		
2013–14	Tottenham H	26	1		
2014–15	Tottenham H	15	0		
2015–16	Tottenham H	33	1		
2016–17	Tottenham H	33	0	**183**	**4**
2017–18	Manchester C	32	0		
2018–19	Manchester C	33	1		
2019–20	Manchester C	29	1		
2020–21	Manchester C	24	1	**118**	**3**

WILSON-ESBRAND, Josh (D) 0 0
b.Hackney 26-12-02
Internationals: England U18.
From West Ham U.

2020–21	Manchester C	0	0		

ZINCHENKO, Alexander (M) 104 2
H: 5 9 W: 9 08 b.Radomyshi 15-12-96
Internationals: Ukraine U16, U17, U18, U19, U21, Full caps.

2014–15	Ufa	7	0		
2015–16	Ufa	24	2	**31**	**2**
2016–17	Manchester C	0	0		
2016–17	*PSV Eindhoven*	12	0	**12**	**0**
2017–18	Manchester C	8	0		
2018–19	Manchester C	14	0		
2019–20	Manchester C	19	0		
2020–21	Manchester C	20	0	**61**	**0**

Scholars
Adam, Josh; Awokoya-Mebude, Adedire Emmanuel; Breckin, Kian; Charles, Shea Emmanuel; Doyle, Callum Craig; Forbs Borges, Carlos Roberto; Griffiths, Harvey Lawson; Gyabi, Darko Boateng; Hamilton, Micah Philippe Jude; Larios Lopez, Juan; Lavia, Romeo; Mbete-Tabu, Luke; McNamara, Joshua Anthony; Nuamah Oduroh, Kwaku; Smith, Liam Kevin; Sodje, Taione Richard Evumena; Van Sas, Mikki Avelon Leander.

MANCHESTER U (50)

ALEX TELLES, Nicolao (D) 244 24
b.Caxias do Sul 15-12-92

2011	Juventide	4	1		
2012	Juventide	9	1	**13**	**2**
2013	Gremio	36	1	**36**	**1**
2013–14	Galatasaray	15	1		
2014–15	Galatasaray	22	1		
2015–16	Galatasaray	2	0	**39**	**2**
2015–16	*Inter Milan*	21	0	**21**	**0**
2016–17	Porto	32	1		
2017–18	Porto	30	3		
2018–19	Porto	33	4		
2019–20	Porto	31	11	**126**	**19**
2020–21	FC Porto	0	0		
2020–21	Manchester U	9	0	**9**	**0**

BAILLY, Eric (D) 106 1
H: 6 2 W: 12 02 b.Bingerville 12-4-94
Internationals: Ivory Coast Full caps.

2014–15	Espanyol	5	0	**5**	**0**
2014–15	Villareal	10	0		
2015–16	Villareal	25	0	**35**	**0**
2016–17	Manchester U	25	0		
2017–18	Manchester U	13	1		
2018–19	Manchester U	12	0		
2019–20	Manchester U	4	0		
2020–21	Manchester U	12	0	**66**	**1**

BERNARD, Di'shon (D) 30 2
b.London 14-10-00
From Chelsea.

2019–20	Manchester U	0	0		
2020–21	Manchester U	0	0		
2020–21	*Salford C*	30	2	**30**	**2**

BISHOP, Nathan (G) 31 0
H: 6 1 W: 11 05 b. 15-10-99
Internationals: England U20.

2016–17	Southend U	0	0		
2017–18	Southend U	1	0		
2018–19	Southend U	18	0		
2019–20	Southend U	12	0	**31**	**0**

2019–20	Manchester U	0	0		
2020–21	Manchester U	0	0		

BRUNO FERNANDES, Miguel (M) 276 84
b.Maia 8-9-94
Internationals: Portugal U19, U20, U21, U23, Full caps.

2012–13	Novara	23	4	**23**	**4**
2013–14	Udinese	24	4		
2014–15	Udinese	31	3		
2015–16	Udinese	31	3	**86**	**10**
2016–17	Sampdoria	33	5	**33**	**5**
2017–18	Sporting Lisbon	33	11		
2018–19	Sporting Lisbon	33	20		
2019–20	Sporting Lisbon	17	8	**83**	**39**
2019–20	Manchester U	14	8		
2020–21	Manchester U	37	18	**51**	**26**

CASTRO, Joel (G) 46 0
H: 6 2 W: 12 13 b. 28-6-96
Internationals: Switzerland U16, U17. Portugal U17, U18, U19, U20, U21.

2015–16	Manchester U	0	0		
2015–16	*Rochdale*	6	0	**6**	**0**
2016–17	Manchester U	1	0		
2016–17	*Belenenses*	8	0	**8**	**0**
2017–18	Manchester U	0	0		
2018–19	Manchester U	0	0		
2018–19	*Vitoria Setubal*	9	0	**9**	**0**
2018–19	*Kortrijk*	0	0		
2019–20	Manchester U	0	0		
2019–20	*Hearts*	20	0	**20**	**0**
2020–21	Manchester U	0	0	**1**	**0**
2020–21	*Huddersfield T*	2	0	**2**	**0**

CAVANI, Edinson (F) 464 269
b.Salto 14-2-87

2005–06	Danubio	10	4		
2006–07	Danubio	15	5	**25**	**9**
2006–07	Palermo	7	2		
2007–08	Palermo	33	5		
2008–09	Palermo	35	14		
2009–10	Palermo	34	13	**109**	**34**
2010–11	Napoli	35	26		
2011–12	Napoli	35	23		
2012–13	Napoli	34	29	**104**	**78**
2013–14	Paris Saint-Germain	30	16		
2014–15	Paris Saint-Germain	35	18		
2015–16	Paris Saint-Germain	32	19		
2016–17	Paris Saint-Germain	36	35		
2017–18	Paris Saint-Germain	32	28		
2018–19	Paris Saint-Germain	21	18		
2019–20	Paris Saint-Germain	14	4	**200**	**138**
2020–21	Manchester U	26	10	**26**	**10**

CHONG, Tahith (F) 28 0
H: 6 1 W: 11 00 b.Willwmstad 1-12-91
Internationals: Netherlands U16, U17, U19, U20, U21.
From Feyenoord.

2018–19	Manchester U	2	0		
2019–20	Manchester U	3	0		
2020–21	Manchester U	0	0	**5**	**0**
2020–21	*Werder Bremen*	13	0	**13**	**0**
2020–21	*Club Brugge*	10	0	**10**	**0**

DALOT, Diogo (D) 47 1
H: 6 0 W: 11 11 b.Braga 18-3-99
Internationals: Portugal U16, U17, U19, U20, U21.

2016–17	Porto	0	0		
2017–18	Porto	6	0	**6**	**0**
2018–19	Manchester U	16	0		
2019–20	Manchester U	4	0		
2020–21	Manchester U	0	0	**20**	**0**
2020–21	*AC Milan*	21	1	**21**	**1**

DE GEA, David (G) 396 0
H: 6 3 W: 12 13 b.Madrid 7-11-90
Internationals: Spain U15, U17, U19, U20, U21, U23, Full caps.

2009–10	Atletico Madrid	19	0		
2010–11	Atletico Madrid	38	0	**57**	**0**
2011–12	Manchester U	29	0		
2012–13	Manchester U	28	0		
2013–14	Manchester U	37	0		
2014–15	Manchester U	37	0		
2015–16	Manchester U	34	0		
2016–17	Manchester U	35	0		
2017–18	Manchester U	37	0		
2018–19	Manchester U	38	0		
2019–20	Manchester U	38	0		
2020–21	Manchester U	26	0	**339**	**0**

DEVINE, Reece (D) 0 0
b.Stourbridge 18-12-01

2020–21	Manchester U	0	0		

DIALLO, Amad (F) 6 1
b.Abidjan 11-7-02

2019–20	Atalanta	3	1		
2020–21	Atalanta	0	0	**3**	**1**
2020–21	Manchester U	3	0	**3**	**0**

ELANGA, Anthony (M) 2 1
b. 27-4-02

2020–21	Manchester U	2	1	**2**	**1**

EMERAN, Noam (F) 0 0
H: 5 10 W: 11 00 b.Paray-le-Monial 24-9-02
Internationals: France U16.
From Amiens.

2020–21	Manchester U	0	0		

FERNANDEZ, Alvaro (D) 0 0
b.El Ferrol 23-3-03
From Real Madrid.

2020–21	Manchester U	0	0		

FISH, William (D) 1 0
b. 17-2-03

2020–21	Manchester U	1	0	**1**	**0**

FOSU-MENSAH, Timothy (D) 49 0
H: 5 10 W: 10 10 b.Amsterdam 3-1-98
Internationals: Netherlands U16, U17, U19, U21, Full caps.

2015–16	Manchester U	8	0		
2016–17	Manchester U	4	0		
2017–18	Manchester U	0	0		
2017–18	*Crystal Palace*	21	0	**21**	**0**
2018–19	Manchester U	0	0		
2018–19	*Fulham*	12	0	**12**	**0**
2019–20	Manchester U	3	0		
2020–21	Manchester U	1	0	**16**	**0**

Transferred to Bayer Leverkusen January 2021.

FRED, Frederico (M) 210 19
H: 5 7 W: 10 10 b.Belo Horizonte 5-3-93
Internationals: Brazil U20, Full caps.

2012	Internacional	28	6		
2013	Internacional	5	1	**33**	**7**
2013–14	Shakhtar Donetsk	23	2		
2014–15	Shakhtar Donetsk	22	1		
2015–16	Shakhtar Donetsk	12	2		
2016–17	Shakhtar Donetsk	18	2		
2017–18	Shakhtar Donetsk	26	3	**101**	**10**
2018–19	Manchester U	17	1		
2019–20	Manchester U	29	0		
2020–21	Manchester U	30	1	**76**	**2**

GALBRAITH, Ethan (M) 0 0
Internationals: Northern Ireland U17, U19, U21, Full caps.
From Linfield.

2019–20	Manchester U	0	0		
2020–21	Manchester U	0	0		

GARNER, James (M) 42 4
b.Birkenhead 13-3-01
Internationals: England U17, U18, U19.

2018–19	Manchester U	1	0		
2019–20	Manchester U	1	0		
2020–21	Manchester U	0	0	**2**	**0**
2020–21	*Watford*	20	0	**20**	**0**
2020–21	*Nottingham F*	20	4	**20**	**4**

GRANT, Lee (G) 468 0
H: 6 3 W: 13 01 b.Hemel Hempstead 27-1-83
Internationals: England U16, U17, U18, U19, U21.

2000–01	Derby Co	0	0		
2001–02	Derby Co	0	0		
2002–03	Derby Co	29	0		
2003–04	Derby Co	36	0		
2004–05	Derby Co	2	0		
2005–06	Derby Co	0	0		
2005–06	*Burnley*	1	0		
2005–06	*Oldham Ath*	16	0	**16**	**0**
2006–07	Derby Co	7	0		
2007–08	Sheffield W	44	0		
2008–09	Sheffield W	46	0		
2009–10	Sheffield W	46	0	**136**	**0**
2010–11	Burnley	25	0		
2011–12	Burnley	43	0		
2012–13	Burnley	46	0	**115**	**0**
2013–14	Derby Co	46	0		
2014–15	Derby Co	40	0		
2015–16	Derby Co	10	0		
2016–17	Derby Co	0	0	**170**	**0**
2016–17	*Stoke C*	28	0		
2017–18	Stoke C	3	0	**31**	**0**
2018–19	Manchester U	0	0		
2019–20	Manchester U	0	0		
2020–21	Manchester U	0	0		

GREENWOOD, Mason (F) 65 17
b. 1-10-01
Internationals: England U17, U18, U21.

2018–19	Manchester U	3	0		
2019–20	Manchester U	31	10		
2020–21	Manchester U	31	7	**65**	**17**

GUADAGNO, Johan (G) 0 0
H: 6 2 b.Milan 21-2-03
Internationals: Sweden U16.

2020–21	Manchester U	0	0		

HARDLEY, Bjorn (D) 0 0
H: 6 2 W: 11 11 b.Tilburg 19-12-02
From NAC Breda.

2020–21	Manchester U	0	0		

HENDERSON, Dean (G) 140 0
H: 6 3 W: 12 13 b.Whitehaven 12-3-97
Internationals: England U16, U17, U20, U21.

2015–16	Manchester U	0	0		
2016–17	Manchester U	0	0		
2016–17	*Grimsby T*	7	0	**7**	**0**
2017–18	Manchester U	0	0		
2017–18	*Shrewsbury T*	38	0	**38**	**0**
2018–19	Manchester U	0	0		
2018–19	*Sheffield U*	46	0		
2019–20	Manchester U	0	0		
2019–20	*Sheffield U*	36	0	**82**	**0**
2020–21	Manchester U	13	0	**13**	**0**

HOOGEWERF, Dillon (F) 0 0
H: 5 5 b.Almere 27-2-03
Internationals: Netherlands U16, U17.
From Ajax.

2020–21	Manchester U	0	0		

HUGILL, Joe (F) 0 0
b.Durham 19-10-03
From Sunderland.

2020–21	Manchester U	0	0		

IGHALO, Odion Jude (F) 298 109
H: 6 2 W: 11 00 b.Lagos 16-6-89
Internationals: Nigeria U20, Full caps.

2007	Lyn	7	3		
2008	Lyn	13	6	**20**	**9**
2008–09	Udinese	6	1		
2009–10	Udinese	0	0		
2010–11	Udinese	0	0		
2010–11	*Cesena*	3	0	**3**	**0**
2010–11	*Granada*	21	4		
2011–12	Udinese	0	0		
2011–12	*Granada*	30	6		
2012–13	Udinese	0	0		
2012–13	*Granada*	28	5		
2013–14	Udinese	0	0		
2013–14	*Granada*	16	2	**95**	**17**
2014–15	Udinese	0	0	**6**	**1**
2014–15	*Watford*	35	20		
2015–16	Watford	37	15		
2016–17	Watford	18	1	**90**	**36**
2017	Changchun Yatai	27	15		
2018	Changchun Yatai	28	21	**55**	**36**
2019	Shanghai Shenhua	17	10	**17**	**10**

On loan from Shanghai Shenhua.

2019–20	Manchester U	11	0		

On loan from Shanghai Shenhua.

2020–21	Manchester U	1	0	**12**	**0**

IQBAL, Zidane (M) 0 0
H: 5 11 b.Manchester 27-4-03

2020–21	Manchester U	0	0		

JAMES, Daniel (M) 81 10
b. 10-11-97
Internationals: Wales U17, U19, U20, U21, Full caps.
Full Hull C.

2015–16	Swansea C	0	0		
2016–17	Swansea C	0	0		
2017–18	Swansea C	0	0		
2017–18	*Shrewsbury T*	0	0		
2018–19	Swansea C	33	4	**33**	**4**
2019–20	Manchester U	33	3		
2020–21	Manchester U	15	3	**48**	**6**

JURADO, Marc (D) 0 0
H: 5 10 b.Sabadell 13-4-04
From Barcelona.

2020–21	Manchester U	0	0		

KOVAR, Matej (G) 18 0
b. 17-5-00
Internationals: Czech Republic U18, U19, U20.
From Slovacko.

2019–20	Manchester U	0	0		
2020–21	Manchester U	0	0		
2020–21	*Swindon T*	18	0	**18**	**0**

LAIRD, Ethan (D) 24 0
b.Basingstoke 5-8-01
Internationals: England U17, U18, U19.

2019–20	Manchester U	0	0		
2020–21	Manchester U	0	0		
2020–21	*Milton Keynes D*	24	0	**24**	**0**

LEVITT, Dylan (M) 10 0
b. 17-11-00
Internationals: Wales U17, U19, U21.
2019–20 Manchester U 0 0
2020–21 Manchester U 0 0
2020–21 *Charlton Ath* 3 0 **3 0**
2020–21 *Istra 1961* 7 0 **7 0**

LINDELOF, Victor (D) 209 5
H: 6 2 W: 12 11 b.Vasteras 17-7-94
Internationals: Sweden U17, U19, U21, Full caps.
2009 Vasteras 1 0
2010 Vasteras 9 0
2011 Vasteras 27 0
2012 Vasteras 13 0 **50 0**
2012–13 Benfica 0 0
2013–14 Benfica 1 0
2014–15 Benfica 0 0
2015–16 Benfica 15 1
2016–17 Benfica 32 1 **48 2**
2017–18 Manchester U 17 0
2018–19 Manchester U 30 1
2019–20 Manchester U 35 1
2020–21 Manchester U 29 1 **111 3**

LINGARD, Jesse (M) 196 38
H: 5 3 W: 11 11 b.Warrington 15-12-92
Internationals: England U17, U21, Full caps.
2011–12 Manchester U 0 0
2012–13 Manchester U 0 0
2012–13 *Leicester C* 5 0 **5 0**
2013–14 Manchester U 0 0
2013–14 *Birmingham C* 13 6 **13 6**
2013–14 *Brighton & HA* 15 3 **15 3**
2014–15 Manchester U 1 0
2014–15 *Derby Co* 14 2 **14 2**
2015–16 Manchester U 25 4
2016–17 Manchester U 25 1
2017–18 Manchester U 33 8
2018–19 Manchester U 27 4
2019–20 Manchester U 22 1
2020–21 Manchester U 0 0 **133 18**
2020–21 *West Ham U* 16 9 **16 9**

MAGUIRE, Harry (D) 345 20
H: 6 2 W: 12 06 b.Mosborough 5-3-93
Internationals: England U21, Full caps.
2010–11 Sheffield U 5 0
2011–12 Sheffield U 44 1
2012–13 Sheffield U 44 3
2013–14 Sheffield U 41 5 **134 9**
2014–15 Hull C 3 0
2014–15 *Wigan Ath* 16 1 **16 1**
2015–16 Hull C 22 0
2016–17 Hull C 29 2 **54 2**
2017–18 Leicester C 38 2
2018–19 Leicester C 31 3
2019–20 Leicester C 0 0 **69 5**
2019–20 Manchester U 38 1
2020–21 Manchester U 34 2 **72 3**

MARTIAL, Anthony (F) 219 66
H: 5 11 W: 12 08 b.Massy 5-12-95
Internationals: France U16, U17, U18, U19, U21, Full caps.
2012–13 Lyon 3 0 **3 0**
2013–14 Monaco 11 2
2014–15 Monaco 35 9
2015–16 Monaco 3 0 **49 11**
2015–16 Manchester U 31 11
2016–17 Manchester U 25 4
2017–18 Manchester U 30 9
2018–19 Manchester U 27 10
2019–20 Manchester U 32 17
2020–21 Manchester U 22 4 **167 55**

MASTNY, Ondrej (G) 0 0
H: 6 0 W: 11 00 b.Trebic 8-3-02
Internationals: Czech Republic U16, U18.
From Vysocina.
2020–21 Manchester U 0 0

MATA, Juan (M) 400 85
H: 5 7 W: 11 00 b.Ocon de Villafranca 28-4-88
Internationals: Spain U16, U17, U19, U20, U21, U23, Full caps.
From Real Oviedo.
2006–07 Real Madrid 0 0
2007–08 Valencia 24 5
2008–09 Valencia 37 11
2009–10 Valencia 35 9
2010–11 Valencia 33 8 **129 33**
2011–12 Chelsea 34 6
2012–13 Chelsea 35 12
2013–14 Chelsea 13 0 **82 18**
2013–14 Manchester U 15 6
2014–15 Manchester U 33 9
2015–16 Manchester U 38 6
2016–17 Manchester U 25 6
2017–18 Manchester U 28 3
2018–19 Manchester U 22 3
2019–20 Manchester U 19 0
2020–21 Manchester U 9 1 **189 34**

MATIC, Nemanja (M) 394 18
H: 6 4 W: 13 02 b.Sabac 1-8-88
Internationals: Serbia U21, Full caps.
2005–06 Jedinstvo 7 0
2006–07 Jedinstvo 9 0 **16 0**
2006–07 Kosice 13 1
2007–08 Kosice 25 1
2008–09 Kosice 29 2 **67 4**
2009–10 Chelsea 2 0
2010–11 Chelsea 0 0
2010–11 *Vitesse* 27 2 **27 2**
2011–12 Benfica 16 1
2012–13 Benfica 26 3
2013–14 Benfica 14 2 **56 6**
2013–14 Chelsea 17 0
2014–15 Chelsea 36 1
2015–16 Chelsea 33 2
2016–17 Chelsea 35 1 **123 4**
2017–18 Manchester U 36 1
2018–19 Manchester U 28 1
2019–20 Manchester U 21 0
2020–21 Manchester U 20 0 **105 2**

McCANN, Charlie (M) 0 0
H: 5 10 W: 10 03 b.Coventry 24-4-02
Internationals: England U16. Republic of Ireland U17, U18.
2020–21 Manchester U 0 0

McNEILL, Charlie (F) 0 0
H: 6 0 b. 9-9-03
Internationals: England U16.
2020–21 Manchester U 0 0

McTOMINAY, Scott (M) 90 10
H: 5 10 W: 10 03 b.Lancaster 8-12-96
Internationals: Scotland Full caps.
2016–17 Manchester U 2 0
2017–18 Manchester U 13 0
2018–19 Manchester U 16 2
2019–20 Manchester U 27 4
2020–21 Manchester U 32 4 **90 10**

MEJBRI, Hannibal (M) 1 0
b. 21-1-03
2020–21 Manchester U 1 0 **1 0**

MEJIA, Mateo (F) 0 0
H: 6 2 b.Zaragoza 31-3-03
From Real Zaragoza.
2020–21 Manchester U 0 0

MENGI, Teden (D) 9 0
b. 30-4-02
Internationals: England U16, U17, U18.
2019–20 Manchester U 0 0
2020–21 Manchester U 0 0
2020–21 *Derby Co* 9 0 **9 0**

PELLISTRI , Facundo (M) 42 1
b.Montevideo 20-12-01
2019 Penarol 18 1
2020 Penarol 12 0
2020–21 Penarol 0 0 **30 1**
2020–21 Manchester U 0 0
2020–21 *Alaves* 12 0 **12 0**

PEREIRA, Andreas (M) 129 9
H: 5 10 W: 10 06 b.Duffel 1-1-96
Internationals: Belgium U16, U17. Brazil U20, U23, Full caps.
From PSV Eindhoven.
2014–15 Manchester U 1 0
2015–16 Manchester U 4 0
2016–17 Manchester U 0 0
2016–17 *Granada* 35 5 **35 5**
2017–18 Manchester U 0 0
2017–18 *Valencia* 23 1 **23 1**
2018–19 Manchester U 15 1
2019–20 Manchester U 25 1
2020–21 Manchester U 0 0 **45 2**
2020–21 *Lazio* 26 1 **26 1**

POGBA, Paul (M) 261 56
H: 6 1 W: 12 08 b.Lagny-sur-Marne 15-3-93
Internationals: France U16, U17, U18, U19, U20, Full caps.
From Le Havre.
2009–10 Manchester U 0 0
2010–11 Manchester U 0 0
2011–12 Manchester U 3 0
2012–13 Juventus 27 5
2013–14 Juventus 36 7
2014–15 Juventus 26 8
2015–16 Juventus 35 8 **124 28**
2016–17 Manchester U 30 5
2017–18 Manchester U 27 6
2018–19 Manchester U 35 13
2019–20 Manchester U 16 1
2020–21 Manchester U 26 3 **137 28**

PYE, Logan (D) 0 0
H: 5 10 b.Sunderland 26-10-03
Internationals: England U16.
From Sunderland.
2020–21 Manchester U 0 0

RASHFORD, Marcus (F) 179 55
H: 5 11 W: 11 00 b.Manchester 31-10-97
Internationals: England U16, U18, U20, U21, Full caps.
2015–16 Manchester U 11 5
2016–17 Manchester U 32 5
2017–18 Manchester U 35 7
2018–19 Manchester U 33 10
2019–20 Manchester U 31 17
2020–21 Manchester U 37 11 **179 55**

ROMERO, Sergio (G) 176 0
H: 6 4 W: 13 01 b.Yrigoyen 22-2-87
Internationals: Argentina U20, Full caps.
2006–07 Racing Club 5 0 **5 0**
2007–08 AZ Alkmaar 12 0
2008–09 AZ Alkmaar 28 0
2009–10 AZ Alkmaar 27 0
2010–11 AZ Alkmaar 23 0 **90 0**
2011–12 Sampdoria 29 0
2012–13 Sampdoria 32 0
2013–14 Sampdoria 0 0
2013–14 *Monaco* 3 0 **3 0**
2014–15 Sampdoria 10 0 **71 0**
2015–16 Manchester U 4 0
2016–17 Manchester U 2 0
2017–18 Manchester U 1 0
2018–19 Manchester U 0 0
2019–20 Manchester U 0 0
2020–21 Manchester U 0 0 **7 0**

SAVAGE, Charlie (M) 0 0
H: 6 0 b.Leicester 2-5-03
Internationals: Wales U17, U18.
2020–21 Manchester U 0 0

SHAW, Luke (D) 188 2
H: 6 1 W: 11 11 b.Kingston 12-7-95
Internationals: England U16, U17, U21, Full caps.
2011–12 Southampton 0 0
2012–13 Southampton 25 0
2013–14 Southampton 35 0 **60 0**
2014–15 Manchester U 16 0
2015–16 Manchester U 5 0
2016–17 Manchester U 11 0
2017–18 Manchester U 11 0
2018–19 Manchester U 29 1
2019–20 Manchester U 24 0
2020–21 Manchester U 32 1 **128 2**

SHORETIRE, Shola (F) 2 0
b. 2-2-04
From Newcastle U.
2020–21 Manchester U 2 0 **2 0**

STANLEY, Connor (M) 0 0
H: 5 9 b.Redditch 30-12-01
From Birmingham C.
2020–21 Manchester U 0 0

SVIDERSKY, Martin (D) 0 0
H: 5 11 W: 10 01 b.Presov 4-10-02
Internationals: Slovakia U17, U21.
2020–21 Manchester U 0 0

TUANZEBE, Axel (D) 49 0
H: 6 0 W: 11 11 b.Bunia 14-11-97
Internationals: England U19, U20, U21.
2015–16 Manchester U 0 0
2016–17 Manchester U 4 0
2017–18 Manchester U 1 0
2017–18 *Aston Villa* 5 0
2018–19 Manchester U 0 0
2018–19 *Aston Villa* 25 0 **30 0**
2019–20 Manchester U 5 0
2020–21 Manchester U 9 0 **19 0**

VAN DE BEEK, Donny (M) 137 29
b.Nijkerkerveen 18-4-97
2015–16 Ajax 8 0
2016–17 Ajax 19 0
2017–18 Ajax 34 11
2018–19 Ajax 34 9
2019–20 Ajax 23 8
2020–21 Ajax 0 0 **118 28**
2020–21 Manchester U 19 1 **19 1**

VITEK, Radek (G) 0 0
H: 6 6 b.Vsetin 24-10-03
Internationals: Czech Republic U17.
From Olomouc.
2020–21 Manchester U 0 0

WAN BISSAKA, Aaron (M) **111** **2**

b. 26-11-97

Internationals: DR Congo U20. England U20, U21.

2016–17	Crystal Palace	0	0		
2017–18	Crystal Palace	7	0		
2018–19	Crystal Palace	35	0	**42**	**0**
2019–20	Manchester U	35	0		
2020–21	Manchester U	34	2	**69**	**2**

WILLIAMS, Brandon (D) **21** **1**

b.Manchester 3-9-00

Internationals: England U20.

2018–19	Manchester U	0	0		
2019–20	Manchester U	17	1		
2020–21	Manchester U	4	0	**21**	**1**

WOOLSTON, Paul (G) **0** **0**

H: 5 11 W: 13 05 b.North Shields 14-8-98

Internationals: England U17, U18.

2020–21	Manchester U	0	0		

Scholars

Bennett, Rhys Joseph Wright; Forson, Omari Nathan; Garnacho Ferreyra, Alejandro; Hansen-Aaroen, Isak; Hughes, Iestyn Tomos; Kambwala Ndengushi, Willy; Mee, Dermot William.

MANSFIELD T (51)

BENNING, Malvind (D) **269** **11**

H: 5 10 W: 12 00 b.Sandwell 2-11-93

2012–13	Walsall	10	0		
2013–14	Walsall	16	2		
2014–15	Walsall	20	0	**46**	**2**
2014–15	*York C*	9	0	**9**	**0**
2015–16	Mansfield T	31	4		
2016–17	Mansfield T	45	1		
2017–18	Mansfield T	28	1		
2018–19	Mansfield T	45	3		
2019–20	Mansfield T	33	0		
2020–21	Mansfield T	32	0	**214**	**9**

BOWERY, Jordan (F) **349** **57**

H: 6 1 W: 12 00 b.Nottingham 2-7-91

2008–09	Chesterfield	3	0		
2009–10	Chesterfield	10	0		
2010–11	Chesterfield	27	1		
2011–12	Chesterfield	40	8		
2012–13	Chesterfield	3	1	**83**	**10**
2012–13	Aston Villa	10	0		
2013–14	Aston Villa	9	0	**19**	**0**
2013–14	*Doncaster R*	3	0	**3**	**0**
2014–15	Rotherham U	33	5		
2015–16	Rotherham U	7	0	**40**	**5**
2015–16	*Bradford C*	3	0	**3**	**0**
2015–16	Oxford U	17	7	**17**	**7**
2016–17	Leyton Orient	17	1	**17**	**1**
2016–17	*Crewe Alex*	19	2		
2017–18	Crewe Alex	45	12		
2018–19	Crewe Alex	44	8	**108**	**22**
2019–20	Milton Keynes D	16	2	**16**	**2**
2020–21	Mansfield T	43	10	**43**	**10**

CAINE, Nathan (F) **0** **0**

2020–21	Mansfield T	0	0		

CAMPBELL, Maison (G) **0** **0**

2019–20	Mansfield T	0	0		
2020–21	Mansfield T	0	0		

CHARLES, Jaden (D) **2** **0**

b. 25-1-02

2020–21	Mansfield T	2	0	**2**	**0**

CHARSLEY, Harry (M) **53** **4**

H: 5 10 W: 10 01 b.Wirral 1-11-96

Internationals: Republic of Ireland U17, U19, U21.

2017–18	Everton	0	0		
2017–18	*Bolton W*	1	0	**1**	**0**
2018–19	Everton	0	0		
2019–20	Mansfield T	9	0		
2020–21	Mansfield T	43	4	**52**	**4**

CLARKE, James (D) **14** **0**

b. 2-4-00

Internationals: Republic of Ireland U18.

2018–19	Burnley	0	0		
2019–20	Mansfield T	12	0		
2020–21	Mansfield T	2	0	**14**	**0**

CLARKE, Ollie (M) **241** **19**

H: 5 11 W: 11 11 b.Bristol 29-6-92

2009–10	Bristol R	0	0		
2010–11	Bristol R	1	0		
2011–12	Bristol R	0	0		
2012–13	Bristol R	5	0		
2013–14	Bristol R	32	2		
2015–16	Bristol R	33	2		
2016–17	Bristol R	30	4		
2017–18	Bristol R	40	1		
2018–19	Bristol R	40	6		
2019–20	Bristol R	27	1	**208**	**16**
2019–20	Mansfield T	0	0		
2020–21	Mansfield T	33	3	**33**	**3**

COOK, Andy (F) **112** **31**

H: 6 0 W: 11 03 b.Bishop Auckland 18-10-90

Internationals: England C.

From Carlisle U, Barrow, Grimsby T, Barrow, Tranmere R.

2018–19	Walsall	43	13	**43**	**13**
2019–20	Mansfield T	23	7		
2019–20	*Tranmere R*	5	0	**5**	**0**
2020–21	Mansfield T	20	3	**43**	**10**
2020–21	*Bradford C*	21	8	**21**	**8**

GORDON, Kellan (M) **82** **6**

b.Burton 25-12-97

From Stoke C.

2017–18	Derby Co	0	0		
2017–18	*Swindon T*	26	3	**26**	**3**
2018–19	Derby Co	0	0		
2018–19	*Lincoln C*	6	2		
2019–20	*Lincoln C*	0	0	**6**	**2**
2019–20	Mansfield T	18	1		
2020–21	Mansfield T	32	0	**50**	**1**

HEWITT, Elliott (D) **269** **10**

H: 5 11 W: 11 10 b.Rhyl 30-5-94

Internationals: Wales U17, U21.

2010–11	Macclesfield T	1	0		
2011–12	Macclesfield T	21	0	**22**	**0**
2012–13	Ipswich T	7	0		
2013–14	Ipswich T	4	0		
2013–14	*Gillingham*	20	0	**20**	**0**
2014–15	Ipswich T	3	0	**14**	**0**
2014–15	*Colchester U*	21	1	**21**	**1**
2015–16	Notts Co	38	0		
2016–17	Notts Co	29	2		
2017–18	Notts Co	43	4		
2018–19	Notts Co	25	2	**135**	**8**
2019–20	Grimsby T	20	0		
2020–21	Grimsby T	37	1	**57**	**1**
2020–21	Mansfield T	0	0		

KNOWLES, Jimmy (F) **5** **1**

2018–19	Mansfield T	0	0		
2019–20	Mansfield T	5	1		
2020–21	Mansfield T	0	0	**5**	**1**

LAPSLIE, George (M) **69** **9**

b. 5-9-97

2016–17	Charlton Ath	0	0		
2017–18	Charlton Ath	1	0		
2018–19	Charlton Ath	27	0		
2019–20	Charlton Ath	10	1		
2020–21	Charlton Ath	2	0	**40**	**1**
2020–21	Mansfield T	29	8	**29**	**8**

LAW, Jason (F) **17** **1**

b. 26-4-99

From Burton Alb, Derby Co, Carlton T.

2015–16	Mansfield T	0	0		
2016–17	Mansfield T	0	0		
2017–18	Mansfield T	0	0		
2018–19	Mansfield T	0	0		
2019–20	Mansfield T	0	0		
2020–21	Mansfield T	17	1	**17**	**1**

MARIS, George (F) **175** **21**

b.Sheffield 6-3-96

2014–15	Barnsley	2	0		
2015–16	Barnsley	1	0	**3**	**0**
2016–17	Cambridge U	23	4		
2017–18	Cambridge U	40	10		
2018–19	Cambridge U	39	5		
2019–20	Cambridge U	30	1	**132**	**20**
2020–21	Mansfield T	40	1	**40**	**1**

MAYNARD, Nicky (F) **426** **133**

H: 5 11 W: 11 00 b.Winsford 11-12-86

2005–06	Crewe Alex	1	1		
2006–07	Crewe Alex	31	16		
2007–08	Crewe Alex	27	14	**59**	**31**
2008–09	Bristol C	43	11		
2009–10	Bristol C	42	20		
2010–11	Bristol C	13	6		
2011–12	Bristol C	27	8	**125**	**45**
2011–12	West Ham U	14	2		
2012–13	West Ham U	0	0	**14**	**2**
2012–13	Cardiff C	4	1		
2013–14	Cardiff C	8	0		
2013–14	*Wigan Ath*	16	4	**16**	**4**
2014–15	Cardiff C	10	1	**22**	**2**
2015–16	Milton Keynes D	35	7		
2016–17	Milton Keynes D	31	2	**66**	**9**
2017–18	Aberdeen	18	0	**18**	**0**
2018–19	Bury	37	21	**37**	**21**
2019–20	Mansfield T	33	14		
2020–21	Mansfield T	17	3	**50**	**17**
2020–21	*Newport Co*	19	2	**19**	**2**

McLAUGHLIN, Stephen (M) **327** **39**

H: 5 9 W: 11 12 b.Derry 14-6-90

2009	Finn Harps	16	1		
2010	Finn Harps	32	1	**48**	**2**
2011	Derry C	33	3		
2012	Derry C	24	10	**57**	**13**
2012–13	Nottingham F	0	0		
2013–14	Nottingham F	3	0		
2013–14	*Bristol C*	5	0	**5**	**0**
2014–15	Nottingham F	6	0	**9**	**0**
2014–15	*Notts Co*	13	0	**13**	**0**
2014–15	*Southend U*	6	1		
2015–16	Southend U	17	1		
2016–17	Southend U	34	7		
2017–18	Southend U	45	6		
2018–19	Southend U	30	1		
2019–20	Southend U	27	4		
2020–21	Southend U	0	0	**159**	**20**
2020–21	Mansfield T	36	4	**36**	**4**

MENAYESE, Rollin (D) **61** **1**

H: 6 3 W: 12 08 b. 4-12-97

Internationals: Wales U17.

From Weston-super-Mare.

2017–18	Bristol R	3	0		
2017–18	*Swindon T*	14	0	**14**	**0**
2018–19	Bristol R	0	0		
2019–20	Bristol R	13	0	**16**	**0**
2020–21	Mansfield T	10	1	**10**	**1**
2020–21	*Grimsby T*	21	0	**21**	**0**

O'DRISCOLL, Aaron (D) **3** **0**

b. 4-4-99

From Manchester C.

2017–18	Southampton	0	0		
2018–19	Southampton	0	0		
2019–20	Southampton	0	0		
2020–21	Mansfield T	3	0	**3**	**0**

O'KEEFFE, Corey (M) **45** **0**

H: 6 1 W: 11 00 b.Birmingham 5-6-88

Internationals: Republic of Ireland U17, U18, U19.

2016–17	Birmingham C	1	0		
2017–18	Birmingham C	0	0		
2018–19	Birmingham C	0	0		
2019–20	Birmingham C	0	0	**1**	**0**
2019–20	*Macclesfield T*	31	0	**31**	**0**
2020–21	Mansfield T	13	0	**13**	**0**

PERCH, James (D) **513** **22**

H: 5 11 W: 11 05 b.Mansfield 29-9-85

2002–03	Nottingham F	0	0		
2003–04	Nottingham F	0	0		
2004–05	Nottingham F	22	0		
2005–06	Nottingham F	38	3		
2006–07	Nottingham F	46	5		
2007–08	Nottingham F	30	0		
2008–09	Nottingham F	37	3		
2009–10	Nottingham F	17	1	**190**	**12**
2010–11	Newcastle U	13	0		
2011–12	Newcastle U	25	0		
2012–13	Newcastle U	27	1	**65**	**1**
2013–14	Wigan Ath	40	0		
2014–15	Wigan Ath	41	3	**81**	**3**
2015–16	QPR	35	0		
2016–17	QPR	32	0		
2017–18	QPR	7	0	**74**	**0**
2018–19	Scunthorpe U	41	2		
2019–20	Scunthorpe U	30	1	**71**	**3**
2020–21	Mansfield T	32	3	**32**	**3**

RAWSON, Farrend (D) **175** **6**

H: 6 1 W: 11 07 b.Nottingham 11-7-96

2014–15	Derby Co	0	0		
2014–15	*Rotherham U*	4	0		
2015–16	Derby Co	0	0		
2015–16	*Rotherham U*	16	2	**20**	**2**
2016–17	Derby Co	0	0		
2016–17	*Coventry C*	14	0	**14**	**0**
2017–18	Derby Co	0	0		
2017–18	*Accrington S*	12	0	**12**	**0**
2017–18	Forest Green R	18	1		
2018–19	Forest Green R	38	0		
2019–20	Forest Green R	30	3	**86**	**4**
2020–21	Mansfield T	43	0	**43**	**0**

REID, Jamie (F) **62** **9**

H: 5 11 W: 11 09 b.Torquay 15-7-94

Internationals: Northern Ireland U21.

2012–13	Exeter C	4	2		
2013–14	Exeter C	6	0		
2014–15	Exeter C	0	0		
2015–16	Exeter C	13	1		
2016–17	Exeter C	0	0	**23**	**3**

From Torquay U.

2020–21	Mansfield T	39	6	**39**	**6**

SCOTT, Josh (F) **0** **0**

b. 20-9-01

2020–21	Mansfield T	0	0		

SINCLAIR, Tyrese (F) 19 3
b. 4-2-01
2018–19 Mansfield T 0 0
2019–20 Radcliffe 0 0
2019–20 Mansfield T 0 0
2020–21 Mansfield T 19 3 **19 3**

SMITH, Alistair (M) 6 0
b. 19-5-99
2018–19 Mansfield T 0 0
2019–20 Mansfield T 5 0
2020–21 Mansfield T 1 0 **6 0**

STECH, Marek (G) 168 0
H: 6 3 W: 14 00 b.Prague 28-1-90
Internationals: Czech Republic U17 U21, Full caps.
From Sparta Prague.
2008–09 West Ham U 0 0
2008–09 *Wycombe W* 2 0 **2 0**
2009–10 West Ham U 0 0
2009–10 *Bournemouth* 1 0 **1 0**
2010–11 West Ham U 0 0
2011–12 West Ham U 0 0
2011–12 *Yeovil T* 5 0
2011–12 *Leyton Orient* 2 0 **2 0**
2012–13 Yeovil T 46 0
2013–14 Yeovil T 26 0 **77 0**
2014–15 Sparta Prague 17 0
2015–16 Sparta Prague 2 0
2016–17 Sparta Prague 0 0 **19 0**
2017–18 Luton T 38 0
2018–19 Luton T 5 0
2019–20 Luton T 0 0 **43 0**
2020–21 Mansfield T 24 0 **24 0**

STONE, Aiden (G) 25 0
b. 20-7-99
2018–19 Burnley 0 0
2019–20 Mansfield T 3 0
2020–21 Mansfield T 22 0 **25 0**

SWEENEY, Ryan (D) 159 8
b.Kingston upon Thames 15-4-97
Internationals: Republic of Ireland U19, U21.
2014–15 AFC Wimbledon 3 0
2015–16 AFC Wimbledon 10 0 **13 0**
2016–17 Stoke C 0 0
2016–17 *Bristol R* 16 0
2017–18 Stoke C 0 0
2017–18 *Bristol R* 23 3 **39 3**
2018–19 Stoke C 0 0
2018–19 *Mansfield T* 38 1
2019–20 Mansfield T 33 1
2020–21 Mansfield T 36 3 **107 5**

WALKER, Aidan (D) 0 0
2020–21 Mansfield T 0 0

WARD, Keaton (M) 7 0
b. 4-5-00
2020–21 Mansfield T 7 0 **7 0**

WRIGHT, Jake (D) 289 0
H: 5 10 W: 11 07 b.Keighley 11-3-86
2005–06 Bradford C 1 0 **1 0**
From Halifax T, Crawley T
2009–10 Brighton & HA 6 0 **6 0**
2010–11 Oxford U 35 0
2011–12 Oxford U 43 0
2012–13 Oxford U 42 0
2013–14 Oxford U 31 0
2014–15 Oxford U 42 0
2015–16 Oxford U 29 0 **222 0**
2016–17 Sheffield U 30 0
2017–18 Sheffield U 17 0
2019–20 Sheffield U 0 0 **47 0**
2019–20 *Bolton W* 11 0 **11 0**
2020–21 Mansfield T 2 0 **2 0**

Scholars
Adams, Joshua Joseph; Bouch, Jonty Charles; Caine, Nathan Ross; Campbell, Maison Scott; Collins, Cody Sam; Cooper, Frank George; Davies, Curtis James Patrick; Deakin, Jack Mark; Edwards, Diego Antonio; Hill, Ethan Thomas; Hill-Smith, Lewis; Hurdis, Max; Lawson, Sha'Mar Malik; Mason, Owen John; Pitts, Freddie Lewis; Reynolds, Colt Mikey; Sketchley, Kian James; Tomlin, Kyle William.

MIDDLESBROUGH (52)

AKPOM, Chuba (F) 174 28
H: 6 0 W: 12 02 b.London 9-10-95
Internationals: England U16, U17, U19, U20, U21.
2012–13 Arsenal 0 0
2013–14 Arsenal 1 0
2013–14 *Brentford* 4 0 **4 0**
2013–14 *Coventry C* 6 0 **6 0**
2014–15 Arsenal 3 0
2014–15 *Nottingham F* 7 0 **7 0**
2015–16 Arsenal 0 0
2015–16 *Hull C* 35 3 **35 3**
2016–17 Arsenal 0 0
2016–17 *Brighton & HA* 10 0 **10 0**
2017–18 Arsenal 0 0 **4 0**
2017–18 *Sint Truidense* 16 6 **16 6**
2018–19 PAOK 20 6
2019–20 PAOK 33 8
2020–21 PAOK 1 0 **54 14**
2020–21 Middlesbrough 38 5 **38 5**

ARCHER, Jordan (G) 199 0
H: 6 1 W: 12 08 b.Walthamstow 12-4-93
Internationals: Scotland U19, U20, U21, Full caps.
2011–12 Tottenham H 0 0
2012–13 Tottenham H 0 0
2012–13 *Wycombe W* 27 0 **27 0**
2013–14 Tottenham H 0 0
2014–15 Tottenham H 0 0
2014–15 *Northampton T* 13 0 **13 0**
2014–15 *Millwall* 0 0
2015–16 Millwall 39 0
2016–17 Millwall 36 0
2017–18 Millwall 45 0
2018–19 Millwall 24 0 **144 0**
2019–20 *Oxford U* 6 0 **6 0**
2019–20 Fulham 0 0
2020–21 Fulham 0 0
2020–21 Motherwell 4 0 **4 0**
2020–21 Middlesbrough 5 0 **5 0**

ASSOMBALONGA, Britt (F) 307 113
H: 5 9 W: 11 13 b.Kinshasa 6-12-92
Internationals: DR Congo Full caps.
2010–11 Watford 0 0
2011–12 Watford 4 0
2012–13 Watford 0 0
2012–13 *Southend U* 43 15 **43 15**
2013–14 Watford 0 0 **4 0**
2013–14 Peterborough U 43 23 **43 23**
2014–15 Nottingham F 29 15
2015–16 Nottingham F 4 1
2016–17 Nottingham F 32 14 **65 30**
2017–18 Middlesbrough 44 15
2018–19 Middlesbrough 42 14
2019–20 Middlesbrough 35 11
2020–21 Middlesbrough 31 5 **152 45**

BALDE, Alberto (F) 0 0
H: 5 10 b.Madrid 21-3-02
From Portadown.
2020–21 Middlesbrough 0 0

BOLA, Marc (D) 119 3
H: 6 1 W: 12 04 b.Greenwich 9-12-97
2016–17 Arsenal 0 0
2016–17 *Notts Co* 13 0 **13 0**
2017–18 Arsenal 0 0
2017–18 *Bristol R* 18 0 **18 0**
2018–19 Blackpool 35 2
2019–20 Middlesbrough 7 0
2019–20 *Blackpool* 5 0 **40 2**
2020–21 Middlesbrough 41 1 **48 1**

BROWNE, Marcus (M) 63 12
b. 18-12-97
2015–16 West Ham U 0 0
2016–17 West Ham U 0 0
2016–17 *Wigan Ath* 0 0
2017–18 West Ham U 0 0
2018–19 West Ham U 0 0
2018–19 *Oxford U* 34 6
2019–20 Middlesbrough 13 0
2019–20 *Oxford U* 11 4 **45 10**
2020–21 Middlesbrough 5 2 **18 2**

BRYNN, Solomon (G) 0 0
2019–20 Middlesbrough 0 0
2020–21 Middlesbrough 0 0

BURRELL, Rumarn (F) 6 0
b.Birmingham 16-12-00
2018–19 Grimsby T 4 0 **4 0**
2019–20 Middlesbrough 0 0
2020–21 Middlesbrough 0 0
2020–21 *Bradford C* 2 0 **2 0**

COBURN, Josh (F) 4 1
b. 6-12-02
2020–21 Middlesbrough 4 1 **4 1**

COULSON, Hayden (D) 66 1
b. 17-6-98
Internationals: England U16, U17, U18, U19.
2018–19 Middlesbrough 0 0
2018–19 *St Mirren* 6 0 **6 0**
2018–19 *Cambridge U* 14 0 **14 0**
2019–20 Middlesbrough 29 1
2020–21 Middlesbrough 17 0 **46 1**

DIJKSTEEL, Anfernee (M) 86 1
b. 27-10-96
Internationals: Netherlands U20.
2016–17 Charlton Ath 0 0
2017–18 Charlton Ath 10 0
2018–19 Charlton Ath 30 1
2019–20 Charlton Ath 1 0 **41 1**
2019–20 Middlesbrough 16 0
2020–21 Middlesbrough 29 0 **45 0**

DODDS, Daniel (D) 0 0
b. 17-1-01
2020–21 Middlesbrough 0 0

FISHER, Darnell (M) 197 2
H: 5 9 W: 11 00 b.Reading 1-5-94
2012–13 Celtic 0 0
2013–14 Celtic 12 0
2014–15 Celtic 5 0
2015–16 Celtic 0 0 **17 0**
2015–16 *St Johnstone* 23 1 **23 1**
2016–17 Rotherham U 34 0 **34 0**
2017–18 Preston NE 34 0
2018–19 Preston NE 35 0
2019–20 Preston NE 28 0
2020–21 Preston NE 14 1 **111 1**
2020–21 Middlesbrough 12 0 **12 0**

FLETCHER, Ashley (F) 145 26
b.Keighley 12-10-95
Internationals: England U20.
2015–16 Manchester U 0 0
2015–16 *Barnsley* 21 5 **21 5**
2016–17 West Ham U 16 0 **16 0**
2017–18 Middlesbrough 16 1
2017–18 *Sunderland* 16 2 **16 2**
2018–19 Middlesbrough 21 5
2019–20 Middlesbrough 43 11
2020–21 Middlesbrough 12 2 **92 19**

FLETCHER, Isaac (M) 0 0
b. 1-6-02
2020–21 Middlesbrough 0 0

FOLARIN, Sam (M) 2 0
b. 23-9-00
From Tooting & Mitcham U.
2020–21 Middlesbrough 2 0 **2 0**

FRY, Dael (D) 132 1
H: 6 1 W: 11 05 b.Middlesbrough 30-8-97
Internationals: England U17, U18, U19, U20, U21.
2015–16 Middlesbrough 7 0
2016–17 Middlesbrough 0 0
2016–17 *Rotherham U* 10 0 **10 0**
2017–18 Middlesbrough 13 0
2018–19 Middlesbrough 34 0
2019–20 Middlesbrough 36 0
2020–21 Middlesbrough 32 1 **122 1**

GIBSON, Joseph (M) 0 0
b.Bishop Auckland 6-9-01
2020–21 Middlesbrough 0 0

GREEN, Harry (F) 0 0
b.Stockton-on-Tees 24-9-01
2020–21 Middlesbrough 0 0

HACKNEY, Hayden (M) 1 0
b. 26-6-02
2019–20 Middlesbrough 0 0
2020–21 Middlesbrough 1 0 **1 0**

HALL, Grant (D) 185 9
H: 5 9 W: 11 02 b.Brighton 29-10-91
From Lewes.
2009–10 Brighton & HA 0 0
2010–11 Brighton & HA 0 0
2011–12 Brighton & HA 1 0 **1 0**
2012–13 Tottenham H 0 0
2013–14 Tottenham H 0 0
2013–14 *Swindon T* 27 0 **27 0**
2014–15 Tottenham H 0 0
2014–15 *Birmingham C* 7 0 **7 0**
2014–15 *Blackpool* 12 1 **12 1**
2015–16 QPR 39 1
2016–17 QPR 34 0
2017–18 QPR 4 0
2018–19 QPR 12 0
2019–20 QPR 30 5 **119 6**
2020–21 Middlesbrough 19 2 **19 2**

HANNAH, Jack (D) 0 0
H: 6 2 b.Stockton-on-Tees 25-12-02
2020–21 Middlesbrough 0 0

HEMMING, Zachary (G) 0 0
b.Bishop Auckland 7-3-00
2020–21 Middlesbrough 0 0

HOWSON, Jonathan (M) 532 50
H: 5 11 W: 12 01 b.Morley 21-5-88
Internationals: England U21.
2006–07 Leeds U 9 1

2007–08	Leeds U	26	3		
2008–09	Leeds U	40	4		
2009–10	Leeds U	45	4		
2010–11	Leeds U	46	10		
2011–12	Leeds U	19	1	**185**	**23**
2011–12	Norwich C	11	1		
2012–13	Norwich C	30	2		
2013–14	Norwich C	27	2		
2014–15	Norwich C	34	8		
2015–16	Norwich C	36	3		
2016–17	Norwich C	38	6	**176**	**22**
2017–18	Middlesbrough	43	3		
2018–19	Middlesbrough	46	1		
2019–20	Middlesbrough	41	0		
2020–21	Middlesbrough	41	1	**171**	**5**

JAMES, Bradley (G) **0 0**
b. 5-7-99

2020–21	Middlesbrough	0	0		

JOHNSON, Marvin (F) **202 14**
H: 5 10 W: 11 09 b.Birmingham 1-12-90
From Solihull Moors, Kidderminster H.

2014–15	Motherwell	11	0		
2015–16	Motherwell	38	5		
2016–17	Motherwell	4	1	**53**	**6**
2016–17	Oxford U	39	3		
2017–18	Oxford U	2	0	**41**	**3**
2017–18	Middlesbrough	17	1		
2018–19	Middlesbrough	0	0		
2018–19	*Sheffield U*	11	0	**11**	**0**
2019–20	Middlesbrough	38	1		
2020–21	Middlesbrough	42	3	**97**	**5**

JONES, Isaiah (M) **11 1**
b. 26-6-99
From Tooting & Mitcham U.

2019–20	Middlesbrough	0	0		
2019–20	*St Johnstone*	0	0		
2020–21	Middlesbrough	0	0		
2020–21	*Queen of the South*	11	1	**11**	**1**

KAVANAGH, Calum (F) **0 0**
b. 5-9-03
Internationals: Republic of Ireland U17.

2020–21	Middlesbrough	0	0		

KOKOLO, Williams (D) **0 0**
b. 9-6-00
From Monaco.

2018–19	Sunderland	0	0		
2019–20	Middlesbrough	0	0		
2020–21	Middlesbrough	0	0		

MALLEY, Connor (M) **11 1**
b.Newcastle upon Tyne 20-3-00

2018–19	Middlesbrough	0	0		
2019–20	Middlesbrough	0	0		
2019–20	*Ayr U*	5	1	**5**	**1**
2020–21	Middlesbrough	3	0	**3**	**0**
2020–21	*Carlisle U*	3	0	**3**	**0**

McNAIR, Paddy (D) **152 13**
H: 5 8 W: 11 05 b.Ballyclare 27-4-95
Internationals: Northern Ireland U16, U17, U19, U21, Full caps.

2011–12	Manchester U	0	0		
2012–13	Manchester U	0	0		
2013–14	Manchester U	0	0		
2014–15	Manchester U	16	0		
2015–16	Manchester U	8	0	**24**	**0**
2016–17	Sunderland	9	0		
2017–18	Sunderland	16	5	**25**	**5**
2018–19	Middlesbrough	16	0		
2019–20	Middlesbrough	41	6		
2020–21	Middlesbrough	46	2	**103**	**8**

MENDEZ-LAING, Nathaniel (M) **283 40**
H: 5 10 W: 11 12 b.Birmingham 15-4-92
Internationals: England U16, U17.

2009–10	Wolverhampton W	0	0		
2010–11	Wolverhampton W	0	0		
2010–11	*Peterborough U*	33	5		
2011–12	Wolverhampton W	0	0		
2011–12	*Sheffield U*	8	1	**8**	**1**
2012–13	Peterborough U	21	3		
2012–13	*Portsmouth*	8	0	**8**	**0**
2013–14	Peterborough U	16	1		
2013–14	*Shrewsbury T*	6	0	**6**	**0**
2014–15	Peterborough U	14	0	**84**	**9**
2014–15	*Cambridge U*	11	1	**11**	**1**
2015–16	Rochdale	33	7		
2016–17	Rochdale	39	8	**72**	**15**
2017–18	Cardiff C	38	6		
2018–19	Cardiff C	20	4		
2019–20	Cardiff C	27	3		
2020–21	Cardiff C	0	0	**85**	**13**
2020–21	Middlesbrough	9	1	**9**	**1**

MORSY, Sam (M) **370 20**
H: 5 9 W: 12 06 b.Wolverhampton 10-9-91
Internationals: Egypt Full caps.

2009–10	Port Vale	1	0		
2010–11	Port Vale	16	1		
2011–12	Port Vale	26	1		
2012–13	Port Vale	28	2	**71**	**4**
2013–14	Chesterfield	34	1		
2014–15	Chesterfield	39	2		
2015–16	Chesterfield	26	4	**99**	**7**
2015–16	Wigan Ath	16	1		
2016–17	Wigan Ath	15	1		
2016–17	*Barnsley*	14	0	**14**	**0**
2017–18	Wigan Ath	41	2		
2018–19	Wigan Ath	40	1		
2019–20	Wigan Ath	43	3	**155**	**8**
2020–21	Middlesbrough	31	1	**31**	**1**

RIDLEY, Joseph (F) **0 0**
b. 12-3-03
Internationals: England U16.

2020–21	Middlesbrough	0	0		

ROBINSON, Jack (D) **1 0**
b. 21-6-01

2020–21	Middlesbrough	1	0	**1**	**0**

SAVILLE, George (M) **273 31**
H: 5 9 W: 11 07 b.Camberley 1-6-93
Internationals: Northern Ireland Full caps.

2010–11	Chelsea	0	0		
2011–12	Chelsea	0	0		
2012–13	Chelsea	0	0		
2012–13	*Millwall*	3	0		
2013–14	Chelsea	0	0		
2013–14	*Brentford*	40	3	**40**	**3**
2014–15	Wolverhampton W	7	0		
2014–15	*Bristol C*	7	1	**7**	**1**
2015–16	Wolverhampton W	19	5		
2015–16	*Millwall*	12	0		
2016–17	Wolverhampton W	24	1	**50**	**6**
2017–18	Millwall	44	10		
2018–19	Millwall	4	0	**63**	**10**
2018–19	*Middlesbrough*	34	4		
2019–20	Middlesbrough	37	1		
2020–21	Middlesbrough	42	6	**113**	**11**

SPENCE, Djed (D) **60 2**
H: 6 0 W: 11 03 b.London 9-8-00
From Fulham.

2018–19	Middlesbrough	0	0		
2019–20	Middlesbrough	22	1		
2020–21	Middlesbrough	38	1	**60**	**2**

STOJANOVIC, Dejan (G) **132 0**
b.Feldkirch 19-7-93
Internationals: Macedonia U21.

2009–10	Lustenau	1	0		
2010–11	Lustenau	23	0	**24**	**0**
2011–12	Bologna	0	0		
2012–13	Bologna	4	0		
2013–14	Bologna	1	0		
2014–15	Bologna	5	0		
2014–15	*Crotone*	2	0	**2**	**0**
2015–16	Bologna	0	0	**10**	**0**
2016–17	St Gallen	4	0		
2017–18	St Gallen	13	0		
2018–19	St Gallen	34	0		
2019–20	St Gallen	18	0	**69**	**0**
2019–20	Middlesbrough	8	0		
2020–21	Middlesbrough	0	0	**8**	**0**
2020–21	*St Pauli*	19	0	**19**	**0**

SYKES, Cain (M) **0 0**
b. 14-8-02

2020–21	Middlesbrough	0	0		

TAVERNIER, Marcus (M) **98 10**
b.Leeds 22-3-99
Internationals: England U19, U20.

2017–18	Middlesbrough	5	1		
2017–18	*Milton Keynes D*	7	0	**7**	**0**
2018–19	Middlesbrough	20	3		
2019–20	Middlesbrough	37	3		
2020–21	Middlesbrough	29	3	**91**	**10**

WALKER, Stephen (F) **43 4**
b.Middlesbrough 11-10-00
Internationals: England U17, U18, U19.

2018–19	Middlesbrough	0	0		
2018–19	*Milton Keynes D*	7	0		
2019–20	Middlesbrough	7	0		
2019–20	*Crewe Alex*	6	1		
2020–21	Middlesbrough	0	0	**7**	**0**
2020–21	*Milton Keynes D*	12	2	**19**	**2**
2020–21	*Crewe Alex*	11	1	**17**	**2**

WATMORE, Duncan (F) **110 15**
H: 5 9 W: 11 05 b.Cheadle Hulme 8-3-94
Internationals: England U20, U21.
From Altrincham.

2013–14	Sunderland	0	0		
2013–14	*Hibernian*	9	1	**9**	**1**
2014–15	Sunderland	0	0		
2015–16	Sunderland	23	3		
2016–17	Sunderland	14	0		
2017–18	Sunderland	6	0		
2018–19	Sunderland	11	1		
2019–20	Sunderland	17	1	**71**	**5**
2020–21	Middlesbrough	30	9	**30**	**9**

WING, Lewis (M) **120 17**
b.Durham 23-5-95
From Tow Law T, Seaham Red Star, Darlington 1883, Newton Aycliffe, Seaham Red Star, Shildon.

2017–18	Middlesbrough	0	0		
2017–18	*Yeovil T*	20	3	**20**	**3**
2018–19	Middlesbrough	28	3		
2019–20	Middlesbrough	40	7		
2020–21	Middlesbrough	12	2	**80**	**12**
2020–21	*Rotherham U*	20	2	**20**	**2**

WOOD-GORDON, Nathan (D) **17 0**
b.Middlesbrough 31-5-02
Internationals: England U16, U17, U19.
From Stockton T.

2018–19	Middlesbrough	0	0		
2019–20	Middlesbrough	1	0		
2020–21	Middlesbrough	4	0	**5**	**0**
2020–21	*Crewe Alex*	12	0	**12**	**0**

Scholars
Beals, Ben Alan; Bulmer, Jacob Martin; Collins, Sam Robert; Cornet, Isiah Jean-Louis Casimir; Doherty, Alfie John; Gitau, George Chilaka; Howe, Lucas Oliver; Hutchinson, Alex Lee; John, Fenton Lorimer; Makiesse Lindo, Afonso Mozinho; Marshall, Joshua Rae; Metcalfe, Max Cameron; Nelson, Andrew James; Popple, Henry James; Reed, Lucas James; Simpson, Nathan Taylor; Stott, Jack Patrick John; Swan, Oliver Jay; Waites, George Arthur Aitcheson; Whelan, Frankie Kevin; Willis, Pharrell Jeremiah Kieran; Wilson, Andrew.

MILLWALL (53)

ALEXANDER, George (F) **1 0**
b. 22-6-01

2018–19	Millwall	1	0		
2019–20	Millwall	0	0		
2020–21	Millwall	0	0	**1**	**0**

BENNETT, Mason (F) **152 15**
H: 5 10 W: 10 02 b.Shirebrook 15-7-96
Internationals: England U16, U17, U19.

2011–12	Derby Co	9	0		
2012–13	Derby Co	6	0		
2013–14	Derby Co	13	1		
2013–14	*Chesterfield*	5	0	**5**	**0**
2014–15	Derby Co	2	0		
2014–15	*Bradford C*	11	1	**11**	**1**
2015–16	Derby Co	0	0		
2015–16	*Burton Alb*	16	1	**16**	**1**
2016–17	Derby Co	2	0		
2017–18	Derby Co	3	0		
2017–18	*Notts Co*	2	1	**2**	**1**
2018–19	Derby Co	30	3		
2019–20	Derby Co	7	0	**72**	**4**
2019–20	*Millwall*	9	2		
2020–21	Millwall	37	6	**46**	**8**

BIALKOWSKI, Bartosz (G) **375 0**
H: 6 3 W: 12 10 b.Braniewo 6-7-87
Internationals: Poland U20, U21, Full caps.

2004–05	Gornik Zabrze	7	0	**7**	**0**
2005–06	Southampton	5	0		
2006–07	Southampton	8	0		
2007–08	Southampton	1	0		
2008–09	Southampton	0	0		
2009–10	Southampton	7	0		
2009–10	*Barnsley*	2	0	**2**	**0**
2010–11	Southampton	0	0		
2011–12	Southampton	1	0	**22**	**0**
2012–13	Notts Co	40	0		
2013–14	Notts Co	44	0	**84**	**0**
2014–15	Ipswich T	31	0		
2015–16	Ipswich T	20	0		
2016–17	Ipswich T	44	0		
2017–18	Ipswich T	45	0		
2018–19	Ipswich T	28	0	**168**	**0**
2019–20	Millwall	46	0		
2020–21	Millwall	46	0	**92**	**0**

BODVARSSON, Jon Dadi (F) **340 57**
H: 6 3 W: 13 05 b.Selfoss 25-5-92
Internationals: Iceland U19, U21, Full caps.

2008	Selfoss	0	0		
2009	Selfoss	16	1		
2010	Selfoss	21	3		
2011	Selfoss	21	7		
2012	Selfoss	22	7	**80**	**18**
2013	Viking	23	1		
2014	Viking	29	5		
2015	Viking	29	9	**81**	**15**
2015–16	Kaiserslautern	15	2	**15**	**2**
2016–17	Wolverhampton W	42	3	**42**	**3**
2017–18	Reading	33	7		

2018–19	Reading	20	7	53	14
2019–20	Millwall	31	4		
2020–21	Millwall	38	1	69	5

BRADSHAW, Tom (F) 328 81
H: 5 5 W: 11 02 b.Shrewsbury 27-7-92
Internationals: Wales U19, U21, Full caps.
From Aberystwyth T.

2009–10	Shrewsbury T	6	3		
2010–11	Shrewsbury T	26	6		
2011–12	Shrewsbury T	8	1		
2012–13	Shrewsbury T	21	0		
2013–14	Shrewsbury T	28	7	89	17
2014–15	Walsall	29	17		
2015–16	Walsall	41	17	70	34
2016–17	Barnsley	42	8		
2017–18	Barnsley	39	9		
2018–19	Barnsley	4	1	85	18
2018–19	*Millwall*	10	0		
2019–20	Millwall	45	8		
2020–21	Millwall	29	4	84	12

BROWN, James (D) 34 0
H: 6 1 W: 12 06 b. 12-1-98

2016–17	Millwall	0	0		
2017–18	Millwall	0	0		
2017–18	*Carlisle U*	27	0	27	0
2018–19	Millwall	0	0		
2018–19	*Livingston*	1	0	1	0
2018–19	*Lincoln C*	0	0		
2019–20	Millwall	1	0		
2020–21	Millwall	0	0	1	0
2020–21	*St Johnstone*	5	0	5	0

BUREY, Tyler (F) 17 0
b. 9-1-01

2018–19	AFC Wimbledon	3	0	3	0
2019–20	Millwall	1	0		
2020–21	Millwall	13	0	14	0

COOPER, Jake (D) 229 20
H: 6 4 W: 13 05 b.Bracknell 3-2-95
Internationals: England U18, U19, U20.

2013–14	Reading	0	0		
2014–15	Reading	15	2		
2015–16	Reading	24	2		
2016–17	Reading	3	0	42	4
2016–17	*Millwall*	15	2		
2017–18	Millwall	38	4		
2018–19	Millwall	46	6		
2019–20	Millwall	46	3		
2020–21	Millwall	42	1	187	16

DAVIS, Jayden (M) 0 0
b. 19-11-01

2020–21	Millwall	0	0		

EVANS, George (M) 163 9
H: 6 0 W: 11 12 b.Cheadle 13-12-94
Internationals: England U16, U17, U19.

2012–13	Manchester C	0	0		
2013–14	Manchester C	0	0		
2013–14	*Crewe Alex*	23	1	23	1
2014–15	Manchester C	0	0		
2014–15	*Scunthorpe U*	16	1	16	1
2015–16	Manchester C	0	0		
2015–16	*Walsall*	12	3	12	3
2015–16	Reading	6	0		
2016–17	Reading	35	2		
2017–18	Reading	18	1	59	3
2018–19	Derby Co	11	0		
2019–20	Derby Co	17	0		
2020–21	Derby Co	6	0	34	0
2020–21	Millwall	19	1	19	1

FERGUSON, Shane (D) 232 8
H: 5 9 W: 10 01 b.Limavady 12-7-91
Internationals: Northern Ireland U17, U19, U21, B, Full caps.

2008–09	Newcastle U	0	0		
2009–10	Newcastle U	0	0		
2010–11	Newcastle U	7	0		
2011–12	Newcastle U	7	0		
2012–13	Newcastle U	9	0		
2012–13	*Birmingham C*	11	1		
2013–14	Newcastle U	0	0		
2013–14	*Birmingham C*	18	0	29	1
2014–15	Newcastle U	0	0		
2014–15	*Rangers*	0	0		
2015–16	Newcastle U	0	0	23	0
2015–16	Millwall	39	3		
2016–17	Millwall	40	2		
2017–18	Millwall	24	0		
2018–19	Millwall	35	2		
2019–20	Millwall	29	0		
2020–21	Millwall	13	0	180	7

FIELDING, Frank (G) 324 0
H: 5 11 W: 12 00 b.Blackburn 4-4-88
Internationals: England U19, U21.

2006–07	Blackburn R	0	0		
2007–08	Blackburn R	0	0		
2007–08	*Wycombe W*	36	0	36	0
2008–09	Blackburn R	0	0		
2008–09	*Northampton T*	12	0	12	0
2008–09	*Rochdale*	23	0		
2009–10	Blackburn R	0	0		
2009–10	*Rochdale*	18	0	41	0
2009–10	*Leeds U*	0	0		
2010–11	Blackburn R	0	0		
2010–11	*Derby Co*	16	0		
2011–12	Derby Co	44	0		
2012–13	Derby Co	16	0	76	0
2013–14	Bristol C	16	0		
2014–15	Bristol C	46	0		
2015–16	Bristol C	21	0		
2016–17	Bristol C	27	0		
2017–18	Bristol C	43	0		
2018–19	Bristol C	5	0	158	0
2019–20	Millwall	1	0		
2020–21	Millwall	0	0	1	0

HUTCHINSON, Shaun (D) 318 21
H: 6 1 W: 12 04 b.Newcastle upon Tyne 23-11-90

2008–09	Motherwell	1	0		
2009–10	Motherwell	5	3		
2010–11	Motherwell	19	1		
2011–12	Motherwell	30	1		
2012–13	Motherwell	31	1		
2013–14	Motherwell	35	1	121	7
2014–15	Fulham	25	2		
2015–16	Fulham	9	0	34	2
2016–17	Millwall	16	2		
2017–18	Millwall	46	2		
2018–19	Millwall	26	1		
2019–20	Millwall	36	6		
2020–21	Millwall	39	1	163	12

KIEFTENBELD, Maikel (M) 396 10
H: 5 10 W: 11 11 b.Lemelerveld 26-6-90
Internationals: Netherlands U21.

2008–09	Go Ahead Eagles	30	1		
2009–10	Go Ahead Eagles	33	2	63	3
2010–11	Groningen	33	0		
2011–12	Groningen	26	1		
2012–13	Groningen	29	1		
2013–14	Groningen	31	0		
2014–15	Groningen	33	0	152	2
2015–16	Birmingham C	42	3		
2016–17	Birmingham C	39	1		
2017–18	Birmingham C	35	0		
2018–19	Birmingham C	36	1		
2019–20	Birmingham C	8	0		
2020–21	Birmingham C	10	0	170	5
2020–21	Millwall	11	0	11	0

LEONARD, Ryan (D) 325 24
H: 6 0 W: 11 01 b.Plympton 24-5-92

2009–10	Plymouth Arg	1	0		
2010–11	Plymouth Arg	0	0	1	0
2011–12	Southend U	17	1		
2012–13	Southend U	22	2		
2013–14	Southend U	43	5		
2014–15	Southend U	41	3		
2015–16	Southend U	37	2		
2016–17	Southend U	43	3		
2017–18	Southend U	25	4	228	20
2017–18	Sheffield U	13	0		
2018–19	Sheffield U	3	0	16	0
2018–19	Millwall	37	2		
2019–20	Millwall	17	1		
2020–21	Millwall	26	1	80	4

MAHONEY, Connor (M) 110 5
H: 5 9 W: 10 08 b.Blackburn 12-2-97
Internationals: England U17, U18, U20.

2013–14	Accrington S	4	0	4	0
2013–14	Blackburn R	0	0		
2014–15	Blackburn R	0	0		
2015–16	Blackburn R	2	0		
2016–17	Blackburn R	14	0	16	0
2017–18	Bournemouth	0	0		
2017–18	*Barnsley*	8	0	8	0
2018–19	Bournemouth	0	0		
2018–19	*Birmingham C*	30	2	30	2
2019–20	Millwall	38	2		
2020–21	Millwall	14	1	52	3

McNAMARA, Danny (D) 59 1
b. 27-12-98
Internationals: Republic of Ireland U21.

2018–19	Millwall	0	0		
2019–20	Millwall	0	0		
2019–20	Millwall	0	0		
2019–20	*Newport Co*	21	0	21	0
2020–21	Millwall	16	0	16	0
2020–21	*St Johnstone*	22	1	22	1

MITCHELL, Alex (D) 0 0
b. 12-2-02

2020–21	Millwall	0	0		

MITCHELL, Billy (M) 24 1
b. 7-4-01

2018–19	Millwall	1	0		
2019–20	Millwall	7	0		
2020–21	Millwall	16	1	24	1

MOSS, Dan (D) 0 0
H: 6 2 b.Worcestershire 4-11-00
From Burnley.

2020–21	Millwall	0	0		

MULLER, Hayden (D) 3 0
b. 7-2-02

2019–20	Millwall	1	0		
2020–21	Millwall	2	0	3	0

O'BRIEN, Sean (F) 0 0
H: 5 11 b. 13-10-01
From QPR.

2020–21	Millwall	0	0		

PEARCE, Alex (D) 377 20
H: 6 0 W: 11 10 b.Wallingford 9-11-88
Internationals: Scotland U19, U21, Full caps.

2006–07	Reading	0	0		
2006–07	*Northampton T*	15	1	15	1
2007–08	Reading	0	0		
2007–08	*Bournemouth*	11	0	11	0
2007–08	*Norwich C*	11	0	11	0
2008–09	Reading	16	1		
2008–09	*Southampton*	9	2	9	2
2009–10	Reading	25	4		
2010–11	Reading	21	1		
2011–12	Reading	46	5		
2012–13	Reading	19	0		
2013–14	Reading	45	3		
2014–15	Reading	40	0	212	14
2015–16	Derby Co	0	0		
2015–16	*Bristol C*	7	0	7	0
2016–17	Derby Co	40	2		
2017–18	Derby Co	7	1		
2018–19	Derby Co	1	0	48	3
2018–19	*Millwall*	11	0		
2019–20	Millwall	29	0		
2020–21	Millwall	24	0	64	0

ROMEO, Mahlon (M) 197 3
H: 5 10 W: 11 05 b.Westminster 19-9-95
Internationals: Antigua and Barbuda Full caps.

2012–13	Gillingham	1	0		
2013–14	Gillingham	0	0		
2014–15	Gillingham	0	0	1	0
2015–16	Millwall	18	1		
2016–17	Millwall	32	0		
2017–18	Millwall	27	1		
2018–19	Millwall	41	0		
2019–20	Millwall	43	0		
2020–21	Millwall	35	1	196	3

SKALAK, Jiri (F) 182 21
H: 5 9 W: 10 10 b.Pardubice 12-3-92
Internationals: Czech Republic U16, U17, U18, U19, U20, U21, Full caps.

2010–11	Sparta Prague	0	0		
2011–12	Sparta Prague	0	0		
2011–12	*MFA Ruzomberok*	27	3	27	3
2012–13	Sparta Prague	7	0		
2012–13	*1.FC Slovacko*	9	0	9	0
2013–14	Sparta Prague	3	0		
2013–14	*Zbrojovka Brno*	24	3	24	3
2014–15	Sparta Prague	0	0	10	0
2014–15	*Mlada Boleslav*	24	6		
2015–16	Mlada Boleslav	16	6	40	12
2015–16	Brighton & HA	12	2		
2016–17	Brighton & HA	31	0		
2017–18	Brighton & HA	0	0	43	2
2018–19	Millwall	14	0		
2019–20	Millwall	12	1		
2020–21	Millwall	3	0	29	1

Transferred to Mlada Boleslav February 2021.

SMITH, Matt (F) 339 75
H: 6 6 W: 14 00 b.Birmingham 7-6-89
From New Mills, Redditch U, Droylsden, Solihull Moors.

2011–12	Oldham Ath	28	3		
2011–12	*Macclesfield T*	8	1	8	1
2012–13	Oldham Ath	34	6	62	9
2013–14	Leeds U	39	12		
2014–15	Leeds U	3	0	42	12
2014–15	Fulham	15	5		
2014–15	*Bristol C*	14	7	14	7
2015–16	Fulham	20	2		
2016–17	Fulham	16	2	51	9
2016–17	QPR	16	4		
2017–18	QPR	41	11		
2018–19	QPR	35	6	92	21
2019–20	Millwall	41	13		
2020–21	Millwall	29	3	70	16

THOMPSON, Ben (M) 163 11
H: 5 11 W: 12 04 b. 3-10-95
2014–15 Millwall 0 0
2015–16 Millwall 28 1
2016–17 Millwall 38 0
2017–18 Millwall 3 0
2018–19 Millwall 0 0
2018–19 *Portsmouth* 23 2 **23 2**
2018–19 Millwall 13 4
2019–20 Millwall 28 1
2020–21 Millwall 30 3 **140 9**

TIENSIA, Junior (D) 0 0
2019–20 Millwall 0 0
2020–21 Millwall 0 0

TOPALLOJ, Besart (D) 0 0
b.Bromley 16-5-01
2020–21 Millwall 0 0

WALLACE, Jed (M) 329 63
H: 5 10 W: 10 12 b.Reading 15-12-93
Internationals: England U19.
2011–12 Portsmouth 0 0
2012–13 Portsmouth 22 6
2013–14 Portsmouth 44 7
2014–15 Portsmouth 44 14 **110 27**
2015–16 Wolverhampton W 9 0
2015–16 *Millwall* 12 1
2016–17 Wolverhampton W 9 0 **18 0**
2016–17 *Millwall* 16 3
2017–18 Millwall 43 6
2018–19 Millwall 42 5
2019–20 Millwall 43 10
2020–21 Millwall 45 11 **201 36**

WALLACE, Murray (D) 296 15
H: 6 2 W: 11 07 b.Glasgow 10-1-93
Internationals: Scotland U20, U21.
2010–11 Falkirk 0 0
2011–12 Falkirk 19 2
2011–12 Huddersfield T 0 0
2011–12 *Falkirk* 15 2 **34 4**
2012–13 Huddersfield T 6 1
2013–14 Huddersfield T 17 0
2014–15 Huddersfield T 26 2
2015–16 Huddersfield T 2 0 **51 3**
2015–16 *Scunthorpe U* 33 2
2016–17 Scunthorpe U 46 2
2017–18 Scunthorpe U 45 1 **124 5**
2018–19 Millwall 21 2
2019–20 Millwall 43 0
2020–21 Millwall 23 1 **87 3**

WILLIAMS, Shaun (M) 448 60
H: 5 9 W: 11 11 b.Dublin 19-10-86
Internationals: Republic of Ireland U21, U23, Full caps.
2007 Drogheda U 0 0
2007 *Dundalk* 19 9 **19 9**
2008 Drogheda U 4 0
2008 *Finn Harps* 14 2 **14 2**
2009 Drogheda U 1 0 **5 0**
2009 Sporting Fingal 13 7
2010 Sporting Fingal 32 5 **45 12**
2011–12 Milton Keynes D 39 8
2012–13 Milton Keynes D 44 3
2013–14 Milton Keynes D 25 8 **108 19**
2013–14 Millwall 17 1
2014–15 Millwall 38 2
2015–16 Millwall 33 2
2016–17 Millwall 44 4
2017–18 Millwall 35 2
2018–19 Millwall 31 5
2019–20 Millwall 32 2
2020–21 Millwall 27 0 **257 18**

WRIGHT, Joe (G) 0 0
b. 10-4-01
2020–21 Millwall 0 0

Scholars
Abdulmalik, Abdulsabur Oluwatosin; Adom-Malaki, Sashiel Nino Junior; Allen, Alfie-John Terence; Bate, Oliver John; Boateng, Nana Osei; Briscoe, Tyrese Owen; Dailly, Bobby Alistair Neil; Gillmore, Jordan James; Hammond, Ryan Thomas; Hefzalla, Ramez Alaa Morsi Mohamed; Leahy, Tomas Raymond; Miller, Ezekiel Ethan Niyah; Okoli, Chinwike Ebubechukwu; Penney, Arthur James; Smith, Kyle Ray; Walker, George Julian Robinson.

MILTON KEYNES D (54)

AGARD, Kieran (F) 325 89
H: 5 10 W: 10 10 b.Newham 10-10-89
2006–07 Everton 0 0
2007–08 Everton 0 0
2008–09 Everton 0 0
2009–10 Everton 1 0
2010–11 Everton 0 0 **1 0**
2010–11 *Kilmarnock* 8 1 **8 1**
2010–11 *Peterborough U* 0 0
2011–12 Yeovil T 29 6 **29 6**
2012–13 Rotherham U 30 6
2013–14 Rotherham U 46 21
2014–15 Rotherham U 2 0 **78 27**
2014–15 Bristol C 39 13
2015–16 Bristol C 25 2 **64 15**
2016–17 Milton Keynes D 42 12
2017–18 Milton Keynes D 41 6
2018–19 Milton Keynes D 43 20
2019–20 Milton Keynes D 19 2
2020–21 Milton Keynes D 0 0 **145 40**

BAILEY, Joshua (M) 0 0
2020–21 Milton Keynes D 0 0

BIRD, Jay (F) 2 0
b. 13-9-00
2017–18 Milton Keynes D 0 0
2018–19 Milton Keynes D 0 0
2019–20 Milton Keynes D 0 0
2020–21 Milton Keynes D 2 0 **2 0**

BLACK, Malaki (D) 0 0
2020–21 Milton Keynes D 0 0

BOATENG, Hiram (M) 161 3
H: 5 7 W: 11 00 b.Wandsworth 8-1-96
2012–13 Crystal Palace 0 0
2013–14 Crystal Palace 0 0
2013–14 *Crawley T* 1 0 **1 0**
2014–15 Crystal Palace 0 0
2015–16 Crystal Palace 1 0
2015–16 *Plymouth Arg* 24 1 **24 1**
2016–17 Crystal Palace 0 0 **1 0**
2016–17 *Bristol R* 9 0 **9 0**
2016–17 *Northampton T* 16 0 **16 0**
2017–18 Exeter C 38 1
2018–19 Exeter C 27 1 **65 2**
2019–20 Milton Keynes D 20 0
2020–21 Milton Keynes D 0 0 **20 0**
2020–21 *Cambridge U* 25 0 **25 0**

BROWN, Charlie (F) 23 3
b.Ipswich 23-9-99
2018–19 Chelsea 0 0
2019–20 Chelsea 0 0
2019–20 *Union SG* 3 0 **3 0**
2020–21 Milton Keynes D 20 3 **20 3**

DARLING, Harry (D) 78 2
H: 5 11 W: 11 11 b. 8-8-99
2016–17 Cambridge U 0 0
2017–18 Cambridge U 3 0
2018–19 Cambridge U 12 0
2019–20 Cambridge U 24 2
2020–21 Cambridge U 16 0 **55 2**
2020–21 Milton Keynes D 23 0 **23 0**

DAVIES, Jack (M) 1 0
b. 3-12-02
2020–21 Milton Keynes D 1 0 **1 0**

DENHOLM, Aidan (M) 0 0
b. 9-11-03
2020–21 Hearts 0 0
2020–21 Milton Keynes D 0 0

FISHER, Andy (G) 39 0
b. 12-2-98
2016–17 Blackburn R 0 0
2017–18 Blackburn R 0 0
2018–19 Blackburn R 0 0
2019–20 Blackburn R 0 0
2019–20 *Northampton T* 0 0
2019–20 *Milton Keynes D* 0 0
2020–21 Blackburn R 0 0
2020–21 Milton Keynes D 39 0 **39 0**

FRASER, Scott (M) 225 39
H: 6 0 W: 10 12 b.Dundee 30-3-95
2013–14 Dundee U 1 0
2014–15 Dundee U 0 0
2014–15 *Airdrieonians* 28 5 **28 5**
2015–16 Dundee U 32 1
2016–17 Dundee U 25 4
2017–18 Dundee U 23 4 **81 9**
2018–19 Burton Alb 42 6
2019–20 Burton Alb 30 5 **72 11**
2020–21 Milton Keynes D 44 14 **44 14**

FREEMAN, John (M) 4 0
b. 4-11-01
2019–20 Milton Keynes D 0 0
2020–21 Milton Keynes D 4 0 **4 0**

GLADWIN, Ben (D) 133 15
H: 6 3 b.Reading 8-6-92
From Hayes & Yeading U, Marlow.
2013–14 Swindon T 13 0
2014–15 Swindon T 34 8
2015–16 QPR 7 0
2015–16 *Swindon T* 13 2
2015–16 *Bristol C* 1 0 **1 0**
2016–17 QPR 7 0 **14 0**
2016–17 *Swindon T* 18 2 **78 12**
2017–18 Blackburn R 5 0
2018–19 Blackburn R 0 0 **5 0**
2019–20 Milton Keynes D 9 1
2020–21 Milton Keynes D 26 2 **35 3**

HARVIE, Daniel (D) 129 7
b.Drumchapel 14-7-98
2015–16 Aberdeen 2 0
2016–17 Aberdeen 0 0
2016–17 *Dumbarton* 34 3 **34 3**
2017–18 Aberdeen 2 0 **4 0**
2018–19 Ayr U 33 0
2019–20 Ayr U 27 1 **60 1**
2020–21 Milton Keynes D 31 3 **31 3**

HOUGHTON, Jordan (M) 183 7
H: 6 2 W: 12 13 b.Chertsey 9-11-95
Internationals: England U16, U17, U20.
2015–16 Chelsea 0 0
2015–16 *Gillingham* 11 1 **11 1**
2015–16 *Plymouth Arg* 10 1 **10 1**
2016–17 Chelsea 0 0
2016–17 *Doncaster R* 32 1
2017–18 Chelsea 0 0
2017–18 *Doncaster R* 37 0 **69 1**
2018–19 Milton Keynes D 44 2
2019–20 Milton Keynes D 30 2
2020–21 Milton Keynes D 19 0 **93 4**

ILUNGA, Brooklyn (F) 1 0
2020–21 Milton Keynes D 1 0 **1 0**

JALLOW, Tali (M) 0 0
2020–21 Milton Keynes D 0 0

JEROME, Cameron (F) 564 134
H: 6 1 W: 13 06 b.Huddersfield 14-8-86
Internationals: England U21.
From Huddersfield T, Grimsby T, Sheffield W, Middlesbrough.
2004–05 Cardiff C 29 6
2005–06 Cardiff C 44 18 **73 24**
2005–06 Birmingham C 0 0
2006–07 Birmingham C 38 7
2007–08 Birmingham C 33 7
2008–09 Birmingham C 43 9
2009–10 Birmingham C 32 11
2010–11 Birmingham C 34 3
2011–12 Birmingham C 1 0 **181 37**
2011–12 Stoke C 23 4
2012–13 Stoke C 26 3
2013–14 Stoke C 1 0 **50 7**
2013–14 *Crystal Palace* 28 2 **28 2**
2014–15 Norwich C 41 18
2015–16 Norwich C 34 3
2016–17 Norwich C 40 16
2017–18 Norwich C 15 1 **130 38**
2017–18 Derby Co 18 5 **18 5**
2018–19 Goztepe 28 5
2019–20 Goztepe 22 3 **50 8**
2020–21 Milton Keynes D 34 13 **34 13**

JOHNSON, Lewis (F) 4 0
b. 9-1-04
From Aston Villa.
2020–21 Milton Keynes D 4 0 **4 0**

JULES, Zak (D) 86 3
b. 2-7-97
Internationals: Scotland U17, U18, U19, U20, U21.
2016–17 Reading 0 0
2016–17 *Motherwell* 10 1 **10 1**
2017–18 Shrewsbury T 0 0
2017–18 *Chesterfield* 6 0 **6 0**
2017–18 *Port Vale* 2 0 **2 0**
2018–19 Macclesfield T 14 0 **14 0**
2019–20 Walsall 17 0
2020–21 Walsall 17 1 **34 1**
2020–21 Milton Keynes D 20 1 **20 1**

KASUMU, David (M) 46 1
b. 5-10-99
2015–16 Milton Keynes D 0 0
2016–17 Milton Keynes D 0 0
2017–18 Milton Keynes D 1 0
2018–19 Milton Keynes D 0 0
2019–20 Milton Keynes D 21 1
2020–21 Milton Keynes D 24 0 **46 1**

LEWINGTON, Dean (D) 724 22
H: 5 11 W: 11 07 b.Kingston 18-5-84
2002–03 Wimbledon 1 0
2003–04 Wimbledon 28 1 **29 1**
2004–05 Milton Keynes D 43 2
2005–06 Milton Keynes D 44 1
2006–07 Milton Keynes D 45 1
2007–08 Milton Keynes D 45 0
2008–09 Milton Keynes D 40 2
2009–10 Milton Keynes D 42 1
2010–11 Milton Keynes D 42 3

2011–12 Milton Keynes D 46 3
2012–13 Milton Keynes D 38 1
2013–14 Milton Keynes D 43 1
2014–15 Milton Keynes D 41 3
2015–16 Milton Keynes D 46 1
2016–17 Milton Keynes D 36 1
2017–18 Milton Keynes D 22 0
2018–19 Milton Keynes D 46 1
2019–20 Milton Keynes D 33 0
2020–21 Milton Keynes D 43 0 **695 21**

MASON, Joe (F) 271 60
H: 5 9 W: 11 11 b.Plymouth 13-5-91
Internationals: Republic of Ireland U18, U19, U21.
2009–10 Plymouth Arg 19 3
2010–11 Plymouth Arg 34 7 **53 10**
2011–12 Cardiff C 39 9
2012–13 Cardiff C 28 6
2013–14 Cardiff C 0 0
2013–14 *Bolton W* 16 6
2014–15 Cardiff C 7 1
2014–15 *Bolton W* 12 4 **28 10**
2015–16 Cardiff C 23 6 **97 22**
2015–16 Wolverhampton W 16 3
2016–17 Wolverhampton W 19 3
2017–18 Wolverhampton W 0 0
2017–18 *Burton Alb* 6 1 **6 1**
2018 *Colorado Rapids* 14 3 **14 3**
2018–19 Wolverhampton W 0 0 **35 6**
2018–19 *Portsmouth* 1 0 **1 0**
2019–20 Milton Keynes D 13 3
2020–21 Milton Keynes D 24 5 **37 8**

McEACHRAN, Josh (D) 199 1
H: 5 10 W: 10 03 b.Oxford 1-3-93
Internationals: England U16, U17, U19, U20, U21.
2010–11 Chelsea 9 0
2011–12 Chelsea 2 0
2011–12 *Swansea C* 4 0 **4 0**
2012–13 Chelsea 0 0
2012–13 *Middlesbrough* 38 0 **38 0**
2013–14 Chelsea 0 0
2013–14 *Watford* 7 0 **7 0**
2013–14 *Wigan Ath* 8 0 **8 0**
2014–15 Chelsea 0 0 **11 0**
2014–15 *Vitesse* 19 0 **19 0**
2015–16 Brentford 14 0
2016–17 Brentford 27 0
2017–18 Brentford 25 0
2018–19 Brentford 24 1 **90 1**
2019–20 Birmingham C 8 0
2020–21 Birmingham C 0 0 **8 0**
2020–21 Milton Keynes D 14 0 **14 0**

NICHOLLS, Lee (G) 210 0
H: 6 3 W: 13 05 b.Huyton 5-10-92
Internationals: England U19.
2009–10 Wigan Ath 0 0
2010–11 Wigan Ath 0 0
2010–11 *Hartlepool U* 0 0
2010–11 *Shrewsbury T* 0 0
2010–11 *Sheffield W* 0 0
2011–12 Wigan Ath 0 0
2011–12 *Accrington S* 9 0 **9 0**
2012–13 Wigan Ath 0 0
2012–13 *Northampton T* 46 0 **46 0**
2013–14 Wigan Ath 6 0
2014–15 Wigan Ath 1 0
2015–16 Wigan Ath 2 0 **9 0**
2015–16 *Bristol R* 15 0 **15 0**
2016–17 Milton Keynes D 8 0
2017–18 Milton Keynes D 41 0
2018–19 Milton Keynes D 40 0
2019–20 Milton Keynes D 35 0
2020–21 Milton Keynes D 7 0 **131 0**

NOMBE, Sam (F) 42 2
H: 5 9 W: 11 00 b. 22-10-98
2016–17 Milton Keynes D 0 0
2017–18 Milton Keynes D 6 0
2018–19 Milton Keynes D 0 0
2019–20 Milton Keynes D 21 2
2020–21 Milton Keynes D 4 0 **31 2**
2020–21 *Luton T* 11 0 **11 0**

O'HORA, Warren (D) 42 2
b.Dublin 19-4-99
2016 Bohemians 0 0
2017 Bohemians 11 0 **11 0**
2018–19 Brighton & HA 0 0
2019–20 Brighton & HA 0 0
2020–21 Brighton & HA 0 0
2020–21 Milton Keynes D 31 2 **31 2**

O'RILEY, Matt (M) 24 3
H: 6 2 W: 12 02 b.Hounslow 21-11-00
Internationals: England U16, U18.
2017–18 Fulham 0 0
2018–19 Fulham 0 0
2019–20 Fulham 1 0 **1 0**
2020–21 Milton Keynes D 23 3 **23 3**

ROWLEY, Tom (M) 0 0
2020–21 Milton Keynes D 0 0

SORINOLA, Matthew (D) 34 1
b. 19-2-01
From Fulham.
2019–20 Milton Keynes D 0 0
2020–21 Milton Keynes D 34 1 **34 1**

SURMAN, Andrew (M) 445 37
H: 5 10 W: 11 06 b.Johannesburg 20-8-86
Internationals: England U21.
2003–04 Southampton 0 0
2004–05 Southampton 0 0
2004–05 *Walsall* 14 2 **14 2**
2005–06 Southampton 12 2
2005–06 *Bournemouth* 24 6
2006–07 Southampton 37 4
2007–08 Southampton 40 2
2008–09 Southampton 44 7
2009–10 Southampton 0 0 **133 15**
2009–10 Wolverhampton W 7 0 **7 0**
2010–11 Norwich C 22 3
2011–12 Norwich C 25 4
2012–13 Norwich C 4 0
2013–14 Norwich C 0 0
2013–14 *Bournemouth* 35 0
2014–15 Norwich C 1 0 **52 7**
2014–15 Bournemouth 41 3
2015–16 Bournemouth 38 0
2016–17 Bournemouth 22 0
2017–18 Bournemouth 25 2
2018–19 Bournemouth 18 0
2019–20 Bournemouth 5 0 **208 11**
2020–21 Milton Keynes D 31 2 **31 2**

WALKER, Laurie (G) 13 0
H: 6 5 W: 11 09 b.Histon 14-10-89
From Oxford C, Brackley T, Hemel Hempstead T.
2020–21 Milton Keynes D 0 0
2020–21 *Oldham Ath* 13 0 **13 0**

Scholars
Bailey, Joshua William; Black, Malaki Jemain Zidane; Carter, Thomas Charles; Crane, Max Ambrose; Deall, Rio Christopher; Holmes, James Simon; Holmes, Ryan John; Ilunga, Brooklyn; Jallow, Momodou Talibeh; Ogundega, Olutobi Jason Taufiq; Riley, Harry Thomas; Rowley, Tom; Smith, Charlie Alex.

MORECAMBE (55)

ANDRE MENDES, Filipe Silva (G) 0 0
2019–20 Morecambe 0 0
2020–21 Morecambe 0 0

CONLAN, Luke (D) 127 0
H: 5 11 W: 11 05 b.Portaferry 31-10-94
Internationals: Northern Ireland U16, U17, U19, U21.
2011–12 Burnley 0 0
2012–13 Burnley 0 0
2013–14 Burnley 0 0
2014–15 Burnley 0 0
2015–16 Burnley 0 0
2015–16 *St Mirren* 3 0 **3 0**
2015–16 *Morecambe* 16 0
2016–17 Morecambe 21 0
2017–18 Morecambe 27 0
2018–19 Morecambe 40 0
2019–20 Morecambe 20 0
2020–21 Morecambe 0 0 **124 0**
Transferred to AFC Fylde September 2020.

DAVIS, Harry (D) 293 21
H: 6 2 W: 12 04 b.Burnley 24-9-91
2009–10 Crewe Alex 1 0
2010–11 Crewe Alex 1 0
2011–12 Crewe Alex 41 5
2012–13 Crewe Alex 42 1
2013–14 Crewe Alex 32 3
2014–15 Crewe Alex 31 1
2015–16 Crewe Alex 11 1
2016–17 Crewe Alex 25 1 **184 12**
2016–17 *St Mirren* 6 2
2017–18 St Mirren 20 3 **26 5**
2018–19 Grimsby T 35 4
2019–20 Grimsby T 21 0 **56 4**
2020–21 Morecambe 27 0 **27 0**

DIAGOURAGA, Toumani (M) 461 20
H: 6 2 W: 11 05 b.Paris 10-6-87
2004–05 Watford 0 0
2005–06 Watford 1 0
2005–06 *Swindon T* 8 0
2006–07 Watford 0 0
2006–07 *Rotherham U* 7 0 **7 0**
2007–08 Watford 0 0 **1 0**
2007–08 *Hereford U* 41 2
2008–09 Hereford U 45 2 **86 4**
2009–10 Peterborough U 19 0 **19 0**
2009–10 *Brentford* 20 0
2010–11 Brentford 32 1
2011–12 Brentford 35 4
2012–13 Brentford 39 1
2013–14 Brentford 19 0
2013–14 *Portsmouth* 8 0 **8 0**
2014–15 Brentford 38 0
2015–16 Brentford 27 0 **210 6**
2015–16 Leeds U 17 2
2016–17 Leeds U 1 0
2016–17 *Ipswich T* 12 0 **12 0**
2017–18 Leeds U 0 0 **18 2**
2017–18 Plymouth Arg 15 3 **15 3**
2017–18 Fleetwood T 17 1 **17 1**
2018–19 Swindon T 12 0
2019–20 Swindon T 0 0 **20 0**
2019–20 Morecambe 12 1
2020–21 Morecambe 36 3 **48 4**

GIBSON, Liam (D) 45 0
H: 6 1 W: 12 08 b.Stanley 25-4-97
2015–16 Newcastle U 0 0
2016–17 Newcastle U 0 0
2017–18 Newcastle U 0 0
2018–19 Newcastle U 0 0
2018–19 *Accrington S* 5 0 **5 0**
2019–20 Newcastle U 0 0
2019–20 *Grimsby T* 17 0 **17 0**
2020–21 Morecambe 23 0 **23 0**

HALSTEAD, Mark (G) 70 0
H: 6 3 W: 14 00 b.Blackpool 1-9-90
2009–10 Blackpool 0 0
2010–11 Blackpool 1 0
2011–12 Blackpool 0 0
2012–13 Blackpool 2 0
2013–14 Blackpool 0 0 **3 0**
2014–15 Shrewsbury T 1 0
2015–16 Shrewsbury T 16 0
2016–17 Shrewsbury T 3 0 **20 0**
From Southport.
2018–19 Morecambe 26 0
2019–20 Morecambe 12 0
2020–21 Morecambe 9 0 **47 0**

HENDRIE, Stephen (D) 184 2
H: 5 10 W: 11 00 b.Glasgow 8-1-95
Internationals: Scotland U17, U19, U20, U21.
2010–11 Hamilton A 0 0
2011–12 Hamilton A 25 0
2012–13 Hamilton A 23 0
2013–14 Hamilton A 22 0
2014–15 Hamilton A 30 0 **100 0**
2015–16 West Ham U 0 0
2015–16 *Southend U* 5 1
2016–17 West Ham U 0 0
2016–17 *Blackburn R* 4 0 **4 0**
2017–18 Southend U 12 0
2017–18 *Motherwell* 6 0 **6 0**
2018–19 Southend U 19 0 **36 1**
2019–20 Kilmarnock 2 0 **2 0**
2020–21 Morecambe 36 1 **36 1**

KENYON, Alex (M) 239 9
H: 5 11 W: 11 12 b.Preston 17-7-92
From Everton, Chorley, Lancaster C, Stockport Co.
2013–14 Morecambe 39 0
2014–15 Morecambe 37 3
2015–16 Morecambe 29 3
2016–17 Morecambe 19 0
2017–18 Morecambe 38 0
2018–19 Morecambe 32 1
2019–20 Morecambe 27 1
2020–21 Morecambe 18 1 **239 9**

KNIGHT-PERCIVAL, Nathaniel (M) 273 13
H: 6 0 W: 11 06 b.Cambridge 31-3-87
Internationals: England C.
From Histon, Wrexham.
2012–13 Peterborough U 31 0
2013–14 Peterborough U 15 1 **46 1**
2014–15 Shrewsbury T 28 1
2015–16 Shrewsbury T 35 5 **63 6**
2016–17 Bradford C 42 0
2017–18 Bradford C 41 4
2018–19 Bradford C 35 2 **118 6**
2019–20 Carlisle U 15 0 **15 0**
2020–21 Morecambe 31 0 **31 0**

LAVELLE, Sam (D) 134 4
H: 6 0 W: 12 00 b. 3-10-96
Internationals: Scotland U18, U19.
2015–16 Blackburn R 0 0
2016–17 Bolton W 0 0
2017–18 Morecambe 27 1
2018–19 Morecambe 31 1

2019–20 Morecambe 31 1
2020–21 Morecambe 45 1 **134 4**

LEITCH-SMITH, AJ (F) 284 51
H: 5 11 W: 12 04 b.Crewe 6-3-90
2008–09 Crewe Alex 0 0
2009 *IBV* 14 4 **14 4**
2009–10 Crewe Alex 1 0
2010–11 Crewe Alex 16 5
2011–12 Crewe Alex 38 8
2012–13 Crewe Alex 28 4
2013–14 Crewe Alex 20 2 **103 19**
2014–15 Yeovil T 33 2 **33 2**
2015–16 Port Vale 37 10 **37 10**
2016–17 Shrewsbury T 16 1
2017–18 Shrewsbury T 0 0 **16 1**
2017–18 *Dundee* 28 6 **28 6**
2018–19 Morecambe 25 6
2019–20 Morecambe 23 2
2020–21 Morecambe 5 1 **53 9**

LETHEREN, Kyle (G) 126 0
H: 6 2 W: 13 00 b.Swansea 26-12-87
Internationals: Wales U21.
2005–06 Swansea C 0 0
2006–07 Barnsley 0 0
2007–08 Barnsley 0 0
2008–09 Barnsley 0 0
2008–09 *Doncaster R* 0 0
2009–10 Plymouth Arg 0 0
2010–11 Kilmarnock 0 0
2011–12 Kilmarnock 2 0
2012–13 Kilmarnock 9 0 **11 0**
2013–14 Dundee 35 0
2014–15 Dundee 15 0 **50 0**
2015–16 Blackpool 5 0
2016–17 Blackpool 0 0 **5 0**
From York C.
2017–18 Plymouth Arg 7 0
2018–19 Plymouth Arg 13 0 **20 0**
2019–20 Salford C 19 0 **19 0**
2020–21 Morecambe 21 0 **21 0**

McALINDEN, Liam (F) 151 18
H: 6 1 W: 11 10 b.Cannock 26-9-93
Internationals: Northern Ireland U21. Republic of Ireland U21.
2010–11 Wolverhampton W 0 0
2011–12 Wolverhampton W 0 0
2012–13 Wolverhampton W 1 0
2013–14 Wolverhampton W 7 1
2013–14 *Shrewsbury T* 9 3
2014–15 Wolverhampton W 6 0
2014–15 *Fleetwood T* 19 4 **19 4**
2015–16 Wolverhampton W 0 0 **14 1**
2015–16 *Shrewsbury T* 8 0 **17 3**
2015–16 *Crawley T* 6 1 **6 1**
2016–17 Exeter C 32 5
2017–18 Exeter C 29 2 **61 7**
2018–19 Cheltenham T 6 0 **6 0**
From FC Halifax T.
2020–21 Morecambe 28 2 **28 2**

MELLOR, Kelvin (D) 314 19
H: 5 10 W: 11 09 b.Copenhagen 25-1-91
From Nantwich T.
2007–08 Crewe Alex 0 0
2008–09 Crewe Alex 0 0
2009–10 Crewe Alex 0 0
2010–11 Crewe Alex 1 0
2011 *IBV* 10 2 **10 2**
2011–12 Crewe Alex 12 1
2012–13 Crewe Alex 35 0
2013–14 Crewe Alex 28 1 **76 2**
2014–15 Plymouth Arg 37 1
2015–16 Plymouth Arg 41 1 **78 2**
2016–17 Blackpool 44 4
2017–18 Blackpool 29 6 **73 10**
2018–19 Bradford C 20 1
2019–20 Bradford C 25 1 **45 2**
2020–21 Morecambe 32 1 **32 1**

MENDES GOMES, Carlos (F) 74 17
b. 14-11-98
From Atletico Madrid, West Didsbury & Chorlton.
2018–19 Morecambe 15 0
2019–20 Morecambe 16 2
2020–21 Morecambe 43 15 **74 17**

O'SULLIVAN, John (M) 197 14
H: 5 11 W: 13 01 b.Birmingham 18-9-93
Internationals: Republic of Ireland U19, U21.
2011–12 Blackburn R 0 0
2012–13 Blackburn R 1 0
2013–14 Blackburn R 0 0
2014–15 Blackburn R 2 0
2014–15 *Accrington S* 13 4
2014–15 *Barnsley* 8 0 **8 0**
2015–16 Blackburn R 2 0
2015–16 *Rochdale* 2 0 **2 0**
2015–16 *Bury* 19 0 **19 0**
2016–17 Blackburn R 0 0 **5 0**
2016–17 *Accrington S* 19 1 **32 5**
2016–17 Carlisle U 17 1
2017–18 Carlisle U 18 1 **35 2**
2018–19 Blackpool 13 0 **13 0**
2018–19 *Dundee* 11 0 **11 0**
2019–20 Morecambe 34 3
2020–21 Morecambe 38 4 **72 7**

PRICE, Freddie (M) 11 1
b. 12-5-02
2018–19 Morecambe 0 0
2020–21 Morecambe 11 1 **11 1**

PRINGLE, Ben (M) 269 24
H: 5 8 W: 11 10 b.Whitley Bay 25-7-88
From Newcastle Blue Star, Morpeth T, Ilkeston T.
2009–10 Derby Co 5 0
2010–11 Derby Co 15 0 **20 0**
2010–11 *Torquay U* 5 0 **5 0**
2011–12 Rotherham U 21 4
2012–13 Rotherham U 41 7
2013–14 Rotherham U 45 5
2014–15 Rotherham U 40 3 **147 19**
2015–16 Fulham 15 2 **15 2**
2015–16 *Ipswich T* 10 2 **10 2**
2016–17 Preston NE 10 0
2017–18 Preston NE 0 0
2017–18 *Oldham Ath* 13 1 **13 1**
2018–19 Preston NE 0 0 **10 0**
2018–19 *Grimsby T* 15 0 **15 0**
2018–19 *Tranmere R* 13 0 **13 0**
2019–20 Gillingham 10 0 **10 0**
2020–21 Morecambe 11 0 **11 0**

SLEW, Jordan (F) 155 12
H: 6 3 W: 12 11 b.Sheffield 7-9-92
Internationals: England U19.
2010–11 Sheffield U 7 2
2011–12 Sheffield U 4 1 **11 3**
2011–12 Blackburn R 1 0
2011–12 *Stevenage* 9 0 **9 0**
2012–13 Blackburn R 0 0
2012–13 *Oldham Ath* 3 0 **3 0**
2012–13 *Rotherham U* 7 0 **7 0**
2013–14 Blackburn R 0 0
2013–14 *Ross Co* 20 1 **20 1**
2014–15 Blackburn R 0 0 **1 0**
2014–15 *Port Vale* 9 2 **9 2**
2014–15 Cambridge U 13 1
2015–16 Cambridge U 10 0 **23 1**
2015–16 Chesterfield 7 0 **7 0**
2016–17 Plymouth Arg 32 4 **32 4**
2017–18 Rochdale 5 0 **5 0**
From Boston U.
2019–20 Morecambe 11 0
2020–21 Morecambe 17 1 **28 1**

SONGO'O, Yann (D) 210 12
H: 6 0 W: 12 00 b.Yaounde 17-11-91
Internationals: France U16. Cameroon U20.
From Real Zaragoza.
2011–12 Sabadell 6 0 **6 0**
2013 Sporting Kansas C 0 0
2013 *Orlando C* 12 1 **12 1**
2013–14 Blackburn R 0 0
2013–14 *Ross Co* 17 3 **17 3**
2014–15 Blackburn R 0 0
2016–17 Plymouth Arg 46 2
2017–18 Plymouth Arg 33 0
2018–19 Plymouth Arg 42 0 **121 2**
2019–20 Scunthorpe U 16 0 **16 0**
2020–21 Morecambe 38 6 **38 6**

STOCKTON, Cole (F) 211 36
H: 6 1 W: 11 11 b.Huyton 13-3-94
2011–12 Tranmere R 1 0
2012–13 Tranmere R 31 3
2013–14 Tranmere R 21 2
2014–15 Tranmere R 22 4
2015–16 Tranmere R 0 0
2015–16 *Morecambe* 7 2
2016–17 Tranmere R 0 0
2016–17 *Morecambe* 19 5
2017–18 Hearts 12 0 **12 0**
2017–18 Carlisle U 12 1 **12 1**
2018–19 Tranmere R 16 1 **91 10**
2019–20 Morecambe 30 5
2020–21 Morecambe 40 13 **96 25**

WILDIG, Aaron (M) 271 24
H: 5 9 W: 11 02 b.Hereford 15-4-92
Internationals: Wales U16.
2009–10 Cardiff C 11 1
2010–11 Cardiff C 2 0
2010–11 *Hamilton A* 3 0 **3 0**
2011–12 Cardiff C 0 0 **13 1**
2011–12 *Shrewsbury T* 12 2
2012–13 Shrewsbury T 21 1
2013–14 Shrewsbury T 30 2
2014–15 Shrewsbury T 1 0 **64 5**
2014–15 *Morecambe* 9 1
2015–16 Morecambe 32 2
2016–17 Morecambe 28 2
2017–18 Morecambe 31 1
2018–19 Morecambe 26 1
2019–20 Morecambe 28 3
2020–21 Morecambe 37 8 **191 18**

Scholars
Connolly, Lewis Michael; Da Silva Mendes, Andre Filipe; Edgar, Lewis Jack; Flitcroft, Bobby Jon; Giwa, Adeyinka Oluwayesi; Greenwood, Jack; Huddleston, Keallen Daniel; Lawton, Joseph Lee; Lowe, Benjamin James; Ly, Bryan Calum; Mayor, Adam Matthew; Morton, Josh; Nicholson, Jamie Gerard; O'Brien, Harry James Kenneth; Pye, Connor Albert Robert; Shogbeni, Abdulmojeed Eniola; Spraggon, Louis Jake.

NEWCASTLE U (56)

ALLAN, Thomas (F) 4 0
b. 23-9-99
2019–20 Newcastle U 0 0
2020–21 Newcastle U 0 0
2020–21 *Accrington S* 4 0 **4 0**

ALMIRON, Miguel (M) 216 38
H: 5 10 W: 11 00 b.Asuncion 13-11-93
Internationals: Paraguay U17, U20, Full caps.
2013 Cerro Porteno 6 1
2014 Cerro Porteno 14 0
2015 Cerro Porteno 19 5 **39 6**
2015 Lanus 10 0
2016 Lanus 25 3 **35 3**
2017 Atalanta 30 9
2018 Atalanta 32 12 **62 21**
2018–19 Newcastle U 10 0
2019–20 Newcastle U 36 4
2020–21 Newcastle U 34 4 **80 8**

ANDERSON, Elliot (M) 1 0
b.Whitley Bay 6-11-02
2020–21 Newcastle U 1 0 **1 0**

ATSU, Christian (F) 196 22
H: 5 8 W: 10 09 b.Ada Foah 10-1-92
Internationals: Ghana Full caps.
2010–11 Porto 0 0
2011–12 Porto 0 0
2011–12 *Rio Ave* 27 6 **27 6**
2012–13 Porto 17 1 **17 1**
2013–14 Chelsea 0 0
2013–14 *Vitesse* 28 5 **28 5**
2014–15 Chelsea 0 0
2014–15 *Everton* 5 0 **5 0**
2015–16 Chelsea 0 0
2015–16 *Bournemouth* 0 0
2015–16 *Malaga* 12 2 **12 2**
2016–17 Chelsea 0 0
2016–17 *Newcastle U* 32 5
2017–18 Newcastle U 28 2
2018–19 Newcastle U 28 1
2019–20 Newcastle U 19 0
2020–21 Newcastle U 0 0 **107 8**

BARRETT, Ryan (D) 0 0
b.Wrexham 5-6-01
Internationals: Wales U17.
2020–21 Newcastle U 0 0

BONDSWELL, Matthew (D) 6 0
b.Nottingham 18-4-02
Internationals: England U16, U17, U18.
2020–21 RB Leipzig 0 0
2020–21 *Dordrecht* 6 0 **6 0**
2020–21 Newcastle U 0 0

BROOKWELL, Niall (M) 0 0
b.Wigan 22-3-02
From Liverpool.
2020–21 Newcastle U 0 0

BROWN, Will (G) 0 0
b.Newcastle upon Tyne 10-1-02
2020–21 Newcastle U 0 0

CARROLL, Andy (F) 298 72
H: 6 4 W: 11 00 b.Gateshead 6-1-89
Internationals: England U19, U21, Full caps.
2006–07 Newcastle U 4 0
2007–08 Newcastle U 4 0
2007–08 *Preston NE* 11 1 **11 1**
2008–09 Newcastle U 14 3
2009–10 Newcastle U 39 17
2010–11 Newcastle U 19 11
2010–11 Liverpool 7 2
2011–12 Liverpool 35 4
2012–13 Liverpool 2 0 **44 6**
2012–13 *West Ham U* 24 7
2013–14 West Ham U 15 2
2014–15 West Ham U 14 5

2015–16 West Ham U 27 9
2016–17 West Ham U 18 7
2017–18 West Ham U 16 3
2018–19 West Ham U 12 0 **126 33**
2019–20 Newcastle U 19 0
2020–21 Newcastle U 18 1 **117 32**

CLARK, Ciaran (D) 235 18
H: 6 2 W: 12 00 b.Harrow 26-9-89
Internationals: England U17, U18, U19, U20. Republic of Ireland Full caps.
2008–09 Aston Villa 0 0
2009–10 Aston Villa 1 0
2010–11 Aston Villa 19 3
2011–12 Aston Villa 15 1
2012–13 Aston Villa 29 1
2013–14 Aston Villa 27 0
2014–15 Aston Villa 25 1
2015–16 Aston Villa 18 1 **134 7**
2016–17 Newcastle U 34 3
2017–18 Newcastle U 20 2
2018–19 Newcastle U 11 3
2019–20 Newcastle U 14 2
2020–21 Newcastle U 22 1 **101 11**

CROSS, Bradley (D) 0 0
H: 6 0 W: 12 02 b.Gauteng 30-1-01
From Schalke 04.
2020–21 Newcastle U 0 0

DARLOW, Karl (G) 193 0
H: 6 1 W: 12 05 b.Northampton 8-10-90
2009–10 Nottingham F 0 0
2010–11 Nottingham F 1 0
2011–12 Nottingham F 0 0
2012–13 Nottingham F 20 0
2012–13 *Walsall* 9 0 **9 0**
2013–14 Nottingham F 43 0
2014–15 Newcastle U 0 0
2014–15 *Nottingham F* 42 0 **106 0**
2015–16 Newcastle U 9 0
2016–17 Newcastle U 34 0
2017–18 Newcastle U 10 0
2018–19 Newcastle U 0 0
2019–20 Newcastle U 0 0
2020–21 Newcastle U 25 0 **78 0**

DUBRAVKA, Martin (G) 304 0
H: 6 3 W: 13 01 b.Zilina 15-1-89
Internationals: Slovakia U19, U21, Full caps.
2008–09 Zilina 1 0
2009–10 Zilina 26 0
2010–11 Zilina 24 0
2011–12 Zilina 8 0
2012–13 Zilina 26 0
2013–14 Zilina 13 0 **98 0**
2013–14 Esbjerg 15 0
2014–15 Esbjerg 33 0
2015–16 Esbjerg 18 0 **66 0**
2016–17 Slovan Liberec 28 0 **28 0**
2017–18 Sparta Prague 11 0 **11 0**
2017–18 *Newcastle U* 12 0
2018–19 Newcastle U 38 0
2019–20 Newcastle U 38 0
2020–21 Newcastle U 13 0 **101 0**

DUMMETT, Paul (D) 218 5
H: 5 10 W: 10 02 b.Newcastle 26-9-91
Internationals: Wales U21, Full caps.
2010–11 Newcastle U 0 0
2011–12 Newcastle U 0 0
2012–13 Newcastle U 0 0
2012–13 *St Mirren* 30 2 **30 2**
2013–14 Newcastle U 18 1
2014–15 Newcastle U 25 0
2015–16 Newcastle U 23 1
2016–17 Newcastle U 45 0
2017–18 Newcastle U 20 0
2018–19 Newcastle U 26 0
2019–20 Newcastle U 16 0
2020–21 Newcastle U 15 1 **188 3**

FERNANDEZ, Federico (D) 310 9
H: 6 3 W: 13 01 b.Tres Algarrobos 21-2-89
Internationals: Argentina U20, Full caps.
2008–09 Estudiantes 14 2
2009–10 Estudiantes 12 1
2010–11 Estudiantes 33 1 **59 4**
2011–12 Napoli 16 0
2012–13 Napoli 2 0
2012–13 *Getafe* 14 1 **14 1**
2013–14 Napoli 26 0 **44 0**
2014–15 Swansea C 28 0
2015–16 Swansea C 32 1
2016–17 Swansea C 27 0
2017–18 Swansea C 30 1
2018–19 Swansea C 1 0 **118 2**
2018–19 Newcastle U 19 0
2019–20 Newcastle U 32 2
2020–21 Newcastle U 24 0 **75 2**

FLAHERTY, Stan (M) 0 0
b.Hillingdon 5-12-01
From Arsenal.
2020–21 Newcastle U 0 0

FRASER, Ryan (M) 240 24
H: 5 4 W: 10 13 b.Aberdeen 24-2-94
Internationals: Scotland U19, U21, Full caps.
2010–11 Aberdeen 2 0
2011–12 Aberdeen 3 0
2012–13 Aberdeen 16 0 **21 0**
2012–13 Bournemouth 5 0
2013–14 Bournemouth 37 3
2014–15 Bournemouth 21 1
2015–16 Bournemouth 0 0
2015–16 *Ipswich T* 18 4 **18 4**
2016–17 Bournemouth 28 3
2017–18 Bournemouth 26 5
2018–19 Bournemouth 38 7
2019–20 Bournemouth 28 1 **183 20**
2020–21 Newcastle U 18 0 **18 0**

GAYLE, Dwight (F) 255 92
H: 5 10 W: 11 07 b.Walthamstow 20-10-89
2011–12 Dagenham & R 0 0
2012–13 Dagenham & R 18 7 **18 7**
2012–13 Peterborough U 29 13 **29 13**
2013–14 Crystal Palace 23 7
2014–15 Crystal Palace 25 5
2015–16 Crystal Palace 16 3 **64 15**
2016–17 Newcastle U 32 23
2017–18 Newcastle U 35 6
2018–19 Newcastle U 0 0
2018–19 *WBA* 39 23 **39 23**
2019–20 Newcastle U 20 4
2020–21 Newcastle U 18 1 **105 34**

GILLESPIE, Mark (G) 241 0
H: 6 3 W: 13 07 b.Newcastle upon Tyne 27-3-92
From Newcastle U.
2009–10 Carlisle U 1 0
2010–11 Carlisle U 0 0
2011–12 Carlisle U 0 0
2012–13 Carlisle U 35 0
2013–14 Carlisle U 15 0
2014–15 Carlisle U 19 0
2015–16 Carlisle U 45 0
2016–17 Carlisle U 46 0 **161 0**
2017–18 Walsall 23 0 **23 0**
2018–19 Motherwell 27 0
2019–20 Motherwell 30 0 **57 0**
2020–21 Newcastle U 0 0

HAYDEN, Isaac (D) 155 6
H: 6 2 W: 12 06 b.Chelmsford 22-3-95
Internationals: England U16, U17, U18, U19, U20, U21.
2011–12 Arsenal 0 0
2012–13 Arsenal 0 0
2013–14 Arsenal 0 0
2014–15 Arsenal 0 0
2015–16 Arsenal 0 0
2015–16 *Hull C* 18 1 **18 1**
2016–17 Newcastle U 33 2
2017–18 Newcastle U 26 1
2018–19 Newcastle U 25 1
2019–20 Newcastle U 29 1
2020–21 Newcastle U 24 0 **137 5**

HENDRICK, Jeff (M) 340 33
H: 6 1 W: 11 11 b.Dublin 31-1-92
Internationals: Republic of Ireland U17, U19, U21, Full caps.
2010–11 Derby Co 4 0
2011–12 Derby Co 42 3
2012–13 Derby Co 45 6
2013–14 Derby Co 30 4
2014–15 Derby Co 41 7
2015–16 Derby Co 32 2
2016–17 Derby Co 2 0 **196 22**
2016–17 Burnley 32 2
2017–18 Burnley 34 2
2018–19 Burnley 32 3
2019–20 Burnley 24 2
2020–21 Burnley 0 0 **122 9**
2020–21 Newcastle U 22 2 **22 2**

JOELINTON, de Lira (F) 170 31
b. 14-8-96
Internationals: Brazil U17.
2014 Sport Recife 7 2
2015 Sport Recife 5 1 **12 3**
2015–16 Hoffenheim 1 0
2016–17 Hoffenheim 0 0
2016–17 *Rapid Vienna* 33 8
2017–18 Hoffenheim 0 0
2017–18 *Rapid Vienna* 27 7 **60 15**
2018–19 Hoffenheim 28 7 **29 7**
2019–20 Newcastle U 38 2
2020–21 Newcastle U 31 4 **69 6**

KRAFTH, Emil (D) 210 5
b.Ljungby 2-8-94
Internationals: Sweden U17, U19, U21, Full caps.
From Lagans.
2011 Osters 24 0 **24 0**
2012 Helsingborgs 9 0
2013 Helsingborgs 27 1
2014 Helsingborgs 28 1
2015 Helsingborgs 12 1 **76 3**
2015–16 Bologna 4 0
2016–17 Bologna 26 0
2017–18 Bologna 12 0 **42 0**
2018–19 Amiens 35 1 **35 1**
2019–20 Newcastle U 17 0
2020–21 Newcastle U 16 1 **33 1**

LANGLEY, Dan (G) 0 0
b.Newcastle upon Tyne 28-12-00
2020–21 Newcastle U 0 0

LASCELLES, Jamaal (D) 234 15
H: 6 2 W: 13 01 b.Derby 11-11-93
Internationals: England U18, U19, U20, U21.
2010–11 Nottingham F 0 0
2011–12 Nottingham F 1 0
2011–12 *Stevenage* 7 1 **7 1**
2012–13 Nottingham F 2 0
2013–14 Nottingham F 29 2
2014–15 Newcastle U 0 0
2014–15 *Nottingham F* 26 1 **58 3**
2015–16 Newcastle U 18 2
2016–17 Newcastle U 43 3
2017–18 Newcastle U 33 3
2018–19 Newcastle U 32 0
2019–20 Newcastle U 24 1
2020–21 Newcastle U 19 2 **169 11**

LEWIS, Jamal (D) 116 1
b. 25-1-98
Internationals: Northern Ireland U19, U21, Full caps.
2017–18 Norwich C 22 0
2018–19 Norwich C 42 0
2019–20 Norwich C 28 1
2020–21 Norwich C 0 0 **92 1**
2020–21 Newcastle U 24 0 **24 0**

LONGELO, Rosaire (M) 0 0
b.Kinshasa 20-10-99
From West Ham U.
2020–21 Newcastle U 0 0

LONGSTAFF, Matthew (M) 14 2
b. 21-3-00
Internationals: England U20.
2019–20 Newcastle U 9 2
2020–21 Newcastle U 5 0 **14 2**

LONGSTAFF, Sean (M) 128 16
H: 5 11 W: 10 03 b.North Shields 30-10-97
2016–17 Newcastle U 0 0
2016–17 *Kilmarnock* 16 3
2016–17 Newcastle U 0 0
2016–17 *Kilmarnock* 16 3 **32 6**
2017–18 Newcastle U 0 0
2017–18 *Blackpool* 42 8 **42 8**
2018–19 Newcastle U 9 1
2019–20 Newcastle U 23 1
2020–21 Newcastle U 22 0 **54 2**

MANQUILLO, Javier (D) 140 1
H: 5 11 W: 12 04 b.Madrid 5-5-94
Internationals: Spain U16, U17, U18, U19, U20, U21.
2012–13 Atletico Madrid 3 0
2013–14 Atletico Madrid 3 0
2014–15 Atletico Madrid 0 0
2014–15 *Liverpool* 10 0 **10 0**
2015–16 Atletico Madrid 0 0
2015–16 *Marseille* 31 0 **31 0**
2016–17 Atletico Madrid 0 0 **6 0**
2016–17 *Sunderland* 20 1 **20 1**
2017–18 Newcastle U 21 0
2018–19 Newcastle U 18 0
2019–20 Newcastle U 21 0
2020–21 Newcastle U 13 0 **73 0**

McENTEE, Oisin (D) 0 0
H: 6 4 W: 12 04 b.New York 5-1-01
Internationals: Republic of Ireland U17, U18, U19, U21.
2020–21 Newcastle U 0 0

MURPHY, Jacob (M) 225 39
H: 5 9 W: 11 03 b.Wembley 24-2-95
Internationals: England U18, U19, U20, U21.
2013–14 Norwich C 0 0
2013–14 *Swindon T* 6 0 **6 0**
2013–14 *Southend U* 7 1 **7 1**
2014–15 Norwich C 0 0
2014–15 *Blackpool* 9 2 **9 2**
2014–15 *Scunthorpe U* 3 0 **3 0**

2014–15 *Colchester U* 11 4 **11 4**
2015–16 Norwich C 0 0
2015–16 *Coventry C* 40 9 **40 9**
2016–17 Norwich C 37 9 **37 9**
2017–18 Newcastle U 25 1
2018–19 Newcastle U 9 0
2018–19 *WBA* 13 2 **13 2**
2019–20 Newcastle U 0 0
2019–20 *Sheffield W* 39 9 **39 9**
2020–21 Newcastle U 26 2 **60 3**

RITCHIE, Matt (M) 446 90
H: 5 8 W: 11 00 b.Gosport 10-9-89
Internationals: Scotland Full caps.
2008–09 Portsmouth 0 0
2008–09 *Dagenham & R* 37 11 **37 11**
2009–10 Portsmouth 2 0
2009–10 *Notts Co* 16 3 **16 3**
2009–10 *Swindon T* 4 0
2010–11 Portsmouth 5 0 **7 0**
2010–11 Swindon T 36 7
2011–12 Swindon T 40 10
2012–13 Swindon T 27 9 **107 26**
2012–13 Bournemouth 17 3
2013–14 Bournemouth 30 9
2014–15 Bournemouth 46 15
2015–16 Bournemouth 37 4 **130 31**
2016–17 Newcastle U 42 12
2017–18 Newcastle U 35 3
2018–19 Newcastle U 36 2
2019–20 Newcastle U 18 2
2020–21 Newcastle U 18 0 **149 19**

SAINT-MAXIMIN, Allan (F) 178 19
b.Chatenay-Malabry 12-3-97
Internationals: France U16, U17, U20, U21.
2013–14 Saint-Etienne 3 0
2014–15 Saint-Etienne 9 0
2015–16 Saint-Etienne 0 0
2015–16 *Hannover 96* 16 1 **16 1**
2016–17 Saint-Etienne 0 0 **12 0**
2016–17 *Bastia* 34 3 **34 3**
2017–18 Monaco 1 0 **1 0**
2017–18 Nice 30 3
2018–19 Nice 34 6 **64 9**
2019–20 Newcastle U 26 3
2020–21 Newcastle U 25 3 **51 6**

SANGARE, Mohammed (M) 2 0
b. 28-12-98
2019–20 Newcastle U 0 0
2020–21 Newcastle U 0 0
2020–21 *Accrington S* 2 0 **2 0**

SCHAR, Fabian (D) 248 24
H: 6 1 W: 13 05 b.Wil 20-12-91
Internationals: Switzerland U20, U21, U23, Full caps.
2009–10 FC Wil 2 0
2010–11 FC Wil 24 4
2011–12 FC Wil 30 1 **56 5**
2012–13 FC Basel 21 4
2013–14 FC Basel 22 4
2014–15 FC Basel 30 1 **73 9**
2015–16 1899 Hoffenheim 24 1
2016–17 1899 Hoffenheim 6 0 **30 1**
2017–18 Deportivo La Coruna 25 2 **25 2**
2018–19 Newcastle U 24 4
2019–20 Newcastle U 22 2
2020–21 Newcastle U 18 1 **64 7**

SHELVEY, Jonjo (M) 337 39
H: 6 1 W: 11 02 b.Romford 27-2-92
Internationals: England U16, U17, U19, U21, Full caps.
2007–08 Charlton Ath 2 0
2008–09 Charlton Ath 16 3
2009–10 Charlton Ath 24 4 **42 7**
2010–11 Liverpool 15 0
2011–12 Liverpool 13 1
2011–12 *Blackpool* 10 6 **10 6**
2012–13 Liverpool 19 1 **47 2**
2013–14 Swansea C 32 6
2014–15 Swansea C 31 3
2015–16 Swansea C 16 1 **79 10**
2015–16 Newcastle U 15 0
2016–17 Newcastle U 42 5
2017–18 Newcastle U 30 1
2018–19 Newcastle U 16 1
2019–20 Newcastle U 26 6
2020–21 Newcastle U 30 1 **159 14**

SWAILES, Jude (D) 0 0
b.Doncaster 1-9-01
2020–21 Newcastle U 0 0

THOMSON, Reagan (M) 0 0
H: 5 8 W: 9 00 b.Glasgow 5-8-03
Internationals: Scotland U17.
From Queen's Park.
2020–21 Newcastle U 0 0

TOURE, Yannick (F) 0 0
H: 6 1 W: 11 11 b.Dakar 29-9-00
Internationals: Switzerland U17, U20.
From Young Boys.
2020–21 Newcastle U 0 0

TURNER, Jake (G) 14 0
b.Wilmslow 25-2-99
Internationals: England U18, U19.
2016–17 Bolton W 0 0
2017–18 Bolton W 0 0
2018–19 Bolton W 0 0
2019–20 Newcastle U 0 0
2020–21 Newcastle U 0 0
2020–21 *Morecambe* 14 0 **14 0**

TURNER-COOKE, Jay (M) 0 0
b. 31-12-02
From Sunderland.
2020–21 Newcastle U 0 0

VILCA, Rodrigo (M) 24 4
H: 5 9 W: 11 00 b.Lima 12-3-99
2018 Deportivo Municipal 1 0
2019 Deportivo Municipal 13 1
2020 Deportivo Municipal 10 3 **24 4**
2020–21 Newcastle U 0 0

WATTS, Kelland (M) 68 3
b. 3-11-99
Internationals: England U19.
2018–19 Newcastle U 0 0
2019–20 *Stevenage* 16 0 **16 0**
2019–20 Newcastle U 1 0
2019–20 *Mansfield T* 7 1 **7 1**
2020–21 Newcastle U 0 0 **1 0**
2020–21 *Plymouth Arg* 44 2 **44 2**

WHITE, Joe (M) 0 0
H: 6 1 W: 11 00 b.Carlisle 1-10-02
Internationals: England U18.
2020–21 Newcastle U 0 0

WILSON, Adam (F) 0 0
b.Ashington 10-4-00
Internationals: England U18.
2020–21 Newcastle U 0 0

WILSON, Callum (M) 246 95
H: 5 11 W: 10 06 b.Coventry 27-2-92
Internationals: England U21, Full caps.
2009–10 Coventry C 0 0
2010–11 Coventry C 1 0
2011–12 Coventry C 0 0
2012–13 Coventry C 11 1
2013–14 Coventry C 37 21 **49 22**
2014–15 Bournemouth 45 20
2015–16 Bournemouth 13 5
2016–17 Bournemouth 20 6
2017–18 Bournemouth 28 8
2018–19 Bournemouth 30 14
2019–20 Bournemouth 35 8
2020–21 Bournemouth 0 0 **171 61**
2020–21 Newcastle U 26 12 **26 12**

WOODMAN, Freddie (G) 118 0
H: 6 1 W: 10 12 b.London 4-3-97
Internationals: England U16, U17, U18, U19, U20, U21.
From Crystal Palace.
2014–15 Newcastle U 0 0
2014–15 *Hartlepool U* 0 0
2015–16 Newcastle U 0 0
2015–16 *Crawley T* 11 0 **11 0**
2016–17 Newcastle U 0 0
2016–17 *Kilmarnock* 14 0 **14 0**
2017–18 Newcastle U 0 0
2017–18 *Aberdeen* 5 0 **5 0**
2018–19 Newcastle U 0 0
2019–20 Newcastle U 0 0
2019–20 *Swansea C* 43 0
2020–21 Newcastle U 0 0
2020–21 *Swansea C* 45 0 **88 0**

YEDLIN, DeAndre (D) 198 5
H: 5 9 W: 11 07 b.Seattle 9-7-93
Internationals: USA U20, Full caps.
2013 Seattle Sounders 33 2
2014 Seattle Sounders 29 0 **62 2**
2014–15 Tottenham H 1 0
2015–16 Tottenham H 0 0 **1 0**
2015–16 *Sunderland* 23 0 **23 0**
2016–17 Newcastle U 27 1
2017–18 Newcastle U 34 0
2018–19 Newcastle U 29 1
2019–20 Newcastle U 16 1
2020–21 Newcastle U 6 0 **112 3**
Transferred to Galatasaray February 2021.

YOUNG, Jack (M) 5 0
b. 21-10-00
2019–20 Newcastle U 0 0
2020–21 Newcastle U 0 0
2020–21 *Tranmere R* 5 0 **5 0**

Scholars
Banda, Piotr; Barclay, Harry; Brannen, Lewis Paul; Carlyon, Nathan Matthew; Chrystal, Liam Jack; Crossley, Kyle; De Bolle, Lucas; Ebanks, Tai Graham; Gilchrist, Josh Gordon; Green, Joel John; Harrison, Joshua; Huntley, James Alan; Marshall, Oliver Joshua; Midgley, Thomas Jack; Miley, Jamie; Ndiweni, Michael Nqobile; Nicholson, Joshua Philip; Oliver, Joe Alexander; Robertson, Nathan James; Scott, Joshua; Stephenson, Dylan Jay; Stewart, Joshua Thomas; Thompson, Max Anthony.

NEWPORT CO (57)

ABRAHAMS, Tristan (F) 110 14
H: 5 9 W: 10 08 b.Lewisham 29-12-98
2016–17 Leyton Orient 9 2
2017–18 Norwich C 0 0
2018–19 Norwich C 0 0
2018–19 *Exeter C* 16 1 **16 1**
2018–19 *Yeovil T* 15 3 **15 3**
2019–20 Newport Co 33 4
2020–21 Newport Co 23 4 **56 8**
2020–21 *Leyton Orient* 14 0 **23 2**

AMOND, Padraig (F) 487 127
H: 5 11 W: 12 05 b.Carlow 15-4-88
Internationals: Republic of Ireland U21.
2006 Shamrock R 9 1
2007 Shamrock R 6 1
2007 *Kildare Co* 13 5 **13 5**
2008 Shamrock R 27 9
2009 Shamrock R 20 4 **62 15**
2010 Sligo R 27 17 **27 17**
2010–11 Pacos 17 0 **17 0**
2011–12 Accrington S 42 7
2012–13 Accrington S 36 9
2013–14 Accrington S 0 0 **78 16**
2013–14 Morecambe 45 11
2014–15 Morecambe 37 8 **82 19**
From Grimsby T.
2016–17 Hartlepool U 46 14 **46 14**
2017–18 Newport Co 43 13
2018–19 Newport Co 45 14
2019–20 Newport Co 33 8
2020–21 Newport Co 41 6 **162 41**

BAKER, Ashley (D) 20 0
b. 30-10-96
Internationals: Wales U19, U21.
2017–18 Sheffield W 1 0
2018–19 Sheffield W 11 0
2019–20 Sheffield W 0 0 **12 0**
2019–20 Newport Co 4 0
2020–21 Newport Co 4 0 **8 0**

BENNETT, Scott (D) 332 25
H: 5 10 W: 12 10 b.Newquay 30-11-90
2008–09 Exeter C 0 0
2009–10 Exeter C 0 0
2010–11 Exeter C 1 0
2011–12 Exeter C 15 3
2012–13 Exeter C 43 6
2013–14 Exeter C 45 6
2014–15 Exeter C 28 3 **132 18**
2015–16 Notts Co 6 0 **6 0**
2015–16 *Newport Co* 12 0
2015–16 *York C* 11 0 **11 0**
2016–17 Newport Co 39 0
2017–18 Newport Co 28 2
2018–19 Newport Co 38 2
2019–20 Newport Co 28 1
2020–21 Newport Co 38 2 **183 7**

BRAIN, Callum (G) 0 0
b. 10-6-03
2020–21 Newport Co 0 0

BRIGHT, Harrison (D) 0 0
2020–21 Newport Co 0 0

COLLINS, Lewis (M) 22 1
b.Newport 9-5-01
Internationals: Wales U17, U19.
2017–18 Newport Co 0 0
2018–19 Newport Co 0 0
2019–20 Newport Co 6 0
2020–21 Newport Co 16 1 **22 1**

DEMETRIOU, Mickey (D) 232 22
b.Durrington 12-3-90
Internationals: England C.
From Bognor Regis T, Eastbourne Bor, Kidderminster H.
2014–15 Shrewsbury T 42 3
2015–16 Shrewsbury T 1 0
2015–16 *Cambridge U* 15 0 **15 0**
2016–17 Shrewsbury T 0 0 **43 3**
2016–17 Newport Co 17 4
2017–18 Newport Co 46 7

2018–19 Newport Co 45 4
2019–20 Newport Co 21 0
2020–21 Newport Co 45 4 **174 19**

DOLAN, Matthew (M) 263 21
b.Hartlepool 11-2-93
2010–11 Middlesbrough 0 0
2011–12 Middlesbrough 0 0
2012–13 Middlesbrough 0 0
2012–13 *Yeovil T* 8 1
2013–14 Middlesbrough 0 0
2013–14 *Hartlepool U* 20 2
2013–14 *Bradford C* 11 0
2014–15 Bradford C 13 0 **24 0**
2014–15 *Hartlepool U* 2 0 **22 2**
2015–16 Yeovil T 39 3
2016–17 Yeovil T 38 4 **85 8**
2017–18 Newport Co 40 3
2018–19 Newport Co 32 2
2019–20 Newport Co 22 0
2020–21 Newport Co 38 6 **132 11**

ELLISON, Kevin (M) 676 131
H: 6 0 W: 12 00 b.Liverpool 23-2-79
From Southport, Chorley, Conwy U, Altrincham.
2000–01 Leicester C 1 0
2001–02 Leicester C 0 0 **1 0**
2001–02 Stockport Co 11 0
2002–03 Stockport Co 23 1
2003–04 Stockport Co 14 1 **48 2**
2003–04 *Lincoln C* 11 0 **11 0**
2004–05 Chester C 24 9
2004–05 Hull C 16 1
2005–06 Hull C 23 1 **39 2**
2006–07 Tranmere R 34 4 **34 4**
2007–08 Chester C 36 11
2008–09 Chester C 39 8 **99 28**
2008–09 Rotherham U 0 0
2009–10 Rotherham U 39 8
2010–11 Rotherham U 23 3 **62 11**
2010–11 *Bradford C* 7 1 **7 1**
2011–12 Morecambe 34 15
2012–13 Morecambe 40 11
2013–14 Morecambe 42 10
2014–15 Morecambe 43 11
2015–16 Morecambe 44 9
2016–17 Morecambe 45 8
2017–18 Morecambe 40 9
2018–19 Morecambe 43 7
2019–20 Morecambe 21 1 **352 81**
2020–21 Newport Co 23 2 **23 2**

EVANS, Jack (M) 3 0
b.Swansea 25-4-98
Internationals: Wales U19, U20, U21.
2019–20 Swansea C 0 0
2019–20 *Mansfield T* 0 0
2020–21 Newport Co 1 0 **1 0**
2020–21 *AE Pafos* 2 0 **2 0**

FARQUHARSON, Priestley (D) 13 0
b. 15-3-97
2020–21 Connah's Quay Nomads0 0
2020–21 Newport Co 13 0 **13 0**

HAYNES, Ryan (D) 173 3
H: 5 7 W: 10 10 b.Northampton 27-9-95
2012–13 Coventry C 1 0
2013–14 Coventry C 2 0
2014–15 Coventry C 26 1
2015–16 Coventry C 9 0
2015–16 *Cambridge U* 10 0 **10 0**
2016–17 Coventry C 19 0
2017–18 Coventry C 21 0 **78 1**
2018–19 Shrewsbury T 16 0 **16 0**
2019–20 Newport Co 32 1
2020–21 Newport Co 37 1 **69 2**

HILLIER, Ryan (F) 0 0
2019–20 Newport Co 0 0
2020–21 Newport Co 0 0

HOWKINS, Kyle (D) 48 1
H: 6 5 W: 12 11 b.Walsall 4-5-96
2015–16 WBA 0 0
2016–17 WBA 0 0
2016–17 *Mansfield T* 15 0 **15 0**
2017–18 WBA 0 0
2017–18 *Cambridge U* 2 0 **2 0**
2017–18 *Port Vale* 10 0
2018–19 WBA 0 0
2018–19 *Port Vale* 3 0 **13 0**
2019–20 Newport Co 16 1
2020–21 Newport Co 2 0 **18 1**

KING, Tom (G) 81 1
H: 6 1 b.Plymouth 9-3-95
Internationals: England U17.
2011–12 Crystal Palace 0 0
2012–13 Crystal Palace 0 0
2013–14 Crystal Palace 0 0
2014–15 Millwall 0 0
2015–16 Millwall 0 0
2016–17 Millwall 11 0
2017–18 Millwall 0 0
2017–18 *Stevenage* 18 0 **18 0**
2018–19 Millwall 0 0 **11 0**
2018–19 *AFC Wimbledon* 12 0 **12 0**
2019–20 Newport Co 31 0
2020–21 Newport Co 9 1 **40 1**

LABADIE, Joss (M) 325 42
H: 5 7 W: 11 02 b.Croydon 31-8-90
2008–09 WBA 0 0
2008–09 *Shrewsbury T* 1 0
2009–10 WBA 0 0
2009–10 *Shrewsbury T* 13 5 **14 5**
2009–10 *Cheltenham T* 11 0 **11 0**
2009–10 *Tranmere R* 9 3
2010–11 Tranmere R 34 2
2011–12 Tranmere R 27 5 **70 10**
2012–13 Notts Co 24 2
2012–13 *Torquay U* 7 4
2013–14 Notts Co 15 1 **39 3**
2013–14 *Torquay U* 10 1 **17 5**
2014–15 Dagenham & R 24 2
2015–16 Dagenham & R 28 4 **52 6**
2016–17 Newport Co 19 3
2017–18 Newport Co 25 3
2018–19 Newport Co 13 0
2019–20 Newport Co 27 3
2020–21 Newport Co 38 4 **122 13**

LEDLEY, Joe (M) 456 53
H: 6 0 W: 11 06 b.Cardiff 23-1-87
Internationals: Wales U17, U19, U21, Full caps.
2004–05 Cardiff C 28 3
2005–06 Cardiff C 42 3
2006–07 Cardiff C 46 2
2007–08 Cardiff C 41 10
2008–09 Cardiff C 40 4
2009–10 Cardiff C 29 3 **226 25**
2010–11 Celtic 29 2
2011–12 Celtic 32 7
2012–13 Celtic 25 7
2013–14 Celtic 20 4 **106 20**
2013–14 Crystal Palace 14 2
2014–15 Crystal Palace 32 2
2015–16 Crystal Palace 19 1
2016–17 Crystal Palace 18 1 **83 6**
2017–18 Derby Co 26 1
2018–19 Derby Co 4 1 **30 2**
2019–20 Charlton Ath 1 0 **1 0**
2020 Newcastle Jets 6 0 **6 0**
2020–21 Newport Co 4 0 **4 0**

LEWIS, Aaron (D) 29 2
H: 6 0 W: 13 05 b.Swansea 26-6-98
Internationals: Wales U20, U21.
2018–19 Swansea C 0 0
2018–19 *Doncaster R* 7 0 **7 0**
2019–20 Lincoln C 2 1
2020–21 Lincoln C 0 0 **2 1**
2020–21 Newport Co 20 1 **20 1**

LEWIS, Sonny (M) 0 0
b. 2-1-05
2020–21 Newport Co 0 0

LIVERMORE, Aneurin (M) 0 0
2020–21 Newport Co 0 0

LONGE-KING, David (D) 11 0
b. 26-1-95
2020–21 Newport Co 11 0 **11 0**

MAHER, Zack (M) 0 0
2020–21 Newport Co 0 0

OVENDALE, Evan (G) 0 0
2020–21 Newport Co 0 0

RYAN-PHILLIP, Callum (M) 0 0
2020–21 Newport Co 0 0

SHEEHAN, Josh (M) 168 15
H: 6 0 W: 11 11 b.Pembrey 30-3-95
Internationals: Wales U19, U21.
2013–14 Swansea C 0 0
2014–15 Swansea C 0 0
2014–15 *Yeovil T* 13 0
2015–16 Swansea C 0 0
2015–16 *Yeovil T* 13 2 **26 2**
2016–17 Swansea C 0 0
2016–17 *Newport Co* 20 5
2017–18 Newport Co 13 2
2018–19 Newport Co 33 1
2019–20 Newport Co 33 2
2020–21 Newport Co 43 3 **142 13**

SHEPHARD, Liam (D) 188 9
H: 5 10 W: 10 08 b.Rhondda 22-11-94
Internationals: Wales U21.
2013–14 Swansea C 0 0
2014–15 Swansea C 0 0
2014–15 *Yeovil T* 20 0
2015–16 Swansea C 0 0
2015–16 *Yeovil T* 6 0
2016–17 Swansea C 0 0
2016–17 *Yeovil T* 38 1 **64 1**
2017–18 Peterborough U 24 0 **24 0**
2018–19 Forest Green R 39 5
2019–20 Forest Green R 19 1 **58 6**
2020–21 Newport Co 42 2 **42 2**

TAYLOR, Ryan (F) 390 55
H: 6 2 W: 10 10 b.Rotherham 4-5-88
2005–06 Rotherham U 1 0
2006–07 Rotherham U 10 0
2007–08 Rotherham U 35 6
2008–09 Rotherham U 33 4
2009–10 Rotherham U 19 0
2009–10 *Exeter C* 7 0 **7 0**
2010–11 Rotherham U 34 11 **132 21**
2011–12 Bristol C 7 1
2012–13 Bristol C 25 1
2013–14 Bristol C 7 0 **39 2**
2013–14 Portsmouth 18 6
2014–15 Portsmouth 37 9 **55 15**
2015–16 Oxford U 22 3
2016–17 Oxford U 21 1 **43 4**
2016–17 Plymouth Arg 18 4
2017–18 Plymouth Arg 21 5
2018–19 Plymouth Arg 33 0
2019–20 Plymouth Arg 17 2 **89 11**
2020–21 Newport Co 25 2 **25 2**

TELFORD, Dominic (F) 121 14
H: 5 9 W: 11 05 b.Burnley 5-12-96
2014–15 Blackpool 14 1
2015–16 Blackpool 0 0 **14 1**
2016–17 Stoke C 0 0
2017–18 Stoke C 0 0
2017–18 *Bristol R* 19 3 **19 3**
2018–19 Bury 38 6 **38 6**
2019–20 Plymouth Arg 19 2
2020–21 Plymouth Arg 16 1 **35 3**
2020–21 Newport Co 15 1 **15 1**

TOWNSEND, Nick (G) 62 0
H: 5 11 W: 13 11 b.Solihull 1-11-94
2012–13 Birmingham C 0 0
2013–14 Birmingham C 0 0
2014–15 Birmingham C 0 0
2015–16 Barnsley 8 0
2016–17 Barnsley 0 0
2017–18 Barnsley 8 0 **16 0**
2018–19 Newport Co 3 0
2019–20 Newport Co 5 0
2020–21 Newport Co 38 0 **46 0**

TWAMLEY, Lewys (F) 0 0
b. 26-5-03
2020–21 Newport Co 0 0

WILLMOTT, Robbie (M) 195 9
H: 5 9 W: 12 00 b.Harlow 16-5-90
Internationals: England C.
From Cambridge U, Luton T, Cambridge U.
2013–14 Newport Co 46 3
2014–15 Newport Co 16 1
From Ebbsfleet U, Chelmsford C.
2017–18 Newport Co 39 2
2018–19 Newport Co 31 2
2019–20 Newport Co 27 0
2020–21 Newport Co 19 0 **178 8**
2020–21 *Exeter C* 17 1 **17 1**

WOODIWISS, Joe (D) 0 0
2019–20 Newport Co 0 0
2020–21 Newport Co 0 0

Scholars
Bates, Luis Andrew; Brain, Callum Johnathon; Bright, Harrison William; Bullock, Charles; Cirotto, Louie John; Evans, Iestyn James; Graham, Connor Rhys; Kabongo, Dixon Diyoka; Karadogan, Jack Can; Lewis-Hillier, Ryan David; Livermore, Aneurin Riley; Maher, Zachary Jamie; Morgan, Ethan Thomas Stephen; Ovendale, Evan Thomas; Pritchard, Kian Troy Wayne; Ryan-Phillips, Callum Rhys; Twamley, Lewys Morgan; Woodiwiss, Joseph Michael.

NORTHAMPTON T (58)

ARNOLD, Steve (G) 71 0
H: 6 1 W: 13 02 b.Welham Green 22-8-89
Internationals: England C.
From Norwich C, Grays Ath, Eastleigh.
2009–10 Wycombe W 0 0
2010–11 Wycombe W 0 0
2011–12 Wycombe W 0 0
2012–13 Stevenage 30 0
2013–14 Stevenage 3 0 **33 0**
From Forest Green R, Dover Ath.
2017–18 Gillingham 0 0

2018–19	Shrewsbury T	23	0	**23**	**0**
2019–20	Northampton T	4	0		
2020–21	Northampton T	11	0	**15**	**0**

ASHLEY-SEAL, Benny (F) 28 0
b.Southwark 21-11-98
From Norwich C.

2018–19	Wolverhampton W	0	0		
2019–20	Wolverhampton W	0	0		
2019–20	*Accrington S*	5	0	**5**	**0**
2019–20	*Famalicao*	0	0		
2020–21	Northampton T	23	0	**23**	**0**

BALLINGER, Jacob (D) 0 0

2019–20	Northampton T	0	0		
2020–21	Northampton T	0	0		

BERRY, Dylan (G) 0 0

2020–21	Northampton T	0	0		

BOLGER, Cian (D) 262 14
H: 6 4 W: 12 05 b.Co. Kildare 12-3-92
Internationals: Republic of Ireland U19, U21.

2009–10	Leicester C	0	0		
2010–11	Leicester C	0	0		
2010–11	*Bristol R*	6	0		
2011–12	Leicester C	0	0		
2011–12	*Bristol R*	39	2		
2012–13	Leicester C	0	0		
2012–13	*Bristol R*	3	0	**48**	**2**
2012–13	Bolton W	0	0		
2013–14	Bolton W	0	0		
2013–14	*Colchester U*	4	0	**4**	**0**
2013–14	*Southend U*	1	0		
2014–15	Southend U	23	1		
2015–16	Southend U	22	0	**46**	**1**
2015–16	*Bury*	9	0	**9**	**0**
2016–17	Fleetwood T	32	5		
2017–18	Fleetwood T	41	3		
2018–19	Fleetwood T	11	1	**84**	**9**
2018–19	Lincoln C	17	1		
2019–20	Lincoln C	28	0	**45**	**1**
2020–21	Northampton T	26	1	**26**	**1**

CHUKWUEMEKA, Caleb (F) 22 1
b. 25-1-02

2019–20	Northampton T	0	0		
2020–21	Northampton T	22	1	**22**	**1**

CROSS, Liam (M) 1 0
b. 8-4-03

2020–21	Northampton T	1	0	**1**	**0**

DYCHE, Max (D) 2 0
b. 22-2-03

2020–21	Northampton T	2	0	**2**	**0**

FLANAGAN, Josh (D) 0 0

2020–21	Northampton T	0	0		

HARRIMAN, Michael (D) 267 10
H: 5 6 W: 11 10 b.Chichester 23-10-92
Internationals: Republic of Ireland U18, U19, U21.

2010–11	QPR	0	0		
2011–12	QPR	1	0		
2012–13	QPR	1	0		
2012–13	*Wycombe W*	20	0		
2013–14	QPR	0	0		
2013–14	*Gillingham*	34	1	**34**	**1**
2014–15	QPR	0	0	**2**	**0**
2014–15	*Luton T*	35	1	**35**	**1**
2015–16	Wycombe W	45	7		
2016–17	Wycombe W	38	0		
2017–18	Wycombe W	18	1		
2018–19	Wycombe W	24	0	**145**	**8**
2019–20	Northampton T	21	0		
2020–21	Northampton T	30	0	**51**	**0**

HORSFALL, Fraser (D) 66 3
H: 6 3 W: 12 13 b. 12-11-96
Internationals: England C.

2015–16	Huddersfield T	0	0		
2016–17	Huddersfield T	0	0		
2017–18	Huddersfield T	0	0		

From Kidderminster H.

2019–20	Macclesfield T	26	0	**26**	**0**
2020–21	Northampton T	40	3	**40**	**3**

HOSKINS, Sam (F) 264 35
H: 5 8 W: 10 07 b.Dorchester 4-2-93

2011–12	Southampton	0	0		
2011–12	*Preston NE*	0	0		
2011–12	*Rotherham U*	8	2	**8**	**2**
2012–13	Southampton	0	0		
2012–13	*Stevenage*	14	1	**14**	**1**
2013–14	Yeovil T	19	0		
2014–15	Yeovil T	12	1	**31**	**1**
2015–16	Northampton T	34	6		
2016–17	Northampton T	25	3		
2017–18	Northampton T	27	2		
2018–19	Northampton T	42	5		
2019–20	Northampton T	37	8		
2020–21	Northampton T	46	7	**211**	**31**

JOHNSTON, Ethan (F) 0 0

2019–20	Northampton T	0	0		
2020–21	Northampton T	0	0		

JONES, Alex (F) 76 18
b. 28-9-94
From WBA.

2015–16	Birmingham C	0	0		
2016–17	Birmingham C	0	0		
2016–17	*Port Vale*	19	9	**19**	**9**
2016–17	Bradford C	15	5		
2017–18	Bradford C	7	0		
2018–19	Bradford C	2	0	**24**	**5**
2018–19	*Cambridge U*	12	1	**12**	**1**
2019–20	Partick Thistle	12	2	**12**	**2**
2020–21	Northampton T	9	1	**9**	**1**

JONES, Lloyd (D) 100 4
H: 6 3 W: 11 11 b.Plymouth 7-10-95
Internationals: Wales U17, U19. England U19, U20.

2012–13	Liverpool	0	0		
2013–14	Liverpool	0	0		
2014–15	Liverpool	0	0		
2014–15	*Cheltenham T*	6	0	**6**	**0**
2014–15	*Accrington S*	11	1	**11**	**1**
2015–16	Liverpool	0	0		
2015–16	*Blackpool*	10	0	**10**	**0**
2016–17	Liverpool	0	0		
2016–17	*Swindon T*	24	2	**24**	**2**
2017–18	Liverpool	0	0		
2017–18	Luton T	1	0		
2018–19	Luton T	1	0		
2018–19	*Plymouth Arg*	9	1	**9**	**1**
2019–20	Luton T	4	0	**6**	**0**
2019–20	*Northampton T*	7	0		
2020–21	Northampton T	27	0	**34**	**0**

KORBOA, Ricky (F) 16 2
b. 2-8-96
From Carshalton Ath.

2020–21	Northampton T	16	2	**16**	**2**

MARSHALL, Mark (M) 334 23
H: 5 7 W: 10 07 b.Jamaica 9-5-86
From Grays Ath, Eastleigh.

2008–09	Swindon T	12	0		
2009–10	Swindon T	7	0	**19**	**0**
2009–10	*Hereford U*	8	0	**8**	**0**
2010–11	Barnet	46	6		
2011–12	Barnet	25	1	**71**	**7**
2013–14	Coventry C	14	0	**14**	**0**
2014–15	Port Vale	46	7	**46**	**7**
2015–16	Bradford C	31	0		
2016–17	Bradford C	42	6	**73**	**6**
2017–18	Charlton Ath	27	1		
2018–19	Charlton Ath	22	1	**49**	**2**
2019–20	Gillingham	18	0	**18**	**0**
2019–20	Northampton T	7	0		
2020–21	Northampton T	29	1	**36**	**1**

McWILLIAMS, Shaun (M) 98 1
b.Northampton 14-8-98

2014–15	Northampton T	0	0		
2015–16	Northampton T	0	0		
2016–17	Northampton T	5	0		
2017–18	Northampton T	19	0		
2018–19	Northampton T	25	0		
2019–20	Northampton T	17	1		
2020–21	Northampton T	32	0	**98**	**1**

MILLS, Joseph (D) 291 15
H: 5 9 W: 11 00 b.Swindon 30-10-89
Internationals: England U17, U18.

2006–07	Southampton	0	0		
2007–08	Southampton	0	0		
2008–09	Southampton	8	0		
2008–09	*Scunthorpe U*	14	0	**14**	**0**
2009–10	Southampton	16	0		
2010–11	Southampton	2	0		
2010–11	*Doncaster R*	18	2	**18**	**2**
2011–12	Southampton	0	0	**26**	**0**
2011–12	Reading	15	0		
2012–13	Reading	0	0	**15**	**0**
2012–13	*Burnley*	10	0		
2013–14	Burnley	0	0	**10**	**0**
2013–14	*Oldham Ath*	11	0		
2013–14	*Shrewsbury T*	13	0	**13**	**0**
2014–15	Oldham Ath	30	0		
2015–16	Oldham Ath	15	1	**56**	**1**
2016–17	Perth Glory	22	1		
2017–18	Perth Glory	22	0	**44**	**1**
2018–19	Forest Green R	44	4		
2019–20	Forest Green R	24	7	**68**	**11**
2020–21	Northampton T	27	0	**27**	**0**

ROBERTS, Morgan (F) 7 0
b. 22-12-00

2017–18	Northampton T	1	0		
2018–19	Northampton T	3	0		
2019–20	Northampton T	1	0		
2020–21	Northampton T	2	0	**7**	**0**

ROSE, Danny (F) 266 61
H: 5 8 W: 9 00 b.Barnsley 10-12-93

2010–11	Barnsley	1	0		
2011–12	Barnsley	4	0		
2012–13	Barnsley	8	1		
2013–14	Barnsley	3	0		
2013–14	*Bury*	6	3		
2014–15	Barnsley	1	0	**17**	**1**
2014–15	*Bury*	35	10		
2015–16	Bury	28	5	**69**	**18**
2016–17	Mansfield T	37	9		
2017–18	Mansfield T	39	14		
2018–19	Mansfield T	34	4		
2019–20	Mansfield T	31	11		
2020–21	Mansfield T	0	0	**141**	**38**
2020–21	Northampton T	39	4	**39**	**4**

SHEEHAN, Alan (D) 395 25
H: 5 11 W: 11 02 b.Athlone 14-9-86
Internationals: Republic of Ireland U21.
From Belvedere.

2004–05	Leicester C	1	0		
2005–06	Leicester C	2	0		
2006–07	Leicester C	0	0		
2006–07	*Mansfield T*	10	0	**10**	**0**
2007–08	Leicester C	20	1	**23**	**1**
2007–08	*Leeds U*	10	1		
2008–09	Leeds U	11	1		
2008–09	*Crewe Alex*	3	0	**3**	**0**
2009–10	Leeds U	0	0	**21**	**2**
2009–10	*Oldham Ath*	8	1	**8**	**1**
2009–10	*Swindon T*	22	1		
2010–11	Swindon T	21	1	**43**	**2**
2011–12	Notts Co	39	2		
2012–13	Notts Co	33	0		
2013–14	Notts Co	42	7		
2014–15	Bradford C	23	1		
2014–15	*Peterborough U*	2	0	**2**	**0**
2015–16	Bradford C	2	0	**25**	**1**
2015–16	*Notts Co*	14	2	**128**	**11**
2015–16	*Luton T*	20	1		
2016–17	Luton T	34	2		
2017–18	Luton T	42	3		
2018–19	Luton T	17	0		
2019–20	Luton T	4	0	**117**	**6**
2019–20	Lincoln C	1	0	**1**	**0**
2020–21	Northampton T	14	1	**14**	**1**

SMITH, Harry (F) 97 18
H: 6 5 b. 18-5-95
From Sittingbourne, Folkestone Invicta.

2016–17	Millwall	9	1		
2017–18	Millwall	0	0	**9**	**1**
2017–18	*Swindon T*	14	2	**14**	**2**
2018–19	Macclesfield T	39	8	**39**	**8**
2019–20	Northampton T	19	4		
2020–21	Motherwell	0	0		
2020–21	Northampton T	16	3	**35**	**7**

SOWERBY, Jack (F) 130 7
b. 23-3-95

2014–15	Fleetwood T	0	0		
2015–16	Fleetwood T	8	0		
2016–17	Fleetwood T	8	1		
2017–18	Fleetwood T	22	2		
2018–19	Fleetwood T	15	0		
2018–19	*Carlisle U*	25	4	**25**	**4**
2019–20	Fleetwood T	24	0		
2020–21	Fleetwood T	0	0	**77**	**3**
2020–21	Northampton T	28	0	**28**	**0**

WARBURTON, Matthew (F) 22 2
b. 24-5-92
From Curzon Ashton, Salford C, Stockport Co.

2019–20	Northampton T	18	1		
2020–21	Northampton T	4	1	**22**	**2**

WATSON, Ryan (M) 149 15
H: 6 1 W: 11 07 b.Crewe 7-7-93

2011–12	Wigan Ath	0	0		
2012–13	Wigan Ath	0	0		
2012–13	*Accrington S*	0	0		
2013–14	Leicester C	0	0		
2014–15	Leicester C	0	0		
2014–15	*Northampton T*	5	0		
2015–16	Leicester C	0	0		
2015–16	*Northampton T*	11	0		
2016–17	Barnet	19	1		
2017–18	Barnet	28	1	**47**	**2**
2018–19	Milton Keynes D	22	0	**22**	**0**
2019–20	Northampton T	25	5		
2020–21	Northampton T	39	8	**80**	**13**

WOODS, Charlie (G) 0 0

2020–21	Northampton T	0	0		

Scholars
Abimbola, Peter Olanrewaju Enibola; Bailey, Richie Dion; Berry, Dylan Andrew; Chukwuemeka, Chigozier Caleb; Connor, Jack Joseph; Cook, Callum David; Cross, Liam James; Curry, Thomas James; Dyche,

Max; Flanagan, Joshua Francis; Gilbert, Lewis George; Lack, Ethan Thomas; Lashley, Courtney John; Ngwa, Miguel Suh Tunfong; Scott, Thomas William; Watkins-Robinson, Kieran Thomas; Woods, Charlie Elliot.

NORWICH C (59)

AARONS, Maximillian (D) 122 4
b.London 4-1-00
Internationals: England U19, U21.
From Luton T.
2018–19 Norwich C 41 2
2019–20 Norwich C 36 0
2020–21 Norwich C 45 2 **122 4**

AHADME, Gassan (F) 0 0
b.Vic 17-11-00
From Oviedo.
2020–21 Norwich C 0 0

BARDEN, Daniel (G) 2 0
b. 2-1-01
From Arsenal.
2020–21 Norwich C 2 0 **2 0**

BLAIR, Sam (G) 0 0
b. 27-12-02
2020–21 Norwich C 0 0

BROOKE, Harry (M) 0 0
From Millwall.
2020–21 Norwich C 0 0

CANTWELL, Todd (M) 104 15
b. 27-2-98
Internationals: England U17, U21.
2017–18 Norwich C 0 0
2017–18 *Fortuna Sittard* 10 2 **10 2**
2018–19 Norwich C 24 1
2019–20 Norwich C 37 6
2020–21 Norwich C 33 6 **94 13**

COKER, Kenny (F) 4 0
b. 10-11-03
2019–20 Southend U 2 0
2020–21 Southend U 2 0 **4 0**
2020–21 Norwich C 0 0

DENNIS, Matthew (M) 0 0
b. 15-4-02
From Arsenal.
2020–21 Norwich C 0 0

DICKSON-PETERS, Thomas (F) 0 0
b.Slough 16-9-02
2020–21 Norwich C 0 0

DOWELL, Kieran (F) 102 21
H: 5 9 W: 9 04 b.Ormskirk 10-10-97
Internationals: England U16, U17, U18, U20, U21.
2014–15 Everton 0 0
2015–16 Everton 2 0
2016–17 Everton 0 0
2017–18 Everton 0 0
2017–18 *Nottingham F* 38 9 **38 9**
2018–19 Everton 0 0
2018–19 *Sheffield U* 16 2 **16 2**
2019–20 Everton 0 0 **2 0**
2019–20 *Derby Co* 10 0 **10 0**
2019–20 *Wigan Ath* 12 5 **12 5**
2020–21 Norwich C 24 5 **24 5**

EMI, Buendia (M) 188 33
H: 5 7 W: 11 05 b.Mar del Plata 25-12-96
Internationals: Spain U19. Argentina U20.
2013–14 Getafe 0 0
2014–15 Getafe 6 0
2015–16 Getafe 17 1
2016–17 Getafe 12 2
2017–18 Getafe 0 0 **35 3**
2017–18 *Cultural Leonesa* 40 6 **40 6**
2018–19 Norwich C 38 8
2019–20 Norwich C 36 1
2020–21 Norwich C 39 15 **113 24**

FAMEWO, Akin (D) 48 0
H: 5 11 W: 10 06 b.Lewisham 9-11-98
2016–17 Luton T 3 0
2017–18 Luton T 3 0
2018–19 Luton T 0 0 **6 0**
2018–19 *Grimsby T* 10 0 **10 0**
2018–19 Norwich C 0 0
2019–20 Norwich C 1 0
2019–20 *St Mirren* 9 0 **9 0**
2020–21 Norwich C 0 0 **1 0**
2020–21 *Charlton Ath* 22 0 **22 0**

FITZPATRICK, Aidan (F) 43 5
b.Glasgow 20-3-01
Internationals: Scotland U17, U18, U19.
2017–18 Partick Thistle 0 0
2018–19 Partick Thistle 21 3 **21 3**
2019–20 Norwich C 0 0
2020–21 Norwich C 0 0
2020–21 *Queen of the South* 22 2 **22 2**

GIANNOULIS, Dimitrios (D) 203 3
b. 17-10-95
2012–13 Vataniakos 14 1
2013–14 Vataniakos 19 2 **33 3**
2014–15 PAOK 0 0
2014–15 *Pierikos* 26 0 **26 0**
2015–16 PAOK 0 0
2015–16 *Veria* 24 0 **24 0**
2016–17 PAOK 0 0
2016–17 *Anorthosis Famagusta* 8 0 **8 0**
2017–18 PAOK 0 0
2017–18 *Atromitos* 27 0
2018–19 PAOK 8 0
2018–19 *Atromitos* 15 0 **42 0**
2019–20 PAOK 34 0
2020–21 PAOK 12 0 **54 0**
2020–21 Norwich C 16 0 **16 0**

HANLEY, Grant (D) 291 11
H: 6 2 W: 12 00 b.Dumfries 20-11-91
Internationals: Scotland U19, U21, Full caps.
From Rangers.
2008–09 Blackburn R 0 0
2009–10 Blackburn R 1 0
2010–11 Blackburn R 7 0
2011–12 Blackburn R 23 1
2012–13 Blackburn R 39 2
2013–14 Blackburn R 38 1
2014–15 Blackburn R 31 1
2015–16 Blackburn R 44 2 **183 7**
2016–17 Newcastle U 10 1
2017–18 Newcastle U 0 0 **10 1**
2017–18 Norwich C 32 1
2018–19 Norwich C 9 1
2019–20 Norwich C 15 0
2020–21 Norwich C 42 1 **98 3**

HERNANDEZ, Onel (M) 178 15
b.Moron 1-2-93
Internationals: Germany U18.
2010–11 Arminia Bielefeld 10 0
2011–12 Arminia Bielefeld 18 0 **28 0**
2012–13 Werder Bremen 0 0
2013–14 Werder Bremen 0 0
2013–14 Wolfsburg 0 0
2014–15 Wolfsburg 0 0
2015–16 Wolfsburg 0 0
2016–17 Eintracht Brauschweig 34 5 **34 5**
2017–18 Eintracht Brauschweig 17 1 **17 1**
2017–18 Norwich C 12 0
2018–19 Norwich C 40 8
2019–20 Norwich C 26 1
2020–21 Norwich C 21 0 **99 9**

HONDERMARCK, William (M) 3 0
b. 21-11-00
From Drogheda U.
2020–21 Norwich C 0 0
2020–21 *Harrogate T* 3 0 **3 0**

HUGILL, Jordan (F) 247 55
H: 6 0 W: 10 01 b.Middlesbrough 4-6-92
From Seaham Red Star, Consett, Whitby T.
2013–14 Port Vale 20 4 **20 4**
2014–15 Preston NE 3 0
2014–15 *Tranmere R* 6 1 **6 1**
2014–15 *Hartlepool U* 8 4 **8 4**
2015–16 Preston NE 29 3
2016–17 Preston NE 44 12
2017–18 Preston NE 27 8 **103 23**
2017–18 West Ham U 3 0
2018–19 West Ham U 0 0
2018–19 *Middlesbrough* 37 6 **37 6**
2019–20 West Ham U 0 0 **3 0**
2019–20 *QPR* 39 13
2020–21 QPR 0 0 **39 13**
2020–21 Norwich C 31 4 **31 4**

HUTCHINSON, Shae (F) 0 0
H: 5 9 W: 11 00 b.Islington 9-10-00
2020–21 Norwich C 0 0

IDAH, Adam (F) 29 3
b. 11-2-01
Internationals: Republic of Ireland U16, U17, U18, U19, U21.
2019–20 Norwich C 12 0
2020–21 Norwich C 17 3 **29 3**

KAMARA, Abu (M) 0 0
b. 21-7-03
2020–21 Norwich C 0 0

KLOSE, Timm (D) 279 21
H: 6 5 W: 13 10 b.Frankfurt am Main 9-5-88
Internationals: Switzerland U21, U23, Full caps.
2009–10 Thun 29 2
2010–11 Thun 30 3 **59 5**
2011–12 Nuremburg 13 0
2012–13 Nuremburg 32 2 **45 2**
2013–14 Wolfsburg 10 0
2014–15 Wolfsburg 12 1
2015–16 Wolfsburg 8 1 **30 2**
2015–16 Norwich C 10 1
2016–17 Norwich C 32 1
2017–18 Norwich C 37 4
2018–19 Norwich C 31 4
2019–20 Norwich C 7 0
2020–21 Norwich C 0 0 **117 10**
2020–21 *FC Basel* 28 2 **28 2**

KRUL, Tim (G) 327 0
H: 6 2 W: 11 08 b.Den Haag 3-4-88
Internationals: Netherlands U16, U17, U19, U20, U21, Full caps.
From ADO Den Haag.
2005–06 Newcastle U 0 0
2006–07 Newcastle U 0 0
2007–08 *Falkirk* 22 0 **22 0**
2007–08 Newcastle U 0 0
2008–09 Newcastle U 0 0
2008–09 *Carlisle U* 9 0 **9 0**
2009–10 Newcastle U 3 0
2010–11 Newcastle U 21 0
2011–12 Newcastle U 38 0
2012–13 Newcastle U 24 0
2013–14 Newcastle U 36 0
2014–15 Newcastle U 30 0
2015–16 Newcastle U 8 0
2016–17 Newcastle U 0 0
2016–17 *Ajax* 0 0
2016–17 *AZ Alkmaar* 18 0 **18 0**
2017–18 Newcastle U 0 0 **160 0**
2017–18 *Brighton & HA* 0 0
2018–19 Norwich C 46 0
2019–20 Norwich C 36 0
2020–21 Norwich C 36 0 **118 0**

MARTIN, Josh (M) 14 1
b. 9-9-01
From Arsenal.
2019–20 Norwich C 5 0
2020–21 Norwich C 9 1 **14 1**

McALEAR, Reece (M) 1 0
b.Glasgow 12-2-02
From Motherwell.
2020–21 Norwich C 1 0 **1 0**

McCALLUM, Sam (D) 74 3
b. 2-9-00
From Herne Bay.
2018–19 Coventry C 7 0
2019–20 Norwich C 0 0
2019–20 *Coventry C* 26 2
2020–21 Norwich C 0 0
2020–21 *Coventry C* 41 1 **74 3**

McCRACKEN, Jon (G) 0 0
b.Wishaw 24-5-00
From Hamilton A.
2020–21 Norwich C 0 0

McGOVERN, Michael (G) 302 0
H: 6 2 W: 13 07 b.Enniskillen 12-7-84
Internationals: Northern Ireland U19, U21, Full caps.
2004–05 Celtic 0 0
2004–05 *Stranraer* 19 0 **19 0**
2005–06 Celtic 0 0
2006–07 Celtic 0 0
2006–07 *St Johnstone* 1 0 **1 0**
2007–08 Celtic 0 0
2008–09 Dundee U 0 0
2009–10 Ross Co 35 0
2010–11 Ross Co 36 0 **71 0**
2011–12 Falkirk 35 0
2012–13 Falkirk 35 0
2013–14 Falkirk 34 0 **104 0**
2014–15 Hamilton A 38 0
2015–16 Hamilton A 37 0 **75 0**
2016–17 Norwich C 20 0
2017–18 Norwich C 0 0
2018–19 Norwich C 0 0
2019–20 Norwich C 2 0
2020–21 Norwich C 10 0 **32 0**

McLEAN, Kenny (M) 372 45
H: 6 0 W: 11 00 b.Rutherglen 8-1-92
Internationals: Scotland U19, U21, Full caps.
2009–10 St Mirren 0 0
2009–10 *Arbroath* 20 1 **20 1**
2010–11 St Mirren 19 0
2011–12 St Mirren 28 4
2012–13 St Mirren 29 3
2013–14 St Mirren 30 6
2014–15 St Mirren 25 7 **131 20**
2014–15 Aberdeen 13 0
2015–16 Aberdeen 38 6
2016–17 Aberdeen 38 4
2017–18 Aberdeen 22 3

2017–18 Norwich C 0 0
2017–18 *Aberdeen* 15 5 **126 18**
2018–19 Norwich C 20 3
2019–20 Norwich C 37 1
2020–21 Norwich C 38 2 **95 6**

MUMBA, Bali (F) 9 0
b. 8-10-01
Internationals: England U16, U17, U18, U19.
2017–18 Sunderland 1 0
2018–19 Sunderland 4 0
2019–20 Sunderland 0 0 **5 0**
2020–21 Norwich C 4 0 **4 0**

NIZET, Rob (D) 0 0
H: 5 10 W: 10 06 b.Banjul 14-4-02
Internationals: Belgium U16, U17, U18, U19.
From Anderlecht.
2020–21 Norwich C 0 0

NYLAND, Orjan (G) 195 0
H: 6 4 W: 12 04 b.Volda 10-9-90
Internationals: Norway U18, U21, Full caps.
2011 Hodd 28 0
2012 Hodd 28 0 **56 0**
2013 Molde 20 0
2014 Molde 28 0
2015 Molde 13 0 **61 0**
2015–16 Ingolstadt 6 0
2016–17 Ingolstadt 12 0
2017–18 Ingolstadt 30 0 **48 0**
2018–19 Aston Villa 23 0
2019–20 Aston Villa 7 0
2020–21 Aston Villa 0 0 **30 0**
2020–21 Norwich C 0 0

OMOBAMIDELE, Andrew (D) 9 0
b.Dublin 23-6-02
2019–20 Norwich C 0 0
2020–21 Norwich C 9 0 **9 0**

OMOTOYE, Tyrese (F) 10 0
b. 23-9-02
From Cray W.
2020–21 Norwich C 3 0 **3 0**
2020–21 *Swindon T* 7 0 **7 0**

PLACHETA, Przemyslaw (M) 97 17
b.Lowicz 23-9-98
2017–18 Sonnenhof Grossaspach 2 0 **2 0**
2017–18 Pogon Siedice 11 2 **11 2**
2018–19 Podbeskidzie 23 6 **23 6**
2019–20 Slask Wroclaw 35 8 **35 8**
2020–21 Norwich C 26 1 **26 1**

PUKKI, Teemu (F) 367 152
H: 5 9 W: 10 06 b.Kotka 29-3-90
Internationals: Finland U17, U19, U21, Full caps.
2006 KooTeePee 5 0
2007 KooTeePee 24 3 **29 3**
2008–09 Sevilla 0 0
2010 HJK Helsinki 7 2
2011 HJK Helsinki 18 11 **25 13**
2011–12 Schalke 04 19 5
2012–13 Schalke 04 17 3
2013–14 Schalke 04 1 0 **37 8**
2013–14 Celtic 25 7
2014–15 Celtic 1 0 **26 7**
2014–15 *Brondby* 27 9
2015–16 Brondby 33 9
2016–17 Brondby 34 20
2017–18 Brondby 36 17 **130 55**
2018–19 Norwich C 43 29
2019–20 Norwich C 36 11
2020–21 Norwich C 41 26 **120 66**

QUINTILLA, Xavi (D) 66 2
b.Lleida 23-8-96
2015–16 Barcelona 0 0
2016–17 Barcelona 0 0
2016–17 *Lleida Esportiu* 29 0 **29 0**
2017–18 Villarreal 0 0
2018–19 Villarreal 7 0
2019–20 Villarreal 19 0
2020–21 Villarreal 0 0 **26 0**
On loan from Villarreal.
2020–21 Norwich C 11 2 **11 2**

RILEY, Regan (M) 1 0
2019–20 Bolton W 1 0
2020–21 Bolton W 0 0 **1 0**
2020–21 Norwich C 0 0

ROSE, Joseph (G) 0 0
H: 6 1 b. 5-11-01
Internationals: England U16.
2020–21 Norwich C 0 0

ROWE, Jonathan (F) 0 0
H: 5 8 b.Westminster 30-4-03
2020–21 Norwich C 0 0

RUPP, Lukas (M) 213 19
b.Heidelberg 8-1-91
2009–10 Karlsruher 2 0
2010–11 Karlsruher 24 3 **26 3**
2011–12 Borussia M'gladbach 3 0
2011–12 *Paderborn* 15 2
2012–13 Borussia M'gladbach 21 0
2013–14 Borussia M'gladbach 10 0 **34 0**
2014–15 Paderborn 31 4 **46 6**
2015–16 Stuttgart 29 5 **29 5**
2016–17 Hoffenheim 14 2
2017–18 Hoffenheim 21 3
2018–19 Hoffenheim 1 0
2019–20 Hoffenheim 7 0 **43 5**
2019–20 Norwich C 12 0
2020–21 Norwich C 23 0 **35 0**

SHIPLEY, Lewis (D) 0 0
b.Cambridge 29-11-03
2020–21 Norwich C 0 0

SINANI, Danel (F) 129 34
H: 6 1 W: 11 00 b.Belgrade 5-4-97
Internationals: Luxembourg U19, U21, Full caps.
2015–16 Racing 23 4
2016–17 Racing 24 6 **47 10**
2017–18 F91 Dudelange 22 0
2018–19 F91 Dudelange 25 7
2019–20 F91 Dudelange 17 14 **64 21**
2020–21 Waasland-Beveren 18 3 **18 3**
2020–21 Norwich C 0 0

SITTI, Melvin (M) 17 0
b. 14-2-00
From Paris FC.
2019–20 Sochaux 17 0 **17 0**
2020–21 Norwich C 0 0
2020–21 *Waasland-Beveren* 0 0

SORENSEN, Jacob (M) 134 6
b. 3-3-98
2016–17 Esbjerg 8 0
2017–18 Esbjerg 29 1
2018–19 Esbjerg 36 3
2019–20 Esbjerg 29 1 **102 5**
2020–21 Norwich C 32 1 **32 1**

SPRINGETT, Tony (M) 0 0
b.Lewisham 22-9-02
Internationals: Republic of Ireland U18.
2020–21 Norwich C 0 0

STEWART, Sean (D) 0 0
H: 5 11 b. 21-1-03
Internationals: Northern Ireland U17, U21.
2020–21 Norwich C 0 0

STIEPERMANN, Marco (F) 284 31
H: 5 11 W: 11 11 b.Dortmund 9-2-91
Internationals: Germany U16, U17, U18, U19, U20.
2008–09 Borussia Dortmund 0 0
2009–10 Borussia Dortmund 3 1
2010–11 Borussia Dortmund 4 0
2011–12 Borussia Dortmund 0 0 **7 1**
2011–12 *Aachen* 21 2 **21 2**
2012–13 Energie Cottbus 27 2
2013–14 Energie Cottbus 29 5 **56 7**
2014–15 Greuther Furth 31 4
2015–16 Greuther Furth 30 5 **61 9**
2016–17 Bochum 31 1 **31 1**
2017–18 VfL Bochum 0 0
2017–18 Norwich C 23 1
2018–19 Norwich C 43 9
2019–20 Norwich C 24 0
2020–21 Norwich C 18 1 **108 11**

TETTEY, Alexander (M) 398 24
H: 5 11 W: 10 09 b.Accra 4-4-86
Internationals: Norway U18, U19, U21, Full caps.
2003 Rosenborg 0 0
2004 Rosenborg 1 0
2005 Rosenborg 2 0
2005 *Skeid* 5 2 **5 2**
2006 Rosenborg 22 2
2007 Rosenborg 23 4
2008 Rosenborg 24 2
2009 Rosenborg 17 5 **89 13**
2009–10 Rennes 24 0
2010–11 Rennes 17 1
2011–12 Rennes 19 1 **60 2**
2012–13 Norwich C 27 0
2013–14 Norwich C 21 1
2014–15 Norwich C 36 2
2015–16 Norwich C 23 2
2016–17 Norwich C 35 0
2017–18 Norwich C 23 0
2018–19 Norwich C 30 1
2019–20 Norwich C 30 1
2020–21 Norwich C 19 0 **244 7**
Transferred to Rosenborg May 2021.

THOMAS, Jordan (D) 2 0
b. 2-1-01
From Huddersfield T.
2019–20 Norwich C 1 0
2020–21 Norwich C 0 0 **1 0**
2020–21 *Leyton Orient* 1 0 **1 0**

THOMPSON, Louis (M) 137 6
H: 5 11 W: 11 10 b.Bristol 19-12-94
Internationals: Wales U19, U21.
2012–13 Swindon T 4 0
2013–14 Swindon T 28 2
2014–15 Norwich C 0 0
2014–15 *Swindon T* 32 2
2015–16 Norwich C 0 0
2015–16 *Swindon T* 28 2 **92 6**
2016–17 Norwich C 3 0
2017–18 Norwich C 0 0
2018–19 Norwich C 6 0
2019–20 Norwich C 0 0
2019–20 *Shrewsbury T* 10 0 **10 0**
2019–20 *Milton Keynes D* 9 0
2020–21 Norwich C 0 0 **9 0**
2020–21 *Milton Keynes D* 17 0 **26 0**

TOMKINSON, Jonathan (D) 0 0
H: 6 3 W: 11 00 b.Plano 11-4-02
Internationals: USA U17.
2020–21 Norwich C 0 0

TRYBULL, Tom (M) 168 5
H: 5 11 W: 11 05 b.Berlin 9-3-93
Internationals: Germany U17, U18, U19, U20.
2010–11 Hansa Rostock 17 0 **17 0**
2011–12 Werder Bremen 15 1
2012–13 Werder Bremen 4 0
2013–14 Werder Bremen 2 0 **21 1**
2013–14 St Pauli 12 0
2014–15 St Pauli 3 0 **15 0**
2015–16 Greuther Furth 0 0
2016–17 ADO Den Haag 23 1 **23 1**
2017–18 Norwich C 20 2
2018–19 Norwich C 31 1
2019–20 Norwich C 16 0
2020–21 Norwich C 0 0 **67 3**
2020–21 *Blackburn R* 25 0 **25 0**

VRANCIC, Mario (M) 282 33
H: 6 1 W: 12 02 b.Slavonski Brod 23-5-89
Internationals: Germany U17, U19, U20. Bosnia-Herzegovina Full caps.
From VfR Kesselstadt.
2006–07 Mainz 05 1 0
2007–08 Mainz 05 5 0
2008–09 Mainz 05 3 0
2009–10 Mainz 05 0 0 **9 0**
2009–10 *Rot Weiss Ahlen* 12 0 **12 0**
2010–11 Borussia Dortmund 0 0
2011–12 Borussia Dortmund 0 0
2012–13 Paderborn 33 5
2013–14 Paderborn 30 5
2014–15 Paderborn 30 2 **93 12**
2015–16 Darmstadt 22 2
2016–17 Darmstadt 23 4 **45 6**
2017–18 Norwich C 35 1
2018–19 Norwich C 36 10
2019–20 Norwich C 20 1
2020–21 Norwich C 32 3 **123 15**

WARNER, Jaden (D) 0 0
b.Hillingdon 28-10-02
2020–21 Norwich C 0 0

ZIMMERMANN, Christoph (D) 118 3
b.Dusseldorf 12-1-93
2011–12 Borussia M'gladbach 0 0
2012–13 Borussia M'gladbach 0 0
2013–14 Borussia M'gladbach 0 0
2014–15 Borussia Dortmund 0 0
2015–16 Borussia Dortmund 0 0
2016–17 Borussia Dortmund 0 0
2017–18 Norwich C 39 1
2018–19 Norwich C 40 2
2019–20 Norwich C 17 0
2020–21 Norwich C 22 0 **118 3**

Scholars
Alidor-Hamilton, Solomon Kabango; Brown, Zak Jazi Theo; Coker, Kenny Temitope Temilade; Duffy, Joseph Daniel; Earley, Saxon Owen; Hills, Bradley; Jackson, Eddie Robert; Khumbeni, Nelson Wilfred; Okeowo, Olatunde A O O I; Pitcher, Harry James; Thorn, Oscar Peter.

NOTTINGHAM F (60)

AMEOBI, Sammy (F) 265 22
H: 6 3 W: 10 04 b.Newcastle upon Tyne 1-5-92
Internationals: Nigeria U20. England U21.
2010–11 Newcastle U 1 0
2011–12 Newcastle U 10 0
2012–13 Newcastle U 8 0
2012–13 *Middlesbrough* 9 1 **9 1**
2013–14 Newcastle U 10 0
2014–15 Newcastle U 25 2
2015–16 Newcastle U 0 0
2015–16 *Cardiff C* 36 1 **36 1**
2016–17 Newcastle U 4 0 **58 2**
2016–17 *Bolton W* 20 2
2017–18 Bolton W 35 4
2018–19 Bolton W 30 4 **85 10**
2019–20 Nottingham F 45 5
2020–21 Nottingham F 32 3 **77 8**

ARTER, Harry (M) 303 31
H: 5 9 W: 11 07 b.Sidcup 28-12-89
Internationals: Republic of Ireland U17, U19, Full caps.
2007–08 Charlton Ath 0 0
2008–09 Charlton Ath 0 0
From Woking.
2010–11 Bournemouth 18 0
2010–11 *Carlisle U* 5 1 **5 1**
2011–12 Bournemouth 34 5
2012–13 Bournemouth 37 8
2013–14 Bournemouth 31 3
2014–15 Bournemouth 43 9
2015–16 Bournemouth 21 1
2016–17 Bournemouth 35 1
2017–18 Bournemouth 13 1
2018–19 Bournemouth 0 0
2018–19 *Cardiff C* 25 0 **25 0**
2019–20 Bournemouth 0 0 **232 28**
2019–20 *Fulham* 28 2 **28 2**
2020–21 Nottingham F 13 0 **13 0**

BACHIROU, Fouad (M) 262 4
b.Valence 15-4-90
2008–09 Paris Saint-Germain 0 0
2009–10 Paris Saint-Germain 0 0
2010–11 Greenock Morton 19 0
2011–12 Greenock Morton 30 1
2012–13 Greenock Morton 33 1
2013–14 Greenock Morton 35 0 **117 2**
2014 Ostersunds 10 0
2015 Ostersunds 29 0
2016 Ostersunds 22 1
2017 Ostersunds 25 1 **86 2**
2018 Malmo 22 0
2019 Malmo 24 0
2020 Malmo 12 0 **58 0**
2020–21 Malmo FF 0 0
2020–21 Nottingham F 1 0 **1 0**

BACK, Finley (M) 0 0
b. 25-9-02
2020–21 Nottingham F 0 0

BARNES, Joshua (M) 0 0
b. 1-11-00
2020–21 Nottingham F 0 0

BLACKETT, Tyler (D) 151 0
H: 6 1 W: 11 12 b.Manchester 2-4-94
Internationals: England U16, U17, U18, U19, U21.
2012–13 Manchester U 0 0
2013–14 Manchester U 0 0
2013–14 *Blackpool* 5 0 **5 0**
2013–14 *Birmingham C* 8 0 **8 0**
2014–15 Manchester U 11 0
2015–16 Manchester U 0 0 **11 0**
2015–16 *Celtic* 3 0 **3 0**
2016–17 Reading 34 0
2017–18 Reading 25 0
2018–19 Reading 31 0
2019–20 Reading 20 0 **110 0**
2020–21 Nottingham F 14 0 **14 0**

BONG, Gaetan (D) 294 3
H: 6 0 W: 11 09 b.Sakbayeme 25-4-88
Internationals: France U21. Cameroon Full caps.
2005–06 Metz 3 0
2006–07 Metz 2 0
2007–08 Metz 11 0
2008–09 Metz 0 0 **16 0**
2008–09 *Tours* 34 0 **34 0**
2009–10 Valenciennes 29 2
2010–11 Valenciennes 22 1
2011–12 Valenciennes 28 0
2012–13 Valenciennes 29 0
2013–14 Valenciennes 1 0 **109 3**
2013–14 Olympiacos 19 0 **19 0**
2014–15 Wigan Ath 14 0 **14 0**
2015–16 Brighton & HA 16 0
2016–17 Brighton & HA 24 0
2017–18 Brighton & HA 25 0
2018–19 Brighton & HA 22 0
2019–20 Brighton & HA 4 0 **91 0**
2019–20 Nottingham F 1 0
2020–21 Nottingham F 10 0 **11 0**

CAFU, Dias (M) 173 11
b.Guimaraes 26-2-93
2012–13 Benfica 0 0
2013–14 Vitoria Guimaraes 0 0
2014–15 Vitoria Guimaraes 29 0
2015–16 Vitoria Guimaraes 32 3 **61 3**
2016–17 Lorient 18 0 **18 0**
2017–18 Metz 10 0
2017–18 *Legia Warzaw* 7 2
2018–19 Metz 0 0 **10 0**
2018–19 *Legia Warzaw* 31 4
2019–20 Legia Warzaw 6 0 **44 6**
2019–20 Olympiacos 7 1
2020–21 Olympiacos 2 1 **9 2**
2020–21 Nottingham F 31 0 **31 0**

COLBACK, Jack (M) 329 17
H: 5 9 W: 11 05 b.Killingworth 24-10-89
Internationals: England U20.
2007–08 Sunderland 0 0
2008–09 Sunderland 0 0
2009–10 Sunderland 1 0
2009–10 *Ipswich T* 37 4
2010–11 Sunderland 11 0
2010–11 *Ipswich T* 13 0 **50 4**
2011–12 Sunderland 35 1
2012–13 Sunderland 35 0
2013–14 Sunderland 33 3 **115 4**
2014–15 Newcastle U 35 4
2015–16 Newcastle U 29 1
2016–17 Newcastle U 29 0
2017–18 Newcastle U 0 0
2017–18 *Nottingham F* 16 1
2018–19 Newcastle U 0 0
2018–19 *Nottingham F* 38 3
2019–20 Newcastle U 0 0 **93 5**
2020–21 Nottingham F 17 0 **71 4**

DAWSON, Michael (D) 469 23
H: 6 2 W: 12 02 b.Leyburn 18-11-83
Internationals: England U21, B, Full caps.
2000–01 Nottingham F 0 0
2001–02 Nottingham F 1 0
2002–03 Nottingham F 38 5
2003–04 Nottingham F 30 1
2004–05 Nottingham F 14 1
2004–05 Tottenham H 5 0
2005–06 Tottenham H 32 0
2006–07 Tottenham H 37 1
2007–08 Tottenham H 27 1
2008–09 Tottenham H 16 1
2009–10 Tottenham H 29 2
2010–11 Tottenham H 24 1
2011–12 Tottenham H 7 0
2012–13 Tottenham H 27 1
2013–14 Tottenham H 32 0 **236 7**
2014–15 Hull C 28 1
2015–16 Hull C 32 1
2016–17 Hull C 22 3
2017–18 Hull C 40 3 **122 8**
2018–19 Nottingham F 10 0
2019–20 Nottingham F 18 1
2020–21 Nottingham F 0 0 **111 8**

DIALLO, Abdoulaye (G) 91 0
b.Reims 30-3-92
2009–10 Rennes 1 0
2010–11 Rennes 0 0
2011–12 Rennes 1 0
2012–13 Rennes 0 0
2013–14 Rennes 0 0
2013–14 *Le Havre* 16 0
2014–15 Rennes 0 0
2014–15 *Le Havre* 34 0 **50 0**
2015–16 Rennes 7 0
2016–17 Rennes 0 0
2016–17 *Caykur Rizespor* 19 0 **19 0**
2017–18 Rennes 3 0
2018–19 Rennes 6 0 **18 0**
2019–20 Genclerbirligi 4 0 **4 0**
2020–21 Nottingham F 0 0

FERNANDES, Baba (D) 0 0
H: 6 2 b.Guinea-Bissau 3-7-00
Internationals: Portugal U17.
From Vitoria Setubal.
2020–21 Nottingham F 0 0

FORNAH, Tyrese (M) 44 0
b. 11-9-99
From Brighton & HA.
2019–20 Nottingham F 0 0
2019–20 *Casa Pia* 5 0 **5 0**
2020–21 Nottingham F 0 0
2020–21 *Plymouth Arg* 39 0 **39 0**

GIBSON-HAMMOND, Alexander (M) 0 0
b. 10-11-02
2020–21 Nottingham F 0 0

GOMIS, Virgil (F) 26 0
b. 16-4-99
2018–19 Nottingham F 0 0
2018–19 *Notts Co* 10 0 **10 0**
2019–20 Nottingham F 0 0
2019–20 *Macclesfield T* 11 0 **11 0**
2020–21 Nottingham F 0 0
2020–21 *Grimsby T* 5 0 **5 0**

GRABBAN, Lewis (F) 460 148
H: 6 0 W: 11 03 b.Croydon 12-1-88
2005–06 Crystal Palace 0 0
2006–07 Crystal Palace 8 1
2006–07 *Oldham Ath* 9 0 **9 0**
2007–08 Crystal Palace 2 0 **10 1**
2007–08 *Motherwell* 6 0 **6 0**
2007–08 Millwall 13 3
2008–09 Millwall 31 6
2009–10 Millwall 11 0
2009–10 *Brentford* 7 2
2010–11 Millwall 1 0 **56 9**
2010–11 Brentford 22 5 **29 7**
2011–12 Rotherham U 43 18 **43 18**
2012–13 Bournemouth 42 13
2013–14 Bournemouth 44 22
2014–15 Norwich C 35 12
2015–16 Norwich C 6 1 **41 13**
2015–16 Bournemouth 15 0
2016–17 Bournemouth 3 0
2016–17 *Reading* 16 3 **16 3**
2017–18 Bournemouth 0 0 **104 35**
2017–18 *Sunderland* 19 12 **19 12**
2017–18 *Aston Villa* 15 8 **15 8**
2018–19 Nottingham F 39 16
2019–20 Nottingham F 45 20
2020–21 Nottingham F 28 6 **112 42**

GUERRERO, Miguel (F) 205 35
b.Toledo 12-7-90
2009–10 Albacete 2 0
2010–11 Albacete 0 0 **2 0**
2011–12 Sporting Gijon 0 0
2012–13 Sporting Gijon 18 2
2013–14 Sporting Gijon 14 1
2014–15 Sporting Gijon 36 11
2015–16 Sporting Gijon 23 2 **91 16**
2016–17 Leganes 31 5
2017–18 Leganes 22 4
2018–19 Olympiacos 23 7
2019–20 Olympiacos 14 2 **37 9**
2019–20 *Leganes* 13 1 **66 10**
2020–21 Nottingham F 9 0 **9 0**
Transferred to Rayo Vallecano February 2021.

HAMMOND, Oliver (M) 0 0
b. 13-11-02
2020–21 Nottingham F 0 0

HARBOTTLE, Riley (D) 0 0
b.Nottingham 26-9-00
2020–21 Nottingham F 0 0

IOANNOU, Nicholas (D) 95 6
b.Limassol 10-11-95
From Manchester U.
2014–15 APOEL 3 0
2015–16 APOEL 5 0
2016–17 APOEL 17 0
2017–18 APOEL 10 1
2018–19 APOEL 25 4
2019–20 APOEL 19 0
2020–21 APOEL 2 0 **81 5**
2020–21 Nottingham F 5 0 **5 0**
2020–21 *Aris* 9 1 **9 1**

JENKINSON, Carl (D) 119 3
H: 6 1 W: 12 02 b.Harlow 8-2-92
Internationals: Finland U19, U21. England U17, U21, Full caps.
2010–11 Charlton Ath 8 0 **8 0**
2010–11 Arsenal 0 0
2011–12 Arsenal 9 0
2012–13 Arsenal 14 0
2013–14 Arsenal 14 1
2014–15 Arsenal 0 0
2014–15 *West Ham U* 32 0
2015–16 Arsenal 0 0
2015–16 *West Ham U* 20 2 **52 2**
2016–17 Arsenal 1 0
2017–18 Arsenal 0 0
2017–18 *Birmingham C* 7 0 **7 0**
2018–19 Arsenal 3 0
2019–20 Arsenal 0 0 **41 1**
2019–20 Nottingham F 8 0
2020–21 Nottingham F 3 0 **11 0**

JOAO CARVALHO, Antonio (M) 116 6
H: 5 8 W: 10 06 b.Castanheira de Pera 9-3-97
Internationals: Portugal U16, U17, U18, U19, U20, U21.
2014–15 Benfica 0 0
2015–16 Benfica 0 0
2016–17 Benfica 0 0
2016–17 *Vitoria Setubal* 15 1 **15 1**
2017–18 Benfica 7 0 **7 0**
2018–19 Nottingham F 38 4
2019–20 Nottingham F 23 1
2020–21 Nottingham F 0 0 **61 5**
2020–21 *Almeria* 33 0 **33 0**

JOHNSON, Brennan (M) 44 10
b.Nottingham 23-5-01
Internationals: England U16, U17. Wales U19, U21.
2019–20 Nottingham F 4 0
2020–21 Nottingham F 0 0 **4 0**
2020–21 *Lincoln C* 40 10 **40 10**

KONATE, Ateef (M) 0 0
H: 5 10 b.Aubervilliers 4-4-01
From Le Havre.
2020–21 Nottingham F 0 0

KROVINOVIC, Filip (M) 197 22
b.Zagreb 29-8-95
Internationals: Croatia U19, U21.
2012–13 NK Zagreb 2 0
2013–14 NK Zagreb 32 7
2014–15 NK Zagreb 35 3
2015–16 NK Zagreb 6 2 **75 12**
2015–16 Rio Ave 9 0
2016–17 Rio Ave 26 5 **35 5**
2017–18 Benfica 13 1
2018–19 Benfica 4 0
2019–20 Benfica 0 0
2019–20 *WBA* 40 3
2020–21 Benfica 0 0 **17 1**
On loan from Benfica.
2020–21 WBA 11 0 **51 3**
On loan from Benfica.
2020–21 Nottingham F 19 1 **19 1**

LARSSON, Julian (F) 0 0
b. 21-4-01
Internationals: Sweden U16, U17, U19.
From AIK Solna.
2020–21 Nottingham F 0 0

LAWRENCE-GABRIEL, Jordan (D) 37 0
b.London 25-9-98
From Southend U.
2019–20 Nottingham F 0 0
2019–20 *Scunthorpe U* 9 0 **9 0**
2020–21 Nottingham F 1 0 **1 0**
2020–21 *Blackpool* 27 0 **27 0**

LOLLEY, Joe (F) 218 33
H: 5 10 W: 11 05 b.Redditch 25-8-92
Internationals: England C.
2013–14 Huddersfield T 6 1
2014–15 Huddersfield T 17 2
2015–16 Huddersfield T 32 4
2015–16 *Scunthorpe U* 6 0 **6 0**
2016–17 Huddersfield T 19 1
2017–18 Huddersfield T 6 1 **80 9**
2017–18 Nottingham F 16 3
2018–19 Nottingham F 46 11
2019–20 Nottingham F 42 9
2020–21 Nottingham F 28 1 **132 24**

MBE SOH, Loic (D) 10 1
b.Souza Gare 13-6-01
2017–18 Paris Saint-Germain 0 0
2018–19 Paris Saint-Germain 2 0
2019–20 Paris Saint-Germain 1 0 **3 0**
2020–21 Nottingham F 7 1 **7 1**

McDONNELL, Jamie (M) 0 0
b. 16-2-04
Internationals: Northern Ireland U17.
From Glentoran.
2020–21 Nottingham F 0 0

McGUANE, Marcus (M) 29 1
b.Greenwich 2-2-99
Internationals: Republic of Ireland U17. England U17, U18, U19.
2017–18 Arsenal 0 0
2018–19 Barcelona 0 0
2019–20 Barcelona 0 0
2019–20 *Telstar* 14 1 **14 1**
2019–20 Nottingham F 0 0
2020–21 Nottingham F 0 0
2020–21 *Oxford U* 15 0 **15 0**

McKENNA, Scott (D) 138 7
b.Kirriemuir 12-11-96
2014–15 Aberdeen 0 0
2014–15 *Ayr U* 12 0
2015–16 Aberdeen 3 0
2015–16 *Alloa Ath* 4 0 **4 0**
2016–17 Aberdeen 0 0
2016–17 *Ayr U* 11 1 **23 1**
2017–18 Aberdeen 30 2
2018–19 Aberdeen 30 2
2019–20 Aberdeen 24 1 **87 5**
2020–21 Nottingham F 24 1 **24 1**

MIGHTEN, Alex (F) 32 3
b.Nottingham 11-4-02
Internationals: England U16, U17, U18.
2019–20 Nottingham F 8 0
2020–21 Nottingham F 24 3 **32 3**

MURRAY, Glenn (F) 522 191
H: 6 1 W: 12 12 b.Maryport 25-9-83
From Barrow.
2005–06 Carlisle U 26 3
2006–07 Carlisle U 1 0 **27 3**
2006–07 *Stockport Co* 11 3 **11 3**
2006–07 Rochdale 31 16
2007–08 Rochdale 23 9 **54 25**
2007–08 Brighton & HA 21 9
2008–09 Brighton & HA 23 11
2009–10 Brighton & HA 32 12
2010–11 Brighton & HA 42 22
2011–12 Crystal Palace 38 6
2012–13 Crystal Palace 42 30
2013–14 Crystal Palace 14 1
2014–15 Crystal Palace 17 7
2014–15 *Reading* 18 8 **18 8**
2015–16 Crystal Palace 2 0 **113 44**
2015–16 Bournemouth 19 3 **19 3**
2016–17 Brighton & HA 45 23
2017–18 Brighton & HA 35 12
2018–19 Brighton & HA 38 13
2019–20 Brighton & HA 23 1
2020–21 *Watford* 5 0 **5 0**
2020–21 Brighton & HA 0 0 **259 103**
2020–21 Nottingham F 16 2 **16 2**

NUNO DA COSTA, Joia (M) 156 39
b. 10-2-91
Internationals: Cape Verde Full caps.
From Aubagne.
2015–16 Valenciennes 23 10
2016–17 Valenciennes 22 9 **45 19**
2017–18 Strasbourg 26 5
2018–19 Strasbourg 34 8
2019–20 Strasbourg 14 1 **74 14**
2019–20 Nottingham F 10 0
2020–21 Nottingham F 2 0 **12 0**
2020–21 *Royal Excel Mouscron* 25 6 **25 6**

PRESTON, Danny (D) 25 0
b. 6-8-00
2019–20 Nottingham F 0 0
2020–21 Nottingham F 0 0
2020–21 *Grimsby T* 25 0 **25 0**

RAMA, Rezart (D) 0 0
H: 6 0 b.Athens 4-12-00
Internationals: Albania U17, U19.
From Olympiacos.
2020–21 Nottingham F 0 0

RICHARDSON, Jayden (D) 50 1
b. 4-9-00
2019–20 Nottingham F 0 0
2019–20 *Exeter C* 18 1 **18 1**
2020–21 Nottingham F 0 0
2020–21 *Forest Green R* 32 0 **32 0**

SAMBA, Brice (G) 131 0
b.Linzolo 25-4-94
2010–11 Le Havre 0 0
2011–12 Le Havre 0 0
2012–13 Le Havre 0 0
2012–13 Marseille 0 0
2013–14 Marseille 1 0
2014–15 Marseille 0 0
2015–16 Marseille 0 0
2015–16 *Nancy* 2 0 **2 0**
2016–17 Marseille 0 0 **1 0**
2017–18 Caen 4 0
2018–19 Caen 38 0
2019–20 Caen 1 0 **43 0**
2019–20 Nottingham F 40 0
2020–21 Nottingham F 45 0 **85 0**

SANDERS, Samuel (F) 0 0
2020–21 Nottingham F 0 0

SARAIVA, Marcelo (M) 0 0
b.Guatemala 17-5-02
Internationals: Guatemala U17, Full caps.
From Internacional.
2020–21 Nottingham F 0 0

SHELVEY, George (G) 0 0
H: 6 2 W: 13 01 b.Nottingham 22-4-01
2020–21 Nottingham F 0 0

SMITH, Jordan (G) 60 0
b.Nottingham 8-8-94
Internationals: Costa Rica U17, U20, Full caps.
2013–14 Nottingham F 0 0
2014–15 Nottingham F 0 0
2015–16 Nottingham F 0 0
2016–17 Nottingham F 15 0
2017–18 Nottingham F 29 0
2018–19 Nottingham F 0 0
2018–19 *Barnsley* 1 0 **1 0**
2018–19 *Mansfield T* 12 0 **12 0**
2019–20 Nottingham F 2 0
2020–21 Nottingham F 1 0 **47 0**

SOW, Samba (M) 261 5
b.Bamako 29-4-89
Internationals: Mali Full caps.
2008–09 Lens 1 0
2009–10 Lens 31 1
2010–11 Lens 10 0
2011–12 Lens 23 0
2012–13 Lens 25 0 **90 1**
2013–14 Kardemir Karabukspor 32 0
2014–15 Kardemir Karabukspor 18 1 **50 1**
2015–16 Kayserispor 16 1
2016–17 Kayserispor 25 2 **41 3**
2017–18 Dynamo Moscow 23 0
2018–19 Dynamo Moscow 17 0 **40 0**
2019–20 Nottingham F 25 0
2020–21 Nottingham F 15 0 **40 0**

SWAN, Will (F) 12 1
b.Mansfield 26-10-00
2020–21 Nottingham F 2 0 **2 0**
2020–21 *Port Vale* 10 1 **10 1**

TAYLOR, Dale (F) 0 0
b. 12-12-03
Internationals: Northern Ireland U17, U21.
From Linfield.
2020–21 Nottingham F 0 0

TAYLOR, Lyle (F) 377 121
H: 6 2 W: 12 00 b.Greenwich 29-3-90
Internationals: Montserrat Full caps.
2007–08 Millwall 0 0
2008–09 Millwall 0 0
From Concord R
2010–11 Bournemouth 11 0
2011–12 Bournemouth 18 0 **29 0**
2011–12 *Hereford U* 8 2 **8 2**
2012–13 Falkirk 34 24 **34 24**
2013–14 Sheffield U 20 2 **20 2**
2013–14 *Partick Thistle* 20 7
2014–15 Scunthorpe U 18 3 **18 3**
2014–15 *Partick Thistle* 15 3 **35 10**
2015–16 AFC Wimbledon 42 20
2016–17 AFC Wimbledon 43 10
2017–18 AFC Wimbledon 46 14 **131 44**
2018–19 Charlton Ath 41 21
2019–20 Charlton Ath 22 11 **63 32**
2020–21 Nottingham F 39 4 **39 4**

TOBIAS FIGUEIREDO, Pereira (D) 137 7
H: 6 2 W: 13 03 b.Satao 2-2-94
Internationals: Portugal U17, U18, U19, U20, U21, U23.
2012–13 Sporting Lisbon 0 0
2013–14 Sporting Lisbon 0 0
2013–14 *Reus* 13 1 **13 1**
2014–15 Sporting Lisbon 14 2
2015–16 Sporting Lisbon 1 0
2016–17 Sporting Lisbon 0 0
2016–17 *Nacional* 22 1 **22 1**
2017–18 Sporting Lisbon 0 0
2017–18 *Nottingham F* 12 0
2018–19 Sporting Lisbon 0 0 **15 2**
2018–19 *Nottingham F* 13 0
2019–20 Nottingham F 30 3
2020–21 Nottingham F 32 0 **87 3**

WORRALL, Joe (D) 165 4
H: 6 3 b.Nottingham 10-1-97
Internationals: England U20, U21.
2015–16 Nottingham F 0 0
2015–16 *Dagenham & R* 14 1 **14 1**
2016–17 Nottingham F 21 0
2017–18 Nottingham F 31 1
2018–19 Nottingham F 0 0
2018–19 *Rangers* 22 0 **22 0**
2019–20 Nottingham F 46 1
2020–21 Nottingham F 31 1 **129 3**

YATES, Ryan (M) 130 11
b.Nottingham 21-11-97
2016–17 Nottingham F 0 0
2016–17 *Shrewsbury T* 12 0 **12 0**
2017–18 Nottingham F 0 0
2017–18 *Notts Co* 25 3 **25 3**
2017–18 *Scunthorpe U* 16 2 **16 2**
2018–19 Nottingham F 16 1

Season	Club	App	Gls	Total	Gls
2019–20	Nottingham F	27	3		
2020–21	Nottingham F	34	2	77	6

YURI RIBEIRO, Oliveira (D) **77 2**
b. 24-1-97
Internationals: Portugal U16, U17, U18, U19, U20, U21.

Season	Club	App	Gls	Total	Gls
2014–15	Benfica	0	0		
2015–16	Benfica	0	0		
2016–17	Benfica	0	0		
2017–18	Benfica	0	0		
2017–18	*Rio Ave*	25	1	25	1
2018–19	Benfica	0	0		
2019–20	Nottingham F	27	0		
2020–21	Nottingham F	25	1	52	1

Scholars
Akers, Alexander Matthew; Amekortu, Francky Arnord; Barker, Lewis Ryan; Bello, Silvio Olabode; Boland, Luke Thomas; Collins, Samuel Haig; Donnelly, Aaron Martin; Doorbar-Baptist, Luca William; Jackson-Davis, Jovel Nii Odartey; Johnson, Pharrell Junior; Korpal, Aaron Jay; Mbakop Fankwe, William Jordan; Perkins, Jack William; Sarantis, Alexandros; Solomon, Osakpolor Clearance.

OLDHAM ATH (61)

ADAMS, Nicky (F) **546 39**
H: 5 10 W: 11 00 b.Bolton 16-10-86
Internationals: Wales U21.

Season	Club	App	Gls	Total	Gls
2005–06	Bury	15	1		
2006–07	Bury	19	1		
2007–08	Bury	43	12		
2008–09	Leicester C	12	0		
2008–09	*Rochdale*	14	1		
2009–10	Leicester C	18	0	30	0
2009–10	*Leyton Orient*	6	0	6	0
2010–11	Brentford	7	0	7	0
2010–11	Rochdale	30	0		
2011–12	Rochdale	41	4	85	5
2012–13	Crawley T	46	8		
2013–14	Crawley T	24	1	70	9
2013–14	Rotherham U	15	1	15	1
2013–14	Bury	0	0		
2014–15	Bury	38	1		
2015–16	Northampton T	39	3		
2016–17	Carlisle U	42	3		
2017–18	Carlisle U	17	0	59	3
2018–19	Bury	46	2	161	17
2019–20	Northampton T	37	1		
2020–21	Northampton T	14	0	90	4
2020–21	Oldham Ath	23	0	23	0

BADAN, Andrea (D) **66 0**
b.Monselice 21-3-98

Season	Club	App	Gls	Total	Gls
2015–16	Verona	0	0		
2016–17	Verona	0	0		
2017–18	Verona	0	0		
2017–18	*Prato*	20	0	20	0
2017–18	*Albino Leffe*	1	0	1	0
2018–19	Verona	0	0		
2018–19	*Alessandria*	25	0	25	0
2019–20	Verona	0	0		
2019–20	*Carrarese*	1	0	1	0
2019–20	*Cavese*	1	0	1	0
2020–21	Oldham Ath	18	0	18	0

BAHAMBOULA, Dylan (M) **130 17**
b.Corbeil Essonnes 22-5-95

Season	Club	App	Gls	Total	Gls
2012–13	Monaco	0	0		
2013–14	Monaco	0	0		
2014–15	Monaco	0	0		
2015–16	Monaco	0	0		
2015–16	*Paris FC*	29	4	29	4
2016–17	Dijon	11	1		
2017–18	Dijon	4	0	15	1
2017–18	*Gazelec Ajaccio*	13	1	13	1
2018–19	Astra Giurgiu	5	1	5	1
2018–19	CS Constantine	12	2		
2019–20	CS Constantine	1	0	13	2
2019–20	Tsarsko Selo	17	2	17	2
2020–21	Oldham Ath	38	6	38	6

BARNES, Marcus (F) **15 0**
b.Reading 1-12-96

Season	Club	App	Gls	Total	Gls
2017–18	Southampton	0	0		
2017–18	*Yeovil T*	8	0	8	0
2018–19	Southampton	0	0		
2019–20	Southampton	0	0		
2020–21	Southampton	0	0		
2020–21	Oldham Ath	7	0	7	0

BARNETT, Jordan (D) **17 0**
H: 5 10 b.Penistone 20-10-99

Season	Club	App	Gls	Total	Gls
2017–18	Burnley	0	0		
2018–19	Barnsley	0	0		
2019–20	Barnsley	0	0		
2020–21	Oldham Ath	17	0	17	0

Transferred to Notts Co February 2021.

BILBOE, Laurence (G) **3 0**
b. 21-2-98

Season	Club	App	Gls	Total	Gls
2016–17	Rotherham U	0	0		
2017–18	Rotherham U	0	0		
2018–19	Rotherham U	0	0		
2019–20	Rotherham U	0	0		
2020–21	Oldham Ath	3	0	3	0

BLACKWOOD, George (F) **96 17**
b.Sydney 4-6-97

Season	Club	App	Gls	Total	Gls
2014–15	Sydney	3	0		
2015–16	Sydney	14	1		
2016–17	Sydney	2	0	19	1
2017–18	Adelaide U	24	5		
2018–19	Adelaide U	19	4		
2019–20	Adelaide U	21	4	64	13
2020–21	Oldham Ath	13	3	13	3

BORTHWICK-JACKSON, Cameron (D) **86 4**
H: 6 3 W: 13 10 b.Manchester 2-2-97
Internationals: England U16, U17, U19, U20.

Season	Club	App	Gls	Total	Gls
2015–16	Manchester U	10	0		
2016–17	Manchester U	0	0		
2016–17	*Wolverhampton W*	6	0	6	0
2017–18	Manchester U	0	0		
2017–18	*Leeds U*	1	0	1	0
2018–19	Manchester U	0	0		
2018–19	*Scunthorpe U*	29	2	29	2
2019–20	Manchester U	0	0	10	0
2019–20	*Tranmere R*	3	0	3	0
2019–20	*Oldham Ath*	6	0		
2020–21	Oldham Ath	31	2	37	2

CHAPMAN, Mackenzie (G) **1 0**

Season	Club	App	Gls	Total	Gls
2020–21	Oldham Ath	1	0	1	0

DA SILVA, Vani (F) **0 0**
b. 27-11-02

Season	Club	App	Gls	Total	Gls
2020–21	Curzon Ashton	0	0		
2020–21	Oldham Ath	0	0		

DEARNLEY, Zachary (M) **32 11**
b. 28-9-98
Internationals: England U16, U18.

Season	Club	App	Gls	Total	Gls
2016–17	Manchester U	0	0		
2017–18	Manchester U	0	0		
2018–19	Manchester U	0	0		
2018–19	*Oldham Ath*	9	1		
2019–20	Oldham Ath	8	4		
2020–21	Oldham Ath	15	6	32	11

DIARRA, Raphael (D) **62 1**
b.Paris 27-5-95

Season	Club	App	Gls	Total	Gls
2013–14	Monaco	0	0		
2014–15	Monaco	0	0		
2015–16	Monaco	0	0		
2016–17	Monaco	0	0		
2016–17	*Cercle Brugge*	15	1	15	1
2017–18	Monaco	0	0		
2018–19	Quevilly-Rouuen	14	0		
2019–20	Quevilly-Rouuen	17	0	31	0
2020–21	Oldham Ath	16	0	16	0

FAGE, Dylan (M) **46 1**
b. 18-3-99

Season	Club	App	Gls	Total	Gls
2016–17	Auxerre	0	0		
2017–18	Auxerre	0	0		
2018–19	Auxerre	0	0		
2019–20	Oldham Ath	12	0		
2020–21	Oldham Ath	34	1	46	1

GRANT, Bobby (M) **359 74**
H: 5 11 W: 12 00 b.Liverpool 1-7-90

Season	Club	App	Gls	Total	Gls
2006–07	Accrington S	1	0		
2007–08	Accrington S	7	0		
2008–09	Accrington S	15	1		
2009–10	Accrington S	42	14		
2010–11	Scunthorpe U	27	0		
2010–11	*Rochdale*	6	2		
2011–12	Scunthorpe U	29	7		
2011–12	*Accrington S*	8	3		
2012–13	Scunthorpe U	3	0	59	7
2012–13	Rochdale	36	15	42	17
2013–14	Blackpool	6	0		
2013–14	*Fleetwood T*	1	0		
2014–15	Blackpool	0	0	6	0
2014–15	*Shrewsbury T*	33	6	33	6
2015–16	Fleetwood T	38	10		
2016–17	Fleetwood T	46	9		
2017–18	Fleetwood T	29	3		
2018–19	Fleetwood T	4	0	118	22

On loan from Wrexham.

Season	Club	App	Gls	Total	Gls
2019–20	Accrington S	5	1	78	19

On loan from Wrexham.

Season	Club	App	Gls	Total	Gls
2020–21	Oldham Ath	23	3	23	3

HOUGH, Ben (M) **0 0**

Season	Club	App	Gls	Total	Gls
2020–21	Oldham Ath	0	0		

JAMESON, Kyle (D) **25 2**
b.Urmston 11-9-98
From Chelsea.

Season	Club	App	Gls	Total	Gls
2017–18	WBA	0	0		
2020–21	Oldham Ath	25	2	25	2

JOMBATI, Sido (D) **289 9**
H: 6 0 W: 11 11 b.Lisbon 20-8-87
From Sporting Lisbon.

Season	Club	App	Gls	Total	Gls
2011–12	Cheltenham T	36	2		
2012–13	Cheltenham T	37	1		
2013–14	Cheltenham T	43	1	116	4
2014–15	Wycombe W	35	0		
2015–16	Wycombe W	34	1		
2016–17	Wycombe W	25	2		
2017–18	Wycombe W	20	1		
2018–19	Wycombe W	33	1		
2019–20	Wycombe W	7	0	154	5
2020–21	Oldham Ath	19	0	19	0

KEILLOR-DUNN, Davis (M) **92 17**
b.Sunderland 2-11-97

Season	Club	App	Gls	Total	Gls
2016–17	Ross Co	0	0		
2017–18	Ross Co	29	3		
2018–19	Ross Co	11	1	40	4
2018–19	*Falkirk*	11	3	11	3

From Wrexham.

Season	Club	App	Gls	Total	Gls
2020–21	Oldham Ath	41	10	41	10

LUAMBA, Junior (F) **2 0**
b. 27-4-03

Season	Club	App	Gls	Total	Gls
2020–21	Oldham Ath	2	0	2	0

McALENY, Conor (F) **167 43**
H: 5 10 W: 12 05 b.Liverpool 12-8-92

Season	Club	App	Gls	Total	Gls
2009–10	Everton	0	0		
2010–11	Everton	0	0		
2011–12	Everton	2	0		
2011–12	*Scunthorpe U*	3	0	3	0
2012–13	Everton	0	0		
2013–14	Everton	0	0		
2013–14	*Brentford*	4	0	4	0
2014–15	Everton	0	0		
2014–15	*Cardiff C*	8	2	8	2
2015–16	Everton	0	0		
2015–16	*Charlton Ath*	8	0	8	0
2015–16	*Wigan Ath*	13	4	13	4
2016–17	Everton	0	0	2	0
2016–17	*Oxford U*	18	10	18	10
2017–18	Fleetwood T	29	5		
2018–19	Fleetwood T	14	0		
2018–19	*Kilmarnock*	11	3	11	3
2019–20	Fleetwood T	12	2	55	7
2019–20	*Shrewsbury T*	5	0	5	0
2020–21	Oldham Ath	40	17	40	17

NTAMBWE, Brice (M) **116 4**
H: 6 1 W: 12 13 b.Brussels 29-4-93
Internationals: Belgium U16, U17, U19, U20, U21.

Season	Club	App	Gls	Total	Gls
2011–12	Birmingham C	0	0		
2012–13	Mons	6	0		
2013–14	Mons	19	0		
2014–15	Mons	2	0	27	0
2014–15	Lierse	1	0		
2015–16	Lierse	0	0		
2016–17	Lierse	18	1		
2017–18	Lierse	21	1	40	2
2017–18	*Oosterwijk*	9	1	9	1
2018–19	Partick Thistle	5	1	5	1
2018–19	Macclesfield T	8	0		
2019–20	Macclesfield T	3	0	11	0
2020–21	Oldham Ath	24	0	24	0

PIERGIANNI, Carl (D) **63 5**
b.Peterborough 3-5-92

Season	Club	App	Gls	Total	Gls
2010–11	Peterborough U	1	0	1	0

From Stockport Co, Corby T, Boston U, South Melbourne.

Season	Club	App	Gls	Total	Gls
2019–20	Salford C	13	0	13	0
2019–20	*Oldham Ath*	11	0		
2020–21	Oldham Ath	38	5	49	5

SUTTON, Will (D) **1 0**

Season	Club	App	Gls	Total	Gls
2020–21	Oldham Ath	1	0	1	0

VAUGHAN, Harry (F) **6 0**

Season	Club	App	Gls	Total	Gls
2020–21	Oldham Ath	6	0	6	0

WHELAN, Callum (M) **31 0**
b.Barnsley 24-9-98

Season	Club	App	Gls	Total	Gls
2018–19	Manchester U	0	0		
2018–19	*Port Vale*	0	0		
2019–20	Watford	0	0		
2020–21	Oldham Ath	31	0	31	0

WOODS, Gary (G) **205 0**
H: 6 1 W: 11 00 b.Kettering 1-10-90
Internationals: England U18.
From Cambridge U, Manchester U.

Season	Club	App	Gls	Total	Gls
2008–09	Doncaster R	1	0		
2009–10	Doncaster R	0	0		
2010–11	Doncaster R	16	0		
2011–12	Doncaster R	14	0		
2012–13	Doncaster R	42	0		
2013–14	Doncaster R	0	0	73	0
2013–14	Watford	0	0		
2014–15	Leyton Orient	17	0		
2015–16	Leyton Orient	0	0	17	0

2015–16	*Ross Co*	12	0	**12**	**0**
2016–17	Hamilton A	21	0		
2017–18	Hamilton A	32	0		
2018–19	Hamilton A	32	0	**85**	**0**
2019–20	Oldham Ath	15	0		
2020–21	Oldham Ath	0	0	**15**	**0**
2020–21	*Aberdeen*	3	0	**3**	**0**

Scholars
Badby, Kane Peter; Chapman, MacKenzie Jon; Danielewcz, Kacper; Edwards, Joseph Dean; Hemmingsen, Gustav Winkler Elmerdahl; Higgins, Sean Michael; Hough, Benjamin Isaac; Hughes, Asa William; Loforte Tique Da Silva, Ivanilson; Luamba, Junior; Modi, Isaac Tombe Wani; Oseh, Robert Oshomoshiofu; Peixoto Couto, Bernado; Simms, James George William; Speed, Callum; Sutton, William Joseph; Turner, Trey Donnelly; Vaughan, Harry Patrick; Williams, Jack Bobby Owen.

OXFORD U (62)

AGYEI, Daniel (F) **98** **16**
H: 6 0 W: 12 02 b.Dansoman 1-6-97

2014–15	AFC Wimbledon	0	0		
2015–16	Burnley	0	0		
2016–17	Burnley	3	0		
2016–17	*Coventry C*	16	4	**16**	**4**
2017–18	Burnley	0	0		
2017–18	*Walsall*	18	4	**18**	**4**
2017–18	*Blackpool*	9	0	**9**	**0**
2018–19	Burnley	0	0		
2019–20	Burnley	0	0	**3**	**0**
2019–20	Oxford U	13	3		
2020–21	Oxford U	39	5	**52**	**8**

ANIFOWOSE, Joshua (M) **0** **0**
b. 3-2-03

2020–21	Oxford U	0	0		

ASONGANYI, Dylan (F) **6** **0**
b. 10-12-00

2017–18	Milton Keynes D	0	0		
2018–19	Milton Keynes D	3	0		
2019–20	Milton Keynes D	3	0	**6**	**0**
2020–21	Oxford U	0	0		

ATKINSON, Robert (D) **39** **1**
b. 13-7-98
From Basingstoke T.

2017–18	Fulham	0	0		
2018–19	Fulham	0	0		

From Eastleigh.

2019–20	Oxford U	0	0		
2020–21	Oxford U	39	1	**39**	**1**

BARKER, Brandon (M) **94** **9**
H: 5 9 W: 10 10 b.Manchester 4-10-96
Internationals: England U18, U19, U20.

2014–15	Manchester C	0	0		
2015–16	Manchester C	0	0		
2015–16	*Rotherham U*	4	1	**4**	**1**
2016–17	Manchester C	0	0		
2016–17	*NAC Breda*	22	2	**22**	**2**
2017–18	Manchester C	0	0		
2017–18	*Hibernian*	27	2	**27**	**2**
2018–19	Manchester C	0	0		
2018–19	*Preston NE*	16	0	**16**	**0**
2019–20	Rangers	6	1		
2020–21	Rangers	0	0	**6**	**1**

On loan from Rangers.

2020–21	Oxford U	19	3	**19**	**3**

BRANNAGAN, Cameron (M) **130** **9**
H: 5 11 W: 11 03 b.Manchester 9-5-96
Internationals: England U18, U20.

2013–14	Liverpool	0	0		
2014–15	Liverpool	0	0		
2015–16	Liverpool	3	0		
2016–17	Liverpool	0	0		
2016–17	*Fleetwood T*	13	0	**13**	**0**
2017–18	Liverpool	0	0	**3**	**0**
2017–18	Oxford U	12	0		
2018–19	Oxford U	41	3		
2019–20	Oxford U	30	5		
2020–21	Oxford U	31	1	**114**	**9**

BREAREY, Eddie (G) **0** **0**
b.Oxford 9-6-04

2020–21	Oxford U	0	0		

CHAMBERS, Leon (M) **3** **0**
b.Luton 5-11-01
From Luton T, Aston Villa.

2020–21	Oxford U	3	0	**3**	**0**

CLARE, Sean (M) **129** **11**
H: 6 3 b.Sheffield 18-9-96

2015–16	Sheffield W	0	0		
2015–16	*Bury*	4	0	**4**	**0**
2016–17	Sheffield W	0	0		
2016–17	*Accrington S*	8	1	**8**	**1**
2017–18	Sheffield W	5	1	**5**	**1**
2017–18	*Gillingham*	21	1	**21**	**1**
2018–19	Hearts	28	3		
2019–20	Hearts	26	4	**54**	**7**
2020–21	Oxford U	17	0	**17**	**0**
2020–21	*Burton Alb*	20	1	**20**	**1**

COOPER, Joel (M) **24** **3**
b.Ballclare 29-2-96
From Glenavon.

2020–21	Oxford U	4	0	**4**	**0**
2020–21	*Linfield*	20	3	**20**	**3**

EASTWOOD, Simon (G) **231** **0**
H: 6 2 W: 10 13 b.Huddersfield 26-6-89
Internationals: England U18, U19.

2005–06	Huddersfield T	0	0		
2006–07	Huddersfield T	0	0		
2007–08	Huddersfield T	0	0		
2008–09	Huddersfield T	1	0		
2009–10	Huddersfield T	0	0	**1**	**0**
2009–10	*Bradford C*	22	0	**22**	**0**
2010–11	Oxford U	0	0		

From FC Halifax T.

2012–13	Portsmouth	27	0	**27**	**0**
2013–14	Blackburn R	7	0		
2014–15	Blackburn R	6	0		
2015–16	Blackburn R	0	0	**13**	**0**
2016–17	Oxford U	46	0		
2017–18	Oxford U	46	0		
2018–19	Oxford U	34	0		
2019–20	Oxford U	29	0		
2020–21	Oxford U	13	0	**168**	**0**

ELECHI, Michael (D) **0** **0**
b.Westminster 10-10-01
From Manchester U.

2020–21	Oxford U	0	0		

FORDE, Anthony (M) **261** **14**
H: 5 9 W: 10 10 b.Limerick 16-11-93
Internationals: Republic of Ireland U19, U21.

2011–12	Wolverhampton W	6	0		
2012–13	Wolverhampton W	12	0		
2012–13	*Scunthorpe U*	8	0	**8**	**0**
2013–14	Wolverhampton W	3	0	**21**	**0**
2014–15	Walsall	37	3		
2015–16	Walsall	41	4	**78**	**7**
2016–17	Rotherham U	32	2		
2017–18	Rotherham U	41	2		
2018–19	Rotherham U	28	1	**101**	**5**
2019–20	Oxford U	18	1		
2020–21	Oxford U	35	1	**53**	**2**

GORRIN, Alejandro (M) **170** **2**
b.Tenerife 1-8-93

2011–12	Sunderland	0	0		
2012–13	Sunderland	0	0		
2013–14	Sunderland	0	0		
2014–15	Wellington Phoenix	25	0		
2015–16	Wellington Phoenix	24	0		
2016–17	Wellington Phoenix	23	1	**72**	**1**
2017–18	Boavista	0	0		
2017–18	Sepsi	12	0	**12**	**0**
2018–19	Motherwell	20	0	**20**	**0**
2019–20	Oxford U	31	0		
2020–21	Oxford U	35	1	**66**	**1**

HALL, Robert (F) **169** **19**
H: 6 2 W: 10 05 b.Aylesbury 20-10-93
Internationals: England U16, U17, U18, U19.

2010–11	West Ham U	0	0		
2011–12	West Ham U	3	0		
2011–12	*Oxford U*	13	5		
2011–12	*Milton Keynes D*	2	0		
2012–13	West Ham U	1	0	**4**	**0**
2012–13	*Birmingham C*	13	0	**13**	**0**
2012–13	*Bolton W*	1	0		
2013–14	Bolton W	22	1		
2014–15	Bolton W	9	0		
2014–15	*Milton Keynes D*	7	3		
2015–16	Bolton W	0	0	**32**	**1**
2015–16	*Milton Keynes D*	27	2	**36**	**5**
2016–17	Oxford U	26	6		
2017–18	Oxford U	13	2		
2018–19	Oxford U	4	0		
2019–20	Oxford U	13	0		
2019–20	*Forest Green R*	6	0	**6**	**0**
2020–21	Oxford U	9	0	**78**	**13**

HANSON, Jamie (F) **107** **1**
H: 6 3 W: 12 06 b.Burton-upon-Trent 10-11-95
Internationals: England U20.

2012–13	Derby Co	0	0		
2013–14	Derby Co	0	0		
2014–15	Derby Co	2	1		
2015–16	Derby Co	18	0		
2016–17	Derby Co	5	0		
2016–17	*Wigan Ath*	17	0	**17**	**0**
2017–18	Derby Co	6	0	**31**	**1**
2018–19	Oxford U	30	0		
2019–20	Oxford U	5	0		
2020–21	Oxford U	24	0	**59**	**0**

HENRY, James (M) **464** **85**
H: 6 1 W: 11 11 b.Reading 10-6-89
Internationals: Scotland U16, U19. England U18, U19.

2006–07	Reading	0	0		
2006–07	*Nottingham F*	1	0	**1**	**0**
2007–08	Reading	0	0		
2007–08	*Bournemouth*	11	4	**11**	**4**
2007–08	*Norwich C*	3	0	**3**	**0**
2008–09	Reading	7	0		
2008–09	*Millwall*	16	3		
2009–10	Reading	3	0	**10**	**0**
2009–10	*Millwall*	9	5		
2010–11	Millwall	42	5		
2011–12	Millwall	39	0		
2012–13	Millwall	35	5		
2013–14	Millwall	5	0	**146**	**18**
2013–14	Wolverhampton W	32	10		
2014–15	Wolverhampton W	37	5		
2015–16	Wolverhampton W	39	7		
2016–17	Wolverhampton W	2	0	**110**	**22**
2016–17	*Bolton W*	30	1	**30**	**1**
2017–18	Oxford U	42	10		
2018–19	Oxford U	44	11		
2019–20	Oxford U	30	12		
2020–21	Oxford U	37	7	**153**	**40**

JONES, Nico (D) **34** **0**
b. 3-2-02
From Fulham.

2018–19	Oxford U	3	0		
2019–20	Oxford U	31	0		
2020–21	Oxford U	0	0	**34**	**0**

KELLY, Liam (M) **112** **7**
b. 22-11-95
Internationals: Republic of Ireland U19, U21.

2014–15	Reading	0	0		
2015–16	Reading	0	0		
2016–17	Reading	28	1		
2017–18	Reading	34	5		
2018–19	Reading	20	1	**82**	**7**
2019–20	Feyenoord	1	0		
2019–20	*Oxford U*	3	0		
2020–21	Feyenoord	0	0	**1**	**0**

On loan from Feyenoord.

2020–21	Oxford U	26	0	**29**	**0**

LOFTHOUSE, Kyran (F) **0** **0**
b.Oxford 21-10-00

2018–19	Oxford U	0	0		
2019–20	Oxford U	0	0		
2020–21	Oxford U	0	0		

LONG, Sam (D) **88** **8**
H: 5 10 W: 11 11 b.Oxford 16-1-95

2012–13	Oxford U	1	0		
2013–14	Oxford U	3	0		
2014–15	Oxford U	10	1		
2015–16	Oxford U	1	0		
2016–17	Oxford U	3	0		
2017–18	Oxford U	0	0		
2018–19	Oxford U	18	0		
2019–20	Oxford U	16	1		
2020–21	Oxford U	36	6	**88**	**8**

McNALLY, Luke (D) **0** **0**
b. 7-2-99
From Drogheda U, St Patricks Ath.

2020–21	Oxford U	0	0		

MOORE, Elliott (D) **118** **13**
b. 16-3-97
Internationals: England U18, U20.

2016–17	Leicester C	0	0		
2017–18	Leicester C	0	0		
2017–18	*OH Leuven*	24	2		
2018–19	Leicester C	0	0		
2018–19	*OH Leuven*	28	5	**52**	**7**
2019–20	Oxford U	20	1		
2020–21	Oxford U	46	5	**66**	**6**

MOUSINHO, John (M) **469** **23**
H: 6 1 W: 12 07 b.Hounslow 30-4-86

2005–06	Brentford	7	0		
2006–07	Brentford	34	0		
2007–08	Brentford	23	2	**64**	**2**
2008–09	Wycombe W	34	2		
2009–10	Wycombe W	39	1	**73**	**3**
2010–11	Stevenage	38	7		
2011–12	Stevenage	19	3		
2012–13	Preston NE	24	1		
2013–14	Preston NE	2	0	**26**	**1**
2013–14	*Gillingham*	4	1	**4**	**1**
2013–14	*Stevenage*	16	1	**73**	**11**
2014–15	Burton Alb	42	2		
2015–16	Burton Alb	46	0		
2016–17	Burton Alb	32	0		
2017–18	Burton Alb	1	0	**121**	**2**
2017–18	Oxford U	40	1		

2018–19	Oxford U	35	2		
2019–20	Oxford U	26	0		
2020–21	Oxford U	7	0	**108**	**3**

NAPA, Malachi (M) 29 0
b. 26-5-99
From Reading.

2017–18	Oxford U	14	0		
2018–19	Oxford U	0	0		
2018–19	*Macclesfield T*	15	0	**15**	**0**
2019–20	Oxford U	0	0		
2020–21	Oxford U	0	0	**14**	**0**

O'DONKOR, Gatlin (F) 0 0
b. 14-10-04

2020–21	Oxford U	0	0		

OSEI YAW, Derick (F) 24 1
b.Toulouse 10-9-98

2016–17	Toulouse	0	0		
2017–18	Toulouse	0	0		
2018–19	Brest	3	0		
2019–20	Brest	0	0	**3**	**0**
2019–20	*Beziers*	7	1	**7**	**1**
2020–21	Oxford U	3	0	**3**	**0**
2020–21	*Walsall*	11	0	**11**	**0**

RUFFELS, Joshua (M) 258 21
H: 5 10 W: 11 11 b.Oxford 23-10-93

2011–12	Coventry C	1	0		
2012–13	Coventry C	0	0	**1**	**0**
2013–14	Oxford U	29	1		
2014–15	Oxford U	33	0		
2015–16	Oxford U	16	0		
2016–17	Oxford U	20	2		
2017–18	Oxford U	38	5		
2018–19	Oxford U	44	4		
2019–20	Oxford U	35	3		
2020–21	Oxford U	42	6	**257**	**21**

SADE LICHTENFELD, Yoav (D) 0 0

2020–21	Oxford U	0	0		

STEPHENS, Jack (G) 35 0
b. 2-8-97

2014–15	Oxford U	0	0		
2015–16	Oxford U	0	0		
2016–17	Oxford U	0	0		
2017–18	Oxford U	0	0		
2018–19	Oxford U	2	0		
2019–20	Oxford U	0	0		
2020–21	Oxford U	33	0	**35**	**0**

SYKES, Mark (M) 64 1
b. 4-8-97
Internationals: Northern Ireland U19, U21.
From Glenavon.

2018–19	Oxford U	9	0		
2019–20	Oxford U	23	1		
2020–21	Oxford U	32	0	**64**	**1**

TAYLOR, Matty (F) 212 81
H: 5 9 W: 11 05 b. 30-3-90
Internationals: England C.
From Oxford U, North Leigh, Forest Green R.

2015–16	Bristol R	46	27		
2016–17	Bristol R	27	16	**73**	**43**
2016–17	Bristol C	15	2		
2017–18	Bristol C	18	1		
2018–19	Bristol C	33	4		
2019–20	Bristol C	1	0	**67**	**7**
2019–20	*Oxford U*	26	13		
2020–21	Oxford U	46	18	**72**	**31**

WINNALL, Sam (F) 252 88
H: 5 9 W: 11 04 b.Wolverhampton 19-1-91

2009–10	Wolverhampton W	0	0		
2010–11	Wolverhampton W	0	0		
2010–11	*Burton Alb*	19	7	**19**	**7**
2011–12	Wolverhampton W	0	0		
2011–12	*Hereford U*	8	2	**8**	**2**
2011–12	*Inverness CT*	2	0	**2**	**0**
2012–13	Wolverhampton W	0	0		
2012–13	*Shrewsbury T*	4	0	**4**	**0**
2013–14	Scunthorpe U	45	23	**45**	**23**
2014–15	Barnsley	32	9		
2015–16	Barnsley	43	21		
2016–17	Barnsley	22	11	**97**	**41**
2016–17	Sheffield W	14	3		
2017–18	Sheffield W	2	1		
2017–18	*Derby Co*	17	6	**17**	**6**
2018–19	Sheffield W	7	0		
2019–20	Sheffield W	13	1	**36**	**5**
2020–21	Oxford U	24	4	**24**	**4**

Scholars
Anifowose, Joshua Ayodele Temitayo; Brearey, Edward Charles; Chambers-Parillon, Leon Nelson; Coe, Elijah Luke; Crook, Callum James; Gardner, Jack David; Golding, James Anthony; Goodrham, Tyler Charlie; Grant, Trey Darnell; Johnson, Samuel Jack; Masters-Spence, Mac; Niemczycki, Damian; Nosakhare, Clinton; Owens, William Robert; Plumley, Kie; Smith, Adam Peter; Sole, Fabio Calogero Antonio; Watt, Benjamin Alexander.

PETERBOROUGH U (63)

BARKER, Kyle (M) 1 0
b. 16-12-00

2019–20	Peterborough U	0	0		
2020–21	Peterborough U	1	0	**1**	**0**

BEEVERS, Mark (D) 482 21
H: 6 4 W: 13 00 b.Barnsley 21-11-89
Internationals: England U19.

2006–07	Sheffield W	2	0		
2007–08	Sheffield W	28	0		
2008–09	Sheffield W	34	0		
2009–10	Sheffield W	35	0		
2010–11	Sheffield W	28	2		
2011–12	Sheffield W	7	0		
2011–12	*Milton Keynes D*	14	1	**14**	**1**
2012–13	Sheffield W	6	0	**140**	**2**
2012–13	Millwall	35	1		
2013–14	Millwall	28	0		
2014–15	Millwall	25	2		
2015–16	Millwall	42	4	**130**	**7**
2016–17	Bolton W	45	7		
2017–18	Bolton W	44	1		
2018–19	Bolton W	32	3	**121**	**11**
2019–20	Peterborough U	32	0		
2020–21	Peterborough U	45	0	**77**	**0**

BLACKMORE, Will (G) 1 0
b. 13-3-03

2020–21	Peterborough U	1	0	**1**	**0**

BLAKE-TRACY, Frazer (D) 23 0
b. 10-9-95
From Dereham T, Lowestoft, King's Lynn T.

2019–20	Peterborough U	14	0		
2020–21	Peterborough U	9	0	**23**	**0**

BODIE, Dave (D) 0 0

2020–21	Peterborough U	0	0		

BROOM, Ryan (M) 108 13
H: 5 10 W: 12 08 b.Newport 4-9-96

2015–16	Bristol R	1	0		
2016–17	Bristol R	5	0		
2017–18	Bristol R	3	0	**9**	**0**
2018–19	Cheltenham T	39	2		
2019–20	Cheltenham T	34	8	**73**	**10**
2020–21	Peterborough U	15	1	**15**	**1**
2020–21	*Burton Alb*	11	2	**11**	**2**

BURROWS, Harrison (M) 25 1
b. 12-1-02

2017–18	Peterborough U	0	0		
2018–19	Peterborough U	0	0		
2019–20	Peterborough U	4	0		
2020–21	Peterborough U	21	1	**25**	**1**

BUTLER, Dan (D) 248 10
b.Cowes 26-8-94

2012–13	Portsmouth	17	0		
2013–14	Portsmouth	1	0		
2014–15	Portsmouth	30	0		
2015–16	Portsmouth	0	0	**48**	**0**
2016–17	Newport Co	40	3		
2017–18	Newport Co	44	1		
2018–19	Newport Co	45	3	**129**	**7**
2019–20	Peterborough U	29	2		
2020–21	Peterborough U	42	1	**71**	**3**

CARTWRIGHT, Samuel (D) 0 0

2017–18	Peterborough U	0	0		
2018–19	Peterborough U	0	0		
2019–20	Peterborough U	0	0		
2020–21	Peterborough U	0	0		

CLARKE, Flynn (M) 4 0
b. 19-12-02

2019–20	Peterborough U	0	0		
2020–21	Peterborough U	4	0	**4**	**0**

CLARKE-HARRIS, Jonson (F) 276 84
H: 6 0 W: 11 01 b.Leicester 21-7-94

2010–11	Coventry C	0	0		
2011–12	Coventry C	0	0		
2012–13	Peterborough U	0	0		
2012–13	*Southend U*	3	0	**3**	**0**
2012–13	*Bury*	12	4	**12**	**4**
2013–14	Oldham Ath	40	6		
2014–15	Oldham Ath	5	1	**45**	**7**
2014–15	Rotherham U	15	3		
2014–15	*Milton Keynes D*	5	0	**5**	**0**
2014–15	*Doncaster R*	9	1	**9**	**1**
2015–16	Rotherham U	35	6		
2016–17	Rotherham U	7	0		
2017–18	Rotherham U	14	0	**71**	**9**
2017–18	*Coventry C*	17	3		
2018–19	Coventry C	27	5	**44**	**8**
2018–19	Bristol R	16	11		
2019–20	Bristol R	26	13	**42**	**24**
2020–21	Peterborough U	45	31	**45**	**31**

COPPING, Bobby (D) 0 0
From Norwich C, Bury.

2019–20	Peterborough U	0	0		
2020–21	Peterborough U	0	0		

DEMBELE, Siriki (M) 141 25
b. 7-9-96
From Dundee U, Ayr U.

2017–18	Grimsby T	36	4	**36**	**4**
2018–19	Peterborough U	38	5		
2019–20	Peterborough U	25	5		
2020–21	Peterborough U	42	11	**105**	**21**

EDWARDS, Ronnie (M) 2 0
b.Harlow 28-3-03
From Barnet.

2020–21	Peterborough U	2	0	**2**	**0**

EISA, Mohamed (F) 106 39
H: 6 0 W: 11 00 b. 12-7-94
From Dartford, VCD Ath, Corinthian, Greenwich Bor.

2017–18	Cheltenham T	45	23	**45**	**23**
2018–19	Bristol C	5	0	**5**	**0**
2019–20	Peterborough U	29	14		
2020–21	Peterborough U	27	2	**56**	**16**

GYIMAH, Nicky (M) 0 0

2020–21	Peterborough U	0	0		

GYOLLAI, Daniel (G) 0 0
b.Bekescsaba 7-4-97
Internationals: Hungary U18, U19, U21.
From Stoke C.

2019–20	Wigan Ath	0	0		
2020–21	Peterborough U	0	0		

HAMILTON, Ethan (M) 74 5
b.Edinburgh 18-10-98
Internationals: Scotland U16, U19.

2017–18	Manchester U	0	0		
2018–19	Manchester U	0	0		
2018–19	*Rochdale*	14	4	**14**	**4**
2019–20	Manchester U	0	0		
2019–20	*Southend U*	14	0	**14**	**0**
2019–20	*Bolton W*	12	1	**12**	**1**
2020–21	Peterborough U	34	0	**34**	**0**

HARRIS, Luke (M) 0 0

2019–20	Peterborough U	0	0		
2020–21	Peterborough U	0	0		

JADE-JONES, Ricky (M) 26 1
b. 24-6-01

2019–20	Peterborough U	11	0		
2020–21	Peterborough U	15	1	**26**	**1**

JONES, Archie (M) 0 0

2019–20	Peterborough U	0	0		
2020–21	Peterborough U	0	0		

KANU, Idris (F) 44 3
b. 5-12-99
From West Ham U, Aldershot T.

2017–18	Peterborough U	18	0		
2018–19	Peterborough U	0	0		
2018–19	*Port Vale*	3	1	**3**	**1**
2019–20	Peterborough U	6	0		
2020–21	Peterborough U	17	2	**41**	**2**

KENT, Frankie (D) 200 8
H: 6 2 W: 12 00 b.Romford 21-11-95

2013–14	Colchester U	1	0		
2014–15	Colchester U	10	0		
2015–16	Colchester U	26	0		
2016–17	Colchester U	13	0		
2017–18	Colchester U	37	2		
2018–19	Colchester U	40	4	**127**	**6**
2019–20	Peterborough U	28	1		
2020–21	Peterborough U	45	1	**73**	**2**

MASON, Niall (M) 154 4
b. 10-1-97

2015–16	Aston Villa	0	0		
2016–17	Aston Villa	0	0		
2016–17	*Doncaster R*	38	0		
2017–18	Doncaster R	40	3		
2018–19	Doncaster R	20	0	**98**	**3**
2019–20	Peterborough U	30	0		
2020–21	Peterborough U	26	1	**56**	**1**

MENSAH, Benjamin (M) 0 0

2019–20	Peterborough U	0	0		
2020–21	Peterborough U	0	0		

NAISMITH, Jason (D) 209 8
H: 6 1 W: 13 02 b.Paisley 25-6-94
Internationals: Scotland U17, U18, U20, U21.

2011–12	St Mirren	2	0		
2012–13	St Mirren	0	0		
2012–13	*Greenock Morton*	4	0	**4**	**0**
2012–13	*Cowdenbeath*	5	0	**5**	**0**

2013–14 St Mirren 27 2
2014–15 St Mirren 38 2
2015–16 St Mirren 5 0
2016–17 St Mirren 21 0 **93 4**
2016–17 Ross Co 16 0
2017–18 Ross Co 35 2 **51 2**
2018–19 Peterborough U 43 1
2019–20 Peterborough U 0 0
2019–20 *Hibernian* 13 1 **13 1**
2020–21 Peterborough U 0 0 **43 1**
Transferred to Ross Co December 2020.

NASCIMENTO, Adler (F) 1 0
2020–21 Peterborough U 1 0 **1 0**

O'CONNELL, Charlie (D) 1 0
b. 19-12-02
From West Ham U.
2020–21 Peterborough U 1 0 **1 0**

POWELL, Aaron (D) 0 0
b. 14-11-02
2020–21 Peterborough U 0 0

PYM, Christy (G) 226 0
H: 6 0 W: 11 09 b.Exeter 24-4-95
Internationals: England U20.
2012–13 Exeter C 0 0
2013–14 Exeter C 9 0
2014–15 Exeter C 25 0
2015–16 Exeter C 0 0
2016–17 Exeter C 28 0
2017–18 Exeter C 46 0
2018–19 Exeter C 43 0 **151 0**
2019–20 Peterborough U 35 0
2020–21 Peterborough U 40 0 **75 0**

REED, Louis (M) 150 6
b. 25-7-97
Internationals: England U18, U19, U20.
2013–14 Sheffield U 1 0
2014–15 Sheffield U 19 0
2015–16 Sheffield U 19 0
2016–17 Sheffield U 0 0
2017–18 Sheffield U 0 0 **39 0**
2017–18 *Chesterfield* 42 4 **42 4**
2018–19 Peterborough U 28 1
2019–20 Peterborough U 24 1
2020–21 Peterborough U 17 0 **69 2**

ROLT, Bradley (F) 0 0
2019–20 Peterborough U 0 0
2020–21 Peterborough U 0 0

SZMIDICS, Sammie (M) 197 54
H: 5 6 W: 10 01 b.Colchester 24-9-95
2013–14 Colchester U 7 0
2014–15 Colchester U 31 4
2015–16 Colchester U 5 0
2016–17 Colchester U 19 5
2017–18 Colchester U 37 12
2018–19 Colchester U 43 14 **142 35**
2019–20 Bristol C 3 0 **3 0**
2019–20 *Peterborough U* 10 4
2020–21 Peterborough U 42 15 **52 19**

TASDEMIR, Serhat (M) 17 0
b. 21-7-00
Internationals: Azerbaijan U19.
From AFC Fylde.
2019–20 Peterborough U 10 0
2020–21 Peterborough U 0 0 **10 0**
2020–21 *Oldham Ath* 7 0 **7 0**

TAYLOR, Jack (D) 99 8
H: 6 1 W: 11 00 b. 23-6-98
Internationals: Republic of Ireland U21.
2016–17 Barnet 14 0
2017–18 Barnet 38 2 **52 2**
From Barnet.
2019–20 Peterborough U 11 2
2020–21 Peterborough U 36 4 **47 6**

THOMPSON, Nathan (D) 288 6
H: 5 7 W: 11 02 b.Chester 9-11-90
2009–10 Swindon T 0 0
2010–11 Swindon T 3 0
2011–12 Swindon T 5 0
2012–13 Swindon T 26 0
2013–14 Swindon T 41 1
2014–15 Swindon T 35 0
2015–16 Swindon T 23 1
2016–17 Swindon T 34 2 **167 4**
2017–18 Portsmouth 36 0
2018–19 Portsmouth 31 0 **67 0**
2019–20 Peterborough U 15 0
2020–21 Peterborough U 39 2 **54 2**

TYLER, Mark (G) 488 0
H: 6 0 W: 12 09 b.Norwich 2-4-77
Internationals: England U18.
From Norwich C.
1994–95 Peterborough U 5 0
1995–96 Peterborough U 0 0
1996–97 Peterborough U 3 0
1997–98 Peterborough U 46 0
1998–99 Peterborough U 27 0
1999–2000 Peterborough U 32 0
2000–01 Peterborough U 40 0
2001–02 Peterborough U 44 0
2002–03 Peterborough U 29 0
2003–04 Peterborough U 43 0
2004–05 Peterborough U 46 0
2005–06 Peterborough U 40 0
2006–07 Peterborough U 41 0
2007–08 Peterborough U 17 0
2008–09 Peterborough U 0 0
2008–09 *Bury* 11 0 **11 0**
2014–15 Luton T 31 0
2015–16 Luton T 27 0 **58 0**
2015–16 *Peterborough U* 3 0
2016–17 Peterborough U 3 0
2017–18 Peterborough U 0 0
2018–19 Peterborough U 0 0
2019–20 Peterborough U 0 0
2020–21 Peterborough U 0 0 **419 0**

WARD, Joe (M) 125 12
b. 9-4-95
Internationals: England C.
From Chelmsford C.
2015–16 Brighton & HA 0 0
2016–17 Brighton & HA 0 0
2017–18 Peterborough U 17 0
2018–19 Peterborough U 43 4
2019–20 Peterborough U 28 3
2020–21 Peterborough U 37 5 **125 12**

Scholars
Chiha, Hisham; Darlington, Lewis Charlie; Gyimah-Bio, Nicky William Adjei; Harris, Luke; Hickinson, Kellan Reece; Keane, Shaun Kyle; Lakin, William John Geoffrey; Lukyamuzi, Theophilus Luke Bamutenda; McGlinchey, Roddy; O'Connell, Charlie; Peters, Connor Troy; Powell, Aaron Jay; Thomas, Harry James Alan; Tonge, Oscar Joseph; Van Lier, William Lewis.

PLYMOUTH ARG (64)

AIMSON, Will (D) 134 6
H: 5 10 W: 11 00 b.Christchurch 1-1-94
From Eastleigh.
2013–14 Hull C 0 0
2014–15 Hull C 0 0
2014–15 *Tranmere R* 2 0 **2 0**
2015–16 Hull C 0 0
2015–16 Blackpool 15 0
2016–17 Blackpool 18 0
2017–18 Blackpool 17 0 **50 0**
2018–19 Bury 37 4 **37 4**
2019–20 Plymouth Arg 5 2
2020–21 Plymouth Arg 40 0 **45 2**

CAMARA, Panutche (F) 145 8
H: 6 1 W: 9 13 b. 28-2-97
From Dulwich Hamlet.
2017–18 Crawley T 30 2
2018–19 Crawley T 45 3
2019–20 Crawley T 29 1 **104 6**
2020–21 Plymouth Arg 41 2 **41 2**

COOMBES, Tyler (G) 0 0
2020–21 Plymouth Arg 0 0

COOPER, George (M) 195 22
H: 5 9 W: 11 05 b.Warrington 2-11-96
2014–15 Crewe Alex 22 3
2015–16 Crewe Alex 27 1
2016–17 Crewe Alex 46 9
2017–18 Crewe Alex 27 1 **122 14**
2017–18 Peterborough U 13 2
2018–19 Peterborough U 21 2
2019–20 Peterborough U 0 0 **34 4**
2019–20 *Plymouth Arg* 27 3
2020–21 Plymouth Arg 12 1 **39 4**

COOPER, Michael (G) 48 0
b. 8-10-99
2017–18 Plymouth Arg 1 0
2018–19 Plymouth Arg 1 0
2019–20 Plymouth Arg 0 0
2020–21 Plymouth Arg 46 0 **48 0**

CRASKE, Finley (D) 1 0
b. 27-1-03
2020–21 Plymouth Arg 1 0 **1 0**

CROCKER, Scott (F) 0 0
2020–21 Plymouth Arg 0 0

EDWARDS, Joe (D) 332 28
H: 5 8 W: 11 07 b.Gloucester 31-10-90
2009–10 Bristol C 0 0
2010–11 Bristol C 2 0
2011–12 Bristol C 2 0
2011–12 *Yeovil T* 4 1
2012–13 Bristol C 0 0 **4 0**
2012–13 Yeovil T 35 2
2013–14 Yeovil T 46 1
2014–15 Yeovil T 34 0 **119 4**
2015–16 Colchester U 42 2 **42 2**
2016–17 Walsall 43 3
2017–18 Walsall 30 7
2018–19 Walsall 20 2 **93 12**
2019–20 Plymouth Arg 34 3
2020–21 Plymouth Arg 40 7 **74 10**

ENNIS, Niall (F) 63 12
H: 5 10 W: 12 00 b.Wolverhampton 20-5-99
Internationals: England U17, U18, U19.
2017–18 Wolverhampton W 0 0
2017–18 *Shrewsbury T* 1 0 **1 0**
2018–19 Wolverhampton W 0 0
2019–20 Wolverhampton W 0 0
2019–20 *Doncaster R* 29 6 **29 6**
2020–21 Wolverhampton W 0 0
2020–21 *Burton Alb* 9 0 **9 0**
2020–21 Plymouth Arg 24 6 **24 6**

GRANT, Conor (M) 139 10
H: 5 9 W: 12 08 b.Fazakerley 18-4-95
Internationals: England U18.
2013–14 Everton 0 0
2014–15 Everton 0 0
2014–15 *Motherwell* 11 1 **11 1**
2015–16 Everton 0 0
2015–16 *Doncaster R* 19 2
2016–17 Everton 0 0
2016–17 *Ipswich T* 6 0 **6 0**
2016–17 *Doncaster R* 21 1 **40 3**
2017–18 Everton 0 0
2017–18 *Crewe Alex* 17 0 **17 0**
2018–19 Plymouth Arg 10 0
2019–20 Plymouth Arg 17 2
2020–21 Plymouth Arg 38 4 **65 6**

HARDIE, Ryan (F) 157 44
b.Stranraer 4-3-97
Internationals: Scotland U16, U17, U19, U20, U21.
2014–15 Rangers 5 2
2015–16 Rangers 1 0
2015–16 *Raith R* 10 6
2016–17 Rangers 0 0
2016–17 *St Mirren* 16 3 **16 3**
2016–17 *Raith R* 18 6 **28 12**
2017–18 Rangers 7 0
2017–18 *Livingston* 16 8
2018–19 Rangers 0 0 **13 2**
2018–19 Livingston 21 7 **37 15**
2019–20 Blackpool 7 0 **7 0**
2019–20 *Plymouth Arg* 13 7
2020–21 Plymouth Arg 43 5 **56 12**

JEPHCOTT, Luke (F) 64 23
b.Truro 26-1-00
Internationals: Wales U19.
2018–19 Plymouth Arg 9 0
2019–20 Plymouth Arg 14 7
2020–21 Plymouth Arg 41 16 **64 23**

LAW, Ryan (D) 4 0
b. 8-9-99
2017–18 Plymouth Arg 0 0
2018–19 Plymouth Arg 0 0
2019–20 Plymouth Arg 0 0
2020–21 Plymouth Arg 4 0 **4 0**

LOLOS, Klaidi (F) 12 0
b. 6-10-00
Internationals: Greece U19.
2017–18 Plymouth Arg 0 0
2018–19 Plymouth Arg 0 0
2019–20 Plymouth Arg 4 0
2020–21 Plymouth Arg 8 0 **12 0**

MACLEOD, Lewis (M) 120 15
H: 5 9 W: 11 05 b.Law 16-6-94
Internationals: Scotland U16, U17, U18, U19, U21.
2012–13 Rangers 21 3
2013–14 Rangers 18 5
2014–15 Rangers 13 3 **52 11**
2014–15 Brentford 0 0
2015–16 Brentford 1 0
2016–17 Brentford 13 0
2017–18 Brentford 10 1
2018–19 Brentford 17 3 **41 4**
2019–20 Wigan Ath 12 0 **12 0**
2020–21 Plymouth Arg 15 0 **15 0**

MAYOR, Danny (M) 365 34
H: 6 0 W: 11 12 b.Leyland 18-10-90
2008–09 Preston NE 0 0
2008–09 *Tranmere R* 3 0 **3 0**
2009–10 Preston NE 7 0
2010–11 Preston NE 21 0
2011–12 Preston NE 36 2

2012–13 Preston NE 0 0 64 2
2012–13 Sheffield W 8 0
2012–13 *Southend U* 5 0 5 0
2013–14 Sheffield W 0 0 8 0
2013–14 *Bury* 39 5
2014–15 Bury 44 8
2015–16 Bury 44 5
2016–17 Bury 21 3
2017–18 Bury 20 1
2018–19 Bury 39 8 207 30
2019–20 Plymouth Arg 34 1
2020–21 Plymouth Arg 44 1 78 2

McCORMICK, Luke (G) 352 0
H: 6 0 W: 13 12 b.Coventry 15-8-83
2000–01 Plymouth Arg 1 0
2001–02 Plymouth Arg 0 0
2002–03 Plymouth Arg 3 0
2003–04 Plymouth Arg 40 0
2004–05 Plymouth Arg 23 0
2005–06 Plymouth Arg 1 0
2006–07 Plymouth Arg 40 0
2007–08 Plymouth Arg 30 0
From Truro C.
2012–13 Oxford U 15 0 15 0
2013–14 Plymouth Arg 27 0
2014–15 Plymouth Arg 46 0
2015–16 Plymouth Arg 40 0
2016–17 Plymouth Arg 46 0
2017–18 Plymouth Arg 9 0
2018–19 Swindon T 17 0
2019–20 Swindon T 12 0 29 0
2020–21 Plymouth Arg 2 0 308 0

MILLER, Charlie (M) 0 0
2020–21 Plymouth Arg 0 0

MITCHELL, Ethan (M) 0 0
2020–21 Plymouth Arg 0 0

MOORE, Byron (M) 464 47
H: 6 0 W: 10 06 b.Stoke 24-8-88
2006–07 Crewe Alex 0 0
2007–08 Crewe Alex 33 3
2008–09 Crewe Alex 36 3
2009–10 Crewe Alex 32 3
2010–11 Crewe Alex 38 6
2011–12 Crewe Alex 42 8
2012–13 Crewe Alex 41 4
2013–14 Crewe Alex 40 3 262 30
2014–15 Port Vale 15 1
2015–16 Port Vale 36 3 51 4
2016–17 Bristol R 27 2
2017–18 Bristol R 20 0 47 2
2018–19 Bury 36 5 36 5
2019–20 Plymouth Arg 30 5
2020–21 Plymouth Arg 38 1 68 6

NOUBLE, Frank (F) 351 49
H: 6 3 W: 12 08 b.Lewisham 24-9-91
Internationals: England U17, U19.
From Chelsea.
2009–10 West Ham U 8 0
2009–10 *WBA* 3 0 3 0
2009–10 *Swindon T* 8 0 8 0
2010–11 West Ham U 2 0
2010–11 *Swansea C* 6 1 6 1
2010–11 *Barnsley* 4 0
2010–11 *Charlton Ath* 9 1 9 1
2011–12 West Ham U 3 1 13 1
2011–12 *Gillingham* 13 5
2011–12 *Barnsley* 6 0 10 0
2012–13 Wolverhampton W 2 0 2 0
2012–13 Ipswich T 17 2
2013–14 Ipswich T 38 2
2014–15 Ipswich T 1 0 56 4
2014–15 Coventry C 31 6 31 6
2015 Tianjin Songjiang 15 3 15 3
2016–17 Gillingham 12 1 25 6
2016–17 Southend U 5 0 5 0
2017–18 Newport Co 45 9 45 9
2018–19 Colchester U 43 9
2019–20 Colchester U 36 5
2020–21 Plymouth Arg 24 1 24 1
2020–21 *Colchester U* 20 3 99 17

PURSALL, Brandon (D) 0 0
2020–21 Plymouth Arg 0 0

RANDELL, Adam (M) 4 0
b.Plymouth 1-10-00
2018–19 Plymouth Arg 0 0
2019–20 Plymouth Arg 4 0
2020–21 Plymouth Arg 0 0 4 0

REEVES, Ben (D) 233 33
H: 5 10 W: 10 07 b.Verwood 19-11-91
Internationals: Northern Ireland Full caps.
2008–09 Southampton 0 0
2009–10 Southampton 0 0
2010–11 Southampton 0 0
2011–12 Southampton 2 0
2011–12 *Dagenham & R* 5 0 5 0
2012–13 Southampton 3 0 5 0
2012–13 *Southend U* 10 1 10 1
2013–14 Milton Keynes D 28 7
2014–15 Milton Keynes D 30 7
2015–16 Milton Keynes D 18 3
2016–17 Milton Keynes D 34 7
2017–18 Charlton Ath 29 3
2018–19 Charlton Ath 29 4 58 7
2019–20 Milton Keynes D 17 1 127 25
2020–21 Plymouth Arg 28 0 28 0

RUDDY, Jack (G) 27 0
H: 6 1 W: 13 01 b.Glasgow 18-5-97
Internationals: Scotland U21.
2014–15 Bury 0 0
2015–16 Bury 1 0
2016–17 Bury 0 0 1 0
2016–17 Wolverhampton W 0 0
2017–18 Wolverhampton W 0 0
2017–18 *Oldham Ath* 5 0 5 0
2017–18 *Ayr U* 11 0 11 0
2018–19 Wolverhampton W 0 0
2018–19 *Jumilla* 4 0 4 0
2018–19 *Reyes* 6 0 6 0
2019–20 Ross Co 0 0
2019–20 Leganes 0 0
2020–21 Plymouth Arg 0 0

SAWYER, Gary (D) 398 7
H: 6 0 W: 11 08 b.Bideford 5-7-85
2004–05 Plymouth Arg 0 0
2005–06 Plymouth Arg 0 0
2006–07 Plymouth Arg 22 0
2007–08 Plymouth Arg 31 1
2008–09 Plymouth Arg 13 3
2009–10 Plymouth Arg 29 1
2009–10 *Bristol C* 2 0 2 0
2010–11 Bristol R 37 0
2011–12 Bristol R 24 0 61 0
2012–13 Leyton Orient 34 1
2013–14 Leyton Orient 22 0
2014–15 Leyton Orient 13 0 69 1
2015–16 Plymouth Arg 43 0
2016–17 Plymouth Arg 21 0
2017–18 Plymouth Arg 46 1
2018–19 Plymouth Arg 33 0
2019–20 Plymouth Arg 28 0
2020–21 Plymouth Arg 0 0 266 6

TOMLINSON, Ollie (D) 2 0
b.Ivybridge 19-5-02
2020–21 Plymouth Arg 2 0 2 0

WILSON, James (D) 247 8
H: 6 2 W: 11 05 b.Chepstow 26-2-89
Internationals: Wales U19, U21, Full caps.
2005–06 Bristol C 0 0
2006–07 Bristol C 0 0
2007–08 Bristol C 0 0
2008–09 Bristol C 2 0
2008–09 *Brentford* 14 0
2009–10 Bristol C 0 0
2009–10 *Brentford* 13 0 27 0
2010–11 Bristol C 2 0
2011–12 Bristol C 21 0
2012–13 Bristol C 6 0
2013–14 Bristol C 0 0 31 0
2013–14 *Cheltenham T* 4 0 4 0
2013–14 Oldham Ath 16 1
2014–15 Oldham Ath 41 1
2015–16 Oldham Ath 43 0 100 2
2016–17 Sheffield U 7 1
2017–18 Sheffield U 0 0 7 1
2017–18 *Walsall* 19 1 19 1
2017–18 Lincoln C 8 1
2018–19 Lincoln C 11 1
2019–20 Lincoln C 0 0 19 2
2019–20 Ipswich T 23 0
2020–21 Ipswich T 17 2 40 2
2020–21 Plymouth Arg 0 0

WOOTTON, Scott (D) 212 5
H: 6 2 W: 13 00 b.Birkenhead 12-9-91
Internationals: England U17.
From Liverpool.
2009–10 Manchester U 0 0
2010–11 Manchester U 0 0
2010–11 *Tranmere R* 7 1 7 1
2011–12 Manchester U 0 0
2011–12 *Peterborough U* 11 0
2011–12 *Nottingham F* 13 0 13 0
2012–13 Manchester U 0 0
2012–13 *Peterborough U* 2 1 13 1
2013–14 Manchester U 0 0
2013–14 Leeds U 20 0
2014–15 Leeds U 23 0
2014–15 *Rotherham U* 7 0 7 0
2015–16 Leeds U 23 0 66 0
2016–17 Milton Keynes D 1 1
2017–18 Milton Keynes D 38 0 39 1
2018–19 Plymouth Arg 9 0
2019–20 Plymouth Arg 35 1
2020–21 Plymouth Arg 10 0 54 1
2020–21 *Wigan Ath* 13 1 13 1

Scholars
Coombes, Tyler Lee; Craske, Finley Thomas; Crocker, Scott Lee; Garside, Carlo Marcel; Mansaray, Alimamy; Massey, Oscar; Medine, Jeremiah; Miller, Charles Louis; Mitchell, Ethan Francis; Moyle, Lewis William; Rutherford, Oscar Thor; Salawu, Jamal Rasaq Michael; Shirley, Rhys Bowles; Waruih, Angel Michael Mathaiya; Wotton, Alfie Samuel.

PORT VALE (65)

AMOO, David (F) 322 37
H: 5 10 W: 12 03 b.Southwark 23-4-91
From Millwall.
2007–08 Liverpool 0 0
2008–09 Liverpool 0 0
2009–10 Liverpool 0 0
2010–11 Liverpool 0 0
2010–11 *Milton Keynes D* 3 0 3 0
2010–11 *Hull C* 7 1 7 1
2011–12 Liverpool 0 0
2011–12 *Bury* 27 4 27 4
2012–13 Preston NE 17 0 17 0
2012–13 Tranmere R 11 1
2013–14 Tranmere R 0 0 11 1
2013–14 Carlisle U 43 8
2014–15 Carlisle U 27 5 70 13
2015–16 Partick Thistle 37 5
2016–17 Partick Thistle 25 1 62 6
2017–18 Cambridge U 24 2
2018–19 Cambridge U 43 5 67 7
2019–20 Port Vale 32 4
2020–21 Port Vale 26 1 58 5

BAILEY, Eden (F) 0 0
2020–21 Port Vale 0 0

BRISLEY, Shaun (M) 352 15
H: 6 2 W: 12 02 b.Macclesfield 6-5-90
2007–08 Macclesfield T 10 2
2008–09 Macclesfield T 38 0
2009–10 Macclesfield T 33 1
2010–11 Macclesfield T 14 0
2011–12 Macclesfield T 29 3 124 6
2011–12 Peterborough U 11 0
2012–13 Peterborough U 28 0
2013–14 Peterborough U 22 0
2014–15 Peterborough U 15 1
2014–15 *Scunthorpe U* 7 0 7 0
2015–16 Peterborough U 2 0 78 1
2015–16 *Northampton T* 9 1 9 1
2015–16 *Leyton Orient* 16 1 16 1
2016–17 Carlisle U 28 2 28 2
2017–18 Notts Co 37 2
2018–19 Notts Co 20 0 57 2
2019–20 Port Vale 9 1
2020–21 Port Vale 24 1 33 2

BROWN, Scott (G) 489 0
H: 6 2 W: 13 01 b.Wolverhampton 26-4-85
From Birmingham C, Welshpool T.
2003–04 Bristol C 0 0
2004–05 Cheltenham T 0 0
2005–06 Cheltenham T 1 0
2006–07 Cheltenham T 11 0
2007–08 Cheltenham T 0 0
2008–09 Cheltenham T 35 0
2009–10 Cheltenham T 46 0
2010–11 Cheltenham T 46 0
2011–12 Cheltenham T 22 0
2012–13 Cheltenham T 46 0
2013–14 Cheltenham T 45 0
2014–15 Aberdeen 25 0
2015–16 Aberdeen 13 0 38 0
2016–17 Wycombe W 3 0
2016–17 *Cheltenham T* 21 0 273 0
2017–18 Wycombe W 46 0 49 0
2018–19 Port Vale 46 0
2019–20 Port Vale 37 0
2020–21 Port Vale 46 0 129 0

BURGESS, Scott (M) 68 5
H: 5 10 W: 11 00 b.Warrington 27-6-96
2013–14 Bury 1 0
2014–15 Bury 0 0
2015–16 Bury 3 0
2016–17 Bury 16 2
2017–18 Bury 0 0
2018–19 Bury 0 0 20 2
2019–20 Port Vale 24 3
2020–21 Port Vale 24 0 48 3

CAMPBELL-GORDON, Ryan (D) 1 0
2018–19 Port Vale 0 0
2019–20 Port Vale 1 0
2020–21 Port Vale 0 0 1 0

CHAMBERS, Luke (M)				**0**	**0**
2020–21	Port Vale	0	0		

COLLINGE, Joseph (G)				**0**	**0**
b. 6-9-03					
2020–21	Port Vale	0	0		

CONLON, Tom (M)				**160**	**16**
H: 5 8 W: 9 11 b.Stoke-on-Trent 3-2-96					
2013–14	Peterborough U	1	0	**1**	**0**
2014–15	Stevenage	13	0		
2015–16	Stevenage	32	2		
2016–17	Stevenage	4	0		
2017–18	Stevenage	12	0	**61**	**2**
2018–19	Port Vale	34	3		
2019–20	Port Vale	22	1		
2020–21	Port Vale	42	10	**98**	**14**

CROOKES, Adam (D)				**49**	**1**
b.Lincoln 18-11-97					
2017–18	Nottingham F	0	0		
2018–19	Nottingham F	0	0		
2018–19	*Lincoln C*	0	0		
2018–19	*Port Vale*	19	0		
2019–20	Port Vale	14	0		
2020–21	Port Vale	16	1	**49**	**1**

CULLEN, Mark (F)				**218**	**43**
H: 5 9 W: 11 11 b.Ashington 21-4-92					
2009–10	Hull C	3	1		
2010–11	Hull C	17	0		
2010–11	*Bradford C*	4	0	**4**	**0**
2011–12	Hull C	4	0		
2011–12	*Bury*	4	0		
2012–13	Hull C	0	0		
2012–13	Hull C	0	0	**24**	**1**
2012–13	*Bury*	10	1	**14**	**1**
2014–15	Luton T	42	13	**42**	**13**
2015–16	Blackpool	41	9		
2016–17	Blackpool	27	9		
2017–18	Blackpool	9	0		
2018–19	Blackpool	12	3	**89**	**21**
2018–19	*Carlisle U*	9	0	**9**	**0**
2019–20	Port Vale	18	5		
2020–21	Port Vale	18	2	**36**	**7**

FITZPATRICK, David (D)				**83**	**3**
H: 5 10 W: 11 07 b.Manchester 22-2-90					
Internationals: England C.					
From Southport.					
2018–19	Macclesfield T	40	3		
2019–20	Macclesfield T	21	0	**61**	**3**
2020–21	Port Vale	22	0	**22**	**0**

GIBBONS, James (D)				**88**	**1**
H: 5 9 W: 9 11 b. 16-3-98					
2016–17	Port Vale	0	0		
2017–18	Port Vale	30	0		
2018–19	Port Vale	15	0		
2019–20	Port Vale	32	1		
2020–21	Port Vale	11	0	**88**	**1**

GUTHRIE, Kurtis (F)				**141**	**30**
H: 5 11 W: 11 00 b.Jersey 21-4-93					
Internationals: England C.					
From St Clement, Trinity.					
2011–12	Accrington S	13	0		
2012–13	Accrington S	0	0	**13**	**0**
From Bath C, Welling U, Forest Green R.					
2016–17	Colchester U	33	12		
2017–18	Colchester U	12	1	**45**	**13**
2018–19	Stevenage	34	11		
2019–20	Stevenage	22	5	**56**	**16**
2019–20	Bradford C	2	0		
2020–21	Bradford C	8	0	**10**	**0**
2020–21	Port Vale	17	1	**17**	**1**

HURST, Alex (M)				**20**	**1**
b. 6-10-99					
From Matlock T, Bradford PA.					
2019–20	Port Vale	0	0		
2020–21	Port Vale	20	1	**20**	**1**

JOYCE, Luke (M)				**506**	**14**
H: 5 11 W: 12 03 b.Bolton 9-7-87					
2005–06	Wigan Ath	0	0		
2005–06	Carlisle U	0	0		
2006–07	Carlisle U	16	1		
2007–08	Carlisle U	3	1		
2008–09	Carlisle U	7	0		
2009–10	Accrington S	41	1		
2010–11	Accrington S	27	1		
2011–12	Accrington S	43	2		
2012–13	Accrington S	44	0		
2013–14	Accrington S	46	1		
2014–15	Accrington S	45	3	**246**	**8**
2015–16	Carlisle U	37	0		
2016–17	Carlisle U	45	1		
2017–18	Carlisle U	38	2	**146**	**5**
2018–19	Port Vale	37	0		
2019–20	Port Vale	36	1		
2020–21	Port Vale	41	0	**114**	**1**

LEGGE, Leon (D)				**394**	**36**
H: 6 1 W: 11 02 b.Bexhill 1-7-85					
From Hailsham T, Lewes, Tonbridge Angels.					
2009–10	Brentford	29	2		
2010–11	Brentford	30	3		
2011–12	Brentford	28	4		
2012–13	Brentford	7	0	**94**	**9**
2012–13	Gillingham	22	2		
2013–14	Gillingham	37	2		
2014–15	Gillingham	22	4	**81**	**8**
2015–16	Cambridge U	39	3		
2016–17	Cambridge U	44	6		
2017–18	Cambridge U	27	2	**110**	**11**
2018–19	Port Vale	35	1		
2019–20	Port Vale	37	4		
2020–21	Port Vale	37	3	**109**	**8**

LENNON, Michael (D)				**0**	**0**
b. 2-5-01					
2020–21	Port Vale	0	0		

McKIRDY, Harry (M)				**75**	**10**
H: 5 9 W: 11 00 b.Stoke-on-Trent 29-3-97					
From Stoke C.					
2016–17	Aston Villa	0	0		
2016–17	*Stevenage*	11	1	**11**	**1**
2017–18	Aston Villa	0	0		
2017–18	*Crewe Alex*	16	3	**16**	**3**
2018–19	Aston Villa	0	0		
2018–19	*Newport Co*	12	1	**12**	**1**
2019–20	Carlisle U	28	5	**28**	**5**
2020–21	Port Vale	8	0	**8**	**0**

MILLS, Zak (D)				**142**	**2**
b. 28-5-92					
From Histon, Boston U.					
2016–17	Grimsby T	30	0		
2017–18	Grimsby T	28	0	**58**	**0**
2018–19	Morecambe	38	1	**38**	**1**
2019–20	Oldham Ath	25	1	**25**	**1**
2020–21	Port Vale	21	0	**21**	**0**

MONTANO, Cristian (F)				**248**	**28**
H: 5 11 W: 12 00 b.Cali 11-12-91					
2010–11	West Ham U	0	0		
2011–12	West Ham U	0	0		
2011–12	*Notts Co*	15	4	**15**	**4**
2011–12	*Swindon T*	4	1	**4**	**1**
2011–12	*Dagenham & R*	10	3	**10**	**3**
2011–12	*Oxford U*	9	2	**9**	**2**
2012–13	Oldham Ath	30	1		
2013–14	Oldham Ath	10	2	**40**	**3**
2015–16	Bristol R	27	2		
2016–17	Bristol R	25	1	**52**	**3**
2017–18	Port Vale	30	4		
2018–19	Port Vale	29	5		
2019–20	Port Vale	30	0		
2020–21	Port Vale	29	3	**118**	**12**

OYELEKE, Emmanuel (M)				**65**	**5**
H: 5 9 W: 11 11 b.Wandsworth 24-12-92					
2011–12	Brentford	1	0		
2012–13	Brentford	0	0		
2012–13	*Northampton T*	2	0	**2**	**0**
2013–14	Brentford	0	0		
2014–15	Brentford	0	0	**1**	**0**
2014–15	Exeter C	0	0		
2015–16	Exeter C	8	0	**8**	**0**
From Aldershot T.					
2018–19	Port Vale	28	3		
2019–20	Port Vale	6	0		
2020–21	Port Vale	20	2	**54**	**5**
Transferred to Chesterfield April 2021.					

POPE, Tom (F)				**488**	**127**
H: 6 3 W: 11 03 b.Stoke 27-8-85					
2005–06	Crewe Alex	0	0		
2006–07	Crewe Alex	4	0		
2007–08	Crewe Alex	26	7		
2008–09	Crewe Alex	26	10	**56**	**17**
2009–10	Rotherham U	35	3		
2010–11	Rotherham U	18	1	**53**	**4**
2010–11	*Port Vale*	13	3		
2011–12	Port Vale	41	5		
2012–13	Port Vale	46	31		
2013–14	Port Vale	43	12		
2014–15	Port Vale	33	8		
2015–16	Bury	36	6		
2016–17	Bury	37	4	**73**	**10**
2016–17	Port Vale	0	0		
2017–18	Port Vale	41	17		
2018–19	Port Vale	38	11		
2019–20	Port Vale	32	6		
2020–21	Port Vale	19	3	**306**	**96**

ROBINSON, Theo (F)				**442**	**102**
H: 5 9 W: 10 03 b.Birmingham 22-1-89					
Internationals: Jamaica Full caps.					
2005–06	Watford	1	0		
2006–07	Watford	1	0		
2007–08	Watford	0	0		
2007–08	*Hereford U*	43	13	**43**	**13**
2008–09	Watford	3	0	**5**	**0**
2008–09	*Southend U*	21	7		
2009–10	Huddersfield T	37	13		
2010–11	Huddersfield T	1	0		
2010–11	Millwall	11	3		
2010–11	*Derby Co*	13	2		
2011–12	Derby Co	39	10		
2012–13	Derby Co	28	8		
2012–13	*Huddersfield T*	6	0	**44**	**13**
2013–14	Millwall	0	0	**11**	**3**
2013–14	Derby Co	0	0	**80**	**20**
2013–14	Doncaster R	31	5		
2014–15	Doncaster R	32	4	**63**	**9**
2014–15	*Scunthorpe U*	8	3	**8**	**3**
2015–16	Motherwell	10	0	**10**	**0**
2015–16	Port Vale	14	2		
2016–17	Southend U	18	2		
2017–18	Southend U	25	5		
2018–19	Southend U	24	4		
2018–19	*Swindon T*	16	7	**16**	**7**
2019–20	Southend U	3	0	**91**	**18**
2019–20	*Colchester U*	28	11	**28**	**11**
2020–21	Port Vale	29	3	**43**	**5**

RODNEY, Devante (F)				**47**	**13**
b.Manchester 19-5-98					
From Sheffield W.					
2016–17	Hartlepool U	4	2	**4**	**2**
From Hartlepool U.					
2019–20	Salford C	3	0	**3**	**0**
2020–21	Port Vale	40	11	**40**	**11**

SCOTT, Tom (G)				**0**	**0**
b. 28-10-00					
2020–21	Manchester C	0	0		
2020–21	Port Vale	0	0		

SMITH, Nathan (D)				**214**	**14**
H: 6 0 W: 11 05 b.Madeley 3-4-96					
2013–14	Port Vale	0	0		
2014–15	Port Vale	0	0		
2015–16	Port Vale	0	0		
2016–17	Port Vale	46	4		
2017–18	Port Vale	46	1		
2018–19	Port Vale	44	0		
2019–20	Port Vale	34	5		
2020–21	Port Vale	44	4	**214**	**14**

TAYLOR, Jake (M)				**43**	**6**
b. 8-9-98					
2019–20	Nottingham F	0	0		
2019–20	*Port Vale*	18	5		
2020–21	Nottingham F	0	0		
2020–21	*Scunthorpe U*	13	0	**13**	**0**
2020–21	Port Vale	12	1	**30**	**6**

TRICKETT-SMITH, Dan (M)				**0**	**0**
Internationals: England U16.					
From Liverpool, Crew Alex, Sacramento Republic, Leek T.					
2017–18	Port Vale	0	0		
2018–19	Port Vale	0	0		
2019–20	Port Vale	0	0		
2020–21	Port Vale	0	0		

VISSER, Dino (G)				**70**	**0**
b.Johannesburg 10-7-89					
2010–11	Platinum Stars	1	0		
2011–12	Platinum Stars	0	0		
2012–13	Bloemfontein Celtic	0	0		
2013–14	Bloemfontein Celtic	0	0		
2013–14	*Black Leopards*	1	0	**1**	**0**
2014–15	Polokwane City	10	0		
2015–16	Polokwane City	0	0	**10**	**0**
2016–17	Engen Santos	23	0	**23**	**0**
2017–18	Platinum Stars	15	0	**16**	**0**
2018–19	Cape Umoya U	20	0	**20**	**0**
2019–20	Exeter C	0	0		
2019–20	Crewe Alex	0	0		
2020–21	Port Vale	0	0		

WHITEHEAD, Danny (M)				**45**	**1**
H: 5 10 W: 10 11 b.Trafford 23-10-93					
From Stockport Co.					
2013–14	West Ham U	0	0		
2014–15	West Ham U	0	0		
2014–15	Accrington S	2	0	**2**	**0**
From Macclesfield T.					
2015–16	Wigan Ath	0	0		
2016–17	Wigan Ath	0	0		
2016–17	*Cheltenham T*	6	0	**6**	**0**
2017–18	Wigan Ath	0	0		
2019–20	Salford C	12	1	**12**	**1**
2019–20	*Macclesfield T*	10	0	**10**	**0**
2020–21	Port Vale	15	0	**15**	**0**

WORRALL, David (M)				**439**	**37**
H: 6 0 W: 11 03 b.Manchester 12-6-90					
2006–07	Bury	1	0		
2007–08	Bury	0	0		
2007–08	WBA	0	0		
2008–09	*Accrington S*	4	0	**4**	**0**
2008–09	*Shrewsbury T*	9	0	**9**	**0**
2009–10	WBA	0	0		

2009–10	Bury	40	4		
2010–11	Bury	40	2		
2011–12	Bury	41	3		
2012–13	Bury	41	2	**163**	**11**
2013–14	Rotherham U	3	1	**3**	**1**
2013–14	*Oldham Ath*	18	1	**18**	**1**
2014–15	Southend U	38	6		
2015–16	Southend U	35	3	**73**	**9**
2016–17	Millwall	33	1	**33**	**1**
2017–18	Port Vale	40	4		
2018–19	Port Vale	25	1		
2019–20	Port Vale	34	4		
2020–21	Port Vale	37	5	**136**	**14**

Scholars
Agho, Nelson Iradia; Bailey, Eden Mark; Barrett, Kenniel Devon Arnold; Bradbury, Thyler Owen; Chambers, Luke George; Chibaya, Tazivaishe Sean; Collinge, Joseph Oliver; Dyer, Ammar Christopher Deacon; Gregors, Thomas Michael; Ilori, Dayo Harrison; Jones, Ellis Raymond; Lake, Louis Jaye; Lennon, Michael Edward; McFarlane, Kamani Lloyd; Okenla, Henry Samuel Kolade; Osman, Abdimajid; Robins, Reece David; Tams, William David Francis.

PORTSMOUTH (66)

BASS, Alex (G) **17 0**
H: 6 2 W: 11 00 b.Southampton 1-1-97

2014–15	Portsmouth	0	0		
2015–16	Portsmouth	0	0		
2016–17	Portsmouth	0	0		
2017–18	Portsmouth	1	0		
2018–19	Portsmouth	0	0		
2019–20	Portsmouth	15	0		
2020–21	Portsmouth	0	0	**16**	**0**
2020–21	*Southend U*	1	0	**1**	**0**

BELL, Charlie (M) **0 0**
b. 24-12-02

2020–21	Portsmouth	0	0		

BOLTON, James (D) **100 4**
H: 5 11 W: 11 11 b.Stone 13-8-94
Internationals: England C.
From Macclesfield T, Halifax T, Gateshead.

2017–18	Shrewsbury T	33	1		
2018–19	Shrewsbury T	31	1	**64**	**2**
2019–20	Portsmouth	23	1		
2020–21	Portsmouth	13	1	**36**	**2**

BRIDGMAN, Alfie (M) **0 0**

2020–21	Portsmouth	0	0		

BROOK, Harrison (M) **0 0**

2020–21	Portsmouth	0	0		

BROWN, Lee (M) **335 22**
H: 6 0 W: 12 06 b.Bromley 10-8-90
Internationals: England C.

2008–09	QPR	0	0		
2009–10	QPR	1	0		
2010–11	QPR	0	0	**1**	**0**
2011–12	Bristol R	42	7		
2012–13	Bristol R	39	3		
2013–14	Bristol R	41	2		
2015–16	Bristol R	46	6		
2016–17	Bristol R	41	0		
2017–18	Bristol R	33	1	**242**	**19**
2018–19	Portsmouth	44	0		
2019–20	Portsmouth	16	1		
2020–21	Portsmouth	32	2	**92**	**3**

BRUCE, Thomas (D) **0 0**

2020–21	Portsmouth	0	0		

CANNON, Andy (M) **164 7**
H: 5 9 W: 11 09 b.Ashton-under-Lyne 14-3-96

2014–15	Rochdale	18	0		
2015–16	Rochdale	25	0		
2016–17	Rochdale	25	2		
2017–18	Rochdale	21	2		
2018–19	Rochdale	12	0	**101**	**4**
2018–19	Portsmouth	2	0		
2019–20	Portsmouth	18	1		
2020–21	Portsmouth	43	2	**63**	**3**

CLOSE, Ben (M) **138 14**
H: 5 9 W: 11 11 b.Portsmouth 8-8-96

2013–14	Portsmouth	0	0		
2014–15	Portsmouth	6	0		
2015–16	Portsmouth	7	0		
2016–17	Portsmouth	0	0		
2017–18	Portsmouth	40	2		
2018–19	Portsmouth	34	8		
2019–20	Portsmouth	29	3		
2020–21	Portsmouth	22	1	**138**	**14**

CURTIS, Ronan (F) **207 50**
H: 6 0 W: 12 02 b.Derry 29-3-96
Internationals: Republic of Ireland U21, Full caps.

2015	Derry C	13	1		
2016	Derry C	24	4		
2017	Derry C	32	8		
2018	Derry C	22	5	**91**	**18**
2018–19	Portsmouth	41	11		
2019–20	Portsmouth	33	11		
2020–21	Portsmouth	42	10	**116**	**32**

DANIELS, Charlie (M) **435 23**
H: 6 1 W: 12 12 b.Harlow 7-9-86

2005–06	Tottenham H	0	0		
2006–07	Tottenham H	0	0		
2006–07	*Chesterfield*	2	0	**2**	**0**
2007–08	Tottenham H	0	0		
2007–08	*Leyton Orient*	31	2		
2008–09	Tottenham H	0	0		
2008–09	*Gillingham*	5	1	**5**	**1**
2008–09	Leyton Orient	21	2		
2009–10	Leyton Orient	41	0		
2010–11	Leyton Orient	42	0		
2011–12	Leyton Orient	13	0	**148**	**4**
2011–12	Bournemouth	21	2		
2012–13	Bournemouth	34	4		
2013–14	Bournemouth	23	0		
2014–15	Bournemouth	42	1		
2015–16	Bournemouth	37	3		
2016–17	Bournemouth	34	4		
2017–18	Bournemouth	35	1		
2018–19	Bournemouth	21	1		
2019–20	Bournemouth	2	0		
2020–21	Bournemouth	0	0	**249**	**16**
2020–21	Shrewsbury T	14	1	**14**	**1**
2020–21	Portsmouth	17	1	**17**	**1**

DOWNING, Paul (D) **283 7**
H: 6 1 W: 12 06 b.Taunton 26-10-91

2009–10	WBA	0	0		
2009–10	*Hereford U*	6	0		
2010–11	WBA	0	0		
2010–11	*Hereford U*	0	0	**6**	**0**
2010–11	*Shrewsbury T*	0	0		
2011–12	WBA	0	0		
2011–12	*Barnet*	26	0	**26**	**0**
2012–13	Walsall	31	1		
2013–14	Walsall	44	1		
2014–15	Walsall	35	1		
2015–16	Walsall	46	3	**156**	**6**
2016–17	Milton Keynes D	37	0		
2017–18	Milton Keynes D	0	0	**37**	**0**
2017–18	Blackburn R	28	1		
2018–19	Blackburn R	3	0	**31**	**1**
2018–19	*Doncaster R*	18	0	**18**	**0**
2019–20	Portsmouth	6	0		
2020–21	Portsmouth	3	0	**9**	**0**

HACKETT-FAIRCHILD, Recco (F) **37 1**
H: 6 3 W: 11 00 b. 30-6-98
From Norwich C.

2017–18	Charlton Ath	5	0		
2018–19	Charlton Ath	7	0	**12**	**0**
2019–20	Portsmouth	0	0		
2020–21	Portsmouth	0	0		
2020–21	*Southend U*	25	1	**25**	**1**

HARNESS, Marcus (M) **174 18**
H: 6 0 W: 11 00 b.Coventry 1-8-94

2013–14	Burton Alb	3	0		
2014–15	Burton Alb	18	0		
2015–16	Burton Alb	5	0		
2016–17	Burton Alb	10	0		
2017–18	Burton Alb	0	0		
2017–18	*Port Vale*	35	1	**35**	**1**
2018–19	Burton Alb	32	5	**68**	**5**
2019–20	Portsmouth	25	5		
2020–21	Portsmouth	46	7	**71**	**12**

HARRISON, Ellis (F) **221 41**
H: 5 11 W: 12 06 b.Newport 1-2-94
Internationals: Wales U21.

2010–11	Bristol R	1	0		
2011–12	Bristol R	0	0		
2012–13	Bristol R	13	3		
2013–14	Bristol R	25	1		
2015–16	Bristol R	30	7		
2015–16	*Hartlepool U*	2	0	**2**	**0**
2016–17	Bristol R	37	8		
2017–18	Bristol R	44	12	**150**	**31**
2018–19	Ipswich T	16	1	**16**	**1**
2019–20	Portsmouth	28	5		
2020–21	Portsmouth	25	4	**53**	**9**

HIWULA, Jordy (F) **201 45**
H: 5 10 W: 11 12 b.Manchester 24-9-94
Internationals: England U18, U19.

2013–14	Manchester C	0	0		
2014–15	Manchester C	0	0		
2014–15	*Yeovil T*	8	0	**8**	**0**
2014–15	*Walsall*	19	9		
2015–16	Huddersfield T	0	0		
2015–16	*Wigan Ath*	14	2	**14**	**2**
2015–16	*Walsall*	13	3	**32**	**12**
2016–17	Huddersfield T	0	0		
2016–17	*Bradford C*	41	9	**41**	**9**
2017–18	Huddersfield T	0	0		
2017–18	*Fleetwood T*	43	8	**43**	**8**
2018–19	Coventry C	39	12		
2019–20	Coventry C	15	2	**54**	**14**
2020–21	Portsmouth	9	0	**9**	**0**

HUGHES, Harvey (D) **0 0**

2020–21	Portsmouth	0	0		

JACOBS, Michael (M) **371 56**
H: 5 9 W: 11 08 b.Rothwell 23-3-92

2009–10	Northampton T	0	0		
2010–11	Northampton T	41	5		
2011–12	Northampton T	46	6	**87**	**11**
2012–13	Derby Co	38	2		
2013–14	Derby Co	3	0	**41**	**2**
2013–14	Wolverhampton W	30	8		
2014–15	Wolverhampton W	12	0	**42**	**8**
2014–15	*Blackpool*	5	1	**5**	**1**
2015–16	Wigan Ath	35	10		
2016–17	Wigan Ath	43	3		
2017–18	Wigan Ath	44	12		
2018–19	Wigan Ath	22	4		
2019–20	Wigan Ath	32	3	**176**	**32**
2020–21	Portsmouth	20	2	**20**	**2**

JEWITT-WHITE, Harry (M) **0 0**
b. 26-3-04

2020–21	Portsmouth	0	0		

JOHNSON, Callum (M) **145 1**
b. 23-10-97
From Middlesbrough.

2017–18	Accrington S	31	1		
2018–19	Accrington S	41	0		
2019–20	Accrington S	33	0	**105**	**1**
2020–21	Portsmouth	40	0	**40**	**0**

KAVANAGH, Harry (D) **0 0**

2020–21	Portsmouth	0	0		

MACGILLIVRAY, Craig (G) **132 0**
H: 6 2 W: 12 04 b.Harrogate 12-1-93
From Stalybridge Celtic, Harrogate T.

2014–15	Walsall	2	0		
2015–16	Walsall	5	0		
2016–17	Walsall	5	0	**12**	**0**
2017–18	Shrewsbury T	8	0	**8**	**0**
2018–19	Portsmouth	46	0		
2019–20	Portsmouth	20	0		
2020–21	Portsmouth	46	0	**112**	**0**

MARQUIS, John (F) **346 111**
H: 6 1 W: 11 03 b.Lewisham 16-5-92

2009–10	Millwall	1	0		
2010–11	Millwall	11	4		
2011–12	Millwall	17	1		
2012–13	Millwall	10	0		
2013–14	Millwall	2	0		
2013–14	*Portsmouth*	5	1		
2013–14	*Torquay U*	5	3	**5**	**3**
2013–14	*Northampton T*	14	2		
2014–15	Millwall	1	0		
2014–15	*Cheltenham T*	13	1	**13**	**1**
2014–15	*Gillingham*	21	8	**21**	**8**
2015–16	Millwall	10	0	**52**	**5**
2015–16	*Leyton Orient*	13	0	**13**	**0**
2015–16	*Northampton T*	15	6	**29**	**8**
2016–17	Doncaster R	45	26		
2017–18	Doncaster R	45	14		
2018–19	Doncaster R	44	21	**134**	**61**
2019–20	Portsmouth	33	8		
2020–21	Portsmouth	41	16	**79**	**25**

MNOGA, Haji (D) **5 0**
b.Portsmouth 16-4-02
Internationals: England U17.

2018–19	Portsmouth	0	0		
2019–20	Portsmouth	0	0		
2020–21	Portsmouth	5	0	**5**	**0**

MORRIS, Bryn (M) **105 4**
H: 6 0 W: 11 01 b.Hartlepool 25-4-96
Internationals: England U16, U17, U18, U19, U20.

2012–13	Middlesbrough	1	0		
2013–14	Middlesbrough	1	0		
2014–15	Middlesbrough	0	0		
2014–15	*Burton Alb*	5	0	**5**	**0**
2015–16	Middlesbrough	0	0		
2015–16	*Coventry C*	6	0	**6**	**0**
2015–16	*York C*	3	0	**3**	**0**
2015–16	*Walsall*	1	0	**1**	**0**
2016–17	Middlesbrough	0	0	**2**	**0**
2016–17	*Shrewsbury T*	13	0		
2017–18	Shrewsbury T	18	0		
2018–19	Shrewsbury T	0	0	**31**	**0**
2018–19	*Wycombe W*	19	3	**19**	**3**
2018–19	Portsmouth	7	1		

2019–20	Portsmouth	0	0		
2020–21	Portsmouth	9	0	**16**	**1**
2020–21	*Northampton T*	22	0	**22**	**0**

NAYLOR, Tom (D) **300** **24**
H: 5 11 W: 11 05 b.Sutton-in-Ashfield 28-6-91
From Mansfield T.

2011–12	Derby Co	8	0		
2012–13	Derby Co	0	0		
2012–13	*Bradford C*	5	0	**5**	**0**
2013–14	Derby Co	0	0		
2013–14	*Newport Co*	33	1	**33**	**1**
2014–15	Derby Co	0	0	**8**	**0**
2014–15	*Cambridge U*	8	0	**8**	**0**
2014–15	*Burton Alb*	17	0		
2015–16	Burton Alb	41	6		
2016–17	Burton Alb	33	3		
2017–18	Burton Alb	33	3	**124**	**12**
2018–19	Portsmouth	43	4		
2019–20	Portsmouth	33	1		
2020–21	Portsmouth	46	6	**122**	**11**

NICOLAISEN, Rasmus (D) **64** **6**
b. 16-3-97

2016–17	Midtjylland	8	1		
2017–18	Midtjylland	2	0		
2018–19	Midtjylland	17	4		
2019–20	Midtjylland	16	1		
2020–21	Midtjylland	0	0	**43**	**6**

On loan from Midtjylland.

2020–21	Portsmouth	21	0	**21**	**0**

RAGGETT, Sean (D) **105** **8**
H: 5 11 W: 12 04 b.Gillingham 17-4-93
Internationals: England C.
From Dover Ath.

2017–18	Lincoln C	25	2	**25**	**2**
2017–18	Norwich C	2	0		
2018–19	Norwich C	0	0		
2018–19	*Rotherham U*	7	1	**7**	**1**
2019–20	Norwich C	0	0	**2**	**0**
2019–20	*Portsmouth*	26	2		
2020–21	Portsmouth	45	3	**71**	**5**

REW, Harvey (D) **0** **0**
b.Portsmouth 25-9-02
Internationals: Wales U17.

2019–20	Portsmouth	0	0		
2020–21	Portsmouth	0	0		

SEOK, Jae-Lee (M) **0** **0**
From Pickwick.

2020–21	Portsmouth	0	0		

SETTERS, David (D) **0** **0**

2020–21	Portsmouth	0	0		

SEYMOUR, Taylor (G) **0** **0**

2020–21	Portsmouth	0	0		

STANLEY, Alfie (F) **0** **0**

2020–21	Portsmouth	0	0		

STOREY, Gerard (M) **0** **0**
b. 5-2-02
From Portadown.

2020–21	Portsmouth	0	0		

TEGGART, Eoin (F) **0** **0**
Internationals: Northern Ireland U17.
From Cliftonville.

2019–20	Portsmouth	0	0		
2020–21	Portsmouth	0	0		

TURNBULL, Duncan (G) **0** **0**

2020–21	Portsmouth	0	0		

WHATMOUGH, Jack (D) **121** **3**
b.Gosport 19-8-96
Internationals: England U18, U19.

2012–13	Portsmouth	0	0		
2013–14	Portsmouth	12	0		
2014–15	Portsmouth	22	0		
2015–16	Portsmouth	2	0		
2016–17	Portsmouth	10	1		
2017–18	Portsmouth	14	0		
2018–19	Portsmouth	26	0		
2019–20	Portsmouth	1	0		
2020–21	Portsmouth	34	2	**121**	**3**

WILLIAMS, Ryan (F) **216** **21**
H: 5 11 W: 12 00 b.Perth 28-10-93
Internationals: Australia U20, U23, Full caps.

2011–12	Portsmouth	4	0		
2011–12	Fulham	0	0		
2012–13	Fulham	0	0		
2012–13	*Gillingham*	0	0		
2013–14	Fulham	0	0		
2013–14	*Oxford U*	36	7	**36**	**7**
2014–15	Fulham	2	0	**2**	**0**
2014–15	*Barnsley*	5	0		
2015–16	Barnsley	5	0		
2016–17	Barnsley	16	1	**26**	**1**
2017–18	Rotherham U	42	4		
2018–19	Rotherham U	39	1	**81**	**5**
2019–20	Portsmouth	26	3		
2020–21	Portsmouth	41	5	**71**	**8**

Scholars
Anderson, Harry James; Bell, Charlie George; Bridgman, Alfie Jack; Brook, Harrison Phillip; Cadman, Daniel Peter; Dawson, Kristian Patrick; Gifford, Daniel Thomas; Hughes, Harvey Russell; Jewitt-White, Harry George; Kaba, Issiaga; Kavanagh, Harry John; Lee, Seokjae; Manderson, Conor Stephen; Setters, David Kevin; Stanley, Alfie Frederick James.

PRESTON NE (67)

BARKHUIZEN, Tom (F) **317** **61**
H: 5 9 W: 11 00 b.Blackpool 4-7-93

2011–12	Blackpool	0	0		
2011–12	*Hereford U*	38	11	**38**	**11**
2012–13	Blackpool	0	0		
2012–13	*Fleetwood T*	13	1	**13**	**1**
2013–14	Blackpool	14	1		
2014–15	Blackpool	7	0	**21**	**1**
2014–15	*Morecambe*	5	0		
2015–16	Morecambe	40	10		
2016–17	Morecambe	14	5	**59**	**15**
2016–17	Preston NE	17	6		
2017–18	Preston NE	46	8		
2018–19	Preston NE	34	6		
2019–20	Preston NE	44	9		
2020–21	Preston NE	45	4	**186**	**33**

BAUER, Patrick (D) **222** **14**
H: 6 4 W: 13 08 b.Backnang 28-10-92
Internationals: Germany U17, U18, U20.

2010–11	Stuttgart	0	0		
2011–12	Stuttgart	0	0		
2012–13	Stuttgart	0	0		
2013–14	Maritimo	16	0		
2014–15	Maritimo	29	2	**45**	**2**
2015–16	Charlton Ath	19	1		
2016–17	Charlton Ath	36	4		
2017–18	Charlton Ath	34	3		
2018–19	Charlton Ath	35	0	**124**	**8**
2019–20	Preston NE	41	3		
2020–21	Preston NE	12	1	**53**	**4**

BAXTER, Jack (M) **9** **2**
b.Chorley 27-10-00

2018–19	Preston NE	0	0		
2019–20	Preston NE	0	0		
2020–21	Preston NE	0	0		
2020–21	*Cork C*	9	2	**9**	**2**

BAYLISS, Tom (M) **74** **9**
b. 6-4-99
Internationals: England U19.

2017–18	Coventry C	24	5		
2018–19	Coventry C	38	3		
2019–20	Coventry C	0	0	**62**	**8**
2019–20	Preston NE	1	0		
2020–21	Preston NE	11	1	**12**	**1**

BODIN, Billy (M) **249** **52**
H: 5 11 W: 11 00 b.Swindon 24-3-92
Internationals: Wales U17, U19, U21, Full caps.

2009–10	Swindon T	0	0		
2010–11	Swindon T	5	0		
2011–12	Swindon T	11	3	**16**	**3**
2011–12	*Torquay U*	17	5		
2011–12	*Crewe Alex*	8	0	**8**	**0**
2012–13	Torquay U	43	5		
2013–14	Torquay U	27	1	**87**	**11**
2014–15	Northampton T	4	0	**4**	**0**
2015–16	Bristol R	38	13		
2016–17	Bristol R	36	13		
2017–18	Bristol R	21	9	**95**	**35**
2017–18	Preston NE	17	1		
2018–19	Preston NE	0	0		
2019–20	Preston NE	18	2		
2020–21	Preston NE	4	0	**39**	**3**

BROWNE, Alan (M) **258** **34**
H: 5 8 W: 11 03 b.Cork 15-4-95
Internationals: Republic of Ireland U19, U21, Full caps.

2013	Cork C	0	0		
2013–14	Preston NE	8	1		
2014–15	Preston NE	20	3		
2015–16	Preston NE	36	3		
2016–17	Preston NE	31	0		
2017–18	Preston NE	44	7		
2018–19	Preston NE	38	12		
2019–20	Preston NE	43	4		
2020–21	Preston NE	38	4	**258**	**34**

COULTON, Lewis (D) **0** **0**
b. 3-3-03

2020–21	Preston NE	0	0		

CUNNINGHAM, Greg (D) **267** **9**
H: 6 0 W: 11 00 b.Galway 31-1-91
Internationals: Republic of Ireland U17, U21, Full caps.

2008–09	Manchester C	0	0		
2009–10	Manchester C	2	0		
2010–11	Manchester C	0	0		
2010–11	*Leicester C*	13	0	**13**	**0**
2011–12	Manchester C	0	0		
2011–12	*Nottingham F*	27	0	**27**	**0**
2012–13	Manchester C	0	0	**2**	**0**
2012–13	Bristol C	30	1		
2013–14	Bristol C	37	1		
2014–15	Bristol C	24	2	**91**	**4**
2015–16	Preston NE	43	2		
2016–17	Preston NE	40	1		
2017–18	Preston NE	20	1		
2018–19	Cardiff C	7	0		
2019–20	Cardiff C	0	0		
2019–20	*Blackburn R*	8	0	**8**	**0**
2020–21	Cardiff C	5	0	**12**	**0**
2020–21	Preston NE	11	1	**114**	**5**

EARL, Joshua (D) **62** **0**
b. 24-10-98

2017–18	Preston NE	19	0		
2018–19	Preston NE	14	0		
2019–20	Preston NE	0	0		
2019–20	*Bolton W*	9	0	**9**	**0**
2019–20	*Ipswich T*	7	0	**7**	**0**
2020–21	Preston NE	5	0	**38**	**0**
2020–21	*Burton Alb*	8	0	**8**	**0**

EVANS, Ched (F) **286** **94**
H: 6 0 W: 12 00 b.Rhyl 28-12-88
Internationals: Wales U21, Full caps.
From Chester.

2006–07	Manchester C	0	0		
2007–08	Manchester C	0	0		
2007–08	*Norwich C*	28	10	**28**	**10**
2008–09	Manchester C	16	1	**16**	**1**
2009–10	Sheffield U	33	4		
2010–11	Sheffield U	34	9		
2011–12	Sheffield U	36	29		
2016–17	Chesterfield	25	5	**25**	**5**
2017–18	Sheffield U	9	0		
2018–19	Sheffield U	0	0	**112**	**42**
2018–19	*Fleetwood T*	39	17		
2019–20	Fleetwood T	28	9		
2020–21	Fleetwood T	17	5	**84**	**31**
2020–21	Preston NE	21	5	**21**	**5**

GALLAGHER, Paul (F) **552** **90**
H: 6 1 W: 11 00 b.Glasgow 9-8-84
Internationals: Scotland U21, B, Full caps.

2002–03	Blackburn R	1	0		
2003–04	Blackburn R	26	3		
2004–05	Blackburn R	16	2		
2005–06	Blackburn R	1	0		
2005–06	*Stoke C*	37	11		
2006–07	Blackburn R	16	1		
2007–08	Blackburn R	0	0		
2007–08	*Preston NE*	19	1		
2007–08	*Stoke C*	7	0	**44**	**11**
2008–09	Blackburn R	0	0		
2008–09	*Plymouth Arg*	40	13	**40**	**13**
2009–10	Blackburn R	1	0	**61**	**6**
2009–10	Leicester C	41	7		
2010–11	Leicester C	41	10		
2011–12	Leicester C	28	8		
2012–13	Leicester C	8	0		
2012–13	Sheffield U	6	1	**6**	**1**
2013–14	Leicester C	0	0		
2013–14	*Preston NE*	28	6		
2014–15	Leicester C	0	0	**118**	**25**
2014–15	*Preston NE*	46	7		
2015–16	Preston NE	41	5		
2016–17	Preston NE	31	1		
2017–18	Preston NE	32	2		
2018–19	Preston NE	40	6		
2019–20	Preston NE	33	6		
2020–21	Preston NE	13	0	**283**	**34**

HARROP, Josh (M) **99** **8**
H: 5 9 W: 11 00 b.Stockport 15-12-95
Internationals: England U20.

2016–17	Manchester U	1	1	**1**	**1**
2017–18	Preston NE	38	2		
2018–19	Preston NE	8	0		
2019–20	Preston NE	32	5		
2020–21	Preston NE	5	0	**83**	**7**
2020–21	*Ipswich T*	15	0	**15**	**0**

HOLLAND-WILKINSON, Jacob (F) **0** **0**
b.Bury 30-10-02

2020–21	Preston NE	0	0		

HUDSON, Matthew (G) **1** **0**
H: 6 4 b.Southport 29-7-98

2014–15	Preston NE	0	0		
2015–16	Preston NE	1	0		
2016–17	Preston NE	0	0		

2017–18 Preston NE 0 0
2018–19 Preston NE 0 0
2018–19 *Bury* 0 0
2019–20 Preston NE 0 0
2020–21 Preston NE 0 0 **1 0**

HUGHES, Andrew (D) 243 9
b.Cardiff 5-6-92
Internationals: Wales U18, U23.
2013–14 Newport Co 26 2
2014–15 Newport Co 16 1
2015–16 Newport Co 25 0 **67 3**
2016–17 Peterborough U 39 1
2017–18 Peterborough U 43 2 **82 3**
2018–19 Preston NE 32 3
2019–20 Preston NE 28 0
2020–21 Preston NE 34 0 **94 3**

HUNTINGTON, Paul (D) 394 22
H: 6 3 W: 12 08 b.Carlisle 17-9-87
Internationals: England U18.
2005–06 Newcastle U 0 0
2006–07 Newcastle U 11 1
2007–08 Newcastle U 0 0 **11 1**
2007–08 Leeds U 17 2
2008–09 Leeds U 4 0
2009–10 Leeds U 0 0 **21 2**
2009–10 Stockport Co 26 0 **26 0**
2010–11 Yeovil T 40 5
2011–12 Yeovil T 37 2 **77 7**
2012–13 Preston NE 37 3
2013–14 Preston NE 23 2
2014–15 Preston NE 32 5
2015–16 Preston NE 38 0
2016–17 Preston NE 33 1
2017–18 Preston NE 44 1
2018–19 Preston NE 22 0
2019–20 Preston NE 9 0
2020–21 Preston NE 21 0 **259 12**

JAKOBSEN, Emil (F) 104 15
b. 24-6-98
2017–18 Derby Co 0 0
2017–18 *VVV-Venlo* 3 0 **3 0**
2018–19 Randers 30 4
2019–20 Randers 33 9 **63 13**
2020–21 Randers FC 0 0
2020–21 Preston NE 38 2 **38 2**

JOHNSON, Daniel (M) 259 48
H: 5 8 W: 10 07 b.Kingston, Jamaica 8-10-92
2010–11 Aston Villa 0 0
2011–12 Aston Villa 0 0
2012–13 Aston Villa 0 0
2012–13 *Yeovil T* 5 0 **5 0**
2013–14 Aston Villa 0 0
2014–15 Aston Villa 0 0
2014–15 *Chesterfield* 11 0 **11 0**
2014–15 *Oldham Ath* 6 3 **6 3**
2014–15 Preston NE 20 8
2015–16 Preston NE 43 8
2016–17 Preston NE 40 4
2017–18 Preston NE 33 3
2018–19 Preston NE 35 6
2019–20 Preston NE 33 12
2020–21 Preston NE 33 4 **237 45**

LEDSON, Ryan (M) 166 6
H: 5 9 W: 10 12 b.Liverpool 19-8-97
Internationals: England U16, U17, U18, U19, U20.
2013–14 Everton 0 0
2014–15 Everton 0 0
2015–16 Everton 0 0
2015–16 *Cambridge U* 27 0 **27 0**
2016–17 Oxford U 22 1
2017–18 Oxford U 44 3 **66 4**
2018–19 Preston NE 24 0
2019–20 Preston NE 13 0
2020–21 Preston NE 36 2 **73 2**

LEIGH, Lewis (M) 0 0
b. 5-12-03
2020–21 Preston NE 0 0

MAGUIRE, Sean (F) 265 81
H: 5 9 W: 11 10 b.Luton 1-5-94
Internationals: Republic of Ireland U19, U21, Full caps.
2010–11 West Ham U 0 0
2011 *Waterford U* 8 1
2011–12 West Ham U 0 0
2012 *Waterford U* 26 13 **34 14**
2012–13 West Ham U 0 0
2013–14 West Ham U 0 0
2014 *Sligo R* 18 1 **18 1**
2014–15 West Ham U 0 0
2014–15 *Accrington S* 33 7 **33 7**
2015 Dundalk 6 0 **6 0**
2016 Cork C 30 18
2017 Cork C 21 20 **51 38**
2017–18 Preston NE 24 10
2018–19 Preston NE 26 3
2019–20 Preston NE 44 5
2020–21 Preston NE 29 3 **123 21**

MOULT, Louis (F) 149 47
H: 6 0 W: 13 05 b.Stoke 14-5-92
2009–10 Stoke C 1 0
2010–11 Stoke C 0 0
2010–11 *Bradford C* 11 1 **11 1**
2011–12 Stoke C 0 0
2011–12 *Accrington S* 4 0 **4 0**
2012–13 Stoke C 0 0 **1 0**
2012–13 Northampton T 13 1 **13 1**
From Nuneaton T, Wrexham.
2015–16 Motherwell 38 15
2016–17 Motherwell 31 15
2017–18 Motherwell 15 8 **84 38**
2017–18 Preston NE 10 2
2018–19 Preston NE 24 4
2019–20 Preston NE 2 1
2020–21 Preston NE 0 0 **36 7**

NUGENT, David (F) 618 155
H: 5 11 W: 12 13 b.Liverpool 2-5-85
Internationals: England U20, U21, Full caps.
2001–02 Bury 5 0
2002–03 Bury 31 4
2003–04 Bury 26 3
2004–05 Bury 26 11 **88 18**
2004–05 Preston NE 18 8
2005–06 Preston NE 32 10
2006–07 Preston NE 44 15
2007–08 Portsmouth 15 0
2008–09 Portsmouth 16 3
2009–10 Portsmouth 3 0
2009–10 *Burnley* 30 6 **30 6**
2010–11 Portsmouth 44 13 **78 16**
2011–12 Leicester C 42 15
2012–13 Leicester C 42 14
2013–14 Leicester C 46 20
2014–15 Leicester C 29 5 **159 54**
2015–16 Middlesbrough 38 8
2016–17 Middlesbrough 4 0 **42 8**
2016–17 Derby Co 17 6
2017–18 Derby Co 37 9
2018–19 Derby Co 31 2 **85 17**
2019–20 Preston NE 24 1
2020–21 Preston NE 0 0 **118 34**
2020–21 *Tranmere R* 18 2 **18 2**

O'REILLY, Adam (M) 15 0
b. 11-5-01
Internationals: Republic of Ireland U17, U19.
2017–18 Preston NE 0 0
2018–19 Preston NE 1 0
2019–20 Preston NE 0 0
2020–21 Preston NE 0 0 **1 0**
2020–21 *Waterford* 14 0 **14 0**

POTTS, Brad (M) 333 43
H: 6 2 W: 12 09 b.Carlisle 3-7-94
Internationals: England U19.
2012–13 Carlisle U 27 0
2013–14 Carlisle U 37 2
2014–15 Carlisle U 39 7 **103 9**
2015–16 Blackpool 45 6
2016–17 Blackpool 42 10 **87 16**
2017–18 Barnsley 37 3
2018–19 Barnsley 22 6 **59 9**
2018–19 Preston NE 10 2
2019–20 Preston NE 32 2
2020–21 Preston NE 42 5 **84 9**

RAFFERTY, Joe (D) 271 4
H: 6 0 W: 11 11 b.Liverpool 6-10-93
Internationals: Republic of Ireland U18, U19.
From Liverpool.
2012–13 Rochdale 21 0
2013–14 Rochdale 31 0
2014–15 Rochdale 31 1
2015–16 Rochdale 31 1
2016–17 Rochdale 40 0
2017–18 Rochdale 33 1
2018–19 Rochdale 27 0 **214 3**
2018–19 Preston NE 6 0
2019–20 Preston NE 29 1
2020–21 Preston NE 22 0 **57 1**

RIPLEY, Connor (G) 140 0
H: 5 11 W: 11 13 b.Middlesbrough 13-2-93
Internationals: England U19, U20.
2010–11 Middlesbrough 1 0
2011–12 Middlesbrough 1 0
2011–12 *Oxford U* 1 0 **1 0**
2012–13 Middlesbrough 0 0
2013–14 Middlesbrough 0 0
2013–14 *Bradford C* 0 0
2014 *Ostersunds* 14 0 **14 0**
2014–15 Middlesbrough 0 0
2015–16 Middlesbrough 0 0
2015–16 *Motherwell* 36 0 **36 0**
2016–17 Middlesbrough 0 0
2016–17 *Oldham Ath* 46 0 **46 0**
2017–18 Middlesbrough 0 0
2017–18 *Burton Alb* 2 0 **2 0**
2017–18 *Bury* 15 0 **15 0**
2018–19 Middlesbrough 0 0 **2 0**
2018–19 *Accrington S* 21 0 **21 0**
2018–19 Preston NE 2 0
2019–20 Preston NE 0 0
2020–21 Preston NE 1 0 **3 0**

RODWELL-GRANT, Joe (F) 0 0
2020–21 Preston NE 0 0

RUDD, Declan (G) 239 0
H: 6 3 W: 12 06 b.Diss 16-1-91
Internationals: England U16, U17, U19, U20, U21, Full caps.
2008–09 Norwich C 0 0
2009–10 Norwich C 7 0
2010–11 Norwich C 1 0
2011–12 Norwich C 2 0
2012–13 Norwich C 0 0
2012–13 *Preston NE* 14 0
2013–14 Norwich C 0 0
2013–14 *Preston NE* 46 0
2014–15 Norwich C 0 0
2015–16 Norwich C 11 0
2016–17 Norwich C 0 0 **21 0**
2016–17 *Charlton Ath* 38 0 **38 0**
2017–18 Preston NE 16 0
2018–19 Preston NE 36 0
2019–20 Preston NE 46 0
2020–21 Preston NE 22 0 **180 0**

SINCLAIR, Scott (F) 371 89
H: 5 10 W: 10 00 b.Bath 26-3-89
Internationals: England U17, U18, U19, U20, U21. Great Britain.
2004–05 Bristol R 2 0 **2 0**
2005–06 Chelsea 0 0
2006–07 Chelsea 2 0
2006–07 *Plymouth Arg* 15 2 **15 2**
2007–08 Chelsea 1 0
2007–08 *QPR* 9 1 **9 1**
2007–08 *Charlton Ath* 3 0 **3 0**
2007–08 *Crystal Palace* 6 2 **6 2**
2008–09 Chelsea 2 0
2008–09 *Birmingham C* 14 0 **14 0**
2009–10 Chelsea 0 0 **5 0**
2009–10 *Wigan Ath* 18 1 **18 1**
2010–11 Swansea C 43 19
2011–12 Swansea C 38 8
2012–13 Swansea C 1 1 **82 28**
2012–13 Manchester C 11 0
2013–14 Manchester C 0 0
2013–14 *WBA* 8 0 **8 0**
2014–15 Manchester C 2 0 **13 0**
2014–15 *Aston Villa* 9 1
2015–16 Aston Villa 27 2 **36 3**
2016–17 Celtic 35 21
2017–18 Celtic 35 10
2018–19 Celtic 33 9
2019–20 Celtic 2 0 **105 40**
2019–20 Preston NE 18 3
2020–21 Preston NE 37 9 **55 12**

STOCKLEY, Jayden (F) 279 79
H: 6 2 W: 12 07 b.Poole 10-10-93
2009–10 Bournemouth 2 0
2010–11 Bournemouth 4 0
2011–12 Bournemouth 10 0
2011–12 *Accrington S* 9 3 **9 3**
2012–13 Bournemouth 0 0
2013–14 Bournemouth 0 0
2013–14 *Leyton Orient* 8 1 **8 1**
2013–14 *Torquay U* 19 1 **19 1**
2014–15 Bournemouth 0 0
2014–15 *Cambridge U* 3 2 **3 2**
2014–15 *Luton T* 13 3 **13 3**
2015–16 Bournemouth 0 0 **16 0**
2015–16 *Portsmouth* 9 2 **9 2**
2015–16 *Exeter C* 22 10
2016–17 Aberdeen 27 5 **27 5**
2017–18 Exeter C 41 19
2018–19 Exeter C 25 16 **88 45**
2018–19 Preston NE 17 4
2019–20 Preston NE 32 4
2020–21 Preston NE 16 1 **65 9**
2020–21 *Charlton Ath* 22 8 **22 8**

STOREY, Jordan (D) 81 4
H: 6 2 W: 12 00 b. 2-9-97
2016–17 Exeter C 0 0
2017–18 Exeter C 13 2 **13 2**
2018–19 Preston NE 28 1
2019–20 Preston NE 10 0
2020–21 Preston NE 30 1 **68 2**

WALKER, Ethan (F) 17 0
b. 28-7-02
2018–19 Preston NE 1 0
2019–20 Preston NE 0 0

2020–21 Preston NE 0 0 **1 0**
2020–21 *Carlisle U* 16 0 **16 0**

WHITEMAN, Ben (M) 187 27
b.Rochdale 17-6-96
2014–15 Sheffield U 0 0
2015–16 Sheffield U 6 0
2016–17 Sheffield U 2 0 **8 0**
2016–17 *Mansfield T* 23 7 **23 7**
2017–18 Doncaster R 42 6
2018–19 Doncaster R 40 3
2019–20 Doncaster R 33 5
2020–21 Doncaster R 18 5 **133 19**
2020–21 Preston NE 23 1 **23 1**

Scholars
Bennett, Aaron James Anthony; Blanchard, Joseph Kirkcaldy; Coulton, Lewis Thomas; De Oliveira Amaral, Dana; Dooley, Ben Michael; Duggan, Declyn; Green, Vaughn Killian; Holland-Wilkinson, Jacob William; Huddart, Harry Lee Joseph; Leigh, Lewis Jack; Lewis, Levi Aaron; Lombard, Oliver Michael; Mfuni, Teddy Mbiya; Nevin, Harry; Nicholson, Kyi Joseph Samuel; O'Neill, Michael; Rodwell-Grant, Joseph Edward.

QPR (68)

ADOMAH, Albert (F) 553 84
H: 6 1 W: 11 08 b.Lambeth 13-12-87
Internationals: Ghana Full caps.
From Harrow Bor.
2007–08 Barnet 22 5
2008–09 Barnet 45 9
2009–10 Barnet 45 5 **112 19**
2010–11 Bristol C 46 5
2011–12 Bristol C 45 5
2012–13 Bristol C 40 7 **131 17**
2013–14 Middlesbrough 42 12
2014–15 Middlesbrough 43 5
2015–16 Middlesbrough 43 6
2016–17 Middlesbrough 2 0 **130 23**
2016–17 Aston Villa 38 3
2017–18 Aston Villa 39 14
2018–19 Aston Villa 36 4 **113 21**
2019–20 Nottingham F 24 2 **24 2**
2019–20 *Cardiff C* 9 0 **9 0**
2020–21 QPR 34 2 **34 2**

ALFA, Ody (F) 0 0
b. 9-3-99
2019–20 QPR 0 0
2020–21 QPR 0 0

AMOS, Luke (M) 59 4
H: 5 10 W: 11 00 b.Hatfield 23-2-97
Internationals: England U18.
2016–17 Tottenham H 0 0
2016–17 *Southend U* 3 0 **3 0**
2017–18 Tottenham H 0 0
2017–18 *Stevenage* 16 2 **16 2**
2018–19 Tottenham H 1 0 **1 0**
2019–20 *QPR* 34 2
2020–21 QPR 5 0 **39 2**

ARMSTRONG, Sinclair (F) 0 0
H: 6 0 b.Dublin 22-6-03
Internationals: Republic of Ireland U17.
From Shamrock R.
2020–21 QPR 0 0

BALL, Dominic (D) 168 3
H: 6 0 W: 12 06 b.Welwyn Garden City 2-8-95
Internationals: Northern Ireland U16, U17, U19, U21. England U19, U20.
2013–14 Tottenham H 0 0
2014–15 Tottenham H 0 0
2014–15 *Cambridge U* 11 0 **11 0**
2015–16 Tottenham H 0 0
2015–16 *Rangers* 21 0 **21 0**
2016–17 Rotherham U 13 0
2016–17 *Peterborough U* 6 1 **6 1**
2017–18 Rotherham U 0 0
2017–18 *Aberdeen* 16 0
2018–19 Rotherham U 0 0 **13 0**
2018–19 *Aberdeen* 31 0 **47 0**
2019–20 QPR 31 1
2020–21 QPR 39 1 **70 2**

BARBET, Yoann (D) 213 10
H: 6 2 W: 12 11 b.Talence 10-5-93
Internationals: France U18.
2013–14 Bordeaux 0 0
2014–15 Chamois Niortais 33 2 **33 2**
2015–16 Brentford 18 1
2016–17 Brentford 23 1
2017–18 Brentford 34 3
2018–19 Brentford 32 1 **107 6**
2019–20 QPR 27 0
2020–21 QPR 46 2 **73 2**

BARNES, Dillon (G) 29 0
H: 6 4 W: 11 11 b. 8-4-96
2014–15 Fulham 0 0
2015–16 Colchester U 0 0
2016–17 Colchester U 0 0
2017–18 Colchester U 2 0
2018–19 Colchester U 22 0 **24 0**
2019–20 QPR 0 0
2020–21 QPR 0 0
2020–21 *Hibernian* 4 0 **4 0**
2020–21 *Burton Alb* 1 0 **1 0**

BETTACHE, Faysal (M) 9 0
b.Westminster 7-7-00
2018–19 QPR 0 0
2019–20 QPR 3 0
2020–21 QPR 6 0 **9 0**

BONNE, Macauley (F) 145 21
H: 5 11 W: 12 00 b.Ipswich 26-10-95
Internationals: Zimbabwe U23, Full caps.
2013–14 Colchester U 14 2
2014–15 Colchester U 10 1
2015–16 Colchester U 33 3
2016–17 Colchester U 18 1 **75 7**
From Leyton Orient.
2019–20 Charlton Ath 33 11
2020–21 Charlton Ath 3 0 **36 11**
2020–21 QPR 34 3 **34 3**

CAMERON, Geoff (D) 373 15
H: 6 3 W: 13 02 b.Attleboro 11-7-85
Internationals: USA Full caps.
From Rhode Island Stingrays.
2008 Houston D 23 1
2009 Houston D 29 2
2010 Houston D 16 3
2011 Houston D 33 5
2012 Houston D 15 0 **116 11**
2012–13 Stoke C 35 0
2013–14 Stoke C 37 2
2014–15 Stoke C 27 0
2015–16 Stoke C 30 0
2016–17 Stoke C 19 0
2017–18 Stoke C 20 0
2018–19 Stoke C 0 0 **168 2**
2018–19 *QPR* 19 1
2019–20 QPR 36 1
2020–21 QPR 34 0 **89 2**
Transferred to Cincinnati May 2021.

CARROLL, Tommy (M) 188 3
H: 5 10 W: 10 00 b.Watford 28-5-92
Internationals: England U19, U21.
2010–11 Tottenham H 0 0
2010–11 *Leyton Orient* 12 0 **12 0**
2011–12 Tottenham H 0 0
2011–12 *Derby Co* 12 1 **12 1**
2012–13 Tottenham H 7 0
2013–14 Tottenham H 0 0
2013–14 *QPR* 26 0
2014–15 Tottenham H 0 0
2014–15 *Swansea C* 13 0
2015–16 Tottenham H 19 1
2016–17 Tottenham H 1 0 **27 1**
2016–17 Swansea C 17 1
2017–18 Swansea C 37 0
2018–19 Swansea C 12 0
2018–19 *Aston Villa* 2 0 **2 0**
2019–20 Swansea C 8 0 **87 1**
2020–21 QPR 22 0 **48 0**

CHAIR, Ilias (M) 112 19
b.Lierse 30-10-97
Internationals: Morocco U23.
2015–16 Lierse 2 0
2016–17 Lierse 0 0 **2 0**
2017–18 QPR 4 1
2018–19 QPR 4 0
2018–19 *Stevenage* 16 6 **16 6**
2019–20 QPR 41 4
2020–21 QPR 45 8 **94 13**

DE SILVA, Dillon (M) 0 0
b. 18-4-02
2020–21 QPR 0 0

DE WIJS, Jordy (D) 119 4
H: 6 2 W: 13 03 b.Vlijmen 8-1-95
Internationals: Netherlands U17, U18, U20, U21.
2014–15 PSV Eindhoven 0 0
2015–16 PSV Eindhoven 1 0
2016–17 PSV Eindhoven 0 0
2016–17 *Excelsior* 15 0
2017–18 PSV Eindhoven 1 0 **2 0**
2017–18 *Excelsior* 19 0 **34 0**
2018–19 Hull C 32 1
2019–20 Hull C 35 2
2020–21 Hull C 7 0 **74 3**
2020–21 QPR 9 1 **9 1**

DICKIE, Rob (D) 168 7
H: 6 0 W: 11 09 b.Wokingham 3-3-96
Internationals: England U18, U19.
2015–16 Reading 1 0
2016–17 Reading 0 0
2016–17 *Cheltenham T* 20 2 **20 2**
2017–18 Reading 0 0 **1 0**
2017–18 *Lincoln C* 18 0 **18 0**
2017–18 Oxford U 15 1
2018–19 Oxford U 37 1
2019–20 Oxford U 34 0 **86 2**
2020–21 QPR 43 3 **43 3**

DIENG, Timothy (G) 101 0
b. 23-11-94
2010–11 Red Star Zurich 0 0
2011–12 Grasshoppers 0 0
2012–13 Grasshoppers 0 0
2012–13 *Grenchen* 3 0 **3 0**
2013–14 Grasshoppers 0 0
2014–15 Grasshoppers 0 0
2015–16 MSV Duisburg 0 0
2016–17 QPR 0 0
2017–18 QPR 0 0
2018–19 QPR 0 0
2018–19 *Stevenage* 13 0 **13 0**
2018–19 *Dundee* 16 0 **16 0**
2019–20 QPR 0 0
2019–20 *Doncaster R* 27 0 **27 0**
2020–21 QPR 42 0 **42 0**

DOMI, Franklin (D) 0 0
H: 6 0 b.London 19-9-00
Internationals: Albania U21.
2020–21 QPR 0 0

DREWE, Aaron (D) 0 0
b. 8-2-01
2020–21 QPR 0 0

DUKE-McKENNA, Stephen (M) 1 0
H: 5 7 b.Liverpool 17-8-00
Internationals: Guyana Full caps.
2017–18 Everton 0 0
2018–19 Bolton W 0 0
2019–20 QPR 0 0
2020–21 QPR 1 0 **1 0**

DYKES, Lyndon (M) 167 32
b.Gold Coast 7-10-95
From Mudgeeraba, Merrimac, Redlands U, Gold Cost C, Surfers Paradise Apollo.
2016–17 Queen of the South 30 2
2017–18 Queen of the South 34 7
2018–19 Queen of the South 36 2 **100 11**
2019–20 Livingston 25 9
2020–21 Livingston 0 0 **25 9**
2020–21 QPR 42 12 **42 12**

FRAILING, Jake (M) 0 0
b. 17-8-01
2020–21 QPR 0 0

GUBBINS, Joseph (D) 1 0
b. 3-8-01
2019–20 QPR 1 0
2020–21 QPR 0 0 **1 0**

HAMALAINEN, Niko (M) 57 0
b.Florida 3-5-97
Internationals: Finland U18, U19, U21, Full caps.
2014–15 QPR 0 0
2015–16 QPR 0 0
2015–16 *Dagenham & R* 1 0 **1 0**
2016–17 QPR 3 0
2017–18 QPR 0 0
2018–19 QPR 0 0
2018–19 *Los Angeles FC* 3 0 **3 0**
2019–20 QPR 0 0
2019–20 *Kilmarnock* 28 0 **28 0**
2020–21 QPR 22 0 **25 0**

KAKAY, Osman (D) 59 1
b.Westminster 25-8-97
Internationals: Sierra Leone Full caps.
2015–16 QPR 0 0
2015–16 *Livingston* 10 0 **10 0**
2016–17 QPR 1 0
2016–17 Chesterfield 8 0
2017–18 Chesterfield 0 0 **8 0**
2017–18 QPR 2 0
2018–19 QPR 3 0
2019–20 *Partick Thistle* 0 0
2019–20 QPR 7 0
2020–21 QPR 28 1 **41 1**

KANE, Todd (D) 215 13
H: 5 11 W: 11 00 b.Huntingdon 17-9-93
Internationals: England U19.
2011–12 Chelsea 0 0
2012–13 Chelsea 0 0
2012–13 *Preston NE* 3 0 **3 0**
2012–13 *Blackburn R* 14 0

2013–14 Chelsea 0 0
2013–14 *Blackburn R* 27 2 **41** **2**
2014–15 Chelsea 0 0
2014–15 *Bristol C* 5 0 **5** **0**
2014–15 *Nottingham F* 8 1 **8** **1**
2015–16 Chelsea 0 0
2015–16 *NEC* 31 1 **31** **1**
2016–17 Chelsea 0 0
2017–18 Chelsea 0 0
2017–18 *FC Groningen* 11 0 **11** **0**
2017–18 *Oxford U* 17 3 **17** **3**
2018–19 Chelsea 0 0
2018–19 *Hull C* 39 3 **39** **3**
2019–20 QPR 32 1
2020–21 QPR 28 2 **60** **3**

KARGBO, Hamzad (F) **0** **0**
H: 6 6 b. 20-1-02
2020–21 QPR 0 0

KEFALAS, Themistoklis (D) **0** **0**
b.Athens 28-5-00
2020–21 QPR 0 0

KELLY, Liam (G) **123** **0**
b.Glasgow 23-1-96
Internationals: Scotland U16, U17, U19, U21.
2015–16 Rangers 0 0
2015–16 *East Fife* 16 0 **16** **0**
2016–17 Rangers 0 0
2016–17 *Livingston* 34 0
2017–18 Rangers 0 0
2018–19 Livingston 36 0 **70** **0**
2019–20 QPR 19 0
2020–21 QPR 0 0 **19** **0**
2020–21 *Motherwell* 18 0 **18** **0**

KELMAN, Charlie (F) **42** **6**
b. 2-11-01
Internationals: USA U18, U20.
2018–19 Southend U 10 1
2019–20 Southend U 18 5
2020–21 Southend U 3 0 **31** **6**
2020–21 QPR 11 0 **11** **0**

KENDALL, Charley (F) **0** **0**
b. 15-12-00
2020–21 QPR 0 0

LITTLE, Max (G) **0** **0**
2020–21 QPR 0 0

LLOYD, Alfie (F) **0** **0**
b. 30-4-03
2020–21 QPR 0 0

LUMLEY, Joe (G) **128** **0**
H: 6 3 W: 11 07 b.Harlow 15-2-95
2013–14 QPR 0 0
2014–15 QPR 0 0
2014–15 *Accrington S* 5 0 **5** **0**
2014–15 *Morecambe* 0 0
2015–16 QPR 1 0
2015–16 *Stevenage* 0 0
2016–17 QPR 0 0
2016–17 *Bristol R* 19 0 **19** **0**
2017–18 QPR 2 0
2017–18 *Blackpool* 17 0 **17** **0**
2018–19 QPR 42 0
2019–20 QPR 27 0
2020–21 QPR 5 0 **77** **0**
2020–21 *Gillingham* 2 0 **2** **0**
2020–21 *Doncaster R* 8 0 **8** **0**

MAHOM, Trent (D) **0** **0**
b. 8-9-01
2020–21 QPR 0 0

MAHONEY, Murphy (G) **0** **0**
2020–21 QPR 0 0

MASTERSON, Conor (D) **21** **1**
b.Dublin 8-9-98
Internationals: Republic of Ireland U16, U17, U18, U19, U21.
2015–16 Liverpool 0 0
2016–17 Liverpool 0 0
2017–18 Liverpool 0 0
2018–19 Liverpool 0 0
2019–20 QPR 12 1
2020–21 QPR 4 0 **16** **1**
2020–21 *Swindon T* 5 0 **5** **0**

MEMA, Armelindo (F) **0** **0**
b. 23-5-02
Internationals: Albania U21.
2020–21 QPR 0 0

MIDDLEHURST, Thomas (G) **0** **0**
2020–21 QPR 0 0

OTEH, Aramide (F) **74** **10**
b.London 10-9-98
From Tottenham H.
2017–18 QPR 6 1
2018–19 QPR 2 0
2018–19 *Walsall* 13 1 **13** **1**
2019–20 *Bradford C* 18 3 **18** **3**
2019–20 QPR 9 0
2020–21 QPR 0 0 **17** **1**
2020–21 *Stevenage* 13 4 **13** **4**
2020–21 *Colchester U* 13 1 **13** **1**

REMY, Shiloh (M) **0** **0**
b. 28-12-00
2020–21 QPR 0 0

SAMUEL, Bright (F) **167** **15**
H: 5 9 W: 11 05 b. 1-2-97
2014–15 Blackpool 6 0
2015–16 Blackpool 23 0
2016–17 Blackpool 31 4
2017–18 Blackpool 4 0 **64** **4**
2017–18 QPR 18 1
2018–19 QPR 27 2
2019–20 QPR 37 5
2020–21 QPR 21 3 **103** **11**
Transferred to Fenerbahce January 2021.

SHODIPO, Olamide (M) **78** **10**
b.Dublin 5-7-97
Internationals: Republic of Ireland U19, U21.
2016–17 QPR 11 0
2016–17 *Port Vale* 6 0 **6** **0**
2017–18 QPR 0 0
2017–18 *Colchester U* 6 0 **6** **0**
2018–19 QPR 4 0
2019–20 QPR 12 0
2020–21 QPR 0 0 **27** **0**
2020–21 *Oxford U* 39 10 **39** **10**

SMYTH, Paul (M) **88** **10**
b. 10-9-97
Internationals: Northern Ireland U19, U21, Full caps.
2017–18 Linfield 0 0
2017–18 QPR 13 2
2018–19 QPR 3 0
2018–19 *Accrington S* 15 3
2019–20 QPR 0 0
2019–20 *Wycombe W* 19 1 **19** **1**
2020–21 QPR 3 0 **19** **2**
2020–21 *Charlton Ath* 14 1 **14** **1**
2020–21 *Accrington S* 21 3 **36** **6**

THOMAS, George (M) **103** **8**
H: 5 8 W: 12 00 b.Leicester 24-3-97
Internationals: Wales U17, U19, U20, U21, Full caps.
2013–14 Coventry C 1 0
2014–15 Coventry C 6 0
2015–16 Coventry C 7 0
2015–16 *Yeovil T* 5 0 **5** **0**
2016–17 Coventry C 28 5 **42** **5**
2017–18 Leicester C 0 0
2018–19 Leicester C 0 0
2018–19 *Scunthorpe U* 37 3 **37** **3**
2019–20 Leicester C 0 0
2019–20 *ADO Den Haag* 2 0 **2** **0**
2020–21 QPR 17 0 **17** **0**

WALLACE, Lee (D) **367** **25**
b.Edinburgh 1-8-87
Internationals: Scotland U19, U20, U21, Full caps.
2004–05 Hearts 13 0
2005–06 Hearts 13 0
2006–07 Hearts 17 0
2007–08 Hearts 21 0
2008–09 Hearts 34 2
2009–10 Hearts 32 1
2010–11 Hearts 9 0 **139** **3**
2011–12 Rangers 28 2
2012–13 Rangers 33 3
2013–14 Rangers 28 3
2014–15 Rangers 31 3
2015–16 Rangers 36 7
2016–17 Rangers 27 3
2017–18 Rangers 5 0
2018–19 Rangers 2 0 **190** **21**
2019–20 QPR 11 0
2020–21 QPR 27 1 **38** **1**

WALSH, Joe (G) **1** **0**
b. 1-4-02
2019–20 Gillingham 0 0
2020–21 Gillingham 1 0 **1** **0**
2020–21 QPR 0 0

WELLS, Ben (D) **0** **0**
b. 29-2-00
From West Ham U.
2020–21 QPR 0 0

WILLIAMS-LOWE, Kayden (D) **0** **0**
b. 4-12-00
2020–21 QPR 0 0

WILLOCK, Chris (M) **52** **5**
H: 5 10 W: 10 08 b.London 31-1-98
Internationals: England U16, U17, U18, U19, U20.
2015–16 Arsenal 0 0
2016–17 Arsenal 0 0
2017–18 Arsenal 0 0
2018–19 Arsenal 0 0
2019–20 Arsenal 0 0
2019–20 *WBA* 0 0
2019–20 *Huddersfield T* 14 2 **14** **2**
2020–21 QPR 38 3 **38** **3**

WOOLLARD-INNOCENT, Kai (D) **0** **0**
b. 28-9-00
2020–21 QPR 0 0

Scholars
Anthony, Elijah Oluwaseyi; Anthony, Micah Oluwapelumi; Aoraha, Alexander; Castillo-Anderson, Matthew William; Cotter, Riley Haslett; Danso, Ferrell Michael Kofi Abiam; Dougui, Adam; Eisa, Omar Mamoun Elaisir Kafi; Evangelista Conte, Raheem; Eze, Chimaechi Nwodim; Ferreira De Paiva, Alison Junio; Griffiths, Lemar Anthony; Hamid, Harun Ar-Rashid Faheem; Harrack, Kayden Michael; Hawkins, Henry; Hayes, Ryan Alexander; Jude-Boyd, Arkell Nicholas Cecil; McLean, Mason Ashley Francis; Murphy, Harrison Thomas; Obeng, Mason Charlie Yaw; Rossi, Ivo Matas; Sacopon, Jaime Alcantara; Woodman, Deonysus Sangai.

READING (69)

ABBEY, Nelson (D) **0** **0**
b. 28-8-03
2020–21 Reading 0 0

AJOSE, Joseph (M) **0** **0**
b.London 21-1-01
From Newcastle U, Port Vale.
2020–21 Reading 0 0

ALUKO, Sone (M) **372** **52**
H: 5 8 W: 9 10 b.Birmingham 19-2-89
Internationals: England U16, U17, U18, U19. Nigeria U20, Full caps.
2005–06 Birmingham C 0 0
2006–07 Birmingham C 0 0
2007–08 Birmingham C 0 0
2007–08 *Aberdeen* 20 3
2008–09 Birmingham C 0 0
2008–09 *Blackpool* 1 0 **1** **0**
2008–09 Aberdeen 32 2
2009–10 Aberdeen 22 3
2010–11 Aberdeen 28 2 **102** **10**
2011–12 Rangers 21 12 **21** **12**
2012–13 Hull C 23 8
2013–14 Hull C 17 1
2014–15 Hull C 25 1
2015–16 Hull C 25 3 **90** **13**
2016–17 Fulham 45 8
2017–18 Fulham 4 0 **49** **8**
2017–18 Reading 39 3
2018–19 Reading 19 1
2019 *Beijing Renhe* 16 3 **16** **3**
2019–20 Reading 2 0
2020–21 Reading 33 2 **93** **6**

ANDERSSON, Jokull (G) **31** **0**
b. 25-8-01
Internationals: Iceland U17, U19.
From Afturelding.
2019–20 Reading 0 0
2020–21 Reading 0 0
2020–21 *Morecambe* 2 0 **2** **0**
2020–21 *Exeter C* 29 0 **29** **0**

ANDRESSON, Jokull (G) **0** **0**
H: 6 4 W: 12 13 b.Mosfellsbaer 25-8-01
Internationals: Iceland U17, U19.
2020–21 Reading 0 0

AZEEZ, Femi (M) **1** **0**
b. 5-6-01
From Wealdstone.
2020–21 Reading 1 0 **1** **0**

BALDOCK, Sam (F) **352** **100**
H: 5 7 W: 10 07 b.Buckingham 15-3-89
Internationals: England U20.
2005–06 Milton Keynes D 0 0
2006–07 Milton Keynes D 1 0
2007–08 Milton Keynes D 5 0
2008–09 Milton Keynes D 40 12
2009–10 Milton Keynes D 20 5
2010–11 Milton Keynes D 30 12
2011–12 Milton Keynes D 4 4 **100** **33**
2011–12 West Ham U 23 5

2012–13 West Ham U 0 0 **23 5**
2012–13 Bristol C 34 10
2013–14 Bristol C 45 24
2014–15 Bristol C 4 0 **83 34**
2014–15 Brighton & HA 20 3
2015–16 Brighton & HA 28 4
2016–17 Brighton & HA 31 11
2017–18 Brighton & HA 2 0 **81 18**
2018–19 Reading 21 5
2019–20 Reading 24 5
2020–21 Reading 20 0 **65 10**

BOYCE-CLARKE, Coniah (G) 0 0
b. 1-3-03
Internationals: England U16, U17.
2019–20 Reading 0 0
2020–21 Reading 0 0

BRISTOW, Ethan (D) 0 0
b. 27-11-01
2020–21 Reading 0 0

CAMARA, Mamadi (F) 1 0
b. 31-12-03
2020–21 Reading 1 0 **1 0**

DORSETT, Jeriel (D) 0 0
Internationals: England U18.
2019–20 Reading 0 0
2020–21 Reading 0 0

EAST, Ryan (M) 1 0
b. 7-8-98
2017–18 Reading 0 0
2018–19 Reading 1 0
2019–20 Reading 0 0
2020–21 Reading 0 0 **1 0**

EJARIA, Oviemuno (M) 117 9
H: 6 0 W: 11 11 b.Southwark 18-11-97
Internationals: England U20, U21.
From Arsenal.
2016–17 Liverpool 2 0
2017–18 Liverpool 0 0
2017–18 *Sunderland* 11 1 **11 1**
2018–19 Liverpool 0 0
2018–19 *Rangers* 14 1 **14 1**
2018–19 *Reading* 16 1
2019–20 Liverpool 0 0 **2 0**
2019–20 *Reading* 36 3
2020–21 Reading 38 3 **90 7**

FELIPE ARARUNA, Hoffmann (M) 33 0
b. 12-3-96
2016 Sao Paulo 0 0
2017 Sao Paulo 8 0
2018 Sao Paulo 11 0
2019 Sao Paulo 0 0 **19 0**
2019 *Fortaleza* 9 0 **9 0**
2019–20 Reading 3 0
2020–21 Reading 2 0 **5 0**

HOLDEN, James (G) 0 0
b. 4-9-01
From Bury.
2020–21 Reading 0 0

HOLMES, Thomas (D) 51 0
b. 12-3-00
2017–18 Reading 1 0
2018–19 Reading 0 0
2019–20 Reading 0 0
2019–20 *KSV Roeselare* 11 0 **11 0**
2020–21 Reading 39 0 **40 0**

LAURENT, Josh (M) 172 9
H: 6 0 W: 11 00 b.Leytonstone 6-5-95
From Wycombe W.
2013–14 QPR 0 0
2014–15 QPR 0 0
2015–16 Brentford 0 0
2015–16 *Newport Co* 3 0 **3 0**
2015–16 Hartlepool U 3 0
2016–17 Hartlepool U 25 1 **28 1**
2016–17 Wigan Ath 1 0
2017–18 Wigan Ath 0 0 **1 0**
2017–18 *Bury* 22 1 **22 1**
2018–19 Shrewsbury T 42 2
2019–20 Shrewsbury T 31 2 **73 4**
2020–21 Reading 45 3 **45 3**

LAWLESS, Conor (M) 0 0
2020–21 Reading 0 0

LUCAS JOAO, Eduardo (F) 257 72
H: 6 4 W: 12 08 b.Luanda 4-9-93
Internationals: Portugal U20, U21, U23, Full caps.
2012–13 Nacional 0 0
2012–13 *Mirandela* 27 12 **27 12**
2013–14 Nacional 16 0
2014–15 Nacional 30 6 **46 6**
2015–16 Sheffield W 40 6
2016–17 Sheffield W 10 0
2016–17 *Blackburn R* 13 3 **13 3**
2017–18 Sheffield W 31 9
2018–19 Sheffield W 31 10
2019–20 Sheffield W 1 1 **113 26**
2019–20 Reading 19 6
2020–21 Reading 39 19 **58 25**

LUZON, Omri (D) 53 0
b.Petah Tikva 7-1-99
Internationals: Israel U16, U17, U18, U19, U21.
2016–17 Maccabi Petah Tikva 1 0
2017–18 Maccabi Petah Tikva 1 0
2018–19 Maccabi Petah Tikva 0 0
2018–19 *Hapoel Hadera* 0 0
2018–19 Hapoel Nof HaGalil 5 0 **5 0**
2018–19 Hapoel Ashkelon 13 0 **13 0**
2019–20 Hapoel Rishon LeZion 33 0 **33 0**
2020–21 Maccabi Petah Tikva 0 0 **2 0**
From Petah Tikva.
2020–21 Reading 0 0

McINTYRE, Tom (D) 38 2
b. 6-11-98
Internationals: Scotland U17, U20, U21.
2018–19 Reading 2 0
2019–20 Reading 10 0
2020–21 Reading 26 2 **38 2**

McNULTY, Marc (M) 303 95
H: 5 10 W: 11 00 b.Edinburgh 14-9-92
Internationals: Scotland Full caps.
2009–10 Livingston 9 1
2010–11 Livingston 5 1
2011–12 Livingston 30 11
2012–13 Livingston 26 7
2013–14 Livingston 35 17 **105 37**
2014–15 Sheffield U 31 9
2015–16 Sheffield U 5 1
2015–16 *Portsmouth* 27 10 **27 10**
2016–17 Sheffield U 4 0 **40 10**
2016–17 *Bradford C* 15 1 **15 1**
2016–17 Coventry C 0 0
2017–18 Coventry C 42 23 **42 23**
2018–19 Reading 13 1
2018–19 *Hibernian* 15 7
2019–20 Reading 0 0
2019–20 *Sunderland* 15 2 **15 2**
2019–20 *Hibernian* 6 1 **21 8**
2020–21 Reading 0 0 **13 1**
2020–21 *Dundee U* 25 3 **25 3**

MEITE, Yakou (M) 148 41
H: 6 0 W: 11 05 b.Paris 11-2-96
Internationals: Ivory Coast U17, U20, U23, Full caps.
2013–14 Paris Saint-Germain 0 0
2014–15 Paris Saint-Germain 0 0
2015–16 Paris Saint-Germain 1 0 **1 0**
2016–17 Reading 14 1
2017–18 Reading 0 0
2017–18 *Sochaux* 31 3 **31 3**
2018–19 Reading 37 12
2019–20 Reading 40 13
2020–21 Reading 25 12 **116 38**

MELVIN-LAMBERT, Nahum (F) 4 1
2020–21 Reading 0 0
2020–21 *St Patricks Ath* 4 1 **4 1**

MOORE, Liam (D) 295 7
H: 6 1 W: 13 08 b.Loughborough 31-1-93
Internationals: England U17, U20, U21.
2011–12 Leicester C 2 0
2011–12 *Bradford C* 17 0 **17 0**
2012–13 Leicester C 16 0
2012–13 *Brentford* 7 0
2013–14 Leicester C 30 1
2014–15 Leicester C 11 0
2014–15 *Brentford* 3 0 **10 0**
2015–16 Leicester C 0 0 **59 1**
2015–16 *Bristol C* 10 0 **10 0**
2016–17 Reading 40 1
2017–18 Reading 46 3
2018–19 Reading 38 1
2019–20 Reading 43 1
2020–21 Reading 32 0 **199 6**

MORRISON, Michael (D) 478 31
H: 6 0 W: 12 00 b.Bury St Edmunds 3-3-88
Internationals: England C.
From Cambridge U.
2008–09 Leicester C 35 3
2009–10 Leicester C 31 2
2010–11 Leicester C 11 0 **77 5**
2010–11 Sheffield W 12 0 **12 0**
2011–12 Charlton Ath 45 4
2012–13 Charlton Ath 44 1
2013–14 Charlton Ath 45 1
2014–15 Charlton Ath 2 0 **136 6**
2014–15 Birmingham C 21 0
2015–16 Birmingham C 46 3
2016–17 Birmingham C 31 3
2017–18 Birmingham C 33 1
2018–19 Birmingham C 43 7 **174 14**
2019–20 Reading 44 2
2020–21 Reading 35 4 **79 6**

OLISE, Michael (M) 67 7
b. 12-12-01
Internationals: France U18.
2018–19 Reading 4 0
2019–20 Reading 19 0
2020–21 Reading 44 7 **67 7**

ONEN, Jayden (M) 1 0
b. 17-2-01
From Arsenal, Crystal Palace, Brighton & HA, Brentford.
2020–21 Reading 1 0 **1 0**

OSORIO, Claudio (M) 0 0
b. 26-9-02
Internationals: England U16.
2020–21 Reading 0 0

PENDLEBURY, Oliver (M) 0 0
b. 19-1-02
2020–21 Reading 0 0

PUSCAS, George (F) 177 49
b.Marghita 8-4-96
Internationals: Romania U17, U19, U21, Full caps.
2012–13 Bihor Oradea 13 2 **13 2**
2013–14 Inter Milan 0 0
2014–15 Inter Milan 4 0
2015–16 Inter Milan 0 0
2015–16 *Bari* 17 5 **17 5**
2016–17 Inter Milan 0 0
2016–17 *Benevento* 21 7
2017–18 Inter Milan 0 0 **4 0**
2017–18 *Benevento* 11 1 **32 8**
2017–18 *Novara* 19 9 **19 9**
2018–19 Palermo 33 9 **33 9**
2019–20 Reading 38 12
2020–21 Reading 21 4 **59 16**

RAFAEL CABRAL, Barbosa (G) 217 0
b.Sorocaba 20-5-90
Internationals: Brazil U23, Full caps.
2010 Santos 32 0
2011 Santos 32 0
2012 Santos 25 0
2013 Santos 5 0 **94 0**
2013–14 Napoli 8 0
2014–15 Napoli 23 0
2015–16 Napoli 0 0
2016–17 Napoli 1 0
2017–18 Napoli 0 0 **32 0**
2018–19 Sampdoria 2 0
2019–20 Sampdoria 0 0 **2 0**
2019–20 Reading 44 0
2020–21 Reading 45 0 **89 0**

RICHARDS, Omar (D) 92 2
H: 6 1 W: 10 12 b. 15-2-98
Internationals: England U21.
2017–18 Reading 13 2
2018–19 Reading 10 0
2019–20 Reading 28 0
2020–21 Reading 41 0 **92 2**
Transferred to Bayern Munich July 2021.

RINOMHOTA, Andy (M) 105 3
b. 21-4-97
From AFC Portchester.
2017–18 Reading 0 0
2018–19 Reading 26 1
2019–20 Reading 37 1
2020–21 Reading 42 1 **105 3**

SACKEY, Lynford (M) 0 0
2020–21 Reading 0 0

SAMUELS, Imari (D) 0 0
2020–21 Reading 0 0

SAMUELS, Imari (D) 0 0
H: 6 2 b. 5-2-03
Internationals: England U16, U17.
2020–21 Reading 0 0

SEMEDO, Alfa (M) 128 10
b.Bissau 30-8-97
2016–17 Benfica 0 0
2016–17 *Vilafranquense* 29 4 **29 4**
2017–18 Morirense 28 2 **28 2**
2018–19 Benfica 5 0
2018–19 *Espanyol* 3 0 **3 0**
2019–20 Benfica 0 0
2019–20 *Nottingham F* 24 2 **24 2**
2020–21 Benfica 0 0 **5 0**
On loan from Benfica.
2020–21 Reading 39 2 **39 2**

SMITH, Sam (F) 80 12
H: 5 11 W: 11 07 b. 8-3-98
2017–18 Reading 8 1
2018–19 Reading 0 0
2018–19 *Oxford U* 15 0 **15 0**

2018–19 *Shrewsbury T* 3 0 3 0
2019–20 Reading 0 0
2019–20 *Cambridge U* 28 7 28 7
2020–21 Reading 0 0 8 1
2020–21 *Tranmere R* 5 0 5 0
2020–21 *Cheltenham T* 21 4 21 4

SOUTHWOOD, Luke (G) 16 0
b. 6-12-97
Internationals: England U19, U20.
2019–20 Reading 0 0
2019–20 *Hamilton A* 15 0 15 0
2020–21 Reading 1 0 1 0

SWIFT, John (M) 198 29
H: 6 0 W: 11 07 b.Portsmouth 23-6-95
Internationals: England U16, U17, U18, U19, U20, U21.
2013–14 Chelsea 1 0
2014–15 Chelsea 0 0
2014–15 *Rotherham U* 3 0 3 0
2014–15 *Swindon T* 18 2 18 2
2015–16 Chelsea 0 0 1 0
2015–16 *Brentford* 27 7 27 7
2016–17 Reading 36 8
2017–18 Reading 24 2
2018–19 Reading 34 3
2019–20 Reading 41 6
2020–21 Reading 14 1 149 20

TETEK, Dejan (M) 7 0
b.Oxford 24-9-02
2020–21 Reading 7 0 7 0

TOMAS ESTEVES, Lago (D) 31 1
b. 3-4-02
2018–19 Porto 0 0
2019–20 Porto 2 0
2020–21 Porto 0 0 2 0
On loan from Porto.
2020–21 Reading 29 1 29 1

WALKER, Sam (G) 280 0
H: 6 5 W: 14 00 b.Gravesend 2-10-91
2009–10 Chelsea 0 0
2010–11 Chelsea 0 0
2010–11 *Barnet* 7 0 7 0
2011–12 Chelsea 0 0
2011–12 *Northampton T* 21 0 21 0
2011–12 *Yeovil T* 20 0 20 0
2012–13 Chelsea 0 0
2012–13 *Bristol R* 11 0 11 0
2012–13 *Colchester U* 19 0
2013–14 Colchester U 46 0
2014–15 Colchester U 45 0
2015–16 Colchester U 0 0
2016–17 Colchester U 46 0
2017–18 Colchester U 44 0 200 0
2018–19 Reading 7 0
2019–20 Reading 0 0
2020–21 Reading 0 0 7 0
2020–21 *Blackpool* 2 0 2 0
2020–21 *AFC Wimbledon* 12 0 12 0

WATSON, Tennai (D) 31 0
b. 4-3-97
2015–16 Reading 0 0
2016–17 Reading 3 0
2017–18 Reading 0 0
2018–19 Reading 0 0
2018–19 *AFC Wimbledon* 24 0 24 0
2019–20 Reading 0 0
2019–20 *Coventry C* 3 0 3 0
2020–21 Reading 1 0 4 0

YIADOM, Andy (M) 240 13
H: 5 11 W: 11 11 b.Camden 9-12-91
Internationals: England C. Ghana Full caps.
From Hayes & Yeading U, Braintree T.
2011–12 Barnet 7 1
2012–13 Barnet 39 3
2015–16 Barnet 40 6 86 10
2016–17 Barnsley 32 0
2017–18 Barnsley 32 0 64 0
2018–19 Reading 45 1
2019–20 Reading 24 1
2020–21 Reading 21 1 90 3

Scholars
Abdel Salam, Hamid Awad; Abrefa, Kelvin Opoku; Addo-Antoine, Jordan Kwesi; Anderson, Alfie Donal; Ashcroft, Tyrell Dean; Clarke, Jahmari Oshown; Collins, Harvey Robert; Ehibhatiomhan, Kelvin Osemudiamen; Hamilton Olise, Jordan Jewel Nkoenye; Holzman, Louie James; Leavy, Kian; Maudner, Harvey James Troy; Nyarko, David; Paul, Samuel Benjamin; Purcell, Benjamin David; Rowley, Matthew Christopher; Sackey, Lynford; Senga-Ngoyi, Jack Michel Dasquela; Stickland, Michael George; Talent Aryeetey, Malachi Stephen; Turkson, Yaw.

ROCHDALE (70)

BAAH, Kwadwo (F) 37 3
b. 27-1-03
2019–20 Rochdale 7 0
2020–21 Rochdale 30 3 37 3

BEESLEY, Jake (F) 41 8
H: 6 1 W: 10 08 b.Sheffield 2-12-96
2013–14 Chesterfield 0 0
2014–15 Chesterfield 0 0
2015–16 Chesterfield 0 0
2016–17 Chesterfield 7 0 7 0
From Chesterfield.
2019–20 Salford C 7 2 7 2
2020–21 Solihull Moors 0 0
2020–21 Rochdale 27 6 27 6

BRADLEY, Lewis (M) 3 0
b. 29-5-01
2018–19 Rochdale 1 0
2019–20 Rochdale 2 0
2020–21 Rochdale 0 0 3 0

BRIERLEY, Ethan (M) 5 0
2019–20 Rochdale 0 0
2020–21 Rochdale 5 0 5 0

CHALTON, Ben (G) 0 0
2020–21 Rochdale 0 0

DONE, Matt (M) 487 45
H: 5 10 W: 10 04 b.Oswestry 22-6-88
2005–06 Wrexham 6 0
2006–07 Wrexham 34 1
2007–08 Wrexham 26 0 66 1
2008–09 Hereford U 36 0
2009–10 Hereford U 20 0 56 0
2010–11 Rochdale 33 5
2011–12 Barnsley 31 4
2012–13 Barnsley 13 0 44 4
2012–13 *Hibernian* 7 0 7 0
2013–14 Rochdale 38 0
2014–15 Rochdale 23 10
2014–15 Sheffield U 15 7
2015–16 Sheffield U 31 4
2016–17 Sheffield U 31 3 77 14
2017–18 Rochdale 46 6
2018–19 Rochdale 36 2
2019–20 Rochdale 24 0
2020–21 Rochdale 37 3 237 26

DOOLEY, Stephen (M) 157 16
H: 5 11 W: 12 08 b.Portstewart 19-10-91
Internationals: Northern Ireland U17, U19.
2014 Derry C 14 1
2015 Derry C 15 2 29 3
2016 Cork C 26 5
2017 Cork C 27 4 53 9
2018–19 Rochdale 22 0
2019–20 Rochdale 22 3
2020–21 Rochdale 31 1 75 4

DUNNE, Joe (D) 0 0
2018–19 Rochdale 0 0
2019–20 Rochdale 0 0
2020–21 Rochdale 0 0

GRANT, Conor (M) 20 1
b. 23-7-01
Internationals: Republic of Ireland U17, U19.
From Shamrock R.
2019–20 Sheffield W 0 0
2020–21 Sheffield W 0 0
2020–21 Rochdale 20 1 20 1

HOPPER, Harrison (M) 2 0
b. 24-12-00
2018–19 Rochdale 0 0
2019–20 Rochdale 1 0
2020–21 Rochdale 1 0 2 0

HUMPHRYS, Stephen (F) 108 29
b.Oldham 15-9-97
2016–17 Fulham 2 0
2016–17 *Shrewsbury T* 14 2 14 2
2017–18 Fulham 0 0
2017–18 *Rochdale* 16 2
2018–19 Fulham 0 0 2 0
2018–19 *Scunthorpe U* 16 4 16 4
2018–19 Southend U 10 5
2019–20 Southend U 21 5
2020–21 Southend U 0 0 31 10
2020–21 Rochdale 29 11 45 13

KEOHANE, Jimmy (M) 235 26
H: 5 11 W: 11 05 b.Wexford 22-1-91
Internationals: Republic of Ireland U19.
2009 Wexford Youths 16 2
2010 Wexford Youths 18 4 34 6
2010–11 Bristol C 0 0
2011–12 Bristol C 0 0
2011–12 Exeter C 4 0
2012–13 Exeter C 33 3
2013–14 Exeter C 20 3
2014–15 Exeter C 23 3 80 9
From Woking.
2016 Sligo R 31 1 31 1
2017 Cork C 10 0 10 0
2018–19 Rochdale 8 0
2019–20 Rochdale 28 0
2020–21 Rochdale 44 10 80 10

LUND, Matthew (M) 263 46
H: 6 0 W: 11 13 b.Manchester 21-11-90
Internationals: Northern Ireland U21, Full caps.
From Crewe Alex.
2009–10 Stoke C 0 0
2010–11 Stoke C 0 0
2010–11 *Hereford U* 2 0 2 0
2011–12 Stoke C 0 0
2011–12 *Oldham Ath* 3 0 3 0
2011–12 *Bristol R* 13 2
2012–13 Stoke C 0 0
2012–13 *Bristol R* 18 2 31 4
2012–13 Southend U 12 1 12 1
2013–14 Rochdale 40 8
2014–15 Rochdale 14 2
2015–16 Rochdale 29 1
2016–17 Rochdale 29 9
2017–18 Burton Alb 12 1 12 1
2017–18 *Bradford C* 10 2 10 2
2018–19 Scunthorpe U 22 2
2019–20 Scunthorpe U 22 4 44 6
2019–20 Rochdale 5 1
2020–21 Rochdale 32 11 149 32

LYNCH, Jay (G) 27 0
H: 6 2 W: 13 04 b.Salford 31-3-93
2012–13 Bolton W 0 0
2013–14 Bolton W 0 0
2014–15 Accrington S 2 0 2 0
From Salford C, AFC Fylde.
2019–20 Rochdale 8 0
2020–21 Rochdale 17 0 25 0

McLAUGHLIN, Ryan (D) 121 3
H: 5 9 W: 10 12 b.Belfast 30-9-94
Internationals: Northern Ireland U16, U17, U19, U21, Full caps.
From Glenavon.
2011–12 Liverpool 0 0
2012–13 Liverpool 0 0
2013–14 Liverpool 0 0
2013–14 *Barnsley* 9 0 9 0
2014–15 Liverpool 0 0
2015–16 Liverpool 0 0
2015–16 *Aberdeen* 4 0 4 0
2016–17 Oldham Ath 36 2
2017–18 Oldham Ath 16 1 52 3
2018–19 Blackpool 6 0 6 0
2018–19 Rochdale 13 0
2019–20 Rochdale 3 0
2020–21 Rochdale 34 0 50 0

McNULTY, Jim (D) 384 7
H: 6 1 W: 12 00 b.Runcorn 13-2-85
Internationals: Scotland U17, U19.
From Everton, Wrexham.
2006–07 Macclesfield T 15 0
2007–08 Macclesfield T 19 1 34 1
2007–08 Stockport Co 11 0
2008–09 Stockport Co 26 1 37 1
2008–09 Brighton & HA 5 1
2009–10 Brighton & HA 8 0
2009–10 *Scunthorpe U* 3 0
2010–11 Brighton & HA 0 0 13 1
2010–11 *Scunthorpe U* 6 0 9 0
2011–12 Barnsley 44 2
2012–13 Barnsley 12 0
2013–14 Barnsley 0 0 56 2
2013–14 *Tranmere R* 12 0 12 0
2013–14 Bury 21 0
2014–15 Bury 25 0 46 0
2015–16 Rochdale 46 0
2016–17 Rochdale 35 0
2017–18 Rochdale 40 1
2018–19 Rochdale 25 1
2019–20 Rochdale 14 0
2020–21 Rochdale 17 0 177 2

McSHANE, Paul (D) 369 14
H: 6 0 W: 11 05 b.Wicklow 6-1-86
Internationals: Republic of Ireland U21, Full caps.
2002–03 Manchester U 0 0
2003–04 Manchester U 0 0
2004–05 Manchester U 0 0
2004–05 *Walsall* 4 1 4 1
2005–06 Manchester U 0 0
2005–06 *Brighton & HA* 38 3 38 3
2006–07 WBA 32 2 32 2
2007–08 Sunderland 21 0
2008–09 Sunderland 3 0

2008–09 *Hull C* 17 1
2009–10 Sunderland 0 0 **24 0**
2009–10 Hull C 27 0
2010–11 Hull C 19 0
2010–11 *Barnsley* 10 1 **10 1**
2011–12 Hull C 1 0
2011–12 *Crystal Palace* 11 0 **11 0**
2012–13 Hull C 25 2
2013–14 Hull C 10 0
2014–15 Hull C 20 1 **119 4**
2015–16 Reading 35 0
2016–17 Reading 30 3
2017–18 Reading 26 0
2018–19 Reading 5 0 **96 3**
2019–20 Rochdale 16 0
2020–21 Rochdale 19 0 **35 0**

MIALKOWSKI, Kacper (D) 0 0
2020–21 Rochdale 0 0

MORLEY, Aaron (M) 72 5
b. 27-2-00
2016–17 Rochdale 2 0
2017–18 Rochdale 0 0
2018–19 Rochdale 3 0
2019–20 Rochdale 23 3
2020–21 Rochdale 44 2 **72 5**

NEWBY, Alex (M) 38 6
b.Barrow-in-Furness 21-11-95
From Barrow, Clitheroe, Chorley.
2020–21 Rochdale 38 6 **38 6**

O'CONNELL, Eoghan (D) 146 5
H: 6 1 W: 12 08 b.Cork 13-8-95
Internationals: Republic of Ireland U19, U21.
2013–14 Celtic 1 0
2014–15 Celtic 3 0
2015–16 Celtic 1 0
2015–16 *Oldham Ath* 2 0 **2 0**
2016 *Cork C* 7 1 **7 1**
2016–17 Celtic 2 0 **7 0**
2016–17 *Walsall* 17 1 **17 1**
2017–18 Bury 12 0
2018–19 Bury 31 2 **43 2**
2019–20 Rochdale 31 0
2020–21 Rochdale 39 1 **70 1**

ODOH, Abraham (M) 2 0
b. 25-1-00
From Tooting & Mitcham U.
2019–20 Charlton Ath 0 0
2020–21 Rochdale 2 0 **2 0**

RATHBONE, Oliver (M) 152 12
H: 5 7 W: 10 06 b.Blackburn 10-10-96
From Manchester U.
2016–17 Rochdale 27 2
2017–18 Rochdale 33 1
2018–19 Rochdale 28 4
2019–20 Rochdale 24 2
2020–21 Rochdale 40 3 **152 12**

RYAN, James (M) 419 38
H: 5 8 W: 11 08 b.Maghull 6-9-88
Internationals: Republic of Ireland U21.
2006–07 Liverpool 0 0
2007–08 Liverpool 0 0
2007–08 *Shrewsbury T* 4 0 **4 0**
2008–09 Accrington S 44 10
2009–10 Accrington S 39 3
2010–11 Accrington S 46 9 **129 22**
2011–12 Scunthorpe U 24 2
2012–13 Scunthorpe U 45 2 **69 4**
2013–14 Chesterfield 39 2
2014–15 Chesterfield 44 4 **83 6**
2015–16 Fleetwood T 43 2
2016–17 Fleetwood T 16 0 **59 2**
2017–18 Blackpool 36 3
2018–19 Blackpool 1 0 **37 3**
2019–20 Rochdale 24 1
2020–21 Rochdale 14 0 **38 1**

SHAUGHNESSY, Conor (M) 60 1
H: 6 3 W: 11 09 b. 30-6-96
Internationals: Republic of Ireland U16, U17, U18, U21, Full caps.
From Reading.
2017–18 Leeds U 9 0
2018–19 Leeds U 0 0
2018–19 *Hearts* 10 0 **10 0**
2019–20 Leeds U 0 0
2019–20 *Mansfield T* 15 0 **15 0**
2019–20 *Burton Alb* 8 0 **8 0**
2020–21 Leeds U 0 0 **9 0**
2020–21 Rochdale 18 1 **18 1**

WADE, Bradley (G) 0 0
b.Gloucester 3-7-00
2018–19 Rochdale 0 0
2019–20 Rochdale 0 0
2020–21 Rochdale 0 0

Scholars
Caldwell, Mikey Lee Ryan; Chalton, Benjamin Barry; Chorlton, Louie Joseph; Clarkson, Louie James; Cullen, Adam James; D'Souza, Louie Isaac; Duarte Gouveia, Joao Vasco; Kelly, Bradley James; Kershaw, Benjamin Joshua; Kinsella, Morgan James; Lee, Harry Mackenzie; Mialkowski, Kacper; Nock, Luke John; Patrick, Oliver Edward; Scanlon, Jordan Michael; Thomas, Peter Anthony; Wright, Joseph Philip.

ROTHERHAM U (71)

BARLASER, Daniel (M) 103 6
H: 6 0 W: 9 11 b.Gateshead 18-1-97
Internationals: Turkey U16, U17. England U18.
2015–16 Newcastle U 0 0
2016–17 Newcastle U 0 0
2017–18 Newcastle U 0 0
2017–18 *Crewe Alex* 4 0 **4 0**
2018–19 Newcastle U 0 0
2018–19 *Accrington S* 39 1 **39 1**
2019–20 Newcastle U 0 0
2019–20 *Rotherham U* 27 2
2020–21 Rotherham U 33 3 **60 5**

CLARKE, Trevor (D) 97 5
b. 26-3-98
Internationals: Republic of Ireland U17, U19, U21.
2016 Shamrock R 26 1
2017 Shamrock R 27 3
2018 Shamrock R 6 0
2019 Shamrock R 21 1 **80 5**
2019–20 Rotherham U 8 0
2020–21 Rotherham U 9 0 **17 0**

CROOKS, Matt (M) 206 36
H: 6 0 W: 11 05 b.Leeds 20-1-94
2011–12 Huddersfield T 0 0
2012–13 Huddersfield T 0 0
2013–14 Huddersfield T 0 0
2014–15 Huddersfield T 1 0 **1 0**
2014–15 *Hartlepool U* 3 0 **3 0**
2014–15 Accrington S 16 0
2015–16 Accrington S 32 6 **48 6**
2016–17 Rangers 2 0 **2 0**
2016–17 *Scunthorpe U* 12 3 **12 3**
2017–18 Northampton T 30 4
2018–19 Northampton T 21 5 **51 9**
2018–19 Rotherham U 16 3
2019–20 Rotherham U 33 9
2020–21 Rotherham U 40 6 **89 18**

GRATTON, Jacob (F) 0 0
2019–20 Rotherham U 0 0
2020–21 Rotherham U 0 0

GREAVES, Jerome (F) 0 0
b. 22-3-03
2020–21 Rotherham U 0 0

HARDING, Wes (D) 97 0
H: 5 11 W: 12 06 b.Leicester 20-10-96
2017–18 Birmingham C 9 0
2018–19 Birmingham C 27 0
2019–20 Birmingham C 15 0 **51 0**
2020–21 Rotherham U 46 0 **46 0**

HULL, Jake (D) 0 0
2020–21 Rotherham U 0 0

IHIEKWE, Michael (D) 192 9
H: 6 1 W: 12 02 b.Liverpool 20-11-92
Internationals: England C.
2011–12 Wolverhampton W 0 0
2012–13 Wolverhampton W 0 0
2013–14 Wolverhampton W 0 0
2013–14 *Cheltenham T* 13 0 **13 0**
2014–15 Tranmere R 38 1 **38 1**
2017–18 Rotherham U 31 1
2018–19 Rotherham U 15 2
2018–19 *Accrington S* 20 1 **20 1**
2019–20 Rotherham U 33 2
2020–21 Rotherham U 42 2 **121 7**

JOHANSSON, Viktor (G) 21 0
b. 14-9-98
From Hammarby.
2017–18 Aston Villa 0 0
2018–19 Leicester C 0 0
2019–20 Leicester C 0 0
2020–21 Rotherham U 21 0 **21 0**

JONES, Billy (M) 484 25
H: 5 11 W: 13 00 b.Shrewsbury 24-3-87
Internationals: England U16, U17, U19, U20.
2003–04 Crewe Alex 27 1
2004–05 Crewe Alex 20 0
2005–06 Crewe Alex 44 6
2006–07 Crewe Alex 41 1
2007–08 Preston NE 29 0
2008–09 Preston NE 44 3
2009–10 Preston NE 44 4
2010–11 Preston NE 43 6 **160 13**
2011–12 WBA 18 0
2012–13 WBA 27 1
2013–14 WBA 21 0 **66 1**
2014–15 Sunderland 14 0
2015–16 Sunderland 24 1
2016–17 Sunderland 27 1
2017–18 Sunderland 22 1 **87 3**
2018–19 Rotherham U 21 0
2019–20 Rotherham U 10 0
2020–21 Rotherham U 5 0 **36 0**
2020–21 *Crewe Alex* 3 0 **135 8**

KAYODE, Joshua (F) 39 11
b. 14-12-00
2017–18 Rotherham U 0 0
2018–19 Rotherham U 0 0
2019–20 Rotherham U 0 0
2019–20 *Carlisle U* 5 3
2020–21 Rotherham U 0 0
2020–21 *Carlisle U* 34 8 **39 11**

LADAPO, Freddie (F) 167 47
H: 6 0 W: 12 06 b.Romford 1-2-93
2011–12 Colchester U 0 0
2012–13 Colchester U 4 0
2013–14 Colchester U 2 0 **6 0**
From Margate.
2015–16 Crystal Palace 0 0
2016–17 Crystal Palace 0 0
2016–17 *Oldham Ath* 17 2 **17 2**
2016–17 *Shrewsbury T* 15 4 **15 4**
2017–18 Crystal Palace 1 0 **1 0**
2017–18 Southend U 10 0 **10 0**
2018–19 Plymouth Arg 45 18 **45 18**
2019–20 Rotherham U 31 14
2020–21 Rotherham U 42 9 **73 23**

LINDSAY, Jamie (M) 172 12
b.Motherwell 11-9-95
Internationals: Scotland U16, U17, U19.
2015–16 Celtic 0 0
2015–16 *Dumbarton* 23 0 **23 0**
2016–17 Celtic 0 0
2016–17 *Greenock Morton* 31 0 **31 0**
2017–18 Celtic 0 0
2017–18 *Ross County* 26 2
2018–19 Ross County 35 6 **61 8**
2019–20 Rotherham U 22 1
2020–21 Rotherham U 35 3 **57 4**

MACDONALD, Angus (D) 127 2
H: 6 0 W: 11 00 b.Winchester 15-10-92
Internationals: England U16, U19, C.
2011–12 Reading 0 0
2011–12 *Torquay U* 2 0
2012–13 Reading 0 0
2012–13 *AFC Wimbledon* 4 0 **4 0**
2012–13 *Torquay U* 14 0 **16 0**
From Salisbury C, Torquay U.
2016–17 Barnsley 39 1
2017–18 Barnsley 11 0 **50 1**
2017–18 Hull C 12 0
2018–19 Hull C 1 0
2019–20 Hull C 5 0 **18 0**
2020–21 Rotherham U 39 1 **39 1**

MACDONALD, Shaun (M) 240 11
H: 6 1 W: 11 04 b.Swansea 17-6-88
Internationals: Wales U19, U21, Full caps.
2005–06 Swansea C 7 0
2006–07 Swansea C 8 0
2007–08 Swansea C 1 0
2008–09 Swansea C 5 0
2008–09 *Yeovil T* 4 2
2009–10 Swansea C 3 0
2009–10 *Yeovil T* 31 3
2010–11 Swansea C 0 0
2010–11 *Yeovil T* 26 4 **61 9**
2011–12 Swansea C 0 0 **24 0**
2011–12 Bournemouth 25 1
2012–13 Bournemouth 28 0
2013–14 Bournemouth 23 0
2014–15 Bournemouth 5 0
2015–16 Bournemouth 3 0 **84 1**
2016–17 Wigan Ath 39 1
2017–18 Wigan Ath 0 0
2018–19 Wigan Ath 0 0 **39 1**
2019–20 Rotherham U 13 0
2020–21 Rotherham U 19 0 **32 0**

MATTOCK, Joe (D) 375 8
H: 5 11 W: 12 05 b.Leicester 15-5-90
Internationals: England U17, U19, U21.
2006–07 Leicester C 4 0
2007–08 Leicester C 31 0
2008–09 Leicester C 31 1
2009–10 Leicester C 0 0 **66 1**
2009–10 WBA 29 0

2010–11 WBA 0 0
2010–11 *Sheffield U* 13 0 **13 0**
2011–12 WBA 0 0 **29 0**
2011–12 *Portsmouth* 7 0 **7 0**
2011–12 *Brighton & HA* 15 1 **15 1**
2012–13 Sheffield W 7 0
2013–14 Sheffield W 23 2
2014–15 Sheffield W 27 0 **57 2**
2015–16 Rotherham U 35 1
2016–17 Rotherham U 36 0
2017–18 Rotherham U 35 1
2018–19 Rotherham U 44 1
2019–20 Rotherham U 24 1
2020–21 Rotherham U 14 0 **188 4**

MILLER, Mickel (F) 79 8
b.Croydon 2-12-95
From Carshalton Ath.
2017–18 Hamilton A 6 0
2018–19 Hamilton A 31 5
2019–20 Hamilton A 21 3 **58 8**
2020–21 Rotherham U 9 0 **9 0**
2020–21 *Northampton T* 12 0 **12 0**

OGBENE, Chiedozie (M) 97 12
H: 5 9 W: 11 11 b. 1-5-97
2015 Cork C 1 0
2016 Cork C 8 3 **9 3**
2017 Limerick 32 8 **32 8**
2017–18 Brentford 2 0
2018–19 Brentford 4 0 **6 0**
2018–19 *Exeter C* 14 0 **14 0**
2019–20 Rotherham U 25 1
2020–21 Rotherham U 11 0 **36 1**

OLOSUNDE, Matthew (D) 64 0
b. 7-3-98
Internationals: USA U17, U20, U23, Full caps.
From Manchester U.
2019–20 Rotherham U 32 0
2020–21 Rotherham U 32 0 **64 0**

PROCTOR, Jamie (F) 289 44
H: 6 2 W: 12 03 b.Preston 25-3-92
2009–10 Preston NE 1 0
2010–11 Preston NE 5 1
2010–11 *Stockport Co* 7 0 **7 0**
2011–12 Preston NE 31 3 **37 4**
2012–13 Swansea C 0 0
2012–13 *Shrewsbury T* 2 0 **2 0**
2012–13 Crawley T 18 7
2013–14 Crawley T 44 6 **62 13**
2014–15 Fleetwood T 41 8
2015–16 Fleetwood T 23 4 **64 12**
2015–16 Bradford C 18 5 **18 5**
2016–17 Bolton W 21 0 **21 0**
2016–17 *Carlisle U* 17 4 **17 4**
2017–18 Rotherham U 4 0
2018–19 Rotherham U 16 2
2019–20 Rotherham U 3 0
2019–20 *Scunthorpe U* 13 1 **13 1**
2020–21 Rotherham U 0 0 **23 2**
2020–21 *Newport Co* 10 1 **10 1**
2020–21 *Wigan Ath* 15 2 **15 2**

ROBERTSON, Clark (D) 239 9
H: 6 2 W: 12 00 b.Aberdeen 5-9-93
Internationals: Scotland U19, U21.
2009–10 Aberdeen 3 0
2010–11 Aberdeen 13 0
2011–12 Aberdeen 9 0
2012–13 Aberdeen 23 0
2013–14 Aberdeen 8 0
2014–15 Aberdeen 1 0 **57 0**
2015–16 Blackpool 38 1
2016–17 Blackpool 44 0
2017–18 Blackpool 39 3 **121 4**
2018–19 Rotherham U 28 3
2019–20 Rotherham U 17 2
2020–21 Rotherham U 16 0 **61 5**

SADLIER, Kieran (F) 170 49
H: 5 10 W: 10 06 b. 14-9-94
Internationals: Republic of Ireland U17, U19, U21.
2013–14 West Ham U 0 0
2014–15 St Mirren 11 1 **11 1**
2015–16 Peterborough U 0 0
2015–16 *FC Halifax T* 0 0
2016 Sligo R 29 8
2017 Sligo R 20 7 **49 15**
2017 Cork C 13 2
2018 Cork C 35 16 **48 18**
2018–19 Doncaster R 14 3
2019–20 Doncaster R 33 11 **47 14**
2020–21 Rotherham U 15 1 **15 1**

SMITH, Michael (F) 361 83
H: 6 4 W: 11 02 b.Wallsend 17-10-91
2009–10 Darlington 7 1
2010–11 Darlington 29 5 **36 6**
2011–12 Charlton Ath 0 0
2011–12 *Accrington S* 6 3 **6 3**
2012–13 Charlton Ath 0 0
2012–13 *Colchester U* 8 1 **8 1**
2013–14 Charlton Ath 0 0
2013–14 *AFC Wimbledon* 23 9 **23 9**
2013–14 Swindon T 20 8
2014–15 Swindon T 40 13
2015–16 Swindon T 5 0 **65 21**
2015–16 *Barnsley* 13 0 **13 0**
2015–16 *Portsmouth* 16 4
2016–17 Portsmouth 18 3 **34 7**
2016–17 *Northampton T* 14 2
2017–18 Northampton T 0 0 **14 2**
2017–18 Bury 19 1 **19 1**
2017–18 Rotherham U 20 6
2018–19 Rotherham U 45 8
2019–20 Rotherham U 34 9
2020–21 Rotherham U 44 10 **143 33**

SOUTHERN-COOPER, Jake (M) 0 0
b. 1-1-00
2018–19 Rotherham U 0 0
2019–20 Rotherham U 0 0
2020–21 Rotherham U 0 0

TILT, Curtis (D) 136 8
H: 6 4 W: 11 11 b. 4-8-91
From Halesowen T, Hednesford T, AFC Telford U, Wrexham.
2017–18 Blackpool 42 1
2018–19 Blackpool 37 4
2019–20 Blackpool 20 0 **99 5**
2019–20 Rotherham U 1 0
2020–21 Rotherham U 0 0 **1 0**
2020–21 *Wigan Ath* 36 3 **36 3**

VASSELL, Kyle (F) 199 36
H: 6 0 W: 12 04 b.Milton Keynes 7-2-93
Internationals: Northern Ireland Full caps.
2013–14 Peterborough U 6 0
2014–15 Peterborough U 17 5
2014–15 *Oxford U* 6 1 **6 1**
2015–16 Peterborough U 5 0 **28 5**
2015–16 *Dagenham & R* 8 0 **8 0**
2015–16 *Shrewsbury T* 13 0 **13 0**
2016–17 Blackpool 34 11
2017–18 Blackpool 29 11 **63 22**
2018–19 Rotherham U 23 0
2019–20 Rotherham U 20 4
2020–21 Rotherham U 12 0 **55 4**
2020–21 *Fleetwood T* 26 4 **26 4**

VICKERS, Josh (G) 93 0
H: 6 0 W: 11 05 b.Billericay 1-12-95
From Arsenal.
2015–16 Swansea C 0 0
2016–17 Swansea C 0 0
2016–17 *Barnet* 23 0 **23 0**
2017–18 Lincoln C 17 0
2018–19 Lincoln C 18 0
2019–20 Lincoln C 35 0 **70 0**
2020–21 Rotherham U 0 0

WILES, Ben (M) 97 5
b. 17-4-99
2017–18 Rotherham U 0 0
2018–19 Rotherham U 20 0
2019–20 Rotherham U 33 3
2020–21 Rotherham U 44 2 **97 5**

WOOD, Richard (D) 493 32
H: 6 3 W: 12 13 b.Ossett 5-7-85
2002–03 Sheffield W 3 1
2003–04 Sheffield W 12 0
2004–05 Sheffield W 34 1
2005–06 Sheffield W 30 1
2006–07 Sheffield W 12 0
2007–08 Sheffield W 27 2
2008–09 Sheffield W 42 0
2009–10 Sheffield W 11 2 **171 7**
2009–10 Coventry C 24 3
2010–11 Coventry C 40 1
2011–12 Coventry C 17 1
2012–13 Coventry C 36 3 **117 8**
2013–14 Charlton Ath 21 0 **21 0**
2014–15 Rotherham U 6 0
2014–15 *Crawley T* 10 3 **10 3**
2015–16 Rotherham U 13 0
2015–16 *Fleetwood T* 6 0 **6 0**
2015–16 *Chesterfield* 5 0 **5 0**
2016–17 Rotherham U 29 3
2017–18 Rotherham U 36 4
2018–19 Rotherham U 26 2
2019–20 Rotherham U 23 3
2020–21 Rotherham U 30 2 **163 14**

Scholars
Booth, Mason Jay; Burnett, Alfie George; Carroll, Billy Fredrick; Durose, Curtis Reece; Ellis, Elliot David Peter; Exton, Nathan John; Greenhouse, Samuel Lewis; Hanley, Samuel Stephen; Kenny, Ethan Morgan; Makwedza, Bolton Bernard; McGuckin, Ciaran Reece; Millen, Josh; Salah, Haroon; Scott, George Henry Christopher; Smith, Charles Oliver; Warne, MacKenzie Cliff; Watson, Nathan Christopher.

SALFORD C (72)

ANDO, Cerny (D) 0 0
b. 24-11-03
2020–21 Salford C 0 0

ANDRADE, Bruno (M) 140 14
H: 5 9 W: 11 09 b.Aveiro 2-10-93
2010–11 QPR 1 0
2011–12 QPR 1 0
2011–12 *Aldershot T* 1 0 **1 0**
2012–13 QPR 0 0
2012–13 *Wycombe W* 23 2 **23 2**
2013–14 QPR 0 0
2013–14 *Stevenage* 13 0
2014–15 QPR 0 0 **2 0**
2014–15 *Stevenage* 16 1 **29 1**
From Woking, Boreham Wood.
2018–19 Lincoln C 42 10
2019–20 Lincoln C 17 1 **59 11**
2019–20 Salford C 7 0
2020–21 Salford C 19 0 **26 0**

ARMSTRONG, Luke (F) 47 4
b. 2-7-96
2015–16 Cowdenbeath 6 0 **6 0**
From Blyth Spartans
2017–18 Middlesbrough 0 0
2018–19 Middlesbrough 0 0
2018–19 *Accrington S* 16 3 **16 3**
2019–20 Salford C 21 1
2020–21 Salford C 4 0 **25 1**

BERKOE, Kevin (D) 0 0
b. 5-7-01
From Wolverhampton W.
2019–20 Oxford U 0 0
2020–21 Salford C 0 0

BOYD, George (M) 500 86
H: 5 10 W: 11 07 b.Chatham 2-10-85
Internationals: Scotland B, Full caps.
From Stevenage Bor.
2006–07 Peterborough U 20 6
2007–08 Peterborough U 46 12
2008–09 Peterborough U 46 9
2009–10 Peterborough U 32 9
2009–10 *Nottingham F* 6 1 **6 1**
2010–11 Peterborough U 43 15
2011–12 Peterborough U 45 7
2012–13 Peterborough U 31 6
2012–13 *Hull C* 13 4
2013–14 Hull C 29 2
2014–15 Hull C 1 0 **43 6**
2014–15 Burnley 35 5
2015–16 Burnley 44 5
2016–17 Burnley 36 2 **115 12**
2017–18 Sheffield W 20 2
2018–19 Sheffield W 20 1 **40 3**
2019–20 Peterborough U 22 0
2020–21 Peterborough U 0 0 **285 64**
2020–21 Salford C 11 0 **11 0**

BURGESS, Luke (M) 17 3
b. 3-3-99
2017–18 Wigan Ath 0 0
2018–19 Wigan Ath 0 0
2019–20 Wigan Ath 0 0
2019–20 Salford C 0 0
2020–21 Salford C 17 3 **17 3**

CAMPBELL, Hayden (M) 0 0
2020–21 Salford C 0 0

CLARKE, Tom (D) 355 17
H: 6 0 W: 11 02 b.Sowerby Bridge 21-12-87
Internationals: England U18, U19.
2004–05 Huddersfield T 12 0
2005–06 Huddersfield T 17 1
2006–07 Huddersfield T 9 0
2007–08 Huddersfield T 3 0
2008–09 Huddersfield T 15 1
2008–09 *Bradford C* 6 0 **6 0**
2009–10 Huddersfield T 21 0
2010–11 Huddersfield T 5 1
2011–12 Huddersfield T 14 0
2011–12 *Leyton Orient* 10 0 **10 0**
2012–13 Huddersfield T 0 0 **96 3**
2013–14 Preston NE 42 4
2014–15 Preston NE 43 1
2015–16 Preston NE 35 0
2016–17 Preston NE 42 4
2017–18 Preston NE 18 2
2018–19 Preston NE 21 1
2019–20 Preston NE 10 0 **211 12**
2020–21 Salford C 32 2 **32 2**

DENNY, Alex (M) 15 0
H: 6 1 W: 12 11 b.Chester 12-4-00
Internationals: England U17, U18.
2017–18 Everton 0 0
2018–19 Everton 0 0
2019–20 Everton 0 0
2020–21 Salford C 9 0 **9 0**
2020–21 *Morecambe* 6 0 **6 0**

DIESERUVWE, Emmanuel (F) 77 4
H: 6 5 W: 11 05 b.Leeds 5-1-94
2013–14 Sheffield W 0 0
2013–14 *Fleetwood T* 4 0 **4 0**
2014–15 Sheffield W 0 0
2014–15 *Chesterfield* 9 0
2015–16 Chesterfield 16 0 **25 0**
2015–16 *Mansfield T* 10 1 **10 1**
From Kidderminster H, Salford C.
2019–20 Salford C 20 3
2019–20 *Oldham Ath* 4 0 **4 0**
2020–21 Salford C 14 0 **34 3**

DITCHFIELD, Harry (D) 0 0
2020–21 Salford C 0 0

DOYLE, Alex (M) 1 0
2019–20 Salford C 1 0
2020–21 Salford C 0 0 **1 0**

EASTHAM, Ashley (D) 332 14
H: 6 3 W: 12 06 b.Preston 22-3-91
2009–10 Blackpool 1 0
2009–10 *Cheltenham T* 20 0
2010–11 Blackpool 0 0
2010–11 *Cheltenham T* 9 0 **29 0**
2010–11 *Carlisle U* 0 0
2011–12 Blackpool 0 0
2011–12 *Bury* 25 2
2012–13 Blackpool 0 0 **1 0**
2012–13 *Fleetwood T* 1 0
2012–13 *Notts Co* 4 0 **4 0**
2012–13 *Bury* 19 0 **44 2**
2013–14 Rochdale 15 0
2014–15 Rochdale 41 2
2015–16 Rochdale 20 2 **76 4**
2016–17 Fleetwood T 35 2
2017–18 Fleetwood T 45 3
2018–19 Fleetwood T 45 2
2019–20 Fleetwood T 9 0 **135 7**
2019–20 Salford C 4 0
2020–21 Salford C 39 1 **43 1**

ELLIOTT, Tom (F) 267 39
H: 6 3 W: 12 00 b.Hunslet 9-11-90
Internationals: England U16, U18.
2006–07 Leeds U 3 0
2007–08 Leeds U 0 0
2008–09 Leeds U 0 0
2008–09 *Macclesfield T* 6 0 **6 0**
2009–10 Leeds U 0 0
2009–10 *Bury* 16 1 **16 1**
2010–11 Leeds U 0 0 **3 0**
2010–11 *Rotherham U* 6 0 **6 0**
2011–12 Hamilton A 7 0 **7 0**
2011–12 Stockport Co 42 7 **42 7**
2014–15 Cambridge U 30 8 **30 8**
2015–16 AFC Wimbledon 39 6
2016–17 AFC Wimbledon 39 9 **78 15**
2017–18 Millwall 24 4
2018–19 Millwall 33 3
2019–20 Millwall 0 0 **57 7**
2019–20 Salford C 8 1
2020–21 Salford C 14 0 **22 1**

EVANS, William (G) 0 0
2019–20 Salford C 0 0
2020–21 Salford C 0 0

FIELDING, Sam (D) 0 0
b.Burton upon Trent 2-11-99
From York C.
2018–19 Barnsley 0 0
2019–20 Barnsley 0 0
2020–21 Salford C 0 0

GIBSON, Darron (M) 181 7
H: 6 0 W: 12 04 b.Derry 25-10-87
Internationals: Republic of Ireland U21, B, Full caps.
2005–06 Manchester U 0 0
2006–07 Manchester U 0 0
2006–07 *Royal Antwerp* 25 1 **25 1**
2007–08 Manchester U 0 0
2007–08 *Wolverhampton W* 21 1 **21 1**
2008–09 Manchester U 3 1
2009–10 Manchester U 15 2
2010–11 Manchester U 12 0
2011–12 Manchester U 1 0 **31 3**
2011–12 Everton 11 1
2012–13 Everton 23 1
2013–14 Everton 1 0
2014–15 Everton 9 0
2015–16 Everton 7 0
2016–17 Everton 0 0 **51 2**
2016–17 Sunderland 12 0
2017–18 Sunderland 15 0 **27 0**
2018–19 Wigan Ath 18 0 **18 0**
2019–20 Salford C 3 0
2020–21 Salford C 5 0 **8 0**

GOLDEN, Tylor (D) 7 0
b.Ipswich 8-11-99
2017–18 Wigan Ath 0 0
2018–19 Wigan Ath 0 0
2019–20 Wigan Ath 0 0
2020–21 Salford C 7 0 **7 0**

HAWKINS, Daniel (F) 0 0
2020–21 Salford C 0 0

HAYES, Nick (G) 0 0
From Ipswich T, Woking, Dunstable, Norwich C.
2020–21 Salford C 0 0

HENDERSON, Ian (F) 593 161
H: 5 10 W: 11 06 b.Thetford 25-1-85
Internationals: England U18, U20.
2002–03 Norwich C 20 1
2003–04 Norwich C 19 4
2004–05 Norwich C 3 0
2005–06 Norwich C 24 1
2006–07 Norwich C 2 0 **68 6**
2006–07 *Rotherham U* 18 1 **18 1**
2007–08 Northampton T 23 0
2008–09 Northampton T 3 0 **26 0**
2008–09 Luton T 19 1 **19 1**
2009–10 Colchester U 13 2
2009–10 *Ankaragucu* 2 0 **2 0**
2010–11 Colchester U 36 10
2011–12 Colchester U 46 9
2012–13 Colchester U 22 3 **117 24**
2012–13 Rochdale 12 3
2013–14 Rochdale 45 11
2014–15 Rochdale 44 22
2015–16 Rochdale 39 13
2016–17 Rochdale 42 15
2017–18 Rochdale 39 13
2018–19 Rochdale 45 20
2019–20 Rochdale 31 15 **297 112**
2020–21 Salford C 46 17 **46 17**

HLADKY, Vaclav (G) 166 0
b. 14-11-90
2010–11 Zbrojovka Brno 0 0
2011–12 Zbrojovka Brno 0 0
2012–13 Zbrojovka Brno 1 0
2013–14 Zbrojovka Brno 25 0
2014–15 Zbrojovka Brno 16 0 **42 0**
2015–16 Slovan Liberec 5 0
2016–17 Slovan Liberec 2 0
2017–18 Slovan Liberec 15 0
2018–19 Slovan Liberec 9 0 **31 0**
2018–19 St Mirren 17 0
2019–20 St Mirren 30 0 **47 0**
2020–21 Salford C 46 0 **46 0**

HUNTER, Ashley (F) 233 43
H: 5 10 W: 10 08 b.Derby 29-9-93
From Ilkeston.
2014–15 Fleetwood T 12 1
2015–16 Fleetwood T 24 5
2016–17 Fleetwood T 44 8
2017–18 Fleetwood T 44 9
2018–19 Fleetwood T 43 8
2019–20 Fleetwood T 14 0 **181 31**
2019–20 *Salford C* 11 5
2020–21 Salford C 41 7 **52 12**

JAMES, Tom (D) 109 9
H: 5 11 W: 11 00 b.Leamington Spa 19-11-88
Internationals: Wales U19.
2013–14 Cardiff C 1 0
2014–15 Cardiff C 0 0
2015–16 Cardiff C 0 0
2016–17 Cardiff C 0 0 **1 0**
2016–17 Yeovil T 2 0
2017–18 Yeovil T 38 0
2018–19 Yeovil T 38 6 **78 6**
2019–20 Hibernian 6 0
2020–21 Hibernian 0 0 **6 0**
On loan from Hibernian.
2020–21 Wigan Ath 20 3 **20 3**
On loan from Hibernian.
2020–21 Salford C 4 0 **4 0**

JONES, Dan (D) 64 1
H: 6 0 W: 12 05 b.Bishop Auckland 14-12-94
Internationals: England C.
2013–14 Hartlepool U 1 0
2014–15 Hartlepool U 25 0
2015–16 Hartlepool U 11 0 **37 0**
2016–17 Grimsby T 3 0 **3 0**
From Barrow.
2019–20 Salford C 3 0
2020–21 Salford C 0 0 **3 0**
2020–21 *Harrogate T* 21 1 **21 1**

JONES, Joey (D) 21 0
b.Kingston upon Thames 15-4-94
Internationals: Northern Ireland U16, U17, U19, U21.
2019–20 Salford C 20 0
2020–21 Salford C 1 0 **21 0**
Transferred to Dagenham & R November 2020.

LOUGHLIN, Liam (M) 0 0
2020–21 Salford C 0 0

LOWE, Jason (M) 298 3
H: 6 0 W: 12 08 b.Wigan 2-9-91
Internationals: England U20, U21.
2009–10 Blackburn R 0 0
2010–11 Blackburn R 1 0
2010–11 *Oldham Ath* 7 2 **7 2**
2011–12 Blackburn R 32 0
2012–13 Blackburn R 36 0
2013–14 Blackburn R 39 1
2014–15 Blackburn R 12 0
2015–16 Blackburn R 10 0
2016–17 Blackburn R 43 0 **173 1**
2017–18 WBA 0 0
2017–18 Birmingham C 9 0 **9 0**
2018–19 Bolton W 35 0
2019–20 Bolton W 29 0 **64 0**
2019–20 Salford C 0 0
2020–21 Salford C 45 0 **45 0**

SARGENT, Matthew (F) 0 0
From Wrexham.
2020–21 Salford C 0 0

SHEPHERD, William (M) 0 0
2020–21 Salford C 0 0

SMITH, Martin (M) 31 1
H: 5 10 W: 11 00 b.Sunderland 25-1-96
2014–15 Sunderland 0 0
2015–16 Sunderland 0 0
2015–16 *Carlisle U* 2 0 **2 0**
2016–17 Kilmarnock 10 1 **10 1**
From Coleraine.
2018–19 Swindon T 11 0 **11 0**
2019–20 Salford C 4 0
2020–21 Salford C 4 0 **8 0**
Transferred to Chesterfield January 2021.

THOMAS-ASANTE, Brandon (F) 84 11
H: 5 11 W: 12 08 b. 29-12-98
2016–17 Milton Keynes D 6 0
2017–18 Milton Keynes D 15 0
2018–19 Milton Keynes D 1 0 **22 0**
2019–20 Salford C 20 6
2020–21 Salford C 42 5 **62 11**

THRELKELD, Oscar (D) 161 4
H: 6 0 W: 12 04 b.Bolton 15-12-94
2013–14 Bolton W 2 0
2014–15 Bolton W 4 0
2015–16 Bolton W 3 0 **9 0**
2015–16 *Plymouth Arg* 25 1
2016–17 Plymouth Arg 36 2
2017–18 Plymouth Arg 24 0
2018–19 Waasland-Beveren 2 0 **2 0**
2018–19 *Plymouth Arg* 12 1 **97 4**
2019–20 Salford C 18 0
2020–21 Salford C 35 0 **53 0**

TOURAY, Ibou (D) 81 5
H: 5 10 W: 10 09 b.Liverpool 24-12-94
Internationals: Gambia Full caps.
2013–14 Everton 0 0
2014–15 Everton 0 0
From Rhyl, Chester.
2019–20 Salford C 35 4
2020–21 Salford C 46 1 **81 5**

TOURAY, Momodou (F) 1 0
H: 5 11 W: 10 06 b. 30-7-99
Internationals: Wales U18, U19, U21.
2016–17 Newport Co 0 0
2017–18 Newport Co 1 0
2018–19 Newport Co 0 0
2019–20 Newport Co 0 0 **1 0**
2020–21 Salford C 0 0

TOWELL, Richie (D) 251 59
H: 5 8 W: 10 06 b.Dublin 17-7-91
Internationals: Republic of Ireland U17, U19, U21.
2010–11 Celtic 1 0
2011–12 Celtic 0 0
2011–12 *Hibernian* 16 0
2012–13 Celtic 0 0 **1 0**
2012–13 *Hibernian* 14 1 **30 1**
2013 Dundalk 31 7
2014 Dundalk 33 11
2015 Dundalk 32 25 **96 43**

2015–16 Brighton & HA 0 0
2016–17 Brighton & HA 1 0
2017–18 Brighton & HA 0 0
2017–18 *Rotherham U* 39 5
2018–19 Brighton & HA 0 0 **1 0**
2018–19 *Rotherham U* 34 4 **73 9**
2019–20 Salford C 26 3
2020–21 Salford C 24 3 **50 6**

TURNBULL, Jordan (D) 240 7
H: 6 1 W: 11 05 b.Trowbridge 30-10-94
Internationals: England U19, U20.
2014–15 Southampton 0 0
2014–15 *Swindon T* 44 1
2015–16 Southampton 0 0
2015–16 *Swindon T* 42 0 **86 1**
2016–17 Coventry C 36 0
2017–18 Coventry C 0 0 **36 0**
2017–18 *Partick Thistle* 0 0
2017–18 Northampton T 14 0
2018–19 Northampton T 31 0
2019–20 Northampton T 31 5 **76 5**
2020–21 Salford C 42 1 **42 1**

WILSON, James (F) 116 22
H: 6 0 W: 12 04 b.Biddulph 1-12-95
Internationals: England U16, U19, U20, U21.
2013–14 Manchester U 1 2
2014–15 Manchester U 13 1
2015–16 Manchester U 1 0
2015–16 *Brighton & HA* 25 5 **25 5**
2016–17 Manchester U 0 0
2016–17 *Derby Co* 4 0 **4 0**
2017–18 Manchester U 0 0
2017–18 *Sheffield U* 8 1 **8 1**
2018–19 Manchester U 0 0 **15 3**
2018–19 *Aberdeen* 24 4
2019–20 Aberdeen 11 0 **35 4**
2019–20 Salford C 5 2
2020–21 Salford C 24 7 **29 9**

Scholars
Bartram, Finlay; Berry, Lucas James; Evans, William Hayden; Finley, Ben David; Ghaly, Ryan Nathan; Jones, Daniel Lee; Kirnon, Lucas William; Lescott, Donovan Joleon; Nmai, Kelly Harmani; Pedro, Djavan Michael; Perry, Philip Edward; Roberts, Charlie Paul; Rose, Bradley Daniel; Rydel, Ben Daniel; Shepherd, Tomas David; Smith, Anton Benjamin Daniel; Timmis, Jaden Robert; Williams, Thomas Max.

SCUNTHORPE U (73)

BAKER, Harry (D) 0 0
b. 11-1-03
2020–21 Scunthorpe U 0 0

BARKS, Charlie (D) 0 0
2020–21 Scunthorpe U 0 0

BEDEAU, Jacob (D) 52 2
H: 6 0 W: 12 04 b.Waltham Forest 24-12-99
2016–17 Bury 7 0 **7 0**
2017–18 Aston Villa 0 0
2018–19 Aston Villa 0 0
2019–20 Scunthorpe U 11 1
2020–21 Scunthorpe U 34 1 **45 2**

BEESTIN, Alfie (F) 77 7
H: 5 10 W: 11 11 b.Leeds 1-10-97
2016–17 Doncaster R 3 0
2017–18 Doncaster R 26 2
2018–19 Doncaster R 5 0 **34 2**
2019–20 Scunthorpe U 3 0
2020–21 Scunthorpe U 40 5 **43 5**

BROWN, Junior (D) 254 21
H: 5 9 W: 10 09 b.Crewe 7-5-89
2006–07 Crewe Alex 0 0
2007–08 Crewe Alex 1 0 **1 0**
From Halifax T, Northwich Vic.
2012–13 Fleetwood T 43 11
2013–14 Fleetwood T 21 1 **64 12**
2013–14 *Tranmere R* 9 1 **9 1**
2014–15 Oxford U 11 0 **11 0**
2014–15 Mansfield T 24 2 **24 2**
2015–16 Shrewsbury T 31 0
2016–17 Shrewsbury T 43 5
2017–18 Shrewsbury T 15 1 **89 6**
2018–19 Coventry C 22 0
2019–20 Coventry C 0 0 **22 0**
2019–20 *Scunthorpe U* 20 0
2020–21 Scunthorpe U 14 0 **34 0**

BUTROID, Lewis (D) 18 0
H: 5 9 W: 10 08 b. 17-9-98
2016–17 Scunthorpe U 0 0
2017–18 Scunthorpe U 7 0
2018–19 Scunthorpe U 6 0
2019–20 Scunthorpe U 4 0
2020–21 Scunthorpe U 1 0 **18 0**

CLARKE, Jordan (D) 283 11
H: 6 0 W: 11 02 b.Coventry 19-11-91
Internationals: England U19, U20.
2009–10 Coventry C 12 0
2010–11 Coventry C 21 1
2011–12 Coventry C 19 1
2012–13 Coventry C 20 0
2013–14 Coventry C 41 1
2014–15 Coventry C 11 1 **124 4**
2014–15 *Yeovil T* 5 2 **5 2**
2014–15 Scunthorpe U 24 0
2015–16 Scunthorpe U 33 2
2016–17 Scunthorpe U 23 1
2017–18 Scunthorpe U 23 0
2018–19 Scunthorpe U 15 1
2019–20 Scunthorpe U 12 0
2020–21 Scunthorpe U 24 1 **154 5**

COLCLOUGH, Ryan (F) 161 25
H: 6 3 W: 13 01 b.Budapest 27-12-94
2012–13 Crewe Alex 18 1
2013–14 Crewe Alex 8 2
2014–15 Crewe Alex 7 2
2015–16 Crewe Alex 27 7 **60 12**
2015–16 Wigan Ath 10 2
2016–17 Wigan Ath 10 0
2016–17 *Milton Keynes D* 18 5 **18 5**
2017–18 Wigan Ath 26 4 **46 6**
2018–19 Scunthorpe U 17 2
2019–20 Scunthorpe U 20 0
2020–21 Scunthorpe U 0 0 **37 2**
Transferred to Altrincham November 2020.

COLLINS, Tom (G) 0 0
2019–20 Scunthorpe U 0 0
2020–21 Scunthorpe U 0 0

DALES, Andy (M) 35 1
b. 13-11-94
Internationals: England C.
2013–14 Derby Co 0 0
From Mickleover Sports.
2018–19 Scunthorpe U 20 1
2018–19 *Dundee* 10 0 **10 0**
2019–20 Scunthorpe U 3 0
2019–20 *Hamilton A* 2 0 **2 0**
2020–21 Scunthorpe U 0 0 **23 1**

DAWSON, Joey (M) 0 0
b. 30-5-03
2019–20 Scunthorpe U 0 0
2020–21 Scunthorpe U 0 0

DUNNWALD, Kenan (F) 34 5
H: 6 2 W: 12 08 b. 14-11-95
From TSG Sprockhovel.
2017–18 Bristol R 1 0 **1 0**
2018–19 Kaan-Marienborn 10 3 **10 3**
2018–19 Wuppertaler 9 2 **9 2**
2019–20 Fortuna 3 0 **3 0**
2019–20 Bonner 6 0 **6 0**
2020–21 Scunthorpe U 5 0 **5 0**

EISA, Abobaker (M) 91 17
b. 5-1-96
From Uxbridge, Wealdstone.
2017–18 Shrewsbury T 5 1
2018–19 Shrewsbury T 4 0
2018–19 *Colchester U* 14 2 **14 2**
2019–20 Shrewsbury T 1 0 **10 1**
2019–20 Scunthorpe U 28 5
2020–21 Scunthorpe U 39 9 **67 14**

GILLIEAD, Alex (F) 210 15
H: 6 0 W: 11 00 b.Shotley Bridge 11-2-96
Internationals: England U16, U17, U18, U20.
2014–15 Newcastle U 0 0
2015–16 Newcastle U 0 0
2015–16 *Carlisle U* 35 5 **35 5**
2016–17 Newcastle U 0 0
2016–17 *Luton T* 18 1 **18 1**
2016–17 *Bradford C* 9 0
2017–18 Newcastle U 0 0
2017–18 *Bradford C* 42 1 **51 1**
2018–19 Shrewsbury T 27 1 **27 1**
2019–20 Scunthorpe U 35 6
2020–21 Scunthorpe U 44 1 **79 7**

GREEN, Devarn (F) 38 3
b. 26-8-96
2014–15 Blackburn R 0 0
2015–16 Blackburn R 0 0
From Tranmere R, Southport.
2019–20 Scunthorpe U 2 0
2020–21 Scunthorpe U 36 3 **38 3**

HALLAM, Jordan (M) 25 3
b. 6-10-98
2016–17 Sheffield U 0 0
2017–18 Sheffield U 0 0
2018 *Viking* 5 0 **5 0**
2018–19 Scunthorpe U 7 1
2019–20 Scunthorpe U 0 0
2020–21 Scunthorpe U 13 2 **20 3**

HIPPOLYTE, Myles (M) 167 17
b.London 9-11-94
2012–13 Brentford 0 0
From Southall, Tamworth, Hayes & Yeading U, Burnham.
2014–15 Livingston 33 2
2015–16 Livingston 17 1 **50 3**
2015–16 Falkirk 12 1
2016–17 Falkirk 30 7
2017–18 Falkirk 10 2 **52 10**
2017–18 St Mirren 8 1 **8 1**
2018–19 Dunfermline Ath 31 2 **31 2**
From Yeovil T.
2020–21 Scunthorpe U 26 1 **26 1**

HORNSHAW, George (M) 8 0
b. 20-1-00
2017–18 Scunthorpe U 0 0
2018–19 Scunthorpe U 0 0
2019–20 Scunthorpe U 0 0
2020–21 Scunthorpe U 8 0 **8 0**

HOWARD, Mark (G) 254 0
H: 6 0 W: 11 13 b.Southwark 21-9-86
2005–06 Arsenal 0 0
2005–06 *Falkirk* 8 0 **8 0**
2006–07 Cardiff C 0 0
2006–07 *Swansea C* 0 0
2007–08 St Mirren 10 0
2008–09 St Mirren 33 0
2009–10 St Mirren 2 0 **45 0**
2010–11 Aberdeen 9 0 **9 0**
2011–12 Blackpool 4 0
2011–12 Sheffield U 0 0
2012–13 Sheffield U 11 0
2013–14 Sheffield U 19 0
2014–15 Sheffield U 35 0
2015–16 Sheffield U 15 0 **80 0**
2016–17 Bolton W 27 0
2017–18 Bolton W 8 0 **35 0**
2018–19 Blackpool 32 0
2019–20 *Salford C* 3 0 **3 0**
2019–20 Blackpool 4 0 **40 0**
2020–21 Scunthorpe U 34 0 **34 0**

JARVIS, Aaron (F) 30 2
H: 6 2 W: 12 08 b. 24-1-98
From Basinstoke T.
2017–18 Luton T 1 0
2018–19 Luton T 4 0 **5 0**
2018–19 *Falkirk* 12 0 **12 0**
From Sutton U.
2020–21 Scunthorpe U 13 2 **13 2**

JESSOP, Harry (F) 3 0
b. 1-8-02
2020–21 Scunthorpe U 3 0 **3 0**

KARACAN, Jem (M) 245 14
H: 5 10 W: 11 13 b.Lewisham 21-2-89
Internationals: Turkey U17, U18, U19, U21.
2007–08 Reading 0 0
2007–08 *Bournemouth* 13 1 **13 1**
2007–08 *Millwall* 7 0
2008–09 Reading 15 1
2009–10 Reading 27 0
2010–11 Reading 40 3
2011–12 Reading 37 3
2012–13 Reading 21 1
2013–14 Reading 7 2
2014–15 Reading 8 1 **155 11**
2015–16 Galatasaray 2 0
2015–16 *Bursaspor* 9 0 **9 0**
2016–17 Galatasaray 0 0 **2 0**
2016–17 Bolton W 5 1
2017–18 Bolton W 16 0 **21 1**
2018–19 Millwall 4 0 **11 0**
2019 Central Coast Mariners 10 1 **10 1**
2020–21 Scunthorpe U 24 0 **24 0**

KELSEY, Adam (G) 0 0
2016–17 Scunthorpe U 0 0
2017–18 Scunthorpe U 0 0
2018–19 Scunthorpe U 0 0
2019–20 Scunthorpe U 0 0
2020–21 Scunthorpe U 0 0

LOFT, Ryan (F) 77 12
H: 6 3 W: 11 07 b.Gravesend 14-9-97
2016–17 Tottenham H 0 0
2016–17 *Stevenage* 9 0 **9 0**
2017–18 Tottenham H 0 0
2017–18 *Exeter C* 1 0 **1 0**
2018–19 Leicester C 0 0
2019–20 Leicester C 0 0
2019–20 *Carlisle U* 26 4 **26 4**
2020–21 Scunthorpe U 41 8 **41 8**

McATEE, John (F) **50 4**
b. 23-7-99

2016–17	Shrewsbury T	1	0		
2017–18	Shrewsbury T	0	0		
2018–19	Shrewsbury T	0	0	**1**	**0**
2019–20	Scunthorpe U	19	3		
2020–21	Scunthorpe U	30	1	**49**	**4**

McGAHEY, Harrison (D) **187 1**
b.Preston 26-9-95

2013–14	Blackpool	4	0	**4**	**0**
2014–15	Sheffield U	15	0		
2014–15	*Tranmere R*	4	0	**4**	**0**
2015–16	Sheffield U	7	0	**22**	**0**
2016–17	Rochdale	36	0		
2017–18	Rochdale	42	0		
2018–19	Rochdale	21	0	**99**	**0**
2018–19	Scunthorpe U	10	0		
2019–20	Scunthorpe U	32	0		
2020–21	Scunthorpe U	16	1	**58**	**1**

MOONEY, Kelsey (F) **8 1**
b. 5-2-99

2018–19	Aston Villa	0	0		
2018–19	*Cheltenham T*	8	1	**8**	**1**

From Hereford.

2020–21	Scunthorpe U	0	0		

O'MALLEY, Mason (D) **29 0**
b. 8-6-01
From Huddersfield T.

2019–20	Scunthorpe U	0	0		
2020–21	Scunthorpe U	29	0	**29**	**0**

OLOMOLA, Olufela (F) **76 15**
H: 5 7 b.London 5-9-97
From Huddersfield T.

2015–16	Southampton	0	0		
2016–17	Southampton	0	0		
2017–18	Southampton	0	0		
2017–18	*Yeovil T*	21	7		
2018–19	Scunthorpe U	6	0		
2018–19	*Yeovil T*	17	3	**38**	**10**
2019–20	Scunthorpe U	0	0		
2019–20	*Carlisle U*	27	5	**27**	**5**
2020–21	Scunthorpe U	5	0	**11**	**0**

ONARIASE, Manny (D) **53 3**
H: 6 1 b. 29-1-95

2014–15	West Ham U	0	0		
2015–16	West Ham U	0	0		
2016–17	Brentford	0	0		
2016–17	*Cheltenham T*	22	1		
2017–18	Rotherham U	0	0		
2017–18	*Cheltenham T*	5	0	**27**	**1**
2018–19	Rotherham U	0	0		

From Dagenham & R.

2020–21	Scunthorpe U	26	2	**26**	**2**

PUGH, Tom (M) **2 0**
b.Doncaster 27-9-00
Internationals: Wales U21.

2018–19	Scunthorpe U	0	0		
2019–20	Scunthorpe U	1	0		
2020–21	Scunthorpe U	1	0	**2**	**0**

ROWE, Jai (D) **26 1**
b. 8-8-01
From Nuneaton, Barwell.

2019–20	Scunthorpe U	1	0		
2020–21	Scunthorpe U	25	1	**26**	**1**

SHRIMPTON, Finley (M) **0 0**

2020–21	Scunthorpe U	0	0		

SPENCE, Lewis (M) **156 4**
b.Kirkcaldy 28-1-96

2013–14	Dunfermline Ath	6	0		
2014–15	Dunfermline Ath	26	0		
2015–16	Dunfermline Ath	0	0		
2015–16	*Brechin C*	13	3		
2016–17	Dunfermline Ath	2	0	**34**	**0**
2016–17	*Brechin C*	7	0	**20**	**3**
2017–18	Dundee	18	0		
2018–19	Dundee	13	0	**31**	**0**
2018–19	Ross Co	15	0		
2019–20	Ross Co	15	0	**30**	**0**
2020–21	Scunthorpe U	41	1	**41**	**1**

TAFT, George (D) **166 6**
H: 5 9 W: 11 09 b.Leicester 29-7-93
Internationals: England U18, U19.

2010–11	Leicester C	0	0		
2011–12	Leicester C	0	0		
2012–13	Leicester C	0	0		
2013–14	Leicester C	0	0		
2013–14	*York C*	3	0	**3**	**0**
2014–15	Burton Alb	30	1		
2015–16	Burton Alb	0	0	**30**	**1**
2015–16	*Cambridge U*	11	1		
2016–17	Mansfield T	13	0		
2017–18	Mansfield T	0	0	**13**	**0**
2017–18	*Cambridge U*	28	1		
2018–19	Cambridge U	37	2		
2019–20	Cambridge U	27	1	**103**	**5**
2019–20	Bolton W	0	0		
2020–21	Bolton W	1	0	**1**	**0**
2020–21	Scunthorpe U	16	0	**16**	**0**

VAN VEEN, Kevin (F) **249 75**
H: 6 1 W: 11 11 b.Eindhoven 1-6-91

2013–14	JVC Cuyk	29	20	**29**	**20**
2014–15	FC Oss	20	16	**20**	**16**
2014–15	Scunthorpe U	20	2		
2015–16	Scunthorpe U	20	2		
2015–16	*Cambuur Leeuwarden*	12	1	**12**	**1**
2016–17	Scunthorpe U	33	10		
2017–18	Scunthorpe U	21	5		
2017–18	Northampton T	10	0		
2018–19	Northampton T	25	7	**35**	**7**
2018–19	Scunthorpe U	13	1		
2019–20	Scunthorpe U	27	10		
2020–21	Scunthorpe U	19	1	**153**	**31**

WATSON, Rory (G) **44 0**
b. 5-2-96

2014–15	Hull C	0	0		
2015–16	Hull C	0	0		
2015–16	*Scunthorpe U*	0	0		
2016–17	Scunthorpe U	0	0		
2017–18	Scunthorpe U	4	0		
2018–19	Scunthorpe U	5	0		
2019–20	Scunthorpe U	23	0		
2020–21	Scunthorpe U	12	0	**44**	**0**

Scholars
Balme, Jake Paul; Crosher, Benjamin James Jack; Dawson, Joey; Franklin, Benjamin James; Gallimore, Daniel James; Kemp, Oliver George; Lewis, Harry James; Lobley, Oliver Shay Sherratt; Moore, Jamie Matthew; Moore-Billam, Jack Billy James; Virgo, Patrick Henry; Wilkinson, Alexander Eric; Wilson, Cameron Harry; Young, Ethan Kai.

SHEFFIELD U (74)

AMISSAH, Jordan (G) **0 0**
H: 6 6 b. 2-8-01
From Borussia Dortmund.

2020–21	Sheffield U	0	0		

ARBLASTER, Oliver (M) **0 0**
H: 5 8 b. 5-5-04

2020–21	Sheffield U	0	0		

BALDOCK, George (M) **279 9**
H: 5 9 W: 10 07 b.Buckingham 26-1-93

2009–10	Milton Keynes D	1	0		
2010–11	Milton Keynes D	2	0		
2011–12	Milton Keynes D	0	0		
2011–12	*Northampton T*	5	0	**5**	**0**
2012–13	Milton Keynes D	2	0		
2013–14	Milton Keynes D	38	2		
2014–15	Milton Keynes D	9	0		
2014–15	*Oxford U*	12	1		
2015–16	Milton Keynes D	15	0		
2015–16	*Oxford U*	27	2	**39**	**3**
2016–17	Milton Keynes D	37	0	**104**	**2**
2017–18	Sheffield U	34	1		
2018–19	Sheffield U	27	1		
2019–20	Sheffield U	38	2		
2020–21	Sheffield U	32	0	**131**	**4**

BASHAM, Chris (M) **396 17**
H: 5 11 W: 12 08 b.Hebburn 20-7-88
From Newcastle U.

2007–08	Bolton W	0	0		
2007–08	*Rochdale*	13	0	**13**	**0**
2008–09	Bolton W	11	1		
2009–10	Bolton W	8	0	**19**	**1**
2010–11	Blackpool	2	0		
2011–12	Blackpool	17	2		
2012–13	Blackpool	26	1		
2013–14	Blackpool	40	2	**85**	**5**
2014–15	Sheffield U	37	0		
2015–16	Sheffield U	44	3		
2016–17	Sheffield U	43	2		
2017–18	Sheffield U	45	2		
2018–19	Sheffield U	41	4		
2019–20	Sheffield U	38	0		
2020–21	Sheffield U	31	0	**279**	**11**

BELEHOUAN, Jean (D) **0 0**
b. 1-9-00

2020–21	Sheffield U	0	0		

BERGE, Sander (M) **146 6**
b.Baerum 14-2-98
Internationals: Norway U16, U17, U18, U19, U21, Full caps.

2013	Asker	1	0		
2014	Asker	7	0	**8**	**0**
2015	Valerenga	11	0		
2016	Valerenga	25	0	**36**	**0**
2016–17	Genk	9	0		
2017–18	Genk	13	0		
2018–19	Genk	28	0		
2019–20	Genk	23	4	**73**	**4**
2019–20	Sheffield U	14	1		
2020–21	Sheffield U	15	1	**29**	**2**

BOGLE, Jayden (D) **93 5**
b. 27-7-00
Internationals: England U20.

2017–18	Derby Co	0	0		
2018–19	Derby Co	40	2		
2019–20	Derby Co	37	1	**77**	**3**
2020–21	Sheffield U	16	2	**16**	**2**

BOYES, Harry (M) **0 0**
b. 2-11-01
From Manchester C.

2020–21	Sheffield U	0	0		

BREWSTER, Rhian (F) **47 10**
b. 1-4-00
Internationals: England U16, U17, U18, U21
From Chelsea.

2016–17	Liverpool	0	0		
2017–18	Liverpool	0	0		
2018–19	Liverpool	0	0		
2019–20	Liverpool	0	0		
2019–20	*Swansea C*	20	10	**20**	**10**
2020–21	Sheffield U	27	0	**27**	**0**

BROADBENT, George (M) **0 0**
b. 30-9-00

2020–21	Sheffield U	0	0		

BROOKS, Andre (M) **0 0**
H: 5 11 b. 20-8-03

2020–21	Sheffield U	0	0		

BRUNT, Zak (M) **0 0**
b. 17-11-01
From Matlock.

2020–21	Sheffield U	0	0		

BRYAN, Kean (M) **63 4**
H: 6 1 b.Manchester 1-11-96
Internationals: England U16, U17, U19, U20.

2016–17	Manchester C	0	0		
2016–17	*Bury*	12	0	**12**	**0**
2017–18	Manchester C	0	0		
2017–18	*Oldham Ath*	32	2	**32**	**2**
2018–19	Sheffield U	0	0		
2019–20	Sheffield U	0	0		
2019–20	*Bolton W*	6	1	**6**	**1**
2020–21	Sheffield U	13	1	**13**	**1**

BURKE, Oliver (M) **142 13**
H: 5 9 W: 11 11 b.Melton Mowbray 7-4-97
Internationals: Scotland U19, U20, Full caps.

2014–15	Nottingham F	2	0		
2014–15	*Bradford C*	2	0	**2**	**0**
2015–16	Nottingham F	18	2		
2016–17	Nottingham F	5	4	**25**	**6**
2016–17	RB Leipzig	25	1	**25**	**1**
2017–18	WBA	15	0		
2018–19	WBA	3	0		
2018–19	*Celtic*	14	4	**14**	**4**
2019–20	WBA	2	0	**20**	**0**
2019–20	*Alaves*	31	1	**31**	**1**
2020–21	Sheffield U	25	1	**25**	**1**

CAPPELLO, Angelo (F) **0 0**
b. 27-1-02
Internationals: Belize Full caps.

2020–21	Sheffield U	0	0		

COULIBALY, Ismaila (M) **49 9**
H: 6 0 b.Mali 25-12-00
Internationals: Mali U20.

2019	Sarpsborg 08	13	0		
2020	Sarpsborg 08	14	4	**27**	**4**
2020–21	Sheffield U	0	0		
2020–21	*Beerschot*	22	5	**22**	**5**

DEWHURST, Marcus (G) **0 0**
b.Kingston upon Hull --
Internationals: England U17, U18, U19.

2019–20	Sheffield U	0	0		
2019–20	*Carlisle U*	0	0		
2020–21	Sheffield U	0	0		
2020–21	*Carlisle U*	0	0		

EASTWOOD, Jake (G) **24 0**
b. 3-10-96

2017–18	Chesterfield	4	0	**4**	**0**
2017–18	Sheffield U	1	0		
2018–19	Sheffield U	0	0		
2019–20	Sheffield U	0	0		
2019–20	*Scunthorpe U*	11	0	**11**	**0**
2020–21	Sheffield U	0	0	**1**	**0**
2020–21	*Kilmarnock*	1	0	**1**	**0**
2020–21	*Grimsby T*	7	0	**7**	**0**

EGAN, John (D) 278 20
H: 6 1 W: 11 11 b.Cork 20-10-92
Internationals: Republic of Ireland U17, U19, U21, Full caps.
2009–10 Sunderland 0 0
2010–11 Sunderland 0 0
2011–12 Sunderland 0 0
2011–12 *Crystal Palace* 1 0 **1 0**
2011–12 *Sheffield U* 1 0
2012–13 Sunderland 0 0
2012–13 *Bradford C* 4 0 **4 0**
2013–14 Sunderland 0 0
2013–14 *Southend U* 13 1 **13 1**
2014–15 Gillingham 45 4
2015–16 Gillingham 36 6 **81 10**
2016–17 Brentford 34 4
2017–18 Brentford 33 2 **67 6**
2018–19 Sheffield U 44 1
2019–20 Sheffield U 36 2
2020–21 Sheffield U 31 0 **112 3**

FLECK, John (M) 401 23
H: 5 9 W: 11 05 b.Glasgow 24-8-91
Internationals: Scotland U17, U19, U21, Full caps.
2007–08 Rangers 1 0
2008–09 Rangers 8 1
2009–10 Rangers 15 1
2010–11 Rangers 13 0
2011–12 Rangers 4 0 **41 2**
2011–12 *Blackpool* 7 0 **7 0**
2012–13 Coventry C 35 3
2013–14 Coventry C 43 1
2014–15 Coventry C 44 0
2015–16 Coventry C 40 4 **162 8**
2016–17 Sheffield U 44 4
2017–18 Sheffield U 41 2
2018–19 Sheffield U 45 2
2019–20 Sheffield U 30 5
2020–21 Sheffield U 31 0 **191 13**

FODERINGHAM, Wesley (G) 276 0
H: 6 1 W: 12 00 b.Hammersmith 14-1-91
Internationals: England U16, U17, U19.
2009–10 Fulham 0 0
2010–11 Crystal Palace 0 0
2011–12 Crystal Palace 0 0
2011–12 Swindon T 33 0
2012–13 Swindon T 46 0
2013–14 Swindon T 41 0
2014–15 Swindon T 44 0 **164 0**
2015–16 Rangers 36 0
2016–17 Rangers 37 0
2017–18 Rangers 33 0
2018–19 Rangers 4 0
2019–20 Rangers 2 0 **112 0**
2020–21 Sheffield U 0 0

FREEMAN, Luke (F) 367 42
H: 6 0 W: 10 00 b.Dartford 22-3-92
Internationals: England U16, U17.
2007–08 Gillingham 1 0 **1 0**
2008–09 Arsenal 0 0
2009–10 Arsenal 0 0
2010–11 Arsenal 0 0
2010–11 *Yeovil T* 13 2 **13 2**
2011–12 Arsenal 0 0
2011–12 Stevenage 26 7
2012–13 Stevenage 39 2
2013–14 Stevenage 45 6 **110 15**
2014–15 Bristol C 46 7
2015–16 Bristol C 41 1
2016–17 Bristol C 18 2 **105 10**
2016–17 QPR 16 2
2017–18 QPR 45 5
2018–19 QPR 43 7 **104 14**
2019–20 Sheffield U 11 0
2020–21 Sheffield U 0 0 **11 0**
2020–21 *Nottingham F* 23 1 **23 1**

GAXHA, Leonardo (F) 0 0
b. 2-3-02
Internationals: Republic of Ireland U16, U17. Albania U18.
2020–21 Sheffield U 0 0

GOMIS, Nicksoen (D) 0 0
b. 15-3-02
Internationals: France U18.
2020–21 Sheffield U 0 0

GORDON, Kyron (D) 0 0
b. 24-5-02
2020–21 Sheffield U 0 0

HACKFORD, Antwoine (F) 1 0
b.Sheffield 20-3-04
2020–21 Sheffield U 1 0 **1 0**

JAGIELKA, Phil (D) 592 32
H: 6 0 W: 13 01 b.Manchester 17-8-82
Internationals: England U20, U21, B, Full caps.
1999–2000 Sheffield U 1 0
2000–01 Sheffield U 15 0
2001–02 Sheffield U 23 3
2002–03 Sheffield U 42 0
2003–04 Sheffield U 43 3
2004–05 Sheffield U 46 0
2005–06 Sheffield U 46 8
2006–07 Sheffield U 38 4
2007–08 Everton 34 1
2008–09 Everton 34 0
2009–10 Everton 12 0
2010–11 Everton 33 1
2011–12 Everton 30 2
2012–13 Everton 36 2
2013–14 Everton 26 0
2014–15 Everton 37 4
2015–16 Everton 21 0
2016–17 Everton 27 3
2017–18 Everton 25 0
2018–19 Everton 7 1 **322 14**
2019–20 Sheffield U 6 0
2020–21 Sheffield U 10 0 **270 18**

JEBBISON, Daniel (F) 4 1
b. 11-7-03
2020–21 Sheffield U 4 1 **4 1**

LOPTATA, Kacper (D) 7 0
H: 6 4 b.Krakow 27-8-01
Internationals: Poland U18, U19.
2019–20 Brighton & HA 0 0
2019–20 *Zaglebie Sosnowiec* 7 0 **7 0**
2020–21 Sheffield U 0 0

LOWE, Max (D) 94 2
H: 5 9 W: 11 09 b.Birmingham 11-5-97
Internationals: England U16, U17, U18, U20.
2013–14 Derby Co 0 0
2014–15 Derby Co 0 0
2015–16 Derby Co 0 0
2016–17 Derby Co 9 0
2017–18 Derby Co 0 0
2017–18 *Shrewsbury T* 12 0 **12 0**
2018–19 Derby Co 3 0
2018–19 *Aberdeen* 33 2 **33 2**
2019–20 Derby Co 29 0 **41 0**
2020–21 Sheffield U 8 0 **8 0**

LUNDSTRAM, John (M) 253 14
H: 5 11 W: 11 09 b.Liverpool 18-2-94
Internationals: England U17, U18, U19, U20.
2011–12 Everton 0 0
2012–13 Everton 0 0
2012–13 *Doncaster R* 14 0 **14 0**
2013–14 Everton 0 0
2013–14 *Yeovil T* 14 2 **14 2**
2013–14 *Leyton Orient* 7 0
2014–15 Everton 0 0
2014–15 *Blackpool* 17 0 **17 0**
2014–15 *Leyton Orient* 4 0 **11 0**
2014–15 *Scunthorpe U* 7 0 **7 0**
2015–16 Oxford U 37 3
2016–17 Oxford U 45 1 **82 4**
2017–18 Sheffield U 36 3
2018–19 Sheffield U 10 0
2019–20 Sheffield U 34 5
2020–21 Sheffield U 28 0 **108 8**

MAGUIRE, Frankie (M) 0 0
b. 29-7-03
2020–21 Sheffield U 0 0

McBURNIE, Oliver (F) 157 41
H: 6 2 W: 10 04 b.Bradford 6-4-96
Internationals: Scotland U19, U21, Full caps.
2013–14 Bradford C 8 0
2014–15 Bradford C 7 0 **15 0**
2015–16 Swansea C 0 0
2015–16 *Newport Co* 3 3 **3 3**
2015–16 *Bristol R* 5 0 **5 0**
2016–17 Swansea C 5 0
2017–18 Swansea C 11 0
2017–18 *Barnsley* 17 9 **17 9**
2018–19 Swansea C 42 22
2019–20 Swansea C 0 0 **58 22**
2019–20 Sheffield U 36 6
2020–21 Sheffield U 23 1 **59 7**

McGOLDRICK, David (F) 446 110
H: 6 1 W: 11 10 b.Nottingham 29-11-87
Internationals: Republic of Ireland Full caps.
2003–04 Notts Co 4 0
2004–05 Notts Co 0 0
2005–06 Southampton 1 0
2005–06 *Notts Co* 6 0 **10 0**
2006–07 Southampton 9 0
2006–07 *Bournemouth* 12 6 **12 6**
2007–08 Southampton 8 0
2007–08 *Port Vale* 17 2 **17 2**
2008–09 Southampton 46 12 **64 12**
2009–10 Nottingham F 33 3
2010–11 Nottingham F 21 5
2011–12 Nottingham F 9 0
2011–12 *Sheffield W* 4 1 **4 1**
2012–13 Nottingham F 0 0 **63 8**
2012–13 *Coventry C* 22 16 **22 16**
2012–13 *Ipswich T* 13 4
2013–14 Ipswich T 31 14
2014–15 Ipswich T 26 7
2015–16 Ipswich T 24 4
2016–17 Ipswich T 30 5
2017–18 Ipswich T 22 6 **146 40**
2018–19 Sheffield U 45 15
2019–20 Sheffield U 28 2
2020–21 Sheffield U 35 8 **108 25**

MOUSSET, Lys (M) 133 23
H: 6 0 W: 12 08 b.Montvilliers 8-2-96
Internationals: France U20, U21.
2013–14 Le Havre 5 0
2014–15 Le Havre 1 0
2015–16 Le Havre 28 14 **34 14**
2016–17 Bournemouth 11 0
2017–18 Bournemouth 23 2
2018–19 Bournemouth 24 1 **58 3**
2019–20 Sheffield U 30 6
2020–21 Sheffield U 11 0 **41 6**

NDIAYE, Iliman-Cheikh (M) 1 0
b.Rouen 6-3-00
From Boreham Wood.
2019–20 Sheffield U 0 0
2020–21 Sheffield U 1 0 **1 0**

NEAL, Harrison (M) 0 0
b. 12-5-01
2020–21 Sheffield U 0 0

NORRINGTON-DAVIES, Rhys (D) 65 2
b. 22-4-99
Internationals: Wales U19, U21.
2017–18 Sheffield U 0 0
2018–19 Sheffield U 0 0
2019–20 Sheffield U 0 0
2019–20 *Rochdale* 27 1 **27 1**
2020–21 Sheffield U 0 0
2020–21 *Luton T* 18 0 **18 0**
2020–21 *Stoke C* 20 1 **20 1**

NORWOOD, Oliver (M) 382 24
H: 5 11 W: 11 13 b.Burnley 12-4-91
Internationals: England U16, U17. Northern Ireland U19, U21, B, Full caps.
2009–10 Manchester U 0 0
2010–11 Manchester U 0 0
2010–11 *Carlisle U* 6 0 **6 0**
2011–12 Manchester U 0 0
2011–12 *Scunthorpe U* 15 1 **15 1**
2011–12 *Coventry C* 18 2 **18 2**
2012–13 Huddersfield T 39 3
2013–14 Huddersfield T 40 5
2014–15 Huddersfield T 1 0 **80 8**
2014–15 Reading 38 1
2015–16 Reading 43 3 **81 4**
2016–17 Brighton & HA 33 0
2017–18 Brighton & HA 0 0 **33 0**
2017–18 *Fulham* 36 5 **36 5**
2018–19 Sheffield U 43 3
2019–20 Sheffield U 38 1
2020–21 Sheffield U 32 0 **113 4**

O'CONNELL, Jack (D) 270 13
H: 6 3 W: 13 05 b.Liverpool 29-3-94
Internationals: England U18, U19.
2012–13 Blackburn R 0 0
2012–13 *Rotherham U* 3 0 **3 0**
2012–13 *York C* 18 0 **18 0**
2013–14 Blackburn R 0 0
2013–14 *Rochdale* 38 0
2014–15 Blackburn R 0 0
2014–15 *Rochdale* 29 5 **67 5**
2014–15 Brentford 0 0
2015–16 Brentford 16 1 **16 1**
2016–17 Sheffield U 44 4
2017–18 Sheffield U 46 0
2018–19 Sheffield U 41 3
2019–20 Sheffield U 33 0
2020–21 Sheffield U 2 0 **166 7**

OSBORN, Ben (D) 249 16
H: 5 9 W: 11 11 b.Derby 5-8-94
Internationals: England U18, U19, U20.
2011–12 Nottingham F 0 0
2012–13 Nottingham F 0 0
2013–14 Nottingham F 8 0
2014–15 Nottingham F 37 3
2015–16 Nottingham F 36 3
2016–17 Nottingham F 46 4
2017–18 Nottingham F 46 4
2018–19 Nottingham F 39 1 **212 15**
2019–20 Sheffield U 13 0
2020–21 Sheffield U 24 1 **37 1**

OSULA, William (F) **0 0**
b. 4-8-03

2020–21	Sheffield U	0	0		

RAMSDALE, Aaron (G) **114 0**
b. 14-5-98
Internationals: England U18, U19, U20, U21.

2015–16	Sheffield U	0	0		
2016–17	Sheffield U	0	0		
2016–17	Bournemouth	0	0		
2017–18	Bournemouth	0	0		
2017–18	*Chesterfield*	19	0	**19**	**0**
2018–19	Bournemouth	0	0		
2018–19	*AFC Wimbledon*	20	0	**20**	**0**
2019–20	Bournemouth	37	0	**37**	**0**
2020–21	Sheffield U	38	0	**38**	**0**

ROBINSON, Jack (D) **190 4**
H: 5 11 W: 10 08 b.Warrington 1-9-93
Internationals: England U16, U17, U18, U19, U21.

2009–10	Liverpool	1	0		
2010–11	Liverpool	2	0		
2011–12	Liverpool	0	0		
2012–13	Liverpool	0	0		
2012–13	*Wolverhampton W*	11	0	**11**	**0**
2013–14	Liverpool	0	0	**3**	**0**
2013–14	*Blackpool*	34	0	**34**	**0**
2014–15	QPR	0	0		
2014–15	*Huddersfield T*	30	0	**30**	**0**
2015–16	QPR	1	0		
2016–17	QPR	7	0		
2017–18	QPR	31	2	**39**	**2**
2018–19	Nottingham F	38	2		
2019–20	Nottingham F	18	0	**56**	**2**
2019–20	Sheffield U	6	0		
2020–21	Sheffield U	11	0	**17**	**0**

RODWELL, Jack (D) **190 12**
H: 6 2 W: 12 08 b.Southport 11-3-91
Internationals: England U16, U17, U19, U21, Full caps.

2007–08	Everton	2	0		
2008–09	Everton	19	0		
2009–10	Everton	26	2		
2010–11	Everton	24	0		
2011–12	Everton	14	2	**85**	**4**
2012–13	Manchester C	11	2		
2013–14	Manchester C	5	0	**16**	**2**
2014–15	Sunderland	23	3		
2015–16	Sunderland	22	1		
2016–17	Sunderland	20	0		
2017–18	Sunderland	2	1	**67**	**5**
2018–19	Blackburn R	21	1	**21**	**1**
2019–20	Sheffield U	1	0		
2020–21	Sheffield U	0	0	**1**	**0**

SERIKI, Femi (F) **1 0**
b. 28-4-02

2018–19	Bury	0	0		
2020–21	Sheffield U	1	0	**1**	**0**

SHARP, Billy (F) **553 233**
H: 5 9 W: 11 00 b.Sheffield 5-2-86

2004–05	Sheffield U	2	0		
2004–05	*Rushden & D*	16	9	**16**	**9**
2005–06	Scunthorpe U	37	23		
2006–07	Scunthorpe U	45	30	**82**	**53**
2007–08	Sheffield U	29	4		
2008–09	Sheffield U	22	4		
2009–10	Sheffield U	0	0		
2009–10	*Doncaster R*	33	15		
2010–11	Doncaster R	29	15		
2011–12	Doncaster R	20	10		
2011–12	Southampton	15	9		
2012–13	Southampton	2	0		
2012–13	*Nottingham F*	39	10	**39**	**10**
2013–14	Southampton	0	0	**17**	**9**
2013–14	*Reading*	10	2	**10**	**2**
2013–14	*Doncaster R*	16	4	**98**	**44**
2014–15	Leeds U	33	5	**33**	**5**
2015–16	Sheffield U	44	21		
2016–17	Sheffield U	46	30		
2017–18	Sheffield U	34	13		
2018–19	Sheffield U	40	23		
2019–20	Sheffield U	25	3		
2020–21	Sheffield U	16	3	**258**	**101**

SLATER, Regan (M) **75 3**
b. 11-9-99

2016–17	Sheffield U	0	0		
2017–18	Sheffield U	1	0		
2018–19	Sheffield U	0	0		
2018–19	*Carlisle U*	35	2	**35**	**2**
2019–20	Sheffield U	0	0		
2019–20	*Scunthorpe U*	12	0	**12**	**0**
2020–21	Sheffield U	0	0	**1**	**0**
2020–21	*Hull C*	27	1	**27**	**1**

SMITH, Tyler (F) **61 13**
b. 4-12-98

2018–19	Sheffield U	0	0		
2018–19	*Doncaster R*	14	2	**14**	**2**
2019–20	Sheffield U	0	0		
2019–20	*Bristol R*	20	3	**20**	**3**
2019–20	*Rochdale*	4	1	**4**	**1**
2020–21	Sheffield U	0	0		
2020–21	*Swindon T*	23	7	**23**	**7**

STEVENS, Enda (D) **380 10**
H: 6 0 W: 12 04 b.Dublin 9-7-90
Internationals: Republic of Ireland U21, Full caps.

2008	UCD	2	0	**2**	**0**
2009	St Patrick's Ath	30	0	**30**	**0**
2010	Shamrock R	18	0		
2011	Shamrock R	28	0	**46**	**0**
2011–12	Aston Villa	0	0		
2012–13	Aston Villa	7	0		
2013–14	Aston Villa	0	0		
2013–14	*Notts Co*	2	0	**2**	**0**
2013–14	*Doncaster R*	13	0		
2014–15	Aston Villa	0	0	**7**	**0**
2014–15	*Northampton T*	4	1	**4**	**1**
2014–15	*Doncaster R*	28	1	**41**	**1**
2015–16	Portsmouth	45	0		
2016–17	Portsmouth	45	1	**90**	**1**
2016–17	Sheffield U	0	0		
2017–18	Sheffield U	45	1		
2018–19	Sheffield U	45	4		
2019–20	Sheffield U	38	2		
2020–21	Sheffield U	30	0	**158**	**7**

VERRIPS, Michael (G) **80 0**
b.Velp 3-12-96
Internationals: Netherlands U19, U21.

2014–15	FC Twente	0	0		
2015–16	FC Twente	0	0		
2016–17	Sparta Rotterdam	1	0		
2017–18	Sparta Rotterdam	0	0	**1**	**0**
2017–18	*MVV Maastricht*	38	0	**38**	**0**
2018–19	Mechelen	27	0		
2019–20	Mechelen	0	0	**27**	**0**
2019–20	Sheffield U	0	0		
2020–21	Sheffield U	0	0		
2020–21	*Emmen*	14	0	**14**	**0**

Scholars
Anderson, Beau James; Angell, Thomas Harry; Ayari, Hassan Ben Kamel; Bailey-Green, Tyrese; Chapman, Joshua Matthew; Cullinan, Harvey; Hackford, Antwoine; Hampshaw, Henry Kit; Hiddleston, Callum; Marsh, Louie; Osula, William Idamudia Daugard; Potter, Finley John; Skerritt, Tristan Devere; Slater, Ethan; Smith, Joshua James; Viggars, Ryan James; Williams, Luther Cornelius Mclachlan; Williams, Theo.

SHEFFIELD W (75)

ADEDOYIN, Korede (F) **0 0**
H: 5 11 W: 11 11 b.Lagos 14-11-00
From Everton.

2020–21	Sheffield W	0	0		

BANNAN, Barry (D) **377 16**
H: 5 10 W: 10 08 b.Glasgow 1-12-89
Internationals: Scotland U21, Full caps.

2008–09	Aston Villa	0	0		
2008–09	*Derby Co*	10	1	**10**	**1**
2009–10	Aston Villa	0	0		
2009–10	*Blackpool*	20	1	**20**	**1**
2010–11	Aston Villa	12	0		
2010–11	*Leeds U*	7	0	**7**	**0**
2011–12	Aston Villa	28	1		
2012–13	Aston Villa	24	0		
2013–14	Aston Villa	0	0	**64**	**1**
2013–14	Crystal Palace	15	1		
2014–15	Crystal Palace	7	0		
2014–15	*Bolton W*	16	0	**16**	**0**
2015–16	Crystal Palace	0	0	**22**	**1**
2015–16	Sheffield W	35	2		
2016–17	Sheffield W	43	1		
2017–18	Sheffield W	29	0		
2018–19	Sheffield W	41	5		
2019–20	Sheffield W	44	2		
2020–21	Sheffield W	46	2	**238**	**12**

BORNER, Julian (M) **234 22**
b.Weimar 21-1-91
Internationals: Germany U16, U17, U18.

2009–10	Energi Cottbus	1	0		
2010–11	Energi Cottbus	0	0		
2011–12	Energi Cottbus	5	0		
2012–13	Energi Cottbus	15	1		
2013–14	Energi Cottbus	16	0	**37**	**1**
2014–15	Arminia Bielefeld	25	4		
2015–16	Arminia Bielefeld	31	2		
2016–17	Arminia Bielefeld	26	4		
2017–18	Arminia Bielefeld	27	4		
2018–19	Arminia Bielefeld	25	3	**134**	**17**
2019–20	Sheffield W	37	1		
2020–21	Sheffield W	26	3	**63**	**4**

BRENNAN, Ciaran (D) **0 0**
b.Kilkenny 5-5-00
Internationals: Republic of Ireland U18.
From Waterford.

2019–20	Sheffield W	0	0		
2020–21	Sheffield W	0	0		

DAWODU, Joshua (D) **0 0**
b. 10-10-00

2020–21	Sheffield W	0	0		

DAWSON, Cameron (G) **68 0**
H: 6 0 W: 10 12 b.Sheffield 7-7-95
Internationals: England U18, U19.

2013–14	Sheffield W	0	0		
2013–14	*Plymouth Arg*	0	0		
2014–15	Sheffield W	0	0		
2015–16	Sheffield W	0	0		
2016–17	Sheffield W	4	0		
2016–17	*Wycombe W*	1	0	**1**	**0**
2017–18	Sheffield W	3	0		
2017–18	*Chesterfield*	2	0	**2**	**0**
2018–19	Sheffield W	26	0		
2019–20	Sheffield W	24	0		
2020–21	Sheffield W	8	0	**65**	**0**

DELE-BASHIRU, Fisayo (M) **8 0**
b. 6-2-01
From Manchester C.

2020–21	Sheffield W	8	0	**8**	**0**

DUNKLEY, Cheyenne (D) **197 20**
H: 6 2 W: 13 05 b.Wolverhampton 13-2-92
Internationals: England C.
From Crewe Alex, Hednesford T, Kidderminster H.

2014–15	Oxford U	9	0		
2015–16	Oxford U	29	4		
2016–17	Oxford U	40	3	**78**	**7**
2017–18	Wigan Ath	43	7		
2018–19	Wigan Ath	38	0		
2019–20	Wigan Ath	26	6	**107**	**13**
2020–21	Sheffield W	12	0	**12**	**0**

ERATT-THOMPSON, Declan (D) **0 0**
From Stocksbridge Park Steels.

2020–21	Sheffield W	0	0		

FARMER, Lewis (M) **0 0**
b. 17-5-02

2020–21	Sheffield W	0	0		

GALVIN, Ryan (D) **0 0**
From Wigan Ath.

2020–21	Sheffield W	0	0		

GREEN, Andre (F) **74 5**
H: 5 11 W: 11 03 b.Solihull 2-5-98
Internationals: England U16, U17, U18, U19, U20.

2014–15	Aston Villa	0	0		
2015–16	Aston Villa	2	0		
2016–17	Aston Villa	15	0		
2017–18	Aston Villa	5	1		
2018–19	Aston Villa	18	1		
2018–19	*Portsmouth*	6	1	**6**	**1**
2019–20	Aston Villa	0	0	**40**	**2**
2019–20	*Preston NE*	4	0	**4**	**0**
2019–20	*Charlton Ath*	13	2	**13**	**2**
2020–21	Sheffield W	11	0	**11**	**0**

HAGAN, Charles (F) **0 0**
b. 6-9-01
From Chelsea.

2020–21	Sheffield W	0	0		

HARRIS, Kedeem (M) **191 10**
H: 5 9 W: 10 08 b.Westminster 8-6-93

2009–10	Wycombe W	2	0		
2010–11	Wycombe W	0	0		
2011–12	Wycombe W	17	0	**19**	**0**
2011–12	Cardiff C	0	0		
2012–13	Cardiff C	0	0		
2013–14	Cardiff C	0	0		
2013–14	*Brentford*	10	1	**10**	**1**
2014–15	Cardiff C	14	1		
2015–16	Cardiff C	3	0		
2015–16	*Barnsley*	11	0	**11**	**0**
2016–17	Cardiff C	37	4		
2017–18	Cardiff C	3	0		
2018–19	Cardiff C	13	1	**70**	**6**
2019–20	Sheffield W	43	3		
2020–21	Sheffield W	38	0	**81**	**3**

HUNT, Alex (M) **9 0**
b.Sheffield 29-5-00

2018–19	Sheffield W	0	0		
2019–20	Sheffield W	6	0		
2020–21	Sheffield W	3	0	**9**	**0**

HUTCHINSON, Sam (M) **185 6**
H: 6 0 W: 11 07 b.Windsor 3-8-89
Internationals: England U18, U19.

2006–07	Chelsea	1	0		
2007–08	Chelsea	0	0		

2008–09	Chelsea	0	0		
2009–10	Chelsea	2	0		
2010–11	Chelsea	0	0		
2011–12	Chelsea	2	0		
2012–13	Chelsea	0	0		
2012–13	*Nottingham F*	9	1	**9**	**1**
2013–14	Chelsea	0	0	**5**	**0**
2013–14	*Vitesse*	1	0	**1**	**0**
2013–14	*Sheffield W*	10	1		
2014–15	Sheffield W	20	0		
2015–16	Sheffield W	25	0		
2016–17	Sheffield W	33	2		
2017–18	Sheffield W	8	0		
2018–19	Sheffield W	24	0		
2019–20	Sheffield W	23	1		
2020–21	Pafos	5	0	**5**	**0**
2020–21	Sheffield W	22	1	**165**	**5**

IORFA, Dominic (D) **177** **6**
H: 6 2 W: 12 04 b.Southend-on-Sea 24-6-95
Internationals: England U18, U20, U21.

2013–14	Wolverhampton W	0	0		
2013–14	*Shrewsbury T*	7	0	**7**	**0**
2014–15	Wolverhampton W	20	0		
2015–16	Wolverhampton W	42	0		
2016–17	Wolverhampton W	22	0		
2017–18	Wolverhampton W	0	0		
2017–18	*Ipswich T*	23	1	**23**	**1**
2018–19	Wolverhampton W	0	0	**84**	**0**
2018–19	Sheffield W	12	3		
2019–20	Sheffield W	41	2		
2020–21	Sheffield W	10	0	**63**	**5**

JACKSON, Luke (G) **0** **0**
b. 18-3-02

2020–21	Sheffield W	0	0		

KACHUNGA, Elias (F) **253** **41**
H: 5 9 W: 10 01 b.Cologne 22-4-92
Internationals: Germany U19, U21, DR Congo Full caps.

2009–10	Borussia M'gladbach	0	0		
2010–11	Borussia M'gladbach	2	0		
2011–12	Borussia M'gladbach	0	0		
2011–12	*Osnabruck*	17	10	**17**	**10**
2012–13	Borussia M'gladbach	0	0	**2**	**0**
2012–13	*Hertha Berlin*	2	0	**2**	**0**
2012–13	*Paderborn*	13	3		
2013–14	Paderborn	33	6		
2014–15	Paderborn	32	6	**78**	**15**
2015–16	Ingolstadt	10	0		
2016–17	Ingolstadt	0	0	**10**	**0**
2016–17	*Huddersfield T*	42	12		
2017–18	Huddersfield T	19	1		
2018–19	Huddersfield T	20	0		
2019–20	Huddersfield T	36	3	**117**	**16**
2020–21	Sheffield W	27	0	**27**	**0**

LEES, Tom (D) **456** **17**
H: 6 1 W: 12 04 b.Warwick 28-11-90
Internationals: England U21.

2008–09	Leeds U	0	0		
2009–10	Leeds U	0	0		
2009–10	*Accrington S*	39	0	**39**	**0**
2010–11	Leeds U	0	0		
2010–11	*Bury*	45	4	**45**	**4**
2011–12	Leeds U	42	2		
2012–13	Leeds U	40	1		
2013–14	Leeds U	41	0	**123**	**3**
2014–15	Sheffield W	44	0		
2015–16	Sheffield W	34	3		
2016–17	Sheffield W	35	1		
2017–18	Sheffield W	29	1		
2018–19	Sheffield W	42	2		
2019–20	Sheffield W	27	2		
2020–21	Sheffield W	38	1	**249**	**10**

LUONGO, Massimo (F) **278** **26**
H: 5 8 W: 11 10 b.Sydney 25-9-92
Internationals: Australia U20, Full caps.

2010–11	Tottenham H	0	0		
2011–12	Tottenham H	0	0		
2012–13	Tottenham H	0	0		
2012–13	*Ipswich T*	9	0	**9**	**0**
2012–13	*Swindon T*	7	1		
2013–14	Swindon T	44	6		
2014–15	Swindon T	34	6	**85**	**13**
2015–16	QPR	30	0		
2016–17	QPR	35	1		
2017–18	QPR	39	6		
2018–19	QPR	41	3	**145**	**10**
2019–20	Sheffield W	27	3		
2020–21	Sheffield W	12	0	**39**	**3**

ODUBAJO, Moses (M) **250** **16**
H: 5 9 W: 11 05 b.Greenwich 28-7-93
Internationals: England U20.

2011–12	Leyton Orient	3	1		
2012–13	Leyton Orient	44	2		
2013–14	Leyton Orient	46	10	**93**	**13**
2014–15	Brentford	45	3		
2015–16	Hull C	42	0		
2016–17	Hull C	0	0		
2017–18	Hull C	0	0	**42**	**0**
2018–19	Brentford	30	0	**75**	**3**
2019–20	Sheffield W	22	0		
2020–21	Sheffield W	18	0	**40**	**0**

PALMER, Liam (M) **308** **2**
H: 6 2 W: 12 10 b.Worksop 19-9-91
Internationals: Scotland U19, U21, Full caps.

2010–11	Sheffield W	9	0		
2011–12	Sheffield W	14	1		
2012–13	Sheffield W	0	0		
2012–13	*Tranmere R*	43	0	**43**	**0**
2013–14	Sheffield W	39	0		
2014–15	Sheffield W	35	0		
2015–16	Sheffield W	15	0		
2016–17	Sheffield W	21	0		
2017–18	Sheffield W	25	0		
2018–19	Sheffield W	35	0		
2019–20	Sheffield W	33	0		
2020–21	Sheffield W	39	1	**265**	**2**

PATERSON, Callum (D) **275** **60**
H: 6 0 W: 12 00 b.London 13-10-94
Internationals: Scotland U18, U19, U21, Full caps.

2012–13	Hearts	22	3		
2013–14	Hearts	37	11		
2014–15	Hearts	29	6		
2015–16	Hearts	29	5		
2016–17	Hearts	20	8	**137**	**33**
2017–18	Cardiff C	32	10		
2018–19	Cardiff C	27	4		
2019–20	Cardiff C	36	5	**95**	**19**
2020–21	Sheffield W	43	8	**43**	**8**

PELUPESSY, Joey (M) **212** **3**
H: 5 8 W: 9 13 b.Nijverdal 15-5-93

2012–13	FC Twente	3	0		
2013–14	FC Twente	0	0	**3**	**0**
2014–15	Heracles	17	1		
2015–16	Heracles	34	0		
2016–17	Heracles	34	1		
2017–18	Heracles	18	0	**103**	**2**
2017–18	Sheffield W	17	1		
2018–19	Sheffield W	33	0		
2019–20	Sheffield W	17	0		
2020–21	Sheffield W	39	0	**106**	**1**

PENNEY, Matt (D) **48** **1**
b.Chesterfield 11-2-98

2016–17	Sheffield W	0	0		
2016–17	*Bradford C*	1	0	**1**	**0**
2017–18	Sheffield W	0	0		
2017–18	*Mansfield T*	2	0	**2**	**0**
2018–19	Sheffield W	16	0		
2019–20	Sheffield W	0	0		
2019–20	*St Pauli*	17	1	**17**	**1**
2020–21	Sheffield W	12	0	**28**	**0**

REACH, Adam (M) **346** **37**
H: 6 1 W: 11 07 b.Gateshead 3-2-93
Internationals: England U19, U20.

2010–11	Middlesbrough	1	1		
2011–12	Middlesbrough	1	0		
2012–13	Middlesbrough	16	2		
2013–14	Middlesbrough	2	0		
2013–14	*Shrewsbury T*	22	3	**22**	**3**
2013–14	*Bradford C*	18	3	**18**	**3**
2014–15	Middlesbrough	39	2		
2015–16	Middlesbrough	4	1		
2015–16	*Preston NE*	35	4	**35**	**4**
2016–17	Middlesbrough	0	0	**63**	**6**
2016–17	Sheffield W	39	3		
2017–18	Sheffield W	46	4		
2018–19	Sheffield W	42	8		
2019–20	Sheffield W	37	1		
2020–21	Sheffield W	44	5	**208**	**21**

RENDER, Joshua (G) **0** **0**

2020–21	Sheffield W	0	0		

RHODES, Jordan (F) **473** **195**
H: 6 1 W: 11 03 b.Oldham 5-2-90
Internationals: Scotland U21, Full caps.

2007–08	Ipswich T	8	1		
2008–09	Ipswich T	2	0	**10**	**1**
2008–09	*Rochdale*	5	2	**5**	**2**
2008–09	*Brentford*	14	7	**14**	**7**
2009–10	Huddersfield T	45	19		
2010–11	Huddersfield T	37	16		
2011–12	Huddersfield T	40	35		
2012–13	Huddersfield T	2	2	**124**	**72**
2012–13	Blackburn R	43	27		
2013–14	Blackburn R	46	25		
2014–15	Blackburn R	45	21		
2015–16	Blackburn R	25	10	**159**	**83**
2015–16	Middlesbrough	18	6		
2016–17	Middlesbrough	6	0	**24**	**6**
2016–17	*Sheffield W*	18	3		
2017–18	Sheffield W	31	5		
2018–19	Sheffield W	0	0		
2018–19	*Norwich C*	36	6	**36**	**6**
2019–20	Sheffield W	16	3		
2020–21	Sheffield W	36	7	**101**	**18**

RICE, Isaac (D) **0** **0**
b.Lincoln 30-9-00

2018–19	Sheffield W	0	0		
2019–20	Sheffield W	0	0		
2020–21	Sheffield W	0	0		

SHAW, Liam (M) **21** **1**
H: 5 10 b. 12-3-01

2018–19	Sheffield W	0	0		
2019–20	Sheffield W	2	0		
2020–21	Sheffield W	19	1	**21**	**1**

URHOGHIDE, Osaze (D) **19** **0**
b. 4-7-00

2017–18	AFC Wimbledon	0	0		
2018–19	AFC Wimbledon	0	0		
2019–20	Sheffield W	3	0		
2020–21	Sheffield W	16	0	**19**	**0**

VAN AKEN, Joost (D) **138** **4**
H: 5 10 W: 11 11 b.Haarlem 13-5-94
Internationals: Netherlands U21.

2013–14	Heerenveen	6	2		
2014–15	Heerenveen	30	0		
2015–16	Heerenveen	20	0		
2016–17	Heerenveen	26	1		
2017–18	Heerenveen	2	0	**84**	**3**
2017–18	Sheffield W	14	0		
2018–19	Sheffield W	1	0		
2019–20	Sheffield W	0	0		
2019–20	*Osnabruck*	22	1	**22**	**1**
2020–21	Sheffield W	17	0	**32**	**0**

Transferred to Zulte Waregem May 2021.

WALDOCK, Liam (M) **0** **0**
b. 25-9-00

2019–20	Sheffield W	0	0		
2020–21	Sheffield W	0	0		

WESTWOOD, Keiren (G) **469** **0**
H: 6 1 W: 13 10 b.Manchester 23-10-84
Internationals: Republic of Ireland Full caps.

2001–02	Manchester C	0	0		
2002–03	Manchester C	0	0		
2003–04	Manchester C	0	0		
2003–04	*Oldham Ath*	0	0		
2004–05	Manchester C	0	0		
2005–06	Manchester C	0	0		
2005–06	Carlisle U	35	0		
2006–07	Carlisle U	46	0		
2007–08	Carlisle U	46	0	**127**	**0**
2008–09	Coventry C	46	0		
2009–10	Coventry C	44	0		
2010–11	Coventry C	41	0	**131**	**0**
2011–12	Sunderland	9	0		
2012–13	Sunderland	0	0		
2013–14	Sunderland	10	0	**19**	**0**
2014–15	Sheffield W	43	0		
2015–16	Sheffield W	34	0		
2016–17	Sheffield W	43	0		
2017–18	Sheffield W	18	0		
2018–19	Sheffield W	20	0		
2019–20	Sheffield W	14	0		
2020–21	Sheffield W	20	0	**192**	**0**

WILDSMITH, Joe (G) **66** **0**
H: 6 0 W: 10 03 b.Sheffield 28-12-95
Internationals: England U20.

2013–14	Sheffield W	0	0		
2014–15	Sheffield W	0	0		
2014–15	*Barnsley*	2	0	**2**	**0**
2015–16	Sheffield W	9	0		
2016–17	Sheffield W	1	0		
2017–18	Sheffield W	26	0		
2018–19	Sheffield W	0	0		
2019–20	Sheffield W	9	0		
2020–21	Sheffield W	19	0	**64**	**0**

WINDASS, Josh (M) **234** **55**
H: 5 9 W: 10 10 b.Hull 9-1-93
From Huddersfield T, Harrogate Railway Ath.

2013–14	Accrington S	10	0		
2014–15	Accrington S	35	6		
2015–16	Accrington S	30	15	**75**	**21**
2016–17	Rangers	21	0		
2017–18	Rangers	33	13		
2018–19	Rangers	1	0	**55**	**13**
2018–19	Wigan Ath	39	5		
2019–20	Wigan Ath	15	4	**54**	**9**
2019–20	*Sheffield W*	9	3		
2020–21	Sheffield W	41	9	**50**	**12**

Scholars
Al-Jahadhmy, Murtadha Fuad; Asfha, Filimon Drar; Ashman, Joshua David; Bonnington, Alex; Curtis, Charlie Luke; Davidson, Leojo Chase Michael; Dutra Aguas, Paulo Jorge; Glaves, Corey Alan; Glover, Jay Michael; Hall, Luke Charles;

Hare, Alexander Charles; Kilheeney, Caelan Michael Carl; Sesay, Fuad; Trueman, William Henry Mangham; Wassell, Daniel Lewis; Whitham, Jenson; Yates, Luke David Richard; Zottos, Basile.

SHREWSBURY T (76)

ARIS, Nigel (M)				**0**	**0**
2020–21	Shrewsbury T	0	0		

BARNETT, Ryan (M)				**8**	**0**
b. 23-9-99					
2016–17	Shrewsbury T	0	0		
2017–18	Shrewsbury T	0	0		
2018–19	Shrewsbury T	1	0		
2019–20	Shrewsbury T	0	0		
2020–21	Shrewsbury T	7	0	**8**	**0**

BEVAN, Jaden (G)				**0**	**0**
2020–21	Shrewsbury T	0	0		

BLOXHAM, Tom (F)				**4**	**0**
b. 1-11-03					
2020–21	Shrewsbury T	4	0	**4**	**0**

BURGOYNE, Harry (G)				**42**	**0**
H: 6 4 W: 13 05 b.Ludlow 28-12-96					
2015–16	Wolverhampton W	0	0		
2016–17	*Barnet*	2	0	**2**	**0**
2016–17	Wolverhampton W	6	0		
2017–18	Wolverhampton W	1	0		
2018–19	Wolverhampton W	0	0		
2018–19	*Falkirk*	15	0	**15**	**0**
2019–20	Wolverhampton W	0	0	**7**	**0**
2019–20	Shrewsbury T	0	0		
2020–21	Shrewsbury T	18	0	**18**	**0**

CATON, Charlie (F)				**3**	**0**
b. 25-11-02					
2019–20	Shrewsbury T	0	0		
2020–21	Shrewsbury T	3	0	**3**	**0**

CLARKE, Leon (F)				**468**	**139**
H: 6 2 W: 14 02 b.Birmingham 10-2-85					
2003–04	Wolverhampton W	0	0		
2003–04	*Kidderminster H*	4	0	**4**	**0**
2004–05	Wolverhampton W	28	7		
2005–06	Wolverhampton W	24	1		
2005–06	*QPR*	1	0		
2005–06	*Plymouth Arg*	5	0	**5**	**0**
2006–07	Wolverhampton W	22	5		
2006–07	Sheffield W	10	1		
2006–07	*Oldham Ath*	5	3	**5**	**3**
2007–08	Sheffield W	8	3		
2007–08	*Southend U*	16	8	**16**	**8**
2008–09	Sheffield W	29	8		
2009–10	Sheffield W	36	6	**83**	**18**
2010–11	QPR	13	0	**14**	**0**
2010–11	*Preston NE*	6	1	**6**	**1**
2011–12	Swindon T	2	0	**2**	**0**
2011–12	*Chesterfield*	14	9	**14**	**9**
2011–12	Charlton Ath	7	0		
2011–12	*Crawley T*	4	1	**4**	**1**
2012–13	Charlton Ath	0	0	**7**	**0**
2012–13	*Scunthorpe U*	15	11	**15**	**11**
2012–13	Coventry C	12	8		
2013–14	Coventry C	23	15	**35**	**23**
2013–14	Wolverhampton W	13	1		
2014–15	Wolverhampton W	16	2	**103**	**16**
2014–15	*Wigan Ath*	10	1		
2015–16	Bury	32	15	**32**	**15**
2016–17	Sheffield U	23	7		
2017–18	Sheffield U	39	19		
2018–19	Sheffield U	24	3		
2018–19	*Wigan Ath*	15	3	**25**	**4**
2019–20	Sheffield U	2	0	**88**	**29**
2020–21	Shrewsbury T	10	1	**10**	**1**

CUMMINGS, Jason (F)				**205**	**69**
H: 5 10 W: 10 10 b.Edinburgh 1-8-95					
Internationals: Scotland U19, U21, Full caps.					
2013–14	Hibernian	16	0		
2014–15	Hibernian	33	18		
2015–16	Hibernian	33	18		
2016–17	Hibernian	32	19	**114**	**55**
2017–18	Nottingham F	14	1		
2017–18	*Rangers*	15	2	**15**	**2**
2018–19	Nottingham F	0	0		
2018–19	*Peterborough U*	22	6	**22**	**6**
2018–19	*Luton T*	5	1	**5**	**1**
2019–20	Nottingham F	0	0	**14**	**1**
2019–20	Shrewsbury T	24	4		
2020–21	Shrewsbury T	11	0	**35**	**4**
Transferred to Dundee January 2021.					

DANIELS, Josh (F)				**19**	**2**
b.Derry 22-2-96					
From Derry C, Glenavon.					
2020–21	Shrewsbury T	19	2	**19**	**2**

DAVIS, David (M)				**301**	**12**
H: 5 8 W: 12 03 b.Smethwick 20-2-91					
2009–10	Wolverhampton W	0	0		
2009–10	*Darlington*	5	0	**5**	**0**
2010–11	Wolverhampton W	0	0		
2010–11	*Walsall*	7	0	**7**	**0**
2010–11	*Shrewsbury T*	19	2		
2011–12	Wolverhampton W	7	0		
2011–12	*Chesterfield*	9	0	**9**	**0**
2012–13	Wolverhampton W	28	0		
2013–14	Wolverhampton W	18	0	**53**	**0**
2014–15	Birmingham C	42	3		
2015–16	Birmingham C	35	1		
2016–17	Birmingham C	41	4		
2017–18	Birmingham C	38	2		
2018–19	Birmingham C	11	0		
2019–20	Birmingham C	15	0		
2019–20	*Charlton Ath*	5	0	**5**	**0**
2020–21	Birmingham C	0	0	**182**	**10**
2020–21	Shrewsbury T	21	0	**40**	**2**

EBANKS-LANDELL, Ethan (M)				**214**	**16**
H: 5 6 W: 11 02 b.Oldbury 16-12-92					
2009–10	Wolverhampton W	0	0		
2010–11	Wolverhampton W	0	0		
2011–12	Wolverhampton W	0	0		
2012–13	Wolverhampton W	0	0		
2012–13	*Bury*	24	0	**24**	**0**
2013–14	Wolverhampton W	7	2		
2014–15	Wolverhampton W	14	2		
2015–16	Wolverhampton W	21	1		
2016–17	Wolverhampton W	0	0		
2016–17	*Sheffield U*	34	5	**34**	**5**
2017–18	Wolverhampton W	0	0		
2017–18	*Milton Keynes D*	29	2	**29**	**2**
2018–19	Wolverhampton W	0	0	**42**	**5**
2018–19	*Rochdale*	16	2	**16**	**2**
2019–20	Shrewsbury T	28	1		
2020–21	Shrewsbury T	41	1	**69**	**2**

EDWARDS, Dave (M)				**504**	**62**
H: 5 11 W: 11 04 b.Shrewsbury 3-2-86					
Internationals: Wales U21, Full caps.					
2002–03	Shrewsbury T	1	0		
2003–04	Shrewsbury T	0	0		
2004–05	Shrewsbury T	27	5		
2005–06	Shrewsbury T	30	2		
2006–07	Shrewsbury T	45	5		
2007–08	Luton T	19	4	**19**	**4**
2007–08	Wolverhampton W	10	1		
2008–09	Wolverhampton W	44	3		
2009–10	Wolverhampton W	20	1		
2010–11	Wolverhampton W	15	1		
2011–12	Wolverhampton W	26	3		
2012–13	Wolverhampton W	24	2		
2013–14	Wolverhampton W	30	9		
2014–15	Wolverhampton W	41	6		
2015–16	Wolverhampton W	29	5		
2016–17	Wolverhampton W	44	10		
2017–18	Wolverhampton W	1	0	**284**	**41**
2017–18	Reading	32	3		
2018–19	Reading	0	0	**32**	**3**
2018–19	Shrewsbury T	6	0		
2019–20	Shrewsbury T	29	1		
2020–21	Shrewsbury T	31	1	**169**	**14**

GOLBOURNE, Scott (M)				**401**	**7**
H: 5 8 W: 11 08 b.Bristol 29-2-88					
Internationals: England U17, U19.					
2004–05	Bristol C	9	0		
2005–06	Bristol C	5	0		
2005–06	Reading	1	0		
2006–07	Reading	0	0		
2006–07	*Wycombe W*	34	1	**34**	**1**
2007–08	Reading	1	0		
2007–08	*Bournemouth*	5	0	**5**	**0**
2008–09	Reading	0	0	**2**	**0**
2008–09	*Oldham Ath*	8	0	**8**	**0**
2009–10	Exeter C	34	0		
2010–11	Exeter C	44	2		
2011–12	Exeter C	26	0	**104**	**2**
2011–12	Barnsley	12	1		
2012–13	Barnsley	31	1		
2013–14	Barnsley	4	0	**47**	**2**
2013–14	Wolverhampton W	40	1		
2014–15	Wolverhampton W	27	0		
2015–16	Wolverhampton W	20	0	**87**	**1**
2015–16	Bristol C	16	0		
2016–17	Bristol C	19	0		
2017–18	Bristol C	0	0	**49**	**0**
2017–18	*Milton Keynes D*	25	0	**25**	**0**
2018–19	Shrewsbury T	15	0		
2019–20	Shrewsbury T	15	1		
2020–21	Shrewsbury T	10	0	**40**	**1**

GOSS, Sean (M)				**67**	**5**
H: 5 10 W: 11 03 b.Wegberg 1-10-95					
2015–16	Manchester U	0	0		
2016–17	Manchester U	0	0		
2016–17	QPR	6	0		
2017–18	QPR	0	0		
2017–18	*Rangers*	13	2	**13**	**2**
2018–19	QPR	0	0		
2018–19	*St Johnstone*	6	0	**6**	**0**
2019–20	QPR	0	0	**6**	**0**
2019–20	Shrewsbury T	22	0		
2020–21	Shrewsbury T	20	3	**42**	**3**

GREGORY, Cameron (G)				**0**	**0**
2017–18	Shrewsbury T	0	0		
2018–19	Shrewsbury T	0	0		
2019–20	Shrewsbury T	0	0		
2020–21	Shrewsbury T	0	0		

LLOYD, Louis (F)				**0**	**0**
From Connah's Quay Nomads.					
2020–21	Shrewsbury T	0	0		

LOVE, Donald (D)				**77**	**0**
H: 5 10 W: 11 05 b.Rochdale 2-12-94					
Internationals: Scotland U17, U19, U21.					
2015–16	Manchester U	1	0	**1**	**0**
2015–16	*Wigan Ath*	7	0	**7**	**0**
2016–17	Sunderland	12	0		
2017–18	Sunderland	11	0		
2018–19	Sunderland	4	0	**27**	**0**
2019–20	Shrewsbury T	28	0		
2020–21	Shrewsbury T	14	0	**42**	**0**

MAIN, Curtis (F)				**280**	**42**
H: 5 9 W: 12 02 b.South Shields 20-6-92					
2007–08	Darlington	1	0		
2008–09	Darlington	18	2		
2009–10	Darlington	26	3		
2010–11	Darlington	0	0	**45**	**5**
2011–12	Middlesbrough	12	2		
2012–13	Middlesbrough	13	3		
2013–14	Middlesbrough	23	1	**48**	**6**
2013–14	*Shrewsbury T*	5	0		
2014–15	Doncaster R	38	8		
2015–16	Doncaster R	10	1	**48**	**9**
2015–16	*Oldham Ath*	18	4	**18**	**4**
2016–17	Portsmouth	12	2		
2017–18	Portsmouth	5	0	**17**	**2**
2017–18	Motherwell	16	5		
2018–19	Motherwell	31	3	**47**	**8**
2019–20	Aberdeen	18	4		
2020–21	Aberdeen	14	2	**32**	**6**
2020–21	Shrewsbury T	20	2	**25**	**2**

MILLAR, Matthew (D)				**157**	**31**
b. 23-8-96					
2013	Dandenong Thunder	9	0		
2014	Dandenong Thunder	25	7	**34**	**7**
2014–15	Melbourne C	0	0		
2015–16	Melbourne C	4	0	**4**	**0**
2016	South Melbourne	26	7		
2017	South Melbourne	25	9		
2018	South Melbourne	14	2	**65**	**18**
2018–19	Central Coast Mariners	21	1	**21**	**1**
2019–20	Newcastle Jets	24	4		
2020–21	Newcastle Jets	0	0	**24**	**4**
On loan from Newcastle Jets.					
2020–21	Shrewsbury T	9	1	**9**	**1**

NORBURN, Oliver (M)				**167**	**19**
H: 6 1 W: 12 13 b.Leicester 26-10-92					
2011–12	Leicester C	0	0		
2011–12	*Bristol R*	5	0		
2012–13	Bristol R	35	3		
2013–14	Bristol R	16	0	**56**	**3**
2014–15	Plymouth Arg	14	0	**14**	**0**
From Guiseley, Macclesfield T, Tranmere R.					
2018–19	Shrewsbury T	41	9		
2019–20	Shrewsbury T	17	3		
2020–21	Shrewsbury T	39	4	**97**	**16**

OGBETA, Nathaniel (D)				**25**	**2**
b. 28-4-01					
2018–19	Manchester C	0	0		
2019–20	Manchester C	0	0		
2020–21	Shrewsbury T	25	2	**25**	**2**

PIERRE, Aaron (D)				**245**	**22**
H: 6 1 W: 13 12 b.Southall 17-2-93					
Internationals: Grenada Full caps.					
2011–12	Brentford	0	0		
2012–13	Brentford	0	0		
2013–14	Brentford	0	0		
2013–14	*Wycombe W*	8	1		
2014–15	Wycombe W	42	4		
2015–16	Wycombe W	40	2		
2016–17	Wycombe W	39	2	**129**	**9**
2017–18	Northampton T	19	0		
2018–19	Northampton T	41	6	**60**	**6**
2019–20	Shrewsbury T	30	3		
2020–21	Shrewsbury T	26	4	**56**	**7**

PUGH, Marc (M)				**461**	**73**
H: 5 11 W: 11 04 b.Bacup 2-4-87					
2005–06	Burnley	0	0		
2005–06	Bury	6	1		
2006–07	Bury	35	3	**41**	**4**
2007–08	Shrewsbury T	37	4		
2008–09	Shrewsbury T	7	0		

2008–09	*Luton T*	4	0	**4**	**0**
2008–09	*Hereford U*	9	1		
2009–10	Hereford U	40	13	**49**	**14**
2010–11	Bournemouth	41	12		
2011–12	Bournemouth	42	8		
2012–13	Bournemouth	40	6		
2013–14	Bournemouth	42	5		
2014–15	Bournemouth	42	9		
2015–16	Bournemouth	26	3		
2016–17	Bournemouth	21	2		
2017–18	Bournemouth	20	0		
2018–19	Bournemouth	0	0	**274**	**45**
2018–19	*Hull C*	14	3	**14**	**3**
2019–20	QPR	27	2	**27**	**2**
2020–21	Shrewsbury T	8	1	**52**	**5**

PYKE, Rekeil (F) **51** **1**
H: 5 10 W: 10 03 b. 1-9-97

2016–17	Huddersfield T	0	0		
2016–17	*Colchester U*	12	0	**12**	**0**
2017–18	Huddersfield T	0	0		
2017–18	*Port Vale*	7	0	**7**	**0**
2018–19	Huddersfield T	0	0		
2018–19	*Rochdale*	6	0		
2019–20	Huddersfield T	1	0	**1**	**0**
2019–20	*Rochdale*	13	1	**19**	**1**
2020–21	Shrewsbury T	12	0	**12**	**0**

ROWLAND, James (M) **0** **0**
b.Walsall 3-12-01
From WBA.

2018–19	Shrewsbury T	0	0		
2019–20	Shrewsbury T	0	0		
2020–21	Shrewsbury T	0	0		

SEARS, Ryan (D) **12** **0**
b. 13-12-98

2016–17	Shrewsbury T	0	0		
2017–18	Shrewsbury T	0	0		
2018–19	Shrewsbury T	5	0		
2019–20	Shrewsbury T	2	0		
2020–21	Shrewsbury T	5	0	**12**	**0**

TRACEY, Shilow (F) **32** **2**
b. 29-4-98
From Ebbsfleet U.

2016–17	Tottenham H	0	0		
2017–18	Tottenham H	0	0		
2018–19	Tottenham H	0	0		
2019–20	Tottenham H	0	0		
2019–20	*Macclesfield T*	7	1	**7**	**1**
2020–21	Tottenham H	0	0		
2020–21	Shrewsbury T	8	0	**8**	**0**
2020–21	*Cambridge U*	17	1	**17**	**1**

UDOH, Daniel (F) **79** **8**
H: 6 0 W: 13 01 b. 30-8-96
Internationals: Nigeria U17.
From Worcester C, North Greenwood U, Grays Ath, Hoddesdon T, Ilkeston.

2015–16	Crewe Alex	6	0		
2016–17	Crewe Alex	9	0	**15**	**0**

From AFC Telford U.

2019–20	Shrewsbury T	25	4		
2020–21	Shrewsbury T	39	4	**64**	**8**

VELA, Joshua (M) **224** **15**
H: 5 11 W: 11 07 b.Salford 14-12-93

2010–11	Bolton W	0	0		
2011–12	Bolton W	3	0		
2012–13	Bolton W	4	0		
2013–14	Bolton W	0	0		
2013–14	*Notts Co*	7	0	**7**	**0**
2014–15	Bolton W	29	0		
2015–16	Bolton W	31	2		
2016–17	Bolton W	46	9		
2017–18	Bolton W	30	1		
2018–19	Bolton W	17	0	**160**	**12**
2019–20	Hibernian	9	0	**9**	**0**
2019–20	Shrewsbury T	4	0		
2020–21	Shrewsbury T	44	3	**48**	**3**

WALKER, Brad (M) **173** **12**
H: 6 1 W: 12 08 b. 25-4-95

2012–13	Hartlepool U	0	0		
2013–14	Hartlepool U	36	3		
2014–15	Hartlepool U	28	5		
2015–16	Hartlepool U	23	1		
2016–17	Hartlepool U	20	1	**107**	**10**
2017–18	Crewe Alex	27	1		
2018–19	Crewe Alex	1	0	**28**	**1**
2019–20	Shrewsbury T	15	0		
2020–21	Shrewsbury T	23	1	**38**	**1**

WHALLEY, Shaun (M) **265** **38**
H: 5 9 W: 10 08 b.Whiston 7-8-87

2004–05	Chester C	3	0	**3**	**0**

From Runcorn, Witton Alb.

2006–07	Accrington S	20	2		
2007–08	Accrington S	31	3	**51**	**5**

From Wrexham, Droylsden, Hyde U, Southport.

2014–15	Luton T	18	3	**18**	**3**
2015–16	Shrewsbury T	24	6		
2016–17	Shrewsbury T	32	3		
2017–18	Shrewsbury T	44	8		
2018–19	Shrewsbury T	32	2		
2019–20	Shrewsbury T	23	2		
2020–21	Shrewsbury T	38	9	**193**	**30**

WILLIAMS, Ro-Shaun (M) **81** **0**
b. 9-3-98
Internationals: England U17, U18, U19.

2015–16	Manchester U	0	0		
2016–17	Manchester u	0	0		
2017–18	Manchester u	0	0		
2018–19	Manchester U	0	0		
2018–19	Shrewsbury T	16	0		
2019–20	Shrewsbury T	25	0		
2020–21	Shrewsbury T	40	0	**81**	**0**

Scholars
Akinwe, Akanni Oluwademilade; Aris, Nigel Achuche Anayo; Barlow, Joshua Daniel; Bell, Jacob Philip; Bevan, Jaden Thomas; Bloxham, Thomas Stanley; Brown, Amarie Solomon; Caton, Charlie George; Cooper, Jenson George; Crompton, Ben Robert; Duberry, Lewis Joseph; Harper, Remmiko Jasiah; Kaninda, Ben Benedict Tshiba; Lloyd, Louis Charles; O'Toole, Ethan David; Sears, Edan Martin; Spiers, James Matthew; Thomas, William Luke; Wilson, Callum Ray.

SOUTHAMPTON (77)

ADAMS, Che (F) **229** **58**
H: 5 10 W: 10 06 b.Leicester 13-7-96
Internationals: England C, U20.
From Ilkeston.

2014–15	Sheffield U	10	0		
2015–16	Sheffield U	36	11		
2016–17	Sheffield U	1	0	**47**	**11**
2016–17	Birmingham C	40	7		
2017–18	Birmingham C	30	5		
2018–19	Birmingham C	46	22	**116**	**34**
2019–20	Southampton	30	4		
2020–21	Southampton	36	9	**66**	**13**

ARMSTRONG, Stuart (M) **317** **53**
H: 6 0 W: 10 10 b.Inverness 30-3-92
Internationals: Scotland U19, U21, Full caps.

2010–11	Dundee U	12	0		
2011–12	Dundee U	23	1		
2012–13	Dundee U	36	3		
2013–14	Dundee U	36	8		
2014–15	Dundee U	20	6	**127**	**18**
2014–15	Celtic	15	1		
2015–16	Celtic	25	4		
2016–17	Celtic	31	15		
2017–18	Celtic	27	3	**98**	**23**
2018–19	Southampton	29	3		
2019–20	Southampton	30	5		
2020–21	Southampton	33	4	**92**	**12**

BEDNAREK, Jan (D) **148** **4**
H: 6 2 W: 12 02 b.Slupca 12-4-96
Internationals: Poland U16, U17, U18, U19, U20, U21, Full caps.

2013–14	Lech Poznan	2	0		
2014–15	Lech Poznan	2	0		
2015–16	Lech Poznan	0	0		
2015–16	*Gornik Leczna*	17	0	**17**	**0**
2016–17	Lech Poznan	27	1	**31**	**1**
2017–18	Southampton	5	1		
2018–19	Southampton	25	0		
2019–20	Southampton	34	1		
2020–21	Southampton	36	1	**100**	**3**

BELLIS, Sam (M) **0** **0**
b.Manchester 30-12-02
From Manchester C.

2020–21	Southampton	0	0		

BERTRAND, Ryan (D) **403** **8**
H: 5 10 W: 11 00 b.Southwark 5-8-89
Internationals: England U17, U18, U19, U20, U21, Full caps. Great Britain.

2006–07	Chelsea	0	0		
2006–07	*Bournemouth*	5	0	**5**	**0**
2007–08	Chelsea	0	0		
2007–08	*Oldham Ath*	21	0	**21**	**0**
2007–08	*Norwich C*	18	0		
2008–09	Chelsea	0	0		
2008–09	*Norwich C*	38	0	**56**	**0**
2009–10	Chelsea	0	0		
2009–10	*Reading*	44	1	**44**	**1**
2010–11	Chelsea	1	0		
2010–11	*Nottingham F*	19	0	**19**	**0**
2011–12	Chelsea	7	0		
2012–13	Chelsea	19	0		
2013–14	Chelsea	1	0	**28**	**0**
2013–14	*Aston Villa*	16	0	**16**	**0**
2014–15	Southampton	34	2		
2015–16	Southampton	32	1		
2016–17	Southampton	28	2		
2017–18	Southampton	35	0		
2018–19	Southampton	24	1		
2019–20	Southampton	32	1		
2020–21	Southampton	29	0	**214**	**7**

BYCROFT, Jack (G) **0** **0**
H: 6 0 W: 11 03 b.Salisbury 21-9-01
Internationals: England U19.

2020–21	Southampton	0	0		

CHAUKE, Kgaogelo (M) **0** **0**
b. 8-1-03
From Thatcham T.

2020–21	Southampton	0	0		

DIALLO, Ibrahima (M) **64** **0**
b. 8-3-99

2017–18	Monaco	0	0		
2018–19	Monaco	0	0		
2018–19	*Brest*	23	0		
2019–20	Brest	19	0		
2020–21	Brest	0	0	**42**	**0**
2020–21	Southampton	22	0	**22**	**0**

DJENEPO, Moussa (F) **94** **12**
b.Bamako 15-1-98
Internationals: Mali U20, Full caps.

2017–18	Standard Liege	17	1		
2018–19	Standard Liege	32	8	**49**	**9**
2019–20	Southampton	18	2		
2020–21	Southampton	27	1	**45**	**3**

FERRY, Will (M) **0** **0**
Internationals: Republic of Ireland U18, U19.

2016–17	Bury	0	0		
2017–18	Southampton	0	0		
2018–19	Southampton	0	0		
2019–20	Southampton	0	0		
2020–21	Southampton	0	0		

FINNIGAN, Ryan (M) **0** **0**
b. 23-9-03

2020–21	Southampton	0	0		

FORSTER, Fraser (G) **331** **0**
H: 6 0 W: 12 00 b.Hexham 17-3-88
Internationals: England Full caps.

2007–08	Newcastle U	0	0		
2008–09	Newcastle U	0	0		
2008–09	*Stockport Co*	6	0	**6**	**0**
2009–10	Newcastle U	0	0		
2009–10	*Bristol R*	4	0	**4**	**0**
2009–10	*Norwich C*	38	0	**38**	**0**
2010–11	Newcastle U	0	0		
2010–11	*Celtic*	36	0		
2011–12	Newcastle U	0	0		
2011–12	*Celtic*	33	0		
2012–13	Celtic	34	0		
2013–14	Celtic	37	0		
2014–15	Southampton	30	0		
2015–16	Southampton	18	0		
2016–17	Southampton	38	0		
2017–18	Southampton	20	0		
2018–19	Southampton	1	0		
2019–20	Southampton	0	0		
2019–20	*Celtic*	28	0	**168**	**0**
2020–21	Southampton	8	0	**115**	**0**

GUNN, Angus (G) **83** **0**
H: 6 0 W: 12 02 b.Norwich 22-1-96
Internationals: England U16, U17, U18, U19, U20, U21.

2013–14	Manchester C	0	0		
2014–15	Manchester C	0	0		
2015–16	Manchester C	0	0		
2016–17	Manchester C	0	0		
2017–18	Manchester C	0	0		
2017–18	*Norwich C*	46	0	**46**	**0**
2018–19	Southampton	12	0		
2019–20	Southampton	10	0		
2020–21	Southampton	0	0	**22**	**0**
2020–21	*Stoke C*	15	0	**15**	**0**

HESKETH, Jake (M) **69** **4**
H: 5 6 W: 9 13 b. 27-3-96

2014–15	Southampton	2	0		
2015–16	Southampton	0	0		
2016–17	Southampton	0	0		
2017–18	Southampton	0	0		
2018–19	Southampton	0	0		
2018–19	Southampton	0	0		
2018–19	*Burton Alb*	16	1	**16**	**1**
2018–19	*Milton Keynes D*	16	2	**16**	**2**
2019–20	Southampton	0	0		
2019–20	*Lincoln C*	20	1	**20**	**1**
2020–21	Southampton	0	0	**2**	**0**
2020–21	*Crawley T*	15	0	**15**	**0**

HOEDT, Wesley (D) **160** **4**
H: 6 2 W: 12 02 b.Alkmaar 6-3-94
Internationals: Netherlands U20, U20, Full caps.

2013–14	AZ Alkmaar	2	0		

2014–15 AZ Alkmaar 24 2 **26 2**
2015–16 Lazio 25 0
2016–17 Lazio 23 2
2017–18 Lazio 0 0
2017–18 Southampton 28 0
2018–19 Southampton 13 0
2018–19 *Celta Vigo* 10 0 **10 0**
2019–20 Southampton 0 0
2019–20 *Royal Antwerp* 18 0 **18 0**
2020–21 Southampton 0 0 **41 0**
2020–21 *Lazio* 17 0 **65 2**
Transferred to Anderlecht June 2021.

INGS, Danny (F) 254 89
H: 5 10 W: 11 07 b.Winchester 16-3-92
Internationals: England U21, Full caps.
2009–10 Bournemouth 0 0
2010–11 Bournemouth 26 7
2011–12 Bournemouth 1 0 **27 7**
2011–12 Burnley 15 3
2012–13 Burnley 32 3
2013–14 Burnley 40 21
2014–15 Burnley 35 11 **122 38**
2015–16 Liverpool 6 2
2016–17 Liverpool 0 0
2017–18 Liverpool 8 1
2018–19 Liverpool 0 0 **14 3**
2018–19 *Southampton* 24 7
2019–20 Southampton 38 22
2020–21 Southampton 29 12 **91 41**

JANKEWITZ, Alexandre (M) 2 0
b.Vevey 25-12-01
Internationals: Switzerland U16, U17, U18, U19.
From Servette.
2019–20 Southampton 0 0
2020–21 Southampton 2 0 **2 0**

LEMINA, Mario (M) 178 8
H: 6 0 W: 12 00 b.Libreville 1-9-93
Internationals: France U20, U21. Gabon Full caps.
2012–13 Lorient 10 0
2013–14 Lorient 4 0 **14 0**
2013–14 Marseille 14 0
2014–15 Marseille 23 2
2015–16 Marseille 4 0 **41 2**
2015–16 Juventus 10 2
2016–17 Juventus 19 1 **29 3**
2017–18 Southampton 25 1
2018–19 Southampton 21 1
2019–20 Southampton 0 0
2019–20 *Galatasaray* 20 0 **20 0**
2020–21 Southampton 0 0 **46 2**
2020–21 *Fulham* 28 1 **28 1**

LEWIS, Harry (G) 30 0
b. 20-12-97
Internationals: England U18.
2015–16 Shrewsbury T 0 0
2016–17 Shrewsbury T 0 0
2016–17 Southampton 0 0
2017–18 Southampton 0 0
2017–18 *Dundee U* 30 0 **30 0**
2018–19 Southampton 0 0
2019–20 Southampton 0 0
2020–21 Southampton 0 0

LONG, Shane (F) 467 96
H: 5 10 W: 11 02 b.Co. Tipperary 22-1-87
Internationals: Republic of Ireland B, U21, Full caps.
2005 Cork C 1 0 **1 0**
2005–06 Reading 11 3
2006–07 Reading 21 2
2007–08 Reading 29 3
2008–09 Reading 37 9
2009–10 Reading 31 6
2010–11 Reading 44 21
2011–12 Reading 1 0 **174 44**
2011–12 WBA 32 8
2012–13 WBA 34 8
2013–14 WBA 15 3 **81 19**
2013–14 Hull C 15 4 **15 4**
2014–15 Southampton 32 5
2015–16 Southampton 28 10
2016–17 Southampton 32 3
2017–18 Southampton 30 2
2018–19 Southampton 26 5
2019–20 Southampton 26 2
2020–21 Southampton 11 0 **185 27**
2020–21 *Bournemouth* 11 2 **11 2**

McCARTHY, Alex (G) 248 0
H: 6 4 W: 11 12 b.Guildford 3-12-89
Internationals: England U21, Full caps.
2008–09 Reading 0 0
2008–09 *Aldershot T* 4 0 **4 0**
2009–10 Reading 0 0
2009–10 *Yeovil T* 44 0 **44 0**
2010–11 Reading 13 0
2010–11 *Brentford* 3 0 **3 0**
2011–12 Reading 0 0
2011–12 *Leeds U* 6 0 **6 0**
2011–12 *Ipswich T* 10 0 **10 0**
2012–13 Reading 13 0
2013–14 Reading 44 0 **70 0**
2014–15 QPR 3 0 **3 0**
2015–16 Crystal Palace 7 0 **7 0**
2016–17 Southampton 0 0
2017–18 Southampton 18 0
2018–19 Southampton 25 0
2019–20 Southampton 28 0
2020–21 Southampton 30 0 **101 0**

MITCHELL, Ramello (M) 0 0
b.Birmingham 1-1-03
From Birmingham C.
2020–21 Southampton 0 0

N'LUNDULU, Daniel (F) 13 0
b. 5-2-99
Internationals: England U16.
2016–17 Southampton 0 0
2017–18 Southampton 0 0
2018–19 Southampton 0 0
2019–20 Southampton 0 0
2020–21 Southampton 13 0 **13 0**

O'CONNOR, Thomas (M) 62 1
b. 21-4-99
Internationals: Republic of Ireland U19, U21.
2019–20 Southampton 0 0
2019–20 *Gillingham* 28 1
2020–21 Southampton 0 0
2020–21 *Gillingham* 34 0 **62 1**

OBAFEMI, Michael (F) 32 4
H: 5 7 W: 11 03 b.Dublin 6-7-00
Internationals: Republic of Ireland U19, Full caps.
From Leyton Orient.
2017–18 Southampton 1 0
2018–19 Southampton 6 1
2019–20 Southampton 21 3
2020–21 Southampton 4 0 **32 4**

OLAIGBE, Kazeem (F) 0 0
b. 2-1-03
Internationals: Belgium U16, U17.
From Anderlecht.
2020–21 Southampton 0 0

OLUFUNWA, Dare (D) 0 0
b.Southampton 29-7-01
2020–21 Southampton 0 0

PAMBOU, Leon (D) 0 0
b. 25-1-04
From Metz.
2020–21 Southampton 0 0

RAMSEY, Kayne (D) 7 0
b. 10-10-00
From Chelsea.
2018–19 Southampton 1 0
2019–20 Southampton 0 0
2019–20 *Shrewsbury T* 5 0 **5 0**
2020–21 Southampton 1 0 **2 0**

REDMOND, Nathan (M) 341 38
H: 5 8 W: 11 11 b.Birmingham 6-3-94
Internationals: England U16, U17, U18, U19, U20, U21, Full caps.
2011–12 Birmingham C 24 5
2012–13 Birmingham C 38 2 **62 7**
2013–14 Norwich C 34 1
2014–15 Norwich C 43 4
2015–16 Norwich C 35 6 **112 11**
2016–17 Southampton 37 7
2017–18 Southampton 31 1
2018–19 Southampton 38 6
2019–20 Southampton 32 4
2020–21 Southampton 29 2 **167 20**

RODRIGUEZ, Jeremi (D) 0 0
From Las Palmas.
2020–21 Southampton 0 0

ROMEU, Oriol (M) 292 6
H: 6 0 W: 12 06 b.Ulldecona 24-9-91
Internationals: Spain U17, U19, U20, U21, U23.
2008–09 Barcelona B 5 0
2009–10 Barcelona B 26 0
2010–11 Barcelona B 18 1 **49 1**
2010–11 Barcelona 1 0 **1 0**
2011–12 Chelsea 16 0
2012–13 Chelsea 6 0
2013–14 Chelsea 0 0
2013–14 *Valencia* 13 0 **13 0**
2014–15 Chelsea 0 0 **22 0**
2014–15 *Stuttgart* 27 0 **27 0**
2015–16 Southampton 29 1
2016–17 Southampton 35 1
2017–18 Southampton 34 1
2018–19 Southampton 31 1
2019–20 Southampton 30 0
2020–21 Southampton 21 1 **180 5**

ROSS-LANG, Fedel (F) 0 0
Internationals: England U17.
From Manchester C.
2020–21 Southampton 0 0

SALISU, Mohammed (D) 43 1
b.Citizenship 17-4-99
2017–18 Real Vallodolid 0 0
2018–19 Real Vallodolid 0 0
2019–20 Real Vallodolid 31 1 **31 1**
2020–21 Valladolid 0 0
2020–21 Southampton 12 0 **12 0**

SIMS, Josh (M) 75 1
b. 28-3-97
Internationals: England U17, U18, U20.
From Portsmouth.
2016–17 Southampton 7 0
2017–18 Southampton 6 0
2018–19 Southampton 7 0
2018–19 *Reading* 17 0 **17 0**
2019–20 Southampton 0 0
2019–20 *New York Red Bulls* 10 0 **10 0**
2020–21 Southampton 0 0 **20 0**
2020–21 *Doncaster R* 28 1 **28 1**

SLATTERY, Callum (M) 15 1
b. 8-2-99
Internationals: England U16, U17, U20.
2018–19 Southampton 3 0
2019–20 Southampton 0 0
2019–20 *De Graafschap* 5 1 **5 1**
2020–21 Southampton 0 0 **3 0**
2020–21 *Gillingham* 7 0 **7 0**

SMALES-BRAITHWAITE, Benni (F) 0 0
b.Leeds 29-4-02
Internationals: England U16.
From Manchester C.
2020–21 Southampton 0 0

SMALLBONE, William (M) 12 0
b. 21-2-00
Internationals: Republic of Ireland U18, U19.
2016–17 Southampton 0 0
2017–18 Southampton 0 0
2018–19 Southampton 0 0
2019–20 Southampton 9 0
2020–21 Southampton 3 0 **12 0**

STEPHENS, Jack (D) 178 5
H: 6 1 W: 13 03 b.Torpoint 27-1-94
Internationals: England U18, U19, U20, U21.
2010–11 Plymouth Arg 5 0 **5 0**
2010–11 Southampton 0 0
2011–12 Southampton 0 0
2012–13 Southampton 0 0
2013–14 Southampton 0 0
2013–14 *Swindon T* 10 0
2014–15 Southampton 0 0
2014–15 *Swindon T* 37 1 **47 1**
2015–16 Southampton 0 0
2015–16 *Middlesbrough* 1 0 **1 0**
2015–16 *Coventry C* 16 0 **16 0**
2016–17 Southampton 17 0
2017–18 Southampton 22 2
2018–19 Southampton 24 1
2019–20 Southampton 28 1
2020–21 Southampton 18 0 **109 4**

TCHAPTCHET, Allan (D) 1 0
b.Besancon 21-12-01
From Auxerre.
2020–21 Southampton 1 0 **1 0**

TELLA, Nathan (F) 19 1
b. 5-7-99
From Arsenal.
2017–18 Southampton 0 0
2018–19 Southampton 0 0
2019–20 Southampton 1 0
2020–21 Southampton 18 1 **19 1**

VALERY, Yann (D) 44 2
H: 5 11 W: 11 00 b.Champigny-sur-Marne 22-2-99
Internationals: France U17, U18.
From Rennes.
2018–19 Southampton 23 2
2019–20 Southampton 11 0
2020–21 Southampton 3 0 **37 2**
2020–21 *Birmingham C* 7 0 **7 0**

VESTERGAARD, Jannik (D) 257 18
H: 6 6 W: 15 02 b.Copenhagen 3-8-92
Internationals: Denmark U18, U19, U20, U21, Full caps.
2010–11 Hoffenheim 1 0
2011–12 Hoffenheim 23 2
2012–13 Hoffenheim 16 0
2013–14 Hoffenheim 25 1

2014–15 Hoffenheim 6 1 **71 4**
2014–15 Werder Bremen 15 1
2015–16 Werder Bremen 33 2 **48 3**
2016–17 Borussia M'gladbach 34 4
2017–18 Borussia M'gladbach 32 3 **66 7**
2018–19 Southampton 23 0
2019–20 Southampton 19 1
2020–21 Southampton 30 3 **72 4**

VOKINS, Jake (D) 6 0
b.Oxford 17-3-00
Internationals: England U17, U18, U19.
2019–20 Southampton 1 0
2020–21 Southampton 1 0 **2 0**
2020–21 *Sunderland* 4 0 **4 0**

WALKER-PETERS, Kyle (F) 52 0
H: 5 8 W: 9 13 b.Edmonton 13-4-97
Internationals: England U18, U19, U20, U21.
2015–16 Tottenham H 0 0
2016–17 Tottenham H 0 0
2017–18 Tottenham H 3 0
2018–19 Tottenham H 6 0
2019–20 Tottenham H 3 0 **12 0**
2019–20 *Southampton* 10 0
2020–21 Southampton 30 0 **40 0**

WARD-PROWSE, James (M) 269 30
H: 5 8 W: 10 06 b.Portsmouth 1-11-94
Internationals: England U17, U19, U20, U21, Full caps.
2011–12 Southampton 0 0
2012–13 Southampton 15 0
2013–14 Southampton 34 0
2014–15 Southampton 25 1
2015–16 Southampton 33 2
2016–17 Southampton 30 4
2017–18 Southampton 30 3
2018–19 Southampton 26 7
2019–20 Southampton 38 5
2020–21 Southampton 38 8 **269 30**

WATTS, Caleb (M) 3 0
b. 16-1-02
From QPR.
2020–21 Southampton 3 0 **3 0**

Scholars
Babic, Goran Gogo; Bailey, Samuel James; Beach, Edward James; Burnett, Ethan Darren; Carson, Matthew; Davey, Teddy Jay; Hall, Matthew Gary; Lillienberg, Gustav Erik; Otseh-Taiwo, Zuriel Jonathan; Payne, Lewis James; Pearce, Luke Edward Andrew; Smith, Jayden Pharell Llamar Mills; Tizzard, William James; Tshaka, Kaya Sean; Turner, Jack Henry; Woods, Harvey James; Wright, Oliver Lennon George.

SOUTHEND U (78)

ACQUAH, Emile (F) 41 3
b. 13-7-00
2018–19 Southend U 3 0
2019–20 Southend U 7 1
2020–21 Southend U 31 2 **41 3**

ADEDOJA, Tayo (F) 0 0
2020–21 Southend U 0 0

AKINOLA, Simeon (F) 72 8
H: 5 10 W: 12 00 b. 6-8-92
From Boreham Wood, Harrow Bor, Braintree T.
2016–17 Barnet 19 2
2017–18 Barnet 29 4 **48 6**
2020–21 Southend U 24 2 **24 2**

BROWN, Cameron (M) 0 0
2020–21 Southend U 0 0

BWOMONO, Elvis (D) 116 2
H: 5 9 W: 9 13 b. 29-11-98
2017–18 Southend U 11 0
2018–19 Southend U 30 0
2019–20 Southend U 34 1
2020–21 Southend U 41 1 **116 2**

CHANDLER, Reiss (D) 0 0
b. 21-5-03
2020–21 Southend U 0 0

CLIFFORD, Tom (D) 37 3
b. 9-2-99
From Tottenham H.
2018–19 Southend U 1 0
2019–20 Southend U 8 0
2020–21 Southend U 28 3 **37 3**

COKER, Oliver (M) 1 0
2020–21 Southend U 1 0 **1 0**

DAVIS, Tommy (D) 0 0
2020–21 Southend U 0 0

DEMETRIOU, Jason (D) 452 33
H: 5 11 W: 10 08 b.Newham 18-11-87
Internationals: Cyprus Full caps.
2005–06 Leyton Orient 3 0
2006–07 Leyton Orient 15 2
2007–08 Leyton Orient 43 3
2008–09 Leyton Orient 43 4
2009–10 Leyton Orient 39 1 **143 10**
2010–11 AEK Larnaca 15 0
2011–12 AEK Larnaca 23 1
2012–13 AEK Larnaca 19 3 **57 4**
2013–14 Anorthis Famagusta 19 1
2014–15 Anorthis Famagusta 25 0 **44 1**
2015–16 Walsall 43 3 **43 3**
2016–17 Southend U 41 1
2017–18 Southend U 42 8
2018–19 Southend U 24 2
2019–20 Southend U 20 3
2020–21 Southend U 38 1 **165 15**

DIENG, Timothee (M) 231 14
H: 5 11 W: 12 00 b.Grenoble 9-4-92
2011–12 Brest 0 0
2012–13 Brest 2 0
2013–14 Brest 4 0 **6 0**
2014–15 Oldham Ath 22 0
2015–16 Oldham Ath 38 1 **60 1**
2016–17 Bradford C 39 3
2017–18 Bradford C 26 2 **65 5**
2018–19 Southend U 43 3
2019–20 Southend U 21 2
2020–21 Southend U 36 3 **100 8**

EGBRI, Terrell (M) 31 2
b. 21-6-01
2019–20 Southend U 6 1
2020–21 Southend U 25 1 **31 2**

FERGUSON, Nathan (M) 59 7
b. 12-10-95
2014–15 Dagenham & R 0 0
2015–16 Burton Alb 0 0
2016–17 Port Vale 0 0
From Bromley, Dulwich Hamlet.
2019–20 Crawley T 31 5
2020–21 Crawley T 9 0 **40 5**
2020–21 Southend U 19 2 **19 2**

GARD, Lewis (M) 7 1
b. 26-8-99
2017–18 Southend U 2 0
2018–19 Southend U 0 0
2019–20 Southend U 2 1
2020–21 Southend U 3 0 **7 1**

GOODSHIP, Brandon (F) 70 5
b. 1-1-86
Internationals: England C.
2013–14 Bournemouth 0 0
2014–15 Bournemouth 0 0
2015–16 Bournemouth 0 0
2015–16 *Yeovil T* 10 1
2016–17 Yeovil T 8 0 **18 1**
From Weymouth.
2019–20 Southend U 23 3
2020–21 Southend U 29 1 **52 4**

GROSSART, Jamie (G) 0 0
2020–21 Southend U 0 0

HALFORD, Greg (D) 472 46
H: 6 4 W: 12 10 b.Chelmsford 8-12-84
Internationals: England U20.
2002–03 Colchester U 1 0
2003–04 Colchester U 18 4
2004–05 Colchester U 44 4
2005–06 Colchester U 45 7
2006–07 Colchester U 28 3 **136 18**
2006–07 Reading 3 0 **3 0**
2007–08 Sunderland 8 0
2007–08 *Charlton Ath* 16 2 **16 2**
2008–09 Sunderland 0 0
2008–09 *Sheffield U* 41 4 **41 4**
2009–10 Sunderland 0 0 **8 0**
2009–10 Wolverhampton W 15 0
2010–11 Wolverhampton W 2 0 **17 0**
2010–11 *Portsmouth* 33 5
2011–12 Portsmouth 42 7 **75 12**
2012–13 Nottingham F 37 3
2013–14 Nottingham F 36 4
2014–15 Nottingham F 0 0 **73 7**
2014–15 *Brighton & HA* 19 0 **19 0**
2015–16 Rotherham U 21 2
2015–16 *Birmingham C* 3 0 **3 0**
2016–17 Rotherham U 14 0 **35 2**
2016–17 Cardiff C 16 0
2017–18 Cardiff C 12 0 **28 0**
2018–19 Aberdeen 2 0 **2 0**
2020–21 Southend U 16 1 **16 1**

HART, Sam (D) 71 1
b. 10-9-96
2016–17 Liverpool 0 0
2016–17 *Port Vale* 11 1
2017–18 Port Vale 0 0 **11 1**
2017–18 Blackburn R 3 0
2017–18 *Rochdale* 3 0
2018–19 Blackburn R 0 0
2018–19 *Rochdale* 11 0 **14 0**
2018–19 *Southend U* 18 0
2019–20 Blackburn R 0 0 **3 0**
2019–20 *Shrewsbury T* 4 0 **4 0**
2020–21 Southend U 21 0 **39 0**

HOBSON, Shaun (D) 44 2
b. 29-6-98
2017–18 Bournemouth 0 0
2018–19 Bournemouth 0 0
2019–20 Bournemouth 0 0
2020–21 Southend U 44 2 **44 2**

HOLMES, Ricky (M) 295 54
H: 6 2 W: 11 11 b.Southend 19-6-87
Internationals: England C.
From Chelmsford C.
2010–11 Barnet 25 2
2011–12 Barnet 41 8
2012–13 Barnet 25 5 **91 15**
2013–14 Portsmouth 40 2
2014–15 Portsmouth 13 0 **53 2**
2014–15 Northampton T 21 5
2015–16 Northampton T 28 9
2016–17 Charlton Ath 35 13
2017–18 Charlton Ath 23 6 **58 19**
2017–18 Sheffield U 5 0
2018–19 Sheffield U 0 0
2018–19 *Oxford U* 16 3 **16 3**
2018–19 *Gillingham* 0 0
2019–20 Sheffield U 0 0 **5 0**
2020–21 Northampton T 9 1 **58 15**
2020–21 Southend U 14 0 **14 0**

HOWARD, Rob (D) 2 0
b. 15-9-99
From Arsenal, Colchester U.
2018–19 Southend U 0 0
2019–20 Southend U 0 0
2020–21 Southend U 2 0 **2 0**

KINALI, Eren (M) 8 0
b. 24-2-00
2019–20 Southend U 6 0
2020–21 Southend U 2 0 **8 0**

KLASS, Michael (M) 12 0
b. 9-2-99
From QPR.
2017–18 Southend U 0 0
2018–19 Southend U 10 0
2019–20 Southend U 0 0
2020–21 Southend U 2 0 **12 0**

KYPRIANOU, Harry (D) 23 1
b. 16-3-97
Internationals: Cyprus U21.
2013–14 Watford 0 0
2014–15 Watford 0 0
2015–16 Watford 0 0
2015–16 Southend U 0 0
2016–17 Southend U 3 1
2017–18 Southend U 13 0
2018–19 Southend U 1 0
2019–20 Southend U 1 0
2020–21 Southend U 5 0 **23 1**

LENNON, Harry (M) 77 5
H: 6 3 W: 11 11 b.Barking 16-12-94
2012–13 Charlton Ath 0 0
2013–14 Charlton Ath 2 0
2014–15 Charlton Ath 0 0
2014–15 *Cambridge U* 2 0 **2 0**
2014–15 *Gillingham* 2 0
2015–16 Charlton Ath 19 2
2015–16 *Gillingham* 6 2 **8 2**
2016–17 Charlton Ath 2 0
2017–18 Charlton Ath 10 0 **33 2**
2018–19 Southend U 9 0
2019–20 Southend U 16 1
2020–21 Southend U 9 0 **34 1**

McCORMACK, Alan (M) 464 26
H: 5 8 W: 11 00 b.Dublin 10-1-84
Internationals: Republic of Ireland U19.
2002–03 Preston NE 0 0
2003–04 Preston NE 5 0
2003–04 *Leyton Orient* 10 0 **10 0**
2004–05 Preston NE 3 0
2004–05 *Southend U* 7 2
2005–06 Preston NE 0 0
2005–06 *Motherwell* 24 2 **24 2**
2006–07 Preston NE 3 0 **11 0**
2006–07 Southend U 22 3
2007–08 Southend U 42 8
2008–09 Southend U 34 2
2009–10 Southend U 41 3
2010–11 Charlton Ath 24 1 **24 1**

2011–12 Swindon T 40 2
2012–13 Swindon T 40 0 **80 2**
2013–14 Brentford 43 1
2014–15 Brentford 18 1
2015–16 Brentford 27 0
2016–17 Brentford 11 0 **99 2**
2017–18 Luton T 16 1
2018–19 Luton T 19 0 **35 1**
2019–20 Northampton T 15 0 **15 0**
2020–21 Southend U 20 0 **166 18**

MELLIS, Jacob (M) 272 18
H: 5 11 W: 10 11 b.Nottingham 8-1-91
Internationals: England U16, U17, U19.
From Sheffield U.
2009–10 Chelsea 0 0
2009–10 *Southampton* 12 0 **12 0**
2010–11 Chelsea 0 0
2010–11 *Barnsley* 15 2
2011–12 Chelsea 0 0
2012–13 Barnsley 36 6
2013–14 Barnsley 30 2 **81 10**
2014–15 Blackpool 13 0 **13 0**
2014–15 *Oldham Ath* 7 0 **7 0**
2015–16 Bury 23 0
2016–17 Bury 35 3 **58 3**
2017–18 Mansfield T 30 1
2018–19 Mansfield T 41 3
2019–20 Mansfield T 13 0 **84 4**
2019–20 Bolton W 6 0 **6 0**
2020–21 Gillingham 8 1 **8 1**
2020–21 Southend U 3 0 **3 0**

MITCHELL-NELSON, Miles (D) 6 0
2017–18 Southend U 0 0
2018–19 Southend U 0 0
2019–20 Southend U 6 0
2020–21 Southend U 0 0 **6 0**

MONTGOMERY, James (G) 22 0
b. 20-4-94
From Guisley, AFC Telford U, Gateshead.
2018–19 Forest Green R 18 0
2019–20 Forest Green R 0 0 **18 0**
From AFC Fylde, Gateshead. On loan from Gateshead.
2020–21 Southend U 4 0 **4 0**

NATHANIEL-GEORGE, Ashley (M) 75 11
b. 14-6-95
From Wealdstone, Potters Bar T, Hendon.
2018–19 Crawley T 30 6
2019–20 Crawley T 16 3 **46 9**
2020–21 Southend U 29 2 **29 2**

OXLEY, Mark (G) 263 1
H: 5 11 W: 11 05 b.Aston 2-6-90
Internationals: England U18.
2007–08 Rotherham U 0 0
2008–09 Hull C 0 0
2009–10 Hull C 0 0
2009–10 *Grimsby T* 3 0 **3 0**
2010–11 Hull C 0 0
2011–12 Hull C 0 0
2012–13 Hull C 1 0
2012–13 *Burton Alb* 3 0 **3 0**
2013–14 Hull C 0 0
2013–14 *Oldham Ath* 36 0 **36 0**
2014–15 Hull C 0 0 **1 0**
2014–15 *Hibernian* 35 1
2015–16 Hibernian 34 0 **69 1**
2016–17 Southend U 20 0
2017–18 Southend U 46 0
2018–19 Southend U 25 0
2019–20 Southend U 19 0
2020–21 Southend U 41 0 **151 0**

PHILLIPS, Harry (M) 3 1
b. 19-9-97
2017–18 Southend U 0 0
2018–19 Southend U 0 0
2019–20 Southend U 2 1
2020–21 Southend U 1 0 **3 1**

RALPH, Nathan (D) 59 2
H: 5 9 W: 11 00 b.Dunmow 14-2-93
From Ipswich T.
2010–11 Peterborough U 0 0
2011–12 Peterborough U 0 0
2012–13 Yeovil T 14 1
2013–14 Yeovil T 0 0
2014–15 Yeovil T 21 0 **35 1**
2015–16 Newport Co 0 0
From Woking.
2019–20 Southend U 17 0
2020–21 Southend U 7 1 **24 1**

RANGER, Nile (F) 147 24
H: 6 2 W: 13 03 b.Wood Green 11-4-91
Internationals: England U19.
2008–09 Newcastle U 0 0
2009–10 Newcastle U 25 2
2010–11 Newcastle U 24 0
2011–12 Newcastle U 0 0
2011–12 *Barnsley* 5 0 **5 0**
2011–12 *Sheffield W* 8 2 **8 2**
2012–13 Newcastle U 2 0 **51 2**
2013–14 Swindon T 23 8 **23 8**
2014–15 Blackpool 14 2
2015–16 Blackpool 0 0 **14 2**
2016–17 Southend U 27 8
2017–18 Southend U 18 2
2020–21 Southend U 1 0 **46 10**

RUSH, Matt (F) 14 1
b. 11-3-01
2019–20 Southend U 7 0
2020–21 Southend U 7 1 **14 1**

SEADEN, Harry (G) 2 0
b.Southend-on-Sea 23-4-01
Internationals: England U16, U17.
2018–19 Southend U 0 0
2019–20 Southend U 1 0
2020–21 Southend U 1 0 **2 0**

STEWART, O'Shane (M) 0 0
b. 21-12-00
2020–21 Southend U 0 0

TAYLOR, Callum (G) 1 0
2019–20 Southend U 1 0
2020–21 Southend U 0 0 **1 0**

TAYLOR, Richard (D) 14 0
b. 2-10-00
2018–19 Burnley 0 0
2019–20 Southend U 2 0
2020–21 Southend U 12 0 **14 0**

WALSH, Louis (M) 5 0
b. 1-3-01
2018–19 Barnsley 0 0
2019–20 Nottingham F 0 0
2020–21 Southend U 5 0 **5 0**

WHITE, John (D) 460 8
H: 6 0 W: 12 01 b.Maldon 26-7-86
2004–05 Colchester U 20 0
2005–06 Colchester U 35 0
2006–07 Colchester U 16 0
2007–08 Colchester U 21 0
2008–09 Colchester U 26 0
2009–10 Colchester U 39 0
2009–10 *Southend U* 5 0
2010–11 Colchester U 22 0
2011–12 Colchester U 26 0
2012–13 Colchester U 22 0 **227 0**
2013–14 Southend U 41 1
2014–15 Southend U 42 0
2015–16 Southend U 29 1
2016–17 Southend U 13 1
2017–18 Southend U 31 2
2018–19 Southend U 33 2
2019–20 Southend U 11 0
2020–21 Southend U 28 1 **233 8**

Scholars
Adedoja, Adetayo Oluwaseun; Anyadike, Damaray Chukwemeka; Arrowsmith, Louie Charles; Brogan, Samuel William Peter; Brown, Cameron Marcel; Burkey, Callum James; Chandler, Reiss Billy; Clayden, Harrison William David; Coker, Oliver; Crowhurst, Jaden; Dabbs, Ben Derek Harry; Davis, Tommy; Eastwood, Freddy John; Garzon, Brian Alexander; Grossart, Jamie William; Lambourne, Thomas John Joseph; Mpenga, Issa Ali; Quamina, Tendi; Reeve, Luke James; Shala, Ergis; Unwin, Robert David; Wallace, Jimmy Terence.

STEVENAGE (79)

AKINWANDE, Femi (F) 10 0
b. 1-5-96
2015–16 Colchester U 2 0
2016–17 Colchester U 1 0 **3 0**
2020–21 Stevenage 7 0 **7 0**

ARAI, Yasin (M) 0 0
2020–21 Stevenage 0 0

CARTER, Charlie (M) 47 8
b. 25-10-96
From Woking.
2019–20 Stevenage 29 5
2020–21 Stevenage 18 3 **47 8**

COKER, Ben (D) 265 4
H: 5 11 W: 11 09 b.Hatfield 17-6-89
From Histon.
2010–11 Colchester U 20 0
2011–12 Colchester U 20 0
2012–13 Colchester U 1 0 **41 0**
2013–14 Southend U 45 2
2014–15 Southend U 32 1
2015–16 Southend U 40 1
2016–17 Southend U 31 0
2017–18 Southend U 22 0
2018–19 Southend U 16 0 **186 4**
2019–20 Lincoln C 0 0
2019–20 *Cambridge U* 0 0
2020–21 Stevenage 38 0 **38 0**

CUTHBERT, Scott (D) 443 21
H: 6 2 W: 14 00 b.Alexandria 15-6-87
Internationals: Scotland U19, U20, U21, B.
2004–05 Celtic 0 0
2005–06 Celtic 0 0
2006–07 Celtic 0 0
2006–07 *Livingston* 4 1 **4 1**
2007–08 Celtic 0 0
2008–09 Celtic 0 0
2008–09 *St Mirren* 29 0 **29 0**
2009–10 Swindon T 39 3
2010–11 Swindon T 41 2 **80 5**
2011–12 Leyton Orient 33 1
2012–13 Leyton Orient 18 0
2013–14 Leyton Orient 44 4
2014–15 Leyton Orient 38 2 **133 7**
2015–16 Luton T 36 0
2016–17 Luton T 38 1
2017–18 Luton T 23 2 **97 3**
2018–19 Stevenage 46 2
2019–20 Stevenage 21 2
2020–21 Stevenage 33 1 **100 5**

DINANGA, Marcus (F) 6 1
b. 30-6-97
2016–17 Burton Alb 0 0
2017–18 Burton Alb 0 0
2018–19 Burton Alb 0 0
From Hartlepool U, AFC Telford U.
2020–21 Stevenage 6 1 **6 1**

DRAPER, Harry (F) 0 0
b.Stevenage 5-10-00
2019–20 Stevenage 0 0
2020–21 Stevenage 0 0

DREYER, Sam (D) 0 0
b. 3-1-04
2020–21 Stevenage 0 0

EFFIONG, Inih (F) 11 1
b.Brent 10-8-90
From St Albans C, Boreham Wood, Chesham U, Dunstable T, Arlesey T, Biggleswade T, Barrow, Woking.
2017–18 Ross Co 2 0 **2 0**
From Dover Ath.
2020–21 Stevenage 9 1 **9 1**

FERNANDEZ, Luis (D) 5 0
b. 28-9-01
2019–20 Stevenage 4 0
2020–21 Stevenage 1 0 **5 0**

GRANVILLE, Max (M) 0 0
2020–21 Stevenage 0 0

IONTTON, Arthur (M) 29 1
b.Enfield 16-12-00
2017–18 Stevenage 2 0
2018–19 Stevenage 18 1
2019–20 Stevenage 7 0
2020–21 Stevenage 2 0 **29 1**

JOHNSON, Billy (G) 0 0
b. 25-9-99
2020–21 Stevenage 0 0

JOHNSON, Finlay (M) 0 0
b. 7-7-04
2020–21 Stevenage 0 0

LINES, Chris (M) 485 38
H: 6 2 W: 12 00 b.Bristol 30-11-88
2005–06 Bristol R 4 0
2006–07 Bristol R 7 0
2007–08 Bristol R 27 3
2008–09 Bristol R 45 4
2009–10 Bristol R 42 10
2010–11 Bristol R 42 3
2011–12 Bristol R 1 0
2011–12 Sheffield W 41 3
2012–13 Sheffield W 6 0 **47 3**
2012–13 *Milton Keynes D* 16 0 **16 0**
2013–14 Port Vale 34 1
2014–15 Port Vale 27 2 **61 3**
2015–16 Bristol R 33 0
2016–17 Bristol R 44 3
2017–18 Bristol R 42 5
2018–19 Bristol R 19 1 **306 29**
2019–20 Northampton T 31 2
2020–21 Northampton T 4 1 **35 3**
2020–21 Stevenage 20 0 **20 0**

LIST, Elliott (M) 150 18
b.Camberwell 12-5-97
From Crystal Palace.

2015–16 Gillingham 6 0
2016–17 Gillingham 15 0
2017–18 Gillingham 23 2
2018–19 Gillingham 37 5
2019–20 Gillingham 4 0 **85 7**
2019–20 Stevenage 21 2
2020–21 Stevenage 44 9 **65 11**

MARSH, Tyrone (F) 42 2
b. 24-12-93
2012–13 Oxford U 2 0
2013–14 Oxford U 5 0 **7 0**
From Ebbsfleet U, Torquay U, Dover Ath.
2018–19 Macclesfield T 25 2 **25 2**
From Boreham Wood.
2020–21 Stevenage 10 0 **10 0**
Transferred to Boreham Wood February 2021.

MARSHALL, Ross (M) 15 0
b. 9-10-99
From Ipswich T, Maidstone U.
2020–21 Stevenage 15 0 **15 0**

MARTIN, Joe (M) 326 15
H: 6 0 W: 12 13 b.Dagenham 29-11-88
Internationals: England U16, U17.
From West Ham U.
2005–06 Tottenham H 0 0
2006–07 Tottenham H 0 0
2007–08 Tottenham H 0 0
2007–08 *Blackpool* 1 0
2008–09 Blackpool 15 0
2009–10 Blackpool 6 0 **22 0**
2010–11 Gillingham 17 1
2011–12 Gillingham 35 1
2012–13 Gillingham 38 2
2013–14 Gillingham 46 2
2014–15 Gillingham 25 2 **161 8**
2015–16 Millwall 29 2
2016–17 Millwall 23 1 **52 3**
2017–18 Stevenage 39 2
2018–19 Bristol R 10 1 **10 1**
2018–19 Stevenage 5 1
2019–20 Northampton T 17 0
2020–21 Northampton T 6 0 **23 0**
2020–21 Stevenage 14 0 **58 3**

NEWTON, Danny (F) 115 26
b.Liverpool 18-3-91
From Hinckley T, Nuneaton T, Barwell, Brackley T, Leamington, Tamworth.
2017–18 Stevenage 45 14
2018–19 Stevenage 25 6
2019–20 Stevenage 10 2
2020–21 Stevenage 35 4 **115 26**

NORRIS, Luke (F) 281 66
H: 6 1 W: 13 05 b.Stevenage 3-6-93
2011–12 Brentford 1 0
2012–13 Brentford 0 0
2013–14 Brentford 1 0 **2 0**
2013–14 *Northampton T* 10 4 **10 4**
2013–14 *Dagenham & R* 19 4 **19 4**
2014–15 Gillingham 37 6
2015–16 Gillingham 33 8 **70 14**
2016–17 Swindon T 39 4
2017–18 Swindon T 35 13 **74 17**
2018–19 Colchester U 34 7
2019–20 Colchester U 32 9
2020–21 Colchester U 17 4 **83 20**
2020–21 Stevenage 23 7 **23 7**

OSBORNE, Elliot (M) 37 2
b. 12-5-96
2016–17 Fleetwood T 0 0
2017–18 Fleetwood T 0 0
2017–18 *Morecambe* 11 0 **11 0**
From Southport, Stockport Co.
2020–21 Stevenage 26 2 **26 2**

PETT, Tom (M) 227 26
H: 5 8 W: 11 00 b. 3-12-91
Internationals: England C.
From Potters Bar T, Wealdstone.
2014–15 Stevenage 34 7
2015–16 Stevenage 40 1
2016–17 Stevenage 40 6
2017–18 Stevenage 27 6
2017–18 Lincoln C 9 1
2018–19 Lincoln C 44 3
2019–20 Lincoln C 2 0 **55 4**
2020–21 Stevenage 31 2 **172 22**

PROSSER, Luke (D) 305 16
H: 6 2 W: 12 04 b.Waltham Cross 28-5-88
From Tottenham H.
2005–06 Port Vale 0 0
2006–07 Port Vale 0 0
2007–08 Port Vale 5 0
2008–09 Port Vale 26 1
2009–10 Port Vale 2 1 **33 2**
2010–11 Southend U 17 1
2011–12 Southend U 21 1
2012–13 Southend U 25 0
2013–14 Southend U 25 3
2014–15 Southend U 30 0
2015–16 Southend U 13 2 **131 7**
2015–16 *Northampton T* 8 0 **8 0**
2016–17 Colchester U 14 0
2017–18 Colchester U 16 1
2018–19 Colchester U 38 2
2019–20 Colchester U 35 3 **103 6**
2020–21 Stevenage 30 1 **30 1**

SMITH, Jack (D) 26 0
b. 15-9-01
2019–20 Stevenage 1 0
2020–21 Stevenage 25 0 **26 0**

SMITH, Timmy (G) 0 0
b. 29-11-03
2020–21 Stevenage 0 0

TINUBU, Sam (F) 0 0
2020–21 Stevenage 0 0

TOWNSEND-WEST, Mackye (D) 0 0
2019–20 Stevenage 0 0
2020–21 Stevenage 0 0

VANCOOTEN, Terence (D) 79 0
H: 6 1 W: 12 04 b. 29-12-97
Internationals: Guyana Full caps.
From Staines T.
2016–17 Reading 0 0
2017–18 Stevenage 22 0
2018–19 Stevenage 12 0
2019–20 Stevenage 16 0
2020–21 Stevenage 29 0 **79 0**

VINCELOT, Romain (M) 399 29
H: 5 9 W: 11 02 b.Poitiers 29-10-85
2004–05 Chamois Niortais 3 0 **3 0**
2005–06 Chemois Niortais 30 1
2006–07 Chemois Niortais 9 0
2007–08 Chemois Niortais 6 0 **45 1**
2008–09 Gueugnon 20 0 **20 0**
2009–10 Dagenham & R 9 1
2010–11 Dagenham & R 46 12 **55 13**
2011–12 Brighton & HA 15 1
2012–13 Brighton & HA 0 0 **15 1**
2012–13 *Gillingham* 9 1 **9 1**
2012–13 Leyton Orient 15 1
2013–14 Leyton Orient 39 0
2014–15 Leyton Orient 27 2 **81 3**
2015–16 Coventry C 45 4 **45 4**
2016–17 Bradford C 45 2
2017–18 Bradford C 38 4 **83 6**
2018–19 Crawley T 12 0 **12 0**
2018–19 Shrewsbury T 3 0
2019–20 Shrewsbury T 2 0 **5 0**
2020–21 Stevenage 26 0 **26 0**

WILDIN, Luther (M) 99 4
b. 3-12-97
Internationals: Antigua and Barbuda U20, Full caps.
2015–16 Notts Co 0 0
2016–17 Notts Co 0 0
From Nuneaton T.
2018–19 Stevenage 39 1
2019–20 Stevenage 21 1
2020–21 Stevenage 39 2 **99 4**

WILLIAMS, Alfie (M) 1 0
b. 20-4-03
2020–21 Stevenage 1 0 **1 0**

Scholars
Aitken, Alexander James; Arai, Yasin; Berman, Jack Louie; Bugyei-Kyei, Kwadwo Ankapong; Bunyan, Jake; Edgeworth, George David; Granville, Max Reece Kai; Halpin, Cian James; Johnson, Finlay Joseph; Lynn, Lewis Stephen; Mahoney, Morgan James; Onyeagwara, Obidinma Chigozie Chibuzo; Siggers, Ben Kenneth; Stevenson, Teddy Dean; Wilson, Jack Robert Michael.

STOKE C (80)

ADEBAMBO, Gabriel (M) 0 0
b. 27-2-02
Internationals: Republic of Ireland U18.
From Dundalk.
2020–21 Stoke C 0 0

AFOBE, Benik (F) 301 73
H: 5 10 W: 11 00 b.Leyton 12-2-93
Internationals: England U16, U17, U19, U21. DR Congo Full caps.
2009–10 Arsenal 0 0
2010–11 Arsenal 0 0
2010–11 *Huddersfield T* 28 5 **28 5**
2011–12 Arsenal 0 0
2011–12 *Reading* 3 0 **3 0**
2012–13 Arsenal 0 0
2012–13 *Bolton W* 20 2 **20 2**
2012–13 *Millwall* 5 0 **5 0**
2013–14 Arsenal 0 0
2013–14 *Sheffield W* 12 2 **12 2**
2014–15 Arsenal 0 0
2014–15 *Milton Keynes D* 22 10 **22 10**
2014–15 Wolverhampton W 21 13
2015–16 Wolverhampton W 25 9
2015–16 Bournemouth 15 4
2016–17 Bournemouth 31 6
2017–18 Bournemouth 17 0 **63 10**
2017–18 *Wolverhampton W* 16 6
2018–19 Wolverhampton W 0 0 **62 28**
2018–19 *Stoke C* 45 8
2019–20 Stoke C 1 0
2019–20 *Bristol C* 12 3 **12 3**
2020–21 Stoke C 0 0 **46 8**
2020–21 *Trabzonspor* 28 5 **28 5**

ALLEN, Joe (M) 389 29
H: 5 6 W: 9 10 b.Carmarthen 14-3-90
Internationals: Wales U17, U19, U21, Full caps. Great Britain.
2006–07 Swansea C 1 0
2007–08 Swansea C 6 0
2008–09 Swansea C 23 1
2009–10 Swansea C 21 0
2010–11 Swansea C 40 2
2011–12 Swansea C 36 4
2012–13 Swansea C 0 0 **127 7**
2012–13 Liverpool 27 0
2013–14 Liverpool 24 1
2014–15 Liverpool 21 1
2015–16 Liverpool 19 2 **91 4**
2016–17 Stoke C 36 6
2017–18 Stoke C 36 2
2018–19 Stoke C 46 6
2019–20 Stoke C 35 4
2020–21 Stoke C 18 0 **171 18**

BATTH, Danny (D) 366 22
H: 6 3 W: 13 05 b.Brierley Hill 21-9-90
2009–10 Wolverhampton W 0 0
2009–10 *Colchester U* 17 1 **17 1**
2010–11 Wolverhampton W 0 0
2010–11 *Sheffield U* 1 0 **1 0**
2010–11 *Sheffield W* 10 0
2011–12 Wolverhampton W 0 0
2011–12 *Sheffield W* 44 2 **54 2**
2012–13 Wolverhampton W 12 1
2013–14 Wolverhampton W 46 2
2014–15 Wolverhampton W 44 4
2015–16 Wolverhampton W 38 2
2016–17 Wolverhampton W 39 4
2017–18 Wolverhampton W 16 1
2018–19 Wolverhampton W 0 0 **195 14**
2018–19 *Middlesbrough* 10 0 **10 0**
2018–19 Stoke C 17 0
2019–20 Stoke C 43 4
2020–21 Stoke C 29 1 **89 5**

BAUER, Moritz (D) 169 0
H: 5 11 W: 11 07 b.Veltheim 25-1-92
Internationals: Switzerland U19, U21. Austria Full caps.
2011–12 Grasshopper Zurich 16 0
2012–13 Grasshopper Zurich 13 0
2013–14 Grasshopper Zurich 15 0
2014–15 Grasshopper Zurich 16 0
2015–16 Grasshopper Zurich 33 0 **93 0**
2016–17 Ruban Kazan 21 0 **21 0**
2017–18 Rubin Kazan 16 0 **16 0**
2017–18 Stoke C 15 0
2018–19 Stoke C 8 0
2019–20 Stoke C 0 0
2019–20 *Celtic* 9 0 **9 0**
2020–21 Stoke C 0 0 **23 0**
2020–21 *Ufa* 7 0 **7 0**

BROOME, Nathan (G) 0 0
b.Manchester 3-1-02
Internationals: England U17, U18.
From Manchester C.
2020–21 Stoke C 0 0

BROWN, Jacob (M) 128 16
H: 5 10 W: 9 11 b. 10-4-98
From Guiseley.
2014–15 Barnsley 0 0
2015–16 Barnsley 0 0
2016–17 Barnsley 2 0
2017–18 Barnsley 0 0
2017–18 *Chesterfield* 13 0 **13 0**
2018–19 Barnsley 32 8
2019–20 Barnsley 40 3 **74 11**
2020–21 Stoke C 41 5 **41 5**

BURSIK, Josef (G) **47 0**
b. 12-7-00
Internationals: England U17, U18, U19, U20.
From AFC Wimbledon.

2019–20	Stoke C	0	0		
2019–20	*Accrington S*	16	0	**16**	**0**
2020–21	Stoke C	15	0	**15**	**0**
2020–21	*Doncaster R*	10	0	**10**	**0**
2020–21	*Peterborough U*	6	0	**6**	**0**
2020–21	*Lincoln C*	0	0		

CAMPBELL, Tyrese (F) **71 20**
b.Derby 16-9-97
Internationals: England U17, U20.
From Manchester C.

2017–18	Stoke C	4	0		
2018–19	Stoke C	3	0		
2018–19	*Shrewsbury T*	15	5	**15**	**5**
2019–20	Stoke C	33	9		
2020–21	Stoke C	16	6	**56**	**15**

CHESTER, James (D) **362 21**
H: 5 11 W: 11 04 b.Warrington 23-1-89
Internationals: Wales Full caps.

2007–08	Manchester U	0	0		
2008–09	Manchester U	0	0		
2008–09	*Peterborough U*	5	0	**5**	**0**
2009–10	Manchester U	0	0		
2009–10	*Plymouth Arg*	3	0	**3**	**0**
2010–11	Manchester U	0	0		
2010–11	*Carlisle U*	18	2	**18**	**2**
2010–11	Hull C	21	1		
2011–12	Hull C	44	2		
2012–13	Hull C	44	1		
2013–14	Hull C	24	1		
2014–15	Hull C	23	2	**156**	**7**
2015–16	WBA	13	0	**13**	**0**
2016–17	Aston Villa	45	3		
2017–18	Aston Villa	46	4		
2018–19	Aston Villa	28	5		
2019–20	Aston Villa	0	0	**119**	**12**
2019–20	*Stoke C*	16	0		
2020–21	Stoke C	32	0	**48**	**0**

CLUCAS, Sam (M) **328 45**
H: 5 10 W: 11 08 b.Lincoln 25-9-90
Internationals: England C.

2009–10	Lincoln C	0	0		
2010–11	Jerez Industrial	20	0	**20**	**0**
2011–12	Hereford U	17	0	**17**	**0**

From Hereford U.

2013–14	Mansfield T	38	8		
2014–15	Mansfield T	5	0	**43**	**8**
2014–15	Chesterfield	41	9	**41**	**9**
2015–16	Hull C	44	6		
2016–17	Hull C	37	3		
2017–18	Hull C	3	0	**84**	**9**
2017–18	Swansea C	29	3	**29**	**3**
2018–19	Stoke C	26	3		
2019–20	Stoke C	44	11		
2020–21	Stoke C	24	2	**94**	**16**

COATES, Kieran (D) **0 0**
b.Smallthorne 9-12-00

2020–21	Stoke C	0	0

COLLINS, Nathan (D) **39 2**
b. 30-4-01
Internationals: Republic of Ireland U17, U19, U21.

2018–19	Stoke C	3	0		
2019–20	Stoke C	14	0		
2020–21	Stoke C	22	2	**39**	**2**

COUSINS, Jordan (D) **225 8**
H: 5 10 W: 11 05 b.Greenwich 6-3-94
Internationals: England U16, U17, U18, U20.

2011–12	Charlton Ath	0	0		
2012–13	Charlton Ath	0	0		
2013–14	Charlton Ath	42	2		
2014–15	Charlton Ath	44	3		
2015–16	Charlton Ath	39	2	**125**	**7**
2016–17	QPR	18	0		
2017–18	QPR	15	0		
2018–19	QPR	28	1	**61**	**1**
2019–20	Stoke C	20	0		
2020–21	Stoke C	19	0	**39**	**0**

DAVIES, Adam (G) **205 0**
H: 6 1 W: 11 11 b.Rinteln 17-7-92
Internationals: Wales Full caps.

2009–10	Everton	0	0		
2010–11	Everton	0	0		
2011–12	Everton	0	0		
2012–13	Sheffield W	0	0		
2013–14	Sheffield W	0	0		
2014–15	Barnsley	23	0		
2015–16	Barnsley	38	0		
2016–17	Barnsley	46	0		
2017–18	Barnsley	35	0		
2018–19	Barnsley	42	0	**184**	**0**
2019–20	Stoke C	4	0		
2020–21	Stoke C	17	0	**21**	**0**

DOUGHTY, Alfie (M) **36 3**
b. 21-12-99

2018–19	Charlton Ath	0	0		
2019–20	Charlton Ath	29	2		
2020–21	Charlton Ath	7	1	**36**	**3**
2020–21	Stoke C	0	0		

EDWARDS, Thomas (D) **62 1**
b. 22-1-99
Internationals: England U20.

2016–17	Stoke C	0	0		
2017–18	Stoke C	6	0		
2018–19	Stoke C	27	1		
2019–20	Stoke C	13	0		
2020–21	Stoke C	0	0	**46**	**1**
2020–21	*Fleetwood T*	11	0	**11**	**0**
2020–21	*New York Red Bulls*	5	0	**5**	**0**

FLETCHER, Steven (F) **519 143**
H: 6 1 W: 12 00 b.Shrewsbury 26-3-87
Internationals: Scotland U20, U21, B, Full caps.

2003–04	Hibernian	5	0		
2004–05	Hibernian	20	5		
2005–06	Hibernian	34	8		
2006–07	Hibernian	31	6		
2007–08	Hibernian	32	13		
2008–09	Hibernian	34	11	**156**	**43**
2009–10	Burnley	35	8	**35**	**8**
2010–11	Wolverhampton W	29	10		
2011–12	Wolverhampton W	32	12	**61**	**22**
2012–13	Sunderland	28	11		
2013–14	Sunderland	20	3		
2014–15	Sunderland	30	5		
2015–16	Sunderland	16	4	**94**	**23**
2015–16	*Marseille*	12	2	**12**	**2**
2016–17	Sheffield W	38	10		
2017–18	Sheffield W	19	2		
2018–19	Sheffield W	40	11		
2019–20	Sheffield W	27	13	**124**	**36**
2020–21	Stoke C	37	9	**37**	**9**

FORRESTER, William (D) **1 1**
b. 29-6-01

2020–21	Stoke C	1	1	**1**	**1**

FOX, Morgan (D) **220 5**
H: 6 1 W: 12 03 b.Chelmsford 21-9-93
Internationals: Wales U21.

2012–13	Charlton Ath	0	0		
2013–14	Charlton Ath	6	0		
2013–14	*Notts Co*	7	1	**7**	**1**
2014–15	Charlton Ath	31	0		
2015–16	Charlton Ath	42	1		
2016–17	Charlton Ath	24	0	**103**	**1**
2016–17	Sheffield W	10	1		
2017–18	Sheffield W	28	0		
2018–19	Sheffield W	25	0		
2019–20	Sheffield W	27	2	**90**	**3**
2020–21	Stoke C	20	0	**20**	**0**

GOODWIN, William (F) **0 0**
H: 6 1 b.Tarporley 11-5-02
From FC Chester.

2020–21	Stoke C	0	0

GREGORY, Lee (F) **261 74**
H: 6 2 b.Sheffield 26-8-88

2014–15	Millwall	39	9		
2015–16	Millwall	41	18		
2016–17	Millwall	37	17		
2017–18	Millwall	43	10		
2018–19	Millwall	44	10	**204**	**64**
2019–20	Stoke C	40	6		
2020–21	Stoke C	6	1	**46**	**7**
2020–21	*Derby Co*	11	3	**11**	**3**

HEMFREY, Robbie (G) **0 0**
H: 6 4 W: 13 05 b.Wishaw 21-2-02
Internationals: Scotland U16, U17.
From Motherwell.

2020–21	Stoke C	0	0

INCE, Tom (M) **355 82**
H: 5 10 W: 10 06 b.Stockport 30-1-92
Internationals: England U17, U19, U21.

2009–10	Liverpool	0	0		
2010–11	Liverpool	0	0		
2010–11	*Notts Co*	6	2	**6**	**2**
2011–12	Blackpool	33	6		
2012–13	Blackpool	44	18		
2013–14	Blackpool	23	7	**100**	**31**
2013–14	*Crystal Palace*	8	1	**8**	**1**
2014–15	*Hull C*	7	0	**7**	**0**
2014–15	*Nottingham F*	6	0	**6**	**0**
2014–15	*Derby Co*	18	11		
2015–16	Derby Co	42	12		
2016–17	Derby Co	45	14	**105**	**37**
2017–18	Huddersfield T	33	2	**33**	**2**
2018–19	Stoke C	38	6		
2019–20	Stoke C	38	3		
2020–21	Stoke C	7	0	**83**	**9**
2020–21	*Luton T*	7	0	**7**	**0**

JAMES-TAYLOR, Douglas (F) **0 0**
H: 6 1 b.Camden 18-11-01
From Salford C.

2020–21	Stoke C	0	0

JARRETT, Patrick (M) **0 0**
H: 5 10 b.Nantwich 23-11-01

2020–21	Stoke C	0	0

JONES, Edward (D) **0 0**
b. 25-10-01
From Bury.

2020–21	Stoke C	0	0

LINDSAY, Liam (D) **203 13**
H: 6 4 W: 12 07 b.Paisley 12-10-95

2012–13	Partick Thistle	1	0		
2013–14	*Alloa Ath*	10	0	**10**	**0**
2013–14	Partick Thistle	1	0		
2014–15	Partick Thistle	1	0		
2014–15	*Airdrieonians*	13	1	**13**	**1**
2015–16	Partick Thistle	25	1		
2016–17	Partick Thistle	36	6	**64**	**7**
2017–18	Barnsley	42	1		
2018–19	Barnsley	41	1	**83**	**2**
2019–20	Stoke C	20	1		
2020–21	Stoke C	0	0	**20**	**1**
2020–21	*Preston NE*	13	2	**13**	**2**

MACARI, Lewis (D) **0 0**

2020–21	Stoke C	0	0

MALONE, Dan (M) **0 0**
b. 9-5-02

2020–21	Stoke C	0	0

MARTINS INDI, Bruno (D) **300 10**
H: 6 1 W: 11 09 b.Barreiro, Portugal 8-2-92
Internationals: Netherlands U17, U19, U21, Full caps.

2010–11	Feyenoord	15	1		
2011–12	Feyenoord	29	1		
2012–13	Feyenoord	32	1		
2013–14	Feyenoord	26	2	**102**	**5**
2014–15	Porto	24	2		
2015–16	Porto	23	0		
2016–17	Porto	0	0	**47**	**2**
2016–17	*Stoke C*	35	1		
2017–18	Stoke C	17	0		
2018–19	Stoke C	37	1		
2019–20	Stoke C	33	0		
2020–21	Stoke C	2	0	**124**	**2**
2020–21	*AZ Alkmaar*	27	1	**27**	**1**

MATONDO, Rabbi (F) **40 3**
b.Liverpool 9-9-00
From Cardiff C.

2017–18	Manchester C	0	0		
2018–19	Manchester C	0	0		
2018–19	Schalke 04	7	0		
2019–20	Schalke 04	20	2		
2020–21	Schalke 04	3	0	**30**	**2**

On loan from Schalke 04.

2020–21	Stoke C	10	1	**10**	**1**

McCLEAN, James (M) **411 48**
H: 5 11 W: 11 00 b.Derry 22-4-89
Internationals: Northern Ireland U21. Republic of Ireland Full caps.

2008	Derry C	1	0		
2009	Derry C	26	1		
2010	Derry C	30	8		
2011	Derry C	21	7	**78**	**16**
2011–12	Sunderland	23	5		
2012–13	Sunderland	36	2		
2013–14	Sunderland	0	0	**59**	**7**
2013–14	Wigan Ath	37	3		
2014–15	Wigan Ath	36	6	**73**	**9**
2015–16	WBA	35	2		
2016–17	WBA	34	1		
2017–18	WBA	30	1	**99**	**4**
2018–19	Stoke C	42	3		
2019–20	Stoke C	36	7		
2020–21	Stoke C	24	2	**102**	**12**

MIKEL, John Obi (M) **362 6**
H: 6 0 W: 13 05 b.Plateau State 22-4-87
Internationals: Nigeria Youth, Full caps.

2005	Lyn	6	1	**6**	**1**
2006–07	Chelsea	22	0		
2007–08	Chelsea	29	0		
2008–09	Chelsea	34	0		
2009–10	Chelsea	25	0		
2010–11	Chelsea	28	0		
2011–12	Chelsea	22	0		
2012–13	Chelsea	22	0		
2013–14	Chelsea	24	1		
2014–15	Chelsea	18	0		
2015–16	Chelsea	25	0		
2016–17	Chelsea	0	0	**249**	**1**
2017	Tianjin Taida	13	1		
2018	Tianjin Taida	18	2	**31**	**3**
2018–19	Middlesbrough	18	1	**18**	**1**

2019–20 Trabzonspor 19 0 **19 0**
2020–21 Stoke C 39 0 **39 0**

NNA NOUKEU, Blondy (G) 0 0
b. 17-9-01
2019–20 Stoke C 0 0
2020–21 Stoke C 0 0

NORTON, Christian (F) 6 0
b. 21-5-01
2020–21 Southampton 0 0
2020–21 Stoke C 6 0 **6 0**

O'DRISCOLL VARIAN, Ethon (F) 0 0
b. 11-8-02
Internationals: Republic of Ireland U21.
2020–21 Stoke C 0 0

OAKLEY-BOOTHE, Tashan (M) 18 0
H: 5 10 W: 11 00 b.Lambeth 14-2-00
Internationals: England U16, U17, U18.
2017–18 Tottenham H 0 0
2018–19 Tottenham H 0 0
2019–20 Tottenham H 0 0
2019–20 Stoke C 2 0
2020–21 Stoke C 16 0 **18 0**

PORTER, Adam (M) 0 0
2019–20 Stoke C 0 0
2020–21 Stoke C 0 0

POWELL, Nick (F) 255 68
H: 6 0 W: 10 05 b.Crewe 23-3-94
Internationals: England U16, U17, U18, U19, U21.
2010–11 Crewe Alex 17 0
2011–12 Crewe Alex 38 14 **55 14**
2012–13 Manchester U 2 1
2013–14 Manchester U 0 0
2013–14 *Wigan Ath* 31 7
2014–15 Manchester U 0 0
2014–15 *Leicester C* 3 0 **3 0**
2015–16 Manchester U 1 0 **3 1**
2015–16 *Hull C* 3 0 **3 0**
2016–17 Wigan Ath 21 6
2017–18 Wigan Ath 39 15
2018–19 Wigan Ath 32 8 **123 36**
2019–20 Stoke C 29 5
2020–21 Stoke C 39 12 **68 17**

SHAWCROSS, Ryan (D) 402 22
H: 6 3 W: 13 13 b.Buckley 4-10-87
Internationals: England U21, Full caps.
2006–07 Manchester U 0 0
2007–08 Manchester U 0 0
2007–08 Stoke C 41 7
2008–09 Stoke C 30 3
2009–10 Stoke C 28 2
2010–11 Stoke C 36 1
2011–12 Stoke C 36 2
2012–13 Stoke C 37 1
2013–14 Stoke C 37 1
2014–15 Stoke C 32 2
2015–16 Stoke C 20 0
2016–17 Stoke C 35 1
2017–18 Stoke C 27 1
2018–19 Stoke C 36 1
2019–20 Stoke C 5 0
2020–21 Stoke C 2 0 **402 22**
Transferred to Inter Miami February 2021.

SMITH, Tommy (D) 247 6
H: 6 1 W: 13 02 b.Warrington 14-4-92
2012–13 Huddersfield T 0 0
2013–14 Huddersfield T 24 0
2014–15 Huddersfield T 41 0
2015–16 Huddersfield T 36 0
2016–17 Huddersfield T 42 4
2017–18 Huddersfield T 24 0
2018–19 Huddersfield T 15 0 **182 4**
2019–20 Stoke C 30 0
2020–21 Stoke C 35 2 **65 2**

SORENSON, Lasse (M) 32 0
b. 21-10-99
From Esbjerg.
2017–18 Stoke C 1 0
2018–19 Stoke C 1 0
2019–20 Stoke C 6 0
2020–21 Stoke C 0 0 **8 0**
2020–21 *Milton Keynes D* 24 0 **24 0**

SOUTAR, Harry (D) 98 6
H: 6 6 W: 12 08 b.Aberdeen 22-6-98
Internationals: Scotland U17, U19. Australia U23, Full caps.
2015–16 Dundee U 2 1
2016–17 Dundee U 0 0 **2 1**
2016–17 Stoke C 0 0
2017–18 Stoke C 0 0
2017–18 *Ross Co* 13 0 **13 0**
2018–19 Stoke C 0 0
2018–19 *Fleetwood T* 11 1
2019–20 Stoke C 0 0
2019–20 *Fleetwood T* 34 3 **45 4**
2020–21 Stoke C 38 1 **38 1**

SPARROW, Tom (M) 0 0
2020–21 Stoke C 0 0

SY, Ibrahima (M) 0 0
b. 16-12-02
Internationals: Senegal U17.
From Reims.
2020–21 Stoke C 0 0

TAYLOR, Connor (D) 1 0
From Stafford R.
2020–21 Stoke C 1 0 **1 0**

THOMPSON, Jordan (M) 154 7
H: 5 9 W: 10 03 b.Belfast 3-1-97
Internationals: Northern Ireland U17, U19, U21, Full caps.
From Manchester U.
2015–16 Rangers 2 0
2015–16 *Airdrieonians* 7 1 **7 1**
2016–17 Rangers 0 0
2016–17 *Raith R* 29 1 **29 1**
2017–18 Rangers 0 0 **2 0**
2017–18 *Livingston* 11 0 **11 0**
2018–19 Blackpool 38 3
2019–20 Blackpool 18 1 **56 4**
2019–20 Stoke C 15 0
2020–21 Stoke C 34 1 **49 1**

TYMON, Josh (D) 51 0
b. 22-5-99
Internationals: England U17, U18, U19, U20.
2015–16 Hull C 0 0
2016–17 Hull C 5 0 **5 0**
2017–18 Stoke C 3 0
2017–18 *Milton Keynes D* 9 0 **9 0**
2018–19 Stoke C 1 0
2019–20 Stoke C 2 0
2019–20 *Famalicao* 5 0 **5 0**
2020–21 Stoke C 26 0 **32 0**

VERLINDEN, Thibaud (M) 26 3
b. 9-7-99
Internationals: Belgium U16, U17, U19.
From Club Bruges.
2016–17 Stoke C 0 0
2017–18 Stoke C 0 0
2017–18 *St Pauli* 0 0
2018–19 Stoke C 5 0
2019–20 Stoke C 5 0
2019–20 *Bolton W* 15 3 **15 3**
2020–21 Stoke C 1 0 **11 0**
Transferred to Fortuna Sittard January 2021.

VOKES, Sam (F) 451 94
H: 6 1 W: 13 10 b.Lymington 21-10-89
Internationals: Wales U21, Full caps.
2006–07 Bournemouth 13 4
2007–08 Bournemouth 41 12 **54 16**
2008–09 Wolverhampton W 36 6
2009–10 Wolverhampton W 5 0
2009–10 *Leeds U* 8 1 **8 1**
2010–11 Wolverhampton W 2 0
2010–11 *Bristol C* 1 0 **1 0**
2010–11 *Sheffield U* 6 1 **6 1**
2010–11 *Norwich C* 4 1 **4 1**
2011–12 Wolverhampton W 4 0
2011–12 *Burnley* 9 2
2011–12 *Brighton & HA* 14 3 **14 3**
2012–13 Wolverhampton W 0 0 **47 6**
2012–13 Burnley 46 4
2013–14 Burnley 39 20
2014–15 Burnley 15 0
2015–16 Burnley 43 15
2016–17 Burnley 37 10
2017–18 Burnley 30 4
2018–19 Burnley 20 3 **239 58**
2018–19 Stoke C 12 3
2019–20 Stoke C 36 5
2020–21 Stoke C 30 0 **78 8**

WOODS, Ryan (M) 307 4
H: 5 8 W: 13 01 b.Norton Canes 13-12-93
2012–13 Shrewsbury T 2 0
2013–14 Shrewsbury T 41 1
2014–15 Shrewsbury T 43 0
2015–16 Shrewsbury T 5 0 **91 1**
2015–16 Brentford 41 2
2016–17 Brentford 42 0
2017–18 Brentford 39 1
2018–19 Brentford 0 0 **122 3**
2018–19 Stoke C 27 0
2019–20 Stoke C 8 0
2019–20 *Millwall* 18 0
2020–21 Stoke C 0 0 **35 0**
2020–21 *Millwall* 41 0 **59 0**

WRIGHT-PHILLIPS, D'Margio (F) 0 0
b.Manchester 24-9-01
Internationals: England U16, U17.
From Manchester C.
2020–21 Stoke C 0 0

Scholars
Cargill, Ted Makinson; Cartwright, Jake Owen; Cooper, Paul Oyemwinmina; Fernandes, Kevin; Godfrinne, Andre Marie Paul; Ireland, Joshua Stephen; Knowles, Samuel James; Lewis, George Samuel; Malbon, Ryanjay Simon; Melbourne, Jamie; Nash, Henry George; Ndene, Julius Kimathi; Nixon, Thomas George Joseph; Okagbue, David Chukwudubem; Parke, Xander Nevis; Robson, Conor Jon; Sparrow, Thomas Lance; Udanoh, Ifeanyi Dunhill; Verma, Jai; Waite, Joshua Morgan; Waldo, Shilo Daniel O'Neil.

SUNDERLAND (81)

ALMOND, Patrick (D) 0 0
2020–21 Sunderland 0 0

BURGE, Lee (G) 186 0
H: 5 11 W: 11 00 b.Hereford 9-1-93
2011–12 Coventry C 0 0
2012–13 Coventry C 0 0
2013–14 Coventry C 0 0
2014–15 Coventry C 18 0
2015–16 Coventry C 9 0
2016–17 Coventry C 33 0
2017–18 Coventry C 40 0
2018–19 Coventry C 40 0 **140 0**
2019–20 Sunderland 5 0
2020–21 Sunderland 41 0 **46 0**

CURRY, Mitchell (F) 10 1
b.Newcastle upon Tyne 14-7-99
2017–18 Middlesbrough 0 0
2018–19 Middlesbrough 0 0
2019–20 Middlesbrough 0 0
2019–20 *Inverness CT* 9 1 **9 1**
2020–21 Sunderland 1 0 **1 0**
Transferred to Fort Lauderdale April 2021.

DIAMOND, Jack (F) 24 1
b.Gateshead 12-1-00
2018–19 Sunderland 0 0
2019–20 Sunderland 0 0
2020–21 Sunderland 24 1 **24 1**

DOBSON, George (M) 144 3
H: 6 1 b.Harold Wood 15-11-97
From Arsenal.
2015–16 West Ham U 0 0
2016–17 West Ham U 0 0
2016–17 *Walsall* 21 1
2017–18 Sparta Rotterdam 5 0 **5 0**
2017–18 Walsall 21 1
2018–19 Walsall 39 0 **81 2**
2019–20 Sunderland 29 0
2020–21 Sunderland 5 0 **34 0**
2020–21 *AFC Wimbledon* 24 1 **24 1**

DUNNE, Cieran (M) 0 0
b. 8-2-00
From Falkirk.
2020–21 Sunderland 0 0

EMBLETON, Elliot (M) 59 4
H: 5 8 W: 10 01 b. 2-4-99
Internationals: England U17, U18, U19, U20.
2016–17 Sunderland 0 0
2017–18 Sunderland 2 0
2018–19 Sunderland 0 0
2018–19 *Grimsby T* 27 3 **27 3**
2019–20 Sunderland 3 0
2020–21 Sunderland 9 0 **14 0**
2020–21 *Blackpool* 18 1 **18 1**

FLANAGAN, Tom (D) 206 9
H: 6 2 W: 11 05 b.Hammersmith 21-10-91
Internationals: Northern Ireland U21, Full caps.
2009–10 Milton Keynes D 1 0
2010–11 Milton Keynes D 2 0
2011–12 Milton Keynes D 21 3
2012–13 Milton Keynes D 0 0
2012–13 *Gillingham* 13 1 **13 1**
2012–13 *Barnet* 9 0 **9 0**
2013–14 Milton Keynes D 7 0
2013–14 *Stevenage* 2 0 **2 0**
2014–15 Milton Keynes D 6 0 **37 3**
2014–15 *Plymouth Arg* 4 0 **4 0**
2015–16 Burton Alb 18 0
2016–17 Burton Alb 30 0
2017–18 Burton Alb 27 2 **75 2**
2018–19 Sunderland 32 2
2019–20 Sunderland 18 1
2020–21 Sunderland 16 0 **66 3**

GOOCH, Lynden (M) 152 20
H: 5 8 W: 10 12 b.Santa Cruz 24-12-95
Internationals: Republic of Ireland U18. USA U20, Full caps.
2015–16 Sunderland 0 0

2015–16	*Doncaster R*	10	0	**10**	**0**
2016–17	Sunderland	11	0		
2017–18	Sunderland	24	1		
2018–19	Sunderland	39	5		
2019–20	Sunderland	30	10		
2020–21	Sunderland	38	4	**142**	**20**

GRAHAM, Danny (F) **558** **153**
H: 5 11 W: 12 05 b.Gateshead 12-8-85
Internationals: England U20.

2003–04	Middlesbrough	0	0		
2003–04	*Darlington*	9	2	**9**	**2**
2004–05	Middlesbrough	11	1		
2005–06	Middlesbrough	3	0		
2005–06	*Derby Co*	14	0	**14**	**0**
2005–06	*Leeds U*	3	0	**3**	**0**
2006–07	Middlesbrough	1	0		
2006–07	*Blackpool*	4	1	**4**	**1**
2006–07	*Carlisle U*	11	7		
2007–08	Carlisle U	45	14		
2008–09	Carlisle U	44	15	**100**	**36**
2009–10	Watford	46	14		
2010–11	Watford	45	23	**91**	**37**
2011–12	Swansea C	36	12		
2012–13	Swansea C	18	3	**54**	**15**
2012–13	Sunderland	13	0		
2013–14	Sunderland	0	0		
2013–14	*Hull C*	18	1	**18**	**1**
2013–14	*Middlesbrough*	18	6	**33**	**7**
2014–15	Sunderland	14	1		
2014–15	*Wolverhampton W*	5	1	**5**	**1**
2015–16	Sunderland	10	0		
2015–16	*Blackburn R*	18	7		
2016–17	Blackburn R	35	12		
2017–18	Blackburn R	42	14		
2018–19	Blackburn R	43	15		
2019–20	Blackburn R	38	4	**176**	**52**
2020–21	Sunderland	14	0	**51**	**1**

GRIGG, Will (M) **377** **118**
H: 5 11 W: 11 00 b.Solihull 3-7-91
Internationals: Northern Ireland U19, U21, Full caps.
From Stratford T.

2008–09	Walsall	1	0		
2009–10	Walsall	0	0		
2010–11	Walsall	28	4		
2011–12	Walsall	29	4		
2012–13	Walsall	41	19	**99**	**27**
2013–14	Brentford	34	5		
2014–15	Brentford	0	0	**34**	**5**
2014–15	*Milton Keynes D*	44	20		
2015–16	Wigan Ath	40	25		
2016–17	Wigan Ath	33	5		
2017–18	Wigan Ath	43	19		
2018–19	Wigan Ath	17	4	**133**	**53**
2018–19	Sunderland	18	4		
2019–20	Sunderland	20	1		
2020–21	Sunderland	9	0	**47**	**5**
2020–21	*Milton Keynes D*	20	8	**64**	**28**

HARRIS, Will (F) **0** **0**
b.South Shields 1-10-00
From Burnley.

2020–21	Sunderland	0	0		

HAWKES, Josh (M) **2** **0**
b.Stockton-on-Tees 28-1-99

2016–17	Hartlepool U	2	0	**2**	**0**

From Hartlepool U.

2020–21	Sunderland	0	0		

HUME, Denver (D) **64** **2**
b. 11-8-96

2017–18	Sunderland	1	0		
2018–19	Sunderland	8	0		
2019–20	Sunderland	32	1		
2020–21	Sunderland	23	1	**64**	**2**

JONES, Jordan (M) **138** **15**
H: 5 8 W: 9 07 b.Kettering 24-10-94

2012–13	Middlesbrough	0	0		
2013–14	Middlesbrough	0	0		
2014–15	Middlesbrough	0	0		
2014–15	*Hartlepool U*	11	0	**11**	**0**
2015–16	Middlesbrough	0	0		
2015–16	*Cambridge U*	1	0	**1**	**0**
2016–17	Kilmarnock	37	3		
2017–18	Kilmarnock	32	4		
2018–19	Kilmarnock	28	4	**97**	**11**
2019–20	Rangers	7	0		
2020–21	Rangers	3	1	**10**	**1**

On loan from Rangers.

2020–21	Sunderland	19	3	**19**	**3**

LEADBITTER, Grant (M) **513** **60**
H: 5 9 W: 11 06 b.Chester-le-Street 7-1-86
Internationals: England U16, U17, U19, U20, U21.

2002–03	Sunderland	0	0		
2003–04	Sunderland	0	0		
2004–05	Sunderland	0	0		
2005–06	Sunderland	12	0		
2005–06	*Rotherham U*	5	1	**5**	**1**
2006–07	Sunderland	44	7		
2007–08	Sunderland	31	2		
2008–09	Sunderland	23	2		
2009–10	Sunderland	1	0		
2009–10	Ipswich T	38	3		
2010–11	Ipswich T	44	5		
2011–12	Ipswich T	34	5		
2012–13	Ipswich T	0	0	**116**	**13**
2012–13	Middlesbrough	42	3		
2013–14	Middlesbrough	39	6		
2014–15	Middlesbrough	43	11		
2015–16	Middlesbrough	41	4		
2016–17	Middlesbrough	13	1		
2017–18	Middlesbrough	32	3		
2018–19	Middlesbrough	2	0	**212**	**28**
2018–19	Sunderland	15	0		
2019–20	Sunderland	14	0		
2020–21	Sunderland	40	7	**180**	**18**

MAGUIRE, Chris (F) **447** **85**
H: 5 7 W: 10 05 b.Bellshill 16-1-89
Internationals: Scotland U16, U19, U21, Full caps.

2005–06	Aberdeen	1	0		
2006–07	Aberdeen	19	1		
2007–08	Aberdeen	28	4		
2008–09	Aberdeen	31	3		
2009–10	Aberdeen	17	1		
2009–10	*Kilmarnock*	14	4	**14**	**4**
2010–11	Aberdeen	35	7	**131**	**16**
2011–12	Derby Co	7	1	**7**	**1**
2011–12	*Portsmouth*	11	3	**11**	**3**
2012–13	Sheffield W	10	1		
2013–14	Sheffield W	27	9		
2013–14	*Coventry C*	3	2	**3**	**2**
2014–15	Sheffield W	42	8	**79**	**18**
2015–16	Rotherham U	14	0	**14**	**0**
2015–16	Oxford U	21	4		
2016–17	Oxford U	42	13	**63**	**17**
2017–18	Bury	24	2	**24**	**2**
2018–19	Sunderland	33	7		
2019–20	Sunderland	35	10		
2020–21	Sunderland	33	5	**101**	**22**

MATTHEWS, Remi (G) **111** **0**
H: 6 0 W: 12 04 b.Gorleston 10-2-94

2014–15	Norwich C	0	0		
2014–15	*Burton Alb*	0	0		
2015–16	Norwich C	0	0		
2015–16	*Burton Alb*	2	0	**2**	**0**
2015–16	*Doncaster R*	9	0	**9**	**0**
2016–17	Norwich C	0	0		
2016–17	*Hamilton A*	17	0	**17**	**0**
2017–18	Norwich C	0	0		
2017–18	*Plymouth Arg*	26	0	**26**	**0**
2018–19	Bolton W	18	0		
2019–20	Bolton W	33	0	**51**	**0**
2020–21	Sunderland	6	0	**6**	**0**

McFADZEAN, Callum (D) **136** **6**
b.Sheffield 16-1-94
Internationals: England U16. Scotland U21.

2010–11	Sheffield U	0	0		
2011–12	Sheffield U	0	0		
2012–13	Sheffield U	8	0		
2013–14	Sheffield U	7	0		
2013–14	*Chesterfield*	4	0	**4**	**0**
2013–14	*Burton Alb*	7	1		
2014–15	Sheffield U	0	0		
2014–15	*Burton Alb*	9	1	**16**	**2**
2015–16	Sheffield U	1	0	**16**	**0**
2015–16	*Stevenage*	6	0	**6**	**0**
2016–17	Kilmarnock	4	0	**4**	**0**

From Alfreton T, Guiseley.

2018–19	Bury	40	0	**40**	**0**
2019–20	Plymouth Arg	25	3	**25**	**3**
2020–21	Sunderland	25	1	**25**	**1**

McGEADY, Aiden (M) **459** **78**
H: 5 10 W: 11 03 b.Glasgow 4-4-86
Internationals: Republic of Ireland Full caps.

2003–04	Celtic	4	1		
2004–05	Celtic	27	4		
2005–06	Celtic	20	4		
2006–07	Celtic	34	5		
2007–08	Celtic	36	7		
2008–09	Celtic	29	3		
2009–10	Celtic	35	7	**185**	**31**
2010–11	Spartak Moscow	11	2		
2011–12	Spartak Moscow	31	3		
2012–13	Spartak Moscow	17	5		
2013–14	Spartak Moscow	13	1	**72**	**11**
2013–14	Everton	16	0		
2014–15	Everton	16	1		
2015–16	Everton	0	0		
2015–16	*Sheffield W*	13	1	**13**	**1**
2016–17	Everton	0	0	**32**	**1**
2016–17	*Preston NE*	34	8	**34**	**8**
2017–18	Sunderland	35	7		
2018–19	Sunderland	34	11		
2019–20	Sunderland	15	4		
2019–20	*Charlton Ath*	10	0	**10**	**0**
2020–21	Sunderland	29	4	**113**	**26**

McLAUGHLIN, Conor (D) **272** **8**
H: 6 0 W: 11 02 b.Belfast 26-7-91
Internationals: Northern Ireland U21, Full caps.

2009–10	Preston NE	0	0		
2010–11	Preston NE	7	0		
2011–12	Preston NE	17	0	**24**	**0**
2011–12	*Shrewsbury T*	4	0	**4**	**0**
2012–13	Fleetwood T	19	0		
2013–14	Fleetwood T	35	0		
2014–15	Fleetwood T	39	1		
2015–16	Fleetwood T	37	2		
2016–17	Fleetwood T	42	4	**172**	**7**
2017–18	Millwall	24	1		
2018–19	Millwall	8	0	**32**	**1**
2019–20	Sunderland	15	0		
2020–21	Sunderland	25	0	**40**	**0**

MGUNGA-KIMPIOKA, Benjamin (M) **8** **1**
b. 21-2-00
Internationals: Sweden U19, U21.
From IK Sirius.

2018–19	Sunderland	4	0		
2019–20	Sunderland	4	1		
2020–21	Sunderland	0	0	**8**	**1**

NEILL, Daniel (M) **2** **0**
b. 30-11-01

2018–19	Sunderland	0	0		
2019–20	Sunderland	0	0		
2020–21	Sunderland	2	0	**2**	**0**

O'BRIEN, Aiden (F) **232** **38**
H: 5 8 W: 10 12 b.Islington 4-10-93
Internationals: Republic of Ireland U17, U19, U21, Full caps.

2010–11	Millwall	0	0		
2011–12	Millwall	0	0		
2012–13	Millwall	0	0		
2012–13	*Crawley T*	9	0	**9**	**0**
2013–14	Millwall	0	0		
2013–14	*Torquay U*	3	0	**3**	**0**
2014–15	Millwall	19	2		
2015–16	Millwall	43	10		
2016–17	Millwall	43	13		
2017–18	Millwall	30	4		
2018–19	Millwall	35	2		
2019–20	Millwall	18	3	**188**	**34**
2020–21	Sunderland	32	4	**32**	**4**

O'NIEN, Luke (M) **212** **26**
b. 21-11-94

2013–14	Watford	1	0		
2014–15	Watford	0	0	**1**	**0**
2015–16	Wycombe W	35	5		
2016–17	Wycombe W	31	3		
2017–18	Wycombe W	35	7	**101**	**15**
2018–19	Sunderland	37	5		
2019–20	Sunderland	35	4		
2020–21	Sunderland	38	2	**110**	**11**

PATTERSON, Anthony (G) **0** **0**
b. 10-5-00

2018–19	Sunderland	0	0		
2019–20	Sunderland	0	0		
2020–21	Sunderland	0	0		

POWER, Max (M) **344** **34**
H: 5 11 W: 11 13 b.Bebington 27-7-93

2010–11	Tranmere R	0	0		
2011–12	Tranmere R	4	0		
2012–13	Tranmere R	27	3		
2013–14	Tranmere R	33	2		
2014–15	Tranmere R	45	7	**109**	**12**
2015–16	Wigan Ath	44	6		
2016–17	Wigan Ath	42	0		
2017–18	Wigan Ath	40	5		
2018–19	Wigan Ath	1	0	**127**	**11**
2018–19	Sunderland	35	4		
2019–20	Sunderland	31	2		
2020–21	Sunderland	42	5	**108**	**11**

RICHARDSON, Adam (G) **0** **0**

2020–21	Sunderland	0	0		

SCOWEN, Josh (M) **329** **17**
H: 5 10 W: 11 09 b.Cheshunt 28-3-93

2010–11	Wycombe W	2	0		
2011–12	Wycombe W	0	0		
2012–13	Wycombe W	34	1		
2013–14	Wycombe W	37	1		
2014–15	Wycombe W	18	1	**91**	**3**
2014–15	Barnsley	21	4		
2015–16	Barnsley	34	4		
2016–17	Barnsley	41	2	**96**	**10**
2017–18	QPR	42	1		
2018–19	QPR	35	2		
2019–20	QPR	18	0	**95**	**3**
2019–20	Sunderland	4	0		
2020–21	Sunderland	43	1	**47**	**1**

STEELS, Vinny (M) **0 0**
b. 9-8-01
From Darlington, York C, Burnley.
2020–21 Sunderland 0 0

STEWART, Ross C (F) **109 34**
b.Glasgow 1-9-96
2016–17 Albion R 25 12 **25 12**
2017–18 St Mirren 9 0
2017–18 *Alloa Ath* 19 7 **19 7**
2018–19 St Mirren 1 0 **10 0**
2018–19 Ross Co 23 6
2019–20 Ross Co 21 7
2020–21 Ross Co 0 0 **44 13**
2020–21 Sunderland 11 2 **11 2**

TAYLOR, Brandon (D) **0 0**
b.Gateshead 10-5-99
2018–19 Sunderland 0 0
2019–20 Sunderland 0 0
2020–21 Sunderland 0 0

WEARNE, Stephen (M) **0 0**
b. 16-12-00
From Newcastle U.
2020–21 Middlesbrough 0 0
2020–21 Sunderland 0 0

WILDING, Samuel (M) **0 0**
From WBA.
2020–21 Sunderland 0 0

WILLIS, Jordan (D) **229 6**
H: 5 11 W: 11 00 b.Coventry 24-8-94
Internationals: England U18, U19.
2011–12 Coventry C 3 0
2012–13 Coventry C 1 0
2013–14 Coventry C 28 0
2014–15 Coventry C 34 0
2015–16 Coventry C 4 0
2016–17 Coventry C 36 3
2017–18 Coventry C 35 0
2018–19 Coventry C 38 1 **179 4**
2019–20 Sunderland 35 2
2020–21 Sunderland 15 0 **50 2**

WINCHESTER, Carl (D) **302 25**
H: 5 10 W: 11 08 b.Belfast 12-4-93
Internationals: Northern Ireland U16, U17, U18, U19, U21, Full caps.
From Linfield.
2010–11 Oldham Ath 6 1
2011–12 Oldham Ath 12 0
2012–13 Oldham Ath 9 0
2013–14 Oldham Ath 12 1
2014–15 Oldham Ath 41 4
2015–16 Oldham Ath 31 1
2016–17 Oldham Ath 9 1 **120 8**
2016–17 Cheltenham T 20 1
2017–18 Cheltenham T 44 5 **64 6**
2018–19 Forest Green R 45 3
2019–20 Forest Green R 35 5
2020–21 Forest Green R 18 2 **98 10**
2020–21 Sunderland 20 1 **20 1**

WRIGHT, Bailey (D) **289 11**
H: 5 9 W: 13 05 b.Melbourne 28-7-92
Internationals: Australia U17, Full caps.
2010–11 Preston NE 2 0
2011–12 Preston NE 13 1
2012–13 Preston NE 38 2
2013–14 Preston NE 43 4
2014–15 Preston NE 27 1
2015–16 Preston NE 38 0
2016–17 Preston NE 18 0 **179 8**
2016–17 Bristol C 21 1
2017–18 Bristol C 36 0
2018–19 Bristol C 12 0
2019–20 Bristol C 3 0 **72 1**
2019–20 *Sunderland* 5 0
2020–21 Sunderland 33 2 **38 2**

WYKE, Charlie (F) **282 96**
b.Middlesbrough 6-12-92
2011–12 Middlesbrough 0 0
2012–13 Middlesbrough 0 0
2012–13 *Hartlepool U* 25 2
2013–14 Middlesbrough 0 0
2013–14 *AFC Wimbledon* 17 2 **17 2**
2014–15 Middlesbrough 0 0
2014–15 *Hartlepool U* 13 4 **38 6**
2014–15 Carlisle U 17 6
2015–16 Carlisle U 34 12
2016–17 Carlisle U 26 14 **77 32**
2016–17 Bradford C 16 7
2017–18 Bradford C 40 15 **56 22**
2018–19 Sunderland 24 4
2019–20 Sunderland 27 5
2020–21 Sunderland 43 25 **94 34**

XHEMAJLI, Arbenit (D) **46 2**
b. 23-4-98
2017–18 Neuchatel Xamax 6 0
2018–19 Neuchatel Xamax 17 0
2019–20 Neuchatel Xamax 23 2
2020–21 Neuchatel Xamax 0 0 **46 2**
2020–21 Sunderland 0 0

YOUNGER, Ollie (D) **1 0**
b. 14-11-99
2017–18 Burnley 0 0
2018–19 Burnley 0 0
2019–20 Burnley 0 0
2020–21 Sunderland 1 0 **1 0**

Scholars
Almond, Patrick Joseph; Armstrong, Jack William; Baggs, Joshua William; Basey, Oliver Paul; Bond, Harrison; Bruce, Ryan; Chapman, Luke; Dicicco, McKenzie Michael; Foster, James Henry; Gardiner, Harry Jay; Gooch, Ryan; Irons, Samuel Alan; Jones, Daniel Alan; Kelly, Caden Christopher; Krakue, Jonathan Kojo; Lohia, Lakhraj Singh; Taylor, Ellis James; Watts, Louis Jake; Wombwell, Ryan Robert.

SWANSEA C (82)

AKANDE, Adrian (F) **0 0**
b. 22-10-03
From Chelsea.
2020–21 Swansea C 0 0

AL-HAMADI, Ali (F) **0 0**
H: 6 1 b.Maysan 1-3-02
Internationals: Iraq U23.
From Tranmere R.
2020–21 Swansea C 0 0

ARRIOLA, Paul (F) **151 18**
b.Chula Vista, California 5-2-95
2013–14 Tijuana 20 1
2014–15 Tijuana 5 0
2015–16 Tijuana 26 1
2016–17 Tijuana 28 2
2017 DC United 11 1
2017–18 Tijuana 1 0 **80 4**
2018 DC United 28 7
2019 DC United 29 6
2020 DC United 1 0 **69 14**
On loan from DC United.
2020–21 Swansea C 2 0 **2 0**

ASORO, Joel (F) **56 6**
H: 5 9 W: 11 11 b. 27-4-99
Internationals: Sweden U17, U21.
2016–17 Sunderland 1 0
2017–18 Sunderland 26 3 **27 3**
2018–19 Swansea C 14 0
2019–20 Swansea C 0 0
2019–20 *Groningen* 15 3 **15 3**
2020–21 Swansea C 0 0 **14 0**
2020–21 *Genoa* 0 0
Transferred to Djurgardens February 2021.

AYEW, Andre (F) **412 108**
H: 5 9 W: 11 05 b.Seclin 17-12-89
Internationals: Ghana U20, Full caps.
2007–08 Marseille 9 0
2008–09 Marseille 0 0
2008–09 *Lorient* 22 3 **22 3**
2009–10 Marseille 0 0
2009–10 *Arles-Avignon* 25 4 **25 4**
2010–11 Marseille 37 11
2011–12 Marseille 26 8
2012–13 Marseille 35 9
2013–14 Marseille 25 6
2014–15 Marseille 28 10 **160 44**
2015–16 Swansea C 34 12
2016–17 West Ham U 25 6
2017–18 West Ham U 18 3 **43 9**
2017–18 Swansea C 12 0
2018–19 Swansea C 0 0
2018–19 *Fenerbahce* 29 5 **29 5**
2019–20 Swansea C 44 15
2020–21 Swansea C 43 16 **133 43**

BENDA, Steven (G) **25 0**
H: 6 4 W: 13 01 b.Stuttgart 1-1-98
From Aalen, Heidenheim, TSV 1860.
2018–19 Swansea C 0 0
2019–20 Swansea C 0 0
2019–20 *Swindon T* 24 0 **24 0**
2020–21 Swansea C 1 0 **1 0**

BENNETT, Ryan (M) **399 16**
H: 6 2 W: 11 00 b.Thurrock 6-3-90
Internationals: England U18, U21.
2006–07 Grimsby T 5 0
2007–08 Grimsby T 40 1
2008–09 Grimsby T 45 5
2009–10 Grimsby T 13 0 **103 6**
2009–10 Peterborough U 22 1
2010–11 Peterborough U 34 4
2011–12 Peterborough U 32 1 **88 6**
2011–12 Norwich C 8 0
2012–13 Norwich C 15 1
2013–14 Norwich C 16 1
2014–15 Norwich C 7 0
2015–16 Norwich C 22 0
2016–17 Norwich C 33 0 **101 2**
2017–18 Wolverhampton W 29 1
2018–19 Wolverhampton W 34 1
2019–20 Wolverhampton W 11 0 **74 2**
2019–20 *Leicester C* 5 0 **5 0**
2020–21 Swansea C 28 0 **28 0**

BIDWELL, Jake (D) **388 6**
H: 6 0 W: 11 00 b.Southport 21-3-93
Internationals: England U16, U17, U18, U19.
2009–10 Everton 0 0
2010–11 Everton 0 0
2011–12 Everton 0 0
2011–12 *Brentford* 24 0
2012–13 Everton 0 0
2012–13 *Brentford* 40 0
2013–14 Brentford 38 0
2014–15 Brentford 43 0
2015–16 Brentford 45 3 **190 3**
2016–17 QPR 36 0
2017–18 QPR 46 2
2018–19 QPR 40 0 **122 2**
2019–20 Swansea C 37 0
2020–21 Swansea C 39 1 **76 1**

BYERS, George (M) **71 4**
H: 5 11 W: 11 07 b.Ilford 29-5-96
Internationals: Scotland U16, U17.
2014–15 Watford 1 0
2015–16 Watford 0 0 **1 0**
2016–17 Swansea C 0 0
2017–18 Swansea C 0 0
2018–19 Swansea C 21 2
2019–20 Swansea C 35 2
2020–21 Swansea C 0 0 **56 4**
2020–21 *Portsmouth* 14 0 **14 0**

CABANGO, Ben (D) **51 5**
b.Cardiff 30-5-00
Internationals: Wales U17, U19, U21.
2018–19 Swansea C 0 0
2019–20 Swansea C 21 1
2020–21 Swansea C 30 4 **51 5**

CAMPBELL, Rio (F) **0 0**
b. 6-10-02
2020–21 Swansea C 0 0

COOPER, Brandon (D) **20 1**
b.Bridgend 14-1-00
Internationals: Wales U21.
2018–19 Swansea C 0 0
2019–20 Swansea C 0 0
2020–21 Swansea C 1 0 **1 0**
2020–21 *Newport Co* 19 1 **19 1**

COOPER, Oliver (M) **3 0**
b. 14-12-99
2020–21 Swansea C 3 0 **3 0**

CULLEN, Liam (F) **19 2**
b.Tenby 23-4-99
Internationals: Wales U16, U17, U19, U20, U21.
2018–19 Swansea C 0 0
2019–20 Swansea C 6 1
2020–21 Swansea C 13 1 **19 2**

DHANDA, Yan (F) **47 5**
H: 5 8 W: 10 03 b.Birmingham 14-12-98
Internationals: England U16, U17.
From Liverpool.
2018–19 Swansea C 5 1
2019–20 Swansea C 16 3
2020–21 Swansea C 26 1 **47 5**

EVANS, Cameron James (D) **15 0**
Internationals: Wales U17, U19.
2019–20 Swansea C 0 0
2020–21 Swansea C 0 0
2020–21 *Waterford* 15 0 **15 0**

FREEMAN, Kieron (D) **203 15**
H: 5 10 W: 12 05 b.Nottingham 21-3-92
Internationals: Wales U17, U19, U21, Full caps.
2010–11 Nottingham F 0 0
2011–12 Nottingham F 0 0
2011–12 *Notts Co* 19 1
2012–13 Derby Co 19 0
2013–14 Derby Co 6 0
2013–14 *Notts Co* 16 0 **35 1**
2013–14 *Sheffield U* 12 0
2014–15 Derby Co 0 0 **25 0**
2014–15 *Mansfield T* 11 0 **11 0**
2014–15 Sheffield U 19 1
2015–16 Sheffield U 19 0
2015–16 *Portsmouth* 7 0 **7 0**

2016–17 Sheffield U 41 10
2017–18 Sheffield U 10 1
2018–19 Sheffield U 20 2
2019–20 Sheffield U 2 0
2020–21 Sheffield U 0 0 **123 14**
2020–21 Swindon T 2 0 **2 0**
2020–21 Swansea C 0 0

FULTON, Jay (M) 144 9
H: 5 10 W: 10 08 b.Bolton 4-4-94
Internationals: Scotland U18, U19, U21.
From Falkirk.
2013–14 Swansea C 2 0
2014–15 Swansea C 2 0
2015–16 Swansea C 2 0
2015–16 *Oldham Ath* 11 0 **11 0**
2016–17 Swansea C 11 0
2017–18 Swansea C 2 0
2017–18 *Wigan Ath* 5 1 **5 1**
2018–19 Swansea C 33 2
2019–20 Swansea C 36 3
2020–21 Swansea C 40 3 **128 8**

GARRICK, Jordan (F) 33 4
b. 15-7-98
From Ossett T.
2019–20 Swansea C 11 2
2020–21 Swansea C 3 0 **14 2**
2020–21 *Swindon T* 19 2 **19 2**

GRIMES, Matt (M) 262 12
H: 5 10 W: 11 00 b.Exeter 15-7-95
Internationals: England U20, U21.
2013–14 Exeter C 35 1
2014–15 Exeter C 23 4 **58 5**
2014–15 Swansea C 3 0
2015–16 Swansea C 1 0
2015–16 *Blackburn R* 13 0 **13 0**
2016–17 Swansea C 0 0
2016–17 *Leeds U* 7 0 **7 0**
2017–18 Swansea C 0 0
2017–18 *Northampton T* 44 4 **44 4**
2018–19 Swansea C 45 1
2019–20 Swansea C 46 0
2020–21 Swansea C 45 2 **140 3**

HAMER, Ben (G) 270 0
H: 5 11 W: 12 04 b.Chard 20-11-87
2006–07 Reading 0 0
2007–08 Reading 0 0
2007–08 *Brentford* 20 0
2008–09 Reading 0 0
2008–09 *Brentford* 45 0
2009–10 Reading 0 0
2010–11 Reading 0 0
2010–11 *Brentford* 10 0 **75 0**
2010–11 *Exeter C* 18 0 **18 0**
2011–12 Charlton Ath 41 0
2012–13 Charlton Ath 41 0
2013–14 Charlton Ath 32 0 **114 0**
2014–15 Leicester C 8 0
2015–16 Leicester C 0 0
2015–16 *Bristol C* 4 0 **4 0**
2016–17 Leicester C 0 0
2017–18 Leicester C 4 0 **12 0**
2018–19 Huddersfield T 7 0
2019–20 *Derby Co* 25 0 **25 0**
2020–21 Huddersfield T 15 0 **22 0**
2020–21 Swansea C 0 0

JOHN, Declan (M) 121 5
H: 5 10 W: 11 10 b.Merthyr Tydfil 30-6-95
Internationals: Wales U17, U19, Full caps.
2010–11 Llanelli 1 0 **1 0**
2011–12 Afan Lido 5 0 **5 0**
2012–13 Cardiff C 0 0
2013–14 Cardiff C 20 0
2014–15 Cardiff C 6 0
2014–15 *Barnsley* 9 0 **9 0**
2015–16 Cardiff C 1 0
2015–16 *Chesterfield* 6 0 **6 0**
2016–17 Cardiff C 15 0
2017–18 Cardiff C 0 0 **42 0**
2017–18 Rangers 26 3 **26 3**
2018–19 Swansea C 10 0
2019–20 Swansea C 1 0
2019–20 *Sunderland* 0 0
2020–21 Swansea C 0 0 **11 0**
2020–21 *Bolton W* 21 2 **21 2**

JONES, Harry (D) 0 0
b. 8-10-02
Internationals: Wales U16, U17, U18.
From Arsenal.
2020–21 Swansea C 0 0

JONES, Jacob (D) 0 0
b. 5-9-01
Internationals: Wales U19.
2020–21 Swansea C 0 0

LATIBEAUDIERE, Joel (D) 13 1
b. 6-1-00
2017–18 Manchester C 0 0
2018–19 Manchester C 0 0
2019–20 Manchester C 0 0
2019–20 *FC Twente* 5 1 **5 1**
2020–21 Swansea C 8 0 **8 0**

LOWE, Jamal (F) 203 45
H: 6 0 W: 12 06 b.Harrow 21-7-94
Internationals: England C.
2012–13 Barnet 8 0 **8 0**
From St Albans C, Hemel Hempstead T, Hampton & Richmond.
2016–17 Portsmouth 14 4
2017–18 Portsmouth 44 6
2018–19 Portsmouth 45 15
2019–20 Portsmouth 0 0 **103 25**
2019–20 Wigan Ath 46 6 **46 6**
2020–21 Swansea C 46 14 **46 14**

MANNING, Ryan (F) 169 24
H: 5 8 W: 10 06 b.Galway 14-6-96
Internationals: Republic of Ireland U17, U19, U21.
2013 Mervue U 26 9 **26 9**
2014 Galway U 21 4 **21 4**
2014–15 QPR 0 0
2015–16 QPR 0 0
2016–17 QPR 18 1
2017–18 QPR 19 2
2018–19 QPR 9 0
2018–19 *Rotherham U* 18 4 **18 4**
2019–20 QPR 41 4
2020–21 QPR 0 0 **87 7**
2020–21 Swansea C 17 0 **17 0**

McFAYDEN, Lincoln (D) 0 0
b. 11-2-02
From Preston NE.
2020–21 Swansea C 0 0

McKAY, Barrie (M) 238 27
H: 5 9 W: 11 00 b.Paisley 30-12-94
Internationals: Scotland U18, U19, U21, Full caps.
From Kilmarnock.
2011–12 Rangers 1 0
2012–13 Rangers 31 1
2013–14 Rangers 2 0
2013–14 *Greenock Morton* 18 3 **18 3**
2014–15 Rangers 0 0
2014–15 *Raith R* 23 1 **23 1**
2015–16 Rangers 34 6
2016–17 Rangers 35 5 **103 12**
2017–18 Nottingham F 26 5 **26 5**
2018–19 Swansea C 30 2
2019–20 Swansea C 4 0
2019–20 *Fleetwood T* 8 2
2020–21 Swansea C 0 0 **34 2**
2020–21 *Fleetwood T* 26 2 **34 4**

MORRIS, Jordan (F) 106 35
b.Seattle 26-10-94
2016 Seattle Sounders 34 12
2017 Seattle Sounders 23 3
2018 Seattle Sounders 0 0
2019 Seattle Sounders 26 10
2020 Seattle Sounders 19 10 **102 35**
On loan from Seattle Sounders.
2020–21 Swansea C 4 0 **4 0**

NAUGHTON, Kyle (M) 380 11
H: 5 11 W: 11 07 b.Sheffield 11-11-88
Internationals: England U21.
2006–07 Sheffield U 0 0
2007–08 *Gretna* 18 0 **18 0**
2007–08 Sheffield U 0 0
2008–09 Sheffield U 40 1
2009–10 Sheffield U 0 0 **40 1**
2009–10 Tottenham H 1 0
2009–10 *Middlesbrough* 15 0 **15 0**
2010–11 Tottenham H 0 0
2010–11 *Leicester C* 34 5 **34 5**
2011–12 Tottenham H 0 0
2011–12 *Norwich C* 32 0 **32 0**
2012–13 Tottenham H 14 0
2013–14 Tottenham H 22 0
2014–15 Tottenham H 5 0 **42 0**
2014–15 Swansea C 10 0
2015–16 Swansea C 27 0
2016–17 Swansea C 31 1
2017–18 Swansea C 34 0
2018–19 Swansea C 35 1
2019–20 Swansea C 32 3
2020–21 Swansea C 30 0 **199 5**

PETERSON, Kristoffer (M) 141 27
b.Gothenburg 28-11-94
Internationals: Sweden U17, U21, Full caps.
2011–12 Liverpool 0 0
2012–13 Liverpool 0 0
2013–14 Liverpool 0 0
2013–14 *Tranmere R* 6 0 **6 0**
2014–15 Utrecht 20 2
2015–16 Utrecht 7 0
2015–16 *Roda* 14 1 **14 1**
2016–17 Heracles 15 4
2017–18 Heracles 33 7
2018–19 Heracles 33 12 **81 23**
2019–20 Swansea C 7 0
2019–20 *Utrecht* 6 1 **33 3**
2020–21 Swansea C 0 0 **7 0**
Transferred to Fortuna Dusseldorf October 2020.

ROBERTS, Connor (D) 181 11
H: 5 9 W: 11 03 b.Neath 23-9-95
Internationals: Wales U19, U21, Full caps.
2014–15 Swansea C 0 0
2015–16 Swansea C 0 0
2015–16 *Yeovil T* 45 0 **45 0**
2016–17 Swansea C 0 0
2016–17 *Bristol R* 2 0 **2 0**
2017–18 Swansea C 4 0
2017–18 *Middlesbrough* 1 0 **1 0**
2018–19 Swansea C 45 5
2019–20 Swansea C 38 1
2020–21 Swansea C 46 5 **133 11**

ROUTLEDGE, Wayne (M) 520 48
H: 5 6 W: 11 02 b.Sidcup 7-1-85
Internationals: England U20, U21.
2001–02 Crystal Palace 2 0
2002–03 Crystal Palace 26 4
2003–04 Crystal Palace 44 6
2004–05 Crystal Palace 38 0 **110 10**
2005–06 Tottenham H 3 0
2005–06 *Portsmouth* 13 0 **13 0**
2006–07 Tottenham H 0 0
2006–07 *Fulham* 24 0 **24 0**
2007–08 Tottenham H 2 0 **5 0**
2007–08 Aston Villa 1 0
2008–09 Aston Villa 1 0 **2 0**
2008–09 *Cardiff C* 9 2 **9 2**
2008–09 QPR 19 1
2009–10 QPR 25 2
2009–10 Newcastle U 17 3
2010–11 Newcastle U 17 0 **34 3**
2010–11 *QPR* 20 5 **64 8**
2011–12 Swansea C 28 1
2012–13 Swansea C 36 5
2013–14 Swansea C 35 2
2014–15 Swansea C 29 3
2015–16 Swansea C 28 2
2016–17 Swansea C 27 3
2017–18 Swansea C 15 0
2018–19 Swansea C 24 5
2019–20 Swansea C 21 4
2020–21 Swansea C 16 0 **259 25**

RUSHESHA, Tivonge (D) 0 0
b. 24-7-02
Internationals: Wales U17.
2019–20 Swansea C 0 0
2020–21 Swansea C 0 0

SEARLE, Jamie (G) 0 0
b. 25-11-00
From Aston Villa.
2020–21 Swansea C 0 0

SMITH, Korey (M) 360 6
H: 5 9 W: 11 01 b.Hatfield 31-1-91
2008–09 Norwich C 2 0
2009–10 Norwich C 37 4
2010–11 Norwich C 28 0
2011–12 Norwich C 0 0
2011–12 *Barnsley* 12 0 **12 0**
2012–13 Norwich C 0 0 **67 4**
2012–13 *Yeovil T* 17 0 **17 0**
2012–13 *Oldham Ath* 10 0
2013–14 Oldham Ath 42 1 **52 1**
2014–15 Bristol C 44 0
2015–16 Bristol C 36 0
2016–17 Bristol C 23 0
2017–18 Bristol C 45 1
2018–19 Bristol C 5 0
2019–20 Bristol C 22 0
2020–21 Bristol C 0 0 **175 1**
2020–21 Swansea C 37 0 **37 0**

THOMAS, Joshua (F) 0 0
H: 5 8 b. 24-9-02
Internationals: Wales U17, U19.
2020–21 Swansea C 0 0

WEBB, Lewis (G) 0 0
b. 12-9-01
2020–21 Swansea C 0 0

WHITTAKER, Morgan (F) **37 2**
b. 7-1-01
Internationals: England U16, U17, U18, U19.

2019–20	Derby Co	16	1		
2020–21	Derby Co	9	0	**25**	**1**
2020–21	Swansea C	12	1	**12**	**1**

WILLIAMS, Daniel (M) **0 0**
b. 19-4-01

2020–21	Swansea C	0	0		

Scholars
Bassett, Ryan David Harry; Butler, Scott James; Clarke, Morgan James; Congreve, Cameron Mark; Davies, Ruben James; Edwards, Jacob Lloyd; Edwards, Joshua; Evans, Andrew Tyler Jay; Hillier, Aaron Jac; Hutchings, Joshua; Jenkins, Kian John; Kenko Djoudie, Erick Ryan; Ludvigsen, Kai; Makokowe, Panashe; Moti, Adnaan Rahim; Murphy, Michael James; Perkins, Dylan Anthony; Williams, Cian Owain.

SWINDON T (83)

BAUDRY, Mathieu (D) **273 17**
H: 6 2 W: 12 08 b.Le Havre 24-2-88
From Le Havre.

2007–08	Troyes	2	1		
2008–09	Troyes	17	0		
2009–10	Troyes	7	0	**26**	**1**
2010–11	Bournemouth	3	1		
2011–12	Bournemouth	7	0	**10**	**1**
2011–12	*Dagenham & R*	11	0	**11**	**0**
2012–13	Leyton Orient	24	3		
2013–14	Leyton Orient	39	2		
2014–15	Leyton Orient	31	1		
2015–16	Leyton Orient	34	2	**128**	**8**
2016–17	Doncaster R	31	5		
2017–18	Doncaster R	22	1	**53**	**6**
2018–19	Milton Keynes D	5	0	**5**	**0**
2019–20	Swindon T	24	0		
2020–21	Swindon T	16	1	**40**	**1**

BROADBENT, Tom (D) **68 1**
H: 6 3 W: 14 02 b. 15-2-92
From Farnborough, Petersfield T, Hayes & Yeading U.

2017–18	Bristol R	22	0		
2018–19	Bristol R	7	0	**29**	**0**
2018–19	Swindon T	12	0		
2019–20	Swindon T	9	0		
2020–21	Swindon T	18	1	**39**	**1**

CADDIS, Paul (D) **353 22**
H: 5 7 W: 10 07 b.Irvine 19-4-88
Internationals: Scotland U19, U21, Full caps.

2007–08	Celtic	2	0		
2008–09	Celtic	5	0		
2008–09	*Dundee U*	11	0	**11**	**0**
2009–10	Celtic	10	0	**17**	**0**
2010–11	Swindon T	38	1		
2011–12	Swindon T	39	4		
2012–13	Swindon T	0	0		
2012–13	*Birmingham C*	27	0		
2013–14	Birmingham C	38	5		
2014–15	Birmingham C	45	6		
2015–16	Birmingham C	39	4		
2016–17	Birmingham C	0	0	**149**	**15**
2016–17	Bury	13	0	**13**	**0**
2017–18	Blackburn R	14	0	**14**	**0**
2018–19	Bradford C	27	1	**27**	**1**
2019–20	Swindon T	19	0		
2020–21	Swindon T	26	1	**122**	**6**

CAMP, Lee (G) **550 0**
H: 5 11 W: 11 11 b.Derby 22-8-84
Internationals: England U21. Northern Ireland Full caps.

2002–03	Derby Co	1	0		
2003–04	Derby Co	0	0		
2003–04	*QPR*	12	0		
2004–05	Derby Co	45	0		
2005–06	Derby Co	40	0		
2006–07	Derby Co	3	0	**89**	**0**
2006–07	*Norwich C*	3	0		
2006–07	*QPR*	11	0		
2007–08	QPR	46	0		
2008–09	QPR	4	0	**73**	**0**
2008–09	*Nottingham F*	15	0		
2009–10	Nottingham F	45	0		
2010–11	Nottingham F	46	0		
2011–12	Nottingham F	46	0		
2012–13	Nottingham F	26	0	**178**	**0**
2012–13	Norwich C	3	0	**6**	**0**
2013–14	WBA	0	0		
2013–14	Bournemouth	33	0		
2014–15	Bournemouth	9	0		
2015–16	Bournemouth	0	0	**42**	**0**
2015–16	Rotherham U	41	0		
2016–17	Rotherham U	18	0	**59**	**0**
2017–18	Cardiff C	0	0		
2017–18	*Sunderland*	12	0	**12**	**0**
2018–19	Birmingham C	44	0		
2019–20	Birmingham C	36	0		
2020–21	Birmingham C	0	0	**80**	**0**
2020–21	Coventry C	0	0		
2020–21	Swindon T	11	0	**11**	**0**

CHESHIRE, Anthony (D) **0 0**

2019–20	Swindon T	0	0		
2020–21	Swindon T	0	0		

CONROY, Dion (D) **78 1**
b.Redhill 11-12-95
From Chelsea.

2016–17	Swindon T	14	0		
2017–18	Swindon T	7	0		
2018–19	Swindon T	27	1		
2019–20	Swindon T	11	0		
2020–21	Swindon T	19	0	**78**	**1**

CURRAN, Taylor (D) **14 1**
b. 7-7-00

2018–19	Southend U	0	0		
2018–19	Swindon T	1	0		
2019–20	Swindon T	2	0		
2020–21	Swindon T	11	1	**14**	**1**

DOUGHTY, Michael (M) **212 24**
H: 6 1 W: 12 10 b.Westminster 20-11-92
Internationals: Wales U19, U21.

2010–11	QPR	0	0		
2011–12	QPR	0	0		
2011–12	*Crawley T*	16	0	**16**	**0**
2011–12	*Aldershot T*	5	0	**5**	**0**
2012–13	QPR	0	0		
2012–13	*St Johnstone*	5	0	**5**	**0**
2013–14	QPR	0	0		
2013–14	*Stevenage*	36	2	**36**	**2**
2014–15	QPR	3	0		
2014–15	*Gillingham*	9	0	**9**	**0**
2015–16	QPR	5	0		
2015–16	*Swindon T*	20	5		
2016–17	QPR	4	0	**12**	**0**
2016–17	*Swindon T*	14	2		
2017–18	Peterborough U	34	1	**34**	**1**
2018–19	Swindon T	30	13		
2019–20	Swindon T	31	1		
2020–21	Swindon T	0	0	**95**	**21**

FRYER, Joe (G) **49 0**
b.Chester-le-Street 14-11-95

2016–17	Middlesbrough	0	0		
2016–17	*Hartlepool U*	14	0	**14**	**0**
2017–18	Middlesbrough	0	0		
2017–18	*Stevenage*	28	0	**28**	**0**
2018–19	Middlesbrough	0	0		
2018–19	*Carlisle U*	5	0	**5**	**0**
2019–20	Middlesbrough	0	0		
2020–21	Swindon T	2	0	**2**	**0**

FRYERS, Zeki (D) **97 2**
H: 6 0 W: 12 00 b.Manchester 9-9-92
Internationals: England U16, U17, U19.

2011–12	Manchester U	2	0	**2**	**0**
2012–13	Standard Liege	7	0	**7**	**0**
2012–13	Tottenham H	0	0		
2013–14	Tottenham H	7	0	**7**	**0**
2014–15	Crystal Palace	1	0		
2014–15	*Rotherham U*	10	0	**10**	**0**
2014–15	*Ipswich T*	3	0	**3**	**0**
2015–16	Crystal Palace	0	0		
2016–17	Crystal Palace	8	0	**9**	**0**
2017–18	Barnsley	22	1		
2018–19	Barnsley	5	0	**27**	**1**
2019–20	Swindon T	22	1		
2020–21	Swindon T	10	0	**32**	**1**

GIAMATTEI, Massimo (M) **0 0**

2019–20	Swindon T	0	0		
2020–21	Swindon T	0	0		

GRANT, Anthony (M) **540 18**
H: 5 10 W: 11 01 b.Lambeth 4-6-87
Internationals: England U16, U17, U19.

2004–05	Chelsea	1	0		
2005–06	Chelsea	0	0		
2005–06	*Oldham Ath*	2	0	**2**	**0**
2006–07	Chelsea	0	0		
2006–07	*Wycombe W*	40	0	**40**	**0**
2007–08	Chelsea	0	0	**1**	**0**
2007–08	*Luton T*	4	0	**4**	**0**
2007–08	*Southend U*	10	0		
2008–09	Southend U	35	1		
2009–10	Southend U	38	0		
2010–11	Southend U	43	8		
2011–12	Southend U	33	1	**159**	**10**
2012–13	Stevenage	41	0	**41**	**0**
2013–14	Crewe Alex	38	2		
2014–15	Crewe Alex	43	2	**81**	**4**
2015–16	Port Vale	38	1		
2016–17	Port Vale	20	0	**58**	**1**
2016–17	Peterborough U	11	0		
2017–18	Peterborough U	38	0	**49**	**0**
2018–19	Shrewsbury T	42	0		
2019–20	*Shrewsbury T*	0	0	**42**	**0**
2019–20	Swindon T	30	0		
2020–21	Swindon T	33	3	**63**	**3**

GRANT, Joel (F) **369 60**
H: 6 0 W: 12 01 b.Acton 26-8-87
Internationals: Jamaica U20, Full caps.

2005–06	Watford	7	0		
2006–07	Watford	0	0	**7**	**0**

From Aldershot T.

2008–09	Crewe Alex	28	2		
2009–10	Crewe Alex	43	9		
2010–11	Crewe Alex	25	5	**96**	**16**
2011–12	Wycombe W	30	4		
2012–13	Wycombe W	41	10	**71**	**14**
2013–14	Yeovil T	34	3		
2014–15	Yeovil T	21	3	**55**	**6**
2015–16	Exeter C	26	4		
2016–17	Exeter C	20	4	**46**	**8**
2017–18	Plymouth Arg	33	6		
2018–19	Plymouth Arg	17	4		
2019–20	Plymouth Arg	24	4	**74**	**14**
2020–21	Swindon T	20	2	**20**	**2**

GROUNDS, Jonathan (D) **380 11**
H: 6 1 W: 13 10 b.Thornaby 2-2-88

2007–08	Middlesbrough	5	0		
2008–09	Middlesbrough	2	0		
2008–09	*Norwich C*	16	3	**16**	**3**
2009–10	Middlesbrough	20	0		
2010–11	Middlesbrough	6	1		
2010–11	*Hibernian*	13	0	**13**	**0**
2011–12	Middlesbrough	0	0	**33**	**1**
2011–12	*Chesterfield*	13	0	**13**	**0**
2011–12	*Yeovil T*	14	0	**14**	**0**
2012–13	Oldham Ath	44	1		
2013–14	Oldham Ath	45	2	**89**	**3**
2014–15	Birmingham C	45	1		
2015–16	Birmingham C	45	1		
2016–17	Birmingham C	42	2		
2017–18	Birmingham C	26	0		
2018–19	Birmingham C	0	0		
2018–19	*Bolton W*	13	0	**13**	**0**
2019–20	Birmingham C	0	0	**158**	**4**
2020–21	Swindon T	31	0	**31**	**0**

HAINES, Luke (M) **0 0**

2019–20	Swindon T	0	0		
2020–21	Swindon T	0	0		

HOLLAND, Toby (M) **0 0**

2019–20	Swindon T	0	0		
2020–21	Swindon T	0	0		

HOPE, Hallam (F) **235 45**
H: 5 10 W: 12 00 b.Manchester 17-3-94
Internationals: England U16, U17, U18, U19. Barbados Full caps.

2010–11	Everton	0	0		
2011–12	Everton	0	0		
2012–13	Everton	0	0		
2013–14	Everton	0	0		
2013–14	*Northampton T*	3	1	**3**	**1**
2013–14	*Bury*	8	5		
2014–15	Everton	0	0		
2014–15	*Sheffield W*	4	0	**4**	**0**
2014–15	Bury	19	0		
2015–16	Bury	6	0		
2015–16	*Carlisle U*	21	4		
2016–17	Bury	33	3	**66**	**8**
2017–18	Carlisle U	41	9		
2018–19	Carlisle U	40	14		
2019–20	Carlisle U	23	2	**125**	**29**
2019–20	Swindon T	5	2		
2020–21	Swindon T	32	5	**37**	**7**

HUNT, Robert (M) **135 2**
H: 5 7 W: 10 08 b.Dagenham 7-7-95

2013–14	Brighton & HA	0	0		
2014–15	Brighton & HA	0	0		
2015–16	Brighton & HA	0	0		
2016–17	Brighton & HA	1	0	**1**	**0**
2016–17	*Oldham Ath*	10	0		
2017–18	Oldham Ath	33	0		
2018–19	Oldham Ath	38	1	**81**	**1**
2019–20	Swindon T	34	1		
2020–21	Swindon T	19	0	**53**	**1**

IANDOLO, Ellis (M) **70 1**
b. 22-8-97
From Maidstone U.

2015–16	Swindon T	12	0		
2016–17	Swindon T	10	0		
2017–18	Swindon T	12	1		
2018–19	Swindon T	15	0		
2019–20	Swindon T	13	0		
2020–21	Swindon T	8	0	**70**	**1**

LYDEN, Jordan (M)				**49**	**2**
H: 5 10 W: 11 00 b.Perth 30-1-96					
Internationals: Australia U20.					
2015–16	Aston Villa	4	0		
2016–17	Aston Villa	0	0		
2017–18	Aston Villa	0	0		
2018–19	Aston Villa	0	0	**4**	**0**
2018–19	*Oldham Ath*	10	1	**10**	**1**
2019–20	Swindon T	21	1		
2020–21	Swindon T	14	0	**35**	**1**

MATTHEWS, Archie (G)				**1**	**0**
b. 2-8-01					
2018–19	Swindon T	0	0		
2019–20	Swindon T	0	0		
2020–21	Swindon T	1	0	**1**	**0**

MISSILOU, Christopher (M)				**168**	**16**
H: 5 11 W: 11 00 b.Auxerre 18-7-92					
Internationals: France U18. Congo Full caps.					
2009–10	Auxerre	0	0		
2010–11	Auxerre	0	0		
2011–12	Auxerre	1	0		
2012–13	Auxerre	0	0	**1**	**0**
2013–14	Evry	11	1	**11**	**1**
2014–15	Stade Brestpos 29	1	0	**1**	**0**
2015–16	Montceau	12	0		
2016–17	Montceau	24	7	**36**	**7**
2017–18	Entente Sannois	6	0	**6**	**0**
2017–18	Le Puy Foot 43	15	3	**15**	**3**
2018–19	Oldham Ath	42	1		
2019–20	Oldham Ath	30	3	**72**	**4**
2020–21	Northampton T	15	1	**15**	**1**
2020–21	Swindon T	11	0	**11**	**0**

ODIMAYO, Akinwale (D)				**34**	**0**
b. 28-11-99					
2019–20	Reading	0	0		
2020	*Waterford*	4	0	**4**	**0**
2020–21	Swindon T	30	0	**30**	**0**

PALMER, Matthew (M)				**227**	**8**
H: 5 10 W: 12 06 b.Derby 1-8-93					
2012–13	Burton Alb	2	0		
2013–14	Burton Alb	40	0		
2014–15	Burton Alb	33	4		
2015–16	Burton Alb	14	0		
2015–16	*Oldham Ath*	14	1	**14**	**1**
2016–17	Burton Alb	36	1		
2017–18	Burton Alb	11	1	**136**	**6**
2017–18	Rotherham U	14	0		
2018–19	Rotherham U	10	0		
2019–20	Rotherham U	0	0	**24**	**0**
2019–20	*Bradford C*	18	0	**18**	**0**
2019–20	Swindon T	1	0		
2020–21	Swindon T	24	1	**25**	**1**
2020–21	*Wigan Ath*	10	0	**10**	**0**

PARSONS, Harry (F)				**2**	**0**
b. 9-10-02					
2019–20	Swindon T	0	0		
2020–21	Swindon T	2	0	**2**	**0**

PAYNE, Jack (M)				**251**	**36**
H: 5 5 W: 9 06 b.Tower Hamlets 25-10-94					
2013–14	Southend U	11	0		
2014–15	Southend U	34	6		
2015–16	Southend U	32	9	**77**	**15**
2016–17	Huddersfield T	23	2		
2017–18	Huddersfield T	0	0		
2017–18	*Oxford U*	28	3	**28**	**3**
2017–18	*Blackburn R*	18	1	**18**	**1**
2018–19	Huddersfield T	0	0	**23**	**2**
2018–19	*Bradford C*	39	9	**39**	**9**
2019–20	Lincoln C	23	2	**23**	**2**
2020–21	Swindon T	43	4	**43**	**4**

PITMAN, Brett (F)				**528**	**177**
H: 6 0 W: 11 00 b.Jersey 31-1-88					
From St Paul's.					
2005–06	Bournemouth	19	1		
2006–07	Bournemouth	29	5		
2007–08	Bournemouth	39	6		
2008–09	Bournemouth	39	17		
2009–10	Bournemouth	46	26		
2010–11	Bournemouth	2	3		
2010–11	Bristol C	39	13		
2011–12	Bristol C	35	7		
2012–13	Bristol C	3	0	**77**	**20**
2012–13	Bournemouth	26	19		
2013–14	Bournemouth	34	5		
2014–15	Bournemouth	34	13	**268**	**95**
2015–16	Ipswich T	42	10		
2016–17	Ipswich T	22	4	**64**	**14**
2017–18	Portsmouth	38	24		
2018–19	Portsmouth	32	11		
2019–20	Portsmouth	11	2	**81**	**37**
2020–21	Swindon T	38	11	**38**	**11**

TWINE, Scott (F)				**69**	**14**
H: 5 9 W: 10 12 b.Swindon 14-7-99					
2015–16	Swindon T	0	0		
2016–17	Swindon T	1	0		
2017–18	Swindon T	4	0		
2018–19	Swindon T	14	1		
2019–20	Swindon T	6	0		
2020–21	Swindon T	25	7	**50**	**8**
2020–21	*Newport Co*	19	6	**19**	**6**

Scholars

Case, Oliver Loddington; Cowmeadow, George Ross; Francis, Christopher Lucius; Francis, Levi Lloyd; Gordon, Donell David; King, William Martin; Lawrence, Charlie Robert; Lynn, Anthony Steven; Minturn, Harrison James; Moore, Thomas Kenneth; Parsons, Harry John; Rendell, Louis William; Storr, Kai Douglas; Weir, Taye Isaac Mark; Whitfield, Max Thomas; Winchcombe, Callum George.

TOTTENHAM H (84)

ALDERWEIRELD, Toby (D)				**339**	**17**
H: 6 1 W: 11 11 b.Wilrijk 2-3-89					
Internationals: Belgium U26, U17, U18, U19, U21, Full caps.					
2008–09	Ajax	5	0		
2009–10	Ajax	31	2		
2010–11	Ajax	26	2		
2011–12	Ajax	29	1		
2012–13	Ajax	32	2		
2013–14	Ajax	4	0	**127**	**7**
2013–14	Atletico Madrid	12	1	**12**	**1**
2014–15	Atletico Madrid	0	0		
2014–15	*Southampton*	26	1	**26**	**1**
2015–16	Tottenham H	38	4		
2016–17	Tottenham H	30	1		
2017–18	Tottenham H	14	0		
2018–19	Tottenham H	34	0		
2019–20	Tottenham H	33	2		
2020–21	Tottenham H	25	1	**174**	**8**

ALLI, Bamidele (M)				**243**	**72**
H: 6 1 W: 11 12 b.Watford 11-4-96					
Internationals: England U17, U18, U19, U21, Full caps.					
2012–13	Milton Keynes D	0	0		
2013–14	Milton Keynes D	33	6		
2014–15	Milton Keynes D	39	16	**72**	**22**
2015–16	Tottenham H	33	10		
2016–17	Tottenham H	37	18		
2017–18	Tottenham H	36	9		
2018–19	Tottenham H	25	5		
2019–20	Tottenham H	25	8		
2020–21	Tottenham H	15	0	**171**	**50**

AURIER, Serge (D)				**254**	**15**
H: 5 9 W: 11 11 b.Paris 24-12-92					
Internationals: Ivory Coast Full caps.					
2009–10	Lens	5	0		
2010–11	Lens	27	0		
2011–12	Lens	16	0	**48**	**0**
2011–12	Toulouse	10	1		
2012–13	Toulouse	28	1		
2013–14	Toulouse	34	6		
2014–15	Toulouse	0	0	**72**	**8**
2014–15	*Paris Saint-Germain*	14	0		
2015–16	Paris Saint-Germain	21	2		
2016–17	Paris Saint-Germain	22	0	**57**	**2**
2017–18	Tottenham H	17	2		
2018–19	Tottenham H	8	0		
2019–20	Tottenham H	33	1		
2020–21	Tottenham H	19	2	**77**	**5**

AUSTIN, Brandon (G)				**15**	**0**
b.Hemel Hempstead 8-1-99					
Internationals: USA U18. England U20, U21.					
2019–20	Tottenham H	0	0		
2019–20	*Viborg*	14	0	**14**	**0**
2020–21	Tottenham H	0	0		
2021	*Orlando C*	1	0	**1**	**0**

BALE, Gareth (D)				**377**	**138**
H: 6 0 W: 11 10 b.Cardiff 16-7-89					
Internationals: Wales Youth, U21, Full caps.					
2005–06	Southampton	2	0		
2006–07	Southampton	38	5	**40**	**5**
2007–08	Tottenham H	8	2		
2008–09	Tottenham H	16	0		
2009–10	Tottenham H	23	3		
2010–11	Tottenham H	30	7		
2011–12	Tottenham H	36	9		
2012–13	Tottenham H	33	21		
2013–14	Tottenham H	0	0		
2013–14	Real Madrid	27	15		
2014–15	Real Madrid	31	13		
2015–16	Real Madrid	23	19		
2016–17	Real Madrid	19	7		
2017–18	Real Madrid	26	16		
2018–19	Real Madrid	29	8		
2019–20	Real Madrid	16	2		
2020–21	Real Madrid	0	0	**171**	**80**
On loan from Real Madrid.					
2020–21	Tottenham H	20	11	**166**	**53**

BERGWIJN, Steven (M)				**147**	**33**
b.Amsterdam 8-10-97					
Internationals: Netherlands U17, U18, U19, U20, U21, Full caps.					
2014–15	PSV Eindhoven	1	0		
2015–16	PSV Eindhoven	5	0		
2016–17	PSV Eindhoven	25	2		
2017–18	PSV Eindhoven	32	8		
2018–19	PSV Eindhoven	33	14		
2019–20	PSV Eindhoven	16	5	**112**	**29**
2019–20	Tottenham H	14	3		
2020–21	Tottenham H	21	1	**35**	**4**

BOWDEN, Jamie (M)				**0**	**0**
b. 9-8-01					
2020–21	Tottenham H	0	0		

CARTER-VICKERS, Cameron (D)				**113**	**2**
H: 6 1 W: 13 08 b.Westcliff on Sea 31-12-97					
Internationals: USA U18, U20, U23, Full caps.					
2015–16	Tottenham H	0	0		
2016–17	Tottenham H	0	0		
2017–18	Tottenham H	0	0		
2017–18	*Sheffield U*	17	1	**17**	**1**
2017–18	*Ipswich T*	17	0	**17**	**0**
2018–19	Tottenham H	0	0		
2018–19	*Swansea C*	30	0	**30**	**0**
2019–20	Tottenham H	0	0		
2019–20	*Stoke C*	12	0	**12**	**0**
2019–20	*Luton T*	16	0	**16**	**0**
2020–21	Tottenham H	0	0		
2020–21	*Bournemouth*	21	1	**21**	**1**

CIRKIN, Dennis (D)				**0**	**0**
Internationals: England U17.					
2019–20	Tottenham H	0	0		
2020–21	Tottenham H	0	0		

CLARKE, Jack (F)				**43**	**2**
b.York 23-11-00					
Internationals: England U20.					
2017–18	Leeds U	0	0		
2018–19	Leeds U	22	2		
2019–20	Tottenham H	0	0		
2019–20	*Leeds U*	1	0	**23**	**2**
2019–20	*QPR*	6	0	**6**	**0**
2020–21	Tottenham H	0	0		
2020–21	*Stoke C*	14	0	**14**	**0**

CRAIG, Matthew (M)				**0**	**0**
b.Barnet 16-4-03					
Internationals: Scotland U16.					
2020–21	Tottenham H	0	0		

CRAIG, Michael (M)				**0**	**0**
b.Barnet 16-4-03					
Internationals: Scotland U16, U17.					
2020–21	Tottenham H	0	0		

DAVIES, Ben (D)				**219**	**6**
H: 5 7 W: 12 00 b.Neath 24-4-93					
Internationals: Wales U19, Full caps.					
2011–12	Swansea C	0	0		
2012–13	Swansea C	37	1		
2013–14	Swansea C	34	2	**71**	**3**
2014–15	Tottenham H	14	0		
2015–16	Tottenham H	17	0		
2016–17	Tottenham H	23	1		
2017–18	Tottenham H	29	2		
2018–19	Tottenham H	27	0		
2019–20	Tottenham H	18	0		
2020–21	Tottenham H	20	0	**148**	**3**

DEVINE, Alfie (M)				**0**	**0**
b.Warrington 1-8-04					
From Wigan Ath.					
2020–21	Tottenham H	0	0		

DIER, Eric (D)				**229**	**11**
H: 6 3 W: 13 08 b.Cheltenham 15-1-94					
Internationals: England U18, U19, U20, U21, Full caps.					
2012–13	Sporting Lisbon	14	1		
2013–14	Sporting Lisbon	13	0	**27**	**1**
2014–15	Tottenham H	28	2		
2015–16	Tottenham H	37	3		
2016–17	Tottenham H	36	2		
2017–18	Tottenham H	34	0		
2018–19	Tottenham H	20	3		
2019–20	Tottenham H	19	0		
2020–21	Tottenham H	28	0	**202**	**10**

DOHERTY, Matthew (M)				**307**	**23**
H: 6 0 W: 12 08 b.Dublin 17-1-92					
Internationals: Republic of Ireland U19, U21, Full caps.					
2010–11	Wolverhampton W	0	0		
2011–12	Wolverhampton W	1	0		
2011–12	*Hibernian*	13	2	**13**	**2**
2012–13	Wolverhampton W	13	1		

2012–13 *Bury* 17 1 **17 1**
2013–14 Wolverhampton W 18 1
2014–15 Wolverhampton W 33 0
2015–16 Wolverhampton W 34 2
2016–17 Wolverhampton W 42 4
2017–18 Wolverhampton W 45 4
2018–19 Wolverhampton W 38 4
2019–20 Wolverhampton W 36 4 **260 20**
2020–21 Tottenham H 17 0 **17 0**

EYOMA, Timothy (D) 39 1
H: 6 1 W: 11 11 b.Hackney 29-1-00
Internationals: England U16, U17, U18, U19.
2018–19 Tottenham H 0 0
2019–20 Tottenham H 0 0
2019–20 *Lincoln C* 0 0
2020–21 Tottenham H 0 0
2020–21 *Lincoln C* 39 1 **39 1**

FERNANDES, Gedson (M) 53 0
b.Sao Tome 9-1-99
Internationals: Portugal U16, U17, U19, U20, U21, Full caps.
2016–17 Benfica 0 0
2017–18 Benfica 0 0
2018–19 Benfica 22 0
2019–20 Benfica 7 0
2019–20 *Tottenham H* 7 0
2020–21 Benfica 0 0 **29 0**
On loan from Benfica.
2020–21 Tottenham H 0 0 **7 0**
On loan from Benfica.
2020–21 *Galatasaray* 17 0 **17 0**

FOYTH, Juan (D) 39 1
H: 5 10 W: 10 12 b.La Plata 12-1-98
Internationals: Argentina U20, Full caps.
2017 Estudiantes 7 0
2017–18 Estudiantes 0 0 **7 0**
2017–18 Tottenham H 0 0
2018–19 Tottenham H 12 1
2019–20 Tottenham H 4 0
2020–21 Tottenham H 0 0 **16 1**
2020–21 *Villarreal* 16 0 **16 0**
Transferred to Villarreal July 2021.

GAZZANIGA, Paulo (G) 103 0
H: 6 5 W: 14 02 b.Santa Fe 2-1-92
Internationals: Argentina Full caps.
2011–12 Gillingham 20 0 **20 0**
2012–13 Southampton 9 0
2013–14 Southampton 8 0
2014–15 Southampton 2 0
2015–16 Southampton 2 0
2016–17 Southampton 0 0 **21 0**
2016–17 *Rayo Vallecano* 32 0 **32 0**
2017–18 Tottenham H 1 0
2018–19 Tottenham H 3 0
2019–20 Tottenham H 18 0
2020–21 Tottenham H 0 0 **22 0**
2020–21 *Elche* 8 0 **8 0**

HART, Joe (G) 439 0
H: 6 3 W: 13 03 b.Shrewsbury 19-4-87
Internationals: England U19, U21, Full caps.
2004–05 Shrewsbury T 6 0
2005–06 Shrewsbury T 46 0 **52 0**
2006–07 Manchester C 1 0
2006–07 *Tranmere R* 6 0 **6 0**
2006–07 *Blackpool* 5 0 **5 0**
2007–08 Manchester C 26 0
2008–09 Manchester C 23 0
2009–10 Manchester C 0 0
2009–10 *Birmingham C* 36 0 **36 0**
2010–11 Manchester C 38 0
2011–12 Manchester C 38 0
2012–13 Manchester C 38 0
2013–14 Manchester C 31 0
2014–15 Manchester C 36 0
2015–16 Manchester C 35 0
2016–17 Manchester C 0 0
2016–17 *Torino* 36 0 **36 0**
2017–18 Manchester C 0 0 **266 0**
2017–18 *West Ham U* 19 0 **19 0**
2018–19 Burnley 19 0
2019–20 Burnley 0 0 **19 0**
2020–21 Tottenham H 0 0

HOJBJERG, Pierre (M) 203 8
H: 6 1 W: 12 11 b. 5-8-95
Internationals: Denmark U16, U17, U19, U21, Full caps.
From Brondby.
2012–13 Bayern Munich 2 0
2013–14 Bayern Munich 7 0
2014–15 Bayern Munich 8 0
2014–15 *Augsburg* 16 2 **16 2**
2015–16 Bayern Munich 0 0 **17 0**
2015–16 *Schalke* 23 0 **23 0**
2016–17 Southampton 22 0
2017–18 Southampton 23 0
2018–19 Southampton 31 4
2019–20 Southampton 33 0 **109 4**
2020–21 Tottenham H 38 2 **38 2**

JOHN, Nile (M) 0 0
2020–21 Tottenham H 0 0

KANE, Harry (F) 298 180
H: 6 0 W: 10 00 b.Chingford 28-7-93
Internationals: England U17, U19, U20, U21, Full caps.
2010–11 Tottenham H 0 0
2010–11 *Leyton Orient* 18 5 **18 5**
2011–12 Tottenham H 0 0
2011–12 *Millwall* 22 7 **22 7**
2012–13 Tottenham H 1 0
2012–13 *Norwich C* 3 0 **3 0**
2012–13 *Leicester C* 13 2 **13 2**
2013–14 Tottenham H 10 3
2014–15 Tottenham H 34 21
2015–16 Tottenham H 38 25
2016–17 Tottenham H 30 29
2017–18 Tottenham H 37 30
2018–19 Tottenham H 28 17
2019–20 Tottenham H 29 18
2020–21 Tottenham H 35 23 **242 166**

LAMELA, Erik (F) 273 40
H: 6 0 W: 10 13 b.Buenos Aires 4-3-92
Internationals: Argentina U20, Full caps.
2008–09 River Plate 1 0
2009–10 River Plate 1 0
2010–11 River Plate 32 4 **34 4**
2011–12 Roma 29 4
2012–13 Roma 33 15 **62 19**
2013–14 Tottenham H 9 0
2014–15 Tottenham H 33 2
2015–16 Tottenham H 34 5
2016–17 Tottenham H 9 1
2017–18 Tottenham H 25 2
2018–19 Tottenham H 19 4
2019–20 Tottenham H 25 2
2020–21 Tottenham H 23 1 **177 17**

LAVINIER, Marcel (D) 0 0
b. 16-12-00
From Chelsea.
2020–21 Tottenham H 0 0

LLORIS, Hugo (G) 516 0
H: 6 2 W: 12 03 b.Nice 26-12-86
Internationals: France U18, U19, U20, U21, Full caps.
2005–06 Nice 5 0
2006–07 Nice 37 0
2007–08 Nice 30 0 **72 0**
2008–09 Lyon 35 0
2009–10 Lyon 36 0
2010–11 Lyon 37 0
2011–12 Lyon 36 0
2012–13 Lyon 2 0 **146 0**
2012–13 Tottenham H 27 0
2013–14 Tottenham H 37 0
2014–15 Tottenham H 35 0
2015–16 Tottenham H 37 0
2016–17 Tottenham H 34 0
2017–18 Tottenham H 36 0
2018–19 Tottenham H 33 0
2019–20 Tottenham H 21 0
2020–21 Tottenham H 38 0 **298 0**

LO CELSO, Giovani (M) 152 17
b.Rosario 9-4-96
Internationals: Argentina U23, Full caps.
2014 Rosario Central 0 0
2015 Rosario Central 13 0
2016 Rosario Central 14 2
2016–17 Paris Saint-Germain 4 0
2016–17 *Rosario Central* 9 1 **36 3**
2017–18 Paris Saint-Germain 33 4
2018–19 Paris Saint-Germain 1 0 **38 4**
2018–19 Real Betis 32 9
2019–20 Real Betis 0 0 **32 9**
2019–20 Tottenham H 28 0
2020–21 Tottenham H 18 1 **46 1**

LUCAS MOURA, Rodrigues (M) 330 70
H: 5 8 W: 10 06 b.Sao Paulo 13-8-92
Internationals: Brazil U20, U23, Full caps.
2010 Sao Paulo 25 4
2011 Sao Paulo 28 9
2012 Sao Paulo 21 6 **74 19**
2012–13 Paris Saint-Germain 10 0
2013–14 Paris Saint-Germain 36 5
2014–15 Paris Saint-Germain 29 7
2015–16 Paris Saint-Germain 36 9
2016–17 Paris Saint-Germain 37 12
2017–18 Paris Saint-Germain 5 1 **153 34**
2017–18 Tottenham H 6 0
2018–19 Tottenham H 32 10
2019–20 Tottenham H 35 4
2020–21 Tottenham H 30 3 **103 17**

LUSALA, Dermi (D) 0 0
b.London 16-1-03
Internationals: England U16.
2020–21 Tottenham H 0 0

LYONS-FRASER, Brooklyn (D) 0 0
b.London 1-12-00
Internationals: England U17.
2020–21 Tottenham H 0 0

MARKANDAY, Dilan (M) 0 0
2020–21 Tottenham H 0 0

MUIR, Marques (D) 0 0
b.London 21-9-02
2020–21 Tottenham H 0 0

MUKENDI, Jeremie (F) 0 0
b.London 12-9-00
2020–21 Tottenham H 0 0

MUNDLE, Romaine (M) 0 0
b.London 24-4-03
2020–21 Tottenham H 0 0

NDOMBELE, Tanguy (M) 153 8
b.Longjumeau 28-12-96
Internationals: France U21, Full caps.
2016–17 Amiens 30 2
2017–18 Amiens 3 0 **33 2**
2017–18 *Lyon* 32 0
2018–19 Lyon 34 1 **66 1**
2019–20 Tottenham H 21 2
2020–21 Tottenham H 33 3 **54 5**

OKEDINA, Jubril (D) 14 0
b.London 26-10-00
2020–21 Tottenham H 0 0
2020–21 *Cambridge U* 14 0 **14 0**

OLUWAYEMI, Oluwaferanmi (G) 0 0
b.London 13-3-01
2020–21 Tottenham H 0 0

OMOLE, Tobi (D) 0 0
b. 17-12-99
From Arsenal.
2020–21 Tottenham H 0 0

PARROTT, Troy (F) 31 2
b. 4-2-02
Internationals: Republic of Ireland U17, U19, U21, Full caps.
From Belvedere.
2019–20 Tottenham H 2 0
2020–21 Tottenham H 0 0 **2 0**
2020–21 *Millwall* 11 0 **11 0**
2020–21 *Ipswich T* 18 2 **18 2**

PASKOTSI, Maksim (D) 0 0
b.Tallinn 19-1-03
Internationals: Estonia U16, U17, Full caps.
From Flora.
2020–21 Tottenham H 0 0

REGUILON, Sergio (D) 111 10
b.Madrid 16-12-96
2015–16 Real Madrid 0 0
2015–16 *Logrones* 9 0
2016–17 Real Madrid 0 0
2016–17 *Logrones* 30 8 **39 8**
2017–18 Real Madrid 0 0
2018–19 Real Madrid 14 0
2019–20 Real Madrid 0 0 **14 0**
2019–20 *Sevilla* 31 2
2020–21 Sevilla 0 0 **31 2**
2020–21 Tottenham H 27 0 **27 0**

ROBSON, Max (M) 0 0
b. 17-10-02
2020–21 Tottenham H 0 0

RODON, Joe (D) 76 0
b.Swansea 22-10-97
Internationals: Wales U20, U21, Full caps.
2015–16 Swansea C 0 0
2016–17 Swansea C 0 0
2017–18 Swansea C 0 0
2017–18 *Cheltenham T* 12 0 **12 0**
2018–19 Swansea C 27 0
2019–20 Swansea C 21 0
2020–21 Swansea C 4 0 **52 0**
2020–21 Tottenham H 12 0 **12 0**

ROLES, Jack (M) 27 5
b.London 26-2-99
Internationals: Cyprus U19, U21, Full caps.
2019–20 Tottenham H 0 0
2019–20 *Cambridge U* 23 5 **23 5**
2020–21 Tottenham H 0 0
2020–21 *Burton Alb* 2 0 **2 0**
2020–21 *Stevenage* 2 0 **2 0**

SANCHEZ, Davinson (D) **159** **7**
H: 6 2 W: 13 01 b.Caloto 12-6-96
Internationals: Columbia U17, U20, U23, Full caps.

2013	Atletico Nacional	3	0		
2014	Atletico Nacional	2	0		
2015	Atletico Nacional	7	0		
2016	Atletico Nacional	14	0	**26**	**0**
2016–17	Ajax	32	6		
2017–18	Ajax	0	0	**32**	**6**
2017–18	Tottenham H	31	0		
2018–19	Tottenham H	23	1		
2019–20	Tottenham H	29	0		
2020–21	Tottenham H	18	0	**101**	**1**

SANTIAGO, Yago (M) **0** **0**
H: 5 10 b.Vigo 15-4-03
From Celta Vigo.

2020–21	Tottenham H	0	0		

SCARLETT, Dane (F) **1** **0**
b.Hillingdon 24-3-04

2020–21	Tottenham H	1	0	**1**	**0**

SESSEGNON, Ryan (D) **135** **24**
H: 5 10 W: 11 02 b.Roehampton 18-5-00
Internationals: England U16, U17, U19, U21.

2016–17	Fulham	25	5		
2017–18	Fulham	46	15		
2018–19	Fulham	35	2		
2019–20	Fulham	0	0	**106**	**22**
2019–20	Tottenham H	6	0		
2020–21	Tottenham H	0	0	**6**	**0**
2020–21	*Hoffenheim*	23	2	**23**	**2**

SISSOKO, Moussa (M) **451** **34**
H: 6 2 W: 13 00 b.Le Blanc Mesnil 16-8-89
Internationals: France U16, U17, U18, U19, U21, Full caps.

2007–08	Toulouse	30	1		
2008–09	Toulouse	35	4		
2009–10	Toulouse	37	7		
2010–11	Toulouse	36	5		
2011–12	Toulouse	35	2		
2012–13	Toulouse	19	1	**192**	**20**
2012–13	Newcastle U	12	3		
2013–14	Newcastle U	35	3		
2014–15	Newcastle U	34	4		
2015–16	Newcastle U	37	1	**118**	**11**
2016–17	Tottenham H	25	0		
2017–18	Tottenham H	33	1		
2018–19	Tottenham H	29	0		
2019–20	Tottenham H	29	2		
2020–21	Tottenham H	25	0	**141**	**3**

SKIPP, Oliver (M) **60** **1**
H: 5 9 W: 11 00 b.Hatfield 16-9-00
Internationals: England U16, U17, U18, U21.

2018–19	Tottenham H	8	0		
2019–20	Tottenham H	7	0		
2020–21	Tottenham H	0	0	**15**	**0**
2020–21	*Norwich C*	45	1	**45**	**1**

SOLBERG, Isak (G) **0** **0**
b.Voss 28-6-03
Internationals: Norway U16, U18.
From Bryne.

2020–21	Tottenham H	0	0		

SON, Heung-Min (M) **332** **111**
H: 6 0 W: 12 00 b.Chuncheon 8-7-92
Internationals: South Korea U17, U23, Full caps.

2010–11	Hamburg	13	3		
2011–12	Hamburg	27	5		
2012–13	Hamburg	33	12	**73**	**20**
2013–14	Bayer Leverkusen	31	10		
2014–15	Bayer Leverkusen	30	11		
2015–16	Bayer Leverkusen	1	0	**62**	**21**
2015–16	Tottenham H	28	4		
2016–17	Tottenham H	34	14		
2017–18	Tottenham H	37	12		
2018–19	Tottenham H	31	12		
2019–20	Tottenham H	30	11		
2020–21	Tottenham H	37	17	**197**	**70**

STERLING, Kazaiah (F) **28** **1**
H: 5 9 W: 11 03 b.Enfield 9-11-98
Internationals: England U17, U18.
From Leyton Orient.

2017–18	Tottenham H	0	0		
2018–19	Tottenham H	0	0		
2018–19	*Sunderland*	8	1	**8**	**1**
2019–20	Tottenham H	0	0		
2019–20	*Doncaster R*	3	0	**3**	**0**
2019–20	*Leyton Orient*	0	0		
2020–21	Tottenham H	0	0		
2020–21	*Southend U*	10	0	**10**	**0**
2020–21	*Greenock Morton*	7	0	**7**	**0**

TANGANGA, Japhet (D) **12** **0**
b. 31-3-99
Internationals: England U16, U17, U18, U19, U20.

2019–20	Tottenham H	6	0		
2020–21	Tottenham H	6	0	**12**	**0**

THORPE, Elliot (M) **0** **0**
H: 5 9 b.Hinchingbrooke 9-11-00
Internationals: Wales U17, U19.

2020–21	Tottenham H	0	0		

VINICIUS, Carlos (F) **111** **48**
b.Rio 22-3-95

2016	Caldense	0	0		
2017	Caldense	0	0		
2017	Gremio Anapolis	2	0	**2**	**0**
2017–18	*Real*	37	19	**37**	**19**
2018–19	Napoli	0	0		
2018–19	*Rio Ave*	14	8	**14**	**8**
2018–19	*Monaco*	16	2	**16**	**2**
2019–20	Benfica	32	18		
2020–21	Benfica	1	0	**33**	**18**

On loan from Benfica.

2020–21	Tottenham H	9	1	**9**	**1**

WHITE, Harvey (M) **21** **1**
b.Maidstone 19-9-01
Internationals: England U18.

2019–20	Tottenham H	0	0		
2020–21	Tottenham H	0	0		
2020–21	*Portsmouth*	21	1	**21**	**1**

WHITEMAN, Alfie (G) **0** **0**
b. 2-10-98
Internationals: England U16, U17, U18, U19.

2016–17	Tottenham H	0	0		
2017–18	Tottenham H	0	0		
2018–19	Tottenham H	0	0		
2019–20	Tottenham H	0	0		
2020–21	Tottenham H	0	0		

WINKS, Harry (M) **109** **2**
H: 5 10 W: 10 03 b.Hemel Hempstead 2-2-96
Internationals: England U17, U18, U19, U20, U21, Full caps.

2013–14	Tottenham H	0	0		
2014–15	Tottenham H	0	0		
2015–16	Tottenham H	0	0		
2016–17	Tottenham H	21	1		
2017–18	Tottenham H	16	0		
2018–19	Tottenham H	26	1		
2019–20	Tottenham H	31	0		
2020–21	Tottenham H	15	0	**109**	**2**

Scholars
Asante, Enock Amponsah; Carrington Alberdi, Eddie; Cassanova, Dante Jamel; Cesay, Kallum; Cooper, Chay; Davies, Jezreel Titus Chinedu; Devine, Alfie Sean; Hackett-Valton, Jordan; Haysman, Khalon Casey; Hayton, Adam Paul; Kurylowicz, Kacper; Kyezu, Jeremy; Lo-Tutala, Thimothee Jacques Orcel; Maguire, Aaron Joseph; Mathurin, Roshaun Andre; Pedder, Rafferty; Torraj, Renaldo; Turner, Oliver; Whittaker, Tarrelle Ricardo Kabirizi.

TRANMERE R (85)

BURTON, Jake (F) **2** **0**
b. 15-11-01

2019–20	Tranmere R	0	0		
2020–21	Tranmere R	2	0	**2**	**0**

CLARKE, Peter (D) **718** **52**
H: 6 0 W: 12 00 b.Southport 3-1-82
Internationals: England U21.

1998–99	Everton	0	0		
1999–2000	Everton	0	0		
2000–01	Everton	1	0		
2001–02	Everton	7	0		
2002–03	Everton	0	0		
2002–03	*Blackpool*	16	3		
2002–03	*Port Vale*	13	1	**13**	**1**
2003–04	Everton	1	0		
2003–04	*Coventry C*	5	0	**5**	**0**
2004–05	Everton	0	0	**9**	**0**
2004–05	Blackpool	38	5		
2005–06	Blackpool	46	6		
2006–07	Southend U	38	2		
2007–08	Southend U	45	4		
2008–09	Southend U	43	4	**126**	**10**
2009–10	Huddersfield T	46	5		
2010–11	Huddersfield T	46	4		
2011–12	Huddersfield T	31	0		
2012–13	Huddersfield T	43	0		
2013–14	Huddersfield T	26	0	**192**	**9**
2014–15	Blackpool	39	2	**139**	**16**
2015–16	Bury	45	1		
2016–17	Oldham Ath	46	5		
2017–18	Oldham Ath	19	2		
2017–18	*Bury*	18	1	**63**	**2**
2018–19	Oldham Ath	42	3	**107**	**10**
2019–20	Fleetwood T	12	1	**12**	**1**
2019–20	Tranmere R	6	0		
2020–21	Tranmere R	46	3	**52**	**3**

DAVIES, Scott (G) **221** **0**
H: 6 0 W: 10 13 b.Blackpool 27-2-87

2007–08	Morecambe	10	0		
2008–09	Morecambe	0	0		
2009–10	Morecambe	1	0		
2012–13	Fleetwood T	45	0		
2013–14	Fleetwood T	28	0		
2014–15	Fleetwood T	0	0	**73**	**0**
2014–15	*Morecambe*	10	0	**21**	**0**
2014–15	*Accrington S*	19	0	**19**	**0**
2018–19	Tranmere R	46	0		
2019–20	Tranmere R	28	0		
2020–21	Tranmere R	34	0	**108**	**0**

ELLIS, Mark (D) **305** **21**
H: 6 2 W: 12 04 b.Kingsbridge 30-9-88

2007–08	Bolton W	0	0		
2009–10	Torquay U	27	3		
2010–11	Torquay U	27	2		
2011–12	Torquay U	35	3	**89**	**8**
2012–13	Crewe Alex	44	5		
2013–14	Crewe Alex	37	1	**81**	**6**
2014–15	Shrewsbury T	32	2		
2015–16	Shrewsbury T	9	1	**41**	**3**
2015–16	Carlisle U	30	0		
2016–17	Carlisle U	7	0		
2017–18	Carlisle U	23	2	**60**	**2**
2018–19	Tranmere R	25	0		
2019–20	Tranmere R	3	2		
2020–21	Tranmere R	6	0	**34**	**2**

FERRIER, Morgan (F) **63** **10**
H: 6 1 W: 12 08 b.London 15-11-94
Internationals: England C.
From Nottingham F, Crystal Palace, Bishop's Stortford, Hemel Hempstead T, Dagenham & R, Boreham Wood.

2018–19	Walsall	33	5	**33**	**5**
2019–20	Tranmere R	20	5		
2020–21	Tranmere R	10	0	**30**	**5**

Transferred to Maccabi Petah Tikva February 2021.

GOULDBOURNE, Ethan (M) **0** **0**
b. 10-10-00

2019–20	Tranmere R	0	0		
2020–21	Tranmere R	0	0		

HAYDE, Kyle (D) **0** **0**

2019–20	Tranmere R	0	0		
2020–21	Tranmere R	0	0		

JOLLEY, Charlie (F) **5** **0**
b.Liverpool 13-1-01

2018–19	Wigan Ath	1	0		
2019–20	Wigan Ath	0	0		
2020–21	Wigan Ath	2	0	**3**	**0**
2020–21	Tranmere R	2	0	**2**	**0**

JONES, Ben (G) **0** **0**

2019–20	Tranmere R	0	0		
2020–21	Tranmere R	0	0		

KHAN, Otis (M) **155** **17**
H: 5 9 W: 11 03 b.Ashton-under-Lyme 5-9-95

2013–14	Sheffield U	2	0		
2014–15	Sheffield U	0	0		
2015–16	Sheffield U	0	0	**2**	**0**
2015–16	Barnsley	3	0	**3**	**0**
2016–17	Yeovil T	29	6		
2017–18	Yeovil T	38	6	**67**	**12**
2018–19	Mansfield T	22	2		
2019–20	Mansfield T	21	1	**43**	**3**
2019–20	*Newport Co*	5	0	**5**	**0**
2020–21	Tranmere R	35	2	**35**	**2**

LEWIS, Paul (M) **124** **15**
H: 6 1 W: 11 00 b. 17-12-94
Internationals: England C.
From Macclesfield T.

2016–17	Cambridge U	13	0		
2017–18	Cambridge U	12	1		
2018–19	Cambridge U	23	4		
2019–20	Cambridge U	36	4	**84**	**9**
2020–21	Tranmere R	40	6	**40**	**6**

LLOYD, Danny (F) **71** **13**
b. 3-12-91
From Stockport Co, Colwyn Bay, Lincoln C, Tamworth, AFC Fylde, Stockport Co.

2017–18	Peterborough U	31	8	**31**	**8**
2019–20	Salford C	9	2	**9**	**2**
2020–21	Tranmere R	31	3	**31**	**3**

MACDONALD, Calum (D) **51 1**
b. 18-12-97
Internationals: Scotland U21.
2016–17 Derby Co 0 0
2017–18 Derby Co 0 0
2018–19 Derby Co 0 0
2019–20 Derby Co 0 0
2019–20 Blackpool 12 0
2020–21 Blackpool 0 0 **12 0**
2020–21 Tranmere R 39 1 **39 1**

MONTHE, Emmanuel (D) **121 3**
H: 6 0 W: 12 08 b. 26-1-95
2013–14 QPR 0 0
From Southport, Whitehawk, Hayes & Yeading, Havant & Waterford, Bath C.
2017–18 Forest Green R 13 0 **13 0**
2018–19 Tranmere R 43 2
2019–20 Tranmere R 31 1
2020–21 Tranmere R 34 0 **108 3**

MORRIS, Kieron (M) **233 23**
H: 5 10 W: 11 01 b.Hereford 3-6-94
2012–13 Walsall 0 0
2013–14 Walsall 2 0
2014–15 Walsall 14 2
2015–16 Walsall 33 3
2016–17 Walsall 35 5
2017–18 Walsall 42 3
2018–19 Walsall 17 2 **143 15**
2018–19 *Tranmere R* 14 1
2019–20 Tranmere R 34 2
2020–21 Tranmere R 42 5 **90 8**

MURPHY, Joe (G) **550 0**
H: 6 2 W: 13 06 b.Dublin 21-8-81
Internationals: Republic of Ireland U21, Full caps.
1999–2000 Tranmere R 21 0
2000–01 Tranmere R 20 0
2001–02 Tranmere R 22 0
2002–03 WBA 2 0
2003–04 WBA 3 0
2004–05 WBA 0 0 **5 0**
2004–05 *Walsall* 25 0
2005–06 Sunderland 0 0
2005–06 *Walsall* 14 0 **39 0**
2006–07 Scunthorpe U 45 0
2007–08 Scunthorpe U 45 0
2008–09 Scunthorpe U 42 0
2009–10 Scunthorpe U 40 0
2010–11 Scunthorpe U 29 0 **201 0**
2011–12 Coventry C 46 0
2012–13 Coventry C 45 0
2013–14 Coventry C 46 0 **137 0**
2014–15 Huddersfield T 2 0
2014–15 *Chesterfield* 0 0
2015–16 Huddersfield T 7 0
2016–17 Huddersfield T 0 0 **9 0**
2016–17 *Bury* 16 0
2017–18 Bury 17 0
2018–19 Bury 46 0 **79 0**
2019–20 Shrewsbury T 4 0 **4 0**
2020–21 Tranmere R 13 0 **76 0**

NELSON, Sid (D) **122 1**
H: 6 1 b.London 1-1-96
2013–14 Millwall 0 0
2014–15 Millwall 14 0
2015–16 Millwall 9 0
2016–17 Millwall 3 0
2016–17 *Newport Co* 14 0 **14 0**
2017–18 Millwall 0 0
2017–18 *Yeovil T* 12 0 **12 0**
2017–18 *Chesterfield* 15 1 **15 1**
2018–19 Millwall 0 0 **26 0**
2018–19 *Swindon T* 20 0 **20 0**
2018–19 *Tranmere R* 7 0
2019–20 Tranmere R 19 0
2020–21 Tranmere R 9 0 **35 0**

NUGENT, George (M) **0 0**
2018–19 Tranmere R 0 0
2019–20 Tranmere R 0 0
2020–21 Tranmere R 0 0

O'CONNOR, Lee (D) **37 0**
b.Waterford 28-7-00
From Waterford.
2019–20 Manchester U 0 0
2019–20 Celtic 0 0
2019–20 *Partick Thistle* 4 0 **4 0**
2020–21 Celtic 0 0
On loan from Celtic.
2020–21 Tranmere R 33 0 **33 0**

RAY, George (D) **163 6**
H: 5 10 W: 11 03 b.Warrington 13-10-93
Internationals: Wales U21.
2011–12 Crewe Alex 0 0
2012–13 Crewe Alex 4 0
2013–14 Crewe Alex 9 0
2014–15 Crewe Alex 35 2
2015–16 Crewe Alex 22 0
2016–17 Crewe Alex 23 1
2017–18 Crewe Alex 12 0
2018–19 Crewe Alex 32 2 **137 5**
2019–20 Tranmere R 15 0
2020–21 Tranmere R 11 1 **26 1**

RIDEHALGH, Liam (D) **210 3**
H: 5 10 W: 11 05 b.Halifax 20-4-91
2009–10 Huddersfield T 0 0
2010–11 Huddersfield T 20 0
2011–12 Huddersfield T 0 0
2011–12 *Swindon T* 11 0 **11 0**
2011–12 *Chesterfield* 20 1
2012–13 Huddersfield T 0 0
2012–13 *Chesterfield* 14 0 **34 1**
2012–13 *Rotherham U* 20 0 **20 0**
2013–14 Huddersfield T 0 0 **20 0**
2013–14 *Tranmere R* 36 1
2014–15 Tranmere R 18 0
2018–19 Tranmere R 18 0
2019–20 Tranmere R 29 1
2020–21 Tranmere R 24 0 **125 2**

SPEARING, Jay (M) **362 19**
H: 5 6 W: 11 01 b.Wallasey 25-11-88
2006–07 Liverpool 0 0
2007–08 Liverpool 0 0
2008–09 Liverpool 0 0
2009–10 Liverpool 3 0
2009–10 *Leicester C* 7 1 **7 1**
2010–11 Liverpool 11 0
2011–12 Liverpool 16 0
2012–13 Liverpool 0 0
2012–13 *Bolton W* 37 2
2013–14 Liverpool 0 0 **30 0**
2013–14 Bolton W 45 2
2014–15 Bolton W 21 1
2014–15 *Blackburn R* 15 1 **15 1**
2015–16 Bolton W 22 2
2016–17 Bolton W 37 3
2017–18 Bolton W 0 0 **162 10**
2017–18 Blackpool 33 0
2018–19 Blackpool 42 4
2019–20 Blackpool 30 2 **105 6**
2020–21 Tranmere R 43 1 **43 1**

TAYLOR, Corey (F) **55 3**
b.Erdington 23-9-97
Internationals: England U17.
2015–16 Aston Villa 0 0
2016–17 Aston Villa 1 0
2017–18 Aston Villa 0 0
2018–19 Aston Villa 0 0 **1 0**
2018–19 *Walsall* 10 0 **10 0**
2019–20 Tranmere R 24 2
2020–21 Tranmere R 20 1 **44 3**

TIMLIN, Jamie (F) **0 0**
2020–21 Tranmere R 0 0

VAUGHAN, James (F) **355 110**
H: 5 11 W: 13 00 b.Birmingham 14-7-88
Internationals: England U17, U19, U21.
2004–05 Everton 2 1
2005–06 Everton 1 0
2006–07 Everton 14 4
2007–08 Everton 8 1
2008–09 Everton 13 0
2009–10 Everton 8 1
2009–10 *Derby Co* 2 0 **2 0**
2010–11 Everton 1 0 **47 7**
2010–11 *Crystal Palace* 30 9 **30 9**
2011–12 Norwich C 5 0
2012–13 Norwich C 0 0 **5 0**
2012–13 *Huddersfield T* 33 14
2013–14 Huddersfield T 23 10
2014–15 Huddersfield T 26 7
2015–16 Huddersfield T 4 0 **86 31**
2015–16 *Birmingham C* 15 0 **15 0**
2016–17 Bury 37 24 **37 24**
2017–18 Sunderland 23 2 **23 2**
2017–18 Wigan Ath 19 3
2018–19 Wigan Ath 19 2 **38 5**
2018–19 *Portsmouth* 10 0 **10 0**
2019–20 Bradford C 25 11 **25 11**
2019–20 *Tranmere R* 8 3
2020–21 Tranmere R 29 18 **37 21**

WALKER-RICE, Danny (F) **1 0**
b. 10-11-00
2018–19 Tranmere R 0 0
2019–20 Tranmere R 0 0
2020–21 Tranmere R 1 0 **1 0**

WOOLERY, Kaiyne (F) **165 22**
H: 5 10 W: 11 07 b.Hackney 11-1-95
From Tamworth.
2014–15 Bolton W 1 0
2014–15 *Notts Co* 5 0 **5 0**
2015–16 Bolton W 17 2
2016–17 Bolton W 1 0 **19 2**
2016–17 Wigan Ath 1 0 **1 0**
2017–18 Swindon T 37 4
2018–19 Swindon T 29 6
2019–20 Swindon T 34 2 **100 12**
2020–21 Tranmere R 40 8 **40 8**

Scholars
Capps, Robbie Jason; Duncan, Oliver Joseph; Farley, Harry James; Ferguson, Cameron Duncan; Fisher, Max Steven; Gouldbourne, Ethan; Haley, Joe Peter; Jones, Benjamin Thomas; Jones, Ethan Robert; Quinn, Michael Sean; Rhami, Joshua Demitrius; Shead, Louis James; Stratulis, Ryan William; Timlin, Jamie Benjamin.

WALSALL (86)

BATES, Alfie (M) **49 1**
b. 3-5-01
2018–19 Walsall 0 0
2019–20 Walsall 13 1
2020–21 Walsall 36 0 **49 1**

CLARKE, James (D) **170 7**
H: 6 0 W: 13 03 b.Aylesbury 17-11-89
From Watford, Oxford U, Oxford C, Salisbury C, Woking.
2015–16 Bristol R 37 0
2016–17 Bristol R 22 0
2017–18 Bristol R 11 0
2018–19 Bristol R 42 2 **112 2**
2019–20 Walsall 27 3
2020–21 Walsall 31 2 **58 5**

COCKERILL-MOLLETT, Callum (D) **21 0**
H: 5 10 W: 11 00 b. 15-1-99
Internationals: Republic of Ireland U18, U19.
2016–17 Walsall 0 0
2017–18 Walsall 1 0
2018–19 Walsall 0 0
2019–20 Walsall 9 0
2020–21 Walsall 11 0 **21 0**

GORDON, Josh (F) **107 21**
H: 5 10 W: 11 00 b.Stoke-on-Trent 19-1-95
From Stafford Rangers.
2017–18 Leicester C 0 0
2018–19 Walsall 37 7
2019–20 Walsall 34 9
2020–21 Walsall 36 5 **107 21**

GUTHRIE, Danny (M) **306 16**
H: 5 9 W: 11 06 b.Shrewsbury 18-4-87
Internationals: England U16.
2004–05 Liverpool 0 0
2005–06 Liverpool 0 0
2006–07 Liverpool 3 0
2006–07 *Southampton* 10 0 **10 0**
2007–08 Liverpool 0 0 **3 0**
2007–08 *Bolton W* 25 0 **25 0**
2008–09 Newcastle U 24 2
2009–10 Newcastle U 38 4
2010–11 Newcastle U 14 0
2011–12 Newcastle U 16 1 **92 7**
2012–13 Reading 21 1
2013–14 Reading 32 4
2014–15 Reading 9 0 **62 5**
2014–15 *Fulham* 6 0 **6 0**
2015–16 Blackburn R 16 0
2016–17 Blackburn R 24 1 **40 1**
2018 Mitra Kukar 29 2 **29 2**
2019–20 Walsall 25 1
2020–21 Walsall 14 0 **39 1**

HOLDEN, Rory (F) **69 7**
H: 5 7 W: 10 10 b.Derry 23-8-97
Internationals: Northern Ireland U21.
2016 Derry C 4 0
2017 Derry C 9 1 **13 1**
2017–18 Bristol C 0 0
2018–19 Bristol C 0 0
2018–19 *Rochdale* 6 0 **6 0**
2019–20 Bristol C 0 0
2019–20 *Walsall* 29 2
2020–21 Walsall 21 4 **50 6**

KINSELLA, Liam (M) **143 1**
b.Colchester 23-2-96
Internationals: Republic of Ireland U19, U21.
2013–14 Walsall 0 0
2014–15 Walsall 4 0
2015–16 Walsall 7 1
2016–17 Walsall 8 0
2017–18 Walsall 19 0
2018–19 Walsall 31 0
2019–20 Walsall 31 0
2020–21 Walsall 43 0 **143 1**

LAVERY, Caolan (F) **201** **37**

H: 5 11 W: 11 12 b.Red Deer 22-10-92

Internationals: Canada U17. Northern Ireland U19, U21.

2012–13	Sheffield W	0	0		
2012–13	*Southend U*	3	0	**3**	**0**
2013–14	Sheffield W	21	4		
2013–14	*Plymouth Arg*	8	3	**8**	**3**
2014–15	Sheffield W	13	2		
2014–15	*Chesterfield*	8	3	**8**	**3**
2015–16	Sheffield W	0	0	**34**	**6**
2015–16	*Portsmouth*	13	4	**13**	**4**
2016–17	Sheffield U	27	4		
2017–18	Sheffield U	3	0		
2017–18	*Rotherham U*	14	2	**14**	**2**
2018–19	Sheffield U	0	0	**30**	**4**
2018–19	*Bury*	23	5	**23**	**5**
2019–20	Walsall	27	4		
2020–21	Walsall	41	6	**68**	**10**

LEAK, Tom (D) **6** **0**

b. 31-10-00

2019–20	Walsall	0	0		
2020–21	Walsall	6	0	**6**	**0**

McDONALD, Wesley (F) **78** **7**

H: 5 9 W: 12 02 b.Lambeth 4-5-97

2015–16	Birmingham C	0	0		
2016–17	Birmingham C	0	0		
2017–18	Birmingham C	0	0		
2018–19	Yeovil T	9	0	**9**	**0**
2019–20	Walsall	28	5		
2020–21	Walsall	41	2	**69**	**7**

NOLAN, Jack (M) **13** **0**

b. 25-5-01

Internationals: England U17.

2018–19	Reading	0	0		
2019–20	Walsall	4	0		
2020–21	Walsall	9	0	**13**	**0**

NORMAN, Cameron (D) **69** **0**

H: 6 2 W: 11 09 b.Norwich 12-10-95

From Norwich C, Concord Rangers, Needham Market, King's Lynn T.

2018–19	Oxford U	7	0	**7**	**0**
2018–19	Walsall	9	0		
2019–20	Walsall	18	0		
2020–21	Walsall	35	0	**62**	**0**

OSAOABE, Emmanuel (M) **124** **10**

b.Dundalk 1-10-96

2015–16	Gillingham	18	2		
2016–17	Gillingham	24	1	**42**	**3**
2017–18	Cambridge U	4	0		
2017–18	*Newport Co*	3	0	**3**	**0**
2018–19	Cambridge U	12	0	**16**	**0**
2019–20	Macclesfield T	25	4	**25**	**4**
2019–20	Southend U	0	0		
2020–21	Walsall	38	3	**38**	**3**

PERRY, Sam (M) **16** **1**

b. 29-12-01

From Aston Villa.

2019–20	Walsall	0	0		
2020–21	Walsall	16	1	**16**	**1**

ROBERTS, Liam (G) **131** **0**

H: 6 0 W: 12 13 b.Walsall 24-11-94

2012–13	Walsall	0	0		
2013–14	Walsall	0	0		
2014–15	Walsall	0	0		
2015–16	Walsall	1	0		
2016–17	Walsall	0	0		
2017–18	Walsall	24	0		
2018–19	Walsall	42	0		
2019–20	Walsall	32	0		
2020–21	Walsall	32	0	**131**	**0**

ROSE, Jack (G) **28** **0**

H: 6 0 W: 11 11 b.Solihull 31-1-95

2014–15	WBA	0	0		
2014–15	*Accrington S*	4	0	**4**	**0**
2015–16	WBA	0	0		
2015–16	*Crawley T*	5	0	**5**	**0**
2016–17	WBA	0	0		
2017–18	Southampton	0	0		
2018–19	Southampton	0	0		
2019–20	Southampton	0	0		
2019–20	*Walsall*	4	0		
2020–21	Walsall	15	0	**19**	**0**

SADLER, Matthew (D) **492** **11**

H: 5 11 W: 11 08 b.Birmingham 26-2-85

Internationals: England U17, U18, U19.

2001–02	Birmingham C	0	0		
2002–03	Birmingham C	2	0		
2003–04	Birmingham C	0	0		
2003–04	*Northampton T*	7	0	**7**	**0**
2004–05	Birmingham C	0	0		
2005–06	Birmingham C	8	0		
2006–07	Birmingham C	36	0		
2007–08	Birmingham C	5	0	**51**	**0**
2007–08	Watford	15	0		
2008–09	Watford	15	0		
2009–10	Watford	0	0		
2009–10	*Stockport Co*	20	0	**20**	**0**
2010–11	Watford	0	0	**30**	**0**
2010–11	*Shrewsbury T*	46	0		
2011–12	Walsall	46	1		
2012–13	Crawley T	46	1		
2013–14	Crawley T	46	1		
2014–15	Rotherham U	0	0		
2014–15	*Crawley T*	10	0	**102**	**2**
2014–15	*Oldham Ath*	8	0	**8**	**0**
2014–15	Shrewsbury T	0	0		
2015–16	Shrewsbury T	24	2		
2016–17	Shrewsbury T	34	2		
2017–18	Shrewsbury T	42	1		
2018–19	Shrewsbury T	29	0	**175**	**5**
2019–20	Walsall	27	2		
2020–21	Walsall	26	1	**99**	**4**

SCARR, Dan (D) **107** **6**

b. 24-12-94

From Reddich U, Stourbridge.

2017–18	Birmingham C	0	0		
2017–18	*Wycombe W*	22	1	**22**	**1**
2018–19	Birmingham C	0	0		
2018–19	Walsall	17	1		
2019–20	Walsall	33	0		
2020–21	Walsall	35	4	**85**	**5**

SINCLAIR, Stuart (M) **158** **7**

H: 5 7 W: 10 08 b.Houghton Conquest 9-11-87

From Luton T, Cambridge C, Bedford T, Dunstable T, Arlesey T, Salisbury C.

2015–16	Bristol R	30	2		
2016–17	Bristol R	38	1		
2017–18	Bristol R	29	2		
2018–19	Bristol R	18	0	**115**	**5**
2019–20	Walsall	26	2		
2020–21	Walsall	17	0	**43**	**2**

WHITE, Hayden (D) **156** **3**

H: 6 1 W: 10 10 b.Greenwich 15-4-95

From Sheffield W.

2013–14	Bolton W	2	0		
2014–15	Bolton W	3	0		
2014–15	*Carlisle U*	8	0	**8**	**0**
2014–15	*Bury*	2	0	**2**	**0**
2014–15	*Notts Co*	3	0	**3**	**0**
2015–16	Bolton W	0	0	**5**	**0**
2015–16	*Blackpool*	29	1	**29**	**1**
2016–17	Peterborough U	6	0	**6**	**0**
2016–17	*Mansfield T*	18	1		
2017–18	Mansfield T	28	1		
2018–19	Mansfield T	19	0		
2019–20	Mansfield T	10	0	**75**	**2**
2020–21	Walsall	28	0	**28**	**0**

WILLIS, Joe (M) **2** **0**

b. 3-10-01

2019–20	Walsall	0	0		
2020–21	Walsall	2	0	**2**	**0**

Scholars

Allamby-John, Jayden Nathaniel Anton; Barry, Oscar Stanley; Campbell, Jayden Vincent Michael; Dallaywaters, Benjamin Kevin Campbell; Derry, Callum Anthony; Foulkes, Joseph James; Francis, Ade Lamarr; Hunter, Ky-Mani Ter; Jackson, Tommy; Lynch, Jack Daniel; Mukadam, Saif Ismail; Perry, Joseph; Sharp, Kyle David; Simcox, Joshua James; Taylor, Bradley Michael; Walker, Lewis; Zona, Luke.

WATFORD (87)

AGYAKWA, Derek (D) **0** **0**

2020–21	Watford	0	0		
2020–21	*Como*	0	0		

ALVARADO, Jamie (M) **34** **0**

H: 5 11 b.Santa Marta 26-7-99

Internationals: Colombia U20, U23.

2017–18	Watford	0	0		
2017–18	*Valladolid*	0	0		
2018–19	Watford	0	0		
2018–19	*Hercules*	11	0		
2019–20	Watford	0	0		
2019–20	*Hercules*	6	0	**17**	**0**
2019–20	*Badalona*	3	0	**3**	**0**
2020–21	Watford	0	0		
2020–21	*Athletico Paranaense*	14	0	**14**	**0**

BACHMANN, Daniel (G) **57** **0**

H: 6 3 W: 12 11 b.Vienna 9-7-94

Internationals: Austria U16, U17, U18, U19, U21.

2011–12	Stoke C	0	0		
2012–13	Stoke C	0	0		
2013–14	Stoke C	0	0		
2014–15	Stoke C	0	0		
2015–16	Stoke C	0	0		
2015–16	*Ross Co*	1	0	**1**	**0**
2015–16	*Bury*	8	0	**8**	**0**
2016–17	Stoke C	0	0		
2017–18	Watford	0	0		
2018–19	Watford	0	0		
2018–19	*Kilmarnock*	25	0	**25**	**0**
2019–20	Watford	0	0		
2020–21	Watford	23	0	**23**	**0**

BARRETT, Mason (D) **0** **0**

From West Ham U.

2019–20	Watford	0	0		
2020–21	Watford	0	0		

CAPOUE, Etienne (M) **365** **23**

H: 6 2 W: 11 10 b.Niort 11-7-88

Internationals: France U18, U19, U21, Full caps.

2006–07	Toulouse	0	0		
2007–08	Toulouse	5	0		
2008–09	Toulouse	32	1		
2009–10	Toulouse	33	0		
2010–11	Toulouse	37	2		
2011–12	Toulouse	33	3		
2012–13	Toulouse	34	7	**174**	**13**
2013–14	Tottenham H	12	1		
2014–15	Tottenham H	12	0	**24**	**1**
2015–16	Watford	33	0		
2016–17	Watford	37	7		
2017–18	Watford	23	1		
2018–19	Watford	33	1		
2019–20	Watford	30	0		
2020–21	Watford	11	0	**167**	**9**

Transferred to Villareal January 2021.

CASSIDY, Ryan (M) **11** **2**

b. 2-3-01

2020–21	Watford	0	0		
2020–21	*Accrington S*	11	2	**11**	**2**

CATHCART, Craig (D) **344** **14**

H: 6 2 W: 11 06 b.Belfast 6-2-89

Internationals: Northern Ireland U16, U17, U20, U21, Full caps.

2005–06	Manchester U	0	0		
2006–07	Manchester U	0	0		
2007–08	Manchester U	0	0		
2007–08	*Antwerp*	13	2	**13**	**2**
2008–09	Manchester U	0	0		
2008–09	*Plymouth Arg*	31	1	**31**	**1**
2009–10	Manchester U	0	0		
2009–10	*Watford*	12	0		
2010–11	Blackpool	30	1		
2011–12	Blackpool	27	0		
2012–13	Blackpool	25	1		
2013–14	Blackpool	30	1	**112**	**3**
2014–15	Watford	29	3		
2015–16	Watford	35	1		
2016–17	Watford	15	0		
2017–18	Watford	7	0		
2018–19	Watford	36	3		
2019–20	Watford	29	0		
2020–21	Watford	25	1	**188**	**8**

CHALOBAH, Nathaniel (D) **178** **12**

H: 6 1 W: 11 11 b.Sierra Leone 12-12-94

Internationals: England U16, U17, U19, U20, U21, Full caps.

2010–11	Chelsea	0	0		
2011–12	Chelsea	0	0		
2012–13	Chelsea	0	0		
2012–13	*Watford*	38	5		
2013–14	Chelsea	0	0		
2013–14	*Nottingham F*	12	2	**12**	**2**
2013–14	*Middlesbrough*	19	1	**19**	**1**
2014–15	Chelsea	0	0		
2014–15	*Burnley*	4	0	**4**	**0**
2014–15	*Reading*	15	1	**15**	**1**
2015–16	Chelsea	0	0		
2015–16	*Napoli*	5	0	**5**	**0**
2016–17	Chelsea	10	0	**10**	**0**
2017–18	Watford	6	0		
2018–19	Watford	9	0		
2019–20	Watford	22	0		
2020–21	Watford	38	3	**113**	**8**

CLEVERLEY, Tom (M) **296** **31**

H: 5 9 W: 10 07 b.Basingstoke 12-8-89

Internationals: England U20, U21, Full caps. Great Britain.

2007–08	Manchester U	0	0		
2008–09	Manchester U	0	0		
2008–09	*Leicester C*	15	2	**15**	**2**
2009–10	Manchester U	0	0		
2009–10	*Watford*	33	11		
2010–11	Manchester U	0	0		
2010–11	*Wigan Ath*	25	3	**25**	**3**
2011–12	Manchester U	10	0		
2012–13	Manchester U	22	2		

2013–14	Manchester U	22	1		
2014–15	Manchester U	1	0	**55**	**3**
2014–15	*Aston Villa*	31	3	**31**	**3**
2015–16	Everton	22	2		
2016–17	Everton	10	0	**32**	**2**
2016–17	*Watford*	17	0		
2017–18	Watford	23	1		
2018–19	Watford	13	1		
2019–20	Watford	18	1		
2020–21	Watford	34	4	**138**	**18**

CRICHLOW, Kane (M) 0 0

From AFC Wimbledon.

2020–21	Watford	0	0		

CUKUR, Tiago (F) 0 0

H: 6 5 b.Amsterdam 30-11-02

Internationals: Turkey U17, U21.

From AZ Alkmaar.

2020–21	Watford	0	0		

DALBY, Sam (F) 18 1

b.Leytonstone 17-1-00

2016–17	Leyton Orient	16	1		
2017–18	Leyton Orient	0	0	**16**	**1**
2018–19	Leeds U	0	0		
2018–19	*Morecambe*	2	0	**2**	**0**
2019–20	Watford	0	0		
2020–21	Watford	0	0		

DAWSON, Craig (D) 348 42

H: 6 0 W: 12 04 b.Rochdale 6-5-90

Internationals: England U21. Great Britain.

2008–09	Rochdale	0	0		
2009–10	Rochdale	42	9		
2010–11	WBA	0	0		
2010–11	*Rochdale*	45	10	**87**	**19**
2011–12	WBA	8	0		
2012–13	WBA	1	0		
2012–13	*Bolton W*	16	4	**16**	**4**
2013–14	WBA	12	0		
2014–15	WBA	29	2		
2015–16	WBA	38	4		
2016–17	WBA	37	4		
2017–18	WBA	28	2		
2018–19	WBA	41	2	**194**	**14**
2019–20	Watford	29	2		
2020–21	Watford	0	0	**29**	**2**
2020–21	*West Ham U*	22	3	**22**	**3**

DEENEY, Troy (F) 510 159

H: 5 11 W: 12 00 b.Solihull 29-6-88

From Chelmsley T.

2006–07	Walsall	1	0		
2007–08	Walsall	35	1		
2008–09	Walsall	45	12		
2009–10	Walsall	42	14	**123**	**27**
2010–11	Watford	36	3		
2011–12	Watford	43	11		
2012–13	Watford	40	19		
2013–14	Watford	44	24		
2014–15	Watford	42	21		
2015–16	Watford	38	13		
2016–17	Watford	37	10		
2017–18	Watford	29	5		
2018–19	Watford	32	9		
2019–20	Watford	27	10		
2020–21	Watford	19	7	**387**	**132**

DELE-BASHIRU, Ayotomiwa (M) 2 0

H: 6 0 W: 10 10 b. 17-9-99

Internationals: England U16, U20.

2017–18	Manchester C	0	0		
2018–19	Manchester C	0	0		
2019–20	Watford	0	0		
2020–21	Watford	2	0	**2**	**0**

ELITIM, Juergen (M) 95 3

H: 5 8 b.Cartagena de Indias 13-7-99

2018–19	Watford	0	0		
2018–19	*Marbella*	32	2		
2019–20	Watford	0	0		
2019–20	*Marbella*	22	1	**54**	**3**

From Grenada.

2020–21	Watford	0	0		
2020–21	*Ponferradina*	41	0	**41**	**0**

ELLIOT, Rob (G) 162 0

H: 6 3 W: 14 10 b.Chatham 30-4-86

Internationals: Republic of Ireland U19, Full caps.

2004–05	Charlton Ath	0	0		
2004–05	*Notts Co*	4	0	**4**	**0**
2005–06	Charlton Ath	0	0		
2006–07	Charlton Ath	0	0		
2006–07	*Accrington S*	7	0	**7**	**0**
2007–08	Charlton Ath	1	0		
2008–09	Charlton Ath	23	0		
2009–10	Charlton Ath	33	0		
2010–11	Charlton Ath	35	0		
2011–12	Charlton Ath	4	0	**96**	**0**
2011–12	Newcastle U	0	0		
2012–13	Newcastle U	10	0		
2013–14	Newcastle U	2	0		
2014–15	Newcastle U	3	0		
2015–16	Newcastle U	21	0		
2016–17	Newcastle U	3	0		
2017–18	Newcastle U	16	0		
2018–19	Newcastle U	0	0		
2019–20	Newcastle U	0	0		
2020–21	Newcastle U	0	0	**55**	**0**
2020–21	Watford	0	0		

FEMENIA, Kiko (M) 274 11

H: 5 9 W: 9 11 b.Sanet i Negrals 2-2-91

Internationals: Spain U18, U19, U20.

2007–08	Hercules	1	0		
2008–09	Hercules	1	0		
2009–10	Hercules	35	3		
2010–11	Hercules	34	1	**71**	**4**
2011–12	Barcelona	0	0		
2012–13	Barcelona	0	0		
2013–14	Real Madrid	0	0		
2014–15	Alcorcon	17	0	**17**	**0**
2015–16	Alaves	38	5		
2016–17	Alaves	31	0	**69**	**5**
2017–18	Watford	23	1		
2018–19	Watford	29	1		
2019–20	Watford	28	0		
2020–21	Watford	37	0	**117**	**2**

FOSTER, Ben (G) 450 0

H: 6 2 W: 12 08 b.Leamington Spa 3-4-83

Internationals: England Full caps.

2000–01	Stoke C	0	0		
2001–02	Stoke C	0	0		
2002–03	Stoke C	0	0		
2003–04	Stoke C	0	0		
2004–05	Stoke C	0	0		
2004–05	*Kidderminster H*	2	0	**2**	**0**
2004–05	*Wrexham*	17	0	**17**	**0**
2005–06	Manchester U	0	0		
2005–06	*Watford*	44	0		
2006–07	Manchester U	0	0		
2006–07	*Watford*	29	0		
2007–08	Manchester U	1	0		
2008–09	Manchester U	2	0		
2009–10	Manchester U	9	0	**12**	**0**
2010–11	Birmingham C	38	0		
2011–12	Birmingham C	0	0	**38**	**0**
2011–12	*WBA*	37	0		
2012–13	WBA	30	0		
2013–14	WBA	24	0		
2014–15	WBA	28	0		
2015–16	WBA	15	0		
2016–17	WBA	38	0		
2017–18	WBA	37	0	**209**	**0**
2018–19	Watford	38	0		
2019–20	Watford	38	0		
2020–21	Watford	23	0	**172**	**0**

GOSLING, Dan (M) 266 25

H: 6 0 W: 11 00 b.Brixham 2-2-90

Internationals: England U17, U18, U19, U21.

2006–07	Plymouth Arg	12	2		
2007–08	Plymouth Arg	10	0	**22**	**2**
2007–08	Everton	0	0		
2008–09	Everton	11	2		
2009–10	Everton	11	2	**22**	**4**
2010–11	Newcastle U	1	0		
2011–12	Newcastle U	12	1		
2012–13	Newcastle U	3	0		
2013–14	Newcastle U	8	0	**24**	**1**
2013–14	*Blackpool*	14	2	**14**	**2**
2014–15	Bournemouth	18	0		
2015–16	Bournemouth	34	3		
2016–17	Bournemouth	27	2		
2017–18	Bournemouth	28	2		
2018–19	Bournemouth	25	2		
2019–20	Bournemouth	24	3		
2020–21	Bournemouth	15	2	**171**	**14**
2020–21	Watford	13	2	**13**	**2**

GRAY, Andre (F) 237 69

H: 5 10 W: 12 06 b.Shrewsbury 26-6-91

Internationals: England C.

2009–10	Shrewsbury T	4	0	**4**	**0**

From Hinckley U, Luton T.

2014–15	Brentford	45	16		
2015–16	Brentford	2	2	**47**	**18**
2015–16	Burnley	41	23		
2016–17	Burnley	32	9	**73**	**32**
2017–18	Watford	31	5		
2018–19	Watford	29	7		
2019–20	Watford	23	2		
2020–21	Watford	30	5	**113**	**19**

HERNANDEZ, Cucho (F) 186 51

H: 5 9 b.Pereira 22-4-99

Internationals: Colombia U20, Full caps.

2015	Deportivo Pereira	22	3		
2016	Deportivo Pereira	33	20	**55**	**23**
2017	Granada	0	0		
2017	*America de Cali*	17	1	**17**	**1**
2017–18	Watford	0	0		
2017–18	*Huesca*	35	16		
2018–19	Watford	0	0		
2018–19	*Huesca*	34	4	**69**	**20**
2019–20	Watford	0	0		
2019–20	*Mallorca*	22	5	**22**	**5**
2020–21	Watford	0	0		
2020–21	*Getafe*	23	2	**23**	**2**

HUGHES, Will (M) 272 16

H: 6 1 W: 11 08 b.Weybridge 7-4-95

Internationals: England U17, U21.

2011–12	Derby Co	3	0		
2012–13	Derby Co	35	2		
2013–14	Derby Co	41	3		
2014–15	Derby Co	42	2		
2015–16	Derby Co	6	0		
2016–17	Derby Co	38	2	**165**	**9**
2017–18	Watford	15	2		
2018–19	Watford	32	2		
2019–20	Watford	30	1		
2020–21	Watford	30	2	**107**	**7**

HUNGBO, Joseph (M) 5 0

b. 15-1-00

2018–19	Crystal Palace	0	0		
2019–20	Watford	0	0		
2020–21	Watford	5	0	**5**	**0**

JOAO PEDRO, de Jesus (F) 66 13

b. 26-9-01

2019	Fluminense	25	4	**25**	**4**
2019–20	Watford	3	0		
2020–21	Watford	38	9	**41**	**9**

KABASELE, Christian (D) 262 21

b.Lubumbashi 24-2-91

Internationals: Belgium U19, U20, Full caps.

2008–09	Eupen	3	0		
2009–10	Eupen	1	0		
2010–11	Eupen	3	0		
2010–11	*Mechelen*	4	1	**4**	**1**
2011–12	Ludogorets	11	3	**11**	**3**
2012–13	Eupen	26	4		
2013–14	Eupen	26	2	**59**	**6**
2014–15	Genk	34	2		
2015–16	Genk	42	4	**76**	**6**
2016–17	Watford	16	2		
2017–18	Watford	28	2		
2018–19	Watford	21	0		
2019–20	Watford	27	0		
2020–21	Watford	20	1	**112**	**5**

LAZAAR, Achraf (D) 141 5

H: 5 8 W: 10 08 b.Casablanca 22-1-92

Internationals: Morocco Full caps.

2011–12	Varese	0	0		
2012–13	Varese	20	0		
2013–14	Varese	17	0	**37**	**0**
2013–14	Palermo	14	0		
2014–15	Palermo	29	2		
2015–16	Palermo	30	1		
2016–17	Palermo	0	0	**73**	**3**
2016–17	Newcastle U	4	0		
2017–18	Newcastle U	0	0		
2017–18	*Benevento*	9	1	**9**	**1**
2018–19	Newcastle U	0	0		
2018–19	*Sheffield W*	4	0	**4**	**0**
2019–20	Newcastle U	0	0		
2019–20	*Cosenza*	9	1		
2020–21	Cosenza	0	0	**9**	**1**
2020–21	Newcastle U	0	0	**4**	**0**
2020–21	Watford	5	0	**5**	**0**

LO-EVERTON, Sonny (F) 0 0

H: 5 7 b.London 15-9-02

Internationals: Scotland U17, U19.

2020–21	Watford	0	0		

MASINA, Adam (D) 192 7

H: 5 10 W: 10 12 b.Khouribga 2-1-94

Internationals: Italy U21.

2013–14	Bologna	0	0		
2014–15	Bologna	28	1		
2015–16	Bologna	33	2		
2016–17	Bologna	32	1		
2017–18	Bologna	34	0	**127**	**4**
2018–19	Watford	14	0		
2019–20	Watford	26	1		
2020–21	Watford	25	2	**65**	**3**

NAVARRO, Marc (D) 43 3

H: 6 2 W: 12 06 b.Barcelona 2-7-85

From Barcelona.

2014–15	Espanyol	0	0		
2015–16	Espanyol	0	0		
2016–17	Espanyol	12	2		
2017–18	Espanyol	19	1	**31**	**3**
2018–19	Watford	2	0		
2019–20	Watford	0	0		
2019–20	*Leganes*	4	0	**4**	**0**
2020–21	Watford	6	0	**8**	**0**

NGAKIA, Jeremy (D) **30 0**
b. 7-9-00

2019–20	West Ham U	5	0	**5**	**0**
2020–21	Watford	25	0	**25**	**0**

PARKES, Adam (G) **0 0**
b. 30-11-99
Internationals: England U17.
From Southampton.

2019–20	Watford	0	0		
2020–21	Watford	0	0		

PENARANDA, Adalberto (F) **81 9**
b.El Vigia 31-5-97
Internationals: Venezuela U17, U20, Full caps.

2013–14	Dep La Guaira	18	1		
2014–15	Dep La Guaira	19	3	**37**	**4**
2015–16	Udinese	0	0		
2015–16	Watford	0	0		
2015–16	*Granada*	23	5	**23**	**5**
2016–17	Watford	0	0		
2016–17	*Malaga*	3	0		
2017–18	Watford	0	0		
2017–18	*Malaga*	13	0	**16**	**0**
2018–19	Watford	0	0		
2019–20	Watford	0	0		
2019–20	*Eupen*	5	0	**5**	**0**
2020–21	Watford	0	0		
2020–21	*CSKA Sofia*	0	0		

PERICA, Stipe (F) **174 37**
H: 6 3 b.Zadar 7-7-95
Internationals: Croatia U19, U20, U21.

2012–13	Zadar	20	8	**20**	**8**
2013–14	Chelsea	0	0		
2013–14	*NAC Breda*	25	6		
2014–15	Chelsea	0	0		
2014–15	*NAC Breda*	10	3	**35**	**9**
2014–15	*Udinese*	9	1		
2015–16	Chelsea	0	0		
2015–16	*Udinese*	11	2		
2016–17	Udinese	27	6		
2017–18	Udinese	22	1		
2018–19	Udinese	0	0		
2018–19	*Frosinone*	7	0	**7**	**0**
2018–19	*Kasimpasa*	12	2	**12**	**2**
2019–20	Udinese	0	0	**69**	**10**
2019–20	*Royal Excel Mouscron*	15	7	**15**	**7**
2020–21	Watford	16	1	**16**	**1**

PHILIPS, Daniel (M) **2 0**
b. 18-1-01
From Chelsea.

2020–21	Watford	2	0	**2**	**0**

POCHETTINO, Maurizio (M) **1 0**
b. 30-3-01
From Southampton, Tottenham H.

2020–21	Watford	1	0	**1**	**0**

PUSSETTO , Ignacio (M) **152 23**
b.Canada Rosquin 21-12-95

2012–13	Atletico de Rafaela	0	0		
2013–14	Atletico de Rafaela	11	0		
2014	Atletico de Rafaela	3	0		
2015	Atletico de Rafaela	19	2		
2016	Atletico de Rafaela	11	2	**44**	**4**
2016–17	Huracan	15	2		
2017–18	Huracan	27	9	**42**	**11**
2018–19	Udinese	35	4		
2019–20	Udinese	12	1		
2019–20	Watford	7	0		
2020–21	Watford	1	0	**8**	**0**
2020–21	*Udinese*	11	3	**58**	**8**

QUINA, Domingos (F) **34 4**
b. 18-11-99
Internationals: Portugal U17, U18, U19, U20.

2016–17	West Ham U	0	0		
2017–18	West Ham U	0	0		
2018–19	Watford	8	1		
2019–20	Watford	4	0		
2020–21	Watford	14	1	**26**	**2**
2020–21	*Granada*	8	2	**8**	**2**

ROBERTS, Myles (G) **0 0**
b. 9-12-01
From Reading.

2020–21	Watford	0	0		

SANCHEZ, Carlos (M) **372 15**
H: 6 0 W: 12 08 b.Quidbo 6-2-86
Internationals: Colombia Full caps.

2005–06	River Plate	14	0		
2006–07	River Plate	26	1	**40**	**1**
2007–08	Valenciennes	34	0		
2008–09	Valenciennes	37	1		
2009–10	Valenciennes	28	5		
2010–11	Valenciennes	28	2		
2011–12	Valenciennes	21	1		
2012–13	Valenciennes	30	2	**178**	**11**
2013–14	Elche	30	0	**30**	**0**
2014–15	Aston Villa	28	1		
2015–16	Aston Villa	20	0		
2016–17	Aston Villa	0	0	**48**	**1**
2016–17	*Fiorentina*	31	1		
2017–18	Fiorentina	9	1	**40**	**2**
2017–18	*Espanyol*	14	0	**14**	**0**
2018–19	West Ham U	7	0		
2019–20	West Ham U	6	0	**13**	**0**
2020–21	Watford	9	0	**9**	**0**

SARR, Ismaila (M) **157 36**
b.Saint-Louis 25-2-98
Internationals: Senegal U23, Full caps.

2016–17	Metz	31	5	**31**	**5**
2017–18	Rennes	24	5		
2018–19	Rennes	35	8	**59**	**13**
2019–20	Watford	28	5		
2020–21	Watford	39	13	**67**	**18**

SEMA, Ken (M) **230 31**
H: 5 10 W: 11 03 b.Norrkoping 30-9-93
Internationals: Sweden U23, Full caps.

2013	IFK Norrkoping	0	0		
2013	*IF Sylvia*	22	4	**22**	**4**
2014	Ljungskile	30	7		
2015	Ljungskile	30	4	**60**	**11**
2016	Ostersunds	23	4		
2017	Ostersunds	24	4		
2018	Ostersunds	11	0	**58**	**8**
2018–19	Watford	17	1		
2019–20	Watford	0	0		
2019–20	*Udinese*	32	2	**32**	**2**
2020–21	Watford	41	5	**58**	**6**

SIERRALTA, Francisco (D) **72 4**
b.Las Condes 6-5-97

2015–16	Universidad Catolica	2	1		
2016–17	Universidad Catolica	0	0	**2**	**1**
2016–17	Palestino	17	1	**17**	**1**
2017–18	Udinese	0	0		
2017–18	*Parma*	10	0		
2018–19	Udinese	0	0		
2018–19	*Parma*	6	0	**16**	**0**
2019–20	Udinese	0	0		
2019–20	*Empoli*	11	1		
2020–21	Empoli	0	0	**11**	**1**
2020–21	Udinese	0	0		
2020–21	Watford	26	1	**26**	**1**

SINCLAIR, Jerome (F) **87 6**
H: 5 8 W: 12 06 b.Birmingham 20-9-96
Internationals: England U16, U17.

2012–13	Liverpool	0	0		
2013–14	Liverpool	0	0		
2014–15	Liverpool	2	0		
2014–15	*Wigan Ath*	1	0	**1**	**0**
2015–16	Liverpool	0	0	**2**	**0**
2016–17	Watford	5	0		
2016–17	*Birmingham C*	5	0	**5**	**0**
2017–18	Watford	4	0		
2018–19	Watford	0	0		
2018–19	*Sunderland*	13	1	**13**	**1**
2018–19	*Oxford U*	16	4	**16**	**4**
2019–20	Watford	0	0		
2019–20	*VVV Venlo*	23	0	**23**	**0**
2020–21	Watford	0	0	**9**	**0**
2020–21	*CSKA Sofia*	18	1	**18**	**1**

STEVENSON, Toby (D) **3 0**
b.Colchester 22-11-99
From Leyton Orient.

2018–19	Charlton Ath	3	0		
2019–20	Charlton Ath	0	0	**3**	**0**
2020–21	Watford	0	0		

SUCCESS, Isaac (F) **122 10**
H: 6 1 W: 11 03 b. 7-1-96
Internationals: Nigeria U17, U20, Full caps.

2014–15	Granada	19	1		
2015–16	Granada	30	6	**49**	**7**
2016–17	Watford	19	1		
2017–18	Watford	0	0		
2017–18	*Malaga*	9	0	**9**	**0**
2018–19	Watford	30	1		
2019–20	Watford	5	0		
2020–21	Watford	10	1	**64**	**3**

TROOST-EKONG, William (D) **199 7**
b.Haarlem 1-9-93

2013–14	Groningen	2	0	**2**	**0**
2013–14	Dordrecht	10	0		
2014–15	Dordrecht	22	0	**32**	**0**
2015	Haugesund	13	0		
2016	Haugesund	24	3	**37**	**3**
2016–17	Gent	3	0	**3**	**0**
2017–18	Bursaspor	27	2	**27**	**2**
2018–19	Busaspor	1	1	**1**	**1**
2018–19	Udinese	35	0		
2019–20	Udinese	30	0		
2020–21	Udinese	0	0	**65**	**0**
2020–21	Watford	32	1	**32**	**1**

WILMOT, Ben (M) **63 3**
H: 6 2 W: 12 08 b. 4-11-99
Internationals: England U19, U20, U21.

2016–17	Stevenage	0	0		
2017–18	Stevenage	10	0	**10**	**0**
2018–19	Watford	2	0		
2018–19	*Udinese*	5	0	**5**	**0**
2019–20	Watford	0	0		
2019–20	*Swansea C*	21	2	**21**	**2**
2020–21	Watford	25	1	**27**	**1**

ZINCKERNAGEL, Philip (F) **231 46**
b. 16-12-94

2012–13	Nordsjaelland	0	0		
2013–14	HB Koge	29	3		
2014–15	HB Koge	27	2	**56**	**5**
2015–16	Helsingor	23	3		
2016–17	Helsingor	6	2	**29**	**5**
2016–17	SonderjyskE	24	1		
2017–18	SonderjyskE	20	3	**44**	**4**
2018	Bodo/Glimt	24	6		
2019	Bodo/Glimt	30	6		
2020	Bodo/Glimt	28	19		
2020–21	Bodo/Glimt	0	0	**82**	**31**
2020–21	Watford	20	1	**20**	**1**

Scholars
Andrews, Ryan Tyler Wayne; Baptiste, Dante Astor Kareem; Broome, Jack David; Burchell, Jack Oliver; Chisholm, Mac Lindsey; Conteh, Kamil Amadu; Forde, Shaqai Tyreece Steven; Hall, William James David; Harrison, Jordan Carter; Horsewood, Thomas Roger; Hunter, Damani Daiaire Morrison; Hutchinson, Dominic Charles; Janjeva, Andi; Lawal, Mohammed Olabosun; Manning, Adian Antoine; Marriott, Alfie Simon Rodney; McKiernan, John Joshua; Moriarty, Freddie; Muwonge, Enoch Michael Apollo; Smith, Ben Robert; Thompson, Max.

WBA (88)

AHEARNE-GRANT, Karlan (F) **175 49**
H: 6 0 b.London 19-12-97
Internationals: England U17, U18, U19.

2014–15	Charlton Ath	5	0		
2015–16	Charlton Ath	17	1		
2015–16	*Cambridge U*	3	0	**3**	**0**
2016–17	Charlton Ath	8	0		
2017–18	Charlton Ath	22	1		
2017–18	*Crawley T*	15	9	**15**	**9**
2018–19	Charlton Ath	28	14	**80**	**16**
2018–19	Huddersfield T	13	4		
2019–20	Huddersfield T	43	19	**56**	**23**
2020–21	WBA	21	1	**21**	**1**

AJAYI, Semi (D) **192 19**
H: 6 4 W: 13 00 b.Croydon 9-11-93
Internationals: Nigeria U20, Full caps.

2012–13	Charlton Ath	0	0		
2013–14	Charlton Ath	0	0		
2014–15	Arsenal	0	0		
2014–15	*Cardiff C*	0	0		
2015–16	Cardiff C	0	0		
2015–16	*AFC Wimbledon*	5	0	**5**	**0**
2015–16	*Crewe Alex*	13	0	**13**	**0**
2016–17	Cardiff C	0	0		
2016–17	*Rotherham U*	17	1		
2017–18	Rotherham U	35	4		
2018–19	Rotherham U	46	7	**98**	**12**
2019–20	WBA	43	5		
2020–21	WBA	33	2	**76**	**7**

AUSTIN, Charlie (F) **349 151**
H: 6 2 W: 13 03 b.Hungerford 5-7-89
From Kintbury Rangers, Hungerford T, Thatcham T, Poole T.

2009–10	Swindon T	33	19		
2010–11	Swindon T	21	12	**54**	**31**
2010–11	Burnley	4	0		
2011–12	Burnley	41	16		
2012–13	Burnley	37	25	**82**	**41**
2013–14	QPR	31	17		
2014–15	QPR	35	18		
2015–16	QPR	16	10		
2015–16	Southampton	7	1		
2016–17	Southampton	15	6		
2017–18	Southampton	24	7		
2018–19	Southampton	25	2		
2019–20	Southampton	0	0	**71**	**16**
2019–20	WBA	34	10		
2020–21	WBA	5	0	**39**	**10**
2020–21	*QPR*	21	8	**103**	**53**

AZAZ, Finn (M) **37 1**
b.Westminster 7-9-00

2020–21	WBA	0	0		
2020–21	*Cheltenham T*	37	1	**37**	**1**

BARTLEY, Kyle (D) 238 16
H: 5 11 W: 11 00 b.Stockport 22-5-91
Internationals: England U16, U17.

2008–09	Arsenal	0	0		
2009–10	Arsenal	0	0		
2009–10	*Sheffield U*	14	0		
2010–11	Arsenal	0	0		
2010–11	*Sheffield U*	21	0	**35**	**0**
2010–11	*Rangers*	5	1		
2011–12	Arsenal	0	0		
2011–12	*Rangers*	19	0	**24**	**1**
2012–13	Arsenal	0	0		
2012–13	Swansea C	2	0		
2013–14	Swansea C	2	0		
2013–14	*Birmingham C*	17	3	**17**	**3**
2014–15	Swansea C	7	0		
2015–16	Swansea C	5	0		
2016–17	Swansea C	0	0		
2016–17	*Leeds U*	45	6	**45**	**6**
2017–18	Swansea C	5	0	**21**	**0**
2018–19	WBA	28	1		
2019–20	WBA	38	2		
2020–21	WBA	30	3	**96**	**6**

BOND, Jonathan (G) 91 0
H: 6 3 W: 13 03 b.Hemel Hempstead 19-5-93
Internationals: Wales U17, U19. England U20, U21.

2010–11	Watford	0	0		
2011–12	Watford	1	0		
2011–12	*Dagenham & R*	5	0	**5**	**0**
2011–12	*Bury*	6	0	**6**	**0**
2012–13	Watford	8	0		
2013–14	Watford	10	0		
2014–15	Watford	3	0	**22**	**0**
2015–16	Reading	14	0		
2016–17	Reading	0	0		
2016–17	*Gillingham*	7	0	**7**	**0**
2017–18	Reading	0	0	**14**	**0**
2017–18	*Peterborough U*	37	0	**37**	**0**
2018–19	WBA	0	0		
2019–20	WBA	0	0		
2020–21	WBA	0	0		

Transferred to LA Galaxy January 2021.

BUTTON, David (G) 294 0
H: 6 3 W: 13 00 b.Stevenage 27-2-89
Internationals: England U16, U17, U19, U20.

2005–06	Tottenham H	0	0		
2006–07	Tottenham H	0	0		
2007–08	*Rochdale*	0	0		
2007–08	Tottenham H	0	0		
2008–09	Tottenham H	0	0		
2008–09	*Bournemouth*	4	0	**4**	**0**
2008–09	*Luton T*	0	0		
2008–09	*Dagenham & R*	3	0	**3**	**0**
2009–10	Tottenham H	0	0		
2009–10	*Crewe Alex*	10	0	**10**	**0**
2009–10	*Shrewsbury T*	26	0	**26**	**0**
2010–11	Tottenham H	0	0		
2010–11	*Plymouth Arg*	30	0	**30**	**0**
2011–12	Tottenham H	0	0		
2011–12	*Leyton Orient*	1	0	**1**	**0**
2011–12	*Doncaster R*	7	0	**7**	**0**
2011–12	*Barnsley*	9	0	**9**	**0**
2012–13	Tottenham H	0	0		
2012–13	Charlton Ath	5	0	**5**	**0**
2013–14	Brentford	42	0		
2014–15	Brentford	46	0		
2015–16	Brentford	46	0	**134**	**0**
2016–17	Fulham	40	0		
2017–18	Fulham	20	0	**60**	**0**
2018–19	Brighton & HA	4	0		
2019–20	Brighton & HA	0	0		
2020–21	Brighton & HA	0	0	**4**	**0**
2020–21	WBA	1	0	**1**	**0**

DELANEY, Zak (D) 0 0
b. 10-1-02
Internationals: Republic of Ireland U17.

2020–21	WBA	0	0		

DIABY, Cheikh (F) 0 0
b.Creteil 7-3-00
From Le Havre.

2020–21	WBA	0	0		

DIAGNE, Mbaye (F) 158 91
b.Dakar 28-10-91
From Bra.

2013–14	Juventus	0	0		
2013–14	*Ajaccio*	0	0		
2013–14	*Lierse*	7	4	**7**	**4**
2014–15	Juventus	0	0		
2014–15	*Al-Shabab*	2	0	**2**	**0**
2014–15	*Westerlo*	5	2	**5**	**2**
2015–16	Juventus	0	0		
2015–16	*Ujpest*	14	11	**14**	**11**
2016	Tianjin Tigers	27	10		
2017	Tianjin Tigers	17	6	**44**	**16**
2017–18	Kasimpasa	17	12		
2018–19	Kasimpasa	17	20	**34**	**32**
2018–19	Galatasaray	12	10		
2019–20	Galatasaray	3	0		
2019–20	*Club Brugge*	6	4	**6**	**4**
2020–21	Galatasaray	15	9	**30**	**19**

On loan from Galatasaray.

2020–21	WBA	16	3	**16**	**3**

DIANGANA, Grady (M) 67 9
b. 19-4-98
Internationals: England U20, U21.

2016–17	West Ham U	0	0		
2017–18	West Ham U	0	0		
2018–19	West Ham U	17	0		
2019–20	West Ham U	0	0	**17**	**0**
2019–20	*WBA*	30	8		
2020–21	WBA	20	1	**50**	**9**

EDWARDS, Kyle (M) 60 3
H: 5 8 W: 10 01 b.Dudley 17-2-98
Internationals: England U16, U17, U20.

2015–16	WBA	0	0		
2016–17	WBA	0	0		
2017–18	WBA	0	0		
2017–18	*Exeter C*	23	0	**23**	**0**
2018–19	WBA	6	1		
2019–20	WBA	26	2		
2020–21	WBA	5	0	**37**	**3**

FIELD, Sam (M) 70 3
b. 8-5-98
Internationals: England U18, U19, U20.

2015–16	WBA	1	0		
2016–17	WBA	8	0		
2017–18	WBA	10	1		
2018–19	WBA	12	1		
2019–20	WBA	0	0		
2019–20	*Charlton Ath*	17	0		
2020–21	Charlton Ath	0	0	**17**	**0**
2020–21	WBA	3	0	**34**	**2**
2020–21	*QPR*	19	1	**19**	**1**

FURLONG, Darnell (D) 185 6
b. 31-10-95

2014–15	QPR	3	0		
2015–16	QPR	0	0		
2015–16	*Northampton T*	10	0	**10**	**0**
2015–16	*Cambridge U*	21	0	**21**	**0**
2016–17	QPR	14	0		
2016–17	*Swindon T*	24	2	**24**	**2**
2017–18	QPR	22	0		
2018–19	QPR	25	1	**64**	**1**
2019–20	WBA	31	2		
2020–21	WBA	35	1	**66**	**3**

GARDNER-HICKMAN, Taylor (D) 0 0

2020–21	WBA	0	0		

GIBBS, Kieran (M) 237 7
H: 5 10 W: 10 02 b.Lambeth 26-9-89
Internationals: England U19, U20, U21, Full caps.

2007–08	Arsenal	0	0		
2007–08	*Norwich C*	7	0	**7**	**0**
2008–09	Arsenal	8	0		
2009–10	Arsenal	3	0		
2010–11	Arsenal	7	0		
2011–12	Arsenal	16	1		
2012–13	Arsenal	27	0		
2013–14	Arsenal	28	0		
2014–15	Arsenal	22	0		
2015–16	Arsenal	15	1		
2016–17	Arsenal	11	0		
2017–18	Arsenal	0	0	**137**	**2**
2017–18	WBA	33	0		
2018–19	WBA	36	4		
2019–20	WBA	14	1		
2020–21	WBA	10	0	**93**	**5**

GRIFFITHS, Joshua (G) 44 0
b.Hereford 5-9-01

2020–21	WBA	0	0		
2020–21	*Cheltenham T*	44	0	**44**	**0**

GROSICKI, Kamil (M) 407 72
H: 5 11 W: 12 04 b.Szczecin 8-6-88
Internationals: Poland U19, U21, Full caps.

2005–06	Pognon Szczecin	2	0		
2006–07	Pognon Szczecin	21	2	**23**	**2**
2007–08	Legia Warsaw	11	1		
2007–08	Sion	8	2	**8**	**2**
2008–09	Legia Warsaw	0	0	**11**	**1**
2008–09	Jagiellonia	13	4		
2009–10	Jagiellonia	30	4		
2010–11	Jagiellonia	15	6	**58**	**14**
2010–11	Sivasspor	17	6		
2011–12	Sivasspor	40	7		
2012–13	Sivasspor	28	2		
2013–14	Sivasspor	5	0	**90**	**15**
2013–14	Rennes	13	0		
2014–15	Rennes	19	0		
2015–16	Rennes	33	9		
2016–17	Rennes	16	4	**81**	**13**
2016–17	Hull C	15	0		
2017–18	Hull C	37	9		
2018–19	Hull C	39	9		
2019–20	Hull C	28	6	**119**	**24**
2019–20	WBA	14	1		
2020–21	WBA	3	0	**17**	**1**

HARMON, George (D) 0 0
b.Birmingham 8-12-00

2020–21	WBA	0	0		

HARPER, Rekeem (M) 51 1
H: 6 0 W: 10 01 b. 8-3-00
Internationals: England U17, U19.

2016–17	WBA	0	0		
2017–18	WBA	1	0		
2017–18	*Blackburn R*	4	0	**4**	**0**
2018–19	WBA	16	1		
2019–20	WBA	10	0		
2020–21	WBA	2	0	**29**	**1**
2020–21	*Birmingham C*	18	0	**18**	**0**

HEGAZI, Ahmed (D) 200 6
H: 6 5 W: 11 03 b.Ismalia 25-1-91
Internationals: Egypt U20, U23, Full caps.

2009–10	Ismaily	12	0		
2010–11	Ismaily	7	0		
2011–12	Ismaily	9	0	**28**	**0**
2012–13	Fiorentina	2	0		
2013–14	Fiorentina	1	0		
2014–15	Fiorentina	0	0	**3**	**0**
2014–15	*Perugia*	10	0	**10**	**0**
2015–16	Al Ahly	29	0		
2016–17	Al Ahly	11	0	**40**	**0**
2017–18	WBA	38	2		
2018–19	WBA	38	1		
2019–20	WBA	16	1		
2020–21	WBA	1	0	**93**	**4**
2020–21	*Al Ittihad*	26	2	**26**	**2**

Transferred to Al-Ittihad October 2020.

IROEGBUNAM, Tim (M) 0 0

2020–21	WBA	0	0		

IVANOVIC, Branislav (M) 492 42
H: 6 0 W: 12 04 b.Sremska Mitreovica 22-2-84
Internationals: Serbia U21, Full caps.

2002–03	Sremska	19	2	**19**	**2**
2003–04	OFK Belgrade	13	0		
2004–05	OFK Belgrade	27	2		
2005–06	OFK Belgrade	15	3	**55**	**5**
2006	Lokomotiv Moscow	28	2		
2007	Lokomotiv Moscow	26	3	**54**	**5**
2007–08	Chelsea	0	0		
2008–09	Chelsea	16	0		
2009–10	Chelsea	28	1		
2010–11	Chelsea	34	4		
2011–12	Chelsea	29	3		
2012–13	Chelsea	34	5		
2013–14	Chelsea	36	3		
2014–15	Chelsea	38	4		
2015–16	Chelsea	33	2		
2016–17	Chelsea	13	0	**261**	**22**
2016–17	Zenit Saint Petersburg	10	1		
2017–18	Zenit Saint Petersburg	27	2		
2018–19	Zenit Saint Petersburg	28	1		
2019–20	Zenit Saint Petersburg	25	4	**90**	**8**
2020–21	WBA	13	0	**13**	**0**

JOHNSTONE, Samuel (G) 269 0
H: 6 0 W: 12 10 b.Preston 25-3-93
Internationals: England U16, U17, U19, U20.

2009–10	Manchester U	0	0		
2010–11	Manchester U	0	0		
2011–12	Manchester U	0	0		
2011–12	*Oldham Ath*	0	0		
2011–12	*Scunthorpe U*	12	0	**12**	**0**
2012–13	Manchester U	0	0		
2012–13	*Walsall*	7	0	**7**	**0**
2013–14	Manchester U	0	0		
2013–14	*Yeovil T*	1	0	**1**	**0**
2013–14	*Doncaster R*	18	0		
2014–15	Manchester U	0	0		
2014–15	*Doncaster R*	10	0	**28**	**0**
2014–15	*Preston NE*	22	0		
2015–16	Manchester U	0	0		
2015–16	*Preston NE*	4	0	**26**	**0**
2016–17	Manchester U	0	0		
2016–17	*Aston Villa*	21	0		
2017–18	Manchester U	0	0		
2017–18	*Aston Villa*	45	0	**66**	**0**
2018–19	WBA	46	0		
2019–20	WBA	46	0		
2020–21	WBA	37	0	**129**	**0**

JOSHUA, Kevin (D) 0 0
b. 30-11-01
From Solihull Moors.

2020–21	WBA	0	0		

KING, Toby (M) 0 0

2020–21	WBA	0	0		

KIPRE, Cedric (D) 115 3
H: 6 3 W: 12 02 b.Paris 9-12-96
Internationals: Ivory Coast U23.
From Paris Saint-Germain.
2014–15 Leicester C 0 0
2015–16 Leicester C 0 0
2016–17 Leicester C 0 0
2017–18 Motherwell 36 1 **36 1**
2018–19 Wigan Ath 38 0
2019–20 Wigan Ath 36 2
2020–21 Wigan Ath 0 0 **74 2**
2020–21 WBA 0 0
2020–21 *Charleroi* 5 0 **5 0**

LIVERMORE, Jake (M) 361 18
H: 5 9 W: 12 08 b.Enfield 14-11-89
Internationals: England Full caps.
2006–07 Tottenham H 0 0
2007–08 Tottenham H 0 0
2007–08 *Milton Keynes D* 5 0 **5 0**
2008–09 Tottenham H 0 0
2008–09 *Crewe Alex* 0 0
2009–10 Tottenham H 1 0
2009–10 *Derby Co* 16 1 **16 1**
2009–10 *Peterborough U* 9 1 **9 1**
2010–11 Tottenham H 0 0
2010–11 *Ipswich T* 12 0 **12 0**
2010–11 *Leeds U* 5 0 **5 0**
2011–12 Tottenham H 24 0
2012–13 Tottenham H 11 0
2013–14 Tottenham H 0 0 **36 0**
2013–14 *Hull C* 36 3
2014–15 Hull C 35 1
2015–16 Hull C 34 4
2016–17 Hull C 21 1 **126 9**
2016–17 WBA 16 0
2017–18 WBA 34 2
2018–19 WBA 39 2
2019–20 WBA 45 3
2020–21 WBA 18 0 **152 7**

LONERGAN, Andrew (G) 353 1
H: 6 4 W: 13 02 b.Preston 19-10-83
Internationals: Republic of Ireland U16. England U20.
2000–01 Preston NE 1 0
2001–02 Preston NE 0 0
2002–03 Preston NE 0 0
2002–03 *Darlington* 2 0 **2 0**
2003–04 Preston NE 8 0
2004–05 Preston NE 23 1
2005–06 Preston NE 0 0
2005–06 *Wycombe W* 2 0 **2 0**
2006–07 Preston NE 13 0
2006–07 *Swindon T* 1 0 **1 0**
2007–08 Preston NE 43 0
2008–09 Preston NE 46 0
2009–10 Preston NE 45 0
2010–11 Preston NE 29 0 **208 1**
2011–12 Leeds U 35 0
2012–13 Bolton W 5 0
2013–14 Bolton W 17 0
2014–15 Bolton W 29 0 **51 0**
2015–16 Fulham 29 0 **29 0**
2016–17 Wolverhampton W 11 0
2017–18 Wolverhampton W 0 0 **11 0**
2017–18 Leeds U 7 0 **42 0**
2018–19 Middlesbrough 0 0
2018–19 *Rochdale* 7 0 **7 0**
2019–20 Liverpool 0 0
2020–21 Stoke C 0 0
2020–21 WBA 0 0

MATHEUS PEREIRA, Fellipe (M) 136 30
b. 5-5-95
2013–14 Sporting Lisbon 0 0
2014–15 Sporting Lisbon 0 0
2015–16 Sporting Lisbon 8 0
2016–17 Sporting Lisbon 7 1
2017–18 Sporting Lisbon 0 0
2017–18 *Chaves* 27 7 **27 7**
2018–19 Sporting Lisbon 0 0
2018–19 *Nuremberg* 19 3 **19 3**
2019–20 Sporting Lisbon 0 0 **15 1**
On loan from Sporting Lisbon.
2019–20 WBA 42 8
2020–21 WBA 33 11 **75 19**

MORTON, Callum (F) 26 7
b. 19-1-00
From Yeovil T.
2019–20 WBA 0 0
2019–20 *Northampton T* 9 5 **9 5**
2020–21 WBA 0 0
2020–21 *Lincoln C* 17 2 **17 2**

O'SHEA, Dara (D) 72 3
b. 4-3-99
Internationals: Republic of Ireland U18, U19, U21.
2018–19 WBA 0 0
2018–19 *Exeter C* 27 0 **27 0**
2019–20 WBA 17 3
2020–21 WBA 28 0 **45 3**

PALMER, Alex (G) 85 0
b. 10-8-96
Internationals: England U16.
2014–15 WBA 0 0
2015–16 WBA 0 0
2016–17 WBA 0 0
2017–18 WBA 0 0
2018–19 WBA 0 0
2018–19 *Oldham Ath* 1 0 **1 0**
2018–19 *Notts Co* 1 0 **1 0**
2019–20 WBA 0 0
2019–20 *Plymouth Arg* 37 0 **37 0**
2020–21 WBA 0 0
2020–21 *Lincoln C* 46 0 **46 0**

PELTIER, Lee (D) 443 5
H: 5 10 W: 12 00 b.Liverpool 11-12-86
Internationals: England U18.
2004–05 Liverpool 0 0
2005–06 Liverpool 0 0
2006–07 Liverpool 0 0
2006–07 *Hull C* 7 0 **7 0**
2007–08 Liverpool 0 0
2007–08 Yeovil T 34 0
2008–09 Yeovil T 35 1 **69 1**
2009–10 Huddersfield T 42 0
2010–11 Huddersfield T 38 1
2011–12 Leicester C 40 2
2012–13 Leicester C 0 0 **40 2**
2012–13 Leeds U 41 0
2013–14 Leeds U 25 1 **66 1**
2013–14 *Nottingham F* 7 0 **7 0**
2014–15 Huddersfield T 11 0 **91 1**
2014–15 Cardiff C 15 0
2015–16 Cardiff C 41 0
2016–17 Cardiff C 28 0
2017–18 Cardiff C 30 0
2018–19 Cardiff C 20 0
2019–20 Cardiff C 25 0 **159 0**
2019–20 WBA 0 0
2020–21 WBA 4 0 **4 0**

PHILLIPS, Matthew (M) 427 59
H: 6 0 W: 12 10 b.Aylesbury 13-3-91
Internationals: England U19, U20. Scotland Full caps.
2007–08 Wycombe W 2 0
2008–09 Wycombe W 37 3
2009–10 Wycombe W 36 5
2010–11 Wycombe W 3 0 **78 8**
2010–11 Blackpool 27 1
2011–12 Blackpool 33 7
2011–12 *Sheffield U* 6 5 **6 5**
2012–13 Blackpool 34 4
2013–14 Blackpool 0 0 **94 12**
2013–14 QPR 21 3
2014–15 QPR 25 3
2015–16 QPR 44 8 **90 14**
2016–17 WBA 27 4
2017–18 WBA 30 2
2018–19 WBA 30 5
2019–20 WBA 39 7
2020–21 WBA 33 2 **159 20**

RICHARDS, Rico (M) 0 0
b. 27-9-03
Internationals: England U16.
2019–20 WBA 0 0
2020–21 WBA 0 0

ROBINSON, Callum (F) 219 44
H: 5 10 W: 11 11 b.Birmingham 2-2-95
Internationals: England U16, U17, U19, U20. Republic of Ireland Full caps.
2013–14 Aston Villa 4 0
2014–15 Aston Villa 0 0
2014–15 *Preston NE* 25 4
2015–16 Aston Villa 0 0 **4 0**
2015–16 *Bristol C* 6 0 **6 0**
2015–16 *Preston NE* 14 2
2016–17 Preston NE 42 10
2017–18 Preston NE 41 7
2018–19 Preston NE 27 12 **149 35**
2019–20 Sheffield U 16 1 **16 1**
2019–20 *WBA* 16 3
2020–21 WBA 28 5 **44 8**

ROBSON-KANU, Hal (F) 383 54
H: 5 7 W: 11 08 b.Acton 21-5-89
Internationals: England U19, U20. Wales U21, Full caps.
2007–08 Reading 0 0
2007–08 *Southend U* 8 3
2008–09 Reading 0 0
2008–09 *Southend U* 14 2 **22 5**
2008–09 *Swindon T* 20 4 **20 4**
2009–10 Reading 17 0
2010–11 Reading 27 5
2011–12 Reading 36 4
2012–13 Reading 25 7
2013–14 Reading 36 4
2014–15 Reading 29 1
2015–16 Reading 28 3
2016–17 Reading 0 0 **198 24**
2016–17 WBA 29 3
2017–18 WBA 21 2
2018–19 WBA 35 4
2019–20 WBA 39 10
2020–21 WBA 19 2 **143 21**

SAWYERS, Romaine (M) 332 23
H: 5 9 W: 11 00 b.Birmingham 2-11-91
Internationals: St Kitts and Nevis U23, Full caps.
2009–10 WBA 0 0
2010–11 WBA 0 0
2010–11 *Port Vale* 1 0 **1 0**
2011–12 WBA 0 0
2011–12 *Shrewsbury T* 7 0 **7 0**
2012–13 WBA 0 0
2012–13 Walsall 4 0
2013–14 Walsall 44 6
2014–15 Walsall 42 4
2015–16 Walsall 46 6 **136 16**
2016–17 Brentford 43 2
2017–18 Brentford 42 4
2018–19 Brentford 42 0 **127 6**
2019–20 WBA 42 1
2020–21 WBA 19 0 **61 1**

SNODGRASS, Robert (M) 494 92
H: 6 0 W: 12 02 b.Glasgow 7-9-87
Internationals: Scotland U20, U21, Full caps.
2003–04 Livingston 0 0
2004–05 Livingston 17 2
2005–06 Livingston 27 4
2006–07 Livingston 6 0
2006–07 *Stirling Alb* 12 5 **12 5**
2007–08 Livingston 31 9 **81 15**
2008–09 Leeds U 42 9
2009–10 Leeds U 44 7
2010–11 Leeds U 37 6
2011–12 Leeds U 43 13 **166 35**
2012–13 Norwich C 37 6
2013–14 Norwich C 30 6 **67 12**
2014–15 Hull C 1 0
2015–16 Hull C 24 4
2016–17 Hull C 20 7 **45 11**
2016–17 West Ham U 15 0
2017–18 West Ham U 0 0
2017–18 *Aston Villa* 40 7 **40 7**
2018–19 West Ham U 33 2
2019–20 West Ham U 24 5
2020–21 West Ham U 3 0 **75 7**
2020–21 WBA 8 0 **8 0**

SOULE, Jamie (F) 1 0
b. 26-11-00
Internationals: England U17.
2019–20 WBA 0 0
2020–21 WBA 0 0
2020–21 *Lincoln C* 1 0 **1 0**

TAYLOR, Caleb (D) 0 0
b. 14-1-03
2020–21 WBA 0 0

TOWNSEND, Conor (D) 193 6
H: 5 4 W: 9 11 b.Hessle 4-3-93
2011–12 Hull C 0 0
2012–13 Hull C 0 0
2012–13 *Chesterfield* 20 1 **20 1**
2013–14 Hull C 0 0
2013–14 *Carlisle U* 12 0 **12 0**
2014–15 Hull C 0 0
2014–15 *Dundee U* 17 0 **17 0**
2014–15 *Scunthorpe U* 6 0
2015–16 Hull C 0 0
2015–16 Scunthorpe U 20 1
2016–17 Scunthorpe U 24 0
2017–18 Scunthorpe U 30 4 **80 5**
2018–19 WBA 12 0
2019–20 WBA 27 0
2020–21 WBA 25 0 **64 0**

TULLOCH, Rayhaan (F) 2 0
b.Birmingham 20-1-01
Internationals: England U16, U17, U18.
2017–18 WBA 0 0
2018–19 WBA 0 0
2019–20 WBA 0 0
2020–21 *Doncaster R* 2 0 **2 0**

WINDSOR, Owen (F) 13 1
b. 17-9-01
From Cirencester T.
2020–21 WBA 0 0
2020–21 *Grimsby T* 12 1 **12 1**
2020–21 *Newport Co* 1 0 **1 0**

YOKUSLU, Okay (M) 293 19
b.Izmir 9-3-94
2009–10 Altay 12 2
2010–11 Altay 21 2 **33 4**
2011–12 Kayserispor 22 2
2012–13 Kayserispor 24 0
2013–14 Kayserispor 25 1
2014–15 Kayserispor 31 4 **102 7**
2015–16 Trabzonspor 27 2
2016–17 Trabzonspor 29 2
2017–18 Trabzonspor 30 2 **86 6**
2018–19 Celta Vigo 30 2
2019–20 Celta Vigo 26 0
2020–21 Celta Vigo 0 0 **56 2**
On loan from Celta Vigo.
2020–21 WBA 16 0 **16 0**

ZOHORE, Kenneth (F) 203 46
H: 6 4 W: 12 06 b.Copenhagen 31-1-94
Internationals: Denmark U17, U18, U19, U21.
2009–10 Copenhagen 1 0
2010–11 Copenhagen 15 1
2011–12 Copenhagen 0 0 **16 1**
2011–12 Fiorentina 0 0
2012–13 Fiorentina 0 0
2013–14 Fiorentina 0 0
2013–14 *Brondby* 25 5 **25 5**
2014 *Gothenburg* 5 2 **5 2**
2014–15 Fiorentina 0 0
2014–15 Odense BK 11 2
2015–16 Odense BK 16 7 **27 9**
2015–16 KV Kortrijk 0 0
2015–16 *Cardiff C* 12 2
2016–17 Cardiff C 29 12
2017–18 Cardiff C 36 9
2018–19 Cardiff C 19 1 **96 24**
2019–20 WBA 17 3
2020–21 WBA 0 0 **17 3**
2020–21 *Millwall* 17 2 **17 2**

Scholars
Andrews, Jamie; Ashworth, Zachary; Boruc, Maksymilian Pawel; Chidi, Mark Onyemaechi; Cleary, Reyes Demar Uriah; Dwyer, Vinnie Conor; Emery, Jamie Lewis; Faal, Modou Lamin; Fellows, Tom Allen; Grant, Ryan Liam; Hall, Reece Daniel; Ingram, Ethan John; Iroegbunam, Timothy Emeka; Lamb, MacKenzie Craig; MacHisa, Leon Tafara; Malcolm, Jovan Anthony; Neto Teixeira, Aurio Clinton; Ngoma Muanda, Daniel; Okoka, Samuel; Shaw, Joshua Aaron; Shepherd, Jacob Lewis; Taylor, Caleb Joaquin.

WEST HAM U (89)

AKINOLA, Tunji (D) 33 0
b. 21-11-98
2020–21 West Ham U 0 0
2020–21 *Leyton Orient* 33 0 **33 0**

ALESE, Ajibola (D) 12 0
b.Islington 17-1-01
Internationals: England U16, U17, U18, U19.
2019–20 West Ham U 0 0
2019–20 *Accrington S* 10 0 **10 0**
2020–21 West Ham U 0 0
2020–21 *Cambridge U* 2 0 **2 0**

ALVES, Frederik (D) 33 0
b.Hvidovre 8-11-99
2018–19 Silkeborg 17 0
2019–20 Silkeborg 16 0
2020–21 Silkeborg 0 0 **33 0**
2020–21 West Ham U 0 0

ALVES, Frederik (D) 41 0
H: 6 2 W: 12 04 b.Hvidovre 8-11-99
Internationals: Denmark U20, U21.
2018–19 Silkeborg 17 0
2019–20 Silkeborg 16 0
2020–21 Silkeborg 8 0 **41 0**
2020–21 West Ham U 0 0

ANTONIO, Michael (M) 367 87
H: 6 0 W: 11 11 b.Wandsworth 28-3-90
From Tooting & Mitcham U.
2008–09 Reading 0 0
2008–09 *Cheltenham T* 9 0 **9 0**
2009–10 Reading 1 0
2009–10 *Southampton* 28 3 **28 3**
2010–11 Reading 21 1
2011–12 Reading 6 0
2011–12 *Colchester U* 15 4 **15 4**
2011–12 *Sheffield W* 14 5
2012–13 Reading 0 0 **28 1**
2012–13 Sheffield W 37 8
2013–14 Sheffield W 27 4 **78 17**
2014–15 Nottingham F 46 14
2015–16 Nottingham F 4 2 **50 16**
2015–16 West Ham U 26 8
2016–17 West Ham U 29 9
2017–18 West Ham U 21 3
2018–19 West Ham U 33 6
2019–20 West Ham U 24 10
2020–21 West Ham U 26 10 **159 46**

APPIAH-FORSON, Keenan (M) 0 0
b. 16-10-01
2020–21 West Ham U 0 0

ASHBY, Harrison (D) 0 0
b.Milton Keynes 14-11-01
2020–21 West Ham U 0 0

BALBUENA, Fabian (D) 289 17
H: 5 11 W: 11 07 b.Ciudad del Este 23-8-91
Internationals: Paraguay Full caps.
2010 Cerro Porteno 7 0
2011 Cerro Porteno 28 4
2012 Cerro Porteno 41 1 **76 5**
2013 Rubio Nu 17 1 **17 1**
2013 Nacional 14 0
2014 Nacional 16 1 **30 1**
2014 Libertad 16 1
2015 Libertad 26 2
2016 Libertad 1 0 **43 3**
2016 Corinthians 29 0
2017 Corinthians 32 4
2018 Corinthians 8 0 **69 4**
2018–19 West Ham U 23 1
2019–20 West Ham U 17 1
2020–21 West Ham U 14 1 **54 3**

BAPTISTE, Jamal (M) 0 0
b. 11-11-03
2020–21 West Ham U 0 0

BENRAHMA, Said (F) 188 44
H: 5 8 W: 10 08 b.Toulouse 10-8-95
Internationals: Algeria Full caps.
2013–14 Nice 5 0
2014–15 Nice 3 1
2015–16 Nice 9 2
2015–16 *Angers* 12 1 **12 1**
2016–17 Nice 0 0
2016–17 *Gazelec Ajaccio* 15 3 **15 3**
2017–18 Nice 0 0 **17 3**
2017–18 *Chateauroux* 31 9 **31 9**
2018–19 Brentford 38 10
2019–20 Brentford 43 17
2020–21 Brentford 2 0 **83 27**
2020–21 West Ham U 30 1 **30 1**

BOWEN, Jarrod (F) 175 61
b.Leominster 1-1-96
2014–15 Hull C 0 0
2015–16 Hull C 0 0
2016–17 Hull C 7 0
2017–18 Hull C 42 14
2018–19 Hull C 46 22
2019–20 Hull C 29 16 **124 52**
2019–20 West Ham U 13 1
2020–21 West Ham U 38 8 **51 9**

CARDOSO, Goncalo (D) 20 0
H: 6 2 W: 12 08 b.Marco de Canaveses 21-10-00
Internationals: Portugal U19, U20.
2018–19 Boavista 15 0 **15 0**
2019–20 West Ham U 0 0
2020–21 West Ham U 0 0
2020–21 *FC Basel* 5 0 **5 0**

CHESTERS, Daniel (F) 0 0
H: 5 10 W: 10 03 b.Hitchin 4-4-02
2020–21 West Ham U 0 0

COUFAL, Vladimir (D) 239 10
b. 22-8-92
2010–11 Hlucin 14 0
2011–12 Hlucin 0 0 **14 0**
2011–12 *Opava* 13 1 **13 1**
2012–13 Slovan Liberec 10 0
2013–14 Slovan Liberec 21 0
2014–15 Slovan Liberec 13 0
2015–16 Slovan Liberec 27 1
2016–17 Slovan Liberec 17 0
2017–18 Slovan Liberec 30 2 **118 3**
2018–19 Slavia Prague 28 3
2019–20 Slavia Prague 32 3
2020–21 Slavia Prague 0 0 **60 6**
2020–21 West Ham U 34 0 **34 0**

COVENTRY, Conor (M) 7 0
b. 25-3-00
Internationals: Republic of Ireland U17, U18, U21.
2018–19 West Ham U 0 0
2019–20 West Ham U 0 0
2019–20 *Lincoln C* 7 0 **7 0**
2020–21 West Ham U 0 0

CRESSWELL, Aaron (D) 426 19
H: 5 7 W: 10 05 b.Liverpool 15-12-89
Internationals: England Full caps.
2008–09 Tranmere R 13 1
2009–10 Tranmere R 14 0
2010–11 Tranmere R 43 4 **70 5**
2011–12 Ipswich T 44 1
2012–13 Ipswich T 46 3
2013–14 Ipswich T 42 2 **132 6**
2014–15 West Ham U 38 2
2015–16 West Ham U 37 2
2016–17 West Ham U 26 0
2017–18 West Ham U 36 1
2018–19 West Ham U 20 0
2019–20 West Ham U 31 3
2020–21 West Ham U 36 0 **224 8**

CULLEN, Josh (M) 133 3
H: 5 8 W: 11 00 b.Southend-on-Sea 4-7-96
Internationals: England U16. Republic of Ireland U19, U21, Full caps.
2014–15 West Ham U 0 0
2015–16 West Ham U 1 0
2015–16 *Bradford C* 15 0
2016–17 West Ham U 0 0
2016–17 *Bradford C* 40 1 **55 1**
2017–18 West Ham U 2 0
2017–18 *Bolton W* 12 0 **12 0**
2018–19 West Ham U 0 0
2018–19 *Charlton Ath* 29 1
2019–20 West Ham U 0 0
2019–20 *Charlton Ath* 34 1
2020–21 *Charlton Ath* 0 0 **63 2**
2020–21 West Ham U 0 0 **3 0**
Transferred to Anderlecht October 2020.

DIALLO, Amadou (F) 0 0
b. 15-2-03
Internationals: England U16, U17.
2020–21 West Ham U 0 0

DIOP, Issa (D) 160 11
H: 6 4 W: 13 03 b.Toulouse 9-1-97
Internationals: France U16, U17, U18, U19, U20, U21.
2015–16 Toulouse 21 1
2016–17 Toulouse 30 2
2017–18 Toulouse 26 2 **77 5**
2018–19 West Ham U 33 1
2019–20 West Ham U 32 3
2020–21 West Ham U 18 2 **83 6**

DJU, Mesaque (F) 0 0
H: 5 10 W: 10 06 b.Bissau 18-3-99
Internationals: Portugal U16, U17, U18, U19, U20.
From Benfica.
2020–21 West Ham U 0 0

EMMANUEL, Mbule (D) 0 0
2020–21 West Ham U 0 0

FABIANSKI, Lukasz (G) 332 0
H: 6 3 W: 13 01 b.Costrzyn nad Odra 18-4-85
Internationals: Poland U21, Full caps.
2004–05 Lech Poznan 0 0
2005–06 Legia Warsaw 30 0
2006–07 Legia Warsaw 23 0 **53 0**
2007–08 Arsenal 3 0
2008–09 Arsenal 6 0
2009–10 Arsenal 4 0
2010–11 Arsenal 14 0
2011–12 Arsenal 0 0
2012–13 Arsenal 4 0
2013–14 Arsenal 1 0 **32 0**
2014–15 Swansea C 37 0
2015–16 Swansea C 37 0
2016–17 Swansea C 37 0
2017–18 Swansea C 38 0 **149 0**
2018–19 West Ham U 38 0
2019–20 West Ham U 25 0
2020–21 West Ham U 35 0 **98 0**

FELIPE ANDERSON, Gomes (M) 266 42
H: 5 10 W: 10 12 b.Brasília 15-4-93
Internationals: Brazil U17, U20, U23, Full caps.
2010 Santos 5 0
2011 Santos 18 1
2012 Santos 35 6
2013 Santos 3 0 **61 7**
2013–14 Lazio 13 0
2014–15 Lazio 32 10
2015–16 Lazio 35 7
2016–17 Lazio 36 4
2017–18 Lazio 21 4 **137 25**
2018–19 West Ham U 36 9
2019–20 West Ham U 25 1
2020–21 West Ham U 2 0 **63 10**
2020–21 *Porto* 5 0 **5 0**

FORNALS, Pablo (M) **198** **19**
b.Castellon de la Plana 22-2-96
Internationals: Spain U21, Full caps.

2015–16	Malaga	27	1		
2016–17	Malaga	32	6	**59**	**7**
2017–18	Villareal	35	3		
2018–19	Villareal	35	2	**70**	**5**
2019–20	West Ham U	36	2		
2020–21	West Ham U	33	5	**69**	**7**

FREDERICKS, Ryan (M) **201** **3**
H: 5 8 W: 11 10 b.Potters Bar 10-10-92
Internationals: England U19.

2010–11	Tottenham H	0	0		
2011–12	Tottenham H	0	0		
2012–13	Tottenham H	0	0		
2012–13	*Brentford*	4	0	**4**	**0**
2013–14	Tottenham H	0	0		
2013–14	*Millwall*	14	1	**14**	**1**
2014–15	Tottenham H	0	0		
2014–15	*Middlesbrough*	17	0	**17**	**0**
2015–16	Bristol C	4	0	**4**	**0**
2015–16	Fulham	32	0		
2016–17	Fulham	30	0		
2017–18	Fulham	44	0	**106**	**0**
2018–19	West Ham U	15	1		
2019–20	West Ham U	27	0		
2020–21	West Ham U	14	1	**56**	**2**

HALLER, Sebastien (F) **240** **81**
b.Ris-Orangis 22-6-94
Internationals: France U16, U17, U18, U19, U20, U21.

2012–13	Auxerre	17	2		
2013–14	Auxerre	25	4		
2014–15	Auxerre	8	0	**50**	**6**
2014–15	Utrecht	17	11		
2015–16	Utrecht	33	17		
2016–17	Utrecht	32	13	**82**	**41**
2017–18	Eintracht Frankfurt	31	9		
2018–19	Eintracht Frankfurt	29	15	**60**	**24**
2019–20	West Ham U	32	7		
2020–21	West Ham U	16	3	**48**	**10**

Transferred to Ajax January 2021.

HEGYI, Krisztian (G) **0** **0**
H: 6 4 W: 13 05 b.Budapest 24-9-02
Internationals: Hungary U16, U17.

2020–21	West Ham U	0	0		

HOLLAND, Nathan (M) **12** **2**
b. 19-6-98
Internationals: England U16, U17, U18, U19.
From Everton.

2016–17	West Ham U	0	0		
2017–18	West Ham U	0	0		
2018–19	West Ham U	0	0		
2019–20	West Ham U	2	0		
2019–20	*Oxford U*	10	2	**10**	**2**
2020–21	West Ham U	0	0	**2**	**0**

JOHNSON, Ben (M) **18** **1**
b. 21-1-00

2017–18	West Ham U	0	0		
2018–19	West Ham U	1	0		
2019–20	West Ham U	3	0		
2020–21	West Ham U	14	1	**18**	**1**

LANZINI, Manuel (M) **275** **44**
H: 5 7 W: 11 00 b.Ituzaingo 15-2-93
Internationals: Argentina U20, Full caps.

2010–11	River Plate	22	0		
2010–11	*Fluminense*	22	2		
2011–12	River Plate	0	0		
2011–12	*Fluminense*	6	1	**28**	**3**
2012–13	River Plate	26	8	**26**	**8**
2013–14	River Plate	36	4	**58**	**4**
2014–15	Al-Jazira	24	8		
2015–16	Al-Jazira	0	0	**24**	**8**
2015–16	*West Ham U*	26	6		
2016–17	West Ham U	35	8		
2017–18	West Ham U	27	5		
2018–19	West Ham U	10	1		
2019–20	West Ham U	24	0		
2020–21	West Ham U	17	1	**139**	**21**

MARTIN, David E (G) **347** **0**
H: 6 1 W: 13 04 b.Romford 22-1-86
Internationals: England U16, U17, U18, U19.

2003–04	Wimbledon	2	0	**2**	**0**
2004–05	Milton Keynes D	15	0		
2005–06	Milton Keynes D	0	0		
2005–06	Liverpool	0	0		
2006–07	Liverpool	0	0		
2006–07	*Accrington S*	10	0	**10**	**0**
2007–08	Liverpool	0	0		
2008–09	Liverpool	0	0		
2008–09	*Leicester C*	25	0	**25**	**0**
2009–10	Liverpool	0	0		
2009–10	*Tranmere R*	3	0	**3**	**0**
2009–10	*Leeds U*	0	0		
2009–10	*Derby Co*	2	0	**2**	**0**
2010–11	Milton Keynes D	43	0		
2011–12	Milton Keynes D	46	0		
2012–13	Milton Keynes D	31	0		
2013–14	Milton Keynes D	40	0		
2014–15	Milton Keynes D	39	0		
2015–16	Milton Keynes D	35	0		
2016–17	Milton Keynes D	40	0	**289**	**0**
2017–18	Millwall	1	0		
2018–19	Millwall	10	0	**11**	**0**
2019–20	West Ham U	5	0		
2020–21	West Ham U	0	0	**5**	**0**

MASUAKU, Arthur (D) **170** **2**
b. 7-11-93
Internationals: France U18, U19. DR Congo Full caps.

2012–13	Valenciennes	0	0		
2013–14	Valenciennes	27	1	**27**	**1**
2014–15	Olympiacos	27	0		
2015–16	Olympiacos	24	1	**51**	**1**
2016–17	West Ham U	13	0		
2017–18	West Ham U	27	0		
2018–19	West Ham U	23	0		
2019–20	West Ham U	17	0		
2020–21	West Ham U	12	0	**92**	**0**

NOBLE, Mark (M) **479** **55**
H: 5 11 W: 12 00 b.West Ham 8-5-87
Internationals: England U16, U17, U18, U19, U21.

2004–05	West Ham U	13	0		
2005–06	West Ham U	5	0		
2005–06	*Hull C*	5	0	**5**	**0**
2006–07	West Ham U	10	2		
2006–07	*Ipswich T*	13	1	**13**	**1**
2007–08	West Ham U	31	3		
2008–09	West Ham U	29	3		
2009–10	West Ham U	27	2		
2010–11	West Ham U	26	4		
2011–12	West Ham U	45	8		
2012–13	West Ham U	28	4		
2013–14	West Ham U	38	3		
2014–15	West Ham U	28	2		
2015–16	West Ham U	37	7		
2016–17	West Ham U	30	3		
2017–18	West Ham U	29	4		
2018–19	West Ham U	31	5		
2019–20	West Ham U	33	4		
2020–21	West Ham U	21	0	**461**	**54**

ODUBEKO, Ademipo (F) **0** **0**
b.Tallaght 21-10-02
From Manchester U.

2020–21	West Ham U	0	0		

OGBONNA, Angelo (D) **376** **8**
H: 6 2 W: 13 08 b.Cassino 23-5-88
Internationals: Italy U21, Full caps.

2006–07	Torino	4	0		
2007–08	Torino	0	0		
2007–08	*Crotone*	22	0	**22**	**0**
2008–09	Torino	19	0		
2009–10	Torino	31	1		
2010–11	Torino	35	0		
2011–12	Torino	39	0		
2012–13	Torino	22	0	**150**	**1**
2013–14	Juventus	16	0		
2014–15	Juventus	25	0	**41**	**0**
2015–16	West Ham U	28	0		
2016–17	West Ham U	20	0		
2017–18	West Ham U	32	1		
2018–19	West Ham U	24	1		
2019–20	West Ham U	31	2		
2020–21	West Ham U	28	3	**163**	**7**

RANDOLPH, Darren (G) **385** **0**
H: 6 1 W: 12 02 b.Dublin 12-5-87
Internationals: Republic of Ireland U21, B, Full caps.

2004–05	Charlton Ath	0	0		
2005–06	Charlton Ath	0	0		
2006–07	Charlton Ath	1	0		
2006–07	*Gillingham*	3	0	**3**	**0**
2007–08	Charlton Ath	1	0		
2007–08	*Bury*	14	0	**14**	**0**
2008–09	Charlton Ath	1	0		
2008–09	*Hereford U*	13	0	**13**	**0**
2009–10	Charlton Ath	11	0	**14**	**0**
2010–11	Motherwell	37	0		
2011–12	Motherwell	38	0		
2012–13	Motherwell	36	0	**111**	**0**
2013–14	Birmingham C	46	0		
2014–15	Birmingham C	45	0	**91**	**0**
2015–16	West Ham U	6	0		
2016–17	West Ham U	22	0		
2017–18	Middlesbrough	46	0		
2018–19	Middlesbrough	46	0		
2019–20	Middlesbrough	14	0	**106**	**0**
2019–20	West Ham U	2	0		
2020–21	West Ham U	3	0	**33**	**0**

REID, Winston (D) **298** **12**
H: 6 3 W: 13 10 b.North Shore 3-7-88
Internationals: Denmark U19, U20, U21. New Zealand Full caps.

2005–06	Midtjylland	9	0		
2006–07	Midtjylland	11	0		
2007–08	Midtjylland	9	0		
2008–09	Midtjylland	25	2		
2009–10	Midtjylland	29	0		
2010–11	Midtjylland	1	0	**84**	**2**
2010–11	West Ham U	7	0		
2011–12	West Ham U	28	3		
2012–13	West Ham U	36	1		
2013–14	West Ham U	22	1		
2014–15	West Ham U	30	1		
2015–16	West Ham U	24	1		
2016–17	West Ham U	30	2		
2017–18	West Ham U	17	0		
2018–19	West Ham U	0	0		
2019–20	West Ham U	0	0		
2020	Sporting Kansas C	10	1	**10**	**1**
2020–21	West Ham U	0	0	**194**	**9**
2020–21	*Brentford*	10	0	**10**	**0**

RICE, Declan (M) **131** **5**
b. 14-1-99
Internationals: Republic of Ireland U16, U17, U19, U21, Full caps.
From Chelsea.

2016–17	West Ham U	1	0		
2017–18	West Ham U	26	0		
2018–19	West Ham U	34	2		
2019–20	West Ham U	38	1		
2020–21	West Ham U	32	2	**131**	**5**

SOUCEK, Tomas (M) **191** **44**
b. 27-2-95
Internationals: Czech Republic U19, U20, U21, Full caps.

2014–15	Slavia Prague	0	0		
2014–15	*Viktoria Zizkov*	14	0	**14**	**0**
2015–16	Slavia Prague	29	7		
2016–17	Slavia Prague	7	0		
2016–17	*Slovan Liberec*	12	0	**12**	**0**
2017–18	Slavia Prague	27	3		
2018–19	Slavia Prague	34	13		
2019–20	Slavia Prague	17	8	**114**	**31**
2019–20	*West Ham U*	13	3		
2020–21	West Ham U	38	10	**51**	**13**

SWYER, Kamarai (M) **0** **0**
b. 4-12-02

2020–21	West Ham U	0	0		

TROTT, Nathan (G) **23** **0**
H: 6 0 W: 11 00 b. 21-11-98
Internationals: Bermuda U17. England U18, U20.

2017–18	West Ham U	0	0		
2018–19	West Ham U	0	0		
2019–20	West Ham U	0	0		
2019–20	*AFC Wimbledon*	23	0	**23**	**0**
2020–21	West Ham U	0	0		

XANDE SILVA, Nascimento (F) **56** **5**
b. 16-3-97
Internationals: Portugal U16, U17, U18, U19, U20.

2014–15	Vitoria Guimaraes	1	0		
2015–16	Vitoria Guimaraes	20	1		
2016–17	Vitoria Guimaraes	4	0		
2017–18	Vitoria Guimaraes	1	0	**26**	**1**
2018–19	West Ham U	1	0		
2019–20	West Ham U	0	0		
2020–21	West Ham U	0	0	**1**	**0**
2020–21	*Aris*	29	4	**29**	**4**

YARMOLENKO, Andriy (M) **302** **113**
H: 6 2 W: 12 00 b.Saint Petersburg 23-10-89
Internationals: Ukraine U19, U21, Full caps.

2006–07	Desna Chernihiv	9	4	**9**	**4**
2007–08	Dynamo Kyiv	1	1		
2008–09	Dynamo Kyiv	10	0		
2009–10	Dynamo Kyiv	28	7		
2010–11	Dynamo Kyiv	26	11		
2011–12	Dynamo Kyiv	28	12		
2012–13	Dynamo Kyiv	27	11		
2013–14	Dynamo Kyiv	26	12		
2014–15	Dynamo Kyiv	26	14		
2015–16	Dynamo Kyiv	23	13		
2016–17	Dynamo Kyiv	28	15		
2017–18	Dynamo Kyiv	5	3	**228**	**99**
2017–18	Borussia Dortmund	18	3	**18**	**3**
2018–19	West Ham U	9	2		
2019–20	West Ham U	23	5		
2020–21	West Ham U	15	0	**47**	**7**

Scholars
Adebayo, Iyiola El-Ameen; Adu, Michael Asare; Coddington, Remy Taye Stephon; Corbett, Kai Michael James; Evans, Isaac Paul Ernest; Fevrier, Jayden Raymond;

Forbes, Michael; Heal, Benjamin Atticus William; Kileba, Gael Mulamba; Knightbridge, Jacob Christopher; Laing, Levi Alexander; Peake, Lennon; Perkins, Sonny Tufail; Potts, Freddie; Roach, Joshua Michael Phillip; Robinson, Carl Junior; Sanneh, Serine; Thomas, Brandon Val; Woods, Archie James.

WIGAN ATH (90)

AASGAARD, Thelo (M) 33 3
b. 2-5-02
2020–21 Wigan Ath 33 3 **33 3**

BANINGIME, Divin (F) 0 0
b. 13-10-00
2017–18 Wigan Ath 0 0
2018–19 Wigan Ath 0 0
2019–20 Wigan Ath 0 0
2020–21 Wigan Ath 0 0

CAMERON, Nathan (D) 220 13
H: 6 2 W: 12 04 b.Birmingham 21-11-91
Internationals: England U20.
2009–10 Coventry C 0 0
2010–11 Coventry C 25 0
2011–12 Coventry C 14 0
2012–13 Coventry C 9 0 **48 0**
2012–13 *Northampton T* 3 0 **3 0**
2013–14 Bury 27 4
2014–15 Bury 46 2
2015–16 Bury 28 3
2016–17 Bury 4 0
2017–18 Bury 21 2 **126 11**
2018–19 Macclesfield T 25 2
2019–20 Macclesfield T 16 0 **41 2**
2020–21 Wigan Ath 2 0 **2 0**
Transferred to Solihull Moors January 2021.

CLOUGH, Zach (F) 117 27
H: 5 7 b.Manchester 8-3-95
2013–14 Bolton W 0 0
2014–15 Bolton W 8 5
2015–16 Bolton W 28 7
2016–17 Bolton W 23 9
2016–17 Nottingham F 14 4
2017–18 Nottingham F 13 0
2017–18 *Bolton W* 9 1 **68 22**
2018–19 Nottingham F 0 0
2018–19 *Rochdale* 9 0 **9 0**
2019–20 Nottingham F 0 0
2020–21 Nottingham F 0 0 **27 4**
2020–21 Wigan Ath 13 1 **13 1**

DARIKWA, Tendayi (M) 230 10
H: 6 2 W: 12 02 b.Nottingham 13-12-91
Internationals: Zimbabwe Full caps.
2010–11 Chesterfield 0 0
2011–12 Chesterfield 2 0
2012–13 Chesterfield 36 5
2013–14 Chesterfield 41 3
2014–15 Chesterfield 46 1 **125 9**
2015–16 Burnley 21 1
2016–17 Burnley 0 0 **21 1**
2017–18 Nottingham F 30 0
2018–19 Nottingham F 28 0
2019–20 Nottingham F 0 0
2020–21 Nottingham F 0 0 **58 0**
2020–21 Wigan Ath 26 0 **26 0**

DODOO, Joseph (F) 92 15
H: 6 0 W: 12 08 b.Nottingham 6-1-95
Internationals: England U18.
2013–14 Leicester C 0 0
2014–15 Leicester C 0 0
2015–16 Leicester C 1 0 **1 0**
2015–16 *Bury* 4 1 **4 1**
2016–17 Rangers 20 3
2017–18 Rangers 0 0
2017–18 *Charlton Ath* 5 1 **5 1**
2018–19 Rangers 0 0 **20 3**
2018–19 *Blackpool* 18 2 **18 2**
2019–20 Bolton W 24 4 **24 4**
2020–21 Wigan Ath 20 4 **20 4**

EVANS, Lee (M) 222 15
H: 6 1 W: 13 12 b.Newport 24-7-94
Internationals: Wales U21, Full caps.
From Newport Co.
2012–13 Wolverhampton W 0 0
2013–14 Wolverhampton W 26 2
2014–15 Wolverhampton W 18 1
2015–16 Wolverhampton W 0 0
2015–16 *Bradford C* 35 4 **35 4**
2016–17 Wolverhampton W 15 0
2017–18 Wolverhampton W 0 0 **59 3**
2017–18 *Wigan Ath* 20 1
2017–18 Sheffield U 19 2
2018–19 Sheffield U 2 0 **21 2**
2018–19 *Wigan Ath* 34 1
2019–20 Wigan Ath 32 2
2020–21 Wigan Ath 21 2 **107 6**

EVANS, Owen (G) 36 0
b. 28-11-96
Internationals: Wales U19, U21.
From Hereford U.
2016–17 Wigan Ath 0 0
2017–18 Wigan Ath 0 0
2018–19 Wigan Ath 0 0
2019–20 Wigan Ath 0 0
2019–20 *Macclesfield T* 24 0 **24 0**
2019–20 *Cheltenham T* 11 0 **11 0**
2020–21 Wigan Ath 1 0 **1 0**

FOX, Danny (D) 434 15
H: 5 11 W: 12 06 b.Winsford 29-5-86
Internationals: England U21. Scotland Full caps.
2004–05 Everton 0 0
2004–05 *Stranraer* 11 1 **11 1**
2005–06 Walsall 33 0
2006–07 Walsall 44 3
2007–08 Walsall 22 3 **99 6**
2007–08 Coventry C 18 1
2008–09 Coventry C 39 5
2009–10 Coventry C 0 0 **57 6**
2009–10 Celtic 15 0 **15 0**
2009–10 Burnley 14 1
2010–11 Burnley 35 0
2011–12 Burnley 1 0 **50 1**
2011–12 Southampton 41 0
2012–13 Southampton 20 1
2013–14 Southampton 3 0 **64 1**
2013–14 *Nottingham F* 14 0
2014–15 Nottingham F 27 0
2015–16 Nottingham F 10 0
2016–17 Nottingham F 23 0
2017–18 Nottingham F 23 0
2018–19 Nottingham F 18 0 **115 0**
2018–19 Wigan Ath 10 0
2019–20 Wigan Ath 11 0
2020–21 Wigan Ath 2 0 **23 0**
Transferred to East Bengal October 2020.

GARDNER, Dan (M) 212 16
H: 6 1 W: 12 05 b.Manchester 5-4-90
2008–09 Celtic 4 0 **4 0**
2009–10 Crewe Alex 2 0 **2 0**
From Droylsden, FC Halifax T
2013–14 Chesterfield 16 3
2014–15 Chesterfield 17 1
2014–15 *Tranmere R* 4 2 **4 2**
2015–16 Chesterfield 30 4
2015–16 *Bury* 6 0 **6 0**
2016–17 Chesterfield 34 2 **97 10**
2017–18 Oldham Ath 43 1
2018–19 Oldham Ath 20 2
2019–20 Oldham Ath 0 0 **63 3**
2019–20 Salford C 0 0
2020–21 Wigan Ath 36 1 **36 1**

GARNER, Joe (F) 435 121
H: 5 10 W: 11 02 b.Blackburn 12-4-88
Internationals: England U16, U17, U19.
2004–05 Blackburn R 0 0
2005–06 Blackburn R 0 0
2006–07 Blackburn R 0 0
2006–07 *Carlisle U* 18 5
2007–08 Carlisle U 31 14
2008–09 Nottingham F 28 7
2009–10 Nottingham F 18 2
2010–11 Nottingham F 0 0
2010–11 *Huddersfield T* 16 0 **16 0**
2010–11 *Scunthorpe U* 18 6 **18 6**
2011–12 Nottingham F 2 0 **48 9**
2011–12 Watford 22 1
2012–13 Watford 2 0 **24 1**
2012–13 *Carlisle U* 16 7 **65 26**
2012–13 Preston NE 14 0
2013–14 Preston NE 35 18
2014–15 Preston NE 37 25
2015–16 Preston NE 41 6
2016–17 Preston NE 2 0 **129 49**
2016–17 Rangers 31 7 **31 7**
2017–18 Ipswich T 32 10 **32 10**
2018–19 Wigan Ath 33 8
2019–20 Wigan Ath 28 2
2020–21 Wigan Ath 11 3 **72 13**
Transferred to APOEL January 2021.

JONES, Bobby (G) 0 0
From Middlesbrough.
2020–21 Wigan Ath 0 0

JONES, Jamie (G) 334 0
H: 6 2 W: 14 05 b.Kirkby 18-2-89
2007–08 Everton 0 0
2008–09 Leyton Orient 20 0
2009–10 Leyton Orient 36 0
2010–11 Leyton Orient 35 0
2011–12 Leyton Orient 6 0
2012–13 Leyton Orient 26 0
2013–14 Leyton Orient 28 0 **151 0**
2014–15 Preston NE 17 0
2014–15 *Coventry C* 4 0 **4 0**
2014–15 *Rochdale* 13 0 **13 0**
2015–16 Preston NE 0 0 **17 0**
2015–16 *Colchester U* 17 0 **17 0**
2015–16 *Stevenage* 17 0
2016–17 Stevenage 36 0 **53 0**
2017–18 Wigan Ath 15 0
2018–19 Wigan Ath 12 0
2019–20 Wigan Ath 7 0
2020–21 Wigan Ath 45 0 **79 0**

JOSEPH, Kyle (F) 18 5
b. 10-9-01
2020–21 Wigan Ath 18 5 **18 5**

KEANE, Will (F) 137 21
H: 6 2 W: 11 05 b.Stockport 11-1-93
Internationals: England U16, U17, U19, U20, U21.
2009–10 Manchester U 0 0
2010–11 Manchester U 0 0
2011–12 Manchester U 1 0
2012–13 Manchester U 0 0
2013–14 Manchester U 0 0
2013–14 *Wigan Ath* 4 0
2013–14 *QPR* 10 0 **10 0**
2014–15 Manchester U 0 0
2014–15 *Sheffield W* 13 3 **13 3**
2015–16 Manchester U 1 0
2015–16 *Preston NE* 20 1 **20 1**
2016–17 Manchester U 0 0 **2 0**
2016–17 Hull C 5 0
2017–18 Hull C 9 1
2018–19 Hull C 8 0 **22 1**
2018–19 *Ipswich T* 11 3
2019–20 Ipswich T 23 3 **34 6**
2020–21 Wigan Ath 32 10 **36 10**

LANG, Callum (F) 129 38
H: 5 11 W: 11 00 b. 8-9-98
2016–17 Wigan Ath 0 0
2017–18 Wigan Ath 0 0
2017–18 *Morecambe* 30 10 **30 10**
2018–19 Wigan Ath 0 0
2018–19 *Oldham Ath* 42 13 **42 13**
2019–20 Wigan Ath 1 0
2019–20 *Shrewsbury T* 16 3 **16 3**
2020–21 Wigan Ath 23 9 **24 9**
2020–21 *Motherwell* 17 3 **17 3**

LONG, Adam (D) 13 0
b. 11-11-00
2017–18 Wigan Ath 0 0
2018–19 Wigan Ath 0 0
2019–20 Wigan Ath 0 0
2020–21 Wigan Ath 13 0 **13 0**

MASSEY, Gavin (F) 334 42
H: 5 11 W: 11 06 b.Watford 14-10-92
2009–10 Watford 1 0
2010–11 Watford 3 0
2011–12 Watford 3 0
2011–12 *Yeovil T* 16 3 **16 3**
2011–12 *Colchester U* 8 0
2012–13 Watford 0 0 **7 0**
2012–13 Colchester U 40 6
2013–14 Colchester U 30 3
2014–15 Colchester U 46 7
2015–16 Colchester U 42 4 **166 20**
2016–17 Leyton Orient 36 8 **36 8**
2017–18 Wigan Ath 42 6
2018–19 Wigan Ath 20 5
2019–20 Wigan Ath 31 0
2020–21 Wigan Ath 16 0 **109 11**

McHUGH, Harry (F) 1 0
b. 14-10-02
From Everton.
2020–21 Wigan Ath 1 0 **1 0**

MERRIE, Christopher (M) 26 0
b.Liverpool 2-11-98
From Everton.
2017–18 Wigan Ath 0 0
2018–19 Wigan Ath 0 0
2019–20 Wigan Ath 0 0
2020–21 Wigan Ath 26 0 **26 0**

O'NEILL, Mackenzie (M) 0 0
b. 20-1-02
2020–21 Wigan Ath 0 0

OBI, Chuckwuemeka (D) 4 0
b. 6-6-01
2016–17 Bury 0 0
2016–17 Liverpool 0 0
2017–18 Liverpool 0 0
2018–19 Liverpool 0 0
2019–20 Wigan Ath 0 0
2020–21 Wigan Ath 4 0 **4 0**
Transferred to AFC Fylde February 2021.

OJO, Funso (M) **273** **4**
H: 5 10 W: 11 03 b.Antwerp 28-8-91
Internationals: Belgium U16, U17, U20, U21.
2008–09 PSV Eindhoven 1 0
2009–10 PSV Eindhoven 3 0
2010–11 PSV Eindhoven 2 0
2010–11 *VVV Venlo* 8 0 **8** **0**
2011–12 PSV Eindhoven 5 0 **11** **0**
2012–13 Beerschott 24 1 **24** **1**
2013–14 Antwerp 8 0 **8** **0**
2013–14 Dordrecht 13 0
2014–15 Dordrecht 19 0 **32** **0**
2015–16 Willem II 32 0
2016–17 Willem II 28 0 **60** **0**
2017–18 Scunthorpe U 41 2
2018–19 Scunthorpe U 39 1 **80** **3**
2019–20 Aberdeen 16 0
2020–21 Aberdeen 11 0 **27** **0**
On loan from Aberdeen.
2020–21 Wigan Ath 23 0 **23** **0**

PEARCE, Tom (D) **46** **2**
b.Ormskirk 12-4-98
Internationals: England U20, U21.
From Everton.
2017–18 Leeds U 5 1
2018–19 Leeds U 2 0 **7** **1**
2018–19 *Scunthorpe U* 9 1 **9** **1**
2019–20 Wigan Ath 7 0
2020–21 Wigan Ath 23 0 **30** **0**

PERRY, Alex (M) **21** **0**
b.Liverpool 4-3-98
2016–17 Bolton W 0 0
2017–18 Bolton W 0 0
2018–19 Wigan Ath 0 0
2019–20 Wigan Ath 0 0
2020–21 Wigan Ath 21 0 **21** **0**

ROBINSON, Luke (D) **25** **0**
b. 20-11-01
From Wrexham.
2020–21 Wigan Ath 25 0 **25** **0**

SMITH, Scott (M) **0** **0**
b. 7-11-01
2020–21 Wigan Ath 0 0

SOLOMON-OTABOR, Viv (M) **135** **11**
H: 5 9 W: 12 02 b.London 2-1-96
From Crystal Palace.
2015–16 Birmingham C 22 1
2016–17 Birmingham C 3 0
2016–17 *Bolton W* 4 0 **4** **0**
2017–18 Birmingham C 0 0
2017–18 *Blackpool* 44 5 **44** **5**
2018–19 Birmingham C 8 1 **33** **2**
2018–19 *Portsmouth* 7 1 **7** **1**
2019–20 CSKA Sofia 19 1 **19** **1**
2020–21 Wigan Ath 28 2 **28** **2**

TICKLE, Sam (G) **0** **0**
b. 31-3-02
2020–21 Wigan Ath 0 0

WEBBER, Patrick (D) **0** **0**
b.Worthing 20-1-99
2016–17 Ipswich T 0 0
2017–18 Ipswich T 0 0
2018–19 Ipswich T 0 0
2019–20 Wigan Ath 0 0
2020–21 Wigan Ath 0 0

WHELAN, Corey (D) **54** **1**
b. 12-12-97
Internationals: Republic of Ireland U17, U21.
2017–18 Liverpool 0 0
2017–18 *Yeovil T* 7 0 **7** **0**
2018–19 Liverpool 0 0
2018–19 *Crewe Alex* 16 1 **16** **1**
2019 Phoenix Rising 7 0
2019 *Tucson* 1 0 **1** **0**
2020 Phoenix Rising 15 0 **22** **0**
2020–21 Wigan Ath 8 0 **8** **0**

Scholars
Adeeko, Babajide Ezekiel; Brooks, Adam James; Brown, Millen Edward; Campbell, Sam Kevin; Carragher, James Lee; Costello, Thomas Anthony; Dobie, Zach Louis; Fulton, Jason Richard; Hughes, Charles Roger; Lloyd, Kieran David; Lomax-Jones, Arthur Michael; McGee, Harry David; McGurk, Sean; McHugh, Harry; Monks, Kian Christopher; Mooney, Owen Charles; Smith, Daniel Alexander; Snell, Marcus James; Sze, Christopher John Bernard; Tickle, Samuel Lloyd; Watson, Thomas George; Welsh, Levi Jordan Joshua.

WOLVERHAMPTON W (91)

AGBOOLA, Michael (D) **0** **0**
H: 6 3 W: 11 11 b.Newham 12-8-01
From Dagenham & R.
2020–21 Wolverhampton W 0 0

AIT NOURI, Rayan (D) **44** **1**
b.Montreuil 18-6-92
2018–19 Angers 3 0
2019–20 Angers 17 0
2020–21 Angers 3 0 **23** **0**
On loan from Angers.
2020–21 Wolverhampton W 21 1 **21** **1**

ARINBJORNSSON, Palmi (G) **0** **0**
H: 6 3 b.Reykjanesbaer 29-11-03
Internationals: Iceland U16, U17.
From Njardvik.
2020–21 Wolverhampton W 0 0

BOLY, Willy (D) **241** **13**
H: 6 1 W: 12 11 b. 3-2-91
Internationals: France U16, U17, U19.
2010–11 Auxerre 8 1
2011–12 Auxerre 33 1
2012–13 Auxerre 25 1
2013–14 Auxerre 30 0
2014–15 Auxerre 1 0 **97** **3**
2014–15 Braga 0 0
2015–16 Braga 22 2
2016–17 Braga 3 0 **25** **2**
2016–17 Porto 4 0
2017–18 Porto 0 0 **4** **0**
2017–18 *Wolverhampton W* 36 3
2018–19 Wolverhampton W 36 4
2019–20 Wolverhampton W 22 0
2020–21 Wolverhampton W 21 1 **115** **8**

BRUNO JORDAO, Andre (M) **36** **5**
b.Marinha Grande 12-10-98
Internationals: Portugal U18, U19, U20, U21.
2015–16 Uniao de Leiria 23 4 **23** **4**
2016–17 Braga 0 0
2017–18 Braga 0 0
2017–18 *Lazio* 0 0
2018–19 Braga 0 0
2018–19 *Lazio* 3 0
2019–20 Lazio 0 0 **3** **0**
2019–20 Wolverhampton W 1 0
2020–21 Wolverhampton W 0 0 **1** **0**
2020–21 *Famalicao* 9 1 **9** **1**

BUENO, Hugo (D) **0** **0**
b.Vigo 18-9-02
2020–21 Wolverhampton W 0 0

BUGARIN, Erik (F) **0** **0**
b. 1-1-03
From Celta Vigo.
2020–21 Wolverhampton W 0 0

BUUR, Oskar (D) **22** **1**
b.Skanderborg 31-3-98
Internationals: Denmark U16, U17, U18, U19.
2014–15 AGF 8 0
2015–16 AGF 1 0
2016–17 AGF 1 0 **10** **0**
2017–18 Wolverhampton W 1 1
2018–19 Wolverhampton W 0 0
2019–20 Wolverhampton W 0 0
2020–21 Wolverhampton W 1 0 **2** **1**
2020–21 *Grasshoppers* 10 0 **10** **0**

CAMPANA, Leonardo (F) **9** **2**
b.Guayaquil 24-7-00
Internationals: Ecuador U20, Full caps.
2016–17 Barcelona 0 0
2017–18 Barcelona 0 0
2018–19 Barcelona 0 0
2019–20 Barcelona 0 0
2019–20 Wolverhampton W 0 0
2020–21 Wolverhampton W 0 0
2020–21 *Famalicao* 9 2 **9** **2**

CARTY, Conor (F) **0** **0**
H: 6 0 W: 11 07 b. 25-5-02
Internationals: Republic of Ireland U16, U17, U18.
2020–21 Wolverhampton W 0 0

COADY, Conor (D) **320** **10**
H: 6 1 W: 11 05 b.Liverpool 25-2-93
Internationals: England U16, U17, U18, U19, U20.
2010–11 Liverpool 0 0
2011–12 Liverpool 0 0
2012–13 Liverpool 1 0
2013–14 Liverpool 0 0 **1** **0**
2013–14 *Sheffield U* 39 5 **39** **5**
2014–15 Huddersfield T 45 3 **45** **3**
2015–16 Wolverhampton W 37 0
2016–17 Wolverhampton W 40 0
2017–18 Wolverhampton W 45 1
2018–19 Wolverhampton W 38 0
2019–20 Wolverhampton W 38 0
2020–21 Wolverhampton W 37 1 **235** **2**

CORBEANU, Theo (M) **1** **0**
b.Burlington 17-5-02
From Toronto.
2020–21 Wolverhampton W 1 0 **1** **0**

CUNDLE, Luke (M) **0** **0**
b.Warrington 26-4-02
2019–20 Wolverhampton W 0 0
2020–21 Wolverhampton W 0 0

CUTRONE, Patrick (F) **114** **19**
b.Como 3-1-98
Internationals: Italy U16, U17, U18, U19, U21, Full caps.
2016–17 AC Milan 1 0
2017–18 AC Milan 28 10
2018–19 AC Milan 34 3 **63** **13**
2019–20 Wolverhampton W 12 2
2019–20 *Fiorentina* 19 4
2020–21 Wolverhampton W 2 0 **14** **2**
2020–21 *Fiorentina* 11 0 **30** **4**
2020–21 *Valencia* 7 0 **7** **0**

DANIEL PODENCE, Castelo (F) **114** **16**
b. 21-10-95
Internationals: Portugal U16, U18, U19, U20, U21.
2012–13 Sporting Lisbon 0 0
2013–14 Sporting Lisbon 0 0
2014–15 Sporting Lisbon 0 0
2015–16 Sporting Lisbon 0 0
2016–17 Sporting Lisbon 13 0
2016–17 *Moreirense* 14 4 **14** **4**
2017–18 Sporting Lisbon 12 0 **25** **0**
2018–19 Olympiacos 27 5
2019–20 Olympiacos 15 3 **42** **8**
2019–20 Wolverhampton W 9 1
2020–21 Wolverhampton W 24 3 **33** **4**

DENDONCKER, Leander (M) **215** **16**
H: 6 2 W: 12 02 b.Passendale 15-4-95
Internationals: Belgium U16, U17, U19, U21, Full caps.
2013–14 Anderlecht 0 0
2014–15 Anderlecht 26 2
2015–16 Anderlecht 23 1
2016–17 Anderlecht 40 5
2017–18 Anderlecht 36 1 **125** **9**
2018–19 *Wolverhampton W* 19 2
2019–20 Wolverhampton W 38 4
2020–21 Wolverhampton W 33 1 **90** **7**

ESTRADA, Pascal (D) **0** **0**
H: 6 1 W: 10 10 b.Leonding 12-3-02
Internationals: Austria U18.
From Lask.
2020–21 Wolverhampton W 0 0

GIBBS-WHITE, Morgan (M) **69** **2**
b. 27-1-00
Internationals: England U16, U17, U18, U19, U21.
2016–17 Wolverhampton W 7 0
2017–18 Wolverhampton W 13 0
2018–19 Wolverhampton W 26 0
2019–20 Wolverhampton W 7 0
2020–21 Wolverhampton W 11 1 **64** **1**
2020–21 *Swansea C* 5 1 **5** **1**

GILES, Ryan (M) **62** **3**
H: 5 10 W: 11 00 b.Telford 26-1-00
Internationals: England U20.
2018–19 Wolverhampton W 0 0
2019–20 Wolverhampton W 0 0
2019–20 *Shrewsbury T* 19 1 **19** **1**
2019–20 *Coventry C* 1 0
2020–21 Wolverhampton W 0 0
2020–21 *Coventry C* 19 0 **20** **0**
2020–21 *Rotherham U* 23 2 **23** **2**

GOMES, Tote (D) **36** **2**
H: 6 2 b.Bissau 16-1-99
2018–19 Estoril 3 0
2019–20 Estoril 0 0 **3** **0**
2020–21 Wolverhampton W 0 0
2020–21 *Grosshopper* 33 2 **33** **2**

HE, Zhenyu (F) **3** **0**
H: 5 11 b.Shenyang 28-6-01
2019–20 Wolverhampton W 0 0
2020–21 Wolverhampton W 0 0
2020–21 *Beijing Guoan* 3 0 **3** **0**

HESKETH, Owen (M) **0** **0**
H: 5 11 W: 10 08 b.Manchester 10-10-02
Internationals: Wales U17.
From Manchester C.
2020–21 Wolverhampton W 0 0

HODNETT, Jack (M) **0 0**
H: 5 6 W: 9 11 b.Telford 17-1-03
Internationals: England U16.

2020–21	Wolverhampton W	0	0		

HOEVER, Ki-Jana (D) **12 0**
b.Amsterdam 18-1-02
Internationals: Netherlands U16, U17, U18.
From Ajax.

2018–19	Liverpool	0	0		
2019–20	Liverpool	0	0		
2020–21	Wolverhampton W	12	0	**12**	**0**

JIMENEZ, Raul (F) **262 82**
H: 6 2 W: 12 04 b.Tepeji 5-5-91
Internationals: Mexico U23, Full caps.

2011–12	America	15	2		
2012–13	America	29	11		
2013–14	America	27	12		
2014–15	America	4	4	**75**	**29**
2014–15	Atletico Madrid	21	1	**21**	**1**
2015–16	Benfica	28	5		
2016–17	Benfica	19	7		
2017–18	Benfica	33	6		
2018–19	Benfica	0	0	**80**	**18**
2018–19	*Wolverhampton W*	38	13		
2019–20	Wolverhampton W	38	17		
2020–21	Wolverhampton W	10	4	**86**	**34**

JOAO MOUTINHO, Felipe (M) **513 37**
H: 5 7 W: 9 08 b.Portimao 8-9-86
Internationals: Portugal U17, U18, U19, U21, B, Full caps.

2004–05	Sporting Lisbon	15	0		
2005–06	Sporting Lisbon	34	4		
2006–07	Sporting Lisbon	29	4		
2007–08	Sporting Lisbon	30	5		
2008–09	Sporting Lisbon	27	3		
2009–10	Sporting Lisbon	28	5	**163**	**21**
2010–11	Porto	27	0		
2011–12	Porto	29	3		
2012–13	Porto	27	1	**83**	**4**
2013–14	Monaco	31	1		
2014–15	Monaco	37	4		
2015–16	Monaco	26	1		
2016–17	Monaco	31	2		
2017–18	Monaco	33	1	**158**	**9**
2018–19	Wolverhampton W	38	1		
2019–20	Wolverhampton W	38	1		
2020–21	Wolverhampton W	33	1	**109**	**3**

JONNY, Castro (D) **258 6**
H: 5 9 W: 11 00 b.Vigo 3-3-94
Internationals: Spain U18, U19, U20, U21, Full caps.

2011–12	Celta Vigo	0	0		
2012–13	Celta Vigo	19	0		
2013–14	Celta Vigo	26	0		
2014–15	Celta Vigo	36	0		
2015–16	Celta Vigo	36	1		
2016–17	Celta Vigo	30	0		
2017–18	Celta Vigo	36	2	**183**	**3**
2018–19	Atletico Madrid	0	0		
2018–19	*Wolverhampton W*	33	1		
2019–20	Wolverhampton W	35	2		
2020–21	Wolverhampton W	7	0	**75**	**3**

KILMAN, Max (D) **22 0**
b.London 23-5-97
From Welling U, Maidenhead U.

2018–19	Wolverhampton W	1	0		
2019–20	Wolverhampton W	3	0		
2020–21	Wolverhampton W	18	0	**22**	**0**

LONWIJK, Nigel (D) **0 0**
b.Goirle 27-10-02
From PSV Eindhoven.

2020–21	Wolverhampton W	0	0		

MARCAL, Fernando (D) **247 5**
b.Sao Paulo 19-2-89

2010	Guaratingueta	3	0	**3**	**0**
2010–11	Torreense	28	2		
2011–12	Torreense	12	1	**40**	**3**
2011–12	Nacional	14	0		
2012–13	Nacional	27	0		
2013–14	Nacional	27	2		
2014–15	Nacional	29	0	**97**	**2**
2015–16	Benfica	0	0		
2015–16	*Gaziantepspor*	21	0	**21**	**0**
2016–17	Benfica	0	0		
2016–17	*Guingamp*	31	0	**31**	**0**
2017–18	Lyon	18	0		
2018–19	Lyon	12	0		
2019–20	Lyon	11	0		
2020–21	Lyon	1	0	**42**	**0**
2020–21	Wolverhampton W	13	0	**13**	**0**

MARQUES, Christian (D) **0 0**
b.Uster 15-1-03
From Grasshopper.

2020–21	Wolverhampton W	0	0		

MATHESON, Luke (D) **25 1**
b.Manchester 3-10-02
Internationals: England U17, U18.

2018–19	Rochdale	3	0		
2019–20	Wolverhampton W	0	0		
2019–20	*Rochdale*	20	1	**23**	**1**
2020–21	Wolverhampton W	0	0		
2020–21	*Ipswich T*	2	0	**2**	**0**

NELSON SEMEDO, Cabral (D) **214 10**
b.Lisbon 16-11-93

2011–12	Sintrense	26	5	**26**	**5**
2012–13	Benfica	0	0		
2012–13	*Fatima*	29	0	**29**	**0**
2013–14	Benfica	0	0		
2014–15	Benfica	0	0		
2015–16	Benfica	12	1		
2016–17	Benfica	31	1	**43**	**2**
2017–18	Barcelona	24	0		
2018–19	Barcelona	26	1		
2019–20	Barcelona	32	1		
2020–21	Barcelona	0	0	**82**	**2**
2020–21	Wolverhampton W	34	1	**34**	**1**

NEVES, Ruben (M) **210 20**
H: 5 11 W: 12 08 b. 13-3-97
Internationals: Portugal U16, U17, U18, U21, U23, Full caps.

2014–15	Porto	24	1		
2015–16	Porto	22	1		
2016–17	Porto	13	1	**59**	**3**
2017–18	Wolverhampton W	42	6		
2018–19	Wolverhampton W	35	4		
2019–20	Wolverhampton W	38	2		
2020–21	Wolverhampton W	36	5	**151**	**17**

NYA, Raphael (D) **0 0**
H: 6 0 W: 10 10 b. 16-6-00
From Paris Saint-Germain.

2020–21	Wolverhampton W	0	0		

O'SHAUGHNESSY, Joseph (G) **0 0**
H: 6 6 b.Warrington 5-1-03
From Burnley.

2020–21	Wolverhampton W	0	0		

OTASOWIE, Owen (M) **6 0**
b. 20-4-01
Internationals: USA U18.

2019–20	Wolverhampton W	0	0		
2020–21	Wolverhampton W	6	0	**6**	**0**

PARDINGTON, James (G) **2 0**
b. 20-7-00
From Rushall.

2018–19	Wolverhampton W	0	0		
2019–20	Wolverhampton W	0	0		
2020–21	Wolverhampton W	0	0		
2020–21	*Mansfield T*	2	0	**2**	**0**

PEDRO NETO, Lomba (M) **67 9**
b.Viana do Castelo 9-3-00
Internationals: Portugal U17, U18, U19, U20, U21.

2016–17	Braga	2	1		
2017–18	Braga	1	0		
2018–19	Braga	0	0	**3**	**1**
2018–19	*Lazio*	4	0	**4**	**0**
2019–20	Wolverhampton W	29	3		
2020–21	Wolverhampton W	31	5	**60**	**8**

PERRY, Taylor (M) **0 0**
b. 15-8-01

2019–20	Wolverhampton W	0	0		
2020–21	Wolverhampton W	0	0		

RICHARDS, Lewis (D) **0 0**
Internationals: Republic of Ireland U19.

2019–20	Wolverhampton W	0	0		
2020–21	Wolverhampton W	0	0		

RUBEN VINAGRE, Goncalo (D) **66 1**
b. 9-4-99
Internationals: Portugal U16, U17, U18, U19, U20, U21.

2016–17	Monaco	0	0		
2017–18	Monaco	0	0		
2017–18	*Wolverhampton W*	9	1		
2018–19	Wolverhampton W	17	0		
2019–20	Wolverhampton W	16	0		
2020–21	Wolverhampton W	2	0	**44**	**1**
2020–21	*Olympiacos*	2	0	**2**	**0**
2020–21	*Famalicao*	20	0	**20**	**0**

RUDDY, John (G) **417 0**
H: 6 3 W: 12 07 b.St Ives 24-10-86
Internationals: England Full caps.

2003–04	Cambridge U	1	0		
2004–05	Cambridge U	38	0	**39**	**0**
2005–06	Everton	1	0		
2005–06	*Walsall*	5	0	**5**	**0**
2005–06	*Rushden & D*	3	0	**3**	**0**
2005–06	*Chester C*	4	0	**4**	**0**
2006–07	Everton	0	0		
2006–07	*Stockport Co*	11	0		
2006–07	*Wrexham*	5	0	**5**	**0**
2006–07	*Bristol C*	1	0	**1**	**0**
2007–08	Everton	0	0		
2007–08	*Stockport Co*	12	0	**23**	**0**
2008–09	Everton	0	0		
2008–09	*Crewe Alex*	19	0	**19**	**0**
2009–10	Everton	0	0	**1**	**0**
2009–10	*Motherwell*	34	0	**34**	**0**
2010–11	Norwich C	45	0		
2011–12	Norwich C	37	0		
2012–13	Norwich C	15	0		
2013–14	Norwich C	38	0		
2014–15	Norwich C	46	0		
2015–16	Norwich C	27	0		
2016–17	Norwich C	27	0	**235**	**0**
2017–18	Wolverhampton W	45	0		
2018–19	Wolverhampton W	1	0		
2019–20	Wolverhampton W	0	0		
2020–21	Wolverhampton W	2	0	**48**	**0**

RUI PATRICIO, Pedro (G) **439 0**
H: 6 2 W: 13 03 b.Marrazes 15-2-88
Internationals: Portugal U16, U17, U18, U19, U20, U21, Full caps.

2006–07	Sporting Lisbon	1	0		
2007–08	Sporting Lisbon	20	0		
2008–09	Sporting Lisbon	26	0		
2009–10	Sporting Lisbon	30	0		
2010–11	Sporting Lisbon	30	0		
2011–12	Sporting Lisbon	28	0		
2012–13	Sporting Lisbon	30	0		
2013–14	Sporting Lisbon	30	0		
2014–15	Sporting Lisbon	33	0		
2015–16	Sporting Lisbon	34	0		
2016–17	Sporting Lisbon	31	0		
2017–18	Sporting Lisbon	34	0	**327**	**0**
2018–19	Wolverhampton W	37	0		
2019–20	Wolverhampton W	38	0		
2020–21	Wolverhampton W	37	0	**112**	**0**

SAISS, Romain (M) **302 21**
H: 6 3 W: 12 00 b.Bourg-de-Peage 26-3-90
Internationals: Morocco Full caps.

2010–11	Valence	13	4	**13**	**4**
2011–12	Clermont	17	1		
2012–13	Clermont	31	0	**48**	**1**
2013–14	Le Havre	27	1		
2014–15	Le Havre	34	2	**61**	**3**
2015–16	Angers	35	2	**35**	**2**
2016–17	Wolverhampton W	24	0		
2017–18	Wolverhampton W	42	4		
2018–19	Wolverhampton W	19	2		
2019–20	Wolverhampton W	33	2		
2020–21	Wolverhampton W	27	3	**145**	**11**

SAMUELS, Austin (F) **12 0**
b. 20-11-00
Internationals: England U16.

2019–20	Wolverhampton W	0	0		
2020–21	Wolverhampton W	0	0		
2020–21	*Bradford C*	12	0	**12**	**0**

SANDERSON, Dion (M) **36 1**
b. 15-12-99

2019–20	Wolverhampton W	0	0		
2019–20	*Cardiff C*	10	0	**10**	**0**
2020–21	Wolverhampton W	0	0		
2020–21	*Sunderland*	26	1	**26**	**1**

SARKIC, Matija (G) **40 0**
H: 6 4 W: 11 07 b.Podgorica 23-6-97
Internationals: Montenegro U17, U19, U21, Full caps.

2014–15	Anderlecht	0	0		
2015–16	Aston Villa	0	0		
2016–17	Aston Villa	0	0		
2017–18	Aston Villa	0	0		
2017–18	*Wigan Ath*	0	0		
2018–19	Aston Villa	0	0		
2019–20	Aston Villa	0	0		
2019–20	*Livingston*	14	0	**14**	**0**
2020–21	Wolverhampton W	0	0		
2020–21	*Shrewsbury T*	26	0	**26**	**0**

SCOTT, Jack (D) **0 0**
H: 6 0 W: 11 11 b. 22-9-02
Internationals: Northern Ireland U17, U21.
From Linfield.

2020–21	Wolverhampton W	0	0		

SHABANI, Meritan (M) **7 0**
b.Munich 15-3-99

2017–18	Bayern Munich	1	0		
2018–19	Bayern Munich	1	0	**2**	**0**
2019–20	Wolverhampton W	0	0		
2020–21	Wolverhampton W	0	0		
2020–21	*VVV Venlo*	5	0	**5**	**0**

SILVA, Fabio (F) **44 5**
b.Porto 19-7-02

2019–20	Porto	12	1	**12**	**1**
2020–21	Wolverhampton W	32	4	**32**	**4**

SONDERGAARD, Andreas (G) **0 0**
b. 17-1-01
Internationals: Denmark U16, U17, U18, U19.
From Odense.

2019–20	Wolverhampton W	0	0		
2020–21	Wolverhampton W	0	0		

TIPTON, Ollie (D) **0 0**
b.Wolverhampton 22-9-03

2020–21	Wolverhampton W	0	0		

TRAORE, Adama (F) **176 12**
H: 5 10 W: 12 00 b.L'Hospitalet de Llobregat 25-1-96
Internationals: Spain U16, U17, U19, U21.

2013–14	Barcelona	1	0		
2014–15	Barcelona	0	0	**1**	**0**
2015–16	Aston Villa	10	0		
2016–17	Aston Villa	1	0	**11**	**0**
2016–17	Middlesbrough	27	0		
2017–18	Middlesbrough	34	5	**61**	**5**
2018–19	Wolverhampton W	29	1		
2019–20	Wolverhampton W	37	4		
2020–21	Wolverhampton W	37	2	**103**	**7**

VITINHA, Ferreira (M) **27 0**
b.Povoa 13-2-00

2019–20	Porto	8	0		
2020–21	Porto	0	0	**8**	**0**

On loan from Porto.

2020–21	Wolverhampton W	19	0	**19**	**0**

WILLIAN JOSE, da Silva (F) **288 78**
b.Porto Calvo 23-11-91

2009	Barueri	7	0		
2010	Barueri	19	6		
2011	Barueri	0	0		
2011	*Sao Paulo*	9	0		
2012	Barueri	0	0		
2012	*Sao Paulo*	19	1	**28**	**1**
2013	Barueri	0	0		
2013	*Gremio*	0	0		
2013	*Santos*	23	5	**23**	**5**
2013–14	Barueri	0	0		
2013–14	*Real Madrid*	1	0	**1**	**0**
2014–15	Barueri	0	0		
2014–15	*Real Zaragoza*	33	7	**33**	**7**
2015–16	Barueri	0	0	**26**	**6**
2015–16	*Las Palmas*	30	9	**30**	**9**
2016–17	Real Sociedad	28	12		
2017–18	Real Sociedad	34	15		
2018–19	Real Sociedad	31	11		
2019–20	Real Sociedad	37	11		
2020–21	Real Sociedad	0	0	**130**	**49**

On loan from Real Sociedad.

2020–21	Wolverhampton W	17	1	**17**	**1**

YOUNG, Joe (G) **0 0**
H: 5 10 W: 11 11 b.Telford 22-9-02
Internationals: England U17.

2020–21	Wolverhampton W	0	0		

Scholars
Birtwistle, Ryan James Harry; Diyawa, Aaron Keto; Forrester, Jaden Joshua; Kandola, Kamran; Lembikisa, Dexter Joeng Woo; Pinnington, Dean Stanley; Roberts, Tyler; Sangare, Faisu.

WYCOMBE W (92)

AKINFENWA, Adebayo (F) **652 195**
H: 5 11 W: 13 07 b.Nigeria 10-5-82

2001	Atlantas	18	4		
2002	Atlantas	4	1	**22**	**5**

From Barry T.

2003–04	Boston U	3	0	**3**	**0**
2003–04	Leyton Orient	1	0	**1**	**0**
2003–04	Rushden & D	0	0		
2003–04	Doncaster R	9	4	**9**	**4**
2004–05	Torquay U	37	14	**37**	**14**
2005–06	Swansea C	34	9		
2006–07	Swansea C	25	5		
2007–08	Swansea C	0	0	**59**	**14**
2007–08	Millwall	7	0	**7**	**0**
2007–08	Northampton T	15	7		
2008–09	Northampton T	33	13		
2009–10	Northampton T	40	17		
2010–11	Gillingham	44	11		
2011–12	Northampton T	39	18		
2012–13	Northampton T	41	16	**168**	**71**
2013–14	Gillingham	34	10	**78**	**21**
2014–15	AFC Wimbledon	45	13		
2015–16	AFC Wimbledon	38	6	**83**	**19**
2016–17	Wycombe W	42	12		
2017–18	Wycombe W	42	17		
2018–19	Wycombe W	36	7		
2019–20	Wycombe W	32	10		
2020–21	Wycombe W	33	1	**185**	**47**

ALLSOP, Ryan (G) **231 2**
H: 6 2 W: 12 06 b.Birmingham 17-6-92
Internationals: England U17.

2009–10	WBA	0	0		
2010–11	WBA	0	0		
2011–12	Millwall	0	0		
2012	Hottur	8	2	**8**	**2**
2012–13	Leyton Orient	20	0	**20**	**0**
2012–13	Bournemouth	10	0		
2013–14	Bournemouth	12	0		
2014–15	Bournemouth	0	0		
2014–15	*Coventry C*	24	0	**24**	**0**
2015–16	Bournemouth	1	0		
2015–16	*Wycombe W*	18	0		
2015–16	*Portsmouth*	0	0		
2016–17	Bournemouth	1	0		
2017–18	Bournemouth	0	0	**24**	**0**
2017–18	*Blackpool*	22	0	**22**	**0**
2017–18	*Lincoln C*	16	0	**16**	**0**
2018–19	Wycombe W	38	0		
2019–20	Wycombe W	32	0		
2020–21	Wycombe W	29	0	**117**	**0**

ANDERSON, Curtis (G) **0 0**
From Manchester C, Charlotte Independence.

2020–21	Wycombe W	0	0		

BLOOMFIELD, Matt (M) **486 39**
H: 5 9 W: 11 00 b.Felixstowe 8-2-84
Internationals: England U19.

2001–02	Ipswich T	0	0		
2002–03	Ipswich T	0	0		
2003–04	Ipswich T	0	0		
2003–04	Wycombe W	12	1		
2004–05	Wycombe W	26	2		
2005–06	Wycombe W	39	5		
2006–07	Wycombe W	41	4		
2007–08	Wycombe W	35	4		
2008–09	Wycombe W	20	0		
2009–10	Wycombe W	14	2		
2010–11	Wycombe W	34	3		
2011–12	Wycombe W	31	2		
2012–13	Wycombe W	2	1		
2013–14	Wycombe W	32	0		
2014–15	Wycombe W	33	1		
2015–16	Wycombe W	27	1		
2016–17	Wycombe W	33	5		
2017–18	Wycombe W	37	3		
2018–19	Wycombe W	28	2		
2019–20	Wycombe W	26	2		
2020–21	Wycombe W	16	1	**486**	**39**

BURLEY, Andre (D) **3 0**

2019–20	Reading	0	0		
2020	*Waterford*	3	0	**3**	**0**
2020–21	Wycombe W	0	0		

CHARLES, Darius (M) **290 18**
H: 6 1 W: 13 05 b.Ealing 10-12-87
Internationals: England C.

2004–05	Brentford	1	0		
2005–06	Brentford	2	0		
2006–07	Brentford	17	1		
2007–08	Brentford	17	0	**37**	**1**

From Ebbsfleet U.

2010–11	Stevenage	28	2		
2011–12	Stevenage	28	4		
2012–13	Stevenage	37	1		
2013–14	Stevenage	22	4		
2014–15	Stevenage	29	2	**144**	**13**
2015–16	Burton Alb	0	0		
2015–16	*AFC Wimbledon*	9	0		
2016–17	AFC Wimbledon	34	2		
2017–18	AFC Wimbledon	31	0	**74**	**2**
2018–19	Wycombe W	5	0		
2019–20	Wycombe W	25	2		
2020–21	Wycombe W	5	0	**35**	**2**

CLARK, James (D) **0 0**
b.Ealing 5-9-01
From Chelsea.

2020–21	Wycombe W	0	0		

FREEMAN, Nick (M) **116 5**
b. 7-11-95
From Histon, Hemel Hempstead T, Biggleswade T.

2016–17	Wycombe W	14	0		
2017–18	Wycombe W	27	3		
2018–19	Wycombe W	27	0		
2019–20	Wycombe W	26	2		
2020–21	Wycombe W	7	0	**101**	**5**
2020–21	*Leyton Orient*	15	0	**15**	**0**

GAPE, Dominic (M) **153 3**
H: 5 11 W: 10 13 b.Southampton 9-9-94

2012–13	Southampton	0	0		
2013–14	Southampton	0	0		
2014–15	Southampton	1	0		
2015–16	Southampton	0	0		
2016–17	Southampton	0	0	**1**	**0**
2016–17	Wycombe W	32	1		
2017–18	Wycombe W	35	1		
2018–19	Wycombe W	43	1		
2019–20	Wycombe W	28	0		
2020–21	Wycombe W	14	0	**152**	**3**

GRIMMER, Jack (M) **192 3**
H: 6 0 W: 12 06 b.Aberdeen 25-1-94
Internationals: Scotland U16, U17, U18, U19, U21.

2009–10	Aberdeen	2	0		
2010–11	Aberdeen	2	0		
2011–12	Aberdeen	0	0	**4**	**0**
2011–12	Fulham	0	0		
2012–13	Fulham	0	0		
2013–14	Fulham	0	0		
2013–14	*Port Vale*	13	1	**13**	**1**
2014–15	Fulham	13	0		
2014–15	*Shrewsbury T*	6	0		
2015–16	Fulham	0	0		
2015–16	*Shrewsbury T*	21	1		
2016–17	Fulham	0	0	**13**	**0**
2016–17	*Shrewsbury T*	24	0	**51**	**1**
2017–18	Coventry C	42	1		
2018–19	Coventry C	11	0	**53**	**1**
2019–20	Wycombe W	18	0		
2020–21	Wycombe W	40	0	**58**	**0**

HORGAN, Daryl (M) **142 9**
H: 5 7 W: 10 10 b.Galway 10-8-92
Internationals: Republic of Ireland U19, U21, Full caps.
From Dundalk.

2016–17	Preston NE	19	2		
2017–18	Preston NE	20	1		
2018–19	Preston NE	1	0	**40**	**3**
2018–19	Hibernian	34	3		
2019–20	Hibernian	28	3		
2020–21	Hibernian	0	0	**62**	**6**
2020–21	Wycombe W	40	0	**40**	**0**

IKPEAZU, Uche (F) **212 41**
H: 6 3 W: 12 04 b.London 28-2-95

2011–12	Reading	0	0		
2012–13	Reading	0	0		
2013–14	Watford	0	0		
2013–14	*Crewe Alex*	15	4		
2014–15	Watford	0	0		
2014–15	*Crewe Alex*	17	2	**32**	**6**
2014–15	*Doncaster R*	7	0	**7**	**0**
2015–16	Watford	0	0		
2015–16	*Port Vale*	21	5	**21**	**5**
2015–16	*Blackpool*	12	0	**12**	**0**
2016–17	Cambridge U	29	6		
2017–18	Cambridge U	40	13	**69**	**19**
2018–19	Hearts	17	3		
2019–20	Hearts	23	2	**40**	**5**
2020–21	Wycombe W	31	6	**31**	**6**

JACOBSON, Joe (D) **496 44**
H: 5 11 W: 12 06 b.Cardiff 17-11-86
Internationals: Wales U21.

2005–06	Cardiff C	1	0		
2006–07	Cardiff C	0	0	**1**	**0**
2006–07	*Accrington S*	6	1		
2006–07	*Bristol R*	11	0		
2007–08	Bristol R	40	1		
2008–09	Bristol R	22	0	**73**	**1**
2009–10	Oldham Ath	15	0		
2010–11	Oldham Ath	1	0	**16**	**0**
2010–11	Accrington S	26	2	**32**	**3**
2011–12	Shrewsbury T	39	1		
2012–13	Shrewsbury T	30	2		
2013–14	Shrewsbury T	41	4	**110**	**7**
2014–15	Wycombe W	42	3		
2015–16	Wycombe W	34	1		
2016–17	Wycombe W	39	3		
2017–18	Wycombe W	46	6		
2018–19	Wycombe W	36	7		
2019–20	Wycombe W	30	9		
2020–21	Wycombe W	37	4	**264**	**33**

KASHKET, Scott (M) **121 23**
H: 5 9 W: 10 06 b.London 6-7-95

2014–15	Leyton Orient	1	0		
2015–16	Leyton Orient	15	1		
2016–17	Leyton Orient	0	0	**16**	**1**
2016–17	Wycombe W	21	10		
2017–18	Wycombe W	9	1		
2018–19	Wycombe W	27	3		
2019–20	Wycombe W	19	4		
2020–21	Wycombe W	29	4	**105**	**22**

LINTON, Malachi (F) **0 0**
From Ipswich T, Crewe Alex, Lowestoft.

2020–21	Wycombe W	0	0		

McCARTHY, Jason (D) **182 12**
H: 6 1 W: 12 08 b.Southampton 7-11-95

2013–14	Southampton	0	0		
2014–15	Southampton	1	0		
2015–16	Southampton	0	0		
2015–16	*Wycombe W*	35	2		

2016–17	Southampton	0	0	**1**	**0**
2016–17	*Walsall*	46	5	**46**	**5**
2017–18	Barnsley	21	0	**21**	**0**
2018–19	Wycombe W	44	2		
2019–20	Millwall	2	0	**2**	**0**
2019–20	*Wycombe W*	9	1		
2020–21	Wycombe W	24	2	**112**	**7**

McCLEARY, Garath (M) **385** **40**
H: 5 10 W: 12 06 b.Oxford 15-5-87
Internationals: Jamaica Full caps.
From Oxford C, Slough T, Bromley.

2007–08	Nottingham F	8	1		
2008–09	Nottingham F	39	1		
2009–10	Nottingham F	24	0		
2010–11	Nottingham F	18	2		
2011–12	Nottingham F	22	9	**111**	**13**
2011–12	Reading	0	0		
2012–13	Reading	31	3		
2013–14	Reading	42	5		
2014–15	Reading	26	1		
2015–16	Reading	34	4		
2016–17	Reading	41	9		
2017–18	Reading	18	0		
2018–19	Reading	31	0		
2019–20	Reading	19	1	**242**	**23**
2020–21	Wycombe W	32	4	**32**	**4**

MEHMETI, Anis (M) **29** **3**
b. 9-1-01

2019–20	Norwich C	0	0		
2020–21	Wycombe W	29	3	**29**	**3**

OBITA, Jordan (M) **211** **10**
H: 5 11 W: 11 08 b.Oxford 8-12-93
Internationals: England U18, U19, U21.

2010–11	Reading	0	0		
2011–12	Reading	0	0		
2011–12	*Barnet*	5	0	**5**	**0**
2011–12	*Gillingham*	6	3	**6**	**3**
2012–13	Reading	0	0		
2012–13	*Portsmouth*	8	1	**8**	**1**
2012–13	*Oldham Ath*	8	0	**8**	**0**
2013–14	Reading	34	1		
2014–15	Reading	43	0		
2015–16	Reading	26	0		
2016–17	Reading	37	2		
2017–18	Reading	2	0		
2018–19	Reading	0	0		
2019–20	Reading	21	2		
2020–21	Reading	0	0	**163**	**5**
2020–21	Oxford U	12	1	**12**	**1**
2020–21	Wycombe W	9	0	**9**	**0**

ONYEDINMA, Fred (M) **222** **27**
H: 6 1 b.London 24-11-96

2013–14	Millwall	4	0		
2014–15	Millwall	2	0		
2014–15	*Wycombe W*	25	8		
2015–16	Millwall	34	4		
2016–17	Millwall	42	3		
2017–18	Millwall	37	1		
2018–19	Millwall	1	0	**120**	**8**
2018–19	*Wycombe W*	21	4		
2019–20	Wycombe W	13	4		
2020–21	Wycombe W	43	3	**102**	**19**

PATTISON, Alex (F) **52** **0**
b. 6-9-97

2016–17	Middlesbrough	0	0		
2017–18	Middlesbrough	0	0		
2018–19	Middlesbrough	0	0		
2018–19	*Yeovil T*	29	0	**29**	**0**
2019–20	Wycombe W	17	0		
2020–21	Wycombe W	6	0	**23**	**0**

PHILLIPS, Giles (D) **11** **0**

2018–19	QPR	0	0		
2019–20	*Wycombe W*	11	0		
2020–21	Wycombe W	0	0	**11**	**0**

SAMUEL, Alex (F) **138** **10**
H: 6 0 W: 11 11 b.Neath 20-9-95
Internationals: Wales U18.
From Aberystwyth T.

2014–15	Swansea C	0	0		
2015–16	Swansea C	0	0		
2015–16	*Greenock Morton*	26	2	**26**	**2**
2016–17	Swansea C	0	0		
2016–17	*Newport Co*	18	2	**18**	**2**
2017–18	Stevenage	22	0	**22**	**0**
2018–19	Wycombe W	30	5		
2019–20	Wycombe W	21	1		
2020–21	Wycombe W	21	0	**72**	**6**

STEWART, Anthony (D) **224** **10**
H: 5 10 W: 12 03 b.Brixton 18-9-92

2011–12	Wycombe W	4	0		
2012–13	Wycombe W	19	1		
2013–14	Wycombe W	33	3		
2014–15	Crewe Alex	10	0	**10**	**0**
2015–16	Wycombe W	27	1		
2016–17	Wycombe W	31	1		
2017–18	Wycombe W	17	1		
2018–19	Wycombe W	17	0		
2019–20	Wycombe W	34	2		
2020–21	Wycombe W	32	1	**214**	**10**

STOCKDALE, David (G) **366** **0**
H: 6 3 W: 13 04 b.Leeds 20-9-85
Internationals: England C.

2002–03	York C	1	0		
2003–04	York C	0	0		
2004–05	York C	0	0		
2005–06	York C	0	0	**1**	**0**
2006–07	Darlington	6	0		
2007–08	Darlington	41	0	**47**	**0**
2008–09	Fulham	0	0		
2008–09	*Rotherham U*	8	0	**8**	**0**
2008–09	*Leicester C*	8	0	**8**	**0**
2009–10	Fulham	1	0		
2009–10	*Plymouth Arg*	21	0	**21**	**0**
2010–11	Fulham	7	0		
2011–12	Fulham	8	0		
2011–12	*Ipswich T*	18	0	**18**	**0**
2012–13	Fulham	2	0		
2012–13	*Hull C*	24	0	**24**	**0**
2013–14	Fulham	21	0	**39**	**0**
2014–15	Brighton & HA	42	0		
2015–16	Brighton & HA	46	0		
2016–17	Brighton & HA	45	0	**133**	**0**
2017–18	Birmingham C	36	0		
2018–19	Birmingham C	0	0	**36**	**0**
2018–19	*Southend U*	3	0	**3**	**0**
2018–19	*Wycombe W*	2	0		
2018–19	*Coventry C*	2	0	**2**	**0**
2019–20	Wycombe W	2	0		
2020–21	Wycombe W	17	0	**21**	**0**
2020–21	*Stevenage*	5	0	**5**	**0**

TAFAZOLLI, Ryan (D) **240** **17**
H: 6 5 W: 12 03 b.Sutton 28-9-91

2010–11	Southampton	0	0		

From Concorde Rangers, Cambridge C.

2013–14	Mansfield T	24	2		
2014–15	Mansfield T	36	1		
2015–16	Mansfield T	44	5	**104**	**8**
2016–17	Peterborough U	31	3		
2017–18	Peterborough U	33	1		
2018–19	Peterborough U	37	1	**101**	**5**
2019–20	Hull C	15	2	**15**	**2**
2020–21	Wycombe W	20	2	**20**	**2**

THOMPSON, Curtis (M) **183** **3**
H: 5 10 W: 12 06 b.Nottingham 2-9-93
From Lincoln C.

2011–12	Notts Co	0	0		
2012–13	Notts Co	2	0		
2013–14	Notts Co	11	0		
2014–15	Notts Co	31	0		
2015–16	Notts Co	26	2		
2016–17	Notts Co	13	0		
2017–18	Notts Co	0	0	**83**	**2**
2017–18	*Wycombe W*	7	0		
2018–19	Wycombe W	39	1		
2019–20	Wycombe W	21	0		
2020–21	Wycombe W	33	0	**100**	**1**

WHEELER, David (M) **259** **44**
H: 5 11 W: 12 00 b.Brighton 4-10-90
From Brighton & HA.

2013–14	Exeter C	35	3		
2014–15	Exeter C	45	7		
2015–16	Exeter C	31	6		
2016–17	Exeter C	38	17		
2017–18	Exeter C	2	0	**151**	**33**
2017–18	QPR	9	1		
2018–19	QPR	0	0	**9**	**1**
2018–19	*Portsmouth*	11	0	**11**	**0**
2018–19	*Milton Keynes D*	19	4	**19**	**4**
2019–20	Wycombe W	31	3		
2020–21	Wycombe W	38	3	**69**	**6**

YATES, Cameron (G) **0** **0**
b.Edinburgh 14-2-99
From Leicester C.

2018–19	Wycombe W	0	0		
2019–20	Wycombe W	0	0		
2020–21	Wycombe W	0	0		

ENGLISH LEAGUE PLAYERS – INDEX

Aarons, Maximillian 59
Aarons, Rolando 40
Aasgaard, Thelo 90
Abbey, Nelson 69
Ablade, Terry 36
Abldeen-Goodridge, Tristan 4
Abraham, Tammy 23
Abraham, Timmy 36
Abrahams, Tristan 57
Abu, Derrick 23
Acquah, Emile 78
Adams, Che 77
Adams, Ebou 35
Adams, Joe 13
Adams, Nicky 61
Adarabioyo, Tosin 36
Adaramola, Omotayo 29
Addai, Alex 24
Addai, Corey 5
Addy, TQ 48
Adebambo, Gabriel 80
Adebayo, Elijah 48
Adebisi, Rio 28
Adebowale, Emmanuel 27
Adeboyejo, Victor 5
Adedoja, Tayo 78
Adedoyin, Korede 75
Adegoke, Prince 23
Adelakun, Hakeeb 15
Adeniran, Dennis 32
Adlard, Luis 38
Adomah, Albert 68
Adrian 47
Adubofour-Poku, Kwame 25
Afobe, Benik 80
Afolayan, Oladapo 10
Agard, Kieran 54
Agboola, Michael 91
Aghatise, Osazee 30
Agnew, Liam 39
Aguero, Sergio 49
Agyakwa, Derek 87
Agyei, Daniel 62
Ahadme, Gassan 59
Ahearne-Grant, Karlan 88
Aidoo, Kasim 22
Aimson, Will 64
Aina, Ola 36
Ainley, Callum 28
Ait Nouri, Rayan 91
Aitchison, Jack 5
Ajayi, Semi 88
Ajose, Joseph 69
Ajose, Nicholas 33
Akande, Adrian 82
Ake, Nathan 49
Akinde, John 37
Akinfenwa, Adebayo 92
Akinola, Simeon 78
Akinola, Tim 3
Akinola, Tunji 89
Akins, Lucas 18
Akinwande, Femi 79
Akpom, Chuba 52
Akrobar-Boateng, David 29
Al-Hamadi, Ali 82
Al-Hussaini, Zaid 27
Albrighton, Marc 44
Alderweireld, Toby 84
Alebiosu, Ryan 3
Alese, Ajibola 89
Alessandra, Lewis 21
Alex Telles, Nicolao 50
Alexander, Cheye 2
Alexander, George 53
Alexander, Matthew 10
Alexander-Arnold, Trent 47
Alfa, Ody 68
Alioski, Ezgjan 43
Alisson, Ramses 47
Allan, Marques 32
Allan, Thomas 56
Allarakhia, Tarryn 27
Allen, Charlie 43
Allen, Jamie 26
Allen, Joe 80
Allen, Taylor 35
Alli, Bamidele 84
Allsop, Ryan 92
Almiron, Miguel 56
Almond, Patrick 81
Alonso, Marcus 23
Aluko, Sone 69
Alvarado, Jamie 87
Alves, Frederik 89
Alves, Frederik 89
Alzate, Steve 14
Amankwah, Yeboah 49
Amartey, Daniel 44
Ameobi, Sammy 60
Ameyaw, Eric 36
Aminu, Mohammed 49
Amissah, Jordan 74
Amoateng, Bright 10
Amond, Padraig 57
Amoo, David 65
Amos, Ben 22
Amos, Danny 31
Amos, Luke 68
Ampadu, Ethan 23
Andersen, Joachim 36
Andersen, Mads 5
Anderson, Curtis 92
Anderson, Elliot 56
Anderson, Harry 46
Anderson, Jevan 18
Anderson, Keshi 9
Anderson, Thomas 31
Andersson, Edwin 23
Andersson, Jokull 69
Anderton, Nick 21
Ando, Cerny 72
Andoh, Levi 42
Andone, Florin 14
Andrade, Bruno 72
Andre, Alexis 16
Andre Gomes, Filipe 32
Andre Mendes, Filipe Silva 55
Andres, Prieto 7
Andresson, Jokull 69
Andrew, Calvin 6
Andrew, Danny 34
Andrews, Corie 2
Andrews, Josh 7
Aneke, Chuks 22
Angol, Lee 45
Angus, Dior 6
Anifowose, Joshua 62
Anjorin, Faustino 23
Annesley, Louie 8
Anthony, Jaidon 11
Antonio, Michael 89
Antwi, Cameron 9
Aouachira, Wassim 22
Appiah, Paul 4
Appiah-Forson, Keenan 89
Apter, Robert 9
Arai, Yasin 79
Arblaster, Oliver 74
Archer, Jordan 52
Archibald, Theo 46
Areola, Alphonse 36
Arinbjornsson, Palmi 91
Aris, Nigel 76
Armer, Jack 21
Armin, Albie 42
Armitage, Tom 18
Armstrong, Adam 8
Armstrong, Jamie 21
Armstrong, Liam 16
Armstrong, Luke 72
Armstrong, Sinclair 68
Armstrong, Stuart 77
Arnold, Steve 58
Arriola, Paul 82
Arrizabalaga, Kepa 23
Arroyo, Anderson 47
Arter, Harry 60
Arthur, Festus 41
Ashby, Harrison 89
Ashby-Hammond, Taye 36
Ashford, Sam 27
Ashley-Seal, Benny 58
Asonganyi, Dylan 62
Asoro, Joel 82
Assal, Ayoub 2
Assarsson, Markus 10
Assombalonga, Britt 52
Astley, Ryan 32
Atangana, Nigel 33
Atkinson, Robert 62
Atsu, Christian 56
Aubameyang, Pierre-Emerick 3
Aurier, Serge 84
Austerfield, Joshua 40
Austin, Brandon 84
Austin, Charlie 88
Awe, Zacharia 3
Awoniyi, Taiwo 47
Ayala, Daniel 8
Ayew, Andre 82
Ayew, Jordan 29
Ayina, Loick 40
Ayling, Luke 43
Ayunga, Jonah 16
Azaz, Finn 88
Azeez, Femi 69
Azeez, Miguel 3
Azpilicueta, Cesar 23
Baah, Kwadwo 70
Bachirou, Fouad 60
Bachmann, Daniel 87
Back, Finley 60
Bacuna, Juninho 40
Bacuna, Leandro 20
Badan, Andrea 61
Bagan, Joel 20
Baggley, Barry 34
Baggott, Elkan 42
Bahamboula, Dylan 61
Bailey, Eden 65
Bailey, Joshua 54
Bailey, Odin 7
Bailly, Eric 50
Bakayoko, Amadou 26
Baker, Ashley 57
Baker, Harry 73
Baker, Nathan 15
Bakinson, Tyreeq 15
Balagizi, James 47
Balbuena, Fabian 89
Balcombe, Ellery 13
Balde, Alberto 52
Baldock, George 74
Baldock, Sam 69
Baldwin, Jack 16
Bale, Gareth 84
Ball, Dominic 68
Ballard, Daniel 3
Ballinger, Jacob 58
Ballo, Thierno 23
Balogun, Folarin 3
Baluta, Tudor 14
Bamba, Souleymane 20
Bamford, Patrick 43
Bange, Ewan 9
Baningime, Beni 32
Baningime, Divin 90
Banks, Oliver 6
Banks, Scott 29
Bannan, Barry 75
Bapaga, Will 26
Baptiste, Alex 10
Baptiste, Jamal 89
Baptiste, Shandon 13
Barbet, Yoann 68
Barclay, Ben 1
Barden, Daniel 59
Bardsley, Phillip 17
Bardwell, Max 30
Barker, Brandon 62
Barker, Charlie 22
Barker, Kyle 63
Barkhuizen, Tom 67
Barkley, Ross 23
Barks, Charlie 73
Barlaser, Daniel 71
Barnes, Ashley 17
Barnes, Dillon 68
Barnes, Harvey 44
Barnes, Joshua 60
Barnes, Marcus 61
Barnes, Samuel 8
Barnett, Jordan 61
Barnett, Josh 21
Barnett, Ryan 76
Barrett, Jack 32
Barrett, Josh 16
Barrett, Mason 87
Barrett, Ryan 56
Barrett, Sam 34
Barry, Bradley 6
Barry, Louie 4
Bartley, Kyle 88
Basham, Chris 74
Bass, Alex 66
Bastien, Sacha 37
Batch, Billy 34
Bate, Lewis 23
Bateman, Joe 30
Bates, Alfie 86
Batshuayi, Michy 23
Battersby, Ollie 38
Batth, Danny 80
Batty, Daniel 34
Baudry, Mathieu 83
Bauer, Moritz 80
Bauer, Patrick 67
Baxter, Jack 67
Baxter, Nathan 23
Bayliss, Tom 67
Bazunu, Gavin 49
Beadling, Tom 6
Beck, Mark 39
Beck, Owen 47
Beckett, Louis 41
Beckles, Omar 28
Beckwith, Sam 48
Bedeau, Jacob 73
Bednarek, Jan 77
Beesley, Jake 70
Beestin, Alfie 73
Beevers, Mark 63
Begovic, Asmir 11
Bela, Jeremie 7
Belehouan, Jean 74
Bell, Amari 8
Bell, Charlie 66
Bell, Finn 35
Bell, Lewis 21
Bell, Sam 15
Bellagambi, Giosue 40
Bellerin, Hector 3
Bellis, Sam 77
Belshaw, James 39
Benarous, Ayman 15
Benda, Steven 82
Benkovic, Filip 44
Bennett, Elliott 8
Bennett, Joe 20
Bennett, Kyle 16
Bennett, Mason 53
Bennett, Rhys 21
Bennett, Ryan 82
Bennett, Scott 57
Bennetts, Keanan 42
Benning, Malvind 51
Benrahma, Said 89
Benson, Josh 17
Benteke, Christian 29
Bentley, Daniel 15
Berardi, Gaetano 43
Berge, Sander 74
Bergstrom, Lucas 23
Bergwijn, Steven 84
Berkoe, Kevin 72
Bernabe, Adrian 49
Bernard, Caldeira 32
Bernard, Di'shon 50
Bernard, Dominic 35
Bernardo, Junior 14
Bernardo Silva, Mota 49
Berry, Dylan 58
Berry, James 41
Berry, Luke 48
Bertrand, Ryan 77
Bettache, Faysal 68
Bettinelli, Marcus 36
Bevan, Jaden 76
Bialkowski, Bartosz 53
Biamou, Maxime 26
Bidstrup, Mads 13
Bidwell, Jake 82
Bielik, Krystian 30
Biggins, Harrison 34
Bilboe, Laurence 61
Biler, Huseyin 2
Billing, Phillip 11
Bilokapic, Nicholas 40
Bilson, Tom 26
Birch, Charlie 21
Bird, Jay 54
Bird, Max 30
Bird, Samuel 34
Bishop, Colby 1
Bishop, Nathan 50
Bishop, Teddy 42
Bissouma, Yves 14
Black, Malaki 54
Blackett, Tyler 60
Blackman, Jamal 23
Blackmore, Will 63
Blackwood, George 61
Blair, Harvey 47
Blair, Matty 24
Blair, Sam 59
Blake-Tracy, Frazer 63
Bloomfield, Matt 92
Bloxham, Tom 76
Blythe, Ben 31
Boateng, Hiram 54
Boateng, Malachi 29
Bobb, Oscar 49
Bodie, Dave 63
Bodin, Billy 67
Bodvarsson, Jon Dadi 53
Bogarde, Lamar 4
Bogle, Jayden 74
Bogle, Omar 31
Bogusz, Mateusz 43
Bohui, Joshua 25
Bola, Marc 52
Bola, Tolaji 3
Bolasie, Yannick 32
Bolger, Cian 58
Bolton, Elliott 2
Bolton, Jack 1
Bolton, James 66
Boly, Willy 91
Bond, Jonathan 88
Bonds, Elliott 41
Bondswell, Matthew 56
Bong, Gaetan 60
Bonham, Jack 37
Bonne, Macauley 68
Booth, Sam 28
Borner, Julian 75
Borthwick-Jackson, Cameron 61
Borwick, Johnathon 34
Bostock, John 31
Bostwick, Michael 18
Bottomley, Ben 31
Bowden, Jamie 84
Bowen, Jarrod 89
Bowen, Sam 20
Bowery, Jordan 51
Bowman, Ryan 33
Bowry, Dan 24
Boyce-Clarke, Coniah 69
Boyd, George 72
Boyd, Louis 38
Boyd-Munce, Caolan 7
Boyes, Harry 74
Boyes, Morgan 47
Boyle, Dylan 34
Boyle, William 24
Braaf, Jayden 49
Bradley, Alex 46
Bradley, Conor 47
Bradley, Lewis 70
Bradley, Sonny 48
Bradley-Morgan, Luke 23
Bradshaw, Tom 53
Brady, Robert 17
Brain, Callum 57
Bramall, Cohen 46
Bramall, Daniel 5
Brannagan, Cameron 62
Branthwaite, Jarrad 32
Bravo, Claudio 49
Brayford, John 18
Brearey, Eddie 62
Bree, James 48
Breeze, Gabriel 21
Brennan, Ciaran 75

Brennan, Luke 8
Brereton, Ben 8
Brewster, Rhian 74
Bridcutt, Liam 46
Bridge, Mungo 4
Bridgman, Alfie 66
Brierley, Ethan 70
Bright, Harrison 57
Bright, Myles 40
Brisley, Shaun 65
Bristow, Ethan 69
Brittain, Callum 5
Britton, Louis 15
Broadbent, George 74
Broadbent, Tom 83
Broadhead, Nathan 32
Brockbank, Harry 10
Broja, Armando 23
Brook, Harrison 66
Brook, Lachlan 13
Brooke, Harry 59
Brooking, Josh 23
Brooks, Andre 74
Brooks, David 11
Brookwell, Niall 56
Broom, Ryan 63
Broome, Nathan 80
Brophy, James 45
Brough, Patrick 6
Brown, Archie 30
Brown, Cameron 78
Brown, Charlie 54
Brown, Ciaron 20
Brown, Connor 6
Brown, Isaiah 23
Brown, Jacob 80
Brown, Jaden 40
Brown, James 53
Brown, Jevani 25
Brown, Jordan 30
Brown, Junior 73
Brown, Lee 66
Brown, Reece 40
Brown, Scott 65
Brown, Will 56
Brown, Zak 42
Browne, Alan 67
Browne, Marcus 52
Brownhill, Josh 17
Bruce, Thomas 66
Bruno Fernandes, Miguel 50
Bruno Jordao, Andre 91
Brunt, Chris 15
Brunt, Zak 74
Bryan, Joe 36
Bryan, Kean 74
Brynn, Solomon 52
Buchanan, Lee 30
Buckley, Jack 1
Buckley, John 8
Bueno, Hugo 91
Bugarin, Erik 91
Bulman, Dannie 27
Bunker, Harvey 35
Bunney, Joe 38
Burchall, Ajani 11
Burey, Tyler 53
Burge, Lee 81
Burgess, Cameron 1
Burgess, Luke 72
Burgess, Scott 65
Burgoyne, Harry 76
Burke, Oliver 74
Burke, Reece 41
Burley, Andre 92
Burn, Dan 14
Burnett, Henry 27
Burns, Bobby 6
Burns, Finley 49
Burns, Samuel 8
Burns, Wes 34
Burrell, Rumarn 52
Burrell, Warren 39
Burroughs, Jack 26
Burrows, Harrison 63
Bursik, Josef 80
Burton, Callum 19
Burton, Jake 85
Buse, William 15
Butcher, Matt 1
Butland, Jack 29
Butler, Andy 31
Butler, Dan 63
Butroid, Lewis 73
Butterfield, Luke 32
Butterworth, Daniel 8
Button, David 88
Buur, Oskar 91
Bwomono, Elvis 78
Bycroft, Jack 77
Byers, George 82
Byrne, Nathan 30
Caballero, Willy 23
Cabango, Ben 82
Cadden, Nicky 35
Caddis, Paul 83
Cafu, Dias 60
Cahill, Gary 29
Caicedo, Moises 14
Cain, Jake 47
Caine, Nathan 51
Cairney, Tom 36
Cairns, Alex 34
Calvert-Lewin, Dominic 32
Camara, Etienne 40
Camara, Mamadi 69
Camara, Panutche 64
Cameron, Geoff 68
Cameron, Nathan 90
Camp, Lee 83
Campana, Leonardo 91
Campbell, Frazier 40
Campbell, Hayden 72
Campbell, Maison 51
Campbell, Rio 82
Campbell, Tahvon 24
Campbell, Tate 7
Campbell, Tyrese 80
Campbell-Gordon, Ryan 65
Camps, Callum 34
Campton-Sturridge, DJ 4
Canavan, Niall 12
Cann, Hayden 46
Cannon, Andy 66
Cannon, Thomas 32
Canos, Sergi 13
Cantwell, Todd 59
Capoue, Etienne 87
Cappello, Angelo 74
Caprice, Jake 33
Caprile, Elia 43
Cardoso, Goncalo 89
Cargill, Baily 35
Carroll, Andy 56
Carroll, Tommy 68
Carson, Scott 30
Carter, Charlie 79
Carter, Hayden 8
Carter, Jack 35
Carter-Vickers, Cameron 84
Cartwright, Harvey 41
Cartwright, Samuel 63
Carty, Conor 91
Carvalho, Fabio 36
Casey, Oliver 43
Cash, Matty 4
Cashin, Eiran 30
Casilla, Francisco 43
Cassidy, Ryan 87
Castagne, Timothy 44
Castillo, Juan 23
Castro, Joel 50
Cathcart, Craig 87
Caton, Charlie 76
Cavani, Edinson 50
Ceballos, Dani 3
Cedric Soares, Ricardo 3
Chadwick, Billy 41
Chadwick, Louis 19
Chair, Ilias 68
Chalobah, Nathaniel 87
Chalton, Ben 70
Chamberlain, Tom 24
Chambers, Calum 3
Chambers, Leon 62
Chambers, Luke 42
Chambers, Luke 65
Chandler, Reiss 78
Chaplin, Conor 5
Chapman, Ellis 24
Chapman, Harry 8
Chapman, Mackenzie 61
Charles, Darius 92
Charles, Dion 1
Charles, Jaden 51
Charsley, Harry 51
Charters, Taylor 21
Chauke, Kgaogelo 77
Cheshire, Anthony 83
Chester, James 80
Chesters, Daniel 89
Chilvers, Noah 25
Chilwell, Ben 23
Chirewa, Tawanda 42
Chislett, Ethan 2
Chong, Tahith 50
Choudhury, Hamza 44
Chrisene, Benjamin 4
Christensen, Andreas 23
Christie, Cyrus 36
Christie, Eli 30
Christie-Davies, Isaac 5
Chukwuemeka, Caleb 58
Chukwuemeka, Carney 4
Cirjan, Catalin 3
Cirkin, Dennis 84
Cisse, Ousseynou 45
Clampin, Ryan 25
Clare, Sean 62
Clark, Ciaran 56
Clark, James 92
Clark, Jordan 48
Clark, Max 41
Clark, Mitchell 44
Clarke, Billy 12
Clarke, Courtney 30
Clarke, Flynn 63
Clarke, Harrison 3
Clarke, Jack 84
Clarke, James 86
Clarke, James 51
Clarke, Jordan 73
Clarke, Leon 76
Clarke, Matthew 14
Clarke, Ollie 51
Clarke, Peter 85
Clarke, Tom 72
Clarke, Trevor 71
Clarke-Harris, Jonson 63
Clarke-Salter, Jake 23
Clarkson, Leighton 47
Clay, Craig 45
Clayden, Charles 22
Clayton, Adam 7
Clements, Chris 24
Cleverley, Tom 87
Clifford, Tom 78
Clifton, Harry 38
Close, Ben 66
Clough, Zach 90
Clucas, Sam 80
Clyne, Nathaniel 29
Coady, Conor 91
Coates, Kieran 80
Coburn, Josh 52
Cochrane, Alex 14
Cockerill-Mollett, Callum 86
Coke, Giles 38
Coker, Ben 79
Coker, Kenny 59
Coker, Oliver 78
Colback, Jack 60
Colclough, Ryan 73
Coleman, Joel 34
Coleman, Seamus 32
Colin, Maxime 7
Collinge, Joseph 65
Collins, Aaron 35
Collins, Archie 33
Collins, Bradley 5
Collins, James S 48
Collins, Lewis 57
Collins, Nathan 80
Collins, Tom 73
Collyer, Toby 14
Colwill, Levi 23
Colwill, Rubin 20
Comley, Brandon 10
Conlan, Luke 55
Conlon, Tom 65
Conneely, Seamus 1
Connolly, Aaron 14
Connolly, Callum 32
Conroy, Dion 83
Conway, Max 10
Conway, Tommy 15
Cook, Andy 51
Cook, Lewis 11
Cook, Steve 11
Cooke, Callum 12
Coombes, Tyler 64
Cooney, Ryan 17
Cooper, Brandon 82
Cooper, George 64
Cooper, Jake 53
Cooper, Joel 62
Cooper, Liam 43
Cooper, Michael 64
Cooper, Oliver 82
Copping, Bobby 63
Coppinger, James 31
Corbeanu, Theo 91
Cordner, Tyler 11
Cork, Jack 17
Cornell, David 42
Corness, Dominic 47
Cornick, Harry 48
Cornish, Sam 25
Cosgrove, Sam 7
Costello, Dara 17
Cottrell, Ben 3
Coufal, Vladimir 89
Coulibaly, Ismaila 74
Coulson, Hayden 52
Coulson, Josh 45
Coulter, Callum 25
Coulton, Lewis 67
Cousin-Dawson, Finn 12
Cousins, Jordan 80
Couto, Yan 49
Coutts, Paul 34
Coventry, Conor 89
Covil, Vaughn 35
Cowan-Hall, Paris 25
Cox, Matthew 2
Cox, Sonny 33
Coyle, Lewie 41
Coyle, Trae 3
Cracknell, Billy 25
Cracknell, Joe 39
Craig, Matthew 84
Craig, Michael 84
Craig, Tony 27
Crama, Tristan 13
Crane, Ross 42
Cranie, Martin 48
Crankshaw, Oliver 12
Craske, Finley 64
Crawford, Ali 10
Crellin, Billy 34
Cresswell, Aaron 89
Cresswell, Cameron 30
Cresswell, Charlie 43
Crichlow, Kane 87
Crichlow-Noble, Romoney 40
Crocker, Scott 64
Crookes, Adam 65
Crooks, Matt 71
Cross, Bradley 56
Cross, Liam 58
Crowe, Dylan 42
Crowley, Daniel 7
Csoka, Daniel 2
Cukur, Tiago 87
Cullen, Josh 89
Cullen, Liam 82
Cullen, Mark 65
Cumming, Jamie 23
Cummings, Jason 76
Cundle, Luke 91
Cundy, Robbie 15
Cunningham, Greg 67
Curran, Taylor 83
Currie, Jack 2
Curry, Mitchell 81
Curtis, Ronan 66
Cuthbert, Scott 79
Cutrone, Patrick 91
Cybulski, Bartosz 30
d'Almeida, Tavio 20
Da Costa, Julien 26
Da Silva, Josh 13
Da Silva, Vani 61
Dabo, Fankaty 26
Dack, Bradley 8
Dacres-Cogley, Josh 7
Dalby, Sam 87
Dale, Owen 28
Dales, Andy 73
Daley, Luke 40
Daley-Campbell, Vontae 44
Dallas, Andrew 19
Dallas, Stuart 43
Dallison, Tom 27
Dalot, Diogo 50
Dalsgaard, Henrik 13
Daly, James 16
Daly, Matty 40
Daniel, Colin 18
Daniel Podence, Castelo 91
Daniels, Charlie 66
Daniels, Donervon 28
Daniels, Josh 76
Daniels, Luke 13
Danjuma, Arnaut 11
Dann, Scott 29
Darcy, Ronan 10
Darikwa, Tendayi 90
Darling, Harry 54
Darlow, Karl 56
Dasilva, Jay 15
Davenport, Jacob 8
Davies, Adam 80
Davies, Archie 27
Davies, Ben 84
Davies, Ben 47
Davies, Curtis 30
Davies, Harvey 47
Davies, Isaak 20
Davies, Jack 54
Davies, Leon 19
Davies, Scott 85
Davies, Tom 16
Davies, Tom 32
Davis, David 76
Davis, Harry 55
Davis, Jayden 53
Davis, Keinan 4
Davis, Leif 43
Davis, Tommy 78
Davison, Joshua 22
Dawodu, Joshua 75
Dawson, Cameron 75
Dawson, Craig 87
Dawson, Joey 73
Dawson, Michael 60
Day, Joe 20
Dayton, James 45
De Bruyne, Kevin 49
De Gea, David 50
De Silva, Dillon 68
De Wijs, Jordy 68
Dean, Harlee 7
Dean, Max 43
Dean, Will 33
Dearnley, Zachary 61
Decordova-Reid, Bobby 36
Deeney, Troy 87
Delaney, Ryan 10
Delaney, Zak 88
Delap, Liam 49
Dele-Bashiru, Ayotomiwa 87
Dele-Bashiru, Fisayo 75
Delfouneso, Nathan 10
Delph, Fabian 32
Dembele, Siriki 63
Demetriou, Jason 78
Demetriou, Mickey 57
Dempsey, Ben 22
Dempsey, Kyle 37
Dendoncker, Lars 14
Dendoncker, Leander 91
Denholm, Aidan 54
Dennis, Louis 45
Dennis, Matthew 59
Dennis, William 11
Denny, Alex 72
Dervisoglu, Halil 13
Desbois, Adam 14
Devine, Alfie 84
Devine, Daniel 21
Devine, Reece 50
Devitt, Jamie 6
Dewhurst, Marcus 74
Dewsbury-Hall, Kiernan 44
Dhanda, Yan 82
Diabate, Cheick 33
Diaby, Cheikh 88
Diagne, Mbaye 88
Diagouraga, Toumani 55
Diakhaby, Adama 40
Diallo, Abdoulaye 60
Diallo, Amad 50
Diallo, Amadou 89
Diallo, Ibrahima 77

Diamond, Jack 81
Diangana, Grady 88
Diarra, Brahima 40
Diarra, Raphael 61
Dias, Ruben 49
Dickenson, Brennan 21
Dickie, Rob 68
Dickson-Peters, Thomas 59
Diedhiou, Famara 15
Dieng, Timothee 78
Dieng, Timothy 68
Dier, Eric 84
Dieseruvwe, Emmanuel 72
Digby, Paul 19
Digne, Lucas 32
Dijksteel, Anfernee 52
Dike, Daryl 5
Dinanga, Marcus 79
Dinzeyi, Jonathan 3
Dionkou, Alpha 49
Diop, Issa 89
Ditchfield, Harry 72
Dixon, Connor 30
Dixon, Joel 6
Dixon, Josh 21
Djenepo, Moussa 77
Dju, Mesaque 89
Dobbin, Lewis 32
Dobbin, Lewis 32
Dobra, Armando 42
Dobson, George 81
Docherty, Greg 41
Dodds, Daniel 52
Dodoo, Joseph 90
Doherty, Josh 27
Doherty, Matthew 84
Dolan, Matthew 57
Dolan, Tyrhys 8
Domi, Franklin 68
Donacien, Janoi 42
Donaghy, Thomas 34
Donaldson, Clayton 12
Done, Matt 70
Donohue, Dion 6
Dooley, Stephen 70
Dorsett, Jeriel 69
Doucoure, Abdoulaye 32
Dougall, Kenneth 9
Doughty, Alfie 80
Doughty, Michael 83
Douglas, Barry 43
Douglas Luiz, de Paulo 4
Dowell, Kieran 59
Downes, Flynn 42
Downing, Paul 66
Downing, Stewart 8
Doyle, Alex 72
Doyle, Eoin 10
Doyle, Tommy 49
Dozzell, Andre 42
Drameh, Cody 43
Draper, Freddie 46
Draper, Harry 79
Drewe, Aaron 68
Dreyer, Sam 79
Drinan, Aaron 42
Driscoll-Glennon, Anthony 17
Drysdale, Declan 26
Dubravka, Martin 56
Duffy, Mark 34
Duhaney, Demeaco 40
Duke-Mckenna, Stephen 68
Dummett, Paul 56
Duncan, Bobby 30
Dunk, Harrison 19
Dunk, Lewis 14
Dunkley, Cheyenne 75
Dunne, Cieran 81
Dunne, Jimmy 17
Dunne, Joe 70
Dunnwald, Kenan 73
Dyche, Max 58
Dyer, Jordan 33
Dykes, Lyndon 68
Ealing, Frankie 4
Eardley, Neal 18
Earl, Joshua 67
East, Ryan 69
Eastham, Ashley 72
Eastham, Jordan 8
Eastman, Tom 25
Eastwood, Jake 74
Eastwood, Simon 62
Eaves, Tom 41
Ebanks, Callum 24
Ebanks-Landell, Ethan 76
Ebosele , Festy 30
Eccles, Josh 26
Ederson, de Moraes 49
Edmonds-Green, Rarmani 40
Edmondson, Ryan 43
Edmundson, Sam 30
Edozie, Samuel 49
Edun, Tayo 46
Edwards, Danny 34
Edwards, Dave 76
Edwards, Gwion 42
Edwards, Joe 64
Edwards, Kyle 88
Edwards, Opi 15
Edwards, Owura 15
Edwards, Ronnie 63
Edwards, Ryan 18
Edwards, Thomas 80
Effiong, Inih 79
Egan, John 74
Egan-Riley, CJ 49
Egbri, Terrell 78
Ehmer, Max 16
Eisa, Abobaker 73
Eisa, Mohamed 63
Eiting, Carel 40
Ejaria, Oviemuno 69
Ekpiteta, Marvin 9
Ekwah, Pierre 23
El Ghazi, Anwar 4
El Mizouni, Idris 42
Elanga, Anthony 50
Elbouzedi, Zak 46
Elder, Callum 41
Elechi, Michael 62
Eliasson, Niclas 15
Elitim, Juergen 87
Elliot, Rob 87
Elliott, Harvey 47
Elliott, Kit 40
Elliott, Tom 72
Ellis, Mark 85
Ellison, Kevin 57
Elmohamady, Ahmed 4
Elneny, Mohamed 3
Elphick, Tommy 40
Embleton, Elliot 81
Emeran, Noam 50
Emerson, dos Santos 23
Emi, Buendia 59
Emmanuel, Josh 41
Emmanuel, Mbule 89
Emmett, Jack 39
Eneme Ella, Ulrick 14
Engels, Bjorn 4
Ennis, Niall 64
Eratt-Thompson, Declan 75
Estrada, Pascal 91
Etheridge, Neil 7
Evans, Antony 28
Evans, Cameron James 82
Evans, Ched 67
Evans, Corry 8
Evans, Gary 12
Evans, George 53
Evans, Jack 57
Evans, Jack 35
Evans, Jonny 44
Evans, Kieron 20
Evans, Lee 90
Evans, Owen 90
Evans, William 72
Eyoma, Timothy 84
Eze, Eberechi 29
Fabianski, Lukasz 89
Fabinho, Henrique 47
Fage, Dylan 61
Falkingham, Joshua 39
Fallowfield, Ryan 39
Famewo, Akin 59
Farman, Paul 21
Farmer, Lewis 75
Farquharson, Priestley 57
Feeney, Josh 34
Feeney, Liam 9
Feeney, Morgan 21
Felipe Anderson, Gomes 89
Felipe Araruna, Hoffmann 69
Femenia, Kiko 87
Fenlon, Rhys-James 1
Ferguson, Nathan 78
Ferguson, Shane 53
Fernandes, Baba 60
Fernandes, Gedson 84
Fernandez, Alvaro 50
Fernandez, Federico 56
Fernandez, Luis 79
Fernandinho, Luis 49
Ferrier, Morgan 85
Ferry, Will 77
Fiabema, Bryan 23
Field, Sam 88
Fielding, Frank 53
Fielding, Sam 72
Finley, Sam 34
Finnegan, Aidan 26
Finney, Oliver 28
Finnigan, Ryan 77
Fiorini, Lewis 49
Firmino, Roberto 47
Fish, William 50
Fishburn, Sam 21
Fisher, Alex 33
Fisher, Andy 54
Fisher, Darnell 52
Fitzhugh, Ethan 44
Fitzpatrick, Aidan 59
Fitzpatrick, David 65
Flaherty, Stan 56
Flanagan, Josh 58
Flanagan, Tom 81
Fleck, John 74
Fleming, Brandon 41
Fletcher, Ashley 52
Fletcher, Isaac 52
Fletcher, Steven 80
Flinders, Scott 24
Flint, Aiden 20
Flores, Jordan 41
Flores, Marcelo 3
Flynn, Shane 44
Foden, Phil 49
Foderingham, Wesley 74
Fofana, Wesley 44
Fojticek, Alex 9
Folami, Ben 42
Folarin, Sam 52
Folivi, Michael 25
Fondop-Talom, Mike 18
Forde, Anthony 62
Fornah, Tyrese 60
Fornals, Pablo 89
Forrester, William 80
Forss, Marcus 13
Forster, Fraser 77
Forster-Caskey, Jake 22
Forsyth, Craig 30
Fossey, Marlon 36
Foster, Ben 87
Foster, Bradley 30
Fosu, Tarique 13
Fosu-Mensah, Timothy 50
Foulds, Matthew 12
Fox, Ben 18
Fox, Danny 90
Fox, Morgan 80
Foyth, Juan 84
Frailing, Jake 68
Francis, Edward 39
Francois, Marlee 15
Francois, Tyrese 36
Francomb, George 27
Fraser, Ryan 56
Fraser, Scott 54
Fred, Frederico 50
Fredericks, Ryan 89
Freeman, John 54
Freeman, Kieron 82
Freeman, Luke 74
Freeman, Nick 92
Freestone, Lewis 24
Freitas Gouveia, Diogo 25
French, Billy 22
French, Tyler 12
Friend, George 7
Frieser, Dominik 5
Frost, Tyler 27
Fry, Dael 52
Fryer, Joe 83
Fryers, Zeki 83
Fuchs, Christian 44
Fulton, Jay 82
Furlong, Darnell 88
Furlong, James 14
Furman, Dean 21
Gabriel, Magalhaes 3
Gabriel Jesus, Fernando 49
Galach, Brian 27
Galbraith, Ethan 50
Gallacher, Owen 18
Gallagher, Conor 23
Gallagher, Paul 67
Gallagher, Sam 8
Galloway, Brendon 48
Galvin, Ryan 75
Gambin, Luke 25
Gape, Dominic 92
Garbutt, Luke 9
Garcia, Eric 49
Garcia Ferreira, Rafael 32
Gard, Lewis 78
Gardner, Dan 90
Gardner, Gary 7
Gardner-Hickman, Taylor 88
Garner, Gerard 34
Garner, James 50
Garner, Joe 90
Garratt, Ben 18
Garrett, Jake 8
Garrick, Jordan 82
Garrity, Ben 9
Gavin, Dylan 22
Gaxha, Leonardo 74
Gayle, Dwight 56
Gazzaniga, Paulo 84
Gbadebo, Camron 49
Gbamin, Jean-Philippe 32
Gelhardt, Joe 43
George, Adan 7
George, Shamal 25
Gerken, Dean 25
German, Ricky 27
Ghandour, Hady 22
Ghoddos, Saman 13
Giamattei, Massimo 83
Giannoulis, Dimitrios 59
Gibbons, James 65
Gibbs, Kieran 88
Gibbs, Liam 42
Gibbs-White, Morgan 91
Gibson, Ben 17
Gibson, Darron 72
Gibson, Joseph 52
Gibson, Lewis 32
Gibson, Liam 55
Gibson, Montel 38
Gibson-Hammond, Alexander 60
Giddings, Jake 29
Gilbert, Alex 13
Gilbey, Alex 22
Giles, Ryan 91
Gilks, Matthew 10
Gillespie, Mark 56
Gilliead, Alex 73
Gilligan, Ciaran 18
Gilmour, Billy 23
Giraud-Hutchinson, Omari 3
Giroud, Olivier 23
Gladwin, Ben 54
Glatzel, Paul 47
Glatzel, Robert 20
Glover, Ryan 11
Gnahoua, Arthur 10
Godden, Matthew 26
Godfrey, Ben 32
Godwin-Malife, Udoka 35
Golbourne, Scott 76
Golden, Tylor 72
Gomes, Claudio 49
Gomes, Madger 31
Gomes, Tote 91
Gomez, Joseph 47
Gomis, Nicksoen 74
Gomis, Virgil 60
Gooch, Lynden 81
Goode, Charlie 13
Goodridge, Mace 17
Goodship, Brandon 78
Goodwin, William 80
Gordon, Anthony 32
Gordon, Josh 86
Gordon, Kaide 47
Gordon, Kellan 51
Gordon, Kyron 74
Gordon, Lewis 13
Gordon, Liam 10
Gordon, Nico 7
Gorrin, Alejandro 62
Gosling, Dan 87
Goss, Sean 76
Gotts, Robbie 43
Gouldbourne, Ethan 85
Grabara, Kamil 47
Grabban, Lewis 60
Graczyk, Hubert 3
Graham, Danny 81
Graham, Jordan 37
Grant, Anthony 83
Grant, Bobby 61
Grant, Conor 64
Grant, Conor 70
Grant, Daniel 40
Grant, Joel 83
Grant, Jorge 46
Grant, Josh 16
Grant, Lee 50
Granville, Max 79
Gratton, Jacob 71
Gray, Andre 87
Gray, Demarai 44
Grayson, Joe 8
Grealish, Jack 4
Greaves, Anthony 31
Greaves, Jacob 41
Greaves, Jerome 71
Green, Andre 75
Green, Devarn 73
Green, Harry 52
Green, Jordan 5
Green, Matt 38
Greenidge, Reiss 10
Greenwood, Mason 50
Greenwood, Sam 43
Gregory, Cameron 76
Gregory, Lee 80
Gretarsson, Daniel 9
Gribbin, Callum 6
Griffiths, Joshua 88
Griffiths, Regan 28
Grigg, Will 81
Grimes, Matt 82
Grimmer, Jack 92
Grist, Ben 38
Grosicki, Kamil 88
Gross, Pascal 14
Grossart, Jamie 78
Grounds, Jonathan 83
Grujic, Marko 47
Guadagno, Johan 50
Guaita, Vicente 29
Gubbins, Joseph 68
Gudmundsson, Johann Berg 17
Guehi, Marc 23
Guerrero, Miguel 60
Guilbert, Frederic 4
Guinness-Walker, Nesta 2
Gundogan, Ilkay 49
Gunn, Angus 77
Gunter, Chris 22
Guthrie, Danny 86
Guthrie, Kurtis 65
Guy, Callum 21
Gwargis, Peter 14
Gyimah, Nicky 63
Gyokeres, Viktor 14
Gyollai, Daniel 63
Habergham, Sam 38
Hackett-Fairchild, Recco 66
Hackford, Antwoine 74
Hackney, Hayden 52
Hagan, Charles 75
Hagan, Harry 32
Haigh, Joe 23
Haines, Luke 83
Halford, Greg 78
Halilovic, Alen 7
Hall, Connor 39
Hall, Grant 52
Hall, Robert 62
Hallam, Jordan 73
Haller, Sebastien 89
Hallett, Luke 35
Halliday, Bradley 31
Halme, Aapo 5
Halstead, Mark 55
Hamalainen, Niko 68
Hamer, Ben 82
Hamer, Gustavo 26
Hamilton, CJ 9

Hamilton, Ethan 63
Hammar, Fredrik 13
Hammond, Oliver 60
Hanlan, Brandon 16
Hanley, Grant 59
Hannah, Jack 52
Hannam, Reece 29
Hannant, Luke 19
Hanson, James 38
Hanson, Jamie 62
Hanson, Ryan 41
Happe, Daniel 45
Harbottle, Riley 60
Hardcastle, Lewis 6
Hardie, Ryan 64
Harding, Wes 71
Hardley, Bjorn 50
Hare, Josh 16
Hargreaves, Cameron 16
Harmon, George 88
Harness, Marcus 66
Harness, Nathan 22
Harper, Rekeem 88
Harratt, Kian 40
Harries, Cian 16
Harriman, Michael 58
Harriott, Callum 25
Harris, Kedeem 75
Harris, Luke 63
Harris, Mark 20
Harris, Max 24
Harris, Will 81
Harrison, Ellis 66
Harrison, Jack 49
Harrison, Shayon 2
Harrop, Josh 67
Hart, Ben 18
Hart, Joe 84
Hart, Sam 78
Hartigan, Anthony 2
Hartridge, Alex 33
Harvey, Nathan 22
Harvie, Daniel 54
Harwood-Bellis, Taylor 49
Hasani, Lirak 31
Hause, Kortney 4
Havertz, Kai 23
Hawkes, Josh 81
Hawkins, Callum 18
Hawkins, Daniel 72
Hawkins, Oliver 42
Hawley, Kyle 55
Hayde, Kyle 85
Hayden, Aaron 21
Hayden, Isaac 56
Hayden, Kaine 4
Hayes, Cian 34
Hayes, Nick 72
Haygarth, Max 13
Haymer, Tom 18
Haynes, Ryan 57
He, Zhenyu 91
Headley, Jaheim 40
Heal, Sam 16
Healy, Matthew 42
Heaton, Tom 4
Hector, Michael 36
Hector-Ingram, Jahmal 30
Hegazi, Ahmed 88
Hegyi, Krisztian 89
Hein, Karl Jakob 3
Helder Costa, Wander 43
Helik, Michal 5
Hemfrey, Robbie 80
Hemming, Zachary 52
Hemmings, Kane 18
Henderson, Dean 50
Henderson, Ian 72
Henderson, Jordan 47
Henderson, Stephen 29
Hendrick, Jeff 56
Hendrie, Luke 38
Hendrie, Stephen 55
Heneghan, Ben 2
Hennessey, Wayne 29
Henry, Aaron 22
Henry, James 62
Henry, Mitchell 10
Henry, Rico 13
Hercules, Wraynel 13
Hernandez, Cucho 87
Hernandez, Onel 59
Hernandez, Pablo 43
Herrera, Yangel 49
Hesketh, Jake 77
Hesketh, Owen 91
Hessenthaler, Jake 27
Hewitt, Elliott 51
Hewlett, Tom 18
Hickey, Jordan 41
Hickman, Jak 10
High, Scott 40
Hill, Cameron 9
Hill, James 34
Hillier, Ryan 57
Hillson, James 3
Hilssner, Marcel 26
Hilton, Joe 8
Hilton, Sonny 36
Hindle, Jack 6
Hinds, Anthony 41
Hippolyte, Myles 73
Hird, Samuel 6
Hirst, George 44
Hiwula, Jordy 66
Hladky, Vaclav 72
Hobson, Shaun 78
Hockenhull, Ben 13
Hodge, Joseph 49
Hodnett, Jack 91
Hoedt, Wesley 77
Hoever, Ki-Jana 91
Hogan, Scott 7
Hogg, Jonathan 40
Hoilett, Junior 20
Hojbjerg, Pierre 84
Holden, James 69
Holden, Rory 86
Holding, Rob 3
Holgate, Harrison 34
Holgate, Mason 32
Holland, Nathan 89
Holland, Toby 83
Holland-Wilkinson, Jacob 67
Holmes, Bradley 9
Holmes, Duane 40
Holmes, Ricky 78
Holmes, Thomas 69
Holtby, Lewis 8
Holy, Tomas 42
Hondermarck, William 59
Honeyman, George 41
Hoogewerf, Dillon 50
Hoolahan, Wes 19
Hope, Hallam 83
Hope, Joseph 38
Hopper, Harrison 70
Hopper, Tom 46
Horgan, Daryl 92
Hornby, Fraser 32
Hornby, Sam 12
Hornshaw, George 73
Horsfall, Fraser 58
Horton, Branden 31
Horton, Grant 24
Hosannah, Bryce 43
Hoskins, Sam 58
Hough, Ben 61
Houghton, Jordan 54
Hourihane, Conor 4
Howard, Mark 73
Howard, Rob 78
Howarth, Ramirez 46
Howe, Teddy 9
Howkins, Kyle 57
Howley, Ryan 26
Howson, Jonathan 52
Hudson, Matthew 67
Hudson-Odoi, Callum 23
Huffer, Will 12
Huggins, Niall 43
Hughes, Andrew 67
Hughes, Caleb 20
Hughes, Harvey 66
Hughes, Liam 47
Hughes, Mark 1
Hughes, Rhys 32
Hughes, Sam 44
Hughes, Will 87
Hugill, Joe 50
Hugill, Jordan 59
Hulbert, Ollie 16
Hull, Jake 71
Hume, Denver 81
Humphreys, Bashir 23
Humphrys, Stephen 70
Hungbo, Joseph 87
Hunt, Alex 75
Hunt, Jack 15
Hunt, MacKenzie 32
Hunt, Max 21
Hunt, Robert 83
Hunter, Ashley 72
Huntington, Paul 67
Hurford-Lockett, Finlay 10
Hurst, Alex 65
Hurst, Kyle 7
Husband, James 9
Hussein, Mustafa 27
Hussey, Chris 24
Hutchinson, Isaac 30
Hutchinson, Jake 25
Hutchinson, Reece 18
Hutchinson, Sam 75
Hutchinson, Shae 59
Hutchinson, Shaun 53
Hutton, Remeao 7
Huws, Emyr 42
Hyam, Dominic 26
Hylton, Danny 48
Iandolo, Ellis 83
Ibe, Jordan 30
Ibrahim, Ola 30
Ibsen Rossi, Zeno 11
Idah, Adam 59
Idehen, Duncan 38
Ideho, Joel 3
Idem, Manny 30
Ighalo, Odion Jude 50
Iheanacho, Kelechi 44
Ihiekwe, Michael 71
Ikpeazu, Uche 92
Iliev, Dejan 3
Ilunga, Brooklyn 54
Imray, Daniel 29
Ince, Tom 80
Ingram, Matt 41
Ings, Danny 77
Inniss, Ryan 22
Ioannou, Nicholas 60
Iontton, Arthur 79
Iorfa, Dominic 75
Iqbal, Zidane 50
Iredale, Jack 19
Iroegbunam, Tim 88
Ironside, Joe 19
Iseguan, Nelson 33
Isgrove, Lloyd 10
Isherwood, Liam 1
Ismail, Zeli 12
Isted, Harry 48
Itakura, Ko 49
Ivan Cavaleiro, Ricardo 36
Ivan Sanchez, Aguayo 7
Ivanovic, Branislav 88
Iversen, Daniel 44
Iversen, Einar 32
Iwobi, Alex 32
Izquierdo, Jose 14
Jaakkola, Anssi 16
Jaaskelainen, William 28
Jach, Jaroslaw 29
Jackson, Adam 46
Jackson, Ben 40
Jackson, Ira 38
Jackson, Kayden 42
Jackson, Luke 75
Jackson, Ryan 37
Jacob, Matty 41
Jacobs, Michael 66
Jacobson, Joe 92
Jade-Jones, Ricky 63
Jagielka, Phil 74
Jagne, Seedy 32
Jahanbakhsh, Alireza 14
Jaiyesimi, Diallang 22
Jakeways, Connor 24
Jakobsen, Emil 67
Jakupovic, Eldin 44
Jallow, Tali 54
James, Bradley 52
James, Daniel 50
James, Luke 6
James, Matthew 44
James, Reece 31
James, Reece 23
James, Tom 72
James-Taylor, Douglas 80
Jameson, Kyle 61
Janelt, Vitaly 13
Jankewitz, Alexandre 77
Janneh, Saikou 15
Jansson, Pontus 13
Jaros, Vitezslav 47
Jarrett, Patrick 80
Jarvis, Aaron 73
Jarvis, Will 41
Jasper, Sylvester 36
Jay, Matt 33
Jay-Hart, Taylor 4
Jeacock, Zach 7
Jeanvier, Julian 13
Jebbison, Daniel 74
Jenkins, Jack 43
Jenkinson, Carl 60
Jenks, Teddy 14
Jensen, Lukas 17
Jensen, Mathias 13
Jephcott, Luke 64
Jerome, Cameron 54
Jessop, Harry 73
Jewitt-White, Harry 66
Jimenez, Raul 91
Jinkinson, Hugo 30
Joao Cancelo, Cavaco 49
Joao Carvalho, Antonio 60
Joao Moutinho, Felipe 91
Joao Pedro, de Jesus 87
Jobello, Wesley 26
Joelinton, de Lira 56
Johansen, Stefan 36
Johansson, Viktor 71
John, Cameron 31
John, Declan 82
John, Kyle 32
John, Nile 84
John-Jules, Tyreece 3
John-Lewis, Lenell 38
Johnson, Ben 89
Johnson, Billy 79
Johnson, Bradley 8
Johnson, Brennan 60
Johnson, Callum 66
Johnson, Daniel 67
Johnson, Danny 45
Johnson, Darnell 44
Johnson, Finlay 79
Johnson, Lewis 54
Johnson, Marvin 52
Johnson, Travis 28
Johnson, Tyreke 37
Johnston, Carl 34
Johnston, Ethan 58
Johnston, George 47
Johnstone, Samuel 88
Jolley, Charlie 85
Jombati, Sido 61
Jones, Alex 58
Jones, Alfie 27
Jones, Alfie 41
Jones, Archie 63
Jones, Avan 48
Jones, Ben 85
Jones, Billy 71
Jones, Bobby 90
Jones, Callum 41
Jones, Curtis 47
Jones, Dan 72
Jones, Edward 80
Jones, Gethin 10
Jones, Harry 82
Jones, Isaiah 52
Jones, Jacob 82
Jones, James 46
Jones, James 6
Jones, Jamie 90
Jones, Joey 72
Jones, Jordan 81
Jones, Lloyd 58
Jones, Louis 31
Jones, Mike 6
Jones, Nico 62
Jones, Patrick 40
Jones, Ryan 16
Jonny, Castro 91
Jorginho, Filho Jorge 23
Joseph, Kyle 90
Joshua, Kevin 88
Jota, Diogo 47
Jota, Ramallo 4
Joyce, Luke 65
Jozefzoon, Florian 30
Jozwiak, Kamil 30
Judd, Myles 45
Judge, Alan 42
Jules, Zak 54
Jurado, Marc 50
Justin, James 44
Jutkiewicz, Lucas 7
Kabak, Ozan 47
Kabasele, Christian 87
Kabore, Issa 49
Kachunga, Elias 75
KaiKai, Sullay 9
Kakay, Osman 68
Kalambayi, Paul 2
Kalas, Tomas 15
Kalinic, Lovre 4
Kamara, Aboubakar 36
Kamara, Abu 59
Kaminski, Thomas 8
Kamwa, Bobby 43
Kane, Harry 84
Kane, Herbie 5
Kane, Todd 68
Kante, Ngolo 23
Kanu, Idris 63
Karacan, Jem 73
Karbownik, Michal 14
Kargbo, Hamzad 68
Kashket, Scott 92
Kastaneer, Gervane 26
Kasumu, David 54
Kavanagh, Calum 52
Kavanagh, Harry 66
Kay, Josh 6
Kayode, Joshua 71
Kazeem, Al-Amin 25
Kazim-Richards, Colin 30
Kean, Moise 32
Keane, Michael 32
Keane, Will 90
Kebano, Neeskens 36
Kefalas, Themistoklis 68
Keillor-Dunn, Davis 61
Keita, Naby 47
Kelleher, Caoimhin 47
Kelly, Liam 26
Kelly, Liam 62
Kelly, Liam 68
Kelly, Lloyd 11
Kelly, Martin 29
Kelly, Michael 16
Kelman, Charlie 68
Kelsey, Adam 73
Kemp, Daniel 45
Kendall, Charley 68
Kendrick, Henry 5
Kenlock, Myles 42
Kenneh, Nohan 43
Kenny, Jonjoe 32
Kensdale, Ollie 25
Kent, Frankie 63
Kenyon, Alex 55
Keogh, Richard 40
Keohane, Jimmy 70
Kerry, Lloyd 39
Key, Josh 33
Khadra, Reda 14
Khaleel, Rafiq 27
Khan, Otis 85
Kherbouche, Nasim 40
Khouri, Evan 38
Kieftenbeld, Maikel 53
Kiernan, Brendan 39
Kilgour, Alfie 16
Kilkenny, Gavin 11
Kilman, Max 91
Kilsby, Max 21
Kinali, Eren 78
King, Josh 32
King, Toby 88
King, Tom 57
Kinsella, Liam 86
Kioso, Peter 48
Kipre, Cedric 88
Kirby, Connor 39
Kirby, Nya 29
Kirk, Alex 3
Kirk, Charlie 28
Kitching, Liam 5
Kite, Harry 33
Klass, Michael 78
Klich, Mateusz 43
Klose, Timm 59

Knibbs, Harvey 19
Knight, Ben 49
Knight, Benjamin 49
Knight, Jason 30
Knight, Josh 44
Knight-Percival, Nathaniel 55
Knockaert, Anthony 36
Knowles, Jimmy 51
Knowles, Tom 19
Knoyle, Kyle 19
Koch, Robin 43
Koiki, Ali 16
Kokolo, Williams 52
Kolasinac, Sead 3
Konate, Ateef 60
Kongolo, Terence 36
Konsa, Ezri 4
Korboa, Ricky 58
Koroma, Josh 40
Kourmetio, Billy 47
Kouyate, Cheikhou 29
Kovacic, Mateo 23
Kovar, Matej 50
Kowalczyk, Szymon 27
Krafth, Emil 56
Kristensen, Sebastian 32
Krovinovic, Filip 60
Krul, Tim 59
Kyprianou, Harry 78
Kyprianou, Hector 45
Labadie, Joss 57
Lacazette, Alexandre 3
Ladapo, Freddie 71
Lafferty, Dan 26
Laird, Ethan 50
Lakin, Charlie 7
Lallana, Adam 14
Lamela, Erik 84
Lamptey, Tariq 14
Lamy, Julien 38
Lancashire, Oliver 28
Lancaster, Will 5
Lang, Callum 90
Langley, Dan 56
Lankester, Jack 42
Lansbury, Henri 15
Lanzini, Manuel 89
Laporte, Aymeric 49
Lapslie, George 51
Lapslie, Tom 25
Larkeche, Ziyad 36
Larouci, Yasser 47
Larsson, Julian 60
Las, Damian 36
Lascelles, Jamaal 56
Latibeaudiere, Joel 82
Latty-Fairweather, Thierry 18
Laurent, Josh 69
Lavelle, Sam 55
Lavery, Caolan 86
Lavinier, Marcel 84
Law, Jason 51
Law, Nicky 33
Law, Ryan 64
Lawless, Conor 69
Lawless, Steven 18
Lawlor, Ian 31
Lawlor, Jake 39
Lawrence, Henry 23
Lawrence, Tom 30
Lawrence-Gabriel, Jordan 60
Lazaar, Achraf 87
Le Fondre, Kian 10
Le Marchand, Maxime 36
Leadbitter, Grant 81
Leahy, Luke 16
Leak, Tom 86
Leake, Jake 41
Leban, Zan-Luk 32
Ledley, Joe 57
Ledson, Ryan 67
Lee, Elliot 48
Lee, Harry 33
Lee, Kieran 10
Lee, Oliver 37
Lees, Tom 75
Legge, Leon 65
Leigh, Lewis 67
Leitch-Smith, AJ 55
Leko, Jonathan 7
Lemina, Mario 77
Lenihan, Darragh 8
Lennon, Harry 78
Lennon, Michael 65
Leno, Bernd 3
Leonard, Marc 14
Leonard, Ryan 53
Lerma, Jefferson 11
Leshabela, Thakgalo 44
Letheren, Kyle 55
Leutwiler, Jayson 40
Levitt, Dylan 50
Lewington, Dean 54
Lewis, Aaron 57
Lewis, Adam 47
Lewis, George 3
Lewis, Harry 77
Lewis, Jamal 56
Lewis, Marcel 23
Lewis, Paul 85
Lewis, Sonny 57
Lewis-Potter, Keane 41
Liddle, Ben 16
Lillis, Josh 6
Lindelof, Victor 50
Lindley, Hayden 4
Lindsay, Jamie 71
Lindsay, Liam 80
Lines, Chris 79
Ling, Sam 45
Lingard, Jesse 50
Linton, Malachi 92
Lintott, Harvey 37
List, Elliott 79
Little, Mark 16
Little, Max 68
Livermore, Aneurin 57
Livermore, Jake 88
Livramento, Valentino 23
Llorente, Diego 43
Lloris, Hugo 84
Lloyd, Alfie 68
Lloyd, Danny 85
Lloyd, George 24
Lloyd, Louis 76
Lo Celso, Giovani 84
Lo-Everton, Sonny 87
Lockyer, Tom 48
Loft, Ryan 73
Lofthouse, Kyran 62
Loftus-Cheek, Ruben 23
Lokilo, Jason 31
Lokko, Kevin 39
Lolley, Joe 60
Lolos, Klaidi 64
Lonergan, Andrew 88
Long, Adam 90
Long, George 41
Long, Kevin 17
Long, Sam 62
Long, Sam 46
Long, Sean 24
Long, Shane 77
Longe-King, David 57
Longelo, Rosaire 56
Longman, Ryan 14
Longridge, Jackson 12
Longstaff, Matthew 56
Longstaff, Sean 56
Lonwijk, Nigel 91
Lookman, Ademola 36
Lopez, Joel 3
Loptata, Kacper 74
Lossl, Jonas 32
Loughlin, Liam 72
Love, Donald 76
Lovick, Harry 41
Low, Joseph 15
Lowe, Jamal 82
Lowe, Jason 72
Lowe, Max 74
Lowery, Tom 28
Lowton, Matt 17
LuaLua, Kazenga 48
Luamba, Junior 61
Lubula, Beryly 9
Lucas Joao, Eduardo 69
Lucas Moura, Rodrigues 84
Ludewig, Kilian 5
Luiz, David 3
Lumley, Joe 68
Lund, Matthew 70
Lundstram, John 74
Lundstram, Josh 28
Luongo, Massimo 75
Lusala, Dermi 84
Luzon, Omri 69
Lyden, Jordan 83
Lynch, Jay 70
Lyons, Brad 8
Lyons-Fraser, Brooklyn 84
Maatsen, Ian 23
Mac Allister, Alexis 14
Macari, Lewis 80
MacDonald, Alex 37
MacDonald, Angus 71
MacDonald, Calum 85
MacDonald, Shaun 71
Macey, Matt 3
MacGillivray, Craig 66
Macleod, Lewis 64
Madden, Patrick 34
Maddison, James 44
Maddison, Marcus 22
Madine, Gary 9
Magennis, Josh 41
Maghoma, Christian 37
Maghoma, Edmond-Paris 13
Magliore, Tyler 8
Maguire, Chris 81
Maguire, Frankie 74
Maguire, Harry 50
Maguire, Joe 1
Maguire, Sean 67
Maguire-Drew, Jordan 45
Maher, Zack 57
Mahom, Trent 68
Mahoney, Connor 53
Mahoney, Murphy 68
Mahrez, Riyad 49
Main, Curtis 76
Maitland-Niles, Ainsley 3
Maja, Josh 36
Makama, Jovon 46
Malley, Connor 52
Malone, Dan 80
Malone, Scott 30
Maloney, Scott 6
Mancienne, Michael 18
Mancini, Anthony 17
Mandron, Mikael 28
Mane, Sadio 47
Manly, Jack 42
Manning, Ryan 82
Manquillo, Javier 56
Mansell, Lewis 1
Marcal, Fernando 91
Marcelo 47
March, Josh 35
March, Solly 14
Marcondes, Emiliano 13
Mariappa, Adrian 15
Mariette, Luke 9
Maris, George 51
Markanday, Dilan 84
Markelo, Nathangelo 32
Marosi, Marko 26
Marques, Christian 91
Marquis, John 66
Marriott, Jack 30
Marsh, Aiden 5
Marsh, Tyrone 79
Marshall, David 30
Marshall, Mark 58
Marshall, Marley 25
Marshall, Ross 79
Martial, Anthony 50
Martin, Aaron 39
Martin, Chris 15
Martin, Dan 1
Martin, David E 89
Martin, Joe 79
Martin, Josh 59
Martinelli, Gabriel 3
Martinez, Damian 4
Martinez, Pablo 16
Martins Indi, Bruno 80
Mascoll, Jamie 10
Masina, Adam 87
Mason, Brandon 26
Mason, Joe 54
Mason, Niall 63
Massengo, Han-Noah 15
Massey, Gavin 90
Masterson, Conor 68
Mastny, Ondrej 50
Masuaku, Arthur 89
Maswanhise, Tawanda 44
Mata, Juan 50
Mateta, Jean-Philippe 29
Matete, Jay 34
Matheson, Luke 91
Matheus Pereira, Fellipe 88
Matic, Nemanja 50
Matip, Joel 47
Matondo, Rabbi 80
Matt, Jamille 35
Matthews, Adam 22
Matthews, Archie 83
Matthews, Remi 81
Matthews, Sam 27
Mattock, Joe 71
Maupay, Neal 14
Mawson, Alfie 36
Maxted, Jonathan 33
Maxwell, Chris 9
May, Adam 19
May, Alfie 24
Mayer, Thomas 41
Maynard, Nicky 51
Maynard-Brewer, Ashley 22
Mayor, Danny 64
Mbe Soh, Loic 60
Mbenza, Isaac 40
Mbete-Tabu, Luke 49
Mbeumo, Bryan 13
Mbuyamba, Xavier 23
McAlear, Reece 59
McAleny, Conor 61
McAlinden, Liam 55
McAllister, Sean 32
McAnuff, Jobi 45
McArdle, Rory 33
McArthur, James 29
McAtee, James 49
Mcatee, John 73
McAvoy, Connor 36
McBride, Connor 8
McBurnie, Oliver 74
McCallum, Sam 59
McCalmont, Alfie 43
McCann, Charlie 50
McCarthy, Alex 77
McCarthy, James 29
McCarthy, Jason 92
McClean, James 80
McCleary, Garath 92
McClelland, Sam 23
McConville, Sean 1
McCormack, Alan 78
McCormick, Luke 23
McCormick, Luke 64
McCoulsky, Shawn 35
McCracken, Jon 59
McDonald, Kevin 36
McDonald, Kornell 30
McDonald, Rod 21
McDonald, Rowan 49
McDonald, Wesley 86
McDonnell, Jamie 60
McEachran, Josh 54
McEntee, Oisin 56
McFadzean, Callum 81
McFadzean, Kyle 26
McFayden, Lincoln 82
McGahey, Harrison 73
McGavin, Brett 42
McGeady, Aiden 81
McGee, Luke 35
McGill, Thomas 14
McGinn, John 4
McGoldrick, David 74
McGovern, Michael 59
McGrandles, Conor 46
McGrath, Jay 26
McGree, Riley 7
McGuane, Marcus 60
McGuinness, Mark 3
McHugh, Harry 90
McIntyre, Tom 69
McJannet, Edward 48
McKay, Barrie 82
McKenna, Scott 60
McKenzie, Robbie 37
McKenzie-Lyle, Kai 19
McKeown, James 38
McKinstry, Stuart 43
McKirdy, Harry 65
McLaughlin, Conor 81
McLaughlin, Ryan 70
McLaughlin, Stephen 51
McLean, Kenny 59
McLeod, Sammie 25
McLoughlin, Sean 41
McLoughlin, Shane 2
McMillan, Max 34
McNair, Paddy 52
McNally, Luke 62
McNamara, Danny 53
McNeil, Dwight 17
McNeill, Charlie 50
McNerney, Joe 27
McNulty, Jim 70
McNulty, Marc 69
McPake, Joshua 39
McShane, Paul 70
McTominay, Scott 50
McWilliams, Shaun 58
Medina, Agus 7
Medley, Zechariah 3
Mee, Ben 17
Mehew, Tom 16
Mehmeti, Anis 92
Meite, Yakou 69
Mejbri, Hannibal 50
Mejia, Mateo 50
Melbourne, Max 46
Mellis, Jacob 78
Mellish, Jon 21
Mellor, Kelvin 55
Melvin-Lambert, Nahum 69
Mema, Armelindo 68
Menayese, Rollin 51
Mendes Gomes, Carlos 55
Mendez-Laing, Nathaniel 52
Mendy, Benjamin 49
Mendy, Edouard 23
Mendy, Nampalys 44
Mengi, Teden 50
Mensah, Benjamin 63
Mepham, Chris 11
Merrie, Christopher 90
Meshino, Ryotaro 49
Meslier, Illan 43
Meyer, Max 29
Mgunga-Kimpioka, Benjamin 81
Mialkowski, Kacper 70
Middlehurst, Thomas 68
Mighten, Alex 60
Mikel, John Obi 80
Miles, Felix 24
Milivojevic, Luka 29
Millar, Liam 47
Millar, Matthew 76
Miller, Amari 7
Miller, Calvin 39
Miller, Charlie 64
Miller, George 5
Miller, Mickel 71
Miller, Shaun 10
Mills, Joseph 58
Mills, Zak 65
Milner, James 47
Mina, Yerry 32
Minamino, Takumi 47
Mingi, Jade 22
Mings, Tyrone 4
Minter, Melvin 39
Missilou, Christopher 83
Mitchell, Alex 53
Mitchell, Billy 53
Mitchell, Demetri 9
Mitchell, Ethan 64
Mitchell, Jonathan 30
Mitchell, Ramello 77
Mitchell, Tyrick 29
Mitchell-Lawson, Jayden 30
Mitchell-Nelson, Miles 78
Mitov, Dimitar 19
Mitrovic, Aleksandar 36
Mlakar, Jan 14
Mnoga, Haji 66
Moder, Jakub 14
Mohammed, Zehn 1
Mohsni, Bilel 38
Moller, Nikolaj 3
Molumby, Jayson 14
Moncur, George 48
Monks, Charles 9
Monlouis, Zane 3
Montano, Cristian 65
Montgomery, James 78
Monthe, Emmanuel 85
Montsma, Lewis 46
Moon, Jasper 5

Mooney, Fionn 29
Mooney, Kelsey 73
Moore, Byron 64
Moore, Elliott 62
Moore, Kieffer 20
Moore, Liam 69
Moore, Stuart 9
Moore, Taylor 15
Moore-Taylor, Jordan 35
Morais, Filipe 38
Moreno, Marlos 49
Moreno , Pablo 49
Morgan, Albie 22
Morgan, David 1
Morgan, Wes 44
Moriah-Welsh, Nathan 11
Morison, Louis 33
Morley, Aaron 70
Morrell, Joe 48
Morris, Bryn 66
Morris, Carlton 5
Morris, Glenn 27
Morris, Jordan 82
Morris, Josh 34
Morris, Kieron 85
Morris, Shayden 34
Morrison, Michael 69
Morrison, Sean 20
Morsy, Sam 52
Morton, Callum 88
Morton, James 15
Morton, Tyler 47
Moses, Victor 23
Moss, Dan 53
Mothersille, Malik 23
Mottley-Henry, Dylan 12
Moult, Louis 67
Mount, Mason 23
Mousinho, John 62
Mousset, Lys 74
Mowatt, Alex 5
Muir, Marques 84
Mukendi, Jeremie 84
Muldoon, Jack 39
Mulgrew, Charlie 8
Muller, Hayden 53
Mullin, Paul 19
Mumba, Bali 59
Mumbongo, Joel 17
Mundle, Romaine 84
Murphy, Jacob 56
Murphy, Joe 85
Murphy, Josh 20
Murphy, Luke 28
Murray, Glenn 60
Muskwe, Admiral 44
Mustafi, Shkodran 3
N'Lundulu, Daniel 77
Nadesan, Ashley 27
Nagy, Adam 15
Naismith, Jason 63
Naismith, Kal 48
Nakamba, Marvelous 4
Napa, Malachi 62
Nartey, Richard 17
Nascimento, Adler 63
Nathaniel-George, Ashley 78
Naughton, Kyle 82
Navarro, Marc 87
Naylor, Tom 66
Ndaba, Corrie 42
Ndiaye, Iliman-Cheikh 74
Ndidi, Onyinye 44
Ndjoli, Mikael 6
Ndombele, Tanguy 84
Neal, Harrison 74
Neal, Joe 19
Neill, Daniel 81
Nelson, Ben 44
Nelson, Curtis 20
Nelson, Reiss 3
Nelson, Sid 85
Nelson, Stuart 27
Nelson Semedo, Cabral 91
Ness, Lukas 22
Neves, Ruben 91
Newby, Alex 70
Newton, Danny 79
Ng, Perry 20
Ngakia, Jeremy 87
Nicholls, Lee 54
Nichols, Tom 27
Nicholson, Sam 16
Nicolaisen, Rasmus 66
Niemczyk, Jakub 18
Nightingale, Will 2
Nippard, Luke 11
Nizet, Rob 59
Nketiah, Eddie 3
Nkounkou, Niels 32
Nmecha, Felix 49
Nna Noukeu, Blondy 80
Noble, Mark 89
Nolan, Eddie 28
Nolan, Jack 86
Nolan, Jon 42
Nolan, Joseph 8
Nombe, Sam 54
Norburn, Oliver 76
Norgaard, Christian 13
Norman, Cameron 86
Norman, Magnus 21
Norrington-Davies, Rhys 74
Norris, Luke 79
Norris, Will 17
Norton, Christian 80
Norton-Cuffy, Brooke 3
Norwood, James 42
Norwood, Oliver 74
Nottingham, Michael 1
Nouble, Frank 64
Novak, Lee 12
Nsiala, Aristote 42
Ntambwe, Brice 61
Ntlhe, Kgosietsile 6
Nugent, David 67
Nugent, George 85
Nunn, George 23
Nuno Da Costa, Joia 60
Nurse, George 15
Nuttall, Joe 9
Nya, Raphael 91
Nyambe, Ryan 8
Nydam, Tristan 42
Nyland, Orjan 59
O'Brien, Aiden 81
O'Brien, Lewis 40
O'Brien, Sean 53
O'Connell, Charlie 63
O'Connell, Eoghan 70
O'Connell, Jack 74
O'Conner, Kane 13
O'Connor, Anthony 12
O'Connor, Lee 85
O'Connor, Paudie 12
O'Connor, Thomas 77
O'Donkor, Gatlin 62
O'Donnell, Richard 12
O'Dowda, Callum 15
O'Driscoll, Aaron 51
O'Driscoll Varian, Ethon 80
O'Hara, Kieran 18
O'Hare, Callum 26
O'Hora, Warren 54
O'Keefe, Stuart 37
O'Keeffe, Corey 51
O'Leary, Max 15
O'Malley, Mason 73
O'Neil, Liam 19
O'Neill, Luke 2
O'Neill, Mackenzie 90
O'Neill, Ollie 36
O'Nien, Luke 81
O'Reilly, Adam 67
O'Riley, Matt 54
O'Rourke, Fidel 47
O'Shaughnessy, Joseph 91
O'Shea, Dara 88
O'Sullivan, John 55
O'Toole, John 18
Oakley-Boothe, Tashan 80
Obafemi, Michael 77
Obi, Chuckwuemeka 90
Obiero, Micah 40
Obita, Jordan 92
Odegaard, Martin 3
Odimayo, Akinwale 83
Odoh, Abraham 70
Odoi, Denis 36
Odour, Clarke 5
Odubajo, Moses 75
Odubeko, Ademipo 89
Odunze, Chituru 44
Offiah, Odel 14
Offord, Luke 28
Ofoborh, Nnamdi 11
Ogbene, Chiedozie 71
Ogbeta, Nathaniel 76
Ogbonna, Angelo 89
Ogie, Shadrach 45
Ogilvie, Connor 37
Ogle, Reagan 1
Ogogo, Abu 16
Ohman, Ludvig 38
Ojo, Funso 90
Ojo, Sheyi 47
Ojrzynski, Jakub 47
Okedina, Jubril 84
Okenabirhie, Fejiri 31
Okonkwo, Arthur 3
Oksanen, Jaako 13
Olagunju, Mustapha 40
Olaigbe, Kazeem 77
Olayinka, James 3
Olise, Michael 69
Oliver, Vadaine 37
Olomola, Olufela 73
Olosunde, Matthew 71
Olsen, Robin 32
Olufunwa, Dare 77
Oluwayemi, Oluwaferanmi 84
Omar, Ali 5
Omilabu, David 29
Omobamidele, Andrew 59
Omole, Tobi 84
Omotoye, Tyrese 59
Onariase, Manny 73
Onen, Jayden 69
Onodi, Akos 4
Onomah, Joshua 36
Onyango, Tyler 32
Onyedinma, Fred 92
Onyeka, Tyreece 28
Opoku, Jerome 36
Origi, Divock 47
Osaghae, Joseph 22
Osaoabe, Emmanuel 86
Osborn, Ben 74
Osborne, Elliot 79
Osei Yaw, Derick 62
Osei-Tutu, Jordi 3
Osew, Paul 2
Oshilaja, Adedeji 22
Osho, Gabriel 48
Osorio, Claudio 69
Ostigard, Leo 14
Osula, William 74
Otamendi, Nicolas 49
Otasowie, Owen 91
Oteh, Aramide 68
Oulad M'Hand, Salah 3
Ovendale, Evan 57
Owers, Josh 15
Oxlade-Chamberlain, Alex 47
Oxley, Mark 78
Oyeleke, Emmanuel 65
Oztumer, Erhun 22
Pablo Mari, Villar 3
Pache, Rudi 5
Pack, Marlon 20
Packham, Sam 14
Page, Jonathon 36
Page, Lewis 33
Pajaziti, Adrion 36
Palaversa, Ante 49
Palmer, Alex 88
Palmer, Cole 49
Palmer, Kasey 15
Palmer, Liam 75
Palmer, Matthew 83
Palmer, Oliver 2
Palmer, Romal 5
Palmer-Brown, Erik 49
Pambou, Leon 77
Papastathopoulos, Sokratis 3
Pardington, James 91
Parker, Josh 18
Parkes, Adam 87
Parkes, Tom 33
Parrott, Troy 84
Parsons, Harry 83
Pask, Josh 26
Paskotsi, Maksim 84
Paterson, Callum 75
Paterson, Jamie 15
Patino, Charlie 3
Patrick, Omari 21
Patten, Keenan 20
Patterson, Anthony 81
Pattison, Alex 92
Payne, Jack 83
Payne, Stefan 38
Peacock-Farrell, Bailey 17
Pearce, Alex 53
Pearce, Jason 22
Pearce, Tom 90
Pears, Aynsley 8
Pearson, Ben 11
Pearson, Matthew 48
Pearson, Sam 15
Pedersen, Kristian 7
Pedro Neto, Lomba 91
Pell, Harry 25
Pellistri , Facundo 50
Peltier, Lee 88
Pelupessy, Joey 75
Penaranda, Adalberto 87
Pendlebury, Oliver 69
Penfold, Morgan 6
Pennant, Terell 44
Penney, Matt 75
Pennington, Matthew 32
Pepe, Nicolas 3
Perch, James 51
Pereira, Andreas 50
Pereira, Dion 48
Perez, Ayoze 44
Perica, Stipe 87
Perritt, Harry 1
Perry, Alex 90
Perry, Sam 86
Perry, Taylor 91
Peterson, Kristoffer 82
Pett, Tom 79
Peupion, Cameron 14
Philips, Daniel 87
Phillips, Adam 17
Phillips, Dillon 20
Phillips, Giles 92
Phillips, Harry 78
Phillips, Kalvin 43
Phillips, Kieran 16
Phillips, Kieran 40
Phillips, Matthew 88
Phillips, Nathaniel 47
Philogene-Bidace, Jayden 4
Pickering, Harry 8
Pickford, Jordan 32
Piergianni, Carl 61
Pierre, Aaron 76
Pierrick, Brandon 29
Pieters, Erik 17
Pigott, Joe 2
Pike, Dan 8
Pinnock, Ethan 13
Pipa, Gonzalo 40
Pitman, Brett 83
Placheta, Przemyslaw 59
Platt, Matt 6
Pochettino, Maurizio 87
Pogba, Paul 50
Pollock, Matthew 38
Pond, Alfie 33
Poole, Regan 46
Pope, Nick 17
Pope, Tom 65
Porro, Pedro 49
Porter, Adam 80
Porter, Chris 28
Potts, Brad 67
Potts, Danny 48
Poveda-Ocampo, Ian 43
Powell, Aaron 63
Powell, Daniel 28
Powell, Jack 27
Powell, Joe 18
Powell, Johl 22
Powell, Nick 80
Power, Max 81
Power, Simon 39
Pozo, Iker 49
Praet, Dennis 44
Pratley, Darren 22
Pressley, Aaron 13
Preston, Danny 60
Price, Freddie 55
Price, Isaac 32
Prieto, Andres 7
Pring, Cameron 15
Pringle, Ben 55
Pritchard, Alex 40
Pritchard, Harry 12
Pritchard, Joe 1
Procter, Archie 2
Proctor, Jamie 71
Propper, Davy 14
Prosser, Luke 79
Pugh, Marc 76
Pugh, Tom 73
Pukki, Teemu 59
Pulisic, Christian 23
Purrington, Ben 22
Pursall, Brandon 64
Puscas, George 69
Pussetto , Ignacio 87
Pye, Logan 50
Pyke, Rekeil 76
Pym, Christy 63
Quansah, Jarell 47
Quigley, Scott 6
Quina, Domingos 87
Quinn, Stephen 18
Quintilla, Xavi 59
Quirk, Sebastian 32
Quitirna, Junior 22
Racic, Luka 13
Rafael Cabral, Barbosa 69
Rafferty, Joe 67
Raffie, Akiel 34
Raggett, Sean 66
Raglan, Charlie 24
Raikhy, Arjan 4
Rak-Sakyi, Jesurun 29
Ralls, Joe 20
Ralph, Nathan 78
Rama, Rezart 60
Ramirez, Fabricio 36
Ramsdale, Aaron 74
Ramsey, Aaron 4
Ramsey, Jacob 4
Ramsey, Kayne 77
Randall, Joel 33
Randell, Adam 64
Randolph, Darren 89
Ranger, Nile 78
Rankin-Costello, Joe 8
Rankine, Dion 23
Raphinha, Raphael 43
Rashford, Marcus 50
Ratcliffe, George 20
Rathbone, Oliver 70
Ravas, Henrich 30
Ravenhill, Liam 31
Rawson, Farrend 51
Ray, George 85
Raya, David 13
Raymond, Jadan 29
Rea, Glen 48
Reach, Adam 75
Read, Arthur 13
Ream, Tim 36
Redmond, Nathan 77
Reed, Harrison 36
Reed, Louis 63
Reeves, Ben 64
Reghba, Ali 44
Reguilon, Sergio 84
Reid, Jamie 51
Reid, Jayden 7
Reid, Josh 26
Reid, Reuben 24
Reid, Winston 89
Reilly, Callum 2
Reilly, Gavin 21
Rekik, Omar 3
Remy, Shiloh 68
Render, Joshua 75
Revan, Dominic 4
Rew, Harvey 66
Rhodes, Jordan 75
Ricardo Pereira, Domingos 44
Rice, Declan 89
Rice, Isaac 75
Rich-Baghuelou, Jay 29
Richards, Dave 28
Richards, Lewis 91
Richards, Omar 69
Richards, Rico 88
Richards, Taylor 14
Richards-Everton, Ben 12
Richardson, Adam 81
Richardson, Jayden 60
Richardson, Lewis 17
Richarlison, de Andrade 32
Richter, Marc 17

Rico, Diego 11
Ridehalgh, Liam 85
Ridley, Joseph 52
Riedewald, Jairo 29
Riley, Joe 21
Riley, Regan 59
Rinomhota, Andy 69
Ripley, Connor 67
Riquelme, Rodrigo 11
Ritaccio, Matteo 47
Ritchie, Matt 56
Ritzmaier, Marcel 5
Robbins, Joe 28
Roberts, Connor 82
Roberts, Gary 1
Roberts, Haydon 14
Roberts, Liam 86
Roberts, Marc 7
Roberts, Mitchell 7
Roberts, Morgan 58
Roberts, Myles 87
Roberts, Patrick 49
Roberts, Tyler 43
Robertson, Andrew 47
Robertson, Clark 71
Robertson, Scott 31
Robertson, Sean 29
Robinson, Antonee 36
Robinson, Callum 88
Robinson, Jack 74
Robinson, Jack 52
Robinson, Luke 90
Robinson, Sammy 49
Robinson, Theo 65
Robinson, Zach 2
Robson, David 41
Robson, Ethan 9
Robson, Max 84
Robson-Kanu, Hal 88
Rodak, Marek 36
Rodari, Davide 27
Rodgers, Harvey 1
Rodman, Alex 16
Rodney, Devante 65
Rodon, Joe 84
Rodri, Rodrigo Hernandez 49
Rodrigo, Moreno 43
Rodriguez, James 32
Rodriguez, Jay 17
Rodriguez, Jeremi 77
Rodwell, Jack 74
Rodwell-Grant, Joe 67
Roerslev Rasmussen, Mads 13
Rogers, Jack 30
Rogers, Morgan 49
Roles, Jack 84
Rolt, Bradley 63
Romeo, Mahlon 53
Romero, Sergio 50
Romeu, Oriol 77
Rooney, Wayne 30
Roos, Kelle 30
Roscrow, Adam 2
Rose, Danny 58
Rose, Danny 38
Rose, Jack 86
Rose, Joseph 59
Rose, Michael 26
Ross, Ethan 46
Ross-Lang, Fedel 77
Rossiter, Jordan 34
Rothwell, Joe 8
Roughan, Sean 46
Routledge, Wayne 82
Rowe, Aaron 40
Rowe, Blaine 26
Rowe, Callum 4
Rowe, Danny 18
Rowe, Danny 12
Rowe, Edward 4
Rowe, Jai 73
Rowe, Jonathan 59
Rowe, Tommy 15
Rowland, James 76
Rowley, Tom 54
Ruben Vinagre, Goncalo 91
Rudd, Declan 67
Ruddock, Pelly 48
Ruddy, Jack 64
Ruddy, John 91
Rudiger, Antonio 23
Rudoni, Jack 2
Ruffels, Joshua 62
Rui Patricio, Pedro 91
Runarsson, Runar 3
Rupp, Lukas 59
Rush, Matt 78
Rushesha, Tivonge 82
Rushworth, Carl 14
Russell, Jonathan 23
Russell, Sam 38
Rutt, Charlie 30
Ryan, James 70
Ryan, Mathew 14
Ryan-Phillip, Callum 57
Rydel, Ryan 34
Saadi, Jalil 8
Sackey, Lynford 69
Sade Lichtenfeld, Yoav 62
Sadler, Matthew 86
Sadlier, Kieran 71
Saint-Maximin, Allan 56
Saiss, Romain 91
Saka, Bukayo 3
Sakho, Mamadou 29
Salah, Mohamed 47
Salam, Ahmed 41
Saliba, William Alain Andre Gabriel 3
Salisu, Mohammed 77
Sama, Stephen 1
Samatta, Mbwana 4
Samba, Brice 60
Samuel, Alex 92
Samuel, Bright 68
Samuel, Dominic 37
Samuels, Austin 91
Samuels, Imari 69
Samuels, Imari 69
Samuelsen, Martin 41
San Jose, Mikel 7
Sanchez, Carlos 87
Sanchez, Davinson 84
Sanchez, Robert 14
Sanders, Max 46
Sanders, Samuel 60
Sanderson, Dion 91
Sang, Tom 20
Sangare, Mohammed 56
Sanogo, Yaya 40
Sanson, Morgan 4
Santiago, Yago 84
Santos, Ricardo 10
Saraiva, Marcelo 60
Sarcevic, Antoni 10
Sargeant, Sam 45
Sargent, Matthew 72
Sarkic, Matija 91
Sarkic, Oliver 9
Sarpeng-Wiredu, Brendan 25
Sarr, Ismaila 87
Sarr, Malang 23
Sarr, Naby 40
Sass-Davies, Billy 28
Saunders, Harvey 34
Savage, Charlie 50
Savage, Remi 47
Saville, George 52
Savin, Toby 1
Sawyer, Gary 64
Sawyers, Romaine 88
Saydee, Christian 11
Sayer, Harvey 25
Scales, Kian 12
Scannell, Sean 38
Scarlett, Dane 84
Scarlett, Miquel 25
Scarr, Dan 86
Schar, Fabian 56
Schindler, Christopher 40
Schlupp, Jeffrey 29
Schmeichel, Kasper 44
Schmidt, Patrick 5
Schofield, Ryan 40
Schwartz, Ronnie 22
Scott, Alex 15
Scott, Cedwyn 21
Scott, Jack 91
Scott, James 41
Scott, Josh 51
Scott, Tom 65
Scowen, Josh 81
Scrimshaw, Jake 11
Scully, Anthony 46
Scully, Thomas 1
Sea, Dimitri 6
Seaden, Harry 78
Seaman, Charlie 31
Searle, Jamie 82
Sears, Freddie 42
Sears, Ryan 76
Seddon, Steve 7
Sema, Ken 87
Semedo, Alfa 69
Semenyo, Antoine 15
Senior, Adam 10
Senior, Courtney 25
Seok, Jae-Lee 66
Sercombe, Liam 24
Seri, Jean 36
Seriki, Femi 74
Sesay, David 27
Sessegnon, Ryan 84
Sessegnon, Steven 36
Setters, David 66
Seymour, Ben 33
Seymour, Taylor 66
Shabani, Brendon 45
Shabani, Meritan 91
Shackleton, Jamie 43
Shade, Tyrese 44
Shakpoke, Ruben 4
Shanks, Connor 12
Shaqiri, Xherdan 47
Sharman-Lowe, Teddy 23
Sharp, Billy 74
Sharrock-Peplow, Sam 40
Shaughnessy, Conor 70
Shaw, Liam 75
Shaw, Luke 50
Shaw, Nathan 9
Shawcross, Ryan 80
Shea, James 48
Sheaf, Ben 3
Sheaf, Max 41
Sheehan, Alan 58
Sheehan, Josh 57
Shelvey, George 60
Shelvey, Jonjo 56
Shephard, Liam 57
Shepherd, William 72
Shepperd, Nathan 13
Sheron, Nathan 34
Sherring, Sam 11
Shinnie, Andrew 22
Shinnie, Graeme 30
Shipley, Jordan 26
Shipley, Lewis 59
Shodipo, Olamide 68
Shonibare, Josh 30
Shoretire, Shola 50
Shrimpton, Finley 73
Sibbick, Toby 25
Sibley, Louie 30
Sierralta, Francisco 87
Sigurdsson, Gylfi 32
Sikora, Jorge 12
Silva, Fabio 91
Simeu, Dynel 23
Simmonds, Keyendrah 7
Simms, Ellis 32
Simoes, Elliot 5
Simons, Xavier 23
Simper, Lewis 19
Simpson, Danny 15
Simpson, Jack 11
Simpson, Steven 5
Simpson, Tyreece 42
Sims, Jack 9
Sims, Josh 77
Sinani, Danel 59
Sinclair, Jerome 87
Sinclair, Scott 67
Sinclair, Sky 9
Sinclair, Stuart 86
Sinclair, Tyrese 51
Sinisalo, Viljami 4
Sisay, Alhagi 38
Sissoko, Moussa 84
Sithole, Gerald 37
Sitti, Melvin 59
Siziba, Zanda 42
Skalak, Jiri 53
Skipp, Oliver 84
Skurek, Harvey 24
Skuse, Cole 42
Slater, Regan 74
Slattery, Callum 77
Slew, Jordan 55
Slicker, Cieran 49
Slimani, Islam 44
Sluga, Simon 48
Smales-Braithwaite, Benni 77
Small, Thierry 32
Smallbone, William 77
Smallwood, Richard 41
Smerdon, Noah 33
Smith, Adam 11
Smith, Alistair 51
Smith, Andy 41
Smith, Harry 58
Smith, Jack 79
Smith, Jonny 18
Smith, Jordan 60
Smith, Korey 82
Smith, Lawrence 34
Smith, Martin 72
Smith, Matt 53
Smith, Matthew 49
Smith, Matthew 3
Smith, Michael 71
Smith, Nathan 65
Smith, Sam 69
Smith, Scott 90
Smith, Timmy 79
Smith, Tommy 25
Smith, Tommy 80
Smith, Tommy 42
Smith, Tyler 74
Smith, Will 39
Smith, Zachary 15
Smith-Rowe, Emile 3
Smithies, Alex 20
Smyth, Paul 68
Snelgrove, McCauley 41
Snodgrass, Robert 88
Sohna, Harrison 4
Solanke, Dominic 11
Solberg, Isak 84
Soldevila, Oriol 7
Sollbauer , Michael 5
Solomon, Harrison 30
Solomon-Otabor, Viv 90
Son, Heung-Min 84
Sondergaard, Andreas 91
Songo'o, Yann 55
Soonsup-Bell, Jude 23
Sorensen, Jacob 59
Sorensen, Mads 13
Sorenson, Lasse 80
Sorinola, Matthew 54
Sotiriou, Ruel 45
Soucek, Tomas 89
Soule, Jamie 88
Soutar, Harry 80
Southern-Cooper, Jake 71
Southwood, Luke 69
Sow, Samba 60
Sowah, Kamal 44
Sowerby, Jack 58
Sowunmi, Omar 25
Soyuncu, Caglar 44
Sparkes, Jack 33
Sparrow, Tom 80
Spearing, Jay 85
Spence, Djed 52
Spence, Lewis 73
Spence, Sion 29
Spencer, Morten 43
Spinelli, Kevin 1
Spokes, Luke 38
Springett, Tony 59
Stacey, Jack 11
Stagg, Thomas 25
Stanislas, Junior 11
Stanley, Alfie 66
Stanley, Connor 50
Starbuck, Joseph 38
Staunton, Reece 12
Stead, Jon 39
Stearman, Richard 40
Stech, Marek 51
Steele, Jason 14
Steels, Vinny 81
Steer, Jed 4
Steffen, Zackary 49
Stephens, Dale 17
Stephens, Jack 77
Stephens, Jack 62
Stergiakis, Antonios 8
Sterling, Kazaiah 84
Sterling, Raheem 49
Stevanovic, Filip 49
Stevens, Enda 74
Stevens, Fin 13
Stevens, Jordan 43
Stevens, Mathew 35
Stevenson, Ben 25
Stevenson, Toby 87
Stewart, Anthony 92
Stewart, Kevin 9
Stewart, O'Shane 78
Stewart, Ross C 81
Stewart, Sean 59
Stiepermann, Marco 59
Stirk, Ryan 7
Stockdale, David 92
Stockley, Jayden 67
Stockton, Cole 55
Stojanovic, Dejan 52
Stokes, Chris 35
Stolarczyk, Jakub 44
Stone, Aiden 51
Stones, John 49
Storey, Gerard 66
Storey, Jordan 67
Stowe, Luke 1
Street, Robert 29
Stretton, Jack 30
Struijk, Pascal 43
Stubbs, Sam 33
Styles, Callum 5
Success, Isaac 87
Suengchitthawon, Thanawat 44
Suklenicki, Oliver 12
Summerville, Crysencio 43
Sunjic, Ivan 7
Surman, Andrew 54
Surridge, Sam 11
Sutcliffe, Ethan 2
Sutton, Levi 12
Sutton, Will 61
Svidersky, Martin 50
Swailes, Jude 56
Swan, Will 60
Sweeney, Dan 35
Sweeney, Jayden 45
Sweeney, Pierce 33
Sweeney, Ryan 51
Swift, John 69
Swinkels, Sil 4
Swyer, Kamarai 89
Sy, Ibrahima 80
Sykes, Cain 52
Sykes, Mark 62
Sykes, Ross 1
Sykes-Kenworthy, George 30
Sylla, Mamadou 4
Szmidics, Sammie 63
Tafazolli, Ryan 92
Taft, George 73
Tait, Michael 4
Takpe, Enoch 34
Talley, Fynn 14
Tanganga, Japhet 84
Tanimowo, Ayo 14
Tanner, George 21
Tarensi, Oscar 49
Targett, Matt 4
Tarkowski, James 17
Tasdemir, Serhat 63
Tau, Percy 14
Tauriainen, Jimi 23
Tavares, Fabio 26
Tavares, Sidnei 44
Tavernier, Marcus 52
Taylor, Brandon 81
Taylor, Caleb 88
Taylor, Callum 78
Taylor, Charlie 17
Taylor, Chris 6
Taylor, Connor 80
Taylor, Corey 85
Taylor, Dale 60
Taylor, Greg 19
Taylor, Jack 63
Taylor, Jake 33
Taylor, Jake 65
Taylor, James 29
Taylor, James 15
Taylor, Jason 6
Taylor, Jon 31
Taylor, Kyle 11
Taylor, Lyle 60
Taylor, Matty 62

Taylor, Neil 4
Taylor, Richard 78
Taylor, Ryan 57
Taylor, Terry 18
Taylor-Crossdale, Martell 36
Tchamadeu, Junior 25
Tchaptchet, Allan 77
te Wierik, Mike 30
Teale, Connor 34
Tedic, Slobodan 49
Teggart, Eoin 66
Telford, Dominic 57
Tella, Nathan 77
Tete, Kenny 36
Tetek, Dejan 69
Tettey, Alexander 59
Thiago, Alcantara 47
Thiago Silva, Emiliano 23
Thomas, Bobby 17
Thomas, Conor 24
Thomas, George 68
Thomas, Jordan 59
Thomas, Joshua 82
Thomas, Lewis 35
Thomas, Luke 5
Thomas, Luke 44
Thomas, Partey 3
Thomas, Sorba 40
Thomas, Terell 2
Thomas-Asante, Brandon 72
Thomason, George 10
Thompson, Adam 45
Thompson, Ben 53
Thompson, Ben 34
Thompson, Cameron 5
Thompson, Curtis 92
Thompson, Dominic 13
Thompson, Jordan 26
Thompson, Jordan 80
Thompson, Liam 30
Thompson, Louis 59
Thompson, Max 17
Thompson, Nathan 63
Thompson, Seb 30
Thompson-Sommers, Kane 7
Thomson, George 39
Thomson, Reagan 56
Thorniley, Jordan 9
Thorpe, Elliot 84
Threlkeld, Oscar 72
Tickle, Sam 90
Tiehi, Jean-Pierre 36
Tielemans, Youri 44
Tiensia, Junior 53
Tierney, Kieran 3
Tilley, James 27
Tilt, Curtis 71
Timlin, Jamie 85
Tinubu, Sam 79
Tipton, Ollie 91
Tobias Figueiredo, Pereira 60
Toffolo, Harry 40
Tolaj, Lorent 14
Tomas Esteves, Lago 69
Tomkins, James 29
Tomkinson, Jonathan 59
Tomlin, Lee 20
Tomlinson, Harvey 38
Tomlinson, Ollie 64
Tomori, Fikayo 23
Toney, Ivan 13
Topalloj, Besart 53
Toral, Jon 7
Torreira, Lucas 3
Torres, Ferran 49
Tosun, Cenk 32
Touray, Ibou 72
Touray, Momodou 72
Toure, Gime 21
Toure, Yannick 56
Tovide, Samson 25
Towell, Richie 72
Towler, Ryley 15
Townsend, Andros 29
Townsend, Conor 88
Townsend, Nick 57
Townsend-West, Mackye 79
Tozer, Ben 24
Tracey, Shilow 76
Trafford, James 49
Traore, Adama 91
Traore, Bertrand 4
Travers, Mark 11
Travis, Lewis 8
Trevitt, Ryan 13
Trezeguet, Mahmoud 4
Trickett-Smith, Dan 65
Troost-Ekong, William 87
Trossard, Leandro 14
Trott, Nathan 89
Trueman, Connal 7
Trybull, Tom 59
Tsaroulla, Nicholas 27
Tsimikas, Konstantinos 47
Tsoungui, Antef 14
Tuanzebe, Axel 50
Tucker, Jack 37
Tulloch, Rayhaan 88
Tunnicliffe, Jordan 27
Tunnicliffe, Ryan 48
Turley, Jamie 45
Turnbull, Duncan 66
Turnbull, Jordan 72
Turner, Jake 56
Turner-Cooke, Jay 56
Turton, Oliver 9
Tutonda, David 16
Tutte, Andrew 10
Twamley, Lewys 57
Tweedley, Matthew 10
Twine, Scott 83
Tyler, Cian 26
Tyler, Mark 63
Tymon, Josh 80
Tyrer, Harry 32
Tzanev, Nikola 2
Udoh, Daniel 76
Under, Cengiz 44
Upson, Edward 16
Urhoghide, Osaze 75
Uwakwe , Tariq 23
Vale, Harvey 23
Vale, Jack 8
Valencia, Joel 13
Valery, Yann 77
Vallejo, Alex 40
Van Aanholt, Patrick 29
van Aken, Joost 75
van de Beek, Donny 50
van den Berg, Sepp 47
Van den Heuvel, Dani 43
van Dijk, Virgil 47
Van Hecke, Jan 14
van Stappershoef, Jordi 16
van Veen, Kevin 73
Vancooten, Terence 79
Vardy, Jamie 44
Varney, Luke 18
Vassell, Kyle 71
Vassilev, Indiana 4
Vaughan, Harry 61
Vaughan, James 85
Vaulks, Will 20
Veale, Jack 33
Vega, Luca 22
Vela, Joshua 76
Veltman, Joel 14
Vennings, James 22
Verlinden, Thibaud 80
Vernam, Charles 12
Verrips, Michael 74
Vestergaard, Jannik 77
Vickers, Josh 71
Vigouroux, Lawrence 45
Vilca, Rodrigo 56
Vincelot, Romain 79
Vincent, Frankie 11
Vincent-Young, Kane 42
Vinicius, Carlos 84
Viral, Allan 42
Virginia, Joao 32
Virtue, Matthew 9
Visser, Dino 65
Vitek, Radek 50
Vitinha, Ferreira 91
Vokes, Sam 80
Vokins, Jake 77
Vrancic, Mario 59
Vydra, Matej 17
Vyner, Zak 15
Wade, Bradley 70
Wady, Ethan 23
Waghorn, Martyn 30
Wagstaff, Scott 35
Wakefield, Charlie 26
Wakeling, Jacob 44
Walcott, Theo 32
Waldock, Liam 75
Walker, Aidan 51
Walker, Brad 76
Walker, Ethan 67
Walker, Jake 4
Walker, Kyle 49
Walker, Laurie 54
Walker, Sam 69
Walker, Stephen 52
Walker, Tom 39
Walker, Tyler 26
Walker, Zain 16
Walker-Peters, Kyle 77
Walker-Rice, Danny 85
Wallace, Jed 53
Wallace, Kieran 18
Wallace, Lee 68
Wallace, Murray 53
Walsh, Joe 46
Walsh, Joe 68
Walsh, Liam 15
Walsh, Louis 78
Walton, Christian 14
Walton, Jack 5
Wan Bissaka, Aaron 50
Warburton, Matthew 58
Ward, Danny 40
Ward, Danny 44
Ward, Grant 9
Ward, Jed 16
Ward, Joe 63
Ward, Joel 29
Ward, Keaton 51
Ward, Lewis 33
Ward, Stephen 42
Ward-Prowse, James 77
Wareham, Jayden 23
Warner, Jaden 59
Warrington, Lewis 32
Washington, Conor 22
Waterfall, Luke 38
Watkins, Marley 15
Watkins, Ollie 4
Watmore, Duncan 52
Watson, Ben 22
Watson, Louis 30
Watson, Rory 73
Watson, Ryan 58
Watson, Tennai 69
Watt, Elliot 12
Watters, Max 20
Watts, Caleb 77
Watts, Kelland 56
Wearne, Stephen 81
Webb, Bradley 15
Webb, Lewis 82
Webber, Oliver 29
Webber, Patrick 90
Webster, Adam 14
Webster, Charlie 23
Weimann, Andreas 15
Weir, Jensen 14
Welbeck, Danny 14
Welch, Reece 32
Welch-Hayes, Miles 25
Wells, Ben 68
Wells, Nahki 15
Werner, Timo 23
Wesley, Moraes 4
Westbrooke, Zain 16
Westwood, Ashley 17
Westwood, Keiren 75
Whalley, Shaun 76
Wharton, Scott 8
Whatmough, Jack 66
Wheeler, David 92
Whelan, Callum 61
Whelan, Corey 90
Whelan, Glenn 34
Whitaker, Charlie 32
White, Albert 42
White, Ben 14
White, Harvey 84
White, Hayden 86
White, Joe 56
White, John 78
White, Tom 8
Whitehall, Isaac 8
Whitehead, Danny 65
Whitehouse, Elliott 35
Whiteman, Alfie 84
Whiteman, Ben 67
Whittaker, Morgan 82
Whyte, Gavin 20
Wickens, George 36
Wickham, Connor 29
Widdowson, Joe 45
Wiggett, Charlie 23
Wijnaldum, Georginio 47
Wildig, Aaron 55
Wildin, Luther 79
Wilding, Samuel 81
Wildsmith, Joe 75
Wiles, Ben 71
Wiles-Richards, Harvey 15
Wilkinson, Conor 45
Wilks, Mallik 41
Williams, Alfie 79
Williams, Andy 24
Williams, Brandon 50
Williams, Charlie 18
Williams, Daniel 82
Williams, Derrick 8
Williams, Dylan 30
Williams, Ed 31
Williams, Euan 22
Williams, George B 16
Williams, George C 38
Williams, Jay 39
Williams, Joe 15
Williams, Jon 20
Williams, Jordan 5
Williams, M Jordan 10
Williams, Morgan 26
Williams, Neco 47
Williams, Randell 33
Williams, Rhys 47
Williams, Ro-Shaun 76
Williams, Ryan 66
Williams, Shaun 53
Williams, Zac 28
Williams-Lowe, Kayden 68
Willian, da Silva 3
Willian Jose, da Silva 91
Willis, Joe 86
Willis, Jordan 81
Willmott, Robbie 57
Willock, Chris 68
Willock, Joe 3
Willock, Matthew 37
Wilmot, Ben 87
Wilshere, Jack 11
Wilson, Adam 56
Wilson, Ben 26
Wilson, Callum 56
Wilson, Harry 47
Wilson, James 64
Wilson, James 72
Wilson, Kane 35
Wilson, Lewis 33
Wilson, Scott 6
Wilson, Tom 21
Wilson, Tyree 30
Wilson-Esbrand, Josh 49
Winchester, Carl 81
Windass, Josh 75
Windsor, Owen 88
Winfield, Charlie 5
Wing, Lewis 52
Winks, Harry 84
Winnall, Sam 62
Wintle, Ryan 28
Wisdom, Andre 30
Wollacott, Jojo 15
Woltman, Max 47
Wood, Charlie 12
Wood, Chris 17
Wood, Connor 12
Wood, Harry 41
Wood, Richard 71
Wood-Gordon, Nathan 52
Woodburn, Ben 47
Woodiwiss, Joe 57
Woodman, Freddie 56
Woodrow, Cauley 5
Woods, Charlie 58
Woods, Gary 61
Woods, Henry 37
Woods, Ryan 80
Woods, Sam 29
Woodthorpe, Nathan 28
Woodyard, Alex 2
Woolery, Kaiyne 85
Woolfenden, Luke 42
Woollard-Innocent, Kai 68
Woolston, Paul 50
Wootton, Scott 64
Worman, Ben 19
Worrall, David 65
Worrall, Joe 60
Wright, Bailey 81
Wright, Callum 44
Wright, Jake 51
Wright, Joe 31
Wright, Joe 53
Wright, Josh 27
Wright, Mark 27
Wright, Max 38
Wright, Tyreik 4
Wright-Phillips, D'Margio 80
Wyke, Charlie 81
Xande Silva, Nascimento 89
Xhaka, Granit 3
Xhemajli, Arbenit 81
Yapi, Romaric 14
Yarmolenko, Andriy 89
Yates, Cameron 92
Yates, Jerry 9
Yates, Matthew 30
Yates, Ryan 60
Yearn, Kai 19
Yedlin, DeAndre 56
Yiadom, Andy 69
Yokuslu, Okay 88
Young, Brad 4
Young, Jack 56
Young, Joe 91
Young, Matt 45
Young , Jake 35
Younger, Ollie 81
Yuri Ribeiro, Oliveira 60
Zaha, Wilfried 29
Zambo, Andre-Franck 36
Zamburek, Jan 13
Zanzala, Offrande 21
Zemura, Jordan 11
Zeqiri, Andi 14
Ziger, Karlo 23
Zimba, Chanka 20
Zimmermann, Christoph 59
Zinchenko, Alexander 49
Zinckernagel, Philip 87
Ziyech, Hakim 23
Zohore, Kenneth 88
Zouma, Kurt 23
Zouma, Yoan 6
Zych, Oliwier 4

NATIONAL LIST OF REFEREES FOR SEASON 2020–21

Adcock, James
Allison, Samuel
Atkinson, Martin
Attwell, Stuart
Backhouse, Anthony
Bankes, Peter
Barrott, Samuel
Bell, James
Bond, Darren
Bourne, Declan
Boyeson, Carl
Bramall, Thomas
Breakspear, Charles
Brook, Carl
Brooks, John
Busby, John
Coggins, Antony
Coote, David
Coy, Martin
Davies, Andy
Dean, Michael
Donohue, Matthew
Doughty, Leigh
Drysdale, Darren
Duncan, Scott
Edwards, Marc
Eltringham, Geoff
England, Darren
Finnie, Will
Friend, Kevin
Gillett, Jarred
Haines, Andy
Hair, Neil
Handley, Darren
Harrington, Tony
Hicks, Craig
Hooper, Simon
Howard, Paul
Huxtable, Brett
Johnson, Kevin
Jones, Robert
Joyce, Ross
Kavanagh, Christopher
Kettle, Trevor
Langford, Oliver
Lewis, Robert
Linington, James
Madley, Andrew
Madley, Bobby
Marriner, Andre
Martin, Stephen
Mason, Lee
Moss, Jonathan
Nield, Tom
Oldham, James
Oldham, Scott
Oliver, Michael
Pawson, Craig
Pollard, Christopher
Purkiss, Sam
Robinson, Tim
Rock, David
Salisbury, Graham
Salisbury, Michael
Sarginson, Christopher
Scott, Graham
Simpson, Jeremy
Smith, Josh
Speedie, Benjamin
Stockbridge, Sebastian
Stroud, Keith
Swabey, Lee
Taylor, Anthony
Tierney, Paul
Toner, Ben
Ward, Gavin
Webb, David
Whitestone, Dean
Woolmer, Andy
Wright, Peter
Yates, Ollie
Young, Alan

ASSISTANT REFEREES

Amey, Justin
Amphlett, Marvyn
Aspinall, Natalie
Atkin, Robert
Avent, David
Aylott, Andrew
Bandara, Damith
Barnard, Nicholas
Bartlett, Richard
Beck, Simon
Begley, Michael
Bennett, Andy
Bennett, Simon
Beswick, Gary
Betts, Lee
Bickle, Oliver
Blunden, Darren
Bonneywell, Dan
Bristow, Matthew
Brown, Conor
Brown, Stephen
Burt, Stuart
Butler, Stuart
Byrne, George
Byrne, Helen
Cann, Darren
Chard, Michael
Cheosiaua, Ravel
Clark, Joe
Clayton, Alan
Clayton, Simon
Cook, Dan
Cook, Daniel
Cooper, Ian
Cooper, Nicholas
Crowhurst, Leigh
Crysell, Adam
Cunliffe, Mark
Da Costa, Anthony
Dabbs, Robert
Dallison, Andrew
Davies, Neil
Denton, Michael
Dermott, Philip
Derrien, Mark
Desborough, Mike
Dwyer, Mark
Eaton, Derek
Evans, Paul
Farmer, Aaron
Farrell, Conor
Finch, Stephen
Fitch-Jackson, Carl
Flynn, Daniel
Flynn, John
Ford, Declan
Fox, Andrew
Freeman, Lee
Fyvie, Graeme
George, Michael
Gill, Bhupinder
Gooch, Peter
Gordon, Barry
Graham, Paul
Gratton, Danny
Greenhalgh, Nick

Grunnill, Wayne
Hall, Bradley
Hanley, Michael
Harty, Thomas
Hatzidakis, Constantine
Hendley, Andrew
Hilton, Gary
Hodskinson, Paul
Holmes, Adrian
Holmes, Martyn
Hopton, Nick
Howick, Kevin
Howson, Akil
Hudson, Shaun
Hughes, Kenwyn
Hunt, David
Hunt, Jonathan
Husband, Christopher
Hussin, Ian
Hyde, Robert
Isherwood, Chris
Jackson, Oliver
Jones, Mark
Jones, Matthew
Kane, Graham
Karaivanov, Hristo
Kelly, Paul
Khan, Abbas
Kidd, Christopher
Kirkup, Peter
Laver, Andrew
Leach, Daniel
Ledger, Scott
Lee, Matthew
Lennard, Harry
Lewis, Sam
Liddle, Geoffrey
Lister, Paul
Long, Simon
Lugg, Nigel
Mainwaring, James
Marks, Louis
Maskell, Garry
Massey-Ellis, Sian
McGrath, Matthew
Mellor, Gareth
Merchant, Robert
Meredith, Steven
Moore, Anthony
Morris, Kevin
Morris, Richard
Mulraine, Kevin
Nelson, Alistair
Newhouse, Paul
Nunn, Adam
Ogles, Samuel
Parry, Matthew
Perry, Marc
Plane, Steven
Pottage, Mark
Rashid, Lisa
Read, Gregory
Rees, Paul
Ricketts, Adam
Robathan, Daniel
Ross, Alasdair
Rushton, Steven
Russell, Geoffrey
Russell, Mark
Scholes, Mark
Sharp, Neil
Shaw, Simon
Simpson, Joe
Smallwood, Billy
Smart, Edward
Smedley, Ian
Smith, Matthew
Smith, Rob
Smith, Wade
Stokes, Joseph
Stonier, Paul
Taylor, Craig
Taylor, Grant
Tranter, Adrian
Treleaven, Dean
Vallance, James
Venamore, Lee
Viccars, Gareth
Wade, Christopher
Wade, Stephen
Ward, Christopher
Waters, Adrian
Webb, Michael
West, Richard
Whitaker, Ryan
Wigglesworth, Richard
Wild, Richard
Wilding, Darren
Wilkes, Matthew
Williams, Andrew
Williams, Ollie
Williams, Scott
Wilson, James
Wilson, Marc
Wood, Timothy
Woodward, Daniel
Woodward, Richard
Yates, Paul

MANAGERS – IN AND OUT 2020–21

SEPTEMBER 2020

3 John Pemberton appointed manager of Chesterfield after being in temporary charge.
11 John Sheridan appointed manager of Wigan Ath.

OCTOBER 2020

6 Sabri Lamouchi sacked as manager of Nottingham F.
6 Chris Hughton appointed manager of Nottingham F.
6 Gerhard Struber leaves as manager of Barnsley to become new head coach of MLS side New York Red Bulls. First-team coach Adam Murray takes temporary charge.
12 Graham Alexander sacked as manager of Salford C. Paul Scholes takes temporary charge.
23 Valerien Ismael appointed manager of Barnsley.
27 Graham Coughlan sacked as manager of Mansfield T. Academy manager Richard Cooper takes temporary charge.
31 Mike Jackson sacked as manager of Tranmere R. Assistant manager Ian Dawes takes temporary charge.

NOVEMBER 2020

4 Richie Wellens leaves as manager of Swindon T to take charge at Salford C. Swindon T assistant manager Noel Hunt takes temporary charge.
6 Nigel Clough appointed manager of Mansfield T.
9 Garry Monk sacked as manager of Sheffield W.
13 Tony Pulis appointed manager of Sheffield W.
13 John Sheridan leaves as manager of Wigan Ath to become manager of Swindon T. Assistant manager Leam Richardson and Academy Coach Gregor Rioch take temporary charge.
14 Phillip Cocu sacked as manager of Derby Co. Wayne Rooney takes temporary charge.
14 Ben Garner sacked as manager of Bristol R. Head of recruitment Tommy Widdrington takes temporary charge.
19 Paul Tisdale appointed manager of Bristol R.
21 Keith Hill appointed as manager of Tranmere R.
25 Sam Ricketts sacked as manager of Shrewsbury T.
27 Steve Cotterill appointed manager of Shrewsbury T.
29 Phil Parkinson sacked as manager of Sunderland. First-team coach Andrew Taylor takes temporary charge.

DECEMBER 2020

5 Lee Johnson appointed manager of Sunderland.
13 Stuart McCall sacked as manager of Bradford C. Youth-team coaches Mark Trueman and Conor Sellars take temporary charge.
13 David Dunn sacked as manager of Barrow. Assistant manager Rob Kelly takes temporary charge.
16 Slaven Bilic sacked as manager of WBA.
16 Sam Allardyce appointed manager of WBA.
19 Vladimir Ivic sacked as manager of Watford.
20 Xisco Munoz appointed manager of Watford.
23 Michael Jolley appointed manager of Barrow.
23 Ian Holloway resigns as manager of Grimsby T. First-team coach Ben Davies takes temporary charge.
28 Tony Pulis sacked as manager of Sheffield W. First-team coach Neil Thompson takes temporary charge.
29 Jake Buxton sacked as manager of Burton Alb.
30 Paul Hurst appointed manager of Grimsby T.

JANUARY 2021

1 Jimmy Floyd Hasselbaink appointed manager of Burton Alb.
4 Joey Barton leaves as manager of Fleetwood T. Youth-team coach Simon Wiles takes temporary charge.
4 John Askey sacked as manager of Port Vale. First-team coach Danny Pugh takes temporary charge.
15 Wayne Rooney appointed manager of Derby Co after being in temporary charge.
21 Neil Harris sacked as manager of Cardiff C.
22 Mick McCarthy appointed manager of Cardiff C until the end of the season.
25 Frank Lampard sacked as manager of Chelsea.
26 Thomas Tuchel appointed manager of Chelsea.
30 Glyn Hodges leaves as manager of AFC Wimbledon by mutual consent. Academy coach Mark Robinson takes temporary charge.
31 Simon Grayson appointed manager of Fleetwood T.

FEBRUARY 2021

3 Jason Tindall sacked as manager of Bournemouth. First-team coach Jonathan Woodgate takes temporary charge.
10 Paul Tisdale sacked as manager of Bristol R. Head of recruitment Tommy Widdrington takes temporary charge.
10 Keith Curle sacked as manager of Northampton T. Youth-team coach Jon Brady takes temporary charge.
15 Darrell Clarke leaves as manager of Walsall and becomes manager of Port Vale. Walsall assistant coach Brian Dutton takes charge until the end of the season.
16 Dean Holden sacked as manager of Bristol C. Assistant head coaches Paul Simpson and Keith Downing take temporary charge.
17 Mark Robinson appointed manager of AFC Wimbledon after being in temporary charge.

21 Jonathan Woodgate appointed manager of Bournemouth until the end of the season.
21 Michael Jolley sacked as manager of Barrow. Assistant manager Rob Kelly takes charge until the end of the season.
22 Nigel Pearson appointed manager of Bristol C.
22 Joey Barton appointed manager of Bristol R.
22 Mark Trueman and Conor Sellars appointed joint managers of Bradford C after being in temporary charge.
23 Steve Ball sacked as manager of Colchester U. Maldon & Tiptree manager and former Colchester U player Wayne Brown takes temporary charge.
27 Ross Embleton sacked as manager of Leyton Orient. Player-coach Jobi McAnuff takes temporary charge.

MARCH 2021
1 Darren Moore leaves as manager of Doncaster R and becomes manager of Sheffield W. Andy Butler appointed manager of Doncaster R until the end of the season.
1 Paul Lambert leaves as manager of Ipswich T by mutual consent.
2 Paul Cook appointed manager of Ipswich T.
7 Harry Kewell sacked as manager of Oldham Ath.
8 Keith Curle appointed manager of Oldham Ath until the end of the season.
13 Chris Wilder leaves as manager of Sheffield U by mutual consent. Under-23 manager Paul Heckingbottom takes charge until the end of the season.
14 Kenny Jackett sacked as manager of Portsmouth.
15 Lee Bowyer resigns as manager of Charlton Ath.
16 Aitor Karanka sacked as manager of Birmingham C. Lee Bowyer appointed manager.
18 Nigel Adkins appointed manager of Charlton Ath.
18 Danny Cowley appointed manager of Portsmouth.
21 Alex Neil sacked as manager of Preston NE. Assistant manager Frankie McAvoy takes charge until the end of the season.
22 Richie Wellens leaves as manager of Salford C by mutual consent.
23 Gary Bowyer appointed manager of Salford C.
31 Wayne Brown sacked as interim manager of Colchester U and assistant Hayden Mullins appointed until the end of the season.

APRIL 2021
9 Mark Molesley sacked as manager of Southend U. Phil Brown appointed manager.
11 Mark Cooper sacked as manager of Forest Green R. Youth-team coach Jimmy Ball takes charge until the end of the season.
18 John Sheridan sacked as manager of Swindon T. Assistant manager Tommy Wright takes charge until the end of the season.
19 Jose Mourinho sacked as manager of Tottenham H. Academy coach Ryan Mason takes charge until the end of the season.
21 Leam Richardson appointed manager of Wigan Ath after being in temporary charge.

MAY 2021
8 Jon Brady appointed manager of Northampton T after being in temporary charge.
10 Frankie McAvoy appointed manager of Preston NE after being in temporary charge.
10 Mark Trueman and Conor Sellars sacked as joint managers of Bradford C.
11 Keith Hill sacked as manager of Tranmere R. Assistant manager Ian Dawes takes temporary charge.
17 Richie Wellens appointed manager of Doncaster R.
18 Roy Hodgson to step down as manager of Crystal Palace at the end of the season.
19 Sam Allardyce to step down as manager of WBA at the end of the season.
19 Matthew Taylor appointed manager of Walsall.
21 Kenny Jackett appointed manager of Leyton Orient.
21 Nuno Espirito Santo to step down as manager of Wolverhampton W at the end of the season.
27 Slavisa Jokanovic appointed manager of Sheffield U.
27 Rob Edwards appointed manager of Forest Green R.
31 Micky Mellon appointed manager of Tranmere R.

JUNE 2021
3 Derek Adams leaves as manager of Morecambe.
4 Derek Adams appointed as manager of Bradford C.
7 Stephen Robinson appointed manager of Morecambe.
9 Bruno Lage appointed manager of Wolverhampton W.
24 Valerien Ismael leaves as manager of Barnsley and becomes manager of WBA.
25 John McGreal leaves as manager of Swindon T.
27 Jonathan Woodgate leaves as manager of Bournemouth.
28 Scott Parker leaves as manager of Fulham and becomes manager of Bournemouth.
29 Markus Schopp appointed manager of Barnsley.
30 Rafael Benitez appointed manager of Everton.
30 Nuno Espirito Santo appointed manager of Tottenham H.
30 Brian Barry-Murphy leaves as manager of Rochdale.

JULY 2021
1 Marco Silva appointed manager of Fulham.
4 Patrick Vieira appointed manager of Crystal Palace.
10 Robbie Stockdale appointed manager of Rochdale.

TRANSFERS 2020–21

**Transfer to be completed at the end of the season.*

JULY 2020

2 Arthur, Festus	Stockport Co	Hull C	Undisclosed
29 Ayunga, Jonah	Havant & Waterlooville	Bristol R	Undisclosed
20 Baldwin, Jack	Sunderland	Bristol R	Free
24 Balogun, Leon	Wigan Ath	Rangers	Free
19 Barrow, Mo	Reading	Jeonbuk Hyundai Motors	Undisclosed
20 Beadling, Tom	Dunfermline Ath	Barrow	Free
20 Bellingham, Jude	Birmingham C	Borussia Dortmund	Undisclosed
3 Cadden, Nicky	Greenock Morton	Forest Green R	Undisclosed
16 Cisse, Ousseynou	Gillingham	Leyton Orient	Free
17 Clarke, Billy	Grimsby T	Bradford C	Free
1 Clarke, Ollie	Bristol R	Mansfield T	Free
14 Clarke, Tom	Preston NE	Salford C	Free
21 Comley, Brandon	Colchester U	Bolton W	Free
25 Cooke, Callum	Peterborough U	Bradford C	Free
7 Costa, Helder	Wolverhampton W	Leeds U	£16m
28 Dele-Bashiru, Fisayo	Manchester C	Sheffield W	Undisclosed
21 Digby, Paul	Stevenage	Cambridge U	Free
10 Doyle, Eoin	Swindon T	Bolton W	Free
21 Ehmer, Max	Gillingham	Bristol R	Free
8 Ekpiteta, Marvin	Leyton Orient	Blackpool	Free
15 Emmerson, Zak	Oldham Ath	Brighton & HA	Undisclosed
7 Evans, Jack	Blackburn R	Forest Green R	Free
17 Foderingham, Wes	Rangers	Sheffield U	Free
3 Gillespie, Mark	Motherwell	Newcastle U	Free
18 Grant, Josh	Chelsea	Bristol R	Free
30 Gyollai, Daniel	Wigan Ath	Peterborough U	Free
31 Hall, Grant	QPR	Middlesbrough	Free
22 Hamilton, CJ	Mansfield T	Blackpool	Undisclosed
27 Harvie, Daniel	Ayr U	Milton Keynes D	Undisclosed
22 Haunstrup, Brandon	Portsmouth	Kilmarnock	Undisclosed
29 Henderson, Ian	Rochdale	Salford C	Free
1 Hornby, Fraser	Everton	Reims	Undisclosed
17 Hunter, Ash	Fleetwood T	Salford C	Undisclosed
31 Jackson, Ryan	Colchester U	Gillingham	Free
27 Jaiyesimi, Diallang	Norwich C	Swindon T	Free
20 James, Luke	Hartlepool U	Barrow	Free
22 Johnson, Billy	Norwich C	Stevenage	Free
31 Jones, James	Altrincham	Barrow	Free
20 Jones, Mike	Carlisle U	Barrow	Free
8 Knockaert, Anthony	Brighton & HA	Fulham	Undisclosed
27 Lallana, Adam	Liverpool	Brighton & HA	Free
28 Laurent, Josh	Shrewsbury T	Reading	Free
13 Lawless, Steven	Livingston	Burton Alb	Free
27 Lovren, Dejan	Liverpool	Zenit St Petersburg	£10.9m
22 Lowe, Jason	Bolton W	Salford C	Free
28 Maris, George	Cambridge U	Mansfield T	Undisclosed
31 Marsh, Tyrone	Boreham Wood	Stevenage	Free
10 Marshall, Ross	Maidstone U	Stevenage	Free
20 Matt, Jamille	Newport Co	Forest Green R	Free
28 McCormick, Luke	Swindon T	Plymouth Arg	Free
15 McGee, Luke	Portsmouth	Forest Green R	Free
27 McGrandles, Conor	Milton Keynes D	Lincoln C	Free
28 Menayese, Rollin	Bristol R	Mansfield T	Undisclosed
5 Miller, Mickel	Hamilton A	Rotherham U	Free
16 Mills, Zak	Oldham Ath	Port Vale	Free
27 Missilou, Christopher	Oldham Ath	Northampton T	Free
21 Moore-Taylor, Jordan	Milton Keynes D	Forest Green R	Free
31 Mulder, Erwin	Swansea C	Heerenveen	Free
20 Mullin, Paul	Tranmere R	Cambridge U	Free
27 Mumba, Bali	Sunderland	Norwich C	Undisclosed
30 O'Brien, Aiden	Millwall	Sunderland	Free
15 O'Hare, Callum	Aston Villa	Coventry C	Free
8 Pinnock, Mitch	AFC Wimbledon	Kilmarnock	Free
29 Platt, Matty	Blackburn R	Barrow	Undisclosed
17 Rawson, Farrend	Forest Green R	Mansfield T	Free
7 Rodney, Devante	Salford C	Port Vale	Free
24 Ross, Ethan	Colchester U	Lincoln C	Free

3 Sane, Leroy	Manchester C	Bayern Munich	£44.7m
15 Sarcevic, Antoni	Plymouth Arg	Bolton W	Free
9 Sarkic, Oliver	Burton Alb	Blackpool	Free
20 Shaughnessy, Joe	Southend U	St Mirren	Free
11 Sutton, Levi	Scunthorpe U	Bradford C	Free
1 Sweeney, Dan	Barnet	Forest Green R	Free
20 Taft, George	Cambridge U	Bolton W	Free
31 Taylor, Matty	Bristol C	Oxford U	Free
27 Thomas, George	Leicester C	QPR	Free
28 Turnbull, Jordan	Northampton T	Salford C	Free
24 Vincelot, Romain	Shrewsbury T	Stevenage	Free
27 Watt, Elliot	Wolverhampton W	Bradford C	Undisclosed
2 Wilks, Mallik	Barnsley	Hull C	Undisclosed
29 Williams, Andy	Northampton T	Cheltenham T	Undisclosed
8 Wilson, Kane	WBA	Forest Green R	Free
21 Yates, Jerry	Rotherham U	Blackpool	Undisclosed
16 Young, Jake	Sheffield U	Forest Green R	Free
1 Zanzala, Offrande	Accrington S	Crewe Alex	Free
AUGUST 2020			
13 Ajeti, Albian	West Ham U	Celtic	£4.5m
6 Ake, Nathan	Bournemouth	Manchester C	£40m
11 Allen, Charlie	Linfield	Leeds U	Undisclosed
17 Amos, Luke	Tottenham H	QPR	Undisclosed
7 Armer, Jack	Preston NE	Carlisle U	Free
18 Asonganyi, Dylan	Milton Keynes D	Oxford U	Free
7 Baptiste, Alex	Doncaster R	Bolton W	Free
28 Bennett, Mason	Derby Co	Millwall	Undisclosed
16 Blackett, Tyler	Reading	Nottingham F	Free
21 Bolger, Cian	Lincoln C	Northampton T	Free
2 Borthwick-Jackson, Cameron	Manchester U	Oldham Ath	Free
6 Bostwick, Michael	Lincoln C	Burton Alb	Free
7 Bridcutt, Liam	Nottingham F	Lincoln C	Free
24 Broom, Ryan	Cheltenham T	Peterborough U	Undisclosed
3 Burgess, Cameron	Scunthorpe U	Accrington S	Free
4 Burns, Bobby	Hearts	Barrow	Free
24 Butcher, Matt	Bournemouth	Accrington S	Undisclosed
7 Camara, Panutche	Crawley T	Plymouth Arg	Free
1 Camps, Callum	Rochdale	Fleetwood T	Free
7 Caprice, Jake	Tranmere R	Exeter C	Free
10 Chester, James	Aston Villa	Stoke C	Free
26 Chilwell, Ben	Leicester C	Chelsea	£45m
12 Chislett, Ethan	Aldershot T	AFC Wimbledon	Free
19 Chrisene, Ben	Exeter C	Aston Villa	Undisclosed
7 Clare, Sean	Hearts	Oxford U	Undisclosed
6 Clark, Jordan	Accrington S	Luton T	Free
27 Clarke-Harris, Jonson	Bristol R	Peterborough U	Undisclosed
11 Colback, Jack	Newcastle U	Nottingham F	Free
20 Coleman, Joel	Huddersfield T	Fleetwood T	Free
25 Connolly, Dylan	AFC Wimbledon	St Mirren	Free
17 Cornell, David	Northampton T	Ipswich T	Free
7 Coyle, Lewie	Fleetwood T	Hull C	Undisclosed
1 Craig, Tony	Bristol R	Crawley T	Free
27 Daniels, Donervon	Luton T	Crewe Alex	Free
3 Daniels, Josh	Glenavon	Shrewsbury T	Undisclosed
1 Davies, Archie	Brighton & HA	Crawley T	Free
2 Davis, Harry	Grimsby T	Morecambe	Free
7 Delfouneso, Nathan	Blackpool	Bolton W	Free
17 Dempsey, Kyle	Fleetwood T	Gillingham	Free
19 Dennis, Kristian	Notts Co	St Mirren	Undisclosed
7 Devine, Danny	Bradford C	Carlisle U	Free
13 Dickenson, Brennan	Exeter C	Carlisle U	Free
21 Dinanga, Marcus	AFC Telford U	Stevenage	Free
12 Dobre, Alex	Bournemouth	Dijon	Undisclosed
20 Docherty, Greg	Rangers	Hull C	Undisclosed
30 Doherty, Matt	Wolverhampton W	Tottenham H	Undisclosed
13 Drameh, Cody	Fulham	Leeds U	Undisclosed
13 Dunkley, Chey	Wigan Ath	Sheffield W	Undisclosed
19 Dykes, Lyndon	Livingston	QPR	Undisclosed
4 Eardley, Neil	Lincoln C	Burton Alb	Free
10 Edwards, Ronnie	Barnet	Peterborough U	Undisclosed
3 Edwards, Ryan	Blackpool	Dundee U	Free
28 Ejaria, Ovie	Liverpool	Reading	Undisclosed
7 Emmanuel, Josh	Bolton W	Hull C	Free

28 Eze, Eberechi	QPR	Crystal Palace	£19.5m
17 Farman, Paul	Stevenage	Carlisle U	Free
21 Feeney, Morgan	Everton	Sunderland	Free
25 Fitzpatrick, David	Macclesfield T	Port Vale	Free
14 Fletcher, Steven	Sheffield W	Stoke C	Free
25 Fojticek, Alex	Manchester U	Blackpool	Free
14 Foulquier, Dimitri	Watford	Granada	Undisclosed
7 Fox, Morgan	Sheffield W	Stoke C	Free
1 Freestone, Lewis	Brighton & HA	Cheltenham T	Free
16 Friend, George	Middlesbrough	Birmingham C	Free
1 Frost, Tyler	Reading	Crawley T	Free
10 Gelhardt, Joe	Wigan Ath	Leeds U	Undisclosed
28 George, Shamal	Liverpool	Colchester U	Free
13 Gibson, Montel	Halesowen T	Grimsby T	Free
12 Gilbey, Alex	Milton Keynes D	Charlton Ath	Undisclosed
7 Gilks, Matt	Fleetwood T	Bolton W	Free
9 Gomes, Angel	Manchester U	Lille	Free
19 Goode, Charlie	Northampton T	Brentford	Undisclosed
1 Gordon, Liam	Dagenham & R	Bolton W	Undisclosed
12 Graham, Jordan	Wolverhampton W	Gillingham	Free
2 Gribbin, Callum	Sheffield U	Barrow	Free
13 Hamilton, Ethan	Manchester U	Peterborough U	Free
20 Harding, Wes	Birmingham C	Rotherham U	Undisclosed
18 Hart, Joe	Burnley	Tottenham H	Free
17 Hawkins, Oli	Portsmouth	Ipswich T	Free
27 Healey, Rhys	Milton Keynes D	Toulouse	Undisclosed
12 Hemmings, Kane	Dundee	Burton Alb	Free
24 Hendrick, Jeff	Burnley	Newcastle U	Free
1 Hendrie, Stephen	West Ham U	Morecambe	Free
7 Hickman, Jak	Coventry C	Bolton W	Free
29 Hippolyte, Myles	Yeovil T	Scunthorpe U	Undisclosed
22 Hladky, Vaclav	St Mirren	Salford C	Free
11 Hojbjerg, Pierre-Emile	Southampton	Tottenham H	Undisclosed
11 Holden, Rory	Bristol C	Walsall	Undisclosed
14 Horsfall, Fraser	Macclesfield T	Northampton T	Free
24 Hugill, Jordan	West Ham U	Norwich C	£5m
17 Ikpeazu, Uche	Hearts	Wycombe W	Undisclosed
14 Iredale, Jack	Carlisle U	Cambridge U	Free
1 Ironside, Joe	Macclesfield T	Cambridge U	Free
11 Jackson, Adam	Hibernian	Lincoln C	Undisclosed
3 Jarvis, Aaron	Luton T	Scunthorpe U	Free
28 John, Cameron	Wolverhampton W	Doncaster R	Undisclosed
2 Jombati, Sido	Wycombe W	Oldham Ath	Free
4 Jones, Gethin	Carlisle U	Bolton W	Free
13 Kapustka, Bartosz	Leicester C	Legia Warsaw	Undisclosed
11 Keillor-Dunn, Davis	Wrexham	Oldham Ath	Free
10 Khan, Otis	Mansfield T	Tranmere R	Free
11 Kirby, Connor	Sheffield W	Harrogate T	Free
3 Knight-Percival, Nat	Carlisle U	Morecambe	Free
28 Leko, Jonathan	WBA	Birmingham C	Undisclosed
17 Lewis, Paul	Cambridge U	Tranmere R	Free
31 Loft, Ryan	Leicester C	Scunthorpe U	Free
2 Lokilo, Jason	Crystal Palace	Doncaster R	Free
14 Lokko, Kevin	Dover Ath	Harrogate T	Free
20 Longe-King, David	St Albans	Newport Co	Free
27 Lowe, Jamal	Wigan Ath	Swansea C	£800,000
14 MacDonald, Alex	Mansfield T	Gillingham	Free
16 MacDonald, Angus	Hull C	Rotherham U	Free
17 Macleod, Lewis	Wigan Ath	Plymouth Arg	Free
1 Mandron, Mikael	Gillingham	Crewe Alex	Free
21 Marshall, David	Wigan Ath	Derby Co	Undisclosed
24 Mascoll, Jamie	Wycombe W	Bolton W	Free
21 Matthews, Remi	Bolton W	Sunderland	Free
18 McAleny, Conor	Fleetwood T	Oldham Ath	Free
4 McAlinden, Liam	FC Halifax T	Morecambe	Free
7 McArdle, Rory	Scunthorpe U	Exeter C	Free
25 McCarthy, Jason	Millwall	Wycombe W	Undisclosed
3 McDonald, Rod	AFC Wimbledon	Carlisle U	Free
21 McKenzie, Robbie	Hull C	Gillingham	Free
10 Mellis, Jacob	Bolton W	Gillingham	Free
13 Mellor, Kelvin	Bradford C	Morecambe	Free
9 Mills, Joseph	Forest Green R	Northampton T	Free
31 Mkhitaryan, Henrikh	Arsenal	Roma	Undisclosed

25 Montoya, Martin	Brighton & HA	Real Betis	Undisclosed
3 Mooney, Kelsey	Aston Villa	Scunthorpe U	Free
13 Moore, Kieffer	Wigan Ath	Cardiff C	£2m
28 Mooy, Aaron	Brighton & HA	Shanghai SIPG	Undisclosed
22 Murphy, Joe	Shrewsbury T	Tranmere R	Free
3 Newby, Alex	Chorley	Rochdale	Free
14 Ngakia, Jeremy	West Ham U	Watford	Free
7 Norman, Magnus	Fulham	Carlisle U	Free
14 Norris, Will	Wolverhampton W	Burnley	Undisclosed
3 Nouble, Frank	Colchester U	Plymouth Arg	Free
18 Odimayo, Akin	Reading	Swindon T	Free
19 O'Driscoll, Aaron	Southampton	Mansfield T	Free
13 O'Keeffe, Corey	Birmingham C	Mansfield T	Free
6 Oliver, Vadaine	Northampton T	Gillingham	Free
3 Onariase, Emmanuel	Dagenham & R	Scunthorpe U	Undisclosed
7 Palmer, Ollie	Crawley T	AFC Wimbledon	Free
13 Perch, James	Scunthorpe U	Mansfield T	Free
20 Phillips, Giles	QPR	Wycombe W	Free
2 Piergianni, Carl	Salford C	Oldham Ath	Undisclosed
10 Pringle, Ben	Gillingham	Morecambe	Free
3 Pyke, Rekeil	Huddersfield T	Shrewsbury T	Free
3 Raggett, Sean	Norwich C	Portsmouth	Free
19 Ramsdale, Aaron	Bournemouth	Sheffield U	£18.5m
30 Reed, Harrison	Southampton	Fulham	Undisclosed
4 Reilly, Gavin	Bristol R	Carlisle U	Free
6 Riley, Joe	Bradford C	Carlisle U	Free
28 Roberto	West Ham U	Real Valladolid	Free
20 Robinson, Antonee	Wigan Ath	Fulham	£2m
24 Robinson, Theo	Southend U	Port Vale	Free
7 Robson, Ethan	Sunderland	Blackpool	Free
31 Rose, Danny	Swindon T	Grimsby T	Free
3 Rossiter, Jordan	Rangers	Fleetwood T	Free
11 Sadlier, Kieran	Doncaster R	Rotherham U	Free
7 Sanchez, Alexis	Manchester U	Internazionale	Undisclosed
3 Santos, Ricardo	Barnet	Bolton W	Free
4 Sercombe, Liam	Bristol R	Cheltenham T	Free
17 Silva, David	Manchester C	Real Sociedad	Free
14 Sisay, Alhagi Touray	Aberystwyth T	Grimsby T	Undisclosed
11 Smallwood, Richie	Blackburn R	Hull C	Free
25 Smith, Tommy	Sunderland	Colchester U	Free
6 Spearing, Jay	Blackpool	Tranmere R	Free
3 Spence, Lewis	Ross Co	Scunthorpe U	Free
3 Tanner, George	Manchester U	Carlisle U	Free
16 Taylor, Lyle	Charlton Ath	Nottingham F	Free
20 Taylor, Ryan	Plymouth Arg	Newport Co	Free
25 Toral, Jon	Hull C	Birmingham C	Free
18 Toure, Gime	Hartlepool U	Carlisle U	Free
28 Tutonda, David	Barnet	Bristol R	Free
12 Varney, Luke	Cheltenham T	Burton Alb	Free
11 Vaughan, James	Bradford C	Tranmere R	Free
14 Vertonghen, Jan	Tottenham H	Benfica	Free
27 Visser, Dino	Crewe Alex	Port Vale	Free
26 Wagstaff, Scott	AFC Wimbledon	Forest Green R	Free
13 Walker, Tom	AFC Fylde	Harrogate T	Undisclosed
28 Walker, Tyler	Nottingham F	Coventry C	Undisclosed
11 Walker-Peters, Kyle	Tottenham H	Southampton	Undisclosed
13 Walsh, Joe	Milton Keynes D	Lincoln C	Free
17 Ward, Danny	Cardiff C	Huddersfield T	Free
17 Ward, Stephen	Stoke C	Ipswich T	Free
13 Washington, Conor	Hearts	Charlton Ath	Undisclosed
3 Westbrooke, Zain	Coventry C	Bristol R	Undisclosed
28 Whelan, Callum	Watford	Oldham Ath	Free
3 Whitehead, Danny	Salford C	Port Vale	Free
10 Whitehouse, Elliott	Grimsby T	Forest Green R	Undisclosed
27 Williams, Ed	Kidderminster H	Doncaster R	Free
20 Williams, Joe	Wigan Ath	Bristol C	Undisclosed
24 Williams, Jordan	Rochdale	Blackpool	Free
14 Willian	Chelsea	Arsenal	Free
7 Woodyard, Alex	Peterborough U	AFC Wimbledon	Free
2 Wright, Bailey	Bristol C	Sunderland	Free
6 Yearwood, Dru	Brentford	New York Red Bulls	Undisclosed
SEPTEMBER 2020			
17 Akinola, Simeon	Barnet	Southend U	Free
22 Arter, Harry	Bournemouth	Nottingham F	Undisclosed

7 Ashley-Seal, Benny	Wolverhampton W	Northampton T	Undisclosed
15 Ayala, Daniel	Middlesbrough	Blackburn R	Free
1 Barnett, Jordan	Barnsley	Oldham Ath	Free
4 Beckles, Omar	Shrewsbury T	Crewe Alex	Free
24 Beesley, Jake	Solihull Moors	Rochdale	Undisclosed
8 Blair, Matty	Doncaster R	Cheltenham T	Free
7 Bogle, Jayden	Derby Co	Sheffield U	Undisclosed
1 Bree, James	Aston Villa	Luton T	Undisclosed
9 Brown, Jacob	Barnsley	Stoke C	Undisclosed
7 Brunt, Chris	WBA	Bristol C	Free
9 Burke, Oliver	WBA	Sheffield U	Swap
11 Butler, Andy	Scunthorpe U	Doncaster R	Free
5 Button, David	Brighton & HA	WBA	Undisclosed
10 Byrne, Nathan	Wigan Ath	Derby Co	Undisclosed
18 Cameron, Nathan	Macclesfield T	Wigan Ath	Free
4 Carroll, Tom	Swansea C	QPR	Free
3 Cash, Matty	Nottingham F	Aston Villa	£16m
9 Celina, Bersant	Swansea C	Dijon	Undisclosed
7 Christie-Davies, Isaac	Liverpool	Barnsley	Free
25 Clarke, Leon	Sheffield U	Shrewsbury T	Free
1 Clayton, Adam	Middlesbrough	Birmingham C	Free
2 Cooper, George	Peterborough U	Plymouth Arg	Undisclosed
12 Csoka, Daniel	Wolverhampton W	AFC Wimbledon	Free
25 Diabate, Fousseni	Leicester C	Trabzonspor	Undisclosed
4 Diangana, Grady	West Ham U	WBA	£18m
1 Dickie, Rob	Oxford U	QPR	Undisclosed
8 Doucoure, Abdoulaye	Watford	Everton	£20m
4 Duffy, Mark	Sheffield U	Fleetwood T	Free
4 Ellison, Kevin	Morecambe	Newport Co	Free
16 Estupinan, Pervis	Watford	Villarreal	£15m
11 Etheridge, Neil	Cardiff C	Birmingham C	Undisclosed
25 Evans, Gareth	Portsmouth	Bradford C	Free
24 Fenlon, Rhys	Burnley	Accrington S	Free
18 Finley, Sam	Accrington S	Fleetwood T	Free
7 Fraser, Ryan	Bournemouth	Newcastle U	Free
9 Fraser, Scott	Burton Alb	Milton Keynes D	Free
22 Garbutt, Luke	Everton	Blackpool	Free
26 Gnahoua, Arthur	Macclesfield T	Bolton W	Free
7 Graham, Danny	Blackburn R	Sunderland	Free
18 Grant, Joel	Plymouth Arg	Swindon T	Free
17 Grounds, Jonathan	Birmingham C	Swindon T	Free
25 Hadergjonaj, Florent	Huddersfield T	Kasimpasa	Undisclosed
10 Hanlan, Brandon	Gillingham	Bristol R	Undisclosed
1 Hessenthaler, Jake	Grimsby T	Crawley T	Free
5 Hobson, Shaun	Bournemouth	Southend U	Undisclosed
19 Hoever, Ki-Jana	Liverpool	Wolverhampton W	£9m
16 Hogan, Scott	Aston Villa	Birmingham C	Undisclosed
2 Horgan, Daryl	Hibernian	Wycombe W	Free
11 Hoti, Florent	Rochdale	Dundee U	Undisclosed
4 Howarth, Remy	Cefn Druids	Lincoln C	Undisclosed
11 Humphrys, Stephen	Southend U	Rochdale	Undisclosed
22 Ibe, Jordon	Bournemouth	Derby Co	Free
26 Isgrove, Lloyd	Swindon T	Bolton W	Free
14 Jacobs, Michael	Wigan Ath	Portsmouth	Free
1 Jameson, Kyle	AFC Fylde	Oldham Ath	Free
2 Johansson, Viktor	Leicester C	Rotherham U	Free
7 Johnson, Callum	Accrington S	Portsmouth	Undisclosed
4 Jones, Alfie	Southampton	Hull C	Undisclosed
19 Jota, Diogo	Wolverhampton W	Liverpool	£41m
2 Kachunga, Elias	Huddersfield T	Sheffield W	Free
4 Kipre, Cedric	Wigan Ath	WBA	Undisclosed
1 Korboa, Ricky	Carshalton Ath	Northampton T	Undisclosed
11 Leutwiler, Jayson	Blackburn R	Fleetwood T	Undisclosed
8 Lewis, Jamal	Norwich C	Newcastle U	Undisclosed
12 Lillis, Josh	Rochdale	Barrow	Free
1 Lockyer, Tom	Charlton Ath	Luton T	Undisclosed
10 Lopes, Leo Da Silva	Hull C	Cercle Bruges	Undisclosed
7 Lowe, Max	Derby Co	Sheffield U	Undisclosed
1 Lubala, Bez	Crawley T	Blackpool	Undisclosed
3 Martin, Chris	Derby Co	Bristol C	Free
16 Martinez, Emiliano	Arsenal	Aston Villa	£17m
4 May, Adam	Portsmouth	Cambridge U	Free
17 McCormack, Alan	Northampton T	Southend U	Free

23 McKenna, Scott	Aberdeen	Nottingham F	Undisclosed
1 McKenzie-Lyle, Kai	Liverpool	Cambridge U	Free
11 McKirdy, Harry	Carlisle U	Port Vale	Free
11 McLaughlin, Stephen	Southend U	Mansfield T	Free
5 Miller, Shaun	Crewe Alex	Bolton W	Free
4 Mitchell, Demetri	Manchester U	Blackpool	Free
11 Morsy, Sam	Wigan Ath	Middlesbrough	Undisclosed
9 Mounie, Steve	Huddersfield T	Stade Brestois	Undisclosed
4 Murphy, Luke	Bolton W	Crewe Alex	Free
7 Nichols, Tom	Bristol R	Crawley T	Free
3 Ntlhe, Kgosi	Scunthorpe U	Barrow	Free
11 O'Hara, Kieran	Manchester U	Burton Alb	Free
29 Otamendi, Nicolas	Manchester C	Benfica	£13.7m
1 Page, Lewis	Charlton Ath	Exeter C	Free
30 Paterson, Callum	Cardiff C	Sheffield W	Undisclosed
28 Pereyra, Roberto	Watford	Udinese	Undisclosed
4 Pitman, Brett	Portsmouth	Swindon T	Free
3 Reeves, Ben	Milton Keynes D	Plymouth Arg	Free
9 Robinson, Callum	Sheffield U	WBA	Swap
3 Ross, Jack	Southampton	Walsall	Free
21 Samuel, Dominic	Blackburn R	Gillingham	Free
11 Sarr, Naby	Charlton Ath	Huddersfield T	Free
2 Scannell, Sean	Blackpool	Grimsby T	Free
2 Scully, Tom	Norwich C	Accrington S	Free
2 Shephard, Liam	Forest Green R	Newport Co	Free
7 Sobhi, Ramadan	Huddersfield T	Pyramids	Undisclosed
23 Songo'o, Yann	Scunthorpe U	Morecambe	Free
22 Sorloth, Alexander	Crystal Palace	RB Leipzig	Undisclosed
18 Sowerby, Jack	Fleetwood T	Northampton T	Undisclosed
24 Stephens, Dale	Brighton & HA	Burnley	Undisclosed
9 Stockdale, David	Birmingham C	Wycombe W	Free
9 Stubbs, Sam	Middlesbrough	Fleetwood T	Undisclosed
8 Szmodics, Sammie	Bristol C	Peterborough U	Undisclosed
2 Tafazolli, Ryan	Hull C	Wycombe W	Free
1 Toney, Ivan	Peterborough U	Brentford	Undisclosed
3 Tutte, Andrew	Morecambe	Bolton W	Free
9 Watkins, Ollie	Brentford	Aston Villa	£28m
25 Watson, Ben	Nottingham F	Charlton Ath	Free
3 White, Hayden	Mansfield T	Walsall	Free
7 Wilson, Callum	Bournemouth	Newcastle U	£20m
4 Wilson, Scott	Burnley	Barrow	Free
2 Windass, Josh	Wigan Ath	Sheffield W	Undisclosed
11 Winnall, Sam	Sheffield W	Oxford U	Free
14 Woolery, Kaiyne	Swindon T	Tranmere R	Free

OCTOBER 2020

5 Adarabioyo, Tosin	Manchester C	Fulham	Undisclosed
5 Adomah, Albert	Nottingham F	QPR	Free
5 Aitchison, Jack	Celtic	Barnsley	Free
8 Baker-Richardson, Courtney	Swansea C	Barrow	Free
2 Barlaser, Dan	Newcastle U	Rotherham U	Undisclosed
16 Bennett, Ryan	Wolverhampton W	Swansea C	Free
16 Benrahma, Said	Brentford	West Ham U	£5 Loan
16 Bilboe, Laurence	Rotherham U	Oldham Ath	Free
2 Bonne, Macauley	Charlton Ath	QPR	Undisclosed
2 Brewster, Rhian	Liverpool	Sheffield U	£23.5m
10 Brittain, Callum	Milton Keynes D	Barnsley	Undisclosed
16 Butland, Jack	Stoke C	Crystal Palace	£1m
5 Carrillo, Guido	Southampton	Elche	Free
15 Chapman, Ellis	Lincoln C	Cheltenham T	Free
16 Coker, Ben	Lincoln C	Stevenage	Undisclosed
2 Cole, Devante	Doncaster R	Motherwell	Free
5 Cullen, Josh	West Ham U	Anderlecht	Undisclosed
2 Eliasson, Niclas	Bristol C	Nimes	Undisclosed
16 Fisher, Andrew	Blackburn R	Milton Keynes D	Free
5 Godfrey, Ben	Norwich C	Everton	£25m
15 Grant, Karlan	Huddersfield T	WBA	£15m
8 Gunter, Chris	Reading	Charlton Ath	Free
13 Inniss, Ryan	Crystal Palace	Charlton Ath	Undisclosed
16 Kane, Herbie	Liverpool	Barnsley	£1.25m
14 Kelman, Charlie	Southend U	QPR	Undisclosed
16 Kongolo, Terence	Huddersfield T	Fulham	£4m
16 Latibeaudiere, Joel	Manchester C	Swansea C	Undisclosed
8 Liddle, Ben	Middlesbrough	Bristol R	Undisclosed

1 Maddison, Marcus	Peterborough U	Charlton Ath	Free
16 Manning, Ryan	QPR	Swansea C	Undisclosed
3 Miller, Calvin	Celtic	Harrogate T	Free
15 Morrell, Joe	Bristol C	Luton T	Undisclosed
5 Nathaniel-George, Ashley	Crawley T	Southend U	Undisclosed
9 Nottingham, Michael	Blackpool	Accrington S	Undisclosed
16 Pears, Aynsley	Middlesbrough	Blackburn R	Undisclosed
5 Peterson, Kristoffer	Swansea C	Fortuna Dusseldorf	Undisclosed
16 Phillips, Dillon	Charlton Ath	Cardiff C	Undisclosed
5 Ramirez, Sandro	Everton	Huesca	Free
16 Rodon, Joe	Swansea C	Tottenham H	£11m
2 Rose, Danny	Mansfield T	Northampton T	Undisclosed
3 Silva, Adrien	Leicester C	Sampdoria	Undisclosed
3 Silva, Tiago	Nottingham F	Olympiacos	Undisclosed
5 Smalling, Chris	Manchester U	Roma	£13.6m
2 Suarez, Luis	Watford	Granada	£10m
5 Taylor, Chris	Bradford C	Barrow	Free
10 Tsaroulla, Nicholas	Brentford	Crawley T	Free
10 Watters, Max	Doncaster R	Crawley T	Free
1 Zouma, Yoan	Bolton W	Barrow	Free
DECEMBER 2020			
30 Capoue, Etienne	Watford	Villarreal	Undisclosed
19 Grant, Danny	Bohemians	Huddersfield T	Undisclosed
JANUARY 2021			
7 Aarons, Rolando	Newcastle U	Huddersfield T	Undisclosed
22 Adams, Nicky	Northampton T	Oldham Ath	Free
31 Andrews, Corie	Kingstonian	AFC Wimbledon	Undisclosed
21 Bancroft, Jacob	Oxford C	Stevenage	Undisclosed
18 Banks, Ollie	Tranmere R	Barrow	Undisclosed
29 Benrahma, Said	Brentford	West Ham U	£20m
29 Bogle, Omar	Charlton Ath	Doncaster R	Free
14 Bond, Jonathan	WBA	LA Galaxy	Undisclosed
13 Brown, Charlie	Chelsea	Milton Keynes D	Undisclosed
12 Canavan, Niall	Plymouth Arg	Bradford C	Undisclosed
7 Cargill, Baily	Milton Keynes D	Forest Green R	Undisclosed
22 Clough, Zach	Nottingham F	Wigan Ath	Free
31 Cosgrove, Sam	Aberdeen	Birmingham C	Undisclosed
11 Darikwa, Tendayi	Nottingham F	Wigan Ath	Free
22 Darling, Harry	Cambridge U	Milton Keynes D	Undisclosed
15 Davis, David	Birmingham C	Shrewsbury T	Free
30 Deulofeu, Gerard	Watford	Udinese	Undisclosed
19 Devitt, Jamie	Blackpool	Barrow	Free
29 Donahue, Dion	Swindon T	Barrow	Free
22 Doughty, Alfie	Charlton Ath	Stoke C	Undisclosed
18 Ennis, Niall	Wolverhampton W	Plymouth Arg	Undisclosed
8 Evans, Jack	Swansea C	Newport Co	Free
29 Farquharson, Priestley	Connah's Quay Nomads	Newport Co	Undisclosed
20 Feeney, Morgan	Sunderland	Carlisle U	Free
29 Ferguson, Nathan	Crawley T	Southend U	Undisclosed
29 Fisher, Darnell	Preston NE	Middlesbrough	Undisclosed
13 Flores, Jordan	Dundalk	Hull C	Undisclosed
13 Fosu-Mensah, Timothy	Manchester U	Bayer Leverkusen	Undisclosed
21 Georgiou, Anthony	Tottenham H	AEL Limassol	Undisclosed
31 Gosling, Dan	Bournemouth	Watford	Undisclosed
31 Gray, Demarai	Leicester C	Bayer Leverkusen	Undisclosed
15 Guthrie, Kurtis	Bradford C	Port Vale	Undisclosed
8 Haller, Sebastien	West Ham U	Ajax	£20.25m
15 Hamer, Ben	Huddersfield T	Swansea C	Undisclosed
29 Hamer, Tom	Oldham Ath	Burton Alb	Undisclosed
29 Hardie, Ryan	Blackpool	Plymouth Arg	Undisclosed
25 Holmes, Duane	Derby Co	Huddersfield T	Undisclosed
7 Huffer, Will	Bradford (Park Avenue)	Bradford C	Undisclosed
12 Irvine, Jackson	Hull C	Hibernian	Undisclosed
20 Johnson, Tyreke	Southampton	Gillingham	Undisclosed
25 Jolley, Charlie	Wigan Ath	Tranmere R	Undisclosed
15 Kemp, Dan	West Ham U	Leyton Orient	Undisclosed
19 Keogh, Richard	Milton Keynes D	Huddersfield T	Undisclosed
25 Kieftenbeld, Maikel	Birmingham C	Millwall	Undisclosed
5 Kitching, Liam	Forest Green R	Barnsley	Undisclosed
29 Lansbury, Henri	Aston Villa	Bristol C	Free
19 Lapslie, George	Charlton Ath	Mansfield T	Undisclosed
26 Letheren, Kyle	Chesterfield	Morecambe	Free
5 Lines, Chris	Northampton T	Stevenage	Undisclosed

19 Longridge, Jackson	Bradford C	Livingston	Free
8 Macey, Matt	Arsenal	Hibernian	Undisclosed
29 Martin, Joe	Northampton T	Stevenage	Free
29 McNally, Luke	St Patrick's Ath	Oxford U	Undisclosed
22 Mejias, Tomas	Middlesbrough	Ankaraspor	Free
6 Morris, Carlton	Norwich C	Barnsley	Undisclosed
19 Ng, Perry	Crewe Alex	Cardiff C	Undisclosed
5 Norris, Luke	Colchester U	Stevenage	Undisclosed
29 Obita, Jordan	Oxford U	Wycombe W	Undisclosed
25 Ogbeta, Nathanael	Manchester C	Shrewsbury T	Undisclosed
18 O'Hora, Warren	Brighton & HA	Milton Keynes D	Undisclosed
24 O'Riley, Matt	Fulham	Milton Keynes D	Undisclosed
24 Osayi-Samuel, Bright	QPR	Fenerbahce	Undisclosed
24 Ozil, Mesut	Arsenal	Fenerbahce	Free
15 Parker, Josh	Wycombe W	Burton Alb	Free
29 Pearson, Ben	Preston NE	Bournemouth	Undisclosed
14 Piazon, Lucas	Chelsea	Braga	Undisclosed
30 Poole, Regan	Milton Keynes D	Lincoln C	Undisclosed
18 Power, Simon	Norwich C	Harrogate T	Undisclosed
29 Reid, Josh	Ross Co	Coventry C	Undisclosed
5 Reilly, Gavin	Carlisle U	Livingston	Free
6 Reilly, Gavin	Carlisle U	Livingston	Free
4 Roberts, Gary	Bala T	Accrington S	Free
25 Rodari, Davide	Hastings	Crawley T	Undisclosed
11 Roscrow, Adam	AFC Wimbledon	The New Saints	Undisclosed
20 Rowe, Danny	Oldham Ath	Bradford C	Undisclosed
20 Scott, Cedwyn	Hebburn T	Carlisle U	Undisclosed
25 Scott, Thomas	Manchester C	Port Vale	Undisclosed
28 Simpson, Jack	Bournemouth	Rangers	Free*
13 Slimani, Islam	Leicester C	Lyon	Free
29 Smith, Jonny	Bristol C	Burton Alb	Undisclosed
8 Snodgrass, Robert	West Ham U	WBA	Undisclosed
31 Stewart, Ross	Ross Co	Sunderland	Undisclosed
21 Stubbs, Sam	Fleetwood T	Exeter C	Free
11 Taylor, Jake	Nottingham F	Port Vale	Undisclosed
19 te Wierik, Mike	Derby Co	FC Groningen	Undisclosed
29 Telford, Dom	Plymouth Arg	Newport Co	Undisclosed
30 Thompson, Adam	Rotherham U	Leyton Orient	Free
15 Tilley, James	Grimsby T	Crawley T	Free
22 Verlinden, Thibaud	Stoke C	Fortuna Sittard	Undisclosed
29 Walsh, Joe	Gillingham	QPR	Undisclosed
16 Watters, Max	Crawley T	Cardiff C	Undisclosed
18 Watters, Max	Crawley T	Cardiff C	Undisclosed
29 White, Jordan	Motherwell	Ross Co	Free
14 Whiteman, Ben	Doncaster R	Preston NE	Undisclosed
7 Williams, Jay	Kettering T	Harrogate T	Undisclosed
10 Winchester, Carl	Forest Green R	Sunderland	Undisclosed
8 Wright, Josh	Leyton Orient	Crawley T	Free
FEBRUARY 2021			
1 Adebayo, Elijah	Walsall	Luton T	Undisclosed
1 Angus, Dior	Barrow	Wrexham	Free
13 Angelino	Manchester C	RB Leipzig	Undisclosed
1 Batty, Dan	Hull C	Fleetwood T	Free
1 Bramall, Cohen	Colchester U	Lincoln C	Undisclosed
12 Coke, Giles	Hereford	Grimsby T	Free
1 Crankshaw, Ollie	Wigan Ath	Bradford C	Undisclosed
1 Davies, Ben	Preston NE	Liverpool	£2m
1 Diakhaby, Adama	Huddersfield T	Amiens	Undisclosed
8 Evans, Ched	Fleetwood T	Preston NE	Undisclosed
1 Evans, George	Derby Co	Millwall	Undisclosed
11 Ferrier, Morgan	Tranmere R	Maccabi Petah Tikva	Undisclosed
1 Freeman, Kieron	Swindon T	Swansea C	Undisclosed
1 Gilmour, Charlie	Norwich C	St Johnstone	Undisclosed
1 Grant, Conor	Sheffield W	Rochdale	Undisclosed
1 Grot, Jay-Roy	Leeds U	VfL Osnabruck	Undisclosed
1 Guerrero, Miguel Angel	Nottingham F	Rayo Vallecano	Undisclosed
1 Jaiyesimi, Diallang	Swindon T	Charlton Ath	Undisclosed
1 John-Lewis, Lenell	Hereford	Forest Green R	Undisclosed
1 Jules, Zak	Walsall	Milton Keynes D	Undisclosed
1 King, Joshua	Bournemouth	Everton	Undisclosed
1 Leutwiler, Jayson	Fleetwood T	Huddersfield T	Free
1 Long, Shane	Southampton	Bournemouth	Undisclosed
1 Lossl, Jonas	Everton	Midtjylland	Undisclosed

1 MacDonald, Calum	Blackpool	Tranmere R	Undisclosed
1 Main, Curtis	Aberdeen	Shrewsbury T	Free
1 Mellis, Jacob	Gillingham	Southend U	Undisclosed
1 Miranda, Roderick	Wolverhampton W	Gaziantep	Free
1 Missilou, Christopher	Northampton T	Swindon T	Undisclosed
1 Morgan, David	Southport	Accrington S	Undisclosed
1 Murray, Glenn	Brighton & HA	Nottingham F	Free
1 Mustafi, Shkodran	Arsenal	Schalke 04	Free
1 Ndjoil, Mikael	Bournemouth	Barrow	Free
1 Pickering, Harry	Crewe Alex	Blackburn R	Undisclosed
Loaned back to Crewe Alex until the end of the season.			
1 Riley, Regan	Bolton W	Norwich C	Undisclosed
2 Rojo, Marcos	Manchester U	Boca Juniors	Undisclosed
1 Sanders, Max	Brighton & HA	Lincoln C	Undisclosed
1 Shaughnessy, Conor	Leeds U	Rochdale	Free
1 Simmonds, Keyendrah	Manchester C	Birmingham C	Undisclosed
1 Simpson, Jack	Bournemouth	Rangers	Undisclosed
1 Taft, George	Bolton W	Scunthorpe U	Free
1 Tavares, Fabio	Rochdale	Coventry C	Undisclosed
1 Taylor, Terry	Wolverhampton W	Burton Alb	Undisclosed
1 Vernam, Charles	Burton Alb	Bradford C	Undisclosed
1 Whittaker, Morgan	Derby Co	Swansea C	Undisclosed
1 Williams, Jonny	Charlton Ath	Cardiff C	Undisclosed
1 Williams, MJ	Blackpool	Bolton W	Free
1 Wiredu, Brendan	Charlton Ath	Colchester U	Undisclosed
1 Yedlin, DeAndre	Newcastle U	Galatasaray	Undisclosed
MARCH 2021			
23 Gibbs, Kieran	WBA	Inter Miami	Free
4 Williams, Derrick	Blackburn R	LA Galaxy	Free
APRIL 2021			
6 Dawson, Craig	Watford	West Ham U	Undisclosed
MAY 2021			
27 Afolayan, Dapo	West Ham U	Bolton W	Free
31 Aguero, Sergio	Manchester C	Barcelona	Free
26 Anderton, Nick	Carlisle U	Bristol R	Free
17 Baah, Kwadwo	Rochdale	Watford	Undisclosed
26 Coutts, Paul	Fleetwood T	Bristol R	Free
13 de Wijs, Jordy	Hull C	QPR	Undisclosed
20 Field, Sam	WBA	QPR	Undisclosed
26 Finley, Sam	Fleetwood T	Bristol R	Free
19 Hewitt, Elliott	Grimsby T	Mansfield T	Free
26 Hughes, Mark	Accrington S	Bristol R	Free
17 Leahy, Luke	Bristol R	Shrewsbury T	Free
25 Long, George	Hull C	Millwall	Free
19 Lumley, Joe	QPR	Middlesbrough	Free
25 Malone, Scott	Derby Co	Millwall	Free
7 McGuane, Marcus	Nottingham F	Oxford U	Undisclosed
12 Montano, Cristian	Port Vale	Livingston	Free
26 Nicholls, Lee	Milton Keynes D	Huddersfield T	Free
25 Onyedinma, Fred	Wycombe W	Luton T	Undisclosed
26 Pattison, Alex	Wycombe W	Harrogate T	Free
20 Pearson, Matty	Luton T	Huddersfield T	Free
14 Pell, Harry	Colchester U	Accrington S	Free
27 Pennington, Matthew	Everton	Shrewsbury T	Free
27 Pollock, Mattie	Grimsby T	Watford	£250,000
24 Read, Arthur	Brentford	Stevenage	Free
21 Rhodes, Jordan	Sheffield W	Huddersfield T	Free
27 Richards, Omar	Reading	Bayern Munich	Free
25 Skuse, Cole	Ipswich T	Colchester U	Free
14 Sorinola, Matthew	Milton Keynes D	Union SG	Undisclosed
18 Walcott, Theo	Everton	Southampton	Free
20 Wilson, James	Ipswich T	Plymouth Arg	Free
28 Wimmer, Kevin	Stoke C	Rapid Vienna	Free
7 Woods, Gary	Oldham Ath	Aberdeen	Free

THE NEW FOREIGN LEGION 2020–21

**Transfer to be completed at the end of the season.*

JULY 2020

6	Dacosta, Julien	Niort	Coventry C	Free
3	Hamer, Gustavo	PEC Zwolle	Coventry C	£1.5m
16	Hilssner, Marcel	Paderborn	Coventry C	Undisclosed
28	Hoolahan, Wes	Newcastle Jets	Cambridge U	Free
23	Meslier, Illan	Lorient	Leeds U	Undisclosed
14	Montsma, Lewis	FC Dordrecht	Lincoln C	Free
22	Nicholson, Sam	Colorado Rapids	Bristol R	Free
22	Placheta, Przemyslaw	Slask Wroclaw	Norwich C	Undisclosed
20	Sorensen, Jacob	Esbjerg	Norwich C	Undisclosed
29	Veltman, Joel	Ajax	Brighton & HA	Undisclosed

AUGUST 2020

26	Bachirou, Fouad	Malmo	Nottingham F	Undisclosed
20	Frieser, Dominik	LASK	Barnsley	Undisclosed
28	Furman, Dean	SuperSport U	Carlisle U	Free
4	Greenidge, Reiss	Arendal	Bolton W	Free
26	Kaminski, Thomas	Gent	Blackburn R	Undisclosed
21	Kelly, Liam	Feyenoord	Oxford U	Loan
29	Koch, Robin	Freiburg	Leeds U	Undisclosed
17	Ludewig, Kilian	Red Bull Salzburg	Barnsley	Loan
26	Maghoma, Christian	Arka Gdynia	Gillingham	Free
17	Pereira, Matheus	Sporting Lisbon	WBA	Undisclosed
28	Prieto, Andres	Espanyol	Birmingham C	Free
18	Quintilla, Xavi	Villarreal	Norwich C	Loan
29	Rodrigo	Valencia	Leeds U	£26m
12	Salisu, Mohammed	Real Valladolid	Southampton	£10.9m
27	Sanchez, Ivan	Elche	Birmingham C	Free
27	Sarr, Malang	Nice	Chelsea	Free
28	Silva, Thiago	Paris Saint-Germain	Chelsea	Free
4	Torres, Ferran	Valencia	Manchester C	£20.9m
10	Tsimikas, Kostas	Olympiacos	Liverpool	£11.7m

SEPTEMBER 2020

11	Aina, Ola	Torino	Fulham	Loan
19	Akpom, Chuba	PAOK	Middlesbrough	Undisclosed
18	Alcantara, Thiago	Bayern Munich	Liverpool	£20m
5	Allan	Napoli	IngsEverton	£21.7m
9	Areola, Alphonse	Paris Saint-Germain	Fulham	Loan
19	Bale, Gareth	Real Madrid	Tottenham H	Loan
6	Blackwood, George	Adelaide U	Oldham Ath	Free
3	Castagne, Timothy	Atalanta	Leicester C	£25m
4	Ceballos, Dani	Real Madrid	Arsenal	Loan
14	Diallo, Abdoulaye	Genclerbirligi	Nottingham F	Undisclosed
29	Dias, Ruben	Benfica	Manchester C	£65m
25	Duncan, Bobby	Fiorentina	Derby Co	Undisclosed
3	Dunnwald-Turan, Kenan	Bonner	Scunthorpe	Free
19	Eiting, Carel	Ajax	Huddersfield T	Loan
21	Ghoddos, Saman	Amiens	Brentford	Loan
4	Guerrero, Miguel Angel	Olympiacos	Nottingham F	Undisclosed
4	Havertz, Kai	Bayer Leverkusen	Chelsea	£72m
9	Helik, Michal	Cracovia	Barnsley	Undisclosed
25	Ioannou, Nicholas	APOEL	Nottingham F	Undisclosed
16	Jozwiak, Kamil	Lech Poznan	Derby Co	Undisclosed
29	Krovinovic, Filip	Benfica	WBA	Loan
24	Llorente, Diego	Real Sociedad	Leeds U	Undisclosed
30	Lookman, Ademola	RB Leipzig	Fulham	Loan
1	Magalhaes, Gabriel	Lille	Arsenal	£27m
6	Marcal	Lyon	Wolverhampton W	£1.78m
14	Mayer, Thomas	Austria Lustenau	Hull C	Free
24	Mendy, Edouard	Rennes	Chelsea	Undisclosed
23	Nicolaisen, Rasmus	FC Midtjylland	Portsmouth	Loan
7	Perica, Stipe	Udinese	Watford	Undisclosed
7	Pipa	Espanyol	Huddersfield T	Undisclosed
19	Reguilon, Sergio	Real Madrid	Tottenham H	Undisclosed
7	Rodriguez, James	Real Madrid	Everton	£12m
21	Runarsson, Runar Alex	Dijon	Arsenal	Undisclosed
21	San Jose, Mikel	Athletic Bilbao	Birmingham C	Free
23	Semedo, Nelson	Barcelona	Wolverhampton W	£27.6m
9	Sierralta, Francisco	Udinese	Watford	Undisclosed

5 Silva, Fabio	Porto	Wolverhampton W	£35.6m
11 Soh, Loic Mbe	Paris Saint-Germain	Nottingham F	Undisclosed
10 Tete, Kenny	Lyon	Fulham	Undisclosed
19 Traore, Bertrand	Lyon	Aston Villa	£17m
29 Troost-Ekong, William	Udinese	Watford	Undisclosed
21 Under, Cengiz	Roma	Leicester C	Loan
2 Van de Beek, Donny	Ajax	Manchester U	£35m
9 Vitinha	Porto	Wolverhampton W	Loan
OCTOBER 2020			
4 Ait-Nouri, Rayan	Angers	Wolverhampton W	Loan
5 Andersen, Joachim	Lyon	Fulham	Loan
2 Bennetts, Keanan	Borussia Moenchengladbach	Ipswich T	Loan
9 Bohui, Josh	NAC Breda	Colchester U	Free
5 Cafu	Olympiacos	Nottingham F	Loan
2 Coufal, Vladimir	Slavia Prague	West Ham U	£5.4m
4 Diallo, Ibrahima	Brest	Southampton	Undisclosed
5 Esteves, Tomas	Porto	Reading	Loan
2 Fofana, Wesley	Saint-Etienne	Leicester C	Undisclosed
5 Gretarsson, Daniel	Aalesunds	Blackpool	Undisclosed
1 Jakobsen, Emil Riis	Randers	Preston NE	Undisclosed
3 Janelt, Vitaly	VfL Bochum	Brentford	Undisclosed
6 Karbownik, Michal	Legia Warsaw	Brighton & HA	Undisclosed
Loaned back to Legia Warsaw until the end of the season.			
5 McGree, Riley	Charlotte	Birmingham C	Loan
5 Millar, Matt	Newcastle Jets	Shrewsbury T	Loan
6 Moder, Jakub	Lech Poznan	Brighton & HA	Undisclosed
Loaned back to Lech Poznan until the end of the season.			
5 Olsen, Robin	Roma	Everton	Loan
5 Partey, Thomas	Atletico Madrid	Arsenal	£45.3m
5 Pellistri, Facundo	Penarol	Manchester U	£9m
5 Raphinha	Rennes	Leeds U	£17m
1 Riquelme, Rodrigo	Atletico Madrid	Bournemouth	Loan
4 Semedo, Alfa	Benfica	Reading	Loan
6 Stergiakis, Antonis	Slavia Sofia	Blackburn R	Undisclosed
5 Telles, Alex	Porto	Manchester U	£13.6m
2 Vinicius, Carlos	Benfica	Tottenham H	Loan
5 Willock, Chris	Benfica	QPR	Undisclosed
1 Zeqiri, Andi	Lausanne-Sport	Brighton & HA	Undisclosed
JANUARY 2021			
29 Diagne, Mbaye	Galatasaray	WBA	Loan
7 Diallo, Amad	Atalanta	Manchester U	£19m
23 Evans, Antony	Paderborn	Crewe Alex	Loan
14 Ghoddos, Saman	Amiens	Brentford	Undisclosed
19 Giannoulis, Dimitris	PAOK Salonika	Norwich C	Loan
25 Hutchinson, Sam	Pafos	Sheffield W	Free
22 Johnston, George	Feyenoord	Wigan Ath	Loan
23 Jose, Willian	Real Sociedad	Wolverhampton W	Loan
22 Krovinovic, Filip	Benfica	Nottingham F	Loan
21 Mateta, Jean-Philippe	Mainz	Crystal Palace	Loan
7 Matondo, Rabbi	Schalke	Stoke C	Loan
22 Morris, Jordan	Seattle Sounders	Swansea C	Loan
26 Sanson, Morgan	Marseille	Aston Villa	Undisclosed
4 Schwartz, Ronnie	FC Midtjylland	Charlton Ath	Undisclosed
2 Zinckernagel, Philip	Bodo/Glimt	Watford	Undisclosed
FEBRUARY 2021			
1 Arriola, Paul	DC United	Swansea C	Loan
1 Caicedo, Moises	Independiente del Valle	Brighton & HA	£4m
1 Clark, Max	Vitesse Arnhem	Hull C	Free
1 Dike, Daryl	Orlando C	Barnsley	Loan
1 Kabak, Ozan	Schalke 04	Liverpool	Loan
1 Maja, Josh	Bordeaux	Fulham	Loan
9 Mancienne, Michael	New England Revolution	Burton Alb	Undisclosed
1 Yokuslu, Okay	Celta Vigo	WBA	Loan
MAY 2021			
28 Konate, Ibrahima	RB Leipzig	Liverpool	£35m

ENGLISH LEAGUE HONOURS 1888–2021

**Won or placed on goal average (ratio), goal difference or most goals scored. ‡Not promoted after play-offs.*
No official competition during 1915–19 and 1939–46, regional leagues operated.

FOOTBALL LEAGUE (1888–89 to 1891–92) – TIER 1

MAXIMUM POINTS: *a* 44; *b* 52.

1	1888–89*a*	Preston NE	40	Aston Villa	29	Wolverhampton W	28
1	1889–90*a*	Preston NE	33	Everton	31	Blackburn R	27
1	1890–91*a*	Everton	29	Preston NE	27	Notts Co	26
1	1891–92*b*	Sunderland	42	Preston NE	37	Bolton W	36

DIVISION 1 (1892–93 to 1991–92)

MAXIMUM POINTS: *c* 60; *d* 68; *e* 76; *f* 84; *g* 126; *h* 120; *k* 114.

1	1892–93*c*	Sunderland	48	Preston NE	37	Everton	36
1	1893–94*c*	Aston Villa	44	Sunderland	38	Derby Co	36
1	1894–95*c*	Sunderland	47	Everton	42	Aston Villa	39
1	1895–96*c*	Aston Villa	45	Derby Co	41	Everton	39
1	1896–97*c*	Aston Villa	47	Sheffield U*	36	Derby Co	36
1	1897–98*c*	Sheffield U	42	Sunderland	37	Wolverhampton W*	35
1	1898–99*d*	Aston Villa	45	Liverpool	43	Burnley	39
1	1899–1900*d*	Aston Villa	50	Sheffield U	48	Sunderland	41
1	1900–01*d*	Liverpool	45	Sunderland	43	Notts Co	40
1	1901–02*d*	Sunderland	44	Everton	41	Newcastle U	37
1	1902–03*d*	The Wednesday	42	Aston Villa*	41	Sunderland	41
1	1903–04*d*	The Wednesday	47	Manchester C	44	Everton	43
1	1904–05*d*	Newcastle U	48	Everton	47	Manchester C	46
1	1905–06*e*	Liverpool	51	Preston NE	47	The Wednesday	44
1	1906–07*e*	Newcastle U	51	Bristol C	48	Everton*	45
1	1907–08*e*	Manchester U	52	Aston Villa*	43	Manchester C	43
1	1908–09*e*	Newcastle U	53	Everton	46	Sunderland	44
1	1909–10*e*	Aston Villa	53	Liverpool	48	Blackburn R*	45
1	1910–11*e*	Manchester U	52	Aston Villa	51	Sunderland*	45
1	1911–12*e*	Blackburn R	49	Everton	46	Newcastle U	44
1	1912–13*e*	Sunderland	54	Aston Villa	50	Sheffield W	49
1	1913–14*e*	Blackburn R	51	Aston Villa	44	Middlesbrough*	43
1	1914–15*e*	Everton	46	Oldham Ath	45	Blackburn R*	43
1	1919–20*f*	WBA	60	Burnley	51	Chelsea	49
1	1920–21*f*	Burnley	59	Manchester C	54	Bolton W	52
1	1921–22*f*	Liverpool	57	Tottenham H	51	Burnley	49
1	1922–23*f*	Liverpool	60	Sunderland	54	Huddersfield T	53
1	1923–24*f*	Huddersfield T*	57	Cardiff C	57	Sunderland	53
1	1924–25*f*	Huddersfield T	58	WBA	56	Bolton W	55
1	1925–26*f*	Huddersfield T	57	Arsenal	52	Sunderland	48
1	1926–27*f*	Newcastle U	56	Huddersfield T	51	Sunderland	49
1	1927–28*f*	Everton	53	Huddersfield T	51	Leicester C	48
1	1928–29*f*	Sheffield W	52	Leicester C	51	Aston Villa	50
1	1929–30*f*	Sheffield W	60	Derby Co	50	Manchester C*	47
1	1930–31*f*	Arsenal	66	Aston Villa	59	Sheffield W	52
1	1931–32*f*	Everton	56	Arsenal	54	Sheffield W	50
1	1932–33*f*	Arsenal	58	Aston Villa	54	Sheffield W	51
1	1933–34*f*	Arsenal	59	Huddersfield T	56	Tottenham H	49
1	1934–35*f*	Arsenal	58	Sunderland	54	Sheffield W	49
1	1935–36*f*	Sunderland	56	Derby Co*	48	Huddersfield T	48
1	1936–37*f*	Manchester C	57	Charlton Ath	54	Arsenal	52
1	1937–38*f*	Arsenal	52	Wolverhampton W	51	Preston NE	49
1	1938–39*f*	Everton	59	Wolverhampton W	55	Charlton Ath	50
1	1946–47*f*	Liverpool	57	Manchester U*	56	Wolverhampton W	56
1	1947–48*f*	Arsenal	59	Manchester U*	52	Burnley	52
1	1948–49*f*	Portsmouth	58	Manchester U*	53	Derby Co	53
1	1949–50*f*	Portsmouth*	53	Wolverhampton W	53	Sunderland	52
1	1950–51*f*	Tottenham H	60	Manchester U	56	Blackpool	50
1	1951–52*f*	Manchester U	57	Tottenham H*	53	Arsenal	53
1	1952–53*f*	Arsenal*	54	Preston NE	54	Wolverhampton W	51
1	1953–54*f*	Wolverhampton W	57	WBA	53	Huddersfield T	51
1	1954–55*f*	Chelsea	52	Wolverhampton W*	48	Portsmouth*	48
1	1955–56*f*	Manchester U	60	Blackpool*	49	Wolverhampton W	49
1	1956–57*f*	Manchester U	64	Tottenham H*	56	Preston NE	56
1	1957–58*f*	Wolverhampton W	64	Preston NE	59	Tottenham H	51
1	1958–59*f*	Wolverhampton W	61	Manchester U	55	Arsenal*	50
1	1959–60*f*	Burnley	55	Wolverhampton W	54	Tottenham H	53
1	1960–61*f*	Tottenham H	66	Sheffield W	58	Wolverhampton W	57
1	1961–62*f*	Ipswich T	56	Burnley	53	Tottenham H	52
1	1962–63*f*	Everton	61	Tottenham H	55	Burnley	54
1	1963–64*f*	Liverpool	57	Manchester U	53	Everton	52
1	1964–65*f*	Manchester U*	61	Leeds U	61	Chelsea	56

1	1965–66*f*	Liverpool	61	Leeds U*	55	Burnley	55
1	1966–67*f*	Manchester U	60	Nottingham F*	56	Tottenham H	56
1	1967–68*f*	Manchester C	58	Manchester U	56	Liverpool	55
1	1968–69*f*	Leeds U	67	Liverpool	61	Everton	57
1	1969–70*f*	Everton	66	Leeds U	57	Chelsea	55
1	1970–71*f*	Arsenal	65	Leeds U	64	Tottenham H*	52
1	1971–72*f*	Derby Co	58	Leeds U*	57	Liverpool*	57
1	1972–73*f*	Liverpool	60	Arsenal	57	Leeds U	53
1	1973–74*f*	Leeds U	62	Liverpool	57	Derby Co	48
1	1974–75*f*	Derby Co	53	Liverpool*	51	Ipswich T	51
1	1975–76*f*	Liverpool	60	QPR	59	Manchester U	56
1	1976–77*f*	Liverpool	57	Manchester C	56	Ipswich T	52
1	1977–78*f*	Nottingham F	64	Liverpool	57	Everton	55
1	1978–79*f*	Liverpool	68	Nottingham F	60	WBA	59
1	1979–80*f*	Liverpool	60	Manchester U	58	Ipswich T	53
1	1980–81*f*	Aston Villa	60	Ipswich T	56	Arsenal	53
1	1981–82*g*	Liverpool	87	Ipswich T	83	Manchester U	78
1	1982–83*g*	Liverpool	82	Watford	71	Manchester U	70
1	1983–84*g*	Liverpool	80	Southampton	77	Nottingham F*	74
1	1984–85*g*	Everton	90	Liverpool*	77	Tottenham H	77
1	1985–86*g*	Liverpool	88	Everton	86	West Ham U	84
1	1986–87*g*	Everton	86	Liverpool	77	Tottenham H	71
1	1987–88*h*	Liverpool	90	Manchester U	81	Nottingham F	73
1	1988–89*k*	Arsenal*	76	Liverpool	76	Nottingham F	64
1	1989–90*k*	Liverpool	79	Aston Villa	70	Tottenham H	63
1	1990–91*k*	Arsenal[1]	83	Liverpool	76	Crystal Palace	69
1	1991–92*g*	Leeds U	82	Manchester U	78	Sheffield W	75

[1] *Arsenal deducted 2pts due to player misconduct in match on 20/10/1990 v Manchester U at Old Trafford.*

PREMIER LEAGUE (1992–93 to 2020–21)

MAXIMUM POINTS: *a* 126; *b* 114.

1	1992–93*a*	Manchester U	84	Aston Villa	74	Norwich C	72
1	1993–94*a*	Manchester U	92	Blackburn R	84	Newcastle U	77
1	1994–95*a*	Blackburn R	89	Manchester U	88	Nottingham F	77
1	1995–96*b*	Manchester U	82	Newcastle U	78	Liverpool	71
1	1996–97*b*	Manchester U	75	Newcastle U*	68	Arsenal*	68
1	1997–98*b*	Arsenal	78	Manchester U	77	Liverpool	65
1	1998–99*b*	Manchester U	79	Arsenal	78	Chelsea	75
1	1999–2000*b*	Manchester U	91	Arsenal	73	Leeds U	69
1	2000–01*b*	Manchester U	80	Arsenal	70	Liverpool	69
1	2001–02*b*	Arsenal	87	Liverpool	80	Manchester U	77
1	2002–03*b*	Manchester U	83	Arsenal	78	Newcastle U	69
1	2003–04*b*	Arsenal	90	Chelsea	79	Manchester U	75
1	2004–05*b*	Chelsea	95	Arsenal	83	Manchester U	77
1	2005–06*b*	Chelsea	91	Manchester U	83	Liverpool	82
1	2006–07*b*	Manchester U	89	Chelsea	83	Liverpool*	68
1	2007–08*b*	Manchester U	87	Chelsea	85	Arsenal	83
1	2008–09*b*	Manchester U	90	Liverpool	86	Chelsea	83
1	2009–10*b*	Chelsea	86	Manchester U	85	Arsenal	75
1	2010–11*b*	Manchester U	80	Chelsea*	71	Manchester C	71
1	2011–12*b*	Manchester C*	89	Manchester U	89	Arsenal	70
1	2012–13*b*	Manchester U	89	Manchester C	78	Chelsea	75
1	2013–14*b*	Manchester C	86	Liverpool	84	Chelsea	82
1	2014–15*b*	Chelsea	87	Manchester C	79	Arsenal	75
1	2015–16*b*	Leicester C	81	Arsenal	71	Tottenham H	70
1	2016–17*b*	Chelsea	93	Tottenham H	86	Manchester C	78
1	2017–18*b*	Manchester C	100	Manchester U	81	Tottenham H	77
1	2018–19*b*	Manchester C	98	Liverpool	97	Chelsea	72
1	2019–20*b*	Liverpool	99	Manchester C	81	Mancheser U*	66
1	2020–21*b*	Manchester C	86	Manchester U	74	Liverpool	69

DIVISION 2 (1892–93 to 1991–92) – TIER 2

MAXIMUM POINTS: *a* 44; *b* 56; *c* 60; *d* 68; *e* 76; *f* 84; *g* 126; *h* 132; *k* 138.

2	1892–93*a*	Small Heath	36	Sheffield U	35	Darwen	30
2	1893–94*b*	Liverpool	50	Small Heath	42	Notts Co	39
2	1894–95*c*	Bury	48	Notts Co	39	Newton Heath*	38
2	1895–96*c*	Liverpool*	46	Manchester C	46	Grimsby T*	42
2	1896–97*c*	Notts Co	42	Newton Heath	39	Grimsby T	38
2	1897–98*c*	Burnley	48	Newcastle U	45	Manchester C	39
2	1898–99*d*	Manchester C	52	Glossop NE	46	Leicester Fosse	45
2	1899–1900*d*	The Wednesday	54	Bolton W	52	Small Heath	46
2	1900–01*d*	Grimsby T	49	Small Heath	48	Burnley	44
2	1901–02*d*	WBA	55	Middlesbrough	51	Preston NE*	42
2	1902–03*d*	Manchester C	54	Small Heath	51	Woolwich A	48
2	1903–04*d*	Preston NE	50	Woolwich A	49	Manchester U	48
2	1904–05*d*	Liverpool	58	Bolton W	56	Manchester U	53
2	1905–06*e*	Bristol C	66	Manchester U	62	Chelsea	53
2	1906–07*e*	Nottingham F	60	Chelsea	57	Leicester Fosse	48
2	1907–08*e*	Bradford C	54	Leicester Fosse	52	Oldham Ath	50
2	1908–09*e*	Bolton W	52	Tottenham H*	51	WBA	51
2	1909–10*e*	Manchester C	54	Oldham Ath*	53	Hull C*	53
2	1910–11*e*	WBA	53	Bolton W	51	Chelsea	49

2	1911–12*e*	Derby Co*	54	Chelsea	54	Burnley	52
2	1912–13*e*	Preston NE	53	Burnley	50	Birmingham	46
2	1913–14*e*	Notts Co	53	Bradford PA*	49	Woolwich A	49
2	1914–15*e*	Derby Co	53	Preston NE	50	Barnsley	47
2	1919–20*f*	Tottenham H	70	Huddersfield T	64	Birmingham	56
2	1920–21*f*	Birmingham*	58	Cardiff C	58	Bristol C	51
2	1921–22*f*	Nottingham F	56	Stoke C*	52	Barnsley	52
2	1922–23*f*	Notts Co	53	West Ham U*	51	Leicester C	51
2	1923–24*f*	Leeds U	54	Bury*	51	Derby Co	51
2	1924–25*f*	Leicester C	59	Manchester U	57	Derby Co	55
2	1925–26*f*	Sheffield W	60	Derby Co	57	Chelsea	52
2	1926–27*f*	Middlesbrough	62	Portsmouth*	54	Manchester C	54
2	1927–28*f*	Manchester C	59	Leeds U	57	Chelsea	54
2	1928–29*f*	Middlesbrough	55	Grimsby T	53	Bradford PA*	48
2	1929–30*f*	Blackpool	58	Chelsea	55	Oldham Ath	53
2	1930–31*f*	Everton	61	WBA	54	Tottenham H	51
2	1931–32*f*	Wolverhampton W	56	Leeds U	54	Stoke C	52
2	1932–33*f*	Stoke C	56	Tottenham H	55	Fulham	50
2	1933–34*f*	Grimsby T	59	Preston NE	52	Bolton W*	51
2	1934–35*f*	Brentford	61	Bolton W*	56	West Ham U	56
2	1935–36*f*	Manchester U	56	Charlton Ath	55	Sheffield U*	52
2	1936–37*f*	Leicester C	56	Blackpool	55	Bury	52
2	1937–38*f*	Aston Villa	57	Manchester U*	53	Sheffield U	53
2	1938–39*f*	Blackburn R	55	Sheffield U	54	Sheffield W	53
2	1946–47*f*	Manchester C	62	Burnley	58	Birmingham C	55
2	1947–48*f*	Birmingham C	59	Newcastle U	56	Southampton	52
2	1948–49*f*	Fulham	57	WBA	56	Southampton	55
2	1949–50*f*	Tottenham H	61	Sheffield W*	52	Sheffield U*	52
2	1950–51*f*	Preston NE	57	Manchester C	52	Cardiff C	50
2	1951–52*f*	Sheffield W	53	Cardiff C*	51	Birmingham C	51
2	1952–53*f*	Sheffield U	60	Huddersfield T	58	Luton T	52
2	1953–54*f*	Leicester C*	56	Everton	56	Blackburn R	55
2	1954–55*f*	Birmingham C*	54	Luton T*	54	Rotherham U	54
2	1955–56*f*	Sheffield W	55	Leeds U	52	Liverpool*	48
2	1956–57*f*	Leicester C	61	Nottingham F	54	Liverpool	53
2	1957–58*f*	West Ham U	57	Blackburn R	56	Charlton Ath	55
2	1958–59*f*	Sheffield W	62	Fulham	60	Sheffield U*	53
2	1959–60*f*	Aston Villa	59	Cardiff C	58	Liverpool*	50
2	1960–61*f*	Ipswich T	59	Sheffield U	58	Liverpool	52
2	1961–62*f*	Liverpool	62	Leyton Orient	54	Sunderland	53
2	1962–63*f*	Stoke C	53	Chelsea*	52	Sunderland	52
2	1963–64*f*	Leeds U	63	Sunderland	61	Preston NE	56
2	1964–65*f*	Newcastle U	57	Northampton T	56	Bolton W	50
2	1965–66*f*	Manchester C	59	Southampton	54	Coventry C	53
2	1966–67*f*	Coventry C	59	Wolverhampton W	58	Carlisle U	52
2	1967–68*f*	Ipswich T	59	QPR*	58	Blackpool	58
2	1968–69*f*	Derby Co	63	Crystal Palace	56	Charlton Ath	50
2	1969–70*f*	Huddersfield T	60	Blackpool	53	Leicester C	51
2	1970–71*f*	Leicester C	59	Sheffield U	56	Cardiff C*	53
2	1971–72*f*	Norwich C	57	Birmingham C	56	Millwall	55
2	1972–73*f*	Burnley	62	QPR	61	Aston Villa	50
2	1973–74*f*	Middlesbrough	65	Luton T	50	Carlisle U	49
2	1974–75*f*	Manchester U	61	Aston Villa	58	Norwich C	53
2	1975–76*f*	Sunderland	56	Bristol C*	53	WBA	53
2	1976–77*f*	Wolverhampton W	57	Chelsea	55	Nottingham F	52
2	1977–78*f*	Bolton W	58	Southampton	57	Tottenham H*	56
2	1978–79*f*	Crystal Palace	57	Brighton & HA*	56	Stoke C	56
2	1979–80*f*	Leicester C	55	Sunderland	54	Birmingham C*	53
2	1980–81*f*	West Ham U	66	Notts Co	53	Swansea C*	50
2	1981–82*g*	Luton T	88	Watford	80	Norwich C	71
2	1982–83*g*	QPR	85	Wolverhampton W	75	Leicester C	70
2	1983–84*g*	Chelsea*	88	Sheffield W	88	Newcastle U	80
2	1984–85*g*	Oxford U	84	Birmingham C	82	Manchester C*	74
2	1985–86*g*	Norwich C	84	Charlton Ath	77	Wimbledon	76
2	1986–87*g*	Derby Co	84	Portsmouth	78	Oldham Ath‡	75
2	1987–88*h*	Millwall	82	Aston Villa*	78	Middlesbrough	78
2	1988–89*k*	Chelsea	99	Manchester C	82	Crystal Palace	81
2	1989–90*k*	Leeds U*	85	Sheffield U	85	Newcastle U‡	80
2	1990–91*k*	Oldham Ath	88	West Ham U	87	Sheffield W	82
2	1991–92*k*	Ipswich T	84	Middlesbrough	80	Derby Co	78

FIRST DIVISION (1992–93 to 2003–04)

MAXIMUM POINTS: 138

2	1992–93	Newcastle U	96	West Ham U*	88	Portsmouth‡	88
2	1993–94	Crystal Palace	90	Nottingham F	83	Millwall‡	74
2	1994–95	Middlesbrough	82	Reading‡	79	Bolton W	77
2	1995–96	Sunderland	83	Derby Co	79	Crystal Palace‡	75
2	1996–97	Bolton W	98	Barnsley	80	Wolverhampton W‡	76
2	1997–98	Nottingham F	94	Middlesbrough	91	Sunderland‡	90

2	1998–99	Sunderland	105	Bradford C	87	Ipswich T‡	86
2	1999–2000	Charlton Ath	91	Manchester C	89	Ipswich T	87
2	2000–01	Fulham	101	Blackburn R	91	Bolton W	87
2	2001–02	Manchester C	99	WBA	89	Wolverhampton W‡	86
2	2002–03	Portsmouth	98	Leicester C	92	Sheffield U‡	80
2	2003–04	Norwich C	94	WBA	86	Sunderland‡	79

FOOTBALL LEAGUE CHAMPIONSHIP (2004–05 to 2020–21)

MAXIMUM POINTS: 138

2	2004–05	Sunderland	94	Wigan Ath	87	Ipswich T‡	85
2	2005–06	Reading	106	Sheffield U	90	Watford	81
2	2006–07	Sunderland	88	Birmingham C	86	Derby Co	84
2	2007–08	WBA	81	Stoke C	79	Hull C	75
2	2008–09	Wolverhampton W	90	Birmingham C	83	Sheffield U‡	80
2	2009–10	Newcastle U	102	WBA	91	Nottingham F‡	79
2	2010–11	QPR	88	Norwich C	84	Swansea C*	80
2	2011–12	Reading	89	Southampton	88	West Ham U	86
2	2012–13	Cardiff C	87	Hull C	79	Watford‡	77
2	2013–14	Leicester C	102	Burnley	93	Derby Co‡	85
2	2014–15	Bournemouth	90	Watford	89	Norwich C	86
2	2015–16	Burnley	93	Middlesbrough*	89	Brighton & HA‡	89
2	2016–17	Newcastle U	94	Brighton & HA	93	Reading‡	85
2	2017–18	Wolverhampton W	99	Cardiff C	90	Fulham	88
2	2018–19	Norwich C	94	Sheffield U	89	Leeds U‡	83
2	2019–20	Leeds U	93	WBA	83	Brentford*‡	81
2	2020–21	Norwich C	97	Watford	91	Brentford	87

DIVISION 3 (1920–1921) – TIER 3

MAXIMUM POINTS: ***a*** **84.**

3	1920–21*a*	Crystal Palace	59	Southampton	54	QPR	53

DIVISION 3—SOUTH (1921–22 to 1957–58)

MAXIMUM POINTS: ***a*** **84;** ***b*** **92.**

3	1921–22*a*	Southampton*	61	Plymouth Arg	61	Portsmouth	53
3	1922–23*a*	Bristol C	59	Plymouth Arg*	53	Swansea T	53
3	1923–24*a*	Portsmouth	59	Plymouth Arg	55	Millwall	54
3	1924–25*a*	Swansea T	57	Plymouth Arg	56	Bristol C	53
3	1925–26*a*	Reading	57	Plymouth Arg	56	Millwall	53
3	1926–27*a*	Bristol C	62	Plymouth Arg	60	Millwall	56
3	1927–28*a*	Millwall	65	Northampton T	55	Plymouth Arg	53
3	1928–29*a*	Charlton Ath*	54	Crystal Palace	54	Northampton T*	52
3	1929–30*a*	Plymouth Arg	68	Brentford	61	QPR	51
3	1930–31*a*	Notts Co	59	Crystal Palace	51	Brentford	50
3	1931–32*a*	Fulham	57	Reading	55	Southend U	53
3	1932–33*a*	Brentford	62	Exeter C	58	Norwich C	57
3	1933–34*a*	Norwich C	61	Coventry C*	54	Reading*	54
3	1934–35*a*	Charlton Ath	61	Reading	53	Coventry C	51
3	1935–36*a*	Coventry C	57	Luton T	56	Reading	54
3	1936–37*a*	Luton T	58	Notts Co	56	Brighton & HA	53
3	1937–38*a*	Millwall	56	Bristol C	55	QPR*	53
3	1938–39*a*	Newport Co	55	Crystal Palace	52	Brighton & HA	49
3	1946–47*a*	Cardiff C	66	QPR	57	Bristol C	51
3	1947–48*a*	QPR	61	Bournemouth	57	Walsall	51
3	1948–49*a*	Swansea T	62	Reading	55	Bournemouth	52
3	1949–50*a*	Notts Co	58	Northampton T*	51	Southend U	51
3	1950–51*b*	Nottingham F	70	Norwich C	64	Reading*	57
3	1951–52*b*	Plymouth Arg	66	Reading*	61	Norwich C	61
3	1952–53*b*	Bristol R	64	Millwall*	62	Northampton T	62
3	1953–54*b*	Ipswich T	64	Brighton & HA	61	Bristol C	56
3	1954–55*b*	Bristol C	70	Leyton Orient	61	Southampton	59
3	1955–56*b*	Leyton Orient	66	Brighton & HA	65	Ipswich T	64
3	1956–57*b*	Ipswich T*	59	Torquay U	59	Colchester U	58
3	1957–58*b*	Brighton & HA	60	Brentford*	58	Plymouth Arg	58

DIVISION 3—NORTH (1921–22 to 1957–58)

MAXIMUM POINTS: ***a*** **76;** ***b*** **84;** ***c*** **80;** ***d*** **92.**

3	1921–22*a*	Stockport Co	56	Darlington*	50	Grimsby T	50
3	1922–23*a*	Nelson	51	Bradford PA	47	Walsall	46
3	1923–24*b*	Wolverhampton W	63	Rochdale	62	Chesterfield	54
3	1924–25*b*	Darlington	58	Nelson*	53	New Brighton	53
3	1925–26*b*	Grimsby T	61	Bradford PA	60	Rochdale	59
3	1926–27*b*	Stoke C	63	Rochdale	58	Bradford PA	55
3	1927–28*b*	Bradford PA	63	Lincoln C	55	Stockport Co	54
3	1928–29*b*	Bradford C	63	Stockport Co	62	Wrexham	52
3	1929–30*b*	Port Vale	67	Stockport Co	63	Darlington*	50
3	1930–31*b*	Chesterfield	58	Lincoln C	57	Wrexham*	54
3	1931–32*c*	Lincoln C*	57	Gateshead	57	Chester	50
3	1932–33*b*	Hull C	59	Wrexham	57	Stockport Co	54
3	1933–34*b*	Barnsley	62	Chesterfield	61	Stockport Co	59

3	1934–35*b*	Doncaster R	57	Halifax T	55	Chester	54
3	1935–36*b*	Chesterfield	60	Chester*	55	Tranmere R	55
3	1936–37*b*	Stockport Co	60	Lincoln C	57	Chester	53
3	1937–38*b*	Tranmere R	56	Doncaster R	54	Hull C	53
3	1938–39*b*	Barnsley	67	Doncaster R	56	Bradford C	52
3	1946–47*b*	Doncaster R	72	Rotherham U	64	Chester	56
3	1947–48*b*	Lincoln C	60	Rotherham U	59	Wrexham	50
3	1948–49*b*	Hull C	65	Rotherham U	62	Doncaster R	50
3	1949–50*b*	Doncaster R	55	Gateshead	53	Rochdale*	51
3	1950–51*d*	Rotherham U	71	Mansfield T	64	Carlisle U	62
3	1951–52*d*	Lincoln C	69	Grimsby T	66	Stockport Co	59
3	1952–53*d*	Oldham Ath	59	Port Vale	58	Wrexham	56
3	1953–54*d*	Port Vale	69	Barnsley	58	Scunthorpe U	57
3	1954–55*d*	Barnsley	65	Accrington S	61	Scunthorpe U*	58
3	1955–56*d*	Grimsby T	68	Derby Co	63	Accrington S	59
3	1956–57*d*	Derby Co	63	Hartlepools U	59	Accrington S*	58
3	1957–58*d*	Scunthorpe U	66	Accrington S	59	Bradford C	57

DIVISION 3 (1958–59 to 1991–92)

MAXIMUM POINTS: 92; 138 FROM 1981–82.

3	1958–59	Plymouth Arg	62	Hull C	61	Brentford*	57
3	1959–60	Southampton	61	Norwich C	59	Shrewsbury T*	52
3	1960–61	Bury	68	Walsall	62	QPR	60
3	1961–62	Portsmouth	65	Grimsby T	62	Bournemouth*	59
3	1962–63	Northampton T	62	Swindon T	58	Port Vale	54
3	1963–64	Coventry C*	60	Crystal Palace	60	Watford	58
3	1964–65	Carlisle U	60	Bristol C*	59	Mansfield T	59
3	1965–66	Hull C	69	Millwall	65	QPR	57
3	1966–67	QPR	67	Middlesbrough	55	Watford	54
3	1967–68	Oxford U	57	Bury	56	Shrewsbury T	55
3	1968–69	Watford*	64	Swindon T	64	Luton T	61
3	1969–70	Orient	62	Luton T	60	Bristol R	56
3	1970–71	Preston NE	61	Fulham	60	Halifax T	56
3	1971–72	Aston Villa	70	Brighton & HA	65	Bournemouth*	62
3	1972–73	Bolton W	61	Notts Co	57	Blackburn R	55
3	1973–74	Oldham Ath	62	Bristol R*	61	York C	61
3	1974–75	Blackburn R	60	Plymouth Arg	59	Charlton Ath	55
3	1975–76	Hereford U	63	Cardiff C	57	Millwall	56
3	1976–77	Mansfield T	64	Brighton & HA	61	Crystal Palace*	59
3	1977–78	Wrexham	61	Cambridge U	58	Preston NE*	56
3	1978–79	Shrewsbury T	61	Watford*	60	Swansea C	60
3	1979–80	Grimsby T	62	Blackburn R	59	Sheffield W	58
3	1980–81	Rotherham U	61	Barnsley*	59	Charlton Ath	59
3	1981–82	Burnley*	80	Carlisle U	80	Fulham	78
3	1982–83	Portsmouth	91	Cardiff C	86	Huddersfield T	82
3	1983–84	Oxford U	95	Wimbledon	87	Sheffield U*	83
3	1984–85	Bradford C	94	Millwall	90	Hull C	87
3	1985–86	Reading	94	Plymouth Arg	87	Derby Co	84
3	1986–87	Bournemouth	97	Middlesbrough	94	Swindon T	87
3	1987–88	Sunderland	93	Brighton & HA	84	Walsall	82
3	1988–89	Wolverhampton W	92	Sheffield U*	84	Port Vale	84
3	1989–90	Bristol R	93	Bristol C	91	Notts Co	87
3	1990–91	Cambridge U	86	Southend U	85	Grimsby T*	83
3	1991–92	Brentford	82	Birmingham C	81	Huddersfield T‡	78

SECOND DIVISION (1992–93 to 2003–04)

MAXIMUM POINTS: 138

3	1992–93	Stoke C	93	Bolton W	90	Port Vale‡	89
3	1993–94	Reading	89	Port Vale	88	Plymouth Arg*‡	85
3	1994–95	Birmingham C	89	Brentford‡	85	Crewe Alex‡	83
3	1995–96	Swindon T	92	Oxford U	83	Blackpool‡	82
3	1996–97	Bury	84	Stockport Co	82	Luton T‡	78
3	1997–98	Watford	88	Bristol C	85	Grimsby T	72
3	1998–99	Fulham	101	Walsall	87	Manchester C	82
3	1999–2000	Preston NE	95	Burnley	88	Gillingham	85
3	2000–01	Millwall	93	Rotherham U	91	Reading‡	86
3	2001–02	Brighton & HA	90	Reading	84	Brentford*‡	83
3	2002–03	Wigan Ath	100	Crewe Alex	86	Bristol C*‡	83
3	2003–04	Plymouth Arg	90	QPR	83	Bristol C‡	82

FOOTBALL LEAGUE ONE (2004–05 to 2020–21)

MAXIMUM POINTS: 138

3	2004–05	Luton T	98	Hull C	86	Tranmere R‡	79
3	2005–06	Southend U	82	Colchester U	79	Brentford‡	76
3	2006–07	Scunthorpe U	91	Bristol C	85	Blackpool	83
3	2007–08	Swansea C	92	Nottingham F	82	Doncaster R*	80
3	2008–09	Leicester C	96	Peterborough U	89	Milton Keynes D‡	87
3	2009–10	Norwich C	95	Leeds U	86	Millwall	85
3	2010–11	Brighton & HA	95	Southampton	92	Huddersfield T‡	87
3	2011–12	Charlton Ath	101	Sheffield W	93	Sheffield U‡	90
3	2012–13	Doncaster R	84	Bournemouth	83	Brentford‡	79
3	2013–14	Wolverhampton W	103	Brentford	94	Leyton Orient‡	86

3	2014–15	Bristol C	99	Milton Keynes D	91	Preston NE			89
3	2015–16	Wigan Ath	87	Burton Alb	85	Walsall‡			84
3	2016–17	Sheffield U	100	Bolton W	86	Scunthorpe U*‡			82
3	2017–18	Wigan Ath	98	Blackburn R	96	Shrewsbury T‡			87
3	2018–19	Luton T	94	Barnsley	91	Charlton Ath*			88
3	2019–20[2]	Coventry C	67	Rotherham U	62	Wycombe W			59

[2] *Season curtailed due to COVID-19 pandemic. League positions decided on points-per-game basis.*

3	2020–21	Hull C	89	Peterborough U	87	Blackpool			80

DIVISION 4 (1958–59 to 1991–92) – TIER 4

MAXIMUM POINTS: 92; 138 FROM 1981–82.

4	1958–59	Port Vale	64	Coventry C*	60	York C	60	Shrewsbury T	58
4	1959–60	Walsall	65	Notts Co*	60	Torquay U	60	Watford	57
4	1960–61	Peterborough U	66	Crystal Palace	64	Northampton T*	60	Bradford PA	60
4	1961–62[3]	Millwall	56	Colchester U	55	Wrexham	53	Carlisle U	52
4	1962–63	Brentford	62	Oldham Ath*	59	Crewe Alex	59	Mansfield T*	57
4	1963–64	Gillingham*	60	Carlisle U	60	Workington	59	Exeter C	58
4	1964–65	Brighton & HA	63	Millwall*	62	York C	62	Oxford U	61
4	1965–66	Doncaster R*	59	Darlington	59	Torquay U	58	Colchester U*	56
4	1966–67	Stockport Co	64	Southport*	59	Barrow	59	Tranmere R	58
4	1967–68	Luton T	66	Barnsley	61	Hartlepools U	60	Crewe Alex	58
4	1968–69	Doncaster R	59	Halifax T	57	Rochdale*	56	Bradford C	56
4	1969–70	Chesterfield	64	Wrexham	61	Swansea C	60	Port Vale	59
4	1970–71	Notts Co	69	Bournemouth	60	Oldham Ath	59	York C	56
4	1971–72	Grimsby T	63	Southend U	60	Brentford	59	Scunthorpe U	57
4	1972–73	Southport	62	Hereford U	58	Cambridge U	57	Aldershot*	56
4	1973–74	Peterborough U	65	Gillingham	62	Colchester U	60	Bury	59
4	1974–75	Mansfield T	68	Shrewsbury T	62	Rotherham U	59	Chester*	57
4	1975–76	Lincoln C	74	Northampton T	68	Reading	60	Tranmere R	58
4	1976–77	Cambridge U	65	Exeter C	62	Colchester U*	59	Bradford C	59
4	1977–78	Watford	71	Southend U	60	Swansea C*	56	Brentford	56
4	1978–79	Reading	65	Grimsby T*	61	Wimbledon*	61	Barnsley	61
4	1979–80	Huddersfield T	66	Walsall	64	Newport Co	61	Portsmouth*	60
4	1980–81	Southend U	67	Lincoln C	65	Doncaster R	56	Wimbledon	55
4	1981–82	Sheffield U	96	Bradford C*	91	Wigan Ath	91	Bournemouth	88
4	1982–83	Wimbledon	98	Hull C	90	Port Vale	88	Scunthorpe U	83
4	1983–84	York C	101	Doncaster R	85	Reading*	82	Bristol C	82
4	1984–85	Chesterfield	91	Blackpool	86	Darlington	85	Bury	84
4	1985–86	Swindon T	102	Chester C	84	Mansfield T	81	Port Vale	79
4	1986–87	Northampton T	99	Preston NE	90	Southend U	80	Wolverhampton W‡	79
4	1987–88	Wolverhampton W	90	Cardiff C	85	Bolton W	78	Scunthorpe U*‡	77
4	1988–89	Rotherham U	82	Tranmere R	80	Crewe Alex	78	Scunthorpe U*‡	77
4	1989–90	Exeter C	89	Grimsby T	79	Southend U	75	Stockport Co‡	74
4	1990–91	Darlington	83	Stockport Co*	82	Hartlepool U	82	Peterborough U	80
4	1991–92[4]	Burnley	83	Rotherham U*	77	Mansfield T	77	Blackpool	76

[3] *Maximum points: 88 owing to Accrington Stanley's resignation.*
[4] *Maximum points: 126 owing to Aldershot being expelled (and only 23 teams started the competition).*

THIRD DIVISION (1992–93 to 2003–04)

MAXIMUM POINTS: *a* 126; *b* 138.

4	1992–93*a*	Cardiff C	83	Wrexham	80	Barnet	79	York C	75
4	1993–94*a*	Shrewsbury T	79	Chester C	74	Crewe Alex	73	Wycombe W	70
4	1994–95*a*	Carlisle U	91	Walsall	83	Chesterfield	81	Bury‡	80
4	1995–96*b*	Preston NE	86	Gillingham	83	Bury	79	Plymouth Arg*	78
4	1996–97*b*	Wigan Ath*	87	Fulham	87	Carlisle U	84	Northampton T	72
4	1997–98*b*	Notts Co	99	Macclesfield T	82	Lincoln C	72	Colchester U*	74
4	1998–99*b*	Brentford	85	Cambridge U	81	Cardiff C	80	Scunthorpe U	74
4	1999–2000*b*	Swansea C	85	Rotherham U	84	Northampton T	82	Darlington‡	79
4	2000–01*b*	Brighton & HA	92	Cardiff C	82	Chesterfield[5]	80	Hartlepool U‡	77
4	2001–02*b*	Plymouth Arg	102	Luton T	97	Mansfield T	79	Cheltenham T	78
4	2002–03*b*	Rushden & D	87	Hartlepool U	85	Wrexham	84	Bournemouth	74
4	2003–04*b*	Doncaster R	92	Hull C	88	Torquay U*	81	Huddersfield T	81

[5] *Chesterfield deducted 9pts for irregularities.*

FOOTBALL LEAGUE TWO (2004–05 to 2020–21)

MAXIMUM POINTS: 138

4	2004–05	Yeovil T	83	Scunthorpe U*	80	Swansea C*	80	Southend U*	80
4	2005–06	Carlisle U	86	Northampton T	83	Leyton Orient	81	Grimsby T‡	78
4	2006–07	Walsall	89	Hartlepool U	88	Swindon T	85	Milton Keynes D‡	84
4	2007–08	Milton Keynes D	97	Peterborough U	92	Hereford U	88	Stockport Co	82
4	2008–09	Brentford	85	Exeter C	79	Wycombe W*	78	Bury‡	78
4	2009–10	Notts Co	93	Bournemouth	83	Rochdale	82	Morecambe*‡	73
4	2010–11	Chesterfield	86	Bury	81	Wycombe W	80	Shrewsbury T‡	79
4	2011–12	Swindon T	93	Shrewsbury T	88	Crawley T	84	Southend U‡	83
4	2012–13	Gillingham	83	Rotherham U	79	Port Vale	78	Burton Alb	76
4	2013–14	Chesterfield	84	Scunthorpe U*	81	Rochdale	81	Fleetwood T	76
4	2014–15	Burton Alb	94	Shrewsbury T	89	Bury	85	Wycombe W*‡	84
4	2015–16	Northampton T	99	Oxford U	86	Bristol R*	85	Accrington S‡	85
4	2016–17	Portsmouth*	87	Plymouth Arg	87	Doncaster R	85	Luton T‡	77
4	2017–18	Accrington S	93	Luton T	88	Wycombe W	84	Exeter C‡	80
4	2018–19	Lincoln C	85	Bury*	79	Milton Keynes D	79	Mansfield T‡	76
4	2019–20[6]	Swindon T*	69	Crewe Alex	69	Plymouth Arg	68	Cheltenham T‡	64

[6] *Season curtailed due to COVID-19 pandemic. League positions decided on points-per-game basis.*

4	2020–21	Cheltenham T	82	Cambridge U	80	Bolton W	79	Morecambe	78

LEAGUE TITLE WINS

DIVISION 1 (1888–89 to 1991–92) – TIER 1
Liverpool 18, Arsenal 10, Everton 9, Aston Villa 7, Manchester U 7, Sunderland 6, Newcastle U 4, Sheffield W 4 (2 as The Wednesday), Huddersfield T 3, Leeds U 3, Wolverhampton W 3, Blackburn R 2, Burnley 2, Derby Co 2, Manchester C 2, Portsmouth 2, Preston NE 2, Tottenham H 2, Chelsea 1, Ipswich T 1, Nottingham F 1, Sheffield U 1, WBA 1.

PREMIER LEAGUE (1992–93 to 2020–21) – TIER 1
Manchester U 13, Chelsea 5, Manchester C 5, Arsenal 3, Blackburn R 1, Leicester C 1, Liverpool 1.

DIVISION 2 (1892–93 TO 1991–92) – TIER 2
Leicester C 6, Manchester C 6, Sheffield W 5 (1 as The Wednesday), Birmingham C 4 (1 as Small Heath), Derby Co 4, Liverpool 4, Ipswich T 3, Leeds U 3, Middlesbrough 3, Notts Co 3, Preston NE 3, Aston Villa 2, Bolton W 2, Burnley 2, Chelsea 2, Grimsby T 2, Manchester U 2, Norwich C 2, Nottingham F 2, Stoke C 2, Tottenham H 2, WBA 2, West Ham U 2, Wolverhampton W 2, Blackburn R 1, Blackpool 1, Bradford C 1, Brentford 1, Bristol C 1, Bury 1, Coventry C 1, Crystal Palace 1, Everton 1, Fulham 1, Huddersfield T 1, Luton T 1, Millwall 1, Newcastle U 1, Oldham Ath 1, Oxford U 1, QPR 1, Sheffield U 1, Sunderland 1.

FIRST DIVISION (1992–93 to 2003–04) – TIER 2
Sunderland 1, Bolton W 1, Charlton Ath 1, Crystal Palace 1, Fulham 1, Manchester C 1, Middlesbrough 1, Newcastle U 1, Norwich C 1, Nottingham F 1, Portsmouth 1.

FOOTBALL LEAGUE CHAMPIONSHIP (2004–05 to 2020–21) – TIER 2
Newcastle U 2, Norwich C 2, Reading 2, Sunderland 2, Wolverhampton W 2, Bournemouth 1, Burnley 1, Cardiff C 1, Leeds U 1, Leicester C 1, QPR 1, WBA 1,

---

DIVISION 3—SOUTH (1920–21 to 1957–58) – TIER 3
Bristol C 3, Charlton Ath 2, Ipswich T 2, Millwall 2, Notts Co 2, Plymouth Arg 2, Swansea T 2, Brentford 1, Brighton & HA 1, Bristol R 1, Cardiff C 1, Coventry C 1, Crystal Palace 1, Fulham 1, Leyton Orient 1, Luton T 1, Newport Co 1, Norwich C 1, Nottingham F 1, Portsmouth 1, QPR 1, Reading 1, Southampton 1.

DIVISION 3—NORTH (1921–22 to 1957–58) – TIER 3
Barnsley 3, Doncaster R 3, Lincoln C 3, Chesterfield 2, Grimsby T 2, Hull C 2, Port Vale 2, Stockport Co 2, Bradford C 1, Bradford PA 1, Darlington 1, Derby Co 1, Nelson 1, Oldham Ath 1, Rotherham U 1, Scunthorpe U 1, Stoke C 1, Tranmere R 1, Wolverhampton W 1.

DIVISION 3 (1958–59 to 1991–92) – TIER 3
Oxford U 2, Portsmouth 2, Aston Villa 1, Blackburn R 1, Bolton W 1, Bournemouth 1, Bradford C 1, Brentford 1, Bristol R 1, Burnley 1, Bury 1, Cambridge U 1, Carlisle U 1, Coventry C 1, Grimsby T 1, Hereford U 1, Hull C 1, Mansfield T 1, Northampton T 1, Oldham Ath 1, Orient 1, Plymouth Arg 1, Preston NE 1, QPR 1, Reading 1, Rotherham U 1, Shrewsbury T 1, Southampton 1, Sunderland 1, Watford 1, Wolverhampton W 1, Wrexham 1.

SECOND DIVISION (1992–93 to 2003–04) – TIER 3
Birmingham C 1, Brighton & HA 1, Bury 1, Fulham 1, Millwall 1, Plymouth Arg 1, Preston NE 1, Reading 1, Stoke C 1, Swindon T 1, Watford 1, Wigan Ath 1.

FOOTBALL LEAGUE ONE (2004–05 to 2020–21) – TIER 3
Luton T 2, Wigan Ath 2, Brighton & HA 1, Bristol C 1, Charlton Ath 1, Coventry C 1, Doncaster R 1, Hull C 1, Leicester C 1, Norwich C 1, Scunthorpe U 1, Sheffield U 1, Southend U 1, Swansea C 1, Wolverhampton W 1.

DIVISION 4 (1958–59 to 1991–92) – TIER 4
Chesterfield 2, Doncaster R 2, Peterborough U 2, Brentford 1, Brighton & HA 1, Burnley 1, Cambridge U 1, Darlington 1, Exeter C 1, Gillingham 1, Grimsby T 1, Huddersfield T 1, Lincoln C 1, Luton T 1, Mansfield T 1, Millwall 1, Northampton T 1, Notts Co 1, Port Vale 1, Reading 1, Rotherham U 1, Sheffield U 1, Southend U 1, Southport 1, Stockport Co 1, Swindon T 1, Walsall 1, Watford 1, Wimbledon 1, Wolverhampton W 1, York C 1.

THIRD DIVISION (1992–93 to 2003–04) – TIER 4
Brentford 1, Brighton & HA 1, Cardiff C 1, Carlisle U 1, Doncaster R 1, Notts Co 1, Plymouth Arg 1, Preston NE 1, Rushden & D 1, Shrewsbury T 1, Swansea C 1, Wigan Ath 1.

FOOTBALL LEAGUE TWO (2004–05 to 2020–21) – TIER 4
Chesterfield 2, Swindon T 2, Accrington S 1, Brentford 1, Burton Alb 1, Carlisle U 1, Cheltenham T 1, Gillingham 1, Lincoln C 1, Milton Keynes D 1, Northampton T 1, Notts Co 1, Portsmouth 1, Walsall 1, Yeovil T 1.

PROMOTED AFTER PLAY-OFFS

1986–87	Charlton Ath to Division 1; Swindon T to Division 2; Aldershot to Division 3
1987–88	Middlesbrough to Division 1; Walsall to Division 2; Swansea C to Division 3
1988–89	Crystal Palace to Division 1; Port Vale to Division 2; Leyton Orient to Division 3
1989–90	Sunderland to Division 1; Notts Co to Division 2; Cambridge U to Division 3
1990–91	Notts Co to Division 1; Tranmere R to Division 2; Torquay U to Division 3
1991–92	Blackburn R to Premier League; Peterborough U to First Division; Blackpool to Second Division
1992–93	Swindon T to Premier League; WBA to First Division; York C to Second Division
1993–94	Leicester C to Premier League; Burnley to First Division; Wycombe W to Second Division
1994–95	Bolton W to Premier League; Huddersfield T to First Division; Wycombe W to Second Division
1995–96	Leicester C to Premier League; Bradford C to First Division; Plymouth Arg to Second Division
1996–97	Crystal Palace to Premier League; Crewe Alex to First Division; Northampton T to Second Division
1997–98	Charlton Ath to Premier League; Grimsby T to First Division; Colchester U to Second Division
1998–99	Watford to Premier League; Manchester C to First Division; Scunthorpe U to Second Division
1999–2000	Ipswich to Premier League; Gillingham to First Division; Peterborough U to Second Division
2000–01	Bolton W to Premier league; Walsall to First Division; Blackpool to Second Division
2001–02	Birmingham C to Premier League; Stoke C to First Division; Cheltenham T to Second Division
2002–03	Wolverhampton W to Premier League; Cardiff C to First Division; Bournemouth to Second Division
2003–04	Crystal Palace to Premier League; Brighton & HA to First Division; Huddersfield T to Second Division
2004–05	West Ham U to Premier League; Sheffield W to Championship; Southend U to Football League One
2005–06	Watford to Premier League; Barnsley to Championship; Cheltenham T to Football League One
2006–07	Derby Co to Premier League; Blackpool to Championship; Bristol R to Football League One
2007–08	Hull C to Premier League; Doncaster R to Championship; Stockport Co to Football League One
2008–09	Burnley to Premier League; Scunthorpe U to Championship; Gillingham to Football League One
2009–10	Blackpool to Premier League; Millwall to Championship; Dagenham & R to Football League One
2010–11	Swansea C to Premier League; Peterborough U to Championship; Stevenage to Football League One
2011–12	West Ham U to Premier League; Huddersfield T to Championship; Crewe Alex to Football League One
2012–13	Crystal Palace to Premier League; Yeovil T to Championship; Bradford C to Football League One
2013–14	QPR to Premier League; Rotherham U to Championship; Fleetwood T to Football League One
2014–15	Norwich C to Premier League; Preston NE to Championship; Southend U to Football League One
2015–16	Hull C to Premier League; Barnsley to Championship; AFC Wimbledon to Football League One
2016–17	Huddersfield T to Premier League; Millwall to Championship; Blackpool to Football League One
2017–18	Fulham to Premier League; Rotherham U to Championship; Coventry C to Football League One
2018–19	Aston Villa to Premier League; Charlton Ath to Championship; Tranmere R to Football League One
2019–20	Fulham to Premier League; Wycombe W to Championship; Northampton T to Football League One
2020–21	Brentford to Premier League; Blackpool to Championship; Morecambe to Football League One

RELEGATED CLUBS

1891–92 League extended. Newton Heath, Sheffield W and Nottingham F admitted. *Second Division formed* including Darwen.
1892–93 In Test matches, Sheffield U and Darwen won promotion in place of Notts Co and Accrington S.
1893–94 In Tests, Liverpool and Small Heath won promotion. Newton Heath and Darwen relegated.
1894–95 After Tests, Bury promoted, Liverpool relegated.
1895–96 After Tests, Liverpool promoted, Small Heath relegated.
1896–97 After Tests, Notts Co promoted, Burnley relegated.
1897–98 Test system abolished after success of Stoke C and Burnley. League extended. Blackburn R and Newcastle U elected to First Division. *Automatic promotion and relegation introduced.*

DIVISION 1 TO DIVISION 2 (1898–99 to 1991–92)

1898–99 Bolton W and Sheffield W
1899–1900 Burnley and Glossop NE
1900–01 Preston NE and WBA
1901–02 Small Heath and Manchester C
1902–03 Grimsby T and Bolton W
1903–04 Liverpool and WBA
1904–05 League extended. Bury and Notts Co, two bottom clubs in First Division, re-elected.
1905–06 Nottingham F and Wolverhampton W
1906–07 Derby Co and Stoke C
1907–08 Bolton W and Birmingham C
1908–09 Manchester C and Leicester Fosse
1909–10 Bolton W and Chelsea
1910–11 Bristol C and Nottingham F
1911–12 Preston NE and Bury
1912–13 Notts Co and Woolwich Arsenal
1913–14 Preston NE and Derby Co
1914–15 Tottenham H and Chelsea*
1919–20 Notts Co and Sheffield W
1920–21 Derby Co and Bradford PA
1921–22 Bradford C and Manchester U
1922–23 Stoke C and Oldham Ath
1923–24 Chelsea and Middlesbrough
1924–25 Preston NE and Nottingham F
1925–26 Manchester C and Notts Co
1926–27 Leeds U and WBA
1927–28 Tottenham H and Middlesbrough
1928–29 Bury and Cardiff C
1929–30 Burnley and Everton
1930–31 Leeds U and Manchester U
1931–32 Grimsby T and West Ham U
1932–33 Bolton W and Blackpool
1933–34 Newcastle U and Sheffield U
1934–35 Leicester C and Tottenham H
1935–36 Aston Villa and Blackburn R
1936–37 Manchester U and Sheffield W
1937–38 Manchester C and WBA
1938–39 Birmingham C and Leicester C
1946–47 Brentford and Leeds U
1947–48 Blackburn R and Grimsby T
1948–49 Preston NE and Sheffield U
1949–50 Manchester C and Birmingham C
1950–51 Sheffield W and Everton
1951–52 Huddersfield T and Fulham
1952–53 Stoke C and Derby Co
1953–54 Middlesbrough and Liverpool
1954–55 Leicester C and Sheffield W
1955–56 Huddersfield T and Sheffield U
1956–57 Charlton Ath and Cardiff C
1957–58 Sheffield W and Sunderland
1958–59 Portsmouth and Aston Villa
1959–60 Luton T and Leeds U
1960–61 Preston NE and Newcastle U
1961–62 Chelsea and Cardiff C
1962–63 Manchester C and Leyton Orient
1963–64 Bolton W and Ipswich T
1964–65 Wolverhampton W and Birmingham C
1965–66 Northampton T and Blackburn R
1966–67 Aston Villa and Blackpool
1967–68 Fulham and Sheffield U
1968–69 Leicester C and QPR
1969–70 Sunderland and Sheffield W
1970–71 Burnley and Blackpool
1971–72 Huddersfield T and Nottingham F
1972–73 Crystal Palace and WBA
1973–74 Southampton, Manchester U, Norwich C
1974–75 Luton T, Chelsea, Carlisle U
1975–76 Wolverhampton W, Burnley, Sheffield U
1976–77 Sunderland, Stoke C, Tottenham H
1977–78 West Ham U, Newcastle U, Leicester C
1978–79 QPR, Birmingham C, Chelsea
1979–80 Bristol C, Derby Co, Bolton W
1980–81 Norwich C, Leicester C, Crystal Palace
1981–82 Leeds U, Wolverhampton W, Middlesbrough
1982–83 Manchester C, Swansea C, Brighton & HA
1983–84 Birmingham C, Notts Co, Wolverhampton W
1984–85 Norwich C, Sunderland, Stoke C
1985–86 Ipswich T, Birmingham C, WBA
1986–87 Leicester C, Manchester C, Aston Villa
1987–88 Chelsea**, Portsmouth, Watford, Oxford U
1988–89 Middlesbrough, West Ham U, Newcastle U
1989–90 Sheffield W, Charlton Ath, Millwall
1990–91 Sunderland and Derby Co
1991–92 Luton T, Notts Co, West Ham U

***Relegated after play-offs.*

**Subsequently re-elected to Division 1 when League was extended after the War.*

PREMIER LEAGUE TO DIVISION 1 (1992–93 to 2003–04)

1992–93 Crystal Palace, Middlesbrough, Nottingham F
1993–94 Sheffield U, Oldham Ath, Swindon T
1994–95 Crystal Palace, Norwich C, Leicester C, Ipswich T
1995–96 Manchester C, QPR, Bolton W
1996–97 Sunderland, Middlesbrough, Nottingham F
1997–98 Bolton W, Barnsley, Crystal Palace
1998–99 Charlton Ath, Blackburn R, Nottingham F
1999–2000 Wimbledon, Sheffield W, Watford
2000–01 Manchester C, Coventry C, Bradford C
2001–02 Ipswich T, Derby Co, Leicester C
2002–03 West Ham U, WBA, Sunderland
2003–04 Leicester C, Leeds U, Wolverhampton W

PREMIER LEAGUE TO CHAMPIONSHIP (2004–05 to 2020–21)

2004–05 Crystal Palace, Norwich C, Southampton
2005–06 Birmingham C, WBA, Sunderland
2006–07 Sheffield U, Charlton Ath, Watford
2007–08 Reading, Birmingham C, Derby Co
2008–09 Newcastle U, Middlesbrough, WBA
2009–10 Burnley, Hull C, Portsmouth
2010–11 Birmingham C, Blackpool, West Ham U
2011–12 Bolton W, Blackburn R, Wolverhampton W
2012–13 Wigan Ath, Reading, QPR
2013–14 Norwich C, Fulham, Cardiff C
2014–15 Hull C, Burnley, QPR
2015–16 Newcastle U, Norwich C, Aston Villa
2016–17 Hull C, Middlesbrough, Sunderland
2017–18 Swansea C, Stoke C, WBA
2018–19 Cardiff C, Fulham, Huddersfield T
2019–20 Bournemouth, Watford, Norwich C
2020–21 Fulham, WBA, Sheffield U

DIVISION 2 TO DIVISION 3 (1920–21 to 1991–92)

1920–21 Stockport Co
1921–22 Bradford PA and Bristol C
1922–23 Rotherham Co and Wolverhampton W
1923–24 Nelson and Bristol C
1924–25 Crystal Palace and Coventry C
1925–26 Stoke C and Stockport Co
1926–27 Darlington and Bradford C
1927–28 Fulham and South Shields
1928–29 Port Vale and Clapton Orient
1929–30 Hull C and Notts Co
1930–31 Reading and Cardiff C
1931–32 Barnsley and Bristol C
1932–33 Chesterfield and Charlton Ath
1933–34 Millwall and Lincoln C
1934–35 Oldham Ath and Notts Co
1935–36 Port Vale and Hull C
1936–37 Doncaster R and Bradford C
1937–38 Barnsley and Stockport Co
1938–39 Norwich C and Tranmere R
1946–47 Swansea T and Newport Co
1947–48 Doncaster R and Millwall
1948–49 Nottingham F and Lincoln C
1949–50 Plymouth Arg and Bradford PA
1950–51 Grimsby T and Chesterfield
1951–52 Coventry C and QPR
1952–53 Southampton and Barnsley
1953–54 Brentford and Oldham Ath
1954–55 Ipswich T and Derby Co
1955–56 Plymouth Arg and Hull C
1956–57 Port Vale and Bury
1957–58 Doncaster R and Notts Co
1958–59 Barnsley and Grimsby T
1959–60 Bristol C and Hull C
1960–61 Lincoln C and Portsmouth
1961–62 Brighton & HA and Bristol R
1962–63 Walsall and Luton T
1963–64 Grimsby T and Scunthorpe U
1964–65 Swindon T and Swansea T
1965–66 Middlesbrough and Leyton Orient
1966–67 Northampton T and Bury
1967–68 Plymouth Arg and Rotherham U
1968–69 Fulham and Bury
1969–70 Preston NE and Aston Villa
1970–71 Blackburn R and Bolton W
1971–72 Charlton Ath and Watford
1972–73 Huddersfield T and Brighton & HA
1973–74 Crystal Palace, Preston NE, Swindon T
1974–75 Millwall, Cardiff C, Sheffield W
1975–76 Oxford U, York C, Portsmouth
1976–77 Carlisle U, Plymouth Arg, Hereford U
1977–78 Blackpool, Mansfield T, Hull C
1978–79 Sheffield U, Millwall, Blackburn R
1979–80 Fulham, Burnley, Charlton Ath
1980–81 Preston NE, Bristol C, Bristol R
1981–82 Cardiff C, Wrexham, Orient
1982–83 Rotherham U, Burnley, Bolton W
1983–84 Derby Co, Swansea C, Cambridge U
1984–85 Notts Co, Cardiff C, Wolverhampton W
1985–86 Carlisle U, Middlesbrough, Fulham
1986–87 Sunderland**, Grimsby T, Brighton & HA
1987–88 Huddersfield T, Reading, Sheffield U**
1988–89 Shrewsbury T, Birmingham C, Walsall
1989–90 Bournemouth, Bradford C, Stoke C
1990–91 WBA and Hull C
1991–92 Plymouth Arg, Brighton & HA, Port Vale

FIRST DIVISION TO SECOND DIVISION (1992–93 to 2003–04)

1992–93 Brentford, Cambridge U, Bristol R
1993–94 Birmingham C, Oxford U, Peterborough U
1994–95 Swindon T, Burnley, Bristol C, Notts Co
1995–96 Millwall, Watford, Luton T
1996–97 Grimsby T, Oldham Ath, Southend U
1997–98 Manchester C, Stoke C, Reading
1998–99 Bury, Oxford U, Bristol C
1999–2000 Walsall, Port Vale, Swindon T
2000–01 Huddersfield T, QPR, Tranmere R
2001–02 Crewe Alex, Barnsley, Stockport Co
2002–03 Sheffield W, Brighton & HA, Grimsby T
2003–04 Walsall, Bradford C, Wimbledon

FOOTBALL LEAGUE CHAMPIONSHIP TO FOOTBALL LEAGUE ONE (2004–05 to 2020–21)

2004–05 Gillingham, Nottingham F, Rotherham U
2005–06 Crewe Alex, Millwall, Brighton & HA
2006–07 Southend U, Luton T, Leeds U
2007–08 Leicester C, Scunthorpe U, Colchester U
2008–09 Norwich C, Southampton, Charlton Ath
2009–10 Sheffield W, Plymouth Arg, Peterborough U
2010–11 Preston NE, Sheffield U, Scunthorpe U
2011–12 Portsmouth, Coventry C, Doncaster R
2012–13 Peterborough U, Wolverhampton W, Bristol C
2013–14 Doncaster R, Barnsley, Yeovil T
2014–15 Millwall, Wigan Ath, Blackpool
2015–16 Charlton Ath, Milton Keynes D, Bolton W
2016–17 Blackburn R, Wigan Ath, Rotherham U
2017–18 Barnsley, Burton Alb, Sunderland
2018–19 Rotherham U, Bolton W, Ipswich T
2019–20 Charlton Ath, Wigan Ath, Hull C
2020–21 Wycombe W, Rotherham U, Sheffield W

DIVISION 3 TO DIVISION 4 (1958–59 to 1991–92)

1958–59 Stockport Co, Doncaster R, Notts Co, Rochdale
1959–60 York C, Mansfield T, Wrexham, Accrington S
1960–61 Tranmere R, Bradford C, Colchester U, Chesterfield
1961–62 Torquay U, Lincoln C, Brentford, Newport Co
1962–63 Bradford PA, Brighton & HA, Carlisle U, Halifax T
1963–64 Millwall, Crewe Alex, Wrexham, Notts Co
1964–65 Luton T, Port Vale, Colchester U, Barnsley
1965–66 Southend U, Exeter C, Brentford, York C
1966–67 Swansea T, Darlington, Doncaster R, Workington
1967–68 Grimsby T, Colchester U, Scunthorpe U, Peterborough U (demoted)
1968–69 Northampton T, Hartlepool, Crewe Alex, Oldham Ath
1969–70 Bournemouth, Southport, Barrow, Stockport Co
1970–71 Reading, Bury, Doncaster R, Gillingham
1971–72 Mansfield T, Barnsley, Torquay U, Bradford C
1972–73 Rotherham U, Brentford, Swansea C, Scunthorpe U
1973–74 Cambridge U, Shrewsbury T, Southport, Rochdale
1974–75 Bournemouth, Tranmere R, Watford, Huddersfield T
1975–76 Aldershot, Colchester U, Southend U, Halifax T
1976–77 Reading, Northampton T, Grimsby T, York C
1977–78 Port Vale, Bradford C, Hereford U, Portsmouth
1978–79 Peterborough U, Walsall, Tranmere R, Lincoln C
1979–80 Bury, Southend U, Mansfield T, Wimbledon
1980–81 Sheffield U, Colchester U, Blackpool, Hull C
1981–82 Wimbledon, Swindon T, Bristol C, Chester
1982–83 Reading, Wrexham, Doncaster R, Chesterfield
1983–84 Scunthorpe U, Southend U, Port Vale, Exeter C
1984–85 Burnley, Orient, Preston NE, Cambridge U
1985–86 Lincoln C, Cardiff C, Wolverhampton W, Swansea C
1986–87 Bolton W**, Carlisle U, Darlington, Newport Co
1987–88 Rotherham U**, Grimsby T, York C, Doncaster R
1988–89 Southend U, Chesterfield, Gillingham, Aldershot
1989–90 Cardiff C, Northampton T, Blackpool, Walsall
1990–91 Crewe Alex, Rotherham U, Mansfield T
1991–92 Bury, Shrewsbury T, Torquay U, Darlington

*** Relegated after play-offs.*

SECOND DIVISION TO THIRD DIVISION (1992–93 to 2003–04)

1992–93 Preston NE, Mansfield T, Wigan Ath, Chester C
1993–94 Fulham, Exeter C, Hartlepool U, Barnet
1994–95 Cambridge U, Plymouth Arg, Cardiff C, Chester C, Leyton Orient
1995–96 Carlisle U, Swansea C, Brighton & HA, Hull C
1996–97 Peterborough U, Shrewsbury T, Rotherham U, Notts Co
1997–98 Brentford, Plymouth Arg, Carlisle U, Southend U
1998–99 York C, Northampton T, Lincoln C, Macclesfield T
1999–2000 Cardiff C, Blackpool, Scunthorpe U, Chesterfield
2000–01 Bristol R, Luton T, Swansea C, Oxford U
2001–02 Bournemouth, Bury, Wrexham, Cambridge U
2002–03 Cheltenham T, Huddersfield T, Mansfield T Northampton T
2003–04 Grimsby T, Rushden & D, Notts Co, Wycombe W

FOOTBALL LEAGUE ONE TO FOOTBALL LEAGUE TWO (2004–05 to 2020–21)

2004–05 Torquay U, Wrexham, Peterborough U, Stockport Co
2005–06 Hartlepool U, Milton Keynes D, Swindon T, Walsall
2006–07 Chesterfield, Bradford C, Rotherham U, Brentford
2007–08 Bournemouth, Gillingham, Port Vale, Luton T
2008–09 Northampton T, Crewe Alex, Cheltenham T, Hereford U
2009–10 Gillingham, Wycombe W, Southend U, Stockport Co
2010–11 Dagenham & R, Bristol R, Plymouth Arg, Swindon T
2011–12 Wycombe W, Chesterfield, Exeter C, Rochdale
2012–13 Scunthorpe U, Bury, Hartlepool U, Portsmouth
2013–14 Tranmere R, Carlisle U, Shrewsbury T, Stevenage
2014–15 Notts Co, Crawley T, Leyton Orient, Yeovil T
2015–16 Doncaster R, Blackpool, Colchester U, Crewe Alex
2016–17 Port Vale, Swindon T, Coventry C, Chesterfield
2017–18 Oldham Ath, Northampton T, Milton Keynes D, Bury
2018–19 Plymouth Arg, Walsall, Scunthorpe U, Bradford C
2019–20 Tranmere R, Southend U, Bolton W
2020–21 Rochdale, Northampton T, Swindon T, Bristol R

LEAGUE STATUS FROM 1986–87

RELEGATED FROM LEAGUE

1986–87 Lincoln C
1987–88 Newport Co
1988–89 Darlington
1989–90 Colchester U
1990–91 —
1991–92 —
1992–93 Halifax T
1993–94 —
1994–95 —
1995–96 —
1996–97 Hereford U
1997–98 Doncaster R
1998–99 Scarborough
1999–2000 Chester C
2000–01 Barnet
2001–02 Halifax T
2002–03 Shrewsbury T, Exeter C
2003–04 Carlisle U, York C
2004–05 Kidderminster H, Cambridge U
2005–06 Oxford U, Rushden & D
2006–07 Boston U, Torquay U
2007–08 Mansfield T, Wrexham
2008–09 Chester C, Luton T
2009–10 Grimsby T, Darlington
2010–11 Lincoln C, Stockport Co
2011–12 Hereford U, Macclesfield T
2012–13 Barnet, Aldershot T
2013–14 Bristol R, Torquay U
2014–15 Cheltenham T, Tranmere R
2015–16 Dagenham & R, York C
2016–17 Hartlepool U, Leyton Orient
2017–18 Barnet, Chesterfield
2018–19 Notts Co, Yeovil T
2019–20 Macclesfield T
2020–21 Southend U, Grimsby T

PROMOTED TO LEAGUE

1986–87 Scarborough
1987–88 Lincoln C
1988–89 Maidstone U
1989–90 Darlington
1990–91 Barnet
1991–92 Colchester U
1992–93 Wycombe W
1993–94 —
1994–95 —
1995–96 —
1996–97 Macclesfield T
1997–98 Halifax T
1998–99 Cheltenham T
1999–2000 Kidderminster H
2000–01 Rushden & D
2001–02 Boston U
2002–03 Yeovil T, Doncaster R
2003–04 Chester C, Shrewsbury T
2004–05 Barnet, Carlisle U
2005–06 Accrington S, Hereford U
2006–07 Dagenham & R, Morecambe
2007–08 Aldershot T, Exeter C
2008–09 Burton Alb, Torquay U
2009–10 Stevenage B, Oxford U
2010–11 Crawley T, AFC Wimbledon
2011–12 Fleetwood T, York C
2012–13 Mansfield T, Newport Co
2013–14 Luton T, Cambridge U
2014–15 Barnet, Bristol R
2015–16 Cheltenham T, Grimsby T
2016–17 Lincoln C, Forest Green R
2017–18 Macclesfield T, Tranmere R
2018–19 Leyton Orient, Salford C
2019–20 Barrow, Harrogate T
2020–21 Sutton U, Hartlepool U

APPLICATIONS FOR RE-ELECTION

FOURTH DIVISION

Eleven: Hartlepool U.
Seven: Crewe Alex.
Six: Barrow (lost League place to Hereford U 1972), Halifax T, Rochdale, Southport (lost League place to Wigan Ath 1978), York C.
Five: Chester C, Darlington, Lincoln C, Stockport Co, Workington (lost League place to Wimbledon 1977).
Four: Bradford PA (lost League place to Cambridge U 1970), Newport Co, Northampton T.
Three: Doncaster R, Hereford U.
Two: Bradford C, Exeter C, Oldham Ath, Scunthorpe U, Torquay U.
One: Aldershot, Colchester U, Gateshead (lost League place to Peterborough U 1960), Grimsby T, Swansea C, Tranmere R, Wrexham, Blackpool, Cambridge U, Preston NE.

Accrington S resigned and Oxford U were elected 1962.
Port Vale were forced to re-apply following expulsion in 1968.
Aldershot expelled March 1992. Maidstone U resigned August 1992.

THIRD DIVISIONS NORTH & SOUTH

Seven: Walsall.
Six: Exeter C, Halifax T, Newport Co.
Five: Accrington S, Barrow, Gillingham, New Brighton, Southport.
Four: Rochdale, Norwich C.
Three: Crystal Palace, Crewe Alex, Darlington, Hartlepool U, Merthyr T, Swindon T.
Two: Aberdare Ath, Aldershot, Ashington, Bournemouth, Brentford, Chester, Colchester U, Durham C, Millwall, Nelson, QPR, Rotherham U, Southend U, Tranmere R, Watford, Workington.
One: Bradford C, Bradford PA, Brighton & HA, Bristol R, Cardiff C, Carlisle U, Charlton Ath, Gateshead, Grimsby T, Mansfield T, Shrewsbury T, Torquay U, York C.

LEAGUE ATTENDANCES SINCE 1946–47

Season	*Matches*	*Total*	*Div. 1*	*Div. 2*	*Div. 3 (S)*	*Div. 3 (N)*
1946–47	1848	35,604,606	15,005,316	11,071,572	5,664,004	3,863,714
1947–48	1848	40,259,130	16,732,341	12,286,350	6,653,610	4,586,829
1948–49	1848	41,271,414	17,914,667	11,353,237	6,998,429	5,005,081
1949–50	1848	40,517,865	17,278,625	11,694,158	7,104,155	4,440,927
1950–51	2028	39,584,967	16,679,454	10,780,580	7,367,884	4,757,109
1951–52	2028	39,015,866	16,110,322	11,066,189	6,958,927	4,880,428
1952–53	2028	37,149,966	16,050,278	9,686,654	6,704,299	4,708,735
1953–54	2028	36,174,590	16,154,915	9,510,053	6,311,508	4,198,114
1954–55	2028	34,133,103	15,087,221	8,988,794	5,996,017	4,051,071
1955–56	2028	33,150,809	14,108,961	9,080,002	5,692,479	4,269,367
1956–57	2028	32,744,405	13,803,037	8,718,162	5,622,189	4,601,017
1957–58	2028	33,562,208	14,468,652	8,663,712	6,097,183	4,332,661
		Total	*Div. 1*	*Div. 2*	*Div. 3*	*Div. 4*
1958–59	2028	33,610,985	14,727,691	8,641,997	5,946,600	4,276,697
1959–60	2028	32,538,611	14,391,227	8,399,627	5,739,707	4,008,050
1960–61	2028	28,619,754	12,926,948	7,033,936	4,784,256	3,874,614
1961–62	2015	27,979,902	12,061,194	7,453,089	5,199,106	3,266,513
1962–63	2028	28,885,852	12,490,239	7,792,770	5,341,362	3,261,481
1963–64	2028	28,535,022	12,486,626	7,594,158	5,419,157	3,035,081
1964–65	2028	27,641,168	12,708,752	6,984,104	4,436,245	3,512,067
1965–66	2028	27,206,980	12,480,644	6,914,757	4,779,150	3,032,429
1966–67	2028	28,902,596	14,242,957	7,253,819	4,421,172	2,984,648
1967–68	2028	30,107,298	15,289,410	7,450,410	4,013,087	3,354,391
1968–69	2028	29,382,172	14,584,851	7,382,390	4,339,656	3,075,275
1969–70	2028	29,600,972	14,868,754	7,581,728	4,223,761	2,926,729
1970–71	2028	28,194,146	13,954,337	7,098,265	4,377,213	2,764,331
1971–72	2028	28,700,729	14,484,603	6,769,308	4,697,392	2,749,426
1972–73	2028	25,448,642	13,998,154	5,631,730	3,737,252	2,081,506
1973–74	2027	24,982,203	13,070,991	6,326,108	3,421,624	2,163,480
1974–75	2028	25,577,977	12,613,178	6,955,970	4,086,145	1,992,684
1975–76	2028	24,896,053	13,089,861	5,798,405	3,948,449	2,059,338
1976–77	2028	26,182,800	13,647,585	6,250,597	4,152,218	2,132,400
1977–78	2028	25,392,872	13,255,677	6,474,763	3,332,042	2,330,390
1978–79	2028	24,540,627	12,704,549	6,153,223	3,374,558	2,308,297
1979–80	2028	24,623,975	12,163,002	6,112,025	3,999,328	2,349,620
1980–81	2028	21,907,569	11,392,894	5,175,442	3,637,854	1,701,379
1981–82	2028	20,006,961	10,420,793	4,750,463	2,836,915	1,998,790
1982–83	2028	18,766,158	9,295,613	4,974,937	2,943,568	1,552,040
1983–84	2028	18,358,631	8,711,448	5,359,757	2,729,942	1,557,484
1984–85	2028	17,849,835	9,761,404	4,030,823	2,667,008	1,390,600
1985–86	2028	16,488,577	9,037,854	3,551,968	2,490,481	1,408,274
1986–87	2028	17,379,218	9,144,676	4,168,131	2,350,970	1,715,441
1987–88	2030	17,959,732	8,094,571	5,341,599	2,751,275	1,772,287
1988–89	2036	18,464,192	7,809,993	5,887,805	3,035,327	1,791,067
1989–90	2036	19,445,442	7,883,039	6,867,674	2,803,551	1,891,178
1990–91	2036	19,508,202	8,618,709	6,285,068	2,835,759	1,768,666
1991–92	2064*	20,487,273	9,989,160	5,809,787	2,993,352	1,694,974
		Total	*Premier*	*Div. 1*	*Div. 2*	*Div. 3*
1992–93	2028	20,657,327	9,759,809	5,874,017	3,483,073	1,540,428
1993–94	2028	21,683,381	10,644,551	6,487,104	2,972,702	1,579,024
1994–95	2028	21,856,020	11,213,168	6,044,293	3,037,752	1,560,807
1995–96	2036	21,844,416	10,469,107	6,566,349	2,843,652	1,965,308
1996–97	2036	22,783,163	10,804,762	6,931,539	3,195,223	1,851,639
1997–98	2036	24,692,608	11,092,106	8,330,018	3,503,264	1,767,220
1998–99	2036	25,435,542	11,620,326	7,543,369	4,169,697	2,102,150
1999–2000	2036	25,341,090	11,668,497	7,810,208	3,700,433	2,161,952
2000–01	2036	26,030,167	12,472,094	7,909,512	3,488,166	2,160,395
2001–02	2036	27,756,977	13,043,118	8,352,128	3,963,153	2,398,578
2002–03	2036	28,343,386	13,468,965	8,521,017	3,892,469	2,460,935
2003–04	2036	29,197,510	13,303,136	8,772,780	4,146,495	2,975,099
		Total	*Premier*	*Championship*	*League One*	*League Two*
2004–05	2036	29,245,870	12,878,791	9,612,761	4,270,674	2,483,644
2005–06	2036	29,089,084	12,871,643	9,719,204	4,183,011	2,315,226
2006–07	2036	29,541,949	13,058,115	10,057,813	4,135,599	2,290,422
2007–08	2036	29,914,212	13,708,875	9,397,036	4,412,023	2,396,278
2008–09	2036	29,881,966	13,527,815	9,877,552	4,171,834	2,304,765
2009–10	2036	30,057,892	12,977,251	9,909,882	5,043,099	2,127,660
2010–11	2036	29,459,105	13,406,990	9,595,236	4,150,547	2,306,332
2011–12	2036	29,454,401	13,148,465	9,784,100	4,091,897	2,429,939
2012–13	2036	29,225,443	13,653,958	9,662,232	3,485,290	2,423,963
2013–14	2036	29,629,309	13,930,810	9,168,922	4,126,701	2,402,876
2014–15	2036	30,052,575	13,746,753	9,838,940	3,884,414	2,582,468
2015–16	2036	30,207,923	13,852,291	9,705,865	3,955,385	2,694,382
2016–17	2036	31,727,248	13,612,316	11,106,918	4,385,178	2,622,836
2017–18	2036	32,656,695	14,560,349	11,313,826	4,303,525	2,478,995
2018–19	2035	32,911,714	14,515,181	11,119,775	4,811,797	2,464,961
2019–20	1572†	25,151,300	11,323,981	8,265,475	3,501,237	2,060,607
2020–21	*Due to the COVID-19 pandemic, the majority of matches were played behind closed doors.*					

**Figures include matches played by Aldershot. †Premier League and Championship games behind closed doors from 17 June 2020. League 1 and 2 curtailed from 9 June 2020.*
Football League official total for their three divisions in 2001–02 was 14,716,162.

LEAGUE CUP FINALS 1961–2021

*Played as a two-leg final until 1966. All subsequent finals played at Wembley except between 2001 and 2007 (inclusive) which were played at Millennium Stadium, Cardiff. *After extra time.*

FOOTBALL LEAGUE CUP

1961	Rotherham U v Aston Villa	2-0
	Aston Villa v Rotherham U	3-0*
	Aston Villa won 3-2 on aggregate.	
1962	Rochdale v Norwich C	0-3
	Norwich C v Rochdale	1-0
	Norwich C won 4-0 on aggregate.	
1963	Birmingham C v Aston Villa	3-1
	Aston Villa v Birmingham C	0-0
	Birmingham C won 3-1 on aggregate.	
1964	Stoke C v Leicester C	1-1
	Leicester C v Stoke C	3-2
	Leicester C won 4-3 on aggregate.	
1965	Chelsea v Leicester C	3-2
	Leicester C v Chelsea	0-0
	Chelsea won 3-2 on aggregate.	
1966	West Ham U v WBA	2-1
	WBA v West Ham U	4-1
	WBA won 5-3 on aggregate.	
1967	QPR v WBA	3-2
1968	Leeds U v Arsenal	1-0
1969	Swindon T v Arsenal	3-1*
1970	Manchester C v WBA	2-1*
1971	Tottenham H v Aston Villa	2-0
1972	Stoke C v Chelsea	2-1
1973	Tottenham H v Norwich C	1-0
1974	Wolverhampton W v Manchester C	2-1
1975	Aston Villa v Norwich C	1-0
1976	Manchester C v Newcastle U	2-1
1977	Aston Villa v Everton	0-0
Replay	Aston Villa v Everton	1-1*
	(at Hillsborough)	
Replay	Aston Villa v Everton	3-2*
	(at Old Trafford)	
1978	Nottingham F v Liverpool	0-0*
Replay	Nottingham F v Liverpool	1-0
	(at Old Trafford)	
1979	Nottingham F v Southampton	3-2
1980	Wolverhampton W v Nottingham F	1-0
1981	Liverpool v West Ham U	1-1*
Replay	Liverpool v West Ham U	2-1
	(at Villa Park)	

MILK CUP

1982	Liverpool v Tottenham H	3-1*
1983	Liverpool v Manchester U	2-1*
1984	Liverpool v Everton	0-0*
Replay	Liverpool v Everton	1-0
	(at Maine Road)	
1985	Norwich C v Sunderland	1-0
1986	Oxford U v QPR	3-0

LITTLEWOODS CUP

1987	Arsenal v Liverpool	2-1
1988	Luton T v Arsenal	3-2
1989	Nottingham F v Luton T	3-1
1990	Nottingham F v Oldham Ath	1-0

RUMBELOWS LEAGUE CUP

1991	Sheffield W v Manchester U	1-0
1992	Manchester U v Nottingham F	1-0

COCA-COLA CUP

1993	Arsenal v Sheffield W	2-1
1994	Aston Villa v Manchester U	3-1
1995	Liverpool v Bolton W	2-1
1996	Aston Villa v Leeds U	3-0
1997	Leicester C v Middlesbrough	1-1*
Replay	Leicester C v Middlesbrough	1-0*
	(at Hillsborough)	
1998	Chelsea v Middlesbrough	2-0*

WORTHINGTON CUP

1999	Tottenham H v Leicester C	1-0
2000	Leicester C v Tranmere R	2-1
2001	Liverpool v Birmingham C	1-1*
	Liverpool won 5-4 on penalties.	
2002	Blackburn R v Tottenham H	2-1
2003	Liverpool v Manchester U	2-0

CARLING CUP

2004	Middlesbrough v Bolton W	2-1
2005	Chelsea v Liverpool	3-2*
2006	Manchester U v Wigan Ath	4-0
2007	Chelsea v Arsenal	2-1
2008	Tottenham H v Chelsea	2-1*
2009	Manchester U v Tottenham H	0-0*
	Manchester U won 4-1 on penalties.	
2010	Manchester U v Aston Villa	2-1
2011	Birmingham C v Arsenal	2-1
2012	Liverpool v Cardiff C	2-2*
	Liverpool won 3-2 on penalties.	

CAPITAL ONE CUP

2013	Swansea C v Bradford C	5-0
2014	Manchester C v Sunderland	3-1
2015	Chelsea v Tottenham H	2-0
2016	Manchester C v Liverpool	1-1*
	Manchester C won 3-1 on penalties.	

EFL CUP

2017	Manchester U v Southampton	3-2

CARABAO CUP

2018	Manchester C v Arsenal	3-0
2019	Manchester C v Chelsea	0-0*
	Manchester C won 4-3 on penalties.	
2020	Manchester C v Aston Villa	2-1
2021	Manchester C v Tottenham H	1-0

LEAGUE CUP WINS

Liverpool 8, Manchester C 8, Aston Villa 5, Chelsea 5, Manchester U 5, Nottingham F 4, Tottenham H 4, Leicester C 3, Arsenal 2, Birmingham C 2, Norwich C 2, Wolverhampton W 2, Blackburn R 1, Leeds U 1, Luton T 1, Middlesbrough 1, Oxford U 1, QPR 1, Sheffield W 1, Stoke C 1, Swansea C 1, Swindon T 1, WBA 1.

APPEARANCES IN FINALS

Liverpool 12, Manchester U 9, Aston Villa 9, Manchester C 9, Tottenham H 9, Arsenal 8, Chelsea 8, Nottingham F 6, Leicester C 5, Norwich C 4, Birmingham C 3, Middlesbrough 3, WBA 3, Bolton W 2, Everton 2, Leeds U 2, Luton T 2, QPR 2, Sheffield W 2, Southampton 2, Stoke C 2, Sunderland 2, West Ham U 2, Wolverhampton W 2, Blackburn R 1, Bradford C 1, Cardiff C 1, Newcastle U 1, Oldham Ath 1, Oxford U 1, Rochdale 1, Rotherham U 1, Swansea C 1, Swindon T 1, Tranmere R 1, Wigan Ath 1.

APPEARANCES IN SEMI-FINALS

Liverpool 17, Manchester U 16, Tottenham H 16, Arsenal 15, Aston Villa 15, Chelsea 14, Manchester C 13, West Ham U 9, Blackburn R 6, Leicester C 6, Nottingham F 6, Birmingham C 5, Everton 5, Leeds U 5, Middlesbrough 5, Norwich C 5, Bolton W 4, Burnley 4, Crystal Palace 4, Ipswich T 4, Sheffield W 4, Sunderland 4, WBA 4, Bristol C 3, QPR 3, Southampton 3, Stoke C 3, Swindon T 3, Wolverhampton W 3, Cardiff C 2, Coventry C 2, Derby Co 2, Luton T 2, Oxford U 2, Plymouth Arg 2, Sheffield U 2, Tranmere R 2, Watford 2, Wimbledon 2, Blackpool 1, Bradford C 1, Brentford 1, Burton Alb 1, Bury 1, Carlisle U 1, Chester C 1, Huddersfield T 1, Hull C 1, Newcastle U 1, Oldham Ath 1, Peterborough U 1, Rochdale 1, Rotherham U 1, Shrewsbury T 1, Stockport Co 1, Swansea C 1, Walsall 1, Wigan Ath 1, Wycombe W 1.

CARABAO CUP 2020–21

▪ *Denotes player sent off.*
Due to COVID-19 pandemic, matches played behind closed doors unless otherwise stated.

FIRST ROUND NORTH

Saturday, 29 August 2020

Blackburn R (1) 3 *(Holtby 30, Rankin-Costello 71, Armstrong 81 (pen))*

Doncaster R (0) 2 *(Okenabirhie 54 (pen), Gomes 63)*

Blackburn R: (433) Fisher; Rankin-Costello, Lenihan, Wharton, Bell; Travis, Holtby (Rothwell 41), Johnson; Chapman (Dolan 65), Armstrong, Brereton.
Doncaster R: (4231) Bursik; Halliday, Wright, Anderson, John; Richards (Hasani 73), Gomes; Taylor (Williams 69), Coppinger (Amos 82), Lokilo; Okenabirhie.
Referee: Anthony Backhouse.

Preston NE (3) 4 *(Barkhuizen 14, Maguire 22, Bauer 28, Harrop 65)*

Mansfield T (0) 0

Preston NE: (4231) Ripley; Browne, Huntington, Bauer, Earl; Bayliss (Rafferty 70), Pearson (Ledson 70); Barkhuizen, Potts, Harrop; Maguire (Sinclair 74).
Mansfield T: (352) Stech; Menayese, Rawson (O'Driscoll 64), Sweeney; O'Keeffe, Perch (Sinclair 63), Maris, Charsley, Benning; Cook, Rose (Reid 76).
Referee: Ross Joyce.

Stoke C (0) 0

Blackpool (0) 0

Stoke C: (442) Davies; Smith, Chester, Batth, Martins Indi; Powell (Oakley-Boothe 74), Clucas, Thompson, McClean; Gregory (Fletcher 63), Afobe (Campbell 63).
Blackpool: (433) Maxwell; Turton, Ekpiteta, Nottingham (Thorniley 73), Husband; Robson, Anderson, Ward (Virtue 73); Hamilton, Yates (Sarkic 83), KaiKai.
Stoke C won 5-4 on penalties.
Referee: James Adcock.

Friday, 4 September 2020

Burton Alb (1) 1 *(Akins 32)*

Accrington S (0) 1 *(Burgess 82)*

Burton Alb: (442) Garratt; Eardley, Brayford, O'Toole, Wallace; Powell, Bostwick, Quinn, Vernam (Lawless 67); Akins, Hemmings.
Accrington S: (3412) Savin; Sykes, Hughes, Burgess; Johnson, Barclay, Butcher, Allan (Spinelli 87); Pritchard; Charles, Cassidy (Sangare 65).
Burton Alb won 4-2 on penalties
Referee: Andy Haines.

Middlesbrough (2) 4 *(Johnson 21, Fletcher A 31, 53, Tavernier 65)*

Shrewsbury T (1) 3 *(High 13, Cummings 60, Pyke 73)*

Middlesbrough: (352) Stojanovic; Dijksteel, Hall, Fry (Wood-Gordon 74); Spence, Howson, Wing (Browne 73), Tavernier, Johnson; Fletcher A, Assombalonga.
Shrewsbury T: (433) Burgoyne; Love (Fossey 82), Williams, Ebanks-Landell, Golbourne; High, Walker, Edwards (Daniels J 74); Cummings, Pyke (Udoh 74), Whalley.
Referee: Michael Salisbury.

Saturday, 5 September 2020

Barnsley (0) 1 *(Woodrow 49)*

Nottingham F (0) 0

Barnsley: (3412) Walton; Sollbauer, Andersen, Williams J; Ludewig, Mowatt, Styles, Ritzmaier (Oduor 46); Woodrow; Adeboyejo (Simoes 46), Chaplin (Frieser 61).
Nottingham F: (4141) Samba; Lawrence-Gabriel, Tobias Figueiredo, Blackett, Yuri Ribeiro; Bachirou; Nuno Da Costa, Yates, Joao Carvalho (Taylor 59), Ameobi (Mighten 59); Grabban (Freeman 69).
Referee: Marc Edwards.

Bolton W (0) 1 *(Sarcevic 47)*

Bradford C (1) 2 *(Novak 26, Pritchard 75)*

Bolton W: (3412) Crellin; Santos, Baptiste, Taft; Jones, Comley (Crawford 68), White, Gordon (Miller 81); Sarcevic; Doyle, Delfouneso.
Bradford C: (3412) O'Donnell; O'Connor A, O'Connor P, Staunton; French, Watt, Cooke, Connor Wood; Clarke (Pritchard 62); Novak, Guthrie (Donaldson 72).
Referee: Martin Coy.

Crewe Alex (0) 1 *(Sass-Davies 55)*

Lincoln C (0) 2 *(Hopper 52, Montsma 66)*

Crewe Alex: (433) Richards; Ng, Lancashire, Sass-Davies, Pickering; Murphy, Wintle, Finney (Ainley 71); Dale, Mandron, Kirk.
Lincoln C: (433) Palmer; Bradley, Eyoma, Montsma, Roughan; McGrandles, Edun (Morton 81), Jones; Scully (Howarth 90), Hopper, Grant.
Referee: Scott Oldham.

Derby Co (0) 0

Barrow (0) 0

Derby Co: (352) Roos; te Wierik, Evans, Clarke (Whittaker 61); Buchanan, Holmes (Shinnie 56), Bird, Knight, Forsyth; Sibley (Wisdom 85), Marriott.
Barrow: (532) Dixon; Brown, Jones J, Platt (Hird 79), Ntlhe, Kay (Wilson 68); Hardcastle, Jones M (Biggins 77), Beadling; Hindle, Angus.
Derby Co won 3-2 on penalties.
Referee: Ollie Yates.

Fleetwood T (1) 3 *(Evans 41, 77, Morris J 64)*

Wigan Ath (2) 2 *(Garner 2, 31 (pen))*

Fleetwood T: (433) Coleman (Cairns 58); Burns, Holgate, Hill, Andrew; Camps, Coutts, Whelan; Saunders (Duffy 46), Garner (Evans 40), Morris J.
Wigan Ath: (4231) Jones; Byrne, Obi, Long, Pearce; Evans L, Merrie (Crankshaw 83); Naismith, Roberts (Gardner 73), Solomon-Otabor; Garner.
Referee: Sebastian Stockbridge.

Grimsby T (1) 1 *(Green 34)*

Morecambe (1) 1 *(Phillips 7)*

Grimsby T: (442) McKeown; Wright, Waterfall, Pollock, Preston; Hewitt, Rose D (Khouri 61), Williams (Edwards 72), Scannell; Green (Gibson 77), Tilley.
Morecambe: (4141) Turner; Mellor, Davis, Knight-Percival, Hendrie; Diagouraga; O'Sullivan, Phillips (McAlinden 71), Mendes Gomes, Slew (Kenyon 57); Stockton (Pringle 85).
Morecambe won 4-3 on penalties.
Referee: Graham Salisbury.

Huddersfield T (0) 0

Rochdale (0) 1 *(O'Connell 51)*

Huddersfield T: (433) Hamer; Rowe, Schindler (Diakhaby 60), Crichlow-Noble, Toffolo; Pritchard, Hogg (Mbenza 69), Jackson; Koroma, Ward (Austerfield 79), Bacuna.
Rochdale: (433) Bazunu; McLaughlin, McShane, O'Connell, Keohane; Ryan (Brierley 90), Morley, Rathbone (Baah 73); Done (Tavares 84), Newby, Dooley.
Referee: Ben Toner.

Oldham Ath (2) 3 *(Garrity 29, Grant 37, McAleny 89)*

Carlisle U (0) 0

Oldham Ath: (4231) Lawlor; Hamer, Jombati, Piergianni, Borthwick-Jackson; Garrity, Whelan; Fage (Dearnley 73), McAleny, Keillor-Dunn (Barnett 81); Grant (Da Silva 90).
Carlisle U: (41212) Farman; Tanner, Hayden, McDonald, Anderton; Furman (Reilly 46); Riley (Charters 71), Mellish (Armer 83); Guy; Toure, Alessandra.
Referee: Carl Boyeson.

Salford C (0) 1 *(Henderson 84 (pen))*

Rotherham U (0) 1 *(Crooks 90)*

Salford C: (433) Hladky; Threlkeld, Clarke, Eastham, Touray I; Gibson, Hunter (Turnbull 87), Lowe; Armstrong (Elliott 63), Henderson, Andrade (Thomas-Asante 79).
Rotherham U: (442) Blackman; Harding (Jones 76), Ihiekwe, Wood, Mattock; Ogbene, MacDonald S, Lindsay (Crooks 71), Sadlier; Ladapo, Smith (Vassell 57).
Salford C won 4-2 on penalties.
Referee: James Oldham.

Scunthorpe U (0) 1 *(Loft 69)*

Port Vale (1) 2 *(Mills 45, Robinson 90)*

Scunthorpe U: (442) Watson; Hornshaw, Cordner, Bedeau, Butroid; Gilliead, Vincent (Pugh 84), Spence, Eisa; Colclough (Green 73), Loft (Jarvis 78).
Port Vale: (433) Brown; Mills, Legge, Smith, Fitzpatrick; Conlon, Joyce, Burgess (Whitehead 77); Worrall, Cullen (Robinson 73), Rodney.
Referee: Neil Hair.

Sunderland (0) 0

Hull C (0) 0

Sunderland: (343) Burge; Willis, Wright, Flanagan; O'Nien, Dobson, Power, Hume; Maguire (Gooch 76), Grigg, O'Brien (Wyke 76).
Hull C: (4231) Ingram; Emmanuel, Burke, De Wijs, Fleming; Smallwood, Docherty; Wilks, Honeyman, Samuelsen; Eaves (Lewis-Potter 31).
Hull C won 5-4 on penalties.
Referee: Thomas Bramall.

Tranmere R (0) 1 *(Vaughan 64)*

Harrogate T (0) 1 *(Kerry 69)*

Tranmere R: (442) Davies; O'Connor, Clarke, Monthe, MacDonald; Khan, Spearing, Lewis (Banks 63), Blackett-Taylor (Morris 42); Ferrier (Payne 61), Vaughan.
Harrogate T: (442) Cracknell; Fallowfield, Smith, Hall, Burrell; Thomson, Falkingham, Kerry, Walker (Stead 73); Martin (Beck 83), Muldoon.
Harrogate T won 8-7 on penalties.
Referee: Tom Nield.

Walsall (0) 0

Sheffield W (0) 0

Walsall: (442) Roberts; Norman, Scarr, Clarke, Jules; Gordon, Kinsella, Bates, McDonald (Nurse 88); Lavery (Adebayo 69), Holden.
Sheffield W: (352) Dawson; Iorfa, Lees, Borner; Odubajo (Penney 60), Dele-Bashiru (Rhodes 78), Luongo, Bannan, Harris; Reach (Windass 66), Brown.
Sheffield W won 4-2 on penalties.
Referee: Peter Wright.

FIRST ROUND SOUTH

Saturday, 29 August 2020

Stevenage (3) 3 *(List 9, Carter 10, Cuthbert 29)*

Portsmouth (2) 3 *(Curtis 21, Evans 45 (pen), Marquis 50)*

Stevenage: (433) Cumming; Wildin, Cuthbert, Prosser, Coker; Osborne, Vincelot (Newton 64), Carter; List (Hutton 79), Effiong, Marsh (Akinwande 53).
Portsmouth: (4231) Bass (MacGillivray 46); Bolton, Downing, Raggett, Brown; Naylor, Morris; Harness (Williams 76), Evans (Cannon 76), Curtis; Marquis.
Portsmouth won 3-1 on penalties.
Referee: Sam Purkiss.

Saturday, 5 September 2020

Birmingham C (0) 0

Cambridge U (1) 1 *(Cundy 18)*

Birmingham C: (4231) Andres; Colin, Dean, Friend, Pedersen; Sunjic (Bailey 85), Kieftenbeld (Clayton 68); Bela, Crowley (Toral 60), Lakin; George.
Cambridge U: (442) Mitov; Knoyle, Cundy, Taylor, Dunk; Hoolahan (Iredale 78), Digby, O'Neil (May 58), Hannant; Mullin (Knibbs 82), Ironside.
Referee: Leigh Doughty.

Bristol C (1) 2 *(Paterson 35, Semenyo 83)*

Exeter C (0) 0

Bristol C: (352) Bentley; Vyner, Moore, Rowe (Morton 89); Hunt, Massengo (Bakinson 81), Paterson, Weimann, Dasilva; Wells, Diedhiou (Semenyo 80).
Exeter C: (4411) Ward; Key, McArdle, Dean, Page (Sparkes 75); Williams, Collins, Atangana (Seymour 84), Randall; Jay (Taylor 61); Bowman.
Referee: Christopher Sarginson.

Crawley T (1) 1 *(Ashford 33)*

Millwall (2) 3 *(Malone 14, Tunnicliffe 31 (og), Smith 59)*

Crawley T: (4231) McGill; Tunnicliffe, McNerney (Galach 79), Craig, Dallison; Bulman, Ferguson; Ashford (German 66), Powell (Sesay 58), Frost; Nadesan.
Millwall: (343) Bialkowski; Hutchinson, Wallace M, Cooper; Leonard, Thompson, Woods (Williams 62), Malone; Mahoney (Bradshaw 72), Smith, Bennett (Wallace J 46).
Referee: David Rock.

Forest Green R (1) 1 *(Happe 23 (og))*

Leyton Orient (0) 2 *(Johnson 49, Wilkinson 52)*

Forest Green R: (3142) McGee; Godwin-Malife, Moore-Taylor, Stokes; Winchester; Wilson, Sweeney, Adams, Cadden; Collins (McCoulsky 81), Matt (Stevens 71).
Leyton Orient: (442) Vigouroux; Ling, Coulson, Happe, Brophy; McAnuff (Wright 84), Clay (Dayton 72), Cisse, Angol; Wilkinson (Widdowson 90), Johnson.
Referee: Craig Hicks.

Gillingham (1) 1 *(Ogilvie 27)*

Southend U (0) 0

Gillingham: (532) Bonham; Jackson■, McKenzie, Maghoma (Tucker 62), Medley, Ogilvie; Dempsey, O'Keefe, MacDonald (Willock 75); Akinde, Oliver (Coyle 68).
Southend U: (442) Oxley; Bwomono, White, Hobson, Taylor R (Humphrys 71); Egbri (Kinali 88), Hutchinson, Dieng (Gard 62), Green; Kelman, Goodship.
Referee: Chris Pollard.

Ipswich T (2) 3 *(Sears 29, 68, Chambers 44)*

Bristol R (0) 0

Ipswich T: (433) Holy; Chambers (Ndaba 81), Nsiala, Woolfenden, Ward; Bishop (Edwards 80), Dozzell, Nolan; Judge, Drinan (Hawkins 69), Sears.
Bristol R: (3421) van Stappershoef; Baldwin (Hare 67), Ehmer, Kilgour; Little (Upson 74), Grant, Westbrooke, Leahy; Hargreaves (Ayunga 46), Nicholson; Mitchell-Lawson.
Referee: Will Finnie.

Luton T (0) 3 *(Collins 79 (pen), 83, 90)*

Norwich C (0) 1 *(Dowell 81)*

Luton T: (433) Shea; Cranie, Pearson, Bradley, Norrington-Davies; Berry, Mpanzu, Rea; Cornick (Clark 72), Collins, Lee (LuaLua 85).
Norwich C: (4231) Barden; Mumba, Zimmermann, Klose (Vrancic 59), McCallum (Sitti 85); Rupp, Tettey; Dowell, Stiepermann, Martin (Hernandez 72); Hugill.
Referee: John Busby.

Milton Keynes D (0) 0

Coventry C (0) 1 *(Walker 82)*

Milton Keynes D: (442) Nicholls; Brittain, Freeman, Lewington, Cargill; Houghton, Kasumu, Sorensen, Sorinola; Morris, Nombe (Mason 73).
Coventry C: (541) Marosi; Pask, Drysdale■, McFadzean, Hyam, Giles; Allen, Hamer (Walker 65), Shipley (Kelly 65), O'Hare; Godden (Bakayoko 74).
Referee: Trevor Kettle.

Newport Co (2) 2 *(Abrahams 7, 45)*

Swansea C (0) 0

Newport Co: (4312) Townsend; Shephard, Howkins, Dolan, Demetriou; Labadie (Willmott 72), Sheehan, Haynes; Twine (Taylor 84); Abrahams, Collins (Amond 72).
Swansea C: (3412) Woodman; Smith (Dhanda 72), Rodon, Naughton; Routledge (Peterson 72), Fulton, Gibbs-White, Bidwell (Asoro 72); Grimes; Ayew, Lowe.
Referee: Kevin Johnson.

Northampton T (1) 3 *(Smith 33 (pen), Warburton 49, Watson 59)*

Cardiff C (0) 0

Northampton T: (3421) Arnold; Racic, Bolger, Horsfall; Harriman, Watson, Missilou, Mills; Korboa (Marshall 90), Warburton (Roberts 71); Smith (Lines 89).
Cardiff C: (4231) Smithies; Nelson, Morrison, Bamba (Sang 67), Bennett (Cunningham 67); Bacuna, Pack; Osei-Tutu, Murphy, Hoilett; Glatzel.
Referee: Darren Drysdale.

Oxford U (0) 1 *(Brannagan 63)*

AFC Wimbledon (0) 1 *(Taylor 67 (og))*

Oxford U: (433) Eastwood; Long (Forde 58), Moore, Atkinson, Ruffels; McGuane, Gorrin (Kelly 58), Brannagan; Henry, Taylor, Sykes (Osei Yaw 85).
AFC Wimbledon: (541) Trueman; Alexander, O'Neill, Thomas, Kalambayi, Guinness-Walker; Longman (Chislett 71), Hartigan, Woodyard, Reilly; Pigott.
Oxford U won 4-3 on penalties.
Referee: Lee Swabey.

Peterborough U (0) 0

Cheltenham T (0) 1 *(Sercombe 59)*

Peterborough U: (3412) Pym; Thompson, Kent, Beevers; Ward (Kanu 60), Taylor, Brown (Hamilton 60), Butler; Broom (Clarke 60); Dembele, Eisa.
Cheltenham T: (352) Griffiths; Raglan, Tozer, Freestone (Boyle 67); Thomas, Sercombe (Lloyd 89), Azaz, Clements, Hussey; Williams, May (Addai 83).
Referee: Alan Young.

Plymouth Arg (1) 3 *(Edwards 32, Mayor 55, Nouble 78)*

QPR (1) 2 *(Manning 2, Kakay 57)*

Plymouth Arg: (352) Cooper M; Aimson, Wootton, Watts; Edwards, Macleod, Grant C, Mayor (Camara 85), Cooper G (Law 89); Hardie (Telford 77), Nouble.
QPR: (4231) Lumley; Kakay, Dickie, Masterson, Manning; Ball (Bettache 77), Carroll (Smyth 64); Amos, Chair, Samuel; Oteh (Shodipo 77).
Referee: Antony Coggins.

Reading (1) 3 *(Lucas Joao 45, 56, 75)*

Colchester U (1) 1 *(Brown 37)*

Reading: (433) Southwood; Felipe Araruna, Morrison, Moore, Bristow; Olise, Aluko, Laurent; McNulty (Rinomhota 46), Lucas Joao (Melvin-Lambert 82), Baldock (Richards 67).
Colchester U: (433) Gerken; Scarlett, Eastman, Smith, Bramall; Chilvers (Senior 71), Pell, Stevenson (Marshall 88); Poku, Brown, Harriott.
Referee: Joshua Smith.

Swindon T (0) 1 *(Smith J 64)*

Charlton Ath (1) 3 *(Bonne 36, Barker 74, Aneke 90)*

Swindon T: (433) Kovar; Hunt, Odimayo, Fryers, Iandolo; Lyden (Smith J 50), Grant A, Doughty; Payne (Hope 73), Smith T (Pitman 79), Jaiyesimi.
Charlton Ath: (4411) Amos; Lapslie, Barker, Oshilaja, Purrington; Oztumer (Aneke 71), Pratley, Forster-Caskey, Doughty; Vennings (Gilbey 60); Bonne (Morgan 86).
Referee: Brett Huxtable.

Sunday, 6 September 2020

Brentford (1) 1 *(Pinnock 32)*

Wycombe W (0) 1 *(Horgan 76)*

Brentford: (433) Daniels; Henry, Goode, Pinnock, Thompson (Valencia 84); Marcondes (Baptiste 72), Jensen, Zamburek; Canos, Toney, Fosu (Forss 77).
Wycombe W: (433) Allsop; Grimmer, Stewart, Charles, Jacobson; Freeman, Gape■, Bloomfield; Wheeler (Onyedinma 75), Samuel (Horgan 65), Parker (Kashket 65).
Brentford won 4-2 on penalties.
Referee: Charles Breakspear.

SECOND ROUND NORTH

Tuesday, 15 September 2020

Bradford C (0) 0

Lincoln C (4) 5 *(French 4 (og), Scully 6, Montsma 29, Jones 41, Morton 90)*

Bradford C: (3412) O'Donnell; O'Connor A, O'Connor P, Richards-Everton (Staunton 46); French (Mottley-Henry 46), Watt, Cooke, Connor Wood; Pritchard; Donaldson, Guthrie.
Lincoln C: (433) Palmer; Eyoma, Jackson, Montsma, Melbourne; McGrandles, Grant, Jones (Bridcutt 84); Anderson (Hopper 72), Morton, Scully (Howarth 67).
Referee: Michael Salisbury.

Burton Alb (1) 1 *(Daniel 2)*

Aston Villa (1) 3 *(Watkins 39, Grealish 88, Davis 90)*

Burton Alb: (433) Sharman-Lowe; Fox, Brayford, Bostwick (Gallacher 25), Wallace; Edwards (Powell 66), Quinn, Daniel; Akins, Hemmings, Lawless (Gilligan 66).
Aston Villa: (433) Nyland; Elmohamady, Hause, Mings, Taylor; Lansbury, Nakamba, Ramsey J (Douglas Luiz 71); El Ghazi (Jota 80), Watkins (Davis 71), Grealish.
Referee: Oliver Langford.

Derby Co (0) 1 *(Knight 51)*

Preston NE (0) 2 *(Barkhuizen 79, Johnson 90 (pen))*

Derby Co: (4231) Roos; Wisdom, te Wierik■, Clarke, Buchanan; Evans (Marriott 89), Shinnie; Whittaker (Brown 68), Sibley (Davies 56), Knight; Rooney.
Preston NE: (4231) Rudd; Fisher, Bauer, Huntington, Rafferty; Bayliss (Barkhuizen 67), Gallagher (Sinclair 75); Maguire, Browne, Harrop (Johnson 75); Stockley.
Referee: Andy Davies.

Fleetwood T (1) 2 *(Madden 13, Morris J 75)*

Port Vale (0) 1 *(Whitehead 49)*

Fleetwood T: (4231) Cairns; Burns, Hill, Stubbs, Andrew; Coutts (Duffy 61), Whelan; Morris J, Camps (Matete 80), Madden; Evans (Saunders 55).
Port Vale: (4231) Visser; Mills, Brisley, Crookes, Montano; Trickett-Smith (Joyce 64), Oyeleke (Burgess 74); McKirdy (Worrall 72), Whitehead, Hurst; Robinson.
Referee: Ross Joyce.

Middlesbrough (0) 0

Barnsley (2) 2 *(Schmidt 22, Williams J 34)*

Middlesbrough: (352) Bettinelli; Dijksteel (McNair 46), Fry, Wood-Gordon; Coulson, Wing, Tavernier, Morsy (Howson 69), Bola; Browne, Fletcher A (Folarin 69).
Barnsley: (343) Collins; Sollbauer (Halme 70), Helik, Andersen; Ludewig (Styles 46), Mowatt, Ritzmaier, Williams J; Thomas (Woodrow 60), Schmidt, Frieser.
Referee: Anthony Backhouse.

Morecambe (1) 1 *(Wildig 22)*

Oldham Ath (0) 0

Morecambe: (4231) Halstead; Cooney, Lavelle, Davis, Hendrie; Wildig (Phillips 67), Kenyon (Diagouraga 67); O'Sullivan, Mendes Gomes (Pringle 67), Slew; McAlinden.
Oldham Ath: (442) Lawlor; Hamer, Jombati, Piergianni, Borthwick-Jackson; Dearnley, Whelan, Garrity (Rowe 83), Badan (Keillor-Dunn 66); Fage (Grant 66), McAleny.
Referee: Ben Toner.

Newcastle U (1) 1 *(Fraser 35)*

Blackburn R (0) 0

Newcastle U: (442) Gillespie; Yedlin, Krafth, Clark, Manquillo; Ritchie (Atsu 80), Barlaser, Longstaff S, Fraser (Murphy 58); Joelinton (Saint-Maximin 73), Almiron.
Blackburn R: (433) Kaminski; Nyambe, Lenihan, Williams, Bell; Travis, Holtby (Buckley 73), Rothwell; Dolan (Chapman 72), Brereton, Rankin-Costello (Armstrong 61).
Referee: Jarred Gillett.

Rochdale (0) 0

Sheffield W (0) 2 *(Kachunga 54, Windass 88)*

Rochdale: (442) Bazunu; O'Connell, Amankwah, McNulty, Keohane; Baah (Dooley 51), Lund (Ryan 71), Morley, Rathbone; Newby (Tavares 80), Done.
Sheffield W: (352) Wildsmith; Brennan (Iorfa 80), Shaw, Borner; Palmer, Dele-Bashiru, Pelupessy (Grant 89), Hunt, Odubajo; Reach, Kachunga (Windass 70).
Referee: Sebastian Stockbridge.

Wednesday, 16 September 2020

Everton (1) 3 *(Keane 8, Sigurdsson 74, Kean 87 (pen))*

Salford C (0) 0

Everton: (4231) Virginia; Kenny, Keane, Branthwaite (Digne 24), Nkounkou; Davies, Sigurdsson; Walcott, Bernard, Gordon; Kean.
Salford C: (433) Hladky; Threlkeld (Gibson 74), Eastham, Turnbull, Touray I; Towell, Lowe, Hunter; Wilson (Andrade 61), Henderson, Thomas-Asante (Elliott 75).
Referee: Marc Edwards.

Leeds U (0) 1 *(Alioski 90)*

Hull C (1) 1 *(Wilks 5)*

Leeds U: (4141) Casilla; Shackleton, Cresswell, Davis, Douglas; Bogusz (Gotts 78); Poveda-Ocampo, Casey (Struijk 46), Roberts, Alioski; Rodrigo.
Hull C: (4231) Ingram; Coyle, Jones A, McLoughlin, Elder; Docherty, Batty; Scott, Honeyman (Jones C 81), Lewis-Potter (Mayer 46); Wilks (Chadwick 72).
Hull C won 9-8 on penalties.
Referee: David Webb.

WBA (2) 3 *(Harper 18, Robson-Kanu 22, Robinson 77)*

Harrogate T (0) 0

WBA: (442) Button; Peltier, Kipre, O'Shea, Townsend; Grosicki (Phillips 55), Field, Harper, Edwards; Austin (Robinson 73), Robson-Kanu (Sawyers 61).
Harrogate T: (442) Cracknell; Fallowfield (Jones 73), Smith, Hall, Burrell; Thomson, Falkingham, Kerry (Kirby 79), Muldoon; Beck (Stead 61), Martin.
Referee: Thomas Bramall.

Thursday, 17 September 2020

Burnley (0) 1 *(Vydra 67)*

Sheffield U (1) 1 *(McGoldrick 4)*

Burnley: (442) Pope; Lowton, Long, Dunne, Taylor; Gudmundsson (Pieters 15), Brownhill, Westwood (Benson 75), Brady; Vydra, Rodriguez (Wood 82).
Sheffield U: (352) Foderingham; Ampadu, Jagielka, Robinson; Bogle (Basham 86), Berge, Norwood, Osborn, Lowe; McGoldrick (McBurnie 62), Burke (Sharp 62).
Burnley won 5-4 on penalties.
Referee: Paul Tierney.

Wolverhampton W (0) 0

Stoke C (0) 1 *(Brown 86)*

Wolverhampton W: (343) Ruddy; Boly, Coady, Saiss; Rasmussen (Jimenez 66), Dendoncker (Daniel Podence 77), Neves, Ruben Vinagre; Traore, Silva, Vitinha (Pedro Neto 60).
Stoke C: (352) Davies; Souttar, Collins, Martins Indi; Smith, Oakley-Boothe, Thompson, Tymon, McClean (Cousins 90); Gregory (Brown 70), Vokes (Fletcher 64).
Referee: Simon Hooper.

SECOND ROUND SOUTH

Tuesday, 15 September 2020

Bournemouth (0) 0

Crystal Palace (0) 0

Bournemouth: (532) Begovic; Stacey (Lerma 62), Ofoborh, Simpson, Kelly, Zemura; Cook L (Gosling 74), Arter (Solanke 83), Billing; Brooks, Surridge.
Crystal Palace: (442) Hennessey; Kelly, Woods (Sakho 61), Inniss, Jach; Kirby (Townsend 70), Milivojevic, Meyer, Eze; Batshuayi, Schlupp (Ayew 60).
Bournemouth won 11-10 on penalties.
Referee: Keith Stroud.

Gillingham (0) 1 *(Graham 90 (pen))*

Coventry C (0) 1 *(Biamou 61)*

Gillingham: (41212) Bonham; Jackson, Maghoma, Tucker, Ogilvie; Robertson; Willock (Coyle 72), O'Keefe (Mellis 45); MacDonald (McKenzie 62); Graham, Oliver.
Coventry C: (3412) Bilson; Rose, Drysdale, Thompson; Dabo (Burroughs 80), Eccles, Sheaf, Mason; Bapaga (Biamou 56); Walker, Bakayoko.
Gillingham won 5-4 on penalties.
Referee: Craig Hicks.

Leyton Orient (0) 3 *(Dennis 55, McAnuff 74, Johnson 90)*

Plymouth Arg (2) 2 *(Camara 19, Watts 34)*

Leyton Orient: (4231) Vigouroux; Thomas, Coulson (Brophy 51), Turley, Widdowson; Wright, McAnuff; Sotiriou, Maguire-Drew, Dennis (Dayton 62); Angol (Johnson 75).
Plymouth Arg: (352) Cooper M; Aimson, Wootton, Watts; Moore B, Camara, Macleod (Grant C 84), Mayor, Cooper G (Edwards 74); Hardie, Telford (Nouble 66).
Referee: Josh Smith.

Millwall (1) 3 *(Leonard 19, Mahoney 49, Smith 62)*

Cheltenham T (0) 1 *(Azaz 69)*

Millwall: (442) Bialkowski; Romeo (Skalak 60), Hutchinson, Cooper, Wallace M; Mahoney, Leonard, Woods, Ferguson (Bennett 79); Smith (Wallace J 71), Bradshaw.
Cheltenham T: (352) Griffiths; Raglan, Tozer, Boyle; Blair (Clements 63), Bonds, Thomas, Sercombe (Azaz 46), Hussey; Reid, May (Addai 65).
Referee: John Busby.

Newport Co (0) 1 *(Twine 80)*

Cambridge U (0) 0

Newport Co: (352) King; Howkins, Cooper, Demetriou; Shephard, Willmott, Sheehan, Twine, Haynes; Abrahams (Taylor 73), Amond (Janneh 69).
Cambridge U: (442) Burton; Knoyle, Cundy, Taylor, Iredale; Davies, Digby, May, Knowles (Dunk 69); Knibbs, Ironside (Mullin 74).
Referee: Lee Swabey.

Oxford U (1) 1 *(Hall 26)*

Watford (0) 1 *(Sema 89)*

Oxford U: (4231) Stevens; Clare (McGuane 65), Moore, Mousinho (Lofthouse 70), Long; Forde, Brannagan (Kelly 66); Agyei, Hall, Cooper; Osei Yaw.
Watford: (532) Bachmann; Navarro, Sierralta, Stevenson, Agyakwa (Kabasele 46), Wilmot; Philips, Chalobah (Sema 46), Quina; Sinclair (Joao Pedro 60), Perica.
Watford won 3-0 on penalties.
Referee: Leigh Doughty.

Reading (0) 0

Luton T (1) 1 *(Clark 24)*

Reading: (433) Southwood; Felipe Araruna, Holmes, McIntyre, Bristow; Tetek, Watson, Aluko (Abbey 89); Baldock, Puscas (Melvin-Lambert 85), McNulty (Sackey 70).
Luton T: (433) Shea; Bree (Kioso 85), Lockyer (Cranie 90), Bradley, Norrington-Davies; Shinnie, Moncur, Tunnicliffe; Clark, Hylton, LuaLua (Lee 72).
Referee: Charles Breakspear.

West Ham U (2) 3 *(Haller 22, 26, Felipe Anderson 80)*

Charlton Ath (0) 0

West Ham U: (4231) Randolph; Johnson (Ashby 84), Balbuena, Diop, Masuaku; Cullen, Snodgrass (Coventry 84); Yarmolenko, Lanzini, Felipe Anderson; Haller.
Charlton Ath: (4411) Amos; Lapslie, Barker, Oshilaja, Purrington; Oztumer, Pratley (Gilbey 77), Levitt, Doughty; Williams (Washington 77); Bonne (Aneke 46).
Referee: Andre Marriner.

Wednesday, 16 September 2020

Bristol C (1) 4 *(Martin 42, Palmer 48, 88, Semenyo 82)*

Northampton T (0) 0

Bristol C: (3142) O'Leary; Vyner, Kalas (Moore 7), Mawson (Rowe 71); Bakinson (Brunt 60); Sessegnon, Nagy, Palmer, Eliasson; Semenyo, Martin.

Northampton T: (3412) Mitchell; Racic (Roberts 46), Bolger, Horsfall; Harriman, Watson, Missilou, Martin; Hoskins (Lines 53); Ashley-Seal (Johnston 56), Chukwuemeka.
Referee: Tom Nield.

Ipswich T (0) 0

Fulham (1) 1 *(Mitrovic 38)*

Ipswich T: (433) Cornell; Donacien, Nsiala, Wilson, Kenlock; Nolan (Judge 69), Dozzell (Downes 58), Huws; Edwards, Hawkins (Norwood 68), Dobra.
Fulham: (4231) Areola; Tete (Bryan 81), Odoi, Le Marchand, Robinson; Zambo (Reed 69), Lemina (Cairney 63); Knockaert, Reid, Kebano; Mitrovic.
Referee: Dean Whitestone.

Southampton (0) 0

Brentford (2) 2 *(Norgaard 40, Dasilva 45)*

Southampton: (442) McCarthy; Walker-Peters, Stephens, Bednarek, Bertrand; Tella (Obafemi 84), Ward-Prowse, Romeu, Redmond (Djenepo 71); Ings, Adams (Long 84).
Brentford: (433) Daniels; Dalsgaard, Goode, Sorensen, Thompson (Henry 71); Dasilva (Marcondes 71), Norgaard, Baptiste; Mbeumo, Forss (Dervisoglu 77), Fosu.
Referee: John Brooks.

Thursday, 17 September 2020

Brighton & HA (1) 4 *(Mac Allister 38, Jahanbakhsh 54, Bernardo 57, Gyokeres 71)*

Portsmouth (0) 0

Brighton & HA: (4231) Steele; Molumby, Veltman (Sanders 68), Burn, Bernardo; Propper, Stephens; Jahanbakhsh (Roberts 68), Gross (Gwargis 77), Mac Allister; Gyokeres.
Portsmouth: (4231) MacGillivray; Bolton, Whatmough (Downing 71), Raggett, Pring; Morris, Naylor; Williams, Harness, Curtis (Cannon 63); Marquis (Harrison 63).
Referee: Matthew Donohue.

THIRD ROUND

Tuesday, 22 September 2020

Leyton Orient

Tottenham H

Tottenham awarded the tie after a number of Leyton Orient players tested positive for COVID-19. The Football League ruled that Leyton Orient should forfeit the tie as they were unable to fulfil the fixture.

Luton T (0) 0

Manchester U (1) 3 *(Mata 44 (pen), Rashford 88, Greenwood 90)*

Luton T: (433) Shea; Kioso, Lockyer, Bradley, Norrington-Davies; Shinnie, Tunnicliffe, Moncur (Lee 76); Clark (Cornick 76), Hylton, LuaLua.
Manchester U: (4231) Henderson; Wan Bissaka, Bailly, Maguire, Williams; Fred, Matic; Mata (Greenwood 78), van de Beek (Bruno Fernandes 78), Lingard; Ighalo (Rashford 79).
Referee: Tim Robinson.

Newport Co (2) 3 *(Abrahams 18 (pen), Labadie 28, Amond 65)*

Watford (0) 1 *(Penaranda 54 (pen))*

Newport Co: (352) Townsend; Cooper, Dolan, Demetriou; Shephard, Labadie (Collins 82), Sheehan, Bennett (Willmott 82), Haynes; Abrahams, Amond.
Watford: (352) Bachmann; Sierralta, Agyakwa, Dawson; Pussetto (Crichlow 84), Philips, Garner, Hungbo (Penaranda 46), Stevenson; Sinclair, Murray (Perica■ 46).
Referee: Charles Breakspear.

WBA (0) 2 *(Robson-Kanu 56 (pen), 66 (pen))*

Brentford (0) 2 *(Marcondes 58, Forss 73 (pen))*

WBA: (4231) Button; Peltier, Kipre, Ivanovic (O'Shea 59), Townsend; Harper, Field; Phillips (Diangana 71), Gallagher, Edwards; Robson-Kanu (Austin 86).
Brentford: (433) Raya; Henry, Goode, Sorensen, Thompson; Zamburek (Dasilva 66), Baptiste, Marcondes (Toney 71); Canos (Norgaard 66), Forss, Fosu.
Brentford won 5-4 on penalties.
Referee: Darren England.

West Ham U (2) 5 *(Snodgrass 18, Haller 45, 90, Yarmolenko 56 (pen), 90)*

Hull C (0) 1 *(Wilks 70)*

West Ham U: (4231) Randolph; Ashby (Emmanuel 69), Balbuena, Alese, Johnson; Wilshere, Snodgrass; Yarmolenko, Lanzini, Felipe Anderson; Haller.
Hull C: (4231) Long; Coyle, Jones A, McLoughlin, Fleming; Batty, Smallwood (Honeyman 17); Scott (Wilks 61), Jones C, Mayer (Lewis-Potter 61); Magennis.
Referee: Simon Hooper.

Wednesday, 23 September 2020

Chelsea (2) 6 *(Abraham 19, Havertz 28, 55, 65, Barkley 49, Giroud 83)*

Barnsley (0) 0

Chelsea: (4231) Caballero; Azpilicueta, Tomori, Thiago Silva (Zouma 61), Emerson Palmieri; Barkley, Kovacic; Hudson-Odoi, Havertz (Chilwell 66), Mount; Abraham (Giroud 72).
Barnsley: (3412) Collins; Sollbauer, Halme, Williams J; Ludewig, Ritzmaier (Oduor 57), Mowatt, Styles; Woodrow (Thomas 46); Schmidt, Frieser (Chaplin 57).
Referee: Darren Bond.

Fleetwood T (0) 2 *(Duffy 48, Camps 58)*

Everton (2) 5 *(Richarlison 22, 34, Iwobi 49, Bernard 73, Kean 90)*

Fleetwood T: (352) Cairns; Hill, Stubbs (Duffy 46), Boyes; Burns, Coutts (Matete 75), Camps, Whelan, Andrew; Evans (Saunders 75), Morris J.
Everton: (433) Pickford; Kenny, Keane, Digne, Nkounkou; Sigurdsson, Delph (Davies 62), Bernard; Iwobi, Calvert-Lewin (Gordon 46), Richarlison (Kean 76).
Referee: Jeremy Simpson.

Fulham (2) 2 *(Kamara 9, Reid 32)*

Sheffield W (0) 0

Fulham: (4231) Rodak; Odoi, Hector, Ream, Robinson; Onomah (Seri 62), Johansen; Knockaert (Carvalho 78), Reid, Kebano; Kamara (Francois 71).
Sheffield W: (352) Wildsmith; Brennan, Shaw, Borner; Palmer (Penney 71), Dele-Bashiru, Pelupessy, Waldock (Rhodes 79), Odubajo; Reach, Kachunga (Hagan 82).
Referee: Lee Mason.

Leicester C (0) 0

Arsenal (0) 2 *(Fuchs 57 (og), Nketiah 90)*

Leicester C: (4231) Ward; Amartey, Morgan, Fuchs, Thomas; Choudhury, Dewsbury-Hall (Perez 76); Albrighton, Maddison (Praet 71), Gray; Iheanacho.
Arsenal: (343) Leno; Holding, Luiz, Kolasinac; Maitland-Niles, Willock (Ceballos 78), Elneny, Saka (Bellerin 87); Pepe, Nketiah, Nelson (Willian 72).
Referee: Peter Bankes.

Millwall (0) 0

Burnley (1) 2 *(Brownhill 45, Vydra 90)*

Millwall: (442) Bialkowski; Romeo (Muller 69), Hutchinson, Wallace M, Ferguson; Mahoney, Thompson (Woods 75), Williams, Bodvarsson; Parrott (Bennett 46), Smith.
Burnley: (442) Peacock-Farrell; Lowton, Thomas, Dunne, Taylor; Pieters, Benson, Brownhill (Westwood 73), McNeil (Driscoll-Glennon 82); Vydra, Rodriguez (Wood 16).
Referee: Andy Davies.

Morecambe (0) 0

Newcastle U (5) 7 *(Joelinton 5, 31, Almiron 20, Murphy 27, Hayden 45, Lascelles 51, Lavelle 90 (og))*

Morecambe: (4231) Halstead; Mellor, Lavelle, Davis, Hendrie; Wildig, Diagouraga■; O'Sullivan, Mendes Gomes (Phillips 35), Slew (Cooney 70); Stockton (McAlinden 57).
Newcastle U: (442) Gillespie; Krafth, Lascelles, Clark (Fraser 46), Yedlin; Ritchie, Longstaff S, Hayden (Barlaser 62), Murphy; Joelinton, Almiron (Carroll 62).
Referee: Darren Drysdale.

Preston NE (0) 0

Brighton & HA (0) 2 *(Jahanbakhsh 57, Mac Allister 75)*

Preston NE: (4231) Ripley; Rafferty, Bauer, Storey, Hughes; Bayliss, Gallagher (Pearson 72); Bodin (Sinclair 71), Potts, Harrop (Maguire 71); Stockley.
Brighton & HA: (4231) Steele; Veltman, Burn, Roberts, Bernardo; Propper, Sanders (Cochrane 87); Jahanbakhsh (Jenks 84), Gross, Mac Allister (Gwargis 80); Gyokeres.
Referee: Stephen Martin.

Stoke C (1) 1 *(Campbell 37)*

Gillingham (0) 0

Stoke C: (343) Davies; Collins, Souttar, Fox; Smith, Oakley-Boothe, Thompson, Tymon; Campbell (Fletcher 67), Gregory (Brown 78), McClean.
Gillingham: (433) Walsh; McKenzie, Maghoma, Medley, Ogilvie; Willock (MacDonald 38), Woods, Robertson (Jackson 72); Graham, Akinde, Coyle (Oliver 70).
Referee: David Webb.

Thursday, 24 September 2020

Bristol C (0) 0

Aston Villa (2) 3 *(El Ghazi 11, Traore 14, Watkins 73)*

Bristol C: (352) O'Leary; Vyner, Moore, Rowe; Sessegnon, Brunt (Bakinson 66), Nagy, Palmer (Massengo 84), Eliasson; Semenyo, Diedhiou (Martin 84).
Aston Villa: (433) Steer; Guilbert, Elmohamady, Hause, Taylor; Lansbury (Hourihane 78), Nakamba, Ramsey J; Traore (Trezeguet 70), Davis (Watkins 70), El Ghazi.
Referee: James Linington.

Lincoln C (0) 2 *(Edun 60, Montsma 66)*

Liverpool (4) 7 *(Shaqiri 9, Minamino 18, 46, Jones 32, 36, Grujic 65, Origi 89)*

Lincoln C: (433) Palmer; Bradley, Eyoma, Montsma, Melbourne; Jones (McGrandles 60), Bridcutt (Hopper 59), Edun; Anderson (Archibald 67), Scully, Grant.
Liverpool: (41212) Adrian; Williams N, Williams R, van Dijk (Fabinho 46), Tsimikas; Grujic; Jones, Shaqiri (Keita 75); Minamino; Elliott (Jota 57), Origi.
Referee: Tony Harrington.

Manchester C (1) 2 *(Delap 18, Foden 75)*

Bournemouth (1) 1 *(Surridge 22)*

Manchester C: (4231) Steffen; Walker, Harwood-Bellis, Garcia, Bernabe (Mendy 36); Doyle (Sterling 67), Rodri (De Bruyne 61); Foden, Mahrez, Torres; Delap.
Bournemouth: (3511) Travers; Ofoborh, Simpson, Kelly (Zemura 28); Smith, Billing, Cook L, Gosling, Rico (Cook S 64); Brooks (Kilkenny 76); Surridge.
Referee: Jonathan Moss.

FOURTH ROUND

Tuesday, 29 September 2020

Tottenham H (0) 1 *(Lamela 83)*

Chelsea (1) 1 *(Werner 19)*

Tottenham H: (352) Lloris; Tanganga (Kane 70), Alderweireld, Dier; Aurier, Fernandes (Hojbjerg 63), Sissoko, Ndombele, Reguilon; Lamela, Bergwijn (Lucas Moura 76).
Chelsea: (4231) Mendy; Azpilicueta, Tomori, Zouma, Chilwell (Emerson Palmieri 66); Jorginho, Kovacic (Kante 70); Hudson-Odoi, Mount, Werner; Giroud (Abraham 76).
Tottenham H won 5-4 on penalties.
Referee: Lee Mason.

Wednesday, 30 September 2020

Brighton & HA (0) 0

Manchester U (1) 3 *(McTominay 44, Mata 73, Pogba 80)*

Brighton & HA: (343) Steele; White, Dunk, Burn; Veltman, Molumby (Sanders 81), Gross, Bernardo; Jahanbakhsh (Maupay 50), Gyokeres (Trossard 63), Mac Allister.
Manchester U: (4231) Henderson; Dalot, Bailly, Lindelof, Williams; McTominay, Fred (Lingard 81); Mata, van de Beek, James (Pogba 69); Ighalo (Rashford 69).
Referee: Graham Scott.

Burnley (0) 0

Manchester C (1) 3 *(Sterling 35, 49, Torres 65)*

Burnley: (442) Peacock-Farrell; Lowton (Bardsley 78), Long, Tarkowski, Taylor; McNeil, Westwood, Brownhill, Pieters; Vydra (Wood 46), Barnes (Benson 69).
Manchester C: (4141) Steffen; Walker (Harwood-Bellis 66), Fernandinho, Laporte, Mendy; Rodri (Ake 74); Torres, De Bruyne (Bernardo Silva 64), Palmer, Mahrez; Sterling.
Referee: Andrew Madley.

Everton (1) 4 *(Calvert-Lewin 11, 78, 84, Richarlison 56)*

West Ham U (0) 1 *(Snodgrass 46)*

Everton: (433) Pickford; Kenny (Coleman 42), Keane, Digne, Nkounkou; Sigurdsson, Allan (Doucoure 69), Delph; Rodriguez, Calvert-Lewin, Richarlison (Iwobi 61).
West Ham U: (4231) Randolph; Johnson, Balbuena, Rice, Cresswell; Noble, Snodgrass; Yarmolenko, Lanzini, Felipe Anderson; Haller.
Referee: Darren England.

Newport Co (1) 1 *(Abrahams 5)*

Newcastle U (0) 1 *(Shelvey 87)*

Newport Co: (4312) Townsend; Shephard, Cooper, Dolan, Demetriou; Sheehan, Bennett (Willmott 80), Haynes; Twine (Collins 90); Abrahams, Amond (Taylor 80).
Newcastle U: (4231) Gillespie; Manquillo, Krafth (Schar 71), Fernandez, Lewis; Longstaff S, Shelvey; Murphy, Almiron (Wilson 62), Fraser; Carroll (Joelinton 62).
Newcastle U won 5-4 on penalties.
Referee: John Brooks.

Thursday, 1 October 2020

Aston Villa (0) 0

Stoke C (1) 1 *(Vokes 26)*

Aston Villa: (433) Steer; Guilbert, Elmohamady, Hause (Konsa 58), Taylor; Lansbury, Nakamba, Ramsey J (Watkins 71); Traore (Jota 77), Davis, El Ghazi.
Stoke C: (343) Davies; Collins, Souttar, Martins Indi; Brown, Thompson, Mikel, Tymon; Campbell (Smith 71), Vokes (Fletcher 70), Powell (Oakley-Boothe 75).
Referee: Robert Jones.

Brentford (1) 3 *(Forss 37, Benrahma 62, 77)*

Fulham (0) 0

Brentford: (433) Raya; Fosu, Pinnock, Sorensen, Thompson; Dasilva (Norgaard 69), Jensen, Marcondes; Ghoddos (Canos 69), Forss, Benrahma (Stevens 80).
Fulham: (4231) Rodak; Aina (Odoi 69), Hector, Le Marchand, Robinson; Seri, Johansen; Knockaert (Mitrovic 69), Onomah (Lookman 46), Kebano; Kamara.
Referee: Jonathan Moss.

Liverpool (0) 0

Arsenal (0) 0

Liverpool: (433) Adrian; Williams N, Williams R, van Dijk (Gomez 61), Milner; Jones, Grujic, Wilson; Salah (Origi 61), Minamino, Jota (Wijnaldum 75).
Arsenal: (433) Leno; Cedric, Holding, Gabriel, Kolasinac; Ceballos (Elneny 68), Xhaka, Saka (Maitland-Niles 86); Willock, Nketiah (Lacazette 82), Pepe.
Arsenal won 5-4 on penalties.
Referee: Kevin Friend.

QUARTER-FINALS

Tuesday, 22 December 2020

Arsenal (1) 1 *(Lacazette 31)*

Manchester C (1) 4 *(Gabriel Jesus 3, Mahrez 54, Foden 59, Laporte 73)*

Arsenal: (343) Runarsson; Mustafi, Gabriel, Kolasinac; Cedric, Elneny (Smith-Rowe 66), Ceballos, Maitland-Niles; Willock, Lacazette (Balogun 77), Martinelli (Pepe 49).
Manchester C: (4231) Steffen; Joao Cancelo, Dias, Laporte, Zinchenko; Rodri (Walker 77), Fernandinho; Mahrez, Bernardo Silva (Torres 70), Foden; Gabriel Jesus (Aguero 74).
Referee: Stuart Attwell.

Brentford (0) 1 *(Dasilva 66)*

Newcastle U (0) 0

Brentford: (433) Daniels; Fosu, Pinnock, Sorensen, Thompson; Dasilva (Jensen 81), Janelt (Norgaard 60), Marcondes; Canos (Toney 69), Forss, Ghoddos.
Newcastle U: (4231) Darlow; Yedlin, Hayden, Clark, Lewis (Carroll 80); Shelvey, Longstaff; Murphy, Almiron (Gayle 65), Fraser (Joelinton 65); Wilson.
Referee: Robert Jones.

Wednesday, 23 December 2020

Everton (0) 0

Manchester U (0) 2 *(Cavani 88, Martial 90)*

Everton: (4231) Olsen; Coleman, Mina, Keane, Godfrey; Doucoure (Tosun 89), Andre Gomes (Davies 58); Iwobi, Sigurdsson, Richarlison (Bernard 56); Calvert-Lewin.
Manchester U: (4231) Henderson; Tuanzebe, Bailly, Maguire, Alex Telles (Shaw 84); Pogba, Matic; Greenwood (Rashford 67), Bruno Fernandes, van de Beek (Martial 67); Cavani.
Referee: Andrew Madley.

Stoke C (0) 1 *(Thompson 53)*

Tottenham H (1) 3 *(Bale 22, Davies 70, Kane 81)*

Stoke C: (343) Lonergan; Collins, Souttar, Batth; Smith, Cousins, Thompson, Fox (Fletcher 34); Oakley-Boothe (Vokes 79), Brown (Powell 71), McClean.
Tottenham H: (4231) Lloris; Doherty, Sanchez, Dier, Davies; Hojbjerg, Winks; Bale (Son 46), Alli (Lamela 66), Lucas Moura (Sissoko 66); Kane.
Referee: Darren England.

SEMI-FINALS

Tuesday, 5 January 2021

Tottenham H (1) 2 *(Sissoko 12, Son 70)*

Brentford (0) 0

Tottenham H: (4231) Lloris; Aurier, Sanchez, Dier, Reguilon (Davies 71); Sissoko, Hojbjerg (Tanganga 86); Lucas Moura (Winks 71), Ndombele, Son (Vinicius 89); Kane.
Brentford: (433) Raya; Dalsgaard, Pinnock, Sorensen, Henry; Dasilva■, Janelt (Marcondes 74), Jensen; Mbeumo (Forss 81), Toney, Canos (Fosu 74).
Referee: Mike Dean.

Wednesday, 6 January 2021

Manchester U (0) 0

Manchester C (0) 2 *(Stones 50, Fernandinho 83)*

Manchester U: (4312) Henderson; Wan Bissaka, Lindelof, Maguire, Shaw; Fred (van de Beek 88), McTominay (Greenwood 75), Pogba; Bruno Fernandes; Rashford, Martial.
Manchester C: (352) Steffen; Stones, Dias, Zinchenko; Sterling, Joao Cancelo, Fernandinho, Gundogan, Foden; De Bruyne, Mahrez (Rodri 79).
Referee: Martin Atkinson.

CARABAO CUP FINAL 2020–21

Sunday, 25 April 2021

(at Wembley Stadium, attendance 7773)

Manchester C (0) 1 Tottenham H (0) 0

Manchester C: (4231) Steffen; Walker, Dias, Laporte, Joao Cancelo; Fernandinho (Rodri 84), Gundogan; Mahrez, De Bruyne (Bernardo Silva 87), Sterling; Foden.
Scorer: Laporte 82.

Tottenham H: (433) Lloris; Aurier (Bergwijn 90), Alderweireld, Dier, Reguilon; Winks, Hojbjerg (Alli 84), Lo Celso (Sissoko 67); Lucas Moura (Bale 67), Kane, Son.

Referee: Paul Tierney.

The Manchester City players celebrate with the Carabao Cup following their 1-0 victory over Tottenham Hotspur at Wembley Stadium on 25 April. (Pool via REUTERS/Carl Recine)

LEAGUE CUP ATTENDANCES 1960–2021

Season	*Attendances*	*Games*	*Average*
1960–61	1,204,580	112	10,755
1961–62	1,030,534	104	9,909
1962–63	1,029,893	102	10,097
1963–64	945,265	104	9,089
1964–65	962,802	98	9,825
1965–66	1,205,876	106	11,376
1966–67	1,394,553	118	11,818
1967–68	1,671,326	110	15,194
1968–69	2,064,647	118	17,497
1969–70	2,299,819	122	18,851
1970–71	2,035,315	116	17,546
1971–72	2,397,154	123	19,489
1972–73	1,935,474	120	16,129
1973–74	1,722,629	132	13,050
1974–75	1,901,094	127	14,969
1975–76	1,841,735	140	13,155
1976–77	2,236,636	147	15,215
1977–78	2,038,295	148	13,772
1978–79	1,825,643	139	13,134
1979–80	2,322,866	169	13,745
1980–81	2,051,576	161	12,743
1981–82	1,880,682	161	11,681
1982–83	1,679,756	160	10,498
1983–84	1,900,491	168	11,312
1984–85	1,876,429	167	11,236
1985–86	1,579,916	163	9,693
1986–87	1,531,498	157	9,755
1987–88	1,539,253	158	9,742
1988–89	1,552,780	162	9,585
1989–90	1,836,916	168	10,934
1990–91	1,675,496	159	10,538
1991–92	1,622,337	164	9,892
1992–93	1,558,031	161	9,677
1993–94	1,744,120	163	10,700
1994–95	1,530,478	157	9,748
1995–96	1,776,060	162	10,963
1996–97	1,529,321	163	9,382
1997–98	1,484,297	153	9,701
1998–99	1,555,856	153	10,169
1999–2000	1,354,233	153	8,851
2000–01	1,501,304	154	9,749
2001–02	1,076,390	93	11,574
2002–03	1,242,478	92	13,505
2003–04	1,267,729	93	13,631
2004–05	1,313,693	93	14,216
2005–06	1,072,362	93	11,531
2006–07	1,098,403	93	11,811
2007–08	1,332,841	94	14,179
2008–09	1,329,753	93	14,298
2009–10	1,376,405	93	14,800
2010–11	1,197,917	93	12,881
2011–12	1,209,684	93	13,007
2012–13	1,210,031	93	13,011
2013–14	1,362,360	93	14,649
2014–15	1,274,413	93	13,690
2015–16	1,430,554	93	15,382
2016–17	1,462,722	93	15,728
2017–18	1,454,912	93	15,644
2018–19	1,275,575	93	13,716
2019–20	1,337,845	92	14,542
2020–21	*Due to the COVID-19 pandemic all games played behind closed doors until the final.*		

FOOTBALL LEAGUE TROPHY FINALS 1984–2021

The 1984 final was played at Boothferry Park, Hull. All subsequent finals played at Wembley except between 2001 and 2007 (inclusive) which were played at Millennium Stadium, Cardiff.

ASSOCIATE MEMBERS' CUP

1984	Bournemouth v Hull C	2-1

FREIGHT ROVER TROPHY

1985	Wigan Ath v Brentford	3-1
1986	Bristol C v Bolton W	3-0
1987	Mansfield T v Bristol C	1-1*
	Mansfield T won 5-4 on penalties	

SHERPA VANS TROPHY

1988	Wolverhampton W v Burnley	2-0
1989	Bolton W v Torquay U	4-1

LEYLAND DAF CUP

1990	Tranmere R v Bristol R	2-1
1991	Birmingham C v Tranmere R	3-2

AUTOGLASS TROPHY

1992	Stoke C v Stockport Co	1-0
1993	Port Vale v Stockport Co	2-1
1994	Swansea C v Huddersfield T	1-1*
	Swansea C won 3-1 on penalties	

AUTO WINDSCREENS SHIELD

1995	Birmingham C v Carlisle U	1-0*
1996	Rotherham U v Shrewsbury T	2-1
1997	Carlisle U v Colchester U	0-0*
	Carlisle U won 4-3 on penalties	
1998	Grimsby T v Bournemouth	2-1
1999	Wigan Ath v Millwall	1-0
2000	Stoke C v Bristol C	2-1

LDV VANS TROPHY

2001	Port Vale v Brentford	2-1
2002	Blackpool v Cambridge U	4-1
2003	Bristol C v Carlisle U	2-0
2004	Blackpool v Southend U	2-0
2005	Wrexham v Southend U	2-0*

FOOTBALL LEAGUE TROPHY

2006	Swansea C v Carlisle U	2-1

JOHNSTONE'S PAINT TROPHY

2007	Doncaster R v Bristol R	3-2*
2008	Milton Keynes D v Grimsby T	2-0
2009	Luton T v Scunthorpe U	3-2*
2010	Southampton v Carlisle U	4-1
2011	Carlisle U v Brentford	1-0
2012	Chesterfield v Swindon T	2-0
2013	Crewe Alex v Southend U	2-0
2014	Peterborough U v Chesterfield	3-1
2015	Bristol C v Walsall	2-0
2016	Barnsley v Oxford U	3-2

EFL CHECKATRADE TROPHY

2017	Coventry C v Oxford U	2-1
2018	Lincoln C v Shrewsbury T	1-0
2019	Portsmouth v Sunderland	2-2*
	Portsmouth won 5-4 on penalties	

PAPA JOHN'S EFL TROPHY

2020	Salford C v Portsmouth	0-0*
	Salford C won 4-2 on penalties	
2021	Sunderland v Tranmere R	1-0

**After extra time. †Due to the COVID-19 pandemic, the final due to be played on Sunday 5 April 2020 was postponed and played on Saturday 13 March 2021.*

FOOTBALL LEAGUE TROPHY WINS

Bristol C 3, Birmingham C 2, Blackpool 2, Carlisle U 2, Port Vale 2, Stoke C 2, Swansea C 2, Wigan Ath 2, Barnsley 1, Bolton W 1, Bournemouth 1, Chesterfield 1, Coventry C 1, Crewe Alex 1, Doncaster R 1, Grimsby T 1, Lincoln C 1, Luton T 1, Mansfield T 1, Milton Keynes D 1, Peterborough U 1, Portsmouth 1, Rotherham U 1, Salford C 1, Southampton 1, Sunderland 1, Tranmere R 1, Wolverhampton W 1, Wrexham 1.

APPEARANCES IN FINALS

Carlisle U 6, Bristol C 5, Brentford 3, Southend U 3, Tranmere R 3, Birmingham C 2, Blackpool 2, Bolton W 2, Bournemouth 2, Bristol R 2, Chesterfield 2, Grimsby T 2, Oxford U 2, Port Vale 2, Portsmouth 2, Shrewsbury T 2, Stockport Co 2, Stoke C 2, Sunderland 2, Swansea C 2, Wigan Ath 2, Barnsley 1, Burnley 1, Cambridge U 1, Colchester U 1, Coventry C 1, Crewe Alex 1, Doncaster R 1, Huddersfield T 1, Hull C 1, Lincoln C 1, Luton T 1, Mansfield T 1, Millwall 1, Milton Keynes D 1, Peterborough U 1, Rotherham U 1, Salford C 1, Scunthorpe U 1, Southampton 1, Swindon T 1, Torquay U 1, Walsall 1, Wolverhampton W 1, Wrexham 1.

PAPA JOHN'S EFL TROPHY 2019–20

PAPA JOHN'S EFL TROPHY FINAL 2019–20

Saturday, 13 March 2021

(at Wembley Stadium, postponed from Saturday 5 April 2020 – behind closed doors)

Salford C (0) 0 Portsmouth (0) 0

Salford C: (4231) Hladky; Clarke (Loughlan 115), Eastham, Turnbull, Touray I; Lowe, Threlkeld; Towell (Dieseruvwe 99), Thomas-Asante, Hunter (Andrade 74); Wilson (Burgess 87).

Portsmouth: (442) MacGillivray; Bolton, Whatmough, Raggett, Daniels (Brown 46); Williams, Naylor, Byers (Close 73), White (Curtis 46); Hiwula (Harness 46), Marquis (Jacobs 105).

aet; Salford C won 4-2 on penalties.

Referee: Carl Boyeson.

PAPA JOHN'S EFL TROPHY 2020–21

▪ *Denotes player sent off.*
Due to COVID-19 pandemic, matches played behind closed doors.
In the group stages drawn matches were decided on a penalty shoot-out. Two points were awarded to the team that won on penalties (DW). The team that lost on penalties were awarded one point (DL).

NORTHERN SECTION GROUP A

Tuesday, 1 September 2020

Carlisle U (1) 1 *(Toure 36)*

Fleetwood T (1) 3 *(Camps 44, Saunders 57, 68)*

Carlisle U: (433) Farman; Tanner, McDonald, Hayden, Anderton; Riley, Devine (Furman 46), Mellish; Reilly, Toure▪, Alessandra.
Fleetwood T: (433) Coleman; Burns, Hill, Holgate, Andrew; Camps (Johnston 76), Coutts, Whelan (Matete 71); Saunders, Garner (Evans 70), Morris J.

Tuesday, 8 September 2020

Sunderland (2) 8 *(Wyke 15, 50, Feeney 21, Scowen 75, Power 77, Graham 82, Dobson 84, O'Brien 90)*

Aston Villa U21 (0) 1 *(Vassilev 47 (pen))*

Sunderland: (352) Matthews; Taylor, Feeney, Xhemajli; Diamond, Power (Dobson 80), Scowen, Leadbitter, Gooch; Neill (O'Brien 70), Wyke (Graham 70).
Aston Villa U21: (433) Sinisalo; Kesler, Revan D, Bridge, Revan S; Chukwuemeka, Ramsey J, Ramsey A (Brunt 68); Wright (Sturridge 82), Vassilev (Archer 56), Philogene-Bidace.

Tuesday, 6 October 2020

Fleetwood T (3) 3 *(Saunders 3, 4, 15)*

Aston Villa U21 (0) 0

Fleetwood T: (433) Leutwiler; Smith, Holgate, Stubbs, Rydel; Duffy, Coutts (Johnston 57), Matete; Morris S (Hayes 69), Saunders, Garner (Raffie 69).
Aston Villa U21: (433) Onodi; Walker (Appiah 70), Revan D, Bridge, Revan S; Chukwuemeka, Ramsey A, Ramsey J; Wright, Sturridge (Young 77), Barry (Farr 80).

Sunderland (2) 5 *(Maguire 26, 54, Hume 37, Wyke 69, Diamond 90)*

Carlisle U (1) 3 *(Alessandra 6 (pen), Mellish 72, 82)*

Sunderland: (3142) Matthews; Taylor (Willis 84), Wright, O'Nien; Dobson; Diamond, Neill (O'Brien 75), Power, Hume; Wyke (Graham 75), Maguire.
Carlisle U: (433) Norman; Tanner, Hunt, Hayden, Armer; Riley, Devine, Malley (Guy 72); Charters (Bell 54), Alessandra, Walker (Mellish 26).

Tuesday, 10 November 2020

Fleetwood T (0) 2 *(McKay 51, Duffy 59)*

Sunderland (1) 1 *(McFadzean 15)*

Fleetwood T: (433) Cairns; Smith, Hill, Holgate, Rydel; Duffy (Boyle 86), Rossiter (Baggley 46), Finley (Barrett 89); Morris J, McKay, Morris S.
Sunderland: (352) Patterson; Taylor, Willis, Younger (Dunne 45); Diamond, Dobson, Neill, Embleton, McFadzean (Wilding 61); Hawkes, O'Brien.

Tuesday, 17 November 2020

Carlisle U (1) 3 *(Obiero 32, Toure 55, Reilly 67)*

Aston Villa U21 (0) 1 *(Sohna 82)*

Carlisle U: (433) Dewhurst (Norman 46); Devine, Bennett, Hunt, Armer; Charters, Obiero, Malley (Dixon 16); Toure, Reilly, Patrick (Bell 55).
Aston Villa U21: (433) Onodi; Revan S, Revan D, Appiah, Rowe (Chrisene 61); Sylla (Sohna 70), Bogarde, Raikhy (Lindley 79); Wright, Young, Farr.
Referee: Marc Edwards.

North Group A	P	W	PW	PL	L	F	A	GD	Pts
Fleetwood T	3	3	0	0	0	8	2	6	9
Sunderland	3	2	0	0	1	14	6	8	6
Carlisle U	3	1	0	0	2	7	9	–2	3
Aston Villa U21	3	0	0	0	3	2	14	–12	0

NORTHERN SECTION GROUP B

Tuesday, 8 September 2020

Morecambe (1) 1 *(Lavelle 23)*

Rochdale (0) 2 *(Tavares 86, Newby 90)*

Morecambe: (4231) Halstead; Cooney, Lavelle, Knight-Percival (Davis 46), Conlan; Phillips (Mendes Gomes 62), Kenyon; O'Sullivan (Price 76), Pringle, Slew; McAlinden.
Rochdale: (442) Lynch; McLaughlin (Keohane 46), Amankwah (Newby 72), McNulty, Dunne; Bradley, Morley, Brierley, Rathbone (Dooley 64); Tavares, Baah.

Wednesday, 9 September 2020

Salford C (0) 0

Manchester U U21 (2) 6 *(Mejbri 8, Puigmal 29, Helm 46, 73, McCann 70, Elanga 74)*

Salford C: (433) Hayes; Golden, Turnbull, Doyle, Loughlan; Hawkins (Ditchfield 81), Denny, Towell; Wilson, Elliott (Touray M 71), Thomas-Asante (Shepherd 81).
Manchester U U21: (4231) Bishop; Laird (Taylor 58), Fish, Bernard, Mengi; McCann, Garner; Puigmal (Haygarth 46), Mejbri (Stanley 85), Elanga; Helm.

Tuesday, 29 September 2020

Rochdale (0) 0

Manchester U U21 (0) 0

Rochdale: (433) Lynch; Keohane, Morley, McNulty, Done; Hopper, Brierley (Mialkowski 83), Lund (Rathbone 60); Tavares, Beesley (Newby 60), Dooley.
Manchester U U21: (4231) Mastny; Ercolani, Fish, Bernard, Pye (Hansen-Aaroen 69); Svidersky, McCann; Wellens, Mejbri, Elanga; Hugill.
Manchester U U21 won 5-4 on penalties.

Salford C (1) 2 *(Wilson 45, Hunter 90)*

Morecambe (0) 0

Salford C: (433) Evans; Golden, Turnbull, Eastham, Touray I; Loughlan (Hunter 84), Smith, Denny; Thomas-Asante (Dieseruvwe 79), Wilson (Fielding 85), Andrade.
Morecambe: (4231) Halstead; Mellor, Knight-Percival, Lavelle, Hendrie; Diagouraga, Songo'o; Slew, Leitch-Smith (Phillips 80), Pringle; McAlinden (Price 73).

Tuesday, 10 November 2020

Rochdale (1) 1 *(Beesley 8)*

Salford C (0) 2 *(Andrade 53, Dieseruvwe 82 (pen))*

Rochdale: (433) Lynch; Keohane, O'Connell, McNulty, Done; Hopper (Baah 65), Brierley (Dunne 83), Rathbone; Dooley, Beesley, Tavares (Morley 65).
Salford C: (433) Hladky; Golden, Fielding, Threlkeld (Campbell 59), Berkoe; Burgess, Smith, Denny; Armstrong (Elliott 69), Andrade (Dieseruvwe 65), Hawkins.

Wednesday, 18 November 2020

Morecambe (3) 4 *(Cooney 24, 28, Davis 34, Price 62)*

Manchester U U21 (0) 0

Morecambe: (4141) Halstead; Mellor (Hendrie 46), Davis, Knight-Percival (Lavelle 46), Cooney; Kenyon; O'Sullivan, Wildig (Mendes Gomes 61), Pringle, Price; Stockton.
Manchester U U21: (4231) Woolston; Neville (Elanga 61), Fish, Mengi, Devine (Bejger 78); Mejbri, McCann (Helm 78); Puigmal, Pellistri, Shoretire; Hugill.

North Group B	P	W	PW	PL	L	F	A	GD	Pts
Salford C	3	2	0	0	1	4	7	–3	6
Manchester U U21	3	1	1	0	1	6	4	2	5
Rochdale	3	1	0	1	1	3	3	0	4
Morecambe	3	1	0	0	2	5	4	1	3

NORTHERN SECTION GROUP C

Tuesday, 8 September 2020

Bolton W (0) 2 *(Delaney 53, Miller 75)*

Crewe Alex (1) 3 *(Mandron 15, 89 (pen), Dale 66)*

Bolton W: (3412) Crellin; Brockbank, Delaney, Taft; Hickman (Jones 76), Sarcevic, White (Comley 66), Gordon; Crawford; Doyle, Delfouneso (Miller 66).
Crewe Alex: (433) Richards; Johnson, Beckles, Sass-Davies, Pickering; Lundstram (Finney 80), Wintle, Ainley; Zanzala (Kirk 65), Mandron, Dale.

Tuesday, 22 September 2020

Shrewsbury T (2) 3 *(High 11, Barnett 18, Cummings 55)*

Newcastle U U21 (0) 0

Shrewsbury T: (433) Sarkic; Love, Golbourne, Sears (Williams 50), Pierre; High, Walker (Norburn 46), Vela; Cummings, Udoh (Bloxham 66), Barnett.
Newcastle U U21: (4411) Brown; Cass, Brookwell, Francillette, Wilson (Stephenson 15); Longelo (Gamblin 85), Thomson (Carlyon 62), Young, Flaherty; Anderson; Toure.

Tuesday, 29 September 2020

Crewe Alex (0) 1 *(Pickering 66)*

Newcastle U U21 (0) 0

Crewe Alex: (433) Richards; Daniels, Lancashire (Ng 30), Sass-Davies, Johnson; Lowery (Murphy 70), Wintle (Pickering 46), Lundstram; Ainley, Zanzala, Kirk.
Newcastle U U21: (4231) Brown; Cass, Francillette, Gamblin, Longelo; Young, Carlyon; Stephenson (Barrett 60), Anderson (Sorensen 67), Flaherty; Toure (Midgeley 67).

Tuesday, 6 October 2020

Shrewsbury T (2) 2 *(Barnett 19, Cummings 43)*

Bolton W (0) 1 *(Senior 64)*

Shrewsbury T: (433) Burgoyne; Golbourne, Walker, Pierre, Fossey; High, Vela (Daniels J 46), Zamburek; Tracey (Millar 80), Cummings, Barnett.
Bolton W: (3412) Crellin; Senior, Delaney (Greenidge 46), Taft; Hickman, White (Riley 37), Comley, Gordon; Darcy; Gnahoua, Hurford-Lockett (Mascoll 69).

Tuesday, 10 November 2020

Crewe Alex (2) 3 *(Powell 34, 60, Zanzala 40)*

Shrewsbury T (2) 4 *(Millar 17, Tracey 25, 76, 82)*

Crewe Alex: (433) Richards; Johnson, Lancashire, Nolan, Adebisi; Ainley, Griffiths, Finney; Dale, Zanzala, Powell.
Shrewsbury T: (343) Burgoyne; Williams, Ebanks-Landell, Pierre; Millar (Love 46), Goss, Zamburek, Vela; Barnett, Daniels J (Caton 81), Tracey (Lloyd 89).

Tuesday, 17 November 2020

Bolton W (1) 3 *(Hickman 44, Gnahoua 69, Mascoll 85)*

Newcastle U U21 (2) 2 *(Anderson 11, 40)*

Bolton W: (3412) Crellin; Greenidge, Taft, Mascoll; Hickman, White (Gnahoua 64), Comley, Gordon; Darcy; Miller (Thomason 74), Isgrove (Henry 73).
Newcastle U U21: (4231) Langley; Swales, Cross, Francillette, Lazaar; Brookwell, Rounsfell; Vilca, Anderson (Longelo 81), Flaherty (Indalecio 89); Toure.

North Group C	P	W	PW	PL	L	F	A	GD	Pts
Shrewsbury T	3	3	0	0	0	9	4	5	9
Crewe Alex	3	2	0	0	1	7	6	1	6
Bolton W	3	1	0	0	2	6	7	–1	3
Newcastle U U21	3	0	0	0	3	2	7	–5	0

NORTHERN SECTION GROUP D

Tuesday, 8 September 2020

Port Vale (0) 0

Tranmere R (0) 0

Port Vale: (433) Visser; Smith, Brisley, Crookes, Fitzpatrick; Oyeleke (Conlon 46), Trickett-Smith, Whitehead; Hurst, Robinson (Cullen 71), Montano (Rodney 46).
Tranmere R: (4411) Murphy; O'Connor, Clarke (Ellis 62), Monthe, Ridehalgh; Morris, Banks, Spearing (Lewis 62), MacDonald (Walker-Rice 79); Khan; Payne.
Port Vale won 4-3 on penalties.

Tuesday, 22 September 2020

Wigan Ath (0) 6 *(Naismith 47, Jolley 59, 66, Crankshaw 79, 90, Garner 81 (pen))*

Liverpool U21 (1) 1 *(Clarkson 44)*

Wigan Ath: (442) Evans O; Crankshaw, Obi, Long, Pearce; Solomon-Otabor (James 46), Perry, Merrie, Gardner (Naismith 46); Jolley, Evans L (Garner 72).
Liverpool U21: (433) Kelleher; Sharif, Clayton, Savage, Beck; Cain (Balagizi 84), Woodburn, Clarkson; Bearne (Dixon-Bonner 64), Millar, Longstaff (O'Rourke 84).

Tuesday, 29 September 2020

Tranmere R (0) 3 *(Vaughan 74, 75, Payne 90)*

Liverpool U21 (0) 2 *(Cain 50, Longstaff 83)*

Tranmere R: (532) Murphy; MacDonald, Nelson, Ellis, Ray, Ridehalgh (Spearing 66); Banks (Khan 77), O'Connor, Lewis; Woolery (Vaughan 46), Payne.
Liverpool U21: (442) Jaros; Sharif (Bradley 79), van den Berg, Clayton, Beck; Clarkson, Woodburn, Cain, Dixon-Bonner (Bearne 79); Longstaff (O'Rourke 88), Millar.

Tuesday, 6 October 2020

Wigan Ath (0) 1 *(Pearce 79)*

Port Vale (2) 3 *(Robinson 13, 30, Montano 55)*

Wigan Ath: (442) Evans O; James (Solomon-Otabor 70), Obi, Johnson, Merrie; Crankshaw, Perry, Gardner, Pearce; Jolley, Evans L (Baningime 62).
Port Vale: (433) Visser; Gibbons, Crookes, Brisley, Montano (Rodney 65); Burgess, Whitehead, Hurst; Amoo (Worrall 7), Pope, Robinson (Fitzpatrick 65).

Tuesday, 10 November 2020

Port Vale (2) 4 *(Cullen 12, Hurst 19, McKirdy 61, Rodney 64)*

Liverpool U21 (2) 2 *(Millar 11, 34)*

Port Vale: (442) Visser; Smith, Brisley, Crookes, Montano; McKirdy, Burgess (Conlon 46), Oyeleke (Joyce 46), Hurst; Robinson (Rodney 62), Cullen.
Liverpool U21: (433) Jaros; Bradley, van den Berg, Koumetio (Beck 69), Savage; Longstaff (Ritaccio 69), Cain, Clarkson; O'Rourke, Glatzel (Hardy 61), Millar.

Wednesday, 11 November 2020

Tranmere R (1) 2 *(Woolery 45, Morris 72)*

Wigan Ath (2) 2 *(Keane 19, McHugh 45)*

Tranmere R: (442) Murphy; Ray, Ellis, Nelson, Ridehalgh (Morris 34); Walker-Rice, Lloyd, Banks, Khan; Woolery (Ferrier 46), Smith.
Wigan Ath: (4231) Evans O; James, Obi, Long, Pearce (Webber 64); Perry, Merrie; McHugh, Aasgaard (Baningime 78), Crankshaw; Keane (Joseph 46).
Tranmere R won 3-1 on penalties.

North Group D	P	W	PW	PL	L	F	A	GD	Pts
Port Vale	3	2	1	0	0	7	3	4	8
Tranmere R	3	1	1	1	0	5	4	1	6
Wigan Ath	3	1	0	1	1	9	6	3	4
Liverpool U21	3	0	0	0	3	5	13	–8	0

NORTHERN SECTION GROUP E

Tuesday, 8 September 2020

Lincoln C (0) 1 *(Anderson 80)*

Scunthorpe U (1) 1 *(Cordner 38)*

Lincoln C: (433) Palmer; Eyoma, Montsma, Jackson, Melbourne; Bradley (Grant 61), Edun, Howarth; Anderson, Morton (Jones 64), Elbouzedi (Scully 75).
Scunthorpe U: (541) Watson; Pugh, McGahey (Hornshaw 65), Cordner, Bedeau, O'Malley; Green (Vincent 52), Gilliead, Spence, Dales (Hippolyte 46); Jarvis.
Lincoln C won 4-2 on penalties.

Mansfield T (0) 0

Manchester C U21 (1) 3 *(Bernabe 25, Delap 89, 90)*

Mansfield T: (3412) Stech; Menayese, O'Driscoll, Sweeney; O'Keeffe, Smith, Clarke O (Scott 61), Benning; Sinclair; Maynard (Gordon 61), Reid (Knowles 83).
Manchester C U21: (4141) Trafford; Robinson, Burns, Mbete-Tabu, Wilson-Esbrand; Egan-Riley; Knight, Nmecha, Bernabe, Edozie (McAtee 69); Delap.

Tuesday, 29 September 2020

Scunthorpe U (0) 0

Manchester C U21 (1) 4 *(Knight 17, 63, Edozie 58, 66)*

Scunthorpe U: (442) Kelsey; Hornshaw (Rowe 46), Cordner (Onariase 46), Bedeau, Butroid; Green, McAtee, Beestin, Eisa; Jarvis (Pugh 74), Colclough.
Manchester C U21: (433) Trafford; Dionkou (Bobb 76), Burns, Mbete-Tabu, Ogbeta; Smith, Egan-Riley, Gomes; Knight (Wright-Phillips 82), McAtee (Gyabi 71), Edozie.

Tuesday, 6 October 2020

Mansfield T (0) 1 *(Menayese 72)*

Lincoln C (1) 3 *(Soule 31, Scully 49, Archibald 62)*

Mansfield T: (3412) Stone; Menayese, O'Driscoll, Sweeney; Gordon, Perch (Smith 57), Charsley, Benning; Sinclair (McLaughlin 58); Reid, Bowery (Maynard 57).
Lincoln C: (4141) Ross; Anderson, Eyoma, Roughan, Edun (Cann 90); Grant; Scully, McGrandles, Howarth, Archibald; Soule.

Tuesday, 10 November 2020

Scunthorpe U (0) 1 *(Olomola 78)*

Mansfield T (2) 2 *(Sweeney 33, Reid 44)*

Scunthorpe U: (442) Watson; Rowe (Hornshaw 81), Onariase, Cordner, O'Malley; Dales, Pugh, Beestin, Hippolyte; van Veen (Hallam 46), Loft (Olomola 65).
Mansfield T: (442) Stone; Clarke J, Menayese, Sweeney, O'Keeffe; Sinclair (Gordon 87), O'Driscoll, Smith (Clarke O 73), Law; Cook, Reid (Caine 88).

Tuesday, 17 November 2020

Lincoln C (0) 1 *(Anderson 76)*

Manchester C U21 (0) 1 *(Simmonds 89)*

Lincoln C: (433) Ross; Anderson, Eyoma, Roughan, Melbourne; Gotts, Bridcutt (Grant 62), Edun; Archibald, Hopper (Jones 70), Howarth (McGrandles 19).
Manchester C U21: (4141) Slicker; Robinson (Sobowale 63), Gomes, Doyle, Bernabe; Lavia; Braaf (Gyabi 58), Nmecha, Knight, Bobb (Hamilton 77); Simmonds.
Lincoln C won 4-3 on penalties.

North Group E	P	W	PW	PL	L	F	A	GD	Pts
Manchester C U21	3	2	0	1	0	8	1	7	7
Lincoln C	3	1	2	0	0	5	3	2	7
Mansfield T	3	1	0	0	2	3	7	–4	3
Scunthorpe U	3	0	0	1	2	2	7	–5	1

NORTHERN SECTION GROUP F

Tuesday, 8 September 2020

Doncaster R (0) 0

Bradford C (0) 0

Doncaster R: (4231) Jones; Halliday, Wright, Anderson, John; Gomes, Whiteman; Richards (Williams 66), Coppinger, Taylor (Lokilo 66); Okenabirhie.
Bradford C: (3412) Hornby; Cousin-Dawson, Sikora, Richards-Everton; Sutton, Scales, Pritchard, Longridge; Shanks (Staunton 80); Mottley-Henry (French 62), Donaldson (Guthrie 77).
Doncaster R won 4-1 on penalties.

Tuesday, 22 September 2020

Oldham Ath (1) 4 *(Rowe 42, Grant 85, McAleny 88, 90)*

Wolverhampton W U21 (0) 0

Oldham Ath: (442) Lawlor; Hamer, Jombati, Piergianni, Badan (McAleny 62); Fage (Keillor-Dunn 77), Hough, Whelan (Garrity 46), Barnett; Grant, Rowe.
Wolverhampton W U21: (343) Young; Lonwijk, Marques, Estrada; Scott (Matheson 81), Cundle, Otasowie (Wan 62), Bueno; Corbeanu, Samuels, Campbell (Carty 64).

Tuesday, 6 October 2020

Bradford C (0) 1 *(Donaldson 83)*

Wolverhampton W U21 (0) 1 *(Samuels 61)*

Bradford C: (4231) Hornby; Hosannah, Sikora, O'Connor P, Longridge; Pritchard, Cousin-Dawson (Staunton 72); Ismail (Shanks 46), Scales, Mottley-Henry; Donaldson.
Wolverhampton W U21: (343) Ruddy; Sanderson, Bennett, Richards; Hoever, Shabani, Otasowie, Bueno; Corbeanu, Samuels, Perry (Campbell 90).
Wolverhampton W U21 won 5-3 on penalties.

Oldham Ath (0) 2 *(Rowe 66, Dearnley 86)*

Doncaster R (0) 0

Oldham Ath: (343) Lawlor; Hamer, Jombati, Piergianni; Fage, Whelan, Keillor-Dunn (Garrity 69), Barnett; Bahamboula (Dearnley 46), Rowe, Grant (Blackwood 82).
Doncaster R: (4231) Jones; Halliday, Wright, Anderson, John; Whiteman, Gomes; Okenabirhie, Richards (Williams 70), Coppinger (Taylor 46); John-Jules.

Tuesday, 10 November 2020

Bradford C (0) 1 *(Sutton 60 (og))*

Oldham Ath (1) 3 *(Keillor-Dunn 7, McCalmont 84, 90)*

Bradford C: (3421) Hornby; Sikora, O'Connor P (Staunton 46), Richards-Everton; French, Sutton (Suklenicki 80), Cousin-Dawson, Longridge; Scales, Shanks (Connor Wood 80); Mottley-Henry.
Oldham Ath: (433) Lawlor; Hamer, Diarra (Jameson 72), Sutton, Jombati; Whelan, McCalmont, Keillor-Dunn; Bahamboula (Da Silva 60), Blackwood (Garrity 72), Rowe.

Doncaster R (1) 1 *(Okenabirhie 23 (pen))*

Wolverhampton W U21 (1) 2 *(Silva 15, 88)*

Doncaster R: (4231) Jones; Halliday (Wright 46), John, Butler, Amos; Ravenhill (Whiteman 86), James; Williams, Coppinger (Richards 61), Lokilo; Okenabirhie.
Wolverhampton W U21: (532) Ruddy; Hoever, Rasmussen, Marques, Richards, Marcal (Bueno 71); Cundle, Perry, Shabani (Hasketh 67); Corbeanu, Silva.

North Group F	P	W	PW	PL	L	F	A	GD	Pts
Oldham Ath	3	3	0	0	0	9	1	8	9
Wolverhampton W U21	3	1	1	0	1	3	6	–3	5
Bradford C	3	0	0	2	1	2	4	–2	2
Doncaster R	3	0	1	0	2	1	4	–3	2

NORTHERN SECTION GROUP G

Tuesday, 8 September 2020

Accrington S (5) 7 *(Uwakwe 5, 22, 72, Burgess 14, Charles 30, Cassidy 38, 55)*

Leeds U U21 (0) 0

Accrington S: (3142) Savin; Sykes, Hughes, Burgess; Conneely; Allan, Sangare, Butcher (Sama 46), Uwakwe; Cassidy (Scully 59), Charles (Spinelli 46).
Leeds U U21: (352) Skerry (Christy 17); Suttcliffe, Moore, Mullen; Pilkintong (Hughes 46), Allen, Leverett, Bray (Littlewood 78), Kachosa; Galloway, Dean.

Blackpool (0) 0

Barrow (0) 0

Blackpool: (433) Maxwell; Howe, Nottingham, Thorniley, Shaw; Williams, Ward, Robson (Anderson 71); Kemp, Madine (Yates 90), Lubala.
Barrow: (4231) Dixon; Jones J (Beadling 46), Ntlhe (Brown 46), Hird, Wilson; Taylor J, Biggins; Penfold, Gribbin, James; Quigley.
Blackpool won 5-3 on penalties.

Monday, 5 October 2020

Barrow (0) 2 *(Angus 62, Taylor J 80)*

Leeds U U21 (2) 2 *(Dean 11, 38)*

Barrow: (352) Lillis; Hird, Zouma, Wilson; Brown (Barry 46), Gribbin (Biggins 81), Taylor J, Taylor C, Kay; Hindle (Angus 59), James.

Leeds U U21: (352) Caprile; Drameh, Casey, Davis; Summerville, Jenkins, Struijk, Shackleton, McKinstry (Gibbon 86); Dean, McMillan (Galloway 75).
Barrow won 4-3 on penalties.

Tuesday, 6 October 2020

Accrington S (0) 1 *(Bishop 79)*

Blackpool (1) 1 *(Anderson 10)*

Accrington S: (352) Savin; Sykes, Sama (Pritchard 53), Burgess; Allan (Uwakwe 73), Scully, Butcher, Barclay, Maguire (Mohammed 46); Charles, Bishop.
Blackpool: (433) Maxwell; Lawrence-Gabriel, Husband, Thorniley, Garbutt (Mitchell 73); Anderson, Williams, Ward; Kemp, Sarkic (Yates 46), Lubala (Robson 81).
Accrington S won 4-3 on penalties.

Tuesday, 10 November 2020

Barrow (0) 0

Accrington S (1) 1 *(Mansell 4)*

Barrow: (3412) Lillis; Zouma, Wilson, Ntlhe (Brough 68); Brown, Taylor J, Taylor C, Kay; Gribbin (Sea 65); Quigley (Biggins 71), Reid.
Accrington S: (352) Baxter; Sykes, Hughes, Burgess; Pritchard, Barclay, Scully, Butcher (Rodgers 46), Uwakwe (Conneely 71); Cassidy, Mansell (Charles 46).

Wednesday, 11 November 2020

Blackpool (2) 3 *(Kemp 9, Drameh 20 (og), Robson 82)*

Leeds U U21 (0) 0

Blackpool: (433) Sims; Lawrence-Gabriel (Howe 69), Turton, Thorniley, Husband; Robson, Ward, Antwi■; Kemp, Yates (Apter 83), Lubala (Anderson 70).
Leeds U U21: (433) Casilla; Drameh, Cresswell, Kenneh, Davis (Huggins 46); Gelhardt, Casey (Jenkins 46), McCarron; Summerville, Greenwood, Poveda-Ocampo (McKinstry 46).

North Group G	P	W	PW	PL	L	F	A	GD	Pts
Accrington S	3	2	1	0	0	9	1	8	8
Blackpool	3	1	1	1	0	4	1	3	6
Barrow	3	0	1	1	1	2	3	–1	3
Leeds U U21	3	0	0	1	2	2	12	–10	1

NORTHERN SECTION GROUP H

Tuesday, 8 September 2020

Grimsby T (1) 2 *(Gibson 36 (pen), Boyd 74)*

Harrogate T (0) 2 *(Kiernan 81, Lokko 85)*

Grimsby T: (343) Russell; Hewitt (Jackson 76), Ohman, Idehen; Starbuck, Taylor, Clifton, Hope (Boyd 67); Spokes (Khouri■ 59), Gibson, Edwards.
Harrogate T: (442) Cracknell; Fallowfield, Smith, Lokko, Burrell; Kiernan, Kerry, Kirby, Walker (Thomson 76); Muldoon (Martin 59), Stead (Beck 65).
Grimsby T won 5-4 on penalties.

Hull C (0) 1 *(Lewis-Potter 66)*

Leicester C U21 (0) 2 *(Wright 50, Hirst 90 (pen))*

Hull C: (433) Cartwright; Arthur (Hickey 79), Greaves, Jones A, McLoughlin; Batty, Sheaf, Jones C; Berry, Samuelsen (Chadwick 63), Lewis-Potter.
Leicester C U21: (433) Stolarczyk; Clark, O'Connor, Hughes, Flynn; Wright, Hulme, Ndukwu; Shade (Pennant 67), Hirst, Reghba (Russ 72).

Tuesday, 6 October 2020

Harrogate T (2) 3 *(Stead 16, Jones 20, Kiernan 58)*

Leicester C U21 (0) 1 *(Suengchitthawon 84)*

Harrogate T: (442) Belshaw; Burrell, Lawlor, Lokko, Jones; Walker (Miller 79), Kerry, Kirby, Emmett; Kiernan, Stead (Martin 87).
Leicester C U21: (442) Stolarczyk; Godsmark-Ford (Nelson 56), O'Connor, Hughes, Flynn; Daley-Campbell, Leshabela, Wright, Shade; Russ (Suengchitthawon 43), Reghba (McAteer 56).

Tuesday, 10 November 2020

Grimsby T (1) 1 *(Pollock 21)*

Leicester C U21 (0) 3 *(Wright 58, Tavares 60, Muskwe 74)*

Grimsby T: (343) Battersby; Idehen, Pollock, Ohman; Starbuck, Rose D, Morton, Preston (Spokes 76); Scannell (Jackson 39), Gibson (Gomis 69), Williams.
Leicester C U21: (4231) Stolarczyk; McAteer (Godsmark-Ford 46), Daley-Campbell, Leathers, Flynn; Hulme (Reghba 46), Tavares; Suengchitthawon (Fitzhugh 82), Leshabela, Wright; Muskwe.

Harrogate T (0) 0

Hull C (0) 2 *(Scott 75, Jones C 85 (pen))*

Harrogate T: (442) Cracknell; Burrell, Lawlor, Lokko, Jones; Walker, Kerry, Kirby, Kiernan; Martin (Stead 78), Beck (Thomson 58).
Hull C: (433) Ingram; Jones C, Jones A, McLoughlin, Fleming; Slater, Batty, Mayer (Scott 58); Adelakun (Salam 78), Eaves (Chadwick 70), Samuelsen.

Tuesday, 17 November 2020

Hull C (2) 3 *(Samuelsen 27, 32, Scott 79)*

Grimsby T (0) 0

Hull C: (433) Long; Coyle, Jones A, McLoughlin, Fleming; Slater, Batty, Jones C (Sheaf 74); Samuelsen, Eaves (Scott 60), Adelakun (Mayer 59).
Grimsby T: (343) McKeown; Ohman, Waterfall, Pollock; Wright (Edwards 54), Rose D, Spokes, Preston; Scannell, Green (Sisay 59), Bennett (Williams 71).

North Group H	P	W	PW	PL	L	F	A	GD	Pts
Hull C	3	2	0	0	1	6	2	4	6
Leicester C U21	3	2	0	0	1	6	5	1	6
Harrogate T	3	1	0	1	1	5	5	0	4
Grimsby T	3	0	1	0	2	3	8	–5	2

SOUTHERN SECTION GROUP A

Tuesday, 8 September 2020

Portsmouth (2) 2 *(Harness 37, 38)*

Colchester U (0) 0

Portsmouth: (4231) MacGillivray; Johnson, Whatmough, Raggett, Pring; Naylor, Morris; Harness (Williams 77), Evans, Curtis (Cannon 76); Marquis (Harrison 82).
Colchester U: (4231) George; Welch-Hayes, Sowunmi, Eastman, Scarlett; Chilvers, Stevenson; Poku (Cowan-Hall 66), Gambin (Marshall 78), Senior; Brown (Taylor-Crossdale 66).

Southend U (1) 1 *(Humphrys 13)*

West Ham U U21 (1) 3 *(Odubeko 2, 84, Coventry 90)*

Southend U: (442) Seaden; Mitchell-Nelson, Taylor R, White (Kyprianou 46), Ralph (Bwomono 46); Kinali, Gard, Phillips, Egbri (Kelman 73); Rush, Humphrys.
West Ham U U21: (442) Anang; Ashby, Akinola, Baptiste, Adarkwa; Ashley, Coventry, Afolayan (Costa Da Rosa 68), Emmanuel; Odubeko, Dju (Goncalo Cardoso 89).

Tuesday, 29 September 2020

Colchester U (0) 0

West Ham U U21 (0) 1 *(Coventry 61)*

Colchester U: (4231) George; Scarlett, Sowunmi, Kensdale, Welch-Hayes (Sayer 66); Gambin, McLeod; Cowan-Hall, Chilvers (Marshall 66), Senior; Norris (Brown 71).
West Ham U U21: (433) Anang; Akinola, Baptiste, Goncalo Cardoso (Ashley 60), Emmanuel; Lewis, Coventry, Costa Da Rosa; Chesters (Adarkwa 90), Dju, Afolayan.

Tuesday, 6 October 2020

Southend U (0) 0

Portsmouth (2) 3 *(Marquis 21 (pen), Curtis 40, 77)*

Southend U: (442) Oxley; Hobson, Dieng (Coker K 46), Taylor R, Clifford; Egbri, Gard (Coker O 52), Phillips, Kyprianou; Acquah (Nathaniel-George 74), Rush.
Portsmouth: (3421) Bass; Bolton, Downing, Nicolaisen; Mnoga, Close, Cannon, Pring; Williams (Morris 88), Curtis (Johnson 80); Marquis.

Tuesday, 10 November 2020

Colchester U (2) 6 *(Brown 16, 38, 57 (pen), Folivi 62, Chilvers 70, Poku 83)*

Southend U (0) 1 *(Sterling 90)*

Colchester U: (4231) George; Scarlett, Sowunmi, Eastman (Welch-Hayes 63), Clampin; Chilvers, Pell (Marshall 58); Poku, Folivi, Bohui; Brown (Tovide 58).
Southend U: (442) Seaden; Hobson, White (Chandler 46), Taylor R, Clifford; Egbri, Phillips, Goodship (Nathaniel-George 46), Acquah (Coker O 71); Sterling, Rush.

Portsmouth (0) 0

West Ham U U21 (1) 1 *(Corbett 4)*

Portsmouth: (442) Bass; Mnoga, Bolton, Downing, Rew; Kavanagh (Brook 67), Bell (Seok 79), Morris, Teggart; Hiwula, Stanley (Jewitt-White 66).
West Ham U U21: (442) Trott; Costa Da Rosa (Forbes 80), Johnson, Greenidge, Emmanuel (Chesters 73); Okotcha, Appiah-Forson, Lewis, Corbett; Afolayan, Simon-Swyer (Adarkwa 83).

South Group A	P	W	PW	PL	L	F	A	GD	Pts
West Ham U U21	3	3	0	0	0	5	1	4	9
Portsmouth	3	2	0	0	1	5	1	4	6
Colchester U	3	1	0	0	2	6	4	2	3
Southend U	3	0	0	0	3	2	12	–10	0

SOUTHERN SECTION GROUP B

Tuesday, 8 September 2020

Gillingham (1) 2 *(Coyle 40, Oliver 50)*

Crawley T (0) 1 *(Ferguson 78)*

Gillingham: (433) Bonham; Jackson, Tucker, Maghoma, Medley (Ogilvie 80); Woods, Mellis, Willock; Graham (MacDonald 83), Akinde (Oliver 46), Coyle.
Crawley T: (433) McGill; Adebowale (Frost 52), McNerney, Tunnicliffe, Doherty; Davies, Ferguson, Francomb (Hessenthaler 69); Allarakhia (Ashford 69), German, Nadesan.

Ipswich T (1) 1 *(Nolan 26)*

Arsenal U21 (1) 2 *(Lewis 45, Balogun 54)*

Ipswich T: (433) Cornell; Chambers, Ndaba, Woolfenden, Kenlock; Bishop (Huws 52), Dozzell, Nolan; Judge, Drinan (Norwood 55), Sears (Edwards 46).
Arsenal U21: (433) Smith; Alebiousu, Oyegoke, McGuinness, Bola; Cottrell, Oulad M'hand (Akinola 65), Olayinka; McEneff (Azeez 46), Balogun (Cirjan 73), Lewis.

Tuesday, 6 October 2020

Ipswich T (0) 2 *(Dobra 57, Folami 75)*

Gillingham (0) 0

Ipswich T: (4231) Cornell; Donacien, Woolfenden, Baggott, Ndaba; McGavin, Gibbs (Viral 90); Dobra (Crane 82), Lankester (Siziba 90), Folami; Simpson.
Gillingham: (433) Walsh; McKenzie, Maghoma, Tucker, Medley; Drysdale, Willock (Samuel 46), Woods; MacDonald (Eccles 71), Akinde, Coyle.

Tuesday, 13 October 2020

Crawley T (1) 1 *(Watters 37)*

Arsenal U21 (1) 2 *(McEneff 15, Azeez 55)*

Crawley T: (352) McGill; McNerney, Dallison, Adebowale; Davies (Al-Hussaini 76), Powell, Ferguson, Matthews (Khaleel 66), Sesay; Galach, Watters (Ashford 55).
Arsenal U21: (433) Okonkwo; Alebiousu, Dinzeyi (Laing 81), Clarke, Lopez (Kirk 70); Olayinka, Akinola, Azeez; McEneff, Cottrell, Taylor-Hart.

Tuesday, 10 November 2020

Crawley T (1) 2 *(Galach 17, 55)*

Ipswich T (0) 0

Crawley T: (442) Nelson; Sesay, McNerney, Adebowale, Dallison; Ashford, Ferguson (Burnett 62), Khaleel, Allarakhia (Tsaroulla 56); German (Al-Hussaini 46), Galach.
Ipswich T: (433) Cornell; Crowe, Andoh, Ndaba, Smith; Viral (Manly 68), Siziba, Gibbs; Crane (Brown 68), Simpson, Bennetts.

Gillingham (0) 1 *(Coyle 55)*

Arsenal U21 (1) 1 *(Cirjan 6)*

Gillingham: (433) Walsh; Jackson (McKenzie 46), Maghoma, Drysdale, Medley; Woods, Eccles, Willock (Dempsey 83); MacDonald, Oliver (Samuel 61), Coyle.
Arsenal U21: (4231) Macey; Monlouis, Chambers (Laing 46), Saliba, Lopez; Cirjan, Akinola; Cottrell, Smith-Rowe, Moller; Balogun.
Arsenal U21 won 4-2 on penalties.

South Group B	P	W	PW	PL	L	F	A	GD	Pts
Arsenal U21	3	2	1	0	0	5	3	2	8
Gillingham	3	1	0	1	1	3	4	–1	4
Crawley T	3	1	0	0	2	4	4	0	3
Ipswich T	3	1	0	0	2	3	4	–1	3

SOUTHERN SECTION GROUP C

Tuesday, 8 September 2020

Milton Keynes D (1) 3 *(Poole 34, Nombe 74, Sorinola 77)*

Northampton T (1) 1 *(Mills 13)*

Milton Keynes D: (442) Walker L; O'Hora, Lewington, Cargill, Sorinola; Poole, Sorensen (Freeman 71), Houghton (Brittain 80), Kasumu; Mason (Morris 61), Nombe.
Northampton T: (532) Mitchell; Harriman, Racic (Martin 46), Bolger, Horsfall, Mills (Roberts 40); Watson, Korboa, Missilou; Smith (Lines 45), Warburton.

Tuesday, 22 September 2020

Stevenage (1) 2 *(Dinanga 45, Marsh 90)*

Southampton U21 (1) 1 *(Slattery 37)*

Stevenage: (433) Cumming; Hutton, Marshall, Vancooten, Fernandez; Smith (Osborne 63), Vincelot, Marsh; Dinanga, Effiong (Read 85), Akinwande.
Southampton U21: (442) Lewis; Valery (Kpohomouh 90), Ramsay, Tchaptchet (O'Connor 59), Ferry; Chauke, Slattery, Jankewitz, Hesketh; Mitchell (Olaigbe 69), N'Lundulu.

Tuesday, 6 October 2020

Northampton T (2) 5 *(Mills 7, Marshall 40, Ashley-Seal 46, 58, Chukwuemeka 50)*

Southampton U21 (0) 0

Northampton T: (343) Mitchell; Harriman, Martin, Mills; Adams (Roberts 54), McWilliams (Sowerby 46), Lines, Marshall; Korboa, Ashley-Seal, Rose (Chukwuemeka 46).
Southampton U21: (451) Lewis; Valery, Ramsay, Tchaptchet, Vokins; Chauke, Agbontohoma (Defise 70), Watts, Hesketh, Tella; Mitchell (Olaigbe 61).

Stevenage (1) 2 *(Thompson 45 (og), Effiong 66 (pen))*

Milton Keynes D (2) 3 *(Morris 32, Bird 38, 84)*

Stevenage: (4231) Johnson; Hutton, Marshall, Townsend-West, Coker (Wildin 46); Vincelot, Smith; Osborne (Cuthbert 46), Newton (Read 67), Akinwande; Effiong.
Milton Keynes D: (352) Walker L; O'Hora (Williams 62), Houghton, Cargill; Brittain, Sorensen, Thompson (Kasumu 67), Freeman, Sorinola; Bird, Nombe (Morris 30).

Wednesday, 11 November 2020

Milton Keynes D (0) 1 *(Sorinola 46)*

Southampton U21 (1) 2 *(Bellis 22, Olaigbe 90)*

Milton Keynes D: (352) Walker L; Denholm, Cargill, Davies; Sorensen, Freeman, Kasumu (Black 61), Fraser (Thompson 46), Sorinola (Bailey 61); Johnson, Morris.
Southampton U21: (442) Lewis; Chauke, Kpohomouh (Keogh 73), Agbontohoma, Tchaptchet; Robise, Johnson, Watts, Finnigan (Mitchell 49); Olaigbe, Bellis (Defise 58).

Tuesday, 17 November 2020

Northampton T (0) 0

Stevenage (0) 0

Northampton T: (3412) Mitchell; Bolger, Sheehan, Horsfall; Harriman, Watson (McWilliams 56), Sowerby, Adams; Holmes (Lines 60); Ashley-Seal (Chukwuemeka 61), Rose.
Stevenage: (442) Cumming; Vancooten (Read 85), Marshall, Prosser, Hutton; List (Carter 70), Iontton, Smith, Marsh; Akinwande, Dinanga (Newton 70).
Northampton T won 4-2 on penalties.

South Group C	P	W	PW	PL	L	F	A	GD	Pts
Milton Keynes D	3	2	0	0	1	7	5	2	6
Northampton T	3	1	1	0	1	6	3	3	5
Stevenage	3	1	0	1	1	4	4	0	4
Southampton U21	3	1	0	0	2	3	8	–5	3

SOUTHERN SECTION GROUP D

Tuesday, 8 September 2020

Bristol R (1) 2 *(Mehew 16, Ayunga 71)*

Walsall (1) 2 *(Jules 29, Gordon 64)*

Bristol R: (343) van Stappershoef; Kilgour, Harries, Kelly; Hare, Mehew (Grant 85), Baldwin, Tutonda; Walker (Daly 70), Ayunga, Hargreaves (Mitchell-Lawson 70).
Walsall: (433) Rose; White (Norman 58), Clarke, Jules, Nurse; Osadebe (Holden 58), Kinsella, Bates; Nolan (McDonald 58), Lavery, Gordon.
Walsall won 4-2 on penalties.

Oxford U (2) 2 *(Agyei 17, Osei Yaw 45)*

Chelsea U21 (0) 1 *(Russell 53)*

Oxford U: (433) Stevens; Clare, Mousinho, Jones, Long; Sykes (Brannagan 58), Kelly (McGuane 59), Forde; Hall (Napa 74), Agyei, Osei Yaw.
Chelsea U21: (4231) Bergstrom; Lawrence, Simeu, Colwill, Maatsen; McEachran, Bate (Russell 46); Livramento, McCormick (Peart-Harris 77), Castillo; Ballo (Nunn 74).

Tuesday, 29 September 2020

Walsall (0) 1 *(McDonald 53)*

Chelsea U21 (0) 1 *(Simeu 69)*

Walsall: (442) Rose; Norman, Scarr, Sadler, Nurse; Nolan (Holden 56), Guthrie (Sinclair 55), Bates, McDonald; Osadebe (Lavery 72), Adebayo.
Chelsea U21: (4312) Bergstrom; Lawrence, Simeu, Colwill, Maatsen; Livramento (Rankine 87), McEachran, Ballo; Peart-Harris (Vale 67); Russell, Nunn (Fiabema 65).
Chelsea U21 won 5-3 on penalties.

Tuesday, 6 October 2020

Oxford U (0) 1 *(Osei Yaw 89)*

Bristol R (1) 1 *(Mehew 12)*

Oxford U: (433) Stevens; Lofthouse (Hanson 62), Long, Atkinson (Jones 67), Elechi; Brannagan, Kelly (Agyei 62), McGuane; Hall, Osei Yaw, Sykes.
Bristol R: (352) van Stappershoef; Kilgour, Baldwin, Kelly; Nicholson (Hare 69), Upson, Hargreaves, Mehew, Leahy; Daly (Phillips 82), Walker.
Oxford U won 4-3 on penalties.

Tuesday, 10 November 2020

Walsall (0) 0

Oxford U (0) 1 *(Osei Yaw 87)*

Walsall: (442) Rose; White, Scarr, Sadler, Cockerill-Mollett; Nolan (Holden 69), Sinclair (Guthrie 69), Bates, Osadebe (McDonald 81); Lavery, Scrimshaw.
Oxford U: (4231) Stevens; Long, Mousinho, Jones, Elechi; Kelly, Henry; Cooper (Chambers 81), Hall, Obita (Agyei 46); Winnall (Osei Yaw 70).

Wednesday, 18 November 2020

Bristol R (2) 4 *(Hanlan 10, Nicholson 15, Westbrooke 57, Hare 90)*

Chelsea U21 (1) 3 *(Anjorin 11, 67, Lewis 62)*

Bristol R: (532) van Stappershoef; Hare, Kilgour, Ehmer, Harries, Tutonda (Leahy 62); Grant, Nicholson (Hargreaves 90), Upson; Daly (Westbrooke 46), Hanlan.
Chelsea U21: (4231) Ziger; Livramento, Simeu, Colwill, Lawrence; Gilmour (Bate 60), Drinkwater; Peart-Harris, Anjorin, Lewis; Brown (Nunn 46).

South Group D	P	W	PW	PL	L	F	A	GD	Pts
Oxford U	3	2	1	0	0	4	2	2	8
Bristol R	3	1	0	2	0	7	6	1	5
Walsall	3	0	1	1	1	3	4	–1	3
Chelsea U21	3	0	1	0	2	5	7	–2	2

SOUTHERN SECTION GROUP E

Tuesday, 8 September 2020

Exeter C (1) 3 *(Ajose 45, Jay 57, Key 67)*

Forest Green R (1) 2 *(Stevens 5, 51)*

Exeter C: (3412) Maxted; Dean (Sweeney 46), Dyer, Parkes (Randall 57); Key, Kite, Taylor, Sparkes; Jay; Bowman (Morison 70), Ajose.
Forest Green R: (3412) Thomas; Godwin-Malife, Bernard, Kitching (Sweeney 56); Covil, Bunker, Allen, Evans; Wagstaff (Young 46); Stevens, McCoulsky.

Swindon T (0) 2 *(Smith T 72, Caddis 75)*

WBA U21 (1) 3 *(Dyce 26, Windsor 47, Gardner-Hickman 74)*

Swindon T: (4231) Kovar; Caddis, Odimayo, Curran, Iandolo; Palmer (Grant A 56), Smith M; Smith J, Payne, Hope (Jaiyesimi 62); Pitman (Smith T 68).
WBA U21: (442) Cann; White, Taylor P, Shotton, Harmon; Gardner-Hickman (Richards 80), Solanke, King (Thorndike 72), Dyce; Brown, Windsor (Faal 85).

Tuesday, 6 October 2020

Forest Green R (3) 3 *(Stokes 17, Stevens 19, Young 29)*

WBA U21 (0) 0

Forest Green R: (343) Thomas; Richardson, Stokes, Bernard; Carter (Covil 61), Whitehouse, Allen, Evans; March (Bell 83), Stevens, Young (Bunker 78).
WBA U21: (3412) Cann; White (Richards 75), Taylor C (Delaney 20), Williams; Gardner-Hickman, King, Solanke, Harmon; Brown; Thorndike (Fellows 61), Malcolm.

Swindon T (0) 3 *(Smith T 61, 85, Palmer 90)*

Exeter C (2) 4 *(Kite 4, Seymour 7 (pen), Atangana 63, Hartridge 68)*

Swindon T: (4231) Fryer; Hunt (Stevens 74), Curran, Grounds, Donohue; Palmer, Grant A; Hope (Payne 64), Grant J (Smith J 64), Jaiyesimi; Smith T.
Exeter C: (3412) Maxted; Sweeney, Dean, Hartridge; Caprice, Kite, Atangana, Sparkes; Ajose; Seymour, Fisher.

Tuesday, 10 November 2020

Forest Green R (0) 0

Swindon T (0) 1 *(Broadbent 90)*

Forest Green R: (3412) Thomas; Sweeney, Stokes, Allen; Wilson (Covil 46), Whitehouse, Evans, Cadden (Richardson 61); Collins; March, Stevens.
Swindon T: (352) Fryer; Curran, Baudry, Hunt; Odimayo, Haines, Stevens, Smith M, Iandolo (Broadbent 20); Smith J, Pitman.

Tuesday, 17 November 2020

Exeter C (1) 4 *(Kite 27, Seymour 48, Sparkes 60, Law 84)*

WBA U21 (0) 0

Exeter C: (442) Andersson; Caprice, McArdle (Wilson 65), Hartridge, Sparkes (Diabate 62); Iseguan, Dean, Kite, Law; Ajose, Seymour (Dyer 50).
WBA U21: (433) French; White, Taylor C, Delaney, Harmon; Solanke (Iroegbunam 72), King, Gardner-Hickman; Dyce (Teixeira 88), Faal (Malcolm 58), Diaby.

South Group E	P	W	PW	PL	L	F	A	GD	Pts
Exeter C	3	3	0	0	0	11	5	6	9
Forest Green R	3	1	0	0	2	5	4	1	3
Swindon T	3	1	0	0	2	6	7	–1	3
WBA U21	3	1	0	0	2	3	9	–6	3

SOUTHERN SECTION GROUP F

Tuesday, 8 September 2020

Newport Co (0) 0

Cheltenham T (0) 1 *(Reid 70)*

Newport Co: (433) King; Baker, Woodiwiss, Cooper, Haynes (Twamley 83); Willmott, Collins, Lewis S (Shephard 69); Amond, Taylor (Hillier 79), Janneh.
Cheltenham T: (343) Griffiths; Horton, Bowry, Boyle; Blair (Clements 46), Chamberlain, Bonds (Azaz 64), Freestone (Tozer 64); Addai, Reid, Lloyd.

Plymouth Arg (1) 2 *(Lolos 39 (pen), Telford 63)*

Norwich C U21 (1) 3 *(Hondermarck 26, Omotoye 54, Dennis 67)*

Plymouth Arg: (3412) Ruddy; Tomlinson, Canavan, Sawyer (Pursall 78); Moore B (Edwards 84), Randell, Camara, Law; Lolos; Jephcott (Hardie 69), Telford.
Norwich C U21: (433) McCracken; Vaughan (Jackson 72), Omobamidele, Tomkinson, Nizet; McAlear, Dronfield, Hondermarck; Giurgi, Dennis (Springett 84), Omotoye.

Tuesday, 6 October 2020

Cheltenham T (0) 2 *(Reid 56, 77)*

Plymouth Arg (0) 0

Cheltenham T: (343) Flinders (Harris 46); Bowry, Raglan, Tozer; Sang, Bonds, Clements, Freestone; Addai (Lloyd 80), Reid, May.
Plymouth Arg: (3142) Ruddy; Aimson, Wootton, Pursall; Fornah; Edwards, Reeves (Opoku 80), Lolos (Grant C 60), Law (Cooper G 64); Telford, Hardie.

Newport Co (0) 0

Norwich C U21 (1) 5 *(Omotoye 2, 49, 75, Dennis 77, Martin 83 (pen))*

Newport Co: (352) King; Ryan-Phillip, Bennett (Maher 32), Webb; Baker, Willmott (Bright 78), Ellison, Woodiwiss, Twamley; Amond (Hillier 68), Janneh.
Norwich C U21: (442) Barden; Mumba, Omobamidele, Tomkinson, Nizet; Hondermarck (Rowe 84), Dronfield (Khumbeni 40), McAlear, Martin; Dennis (Giurgi 79), Omotoye.

Tuesday, 10 November 2020

Cheltenham T (0) 1 *(Lloyd 67)*

Norwich C U21 (0) 0

Cheltenham T: (433) Flinders; Horton, Bowry, Raglan, Freestone; Sang, Clements, Chapman (Chamberlain 61); Lloyd (Blair 80), Reid (Ebanks 77), Addai.
Norwich C U21: (433) McCracken; Vaughan, Omobamidele, Tomkinson, Nizet; Giurgi, McAlear, Dronfield; Dennis (Dickson-Peters 78), Omotoye, Hondermarck (Hutchinson 87).

Plymouth Arg (1) 3 *(Reeves 30, Woodiwiss 48 (og), Cooper G 59)*

Newport Co (0) 1 *(Amond 64)*

Plymouth Arg: (3412) McCormick; Wootton, Canavan (Mitchell 79), Pursall; Cooper G, Grant C (Craske 76), Reeves, Law; Telford; Nouble (Crocker 67), Abraham.
Newport Co: (3412) Brain; Woodiwiss (Lewis S 54), Bennett (Bright 46), Webb; Baker, Livermore, Ryan-Phillip, Twamley; Twine (Hillier 67); Amond, Ellison.

South Group F	P	W	PW	PL	L	F	A	GD	Pts
Cheltenham T	3	3	0	0	0	4	0	4	9
Norwich C U21	3	2	0	0	1	8	3	5	6
Plymouth Arg	3	1	0	0	2	5	6	–1	3
Newport Co	3	0	0	0	3	1	9	–8	0

SOUTHERN SECTION GROUP G

Tuesday, 1 September 2020

AFC Wimbledon (0) 2 *(Roscrow 46, Thomas 58)*

Charlton Ath (1) 1 *(Oztumer 22)*

AFC Wimbledon: (352) Trueman; Thomas, Nightingale, Kalambayi (Procter 63); McLoughlin, Chislett, Hartigan, Reilly (Woodyard 76), Osew; Roscrow, Longman (Pigott 62).
Charlton Ath: (451) Maynard-Brewer; Dempsey, Barker, Oshilaja, Purrington (Doughty 61); Lapslie, Vennings, Henry, Oztumer (Bonne 62), Morgan (Forster-Caskey 62); Davison.

Tuesday, 8 September 2020

Leyton Orient (1) 3 *(Ling 36, Johnson 55, Wilkinson 90)*

Brighton & HA U21 (0) 2 *(Wilson 84, 88)*

Leyton Orient: (433) Sargeant; Thomas, Turley, Widdowson, Ogie; Dayton (Wilkinson 65), Ling (Clay 58), Wright; Maguire-Drew, Johnson (Angol 58), Sotiriou.
Brighton & HA U21: (4231) Rushworth; Yapi, Dendoncker, Roberts (Tsoungui 77), Cochrane; Crofts, Weir; Gwargis, Jenks, Spong (Wilson 58); Cashman (Vukoje 72).

Tuesday, 22 September 2020

AFC Wimbledon (1) 2 *(Robinson 20, Roscrow 87 (pen))*

Brighton & HA U21 (0) 0

AFC Wimbledon: (352) Tzanev; Kalambayi (Thomas 77), Nightingale, Csoka; Alexander, Woodyard (Chislett 62), Hartigan, Oksanen, Osew; Robinson (Assal 62), Roscrow.
Brighton & HA U21: (4231) Rushworth; Packham, Baluta (Turns 46), Tsoungui, Furlong; Leonard (Spong 64), Crofts; Vukoje, Weir, Cashman; Wilson (Eneme 69).

Wednesday, 30 September 2020

Charlton Ath (0) 1 *(Morgan 48)*

Brighton & HA U21 (1) 1 *(Lapslie 30 (og))*

Charlton Ath: (433) Maynard-Brewer; Lapslie, Barker, Mingi, Vega (Ness 55); Watson (Quitirna 61), Vennings, Forster-Caskey; Morgan, Davison, Williams (Henry 46).
Brighton & HA U21: (4231) Rushworth; Packham, Baluta (Tsoungui 63), Turns, Furlong; Spong, Weir; Yapi, Cashman (Leonard 24), Vukoje; Wilson (Eneme 63).
Charlton Ath won 4-1 on penalties.

Tuesday, 6 October 2020

Leyton Orient (1) 2 *(Angol 32 (pen), Wilkinson 75)*

AFC Wimbledon (0) 0

Leyton Orient: (433) Sargeant; Judd (Sweeney 71), Coulson, Happe, Widdowson; Dayton, Clay, Wright; Maguire-Drew, Angol (Wilkinson 52), Brophy (Dennis 62).
AFC Wimbledon: (352) Tzanev; Kalambayi, Nightingale, Csoka; Alexander, Chislett, Hartigan, Reilly (Rudoni 46), Guinness-Walker; Longman (Robinson 46), Roscrow.

Tuesday, 10 November 2020

Charlton Ath (1) 3 *(Aouachira 12, Mingi 64, Maddison 74)*

Leyton Orient (0) 1 *(Dennis 67)*

Charlton Ath: (433) Maynard-Brewer; Matthews, Pearce (Mingi 46), Barker, Aidoo; Vennings (Powell 72), Henry, Morgan; Aouachira (Gavin 72), Maddison, Ghandour.
Leyton Orient: (343) Sargeant; Ling, Turley, Widdowson; Thomas, Kyprianou (Cisse 78), Wright, Sweeney (Brophy 83); Dennis (Johnson 83), Maguire-Drew, Dayton.

South Group G	P	W	PW	PL	L	F	A	GD	Pts
Leyton Orient	3	2	0	0	1	6	5	1	6
AFC Wimbledon	3	2	0	0	1	4	3	1	6
Charlton Ath	3	1	1	0	1	5	4	1	5
Brighton & HA U21	3	0	0	1	2	3	6	–3	1

SOUTHERN SECTION GROUP H

Tuesday, 8 September 2020

Cambridge U (1) 2 *(Knowles 24, Mullin 84)*

Fulham U21 (0) 0

Cambridge U: (442) Burton; Knoyle (Mullin 78), Taylor, Iredale, Dunk; Davies, Digby, May (Simper 43), Knowles; Dallas, Knibbs (Ironside 81).
Fulham U21: (4321) Ashby-Hammond; Harris, McAvoy, Mundle-Smith, Larkeche; Davis (Tiehi 81), De Havilland, Pajaziti (Ablade 67); Carvalho, Jasper; Stansfield.

Peterborough U (2) 3 *(Clarke 3, Reed 23, Mason 68)*

Burton Alb (1) 3 *(Lawless 44, Powell 52, 55)*

Peterborough U: (3412) Gyollai; Mason, Edwards, Kent; Kanu, Reed, Hamilton, Burrows; Clarke; Clarke-Harris (Eisa 46), Tasdemir.
Burton Alb: (532) Sharman-Lowe; Eardley (Quinn 61), Wallace, Bostwick, O'Toole, Daniel; Fox, Gilligan, Powell; Hemmings (Hewlett 75), Lawless (Niemczyk 70).
Peterborough U won 5-4 on penalties.

Tuesday, 6 October 2020

Burton Alb (2) 2 *(Akins 3, Powell 4)*

Cambridge U (2) 4 *(Knibbs 27, Hannant 31, 86, Darling 79)*

Burton Alb: (4321) O'Hara; Brayford, Wallace, O'Toole (Niemczyk 59), Gallacher; Gilligan, Fox, Powell (Anderson 55); Akins (Edwards 46), Daniel; Hemmings.
Cambridge U: (442) Burton; Davies, Darling, Taylor, Iredale; Hannant, Digby, El Mizouni (May 74), Knowles (Dunk 74); Ironside, Knibbs.

Peterborough U (1) 4 *(Eisa 24, Szmodics 49, Clarke 56, Boyd 76)*

Fulham U21 (0) 2 *(Harris 52, Tiehi 71)*

Peterborough U: (3412) Gyollai; Mason, Naismith, Blake-Tracy; Kanu (Mensah 71), Hamilton, Brown, Burrows; Boyd; Eisa (Clarke 46), Szmodics (Tasdemir 59).
Fulham U21: (433) Wickens; Harris, McAvoy, Murphy, Mundle-Smith; Davis, Francois, De Havilland (Pajaziti 72); Carvalho, Tiehi, O'Neill (Ablade 59).

Tuesday, 10 November 2020

Burton Alb (1) 1 *(Edwards 34)*

Fulham U21 (1) 1 *(Hemmings 10 (og))*

Burton Alb: (4141) Sharman-Lowe; Eardley (Latty-Fairweather 46), Brayford (Armitage 46), O'Toole, Gallacher; Edwards; Hart, Lawless, Gilligan, Hutchinson; Hemmings.
Fulham U21: (433) Wickens; Aina, McAvoy, Harris, Duru; Mundle-Smith (Murphy 73), Page, Pajaziti; Ablade, Tiehi (Biereth 77), De Havilland.
Burton Alb won 4-1 on penalties.

Cambridge U (0) 1 *(Worman 86)*

Peterborough U (0) 1 *(Clarke 48)*

Cambridge U: (442) Burton; Davies, Darling, Cundy, Dunk; El Mizouni, Boateng (Worman 67), May, Knowles; Dallas, Knibbs (Neal 79).
Peterborough U: (3412) Gyollai; Naismith, Edwards, Blake-Tracy; Kanu (Mensah 74), Hamilton, Barker, Burrows; Clarke; Eisa, Tasdemir.
Cambridge U won 3-1 on penalties.

South Group H	P	W	PW	PL	L	F	A	GD	Pts
Cambridge U	3	2	1	0	0	7	3	4	8
Peterborough U	3	1	1	1	0	8	6	2	6
Burton Alb	3	0	1	1	1	6	8	–2	3
Fulham U21	3	0	0	1	2	3	7	–4	1

NORTHERN SECTION SECOND ROUND

Tuesday, 8 December 2020

Accrington S (1) 3 *(Burgess 8, Pritchard 67, 85)*

Manchester U U21 (1) 2 *(Pellistri 40, Elanga 61)*

Accrington S: (352) Baxter; Mohammed, Sama, Burgess; Pritchard, Butcher, McConville, Barclay (Fenlon 69), Uwakwe (Bishop 67); Mansell (Charles 46), Cassidy.
Manchester U U21: (4231) Woolston; Fernandez, Fish, Mengi, Devine; Galbraith, Puigmal (Hugill 45); Pellistri (Helm 78), Mejbri, Elanga; Shoretire.

Fleetwood T (0) 0

Blackpool (0) 0

Fleetwood T: (343) Cairns; Hill, Stubbs, Boyes; Morris S (Whelan 77), Coutts, Matete (McKay 77), Rydel; Duffy, Evans, Saunders (Madden 73).
Blackpool: (433) Sims; Lawrence-Gabriel, Turton, Thorniley (Gretarsson 74), Garbutt; Virtue (Williams 46), Anderson (Mitchell 64), Robson; Kemp, Sarkic, Lubala.
Fleetwood T won 5-4 on penalties.

Hull C (0) 0

Crewe Alex (0) 0

Hull C: (433) Long; Coyle, Arthur, McLoughlin, Fleming; Docherty, Slater, Sheaf (Adelakun 72); Mayer (Chadwick 63), Eaves (Wilks 36), Scott.
Crewe Alex: (433) Richards; Johnson, Sass-Davies, Nolan, Adebisi; Ng, Griffiths, Finney; Zanzala, Porter, Kirk.
Hull C won 3-2 on penalties.

Oldham Ath (1) 1 *(Grant 13)*

Sunderland (1) 2 *(Maguire 30, Scowen 64)*

Oldham Ath: (4141) Lawlor; Jombati, Diarra, Piergianni, Barnett; Ntambwe; Bahamboula (McAleny 67), Whelan (Garrity 67), Keillor-Dunn, Grant; Rowe (Fage 57).
Sunderland: (433) Patterson; McLaughlin, Wright, Flanagan, McFadzean; Scowen, Leadbitter (Dobson 70), Power; Diamond, Grigg (Wyke 64), Maguire (McGeady 64).

Port Vale (1) 2 *(McKirdy 27, Mills 80)*

Wolverhampton W U21 (1) 1 *(Perry 20)*

Port Vale: (442) Visser; Mills, Smith, Brisley, Fitzpatrick; McKirdy (Worrall 69), Burgess, Conlon (Joyce 46), Hurst; Cullen (Robinson 46), Pope.
Wolverhampton W U21: (352) Sondergaard; Rasmussen (Lonwijk 81), Marques, Richards; Hoever, Cundle, Perry, Shabani, Bueno; Corbeanu, Carty (Hasketh 78).

Salford C (1) 3 *(Thomas-Asante 24, Dieseruvwe 59, 78)*

Leicester C U21 (0) 3 *(Muskwe 64, 69, Flynn 83)*

Salford C: (4231) Hladky; Golden, Fielding, Turnbull, Berkoe; Smith, Sargent (Campbell 61); Andrade (Loughlan 46), Thomas-Asante, Hawkins; Elliott (Dieseruvwe 46).
Leicester C U21: (4231) Stolarczyk; Daley-Campbell (McAteer 70), O'Connor, Nelson, Flynn; Hulme, Leshabela; Ndukwu (Suengchitthawon 46), Muskwe, Wright; Reghba.
Leicester C U21 won 6-5 on penalties.

Shrewsbury T (1) 1 *(Tracey 44)*

Lincoln C (2) 4 *(Scully 18, Elbouzedi 40, Howarth 67, Grant 78 (pen))*

Shrewsbury T: (3412) Burgoyne; Love, Ebanks-Landell (Williams 46), Golbourne; Daniels J, Edwards, Goss, Zamburek; High (Barnett 65); Tracey, Cummings (Caton 85).
Lincoln C: (433) Palmer; Gotts, Eyoma (Cann 83), Melbourne, Roughan; Howarth, McGrandles (Grant 46), Johnson; Anderson, Scully, Elbouzedi.

Tranmere R (1) 2 *(Lloyd 27, Banks 88 (pen))*

Manchester C U21 (1) 1 *(Delap 17)*

Tranmere R: (4141) Murphy; MacDonald, Nelson, Monthe, Ridehalgh; Banks; Woolery (Khan 63), Lewis, Lloyd, Smith; Ferrier (Morris 71).
Manchester C U21: (433) Slicker; Egan-Riley, Harwood-Bellis, Mbete-Tabu■, Ogbeta; Knight (Robertson 44), Lavia, McAtee; Rogers (Gyabi 76), Delap, Edozie (Doyle 57).

SOUTHERN SECTION SECOND ROUND

Tuesday, 8 December 2020

AFC Wimbledon (0) 3 *(Longman 67, Osew 73, Pigott 90)*

Arsenal U21 (0) 0

AFC Wimbledon: (352) Tzanev; Kalambayi, Nightingale, Thomas; Seddon, McLoughlin, Reilly, Chislett, Osew; Palmer (Pigott 75), Roscrow (Longman 67).
Arsenal U21: (433) Hein; Alebiousu, Papastathopoulos, Saliba■, Lopez; Cirjan, Akinola■, Azeez (Ideho 78); Moller, Cottrell (Norton-Cuffy 78), Martinelli (Taylor-Hart 46).

Cambridge U (0) 2 *(Mullin 67 (pen), Hannant 79)*

Gillingham (0) 0 724

Cambridge U: (442) Burton; Knoyle, Darling, Cundy, Dunk; Hannant (Iredale 90), Taylor (May 85), Digby, Davies; Mullin (Knibbs 80), El Mizouni.
Gillingham: (433) Walsh; Jackson, Drysdale, Tucker, Medley; Woods, Willock, Robertson (McKenzie 46); MacDonald, Akinde, Coyle.

Cheltenham T (0) 0

Portsmouth (2) 3 *(Mnoga 15, Hiwula 29, 50)*

Cheltenham T: (343) Flinders; Bowry, Tozer (Lloyd 46), Freestone; Sang, Azaz (Miles 77), Chamberlain, Chapman; May (Blair 46), Reid, Williams.
Portsmouth: (3412) Bass; Bolton, Downing, Nicolaisen; Mnoga, Morris, Close, Pring; Bell (Storey 62); Stanley (Seok 77), Hiwula.

Exeter C (0) 1 *(Atangana 51)*

Northampton T (1) 2 *(Rose 22, Ashley-Seal 82)*

Exeter C: (352) Maxted; Dyer, McArdle, Hartridge; Caprice (Randall 86), Kite, Atangana (Taylor 76), Law, Sparkes; Fisher, Seymour (Ajose 67).
Northampton T: (343) Mitchell; Harriman, Horsfall, Martin; Marshall (Korboa 53), McWilliams, Watson, Roberts (Chukwuemeka 74); Lines, Smith (Ashley-Seal 54), Rose.

Leyton Orient (1) 1 *(Baldwin 27 (og))*

Bristol R (2) 2 *(Koiki 12, Sargeant 29 (og))* 924

Leyton Orient: (433) Sargeant; Ling, Turley■, Happe, Widdowson (Brophy 46); Clay, Kyprianou, Dayton (Wright 67); Maguire-Drew, Angol (Johnson 61), Sotiriou.
Bristol R: (4231) Jaakkola (van Stappershoef 46); Hare, Kilgour, Baldwin, Leahy; Upson, Westbrooke; Walker (Liddle 75), Hargreaves, Koiki; Hanlan (Ayunga 74).

Milton Keynes D (1) 6 *(Agard 33, 75, Sorensen 56, Poole 59, 80, Walker S 68)*

Norwich C U21 (0) 0

Milton Keynes D: (442) Nicholls; Poole, Williams (Davies 69), Cargill, Harvie; Sorensen, Kasumu (Surman 58), Freeman (Johnson 72), Sorinola; Walker S, Agard.
Norwich C U21: (442) McCracken; Vaughan, Tomkinson, Dronfield, Nizet; Giurgi (Kamara 81), McAlear, Khumbeni, Hondermarck (Springett 73); Dennis (Rowe 69), Dickson-Peters.

Oxford U (0) 1 *(Shodipo 64)*

Forest Green R (1) 1 *(Bailey 45)* 1036

Oxford U: (433) Eastwood; Clare, Mousinho, Jones, Obita (Chambers 63); Forde, Hanson (Osei Yaw 81), Sykes; Hall, Agyei (O'Donkor 86), Shodipo.
Forest Green R: (3412) McGee; Godwin-Malife, Sweeney, Moore-Taylor (Bernard 39); Wilson (Wagstaff 68), Winchester, Adams, Cadden; Bailey; Stevens, Matt (Collins 76).
Oxford U won 4-1 on penalties.

Peterborough U (0) 3 *(Eisa 56, 83, Tasdemir 71)*

West Ham U U21 (0) 0

Peterborough U: (3412) Gyollai; Mason, Edwards, Blake-Tracy; Kanu (Mensah 82), Brown (Barker 82), Hamilton, Burrows; Clarke; Tasdemir, Eisa.
West Ham U U21: (352) Trott; Baptiste, Dawson, Goncalo Cardoso; Yarmolenko, Emmanuel (Corbett 66), Appiah-Forson, Lewis, Costa Da Rosa (Chesters 42); Afolayan, Holland (Fevrier 46).

NORTHERN SECTION THIRD ROUND

Tuesday, 12 January 2021

Hull C (0) 3 *(Wilks 78, Lewis-Potter 80, Coyle 90)*

Fleetwood T (1) 2 *(Madden 8, Burns 53)*

Hull C: (433) Ingram; Coyle, Smith, McLoughlin, Elder; Slater, Batty (Honeyman 46), Jones A; Mayer (Wilks 46), Magennis (Salam 65), Scott (Lewis-Potter 46).
Fleetwood T: (433) Hilton; Burns (Saunders 72), Hill, Connolly, Rydel; Camps, Coutts, Whelan (Duffy 61); Morris S (Matete 75), Madden, Morris J.

Lincoln C (1) 4 *(Elbouzedi 32, Gotts 53, Johnson 62, Grant 90)*

Accrington S (0) 0

Lincoln C: (433) Palmer; Eyoma, Jackson, Melbourne, Edun; Grant, Bridcutt, Gotts; Scully, Johnson (Howarth 63), Elbouzedi.
Accrington S: (352) Savin; Mohammed, Hughes (Bolton 80), Sama; Perritt, Uwakwe (Bishop 61), Barclay, Roberts (Butcher 55), Maguire (Pritchard 60); Fenlon (Charles 60), Cassidy.

Sunderland (1) 2 *(O'Brien 21, McGeady 90 (pen))*

Port Vale (0) 0

Sunderland: (433) Matthews; Power, Willis (Younger 72), Wright, McFadzean; Scowen, Neill (Leadbitter 46), Maguire (McGeady 71); O'Brien, Gooch (Wyke 72), Embleton (Diamond 78).
Port Vale: (442) Visser; Mills, Legge, Smith, Crookes (Fitzpatrick 72); Whitehead (Taylor 57), Burgess (Cullen 73), Conlon, Hurst (Montano 20); Amoo, Robinson (Pope 72).

Wednesday, 13 January 2021

Tranmere R (3) 4 *(Ferrier 4, Lloyd 37, 45, Blackett-Taylor 53)*

Leicester C U21 (1) 2 *(Wakeling 36, Suengchitthawon 56)*

Tranmere R: (433) Murphy; Khan, Ray, Monthe, Morris; Banks, Spearing (Woolery 70), Lewis; Lloyd (Hayde 75), Ferrier (Vaughan 70), Blackett-Taylor (Nugent G 75).
Leicester C U21: (3412) Stolarczyk; Daley-Campbell, O'Connor, Godsmark-Ford (McAteer 64); Hulme, Tavares (Arlott-John 46), Wright, Flynn; Suengchitthawon (Fitzhugh 85); Wakeling, Reghba (Pennant 64).

SOUTHERN SECTION THIRD ROUND

Tuesday, 12 January 2021

Bristol R (0) 0

AFC Wimbledon (0) 1 *(Rudoni 61)*

Bristol R: (433) Day; Little (Hare 62), Kilgour, Harries, Kelly; Ogogo, Grant (Upson 62), Westbrooke (Ayunga 62); Rodman (Hargreaves 76), Barrett (Walker 71), Koiki.
AFC Wimbledon: (41212) Walker; McLoughlin (Alexander 69), Nightingale, Csoka, Guinness-Walker; Oksanen; Woodyard, Rudoni; Chislett (Reilly 69); Longman, Palmer (Pigott 69).

Northampton T (0) 0

Milton Keynes D (1) 2 *(Walker S 27, 83 (pen))*

Northampton T: (343) Mitchell; Harriman, Bolger, Horsfall; Hoskins, McWilliams, Watson, Sowerby (Missilou 87); Mills (Chukwuemeka 80), Rose (Korboa 46), Ashley-Seal (Smith 64).
Milton Keynes D: (352) Nicholls; Poole, Keogh, Lewington; Sorinola, Sorensen, Surman (Gladwin 71), Fraser (Johnson 80), Harvie (Davies 89); Walker S, Mason (Jerome 71).

Oxford U (0) 1 *(Hall 74)*

Cambridge U (0) 0

Oxford U: (433) Eastwood; Forde, Moore, Long, Obita; Sykes (Gorrin 81), Hanson (Kelly 61), Brannagan (McGuane 61); Hall, Winnall (Osei Yaw 61), Agyei (Shodipo 61).
Cambridge U: (442) Burton; Okedina, Cundy, Darling, Iredale; Davies (Knoyle 74), Digby, May (O'Neil 81), Hannant (Dunk 74); Knibbs (Worman 74), Ironside (Dallas 81).

Peterborough U (3) 5 *(Taylor 15, Clarke-Harris 29, Kent 45, Dembele 52, Hamilton 87)*

Portsmouth (0) 1 *(Harrison 90)*

Peterborough U: (3412) Pym; Kent, Thompson, Beevers (Mason 69); Ward (Kanu 46), Hamilton, Taylor, Butler (Burrows 63); Szmodics; Clarke-Harris (Jade-Jones 57), Dembele (Eisa 58).
Portsmouth: (352) Turnbull (Seymour 61); Bolton, Downing (Johnson 72), Nicolaisen; Kavanagh, Morris, Close, Jewitt-White (Bell 61), Rew (Bridgman 81); Harrison, Hiwula.

Oxford U (2) 3 *(Winnall 13, 29, Shodipo 52)*

AFC Wimbledon (0) 1 *(Chislett 78)*

Oxford U: (433) Eastwood; Forde, Hanson, Moore, Ruffels; Kelly (Henry 66), Gorrin (Grayson 46), Sykes; Hall (Long 83), Winnall (Taylor 66), Shodipo (Brannagan 66).
AFC Wimbledon: (433) Walker; Alexander (Biler 69), O'Neill, Procter, Osew (Assal 60); McLoughlin (Reilly 28), Oksanen, Chislett; Rudoni (Robinson 46), Pigott (Currie 60), Longman.

Tranmere R (1) 2 *(Lloyd 38, Lewis 82)*

Peterborough U (0) 1 *(Clarke-Harris 90 (pen))*

Tranmere R: (3412) Murphy; Nelson, Ray, Ridehalgh; Khan, O'Connor, Kirby (Hayde 80), MacDonald; Lewis; Morris (Walker-Rice 90), Lloyd (Woolery 58).
Peterborough U: (3412) Pym; Mason, Thompson (Beevers 46), Blake-Tracy; Kanu (Ward 46), Hamilton, Reed (Brown 69), Burrows (Clarke-Harris 69); Clarke (Szmodics 46); Eisa, Jade-Jones.

QUARTER-FINALS

Tuesday, 2 February 2021

Hull C (0) 1 *(Docherty 60)*

Lincoln C (1) 1 *(Anderson 7)*

Hull C: (433) Ingram; Emmanuel, Burke, McLoughlin, Elder; Slater (Chadwick 61), Smallwood, Docherty; Crowley (Flores 76), Magennis (Scott 61), Lewis-Potter.
Lincoln C: (433) Palmer; Eyoma, Montsma, Walsh, Edun; Jones, Johnson, Grant; Anderson, Scully, Howarth (Hopper 64).
Lincoln C won 4-3 on penalties.

Milton Keynes D (0) 0

Sunderland (1) 3 *(Lewington 12 (og), McGeady 76, Wyke 82)*

Milton Keynes D: (3511) Nicholls; O'Hora, Thompson (Gladwin 60), Lewington (Davies 79); Sorinola, Sorensen, Johnson (Jerome 59), O'Riley (Denholm 80), Harvie; Fraser (Freeman 80); Mason.
Sunderland: (442) Matthews; Power, Willis (McGeady 60), Flanagan, McFadzean (Neill 26); Diamond, O'Nien, Scowen (Wyke 61), Jones (Younger 60); Gooch, O'Brien (Leadbitter 60).

SEMI-FINALS

Tuesday, 16 February 2021

Oxford U (0) 0

Tranmere R (1) 2 *(Woolery 35, Morris 66)*

Oxford U: (433) Eastwood; Hanson (Barker 69), Moore, Grayson (Atkinson 46), Ruffels; Henry (Winnall 69), Gorrin (Brannagan 46), Sykes; Hall (Forde 56), Taylor, Shodipo.
Tranmere R: (41212) Davies; Khan (Ridehalgh 70), Ray, Monthe, MacDonald; O'Connor; Morris (Clarke 90), Kirby (Vaughan 59); Lewis; Woolery (Feeney 71), Lloyd (Spearing 71).

Wednesday, 17 February 2021

Sunderland (0) 1 *(Wyke 75)*

Lincoln C (0) 1 *(Scully 64)*

Sunderland: (433) Burge; Power, Wright (McLaughlin 46), O'Nien, McFadzean; Scowen (Diamond 60), Leadbitter, Neill (Maguire 61); Gooch (O'Brien 83), Wyke, McGeady.
Lincoln C: (433) Palmer; Eyoma, Montsma, Jackson, Edun (Howarth 75); McGrandles, Grant, Sanders (Bramall 58); Scully, Hopper (Jones 75), Johnson.
Sunderland won 5-3 on penalties.

EFL PAPA JOHN'S TROPHY FINAL 2020–21

Sunday, 14 March 2021

(at Wembley Stadium, behind closed doors)

Sunderland (0) 1 Tranmere R (0) 0

Sunderland: (4222) Burge; Power, Flanagan (McLaughlin 44), O'Nien, McFadzean; Leadbitter, Scowen; Maguire (Diamond 63), McGeady; Gooch, Wyke.
Scorer: Gooch 57.

Tranmere R: (4231) Davies; Khan, Clarke, Ray, MacDonald; Feeney, Spearing; Woolery, Morris (Burton 90), Lloyd (Nugent D 65); Lewis (Blackett-Taylor 65).

Referee: Charles Breakspear.

FA CUP FINALS 1872–2021

VENUES

1872 and 1874–92	Kennington Oval
1873	Lillie Bridge
1893	Fallowfield, Manchester
1894	Everton
1923–2000	Wembley Stadium (old)
1895–1914	Crystal Palace
1915	Old Trafford, Manchester
1920–22	Stamford Bridge
2001–06	Millennium Stadium, Cardiff
2007 to date	Wembley Stadium (new)

THE FA CUP

1872 Wanderers v Royal Engineers 1-0
1873 Wanderers v Oxford University 2-0
1874 Oxford University v Royal Engineers 2-0
1875 Royal Engineers v Old Etonians 1-1*
Replay Royal Engineers v Old Etonians 2-0
1876 Wanderers v Old Etonians 1-1*
Replay Wanderers v Old Etonians 3-0
1877 Wanderers v Oxford University 2-1*
1878 Wanderers v Royal Engineers 3-1
Wanderers won the cup outright, but it was restored to the Football Association.
1879 Old Etonians v Clapham R 1-0
1880 Clapham R v Oxford University 1-0
1881 Old Carthusians v Old Etonians 3-0
1882 Old Etonians v Blackburn R 1-0
1883 Blackburn Olympic v Old Etonians 2-1*
1884 Blackburn R v Queen's Park, Glasgow 2-1
1885 Blackburn R v Queen's Park, Glasgow 2-0
1886 Blackburn R v WBA 0-0
Replay Blackburn R v WBA 2-0
(at Racecourse Ground, Derby Co)
A special trophy was awarded to Blackburn R for third consecutive win.
1887 Aston Villa v WBA 2-0
1888 WBA v Preston NE 2-1
1889 Preston NE v Wolverhampton W 3-0
1890 Blackburn R v The Wednesday 6-1
1891 Blackburn R v Notts Co 3-1
1892 WBA v Aston Villa 3-0
1893 Wolverhampton W v Everton 1-0
1894 Notts Co v Bolton W 4-1
1895 Aston Villa v WBA 1-0
FA Cup was stolen from a shop window in Birmingham and never found.
1896 The Wednesday v Wolverhampton W 2-1
1897 Aston Villa v Everton 3-2
1898 Nottingham F v Derby Co 3-1
1899 Sheffield U v Derby Co 4-1
1900 Bury v Southampton 4-0
1901 Tottenham H v Sheffield U 2-2
Replay Tottenham H v Sheffield U 3-1
(at Burnden Park, Bolton W)
1902 Sheffield U v Southampton 1-1
Replay Sheffield U v Southampton 2-1
1903 Bury v Derby Co 6-0
1904 Manchester C v Bolton W 1-0
1905 Aston Villa v Newcastle U 2-0
1906 Everton v Newcastle U 1-0
1907 The Wednesday v Everton 2-1
1908 Wolverhampton W v Newcastle U 3-1
1909 Manchester U v Bristol C 1-0
1910 Newcastle U v Barnsley 1-1
Replay Newcastle U v Barnsley 2-0
(at Goodison Park, Everton)
1911 Bradford C v Newcastle U 0-0
Replay Bradford C v Newcastle U 1-0
(at Old Trafford, Manchester U)
Trophy was given to Lord Kinnaird – he made nine FA Cup Final appearances – for services to football.
1912 Barnsley v WBA 0-0
Replay Barnsley v WBA 1-0
(at Bramall Lane, Sheffield U)
1913 Aston Villa v Sunderland 1-0
1914 Burnley v Liverpool 1-0
1915 Sheffield U v Chelsea 3-0
1920 Aston Villa v Huddersfield T 1-0*
1921 Tottenham H v Wolverhampton W 1-0
1922 Huddersfield T v Preston NE 1-0
1923 Bolton W v West Ham U 2-0
1924 Newcastle U v Aston Villa 2-0
1925 Sheffield U v Cardiff C 1-0
1926 Bolton W v Manchester C 1-0
1927 Cardiff C v Arsenal 1-0
1928 Blackburn R v Huddersfield T 3-1
1929 Bolton W v Portsmouth 2-0
1930 Arsenal v Huddersfield T 2-0
1931 WBA v Birmingham 2-1
1932 Newcastle U v Arsenal 2-1
1933 Everton v Manchester C 3-0
1934 Manchester C v Portsmouth 2-1
1935 Sheffield W v WBA 4-2
1936 Arsenal v Sheffield U 1-0
1937 Sunderland v Preston NE 3-1
1938 Preston NE v Huddersfield T 1-0*
1939 Portsmouth v Wolverhampton W 4-1
1946 Derby Co v Charlton Ath 4-1*
1947 Charlton Ath v Burnley 1-0*
1948 Manchester U v Blackpool 4-2
1949 Wolverhampton W v Leicester C 3-1
1950 Arsenal v Liverpool 2-0
1951 Newcastle U v Blackpool 2-0
1952 Newcastle U v Arsenal 1-0
1953 Blackpool v Bolton W 4-3
1954 WBA v Preston NE 3-2
1955 Newcastle U v Manchester C 3-1
1956 Manchester C v Birmingham C 3-1
1957 Aston Villa v Manchester U 2-1
1958 Bolton W v Manchester U 2-0
1959 Nottingham F v Luton T 2-1
1960 Wolverhampton W v Blackburn R 3-0
1961 Tottenham H v Leicester C 2-0
1962 Tottenham H v Burnley 3-1
1963 Manchester U v Leicester C 3-1
1964 West Ham U v Preston NE 3-2
1965 Liverpool v Leeds U 2-1*
1966 Everton v Sheffield W 3-2
1967 Tottenham H v Chelsea 2-1
1968 WBA v Everton 1-0*
1969 Manchester C v Leicester C 1-0
1970 Chelsea v Leeds U 2-2*
Replay Chelsea v Leeds U 2-1
(at Old Trafford, Manchester U)
1971 Arsenal v Liverpool 2-1*
1972 Leeds U v Arsenal 1-0
1973 Sunderland v Leeds U 1-0
1974 Liverpool v Newcastle U 3-0
1975 West Ham U v Fulham 2-0
1976 Southampton v Manchester U 1-0
1977 Manchester U v Liverpool 2-1
1978 Ipswich T v Arsenal 1-0
1979 Arsenal v Manchester U 3-2
1980 West Ham U v Arsenal 1-0
1981 Tottenham H v Manchester C 1-1*
Replay Tottenham H v Manchester C 3-2

1982	Tottenham H v QPR	1-1*
Replay	Tottenham H v QPR	1-0
1983	Manchester U v Brighton & HA	2-2*
Replay	Manchester U v Brighton & HA	4-0
1984	Everton v Watford	2-0
1985	Manchester U v Everton	1-0*
1986	Liverpool v Everton	3-1
1987	Coventry C v Tottenham H	3-2*
1988	Wimbledon v Liverpool	1-0
1989	Liverpool v Everton	3-2*
1990	Manchester U v Crystal Palace	3-3*
Replay	Manchester U v Crystal Palace	1-0
1991	Tottenham H v Nottingham F	2-1*
1992	Liverpool v Sunderland	2-0
1993	Arsenal v Sheffield W	1-1*
Replay	Arsenal v Sheffield W	2-1*
1994	Manchester U v Chelsea	4-0

THE FA CUP SPONSORED BY LITTLEWOODS POOLS

1995	Everton v Manchester U	1-0
1996	Manchester U v Liverpool	1-0
1997	Chelsea v Middlesbrough	2-0
1998	Arsenal v Newcastle U	2-0

THE AXA-SPONSORED FA CUP

1999	Manchester U v Newcastle U	2-0
2000	Chelsea v Aston Villa	1-0
2001	Liverpool v Arsenal	2-1
2002	Arsenal v Chelsea	2-0

THE FA CUP

2003	Arsenal v Southampton	1-0
2004	Manchester U v Millwall	3-0
2005	Arsenal v Manchester U	0-0*
	Arsenal won 5-4 on penalties.	
2006	Liverpool v West Ham U	3-3*
	Liverpool won 3-1 on penalties.	

THE FA CUP SPONSORED BY E.ON

2007	Chelsea v Manchester U	1-0*
2008	Portsmouth v Cardiff C	1-0
2009	Chelsea v Everton	2-1
2010	Chelsea v Portsmouth	1-0
2011	Manchester C v Stoke C	1-0

THE FA CUP WITH BUDWEISER

2012	Chelsea v Liverpool	2-1
2013	Wigan Ath v Manchester C	1-0
2014	Arsenal v Hull C	3-2*

THE FA CUP

2015	Arsenal v Aston Villa	4-0

THE EMIRATES FA CUP

2016	Manchester U v Crystal Palace	2-1*
2017	Arsenal v Chelsea	2-1
2018	Chelsea v Manchester U	1-0
2019	Manchester C v Watford	6-0
2020	Arsenal v Chelsea	2-1
2021	Leicester C v Chelsea	1-0

**After extra time.*

FA CUP WINS

Arsenal 14, Manchester U 12, Chelsea 8, Tottenham H 8, Aston Villa 7, Liverpool 7, Blackburn R 6, Manchester C 6, Newcastle U 6, Everton 5, The Wanderers 5, WBA 5, Bolton W 4, Sheffield U 4, Wolverhampton W 4, Sheffield W 3, West Ham U 3, Bury 2, Nottingham F 2, Old Etonians 2, Portsmouth 2, Preston NE 2, Sunderland 2, Barnsley 1, Blackburn Olympic 1, Blackpool 1, Bradford C 1, Burnley 1, Cardiff C 1, Charlton Ath 1, Clapham R 1, Coventry C 1, Derby Co 1, Huddersfield T 1, Ipswich T 1, Leeds U 1, Leicester C 1, Notts Co 1, Old Carthusians 1, Oxford University 1, Royal Engineers 1, Southampton 1, Wigan Ath 1, Wimbledon 1.

APPEARANCES IN FINALS

Arsenal 21, Manchester U 20, Chelsea 15, Liverpool 14, Everton 13, Newcastle U 13, Aston Villa 11, Manchester C 11, WBA 10, Tottenham H 9, Blackburn R 8, Wolverhampton W 8, Bolton W 7, Preston NE 7, Old Etonians 6, Sheffield U 6, Sheffield W 6, Huddersfield T 5, Leicester C 5, Portsmouth 5, *The Wanderers 5, West Ham U 5, Derby Co 4, Leeds U 4, Oxford University 4, Royal Engineers 4, Southampton 4, Sunderland 4, Blackpool 3, Burnley 3, Cardiff C 3, Nottingham F 3, Barnsley 2, Birmingham C 2, *Bury 2, Charlton Ath 2, Clapham R 2, Crystal Palace 2, Notts Co 2, Queen's Park (Glasgow) 2, Watford 2, *Blackburn Olympic 1, *Bradford C 1, Brighton & HA 1, Bristol C 1, *Coventry C 1, Fulham 1, Hull C 1, *Ipswich T 1, Luton T 1, Middlesbrough 1, Millwall 1, *Old Carthusians 1, QPR 1, Stoke C 1, *Wigan Ath 1, *Wimbledon 1.
* *Denotes undefeated in final.*

APPEARANCES IN SEMI-FINALS

Arsenal 30, Manchester U 30, Everton 26, Chelsea 25, Liverpool 24, Aston Villa 21, Tottenham H 21, WBA 20, Blackburn R 18, Newcastle U 17, Manchester C 16, Sheffield W 16, Wolverhampton W 15, Bolton W 14, Sheffield U 14, Derby Co 13, Southampton 13, Nottingham F 12, Sunderland 12, Preston NE 10, Birmingham C 9, Burnley 8, Leeds U 8, Leicester C 8, Huddersfield T 7, Portsmouth 7, West Ham U 7, Watford 7, Fulham 6, Old Etonians 6, Oxford University 6, Millwall 5, Notts Co 5, The Wanderers 5, Cardiff C 4, Crystal Palace (professional club) 4, Luton T 4, Queen's Park (Glasgow) 4, Royal Engineers 4, Stoke C 4, Barnsley 3, Blackpool 3, Clapham R 3, Ipswich T 3, Middlesbrough 3, Norwich C 3, Old Carthusians 3, Oldham Ath 3, The Swifts 3, Blackburn Olympic 2, Brighton & HA 2, Bristol C 2, Bury 2, Charlton Ath 2, Grimsby T 2, Hull C 2, Reading 2, Swansea T 2, Swindon T 2, Wigan Ath 2, Wimbledon 2, Bradford C 1, Cambridge University 1, Chesterfield 1, Coventry C 1, Crewe Alex 1, Crystal Palace (amateur club) 1, Darwen 1, Derby Junction 1, Glasgow R 1, Marlow 1, Old Harrovians 1, Orient 1, Plymouth Arg 1, Port Vale 1, QPR 1, Shropshire W 1, Wycombe W 1, York C 1.

FA CUP ATTENDANCES 1969–2021

	1st Round	*2nd Round*	*3rd Round*	*4th Round*	*5th Round*	*6th Round*	*Semi-finals & Final*	*Total*	*No. of matches*	*Average per match*
1969–70	345,229	195,102	925,930	651,374	319,893	198,537	390,700	3,026,765	170	17,805
1970–71	329,687	230,942	956,683	757,852	360,687	304,937	279,644	3,220,432	162	19,879
1971–72	277,726	236,127	986,094	711,399	486,378	230,292	248,546	3,158,562	160	19,741
1972–73	259,432	169,114	938,741	735,825	357,386	241,934	226,543	2,928,975	160	18,306
1973–74	214,236	125,295	840,142	747,909	346,012	233,307	273,051	2,779,952	167	16,646
1974–75	283,956	170,466	914,994	646,434	393,323	268,361	291,369	2,968,903	172	17,261
1975–76	255,533	178,099	867,880	573,843	471,925	206,851	205,810	2,759,941	161	17,142
1976–77	379,230	192,159	942,523	631,265	373,330	205,379	258,216	2,982,102	174	17,139
1977–78	258,248	178,930	881,406	540,164	400,751	137,059	198,020	2,594,578	160	16,216
1978–79	243,773	185,343	880,345	537,748	243,683	263,213	249,897	2,604,002	166	15,687
1979–80	267,121	204,759	804,701	507,725	364,039	157,530	355,541	2,661,416	163	16,328
1980–81	246,824	194,502	832,578	534,402	320,530	288,714	339,250	2,756,800	169	16,312
1981–82	236,220	127,300	513,185	356,987	203,334	124,308	279,621	1,840,955	160	11,506
1982–83	191,312	150,046	670,503	452,688	260,069	193,845	291,162	2,209,625	154	14,348
1983–84	192,276	151,647	625,965	417,298	181,832	185,382	187,000	1,941,400	166	11,695
1984–85	174,604	137,078	616,229	320,772	269,232	148,690	242,754	1,909,359	157	12,162
1985–86	171,142	130,034	486,838	495,526	311,833	184,262	192,316	1,971,951	168	11,738
1986–87	209,290	146,761	593,520	349,342	263,550	119,396	195,533	1,877,400	165	11,378
1987–88	204,411	104,561	720,121	443,133	281,461	119,313	177,585	2,050,585	155	13,229
1988–89	212,775	121,326	690,199	421,255	206,781	176,629	167,353	1,966,318	164	12,173
1989–90	209,542	133,483	683,047	412,483	351,423	123,065	277,420	2,190,463	170	12,885
1990–91	194,195	121,450	594,592	530,279	276,112	124,826	196,434	2,038,518	162	12,583
1991–92	231,940	117,078	586,014	372,576	270,537	155,603	201,592	1,935,340	160	12,095
1992–93	241,968	174,702	612,494	377,211	198,379	149,675	293,241	2,047,670	161	12,718
1993–94	190,683	118,031	691,064	430,234	172,196	134,705	228,233	1,965,146	159	12,359
1994–95	219,511	125,629	640,017	438,596	257,650	159,787	174,059	2,015,249	161	12,517
1995–96	185,538	115,669	748,997	391,218	274,055	174,142	156,500	2,046,199	167	12,252
1996–97	209,521	122,324	651,139	402,293	199,873	67,035	191,813	1,843,998	151	12,211
1997–98	204,803	130,261	629,127	455,557	341,290	192,651	172,007	2,125,696	165	12,883
1998–99	191,954	132,341	609,486	431,613	359,398	181,005	202,150	2,107,947	155	13,599
1999–2000	181,485	127,728	514,030	374,795	182,511	105,443	214,921	1,700,913	158	10,765
2000–01	171,689	122,061	577,204	398,241	256,899	100,663	177,778	1,804,535	151	11,951
2001–02	198,369	119,781	566,284	330,434	249,190	173,757	171,278	1,809,093	148	12,224
2002–03	189,905	104,103	577,494	404,599	242,483	156,244	175,498	1,850,326	150	12,336
2003–04	162,738	117,967	624,732	347,964	292,521	156,780	167,401	1,870,103	149	12,551
2004–05	161,197	98,702	602,152	477,472	339,082	127,914	193,233	1,999,752	146	13,697
2005–06	188,876	107,456	654,570	388,339	286,225	163,449	177,723	1,966,638	160	12,291
2006–07	168,884	113,924	708,628	478,924	340,612	230,064	177,810	2,218,846	158	14,043
2007–08	175,195	99,528	704,300	356,404	276,903	142,780	256,210	2,011,320	152	13,232
2008–09	161,526	96,923	631,070	529,585	297,364	149,566	264,635	2,131,669	163	13,078
2009–10	147,078	100,476	613,113	335,426	288,604	144,918	254,806	1,884,421	151	12,480
2010–11	169,259	101,291	637,202	390,524	284,311	164,092	250,256	1,996,935	150	13,313
2011–12	155,858	92,267	640,700	391,214	250,666	194,971	262,064	1,987,740	151	13,164
2012–13	135,642	115,965	645,676	373,892	288,509	221,216	234,210	2,015,110	156	12,917
2013–14	144,709	75,903	668,242	346,706	254,084	156,630	243,350	1,889,624	149	12,682
2014–15	156,621	111,434	609,368	515,229	208,908	233,341	258,780	2,093,681	153	13,684
2015–16	134,914	94,855	755,187	397,217	235,433	227,262	253,793	2,098,661	149	14,085
2016–17	147,448	97,784	685,467	409,084	212,842	163,620	261,552	1,977,797	156	12,678
2017–18	125,978	87,075	712,036	371,650	210,328	140,641	245,730	1,893,438	149	12,708
2018–19	146,449	92,928	655,501	402,836	146,476	86,028	237,467	1,767,685	150	11,785
2019–20*	160,471	91,200	697,152	489,571	233,190			1,671,584	149	11,219

2020–21 *Due to the COVID-19 pandemic most games were played behind closed doors.*

**Due to the COVID-19 pandemic, the 6th Round, Semi-finals and Final were played behind closed doors.*

THE EMIRATES FA CUP 2020–21

PRELIMINARY AND QUALIFYING ROUNDS

**After extra time.*

EXTRA PRELIMINARY ROUND

Penrith v Pickering T 3-2
Northallerton T v Billingham T 1-4
Sunderland RCA v Durham C 3-1
Whickham v West Allotment Celtic 0-0
West Allotment Celtic won 4-2 on penalties
Thornaby v Bridlington T 2-0
Crook T v Yorkshire Amateur 1-1
Crook T won 5-4 on penalties
Guisborough T v Newton Aycliffe 1-0
Glasshoughton Welfare v Knaresborough T 1-1
Knaresborough T won 4-2 on penalties
Hebburn T v Hemsworth MW 4-1
Consett v Sunderland Ryhope CW 3-2
Marske U v North Shields 3-0
Stockton T v Shildon 3-0
Garforth T v Whitley Bay 0-3
Newcastle Benfield v Seaham Red Star 1-1
Newcastle Benfield won 4-3 on penalties
Ashington v Goole 2-1
Heaton Stannington v West Auckland T 2-3
Bishop Auckland v Hall Road Rangers 1-0
1874 Northwich v Warrington Rylands 1-6
St Helens T v Cammell Laird 1907 1-1
St Helens T won 5-4 on penalties
Longridge T v Winsford U 2-1
Wythenshawe Amateurs v Shelley 1-1
Wythenshawe Amateurs won 4-2 on penalties
Avro v Bootle 1-2
Runcorn T v Thackley 2-1
Litherland Remyca v Ashton Ath 3-0
Eccleshill U v Silsden 0-3
AFC Darwen v Barnoldswick T 2-4
Northwich Vic v Padiham 1-0
Skelmersdale U v Penistone Church 3-2
Daisy Hill v Colne 0-2
Campion v Albion Sports 0-1
Athersley Recreation v Charnock Richard 1-4
Irlam v Liversedge 2-1
Maine Road v Squires Gate 0-5
Congleton T v Burscough 1-1
Congleton T won 3-2 on penalties
Hanley T v Lye T 3-1
Rugby T v Worcester C 0-2
Sporting Khalsa v Boldmere St Michaels 2-1
Highgate U v AFC Bridgnorth 0-3
Stourport Swifts v Coventry U 1-3
Gresley R v Wellington 2-0
Stone Old Alleynians v Tividale 0-0
Tividale won 4-1 on penalties
Bewdley T v OJM Black Country 1-5
Romulus v Coventry Sphinx 0-0
Coventry Sphinx won 4-3 on penalties
Chelmsley T v Shifnal T 0-3
Westfields v Brocton 2-0
Heather St Johns v Walsall Wood 0-1
Whitchurch Alport v Haughmond 3-1
Racing Club Warwick v AFC Wulfrunians 3-0
Anstey Nomads v Sleaford T 3-0
Lutterworth T v Staveley MW 2-0
Carlton T v Loughborough University 1-1
Carlton T won 4-2 on penalties
Bottesford T v Selston 2-1
Radford v Shepshed Dynamo 1-1
Shepshed Dynamo won 4-3 on penalties
Spalding U v Barton T 1-3
Quorn v Melton T 2-0
AFC Mansfield v Sherwood Colliery 2-1
Holbeach U v Kirby Muxloe 1-0
Long Eaton U v Grimsby Bor 3-1
Newark v Deeping Rangers 4-0
Maltby Main v Handsworth 2-1
Blackstones v Boston T 2-3
West Bridgford v Dunkirk 1-1
West Bridgford won 5-3 on penalties
Leicester Nirvana v GNG Oadby T 1-3
Long Melford v Northampton ON Chenecks 3-2
Whitton U v Ipswich W 4-3
Newmarket T (walkover) v Walsham Le Willows
Hadleigh U v Mildenhall T 3-4
Peterborough Northern Star v Potton U 0-1
Kirkley & Pakefield v Cogenhoe U 1-2
Diss T v Framlingham T 1-0
Thetford T v Wellingborough T 2-0
Pinchbeck U v St Neots T 0-4
Burton Park W v AFC Sudbury (walkover)
Gorleston v Swaffham T 5-0
Haverhill R v Norwich U 2-1
Eynesbury R v Desborough T 7-3
Wellingborough Whitworths v Harborough T 1-6
Woodbridge T v Biggleswade U 2-2
Biggleswade U won 7-6 on penalties
Stowmarket T v Rothwell Corinthians 2-1
Wroxham v Arlesey T 5-0
Godmanchester R v Ely C 1-1
Ely C won 4-2 on penalties
Redbridge v Harpenden T 0-2
Park View v Hashtag U 1-2
Harlow T v Enfield 5-1
Clapton v Sporting Bengal U 2-2
Sporting Bengal U won 6-5 on penalties
Hoddesdon T v FC Clacton 1-2
New Salamis v Colney Heath 1-0
Southend Manor v Ware 0-5
Walthamstow v London Lions 3-2
Saffron Walden T v Little Oakley 4-2
Baldock T v St Margaretsbury 2-2
St Margaretsbury won 4-2 on penalties
Stansted v Takeley 3-2
Cockfosters v Stanway R 4-2
Hullbridge Sports v Hadley 0-2
Sawbridgeworth T v Romford 2-1
Brantham Ath v Benfleet 1-1
Brantham Ath won 3-2 on penalties
Woodford T v London Colney 3-1
West Essex v Crawley Green 6-3
Ilford v Halstead T 1-3
Oxhey Jets v Bishop's Cleeve 1-0
Clanfield 85 v Long Crendon 0-1
Leverstock Green v Wembley 3-1
Tuffley R v Harefield U 2-5
Holmer Green v Shrivenham 3-2
Winslow U v Newport Pagnell T 2-1
Cribbs v Newent T 3-1
Easington Sports v Tring Ath 2-0
Aylesbury Vale Dynamos v Windsor 1-2
Ardley U v Edgware T 0-0
Edgware T won 6-5 on penalties
Lydney T v Fairford T 0-1
Risborough Rangers v Longlevens 4-1
Leighton T v Abingdon U 3-0
AFC Dunstable v Hallen 4-0
Roman Glass St George v Flackwell Heath 1-2
Royal Wootton Bassett T v Chipping Sodbury T 2-2
Royal Wootton Bassett T won 4-1 on penalties
Burnham v Cheltenham Saracens 0-0
Burnham won 5-3 on penalties
Dunstable T v Thame Rangers 1-1
Dunstable T won 4-3 on penalties

North Greenford U v Brimscombe & Thrupp	1-2
CB Hounslow U v Banstead Ath	6-1
East Preston v Chatham T	0-2
Billingshurst v Westside	0-2
Lordswood v Hanworth Villa	2-3
Molesey v Southall	0-7
AFC Croydon Ath v Sutton Common R	0-3
Glebe v Whyteleafe	1-3
Broadbridge Heath v Raynes Park Vale	3-1
Alfold v Shoreham	9-1
Saltdean U v Eastbourne T	1-3
Colliers Wood U v Hollands & Blair	0-1
Kennington v Erith & Belvedere	0-1
Langney W v Tower Hamlets	3-1
Stansfeld v Punjab U	3-3
Stansfeld won 4-3 on penalties	
Abbey Rangers v Welling T	3-1
Oakwood v Cobham	0-2
Tunbridge Wells v Erith T	1-0
Newhaven v Lingfield	1-1
Newhaven won 4-2 on penalties	
Broadfields U v Loxwood	3-0
Crowborough Ath v Crawley Down Gatwick	3-4
Redhill v Egham T (walkover)	
Fisher v Horsham YMCA	2-0
Corinthian v Sheerwater	2-1
Guildford C v Canterbury C	3-2
K Sports v Steyning T	0-2
AFC Uckfield T v Little Common	0-1
Mile Oak v Beckenham T	0-4
Lancing v Phoenix Sports	3-3
Phoenix Sports won 11-10 on penalties	
Eastbourne U v Horley T	0-1
Balham v Hassocks	2-2
Hassocks won 5-3 on penalties	
Knaphill v Deal T	0-4
Bearsted v Peacehaven & Telscombe	3-5
Tie awarded to Bearsted – Peacehaven & Telscombe removed	
Spelthorne Sports v Virginia Water	1-0
Sheppey U v Sutton Ath	1-0
Pagham v Fleet T	2-1
Corsham T v Farnham T	2-2
Corsham T won 4-3 on penalties	
Hamworthy U v Calne T	3-0
Badshot Lea v Amesbury T	4-0
Hamble Club v Reading C	2-1
Frimley Green v Fareham T	1-0
Bashley v Whitchurch U	8-2
Brockenhurst v Lymington T	0-1
Baffins Milton R v AFC Stoneham	1-2
Cowes Sports v Totton & Eling	1-0
Basingstoke T v Bournemouth	1-1
Basingstoke T won 5-4 on penalties	
Camberley T v Blackfield & Langley	0-0
Camberley T won 5-4 on penalties	
Shaftesbury v Fawley	2-2
Fawley won 6-5 on penalties	
Tadley Calleva v Alresford T	1-0
Westbury U v Binfield	0-2
Bemerton Heath Harlequins v Horndean	2-1
Christchurch v Ascot U	1-1
Christchurch won 7-6 on penalties	
AFC Portchester v Sandhurst T	4-0
Keynsham T v Exmouth T	1-3
Tavistock v Bradford T	2-0
Odd Down v Helston Ath	1-4
Buckland Ath v Bitton	1-1
Bitton won 5-3 on penalties	
Wells C v Bovey Tracey	2-0
Willand R v Bridport	2-1
Shepton Mallet v Torrington	3-0
Wellington v Bodmin T	2-2
Bodmin T won 4-3 on penalties	
Plymouth Parkway v Saltash U	1-1
Saltash U won 5-4 on penalties	
Millbrook v Bridgwater T	0-1
Portland v Clevedon T	0-1
Sherborne T v Street	2-1
Brislington v Cadbury Heath	0-2
Newton Abbot Spurs v AFC St Austell	3-0

PRELIMINARY ROUND

Whitley Bay (walkover) v Dunston UTS	
Penrith v West Allotment Celtic	1-3
Kendal T v Bishop Auckland	0-5
West Auckland T v Ashington	3-3
West Auckland T won 3-0 on penalties	
Billingham T v Stockton T	1-2
Knaresborough T v Workington	1-3
Crook T v Marske U	0-2
Thornaby v Sunderland RCA	0-2
Frickley Ath v Newcastle Benfield	3-1
Hebburn T v Pontefract Collieries	2-2
Pontefract Collieries won 5-3 on penalties	
Guisborough T v Tadcaster Alb	1-2
Consett v Ossett U	2-2
Consett won 5-4 on penalties	
Congleton T v Skelmersdale U	1-2
Glossop North End v City of Liverpool	0-3
Ramsbottom U v Irlam	4-1
Ashton U v Squires Gate	2-0
Wythenshawe Amateurs v Trafford	1-4
Runcorn Linnets v Albion Sports	2-0
Droylsden v Litherland Remyca (walkover)	
Silsden v Bootle	2-5
Mossley v St Helens T	3-0
Stocksbridge Park Steels v Stalybridge Celtic	1-3
Northwich Vic v Charnock Richard	2-2
Charnock Richard won 5-4 on penalties	
Colne v Prescot Cables	0-2
Runcorn T v Brighouse T	1-1
Runcorn T won 5-4 on penalties	
Warrington Rylands v Clitheroe	1-0
Marine v Barnoldswick T	2-1
Widnes v Longridge T	2-3
Worcester C v Walsall Wood	2-1
OJM Black Country v Matlock T	0-1
Coventry Sphinx v Coleshill T	0-0
Coventry Sphinx won 4-3 on penalties	
Sutton Coldfield T v Belper T	0-1
Kidsgrove Ath v Chasetown	0-1
Leek T v Sporting Khalsa	2-1
Westfields v Whitchurch Alport	2-0
Racing Club Warwick v Bedworth U	1-1
Bedworth U won 3-2 on penalties	
Market Drayton T v Tividale	0-1
Newcastle T v Halesowen T	1-2
Evesham U (walkover) v Coventry U	
Hanley T v Gresley R	5-1
Shifnal T v AFC Bridgnorth	4-1
Cleethorpes T v AFC Mansfield	0-1
Boston T v Coalville T	0-3
Anstey Nomads v Worksop T	1-2
Holbeach U v Sheffield	0-4
Quorn v Barton T	2-0
Maltby Main v Newark	0-4
West Bridgford (walkover) v Lincoln U	
Ilkeston T v Shepshed Dynamo	3-0
Long Eaton U v Bottesford T	1-1
Long Eaton U won 4-2 on penalties	
GNG Oadby T v Carlton T (walkover)	
Lutterworth T v Loughborough Dynamo	0-6
Wroxham v Gorleston	3-1
Biggleswade v Histon	1-0
Cambridge C v Biggleswade U	4-0
Yaxley v Stowmarket T	1-2
Mildenhall T v Corby T	1-1
Mildenhall T won 4-3 on penalties	
Ely C v Eynesbury R	3-1
Stamford v Diss T	4-0
Thetford T v Potton U	0-2

Dereham T v Whitton U 3-2
Daventry T v Bedford T 1-0
AFC Sudbury v Harborough T 4-2
Haverhill R v Wisbech T 4-3
Cogenhoe U v Bury T 0-1
Long Melford v Kempston R 0-0
Long Melford won 4-2 on penalties
Soham T Rangers v St Neots T 3-2
Royston T v Newmarket T 6-0
Great Wakering R v Brantham Ath 0-1
Welwyn Garden C v Saffron Walden T 2-0
Grays Ath v Witham T 1-0
Coggeshall T v Tilbury 2-0
Walthamstow v Cockfosters 1-1
Walthamstow won 3-2 on penalties
Sawbridgeworth T v St Margaretsbury 1-3
FC Romania v Brentwood T 0-1
Barking v Heybridge Swifts 2-0
FC Clacton v Hadley 1-1
FC Clacton won 10-9 on penalties
Hertford T v Maldon & Tiptree 0-1
Bowers & Pitsea v Barton R 5-1
Stansted v Basildon U 2-0
Harlow T v Sporting Bengal U 3-0
Harpenden T v Aveley 0-3
Canvey Island v Ware 2-0
Leiston v Halstead T 5-0
New Salamis v West Essex 5-1
Hashtag U v Felixstowe & Walton U 1-1
Hashtag U won 13-12 on penalties
Waltham Abbey v Woodford T 1-0
Oxhey Jets v Chalfont St Peter 0-1
Aylesbury U v Long Crendon 3-0
Risborough Rangers v Winslow U 2-1
Flackwell Heath v Cirencester T 0-3
Didcot T v Royal Wootton Bassett T 1-2
Holmer Green v Highworth T 0-2
Dunstable T v Easington Sports 1-1
Dunstable T won 7-6 on penalties
Kidlington v Thame U 1-0
Cribbs v Berkhamsted 2-0
Harefield U v Leighton T 1-2
Brimscombe & Thrupp v Cinderford T 1-2
Fairford T v Edgware T 2-2
Fairford T won 4-2 on penalties
Northwood v Slimbridge 1-1
Northwood won 4-2 on penalties
Wantage T v Windsor 3-2
Marlow v North Leigh 2-0
Thatcham T v AFC Dunstable 1-5
Leverstock Green v Burnham 1-4
Tunbridge Wells v Beckenham T 1-1
Tunbridge Wells won 4-1 on penalties
Cray Valley PM v VCD Ath 6-0
Hanwell T v Spelthorne Sports 4-1
Sevenoaks T v CB Hounslow U 3-0
Tie awarded to Sevenoaks T
Southall v Ashford T (Middlesex) 2-1
Chertsey T v Abbey Rangers 2-0
Staines T v Guildford C 2-1
East Grinstead T v Phoenix Sports 3-2
Langney W v Harrow Bor 1-1
Harrow Bor won 3-2 on penalties
Hastings U v Herne Bay 1-0
Ramsgate v Chipstead 0-3
Sutton Common R v Broadfields U 4-0
Carshalton Ath v Whitstable T 5-1
Bedfont Sports v Hassocks 3-1
Deal T v Sittingbourne 4-1
Newhaven v Corinthian 1-2
Erith & Belvedere v Alfold 1-1
Erith & Belvedere won 4-3 on penalties
Kingstonian v Horley T 4-1
Westside v Chatham T 0-2
Cobham v Three Bridges 1-1
Cobham won 4-3 on penalties

Whyteleafe v Bearsted 4-0
Egham T v Crawley Down Gatwick 1-3
Steyning T v Hanworth Villa 2-1
Broadbridge Heath v Haywards Heath T (walkover)
Sheppey U v Uxbridge 4-1
Hythe T v South Park 1-2
Tooting & Mitcham U v Fisher 2-2
Fisher won 3-1 on penalties
Stansfeld v Little Common 2-3
Faversham T v Eastbourne T 1-1
Faversham T won 6-5 on penalties
Ashford U v Whitehawk 2-0
Burgess Hill T (walkover) v Hollands & Blair
Farnborough v Lymington T 0-0
Farnborough won 4-3 on penalties
Basingstoke T v Chichester C 2-2
Chichester C won 3-1 on penalties
Hartley Wintney v Hamworthy U 1-0
Bashley v Christchurch 0-2
Westfield v Frimley Green 2-2
Frimley Green won 5-3 on penalties
Fawley v Tadley Calleva 0-1
Moneyfields v Camberley T 4-2
Winchester C v Corsham T 2-0
Cowes Sports v Hamble Club 1-0
Badshot Lea v Bracknell T 0-2
Binfield v AFC Totton 5-1
Bemerton Heath Harlequins v Sholing 0-1
Wimborne T v AFC Portchester 3-0
AFC Stoneham v Pagham 3-0
Frome T v Bodmin T 3-0
Cadbury Heath v Bristol Manor Farm 1-5
Exmouth T v Melksham T 0-2
Saltash U v Paulton R 1-0
Shepton Mallet v Willand R 1-0
Sherborne T v Clevedon T 1-2
Newton Abbot Spurs v Larkhall Ath 0-4
Bideford v Wells C 3-0
Bridgwater T v Bitton 2-3
Barnstaple T v Helston Ath 2-0
Tavistock v Mangotsfield U 2-1

FIRST QUALIFYING ROUND

Sunderland RCA v Prescot Cables 0-4
Lancaster C v Runcorn T 0-0
Lancaster C won 4-3 on penalties
Warrington T v South Shields 0-0
South Shields won 6-5 on penalties
Marske U v Trafford 1-0
Mossley v Ramsbottom U 2-1
West Allotment Celtic v Hyde U 1-5
Skelmersdale U v Bootle 2-1
West Auckland T v Runcorn Linnets 0-0
Runcorn Linnets won 3-2 on penalties
Whitley Bay v Witton Alb 3-2
Radcliffe v Workington 5-3
Scarborough Ath v Ashton U 0-2
Frickley Ath v Marine 0-1
Whitby T v Warrington Rylands 1-1
Warrington Rylands won 4-3 on penalties
City of Liverpool v Morpeth T 0-3
Atherton Colleries (walkover) v Bamber Bridge
Longridge T v Charnock Richard 2-0
Stalybridge Celtic v Bishop Auckland 3-0
Consett v Stockton T 1-0
FC United of Manchester v Pontefract Collieries 6-2
Tadcaster Alb v Litherland Remyca 7-2
Hednesford T v Long Eaton U 3-2
Tamworth v Stourbridge 3-3
Tamworth won 5-4 on penalties
Worcester C v Stafford Rangers 2-3
Quorn v Matlock T 0-2
Leek T v Mickleover 1-2
Grantham T v Rushall Olympic 2-2
Grantham T won 3-1 on penalties
Nuneaton Bor v Loughborough Dynamo 2-1

Westfields v Worksop T	1-3
West Bridgford v Halesowen T	0-1
Coventry Sphinx v Ilkeston T	0-2
Banbury U v Carlton T	1-0
Chasetown v Basford U	2-1
Tividale v Nantwich T	2-4
Barwell v Bedworth U	3-1
AFC Mansfield v Gainsborough Trinity	3-0
Coalville T v Sheffield	2-0
Buxton v Belper T	7-0
Daventry T v Evesham U	0-2
AFC Rushden & Diamonds v Newark	0-5
Shifnal T v Alvechurch	0-2
Bromsgrove Sporting v Stratford T	1-2
Hanley T v Redditch U	3-2
Ely C v Biggleswade	1-2
Haverhill R v Maldon & Tiptree	0-3
Walthamstow v St Margaretsbury	0-0
Walthamstow won 4-3 on penalties	
Bury T v Brightlingsea Regent	2-1
Dereham T v Canvey Island	0-2
Kings Langley v FC Clacton	1-1
Kings Langley won 4-2 on penalties	
Stamford v AFC Sudbury	4-0
Hitchin T v Needham Market	3-0
Bowers & Pitsea v Hornchurch	0-3
Grays Ath v Potton U	3-1
Long Melford v Cheshunt	1-3
Hashtag U v Soham T Rangers	1-1
Hashtag U won 4-2 on penalties	
Leiston v Biggleswade T	5-1
Cambridge C v Stowmarket T	1-1
Cambridge C won 4-2 on penalties	
Lowestoft T v Aveley	2-3
Peterborough Sports v Enfield T	2-2
Peterborough Sports won 5-4 on penalties	
Potters Bar T v East Thurrock U	1-0
Harlow T v Waltham Abbey	0-1
Royston T v Wroxham	2-0
Leighton T v Mildenhall T	4-0
Welwyn Garden C v Bishop's Stortford	1-1
Bishop's Stortford won 4-3 on penalties	
Coggeshall T v Stansted	0-1
Barking v Dunstable T	6-1
Brantham Ath v St Ives T	1-0
New Salamis v Brentwood T	1-2
Burnham v Northwood	1-0
Horsham v Kingstonian	2-1
Corinthian v Sevenoaks T	3-1
Hartley Wintney v Erith & Belvedere	5-0
Whyteleafe v Binfield	2-0
Chipstead v Deal T	1-1
Chipstead won 4-2 on penalties	
Staines T v Walton Casuals	1-2
Frimley Green v Marlow	1-1
Marlow won 4-1 on penalties	
Little Common v Corinthian Casuals	0-3
Haringey Bor v Tunbridge Wells	5-1
Haywards Heath T v Hanwell T	0-1
Sutton Common R v Metropolitan Police	1-3
Cobham v Risborough Rangers	1-3
Ashford U v Bracknell T	1-4
Bedfont Sports v Lewes	3-1
Crawley Down Gatwick v Hendon	1-2
Wingate & Finchley v Folkestone Invicta	1-4
Hastings U v Chesham U	0-0
Hastings U won 6-5 on penalties	
Cray W v Fisher	3-1
Steyning T v Sheppey U	0-5
East Grinstead T v Worthing	3-3
East Grinstead T won 4-3 on penalties	
South Park v Bognor Regis T	2-2
Bognor Regis T won 4-2 on penalties	
Merstham v AFC Dunstable	2-2
AFC Dunstable won 7-6 on penalties	
Chertsey T v Leatherhead	0-0
Chertsey T won 5-4 on penalties	
Cray Valley PM v Burgess Hill T	3-1
Beaconsfield T v Harrow Bor	0-2
Chatham T v Southall	3-2
Chalfont St Peter v Farnborough	2-3
Margate v Hayes & Yeading U	1-2
Carshalton Ath v Faversham T	5-0
Tavistock v Gosport Bor	2-2
Gosport Bor won 5-3 on penalties	
Fairford T v Sholing	1-2
Cinderford T v Royal Wootton Bassett T	2-2
Royal Wootton Bassett T won 6-5 on penalties	
Chichester C v Cribbs	3-1
Cowes Sports v Weston-super-Mare	0-5
Kidlington v Salisbury	1-1
Kidlington won 4-2 on penalties	
Aylesbury U v Moneyfields	2-2
Moneyfields won 4-3 on penalties	
Taunton T v Wantage T	5-0
Winchester C v Clevedon T	3-2
Larkhall Ath v Bitton	3-2
Tiverton T v Bideford	2-0
Tadley Calleva v Truro C	0-1
Barnstaple T v Wimborne T	2-3
Yate T v Bristol Manor Farm	1-2
Highworth T v Melksham T	1-1
Melksham T won 5-4 on penalties	
Merthyr T v Poole T (walkover)	
Frome T v AFC Stoneham	4-1
Christchurch v Dorchester T	2-1
Swindon Supermarine v Shepton Mallet	3-0
Saltash U v Cirencester T	3-1

SECOND QUALIFYING ROUND

Guiseley v Atherton Colleries	4-0
Mossley v Tadcaster Alb	1-1
Tadcaster Alb won 4-3 on penalties	
Chorley v Gateshead	2-1
Southport v Morpeth T	2-1
Stalybridge Celtic v Longridge T	2-3
Whitley Bay v Blyth Spartans	2-4
Farsley Celtic v Radcliffe	2-1
Runcorn Linnets v Marine	1-1
Marine won 4-3 on penalties	
Ashton U v South Shields	0-4
Curzon Ashton v FC United of Manchester	1-2
Darlington v Prescot Cables	2-2
Darlington won 5-4 on penalties	
Bradford (Park Avenue) v Spennymoor T	1-3
Warrington Rylands v York C	0-1
Hyde U v AFC Fylde	2-4
Marske U v Consett	6-0
Skelmersdale U v Lancaster C	2-1
Boston U v AFC Mansfield	4-2
Hednesford T v Halesowen T	0-0
Halesowen T won 5-3 on penalties	
Coalville T v Alfreton T	1-2
Tamworth v Evesham U	3-1
Chasetown v AFC Telford U	1-1
AFC Telford U won 5-4 on penalties	
Alvechurch v Kidderminster H	2-2
Alvechurch won 4-2 on penalties	
Nantwich T v Barwell	1-0
Mickleover v Newark	4-1
Buxton v Stafford Rangers	0-0
Stafford Rangers won 4-2 on penalties	
Grantham T v Matlock T	0-1
Leamington v Banbury U	0-1
Worksop T v Chester	2-2
Chester won 5-3 on penalties	
Nuneaton Bor v Stratford T	2-1
Ilkeston T v Hanley T	4-1
AFC Dunstable v Hemel Hempstead T	1-2
Brackley T v Billericay T	2-2
Brackley T won 4-2 on penalties	

Maldon & Tiptree v Grays Ath 2-2
Maldon & Tiptree won 5-4 on penalties
Canvey Island v Biggleswade 2-2
Canvey Island won 4-3 on penalties
Cheshunt v Cambridge C 1-2
Royston T v Stamford 2-2
Royston T won 4-2 on penalties
Barking v Kings Langley 2-2
Barking won 3-2 on penalties
Hashtag U v Braintree T 1-1
Braintree T won 7-6 on penalties
St Albans C v Hitchin T 5-0
Bishop's Stortford v Brentwood T 1-0
Concord Rangers v Potters Bar T 2-1
Walthamstow v Hornchurch 0-2
Leighton T v Leiston 1-2
Brantham Ath v Aveley 0-3
Kettering T v Chelmsford C 2-0
Peterborough Sports v Stansted 4-2
Bury T v Waltham Abbey 4-1
Havant & Waterlooville v Horsham 2-1
Hayes & Yeading U v Bognor Regis T 5-0
Dartford v Slough T 0-1
Farnborough v Tonbridge Angels 0-1
Harrow Bor v Cray Valley PM 1-5
Chipstead v East Grinstead T 1-0
Chichester C v Risborough Rangers 2-1
Corinthian Casuals v Dulwich Hamlet 2-2
Dulwich Hamlet won 3-1 on penalties
Haringey Bor v Chertsey T 2-0
Folkestone Invicta v Chatham T 0-3
Hendon v Maidstone U 0-1
Hanwell T v Hartley Wintney 3-5
Moneyfields v Cray W 2-6
Ebbsfleet U v Hastings U 2-2
Ebbsfleet U won 4-1 on penalties
Sheppey U v Welling U 2-0
Corinthian v Hampton & Richmond Bor 0-1
Bedfont Sports v Carshalton Ath 2-0
Dorking W v Eastbourne Bor 3-3
Eastbourne Bor won 4-3 on penalties
Bracknell T v Marlow 2-2
Bracknell T won 4-3 on penalties
Metropolitan Police v Walton Casuals 1-2
Burnham v Whyteleafe 1-3
Weston-super-Mare v Swindon Supermarine 2-2
Weston-super-Mare won 4-2 on penalties
Truro C v Hungerford T 4-0
Saltash U v Sholing 1-3
Frome T v Larkhall Ath 1-1
Larkhall Ath won 4-3 on penalties
Christchurch v Gloucester C 1-1
Christchurch won 6-5 on penalties
Tiverton T v Taunton T 3-5
Gosport Bor v Hereford 1-3
Bath C v Winchester C 3-2
Wimborne T v Melksham T 0-0
Wimborne T won 5-4 on penalties
Kidlington v Bristol Manor Farm 1-1
Bristol Manor Farm won 7-6 on penalties
Royal Wootton Bassett T v Oxford C 1-2
Chippenham T v Poole T 2-2
Chippenham T won 5-4 on penalties

THIRD QUALIFYING ROUND
Southport v South Shields 1-1
South Shields won 4-2 on penalties
Longridge T v Skelmersdale U 0-1
Chester v Spennymoor T 3-1
Marske U v Blyth Spartans 1-0
Farsley Celtic v AFC Fylde 1-3
Darlington v Tadcaster Alb 6-1
Marine v Nantwich T 4-1
Chorley v York C 1-0
Guiseley v Matlock T 2-0
FC United of Manchester (walkover) v Alfreton T
St Albans C v Mickleover 1-1
St Albans C won 4-3 on penalties
Braintree T v Maldon & Tiptree 0-1
Ilkeston T v Alvechurch 1-0
Bishop's Stortford v Royston T 3-0
Stafford Rangers v Hereford 3-1
Peterborough Sports v Banbury U 1-1
Banbury U won 7-6 on penalties
Leiston v AFC Telford U 0-0
Leiston won 9-8 on penalties
Brackley T (walkover) v Kettering T
Cambridge C v Halesowen T 2-0
Oxford C v Tamworth 6-1
Bury T v Nuneaton Bor 2-0
Boston U v Hemel Hempstead T (walkover)
Haringey Bor v Bracknell T 5-1
Havant & Waterlooville v Chatham T 4-1
Bedfont Sports v Canvey Island 0-2
Cray Valley PM v Aveley 2-0
Hartley Wintney v Barking 3-1
Bristol Manor Farm v Cray W 3-3
Cray W won 4-2 on penalties
Eastbourne Bor v Sheppey U 3-1
Hayes & Yeading U v Chipstead 0-0
Hayes & Yeading U won 4-2 on penalties
Slough T v Bath C 0-1
Taunton T v Truro C 4-2
Christchurch v Dulwich Hamlet 1-1
Dulwich Hamlet won 3-1 on penalties
Wimborne T v Maidstone U 2-2
Wimborne T won 3-1 on penalties
Sholing v Walton Casuals 5-2
Chichester C v Tonbridge Angels 1-2
Weston-super-Mare v Larkhall Ath 6-0
Hampton & Richmond Bor v Hornchurch 2-2
Hampton & Richmond Bor won 4-3 on penalties
Whyteleafe v Concord Rangers 1-2
Ebbsfleet U v Chippenham T 1-1
Chippenham T won 9-8 on penalties

FOURTH QUALIFYING ROUND
Darlington v Cambridge C 2-0
Stafford Rangers v Skelmersdale U 1-4
Solihull Moors v Wrexham 4-0
Banbury U v Bury T 2-1
South Shields v FC Halifax T 2-0
Ilkeston T v Hartlepool U 0-6
FC United of Manchester v Guiseley 2-1
Brackley T v Marske U 5-1
King's Lynn T (walkover) v Notts Co
Stockport Co v Chesterfield 4-0
AFC Fylde v Altrincham 2-1
Chester v Marine 0-1
Maidenhead U v Cray Valley PM 2-3
Canvey Island v Cray W 3-2
Wealdstone v Hayes & Yeading U 0-2
Sutton U v Bromley 0-1
Tonbridge Angels v Taunton T 5-0
Hemel Hempstead T v Hampton & Richmond Bor 0-1
Aldershot T v Woking 1-2
Maldon & Tiptree v Haringey Bor 1-0
Dagenham & R v Hartley Wintney 1-0
Leiston v Barnet 2-3
Weymouth v Oxford C 2-3
Eastbourne Bor v Dulwich Hamlet 1-0
Eastleigh v Weston-super-Mare 3-1
Sholing v Torquay U 0-2
Bath C v Havant & Waterlooville 0-3
Boreham Wood v Wimborne T 2-0
Yeovil T v Dover Ath 3-3
Yeovil T won 7-6 on penalties
Bishop's Stortford v St Albans C 2-0
Concord Rangers v Chippenham T 2-1
Chorley (bye)

THE EMIRATES FA CUP 2020–21

COMPETITION PROPER

▪ *Denotes player sent off.*
Due to COVID-19 pandemic, matches played behind closed doors unless otherwise stated.

FIRST ROUND

Friday, 6 November 2020

Harrogate T (2) 4 *(Miller 1, Beck 45, Lawlor 68, Martin 73)*

Skelmersdale U (0) 1 *(Mitchley 89)*

Harrogate T: (442) Cracknell; Burrell, Lawlor, Lokko, Jones; Walker (Thomson 63), Kirby, Falkingham, Miller (Kiernan 63); Muldoon (Martin 69), Beck.
Skelmersdale U: (451) Barnes; Griffiths, Murphy, Herbert, Preston; Grimshaw (Ellis 75), Grogan, Peet (Croughan 69), Ellams, Adegbenro (Brodie 75); Mitchley.
Referee: Robert Madley.

Saturday, 7 November 2020

Banbury U (0) 1 *(Johnson 68)*

Canvey Island (1) 2 *(Hubble 23, Ronto 71)*

Banbury U: (433) Harding; Roberts, Langmead, Westbrook, Brown; Self, Haysham (Finch 65 (Constable 81)), Rasulo; Landers, Johnson, Morrison (Awadh 56).
Canvey Island: (4132) Mason; Humphreys, Finneran, Hall, Sampayo; Salmon; Ronto, Chatting (Girdlestone 84), Hubble; Joseph, Kouassi (Siva 89).
Referee: Lewis Smith.

Bolton W (1) 2 *(Delfouneso 37, 78)*

Crewe Alex (1) 3 *(Mandron 29, Finney 70, Kirk 75)*

Bolton W: (343) Crellin; Baptiste, Santos, Delaney; Kioso, Sarcevic, White (Tutte 76), Gordon; Darcy (Miller 61), Crawford (Isgrove 68), Delfouneso.
Crewe Alex: (433) Jaaskelainen; Ng (Johnson 80), Beckles, Offord, Pickering; Finney (Ainley 70), Wintle, Lowery; Powell (Dale 70), Mandron, Kirk.
Referee: Robert Lewis.

Boreham Wood (1) 3 *(Fyfield 8, Ricketts 51, Tshimanga 93 (pen))*

Southend U (0) 3 *(Goodship 59, Egbri 62, Olayinka 100)*

Boreham Wood: (352) Ashmore; Champion, Fyfield, Ilesanmi (Coulthirst 120); Smith, Mafuta, Ricketts (Stephens 90), Whitely (Mingoia 89), Thomas; Rhead, Tshimanga.
Southend U: (541) Oxley; Bwomono, Hobson, Dieng, Lennon (Sterling 120), Clifford; Nathaniel-George, Demetriou, Olayinka, Goodship (Rush 117); Acquah (Egbri 58).
aet; Boreham Wood won 4-3 on penalties.
Referee: Ben Toner.

Brackley T (2) 3 *(Ndlovu 14, Lowe 21, Mitford 69)*

Bishop's Stortford (0) 3 *(Foxley 65, 87, Richardson 72)*

Brackley T: (442) Lewis; Myles, Coleman, Walker (Flowers 105), Franklin (Dean 69); Lowe, Byrne, Murombedzi, Chambers (York 57); Mitford (Armson 84), Ndlovu.
Bishop's Stortford: (4411) Giddens; Robbins, Henshaw, Haines, Mvemba; Foxley (Johnson 105), Thomas, Jones, Greene (Davidson 46); Marlow (Richardson 46); Merrifield.
aet; Brackley T won 3-2 on penalties.
Referee: Adrian Quelch.

Bromley (0) 0

Yeovil T (0) 1 *(Rogers 120)*

Bromley: (4231) Cousins; Kizzi, Bush, Roberts, Kyprianou (Holland 66); Trotter (Bingham 55), Raymond; Williamson (Alabi 73), Hackett-Fairchild (L'Ghoul 112), Forster▪; Cheek.
Yeovil T: (41212) Smith A; Bradley, Wilkinson, Williams, Dickinson; Lee; Skendi, D'Ath (Rogers 106); Warburton (Smith J 98); Quigley, Murphy.
aet.
Referee: Antony Coggins.

Cambridge U (0) 0

Shrewsbury T (0) 2 *(Daniels C 47, Walker 89)*

Cambridge U: (451) Mitov; Knoyle, Cundy, Taylor, Dunk; Hannant, May (Hoolahan 67), El Mizouni (Dallas 76), Boateng, Iredale (Knowles 76); Knibbs.
Shrewsbury T: (433) Burgoyne; Williams, Walker, Pierre, Daniels C; High, Edwards (Ebanks-Landell 83), Norburn; Daniels J (Barnett 69), Udoh, Pugh (Millar 90).
Referee: Peter Wright.

Charlton Ath (0) 0

Plymouth Arg (0) 1 *(Jephcott 60)*

Charlton Ath: (4231) Maynard-Brewer; Matthews, Inniss, Barker, Purrington; Forster-Caskey (Maatsen 84), Levitt; Maddison (Vennings 65), Morgan, Williams; Aneke (Washington 65).
Plymouth Arg: (352) Cooper M; Aimson, Opoku, Watts; Edwards, Camara (Grant C 90), Fornah, Mayor, Moore B; Jephcott (Nouble 75), Hardie (Telford 75).
Referee: Neil Hair.

Cheltenham T (1) 3 *(May 12, 53, Sercombe 62)*

South Shields (1) 1 *(Osei 18)*

Cheltenham T: (352) Griffiths; Tozer, Boyle, Freestone (Addai 79); Blair, Sercombe, Thomas, Chapman, Hussey; Reid (Williams 79), May.
South Shields: (3412) Boney; Baxter (Lowe 60), Morse, Adams; Hunter, Turnbull, Ross, Kempster (Gillies 69); Briggs; Osei (McCamley 21), Gilchrist.
Referee: Martin Woods.

Colchester U (0) 1 *(Pell 64)*

Marine (1) 1 *(Miley 22)*

Colchester U: (4231) Gerken; Welch-Hayes (Smith 61), Eastman, Sowunmi, Bramall; Pell, Chilvers; Senior, Poku (Folivi 81), Harriott (Bohui 18); Brown.
Marine: (433) Passant; Solomon-Davies, Miley, Raven, Joyce; Hmami (Howard 82), Doyle (Devine 86), Barrigan (Hughes 99); Kengni-Kuemo, Cummins (Strickland 105), Touray.
aet; Marine won 5-3 on penalties.
Referee: Sam Allison.

Dagenham & R (1) 3 *(Wilson 10, 90, Brundle 90 (pen))*

Grimsby T (0) 1 *(Windsor 60 (pen))*

Dagenham & R: (442) Justham; Wright, Croll, Clark, Johnson; Weston, Brundle, Ogogo (Adams 85), Deering; Wilson (McQueen 90), Balanta (Saunders 66).
Grimsby T: (433) McKeown; Hendrie, Pollock, Waterfall, Preston; Clifton, Rose (Scannell 87), Morton; Windsor (Gibson 81), Green (Williams 68), Bennett.
Referee: Craig Hicks.

Exeter C (2) 2 *(Jay 26, Hartridge 33)*

AFC Fylde (1) 1 *(Hulme 11)*

Exeter C: (352) Andersson; Sweeney, Hartridge, McArdle; Caprice (Key 82), Kite (Taylor 62), Law, Jay, Sparkes; Seymour, Bowman (Randall 67).
AFC Fylde: (442) Neal; Burke, Sanders, Whitmore, Conlan; Shaw (Mondal 89), Lussey (Perkins 67), Philliskirk, Tollitt; Haughton (Willoughby 81), Hulme.
Referee: Tom Reeves.

FC United of Manchester (1) 1 *(Linney 30)*

Doncaster R (4) 5 *(Okenabirhie 13, Whiteman 21, Sims 33, 50, Coppinger 42)*

FC United of Manchester: (4141) Lavercombe; Donohue, Jones, Doyle, Dodd; Simpson (Morris 57); Linney, Griffiths, Potts, Sinclair-Smith (Fowler 57); Ennis (Cockerline 74).
Doncaster R: (4231) Jones; Halliday, Wright, Anderson, James; Smith, Whiteman; Williams (Lokilo 58), Coppinger (Ravenhill 82), Sims (John 66); Okenabirhie.
Referee: Thomas Bramall.

Gillingham (0) 3 *(Samuel 59, 68, Oliver 79)*

Woking (1) 2 *(Kretzschmar 23, Davison 55)*

Gillingham: (433) Bonham; Jackson, Tucker, Drysdale, Ogilvie; McKenzie, Dempsey, O'Connor (Coyle 59); Samuel, Akinde (Oliver 46), Graham.
Woking: (4312) Ross; Reid, Cook, Shotton, Casey; Dempsey (Tarpey 83), Cooper, Ferdinand; Kretzschmar (Wareham 86); Spasov, Davison.
Referee: Christopher Sarginson.

Hull C (1) 2 *(Magennis 31, Burke 63)*

Fleetwood T (0) 0

Hull C: (433) Long; Emmanuel, Burke, Greaves, Elder; Jones A, Honeyman (Slater 75), Smallwood; Wilks (Mayer 80), Magennis, Scott (Lewis-Potter 61).
Fleetwood T: (433) Leutwiler; Edwards (Finley 64), Connolly, Holgate, Andrew; Coutts, Camps, Whelan; Saunders (Morris J 46), Evans (Burns 12), Madden.
Referee: Marc Edwards.

Ipswich T (1) 2 *(Nolan 43, Norwood 66)*

Portsmouth (2) 3 *(Curtis 11, Naylor 13, Raggett 111)*

Ipswich T: (433) Cornell; Donacien, Nsiala, McGuinness, Kenlock; Nolan, McGavin, Huws (Judge 102); Bennetts (Edwards 68), Hawkins (Norwood 62), Sears (Lankester 94).
Portsmouth: (442) MacGillivray; Johnson (Mnoga 51), Raggett, Nicolaisen, Pring; Harness, Cannon (Close 23), Naylor, Curtis (Harrison 74); Marquis (Morris 91), Williams.
aet.
Referee: Andy Haines.

Leyton Orient (1) 1 *(Kyprianou 40)*

Newport Co (1) 2 *(Baker 37, Devitt 77)*

Leyton Orient: (433) Vigouroux; Widdowson (Maguire-Drew 81), Turley, Coulson, Akinola; McAnuff, Kyprianou, Dayton (Clay 64); Wilkinson (Brophy 68), Johnson, Dennis.
Newport Co: (3412) Townsend; Demetriou, Dolan, Cooper; Baker, Bennett, Sheehan, Haynes; Devitt (Willmott 85); Proctor (Ellison 85), Abrahams (Amond 90).
Referee: James Adcock.

Lincoln C (2) 6 *(Grant 17, 24 (pen), Johnson 64, Scully 78, 88, Jones 90)*

Forest Green R (0) 2 *(Whitehouse 82, Young 90)*

Lincoln C: (433) Palmer; Anderson, Jackson, Roughan, Melbourne; Gotts, Grant (McGrandles 72), Edun (Jones 72); Scully, Johnson, Archibald (Elbouzedi 77).
Forest Green R: (3412) Thomas; Godwin-Malife, Sweeney (Moore-Taylor 62), Kitching; Wilson, Whitehouse, Winchester, Cadden (Collins 65); Bailey; Young, Stevens (March 72).
Referee: Sam Barrott.

Oxford U (1) 1 *(Ruffels 45)*

Peterborough U (1) 2 *(Dembele 23, Taylor 63)*

Oxford U: (433) Stevens; Forde, Moore, Long, Ruffels; Sykes, Kelly, McGuane (Asonganyi 86); Hall (Cooper 75), Taylor (Winnall 65), Shodipo.
Peterborough U: (3412) Pym; Kent, Mason, Blake-Tracy; Thompson (Edwards 43), Reed (Brown 87), Taylor, Broom; Hamilton (Clarke-Harris 75); Dembele, Eisa.
Referee: Ben Speedie.

Port Vale (0) 0

King's Lynn T (0) 1 *(Carey 82)*

Port Vale: (433) Brown; Clark, Legge, Smith, Crookes; Conlon (McKirdy 76), Joyce, Burgess; Amoo, Pope, Worrall (Robinson 85).
King's Lynn T: (451) Mair; Barrows, McAuley, Lupano, Brown; Power (Marriott 68), Clunan, Jarvis, Richards, Loza (Carey 69); Southwell (Smith 89).
Referee: David Richardson.

Rochdale (1) 1 *(Lund 22)*

Stockport Co (2) 2 *(Rooney 7, Reid 14)*

Rochdale: (433) Bazunu; Keohane, O'Connell, McNulty, Bola (Dooley 74); Morley, Ryan (Tavares 72), Lund; Newby, Beesley, Rathbone.
Stockport Co: (442) Hinchliffe; Hogan, Keane, Palmer, Stott; Thomas, Croasdale (Williams 75), Rooney (Maynard 69), Kitching; Reid (Britton 86), Jennings.
Referee: Scott Oldham.

Salford C (0) 2 *(Andrade 105, Dieseruvwe 120)*

Hartlepool U (0) 0

Salford C: (442) Hladky; Bernard, Eastham (Clarke 65), Turnbull, Touray I; Hunter, Boyd (Threlkeld 64), Lowe, Thomas-Asante; Wilson (Andrade 78), Henderson (Dieseruvwe 113).
Hartlepool U: (541) Ravas; Donaldson, Cass, Magloire, Johnson, Ferguson; MacDonald (Parkhouse 57), Featherstone, Crawford (Bloomfield 106), Ofosu (Holohan 96); Oates (Molyneux 72).
aet.
Referee: Carl Boyeson.

Stevenage (1) 2 *(Coker 28, Newton 99)*

Concord Rangers (1) 2 *(Wall 43, Martin 109)*

Stevenage: (433) Cumming; Wildin, Cuthbert (Marshall 53), Prosser, Coker; Carter, Read, Pett (Osborne 110); Dinanga (Oteh 77), Effiong (Newton 66), List.
Concord Rangers: (451) Haigh; Popo, Scott, Sterling (Hanfrey 100), Pollock; Babalola (Reynolds 90), Martin, Shabani, Blackman, Raad (Bridge 81); Wall (Hughes 73).
aet; Stevenage won 5-4 on penalties.
Referee: John Busby.

Sunderland (0) 0

Mansfield T (0) 1 *(Lapslie 49)*

Sunderland: (3412) Matthews; Sanderson, McLaughlin, Flanagan; Diamond, Power, Dobson, McFadzean (O'Brien 75); Maguire (Embleton 65); Graham (Wyke 66), Grigg.
Mansfield T: (433) Stech; Gordon, Rawson, Perch, Benning; Charsley, Lapslie, Maris; Bowery, Maynard (O'Keeffe 81), McLaughlin.
Referee: Anthony Backhouse.

Swindon T (1) 1 *(Pitman 41)*

Darlington (1) 2 *(Campbell 31, 60)*

Swindon T: (4231) Kovar; Caddis, Grounds, Odimayo, Stevens (Hunt 77); Grant A, Smith M; Grant J, Payne (Hope 66), Iandolo; Pitman.
Darlington: (4321) Saltmer; Hedley, Storey, Hunt, Liddle; Reid, Wheatley, Holness (Atkinson 79); Campbell, Rivers; Charman.
Referee: Declan Bourne.

Tonbridge Angels (0) 0

Bradford C (3) 7 *(O'Connor A 6, Clarke 14, 44, Donaldson 55, Samuels 68, Pritchard 83, Connor Wood 90)*

Tonbridge Angels: (442) Henly; Parter, Miles, Lee, Campbell; Turner, Theobalds, Parkinson (Beere 51), Greenhalgh (Da Costa 58); Akrofi, Wood (Splatt 63).
Bradford C: (3412) O'Donnell; O'Connor A, O'Connor P, Staunton; Hosannah (French 62), Cooke, Watt, Connor Wood; Pritchard; Clarke (Mottley-Henry 74), Donaldson (Samuels 62).
Referee: James Oldham.

Tranmere R (1) 2 *(Blackett-Taylor 13, Clarke 84)*

Accrington S (1) 1 *(Bishop 24)*

Tranmere R: (4231) Davies; O'Connor, Clarke, Monthe, Ridehalgh; Spearing, Lewis (Khan 7); Feeney, Morris (Banks 90), Blackett-Taylor (Woolery 61); Vaughan.
Accrington S: (352) Baxter; Sykes, Hughes, Burgess; Nottingham, Russell, Butcher, Pritchard (Uwakwe 87), Conneely (Cassidy 87); Charles (Allan 72), Bishop.
Referee: Graham Salisbury.

Walsall (0) 1 *(Lavery 87)*

Bristol R (2) 2 *(Baldwin 33, Hanlan 39)*

Walsall: (442) Roberts; Norman, Scarr, Sadler (Cockerill-Mollett 58), Jules; Holden, Sinclair (Bates 58), Kinsella, McDonald; Lavery, Adebayo (Scrimshaw 63).
Bristol R: (3511) Jaakkola; Kilgour, Ehmer, Baldwin; Nicholson (Hare 76), Westbrooke (Grant 87), Upson (Liddle 74), McCormick, Koiki; Oztumer; Hanlan.
Referee: Ross Joyce.

Sunday, 8 November 2020

Barnet (1) 1 *(Fonguck 10)*

Burton Alb (0) 0

Barnet: (4231) Loach; McQueen, Nugent, Preston■, Binnom-Williams; Taylor H, Fonguck; Mason-Clarke, Petrasso (Hernandez 82), Richards (Pascal 63); Hooper (Pavey 90).
Burton Alb: (433) O'Hara; Eardley, Brayford, Hughes, Wallace (Roles 79); Edwards (Vernam 64), Powell, Daniel; Akins, Hemmings, Ennis.
Referee: Trevor Kettle.

Eastbourne Bor (0) 0

Blackpool (0) 3 *(Madine 58, 68, Yates 90)*

Eastbourne Bor: (4231) Ravizzoli; Vaughan, James, Dickenson, Cox (Rollinson 66); Hammond, Woollard-Innocent; Ferry, Walker (Gravata 81), Whelpdale (Kendall 56); Luer.
Blackpool: (442) Maxwell; Lawrence-Gabriel, Ekpiteta, Gretarsson, Husband; Hamilton (Kemp 71), Dougall (Ward 85), Turton, KaiKai; Yates, Madine (Lubala 83).
Referee: David Rock.

Eastleigh (0) 0

Milton Keynes D (0) 0

Eastleigh: (3412) McDonnell; Wynter, Boyce, Tomlinson; Smart (Bird 106), Payne (Bearwish 106), Hollands, Green; Miley; House, Smith (Barnett 76).
Milton Keynes D: (352) Nicholls; O'Hora (Sorinola 68), Cargill, Lewington; Poole, Sorensen (Bird 96), Kasumu, Thompson (Fraser 68), Harvie (Gladwin 62); Walker S, Morris.
aet; Milton Keynes D won 4-3 on penalties.
Referee: Alan Young.

Hampton & Richmond Bor (1) 2 *(Deadfield 30 (pen), 75)*

Oldham Ath (2) 3 *(Garrity 6, Grant 40, Rowe 49)*

Hampton & Richmond Bor: (4141) Julian; Steer (Minhas 89), Inman, Smith, Farrell; Miller-Rodney■; Carvalho (Coleman 65), Gray, Deadfield, Donaldson (Bassett 81); Muir.
Oldham Ath: (4141) Lawlor; Fage, Clarke, Jameson, Borthwick-Jackson; Ntambwe; Bahamboula, Garrity (Barnett 69), McCalmont, Grant; Rowe.
Referee: Sam Purkiss.

Havant & Waterlooville (1) 1 *(Gomis 18)*

Cray Valley PM (0) 0

Havant & Waterlooville: (352) Worner; Magri, Gomis, Diarra; Read, Taylor, Poku■, Deacon (Sinclair 84), McLennan (Straker 46); Wright, Iaciofano (Robson 67).
Cray Valley PM: (442) Walker; Tumkaya, Sains, Dymond, Hickey (Moraith-Gibbs 64); Gayle, A-Warren, Ibrahiym, McCann (Babalola 70); Adeyemo (Hill 79), Yusuff.
Referee: James Durkin.

Hayes & Yeading U (0) 2 *(Rowe 104, Nasha 108)*

Carlisle U (0) 2 *(Mellish 118, 120)*

Hayes & Yeading U: (4231) Smith; Downing (Johnson-Schuster 116), Robinson, McDevitt, Norville-Williams; Sheppard (Gafaiti 110), Williams; Rowe, Cunningham (Donnelly 69 (Nasha 95)), Odelusi; Amartey.
Carlisle U: (433) Dewhurst; Tanner, Hayden, Hunt, Armer (Anderton 90); Riley (Alessandra 102), Furman (Guy 78), Mellish; Kayode, Reilly, Patrick (Obiero 83).
aet; Carlisle U won 4-3 on penalties.
Referee: Ollie Yates.

Maldon & Tiptree (0) 0

Morecambe (1) 1 *(Phillips 43 (pen))*

Maldon & Tiptree: (433) McNamara; Butler, Cracknell, Stokes, Ryan-Khanye; William-Bushell (Hasanally 66), Coombes, McClenaghan (Stagg 84); Kaid, Barnwell, Kemp (Vyse 79).
Morecambe: (4231) Turner; Mellor, Lavelle, Knight-Percival, Hendrie (Cooney 19); Wildig, Songo'o; Pringle (O'Sullivan 70), Mendes Gomes, Phillips; Slew (Stockton 71).
Referee: Will Finnie.

Scunthorpe U (1) 2 *(McAtee 14, van Veen 84)*

Solihull Moors (1) 3 *(Gleeson 4 (pen), 80 (pen), Pearce 51)*

Scunthorpe U: (352) Howard; Cordner■, Bedeau, Butroid; Green, Taylor (Hallam 71), Gilliead, Spence, Brown; McAtee (Olomola 72), Dunnwald (van Veen 71).
Solihull Moors: (3421) Boot; Williams, Pearce, Hancox; Coxe, Gleeson, Storer, Cranston (Carter 72); Sbarra, Maycock (Osborne 72); Hudlin (Ward 80).
Referee: James Bell.

Torquay U (2) 5 *(Nemane 18, Whitfield 24, Umerah 90, Hall 102 (pen), 107 (pen))*

Crawley T (0) 6 *(Nichols 83 (pen), 108, 113, Tunnicliffe 90, Watters 90, Nadesan 118)*

Torquay U: (4231) Lucas Covolan; Wynter, Cameron, Sherring, Moxey; Hall, Randell; Nemane (Warren 90), Lemonheigh-Evans (Little 84), Whitfield (Waters 109); Wright (Umerah 84).
Crawley T: (433) McGill (Nelson 64); Davies, Doherty, Powell (Allarakhia 81), Craig; Hessenthaler, Tunnicliffe, Bulman (Ashford 103); Frost (Watters 73), Nadesan, Nichols.
aet.
Referee: Charles Breakspear.

Wigan Ath (2) 2 *(Garner 19, James 34)*

Chorley (0) 3 *(Newby 48, Cardwell 60, Hall 91)*

Wigan Ath: (442) Evans; James, Obi, Long■, Pearce; Massey, Perry (McHugh 110), Merrie (Crankshaw 44), Gardner (Keane 106); Garner, Joseph (Aasgaard 64).
Chorley: (4132) Urwin; Birch, Leather, Halls, Baines; Walker; Newby (Putnam 120), Calveley, Shenton (Smith 111); Cardwell (Reilly 99), Hall (Marah 106).
aet.
Referee: Martin Coy.

Monday, 9 November 2020

Oxford C (1) 2 *(Roberts 12, Ashby 68 (pen))*

Northampton T (1) 1 *(Hoskins 7)*

Oxford C: (4411) Dudzinski; Drewe, Fernandez, Oastler, Hall; Roberts, Ashby, Fleet, McEachran (Martinez 75); Coyle (Owusu 86); Bradbury (Benyon 66).
Northampton T: (352) Mitchell; Racic, Horsfall, Martin; Marshall (Rose 64), Korboa, Hoskins, Missilou, Roberts (Holmes 72); Chukwuemeka (Smith 64), Ashley-Seal.
Referee: Paul Howard.

Thursday, 26 November 2020

Barrow (0) 0

AFC Wimbledon (0) 0

Barrow: (4312) Lillis; Hird, Zouma (Brough 77), Wilson, Ntlhe (Brown 91); Gribbin, Taylor C, Kay; Sea (James 71); Angus, Reid (Quigley 86).
AFC Wimbledon: (352) Tzanev; Rudoni, Nightingale, Csoka; Alexander (McLoughlin 90), Woodyard, Hartigan, Chislett (Longman 90), Thomas; Palmer (Pigott 65), Guinness-Walker (Seddon 106).
aet; AFC Wimbledon won 4-2 on penalties.
Referee: Sebastian Stockbridge.

SECOND ROUND

Friday, 27 November 2020

Tranmere R (0) 1 *(Woolery 67)*

Brackley T (0) 0

Tranmere R: (41212) Davies; MacDonald, Clarke, Monthe, Ridehalgh; Spearing; Morris, Khan (Lewis 60); Feeney (Woolery 60); Vaughan, Blackett-Taylor (Lloyd 82).

Brackley T: (442) Lewis; McNally, Dean, Coleman (Flowers 90), Franklin (Chambers 77); Lowe, Byrne, Murombedzi, Armson; Ndlovu, Mitford (York 71).
Referee: Tom Nield.

Saturday, 28 November 2020

Bradford C (1) 1 *(Donaldson 11 (pen))*

Oldham Ath (1) 2 *(McAleny 18, Rowe 47)*

Bradford C: (3412) O'Donnell; O'Connor A, O'Connor P, Richards-Everton; Hosannah (Evans 46), Clarke (Cooke 73), Watt, Connor Wood; Ismail (Mottley-Henry 16); Donaldson, Samuels.
Oldham Ath: (4141) Lawlor; Clarke, Garrity, Piergianni, Borthwick-Jackson; Ntambwe; McAleny (Barnett 71), Fage (Jombati 78), McCalmont, Keillor-Dunn; Rowe.
Referee: Martin Coy.

Cheltenham T (1) 2 *(Azaz 2, Lloyd 94)*

Crewe Alex (0) 1 *(Porter 63)*

Cheltenham T: (352) Flinders; Raglan, Tozer, Freestone (Boyle 84); Blair, Clements, Sercombe, Azaz (Sang 74), Hussey; Lloyd (Williams 105), May.
Crewe Alex: (433) Jaaskelainen; Ng, Offord, Lancashire, Pickering; Ainley (Finney 6 (Lowery 100)), Wintle, Murphy (Zanzala 106); Powell (Dale 64), Porter, Kirk.
aet.
Referee: James Adcock.

Gillingham (1) 2 *(Oliver 21, Samuel 80)*

Exeter C (3) 3 *(Law 29, Randall 35, 40)*

Gillingham: (442) Bonham; Jackson (Akinde 84), Tucker, Maghoma (Drysdale 46), Ogilvie; Graham, McKenzie, Dempsey, MacDonald (Robertson 46); Oliver, Samuel.
Exeter C: (442) Andersson; Key, McArdle, Hartridge, Page (Sparkes 25); Williams (Taylor 79), Atangana (Sweeney 79), Collins, Law; Randall, Bowman.
Referee: Alan Young.

Harrogate T (0) 0

Blackpool (0) 4 *(Falkingham 50 (og), Ward 60, Lawrence-Gabriel 85, Kemp 90)*

Harrogate T: (442) Belshaw; Burrell, Lawlor, Lokko■, Hall; Thomson, Kerry, Falkingham (Kirby 88), Miller (Kiernan 63); Muldoon, Beck.
Blackpool: (442) Maxwell; Lawrence-Gabriel, Ekpiteta, Ballard, Garbutt; Hamilton (Mitchell 85), Dougall, Ward, Woodburn (Lubala 61); Anderson (Kemp 79), Madine.
Referee: James Oldham.

Morecambe (0) 4 *(Stockton 53, 59, O'Sullivan 95, Hancox 108 (og))*

Solihull Moors (1) 2 *(Hudlin 19, Cranston 69)*

Morecambe: (4141) Turner (Halstead 46); Mellor, Lavelle, Davis, Cooney; Songo'o; Mendes Gomes (Leitch-Smith 118), Wildig, Phillips (O'Sullivan 83), Slew (Hendrie 46); Stockton.
Solihull Moors: (343) Boot; Williams, Pearce, Hancox; Coxe, Storer, Gleeson (Ball 102), Cranston; Sbarra (Maycock 30), Hudlin (Archer 60), Osborne (Ward 70).
aet.
Referee: Ben Speedie.

Newport Co (0) 3 *(Proctor 56, Amond 75 (pen), Janneh 90)*

Salford C (0) 0

Newport Co: (3412) King; Cooper, Bennett, Demetriou; Shephard, Sheehan, Twine, Haynes (Janneh 53); Devitt (Ellison 66); Willmott, Proctor (Amond 72).
Salford C: (442) Hladky; Golden, Eastham, Turnbull, Berkoe; Fielding, Boyd (Andrade 64), Threlkeld, Thomas-Asante■; Dieseruvwe (Armstrong 69), Hawkins (Hunter 64).
Referee: Kevin Johnson.

Peterborough U (1) 1 *(Taylor 2)*

Chorley (0) 2 *(Hall 60, Calveley 62)*

Peterborough U: (3412) Pym; Kent, Beevers, Blake-Tracy; Broom (Kanu 69), Taylor, Brown, Butler (Mason 65); Szmodics (Clarke 58); Eisa, Dembele.
Chorley: (532) Urwin; Birch, Leather, Smith, Halls, Baines; Shenton (Henley 90), Calveley, Newby; Cardwell (Reilly 90), Hall (Tomlinson 86).
Referee: Darren Drysdale.

Plymouth Arg (1) 2 *(Jephcott 6, Reeves 55)*

Lincoln C (0) 0

Plymouth Arg: (352) Cooper M; Wootton, Canavan, Watts; Edwards, Grant C (Camara 72), Fornah, Reeves, Cooper G (Opoku 81); Nouble, Jephcott (Hardie 86).
Lincoln C: (433) Palmer; Anderson, Eyoma, Walsh (Grant 61), Melbourne; Gotts, Archibald (Jones 68), Edun; Scully, Johnson, McGrandles.
Referee: David Rock.

Portsmouth (2) 6 *(Nicolaisen 2, Naylor 30, Raggett 51, Harness 58, Harrison 72 (pen), Hiwula 80)*

King's Lynn T (0) 1 *(Southwell 68)*

Portsmouth: (442) Bass; Johnson, Raggett, Nicolaisen, Pring; Williams, Close, Naylor (Morris 66), Curtis (Hiwula 59); Harness, Harrison (Marquis 81).
King's Lynn T: (541) Mair; Barrows, Callan-McFadden, Smith, McAuley, Brown; Power (Gash 81), Clunan, Loza (King 63), Carey; Marriott (Southwell 63).
Referee: Will Finnie.

Sunday, 29 November 2020

AFC Wimbledon (1) 1 *(Pigott 22)*

Crawley T (1) 2 *(Nadesan 30, Watters 49)*

AFC Wimbledon: (352) Trueman; Thomas, Heneghan, Csoka; McLoughlin (Alexander 82), Chislett (Rudoni 71), Hartigan, Reilly, Seddon; Palmer (Longman 62), Pigott.
Crawley T: (532) Morris; Sesay, Tunnicliffe, Craig, Dallison, Tsaroulla (Frost 76); Hessenthaler, Bulman, Powell; Watters (Ashford 88), Nadesan.
Referee: Rob Lewis.

Barnet (0) 0

Milton Keynes D (0) 1 *(Jerome 82)*

Barnet: (4321) Loach; McQueen, Taylor H, Nugent, Binnom-Williams; Petrasso (Faal 57), Dunne, Wordsworth; Fonguck (Vasiliou 80), Mason-Clarke; Hooper.
Milton Keynes D: (352) Nicholls; Poole, Keogh, Lewington; Harvie, Freeman (Jerome 67), Houghton (Sorensen 14), Surman (Fraser 67), Williams; Morris, Walker S.
Referee: Ben Toner.

Bristol R (4) 6 *(Daly 29, Hare 38, Leahy 44 (pen), 53 (pen), Oztumer 45, Nicholson 59)*

Darlington (0) 0

Bristol R: (4231) Jaakkola; Hare, Ehmer (Kilgour 63), Baldwin, Leahy; Grant, Liddle (Harries 78); McCormick, Oztumer, Nicholson (Westbrooke 63); Daly.
Darlington: (4321) Saltmer; McMahon, Hunt, Atkinson, Watson; Hatfield (Hudson 87), Wheatley, Reid (O'Neill 46); Rivers, Campbell; Charman (Holness 63).
Referee: Brett Huxtable.

Carlisle U (0) 1 *(Mellish 78)*

Doncaster R (2) 2 *(Whiteman 32, 40)*

Carlisle U: (433) Farman; Tanner, Hayden, Bennett, Anderton; Riley (Dixon 70 (Reilly 90)), Mellish, Guy; Toure (Alessandra 70), Kayode, Patrick.
Doncaster R: (4231) Lumley; Halliday, Anderson, Wright, Amos (Lokilo 52); Whiteman, James; Richards (Gomes 63), Smith, Sims (John-Jules 75); Okenabirhie.
Referee: Scott Oldham.

Mansfield T (1) 2 *(Charsley 25, Maynard 120)*

Dagenham & R (1) 1 *(McCallum 19)*

Mansfield T: (442) Stech (Stone 120); Gordon, Rawson, Sweeney, Benning; Charsley (Maynard 115), Lapslie, Clarke O, McLaughlin (Maris 57); Bowery, Cook (Reid 76).
Dagenham & R: (442) Justham; Ogogo, Wright, Croll, Johnson; Weston (Balanta 75), Rance (Adams 110), Brundle, Deering; McCallum, Wilson (Saunders 87).
aet.
Referee: Lee Swabey.

Marine (0) 1 *(Cummins 120)*

Havant & Waterlooville (0) 0

Marine: (433) Passant; Solomon-Davies (Strickland 108), Miley, Raven, Joyce; Hmami (Wignall 104), Doyle (Devine 46), Barrigan; Kengni-Kuemo, Cummins, Touray (Hughes 120).
Havant & Waterlooville: (532) Worner; Read, Diarra, Gomis (Sinclair 81), Magri, Straker■; Deacon, Clifford (Widdrington 60 (McLennan 91)), Robson (Iaciofano 72); Taylor, Wright.
aet.
Referee: Ross Joyce.

Shrewsbury T (0) 1 *(Udoh 108)*

Oxford C (0) 0

Shrewsbury T: (3412) Sarkic; Williams, Ebanks-Landell (Golbourne 46), Pierre■; Vela, Goss (Udoh 79), Norburn, Daniels C; Edwards (Millar 57); Whalley (Cummings 91), Pugh.
Oxford C: (4411) Dudzinski; Drewe, Gerring (Matsuzaka 75), Fernandez, Hall; Roberts■, Fleet, Ashby, Coyle (Bancroft 103); McEachran (Bradbury 90); Owusu (Benyon 60).
aet.
Referee: Chris Pollard.

Stevenage (0) 1 *(List 79)*

Hull C (0) 1 *(Eaves 52 (pen))*

Stevenage: (41212) Cumming; Hutton, Vancooten, Prosser, Coker; Iontton (Read 67); Marsh (List 72), Carter (Vincelot 88); Pett; Newton, Oteh (Smith 97).
Hull C: (433) Long; Coyle, Jones A, De Wijs (Fleming 82), McLoughlin; Slater, Batty, Samuelsen (Jones C 91); Mayer (Lewis-Potter 60), Eaves, Scott (Chadwick 79).
aet; Stevenage won 6-5 on penalties.
Referee: Sam Allison.

Stockport Co (1) 3 *(Rooney 41 (pen), Palmer 76, Jennings C 100)*

Yeovil T (1) 2 *(Warburton 2, Wilkinson 70)*

Stockport Co: (442) Hinchliffe; Hogan, Keane, Palmer, Stott; Thomas (Bennett 75), Croasdale (Minihan 46), Rooney, Kitching (Williams 75); Reid, Jennings C (Maynard 106).
Yeovil T: (433) Smith A; Bradley (Leadbitter 56), Wilkinson, Staunton, Dickinson; Warburton (Smith J 99), Skendi, Lee; Quigley, Dagnall (Murphy 78), Duffus (Rogers 91).
aet.
Referee: Thomas Bramall.

Monday, 30 November 2020

Canvey Island (0) 0

Boreham Wood (2) 3 *(Tshimanga 8, Smith 28, Rhead 83)*

Canvey Island: (532) Mason; Humphreys, Finneran, Girdlestone (Chatting 64), Hall, Siva; Hubble (Lacey 90), Salmon, Ronto; Joseph (Charles 78), Kouassi.
Boreham Wood: (3412) Ashmore; Champion, Fyfield, Ilesanmi; Smith, Murtagh (McDonnell 90), Mafuta, Francis-Angol; Thomas; Rhead, Tshimanga.
Referee: Ollie Yates.

THIRD ROUND

Friday, 8 January 2021

Aston Villa (1) 1 *(Barry 41)*

Liverpool (1) 4 *(Mane 4, 63, Wijnaldum 60, Salah 65)*

Aston Villa: (451) Onodi; Walker (Rowe E 75), Revan, Bridge, Rowe C (Swinkels 75); Kesler, Raikhy (Sohna 65), Sylla, Bogarde (Lindley 66), Chrisene (Young 61); Barry.
Liverpool: (433) Kelleher; Williams N, Williams R, Fabinho, Milner; Jones (Firmino 61), Henderson (Thiago 46), Wijnaldum; Salah (Oxlade-Chamberlain 74), Mane (Origi 74), Minamino (Shaqiri 61).
Referee: Craig Pawson.

Wolverhampton W (1) 1 *(Traore 35)*

Crystal Palace (0) 0

Wolverhampton W: (433) Ruddy; Nelson Semedo, Coady, Saiss, Ait Nouri; Dendoncker (Hoever 85), Neves, Joao Moutinho; Traore (Gibbs-White 69), Silva (Cutrone 78), Pedro Neto.
Crystal Palace: (442) Butland; Clyne, Tomkins, Sakho (Kouyate 46), van Aanholt; Ayew, McCarthy (Mitchell 70), Riedewald, Eze; Benteke (Zaha 70), Batshuayi (Townsend 85).
Referee: David Coote.

Saturday, 9 January 2021

Arsenal (0) 2 *(Smith-Rowe 109, Aubameyang 117)*

Newcastle U (0) 0

Arsenal: (4231) Leno; Cedric (Maitland-Niles 120), Luiz, Pablo Mari, Tierney; Elneny, Willock (Xhaka 66); Pepe (Lacazette 106), Willian (Saka 66), Nelson (Smith-Rowe 56); Aubameyang.
Newcastle U: (541) Dubravka; Krafth (Murphy 68), Hayden, Lascelles (Ritchie 46), Clark, Dummett; Almiron (Yedlin 81), Longstaff S, Hendrick, Joelinton (Anderson 81); Carroll (Gayle 106).
aet.
Referee: Chris Kavanagh.

Blackburn R (0) 0

Doncaster R (1) 1 *(Richards 42)*

Blackburn R: (433) Pears; Buckley, Lenihan, Johnson, Bell (Douglas 46); Travis (Elliott 59), Trybull (Armstrong 64), Downing (Rothwell 59); Dolan, Dack (Davenport 73), Brereton.
Doncaster R: (4231) Balcombe; Wright, Anderson, Butler, John; Halliday, James; Okenabirhie (Amos 80), Richards (Lokilo 67), Simoes; John-Jules.
Referee: Sam Barrott.

Blackpool (1) 2 *(Yates 40, Madine 66)*

WBA (0) 2 *(Ajayi 52, Matheus Pereira 80 (pen))*

Blackpool: (442) Maxwell; Turton, Ballard (Ekpiteta 91), Gretarsson (Mitchell 99), Husband; Kemp (Virtue 82), Ward (Robson 115), Dougall, Lubala (KaiKai 75); Madine, Yates.
WBA: (4141) Button; Peltier (O'Shea 96), Bartley (Sawyers 61), Ivanovic (Kipre 72), Gibbs (Furlong 46); Ajayi; Krovinovic, Livermore, Gallagher (Edwards 61), Grosicki; Matheus Pereira.
aet; Blackpool won 3-2 on penalties.
Referee: John Brooks.

Boreham Wood (0) 0

Millwall (1) 2 *(Zohore 31, Hutchinson 74)*

Boreham Wood: (343) Ashmore; Stephens, Fyfield, Ilesanmi; Smith, Mafuta, Murtagh (Mingoia 87), Thomas; Tshimanga (Coulthirst 79), Rhead (McDonnell 87), Morias (Whitely 69).
Millwall: (343) Fielding; Hutchinson, Pearce, Cooper; McNamara, Leonard, Woods (Thompson 87), Malone; Burey (Bradshaw 60), Zohore (Bodvarsson 61), Parrott (Smith 81).
Referee: Ben Speedie.

Brentford (1) 2 *(Dervisoglu 35, Ghoddos 64)*

Middlesbrough (0) 1 *(Folarin 48)*

Brentford: (433) Daniels; Roerslev, Pinnock, Sorensen, Gordon (Haygarth 71); Ghoddos, Stevens, Gilbert; Dervisoglu (Goode 71), Forss, Fosu.
Middlesbrough: (4231) Archer; Spence, Wood-Gordon, Bola, Coulson; Wing, Hackney; Tavernier (Jones 90), Roberts, Browne (Folarin 45); Akpom (Burrell 90).
Referee: Tim Robinson.

Bristol R (1) 2 *(Kilgour 21, Ehmer 62)*

Sheffield U (1) 3 *(Day 6 (og), Burke 59, Bogle 63)*

Bristol R: (4312) Day; Ehmer, Kilgour, Baldwin, Leahy; Westbrooke, Upson (Rodman 80), McCormick; Oztumer (Grant 60); Hanlan, Ayunga (Barrett 60).
Sheffield U: (352) Ramsdale; Basham, Egan, Ampadu; Bogle, Lundstram (Bryan 74), Norwood, Fleck (Lowe 86), Osborn; McGoldrick, Mousset (Burke 53).
Referee: Keith Stroud.

Burnley (0) 1 *(Vydra 90)*

Milton Keynes D (1) 1 *(Jerome 29)*

Burnley: (442) Norris; Bardsley, Tarkowski, Mee, Pieters; Gudmundsson (Mumbongo 83), Stephens, Cork (Benson 72), Brady (Lowton 99); Barnes (Driscoll-Glennon 83), Wood (Vydra 77).
Milton Keynes D: (3511) Nicholls; Williams (Laird 62), Keogh, Lewington; Poole, Sorensen, Gladwin, Fraser, Harvie (Sorinola 68); Walker S (Mason 62); Jerome (Johnson 81).
aet; Burnley won 4-3 on penalties.
Referee: Jonathan Moss.

Chorley (1) 2 *(Hall 10, Calveley 84)*

Derby Co (0) 0

Chorley: (4132) Urwin; Birch, Leather, Halls (Henley 71), Baines; Tomlinson; Newby, Calveley, Shenton (Smith 77); Hall (Reilly 80), Cardwell.
Derby Co: (352) Yates; Jinkinson, Bateman, Solomon; Bardwell (Cybulski 73), Hutchinson, Thompson (Ibrahim 84), Aghatise (Ebosele 64), Williams; Cresswell, Duncan.
Referee: Kevin Friend.

Everton (1) 2 *(Tosun 9, Doucoure 93)*

Rotherham U (0) 1 *(Olosunde 56)*

Everton: (4231) Olsen; Coleman, Godfrey, Keane, Digne (Mina 66); Davies (Sigurdsson 66), Andre Gomes; Iwobi (Doucoure 61), Rodriguez (Nkounkou 95), Gordon (Bernard 61); Tosun.
Rotherham U: (541) Blackman; Olosunde (Jones 91), Ihiekwe, Wood, MacDonald A, Harding (Clarke 83); Lindsay (Jozefzoon 76), Barlaser, Crooks (Vassell 67), Wiles; Smith (Hirst 77).
aet.
Referee: Stuart Attwell.

Exeter C (0) 0

Sheffield W (1) 2 *(Reach 27, Paterson 90)*

Exeter C: (442) Ward; Caprice, McArdle, Parkes, Page (Sparkes 46); Key, Taylor (Atangana 77), Collins, Randall (Ajose 77); Bowman (Seymour 61), Jay (Law 61).
Sheffield W: (433) Wildsmith; Odubajo, Brennan, Shaw, Galvin (Eratt-Thompson 90); Hunt (Dele-Bashiru 64), Pelupessy, Bannan; Reach, Paterson (Rice 90), Harris.
Referee: Dean Whitestone.

Huddersfield T (2) 2 *(Crichlow-Noble 4, Rowe 32)*

Plymouth Arg (2) 3 *(Hardie 24, Camara 42, Edwards 70)*

Huddersfield T: (433) Hamer; Rowe, Olagunju (Diarra 77), Crichlow-Noble, Brown (Jackson 77); Duhaney, Vallejo, Austerfield (Camara 83); Phillips, Daly (Bright 83), Jones (Aarons 71).
Plymouth Arg: (352) Cooper M; Aimson, Opoku, Watts; Edwards, Camara, Fornah (Wootton 85), Mayor, Grant C (Moore B 85); Jephcott (Telford 82), Hardie (Nouble 78).
Referee: Martin Coy.

Luton T (1) 1 *(Moncur 30)*

Reading (0) 0

Luton T: (433) Sluga; Bree (Clark 58), Osho, Potts, Galloway (Norrington-Davies 74); Tunnicliffe, Morrell, Moncur; Lee (Berry 74), Hylton, Nombe (LuaLua 81).
Reading: (4231) Southwood; Tomas Esteves, McIntyre, Dorsett, Bristow; Pendlebury, Semedo (Lawless 77); Aluko (Tetek 72), Olise (Melvin-Lambert 78), Onen; Baldock (Camara 78).
Referee: Darren Bond.

Manchester U (1) 1 *(McTominay 5)*

Watford (0) 0

Manchester U: (4231) Henderson; Williams, Bailly (Maguire 45), Tuanzebe, Alex Telles; McTominay, van de Beek; Mata, Lingard (Matic 80), James (Rashford 69); Greenwood (Martial 69).
Watford: (442) Bachmann; Navarro, Troost-Ekong (Wilmot 76), Sierralta, Masina (Ngakia 58); Sarr (Sema 58), Chalobah (Philips 84), Hughes, Zinckernagel (Hungbo 76); Joao Pedro, Gray.
Referee: Andrew Madley.

Norwich C (2) 2 *(McLean 6, Hugill 7)*

Coventry C (0) 0

Norwich C: (4141) Barden; Mumba (Aarons 62), Zimmermann (Hanley 46), Gibson, Quintilla; Tettey; Cantwell (Emi 72), Sorensen (Skipp 88), McLean, Placheta; Hugill (Pukki 72).
Coventry C: (3421) Wilson; Ostigard, McFadzean, Hyam; Da Costa, Hamer (Bapaga 78), Sheaf (James 69), Giles; O'Hare, Shipley (Eccles 79); Biamou (Bakayoko 68).
Referee: Darren Drysdale.

Nottingham F (1) 1 *(Taylor 3)*

Cardiff C (0) 0

Nottingham F: (4231) Smith; Jenkinson, Worrall, McKenna, Bong; Arter (Sow 85), Cafu; Lolley, Guerrero (Yates 66), Ameobi (Mighten 60); Taylor.
Cardiff C: (4231) Phillips; Bacuna, Nelson, Bennett, Bagan; Vaulks (Hoilett 63), Pack (Harris 84); Wilson, Ralls, Murphy (Ojo 78); Glatzel.
Referee: David Webb.

Oldham Ath (1) 1 *(Bahamboula 45 (pen))*

Bournemouth (1) 4 *(Brooks 43, Riquelme 49, King 74, 86)*

Oldham Ath: (3421) Lawlor; Diarra (Dearnley 71), Piergianni, Clarke; Hamer, Ntambwe (McAleny 67), McCalmont, Barnett; Garrity (Whelan 78), Keillor-Dunn; Bahamboula.
Bournemouth: (433) Dennis; Stacey (Smith 67), Carter-Vickers, Simpson, Zemura (Lerma 79); Billing (Surridge 79), Kilkenny, Gosling (Rico 46); Brooks (Anthony 67), King, Riquelme.
Referee: Andy Woolmer.

QPR (0) 0

Fulham (0) 2 *(Reid 104, Kebano 105)*

QPR: (532) Dieng; Kane, Dickie, Cameron (Masterson 91), Barbet, Samuel (Hamalainen 91); Ball, Chair (Thomas 82), Carroll (Bettache 82); Dykes, Bonne (Kelman 73).
Fulham: (3142) Rodak; Aina, Ream, Kongolo (Hector 67); Reed (Kebano 78); Tete (Odoi 91), Onomah, Loftus-Cheek (Robinson 91), Bryan; Ivan Cavaleiro (Reid 67), Mitrovic.
aet.
Referee: Simon Hooper.

Stevenage (0) 0

Swansea C (1) 2 *(Routledge 7, Gyokeres 50)*

Stevenage: (442) Cumming; Wildin, Vancooten, Cuthbert, Coker; Smith (Vincelot 76), Lines (Oteh 63), Read, Pett (Norris 46); Carter, Newton (Aitchison 63).
Swansea C: (3412) Woodman; Naughton, Cabango, Evans (Bidwell 72); Garrick (Cooper 83), Fulton (Smith 46), Dhanda, Manning; Byers; Routledge (Cullen 65), Gyokeres.
Referee: Michael Salisbury.

Stoke C (0) 0

Leicester C (1) 4 *(Justin 34, Albrighton 59, Perez 79, Barnes 81)*

Stoke C: (352) Bursik; Souttar, Shawcross, Batth (Matondo 65); Smith (Collins 65), Allen, Mikel, Clucas, McClean (Thompson 65); Brown, Vokes.
Leicester C: (451) Schmeichel; Castagne, Fofana (Soyuncu 80), Evans, Justin; Albrighton, Tielemans, Ndidi, Praet (Mendy 90), Barnes (Iheanacho 82); Perez.
Referee: Tony Harrington.

Wycombe W (3) 4 *(Onyedinma 3, Jacobson 9 (pen), Knight 25, Samuel 82)*

Preston NE (1) 1 *(Jakobsen 43 (pen))*

Wycombe W: (433) Allsop; McCarthy, Knight, Tafazolli, Jacobson; Wheeler, Adeniran (Gape 66), Bloomfield (Horgan 57); Muskwe (Samuel 75), Ikpeazu (Akinfenwa 76), Onyedinma.
Preston NE: (442) Ripley; Rafferty (Fisher 74), Storey, Hughes, Earl (Huntington 46); Potts, Molumby (Maguire 75), Ledson, Bayliss (Browne 46); Jakobsen, Stockley.
Referee: Matthew Donohue.

Sunday, 10 January 2021

Barnsley (0) 2 *(Helik 59, Woodrow 90 (pen))*

Tranmere R (0) 0

Barnsley: (343) Collins; Sollbauer (Sibbick 63), Helik, Andersen; Brittain (Williams J 79), Kane, Mowatt (Palmer 72), Styles; Frieser (Thomas 46), Woodrow, Chaplin (Adeboyejo 63).
Tranmere R: (442) Davies; O'Connor, Ray, Monthe, Ridehalgh (Burton 76); Woolery, Lewis, Spearing, Khan (Morris 81); Ferrier (Blackett-Taylor 67), Vaughan.
Referee: Oliver Langford.

Bristol C (1) 2 *(Diedhiou 19, Martin 83)*

Portsmouth (1) 1 *(Johnson 45)*

Bristol C: (442) Bentley; Mariappa, Kalas, Mawson (Moore 66), Rowe; Semenyo, Nagy (Massengo 77), Bakinson (Vyner 81), Adelakun (Wells 66); Martin, Diedhiou.
Portsmouth: (442) MacGillivray; Johnson, Raggett, Nicolaisen (Whatmough 46), Brown; Harness, Naylor, Cannon, Jacobs (Hiwula 86); Williams, Marquis (Harrison 65).
Referee: Jarred Gillett.

Chelsea (2) 4 *(Mount 18, Werner 44, Hudson-Odoi 49, Havertz 85)*

Morecambe (0) 0

Chelsea: (433) Arrizabalaga; Azpilicueta, Zouma (Tomori 80), Rudiger, Emerson Palmieri; Havertz, Gilmour, Mount (Abraham 74); Ziyech (Pulisic 68), Werner (Giroud 68), Hudson-Odoi (Anjorin 80).
Morecambe: (4231) Halstead; Cooney (Mellor 62), Davis, Knight-Percival, Hendrie (Gibson 62); Wildig, Songo'o; Slew (O'Sullivan 62), Phillips, Mendes Gomes (Lyons 74); Stockton (McAlinden 86).
Referee: Darren England.

Cheltenham T (0) 2 *(May 73, Boyle 110)*

Mansfield T (1) 1 *(McLaughlin 3)*

Cheltenham T: (3412) Griffiths; Raglan (Addai 71), Tozer, Boyle; Blair, Thomas, Chapman (Clements 106), Hussey (Freestone 46); May; Williams (Campbell 112), Lloyd (Azaz 57).
Mansfield T: (4132) Stech; O'Keeffe, Rawson, Sweeney, Benning (Clarke J 115); Maris (O'Driscoll 108); Charsley, Lapslie, McLaughlin (Cook 79); Reid, Bowery.
aet.
Referee: Tom Nield.

Crawley T (0) 3 *(Tsaroulla 50, Nadesan 53, Tunnicliffe 70)*

Leeds U (0) 0

Crawley T: (442) Morris; Francomb, Tunnicliffe, Craig, Dallison (Wright M 90); Matthews (Davies 71), Hessenthaler (Doherty 90), Powell, Tsaroulla (Wright J 72); Nadesan (Watters 72), Nichols.
Leeds U: (343) Casilla; Phillips, Cooper (Casey 46), Davis (Greenwood 58); Shackleton, Struijk (Jenkins 46), Hernandez, Alioski; Poveda-Ocampo (Raphinha 58), Rodrigo (Harrison 46), Helder Costa.
Referee: Peter Bankes.

Manchester C (3) 3 *(Bernardo Silva 8, 15, Foden 33)*

Birmingham C (0) 0

Manchester C: (4141) Steffen; Joao Cancelo (Harwood-Bellis 46), Walker, Dias (Stones 46), Mendy; Rodri (Fernandinho 67); Mahrez, De Bruyne (Nmecha 46), Bernardo Silva, Foden; Gabriel Jesus (Delap 75).
Birmingham C: (4231) Andres; Colin, San Jose, Clarke-Salter, Friend; Kieftenbeld, Sunjic (Bela 67); Toral (Clayton 46), Ivan Sanchez, Leko (Jutkiewicz 68); Hogan (Roberts 46).
Referee: Robert Jones.

Marine (0) 0

Tottenham H (4) 5 *(Vinicius 24, 30, 37, Lucas Moura 32, Devine 60)*

Marine: (532) Passant; Solomon-Davies, Raven (Shaw 81), Miley, Hughes (Howard 46), Joyce; Hmami (Doyle 67), Devine (Strickland 75), Barrigan; Cummins (Wignall 75), Kengni-Kuemo.
Tottenham H: (4231) Hart; Doherty, Alderweireld (Tanganga 46), Rodon, Davies (Reguilon 71); Sissoko (Devine 46), White; Fernandes, Alli (Bale 64), Lucas Moura (Clarke 65); Vinicius.
Referee: Michael Oliver.

Newport Co (0) 1 *(Webster 90 (og))*

Brighton & HA (0) 1 *(March 90)*

Newport Co: (3421) King; Longe-King, Dolan (Ellison 90), Demetriou; Shephard, Bennett, Sheehan, Haynes; Willmott (Labadie 39), Devitt (Collins 63 (Proctor 90)); Amond (Taylor 62).
Brighton & HA: (343) Steele; White (Veltman 108), Webster, Dunk; Jahanbakhsh (Tau 71), Gross, Bissouma, March (Bernardo 90); Zeqiri (Propper 63), Maupay, Mac Allister (Trossard 63).
aet; Brighton & HA won 4-3 on penalties.
Referee: Lee Mason.

Monday, 11 January 2021

Stockport Co (0) 0

West Ham U (0) 1 *(Dawson 83)*

Stockport Co: (4231) Hinchliffe; Minihan (Palmer 86), Keane, Hogan, Kitching; Croasdale, Maynard; Jennings C (Southam-Hales 82), Rooney (Hinchy 86), Williams (Thomas 86); Reid (Bennett 62).
West Ham U: (4231) Randolph; Coufal, Dawson, Ogbonna, Johnson (Cresswell 73); Noble, Rice; Yarmolenko (Bowen 68), Lanzini (Soucek 68), Benrahma (Fornals 90); Antonio (Odubeko 90).
Referee: Mike Dean.

Tuesday, 19 January 2021

Southampton (1) 2 *(N'Lundulu 17, Ward-Prowse 89)*

Shrewsbury T (0) 0

Southampton: (442) Forster; Valery, Bednarek, Stephens, Vokins; Chauke (Armstrong 79), Ward-Prowse, Diallo (Finnigan 90), Watts (Jankewitz 85); Long (Adams 79), N'Lundulu.
Shrewsbury T: (3412) Sarkic; Ebanks-Landell, Pierre, Pennington (Cummings 84); Williams, Norburn (Edwards 74), Vela, Golbourne (Sears 73); Chapman (Tracey 63); Whalley, Udoh (Pyke 73).
Referee: Simon Hooper.

FOURTH ROUND

Friday, 22 January 2021

Chorley (0) 0

Wolverhampton W (1) 1 *(Vitinha 12)*

Chorley: (532) Urwin; Birch, Halls, Leather, Baines (Miller 84), Shenton (Henley 84); Calveley, Tomlinson, Newby; Hall (Smith 87), Cardwell.
Wolverhampton W: (3412) Ruddy; Boly, Coady, Kilman; Hoever, Dendoncker, Joao Moutinho (Neves 68), Ait Nouri; Vitinha (Traore 69); Silva, Cutrone (Pedro Neto 69).
Referee: Anthony Taylor.

Saturday, 23 January 2021

Barnsley (0) 1 *(Styles 56)*

Norwich C (0) 0

Barnsley: (343) Collins; Sibbick (Sollbauer 64), Helik, Andersen; Brittain, Mowatt, Palmer (Kane 46), Styles; Frieser (Miller 79), Woodrow (Schmidt 79), Adeboyejo (Chaplin 57).
Norwich C: (4231) Krul; Aarons, Hanley, Gibson, Sorensen; Tettey (Skipp 63), Rupp (Vrancic 77); Hernandez (Emi 64), Dowell (Martin 77), Placheta; Hugill (Omotoye 65).
Referee: John Brooks.

Brighton & HA (1) 2 *(Bissouma 27, Alzate 58)*

Blackpool (1) 1 *(Madine 45)*

Brighton & HA: (3421) Walton; Webster, Dunk, Burn; Veltman, Propper, Bissouma, Alzate (March 61); Tau (Maupay 61), Mac Allister (Trossard 61); Zeqiri (Gross 76).
Blackpool: (532) Maxwell; Lawrence-Gabriel, Ekpiteta, Thorniley (KaiKai 77), Husband, Garbutt; Virtue (Lubala 77), Williams, Robson; Madine (Sarkic 77), Yates (Simms 66).
Referee: Darren England.

Cheltenham T (0) 1 *(May 59)*

Manchester C (0) 3 *(Foden 81, Gabriel Jesus 84, Torres 90)*

Cheltenham T: (352) Griffiths; Raglan, Tozer, Boyle; Blair, Azaz (Williams 81), Thomas, Clements (Addai 88), Freestone; May, Lloyd (Long 68).
Manchester C: (442) Steffen; Harwood-Bellis (Dias 67), Garcia, Laporte, Mendy (Joao Cancelo 77); Mahrez, Doyle (Gundogan 68), Fernandinho, Foden; Torres, Gabriel Jesus.
Referee: Stuart Attwell.

Millwall (0) 0

Bristol C (1) 3 *(Diedhiou 32 (pen), Wells 58, Semenyo 72)*

Millwall: (442) Fielding; Romeo, Pearce, Cooper, Ferguson; Bradshaw, Leonard, Thompson (Woods 76), Bennett (Skalak 76); Zohore (Smith 63), Parrott (Burey 63).
Bristol C: (442) O'Leary; Mariappa, Kalas, Moore, Rowe; Semenyo (Adelakun 76), Vyner (Edwards 80), Bakinson, Palmer (Massengo 75); Diedhiou (Martin 76), Wells (Bell 87).
Referee: Tony Harrington.

Sheffield U (1) 2 *(Basham 39, Sharp 47)*

Plymouth Arg (0) 1 *(Camara 75)*

Sheffield U: (352) Ramsdale; Basham, Egan, Ampadu; Bogle (Baldock 71), Lundstram, Norwood (Bryan 72), Fleck, Stevens; Brewster (McGoldrick 79), Sharp (Burke 79).
Plymouth Arg: (352) Cooper M; Aimson, Opoku, Watts; Edwards, Camara (Nouble 88), Fornah (Reeves 59), Mayor, Grant C; Jephcott (Moore B 64), Hardie (Telford 64).
Referee: Lee Mason.

Southampton (1) 1 *(Gabriel 24 (og))*

Arsenal (0) 0

Southampton: (442) Forster; Walker-Peters, Bednarek, Stephens, Bertrand; Armstrong, Ward-Prowse, Diallo, Walcott; Ings (Long 85), Adams (N'Lundulu 78).
Arsenal: (4231) Leno; Bellerin (Lacazette 72), Holding, Gabriel, Cedric; Elneny (Thomas 57), Xhaka; Pepe, Willian, Martinelli (Saka 58); Nketiah.
Referee: Peter Bankes.

Swansea C (2) 5 *(Cullen 7, 67, Grimes 29, 61 (pen), Cooper 84)*

Nottingham F (0) 1 *(Knockaert 56)*

Swansea C: (3412) Woodman; Latibeaudiere, Bennett, Guehi (Bidwell 66); Roberts (Garrick 76), Hourihane (Cooper 66), Grimes (Fulton 65), Manning; Dhanda; Routledge (Lowe 20), Cullen.
Nottingham F: (4231) Smith; Jenkinson, Tobias Figueiredo, Worrall, Bong (Blackett 76); Mbe Soh, Bachirou (Cafu 46); Knockaert (Mighten 76), Freeman (Guerrero 46), Lolley; Taylor.
Referee: Kevin Friend.

West Ham U (2) 4 *(Fornals 2, Yarmolenko 32, Butler 53 (og), Afolayan 78)*

Doncaster R (0) 0

West Ham U: (4231) Fabianski (Trott 83); Fredericks (Baptiste 83), Balbuena, Diop, Johnson; Noble, Soucek (Afolayan 70); Fornals, Lanzini, Benrahma; Yarmolenko.
Doncaster R: (4231) Balcombe; Wright (Amos 79), Anderson, Butler, John; Halliday, Smith (Richards 64); Taylor (Williams 70), James, Lokilo (Simoes 64); Okenabirhie.
Referee: Rob Jones.

Sunday, 24 January 2021

Brentford (1) 1 *(Sorensen 7)*

Leicester C (0) 3 *(Under 46, Tielemans 51 (pen), Maddison 71)*

Brentford: (4231) Daniels; Roerslev, Pinnock, Sorensen, Stevens; Janelt (Jensen 64), Ghoddos (Gilbert 79); Canos (Pressley 64), Zamburek (Haygarth 84), Fosu; Forss.
Leicester C: (4231) Ward; Ricardo Pereira (Castagne 69), Amartey, Soyuncu, Thomas; Mendy (Ndidi 70), Tielemans; Under (Iheanacho 76), Maddison, Barnes; Perez (Albrighton 81).
Referee: Michael Oliver.

Chelsea (2) 3 *(Abraham 11, 17, 74)*

Luton T (1) 1 *(Clark 30)*

Chelsea: (4231) Arrizabalaga; James, Christensen, Zouma, Emerson Palmieri; Mount (Kovacic 84), Gilmour; Ziyech (Havertz 77), Werner, Pulisic (Hudson-Odoi 70); Abraham (Giroud 77).
Luton T: (532) Sluga; Bree (LuaLua 61), Lockyer, Rea (Potts 46), Bradley, Naismith (Moncur 75); Tunnicliffe (Berry 61), Dewsbury-Hall, Clark; Cornick (Collins 60), Mpanzu.
Referee: David Coote.

Everton (1) 3 *(Calvert-Lewin 29, Richarlison 59, Mina 62)*

Sheffield W (0) 0

Everton: (4231) Olsen; Coleman, Mina, Holgate, Godfrey (Kenny 76); Doucoure, Andre Gomes (Onyango 85); Rodriguez (Small 85), Sigurdsson, Richarlison (Gordon 76); Calvert-Lewin (Bernard 67).
Sheffield W: (3421) Wildsmith; Urhoghide, Brennan, Borner; Harris, Pelupessy, Bannan (Dele-Bashiru 68), Galvin (Penney 60); Reach (Marriott 80), Green (Windass 46); Paterson (Brown 60).
Referee: Graham Scott.

Fulham (0) 0

Burnley (1) 3 *(Rodriguez 31, 71 (pen), Long 81)*

Fulham: (3142) Rodak; Hector, Ream, Adarabioyo (Odoi 82); Onomah; Reid (Kebano 68), Lemina (Carvalho 82), Zambo (Loftus-Cheek 68), Bryan; Kamara, Mitrovic.
Burnley: (442) Peacock-Farrell; Bardsley, Long, Tarkowski (Dunne 86), Pieters (Lowton 87); Gudmundsson, Stephens, Cork, McNeil (Benson 86); Rodriguez (Mumbongo 89), Vydra.
Referee: Andrew Madley.

Manchester U (1) 3 *(Greenwood 26, Rashford 48, Bruno Fernandes 78)*

Liverpool (1) 2 *(Salah 18, 58)*

Manchester U: (4231) Henderson; Wan Bissaka, Lindelof, Maguire, Shaw; McTominay, Pogba; Greenwood (Fred 66), van de Beek (Bruno Fernandes 66), Rashford (Martial 86); Cavani.
Liverpool: (433) Alisson; Alexander-Arnold, Williams R, Fabinho, Robertson; Wijnaldum (Mane 62), Thiago (Shaqiri 81), Milner; Salah, Firmino (Origi 81), Jones.
Referee: Craig Pawson.

Monday, 25 January 2021

Wycombe W (1) 1 *(Onyedinma 25)*

Tottenham H (1) 4 *(Bale 45, Winks 86, Ndombele 87, 90)*

Wycombe W: (4231) Allsop; McCarthy, Grimmer, Knight, Jacobson (Charles 34); Bloomfield (McCleary 61), Thompson; Wheeler, Muskwe (Kashket 73), Onyedinma; Ikpeazu (Akinfenwa 72).
Tottenham H: (4231) Hart; Tanganga (Hojbjerg 46), Sanchez, Alderweireld, Davies (Rodon 90); Winks, Sissoko; Bale, Lamela (Ndombele 68), Lucas Moura (Son 68); Vinicius (Kane 58).
Referee: Jonathan Moss.

Tuesday, 26 January 2021

Bournemouth (1) 2 *(Wilshere 24, King 65)*

Crawley T (0) 1 *(Nichols 59)*

Bournemouth: (433) Begovic; Stacey (Smith 66), Cook S, Kelly, Rico; Cook L, Wilshere (Solanke 67), Billing (Lerma 67); Brooks, King (Surridge 83), Danjuma (Riquelme 78).
Crawley T: (442) Morris; Adebowale (Sesay 51), Tunnicliffe, McNerney, Dallison; Matthews (Rodari 69), Hessenthaler, Powell, Tsaroulla (Wright J 29); Nadesan, Nichols.
Referee: Andre Marriner.

FIFTH ROUND

Tuesday, 9 February 2021

Burnley (0) 0

Bournemouth (1) 2 *(Surridge 21, Stanislas 88 (pen))*

Burnley: (442) Peacock-Farrell; Bardsley, Long, Dunne, Driscoll-Glennon; Gudmundsson (Lowton 74), Stephens, Benson (Westwood 65), McNeil; Rodriguez (Barnes 74), Vydra (Mumbongo 74).
Bournemouth: (433) Begovic; Stacey (Mepham 46), Carter-Vickers, Cook S, Rico; Pearson, Lerma, Billing; Brooks (Cook L 63), Surridge, Stanislas.
Referee: Darren England.

Manchester U (0) 1 *(McTominay 97)*

West Ham U (0) 0

Manchester U: (4231) Henderson; Wan Bissaka (Williams 91), Lindelof, Maguire, Alex Telles (Shaw 91); Fred, Matic (McTominay 73); Greenwood (Cavani 86), van de Beek (Bruno Fernandes 73), Rashford; Martial.
West Ham U: (4231) Fabianski; Coufal, Dawson, Ogbonna (Diop 16 (Fredericks 46)), Cresswell; Noble, Rice; Bowen (Johnson 46), Soucek, Fornals (Benrahma 88); Yarmolenko (Odubeko 54 (Lanzini 112)).
aet.
Referee: Paul Tierney.

Wednesday, 10 February 2021

Everton (3) 5 *(Calvert-Lewin 36, Richarlison 38, 68, Sigurdsson 43 (pen), Bernard 97)*

Tottenham H (2) 4 *(Sanchez 4, Lamela 45, Sanchez 57, Kane 83)*

Everton: (4231) Olsen; Godfrey, Mina, Keane, Digne (Holgate 107); Doucoure, Davies; Iwobi (Bernard 70), Sigurdsson, Richarlison; Calvert-Lewin (Coleman 55).
Tottenham H: (4231) Lloris; Doherty (Sissoko 98), Sanchez, Alderweireld, Davies; Ndombele (Winks 91), Hojbjerg; Lamela (Vinicius 98), Lucas Moura (Alli 77), Bergwijn (Kane 53); Son.
aet.
Referee: David Coote.

Leicester C (0) 1 *(Iheanacho 90)*

Brighton & HA (0) 0

Leicester C: (343) Ward; Amartey, Soyuncu, Justin (Fuchs 75); Daley-Campbell, Ndidi (Choudhury 62), Tielemans, Thomas; Under, Vardy (Iheanacho 62), Perez (Maddison 62).
Brighton & HA: (352) Walton; White (Veltman 71), Dunk, Burn; Karbownik, Gross, Lallana (Bissouma 79), Moder, Alzate (Mac Allister 79); Tau, Zeqiri.
Referee: Mike Dean.

Sheffield U (0) 1 *(Sharp 66 (pen))*

Bristol C (0) 0

Sheffield U: (3412) Ramsdale; Basham, Egan, Ampadu; Bogle, Lundstram, Fleck, Lowe; McGoldrick; Brewster (Burke 83), Sharp (Norwood 73).
Bristol C: (3412) O'Leary; Moore, Kalas, Mawson■; Hunt, Paterson (Palmer 76), Vyner, Towler; Williams (Nagy 57); Wells (Massengo 73), Diedhiou (Semenyo 76).
Referee: Rob Jones.

Swansea C (0) 1 *(Whittaker 77)*

Manchester C (1) 3 *(Walker 30, Sterling 47, Gabriel Jesus 50)*

Swansea C: (3412) Woodman; Latibeaudiere, Cabango, Guehi (Bidwell 66); Roberts (Freeman 66), Fulton, Grimes, Manning; Dhanda (Hourihane 76); Lowe (Arriola 65), Morris (Whittaker 66).
Manchester C: (433) Steffen; Walker, Garcia, Laporte, Mendy; Bernardo Silva (Foden 66), Rodri (Gomes 72), Gundogan (Doyle 57); Torres, Gabriel Jesus, Sterling (Mahrez 56).
Referee: Peter Banks.

Thursday, 11 February 2021

Barnsley (0) 0

Chelsea (0) 1 *(Abraham 64)*

Barnsley: (343) Collins; Sibbick (Sollbauer 76), Helik, Andersen; Brittain (Williams 73), Kane (Palmer 73), Mowatt, Styles; Adeboyejo (Dike 59), Woodrow, Chaplin (Frieser 59).
Chelsea: (343) Arrizabalaga; Christensen (Rudiger 46), Zouma, Emerson Palmieri; Hudson-Odoi, Kante, Gilmour, Alonso (James 46); Ziyech (Anjorin 69), Abraham, Pulisic (Kovacic 80).
Referee: Martin Atkinson.

Wolverhampton W (0) 0

Southampton (0) 2 *(Ings 49, Armstrong 90)*

Wolverhampton W: (343) Ruddy; Dendoncker, Saiss, Kilman; Hoever, Neves, Joao Moutinho, Jonny (Ait Nouri 46); Gibbs-White (Traore 63), Silva (Willian Jose 64), Vitinha (Pedro Neto 69).
Southampton: (442) Forster; Walker-Peters, Bednarek, Salisu, Bertrand; Armstrong, Ward-Prowse, Romeu, Djenepo (Tella 87); Redmond, Ings (Adams 83).
Referee: Jonathan Moss.

SIXTH ROUND

Saturday, 20 March 2021

Bournemouth (0) 0

Southampton (2) 3 *(Djenepo 37, Redmond 45, 59)*

Bournemouth: (4231) Begovic; Stacey, Carter-Vickers, Cook S, Rico (Mepham 67); Wilshere, Pearson (Surridge 56); Riquelme (Anthony 56), Billing (Kilkenny 77), Danjuma; Solanke.
Southampton: (442) Forster; Walker-Peters (Ramsay 89), Bednarek (Stephens 77), Vestergaard (Salisu 77), Bertrand; Armstrong, Ward-Prowse, Diallo, Djenepo (Tella 85); Adams (N'Lundulu 90), Redmond.
Referee: Martin Atkinson.

Everton (0) 0

Manchester C (0) 2 *(Gundogan 84, De Bruyne 90)*

Everton: (532) Virginia; Coleman, Holgate (Iwobi 87), Mina, Godfrey, Digne; Sigurdsson, Allan, Andre Gomes; Calvert-Lewin, Richarlison.
Manchester C: (433) Steffen; Walker, Dias, Laporte, Zinchenko; Bernardo Silva (Mahrez 64), Fernandinho, Gundogan (Rodri 90); Foden, Gabriel Jesus, Sterling (De Bruyne 80).
Referee: Michael Oliver.

Sunday, 21 March 2021

Chelsea (1) 2 *(Norwood 24 (og), Ziyech 90)*

Sheffield U (0) 0

Chelsea: (3421) Arrizabalaga; Christensen (Azpilicueta 63), Zouma, Emerson Palmieri; Hudson-Odoi (Havertz 72), Gilmour (Ziyech 72), Kovacic, Chilwell; Mount, Pulisic (Kante 83); Giroud (James 63).
Sheffield U: (352) Ramsdale; Baldock, Jagielka, Stevens; Bogle (Mousset 90), Lundstram, Norwood (Brewster 79), Fleck, Osborn; McBurnie (Burke 75), McGoldrick.
Referee: Andrew Madley.

Leicester C (1) 3 *(Iheanacho 24, 78, Tielemans 52)*

Manchester U (1) 1 *(Greenwood 38)*

Leicester C: (3412) Schmeichel; Fofana, Evans, Soyuncu; Albrighton, Tielemans, Ndidi, Castagne; Perez (Praet 73); Iheanacho, Vardy (Choudhury 83).
Manchester U: (4231) Henderson; Wan Bissaka, Lindelof, Maguire, Alex Telles (Shaw 64); Fred (Diallo 84), Matic (Bruno Fernandes 64); Greenwood, van de Beek (Cavani 64), Pogba (McTominay 64); Martial.
Referee: Craig Pawson.

SEMI-FINALS

Saturday, 17 April 2021

Chelsea (0) 1 *(Ziyech 55)*

Manchester C (0) 0

Chelsea: (3421) Arrizabalaga; Azpilicueta, Thiago Silva (Zouma 88), Rudiger; James, Kante, Jorginho, Chilwell; Ziyech (Emerson Palmieri 79), Mount (Pulisic 70); Werner (Havertz 79).
Manchester C: (4231) Steffen; Joao Cancelo, Dias, Laporte, Mendy; Fernandinho, Rodri; Torres (Gundogan 64), De Bruyne (Foden 48), Sterling; Gabriel Jesus.
Referee: Mike Dean.

Sunday, 18 April 2021

Leicester C (0) 1 *(Iheanacho 55)*

Southampton (0) 0 4000

Leicester C: (3412) Schmeichel; Fofana, Evans, Soyuncu; Castagne, Ndidi, Tielemans, Ricardo Pereira (Albrighton 60); Perez (Maddison 69); Iheanacho, Vardy.
Southampton: (442) Forster; Walker-Peters (Tella 84), Bednarek, Vestergaard, Bertrand (Salisu 85); Armstrong, Ward-Prowse, Diallo, Djenepo (Walcott 72); Redmond (Adams 59), Ings.
Referee: Chris Kavanagh.

THE EMIRATES FA CUP FINAL 2020–21

Saturday, 15 May 2021

(at Wembley Stadium, attendance 20,000)

Chelsea (0) 0 Leicester C (0) 1

Chelsea: (3421) Arrizabalaga; James, Thiago Silva, Rudiger; Azpilicueta (Hudson-Odoi 76), Kante, Jorginho (Havertz 75), Alonso (Chilwell 68); Ziyech (Pulisic 68), Mount; Werner (Giroud 82).

Leicester C: (3412) Schmeichel; Fofana, Evans (Albrighton 34), Soyuncu; Castagne, Tielemans, Ndidi, Thomas (Morgan 82); Perez (Choudhury 82); Iheanacho (Maddison 67), Vardy.
Scorer: Tielemans 63.

Referee: Michael Oliver.

Leicester City's Youri Tielemans scores the spectacular goal that clinched the FA Cup against Chelsea at Wembley Stadium on 15 May. It was the Foxes' first victory in five Final appearances. (Pool via REUTERS/Matthew Childs)

NATIONAL LEAGUE 2020–21

NATIONAL LEAGUE TABLE 2020–21

			Home					Away					Total						
		P	*W*	*D*	*L*	*F*	*A*	*W*	*D*	*L*	*F*	*A*	*W*	*D*	*L*	*F*	*A*	*GD*	*Pts*
1	Sutton U	42	14	4	3	43	16	11	5	5	29	20	25	9	8	72	36	36	84
2	Torquay U	42	11	6	4	34	20	12	5	4	34	19	23	11	8	68	39	29	80
3	Stockport Co	42	8	11	2	31	16	13	3	5	38	16	21	14	7	69	32	37	77
4	Hartlepool U¶	42	14	3	4	36	19	8	7	6	30	24	22	10	10	66	43	23	76
5	Notts Co	42	11	3	7	33	20	9	7	5	29	21	20	10	12	62	41	21	70
6	Chesterfield	42	10	3	8	32	19	11	3	7	28	24	21	6	15	60	43	17	69
7	Bromley	42	8	6	7	30	28	11	6	4	33	25	19	12	11	63	53	10	69
8	Wrexham	42	10	6	5	32	17	9	5	7	32	26	19	11	12	64	43	21	68
9	Eastleigh	42	11	6	4	25	12	7	6	8	24	28	18	12	12	49	40	9	66
10	FC Halifax T	42	9	4	8	33	30	10	4	7	30	24	19	8	15	63	54	9	65
11	Solihull Moors	42	15	2	4	37	16	4	5	12	21	32	19	7	16	58	48	10	64
12	Dagenham & R	42	9	6	6	27	22	8	3	10	26	26	17	9	16	53	48	5	60
13	Maidenhead U	42	7	4	10	30	34	8	7	6	32	26	15	11	16	62	60	2	56
14	Boreham Wood	42	5	9	7	26	28	8	7	6	26	20	13	16	13	52	48	4	55
15	Aldershot T	42	8	3	10	30	33	7	4	10	29	33	15	7	20	59	66	–7	52
16	Yeovil T	42	10	3	8	31	25	5	4	12	27	43	15	7	20	58	68	–10	52
17	Altrincham	42	6	6	9	25	28	6	5	10	21	32	12	11	19	46	60	–14	47
18	Weymouth	42	7	2	12	25	36	4	4	13	20	35	11	6	25	45	71	–26	39
19	Wealdstone	42	7	2	12	32	51	3	5	13	17	48	10	7	25	49	99	–50	37
20	Woking	42	5	6	10	27	36	3	3	15	15	33	8	9	25	42	69	–27	33
21	King's Lynn T†	42	4	8	9	28	39	3	2	16	22	59	7	10	25	50	98	–48	31
22	Barnet†	42	5	2	14	16	39	3	5	13	21	49	8	7	27	37	88	–51	31
23	Dover Ath*	0	0	0	0	0	0	0	0	0	0	0	0	0	0	0	0	0	0

Macclesfield Town suspended after being wound up by the High Court.
¶Hartlepool U promoted via play-offs.
**Dover Ath record for season 2020–21 expunged after failing to fufill their fixtures. The National League has imposed a 12-point deduction on them for the start of 2021–22 season.*
†As Macclesfield T were suspended and Dover Ath's results expunged, King's Lynn T and Barnet were reprieved from relegation for numerical reasons.

NATIONAL LEAGUE PLAY-OFFS 2020–21

NATIONAL LEAGUE PLAY-OFF ELIMINATORS

Saturday, 5 June 2021

Notts Co (1) 3 *(Wootton 30, 71, Ellis 90)*

Chesterfield (2) 2 *(Rowe 27, Mandeville 42)* 4569

Notts Co: (442) Slocombe; Miller, Chicksen, Ellis, Rawlinson (Knowles 46); Brindley, Doyle, Reeves (Kelly-Evans 90), Boldewijn; Rodrigues, Wootton.
Chesterfield: (442) Montgomery; Carline, Evans, Gunning, Maguire; Whittle (Taylor 78), Weston, Oyeleke (McCourt 58), Clarke; Mandeville, Rowe (Tyson 66).
Referee: Tom Reeves.

Sunday, 6 June 2021

Hartlepool U (3) 3 *(Oates 17, 24, Armstrong 20)*

Bromley (0) 2 *(Alabi 48, Webster 90)* 1700

Hartlepool U: (442) James; Sterry, Odusina, Liddle, Johnson; Ferguson (Donaldson 83), Featherstone, Holohan (Francis-Angol 80), Shelton; Armstrong, Oates (Elliott 88).
Bromley: (442) Cousins; Kizzi, Mitchell, Bush, Fox (Alabi 46); Bingham, Arthurs, Bridge, Williamson (Webster 46); Forster (Campbell 69), Cheek.
Referee: Lewis Smith.

NATIONAL LEAGUE PLAY-OFF SEMI-FINALS

Saturday, 12 June 2021

Torquay U (1) 4 *(Wright 1, 48, Hall 102, Moxey 105 (pen))*

Notts Co (1) 2 *(Rodrigues 39, Chicksen 51)* 1709

Torquay U: (433) Lucas Covolan; Wynter, Cameron (Andrews 79), Lewis, Sherring; Moxey, Hall (Buse 106), Little (Waters 95); Randell, Wright (Mbunga-Kimpioka 91), Lemonheigh-Evans.
Notts Co: (433) Slocombe; Brindley, Ellis, Miller (Barnett 85), Reeves (Griffiths 105); Chicksen (Rawlinson 105), Kelly-Evans, Doyle; Wootton, Rodrigues, Boldewijn (Knowles 73).
aet.
Referee: Andrew Kitchen.

Sunday, 13 June 2021

Stockport Co (0) 0

Hartlepool U (0) 1 *(Oates 76)* 2758

Stockport Co: (433) Hinchliffe; Jennings, Hogan, Palmer, Rooney; Southam-Hales, Croasdale, Collar (Newby 59); Walker (Bennett 81), Cardwell (Reid 73), Madden.
Hartlepool U: (442) James; Sterry, Odusina, Liddle, Johnson; Ferguson, Featherstone, Holohan (Molyneux 77), Shelton (Donaldson 88); Armstrong, Oates.
Referee: David Richardson.

FINAL (at Ashton Gate, Bristol)

Sunday, 20 June 2021

Hartlepool U (1) 1 *(Armstrong 35)*

Torquay U (0) 1 *(Lucas Covolan 90)* 6606

Hartlepool U: (532) James; Sterry, Odusina (Molyneux 120), Liddle, Johnson, Ferguson (Francis-Angol 76); Featherstone, Holohan (Donaldson 90), Shelton; Armstrong, Oates (Elliott 72).
Torquay U: (442) Lucas Covolan; Wynter, Cameron (Mbunga-Kimpioka 77), Lewis, Sherring; Moxey (Andrews 84 (Buse 105)), Hall, Little, Randell (Waters 89); Lemonheigh-Evans, Wright.
aet; Hartlepool U won 5-4 on penalties.
Referee: Simon Mather.

NATIONAL LEAGUE LEADING GOALSCORERS 2020–21

Player (Team)	*League*	*FA Cup*	*FA Trophy*	*Play-Offs*	*Total*
Michael Cheek (Bromley)	23	1	1	0	25
Kabongo Tshimanga (Boreham Wood)	19	3	0	0	22
Danilo Orsi-Dadomo (Maidenhead U)	19	0	2	0	21
Alex Reid (Stockport Co)	17	2	2		21
John Rooney (Stockport Co)	16	4	1		21
Kyle Wootton (Notts Co)	15	0	2	2	19
Akwasi Asante (Chesterfield)	18	0	0	0	18
Includes 8 National League North goals for Gloucester C.					
Paul McCallum (Dagenham & R)	16	1	1	0	18
Rhys Oates (Hartlepool U)	15	0	0	3	18
Isaac Olaofe (Sutton U)	14	0	2	0	16
On loan from Millwall.					
Sam Barratt (Maidenhead U)	15	0	0	0	15
Luke Armstrong (Hartlepool U)	13	0	0	2	15
On loan from Salford C.					
Asa Hall (Torquay U)	10	3	1	1	15
Rhys Murphy (Yeovil T)	13	2	0	0	15
Joe Quigley (Yeovil T)	12	1	1	0	14
Includes 1 FA Trophy goal for Dagenham & R.					
Angelo Balanta (Dagenham & R)	12	0	1	0	13
Josh Rees (Aldershot T)	12	0	1	0	13
Rúben Rodrigues (Notts Co)	11	0	1	1	13
Tyrone Barnett (Eastleigh)	12	0	0	0	12
Harry Beautyman (Sutton U)	11	0	1	0	12
Andrew Dallas (Weymouth)	12	0	0	0	12
On loan from Cambridge U.					
Josh Hancock (Altrincham)	12	0	0	0	12
Kyle Hudlin (Solihull Moors)	9	1	2	0	12
Jake Hyde (FC Halifax T)	12	0	0	0	12
Harry Panayiotou (Aldershot T)	12	0	0	0	12
Joseph Tomlinson (Eastleigh)	12	0	0	0	12
Luke Young (Wrexham)	12	0	0	0	12
Connor Lemenheigh-Evans (Torquay U)	10	0	1	0	11
Danny Wright (Torquay U)	9	0	0	2	11
Jimmy Ball (Solihull Moors)	9	0	1	0	10
Ben House (Eastleigh)	9	1	0	0	10
Jacob Mendy (Wealdstone)	9	0	1	0	10
Scott Boden (Chesterfield)	9	0	0	0	9
Includes 6 National League goals on loan at Torquay U.					
Tom Denton (Chesterfield)	9	0	0	0	9
Courtney Duffus (Bromley)	9	0	0	0	9
Includes 4 National League goals for Yeovil T.					
Kwame Thomas (Wrexham)	9	0	0	0	9

NATIONAL LEAGUE PROMOTED TEAMS ROLL CALL 2020–21

HARTLEPOOL UNITED

Player	*H*	*W*	*DOB*
Armstrong, Luke (F)	6 1	11 00	02/07/1996
Bloomfield, Mason, (F)	6 3	12 02	06/11/1996
Cooper, Jake, (M)	6 0	11 09	02/01/2001
Crawford, Tom (M)	6 1	11 05	30/05/1999
Donaldson, Ryan (M)	6 4	14 11	01/05/1991
Elliott, Danny (F)	6 0	11 11	29/09/1995
Featherstone, Nicky (M)	5 9	11 03	22/09/1988
Ferguson, David (D)	5 10	12 00	07/06/1994
Francis-Angol, Zaine (D)	5 8	12 04	30/06/1993
Grey, Joe (F)	5 9	11 00	04/05/2003
Holohan, Gavan (M)	5 11	11 11	15/12/1991
Johnson, Ryan (D)	6 2	13 05	02/10/1996
Killip, Ben (G)	6 2	11 09	24/11/1995
Liddle, Gary (D)	6 1	11 11	15/06/1986
MacDonald, Josh (M)	6 0	10 08	05/06/1998
Molyneux, Luke (M)	5 11	11 09	29/03/1998
Oates, Rhys (F)	6 0	11 09	04/12/1994
Odusina, Timi (D)	6 1	11 09	28/10/1999
Ofosu, Claudio (F)	6 0	12 06	27/09/1998
Shelton, Mark (M)	6 0	11 00	12/09/1996
Sterry, Jamie (D)	5 11	11 00	21/11/1995
White, Tom (M)	5 11	10 06	09/05/1997
Williams, Luke (F)	6 1	11 09	11/06/1993

SUTTON UNITED

Player	*H*	*W*	*DOB*
Ajiboye, David (M)	–	–	28/09/1990
Barden, Jonathan (M)	6 0	12 04	09/11/1992
Beautyman, Harry (M)	5 10	11 09	01/04/1992
Bouzanis, Dean (G)	6 0	12 08	02/10/1990
Browne, Stephen Rhys (M)	5 10	12 08	16/11/1995
Bugiel, Omar (F)	6 0	12 02	25/09/1994
Chalupniczak, Filip (G)	6 2	13 10	15/02/2001
Davis, Kenny (M)	5 8	11 03	17/04/1988
Dundas, Craig (F)	–	–	16/02/1981
Eastmond, Craig (M)	5 8	11 11	09/12/1990
Goodliffe, Ben (D)	6 2	12 08	19/06/1999
House, Brad (G)	6 2	12 04	19/10/1998
John, Louis (D)	6 3	13 05	19/04/1994
Kealy, Callum (F)	–	–	26/09/1998
Mason, Jude (D)	–	–	10/01/2001
Milsom, Robert (M)	5 10	11 05	02/01/1987
Nembhard, Joash (D)	–	–	13/03/1998
Randall, Will (M)	5 11	10 03	02/05/1997
Rowe, Coby (D)	6 3	13 05	02/10/1995
Sho-Silva, Tobi (F)	6 0	11 11	27/03/1995
Simpson, Aaron (D)	–	–	04/07/1997
Tiensia, Junior (D)	–	–	25/12/2000
Wyatt, Ben (D)	5 8	10 01	04/02/1996

NATIONAL LEAGUE NORTH 2020–21

Due to COVID-19 national lockdown restrictions, a resolution from the National League board to declare the 2020–21 National League North season null and void was passed on 18 February 2021. National League North clubs voted 15 for and 7 against the resolution to declare the season null and void (combined total vote 24-19), and, with a minimum of 51% required, the resolution was passed. The FA ratified the decision on 12 March 2021. No teams will be promoted or relegated and all records are to be expunged.

NATIONAL LEAGUE NORTH TABLE 2020–21

(R) *Relegated into division at end of 2019–20 season. Due to the COVID-19 pandemic no teams were promoted into the National League North from Tier 3.*

			Home					Away					Total						
		P	*W*	*D*	*L*	*F*	*A*	*W*	*D*	*L*	*F*	*A*	*W*	*D*	*L*	*F*	*A*	*GD*	*Pts*
1	Gloucester C	18	6	3	1	25	13	4	2	2	11	9	10	5	3	36	22	14	35
2	AFC Fylde (R)	15	6	1	0	16	6	3	2	3	10	10	9	3	3	26	16	10	30
3	Chester	17	6	0	2	19	10	2	4	3	13	14	8	4	5	32	24	8	28
4	Brackley T	16	5	3	1	14	10	2	3	2	8	9	7	6	3	22	19	3	27
5	Kidderminster H	15	3	3	2	11	8	4	1	2	13	9	7	4	4	24	17	7	25
6	Boston U	13	2	3	1	8	7	4	2	1	12	3	6	5	2	20	10	10	23
7	Chorley (R)	18	3	1	3	10	10	3	4	4	11	15	6	5	7	21	25	–4	23
8	York C	13	4	2	1	10	6	2	2	2	12	11	6	4	3	22	17	5	22
9	Leamington	15	2	5	1	10	12	3	2	2	12	8	5	7	3	22	20	2	22
10	Gateshead	14	4	1	3	10	8	2	2	2	7	7	6	3	5	17	15	2	21
11	Farsley Celtic	17	3	4	1	10	10	2	2	5	11	16	5	6	6	21	26	–5	21
12	Hereford	13	3	2	2	12	10	2	3	1	8	6	5	5	3	20	16	4	20
13	Spennymoor T	13	3	2	1	11	9	2	3	2	7	5	5	5	3	18	14	4	20
14	AFC Telford U	17	3	2	4	9	8	2	2	4	8	15	5	4	8	17	23	–6	19
15	Bradford (Park Avenue)	16	2	3	4	13	15	2	3	2	13	15	4	6	6	26	30	–4	18
16	Curzon Ashton	17	3	1	4	8	12	1	4	4	10	14	4	5	8	18	26	–8	17
17	Southport	14	1	3	4	6	10	3	1	2	10	9	4	4	6	16	19	–3	16
18	Kettering T	14	2	2	2	7	6	1	4	3	14	17	3	6	5	21	23	–2	15
19	Darlington	11	1	1	3	8	6	3	0	3	9	5	4	1	6	17	11	6	13
20	Guiseley	15	2	1	4	13	14	1	2	5	4	8	3	3	9	17	22	–5	12
21	Alfreton T	15	1	4	2	9	11	1	2	5	6	16	2	6	7	15	27	–12	12
22	Blyth Spartans	14	0	3	4	4	14	1	0	6	6	22	1	3	10	10	36	–26	6

NATIONAL LEAGUE NORTH TOP GOALSCORERS

Player	*Club*	*Goals*
Matt McClure	Gloucester C	12
Lenell John-Lewis	Hereford	9
Lewis Knight	Bradford (Park Avenue)	9
Sam Osborne	Leamington	9
Akwasi Asante	Gloucester C	8
Glen Taylor	Spennymoor T	8
Danny Elliott	Chester	7
Dominic Knowles	Curzon Ashton	7
Sean Newton	York C	7
Shane Byrne	Brackley T	6
Nick Haughton	AFC Fylde	6
Ashley Hemmings	Kidderminster H	6
Connor Kennedy	Kettering T	6
Callum Powell	Kettering T	6
Jimmy Spencer	Farsley Celtic	6
Ben Tollitt	AFC Fylde	6

NATIONAL LEAGUE NORTH PLAYER OF THE MONTH AWARDS

Month	*Player of the Month*	*Club*
October 2020	Matt McClure	Gloucester C
November 2020	Sam Osborne	Leamington
December 2020	Ross Fitzsimons	Boston U
January 2021	George Glendon	Chester

NATIONAL LEAGUE NORTH MANAGER OF THE MONTH AWARDS

Month	*Manager of the Month*	*Club*
October 2020	Jim Bentley	AFC Fylde
November 2020	Jamie Vermiglio	Chorley
December 2020	Kevin Wilkin	Brackley T
January 2021	Paul Holleran	Leamington

NATIONAL LEAGUE SOUTH 2020–21

Due to COVID-19 national lockdown restrictions, a resolution from the National League board to declare the 2020–21 National League South season null and void was passed on 18 February 2021. National League South clubs voted 9 for and 12 against the resolution to declare the season null and void (combined total vote 24-19), and, with a minimum of 51% required, the resolution was passed. The FA ratified the decision on 12 March 2021. No teams will be promoted or relegated and all records are to be expunged.

NATIONAL LEAGUE SOUTH TABLE 2020–21

(R) *Relegated into division at end of 2019–20 season. Due to the COVID-19 pandemic no teams were promoted into the National League South from Tier 3.*

			Home					*Away*					*Total*						
		P	*W*	*D*	*L*	*F*	*A*	*W*	*D*	*L*	*F*	*A*	*W*	*D*	*L*	*F*	*A*	*GD*	*Pts*
1	Dorking W	18	6	2	2	22	10	6	1	1	18	7	12	3	3	40	17	23	39
2	Dartford	19	6	3	3	15	9	4	1	2	11	8	10	4	5	26	17	9	34
3	Eastbourne Bor	19	5	3	3	21	16	4	3	1	15	10	9	6	4	36	26	10	33
4	Oxford C	17	5	4	1	17	5	4	1	2	18	12	9	5	3	35	17	18	32
5	St Albans C	15	5	2	1	13	7	4	3	0	9	3	9	5	1	22	10	12	32
6	Hampton & Richmond Bor	17	2	2	4	6	11	7	0	2	18	5	9	2	6	24	16	8	29
7	Hungerford T	19	4	0	4	10	11	5	2	4	17	17	9	2	8	27	28	–1	29
8	Ebbsfleet U (R)	18	3	2	2	8	9	5	2	4	18	15	8	4	6	26	24	2	28
9	Havant and Waterlooville	14	4	2	3	18	14	2	0	3	7	7	6	2	6	25	21	4	20
10	Hemel Hempstead T	18	1	1	7	11	23	5	1	3	17	15	6	2	10	28	38	–10	20
11	Maidstone U	13	3	1	2	13	7	2	3	2	11	11	5	4	4	24	18	6	19
12	Dulwich Hamlet	13	1	1	2	3	7	3	3	3	12	10	4	4	5	15	17	–2	16
13	Chelmsford C	16	2	1	5	9	13	2	3	3	12	12	4	4	8	21	25	–4	16
14	Tonbridge Angels	14	2	1	4	9	11	3	0	4	7	12	5	1	8	16	23	–7	16
15	Billericay T	17	3	2	6	17	22	1	2	3	9	13	4	4	9	26	35	–9	16
16	Chippenham T	14	1	3	3	7	11	3	1	3	6	11	4	4	6	13	22	–9	16
17	Concord Rangers	14	1	3	1	8	9	2	2	5	8	15	3	5	6	16	24	–8	14
18	Bath C	13	2	0	3	6	9	2	1	5	10	14	4	1	8	16	23	–7	13
19	Braintree T	16	2	1	5	9	17	2	0	6	10	17	4	1	11	19	34	–15	13
20	Slough T	12	3	1	3	13	15	0	2	3	3	9	3	3	6	16	24	–8	12
21	Welling U	14	1	1	3	6	12	1	5	3	12	18	2	6	6	18	30	–12	12

NATIONAL LEAGUE SOUTH TOP GOALSCORERS

Player	*Club*	*Goals*
Jason Prior	Dorking W	15
Ryan Seager	Hungerford T	14
Jake Robinson	Billericay T	12
James Roberts	Oxford C	11
Chris Whelpdale	Eastbourne Bor	11
Rakish Bingham	Ebbsfleet U	9
Shaun Jeffers	St Albans C	9
Charlie Sheringham	Dartford	9
(Includes 5 goals on loan at Chelmsford C)		
Harvey Bradbury	Oxford C	8
Alex Wall	Concord Rangers	7
Tommy Wright	Havant & Waterlooville	7

NATIONAL LEAGUE SOUTH PLAYER OF THE MONTH AWARDS

Month	*Player of the Month*	*Club*
October 2020	Mike Jones	Hungerford T
November 2020	Jason Prior	Dorking W
December 2020	Tommy Wright	Havant & Waterlooville
January 2021	Ben Dudzinski	Oxford C

NATIONAL LEAGUE SOUTH MANAGER OF THE MONTH AWARDS

Month	*Manager of the Month*	*Club*
October 2020	Steve King	Dartford
November 2020	Ian Allinson	St Albans C
December 2020	David Oldfield	Oxford C
January 2021	Robbie Simpson	Chelmsford C

ALDERSHOT TOWN

Ground: The EBB Stadium at the Recreation Ground, High Street, Aldershot, Hampshire GU11 1TW.
Tel: (01252) 320 211. *Website:* www.theshots.co.uk *Email:* admin@theshots.co.uk *Year Formed:* 1926.
Record Attendance: 19,138 v Carlisle U, FA Cup 4th rd (replay), 28 January 1970. *Nickname:* 'The Shots'.
Manager: Danny Searle. *Colours:* Red shirts with blue trim, blue shorts, red socks with blue trim.

ALDERSHOT TOWN – NATIONAL LEAGUE 2020–21 LEAGUE RECORD

Match No.	*Date*		*Venue*	*Opponents*	*Result*		*H/T Score*	*Lg Pos.*	*Goalscorers*	*Attendance*
1	Oct	3	A	Hartlepool U	L	1-2	0-1	12	Tanner 63	0
2		6	H	Sutton U	L	1-2	0-1	18	Bettamer 75	0
3		17	A	Eastleigh	D	2-2	1-1	22	Tanner 45, Whittingham 61	0
4		27	H	Torquay U	L	1-4	1-1	22	Tanner 8	0
5	Nov	7	H	Notts Co	W	1-0	0-0	20	Panayiotou 64	0
6		14	A	Altrincham	W	2-1	1-0	15	Edser 13, Kandi 79	0
7		17	H	Maidenhead U	D	0-0	0-0	15		0
8		21	A	Wrexham	L	0-1	0-0	16		0
9	Dec	1	A	Chesterfield	D	0-0	0-0	17		0
10		5	H	Dagenham & R	W	2-1	2-0	16	Bettamer 7, Panayiotou 31	920
11		8	H	FC Halifax T	L	1-3	1-0	18	Bettamer (pen) 36	0
12		12	A	Boreham Wood	L	2-3	1-2	18	Ogie 28, Fyfield (og) 53	650
13		26	H	Woking	W	3-0	3-0	17	Panayiotou 32, Anderson 2 34, 38	0
14		28	A	Yeovil T	L	0-3	0-1	18		0
15	Jan	2	A	Woking	W	1-0	0-0	17	Ricky Miller 72	0
16		23	A	Wealdstone	W	4-3	3-2	12	Nouble 6, Anderson 38, Kandi 42, Rees 75	0
17		26	H	Weymouth	L	0-2	0-2	14		0
18		30	A	Bromley	L	0-2	0-1	15		0
19	Feb	2	H	Barnet	W	2-1	0-0	13	Sendles-White 61, Bettamer 72	0
20		13	A	Stockport Co	D	0-0	0-0	13		0
21		16	H	Solihull Moors	L	1-3	0-2	14	Rees 87	0
22		20	H	Wrexham	W	3-0	1-0	12	Nouble 2 26, 47, Anderson 68	0
23		23	A	Maidenhead U	W	4-2	3-1	10	Ricky Miller 6, Rees 3 27, 39, 90	0
24	Mar	13	H	Altrincham	W	2-1	1-0	14	Nouble 43, Kandi 88	0
25		16	A	FC Halifax T	L	0-1	0-0	15		0
26		20	H	Boreham Wood	D	3-3	0-1	13	Edser 54, Rees 2 64, 78	0
27		23	H	Chesterfield	L	0-1	0-1	15		0
28		27	A	Solihull Moors	L	0-1	0-1	16		0
29		30	A	Notts Co	W	1-0	1-0	15	Panayiotou (pen) 4	0
30	Apr	2	H	Stockport Co	L	1-2	0-1	16	Rees 74	0
31		5	A	Dagenham & R	W	2-0	1-0	12	Bettamer (pen) 43, Nouble 46	0
32		13	A	Weymouth	W	3-0	1-0	12	Rees 2 34, 88, Panayiotou 56	0
33		17	A	Barnet	L	1-3	1-1	12	Panayiotou 37	0
34		20	H	King's Lynn T	D	1-1	1-0	12	Ricky Miller 31	0
35		24	H	Wealdstone	W	2-0	1-0	11	Panayiotou 35, Kandi 90	0
36		27	A	Torquay U	L	1-2	1-1	11	Lyons-Foster 17	0
37	May	1	A	Sutton U	L	1-3	1-2	14	Ricky Miller 23	0
38		11	H	Yeovil T	W	2-0	0-0	15	Kandi 51, Panayiotou 83	0
39		15	H	Hartlepool U	L	1-3	0-0	15	Bettamer (pen) 87	0
40		18	H	Eastleigh	L	1-3	0-1	16	Panayiotou 53	1073
41		22	H	Bromley	L	2-3	0-1	16	Panayiotou 2 72, 83	1175
42		29	A	King's Lynn T	D	4-4	2-1	15	Edser 20, Kandi 38, Lyons-Foster 2 62, 73	881

Final League Position: 15

GOALSCORERS

League (59): Panayiotou 11 (1 pen), Rees 10, Bettamer 6 (3 pens), Kandi 6, Nouble 5, Anderson 4, Ricky Miller 4, Edser 3, Lyons-Foster 3, Tanner 3, Ogie 1, Sendles-White 1, Whittingham 1, own goal 1.
FA Cup (1): Bettamer 1.
FA Trophy (9): Bettamer 3 (1 pen), Edser 1, Finney 1, Fondop-Talum 1, Kandi 1, Ogie 1, Rees 1.

Walker 27	Fowler 28 + 1	Finney 9 + 1	Sendles-White 25 + 3	Lyons-Foster 35 + 4	Rees 38	Bettamer 25 + 14	Nouble 27 + 4	Edser 37 + 5	Ogie 26 + 2	Tanner 10 + 5	Panayiotou 30 + 6	Colombie 8 + 4	Rowe 8 + 7	Whittingham 17 + 6	McCormack — + 1	Kandi 19 + 16	James 11 + 1	Hungbo 2 + 4	Phillips 18	Fondop-Talom 2 + 2	Anderson 28 + 3	Miller Ricky 14 + 7	Gillela 3	Shroll 1	Hall 4	Kinsella 9 + 4	Hinds 1 + 6	Wylie — + 2	Miller Reece — + 1	Rabbetts — + 1	Match No.
1	2	3	4	5^{3}	6	7^{1}	8^{2}	9	10	11	12	13	14																		1
1	2	3	4	5^{1}	6	7	8^{2}	9^{3}	10	11		13	12	14																	2
1	3		5	4	8	9		13	2	11	10^{2}		7^{1}	6	12																3
1	2	13^{3}	4	3	6^{1}	7		12	10	11		14	5^{2}	9		8															4
	2		3	4	5	6		12	10	11	8^{1}			9		7	1														5
	2			3	4			8	10		5^{2}		13	6		12	1	7^{1}	9	11											6
	2			3	4	13		8	10		6^{1}			7		5^{2}	1	12	9	11■											7
	2			3	6	11	14	9^{1}	5		10		12	7^{2}		13	1	8^{3}	4												8
	2		13	3	4	5^{1}		9	11		7^{2}			8■		6	1	12	10												9
	2		14	3	5	6		9^{1}	11		8		4^{3}			7^{2}	1	13	10		12										10
	2			3	5	6		9	11		8^{2}		4^{3}			7^{1}	1	12	10	14	13										11
				2	4	5		8	11		7^{2}	10	3^{1}			6	1		9	12	13										12
	2		3^{3}	13	4	5	14	9^{1}	11		7			12		6^{2}	1		10		8										13
	2	3			4	5	12	9	11		7					6^{1}	1		10		8■										14
1	2			3	4	5	8^{1}	9	11		6			7		13			10			12^{2}									15
1	2	3		4	5	6	8^{2}	10	11			13		12		7^{1}					9										16
1■		2	3	14	4	5	7^{3}	9	11			10^{2}		13		6^{1}	12				8										17
		3		4	5	11^{2}	9^{3}	8^{1}	2		10		14	6		13	1				7	12									18
1		2	3	4	5	12	7	10			6^{2}					13					8	11^{1}	9								19
1		2	3	4	5	11	10	8^{1}			13					12					6	9^{2}	7								20
1		2^{1}	3	4	5	11	10	8^{3}	12				14			13					6	9^{2}	7								21
1			2		4	13	7^{3}	14			12	10	3	6		5^{2}					8	11^{1}		9							22
1			3	13	5	14	11^{2}	12				8■	4	6		9^{3}			2		7	10^{1}									23
			14	3	4	11^{2}	10^{3}	7			13	8		5		12			2		6	9^{1}			1						24
				3	4	11^{2}	10	7			12	8		5		13			2		6	9^{1}			1						25
				3	4	12	10	7	14		11^{3}	8^{2}		5		13			2		6	9^{1}			1						26
1	4^{3}			5	6	11	9^{1}	8	2		10^{2}			14		12			3		7	13									27
1	4^{2}			5	7	12	11	9	3		14		6^{1}			13			2		8	10^{3}									28
1			2	14	3	12	7^{2}	9	11		5^{1}			6		4^{3}			10		8					13					29
1	12		2		3	4^{3}	7	9	11^{1}		5			6^{2}					10		8					14	13				30
1	3		4	5	6	11^{2}	9	8	2		10^{1}										7	13				12					31
1	2		3	4	6		11	8^{2}	5	12	10^{3}					9^{1}					7	14				13					32
1	2^{2}		3	4	6	12	11	8	5	14	10^{3}					9^{1}					7	13									33
1			3	4	5	12	10^{2}	7		13	11^{3}	8	14								6	9^{1}				2					34
1	2		3	4	5		7	9^{2}		14	6^{1}					12					8	11^{3}				10	13				35
1	3		4	5	6	13	10^{2}	8			11					12					7	9^{1}				2					36
1	2		3	4	5	12	7	9^{2}		13	6^{3}										8	11^{1}				10	14				37
1	2		3	4	5^{2}	14	12	9		11^{1}	7					6^{3}					8					10	13				38
1	2		3	4		13		7		10^{3}	9					8^{1}					6	11^{2}				5	12	14			39
1	2		3	4		5^{2}	7	9		11^{3}	6^{1}					13					8	12				10	14				40
	2		3	4		13	9	7		10^{1}	8			12		14					6^{2}				1	5	11^{3}				41
1	2			3		8		7^{1}	4	11^{3}	10^{2}			6		9										5		12	13	14	42

FA Cup

Fourth Qualifying	Woking	(h)	1-2

FA Trophy

Third Round	Welwyn Garden C	(a)	5-1
Fourth Round	Solihull Moors	(h)	3-2
Fifth Round	Chesterfield	(h)	

Aldershot T awarded a walkover due to the positive COVID-19 test of a Chesterfield player.

Quarter-Finals	Hereford	(h)	1-1

(Hereford won 5-3 on penalties)

ALTRINCHAM

Ground: J. Davidson Stadium, Moss Lane, Altrincham WA15 8AP. *Tel:* (0161) 928 1045.
Website: www.altrinchamfc.co.uk *Email:* see website. *Year Formed:* 1903.
Record Attendance: 10,275 (Altrincham Boys v Sunderland Boys, ESFA Shield, 28 February 1925).
Nickname: 'The Robins'. *Manager:* Phil Parkinson.
Colours: Red shirts with white front panel, black shorts with red trim, white socks with red trim.

ALTRINCHAM – NATIONAL LEAGUE 2020–21 LEAGUE RECORD

Match No.	*Date*		*Venue*	*Opponents*	*Result*		*H/T Score*	*Lg Pos.*	*Goalscorers*	*Attendance*
1	Oct	3	H	Weymouth	D	0-0	0-0	10		0
2		7	A	Notts Co	L	1-3	0-2	16	Mooney ^{77}	0
3		10	A	Eastleigh	D	1-1	1-1	16	Ceesay ^{10}	0
4		27	A	Hartlepool U	D	1-1	0-1	21	Peers ^{85}	0
5	Nov	7	A	Wealdstone	L	0-1	0-0	22		0
6		11	H	Solihull Moors	L	0-2	0-2	22		0
7		14	H	Aldershot T	L	1-2	0-1	22	Peers ^{89}	0
8		17	H	Chesterfield	W	3-2	1-1	21	Adarabioyo ^{29}, Hancock 2 (1 pen) $^{62 (p), 89}$	0
9		21	A	Boreham Wood	W	1-0	0-0	15	McDonald ^{86}	0
10		24	H	Bromley	L	0-1	0-1	15		0
11		28	H	Maidenhead U	W	2-0	0-0	12	Hancock (pen) ^{63}, Peers ^{80}	0
12	Dec	1	A	Wrexham	W	1-0	1-0	11	Sutton ^{44}	0
13		12	A	Dagenham & R	W	1-0	1-0	8	Moult ^{39}	773
14		26	H	Stockport Co	D	1-1	1-0	11	Ceesay ^{25}	0
15		28	A	FC Halifax T	L	2-3	1-2	13	Hancock ^{31}, Mooney ^{70}	0
16	Jan	2	A	Stockport Co	D	2-2	0-1	12	Ceesay ^{70}, Colclough ^{75}	0
17		9	A	Sutton U	D	2-2	1-2	10	Mullarkey ^{16}, Hampson ^{90}	0
18		23	A	Barnet	W	2-1	1-1	8	Kosylo ^{35}, Hancock ^{90}	0
19		26	H	Wealdstone	W	2-0	1-0	5	Hancock ^{39}, Smith ^{79}	0
20	Feb	2	A	Torquay U	W	2-1	2-1	6	Hancock (pen) ^{33}, Colclough ^{45}	0
21		9	H	Wrexham	L	1-2	0-1	8	Colclough ^{51}	0
22		13	A	Yeovil T	L	0-2	0-0	8		0
23		20	H	Boreham Wood	L	2-3	0-2	11	Kosylo ^{59}, Peers ^{86}	0
24		23	A	Chesterfield	L	0-1	0-0	13		0
25		27	A	Bromley	L	1-3	1-3	14	Moult ^{36}	0
26	Mar	2	H	Woking	W	1-0	0-0	10	Kosylo ^{69}	0
27		9	H	Hartlepool U	D	1-1	1-1	12	Colclough ^{45}	0
28		13	A	Aldershot T	L	1-2	0-1	15	Hancock (pen) ^{47}	0
29		16	A	Woking	D	1-1	0-1	14	Hancock (pen) ^{90}	0
30		20	H	Dagenham & R	L	0-1	0-0	15		0
31		23	H	King's Lynn T	W	3-0	1-0	13	Hancock 2 $^{16, 57}$, Hardy ^{59}	0
32		27	A	Maidenhead U	W	1-0	0-0	11	Colclough ^{64}	0
33	Apr	5	A	King's Lynn T	L	0-2	0-0	13		0
34		10	H	FC Halifax T	L	0-1	0-1	13		0
35		17	H	Sutton U	L	0-4	0-2	17		0
36		24	H	Barnet	L	2-3	2-1	17	Colclough ^{4}, Smith ^{16}	0
37	May	1	H	Notts Co	D	1-1	1-1	17	Smith ^{24}	0
38		3	A	Solihull Moors	L	0-4	0-1	17		0
39		15	A	Weymouth	L	1-2	0-1	17	Colclough ^{50}	0
40		22	H	Yeovil T	W	4-3	2-0	17	Kirby ^{19}, Mooney ^{45}, Peers ^{85}, Hancock ^{90}	600
41		25	H	Eastleigh	D	1-1	0-0	17	Colclough ^{78}	600
42		29	H	Torquay U	D	0-0	0-0	17		1032

Final League Position: 17

GOALSCORERS

League (46): Hancock 12 (5 pens), Colclough 8, Peers 5, Ceesay 3, Kosylo 3, Mooney 3, Smith 3, Moult 2, Adarabioyo 1, Hampson 1, Hardy 1, Kirby 1, McDonald 1, Mullarkey 1, Sutton 1.
FA Cup (1): Peers 1.
FA Trophy (2): Peers 1, Senior 1.

Thompson 41	Densmore 6 + 6	White 10 + 3	Mullarkey 27 + 4	Hannigan 32	Moult 37 + 1	Kosylo 28 + 3	Williams 10 + 4	Peers 12 + 20	Hancock 32 + 3	Ceesay 23 + 8	Miller — + 6	Richman 4 + 7	Clayton — + 1	Mooney 11 + 8	Senior 38 + 1	Sutton 14 + 2	Adarabioyo 7 + 1	Hampson 17 + 1	Robbins 3 + 1	Sass-Davies 5 + 2	Dales 3	Smith 29 + 1	McDonald — + 3	Colclough 23 + 5	Holgate 2	Blyth 1 + 2	Harrison 7 + 1	Piggott 8 + 3	Hardy 5 + 6	Zouma 5	Ogle 11 + 1	Gibson 2	Bell 3 + 6	Kirby 5 + 2	Gould 1	*Match No.*
1	2	3	4	5	6	7^{3}	8	9	10^{1}	11^{2}	12	13	14																							1
1	4	2	9	3	5	10^{1}	6^{2}	11	7	8^{3}	14	13		12																						2
1		4	6		5	10	7^{1}	11	9	8^{2}		12		13	2	3																				3
1		5	3^{3}	4	6	14		8	9^{2}	10		7^{1}		13	2	12	11																			4
1				4	6	9		13	8	11^{3}	14				3	5^{1}	10^{2}	2	7	12																5
1				5	6	7		9	10		12			11^{1}	2			3	8	4																6
1				4	6	8		9			14				2		11^{1}	5	7^{3}	3	10^{2}	12	13													7
1	2			5	6	7			10		12					13	11^{1}	3		4	8^{2}	9														8
1				4	6	9			8^{2}	12					2		10^{1}	3	14	5	11^{3}	7	13													9
1	2				6	7▪			10	8^{1}					12	5	11^{2}	3^{3}		4		9	14	13												10
1	14	2		4	6	8		13	9^{3}	10^{1}					5	3	11^{2}					7		12												11
1	13	5		4	6	10		12	8^{3}	9^{1}					2	3				14		7		11^{2}												12
1	14	5		4	6	11		13	8	9^{3}		12			2	3^{1}						7		10^{2}												13
1				4		8^{2}		11	9	10^{1}		6		12	2			5				7			3	13										14
1				3	4	7^{1}		8^{2}	5	6^{3}				12	9			2				10		14	11	13										15
1			13	3	6			14	12	10				9^{2}	2	4^{1}		5				7		8		11^{3}										16
1			3		6	10			9^{2}	11^{1}				13	2	4		5				7		8			12									17
1		14	7	4		10		12	6	13				9^{2}	5	3		2^{1}				8					11^{3}									18
1			4	3	6	8^{1}		13	9					10	2			5				7		12			11^{2}									19
1		13	7	3	5▪	10			6	14				9^{1}	4			2^{3}				8		12			11^{2}									20
1		5	6	4		8			9	13					2	3^{1}						7		10			11^{2}	12								21
1		3	7	4	6	9^{2}		10^{1}	8	12					2							5		11				13								22
1		13	14	4	6	9^{3}		12		10					2	3		5▪				7		8^{2}			11^{1}									23
1	14	5^{2}	4	3	6	9		8^{1}		10					2							7					11^{3}	12	13							24
1	12		14	4	6	10		13		7					5	3		2^{3}				8					11^{2}		9^{1}							25
1			12	3▪	6	9		13		10^{1}					2			14				7		8^{2}						4	5	11^{3}				26
1			3		6	9^{3}		12		10^{2}				13	2							7		8					14	4	5	11^{1}				27
1			8		5			11	6^{1}	7					2							9		10					12	4	3					28
1			8	5	12	10^{3}	6		7	13					2									9				11^{1}		4^{2}	3		14			29
1			4	3	7		6	14	9	10^{3}		12			2									8				11^{2}			5^{1}		13			30
1			4	3	7		13		9^{3}			2^{2}			5							6		8				11^{1}	10		14		12			31
1			7	4	5		14	13	6^{1}						2			3				8		10				11^{3}	9^{2}				12			32
1			8	4	5		6^{2}	12	7	13		14			2			3						10				11^{1}	9^{3}							33
1			9	4	5		6		7^{2}	8					2									10				11^{1}	13		3		12			34
1			4	3^{1}	6		7		9^{2}	10		14		12	2									8				11^{3}			5		13			35
1			4		6			12		13				8^{2}	2	3						7		10							5		11^{1}	9		36
1			6		3			12	13					11^{1}	5	2						7		9							4		10^{2}	8		37
	12		8				2	6	4	5		9^{3}			7		13											3^{1}	10^{2}	11				14	1	38
1			4		3	13	7^{3}	14	12					11^{2}	2							6		9							5		10^{1}	8		39
1			6		4	10^{1}	12	13	5					9^{2}	3							7		11					14		2			8^{3}		40
1	2		5	3	6	12	14	13	9^{3}					10^{1}	4							8^{2}		11										7		41
1	2		4	3	6	9^{1}		12	8^{3}					10^{2}	5							7		11					13					14		42

FA Cup
Fourth Qualifying AFC Fylde (a) 1-2

FA Trophy
Third Round Chester (h) 2-1
Fourth Round Havant & Waterlooville (a)
Havant & Waterlooville awarded a walkover due to the positive COVID-19 test of an Altrincham player.

BARNET

Ground: The Hive Stadium, Camrose Avenue, Edgware, London HA8 6AG. *Tel:* (020) 8381 3800.
Website: www.barnetfc.com *Email:* tellus@barnetfc.com *Year Formed:* 1888.
Record Attendance: 11,026 v Wycombe Wanderers, FA Amateur Cup 4th rd, 2 February 1952 (at Underhill); 6,215 v Brentford, FA Cup 4th rd, 28 January 2019 (at The Hive Stadium). *Nickname:* 'The Bees'.
Manager: Harry Kewell. *Colours:* Amber shirts with black trim, black shorts, black socks.

BARNET – NATIONAL LEAGUE 2020–21 LEAGUE RECORD

Match No.	*Date*	*Venue*	*Opponents*	*Result*	*H/T Score*	*Lg Pos.*	*Goalscorers*	*Attendance*
1	Oct 3	H	Eastleigh	L 1-5	1-1	18	Fonguck 39	0
2	6	A	Dagenham & R	W 2-1	0-1	11	Hooper (pen) 85, Richards 88	0
3	10	A	Notts Co	L 2-4	1-3	14	Hooper 2 45, 75	0
4	13	H	Weymouth	W 1-0	1-0	10	Fonguck 45	0
5	27	A	Wrexham	D 0-0	0-0	13		0
6	Nov 14	H	Bromley	L 1-3	0-2	17	Petrasso 68	0
7	17	H	King's Lynn T	L 0-2	0-1	19		0
8	21	A	Woking	L 1-4	0-2	20	Petrasso (pen) 88	0
9	24	H	Hartlepool U	D 0-0	0-0	18		0
10	Dec 2	A	FC Halifax T	L 2-5	0-3	20	Faal 68, Effiong 85	0
11	5	H	Wealdstone	D 0-0	0-0	20		0
12	8	H	Stockport Co	L 1-2	0-1	20	Mason-Clarke 48	0
13	12	A	Chesterfield	L 0-6	0-1	20		0
14	Jan 2	H	Boreham Wood	L 0-3	0-3	22		0
15	23	H	Altrincham	L 1-2	1-1	22	Hooper 14	0
16	30	H	Torquay U	L 0-2	0-1	22		0
17	Feb 2	A	Aldershot T	L 1-2	0-0	22	Petrasso 53	0
18	16	H	FC Halifax T	W 2-1	2-1	22	Petrasso 32, Wordsworth 45	0
19	20	H	Woking	L 0-2	0-1	22		0
20	23	A	King's Lynn T	L 1-5	1-2	22	Hooper 28	0
21	27	A	Hartlepool U	L 0-1	0-1	22		0
22	Mar 2	H	Yeovil T	L 1-4	1-2	22	Hooper 14	0
23	9	H	Wrexham	L 0-2	0-1	22		0
24	13	A	Bromley	D 2-2	1-1	22	Baker-Richardson (pen) 13, Petrasso 63	0
25	16	A	Stockport Co	L 1-2	0-1	22	McQueen 62	0
26	20	H	Chesterfield	L 0-2	0-1	22		0
27	27	A	Yeovil T	L 1-3	0-3	22	Kefalas 68	0
28	Apr 2	H	Solihull Moors	L 0-2	0-1	22		0
29	5	A	Wealdstone	L 1-5	0-2	22	Baker-Richardson 46	0
30	10	A	Maidenhead U	D 0-0	0-0	22		0
31	17	H	Aldershot T	W 3-1	1-1	22	Hooper 30, Mason-Clarke (pen) 71, Adeloye 90	0
32	20	A	Boreham Wood	D 0-0	0-0	22		0
33	24	A	Altrincham	W 3-2	1-2	22	Baker-Richardson 45, Mason-Clarke 88, Adeloye 89	0
34	27	A	Sutton U	L 0-1	0-0	22		0
35	May 1	H	Dagenham & R	L 0-2	0-1	22		0
36	3	A	Weymouth	W 2-0	1-0	22	Richards-Everton 34, Adeloye 79	0
37	8	H	Notts Co	L 1-4	0-1	22	Petrasso 89	0
38	15	A	Eastleigh	L 0-3	0-1	22		0
39	19	A	Solihull Moors	L 0-1	0-0	22		0
40	22	A	Torquay U	D 2-2	1-2	22	Petrasso (pen) 37, Kefalas 54	1561
41	25	H	Maidenhead U	W 2-0	0-0	22	Taylor, H 57, Wordsworth 64	562
42	29	H	Sutton U	W 2-0	0-0	22	Simpson (og) 61, Walker 90	686

Final League Position: 22

GOALSCORERS

League (37): Hooper 7 (1 pen), Petrasso 7 (2 pens), Adeloye 3, Baker-Richardson 3 (1 pen), Mason-Clarke 3 (1 pen), Fonguck 2, Kefalas 2, Wordsworth 2, Effiong 1, Faal 1, McQueen 1, Richards 1, Richards-Everton 1, Taylor, H 1, Walker 1, own goal 1.
FA Cup (4): Petrasso 2, Fonguck 1, Hooper 1 (1 pen).
FA Trophy (1): Fox 1.

Loach 23	Preston 15	Dunne 21	McQueen 31 + 3	Richards 3	Hooper 21 + 2	Taylor H 40 + 1	Fonguck 10 + 1	Binnom-Williams 19	Mason-Clarke 34 + 7	Nugent 19 + 2	Duffus 2 + 2	Pavey 3 + 6	Walker 2 + 4	Vasiliou 1 + 11	Azaze 11 + 1	Pascal 2 + 1	Connors 6	Petrasso 18 + 9	Faal 6 + 13	Wordsworth 18	McBurnie 5 + 13	Effiong 5	Mohsni 3	Parrett 1 + 1	Judd 8	Kefalas 19 + 2	Richards-Everton 19 + 3	Daly 18	Baker-Richardson 14 + 3	Taylor R 3 + 1	Adeloye 11 + 6	Vaughan 20	Beard 11	Skeffington 12	Callan — + 1	Parkes 8	*Match No.*
1	2[1]	3	4	5[2]	6	7	8	9	10	11	12	13																									1
1	2	7	3	10[2]	11	4	8	5	9[1]	6	13	12																									2
1	3	4	5		6	7[2]	8[1]	9	10	11	2	13	12																								3
1		3	4		6	7	8	9	10	11	2	5[1]		12																							4
	4	5	6	7	9	10						12	11		1	2	3	8[1]																			5
1			3			6	7[2]	8	9[3]	10		13		12		2		4	5[1]	11	14																6
1	2		3		5	6	7[1]	8	9	10				13				4[2]	12	11																	7
1			3[3]		4	5	6[1]	8	9	10				14			2[2]	12	13	11	7																8
1		6	2		11	3	12	4	9	5								7[1]	13	10	8[2]																9
1		6	4			5	7	3	8	2						12			11	9[1]		10															10
1		6	2			3	7		8	4				12			5		10[1]	9		11															11
1		3	4			6	8[1]		9	10							2		12	11▪		7	5														12
1		3	4		12	7		10	11								2		5[1]			8	6	9													13
1		7	12			3		4	8[2]	6		11[1]	9[3]	14								10	2	13	5▪												14
1		8	2[2]		11	4		6	9[1]			10						12	13							3	5	7									15
1		2			3	4		7	8[3]			13						12		11[2]	14				9		5	10	6[1]								16
1		7			11	3[2]		2	12									6[1]		9	13				4		5	8	10								17
1		7			10[2]	2		4	12									8[1]	13	9	14				5		3	6	11[3]								18
1		6	12		10			5[1]	13									7[3]	14	9	8[2]				4	3		2	11								19
1		3	12		5	7			13								2[2]	4		11[1]	14				9	6		10	8[3]								20
1		6	7		10	3			13									9[1]							5		4	2	12	8	11[2]						21
1		8[2]	2		10[3]	3			14									9[1]	13						5	12	4	7		6	11▪						22
1		9[3]	2		10	13			14										12	8[2]						3	4	7	11[1]	6		5					23
1[1]		8▪	5			4		2	10[3]						12			9	14							13	3	6[2]	11			7					24
			7			5		3	9						1			8	11[1]		12						2	6	10			4					25
			2[3]			6		9	10					12	1			3	4		13					5	7▪		8[2]	14		11[1]					26
	2				10[2]	4			9[1]					13	1			7	12		8					3		6			11	5					27
	2		3		5	7			8					12	1			4[2]		11[3]	13					6▪		10			14	9[1]					28
	2		3[3]		14	4			7					9[1]	1				12	11	5[2]							10	6▪		13	8					29
	4		5		11	7			10	12					1											6		3				2	8[1]	9			30
	2		3		11[1]	5[2]			10						1											4	13	7			12	6	8	9			31
	2		3			5[1]			10						1				12							4	13	7			11[2]	6	8	9			32
	2		3			5			9						1			12								4[3]	14	11	6[2]		13	10	7	8[1]			33
	2		3			6			10						1[2]			14								4	7		11[1]		13	5	8	9[3]	12		34
	2		3			6			10[2]	12				13				4[3]								5	7		8		14	11	9[1]			1	35
			5			9			6[2]	4								12		10▪						7	3		13		11[1]	2		8		1	36
	2[2]		3			5			10	8								12			13					4[1]	6				11	7		9		1	37
			2[1]			4			9	11								12								3	5				6	10	7	8		1	38
						4			9	3				13				7[2]			12						5		11[1]		10	2	6	8		1	39
						3			10[1]	6			12					7[2]			13					2	4				11	5	8	9		1	40
						5			9	4			12					13		10[1]	14					3	6				11[3]	2	7	8[2]		1	41
						3[2]			8	10			12							11	14					2[1]	4		13		5[3]	9	6	7		1	42

FA Cup

Fourth Qualifying	Leiston	(a)	3-2
First Round	Burton Alb	(h)	1-0
Second Round	Milton Keynes D	(h)	0-1

FA Trophy

Third Round	Dorking W	(a)	1-3

BOREHAM WOOD

Ground: Meadow Park, Broughinge Road, Borehamwood, Hertfordshire WD6 5AL. *Tel:* (02089) 535 097.
Website: borehamwoodfootballclub.co.uk *Email:* see website. *Year Formed:* 1948.
Record Attendance: 4,030 v Arsenal, Friendly, 13 July 2001. *Nickname:* 'The Wood' *Manager:* Luke Garrard.
Colours: White shirts, white shorts, white socks.

BOREHAM WOOD – NATIONAL LEAGUE 2020–21 LEAGUE RECORD

Match No.	*Date*	*Venue*	*Opponents*	*Result*	*H/T Score*	*Lg Pos.*	*Goalscorers*	*Attendance*
1	Oct 3	A	Wrexham	L 1-2	0-1	12	Murtagh [60]	0
2	10	H	FC Halifax T	D 0-0	0-0	18		0
3	13	A	King's Lynn T	W 3-0	2-0	12	Rhead [28], Tshimanga 2 (1 pen) [32 (p), 63]	0
4	17	A	Solihull Moors	L 0-1	0-0	13		0
5	27	H	Woking	W 1-0	1-0	11	Mafuta [33]	0
6	Nov 10	H	Dagenham & R	L 0-1	0-0	11		0
7	14	A	Torquay U	D 1-1	1-1	11	Thomas [45]	0
8	17	A	Bromley	D 1-1	1-1	13	Thomas [5]	0
9	21	H	Altrincham	L 0-1	0-0	14		0
10	Dec 5	A	Hartlepool U	W 2-1	1-1	15	Mafuta 2 [36, 68]	0
11	8	A	Notts Co	W 1-0	0-0	13	Fyfield [71]	0
12	12	H	Aldershot T	W 3-2	2-1	7	Tshimanga (pen) [12], Mafuta [21], Thomas [87]	650
13	Jan 2	A	Barnet	W 3-0	3-0	7	Tshimanga 2 (1 pen) [19, 29 (p)], Champion [43]	0
14	23	A	Stockport Co	D 1-1	0-1	10	Tshimanga [60]	0
15	26	H	Chesterfield	D 0-0	0-0	11		0
16	30	H	Eastleigh	L 1-2	1-0	12	Smith [12]	0
17	Feb 2	H	Weymouth	W 1-0	0-0	10	Tshimanga [71]	0
18	6	A	Maidenhead U	W 1-0	0-0	8	Marsh [52]	0
19	13	A	Sutton U	L 0-2	0-1	9		0
20	16	H	Yeovil T	L 2-3	0-3	10	Tshimanga (pen) [47], Mafuta [78]	0
21	20	A	Altrincham	W 3-2	2-0	7	Smith [7], Tshimanga [30], Whitely [48]	0
22	23	H	Bromley	D 1-1	1-0	7	Marsh [29]	0
23	27	H	Solihull Moors	D 2-2	1-1	8	Tshimanga (pen) [40], Morias [53]	0
24	Mar 2	A	Wealdstone	L 0-1	0-1	8		0
25	6	A	Dagenham & R	D 2-2	1-0	9	Whitely [44], Coulthirst [49]	0
26	9	A	Woking	D 0-0	0-0	10		0
27	13	H	Torquay U	D 0-0	0-0	9		0
28	16	H	Notts Co	D 2-2	1-0	11	Marsh [1], Tshimanga [54]	0
29	20	A	Aldershot T	D 3-3	1-0	12	Phillips (og) [14], Whitely [56], Tshimanga (pen) [59]	0
30	Apr 2	H	Sutton U	D 0-0	0-0	12		0
31	5	H	Hartlepool U	D 2-2	2-1	11	Marsh [4], Whitely [26]	0
32	10	H	Wealdstone	W 3-1	0-0	11	Fyfield [72], Tshimanga 2 [84, 90]	0
33	13	A	Chesterfield	D 0-0	0-0	11		0
34	17	A	Yeovil T	L 0-1	0-1	11		0
35	20	H	Barnet	D 0-0	0-0	11		0
36	24	H	Stockport Co	L 0-3	0-2	13		0
37	May 3	H	King's Lynn T	W 5-1	1-1	13	Mafuta [6], Tshimanga 3 [51, 58, 73], Smith [67]	0
38	8	A	FC Halifax T	W 1-0	0-0	13	Ilesanmi [67]	0
39	15	H	Wrexham	L 2-3	2-0	13	Smith [18], Tshimanga [45]	0
40	18	A	Weymouth	W 3-1	2-0	12	Marsh [22], Smith [33], Whitely [85]	545
41	22	A	Eastleigh	L 0-1	0-0	13		1500
42	29	H	Maidenhead U	L 1-4	0-2	14	Marsh [46]	651

Final League Position: 14

GOALSCORERS

League (52): Tshimanga 18 (6 pens), Mafuta 6, Marsh 6, Smith 5, Whitely 5, Thomas 3, Fyfield 2, Champion 1, Coulthirst 1, Ilesanmi 1, Morias 1, Murtagh 1, Rhead 1, own goal 1.
FA Cup (8): Tshimanga 3, Fyfield 2, Rhead 1, Ricketts 1, Smith 1.
FA Trophy (0).

Ashmore 42	Champion 24 + 2	Ilesanmi 39	Fyfield 41	Ricketts 26	Murtagh 32 + 3	Whitely 30 + 4	Thomas 10	Smith 42	Rhead 14 + 12	Tshimanga 41	Coulthirst 3 + 13	Mingoia 6 + 1	Mafuta 39 + 1	Francis-Angol 10 + 5	Stephens 4 + 7	McDonnell 4 + 3	Woodards 1 + 3	Pearce 20 + 1	Morias 10 + 2	Marsh 23	Jallow 1 + 1	Green — + 1	*Match No.*
1	2	3	4	5	6	7^{1}	8	9	10	11	12												1
1	2	4	3	5	6^{3}	13	8	9	12	11	10^{1}	7^{2}	14										2
1	6	2	3	7		9^{3}		5	10^{1}	11	13	12	8	4^{2}	14								3
1	6	3	2	7		9		5	10	11	12		8	4^{1}									4
1	2	4	3	5	12	7	8	9	10	11^{1}			6										5
1	2	4	3				8	9	12	10	11^{1}	7^{2}	6	13	14	5^{3}							6
1	2	4	3				8	9	11	10^{1}	12	7	6			5							7
1	5	3	2				9	4	11	10		8	7		12	6^{1}							8
1	2	4	3				8	9	11	10	12	7	6			5^{1}							9
1	2	4	3		5^{1}		7	8	11	10			6	9		12							10
1	6	3	2		7		9	4	11	10			8	5									11
1	2	4	3		5^{1}		7	8	11	10			6	9		12							12
1	5	4	3		6	8		2^{2}	11	10^{1}	12	9	7^{3}			14	13						13
1		4	3	5	9	12		7		10			6	8^{1}				2	11				14
1	12	6	5	7	9^{2}	13		4	14	10^{1}			8	3^{3}				2	11				15
1		4	3	7^{2}	12	9		5	10		13		6	8^{1}				2	11				16
1	2^{2}	8	4		7	9		5	12	11^{3}	14		6	13				3	10^{1}				17
1		4	3		7			5	12	10			6	8				2	9^{1}	11			18
1		4	3		6	13		5	12	10			7	8^{1}				2	9^{2}	11			19
1		4	3		6	8		5	10^{1}	11			7					2	12	9			20
1		4	3		6	8		5		11	12		7					2	10^{1}	9			21
1		4	3		6	8		5		11	12		7					2	10^{1}	9			22
1		4	3		6	8		5		10			7					2	11	9			23
1		4	3		6	8		5		10	12		7					2	11^{1}	9			24
1		4	3	6^{2}	13	8		5		11	10^{1}		7					2	12	9			25
1		4	3	7	6	8		5		11	12		9^{1}	13	2					10^{2}			26
1		4	3	7	6^{2}	8^{1}		5		11	13		9	12				2		10			27
1		4	3	7	6	8		5		11			9					2		10			28
1		4	3	7	6^{1}	8		5	12	11			9	13				2		10^{2}			29
1	3	2	4	5	7^{1}	8		9	12	10			6							11			30
1	3	2	4	5	7^{1}	8		9	12	10			6							11			31
1	3	2	4	5	7	8		9		10			6							11			32
1	5	2	3	6	8^{1}	9		4	12	10			7							11			33
1	3	2	4	5	7^{1}	8		9	12	10			6		13					11^{2}			34
1		2	3	5		8		9	11	10			6					4		7			35
1	3	2	4^{1}	5	7^{2}	8		9	12	10			6					13		11			36
1	12	2	8^{2}	3	6	7		10		5^{1}			4^{3}		14			9		11	13		37
1	8	2	3	6	7	9		5		10					12			4			11^{1}		38
1	7■	5	2	6	8^{1}	10		4		11			9		12			3					39
1			4	5	6	8		9		10			7		3		2			11			40
1	2		4	5	6	8		9^{1}		10			7		3		12			11			41
1^{2}	5			6	7	9		4		10			8		2		12	3^{1}		11		13	42

FA Cup

Fourth Qualifying	Wimborne T	(h)	2-0
First Round	Southend U	(h)	3-3
(aet; Boreham Wood won 4-3 on penalties)			
Second Round	Canvey Island	(a)	3-0
Third Round	Millwall	(h)	0-2

FA Trophy

Third Round	Yeovil T	(h)	
Boreham Wood awarded a walkover due to the positive COVID-19 test of a Yeovil T player.			
Fourth Round	Torquay U	(h)	0-4

BROMLEY

Ground: Westminster Waste Stadium, Hayes Lane, Bromley, Kent BR2 9EF. *Tel:* (02084) 605 291.
Website: bromleyfc.tv *Email:* info@bromleyfc.co.uk *Year Formed:* 1892.
Record Attendance: 10,798 v Nigeria, Friendly, 24 September 1949. *Nickname:* 'The Ravens', 'The Lillywhites'.
Manager: Andy Woodman. *Colours:* White shirts with black and gold trim, white shorts with black and gold trim, white socks with black and gold trim.

BROMLEY – NATIONAL LEAGUE 2020–21 LEAGUE RECORD

Match No.	*Date*	*Venue*	*Opponents*	*Result*		*H/T Score*	*Lg Pos.*	*Goalscorers*	*Attendance*
1	Oct 10	H	Torquay U	L	1-2	1-0	20	Webster 17	0
2	13	A	Hartlepool U	D	0-0	0-0	19		0
3	27	H	Weymouth	W	3-2	1-1	15	Cheek (pen) 35, L'Ghoul 47, Williamson 67	0
4	31	H	Eastleigh	L	1-2	0-0	18	Alabi 85	0
5	Nov 14	A	Barnet	W	3-1	2-0	12	Kizzi 12, Alabi 25, Cheek 57	0
6	17	H	Boreham Wood	D	1-1	1-1	14	Cheek 45	0
7	21	A	Maidenhead U	D	2-2	0-1	13	Hackett-Fairchild 58, Bush 90	0
8	24	A	Altrincham	W	1-0	1-0	11	Alabi 4	0
9	28	H	Wrexham	D	1-1	1-0	11	Cheek 45	0
10	Dec 1	A	King's Lynn T	W	4-1	3-0	9	Alabi 21, Cheek 42, Trotter 45, Hackett-Fairchild 55	0
11	5	H	Stockport Co	L	0-2	0-1	9		0
12	8	H	Yeovil T	L	1-2	0-2	12	Cheek 70	0
13	12	A	Solihull Moors	W	1-0	1-0	6	Cheek 45	0
14	Jan 23	H	FC Halifax T	L	1-2	1-1	16	Cheek (pen) 15	0
15	26	H	Woking	D	2-2	1-0	16	Roberts 30, Wakefield 62	0
16	30	H	Aldershot T	W	2-0	1-0	13	Bridge 21, Cheek 79	0
17	Feb 6	A	Weymouth	L	1-2	1-2	14	Kizzi 33	0
18	9	H	King's Lynn T	W	2-0	1-0	12	Duffus 2 40, 68	0
19	16	A	Dagenham & R	L	0-1	0-1	12		0
20	20	H	Maidenhead U	D	2-2	2-0	14	Coulson 12, Cheek 33	0
21	23	A	Boreham Wood	D	1-1	0-1	14	Duffus 54	0
22	27	H	Altrincham	W	3-1	3-1	10	Cheek 2 (1 pen) 5, 40 (p), Kizzi 37	0
23	Mar 2	A	Sutton U	L	2-3	1-0	14	Cheek 14, Duffus 65	0
24	6	A	Eastleigh	W	2-1	0-0	11	Holland 64, Duffus 86	0
25	13	H	Barnet	D	2-2	1-1	12	Trotter 8, Cheek (pen) 61	0
26	16	A	Yeovil T	W	2-1	0-0	10	Cheek 56, Reid (og) 90	0
27	20	H	Solihull Moors	W	1-0	0-0	9	Kizzi 79	0
28	23	H	Sutton U	L	1-3	0-1	10	Bridge 79	0
29	27	A	Wrexham	L	0-3	0-2	10		0
30	Apr 2	H	Wealdstone	D	2-2	1-2	10	Webster 25, Cheek 74	0
31	5	A	Stockport Co	D	0-0	0-0	10		0
32	10	H	Dagenham & R	W	1-0	1-0	10	Cheek 32	0
33	13	A	Woking	W	4-3	1-2	9	Bridge 3, Cook (og) 88, Cheek 79, Alabi 83	0
34	17	A	Chesterfield	W	2-1	1-0	9	Cheek 19, Kizzi 84	0
35	24	A	FC Halifax T	W	2-1	1-0	6	Cheek (pen) 13, Alabi 90	0
36	27	H	Chesterfield	L	1-2	0-0	8	Arthurs 67	0
37	May 3	H	Hartlepool U	W	1-0	1-0	7	Arthurs 41	0
38	8	A	Torquay U	D	0-0	0-0	9		0
39	11	A	Wealdstone	W	1-0	0-0	8	Kizzi 60	0
40	15	A	Notts Co	D	2-2	1-0	8	Ellis (og) 27, Campbell 75	0
41	22	A	Aldershot T	W	3-2	1-0	8	Cheek 28, Alabi 76, Kizzi 90	1175
42	29	H	Notts Co	W	1-0	0-0	7	Williamson 64	1344

Final League Position: 7

GOALSCORERS

League (63): Cheek 21 (5 pens), Alabi 7, Kizzi 7, Duffus 5, Bridge 3, Arthurs 2, Hackett-Fairchild 2, Trotter 2, Webster 2, Williamson 2, Bush 1, Campbell 1, Coulson 1, Holland 1, L'Ghoul 1, Roberts 1, Wakefield 1, own goals 3.
FA Cup (1): Cheek 1 (1 pen).
FA Trophy (3): Forster 2, Cheek 1 (1 pen).
National League Play-Offs (2): Alibi 1, Webster 1.

Cousins 42	Webster 26	Bush 35	Holland 14 + 11	Roberts 18 + 3	Raymond 24 + 10	Bingham 26 + 1	Kizzi 38	Forster 6 + 7	Williamson 24 + 10	Cheek 42	Trotter 27 + 6	Alabi 8 + 28	Maloney 15 + 2	L'Ghoul 3 + 1	Coulson 19 + 6	Kyprianou 2 + 1	Hackett-Fairchild 9 + 2	Bridge 28	Duffus 14 + 4	Wakefield 4 + 8	Arthurs 12 + 3	Purrington 1	Vincent 4 + 3	Fox 12	Mitchell 9	Campbell — + 4	*Match No.*
1	2	3	4	5	6^{3}	7^{2}	8	9	10^{1}	11	12	13	14														1
1	4	5	3^{3}	2	6			8^{2}	11	10	7	13	14	9^{1}	12												2
1		3	14	4				8^{3}	9	11^{1}	6	13	7	10^{2}	2	5	12										3
1		3	4	6	14			10^{1}	9	5	8	13	7^{2}	11^{3}		2	12										4
1	3	5		4	7	8	2		9	11		10				12	6^{1}										5
1	5	3		4	7^{1}	6	2		11	8	12	9					10										6
1	3	5	14	4^{1}	7^{2}	8	2		6^{3}	11	12	10		13			9										7
1	3	5	13	4		7	2		8■	11	6	10^{1}			12		9^{2}										8
1	3	5		4		8	2	12		11	7	10^{1}			6		9										9
1	4^{1}	5	12	3	14	7	2	13		11^{2}	8	10			9		6^{3}										10
1	3	5	12	4^{2}		8	2	13		11	7	10^{1}			6		9										11
1	11		4	9^{2}	13	3	2		12	6	10	7^{1}			5		8										12
1	3	5	13	4	14	7	2		9^{2}	10^{3}	8	12			6		11^{1}										13
1	3	5		4	14	6	2	8^{2}	12	11	7■							9^{3}	10^{1}	13							14
1	4	2	13	3	6				11	10			7					8^{2}	12	9^{1}	5						15
1	3		12	4	5	6	2		10^{1}	11^{3}		13	7					9^{2}	14	8							16
1	3	5■	13	4	6		2		10^{1}	11		14	7^{2}					9^{3}	12	8■							17
1	10		4		5	3	2		12	6^{2}	9	13						11	7^{3}			8^{1}	14				18
1	3	5	4		7^{2}	14	2^{3}	6^{1}	12	11	8				13			9	10								19
1	3	5	4	13		7	2		14	10	8	12			9^{2}			6^{3}	11^{1}								20
1		3	5		6	7	2			11	8				4			9^{1}	10	12							21
1		4■	5		7	3	2		13	8^{1}	10	14			6^{3}			11^{2}	9	12							22
1	4		3		5	7	2		12	11^{1}	8	14			6^{2}			9^{3}	10	13							23
1	4		3		5		2			11	8	12	7		6			9^{2}	10^{1}	13							24
1	4		3		5		2■		12	11^{3}	8	14	7		6			9^{2}	10^{1}	13							25
1	4		3^{3}	13	5		2			11^{1}	8	14	7		6			9^{2}	10	12							26
1	3^{2}	4		13	5		2			11	8	12	7		6			9	10^{1}								27
1		3		4^{1}	6		2		14	10^{2}	8	13	7		5			9	11^{3}	12							28
1	3	4			8^{2}		2		13	11^{1}	7		6		5^{3}			9	10		14		12				29
1	3	4			13		2		10^{1}	11	7	14	6^{2}		12			8			9^{3}		5				30
1	3^{2}	4			8		2		10	11			7		12			9			13		6^{1}	5			31
1		4	5^{1}		6		2		10^{3}	11		14	7		12■			9			13		8^{2}	3			32
1		4			12		3			11	8^{3}	14	7^{1}					9	10	6^{2}	2		13	5			33
1		4			14	7	2		10	11^{2}		12						9	13		8^{1}		6^{3}	5	3		34
1		4				7	2		10	11^{3}	13	12			6			9^{2}			8^{1}			5	3	14	35
1		4			12	7	2		11^{2}	10		13			5^{1}			9			8			3	6		36
1		4	14		6^{1}	7	2		10^{3}	11	13	12						9^{2}			8			5	3		37
1		4			13	6	2		10	11^{1}	7	14			9^{2}						8^{3}			5	3	12	38
1		4	12		6	7	2	14	10^{3}	11		13						9^{1}			8			5	3^{2}		39
1		4				7	2	14	10^{1}	11	6	13						9^{3}			8^{2}			5	3	12	40
1		4				7	2	12	10^{3}	11	6	13						9^{1}			8^{2}			5	3	14	41
1		4			6^{3}	7	2	12	10^{1}	11	14	13						9			8^{2}			5	3		42

FA Cup

Fourth Qualifying	Sutton U	(a)	1-0
First Round	Yeovil T	(h)	0-1

(aet.)

FA Trophy

Third Round	Hemel Hempstead T	(h)	2-0
Fourth Round	Woking	(h)	1-1

(Woking won 7-6 on penalties)

National League Play-Offs

Eliminator	Hartlepool U	(a)	2-3

CHESTERFIELD

Ground: Technique Stadium, 1866 Sheffield Road, Whittington Moor, Chesterfield, Derbyshire S41 8NZ.
Tel: (01246) 269 300. *Website:* www.chesterfield-fc.co.uk *Email:* reception@chesterfield-fc.co.uk *Year Formed:* 1866.
Record Attendance: 30,968 v Newcastle U, Division 2, 7 April 1939 (at Saltergate); 10,089 v Rotherham U, FL 2, 18 March 2011 (at b2net Stadium (now called the Technique Stadium)). *Nickname:* 'The Blues', 'The Spireites'.
Manager: James Rowe. *Colours:* Blue shirts with white trim, white shorts with blue trim, blue socks with white trim.

CHESTERFIELD – NATIONAL LEAGUE 2020–21 LEAGUE RECORD

Match No.	Date	Venue	Opponents	Result	H/T Score	Lg Pos.	Goalscorers	Attendance
1	Oct 6	H	Hartlepool U	L 1-2	0-0	16	Tom Denton (pen) [53]	0
2	10	H	Woking	W 4-0	1-0	11	Tom Denton [4], Rawson 2 [84, 90], Kiwomya [87]	0
3	13	A	Torquay U	L 1-2	1-1	14	Tom Denton [43]	0
4	17	H	Stockport Co	L 1-2	1-1	19	Cropper [36]	0
5	20	A	Wealdstone	L 2-3	1-2	19	Tom Denton 2 (1 pen) [3 (p), 83]	0
6	31	A	Yeovil T	W 1-0	0-0	16	Tom Denton [69]	0
7	Nov 14	H	Maidenhead U	L 1-2	1-0	19	Boden [30]	0
8	17	A	Altrincham	L 2-3	1-1	20	Boden [13], Cropper [63]	0
9	21	H	Notts Co	L 2-3	1-1	21	Smith, J [33], Tom Denton [78]	0
10	28	A	Weymouth	W 2-1	1-1	16	Asante [45], Tom Denton [60]	0
11	Dec 1	H	Aldershot T	D 0-0	0-0	14		0
12	8	A	Sutton U	W 1-0	1-0	16	Hollis [39]	776
13	12	H	Barnet	W 6-0	1-0	14	Asante 3 [40, 74, 78], Boden [56], Hollis [64], McCourt [89]	0
14	Jan 2	H	Solihull Moors	W 1-0	1-0	13	Whelan [43]	0
15	5	A	Solihull Moors	L 1-2	1-0	14	Tom Denton [34]	0
16	23	H	Wrexham	W 2-1	1-1	9	Asante 2 [9, 89]	0
17	26	A	Boreham Wood	D 0-0	0-0	9		0
18	30	A	Dagenham & R	D 2-2	2-1	10	Evans [17], Asante [40]	0
19	Feb 20	A	Notts Co	W 1-0	1-0	13	Gunning [32]	0
20	23	H	Altrincham	W 1-0	0-0	11	Asante [49]	0
21	27	A	Stockport Co	L 0-2	0-0	13		0
22	Mar 2	H	Eastleigh	W 1-0	0-0	9	Asante [85]	0
23	6	H	Yeovil T	W 3-0	0-0	8	Asante [48], Whelan [68], McCourt [78]	0
24	13	A	Maidenhead U	L 0-2	0-1	10		0
25	16	H	Sutton U	L 0-1	0-1	12		0
26	20	A	Barnet	W 2-0	1-0	10	Whelan [10], Yussuf [47]	0
27	23	A	Aldershot T	W 1-0	1-0	9	Whittle [27]	0
28	27	H	Weymouth	W 1-0	1-0	7	Whelan [37]	0
29	Apr 2	A	Eastleigh	W 1-0	0-0	6	Mandeville [61]	0
30	10	A	King's Lynn T	W 2-1	0-1	6	Tyson [74], Whelan [75]	0
31	13	H	Boreham Wood	D 0-0	0-0	5		0
32	17	H	Bromley	L 1-2	0-1	7	Maguire [74]	0
33	20	H	FC Halifax T	L 1-2	0-2	7	Mitchell [71]	0
34	24	A	Wrexham	D 0-0	0-0	8		0
35	27	A	Bromley	W 2-1	0-0	6	Clarke [51], Carline [76]	0
36	May 1	A	Hartlepool U	L 1-3	0-3	7	Kerr [60]	0
37	3	H	Torquay U	L 0-2	0-1	8		0
38	8	A	Woking	W 4-1	3-1	8	Gunning [7], Dinanga [20], Carline [40], Clarke [88]	0
39	11	H	King's Lynn T	W 4-1	2-1	6	Yussuf [28], Carline [33], Yarney [47], Rowe [54]	0
40	15	H	Wealdstone	D 0-0	0-0	7		0
41	22	H	Dagenham & R	W 2-1	1-1	7	Rowe 2 (1 pen) [38, 86 (p)]	2950
42	29	A	FC Halifax T	W 2-1	1-1	6	Mandeville [14], Tyson [79]	843

Final League Position: 6

GOALSCORERS

League (60): Asante 10, Tom Denton 9 (2 pens), Whelan 5, Boden 3, Carline 3, Rowe 3 (1 pen), Clarke 2, Cropper 2, Gunning 2, Hollis 2, Mandeville 2, McCourt 2, Rawson 2, Tyson 2, Yussuf 2, Dinanga 1, Evans 1, Kerr 1, Kiwomya 1, Maguire 1, Mitchell 1, Smith, J 1, Whittle 1, Yarney 1.
FA Cup (1): Butterfield 1 *(Milan Butterfield scored in the 1-1 draw with Stockport Co. However the FA ordered that the game be replayed because Chesterfield fielded an ineligible player).*
FA Trophy (1): Hollis 1.
National League Play-Offs (2): Mandeville 1, Rowe 1.

Letheren 13	Cropper 10 + 2	Yarney 10 + 6	Evans 24 + 1	Maguire 40	Buchanan 10	Smith J 10 + 1	Weston 37	Butterfield 5 + 2	Boden 5 + 4	Denton Tom 14 + 1	Mandeville 14 + 20	Rawson 1 + 7	Rowley 5 + 6	Sharman 6	Kiwomya 3 + 2	Denton Tyler 2 + 3 / Rowe 9	McKay — + 1	Tyson 4 + 14	Hollis 17 + 1	Addai 2	Asante 22	Whelan 17 + 10	McCourt 14 + 5	Taylor 12 + 4	Carline 30	Dinanga 5 + 7	Przybek 3	Whittle 17 + 2	Gunning 17 + 1	Smith M 8 + 3	Smith G 18	Clarke 12 + 8	Yussuf 6 + 4	Kerr 16	Oyeleke 12	Mitchell 6 + 2	Montgomery 6	Match No.
1	2	3	4	5^{2}	6	7	8^{1}	9	10■	11^{3}	12	13	14																									1
1	6		4	3^{1}	2	7	8	9^{2}		11^{3}	14	13		5	10	12																						2
1	11		3	4	2	9	5	14		10^{1}	6^{2}	12		8	7^{3}		13																					3
1	2		4	5	6^{1}	8	7^{2}	13		11	9	10^{3}		3	14			12																				4
1	2	13	4			7	8		14	11	9^{2}	12		3^{3}		6		10^{1}	5																			5
1			4	3	2^{3}	6^{2}	8	7		10	13	12		5	9	14		11^{1}																				6
1	2		4	5	6		8	7	10	11		12	9^{2}	3^{1}	13																							7
	2	3	4	5	6^{1}	9^{2}	8	7	10^{3}	11		13	12			14				1																		8
	8	7	3	4	2	6	5		10	11						9				1																		9
1	3^{2}	14	5	6	4	9	8		13	10	12		7^{1}						2		11^{3}																	10
1	11		3	4	2	8^{2}	5		14	9	7^{1}								10		6^{3}	12	13															11
1	12		3	2			9^{3}		14	11	13								5		10^{1}	6	7	4^{2}	8													12
1	13	3		5			7		11^{3}	12	14								4		10^{2}	9	8	6	2^{1}													13
1		14	3	4		13	7			10^{1}	12								5		11	9^{2}	8^{3}	6	2■													14
1		2	3	4			7			10^{2}	12								5		11	9^{1}	8	6		13												15
		13	3	4			7				14		12						5		11	9^{2}	8		2	10^{1}	1	6^{3}										16
			3	4			7				12		10^{2}						5		11	9^{1}	8		2		1	6	13									17
			2	3			8				12								4		11	9■			7	10^{1}	1	5	6^{2}	13								18
			2	3			8				12								4		11^{1}		9	5	7	10^{3}			6^{2}		1	13	14					19
			3	4			7				9^{3}								5		11		8	13	2	12		6^{2}			1	14	10^{1}					20
			2	3			8				12								4		11		9^{2}	5	7	10^{3}			6^{1}	14	1		13					21
				3			7				12							14			11	9^{1}	13		2			6	5	10^{3}	1	8^{2}		4				22
				5			7				9^{3}							13			11^{2}	10	8	12	2			6^{1}	4		1	14		3				23
			3	2							11^{3}							13			10	8	7	14	6			5^{1}	4	9^{2}	1		12					24
				5			7											13	14		11	10^{1}	8	6	2			12	4^{2}		1	9		3^{3}				25
				3			4						14					12	8		5^{2}	7^{1}			2	13		9			1	6	11^{3}	10				26
				3			7				14								4		11^{2}	12			2	13		6		8	1	9^{3}	10^{1}	5				27
		12		5^{1}			8				14							10^{2}	4		11	9^{3}			2	13		6		7	1			3				28
		5					8				12		10^{3}					13	4^{2}		11	9^{1}			2			6		7	1	14		3				29
				5			8				9^{2}							12			11	13			2			6	4	7^{3}	1	14	10^{1}	3				30
				3			7				13							12			11^{1}	9^{2}			2			6	4		1			5	8	10		31
		4		3			7^{2}				10^{1}							12				13			6			2		14	1	9^{3}		5	8	11		32
				5			7				10^{2}							12				9^{3}		13	2			6^{1}	4			14		3	8	11	1	33
				2			7									11		12				13		3	6				5		1	8^{1}		4	10	9^{2}		34
		14		2												11		12				13		3	6				5^{2}	8	1	7^{1}		4	10	9^{3}		35
		3		4			7				12		13			11		10^{3}						6^{2}	2						1	8^{1}		5	9	14		36
				3							4^{3}					10						14			2			6	8	5^{1}	1	13	12	7	11	9^{2}		37
				5			7				13		6^{1}			11						9^{3}	12		2	10			4			14		3^{2}	8		1	38
		2	14	4												11						13	7^{3}		6	12		5^{2}	3			9	10^{1}		8		1	39
		2	3	4							9^{3}					11						13	6^{1}		5	12						8	10^{2}		7	14	1	40
			2	4			8^{1}				10^{3}		12			11						14	13	5	7				3			9^{2}			6		1	41
			2	3			7				10^{1}					11^{2}		12					14	4^{3}	6			13	5			8			9		1	42

FA Cup

Fourth Qualifying Stockport Co (a) 1-1
(Chesterfield won 7-6 on penalties but the FA ordered the game to be replayed because Chesterfield fielded an ineligible player)
Fourth Qualifying Stockport Co (a) 0-4

National League Play-Offs

Eliminator Notts Co (a) 2-3

FA Trophy

Third Round Brackley T (h) 0-0
(Chesterfield won 4-3 on penalties)
Fourth Round Boston U (a) 1-1
(Chesterfield won 4-1 on penalties)
Fifth Round Aldershot T (a)
Aldershot T awarded a walkover due to the positive COVID-19 test of a Chesterfield player.

DAGENHAM & REDBRIDGE

Ground: Chigwell Construction Stadium, Victoria Road, Dagenham, Essex RM10 7XL.
Tel: (020) 8592 1549. *Website:* www.daggers.co.uk *Email:* info@daggers.co.uk *Year Formed:* 1992.
Record Attendance: 5,949 v Ipswich T, FA Cup 3rd rd, 5 January 2002. *Nickname:* 'The Daggers'.
Manager: Daryl McMahon. *Colours:* Red shirts with blue trim, blue shorts with white trim, blue socks.

DAGENHAM & REDBRIDGE – NATIONAL LEAGUE 2020–21 LEAGUE RECORD

Match No.	*Date*	*Venue*	*Opponents*	*Result*		*H/T Score*	*Lg Pos.*	*Goalscorers*	*Attendance*
1	Oct 3	A	FC Halifax T	L	0-2	0-1	16		0
2	6	H	Barnet	L	1-2	1-0	19	Balanta [30]	0
3	10	H	Wealdstone	W	1-0	0-0	13	Balanta [65]	0
4	13	A	Woking	L	0-2	0-2	16		0
5	17	H	Yeovil T	D	0-0	0-0	17		0
6	27	A	Maidenhead U	L	1-2	1-0	18	Deering [45]	0
7	Nov 10	A	Boreham Wood	W	1-0	0-0	15	Weston [58]	0
8	17	A	Sutton U	D	1-1	0-1	16	McCallum [66]	0
9	Dec 2	H	Notts Co	D	0-0	0-0	19		0
10	5	A	Aldershot T	L	1-2	0-2	19	Rance [89]	920
11	8	A	Weymouth	W	3-2	2-1	17	Brundle 2 (1 pen) [26, 71 (p)], McCallum [27]	438
12	12	H	Altrincham	L	0-1	0-1	17		773
13	15	A	Torquay U	W	1-0	1-0	17	McCallum [14]	1165
14	Jan 19	H	Stockport Co	L	0-2	0-0	19		0
15	23	H	King's Lynn T	W	3-2	0-2	18	Reynolds [72], Eleftheriou [78], Brundle [90]	0
16	26	A	Eastleigh	L	0-3	0-1	18		0
17	30	H	Chesterfield	D	2-2	1-2	18	Wilson [20], Deering [53]	0
18	Feb 6	A	Wrexham	D	2-2	0-1	18	Robinson [77], Rance [90]	0
19	9	A	Notts Co	L	1-3	0-3	18	Robinson [90]	0
20	16	H	Bromley	W	1-0	1-0	17	Gordon [25]	0
21	23	H	Sutton U	L	1-2	0-1	18	Gordon [62]	0
22	27	A	Yeovil T	L	0-1	0-0	18		0
23	Mar 2	A	Solihull Moors	W	1-0	0-0	17	McCallum [57]	0
24	6	H	Boreham Wood	D	2-2	0-1	17	Balanta 2 [73, 89]	0
25	9	H	Maidenhead U	W	2-1	2-0	16	McCallum 2 [14, 16]	0
26	16	H	Weymouth	D	1-1	1-0	16	Gordon [43]	0
27	20	A	Altrincham	W	1-0	0-0	16	Wright [79]	0
28	23	H	Hartlepool U	L	0-1	0-1	16		0
29	27	H	Torquay U	W	1-0	0-0	15	Balanta [80]	0
30	Apr 2	A	Hartlepool U	L	1-2	1-1	17	Robinson [32]	0
31	5	H	Aldershot T	L	0-2	0-1	17		0
32	10	A	Bromley	L	0-1	0-1	17		0
33	13	H	Eastleigh	W	2-0	1-0	16	Balanta [23], McCallum [65]	0
34	17	H	Solihull Moors	W	3-2	2-1	13	Saunders [29], Balanta (pen) [41], Robinson [50]	0
35	24	A	King's Lynn T	W	3-0	2-0	14	McCallum [16], Balanta [39], Robinson [46]	0
36	May 1	A	Barnet	W	2-0	1-0	11	McCallum [38], Robinson [56]	0
37	3	H	Woking	W	3-1	2-0	11	McCallum 2 (1 pen) [8, 27 (p)], Balanta [81]	0
38	8	A	Wealdstone	W	5-0	4-0	11	Balanta [1], Robinson 2 [4, 90], McCallum 2 [21, 36]	0
39	11	A	Stockport Co	D	1-1	1-1	11	McCallum [43]	0
40	15	H	FC Halifax T	W	3-0	2-0	11	Vilhete [34], McCallum [45], Balanta [55]	0
41	22	A	Chesterfield	L	1-2	1-1	12	Gordon [29]	2950
42	29	H	Wrexham	D	1-1	0-0	12	McCallum [51]	1278

Final League Position: 12

GOALSCORERS

League (53): McCallum 16 (1 pen), Balanta 11 (1 pen), Robinson 8, Gordon 4, Brundle 3 (1 pen), Deering 2, Rance 2, Eleftheriou 1, Reynolds 1, Saunders 1, Vilhete 1, Weston 1, Wilson 1, Wright 1.
FA Cup (5): Brundle 2 (2 pens), McCallum 1, Wilson 2.
FA Trophy (6): McQueen 2, Balanta 1, McCallum 1, Reynolds 1, Wilson 1.

Justham 42	Eleftheriou 16 + 2	Reynolds 18 + 2	Clark 33	Johnson 36 + 1	Brundle 17	Rance 24 + 2	Robinson 24 + 2	Balanta 30 + 4	McQueen 7 + 15	McCallum 32 + 4	Croll 17 + 4	Deering 13 + 5	Clifton — + 6	Weston 22 + 4	Adams 7 + 3	Brown 3	Wright 26 + 5	Thompson-Brissett — + 2	Saunders 14 + 10	Ogogo 8	Wilson 13 + 14	Jones 14 + 3	Gordon 17 + 5	Sagaf 9 + 4	Smith 1 + 6	Vilhete 10 + 4	Khan 9 + 2	*Match No.*
1	2	3	4	5	6^{2}	7	8^{3}	9	10^{1}	11	12	13	14															1
1	12	3	4	5	6	7^{3}	13	10	14	11	2■	9^{2}		8^{1}														2
1	2	3^{3}	4	5	7			10		11^{2}		13	14	8^{1}	6	9	12											3
1	2		3	5	7			10	13	11^{1}	4	8	12^{3}		6	9^{2}		14										4
1	3^{2}		4	6	2			11	10		5	8			7	9^{1}	13		12									5
1	12		3	5	6			10	13		4	8					2		9^{2}	7^{1}	11							6
1			4	6	8			13		10^{3}	5	9^{1}		12	14		2^{2}			7	11	3						7
1			4■	6	8			10^{3}		12	5	9^{1}		2	14		13			7	11	3^{2}						8
1			3	5	8			12		11	4	9		6^{1}			2			7	10							9
1			3	5	6	12		8^{3}	14	11	4	9^{1}		13			2			7	10^{2}							10
1			3	5	8	6			11^{1}	10	4			9			2			7	12							11
1			4	6	2	7		12	11^{1}		5			9			3^{2}	13		8	10							12
1	2		3	5^{3}	8■	7			9^{1}	10^{2}	4			11	12		13			6	14							13
1	2	4		12	7^{3}		8	10	14	11	5	9									13	3^{2}	6^{1}					14
1	2	3		5^{3}	6	7		9	14	11^{2}	4	10							8^{1}		13		12					15
1	2	3		5^{2}	6	7	14	9^{1}		11	4	10							8^{3}		13		12					16
1	5^{1}	3	2		6	7				10	4	12		8^{3}					14		11		13	9^{2}				17
1	2	14	3	5^{1}		8	7		10	12	4	9		13					6^{2}		11^{3}							18
1	5^{1}	2	4			6	7		11^{3}	10	3	9^{2}		8					14		13		12					19
1		3	2	4		8	6		12		14	13		5	7^{3}				10^{1}		11^{2}		9					20
1		3	2	4		9	7		14	12		13		5	8^{1}				10^{2}		11^{3}		6					21
1		3■	4	2		6	7	12		11^{2}				9	8^{3}		14		10^{1}		13		5					22
1			3	4		8	6	10^{2}		11				5			2		13			12	9		7^{1}			23
1			3	2		7	6	11		10^{1}				9			4		12		13	8^{2}	5					24
1			3	2		7	6^{2}	11		10^{3}				9			4		8^{1}		14	12	5	13				25
1			3	4		7		10					12	5	6		2				11^{1}		9	8^{2}		13		26
1			3	4		7		11	14				13	5			2				10^{3}		9	6^{2}		12	8^{1}	27
1			3	4		7^{2}		10	13	12				5			2				11^{1}		9	8		6^{3}	14	28
1			3	2		7	6	11		10				9			4		12				5	8^{1}				29
1			3			7	8	10	13	11^{1}				5			2		12			4	9			6^{2}		30
1	5^{3}	12	4			7	8	10	14	11							3		9^{1}			6^{2}	2			13		31
1			5	4		7	6^{1}	10		11			14				3		8				2^{3}	12		13	9^{2}	32
1			4	5			6	10		11							3		7			2^{1}		8	12	9		33
1			4	3			6	11^{2}		10							5		7^{1}		14	2^{3}	12	8	13	9		34
1			3	4		14	9	10^{1}		11							2				12	5^{2}	6	13		7	8^{3}	35
1	5	3		4		7^{2}	8	10^{1}		11							2		14			12		6^{3}		9	13	36
1	5	3		4			8	10^{2}		11	14						2				13	7^{3}			12	9	6^{1}	37
1	5	3		4			8	10^{1}	14	11	12						2					7^{2}			13	9	6^{3}	38
1	5	3		4			8	10^{1}		11							2		12			7				9	6	39
1		3		4			8	10^{2}	13	11				12			2		6			5^{1}			14	9^{3}	7	40
1		3		4			8			11^{2}				10			2		5^{3}		12	6■	9	13	14		7^{1}	41
1		4	3				8	10^{1}	13	11^{2}				5^{3}			2		12		14		9	7			6	42

FA Cup

Fourth Qualifying	Hartley Wintney	(h)	1-0
First Round	Grimsby T	(h)	3-1
Second Round	Mansfield T	(a)	1-2

(aet.)

FA Trophy

Third Round	Ebbsfleet U	(h)	5-2
Fourth Round	Sutton U	(a)	1-3

DOVER ATHLETIC

Ground: Crabble Athletic Ground, Lewisham Road, Dover, Kent CT17 0JB. *Tel:* (01304) 822 373.
Website: doverathletic.com *Email:* enquiries@doverathletic.com *Year Formed:* 1894 as Dover FC, reformed as Dover Ath 1983. *Record Attendance:* 7,000 v Folkestone, 13 October 1951 (Dover FC); 5,645 v Crystal Palace, FA Cup 3rd rd, 4 January 2015 (Dover Ath). *Nickname:* 'The Whites'. *Manager:* Andy Hessenthaler.
Colours: White shirts with black trim, black shorts with white trim, black socks.

National League Statement of 26 March 2021.

An Independent Panel has ruled that Dover Athletic are deemed guilty of four breaches of Rule 8.39 for failing to meet fixture obligations between February 16th and February 27th.

The Club will play no further part in the 2020–21 Playing Season, with the Club's existing National League (Step One) results expunged. A 12-point deduction for the 2021–22 Playing Season and fine of £40,000 have additionally been issued.

The following matches are those completed and those postponed for the 2020–21 season. The League record for 2020–21 was expunged from the records.

DOVER ATHLETIC – NATIONAL LEAGUE 2020–21 LEAGUE RECORD

Match No.	Date	Venue	Opponents	Result	H/T Score	Goalscorers
1	Oct 3	H	Notts Co	W 1-0	0-0	Ransom 89
2	6	A	Bromley	L 1-4	0-1	Wood 60
3	10	A	Stockport Co	L 0-3	0-0	
4	13	H	Aldershot T	L 0-5	0-3	
5	17	A	Torquay U	L 0-2	0-2	
6	27	H	Eastleigh	W 3-2	2-1	Wood 24, Collins 29, Azeez 80
7	31	H	Altrincham	L 0-1	0-1	
8	Nov 17	H	Woking	L 1-5	0-3	Gobern 65
9	21	A	King's Lynn T	L 0-2	0-1	
10	Dec 26	H	Dagenham & R	L 0-1	0-0	
11	Jan 9	H	Weymouth	P-P		
12	12	H	Boreham Wood	D 1-1	0-1	Bramble 61
13	16	A	Wrexham	L 1-3	1-1	Rose 43
14	23	H	Solihull Moors	L 0-2	0-1	
15	26	H	Barnet	W 3-1	3-0	De Havilland 2 17, 19, Rose 35
16	30	A	Yeovil T	L 1-3	1-1	Azeez 13
17	Feb 6	H	Hartlepool U	P-P		
18	9	H	Maidenhead U	P-P		
19	13	A	FC Halifax T	P-P		
20	16	A	Sutton U	P-P		
21	20	H	King's Lynn T	P-P		
22	23	A	Woking	P-P		
23	27	H	Maidenhead U	P-P		
24	27	H	Torquay U	P-P		
25	Mar 2	A	Maidenhead U	P-P		
26	6	A	Altrincham	P-P		
27	9	A	Eastleigh	P-P		
28	13	H	Wealdstone	P-P		
29	16	A	Solihull Moors	P-P		
30	20	H	Wrexham	P-P		
31	23	H	Chesterfield	P-P		
32	27	A	Boreham Wood	P-P		
33	30	A	Dagenham & R	P-P		
34	Apr 2	H	FC Halifax T	P-P		
35	5	A	Chesterfield	P-P		
36	10	H	Sutton U	P-P		
37	13	A	Barnet	P-P		
38	17	A	Weymouth	P-P		
39	20	H	Weymouth	P-P		
40	27	A	Wealdston	P-P		
41	May 1	H	Bromley	P-P		
42	3	A	Aldershot T	P-P		
43	8	H	Stockport Co	P-P		
44	15	A	Notts Co	P-P		
45	22	H	Yeovil T	P-P		
46	29	A	Hartlepool U	P-P		

CUP RESULTS 2020–21

FA Cup				**FA Trophy**			
Fourth Qualifying	Yeovil T	(a)	3-3	Third Round	Woking	(a)	1-2

(aet; Yeovil T won 7-6 on penalties

CUP GOALSCORERS 2020–21

FA Cup (3): Collins 2, Bramble 1.

FA Trophy (1): Azeez 1.

EASTLEIGH

Ground: The Silverlake Stadium, Ten Acres, Stoneham Lane, Eastleigh, Hampshire SO50 9HT. *Tel:* (02380) 613 361.
Website: eastleighfc.com *Email:* admin@eastleighfc.com *Year Formed:* 1946.
Record Attendance: 5,250 v Bolton W, FA Cup 3rd rd, 9 January 2016. *Nickname:* 'Spitfires'.
Manager: Ben Strevens. *Colours:* Blue shirts with white trim, blue shorts with white trim, blue socks with white trim.

EASTLEIGH – NATIONAL LEAGUE 2020–21 LEAGUE RECORD

Match No.	*Date*	*Venue*	*Opponents*	*Result*		*H/T Score*	*Lg Pos.*	*Goalscorers*	*Attendance*
1	Oct 3	A	Barnet	W	5-1	1-1	1	Barnett 5, Wynter 53, House 56, Miley 64, Bell-Baggie 75	0
2	6	H	Torquay U	W	2-1	0-1	1	House 2 73, 82	0
3	10	H	Altrincham	D	1-1	1-1	3	Miley 45	0
4	17	H	Aldershot T	D	2-2	1-1	8	Tomlinson (pen) 42, Wynter 90	0
5	31	A	Bromley	W	2-1	0-0	4	House 2 59, 66	0
6	Nov 17	H	Wealdstone	W	2-0	0-0	5	Miley 68, Smart 90	0
7	Dec 1	A	Yeovil T	W	3-1	2-0	3	Barnett 7, Tomlinson (pen) 34, House 59	0
8	5	H	Maidenhead U	L	0-1	0-0	6		776
9	22	A	FC Halifax T	L	1-3	0-2	13	Barnett 54	0
10	26	H	Weymouth	D	0-0	0-0	12		0
11	28	A	Woking	D	0-0	0-0	10		0
12	Jan 2	A	Weymouth	D	1-1	1-0	10	Green 11	0
13	19	H	King's Lynn T	L	0-1	0-1	12		0
14	23	A	Sutton U	L	0-3	0-2	14		0
15	26	H	Dagenham & R	W	3-0	1-0	10	Hill 9, Tomlinson 2 (2 pens) 50, 67	0
16	30	A	Boreham Wood	W	2-1	0-1	9	Barnett 71, Smith 90	0
17	Feb 2	H	Wrexham	D	1-1	0-1	9	Tomlinson (pen) 71	0
18	6	H	Solihull Moors	D	1-1	1-0	9	Barnett 22	0
19	9	H	Yeovil T	W	1-0	1-0	5	Hill 42	0
20	16	H	Hartlepool U	W	2-1	2-0	5	House 1, Barnett 27	0
21	20	H	Stockport Co	W	1-0	0-0	4	Tomlinson (pen) 54	0
22	23	A	Wealdstone	D	0-0	0-0	4		0
23	Mar 2	A	Chesterfield	L	0-1	0-0	5		0
24	6	H	Bromley	L	1-2	0-0	5	Barnett 56	0
25	13	A	Hartlepool U	D	0-0	0-0	8		0
26	16	A	Wrexham	D	2-2	1-1	8	Tomlinson 2 (1 pen) 11, 50 (p)	0
27	20	H	FC Halifax T	W	1-0	0-0	8	Barnett 59	0
28	23	A	Stockport Co	L	0-3	0-1	8		0
29	27	A	King's Lynn T	L	1-2	1-0	9	Payne 1	0
30	Apr 2	H	Chesterfield	L	0-1	0-0	9		0
31	5	A	Maidenhead U	W	1-0	0-0	9	House 87	0
32	10	H	Woking	D	0-0	0-0	9		0
33	13	A	Dagenham & R	L	0-2	0-1	10		0
34	17	A	Notts Co	W	1-0	1-0	10	House 45	0
35	24	H	Sutton U	W	1-0	1-0	10	Marriott 43	0
36	27	H	Notts Co	W	2-0	0-0	7	Boyce 57, Tomlinson 75	0
37	May 1	A	Torquay U	L	1-3	0-1	8	Barnett 59	0
38	15	H	Barnet	W	3-0	1-0	10	Barnett 9, Tomlinson (pen) 72, Smart 83	0
39	18	A	Aldershot T	W	3-1	1-0	9	Wynter 29, Boyce 73, Tomlinson 84	1073
40	22	H	Boreham Wood	W	1-0	0-0	9	Tomlinson (pen) 90	1500
41	25	A	Altrincham	D	1-1	0-0	8	Barnett 51	600
42	29	A	Solihull Moors	L	0-2	0-2	9		550

Final League Position: 9

GOALSCORERS

League (49): Tomlinson 12 (9 pens), Barnett 11, House 9, Miley 3, Wynter 3, Boyce 2, Hill 2, Smart 2, Bell-Baggie 1, Green 1, Marriott 1, Payne 1, Smith 1.
FA Cup (3): Bearwish 1, House 1, Smith 1 (1 pen).
FA Trophy (3): Hill 2, Boyce 1.

McDonnell 42	Smart 27 + 14	Partington 29 + 1	Wynter 16 + 2	Boyce 42	Tomlinson 37 + 3	Payne 40	Miley 29 + 6	Bell-Baggie 12 + 7	House 34 + 3	Barnett 32 + 3	Green 22 + 11	Smith 9 + 27	Hollands 26 + 4	Bearwish 2 + 8	Hill 21 + 10	Blair 9 + 12	Bird 28 + 1	Marriott 5 + 6	Match No.
1	2^1	3	4	5	6	7	8	9^2	10	11^3	12	13	14						1
1	2	3	4	5	6^1	7	8	9^3	10	11^2	12	13	14						2
1	6	2	3	4	14	7	8	9^1	10	11^3	5^2	12		13					3
1	7^2	2	3	4^1	5	6	8	9^3	10	11	14	12	13						4
1	6		7	4	8	5	3		9		2	11	10						5
1	2		3	4	5	8	9^3		11^2	10^1	6■	12	7		13	14			6
1	6^2	2	3	4	5	8	9		11^3	10^1		12	7		13	14			7
1	7	2	8	4	9^1	5	3		10	6^3		12	11^2	14	13				8
1	2^3	4	3	5	6^1	9	8		10	11	12	14	7^2		13				9
1	12	2^1	4	3	6	8	7	13	11	14	5	10^3			9^2				10
1	12		4	3	5	8	7		13	11	6		9		10^1	2^2			11
1	2^2		4	3	5	8	7^3		11	10^1	6	13	9		14	12			12
1	12		4	3	5	7	8		10	13	6^1	11		14	9^3	2^2			13
1	5	12	6^2	4	7		3■			11	2	10^1	8		9^3	13	14		14
1	6^3	2		3	5	8		13	11^1	10^2	14	12	7		9		4		15
1	6^2	2		3	5	8		12	11	10^3		13	7	14	9^1		4		16
1	6^2	2		3	5	8			11	10^1		12		7	9	13	4		17
1	6^3	2■		3	5	8	12		11	10^1	13	14	7		9^2		4		18
1	6^3			3	2	8	12		11	10^2	5	13	7		9^1	14	4		19
1	6^1			3	2	8	12		11^3	10^2	5	14	7		9	13	4		20
1	6			3	2	8	12		11^3	10^2	5	13	7		9^1	14	4		21
1	6^1			3	2		8		11	10^2	5	12	7		9	13	4		22
1	6^1			3	2	8	12	13	11	10^3	5	14	7		9^2		4		23
1	12			3	2	8		14	11	10^2	5^1	13	7		9^3	6	4		24
1	12	3		5	2	6		13	10	11^2		14	7		8^3	9^1	4		25
1	13	2		3	5	8		9^1	11	10	14	12	7			6^2	4^3		26
1	12	3		4	6	8		9^1	11	10^3		13	7	14		2^2	5		27
1	12	2		5	10	7	3	6			13	8		9^2		11^1	4		28
1	12	3^1		4	6	8	9	10				11	7	13		2^2	5		29
1	6^1	2		4	5	7	13	9				11	8^2	14	10^3	12	3		30
1		2		3	5	8	7	9^2	12		13	11		14	10^1	6^3	4		31
1	12	2		3	5	7	8	9^3	11			10			6^2	13	4^1	14	32
1	6^3	2		3	5^1	8	7	9^2	11		12				10	14	4	13	33
1	2^1	3		4		8	9		11	12	6	14	7^2		13		5	10^3	34
1	2^2	3	14	4		7	8		9^1	10^3	6	13			12		5	11	35
1	2	3		4	12	7	8	14		10^1	6	13			9^2		5	11^3	36
1	8	2^3	12	5	13	7	6		14	11	3^1				9^2		4	10	37
1	13		3	4	2	8	7		9^3	10	6^2		12		14		5	11^1	38
1	12	2	5^2	3	6	8	7		11^1	10^3	13		9				4	14	39
1	12	3		4	2	8	7		11^2	10^3	6	14	9^1				5	13	40
1	14	3		4	2	8	7		11	10^1	6^3		9^2		13		5	12	41
1	7^1	2		3	6	8	9		10	11	5^3	14			13		4^2	12	42

FA Cup

Fourth Qualifying	Weston-super-Mare	(h)	3-1
First Round	Milton Keynes D	(h)	0-0

(aet; Milton Keynes D won 4-3 on penalties)

FA Trophy

Third Round	Wealdstone	(a)	3-4

FC HALIFAX TOWN

Ground: The MBi Shay Stadium, Halifax HX1 2YT. *Tel:* (01422) 341 222.
Website: fchalifaxtown.com *Email:* tonyallan@fchalifaxtown.com *Year Formed:* 1911 (Reformed 2008).
Record Attendance: 36,855 v Tottenham H, FA Cup 5th rd, 15 February 1953. *Nickname:* 'The Shaymen'.
Manager: Pete Wild. *Colours:* Blue shirts with white trim, blue shorts with white trim, blue socks with white trim.

FC HALIFAX TOWN – NATIONAL LEAGUE 2020–21 LEAGUE RECORD

Match No.	*Date*		*Venue*	*Opponents*	*Result*		*H/T Score*	*Lg Pos.*	*Goalscorers*	*Attendance*
1	Oct	3	H	Dagenham & R	W	2-0	1-0	3	Summerfield (pen) [45], Earing [67]	0
2		6	A	Stockport Co	L	1-2	1-1	6	Earing [12]	0
3		10	A	Boreham Wood	D	0-0	0-0	9		0
4		13	H	Yeovil T	D	1-1	1-0	11	King [6]	0
5		17	A	Woking	D	0-0	0-0	9		0
6	Nov	10	H	Wealdstone	L	0-1	0-0	18		0
7		17	H	Notts Co	D	1-1	0-1	17	Allen [90]	0
8		21	H	Torquay U	L	1-2	0-1	18	Allen [53]	0
9		28	A	Sutton U	L	0-1	0-1	20		0
10	Dec	2	H	Barnet	W	5-2	3-0	14	King [1], Bell [21], Hyde [44], Earing [47], Woods [57]	0
11		5	A	Weymouth	W	5-1	2-0	13	Williams [10], Maher [22], Nepomuceno [71], Bradbury [79], Hyde [82]	800
12		8	A	Aldershot T	W	3-1	0-1	9	Hyde 2 (1 pen) [63, 70 (p)], Bell [66]	0
13		15	A	Solihull Moors	L	1-2	1-1	15	Woods [21]	0
14		22	H	Eastleigh	W	3-1	2-0	8	Allen [33], Green [45], Bell [84]	0
15		26	A	Hartlepool U	L	1-3	1-1	8	Chadwick [13]	0
16		28	H	Altrincham	W	3-2	2-1	6	Summerfield (pen) [17], Chadwick [30], Woods [46]	0
17	Jan	9	A	King's Lynn T	D	1-1	0-1	4	Mansell [51]	0
18		23	A	Bromley	W	2-1	1-1	4	Summerfield (pen) [22], Allen [48]	0
19		26	A	Wrexham	D	0-0	0-0	4		0
20		30	H	Maidenhead U	L	2-3	1-2	7	Green [38], Bradbury [77]	0
21	Feb	16	A	Barnet	L	1-2	1-2	11	King [45]	0
22		20	A	Torquay U	W	3-2	1-1	10	Sherring (og) [34], Earing [78], King [88]	0
23	Mar	2	H	Hartlepool U	D	1-1	0-1	13	Green [77]	0
24		6	A	Wealdstone	W	2-1	0-1	10	Hyde [57], Earing [82]	0
25		9	A	Notts Co	W	2-1	1-0	8	Hyde [28], Campbell [83]	0
26		13	H	Solihull Moors	W	1-0	0-0	7	Woods (pen) [48]	0
27		16	H	Aldershot T	W	1-0	0-0	6	Allen [84]	0
28		20	A	Eastleigh	L	0-1	0-0	7		0
29		27	H	Sutton U	D	2-2	1-0	8	Chadwick [18], Earing [61]	0
30	Apr	5	H	Weymouth	W	3-2	2-1	7	Hyde 2 [2, 47], Bradbury [30]	0
31		10	A	Altrincham	W	1-0	1-0	7	Earing [12]	0
32		13	H	Wrexham	L	0-4	0-4	8		0
33		17	H	King's Lynn T	W	4-2	2-2	6	Chadwick [42], Hyde [45], Summerfield [50], Earing [57]	0
34		20	A	Chesterfield	W	2-1	2-0	5	King [8], Hyde [29]	0
35		24	H	Bromley	L	1-2	0-1	5	Byrne [90]	0
36		27	H	Woking	W	1-0	0-0	5	Hyde [74]	0
37	May	1	H	Stockport Co	L	0-1	0-1	5		0
38		3	A	Yeovil T	W	3-0	1-0	5	Summerfield [14], Green [84], Hyde [90]	0
39		8	H	Boreham Wood	L	0-1	0-0	5		0
40		15	A	Dagenham & R	L	0-3	0-2	9		0
41		22	A	Maidenhead U	W	2-1	1-0	10	Hyde [44], King [60]	845
42		29	H	Chesterfield	L	1-2	1-1	10	Stephenson [31]	843

Final League Position: 10

GOALSCORERS

League (63): Hyde 13 (1 pen), Earing 8, King 6, Allen 5, Summerfield 5 (3 pens), Chadwick 4, Green 4, Woods 4 (1 pen), Bell 3, Bradbury 3, Byrne 1, Campbell 1, Maher 1, Mansell 1, Nepomuceno 1, Stephenson 1, Williams 1, own goal 1.
FA Cup (0).
FA Trophy (4): Chadwick 1, Earing 1, Nepomueno 1, Summerfield 1 (1 pen).

Johnson 42	King 35	Williams 25 + 4	Byrne 40	Clarke 23	Bradbury 35	Summerfield 30 + 1	Woods 31 + 5	Earing 23 + 9	Omotayo 4	Nepomuceno 4 + 9	Green 32 + 9	Allen 22 + 9	Benn — + 2	Senior 21 + 10	Maher 36 + 1	Hyde 22 + 5	Stenson 1	Tear 1 + 9	Danns 2 + 3	Bell 5 + 2	Chadwick 13 + 4	Leroy-Belehouan 1	Mansell 2	Campbell 9 + 6	Spence 1 + 7	Obiero — + 1	Stephenson 2 + 2	Match No.
1	2	3	4	5	6	7	8^3	9^2	10	11^1	12	13	14															1
1	2	3	4	5	6	7	8^1	9	10^2	13	12	11																2
1	2^1	3^2	4	6	5	8	12	9	11^3		7	10		13	14													3
1	7		3	5	4	6	8	13	11^1	12	9^2	10		2														4
1	5	7^2	3	4		8	6	9^3		11^1	12	10		14	2	13												5
1	2■	3■	4	5	6	8	7				9		13			10^2	11^1	12										6
1			2	3	4	8	7	12		13	9^2	11		5	6	10^1												7
1			2	3	4	8	7	12		13	9^2	11		5	6^1	10												8
1		6	3	5^1	4	7	8^3	12		10	14	11			2				9^2	13								9
1	5	6^2	2		4	7	8^1	9		12				14	3	10			13	11^3								10
1	5	6^3	2		4	7	8	14		12	9^1			13	3	10				11^2								11
1	5	6	2		4	7	8^3	12		13	9^2				3	10			14	11^1								12
1	5	6	2		4^2	7	8	9^1		12	14			13	3	10^3				11								13
1		2	6		4	7		13		14	9	10^2		3	5				8^3	12	11^1							14
1		5			3	7	8	12		6^1	4			2	9					11■	10							15
1	2	3	6		4	7	8	10			9^1				5				12		11							16
1	2	3			6	7	8^2	9			12	14		13	5						10	4^3	11^1					17
1	2	6^1	3		4	7		9			8	10		12	5			13						11^2				18
1	2		6		4	7		9			8	10		3	5									11				19
1	9		4		6		12	7			8	13		3	5			2^1					11^2	10				20
1	2	13	5		4^1		7	9^3			8	11		3	6	12		14						10^2				21
1	2	9^1	5		4			8			7	10		3	6	12								11				22
1	2	12■	4		3		13	8			6	10		5^3	7	11^1		14						9^2				23
1	6^1		4		3		8	9			7	13		2	5	11^3		14			12			10^2				24
1	2		5		4		8	9^3			7	10^1		3^2	6	11		14			12			13				25
1	5^2	8	3		2		9	7			6	13			4	11^1					10			12				26
1	2		4		5		8	7			6	10			3			13			9^2			11^1	12			27
1	2		6	5	4^1		8				9	11		3	7						10				12			28
1	8	9^1	2	4	3			10^2			7			5	6	12					11				13			29
1	2^2	13	6	5	7			9^1			8	11		4^3	3	10									14	12		30
1	2^2	6^1	3	4	5	12	13	10			7^3	9		14	8	11												31
1	2		5	4	3^1	7	12	9^2			14	10		6	8	11^3					13							32
1	5	6	4		3^1	8	7^2	9^3			12	14		13	2	11					10							33
1	5	6	4	3		7	9^2				8	13			2	11					10^1				12			34
1	2	3^1	6	5		7	9				8	12		13	4	11					10^2							35
1		14	2	4	5	6	7				12	10^3		3		11					9^1			13	8^2			36
1		8	4	3		9	10				6	5^1		2	11	7					12							37
1	2	11	4	5	3^2	9	8				7				6	12					10^1						13	38
1	5^2	6■	2	3		8	7	13^3			9^1	10			4	11								12	14			39
1	9		2	5	3	7	6				8^3			10^2	4			13						11^1	14		12	40
1	9^1		2	4		6	7				8^2			5	3	11		12						13			10	41
1	9		2	4		6	7				8	12		5^1	3	11								13			10^2	42

FA Cup
Fourth Qualifying South Shields (a) 0-2

FA Trophy
Third Round Hartlepool U (h) 3-3
(FC Halifax T won 4-2 on penalties)
Fourth Round Southport (h) 1-2

HARTLEPOOL UNITED

Ground: Victoria Park, Clarence Road, Hartlepool TS24 8BZ. *Tel:* (01429) 272 584.
Website: www.hartlepoolunited.co.uk *Email:* enquires@hartlepoolunited.co.uk
Year Formed: 1908. *Record Attendance:* 17,426 v Manchester U, FA Cup 3rd rd, 5 January 1957.
Nickname: 'The Pool', 'Monkey Hangers'. *Manager:* Dave Challinor.
Colours: Blue shirts with white trim, blue shorts with white trim, blue socks with white trim.

HARTLEPOOL UNITED – NATIONAL LEAGUE 2020–21 LEAGUE RECORD

Match No.	*Date*		*Venue*	*Opponents*	*Result*		*H/T Score*	*Lg Pos.*	*Goalscorers*	*Attendance*
1	Oct	3	H	Aldershot T	W	2-1	1-0	4	Featherstone (pen) ^{34}, Oates ^{86}	0
2		6	A	Chesterfield	W	2-1	0-0	3	Evans (og) ^{64}, Johnson ^{69}	0
3		10	A	Maidenhead U	W	4-0	1-0	1	Massey (og) ^{45}, Ofosu ^{47}, Johnson ^{51}, Holohan ^{83}	0
4		13	H	Bromley	D	0-0	0-0	1		0
5		27	H	Altrincham	D	1-1	1-0	3	Parkhouse ^{30}	0
6		31	H	Torquay U	L	0-5	0-3	5		0
7	Nov	17	H	Wrexham	L	0-1	0-0	7		0
8		21	A	Yeovil T	W	3-1	3-1	6	Molyneux ^{2}, Holohan ^{36}, Magloire ^{43}	0
9		24	A	Barnet	D	0-0	0-0	6		0
10	Dec	1	A	Solihull Moors	L	0-2	0-0	10		0
11		5	H	Boreham Wood	L	1-2	1-1	10	Bloomfield ^{45}	0
12		8	H	King's Lynn T	W	2-0	1-0	5	Armstrong 2 $^{22, 52}$	0
13		12	A	Woking	L	0-3	0-2	9		799
14		22	H	Stockport Co	W	4-0	1-0	4	Oates ^{6}, Johnson ^{47}, Armstrong 2 $^{50, 90}$	0
15		26	H	FC Halifax T	W	3-1	1-1	3	Johnson ^{7}, Oates ^{57}, Bloomfield ^{89}	0
16		28	A	Notts Co	W	1-0	1-0	2	Armstrong ^{19}	0
17	Jan	9	H	Wealdstone	W	3-1	1-0	2	Armstrong ^{34}, Oates ^{54}, Featherstone ^{58}	0
18		23	A	Weymouth	L	0-1	0-1	3		0
19		30	H	Sutton U	W	1-0	0-0	2	Oates ^{53}	0
20	Feb	9	H	Solihull Moors	W	2-0	1-0	2	Armstrong ^{11}, Ferguson ^{57}	0
21		16	A	Eastleigh	L	1-2	0-2	4	Grey ^{90}	0
22		20	H	Yeovil T	W	2-1	0-0	3	Armstrong ^{72}, Holohan ^{90}	0
23		23	A	Wrexham	D	0-0	0-0	3		0
24		27	H	Barnet	W	1-0	1-0	3	Armstrong ^{32}	0
25	Mar	2	A	FC Halifax T	D	1-1	1-0	3	Shelton ^{12}	0
26		6	A	Torquay U	W	1-0	1-0	2	Molyneux ^{14}	0
27		9	A	Altrincham	D	1-1	1-1	2	Oates ^{33}	0
28		13	H	Eastleigh	D	0-0	0-0	2		0
29		16	A	King's Lynn T	D	2-2	1-2	2	Armstrong ^{37}, Oates ^{64}	0
30		20	H	Woking	W	1-0	0-0	2	Oates ^{80}	0
31		23	A	Dagenham & R	W	1-0	1-0	2	Armstrong ^{43}	0
32		27	A	Stockport Co	D	1-1	0-0	2	Holohan ^{47}	0
33	Apr	2	H	Dagenham & R	W	2-1	1-1	2	Oates ^{21}, Holohan ^{61}	0
34		5	A	Boreham Wood	D	2-2	1-2	2	Holohan ^{5}, Bennett ^{77}	0
35		10	H	Notts Co	W	2-0	1-0	1	Holohan ^{45}, Bennett ^{86}	0
36		17	A	Wealdstone	W	7-2	3-0	1	Oates 2 $^{25, 47}$, Bennett 3 (1 pen) $^{38, 41, 81 (p)}$, Featherstone (pen) ^{63}, Shelton ^{76}	0
37	May	1	H	Chesterfield	W	3-1	3-0	3	Oates ^{5}, Yarney (og) ^{39}, Armstrong ^{43}	0
38		3	A	Bromley	L	0-1	0-1	4		0
39		8	H	Maidenhead U	L	2-4	1-2	4	Oates ^{29}, Elliott ^{85}	0
40		15	A	Aldershot T	W	3-1	0-0	3	Armstrong ^{59}, Oates ^{77}, Featherstone (pen) ^{90}	0
41		23	A	Sutton U	L	0-3	0-1	4		1050
42		29	H	Weymouth	W	4-0	2-0	4	Johnson ^{7}, Oates ^{33}, Shelton ^{63}, Holohan ^{78}	1730

Final League Position: 4

GOALSCORERS

League (66): Oates 15, Armstrong 13, Holohan 8, Bennett 5 (1 pen), Johnson 5, Featherstone 4 (3 pens), Shelton 3, Bloomfield 2, Molyneux 2, Elliott 1, Ferguson 1, Grey 1, Magloire 1, Ofosu 1, Parkhouse 1, own goals 3.
FA Cup (6): Crawford 1, Enigbokan-Bloomfield 1, Grey 1, Holohan 1, Molyneux 1, Parkhouse 1.
FA Trophy (3): Featherstone 1 (1 pen), Holohan 1, Williams 1 (1 pen).
National League Play-Offs (5): Oates 3, Armstrong 2.

Killip 29	Cass 33 + 1	Ferguson 39	Liddle 22 + 1	Odusina 26 + 2	Shelton 34 + 2	Featherstone 37	Holohan 36 + 4	Ofosu 4 + 7	Donaldson 14 + 12	Parkhouse 3 + 3	Oates 27 + 10	Bloomfield 6 + 16	Johnson 31 + 2	Crawford 8 + 9	Grey 2 + 11	Molyneux 15 + 10	Ravas 10	Magloire 9	Bunney 2 + 2	Armstrong 28	Sterry 27	Williams 1 + 7	White 8 + 2	Cooper 2	Bennett 2 + 2	Elliott 1 + 4	Francis-Angol 1 + 3	Saunders 2 + 1	James 3	*Match No.*
1	2	3	4	5	6	7	8	9^{1}	10	11^{2}	12	13																		1
1	2	3	4^{3}	5	6	7	8	10^{1}	9		13	11^{2}	12	14																2
1	2	3		5	6^{1}	7	8	9^{2}	10^{3}		12	11	4	13	14															3
1	2	3		5	6^{2}	7	8	11^{1}	9		10^{3}	14	4		13	12														4
1	2	3		4	6	7	8^{1}	12	10	11^{3}		13	5	14		9^{2}														5
1	2	3		4^{1}	6^{3}	7	8^{2}		10	11		13	5	14	12	9														6
	2	3				7	8	14	10^{2}	12	13	11^{1}	5	6^{3}		9	1	4												7
	2	3			12	7	8		10	13	11^{1}		5	6		9^{2}	1	4												8
	2	3				7	8	12	10^{2}	13	11^{1}		5	6		9	1	4												9
	2			5■		7	8	13	10			11^{3}	12	6	14	9^{2}	1	4	3^{1}											10
	2	3				7	8	12	10^{2}		13	11	5	6^{1}	14	9^{3}	1	4												11
1	2	3		4	6	7	8				9^{3}	14	5		10^{2}	13			12	11^{1}										12
1	2	3		4^{1}	6	7	8	13	14		9^{3}	10^{2}	5		12					11										13
1		3		5	7	8	9^{2}		14		10^{1}		4	12	13			6		11	2^{3}									14
1		3^{2}		4	7	8	9				10^{1}	13	5					6	12	11	2									15
1				4		8	9^{1}		12		10^{2}	13	5	7	14			6	3	11^{3}	2									16
1		3		5	7	8	9^{3}				10^{2}	13	6			14		4		11^{1}	2	12								17
1	5	3		6^{2}	7^{3}	8	9				10^{1}	14	4			12■				11	2	13								18
1	4	3		5	7	8	9^{2}				10^{1}	12	6	13						11	2									19
1	4	3	12	5	7				13		10^{2}		6	9	14					11^{1}	2		8^{3}							20
1	5^{3}	3		6	7^{1}		9		14		10^{2}	13	4		12					11	2		8							21
1	4	3	5		7		9		2^{2}		10^{3}	14	6	12	13					11			8^{1}							22
1	5	3	6		7		9				12		4	13	10^{2}					11	2		8^{1}							23
1	3	5	4		7		9				10^{1}		6			12				11	2		8							24
1	5	3	6	4	7	8	9^{1}				12	13		14		10^{2}				11	2^{3}									25
1	5	3	6		7	8	12				10^{2}	13	4			9^{1}				11	2									26
1	2■	5	4	12	6	7	13				9^{1}	14	3	8		10^{3}				11^{2}										27
1		6	4	3■	9^{2}	7					12	13				10				11^{1}	2		8	5						28
1		6	4		9^{2}	7	13				12		5			10^{1}				11	2	14	8	3^{3}						29
1		5	3		13	6	12		14		9		4			10^{2}				11	2	8^{3}	7^{1}							30
1	3	6	4	14	8^{2}	7	9^{1}				10^{3}		5			13				11	2		12							31
1	3	6	4		8	7	9	13	12				5			10				11^{1}	2^{2}									32
1	3	6	4	5	9^{3}	7	8				10^{2}									11^{1}	2	12	14		13					33
1^{2}	3	6	4	5	9^{1}	7	8				10					13				11	2				12					34
	3	6	4	5	9	7	8		12								1			11^{1}	2				10					35
	3^{2}	6	4	5	9	7	8^{3}		14		10^{1}						1				2	13			11	12				36
	3^{3}	6	4	5	8	7	9		14		11^{1}						1			10^{2}	2						12	13		37
		5^{1}	3■	4	9^{3}	7	8		6		13					12	1			11	2					14		10^{2}		38
	12	5		3^{2}	8^{1}	6	7^{3}				10		4			9	1				2	13				14		11		39
	3	6^{2}	4		9^{3}	7	8		12		11^{1}		5							10	2					13	14		1	40
	3^{2}		4			7	9		8^{1}		10		5			13				11	2	12					6		1	41
	3	6	4^{3}		9	7	8		12		10^{1}		5			13					2^{2}					11	14		1	42

FA Cup

Fourth Qualifying	Ilkeston T	(a)	6-0
First Round	Salford C	(a)	0-2

(aet.)

FA Trophy

Third Round	FC Halifax T	(a)	3-3

(FC Halifax T won 4-2on penalties)

National League Play-Offs

Eliminator	Bromley	(h)	3-2
Semi-Finals	Stockport Co	(a)	1-0
Final	Torquay	(Ashton Gate)	1-1

(aet; Hartlepool U won 5-4 on penalties)

KING'S LYNN TOWN

Ground: The Walks Stadium, Tennyson Road, King's Lynn PE30 5PB. *Tel:* (01553) 760 060.
Website: www.kltown.co.uk *Email:* office@kltown.co.uk *Year Formed:* 1881 (reformed 2010).
Record Attendance: 12,937 v Exeter C, FA Cup First Round, 24 November 1951.
Nickname: 'The Linnets'. *Manager:* Ian Culverhouse.
Colours: Blue shirts with yellow and dark blue diagonal stripes, blue shorts, blue socks.

KING'S LYNN TOWN – NATIONAL LEAGUE 2020–21 LEAGUE RECORD

Match No.	*Date*	*Venue*	*Opponents*	*Result*		*H/T Score*	*Lg Pos.*	*Goalscorers*	*Attendance*
1	Oct 3	H	Yeovil T	D	2-2	0-0	8	Southwell [76], Marriott [87]	0
2	6	A	Maidenhead U	W	3-2	1-1	5	Power [40], Southwell [82], Jones, A [90]	0
3	10	A	Solihull Moors	L	0-5	0-1	10		0
4	13	H	Boreham Wood	L	0-3	0-2	13		0
5	17	A	Weymouth	L	1-2	0-1	18	Marriott [52]	0
6	27	H	Wealdstone	L	2-3	0-1	19	Mitchell 2 [48, 70]	0
7	31	H	Woking	W	3-2	1-2	15	Marriott [27], Loza 2 [81, 88]	0
8	Nov 14	A	Sutton U	L	1-5	0-1	18	Southwell [78]	0
9	17	A	Barnet	W	2-0	1-0	12	Loza 2 [6, 60]	0
10	Dec 1	H	Bromley	L	1-4	0-3	15	Power [52]	0
11	8	A	Hartlepool U	L	0-2	0-1	19		0
12	12	H	Torquay U	D	0-0	0-0	19		625
13	Jan 9	H	FC Halifax T	D	1-1	1-0	20	Kiwomya [38]	0
14	19	A	Eastleigh	W	1-0	1-0	20	Marriott (pen) [39]	0
15	23	A	Dagenham & R	L	2-3	2-0	20	Kiwomya [31], Gash [45]	0
16	30	H	Wrexham	L	0-2	0-2	21		0
17	Feb 9	A	Bromley	L	0-2	0-1	21		0
18	16	H	Notts Co	L	0-1	0-0	21		0
19	23	H	Barnet	W	5-1	2-1	21	Gash 2 [8, 20], King [63], Southwell [87], Marriott [88]	0
20	27	H	Weymouth	D	2-2	2-2	21	Denton [29], King [35]	0
21	Mar 2	A	Notts Co	D	2-2	1-2	21	Carey [1], Mitchell [90]	0
22	6	A	Woking	L	0-3	0-1	21		0
23	9	A	Wealdstone	L	1-3	0-2	21	Mitchell [80]	0
24	13	H	Sutton U	L	0-1	0-0	21		0
25	16	H	Hartlepool U	D	2-2	2-1	21	Mitchell [16], Gyasi [45]	0
26	20	A	Torquay U	L	0-1	0-0	21		0
27	23	A	Altrincham	L	0-3	0-1	21		0
28	27	H	Eastleigh	W	2-1	0-1	21	Gyasi [50], Jackson (pen) [71]	0
29	Apr 5	H	Altrincham	W	2-0	0-0	21	Mitchell 2 (1 pen) [80, 86 (p)]	0
30	10	H	Chesterfield	L	1-2	1-0	21	Carey [39]	0
31	13	A	Stockport Co	L	0-4	0-1	21		0
32	17	A	FC Halifax T	L	2-4	2-2	21	Gash [13], Carey [25]	0
33	20	A	Aldershot T	D	1-1	0-1	21	Gash [62]	0
34	24	H	Dagenham & R	L	0-3	0-2	21		0
35	27	H	Stockport Co	L	0-4	0-4	21		0
36	May 1	H	Maidenhead U	D	0-0	0-0	21		0
37	3	A	Boreham Wood	L	1-5	1-1	21	Gash [4]	0
38	11	A	Chesterfield	L	1-4	1-2	21	Carey [31]	0
39	15	A	Yeovil T	L	1-3	1-2	21	Jackson (pen) [23]	0
40	22	A	Wrexham	L	3-5	1-3	21	Carey [21], Jackson 2 [58, 69]	0
41	25	H	Solihull Moors	D	1-1	1-0	21	Barrows [30]	613
42	29	H	Aldershot T	D	4-4	1-2	21	Gash [43], Jackson 2 (1 pen) [58 (p), 66], Fleming [90]	881

Final League Position: 21

GOALSCORERS

League (50): Gash 7, Mitchell 7 (1 pen), Jackson 6 (3 pens), Carey 5, Marriott 5 (1 pen), Loza 4, Southwell 4, Gyasi 2, King 2, Kiwomya 2, Power 2, Barrows 1, Denton 1, Fleming 1, Jones, A 1.
FA Cup (2): Carey 1, Southwell 1.
FA Trophy (4): Marriott 2, Barrows 1, Mitchell 1.

Street 2	Jones A 10	Brown 12	Smith 24 + 1	McAuley 14	Richards 23 + 1	Jarvis 16 + 2	King 19 + 2	Kelly 4 + 3	Southwell 8 + 8	Power 6 + 5	Marriott 12 + 6	Carey 29 + 12	Hawkins — + 1	Clunan 30 + 3	Mair 22	Barrows 17 + 1	Loza 4 + 4	Barker — + 1	Lupano 4	Mitchell 11 + 8	Callan-McFadden 30	Fleming 18 + 1	Gash 25 + 4	Kiwomya 15 + 9	Denton 27 + 1	Gyasi 13 + 9	Hickman 1	Jackson 6 + 11	Payne 4 + 10	Richardson 18	Davies — + 3	Baggott 7	Howard 16	Coleman 9	Gascoigne 1 + 1	Babos 5 + 5	Tsagium — + 1	Match No.
1	2	3	4	5	6	7	8^{3}	9^{1}	10	11^{2}	12	13	14																									1
1	2	3	4	5	6	8	9^{3}	14	10	11^{2}	7^{1}	13		12																								2
	2	3	4	6	7	8^{3}	9^{2}		10		11^{1}	13		12	1	5	14																					3
	2	3	4	5	7			8^{3}	11^{1}	9	12	14		6^{2}	1		10■	13																				4
	2	3	4	5■	7	8^{1}	9^{3}		11	13	10^{2}	14		6	1	12																						5
		5	3		8^{2}	7		12		13	9^{3}	10^{1}		6	1	2	14		4	11																		6
		5^{3}		3	6		8^{1}		14	13	10	9		7	1	2	12		4	11^{2}																		7
		5		3		6^{2}		14	10	12	11^{1}	8		7	1	2	9^{3}		4	13																		8
		6	4	3		8	13	9	14			12		7	1	2	11^{3}		5^{2}	10^{1}																		9
		2	4		6	7	8^{1}		13	11		14		5	1	10				9^{3}	3^{2}	12																10
		4^{3}	6		8					13	11	9^{1}		7	1	2	14			12	5	3	10^{2}															11
	3		5		7	8			10^{3}	6	13	14			1	2	9^{2}			12	4		11^{1}															12
		2	4		5	7			8^{3}	11^{1}	12	13			1	9				14	3		6	10^{2}														13
	2		4		5	8	9^{2}		13		7^{3}	12			1	10				14	3		6	11^{1}														14
	2		4		6	7	8^{1}				11^{2}	12			1	5				14	3		10	9^{3}	13													15
	2		4		6	9^{3}	10		12		8^{1}			5^{2}	1					14	3		7		11	13												16
	2		4^{2}	5	6		8	9^{3}	14		13	12			1						3		7	10^{1}	11													17
			3	4^{2}	6	7^{1}	8				13	5			1	10				9^{3}	2		12	14	11													18
			12	3^{3}		13	7		14		6	10		4	1	8					2^{2}		5	9^{1}	11													19
			3		13		7		12		11^{1}	9		6	1						2	4	10	8^{2}	5													20
			2		7	8^{2}	9^{1}					11		6	1	5^{3}				10		3	12	13	4	14												21
			4		10^{2}	13	6^{3}					9		12	1					7	3	5	11	8^{1}	2	14												22
			3		5^{2}							9		4	1					7	2	6^{3}		8	10	13	11^{1}	12	14									23
			3		5							8		4^{2}	1					12	2	6		7	9	13		11	10^{1}									24
			5		7							10		6						9	4	2			3	8^{1}		12	11	1								25
			3		7^{2}							10		6						9	2	4	12		5	8^{1}		13	11^{3}	1	14							26
			5^{2}		8^{3}							9		7							4		11		6	12		10^{1}	14	1	13	2	3					27
												9		6^{1}							5	4	11	8	2	7^{3}		13	12	1	14		3	10^{2}				28
							12					8								7	5		13		4	6^{2}			9	1		3	2	10	11^{1}			29
							7^{1}					8									5^{2}	4	11	14	3	6		12	13	1			2	10		9^{3}		30
												6		3^{1}							2		4	13	7	5^{3}		14	12	1		10	11	9		8^{2}		31
							7^{3}					8		6							2		10	12	3	13		11^{2}		1		4	5	9^{1}		14		32
							10^{1}					8		7							6	4^{2}	11	13	5	12				1		3	2	9				33
							8^{3}					9		7							2^{1}	3^{2}	11		4	14		13		1		5	6	10		12		34
												9		6							3	4	11	8	5	7				1			2	10				35
				5								9		6^{2}							2		11	8^{3}	4	7^{1}		13	12	1			3	10		14		36
				3^{3}								7		4							2		11	6^{1}	8	5^{2}		12	14	1		9	10			13		37
				6		8^{1}						10		7							2	3	11	9^{2}	5			13	12	1			4					38
												9		6							5	3	11	8^{1}	4	7^{2}		10	12	1			2			13		39
												8		7		5					6^{1}	4	11	13	2	10^{3}		12	14	1			3			9^{2}		40
												8		6		5						3	11	12	4	7^{1}		10		1			2			9		41
												8		6		3						2	10^{2}	12	4	7		11^{1}		1			5		13	9^{3}	14	42

FA Cup

Fourth Qualifying	Notts Co	(h)	

King's Lynn T awarded a walkover due to the positive COVID-19 test of a Notts Co player.

First Round	Port Vale	(a)	1-0
Second Round	Portsmouth	(a)	1-6

FA Trophy

Third Round	Alfreton T	(a)	3-1
Fourth Round	Hornchurch	(a)	1-1

(Hornchurch won 3-0 on penalties)

MAIDENHEAD UNITED

Ground: York Road, Maidenhead, Berkshire SL6 1SF. *Tel:* (01628) 636 314.
Website: pitchero.com/clubs/maidenheadunited *Email:* social@maidenheadunitedfc.org *Year Formed:* 1870.
Record Attendance: 7,920 v Southall, FA Amateur Cup quarter-final, 7 March 1936. *Nickname:* 'The Magpies'.
Manager: Alan Devonshire. *Colours:* White shirts with black trim, black shorts with white trim, black socks with white trim.

MAIDENHEAD UNITED – NATIONAL LEAGUE 2020–21 LEAGUE RECORD

Match No.	Date	Venue	Opponents	Result		H/T Score	Lg Pos.	Goalscorers	Attendance
1	Oct 3	A	Sutton U	L	0-3	0-2	17		0
2	6	H	King's Lynn T	L	2-3	1-1	20	Barratt 2 (2 pens) [7, 54]	0
3	10	H	Hartlepool U	L	0-4	0-1	22		0
4	12	A	Wrexham	W	1-0	1-0	15	Coley [33]	0
5	17	A	Notts Co	W	3-2	1-2	12	Barratt 2 [14, 64], Orsi-Dadamo [75]	0
6	27	H	Dagenham & R	W	2-1	0-1	9	Blissett [56], Coley [75]	0
7	31	H	Solihull Moors	W	3-1	0-0	3	Barratt 3 (2 pens) [56, 82 (p), 90 (p)]	0
8	Nov 14	A	Chesterfield	W	2-1	0-1	4	Barratt 2 [54, 71]	0
9	17	A	Aldershot T	D	0-0	0-0	4		0
10	21	H	Bromley	D	2-2	1-0	4	Orsi-Dadamo [30], Donnellan [46]	0
11	28	A	Altrincham	L	0-2	0-0	5		0
12	Dec 5	A	Eastleigh	W	1-0	0-0	4	Addai [47]	776
13	8	A	Torquay U	L	1-2	0-1	4	Donnellan [83]	980
14	26	H	Wealdstone	W	4-0	2-0	5	Upward [4], Coley [38], Orsi-Dadamo (pen) [49], Blissett [53]	0
15	Jan 23	A	Woking	D	0-0	0-0	7		0
16	27	H	Yeovil T	W	4-2	1-1	6	Orsi-Dadamo 2 (1 pen) [31, 88 (p)], Parry [49], Sparkes [69]	0
17	30	A	FC Halifax T	W	3-2	2-1	5	Orsi-Dadamo 2 [24, 45], Coley [85]	0
18	Feb 6	H	Boreham Wood	L	0-1	0-0	6		0
19	16	H	Stockport Co	D	0-0	0-0	8		0
20	20	A	Bromley	D	2-2	0-2	8	Upward [49], Wiltshire [90]	0
21	23	H	Aldershot T	L	2-4	1-3	9	Orsi-Dadamo 2 [43, 50]	0
22	Mar 6	A	Solihull Moors	D	1-1	1-0	12	Blissett [29]	0
23	9	A	Dagenham & R	L	1-2	0-2	13	Clerima [76]	0
24	13	H	Chesterfield	W	2-0	1-0	11	Blissett [20], Sparkes [52]	0
25	16	H	Torquay U	W	4-1	2-0	9	Coley [6], Blissett 2 [42, 49], Orsi-Dadamo [55]	0
26	27	H	Altrincham	L	0-1	0-0	13		0
27	Apr 2	A	Weymouth	L	1-2	0-0	13	Barratt [50]	0
28	5	H	Eastleigh	L	0-1	0-0	14		0
29	10	H	Barnet	D	0-0	0-0	14		0
30	17	A	Stockport Co	D	2-2	1-1	16	Parry [26], Orsi-Dadamo [74]	0
31	20	A	Wealdstone	W	6-0	1-0	13	Barratt [34], Orsi-Dadamo 3 [64, 69, 71], Sparkes 2 [81, 85]	0
32	24	H	Woking	W	2-1	2-0	12	Orsi-Dadamo 2 [16, 26]	0
33	27	H	Weymouth	L	0-1	0-1	12		0
34	May 1	A	King's Lynn T	D	0-0	0-0	12		0
35	3	H	Wrexham	D	2-2	2-0	12	Barratt [15], Comley [32]	0
36	8	A	Hartlepool U	W	4-2	2-1	12	Orsi-Dadamo [15], Barratt 3 [38, 47, 55]	0
37	11	H	Notts Co	L	0-4	0-1	13		0
38	15	H	Sutton U	L	0-3	0-0	14		0
39	18	A	Yeovil T	D	0-0	0-0	14		1497
40	22	H	FC Halifax T	L	1-2	0-1	14	Orsi-Dadamo [63]	845
41	25	A	Barnet	L	0-2	0-0	14		562
42	29	A	Boreham Wood	W	4-1	2-0	13	Smith [10], Kelly [45], Orsi-Dadamo [54], Lovett [90]	651

Final League Position: 13

GOALSCORERS

League (62): Orsi-Dadamo 19 (2 pens), Barratt 15 (4 pens), Blissett 6, Coley 5, Sparkes 4, Donnellan 2, Parry 2, Upward 2, Addai 1, Clerima 1, Comley 1, Kelly 1, Lovett 1, Smith 1, Wiltshire 1.
FA Cup (2): Parry 1, Sparkes 1.
FA Trophy (2): Orsi-Dadomo 2.

Ashby-Hammond 33	Massey 40	Wells 34	Donnellan 12 + 1	Parry 39	Coley 25 + 12	Comley 27 + 1	Upward 38	Barratt 24 + 5	Sheckelford 25 + 3	Orsi-Dadamo 32 + 7	Sparkes 28 + 4	Smile 2 + 9	Blissett 22 + 2	Nana Ofori-Twumasi 10 + 16	Wiltshire 8 + 7	Clerima 15	Kelly 2 + 17	Ince 29 + 1	Addai 3 + 2	Oluwayemi — + 1	Keetch 1 + 7	Smith 2 + 4	Egan 2 + 8	Lovett 4 + 1	Holden 5	Match No.
1	2	3	4	5	6	7	8^{1}	9^{2}	10	11	12	13														1
1	2	3	10	4	14	7^{1}	8	9^{3}	5^{2}		6	13	11	12												2
1	2	3	9		14		8^{2}	12		10	6	7	11^{1}	13	4	5^{3}										3
1	2	3	5^{1}	4	8^{3}	7	9	10		12	14		11^{2}	13		6										4
1	2	3		4	8^{3}	7	9	10^{2}		11^{1}	6	12		14		5	13									5
1	2	3	6	4	9^{1}	8	10	12	5		7^{2}		11	13												6
1	2	3	10	4	7^{2}	6■	8	9		13	5^{1}	12	11													7
1	3	4^{2}	2	5	7^{1}		9	10		13	6^{3}		11	12	14			8								8
1	2		10	3	12		8	9^{1}	5	13	7^{2}	14	11	6				4^{3}								9
1	2		10	3	7^{2}		8	9	4	11^{1}		13		5				6	12							10
1^{3}	2		10	3	7		8^{1}	9	5	11^{2}			13	6				4	14	12						11
1	2	3	13	4	8■		9	10^{2}		14			11	12		5^{1}		6	7^{3}							12
1		2	10	4			8^{2}	9	6	12		13	11		3			5	7^{1}							13
1	2	3	9^{1}	4	7^{2}	12	8		5	10^{3}		13	11						6		14					14
1		2		4	12		8	9^{1}	5	10^{2}	6	13	11		3			7								15
1	2	3		4	13	7^{2}	9^{3}	10	5	11	6^{1}			12	14			8								16
1	2	3		4	12	7^{3}	9	10	5	11^{1}	6^{2}			14			13	8								17
1	2	3		4	9	7			5	11	6	10^{1}	13				12^{2}	8								18
1	2	3		4	12	7	9		5	10^{2}	6^{1}		11				13	8								19
1	2	3		4	12	7^{1}	9		5	10^{3}	6		11^{2}		14		13	8								20
1	2	3		4	6	7^{2}	9^{1}		5^{3}	10			11	12			13	8			14					21
1	2	3		4	12	7	9^{2}			10^{1}	6		11	13		5		8								22
1	2	3			7^{2}	6	9		5	10^{1}			11			4		8			13	12				23
1	2	3		4	8^{2}	7^{1}	10	12			6		11	13		5		9								24
1	2			3	7^{2}	6^{1}	9	12	4	10^{3}			11	5			14	8			13					25
1	3	2		4	9		6	12		10			11	7^{1}		5	13						8^{2}			26
1	3	2		4■	12	7^{3}	8	9^{1}	6	10^{2}			11	13		5							14			27
1	3	2		4	10■		7	8^{2}	5	12	9^{1}		11	13		6										28
1	2	3		4			8	9	13	10	6^{1}		11			5^{2}	12	7								29
1	2	3		4		8^{2}	9	10		11^{3}	6^{1}				14	5	12	7					13			30
1	2	3^{2}		4		8	9	10^{3}		11^{1}	6			12		5	13	7					14			31
1	2			3		8^{3}	9	10	13	11^{2}	6^{1}			5		4	12	7					14			32
1	2			3^{2}	10^{1}	8	9		13	11	6			5■	14	4^{3}	12	7								33
	10			2	12		8	11	6	3^{2}	4				13		9^{1}	5					7	1		34
	10			3	4^{2}	5	9	11	8	6^{1}	7				2		12	13						1		35
	2	3		4	14	9		10^{3}	5■	11^{1}	7^{2}				6		13	8					12	1		36
	2	3		4	5	9				11	7^{1}			10	6^{2}		13	8				14	12	1^{3}		37
	2	3		4	6^{2}	9^{1}	10			11	7^{3}			5				8			14	13	12		1	38
	2	3		4	6^{2}	9^{1}	10			11	12			5				8			13	7^{3}	14		1	39
	2	3		4	6^{2}		10■	9^{1}	5	11	7				13			8			12				1	40
	2	3			7^{1}	8			5	11	9				4		12	10			6^{2}	13			1	41
	3	4		5	9		8		6^{1}	11	13			12	2^{2}		10^{3}					7		14	1	42

FA Cup
Fourth Qualifying Cray Valley PM (h) 2-3

FA Trophy
Third Round Weymouth (a) 2-3

NOTTS COUNTY

Ground: Meadow Lane Stadium, Meadow Lane, Nottingham NG2 3HJ. *Tel:* (0115) 952 9000.
Website: www.nottscountyfc.co.uk *Email:* office@nottscountyfc.co.uk *Year Formed:* 1862.
Record Attendance: 47,310 v York C, FA Cup 6th rd, 12 March 1955. *Nickname:* 'The Magpies'.
Manager: Ian Burchnall. *Colours:* Black and white striped shirts, black shorts with white trim, white socks with black trim.

NOTTS COUNTY – NATIONAL LEAGUE 2020–21 LEAGUE RECORD

Match No.	*Date*		*Venue*	*Opponents*	*Result*		*H/T Score*	*Lg Pos.*	*Goalscorers*	*Attendance*
1	Oct	7	H	Altrincham	W	3-1	2-0	6	Wootton 2 [15, 26], Reeves [64]	0
2		10	H	Barnet	W	4-2	3-1	5	Roberts [14], Wootton [17], Boldewijn [23], Doyle [90]	0
3		13	A	Sutton U	W	1-0	0-0	2	Wootton [90]	0
4		17	H	Maidenhead U	L	2-3	2-1	4	Knowles [3], Rodrigues [29]	0
5	Nov	7	A	Aldershot T	L	0-1	0-0	10		0
6		17	A	FC Halifax T	D	1-1	1-0	9	Sam [6]	0
7		21	A	Chesterfield	W	3-2	1-1	9	Boldewijn [22], Wootton [90], Rodrigues [90]	0
8		27	H	Wealdstone	W	3-0	2-0	5	Boldewijn [15], Sam [19], Knowles [89]	0
9	Dec	2	A	Dagenham & R	D	0-0	0-0	4		0
10		5	H	Woking	W	1-0	0-0	3	Wootton [80]	0
11		8	H	Boreham Wood	L	0-1	0-0	3		0
12		15	H	Stockport Co	W	1-0	1-0	3	Reeves [35]	0
13		28	H	Hartlepool U	L	0-1	0-1	4		0
14	Jan	23	H	Torquay U	D	0-0	0-0	6		0
15		27	H	Solihull Moors	W	2-0	0-0	4	Wootton 2 [79, 87]	0
16		30	A	Weymouth	W	1-0	0-0	4	Sam [51]	0
17	Feb	9	H	Dagenham & R	W	3-1	3-0	4	Wootton 2 [10, 45], Rodrigues [34]	0
18		16	A	King's Lynn T	W	1-0	0-0	3	Reeves [54]	0
19		20	H	Chesterfield	L	0-1	0-1	5		0
20		23	A	Stockport Co	D	0-0	0-0	5		0
21	Mar	2	H	King's Lynn T	D	2-2	2-1	4	Wootton 2 [39, 43]	0
22		9	H	FC Halifax T	L	1-2	0-1	6	Boldewijn [75]	0
23		13	A	Wealdstone	W	1-0	0-0	5	Ellis [63]	0
24		16	A	Boreham Wood	D	2-2	0-1	7	Lacey [75], Effiong (pen) [88]	0
25		20	H	Yeovil T	W	2-0	1-0	4	Reeves [40], Barnett [78]	0
26		23	A	Yeovil T	D	2-2	0-2	5	Boldewijn [78], Rodrigues [86]	0
27		30	H	Aldershot T	L	0-1	0-1	6		0
28	Apr	2	H	Wrexham	W	1-0	0-0	5	Ellis [80]	0
29		5	A	Woking	W	4-2	1-2	5	Ellis [20], Knowles 3 [60, 66, 79]	0
30		10	A	Hartlepool U	L	0-2	0-1	5		0
31		13	A	Solihull Moors	L	1-2	1-0	6	Knowles [11]	0
32		17	H	Eastleigh	L	0-1	0-1	8		0
33		24	A	Torquay U	D	2-2	1-0	9	Kelly-Evans [38], Ellis [49]	0
34		27	A	Eastleigh	L	0-2	0-0	10		0
35	May	1	A	Altrincham	D	1-1	1-1	10	Rodrigues [45]	0
36		4	H	Sutton U	W	3-2	1-1	8	Rodrigues 2 (1 pen) [8, 90 (p)], Wootton [48]	0
37		8	A	Barnet	W	4-1	1-0	7	Ellis [45], Rodrigues [46], Nugent (og) [54], Boldewijn [85]	0
38		11	A	Maidenhead U	W	4-0	1-0	5	O'Brien 3 (1 pen) [10, 65, 75 (p)], Rodrigues [83]	0
39		15	H	Bromley	D	2-2	0-1	6	Wootton [53], Rodrigues [62]	0
40		18	A	Wrexham	W	1-0	1-0	5	Reeves [26]	0
41		22	H	Weymouth	W	3-0	2-0	5	Rodrigues (pen) [25], Wootton [29], Boldewijn [64]	4197
42		29	A	Bromley	L	0-1	0-0	5		1344

Final League Position: 5

GOALSCORERS

League (62): Wootton 15, Rodrigues 11 (2 pens), Boldewijn 7, Knowles 6, Ellis 5, Reeves 5, O'Brien 3 (1 pen), Sam 3, Barnett 1, Doyle 1, Effiong 1 (1 pen), Kelly-Evans 1, Lacey 1, Roberts 1, own goal 1.
FA Cup (0).
FA Trophy (13): Knowles 4 (1 pen), Sam 4, Wootton 2, Graham 1, Rodrigues 1, Wolfe 1.
National League Play-Offs (5): Wootton 2, Chickson 1, Ellis 1, Rodrigues 1.

Slocombe 36	Brindley 17 + 3	Rawlinson 37	Kelly-Evans 30 + 3	Lacey 20	Reeves 40	O'Brien 22 + 10	Doyle 36	Wootton 41	Roberts 3 + 5	Thomas 2 + 1	Boldewijn 28 + 10	Sam 10 + 16	Rodrigues 26 + 9	Graham 2	McCrory 2 + 1	Knowles 12 + 14	Chicksen 17 + 1	Wolfe 1 + 2	Turner 12 + 6	Walker 3 + 2	Effiong 5 + 7	Miller 13 + 4	Barnett 12	Pilling 3	Richardson 1	Ellis 19	Griffiths 6 + 5	Knight 3 + 5	Steele 3	Match No.
1	2	3	4	5	6	7	8	9[2]	10[1]	11[3]	12	13	14																	1
1	14	8	10		3	13	4	5	6[1]	12	7[2]		11[3]	2	9															2
1	2	3	4	5	6	7	8	9	12		11[2]		10[1]			13														3
1		2		4[1]	5		6	7			9[3]	13	11[2]		8	10	3	12	14											4
1	2			11	4	5	7	8		6[3]	12	14	9[2]	3[1]			10		13											5
1	2	3	4	5[1]	6	7	8	9	13		10	11[2]							12											6
1	2	10	11		3	5[1]	6	7	8		9[2]	13	12						4											7
1	2	8	9		3	12	5	6			7	10[1]	11[2]			13			4											8
1		3	4		8	14	6	7			11[3]	10[2]	9[1]			13	2		5	12										9
1	2	7	8		3	13	5	6			12	9[3]	10[1]			14			4	11[2]										10
1	2	4	5		6	7[1]	8	9			11	13	12						3	10[2]										11
1	3	4	2		9	6	7	8			11		10[1]						5	12										12
1	2	8	9		3		5	6			7.	12	10[1]			13			4▮	11[2]										13
1	3[3]	4	2	5	6	13	8	9			10[1]	12	7								11[2]	14								14
1		2	3	4	6	7[2]	8	9			11		12			13					10[1]	5								15
1		6	7	10	2	12	3	4			5	8[2]	9[1]								13	11								16
1▮		7	8	11	2		4	5			6		10			9[1]					12		3							17
		7	8	11	2		4	5			6[3]		10[1]			9[2]			13		14	12	3	1						18
		2	3	4	6		7	8			10	11[2]	9			12					13	5[1]		1						19
		7	8	11		2	4	5	13		6		10[2]			12		9[1]					3	1						20
1		4	5	3	8	12	7	9			10[3]		6[2]			11[1]		14			13		2							21
1		4		3	7		6	11			9	12	8			10[1]							2		5					22
1		5	6	3		9	8	10			7	12									11[1]	2				4				23
1		5[2]		3	9	14	8	10			6	11[3]	7[1]			12					13	2				4				24
1		4		2[1]	7	8	6	9			10					13			12		11[2]		5			3				25
1		5	12		8	9[1]	7	11			6		14			13			3[2]		10[3]		2			4				26
1			5		6	7		11			9[2]	10[3]	13			12			3		14	8[1]	2			4				27
1		5			7	8[1]		11▮	13		6					10[2]	3						2			4	9	12		28
1		5	14		7	8					6[1]	11[3]	12			10	3						2			4	9[2]	13		29
1		5	13		7	8		10	14		6[1]					11	3						2[3]			4	9[2]	12		30
1		5	6	3	7			9			14	12	13			11[3]	2									4[1]	8	10[2]		31
1		5	6	3	7	14		10			12					9	2		4[3]			13					8[1]	11[2]		32
		3	6	5[1]	8	9[3]	7	10								11[2]	2					12				4	14	13	1	33
		5	6		8		7	10			12		13			14	2		3							4[2]	9[3]	11[1]	1	34
	5	3			7		8	9			11		10[1]			14	13		2[3]				4[2]			6		12	1	35
1	13	5	6▮		8		7	10				12	9[3]			11[1]	3		14			2[2]				4				36
1	6	5			7	14	8[2]	10[3]			13	11	9[1]				3					2				4	12			37
1	14	5	6		8	9	7[3]	11				13	10[2]				3					2[1]				4	12			38
1	5		6[1]		8	9[2]	7	11			12	13	10				3					2				4				39
1	5		6		8	9	7	11				12	10[2]		13		3					2[1]				4				40
1	5		6[2]		9[1]	8	7	11			12	13	10[3]				3					2				4	14			41
1	6	5			9[1]	8	7	11			12	13	10[2]				3					2[3]				4	14			42

FA Cup
Fourth Qualifying King's Lynn T (a)
King's Lynn T awarded a walkover due to the positive COVID-19 test of a Notts Co player.

National League Play-Offs

Eliminator	Chesterfield	(h)	3-2
Semi-Finals	Torquay	(a)	2-4

(aet.)

FA Trophy

Third Round	Morpeth T	(a)	3-0
Fourth Round	Stockport Co	(a)	2-1
Fifth Round	Havant & Waterlooville	(a)	2-2
(Notts Co won 4-2 on penalties)			
Quarter-Finals	Oxford C	(h)	3-1
Semi-Finals	Hornchurch	(h)	3-3
(Hornchurch won 5-3 on penalties)			

SOLIHULL MOORS

Ground: SportNation.bet Stadium, Damson Parkway, Solihull, West Midlands B91 2PP (satnav B92 9EJ).
Tel: (0121) 705 6770. *Website:* www.solihullmoorsfc.co.uk *Email:* info@solihullmoorsfc.co.uk *Year Formed:* 2007.
Record Attendance: 3,681 v Leyton Orient, National League, 22 April 2019; 3,681 v AFC Fylde, National League Play-offs Semi-Final, 4 May 2019. *Nickname:* 'Moors'. *Manager:* Neil Ardley.
Colours: Yellow shirts with blue trim, blue shorts with yellow trim, yellow socks with blue trim.

SOLIHULL MOORS – NATIONAL LEAGUE 2020–21 LEAGUE RECORD

Match No.	*Date*	*Venue*	*Opponents*	*Result*		*H/T Score*	*Lg Pos.*	*Goalscorers*	*Attendance*
1	Oct 3	A	Woking	L	1-2	1-0	12	Ward (pen) 18	0
2	6	H	Wrexham	W	1-0	0-0	7	Ball 56	0
3	10	H	King's Lynn T	W	5-0	1-0	4	Sbarra 39, Archer 2 47, 71, Osborne 64, Howe 81	0
4	17	H	Boreham Wood	W	1-0	0-0	3	Rooney 75	0
5	27	A	Stockport Co	D	0-0	0-0	4		0
6	31	A	Maidenhead U	L	1-3	0-0	6	Gleeson (pen) 49	0
7	Nov 11	A	Altrincham	W	2-0	2-0	3	Sbarra 18, Osborne 22	0
8	Dec 1	H	Hartlepool U	W	2-0	0-0	7	Pearce 62, Ball 81	0
9	5	A	Sutton U	L	1-4	0-2	8	Ball 47	934
10	12	H	Bromley	L	0-1	0-1	16		0
11	15	H	FC Halifax T	W	2-1	1-1	7	Ball 24, Hudlin 56	0
12	Jan 2	A	Chesterfield	L	0-1	0-1	14		0
13	5	H	Chesterfield	W	2-1	0-1	7	Sbarra 61, Hudlin 90	0
14	27	A	Notts Co	L	0-2	0-0	12		0
15	Feb 6	A	Eastleigh	D	1-1	0-1	15	Sbarra 90	0
16	9	A	Hartlepool U	L	0-2	0-1	15		0
17	16	A	Aldershot T	W	3-1	2-0	13	Ward 18, Gudger 45, Rooney 62	0
18	20	A	Weymouth	D	0-0	0-0	15		0
19	23	H	Torquay U	L	1-2	0-1	15	Gudger 90	0
20	27	A	Boreham Wood	D	2-2	1-1	16	Gudger 1, Rooney (pen) 59	0
21	Mar 2	H	Dagenham & R	L	0-1	0-0	16		0
22	6	H	Maidenhead U	D	1-1	0-1	16	Ward 83	0
23	9	H	Stockport Co	L	0-5	0-4	17		0
24	13	A	FC Halifax T	L	0-1	0-0	17		0
25	20	A	Bromley	L	0-1	0-0	17		0
26	23	A	Torquay U	L	0-2	0-2	18		0
27	27	H	Aldershot T	W	1-0	1-0	17	Archer 31	0
28	30	H	Wealdstone	W	3-0	1-0	17	Barnett 29, McNally 48, Sbarra 59	0
29	Apr 2	A	Barnet	W	2-0	1-0	15	Williams 45, Hudlin 77	0
30	5	H	Sutton U	D	0-0	0-0	15		0
31	13	H	Notts Co	W	2-1	0-1	13	Ball 65, Hudlin 79	0
32	17	A	Dagenham & R	L	2-3	1-2	14	Cranston 11, Rooney 90	0
33	24	H	Yeovil T	W	5-1	1-0	15	Donawa 3 26, 58, 90, Hudlin 62, Ball 83	0
34	27	A	Yeovil T	L	0-3	0-1	15		0
35	May 1	A	Wrexham	L	1-2	0-2	16	Rooney (pen) 80	0
36	3	H	Altrincham	W	4-0	1-0	14	Thompson 38, Densmore (og) 56, Hudlin 65, Archer 88	0
37	11	H	Weymouth	W	2-1	1-1	14	Hudlin 31, Rooney 63	0
38	15	H	Woking	W	2-1	1-0	12	Rooney 5, Hudlin 83	0
39	19	H	Barnet	W	1-0	0-0	12	Ball 50	0
40	22	A	Wealdstone	W	4-1	2-0	11	Williams 21, Addai 30, Ball 57, Donawa 80	550
41	25	A	King's Lynn T	D	1-1	0-1	11	Rooney 54	613
42	29	H	Eastleigh	W	2-0	2-0	11	Ball 29, Sbarra 45	550

Final League Position: 11

GOALSCORERS

League (58): Ball 9, Hudlin 8, Rooney 8 (2 pens), Sbarra 6, Archer 4, Donawa 4, Gudger 3, Ward 3 (1 pen), Osborne 2, Williams 2, Addai 1, Barnett 1, Cranston 1, Gleeson 1 (1 pen), Howe 1, McNally 1, Pearce 1, Thompson 1, own goal 1.
FA Cup (9): Gleeson 2 (2 pens), Sbarra 2, Archer 1, Cranston 1, Hudlin 1, Pearce 1, Rooney 1 (1 pen).
FA Trophy (6): Hudlin 2, Archer 1, Ball 1, Hancox 1, Pearce 1.

Boot 42	Williams 36	Cranston 39 + 1	Storer 38 + 1	Howe 4	Gudger 9	Sbarra 25 + 8	Gleeson 19 + 1	Ward 12 + 6	Coxe 18 + 4	Ball 27 + 2	Archer 11 + 15	Carter 10 + 1	Hancox 9 + 11	Maycock 31 + 8	Osborne 6 + 3	Usher-Shipway 12 + 4	Piggott 12 + 4	Rooney 18 + 11	Hudlin 19 + 15	Pearce 6	Donawa 10 + 14	Clayton-Phillips — + 1	Cameron 13	Howkins 5 + 1	McNally 9	Barnett 5	Addai 9 + 1	Thompson 8	Match No.
1	2	3	4	5	6	7	8	9^1	10	11	12																		1
1	2	3	4	5	6^2	7^1	8			9^3	11	10	12	13	14														2
1	2	3^2		4		5	6			8^1	11^3	9	10	7	12	13	14												3
1	2	3	6	4		7^1	8^2		5	9^3	14	10■	13	12				11											4
1	2	3	5			6			4	8^1	11	9	10	7	12														5
1	2	3	4			12	5		7			9		8	6^2				10^1	11	13								6
1	2		5			6^3	7	13				9	10	14	8^2		4		11^1	3	12								7
1	2	6	7		3		8	12	4^3	10	11^2			14	9^1				13	5									8
1	2	3	13				4	5		7	9^1		8	6^2					14	11	10^3	12							9
1	.2	3	4			5^1	6	13	9		12	10^3		14	8			7^2		11									10
1	2	3	6			12	7		5	9			10		8^1				11	4									11
1	2	3^1			4^3	6	7	10	13		11^2		12	9	8		5		14										12
1	2	3	6			7^1		12	4			9		8					11		10		5						13
1	6	3	8			12		11^2	5^1	9			14	7				13	10^3				4	2					14
1	2	3	4^2		5^1	13	6	7^3						8				12	10		14		11	9					15
1	2	3	4		5^2	6^3	14	8	9^1					10				7	12				11	13					16
1	5	6	7^3		3^1	13	8	10^2	2					9			14	11	12					4					17
1	2	3	7			12	8		4^1					9				10	11^2		13		6	5					18
1		2	7		3	8	9^3		4^2					10		13		11	12		14		6^1	5					19
1	2				3	12	5		13	7^1			8■	6		10		9	14		11^2		4^3						20
1	3	4	5			6^3			12	8^2	13	9		7		11^1	2	10	14										21
1	3	4	5^3				6	12		8	13	9		7^2		10^1	2	11	14										22
1	2■	3	4				5	7^3	8	10		13		12		14	9	6^1	11^2										23
1		5	6					11	4^2	8^1	14		9	7^3		13		10	12				2		3				24
1	2	3	6					10	5^1	7	13		8^2					11			12				4	9			25
1	2	3	4^3			5^1		6	7	14				12				13	10^2		9				8	11			26
1	3	12	4							6■	9^1		7■	5		10		11^3	14		13				2	8^2			27
1	2	3	4			5			14		10^3			7		9		6^1	12		13				8	11^2			28
1	2	3	4			5		12			9^3			6		8^1	14		10		13				7	11^2			29
1	2	3	4			5		6			10^2			7		9	13		11		12				8^1				30
1	2	4	5			6^3				12	10^2			7		9	3	13	11		14						8^1		31
1	3■	4	5			6^1				8	14		13	7^3		10	2	12	11								9^2		32
1		2	3			4^1				8^2	14		12	5		9	7	13	11^3		10				6				33
1		2	5^1			6^2				8			14	7		9	4	12	11^3		10				3		13		34
1		2	6			14	7^2		3^1	8^3				12				10	13		11		4				9	5	35
1		2^2	3			4^1				7	12		13	5		8^3	6	14	10		9							11	36
1	2	3	4							7	13			5			6	12	9^2		8						10^1	11	37
1	2	3	6							8	12			7			4	10^2	13		11						9^1	5	38
1	4	5	6			7^2				9	14			8				13	11^1		12		2				10^3	3	39
1	4	5	6			7^3				9	14		13	8				11^1			12		2				10^2	3	40
1	4	5	6^3			7				9^1	13		14	8				11^2	12				2				10	3	41
1	2	3	6			7^1				9			13	8				14	11^3		12		4				10^2	5	42

FA Cup

Fourth Qualifying	Wrexham	(h)	4-0
First Round	Scunthorpe U	(a)	3-2
Second Round	Morecambe	(a)	2-4

(aet.)

FA Trophy

Third Round	Farsley Celtic	(h)	4-0
Fourth Round	Aldershot T	(a)	2-3

STOCKPORT COUNTY

Ground: Edgeley Park, Hardcastle Road, Edgeley, Stockport, Cheshire SK3 9DD. *Tel:* (0161) 286 8888.
Website: www.stockportcounty.com *Email:* see website *Year Formed:* 1883.
Record Attendance: 27,833 v Liverpool, FA Cup 5th rd, 11 February 1950. *Nickname:* 'County' or 'The Hatters'.
Manager: Simon Rusk. *Colours:* Blue shirts, blue shorts, blue socks.

STOCKPORT COUNTY – NATIONAL LEAGUE 2020–21 LEAGUE RECORD

Match No.	Date		Venue	Opponents	Result		H/T Score	Lg Pos.	Goalscorers	Attendance
1	Oct	3	A	Torquay U	L	0-1	0-0	15		0
2		6	H	FC Halifax T	W	2-1	1-1	9	Kitching [23], Thomas [80]	0
3		13	A	Wealdstone	W	5-2	1-1	8	Rooney 3 (1 pen) [22 (p), 84, 88], Bennett [77], Maynard [79]	0
4		17	A	Chesterfield	W	2-1	1-1	5	Kitching [20], Reid [85]	0
5		27	H	Solihull Moors	D	0-0	0-0	5		0
6		31	H	Weymouth	L	1-2	1-0	7	Palmer [14]	0
7	Dec	5	A	Bromley	W	2-0	1-0	14	Reid [16], Rooney [60]	0
8		8	A	Barnet	W	2-1	1-0	10	Reid 2 [43, 73]	0
9		15	A	Notts Co	L	0-1	0-1	16		0
10		22	A	Hartlepool U	L	0-4	0-1	16		0
11		26	A	Altrincham	D	1-1	0-1	14	Jennings, C [82]	0
12		28	H	Wrexham	W	2-0	2-0	8	Bennett [12], Keane [15]	0
13	Jan	2	H	Altrincham	D	2-2	1-0	8	Reid [5], Rooney [55]	0
14		19	A	Dagenham & R	W	2-0	0-0	4	Bennett [51], Reid [68]	0
15		23	H	Boreham Wood	D	1-1	1-0	5	Rooney [6]	0
16		30	A	Woking	W	4-1	3-0	6	Jennings, C [3], Rooney [37], Southam-Hales [45], Reid [65]	0
17	Feb	2	H	Sutton U	L	0-2	0-1	7		0
18		6	H	Yeovil T	W	1-0	1-0	4	Reid [23]	0
19		13	H	Aldershot T	D	0-0	0-0	5		0
20		16	A	Maidenhead U	D	0-0	0-0	6		0
21		20	A	Eastleigh	L	0-1	0-0	6		0
22		23	H	Notts Co	D	0-0	0-0	6		0
23		27	H	Chesterfield	W	2-0	0-0	6	Jennings, J [59], Reid [80]	0
24	Mar	6	A	Weymouth	L	0-1	0-1	6		0
25		9	A	Solihull Moors	W	5-0	4-0	4	Rooney 2 (1 pen) [18 (p), 20], Cardwell [24], Walker [28], Stretton [80]	0
26		16	H	Barnet	W	2-1	1-0	5	Hogan [9], Stretton [83]	0
27		20	A	Sutton U	D	1-1	0-0	5	Jennings, J [90]	0
28		23	H	Eastleigh	W	3-0	1-0	4	Cardwell [23], Collar [54], Reid [90]	0
29		27	H	Hartlepool U	D	1-1	0-0	4	Madden [78]	0
30	Apr	2	A	Aldershot T	W	2-1	1-0	4	Stretton [37], Palmer [68]	0
31		5	H	Bromley	D	0-0	0-0	4		0
32		10	A	Wrexham	W	3-0	2-0	4	Reid 2 [14, 26], Rooney (pen) [70]	0
33		13	H	King's Lynn T	W	4-0	1-0	4	Reid [14], Rooney [65], Madden 2 [71, 84]	0
34		17	H	Maidenhead U	D	2-2	1-1	4	Cardwell [38], Madden [78]	0
35		24	A	Boreham Wood	W	3-0	2-0	4	Palmer [16], Rooney [32], Reid [70]	0
36		27	A	King's Lynn T	W	4-0	4-0	4	Madden [9], Gash (og) [14], Cardwell 2 [37, 43]	0
37	May	1	A	FC Halifax T	W	1-0	1-0	4	Madden [44]	0
38		3	H	Wealdstone	W	4-0	0-0	3	Croasdale [53], Reid 2 [55, 86], Rooney [90]	0
39		11	H	Dagenham & R	D	1-1	1-1	3	Madden [34]	0
40		16	H	Torquay U	D	2-2	1-1	3	Southam-Hales [34], Palmer [64]	0
41		22	H	Woking	D	1-1	1-1	3	Gerring (og) [45]	2273
42		29	A	Yeovil T	W	1-0	1-0	3	Rooney [23]	1689

Final League Position: 3

GOALSCORERS

League (69): Reid 16, Rooney 14 (3 pens), Madden 7, Cardwell 5, Palmer 4, Bennett 3, Stretton 3, Jennings, C 2, Jennings, J 2, Kitching 2, Southam-Hales 2, Collar 1, Croasdale 1, Hogan 1, Keane 1, Maynard 1, Thomas 1, Walker 1, own goals 2.
FA Cup (10): Rooney 4 (3 pens), Reid 2, Bennett 1, Hogan 1 (*Liam Hogan scored in the 1-1 draw with Chesterfield. However the FA ordered that the game be replayed because Chesterfield fielded an ineligible player*), Jennings C 1, Palmer 1.
FA Trophy (4): Reid 2, Palmer 1, Rooney 1.
National League Play-Offs (0).

Hinchliffe 42	Minihan 25 + 13	Hogan 39	Palmer 30 + 2	Jennings J 26 + 4	Kitching 14 + 2	Maynard 20 + 3	Rooney 34 + 1	Jennings C 13 + 3	Reid 33 + 7	Bennett 17 + 13	Keane 22 + 4	Bell — + 2	Thomas 3 + 9	Stott 10	Southam-Hales 20 + 8	Croasdale 31 + 3	Britton — + 4	Williams 6 + 11	Walker 20 + 1	Collar 9 + 5	Gilmour 3	Dalby 3 + 1	Cardwell 15 + 3	Newby 9 + 6	Stretton 2 + 3	Madden 13 + 1	Shaw 1 + 1	Rydel 2 + 2	*Match No.*
1	2	3	4	5	6	7	8	9^{3}	10^{2}	11^{1}	12	13	14																1
1	2		3	13	6^{3}	7	9	10^{2}	14	11	8		12	4	5^{1}														2
1	2	4	5	3^{1}	12	6	7^{2}	9	11^{3}	8	10		13			14													3
1	2^{1}	3	4	13	6^{3}	5	9	11	12	10	8		14	7^{2}															4
1	2	3					7	10^{1}	11	9^{2}	5	13	6	4	12	8													5
1	2	3	4		8	5	6	14	11^{2}	7^{1}			13	9^{3}		10	12												6
1	12	5		4	3^{2}	6	8	10	11^{3}	9^{1}	2		7				13	14											7
1	2	4		3	12	5	6	8^{1}	11	7^{3}	10		14				13	9^{2}											8
1	2	3	4		9^{2}	5	6	13	11	7	10^{1}		12^{3}			14		8											9
1	2	3	4■		8		5■		11	6^{1}	9				12	10		7											10
1	2	3			8	4		6	11		9		5^{1}		12	10		7											11
1	12	2			4	3		10	11^{1}	9^{3}	6			5	7^{2}	8	14	13											12
1	12	3			6	8	9		10^{2}	11^{1}	4		14	5	2^{3}	7		13											13
1	2	3			7	4	5	14	11^{1}	6^{3}	9		12	8^{2}		10		13											14
1		2	3		8^{2}	4	5	7	11^{1}	6	9				10	13		12											15
1	2	3	14		5	4	7^{2}	10	11^{3}	12	6				8^{1}	9		13											16
1	2	3■	13		5^{3}	4^{2}	7	10	11^{1}	14	6				8	9		12											17
1	12	2	3	13			5	10	11^{1}	9				4	7	8		6^{2}											18
1	13	3	4	2		5	6		10^{2}	11					9			7	8^{1}	12									19
1	13	2	3			4^{3}	5		9	12	7			6	8			14	11^{1}	10^{2}									20
1	2	4	5	12			6		10	11^{3}				3^{1}	7			14		9^{2}	8■	13							21
1	2	4	5	3			6		8^{1}	12						7			11^{2}	13	9	10							22
1	2	4	5	3			6^{2}		10		14					7			9^{3}	13	8	11^{1}	12						23
1	2	4	5^{1}	3					10	14	13					6			8^{3}	7		11^{2}	12	9					24
1	2	4		3		5	6^{2}		9^{3}	14	7					8			10				11^{1}	13	12				25
1	2	4		3		5			11		6					7			8^{3}	13			10^{1}	9^{2}	14	12			26
1	2	3		5		6^{2}			9	14	4				13	7			12					8^{3}	10^{1}	11			27
1	2		4	3					12		5				14	6			8^{2}	7			9	10^{1}		11^{3}	13		28
1	2^{3}		4	3					11^{2}		5				12	6				7			13	8	14	10	9^{1}		29
1	2	4	5	3			12		14						13	6			8^{1}	7^{2}			9		10^{3}	11			30
1	13	3	4	2			5								6	7			9^{1}	8^{2}			10	12		11			31
1	14	3	4	2		13	5^{2}		9						6	7			8				10^{1}	12		11^{3}			32
1	13	3	4	2			5		8^{3}						6^{2}	7		14	9	12			10^{1}			11			33
1	13	3	4	2			5		8^{1}						6	7			9^{2}				10	12		11			34
1		3	4	2		13	5^{2}		12						6	7^{1}			9	8			10^{3}	14		11			35
1	2	4^{2}	5	3			6		14						12	7			8^{3}				11^{1}	9		10		13	36
1	14	3	4	2		12	5			13					6	7			9^{1}	8^{2}			10^{3}			11			37
1	2	4	5	3^{2}			6		8	13						7			9^{3}				10^{1}	12		11		14	38
1		3	4	2			5		12	13					6	7							8	9		11^{2}		10^{1}	39
1	12	3	4	2			5		8^{2}	14	13				6	7			9^{1}				10^{3}	11					40
1		3	4	2			6		11	12					7	8		13	9^{1}					10				5^{2}	41
1	13	3	4	2			7		11^{2}	12	5				6	8			9				10^{1}						42

FA Cup

Fourth Qualifying	Chesterfield	(h)	1-1

(Chesterfield won 7-6 on penalties but the FA ordered the game to be replayed because Chesterfield fielded an ineligible player)

Fourth Qualifying	Chesterfield	(h)	4-0
First Round	Rochdale	(a)	2-1
Second Round	Yeovil T	(h)	3-2

(aet.)

Third Round	West Ham U	(h)	0-1

FA Trophy

Third Round	Guiseley	(h)	3-1
Fourth Round	Notts Co	(h)	1-2

National League Play-Offs

Semi-Finals	Hartlepool U	(h)	0-1

SUTTON UNITED

Ground: The Borough Sports Ground, Gander Green Lane, Sutton, Surrey SM1 2EY. *Tel:* (0208) 644 4440.
Website: www.suttonunited.net *Email:* info@suttonunited.net *Year Formed:* 1898.
Record Attendance: 14,000 v Leeds U, FA Cup 4th rd, 24 January 1970. *Nickname:* 'The U's'.
Manager: Matt Gray. *Colours:* Amber shirts with chocolate trim, amber shorts with chocolate trim, amber socks with chocolate trim.

SUTTON UNITED – NATIONAL LEAGUE 2020–21 LEAGUE RECORD

Match No.	*Date*	*Venue*	*Opponents*	*Result*		*H/T Score*	*Lg Pos.*	*Goalscorers*	*Attendance*
1	Oct 3	H	Maidenhead U	W	3-0	2-0	2	Bugiel [17], Donnellan (og) [35], Kealy [82]	0
2	6	A	Aldershot T	W	2-1	1-0	2	Eastmond [39], Finney (og) [85]	0
3	10	A	Weymouth	W	1-0	0-0	2	Randall [81]	0
4	13	H	Notts Co	L	0-1	0-0	3		0
5	27	A	Yeovil T	W	2-1	1-1	2	Beautyman 2 (1 pen) [10, 49 (p)]	0
6	Nov 14	H	King's Lynn T	W	5-1	1-0	3	Olaofe 3 [25, 53, 69], Sho-Silva [68], Beautyman [89]	0
7	17	H	Dagenham & R	D	1-1	1-0	2	Bugiel [14]	0
8	21	A	Wealdstone	D	3-3	2-0	2	Olaofe [4], Bugiel [11], Eastmond [90]	0
9	24	A	Wrexham	L	0-4	0-2	2		0
10	28	H	FC Halifax T	W	1-0	1-0	1	Beautyman (pen) [9]	0
11	Dec 1	A	Woking	W	1-0	1-0	1	Beautyman (pen) [45]	0
12	5	H	Solihull Moors	W	4-1	2-0	1	Boot (og) [22], Sho-Silva [42], Ajiboye [73], Simpson [85]	934
13	8	H	Chesterfield	L	0-1	0-1	2		776
14	Jan 9	H	Altrincham	D	2-2	2-1	3	Ajiboye [33], Olaofe [40]	0
15	23	H	Eastleigh	W	3-0	2-0	2	Milsom [37], Ajiboye [42], Eastmond [70]	0
16	26	A	Torquay U	D	0-0	0-0	2		0
17	30	A	Hartlepool U	L	0-1	0-0	3		0
18	Feb 2	A	Stockport Co	W	2-0	1-0	2	Hinchliffe (og) [31], Olaofe [68]	0
19	13	H	Boreham Wood	W	2-0	1-0	2	John [32], Randall [48]	0
20	20	H	Wealdstone	W	4-1	3-0	2	Olaofe [20], Goodliffe [41], John [45], Sho-Silva [82]	0
21	23	A	Dagenham & R	W	2-1	1-0	2	Beautyman 2 (2 pens) [24, 90]	0
22	Mar 2	H	Bromley	W	3-2	0-1	1	Eastmond [55], Beautyman [86], Webster (og) [90]	0
23	6	H	Wrexham	D	0-0	0-0	1		0
24	9	H	Yeovil T	W	2-1	1-0	1	Olaofe [32], Beautyman [82]	0
25	13	A	King's Lynn T	W	1-0	0-0	1	Wilson [55]	0
26	16	A	Chesterfield	W	1-0	1-0	1	Wilson [35]	0
27	20	H	Stockport Co	D	1-1	0-0	1	Beautyman [56]	0
28	23	A	Bromley	W	3-1	1-0	1	Cousins (og) [6], Beautyman (pen) [48], Olaofe [70]	0
29	27	A	FC Halifax T	D	2-2	0-1	1	Olaofe [75], Eastmond [85]	0
30	Apr 2	A	Boreham Wood	D	0-0	0-0	1		0
31	5	A	Solihull Moors	D	0-0	0-0	1		0
32	13	H	Torquay U	L	0-1	0-0	2		0
33	17	A	Altrincham	W	4-0	2-0	2	Milsom [7], Wilson 2 [31, 64], Sho-Silva [55]	0
34	24	A	Eastleigh	L	0-1	0-1	3		0
35	27	H	Barnet	W	1-0	0-0	2	Bugiel [70]	0
36	May 1	H	Aldershot T	W	3-1	2-1	2	Wilson [8], John [45], Olaofe [73]	0
37	4	A	Notts Co	L	2-3	1-1	2	Olaofe [20], Bugiel [62]	0
38	8	H	Weymouth	W	2-0	1-0	2	Eastmond [14], Wilson [51]	0
39	11	H	Woking	W	3-2	1-1	1	John [6], Wilson [51], Ajiboye [58]	0
40	15	A	Maidenhead U	W	3-0	0-0	1	Ajiboye [65], Olaofe [79], John [90]	0
41	23	H	Hartlepool U	W	3-0	1-0	1	Milsom [35], John [73], Olaofe [80]	1050
42	29	A	Barnet	L	0-2	0-0	1		686

Final League Position: 1

GOALSCORERS

League (72): Olaofe 14, Beautyman 11 (6 pens), Wilson 7, Eastmond 6, John 6, Ajiboye 5, Bugiel 5, Sho-Silva 4, Milsom 3, Randall 2, Goodliffe 1, Kealy 1, Simpson 1, own goals 6.
FA Cup (0).
FA Trophy (5): Olaofe 2, Beautyman 1, Bugiel 1, Randall 1.

Bouzanis 42	Rowe 9 + 1	Wyatt 13 + 4	Ajiboye 38 + 1	Barden 36 + 2	Milsom 35 + 1	Beautyman 39 + 1	Randall 22 + 2	Eastmond 41	Bugiel 34 + 3	Sho-Silva 11 + 24	Simpson 4 + 8	Dundas — + 12	Kealy — + 9	Davis 21 + 5	Olaofe 35 + 2	Goodliffe 33 + 1	John 35	Adebayo-Smith — + 1	Browne — + 12	Wilson 11 + 5	Nembhard 2 + 2	Tiensia — + 1	Lovatt 1	*Match No.*
1	2	3	4	5^{3}	6	7	8	9	10^{1}	11^{2}	12	13	14											1
1	4	3	8	2^{1}	5	6	9	7	10^{2}	11	13	12												2
1	4	3	8	2		7	9	5		10^{1}		13	12	6	11^{2}									3
1	3	2	8	4	6	7	9	5	12	10^{1}		13			11^{2}									4
1	3	5	6	2^{1}	8	7	9	4	10^{2}	14		13			11^{3}	12								5
1			4		10	7	8	9	6^{1}	12			13	5	11^{2}	2	3							6
1			4	13	10	7	8^{2}	9	6^{1}	12			14	5	11^{3}	2	3							7
1			6	5	4	7		9	10^{1}	12			13	8	11^{2}	2	3							8
1		3^{1}	6	2	9	7		8	11	10^{2}				13	12	4	5							9
1		14	4^{1}	12	9	6	7^{2}	8	13	11^{3}				5	10	2	3							10
1		5		2	9^{1}	8		6	11[illegible]	13	12			7	10^{2}	3	4							11
1		3	6	2	12^{3}	8		9		10^{1}	13	14		7^{2}	11	4	5							12
1		4	8	9		6		7		11^{2}	5^{1}	13	14		10^{3}	2	3	12						13
1			9	2	5	7	8^{2}	4	10^{1}	13				6	11	3			12					14
1			5	2	9	7	8	6^{3}	10^{2}	12				13	11^{1}	3	4		14					15
1			9	2	5	7	8	6	10^{1}			13			11^{2}	3	4		12					16
1			9	2	5	7	8^{3}		10^{1}	13		14		6	11^{2}	3	4		12					17
1		14	9	2	5	7		8	10^{1}	13				6^{2}	11^{3}	3	4		12					18
1			9	2	5	6	8	7	10^{2}	12		13			11^{1}	4	3							19
1		12	9	4	5^{2}	6	8	7	10^{1}	13					11^{3}	3	2		14					20
1			9	2	5	6	8	7	10^{1}	12				13	11^{2}	4	3							21
1			9	2	5	6	8	7	10						11^{1}	4	3		12					22
1			9^{1}	2	5	6	8	7	10						11^{2}	4	3		13	12				23
1			9	2	5	6		7	10					8	11^{1}	4	3			12				24
1				2	5	6^{1}	9	7	10	12	13			8		4	3			11^{2}				25
1				2^{2}	5	6	9	7	10^{3}	14	12			8	13	4	3			11^{1}				26
1			12		5	6	9^{3}	7	10^{2}	14	2			8	11^{1}	4	3			13				27
1		13	9		5	6^{2}		7	10^{1}	12	2			8	11	4	3							28
1			6	2	5	8		9	11	13			12	7^{1}	10^{2}	3	4							29
1			9	2	5	6	8^{2}	7	10^{1}	13					11	4	3				12			30
1			9	2	5	6		7	10						11^{1}	4	3			12	8			31
1			8	2	5	6		7	10^{2}	14					11	4	3			13	9^{1}	12^{3}		32
1	12		8	2	5	6		7		10^{1}		14	13		11	4^{2}	3			9^{3}				33
1	4		8	2^{2}	5	6		7	12	10^{3}	14				11^{1}		3		13	9				34
1	4		8^{3}	2	5	6		7	10^{2}	13				14	11		3		12	9^{1}				35
1	3		4	6	8^{1}	5		7	11		12			13	9		2			10^{2}				36
1		5	8	2		6		7	10^{1}	13					11^{2}	4	3		12	9				37
1		4	8^{2}	5		6		7	11^{1}	12				9		3	2		13	10				38
1		5	9	2		6		7	11^{1}	12				8		4	3			10				39
1			9	2	5		12	7	11					8	6^{1}	4	3			10				40
1			8^{3}	2	5	13	12	6	11^{2}	14				7	9	4	3			10^{1}				41
1	6^{2}	2	3				5	7		8^{1}	11	14	12	4	10^{3}						13		9	42

FA Cup

Fourth Qualifying	Bromley	(h)	0-1

FA Trophy

Third Round	St Albans C	(a)	2-0
Fourth Round	Dagenham & Redbridge	(h)	3-1
Fifth Round	Woking	(h)	0-1

TORQUAY UNITED

Ground: Plainmoor, Marnham Road, Torquay, Devon TQ1 3PS. *Tel:* (01803) 328 666.
Website: www.torquayunited.com *Email:* reception@torquayunited.com *Year Formed:* 1899.
Record Attendance: 21,908 v Huddersfield T, FA Cup 4th rd, 29 January 1955. *Nickname:* 'The Gulls'.
Manager: Gary Johnson. *Colours:* Yellow shirts with blue trim, blue shorts, white socks.

TORQUAY UNITED – NATIONAL LEAGUE 2020–21 LEAGUE RECORD

Match No.	*Date*		*Venue*	*Opponents*	*Result*		*H/T Score*	*Lg Pos.*	*Goalscorers*	*Attendance*
1	Oct	3	H	Stockport Co	W	1-0	0-0	7	Lemonheigh-Evans 90	0
2		6	A	Eastleigh	L	1-2	1-0	7	Sherring 24	0
3		10	A	Bromley	W	2-1	0-1	6	Randell 61, Wright (pen) 90	0
4		13	H	Chesterfield	W	2-1	1-1	4	Britton 9, Wynter 90	0
5		27	A	Aldershot T	W	4-1	1-1	1	Wynter 43, Wright 2 47, 90, Whitfield 51	0
6		31	A	Hartlepool U	W	5-0	3-0	1	Wright 3 11, 15, 55, Whitfield 36, Warren 87	0
7	Nov	14	H	Boreham Wood	D	1-1	1-1	1	Sherring 16	0
8		21	A	FC Halifax T	W	2-1	1-0	1	Hall 17, Lemonheigh-Evans 83	0
9	Dec	1	A	Wealdstone	W	2-1	0-1	2	Waters 2 59, 89	0
10		5	H	Wrexham	W	3-1	2-1	2	Whitfield 5, Hall (pen) 17, Lemonheigh-Evans 74	975
11		8	H	Maidenhead U	W	2-1	1-0	1	Whitfield 45, Wright 59	980
12		12	A	King's Lynn T	D	0-0	0-0	1		625
13		15	H	Dagenham & R	L	0-1	0-1	1		1165
14		26	H	Yeovil T	W	6-1	4-0	1	Little 5, Wright 9, Lee (og) 21, Nemane 36, Lemonheigh-Evans 53, Cameron 83	1323
15		28	A	Weymouth	W	4-3	2-1	1	Hall 15, Umerah 24, Nemane 46, Lemonheigh-Evans 87	575
16	Jan	2	A	Yeovil T	L	1-2	0-0	1	Nemane 46	0
17		23	A	Notts Co	D	0-0	0-0	1		0
18		26	H	Sutton U	D	0-0	0-0	1		0
19		30	A	Barnet	W	2-0	1-0	1	Whitfield 7, Andrews 82	0
20	Feb	2	H	Altrincham	L	1-2	1-2	1	Cameron 22	0
21		9	H	Wealdstone	D	1-1	0-1	1	Waters 90	0
22		20	H	FC Halifax T	L	2-3	1-1	1	Hall 2 (2 pens) 41, 71	0
23		23	A	Solihull Moors	W	2-1	1-0	1	Hall (pen) 17, Waters 63	0
24	Mar	6	H	Hartlepool U	L	0-1	0-1	3		0
25		13	A	Boreham Wood	D	0-0	0-0	3		0
26		16	A	Maidenhead U	L	1-4	0-2	3	Boden (pen) 89	0
27		20	H	King's Lynn T	W	1-0	0-0	3	Boden 46	0
28		23	H	Solihull Moors	W	2-0	2-0	3	Andrews 9, Randell 40	0
29		27	A	Dagenham & R	L	0-1	0-0	3		0
30	Apr	2	H	Woking	W	1-0	0-0	3	Wright 83	0
31		5	A	Wrexham	W	1-0	0-0	3	Sherring 90	0
32		10	H	Weymouth	W	2-1	0-1	3	Andrews 59, Lemonheigh-Evans 85	0
33		13	A	Sutton U	W	1-0	0-0	3	Hall 81	0
34		20	A	Woking	W	2-0	2-0	3	Boden 14, Lemonheigh-Evans 15	0
35		24	H	Notts Co	D	2-2	0-1	1	Lemonheigh-Evans 75, Wynter 90	0
36		27	H	Aldershot T	W	2-1	1-1	1	Hall 12, Boden 90	0
37	May	1	H	Eastleigh	W	3-1	1-0	1	Waters 6, Hall 48, Andrews 75	0
38		3	A	Chesterfield	W	2-0	1-0	1	Lemonheigh-Evans 11, Waters 76	0
39		8	H	Bromley	D	0-0	0-0	1		0
40		16	A	Stockport Co	D	2-2	1-1	2	Boden 2 (1 pen) 40 (p), 57	0
41		22	H	Barnet	D	2-2	2-1	2	Andrews 13, Lemonheigh-Evans 23	1561
42		29	A	Altrincham	D	0-0	0-0	2		1032

Final League Position: 2

GOALSCORERS

League (68): Lemonheigh-Evans 10, Hall 9 (4 pens), Wright 9 (1 pen), Boden 6 (2 pens), Waters 6, Andrews 5, Whitfield 5, Nemane 3, Sherring 3, Wynter 3, Cameron 2, Randell 2, Britton 1, Little 1, Umerah 1, Warren 1, own goal 1.
FA Cup (7): Hall 3 (3 pens), Umerah 2, Nemane 1, Whitfield 1.
FA Trophy (7): Umerah 2, Waters 2, Hall 1, Lemonheigh-Evans 1, Randell 1.
National League Play-Offs (5): Wright 2, Hall 1, Lucas Covolan 1, Moxey 1 (1 pen).

Lucas Covolan 11	Wynter 30	Cameron 23 + 3	Lemonheigh-Evans 41	Wright 17 + 1	Andrews 26 + 12	Buse 5 + 8	Sherring 41	Nemane 20	Whitfield 25 + 1	Umerah 8 + 19	Randell 39 + 2	Hall 34 + 3	Britton 2 + 2	Warren 7 + 8	Koszela — + 6	Moxey 20 + 2	Little 17 + 7	MacDonald 19	Waters 11 + 17	Kerr 5 + 2	Sheaf 2 + 1	Lewis 23	Street 1 + 4	Boden 14 + 4	Hamon — + 1	Law 6 + 2	Covolan 12	Mbunga-Kimpioka 3 + 5	Tomlinson — + 2	*Match No.*
1	2	3	4	5	6^{1}	7^{3}	8	9	10	11^{2}	12	13	14																	1
1	2	3	4^{2}	6	7	13	8	9	10	11^{3}	12	5^{1}	14																	2
1	2	3	4	5	6^{2}		8	10	11		7		9^{1}	12	13															3
1	2	3	4	5^{2}	13		7	10	11		6	14	8^{3}		12	9^{1}														4
1	2	3	4	5			7	9	10	11^{2}	6^{1}	12		14		8^{3}	13													5
1	2	4	10	11	13		3	8	9^{3}		7	6^{2}		14		5^{1}	12													6
	2	3	4	6			8	10	11		7■	5		12		9^{1}		1												7
	2	4	10	11^{2}	13		3	7	8	12		6		5				1	9^{1}											8
	2	3	4	6^{2}	7^{1}		9	10	11	12	8^{3}	5						1	13	14										9
		4	10^{3}	11^{2}	5	14	2	6	9	12	8	7						1	13	3^{1}										10
		2	4^{1}	6^{3}	7	14	9	10	11^{2}	12	8	5						1	13	3										11
		2	10	11^{2}	9		3^{1}	7	8	12	6^{3}	5■		14				1	13	4										12
		2	9	10	11	6^{2}		7^{1}	8	14	5			4			13	1	12	3^{3}										13
		2	4	5^{3}	13		8	10	11	12	7			3		9^{1}	6^{2}	1		14										14
		2	10		13	14	4	8	9^{3}	11^{1}	7	6		12		5^{2}		1		3										15
1		2	4				7	9	10	11	6	5		3^{1}		8			12											16
		2	10		14		4	6	9	12	7			3^{1}		5	13	1	11^{3}		8^{2}									17
		3	11		13		4	8	9	10^{1}	7					5■	6^{2}	1				2	12							18
		2	3		13		7	9	11		6	4^{2}					5^{3}	1	12		14	10	8^{1}							19
		2	11		14		3	9^{3}	10		8	6^{1}				4	7^{2}	1	12			5	13							20
		2			4^{2}		6		10	11	5	3			12			1	7		9^{1}	8	13							21
	4	5^{1}	11		12		2		8	9^{2}	7	6						1	10			3	13							22
	4		10		9	7	2		8^{1}		6	5						1■	11^{2}			3		12	13					23
	2		9		10		3		8	13	7	5					6^{2}	1	12			4		11^{1}						24
	2		3			12	7		11^{2}	13	6	4			14		5^{1}	1	9			10		8^{3}						25
	2		9		5		3			12	8	6^{1}			14		7^{2}	1	11^{3}			4		10		13				26
1	2		9		10	13	3			12	8	6					7^{2}					5		11^{1}		4				27
	2		3		6		8			12	7	4					5^{1}		13			11		9^{2}		10	1			28
	5		10		9^{3}		4			13	8	6				14	7					2		11^{1}		3^{2}	1	12		29
	2		10	12	13		5				8	6^{3}					7		14			4		11^{1}		3	1	9^{2}		30
	2		3^{1}	5^{2}	13		8				7	4					6		12			11		14		9	1	10^{3}		31
	2		9	10^{3}	11		3				8	6				12	7^{2}		13			5		14		4^{1}	1			32
	2	12	3	5^{1}	7^{2}		9				8	4				10^{3}	6					11		14		13	1			33
	2		9		10^{3}	8	4			14	7	6		13		3^{1}			12			5		11^{2}			1			34
	2		3		5^{2}	7^{3}	8			13■	6	4				10			14			11		9^{1}			1		12	35
	5		6		9		4				8	7		12	14	3^{1}			11^{3}			2^{2}		10			1		13	36
	4		11		10		3				7	6		5		2	13		9^{1}					8^{2}			1	12		37
	2		4		6^{1}	13	8			14	7	5		3^{2}		9	12		10								1	11^{3}		38
	2		3		5^{1}		7			14	6	4				9	13		10^{3}			11		8^{2}			1	12		39
1	2	14	9		10^{3}		4		13		8	6				3	7^{2}					5		11^{1}				12		40
1	2	12	9		10		3^{1}				8	6				4	7^{3}		13			5		11^{2}				14		41
1	2	3^{2}	10		11^{1}	12	4			14	9	7^{3}				5	8		13			6								42

FA Cup

Fourth Qualifying	Sholing	(a)	2-0
First Round	Crawley T	(h)	5-6

(aet.)

FA Trophy

Third Round	Chesham U	(a)	1-0
Fourth Round	Boreham Wood	(a)	4-0
Fifth Round	Southport	(a)	2-0
Quarter-Finals	Woking	(a)	0-1

National League Play-Offs

Semi-Finals	Notts Co	(h)	4-2
Final	Hartlepool U (Ashton Gate)		1-1

(aet; Hartlepool U won 5-4 on penalties)

WEALDSTONE

Ground: Grosvenor Vale, Ruislip, Middlesex HA4 6JQ. *Tel:* (07790) 038 095.
Website: www.wealdstone-fc.com *Email:* see website. *Year Formed:* 1899.
Record Attendance: 13,504 v Leytonstone, FA Amateur Cup, 4th rd replay, 5 March 1949.
Nicknames: 'The Stones', 'The Royals'. *Manager:* Stuart Maynard.
Colours: Royal blue shirts with yellow trim and white sleeves, white shorts with royal blue trim, royal blue socks.

WEALDSTONE – NATIONAL LEAGUE 2020–21 LEAGUE RECORD

Match No.	Date		Venue	Opponents	Result		H/T Score	Lg Pos.	Goalscorers	Attendance
1	Oct	6	A	Yeovil T	D	2-2	1-0	13	Emmanuel (pen) 26, Phillips 73	0
2		10	A	Dagenham & R	L	0-1	0-0	17		0
3		13	H	Stockport Co	L	2-5	1-1	21	Slew 16, Lafayette 48	0
4		17	H	Wrexham	W	4-3	2-2	16	Wakefield 15, Mendy 22, Dyer 57, Efete 63	0
5		20	H	Chesterfield	W	3-2	2-1	9	Emmanuel 2 13, 16, Mendy 81	0
6		27	A	King's Lynn T	W	3-2	1-0	6	Parish 3 6, 67, 74	0
7	Nov	7	H	Altrincham	W	1-0	0-0	2	Emmanuel 64	0
8		10	A	FC Halifax T	W	1-0	0-0	1	Parish 86	0
9		17	A	Eastleigh	L	0-2	0-0	3		0
10		21	H	Sutton U	D	3-3	0-2	3	Lafayette 2 46, 66, Mendy 88	0
11		27	A	Notts Co	L	0-3	0-2	4		0
12	Dec	1	H	Torquay U	L	1-2	1-0	6	Parish 27	0
13		5	A	Barnet	D	0-0	0-0	5		0
14		12	H	Weymouth	W	2-1	1-1	3	Lewis 45, Cawley 47	772
15		26	A	Maidenhead U	L	0-4	0-2	6		0
16	Jan	9	A	Hartlepool U	L	1-3	0-1	11	Mendy 75	0
17		23	H	Aldershot T	L	3-4	2-3	13	Lewis 18, Dyer 27, Emmanuel (pen) 82	0
18		26	A	Altrincham	L	0-2	0-1	15		0
19	Feb	9	A	Torquay U	D	1-1	1-0	16	Mendy 36	0
20		20	A	Sutton U	L	1-4	0-3	19	Parish 55	0
21		23	H	Eastleigh	D	0-0	0-0	19		0
22		27	A	Wrexham	L	1-4	1-0	19	Parish 34	0
23	Mar	2	H	Boreham Wood	W	1-0	1-0	18	Smith, C 26	0
24		6	H	FC Halifax T	L	1-2	1-0	19	Lewis 29	0
25		9	H	King's Lynn T	W	3-1	2-0	18	Green 8, Lafayette 36, Mendy 65	0
26		13	H	Notts Co	L	0-1	0-0	18		0
27		20	A	Weymouth	L	0-4	0-1	18		0
28		23	H	Woking	L	0-1	0-0	19		0
29		30	A	Solihull Moors	L	0-3	0-1	19		0
30	Apr	2	A	Bromley	D	2-2	2-1	20	Gondoh 5, Smith, C 18	0
31		5	H	Barnet	W	5-1	2-0	18	Okimo 5, Lewis 2 29, 76, Fasanmade 69, Mendy (pen) 72	0
32		10	A	Boreham Wood	L	1-3	0-0	18	Mendy 82	0
33		17	H	Hartlepool U	L	2-7	0-3	18	Lo-Everton 87, Gondoh 90	0
34		20	H	Maidenhead U	L	0-6	0-1	18		0
35		24	A	Aldershot T	L	0-2	0-1	18		0
36	May	1	H	Yeovil T	L	0-2	0-2	19		0
37		3	A	Stockport Co	L	0-4	0-0	19	0	
38		8	H	Dagenham & R	L	0-5	0-4	19		0
39		11	H	Bromley	L	0-1	0-0	19		0
40		15	A	Chesterfield	D	0-0	0-0	19		0
41		22	H	Solihull Moors	L	1-4	0-2	19	Mendy (pen) 87	550
42		29	A	Woking	W	4-2	1-1	19	Hughes 32, Gondoh 2 (1 pen) 68 (p), 74, Lo-Everton 76	600

Final League Position: 19

GOALSCORERS

League (49): Mendy 9 (2 pens), Parish 7, Emmanuel 5 (2 pens), Lewis 5, Gondoh 4 (1 pen), Lafayette 4, Dyer 2, Lo-Everton 2, Smith, C 2, Cawley 1, Efete 1, Fasanmade 1, Green 1, Hughes 1, Okimo 1, Phillips 1, Slew 1, Wakefield 1.
FA Cup (0).
FA Trophy (8): Emmanuel 2 (1 pen), Cawley 1, Dyer 1, Green 1 (1 pen), Lewis 1, Mendy 1, Wakefield 1.

Isted 23	Efete 22	Phillips 32 + 2	Okimo 42	Mendy 41	Smith C 30 + 2	Green 30 + 6	Benyu 6 + 6	Wakefield 8 + 3	Lewis 36 + 4	Emmanuel 10 + 4	Slew 2 + 6	Parish 15 + 12	Lafayette 10 + 10	Dyer 29 + 5	Cawley 26 + 5	Charles 19 + 3	Wishart 9 + 6	Parrett 2 + 2	Moore 7	Hughes 7 + 7	Lench 1 + 3	Browne Stephen Rhys — + 1	Debayo — + 1	Kougun — + 1 / Shrowder — + 2	Meekings 2 + 1	Olowu 13	Langston 1	Dalling — + 1 / Stevens — + 1	Bowry 1 + 2	Harbottle 11	Gondoh 7 + 7	Fasanmade — + 4	Tavares 1	Askew 7 + 1	Hearn — + 2	Shelvey 5	Lo-Everton 7 + 3	*Match No.*
1	2	3	4	5	6	7	8^{1}	9^{3}	10	11^{2}	12	13	14																									1
1	2	3	4	5	6	7	8^{3}	9^{2}	10	11^{1}	12		14	13																								2
1	2	3	4	5	6		8^{3}	9			10	14	11^{1}	7^{2}	12	13																						3
1	2	4^{2}	3	10	5	13	7^{1}	8	9	14			11^{3}	6	12																							4
1	2		5	3	4	12	7	6^{2}	11	10^{3}	14		13	9^{1}	8																							5
1	2	6	3	5		7	14		10	12		9^{3}	11^{2}	8^{1}	4		13																					6
1	2	6	3	5	13	7			10	11^{1}		9^{2}	12	8^{3}	4		14																					7
1	2	4	6	3	7	12			11	13	9^{2}	14	10	8^{3}	5^{1}																							8
1	2	5	3	10	6	7^{1}	13		8^{3}	11^{2}	14	9	12		4																							9
1	2	4	3	11	6	7^{1}	12	13	5	10^{2}		8^{3}	9					14																				10
1	2	6^{2}	3	5	7	8^{1}	14	9	13			10	11^{3}		4			12																				11
	2	4	6	3^{1}	7	10		14	11			8^{2}		12	5			9^{3}	1	13																		12
	4	5	3		7	9^{3}	13	10^{1}	11		12			6	2			8^{2}	1	14																		13
	2	3^{3}	4	5	6	9	8^{2}	14	10		13			7	12				1	11^{1}																		14
	2		6	3^{2}	7	10		8^{1}	11	9^{3}				5	4				1		12	13	14															15
	2	3	4	10	6	7	13		9	11							5^{1}		1		8^{2}			12														16
	2	7	4	5	6	9^{2}			10	11				8	12				1		13				3^{1}													17
	2	7^{1}	3	5	6	9			10	11				8^{2}	4		13		1	12																		18
1			5	10	8				11^{1}	13				9	4	7	6^{2}				12					2	3											19
1		12	3	10		7			9^{1}			11^{3}	14	8	4	6■	5^{2}								13	2												20
1		8	3	6	9	10			11				12	7	4										5^{1}	2												21
1	2^{2}	3	5	9	6	7			10^{1}			11	14	8^{3}	4	12												13										22
1	2	7	3	10^{3}	8^{1}	9			12			14	11^{2}	13	4	6	5																					23
1		5	2	10		8			9^{3}			11^{1}	13	7	3	6	4^{2}			14									12■									24
1	2	7	3	5		9^{1}			10			12	11^{2}	8^{3}	4	6	13			14																		25
1	2	8	3	6		9^{2}			10^{1}			11^{3}	13	7	4	5	14			12																		26
1		7	4	2^{2}	13	10			11^{1}			14	9	8	3	6^{3}														5	12							27
1		7	4	9^{1}	8	13			12			10^{2}	11^{3}		3	6													5	2		14						28
1		7^{3}	4	9	8	12			11			13			3	6													14	2	10^{2}		5^{1}					29
1		7^{2}	4	5	8	9			11^{1}					12	3	6■														2	10	13						30
		7	4^{2}	5	8^{3}	9			11			13		6	3															2	10^{1}	12		1	14			31
		7	4	5	8^{2}	9			11			13		6	3															2	10^{1}	12■				1		32
		7	4	5	8^{3}	9^{1}			11			14		6	3	12										2^{2}					10					1	13	33
			3	5		12			10			11		7	4	9										2					6^{1}			1			8	34
		2	4	10	7	9			11^{3}			12		8^{1}		6	5^{2}									3					13			1			14	35
		4	3	9	8	10			11^{1}					7^{2}		6	5^{3}			13						2					14			1			12	36
		4^{3}	3	10	5	6										2	8^{1}			7^{2}				13		11					12			1	14		9	37
			4	5	7^{1}	9^{2}			10^{3}			13		14		6	12			11						3				2				1			8	38
		12	4	5					13			10		7		6	9^{2}			11^{3}						2^{1}				3	14			1			8	39
			4	9					8			10^{1}		6		5				11						2				3	12					1	7	40
			4	11					8			9^{1}		6	13	5				10						2				3^{2}	12					1	7	41
			4	10					5					9		3				11				14		2^{2}		13		6	7^{1}			12		1^{3}	8	42

FA Cup

Fourth Qualifying	Hayes & Yeading U	(h)	0-2

FA Trophy

Third Round	Eastleigh	(h)	4-3
Fourth Round	Gloucester C	(h)	3-1
Fifth Round	Darlington	(a)	1-4

WEYMOUTH

Ground: Bob Lucas Stadium, Radipole Lane, Weymouth, Dorset DT4 9XJ. *Tel:* (01305) 785 558.
Year formed: 1890. *Website:* www.uptheterrars.co.uk *Email:* info@theterrars.co.uk
Record Attendance: 6,680 v Nottingham F, FA Cup 1st rd replay, 14 November 2005.
Nickname: The Terras. *Manager:* Brian Stock.
Colours: Claret shirts with sky blue sleeves, sky blue shorts with white trim, sky blue socks with white trim.

WEYMOUTH – NATIONAL LEAGUE 2020–21 LEAGUE RECORD

Match No.	*Date*	*Venue*	*Opponents*	*Result*		*H/T Score*	*Lg Pos.*	*Goalscorers*	*Attendance*
1	Oct 3	A	Altrincham	D	0-0	0-0	10		0
2	6	H	Woking	L	0-1	0-1	15		0
3	10	H	Sutton U	L	0-1	0-0	19		0
4	13	A	Barnet	L	0-1	0-1	20		0
5	17	H	King's Lynn T	W	2-1	1-0	15	Cooke [38], Whelan (pen) [86]	0
6	27	A	Bromley	L	2-3	1-1	17	Wakefield [23], Whelan (pen) [86]	0
7	31	A	Stockport Co	W	2-1	0-1	13	Brooks [51], Whelan [85]	0
8	Nov 28	H	Chesterfield	L	1-2	1-1	21	Shields [40]	0
9	Dec 5	H	FC Halifax T	L	1-5	0-2	21	McQuoid [65]	800
10	8	H	Dagenham & R	L	2-3	1-2	22	McQuoid [14], McCarthy [83]	438
11	12	A	Wealdstone	L	1-2	1-1	22	Thomson [25]	772
12	15	H	Wrexham	L	2-3	2-0	22	McQuoid [3], McCarthy [26]	0
13	26	A	Eastleigh	D	0-0	0-0	21		0
14	28	H	Torquay U	L	3-4	1-2	22	Cooke [31], Murray [49], McQuoid (pen) [62]	575
15	Jan 2	H	Eastleigh	D	1-1	0-1	21	Ngalo [74]	0
16	5	H	Yeovil T	L	0-3	0-2	21		0
17	23	H	Hartlepool U	W	1-0	1-0	21	McQuoid [40]	0
18	26	A	Aldershot T	W	2-0	2-0	20	Dallas 2 [12, 41]	0
19	30	H	Notts Co	L	0-1	0-0	20		0
20	Feb 2	A	Boreham Wood	L	0-1	0-0	20		0
21	6	H	Bromley	W	2-1	2-1	19	Dallas 2 (1 pen) [3 (p), 7]	0
22	20	H	Solihull Moors	D	0-0	0-0	20		0
23	23	A	Yeovil T	L	1-3	1-1	20	Mensah [23]	0
24	27	A	King's Lynn T	D	2-2	2-2	20	Dallas [13], Robinson [30]	0
25	Mar 6	H	Stockport Co	W	1-0	1-0	20	Dallas [4]	0
26	13	A	Wrexham	L	0-2	0-0	20		0
27	16	A	Dagenham & R	D	1-1	0-1	20	McCarthy [90]	0
28	20	H	Wealdstone	W	4-0	1-0	20	McQuoid [21], Camp [59], Shields 2 [82, 84]	0
29	27	A	Chesterfield	L	0-1	0-1	20		0
30	Apr 2	H	Maidenhead U	W	2-1	0-0	19	Shields [86], Dallas (pen) [90]	0
31	5	A	FC Halifax T	L	2-3	1-2	20	McCarthy 2 [22, 90]	0
32	10	A	Torquay U	L	1-2	1-0	20	Dallas (pen) [42]	0
33	13	H	Aldershot T	L	0-3	0-1	20		0
34	27	A	Maidenhead U	W	1-0	1-0	18	Brooks [30]	0
35	May 1	A	Woking	W	4-2	1-1	18	Dallas 2 [44, 61], McCarthy [89], Shields [90]	0
36	3	H	Barnet	L	0-2	0-1	18		0
37	8	A	Sutton U	L	0-2	0-1	18		0
38	11	A	Solihull Moors	L	1-2	1-1	18	McQuoid [9]	0
39	15	H	Altrincham	W	2-1	1-0	18	Dallas 2 [22, 78]	0
40	18	H	Boreham Wood	L	1-3	0-2	18	McCarthy [64]	545
41	22	A	Notts Co	L	0-3	0-2	18		4197
42	29	A	Hartlepool U	L	0-4	0-2	18		1730

Final League Position: 18

GOALSCORERS

League (45): Dallas 12 (3 pens), McCarthy 7, McQuoid 7 (1 pen), Shields 5, Whelan 3 (2 pens), Brooks 2, Cooke 2, Camp 1, Mensah 1, Murray 1, Ngalo 1, Robinson 1, Thomson 1, Wakefield 1.
FA Cup (2): Robinson 1, own goal 1.
FA Trophy (3): Cooke 1, Jordan 1, McQuoid 1 (1 pen).

Bycroft 14	Camp 31 + 2	Jordan 11	Wakefield 10 + 6	McCarthy 35 + 5	McQuoid 29 + 2	Robinson 26 + 5	Brooks 38 + 1	Cooke 11 + 6	Murray 12 + 13	Harfield 39 + 1	Hoey 2 + 5	Thomson 9 + 15	Ngalo 17 + 5	Leslie-Smith 11 + 6	Whelan 5 + 2	Santos 2 + 4	Mullings 2 + 3	Shields 31 + 2	Benfield 2	Al-Hussaini 2 + 1	Anderson 1 + 1	Saydee 1 + 2	Dickson 2 + 3	Ross 26	Dallas 25	Mensah 26	Revan 16	Luque 7 + 3	Fonkeu 6 + 9	Morgan 5	Worman 8 + 1	*Match No.*
1	2	3	4	5	6^2	7	8	9	10^1	11	12	13																				1
1	2		12	4^3	6^1	14	8	9		11		5	3^2	7	10	13																2
1	2		3	13		6	7	8	9	11	12			5	10^2	4^1																3
1	2	3^2	4^3	5		7^1	8	9	13	10				6	14		11	12														4
1	2	3	9	4^2		8	6	10		7	12			5^1	13			11														5
1	2	3	6^2		10^1	7	5		12	13	14	9		4^3	8			11														6
1	2^3	3	4^1	14	5	6	7	8^2		10		12		13	9			11														7
	4	5		6	9^2	7	2	11^3	13	3		14			8^1		12	10	1													8
1	2	3		4	11^3	8	6^1	13	14	7		12		5			9^2	10														9
1	2	3	4▮	12	6^3	7^1	8		9^2	10		5		13				11		14												10
1	2	3		5	7^1			14			13	6^3	4	9			12	11		10^2	8											11
1		2		3	10^1		5	14		6		9^2	7	4^3			13▮	11		8	12											12
1	12	2^3	13	5	6^1		7	9		10	8		3			4^2		11				14										13
1			5	2	9		3	10	8	4			6			12						11	7^1									14
1	2		12	4	5^3		6	8	9^2	10	7^1		3			14		11					13									15
	2		6	4▮	9		5	11	8^1	3			7			12		10						1								16
				3	4^1	13	5		12	9			2					11						1	6	7	8	10^2				17
				3	4^2	12	5		13	9			2					11				14		1	6^1	7	8	10^3				18
				3	4^1		5		13	9			2					11						1	6	7	8	10^2	12			19
	2^1			4	9^2		14		13	7			6					11						1	10	3	5	12	8^3			20
	2			3		12	4			7		13	8▮					11						1	10^1	5	6	9^2				21
	2			3		8	4	12		6		13						11						1	10^1	5	7	9^2				22
	2^3			4		6	7^2	14				12	3^1	5				11						1	8	9	10		13			23
	2			3		8	4^2	13		7		9^1						11						1	10	5	6	12				24
	2			3	4^2	5	6^1			10		12						11						1	7	8	9	13				25
	2		14	3	9^3	7			12	6		13												1	10	4	5	8^1	11^2			26
	2			6	9	7				5		12												1	10	3	4	8^1	11			27
	2			3	9^2	8	4^1			7		12	14					11						1	10^3	5	6		13			28
	2			3	11^2		4			7		12	8					9						1	10	5^1	6		13			29
			12	2			3		13	6		9	7^2					11						1	10	4	5		8^1			30
			7^1	2		8	6		9^2	5		12		13				10						1	11	3	4					31
				2		8	4			7		9						11						1	10	5	6			3		32
	2		13	6^1		14	8			5		12	7^2					10						1	11	4			9	3^3		33
	5			6	12	8	4		14	2		11^3	13					10^1						1		3				7	9^2	34
	2			3	12	8	5^3		13	7			14					11						1	10^1	6				4	9^2	35
	13			12	10		3		8	5			6^2					14					7^1	1	11	4				2^3	9	36
	2			3	9^3	7	4			5		13		12				11						1	10^1	6^2			14		8	37
	2			3	10	7^1	8^2		14	5				4^3				11						1	9	6			12		13	38
	3			12	10^3	6	4^2		7^1	2								9					13	1	11	5			14		8	39
	3			4	11	9	5^3		7^1	2				14									13	1	10	6			12		8^2	40
	2^2			3	4^3	5^1	6		9	10			13	14										1	7	8			12		11	41
					9^1	6	3		7	5			12	2					1						10	4			11		8	42

FA Cup
Fourth Qualifying Oxford C (h) 2-3

FA Trophy
Third Round Maidenhead U (h) 3-2
Fourth Round Darlington (h) 0-1

WOKING

Ground: The Laithwaite Community Stadium, Kingfield, Woking, Surrey GU22 9AA. *Tel:* (01483) 722 470.
Website: wokingfc.co.uk *Email:* see website *Year Formed:* 1889.
Record Attendance: 7,020 v Finchley, FA Amateur Cup 4th rd, 1957–58. *Nickname:* 'The Cardinals'.
Manager: Alan Dowson. *Colours:* Red shirts with black and white trim, black shorts with red trim, black socks with red trim.

WOKING – NATIONAL LEAGUE 2020–21 LEAGUE RECORD

Match No.	Date		Venue	Opponents	Result		H/T Score	Lg Pos.	Goalscorers	Attendance
1	Oct	3	H	Solihull Moors	W	2-1	0-1	4	Kretzschmar 53, Ferdinand 60	0
2		6	A	Weymouth	W	1-0	1-0	4	Spasov 45	0
3		10	A	Chesterfield	L	0-4	0-1	8		0
4		13	H	Dagenham & R	W	2-0	2-0	5	Cook 20, Napa 32	0
5		17	H	FC Halifax T	D	0-0	0-0	2		0
6		27	A	Boreham Wood	L	0-1	0-1	7		0
7		31	A	King's Lynn T	L	2-3	2-1	9	Ferdinand 40, Davison 45	0
8	Nov	14	H	Yeovil T	D	1-1	0-1	8	Davison 89	0
9		21	H	Barnet	W	4-1	2-0	7	Ferdinand 7, Binnom-Williams (og) 17, Kretzschmar 63, Tarpey 82	0
10	Dec	1	H	Sutton U	L	0-1	0-1	12		0
11		5	A	Notts Co	L	0-1	0-0	12		0
12		12	H	Hartlepool U	W	3-0	2-0	11	Jarvis 2, Cook 17, Spasov 59	799
13		26	A	Aldershot T	L	0-3	0-3	15		0
14		28	H	Eastleigh	D	0-0	0-0	15		0
15	Jan	2	H	Aldershot T	L	0-1	0-0	16		0
16		23	H	Maidenhead U	D	0-0	0-0	17		0
17		26	A	Bromley	D	2-2	0-1	17	Wareham 2 72, 86	0
18		30	H	Stockport Co	L	1-4	0-3	17	Diarra 52	0
19	Feb	16	A	Wrexham	L	0-2	0-1	19		0
20		20	A	Barnet	W	2-0	1-0	16	Loza 28, Diarra 67	0
21	Mar	2	A	Altrincham	L	0-1	0-0	19		0
22		6	H	King's Lynn T	W	3-0	1-0	18	Ashford 28, Loza 81, Gerring 90	0
23		9	H	Boreham Wood	D	0-0	0-0	19		0
24		13	A	Yeovil T	L	1-2	0-1	19	Kretzschmar 65	0
25		16	H	Altrincham	D	1-1	1-0	19	Lofthouse 18	0
26		20	A	Hartlepool U	L	0-1	0-0	19		0
27		23	A	Wealdstone	W	1-0	0-0	17	Diarra 86	0
28	Apr	2	A	Torquay U	L	0-1	0-0	18		0
29		5	H	Notts Co	L	2-4	2-1	19	Kretzschmar (pen) 28, Ashford 33	0
30		10	A	Eastleigh	D	0-0	0-0	19		0
31		13	H	Bromley	L	3-4	2-1	19	Diarra 17, Cook 21, Dalby 81	0
32		17	H	Wrexham	L	0-4	0-1	19		0
33		20	H	Torquay U	L	0-2	0-2	19		0
34		24	A	Maidenhead U	L	1-2	0-2	19	Ferdinand 46	0
35		27	A	FC Halifax T	L	0-1	0-0	20		0
36	May	1	H	Weymouth	L	2-4	1-1	20	Cooper 31, Ashford 47	0
37		3	A	Dagenham & R	L	1-3	0-2	20	Ashford 73	0
38		8	H	Chesterfield	L	1-4	1-3	20	Cooper (pen) 28	0
39		11	A	Sutton U	L	2-3	1-1	20	Cooper (pen) 24, Leslie 87	0
40		15	A	Solihull Moors	L	1-2	0-1	20	Collier 79	0
41		22	A	Stockport Co	D	1-1	1-1	20	Kretzschmar 44	2273
42		29	H	Wealdstone	L	2-4	1-1	20	Dyer (og) 18, Gerring 50	600

Final League Position: 20

GOALSCORERS

League (42): Kretzschmar 5 (1 pen), Ashford 4, Diarra 4, Ferdinand 4, Cook 3, Cooper 3 (2 pens), Davison 2, Gerring 2, Loza 2, Spasov 2, Wareham 2, Collier 1, Dalby 1, Jarvis 1, Leslie 1, Lofthouse 1, Napa 1, Tarpey 1, own goals 2.
FA Cup (4): Davison 2, Kretzschmar 2.
FA Trophy (5): Cooper 1 (1 pen), Kretzschmar 1, Loza 1, Napa 1, Spasov 1.

Ross 38	Cook 34	Casey 22 + 1	Cooper 35 + 2	Shotton 14	Ferdinand 33 + 1	Kretzschmar 22 + 8	Collier 14	Spasov 10 + 8	Napa 11 + 8	Block 15 + 1	Goddard 6 + 1	Tarpey 4 + 5	Wareham 3 + 11	Hall — + 4	Jarvis 8 + 12	Dempsey 23 + 2	Lofthouse 35	Reid 3	Davison 10	Skinner 1 + 5	Loza 11 + 1	Gerring 22	Smith J 5 + 7	Diarra 21	Muir 4 + 1	Ashford 14	Smith M 4	Dalby 9 + 5	Hodges 4 + 10	Hamblin 8 + 2	Robinson 9 + 1	Evans — + 3	Freeman 8	Leslie 2 + 5	Saied — + 2	*Match No.*
1	2	3	4	5	6	7^{3}	8	9^{1}	10^{2}	11	12	13	14																							1
1	2	3	4	5	6		7	8^{1}	9	10	11			12																						2
1	3	4	5	2	6	12	7^{2}	11	10	8^{3}	9^{1}			14	13																					3
1	2	3	4	5	7	12	8	9^{1}	11^{3}			6^{2}		14	13	10																				4
1	2	3	5	4	6	14	7	10^{1}			8^{2}	11^{3}		13	12	9																				5
1	2	3	12	4	5	13		14		10^{3}					6	8^{1}	7^{2}	9	11																	6
1	2	3	4	5	6	12		13		10^{2}		14			7^{1}		8	9	11^{3}																	7
1	2	3	4	5	6	7		8				12				10^{1}	9		11																	8
1	2	3	4■	5	7	8		12				6				10	9		11^{1}																	9
1	2	3		4	6	7	8^{1}	13				5^{2}	14		12	10^{3}	9		11																	10
1	2	3	4	5	6^{2}	7		8^{3}				12	14		13	10^{1}	9		11																	11
1	2	3	5	4		6■		10^{2}		12			14		7^{3}	9	8		11^{1}	13																12
1		2	3	4	5		6	7^{1}				13	14		12	9^{2}	8		10		11^{3}															13
1		2	3	4	12		6	13		9					5^{1}	8^{2}	7		10		11															14
1	2	3	4^{3}		5	6	7	14		9^{1}					13	12	8		10		11^{2}															15
1	2	3	4		6	7^{1}		8^{2}	14		11^{3}				13	10	9					5	12													16
1	2		6		5	7^{3}		14	13		10		12			9^{1}	8					3	11^{2}	4												17
1	2				6			13	14	8	9^{2}		10		12		7	4^{3}				3	11^{1}	5												18
1	2		3		6	7			12				11^{2}		8^{3}	10^{1}	9				14	4	13	5												19
1	2		3		6	7			9^{1}						12	13	8				10^{2}	4	11	5												20
1	2				5	12			11^{2}	8^{1}			9^{3}		14	7	6				10	3	13	4												21
1	2		3		6	7			13				12				8				11	4		5	9^{2}	10^{1}										22
1	2		3			6							12		13	8	7				11	4		5	9^{2}	10^{1}										23
1	2^{2}	12	5			6			14				13			8	7				11	3		4	9^{3}	10^{1}										24
1		2	3		6	13							12		7^{1}	9	8				11	4		5		10^{2}										25
		2			5	12			10				13		6	8	7					3		4	9^{2}	11^{1}	1									26
1		2	5			6			10^{2}	9					7^{1}	8						3	13	4	14			11^{3}	12							27
		2	5		6	7				10						9^{2}	8^{3}			14		3	12	4			1	11^{1}	13							28
	2	3			5	7				9						8					11^{2}		6^{1}	4		10	1	12	13							29
1	2		14		4	5				8■						7	6				10^{2}		12^{3}	3		9^{1}		11		13						30
1	2	3	4		6	7										9^{1}	8			12				5				11			10					31
1	2		3		6	7^{1}				10^{2}							8					4	14	5				11	12		9^{3}	13				32
1	2		6		5					9^{2}							8			12		3	11^{1}	4^{3}				10	14	13			7			33
1	2		5		6												9			8^{1}		3		4				10	11			12	7^{2}	13		34
1	2		7		6												9					3		4				11	12	5	10		8^{1}			35
1			5		6												8					2^{1}		3		10^{3}		13	11^{2}	4	9		7	12	14	36
1			2		4				13								6							3		8		10^{1}	11^{2}	7	12	14	5	9^{3}		37
1	3		4		5		6		10^{2}								8									11^{1}		12	14	2	9		7^{3}	13		38
1	3		5				6		9^{1}								7					4				10			11^{2}	2	8			12	13	39
	2		5				6		9^{1}								7					3				10	1	12	13	4	8^{2}			11		40
1	2		5			6^{2}	7		12								9			13		3				11			14	4	10^{3}		8^{1}			41
1	2^{3}		4			6	7										9					5				11		14	12	3	10^{2}		8^{1}	13		42

FA Cup

Fourth Qualifying	Aldershot T	(a)	2-1
First Round	Gillingham	(a)	2-3

FA Trophy

Third Round	Dover Ath	(h)	2-1
Fourth Round	Bromley	(a)	1-1
(Woking won 7-6 on penalties)			
Fifth Round	Sutton U	(a)	1-0
Quarter-Finals	Torquay U	(h)	1-0
Semi-Finals	Hereford	(a)	0-1

WREXHAM

Ground: Racecourse Ground, Mold Road, Wrexham, Wales LL11 2AH. *Tel:* (01978) 891 864.
Website: wrexhamafc.co.uk *Email:* info@wrexhamfc.tv *Year Formed:* 1872.
Record Attendance: 34,445 v Manchester U, FA Cup 4th rd, 26 January 1957. *Nickname:* 'Red Dragons'.
Manager: Phil Parkinson. *Colours:* Red shirts with white trim, white shorts with red trim, white socks with red trim.

WREXHAM – NATIONAL LEAGUE 2020–21 LEAGUE RECORD

Match No.	*Date*	*Venue*	*Opponents*	*Result*		*H/T Score*	*Lg Pos.*	*Goalscorers*	*Attendance*
1	Oct 3	H	Boreham Wood	W	2-1	1-0	4	Hall-Johnson 27, Young 70	0
2	6	A	Solihull Moors	L	0-1	0-0	9		0
3	10	A	Yeovil T	W	1-0	1-0	7	Thomas 10	0
4	12	H	Maidenhead U	L	0-1	0-1	7		0
5	17	A	Wealdstone	L	3-4	2-2	10	Okimo (og) 16, Yussuf 2 18, 90	0
6	27	H	Barnet	D	0-0	0-0	12		0
7	Nov 17	A	Hartlepool U	W	1-0	0-0	11	Durrell 54	0
8	21	H	Aldershot T	W	1-0	0-0	10	Young 64	0
9	24	H	Sutton U	W	4-0	2-0	5	Thomas 2 27, 78, Harris 42, Yussuf 73	0
10	28	A	Bromley	D	1-1	0-1	3	Yussuf 77	0
11	Dec 1	H	Altrincham	L	0-1	0-1	4		0
12	5	A	Torquay U	L	1-3	1-2	7	Vassell 19	975
13	15	A	Weymouth	W	3-2	0-2	5	Vassell 2 72, 73, Hall-Johnson 90	0
14	28	A	Stockport Co	L	0-2	0-2	9		0
15	Jan 23	A	Chesterfield	L	1-2	1-1	15	Young (pen) 20	0
16	26	H	FC Halifax T	D	0-0	0-0	13		0
17	30	A	King's Lynn T	W	2-0	2-0	11	Reckord 9, Yussuf 26	0
18	Feb 2	A	Eastleigh	D	1-1	1-0	11	Thomas 45	0
19	6	H	Dagenham & R	D	2-2	1-0	11	Reckord 30, Hall-Johnson 58	0
20	9	A	Altrincham	W	2-1	1-0	10	Thomas 2 36, 68	0
21	16	H	Woking	W	2-0	1-0	7	Angus 44, Young (pen) 65	0
22	20	A	Aldershot T	L	0-3	0-1	9		0
23	23	H	Hartlepool U	D	0-0	0-0	8		0
24	27	H	Wealdstone	W	4-1	0-1	7	Thomas 2 46, 68, Young 53, Angus 75	0
25	Mar 6	A	Sutton U	D	0-0	0-0	7		0
26	9	A	Barnet	W	2-0	1-0	5	Young 41, Durrell 80	0
27	13	H	Weymouth	W	2-0	0-0	4	Vassell 66, Ponticelli 78	0
28	16	H	Eastleigh	D	2-2	1-1	4	Hall-Johnson 45, Thomas 71	0
29	27	H	Bromley	W	3-0	2-0	5	Davies 32, Angus 2 38, 67	0
30	Apr 2	A	Notts Co	L	0-1	0-0	7		0
31	5	H	Torquay U	L	0-1	0-0	8		0
32	10	H	Stockport Co	L	0-3	0-2	8		0
33	13	A	FC Halifax T	W	4-0	4-0	7	Davies 3 4, 32, 35, Angus 22	0
34	17	A	Woking	W	4-0	1-0	5	Young (pen) 37, Hall-Johnson 51, Davies 90, Omotayo 90	0
35	24	H	Chesterfield	D	0-0	0-0	7		0
36	May 1	H	Solihull Moors	W	2-1	2-0	6	Young 2 (2 pens) 27, 32	0
37	3	A	Maidenhead U	D	2-2	0-2	6	Davies 55, Angus 78	0
38	8	H	Yeovil T	W	3-0	3-0	6	Pearson 9, Young 20, Davies 29	0
39	15	A	Boreham Wood	W	3-2	0-2	5	Hall-Johnson 2 59, 88, Ponticelli 86	0
40	18	H	Notts Co	L	0-1	0-1	6		0
41	22	H	King's Lynn T	W	5-3	3-1	6	Young (pen) 18, Davies 34, Omotayo 2 42, 82, Ponticelli 64	0
42	29	A	Dagenham & R	D	1-1	0-0	8	Ponticelli 90	1278

Final League Position: 8

GOALSCORERS

League (64): Young 11 (6 pens), Thomas 9, Davies 8, Hall-Johnson 7, Angus 6, Yussuf 5, Ponticelli 4, Vassell 4, Omotayo 3, Durrell 2, Reckord 2, Harris 1, Pearson 1, own goal 1.
FA Cup (0).
FA Trophy (0).

Lainton 24	Hall-Johnson 32 + 1	Vassell 30	Kelleher 40 + 1	Reckord 33	Durrell 16 + 10	Harris 26 + 5	Young 42	Jeffrey 4 + 4	Thomas 27 + 1	Yussuf 7 + 8	Bickerstaff 3 + 2	Rutherford 14 + 12	Horsfield 11 + 4	Davies 32 + 5	Ponticelli 11 + 16	Jarvis 8 + 12	Dibble 18 + 1	Pearson 14 + 1	Redmond — + 2	Carrington 16 + 1	French 14 + 3	Angus 22 + 3	Marsh-Brown 1 + 2	Omotayo 10 + 1	Sang 1 + 2	Green 6	*Match No.*
1	2	3	4	5	6^{2}	7	8	9^{1}	10	11^{3}	12	13	14														1
1	2	3	4	5	13	7^{1}	8	12	10		11^{3}	6^{2}		9	14												2
1	2	3	4	5	12	7	8	11^{1}	10			9		6^{2}	13												3
1	6	2	3	5	7^{3}	8^{2}	9		10^{1}	12		13		4	11	14											4
1	5	2	3	4	6	7	8		10	11		9^{1}				12											5
1	2^{1}	3^{2}	4	5	6	7	8	9	10	12	11^{3}		13	14													6
1	13	3	4	5	6^{2}	7	8		10	12		9	2		11^{1}												7
1		3	4	5	6	7	8		10	12		9	2		11^{1}												8
1		5	3	4	8^{3}	6^{1}	9	13	11	12		7	2	14	10^{2}												9
1^{2}		3	4	5	13	7^{1}	8	6^{3}	10	11		9	2	14			12										10
	2	3	4	5	6^{3}		8	12	10	11^{1}	14	9^{2}		7		13	1										11
		3	4	5	6	7	8	13	10^{2}	12	11^{1}	9	2				1										12
1	2	3	4	6^{3}	7^{2}	8	9		11^{1}	13				12	10	14		5									13
1	2	3	4		7^{2}	8^{3}	9		11^{1}	12		14		6	10	13		5									14
1	2^{3}	3	4		13	8	9			11		14	5	6	10^{1}	7^{2}			12								15
1	5	4	2		13	6	7		12	10			9	3	11^{2}	8^{1}											16
	2^{2}		4	6		8	9		10	11^{1}		13	5	7	12		1			3							17
			4	6		8	9		10				5	7	12		1			2	3■	11^{1}					18
	5		2	3		7	8		10			13		4	12	9^{1}	1			6		11^{2}					19
	2		4	5		8	9		11					7			1			6	3	10					20
	2		3	6	12		7		10					5		8^{1}	1			9	4	11					21
	2^{2}		4	6	12		9		11				8^{1}	7^{3}	14	13	1			5	3	10					22
	2^{3}		4	6	13		9		11				12	7	14	8^{2}	1			5	3	10^{1}					23
		5■	4	6	9^{1}		8		11			13	12	7^{2}	14		1			2	3	10^{3}					24
	2		5	6	9		8		11					7			1			3	4	10					25
		4	5	6	9^{2}	13	8		11					7	12		1			3	2	10^{1}					26
	6	2	3	4	9^{2}	14	8		11					5^{3}	12	13	1			7		10^{1}					27
	2	4	5■	6	9^{2}	7	8		11					13	12		1			3		10^{1}					28
1	7^{3}	3		5	13	8	9		11					6^{1}	12			2		14	4	10^{2}					29
1	2	4	14	6	12	7^{2}	8							9^{1}	11^{3}	13		3			5	10					30
	2		4	6		7	8					12		9^{2}		10^{1}	1	13		3	5	11					31
	6		2	4			9					13		5		8^{1}	1			7	3	11	10^{2}	12			32
			4	6			8					7		9			1	3	12	2	5	11^{2}		10^{1}	13		33
	2^{2}		5	6		12	8					7^{1}		9			1	4		3	13	11^{3}		10	14		34
1	2	3	5	6^{2}		12	8					7		9				4				11^{1}	13	10			35
1	7	2	5			8^{2}	9					13		6	12			3				11^{1}		10		4	36
1		3	8	2		13	5					7^{2}		11				4			9	12		6	10^{1}		37
1	9	2	4			7^{3}	8					12		6^{1}	13	14		3				11^{2}		10		5	38
1	8	2	4				9					7^{2}		6	12	13		3				11		10^{1}		5	39
1	2	3	5^{1}				8							9	13	7^{3}		4			12	11^{2}	14	10		6	40
1	7^{3}	3	5			8^{1}	9							2	11^{2}	13		4			12	14		10		6	41
1	2	3	5^{3}				8					12■	7^{1}	9	11	14		4				13		10^{2}		6	42

FA Cup
Fourth Qualifying Solihull Moors (a) 0-4

FA Trophy
Third Round Leamington (h) 0-0
(Leamington won 6-5 on penalties)

YEOVIL TOWN

Ground: Huish Park, Lufton Way, Yeovil, Somerset BA22 8YF. *Tel:* (01935) 423 662. *Website:* www.ytfc.net
Email: info@ytfc.net *Year Formed:* 1895. *Record Attendance:* 16,318 v Sunderland, FA Cup 4th rd, 29 January 1949 (at Huish); 9,527 v Leeds U, FL 1, 25 April 2008 (at Huish Park). *Nickname:* 'The Glovers'.
Manager: Darren Sarll. *Colours:* Green shirts with dark green trim, white shorts with green trim, white socks with green trim.

YEOVIL TOWN – NATIONAL LEAGUE 2020–21 LEAGUE RECORD

Match No.	Date		Venue	Opponents	Result		H/T Score	Lg Pos.	Goalscorers	Attendance
1	Oct	3	A	King's Lynn T	D	2-2	0-0	8	Wilkinson 46, Duffus 81	0
2		6	H	Wealdstone	D	2-2	0-1	12	Murphy 46, Lee 60	0
3		10	H	Wrexham	L	0-1	0-1	15		0
4		13	A	FC Halifax T	D	1-1	0-1	15	Duffus 53	0
5		17	A	Dagenham & R	D	0-0	0-0	14		0
6		27	H	Sutton U	L	1-2	1-1	16	Quigley 45	0
7		31	H	Chesterfield	L	0-1	0-0	19		0
8	Nov	14	A	Woking	D	1-1	1-0	21	Warburton 44	0
9		21	H	Hartlepool U	L	1-3	1-3	22	Quigley 45	0
10	Dec	1	H	Eastleigh	L	1-3	0-2	22	Quigley 68	0
11		8	A	Bromley	W	2-1	2-0	21	Murphy 7, Quigley 45	0
12		26	A	Torquay U	L	1-6	0-4	22	Skendi 49	1323
13		28	H	Aldershot T	W	3-0	1-0	19	Duffus 2 15, 78, Skendi 87	0
14	Jan	2	H	Torquay U	W	2-1	0-0	19	Neufville 87, Wilkinson 90	0
15		5	A	Weymouth	W	3-0	2-0	18	Neufville 14, Skendi 19, Quigley (pen) 88	0
16		27	A	Maidenhead U	L	2-4	1-1	19	Skendi 2 19, 75	0
17	Feb	6	A	Stockport Co	L	0-1	0-1	20		0
18		9	A	Eastleigh	L	0-1	0-1	20		0
19		13	H	Altrincham	W	2-0	0-0	18	Murphy 64, Dagnall 80	0
20		16	A	Boreham Wood	W	3-2	3-0	16	Murphy 14, Reid (pen) 33, Neufville 40	0
21		20	A	Hartlepool U	L	1-2	0-0	17	Knowles 54	0
22		23	H	Weymouth	W	3-1	1-1	16	Murphy 3 2, 52, 82	0
23		27	H	Dagenham & R	W	1-0	0-0	15	Knowles 89	0
24	Mar	2	A	Barnet	W	4-1	2-1	11	Smith, J 11, Sass-Davies 13, Murphy 58, Neufville 80	0
25		6	A	Chesterfield	L	0-3	0-0	14		0
26		9	A	Sutton U	L	1-2	0-1	14	Reid 55	0
27		13	H	Woking	W	2-1	1-0	13	Murphy 2 31, 59	0
28		16	H	Bromley	L	1-2	0-0	13	Murphy (pen) 64	0
29		20	A	Notts Co	L	0-2	0-1	14		0
30		23	H	Notts Co	D	2-2	2-0	14	Smith, J 29, Reid (pen) 38	0
31		27	H	Barnet	W	3-1	3-0	14	Knowles 10, Lee 24, Neufville 34	0
32	Apr	17	H	Boreham Wood	W	1-0	1-0	15	Knowles 28	0
33		24	A	Solihull Moors	L	1-5	0-1	16	Murphy 54	0
34		27	H	Solihull Moors	W	3-0	1-0	16	Quigley 3 27, 53, 71	0
35	May	1	A	Wealdstone	W	2-0	2-0	13	Knowles 14, Quigley 23	0
36		3	H	FC Halifax T	L	0-3	0-1	16		0
37		8	A	Wrexham	L	0-3	0-3	16		0
38		11	A	Aldershot T	L	0-2	0-0	16		0
39		15	H	King's Lynn T	W	3-1	2-1	16	Knowles 2 8, 11, Sonupe 84	0
40		18	H	Maidenhead U	D	0-0	0-0	15		1497
41		22	A	Altrincham	L	3-4	0-2	15	Sonupe 56, Quigley 69, Lee 72	600
42		29	H	Stockport Co	L	0-1	0-1	16		1689

Final League Position: 16

GOALSCORERS

League (58): Murphy 12 (1 pen), Quigley 10 (1 pen), Knowles 7, Neufville 5, Skendi 5, Duffus 4, Lee 3, Reid 3 (2 pens), Smith, J 2, Sonupe 2, Wilkinson 2, Dagnall 1, Sass-Davies 1, Warburton 1.
FA Cup (6): Murphy 2, Quigley 1, Rogers 1, Warburton 1, Wilkinson 1.
FA Trophy (0).

Smith A 42	Leadbitter 9 + 1	Collins 5 + 2	Wilkinson 18	Dickinson 32 + 2	Lee 26 + 4	Staunton 6	Worthington 21 + 5	Clarke 2 + 1	Duffus 6 + 4	Murphy 20 + 8	D'Ath 11 + 3	Smith J 19 + 7	Burke 3 + 2	Rogers 2 + 5	Skendi 35	Warburton 10 + 6	Quigley 21 + 16	Williams 3	Bradley 19 + 2	Lloyd — + 1	Osho 4	Knowles 23 + 9	Dagnall 12 + 11	Sonupe 3 + 12	Neufville 26 + 4	Hunt 20 + 3	Reid 24 + 2	Kelly 18 + 2	Sass-Davies 22	Stephens — + 5	Match No.
1	2	3	4	5	6^{3}	7	8^{1}	9^{2}	10	11	12	13	14																		1
1	2	14	4	5	7	3	8	6^{1}	11	12	10^{3}	9^{2}		13																	2
1	2	3	4	5^{1}	7		6^{3}		12	11		9^{2}	13	14	8	10															3
1	2	3	4		6	7			9	11^{1}			5^{2}	12	8	10	13														4
1	2	3^{1}	5▮	12	8	4	13			11^{2}		14		6^{3}	7	9	10														5
1	2		4	12	7^{2}	3^{1}		14		11	8	13		5	6	9^{3}	10														6
1	2		4	5	7		8^{3}			13		14	6^{2}	12	10	9^{1}	11	3													7
1			4	5	6					11	7				9	8	10	3	2												8
1			4						12	11	6^{3}	7^{1}	5	13	8	9	10	3^{2}	2	14											9
1	13		4	5	6	3^{1}			11	14					7	9	12				2	8^{2}	10^{3}								10
1	2		4	5	6				12	11^{3}					7	8^{1}	10				3	13		9^{2}	14						11
1	2			3	8^{3}				12		14				6	4^{1}	7				5	13	11^{2}	9		10					12
1			4	5	6^{3}		9^{1}		11^{2}		7				8		10▮				3	13		14	12	2					13
1			4	5	6^{2}		9^{1}		11^{3}		7				8	14			2			13		12	10	3					14
1			4	5			7				6				8^{3}		9		2			14	13	12	10^{1}	3	11^{2}				15
1		12		4	5^{3}		7			13		6			9		10^{2}		2			14			8^{1}	3	11				16
1		4▮					7			12					8	13	10^{2}		2^{1}			6^{3}	14		9	3	11	5			17
1					6^{2}		7			10					9	14	12		2^{3}				13		8	3	11^{1}	5	4		18
1				5						12		7^{2}			8	14	10^{1}		2			6	13		9	3	11^{3}		4		19
1				5			12			10		6			9		14		2			8	13		7^{1}	3	11^{2}		4^{3}		20
1				5			9			10^{1}		7^{3}			4	14	12		2			6^{2}	13		8	3	11				21
1				5			7			10^{2}		6			9		14		2			13	12		8^{1}	3	11^{3}		4		22
1				5^{1}			7^{2}			10^{3}		6			9		14		2			12			8	3	11	13	4		23
1					14					10		6			9^{3}		13		2			7	12		8^{2}	3	11^{1}	5	4		24
1					13		12			10		6^{3}			9		14		2			7			8^{1}	3	11^{2}	5	4		25
1							7^{1}			10^{3}		6			9		14		2			8^{2}	13		12	3	11	5	4		26
1				3	6		12			7^{2}					10		14		2^{3}			5	13		8	4	11^{1}		9		27
1				5	6^{2}		7^{1}			10		14			9		11^{3}		2			12			8	3	13		4		28
1				5^{3}			2			10^{1}		6			8		13					7^{2}	12		9	3	11	14	4		29
1				3	6		5^{1}					7			10	12	13					8			9	2	11^{2}	4			30
1				3	7		6					14			4		12					8^{3}	10	13	9^{1}	2	11^{2}	5			31
1			3	2	12		7^{3}			13		10			9^{2}		14					6			8		11^{1}	5	4		32
1			3^{1}	2	14		8			11		6^{3}			9							7^{2}			13	12	10	5	4		33
1				2	7^{1}		12			14		6			4		11					8^{3}	10^{2}	13	9			5	3		34
1				3	6							8			7		10^{1}		14			5^{3}	11	12	9^{2}		13	4	2		35
1				2								6^{2}			4^{3}		10		12			8	9^{1}	13	7	14	11	5	3		36
1				2			4^{2}								6^{3}		8					7^{1}	11	13	9	12	10	5	3	14	37
1					5						12						10		2▮			6	9^{1}	7^{2}	8		11	4	3	13	38
1			3	5	6						9^{1}						12					7	11	13	8^{2}		10^{3}	2	4	14	39
1			3▮	2	6						9						11					7	10	12	8^{1}			5	4		40
1				2	4						6						10					7	9	12	8^{1}		11^{2}	5	3	13	41
1				2	5						8^{3}	12					10		4			7	9^{1}	13			11^{2}	6	3	14	42

FA Cup

Fourth Qualifying	Dover Ath	(h)	3-3
(aet; Yeovil T won 7-6 on penalties)			
First Round	Bromley	(a)	1-0
(aet.)			
Second Round	Stockport Co	(a)	2-3
(aet.)			

FA Trophy

Third Round	Boreham Wood	(a)

Boreham Wood awarded a walkover due to the positive COVID-19 test of a Yeovil T player.

SCOTTISH LEAGUE TABLES 2020–21

(P) *Promoted into division at end of 2019–20 season.* (R) *Relegated into division at end of 2019–20 season.*

SPFL PREMIERSHIP 2020–21

			Home					*Away*					*Total*						
		P	*W*	*D*	*L*	*F*	*A*	*W*	*D*	*L*	*F*	*A*	*W*	*D*	*L*	*F*	*A*	*GD*	*Pts*
1	Rangers	38	19	0	0	57	4	13	6	0	35	9	32	6	0	92	13	79	102
2	Celtic	38	13	4	2	41	11	9	7	3	37	18	22	11	5	78	29	49	77
3	Hibernian	38	7	6	6	21	21	11	3	5	27	14	18	9	11	48	35	13	63
4	Aberdeen	38	9	5	5	23	18	6	6	7	13	20	15	11	12	36	38	–2	56
5	St Johnstone	38	5	6	8	9	15	6	6	7	27	31	11	12	15	36	46	–10	45
6	Livingston	38	6	4	9	20	25	6	5	8	22	29	12	9	17	42	54	–12	45
7	St Mirren	38	4	8	7	15	23	7	4	8	22	22	11	12	15	37	45	–8	45
8	Motherwell	38	6	3	10	20	31	6	6	7	19	24	12	9	17	39	55	–16	45
9	Dundee U (P)	38	6	6	7	21	24	4	8	7	11	26	10	14	14	32	50	–18	44
10	Ross Co	38	5	4	10	19	35	6	2	11	16	31	11	6	21	35	66	–31	39
11	Kilmarnock®	38	6	5	8	30	27	4	1	14	13	27	10	6	22	43	54	–11	36
12	Hamilton A	38	2	6	11	13	29	5	3	11	21	38	7	9	22	34	67	–33	30

Top 6 teams split after 33 games, teams in the bottom six cannot pass teams in the top six after the split.
®Kilmarnock relegated after play-offs.

SPFL PREMIERSHIP TOP GOALSCORERS 2020–21 (LEAGUE ONLY)

Odsonne Edouard (Celtic) 18
Kevin Nisbet (Hibernian) 14
Kemar Roofe (Rangers) 14
Martin Boyle (Hibernian) 12
Alfredo Morelos (Rangers) 12
James Tavernier (Rangers) 12
Devante Cole (Motherwell) 11
Mohammed Elyounoussi (Celtic) 10
Ryan Kent (Rangers) 10
Jamie McGrath (St Mirren) 10
Chris Burke (Kilmarnock) 9
Ross Callachan (Hamilton A) 9
Lewis Ferguson (Aberdeen) 9
David Turnbull (Celtic) 9
(includes 1 Premiership goal for Motherwell)
Nicholas Clark (Dundee U) 8
Kyle Lafferty (Kilmarnock) 8
Lawrence Shankland (Dundee U) 8
Joe Aribo (Rangers) 7
Christian Doidge (Hibernian) 7
Ianis Hagi (Rangers) 7
Albian Ajeti (Celtic) 6
Leigh Griffiths (Celtic) 6
Greg Kiltie (Kilmarnock) 6
Scott Pittman (Livingston) 6
Oliver Shaw (Ross Co) 6
Ryan Christie (Celtic) 5
Jay Emmanuel-Thomas (Livingston) 5
Jon Guthrie (Livingston) 5
Ryan Hedges (Aberdeen) 5
Nicke Kabamba (Kilmarnock) 5
Stevie May (St Johnstone) 5
Billy McKay (Ross Co) 5
Guy Melamed (St Johnstone) 5
Jonathan Obika (St Mirren) 5
Mark O'Hara (Motherwell) 5

SPFL CHAMPIONSHIP 2020–21

			Home					*Away*					*Total*						
		P	*W*	*D*	*L*	*F*	*A*	*W*	*D*	*L*	*F*	*A*	*W*	*D*	*L*	*F*	*A*	*GD*	*Pts*
1	Hearts (R)	27	11	1	2	44	16	6	5	2	19	8	17	6	4	63	24	39	57
2	Dundee¶	27	8	3	2	25	17	4	6	4	24	23	12	9	6	49	40	9	45
3	Raith R (P)	27	6	3	4	24	18	6	4	4	21	18	12	7	8	45	36	9	43
4	Dunfermline Ath	27	9	3	2	24	13	1	6	6	14	21	10	9	8	38	34	4	39
5	Inverness CT	27	3	8	2	16	13	5	4	5	20	18	8	12	7	36	31	5	36
6	Queen of the South	27	4	3	6	17	24	5	2	7	21	27	9	5	13	38	51	–13	32
7	Arbroath	27	5	6	3	16	11	2	3	8	12	23	7	9	11	28	34	–6	30
8	Ayr U	27	3	6	4	11	12	3	5	6	20	25	6	11	10	31	37	–6	29
9	Greenock Morton	27	4	5	5	14	18	2	6	5	8	15	6	11	10	22	33	–11	29
10	Alloa Ath	27	3	5	6	18	29	2	2	9	12	31	5	7	15	30	60	–30	22

¶Dundee promoted after play-offs. Greenock Morton not relegated after play-offs.

SPFL CHAMPIONSHIP TOP GOALSCORERS 2020–21 (LEAGUE ONLY)

Liam Boyce (Hearts) 14
Jack Hamilton (Arbroath on loan from Livingston) 9
(includes 1 Premiership goal for Livingston)
Declan McManus (Dunfermline Ath) 9
Ayo Obileye (Queen of the South) 9
Nikolay Todorov (Inverness CT) 9
Craig Wighton (Hearts) 9
(includes 6 goals on loan at Dunfermline Ath)
Jason Cummings (Dundee) 8
Kevin O'Hara (Dunfermline Ath) 8
Connor Shields (Queen of the South) 8
Osman Sow (Dundee) 8
Innes Cameron (Alloa Ath on loan from Kilmarnock) 7
(includes 1 Premiership goal for Kilmarnock)
Daniel Mackay (Inverness CT) 7
Jamie Walker (Hearts) 7
Danny Armstrong (Raith R) 6
Steven Naismith (Hearts) 6
Cameron Smith (Ayr U) 6
Charlie Adam (Dundee) 5
Lee Ashcroft (Dundee) 5
Kevin Cawley (Alloa Ath) 5
Immanuelson Duku (Raith R) 5
Armand Gnanduillet (Hearts) 5
Luke McCowan (Ayr U) 5
Daniel Mullen (Dundee) 5
Alan Trouten (Alloa Ath) 5
Max Anderson (Dundee) 4
Liam Fontaine (Dundee) 4
James Gullan (Raith R) 4
Stephen Kingsley (Hearts) 4
Gary Mackay-Steven (Hearts) 4
Michael Miller (Ayr U) 4
Fraser Murray (Dunfermline Ath) 4
Aidan Nesbitt (Greenock Morton) 4

SPFL LEAGUE ONE 2020–21

			Home					Away					Total						
		P	W	D	L	F	A	W	D	L	F	A	W	D	L	F	A	GD	Pts
1	Partick Thistle (R)	22	6	4	1	22	7	5	3	3	18	11	11	7	4	40	18	22	40
2	Airdrieonians	22	7	1	3	21	11	5	1	5	14	13	12	2	8	35	24	11	38
3	Cove Rangers (P)	22	7	1	3	18	10	3	5	3	10	8	10	6	6	28	18	10	36
4	Montrose	22	5	3	3	19	14	4	3	4	14	19	9	6	7	33	33	0	33
5	Falkirk	22	5	4	2	14	9	4	1	6	15	17	9	5	8	29	26	3	32
6	East Fife	22	7	3	1	18	11	3	0	8	12	22	10	3	9	30	33	–3	33
7	Peterhead	22	5	1	5	10	12	4	1	6	14	15	9	2	11	24	27	–3	29
8	Clyde	22	5	1	5	15	17	3	1	7	12	21	8	2	12	27	38	–11	26
9	Dumbarton	22	5	1	5	8	11	2	3	6	6	13	7	4	11	14	24	–10	25
10	Forfar Ath	22	1	2	8	10	21	3	3	5	8	16	4	5	13	18	37	–19	17

Top 5 teams split after 18 games, teams in the bottom six cannot pass teams in the top six after the split.
Airdrieonians not promoted after play-offs. Dumbarton not relegated after play-offs.

SPFL LEAGUE ONE TOP GOALSCORERS 2020–21 (LEAGUE ONLY)

Mitchel Megginson (Cove Rangers) 14
David Goodwillie (Clyde) 11
Brian Graham (Partick Thistle) 11
Dale Carrick (Airdrieonians) 9
Graham Webster (Montrose) 8
Jack Hamilton (East Fife) 7
Russell McLean (Montrose) 7
Scott Tiffoney (Partick Thistle) 7
Kyle Connell (Airdrieonians) 6
Calum Gallagher (Airdrieonians) 6
Callum Morrison (Falkirk) 6
Zak Rudden (Partick Thistle) 6
Cameron Ballantyne (Montrose) 5
Scott Brown (Peterhead) 5
Joe Cardle (Partick Thistle) 5
Daniel Denholm (East Fife) 5
Rory McAllister (Cove Rangers) 5
Ben Armour (Peterhead) 4
Scott Fenwick (Forfar Ath) 4
Lewis Jamieson (Clyde) 4
Hamish Ritchie (Peterhead) 4
Kevin Smith (East Fife) 4
Charles Telfer (Falkirk) 4
Ryan Wallace (East Fife) 4
Jamie Wilson (Dumbarton) 4
Jordan Allan (Forfar Ath) 3
Blair Alston (Falkirk) 3
Lyall Cameron (Peterhead) 3
Ally Love (Clyde) 3
Jamie Masson (Cove Rangers) 3
Lewis Milne (Montrose) 3
Connor Murray (Partick Thistle) 3
Thomas Roberts (Airdrieonians) 3
Alistair Roy (Airdrieonians) 3
Conor Sammon (Falkirk) 3
Daniel Scally (Forfar Ath) 3

SPFL LEAGUE TWO 2020–21

			Home					Away					Total						
		P	W	D	L	F	A	W	D	L	F	A	W	D	L	F	A	GD	Pts
1	Queen's Park	22	8	2	1	21	5	9	1	1	22	8	17	3	2	43	13	30	54
2	Edinburgh C	22	5	1	5	18	14	7	1	3	22	13	12	2	8	40	27	13	38
3	Elgin C	22	7	1	3	23	15	5	1	5	16	13	12	2	8	39	28	11	38
4	Stranraer (R)	22	6	1	4	20	13	5	4	2	16	12	11	5	6	36	25	11	38
5	Stirling Alb	22	4	3	4	9	9	6	3	2	23	13	10	6	6	32	22	10	36
6	Stenhousemuir	22	5	2	4	15	13	2	3	6	10	22	7	5	10	25	35	–10	26
7	Albion R	22	2	3	6	8	16	5	1	5	17	22	7	4	11	25	38	–13	25
8	Annan Ath	22	2	4	5	15	18	3	3	5	10	9	5	7	10	25	27	–2	22
9	Cowdenbeath	22	3	2	6	9	19	2	4	5	6	13	5	6	11	15	32	–17	21
10	Brechin C®	22	0	3	8	6	27	2	1	8	7	19	2	4	16	13	46	–33	10

Top 5 teams split after 18 games, teams in the bottom six cannot pass teams in the top six after the split.
Edinburgh C not promoted after play-offs. ®Brechin C relegated after play-offs.

SPFL LEAGUE TWO TOP GOALSCORERS 2020–21 (LEAGUE ONLY)

Kane Hester (Elgin C) 14
Matthew Aitken (Albion R) 10
Andy Ryan (Stirling Alb) 10
Thomas Orr (Stranraer) 8
Josh Campbell (Edinburgh C) 7
Botti Biabi (Stenhousemuir) 6
Brian Cameron (Elgin C) 6
Mark McGuigan (Stenhousemuir) 6
Robert McHugh (Queen's Park) 6
Simon Murray (Queen's Park) 6
Ruari Paton (Stranraer) 6
Willam Baynham (Queen's Park) 5
Russell Dingwall (Elgin C) 5
Darryl Duffy (Stranraer) 5
Blair Henderson (Edinburgh C) 5
Liam Henderson (Edinburgh C) 5
Tony Wallace (Annan Ath) 5
Liam Brown (Edinburgh C) 4
Declan Byrne (Stirling Alb) 4
Kyle Doherty (Albion R) 4
Nathan Flanagan (Annan Ath) 4
Jack Leitch (Stirling Alb) 4
Darren Lyon (Queen's Park) 4
Ouzy See (Edinburgh C) 4
Aiden Sopel (Elgin C) 4
Greig Spence (Stenhousemuir) 4
Andrew Stirling (Stranraer) 4
Max Wright (Annan Ath) 4
Iain Anderson (Annan Ath) 3
Luca Connell (Queen's Park) 3
Raffaele De Vita (Edinburgh C) 3
James Hilton (Stranraer) 3
Salim Kouider-Aissa (Queen's Park) 3
Louis Longridge (Queen's Park) 3
Dylan Mackin (Stirling Alb) 3
Conor O'Keefe (Elgin C) 3

ABERDEEN

Year Formed: 1903. *Ground & Address:* Pittodrie Stadium, Pittodrie St, Aberdeen AB24 5QH. *Telephone:* 01224 650400. *Fax:* 01224 644173. *E-mail:* feedback@afc.co.uk *Website:* afc.co.uk
Ground Capacity: 20,866 (all seated). *Size of Pitch:* 105m × 66m.
Chairman: Dave Cormack.
Manager: Stephen Glass. *Assistant Manager:* Allan Russell. *Reserve Team Manager:* Paul Sheerin.
Club Nicknames: 'The Dons'; 'The Reds'; 'The Dandies'.
Record Attendance: 45,061 v Hearts, Scottish Cup 4th rd, 13 March 1954.
Record Transfer Fee received: £1,750,000 for Eoin Jess to Coventry C (February 1996).
Record Transfer Fee paid: £1,000,000 for Paul Bernard from Oldham Ath (September 1995).
Record Victory: 13-0 v Peterhead, Scottish Cup 3rd rd, 10 February 1923.
Record Defeat: 0-9 v Celtic, Premier League, 6 November 2010.
Most Capped Player: Alex McLeish, 77 (Scotland).
Most League Appearances: 556: Willie Miller, 1973-90.
Most League Goals in Season (Individual): 38: Benny Yorston, Division I, 1929-30.
Most Goals Overall (Individual): 199: Joe Harper, 1969-72; 1976-81.

ABERDEEN – SPFL PREMIERSHIP 2020–21 LEAGUE RECORD

Match No.	Date	Venue	Opponents	Result		H/T Score	Lg Pos.	Goalscorers	Attendance
1	Aug 1	H	Rangers	L	0-1	0-1	7		0
2	20	A	St Johnstone	W	1-0	0-0	8	Hedges 82	0
3	23	H	Livingston	W	2-1	0-0	7	Ferguson (pen) 49, Wright 55	0
4	30	A	Hibernian	W	1-0	1-0	4	Ferguson (pen) 39	0
5	Sept 12	H	Kilmarnock	W	1-0	1-0	4	McCrorie 16	0
6	20	H	Motherwell	L	0-3	0-3	4		0
7	27	A	Ross Co	W	3-0	1-0	4	Watkins 42, Ferguson 2 (2 pens) 60, 76	0
8	Oct 2	H	St Mirren	W	2-1	0-0	4	Watkins 71, Ferguson 90	0
9	17	A	Dundee U	D	0-0	0-0	4		0
10	20	H	Hamilton A	W	4-2	4-1	3	Hoban 14, Ferguson 21, Edmondson 2 24, 31	0
11	25	H	Celtic	D	3-3	1-0	4	Ferguson 2 (2 pens) 43, 90, Hedges 65	0
12	Nov 6	H	Hibernian	W	2-0	2-0	3	Wright 5, Cosgrove 12	0
13	22	A	Rangers	L	0-4	0-2	3		0
14	25	A	Hamilton A	D	1-1	1-0	3	Hedges 19	0
15	Dec 5	A	St Mirren	D	1-1	1-1	4	Hayes 37	0
16	12	H	Ross Co	W	2-0	1-0	4	Main 2 5, 57	0
17	20	A	Kilmarnock	W	2-0	0-0	3	Hedges 52, Cosgrove 90	0
18	23	A	Motherwell	D	0-0	0-0	4		0
19	26	H	St Johnstone	W	2-1	1-1	3	Cosgrove (pen) 45, Taylor 54	0
20	Jan 2	H	Dundee U	D	0-0	0-0	3		0
21	10	H	Rangers	L	1-2	0-1	3	Kennedy 67	0
22	16	A	Ross Co	L	1-4	1-2	4	Iacovitti (og) 45	0
23	23	H	Motherwell	W	2-0	1-0	3	Hoban 15, Considine 77	0
24	27	A	St Johnstone	D	0-0	0-0	3		0
25	30	A	Livingston	D	0-0	0-0	3		0
26	Feb 2	H	Livingston	L	0-2	0-2	4		0
27	6	A	Hibernian	L	0-2	0-1	4		0
28	13	H	St Mirren	D	0-0	0-0	4		0
29	17	A	Celtic	L	0-1	0-1	4		0
30	20	H	Kilmarnock	W	1-0	1-0	4	Hendry 21	0
31	27	A	Celtic	L	0-1	0-1	4		0
32	Mar 6	H	Hamilton A	D	0-0	0-0	4		0
33	20	A	Dundee U	L	0-1	0-0	4		0
34	Apr 10	A	St Johnstone	W	1-0	0-0	4	Hayes 52	0
35	21	H	Celtic	D	1-1	1-0	4	Ferguson 17	0
36	May 1	A	Livingston	W	2-1	0-0	4	Hendry 52, Hedges 74	0
37	12	H	Hibernian	L	0-1	0-1	4		0
38	15	A	Rangers	L	0-4	0-2	4		0

Final League Position: 4

Honours
League Champions: Division I 1954-55; Premier Division 1979-80, 1983-84, 1984-85.
Runners-up: Premiership 2014-15, 2015-16, 2016-17, 2017-18; Division I 1910-11, 1936-37, 1955-56, 1970-71, 1971-72; Premier Division 1977-78, 1980-81, 1981-82, 1988-89, 1989-90, 1990-91, 1992-93, 1993-94.
Scottish Cup Winners: 1947, 1970, 1982, 1983, 1984, 1986, 1990; *Runners-up:* 1937, 1953, 1954, 1959, 1967, 1978, 1993, 2000, 2017.
League Cup Winners: 1955-56, 1976-77, 1985-86, 1989-90, 1995-96, 2013-14; *Runners-up:* 1946-47, 1978-79, 1979-80, 1987-88, 1988-89, 1992-93, 1999-2000, 2016-17, 2018-19.
Drybrough Cup Winners: 1971, 1980.

European: *European Cup:* 12 matches (1980-81, 1984-85, 1985-86); *Cup Winners' Cup:* 39 matches (1967-68, 1970-71, 1978-79, 1982-83 winners, 1983-84 semi-finals, 1986-87, 1990-91, 1993-94); *UEFA Cup:* 56 matches (*Fairs Cup:* 1968-69. *UEFA Cup:* 1971-72, 1972-73, 1973-74, 1977-78, 1979-80, 1981-82, 1987-88, 1988-89, 1989-90, 1991-92, 1994-95, 1996-97, 2000-01, 2002-03, 2007-08). *Europa League:* 35 matches (2009-10, 2014-15, 2015-16, 2016-17, 2017-18, 2018-19, 2019-20, 2020-21).

Club colours: All: Red with white trim.

Goalscorers: *League (36):* Ferguson 9 (6 pens), Hedges 5, Cosgrove 3 (1 pen), Edmondson 2, Hayes 2, Hendry 2, Hoban 2, Main 2, Watkins 2, Wright 2, Considine 1, Kennedy 1, McCrorie 1, Taylor 1, own goal 1.
William Hill Scottish Cup (3): Hendry 1, Kamberi 1, McGinn 1.
Betfred Scottish League Cup (1): McGinn 1.
UEFA Europa League (0).

Lewis J 35	Hernandez R 2 + 2	Taylor A 30 + 1	McKenna S 4	Considine A 36	Hayes J 34	Ferguson L 35	Ojo F 6 + 5	Kennedy M 22 + 9	Bryson C 1 + 1	Anderson B 1 + 5	Edmondson R 3 + 11	Campbell D 12 + 8	McGinn N 12 + 13	Hedges R 25 + 3	McCrorie R 28 + 1	Hoban T 35 + 2	Wright S 14 + 3	McLennan C 13 + 14	Logan S 2 + 10	Watkins M 9	McGeouch D 7 + 8	Main C 8 + 6	Cosgrove S 9 + 5	Leigh G 6 + 2	Duncan R — + 1	Devlin M — + 1	Ngwenya K — + 2	Virtanen M — + 2	Hornby F 5 + 5	Hendry C 5 + 7	Kamberi F 11	Ross E — + 2	Ruth M — + 1	MacKenzie J 5 + 1	Ramsay C — + 4	Woods G 3	*Match No.*
1	2	3	4	5▮	6	7	8^{4}	9^{1}	10^{3}	11^{2}	12	13	14	15																							1
1	5^{2}	3			9	10	7^{5}	13	14			8^{4}	11^{3}	15	2	4	6^{1}	12	16																		2
1		2	3^{3}		9	7	12	6^{4}						8^{1}	4	16	10^{2}	14	5	11^{5}	13	15															3
1			3	4	8	6		5					14	10^{1}	7	2	11^{3}			9^{2}	12	13															4
1		15	3	4	8	6		5^{4}					14	9^{2}	7^{1}	2	10^{3}		12	11	13																5
1		3^{2}		4	8	6	7^{3}			16	14		5^{5}	11	2	12	9^{1}	15	13	10^{4}																	6
1	14	3		4	8	6				16	15		11^{2}	5^{3}	7	2^{1}	9^{5}	13		10^{4}	12																7
1		3^{1}		4	8	7				14	12		11^{3}	5^{4}	6	2	9^{2}	13		10	15																8
1		3		4	8	7					12		13	10	6	2	9^{1}	5^{2}		11																	9
1		3		4	8^{1}	6	14				10^{4}		15	5	13	2	9^{3}	12		11	7^{2}																10
1		3		4	9	7					11^{2}			10	6	2	13	12		8^{3}	5^{1}		14														11
1		3		4		7		8^{3}						9	6	2	10	5^{2}	14			12	11^{1}	13													12
1	15	2		3			6	8			10^{2}	13		9		4			5^{1}			12	11^{4}	7^{3}	14												13
1		3		4			6	5			12	7	13	9		2						10^{2}	11	8^{1}													14
1		4^{5}		3	6^{4}	8▮	13	9^{1}			15			10^{3}	7	2			12			14	11^{2}	5		16											15
1		3		4	8^{3}		16	9^{4}				7^{1}	15	10	6	2		5^{5}	12			11^{2}	13				14										16
1		3		4	8	7		5				12		9	6	2^{3}		11^{1}	13			10^{2}	14														17
1		3		4	8	7		5			13			9	6	2		11^{1}				10^{2}	12														18
1		3		4	8	6	13	5			12	7		9		2						10^{2}	11^{1}														19
1		3		4	8	7		11^{4}			15	14	9^{1}	5	6^{2}	2	12					10^{3}	13														20
1		3^{1}		4	8	7		13			14	6		5▮		2	9^{3}		12			10^{2}	11														21
1		3^{1}		4	5^{3}	7		8		14					6	2	9		12			10^{2}	11				13										22
1		3		4	8^{5}	6	7^{2}	10^{4}				12		5		2	9^{1}	13				15	11^{3}	16				14									23
1		3		4	5	6		8				12		10	7	2^{2}	9^{1}	13					11														24
1		3		4	11	6		7^{2}		13				5	9	2	12	10^{1}						8													25
1		3^{3}		4	10	7		12				13	15	9^{4}	6	2		5^{1}						8					11^{2}	14							26
1		3^{3}		4	10	9		5					13		7	2		12^{4}	15		6^{2}			8^{1}					11	14							27
1				3	4	6		8^{3}				7	9^{2}		5	2		12											11^{1}	13	10	14					28
1		3		4	9^{1}	7		5^{4}				8^{2}	13		6	2		12			15								10^{3}	14	11						29
1		3		4		7		13				8^{2}	9^{1}		6	2		5										14	10^{3}	12	11						30
1		3		4	9	7		13				8^{2}	10^{1}		6	2		5^{3}			14									12	11						31
1		3^{3}		4	8	9		13					7^{2}		5	2		12			6									10^{1}	11		14				32
1		3		4	11^{2}	8		14				7^{4}	12		6	2^{5}		9^{1}											13	15	10^{3}			5	16		33
1				4	9^{1}	7		6^{3}				8	10^{4}		2	3		13											12		11^{2}	15		5	14		34
				4	5	7		6				8	9^{3}		2^{2}	3					13									11^{1}	10			14	12	1	35
				4	8	6		14					10^{1}	13		3		2			7								12^{3}	11^{2}	9			5		1	36
				4	10^{2}	6		12					13	8^{3}		3		2			7								14	11^{1}	9			5		1	37
1				4	9^{4}	8						13	14	7^{3}		3		2			6								12	11^{2}	10^{1}			5	15		38

AIRDRIEONIANS

Year Formed: 2002. *Ground & Address:* The Penny Cars Stadium, New Broomfield, Craigneuk Avenue, Airdrie ML6 8QZ. *Telephone:* (Stadium) 01236 622000. *Fax:* 01236 622001.
E-mail: enquiries@airdriefc.com *Website:* airdriefc.com
Ground Capacity: 10,101 (all seated). *Size of Pitch:* 105m × 67m.
Chairman: Martin Ferguson.
Manager: Ian Murray. *First Team Coach:* Bryan Prunty.
Club Nickname: 'The Diamonds'.
Record Attendance: 9,044 v Rangers, League 1, 23 August 2013.
Record Victory: 11-0 v Gala Fairydean, Scottish Cup 3rd rd, 19 November 2011.
Record Defeat: 0-7 v Partick Thistle, First Division, 20 October 2012.
Most Capped Player: Simon Vella, 3 (Malta).
Most League Appearances: 222: Paul Lovering, 2004-12.
Most League Goals in Season (Individual): 23: Andy Ryan, 2016-17.
Most Goals Overall (Individual): 43: Bryan Prunty, 2005-08, 2015-16.

AIRDRIEONIANS – SPFL LEAGUE ONE 2020–21 LEAGUE RECORD

Match No.	*Date*	*Venue*	*Opponents*	*Result*	*H/T Score*	*Lg Pos.*	*Goalscorers*	*Attendance*
1	Oct 17	H	Peterhead	W 2-0	1-0	3	Carrick (pen) ^{43}, Fordyce ^{71}	0
2	24	A	Partick Thistle	L 1-2	1-1	3	Carrick ^{36}	0
3	31	H	Dumbarton	L 0-2	0-1	5		0
4	Nov 7	H	Clyde	W 5-0	3-0	5	Gallagher 2 $^{24, 44}$, Carrick 2 (1 pen) $^{30, 52 (p)}$, Connell ^{81}	0
5	21	A	Forfar Ath	W 3-1	3-1	3	Robert ^{6}, Carrick (pen) ^{21}, Connell ^{27}	0
6	28	H	Cove R	D 1-1	0-1	3	Robert ^{57}	0
7	Dec 5	A	East Fife	L 0-2	0-1	4		0
8	12	H	Montrose	L 0-1	0-0	6		0
9	20	A	Falkirk	W 1-0	0-0	4	Connell ^{82}	0
10	26	A	Clyde	W 4-2	3-1	3	Robert ^{8}, Carrick 2 $^{16, 54}$, Kerr ^{20}	0
11	Mar 20	A	Peterhead	L 0-1	0-0	4		0
12	27	H	Partick Thistle	L 2-4	1-1	7	McKay, J ^{2}, Roy ^{72}	0
13	30	A	Cove R	L 0-2	0-0	7		0
14	Apr 1	A	Dumbarton	W 1-0	0-0	6	Roy ^{79}	0
15	6	H	Falkirk	W 2-1	1-1	4	Roy ^{9}, Carrick (pen) ^{81}	0
16	10	A	Montrose	D 2-2	0-2	6	Gallagher ^{51}, Lennox (og) ^{90}	0
17	13	H	Forfar Ath	W 3-1	1-1	4	Thomson (og) ^{2}, Gallagher ^{82}, Connell ^{90}	0
18	20	H	East Fife	W 2-0	0-0	4	Gallagher ^{66}, Carrick ^{77}	0
19	24	A	Partick Thistle	L 0-1	0-1	4		0
20	27	H	Montrose	W 2-1	1-0	4	Connell 2 $^{9, 56}$	0
21	May 1	A	Cove R	W 2-0	0-0	3	Gallagher ^{49}, Ritchie ^{90}	0
22	4	H	Falkirk	W 2-0	0-0	2	Thomson ^{88}, Turner ^{90}	0

Final League Position: 2

Honours
League Champions: Second Division 2003-04.
Runners-up: Second Division 2007-08; League One 2020-21.
League Challenge Cup Winners: 2008-09; *Runners-up:* 2003-04.

Club colours: Shirt: White with red diamond. Shorts: Red with white trim. Socks: Red with white trim.

Goalscorers: *League (35):* Carrick 9 (4 pens), Connell 6, Gallagher 6, Robert 3, Roy 3, Fordyce 1, Kerr 1, McKay J 1, Ritchie 1, Thomson 1, Turner 1, own goals 2.
William Hill Scottish Cup (0).
Betfred Scottish League Cup (3): McKay P 1, Robert 1, Thomson 1.
Scottish League Play-Offs (4): Gallagher 2, McKay J 1, own goal 1.

Currie M 20	MacDonald K 8 + 1	Crighton S 17	Fordyce C 22	McCann L 20 + 1	McKay P 21	Kerr J 13 + 1	Carrick D 18 + 4	Sabatini G 8 + 4	Thomson C 5 + 16	Gallagher C 19 + 2	O'Reilly E 8 + 8	Connell K 11 + 11	Stokes E — + 9	Robert T 10 + 8	Hutton D 2	Ritchie D 6 + 6	Walker S 5 + 2	Roy A 6 + 7	McKay J 7 + 1	Turner K 10	Paton P 6	Mbayo H — + 1	Pyott P — + 2	*Match No.*
1	2	3	4	5	6^{1}	7	8	9	10^{3}	11^{2}	12	13	14											1
1	2	3	4	5	9	7	10^{2}	6^{1}	8	11^{3}		12	14	13										2
	2^{3}	3	4	5	7	8^{2}	9	12	6^{1}	11	15	10^{4}	13	14	1									3
	15	3	4	5	2	7	8^{5}	6^{3}	12	11^{4}	16	9^{2}	13	10^{1}	1	14								4
1	2	3	4	5	6	7	9^{3}	12	13	11^{2}	14	10		8^{1}										5
1		4	3	5	7	8	11^{1}	6	13	10^{3}		12	15	9^{2}		14	2^{4}							6
1	2^{2}	3	4	5	7	6	11^{3}	8	13	12	14	10^{1}		9										7
1	2^{2}	3	4	5	9	7	10^{1}	6^{4}	12	11	13	14	15	8^{3}										8
1	5	3	4		2	7	12	9^{2}	13	11^{1}	14	10		8^{3}		6								9
1	5	3	4	12	2	6	11^{1}	13	8			9^{2}		10^{3}		7		14						10
1		3	4	5			9^{4}	14	15	10	12	11^{3}		8^{1}		6^{2}		13	2	7■				11
1		3■	4	5	7		9^{1}		12	11^{4}	8	13		10^{2}				14	2^{3}		6	15		12
1			4	5	3		9^{2}	6^{3}	7^{5}	12	8^{1}	11		14		13	15	10^{4}	2				16	13
1			4	5	3		12		14	11^{4}	9	13		10^{1}		8	2^{3}	15	6^{2}	7				14
1		4	3	5	7		13		12	10^{1}	9	14		15		8^{2}		11^{4}	6^{3}	2				15
1		4	3	5	7		8^{3}		13	10	9	12	14					11^{1}	6^{2}	2				16
1		4	3	5	7		11^{2}		12	10	6	13		14				9^{1}	8^{3}	2				17
1		4	3	5	7		11^{2}		13	10^{4}	6^{3}	12	14			15	16	9^{1}		2	8^{5}			18
1		3	4	5^{3}	2	15	9^{2}		12	10	6	13		14				11^{4}		8	7^{1}			19
1			4	5	9	3	8^{1}			11^{2}		10^{3}	12			13	2	14		6	7			20
1			4	9	2	3	8^{2}		16	11^{3}		10^{4}		12		15	5^{5}	13	14	6	7^{1}			21
1			4	9	2	3	15		14	10^{3}		11^{4}		13		8^{1}	6^{2}	16		7	5		12^{5}	22

ALBION ROVERS

Year Formed: 1882. *Ground & Address:* Reigart Stadium, Main St, Coatbridge ML5 3RB. *Telephone/Fax:* 01236 606334.
E-mail: secretary@albionroversfc.com *Website:* albionroversfc.com
Ground capacity: 1,572 (seated: 489). *Size of Pitch:* 101m × 66m.
Chairman (Interim): Ian Benton.
Manager: Brian Reid. *Assistant Manager:* Scott MacKenzie.
Club Nickname: 'The Wee Rovers'.
Previous Grounds: Cowheath Park, Meadow Park, Whifflet.
Record Attendance: 27,381 v Rangers, Scottish Cup 2nd rd, 8 February 1936.
Record Transfer Fee received: £40,000 from Motherwell for Bruce Cleland (1979).
Record Transfer Fee paid: £7,000 for Gerry McTeague to Stirling Alb, September 1989.
Record Victory: 12-0 v Airdriehill, Scottish Cup 1st rd, 3 September 1887.
Record Defeat: 1-11 v Partick Thistle, League Cup 2nd rd, 11 August 1993.
Most Capped Player: Jock White, 1 (2), Scotland.
Most League Appearances: 399: Murdy Walls, 1921-36.
Most League Goals in Season (Individual): 41: Jim Renwick, Division II, 1932-33.
Most Goals Overall (Individual): 105: Bunty Weir, 1928-31.

ALBION ROVERS – SPFL LEAGUE TWO 2020–21 LEAGUE RECORD

Match No.	*Date*	*Venue*	*Opponents*	*Result*		*H/T Score*	*Lg Pos.*	*Goalscorers*	*Attendance*
1	Oct 17	H	Stenhousemuir	L	1-3	0-1	7	Doherty ^{89}	0
2	24	A	Queen's Park	L	0-2	0-2	9		0
3	31	H	Brechin C	L	0-2	0-1	10		0
4	Nov 7	A	Annan Ath	W	3-2	0-0	9	Baker (pen) ^{61}, Aitken 2 $^{86, 88}$	0
5	28	H	Stirling Alb	L	0-1	0-1	9		0
6	Dec 5	A	Edinburgh C	L	2-5	1-4	9	Doherty ^{12}, Aitken ^{48}	0
7	12	H	Elgin C	W	3-1	0-1	8	Aitken 2 $^{53, 71}$, Moore ^{90}	0
8	19	A	Stranraer	L	0-4	0-0	9		0
9	Mar 20	A	Stenhousemuir	L	0-2	0-1	9		0
10	23	H	Edinburgh C	L	1-2	0-1	9	McGowan ^{57}	0
11	27	H	Annan Ath	D	1-1	0-0	9	Jamieson ^{90}	0
12	30	H	Queen's Park	L	0-3	0-2	9		0
13	Apr 3	A	Cowdenbeath	W	1-0	1-0	8	Ryan Stevenson (pen) ^{11}	0
14	6	A	Stirling Alb	D	1-1	1-0	8	Aitken ^{41}	0
15	10	A	Brechin C	W	4-2	2-1	7	Wilson, L ^{3}, Gallacher ^{34}, Ryan Stevenson ^{51}, Wilson, C ^{56}	0
16	13	H	Cowdenbeath	D	0-0	0-0	7		0
17	17	A	Elgin C	W	5-2	2-1	7	Aitken 2 $^{11, 58}$, McHale (og) ^{29}, Doherty 2 $^{66, 74}$	0
18	20	H	Stranraer	L	0-2	0-1	7		0
19	24	H	Annan Ath	W	1-0	0-0	7	Leslie ^{60}	0
20	29	A	Stenhousemuir	W	1-0	1-0	6	Aitken ^{31}	0
21	May 1	H	Brechin C	D	1-1	0-0	6	Aitken (pen) ^{85}	0
22	4	A	Cowdenbeath	L	0-2	0-1	7		0

Final League Position: 7

Honours
League Champions: Division II 1933-34; Second Division 1988-89; League Two 2014-15.
Runners-up: Division II 1913-14, 1937-38, 1947-48; Third Division 2010-11.
Promoted via play-offs: 2010-11 (to Second Division).
Scottish Cup Runners-up: 1920.

Club colours: Shirt: Yellow with red trim. Shorts: Red. Socks: Red with yellow tops.

Goalscorers: *League (25):* Aitken 10 (1 pen), Doherty 4, Ryan Stevenson 2 (1 pen), Baker 1 (1 pen), Gallacher 1, Jamieson 1, Leslie 1, McGowan 1, Moore 1, Wilson L 1, Wilson C 1, own goal 1.
William Hill Scottish Cup (0).
Betfred Scottish League Cup (5): Aitken 2 (1 pen), Dolan 1, Fotheringham 1, Jamieson 1.

Goodfellow R 6	Lynas A 20 + 1	Burke J 4	Fagan S 6 + 2	Ecrepont F 10 + 7	Fotheringham G 4 + 2	Wilson C 18 + 2	Skeoch G 2 + 2	Moore J 1 + 5	Aitken M 20	Jamieson S 7 + 8	Glover S 8 + 1	Doherty K 10 + 10	Wilson L 14 + 2	Allan P 7	Leslie J 13 + 8	Baker L 4 + 6	Cairney P — + 1	Dolan K 1 + 3	Henry C 3	Moran D — + 2	Stone H 13	Robinson A 9	Sideserf M 13	McKernon J 13	Cox D 4 + 1	Stevenson Ryan 9 + 1	Gallacher P 8	McGowan J 9 + 1	Kidd L 6 + 2	Kouame J — + 1	Match No.
1	2	3^{3}	4	5	6	7	8^{2}	9^{1}	10	11	12	13	14																		1
1	2^{1}		3	5	6^{2}	7	13	14	10		8	11^{3}	4	9	12																2
1	6^{1}	3	2	5		11	15	12	10	9^{4}	7			4^{2}	8^{3}	13	14														3
1	6		2	5		11	9^{2}		10		3	13		4	8	7^{1}		12													4
1	2			5	8^{2}	6			9	12	3	11	4	7	13	10^{1}															5
1	2			5	8^{2}	6		14	9	12	3	11^{1}	4	7	13	10^{3}															6
	2	3		14	13	6		12	11^{2}	10^{1}	4	9	5■	7	8^{3}				1												7
	2^{1}	4	16	5	14	6^{3}		13	10^{2}	11^{4}	3	9		7^{5}	8	12			1	15											8
	2	3				6^{3}			10^{2}	15	7^{4}	12			14	13					1	4	5	8	9	11^{1}					9
	2					6^{2}			11^{1}	13		12			8						1		5	4	9	10	3	7			10
	2			13		6^{2}			11^{1}	12		14			7						1		5	8	9^{3}	10	4	3			11
	14			9						11		10	5		13	15					1	2		7^{2}	6^{4}	12	4	3^{1}	8^{3}		12
	2			9^{3}		14				10^{2}		12	13		7						1	4	3	8^{1}		11	5		6		13
	2					6			10			12	9^{1}		7						1	4	3	8		11	5				14
	2			13		6^{3}			10			14	9^{2}		7						1	4	5	8		11^{1}	3		12		15
	2					6			11				9		8^{2}						1	3	5	7		10	4^{1}	12	13		16
	2			12		6^{3}			11^{4}			13	9		15	14					1	3^{1}	5	8		10^{2}		4	7		17
	2			15		6			11	14		12	9^{3}		13						1	3	5	7^{1}		10^{4}		4	8^{2}		18
	2			14		7^{2}			11^{4}	13		10^{3}	9		12			16			1	3^{1}	5	8	15			4	6^{5}		19
	2								11	12		10	9		7						1		5	8			3	4	6^{1}		20
	2■		12	9^{2}		14			11	6^{1}		10	5^{4}		8	13		15			1		4	7^{3}				3			21
			2	12		7			11			9	5^{3}		6	10^{1}		8^{2}	1	13			4					3■		14	22

ALLOA ATHLETIC

Year Formed: 1878. *Ground & Address:* Indodrill Stadium, Recreation Park, Clackmannan Rd, Alloa FK10 1RY. *Telephone:* 01259 722695. *Fax:* 01259 210886. *E-mail:* fcadmin@alloaathletic.co.uk *Website:* alloaathletic.co.uk
Ground Capacity: 3,100 (seated: 919). *Size of Pitch:* 102m × 69m.
Chairman: Mike Mulraney. *Secretary:* Ewen Cameron.
Manager: Barry Ferguson. *Assistant Manager:* Paddy Connolly.
Club Nicknames: 'The Wasps'; 'The Hornets'.
Previous Grounds: West End Public Park: Gabberston Park; Bellevue Park.
Record Attendance: 15,467 v Celtic, Scottish Cup 5th rd, 5 February 1955.
Record Transfer Fee received: £100,000 for Martin Cameron to Bristol R (July 2000).
Record Transfer Fee paid: £26,000 for Ross Hamilton from Stenhousemuir (July 2000).
Record Victory: 9-0 v Selkirk, Scottish Cup 1st rd, 28 November 2005.
Record Defeat: 0-10 v Dundee, Division II, 8 March 1947; v Third Lanark, League Cup, 8 August 1953.
Most Capped Player: Jock Hepburn, 1, Scotland.
Most League Appearances: 239: Peter Smith 1960-69.
Most League Goals in Season (Individual): 49: 'Wee' Willie Crilley, Division II, 1921-22.
Most Goals Overall (Individual): 91: Willie Irvine, 1996-2001.

ALLOA ATHLETIC – SPFL CHAMPIONSHIP 2020–21 LEAGUE RECORD

Match No.	Date	Venue	Opponents		Result	H/T Score	Lg Pos.	Goalscorers	Attendance
1	Oct 17	A	Greenock Morton	L	0-1	0-1	7		0
2	24	H	Dunfermline Ath	L	1-4	1-1	9	Cawley 45	0
3	Nov 6	H	Dundee	D	3-3	1-0	8	Thomson 31, Trouten 2 51, 63	0
4	21	A	Queen of the South	L	0-2	0-1	10		0
5	24	A	Hearts	L	0-3	0-3	10		0
6	Dec 5	H	Ayr U	L	0-2	0-1	10		0
7	12	A	Arbroath	W	1-0	0-0	8	Scougall 79	0
8	19	H	Inverness CT	W	2-1	0-1	8	Murray 61, Thomson 78	0
9	26	H	Raith R	L	2-5	0-2	8	Buchanan 2 (1 pen) 75, 89 (p)	0
10	29	A	Dundee	L	1-3	1-0	9	Hetherington 11	0
11	Jan 2	H	Greenock Morton	D	1-1	0-0	9	Thomson 83	0
12	16	H	Hearts	L	1-3	0-2	9	Cawley 87	0
13	30	A	Ayr U	L	1-4	1-2	10	Trouten 11	0
14	Feb 6	H	Queen of the South	W	2-1	1-1	10	Graham 23, Cawley 61	0
15	13	H	Arbroath	D	1-1	0-1	10	Cameron 90	0
16	20	A	Dunfermline Ath	L	1-2	1-1	10	Cawley 44	0
17	23	A	Inverness CT	D	2-2	1-0	10	Cameron 20, Trouten (pen) 87	0
18	27	A	Raith R	L	1-3	1-0	10	Cameron 14	0
19	Mar 6	H	Inverness CT	D	1-1	1-1	10	Cameron 17	0
20	13	A	Queen of the South	W	3-2	2-2	10	Murray 20, Connelly 44, Buchanan 77	0
21	19	H	Dundee	L	0-3	0-1	10		0
22	27	H	Ayr U	D	2-2	1-1	10	Cameron 31, Williamson 46	0
23	Apr 3	A	Arbroath	L	1-2	0-0	10	Trouten 64	0
24	9	A	Hearts	L	0-6	0-2	10		0
25	17	H	Raith R	L	1-2	1-0	10	Cawley 23	0
26	24	A	Greenock Morton	D	1-1	0-0	10	Cameron 49	0
27	30	H	Dunfermline Ath	W	1-0	0-0	10	Dick 47	0

Final League Position: 10

Honours
League Champions: Division II 1921-22; Third Division 1997-98, 2011-12.
Runners-up: Division II 1938-39; Second Division 1976-77, 1981-82, 1984-85, 1988-89, 1999-2000, 2001-02, 2009-10, 2012-13; League One 2016-17.
Promoted via play-offs: 2012-13 (to First Division); 2017-18 (to Championship).
League Challenge Cup Winners: 1999-2000; *Runners-up:* 2001-02, 2014-15.

Club colours: Shirt: Gold and black hoops. Shorts: Black. Socks: Black with gold trim.

Goalscorers: *League (30):* Cameron 6, Cawley 5, Trouten 5 (1 pen), Buchanan 3 (1 pen), Thomson 3, Murray 2, Connelly 1, Dick 1, Graham 1, Hetherington 1, Scougall 1, Williamson 1.
William Hill Scottish Cup (2): O'Donnell 1, Trouten 1 (1 pen).
Betfred Scottish League Cup (11): Buchanan 3 (1 pen), Thomson 3, Trouten 2 (2 pens), Hetherington 1, Scougall 1, own goal 1.

Wilson R 4 + 2	Robertson J 24 + 1	Taggart S 21	Lynch E 4	Dick L 24	Grant R 24	Hetherington S 24	Cawley K 27	Trouten A 18 + 1	Connelly L 7 + 5	Thomson R 6 + 10	Scougall S 8 + 8	Buchanan L 6 + 13	Murray I 12 + 4	Graham A 25	Brown A 2 + 5	Parry N 23	Jamieson N 10 + 2	O'Donnell C 4 + 2	Malcolm B — + 2	Williamson L 9	Evans L — + 1	Cameron I 15	*Match No.*
1	2	3	4	5	6	7■	8	9	10^{2}	11^{1}	12	13											1
1	2	3	4	5	6		8	9	10^{1}	11	12	13	7^{2}										2
1	2	3		5	7	6	8	9	12	11^{2}			13	4	10^{1}								3
	2	3		5	7	6	8	9		11^{2}	12	13		4	10^{1}	1							4
	2	3		5	7	9	6^{2}	10	14	11^{3}	13	12	8^{1}	4		1							5
	2	4		5	6	7	8^{1}	9	12	13		11	10^{2}	3		1							6
	7	2^{2}		5		8	6^{1}	10		14	9	11^{3}	12	4	13	1	3						7
	2			5		7	8		6^{2}	12		11^{1}	10	3		1	4	9	13				8
12	2			4	5	6	8^{2}			13		11	10	3		1^{1}	9	7					9
1	2			5^{3}	9	8	6		12	14		10^{2}	11	4			3	7^{1}	13				10
	2			5	6	9	10			12		11	8	3		1	4	7^{1}					11
	2				6	7	8			11^{3}	9^{1}	13	10^{2}	3	12	1	4			5■	14		12
			2	5	6	7	10	9			8^{1}	12		3		1	4					11	13
	12	2		5	6	7	8	11				13	10^{2}	3		1	4^{1}					9	14
	2^{2}	4		5	6■	7	8	9		13	12			3		1				10^{1}		11	15
	2^{1}	4		5		6	10	9		13	8			3	12	1				7^{2}		11	16
	2	4		5	7	6	10^{2}	9^{1}			8^{3}	13	12	3		1	14					11	17
	7	2		4	6^{1}	5	10	9			8	12		3		1						11	18
	2	4		5	6	7	8	9■	10^{1}					3		1		12				11	19
	2	4	9		6		8		10^{1}			12	5^{2}	3		1	14	13		7^{3}		11	20
	2	4		5	6	7	8		9^{2}			12	10^{1}	3	13	1						11	21
	2	4		5	6^{2}	7	8	13	9^{1}		12			3		1				10		11	22
	5	2		4	6^{2}	7	9	11		12	13			3		1				8^{1}		10	23
	2	3		5	6	7	8	9^{2}			13		12	4		1				10^{1}		11	24
12	2	4		5	6^{3}	7	10	9		14	8^{1}	13		3		1■						11^{2}	25
	5^{2}	2			6	7	10	9^{1}				12		3	13	1	4			8		11	26
		2		5	6		8		12		9		7^{1}	3		1	4			10		11	27

ANNAN ATHLETIC

Year Formed: 1942. *Ground & Address:* Galabank, North Street, Annan DG12 5DQ. *Telephone:* 01461 204108.
E-mail: annanathletic.enquiries@btconnect.com *Website:* annanathleticfc.com
Ground capacity: 2,517 (seated: 500). *Size of Pitch:* 100m × 62m.
Chairman: Philip Jones. *Vice-Chairman:* Russell Brown.
Secretary: Alan Irving.
Manager: Peter Murphy.
Assistant Manager: Colin McMenamin.
Club Nicknames: 'Galabankies'; 'Black and Golds'.
Previous Ground: Mafeking Park.
Record attendance: 2,517, v Rangers, Third Division, 15 September 2012.
Record Victory: 6-0 v Elgin C, Third Division, 7 March 2009; 6-0 v Berwick Rangers, League Two, 6 April 2019.
Record Defeat: 1-8 v Inverness CT, Scottish Cup 3rd rd, 24 January 1998.
Most League Appearances: 285: Peter Watson, 2008-18.
Most League Goals in Season (Individual): 22: Peter Weatherson, 2014-15.
Most Goals Overall (Individual): 56: Peter Weatherson, 2013-17.

ANNAN ATHLETIC – SPFL LEAGUE TWO 2020–21 LEAGUE RECORD

Match No.	*Date*	*Venue*	*Opponents*	*Result*		*H/T Score*	*Lg Pos.*	*Goalscorers*	*Attendance*
1	Oct 17	A	Cowdenbeath	W	3-0	2-0	3	Flanagan 21, Anderson 28, Purdue 62	0
2	24	H	Stranraer	D	1-1	1-1	2	Moxon 45	0
3	31	A	Stirling Alb	L	0-1	0-1	6		0
4	Nov 7	H	Albion R	L	2-3	0-0	6	Currie 84, Wright 90	0
5	21	A	Stenhousemuir	W	2-1	1-0	5	Wright 2 45, 90	0
6	28	H	Edinburgh C	L	0-4	0-2	7		0
7	Dec 5	A	Elgin C	L	0-1	0-0	7		0
8	19	H	Queen's Park	L	1-2	0-0	7	Currie (pen) 90	0
9	22	A	Brechin C	D	0-0	0-0	7		0
10	Jan 2	A	Stranraer	L	0-2	0-0	7		0
11	Mar 20	H	Cowdenbeath	D	0-0	0-0	7		0
12	27	A	Albion R	D	1-1	0-0	7	Anderson 70	0
13	Apr 3	H	Elgin C	L	0-3	0-2	7		0
14	6	A	Edinburgh C	D	1-1	0-0	7	Wallace (pen) 65	0
15	10	H	Stirling Alb	L	1-2	0-1	9	Wright 59	0
16	13	A	Queen's Park	L	0-1	0-1	9		0
17	17	H	Brechin C	W	3-0	3-0	8	Smith 6, Flanagan 38, Wallace 44	0
18	20	H	Stenhousemuir	W	5-1	3-1	8	Flanagan 8, Wallace 2 10, 27, Smith 72, Christie 90	0
19	24	A	Albion R	L	0-1	0-0	8		0
20	27	H	Stenhousemuir	D	1-1	0-0	8	Wallace 50	0
21	29	A	Brechin C	W	3-0	1-0	8	Anderson 29, Christie 71, Flanagan 81	0
22	May 1	H	Cowdenbeath	D	1-1	0-0	8	Fleming 89	0

Final League Position: 8

Honours
League Two Runners-up: 2013-14.
League Challenge Cup: Semi-finals: 2009-10, 2011-12.

Club colours: Shirt: Gold with black trim. Shorts: Black. Socks: Gold.

Goalscorers: *League (25):* Wallace 5 (1 pen), Flanagan 4, Wright 4, Anderson 3, Christie 2, Currie 2 (1 pen), Smith 2, Fleming 1, Moxon 1, Purdue 1.
William Hill Scottish Cup (3): Smith 2, Lowdon 1.
Betfred Scottish League Cup (9): Fleming 2, Wright 2, Docherty 1 (1 pen), Fulton 1, Moxon 1, Purdue 1, Swinglehurst 1.

Pettigrew J 5	Hunter L 17 + 3	Swinglehurst S 11 + 1	Douglas M 21	Clark C 16	Purdue J 2	Splaine A 7 + 2	Moxon O 16 + 2	Flanagan N 12 + 5	Anderson I 14 + 7	Wright M 11 + 1	Smith A 18 + 4	Docherty M 12 + 5	Fleming K 12 + 6	Currie R — + 11	Mitchell A 14	Fulton T 10 + 3	Love R 11 + 1	Lowdon J 7 + 1	Emerson H — + 1	Wallace T 10 + 1	McCaw A 1 + 4	Sinnamon R 6 + 1	Christie D 4 + 5	Watson D 2 + 3	Kinnear B 1	Munro R 2	Murphy P — + 1	*Match No.*
1	2	3	4	5	6^2	7	8	9^3	10^1	11	12	13	14															1
1	2^2	4	3	5	9^1	8	7	6	11	10	12	13																2
1	2	4	3	5		8	7	9	11^1	10	6		12															3
1	2	4	3	5		8^2	7	9	11	10	6^1		12	13														4
	2	7	3	5		4	9		12	11	10^1	8	6		1													5
1	2	4	3	5		6^3	8	12	13	11	10^4	7^1	9^2	14		15												6
	12		3	5		6^2	8		11^1	10^5	14	7	9^3	15	1	2^4	4	13	16									7
			3	5		12	8		11	10	9	7^2	6^1	13	1	2	4											8
	6		3	5			8^1		11	10	9	7		12	1	2	4											9
		4	3	2		13	8■	12	11^3	10^1	9	7	6^2		1		14	5										10
	8		3	4				6■	11^1		10	7			1	2		5		9	12							11
	7		3	4			13		11		10	8^2	12		1	2		5■		6	9^1							12
	7^1		3	4			12	6^3	10		11^4	8^2	13	14	1	2	5^5			9	16	15						13
	7		3	4			8^1	6^3	11^4	14	10^2		12		1			5		9		2	13	15				14
	7^3		3	4			6	12	14	10^1	11	13			1			5		8■		2	9^2					15
	7		3				8	12	11		10^2		9^3	14			4	5				2	6^1	13	1			16
	7^3	13	3				6	9^5			10^4	14	8	15	1	12	4	5^2		11		2^1	16					17
	7^2		3	5			6^3	9^1	12		10^4	15	8	13	1	2	4			11^5			14	16				18
	13	4	3				9■	6^4	12		11^2	7	8	15	1	2	5^1			10^3			14					19
	6	4	3					9^1	13		10		8			2	5			11			12	7^2		1		20
	7	4						12	10^3		16	8	6			3^4	5			13	15	2^2	11^1	9^5		1	14	21
	14	4	3					9	13		10	7^1	6	16	1	12	5^4			8^3	15	2^5	11^2					22

ARBROATH

Year Formed: 1878. *Ground & Address:* Gayfield Park, Arbroath DD11 1QB. *Telephone:* 01241 872157. *Fax:* 01241 431125. *E-mail:* arbroathfc@outlook.com *Website:* arbroathfc.co.uk
Ground Capacity: 6,600 (seated: 861). *Size of Pitch:* 105m × 65m.
Chairman: Mike Caird. *Secretary:* Dr Gary Callon.
Manager: Dick Campbell. *Assistant Manager:* Ian Campbell.
Club Nickname: 'The Red Lichties'.
Previous Ground: Lesser Gayfield.
Record Attendance: 13,510 v Rangers, Scottish Cup 3rd rd, 23 February 1952.
Record Transfer Fee received: £120,000 for Paul Tosh to Dundee (August 1993).
Record Transfer Fee paid: £20,000 for Douglas Robb from Montrose (1981).
Record Victory: 36-0 v Bon Accord, Scottish Cup 1st rd, 12 September 1885.
Record Defeat: 0-8 v Kilmarnock, Division II, 3 January 1949; 1-9 v Celtic, League Cup 3rd rd, 25 August 1993.
Most Capped Player: Ned Doig, 2 (5), Scotland.
Most League Appearances: 445: Tom Cargill, 1966-81.
Most League Goals in Season (Individual): 45: Dave Easson, Division II, 1958-59.
Most Goals Overall (Individual): 120: Jimmy Jack, 1966-71.

ARBROATH – SPFL CHAMPIONSHIP 2020–21 LEAGUE RECORD

Match No.	*Date*	*Venue*	*Opponents*	*Result*		*H/T Score*	*Lg Pos.*	*Goalscorers*	*Attendance*
1	Oct 17	A	Raith R	L	0-3	0-3	9		0
2	23	H	Hearts	L	0-1	0-0	10		0
3	31	A	Inverness CT	L	1-3	1-0	10	Doolan 24	0
4	Nov 7	H	Queen of the South	D	1-1	0-1	10	Linn 48	0
5	21	H	Greenock Morton	D	0-0	0-0	9		0
6	Dec 5	A	Dundee	L	0-1	0-1	9		0
7	12	H	Alloa Ath	L	0-1	0-0	10		0
8	19	H	Ayr U	W	2-1	2-0	9	Craigen 2 36, 39	0
9	26	A	Dunfermline Ath	L	0-1	0-0	9		0
10	29	A	Hearts	L	1-3	0-3	10	Doolan 48	0
11	Jan 16	A	Queen of the South	D	2-2	0-0	10	Stewart 63, O'Brien 65	0
12	22	H	Dundee	D	1-1	0-1	10	Little 65	0
13	30	A	Greenock Morton	W	1-0	0-0	9	Hamilton, J 77	0
14	Feb 3	H	Inverness CT	D	1-1	1-0	9	Hamilton, J 45	0
15	6	H	Dunfermline Ath	W	2-0	2-0	8	O'Brien 27, Hilson 36	0
16	13	A	Alloa Ath	D	1-1	1-0	7	Hamilton, J 24	0
17	20	H	Raith R	W	1-0	0-0	6	Doolan 60	0
18	27	A	Ayr U	W	1-0	0-0	6	McKenna 63	0
19	Mar 6	H	Queen of the South	L	2-4	2-3	6	Hamilton, J 11, McKenna (pen) 22	0
20	13	A	Dundee	L	0-2	0-0	9		0
21	20	H	Hearts	D	0-0	0-0	9		0
22	27	A	Inverness CT	L	0-1	0-0	9		0
23	Apr 3	H	Alloa Ath	W	2-1	0-0	9	Hamilton, J 59, Gold 83	0
24	10	A	Raith R	D	2-2	0-1	8	Hamilton, J 72, Little 84	0
25	17	H	Ayr U	W	4-0	3-0	7	Little 11, Williamson 24, Hamilton, J 27, Hilson 65	0
26	24	A	Dunfermline Ath	L	3-4	2-2	7	Hamilton, J 33, Low (pen) 35, Stewart 82	0
27	30	H	Greenock Morton	D	0-0	0-0	7		0

Final League Position: 7

Honours
League Champions: League One 2018-19. Third Division 2010-11; League Two 2016-17.
Runners-up: Division II 1934-35, 1958-59, 1967-68, 1971-72; Second Division 2000-01; Third Division 1997-98, 2006-07.
Promoted via play-offs: 2007-08 (to Second Division).
Scottish Cup: Semi-finals 1947, Quarter-finals 1993.

Club colours: Shirt: Maroon with white trim. Shorts: White. Socks: Maroon.

Goalscorers: *League (28):* Hamilton J 8, Doolan 3, Little 3, Craigen 2, Hilson 2, McKenna 2 (1 pen), O'Brien 2, Stewart 2, Gold 1, Linn 1, Low 1 (1 pen), Williamson 1.
William Hill Scottish Cup (1): Own goal 1.
Betfred Scottish League Cup (10): Gold 2, Hilson 2, O'Brien 2, Donnelly 1, Stewart 1, Swankie 1, Thomson 1.

Gaston D 27	Thomson J 25	Little R 26	O'Brien T 26	Craigen J 16 + 4	McKenna M 15 + 11	Virtanen M 8 + 1	Swankie G 4	Stewart S 9 + 13	Donnelly L 4 + 11	Hilson D 22 + 4	Linn B 13 + 6	Smith Connor 1 + 2	Ruth M 4 + 7	Hamilton C 24	Doolan K 14 + 6	Gold D 16 + 7	Whatley M 2 + 3	Davidson J 1	Williamson B 17	Hamilton J 14	Moore L 3 + 4	Pignatiello C 1 + 2	Low N 5 + 1	*Match No.*
1	2	3	4■	5^{1}	6^{3}	7	8	9^{2}	10	11	12	13	14											1
1	2	3		5	8	9	7^{3}		13	10^{1}	12		6	4	11^{2}	14								2
1	2	4	3		14	10			13	12	6^{2}	8^{3}	9	5	11^{1}	7								3
1	2	3	4		8	9	7^{3}	5	12	6	10^{1}		14		11^{2}	13								4
1	2^{3}	3	4	9	8	12		14	13	10^{1}	6			5	11^{2}	7								5
1	2	3	4	8	12	9^{2}		13	14	10	6^{1}		11^{3}	5		7								6
1	2	3	4	7	13					9	6^{1}	14	12	5	11	10^{2}	8^{3}							7
1	2	3	4	8^{1}	11	6		14	10^{2}	9^{3}			13	5	12	7								8
1	2	3	4	9	8^{1}	6		12	11^{3}	10^{2}			14	5	13	7								9
1	2	3	4	8^{1}	14	6	10^{2}	13	11^{3}		12			5	9	7								10
1	2		4	9				12		10	13		14	5	11^{1}	7	6^{3}	3^{2}	8					11
1	2	3	4	9^{2}	13			6^{1}	14	10	12		11	5		7^{3}			8					12
1	2	3	4	13	8				14	6^{3}	10^{1}		12	5		7^{2}			9	11				13
1	2	3	4	7	8			12	14	6^{3}	10^{2}			5	13				9	11^{1}				14
1	5	3	4	8	7			2	13	11^{3}	6^{2}					12	14		9	10^{1}				15
1	2	4	3	8■	7			12		11^{2}	6^{1}			5	14	13			9^{3}	10				16
1	2	4	3		7^{2}			6		11	9^{1}			5	10^{3}	13	14		8		12			17
1	2	3	4	13	7^{1}			6		10	9^{3}			5	14				8	11^{2}	12			18
1	2	4	3		7^{2}			6^{1}		10	9^{3}			5		14			8	11	12	13		19
1	2	3	4	9	7^{3}			6		10	13			5	14				8^{2}	11^{1}	12			20
1		3	4	9	12			14		13	6^{1}			5	10^{2}	7^{3}			8	11		2		21
1		4	3	7^{2}	6^{1}			12		11				5		2	13		8^{3}	10	9		14	22
1	2	3	4	14	13					12				5	10^{2}	6			7	11	9^{3}		8^{1}	23
1	2	4	3		14			13		12				5	10^{1}	6			7^{3}	11	9^{2}	15	8^{4}	24
1	2	3	4	14	13			12		9				5	10^{2}	6^{1}			7	11			8^{3}	25
1	2	3	4		13			12	14	9^{2}				5	10^{1}	6^{3}			7	11			8	26
1	2^{2}	3	4		13			6	14	9				5	11^{1}	12			8	10^{3}			7	27

AYR UNITED

Year Formed: 1910. *Ground & Address:* Somerset Park, Tryfield Place, Ayr KA8 9NB. *Telephone:* 01292 263435. *Fax:* 01292 281314. *E-mail:* info@ayrunitedfc.co.uk *Website:* ayrunitedfc.co.uk
Ground Capacity: 10,185 (seated: 1,597). *Size of Pitch:* 101m × 66m.
Chairman: David Smith.
Manager: David Hopkin. *Assistant Manager:* David Timmins.
Club Nickname: 'The Honest Men'.
Record Attendance: 25,225 v Rangers, Division I, 13 September 1969.
Record Transfer Fee received: £300,000 for Steve Nicol to Liverpool (October 1981).
Record Transfer Fee paid: £90,000 for Mark Campbell from Stranraer (March 1999).
Record Victory: 11-1 v Dumbarton, League Cup, 13 August 1952.
Record Defeat: 0-9 in Division I v Rangers (1929); v Hearts (1931); B Division v Third Lanark (1954).
Most Capped Player: Jim Nisbet, 3, Scotland.
Most League Appearances: 459: John Murphy, 1963-78.
Most League League and Cup Goals in Season (Individual): 66: Jimmy Smith, 1927-28.
Most League and Cup Goals Overall (Individual): 213: Peter Price, 1955-61.

AYR UNITED – SPFL CHAMPIONSHIP 2020–21 LEAGUE RECORD

Match No.	Date	Venue	Opponents	Result		H/T Score	Lg Pos.	Goalscorers	Attendance
1	Oct 17	H	Queen of the South	W	2-1	2-0	4	Miller, M 2 13, 18	0
2	24	A	Inverness CT	D	1-1	0-0	4	Cameron 57	0
3	31	A	Greenock Morton	L	2-3	1-0	5	Strapp (og) 32, Smith, C 74	0
4	Nov 7	H	Dunfermline Ath	D	0-0	0-0	5		0
5	21	H	Dundee	W	2-0	2-0	4	Smith, C 3, Moffat 16	0
6	Dec 5	A	Alloa Ath	W	2-0	1-0	4	McCowan 38, Murdoch 61	0
7	11	H	Raith R	D	0-0	0-0	4		0
8	19	A	Arbroath	L	1-2	0-2	5	Baird 88	0
9	26	A	Hearts	L	3-5	0-1	6	Smith, C 57, McCowan 60, Walsh 90	0
10	29	H	Greenock Morton	D	1-1	1-1	6	McCowan 38	0
11	Jan 2	A	Queen of the South	L	2-3	1-2	6	Reading 7, Miller, M 90	0
12	23	A	Dunfermline Ath	D	0-0	0-0	6		0
13	30	H	Alloa Ath	W	4-1	2-1	5	Walsh 6, McCowan 2 30, 69, Muirhead (pen) 61	0
14	Feb 5	H	Hearts	L	0-1	0-0	5		0
15	20	H	Inverness CT	L	0-2	0-1	9		0
16	27	H	Arbroath	L	0-1	0-0	9		0
17	Mar 6	A	Greenock Morton	W	2-0	0-0	8	Smith, C 2 55, 87	0
18	9	A	Raith R	D	0-0	0-0	7		0
19	13	A	Hearts	L	0-2	0-0	8		0
20	16	A	Dundee	W	3-1	1-0	7	McKenzie 2 18, 84, Smith, C 49	0
21	20	H	Raith R	D	1-1	0-0	7	Muirhead 72	0
22	27	A	Alloa Ath	D	2-2	1-1	7	Walsh 15, Robertson (og) 76	0
23	Apr 6	H	Dundee	L	0-3	0-0	7		0
24	10	H	Dunfermline Ath	D	1-1	1-1	7	Miller, M 24	0
25	17	A	Arbroath	L	0-4	0-3	8		0
26	24	H	Queen of the South	D	0-0	0-0	8		0
27	30	A	Inverness CT	D	2-2	1-1	8	Muirhead (pen) 39, Todd 67	0

Final League Position: 8

Honours
League Champions: Division II 1911-12, 1912-13, 1927-28, 1936-37, 1958-59, 1965-66; Second Division 1987-88, 1996-97; League One 2017-18.
Runners-up: Division II 1910-11, 1955-56, 1968-69; Second Division 2008-09; League One 2015-16.
Promoted via play-offs: 2008-09 (to First Division); 2010-11 (to First Division); 2015-16 (to Championship).
Scottish Cup: Semi-finals 2002.
League Cup: Runners-up: 2001-02.
League Challenge Cup Runners-up: 1990-91, 1991-92.

Club colours: Shirt: White with black trim. Shorts: Black. Socks: White.

Goalscorers: *League (31):* Smith C 6, McCowan 5, Miller M 4, Muirhead 3 (2 pens), Walsh 3, McKenzie 2, Baird 1, Cameron 1, Moffat 1, Murdoch 1, Reading 1, Todd 1, own goals 2.
William Hill Scottish Cup (4): McCowan 2, Chalmers 1, Moffat 1.
Betfred Scottish League Cup (8): Anderson 2, McCowan 2, Moffat 2 (1 pen), Walsh 1, Zanatta 1.

Sinisalo V 22	Muirhead A 24	Baird J 27	Roscoe S 14	Reading P 21	Chalmers J 21 + 3	Murdoch A 21 + 3	McCowan L 26	Moffat M 16 + 9	Miller M 16 + 5	Anderson B 7 + 2	McKenzie M 6 + 14	Smith C 19 + 1	Cameron I — + 5	Houston J 17 + 2	Hewitt M — + 4	Zanatta D 3 + 10	Walsh T 10 + 8	Kerr M 1	Ndaba C 13	Wright A 3 + 2	McGavin B — + 1	Urminsky P 1	Barjonas J 2 + 2	Todd J 3 + 1	Morrison Peter 4	Match No.
1	2	3	4	5	6	7	8■	9	10	11^{1}	12															1
1	2	3	4	5	7^{3}	6		9^{2}	10	11		8^{1}	12	13	14											2
1	2■	3	4	5	7	6	8	10^{3}	14	11^{2}		9^{1}	13	12												3
1		4	3	5	8	6^{3}	9^{2}	11	14	10^{1}		7	13	2		12										4
1		4	3	5	9	8	7^{1}	11^{2}	6		12	10^{3}	13	2		14										5
1	2	3	4		8	6	9	10^{2}	12	11^{1}	13	7■		5												6
1	2	4	3		9^{2}	7	8^{1}	10	6	11			13	5		12										7
1	2	4	3	5	9	8^{3}	6	10	7^{1}	11^{2}	13	14				12										8
1	2	3	4	5	9^{3}	7	6	11^{1}	8	12		10^{2}				13	14									9
1	3	4		5	8	6	9^{2}	10^{3}		14		11^{1}		2		12	13	7								10
1		4	3	5	6	2^{3}	10	12	8		13	7			14	11^{2}	9^{1}									11
1	4	3			7	6	8	12	2			10				11^{1}	9		5							12
1	4	3			7	6	8	12	2		14	9^{1}				13	10^{3}		5	11^{2}						13
1	3	4			6^{3}	7	10	12	2^{1}		14	9					8^{2}		5	11	13					14
1	3	4			7	6	8	11	2^{2}		12	9^{3}			13	14	10^{1}		5							15
	3	4		5	6	12	9	14			13	8^{1}		2^{3}		11	10^{2}		7			1				16
1	4	3		5	14	6	8	13	12		11^{1}	9		2^{3}			10^{2}		7							17
1	6	4		5	13	7	8	11^{3}	12		14	9^{1}		2^{2}			10		3							18
1	7	3		5	12	6	8	11^{3}			14	9^{1}		2		13	10^{2}		4							19
1	7	3		5	11	12	6^{3}	13	8^{2}		10	9^{1}		2			14		4							20
1	6	3		5	10^{1}	8	9	12			11^{2}	7		2			13		4							21
1	4	3		5		9^{1}	8	11^{2}	6		12	7		2	14		10						13^{3}			22
1	6	4		5	10^{1}	9^{2}	8^{4}	15			11			2			12		3	13			14	7^{3}		23
	8	3	4	6			10^{1}		7		11			2					5	12			9		1	24
	8	3	4^{3}	6			10		7		12			2			14		5	11^{1}			9^{2}	13	1	25
	7	3	4	5	6^{1}		9	11^{2}			10			2		12	13							8	1	26
	6	3	4	5	9	14	7^{2}	11^{1}	8^{3}		12			2			13							10	1	27

BRECHIN CITY

Year Formed: 1906. *Ground & Address:* Glebe Park, Trinity Rd, Brechin, Angus DD9 6BJ. *Telephone:* 01356 622856.
Fax: 01382 206331. *E-mail:* secretary@brechincityfc.com *Website:* brechincity.com
Ground Capacity: 4,123 (seated: 1,528). *Size of Pitch:* 101m × 61m.
Chairman: Ken Ferguson. *Vice-Chairman:* Martin Smith. *Secretary:* Grant Hood.
Player/Manager: Michael Paton. *Assistant Manager:* Gerry McCabe.
Club Nicknames: 'The City'; 'The Hedgemen'.
Previous Ground: Nursery Park.
Record Attendance: 8,122 v Aberdeen, Scottish Cup 3rd rd, 3 February 1973.
Record Transfer Fee received: £100,000 for Scott Thomson to Aberdeen (1991) and Chris Templeman to Morton (2004).
Record Transfer Fee paid: £16,000 for Sandy Ross from Berwick Rangers (1991).
Record Victory: 12-1 v Thornhill, Scottish Cup 1st rd, 28 January 1926.
Record Defeat: 0-10 v Airdrieonians, Albion R and Cowdenbeath, all in Division II, 1937-38.
Most League Appearances: 459: David Watt, 1975-89.
Most League Goals in Season (Individual): 26: Ronald McIntosh, Division II, 1959-60.
Most Goals Overall (Individual): 131: Ian Campbell, 1977-85.

BRECHIN CITY – SPFL LEAGUE TWO 2020–21 LEAGUE RECORD

Match No.	Date	Venue	Opponents	Result		H/T Score	Lg Pos.	Goalscorers	Attendance
1	Oct 17	H	Edinburgh C	L	1-5	0-1	10	Scott 48	0
2	24	A	Elgin C	L	0-3	0-1	10		0
3	31	A	Albion R	W	2-0	1-0	8	Makovora 23, Todd 68	0
4	Nov 7	H	Stirling Alb	L	0-5	0-2	10		0
5	21	A	Queen's Park	L	0-3	0-2	10		0
6	28	H	Stranraer	L	1-4	1-1	10	Bollan 38	0
7	Dec 5	A	Stenhousemuir	L	1-2	0-2	10	Paton C 62	0
8	19	A	Cowdenbeath	L	0-2	0-1	10		0
9	22	H	Annan Ath	D	0-0	0-0	10		0
10	Mar 20	A	Stirling Alb	L	0-1	0-0	10		0
11	23	A	Stranraer	L	0-2	0-0	10		0
12	27	H	Queen's Park	L	0-2	0-2	10		0
13	30	H	Elgin C	L	1-2	1-0	10	Barron 29	0
14	Apr 6	H	Stenhousemuir	D	1-1	1-1	10	Inglis 12	0
15	10	H	Albion R	L	2-4	1-2	10	Currie 36, Paton, M 90	0
16	13	A	Edinburgh C	L	1-2	1-1	10	Barr 14	0
17	17	A	Annan Ath	L	0-3	0-3	10		0
18	20	H	Cowdenbeath	D	0-0	0-0	10		0
19	27	A	Cowdenbeath	W	2-0	1-0	10	McKee 9, Barr 55	0
20	29	H	Annan Ath	L	0-3	0-1	10		0
21	May 1	A	Albion R	D	1-1	0-0	10	Inglis (pen) 54	0
22	4	H	Stenhousemuir	L	0-1	0-0	10		0

Final League Position: 10

Honours
League Champions: Second Division 1982-83, 1989-90, 2004-05; Third Division 2001-02; C Division 1953-54.
Runners-up: Second Division 1992-93, 2002-03; Third Division 1995-96.
Promoted via play-offs: 2016-17 (to Championship).
Scottish Cup: Quarter-finals 2011.
League Cup: Semi-finals 1957.
League Challenge Cup Runners-up: 2002-03.

Club colours: Shirt: Red with white trim. Shorts: Red with white trim. Socks: Red.

Goalscorers: *League (13):* Barr 2, Inglis 2 (1 pen), Barron 1, Bollan 1, Currie 1, Makovora 1, McKee 1, Paton C 1, Paton M 1, Scott 1, Todd 1.
William Hill Scottish Cup (2): Currie 1, Inglis 1.
Betfred Scottish League Cup (3): Inglis 2 (1 pen), Currie 1.
Scottish League Play-Offs (1): Page 1.

McMinn L 6	McIntosh S 10 + 2	Page J 6 + 3	Jordan G 11 + 4	McKay D 7	Todd M 9	Inglis K 10 + 8	Cusick S 2 + 2	Makovora L 3 + 1	Currie R 14 + 3	Scott M 6 + 1	Paton M 14 + 2	Brown R 2 + 1	Nawrocki P 1 + 3	Bollan L 9	Barron C 13	Reekie S 11 + 4	McLevy E 12 + 1	Coupe C 8 + 7	Luissint B — + 2	O'Neil P 5	Motherwell L 1	Paton C 4 + 8	Hutton D 11	McLauchlan G 3 + 1	Hussain Y 11 + 1	O'Connor H 12	Osman A 6 + 2	Barr B 9 + 2	McKee C 10 + 2	Slaven S 8 + 5	Devine A 8 + 3	*Match No.*
1	2	3^{2}	4	5	6	7	8	9^{1}	10	11^{3}	12	13	14																			1
1	2^{2}	4		5	6	7^{1}	9^{3}	13	10	14	11			3	8	12																2
1			2	5	6	13		9^{1}	10	8	11^{2}	3	12	4	7																	3
1	12		2■	5	6^{3}	14		9^{2}	10^{1}	8	11	3	13	4	7																	4
1				5	7	9^{1}				10	6		11^{2}	3	8	4	2	12	13													5
1			4	5	6^{1}	8^{2}	13		10		9			3	7		2	11				12										6
			4	5	6				10		7			3^{1}	8	12	2	13		1	11	9^{2}										7
			5		6				11^{2}	8	7			3	9	4	2	10^{1}	13	1		12										8
		4	3		9		13		12	11^{1}	8				7	5	2	10		1		6^{2}										9
			16			15			14		7^{4}				6		2	12				13	1	3^{5}	4	5	8^{3}	9^{2}	10	11^{1}		10
		13				15			10						7	5		14					1	12^{4}	3	4	8^{1}	9^{2}	6	11	2^{3}	11
	9^{2}		13			7^{3}			14						6	2	5	10					1		4	3^{1}		8■	12	11^{4}	15	12
		12	2^{2}						10						7	9	5					13	1		4■	3			8	11^{1}	6	13
	4		2			8									7	9	5					12	1			3			11	10^{1}	6	14
	2					8^{1}			11		13						5						1		4	3	12	9	7■	10	6^{2}	15
	2	7				13			11^{1}		8^{3}					5		14					1		4	3	9^{2}	10		12	6	16
	2^{1}	6	12			15					7^{4}					13		14				16	1		4^{5}	3	8■	9	11^{2}	10^{3}	5	17
	5	2				6^{1}					7^{3}					9	14	10^{2}				13	1		4	3		8	11	12		18
	2					12			10^{1}		7^{3}							6^{4}				14	1	3	4	5	8	9^{2}	11	13	15	19
	2		13			12			11^{5}		9^{3}					16		6^{2}					1	3^{1}	4	5	8	10	7^{4}	15	14	20
			8			7^{4}								3		4	5	13		1		6^{1}			12	2^{3}	14	15	11^{2}	10	9	21
	14	13	2			8			11^{4}					3^{3}		5	7	6		1		10^{2}			4^{1}			12	16	15	9^{5}	22

CELTIC

Year Formed: 1888. *Ground & Address:* Celtic Park, Glasgow G40 3RE. *Telephone:* 0871 226 1888. *Fax:* 0141 551 8106.
E-mail: customerservices@celticfc.co.uk *Website:* celticfc.net
Ground Capacity: 60,832 (all seated). *Size of Pitch:* 105m × 68m.
Chairman: Ian Bankier. *Chief Executive:* Dominic McKay.
Manager: Ange Postecoglou. *Assistant Manager:* John Kennedy.
Club Nicknames: 'The Bhoys'; 'The Hoops'; 'The Celts'.
Record Attendance: 92,000 v Rangers, Division I, 1 January 1938.
Record Transfer Fee received: £25,000,000 for Kieran Tierney to Arsenal (August 2019).
Record Transfer Fee paid: £9,000,000 for Odsonne Édouard from Paris Saint-Germain (June 2018).
Record Victory: 11-0 Dundee, Division I, 26 October 1895. *Record Defeat:* 0-8 v Motherwell, Division I, 30 April 1937.
Most Capped Player: Pat Bonner, 80, Republic of Ireland. *Most League Appearances:* 486: Billy McNeill, 1957-75.
Most League Goals in Season (Individual): 50: James McGrory, Division I, 1935-36.
Most League Goals Overall (Individual): 397: James McGrory, 1922-39.

Honours

League Champions: (51 times) Division I 1892-93, 1893-94, 1895-96, 1897-98, 1904-05, 1905-06, 1906-07, 1907-08, 1908-09, 1909-10, 1913-14, 1914-15, 1915-16, 1916-17, 1918-19, 1921-22, 1925-26, 1935-36, 1937-38, 1953-54, 1965-66, 1966-67, 1967-68, 1968-69, 1969-70, 1970-71, 1971-72, 1972-73, 1973-74; Premier Division 1976-77, 1978-79, 1980-81, 1981-82, 1985-86, 1987-88, 1997-98, 2000-01, 2001-02, 2003-04, 2005-06, 2006-07, 2007-08, 2011-12, 2012-13; Premiership 2013-14, 2014-15, 2015-16, 2016-17, 2017-18, 2018-19, 2019-20. *Runners-up:* 32 times.
Scottish Cup Winners: (40 times) 1892, 1899, 1900, 1904, 1907, 1908, 1911, 1912, 1914, 1923, 1925, 1927, 1931, 1933, 1937, 1951, 1954, 1965, 1967, 1969, 1971, 1972, 1974, 1975, 1977, 1980, 1985, 1988, 1989, 1995, 2001, 2004, 2005, 2007, 2011, 2013, 2017, 2018, 2019, 2020. *Runners-up:* 18 times.
League Cup Winners: (19 times) 1956-57, 1957-58, 1965-66, 1966-67, 1967-68, 1968-69, 1969-70, 1974-75, 1982-83, 1997-98, 1999-2000, 2000-01, 2005-06, 2008-09, 2014-15, 2016-17, 2017-18, 2018-19, 2019-20. *Runners-up:* 15 times.

CELTIC – SPFL PREMIERSHIP 2020–21 LEAGUE RECORD

Match No.	Date	Venue	Opponents	Result	H/T Score	Lg Pos.	Goalscorers	Attendance
1	Aug 2	H	Hamilton A	W 5-1	2-1	1	Edouard 3 [20, 49, 53], Frimpong [31], Klimala [90]	0
2	9	A	Kilmarnock	D 1-1	1-1	4	Christie [11]	0
3	22	A	Dundee U	W 1-0	0-0	4	Ajeti [83]	0
4	30	H	Motherwell	W 3-0	1-0	3	Forrest [40], Ajeti [74], Jullien [90]	0
5	Sept 12	A	Ross Co	W 5-0	2-0	3	Edouard (pen) [4], Ajeti [20], Duffy [59], Ajer [64], Klimala [75]	0
6	16	A	St Mirren	W 2-1	2-1	2	Duffy [21], Forrest [36]	0
7	19	H	Livingston	W 3-2	2-1	1	McGregor [20], Christie [23], Ajeti [52]	0
8	27	H	Hibernian	W 3-0	2-0	2	McGregor [7], Ajeti [35], Elyounoussi [79]	0
9	Oct 4	A	St Johnstone	W 2-0	0-0	2	Klimala [90], Griffiths [90]	0
10	17	H	Rangers	L 0-2	0-1	2		0
11	25	A	Aberdeen	D 3-3	0-1	2	McGregor [52], Griffiths [76], Christie (pen) [78]	0
12	Nov 8	A	Motherwell	W 4-1	2-0	2	Elyounoussi 3 [8, 27, 76], Ntcham [86]	0
13	21	A	Hibernian	D 2-2	0-0	2	Edouard (pen) [79], Laxalt [90]	0
14	Dec 6	H	St Johnstone	D 1-1	0-0	2	Elyounoussi [83]	0
15	13	H	Kilmarnock	W 2-0	0-0	2	Elyounoussi [57], Duffy [70]	0
16	23	H	Ross Co	W 2-0	1-0	2	Turnbull [24], Griffiths [61]	0
17	26	A	Hamilton A	W 3-0	0-0	2	Edouard (pen) [49], Griffiths [54], Turnbull [74]	0
18	30	H	Dundee U	W 3-0	2-0	2	Soro [23], Turnbull [40], Edouard [76]	0
19	Jan 2	A	Rangers	L 0-1	0-0	2		0
20	11	H	Hibernian	D 1-1	0-0	2	Turnbull [82]	0
21	16	H	Livingston	D 0-0	0-0	2		0
22	20	A	Livingston	D 2-2	2-1	2	Elyounoussi [28], Bitton [38]	0
23	27	H	Hamilton A	W 2-0	1-0	2	Griffiths [12], Edouard [48]	0
24	30	H	St Mirren	L 1-2	1-2	2	Edouard [32]	0
25	Feb 2	A	Kilmarnock	W 4-0	1-0	2	Brown [29], Edouard 2 (1 pen) [53 (p), 62], Ajeti [86]	0
26	6	H	Motherwell	W 2-1	1-0	2	Welsh [2], Edouard [50]	0
27	10	A	St Mirren	W 4-0	1-0	2	Rogic [16], Edouard (pen) [79], Christie [82], Turnbull [83]	0
28	14	A	St Johnstone	W 2-1	0-0	2	Edouard 2 [60, 62]	0
29	17	H	Aberdeen	W 1-0	1-0	2	Turnbull [14]	0
30	21	A	Ross Co	L 0-1	0-0	2		0
31	27	H	Aberdeen	W 1-0	1-0	2	Edouard [8]	0
32	Mar 7	A	Dundee U	D 0-0	0-0	2		0
33	21	H	Rangers	D 1-1	1-1	2	Elyounoussi [23]	0
34	Apr 10	H	Livingston	W 6-0	2-0	2	Forrest [30], Turnbull [38], Fitzwater (og) [50], Elyounoussi 2 [54, 66], Christie [87]	0
35	21	A	Aberdeen	D 1-1	0-1	2	Griffiths [90]	0
36	May 2	A	Rangers	L 1-4	1-2	2	Edouard [30]	0
37	12	H	St Johnstone	W 4-0	2-0	2	Turnbull [23], Edouard [24], Ajer [79], Dembele [85]	0
38	15	A	Hibernian	D 0-0	0-0	2		0

Final League Position: 2

European: *European Cup/Champions League:* 214 matches (1966-67 winners, 1967-68, 1968-69, 1969-70 runners-up, 1970-71, 1971-72, 1972-73, 1973-74 semi-finals, 1974-75, 1977-78, 1979-80, 1981-82, 1982-83, 1986-87, 1988-89, 1998-99, 2001-02, 2002-03, 2003-04, 2004-05, 2005-06, 2006-07, 2007-08, 2008-09, 2009-10, 2010-11, 2012-13, 2013-14, 2014-15, 2015-16, 2016-17, 2017-18, 2018-19, 2019-20, 2020-21). *Cup Winners' Cup:* 38 matches (1963-64 semi-finals, 1965-66 semi-finals, 1975-76, 1980-81, 1984-85, 1985-86, 1989-90, 1995-96). *UEFA Cup:* 75 matches (*Fairs Cup:* 1962-63, 1964-65. *UEFA Cup:* 1976-77, 1983-84, 1987-88, 1991-92, 1992-93, 1993-94, 1996-97, 1997-98, 1998-99, 1999-2000, 2000-01, 2001-02, 2002-03 runners-up, 2003-04 quarter-finals). *Europa League:* 60 matches (2009-10, 2010-11, 2011-12, 2014-15, 2015-16, 2017-18, 2018-19, 2019-20, 2020-21).

Club colours: Shirt: Green and white hoops. Shorts: White. Socks: White with green hoops.

Goalscorers: *League (78):* Edouard 18 (5 pens), Elyounoussi 10, Turnbull 8, Ajeti 6, Griffiths 6, Christie 5 (1 pen), Duffy 3, Forrest 3, Klimala 3, McGregor 3, Ajer 2, Bitton 1, Brown 1, Dembele 1, Frimpong 1, Jullien 1, Laxalt 1, Ntcham 1, Rogic 1, Soro 1, Welsh 1, own goal 1.
William Hill Scottish Cup (3): Christie 1, Elyounoussi 1, Forrest 1.
Betfred Scottish League Cup (0).
UEFA Champions League (7): Elyounoussi 2, Christie 1, Edouard 1, Jullien 1, Taylor 1, own goal 1.
UEFA Europa League (10): Elyounoussi 3, Edouard 2, Griffiths 1, Jullien 1, McGregor 1 (1 pen), Rogic 1, Turnbull 1.

Bain S 18	Frimpong J 19 + 3	Jullien C 9	Ajer K 34 + 1	Taylor G 23 + 3	Brown S 25 + 6	McGregor C 37	Forrest J 8 + 5	Christie R 26 + 8	Elyounoussi M 21 + 13	Edouard O 28 + 3	Ntcham J 7 + 7	Klimala P 3 + 14	Dembele K — + 5	Elhamed H 4 + 4	Barkas V 15	Bolingoli Mbombo B — + 1	Bitton N 12 + 2	Ajeti A 10 + 10	Duffy S 14 + 4	Turnbull D 25 + 6	Soro I 11 + 8	Griffiths L 7 + 15	Rogic T 10 + 13	Welsh S 15 + 1	Laxalt D 13 + 4	Hazard C 5	Johnston M 2 + 8	Harper C 1	Okoflex A — + 2	Henderson E — + 2	Ralston A 1	Kenny J 14	Montgomery A 1 + 1	*Match No.*
1	2^2	3	4	5	6	7	8	9^3	10^1	11^4	12	13	14	15																				1
	2^3	3	4	5^4	6^2	7	8	9	10^1	11	14	12		13	1	15																		2
	2	3	14	5^4	6	7	12	8	10^1	11^3	9^2	15			1		4	13																3
	13	3	4	5^1	6	7	8	11	10^3		9^2	12		2	1			14																4
	6	3	4		5^5	8^3	9	14	13	11^4	7^1	12			1			10^2	2	15	16													5
	14		4	9	7	8	5^1	6		11^3	13	10^2		2	1			12	3															6
	5^4		4	9	6	8	12	11^5	16		7^1	14		2^3	1		13	10^2	3	15														7
	5		4	9	7^4	8^3		6^5	10^1	12	14	15			1		2	11^2	3	13	16													8
	5		4	8^4	16	7		12	10^2	11^5	6^3	13		2	1				3	9^1		14	15											9
	5		4	16	6	8			11^5		7^3	10^2			1			12	3	15		13	14	2^1	9^4									10
1	2		4		13	6		8	10		7^1							11^2	3	14		12	9^3		5									11
1	2^1		4^3		6	7		8	10	12	15			13			3	11^4	14				9^2		5									12
1	2		4		6^4	7		8	10^3	12	15						3	11^1	14			13	9^2		5									13
	5	3	4^2	12	7^4	8		6	15	11					1		2			14		13	10^3		9^1									14
	5^5	3	2	8^4		7		13	10^2	11^1		12							4	9^3	6		15		14	1	16							15
	2	3	4			9		7^1		11^3	12							15		8^2	6	10^4	14		5	1	13							16
	2		4	5		7		8^2	15	10^1		13					3	12		9^4	6	11^3				1	14							17
	2	3^1	4		16	9		7	15	11^4					1		12	13		8^2	6^3	10^5	14		5									18
	2		3		14	9^5		7^2	12	11				15	1		4▮		13	8^4	6^1	10^3	16		5									19
	2					7							14						4	8	6		9^2	3	5	1	10^3	11^1	12	13				20
	8					6											3		4	9	7		11^1		5	1	10^2		13	12	2			21
	13		2^4	5	14▮	8		6	11			12			1		3		4	9^2	7^3	10^1					15							22
1			2	5		8		13	9	11^2							3	12	4	6^1	7	10^3	14											23
1			2	5		9		15	8^3	11							3^4	14	4	7^1	6^5	10^2	13	12			16							24
1			4	5^2	6	8		7^3	12	11^4		13						10		9^1				3	15		14					2		25
1			4	5^2	6^1	8			15	11								10^3		7^4	13	12	9	3	14							2		26
1			4	5	6	8		12	15	11^1		14						10^3	13	9^4		16	7^2	3^5								2		27
1			4	5	6	7		9	12	11									3	10^1		13	8^2									2		28
1			4	5	13	9		7	15	10^4		14						11^3		8^1	6^2		12	3								2		29
1			4	5^3	6	9		10^1	14	11										8		13	7^2	3	12							2		30
1			4		6	8		9	12	11		10^1								7^2	13			3	5							2		31
1			4		7^1	8	13	9	10^3	11										6^2		14	12	3	5							2		32
1			4		6^3	7	12	8	10^1	11^2										9^4	14	15	13	3	5							2		33
1			4	5	7^4	8	9^2	12	11^5	10^1								13		6^3	15	16	14	3								2		34
1				5	6^2	7		8^1	10	11^3			14				4			9		12	13	3								2		35
1			4	5	6^3	7▮	8^1	13	10	11^2										9	12			3			14					2		36
			3	13	6^3		7^1	8	10^4	11^5			16		1					9	12	15		4			14					2	5^2	37
			4	5^2	6	7	12	8^1	10^3	11^4			15		1					9		13		3								2	14	38

CLYDE

Year Formed: 1877. *Ground & Address:* Broadwood Stadium, Cumbernauld, G68 9NE. *Telephone:* 01236 451511. *Fax:* 01236 733490. *E-mail:* info@clydefc.co.uk *Website:* clydefc.co.uk
Ground Capacity: 8,086 (all seated). *Size of Pitch:* 100m × 68m.
Chairman: John Taylor. *Vice Chairman:* Gordon Thomson.
Manager: Danny Lennon. *Assistant Manager:* Allan Moore.
Club Nickname: 'The Bully Wee'.
Previous Grounds: Barrowfield Park 1877-98; Shawfield Stadium 1898-1986; Firhill Stadium 1986-91; Douglas Park 1991-94.
Record Attendance: 52,000 v Rangers, Division I, 21 November 1908.
Record Transfer Fee received: £200,000 from Blackburn R for Gordon Greer (May 2001).
Record Transfer Fee paid: £14,000 for Harry Hood from Sunderland (1966).
Record Victory: 11-1 v Cowdenbeath, Division II, 6 October 1951.
Record Defeat: 0-11 v Dumbarton, Scottish Cup 4th rd, 22 November, 1879; v Rangers, Scottish Cup 4th rd, 13 November 1880.
Most Capped Player: Tommy Ring, 12, Scotland.
Most League Appearances: 420: Brian Ahern, 1971-81; 1987-88.
Most League Goals in Season (Individual): 32: Bill Boyd, 1932-33.
Most Goals Overall (Individual): 124: Tommy Ring, 1950-60.

CLYDE – SPFL LEAGUE ONE 2020–21 LEAGUE RECORD

Match No.	*Date*	*Venue*	*Opponents*	*Result*		*H/T Score*	*Lg Pos.*	*Goalscorers*	*Attendance*
1	Oct 17	H	Partick Thistle	W	1-0	0-0	4	Love 70	0
2	31	H	Peterhead	L	0-2	0-0	7		0
3	Nov 3	A	Dumbarton	L	0-1	0-1	8		0
4	7	A	Airdrieonians	L	0-5	0-3	9		0
5	21	H	Montrose	W	3-2	1-1	8	Goodwillie 3 8, 59, 79	0
6	Dec 12	H	Falkirk	L	0-3	0-1	9		0
7	19	A	Cove R	W	3-2	1-2	9	Goodwillie 2 (2 pens) 12, 56, Lamont 90	0
8	26	H	Airdrieonians	L	2-4	1-3	9	Cuddihy 38, Love 61	0
9	Mar 20	H	East Fife	L	1-3	0-1	10	Goodwillie 90	0
10	27	A	Montrose	D	2-2	2-2	9	Jamieson 2 32, 36	0
11	30	A	Peterhead	W	2-0	0-0	8	Howie 62, Cunningham 73	0
12	Apr 1	A	East Fife	L	0-1	0-1	8		0
13	6	H	Cove R	D	1-1	0-0	8	Goodwillie 78	0
14	8	H	Forfar Ath	W	3-0	2-0	8	Goodwillie 2 18, 44, Howie 51	0
15	10	A	Falkirk	L	1-2	0-1	8	Jack 84	0
16	13	A	Partick Thistle	L	0-2	0-0	8		0
17	15	H	Dumbarton	L	0-1	0-1	9		0
18	20	A	Forfar Ath	W	3-1	1-1	8	Jamieson 2 39, 61, Jack 82	0
19	24	A	Peterhead	L	0-3	0-0	8		0
20	29	A	Forfar Ath	L	1-2	1-1	9	Goodwillie 11	0
21	May 1	H	Dumbarton	W	2-0	1-0	8	Lamont 31, Cunningham 75	0
22	6	H	East Fife	W	2-1	1-0	8	Love 41, Goodwillie 82	0

Final League Position: 8

Honours
League Champions: Division II 1904-05, 1951-52, 1956-57, 1961-62, 1972-73; Second Division 1977-78, 1981-82, 1992-93, 1999-2000.
Runners-up: Division II 1903-04, 1905-06, 1925-26, 1963-64; First Division 2002-03, 2003-04; League Two 2018-19.
Promoted via play-offs: 2018-19 (to League Two).
Scottish Cup Winners: 1939, 1955, 1958; *Runners-up:* 1910, 1912, 1949.
League Cup: Semi-finals 1956, 1957, 1968.
League Challenge Cup Runners-up: 2006-07.

Club colours: Shirt: White with red trim. Shorts: Black. Socks: White.

Goalscorers: *League (27):* Goodwillie 11 (2 pens), Jamieson 4, Love 3, Cunningham 2, Howie 2, Jack 2, Lamont 2, Cuddihy 1.
William Hill Scottish Cup (3): Cuddihy 1, Goodwillie 1, Rumsby 1.
Betfred Scottish League Cup (6): Goodwillie 2 (1 pen), Cuddihy 1, Cunningham 1, Lamont 1, Love 1.

Mitchell D 17	Bain J 11 + 1	Lang T 14 + 1	McNiff M 12 + 6	Shiels M 6	Syvertsen K 5 + 2	Cunningham R 17 + 1	Cuddihy B 19 + 3	Love A 17 + 4	Jack J 6 + 11	Goodwillie D 19 + 1	Howie C 12 + 4	Lamont M 7 + 12	Johnston C 1 + 3	Palmer Cameron 1 + 2	Henderson J 1 + 3	Robertson L 5 + 6	Rumsby S 17 + 2	Vajs M 1	Nicoll K 10 + 2	Jamieson L 8 + 4	Thomson J 6 + 7	McGlinchey M 7 + 3	Munro M 8 + 3	Ritchie-Hosler K — + 5	Otoo E 11 + 2	Wilson D 4	Butterworth Z — + 4	*Match No.*
1	2	3	4	5	6^{2}	7	8	9^{1}	10^{3}	11	12	13	14															1
1	2	3	4	5	6^{4}	7^{1}	8	9^{3}	11^{2}	10		12	15	13^{5}	14	16												2
1	2^{2}	3	4	5	12		8	9	7^{1}	11		10^{4}	13		6^{3}	14	15											3
1	5	3^{2}	4	8	10^{1}		7	12	15	11		14	9^{3}		13	6^{4}	2											4
1	13	4	15	5^{3}	12	9	7	8	14	11	2^{2}	10^{4}				6^{1}	3											5
	2^{1}	3		5	8^{5}	9^{3}	7	10^{2}	12	11	14	6^{4}			15	16	4	1	13									6
1	5	3			8	6^{2}	7	10	9^{1}	11	2	13		12			4											7
1	2	3	5			9^{1}	6	10		11	13	12		8			4		7^{2}									8
1		3	4			11	7^{3}		13	10	2	8^{2}				15				5^{1}	6^{4}	9	12	14				9
1		3^{2}	4			13	7^{4}	12	15	11^{3}							14		8	6^{1}	9	10	2		5			10
1			4			11^{2}	16	9^{1}	13		12	14					3		8	10^{3}	7^{4}	6^{5}	2	15	5			11
1	2^{5}		4^{4}			10	7^{2}	12	11^{3}		8	6^{1}					3		13	15	14	9		16	5			12
1		14				11	12	9^{1}		13	8	15					3		7^{3}	10^{4}	6	5^{2}	2		4			13
1		4	14			10^{5}	8^{4}	9^{1}		11^{3}	6	16				12	3		7^{2}	15		13	2		5			14
1		4	16			9^{4}	8^{2}	13	12	10	6	15					3		7^{5}	11^{1}	14		2		5^{3}			15
	2	3	5				13	11^{1}	9^{4}	10		16				6^{5}	4			14	7^{3}	8^{2}		15	12	1		16
		3					9	5^{1}	15	11	7	12					4		8^{2}	6^{4}	13		2^{3}		10	1	14	17
1			13			6^{3}	8	9^{2}	14	10	3						4		7	11^{1}	15		2		5^{4}		12	18
1			16			6	8^{4}	9^{1}	15	10^{2}	3					13	4		7^{3}	11	12		2	14	5^{5}			19
			15			9^{1}	2	11^{3}		10	4	13					3		7		6^{4}	8^{2}	12■		5	1	14	20
	2		5			8	7	10^{3}		11	3^{4}	6^{1}				9^{2}	4				14	13			12	1	15	21
1	2		3			11^{4}	8^{5}	9^{1}	14	10		7^{3}				6^{2}	4			13	15	12	16		5			22

COVE RANGERS

Year Formed: 1922. *Ground & Address:* Balmoral Stadium, Wellington Circle, Altens, Aberdeen AB12 3JG. *Telephone:* 01224 392 111. *Fax:* 01224 392 858. *E-mail:* info@coverangersfc.com *Website:* coverangersfc.com
Ground Capacity: 2322 (356 seated). *Size of Pitch:* 105yd × 68yd.
Chairman: Keith Moorhouse. *Vice Chairman:* Graeme Reid. *Secretary:* Duncan Little.
Manager: Paul Hartley. *Assistant Manager:* Gordon Young.
Club Nickname: 'Wee Rangers', 'Toonsers'.
Previous Grounds: Allan Park.
Record Attendance: 2,100 v Deveronvale, 2009, Highland League.
Record Transfer Fee received: Scott Paterson, £25,000 from Liverpool March 1992.
Record Transfer Fee paid: £14,000 for Harry Hood from Sunderland (1966).
Record Victory: 7-1 v Stirling Albion, League Two, 10 March 2020.
Record Defeat: 0-7 v Ross County, League Cup Group rd, 30 July 2016.
Most League Appearances: 58: Stuart McKenzie and Connor Scully 2019-21.
Most League Goals in Season (Individual): 24: Mitch Megginson, 2019-20.
Most Goals Overall (Individual): 39: Mitch Megginson, 2019-21.

COVE RANGERS – SPFL LEAGUE ONE 2020–21 LEAGUE RECORD

Match No.	Date	Venue	Opponents	Result		H/T Score	Lg Pos.	Goalscorers	Attendance
1	Oct 17	H	East Fife	W	3-1	1-0	—	Megginson 2 39, 59, McIntosh 73	0
2	24	A	Peterhead	W	2-0	1-0	—	Megginson 33, Milne 55	0
3	31	H	Partick Thistle	W	1-0	0-0	—	McAllister 90	0
4	Nov 7	H	Forfar Ath	W	3-0	2-0	—	McAllister 4, Megginson 2 (1 pen) 43 (p), 61	0
5	21	A	Falkirk	L	0-1	0-0	—		0
6	28	A	Airdrieonians	D	1-1	1-0	—	Masson 26	0
7	Dec 5	H	Montrose	L	1-2	1-0	—	Milne 38	0
8	12	A	Dumbarton	L	0-1	0-0	—		0
9	19	H	Clyde	L	2-3	2-1	—	Megginson 2 27, 32	0
10	26	A	Forfar Ath	W	1-0	0-0	—	Megginson 64	0
11	Jan 2	H	Peterhead	W	1-0	1-0	—	McAllister 2	0
12	Mar 20	A	Partick Thistle	D	1-1	0-0	—	Megginson 82	0
13	27	A	East Fife	D	0-0	0-0	—		0
14	30	H	Airdrieonians	W	2-0	0-0	—	Masson 2 65, 71	0
15	Apr 6	A	Clyde	D	1-1	0-0	—	Scully 76	0
16	10	H	Dumbarton	W	1-0	0-0	—	McAllister 54	0
17	17	H	Falkirk	W	2-0	1-0	—	Megginson 2 12, 48	0
18	20	A	Montrose	L	0-1	0-1	—		0
19	24	A	Falkirk	D	2-2	1-1	—	McIntosh 36, Megginson 76	0
20	27	H	Partick Thistle	D	2-2	1-1	—	McAllister (pen) 21, Strachan 75	0
21	29	A	Montrose	W	2-0	1-0	—	Megginson 2 44, 51	0
22	May 1	H	Airdrieonians	L	0-2	0-0	—		0

Final League Position: 3

Honours
League Champions: League Two 2019-20.
Scottish Highland League Champions: 2000-01, 2007-08, 2008-09, 2012-13, 2015-16, 2017-18, 2018-19.
Promoted via play-offs: 2018-19.

Club colours: Shirts: Blue with white trim. Shorts: Blue. Socks: Blue.

Goalscorers: *League (28):* Megginson 14 (1 pen), McAllister 5 (1 pen), Masson 3, McIntosh 2, Milne 2, Scully 1, Strachan 1.
William Hill Scottish Cup (3): Masson 1, McAllister 1, Strachan 1.
Betfred Scottish League Cup (4): McAllister 2 (1 pen), Higgins 1, Semple 1.
Scottish League Play-Offs (3): McAllister 1, McIntosh 1, Megginson 1.

McKenzie S 22	Ross Scott 18 + 1	Strachan R 21	Higgins D 9	Milne H 11	McIntosh L 18 + 3	Yule B 22	Scully C 18 + 1	Masson J 12 + 1	Semple J 2 + 3	Megginson M 19	Watson B 3 + 10	Ross Sebastian 5 + 9	McAllister R 11 + 9	Livingstone A 8 + 3	Graham R 14 + 1	Fyvie F 17 + 1	Logan C 4 + 2	Smith C 4 + 6	Hanratty K — + 4	Ngwenya K 4 + 1	*Match No.*
1	2	3	4	5	6	7	8^{2}	9	10^{3}	11^{1}	12	13	14								1
1	2	3	4	5	6^{3}	7	8	9	10^{2}	11^{1}	13	12	14								2
1	2	3	4^{3}	5	6	7	8	10		11^{1}		14	12	9^{2}	13						3
1	2	3		5	6	7	8	9		10	12		11^{1}		4						4
1	2	3		5	6	7	8		12	11	13		10^{1}	4^{2}		9					5
1	4	3		5	11	8	7	9		10					2	6					6
1	2	3	4	5^{4}	8	6	7^{3}	10^{1}	14		15	13	11^{2}	12		9					7
1	2	3	4	5	11	6	7^{2}	10	13		8^{1}	12				9					8
1		4	3	5	8	2	6	10		11		9^{1}	12			7					9
1	2	3		5	6	7		9		10			11		4	8					10
1	2	3		5	6	7		9		11			10		4	8					11
1		3			10^{2}	8	6^{3}	9		11	14		13	5	4	7	2^{1}	12			12
1	2^{3}	3			6^{5}	7		9^{2}		11	12	14	15	5^{1}	4	8		10^{4}	13	16	13
1	2	3			10^{3}	6^{5}	8	13		11^{1}	16	9^{4}	12		4	7	14	15		5^{2}	14
1		4				6	8				10^{2}	9^{1}	11		3	7	2	12	13	5	15
1	2	3			9^{1}	6	8			11			10	5	4	7		12			16
1	2	3			13	6	8			10		14	11^{1}		4	7	12	9^{2}		5^{3}	17
1	2^{3}	3■			12	6	8			10^{5}	15	14	11^{2}	13	4	7	5^{4}	9^{1}	16		18
1	2		4		10	6	8			11		9^{1}	12	5	3	7					19
1	2	3			9	6	8			10			11^{1}	5	4	7		12			20
1	2	3	4		9^{4}	7	16			10^{1}	11	14	12	13		8^{2}		6^{5}	15	5^{3}	21
1	14	3	2		16	6	7^{5}			10	12	9^{3}	11	8^{4}	4^{1}	15	5^{2}	13			22

COWDENBEATH

Year Formed: 1882. *Ground & Address:* Central Park, Cowdenbeath KY4 9QQ. *Telephone:* 01383 610166. *Fax:* 01383 512132.
E-mail: office@cowdenbeathfc.com *Website:* cowdenbeathfc.com
Ground Capacity: 4,370 (seated: 1,431). *Size of Pitch:* 95m × 60m.
Chairman: Donald Findlay QC. *Finance Director and Secretary:* David Allan.
Club Nicknames: 'The Blue Brazil'; 'Cowden'; 'The Miners'.
Manager: Gary Bollan. *Assistant Manager:* Craig Easton. *First-Team Coach:* Ian Flaherty.
Previous Ground: North End Park.
Record Attendance: 25,586 v Rangers, League Cup quarter-final, 21 September 1949.
Record Transfer Fee received: £30,000 for Nicky Henderson to Falkirk (March 1994).
Record Victory: 12-0 v Johnstone, Scottish Cup 1st rd, 21 January 1928.
Record Defeat: 1-11 v Clyde, Division II, 6 October 1951; 0-10 v Hearts, Championship, 28 February 2015.
Most Capped Player: Jim Paterson, 3, Scotland.
Most League and Cup Appearances: 491, Ray Allan 1972-75, 1979-89.
Most League Goals in Season (Individual): 54, Rab Walls, Division II, 1938-39.
Most Goals Overall (Individual): 127, Willie Devlin, 1922-26, 1929-30.

COWDENBEATH – SPFL LEAGUE TWO 2020–21 LEAGUE RECORD

Match No.	*Date*	*Venue*	*Opponents*	*Result*		*H/T Score*	*Lg Pos.*	*Goalscorers*	*Attendance*
1	Oct 17	H	Annan Ath	L	0-3	0-2	9		0
2	24	A	Edinburgh C	W	1-0	0-0	6	Smith 78	0
3	31	H	Stenhousemuir	D	1-1	0-0	7	Smith 60	0
4	Nov 7	A	Stranraer	L	0-2	0-1	8		0
5	28	A	Elgin C	L	2-5	0-2	8	Miller, K 55, Kavanagh 90	0
6	Dec 5	H	Queen's Park	L	0-3	0-1	8		0
7	12	A	Stirling Alb	L	0-1	0-0	9		0
8	19	H	Brechin C	W	2-0	1-0	8	Barr 14, Russell 52	0
9	Mar 20	A	Annan Ath	D	0-0	0-0	8		0
10	27	H	Stranraer	D	1-1	1-0	8	Morrison 14	0
11	30	H	Edinburgh C	L	1-3	1-2	8	Swan 26	0
12	Apr 3	H	Albion R	L	0-1	0-1	9		0
13	6	A	Queen's Park	L	0-3	0-1	9		0
14	8	A	Stenhousemuir	L	0-1	0-0	9		0
15	10	H	Elgin C	W	1-0	1-0	8	Renton 19	0
16	13	A	Albion R	D	0-0	0-0	8		0
17	17	H	Stirling Alb	L	1-5	1-3	9	Barr 17	0
18	20	A	Brechin C	D	0-0	0-0	9		0
19	24	A	Stenhousemuir	W	2-0	0-0	9	Renton 77, Todd 84	0
20	27	H	Brechin C	L	0-2	0-1	9		0
21	May 1	A	Annan Ath	D	1-1	0-0	9	Buchanan 50	0
22	4	H	Albion R	W	2-0	1-0	9	Miller, K 13, Russell (pen) 90	0

Final League Position: 9

Honours
League Champions: Division II 1913-14, 1914-15, 1938-39; Second Division 2011-12; Third Division 2005-06.
Runners-up: Division II 1921-22, 1923-24, 1969-70; Second Division 1991-92; Third Division 2000-01, 2008-09.
Promoted via play-offs: 2009-10 (to First Division).
Scottish Cup: Quarter-finals 1931.
League Cup: Semi-finals 1959, 1970.

Club colours: Shirt: Royal blue with white sleeves. Shorts: White. Socks: Black with red tops.

Goalscorers: *League (15):* Barr 2, Miller K 2, Renton 2, Russell 2 (1 pen), Smith 2, Buchanan 1, Kavanagh 1, Morrison 1, Swan 1, Todd 1.
William Hill Scottish Cup (2): Barr 1, Renton 1.
Betfred Scottish League Cup (0).

Sinclair R 4	Pollock R 1 + 1	Barr C 20 + 1	Hay G 3	Clarke R 5	Taylor G 16 + 5	Miller K 20 + 1	Smith B 3	Hamilton O 3 + 3	Cox D 2	Kavanagh C 2 + 2	Swan H 17 + 3	Whyte M 1	Mullen F 16 + 1	Todd J 21	Buchanan R 19 + 1	Herd M 4 + 4	McGurn D 1	Glass J 1 + 4	Russell I 6 + 8	Renton K 15 + 2	Munro R 2	Morrison G 14 + 1	Hogarth N 14	Finnie R 14	Miller Z 4 + 6	Hutton K 11 + 1	Sandison J 1	Pyper J 2	Watson L — + 1	*Match No.*
1	2	3	4	5	6	7	8	9[1]	10	11	12																			1
		4	6	5	9	8	11		10■			1	2	3	7															2
1		4	8	5	9	7	10	12		11[1]			2	3	6															3
1		4		5	9	7		11			8		2	3	6■	10														4
	15	4		9[4]	6	8		10[2]		12	13		2	3[1]		7[3]	1	5	11	14										5
1		4			9	7		12			5		2	3	6	8			11[1]	10										6
		4			9	8[1]					5		2	3	6	10			12	11	1	7								7
		3			9	8				12	5		2	4	6				11[1]	10	1	7								8
		3			10	9					5[1]		2	4	7				12	11		8	1	6						9
		3			9	7[1]					5			4	6				13	10[2]		8	1	2	11	12				10
		3			10[1]	8					5			4	6[2]			14	13	12		9	1	2	11[3]	7				11
		4[1]			10[4]	6					5			3	13	15		14	12	11		9[3]	1	2	7[2]	8				12
					10[3]	14					8		2	4	6			12	13	11		9[2]	1	3		7	5[1]			13
		3			13	9					8		2	4	6				11[2]			12	1	5	10	7[1]				14
		3			12	6					10		2	4	7[1]					11		9	1	5		8				15
		3			12	6					10[1]		2	4	7[2]					11		9	1	5	13	8				16
		3			13	6		16			10[4]		2	4	7[3]	14			15	11[1]		9[2]	1	5	12	8[5]				17
		3			9[1]	7					13		2	4	6				11[2]	10			1	5	12	8				18
		4			11[1]	6					5			3	9	12				10		8	1	2		7				19
		4			10[2]	6					5		13	3	7					11		9	1	2	12	8[1]				20
		14			12						9[1]		2	3	6				11[3]	10[2]		8	1	5	13	7■		4		21
		4[5]				9					10[4]		2	3	7	12		15	16	11[3]		8[2]	1	5	13			6[1]	14	22

DUMBARTON

Year Formed: 1872. *Ground:* C&G Systems Stadium, Castle Road, Dumbarton G82 1JJ. *Telephone/Fax:* 01389 762569.
E-mail: office@dumbartonfc.com *Website:* dumbartonfootballclub.com
Ground Capacity: total: 2,025 (all seated). *Size of Pitch:* 98m × 67m.
Chairman: John Steele. *Vice-Chairman:* Colin Hosie.
Manager: Stevie Farrell. *Assistant Manager:* Frank McKeown.
Club Nicknames: 'The Sons'; 'Sons of the Rock'.
Previous Grounds: Broadmeadow; Ropework Lane; Townend Ground; Boghead Park; Cliftonhill Stadium.
Record Attendance: 18,000 v Raith R, Scottish Cup, 2 March 1957.
Record Transfer Fee received: £300,000 for Neill Collins to Sunderland (July 2004).
Record Transfer Fee paid: £50,000 for Charlie Gibson from Stirling Alb (1989).
Record Victory: 13-1 v Kirkintilloch Central, Scottish Cup 1st rd, 1 September 1888.
Record Defeat: 1-11 v Albion R, Division II, 30 January 1926: v Ayr U, League Cup, 13 August 1952.
Most Capped Player: James McAulay, 9, Scotland.
Most League Appearances: 298: Andy Jardine, 1957-67.
Most Goals in Season (Individual): 38: Kenny Wilson, Division II, 1971-72. *(League and Cup):* 46 Hughie Gallacher, 1955-56.
Most Goals Overall (Individual): 202: Hughie Gallacher, 1954-62

DUMBARTON – SPFL LEAGUE ONE 2020–21 LEAGUE RECORD

Match No.	Date	Venue	Opponents	Result		H/T Score	Lg Pos.	Goalscorers	Attendance
1	Oct 17	A	Forfar Ath	D	0-0	0-0	5		0
2	31	A	Airdrieonians	W	2-0	1-0	3	Wilson, J 22, McCann (og) 60	0
3	Nov 3	H	Clyde	W	1-0	1-0	3	Frizzell 13	0
4	7	A	East Fife	L	1-2	0-1	3	Wilson, J 61	0
5	21	A	Peterhead	L	0-1	0-1	5		0
6	24	H	Falkirk	L	0-3	0-2	6		0
7	Dec 5	A	Partick Thistle	D	0-0	0-0	6		0
8	12	H	Cove R	W	1-0	0-0	5	Wedderburn 51	0
9	19	A	Montrose	L	0-4	0-3	6		0
10	Mar 20	H	Forfar Ath	L	0-1	0-0	8		0
11	27	H	Peterhead	L	0-1	0-0	8		0
12	30	A	Falkirk	D	1-1	0-0	9	Omar 68	0
13	Apr 1	H	Airdrieonians	L	0-1	0-0	9		0
14	6	H	Montrose	D	0-0	0-0	9		0
15	8	H	East Fife	W	2-1	1-0	9	McGeever 3, Frizzell 68	0
16	10	A	Cove R	L	0-1	0-0	9		0
17	15	A	Clyde	W	1-0	1-0	8	Wedderburn 45	0
18	20	H	Partick Thistle	L	0-2	0-0	9		0
19	24	A	East Fife	L	1-2	0-1	9	Crossan 80	0
20	27	H	Forfar Ath	W	1-0	0-0	8	Duthie 88	0
21	May 1	A	Clyde	L	0-2	0-1	9		0
22	4	H	Peterhead	W	3-2	1-1	9	Wilson, J 2 21, 90, Neill 80	0

Final League Position: 9

Honours
League Champions: Division I 1890-91 (shared with Rangers), 1891-92; Division II 1910-11, 1971-72; Second Division 1991-92; Third Division 2008-09.
Runners-up: First Division 1983-84; Division II 1907-08; Second Division 1994-95; Third Division 2001-02.
Promoted via play-offs: 2011-12 (Second Division).
Scottish Cup Winners: 1883; *Runners-up:* 1881, 1882, 1887, 1891, 1897.
League Challenge Cup: Runners-up: 2017-18.

Club colours: Shirt: Yellow and black vertical stripes. Shorts: Black. Socks: Yellow with black tops.

Goalscorers: *League (14):* Wilson J 4, Frizzell 2, Wedderburn 2, Crossan 1, Duthie 1, McGeever 1, Neill 1, Omar 1, own goal 1.
William Hill Scottish Cup (4): Wilson J 2, Forbes 1, McGeever 1.
Betfred Scottish League Cup (2): Hamilton 1, Jones 1.
Scottish League Play-Offs (4): Brindley 1, McGeever 1, Neill 1, Wilson J 1.

Dabrowski M 8	Wardrop S 17	McGeever R 18	Neill M 22	Quitongo R 17	Wedderburn N 15 + 3	Carswell S 15 + 3	Forbes R 19 + 1	Johnstone D 2 + 5	Jones R 10 + 12	Wilson J 13 + 7	Langan R 4 + 9	Smith C 2	Hamilton C 7	Reilly M 1 + 4	Frizzell A 16 + 2	Church D 5	Crossan P 5 + 9	Morrison D — + 2	McCluskey S — + 3	Ramsbottom S 12	Brindley T 10 + 2	McAllister Nicholas 10	Omar R 7 + 4	Wallace J 5 + 5	Duthie C 1 + 8	Layne I 1 + 1	Match No.
1	2	3	4	5	6	7	8	9	11^{2}	12	13			10^{1}													1
	2	3	4	5	7	8	9		11	10^{1}	12	1	6^{2}	13													2
1	2	4	3	5	8	7	6		12	11^{3}	14		9^{1}	13	10^{2}												3
1	2	3	4	5^{2}	7	8^{1}	6	12	13	10			9		11												4
1	2	3	4		8^{3}	7	6^{2}	13	12	11^{1}			9	14	10	5											5
1	2	3^{2}	4	5^{4}	8^{1}	7		12	14	11	6				10^{3}	9	13	15									6
1	2		4	5	8	3	6^{3}	14	10^{2}		13		7		11^{1}	9	12										7
1	2		4	5	7	3	6	13	15	11^{3}			8^{4}		10^{1}	9^{2}	12		14								8
1	2		4	5	7	3^{1}	6^{2}	11^{4}	14	13	15		8		10^{3}	9^{5}		16	12								9
	2	3	4		8^{3}	7	5		11^{1}	10^{2}				14	9		13		12	1	6						10
	2	4	3			7^{3}	6		14	11^{5}	16	1			10^{2}		12				5	8^{1}	9^{4}	13	15		11
	2	4	3		8	12	13		11^{4}	14					10^{2}		6^{3}			1	7^{1}	5	9			15	12
	2		4		14	7	6■		13	11^{4}	9^{2}						12			1	5	3	15	10^{3}	8^{1}		13
		4	3	5	7	8			12	10^{1}							9			1	6^{2}	2	11	13			14
	2	3	4	5	8^{3}	15	7		11^{4}	13	6^{1}				10		14			1			12	9^{2}			15
	2^{4}	3	4	5	13		6		14	10^{5}					12		11^{3}			1	8^{2}	7	9^{1}	15	16		16
	2	3	4	5^{3}	7		8		11^{1}	13					10^{4}		9^{2}			1	12	6		15	14		17
	2^{2}	3	4	5	8^{3}		7		11^{1}	13					12					1	9	6	10		14		18
		3	4	5^{3}			8		11^{1}	10	14				7^{4}		9			1	6^{2}	2	13	12	15		19
		4	3	5		12	6		15		7^{5}				8^{4}		13			1	9^{2}	2^{1}	14	11	16	10^{3}	20
		3	4	5		2^{2}	7		11^{4}	13	14				10		12			1	8^{3}		6^{1}	9	15		21
		4^{3}	3	5^{2}	12	7	8		13	10	15				9^{1}					1	14	2	6^{5}	11^{4}	16		22

DUNDEE

Year Formed: 1893. *Ground & Address:* Kilmac Stadium at Dens Park, Sandeman St, Dundee DD3 7JY. *Telephone:* 01382 889966. *Fax:* 01382 832284. *E-mail:* reception@dundeefc.co.uk *Website:* dundeefc.co.uk
Ground Capacity: 11,850 (all seated). *Size of Pitch:* 101m × 66m.
Chairmain: Tim Keyes. *Managing Director:* John Nelms. *Technical Director:* Gordon Strachan.
Manager: James McPake. *Assistant Manager:* Dave Mackay.
Club Nicknames: 'The Dark Blues'; 'The Dee'.
Previous Ground: Carolina Port 1893-98.
Record Attendance: 43,024 v Rangers, Scottish Cup 2nd rd, 7 February 1953.
Record Transfer Fee received: £1,500,000 for Jack Hendry to Celtic (January 2018); £1,500,000 for Robert Douglas to Celtic (October 2000).
Record Transfer Fee paid: £600,000 for Fabian Caballero from Sol de América (Paraguay) (July 2000).
Record Victory: 10-0 Division II v Alloa Ath, 9 March 1947 and v Dunfermline Ath, 22 March 1947.
Record Defeat: 0-11 v Celtic, Division I, 26 October 1895.
Most Capped Player: Alex Hamilton, 24, Scotland.
Most League Appearances: 400: Barry Smith, 1995-2006.
Most League Goals in Season (Individual): 32: Alan Gilzean, 1963-64.
Most Goals Overall (Individual): 169: Alan Gilzean 1960-64.

DUNDEE – SPFL CHAMPIONSHIP 2020–21 LEAGUE RECORD

Match No.	Date	Venue	Opponents	Result		H/T Score	Lg Pos.	Goalscorers	Attendance
1	Oct 16	A	Hearts	L	2-6	1-4	2	Adam 27, Mullen 68	0
2	24	H	Greenock Morton	W	1-0	1-0	6	Afolabi 5	0
3	31	H	Raith R	D	1-1	1-0	7	Adam 41	0
4	Nov 6	A	Alloa Ath	D	3-3	0-1	5	McDaid 47, Kerr 76, Adam (pen) 84	0
5	21	A	Ayr U	L	0-2	0-2	7		0
6	Dec 5	H	Arbroath	W	1-0	1-0	6	McGowan 35	0
7	12	A	Inverness CT	D	2-2	1-0	7	Fontaine 37, McGhee 82	300
8	19	H	Dunfermline Ath	D	3-3	1-0	7	Adam 35, Sow 50, Fontaine 70	0
9	26	A	Queen of the South	W	3-1	2-0	4	Sow 3 13, 21, 54	0
10	29	H	Alloa Ath	W	3-1	0-1	3	Sow 2 49, 73, Fontaine 54	0
11	Jan 2	H	Hearts	W	3-1	2-0	3	McGhee 14, Mullen 36, Afolabi (pen) 84	0
12	22	A	Arbroath	D	1-1	1-0	3	Adam (pen) 8	0
13	30	A	Raith R	L	1-3	1-1	4	Sow 5	0
14	Feb 20	H	Queen of the South	L	2-3	0-2	5	Cummings 51, Marshall 82	0
15	27	A	Greenock Morton	D	2-2	0-1	5	Cummings 65, Mullen 81	0
16	Mar 2	H	Inverness CT	W	2-1	2-0	4	Anderson 10, Cummings 45	0
17	6	A	Hearts	L	1-2	0-1	5	Cummings (pen) 63	0
18	13	H	Arbroath	W	2-0	0-0	4	Mullen 55, Anderson 82	0
19	16	H	Ayr U	L	1-3	0-1	4	Sow 86	0
20	19	A	Alloa Ath	W	3-0	1-0	3	Ashcroft 2 42, 57, Anderson 80	0
21	27	H	Dunfermline Ath	W	3-2	1-2	3	Cummings 30, Mullen 54, Ashcroft 56	0
22	Apr 6	A	Ayr U	W	3-0	0-0	3	Anderson 68, Afolabi 74, McGowan 87	0
23	10	H	Greenock Morton	D	1-1	0-0	3	Ashcroft 88	0
24	13	A	Dunfermline Ath	D	0-0	0-0	3		0
25	20	A	Inverness CT	D	1-1	0-0	3	Ashcroft 86	0
26	24	H	Raith R	W	2-1	2-0	3	Cummings (pen) 13, Fontaine 34	0
27	30	A	Queen of the South	W	2-0	2-0	2	Cummings 2 17, 34	0

Final League Position: 2

Honours
League Champions: Division I 1961-62; First Division 1978-79, 1991-92, 1997-98; Championship 2013-14; Division II 1946-47, 1947-48.
Runners-up: Division I 1902-03, 1906-07, 1908-09, 1948-49; First Division 1980-81, 2007-08, 2009-10, 2011-12; Championship: 2020-21.
Promoted via play-offs: 2020-21 (to Premiership).
Scottish Cup Winners: 1910; *Runners-up:* 1925, 1952, 1964, 2003.
League Cup Winners: 1951-52, 1952-53, 1973-74; *Runners-up:* 1967-68, 1980-81, 1995-96.
League Challenge Cup Winners: 1990-91, 2009-10; *Runners-up:* 1994-95.

European: *European Cup:* 8 matches (1962-63 semi-finals). *Cup Winners' Cup:* 2 matches: (1964-65).
UEFA Cup: 22 matches: (*Fairs Cup:* 1967-68 semi-finals. *UEFA Cup:* 1971-72, 1973-74, 1974-75, 2003-04).

Club colours: Shirt: Navy blue with white sleeves. Shorts: White. Socks: Navy blue.

Goalscorers: *League (49):* Cummings 8 (2 pens), Sow 8, Adam 5 (2 pens), Ashcroft 5, Mullen 5, Anderson 4, Fontaine 4, Afolabi 3 (1 pen), McGhee 2, McGowan 2, Kerr 1, Marshall 1, McDaid 1.
William Hill Scottish Cup (3): Afolabi 1, Ashcroft 1, Sow 1.
Betfred Scottish League Cup (6): Mullen 2, Adam 1 (1 pen), Dorrans 1, Elliot 1, McGowan 1.
Scottish League Play-Offs (7): McGhee 3, Adam 1, Ashcroft 1, Mullen 1, Sow 1.

Hamilton J 13	McGhee J 15	Forster J 1 + 2	Ashcroft L 25	Kerr C 10 + 2	Dorrans G 3	Robertson F 2 + 4	Adam C 17 + 5	Marshall J 24	McGowan P 23 + 2	Sow O 11 + 10	Afolabi J 4 + 15	Mullen D 18 + 7	Anderson M 11 + 8	Ferrie C 3	Byrne S 18 + 4	McDaid D 13 + 7	Elliot C 22 + 3	Legzdins A 11	Jakubiak A 2 + 2	Fontaine L 17 + 1	Walcott M 2	Fisher S 3 + 1	Moore C 1	McMullan P 15	Cummings J 13 + 2	Cameron L — + 1	*Match No.*
1	2	3^{1}	4	5	6	7^{2}	8	9	10	11^{3}	12	13	14														1
	3		4	2	8		7^{1}	5	13		10	11^{2}		1	6	9	12										2
	3		4	2	8		7^{1}	5	13		11	10^{2}	14	1	6	9^{3}	12										3
	4			3		14	7	5	11	12^{3}	10^{2}	9	13	1	6^{1}	8	2										4
	4^{1}		3	2^{2}			6	5	11	10^{3}			8		7	13	9	1	12	14							5
1			3				7	5	9	13		10	8^{1}		6	12	2		11^{2}	4							6
1	5		3				7	8	9^{3}	12		10^{2}	14		6	13	2		11^{1}	4							7
1	5	14	3				7^{1}	8	9	11^{2}	12	10^{3}	13		6		2			4							8
1	6		4			14	8^{1}	5	9	10^{3}	13	11^{2}			7	12	2			3							9
1	7		4			14	8^{3}	5	9^{2}	11	13	12			6	10^{1}	2			3							10
1	6		4	14		13	8^{3}	5	9	10^{2}	12	11^{1}			7		2			3							11
1	6^{2}	14	4	12			8	5	9	10	13	11^{3}			7		2			3^{1}							12
1							8	5	9	10		13			7^{1}		2				3	4	6	11^{2}	12		13
1			4	2			8	5	9	10^{1}	13	12			7^{2}					3				6	11		14
1			3			6^{2}		5	8	10^{3}		13	12		7^{1}	14	2			4				9	11		15
1			3					5	8	12	14	10^{3}	7^{2}		13	9	2			4				6	11^{1}		16
1			3					5	7	12	13	10^{1}	8^{2}			9	2			4				6	11		17
			3				12	5	8	14		10^{3}	7			9	2	1			4^{1}	13		6	11^{2}		18
			3				8	5	9^{1}	12	14	10^{2}	7			13	2	1				4		6	11^{3}		19
			4				13	5	7^{2}		14	10^{1}	8		12	9	2	1				3		6	11^{3}		20
			3					5	8	10^{3}	14	12	7^{2}		13	9	2	1		4				6	11^{1}		21
			3				15	5	7^{1}		12	9	6^{3}		13	8	2	1		4				10^{2}	11^{4}	14	22
			3				14	5	7	13	12	9^{1}	6^{3}			8	2	1		4				10	11^{2}		23
	8		3	2				5^{2}		13	14	10			7	9^{1}	12	1		4				6	11^{3}		24
	6		3	5			12				11^{2}	9^{1}	14		7^{3}	10	2	1		4				8	13		25
	6		3	5			8		11			13	12		7		2	1	14	4^{1}				9^{2}	10^{3}		26
	6		3	5			8		11	13			4		7	12	2	1						9^{2}	10^{1}		27

DUNDEE UNITED

Year Formed: 1909 (1923). *Ground & Address:* Tannadice Park, Tannadice St, Dundee DD3 7JW. *Telephone:* 01382 833166. *Fax:* 01382 889398. *E-mail:* admin@dundeeunited.co.uk *Website:* dundeeunitedfc.co.uk
Ground Capacity: 14,223 (all seated). *Size of Pitch:* 100m × 66m.
Chairman: Mark Ogren. *Chief Executive:* Jamie Kirk.
Head Coach: Thomas Courts. *Assistant Head Coach:* Liam Fox.
Club Nicknames: 'The Terrors'; 'The Arabs'.
Previous Name: Dundee Hibernian (up to 1923).
Record Attendance: 28,000 v Barcelona, Fairs Cup, 16 November 1966.
Record Transfer Fee received: £4,000,000 for Duncan Ferguson from Rangers (July 1993).
Record Transfer Fee paid: £750,000 for Steven Pressley from Coventry C (July 1995).
Record Victory: 14-0 v Nithsdale Wanderers, Scottish Cup 1st rd, 17 January 1931.
Record Defeat: 1-12 v Motherwell, Division II, 23 January 1954.
Most Capped Player: Maurice Malpas, 55, Scotland.
Most League Appearances: 618: Maurice Malpas, 1980-2000.
Most Appearances in European Matches: 76: Dave Narey (record for Scottish player at the time).
Most League Goals in Season (Individual): 40: John Coyle, Division II, 1955-56.
Most Goals Overall (Individual): 199: Peter McKay, 1947-54.

DUNDEE UNITED – SPFL PREMIERSHIP 2020–21 LEAGUE RECORD

Match No.	Date	Venue	Opponents	Result		H/T Score	Lg Pos.	Goalscorers	Attendance
1	Aug 1	H	St Johnstone	D	1-1	1-0	4	Clark (pen) 6	0
2	8	A	Motherwell	W	1-0	0-0	3	Reynolds 52	0
3	11	H	Hibernian	L	0-1	0-0	5		0
4	15	A	Ross Co	W	2-1	1-1	4	Pawlett 40, Clark 79	0
5	22	H	Celtic	L	0-1	0-0	5		0
6	29	A	Kilmarnock	L	0-4	0-2	7		0
7	Sept 12	A	Rangers	L	0-4	0-2	8		0
8	19	H	St Mirren	W	2-1	1-0	6	Shankland 33, Sporle 52	0
9	26	A	Hamilton A	D	1-1	1-0	7	Shankland 4	0
10	Oct 2	H	Livingston	L	1-2	1-0	8	Clark 18	0
11	17	H	Aberdeen	D	0-0	0-0	6		0
12	24	A	St Johnstone	D	0-0	0-0	6		0
13	31	H	Ross Co	W	2-1	1-0	5	Clark 2 (1 pen) 19 (p), 51	0
14	Nov 6	A	St Mirren	D	0-0	0-0	5		0
15	21	H	Hamilton A	W	2-1	0-0	5	Clark 2 76, 80	0
16	Dec 5	A	Livingston	L	0-2	0-0	5		0
17	13	H	Rangers	L	1-2	1-2	5	Smith, L 33	0
18	19	A	Hibernian	D	1-1	0-1	5	Bolton 90	0
19	23	H	Kilmarnock	W	2-0	2-0	5	McNulty 25, Shankland 28	0
20	26	H	Motherwell	D	1-1	0-1	5	Clark 90	0
21	30	A	Celtic	L	0-3	0-2	5		0
22	Jan 2	A	Aberdeen	D	0-0	0-0	6		0
23	12	H	St Johnstone	D	2-2	1-2	6	Appere 9, Shankland 53	0
24	16	A	Hamilton A	D	0-0	0-0	6		0
25	27	H	St Mirren	L	1-5	0-3	6	Harkes 54	0
26	30	H	Hibernian	L	0-2	0-1	7		0
27	Feb 3	A	Motherwell	L	1-2	0-2	7	Edwards 80	0
28	6	A	Ross Co	W	2-0	0-0	7	Shankland 63, Edwards 76	0
29	13	H	Livingston	W	3-0	2-0	6	Sporle 1, Shankland 2 35, 83	0
30	21	A	Rangers	L	1-4	0-2	7	McNulty 86	0
31	27	A	Kilmarnock	D	1-1	1-0	7	Sporle 18	0
32	Mar 7	H	Celtic	D	0-0	0-0	8		0
33	20	H	Aberdeen	W	1-0	0-0	8	Sporle 61	0
34	Apr 10	A	Hamilton A	W	1-0	1-0	7	McNulty 6	0
35	21	A	Kilmarnock	L	0-3	0-3	7		0
36	May 1	H	Ross Co	L	0-2	0-2	9		0
37	12	H	Motherwell	D	2-2	2-0	9	Shankland 13, Meekison 34	0
38	16	A	St Mirren	D	0-0	0-0	9		0

Final League Position: 9

Honours: *League Champions:* Premier Division 1982-83; Championship 2019-20; Division II 1924-25, 1928-29.
Runners-up: Division II 1930-31, 1959-60; First Division 1995-96; Championship 2018-19.
Scottish Cup Winners: 1994, 2010; *Runners-up:* 1974, 1981, 1985, 1987, 1988, 1991, 2005, 2014.
League Cup Winners: 1979-80, 1980-81; *Runners-up:* 1981-82, 1984-85, 1997-98, 2007-08, 2014-15.
League Challenge Cup Winners, 2016-17; *Runners-up:* 1995-96.

European: *European Cup:* 8 matches (1983-84, semi-finals). *Cup Winners' Cup:* 10 matches (1974-75, 1988-89, 1994-95). *UEFA Cup:* 86 matches (*Fairs Cup:* 1966-67, 1969-70, 1970-71. *UEFA Cup:* 1975-76, 1977-78, 1978-79, 1979-80, 1980-81, 1981-82, 1982-83, 1984-85, 1985-86, 1986-87 runners-up, 1987-88, 1989-90, 1990-91, 1993-94, 1997-98, 2005-06). *Europa League:* 6 matches (2010-2011, 2011-12, 2012-13).

Club colours: Shirt: Tangerine with black trim. Shorts: Black. Socks: Black with tangerine tops.

Goalscorers: *League (32):* Clark 8 (2 pens), Shankland 8, Sporle 4, McNulty 3, Edwards 2, Appere 1, Bolton 1, Harkes 1, Meekison 1, Pawlett 1, Reynolds 1, Smith L 1.
William Hill Scottish Cup (6): McNulty 2, Clark 1, Edwards 1, Pawlett 1, Shankland 1.
Betfred Scottish League Cup (7): Clark 2, Smith C 2, Butcher 1, Edwards 1, Harkes 1.

Siegrist B 32	Neilson L 7 + 2	Connolly M 23 + 2	Reynolds M 33 + 1	Smith L 28 + 2	Harkes I 30 + 5	Butcher C 27 + 1	Pawlett P 15 + 11	Robson J 34 + 2	Clark N 24 + 7	Shankland L 30 + 2	Bolton L 18 + 6	Smith C — + 4	Chalmers L 9 + 6	Appere L 11 + 11	Sporle A 15 + 9	Powers D 6 + 8	Edwards R 24	Freeman K 1 + 2	McMullan P 3 + 5	Glass D — + 1	Mehmet D 4	McNulty M 17 + 8	Fuchs J 19 + 1	Watson D — + 1	Fotheringham K — + 1	Smith K 3 + 2	Hoti F 1 + 3	Meekison A 2 + 1	Doohan R 2	Match No.
1	2³	3	4	5	6	7	8	9²	10¹	11	12	13	14																	1
1		3	4	2	8³	6	10⁴	5	15		7¹	12	9²	11	13	14														2
1	13	3	4		6	7	8	9¹	11³		5²	15	14	10	12		2⁴													3
1	12	3	4		7	8⁴	9		13		6³	14	10	11²	5	15		2¹												4
1	2⁴	3	4		8	6	9	5	11²		7¹		10³	14	13			12	15											5
1	2¹	3	4		8	6	9²	5	11		7		10	12					13											6
1	2³		4		11	7	8	9	10²	13	5⁴		12		15	6¹	3	14												7
1			4		8	7	12	5	10²	11	2		6¹		9		3			13										8
1		12	4		8	7³	13	5	10	11	2		6²		9¹	14	3													9
		4			8	7	13	5	10	11	2		6¹	12	9²		3				1									10
1		2	4⁴	13	8	7²	6¹	9	10³	11	5		15			14	3					12								11
1		2	4	12	7			8	9	11	5					6	3					10¹								12
1			4	2	8²	7	9³	5	10¹	11	6			14	12		3						13							13
1			4	2	7³	6	8²	9	11	10	5¹					13	3		14			12								14
1		3	5⁴	2	14	9		15	10	12	13				6¹		4		8²			11	7³							15
1		2	4	5	8					11				12	9	7¹	3					10	6							16
1		3	5	2	8			6		11					10¹		4					7	9	12						17
1		2	4	5		6	14	9	7¹	11	13						3²		12			10	8³							18
1		3	4	2		7²	12	5	13	11	9¹				14				6			10³	8							19
1		3	4	2		7²	12	5³	14	11	9				13				6¹			10	8							20
1		3	5	2⁴	8		9²	6¹	7	11³	15				14	13	4		12			10								21
1	2	3	4	5	7		8¹	9	6	11				10		12														22
1	2¹	3	4	5	8			9	6	10	12			11²		7						13								23
1	2	3	4	5	8			9	6	11				10¹		7						12								24
		3	4	2	9			5	8	11	7²			13		6¹					1	10			12					25
1		3	4	2	13	7	12	5	10	11	9¹											6	8²							26
1				5	8	3	12	4	6¹	11					9		2					10	7							27
1			4	2	13	7³	6	5		10	12				9²	14	3					11	8¹							28
1			4	2	12	7	9■	5		11				8¹	10²		3					13	6							29
1			4	2	8²	6		5	9	10				11¹			3					12	7			13				30
1		13	4	2	6	8		5	14	11				12³	9²		3					10	7¹							31
1			4	2	8¹	6	12	5	9³	11			14	13			3					10²	7							32
1			4	2	8	7²		5	13	10				12	11¹		3					9	6							33
1			4	2	8²	7	13	5	12	10⁴				15	9¹		3					11	6³				14			34
		4		2	6			5			9			10	11						1		7			3	8¹	12		35
			3⁴	2	6⁵	7	12	5	11	10¹			14	13			4				1	9²	8³			15	16			36
		4		2	12	13	6²	14		10			9¹	11³	5							15	7			3		8⁴	1	37
			15	2	8³			5■		10			9⁴	11	14		4					13	7			3¹	12	6²	1	38

DUNFERMLINE ATHLETIC

Year Formed: 1885. *Ground & Address:* East End Park, Halbeath Road, Dunfermline KY12 7RB.
Telephone: 01383 724295. *Fax:* 01383 745 959. *E-mail:* enquiries@dafc.co.uk
Website: dafc.co.uk
Ground Capacity: 11,380 (all seated). *Size of Pitch:* 105m × 65m.
Chairman: Ross McArthur. *Vice-Chairman:* Billy Braisby.
Manager: Peter Grant. *First Team Coach:* Greg Shields.
Club Nickname: 'The Pars'.
Record Attendance: 27,816 v Celtic, Division I, 30 April 1968.
Record Transfer Fee received: £650,000 for Jackie McNamara to Celtic (October 1995).
Record Transfer Fee paid: £540,000 for Istvan Kozma from Bordeaux (September 1989).
Record Victory: 11-2 v Stenhousemuir, Division II, 27 September 1930.
Record Defeat: 1-13 v St. Bernard's, Scottish Cup 1st rd, 15 September 1883.
Most Capped Player: Colin Miller 16 (61), Canada.
Most League Appearances: 497: Norrie McCathie, 1981-96.
Most League Goals in Season (Individual): 53: Bobby Skinner, Division II, 1925-26.
Most Goals Overall (Individual): 212: Charles Dickson, 1954-64.

DUNFERMLINE ATHLETIC – SPFL CHAMPIONSHIP 2020–21 LEAGUE RECORD

Match No.	Date	Venue	Opponents	Result	H/T Score	Lg Pos.	Goalscorers	Attendance
1	Oct 17	H	Inverness CT	W 3-1	1-1	3	Murray, E 23, Dow 78, McManus 84	0
2	24	A	Alloa Ath	W 4-1	1-1	2	Dow 7, O'Hara 3 (1 pen) 67, 77, 90 (p)	0
3	31	H	Queen of the South	W 3-2	2-0	1	Murray, E 21, McManus (pen) 43, Watson 60	0
4	Nov 7	A	Ayr U	D 0-0	0-0	2		0
5	20	H	Hearts	W 2-1	0-0	1	Thomas 49, Murray, E 54	0
6	Dec 5	A	Raith R	D 2-2	0-1	2	Murray, F 73, McManus 74	0
7	12	H	Greenock Morton	L 1-2	0-1	2	McManus (pen) 74	0
8	19	A	Dundee	D 3-3	0-1	2	Watson 78, McManus 2 (1 pen) 82 (p), 90	0
9	26	H	Arbroath	W 1-0	0-0	2	O'Hara 90	0
10	29	A	Inverness CT	D 1-1	1-0	2	Turner 23	0
11	Jan 15	A	Greenock Morton	D 0-0	0-0	2		0
12	23	H	Ayr U	D 0-0	0-0	2		0
13	30	A	Hearts	L 0-1	0-0	3		0
14	Feb 3	H	Raith R	W 4-1	1-0	2	McManus 44, Comrie 51, Murray, F 2 66, 87	0
15	6	A	Arbroath	L 0-2	0-2	3		0
16	20	H	Alloa Ath	W 2-1	1-1	2	Wighton 2 14, 58	0
17	27	A	Queen of the South	L 0-1	0-0	3		0
18	Mar 13	H	Greenock Morton	W 1-0	1-0	2	Wighton 44	0
19	20	H	Inverness CT	L 0-1	0-0	3		0
20	27	A	Dundee	L 2-3	2-1	4	O'Hara 3, Wighton 6	0
21	30	A	Raith R	L 1-5	1-3	5	O'Hara 22	0
22	Apr 3	H	Hearts	D 0-0	0-0	4		0
23	10	A	Ayr U	D 1-1	1-1	5	McManus 12	0
24	13	H	Dundee	D 0-0	0-0	5		0
25	17	H	Queen of the South	W 3-1	1-0	4	O'Hara 10, Murray, F 82, Henderson 90	0
26	24	H	Arbroath	W 4-3	2-2	4	McManus (pen) 10, O'Hara 15, Wighton 2 57, 75	0
27	30	A	Alloa Ath	L 0-1	0-0	4		0

Final League Position: 4

Honours
League Champions: First Division 1988-89, 1995-96, 2010-11; Division II 1925-26; Second Division 1985-86; League One 2015-16.
Runners-up: First Division 1986-87, 1993-94, 1994-95, 1999-2000; Division II 1912-13, 1933-34, 1954-55, 1957-58, 1972-73; Second Division 1978-79; League One 2013-14.
Scottish Cup Winners: 1961, 1968; *Runners-up:* 1965, 2004, 2007.
League Cup Runners-up: 1949-50, 1991-92, 2005-06.
League Challenge Cup Runners-up: 2007-08.

European: *Cup Winners' Cup:* 14 matches (1961-62, 1968-69 semi-finals). *UEFA Cup:* 32 matches (*Fairs Cup:* 1962-63, 1964-65, 1965-66, 1966-67, 1969-70. *UEFA Cup:* 2004-05, 2007-08).

Club colours: Shirt: Black and white stripes. Shorts: Black. Socks: Black with white tops.

Goalscorers: *League (38):* McManus 9 (4 pens), O'Hara 8 (1 pen), Wighton 6, Murray F 4, Murray E 3, Dow 2, Watson 2, Comrie 1, Henderson 1, Thomas 1, Turner 1.
William Hill Scottish Cup (0).
Betfred Scottish League Cup (13): Murray E 4, O'Hara 3 (3 pens), Murray F 2, Dow 1, McManus 1, Watson 1, Wilson 1.
Scottish League Play-Offs (0).

Fon Williams O 26	Comrie A 20 + 2	Watson P 21 + 2	Murray E 24	Edwards J 25	Wilson I 15 + 5	Dow R 11 + 2	Turner K 10 + 3	Thomas D 20 + 1	McManus D 22 + 5	O'Hara K 13 + 11	Murray F 12 + 11	McInroy K 11 + 5	Whittaker S 15 + 3	Mayo L 17 + 5	McCann L 3 + 8	Banks S 6 + 5	Todd M — + 1	Wighton C 9 + 1	MacDonald K 4 + 1	Gaspuitis V 5 + 2	Henderson E 6 + 2	Gill C 1	Allan P 1	McGill G — + 1	Match No.
1	2	3	4	5	6	7	8^1	9	10	11^2	12	13													1
1	2	3^3	4	5	8^1	11^2	14	9	10	13	7		6	12											2
1	2^1	3	4	5	12		8	7	10	11^2	13	9	6												3
1		4	3	5	13	12	9^3	7	11^1	14	8^2	10	6	2											4
1		3	4	5		7	8	10^1	11^2	12	13	9	6	2											5
1	12	3	4	5	6^3	7	8	10	11	14	13	9^1		2^2											6
1	2	3	4	5		6	7	9	11	10^2	12	8^1			13										7
1		3	4	5	12	7	9	10^2	11	13		8^3	6^1	2	14										8
1	13	3	4	5	9^1	7	8	10	11	14		12	6^3	2^2											9
1	2	3	4	5	8	12	7	14	13	10^2		9^3		6	11^1										10
1	2	3	4	5	8^2	6	12	9^1	11	14	13		7		10^3										11
1	2	3	4	5	7	8	9^2	10^1	11		14		6^3	13	12										12
1	2	3	4	5	8	7			11^1	13	10^3		6^2	9	14	12									13
1	2	3	4^1	5	8	6^2			11	12	9	13	14	7		10^3									14
1	2^2	3	4	5	8^3				11	10	9	6		7^1	12	13	14								15
1	2^1	3	4	5	7				11^3	14	10		13	6		9^2		8	12						16
1		3		5	12			10^2	11^3	13	4	9	7^1	6		14		8	2						17
1	2	3	4		9		12	10^1	13		7		6			8^2		11^3	5	14					18
1	5	3^1	4		7^2			10	13		9		6	12		8^3		11	2	14					19
1	2	3^2	4	5	7			10^3	14	8^1	9			6		13		11			12				20
1	2		4	5	13				14	10	9	8^3		3	12	6^2		11			7^1				21
1	2		4	5	8			9	11^2	10^1	12			7	14	6^3				3	13				22
1	2	12	4^3	5				8^1	11	10	9^2		14	6				13		3	7				23
1	2		4	5				10	9	8^2	13		6^1	12	14			11^3		3	7				24
1	2			5				10	8^1	11	12	13	6	3				7^2		4	9				25
1	2	13		5				7	8^3	11	14	12	6	4				10		3^2	9^1				26
		3	4^2	5					8^3	11		9		12	10	13			2		6^1	1	7	14	27

EAST FIFE

Year Formed: 1903. *Ground & Address:* Locality Hub Bayview Stadium, Harbour View, Methil, Fife KY8 3RW. *Telephone:* 01333 426323. *Fax:* 01333 426376. *E-mail:* office@eastfifefc.info. *Website:* eastfifefc.info
Ground Capacity: 1,992. *Size of Pitch:* 105m × 65m.
Chairman: Jim Stevenson. *Vice-Chairman:* David Marshall.
Manager: Darren Young. *Assistant Manager:* Tony McMinn.
Club Nickname: 'The Fifers'.
Previous Ground: Bayview Park.
Record Attendance: 22,515 v Raith Rovers, Division I, 2 January 1950 (Bayview Park); 4,700 v Rangers, League One, 26 October 2013 (Bayview Stadium).
Record Transfer Fee received: £150,000 for Paul Hunter from Hull C (March 1990).
Record Transfer Fee paid: £70,000 for John Sludden from Kilmarnock (July 1991).
Record Victory: 13-2 v Edinburgh C, Division II, 11 December 1937.
Record Defeat: 0-9 v Hearts, Division I, 5 October 1957.
Most Capped Player: George Aitken, 5 (8), Scotland.
Most League Appearances: 517: David Clarke, 1968-86.
Most League Goals in Season (Individual): 41: Jock Wood, Division II; 1926-27 and Henry Morris, Division II, 1947-48.
Most Goals Overall (Individual): 225: Phil Weir, 1922-35.

EAST FIFE – SPFL LEAGUE ONE 2020–21 LEAGUE RECORD

Match No.	Date	Venue	Opponents	Result	H/T Score	Lg Pos.	Goalscorers	Attendance
1	Oct 17	A	Cove R	L 1-3	0-1	8	Hamilton 62	0
2	24	H	Montrose	D 2-2	2-1	8	Hamilton 25, Smith 29	0
3	31	A	Falkirk	L 0-2	0-1	10		0
4	Nov 7	H	Dumbarton	W 2-1	1-0	7	Hamilton 17, Wallace 69	0
5	21	A	Partick Thistle	L 0-2	0-1	9		0
6	Dec 5	H	Airdrieonians	W 2-0	1-0	7	Hamilton 2 30, 56	0
7	12	A	Peterhead	L 1-2	1-1	8	Denholm 34	0
8	19	H	Forfar Ath	W 2-0	1-0	8	Hamilton 28, Denholm 59	0
9	Jan 2	H	Falkirk	W 2-1	1-0	6	Smith 20, Hamilton 69	0
10	Mar 20	A	Clyde	W 3-1	1-0	6	Austin 41, Denholm 56, Wallace 68	0
11	27	H	Cove R	D 0-0	0-0	6		0
12	30	A	Montrose	L 0-3	0-2	6		0
13	Apr 1	H	Clyde	W 1-0	1-0	5	Denholm 4	0
14	6	H	Partick Thistle	D 2-2	2-0	6	Wallace (pen) 14, Smith 17	0
15	8	A	Dumbarton	L 1-2	0-1	6	Dunlop 90	0
16	10	A	Forfar Ath	W 2-1	1-0	5	Wallace 25, Smith 61	0
17	17	H	Peterhead	W 2-1	0-1	4	Denholm 71, Agnew 78	0
18	20	A	Airdrieonians	L 0-2	0-0	6		0
19	24	H	Dumbarton	W 2-1	1-0	6	Dunsmore 28, Steele 67	0
20	29	H	Peterhead	L 1-3	1-1	6	Dunsmore 18	0
21	May 4	A	Forfar Ath	W 3-2	1-1	6	Davidson 14, Murdoch 50, Brown 90	0
22	6	A	Clyde	L 1-2	0-1	6	Agnew (pen) 49	0

Final League Position: 6

Honours
League Champions: Division II 1947-48; Third Division 2007-08; League Two 2015-16.
Runners-up: Division II 1929-30, 1970-71; Second Division 1983-84, 1995-96; Third Division 2002-03.
Scottish Cup Winners: 1938; *Runners-up:* 1927, 1950.
League Cup Winners: 1947-48, 1949-50, 1953-54.

Club colours: Shirt: Gold with black checks. Shorts: Black. Socks: Black.

Goalscorers: *League (30):* Hamilton 7, Denholm 5, Smith 4, Wallace 4 (1 pen), Agnew 2 (1 pen), Dunsmore 2, Austin 1, Brown 1, Davidson 1, Dunlop 1, Murdoch 1, Steele 1.
William Hill Scottish Cup (6): Smith 3, Agnew 2 (1 pen), Watson 1.
Betfred Scottish League Cup (5): Hamilton 2, Wallace 2, Newton 1.

Long B 15	Murdoch S 16+1	Dunlop R 13+3	Higgins C 18	Slattery P 15+1	Dunsmore A 11+6	Newton L 7+4	Agnew S 18	Denholm D 13+5	Wallace R 13+2	Hamilton J 9	Watson C 15+5	Collins T —+5	Smith K 9+8	Watt L 11+7	Davidson R 18+1	Swanson D 9+6	Mackenzie J —+2	Hart J 7	Austin N 3	Mckinnon C 5+4	Brown S 4+6	Fenton M 4+2	Spence G 5+4	Steele A 4+1	Dow C —+1	Healy J —+2	*Match No.*
1	2	3^{3}	4	5	6■	7^{2}	8	9■	10^{4}	11^{1}	12	13	14	15													1
1	2		4	5			8			11	3	12	10^{2}	6	7	9^{1}	13										2
1	2	3	4	5			8		10	11	13	12	9^{2}	6^{1}	7												3
	2	3	4	5	6^{1}		8	12	10	11	13		9^{2}		7			1									4
	2	3	4	5	6^{4}	13	8^{3}	9^{1}		11		15	10^{2}	12	7	14		1									5
1	2		4	5	6^{1}	9^{3}	8	12	11^{2}	10	3		14	13	7												6
1	2		4	5^{3}		9^{1}	8	6^{2}	11	10	3	14	13		7	12											7
1	2		4	5		13	8^{1}	6^{2}	10	11	3		12	9	7												8
1	2	12	4	5			8	6^{1}		11	3		10	9	7												9
1	2		4	8	13		7^{3}	5^{5}	9^{1}		3		12	11^{4}	6	14			10^{2}	15	16						10
1	2		4	5	15	14	8^{4}	6^{1}	11		3		12	9^{2}	7	13			10^{3}								11
1	2	14	4	5^{2}	6^{4}		8		10		3		9^{1}		7	12			11^{3}		15	13					12
		3	4^{3}	16	2	8		6^{1}	14		12			9^{4}	13	11^{5}		1		7	10^{2}	5	15				13
1	2	16	4	5	12	14		6^{4}	10^{1}		3^{2}		11^{5}	15	9	7^{3}				8			13				14
		3	4		2	9^{2}	8	14	12		15		13	6^{4}		16		1		7	10^{1}	5^{3}	11^{5}				15
1	2	3	5		13		8	7^{3}	10		4		11^{2}	12	6	9^{1}					14						16
1	2	3	5		14		8	6^{2}	10		4■		11^{1}		7	9^{3}				13			12				17
1		3	4^{1}	5^{2}	2		6	9	10^{3}					13		8				7	11		12	14			18
		3		5^{3}	6	7^{2}					4			9	8	11^{1}		1		14	13	12	10	2			19
	12	3			8^{1}		10^{2}	14			4		15	16	6	9^{3}		1		7	13	5	11^{5}	2^{4}			20
1	2	3			14	8^{4}		7^{3}			5			10^{1}	6	9					13		11^{2}	4	12	15	21
		3			6		7	12			4			9	8		15	1		14	11^{2}	5^{4}	10^{1}	2^{3}		13	22

EDINBURGH CITY

Year formed: 1928 (disbanded 1955, reformed from Postal United in 1986).
Ground & Address: Meadowbank Stadium, Edinburgh EH7 6AE. *Telephone:* 0845 463 1932.
E-mail: admin@edinburghcityfc.com *Website:* edinburghcityfc.com
Ground Capacity: 500 (seated 500). *Size of Pitch:* 96m × 66m
Chairman: Jim Brown. *Sporting Director:* James McDonaugh.
Manager: Gary Naysmith.
Previous name: Postal United.
Club Nickname: 'The Citizens'.
Previous Grounds: City Park 1928-55; Fernieside 1986-95; Meadowbank Stadium 1996-2017; Ainslie Park 2018-2020.
Record victory: 5-0 v King's Park, Division II (1935-36); 6-1 and 7-2 v Brechin City, Division II (1937-38).
Record defeat: 1-11 v Rangers, Scottish Cup, 19 January 1929.
Most League Appearances: 129: Marc Laird, 2016-21.
Most League Goals in Season (Individual): 30: Blair Henderson, League Two, 2018-19.
Most Goals Overall (Individual): 56: Blair Henderson, 2018-21.

EDINBURGH CITY – SPFL LEAGUE TWO 2020–21 LEAGUE RECORD

Match No.	*Date*	*Venue*	*Opponents*	*Result*		*H/T Score*	*Lg Pos.*	*Goalscorers*	*Attendance*
1	Oct 17	A	Brechin C	W	5-1	1-0	1	Balatoni [39], Brown [47], Henderson, B (pen) [55], Campbell [78], Jardine [82]	0
2	24	H	Cowdenbeath	L	0-1	0-0	5		0
3	31	H	Elgin C	W	1-0	1-0	3	McGill [22]	0
4	Nov 7	A	Stenhousemuir	L	0-2	0-0	5		0
5	21	H	Stranraer	L	0-1	0-1	7		0
6	28	A	Annan Ath	W	4-0	2-0	5	Henderson, L [32], Campbell [36], Henderson, B 2 [56, 62]	0
7	Dec 5	H	Albion R	W	5-2	4-1	3	Henderson, L 3 [7, 10, 16], Thomson 2 [18, 62]	0
8	12	A	Queen's Park	D	3-3	1-0	4	Campbell 2 [15, 57], McGill [85]	0
9	19	H	Stirling Alb	L	2-3	0-3	5	McIntyre [67], Brown [77]	0
10	Mar 20	A	Elgin C	W	2-1	2-1	5	Campbell [3], McIntyre [12]	0
11	23	A	Albion R	W	2-1	1-0	4	See 2 [12, 74]	0
12	27	H	Stenhousemuir	W	3-1	1-0	2	De Vita 2 [16, 62], Handling [90]	0
13	30	A	Cowdenbeath	W	3-1	2-1	2	Henderson, B 2 [15, 36], Hamilton [60]	0
14	Apr 6	H	Annan Ath	D	1-1	0-0	3	See [70]	0
15	10	A	Stranraer	W	1-0	1-0	2	Brown [6]	0
16	13	H	Brechin C	W	2-1	1-1	2	Handling [2], De Vita [71]	0
17	17	H	Queen's Park	L	2-3	0-1	2	Henderson, L [54], Campbell [65]	0
18	20	A	Stirling Alb	W	1-0	1-0	2	See [35]	0
19	24	H	Stirling Alb	L	0-1	0-1	2		0
20	29	A	Queen's Park	L	0-2	0-1	2		0
21	May 1	H	Elgin C	W	2-0	2-0	2	Campbell [6], Brown [38]	0
22	4	A	Stranraer	L	1-2	1-2	2	Robertson (og) [27]	0

Final League Position: 2

Honours
League Champions: Scottish Lowland League Champions: 2014-15, 2015-16. *Runners-up:* League Two 2019-20, 2020-21.
Promoted via play-offs: 2015-16 (to League Two).
League Challenge Cup: Semi-finals 2018-19.

Club colours: Shirt: White. Shorts: Black. Socks: White.

Goalscorers: *League (40):* Campbell 7, Henderson B 5 (1 pen), Henderson L 5, Brown 4, See 4, De Vita 3, Handling 2, McGill 2, McIntyre 2, Thomson 2, Balatoni 1, Hamilton 1, Jardine 1, own goal 1.
William Hill Scottish Cup (6): See 2, Campbell 1, Hamilton 1, McIntyre 1, own goal 1.
Betfred Scottish League Cup (5): Henderson B 3, De Vita 1, Handling 1 (1 pen).
Scottish League Play-Offs (5): Campbell 2, Handling 1, McIntyre 1, See 1.

Antell C 21	Thomson C 19	Balatoni C 13	Henderson L 14	Black A 16 + 3	Brown L 17 + 5	Campbell J 19 + 1	Newman S 7 + 5	Handling D 12 + 4	Henderson B 8 + 5	De Vita R 14 + 5	See O 13 + 9	Jardine D 9 + 10	McGill G 4 + 4	Cunningham M — + 3	Laird M 11 + 5	Harris A 3 + 4	Butterworth Z — + 1	Hamilton L 13	Crane C 10 + 2	McIntyre R 11 + 4	Smith D — + 2	Denham S 3 + 1	Tapping J 3	Dishington J 1 + 5	Goodfellow R 1	Jarron J — + 1	*Match No.*
1	2	3	4	5	6	7^3	8	9^1	10^4	11^2	12	13	14	15													1
1	2	3	4	7^1	6^4	8	5	9^3	10	11^2	12	15	14		13												2
1	2	3	4		13	8	5	6		11^1	9		10^2		7	12											3
1	2	3	4		14	8	5	6	12	11^3	9^1		10^2	13	7^4		15										4
1	2	4	5	7^4	8^1	6	9^3	10^2	11	13	15	14	12					3									5
1	2	3	4	6^2	9^3	8	15		11^5	14	13	16	10^4		7^1			5	12								6
1	2	4	5	7	8^1	9			10^3	6^5	13	16	11^2	15		14		3^4	12								7
1		3	4	7^2	9^3	10	15		13		11^5	16	14		8	6^4		2	5^1	12							8
1	2	3	5	7^1	6	9			10	14	12	15			8^2	11^3		4^4		13							9
1	2		4	12	7^1	10^3			13	6^2	11^4				8	14		3	5	9	15						10
1	2		4	7	8^2			10^1		12	11	14				6^3		3	9	5	13						11
1	2		4	6	7^2			15	14	9^3	11^4	10				13		3^1	8	5		12					12
1	2		4	7	8^1	10	14		6^2	9^3	12	11			13			3		5							13
1	2			14	12	9		10^3		8^2	11	6			7^1			3		5			4	13			14
1	2			8	7^1	10^3		14		13	11	6^2			12			4	9	5			3				15
1	2			6	8^5	9	16	10^2		11^3	13	14			7^4			3	5	12			4^1	15			16
1	2		4^1	6^2	12	9		7^3			11	8			13				5	10		3		14			17
1		3		14	7^2	13	12	8^1		11	10	6			4				2^3	5		9					18
1	2	3		7	12	10	8	9		5^2	11	6^1								4				13			19
1	2	3			8	11		12		9^1	10^2	7			6				5	4				13			20
1	2			6	8	10		9^2	13		11^1	7			12			3	5	4							21
		3		9	8	11	4^5	14	10^4	5^2	12	15			6^3					13		2		7^1	1	16	22

ELGIN CITY

Year Formed: 1893. *Ground and Address:* Borough Briggs, Borough Briggs Road, Elgin IV30 1AP.
Telephone: 01343 551114. *Fax:* 01343 547921. *E-mail:* elgincityfc@btconnect.com *Website:* elgincity.net
Ground Capacity: 3,927 (seated: 478). *Size of pitch:* 102m × 68m.
Chairman: Graham Tatters.
Manager: Gavin Price. *Assistant Manager:* Keith Gibson.
Previous name: Elgin City United 1900-03.
Club Nicknames: 'City'; 'The Black & Whites'.
Previous Grounds: Association Park 1893-95; Milnfield Park 1895-1909; Station Park 1909-19; Cooper Park 1919-21.
Record Attendance: 12,608 v Arbroath, Scottish Cup, 17 February 1968.
Record Transfer Fee received: £32,000 for Michael Teasdale to Dundee (January 1994).
Record Transfer Fee paid: £10,000 for Russell McBride from Fraserburgh (July 2001).
Record Victory: 18-1 v Brora Rangers, North of Scotland Cup, 6 February 1960.
Record Defeat: 1-14 v Hearts, Scottish Cup, 4 February 1939.
Most League Appearances: 306: Mark Nicholson, 2007-17.
Most League Goals in Season (Individual): 21: Craig Gunn, 2015-16.
Most Goals Overall (Individual): 128: Craig Gunn, 2009-17.

ELGIN CITY – SPFL LEAGUE TWO 2020–21 LEAGUE RECORD

Match No.	*Date*	*Venue*	*Opponents*	*Result*		*H/T Score*	*Lg Pos.*	*Goalscorers*	*Attendance*
1	Oct 17	A	Stranraer	W	4-1	1-0	2	Dingwall, R 2 (1 pen) [9, 81 (p)], Hester [47], O'Keefe [65]	0
2	24	H	Brechin C	W	3-0	1-0	1	Cameron [17], Hester 2 [60, 65]	0
3	31	A	Edinburgh C	L	0-1	0-1	2		0
4	Nov 7	H	Queen's Park	L	0-1	0-1	4		0
5	21	A	Stirling Alb	W	2-1	1-0	2	Bronsky [39], Sopel [51]	0
6	28	H	Cowdenbeath	W	5-2	2-0	2	Sopel [26], Hester 3 [38, 63, 77], O'Keefe [90]	0
7	Dec 5	H	Annan Ath	W	1-0	0-0	2	Dingwall, R [57]	0
8	12	A	Albion R	L	1-3	1-0	2	Cooper [28]	0
9	19	H	Stenhousemuir	W	2-0	2-0	2	Hester [39], Cameron [44]	0
10	Mar 20	H	Edinburgh C	L	1-2	1-2	3	Peters [40]	0
11	27	H	Stirling Alb	D	1-1	0-0	5	McHardy [72]	0
12	30	A	Brechin C	W	2-1	0-1	4	Hester (pen) [47], McHardy [83]	0
13	Apr 3	A	Annan Ath	W	3-0	2-0	3	Dingwall, T [37], Cameron [41], Osadolor [90]	0
14	6	H	Stranraer	W	2-1	0-0	2	Dingwall, R [55], Hester [58]	0
15	10	A	Cowdenbeath	L	0-1	0-1	4		0
16	13	A	Stenhousemuir	L	0-2	0-0	4		0
17	17	H	Albion R	L	2-5	1-2	5	Hester [15], O'Keefe [90]	0
18	20	A	Queen's Park	D	0-0	0-0	5		0
19	27	A	Stranraer	W	4-1	4-0	5	Sopel [3], Hester 2 [7, 19], Cameron [10]	0
20	29	H	Stirling Alb	W	3-1	2-0	3	Sopel [16], Dingwall, R [17], Cameron [64]	0
21	May 1	A	Edinburgh C	L	0-2	0-2	4		0
22	4	H	Queen's Park	W	3-2	0-0	3	Hester 2 [49, 76], Cameron [51]	0

Final League Position: 3

Honours
League Runners-up: League Two 2015-16.
Scottish Cup: Quarter-finals 1968.
Highland League Champions: winners 15 times.

Club colours: Shirt: Black and white stripes. Shorts: Black. Socks: Black.

Goalscorers: *League (39):* Hester 14 (1 pen), Cameron 6, Dingwall R 5 (1 pen), Sopel 4, O'Keefe 3, McHardy 2, Bronsky 1, Cooper 1, Dingwall T 1, Osadolor 1, Peters 1.
William Hill Scottish Cup (4): Hester 3, Dingwall R 1.
Betfred Scottish League Cup (5): Cameron 1, Dingwall R 1 (1 pen), Hester 1, O'Keefe 1, Peters 1.
Scottish League Play-Offs (2): McHardy 2.

McHale T 22	Cooper M 20	Bronsky S 19 + 1	Mailer A 6 + 11	Spark E 22	Dingwall R 22	McDonald A 9	Cameron B 22	Osadolor S 5 + 13	Hester K 20 + 1	O'Keefe C 10 + 10	MacEwan R 11 + 6	Sopel A 13 + 8	Wilson D 4 + 2	Peters J 8 + 12	McHardy D 12 + 6	MacBeath J 1 + 6	Dingwall T 4 + 6	MacPhee A 7 + 2	Brown C 5 + 5	Miller M — + 1	*Match No.*
1	2	3	4^{4}	5	6	7	8	9^{2}	10^{3}	11^{1}	12	13	14	15							1
1	2	3		5^{2}	6	4	7	11^{3}	10	9^{1}	8^{4}	12		14	13	15					2
1	2	3	15	5^{2}	6	4^{4}	7	10^{1}	11	9	8^{3}	12		13	14						3
1	2	3		5	6	4	9	12	11■	8^{1}	7^{3}	10^{2}		13		14					4
1	2	4	13	5	6	3	7	12			8^{3}	9^{2}		10^{1}	14	11					5
1	2	3	13	5	6	4	9	12	11^{2}	15	7^{3}	10^{4}		8^{1}		14					6
1	2	3^{1}	14	5	6^{4}	4	7	15	10	12	8^{3}	9		11^{2}	13						7
1	2	3	13	5	6^{3}	4^{1}	7	16	10	15	8^{2}	9^{5}		11^{4}	14	12					8
1	2	3	13	5	6	4	7		10^{1}	9^{4}	8^{2}	12		11^{3}		15	14				9
1	2	3^{1}		4	8^{3}		7	13	10	12	16	9^{4}		11^{5}	14		6^{2}	5	15		10
1	2	3		5	6		7	11^{1}	12	13	8	9^{2}		10^{3}	4				14		11
1	2	3	16	5	6^{3}		8	12	10^{4}	9^{1}	7^{2}			15	4		13	14	11^{5}		12
1	2	4	15	5	6^{1}		7	12	11^{3}	9^{2}		14		13	3		10^{4}	8			13
1	2	3	15	5	6^{2}		7	12	10	11^{1}		14	13		4^{3}		9^{4}	8			14
1	2	3	15	5^{2}	6^{3}		7	11^{4}	10	9		13		12	4	14		8^{1}			15
1	2	4		5	6		7	14	11	9^{3}		13		12	3^{1}		10^{2}	8^{4}	15		16
1		3	15	2^{5}	6^{3}		7	14	10	12	8^{4}	9^{1}		11^{2}	4		13	5	16		17
1		3	7	5	6^{1}		9		11^{3}	12	13	10^{2}	2	14	4		15		8^{4}		18
1	3		7	5	6^{1}		9^{2}	15	11^{4}		16	10^{5}	2	14	4		13		8^{3}	12	19
1	3	12	6	5	8		9^{4}	14	11	15	13	10^{3}	2		4^{1}				7^{2}		20
1	3		5^{3}	9	6^{4}		10		11	13		8^{1}	2	15	4		14	12	7^{2}		21
1	2	4	5	6	7^{3}		8		11^{1}	14	13	10^{2}		15	3			9^{4}	12		22

FALKIRK

Year Formed: 1876. *Ground & Address:* The Falkirk Stadium, 4 Stadium Way, Falkirk FK2 9EE. *Telephone:* 01324 624121. *Fax:* 01324 612418. *Email:* post@falkirkfc.co.uk *Website:* falkirkfc.co.uk
Ground Capacity: 8,750 (all seated). *Size of Pitch:* 105m × 68m.
Chairman: Gary Deans.
Head Coach: Paul Sheerin.
Club Nickname: 'The Bairns'.
Previous Grounds: Randyford 1876-81; Blinkbonny Grounds 1881-83; Brockville Park 1883-2003.
Record Attendance: 23,100 v Celtic, Scottish Cup 3rd rd, 21 February 1953.
Record Transfer Fee received: £945,000 for Conor McGrandles to Norwich C (August 2014).
Record Transfer Fee paid: £225,000 to Chelsea for Kevin McAllister (August 1991).
Record Victory: 11-1 v Tillicoultry, Scottish Cup 1st rd, 7 Sep 1889.
Record Defeat: 1-11 v Airdrieonians, Division I, 28 April 1951.
Most Capped Player: Alex Parker, 14 (15), Scotland.
Most League Appearances: 451: Tom Ferguson, 1919-32.
Most League Goals in Season (Individual): 43: Evelyn Morrison, Division I, 1928-29.
Most Goals Overall (Individual): 154: Kenneth Dawson, 1934-51.

FALKIRK – SPFL LEAGUE ONE 2020–21 LEAGUE RECORD

Match No.	*Date*	*Venue*	*Opponents*	*Result*		*H/T Score*	*Lg Pos.*	*Goalscorers*	*Attendance*
1	Oct 17	A	Montrose	W	3-1	1-0	1	Francis 43, Morrison, C (pen) 85, Leitch 90	0
2	24	H	Forfar Ath	D	1-1	1-0	2	Dowds 15	0
3	31	H	East Fife	W	2-0	1-0	2	Leitch 39, Francis 47	0
4	Nov 7	A	Partick Thistle	D	2-2	1-0	2	Penrice (og) 13, Telfer 88	0
5	21	H	Cove R	W	1-0	0-0	2	Morrison, C 49	0
6	24	A	Dumbarton	W	3-0	2-0	1	Morrison, C 16, Alston 33, Connolly, A 77	0
7	Dec 5	H	Peterhead	W	2-1	2-0	1	Alston 25, Sammon 45	0
8	12	A	Clyde	W	3-0	1-0	1	Telfer 30, Mercer 55, Hall 59	0
9	20	H	Airdrieonians	L	0-1	0-0	1		0
10	26	H	Partick Thistle	D	0-0	0-0	1		0
11	Jan 2	A	East Fife	L	1-2	0-1	1	Morrison, C 47	0
12	Mar 20	H	Montrose	W	2-0	1-0	1	Durnan 12, Morrison, C 90	0
13	27	A	Forfar Ath	W	2-0	1-0	1	Telfer 25, Alston 48	0
14	30	H	Dumbarton	D	1-1	0-0	1	Dowds 74	0
15	Apr 6	A	Airdrieonians	L	1-2	1-1	1	Telfer 35	0
16	10	H	Clyde	W	2-1	1-0	1	Hall 9, Keena 68	0
17	17	A	Cove R	L	0-2	0-1	1		0
18	20	A	Peterhead	L	0-1	0-0	2		0
19	24	H	Cove R	D	2-2	1-1	2	Morrison, C (pen) 19, Sammon 86	0
20	29	A	Partick Thistle	L	0-5	0-3	4		0
21	May 1	H	Montrose	L	1-2	1-1	4	Sammon 5	0
22	4	A	Airdrieonians	L	0-2	0-0	5		0

Final League Position: 5

Honours
League Champions: Division II 1935-36, 1969-70, 1974-75; First Division 1990-91, 1993-94, 2002-03, 2004-05; Second Division 1979-80;
Runners-up: Division I 1907-08, 1909-10; First Division 1985-86, 1988-89, 1997-98, 1998-99; Division II 1904-05, 1951-52, 1960-61; Championship: 2015-16, 2016-17; League One 2019-20.
Scottish Cup Winners: 1913, 1957; *Runners-up:* 1997, 2009, 2015.
League Cup Runners-up: 1947-48.
League Challenge Cup Winners: 1993-94, 1997-98, 2004-05, 2011-12.

European: *Europa League:* 2 matches (2009-10).

Club colours: Shirts: Navy blue with red trim. Shorts: White. Socks: Red.

Goalscorers: *League (29):* Morrison C 6 (2 pens), Telfer 4, Alston 3, Sammon 3, Dowds 2, Francis 2, Hall 2, Leitch 2, Connolly A 1, Durnan 1, Keena 1, Mercer 1, own goal 1.
William Hill Scottish Cup (2): Fotheringham 1, Telfer 1.
Betfred Scottish League Cup (6): Morrison C 3 (1 pen), Dowds 1, Keena 1, Sammon 1.

Mutch R 17	Mercer S 15 + 1	Durnan M 11 + 1	Hall B 16	Dixon P 16	Dowds A 10 + 7	Alston B 20 + 1	Miller G 14 + 4	Morrison C 21 + 1	Todd J 3 + 5	Francis A 4 + 13	Leitch R 10 + 11	Gomis M 16 + 2	Miller L — + 6	Sammon C 14 + 5	Morrison Peter 5 + 1	Deveney E 1 + 3	Kelly S 11 + 3	Telfer C 7 + 6	Connolly A 2 + 3	Keena A 7 + 4	Fotheringham K 10 + 1	Neilson L 7 + 1	McClelland D 5 + 1	*Match No.*
1	2	3	4	5	6^{2}	7^{1}	8	9	10^{3}	11^{4}	12	13	14	15										1
1■	2	3	4	5	11^{1}	9^{2}	7	6		10^{4}	13	8^{3}		14	12	15								2
	2	3	4	5	11	7	8	6	12	10^{2}	9^{1}				1		13							3
	2	3	4	5	11^{1}	8^{3}	7	6	12	10^{4}	9^{2}			15	1		13	14						4
			3	4	11^{4}	7	2	6^{3}		14	9^{2}	8	12	10^{1}	1		5	13	15					5
			3	4	10^{1}	7	2	6^{3}	15	13	9^{4}	8^{2}		11	1		5	12	14					6
	2		4	3	10^{1}	7		6	12		14	8^{2}		11	1		5	9^{3}	13					7
1	2		3	4	11^{2}		15	6^{1}	14	12	13	8		10^{3}		16	5	9^{4}	7^{5}					8
1	2		3	4	10^{3}	13		12		15	8^{1}	7	14	11^{4}			5	6^{2}	9					9
1	2		4	3	12	9^{2}	7^{1}	8	10^{4}	14	13	6		11^{3}			5	15						10
1	2		3	4	10^{2}	7^{3}	16	6	9^{4}		13	8^{5}	14	11^{1}			5	15		12				11
1		4	3	5	13	6	2	9		12	8^{2}	7						14		10^{3}	11^{1}			12
1		3	4	5	13	6	2	9		12	14	7^{2}						8		10^{3}	11^{1}			13
1		4■	3	5	13	6	2	10^{4}		15	7^{3}	8^{1}		14				9^{5}		11^{2}	12	16		14
1	2^{1}		3	5		8		11		12		7	13	14				6		10^{2}	9^{3}	4		15
1		4	3^{4}	5^{2}		6	16	11		14	13			10		15		7^{5}		9^{1}	8^{3}	2	12	16
1	12	3				7	5	6			13	8	14	11^{3}						10	9^{2}	2^{1}	4	17
1	2	3^{2}				7	15	6		14	13	8■		11		5^{3}	12			10^{4}	9^{1}		4	18
1	2					7	8	6		13	9^{1}			11			5			12	10^{2}	4	3	19
1	2^{3}	12			13	7	8	6^{2}		16	9^{4}	14		11^{1}			5			15	10	3^{5}	4	20
1	2				12	7		10			9^{2}	8		11			5			13	6^{1}	3	4	21
1	2^{2}	4			13	9	7	10			12	6		11			5				8^{1}	3		22

FORFAR ATHLETIC

Year Formed: 1885. *Ground & Address:* Station Park, Carseview Road, Forfar DD8 3BT. *Telephone:* 01307 463576.
Fax: 01307 466956. *E-mail:* david.mcgregor@forfarathletic.co.uk *Website:* forfarathletic.co.uk
Ground Capacity: 6,777 (seated: 739). *Size of Pitch:* 103m × 64m.
Chairman: Ross Graham. *Secretary:* David McGregor.
Manager: Gary Irvine. *Assistant Manager:* Tony Docherty.
Club Nicknames: 'The Loons'; 'The Sky Blues'.
Record Attendance: 10,780 v Rangers, Scottish Cup 2nd rd, 2 February 1970.
Record Transfer Fee received: £65,000 for David Bingham to Dunfermline Ath (September 1995).
Record Transfer Fee paid: £50,000 for Ian McPhee from Airdrieonians (1991).
Record Victory: 14-1 v Lindertis, Scottish Cup 1st rd, 1 September 1888.
Record Defeat: 2-12 v King's Park, Division II, 2 January 1930.
Most League Appearances: 463: Ian McPhee, 1978-88 and 1991-98.
Most League Goals in Season (Individual): 46: Dave Kilgour, Division II, 1929-30.
Most Goals Overall: 125: John Clark, 1978-91.

FORFAR ATHLETIC – SPFL LEAGUE ONE 2020–21 LEAGUE RECORD

Match No.	Date	Venue	Opponents	Result		H/T Score	Lg Pos.	Goalscorers	Attendance
1	Oct 17	H	Dumbarton	D	0-0	0-0	5		0
2	24	A	Falkirk	D	1-1	0-1	6	Allan (pen) 66	0
3	31	H	Montrose	L	2-3	0-1	9	Allan 60, Antoniazzi 80	0
4	Nov 7	A	Cove R	L	0-3	0-2	10		0
5	21	H	Airdrieonians	L	1-3	1-3	10	Antoniazzi 23	0
6	28	A	Peterhead	W	1-0	1-0	9	Barr 44	0
7	Dec 12	H	Partick Thistle	L	0-2	0-0	10		0
8	19	A	East Fife	L	0-2	0-1	10		0
9	26	H	Cove R	L	0-1	0-0	10		0
10	Jan 2	A	Montrose	D	0-0	0-0	10		0
11	Mar 20	A	Dumbarton	W	1-0	0-0	9	McGeever (og) 57	0
12	27	H	Falkirk	L	0-2	0-1	10		0
13	30	A	Partick Thistle	D	2-2	2-1	10	Fenwick 2 2, 44	0
14	Apr 6	H	Peterhead	D	1-1	0-0	10	Scott 86	0
15	8	A	Clyde	L	0-3	0-2	10		0
16	10	H	East Fife	L	1-2	0-1	10	Allan 53	0
17	13	A	Airdrieonians	L	1-3	1-1	10	Anderson, G 43	0
18	20	H	Clyde	L	1-3	1-1	10	Fenwick 38	0
19	27	A	Dumbarton	L	0-1	0-0	10		0
20	29	H	Clyde	W	2-1	1-1	10	Scally 2 35, 90	0
21	May 1	A	Peterhead	W	2-1	0-0	10	Strachan (og) 56, Shepherd 79	0
22	4	H	East Fife	L	2-3	1-1	10	Fenwick 11, Scally 48	0

Final League Position: 10

Honours
League Champions: Second Division 1983-84; Third Division 1994-95; C Division 1948-49.
Runners-up: League One 2018-19; Third Division 1996-97, 2009-10; League Two 2016-17.
Promoted via play-offs: 2009-10 (to Second Division); 2016-17 (to League One).
Scottish Cup: Semi-finals 1982.
League Cup: Semi-finals 1977-78.
League Challenge Cup: Semi-finals 2004-05.

Club colours: Shirt: Sky blue. Shorts: Navy blue. Socks: Sky blue and navy blue hoops.

Goalscorers: *League (18):* Fenwick 4, Allan 3 (1 pen), Scally 3, Antoniazzi 2, Anderson G 1, Barr 1, Scott 1, Shepherd 1, own goals 2.
William Hill Scottish Cup (6): Allan 3, Fotheringham 1, MacKintosh 1, Nditi 1.
Betfred Scottish League Cup (3): MacKintosh 2, Allan 1 (1 pen).

McCallum M 19	MacKintosh M 19 + 2	Fisher S 6	Meechan R 22	MacKenzie J 10	Scally D 13 + 1	Irvine G 17	Thomas A 7 + 1	Barr B 10	Robertson J 6 + 1	Shepherd S 13 + 8	Antoniazzi C 2 + 6	Allan J 8 + 10	Hoti F 4 + 2	Doris S 2 + 10	Breadner C — + 4	Hoban D 3 + 1	Coll B 17	Hill M 2	Anderson S 1	Fotheringham M — + 1	Dalling K 1	Nditi R 9	Munro A 6 + 1	Moore C 11 + 1	Anderson G 10 + 2	Scott M 4 + 4	Northcott J 1 + 5	Holmes G 6 + 4	Fenwick S 10 + 1	Thomson H 2 + 1	Andersen M 1 + 3	*Match No.*
1	2	3	4	5	6	7	8^4	9^2	10^3	11^1	12	13	14	15																		1
1	2	3	4	5		6	8^2	10	7^1	11^3		12	9	14	13																	2
1^3	2	3	4	5		7	8^4	6	10^1	11^2	15	9		13	14	12																3
	2	3	4	5		7		8	6	9	13	10^2		11^1	12	1																4
1	12	3	5	4	14	2	7	8		13	11^2	10	6^3				9^1															5
1	2		4	5	8^1	3	12	7		10	13	11					9	6^2														6
1	2		3	5	6		7	9	13	10^1	14	11^3			12^4		8		4^2	15												7
1	2		3	5	6			9	10^2	11		13	12				8	7^1			4											8
1	2		3	5		4	7	9	11^2	13	10	12	6				8^1															9
1	2	3	4	6		5	8^1	10		11	12		7				9															10
1	6		4			7				12		14					5					2^1	3	8	9^2	10	11^3	13				11
1	6		3			7^2				13							5^4					2	4	9	12	11^1	15	8^3	10	14		12
	4		2		6^1					11^2		13				1	5					7	3	8	9^3	14	12	15	10^4			13
1	8		3		6^3	4				11^1				15			5					2		7	9^4	12		13	10^2		14	14
1	7^3		3									13		12			5						4	8	9^1	11	14	2	10^2		6	15
1	8		2		6^3					14		11^2		12			5■						4	7	9^1				10	3	13	16
1	6^1		2		9	5				15				13									4	8^2	10^4	12		7	11^3	3	14	17
1	7^4		3		9	4^5				16		11^3		13			5					2	15	14	6^2	12		8	10^1			18
1	8^2		3		6^4	4				15		13		12			5					2		7	9	10^1	14		11^3			19
			3		9	4				6		11^2		10^1		1	5					2		8	13			7	12			20
1	6		4		8^1	3				9^3		13					5					2		7	10^2		14	12	11			21
1	14		3		8	4				11^2		13		12			5					2		7	10			6^1	9^3			22

GREENOCK MORTON

Year Formed: 1874. *Ground & Address:* Cappielow Park, Sinclair St, Greenock PA15 2TU. *Telephone:* 01475 723571. *Fax:* 01475 781084. *E-mail:* admin@gmfc.net *Website:* gmfc.net
Ground Capacity: 11,612 (seated: 6,062). *Size of Pitch:* 100m × 65m.
Chairman: Crawford Rae.
Manager: Gus MacPherson. *Assistant Manager:* Anton McElhone.
Club Nickname: 'The Ton'.
Previous Grounds: Grant Street 1874; Garvel Park 1875; Cappielow Park 1879; Ladyburn Park 1882; Cappielow Park 1883.
Record Attendance: 23,500 v Celtic, 29 April 1922.
Record Transfer Fee received: £500,000 for Derek Lilley to Leeds U (March 1997).
Record Transfer Fee paid: £250,000 for Janne Lindberg and Marko Rajamäki from MyPa, Finland (November 1994).
Record Victory: 11-0 v Carfin Shamrock, Scottish Cup 4th rd, 13 November 1886.
Record Defeat: 1-10 v Port Glasgow Ath, Division II, 5 May, 1894 and v St Bernards, Division II, 14 October 1933.
Most Capped Player: Jimmy Cowan, 25, Scotland.
Most League Appearances: 534: Derek Collins, 1987-98, 2001-05.
Most League Goals in Season (Individual): 58: Allan McGraw, Division II, 1963-64.
Most Goals Overall (Individual): 136: Andy Ritchie, 1976-83.

GREENOCK MORTON – SPFL CHAMPIONSHIP 2020–21 LEAGUE RECORD

Match No.	Date	Venue	Opponents	Result		H/T Score	Lg Pos.	Goalscorers	Attendance
1	Oct 17	H	Alloa Ath	W	1-0	1-0	5	Salkeld 10	0
2	24	A	Dundee	L	0-1	0-1	5		0
3	31	H	Ayr U	W	3-2	0-1	4	Strapp 88, Oliver 83, Blues 85	0
4	Nov 7	A	Raith R	L	0-5	0-2	4		0
5	21	A	Arbroath	D	0-0	0-0	6		0
6	Dec 5	H	Hearts	L	0-2	0-1	7		0
7	12	A	Dunfermline Ath	W	2-1	1-0	6	McAlister 24, McGuffie 79	0
8	19	H	Queen of the South	W	2-0	1-0	3	Orsi 2 41, 76	0
9	29	A	Ayr U	D	1-1	1-1	5	Nesbitt (pen) 26	0
10	Jan 2	A	Alloa Ath	D	1-1	0-0	5	Fjortoft 69	0
11	15	H	Dunfermline Ath	D	0-0	0-0	4		0
12	23	A	Queen of the South	L	1-2	0-2	5	Orsi 58	0
13	27	H	Inverness CT	D	2-2	1-2	5	McGinty 3, Blues 66	0
14	30	H	Arbroath	L	0-1	0-0	6		0
15	Feb 6	H	Raith R	L	0-1	0-1	6		0
16	20	A	Hearts	D	1-1	0-0	6	McGuffie 53	0
17	27	H	Dundee	D	2-2	1-0	8	McGuffie 41, Colville 69	0
18	Mar 6	H	Ayr U	L	0-2	0-0	9		0
19	9	A	Inverness CT	W	1-0	0-0	6	Nesbitt 56	0
20	13	A	Dunfermline Ath	L	0-1	0-1	6		0
21	20	H	Queen of the South	W	2-1	1-1	8	Nesbitt 19, Oliver 61	0
22	27	A	Raith R	L	0-1	0-0	8		0
23	Apr 6	H	Inverness CT	L	1-4	0-2	9	Muirhead 61	0
24	10	A	Dundee	D	1-1	0-0	9	Nesbitt 78	0
25	20	H	Hearts	D	0-0	0-0	9		0
26	24	H	Alloa Ath	D	1-1	0-0	9	Fjortoft 55	0
27	30	A	Arbroath	D	0-0	0-0	9		0

Final League Position: 9

Honours
League Champions: First Division 1977-78, 1983-84, 1986-87; Division II 1949-50, 1963-64, 1966-67; Second Division 1994-95, 2006-07; League One 2014–15; Third Division 2002-03.
Runners-up: Division 1 1916-17; First Division 2012-13; Second Division 2005-06;. Division II 1899-1900, 1928-29, 1936-37.
Scottish Cup Winners: 1922; *Runners-up:* 1948.
League Cup Runners-up: 1963-64.
League Challenge Cup Runners-up: 1992-93.

European: *UEFA Cup:* 2 matches (*Fairs Cup:* 1968-69).

Club colours: Shirt: Blue and white hoops. Shorts: White. Socks: White with blue tops.

Goalscorers: *League (22):* Nesbitt 4 (1 pen), McGuffie 3, Orsi 3, Blues 2, Fjortoft 2, Oliver 2, Colville 1, McAlister 1, McGinty 1, Muirhead 1, Salkeld 1, Strapp 1.
William Hill Scottish Cup (3): Fjortoft 1, McGinty 1 (1 pen), Muirhead 1.
Betfred Scottish League Cup (4): Blues 1, MacIver 1, McGinty 1, Nesbitt 1.
Scottish League Play-Offs (8): Muirhead 3, Oliver 3, McGuffie 1, Salkeld 1.

McAdams A 27	Fjortoft M 17	McLean B 23	McGinty S 27	Salkeld C 12 + 7	Jacobs K 14 + 2	McAlister J 11 + 1	Muirhead R 10 + 3	McPake J 6	Orsi K 13 + 6	Nesbitt A 21 + 4	Maciver R 2 + 4	Blues C 9 + 3	McGuffie C 9 + 9	Ledger M 21 + 1	Oliver G 8 + 12	Strapp L 22 + 1	Omar R 3 + 8	Lyon R 11 + 8	Colville L 16 + 1	Millar C 2 + 2	Sterling K 2 + 5	Johnson J — + 2	McGinn S 8	Hynes D 3 + 1	Easdale A — + 1	*Match No.*
1	2	3	4	5^3	6	7	8	9■	10^2	11^1	12	13	14													1
1	5	3	4	6^3	7^1	8	10■		11^2	12	13	9		2	14											2
1	2	3	4	5^2		7		9	10^1	11^3	13	6	12		14	8										3
1	2	4	3	12	6^1	8■		5^2	11^3			7			10	9	13	14								4
1	2	3^3	4	13	6	7					11^1			5	14	9	12	8^2	10							5
1	2	3^1	4	12	6	7	10^3	5		14	11^2				13	9	8									6
1		2	4	5	3^3	7	11^2	6^1	10	13			14			9	12	8								7
1		3	4	6^3		8^1	9	10^2	11	12				2	14	5	13	7								8
1		3	4	6^2		8	9^3		11	10^1	14		13	2	12	5		7								9
1	3		4	8^1		7			11	10				2	12	5	13	6^3	9^2	14						10
1	3		4	6	14				11^1	10			13	2	12	5	8^2	7^3	9							11
1	3		4	6^3		8			11	10			13	2	14	5^2	12	7^1	9							12
1	3		4	14						9		6^1	8^3	2	11^2	5	7■	13	10	12						13
1		3	4			14	10		13	9		7	8^2	2	11^3	5		12		6^1						14
1		3	4	14						9		7^2	8^3	2	11	5	12		10	6^1	13					15
1		3	4	11^1	6		12		13	9		7	8^2	2		5		14	10^3							16
1		3	4	11^2	6				12	7		8	10^3	2		5		14	9^1			13				17
1		3	4	11	6		12			10		9	7^1	2		5^2			8^3		13	14				18
1	5	3	4	13	6					7^1		12	10	2			14	8^2	9^3		11					19
1	5	4	3	13					14	10			7^2	2	12			9^1	8		11^3		6			20
1	2^2	3	4						10^3	9				12	11^1	8		14	7		13		6	5		21
1		3	4		12				13	11			14	2	10^2	9		8^1	6^3				7	5		22
1		3	4				11^3		12	9			14	2^1	10^2	8			7		13		6	5		23
1	2	3	4		7		11^1			10		14		5		9		12	8^3		13		6^2			24
1	3	4	5		7^2				11^3	8				2	12	10		9^1	13				6		14	25
1	3	4	5		8		11^1		10^3	6			13	2	12	9^2							7	14		26
1	3	4	5■		7		14			6^1			10^2	2	11	12		13	9^3				8			27

HAMILTON ACADEMICAL

Year Formed: 1874. *Ground:* Hope Stadium, New Douglas Park, Cadzow Avenue, Hamilton ML3 0FT. *Telephone:* 01698 368652. *Fax:* 01698 285422. *E-mail:* office@acciesfc.co.uk *Website:* hamiltonacciesfc.co.uk
Ground Capacity: 6,078 (all seated). *Size of Pitch:* 105m × 68m.
Chairman: Allan Maitland. *Vice-Chairman:* Les Gray.
Head Coach: Brian Rice. *First-Team Coach:* Guillaume Beuzelin.
Club Nickname: 'The Accies'.
Previous Grounds: Bent Farm; South Avenue; South Haugh; Douglas Park; Cliftonhill Stadium; Firhill Stadium.
Record Attendance: 28,690 v Hearts, Scottish Cup 3rd rd, 3 March 1937 (at Douglas Park); 5,895 v Rangers, 28 February 2009 (at New Douglas Park).
Record Transfer Fee received: £1,200,000 (rising to £3,200,000) for James McCarthy to Wigan Ath (July 2009).
Record Transfer Fee paid: £180,000 for Tomas Cerny from Sigma Olomouc (July 2009).
Record Victory: 10-2 v Greenock Morton, Scottish Championship, 3 May 2014.
Record Defeat: 1-11 v Hibernian, Division I, 6 November 1965.
Most Capped Player: Colin Miller, 29 (61), Canada, 1988-94.
Most League Appearances: 452: Rikki Ferguson, 1974-88.
Most League Goals in Season (Individual): 35: David Wilson, Division I; 1936-37.
Most Goals Overall (Individual): 246: David Wilson, 1928-39.

HAMILTON ACADEMICAL – SPFL PREMIERSHIP 2020–21 LEAGUE RECORD

Match No.	Date	Venue	Opponents	Result		H/T Score	Lg Pos.	Goalscorers	Attendance
1	Aug 2	A	Celtic	L	1-5	1-2	10	Jullien (og) 34	0
2	8	H	Ross Co	L	0-1	0-0	12		0
3	15	H	St Mirren	L	0-1	0-1	12		0
4	22	A	Motherwell	W	1-0	0-0	9	Odofin 86	0
5	29	H	Rangers	L	0-2	0-2	11		0
6	Sept 12	A	Livingston	W	2-1	0-1	9	Templeton 57, Munro 85	0
7	19	A	Kilmarnock	L	1-2	1-1	10	Odofin 18	0
8	26	H	Dundee U	D	1-1	0-1	10	Odofin 75	0
9	Oct 2	A	Hibernian	L	2-3	0-2	11	Callachan (pen) 75, Porteous (og) 84	0
10	17	H	St Johnstone	L	3-5	2-3	12	Hughes 2 40, 79, Ogboe 44	0
11	20	A	Aberdeen	L	2-4	1-4	12	Moyo 32, Callachan (pen) 68	0
12	Nov 8	A	Rangers	L	0-8	0-4	12		0
13	21	A	Dundee U	L	1-2	0-0	12	Callachan 65	0
14	25	H	Aberdeen	D	1-1	0-1	12	Ogboe 49	0
15	Dec 5	H	Kilmarnock	W	1-0	0-0	12	Callachan (pen) 73	0
16	12	H	Hibernian	L	0-4	0-2	12		0
17	19	A	Ross Co	W	2-0	1-0	11	Callachan 22, Martin, S 62	0
18	23	H	Livingston	L	0-2	0-0	11		0
19	26	H	Celtic	L	0-3	0-0	11		0
20	30	A	St Johnstone	D	0-0	0-0	12		0
21	Jan 2	H	Motherwell	W	3-0	1-0	10	Hodson 10, Callachan 49, Smith, C 65	0
22	9	A	Kilmarnock	L	0-2	0-1	11		0
23	16	H	Dundee U	D	0-0	0-0	11		0
24	27	A	Celtic	L	0-2	0-1	12		0
25	Feb 3	H	Ross Co	L	1-2	1-0	12	Kelly (og) 16	0
26	7	H	Rangers	D	1-1	0-0	12	McGregor (og) 90	0
27	13	A	Motherwell	W	4-1	3-0	11	Anderson 7, Callachan (pen) 19, Ogboe 31, Moyo 64	0
28	17	A	St Mirren	D	1-1	0-0	11	Anderson 68	0
29	20	A	Hibernian	L	0-2	0-1	11		0
30	Mar 3	H	St Johnstone	D	1-1	1-0	12	Callachan 36	0
31	6	A	Aberdeen	D	0-0	0-0	11		0
32	13	A	Livingston	L	1-2	1-2	11	Smith, C 30	0
33	20	H	St Mirren	D	1-1	0-1	12	Munro 89	0
34	Apr 10	H	Dundee U	L	0-1	0-1	12		0
35	21	H	Motherwell	L	0-1	0-1	12		0
36	May 1	A	St Mirren	W	2-1	1-0	12	Callachan 28, Moyo 57	0
37	12	A	Ross Co	L	1-2	1-1	12	McMann 26	0
38	16	H	Kilmarnock	L	0-2	0-2	12		0

Final League Position: 12

Honours
League Champions: Division II 1903-04; First Division 1985-86, 1987-88, 2007-08; Third Division 2000-01.
Runners-up: Division II 1952-53, 1964-65; Second Division 1996-97, 2003-04; Championship 2013-14.
Promoted via play-offs: 2013-14 (to Premiership).
Scottish Cup Runners-up: 1911, 1935. *League Cup:* Semi-finalists three times.
League Challenge Cup Winners: 1991-92, 1992-93; *Runners-up:* 2005-06, 2011-12.

Club colours: Shirt: Red and white hoops. Shorts: White. Socks: White.

Goalscorers: *League (34):* Callachan 9 (4 pens), Moyo 3, Odofin 3, Ogboe 3, Anderson 2, Hughes 2, Munro 2, Smith C 2, Hodson 1, Martin S 1, McMann 1, Templeton 1, own goals 4.
William Hill Scottish Cup (0).
Betfred Scottish League Cup (4): McMann 1, Odofin 1, Ogboe 1, Trafford 1.

Fulton R 28	Odofin H 37	Hamilton J 21 + 6	Want S 11	McMann S 36	Smith L 4 + 5	Callachan R 32 + 1	Martin S 21 + 3	Hughes R 7 + 9	Moyo D 23 + 10	Winter A 10 + 12	Ogboe M 15 + 5	McKenna C — + 1	Trafford C 9 + 7	Fjortoft M 1 + 1	Smith C 8 + 15	Templeton D 7 + 1	Johnson J 1 + 4	Owolabi T 1 + 6	Hodson L 33	Minnaugh R 8 + 9	Munro K 9 + 7	Collar W 5 + 1	Gourlay K 9 + 1	Stirling B 16 + 4	Easton B 24	Martin A 24	Thomas N 3 + 7	Stanger G 1 + 4	Anderson B 13	Smith J 1	Redfern M — + 1	*Match No.*
1	2^2	3	4	5	6	7^1	8	9^3	10	11	12	13	14																			1
1	2	15	4^3	5	6^2	7^5	8		10	11^1			12	3	9^4	13	14	16														2
1	3		4	5	6^3	7^1	8		10^2	9	13					11	12		2	14												3
1	3		4	5	12	7	8^3		9^4	15	10^1		13		16	11^5	6^2		2	14												4
1	3	12	4	5■		10	6		15	9^2	11^1		7^3		14				2	8^4	13											5
1	3		4			7	2		11	12	10^3		13	14		9^1				8	5	6^2										6
1	3	2^2	4	5			7^4		11	14	10^1		15		12	9	13			8		6^3										7
1	3	14	2	4		12	6			11^1	13				15	9		10^3	5^2	7^4	8^5	16										8
	3	2	4^4	5		9	8^3			11^1	13				15	10^2		14	6		12	7	1									9
1	3		4	5		7	9	12	11		10				13	8^2			2^3		6^1			14								10
1	3		4	5		6^1	7^4	9^2	11		10		12		15				2	13		8^3		14								11
1	3			9	13	6^2		8^1	11	12	10^3								5	14		7		2	4							12
1	7			9		5	8		12		10				11				6					2	4^1	3						13
1	6			8		9	7		12	13	11^2				10^1				5					2	4	3						14
1	7			9		6	8		10						11^1			13	2^2					3	5	4	12					15
1		15		6		7	8		11^2	14			9^3		10^1			12	2^4					3	5	4	13					16
1	6	14		8		9	7^3	13	11^4	15									5		12			2^1	4	3	10^2					17
1^3	6	15		8				7^1	11^4	14							12		5	10	9		13	2	4^2	3						18
	5	2		9					11^1	10^2			8					12	6	13	14		1	7^3	4	3						19
	6	2		8					11	10								13	5				1	7	4^2	3	9^1	12				20
	7	3		6		9^4			11^1	10^3			15		13				2		14		1	8	5^2	4		12				21
	6	2		8		9			11^1	10			7		12				5				1	4				3				22
1	6	2		8		9			11^2	13	12				10^1				5					7	4	3						23
1	6	2		8		9^3	12		10	13	11^1								5	14				7^2	4	3						24
1	6	2		8		9			14	13	11^2								5	12				7^1	4^4	3	15		10^3			25
1	6	2		8		9		12			11		7^1						5						4	3			10			26
1	6	2		8		9	12		13	14	11^3		7^2						5					15	4^4	3			10^1			27
1	6	2		8		9	12	13	14		10		7^1						5						4	3^3			11^2			28
1	3	2■		9		6	8^2	14	12		11^1		7^3		15				5	13					4				10^4			29
1	2			9		6	8^2	12	10				7^1						5					13	4	3			11			30
1	7	2		9		8	6	14	11^2						12				5		13				4^1	3	10^3					31
1	6	2				7	8	12	13						10^1				5^2		9				4	3			11			32
1	6			8		9	7	13	12						10^1				5		14			2^3	4	3^2			11			33
	7	2		9		6		8							12				5		10		1		4^1	3			11			34
	6	2		8	12	9^3		7■											5^1	13	10		1		4^2	3	14		11			35
	5	2		4	12	7^3			10						13				6	8^1	9^4		1			3	15	14	11^2			36
	5	2		4	14	7			11						13				6	8^2			1		9^3	3	12		10^1			37
	7	2		4	5^4			8	15						14					9^3	10^1			6^2		3	13	12	11^5	1	16	38

HEART OF MIDLOTHIAN

Year Formed: 1874. *Ground & Address:* Tynecastle Stadium, McLeod Street, Edinburgh EH11 2NL. *Telephone:* 0333 043 1874. *Fax:* 0131 200 7222. *E-mail:* supporterservices@homplc.co.uk *Website:* heartsfc.co.uk
Ground Capacity: 20,099. *Size of Pitch:* 100m × 64m.
Chairman: Ann Budge. *Chief Executive:* Andrew McKinlay
Manager: Robbie Neilson. *Assistant Managers:* Gordon Forrest, Lee McCulloch.
Club Nicknames: 'Hearts'; 'Jam Tarts'; 'Jambos'.
Previous Grounds: The Meadows 1874; Powderhall 1878; Old Tynecastle 1881; Tynecastle Park 1886.
Record Attendance: 53,396 v Rangers, Scottish Cup 3rd rd, 13 February 1932 (57,857 v Barcelona, 28 July 2007 at Murrayfield).
Record Transfer Fee received: £9,000,000 for Craig Gordon to Sunderland (August 2008).
Record Transfer Fee paid: £850,000 for Mirsad Beslija from Genk (January 2006).
Record Victory: 15-0 v King's Park, Scottish Cup 2nd rd, 13 February 1937 (21-0 v Anchor, EFA Cup, 30 October 1880).
Record Defeat: 1-8 v Vale of Leven, Scottish Cup 3rd rd, 1883; 0-7 v Celtic, Scottish Cup 4th rd, 1 December 2013.
Most Capped Player: Steven Pressley, 32, Scotland.
Most League Appearances: 515: Gary Mackay, 1980-97.
Most League Goals in Season (Individual): 44: Barney Battles, 1930-31.
Most Goals Overall (Individual): 214: John Robertson, 1983-98.

HEART OF MIDLOTHIAN – SPFL CHAMPIONSHIP 2020–21 LEAGUE RECORD

Match No.	Date	Venue	Opponents	Result		H/T Score	Lg Pos.	Goalscorers	Attendance
1	Oct 16	H	Dundee	W	6-2	4-1	1	Smith ^{4}, Ginnelly ^{25}, Boyce (pen) ^{34}, Kingsley 2 $^{45, 84}$, Halliday ^{90}	0
2	23	A	Arbroath	W	1-0	0-0	1	Wighton ^{70}	0
3	Nov 7	H	Inverness CT	W	2-1	0-0	3	Naismith ^{47}, Boyce ^{70}	0
4	20	A	Dunfermline Ath	L	1-2	0-0	3	Kingsley ^{84}	0
5	24	H	Alloa Ath	W	3-0	3-0	2	Smith ^{6}, Halliday ^{24}, Haring ^{37}	0
6	Dec 5	A	Greenock Morton	W	2-0	1-0	1	Walker 2 $^{37, 48}$	0
7	12	H	Queen of the South	W	6-1	2-0	1	Naismith ^{20}, Boyce 2 $^{45, 46}$, Walker ^{76}, Frear ^{82}, Ginnelly ^{90}	0
8	26	H	Ayr U	W	5-3	1-0	1	Kingsley ^{11}, Wighton 2 $^{68, 74}$, Lee ^{71}, Boyce ^{81}	0
9	29	H	Arbroath	W	3-1	3-0	1	Naismith 3 (1 pen) $^{30, 33, 36 (p)}$	0
10	Jan 2	A	Dundee	L	1-3	0-2	1	Irving ^{56}	0
11	16	A	Alloa Ath	W	3-1	2-0	1	Irving ^{35}, Frear ^{45}, Ginnelly ^{90}	0
12	23	H	Raith R	L	2-3	0-1	1	Boyce 2 $^{58, 90}$	0
13	26	A	Raith R	W	4-0	2-0	1	Boyce ^{36}, Henderson ^{39}, Gnanduillet 2 $^{84, 90}$	0
14	30	H	Dunfermline Ath	W	1-0	0-0	1	Walker ^{81}	0
15	Feb 5	A	Ayr U	W	1-0	0-0	1	Boyce (pen) ^{48}	0
16	12	A	Queen of the South	D	1-1	0-1	1	Boyce (pen) ^{90}	0
17	20	H	Greenock Morton	D	1-1	0-0	1	Walker ^{71}	0
18	26	A	Inverness CT	D	1-1	1-1	1	Boyce ^{36}	0
19	Mar 6	H	Dundee	W	2-1	1-0	1	Halliday ^{35}, Gnanduillet ^{58}	0
20	13	H	Ayr U	W	2-0	0-0	1	Gnanduillet ^{72}, Walker ^{86}	0
21	20	A	Arbroath	D	0-0	0-0	1		0
22	27	H	Queen of the South	L	2-3	1-2	1	Popescu ^{34}, Gnanduillet ^{72}	0
23	Apr 3	A	Dunfermline Ath	D	0-0	0-0	1		0
24	9	H	Alloa Ath	W	6-0	2-0	1	Boyce 3 (1 pen) $^{26, 32 (p), 53}$, Henderson ^{51}, McEneff ^{71}, Walker ^{88}	0
25	20	A	Greenock Morton	D	0-0	0-0	1		0
26	24	H	Inverness CT	W	3-0	3-0	1	Mackay-Steven 2 $^{6, 31}$, McEneff ^{9}	0
27	30	A	Raith R	W	4-0	1-0	1	Mackay-Steven 2 $^{11, 73}$, Henderson ^{57}, Naismith ^{70}	0

Final League Position: 1

Honours
League Champions: Division I 1894-95, 1896-97, 1957-58, 1959-60; First Division 1979-80; Championship 2014-15, 2020-21
Runners-up: Division I 1893-94, 1898-99, 1903-04, 1905-06, 1914-15, 1937-38, 1953-54, 1956-57, 1958-59, 1964-65; Premier Division 1985-86, 1987-88, 1991-92, 2005-06; First Division 1977-78, 1982-83.
Scottish Cup Winners: 1891, 1896, 1901, 1906, 1956, 1998, 2006, 2012; *Runners-up:* 1903, 1907, 1968, 1976, 1986, 1996, 2019, 2020.
League Cup Winners: 1954-55, 1958-59, 1959-60, 1962-63; *Runners-up:* 1961-62, 1996-97, 2012-13.

European: *European Cup:* 8 matches (1958-59, 1960-61, 2006-07). *Cup Winners' Cup:* 10 matches (1976-77, 1996-97, 1998-99). *UEFA Cup:* 46 matches (*Fairs Cup:* 1961-62, 1963-64, 1965-66. *UEFA Cup:* 1984-85, 1986-87, 1988-89, 1990-91, 1992-93, 1993-94, 2000-01, 2003-04, 2004-05, 2006-07). *Europa League:* 12 matches (2010-11, 2011-12, 2012-13, 2016-17).

Club colours: Shirt: Maroon. Shorts: White with maroon trim. Socks: Maroon.

Goalscorers: *League (63):* Boyce 14 (4 pens), Walker 7, Naismith 6 (1 pen), Gnanduillet 5, Kingsley 4, Mackay-Steven 4, Ginnelly 3, Halliday 3, Henderson 3, Wighton 3, Frear 2, Irving 2, McEneff 2, Smith 2, Haring 1, Lee 1, Popescu 1.
William Hill Scottish Cup (1): Berra 1.
Betfred Scottish League Cup (8): Wighton 3 (2 pens), Lee 2, Halkett 1, Irving 1, Walker 1 (1 pen).

Gordon C 26	Smith M 25	Halkett C 27	Popescu M 14 + 4	Kingsley S 20	Lee O 9 + 1	Irving A 16 + 7	Ginnelly J 3 + 3	Walker J 10 + 11	Roberts J 4 + 2	Boyce L 24 + 1	Haring P 9 + 5	Halliday A 24 + 2	Wighton C 5 + 3	Frear E 5 + 3	White A 3 + 7	Naismith S 11 + 9	Berra C 9	Brandon J 1	Henderson E 6 + 4	Mackay-Steven G 14 + 3	Gnanduillet A 8 + 5	McEneff A 11 + 2	Kastaneer G 3 + 3	Stewart R 1	Logan S 5	Souttar J 4	McGill S — + 1	Pollock F — + 2	Match No.
1	2	3	4	5	6	7^1	8^2	9	10	11^3	12	13	14																1
1	2	3	4	5	7		8^2	9^1		11	14	6	12	10^3	13														2
1	2	3	4	5	9	12				11^3	6^1	8	7	14	13	10^2													3
1	2	3	4	5	6^2	14		12	13	11		7	8^1	10^3		9													4
1	2^2	3	13	5	14			8	10^1	11	6	7^3			12	9	4												5
1	2	3		5	8	7^2		6	13		12	9	11^1			10	4												6
1	2	3		5	6^1	7	12	8		11		14		13	10^2	9^3	4												7
1	2	3		5^2	6	7			9^1	10	14	8	13	11^3		12	4												8
1	2	3	14		7^3	8		12		11^2	6	5	10	13		9	4^1												9
1		3		5	6	12		8			7^1	9	11^2			10	4	2	13										10
1	2	3		5		7	14	6	9^3	13		8		11^1			4		10^2	12									11
1	2	3	12	5		7	13	14		10		8^1		9^3		11	4^2			6									12
1	2	4	3	5		7	8^3	9		11^2		6				14			12	10^1	13								13
1	2	4	3	5		7		14		11		6			12	9^3			10^2	8^1	13								14
1	2	4	3	5		7^2		8		11		6				14				9^1	10^3	12	13						15
1	2	4	3	5		7^1		10		11		6^3				14			13	8		12	9^2						16
1	2	4	3	5		14		13		11		7^1				9				10^3	12	6	8^2						17
1	2^3	4	3	5		14		13		11		6				9^1				10	12	7	8^2						18
1	2	3	4	5		6^3		12		11	14■	8			13					9^2	10^1	7							19
1	2	4	3	5		6		12		10		8			14					9^1	11^2	7^3	13						20
1	2	4	3	5^2		7		14		10		8			12					9^1	11	6^3	13						21
		2	3			7		12		9		6			5		4		13	10^1	11	8^2		1					22
1	3	4	12			7				11	6				5^1	13			8^3	10	14	9^2			2				23
1	2	3						14		10^3	6	8				12			11^2	13	9	7			5	4^1			24
1	2	3								9	6	8				13			10^1	12	11	7^2			5^3	4	14		25
1	2	4				12				9	7^2	8				13				11^3	10^1	6			5	3		14	26
1	2^1	3				12				9	7	8				13			10^3	11		6^2			5	4		14	27

HIBERNIAN

Year Formed: 1875. *Ground & Address:* Easter Road Stadium, 12 Albion Place, Edinburgh EH7 5QG. *Telephone:* 0131 661 2159. *Fax:* 0131 659 6488. *E-mail:* club@hibernianfc.co.uk *Website:* hibernianfc.co.uk
Ground Capacity: 20,421 (all seated). *Size of Pitch:* 105m × 68m.
Chairman: Ronald Gordon.
Manager: Jack Ross. *Assistant Head Coach:* John Potter.
Club Nickname: 'Hibs'; 'Hibees'.
Previous Grounds: Meadows 1875-78; Powderhall 1878-79; Mayfield 1879-80; First Easter Road 1880-92; Second Easter Road 1892.
Record Attendance: 65,860 v Hearts, Division I, 2 January 1950.
Record Transfer Fee received: £4,400,000 for Scott Brown from Celtic (2007).
Record Transfer Fee paid: £700,000 for Ulises de la Cruz to LDU Quito (2001).
Record Victory: 15-1 v Pebbles Rovers, Scottish Cup 2nd rd, 11 February 1961.
Record Defeat: 0-10 v Rangers, Division I, 24 December 1898.
Most Capped Player: Lawrie Reilly, 38, Scotland.
Most League Appearances: 446: Arthur Duncan, 1969-84.
Most League Goals in Season (Individual): 42: Joe Baker, 1959-60.
Most Goals Overall (Individual): 233: Lawrie Reilly, 1945-58.

HIBERNIAN – SPFL PREMIERSHIP 2020–21 LEAGUE RECORD

Match No.	Date	Venue	Opponents	Result		H/T Score	Lg Pos.	Goalscorers	Attendance
1	Aug 1	H	Kilmarnock	W	2-1	2-1	1	Boyle 2 [5, 34]	0
2	8	A	Livingston	W	4-1	3-0	1	Nisbet 3 (1 pen) [24, 37, 88 (p)], Doidge [41]	0
3	11	A	Dundee U	W	1-0	0-0	1	Doidge [65]	0
4	15	H	Motherwell	D	0-0	0-0	1		0
5	23	A	St Johnstone	W	1-0	0-0	2	Mallan (pen) [90]	0
6	30	H	Aberdeen	L	0-1	0-1	2		0
7	Sept 12	A	St Mirren	W	3-0	2-0	2	Nisbet [14], Newell [17], Boyle [59]	0
8	20	H	Rangers	D	2-2	1-1	3	Wright [22], Doidge [71]	0
9	27	A	Celtic	L	0-3	0-2	3		0
10	Oct 2	H	Hamilton A	W	3-2	2-0	3	Nisbet 2 [19, 35], Hanlon [63]	0
11	17	A	Ross Co	D	0-0	0-0	3		0
12	24	A	Kilmarnock	W	1-0	1-0	3	Nisbet (pen) [27]	0
13	Nov 6	A	Aberdeen	L	0-2	0-2	4		0
14	21	H	Celtic	D	2-2	0-0	4	Murphy [52], Nisbet [59]	0
15	24	H	St Johnstone	D	2-2	1-1	3	McGinn, P 2 [36, 83]	0
16	Dec 5	A	Motherwell	W	3-0	0-0	3	Boyle [59], Doidge [88], McGinn, S [90]	0
17	12	A	Hamilton A	W	4-0	2-0	2	Boyle (pen) [10], Doidge [39], McGinn, P [65], Nisbet [68]	0
18	19	H	Dundee U	D	1-1	1-0	3	Magennis [13]	0
19	23	H	St Mirren	W	1-0	1-0	3	Nisbet [18]	0
20	26	A	Rangers	L	0-1	0-1	4		0
21	30	H	Ross Co	L	0-2	0-1	4		0
22	Jan 2	H	Livingston	L	0-3	0-2	4		0
23	11	A	Celtic	D	1-1	0-0	4	Nisbet [90]	0
24	16	H	Kilmarnock	W	2-0	0-0	3	Power (og) [51], Gogic [80]	0
25	27	H	Rangers	L	0-1	0-0	4		0
26	30	A	Dundee U	W	2-0	1-0	4	McGregor [21], Boyle [69]	0
27	Feb 2	A	St Mirren	W	2-1	0-0	3	Porteous [55], Boyle (pen) [71]	0
28	6	H	Aberdeen	W	2-0	1-0	3	Boyle 2 (1 pen) [27 (p), 67]	0
29	20	H	Hamilton A	W	2-0	1-0	3	Boyle [13], Doig [70]	0
30	27	H	Motherwell	L	0-2	0-1	3		0
31	Mar 6	A	St Johnstone	L	0-1	0-1	3		0
32	13	A	Ross Co	W	2-1	0-0	3	Boyle (pen) [52], Nisbet [60]	0
33	20	A	Livingston	D	1-1	1-1	3	Doidge [41]	0
34	Apr 11	A	Rangers	L	1-2	0-1	3	Nisbet [78]	0
35	21	H	Livingston	W	2-1	2-0	3	Nisbet [8], Boyle (pen) [26]	0
36	May 1	H	St Johnstone	L	0-1	0-1	3		0
37	12	A	Aberdeen	W	1-0	1-0	3	Doidge [41]	0
38	15	H	Celtic	D	0-0	0-0	3		0

Final League Position: 3

Honours
League Champions: Division I 1902-03, 1947-48, 1950-51, 1951-52; First Division 1980-81, 1998-99; Championship 2016-17; Division II 1893-94, 1894-95, 1932-33.
Runners-up: Division I 1896-97, 1946-47, 1949-50, 1952-53, 1973-74, 1974-75; Championship 2014-15.
Scottish Cup Winners: 1887, 1902, 2016; *Runners-up:* 1896, 1914, 1923, 1924, 1947, 1958, 1972, 1979, 2001, 2012, 2013, 2021.
League Cup Winners: 1972-73, 1991-92, 2006-07; *Runners-up:* 1950-51, 1968-69, 1974-75, 1985-86, 1993-94, 2003-04, 2015-16.
Drybrough Cup Winners: 1972-73, 1973-74.

European: *European Cup:* 6 matches (1955-56 semi-finals). *Cup Winners' Cup:* 6 matches (1972-73). *UEFA Cup:* 64 matches (*Fairs Cup:* 1960-61 semi-finals, 1961-62, 1962-63, 1965-66, 1967-68, 1968-69, 1970-71. *UEFA Cup:* 1973-74, 1974-75, 1975-76, 1976-77, 1978-79, 1989-90, 1992-93, 2001-02, 2005-06. *Europa League:* 10 matches 2010-11, 2013-14, 2018-19).

Club colours: Shirt: Green with white sleeves. Shorts: White. Socks: Green.

Goalscorers: *League (48):* Nisbet 14 (2 pens), Boyle 12 (5 pens), Doidge 7, McGinn P 3, Doig 1, Gogic 1, Hanlon 1, Magennis 1, Mallan 1 (1 pen), McGinn S 1, McGregor 1, Murphy 1, Newell 1, Porteous 1, Wright 1, own goal 1.
William Hill Scottish Cup (11): Doidge 5, Boyle 3 (1 pen), Nisbet 2, Irvine 1.
Betfred Scottish League Cup (13): Mallan 3, Gullan 2, Nisbet 2, Doidge 1, Gray 1, Hallberg 1, Hanlon 1, Murphy 1, own goal 1.

Marciano O 32	McGinn P 37 + 1	Porteous R 32 + 2	Hanlon P 36 + 1	Wright D 11 + 9	Allan S 3 + 5	Gogic A 30 + 4	Newell J 32	Doig J 25 + 3	Boyle M 35 + 1	Nisbet K 28 + 5	Horgan D 4 + 1	Stevenson L 11 + 11	Doidge C 29 + 7	Hallberg M 12 + 13	Gullan J — + 14	Mallan S 4 + 10	Murphy J 14 + 5	Shanley R — + 1	Magennis K 4 + 10	Mackie S 2	Gray D 1 + 1	McGinn S — + 5	McGregor D 8 + 2	Bradley S — + 2	Barnes D 3 + 1	Macey M 3	Irvine J 14 + 1	Cadden C 8 + 2	*Match No.*
1	2	3	4	5^{4}	6^{3}	7	8	9^{1}	10	11^{2}	12	13	14	15															1
1	2	3	4			7	8	5	6	11^{1}	9^{2}		10	12	13														2
1	2	3	4		12	7	8^{1}	5	6	11	9^{2}		10	13															3
1	2	3	4		12	7	8^{1}	5^{2}	6	10	9^{3}	14	11	13															4
1	2	3	4	12	10^{1}	7	8^{4}	5^{3}	6		9^{2}		11	14	15	13													5
1	2	3	4	10	9^{1}		7	8^{3}	5				11	6^{2}	14	13	12												6
1	2	3	4	13		7	8^{2}	5	6^{3}	11^{1}			10		12	14	9^{4}	15											7
1	2	3	4	6^{1}		7	8	9^{2}	5	11		12	10	13															8
1	2	3	4	6^{1}		7	8	9^{3}	5	11		12	10^{2}			14	13												9
1	2	3	4	13		7	8^{1}		6	10^{2}		5	11	12		14	9^{3}												10
1	2	3	4			6	8		7	10		5^{1}	11		13	12			9^{2}										11
1	2	3	4			7	8	12	6	10^{3}		5^{1}	11	14		9^{2}			13										12
1	2	3	4	13		7	8^{1}	5	6	11^{3}			10		14	12	9^{2}												13
1	2	3	4			8	9^{1}		6	11				13		7^{2}	10^{3}			5	12	14							14
1	2	3	4^{2}			8^{1}	9		6	11^{3}			13		14	7	10			5			12						15
1	2	3	4	10^{1}			8		6	11		5	12	7^{3}	14		9^{2}					13							16
1	2	3	4	9^{4}			8^{5}		6^{1}	10^{3}		5	11	7^{2}	12	13			14			15		16					17
1	2	3	4	12		13	8		6	10		5	11	7^{1}					9^{2}										18
1^{3}	2	3	4	12		15	7		6	10^{2}		5	11■	8^{1}	14				9^{4}						13				19
	3	4	5	2^{1}		8	7	6	10	11				9	12										1				20
	2	3	4	9^{2}			8	5^{3}	6	10		13	11	7^{1}	12							14			1				21
	2	3	4	15		6^{1}	10	13	7	9		5^{2}	11^{3}		14^{4}	8	12								1				22
	2	3	4	7^{1}		6	9^{4}	5^{2}		10		12	13	8^{3}		14	11					15				1			23
	2	3	4			6		5	8^{4}	11^{1}			12	7	15	14	10^{3}									1	9^{2}	13	24
1	2	4^{4}	13		15	7^{1}		9^{2}	12	11			10	8^{3}					14				3				6	5	25
1	2		4	13		6		8	11^{1}				10				9^{2}		12				3				7	5	26
1	2	12	4			7		5	9	13			10				11^{2}		14				3^{3}				8	6^{1}	27
1	2		4			6		8^{4}	10	15		13	11^{3}	14			9^{2}		12				3				7^{1}	5	28
1	2		4		13	15	6^{4}	8^{3}	10	12		14	11^{2}				9^{1}						3				7	5	29
1	2	12	4		15	14	7		10	13		8^{1}	11				9^{2}						3^{3}				6^{4}	5	30
1	2	3	4			8	9^{3}	5	10	11			12	14			13										7^{2}	6^{1}	31
1	3	4	5			8	9	6^{3}	10	12		13	11^{2}										14				7	2^{1}	32
1	2	3	4			7	5	9	6	10			11														8		33
1	2	3	4			5^{3}	8	9	6	10			11^{1}	14					13								7^{2}	12	34
1	2	3	4	12		7	8^{2}		6	10		5	11^{1}						13								9		35
1	2	3	4	6^{4}		7^{2}	8^{1}	5^{3}	10			15	11	13					12					14			9		36
	2		4			8		5^{3}	6	11^{2}		14	10	7^{1}			13		12				3			1	9		37
1	14	4		11^{3}		6	7	15				5	13	9^{2}			10^{4}		8		2^{1}		3				12		38

INVERNESS CALEDONIAN THISTLE

Year Formed: 1994. *Ground & Address:* Caledonian Stadium, Stadium Road, Inverness IV1 1FF. *Telephone:* 01463 222880. *Fax:* 01463 227479. *E-mail:* info@ictfc.co.uk *Website:* ictfc.com
Ground Capacity: 7,780 (all seated). *Size of Pitch:* 105m × 68m.
Chairman: Ross Morrison. *Chief Executive:* Scot Gardiner.
Manager: Billy Dodds. *Assistant Manager:* Scott Kellacher.
Club Nicknames: 'Caley Thistle'; 'Caley Jags'; 'ICT'.
Record Attendance: 7,753 v Rangers, SPL, 20 January 2008.
Record Transfer Fee received: £400,000 for Marius Niculae to Dinamo Bucharest (July 2008).
Record Transfer Fee paid: £65,000 for John Rankin from Ross Co (July 2006).
Record Victory: 8-1 v Annan Ath, Scottish Cup 3rd rd, 24 January 1998; 7-0 v Ayr U, First Division, 24 April 2010; 7-0 v Arbroath, League Cup Northern Section Group C, 30 July 2016.
Record Defeats: 0-6 v Airdrieonians, First Division, 21 Sep 2000; 0-6 v Celtic, League Cup 3rd rd, 22 Sep 2010; 0-6 v Celtic, Scottish Premiership, 27 April 2014; 0-6 v Celtic, Scottish Cup 5th rd, 11 February 2017.
Most Capped Player: Richard Hastings, 38 (59), Canada.
Most League Appearances: 490: Ross Tokely, 1995-2012.
Most League Goals in Season: 27: Iain Stewart, 1996-97; Denis Wyness, 2002-03.
Most Goals Overall (Individual): 118: Denis Wyness, 2000-03, 2005-08.

INVERNESS CALEDONIAN TH – SPFL CHAMPIONSHIP 2020–21 LEAGUE RECORD

Match No.	*Date*	*Venue*	*Opponents*	*Result*		*H/T Score*	*Lg Pos.*	*Goalscorers*	*Attendance*
1	Oct 17	A	Dunfermline Ath	L	1-3	1-1	8	Todorov 2	0
2	24	H	Ayr U	D	1-1	0-0	7	Todorov 86	0
3	31	H	Arbroath	W	3-1	0-1	5	Mackay, D 47, Allardice 71, Todorov 79	0
4	Nov 7	A	Hearts	L	1-2	0-0	7	Doran 86	0
5	21	H	Raith R	W	2-0	1-0	5	Keatings 19, Allardice 68	0
6	Dec 4	A	Queen of the South	W	3-0	1-0	4	Kennedy 21, MacGregor 50, Storey 80	0
7	12	H	Dundee	D	2-2	0-1	5	Deas 72, Keatings 75	300
8	19	A	Alloa Ath	L	1-2	1-0	6	McKay 7	0
9	29	H	Dunfermline Ath	D	1-1	0-1	7	Storey 67	0
10	Jan 27	A	Greenock Morton	D	2-2	2-1	8	Sutherland 4, Mackay, D 15	0
11	Feb 3	A	Arbroath	D	1-1	0-1	7	Sutherland 48	0
12	17	H	Queen of the South	L	0-1	0-0	9		0
13	20	A	Ayr U	W	2-0	1-0	8	Mackay, D 31, Sutherland 54	0
14	23	H	Alloa Ath	D	2-2	0-1	6	Duffy 77, Keatings 78	0
15	26	H	Hearts	D	1-1	1-1	6	Storey 10	0
16	Mar 2	A	Dundee	L	1-2	0-2	7	Todorov 75	0
17	6	A	Alloa Ath	D	1-1	1-1	7	Todorov 27	0
18	9	H	Greenock Morton	L	0-1	0-0	9		0
19	12	H	Raith R	D	0-0	0-0	7		0
20	16	A	Raith R	W	1-0	0-0	6	Mackay, D 50	0
21	20	A	Dunfermline Ath	W	1-0	0-0	5	Carson 81	0
22	27	H	Arbroath	W	1-0	0-0	5	Todorov 69	0
23	Apr 6	A	Greenock Morton	W	4-1	2-0	4	Allardice 38, Todorov 2 40, 71, Mackay, D 80	0
24	10	A	Queen of the South	D	1-1	0-0	4	Todorov 68	0
25	20	H	Dundee	D	1-1	0-0	5	Mackay, D 84	0
26	24	A	Hearts	L	0-3	0-3	5		0
27	30	H	Ayr U	D	2-2	1-1	5	Mackay, D 6, Welsh (pen) 47	0

Final League Position: 5

Honours
League Champions: First Division 2003-04, 2009-10; Third Division 1996-97.
Runners-up: Championship 2019-20; Second Division 1998-99.
Scottish Cup Winners: 2015; Semi-finals 2003, 2004, 2019.
League Cup Runners-up: 2013-14.
League Challenge Cup Winners: 2003-04, 2017-18; *Runners-up:* 1999-2000, 2009-10.

European: *Europa League:* 4 matches (2015-16).

Club colours: Shirt: Blue and red vertical stripes. Shorts: Blue. Socks: Blue.

Goalscorers: *League (36):* Todorov 9, Mackay D 7, Allardice 3, Keatings 3, Storey 3, Sutherland 3, Carson 1, Deas 1, Doran 1, Duffy 1, Kennedy 1, MacGregor 1, McKay 1, Welsh 1 (1 pen).
William Hill Scottish Cup (7): Mackay D 2, Todorov 2, Keatings 1, Sutherland 1, Welsh 1.
Betfred Scottish League Cup (4): Sutherland 2, Keatings 1 (1 pen), MacGregor 1.

Ridgers M 27	Duffy W 13	Deas R 26	McKay B 19 + 2	McHattie K 1 + 3	Mackay D 19 + 5	Welsh S 17 + 4	Allardice S 23 + 2	MacGregor R 20 + 4	Keatings J 11 + 6	Todorov N 18 + 8	Vincent J 3 + 3	Harper C 19 + 4	Devine D 21 + 2	Kennedy K 6 + 2	Fyffe R — + 1	Doran A 2 + 9	Sutherland S 20 + 4	Storey M 13 + 7	Carson D 14 + 2	Allan S 5 + 1	Lyall A — + 2	*Match No.*
1	2	3	4	5	6	7	8	9^2	10	11^1	12	13										1
1	5	4	2^1		6		7	8	11^2	10		9	3	12	13							2
1	2	11	8		10	5	4	7^2	12	9^1		3	14	6^3		13						3
1	2	4	3		10^1	6	7	9^3	14	11		5		8^2		13	12					4
1		4	2		13	12	7	8	11^3			5	3	6^1		14	10	9^2				5
1		4	2			12	7	8	11^2	14		5	3	6^1		13	10^3	9				6
1		4	2				7	8	10	13		5	3	9^1		12	6^2	11				7
1		4	2			12	6	7	9^3	14		5	3	8^1		13	10^2	11				8
1		4	2		14	9	7			13	8	5	3	12		10^2	6^1	11^3				9
1	2	4			8^3	6	9^2	14	13	12	7	5	3			10^1	11					10
1	2		4		8^2	6	12		10^1	3	7	5				13	9	11				11
1	2	4	3		8^2	6^1	7	13	9^3	12		5					11	10	14			12
1	2	4	14		8^1	13	6	9^3		10^2		5	3				11	12	7			13
1	2	4			8^1		6	9^2	13	10		5	3				11	12	7			14
1	2	4			12	6	13	10^3	9^2	14		5	3				11	8	7^1			15
1	2	4	14		9^2	7	8^3		6	13		5	3^1				11	10	12			16
1	2	4	3		13	7		6	14	10^2		5^3	12				9	11^1	8			17
1	2	5	3		13		7	10	9^1	11			4			12	8		6^2			18
1		5	3		9	7	8	6		11			4				10		2			19
1		5	4	14	9	8^2	7	6	13^3	11			3				10^1	12	2			20
1		5	3	13	9^1	7	8	6		11^2			4				10	12	2			21
1		4		14	10	6	7	8^3		11^1		5	3				9^2	13	2	12		22
1		5	3		10^2		7	6		11	13	14	4				12	8^1	2	9^3		23
1		5	3		10		7	6^1		11^2	12	14	4				13	8	2	9^3		24
1		5	3■		6	7	8■	13		11^2		14	4				9^3	12	2	10^1		25
1		4			8	6	7^3	12		11^1		5	3				14	10^2	2	9	13	26
1		4			8^3	6		7		11^1		5	3			13	10^2	14	2	9	12	27

KILMARNOCK

Year Formed: 1869. *Ground & Address:* The BBSP Stadium, Rugby Park, Kilmarnock KA1 2DP. *Telephone:* 01563 545300. *Fax:* 01563 522181. *E-mail:* info@kilmarnockfc.co.uk *Website:* kilmarnockfc.co.uk
Ground Capacity: 18,128 (all seated). *Size of Pitch:* 102m × 67m.
Director: Billy Bowie.
Manager: Tommy Wright. *Assistant Manager:* Paul Stephenson.
Club Nickname: 'Killie'.
Previous Grounds: Rugby Park (Dundonald Road); The Grange; Holm Quarry; Rugby Park 1899.
Record Attendance: 35,995 v Rangers, Scottish Cup Quarter-final, 10 March 1962.
Record Transfer Fee received: £2,200,000 for Greg Taylor to Celtic (August 2019).
Record Transfer Fee paid: £340,000 for Paul Wright from St Johnstone (1995).
Record Victory: 11-1 v Paisley Academical, Scottish Cup 1st rd, 18 January 1930.
Record Defeat: 1-9 v Celtic, Division I, 13 August 1938.
Most Capped Player: Joe Nibloe, 11, Scotland.
Most League Appearances: 481: Alan Robertson, 1972-88.
Most League Goals in Season (Individual): 34: Harry 'Peerie' Cunningham 1927-28; Andy Kerr 1960-61.
Most Goals Overall (Individual): 148: Willy Culley, 1912-23.

KILMARNOCK – SPFL PREMIERSHIP 2020–21 LEAGUE RECORD

Match No.	Date	Venue	Opponents	Result		H/T Score	Lg Pos.	Goalscorers	Attendance
1	Aug 1	A	Hibernian	L	1-2	1-2	6	Burke 44	0
2	9	H	Celtic	D	1-1	1-1	8	Burke (pen) 24	0
3	12	A	Ross Co	D	2-2	0-1	7	Power 59, Burke 66	0
4	15	H	St Johnstone	L	1-2	0-0	8	Tshibola 61	0
5	22	A	Rangers	L	0-2	0-0	11		0
6	29	H	Dundee U	W	4-0	2-0	9	Kabamba 2 30, 78, Brophy 45, McKenzie 86	0
7	Sept 12	A	Aberdeen	L	0-1	0-1	10		0
8	19	H	Hamilton A	W	2-1	1-1	7	Kiltie 10, Kabamba 57	0
9	26	A	St Mirren	W	1-0	1-0	5	Kabamba 28	0
10	Oct 17	A	Livingston	W	3-1	2-1	5	Tshibola 24, Burke (pen) 37, Kiltie 57	0
11	24	H	Hibernian	L	0-1	0-1	5		0
12	Nov 1	H	Rangers	L	0-1	0-1	6		0
13	6	A	St Johnstone	L	0-1	0-0	6		0
14	21	H	Ross Co	W	3-1	1-1	6	Brophy 14, Kabamba (pen) 68, Burke 90	0
15	Dec 5	A	Hamilton A	L	0-1	0-0	6		0
16	13	A	Celtic	L	0-2	0-0	7		0
17	20	H	Aberdeen	L	0-2	0-0	8		0
18	23	A	Dundee U	L	0-2	0-2	8		0
19	26	H	Livingston	L	1-2	0-0	8	Burke (pen) 48	0
20	30	A	Motherwell	W	2-0	1-0	8	Kiltie 41, Whitehall (pen) 53	0
21	Jan 2	H	St Mirren	D	1-1	1-0	8	Whitehall 12	0
22	9	H	Hamilton A	W	2-0	1-0	7	Kiltie 2 36, 63	0
23	16	A	Hibernian	L	0-2	0-0	7		0
24	27	A	Livingston	L	0-2	0-0	8		0
25	30	H	St Johnstone	L	2-3	2-0	9	Burke 5, Tshibola 32	0
26	Feb 2	H	Celtic	L	0-4	0-1	9		0
27	6	A	St Mirren	L	0-2	0-1	10		0
28	10	H	Motherwell	L	0-1	0-0	10		0
29	13	A	Rangers	L	0-1	0-1	10		0
30	20	A	Aberdeen	L	0-1	0-1	10		0
31	27	H	Dundee U	D	1-1	0-1	11	Medley 64	0
32	Mar 6	A	Ross Co	L	2-3	1-1	12	Lafferty 2 (1 pen) 18, 77 (p)	0
33	20	H	Motherwell	W	4-1	1-1	11	Lafferty 1, McKenzie 55, Burke 57, Pinnock 83	0
34	Apr 10	H	Ross Co	D	2-2	2-1	11	Burke 3, Pinnock 16	0
35	21	H	Dundee U	W	3-0	3-0	10	Lafferty 3 (1 pen) 32, 35, 43 (p)	0
36	May 1	A	Motherwell	L	0-2	0-0	11		0
37	12	H	St Mirren	D	3-3	1-0	11	Lafferty 2 8, 61, Kiltie 81	0
38	16	A	Hamilton A	W	2-0	2-0	11	Pinnock 2 9, 44	0

Final League Position: 11

Honours
League Champions: Division I 1964-65;. Division II 1897-98, 1898-99.
Runners-up: Division I 1959-60, 1960-61, 1962-63, 1963-64; First Division 1975-76, 1978-79, 1981-82, 1992-93; Division II 1953-54, 1973-74; Second Division 1989-90.
Scottish Cup Winners: 1920, 1929, 1997; *Runners-up:* 1898, 1932, 1938, 1957, 1960.
League Cup Winners: 2011-12; *Runners-up:* 1952-53, 1960-61, 1962-63, 2000-01, 2006-07.

European: *European Cup:* 4 matches (1965-66). *Cup Winners' Cup:* 4 matches (1997-98). *UEFA Cup:* 32 matches (*Fairs Cup:* 1964-65, 1966-67 semi-finals, 1969-70, 1970-71. *UEFA Cup:* 1998-99, 1999-2000, 2001-02).

Club colours: Shirt: Blue with white stripes. Shorts: White. Socks: White with blue tops.

Goalscorers: *League (43):* Burke 9 (3 pens), Lafferty 8 (2 pens), Kiltie 6, Kabamba 5 (1 pen), Pinnock 4, Tshibola 3, Brophy 2, McKenzie 2, Whitehall 2 (1 pen), Medley 1, Power 1.
William Hill Scottish Cup (10): Lafferty 4 (1 pen), Kiltie 2, Millen 1 (1 pen), Oakley 1, Rossi 1, own goal 1.
Betfred Scottish League Cup (4): Whitehall 2, Brophy 1, Pinnock 1.
Scottish League Play-Offs (2): Haunstrup 1, Lafferty 1 (1 pen).

Eastwood J 1	Millen R 18 + 1	Broadfoot K 31	Findlay S 21 + 1	Waters C 18	Power A 32	Tshibola A 26 + 5	Burke C 28 + 9	Kiltie G 23 + 6	McKenzie R 23 + 6	Kabamba N 21 + 12	Rogers D 26 + 1	Brophy E 8 + 7	Whitehall D 5 + 12	Dicker G 26	Haunstrup B 21 + 6	Pinnock M 17 + 13	McGowan A 15 + 3	Brindley T — + 1	Rossi Z 11 + 3	Dikamona C 10 + 2	Mulumbu Y 6 + 11	Dabo D 1 + 5	Oakley G 3 + 3	Doyle C 11	Pierrick B 1 + 2	Medley Z 7 + 1	Lafferty K 8 + 1	Match No.
1^{1}	2	3	4	5	6	7^{3}	8	9^{2}	10	11	12	13	14															1
	2	3	4	5	6	8	9^{1}	13	11^{2}	10	1			7	12													2
	2	3	4	5	6	8	9			10	1			7	12	11^{1}												3
	2■	3	4	5	6	8	9^{3}	14		10^{2}	1	13		7		11^{1}	12											4
		3	4	5	6^{2}	8	9	13		12	1	10^{4}		7^{1}	11^{3}	14	2	15										5
		3	4^{5}	5^{3}		7^{2}	6^{1}	9	13	11	1	10^{4}		8	16	14			2	12	15							6
	2	3^{1}	4	5^{4}		7	6^{2}	9	13	11	1	10^{3}	15	8		14			16	12^{5}								7
	2	3	4	5		7	6^{2}	9^{1}	12	11	1	10■		8		13												8
	2^{1}	3	4	5	6	9	8^{2}	10	12	11	1			7					13									9
		3		5	6	7^{2}	9^{1}	11^{4}	12	10^{3}	1	13		8		14			2	4	15							10
		3	12	5	8	6^{4}	9	11^{3}		10	1	14		7^{1}		13			2	4^{2}	15							11
	2	3	4	5	6	8^{3}	9^{1}		11	10^{2}	1	12		7		13					14							12
	2	3	4	5^{2}	6	8^{3}	9	11^{1}		10	1	13	14	7		12												13
		3	4■			8	14		6	11^{2}	1	10^{3}	13	7	5	9^{1}	2		12									14
		3			7	6		11^{1}		10	1	9	12		5	8	2			4■								15
		3	4		8	7	12	6^{1}	9	11^{3}	1	14			5	10^{2}	2				13							16
		3	4^{3}	5	7	8	6	12	9	11^{2}	1	10	13		14■		2^{1}											17
		3	4	8	6^{3}	7	9	11^{4}	5	13	1	10^{1}	14			12				2^{2}	15							18
		3	4	5	7	8	6		9	11	1						2				10							19
		3	4	5^{4}	6	7^{3}	15	9	10^{2}	14	1		11^{1}		12	8	2				13							20
		3	4		8		6	10	9	12	1		11^{1}		5		2				7							21
		3	4		7^{3}	15	6^{4}	10	9	12	1		11^{2}		5	13	2				8^{1}	14						22
			4		8	9^{1}	12	10		13	1		11^{3}		5	7	2^{2}			3	6	14						23
	12		4^{2}		7	8	6^{3}		10	14	1				5	9	2		3			13	11^{1}					24
	2				7	8	6		9	11	1		12		5				4	3			10^{1}					25
	2				6	8	9^{1}		11	13				7^{2}	5	14			3	4			10^{3}	1	12			26
					6	7^{1}	12	9^{2}	8	14			11^{4}	3	5	15			2		13			1	10^{3}	4		27
					7^{3}		6	10^{1}	9^{2}	11				8	5	13	2			3	14		12	1		4		28
						6^{1}	12	9	11^{3}	10			13	7^{2}	5		2			3	8	14		1		4		29
	2	3					6^{2}	16		11^{3}			15	8	5^{1}	10	13			4^{5}	9	7^{4}		1		12	14	30
	2	3			7		12	10	6^{1}	13				8	5	9^{2}								1		4	11	31
	2■	3			7	16	14	10^{4}	6^{5}	13				8^{2}	5	9^{3}	12					15		1		4^{1}	11	32
		3			7		6^{2}		10				14	8	5	9^{3}	2				12			1	13	4	11^{1}	33
		3			7		6	12	10^{1}					8	5	9	2							1		4	11	34
	2	3			8	12	6^{1}		10	13				7	5	9			4					1			11^{2}	35
	2	3			7^{3}	12	13	10^{1}	6^{2}		1			8	5	9			4				14				11	36
	2	3		5^{1}	7		6	11^{2}			1		13	8	12	9			4								10	37
	2	3			6	13	8^{4}	9^{2}	12					7^{1}	5	10			4		15		14	1			11^{3}	38

LIVINGSTON

Year Formed: 1974. *Ground:* Tony Macaroni Arena, Almondvale Stadium, Alderstone Road, Livingston EH54 7DN.
Telephone: 01506 417000. *Fax:* 01506 429948.
E-mail: lfcreception@livingstonfc.co.uk *Website:* livingstonfc.co.uk
Ground Capacity: 9,865 (all seated). *Size of Pitch:* 98m × 69m.
Chairman: Robert Wilson. *Chief Executive:* John Ward.
Manager: David Martindale. *Assistant Manager:* Marvin Bartley.
Club Nickname: 'Livi Lions'.
Previous Ground: Meadowbank Stadium (as Meadowbank Thistle).
Record Attendance: 10,024 v Celtic, Premier League, 18 August 2001.
Record Transfer Fee received: £2,000,000 for Lyndon Dykes to QPR (August 2020).
Record Transfer Fee paid: £225,000 for Lyndon Dykes from Queen of the South (January 2019).
Record Victory: 8-0 v Stranraer, League Cup, 1st rd, 31 July 2012.
Record Defeat: 0-8 v Hamilton A. Division II, 14 December 1974.
Most League Appearances: 446: Walter Boyd, 1979-89.
Most League Goals in Season (Individual): 22: Leigh Griffiths, 2008-09; Iain Russell, 2010-11; Liam Buchanan, 2016-17.
Most Goals Overall (Individual): 64: David Roseburgh, 1986-93.

LIVINGSTON – SPFL PREMIERSHIP 2020–21 LEAGUE RECORD

Match No.	Date	Venue	Opponents	Result		H/T Score	Lg Pos.	Goalscorers	Attendance
1	Aug 1	A	St Mirren	L	0-1	0-1	7		0
2	8	H	Hibernian	L	1-4	0-3	11	Dykes (pen) 60	0
3	12	A	Motherwell	D	2-2	1-2	10	Dykes (pen) 11, Forrest 69	0
4	16	H	Rangers	D	0-0	0-0	10		0
5	23	A	Aberdeen	L	1-2	0-0	12	Pitman 69	0
6	29	H	Ross Co	W	1-0	0-0	10	Guthrie 64	0
7	Sept 12	H	Hamilton A	L	1-2	1-0	11	Want (og) 1	0
8	19	A	Celtic	L	2-3	1-2	12	Holt (pen) 17, Serrano 78	0
9	26	H	St Johnstone	W	2-0	2-0	9	Tiffoney 34, Forrest 35	0
10	Oct 2	A	Dundee U	W	2-1	0-1	6	Guthrie 53, Forrest 90	0
11	17	H	Kilmarnock	L	1-3	1-2	8	Pitman 11	0
12	25	A	Rangers	L	0-2	0-2	9		0
13	31	H	Motherwell	L	0-2	0-2	10		0
14	Nov 6	A	Ross Co	D	1-1	0-1	10	Devlin 56	0
15	21	H	St Mirren	L	0-1	0-0	10		0
16	Dec 5	H	Dundee U	W	2-0	0-0	9	Pitman 57, Bartley 73	0
17	12	A	St Johnstone	W	2-1	0-0	6	Guthrie 48, Robinson 65	0
18	23	A	Hamilton A	W	2-0	0-0	6	Guthrie 51, Mullin 90	0
19	26	A	Kilmarnock	W	2-1	0-0	6	Emmanuel-Thomas 51, Robinson 90	0
20	Jan 2	A	Hibernian	W	3-0	2-0	5	Mullin 9, Guthrie 16, Robinson 47	0
21	10	H	Ross Co	W	3-1	1-1	5	Robinson 9, Forrest 81, Hamilton 90	0
22	16	A	Celtic	D	0-0	0-0	5		0
23	20	H	Celtic	D	2-2	1-2	5	Brown 15, Emmanuel-Thomas 60	0
24	27	H	Kilmarnock	W	2-0	0-0	5	Kabia 89, Pitman 90	0
25	30	H	Aberdeen	D	0-0	0-0	5		0
26	Feb 2	A	Aberdeen	W	2-0	2-0	5	Lewis (og) 7, Devlin 16	0
27	6	H	St Johnstone	L	1-2	0-1	5	Pitman 83	0
28	13	A	Dundee U	L	0-3	0-2	5		0
29	20	A	St Mirren	D	1-1	1-1	5	McCarthy (og) 8	0
30	Mar 3	H	Rangers	L	0-1	0-0	5		0
31	6	A	Motherwell	L	1-3	0-1	5	Fitzwater 60	0
32	13	H	Hamilton A	W	2-1	2-1	5	Emmanuel-Thomas 16, Pitman 36	0
33	20	H	Hibernian	D	1-1	1-1	5	Sibbald 28	0
34	Apr 10	A	Celtic	L	0-6	0-2	5		0
35	21	A	Hibernian	L	1-2	0-2	5	Emmanuel-Thomas (pen) 85	0
36	May 1	H	Aberdeen	L	1-2	0-0	6	Emmanuel-Thomas 80	0
37	12	H	Rangers	L	0-3	0-1	6		0
38	15	A	St Johnstone	D	0-0	0-0	6		0

Final League Position: 6

Honours
League Champions: First Division 2000-01; Second Division 1986-87, 1998-99, 2010-11; League One 2016-17; Third Division 1995-96, 2009-10.
Runners-up: Second Division 1982-83; First Division 1987-88; Championship 2017-18.
Promoted via play-offs: 2017-18 (to Premiership).
Scottish Cup: Semi-finals 2001, 2004.
League Cup Winners: 2003-04. Semi-finals 1984-85.
League Challenge Cup Winners: 2014-15; *Runners-up:* 2000-01.

European: *UEFA Cup:* 4 matches (2002-03).

Club colours: All: Amber with black trim.

Goalscorers: *League (42):* Pitman 6, Emmanuel-Thomas 5 (1 pen), Guthrie 5, Forrest 4, Robinson 4, Devlin 2, Dykes 2 (2 pens), Mullin 2, Bartley 1, Brown 1, Fitzwater 1, Hamilton 1, Holt 1 (1 pen), Kabia 1, Serrano 1, Sibbald 1, Tiffoney 1, own goals 3.
William Hill Scottish Cup (4): Emmanuel-Thomas 2 (1 pen), Fitzwater 1, Poplatnik 1.
Betfred Scottish League Cup (22): Forrest 7, Mullin 3, Emmanuel-Thomas 2 (1 pen), Fitzwater 2, Poplatnik 2, Robinson 2, Lokotsch 1, Sibbald 1, Taylor-Sinclair 1, own goal 1.

McCrorie R 16	Fitzwater J 20	Guthrie J 36	Taylor-Sinclair A 5 + 1	Devlin N 35 + 1	Bartley M 32 + 1	Sibbald C 29 + 3	Ambrose E 17 + 5	Pitman S 37 + 1	Forrest A 21 + 9	Dykes L 3	Kouider-Aisser S — + 4	Robinson S 16 + 10	Souda A — + 2	Brown C 13 + 3	Poplatnik M 5 + 14	Tiffoney S 4 + 8	McMillan J 4 + 4	Stryjek M 22	Holt J 27 + 3	Hamilton J 2 + 3	Crawford R — + 1	Serrano J 19 + 5	Lokotsch L 2 + 2	Pignatiello C — + 1	Lawson S 7 + 8	Emmanuel-Thomas J 14 + 10	Mullin J 16 + 6	Kabia J 1 + 7	Reilly G 3 + 2	Longridge J 9 + 1	Diani D 2 + 2	Lithgow A 1 + 1	*Match No.*
1	2	3	4^{1}	5	6	7^{3}	8	9	10^{2}	11	12	13	14																				1
1	2^{4}	3		5^{3}	6	7^{1}	8	9	12	11	15	10^{2}		4	13	14																	2
1	2	3	4^{1}		6	7	12	9	10	11		5^{2}	13	8^{3}			14																3
	3	4		2	8^{3}	9		6	10^{2}		15	14			13^{4}		5	1	7	11^{1}	12												4
1	3^{2}	4		2	7	9^{3}	12	6	8^{1}			10				15	5^{4}		11	13		14											5
1		4		2	6	7^{1}	3	9	10			8				13			12			5	11^{2}										6
1		4		2	6	13	3	8	10		14	7^{1}				12			9^{3}			5	11^{2}										7
1		4		2	8^{4}	9^{2}	3	10	14			13		5^{3}		11^{1}			7			6	12	15									8
1		4		2	6		3	9	10^{1}			8^{3}		14		11^{2}			7			5	13		12								9
1		4		2	6		3	9	10^{1}			8			12	11^{2}	13		7			5											10
1		4		2	6	14	3	9	10^{3}			8^{1}			13	11^{2}			7			5				12							11
		3		5	6	7^{2}	2^{3}	9	13					4	14			1	11			8				10^{1}	12						12
		4		2	7	11^{1}		6	12					3		14		1	8^{2}			5			13	10	9^{3}						13
		4		2	7	6^{1}	13	10	9			8		3^{2}	12			1							5	11							14
		3		2	6	8^{3}		9^{1}	10					4	14			1	7			12			5^{2}	11	13						15
	3	4		2	6	9^{1}		7	10^{3}			13		14	11^{2}			1				5				12	8						16
	3	4		2	6	7		9	10^{2}			13		14	11^{3}	12^{4}		1	15			5					8^{1}						17
	3	4		2		7		9	10^{1}			11						1	6			5				12	8						18
	3	4		2	7	9^{1}		10				12			13			1	6			5				11^{2}	8						19
		4		2	6	10^{3}	3	9				11^{2}		5				1	7			13			12	14	8^{1}						20
		4		2	6	10^{2}	3	9	12			11^{1}		5				1	7	13						14	8^{3}						21
		4		2	7	10^{2}	3	9	12			11^{1}		5				1		13					6		8						22
1	2	3		14				7	10^{4}			15		4			5^{2}			11^{3}		8			6	9^{1}		12	13				23
	3	4		2	6^{4}	14		9	10^{2}			13		5				1	7							12	8^{1}	15	11^{3}				24
		3		5	6	10^{3}	2	9				11^{2}		4				1	7			8^{1}			14	12				13			25
			3	5			2	10				13						1	7			8			6	11^{1}	9^{2}		12	4			26
			4	2	6		3	9	10^{1}			11						1	7						8^{2}	12		13		5			27
	3■	4		2	7^{1}	11^{3}		6^{2}				10^{4}			14			1	8			5			15	12	9	13					28
1		4	12	2		6^{4}	3	9	10^{1}										7			5			14	15	8^{3}	13	11^{2}				29
	3	4		2	7	9		10				12^{3}				14		1	6^{1}			5			13		8		11^{2}				30
1	3	4	5^{2}	2	7^{1}	9		13	12						11	14						10			6^{3}		8						31
1	3	4		2	7	8^{3}		9	10^{1}						14				6			13				11^{2}	12			5			32
1	4	5		2	6	8		9	10^{1}						14				7			12			13	11^{2}				3^{3}			33
1	3^{2}	4		2	6^{3}	7^{4}	14	9	10^{5}						13				8							11^{1}	12			5	15	16	34
		4		2		7^{4}	5^{3}	9	13						14		12	1	8							11	10^{1}			6^{2}	15	3	35
	3	4		2	6	10^{2}		9							11^{1}			1	7							8	13	12		5			36
	3^{4}	4		2	13	8^{2}	16	6							15		14	1	7^{3}							11^{1}	10^{5}	12		5	9		37
	3	4			6^{2}			9	12						11^{3}		2	1	13							8	14	10^{1}		5	7		38

MONTROSE

Year Formed: 1879. *Ground & Address:* Links Park, Wellington St, Montrose DD10 8QD. *Telephone:* 01674 673200.
Fax: 01674 677311. *E-mail:* office@montrosefc.co.uk *Website:* montrosefc.co.uk
Ground Capacity: total: 4,936, (seated: 1,338). *Size of Pitch:* 100m × 64m.
Chairman: John Crawford. *Secretary:* Brian Petrie.
Manager: Stewart Petrie. *Assistant Manager:* Ross Campbell.
Club Nickname: 'The Gable Endies'.
Record Attendance: 8,983 v Dundee, Scottish Cup 3rd rd, 17 March 1973.
Record Transfer Fee received: £50,000 for Gary Murray to Hibernian (December 1980).
Record Transfer Fee paid: £17,500 for Jim Smith from Airdrieonians (February 1992).
Record Victory: 12-0 v Vale of Leithen, Scottish Cup 2nd rd, 4 January 1975.
Record Defeat: 0-13 v Aberdeen, 17 March 1951.
Most Capped Player: Alexander Keillor, 2 (6), Scotland.
Most League Appearances: 432: David Larter, 1987-98.
Most League Goals in Season (Individual): 28: Brian Third, Division II, 1972-73.
Most Goals Overall (Individual): 126: Bobby Livingstone, 1967-79.

MONTROSE – SPFL LEAGUE ONE 2020–21 LEAGUE RECORD

Match No.	*Date*	*Venue*	*Opponents*	*Result*		*H/T Score*	*Lg Pos.*	*Goalscorers*	*Attendance*
1	Oct 17	H	Falkirk	L	1-3	0-1	8	Quinn [50]	0
2	24	A	East Fife	D	2-2	1-2	8	Milne [34], Webster (pen) [69]	0
3	31	A	Forfar Ath	W	3-2	1-0	4	Watson 2 [30, 65], Callaghan [90]	0
4	Nov 7	H	Peterhead	W	3-2	1-1	4	McLean 2 [39, 46], Webster (pen) [71]	0
5	21	A	Clyde	L	2-3	1-1	6	McLean [17], Mochrie [69]	0
6	28	H	Partick Thistle	L	0-1	0-1	5		0
7	Dec 5	A	Cove R	W	2-1	0-1	5	Webster (pen) [57], McLean [63]	0
8	12	A	Airdrieonians	W	1-0	0-0	4	McLean [51]	0
9	19	H	Dumbarton	W	4-0	3-0	2	Steeves [8], Cameron Ballantyne 2 [24, 85], McLean [40]	0
10	22	A	Peterhead	D	1-1	0-1	2	Webster (pen) [68]	0
11	Jan 2	H	Forfar Ath	D	0-0	0-0	3		0
12	Mar 20	A	Falkirk	L	0-2	0-1	3		0
13	27	H	Clyde	D	2-2	2-2	4	Webster 2 (1 pen) [31 (p), 42]	0
14	30	H	East Fife	W	3-0	2-0	3	Webster [16], Steeves [39], Milne [59]	0
15	Apr 6	A	Dumbarton	D	0-0	0-0	3		0
16	10	H	Airdrieonians	D	2-2	2-0	4	Cameron Ballantyne [30], Crighton (og) [45]	0
17	15	A	Partick Thistle	L	0-5	0-2	5		0
18	20	H	Cove R	W	1-0	1-0	5	Fyvie (og) [15]	0
19	27	A	Airdrieonians	L	1-2	0-1	5	Webster [80]	0
20	29	H	Cove R	L	0-2	0-1	5		0
21	May 1	A	Falkirk	W	2-1	1-1	5	Cameron Ballantyne [45], Milne [62]	0
22	4	H	Partick Thistle	W	3-2	2-1	4	Rennie [19], McLean [36], Cameron Ballantyne [87]	0

Final League Position: 4

Honours
League Champions: Second Division 1984-85; League Two 2017-18.
Runners-up: Second Division 1990-91; Third Division 1994-95.
Scottish Cup: Quarter-finals 1973, 1976.
League Cup: Semi-finals 1975-76.
League Challenge Cup: Semi-finals 1992-93, 1996-97.

Club colours: Shirt: Blue with white sleeves. Shorts: Blue. Socks: White.

Goalscorers: *League (33):* Webster 8 (5 pens), McLean 7, Cameron Ballantyne 5, Milne 3, Steeves 2, Watson 2, Callaghan 1, Mochrie 1, Quinn 1, Rennie 1, own goals 2.
William Hill Scottish Cup (12): Johnston 3, McLean 2, Quinn 2, Cammy Ballantyne 1, Hawke 1, Milne 1, Mochrie 1, Webster 1.
Betfred Scottish League Cup (5): Webster 2, Cammy Ballantyne 1, Hawke 1, Steeves 1.
Scottish League Play-Offs (3): McLean 2, Webster 1.

Lennox A 10	Quinn A 13 + 3	Dillon S 18 + 1	Waddell K 11	Webster G 20 + 2	Ballantyne Cameron 20 + 1	Watson P 7 + 9	Milne L 20 + 2	Steeves A 20	Mochrie C 13 + 7	Johnston C 9 + 11	Rennie M 3 + 10	Campbell R 1 + 12	Hawke L — + 3	Campbell I 4	Callaghan L 6 + 11	McLean R 16 + 3	Cochrane H 11 + 2	Ballantyne Cammy 18	Fleming A 12	Allan M 1 + 2	Masson T 8 + 3	McGale R — + 3	Antoniazzi C 1 + 5	MacFarlane S — + 2	*Match No.*
1	2	3	4	5	6	7^{1}	8	9	10^{3}	11^{2}	12	13	14												1
1	4		2^{1}	5	7	8^{4}	6		11^{2}	9	10^{3}	13	14	3	12	15									2
1	3			2		6^{2}	10^{3}	5	7	11^{1}	12		15	4	14	13	8^{4}	9							3
1	3			2	8	7^{1}	11^{4}	5	9	13	12	15		4	14	10^{3}	6^{2}								4
1		13		8^{5}	10	12	9	5	7^{3}	14	16	15		4	6^{1}	11^{2}	3^{4}	2							5
		4	3^{1}	9	6	7^{4}	8^{3}	5	11	13		14			15	10^{2}	12	2	1						6
		4	3	7^{2}	8^{1}	6^{4}	10	5	12	14		15			13	11^{3}	9	2	1						7
		3	4	9	7^{2}	13	8^{3}	5	11^{4}	12		15			14	10^{1}	6	2	1						8
	16	4^{5}	3^{2}	9^{3}	2	12	8^{4}	5	11	15					13	10	7^{1}	6	1	14					9
		4	3	6	10^{1}	13	7	5		9					12	11	8^{2}	2	1						10
		4	3	9	6^{3}	12	8	5	11^{1}	10		14			13		7^{2}	2	1						11
1	13	4	3^{4}	10^{3}	9^{2}	15	6^{1}	5	8^{5}	14	16					11	12	2			7				12
1	13	4^{3}	3	9^{4}	8	7^{5}	15	5	12	11	16					10^{1}	6^{2}	2			14				13
1	2	4	3^{2}	5	8	13	12	9	14	10^{4}	15				6^{1}	11^{5}					7^{3}	16			14
1	3	4		6	7^{1}		8	5	12	10^{2}	11^{4}				9^{3}	14		2			13		15		15
1	3	4		8^{3}	7	13	9^{4}	5	10^{1}	12	14				15	11^{2}		2			6^{5}			16	16
	4	3^{2}		9^{5}	7	16	8^{4}	5		12		15			13	10^{3}		2	1		6^{1}	14	11		17
	3	4		13	8		9	5	11^{1}			15			6^{2}	10^{4}	7^{3}	2	1		12		14		18
	3	4		13	6^{4}		8	5^{3}	15	16		11^{2}			10^{1}		7^{5}	2	1	12	9		14		19
	3^{4}	4		9^{5}	13		6	5	11^{3}		16				8^{1}	10		2^{2}	1		7	14	12	15	20
	4^{3}	3		10^{4}	6^{2}		8	9	12	13	14	15				11^{1}		5	1	2	7				21
	4	3		2	6		8^{1}		12	9^{3}	11^{2}	14				10		5	1		7		13		22

MOTHERWELL

Year Formed: 1886. *Ground & Address:* Fir Park Stadium, Motherwell ML1 2QN. *Telephone:* 01698 333333. *Fax:* 01698 338001.
E-mail: mfcenquiries@motherwellfc.co.uk *Website:* motherwellfc.co.uk
Ground Capacity: 13,742 (all seated). *Size of Pitch:* 105m × 65m.
Chairman: James McMahon. *Chief Executive:* Alan Burrows.
Manager: Graham Alexander. *Assistant Manager:* Keith Lasley.
Club Nicknames: 'The Well'; 'The Steelmen'.
Previous Grounds: The Meadows; Dalziel Park.
Record Attendance: 35,632 v Rangers, Scottish Cup 4th rd replay, 12 March 1952.
Record Transfer Fee received: £3,000,000 (rising to £3,250,000) for David Turnbull to Celtic (August 2020).
Record Transfer Fee paid: £500,000 for John Spencer from Everton (January 1999).
Record Victory: 12-1 v Dundee U, Division II, 23 January 1954.
Record Defeat: 0-8 v Aberdeen, Premier Division, 26 March 1979.
Most Capped Player: Stephen Craigan, 54, Northern Ireland.
Most League Appearances: 626: Bobby Ferrier, 1918-37.
Most League Goals in Season (Individual): 52: Willie McFadyen, Division I, 1931-32.
Most Goals Overall (Individual): 283: Hugh Ferguson, 1916-25.

MOTHERWELL – SPFL PREMIERSHIP 2020–21 LEAGUE RECORD

Match No.	Date	Venue	Opponents	Result		H/T Score	Lg Pos.	Goalscorers	Attendance
1	Aug 3	A	Ross Co	L	0-1	0-1	9		0
2	8	H	Dundee U	L	0-1	0-0	10		0
3	12	H	Livingston	D	2-2	2-1	8	Turnbull[8], Campbell[35]	0
4	15	A	Hibernian	D	0-0	0-0	9		0
5	22	H	Hamilton A	L	0-1	0-0	10		0
6	30	A	Celtic	L	0-3	0-1	12		0
7	Sept 12	H	St Johnstone	W	1-0	1-0	12	Campbell[4]	0
8	20	A	Aberdeen	W	3-0	3-0	8	O'Hara (pen)[4], Long[9], Mugabi[23]	0
9	27	H	Rangers	L	1-5	0-3	9	Edmundson (og)[87]	0
10	Oct 24	H	Ross Co	W	4-0	1-0	8	Watt[37], O'Hara (pen)[54], Lang[64], Cole[72]	0
11	31	A	Livingston	W	2-0	2-0	7	Lang[22], Watt[45]	0
12	Nov 8	H	Celtic	L	1-4	0-2	7	Gallagher[72]	0
13	21	A	St Johnstone	D	1-1	1-1	7	O'Hara[17]	0
14	Dec 5	H	Hibernian	L	0-3	0-0	8		0
15	12	H	St Mirren	L	0-1	0-1	9		0
16	19	A	Rangers	L	1-3	1-0	10	Lang[6]	0
17	23	H	Aberdeen	D	0-0	0-0	10		0
18	26	A	Dundee U	D	1-1	1-0	9	Watt[9]	0
19	30	H	Kilmarnock	L	0-2	0-1	10		0
20	Jan 2	A	Hamilton A	L	0-3	0-1	11		0
21	9	A	St Mirren	D	1-1	1-0	10	Cole[27]	0
22	17	H	Rangers	D	1-1	1-0	11	Cole[21]	0
23	23	A	Aberdeen	L	0-2	0-1	11		0
24	27	A	Ross Co	W	2-1	0-1	10	Cole[51], Mugabi[72]	0
25	Feb 3	H	Dundee U	W	2-1	2-0	9	Cole[23], Long[28]	0
26	6	A	Celtic	L	1-2	0-1	9	Campbell[66]	0
27	10	A	Kilmarnock	W	1-0	0-0	9	Campbell[71]	0
28	13	H	Hamilton A	L	1-4	0-3	9	O'Hara (pen)[68]	0
29	20	H	St Johnstone	L	0-3	0-2	9		0
30	24	A	St Mirren	D	0-0	0-0	9		0
31	27	A	Hibernian	W	2-0	1-0	9	Roberts[25], Cole[46]	0
32	Mar 6	H	Livingston	W	3-1	1-0	9	Cole 2 (1 pen)[31 (p), 59], Long[69]	0
33	20	A	Kilmarnock	L	1-4	1-1	9	Maguire[8]	0
34	Apr 10	H	St Mirren	W	1-0	0-0	9	Cole[62]	0
35	21	A	Hamilton A	W	1-0	1-0	9	O'Hara[37]	0
36	May 1	H	Kilmarnock	W	2-0	0-0	7	Cole[47], O'Donnell[85]	0
37	12	A	Dundee U	D	2-2	0-2	7	Long[54], Cole[90]	0
38	16	H	Ross Co	L	1-2	1-0	8	Foley[7]	0

Final League Position: 8

Honours
League Champions: Division I 1931-32;. First Division 1981-82, 1984-85; Division II 1953-54, 1968-69.
Runners-up: Premier Division 1994-95, 2012-13; Premiership 2013-14; Division I 1926-27, 1929-30, 1932-33, 1933-34; Division II 1894-95, 1902-03.
Scottish Cup: 1952, 1991; *Runners-up:* 1931, 1933, 1939, 1951, 2011, 2018.
League Cup Winners: 1950-51; *Runners-up:* 1954-55, 2004-05, 2017-18.

European: *Champions League:* 2 matches (2012-13). *Cup Winners' Cup:* 2 matches (1991-92). *UEFA Cup:* 8 matches (1994-95, 1995-96, 2008-09). *Europa League:* 21 matches (2009-10, 2010-11, 2012-13, 2013-14, 2014-15, 2020-21).

Club colours: Shirt: Amber with maroon band. Shorts: Maroon with amber trim. Socks: Amber and maroon bands.

Goalscorers: *League (39):* Cole 11 (1 pen), O'Hara 5 (3 pens), Campbell 4, Long 4, Lang 3, Watt 3, Mugabi 2, Foley 1, Gallagher 1, Maguire 1, O'Donnell 1, Roberts 1, Turnbull 1, own goal 1.
William Hill Scottish Cup (8): Roberts 2, Campbell 1, Cole 1, Lamie 1, Long 1, O'Donnell 1, Watt 1.
Betfred Scottish League Cup (1): Watt 1.
UEFA Europa League (0).

Carson T 12	Grimshaw L 12 + 2	Gallagher D 27 + 2	Lamie R 27 + 4	McGinley N 12 + 7	O'Hara M 23 + 4	Donnelly L 1	Hastie J 7 + 7	Polworth L 18 + 3	Turnbull D 5	Long C 19 + 10	Lang C 12 + 5	Seedorf S 6 + 4	White J 3 + 15	Watt T 28 + 7	Mugabi B 21 + 2	Campbell A 34	Hylton J — + 5	Robinson H — + 1	O'Donnell S 34	Maguire B 14 + 10	Cole D 24 + 3	Chapman A 4 + 2	Crawford Robert 19 + 3	Archer J 4	Cornelius D — + 1	Carroll J 14 + 1	Kelly L 18	Lawless S 3 + 4	Maciver R — + 1	Smith H — + 5	Foley S 3 + 1	Roberts J 5 + 2	Magloire T 8 + 2	Johnston M 1 + 1	*Match No.*
1	2	3	4	5	6^{3}	7	8^{1}	9	10^{4}	11^{2}	12■	13	14	15																					1
1	2	3	5		7		6^{1}		9	10^{3}		11^{4}	13	12	4	8^{2}	14	15																	2
1	2	3	5		7		13	14	9^{1}	10^{3}		6^{2}	11		4	8	12																		3
1	15	3	5		7				8	13	11^{4}	9^{2}	10^{3}	14	4	6	12		2^{1}																4
1		3	5		7		14		8	13	11^{4}	9^{1}	10^{2}	15	4	6^{3}	12		2																5
1	6	3	5^{1}		8			9		10^{2}	12		13	11^{3}	4	7	14		2																6
1	13	3	5	6^{1}	8			9		14	10		12^{3}	11^{2}	4	7			2																7
1	9	3	5		6			8^{1}		11^{2}	13		12	10^{3}	4	7			2	14															8
1	9	2	4		7			8^{4}		12	11^{2}	14	15	10^{3}	3	6			5^{1}	13															9
1^{2}		4		5	3		15	8^{1}		11^{3}	13			10		6			2	7	9^{4}	12	14												10
		4		5	3			8		13	9^{1}		12	10		6			2	7	11^{2}	1													11
		4		5	3			8		13	9		14	10^{3}		6			2	7^{2}	11^{1}	1	12												12
		4	13	5	6			8		12^{3}	9^{1}		14	10	3				2		11^{2}	1	7												13
		4		5	6		13	8^{2}		9^{1}	11	12		10	3	7			2					1											14
	5	4	15		7^{4}		12	14		9^{2}	11^{3}			10	3^{1}	6			2	8	13			1											15
	6^{3}	4	5^{4}	12	9			16			11^{5}	15	13	10^{2}	3	7			2		14		8^{1}	1											16
	6	4	5		3			8			11^{1}		14	10^{3}		9			2	13	12		7^{2}	1											17
1	9	3	4		2			8			11^{1}		12	10		6			5				7^{2}		13										18
1^{3}	9^{1}	3	4		2■			6			14		15	11		8			5		10^{2}	13	7^{4}			12									19
	7	3					9^{1}	8					12	11	4	6			2	13	10^{2}	1				5									20
		4			7		9^{2}	8					12	11	3	6			2	13	10^{1}					5	1								21
		4	14					8^{2}				9^{4}		11^{3}	3	6			2	15	10		7^{1}			5	1	12	13						22
		4		15			14	8■		12		9^{1}		11^{3}	3	6			2	16	10^{5}		7^{2}			5^{4}	1			13					23
		4	13	14						9^{1}				11^{2}	3	7			2	6	10^{3}		8			5	1			12					24
			4	13^{3}						9^{1}				11^{2}	3	6			2	8	10		7			5	1			12	14				25
			4		12					9				11^{2}	3	6			2	8^{3}	10		7^{1}			5	1			14		13			26
			4		12					9^{3}				11	3	6			2	8	10^{1}		7^{2}			5	1			13			14		27
			4		7					9^{1}				10	3^{2}	6			2■	8	11					5	1						12	13	28
			4	13			12	8		9^{1}				11						6^{2}	10		7			5^{3}	1					14	3	2	29
			4											11		8			2	6	10		7			5	1					9	3		30
		13	4	12										11^{2}		8			2	6	10		7			5^{1}	1	14				9^{3}	3		31
		13	4	14						12^{3}				11^{1}		6			2	8	10		7			5	1					9^{2}	3		32
			4							13				11		6			2	8^{2}	10^{1}		7			5	1	12				9	3		33
		3	4	5	13					10^{1}					14	7			2	12	9		6				1	8^{2}				11^{3}			34
		3	4	9	8					11^{1}						6			5	12	10		7				1						2		35
		3	4	5			9^{3}			11^{2}				12	13	6			2	14	10						1	7^{1}			8				36
			4	5	14		8			10				13		6^{2}			2		11		12				1	9^{3}			7^{1}		3		37
			4	5	6		9^{1}			10				13					2		11		7^{2}				1	12			8		3		38

PARTICK THISTLE

Year Formed: 1876. *Ground & Address:* Energy Check Stadium at Firhill, 80 Firhill Rd, Glasgow G20 7AL. *Telephone:* 0141 579 1971. *Fax:* 0141 945 1525. *E-mail:* mail@ptfc.co.uk *Website:* ptfc.co.uk
Ground Capacity: 10,102 (all seated). *Size of Pitch:* 105m × 68m.
Chairman: Jacqui Low. *Chief Executive:* Gerry Britton.
Manager: Ian McCall. *Assistant Managers:* Alan Archibald and Neil Scally.
Club Nickname: 'The Jags'.
Previous Grounds: Overnewton Park; Jordanvale Park; Muirpark; Inchview; Meadowside Park.
Record Attendance: 49,838 v Rangers, Division I, 18 February 1922. *Ground Record:* 54,728, Scotland v Ireland, 25 February 1928.
Record Transfer Fee received: £350,000 for Liam Lindsay to Barnsley (June 2017); £350,000 for Aidan Fitzpatrick to Norwich C (July 2019).
Record Transfer Fee paid: £85,000 for Andy Murdoch from Celtic (February 1991).
Record Victory: 16-0 v Royal Albert, Scottish Cup 1st rd, 17 January 1931.
Record Defeat: 0-10 v Queen's Park, Scottish Cup 5th rd, 3 December 1881.
Most Capped Player: Alan Rough, 51 (53), Scotland.
Most League Appearances: 410: Alan Rough, 1969-82.
Most League Goals in Season (Individual): 41: Alex Hair, Division I, 1926-27.
Most Goals Overall (Individual): 229: Willie Sharp, 1939-57.

PARTICK THISTLE – SPFL LEAGUE ONE 2020–21 LEAGUE RECORD

Match No.	*Date*	*Venue*	*Opponents*	*Result*	*H/T Score*	*Lg Pos.*	*Goalscorers*	*Attendance*
1	Oct 17	A	Clyde	L 0-1	0-0	7		0
2	24	H	Airdrieonians	W 2-1	1-1	5	Graham ^{40}, Spittal ^{60}	0
3	31	A	Cove R	L 0-1	0-0	6		0
4	Nov 7	H	Falkirk	D 2-2	0-1	6	Cardle ^{66}, Graham ^{68}	0
5	21	H	East Fife	W 2-0	1-0	4	Graham 2 (1 pen) $^{17 (p), 78}$	0
6	28	A	Montrose	W 1-0	1-0	4	Murray ^{6}	0
7	Dec 5	H	Dumbarton	D 0-0	0-0	3		0
8	12	A	Forfar Ath	W 2-0	0-0	2	Gordon ^{52}, Docherty ^{78}	0
9	19	H	Peterhead	L 0-1	0-1	3		0
10	26	A	Falkirk	D 0-0	0-0	5		0
11	Mar 20	H	Cove R	D 1-1	0-0	5	Cardle ^{70}	0
12	27	A	Airdrieonians	W 4-2	1-1	3	Tiffoney 2 $^{35, 62}$, Graham ^{47}, Murray ^{49}	0
13	30	H	Forfar Ath	D 2-2	1-2	4	Murray ^{16}, Graham ^{66}	0
14	Apr 6	A	East Fife	D 2-2	0-2	5	Graham ^{72}, Tiffoney ^{90}	0
15	10	A	Peterhead	W 3-0	1-0	3	Cardle ^{39}, Tiffoney ^{52}, Graham ^{60}	0
16	13	H	Clyde	W 2-0	0-0	3	Rudden 2 $^{65, 90}$	0
17	15	H	Montrose	W 5-0	2-0	2	Rudden 2 $^{20, 38}$, Bannigan ^{52}, Tiffoney ^{55}, Gordon ^{77}	0
18	20	A	Dumbarton	W 2-0	0-0	1	Rudden ^{80}, MacIver ^{89}	0
19	24	H	Airdrieonians	W 1-0	1-0	1	Graham ^{31}	0
20	27	A	Cove R	D 2-2	1-1	1	Scott Ross (og) ^{7}, Tiffoney ^{77}	0
21	29	H	Falkirk	W 5-0	3-0	1	Rudden ^{30}, Tiffoney ^{32}, Graham 2 $^{41, 59}$, Cardle ^{72}	0
22	May 4	A	Montrose	L 2-3	1-2	1	MacIver ^{25}, Cardle ^{62}	0

Final League Position: 1

Honours
League Champions: First Division 1975-76, 2001-02, 2012-13; League One: 2020-21; Division II 1896-97, 1899-1900, 1970-71; Second Division 2000-01.
Runners-up: First Division 1991-92, 2008-09; Division II 1901-02.
Promoted via play-offs: 2005-06 (to First Division).
Scottish Cup Winners: 1921; *Runners-up:* 1930.
League Cup Winners: 1971-72; *Runners-up:* 1953-54, 1956-57, 1958-59.
League Challenge Cup Runners-up: 2012-13.

European: *Fairs Cup:* 4 matches (1963-64). *UEFA Cup:* 2 matches (1972-73). *Intertoto Cup:* 4 matches (1995-96).

Club colours: Shirt: Yellow with red stripes. Shorts: Black. Socks: Black.

Goalscorers: *League (40):* Graham 11 (1 pen), Tiffoney 7, Rudden 6, Cardle 5, Murray 3, Gordon 2, MacIver 2, Bannigan 1, Docherty 1, Spittal 1, own goal 1.
William Hill Scottish Cup (4): Gordon 1, Murray 1, Rudden 1, Tiffoney 1.
Betfred Scottish League Cup (3): Cardle 2, Spittal 1.

Sneddon J 10	Foster R 20	Brownlie D 20 + 1	McKenna C 9 + 2	Penrice J 14 + 4	Cardle J 14 + 6	Gordon S 11 + 10	Bannigan S 19	Docherty R 19	Kouider-Aisser S 1	Murray C 16 + 4	Spittal B 3 + 1	Lyons B 1 + 9	Niang M 12 + 5	Williamson R 12 + 2	Reilly C 1 + 1	Wright K 12	Breen R 3 + 1	Graham B 18 + 1	Lyon J — + 2	Rudden Z 7 + 6	Maciver R 3 + 4	Erskine C — + 2	Tiffoney S 9 + 2	Bell S 8 + 2	Geggan A — + 5	Owens B — + 1	Match No.
1	2[5]	3	4	5	6[4]	7[1]	8[2]	9	10[3]	11	12	13	14	15	16												1
	2	3		5		6	8	7		11[1]	9[2]	12	13			1	4	10									2
	2	3		5		7	8	6			10		9			1	4	11									3
		3		5	9[1]	13	8	6		11[2]	7	12		2		1	4	10									4
	5	4		9	6	12	8	7		10[1]			3	2		1		11									5
	5	4		9	6	12	8	7		10[1]			3	2		1		11									6
	5	4		9[1]	6	12	8	7		10[2]		13	3	2		1		11									7
	5	4		9[2]	6[3]	12	8	7		10[1]		13	3	2		1		11	14								8
	5	4		9[3]	6	12	8[1]	7		10[2]		14	3	2		1	15	11[4]		13							9
	5	4	2	9	6[2]	12	7	8[1]		10		13	3			1				11■							10
	5	4	2	9	12	8	7			6[1]			3			1		11			10[2]	13					11
	5	4[4]	14	12	8[5]	6	7[1]			9			3	2[2]		1		11		13			10[3]	15	16		12
1		13		5	6[1]	14	8	7[5]		9			3[4]	2				12		11[2]	10[3]	16	15	4			13
1	5[1]	3	14	15	16	6[2]	9	7		10[4]			4[5]	2[3]				11		12			8	13			14
1	5	3	2	14	6[2]		7	8[5]		11[1]		16						10[4]		15	12		9[3]	4	13		15
1	5	4	2[2]		8[3]	14	7	6		9[1]				13				11		12			10	3			16
1	5	3			12	6[1]	8	7[3]		14		16		2				10[5]		11[2]	13		9[4]	4	15		17
1	5	3	2		13	6[2]	7	8										11[1]		10	12		9	4			18
1	5	3	2		6[2]	8		7		12			13					11		10[3]			9[1]	4	14		19
1	5	3	2	13	12	8		7		6[4]			15					10[1]		11[2]	14		9[3]	4			20
1	5	3		6	13	12	8[5]	7[1]		14			16	2				10		11[3]			9[2]	4[4]	15		21
	5		4	8	9[1]	7[4]				15		11[2]	3	2	6[3]	1			12	13	10[5]		14			16	22

PETERHEAD

Year Formed: 1891. *Ground and Address:* Balmoor Stadium, Balmoor Terrace, Peterhead AB42 1EQ.
Telephone: 01779 478256. *Fax:* 01779 490682. *E-mail:* office@peterheadfc.co.uk *Website:* peterheadfc.org
Ground Capacity: 3,150 (seated: 1,000). *Size of Pitch:* 101m × 64m.
Chairman: Rodger Morrison.
Manager: Jim McInally. *Assistant Manager:* David Nicholls.
Club Nickname: 'Blue Toon'.
Previous Ground: Recreation Park.
Record Attendance: 8,643 v Raith R, Scottish Cup 4th rd replay, 25 February 1987 (Recreation Park); 4,855 v Rangers, Third Division, 19 January 2013 (at Balmoor).
Record Victory: 9-0 v Colville Park, Scottish Cup 2nd rd, 14 October 2017.
Record Defeat: 0-13 v Aberdeen, Scottish Cup 3rd rd, 10 February 1923.
Most League Appearances: 275: Martin Bavidge, 2003-13.
Most League Goals in Season (Individual): 32: Rory McAllister, 2013-14.
Most Goals Overall (Individual): 194: Rory McAllister, 2008, 2011-19.

PETERHEAD – SPFL LEAGUE ONE 2020–21 LEAGUE RECORD

Match No.	Date	Venue	Opponents	Result		H/T Score	Lg Pos.	Goalscorers	Attendance
1	Oct 17	A	Airdrieonians	L	0-2	0-1	10		0
2	24	H	Cove R	L	0-2	0-1	10		0
3	31	A	Clyde	W	2-0	0-0	8	Cameron 55, Brown, S 71	0
4	Nov 7	A	Montrose	L	2-3	1-1	8	Armour 2 12, 51	0
5	21	H	Dumbarton	W	1-0	1-0	7	Armour 5	0
6	28	H	Forfar Ath	L	0-1	0-1	7		0
7	Dec 5	A	Falkirk	L	1-2	0-2	8	Cameron 77	0
8	12	H	East Fife	W	2-1	1-1	7	Cameron 20, Brown, S 50	0
9	19	A	Partick Thistle	W	1-0	1-0	5	Brown, S 30	0
10	22	H	Montrose	D	1-1	1-0	6	Layne (pen) 21	0
11	Jan 2	A	Cove R	L	0-1	0-1	7		0
12	Mar 20	H	Airdrieonians	W	1-0	0-0	7	Jordon Brown 66	0
13	27	A	Dumbarton	W	1-0	0-0	5	Armour 54	0
14	30	H	Clyde	L	0-2	0-0	5		0
15	Apr 6	A	Forfar Ath	D	1-1	0-0	7	Ritchie 61	0
16	10	H	Partick Thistle	L	0-3	0-1	7		0
17	17	A	East Fife	L	1-2	1-0	7	Ritchie 24	0
18	20	H	Falkirk	W	1-0	0-0	7	Jason Brown 81	0
19	24	H	Clyde	W	3-0	0-0	7	Brown, S (pen) 54, Ritchie 2 56, 73	0
20	29	A	East Fife	W	3-1	1-1	7	Lyle 42, McDonald 47, Strachan 77	0
21	May 1	H	Forfar Ath	L	1-2	0-0	7	Brown, S 64	0
22	4	A	Dumbarton	L	2-3	1-1	7	Boyd 34, Lyle 62	0

Final League Position: 7

Honours
League Champions: League Two 2013-14, 2018-19.
Runners up: Third Division 2004-05, 2012-13; League Two 2017-18.
Scottish Cup: Quarter-finals 2001.
League Challenge Cup: Runners up: 2015-16.

Club colours: Shirt: Royal blue with white trim. Shorts: Royal blue with white trim. Socks: Royal blue.

Goalscorers: *League (24):* Brown S 5 (1 pen), Armour 4, Ritchie 4, Cameron 3, Lyle 2, Boyd 1, Jordon Brown 1, Jason Brown 1, Layne 1 (1 pen), McDonald 1, Strachan 1.
William Hill Scottish Cup (0).
Betfred Scottish League Cup (6): Boyd 2, Layne 2, Fraser 1, own goal 1.

Rae J 18	Bailey K 15 + 3	Brown Jason 20	MacKenzie G 5 + 1	Conroy R 15	Freeman K 22	Ferry S 13	Brown S 22	Boyd S 18 + 2	McCarthy A 19	Layne I 3 + 3	Cook A 7 + 6	Lyle D 3 + 13	Cameron L 7 + 4	Kesson D 1 + 13	Fraser G 8	Armour B 7 + 5	Bakar H — + 3	Brown Jordon 5 + 5	Ritchie H 10 + 1	Payne N 7 + 3	Strachan D 6 + 2	McDonald A 7 + 1	McGrath K — + 7	Wilson L 4	*Match No.*
1	2	3	4^{2}	5	6	7^{1}	8	9^{3}	10	11^{4}	12	13	14	15											1
1	3	4		5	2		8	10	7		9	11^{1}	6	12											2
1	3	4		5	2		9	11^{3}	8		10^{2}	12	6^{1}	14	7		13								3
1	3	4■		5^{2}	2		9		8^{1}		10	12	6	14	7	11^{3}	13								4
1	2			5	3	4^{3}	8	9	7	13^{4}	11^{2}	14	12		6	10^{1}	15								5
1	2^{1}	3	12	5	4		7	10	9^{3}		13	14	6		8^{2}	11									6
1	2	4	3^{1}	6	5		8	10	9^{2}		11	12	13		7										7
1	2	4	3	9	5		8	11^{2}	7^{3}	13	12	14	10^{1}		6■										8
1	2	4	3^{3}	9	5	7	8	10		11^{2}	12	14	13		6^{1}										9
1	2	4	3^{1}		5	8	10	11		12^{3}	9	13	6	14	7^{2}										10
1		3		5	2	4■	7	11■	8		9		6	12				10^{1}							11
1	2	3		5	4		7		9	11^{3}				13		12		8^{2}	6	10^{1}	14				12
1		3		5	2	7^{2}	8	13	9^{5}					15		11^{4}		14	6^{3}	10^{1}	16	4	12		13
1		4		5	2^{4}	6	7	9^{1}	10			15		14		11^{2}		12	8^{3}	13		3			14
1		3		5	2	7	8	11^{1}	9							10^{3}		13	6^{2}	12		4	14		15
1	12	3		5^{4}	2	7^{2}	8	11^{5}				15		16		14		9^{3}	6	10^{1}		4	13		16
1	13	3			5	7^{1}	8	11^{3}	9			10^{2}				12			6		2	4■	14		17
	3	4			5		7	10	8					12				9^{1}	6	11^{2}	2		13	1	18
	4	5■			2	6	7	9^{3}	11^{2}			14						13	10	8^{1}	3	12		1	19
	4				5		8	15	7			11^{1}		9^{3}		10^{4}		6^{2}	14	13	2	3	12	1	20
1	3^{2}	4			5	6	7	10^{5}	9^{1}		16			13		15		12	8^{3}	11^{4}	2		14		21
	14	4^{2}			5	6^{1}	7	10^{5}	9		13	12		16		15			8^{4}	11^{3}	2	3		1	22

QUEEN OF THE SOUTH

Year Formed: 1919. *Ground & Address:* Palmerston Park, Dumfries DG2 9BA. *Telephone:* 01387 254853.
Fax: 01387 240470. *E-mail:* admin@qosfc.com *Website:* qosfc.com
Ground Capacity: 8,690 (seated: 3,377) *Size of Pitch:* 102m × 66m.
Chairman: Billy Hewitson. *Vice-Chairman:* Craig Paterson.
Manager: Allan Johnston. *Assistant Manager:* Sandy Clark.
Club Nickname: 'The Doonhamers'.
Record Attendance: 26,552 v Hearts, Scottish Cup 3rd rd, 23 February 1952.
Record Transfer Fee received: £250,000 for Andy Thomson to Southend U (July 1994).
Record Transfer Fee paid: £30,000 for Jim Butter from Alloa Ath (1995).
Record Victory: 11-1 v Stranraer, Scottish Cup 1st rd, 16 January 1932.
Record Defeat: 2-10 v Dundee, Division I, 1 December 1962.
Most Capped Player: Billy Houliston, 3, Scotland.
Most League Appearances: 731: Allan Ball, 1963-82.
Most League Goals in Season (Individual): 37: Jimmy Gray, Division II, 1927-28.
Most Goals in Season: 43: Stephen Dobbie, 2018-19.
Most Goals Overall (Individual): 251: Jim Patterson, 1949-63.

QUEEN OF THE SOUTH – SPFL CHAMPIONSHIP 2020–21 LEAGUE RECORD

Match No.	Date	Venue	Opponents	Result		H/T Score	Lg Pos.	Goalscorers	Attendance
1	Oct 17	A	Ayr U	L	1-2	0-2	6	Dobbie (pen) 56	0
2	24	H	Raith R	L	2-5	1-3	8	Dobbie (pen) 5, Obileye 60	0
3	31	A	Dunfermline Ath	L	2-3	0-2	9	McKee 51, Dobbie (pen) 74	0
4	Nov 7	A	Arbroath	D	1-1	1-0	9	Maxwell 32	0
5	21	H	Alloa Ath	W	2-0	1-0	8	Buchanan 39, McKee 47	0
6	Dec 4	H	Inverness CT	L	0-3	0-1	8		0
7	12	A	Hearts	L	1-6	0-2	9	Obileye 72	0
8	19	A	Greenock Morton	L	0-2	0-1	10		0
9	26	H	Dundee	L	1-3	0-2	10	Shields 84	0
10	29	A	Raith R	W	2-0	1-0	8	Shields 18, Goss 90	0
11	Jan 2	H	Ayr U	W	3-2	2-1	8	Obileye (pen) 29, Shields 2 32, 90	0
12	16	H	Arbroath	D	2-2	0-0	8	Shields 2 46, 52	0
13	23	H	Greenock Morton	W	2-1	2-0	7	Obileye 15, Fitzpatrick 27	0
14	Feb 6	A	Alloa Ath	L	1-2	1-1	9	Jones 8	0
15	12	H	Hearts	D	1-1	1-0	7	Obileye (pen) 43	0
16	17	A	Inverness CT	W	1-0	0-0	5	Nortey 63	0
17	20	A	Dundee	W	3-2	2-0	4	Obileye (pen) 2, Hamilton, J (og) 37, Gibson 78	0
18	27	H	Dunfermline Ath	W	1-0	0-0	4	Gibson 50	0
19	Mar 6	A	Arbroath	W	4-2	3-2	4	Obileye 2 33, 50, Maxwell 38, Mebude 45	0
20	13	H	Alloa Ath	L	2-3	2-2	5	Mebude 11, East 37	0
21	20	A	Greenock Morton	L	1-2	1-1	6	Obileye 45	0
22	27	A	Hearts	W	3-2	2-1	6	Shields 2 2, 22, Irving (og) 82	0
23	Apr 10	H	Inverness CT	D	1-1	0-0	6	Fitzpatrick 65	0
24	13	H	Raith R	L	0-1	0-1	6		0
25	17	A	Dunfermline Ath	L	1-3	0-1	6	Maxwell 87	0
26	24	A	Ayr U	D	0-0	0-0	6		0
27	30	H	Dundee	L	0-2	0-2	6		0

Final League Position: 6

Honours
League Champions: Division II 1950-51; Second Division 2001-02, 2012-13.
Runners-up: Division II 1932-33, 1961-62, 1974-75; Second Division 1980-81, 1985-86; Division Three 1924-25.
Scottish Cup Runners-up: 2007-08.
League Cup: semi-finals 1950-51, 1960-61.
League Challenge Cup Winners: 2002-03, 2012-13; *Runners-up:* 1997-98, 2010-11.

European: *UEFA Cup:* 2 matches (2008-09).

Club colours: All: Royal blue with white trim.

Goalscorers: *League (38):* Obileye 9 (3 pens), Shields 8, Dobbie 3 (3 pens), Maxwell 3, Fitzpatrick 2, Gibson 2, McKee 2, Mebude 2, Buchanan 1, East 1, Goss 1, Jones 1, Nortey 1, own goals 2.
William Hill Scottish Cup (4): Fitzpatrick 1, Gibson 1, Maxwell 1, Shields 1.
Betfred Scottish League Cup (7): Shields 2, Dobbie 1, East 1, Fitzpatrick 1, Joseph 1, Maxwell 1.

Ferguson R 21	Nortey N 7 + 3	Buchanan G 25	Obileye A 27	Maxwell J 26	McCabe R 20 + 2	McKee J 10	Robinson H 1 + 2	Dobbie S 12 + 5	East E 18 + 5	Fitzpatrick A 16 + 6	Gibson W 26 + 1	Goss T 2 + 10	Shields C 21 + 1	McGorry C 6 + 4	Pybus D 13 + 3	Leighfield J 5	Joseph N 5 + 7	McKechnie K — + 1	Cowie C 1	Breen R 15	Mebude D 6 + 5	Jones I 9 + 2	McMahon D — + 1	Dickson C 5	*Match No.*
1	2	3	4	5■	6	7	8^{2}	9	10^{1}	11	12	13													1
1	5	3	4		8	7^{3}		11	10^{2}	9	2	14	6^{1}	12	13										2
1	13	2^{1}	3	4		8	14	10	12	5	9		11^{3}	7^{2}	6										3
		3	4	5		7		11	10^{1}	9	2	13	6^{2}		8	1	12								4
		3	4	5		8		11^{1}	12	6	2		10		7	1	9								5
	13	3	4	5	14	8		11	12	6^{2}	2^{1}		10		7	1	9^{3}								6
	8	3	4	5	7^{2}			11^{1}	12	9^{3}	2		10	14	6	1		13							7
1	6	3	4	5	7			9^{2}	10	12	2	11^{1}	8		13										8
1		3	4	5	9	7^{2}	13		11	6^{1}	2	12	10		8										9
		4	3	5	9	8			11	6	2	12	10^{1}		7				1						10
1		3	4	5	6	7			11	9^{1}	2	12	10		8										11
1		3	4	5	10	7^{1}		12	11	9	2		6		8										12
1			4	5	7				8	10^{1}	2		11	6	9					3	12				13
1			4	5^{1}	6				9	8^{2}	2	14	11^{3}		7		13			3	12	10			14
1	6	3	7	5					10		2	13		12	9^{1}		14			4	11^{2}	8^{3}			15
1	6	3	7	5				11^{2}	10		2	13		9^{1}			12			4		8^{3}	14		16
1	6	3	7	5	12			13	11		2			9^{1}			10^{2}			4		8			17
1		3	6	5	9				7		2			8			11^{1}			4	12	10			18
1		3	7	5	6			14	10	13	2		11^{2}							4	12	8^{1}		9^{3}	19
1		3	6■	5	8■				9^{2}	7^{1}	2	13	10	12						4	11				20
1		3	6	5	8			12	7^{2}	14	2		11	10^{3}			13			4	9^{1}				21
1		4	3	6	8			10^{1}	13		2		11^{2}				9			5	12			7	22
1		3	6	5	8					12	2		10							4	9	11^{1}		7	23
1		3	6	5	8					9^{2}	2		10				13			4	11	12		7^{1}	24
1		3	6^{1}	5	9			12		13	2		11		14					4	7	10^{2}		8^{3}	25
1		4	7	5	9			10^{1}	6^{2}	12	2		11		8					3		13			26
	12	3	6	5	8			11^{1}		7	2	10^{2}	13			1	14			4^{3}		9			27

QUEEN'S PARK

Year Formed: 1867. *Ground & Address:* Lesser Hampden, Mount Florida, Glasgow G42 9BA (2021-22 groundshare at Firhill Stadium). *Telephone:* 0141 632 1275. *Fax:* 0141 636 1612. *E-mail:* secretary@queensparkfc.co.uk *Website:* queensparkfc.co.uk
Ground Capacity: 10,102 (Firhill) (all seated). *Size of Pitch:* 105m × 68m.
President: David Hunter. *Chief Executive:* Leeann Dempster.
Head Coach: Laurie Ellis. *Assistant Head Coach:* Grant Murray.
Club Nickname: 'The Spiders'.
Previous Grounds: 1st Hampden (Recreation Ground); (Titwood Park was used as an interim measure between 1st & 2nd Hampdens); 2nd Hampden (Cathkin); 3rd Hampden, Hampden Park.
Record Attendance: 95,772 v Rangers, Scottish Cup 1st rd, 18 January 1930.
Record for Ground: 149,547 Scotland v England, 1937.
Record Transfer Fees: Not applicable due to amateur status from 1867-2019.
Record Victory: 16-0 v St. Peter's, Scottish Cup 1st rd, 12 Sep 1885.
Record Defeat: 0-9 v Motherwell, Division I, 26 April 1930.
Most Capped Player: Walter Arnott, 14, Scotland.
Most League Appearances: 532: Ross Caven, 1982-2002.
Most League Goals in Season (Individual): 30: William Martin, Division I, 1937-38.
Most Goals Overall (Individual): 163: James B. McAlpine, 1919-33.

QUEEN'S PARK – SPFL LEAGUE TWO 2020–21 LEAGUE RECORD

Match No.	Date	Venue	Opponents	Result	H/T Score	Lg Pos.	Goalscorers	Attendance
1	Oct 17	A	Stirling Alb	D 0-0	0-0	5		0
2	24	H	Albion R	W 2-0	2-0	4	Willam Baynham 2 5, 12	0
3	31	A	Stranraer	W 1-0	0-0	1	MacLean 83	0
4	Nov 7	A	Elgin C	W 1-0	1-0	1	Lyon 35	0
5	21	H	Brechin C	W 3-0	2-0	1	Quitongo 6, McHugh 24, Lyon 69	0
6	28	H	Stenhousemuir	W 3-1	1-1	1	Kilday 39, McHugh 87, Murray 90	0
7	Dec 5	A	Cowdenbeath	W 3-0	1-0	1	Grant 17, Gillespie 58, Murray 90	0
8	12	H	Edinburgh C	D 3-3	0-1	1	MacLean 49, McHugh (pen) 53, Willam Baynham 72	0
9	19	A	Annan Ath	W 2-1	0-0	1	McHugh 58, Slater 66	0
10	Mar 20	H	Stranraer	W 3-0	2-0	1	Doyle 20, Kilday 30, McHugh (pen) 65	0
11	27	A	Brechin C	W 2-0	2-0	1	O'Connor (og) 4, Longridge 15	0
12	30	A	Albion R	W 3-0	2-0	1	Lyon 7, Connell 31, Kouider-Aisser 63	0
13	Apr 3	H	Stirling Alb	W 1-0	1-0	1	Meggatt (og) 34	0
14	6	H	Cowdenbeath	W 3-0	1-0	1	Quitongo 16, Lyon 47, Willam Baynham 61	0
15	10	A	Stenhousemuir	W 3-1	2-0	1	Murray 5, McHugh 32, Longridge 48	0
16	13	H	Annan Ath	W 1-0	1-0	1	Murray 41	0
17	17	A	Edinburgh C	W 3-2	1-0	1	Grant 26, Murray 2 78, 85	0
18	20	H	Elgin C	D 0-0	0-0	1		0
19	23	H	Stranraer	L 0-1	0-1	1		0
20	27	A	Stirling Alb	W 2-1	1-0	1	Kouider-Aisser 2 45, 65	0
21	29	H	Edinburgh C	W 2-0	1-0	1	Longridge 8, Connell 59	0
22	May 4	A	Elgin C	L 2-3	0-0	1	Willam Baynham 54, Connell 87	0

Final League Position: 1

Honours
League Champions: Division II 1922-23; B Division 1955-56; Second Division 1980-81; Third Division 1999-2000; League Two: 2020-21.
Runners-up: Third Division 2011-12; League Two 2014-15.
Promoted via play-offs: 2006-07 (to Second Division); 2015-16 (to League One).
Scottish Cup Winners: 1874, 1875, 1876, 1880, 1881, 1882, 1884, 1886, 1890, 1893; *Runners-up:* 1892, 1900.
FA Cup Runners-up: 1884, 1885.
FA Charity Shield: 1899 (shared with Aston Villa).

Club colours: Shirt: Black and white thin hoops. Shorts: White. Socks: Black with white tops.

Goalscorers: *League (43):* McHugh 6 (2 pens), Murray 6, Willam Baynham 5, Lyon 4, Connell 3, Kouider-Aisser 3, Longridge 3, Grant 2, Kilday 2, MacLean 2, Quitongo 2, Doyle 1, Gillespie 1, Slater 1, own goals 2.
William Hill Scottish Cup (3): Longridge 1, Murray 1, Quitongo 1.
Betfred Scottish League Cup (1): Quitongo 1.

Muir W 21	Doyle M 22	Kilday L 22	Grant P 15	Robson T 13 + 1	Lyon D 13 + 5	Gillespie G 13 + 6	MacLean R 9 + 13	Longridge L 15 + 4	Baynham Willam 9 + 8	McHugh B 18 + 3	Galt D 11 + 10	Morrison S 7 + 8	Slater C 3 + 1	Paterson B 9 + 2	Quitongo J 9 + 6	McGlinchey M 1 + 2	Carroll C 8 + 3	Biggar C 1 + 2	Murray S 6 + 4	Connell L 9 + 2	Kouider-Aisser S 6 + 7	Mullen R 1	Herraghty J — + 1	Gillies M 1 + 1	*Match No.*
1	2	3	4	5	6	7	8^1	9	10	11^2	12				13										1
1	2	3^3	4	5^1	6^5	7	14	9	10	11^2	8^4	12	13	15	16										2
1	2	5	7	3		8	12	4^1	9	10^2	11^3	14	6		13										3
1	2	4	3	5	7^4	16	8	12^5	15	11^1	10^3		6		14	9^2	13								4
1	2	4		5^3	7		12		10^1	11	9^2	3		14	8^4	13	6	15							5
1	2	4		5	8	6	12		11^2	10	7	3			9^1				13						6
1	2	3	4	5	7	6	10			11	9				8^1				12						7
1	2	3	4^4	5		8	12	13	14	10	7^3	15			9^1		6		11^2						8
1	2	3	4	5	15		11^1	6^3	10	9^2	12		8^4			14	7		13						9
1	2	3	4	5	12	14	8^2	16		9^3	10^5				15		6^1		11	7^4	13				10
1	2	3^4	4		8	7	12	9	15	11^3	14	13		5	6^2						10^1				11
1	2	3^2	4		7^4	14	12	9^5	16	10	13	15		5	6^1					8	11^3				12
1	2	3	4		7^4	15	6^2	9	14	10^3	13			5	12					8	11^1				13
1	2^2	3	4		12	6	14	10^1	11^5		9	16		5	8^4				15	7^3	13				14
1	2	3	4■		8^4	7	14	9^5		11^1	16	12		5	6^3		15		10^2		13				15
1	2	4		5	14	16	15	9^4		13	12	3			6^3		7^1		11	8^5	10^2				16
1	2	4	3		6^1	7	12	9	13	10^2				5					11^3	8	14				17
1	2	3	4^4			7	6^2	9	13	10^1	15	12		5					11^3	8	14				18
	2	3		5	7		13	8	11^5	16	10^4	4					6^3	9^1		15	14	1^2	12		19
1	2	3				7	10^2	8^3		13	12	4		5			6	15		9^1	11^4			14	20
1	2	3		5	15	13	12	9^5	11^2	10	14	4					7^4			8^1	16			6^3	21
1	2	3		14	8^2	7^5	6	16	15	10	9^3	4		5^1			13			12	11^4				22

RAITH ROVERS

Year Formed: 1883. *Ground & Address:* Stark's Park, Pratt St, Kirkcaldy KY1 1SA. *Telephone:* 01592 263514. *Fax:* 01592 642833. *E-mail:* info@raithrovers.net *Website:* raithrovers.net
Ground Capacity: 8,473 (all seated). *Size of Pitch:* 103m × 64m.
Chairman: John Sim. *Vice Chairmen:* Steven MacDonald and David Sinton.
Manager: John McGlynn. *Assistant Manager:* Paul Smith.
Club Nickname: 'Rovers'.
Previous Grounds: Robbie's Park.
Record Attendance: 31,306 v Hearts, Scottish Cup 2nd rd, 7 February 1953.
Record Transfer Fee received: £900,000 for Steve McAnespie to Bolton W (September 1995).
Record Transfer Fee paid: £225,000 for Paul Harvey from Airdrieonians (July 1996).
Record Victory: 10-1 v Coldstream, Scottish Cup 2nd rd, 13 February 1954.
Record Defeat: 2-11 v Morton, Division II, 18 March 1936.
Most Capped Player: David Morris, 6, Scotland.
Most League Appearances: 430: Willie McNaught, 1946-51.
Most League Goals in Season (Individual): 38: Norman Haywood, Division II, 1937-38.
Most Goals Overall (Individual): 154: Gordon Dalziel (League), 1987-94.

RAITH ROVERS – SPFL CHAMPIONSHIP 2020–21 LEAGUE RECORD

Match No.	*Date*	*Venue*	*Opponents*	*Result*	*H/T Score*	*Lg Pos.*	*Goalscorers*	*Attendance*
1	Oct 17	H	Arbroath	W 3-0	3-0	2	Armstrong 31, Tumilty 36, Hendry (pen) 44	0
2	24	A	Queen of the South	W 5-2	3-1	1	Matthews 2, Duku 2 12, 85, Armstrong 27, Tait 69	0
3	31	A	Dundee	D 1-1	0-1	2	Musonda 86	0
4	Nov 7	H	Greenock Morton	W 5-0	2-0	1	Armstrong (pen) 20, Musonda 24, Matthews 2 48, 54, Mendy 82	0
5	21	A	Inverness CT	L 0-2	0-1	2		0
6	Dec 5	H	Dunfermline Ath	D 2-2	1-0	3	Duku 28, Musonda 65	0
7	11	A	Ayr U	D 0-0	0-0	3		0
8	26	A	Alloa Ath	W 5-2	2-0	3	Duku 17, Armstrong 33, Lokotsch 84, Ross 2 90, 90	0
9	29	H	Queen of the South	L 0-2	0-1	4		0
10	Jan 23	A	Hearts	W 3-2	1-0	4	Ugwu 5, Duku (pen) 47, Tumilty 52	0
11	26	H	Hearts	L 0-4	0-2	4		0
12	30	H	Dundee	W 3-1	1-1	2	Benedictus 22, Tumilty 54, Kennedy 60	0
13	Feb 3	A	Dunfermline Ath	L 1-4	0-1	3	Spencer 64	0
14	6	A	Greenock Morton	W 1-0	1-0	2	Davidson 12	0
15	20	A	Arbroath	L 0-1	0-0	3		0
16	27	H	Alloa Ath	W 3-1	0-1	2	Davidson 68, Hendry 84, Gullan 90	0
17	Mar 9	H	Ayr U	D 0-0	0-0	2		0
18	12	A	Inverness CT	D 0-0	0-0	2		0
19	16	H	Inverness CT	L 0-1	0-0	3		0
20	20	A	Ayr U	D 1-1	0-0	2	Benedictus 57	0
21	27	H	Greenock Morton	W 1-0	0-0	2	Gullan 82	0
22	30	H	Dunfermline Ath	W 5-1	3-1	2	Hendry 17, Vaughan 2 31, 40, Gullan 2 48, 77	0
23	Apr 10	H	Arbroath	D 2-2	1-0	2	Armstrong 2 29, 70	0
24	13	A	Queen of the South	W 1-0	1-0	2	Ugwu 17	0
25	17	A	Alloa Ath	W 2-1	0-1	2	Ugwu (pen) 56, Tait 61	0
26	24	A	Dundee	L 1-2	0-2	2	Benedictus 88	0
27	30	H	Hearts	L 0-4	0-1	3		0

Final League Position: 3

Honours
League Champions: First Division 1992-93, 1994-95; League One 2019-20; Second Division 2002-03, 2008-09; Division II 1907-08, 1909-10 (shared with Leith Ath), 1937-38, 1948-49.
Runners-up: Division II 1908-09, 1926-27, 1966-67;. Second Division 1975-76, 1977-78, 1986-87; League One 2017-18.
Scottish Cup Runners-up: 1913.
League Cup Winners: 1994-95; *Runners-up:* 1948-49.
League Challenge Cup Winners: 2013-14.

European: *UEFA Cup:* 6 matches (1995-96).

Club colours: Shirt: Navy with light blue trim. Shorts: Navy. Socks: Navy with white tops.

Goalscorers: *League (45):* Armstrong 6 (1 pen), Duku 5 (1 pen), Gullan 4, Benedictus 3, Hendry 3 (1 pen), Matthews 3, Musonda 3, Tumilty 3, Ugwu 3 (1 pen), Davidson 2, Ross 2, Tait 2, Vaughan 2, Kennedy 1, Lokotsch 1, Mendy 1, Spencer 1.
William Hill Scottish Cup (3): Tait 1, Ugwu 1, Vaughan 1.
Betfred Scottish League Cup (7): Duku 5, Hendry 1 (1 pen), own goal 1.
Scottish League Play-Offs (3): Vaughan 2, Ugwu 1.

MacDonald J 26	Tumilty R 27	Davidson I 14+2	Benedictus K 25	MacDonald K 22	Hendry R 25	Armstrong D 23+3	Matthews R 15+2	Tait D 17+6	Ross E 9+2	Duku I 12+8	Musonda F 17+5	Anderson G —+1	Spencer B 14+8	Mendy F 4+3	Lokotsch L 2+5	Coulson Q —+1	Thomson R 1+2	Ugwu G 9+4	Kennedy K 14+2	Vaughan L 7+3	Abraham T 2+5	King A 5+5	Gullan J 7+5	Cooney N —+2	Smith J —+1	*Match No.*
1	2^{2}	3	4	5	6	7	8	9	10	11^{1}	12	13														1
1	2	3	4^{1}	5^{2}	6	7	8	9	10^{3}	11	13		12	14												2
1	2	4^{2}	3	5^{1}	6	7	8	9	10^{3}		12		13	14	11											3
1	2	3^{1}	4		6	7	8^{3}	9	10^{2}		5		13	12	11	14										4
1	2		4	5	6	7	8	10^{2}	9^{1}	11	3		13		12											5
1	2		4	5	6	8	7	9	10^{2}	11^{1}	3		12		13											6
1	2		4	5	6	8	9	7	10^{1}	11^{2}	3		13		12											7
1^{3}	2		4		6	7	8	9^{1}	10	11^{2}	3		14	5	13		12									8
	2		4		6	7^{3}	8	9^{1}	10^{2}	11	5		13	3	12		1	14								9
1	2		4	5	7	8	6^{3}	13	14	12	3		9					11^{2}	10^{1}							10
1	2	13	4	5	8■	6^{3}		12	14	11^{2}	3		7						9	10^{1}						11
1	2	12	4^{2}	5		6^{1}		8		14	3		7						9	10	11^{3}	13				12
1	2	3		5		6^{3}		8^{1}		14	4		7						9	10^{2}	11	13	12			13
1^{3}	5	3		8	7	9					4		6	2			12	10^{2}	14		13		11^{1}			14
1	2	3	4	5	7	6		8^{1}		13								10^{3}	9		14	12	11^{2}			15
1	2^{1}	3	4	5	7	8	6			11^{2}	14		9					12	10^{3}				13			16
1	2	3	4	5	8	6^{1}	7	13		11^{3}			10^{2}					12	9				14			17
1	2		4	5	7	12	13	9		14	3							11^{2}	10			6^{1}	8^{3}			18
1	2	3■	4	5	6	7^{1}	8				12		9^{2}					11	10^{3}	14			13			19
1	2		4	5	7	6^{2}	8	14		11^{3}	3								13	10^{1}	12		9			20
1	2		4	5	7	6^{2}	14	8		11	3							10^{1}		12		9^{3}	13			21
1	2		4	5^{1}	7	12	6	13		14	3		8						10^{3}	9^{2}			11			22
1	2		3	5	6	7^{1}		9^{2}			4		8						10	11		13		12		23
1	2	3	4		6	8^{2}		12		13	5		7					11^{3}	10^{1}		14	9				24
1	2	3	4		8	5		10		12			7					11^{2}	9^{3}		14	6^{1}			13	25
1	2	3	4	5	7			6■					9					10^{1}	8^{2}	12		13	11			26
1	5	2■	4	9	6	12							8	3^{3}				14		10^{1}		7	11^{2}	13		27

RANGERS

Year Formed: 1873. *Ground & Address:* Ibrox Stadium, 150 Edmiston Drive, Glasgow G51 2XD.
Telephone: 0871 702 1972. *Fax:* 0870 600 1978. *Website:* rangers.co.uk
Ground Capacity: 51,082 (all seated). *Size of Pitch:* 105m × 68m.
Chairman: Douglas Park. *Deputy Chairman:* John Bennett.
Manager: Steven Gerrard. *Assistant Manager:* Gary McAllister.
Club Nickname: 'The Gers'; 'The Teddy Bears'.
Previous Grounds: Flesher's Haugh, Burnbank, Kinning Park, Old Ibrox.
Record Attendance: 118,567 v Celtic, Division I, 2 January 1939.
Record Transfer Fee received: £9,000,000 for Alan Hutton to Tottenham H (January 2008).
Record Transfer Fee paid: £12,000,000 for Tore Andre Flo from Chelsea (November 2000).
Record Victory: 13-0 v Possilpark, Scottish Cup 1st rd, 6 October 1877; v Uddingston, Scottish Cup 3rd rd, 10 November 1877; v Kelvinside Athletic, Scottish Cup 2nd rd, 28 September 1889.
Record Defeat: 1-7 v Celtic, League Cup Final, 19 October 1957.
Most Capped Player: Ally McCoist, 60, Scotland. *Most League Appearances:* 496: John Greig, 1962-78.
Most League Goals in Season (Individual): 44: Sam English, Division I, 1931-32.
Most Goals Overall (Individual): 355: Ally McCoist; 1985-98.

Honours
League Champions: (55 times) Division I 1890-91 (shared with Dumbarton), 1898-99, 1899-1900, 1900-01, 1901-02, 1910-11, 1911-12, 1912-13, 1917-18, 1919-20, 1920-21, 1922-23, 1923-24, 1924-25, 1926-27, 1927-28, 1928-29, 1929-30, 1930-31, 1932-33, 1933-34, 1934-35, 1936-37, 1938-39, 1946-47, 1948-49, 1949-50, 1952-53, 1955-56, 1956-57, 1958-59, 1960-61, 1962-63, 1963-64, 1974-75. Premier Division: 1975-76, 1977-78, 1986-87, 1988-89, 1989-90, 1990-91, 1991-92, 1992-93, 1993-94, 1994-95, 1995-96, 1996-97, 1998-99, 1999-2000, 2002-03, 2004-05, 2008-09, 2009-10, 2010-11, 2020-21. *Runners-up, tier 1:* 32 times. Championship 2015-16. League One 2013-14. Third Division 2012-13.
Scottish Cup Winners: (33 times) 1894, 1897, 1898, 1903, 1928, 1930, 1932, 1934, 1935, 1936, 1948, 1949, 1950, 1953, 1960, 1962, 1963, 1964, 1966, 1973, 1976, 1978, 1979, 1981, 1992, 1993, 1996, 1999, 2000, 2002, 2003, 2008, 2009; *Runners-up:* 18 times.

RANGERS – SPFL PREMIERSHIP 2020–21 LEAGUE RECORD

Match No.	Date	Venue	Opponents	Result	H/T Score	Lg Pos.	Goalscorers	Attendance
1	Aug 1	A	Aberdeen	W 1-0	1-0	2	Kent 21	0
2	9	H	St Mirren	W 3-0	1-0	2	McCarthy (og) 23, Morelos 2 69, 74	0
3	12	H	St Johnstone	W 3-0	2-0	1	Barisic 21, Kent 45, Aribo 49	0
4	16	A	Livingston	D 0-0	0-0	1		0
5	22	H	Kilmarnock	W 2-0	0-0	1	Roofe 50, Kent 77	0
6	29	A	Hamilton A	W 2-0	2-0	1	Hagi 15, Tavernier 20	0
7	Sept 12	H	Dundee U	W 4-0	2-0	1	Kent 13, Tavernier 39, Roofe 68, Arfield 87	0
8	20	A	Hibernian	D 2-2	1-1	1	Morelos 45, Arfield 57	0
9	27	A	Motherwell	W 5-1	3-0	1	Tavernier 2 (2 pens) 12, 37, Jones 28, Itten 2 75, 80	0
10	Oct 4	H	Ross Co	W 2-0	1-0	1	Tavernier (pen) 17, Barker 88	0
11	17	A	Celtic	W 2-0	1-0	1	Goldson 2 9, 54	0
12	25	H	Livingston	W 2-0	2-0	1	Aribo 9, Defoe 16	0
13	Nov 1	A	Kilmarnock	W 1-0	1-0	1	Tavernier (pen) 19	0
14	8	H	Hamilton A	W 8-0	4-0	1	Arfield 16, Roofe 2 18, 54, Aribo 2 19, 36, Barker 62, Tavernier 2 (1 pen) 65 (p), 69	0
15	22	H	Aberdeen	W 4-0	2-0	1	Kent 15, Roofe 29, Arfield 49, Tavernier (pen) 53	0
16	Dec 6	A	Ross Co	W 4-0	1-0	1	Roofe 28, Tavernier 56, Morris (og) 72, Defoe 90	0
17	13	A	Dundee U	W 2-1	2-1	1	Tavernier 26, Goldson 44	0
18	19	H	Motherwell	W 3-1	0-1	1	Roofe 2 73, 90, Itten 82	0
19	23	A	St Johnstone	W 3-0	2-0	1	Roofe 24, Kamara 31, Hagi 47	0
20	26	H	Hibernian	W 1-0	1-0	1	Hagi 33	0
21	30	A	St Mirren	W 2-0	2-0	1	Roofe 27, Morelos 33	0
22	Jan 2	H	Celtic	W 1-0	0-0	1	McGregor (og) 70	0
23	10	A	Aberdeen	W 2-1	1-0	1	Morelos 2 32, 50	0
24	17	A	Motherwell	D 1-1	0-1	1	Itten 72	0
25	23	H	Ross Co	W 5-0	3-0	1	Kent 6, Helander 28, Aribo 37, Jack 66, Goldson 81	0
26	27	A	Hibernian	W 1-0	0-0	1	Morelos 51	0
27	Feb 3	H	St Johnstone	W 1-0	0-0	1	Hagi 52	0
28	7	A	Hamilton A	D 1-1	0-0	1	Easton (og) 80	0
29	13	H	Kilmarnock	W 1-0	1-0	1	Jack 38	0
30	21	H	Dundee U	W 4-1	2-0	1	Hagi 35, Kent 38, Aribo 48, Morelos 64	0
31	Mar 3	A	Livingston	W 1-0	0-0	1	Morelos 87	0
32	6	H	St Mirren	W 3-0	2-0	1	Kent 14, Morelos 16, Hagi 46	0
33	21	A	Celtic	D 1-1	1-1	1	Morelos 38	0
34	Apr 11	H	Hibernian	W 2-1	1-0	1	Aribo 20, Kent 62	0
35	21	A	St Johnstone	D 1-1	0-0	1	Wright 55	0
36	May 2	H	Celtic	W 4-1	2-1	1	Roofe 2 26, 57, Morelos 33, Defoe 90	0
37	12	A	Livingston	W 3-0	1-0	1	Tavernier (pen) 42, Kent 57, Hagi 83	0
38	15	H	Aberdeen	W 4-0	2-0	1	Lewis (og) 5, Roofe 2 34, 60, Defoe 88	0

Final League Position: 1

League Cup Winners: (27 times) 1946-47, 1948-49, 1960-61, 1961-62, 1963-64, 1964-65, 1970-71, 1975-76, 1977-78, 1978-79, 1981-82, 1983-84, 1984-85, 1986-87, 1987-88, 1988-89, 1990-91, 1992-93, 1993-94, 1996-97, 1998-99, 2001-02, 2002-03, 2004-05, 2007-08, 2009-10, 2010-11; *Runners-up:* 8 times.
League Challenge Cup Winners: 2015-16; *Runners-up:* 2013-14.

European: *European Cup:* 161 matches (1956-57, 1957-58, 1959-60 semi-finals, 1961-62, 1963-64, 1964-65, 1975-76, 1976-77, 1978-79, 1987-88, 1989-90, 1990-91, 1991-92, 1992-93 final pool, 1993-94, 1994-95, 1995-96; 1996-97, 1997-98, 1999-2000, 2000-01, 2001-02, 2003-04, 2004-05, 2005-06, 2007-08, 2008-09, 2009-10, 2010-11, 2011-12).
Cup Winners' Cup: 54 matches (1960-61 runners-up, 1962-63, 1966-67 runners-up, 1969-70, 1971-72 winners, 1973-74, 1977-78, 1979-80, 1981-82, 1983-84).
UEFA Cup: 88 matches (*Fairs Cup:* 1967-68, 1968-69 semi-finals, 1970-71. *UEFA Cup:* 1982-83, 1984-85, 1985-86, 1986-87, 1988-89, 1997-98, 1998-99, 1999-2000, 2000-01, 2001-02, 2002-03, 2004-05, 2006-07, 2007-08 runners-up). *Europa League:* 31 matches (2010-11, 2011-12, 2017-18, 2019-20, 2020-21).

Club colours: Shirt: Royal blue with red and white trim. Shorts: White. Socks: Black with red tops.

Goalscorers: *League (92):* Roofe 14, Morelos 12, Tavernier 12 (7 pens), Kent 10, Aribo 7, Hagi 7, Arfield 4, Defoe 4, Goldson 4, Itten 4, Barker 2, Jack 2, Barisic 1, Helander 1, Jones 1, Kamara 1, Wright 1, own goals 5.
William Hill Scottish Cup (7): Roofe 2, Davis 1, Defoe 1, Patterson 1, Tavernier 1, own goal 1.
Betfred Scottish League Cup (6): Barisic 1, Bassey 1, Davis 1, Defoe 1, Goldson 1, Tavernier 1.
UEFA Europa League (23): Barisic 3 (3 pens), Morelos 3, Arfield 2, Itten 2 (1 pen), Kent 2, Roofe 2, Tavernier 2 (2 pens), Aribo 1, Goldson 1, Hagi 1, Helander 1, Kamara 1, Patterson 1, own goal 1.

McGregor A 27	Tavernier J 33	Goldson C 38	Balogun L 15 + 4	Barisic B 33	Kamara G 28 + 5	Jack R 16 + 3	Aribo J 27 + 4	Hagi I 23 + 10	Morelos A 26 + 3	Kent R 36 + 1	Arfield S 11 + 17	McLaughlin J 11	Davis S 29 + 6	Itten C 5 + 22	Barker B 4 + 6	Bassey C 3 + 5	Helander F 21 + 1	Roofe K 18 + 6	Patterson N 3 + 4	Stewart G — + 5	Defoe J 3 + 12	Jones J 2 + 1	Edmundson G — + 1	Zungu B 1 + 13	Wright S 1 + 8	Simpson J 4 + 1	King L — + 1	*Match No.*
1	2	3	4	5	6	7	8	9^{1}	10	11	12																	1
	2	3	4	5^{5}	8	7^{3}	6^{1}	9	10^{4}	11^{2}	13	1	12	14	15	16												2
	2	3	4^{1}	5	7	6^{2}	9^{4}	8	11^{5}	10^{3}	16	1	14	15			12	13										3
	2	3		5	6	7		9^{3}	10^{2}	11	8^{1}	1		14	13		4	12										4
	2^{3}	3		5	13	6		14		8^{1}	12	1	7^{2}	10	9^{5}		4	11^{4}	15	16								5
	2	3		5		6		10^{1}		9	12	1	7		8		4	11^{2}		13								6
	2	3		5^{1}	12	7^{2}		9	13^{4}	10	14	1	6		8^{3}	15	4	11										7
	2	3		5	7^{2}			11^{1}	10	9	8	1	6	13			4				12							8
1	2	3	12		7			14	10^{5}	11^{2}	8		6^{3}	13		5	4^{4}				15	9^{1}	16					9
	2	3	4	5^{3}	6	7^{2}		12	11	10^{4}	9	1	15		14	13						8^{1}						10
1	2	3		5	8	12	14		10^{3}	11	6^{1}		7	13	9^{2}		4											11
1	2	3				7	8^{2}	9^{1}		10^{3}	14		6	13		5	4	12			11^{4}	15						12
1	2	3	13	5		7	8^{2}		10^{1}	11	6		12	9			4											13
	2	3	4	5^{5}		7^{2}	8^{1}	15		11^{3}	6^{4}	1		16	14	13		9			10			12				14
1	2	3	4	5	13	7^{4}	8^{5}	15	10^{2}	11^{3}	6		12	16				9^{1}			14							15
1	2	3	4		8^{2}		6^{4}	14	10^{5}	11^{3}	12		7	16		5		9^{1}			13			15				16
1	2	3	4	5	8^{2}		14		10^{3}	11^{1}	6		7	12				9						13				17
1	2	3		5	8^{4}		12	13		11^{2}	6^{3}		7	14			4	9			10^{1}			15				18
1	2	3		5	8		6	9^{4}	12	11^{1}	15		7^{3}	14			4	10^{2}						13				19
1	2	3	4	5	8		6	9^{1}	14	11	12^{3}		7					10^{2}						13				20
1	2^{2}	3	14	5	8		6	9^{3}	10	12			7				4	11^{1}						13				21
1	2	3	4	5	8		6^{3}	12	10^{4}	11^{1}			7	13	15			9^{2}						14				22
1	2	3	4	5	8		6	9^{1}	10	11			7											12				23
1	2	3	4	5	6		8	9^{3}	10^{2}	11^{1}			7	12	14						13							24
1	2^{5}	3		5	7^{4}	12	9^{2}	8	11^{3}	10			6^{1}	15			4		16		14			13				25
1	2	3		5	6	7^{2}	9^{3}		10^{1}	11			8	14			4	12						13				26
1	2	3		5	13	6	8	9^{1}		11			7	12			4	10^{2}										27
1	2	3		5	8^{1}	12	6	9^{2}		11			14	10^{3}			4	13						7^{4}	15			28
1	2	3	4	5		7	6	9^{1}		11^{2}	13		8	10											12			29
1		3	2	5	12	6^{2}	8	9^{5}	10^{3}	11	14		7^{1}				4^{4}				15				13	16		30
1		3		5	8		9		10	11^{1}	6^{2}		7	12			4		2					13				31
1		3	12	5	6		8	9^{5}	10^{4}	11^{1}	13		7^{2}				4^{3}		2	16	14				15			32
1		3	2^{3}	5	6		8^{4}	9^{2}	10^{1}	11	13		7				4	14	12						15			33
1		3		5	8		6^{4}	12	10^{1}	11	13		7^{2}	15			4	9^{3}	2					14				34
	2^{4}	3		5^{5}	7		13	6^{1}			14	1	8^{3}	11		16		10	12		15				9^{2}	4		35
1	2	3		5^{3}	6		8	13	11^{2}	9			7					10^{1}			14				12	4		36
	2	3			6		5^{1}	7^{4}	10^{5}	11^{2}		1	8	13				9^{3}		16	12				14	4	15	37
1	2	3			8		5^{2}	6^{1}	10^{5}	11^{3}	12		7	16				9^{4}		15	13				14	4		38

ROSS COUNTY

Year Formed: 1929. *Ground & Address:* The Global Energy Stadium, Victoria Park, Dingwall IV15 9QZ. *Telephone:* 01349 860860. *Fax:* 01349 866277. *E-mail:* info@rosscountyfootballclub.co.uk
Website: rosscountyfootballclub.co.uk
Ground Capacity: 6,700 (all seated). *Size of Ground:* 105 × 68m.
Chairman: Roy MacGregor. *Chief Executive:* Steven Ferguson.
Manager: Malky Mackay. *Assistant Manager:* Don Cowie.
Club Nickname: 'The Staggies'.
Record Attendance: 6,110 v Celtic, Premier League, 18 August 2012.
Record Transfer Fee received: £500,000 for Liam Boyce to Burton Albion (June 2017).
Record Transfer Fee paid: £100,000 for Ross Draper from Inverness CT (August 2017).
Record Victory: 11-0 v St Cuthbert Wanderers, Scottish Cup 1st rd, 11 December 1993.
Record Defeat: 0-7 v Kilmarnock, Scottish Cup 3rd rd, 17 February 1962.
Most League Appearances: 308: Michael Gardyne, 2006-07, 2008-12, 2014-19.
Most League Goals in Season: 24: Andrew Barrowman, 2007-08.
Most League Goals (Overall): 48: Liam Boyce, 2014-17.

ROSS COUNTY – SPFL PREMIERSHIP 2020–21 LEAGUE RECORD

Match No.	*Date*	*Venue*	*Opponents*	*Result*	*H/T Score*	*Lg Pos.*	*Goalscorers*	*Attendance*
1	Aug 3	H	Motherwell	W 1-0	1-0	3	Stewart (pen) 24	0
2	8	A	Hamilton A	W 1-0	0-0	2	McKay 76	0
3	12	H	Kilmarnock	D 2-2	1-0	3	Draper 15, Stewart (pen) 80	0
4	15	H	Dundee U	L 1-2	1-1	3	Donaldson 29	0
5	22	A	St Mirren	D 1-1	0-1	3	Sheron (og) 70	0
6	29	A	Livingston	L 0-1	0-0	3		0
7	Sept 12	H	Celtic	L 0-5	0-2	5		0
8	19	A	St Johnstone	W 1-0	1-0	5	Vigurs 42	0
9	27	H	Aberdeen	L 0-3	0-1	6		0
10	Oct 4	A	Rangers	L 0-2	0-1	8		0
11	17	H	Hibernian	D 0-0	0-0	7		0
12	24	A	Motherwell	L 0-4	0-1	7		0
13	31	A	Dundee U	L 1-2	0-1	8	Shaw 81	0
14	Nov 6	H	Livingston	D 1-1	1-0	9	Shaw 28	0
15	21	A	Kilmarnock	L 1-3	1-1	9	Grivosti 42	0
16	Dec 6	H	Rangers	L 0-4	0-1	10		0
17	12	A	Aberdeen	L 0-2	0-1	11		0
18	19	H	Hamilton A	L 0-2	0-1	12		0
19	23	A	Celtic	L 0-2	0-1	12		0
20	26	H	St Mirren	L 0-2	0-0	12		0
21	30	A	Hibernian	W 2-0	1-0	11	Paton 25, Shaw 76	0
22	Jan 2	H	St Johnstone	D 1-1	1-1	12	Draper 21	0
23	10	A	Livingston	L 1-3	1-1	12	Lakin 28	0
24	16	H	Aberdeen	W 4-1	2-1	10	Shaw 2 1, 84, Lakin 20, Hylton 90	0
25	23	A	Rangers	L 0-5	0-3	10		0
26	27	H	Motherwell	L 1-2	1-0	11	Shaw 14	0
27	Feb 3	A	Hamilton A	W 2-1	0-1	11	White 81, McKay 85	0
28	6	H	Dundee U	L 0-2	0-0	11		0
29	21	H	Celtic	W 1-0	0-0	10	White 71	0
30	27	A	St Mirren	L 0-1	0-0	10		0
31	Mar 6	H	Kilmarnock	W 3-2	1-1	10	McKay 2 38, 49, Hjelde 47	0
32	13	H	Hibernian	L 1-2	0-0	10	McKay 50	0
33	20	A	St Johnstone	L 0-1	0-0	10		0
34	Apr 10	A	Kilmarnock	D 2-2	1-2	10	Gardyne 5, Iacovitti 54	0
35	21	H	St Mirren	L 1-3	1-0	11	White 18	0
36	May 1	A	Dundee U	W 2-0	2-0	10	White 24, Iacovitti 28	0
37	12	H	Hamilton A	W 2-1	1-1	10	Spittal 28, Lakin 70	0
38	16	A	Motherwell	W 2-1	0-1	10	Vigurs 49, Gardyne 65	0

Final League Position: 10

Honours
League Champions: First Division 2011-12; Championship 2018-19; Second Division 2007-08; Third Division 1998-99.
Scottish Cup Runners-up: 2010.
League Cup Winners: 2015-16.
League Challenge Cup Winners: 2006-07, 2010-11, 2018-19; *Runners-up:* 2004-05, 2008-09.

Club colours: Shirt: Navy blue with red and white trim. Shorts: Navy blue. Socks: Navy blue with red tops.

Goalscorers: *League (35):* Shaw 6, McKay 5, White 4, Lakin 3, Draper 2, Gardyne 2, Iacovitti 2, Stewart 2 (2 pens), Vigurs 2, Donaldson 1, Grivosti 1, Hjelde 1, Hylton 1, Paton 1, Spittal 1, own goal 1.
William Hill Scottish Cup (1): McKay 1.
Betfred Scottish League Cup (14): Stewart 4 (3 pens), Charles-Cook 2, Iacovitti 2, Shaw 2, Grivosti 1, Lakin 1, McKay 1, Paton 1.

Laidlaw R 33	Randall C 13 + 2	Donaldson C 26 + 2	Iacovitti A 34 + 2	Reid J 17 + 3	Paton H 25 + 10	Vigurs I 28 + 2	Tillson J 20 + 12	Erwin L 2 + 2	McKay B 14 + 14	Stewart R 19	Gardyne M 21 + 10	Charles-Cook R 9 + 17	Draper R 13 + 8	Shaw O 12 + 13	Mullin J 1 + 4	Tremarco C 8 + 4	Watson K 17 + 6	Kelly S 16 + 9	Morris C 12	Hylton J 7 + 11	Doohan R 5	Lakin C 14 + 5	Grivosti T 3 + 2	Wright M — + 2	Naismith J 17	Andreu T 4 + 2	Hjelde L 10 + 1	Spittal B 7 + 2	White J 11 + 1	*Match No.*
1	2	3	4	5	6^2	7	8^3	9^1	10^4	11	12	13	14	15																1
1	2	3	4	5	6^1	7	8^3	9^4	10^2	11	13	14	15		12															2
1	2	3	4	5	14	7	15	13	12	11^5	10^2	9^1	6^3	16	8^4															3
1	2	3	4	5^4	9^5	7	13	12	11^2	10	8^3	16	6^1		14	15														4
1	2^3	3^2	4	5^4	9^5	7^1			11	10	8	14	6		16	13	12	15												5
1	5^1	2	4	12		7^4	14		10^3	11	6^2		8^5	15	13	9■	3	16												6
1	2	3	4	5	9	6^4	8^2		11^3	10	7^1	14	13	12				15												7
1	2^2	3	4	5	10^1	6	8			7	9^3	13		11			12	14												8
1		3	4	5	9	6■	8^2		14	7	10^3	12		11^1			2	13												9
1		3	5	6	7		8		13	11	10^1	2^2	9^3	14					4	12										10
	2■	3^1	4		9^2	6	15		14	11	10^3	7					5	13			1	8^4	12							11
		3	5	6	7^1	8^2	15		12	10	11^3	2						14		13	1	9	4^4							12
	2^3	3	4	5	14	9^4			11^1	10	13	6^2		15				8			1	7	12							13
		3	4	5	6		13			9	10^2	12		11				7			1	8^1	2							14
		3	4	5	9^2		8^3		12	11		7					13	6		14	1	10	2^1							15
1	12	3	5	6^4	8	9	7^1			11	10^3	13					2^2		4	14				15						16
1	2^4	3	5^2	12	7^1	8	10^3		13	11	14	9						6	4	15										17
1			4	8	12	9	7^1		10^2	5	6			11			2		3					13						18
1			4	5	6	8^2	15		14	11^3	10^4		7^1	12			2	9	3	13										19
1		15	4	5■	7	6^2	13		14				8■	11		12^4	2^1	9	3	10^3										20
1	12	3	4		6	8^1	7							11		5	2	9		10										21
1		4		13	7^3	6^2	14		15		12		8	11^1			3	9		10^4		5			2					22
1		4	5		10^3	14	6^2		13			12	9	11			3	8^1				7^4			2	15				23
1	5		4		6	7			13			9^1	12	10^2					3	11		8			2					24
1	9^4		3		10^1	7^2	16					14	6^3	11			12		2	13		8^5			5	15	4			25
1			4		9	8^2			14		13	6^1	7	11^3					3	10					2		5	12		26
1			3^1		10^2	7^3			14		16			11^5		13		6	2	9^4		15			5	8	4		12	27
1			15		8^3				11^5		14		16	12		5^2		7^4	3	9^1		13			2	6	4		10	28
1			4		13		14				9^2	15	16			5	12	7^1	3^3			8			2	10^5		6^4	11	29
1		14	12		16		15				9^3			13		5^2	3	7				8^1			2	10^4	4	6^5	11	30
1		2	4		13		8^5		10^2				15	16		9^3	3	14				7^4			5		12	6^1	11	31
1		2^2	4^1		13		7^4		10		14		15	16			3			12		8^3			5		9	6^5	11	32
1		2^4	4		6^3	13	7		10^2		12			14			3			15		8^1			5		9		11	33
1			4		12	7^3	6^1		10^4		9^2	15	8			5	3	13		14					2				11	34
1			4		13	7^2	6		10^1		9^3	14	8^4	16			3			12					2^5		5	15	11	35
1		3	4			7	8				10^1	12						9				13			2		5	6^2	11	36
1		3	4^4		14	7	6				11^3	15					12	8				13			2		5^2	9^1	10	37
1		4				7	6				11^2	13				5^1	3	8				12			2			9	10	38

ST JOHNSTONE

Year Formed: 1884. *Ground & Address:* McDiarmid Park, Crieff Road, Perth PH1 2SJ. *Telephone:* 01738 459090. *Fax:* 01738 625 771. *E-mail:* enquiries@perthsaints.co.uk *Website:* perthstjohnstonefc.co.uk
Ground Capacity: 10,673 (all seated). *Size of Pitch:* 105m × 68m.
Chairman: Steve Brown. *Vice-Chairman:* Charlie Fraser.
Manager: Callum Davidson. *Assistant Manager:* Alec Cleland.
Club Nickname: 'Saints'.
Previous Grounds: Recreation Grounds; Muirton Park.
Record Attendance: 29,972 v Dundee, Scottish Cup 2nd rd, 10 February 1951 (Muirton Park): 10,545 v Dundee, Premier Division, 23 May 1999 (McDiarmid Park).
Record Transfer Fee received: £1,750,000 for Callum Davidson to Blackburn R (March 1998).
Record Transfer Fee paid: £400,000 for Billy Dodds from Dundee (January 1994).
Record Victory: 9-0 v Albion R, League Cup, 9 March 1946.
Record Defeat: 1-10 v Third Lanark, Scottish Cup 1st rd, 24 January 1903.
Most Capped Player: Nick Dasovic, 26, Canada.
Most League Appearances: 362: Steven Anderson, 2004-19.
Most League Goals in Season (Individual): 36: Jimmy Benson, Division II, 1931-32.
Most Goals Overall (Individual): 140: John Brogan, 1977-83.

ST JOHNSTONE – SPFL PREMIERSHIP 2020–21 LEAGUE RECORD

Match No.	Date	Venue	Opponents	Result		H/T Score	Lg Pos.	Goalscorers	Attendance
1	Aug 1	A	Dundee U	D	1-1	0-1	4	Craig 55	0
2	12	A	Rangers	L	0-3	0-2	9		0
3	15	A	Kilmarnock	W	2-1	0-0	7	Wotherspoon 85, O'Halloran 90	0
4	20	H	Aberdeen	L	0-1	0-0	7		0
5	23	H	Hibernian	L	0-1	0-0	8		0
6	29	H	St Mirren	W	1-0	0-0	6	May 72	0
7	Sept 12	A	Motherwell	L	0-1	0-1	6		0
8	19	H	Ross Co	L	0-1	0-1	8		0
9	26	A	Livingston	L	0-2	0-2	11		0
10	Oct 4	H	Celtic	L	0-2	0-0	12		0
11	17	A	Hamilton A	W	5-3	3-2	9	May 2 1, 33, Wotherspoon 14, Conway 2 69, 82	0
12	24	H	Dundee U	D	0-0	0-0	10		0
13	Nov 6	H	Kilmarnock	W	1-0	0-0	8	McNamara 70	0
14	21	H	Motherwell	D	1-1	1-1	8	May (pen) 34	0
15	24	A	Hibernian	D	2-2	1-1	7	McCann 35, Wotherspoon 76	0
16	Dec 6	A	Celtic	D	1-1	0-0	7	Kane 79	0
17	12	H	Livingston	L	1-2	0-0	8	Kane 54	0
18	19	A	St Mirren	L	2-3	2-1	9	May (pen) 22, Tanser 44	0
19	23	H	Rangers	L	0-3	0-2	9		0
20	26	A	Aberdeen	L	1-2	1-1	10	Gordon 38	0
21	30	H	Hamilton A	D	0-0	0-0	9		0
22	Jan 2	A	Ross Co	D	1-1	1-1	9	Conway (pen) 26	0
23	12	A	Dundee U	D	2-2	2-1	9	Melamed 16, Kane 38	0
24	16	H	St Mirren	W	1-0	0-0	9	Kane 46	0
25	27	H	Aberdeen	D	0-0	0-0	9		0
26	30	A	Kilmarnock	W	3-2	0-2	8	Melamed 53, Davidson 68, McCann 72	0
27	Feb 3	A	Rangers	L	0-1	0-0	8		0
28	6	A	Livingston	W	2-1	1-0	8	Tanser 45, Rooney 51	0
29	14	H	Celtic	L	1-2	0-0	8	Rooney 50	0
30	20	A	Motherwell	W	3-0	2-0	8	Melamed 2 (1 pen) 19, 50 (p), Kerr 45	0
31	Mar 3	A	Hamilton A	D	1-1	0-1	8	Melamed 87	0
32	6	H	Hibernian	W	1-0	1-0	7	Craig 16	0
33	20	H	Ross Co	W	1-0	0-0	6	Middleton 86	0
34	Apr 10	H	Aberdeen	L	0-1	0-0	6		0
35	21	H	Rangers	D	1-1	0-0	6	Craig (pen) 90	0
36	May 1	A	Hibernian	W	1-0	1-0	5	Middleton 22	0
37	12	A	Celtic	L	0-4	0-2	5		0
38	15	H	Livingston	D	0-0	0-0	5		0

Final League Position: 5

Honours
League Champions: First Division 1982-83, 1989-90, 1996-97, 2008-09; Division II 1923-24, 1959-60, 1962-63.
Runners-up: Division II 1931-32; First Division 2005-06, 2006-07; Second Division 1987-88.
Scottish Cup Winners: 2014, 2021.
League Cup Winners: 2020-21; *Runners-up:* 1969-70, 1998-99.
League Challenge Cup Winners: 2007-08; *Runners-up:* 1996-97.

European: *UEFA Cup:* 10 matches (1971-72, 1999-2000). *Europa League:* 14 matches (2012-13, 2013-14, 2014-15, 2015-16, 2017-18).

Club colours: Shirt: Blue with white trim. Shorts: White with blue trim. Socks: Blue and white hoops.

Goalscorers: *League (36):* May 5 (2 pens), Melamed 5 (1 pen), Kane 4, Conway 3 (1 pen), Craig 3 (1 pen), Wotherspoon 3, McCann 2, Middleton 2, Rooney 2, Tanser 2, Davidson 1, Gordon 1, Kerr 1, McNamara 1, O'Halloran 1.
William Hill Scottish Cup (7): Kane 2, Melamed 2, Middleton 1, O'Halloran 1, Rooney 1.
Betfred Scottish League Cup (19): May 5 (2 pens), Rooney 3, Wotherspoon 3, Hendry 2 (1 pen), Kane 2, Kerr 2, Conway 1, Davidson 1.

Parish E 9	Kerr J 31	Gordon L 35 + 1	McCart J 37	McNamara D 22	McCann A 32 + 2	Craig L 18 + 5	Booth C 15 + 3	O'Halloran M 13 + 12	Hendry C 8 + 8	Wotherspoon D 28 + 9	May S 17 + 17	Conway C 19 + 9	Tanser S 23 + 7	Olaofe I — + 2	Rooney S 20 + 7	Robertson J — + 5	Davidson M 14 + 7	Kane C 17 + 11	Clark Z 27	Bryson C 12 + 8	Melamed G 11 + 7	Middleton G 3 + 6	Brown J 4 + 1	Gilmour C 1 + 1	Zlamal Z 2	Ferguson A — + 1	Match No.
1	2	3	4	5	6	7	8^{3}	9■	10^{2}	11^{1}	12	13	14														1
1	2	3	4	5	6	7^{1}	8^{2}		11^{4}	10		9^{3}	15	12	13	14											2
1	4	3		7	9	6	13	10	11	12		8^{2}	5^{1}		2^{3}	14											3
1	2	3^{1}	4	5^{4}	6	7		10	11^{2}	9^{3}		12	8	13	15	14											4
1	2	3	4	7	9	6■		10^{2}	11^{3}	13	12	8^{1}	5			14											5
1	2	3	4	5	6			9^{3}	11^{2}	7	12	10^{1}	8				13	14									6
1	3	4^{3}	5	2	7	14		11^{2}	10^{1}	8^{4}	13	9	6				15	12									7
1	3	4	5	2^{4}	8	7^{2}		15	10^{1}	9^{3}	11	13	6				14	12									8
	3^{1}	12	4	2^{4}	8	6^{2}		10	13	14	11	7^{3}	5		15		9		1								9
	2^{1}	3	4	5	6			12	13	10^{2}	11	9	8				7		1								10
	2	3	4	5	7^{1}		14			10^{2}	11^{3}	9	8				6	13	1	12							11
	2	3	4	5	14			13	12	10	11^{1}	9^{3}	8				7		1	6^{2}							12
	2	3	4	5	6			12		10^{2}	11^{1}	9	8				7	13	1								13
	2	3	4	5	6			13		10	11^{2}	9^{3}	8				7^{1}	14	1	12							14
		3	4	5	7	6		10		12	11^{2}		8		2			13	1		9^{1}						15
		3	4	5	6	13		9^{2}		10	11		8		2			12	1	7^{1}							16
	2^{4}	3	4	5	7				12	9	10^{3}		8		14		15	11^{1}	1	6^{2}	13						17
	2■	3	4	5	6				13	10^{2}	11^{1}	9^{3}	8		12		7^{4}		1	14	15						18
		3	4	5^{2}	13	15	8	14■		10	12	9^{3}			2		7^{1}	11^{5}	1	6^{4}	16						19
		3	4	5	6	7^{3}	12		13■	8	10		9^{2}		2			11^{1}	1		14						20
		3	4	5	6	7^{2}	8	14		9^{3}	10^{1}	12			2		13	11	1								21
		3	4	5	6		8	9^{1}		12	13	11^{2}			2		7	10^{3}	1	14							22
		3	4		5	6	8^{2}		15	11^{1}	12	14	13		2		7	10^{3}	1		9^{4}						23
	2	3	4		7	15			14	9^{3}	13		8		5		12	11^{2}	1	6^{1}	10^{4}						24
	2	3	4					9^{3}		12	13	10^{2}	8		5		6	11^{1}	1	7		14					25
	2	3	4		7					11^{3}	12	13	8		5		6	10^{1}	1	14	9^{2}						26
	2	3	4		9	12					11^{4}	10^{3}	8		14		6^{1}	13	1	7	15		5^{2}				27
	2	3	4		7	6		13		10	12		8		5			11^{2}	1		9^{1}						28
	2^{3}	3	4		6		8	14		10	13	9^{1}			5			11^{2}	1	7		12					29
	2	3	4		6^{3}	7	8			10^{1}	13				5			11^{4}	1	12	9^{2}	14		15			30
	2	3	4			7		14		10	11^{2}		8		5^{1}				1	6^{3}	9	13	12				31
	2	3	4		6	7	8	5		9^{2}	13	12	14					10^{1}	1		11^{3}						32
	2	3	4		6	7	8^{1}			9	12		14		5			11^{3}	1		10^{2}	13					33
	2	3	4		6		8^{1}	16		13	12	10^{2}	14		5			11^{5}	1	7^{3}	15	9^{4}					34
	2	3	4		6	7	8^{4}	14		9^{3}	10^{1}		13		5			12	1	15	11^{2}						35
1	2	3	4		6		8	9^{4}		14	13	12			15		16	11^{1}		7^{3}		10^{5}	5^{2}				36
	3		4				8			12		11^{1}			2	15		10^{4}		6	14	9^{2}	5	7^{3}	1	13	37
	4		5			8	6^{3}			9^{2}	11^{4}	14			3		7	13		15	10^{1}	12	2		1		38

ST MIRREN

Year Formed: 1877. *Ground & Address:* The Simple Digital Arena, St Mirren Park, Greenhill Road, Paisley PA3 1RU.
Telephone: 0141 889 2558. *Fax:* 0141 848 6444. *E-mail:* info@stmirren.com *Website:* stmirren.com
Ground Capacity: 7,937 (all seated). *Size of Pitch:* 105m × 68m.
Chairman: Gordon Scott. *Chief Executive:* Tony Fitzpatrick.
Manager: Jim Goodwin. *Assistant Manager:* Lee Sharp.
Club Nickname: 'The Buddies'.
Previous Grounds: Shortroods 1877-79, Thistle Park Greenhill 1879-83, Westmarch 1883-94, Love Street 1894-2009.
Record Attendance: 47,438 v Celtic, League Cup, 20 August 1949.
Record Transfer Fee received: £850,000 for Ian Ferguson to Rangers (February 1988).
Record Transfer Fee paid: £400,000 for Thomas Stickroth from Bayer Uerdingen (March 1990).
Record Victory: 15-0 v Glasgow University, Scottish Cup 1st rd, 30 January 1960.
Record Defeat: 0-9 v Rangers, Division I, 4 December 1897.
Most Capped Player: Godmundur Torfason, 29, Iceland.
Most League Appearances: 403: Hugh Murray, 1997-2012.
Most League Goals in Season (Individual): 45: Dunky Walker, Division I, 1921-22.
Most League Goals Overall (Individual): 222: David McCrae, 1923-34.

ST MIRREN – SPFL PREMIERSHIP 2020–21 LEAGUE RECORD

Match No.	Date	Venue	Opponents	Result	H/T Score	Lg Pos.	Goalscorers	Attendance
1	Aug 1	H	Livingston	W 1-0	1-0	2	Tait 30	0
2	9	A	Rangers	L 0-3	0-1	6		0
3	15	A	Hamilton A	W 1-0	1-0	5	Obika 19	0
4	22	H	Ross Co	D 1-1	1-0	6	Obika 14	0
5	29	A	St Johnstone	L 0-1	0-0	5		0
6	Sept 12	H	Hibernian	L 0-3	0-2	7		0
7	16	H	Celtic	L 1-2	1-2	7	Erwin 3	0
8	19	A	Dundee U	L 1-2	0-1	9	Connolly 64	0
9	26	H	Kilmarnock	L 0-1	0-1	12		0
10	Oct 2	A	Aberdeen	L 1-2	0-0	12	Erhahon 54	0
11	Nov 6	H	Dundee U	D 0-0	0-0	11		0
12	21	A	Livingston	W 1-0	0-0	11	Doyle-Hayes 56	0
13	Dec 5	H	Aberdeen	D 1-1	1-1	11	McGrath (pen) 44	0
14	12	A	Motherwell	W 1-0	1-0	10	McGrath 13	0
15	19	H	St Johnstone	W 3-2	1-2	6	Erhahon 38, Erwin 82, Obika 87	0
16	23	A	Hibernian	L 0-1	0-1	7		0
17	26	A	Ross Co	W 2-0	0-0	7	Fraser 76, Dennis 85	0
18	30	H	Rangers	L 0-2	0-2	7		0
19	Jan 2	A	Kilmarnock	D 1-1	0-1	7	Rogers (og) 90	0
20	9	H	Motherwell	D 1-1	0-1	8	McGrath (pen) 79	0
21	16	A	St Johnstone	L 0-1	0-0	8		0
22	27	A	Dundee U	W 5-1	3-0	7	Shaughnessy 30, McGrath 2 (2 pens) 42, 45, Connolly 80, Dennis 85	0
23	30	A	Celtic	W 2-1	2-1	6	Dennis 18, Durmus 37	0
24	Feb 2	H	Hibernian	L 1-2	0-0	6	Obika 74	0
25	6	H	Kilmarnock	W 2-0	1-0	6	McAllister, K 38, Obika 61	0
26	10	H	Celtic	L 0-4	0-1	6		0
27	13	A	Aberdeen	D 0-0	0-0	7		0
28	17	H	Hamilton A	D 1-1	0-0	6	Durmus 53	0
29	20	H	Livingston	D 1-1	1-1	6	MacPherson 32	0
30	24	H	Motherwell	D 0-0	0-0	6		0
31	27	H	Ross Co	W 1-0	0-0	6	McGrath (pen) 82	0
32	Mar 6	A	Rangers	L 0-3	0-2	6		0
33	20	A	Hamilton A	D 1-1	1-0	7	McGrath (pen) 33	0
34	Apr 10	A	Motherwell	L 0-1	0-0	8		0
35	21	A	Ross Co	W 3-1	0-1	8	Erwin 50, Durmus 71, McGrath (pen) 90	0
36	May 1	H	Hamilton A	L 1-2	0-1	8	McGrath 71	0
37	12	A	Kilmarnock	D 3-3	0-1	8	McGrath 63, MacPherson 78, Quaner 83	0
38	16	H	Dundee U	D 0-0	0-0	7		0

Final League Position: 7

Honours
League Champions: First Division 1976-77, 1999-2000, 2005-06; Division II 1967-68; Championship 2017-18.
Runners-up: First Division 2004-05; Division II 1935-36.
Scottish Cup Winners: 1926, 1959, 1987; *Runners-up:* 1908, 1934, 1962.
League Cup Winners: 2012-13; *Runners-up:* 1955-56, 2009-10.
League Challenge Cup Winners: 2005-06; *Runners-up:* 2016-17.
B&Q Cup Runners-up: 1993-94. *Anglo-Scottish Cup:* 1979-80.

European: *Cup Winners' Cup:* 4 matches (1987-88). *UEFA Cup:* 10 matches (1980-81, 1983-84, 1985-86).

Club colours: Shirt: Black and white stripes. Shorts: Black. Socks: Black with white tops.

Goalscorers: *League (37):* McGrath 10 (7 pens), Obika 5, Dennis 3, Durmus 3, Erwin 3, Connolly 2, Erhahon 2, MacPherson 2, Doyle-Hayes 1, Fraser 1, McAllister K 1, Quaner 1, Shaughnessy 1, Tait 1, own goal 1.
William Hill Scottish Cup (9): McGrath 3 (2 pens), Dennis 2, Fraser 1, McCarthy 1, Shaughnessy 1, own goal 1.
Betfred Scottish League Cup (13): McGrath 4 (1 pen), Obika 3, Connolly 1, Durmus 1, Fraser 1, McCarthy 1, Tait 1, own goal 1.

Alnwick J 34	Fraser M 37	McCarthy C 37	Shaughnessy J 33	Tait R 31 + 2	Foley S 10 + 1	MacPherson C 14 + 18	McAllister K 12 + 23	McGrath J 34 + 1	Durmus I 23 + 8	Obika J 21 + 13	Morias J 7 + 7	Thorvaldsson I — + 2	Sheron N 6 + 1	Erhahon E 28 + 3	Jamieson L — + 2	Dennis K 6 + 11	Connolly D 18 + 11	Zlamal Z 3	Erwin L 17 + 10	Doyle-Hayes J 21 + 1	Mason B 5 + 2	Flynn R 8 + 6	Brophy E 4 + 2	Quaner C 2 + 4	Lyness D 1 + 1	Reid D — + 1	Henderson J 4 + 1	Finlayson D 2 + 1	*Match No.*
1	2	3	4	5	6	7	8^{1}	9	10^{2}	11	12	13																	1
1	2	3	4	5	9^{3}	7^{2}	13	8	10^{1}	11^{4}	12	14	6^{5}	15	16														2
1	2		4	5	3	6	9^{1}	8	12	11	10		7																3
1	2	3	4■	5	8	12	6^{1}	9		11^{2}	10		7			13													4
1	2^{2}	3		4	8	12	7^{1}	6	9	11	10^{4}		5^{3}		15	14	13												5
	2	3		5	4	15	14	6^{1}	9^{5}	11^{4}	16		7^{3}	8		10^{2}	13	1	12										6
	2	3	4	5	9^{2}		12	8	14	13	7^{1}			6			10^{3}	1	11										7
	2	3	4	5■	8	14	7^{1}	9^{4}	12	10^{3}	15			6^{2}			13	1	11										8
1	5	3	4		9^{4}	2	15	8^{3}	7^{1}	13	10		12	6^{2}			14		11										9
1	2	3	4			8		9		11	5		6	7					10										10
1	2	3	4	5	14	9^{3}		11^{4}		13	15			7		10^{1}			12	6	8^{2}								11
1	2	3		5	4	14	12	7^{1}		11^{2}				9			6^{3}		13	8	10								12
1	2	3	4	5		13	14	7	10^{3}	11^{1}				9^{4}		15	6^{2}		12	8									13
1	2	3	4	5^{1}		13		9	10	11^{3}				8			7^{2}		12	6	14								14
1	2^{4}	3	4	5		14	13	7	10^{1}	12	16			9^{2}			6^{3}		11^{5}	8	15								15
1	2	3	4	5^{1}		7^{4}	16	8^{5}	12	13	14			9		15	6^{2}		11^{3}		10■								16
1	2^{4}	3	4	5		14	6^{3}	7^{2}	12	13	10			9^{5}		15			11^{1}	8		16							17
1	2	3	4	5		15	14	8^{4}	12	11				9^{1}		13	6^{2}			7	10^{3}								18
1	2	3	4	5^{1}		15	12	7		11^{3}				9^{2}		14	6^{4}		13	8	10								19
1	2	3	4	5			6^{1}	7	13					9^{2}			10		11	8			12						20
1	2	3	4	5		6■	15	8		14				12			9^{2}		11^{1}	7			10^{3}	13^{4}					21
1	2	3	4	5			14	6	9^{1}	10^{3}				8		12	13					7	11^{2}						22
1	2	3	4	15		6^{3}	10^{1}	8	9	14				7		11^{4}	5^{2}			12			13						23
1■	2	3	4	5^{1}			15	6	9^{3}	13						11^{2}	14			8		7	10^{4}		12				24
	2	3	4	5			9^{1}	10	8^{2}	11				7			12			6		13			1				25
1	2	3	4			13	12	10^{3}	9	11				8			5^{1}		14	7		6^{2}							26
1	2	3	4	5		12	14		9	13				8			10^{2}		11^{1}	7^{3}		6							27
1	2	3	4	5^{1}		6	9		8	10				7			13		11^{2}			12							28
1	2	3	4	5		6^{1}	12		9	11				8			10^{2}		13			7							29
1	2	3	4	5^{3}		9^{2}	13	10	8	11^{1}				7			14		12	6									30
1	2	3	4^{5}	12		14	10	9	8^{2}	13				7^{3}			5^{4}		11^{1}	6		16		15					31
1	2	3	4	5		14	13	9^{1}	10^{3}	12				7^{4}			8^{5}			6		15		11^{2}		16			32
1	2	3	4	5			8^{1}	7	9	11^{3}				12			13		10^{2}	6		14							33
1	2	3	4^{2}			12	13	11	9					7^{1}		14	5		10^{3}	8		6^{4}					15		34
1	2	3	4	8^{2}		9	13	7	5							11^{3}			10					12			6^{1}	14	35
1		2	4	8^{1}		9^{2}	15	12	14					7		10^{3}			13	6				11^{4}			5	3	36
1	2	4				13	16	9	8^{1}	10^{3}						15	12		11^{2}	6^{4}		7		14			5	3^{5}	37
1	2	4		3		12	15	9		13				7		14	5^{4}		10^{3}			6^{2}	11^{1}				8		38

STENHOUSEMUIR

Year Formed: 1884. *Ground & Address:* Ochilview Park, Gladstone Rd, Stenhousemuir FK5 4QL. *Telephone:* 01324 562992. *Fax:* 01324 562980. *E-mail:* info@stenhousemuirfc.com *Website:* stenhousemuirfc.com
Ground Capacity: 3,776 (seated: 626). *Size of Pitch:* 101m × 66m.
Chairman: Iain McMenemy. *Vice-Chairman:* David Reid. *Chief Executive:* Jamie Swinney.
Manager: Stephen Swift. *Assistant Manager:* Frazer Wright.
Club Nickname: 'The Warriors'.
Previous Grounds: Tryst Ground 1884-86; Goschen Park 1886-90.
Record Attendance: 12,500 v East Fife, Scottish Cup quarter-final, 11 March 1950.
Record Transfer Fee received: £70,000 for Euan Donaldson to St Johnstone (May 1995).
Record Transfer Fee paid: £20,000 to Livingston for Ian Little (June 1995); £20,000 to East Fife for Paul Hunter (September 1995).
Record Victory: 9-2 v Dundee U, Division II, 16 April 1937.
Record Defeat: 2-11 v Dunfermline Ath, Division II, 27 September 1930.
Most League Appearances: 434: Jimmy Richardson, 1957-73.
Most League Goals in Season (Individual): 32: Robert Taylor, Division II, 1925-26.

STENHOUSEMUIR – SPFL LEAGUE TWO 2020–21 LEAGUE RECORD

Match No.	Date	Venue	Opponents	Result		H/T Score	Lg Pos.	Goalscorers	Attendance
1	Oct 17	A	Albion R	W	3-1	1-0	4	Spence 31, Little 72, Biabi 85	0
2	24	H	Stirling Alb	D	2-2	0-1	3	Biabi 75, Spence (pen) 83	0
3	31	A	Cowdenbeath	D	1-1	0-0	4	Graham 85	0
4	Nov 7	H	Edinburgh C	W	2-0	0-0	3	Spence 2 (1 pen) 46, 70 (p)	0
5	21	H	Annan Ath	L	1-2	0-1	4	McGuigan 56	0
6	28	A	Queen's Park	L	1-3	1-1	6	Biabi 11	0
7	Dec 5	H	Brechin C	W	2-1	2-0	5	Munro 7, McGuigan 32	0
8	12	H	Stranraer	D	2-2	0-2	5	Biabi 60, Graham 88	0
9	19	A	Elgin C	L	0-2	0-2	6		0
10	Mar 20	H	Albion R	W	2-0	1-0	6	Biabi 29, McGuigan 46	0
11	27	A	Edinburgh C	L	1-3	0-1	6	McGuigan 73	0
12	30	A	Stirling Alb	L	0-1	0-0	6		0
13	Apr 6	A	Brechin C	D	1-1	1-1	6	Hodge, J 36	0
14	8	H	Cowdenbeath	W	1-0	0-0	6	Yeats 50	0
15	10	H	Queen's Park	L	1-3	0-2	6	Muir (pen) 69	0
16	13	H	Elgin C	W	2-0	0-0	6	Muir 47, Biabi 85	0
17	15	A	Stranraer	L	0-4	0-3	6		0
18	20	A	Annan Ath	L	1-5	1-3	6	McGuigan 7	0
19	24	H	Cowdenbeath	L	0-2	0-0	6		0
20	27	A	Annan Ath	D	1-1	0-0	6	Hopkirk 82	0
21	29	H	Albion R	L	0-1	0-1	7		0
22	May 4	A	Brechin C	W	1-0	0-0	6	McGuigan 80	0

Final League Position: 6

Honours
League Runners-up: Third Division 1998-99.
Promoted via play-offs: 2008-09 (to Second Division); 2017-18 (to League One).
Scottish Cup: Semi-finals 1902-03. Quarter-finals 1948-49, 1949-50, 1994-95.
League Cup: Quarter-finals 1947-48, 1960-61, 1975-76.
League Challenge Cup Winners: 1995-96.

Club colours: Shirt: Maroon with white trim. Shorts: White. Socks: Maroon.

Goalscorers: *League (25):* Biabi 6, McGuigan 6, Spence 4 (2 pens), Graham 2, Muir 2 (1 pen), Hodge J 1, Hopkirk 1, Little 1, Munro 1, Yeats 1.
William Hill Scottish Cup (5): McGuigan 3, Hodge 1, Tiffoney 1.
Betfred Scottish League Cup (4): Biabi 1, Graham 1, Spence 1 (1 pen), Tapping 1.

Smith G 2	Tiffoney J 15	Munro A 9	Little C 18 + 1	Yeats C 12	Brown P 5 + 2	Tapping C 17	Hodge J 15 + 3	Spence G 8 + 3	Hopkirk D 9 + 5	Muir T 14 + 3	Biabi B 14 + 7	McGuigan M 13 + 7	Fairley J — + 6	Grigor J 6 + 4	Blair R 19 + 2	Erskine C — + 1	Martin Patrick 29	Halleran T 3 + 8	Graham C 1 + 5	Watters R 5	Hodge B 1	McQueen C 1 + 2	Corbett A 10 + 1	Collins T 4 + 6	Kane C 7 + 2	Howarth J 4 + 1	Brydon J 9	McCracken A 1 + 1	Shiels M — + 1	*Match No.*
1	2^4	3	4	5	6^2	7	8	9^3	10	11^1	12	13	14	15																1
1^3	2	3	4	5	9^4	6	15	11	7^1	10^2	13	14			8	12														2
	2	3	4	5		8	14	10^3		11^2	9	12			7		1	6^1	13											3
	2	3	4	5	13	8	6^1	10^2		11	9^3	12			7		1		14											4
		3		4		8	5	10		2	9	11		12	6		1		7^1											5
	2^1	3	4			8		9		10^2	11^3	12		14	7		1		13	5	6									6
	2	3	8			7	6^2	13			11^1	10		4	9		1	12		5										7
		3	4			7■	6	9^1			11^2	10	13	2	8		1		12	5										8
	2^1	3	4^3				6^4	9			11^5	10	14	7■	8		1	15	13	5^2		12						16		9
	2		4		5	7		13	9	11^2	6^1	10			8		1						3	12						10
	2		4■		5^1	7			9^3	11^2	6	10	14		8		1						13		3	12				11
	7			5		8		14	13	12■	10	11			9^2		1						2^1	6^3	3		4			12
	5^2		4	9		7	8^1		13		12	11^4			6		1	14					3	15		10^3	2			13
	7		4	9			8^3		14	11^4	5^1	12			6		1	15					2	13		10^2	3			14
	8^1		4		15	5	7^5		13	11^2	9^4	10	12		6^3		1	14					2	16			3			15
			4	9	8^1	5	6			10	13				7		1						2		12	11^2	3			16
			4	9		6	7		13	10^2	12	14	15	16	8^5		1						2^1		5^3	11^4	3			17
			4	9		5	6^4		11	12	13	10^2			14		1	15					2	8^3	7^1		3			18
			13	9^1		7	6^4		5	11	8^3	10			12		1	15					4^2	14	3		2			19
	2^2		4				6		11	13	10^3			8	9		1	14		5^1				12	7		3			20
	4						12		3	11	13	10		6	7		1	8				14	2^3	9^1	5^2					21
			3				6^1		11			10		2	7		1	8				4^2		9	12			5	13	22

STIRLING ALBION

Year Formed: 1945. *Ground & Address:* Forthbank Stadium, Springkerse, Stirling FK7 7UJ. *Telephone:* 01786 450399. *Fax:* 01786 448592. *E-mail:* office@stirlingalbionfc.co.uk *Website:* stirlingalbionfc.co.uk
Ground Capacity: 3,808 (seated: 2,508). *Size of Pitch:* 101m × 68m.
Chairman and Operations Director: Stuart Brown.
Manager: Kevin Rutkiewicz. *Assistant Manager:* James Creaney.
Club Nickname: 'The Binos'.
Previous Ground: Annfield 1945-92.
Record Attendance: 26,400 v Celtic, Scottish Cup 4th rd, 14 March 1959 (Annfield); 3,808 v Aberdeen, Scottish Cup 4th rd, 15 February 1996 (Forthbank).
Record Transfer Fee received: £90,000 for Stephen Nicholas to Motherwell (March 1999).
Record Transfer Fee paid: £25,000 for Craig Taggart from Falkirk (August 1994).
Record Victory: 20-0 v Selkirk, Scottish Cup 1st rd, 8 December 1984.
Record Defeat: 0-9 v Dundee U, Division I, 30 December 1967; 0-9 v Ross Co, Scottish Cup 5th rd, 6 February 2010.
Most League Appearances: 504: Matt McPhee, 1967-81.
Most League Goals in Season (Individual): 27: Joe Hughes, Division II, 1969-70.
Most Goals Overall (Individual): 129: Billy Steele, 1971-83.

STIRLING ALBION – SPFL LEAGUE TWO 2020–21 LEAGUE RECORD

Match No.	Date	Venue	Opponents	Result		H/T Score	Lg Pos.	Goalscorers	Attendance
1	Oct 17	H	Queen's Park	D	0-0	0-0	5		0
2	24	A	Stenhousemuir	D	2-2	1-0	7	Wilson 18, Leitch 90	0
3	31	H	Annan Ath	W	1-0	1-0	5	Ryan 40	0
4	Nov 7	A	Brechin C	W	5-0	2-0	2	Leitch 21, Wilson 45, Ryan 49, Roberts, S 58, Byrne 66	0
5	21	H	Elgin C	L	1-2	0-1	3	Roberts, K 48	0
6	28	A	Albion R	W	1-0	1-0	3	Ryan 9	0
7	Dec 5	A	Stranraer	D	2-2	2-1	4	Ryan (pen) 16, McManus (og) 35	0
8	12	H	Cowdenbeath	W	1-0	0-0	3	Byrne 71	0
9	19	A	Edinburgh C	W	3-2	3-0	3	Leitch 25, Byrne 35, Ryan 40	0
10	Mar 20	H	Brechin C	W	1-0	0-0	2	Moore 65	0
11	27	A	Elgin C	D	1-1	0-0	3	Ryan 62	0
12	30	H	Stenhousemuir	W	1-0	0-0	3	Leitch 49	0
13	Apr 3	A	Queen's Park	L	0-1	0-1	4		0
14	6	H	Albion R	D	1-1	0-1	4	Ryan (pen) 67	0
15	10	A	Annan Ath	W	2-1	1-0	3	Mackin 18, Ryan (pen) 55	0
16	13	H	Stranraer	L	0-1	0-0	3		0
17	17	A	Cowdenbeath	W	5-1	3-1	3	Ryan 2 (1 pen) 4, 20 (p), Hamilton 37, Banner 48, Mackin 65	0
18	20	H	Edinburgh C	L	0-1	0-1	3		0
19	24	A	Edinburgh C	W	1-0	1-0	3	Mackin 45	0
20	27	H	Queen's Park	L	1-2	0-1	3	Heaver 82	0
21	29	A	Elgin C	L	1-3	0-2	4	Bikey 81	0
22	May 1	H	Stranraer	D	2-2	1-1	5	McGeachie 44, Byrne 90	0

Final League Position: 5

Honours
League Champions: Division II 1952-53, 1957-58, 1960-61, 1964-65; Second Division 1976-77, 1990-91, 1995-96, 2009-10; Division C 1946-47.
Runners-up: Division II 1948-49, 1950-51; Second Division 2006-07; Third Division 2003-04.
Promoted via play-offs: 2006-07 (to First Division); 2013-14 (to League One).
League Cup: Semi-finals 1961-62.
League Challenge Cup: Semi-finals 1995-96, 1999-2000.

Club colours: Shirt: Red with white sleeves. Shorts: Red with white trim. Socks: Red and white hoops.

Goalscorers: *League (32):* Ryan 10 (4 pens), Byrne 4, Leitch 4, Mackin 3, Wilson 2, Banner 1, Bikey 1, Hamilton 1, Heaver 1, McGeachie 1, Moore 1, Roberts S 1, Roberts K 1, own goal 1.
William Hill Scottish Cup (3): Byrne 1, Roberts 1, Ryan 1.
Betfred Scottish League Cup (3): Heaver 1, Mackin 1, Ryan 1.

Stone H 1	McGeachie R 19 + 1	McGregor J 18	McLean P 7	Banner K 20	Roberts K 19 + 1	Wilson D 13 + 3	Leitch J 18 + 2	Moore K 11 + 6	Ryan A 18 + 1	Mackin D 9 + 7	Roberts S 11 + 7	Byrne D 12 + 9	Binnie C 14	El-Zubaidi A 9 + 2	Heaver S 3 + 7	Docherty D 5 + 4	Magee L — + 2	Thomson C 1 + 3	Creaney J 1 + 2	Mitchell J — + 1	Hamilton C 6 + 4	Kirkpatrick J 2 + 5	Allan J 7 + 3	Meggatt D 3 + 1	Eadie C 6 + 2	Currie B 7	Bikey D 2 + 4	Greenhorn W — + 1	*Match No.*
1	2	3	4	5	6	7	8	9^1	10	11^2	12	13																	1
	2	4	3^2	5	8^1	7	6		10		9	11	1	12	13														2
	2	3		4	7	8	6		10		9	11	1	5															3
	2^1	3		4	7	8^2	9^3		10^5	14	6	11	1	5^4	12	13	15	16											4
	2	4		5	8	7	6	13	10	12	9^1	11^2	1	3															5
	12	4	2	6	7		8	5^1	11	10^3	9^2	13	1	3					14										6
		4^3	3	2	8	7	6	9	11	14	12	10^2	1	13					5^1										7
	2	3	4	5	8	7^1	12	9^4	10		13	14	1		11^2	6^3	15												8
	5	3	2	8	6		7^2	12	10^1	14	9^3	11^4	1	4		13				15									9
	5	2	3^1	6	7	12		13	10		9^3	11	1	4		8^2					14								10
	2	4		3	6^1	7	8^2	9^5	11			10^4	1	5^3	15						16	12	13	14					11
		3^2		2	6	7	8	5	11^1	13		10^3	1		14								9	4	12				12
	2			3	8		9	13	15	11^1	10^2	14	1		6^3						7^4	12	5	4					13
	5^3	2		3	15	7^1	6	9	10	12	13	11^4										8		4^2	14	1			14
	5	2		3	6^4	7	8^3		10	11^1	9^2	14									12	15	13		4	1			15
	5^4	2		3	6	7^1	12	13		11	9^2	10^3			14							8^5	16		4	1	15		16
	5			3			8^3	9^2	11^4	10^1	16		1		14	7		13			2	12	6^5		4		15		17
	2			3			9	5^1	10^4	11	12	15	1			8^2					6	13	7^3		4		14		18
	5	2		3	6	14^4	8^1	13	10	11^2		12				15					7		9^3		4	1			19
	2^1	3			8^5	14		6^2			9	10^3			13	7		5	16		12				4^4	1	11	15	20
	4			2	6		8^2	5^3	11^1	10	12^4	15		3				14			7		9			1	13		21
	2	4			7	8^1	6^3			13		14		3	10	12					9		5			1	11^2		22

STRANRAER

Year Formed: 1870. *Ground & Address:* Stair Park, London Rd, Stranraer DG9 8BS. *Telephone and Fax:* 01776 703271.
E-mail: secretary@stranraerfc.org *Website:* stranraerfc.org
Ground Capacity: 4,178 (seated: 1,830). *Size of Pitch:* 103m × 64m.
Chairman: Shaun Niven.
Manager: Jamie Hamill. *Assistant Manager:* Daryl Duffy.
Club Nicknames: 'The Blues'; 'The Clayholers'.
Record Attendance: 6,500 v Rangers, Scottish Cup 1st rd, 24 January 1948.
Record Transfer Fee received: £90,000 for Mark Campbell to Ayr U (1999).
Record Transfer Fee paid: £35,000 for Michael Moore from St Johnstone (March 2005).
Record Victory: 9-0 v St Cuthbert Wanderers, Scottish Cup 2nd rd, 23 October 2010; 9-0 v Wigtown & Bladnoch, Scottish Cup 2nd rd, 22 October 2011.
Record Defeat: 1-11 v Queen of the South, Scottish Cup 1st rd, 16 January 1932.
Most League Appearances: 301: Keith Knox, 1986-90; 1999-2001.
Most League Goals in Season (Individual): 27: Derek Frye, 1977-78.
Most Goals Overall (Individual): 136: Jim Campbell, 1965-75.

STRANRAER – SPFL LEAGUE TWO 2020–21 LEAGUE RECORD

Match No.	*Date*	*Venue*	*Opponents*	*Result*		*H/T Score*	*Lg Pos.*	*Goalscorers*	*Attendance*
1	Oct 17	H	Elgin C	L	1-4	0-1	—	Devitt 77	0
2	24	A	Annan Ath	D	1-1	1-1	8	Stirling 38	0
3	31	H	Queen's Park	L	0-1	0-0	9		0
4	Nov 7	H	Cowdenbeath	W	2-0	1-0	7	Orr 36, Vitoria 80	0
5	21	A	Edinburgh C	W	1-0	1-0	6	Duffy 26	0
6	28	A	Brechin C	W	4-1	1-1	4	Paton 9, Orr 55, Duffy 58, Hilton 84	0
7	Dec 5	H	Stirling Alb	D	2-2	1-2	6	Orr 8, Duffy 56	0
8	12	A	Stenhousemuir	D	2-2	2-0	6	Cummins 22, Paton (pen) 36	0
9	19	H	Albion R	W	4-0	0-0	4	Paton 47, Orr 53, Duffy 62, Elliott 82	0
10	Jan 2	H	Annan Ath	W	2-0	0-0	3	Orr 64, Paton (pen) 78	0
11	Mar 20	A	Queen's Park	L	0-3	0-2	4		0
12	23	H	Brechin C	W	2-0	0-0	3	Stirling 62, Orr 74	0
13	27	A	Cowdenbeath	D	1-1	0-1	4	Sonkur 66	0
14	Apr 6	A	Elgin C	L	1-2	0-0	5	Matt Yates (pen) 70	0
15	10	H	Edinburgh C	L	0-1	0-1	5		0
16	13	A	Stirling Alb	W	1-0	0-0	5	Stirling 57	0
17	15	H	Stenhousemuir	W	4-0	3-0	4	Hilton 17, Orr 19, Paton 2 21, 73	0
18	20	A	Albion R	W	2-0	1-0	4	Hilton 43, Vitoria 84	0
19	23	A	Queen's Park	W	1-0	1-0	3	Matt Yates 32	0
20	27	H	Elgin C	L	1-4	0-4	4	Elliott 72	0
21	May 1	A	Stirling Alb	D	2-2	1-1	5	Allan (og) 28, Duffy 89	0
22	4	H	Edinburgh C	W	2-1	2-1	4	Stirling 20, Orr 45	0

Final League Position: 4

Honours
League Champions: Second Division 1993-94, 1997-98; Third Division 2003-04.
Runners-up: Second Division 2004-05; Third Division 2007-08; League One 2014-15.
Promoted via play-offs: 2011-12 (to Second Division).
Scottish Cup: Quarter-finals 2003.
League Cup: Quarter-finals 1968-69.
League Challenge Cup Winners: 1996-97. Semi-finals: 2000-01, 2014-15.

Club colours: Shirt: Blue with light blue trim. Shorts: White with blue trim. Socks: Blue with red tops.

Goalscorers: *League (36):* Orr 8, Paton 6 (2 pens), Duffy 5, Stirling 4, Hilton 3, Elliott 2, Vitoria 2, Matt Yates 2 (1 pen), Cummins 1, Devitt 1, Sonkur 1, own goal 1.
William Hill Scottish Cup (11): Yates 3, Orr 2, Paton 2 (1 pen), Cummins 1, Duffy 1, Robertson 1, own goal 1.
Betfred Scottish League Cup (6): Duffy 2, Paton 2, Orr 1, Sonkur 1.
Scottish League Play-Offs (0).

Fleming G 22	Burns S 12 + 1	McManus C 20 + 1	Devitt T 4 + 3	Cummins A 14 + 2	Gallagher G 14	Millar K 19	Robertson S 22	Stirling A 15 + 4	Duffy D 13 + 7	Paton R 17 + 4	Elliott C 3 + 10	Orr T 19 + 3	Vitoria J 9 + 8	Hamill J 10 + 1	Hilton J 8 + 10	Yates Matt 3 + 11	Sonkur A 17	Walker Josh — + 5	Taylor A 1 + 3	*Match No.*
1	2	3	4	5^{3}	6	7■	8	9	10^{1}	11^{2}	12	13	14							1
1	5	7	4	12	8■		3	6	10^{1}	9		11		2						2
1	5	4^{2}	7	14		8	2	6	9^{1}	10^{3}		11		3	12	13				3
1	5	7		4		8	3	6	12	10^{1}		11^{2}	9	2	13					4
1		8		5	2	7	4		10^{1}	6^{2}		11	9^{3}		13	12	3	14		5
1		8		5	2	7	4		10^{1}	6^{2}		11	9^{3}		12	13	3	14		6
1		8		5	2	7	3	12	11^{2}	6^{1}		10	9			13	4			7
1		8		5	2^{3}	7	4	13	10^{1}	6^{2}		11	9	12	14		3			8
1	16	7		5^{2}		6	3	13	10^{1}	9^{5}	14	11^{3}	8^{4}	2	12	15	4			9
1		7		5	2	8	4	6	10^{2}	11^{1}	13	9^{3}	14			12	3			10
1		7^{2}		5	2	6■	3	8^{5}	10^{3}	9^{4}	15	11^{1}	13		12	16	4		14	11
1		8	12	5	7		3^{5}	6^{3}	11^{1}	13	15	10^{2}	9^{4}	2	14	16	4			12
1	5	8			2	7	4		12	6	9^{2}	11	13		10^{1}		3			13
1	5^{1}			2	7		4	9	14	12		10	13		6^{3}	11	3		8^{2}	14
1	5	14	3	2^{1}	8	7^{5}	4	9^{4}	12	16	13	10	6^{3}		15	11^{2}				15
1	5	7		2		6	4	8	10^{1}	11^{2}	13	12			9		3			16
1	5^{4}	7		2		8	4	9^{1}		11		10^{3}	14		6^{2}	12	3	13	15	17
1		8			5	7^{5}	4	9^{3}	14	6^{2}	15	11^{4}	13	2	10^{1}	12	3	16		18
1		8	12		5^{3}	7	4	13		6^{1}	15	14	9■	2	10^{4}	11^{2}	3			19
1	5	7				8^{1}	4	9^{4}	12	11■	14	10^{5}		2^{3}	6^{2}	13	3	16	15	20
1	5	7	13			8	3	9	12		6	10^{2}		2	11^{1}		4			21
1	5	7				8	4	6	10^{2}	13	9^{1}	11^{3}	14	2	12		3			22

SCOTTISH LEAGUE HONOURS 1890–2021

*=Until 1921–22 season teams were equal if level on points, unless a play-off took place. §Not promoted after play-offs. *Won or placed on goal average (ratio), goal difference or most goals scored (goal average from 1921–22 until 1971–72 when it was replaced by goal difference). No official competition during 1939–46; regional leagues operated.*

DIVISION 1 (1890–91 to 1974–75) – TIER 1

Tier	*Season*	*Max Pts*	*First*	*Pts*	*Second*	*Pts*	*Third*	*Pts*
1	1890–91	36	Dumbarton=	29	Rangers=	29	Celtic	21
	Dumbarton and Rangers held title jointly after indecisive play-off ended 2-2. Celtic deducted 4 points for fielding an ineligible player.							
1	1891–92	44	Dumbarton	37	Celtic	35	Hearts	34
1	1892–93	36	Celtic	29	Rangers	28	St Mirren	20
1	1893–94	36	Celtic	29	Hearts	26	St Bernard's	23
1	1894–95	36	Hearts	31	Celtic	26	Rangers	22
1	1895–96	36	Celtic	30	Rangers	26	Hibernian	24
1	1896–97	36	Hearts	28	Hibernian	26	Rangers	25
1	1897–98	36	Celtic	33	Rangers	29	Hibernian	22
1	1898–99	36	Rangers	36	Hearts	26	Celtic	24
1	1899–1900	36	Rangers	32	Celtic	25	Hibernian	24
1	1900–01	40	Rangers	35	Celtic	29	Hibernian	25
1	1901–02	36	Rangers	28	Celtic	26	Hearts	22
1	1902–03	44	Hibernian	37	Dundee	31	Rangers	29
1	1903–04	52	Third Lanark	43	Hearts	39	Celtic / Rangers=	38
1	1904–05	52	Celtic=	41	Rangers=	41	Third Lanark	35
	Celtic won title after beating Rangers 2-1 in play-off.							
1	1905–06	60	Celtic	49	Hearts	43	Airdrieonians	38
1	1906–07	68	Celtic	55	Dundee	48	Rangers	45
1	1907–08	68	Celtic	55	Falkirk	51	Rangers	50
1	1908–09	68	Celtic	51	Dundee	50	Clyde	48
1	1909–10	68	Celtic	54	Falkirk	52	Rangers	46
1	1910–11	68	Rangers	52	Aberdeen	48	Falkirk	44
1	1911–12	68	Rangers	51	Celtic	45	Clyde	42
1	1912–13	68	Rangers	53	Celtic	49	Hearts / Airdrieonians=	41
1	1913–14	76	Celtic	65	Rangers	59	Hearts / Morton=	54
1	1914–15	76	Celtic	65	Hearts	61	Rangers	50
1	1915–16	76	Celtic	67	Rangers	56	Morton	51
1	1916–17	76	Celtic	64	Morton	54	Rangers	53
1	1917–18	68	Rangers	56	Celtic	55	Kilmarnock / Morton=	43
1	1918–19	68	Celtic	58	Rangers	57	Morton	47
1	1919–20	84	Rangers	71	Celtic	68	Motherwell	57
1	1920–21	84	Rangers	76	Celtic	66	Hearts	50
1	1921–22	84	Celtic	67	Rangers	66	Raith R	51
1	1922–23	76	Rangers	55	Airdrieonians	50	Celtic	46
1	1923–24	76	Rangers	59	Airdrieonians	50	Celtic	46
1	1924–25	76	Rangers	60	Airdrieonians	57	Hibernian	52
1	1925–26	76	Celtic	58	Airdrieonians*	50	Hearts	50
1	1926–27	76	Rangers	56	Motherwell	51	Celtic	49
1	1927–28	76	Rangers	60	Celtic*	55	Motherwell	55
1	1928–29	76	Rangers	67	Celtic	51	Motherwell	50
1	1929–30	76	Rangers	60	Motherwell	55	Aberdeen	53
1	1930–31	76	Rangers	60	Celtic	58	Motherwell	56
1	1931–32	76	Motherwell	66	Rangers	61	Celtic	48
1	1932–33	76	Rangers	62	Motherwell	59	Hearts	50
1	1933–34	76	Rangers	66	Motherwell	62	Celtic	47
1	1934–35	76	Rangers	55	Celtic	52	Hearts	50
1	1935–36	76	Celtic	66	Rangers*	61	Aberdeen	61
1	1936–37	76	Rangers	61	Aberdeen	54	Celtic	52
1	1937–38	76	Celtic	61	Hearts	58	Rangers	49
1	1938–39	76	Rangers	59	Celtic	48	Aberdeen	46
1	1946–47	60	Rangers	46	Hibernian	44	Aberdeen	39
1	1947–48	60	Hibernian	48	Rangers	46	Partick Thistle	36
1	1948–49	60	Rangers	46	Dundee	45	Hibernian	39
1	1949–50	60	Rangers	50	Hibernian	49	Hearts	43
1	1950–51	60	Hibernian	48	Rangers*	38	Dundee	38
1	1951–52	60	Hibernian	45	Rangers	41	East Fife	37
1	1952–53	60	Rangers*	43	Hibernian	43	East Fife	39
1	1953–54	60	Celtic	43	Hearts	38	Partick Thistle	35
1	1954–55	60	Aberdeen	49	Celtic	46	Rangers	41
1	1955–56	68	Rangers	52	Aberdeen	46	Hearts*	45
1	1956–57	68	Rangers	55	Hearts	53	Kilmarnock	42
1	1957–58	68	Hearts	62	Rangers	49	Celtic	46
1	1958–59	68	Rangers	50	Hearts	48	Motherwell	44
1	1959–60	68	Hearts	54	Kilmarnock	50	Rangers*	42
1	1960–61	68	Rangers	51	Kilmarnock	50	Third Lanark	42
1	1961–62	68	Dundee	54	Rangers	51	Celtic	46
1	1962–63	68	Rangers	57	Kilmarnock	48	Partick Thistle	46
1	1963–64	68	Rangers	55	Kilmarnock	49	Celtic*	47
1	1964–65	68	Kilmarnock*	50	Hearts	50	Dunfermline Ath	49
1	1965–66	68	Celtic	57	Rangers	55	Kilmarnock	45
1	1966–67	68	Celtic	58	Rangers	55	Clyde	46
1	1967–68	68	Celtic	63	Rangers	61	Hibernian	45

Tier	Season	Max Pts	First	Pts	Second	Pts	Third	Pts
1	1968–69	68	Celtic	54	Rangers	49	Dunfermline Ath	45
1	1969–70	68	Celtic	57	Rangers	45	Hibernian	44
1	1970–71	68	Celtic	56	Aberdeen	54	St Johnstone	44
1	1971–72	68	Celtic	60	Aberdeen	50	Rangers	44
1	1972–73	68	Celtic	57	Rangers	56	Hibernian	45
1	1973–74	68	Celtic	53	Hibernian	49	Rangers	48
1	1974–75	68	Rangers	56	Hibernian	49	Celtic*	45

PREMIER DIVISION (1975–76 to 1997–98)

Tier	Season	Max Pts	First	Pts	Second	Pts	Third	Pts
1	1975–76	72	Rangers	54	Celtic	48	Hibernian	43
1	1976–77	72	Celtic	55	Rangers	46	Aberdeen	43
1	1977–78	72	Rangers	55	Aberdeen	53	Dundee U	40
1	1978–79	72	Celtic	48	Rangers	45	Dundee U	44
1	1979–80	72	Aberdeen	48	Celtic	47	St Mirren	42
1	1980–81	72	Celtic	56	Aberdeen	49	Rangers*	44
1	1981–82	72	Celtic	55	Aberdeen	53	Rangers	43
1	1982–83	72	Dundee U	56	Celtic*	55	Aberdeen	55
1	1983–84	72	Aberdeen	57	Celtic	50	Dundee U	47
1	1984–85	72	Aberdeen	59	Celtic	52	Dundee U	47
1	1985–86	72	Celtic*	50	Hearts	50	Dundee U	47
1	1986–87	88	Rangers	69	Celtic	63	Dundee U	60
1	1987–88	88	Celtic	72	Hearts	62	Rangers	60
1	1988–89	72	Rangers	56	Aberdeen	50	Celtic	46
1	1989–90	72	Rangers	51	Aberdeen*	44	Hearts	44
1	1990–91	72	Rangers	55	Aberdeen	53	Celtic*	41
1	1991–92	88	Rangers	72	Hearts	63	Celtic	62
1	1992–93	88	Rangers	73	Aberdeen	64	Celtic	60
1	1993–94	88	Rangers	58	Aberdeen	55	Motherwell	54
1	1994–95	108	Rangers	69	Motherwell	54	Hibernian	53
1	1995–96	108	Rangers	87	Celtic	83	Aberdeen*	55
1	1996–97	108	Rangers	80	Celtic	75	Dundee U	60
1	1997–98	108	Celtic	74	Rangers	72	Hearts	67

PREMIER LEAGUE (1998–99 to 2012–13)

Tier	Season	Max Pts	First	Pts	Second	Pts	Third	Pts
1	1998–99	108	Rangers	77	Celtic	71	St Johnstone	57
1	1999–2000	108	Rangers	90	Celtic	69	Hearts	54
1	2000–01	114	Celtic	97	Rangers	82	Hibernian	66
1	2001–02	114	Celtic	103	Rangers	85	Livingston	58
1	2002–03	114	Rangers*	97	Celtic	97	Hearts	63
1	2003–04	114	Celtic	98	Rangers	81	Hearts	68
1	2004–05	114	Rangers	93	Celtic	92	Hibernian*	61
1	2005–06	114	Celtic	91	Hearts	74	Rangers	73
1	2006–07	114	Celtic	84	Rangers	72	Aberdeen	65
1	2007–08	114	Celtic	89	Rangers	86	Motherwell	60
1	2008–09	114	Rangers	86	Celtic	82	Hearts	59
1	2009–10	114	Rangers	87	Celtic	81	Dundee U	63
1	2010–11	114	Rangers	93	Celtic	92	Hearts	63
1	2011–12	114	Celtic	93	Rangers	73	Motherwell	62
	Rangers deducted 10 points for entering administration.							
1	2012–13	114	Celtic	79	Motherwell	63	St Johnstone	56

SPFL SCOTTISH PREMIERSHIP (2013–14 to 2020–21)

Tier	Season	Max Pts	First	Pts	Second	Pts	Third	Pts
1	2013–14	114	Celtic	99	Motherwell	70	Aberdeen	68
1	2014–15	114	Celtic	92	Aberdeen	75	Inverness CT	65
1	2015–16	114	Celtic	86	Aberdeen	71	Hearts	65
1	2016–17	114	Celtic	106	Aberdeen	76	Rangers	67
1	2017–18	114	Celtic	82	Aberdeen	73	Rangers	70
1	2018–19	114	Celtic	87	Rangers	78	Kilmarnock*	67
1	2019–20	114	Celtic	80	Rangers	67	Motherwell	46
	The 2019–20 season was curtailed due to the COVID-19 pandemic and positions awarded on a points-per-game basis.							
1	2020–21	114	Rangers	102	Celtic	77	Hibernian	63

DIVISION 2 (1893–93 to 1974–75) – TIER 2

Tier	*Season*	*Max Pts*	*First*	*Pts*	*Second*	*Pts*	*Third*	*Pts*
2	1893–94	36	Hibernian	29	Cowlairs	27	Clyde	24
2	1894–95	36	Hibernian	30	Motherwell	22	Port Glasgow Ath	20
2	1895–96	36	Abercorn	27	Leith Ath	23	Renton / Kilmarnock=	21
2	1896–97	36	Partick Thistle	31	Leith Ath	27	Airdrieonians / Kilmarnock=	21
2	1897–98	36	Kilmarnock	29	Port Glasgow Ath	25	Morton	22
2	1898–99	36	Kilmarnock	32	Leith Ath	27	Port Glasgow Ath	25
2	1899–1900	36	Partick Thistle	29	Morton	28	Port Glasgow Ath	20
2	1900–01	36	St Bernard's	26	Airdrieonians	23	Abercorn	21
2	1901–02	44	Port Glasgow Ath	32	Partick Thistle	30	Motherwell	26
2	1902–03	44	Airdrieonians	35	Motherwell	28	Ayr U / Leith Ath=	27
2	1903–04	44	Hamilton A	37	Clyde	29	Ayr U	28
2	1904–05	44	Clyde	32	Falkirk	28	Hamilton A	27
2	1905–06	44	Leith Ath	34	Clyde	31	Albion R	27
2	1906–07	44	St Bernard's	32	Vale of Leven=	27	Arthurlie=	27
2	1907–08	44	Raith R	30	Dumbarton=	27	Ayr U=	27
	Dumbarton deducted 2 points for registration irregularities.							
2	1908–09	44	Abercorn	31	Raith R=	28	Vale of Leven=	28
2	1909–10	44	Leith Ath=	33	Raith R=	33	St Bernard's	27
	Leith Ath and Raith R held title jointly, no play-off game played.							

Div	Season	Max	First	Pts	Second	Pts	Third	Pts
2	1910–11	44	Dumbarton	31	Ayr U	27	Albion R	25
2	1911–12	44	Ayr U	35	Abercorn	30	Dumbarton	27
2	1912–13	52	Ayr U	34	Dunfermline Ath	33	East Stirlingshire	32
2	1913–14	44	Cowdenbeath	31	Albion R	27	Dunfermline Ath / Dundee U=	26
2	1914–15	52	Cowdenbeath=	37	St Bernard's=	37	Leith Ath=	37
	Cowdenbeath won title after a round robin tournament between the three tied clubs.							
2	1921–22	76	Alloa Ath	60	Cowdenbeath	47	Armadale	45
2	1922–23	76	Queen's Park	57	Clydebank	50	St Johnstone	48
	Clydebank and St Johnstone both deducted 2 points for fielding an ineligible player.							
2	1923–24	76	St Johnstone	56	Cowdenbeath	55	Bathgate	44
2	1924–25	76	Dundee U	50	Clydebank	48	Clyde	47
2	1925–26	76	Dunfermline Ath	59	Clyde	53	Ayr U	52
2	1926–27	76	Bo'ness	56	Raith R	49	Clydebank	45
2	1927–28	76	Ayr U	54	Third Lanark	45	King's Park	44
2	1928–29	72	Dundee U	51	Morton	50	Arbroath	47
2	1929–30	76	Leith Ath*	57	East Fife	57	Albion R	54
2	1930–31	76	Third Lanark	61	Dundee U	50	Dunfermline Ath	47
2	1931–32	76	East Stirlingshire*	55	St Johnstone	55	Raith R*	46
2	1932–33	68	Hibernian	54	Queen of the South	49	Dunfermline Ath	47
	Armadale and Bo'ness were expelled for failing to meet match guarantees. Their records were expunged.							
2	1933–34	68	Albion R	45	Dunfermline Ath*	44	Arbroath	44
2	1934–35	68	Third Lanark	52	Arbroath	50	St Bernard's	47
2	1935–36	68	Falkirk	59	St Mirren	52	Morton	48
2	1936–37	68	Ayr U	54	Morton	51	St Bernard's	48
2	1937–38	68	Raith R	59	Albion R	48	Airdrieonians	47
2	1938–39	68	Cowdenbeath	60	Alloa Ath*	48	East Fife	48
2	1946–47	52	Dundee	45	Airdrieonians	42	East Fife	31
2	1947–48	60	East Fife	53	Albion R	42	Hamilton A	40
2	1948–49	60	Raith R*	42	Stirling Alb	42	Airdrieonians*	41
2	1949–50	60	Morton	47	Airdrieonians	44	Dunfermline Ath*	36
2	1950–51	60	Queen of the South*	45	Stirling Alb	45	Ayr U*	36
2	1951–52	60	Clyde	44	Falkirk	43	Ayr U	39
2	1952–53	60	Stirling Alb	44	Hamilton A	43	Queen's Park	37
2	1953–54	60	Motherwell	45	Kilmarnock	42	Third Lanark*	36
2	1954–55	60	Airdrieonians	46	Dunfermline Ath	42	Hamilton A	39
2	1955–56	72	Queen's Park	54	Ayr U	51	St Johnstone	49
2	1956–57	72	Clyde	64	Third Lanark	51	Cowdenbeath	45
2	1957–58	72	Stirling Alb	55	Dunfermline Ath	53	Arbroath	47
2	1958–59	72	Ayr U	60	Arbroath	51	Stenhousemuir	46
2	1959–60	72	St Johnstone	53	Dundee U	50	Queen of the South	49
2	1960–61	72	Stirling Alb	55	Falkirk	54	Stenhousemuir	50
2	1961–62	72	Clyde	54	Queen of the South	53	Morton	44
2	1962–63	72	St Johnstone	55	East Stirlingshire	49	Morton	48
2	1963–64	72	Morton	67	Clyde	53	Arbroath	46
2	1964–65	72	Stirling Alb	59	Hamilton A	50	Queen of the South	45
2	1965–66	72	Ayr U	53	Airdrieonians	50	Queen of the South	47
2	1966–67	76	Morton	69	Raith R	58	Arbroath	57
2	1967–68	72	St Mirren	62	Arbroath	53	East Fife	49
2	1968–69	72	Motherwell	64	Ayr U	53	East Fife*	48
2	1969–70	72	Falkirk	56	Cowdenbeath	55	Queen of the South	50
2	1970–71	72	Partick Thistle	56	East Fife	51	Arbroath	46
2	1971–72	72	Dumbarton*	52	Arbroath	52	Stirling Alb*	50
2	1972–73	72	Clyde	56	Dumfermline Ath	52	Raith R*	47
2	1973–74	72	Airdrieonians	60	Kilmarnock	58	Hamilton A	55
2	1974–75	76	Falkirk	54	Queen of the South*	53	Montrose	53

Elected to First Division: 1894 Clyde; 1895 Hibernian; 1896 Abercorn; 1897 Partick Thistle; 1899 Kilmarnock; 1900 Morton and Partick Thistle; 1902 Port Glasgow and Partick Thistle; 1903 Airdrieonians and Motherwell; 1905 Falkirk and Aberdeen; 1906 Clyde and Hamilton A; 1910 Raith R; 1913 Ayr U and Dumbarton.

FIRST DIVISION (1975–76 to 2012–13)

Div	Season	Max	First	Pts	Second	Pts	Third	Pts
2	1975–76	52	Partick Thistle	41	Kilmarnock	35	Montrose	30
2	1976–77	78	St Mirren	62	Clydebank	58	Dundee	51
2	1977–78	78	Morton*	58	Hearts	58	Dundee	57
2	1978–79	78	Dundee	55	Kilmarnock*	54	Clydebank	54
2	1979–80	78	Hearts	53	Airdrieonians	51	Ayr U*	44
2	1980–81	78	Hibernian	57	Dundee	52	St Johnstone	51
2	1981–82	78	Motherwell	61	Kilmarnock	51	Hearts	50
2	1982–83	78	St Johnstone	55	Hearts	54	Clydebank	50
2	1983–84	78	Morton	54	Dumbarton	51	Partick Thistle	46
2	1984–85	78	Motherwell	50	Clydebank	48	Falkirk	45
2	1985–86	78	Hamilton A	56	Falkirk	45	Kilmarnock*	44
2	1986–87	88	Morton	57	Dunfermline Ath	56	Dumbarton	53
2	1987–88	88	Hamilton A	56	Meadowbank Thistle	52	Clydebank	49
2	1988–89	78	Dunfermline Ath	54	Falkirk	52	Clydebank	48
2	1989–90	78	St Johnstone	58	Airdrieonians	54	Clydebank	44
2	1990–91	78	Falkirk	54	Airdrieonians	53	Dundee	52
2	1991–92	88	Dundee	58	Partick Thistle*	57	Hamilton A	57
2	1992–93	88	Raith R	65	Kilmarnock	54	Dunfermline Ath	52
2	1993–94	88	Falkirk	66	Dunfermline Ath	65	Airdrieonians	54
2	1994–95	108	Raith R	69	Dunfermline Ath*	68	Dundee	68
2	1995–96	108	Dunfermline Ath	71	Dundee U*	67	Greenock Morton	67
2	1996–97	108	St Johnstone	80	Airdrieonians	60	Dundee*	58
2	1997–98	108	Dundee	70	Falkirk	65	Raith R*	60
2	1998–99	108	Hibernian	89	Falkirk	66	Ayr U	62

Tier	Season	Max Pts	First	Pts	Second	Pts	Third	Pts
2	1999–2000	108	St Mirren	76	Dunfermline Ath	71	Falkirk	68
2	2000–01	108	Livingston	76	Ayr U	69	Falkirk	56
2	2001–02	108	Partick Thistle	66	Airdrieonians	56	Ayr U*	52
2	2002–03	108	Falkirk	81	Clyde	72	St Johnstone	67
2	2003–04	108	Inverness CT	70	Clyde	69	St Johnstone	57
2	2004–05	108	Falkirk	75	St Mirren*	60	Clyde	60
2	2005–06	108	St Mirren	76	St Johnstone	66	Hamilton A	59
2	2006–07	108	Gretna	66	St Johnstone	65	Dundee*	53
2	2007–08	108	Hamilton A	76	Dundee	69	St Johnstone	58
2	2008–09	108	St Johnstone	65	Partick Thistle	55	Dunfermline Ath	51
2	2009–10	108	Inverness CT	73	Dundee	61	Dunfermline Ath	58
2	2010–11	108	Dunfermline Ath	70	Raith R	60	Falkirk	58
2	2011–12	108	Ross Co	79	Dundee	55	Falkirk	52
2	2012–13	108	Partick Thistle	78	Greenock Morton	67	Falkirk	53

SPFL SCOTTISH CHAMPIONSHIP (2013–14 to 2020–21)

Tier	Season	Max Pts	First	Pts	Second	Pts	Third	Pts
2	2013–14	108	Dundee	69	Hamilton A	67	Falkirk§	66
2	2014–15	108	Hearts	91	Hibernian§	70	Rangers§	67
2	2015–16	108	Rangers	81	Falkirk*§	70	Hibernian§	70
2	2016–17	108	Hibernian	71	Falkirk§	60	Dundee U§	57
2	2017–18	108	St Mirren	74	Livingston	62	Dundee U§	61
2	2018–19	108	Ross Co	71	Dundee U§	65	Inverness CT§	56
2	2019–20	108	Dundee U	59	Inverness CT	45	Dundee	41
	The 2019–20 season was curtailed due to the COVID-19 pandemic and positions awarded on a points-per-game basis.							
2	2020–21	81	Hearts	57	Dundee	45	Raith R§	43

SECOND DIVISION (1975–76 to 2012–13) – TIER 3

Tier	Season	Max Pts	First	Pts	Second	Pts	Third	Pts
3	1975–76	52	Clydebank*	40	Raith R	40	Alloa Ath	35
3	1976–77	78	Stirling Alb	55	Alloa Ath	51	Dunfermline Ath	50
3	1977–78	78	Clyde*	53	Raith R	53	Dunfermline Ath*	48
3	1978–79	78	Berwick Rangers	54	Dunfermline Ath	52	Falkirk	50
3	1979–80	78	Falkirk	50	East Stirlingshire	49	Forfar Ath	46
3	1980–81	78	Queen's Park	50	Queen of the South	46	Cowdenbeath	45
3	1981–82	78	Clyde	59	Alloa Ath*	50	Arbroath	50
3	1982–83	78	Brechin C	55	Meadowbank Thistle	54	Arbroath	49
3	1983–84	78	Forfar Ath	63	East Fife	47	Berwick Rangers	43
3	1984–85	78	Montrose	53	Alloa Ath	50	Dunfermline Ath	49
3	1985–86	78	Dunfermline Ath	57	Queen of the South	55	Meadowbank Thistle	49
3	1986–87	78	Meadowbank Thistle	55	Raith R*	52	Stirling Alb*	52
3	1987–88	78	Ayr U	61	St Johnstone	59	Queen's Park	51
3	1988–89	78	Albion R	50	Alloa Ath	45	Brechin C	43
3	1989–90	78	Brechin C	49	Kilmarnock	48	Stirling Alb	47
3	1990–91	78	Stirling Alb	54	Montrose	46	Cowdenbeath	45
3	1991–92	78	Dumbarton	52	Cowdenbeath	51	Alloa Ath	50
3	1992–93	78	Clyde	54	Brechin C*	53	Stranraer	53
3	1993–94	78	Stranraer	56	Berwick Rangers	48	Stenhousemuir*	47
3	1994–95	108	Greenock Morton	64	Dumbarton	60	Stirling Alb	58
3	1995–96	108	Stirling Alb	81	East Fife	67	Berwick Rangers	60
3	1996–97	108	Ayr U	77	Hamilton A	74	Livingston	64
3	1997–98	108	Stranraer	61	Clydebank	60	Livingston	59
3	1998–99	108	Livingston	77	Inverness CT	72	Clyde	53
3	1999–2000	108	Clyde	65	Alloa Ath	64	Ross Co	62
3	2000–01	108	Partick Thistle	75	Arbroath	58	Berwick Rangers*	54
3	2001–02	108	Queen of the South	67	Alloa Ath	59	Forfar Ath	53
3	2002–03	108	Raith R	59	Brechin C	55	Airdrie U	54
3	2003–04	108	Airdrie U	70	Hamilton A	62	Dumbarton	60
3	2004–05	108	Brechin C	72	Stranraer	63	Greenock Morton	62
3	2005–06	108	Gretna	88	Greenock Morton§	70	Peterhead*§	57
3	2006–07	108	Greenock Morton	77	Stirling Alb	69	Raith R§	62
3	2007–08	108	Ross Co	73	Airdrie U	66	Raith R§	60
3	2008–09	108	Raith R	76	Ayr U	74	Brechin C§	62
3	2009–10	108	Stirling Alb*	65	Alloa Ath§	65	Cowdenbeath	59
3	2010–11	108	Livingston	82	Ayr U*	59	Forfar Ath§	59
3	2011–12	108	Cowdenbeath	71	Arbroath§	63	Dumbarton	58
3	2012–13	108	Queen of the South	92	Alloa Ath	67	Brechin C	61

SPFL SCOTTISH LEAGUE ONE (2013–14 to 2020–21)

Tier	Season	Max Pts	First	Pts	Second	Pts	Third	Pts
3	2013–14	108	Rangers	102	Dunfermline Ath§	63	Stranraer§	51
3	2014–15	108	Greenock Morton	69	Stranraer§	67	Forfar Ath	66
3	2015–16	108	Dunfermline Ath	79	Ayr U	61	Peterhead§	59
3	2016–17	108	Livingston	81	Alloa Ath§	62	Airdrieonians§	52
3	2017–18	108	Ayr U	76	Raith R§	75	Alloa Ath	60
3	2018–19	108	Arbroath	70	Forfar Ath§	63	Raith R§	60
3	2019–20	108	Raith R	53	Falkirk	52	Airdrieonians	48
	The 2019–20 season was curtailed due to the COVID-19 pandemic and positions awarded on a points-per-game basis.							
3	2020–21	66	Partick Thistle	40	Airdrieonians§	38	Cove Rangers§	36

THIRD DIVISION (1994–95 to 2012–13) – TIER 4

Tier	Season	Max Pts	First	Pts	Second	Pts	Third	Pts
4	1994–95	108	Forfar Ath	80	Montrose	67	Ross Co	60
4	1995–96	108	Livingston	72	Brechin C	63	Inverness CT	57
4	1996–97	108	Inverness CT	76	Forfar Ath*	67	Ross Co	67
4	1997–98	108	Alloa Ath	76	Arbroath	68	Ross Co	67

4	1998–99	108	Ross Co	77	Stenhousemuir	64	Brechin C	59
4	1999–2000	108	Queen's Park	69	Berwick Rangers	66	Forfar Ath	61
4	2000–01	108	Hamilton A*	76	Cowdenbeath	76	Brechin C	72
4	2001–02	108	Brechin C	73	Dumbarton	61	Albion R	59
4	2002–03	108	Greenock Morton	72	East Fife	71	Albion R	70
4	2003–04	108	Stranraer	79	Stirling Alb	77	Gretna	68
4	2004–05	108	Gretna	98	Peterhead	78	Cowdenbeath	51
4	2005–06	108	Cowdenbeath*	76	Berwick Rangers§	76	Stenhousemuir§	73
4	2006–07	108	Berwick Rangers	75	Arbroath§	70	Queen's Park	68
4	2007–08	108	East Fife	88	Stranraer	65	Montrose§	59
4	2008–09	108	Dumbarton	67	Cowdenbeath	63	East Stirlingshire§	61
4	2009–10	108	Livingston	78	Forfar Ath	63	East Stirlingshire§	61
4	2010–11	108	Arbroath	66	Albion R	61	Queen's Park*§	59
4	2011–12	108	Alloa Ath	77	Queen's Park§	63	Stranraer	58
4	2012–13	108	Rangers	83	Peterhead§	59	Queen's Park§	56

SPFL SCOTTISH LEAGUE TWO (2013–14 to 2020–21)

4	2013–14	108	Peterhead	76	Annan Ath§	63	Stirling Alb	57
4	2014–15	108	Albion R	71	Queen's Park§	61	Arbroath§	56
4	2015–16	108	East Fife	62	Elgin C§	59	Clyde§	56
4	2016–17	108	Abroath	66	Forfar Ath	64	Annan Ath§	58
4	2017–18	108	Montrose	77	Peterhead§	76	Stirling Alb§	55
4	2018–19	108	Peterhead	79	Clyde	74	Edinburgh C§	67
4	2019–20	108	Cove Rangers	68	Edinburgh C	55	Elgin C	43
	The 2019–20 season was curtailed due to the COVID-19 pandemic and positions awarded on a points-per-game basis.							
4	2020–21	66	Queen's Park	54	Edinburgh C*	38	Elgin C*§	38

RELEGATED CLUBS

RELEGATED FROM DIVISION I (1921–22 to 1973–74)

1921–22 *Dumbarton, Queen's Park, Clydebank
1922–23 Albion R, Alloa Ath
1923–24 Clyde, Clydebank
1924–25 Ayr U, Third Lanark
1925–26 Raith R, Clydebank
1926–27 Morton, Dundee U
1927–28 Bo'ness, Dunfermline Ath
1928–29 Third Lanark, Raith R
1929–30 Dundee U, St Johnstone
1930–31 Hibernian, East Fife
1931–32 Dundee U, Leith Ath
1932–33 Morton, East Stirlingshire
1933–34 Third Lanark, Cowdenbeath
1934–35 St Mirren, Falkirk
1935–36 Airdrieonians, Ayr U
1936–37 Dunfermline Ath, Albion R
1937–38 Dundee, Morton
1938–39 Queen's Park, Raith R
1946–47 Kilmarnock, Hamilton A
1947–48 Airdrieonians, Queen's Park
1948–49 Morton, Albion R
1949–50 Queen of the South, Stirling Alb
1950–51 Clyde, Falkirk
1951–52 Morton, Stirling Alb
1952–53 Motherwell, Third Lanark
1953–54 Airdrieonians, Hamilton A
1954–55 *No clubs relegated as league extended to 18 teams*
1955–56 Clyde, Stirling Alb
1956–57 Dunfermline Ath, Ayr U
1957–58 East Fife, Queen's Park
1958–59 Falkirk, Queen of the South
1959–60 Stirling Alb, Arbroath
1960–61 Clyde, Ayr U
1961–62 St Johnstone, Stirling Alb
1962–63 Clyde, Raith R
1963–64 Queen of the South, East Stirlingshire
1964–65 Airdrieonians, Third Lanark
1965–66 Morton, Hamilton A
1966–67 St Mirren, Ayr U
1967–68 Motherwell, Stirling Alb
1968–69 Falkirk, Arbroath
1969–70 Raith R, Partick Thistle
1970–71 St Mirren, Cowdenbeath
1971–72 Clyde, Dunfermline Ath
1972–73 Kilmarnock, Airdrieonians
1973–74 East Fife, Falkirk

**Season 1921–22 – only 1 club promoted, 3 clubs relegated.*

RELEGATED FROM PREMIER DIVISION (1974–75 to 1997–98)

1974–75 *No relegation due to League reorganisation*
1975–76 Dundee, St Johnstone
1976–77 Hearts, Kilmarnock
1977–78 Ayr U, Clydebank
1978–79 Hearts, Motherwell
1979–80 Dundee, Hibernian
1980–81 Kilmarnock, Hearts
1981–82 Partick Thistle, Airdrieonians
1982–83 Morton, Kilmarnock
1983–84 St Johnstone, Motherwell
1984–85 Dumbarton, Morton
1985–86 *No relegation due to League reorganisation*
1986–87 Clydebank, Hamilton A
1987–88 Falkirk, Dunfermline Ath, Morton
1988–89 Hamilton A
1989–90 Dundee
1990–91 *No clubs relegated*
1991–92 St Mirren, Dunfermline Ath
1992–93 Falkirk, Airdrieonians
1993–94 St Johnstone, Raith R, Dundee
1994–95 Dundee U
1995–96 Partick Thistle, Falkirk
1996–97 Raith R
1997–98 Hibernian

RELEGATED FROM PREMIER LEAGUE (1998–99 to 2012–13)

1998–99 Dunfermline Ath
1999–2000 *No relegation due to League reorganisation*
2000–01 St Mirren
2001–02 St Johnstone
2002–03 *No clubs relegated*
2003–04 Partick Thistle
2005–06 Livingston
2006–07 Dunfermline Ath
2007–08 Gretna
2008–09 Inverness CT
2009–10 Falkirk
2010–11 Hamilton A
2011–12 Dunfermline Ath, Rangers (demoted to Third Division)
2012–13 Dundee

RELEGATED FROM SPFL SCOTTISH PREMIERSHIP (2013–14 to 2020–21)

2013–14 Hibernian, Hearts
2014–15 St Mirren
2015–16 Dundee U
2016–17 Inverness CT
2017–18 Ross Co, Partick Thistle
2018–19 Dundee
2019–20 Hearts
2020–21 Hamilton A, Kilmarnock

RELEGATED FROM FIRST DIVISION (1975–76 to 2012–13)

1975–76 Dunfermline Ath, Clyde
1976–77 Raith R, Falkirk
1977–78 Alloa Ath, East Fife
1978–79 Montrose, Queen of the South
1979–80 Arbroath, Clyde
1980–81 Stirling Alb, Berwick Rangers
1981–82 East Stirlingshire, Queen of the South
1982–83 Dunfermline Ath, Queen's Park
1983–84 Raith R, Alloa Ath
1984–85 Meadowbank Thistle, St Johnstone
1985–86 Ayr U, Alloa Ath
1986–87 Brechin C, Montrose
1987–88 East Fife, Dumbarton
1988–89 Kilmarnock, Queen of the South
1989–90 Albion R, Alloa Ath
1990–91 Clyde, Brechin C
1991–92 Montrose, Forfar Ath
1992–93 Meadowbank Thistle, Cowdenbeath
1993–94 Dumbarton, Stirling Alb, Clyde, Morton, Brechin C
1994–95 Ayr U, Stranraer
1995–96 Hamilton A, Dumbarton
1996–97 Clydebank, East Fife
1997–98 Partick Thistle, Stirling Alb
1998–99 Hamilton A, Stranraer
1999–2000 Clydebank
2000–01 Greenock Morton, Alloa Ath
2001–02 Raith R
2002–03 Alloa Ath, Arbroath
2003–04 Ayr U, Brechin C
2004–05 Partick Thistle, Raith R
2005–06 Stranraer, Brechin C
2006–07 Airdrie U, Ross Co
2007–08 Stirling Alb
2008–09 Livingstone *(for breaching rules)*, Clyde
2009–10 Airdrie U, Ayr U
2010–11 Cowdenbeath, Stirling Alb
2011–12 Ayr U, Queen of the South
2012–13 Dunfermline Ath, Airdrie U

RELEGATED FROM SPFL SCOTTISH CHAMPIONSHIP (2013–14 to 2020–21)

2013–14 Greenock Morton
2014–15 Cowdenbeath
2015–16 Livingston, Alloa Ath
2016–17 Raith R, Ayr U
2017–18 Brechin C, Dumbarton
2018–19 Falkirk
2019–20 Partick Thistle
2020–21 Alloa Ath

RELEGATED FROM SECOND DIVISION (1993–94 to 2012–13)

1993–94 Alloa Ath, Forfar Ath, East Stirlingshire, Montrose, Queen's Park, Arbroath, Albion R, Cowdenbeath
1994–95 Meadowbank Thistle, Brechin C
1995–96 Forfar Ath, Montrose
1996–97 Dumbarton, Berwick Rangers
1997–98 Stenhousemuir, Brechin C
1998–99 East Fife, Forfar Ath
1999–2000 Hamilton A *(after being deducted 15 points)*
2000–01 Queen's Park, Stirling Alb
2001–02 Greenock Morton
2002–03 Stranraer, Cowdenbeath
2003–04 East Fife, Stenhousemuir
2004–05 Arbroath, Berwick Rangers
2005–06 Dumbarton
2006–07 Stranraer, Forfar Ath
2007–08 Cowdenbeath, Berwick Rangers
2008–09 Queen's Park, Stranraer
2009–10 Arbroath, Clyde
2010–11 Alloa Ath, Peterhead
2011–12 Stirling Alb
2012–13 Albion R

RELEGATED FROM SPFL SCOTTISH LEAGUE ONE (2013–14 to 2020–21)

2013–14 East Fife, Arbroath
2014–15 Stirling Alb
2015–16 Cowdenbeath, Forfar Ath
2016–17 Peterhead, Stenhousmuir
2017–18 Albion R, Queen's Park
2018–19 Stenhousemuir, Brechin C
2019–20 Stranraer
2020–21 Forfar Ath

RELEGATED FROM SPFL SCOTTISH LEAGUE TWO (2015–16 to 2020–21)

2015–16 East Stirlingshire
2016–17 None
2017–18 None
2018–19 Berwick Rangers
2019–20 None
2020–21 Brechin C

SCOTTISH LEAGUE CHAMPIONSHIP WINS

Rangers 55, Celtic 51, Aberdeen 4, Hearts 4, Hibernian 4, Dumbarton 2, Dundee 1, Dundee U 1, Kilmarnock 1, Motherwell 1, Third Lanark 1.

The totals for Rangers and Dumbarton each include the shared championship of 1890–91.

Since the formation of the Scottish Football League in 1890, there have been periodic reorganisations of the leagues to allow for expansion, improve competition and commercial aspects of the game. The table below lists the league names by tier and chronology. This table can be used to assist when studying the records.

Tier	Division	
1	Scottish League Division I	1890–1939
	Scottish League Division A	1946–1956
	Scottish League Division I	1956–1975
	Premier Division	1975–1998
	Scottish Premier League	1998–2013
	SPFL Premiership	2013–
2	Scottish League Division II	1893–1939
	Scottish League Division B	1946–1956
	Scottish League Division II	1956–1975
	First Division	1975–2013
	SPFL Championship	2013–
3	Scottish League Division III	1923–1926
	Scottish League Division C	1946–1949
	Second Division	1975–2013
	SPFL League One	2013–
4	Third Division	1994–2013
	SPFL League Two	2013–

In 2013–14 the SPFL introduced play-offs to determine a second promotion/relegation place for the Premiership, Championship and League One.

The team finishing second bottom of the Premiership plays two legs against the team from the Championship that won the eliminator games played between the teams finishing second, third and fourth.

For both the Championship and League One, the team finishing second bottom joins the teams from second, third and fourth places of the lower league in a play-off series of two-legged semi-finals and finals.

In 2014–15 a play-off was introduced for promotion/relegation from League Two. The team finishing bottom of League Two plays two legs against the victors of the eliminator games between the winners of the Highland and Lowland leagues.

SCOTTISH LEAGUE PLAY-OFFS 2020–21

▪ *Denotes player sent off. Due to COVID-19 pandemic, matches played behind closed doors unless otherwise stated.*

PREMIERSHIP QUARTER-FINAL FIRST LEG

Tuesday, 4 May 2021

Dunfermline Ath (0) 0

Raith R (0) 0

Dunfermline Ath: (4132) Fon Williams; Comrie, Watson, Murray E, Edwards; Whittaker; Thomas (Banks 80), McManus (McInroy 73), Henderson; O'Hara, Wighton.
Raith R: (4231) MacDonald J; Tumilty, Davidson, Benedictus, MacDonald K; Matthews (King 82), Hendry; Spencer, Vaughan (Duku 85), Kennedy; Gullan (Ugwu 87).
Referee: Steven Kirkland.

PREMIERSHIP QUARTER-FINAL SECOND LEG

Saturday, 8 May 2021

Raith R (0) 2 *(Vaughan 64, Ugwu 89)*

Dunfermline Ath (0) 0

Raith R: (4231) MacDonald J; Tumilty, Davidson (Mendy 85), Benedictus, MacDonald K; Spencer, Hendry; Matthews (Tait 76), Vaughan, Armstrong; Gullan (Ugwu 82).
Dunfermline Ath: (442) Fon Williams; Comrie, Watson, Murray E (Murray F 85), Edwards; Thomas, Mayo (McManus 70), Whittaker, Henderson; O'Hara, Wighton (Banks 70).
Raith R won 2-0 on aggregate.
Referee: Greg Aitken.

PREMIERSHIP SEMI-FINAL FIRST LEG

Wednesday, 12 May 2021

Raith R (0) 0

Dundee (1) 3 *(McGhee 22, 55, Sow 84)*

Raith R: (4231) MacDonald J; Tumilty, Davidson, Benedictus, MacDonald K; Spencer (Ugwu 66), Hendry; Armstrong (Duku 85), Matthews (Tait 80), Vaughan; Gullan.
Dundee: (4321) Legzdins; Elliot, Ashcroft, Fontaine (Anderson 73), Kerr; McGhee, Byrne, Adam; McMullan (Sow 81), McGowan; Cummings (Mullen 66).
Referee: Nick Walsh.

PREMIERSHIP SEMI-FINAL SECOND LEG

Saturday, 15 May 2021

Dundee (0) 0

Raith R (1) 1 *(Vaughan 21)*

Dundee: (4321) Legzdins; Elliot, Ashcroft, McGhee, Kerr; Anderson, Byrne, Adam (Mullen 75); McMullan (McDaid 64), McGowan; Cummings (Sow 56).
Raith R: (442) MacDonald J; Tumilty, Mendy, Benedictus, MacDonald K; Matthews (Spencer 82), Hendry, Vaughan, Armstrong (Tait 82); Ugwu, Gullan (Duku 75).
Dundee won 3-1 on aggregate.
Referee: Don Robertson.

PREMIERSHIP FINAL FIRST LEG

Thursday, 20 May 2021

Dundee (1) 2 *(McGhee 6, Adam 47)*

Kilmarnock (0) 1 *(Haunstrup 77)* 500

Dundee: (4231) Legzdins; Elliot (Marshall 67), Ashcroft, Fontaine, Kerr; McGhee, Byrne; McGowan, Adam, McMullan (Sow 73); Mullen (McDaid 80).
Kilmarnock: (4231) Doyle; Millen, Broadfoot, Rossi, Haunstrup; Power, Dicker; Burke, Kiltie (McKenzie 57), Pinnock; Lafferty.
Referee: John Beaton.

PREMIERSHIP FINAL SECOND LEG

Monday, 24 May 2021

Kilmarnock (0) 1 *(Lafferty 69 (pen))*

Dundee (2) 2 *(Mullen 7, Ashcroft 12)* 500

Kilmarnock: (4411) Doyle; Millen, Broadfoot, Rossi, Haunstrup (Whitehall 33); Burke (Kiltie 58), Power, Tshibola, Pinnock; McKenzie; Lafferty.
Dundee: (4231) Legzdins; Kerr, Ashcroft, Fontaine, Marshall; Byrne, Adam; McMullan, McGhee, McGowan (McDaid 78); Mullen (Sow 71).
Dundee won 4-2 on aggregate.
Referee: Bobby Madden.

CHAMPIONSHIP SEMI-FINALS FIRST LEG

Saturday, 8 May 2021

Cove R (0) 1 *(McIntosh 66)*

Airdrieonians (0) 1 *(Graham 55 (og))*

Cove R: (442) McKenzie; Scott Ross, Strachan, Graham, Ngwenya; Yule, Fyvie, Scully, McIntosh; Megginson, McAllister.
Airdrieonians: (3142) Currie; McKay P, Kerr, Fordyce; Paton; Walker (McKay J 71), Turner, Carrick (Ritchie 83), McCann; Gallagher (Roy 86), Connell.
Referee: David Dickinson.

Montrose (0) 2 *(McLean 57, Webster 77)*

Greenock Morton (1) 1 *(Oliver 5)*

Montrose: (433) Fleming; Cammy Ballantyne, Waddell, Dillon, Steeves; Cameron Ballantyne, Masson, Milne; Webster, McLean, Rennie (Antoniazzi 75).
Greenock Morton: (4411) McAdams; Ledger, Fjortoft, McLean, Strapp; Nesbitt (Blues 79), Jacobs, McGinn, McGuffie; Orsi (Muirhead 78); Oliver.
Referee: Grant Irvine.

CHAMPIONSHIP SEMI-FINALS SECOND LEG

Tuesday, 11 May 2021

Airdrieonians (1) 3 *(Gallagher 19, 108, McKay J 90)*

Cove R (1) 2 *(Megginson 15, McAllister 90)*

Airdrieonians: (352) Currie; McKay P, Kerr (Crighton 46), Fordyce; Walker, Turner, Paton (Connell 6 (McKay J 84)), Ritchie (Robert 67), McCann; Gallagher, Carrick (Thomson 99).
Cove R: (442) McKenzie; Scott Ross, Strachan, Graham, Ngwenya; Yule, Fyvie, Scully, McIntosh (Watson 73); Megginson (Smith 24), McAllister.
aet; Airdrieonians won 4-3 on aggregate.
Referee: Colin Steven.

Greenock Morton (2) 3 *(Oliver 5, Salkeld 19, McGuffie 120)*

Montrose (1) 1 *(McLean 35)*

Greenock Morton: (433) McAdams; Strapp, McLean, Fjortoft, Millar (Ledger 94); Jacobs, McGinn, Blues (Lyon 74); Salkeld, Muirhead (McGuffie 90), Oliver (Nesbitt 86).
Montrose: (433) Fleming; Cammy Ballantyne, Waddell, Dillon, Steeves; Cameron Ballantyne (Johnston 95), Masson, Milne; Webster (Callaghan 104), McLean, Rennie (Mochrie 66).
aet; Greenock Morton won 4-3 on aggregate.
Referee: Euan Anderson.

CHAMPIONSHIP FINAL FIRST LEG

Tuesday, 18 May 2021

Airdrieonians (0) 0

Greenock Morton (0) 1 *(Muirhead 90)*

Airdrieonians: (352) Currie; McKay P (Robert 78), Crighton, Fordyce; Walker (Roy 85), McKay J, Turner, Carrick (Thomson 51), McCann; Gallagher, O'Reilly.
Greenock Morton: (433) Fox; Ledger, Fjortoft, McLean, Strapp; Jacobs (Lyon 26), McGinn, Blues; Oliver, Salkeld (Nesbitt 80), Muirhead.
Referee: David Munro.

CHAMPIONSHIP FINAL SECOND LEG

Friday, 21 May 2021

Greenock Morton (2) 3 *(Muirhead 12, 78, Oliver 44)*

Airdrieonians (0) 0

Greenock Morton: (433) Fox; Ledger, Fjortoft, McLean, Strapp; Lyon (Colville 86), McGinn, Blues; Oliver (McGuffie 81), Salkeld (Nesbitt 69), Muirhead.
Airdrieonians: (3421) Currie; Kerr (Thomson 30), Crighton, Fordyce; Walker (Ritchie 83), O'Reilly, Turner, McCann; McKay J (Roy 59), Robert; Gallagher.
Greenock Morton won 4-0 on aggregate.
Referee: Alan Muir.

LEAGUE ONE SEMI-FINALS FIRST LEG

Saturday, 8 May 2021

Elgin C (0) 0

Edinburgh C (1) 1 *(Campbell 45)*

Elgin C: (4411) McHale; Cooper, Bronsky, McHardy, Spark; Dingwall R (Peters 69), Mailer (Brown 54), MacPhee, Sopel (O'Keefe 66); Cameron; Hester.
Edinburgh C: (4231) Antell; Thomson, Hamilton, McIntyre, Crane; Black, Jardine; Handling (De Vita 80), Brown, Campbell; See (Henderson B 88).
Referee: Alan Newlands.

Stranraer (0) 0

Dumbarton (0) 0

Stranraer: (442) Fleming; Hamill, Robertson, Sonkur, Burns; Elliott (Hilton 71), McManus, Millar, Stirling (Vitoria 71); Duffy (Paton 64), Orr.
Dumbarton: (4411) Ramsbottom; Nicholas McAllister, Wedderburn, Neill, Quitongo; Omar, Carswell, Langan (Wallace 61), Forbes; Frizzell (Jones 81); Wilson J (Duthie 81).
Referee: Chris Graham.

LEAGUE ONE SEMI-FINALS SECOND LEG

Tuesday, 11 May 2021

Dumbarton (1) 1 *(Wilson J 36)*

Stranraer (0) 0

Dumbarton: (442) Ramsbottom; Nicholas McAllister, Neill, Carswell, Quitongo; Forbes, Wedderburn, Brindley, Wallace (Duthie 78); Wilson J (Omar 67), Jones.
Stranraer: (4411) Fleming; Gallagher, Robertson, Sonkur, Burns; Elliott (Duffy 74), McManus, Millar, Stirling (Hilton 65); Paton (Matt Yates 74); Orr.
Dumbarton won 1-0 on aggregate.
Referee: Gavin Duncan.

Edinburgh C (1) 2 *(Handling 26, Campbell 88)*

Elgin C (2) 2 *(McHardy 22, 42)*

Edinburgh C: (4132) Antell; Thomson, Hamilton, McIntyre, Crane (Balatoni 86); Black (Dishington 78); Jardine, Brown, Campbell; Handling, See.
Elgin C: (4231) McHale; Cooper, Bronsky, McHardy, Spark; MacPhee (Peters 79), MacEwan (Brown 61); Dingwall R, Cameron, O'Keefe (Sopel 77); Hester.
Edinburgh C won 3-2 on aggregate.
Referee: Craig Napier.

LEAGUE ONE FINAL FIRST LEG

Monday, 17 May 2021

Edinburgh C (1) 1 *(McIntyre 44)*

Dumbarton (0) 3 *(McGeever 53, Brindley 67, Neill 82)*

Edinburgh C: (442) Antell; Thomson, Hamilton, McIntyre, Henderson L; Black (De Vita 74), Brown, Jardine, Campbell; Handling (Henderson B 79), See.
Dumbarton: (442) Ramsbottom; McGeever, Neill, Quitongo, Nicholas McAllister; Forbes, Wedderburn, Carswell, Brindley; Frizzell (Wallace 84), Jones (Omar 85).
Referee: Colin Steven.

LEAGUE ONE FINAL SECOND LEG

Thursday, 20 May 2021

Dumbarton (0) 0

Edinburgh C (0) 1 *(See 52)* 398

Dumbarton: (442) Ramsbottom; McGeever, Neill, Quitongo, Nicholas McAllister; Forbes, Wedderburn (Omar 83), Carswell, Brindley; Frizzell (Duthie 90), Jones.
Edinburgh C: (433) Antell; Balatoni, Thomson, Hamilton (Harris 69), Henderson L■; Brown, Jardine, Campbell (Dishington 84); Handling (Henderson B 69), McIntyre, See.
Dumbarton won 3-2 on aggregate.
Referee: Alan Newlands.

LEAGUE TWO SEMI-FINAL FIRST LEG

Tuesday, 4 May 2021

Brora R (0) 0

Kelty Hearts (1) 2 *(Easton 22, Higginbotham 56 (pen))*

Brora R: Malin; MacDonald A, Williamson, Nicolson, Gillespie, Morrison, MacLean, MacRae J, MacRae A, Kelly, Wagenaar.
Kelty Hearts: Jamieson; Stevenson, Boyle, Hooper, Hill, Reilly, Higginbotham, Tidser, Austin, Easton, Philip.
Referee: Grant Irvine.

LEAGUE TWO SEMI-FINAL SECOND LEG

Saturday, 8 May 2021

Kelty Hearts (1) 4 *(Austin 29, 58, 65, Easton 90)*

Brora R (1) 1 *(Morrison 27)*

Kelty Hearts: (4231) Jamieson; Stevenson, Hooper, Hill (Reid 18), Boyle; Tidser, Reilly; Philip, Higginbotham (Rodgers 82), Easton; Austin (Russell 62).
Brora R: (433) Malin; Pickles, Nicolson (Gamble 80), Williamson, MacDonald A; MacLean, Gillespie, Wagenaar (MacDonald G 77); Sutherland, Morrison, MacRae A (MacRae J 77).
Kelty Hearts won 6-1 on aggregate.
Referee: Euan Anderson.

LEAGUE TWO FINAL FIRST LEG

Tuesday, 18 May 2021

Kelty Hearts (2) 2 *(Higginbotham 16, Russell 45)*

Brechin C (1) 1 *(Page 23)*

Kelty Hearts: (4231) Jamieson; Stevenson (Russell 26), Reid, Hooper, Boyle; Reilly, Tidser; Philp, Higginbotham, Easton; Austin.
Brechin C: (442) Hutton; McIntosh, Page, Hussain (Jordan 37), Reekie; Coupe, Inglis, Osman, Barr (McLevy 90); Currie (Slaven 77), McKee.
Referee: Gavin Duncan.

LEAGUE TWO FINAL SECOND LEG

Sunday, 23 May 2021

Brechin C (0) 0

Kelty Hearts (0) 1 *(Tidser 88)* 250

Brechin C: (4141) Hutton; McIntosh, Reekie, Page, Jordan (Paton C 74); Osman; McKee■, Inglis, Barr (McLevy 90), Coupe (Currie 62); Paton M.
Kelty Hearts: (4231) Jamieson; Reid, Boyle, Hooper■, Hill; Tidser, Philp; Reilly, Higginbotham, Easton (Rodgers 81); Austin (Russell 70 (McNab 87)).
Kelty Hearts won 3-1 on aggregate.
Referee: Craig Napier.

SCOTTISH LEAGUE CUP FINALS 1946–2021

SCOTTISH LEAGUE CUP

1946–47	Rangers v Aberdeen	4-0
1947–48	East Fife v Falkirk	0-0*
Replay	East Fife v Falkirk	4-1
1948–49	Rangers v Raith R	2-0
1949–50	East Fife v Dunfermline Ath	3-0
1950–51	Motherwell v Hibernian	3-0
1951–52	Dundee v Rangers	3-2
1952–53	Dundee v Kilmarnock	2-0
1953–54	East Fife v Partick Thistle	3-2
1954–55	Hearts v Motherwell	4-2
1955–56	Aberdeen v St Mirren	2-1
1956–57	Celtic v Partick Thistle	0-0*
Replay	Celtic v Partick Thistle	3-0
1957–58	Celtic v Rangers	7-1
1958–59	Hearts v Partick Thistle	5-1
1959–60	Hearts v Third Lanark	2-1
1960–61	Rangers v Kilmarnock	2-0
1961–62	Rangers v Hearts	1-1*
Replay	Rangers v Hearts	3-1
1962–63	Hearts v Kilmarnock	1-0
1963–64	Rangers v Morton	5-0
1964–65	Rangers v Celtic	2-1
1965–66	Celtic v Rangers	2-1
1966–67	Celtic v Rangers	1-0
1967–68	Celtic v Dundee	5-3
1968–69	Celtic v Hibernian	6-2
1969–70	Celtic v St Johnstone	1-0
1970–71	Rangers v Celtic	1-0
1971–72	Partick Thistle v Celtic	4-1
1972–73	Hibernian v Celtic	2-1
1973–74	Dundee v Celtic	1-0
1974–75	Celtic v Hibernian	6-3
1975–76	Rangers v Celtic	1-0
1976–77	Aberdeen v Celtic	2-1*
1977–78	Rangers v Celtic	2-1*
1978–79	Rangers v Aberdeen	2-1

BELL'S LEAGUE CUP

1979–80	Dundee U v Aberdeen	0-0*
Replay	Dundee U v Aberdeen	3-0
1980–81	Dundee U v Dundee	3-0

SCOTTISH LEAGUE CUP

1981–82	Rangers v Dundee U	2-1
1982–83	Celtic v Rangers	2-1
1983–84	Rangers v Celtic	3-2*

SKOL CUP

1984–85	Rangers v Dundee U	1-0
1985–86	Aberdeen v Hibernian	3-0
1986–87	Rangers v Celtic	2-1
1987–88	Rangers v Aberdeen	3-3*
	Rangers won 5-3 on penalties.	
1988–89	Rangers v Aberdeen	3-2
1989–90	Aberdeen v Rangers	2-1*
1990–91	Rangers v Celtic	2-1*
1991–92	Hibernian v Dunfermline Ath	2-0
1992–93	Rangers v Aberdeen	2-1*

SCOTTISH LEAGUE CUP

1993–94	Rangers v Hibernian	2-1

COCA-COLA CUP

1994–95	Raith R v Celtic	2-2*
	Raith R won 6-5 on penalties.	
1995–96	Aberdeen v Dundee	2-0
1996–97	Rangers v Hearts	4-3
1997–98	Celtic v Dundee U	3-0

SCOTTISH LEAGUE CUP

1998–99	Rangers v St Johnstone	2-1

CIS INSURANCE CUP

1999–2000	Celtic v Aberdeen	2-0
2000–01	Celtic v Kilmarnock	3-0
2001–02	Rangers v Ayr U	4-0
2002–03	Rangers v Celtic	2-1
2003–04	Livingston v Hibernian	2-0
2004–05	Rangers v Motherwell	5-1
2005–06	Celtic v Dunfermline Ath	3-0
2006–07	Hibernian v Kilmarnock	5-1
2007–08	Rangers v Dundee U	2-2*
	Rangers won 3-2 on penalties.	

CO-OPERATIVE INSURANCE CUP

2008–09	Celtic v Rangers	2-0*
2009–10	Rangers v St Mirren	1-0
2010–11	Rangers v Celtic	2-1*

SCOTTISH COMMUNITIES LEAGUE CUP

2011–12	Kilmarnock v Celtic	1-0
2012–13	St Mirren v Hearts	3-2
2013–14	Aberdeen v Inverness CT	0-0*
	Aberdeen won 4-2 on penalties.	

SCOTTISH LEAGUE CUP PRESENTED BY QTS

2014–15	Celtic v Dundee U	2-0
2015–16	Ross Co v Hibernian	2-1

BETFRED SCOTTISH LEAGUE CUP

2016–17	Celtic v Aberdeen	3-0
2017–18	Celtic v Motherwell	2-0
2018–19	Celtic v Aberdeen	1-0
2019–20	Celtic v Rangers	1-0
2020–21	St Johnstone v Livingston	1-0

**After extra time.*

SCOTTISH LEAGUE CUP WINS

Rangers 27, Celtic 19, Aberdeen 6, Hearts 4, Dundee 3, East Fife 3, Hibernian 3, Dundee U 2, Kilmarnock 1, Livingston 1, Motherwell 1, Partick Thistle 1, Raith R 1, Ross Co 1, St Johnstone 1, St Mirren 1.

APPEARANCES IN FINALS

Rangers 35, Celtic 34, Aberdeen 15, Hibernian 10, Dundee U 7, Hearts 7, Dundee 6, Kilmarnock 6, Motherwell 4, Partick Thistle 4, Dunfermline Ath 3, East Fife 3, St Johnstone 3, St Mirren 3, Livingston 2, Raith R 2, Ayr U 1, Falkirk 1, Inverness CT 1, Morton 1, Ross Co 1, Third Lanark 1.

BETFRED SCOTTISH LEAGUE CUP 2020–21

■ *Denotes player sent off.*
PW = Drawn match won on penalties (2 pts).
PL = Drawn match lost on penalties (1 pt).
* *Qualified for Second Round as best runners-up.*
Due to COVID-19 pandemic, all matches played behind closed doors.

NORTHERN SECTION

FIRST ROUND – GROUP A

Tuesday, 6 October 2020

East Fife (0) 2 *(Hamilton 70, Wallace 82)*

Cowdenbeath (0) 0

East Fife: (442) Long; Murdoch (Newton 88), Dunlop, Higgins, Slattery; Dunsmore (Denholm 42), Davidson, Agnew (Watson 87), Swanson (Smith 79); Wallace, Hamilton (Watt 78).
Cowdenbeath: (442) Sinclair; Mullen, Todd, Barr, Clarke; Buchanan, Miller K, Taylor, Hamilton; Renton (Kavanagh 51), Herd (Swan 58).

Hearts (0) 1 *(Walker 62 (pen))*

Inverness CT (0) 0

Hearts: (4231) Gordon; Brandon, Halkett, Popescu, White; Lee (Haring 82), Irving (Halliday 63); Ginnelly (Henderson 83), Naismith (Kingsley 74), Walker; Wighton (Roberts 63).
Inverness CT: (451) Ridgers; Duffy (Hyde 66), McKay, Deas, Harper; Storey, Welsh, MacGregor, Allardice, Mackay D (Keatings 80); Sutherland (Todorov 45).

Saturday, 10 October 2020

Cowdenbeath (0) 0

Hearts (0) 1 *(Halkett 78)*

Cowdenbeath: (442) Sinclair; Pollock, Barr, Todd, Clarke; Taylor, Miller K, Herd, Hamilton; Kavanagh, Renton (Cox 58).
Hearts: (4411) Gordon; Brandon, Popescu, Halkett, White; Ginnelly, Lee (Haring 82), McGill (Frear 64), Walker; Roberts; Naismith (Wighton 46).

Raith R (1) 2 *(Hendry 45 (pen), Duku 87)*

East Fife (1) 1 *(Newton 15)*

Raith R: (4141) MacDonald J; Tumilty, Davidson, Benedictus, MacDonald K; Hendry; Armstrong, Matthews, Tait, Ross (Anderson 83); Duku.
East Fife: (451) Hart; Watson, Dunlop, Higgins, Slattery; Denholm (Dunsmore 73), Newton (Hamilton 82), Davidson, Watt (Collins 71), Agnew; Wallace.

Tuesday, 13 October 2020

Hearts (2) 3 *(Wighton 2 (pen), 40 (pen), 87)*

Raith R (0) 1 *(Duku 54)*

Hearts: (4231) Stewart; Brandon, Haring, Kingsley, White (Roberts 53); Cochrane, McGill (Lee 61); Moore (Ginnelly 71), Henderson (Popescu 61), Frear (Walker 71); Wighton.
Raith R: (541) MacDonald J; Tumilty, Davidson, Mendy (Ross 53), Benedictus, MacDonald K; Matthews, Hendry, Tait (Anderson 70), Spencer (Vaughan 67); Duku (Armstrong 67).

Inverness CT (0) 0

Cowdenbeath (0) 0

Inverness CT: (442) Mackay C; Duffy (Devine 77), McHattie (Harper 65), Welsh, McKay; Vincent (Allardice 65), Deas, Keatings, Storey (Todorov 13); Mackay D, MacGregor.
Cowdenbeath: (442) Sinclair; Pollock, Glass, Miller K, Clarke; Taylor, Todd, Kavanagh, Hamilton; Herd (Swan 53), Cox (Renton 90).
Inverness CT won 4-2 on penalties.

Tuesday, 10 November 2020

East Fife (1) 2 *(Hamilton 39, Wallace 64)*

Hearts (2) 3 *(Lee 1, 3, Irving 62)*

East Fife: (442) Hart; Murdoch, Dunlop, Higgins, Slattery; Dunsmore (Watt 82), Davidson, Agnew, Denholm (Collins 76); Wallace, Hamilton (Smith 76).
Hearts: (4231) Stewart; Brandon, Popescu, Berra (Kingsley 71), White; Irving, Lee (Naismith 49); Henderson, McGill, Frear; Wighton.

Raith R (1) 3 *(Duku 11, 90, Devine 59 (og))*

Inverness CT (1) 3 *(Sutherland 24, Keatings 67 (pen), MacGregor 69)*

Raith R: (4231) Thomson; Tumilty, Mendy, Benedictus, Musonda; Matthews, Hendry; Armstrong, Spencer, Ross; Duku.
Inverness CT: (4231) Ridgers; Duffy, McKay (Deas 45), Devine, Harper; Vincent (MacGregor 33), Allardice; Doran (Todorov 85), Keatings, Kennedy; Sutherland.
Raith R won 3-2 on penalties.

Saturday, 14 November 2020

Cowdenbeath (0) 0

Raith R (1) 1 *(Duku 36)*

Cowdenbeath: (4141) Sinclair; Mullen, Barr, Todd (Miller K 40), Clarke (Pyper 54); Glass; Hamilton (Taylor 67), Herd (Swan 67), Smith, Kavanagh; Russell.
Raith R: (4141) Thomson; Tumilty, Mendy, Musonda, Ross (Coulson 76); Hendry; Armstrong, Matthews, Spencer, Tait; Duku.

Inverness CT (0) 1 *(Sutherland 64)*

East Fife (0) 0

Inverness CT: (442) Mackay C; Nicolson, Devine, Deas, Harper; MacGregor, Allardice, Kennedy (Keatings 78), Doran (Mackay D 65); Todorov (Storey 65), Sutherland.
East Fife: (442) Hart; Murdoch (Watson 69), Higgins, Dunlop, Slattery; Denholm (Dunsmore 61), Davidson, Agnew (Newton 75), Smith (Watt 69); Hamilton, Wallace (Collins 46).

Group A Table	P	W	PW	PL	L	F	A	GD	Pts
Hearts	4	4	0	0	0	8	3	5	12
Raith R	4	2	1	0	1	7	7	0	8
Inverness CT	4	1	1	1	1	4	4	0	6
East Fife	4	1	0	0	3	5	6	–1	3
Cowdenbeath	4	0	0	1	3	0	4	–4	1

FIRST ROUND - GROUP B

Tuesday, 6 October 2020

Dundee 3

Forfar Ath 0

Match awarded 3-0 to Dundee due to Forfar Ath being unable to fulfil the fixture after one of their players tested positive for COVID-19.

Wednesday, 7 October 2020

Hibernian (2) 3 *(Mallan 8, 12, Hanlon 89)*

Brora R (0) 1 *(Gillespie 61)*

Hibernian: (433) Barnes; Gray, McGregor, Hanlon, Stevenson; Mallan, Hallberg (Nisbet 78), McGinn S (Magennis 61); Wright (Doidge 61), Gullan, Murphy (Boyle 50).
Brora R: (451) Malin; Pickles (MacDonald N 90), Nicolson, Williamson (Gamble 89), MacDonald A; Kelly, MacLean, Gillespie (MacDonald G 83), MacRae A (Wagenaar 83), Morrison (Brindle 74); MacRae J.

Saturday, 10 October 2020

Brora R (0) 0

Dundee (2) 2 *(Dorrans 11, Mullen 27)*

Brora R: (4411) Malin; Pickles, Nicolson, Williamson, MacDonald A; Kelly, Gillespie (MacDonald G 75), MacLean, Morrison (Brindle 41); MacRae A; MacRae J (Wagenaar 67).
Dundee: (352) Hamilton J; McGhee, Forster, Ashcroft; Elliot (Kerr 79), Anderson (Robertson 60), Adam (Byrne 79), Dorrans, Marshall; McGowan (McDaid 79), Mullen (Sow 58).

Cove R (1) 1 *(Higgins 17)*

Hibernian (0) 2 *(Gullan 49, Nisbet 60)*

Cove R: (4411) McKenzie; Scott Ross, Higgins, Graham, Milne; McIntosh, Scully, Yule, Livingstone (Semple 72); Masson; Megginson.
Hibernian: (352) Barnes; Gray, McGregor, Stevenson; Boyle, Hallberg, McGinn S (Magennis 59), Mallan, Wright (Gullan 46); Nisbet, Doidge.

Tuesday, 13 October 2020

Brora R (1) 2 *(MacLean 29, Wagenaar 72)*

Cove R (2) 2 *(McAllister 18, Semple 28)*

Brora R: (442) Malin; Pickles, Nicolson, Williamson, MacDonald A; Brindle, MacDonald G (Gamble 69), Gillespie (MacRae J 46), Wagenaar; MacRae A, MacLean.
Cove R: (4411) McKenzie; Leighton (Scott Ross 73), Higgins, Graham, Milne; Watson, Scully, Semple, Livingstone; Brown (Yule 73); McAllister (McIntosh 69).
Cove R won 6-5 on penalties.

Forfar Ath (0) 0

Hibernian (0) 1 *(Gray 87)*

Forfar Ath: (442) McCallum; Meechan, Fisher (Coll 66), Whyte (Thomas 39), MacKenzie; Scally, Irvine, MacKintosh, Barr; Shepherd, Robertson (Allan 63).
Hibernian: (442) Barnes; Hallberg, Gray, McGregor, Mackie; Magennis (Boyle 61), Mallan, McGinn S, Gullan; Shanley (Nisbet 61), Doidge (Bradley 88).

Tuesday, 10 November 2020

Dundee (1) 3 *(McGowan 6, Mullen 84, Adam 87 (pen))*

Cove R (0) 0

Dundee: (433) Hamilton J; Elliot, Kerr, McGhee (Hamilton N 89), Marshall; Adam, Byrne (Robertson 74), Anderson (Blacklock 89); McGowan, Mullen (Wilkie 88), McDaid.
Cove R: (442) McKenzie; Livingstone, Scott Ross, Strachan, Semple (Graham 46); Sebastian Ross (Ritchie 67), Yule■, Brown (Scully 67), Masson■; Megginson (McAllister 70), McIntosh (Watson 69).

Forfar Ath (1) 3 *(MacKintosh 34, 81, Allan 87 (pen))*

Brora R (1) 3 *(Irvine 42 (og), MacLean 52, MacRae J 84)*

Forfar Ath: (442) Hoban; MacKintosh, Fisher, Coll (Breadner 86), MacKenzie; Hoti (Shepherd 66), Irvine, Barr, Antoniazzi; Robertson (Allan 66), Hill (Thomas 54).
Brora R: (442) Beattie; Kelly, Nicolson, Gamble, MacDonald A; Morrison, Gillespie (MacDonald G 88), MacLean, Wagenaar (Brindle 70); MacRae J, MacRae A.
Forfar Ath won 4-3 on penalties.

Saturday, 14 November 2020

Cove R (0) 1 *(McAllister 68 (pen))*

Forfar Ath (0) 0

Cove R: (442) McKenzie; Scott Ross, Strachan, Graham, Livingstone; Watson (Semple 66), Scully, Fyvie (Brown 66), Sebastian Ross; Megginson, McAllister.
Forfar Ath: (352) Hoban; Irvine, Fisher■, MacKenzie; MacKintosh, Hoti, Thomas, Barr (Starrs 81), Coll; Shepherd (Allan 73), Antoniazzi.

Sunday, 15 November 2020

Hibernian (1) 4 *(Mallan 10, Nisbet 76, Gullan 80, Hallberg 82)*

Dundee (0) 1 *(Elliot 71)*

Hibernian: (442) Barnes; McGinn P, McGregor, Hanlon, Doig (Mackie 73); Wright (Gullan 73), Mallan (McGinn S 87), Newell, Murphy (Hallberg 80); Boyle (Bradley 88), Nisbet.
Dundee: (433) Hamilton J; Elliot, Kerr, McGhee, Marshall; Adam, Byrne, McGowan; Robertson, Mullen, McDaid.

Group B Table	P	W	PW	PL	L	F	A	GD	Pts
Hibernian	4	4	0	0	0	10	3	7	12
Dundee*	4	3	0	0	1	9	4	5	9
Cove Rangers	4	1	1	0	2	4	7	−3	5
Brora Rangers	4	0	0	2	2	6	10	−4	2
Forfar Ath	4	0	1	0	3	3	8	−5	2

FIRST ROUND - GROUP C

Wednesday, 7 October 2020

Brechin C (0) 2 *(Inglis 52 (pen), Currie 54)*

Dundee U (3) 6 *(Clark 15, 18, Butcher 40, Harkes 47, Smith C 60, 90)*

Brechin C: (442) McMinn; McIntosh, Jordan, Page, McKay; Todd (Luissint 81), Scott (Nawrocki 72), Inglis, Cusick (Paton M 64); Makovora, Currie.
Dundee U: (442) Mehmet; Neilson (Fotheringham 63), Edwards (Connolly 61), Reynolds, Robson; Bolton, Butcher (Powers 50), Harkes (Pawlett 64), McMullan; Clark (Smith C 50), Appere.

Kelty Hearts (0) 1 *(Tidser 71)*

St Johnstone (1) 2 *(Kerr 45, Kane 60)*

Kelty Hearts: (442) Jamieson; Stevenson, Reid, Hooper, Boyle; Higginbotham, Reilly, Tidser, Philp; Russell (Flynn 62), Easton (McNab 82).
St Johnstone: (442) Parish; Rooney, Kerr, Gordon, Booth; Conway (Davidson 81), Craig (Bryson 70), Wotherspoon, Tanser; Hendry (May 90), Kane.

Saturday, 10 October 2020

Dundee U (0) 0

Peterhead (0) 1 *(Boyd 51)*

Dundee U: (4231) Mehmet; Smith L (Appere 54), Connolly, Edwards, Robson; Harkes, Butcher (Powers 76); Bolton, Pawlett, McMullan (Fotheringham 66); Smith C.
Peterhead: (442) Rae; Bailey, Ferry, Jason Brown, Conroy; Mulligan (Fraser 9), McCarthy, Brown S, Boyd; Layne (Cook 33), Armour (Cameron 64).

St Johnstone (2) 7 *(May 3, 58, 62, Wotherspoon 25, 56, Hendry 88 (pen), Davidson 90)*

Brechin C (0) 0

St Johnstone: (4321) Clark; Rooney, Gordon, McCart, Booth; Bryson (Hendry 65), Davidson, Craig; Conway (Ferguson 74), Wotherspoon; May (Kane 65).
Brechin C: (442) McMinn; McIntosh (Bollan 70), Brown, Jordan, McKay (Reekie 46); Paton M, Todd, Inglis, Cusick; Currie (Luissint 61), Makovora (Scott 13).

Tuesday, 13 October 2020

Dundee U (1) 1 *(Edwards 45)*

Kelty Hearts (0) 0

Dundee U: (532) Mehmet; Bolton, Edwards, Connolly (Powers 69), Reynolds, Robson; Pawlett (Mochrie 77), Butcher, Harkes; Appere (Smith C 68), Clark.
Kelty Hearts: (442) Jamieson; Stevenson, Reid (Scobbie 24), Hooper, Boyle; Higginbotham, Tidser, Reilly, Philp (Russell 61); McNab (Flynn 46), Easton.

Peterhead (3) 3 *(Layne 13, 17, Boyd 24)*

Brechin C (0) 1 *(Inglis 46)*

Peterhead: (442) Rae; Bailey, Jason Brown, MacKenzie (Freeman 62), Conroy; McCarthy (Cameron 73), Ferry, Brown S, Boyd (Kesson 73); Layne (Lyle 61), Armour (Cook 10).
Brechin C: (352) O'Neil; Reekie, Page, Bollan; McIntosh (Inglis 46), Todd (Cusick 46), Luissint (Makovora 70), Scott (Currie 61), McKay; Paton M, Nawrocki.

Tuesday, 10 November 2020

Kelty Hearts (0) 1 *(Stevenson 66)*

Peterhead (0) 1 *(Fraser 49)*

Kelty Hearts: (4231) Jamieson; Stevenson, Hooper, Hill, Boyle; Tidser, Reilly; Higginbotham, Philp, Easton; Flynn (McNab 86).
Peterhead: (451) Wilson; Bailey, Freeman, Jason Brown, Conroy; Cameron (Boyd 46), McCarthy (Bakar 81), Fraser, Brown S, Cook (Lyle 46); Armour (Ferry 63).
Peterhead won 5-3 on penalties.

St Johnstone (0) 0

Dundee U (0) 0

St Johnstone: (442) Clark; Rooney, Kerr, Gordon, Booth; Wotherspoon (O'Halloran 74), Bryson (Davidson 77), Craig, Tanser; Hendry (May 67), Kane (Conway 74).

Dundee U: (3412) Mehmet; Connolly, Edwards, Reynolds; Smith L, Butcher, Fuchs (Harkes 62), Sporle (Bolton 84); McMullan (Appere 78); McNulty, Clark.
Dundee U won 4-3 on penalties.

Saturday, 14 November 2020

Brechin C (0) 0

Kelty Hearts (0) 2 *(Easton 48, McNab 79)*

Brechin C: (4411) McMinn; McLevy, Jordan, Bollan, Reekie; Todd, Barron, Inglis (Nawrocki 84), Makovora (Currie 71); Paton M; Scott.
Kelty Hearts: (4231) Jamieson; Reid (Scobbie 53), Hooper, Hill (Cooney 28), Boyle; Stevenson, Tidser; Higginbotham, Philp (McNab 52), Easton; Flynn (Austin 52).

Peterhead (0) 1 *(Rooney 78 (og))*

St Johnstone (0) 3 *(May 49 (pen), 60 (pen), Kane 77)*

Peterhead: (4231) Wilson; Bailey, Freeman, Jason Brown (Lyle 63), Conroy; Brown S, Ferry; McCarthy, Fraser (Cameron 68), Boyd; Armour (Cook 29).
St Johnstone: (3412) Clark; Rooney, Kerr, McCart; O'Halloran, Davidson, Craig, Booth; Conway (Bryson 61); May (Kane 73), Melamed (Hendry 61).

Group C Table	P	W	PW	PL	L	F	A	GD	Pts
St Johnstone	4	3	0	1	0	12	2	10	10
Dundee U	4	2	1	0	1	7	3	4	8
Peterhead	4	2	1	0	1	6	5	1	8
Kelty Hearts	4	1	0	1	2	4	4	0	4
Brechin C	4	0	0	0	4	3	18	–15	0

FIRST ROUND - GROUP D

Tuesday, 6 October 2020

Stirling Alb (0) 1 *(Ryan 76)*

Arbroath (2) 2 *(Donnelly 14, O'Brien 32)*

Stirling Alb: (442) Binnie; Banner, McLean, McGregor, Creaney; Ryan, Roberts K (Roberts S 71), Wilson, Leitch; Moore (Thomson 77), Mackin (Byrne 88).
Arbroath: (4141) Gaston; Thomson, Little, O'Brien, Hamilton C; Virtanen; Gold (Swankie 67), Linn (Ruth 59), McKenna (Connor Smith 67), Hilson (Stewart 59); Donnelly (Doolan 71).

Wednesday, 7 October 2020

Montrose (0) 3 *(Webster 63, Cammy Ballantyne 67, Steeves 89)*

Ross Co (2) 3 *(Shaw 13, McKay 15, Charles-Cook 52)*

Montrose: (352) Fleming; Dillon, Allan (Milne 63), Waddell (Rennie 62); Cammy Ballantyne, Cameron Ballantyne, Watson, Webster, Steeves; Hawke (Campbell R 62), Johnston (Quinn 62).
Ross Co: (433) Laidlaw; Watson, Morris, Iacovitti, Tremarco; Charles-Cook, Paton, Vigurs (Gardyne 90); Shaw (Stewart 79), Hylton (Lakin 67), McKay.
Ross Co won 5-4 on penalties.

Saturday, 10 October 2020

Arbroath (2) 3 *(Swankie 27, Thomson 43, O'Brien 86)*

Montrose (1) 1 *(Webster 10)*

Arbroath: (451) Gaston; Thomson, Little, O'Brien, Hamilton C (Gold 46); Ruth (Linn 79), Craigen (McKenna 72), Swankie, Connor Smith (Hilson 80), Stewart; Doolan (Donnelly 79).
Montrose: (433) Lennox; Cammy Ballantyne, Quinn, Waddell, Steeves; Cameron Ballantyne, Allan (Watson 66), Milne; Rennie (Campbell R 72), Johnston (Hawke 66), Webster.

Elgin C (0) 2 *(Hester 67, Dingwall R 81 (pen))*

Stirling Alb (0) 0

Elgin C: (442) McHale; Wilson (McDonald 46), Cooper, Bronsky, Spark; O'Keefe (Jamieson 90), Cameron, Dingwall R, Sopel (MacBeath 68); Hester■, Osadolor (Mailer 76).
Stirling Alb: (352) Binnie; McGregor, McLean, Banner; Roberts S (Moore 70), Roberts K (Thomson 62), Wilson (Docherty 75), Leitch, Creaney (Heaver 75); Ryan, Byrne.

Tuesday, 13 October 2020

Montrose (0) 0

Elgin C (2) 2 *(O'Keefe 27, Peters 36)*

Montrose: (352) Fleming; Quinn (Milne 46), Dillon (Campbell I 58), Allan; Cammy Ballantyne (Waddell 55), Webster, Watson (Campbell R 58), Cameron Ballantyne, Steeves; Hawke (Johnston 46), Rennie.
Elgin C: (433) McHale; Cooper, McDonald, Bronsky, Spark (Wilson 84); Cameron, Mailer, Dingwall R; Osadolor, Peters (MacBeath 65), O'Keefe (Sopel 88).

Ross Co (0) 2 *(Stewart 65, 68 (pen))*

Arbroath (0) 1 *(Hilson 49)*

Ross Co: (433) Laidlaw; Randall, Donaldson, Morris (Iacovitti 19), Tremarco; Charles-Cook, Lakin, Tillson (Paton 58); Stewart, McKay (Shaw 83), Hylton (Gardyne 58).
Arbroath: (451) Gaston; Gold (Ruth 52), Little, O'Brien, Thomson; Hilson, Stewart (Swankie 75), Virtanen, McKenna (Connor Smith 74), Linn (Craigen 52); Donnelly (Doolan 75).

Tuesday, 10 November 2020

Elgin C (0) 1 *(Cameron 80)*

Ross Co (2) 4 *(Grivosti 5, Iacovitti 45, Paton 51, Lakin 77)*

Elgin C: (442) McHale; Cooper, Bronsky, MacEwan (Mailer 73), Spark (McHardy 66); Dingwall R, McDonald, Cameron, O'Keefe (Sopel 62); Osadolor (MacBeath 73), Hester (Peters 62).
Ross Co: (442) Laidlaw; Tremarco (Reid 7), Grivosti (Williamson 81), Hylton, Shaw (Lakin 69); Iacovitti, McKay, Charles-Cook, Donaldson; Paton (O'Connor 82), Kelly (Tillson 81).

Stirling Alb (2) 2 *(Heaver 35, Mackin 41)*

Montrose (1) 1 *(Hawke 20)*

Stirling Alb: (41212) Binnie; McGeachie, Wilson (Mitchell 90), McGregor (Magee 55), Banner; El-Zubaidi; Leitch (Roberts K 90), Roberts S (Creaney 80); Docherty; Mackin (Byrne 81), Heaver.
Montrose: (442) Fleming; Campbell R, Quinn, Campbell I, Rennie; Cameron Ballantyne, McCormick (Rollo 69), Callaghan (Watson 61), Johnston; Hawke (McLean 66), Milne.

Saturday, 14 November 2020

Arbroath (2) 3 *(Gold 30, 39, Stewart 82)*

Elgin C (0) 0

Arbroath: (451) Gaston; Thomson, Little, O'Brien, Hamilton C; Linn (Ruth 69), Craigen (Swankie 73), McKenna (Connor Smith 69), Gold, Hilson (Stewart 80); Doolan (Donnelly 69).
Elgin C: (442) McHale; Wilson (MacEwan 36), Bronsky, Cooper, Spark (McHardy 78); Dingwall R (MacBeath 71), McDonald, Cameron, O'Keefe (Peters 46); Osadolor (Sopel 46), Hester.

Ross Co (1) 3 *(Shaw 21, Stewart 50 (pen), Charles-Cook 71)*

Stirling Alb (0) 0

Ross Co: (442) Laidlaw; Grivosti, Donaldson (Morris 74), Iacovitti (Williamson 81), Reid; Charles-Cook (Wright 82), Tillson, Vigurs, Hylton; Shaw (McKay 43), Stewart (Mackinnon 82).
Stirling Alb: (352) Binnie; Banner, El-Zubaidi, McGregor; McGeachie, Roberts K, Docherty (Mackin 68), Wilson (Magee 76), Creaney (Moore 68); Byrne (Ryan 83), Leitch (Heaver 82).

Group D Table	P	W	PW	PL	L	F	A	GD	Pts
Ross Co	4	3	1	0	0	12	5	7	11
Arbroath	4	3	0	0	1	9	4	5	9
Elgin C	4	2	0	0	2	5	7	–2	6
Stirling Alb	4	1	0	0	3	3	8	–5	3
Montrose	4	0	0	1	3	5	10	–5	1

SOUTHERN SECTION

FIRST ROUND – GROUP E

Tuesday, 6 October 2020

Dumbarton (0) 0

Dunfermline Ath (1) 1 *(O'Hara 26 (pen))*

Dumbarton: (442) Dabrowski; Wardrop, Neill, McGeever, Quitongo; Langan (Jones 66), Carswell, Wedderburn, Crossan; McCluskey (Hamilton 52), Johnstone.
Dunfermline Ath: (4411) Fon Williams; Comrie, Murray E, Watson, Edwards; Dow (Murray F 64), Whittaker, McInroy, Thomas; Turner (McManus 73); O'Hara (Wilson 73).

Falkirk 3 Kilmarnock 0

Match awarded 3-0 to Falkirk due to Kilmarnock being unable to fulfil the fixture after several of their players tested positive for COVID-19.

Friday, 9 October 2020

Dunfermline Ath (0) 2 *(Murray E 58, 65)*

Falkirk (0) 0

Dunfermline Ath: (4132) Fon Williams; Comrie, Watson, Murray E, Edwards; Whittaker (Wilson 76); Dow (McCann 84), Murray F (Turner 66), Thomas; McManus, O'Hara.
Falkirk: (442) Mutch; Mercer, Durnan, Hall, Dixon; Morrison C, Miller, Gomis, Leitch (Todd 60); Dowds (Sammon 84), Keena (Francis 70).

Saturday, 10 October 2020

Clyde (3) 3 *(Cuddihy 10, Goodwillie 22 (pen), Cunningham 45)*

Dumbarton (1) 2 *(Hamilton 40, Jones 55)*

Clyde: (433) Mitchell; Bain, Lang, McNiff, Shiels; Cuddihy, Jack (Robertson 84), Love (Syvertsen 65); Johnston (Lamont 65), Goodwillie, Cunningham.
Dumbarton: (4231) Dabrowski; Wardrop (Johnstone 67), McGeever, Neill, Quitongo; Wedderburn, Carswell; Hamilton■, Crossan, Forbes (Langan 77); Jones.

Tuesday, 13 October 2020

Falkirk (1) 2 *(Keena 13, Morrison C 47 (pen))*

Clyde (1) 1 *(Goodwillie 17)*

Falkirk: (451) Mutch; Mercer, Durnan, Hall, Dixon; Dowds, Morrison C, Todd (Sammon 83), Gomis, Leitch (Alston 56); Keena (Francis 37).
Clyde: (451) Vajs; Howie (Johnston 68), Rumsby, Lang (Bain 79), Shiels; Cunningham, Robertson (McNiff 80), Lamont (Jack 59), Cuddihy, Love (Syvertsen 59); Goodwillie.

Kilmarnock (0) 0

Dunfermline Ath (0) 3 *(Murray E 56, Murray F 73, 83)*

Kilmarnock: (4231) Doyle; Sloan, Ross, Dicker, Deveney; McKenzie, Haunstrup (Russell 76); Burke (Dee 89), Warnock (Smith 89), Cameron (Rennie 64); Kabamba (Mullen 89).
Dunfermline Ath: (442) Gill; Whittaker, Watson, Murray E, Edwards; Murray F, Turner (Allan 73), Wilson, Thomas (McCann 80); McManus (McGill 80), O'Hara (Dow 66).

Tuesday, 10 November 2020

Clyde (0) 0

Kilmarnock (1) 2 *(Whitehall 44, 49)*

Clyde: (4411) Mitchell; Bain, Rumsby, McNiff, Shiels; Robertson (Jack 65), Cunningham (Henderson 64), Cuddihy, Love (Syvertsen 78); Lamont; Goodwillie.
Kilmarnock: (442) Doyle; McGowan, Rossi, Findlay, Haunstrup; McKenzie, Mulumbu, Brindley, Pinnock; Brophy, Whitehall.

Dumbarton (0) 0

Falkirk (1) 4 *(Morrison C 12, 49, Sammon 73, Dowds 82)*

Dumbarton: (442) Dabrowski (Calder 79); Morrison, McGeever, Wardrop, Quitongo (Frizzell 59); Wilson J, Forbes, Reilly, Langan; Johnstone, Jones.
Falkirk: (442) Peter Morrison; Miller, Hall, Dixon, Kelly; Leitch (Telfer 66), Alston (Gomis 65), Todd, Morrison C (Laverty 83); Sammon, Francis (Dowds 65).

Saturday, 14 November 2020

Dunfermline Ath (0) 3 *(O'Hara 60 (pen), McManus 87, Watson 90)*

Clyde (1) 2 *(Love 35, Lamont 51)*

Dunfermline Ath: (4132) Gill; Bowman (McCann 84), Watson, Murray E, Edwards; Wilson (Turner 53); Dow, Murray F (Thomas 67), McInroy; O'Hara, McManus.
Clyde: (4231) Vajs; Howie (Bain 67), Rumsby, McNiff, Shiels; Cuddihy, Robertson; Love (Henderson 78), Lamont, Cunningham; Goodwillie.

Kilmarnock (2) 2 *(Brophy 3, Pinnock 45)*

Dumbarton (0) 0

Kilmarnock: (442) Eastwood; McGowan, Broadfoot, Rossi, Haunstrup; McKenzie, Mulumbu, Power, Pinnock; Brophy, Whitehall.
Dumbarton: (442) Dabrowski; Wardrop, McGeever (Johnstone 21), Neill, Church; Hamilton, Wedderburn, Forbes, Langan (Reilly 82); Wilson J, Frizzell (Morrison 88).

Group E Table	*P*	*W*	*PW*	*PL*	*L*	*F*	*A*	*GD*	*Pts*
Dunfermline Ath	4	4	0	0	0	9	2	7	12
Falkirk*	4	3	0	0	1	9	3	6	9
Kilmarnock	4	2	0	0	2	4	6	–2	6
Clyde	4	1	0	0	3	6	9	–3	3
Dumbarton	4	0	0	0	4	2	10	–8	0

FIRST ROUND - GROUP F

Tuesday, 6 October 2020

Albion R (2) 2 *(Aitken 23 (pen), 38)*

Ayr U (3) 5 *(McCowan 30, Walsh 35, Anderson 40, 82, Zanatta 59)*

Albion R: (433) Goodfellow; Burke, Fernie, Fagan, Wilson L■; Lynas (Leslie 84), Fotheringham (Trialist 85), Wilson C; Jamieson (Moran 80), Aitken, Doherty (Baker 73).
Ayr U: (442) Sinisalo; Muirhead, Baird, Roscoe, Chalmers; Walsh (Zanatta 49), Murdoch (Hewitt 74), Miller M, McCowan (McKenzie 84); Moffat (Smith P 84), Anderson.

Annan Ath (3) 3 *(Swinglehurst 31, Fulton 38, Purdue 43)*

Hamilton A (0) 1 *(McMann 51)*

Annan Ath: (433) Pettigrew; Fulton, Douglas, Swinglehurst, Clark; Flanagan (Currie 87), Moxon, Hunter; Purdue (Splaine 80), Anderson (Smith 64), Wright.
Hamilton A: (442) Gourlay; Hodson, Odofin, McMann, Munro; Smith C, Callachan, Stirling, Templeton (Johnson 59); Owolabi (Moyo 80), Ogboe.

Saturday, 10 October 2020

Annan Ath (0) 1 *(Moxon 55)*

Stranraer (1) 1 *(Paton 37)*

Annan Ath: (442) Mitchell; Fulton (Docherty 21), Douglas, Swinglehurst, Clark; Flanagan (Wright 73), Moxon, Hunter, Purdue (Fleming 79); Smith (Anderson 73), Splaine.
Stranraer: (442) Fleming; Robertson, Sonkur, Devitt, Burns; Stirling, Gallagher, Millar, Vitoria (Elliott 58); Duffy (Orr 82), Paton (McManus 77).
Stranraer won 5-4 on penalties.

Hamilton A (2) 2 *(Ogboe 19, Trafford 36)*

Ayr U (0) 1 *(Moffat 68)*

Hamilton A: (442) Fulton; Hodson, Odofin, Stirling, McMann; Callachan (Martin S 59), Mimnaugh, Trafford, Smith C (Moyo 74); Templeton (Munro 90), Ogboe.
Ayr U: (4231) Sinisalo; Muirhead, Roscoe, Baird, Chalmers; Miller M (Hewitt 24), Murdoch; McKenzie (Smith P 80), Moffat, McCowan; Zanatta.

Tuesday, 13 October 2020

Ayr U (1) 1 *(Moffat 24 (pen))*

Annan Ath (0) 0

Ayr U: (4231) Sinisalo; Muirhead, Baird, Roscoe, Hewitt; Murdoch (Houston 56), Chalmers; McKenzie, Moffat, McCowan; Zanatta (Smith P 43).
Annan Ath: (442) Mitchell; Hunter, Douglas (Watson 84), Swinglehurst, Clark; Flanagan (Emerson 75), Docherty, Splaine, Fleming (Purdue 60); Anderson (Wright 60), Smith (Currie 75).

Stranraer (1) 2 *(Sonkur 18, Paton 58)*

Albion R (2) 2 *(Jamieson 29, Fotheringham 44)*

Stranraer: (442) Fleming; Robertson, Sonkur (Cummins 46), Devitt, Burns; Hilton (Elliott 66), McManus, Millar, Stirling; Duffy (Orr 73), Paton.
Albion R: (433) Goodfellow; Burke, Lynas, Fagan, Ecrepont; Skeoch, Fotheringham, Wilson C; Moore (Doherty 63), Aitken, Jamieson (Leslie 88).
Albion R won 15-14 on penalties.

Tuesday, 10 November 2020

Albion R (0) 1 *(Dolan 90)*

Annan Ath (4) 5 *(Wright 16, 21, Fleming 28, 76, Docherty 35 (pen))*

Albion R: (442) Henry; Lynas, Fagan, Glover, Ecrepont (Wilson L 46); Wilson C (Cairney 71), Leslie, Moran (Fotheringham 46), Skeoch (Dolan 46); Baker, Doherty (Moore 70).
Annan Ath: (442) Mitchell; Hunter, Douglas, Swinglehurst, Love; Fleming, Moxon (Emerson 80), Docherty, Clark (Flanagan 80); Wright (Currie 59), Smith (Anderson 87).

Wednesday, 11 November 2020

Stranraer (1) 2 *(Orr 34, Duffy 81)*

Hamilton A (0) 1 *(Odofin 71)*

Stranraer: (442) Fleming; Gallagher, Robertson, Sonkur, Cummins; Stirling (Hilton 58), Millar, McManus, Vitoria; Paton, Orr (Duffy 75).
Hamilton A: (451) Fulton; Martin A, Odofin, Easton, McMann; Thomas (Munro 46), Callachan (Hughes 59), Smith C, Martin S (Mimnaugh 73), Smith L (Johnson 73); Winter (Owolabi 64).

Saturday, 14 November 2020

Ayr U (0) 1 *(McCowan 47)*

Stranraer (1) 1 *(Duffy 2)*

Ayr U: (4231) Sinisalo; Houston, Roscoe, Baird, Hewitt (Kerr 82); Chalmers, Miller M; McCowan, Moffat, Zanatta (McKenzie 62); Anderson.
Stranraer: (442) Fleming; McIntyre, Sonkur, Robertson, Cummins; Paton, Gallagher, Hilton, Vitoria; Orr, Duffy.
Ayr U won 6-5 on penalties.

Hamilton A 3

Albion R 0

Match awarded 3-0 to Hamilton A due to Albion R being unable to fulfil the fixture after several of their players tested positive for COVID-19.

Group F Table	P	W	PW	PL	L	F	A	GD	Pts
Ayr U	4	2	1	0	1	8	5	3	8
Annan Ath	4	2	0	1	1	9	4	5	7
Stranraer	4	1	1	2	0	6	5	1	7
Hamilton A*	4	2	0	0	2	7	6	1	6
Albion R	4	0	1	0	3	5	15	–10	2

FIRST ROUND - GROUP G

Tuesday, 6 October 2020

Greenock Morton (1) 2 *(McGinty 18, Nesbitt 68)*

Queen of the South (0) 2 *(Dobbie 53, Shields 79)*

Greenock Morton: (442) McAdams; Omar, McLean, McGinty, Strapp; McPake, Jacobs, McAlister, Nesbitt (Colville 73); Orsi (Salkeld 61), MacIver (Muirhead 70).
Queen of the South: (433) Ferguson; Gibson, Buchanan, Obileye, Maxwell; McCabe, McKee, Pybus (Fitzpatrick 31); Dobbie (Robinson 74), East (Joseph 86), Shields.
Queen of the South won 4-2 on penalties.

Wednesday, 7 October 2020

St Mirren (1) 4 *(Tait 45, Obika 74, Breen 81 (og), Connolly 82)*

Partick Thistle (0) 1 *(Spittal 66)*

St Mirren: (352) Alnwick; Fraser, Shaughnessy, Tait; Morias (McAllister K 59), MacPherson (Foley 77), Sheron (Connolly 59), Erhahon, McGrath; Erwin (Durmus 77), Obika (Jamieson 84).
Partick Thistle: (433) Sneddon; Williamson (McKenna 75), Brownlie, Breen, Penrice; Bannigan, Gordon, Docherty; Cardle (Spittal 61), Graham (Kouider-Aisser 84), Murray (Lyons 75).

Saturday, 10 October 2020

Partick Thistle (0) 2 *(Cardle 66, 81)*

Queen's Park (0) 0

Partick Thistle: (4312) Sneddon; Foster (Williamson 46), Brownlie, McKenna, Penrice; Gordon (Niang 79), Docherty, Bannigan; Spittal (Murray 63); Rudden (Cardle 46), Graham.
Queen's Park: (4231) Muir; Doyle (Kilday 82), Morrison, Grant, Robson; Lyon, Gillespie; MacLean (Willam Baynham 70), Longridge, Paterson (Galt 62); McHugh.

Queen of the South (2) 2 *(Shields 8, Fitzpatrick 12)*

St Mirren (0) 2 *(McGrath 51, Fraser 89)*

Queen of the South: (442) Ferguson; Gibson, Buchanan, Obileye, Maxwell; Fitzpatrick, McKee, Pybus, Shields; East (Goss 85), Dobbie (McGorry 87).
St Mirren: (352) Alnwick; Tait, Shaughnessy, Fraser; Sheron (Obika 46), McGrath, Foley, Durmus (MacPherson 71), Erhahon; Erwin (Connolly 59), McAllister K (Morias 59).
St Mirren won 4-2 on penalties.

Tuesday, 13 October 2020

Greenock Morton (0) 1 *(Blues 51)*

Queen's Park (0) 0

Greenock Morton: (3412) McAdams; Ledger, Fjortoft, McGinty; Salkeld (McPake 70), Blues (Nesbitt 70), Lyon (Jacobs 52), Colville; McGuffie (Wallace 56); Muirhead, Oliver (Orsi 56).
Queen's Park: (4231) Muir; Doyle, Kilday, Grant, Robson (Paterson 68); Lyon, Gillespie; Galt (Biggar 82), Longridge, Willam Baynham (MacLean 73); McHugh.

Queen of the South (0) 0

Partick Thistle (0) 0

Queen of the South: (442) Ferguson; Nortey, Buchanan, Obileye, Maxwell; Fitzpatrick, McGorry, McCabe, Joseph (Goss 72); Shields, Robinson (Gibson 81).
Partick Thistle: (442) Sneddon; Penrice, Foster, Cardle (Niang 46), Brownlie; Bannigan (Kouider-Aisser 83), McKenna, Gordon (Spittal 78), Murray (Rudden 46); Graham■, Docherty.
Partick Thistle won 3-2 on penalties.

Tuesday, 10 November 2020

Queen's Park (1) 1 *(Quitongo 2)*

Queen of the South (2) 3 *(East 22, Joseph 32, Maxwell 80)*

Queen's Park: (4231) Muir; Doyle, Kilday (Grant 59), Morrison, Paterson; Carroll, Gillespie (McHugh 73); Lyon (Biggar 73), Slater (McGlinchey 55), Quitongo (Galt 59); Willam Baynham.
Queen of the South: (4231) Leighfield; Nortey, Buchanan, Obileye, Maxwell; Pybus, McKee; Shields, Joseph, Fitzpatrick; East.

Wednesday, 11 November 2020

St Mirren (1) 1 *(Obika 39)*

Greenock Morton (0) 1 *(Maciver 60)*

St Mirren: (3412) Alnwick; Fraser, McCarthy (McGrath 77), Shaughnessy; Tait, Foley, Erhahon (Doyle-Hayes 46), Mason; McAllister K (Erwin 59); Obika (Connolly 72), Morias (Dennis 59).
Greenock Morton: (352) McAdams; Fjortoft, McLean (McGuffie 86), McGinty; Ledger, Nesbitt (MacIver 60), Blues (Jacobs 46), Omar, Strapp; Salkeld (McPake 75), Muirhead (Oliver 75).
St Mirren won 6-5 on penalties.

Saturday, 14 November 2020

Partick Thistle (0) 0

Greenock Morton (0) 0

Partick Thistle: (433) Wright; Williamson, Brownlie, Breen, Foster; Gordon (Niang 70), Bannigan, Penrice; Cardle, Murray (Reilly 77), Spittal (Lyons 24).
Greenock Morton: (3421) McAdams; Fjortoft, McLean (Wallace 80), McGinty; Ledger, Jacobs, Lyon (Omar 73), Strapp; McGuffie (Salkeld 56), Colville (Muirhead 73); MacIver (McPake 80).
Partick Thistle won 4-2 on penalties.

Queen's Park (0) 0

St Mirren (0) 1 *(Obika 81)*

Queen's Park: (3412) Muir; Morrison, Kilday (Biggar 75), Grant; Doyle, Carroll, Lyon (Gillespie 74), Robson; Galt (MacLean 62); McHugh (McGlinchey 82), Willam Baynham (Quitongo 63).
St Mirren: (3412) Alnwick; Fraser, McCarthy, Shaughnessy■; Tait, Doyle-Hayes, Erhahon, McGrath (Flynn 70); MacPherson (Mason 46); Connolly (McAllister K 70), Dennis (Obika 54).

Group G Table	P	W	PW	PL	L	F	A	GD	Pts
St Mirren	4	2	2	0	0	8	4	4	10
Queen of the South	4	1	1	2	0	7	5	2	7
Partick Thistle	4	1	2	0	1	3	4	–1	7
Greenock Morton	4	1	0	3	0	4	3	1	6
Queen's Park	4	0	0	0	4	1	7	–6	0

FIRST ROUND - GROUP H

Tuesday, 6 October 2020

Edinburgh C (0) 1 *(Handling 70 (pen))*

Livingston (3) 5 *(Robinson 7, Mullin 22, 40, Poplatnik 65, Lokotsch 77)*

Edinburgh C: (451) Antell; Thomson, Brown, Handling (Hamilton 86), Black (Jardine 76); Crane, Balatoni, Henderson L, Campbell, Harris (Butterworth 20); See (Henderson B 76).
Livingston: (451) Stryjek; McMillan (Devlin 71), Fitzwater (Ambrose 80), Guthrie, Serrano (Taylor-Sinclair 66); Robinson, Mullin, Pitman, Holt, Forrest (Lokotsch 71); Tiffoney (Poplatnik 46).

Wednesday, 7 October 2020

Airdrieonians (0) 0

Alloa Ath (1) 2 *(Trouten 14 (pen), Thomson 69)*

Airdrieonians: (4231) Currie; MacDonald (Robert 67), Crighton, Fordyce, McCann; Sabatini, Kerr; Thomson (Stokes 78), McKay, Carrick (O'Reilly 78); Roy (Gallagher 41).
Alloa Ath: (442) Parry; Robertson, Taggart, Lynch, Dick; Cawley (Thomson 59), Grant (O'Donnell 82), Hetherington, Brown (Connelly 59); Trouten (Evans 82), Buchanan (Scougall 59).

Saturday, 10 October 2020

Edinburgh C (1) 2 *(Henderson B 43, De Vita 52)*

Stenhousemuir (1) 2 *(Biabi 9, Tapping 85)*

Edinburgh C: (451) Antell; Thomson, Balatoni, Henderson L, Crane (Hamilton 24); Jardine (Butterworth 80), Black (De Vita 46), Brown, Campbell, Handling (See 87); Henderson B.
Stenhousemuir: (4132) Erskine; Tiffoney, Munro, Little, Yeats; Tapping; Hopkirk, Blair, Spence; Biabi (Hodge J 73), McGuigan.
Stenhousemuir won 4-2 on penalties.

Livingston (0) 2 *(Forrest 46, Mullin 50)*

Alloa Ath (1) 1 *(Thomson 31)*

Livingston: (4231) Stryjek; Devlin, Ambrose, Taylor-Sinclair, Serrano; Bartley, Sibbald; Mullin (Holt 78), Pitman, Forrest; Emmanuel-Thomas.
Alloa Ath: (4231) Parry; Robertson, Taggart, Lynch, Dick; Grant, Hetherington; Murray (Cawley 52), Trouten, Malcolm (Scougall 61); Thomson (Buchanan 51).

Tuesday, 13 October 2020

Alloa Ath (1) 2 *(Scougall 18, Thomson 85)*

Edinburgh C (0) 1 *(Henderson B 81)*

Alloa Ath: (442) Parry (Wilson 44); Robertson, Taggart, Lynch (Graham 56), Dick; Cawley, Scougall (Trouten 56), Grant (Hetherington 46), Murray; Connelly (Thomson 78), Buchanan.
Edinburgh C: (442) Antell; Thomson, Balatoni, Black (Henderson B 75), See; Jardine (Handling 69), Brown, Campbell, Newman; Henderson L, De Vita (Hamilton 82).

Stenhousemuir (0) 0

Airdrieonians (0) 2 *(McKay P 47, Thomson 87)*

Stenhousemuir: (442) Erskine; Tiffoney, McQueen (Brown 66), Munro, Little; Yeats, Tapping, Hodge J (Watters 85), Spence (Fairley 79); Hopkirk (Biabi 67), Muir (McGuigan 79).

Airdrieonians: (442) Currie; MacDonald, Kerr, Crighton, McCann; O'Reilly (Carrick 65), Fordyce, McKay P, Ritchie (Sabatini 84); Gallagher (Stokes 79), Robert (Thomson 65).

Tuesday, 10 November 2020

Stenhousemuir (0) 0

Livingston (3) 4 *(Forrest 1, 8, Poplatnik 30, Taylor-Sinclair 65)*

Stenhousemuir: (4231) Martin; Tiffoney, Munro, McQueen, Yeats; Blair, Tapping; Fairley (Hodge J 62), Brown (Muir 54), Graham (Biabi 74); McGuigan.
Livingston: (4411) Maley; Devlin (Taylor-Sinclair 60), Fitzwater, Ambrose, McMillan (Pignatiello 77); Mullin, Holt, Poplatnik, Forrest; Pitman (Sibbald 60); Emmanuel-Thomas.

Wednesday, 11 November 2020

Airdrieonians (0) 0

Edinburgh C (1) 1 *(Henderson B 5)*

Airdrieonians: (4231) Hutton; McKay P (MacDonald 69), Mbayo, Fordyce, McCann; Sabatini, Kerr (Crighton 86); Robert, Carrick, Connell (Thomson 69); Stokes (O'Reilly 69).
Edinburgh C: (442) Antell; Thomson, Hamilton, Balatoni, Henderson L; Black, Newman (De Vita 84), Campbell, Brown; Henderson B, Cunningham (Handling 57).

Saturday, 14 November 2020

Alloa Ath (0) 4 *(Buchanan 64, 70 (pen), 78, Hetherington 90)*

Stenhousemuir (2) 2 *(Graham 33, Spence 37 (pen))*

Alloa Ath: (352) Wilson R; Jamieson, Graham, Williamson; Murray (Hetherington 60), O'Donnell, Scougall, Malcolm, Brown; Buchanan, Evans (Grant 61).
Stenhousemuir: (343) Martin; Muir, Grigor, McQueen; Hodge J, Tapping, Blair, Yeats (Watters 76); Spence, McGuigan, Graham (Halleran 67).

Livingston (0) 4 *(Forrest 57, 83, Emmanuel-Thomas 58 (pen), 67)*

Airdrieonians (0) 1 *(Robert 52)*

Livingston: (4231) Maley; Devlin, Guthrie, Taylor-Sinclair (Ambrose 61), Serrano (Pignatiello 77); Bartley, Sibbald; Mullin (Holt 61), Robinson, Forrest; Emmanuel-Thomas.
Airdrieonians: (4231) Hutton; MacDonald, Fordyce, Crighton, McCann; Sabatini (Stokes 84), Kerr; Robert (Ritchie 84), McKay P, Connell (O'Reilly 74); Carrick (Thomson 73).

Group H Table	P	W	PW	PL	L	F	A	GD	Pts
Livingston	4	4	0	0	0	15	3	12	12
Alloa Ath	4	3	0	0	1	9	5	4	9
Edinburgh C	4	1	0	1	2	5	9	–4	4
Airdrieonians	4	1	0	0	3	3	7	–4	3
Stenhousemuir	4	0	1	0	3	4	12	–8	2

SECOND ROUND

Saturday, 28 November 2020

Alloa Ath (0) 1 *(Trouten 109 (pen))*

Hearts (0) 0

Alloa Ath: (4231) Parry; Taggart, Graham, Jamieson, Dick; Hetherington, Grant; Cawley, Trouten, Murray (Connelly 94); Buchanan (Thomson 101).
Hearts: (4231) Gordon; Smith, Popescu, Berra, Kingsley; Haring (Henderson 112), Lee (Irving 112); Walker, Halliday (Roberts 81), White (Wighton 59); Boyce (Naismith 62).
aet.

Arbroath (0) 1 *(Hilson 65)*

Dunfermline Ath (2) 3 *(Dow 28, Murray E 36, O'Hara 82 (pen))*

Arbroath: (352) Gaston; Thomson, Little, Hamilton C; Stewart (Linn 46), McKenna (Hilson 46), Craigen, Virtanen, Swankie (Whatley 66); Donnelly (Doolan 66), Ruth.

Dunfermline Ath: (4141) Fon Williams; Mayo, Watson, Murray E, Edwards; Wilson; Dow, McInroy, Turner (Comrie 84), Thomas (Murray F 90); McManus (O'Hara 75).

Hibernian (1) 1 *(Murphy 44)*

Dundee (0) 0

Hibernian: (442) Marciano; McGinn P, McGregor, Porteous, Mackie; Boyle, Mallan (Hallberg 51), Newell, Murphy (Wright 80); Nisbet (Gullan 73), Doidge.
Dundee: (433) Hamilton J; Elliot, Ashcroft, Fontaine, Marshall; Byrne, Adam, Anderson (McDaid 62); McGowan, Afolabi (Sow 69), Jakubiak.

Livingston (4) 4 *(Chalmers 4 (og), Fitzwater 6, 12, Forrest 44)*

Ayr U (0) 0

Livingston: (4231) Stryjek; Devlin (McMillan 75), Guthrie (Brown 75), Fitzwater, Lawson; Bartley (Serrano 65), Sibbald; Mullin (Emmanuel-Thomas 65), Pitman, Forrest; Poplatnik (Tiffoney 64).
Ayr U: (4141) Sinisalo; Houston (McKenzie 76), Roscoe, Baird, Reading; Miller M; McCowan, Murdoch (Zanatta 55), Chalmers, Cameron (Muirhead 63); Moffat (Anderson 76).

Motherwell (0) 1 *(Watt 61)*

St Johnstone (0) 2 *(Hendry 68, Wotherspoon 77)*

Motherwell: (433) Chapman; O'Donnell, Mugabi, Gallagher, Lamie (Grimshaw 77); O'Hara, Crawford, Polworth (White 77); Lang, Watt, Cole (Seedorf 46).
St Johnstone: (3421) Clark; Rooney, Gordon, McCart; Wotherspoon, McCann, Craig, Booth; O'Halloran, Hendry (Kane 77); May.

St Mirren (1) 2 *(Durmus 4, McGrath 88)*

Aberdeen (1) 1 *(McGinn 43)*

St Mirren: (451) Alnwick; Fraser, McCarthy, Foley, Tait; Connolly (Morias 83), MacPherson, Doyle-Hayes, McGrath, Durmus (McAllister K 72); Obika (Erwin 72).
Aberdeen: (3421) Lewis; Hoban, Considine, Leigh; Kennedy, Ojo, Campbell (Edmondson 90), Hayes; Hedges, McGinn (Devlin 46); Cosgrove (Main 46).

Sunday, 29 November 2020

Celtic (0) 0

Ross Co (1) 2 *(Stewart 39 (pen), Iacovitti 84)*

Celtic: (3412) Barkas; Bitton (McGregor 68), Jullien, Ajer; Elhamed (Duffy 79), Brown, Christie, Laxalt; Rogic (Klimala 84); Ajeti (Elyounoussi 68), Edouard.
Ross Co: (541) Laidlaw; Watson, Donaldson, Morris, Iacovitti, Reid (Randall 77); Paton (McKay 89), Kelly, Vigurs, Lakin (Tillson 13); Stewart.

Falkirk (0) 0

Rangers (3) 4 *(Defoe 6, Bassey 30, Barisic 41, Tavernier 51)*

Falkirk: (3511) Peter Morrison; Hall, Durnan, Dixon; Todd (Deveney 81), Alston, Gomis, Telfer (Leitch 74), Kelly; Morrison C (Connolly A 62); Sammon (Dowds 62).
Rangers: (4231) McLaughlin; Tavernier (King 71), Bassey, Goldson, Barisic (Middleton 55); Arfield (Dickson 55), Zungu (Stewart 71); Itten, Hagi, Barker (Kamara 26); Defoe.

QUARTER-FINALS

Tuesday, 15 December 2020

Alloa Ath (1) 1 *(Hanlon 34 (og))*

Hibernian (0) 2 *(Doidge 62, Jamieson 83 (og))*

Alloa Ath: (4231) Parry; Robertson, Graham, Jamieson, Dick; Connelly, Hetherington; Cawley, Trouten (Evans 86), Scougall (O'Donnell 67); Buchanan (Thomson 60).
Hibernian: (442) Marciano; McGinn P, Porteous, Hanlon, Stevenson; Boyle, Hallberg (Magennis 52), Newell, Wright (Mallan 52); Gullan, Doidge.

Dunfermline Ath (0) 1 *(Wilson 113)*

St Johnstone (0) 1 *(Rooney 94)*

Dunfermline Ath: (4141) Fon Williams; Comrie (Mayo 64), Watson, Murray E, Edwards; McInroy; Dow, Murray F (Wilson 106), Turner, Thomas (McCann 104); McManus (O'Hara 71).
St Johnstone: (3421) Clark; Kerr, Gordon, Booth; Rooney, Davidson (Conway 69), Craig, Tanser (McCart 115); Wotherspoon (Hendry 78), McCann; Kane (May 60).
aet; St Johnstone won 4-3 on penalties.

Wednesday, 16 December 2020

Livingston (2) 2 *(Sibbald 4, Forrest 24)*

Ross Co (0) 0

Livingston: (4231) Stryjek; Devlin, Fitzwater, Guthrie, Serrano; Bartley, Sibbald; Mullin (Holt 62), Pitman, Forrest (Brown 47); Robinson (Poplatnik 76).
Ross Co: (442) Laidlaw; Kelly (Draper 61), Morris, Iacovitti, Reid; Charles-Cook (Donaldson 23), Paton (Shaw 82), Vigurs, Gardyne; Stewart, McKay.

St Mirren (1) 3 *(McGrath 40 (pen), 53, McCarthy 90)*

Rangers (1) 2 *(Goldson 7, Davis 88)*

St Mirren: (451) Alnwick; Fraser, McCarthy, Shaughnessy, Tait; Connolly (MacPherson 82), McGrath, Doyle-Hayes, Erhahon, Mason; Obika (Erwin 90).
Rangers: (433) McGregor; Tavernier, Goldson, Balogun (Hagi 84), Bassey (Barisic 57); Arfield (Davis 57), Zungu (Kamara 72), Aribo; Roofe, Itten (Defoe 72), Kent.

SEMI-FINALS

Saturday, 23 January 2021

St Johnstone (1) 3 *(Kerr 35, Rooney 49, Conway 63)*

Hibernian (0) 0

St Johnstone: (3412) Clark; Kerr, Gordon, McCart; Rooney, Davidson, McCann, Tanser; Wotherspoon; Conway, Kane (May 77).
Hibernian: (442) Marciano; McGinn P, Porteous, Hanlon, Doig; Cadden (Doidge 51), Irvine, Gogic (Magennis 65), Murphy (Allan 66); Boyle, Nisbet.

Sunday, 24 January 2021

Livingston (1) 1 *(Robinson 10)*

St Mirren (0) 0

Livingston: (451) Stryjek; Devlin, Ambrose, Guthrie, Serrano; Mullin (Reilly 73), Holt, Bartley, Pitman, Sibbald (Longridge 86); Robinson (Fitzwater 81).
St Mirren: (451) Alnwick; Fraser, McCarthy, Shaughnessy, Tait; Connolly (McAllister K 57), McGrath, MacPherson (Obika 68), Erhahon, Mason (Durmus 68); Brophy (Dennis 81).

BETFRED SCOTTISH LEAGUE CUP FINAL 2020–21

Sunday, 28 February 2021

(at Hampden Park, behind closed doors)

Livingston (0) 0 St Johnstone (1) 1

Livingston: (4231) McCrorie; Devlin, Ambrose, Guthrie, Serrano; Lawson (Sibbald 60), Holt (Emmanuel-Thomas 71); Mullin (Forrest 65), Pitman (Reilly 65), Bartley; Robinson.

St Johnstone: (3421) Clark; Kerr, Gordon, McCart; Rooney, McCann, Craig, Booth; Conway (May 77), Wotherspoon; Kane.
Scorer: Rooney 32.

Referee: Don Robertson.

SCOTTISH CUP FINALS 1874–2021

SCOTTISH FA CUP

1874	Queen's Park v Clydesdale	2-0
1875	Queen's Park v Renton	3-0
1876	Queen's Park v Third Lanark	1-1
Replay	Queen's Park v Third Lanark	2-0
1877	Vale of Leven v Rangers	1-1
Replay	Vale of Leven v Rangers	1-1
2nd Replay	Vale of Leven v Rangers	3-2
1878	Vale of Leven v Third Lanark	1-0
1879	Vale of Leven v Rangers	1-1
	Vale of Leven awarded cup, Rangers failing to appear for replay.	
1880	Queen's Park v Thornliebank	3-0
1881	Queen's Park v Dumbarton	2-1
Replay	Queen's Park v Dumbarton	3-1
	After Dumbarton protested the first game.	
1882	Queen's Park v Dumbarton	2-2
Replay	Queen's Park v Dumbarton	4-1
1883	Dumbarton v Vale of Leven	2-2
Replay	Dumbarton v Vale of Leven	2-1
1884	Queen's Park v Vale of Leven	
	Queen's Park awarded cup, Vale of Leven failing to appear.	
1885	Renton v Vale of Leven	0-0
Replay	Renton v Vale of Leven	3-1
1886	Queen's Park v Renton	3-1
1887	Hibernian v Dumbarton	2-1
1888	Renton v Cambuslang	6-1
1889	Third Lanark v Celtic	3-0
Replay	Third Lanark v Celtic	2-1
	Replay by order of Scottish FA because of playing conditions in first match.	
1890	Queen's Park v Vale of Leven	1-1
Replay	Queen's Park v Vale of Leven	2-1
1891	Hearts v Dumbarton	1-0
1892	Celtic v Queen's Park	1-0
Replay	Celtic v Queen's Park	5-1
	After mutually protested first match.	
1893	Queen's Park v Celtic	0-1
Replay	Queen's Park v Celtic	2-1
	Replay by order of Scottish FA because of playing conditions in first match.	
1894	Rangers v Celtic	3-1
1895	St Bernard's v Renton	2-1
1896	Hearts v Hibernian	3-1
1897	Rangers v Dumbarton	5-1
1898	Rangers v Kilmarnock	2-0
1899	Celtic v Rangers	2-0
1900	Celtic v Queen's Park	4-3
1901	Hearts v Celtic	4-3
1902	Hibernian v Celtic	1-0
1903	Rangers v Hearts	1-1
Replay	Rangers v Hearts	0-0
2nd Replay	Rangers v Hearts	2-0
1904	Celtic v Rangers	3-2
1905	Third Lanark v Rangers	0-0
Replay	Third Lanark v Rangers	3-1
1906	Hearts v Third Lanark	1-0
1907	Celtic v Hearts	3-0
1908	Celtic v St Mirren	5-1
1909	Celtic v Rangers	2-2
Replay	Celtic v Rangers	1-1
	Owing to riot, the cup was withheld.	
1910	Dundee v Clyde	2-2
Replay	Dundee v Clyde	0-0*
2nd Replay	Dundee v Clyde	2-1
1911	Celtic v Hamilton A	0-0
Replay	Celtic v Hamilton A	2-0
1912	Celtic v Clyde	2-0
1913	Falkirk v Raith R	2-0
1914	Celtic v Hibernian	0-0
Replay	Celtic v Hibernian	4-1
1920	Kilmarnock v Albion R	3-2
1921	Partick Thistle v Rangers	1-0
1922	Morton v Rangers	1-0
1923	Celtic v Hibernian	1-0
1924	Airdrieonians v Hibernian	2-0
1925	Celtic v Dundee	2-1
1926	St Mirren v Celtic	2-0
1927	Celtic v East Fife	3-1
1928	Rangers v Celtic	4-0
1929	Kilmarnock v Rangers	2-0
1930	Rangers v Partick Thistle	0-0
Replay	Rangers v Partick Thistle	2-1
1931	Celtic v Motherwell	2-2
Replay	Celtic v Motherwell	4-2
1932	Rangers v Kilmarnock	1-1
Replay	Rangers v Kilmarnock	3-0
1933	Celtic v Motherwell	1-0
1934	Rangers v St Mirren	5-0
1935	Rangers v Hamilton A	2-1
1936	Rangers v Third Lanark	1-0
1937	Celtic v Aberdeen	2-1
1938	East Fife v Kilmarnock	1-1
Replay	East Fife v Kilmarnock	4-2*
1939	Clyde v Motherwell	4-0
1947	Aberdeen v Hibernian	2-1
1948	Rangers v Morton	1-1*
Replay	Rangers v Morton	1-0*
1949	Rangers v Clyde	4-1
1950	Rangers v East Fife	3-0
1951	Celtic v Motherwell	1-0
1952	Motherwell v Dundee	4-0
1953	Rangers v Aberdeen	1-1
Replay	Rangers v Aberdeen	1-0
1954	Celtic v Aberdeen	2-1
1955	Clyde v Celtic	1-1
Replay	Clyde v Celtic	1-0
1956	Hearts v Celtic	3-1
1957	Falkirk v Kilmarnock	1-1
Replay	Falkirk v Kilmarnock	2-1*
1958	Clyde v Hibernian	1-0
1959	St Mirren v Aberdeen	3-1
1960	Rangers v Kilmarnock	2-0
1961	Dunfermline Ath v Celtic	0-0
Replay	Dunfermline Ath v Celtic	2-0
1962	Rangers v St Mirren	2-0
1963	Rangers v Celtic	1-1
Replay	Rangers v Celtic	3-0
1964	Rangers v Dundee	3-1
1965	Celtic v Dunfermline Ath	3-2
1966	Rangers v Celtic	0-0
Replay	Rangers v Celtic	1-0
1967	Celtic v Aberdeen	2-0
1968	Dunfermline Ath v Hearts	3-1
1969	Celtic v Rangers	4-0
1970	Aberdeen v Celtic	3-1
1971	Celtic v Rangers	1-1
Replay	Celtic v Rangers	2-1
1972	Celtic v Hibernian	6-1
1973	Rangers v Celtic	3-2
1974	Celtic v Dundee U	3-0
1975	Celtic v Airdrieonians	3-1
1976	Rangers v Hearts	3-1
1977	Celtic v Rangers	1-0
1978	Rangers v Aberdeen	2-1
1979	Rangers v Hibernian	0-0
Replay	Rangers v Hibernian	0-0*
2nd Replay	Rangers v Hibernian	3-2*
1980	Celtic v Rangers	1-0*
1981	Rangers v Dundee U	0-0*
Replay	Rangers v Dundee U	4-1
1982	Aberdeen v Rangers	4-1*
1983	Aberdeen v Rangers	1-0*
1984	Aberdeen v Celtic	2-1*
1985	Celtic v Dundee U	2-1
1986	Aberdeen v Hearts	3-0
1987	St Mirren v Dundee U	1-0*
1988	Celtic v Dundee U	2-1
1989	Celtic v Rangers	1-0

TENNENTS SCOTTISH CUP

1990	Aberdeen v Celtic *Aberdeen won 9-8 on penalties.*	0-0*
1991	Motherwell v Dundee U	4-3*
1992	Rangers v Airdrieonians	2-1
1993	Rangers v Aberdeen	2-1
1994	Dundee U v Rangers	1-0
1995	Celtic v Airdrieonians	1-0
1996	Rangers v Hearts	5-1
1997	Kilmarnock v Falkirk	1-0
1998	Hearts v Rangers	2-1
1999	Rangers v Celtic	1-0
2000	Rangers v Aberdeen	4-0
2001	Celtic v Hibernian	3-0
2002	Rangers v Celtic	3-2
2003	Rangers v Dundee	1-0
2004	Celtic v Dunfermline Ath	3-1
2005	Celtic v Dundee U	1-0
2006	Hearts v Gretna *Hearts won 4-2 on penalties.*	1-1*
2007	Celtic v Dunfermline Ath	1-0

SCOTTISH FA CUP

2008	Rangers v Queen of the South	3-2

HOMECOMING SCOTTISH CUP

2009	Rangers v Falkirk	1-0

ACTIVE NATION SCOTTISH CUP

2010	Dundee U v Ross Co	3-0

SCOTTISH FA CUP

2011	Celtic v Motherwell	3-0

WILLIAM HILL SCOTTISH CUP

2012	Hearts v Hibernian	5-1
2013	Celtic v Hibernian	3-0
2014	St Johnstone v Dundee U	2-0
2015	Inverness CT v Falkirk	2-1
2016	Hibernian v Rangers	3-2
2017	Celtic v Aberdeen	2-1
2018	Celtic v Motherwell	2-0
2019	Celtic v Hearts	2-1
2020	Celtic v Hearts *Celtic won 4-3 on penalties*	3-3*
2021	St Johnstone v Hibernian	1-0

**After extra time.*

SCOTTISH CUP WINS

Celtic 40, Rangers 33, Queen's Park 10, Hearts 8, Aberdeen 7, Clyde 3, Hibernian 3, Kilmarnock 3, St Mirren 3, Vale of Leven 3, Dundee U 2, Dunfermline Ath 2, Falkirk 2, Motherwell 2, Renton 2, St Johnstone 2, Third Lanark 2, Airdrieonians 1, Dumbarton 1, Dundee 1, East Fife 1, Inverness CT 1, Morton 1, Partick Thistle 1, St Bernard's 1.

APPEARANCES IN FINAL

Celtic 59, Rangers 52, Aberdeen 16, Hearts 16, Hibernian 15, Queen's Park 12, Dundee U 10, Kilmarnock 8, Motherwell 8, Vale of Leven 7, Clyde 6, Dumbarton 6, St Mirren 6, Third Lanark 6, Dundee 5, Dunfermline Ath 5, Falkirk 5, Renton 5, Airdrieonians 4, East Fife 3, Hamilton A 2, Morton 2, Partick Thistle 2, St Johnstone 2, Albion R 1, Cambuslang 1, Clydesdale 1, Gretna 1, Inverness CT 1, Queen of the South 1, Raith R 1, Ross Co 1, St Bernard's 1, Thornliebank 1.

LEAGUE CHALLENGE FINALS 1990–2020

B&Q CENTENARY CUP

1990–91	Dundee v Ayr U	3-2*

B&Q CUP

1991–92	Hamilton A v Ayr U	1-0
1992–93	Hamilton A v Morton	3-2
1993–94	Falkirk v St Mirren	3-0
1994–95	Airdrieonians v Dundee	3-2*

SCOTTISH LEAGUE CHALLENGE CUP

1995–96	Stenhousemuir v Dundee U *Stenhousemuir won 5-4 on penalties.*	0-0*
1996–97	Stranraer v St Johnstone	1-0
1997–98	Falkirk v Queen of the South	1-0
1998–99	*No competition.* *Suspended due to lack of sponsorship.*	

BELL'S CHALLENGE CUP

1999–2000	Alloa Ath v Inverness CT *Alloa Ath won 5-4 on penalties.*	4-4*
2000–01	Airdrieonians v Livingston *Airdrieonians won 3-2 on penalties.*	2-2*
2001–02	Airdrieonians v Alloa Ath	2-1

BELL'S CUP

2002–03	Queen of the South v Brechin C	2-0
2003–04	Inverness CT v Airdrie U	2-0
2004–05	Falkirk v Ross Co	2-1
2005–06	St Mirren v Hamilton A	2-1

SCOTTISH LEAGUE CHALLENGE CUP

2006–07	Ross Co v Clyde *Ross Co won 5-4 on penalties.*	1-1*
2007–08	St Johnstone v Dunfermline Ath	3-2

ALBA CHALLENGE CUP

2008–09	Airdrie U v Ross Co *Airdrie U won 3-2 on penalties.*	2-2*
2009–10	Dundee v Inverness CT	3-2
2010–11	Ross Co v Queen of the South	2-0

RAMSDENS CUP

2011–12	Falkirk v Hamilton A	1-0
2012–13	Queen of the South v Partick Thistle *Queen of the South won 6-5 on penalties.*	1-1*
2013–14	Raith R v Rangers	1-0*

PETROFAC TRAINING SCOTTISH LEAGUE CHALLENGE CUP

2014–15	Livingston v Alloa Athletic	4-0
2015–16	Rangers v Peterhead	4-0

IRN-BRU SCOTTISH LEAGUE CHALLENGE CUP

2016–17	Dundee U v St Mirren	2-1
2017–18	Inverness CT v Dumbarton	1-0
2018–19	Ross Co v Connah's Quay Nomads	3-1

TUNNOCK'S CARAMEL WAFER SCOTTISH LEAGUE CHALLENGE CUP

2019–20†	Raith R v Inverness CT	Joint winners
2020–21	*No competition due to COVID-19 pandemic*	

**After extra time. †Due to the COVID-19 pandemic, the final due to be played on Sunday 8 March 2020 was postponed.*

WILLIAM HILL SCOTTISH FA CUP 2019–20

Competition delayed due to COVID-19 Pandemic.

SEMI-FINALS

Saturday, 31 October 2020

Hearts (0) 2 *(Wighton 60, Boyce 111 (pen))*

Hibernian (0) 1 *(Doidge 67)*

Hearts: (4231) Gordon; Smith, Halkett, Popescu, Kingsley; Lee (Henderson 97), Halliday (Irving 117); Wighton (White 83), Walker (Naismith 56), Roberts (Haring 56); Boyce.
Hibernian: (442) Marciano; McGinn, Porteous, Hanlon, Doig (Mackie 87); Boyle, Gogic (Mallan 115), Newell, Magennis (Murphy 61); Doidge, Nisbet.
aet.
Referee: William Collum.

Sunday, 1 November 2020

Celtic (2) 2 *(Christie 18, Elyounoussi 23)*

Aberdeen (0) 0

Celtic: (4231) Bain; Frimpong, Duffy, Bitton, Laxalt; Brown, McGregor; Christie (Elhamed 73), Rogic (Ntcham 84), Elyounoussi (Ajeti 73); Edouard (Griffiths 73).
Aberdeen: (3421) Lewis; Hoban, Taylor (Leigh 64), Considine; Hedges, McCrorie, Ferguson, Kennedy (McGinn 85); Wright, Watkins (Main 79); Cosgrove (McLennan 64).
Referee: Don Robertson.

WILLIAM HILL SCOTTISH FA CUP FINAL 2019–20

Sunday, 20 December 2020

(at Hampden Park, behind closed doors)

Celtic (2) 3 Hearts (0) 3

Celtic: (4231) Hazard; Ajer, Jullien, Duffy (Johnston 91), Taylor (Laxalt 83); Brown (Soro 106), McGregor; Christie, Turnbull (Rogic 68), Elyounoussi (Frimpong 83); Edouard (Griffiths 97).
Scorers: Christie 19, Edouard 29 (pen), Griffiths 105.

Hearts: (4231) Gordon; Smith, Halkett, Berra, Kingsley; Irving (Frear 109), Halliday (Haring 91); Walker (Ginnelly 57), Naismith, White (Lee 82); Boyce (Wighton 70).
Scorers: Boyce 48, Kingsley 67, Ginnelly 111.

aet; Celtic won 4-3 on penalties.

Referee: John Beaton.

WILLIAM HILL SCOTTISH FA CUP 2020–21

■ *Denotes player sent off. *After extra time.*
Due to the COVID-19 pandemic, all matches played behind closed doors.

FIRST PRELIMINARY ROUND

Lothian Thistle Hutchinson Vale v St Cuthbert W	2-1*
Penicuik Ath v Musselburgh Ath	2-3*

SECOND PRELIMINARY ROUND

Banks O'Dee v Vale Of Leithen	6-1
Blackburn U v Civil Service Strollers	1-1*
(Civil Service Strollers won 4-2 on penalties)	
BSC Glasgow v Haddington Ath	2-3
Clachnacuddin v Caledonian Braves	1-2
Deveronvale v Camelon Juniors	1-4
Dundonald Bluebell v Easthouses Lily MW	4-2
Dunipace v Berwick R	1-3
East Stirlingshire v Inverurie Loco Works	5-0
Edinburgh Uni v Tranent Juniors	1-2
Gala Fairydean R v Wigtown & Bladnoch	6-0
Hill Of Beath Hawthorn v Whitehill Welfare	2-1
Huntly v Dalbeattie Star	3-0
Jeanfield Swifts v Stirling Uni	3-1
Keith v Fort William	5-1
Lothian Thistle Hutchison Vale v Lossiemouth	4-4*
(Lothian Thistle Hutchinson Vale won 4-2 on penalties)	
Nairn Co v Threave R	4-0
Newton Stewart v Broxburn Ath	0-3
Newtongrange Star v Rothes	0-4
The Spartans v East Kilbride	2-1
Strathspey Thistle v Buckie Thistle	0-4
Tynecastle v Cumbernauld Colts	2-3
Glasgow Uni v Linlithgow Rose	1-2
Coldstream v Bo'ness U	0-2
Preston Ath v Hawick Royal Albert	3-2
Formartine U v Turriff U	2-1
Wick Academy v Musselburgh Ath	3-1*

FIRST ROUND

Albion R v Buckie Thistle	0-3
Berwick R v Stirling Alb	0-3
Brechin C v Linlithgow Rose	2-3
Cowdenbeath v Wick Academy	2-0
Edinburgh C v Caledonian Braves	3-1
Elgin C v Civil Service Strollers	4-0
Gala Fairydean R v Annan Ath	1-2
Haddington Ath v Formartine U	1-2
Keith v Hill Of Beath Hawthorn	4-2*
Kelty Hearts v Jeanfield Swifts	2-1
Lothian Thistle Hutchinson Vale v Banks O'Dee	0-3
Nairn Co v Broxburn Ath	0-0*
(Nairn Co won 4-3 on Penalties)	
Rothes v Fraserburgh	1-3
Stenhousemuir v Preston Ath	4-1
Stranraer v The Spartans	5-0
Tranent Juniors v East Stirlingshire	4-1
Dundonald Bluebell v Queen's Park	1-3*
Bonnyrigg Rose Ath v Bo'ness U	5-2
Huntly v Cumbernauld Colts	3-1
Camelon Juniors v Brora Rangers	1-2

SECOND ROUND

Friday, 8 January 2021

Queen's Park (0) 0

Queen of the South (1) 3 *(Gibson 45, Fitzpatrick 66, Shields 82)*

Queen's Park: (433) Muir; Doyle, Kilday, Grant, Robson; Gillespie (Willam Baynham 78), Carroll, Longridge (Galt 58); MacLean (Quitongo 58), McHugh, Murray.
Queen of the South: (4231) Ferguson; Gibson, Buchanan, Obileye, Maxwell; McKee, McCabe; Fitzpatrick, Pybus (McGorry 86), East; Shields (Goss 86).
Referee: Euan Anderson.

Saturday, 9 January 2021

Alloa Ath (2) 2 *(Trouten 28 (pen), O'Donnell 39)*

Cove R (1) 3 *(Masson 38, McAllister 76, Strachan 90)*

Alloa Ath: (4231) Parry; Robertson, Graham, Jamieson, Dick; Grant, Hetherington; Cawley, Trouten (Scougall 46), O'Donnell (Murray 64); Buchanan (Thomson 61).

Cove R: (442) McKenzie; Scott Ross, Strachan, Graham, Milne; Fyvie, Scully, Yule, Masson; McAllister (McIntosh 83), Megginson.
Referee: David Dickinson.

Dundee (0) 3 *(Afolabi 90, Ashcroft 107, Sow 112)*

Bonnyrigg Rose Ath (1) 2 *(Currie 25 (pen), 105 (pen))*

Dundee: (4312) Hamilton J; Fontaine, Forster, Ashcroft, Marshall; Robertson (Afolabi 56), Byrne (Anderson 71), Adam; McGowan; Sow, Mullen (Moore 120).
Bonnyrigg Rose Ath: (352) Weir; Young, Horne, Martyniuk; Brett, Currie, Stewart (Turner 74), Gray S (Barrett 100), Hoskins; Hunter (Gray R 76), McGachie (Wilson 87).
aet.
Referee: Gavin Duncan.

East Fife (2) 5 *(Agnew 40 (pen), 58, Watson 45, Smith 55, 62)*

Tranent Juniors (1) 1 *(Thomson 4)*

East Fife: (442) Long; Murdoch, Watson, Higgins, Slattery; Denholm (Dunsmore 60), Davidson, Agnew, Watt (Newton 76); Wallace, Smith (Swanson 63).
Tranent Juniors: (4231) Adams; Whitson, McKenzie, Miller R, Greig; Craigie, Miller B (Lander 64); Watson (Renton 82), Murphy, Thomson; Paterson (Ponton 67).
Referee: Barry Cook.

Forfar Ath (1) 4 *(MacKintosh 14, Fotheringham 95, Allan 101, 103)*

Linlithgow Rose (1) 1 *(Wilson K 11)*

Forfar Ath: (442) McCallum; Coll (Allan 90), Irvine, Meechan, MacKenzie; Barr, MacKintosh, Hoti, Thomas (Scally 46); Doris (Fotheringham 85 (Antoniazzi 103)), Shepherd.
Linlithgow Rose: (451) Schwake; Stevenson, Thom (Nimmo 115), Brownlie, Wilson A; Ronald, MacLennan, Cairns, Bembo (Watt 58), Wilson K (Hare 75); Coyne.
aet.
Referee: Kevin Graham.

Fraserburgh (0) 2 *(Barbour 71, Beagrie 80)*

Banks O'Dee (0) 1 *(Phillipson 54)*

Fraserburgh: (442) Leask; Cairns, Campbell G, Hay, Cowie; Campbell P (Harris 66), Young, Beagrie, West (Butcher 66); Duncan (Combe 90), Barbour.
Banks O'Dee: (442) Sweeney; Allan, Alexander, Gilmour, Lawrie; Duguid (Macleod H 87), Duff (Armstrong 82), Winton, Phillipson; MacLeod L (Buglass 87), Henderson.
Referee: Chris Graham.

Kelty Hearts (2) 2 *(Austin 25, Higginbotham 37 (pen))*

Stranraer (0) 3 *(Orr 48, Robertson 63, Paton 90 (pen))*

Kelty Hearts: (4231) Jamieson; Stevenson, Hooper, Hill, Boyle; Reilly, Tidser; Higginbotham, Philp (Anderson 86), Easton; Austin.
Stranraer: (442) Fleming; Gallagher, Robertson, Sonkur, Cummins; Paton, Millar, McManus (Hilton 89), Stirling; Duffy (Vitoria 74), Orr.
Referee: Lorraine Watson.

Sunday, 10 January 2021

Airdrieonians (0) 0

Edinburgh C (0) 1 *(See 65)*

Airdrieonians: (4231) Currie; McKay P, Crighton, Fordyce, MacDonald; Kerr, Carrick; Thomson (O'Reilly 70), Stokes (Roy 70), Robert; Connell (Sabatini 70).
Edinburgh C: (4231) Antell; Thomson, Hamilton, Henderson L, McIntyre; Black (Crane 82), Laird; De Vita (Balatoni 90), Brown, Campbell; See.
Referee: David Lowe.

Tuesday, 23 March 2021

Arbroath (1) 1 *(Mutch 8 (og))*

Falkirk (1) 2 *(Telfer 42, Fotheringham 87)*

Arbroath: (442) Gaston; Pignatiello (Gold 46), Little, O'Brien, Hamilton C; Moore, Craigen, Stewart (McKenna 85), Linn (Williamson 31); Hamilton J, Hilson.
Falkirk: (433) Mutch; Deveney, Hall, McClelland (Dixon 79), Neilson; Gomis (Fotheringham 71), Leitch, Telfer; Dowds, Sammon, Francis.
Referee: David Munro.

Brora Rangers (1) 2 *(MacRae J 12, MacLean 75)*

Hearts (0) 1 *(Berra 70)*

Brora Rangers: (442) Malin; Kelly, Nicolson, Williamson, MacDonald A; Wagenaar (MacDonald G 82), Gillespie, MacLean, Gamble (Morrison 65); MacRae A (Brindle 65), MacRae J.
Hearts: (442) Stewart; Haring, Berra, Halkett, White; McEneff (Henderson 59), Irving, Kastaneer (Boyce 46), Mackay-Steven; Gnanduillet, Walker.
Referee: Peter Stuart.

Buckie Thistle (1) 2 *(Murray J 16, Murray C 84)*

Inverness CT (2) 3 *(Keatings 3, Welsh 28, Mackay D 86)*

Buckie Thistle: (442) Bell; Munro, MacKinnon (Morrison 69), Murray J, McLauchlan; Fraser, Pugh, Barry, Urquhart; MacLeod (Murray C 75), Cowie.
Inverness CT: (442) Mackay C; Fyffe, Nicolson, Deas, McHattie (Harper 60); MacGregor, Welsh, Allardice, Mackay D (Lyall 90); Storey, Keatings (Sutherland 75).
Referee: Steven Reid.

Dumbarton (2) 4 *(Wilson J 31, 69, McGeever 40, Forbes 75)*

Huntly (0) 0

Dumbarton: (4411) Smith; Wardrop, McGeever, Neill, Nicholas McAllister (Brindley 72); Forbes, Carswell, Wedderburn (Langan 72), Crossan (Duthie 78); Frizzell; Wilson J.
Huntly: (442) Storrier; Thoirs (McKeown 46), Bowden, Johnstone, Gauld; Thomas, Murison, Booth (Elphinstone 60), Matthew (MacDonald 84); Still, McGowan.
Referee: Matthew MacDermid.

Elgin C (0) 0

Ayr U (4) 4 *(Chalmers 5, Moffat 18, McCowan 25, 43)*

Elgin C: (4231) McHale; Cooper, Bronsky, Spark, MacPhee (McHardy 46); Mailer (Sopel 46), MacEwan; Dingwall R, Cameron, Dingwall T (Peters 63); Osadolor.
Ayr U: (4141) Sinisalo; Houston, Baird, Ndaba (Roscoe 39), Reading; Miller M; McCowan, Walsh, Chalmers, Smith C (Barjonas 67); Moffat (McKenzie 77).
Referee: Craig Napier.

Formartine U (1) 1 *(Smith S 17)*

Annan Ath (1) 1 *(Smith 9)*

Formartine U: (442) Main; Crawford, Smith S, Anderson S, McKeown; Rodger, Kelly, Smith J, Park (Lisle 79); Norris (Greig 68), Wood (Gethins 91).
Annan Ath: (442) Kinnear; Fulton, Clark, Fleming, Douglas; Wallace (Currie 101), Hunter, Lowdon (Love 46), McCaw (Docherty 76); Wright (Anderson 61), Smith.
aet; Formartine U won 3-1 on penalties.
Referee: Calum Scott.

Greenock Morton (0) 0

Dunfermline Ath (0) 0

Greenock Morton: (3421) McAdams; McGinty, McLean, Ledger; Strapp, Lyon, Jacobs (Blues 95), Hynes; McGuffie (Oliver 72), Nesbitt (Muirhead 105); Sterling (Orsi 70).
Dunfermline Ath: (4321) Fon Williams; Comrie, Mayo, Murray E, Edwards; McInroy (Wilson 65), Whittaker (Thomas 76), Todd (Murray F 60); McManus (Wighton 102), O'Hara; McCann.
aet; Greenock Morton won 6-5 on penalties.
Referee: Don Robertson.

Keith (0) 0

Clyde (2) 2 *(Goodwillie 21, Rumsby 33)*

Keith: (442) Simpson; Young, Spink, Robertson, Smith; Brownie, Strachan, Yunus, Duncan; Keith (Watt 70), Selfridge (Gray 31).
Clyde: (433) Mitchell; Bain (Jack 69), Howie, Rumsby, Otoo; Cuddihy, Nicoll, Lamont (Jamieson 65); Cunningham, Goodwillie, Love (Thomson 65).
Referee: Steven Kirkland.

Nairn Co (0) 1 *(Maclennan 56)*

Montrose (4) 7 *(Quinn 11, 25, Johnston 15, 60, 80, McLean 44, Hawke 70)*

Nairn Co: (4231) MacLean D; Maclean C, Dingwall, Porritt, McKenzie; MacLennan, Ramsey; Ewan, Davidson (McConaghy 80), McNab (Main 46); Shewan (Mackenzie 62).

Montrose: (4312) Fleming; Cammy Ballantyne (Callaghan 51), Quinn, Dillon, Steeves; Cochrane, Mochrie, Masson (Rennie 54); Milne; McLean (Hawke 46), Johnston.
Referee: Gavin Ross.

Partick Thistle (1) 3 *(Gordon 7, Rudden 52, Murray 66)*

Cowdenbeath (0) 0

Partick Thistle: (442) Wright; Williamson (McKenna 65), Niang, Brownlie, Tiffoney; Cardle (Murray 64), Gordon, Bannigan, Penrice; Rudden (Lyon 76), MacIver (Graham 69).
Cowdenbeath: (442) Hogarth; Mullen, Barr (Todd 46), Glass, Swan (Morrison 63); Buchanan (Miller K 63), Herd, Pollock, Taylor (Watson 75); Russell, Hamilton (Renton 63).
Referee: Graham Grainger.

Peterhead (0) 0

Stenhousemuir (1) 1 *(McGuigan 18)*

Peterhead: (442) Rae; Bailey (Strachan 80), Jason Brown, Freeman, Conroy; Kesson, Brown S (Armour 23), McDonald, McCarthy; Payne, Layne (McGrath 73).
Stenhousemuir: (433) Martin; Tiffoney, Kane, Little, Brown; Biabi, Tapping, Blair; Hopkirk, McGuigan (Collins 76), Muir (Spence 75).
Referee: Mike Roncone.

Stirling Alb (0) 0

Raith R (1) 2 *(Ugwu 45, Tait 70)*

Stirling Alb: (442) Currie; McGeachie (Allan 56), Banner, Hamilton, El-Zubaidi; Heaver, Meggatt, Wilson (Kirkpatrick 56), Moore (Roberts S 79); Leitch, Mackin.
Raith R: (442) MacDonald J; Tumilty, MacDonald K, Benedictus, Spencer; Musonda, Tait, Kennedy (Armstrong 82), Ugwu (Vaughan 71); King, Gullan (Abraham 90).
Referee: Alan Newlands.

THIRD ROUND

Friday, 2 April 2021

Ross Co (1) 1 *(McKay 38)*

Inverness CT (1) 3 *(Todorov 40, Mackay D 54, Sutherland 87)*

Ross Co: (442) Laidlaw; Naismith, Donaldson, Watson, Hjelde; Gardyne (Charles-Cook 64), Kelly, Vigurs (Hylton 63), Lakin; McKay, Shaw (White 64).
Inverness CT: (4231) Ridgers; Carson, McKay, Devine, Deas; Welsh, Allardice; Mackay D (Harper 83), Allan (Sutherland 72), Storey; Todorov (MacGregor 72).
Referee: Nick Walsh.

Saturday, 3 April 2021

Ayr U (0) 0

Clyde (1) 1 *(Cuddihy 4)*

Ayr U: (4132) Sinisalo; Miller M (Barjonas 87), Baird, Roscoe, Reading; Muirhead; McCowan, Chalmers, Walsh (Todd 71); Moffat (Wright 71), McKenzie.
Clyde: (451) Mitchell; Cuddihy, Howie, Rumsby, Munro; Cunningham (Bain 78), Robertson (McNiff 46), Nicoll, Thomson, Love; Jamieson (Goodwillie 68).
Referee: David Munro.

Brora Rangers (1) 1 *(Gillespie 26 (pen))*

Stranraer (0) 3 *(Malin 88 (og), Matt Yates 100, Orr 107)*

Brora Rangers: (442) Malin; Kelly, Nicolson, Williamson, MacDonald A; Morrison (Pickles 85), Gillespie, MacLean, Wagenaar (MacDonald G 95); MacRae A (Brindle 65), MacRae J.
Stranraer: (433) Fleming; Gallagher, Sonkur, Robertson (Devitt 110), Cummins; Stirling, McManus (Hilton 63), Millar; Orr, Duffy (Matt Yates 63), Paton (Vitoria 68).
aet. Referee: Scott Lambie.

Celtic (0) 3 *(Forrest 56, Christie 58, Elyounoussi 79)*

Falkirk (0) 0

Celtic: (4231) Bain; Kenny, Welsh, Ajer, Laxalt; Brown, Turnbull; Forrest (Elyounoussi 74), Rogic (Soro 72), Christie; Griffiths (Ajeti 62).
Falkirk: (352) Mutch; Mercer, Neilson, McClelland; Francis, Fotheringham (Telfer 64), Miller, Leitch (Alston 64), Deveney; Dowds (Keena 51), Sammon.
Referee: John Beaton.

Dumbarton (0) 0

Aberdeen (0) 1 *(Hendry 84)*

Dumbarton: (4231) Ramsbottom; Wardrop, McGeever, Neill, Nicholas McAllister; Carswell, Wedderburn; Frizzell (Quitongo 88), Brindley (Omar 46), Wilson J; Jones (Crossan 88).
Aberdeen: (4231) Lewis; Ramsay (Kennedy 63), Hoban, Considine, Hayes; Ferguson, Campbell; Ross (McLennan 79), McCrorie, McGinn; Kamberi (Hendry 55).
Referee: Don Robertson.

Dundee (0) 0

St Johnstone (1) 1 *(Melamed 20)*

Dundee: (451) Legzdins; Kerr, Ashcroft (McGowan 68), Fontaine, Marshall; McMullan, Anderson (Cummings 70), Byrne, Adam (Afolabi 82), McDaid; Mullen.
St Johnstone: (3412) Clark; Kerr, Gordon, McCart; Rooney, McCann, Craig (Bryson 64), Booth; Wotherspoon; Melamed (Kane 65), May (Middleton 78).
Referee: Craig Napier.

Dundee U (0) 2 *(Shankland 78, Clark 90)*

Partick Thistle (1) 1 *(Tiffoney 25)*

Dundee U: (4321) Mehmet; Bolton, Edwards, Reynolds, Robson (Chalmers 62); Butcher, Fuchs (Clark 67), Harkes; Sporle, McNulty (Pawlett 86); Shankland.
Partick Thistle: (4411) Wright; McKenna, Brownlie, Niang, Foster; Cardle (Murray 57), Docherty, Gordon, Tiffoney (Penrice 74); Bannigan; Graham (Rudden 81).
Referee: Steven McLean.

East Fife (0) 1 *(Smith 59)*

Greenock Morton (0) 2 *(McGinty 90 (pen), Muirhead 112)*

East Fife: (442) Long; Murdoch, Dunlop, Watson, Slattery (Fenton 114); Dunsmore (Swanson 83), Davidson, Newton (McKinnon 78), Agnew; Smith (Denholm 90), Watt.
Greenock Morton: (352) McAdams; Ledger (Muirhead 70), McLean, McGinty; Hynes, Lyon, Jacobs, Blues (Oliver 78), Strapp; McGuffie (Nesbitt 64), Orsi (Sterling 101).
aet.
Referee: Alan Muir.

Forfar Ath (1) 2 *(Allan 13, Nditi 90)*

Edinburgh C (2) 2 *(See 6, Hamilton 25)*

Forfar Ath: (442) Hoban; Nditi, Meechan, Thomson■, Irvine; Scally, MacKintosh, Holmes (Coll 102), Allan (Shepherd 72); Fenwick, Northcott (Doris 84).
Edinburgh C: (442) Antell; Denham (Thomson 70), Hamilton, Henderson L, Crane; Harris (De Vita 58), Campbell, Laird, Jardine (Brown 107); Handling (Black 79), See.
aet; Forfar Ath won 5-3 on penalties.
Referee: Steven Kirkland.

Formartine U (0) 0

Motherwell (2) 5 *(Long 34, Roberts 41, 52, Cole 63, Campbell 76)*

Formartine U: (4141) Main; Crawford, Kelly, McKeown, Smith S; Anderson S; Park (Lawrence 77), Rodger, Anderson C (Norris 30), Wood; Smith J (Greig 56).
Motherwell: (433) Kelly; O'Donnell, Magloire, Gallagher, McGinley; Campbell (Lamie 77), Crawford (Foley 67), Lawless; Roberts (Hastie 67), Cole, Long.
Referee: Mike Roncone.

Fraserburgh (2) 2 *(Harris 19 (pen), Barbour 22)*

Montrose (2) 4 *(Mochrie 2, Webster 31, McLean 69, Milne 90)*

Fraserburgh: (352) Leask; Hay, Simpson (Duncan 75), West; Cairns, Beagrie, Young, Campbell G (Butcher 85), Cowie; Barbour, Harris (Campbell P 69).
Montrose: (4231) Lennox; Cammy Ballantyne, Waddell (Quinn 22), Dillon, Steeves; Masson, Watson (Johnston 65); Webster, Milne, Mochrie (Cameron Ballantyne 79); McLean.
Referee: Grant Irvine.

Hamilton A (0) 0

St Mirren (1) 3 *(McGrath 4, 79 (pen), Dennis 74)*

Hamilton A: (41212) Fulton; Hodson, Martin A, Easton, McMann; Odofin; Martin S (Hamilton 36), Hughes (Munro 78); Callachan; Anderson, Moyo.
St Mirren: (352) Alnwick; Fraser, McCarthy, Shaughnessy; Connolly (Dennis 63), McGrath, Doyle-Hayes, Erhahon, Durmus (Henderson 85); Erwin (Flynn 54), Obika.
Referee: Euan Anderson.

Livingston (0) 2 *(Fitzwater 70, Poplatnik 109)*

Raith R (1) 1 *(Vaughan 13)*

Livingston: (4231) McCrorie; Devlin, Fitzwater, Guthrie, Longridge; Bartley, Holt; Sibbald (Kabia 113), Pitman (Diani 113), Forrest (Mullin 62); Emmanuel-Thomas (Poplatnik 71).
Raith R: (4231) MacDonald J; Tumilty, Davidson, Benedictus, Musonda; Hendry, Spencer; Gullan (Duku 40), Tait (King 112), Kennedy (Armstrong 89); Vaughan (Ugwu 89).
aet.
Referee: Bobby Madden.

Stenhousemuir (0) 0

Kilmarnock (2) 4 *(Lafferty 38 (pen), 45, 56, Oakley 87)*

Stenhousemuir: (352) Martin; Tiffoney, Kane (Halleran 70), Yeats; Hopkirk, Blair (Grigor 70), Tapping, Hodge, Collins; McGuigan (McQueen 46), Biabi (Fairley 64).
Kilmarnock: (4231) Doyle; Millen, Medley (Rossi 30), Broadfoot, Haunstrup; Power, Dicker; Burke (Tshibola 66), McKenzie (Warnock 75), Pinnock; Lafferty (Oakley 61).
Referee: Greg Aitken.

Sunday, 4 April 2021

Rangers (4) 4 *(Defoe 24, Roofe 31, 32, Patterson 43)*

Cove Rangers (0) 0

Rangers: (433) McLaughlin; Patterson, Goldson, Helander, Bassey; Arfield, Davis (Hagi 46), Kamara; Wright, Defoe (Stewart 73), Roofe (Itten 63).
Cove Rangers: (4411) McKenzie; Scott Ross, Graham, Higgins, Livingstone; Watson (McIntosh 65), Fyvie, Scully, Smith; Masson (Hanratty 67); Megginson (McAllister 46).
Referee: Kevin Clancy.

Monday, 5 April 2021

Queen of the South (0) 1 *(Maxwell 80)*

Hibernian (1) 3 *(Doidge 42, 67, Boyle 70)*

Queen of the South: (4132) Ferguson; Gibson, Buchanan, Breen, Maxwell; Obileye; Joseph (Jones 56), McCabe, Dickson; Shields (Mebude 76), Dobbie (McKee 77).
Hibernian: (3142) Macey; McGinn P, Porteous, Hanlon; Newell; Boyle (Cadden 78), Gogic, Irvine (Magennis 75), Doig; Nisbet, Doidge (Wright 86).
Referee: William Collum.

FOURTH ROUND

Friday, 16 April 2021

Forfar Ath (0) 0

Dundee U (0) 1 *(Pawlett 56)*

Forfar Ath: (442) McCallum; Nditi, Meechan, Irvine, Coll; Shepherd (Northcott 73), MacKintosh, Holmes, Scally; Doris (Fenwick 60), Allan.
Dundee U: (41212) Mehmet; Smith, Edwards, Reynolds, Robson; Butcher (Harkes 71); Pawlett (Fuchs 81), Sporle; Clark; McNulty, Shankland (Appere 71).
Referee: Don Robertson.

Motherwell (0) 1 *(O'Donnell 120)*

Greenock Morton (0) 1 *(Fjortoft 120)*

Motherwell: (433) Kelly; O'Donnell, Gallagher, Lamie, McGinley; Campbell (O'Hara 118), Maguire (Hastie 81), Crawford; Cole, Long, Lawless (Mugabi 120).
Greenock Morton: (4231) McAdams; Ledger, McLean, Fjortoft, McGinty; Jacobs, McGinn; McGuffie (Easdale 120), Lyon (McGrattan 85), Nesbitt (Strapp 105); Muirhead (Orsi 73).
aet; Motherwell won 5-3 on penalties.
Referee: William Collum.

St Mirren (0) 2 *(Dennis 50, Fraser 89)*

Inverness CT (0) 1 *(Todorov 48)*

St Mirren: (3142) Alnwick; Fraser, McCarthy, Shaughnessy; Doyle-Hayes (Tait 41); Connolly, McGrath, McAllister K (MacPherson 46), Durmus; Dennis (Mason 75), Obika.
Inverness CT: (4231) Ridgers; Carson, McKay, Devine, Deas; Welsh (Lyall 90), Allardice; Mackay D, Allan, Storey; Todorov (Sutherland 87).
Referee: John Beaton.

Saturday, 17 April 2021

Aberdeen (0) 2 *(McGinn 77, Kamberi 95)*

Livingston (1) 2 *(Emmanuel-Thomas 37, 93 (pen))*

Aberdeen: (442) Lewis (Woods 36); McCrorie, Hoban, Considine, Hayes; Kennedy, Ferguson, Campbell, McLennan (Hendry 72); Hornby (Kamberi 59), McGinn (Ross 105).
Livingston: (4231) Stryjek; Devlin, Fitzwater (Taylor-Sinclair 108), Guthrie, Longridge (McMillan 106); Bartley, Holt; Emmanuel-Thomas, Pitman, Sibbald (Lithgow 91); Forrest (Poplatnik 84).
aet; Aberdeen won 5-3 on penalties.
Referee: Colin Steven.

Kilmarnock (2) 3 *(Lafferty 6, Steeves 24 (og), Kiltie 61)*

Montrose (0) 1 *(Cammy Ballantyne 82)*

Kilmarnock: (442) Doyle; Millen, Medley, Broadfoot, Waters; Pinnock, Power (Tshibola 64), Mulumbu, Burke (McKenzie 66); Kiltie, Lafferty (Oakley 73).
Montrose: (451) Fleming; Cammy Ballantyne, Quinn, Dillon, Steeves; Milne, Cochrane (Hawke 85), Watson (Cameron Ballantyne 43), Mochrie (Masson 69), Callaghan; McLean.
Referee: Nick Walsh.

St Johnstone (2) 2 *(Melamed 6, O'Halloran 21)*

Clyde (0) 0

St Johnstone: (343) Parish; Kerr, Gordon, McCart; Brown, Wotherspoon (Gilmour 67), Craig (McCann 79), Tanser; O'Halloran, Melamed (Middleton 71), May.
Clyde: (451) Vajs; Bain, Howie, McNiff, Otoo; Munro (Butterworth 56), Lamont (Jamieson 72), Thomson, Robertson, Cunningham (Ritchie-Hosler 64); Jack.
Referee: Steven Kirkland.

Sunday, 18 April 2021

Rangers (2) 2 *(Davis 10, Kenny 34 (og))*

Celtic (0) 0

Rangers: (442) McGregor; Patterson, Goldson, Helander, Barisic; Aribo, Arfield, Davis, Kamara; Morelos (Roofe 80), Kent.
Celtic: (433) Bain; Kenny, Welsh, Ajer, Laxalt (Taylor 46); Christie (Griffiths 73), Brown, McGregor; Turnbull, Edouard, Elyounoussi (Ajeti 86).
Referee: Bobby Madden.

Stranraer (0) 0

Hibernian (1) 4 *(Doidge 37, Nisbet 64, Boyle 71, 84 (pen))*

Stranraer: (3412) Fleming; Sonkur, McManus, Robertson; Gallagher, Millar, Hilton, Burns (Hamill 51); Stirling; Duffy (Paton 68), Orr (Matt Yates 69).
Hibernian: (3142) Macey; McGinn P, Hanlon, Porteous; Newell (Hallberg 74); Boyle, Irvine, Magennis (Wright 68), Doig (Stevenson 72); Nisbet, Doidge.
Referee: David Munro.

QUARTER-FINALS

Saturday, 24 April 2021

Hibernian (0) 2 *(Doidge 52, Irvine 80)*

Motherwell (0) 2 *(Lamie 82, Watt 88)*

Hibernian: (442) Macey; McGinn P, Porteous, Hanlon, Doig (Stevenson 106); Boyle, Gogic■, Newell (Hallberg 102), Irvine; Doidge (Wright 102), Nisbet.
Motherwell: (352) Kelly; Magloire (Watt 68), Gallagher, Lamie; O'Donnell, Campbell (Maguire 120), Crawford (Lawless 78), O'Hara, McGinley; Cole, Long.
aet; Hibernian won 4-2 on penalties.
Referee: John Beaton.

Sunday, 25 April 2021

Aberdeen (0) 0

Dundee U (2) 3 *(McNulty 18, 54, Edwards 37)*

Aberdeen: (4411) Woods; Ramsay, Hoban, Considine, Hayes; Kennedy, Ferguson, Campbell (McGeouch 62), Kamberi; McGinn (Ross 62); Hendry (Ruth 77).
Dundee U: (433) Mehmet; Smith, Edwards, Reynolds, Robson; Fuchs, Butcher (Pawlett 83), Harkes; McNulty, Shankland (Appere 88), Clark (Bolton 88).
Referee: Kevin Clancy.

Rangers (0) 1 *(Tavernier 117)*

St Johnstone (0) 1 *(Kane 120)*

Rangers: (433) McGregor; Tavernier, Goldson, Helander (Simpson 111), Barisic; Aribo, Kamara, Davis (Defoe 120); Hagi (Wright 68), Morelos (Roofe 81), Kent.
St Johnstone: (352) Clark; Kerr, Gordon, McCart; Rooney, McCann, Craig, Wotherspoon (Bryson 71), Tanser (Booth 101); May (O'Halloran 75), Melamed (Kane 58).
aet; St Johnstone won 4-2 on penalties.
Referee: Alan Muir.

Monday, 26 April 2021

Kilmarnock (2) 3 *(Rossi 37, Kiltie 44, Millen 101 (pen))*

St Mirren (1) 3 *(Doyle 25 (og), Shaughnessy 84, McGrath 119 (pen))*

Kilmarnock: (442) Doyle; Millen, Broadfoot, Rossi, Haunstrup; Burke (Dicker 91), Mulumbu (Tshibola 76), Power, Pinnock; Kiltie (McKenzie 91), Oakley (Kabamba 81).
St Mirren: (442) Alnwick; Fraser (MacPherson 106), McCarthy, Shaughnessy, Tait; Henderson, McGrath, Doyle-Hayes, Durmus (McAllister K 72); Dennis (Quaner 61), Erwin (Erhahon 61).
aet; St Mirren won 5-4 on penalties.
Referee: Don Robertson.

SEMI-FINALS

Saturday, 8 May 2021

Dundee U (0) 0

Hibernian (1) 2 *(Nisbet 27, Doidge 58)*

Dundee U: (433) Mehmet; Smith, Edwards, Reynolds, Robson; Harkes (Pawlett 60), Butcher, Fuchs; McNulty, Shankland, Clark (Sporle 53).
Hibernian: (442) Macey; McGinn P, Porteous (McGregor 73), Hanlon, Doig; Boyle, Hallberg, Newell (Magennis 60), Irvine; Nisbet (Murphy 84), Doidge.
Referee: Bobby Madden.

Sunday, 9 May 2021

St Mirren (0) 1 *(McCarthy 86)*

St Johnstone (0) 2 *(Kane 72, Middleton 74)*

St Mirren: (352) Alnwick; Fraser, McCarthy, Shaughnessy; Tait (Connolly 68), McGrath, Doyle-Hayes, Erhahon (Brophy 77), Durmus; Erwin, Dennis (Quaner 57).
St Johnstone: (352) Clark; Kerr, Gordon, McCart; Rooney, McCann, Wotherspoon, Bryson, Booth; Kane (O'Halloran 86), Melamed (Middleton 65).
Referee: William Collum.

WILLIAM HILL SCOTTISH CUP FINAL 2020–21

Saturday, 22 May 2021

(at Hampden Park, behind closed doors)

St Johnstone (1) 1 Hibernian (0) 0

St Johnstone: (3421) Clark; Kerr, Gordon, McCart; Rooney (Brown 79), McCann, Bryson (Davidson 64), Booth; Middleton (O'Halloran 82), Wotherspoon; Kane.
Scorer: Rooney 32.

Hibernian: (442) Macey; McGinn P, Porteous, Hanlon, Doig (Stevenson 76); Boyle, Gogic (Murphy 56), Newell (Hallberg 72), Irvine; Doidge, Nisbet.

Referee: Nick Walsh.

St Johnstone beat Hibernian in the Scottish Cup Final at Hampden Park on 22 May. Here Shaun Rooney scores the only goal of the game. (Andrew Milligan/PA Wire/PA Images)

SCOTTISH FOOTBALL PYRAMID 2020–21

FIFTH TIER

BREEDON HIGHLAND LEAGUE

	P	*W*	*D*	*L*	*F*	*A*	*GD*	*Pts*	*PPG*
Brora Rangers	3	3	0	0	20	1	19	9	3.00
Fraserburgh	3	3	0	0	16	1	15	9	3.00
Buckie Thistle	2	2	0	0	8	3	5	6	3.00
Formartine U	2	2	0	0	7	2	5	6	3.00
Inverurie Loco Works	2	2	0	0	6	2	4	6	3.00
Keith	2	1	0	1	2	3	–1	3	1.50
Rothes	2	1	0	1	2	5	–3	3	1.50
Huntly	3	0	2	1	3	4	–1	2	0.67
Lossiemouth	2	0	1	1	2	4	–2	1	0.50
Deveronvale	3	0	1	2	2	8	–6	1	0.33
Strathspey Thistle	0	0	0	0	0	0	0	0	—
Clachnacuddin	1	0	0	1	2	4	–2	0	0.00
Nairn Co	2	0	0	2	1	3	–2	0	0.00
Wick Academy	2	0	0	2	3	8	–5	0	0.00
Fort William	1	0	0	1	0	10	–10	0	0.00
Turriff U	2	0	0	2	2	18	–16	0	0.00

League suspended due to COVID-19 pandemic on 11 January 2021. Brora Rangers declared champions on points per game basis by the SFA Board on 30 March 2021.

GEOSONIC LOWLAND LEAGUE

	P	*W*	*D*	*L*	*F*	*A*	*GD*	*Pts*	*PPG*
Kelty Hearts	13	12	0	1	40	4	36	36	2.77
East Kilbride	12	9	2	1	32	6	26	29	2.42
Bonnyrigg Rose Ath	12	9	2	1	29	6	23	29	2.42
BSC Glasgow	13	9	3	1	38	16	22	30	2.31
East Stirlingshire	12	8	2	2	30	12	18	26	2.17
Gala Fairydean R	12	7	1	4	22	20	2	22	1.83
Bo'ness U	10	5	3	2	22	13	9	18	1.80
The Spartans	12	6	0	6	27	22	5	18	1.50
University of Stirling	15	7	1	7	31	25	6	22	1.47
Berwick Rangers	13	5	1	7	12	16	–4	16	1.23
Civil Service Strollers	14	4	5	5	14	16	–2	17	1.21
Caledonian Braves	14	4	1	9	22	28	–6	13	0.93
Gretna 2008	11	3	1	7	15	25	–10	10	0.91
Cumbernauld Colts	14	3	2	9	17	30	–13	11	0.79
Dalbeattie Star	10	1	2	7	12	24	–12	5	0.50
Edinburgh University	15	1	2	12	7	54	–47	5	0.33
Vale of Leithen	12	0	0	12	5	58	–53	0	0.00

League suspended due to COVID-19 pandemic on 11 January 2021. Kelty Hearts declared champions on points per game basis by the SFA Board.

SIXTH TIER

MCBOOKIE.COM EAST REGION PREMIERSHIP

	P	*W*	*D*	*L*	*F*	*A*	*GD*	*Pts*
Lochee U	5	5	0	0	22	2	20	15
Tayport	4	4	0	0	14	2	12	12
Broughty Ath	5	4	0	1	14	6	8	12
East Craigie	4	3	0	1	24	4	20	9
Carnoustie Panmure	4	3	0	1	20	7	13	9
Arbroath Victoria	3	3	0	0	12	2	10	9
Downfield	3	2	1	0	5	2	3	7
Brechin Victoria	5	1	2	2	8	15	–7	5
Dundee Violet	3	1	1	1	4	5	–1	4
Forfar West End	4	1	1	2	5	9	–4	4
Forfar U	5	1	1	3	8	13	–5	4
Kirriemuir Thistle	4	1	0	3	6	8	–2	3
Dundee North End	3	0	2	1	4	6	–2	2
Blairgowrie	4	0	0	4	3	10	–7	0
Scone Thistle	3	0	0	3	1	16	–15	0
Lochee Harp	5	0	0	5	2	22	–20	0
Coupar Angus	2	0	0	2	0	23	–23	0

League suspended due to COVID-19 pandemic on 7 January 2021 by the Scottish FA. On 16 March 2021 the management committee declared the season null and void. League table as of 16 March 2021.

NORTH CALEDONIAN LEAGUE

League 1	*P*	*W*	*D*	*L*	*F*	*A*	*GD*	*Pts*
Golspie Sutherland	9	6	1	2	19	9	10	19
Invergordon	9	4	3	2	14	10	4	15
St Duthus	10	4	3	3	21	19	2	15
Thurso	9	4	3	2	16	16	0	11
Orkney	9	0	3	6	12	20	–8	8
Halkirk U	10	3	1	6	13	21	–8	7

Thurso deducted 8 pts; Orkney awarded 5 pts; Halkirk U deducted 3.

League 2	*P*	*W*	*D*	*L*	*F*	*A*	*GD*	*Pts*
Alness U	10	8	1	1	46	11	35	25
Nairn Co A	10	7	0	3	32	21	11	21
Inverness Ath	10	5	2	3	20	10	10	17
Loch Ness	10	4	3	3	30	17	13	15
Bonar Bridge	10	3	0	7	14	37	–23	9
Scourie	10	0	0	10	3	49	–46	0

League suspended due to COVID-19 pandemic on 7 January 2021 by the Scottish FA. On 24 June, the season's two remaining fixtures were cancelled. League table as of 24 June 2021.

CENTRAL TAXIS EAST OF SCOTLAND LEAGUE

	P	*W*	*D*	*L*	*F*	*A*	*GD*	*Pts*
Tranent Juniors	12	8	4	0	36	15	21	28
Jeanfield Swifts	9	7	2	0	27	7	20	23
Linlithgow Rose	11	6	4	1	23	13	10	22
Musselburgh Ath	11	7	1	3	32	25	7	22
Camelon Juniors	10	6	2	2	33	13	20	20
Lothian Thistle Hutchison Vale	10	6	1	3	22	20	2	19
Penicuik Ath	8	5	1	2	20	10	10	16
Dundonald Bluebell	8	5	1	2	13	9	4	16
Newtongrange Star	12	5	1	6	24	22	2	16
Broxburn Ath	11	5	1	5	25	24	1	16
Sauchie Juniors	11	4	3	4	23	18	5	15
Hill of Beath Hawthorn	10	5	0	5	16	18	–2	15
Tynecastle	11	4	2	5	25	25	0	14
Dunbar U	13	3	2	8	12	30	–18	11
Crossgates Primrose	11	2	4	5	15	25	–10	10
Blackburn U	12	1	0	11	15	39	–24	3
Inverkeithing Hillfield Swifts	10	1	0	9	8	34	–26	3
Whitehill Welfare	10	0	1	9	10	32	–22	1

League suspended due to COVID-19 pandemic on 11 January 2021 by the Scottish FA. On 11 April 2021 the clubs voted to declare the season null and void. League table as of 11 April 2021.

SOUTH OF SCOTLAND FOOTBALL LEAGUE

	P	*W*	*D*	*L*	*F*	*A*	*GD*	*Pts*
Stranraer Res	11	8	2	1	40	13	27	26
Threave R	7	6	0	1	33	10	23	18
St Cuthbert W	7	5	1	1	17	7	10	16
Newton Stewart	9	4	3	2	27	20	7	15
Nithsdale W	8	5	0	3	28	25	3	15
Abbey Vale	8	4	2	2	19	13	6	14
Upper Annandale	9	4	0	5	19	21	–2	12
Wigtown & Bladnoch	8	4	0	4	12	17	–5	12
Caledonian Braves Res	6	3	1	2	19	14	5	10
Lochar Thistle	11	3	1	7	20	26	–6	10
Lochmaben	8	1	3	4	14	29	–15	6
Mid-Annandale	7	1	1	5	13	24	–11	4
Heston R	10	1	1	8	13	34	–21	4
Creetown	7	1	1	5	10	31	–21	4

League suspended due to COVID-19 pandemic on 11 January 2021 by the Scottish FA. On 1 April 2021 the clubs voted to declare the season null and void. League table as of 1 April 2021.

WEST OF SCOTLAND FOOTBALL LEAGUE

	P	*W*	*D*	*L*	*F*	*A*	*GD*	*Pts*
Clydebank	7	6	1	0	20	3	17	19
Troon	7	5	1	1	14	9	5	16
Kilwinning Rangers	7	5	0	2	14	9	5	15
Irvine Meadow XI	7	4	1	2	10	7	3	13
Darvel	5	4	0	1	15	3	12	12
Largs Thistle	7	3	2	2	11	7	4	11
Blantyre Vic	7	3	1	3	17	17	0	10
Hurlford U	7	3	1	3	10	14	–4	10
Rossvale	9	2	3	4	14	15	–1	9
Beith Juniors	5	1	4	0	7	6	1	7
Kirkintilloch Rob Roy	7	2	0	5	10	16	–6	6
Bonnyton Thistle	8	2	0	6	9	21	–12	6
Rutherglen Glencairn	6	1	0	5	5	13	–8	3
Cumbernauld U	7	0	0	7	8	24	–16	0
Benburb	0	0	0	0	0	0	0	0

League suspended due to COVID-19 pandemic on 7 January 2021 by the Scottish FA. On 17 March 2021 the board declared the season null and void. League table as of 17 March 2021.

NORTH SUPER LEAGUE

No competition for 2020–21 season.

BARCLAYS FA WOMEN'S SUPER LEAGUE 2020–21

		Home						Away					Total						
	P	W	D	L	F	A	W	D	L	F	A	W	D	L	F	A	GD	Pts
1 Chelsea	22	10	0	1	42	6	8	3	0	27	4	18	3	1	69	10	59	57
2 Manchester C	22	9	2	0	36	5	8	2	1	29	8	17	4	1	65	13	52	55
3 Arsenal	22	8	2	1	30	6	7	1	3	33	9	15	3	4	63	15	48	48
4 Manchester U	22	8	2	1	26	7	7	0	4	18	13	15	2	5	44	20	24	47
5 Everton	22	4	3	4	16	16	5	2	4	23	14	9	5	8	39	30	9	32
6 Brighton & HA	22	5	0	6	11	24	3	3	5	10	17	8	3	11	21	41	–20	27
7 Reading	22	2	5	4	11	20	3	4	4	14	21	5	9	8	25	41	–16	24
8 Tottenham H	22	3	3	5	11	17	2	2	7	7	24	5	5	12	18	41	–23	20
9 West Ham U	22	0	4	7	6	22	3	2	6	15	17	3	6	13	21	39	–18	15
10 Aston Villa	22	1	3	7	5	25	2	3	6	10	22	3	6	13	15	47	–32	15
11 Birmingham C	22	0	4	7	6	24	3	2	6	9	20	3	6	13	15	44	–29	14
12 Bristol C	22	2	1	8	8	33	0	5	6	10	39	2	6	14	18	72	–54	12

BARCLAYS FA WOMEN'S SUPER LEAGUE LEADING GOALSCORERS 2020–21

Player	Team	Goals
Sam Kerr	Chelsea	21
Vivianne Miedema	Arsenal	18
Fran Kirby	Chelsea	16
Caitlin Foord	Arsenal	10
Chloe Kelly	Manchester C	10
Ellen White	Manchester C	10
Pernille Harder	Chelsea	9
Ella Toone	Manchester U	9
Inessa Kaagman	Brighton & HA	8
Caroline Weir	Manchester C	8
Samantha Mewis	Manchester C	7
Jill Roord	Arsenal	7
Izzy Christiansen	Everton	6
Beth England	Chelsea	6
Leah Galton	Manchester U	6
Simone Magill	Everton	6
Lauren Hemp	Manchester C	6
Ebony Salmon	Bristol C	6

FA WOMEN'S CHAMPIONSHIP 2020–21

		Home						Away					Total						
	P	W	D	L	F	A	W	D	L	F	A	W	D	L	F	A	GD	Pts
1 Leicester C	20	9	1	0	22	4	7	1	2	32	12	16	2	2	54	16	38	50
2 Durham	20	6	3	1	18	5	6	3	1	16	10	12	6	2	34	15	19	42
3 Liverpool	20	6	3	1	24	6	5	3	2	13	9	11	6	3	37	15	22	39
4 Sheffield U	20	4	4	2	16	7	7	1	2	21	8	11	5	4	37	15	22	38
5 Lewes	20	5	2	3	12	12	3	2	5	7	10	8	4	8	19	22	–3	28
6 London C Lionesses	20	4	2	4	12	9	2	4	4	7	10	6	6	8	19	19	0	24
7 Crystal Palace	20	3	2	5	15	16	2	3	5	12	20	5	5	10	27	36	–9	20
8 Charlton Ath	20	2	4	4	13	15	2	3	5	6	14	4	7	9	19	29	–10	19
9 Blackburn R	20	2	2	6	9	14	2	4	4	11	17	4	6	10	20	31	–11	18
10 Coventry U	20	3	0	7	14	25	2	1	7	7	26	5	1	14	21	51	–30	16
11 London Bees	20	3	2	5	10	23	0	0	10	4	29	3	2	15	14	52	–38	11

FA WOMEN'S CHAMPIONSHIP LEADING GOALSCORERS 2020–21

Player	Team	Goals
Katie Wilkinson	Sheffield U	19
Natasha Flint	Leicester C	17
Beth Hepple	Durham	10
Bianca Baptiste	Crystal Palace	8
Lachante Paul	Leicester C	7
Jessica King	Charlton Ath	6
Emily Roberts	Durham	6
Remi Allen	Leicester C	5
Rinsola Babajide	Liverpool	5
Paige Bailey-Gayle	Leicester C	5
Rachel Furness	Liverpool	5
Bridget Galloway	Durham	5
Coral-Jade Haines	Crystal Palace	5
Lois Heuchan	Charlton Ath	5
Elise Hughes	Blackburn R	5
Melissa Johnson	Sheffield U	5
Cherelle Khassal	Crystal Palace	5
Courtney Sweetman-Kirk	Sheffield U	5
Iniabasi Umotong	Lewes	5

FA WOMEN'S CONTINENTAL TYRES LEAGUE CUP 2020–21

**After extra time.*

GROUP STAGE

GROUP A

Durham v Coventry U 5-2
Aston Villa v Sheffield U 1-0
Sheffield U v Durham 0-6
Coventry U v Aston V 0-9
Durham v Aston Villa 1-1
Aston Villa won 4-2 on penalties.
Coventry U v Sheffield U 0-4

Group A Table	P	W	WP	LP	L	F	A	GD	Pts
Aston Villa	3	2	1	0	0	11	1	10	8
Durham	3	2	0	1	0	12	3	9	7
Sheffield U	3	1	0	0	2	4	7	–3	3
Coventry U	3	0	0	0	3	2	18	–16	0

GROUP B

Tottenham H v London C Lionesses 4-0
Chelsea v Arsenal 4-1
Chelsea v Tottenham H 2-0
London C Lionesses v Arsenal 0-4
London C Lionesses v Chelsea
Match postponed following positive COVID-19 tests. Fixture not rescheduled as result would not affect qualification.
Arsenal v Tottenham H 2-2
Arsenal won 5-4 on penalties.

Group B Table	P	W	WP	LP	L	F	A	GD	Pts
Chelsea	2	2	0	0	0	6	1	5	6
Arsenal	3	1	1	0	1	7	6	1	5
Tottenham H	3	1	0	1	1	6	4	2	4
London C Lionesses	2	0	0	0	2	0	8	–8	0

GROUP C

Liverpool v Manchester U 3-1
Manchester C v Everton 3-1
Liverpool v Manchester C 0-3
Everton v Liverpool 1-0
Manchester U v Manchester C 0-0
Manchester U won 4-3 on penalties.
Everton v Manchester U 1-0

Group C Table	P	W	WP	LP	L	F	A	GD	Pts
Manchester C	3	2	0	1	0	6	1	5	7
Everton	3	2	0	0	1	3	3	0	6
Liverpool	3	1	0	0	2	3	5	–2	3
Manchester U	3	0	1	0	2	1	4	–3	2

GROUP D

Reading v Charlton Ath 4-0
Brighton & HA v West Ham U 2-2
West Ham U won 4-2 on penalties.
West Ham U v Reading 3-0
Charlton Ath v Brighton & HA
Match postponed following positive COVID-19 tests. Fixture not rescheduled as result would not affect qualification.
Brighton & HA v Reading 0-2
Charlton Ath v West Ham U 0-4

Group D Table	P	W	WP	LP	L	F	A	GD	Pts
West Ham U	3	2	1	0	0	9	2	7	8
Reading	3	2	0	0	1	6	3	3	6
Brighton & HA	2	0	0	1	1	2	4	–2	1
Charlton Ath	2	0	0	0	2	0	8	–8	0

GROUP E

Blackburn R v Birmingham C 0-1
Leicester C v Blackburn R 5-2
Birmingham C v Leicester C 0-0
Leicester C won 6-5 on penalties.

Group E Table	P	W	WP	LP	L	F	A	GD	Pts
Leicester C	2	1	1	0	0	5	2	3	5
Birmingham C	2	1	0	1	0	1	0	1	4
Blackburn R	2	0	0	0	2	2	6	–4	0

GROUP F

Bristol C v London Bees 4-0
Lewes v Crystal Palace 1-2
London Bees v Lewes 1-0
Crystal Palace v Bristol C 2-4
Lewes v Bristol C 1-3
Crystal Palace v London Bees 6-1

Group F Table	P	W	WP	LP	L	F	A	GD	Pts
Bristol C	3	3	0	0	0	11	3	8	9
Crystal Palace	3	2	0	0	1	10	6	4	6
London Bees	3	1	0	0	2	2	10	–8	3
Lewes	3	0	0	0	3	2	6	–4	0

KNOCK-OUT ROUNDS

QUARTER-FINALS

Bristol C v Aston Villa 2-1
Crystal Palace v Leicester C 0-1
Manchester C v Chelsea 2-4*
West Ham U v Durham 3-0

SEMI-FINALS

Chelsea v West Ham U 6-0
Bristol C v Leicester C 1-0

FA WOMEN'S CONTINENTAL TYRES LEAGUE CUP FINAL 2020–21

Watford, Saturday 14 March 2021

Chelsea (4) 6 *(Kerr 2, 10, 48, Kirby 28, 38, Reiten 54)*

Bristol C (0) 0

Chelsea: Berger; Mjelde, Bright, Eriksson, Andersson (Blundell 46), Leupolz (Cuthbert 46), Ingle (Spence 46), Kirby (Charles 60), Fleming, Reiten, Kerr (Carter 60).
Bristol C: Baggaley; Bryson, Skeels (Layzell 85), Evans (Rafferty 80), Purfield, Humphrey (Palmer 66), Bissell (Harrison 46), Mastrantonio, Wellings, Daniels, Salmon.
Referee: Abi Byrne.

FA WOMEN'S NATIONAL LEAGUE 2020–21

On 4 January 2021, all divisions of the FA Women's National League were suspended due to the COVID-19 pandemic. On 15 March 2021, the season was curtailed for a second successive season without promotion and relegation. These league tables are as at the time of the curtailment.

FA WOMEN'S NATIONAL LEAGUE NORTHERN PREMIER DIVISION 2020–21

			Home					*Away*					*Total*						
		P	*W*	*D*	*L*	*F*	*A*	*W*	*D*	*L*	*F*	*A*	*W*	*D*	*L*	*F*	*A*	*GD*	*Pts*
1	Huddersfield T	10	5	1	0	22	9	3	0	1	9	6	8	1	1	31	15	16	25
2	Fylde	8	4	0	0	19	3	2	1	1	10	8	6	1	1	29	11	18	19
3	WBA	9	1	1	1	6	6	4	0	2	18	8	5	1	3	24	14	10	16
4	Derby Co	9	3	1	1	14	11	2	0	2	13	9	5	1	3	27	20	7	16
5	Sunderland	9	5	0	1	15	10	0	0	3	2	7	5	0	4	17	17	0	15
6	Nottingham F	9	3	1	1	16	5	1	1	2	6	7	4	2	3	22	12	10	14
7	Stoke C	8	2	0	1	7	6	1	2	2	8	16	3	2	3	15	22	–7	11
8	Burnley	7	1	1	1	4	4	2	0	2	7	7	3	1	3	11	11	0	10
9	Middlesbrough	9	1	1	2	6	10	1	0	4	9	14	2	1	6	15	24	–9	7
10	Sheffield	9	1	0	3	5	13	1	0	4	6	16	2	0	7	11	29	–18	6
11	Hull C	7	1	0	3	4	10	0	2	1	5	7	1	2	4	9	17	–8	5
12	Loughborough Foxes	8	0	1	3	4	10	0	1	3	4	17	0	2	6	8	27	–19	2

FA WOMEN'S NATIONAL LEAGUE SOUTHERN PREMIER DIVISION 2020–21

			Home					*Away*					*Total*						
		P	*W*	*D*	*L*	*F*	*A*	*W*	*D*	*L*	*F*	*A*	*W*	*D*	*L*	*F*	*A*	*GD*	*Pts*
1	Watford	8	4	1	0	21	2	2	0	1	7	4	6	1	1	28	6	22	19
2	Oxford U	7	3	0	0	10	3	3	0	1	12	3	6	0	1	22	6	16	18
3	Portsmouth	8	4	0	0	16	2	1	1	2	5	6	5	1	2	21	8	13	16
4	Milton Keynes D	8	3	0	2	13	7	2	0	1	10	4	5	0	3	23	11	12	15
5	Crawley Wasps	7	3	0	1	6	1	2	0	1	8	4	5	0	2	14	5	9	15
6	Cardiff C	4	1	0	0	6	0	2	0	1	11	6	3	0	1	17	6	11	9
7	Chichester & Selsey	6	2	0	2	11	5	1	0	1	3	5	3	0	3	14	10	4	9
8	Yeovil U	5	0	1	1	4	5	2	1	0	5	3	2	2	1	9	8	1	8
9	Keynsham T	7	1	0	2	8	6	1	0	3	5	9	2	0	5	13	15	–2	6
10	Gillingham	7	1	0	3	5	7	1	0	2	5	7	2	0	5	10	14	–4	6
11	Plymouth Arg	7	0	0	3	1	18	0	0	4	1	24	0	0	7	2	42	–40	0
12	Hounslow	8	0	0	3	0	16	0	0	5	0	26	0	0	8	0	42	–42	0

FA WOMEN'S NATIONAL LEAGUE DIVISION ONE NORTH 2020–21

			Home					*Away*					*Total*						
		P	*W*	*D*	*L*	*F*	*A*	*W*	*D*	*L*	*F*	*A*	*W*	*D*	*L*	*F*	*A*	*GD*	*Pts*
1	Chester-le-Street T	6	2	1	0	11	5	2	1	0	4	2	4	2	0	15	7	8	14
2	Brighouse T	5	1	1	0	1	0	2	0	1	8	3	3	1	1	9	3	6	10
3	Norton & Stockton Ancients	6	2	0	1	5	3	0	2	1	4	5	2	2	2	9	8	1	8
4	Leeds U	6	1	1	1	2	2	1	1	1	6	6	2	2	2	8	8	0	8
5	Durham Cestria	5	1	1	0	7	0	1	0	2	3	8	2	1	2	10	8	2	7
6	Liverpool Feds	3	0	0	0	0	0	2	0	1	4	2	2	0	1	4	2	2	6
7	Stockport Co	4	2	0	2	8	7	0	0	0	0	0	2	0	2	8	7	1	6
8	Newcastle U	3	1	0	0	1	0	0	1	1	2	3	1	1	1	3	3	0	4
9	Barnsley	6	1	1	2	10	9	0	0	2	0	3	1	1	4	10	12	–2	4
10	Chorley	3	1	0	1	1	4	0	1	0	0	0	1	1	1	1	4	–3	4
11	Bradford C	4	0	2	1	3	4	0	1	0	1	1	0	3	1	4	5	–1	3
12	Bolton W	3	0	0	0	0	0	0	0	3	2	16	0	0	3	2	16	–14	0

FA WOMEN'S NATIONAL LEAGUE DIVISION ONE MIDLANDS 2020–21

		Home						Away					Total						
		P	W	D	L	F	A	W	D	L	F	A	W	D	L	F	A	GD	Pts
1	Wolverhampton W	6	2	0	0	17	1	4	0	0	20	2	6	0	0	37	3	34	18
2	Doncaster R Belles	8	2	1	0	8	2	2	2	1	12	10	4	3	1	20	12	8	15
3	Lincoln C	6	2	1	1	18	4	2	0	0	9	4	4	1	1	27	8	19	13
4	Solihull Moors	6	3	1	0	18	2	0	1	1	2	9	3	2	1	20	11	9	11
5	Long Eaton U	7	3	1	0	14	4	0	1	2	1	5	3	2	2	15	9	6	11
6	Boldmere St Michaels	4	2	1	0	14	3	1	0	0	2	1	3	1	0	16	4	12	10
7	Sporting Khalsa	6	1	1	1	5	9	1	1	1	4	2	2	2	2	9	11	–2	8
8	Bedworth U	7	2	0	2	7	7	0	0	3	1	11	2	0	5	8	18	–10	6
9	Wem T	4	1	1	1	3	8	0	0	1	1	2	1	1	2	4	10	–6	4
10	Holwell Sports	6	0	0	3	4	11	1	1	1	5	7	1	1	4	9	18	–9	4
11	Burton Alb	7	1	0	1	3	5	0	0	5	3	42	1	0	6	6	47	–41	3
12	Leafield Ath	7	0	0	2	0	10	0	1	4	6	16	0	1	6	6	26	–20	1

FA WOMEN'S NATIONAL LEAGUE DIVISION ONE SOUTH EAST 2020–21

		Home						Away					Total						
		P	W	D	L	F	A	W	D	L	F	A	W	D	L	F	A	GD	Pts
1	Ipswich T	4	3	0	0	15	0	1	0	0	3	0	4	0	0	18	0	18	12
2	Hashtag U	5	2	0	0	9	1	2	0	1	7	6	4	0	1	16	7	9	12
3	Enfield T	6	1	1	0	4	2	2	1	1	8	3	3	2	1	12	5	7	11
4	Actonians	4	2	1	0	7	1	1	0	0	2	1	3	1	0	9	2	7	10
5	Norwich C	4	3	0	0	9	3	0	0	1	1	4	3	0	1	10	7	3	9
6	AFC Wimbledon	5	1	1	1	6	6	1	0	1	7	3	2	1	2	13	9	4	7
7	Cambridge U	6	2	0	1	6	4	0	1	2	4	16	2	1	3	10	20	–10	7
8	Kent Football U	6	0	0	0	0	0	1	3	2	7	8	1	3	2	7	8	–1	6
9	Leyton Orient	3	0	1	0	1	1	1	0	1	4	3	1	1	1	5	4	1	4
10	Cambridge C	7	1	1	2	9	11	0	0	3	1	13	1	1	5	10	24	–14	4
11	Billericay T	3	0	0	2	3	7	1	0	0	4	0	1	0	2	7	7	0	3
12	Stevenage	7	0	0	4	0	13	0	0	3	1	12	0	0	7	1	25	–24	0

FA WOMEN'S NATIONAL LEAGUE DIVISION ONE SOUTH WEST 2020–21

		Home						Away					Total						
		P	W	D	L	F	A	W	D	L	F	A	W	D	L	F	A	GD	Pts
1	Southampton FC	4	2	0	0	8	1	2	0	0	11	1	4	0	0	19	2	17	12
2	Chesham U	5	2	0	0	11	2	2	0	1	12	6	4	0	1	23	8	15	12
3	Swindon T	4	2	0	0	8	4	1	0	1	5	4	3	0	1	13	8	5	9
4	Buckland Ath	5	2	0	1	6	7	1	0	1	5	5	3	0	2	11	12	–1	9
5	Exeter C	6	1	2	1	10	14	1	0	1	6	4	2	2	2	16	18	–2	8
6	Cheltenham T	5	1	0	1	2	2	1	1	1	10	6	2	1	2	12	8	4	7
7	Larkhall Ath	5	0	2	0	5	5	1	1	1	10	10	1	3	1	15	15	0	6
8	Maidenhead U	3	0	0	1	2	3	1	1	0	4	3	1	1	1	6	6	0	4
9	Southampton Women	4	1	0	1	7	6	0	1	1	1	3	1	1	2	8	9	–1	4
10	Brislington	3	0	0	2	3	9	0	0	1	0	7	0	0	3	3	16	–13	0
11	Poole T	6	0	0	3	1	14	0	0	3	3	14	0	0	6	4	28	–24	0

THE WOMEN'S FA CUP 2019–20

**After extra time.*
Delayed due to COVID-19 pandemic.

QUARTER-FINALS

Brighton & HA v Birmingham C	2-2*
Birmingham C won 4-2 on penalties.	
Everton v Chelsea	2-1
Arsenal v Tottenham H	4-0
Leicester C v Manchester C	1-2

SEMI-FINALS

Birmingham C v Everton	0-3
Manchester C v Arsenal	2-1

THE WOMEN'S FA CUP FINAL 2019-20

Saturday, 1 November 2020
(at Wembley, behind closed doors)

Manchester C (1) 3 *(Mewis 40, Stanway 111, Beckie 120)*

Everton (0) 1 *(Gauvin 60)*

Manchester C: Roebuck; Bronze, Houghton, Greenwood, Stokes, Mewis, Walsh, Weir, Kelly (Beckie 118), White (Stanway 63), Lavelle (Park 70).
Everton: MacIver; Wold, Finnigan, Sevecke (Pattinson 90), Turner, Graham (Pike 90), Egurrola (Stringer 99), Raso (Boye-Hlorkah 76), Christiansen, Sorensen, Gauvin (Magill 90).
After extra time.
Referee: Rebecca Welch (Durham).

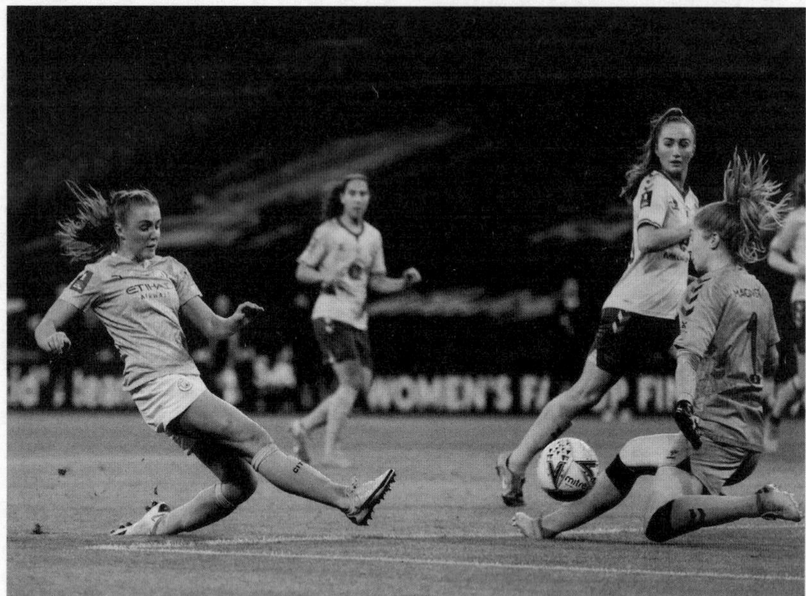

Georgia Stanway scores Manchester City's second goal in their 3-1 victory over Everton in the FA Cup Final at Wembley in November. (Pool via REUTERS/Kirsty Wigglesworth)

THE VITALITY WOMEN'S FA CUP 2020–21

**After extra time.*

EXTRA PRELIMINARY ROUND

Boro Rangers v Workington Reds 0-1
Birtley T v Bishop Auckland 0-3
Stanwix v South Shields 0-6
Wallsend Boys Club v Hartlepool U 6-1
Gateshead Leam Rangers v CLS Amazons 1-3
Appleby Frodingham v South Cave Sporting Club 4-3
Harworth Colliery v Silsden 6-1
Wakefield Trinity v Hepworth U 5-0
Harrogate T v Farsley Celtic 3-1
Yorkshire Amateur v Altofts (walkover)
Rotherham U v Oughtibridge War Memorial 3-3
Rotherham U won 3-0 on penalties
Crewe Alex v West Didsbury & Chorlton 1-0
Tranmere R v Fleetwood T Wrens 2-3
Cheadle T Stingers v Chester 5-1
Curzon Ashton v Haslingden Girls & 7-2
Merseyrail v Mossley 5-0
Didsbury v Northwich Vixens 1-2
FC United of Manchester v West Kirby 13-0
Mossley Hill v Ashton U 12-0
AFC Darwen v Nelson 9-0
Grimsby Bor (walkover) v Pride Park
Notts Co v Lincoln U 4-4
Lincoln U won 3-2 on penalties
AFC Leicester v Woodlands 0-5
Sherwood (walkover) v HBW U
Rise Park v Asfordby Amateurs 3-0
Dronfield T v Arnold Eagles 2-1
Arnold T v Allexton & New Parks (walkover)
Beaumont Park v Groby 6-2
Coalville T v Oadby & Wigston 2-7
Darlaston T (1874) v Shifnal T 2-6
Kingfisher v Knowle 0-3
Sutton Coldfield T v Coventrians 5-0
Westfields v Leamington Lions 2-1
Shrewsbury Juniors v Lye T 0-5
Coventry Sphinx v Sandwell 3-0
Tamworth v Doveridge 8-0
Solihull Sporting v Kidderminster H 1-4
Cookley Sports v Coundon Court 2-1
Hereford Pegasus v Rugby Bor 1-0
Stourbridge v Port Vale 8-0
Walsall Wood v Redditch U 0-6
Tamworth Academy v Worcester C 0-15
Balls To Cancer v Stockingford AA Pavilion 1-9
Rugby T v Sedgley & Gornal U 2-6
St Ives T v Hartham U 12-0
Newmarket T v Wymondham T 3-3
Newmarket T won 4-2 on penalties
Whittlesey Ath v Peterborough U 1-3
Wroxham v Kettering T 10-0
Bedford v Corby T 12-0
Henley Ath v March T U 4-4
March T U won 5-4 on penalties
Northampton T v Haverhill R 5-0
Aylesford v Ashford 1-3
Herne Bay v Whyteleafe 5-1
Dulwich Hamlet v Margate 6-1
New London Lionesses v Parkwood 4-2
Hastings U v Hackney 0-2
Tunbridge Wells Foresters v Ramsgate 1-1
Ramsgate won 5-4 on penalties
Runwell Sports v Harlow T 0-6
Rayleigh T (walkover) v Hoddesdon T
Chelmsford C v Frontiers 3-2
Colney Heath v Herts Vipers 2-1
Hemel Hempstead T v Garston 1-3
Abingdon T v Abingdon U 0-4
Banbury U v Swindon Supermarine 1-2
Woodley U v Wargrave 5-2
Royal Wootton Bassett T v Brentford 1-1
Brentford won 7-6 on penalties
Wycombe W v Oxford C 4-0
Eastbourne U v Pagham 1-0
Badshot Lea v Oakwood 7-3
Walton Casuals v AFC Littlehampton 4-0
Mole Valley v AFC Acorns 0-11
Roffey v Chichester C 1-4
Seaford T v Newhaven 1-1
Seaford T won 3-1 on penalties
Burgess Hill T v Saltdean U 0-10
AFC Stoneham v Merley Cobham Sports 10-0
Eastleigh v Bournemouth 1-10
Bournemouth Sports v Redlands 21-0
Alton v Meon Milton 13-0
Longwell Green v Paulton R 2-2
Paulton R won 6-5 on penalties
FC Chippenham v Oldland Abbotonians 0-6
Bristol Union v Middlezoy R 1-1
Middlezoy R won 4-2 on penalties
Downend Flyers v AEK Boco 1-2
Bristol R v Bristol & West 6-0
Banwell v Ilminster T 0-10
St Agnes v Saltash U 0-1
Marine Academy Plymouth v Ottery St Mary 21-0
AFC St Austell v Feniton 7-0

PRELIMINARY ROUND

Lumley v Spennymoor T 0-1
South Shields v Gateshead Rutherford 3-1
Blyth T v Guisborough T 7-1
Washington v Alnwick T 0-7
Sunderland West End v Carlisle U 7-0
Durham U v Workington Reds 3-4
CLS Amazons v Penrith 1-2
Hartlepool Pools Youth v Wallsend Boys Club 0-9
Redcar T v Bishop Auckland 6-1
Thackley v Ripon C 3-3
Ripon C won 4-3 on penalties
Hull U v Millmoor Juniors 2-1
Bradford (Park Avenue) v Ossett U 1-4
Sheffield W v Harworth Colliery 3-2
Farsley Celtic Juniors v Harrogate T 2-2
Farsley Celtic Juniors won 3-1 on penalties
Brighouse Sports v Appleby Frodingham 6-1
York C v Rotherham U 4-0
Altofts v Wakefield Trinity 3-4
Curzon Ashton v Blackburn Community Sports Club 2-5
Morecambe v Salford C Lionesses 3-0
Rylands v Fleetwood T Wrens 0-14
AFC Darwen v Sir Tom Finney 6-4
FC United of Manchester v Ashton T 9-0
Altrincham v Northwich Vixens 0-5
Mossley Hill v Wythenshawe Amateurs 1-2
Merseyrail v Cheadle T Stingers 7-3
SK Vipers v Warrington Wolves Foundation 0-8
Crewe Alex v Accrington S Community Trust 14-1
Leicester C v Oakham U 7-1
Woodlands v Oadby & Wigston 0-2
St Joseph's Rockware of Worksop v Lincoln Moorlands Railway 1-1
Lincoln Moorlands Railway won 3-1 on penalties
Grimsby T v Ollerton T 5-1
Cleethorpes T v Dronfield T 1-2
Beaumont Park v Grimsby Bor 2-1
Rise Park (walkover) v Allexton & New Parks
Belper T v Sherwood 0-3
Nottingham Trent University v Lincoln U 1-2
Westfields v Worcester C 1-2
Stockingford AA Pavilion v Droitwich Spa 0-3
AFC Telford U v Knowle 2-3
Cookley Sports v Sedgley & Gornal U 2-1
Tamworth v Solihull U 3-2
Hereford Pegasus v Coventry Sphinx 0-7
Kidderminster H v Crusaders 0-1
Lye T v Sutton Coldfield T 1-4
Stourbridge v Wyrley 8-1
Shifnal T v Redditch U 3-3
Redditch U won 5-3 on penalties
Desborough v Netherton U 0-10
Peterborough U v Royston T 4-4
Royston T won 4-2 on penalties
Waveney v Brett Vale 2-2
Brett Vale won 5-4 on penalties
AFC Sudbury v Needham Market 3-1
Peterborough Northern Star v March T U 13-1
Histon v St Ives T 2-4
Bedford v Northampton T 1-3
King's Lynn T v Wroxham 3-7

Bungay T v Newmarket T	0-5
Bexhill U v Sutton U	0-0
Sutton U won 4-1 on penalties	
Regents Park Rangers v Phoenix Sports	2-1
Haringey Bor v Fulham	1-2
Comets v Herne Bay	1-1
Comets won 4-3 on penalties	
Millwall Lionesses v New London Lionesses	0-8
Islington Bor v Ashford	1-4
Dartford v Ramsgate	8-0
Hackney v Dulwich Hamlet	2-6
Southend U Community SC v Houghton Ath	1-1
Southend U Community SC won 3-1 on penalties	
Wodson Park v Watford Development	1-2
Chelmsford C v Leigh Ramblers	1-2
Rayleigh T v Luton T	1-9
Bowers & Pitsea v Garston	5-0
Colney Heath v Harlow T	3-4
Denham U v QPR	2-2
Denham U won 5-3 on penalties	
Ascot U v Swindon Supermarine	6-0
Brentford v Ashford T (Middlesex)	1-6
Wycombe W v Eversley & California	2-1
Tilehurst Panthers v Slough T	7-1
Abingdon U v Newbury	6-0
Woodley U v Milton U	5-3
Steyning T v Worthing	1-8
Seaford T v Badshot Lea	1-2
AFC Acorns v Lancing	2-2
Lancing won 5-4 on penalties	
Chichester C v Eastbourne T	0-3
Woking (walkover) v Godalming Twn	
Eastbourne U v Dorking W	0-2
Walton Casuals v Saltdean U	3-5
Sherborne T v Bournemouth Sports	3-0
Alton v AFC Stoneham	2-5
Shanklin v Moneyfields	0-8
New Milton T v Winchester C Flyers	0-5
United Services Portsmouth v Bournemouth	0-9
Pen Mill v Ilminster T (walkover)	
Weston-super-Mare v Portishead T	2-3
Middlezoy R v Bishops Lydeard	4-3
Oldland Abbotonians v Almondsbury	2-0
Chipping Sodbury T v Bristol R	2-4
AEK Boco v Paulton R	4-3
Helston Ath v Saltash U	5-4
Callington T v Bideford	2-1
Torquay U v RNAS Culdrose	4-0
AFC St Austell v Marine Academy Plymouth	1-6

FIRST QUALIFYING ROUND

Penrith v South Shields	1-2
FC United of Manchester v Wakefield Trinity	4-1
Fleetwood T Wrens v AFC Darwen	1-1
Fleetwood T Wrens won 5-4 on penalties	
Brighouse Sports v Blyth T	2-3
Hull U v Sunderland West End	1-2
Farsley Celtic Juniors v Warrington Wolves Foundation	1-2
Morecambe v Workington Reds	5-2
Blackburn Community Sports Club v Alnwick T	3-2
Wallsend Boys Club v York C	2-1
Spennymoor T v Wythenshawe Amateurs	3-3
Spennymoor T won 4-3 on penalties	
Redcar T v Ossett U	0-4
Ripon C v Merseyrail	1-4
Sutton Coldfield T v Lincoln U	1-0
Worcester C v Droitwich Spa	4-1
Lincoln Moorlands Railway v Beaumont Park	2-3
Oadby & Wigston v Rise Park	5-2
Crusaders v Cookley Sports	4-0
Tamworth v Dronfield T	1-2
Leicester C v Grimsby T	0-9
Sheffield W v Northwich Vixens	1-1
Northwich Vixens won 5-4 on penalties	
Crewe Alex v Coventry Sphinx	1-4
Knowle v Stourbridge	0-6
Redditch U v Sherwood	4-0
Netherton U v Leigh Ramblers	5-4
Northampton T v St Ives T	0-1
Bowers & Pitsea v Harlow T	0-1
Royston T v Brett Vale	8-0
Peterborough Northern Star v Southend U Community SC	10-0
Luton T v Wroxham	5-0
AFC Sudbury v Newmarket T	3-3
Newmarket T won 4-2 on penalties	
Dartford v Winchester C Flyers	7-1
Ascot U v Denham U	0-3
Moneyfields v Bournemouth	1-1
Bournemouth won 4-3 on penalties	
Lancing v Dulwich Hamlet	0-1
Watford Development v Ashford	1-9
Eastbourne T v Tilehurst Panthers	2-0
Badshot Lea v Saltdean U	1-6
Comets v Wycombe W	0-1
Worthing v Sutton U	6-0
Woking v Abingdon U	1-2
Regents Park Rangers v New London Lionesses	0-5
Dorking W v Ashford T (Middlesex)	1-7
Fulham v Woodley U	5-0
Callington T v Ilminster T	1-2
Bristol R v AEK Boco	1-1
AEK Boco won 4-3 on penalties	
Torquay U v Portishead T	0-12
Sherborne T v Oldland Abbotonians	2-1
Marine Academy Plymouth v Helston Ath	3-5
Middlezoy R v AFC Stoneham	2-2
AFC Stoneham won 3-1 on penalties	

SECOND QUALIFYING ROUND

Merseyrail v Bolton	3-2
Stockport Co v Leeds U	0-2
Ossett U v Liverpool Feds	0-5
Brighouse T v Spennymoor T	6-0
Warrington Wolves Foundation v Durham Cestria	2-3
Blyth T v Barnsley	0-5
Norton & Stockton Ancients v FC United of Manchester	2-5
Chorley (walkover) v Wallsend Boys Club	
Chester-le-Street T v South Shields	9-0
Bradford C v Sunderland West End	0-2
Morecambe v Fleetwood T Wrens	1-2
Newcastle U v Blackburn Community Sports Club	11-0
Dronfield T v Coventry Sphinx	1-2
Worcester C v Stourbridge	0-5
Sporting Khalsa v Leafield Ath	4-2
Sutton Coldfield T v Wolverhampton W	0-2
Lincoln C v Burton Alb	10-1
Oadby & Wigston v Crusaders	2-3
Beaumont Park v Boldmere St Michaels	1-2
Solihull Moors v Bedworth U	2-2
Solihull Moors won 3-2 on penalties	
Holwell Sports v Grimsby T	7-2
Redditch U v Doncaster R Belles	1-1
Redditch U won 4-1 on penalties	
Long Eaton U v Netherton U	7-1
Northwich Vixens v Wem T	1-2
Harlow T v St Ives T	5-1
Newmarket T v Norwich C	1-5
Billericay T v Cambridge U	4-1
Luton T v Cambridge C	1-0
Hashtag U v Enfield T	0-2
Stevenage v Royston T	3-3
Royston T won 5-3 on penalties	
Ipswich T v Peterborough Northern Star	10-0
AFC Wimbledon v Ashford	6-0
Actonians v Saltdean U	6-2
New London Lionesses v Worthing	1-1
Worthing won 4-3 on penalties	
Dartford v Eastbourne T	1-1
Eastbourne T won 3-2 on penalties	
Dulwich Hamlet v Leyton Orient	0-1
Fulham v Wycombe W	1-0
Maidenhead U v Denham U	1-0
Abingdon U v Chesham U	1-3
Ashford T (Middlesex) v Kent Football U	2-2
Kent Football U won 5-4 on penalties	
AEK Boco v Larkhall Ath	4-3
Portishead T v Sherborne T	2-0
Cheltenham T v Brislington	3-0
Exeter C v Swindon T	2-1
AFC Stoneham v Buckland Ath	1-6
Ilminster T v Poole T	4-1
Helston Ath v Southampton FC Women	0-11
Southampton Women's FC v Bournemouth	1-3

THIRD QUALIFYING ROUND

Fleetwood T Wrens v Liverpool Feds	0-3
FC United of Manchester v Chorley	2-1
Barnsley v Leeds U	4-1
Brighouse T v Merseyrail	3-0
Newcastle U v Sunderland West End	4-1

Chester-le-Street T v Durham Cestria	3-2
Solihull Moors v Sporting Khalsa	3-0
Holwell Sports v Lincoln C	0-2
Stourbridge v Crusaders	3-0
Wem T v Coventry Sphinx	4-3
Long Eaton U v Wolverhampton W	0-1
Redditch U v Boldmere St Michaels	1-2
Luton T v Enfield T	1-2
Harlow T v Royston T	3-3
Harlow T won 4-2 on penalties	
Billericay T v Chesham U	2-1
Norwich C v Ipswich T	1-3
Actonians v Worthing	4-0
Fulham v Maidenhead U	1-2
Kent Football U v AFC Wimbledon	2-1
Eastbourne T v Leyton Orient	1-4
Exeter C v AEK Boco	7-0
Cheltenham T v Portishead T	3-1
Bournemouth v Buckland Ath	3-1
Ilminster T v Southampton FC Women	0-4

FIRST ROUND

FC United of Manchester v Liverpool Feds	1-2
Chester-le-Street T v Brighouse T	0-3
Newcastle U v Barnsley	3-1
Wolverhampton W v Stourbridge	3-0
Lincoln C v Solihull Moors	3-1
Wem T v Boldmere St Michaels	4-3
Harlow T v Ipswich T	2-9
Kent Football U v Enfield T	1-1
Kent Football U won 4-3 on penalties.	
Billericay T v Maidenhead U	4-0
Leyton Orient v Actonians	2-1
Bournemouth v Southampton FC Women	0-5
Exeter C v Cheltenham T	1-1
Cheltenham T won 4-3 on penalties	

SECOND ROUND

Sunderland v Sheffield	5-1
Liverpool Feds v Huddersfield T	2-3*
(1-1 at the end of normal time)	
Brighouse T v Newcastle U	3-0*
(0-0 at the end of normal time)	
Middlesbrough v Hull C	3-1
Burnley v Fylde	1-0*
(0-0 at the end of normal time)	
Wolverhampton W v Nottingham F	2-2*
Wolverhampton W won 6-5 on penalties	
WBA v Lincoln C	5-2
Loughborough Foxes v Derby Co	0-6
Stoke C v Wem T (walkover)	
Crawley Wasps v Gillingham	2-3
Billericay T v Ipswich T	2-1
Hounslow v Leyton Orient	0-4
Watford v Milton Keynes D	3-1
Chichester & Selsey v Kent Football U	3-1
Portsmouth v Cheltenham T	2-0
Tie awarded to Cheltenham T after Portsmouth fielded an ineligible player	
Southampton v Plymouth Arg	3-0
Keynsham T v Yeovil U	0-1
Cardiff C v Oxford U	0-1

THIRD ROUND

Huddersfield T v Brighouse T	1-1*
Huddersfield T won 5-3 on penalties	
Middlesbrough v Wem T	4-0
Burnley v Sunderland	0-0*
Burnley won 3-1 on penalties	
Oxford U v Billericay T	3-1
WBA v Derby Co	1-4
Watford v Wolverhampton W	1-4
Cheltenham T v Gillingham	1-2*
(1-1 at the end of normal time)	
Southampton v Yeovil U	3-0
Leyton Orient v Chichester & Selsey	1-2

FOURTH ROUND

Leicester C v Liverpool	1-0
Middlesbrough v Sheffield U	0-9
Birmingham C v Coventry U	5-1
Burnley v Manchester U	0-6
Everton v Durham	2-1
Manchester C v Aston Villa	8-0
Wolverhampton W v Blackburn R	2-5
Huddersfield T v Derby Co	3-2
Reading v Tottenham H	2-3*
(2-2 at the end of normal time)	
Oxford U v Charlton Ath	1-2*
(1-1 at the end of normal time)	
Arsenal v Gillingham	10-0
Chelsea v London C Lionesses	5-0
Lewes v Southampton	1-2
Brighton & HA v Bristol C	1-0
West Ham U v Chichester & Selsey	11-0
Crystal Palace v London Bees	3-0

FIFTH ROUND

Birmingham C v Southampton	3-2
Brighton & HA v Huddersfield T	6-0
Arsenal v Crystal Palace	9-0
Blackburn R v Charlton Ath	0-1
Manchester C v West Ham U	5-1
Chelsea v Everton	3-0
Manchester U v Leicester C	2-3
Tottenham H v Sheffield U	2-1*
(1-1 at the end of normal time)	

The final stages of the competition will be started in September 2021.

UEFA WOMEN'S CHAMPIONS LEAGUE 2020–21

**After extra time.*

FIRST QUALIFYING ROUND

Sarajevo v Ramat HaSharon	4-0
Vllaznia v ALG Spor	3-3
Vllaznia won 3-2 on penalties	
Olimpia Cluj v Birkirkara	2-1
Ferencvaros v Racing Union	6-1
Okzhetpes v Lanchkhuti	1-2*
FC Minsk v Rigas FS	3-0
NSA Sofia v Kamenica Sasa	3-1
Zhytlobud-2 Kharkiv v Alashkert	9-0
Pomurje v Breznica	3-0
PAOK v Benfica	1-3
Gintra v Slovan Bratislava	4-0
Apollon Limassol v Swansea C	3-0
CSKA Moscow v Flora	2-0
St Polten v Mitrovica	2-0
Valur v HJK	3-0
Gornik Leczna v Split	4-1
Valerenga v KI Klaksvik	7-0
Spartak Subotica v Anenii Noi	4-0
Anderlecht v Linfield	8-0
Glasgow C v Peamount U	0-0*
Glasgow C won 6-5 on penalties	

SECOND QUALIFYING ROUND

NSA Sofia v Spartak Subotica	0-7
Pomurje v Ferencvaros	4-1
Valur v Glasgow C	1-1*
Glasgow C won 4-3 on penalties	
Gornik Leczna v Apollon Limassol	2-1
Anderlecht v Benfica	1-2
Gintra v Valerenga	0-7
Sarajevo v Zhytlobud-2 Kharkiv	0-2
Olimpia Cluj v Lanchkhuti	0-1
Vllaznia v FC Minsk	0-2
St Polten v CSKA Moscow	1-0

ROUND OF 32 – 1ST LEG

Lanchkhuti v Rosengaard	0-7
FC Minsk v LSK	0-2
Zhytlobud-2 Kharkiv v BIIK-Kazygurt	2-1
Pomurje v Fortuna Hjorring	0-3
Spartak Subotica v VfL Wolfsburg	0-5
Juventus v Lyon	2-3
Sparta Prague v Glasgow C	2-1
Benfica v Chelsea	0-5
Gothenburg v Manchester C	1-2
PSV Eindhoven v Barcelona	1-4
St Polten v Zurich	2-0

Servette Chenois v Atletico Madrid	2-4
Fiorentina v Slavia Prague	2-2
Gornik Leczna v Paris Saint-Germain	0-2
Ajax v Bayern Munich	1-3
Valerenga v Brondby	

Match cancelled due to quaratine restrictions in Norway. The tie was played as a one-legged match.

ROUND OF 32 – 2ND LEG

		(agg)
Lyon v Juventus	3-0	6-2
Atletico Madrid v Servette Chenois	5-0	9-2
BIIK-Kazygurt v Zhytlobud-2 Kharkiv	1-0	2-2
BIIK-Kazygurt won on away goals		
Slavia Prague v Fiorentina	0-1	2-3
Paris Saint-Germain v Gornik Leczna	6-1	8-1
Manchester C v Gothenburg	3-0	5-1
Barcelona v PSV Eindhoven	4-1	8-2
Bayern Munich v Ajax	3-0	6-1
VfL Wolfsburg v Spartak Subotica	2-0	7-0
Rosengaard v Lanchkhuti	10-0	17-0
LSK v FC Minsk	0-1	2-1
Fortuna Hjorring v Pomurje	3-2	6-2
Chelsea v Benfica	3-0	8-0
Glasgow C v Sparta Prague	0-1	1-3
Zurich v St Polten	0-1	0-3
Brondby v Valerenga		1-1*

The tie was played as a one-legged match after the first leg was cancelled due to quaratine restrictions in Norway. Brondby won 5-4 on penalties.

ROUND OF 16 – FIRST LEG

Barcelona v Fortuna Hjorring	4-0
Manchester C v Fiorentina	3-0
Rosengaard v St Polten	2-2
VfL Wolfsburg v LSK	2-0
Chelsea v Atletico Madrid	2-0
BIIK-Kazygurt v Bayern Munich	1-6
Lyon v Brondby	2-0
Paris Saint-Germain v Sparta Prague	5-0

ROUND OF 16 – 2ND LEG

		(agg)
Atletico Madrid v Chelsea	1-1	1-3
Brondby v Lyon	1-3	1-5
LSK v VfL Wolfsburg	0-2	0-4
Fortuna Hjorring v Barcelona	0-5	0-9
Bayern Munich v BIIK-Kazygurt	3-0	9-1
St Polten v Rosengaard	0-2	2-4
Fiorentina v Manchester C	0-5	0-8
Sparta Prague v Paris Saint-Germain	3-0†	3-5

†The second leg could not be played due to the quaratine of the Paris Saint-Germain players. Sparta Prague awarded a 3-0 win.

QUARTER-FINALS – 1ST LEG

Barcelona v Manchester C	3-0
Chelsea v VfL Wolfsburg	2-1
Paris Saint-Germain v Lyon	0-1
Bayern Munich v Rosengaard	3-0

QUARTER-FINALS – 2ND LEG

		(agg)
VfL Wolfsburg v Chelsea	0-3	1-5
Manchester C v Barcelona	2-1	2-4
Lyon v Paris Saint-Germain	1-2	2-2
Paris Saint-Germain won on away goals		
Rosengaard v Bayern Munich	0-1	0-4

SEMI-FINALS – 1ST LEG

Paris Saint-Germain v Barcelona	1-1
Bayern Munich v Chelsea	2-1

SEMI-FINALS – 2ND LEG

		(agg)
Barcelona v Paris Saint-Germain	2-1	3-2
Chelsea v Bayern Munich	4-1	5-3

UEFA WOMEN'S CHAMPIONS LEAGUE FINAL 2020–21

Gothenburg, Sunday 16 May 2021

Barcelona (4) 4 *(Leupolz 1 (og), Putellas 14 (pen), Bonmati 21, Hansen 36)*

Chelsea (0) 0

Barcelona: Panos; Torrejon (Crnogorcevic 82), Guijarro, Leon, Ouahabi (Serrano 82), Bonmati, Hamraoui, Putellas (Losada 71), Hansen (Caldentey 62), Hermoso (Oshoala 71), Martens.

Chelsea: Berger; Carter, Bright, Eriksson, Charles, Leupolz (Reiten 46), Ingle, Ji So-yun (Cuthbert 73), Kirby, Harder, Kerr (England 73).

Referee: Riem Hussein (Germany).

Aitana Bonmati (centre) scores her side's third goal of the game during the UEFA Women's Champions League Final in Gothenburg on 16 May. Barcelona defeated Chelsea 4-0. (Adam Ihse/PA Wire/PA Images)

UEFA WOMEN'S EURO 2022

QUALIFYING

GROUP A

Estonia v Netherlands	0-7
Slovenia v Russia	0-1
Kosovo v Turkey	2-0
Slovenia v Kosovo	5-0
Russia v Estonia	4-0
Netherlands v Turkey	3-0
Turkey v Estonia	0-0
Slovenia v Netherlands	2-4
Turkey v Slovenia	1-6
Estonia v Kosovo1-2	
Netherlands v Russia	2-0
Turkey v Netherlands	0-8
Netherlands v Slovenia	4-1
Kosovo v Russia	0-5
Kosovo v Slovenia	0-3
Russia v Netherlands	0-1
Kosovo v Estonia	2-0
Slovenia v Turkey	3-1
Estonia v Russia	0-3
Russia v Slovenia	1-0
Turkey v Kosovo	0-0
Netherlands v Estonia	7-0
Russia v Turkey	4-2
Kosovo v Netherlands	0-6
Estonia v Turkey	0-4
Russia v Kosovo	3-0
Turkey v Russia	1-2
Slovenia v Estonia	2-0
Netherlands v Kosovo	6-0
Estonia v Slovenia	0-9

Group A Table	P	W	D	L	F	A	GD	Pts
Netherlands	10	10	0	0	48	3	45	30
Russia	10	8	0	2	23	6	17	24
Slovenia	10	6	0	4	31	12	19	18
Kosovo	10	3	1	6	6	29	–23	10
Turkey	10	1	2	7	9	28	–19	5
Estonia	10	0	1	9	1	40	–39	1

GROUP B

Israel v Italy	2-3
Denmark v Malta	8-0
Bosnia-Herzegovina v Georgia	7-1
Georgia v Italy	0-1
Bosnia-Herzegovina v Malta	2-0
Israel v Denmark	0-3
Denmark v Bosnia-Herzegovina	2-0
Malta v Italy	0-2
Italy v Bosnia-Herzegovina	2-0
Georgia v Denmark	0-2
Malta v Israel	1-1
Italy v Georgia	6-0
Italy v Malta	5-0
Israel v Bosnia-Herzegovina	1-3
Denmark v Georgia	14-0
Bosnia-Herzegovina v Israel	1-0
Malta v Georgia	2-1
Israel v Georgia	4-0
Malta v Bosnia-Herzegovina	2-3
Bosnia-Herzegovina v Denmark	0-4
Bosnia-Herzegovina v Italy	0-5
Malta v Denmark	0-8
Denmark v Israel	4-0
Georgia v Israel	1-2
Italy v Denmark	1-3
Georgia v Malta	0-4
Georgia v Bosnia-Herzegovina	0-3
Israel v Malta	0-2
Denmark v Italy	0-0
Italy v Israel	12-0

Group B Table	P	W	D	L	F	A	GD	Pts
Denmark	10	9	1	0	48	1	47	28
Italy	10	8	1	1	37	5	32	25
Bosnia-Herzegovina	10	6	0	4	19	17	2	18
Malta	10	3	1	6	11	30	–19	10
Israel	10	2	1	7	10	30	–20	7
Georgia	10	0	0	10	3	45	–42	0

GROUP C

Faroe Islands v Wales	0-6
Northern Ireland v Norway	0-6
Belarus v Faroe Islands	6-0
Wales v Northern Ireland	2-2
Belarus v Norway	1-7
Faroe Islands v Norway	0-13
Belarus v Wales	0-1
Norway v Northern Ireland	6-0
Northern Ireland v Wales	0-0
Faroe Islands v Northern Ireland	0-6
Norway v Wales	1-0
Faroe Islands v Belarus	0-2
Wales v Faroe Islands	4-0
Wales v Norway	0-1
Belarus v Northern Ireland	0-1
Norway v Faroe Islands	Cancelled
Northern Ireland v Belarus	3-2
Northern Ireland v Faroe Islands	5-1
Wales v Belarus	3-0
Norway v Belarus	Cancelled

Group C Table	P	W	D	L	F	A	GD	Pts
Norway	6	6	0	0	34	1	33	18
Northern Ireland	8	4	2	2	17	17	0	14
Wales	8	4	2	2	16	4	12	14
Belarus	7	2	0	5	11	15	–4	6
Faroe Islands	7	0	0	7	1	42	–41	0

GROUP D

Moldova v Czech Republic	0-7
Spain v Azerbaijan	4-0
Czech Republic v Spain	1-5
Azerbaijan v Czech Republic	0-4
Moldova v Azerbaijan	3-1
Poland v Spain	0-0
Poland v Moldova	5-0
Azerbaijan v Poland	0-5
Czech Republic v Poland	0-0
Moldova v Spain	0-9
Poland v Czech Republic	0-2
Poland v Azerbaijan	3-0
Spain v Czech Republic	4-0
Moldova v Poland	0-3
Czech Republic v Azerbaijan	3-0
Spain v Moldova	10-0
Czech Republic v Moldova	7-0
Azerbaijan v Spain	0-13
Azerbaijan v Moldova	1-0
Spain v Poland	3-0

Group D Table	P	W	D	L	F	A	GD	Pts
Spain	8	7	1	0	48	1	47	22
Czech Republic	8	5	1	2	24	9	15	16
Poland	8	4	2	2	16	5	11	14
Moldova	8	1	0	7	3	43	–40	3
Azerbaijan	8	1	0	7	2	35	–33	3

GROUP E

Scotland v Cyprus	8-0
Albania v Finland	0-3
Albania v Portugal	0-1
Finland v Albania	8-1
Finland v Cyprus	4-0
Albania v Scotland	0-5
Portugal v Finland	1-1
Cyprus v Albania	0-2

Cyprus v Portugal 0-3
Scotland v Albania 3-0
Finland v Scotland 1-0
Portugal v Cyprus 1-0
Albania v Cyprus 4-0
Portugal v Scotland 1-0
Portugal v Albania 1-0
Scotland v Finland 0-1
Cyprus v Scotland 0-10
Finland v Portugal 1-0
Scotland v Portugal 0-2
Cyprus v Finland 0-5

Group E Table	*P*	*W*	*D*	*L*	*F*	*A*	*GD*	*Pts*
Finland	8	7	1	0	24	2	22	22
Portugal	8	6	1	1	10	2	8	19
Scotland	8	4	0	4	26	5	21	12
Albania	8	2	0	6	7	21	–14	6
Cyprus	8	0	0	8	0	37	–37	0

GROUP F
Iceland v Hungary 4-1
Iceland v Slovakia 1-0
Latvia v Sweden 1-4
Latvia v Slovakia 1-2
Hungary v Sweden 0-5
Sweden v Slovakia 7-0
Latvia v Iceland 0-6
Slovakia v Hungary 0-0
Hungary v Latvia 4-0
Sweden v Hungary 8-0
Iceland v Latvia 9-0
Latvia v Hungary 0-5
Iceland v Sweden 1-1
Sweden v Latvia 7-0
Hungary v Slovakia 1-2
Slovakia v Latvia 2-0
Sweden v Iceland 2-0
Slovakia v Iceland 1-3
Hungary v Iceland 0-1
Slovakia v Sweden 0-6

Group F Table	*P*	*W*	*D*	*L*	*F*	*A*	*GD*	*Pts*
Sweden	8	7	1	0	40	2	38	22
Iceland	8	6	1	1	25	5	20	19
Slovakia	8	3	1	4	7	19	–12	10
Hungary	8	2	1	5	11	20	–9	7
Latvia	8	0	0	8	2	39	–37	0

GROUP G
Kazakhstan v Serbia 0-3
Austria v North Macedonia 3-0
North Macedonia v Kazakhstan 4-1
North Macedonia v Serbia 0-6
Kazakhstan v France 0-3
Serbia v Austria 0-1
North Macedonia v Austria 0-3
France v Serbia 6-0
Austria v Kazakhstan 9-0
Serbia v North Macedonia 8-1
Serbia v France 0-2
Kazakhstan v Austria 0-5
North Macedonia v France 0-7
France v North Macedonia 11-0
Serbia v Kazakhstan 4-1
Austria v France 0-0
Kazakhstan v North Macedonia 0-3
France v Austria 3-0
Austria v Serbia 1-0
France v Kazakhstan 12-0

Group G Table	*P*	*W*	*D*	*L*	*F*	*A*	*GD*	*Pts*
France	8	7	1	0	44	0	44	22
Austria	8	6	1	1	22	3	19	19
Serbia	8	4	0	4	21	12	9	12
North Macedonia	8	2	0	6	8	39	–31	6
Kazakhstan	8	0	0	8	2	43	–41	0

GROUP H
Lithuania v Croatia 1-2
Switzerland v Lithuania 4-0
Belgium v Croatia 6-1
Lithuania v Switzerland 0-3
Romania v Belgium 0-1
Switzerland v Croatia 2-0
Romania v Lithuania 3-0
Croatia v Belgium 1-4
Switzerland v Romania 6-0
Belgium v Lithuania 6-0
Belgium v Romania 6-1
Croatia v Switzerland 1-1
Romania v Croatia 4-1
Switzerland v Belgium 2-1
Lithuania v Romania 0-4
Romania v Switzerland 0-2
Lithuania v Belgium 0-9
Croatia v Lithuania 1-0
Belgium v Switzerland 4-0
Croatia v Romania 0-1

Group H Table	*P*	*W*	*D*	*L*	*F*	*A*	*GD*	*Pts*
Belgium	8	7	0	1	37	5	32	21
Switzerland	8	6	1	1	20	6	14	19
Romania	8	4	0	4	13	16	–3	12
Croatia	8	2	1	5	7	19	–12	7
Lithuania	8	0	0	8	1	32	–31	0

GROUP I
Germany v Montenegro 10-0
Ukraine v Germany 0-8
Republic of Ireland v Montenegro 2-0
Germany v Ukraine 8-0
Greece v Germany 0-5
Republic of Ireland v Ukraine 3-2
Montenegro v Greece 0-4
Greece v Republic of Ireland 1-1
Republic of Ireland v Greece 1-0
Montenegro v Republic of Ireland 0-3
Montenegro v Ukraine 1-3
Germany v Republic of Ireland 3-0
Montenegro v Germany 0-3
Ukraine v Greece 4-0
Greece v Montenegro 1-0
Ukraine v Republic of Ireland 1-0
Greece v Ukraine 0-4
Germany v Greece 6-0
Ukraine v Montenegro 2-1
Republic of Ireland v Germany 1-3

Group I Table	*P*	*W*	*D*	*L*	*F*	*A*	*GD*	*Pts*
Germany	8	8	0	0	46	1	45	24
Ukraine	8	5	0	3	16	21	–5	15
Republic of Ireland	8	4	1	3	11	10	1	13
Greece	8	2	1	5	6	21	–15	7
Montenegro	8	0	0	8	2	28	–26	0

PLAY-OFFS – FIRST LEG
Ukraine v Northern Ireland 1-2
Portugal v Russia 0-1
Czech Republic v Switzerland 1-1

PLAY-OFFS – SECOND LEG
Northern Ireland v Ukraine 2-0 4-1
Russia v Portugal 0-0 1-0
Switzerland v Czech Republic 1-1 1-1
aet; Switzerland won 3-2 on penalties

The final competition was scheduled to be played in England between 7 July and 1 August 2021 but due to the COVID-19 pandemic has been delayed until 2022. It is scheduled to take place between 6 and 31 July 2022.

ENGLAND WOMEN'S INTERNATIONALS 2020–21

FRIENDLIES

Wiesbaden, Tuesday 27 October 2020

Germany

England

Cancelled due to a positive COVID-19 test in England Women's backroom staff.

Sheffield, Tuesday 1 December 2020

England

Norway

Cancelled due to COVID-19 travel restrictions in Norway.

Burton, Tuesday 23 February 2021

England (3) 6 *(White 18, 23, 49, Bronze 29, Daly 67, Toone 75 (pen))*

Northern Ireland (0) 0

England: Roebuck (McIver 61); Bronze, Houghton, Williamson (Wubben-Moy 75), Greenwood, Scott, Stanway, Daly (Salmon 84), Nobbs (Toone 46), Hemp (Kelly 61), White (England 76).
Northern Ireland: Flaherty; Magee, Nelson, Robson (Kelly 84), Holloway (Finnegan 83), Wade (McDaniel 73), McCarron (McKenna 57), Caldwell (Burrows 84), Callaghan (Watling 58), Furness, Magill.
Referee: Lorraine Watson.

Caen, Friday 9 April 2021

France (1) 3 *(Baltimore 32, Asseyi 63 (pen), Katoto 82)*

England (0) 1 *(Kirby 79 (pen))*

France: Peyraud-Magnin; Torrent (Perisset 85), Tounkara, De Almeida, Morroni, Diani (Dali 85), Geyoro, Palis (Jaurena 60), Baltimore, Katoto, Gauvin (Asseyi 59).
England: Roebuck; Daly, Bright, Williamson (Wubben-Moy 64), Greenwood (Charles 46), Scott (Nobbs 73), Walsh, Parris (Kelly 46), Kirby, Mead (Hemp 64), White (England 74).
Referee: Sara Persson.

Burton, Tuesday 13 April 2021

England (0) 0

Canada (1) 2 *(Viens 3, Prince 86)*

England: Telford (Bardsley 46); Daly (Bronze 64), Bright, Williamson, Stokes (Greenwood 32), Parris (White 80), Nobbs, Stanway, Hemp, England (Kelly 64), Kirby (Toone 46).
Canada: Labbe; Lawrence, Gilles, Zadorsky, Chapman, Scott (Riviere 66), Quinn (Schmidt 82), Beckie, Fleming, Rose (Prince 59), Viens (Huitema 59).
Referee: Cheryl Foster.

From the penalty spot, Ella Toone scores England's last goal in their 6-0 friendly victory over Northern Ireland at St George's Park in February. (Getty Images/Catherine Ivhill – The FA)

ENGLAND WOMEN'S INTERNATIONAL MATCHES 1972–2021

Note: In the results that follow, WC = World Cup; EC = European (UEFA) Championships; M = Mundialito; CC = Cyprus Cup; AC = Algarve Cup. * = After extra time. Games were organised by the Women's Football Association from 1971 to 1992 and the Football Association from 1993 to date. **Bold type** indicates matches played in season 2020–21.

v ARGENTINA

wc2007	17 Sept	Chengdu	6-1
wc2019	14 June	Le Havre	1-0

v AUSTRALIA

2003	3 Sept	Burnley	1-0
cc2015	6 Mar	Nicosia	3-0
2015	27 Oct	Yongchuan	1-0
2018	9 Oct	Fulham	1-1

v AUSTRIA

wc2005	1 Sept	Amstetten	4-1
wc2006	20 Apr	Gillingham	4-0
wc2010	25 Mar	Shepherd's Bush	3-0
wc2010	21 Aug	Krems	4-0
2017	10 Apr	Milton Keynes	3-0
2018	8 Nov	Vienna	3-0

v BELARUS

EC2007	27 Oct	Walsall	4-0
EC2008	8 May	Minsk	6-1
wc2013	21 Sept	Bournemouth	6-0
wc2014	14 June	Minsk	3-0

v BELGIUM

1978	31 Oct	Southampton	3-0
1980	1 May	Ostende	1-2
M1984	20 Aug	Jesolo	1-1
M1984	25 Aug	Caorle	2-1
1989	14 May	Epinal	2-0
EC1990	17 Mar	Ypres	3-0
EC1990	7 Apr	Sheffield	1-0
EC1993	6 Nov	Koksijde	3-0
EC1994	13 Mar	Nottingham	6-0
EC2016	8 Apr	Rotherham	1-1
EC2016	20 Sept	Leuven	2-0
2019	29 Aug	Leuven	3-3

v BOSNIA-HERZEGOVINA

EC2015	29 Nov	Bristol	1-0
EC2016	12 Apr	Zenica	1-0
wc2017	24 Nov	Walsall	4-0
wc2018	10 Apr	Zenica	2-0

v BRAZIL

2018	6 Oct	Nottingham	1-0
2019	27 Feb	Philadelphia	2-1
2019	5 Oct	Middlesbrough	1-2

v CAMEROON

wc2019	23 June	Valenciennes	3-0

v CANADA

wc1995	6 June	Helsingborg	3-2
2003	19 May	Montreal	0-4
2003	22 May	Ottawa	0-4
cc2009	12 Mar	Nicosia	3-1
cc2010	27 Feb	Nicosia	0-1
cc2011	7 Mar	Nicosia	0-2
cc2013	13 Mar	Nicosia	1-0
2013	7 Apr	Rotherham	1-0
cc2014	10 Mar	Nicosia	2-0
cc2015	11 Mar	Larnaca	1-0
2015	29 May	Hamilton	0-1
wc2015	27 June	Vancouver	2-1
2019	5 Apr	Manchester	0-1
2021	**13 Apr**	**Stoke**	**0-2**

v CHINA PR

AC2005	15 Mar	Guia	0-0*
2007	26 Jan	Guangzhou	0-2
2015	9 Apr	Manchester	2-1
2015	23 Oct	Yongchuan	1-2

v COLOMBIA

wc2015	17 June	Montreal	2-1

v CROATIA

EC1995	19 Nov	Charlton	5-0
EC1996	18 Apr	Osijek	2-0
EC2012	31 Mar	Vrbovec	6-0
EC2012	19 Sept	Walsall	3-0

v CZECH REPUBLIC

2005	26 May	Walsall	4-1
EC2008	20 Mar	Doncaster	0-0
EC2008	28 Sept	Prague	5-1
2019	12 Nov	Ceske Budejovice	3-2

v DENMARK

1979	19 May	Hvidovre	1-3
1979	13 Sept	Hull	2-2
1981	9 Sept	Tokyo	0-1
EC1984	8 Apr	Crewe	2-1
EC1984	28 Apr	Hjorring	1-0
M1985	19 Aug	Caorle	0-1
EC1987	8 Nov	Blackburn	2-1
EC1988	8 May	Herning	0-2
1991	28 June	Nordby	0-0
1991	30 June	Nordby	3-3
1999	22 Aug	Odense	1-0
2001	23 Aug	Northampton	0-3
2004	19 Feb	Portsmouth	2-0
EC2005	8 June	Blackburn	1-2
2009	22 July	Swindon	1-0
2017	1 July	Copenhagen	2-1
2019	25 May	Walsall	2-0

v ESTONIA

2015	21 Sept	Tallinn	8-0
EC2016	15 Sept	Nottingham	5-0

v FINLAND

1979	19 July	Sorrento	3-1
EC1987	25 Oct	Kirkkonummi	2-1
EC1988	4 Sept	Millwall	1-1
EC1989	1 Oct	Brentford	0-0
EC1990	29 Sept	Tampere	0-0
2000	28 Sept	Leyton	2-1
EC2005	5 June	Manchester	3-2
2009	9 Feb	Larnaca	2-2
2009	11 Feb	Larnaca	4-1
EC2009	3 Sept	Turku	3-2
cc2012	28 Feb	Nicosia	3-1
cc2014	7 Mar	Larnaca	3-0
cc2015	4 Mar	Larnaca	3-1

v FRANCE

1973	22 Apr	Brion	3-0
1974	7 Nov	Wimbledon	2-0
1977	26 Feb	Longjumeau	0-0
M1988	22 July	Riva del Garda	1-1
1998	15 Feb	Alencon	2-3
1999	15 Sept	Yeovil	0-1
2000	16 Aug	Marseilles	0-1
wc2002	17 Oct	Crystal Palace	0-1
wc2002	16 Nov	St Etienne	0-1
wc2006	26 Mar	Blackburn	0-0
wc2006	30 Sept	Rennes	1-1
cc2009	7 Mar	Paralimni	2-2
wc2011	9 July	Leverkusen	1-1*
cc2012	4 Mar	Paralimni	0-3
2012	20 Oct	Paris	2-2
EC2013	18 July	Linkoping	0-3
cc2014	12 Mar	Nicosia	0-2
wc2015	9 June	Moncton	0-1
2016	9 Mar	Boca Raton	0-0
2016	21 Oct	Doncaster	0-0
2017	1 Mar	Pennsylvania	1-2
2017	30 July	Deventer	1-0
2017	20 Oct	Valenciennes	0-1
2018	1 Mar	Columbus	4-1
2021	**9 Apr**	**Caen**	**1-3**

v GERMANY

EC1990	25 Nov	High Wycombe	1-4
EC1990	16 Dec	Bochum	0-2
EC1994	11 Dec	Watford	1-4
EC1995	23 Feb	Bochum	1-2
wc1995	13 June	Vasteras	0-3
1997	27 Feb	Preston	4-6
wc1997	25 Sept	Dessau	0-3
wc1998	8 Mar	Millwall	0-1
EC2001	30 June	Jena	0-3
wc2001	27 Sept	Kassel	1-3
wc2002	19 May	Crystal Palace	0-1
2003	11 Sept	Darmstadt	0-4
2006	25 Oct	Aalen	1-5
2007	30 Jan	Guangzhou	0-0
wc2007	14 Sept	Shanghai	0-0
2008	17 July	Unterhaching	0-3
EC2009	10 Sept	Helsinki	2-6
2014	23 Nov	Wembley	0-3
wc2015	4 July	Vancouver	1-0*
2015	26 Nov	Duisburg	0-0
2016	6 Mar	Nashville	1-2
2017	7 Mar	Washington	0-1
2018	4 Mar	New Jersey	2-2
2019	9 Nov	Wembley	1-2

v HUNGARY

wc2005	27 Oct	Tapolca	13-0
wc2006	11 May	Southampton	2-0

v ICELAND

EC1992	17 May	Yeovil	4-0
EC1992	19 July	Kopavogur	2-1
EC1994	8 Oct	Reykjavik	2-1
EC1994	30 Oct	Brighton	2-1
wc2002	16 Sept	Reykjavik	2-2
wc2002	22 Sept	Birmingham	1-0
2004	14 May	Peterborough	1-0
2006	9 Mar	Norwich	1-0
2007	17 May	Southend	4-0
2009	16 July	Colchester	0-2

v ITALY

1976	2 June	Rome	0-2
1976	4 June	Cesena	1-2
1977	15 Nov	Wimbledon	1-0
1979	25 July	Naples	1-3
1982	11 June	Pescara	0-2
M1984	24 Aug	Jesolo	1-1
M1985	20 Aug	Caorle	1-1
M1985	25 Aug	Caorle	3-2
EC1987	13 June	Drammen	1-2
M1988	30 July	Arco di Trento	2-1
1989	1 Nov	High Wycombe	1-1
1990	18 Aug	Wembley	1-4
EC1992	17 Oct	Solofra	2-3
EC1992	7 Nov	Rotherham	0-3
1995	25 Jan	Florence	1-1
EC1995	1 Nov	Sunderland	1-1
EC1996	16 Mar	Cosenza	1-2
1997	23 Apr	Turin	0-2
1998	21 Apr	West Bromwich	1-2
1999	26 May	Bologna	1-4
2003	25 Feb	Viareggio	0-1
2005	17 Feb	Milton Keynes	4-1
EC2009	25 Aug	Lahti	1-2
cc2010	3 Mar	Nicosia	3-2
cc2011	2 Mar	Larnaca	2-0
cc2012	6 Mar	Paralimni	1-3
cc2013	6 Mar	Nicosia	4-2
EC2014	5 Mar	Larnaca	2-0
2017	7 Apr	Port Vale	1-1

v JAPAN

1981	6 Sept	Kobe	4-0
wc2007	11 Sept	Shanghai	2-2
wc2011	5 July	Augsburg	2-0
2013	26 June	Burton	1-1
wc2015	1 July	Edmonton	1-2
2019	5 Mar	Tampa	3-0
wc2019	19 June	Nice	2-0
2020	8 Mar	New Jersey	1-0

v KAZAKHSTAN

wc2017	28 Nov	Colchester	5-0
wc2018	4 Sept	Pavlodar	6-0

v KOREA REPUBLIC

2010	19 Oct	Suwon	0-0
cc2011	9 Mar	Larnaca	2-0

v MALTA

wc2009	25 Oct	Blackpool	8-0
wc2010	20 May	Ta'Qali	6-0

v MEXICO

AC2005	13 Mar	Lagos	5-0
wc2011	27 June	Wolfsburg	1-1
wc2015	13 June	Moncton	2-1

v MONTENEGRO

wc2014	5 Apr	Brighton	9-0
wc2014	17 Sept	Petrovac	10-0

v NETHERLANDS

1973	9 Nov	Reading	1-0
1974	31 May	Groningen	0-3
1976	2 May	Blackpool	2-0
1978	30 Sept	Vlissingen	1-3
1989	13 May	Epinal	0-0
wc1997	30 Oct	West Ham	1-0
wc1998	23 May	Waalwijk	1-2
wc2001	4 Nov	Grimsby	0-0
wc2002	23 Mar	Den Haag	4-1
2004	18 Sept	Heerhugowaard	2-1
2004	22 Sept	Tuitjenhoorn	1-0
wc2005	17 Nov	Zwolle	1-0
wc2006	31 Aug	Charlton	4-0
2007	14 Mar	Swindon	0-1

EC2009	6 Sept	Tampere	2-1*
EC2011	27 Oct	Zwolle	0-0
EC2012	17 June	Salford	1-0
CC2015	9 Mar	Nicosia	1-1
2016	29 Nov	Tilburg	1-0
2017	3 Aug	Enschede	0-3

v NEW ZEALAND

2010	21 Oct	Suwon	0-0
WC2011	1 July	Dresden	2-1
CC2013	11 Mar	Larnaca	3-1
2019	1 June	Brighton	0-1

v NIGERIA

WC1995	10 June	Karlstad	3-2
2002	23 July	Norwich	0-1
2004	22 Apr	Reading	0-3

v NORTHERN IRELAND

1973	7 Sept	Bath	5-1
EC1982	19 Sept	Crewe	7-1
EC1983	14 May	Belfast	4-0
EC1985	25 May	Antrim	8-1
EC1986	16 Mar	Blackburn	10-0
1987	11 Apr	Leeds	6-0
AC2005	9 Mar	Paderne	4-0
EC2007	13 May	Gillingham	4-0
EC2008	6 Mar	Lurgan	2-0
2021	**23 Feb**	**Burton**	**6-0**

v NORWAY

1981	25 Oct	Cambridge	0-3
EC1988	21 Aug	Klep-pe	0-2
EC1988	18 Sept	Blackburn	1-3
EC1990	27 May	Klep-pe	0-2
EC1990	2 Sept	Old Trafford	0-0
WC1995	8 June	Karlstad	3-2
1997	8 June	Lillestrom	0-4
WC1998	14 May	Oldham	1-2
WC1998	15 Aug	Lillestrom	0-2
EC2000	7 Mar	Norwich	0-3
EC2000	4 June	Moss	0-8
AC2002	1 Mar	Albufeira	1-3
2005	6 May	Barnsley	1-0
2008	14 Feb	Larnaca	2-1
2009	23 Apr	Shrewsbury	3-0
2014	17 Jan	La Manga	1-1
WC2015	22 June	Ottawa	2-1
2017	22 Jan	La Manga	0-1
WC2019	27 June	Le Havre	3-0
2019	3 Sept	Bergen	1-2

v PORTUGAL

EC1996	11 Feb	Benavente	5-0
EC1996	19 May	Brentford	3-0
EC2000	20 Feb	Barnsley	2-0
EC2000	22 Apr	Sacavem	2-2
WC2001	24 Nov	Gafanha da Nazare	1-1
WC2002	24 Feb	Portsmouth	3-0
AC2005	11 Mar	Faro	4-0
2017	27 July	Tilburg	2-1
2019	8 Oct	Setubal	1-0

v REPUBLIC OF IRELAND

1978	2 May	Exeter	6-1
1981	2 May	Dublin	5-0
EC1982	7 Nov	Dublin	1-0
EC1983	11 Sept	Reading	6-0
EC1985	22 Sept	Cork	6-0
EC1986	27 Apr	Reading	4-0
1987	29 Mar	Dublin	1-0

v ROMANIA

EC1998	12 Sept	Campina	4-1
EC1998	11 Oct	High Wycombe	2-1

v RUSSIA

EC2001	24 June	Jena	1-1
2003	21 Oct	Moscow	2-2
2004	19 Aug	Bristol	1-2
2007	8 Mar	Milton Keynes	6-0
EC2009	28 Aug	Helsinki	3-2
EC2013	15 July	Linkoping	1-1
WC2017	19 Sept	Tranmere	6-0
WC2018	8 June	Moscow	3-1

v SCOTLAND

1972	18 Nov	Greenock	3-2
1973	23 June	Nuneaton	8-0
1976	23 May	Enfield	5-1
1977	29 May	Dundee	1-2
EC1982	3 Oct	Dumbarton	4-0
EC1983	22 May	Leeds	2-0
EC1985	17 Mar	Preston	4-0
EC1986	12 Oct	Kirkcaldy	3-1
1989	30 Apr	Kirkcaldy	3-0
1990	6 May	Paisley	4-0
1990	12 May	Wembley	4-0
1991	20 Apr	High Wycombe	5-0
EC1992	17 Apr	Walsall	1-0
EC1992	23 Aug	Perth	2-0
1997	9 Mar	Sheffield	6-0
1997	23 Aug	Livingston	4-0
2001	27 May	Bolton	1-0
AC2002	7 Mar	Quarteira	4-1
2003	13 Nov	Preston	5-0
2005	21 Apr	Tranmere	2-1
2007	11 Mar	High Wycombe	1-0
CC2009	10 Mar	Larnaca	3-0
CC2011	4 Mar	Nicosia	0-2
CC2013	8 Mar	Larnaca	4-4
EC2017	19 July	Utrecht	6-0
WC2019	9 June	Nice	2-1

v SERBIA

EC2011	17 Sept	Belgrade	2-2
EC2011	23 Nov	Doncaster	2-0
EC2016	4 June	Wycombe	7-0
EC2016	7 June	Stara Pazova	7-0

v SLOVENIA

EC1993	25 Sept	Ljubljana	10-0
EC1994	17 Apr	Brentford	10-0
EC2011	22 Sept	Swindon	4-0
EC2012	21 June	Velenje	4-0

v SOUTH AFRICA

CC2009	5 Mar	Larnaca	6-0
CC2010	24 Feb	Larnaca	1-0

v SPAIN

EC1993	19 Dec	Osuna	0-0
EC1994	20 Feb	Bradford	0-0
EC1996	8 Sept	Montilla	1-2
EC1996	29 Sept	Tranmere	1-1
2001	22 Mar	Luton	4-2
EC2007	25 Nov	Shrewsbury	1-0
EC2008	2 Oct	Zamora	2-2
WC2010	1 Apr	Millwall	1-0
WC2010	19 June	Aranda de Duero	2-2
EC2013	12 July	Linkoping	2-3
2016	25 Oct	Guadalajara	2-1
EC2017	23 July	Breda	2-0
2019	9 Apr	Swindon	2-1
2020	11 Mar	Frisco (TX)	0-1

v SWEDEN

1975	15 June	Gothenburg	0-2
1975	7 Sept	Wimbledon	1-3
1979	27 July	Scafati	0-0*
1980	17 Sept	Leicester	1-1
1982	26 May	Kinna	1-1
1983	30 Oct	Charlton	2-2
EC1984	12 May	Gothenburg	0-1
EC1984	27 May	Luton	1-0
EC1987	11 June	Moss	2-3*
1989	23 May	Wembley	0-2
1995	13 May	Halmstad	0-4
1998	26 July	Dagenham	0-1
EC2001	27 June	Jena	0-4
2002	25 Jan	La Manga	0-5
AC2002	5 Mar	Lagos	3-6
EC2005	11 June	Blackburn	0-1
2006	7 Feb	Larnaca	0-0
2006	9 Feb	Achna	1-1
2008	12 Feb	Larnaca	0-2
EC2009	31 Aug	Turku	1-1
2011	17 May	Oxford	2-0
2013	4 July	Ljungskile	1-4
2014	3 Aug	Hartlepool	4-0
2017	24 Jan	La Manga	0-0
2018	11 Nov	Rotherham	0-2
wc2019	6 July	Nice	1-2

v SWITZERLAND

1975	19 Apr	Basel	3-1
1977	28 Apr	Hull	9-1
1979	23 July	Sorrento	2-0
EC1999	16 Oct	Zofingen	3-0
EC2000	13 May	Bristol	1-0
CC2010	1 Mar	Nicosia	2-2
wc2010	12 Sept	Shrewsbury	2-0
wc2010	16 Sept	Wohlen	3-2
CC2012	1 Mar	Larnaca	1-0
2017	10 June	Biel	4-0

v TURKEY

wc2009	26 Nov	Izmir	3-0
wc2010	29 July	Walsall	3-0
wc2013	26 Sept	Portsmouth	8-0
wc2013	31 Oct	Adana	4-0

v UKRAINE

EC2000	30 Oct	Kiev	2-1
EC2000	28 Nov	Leyton	2-0
wc2014	8 May	Shrewsbury	4-0
wc2014	19 June	Lviv	2-1

v USA

M1985	23 Aug	Caorle	3-1
M1988	27 July	Riva del Garda	2-0
1990	9 Aug	Blaine	0-3
1991	25 May	Hirson	1-3
1997	9 May	San Jose	0-5
1997	11 May	Portland	0-6
AC2002	3 Mar	Ferreiras	0-2
2003	17 May	Birmingham (Alabama)	0-6
2007	28 Jan	Guangzhou	1-1
wc2007	22 Sept	Tianjin	0-3
2011	2 Apr	Leyton	2-1
2015	13 Feb	Milton Keynes	0-1
2016	4 Mar	Tampa	0-1
2017	4 Mar	New Jersey	1-0
2018	8 Mar	Orlando	0-1
2019	2 Mar	Nashville	2-2
wc2019	2 July	Lyon	1-2
2020	5 Mar	Orlando	0-2

v USSR

1990	11 Aug	Blaine	1-1
1991	20 July	Dmitrov	2-1
1991	21 July	Kashira	2-0
1991	7 Sept	Southampton	2-0
1991	8 Sept	Brighton	1-3

v WALES

1974	17 Mar	Slough	5-0
1976	22 May	Bedford	4-0
1976	17 Oct	Ebbw Vale	2-1
1977	18 Sept	Warminster	5-0
1980	1 June	Warminster	6-1
1985	17 Aug	Ramsey (Isle of Man)	6-0
wc2013	26 Oct	Millwall	2-0
wc2014	21 Aug	Cardiff	4-0
wc2018	6 Apr	Southampton	0-0
wc2018	31 Aug	Newport	3-0

v WEST GERMANY

M1984	22 Aug	Jesolo	0-2
1990	5 Aug	Blaine	1-3

OTHER MATCHES

v ITALY B

1984	27 Aug	Monfalcone	3-1
M1988	20 July	Riva del Garda	3-0

v USA B

1990	7 Aug	Blaine	1-0

WELSH FOOTBALL 2020–21

JD CYMRU PREMIER LEAGUE 2020–21

		Home						*Away*					*Total*						
		P	*W*	*D*	*L*	*F*	*A*	*W*	*D*	*L*	*F*	*A*	*W*	*D*	*L*	*F*	*A*	*GD*	*Pts*
1	Connah's Quay Nomads[1]	32	13	2	1	30	8	12	2	2	40	12	25	4	3	70	20	50	79
2	The New Saints[2]	32	13	2	1	42	10	11	3	2	42	7	24	5	3	84	17	67	77
3	Bala T[2]	32	11	1	4	40	18	7	5	4	27	24	18	6	8	67	42	25	60
4	Penybont	32	7	3	6	22	22	6	4	6	20	18	13	7	12	42	40	2	46
5	Barry Town U	32	8	3	5	31	29	5	1	10	11	24	13	4	15	42	53	–11	43
6	Caernarfon T	32	4	5	7	21	31	6	2	8	22	36	10	7	15	43	67	–24	37
7	Newtown¶	32	7	2	7	31	31	5	4	7	26	22	12	6	14	57	53	4	42
8	Cardiff Metropolitan	32	6	5	5	29	18	5	2	9	18	28	11	7	14	47	46	1	40
9	Haverfordwest Co	32	6	5	5	17	22	4	2	10	21	34	10	7	15	38	56	–18	37
10	Aberystwyth T	32	5	4	7	27	25	3	5	8	20	28	8	9	15	47	53	–6	33
11	Flint Town U	32	5	1	10	15	20	5	1	10	23	38	10	2	20	38	58	–20	32
12	Cefn Druids	32	2	1	13	13	48	2	3	11	12	47	4	4	24	25	95	–70	16

Top 6 teams split after 22 games. [1]Connah's Quay Nomads qualify for the UEFA Champions League first qualifying round. [2]The New Saints and Bala T qualify for the Europa Conference League first qualifying round. ¶Newtown qualify for the Europa Conference League first qualifying round after play-offs.
Due to the cancellation of JD Cymru North and South Leagues there was no promotion or relegation.

UEFA CONFERENCE PLAY-OFF SEMI-FINALS

Penybont v Newtown 0-1
Barry Town U v Caernarfon T 1-3

UEFA CONFERENCE PLAY-OFF FINAL

Caernarfon T v Newtown 3-5

PREVIOUS WELSH LEAGUE WINNERS

1993 Cwmbran Town
1994 Bangor City
1995 Bangor City
1996 Barry Town
1997 Barry Town
1998 Barry Town
1999 Barry Town
2000 TNS
2001 Barry Town
2002 Barry Town
2003 Barry Town
2004 Rhyl
2005 TNS
2006 TNS
2007 TNS
2008 Llanelli
2009 Rhyl
2010 The New Saints
2011 Bangor C
2012 The New Saints
2013 The New Saints
2014 The New Saints
2015 The New Saints
2016 The New Saints
2017 The New Saints
2018 The New Saints
2019 The New Saints
2020 Connah's Quay Nomads
2021 Connah's Quay Nomads

JD CYMRU NORTH LEAGUE 2020–21

Due to the COVID-19 pandemic and national restrictions, the FAW cancelled the JD Cymru North division for the 2021 season on 18 March 2021.

The clubs due to take part in the 2020–21 season were:

Airbus UK Broughton
Bangor C
Buckley T
Colwyn Bay
Conwy Bor
Gresford Ath
Guilsfield
Holyhead Hotspur
Holywell T
Llandudno
Llangefni T
Llanidloes T
Llanrhaeadr
Penrhyncoch
Prestatyn T
Ruthin T

JD CYMRU SOUTH LEAGUE 2020–21

Due to the COVID-19 pandemic and national restrictions, the FAW cancelled the JD Cymru South division for the 2021 season on 18 March 2021.

The clubs due to take part in the 2020–21 season were:

Afan Lido
Ammanford
Briton Ferry Llansawel
Cambrian & Clydach Vale BGC
Carmarthen T
Cwmbran Celtic
Goytre U
Llanelli T
Llantwit Major
Pontypridd T
Port Talbot T
Risca U
Swansea University
Taff's Well
Trefelin BGC
Undy Ath

JD WELSH FA CUP 2020–21

**Due to the COVID-19 pandemic and National restrictions the JD Welsh FA Cup for 2020–21 was cancelled by The Football Association of Wales National Cup Board (NLB).*

PREVIOUS WELSH CUP WINNERS

1878 Wrexham
1879 Newtown White Stars
1880 Druids
1881 Druids
1882 Druids
1883 Wrexham
1884 Oswestry White Stars
1885 Druids
1886 Druids
1887 Chirk
1888 Chirk
1889 Bangor
1890 Chirk
1891 Shrewsbury T
1892 Chirk
1893 Wrexham
1894 Chirk
1895 Newtown
1896 Bangor
1897 Wrexham
1898 Druids
1899 Druids
1900 Aberystwyth T
1901 Oswestry U
1902 Wellington T
1903 Wrexham
1904 Druids
1905 Wrexham
1906 Wellington T
1907 Oswestry U
1908 Chester
1909 Wrexham
1910 Wrexham
1911 Wrexham
1912 Cardiff C
1913 Swansea T
1914 Wrexham
1915 Wrexham
1920 Cardiff C
1921 Wrexham
1922 Cardiff C
1923 Cardiff C
1924 Wrexham
1925 Wrexham
1926 Ebbw Vale
1927 Cardiff C
1928 Cardiff C
1929 Connah's Quay
1930 Cardiff C
1931 Wrexham
1932 Swansea T
1933 Chester
1934 Bristol C
1935 Tranmere R
1936 Crewe Alex
1937 Crewe Alex
1938 Shrewsbury T
1939 South Liverpool
1940 Wellington T
1947 Chester
1948 Lovell's Ath
1949 Merthyr Tydfil
1950 Swansea T
1951 Merthyr Tydfil
1952 Rhyl
1953 Rhyl
1954 Flint Town U
1955 Barry T
1956 Cardiff C
1957 Wrexham
1958 Wrexham
1959 Cardiff C
1960 Wrexham
1961 Swansea T
1962 Bangor C
1963 Borough U
1964 Cardiff C
1965 Cardiff C
1966 Swansea T
1967 Cardiff C
1968 Cardiff C
1969 Cardiff C
1970 Cardiff C
1971 Cardiff C
1972 Wrexham
1973 Cardiff C
1974 Cardiff C
1975 Wrexham
1976 Cardiff C
1977 Shrewsbury T
1978 Wrexham
1979 Shrewsbury T
1980 Newport Co
1981 Swansea C
1982 Swansea C
1983 Swansea C
1984 Shrewsbury T
1985 Shrewsbury T
1986 Wrexham
1987 Merthyr Tydfil
1988 Cardiff C
1989 Swansea C
1990 Hereford U
1991 Swansea C
1992 Cardiff C
1993 Cardiff C
1994 Barry T
1995 Wrexham
1996 TNS
1997 Barry T
1998 Bangor C
1999 Inter Cable-Tel
2000 Bangor C
2001 Barry T
2002 Barry T
2003 Barry T
2004 Rhyl
2005 TNS
2006 Rhyl
2007 Carmarthen T
2008 Bangor C
2009 Bangor C
2010 Bangor C
2011 Llanelli
2012 The New Saints
2013 Prestatyn T
2014 The New Saints
2015 The New Saints
2016 The New Saints
2017 Bala T
2018 Connah's Quay Nomads
2019 The New Saints
2020 *Competition cancelled due to COVID-19 pandemic.*
2021 *Competition cancelled due to COVID-19 pandemic.*

NATHANIEL MG LEAGUE CUP 2020–21

**Due to the COVID-19 pandemic and National restrictions the Nathaniel MG League Cup for 2020–21 was cancelled by The Football Association of Wales National League Board (NCB).*

NATHANIEL MG LEAGUE CUP FINALS 1992–93 to 2020–21

**After extra time.*

1992–93	Afan Lido v Caersws	1-1
	Afan Lido won 4-3 on penalties	
1993–94	Afan Lido v Bangor C	1-0
1994–95	Llansantffraid v Ton Pentre	2-1
1995–96	Connah's Quay Nomads v Ebbw Vale	1-0
1996–97	Barry T v Bangor C	2-2
	Barry T won 4-2 on penalties	
1997–98	Barry T v Bangor C	1-1
	Barry T won 5-4 on penalties	
1998–99	Barry T v Caernarfon T	3-0
1999–2000	Barry T v Bangor C	6-0
2000–01	Caersws v Barry T	2-0
2001–02	Caersws v Cwmbran T	2-1
2002–03	Rhyl v Bangor C	2-2
	Rhyl won 4-3 on penalties	
2003–04	Rhyl v Carmarthen T	4-0
2004–05	Carmarthen T v Rhyl	2-0*
2005–06	Total Network Solutions v Port Talbot T	4-0
2006–07	Caersws v Rhyl	1-1
	Caersws won 3-1 on penalties	
2007–08	Llanelli v Rhyl	2-0
2008–09	The New Saints v Bangor C	2-0
2009–10	The New Saints v Rhyl	3-1
2010–11	The New Saints v Llanelli	4-3*
2011–12	Afan Lido v Newtown	1-1
	Afan Lido won 3–2 on penalties	
2012–13	Carmarthen T v The New Saints	3-3
	Carmarthen T won 3-1 on penalties	
2013–14	Carmarthen T v Bala T	0-0
	Carmarthen T won 3-1 on penalties	
2014–15	The New Saints v Bala T	3-0
2015–16	The New Saints v Denbigh T	2-0
2016–17	The New Saints v Barry Town U	4-0
2017–18	The New Saints v Cardiff Metropolitan University	1-0
2018–19	Cardiff Metropolitan University v Cambrian & Clydach Vale	2-0
2019–20	Connah's Quay Nomads v STM Sports	3-0
2020–21	*Competition cancelled due to COVID-19 pandemic.*	

THE FAW TROPHY 2020–21

**Due to the COVID-19 pademic and National restrictions the FAW Trophy for 2020–21 was cancelled by The Football Association of Wales National League Board (NCB).*

THE FAW TROPHY FINALS 1993–94 to 2020–21

1993–94	Barry T v Aberaman	2-1
1994–95	Rhydymwyn v Taffs Well	1-0
1995–96	Rhydymwyn v Penrhyncoch	2-1
1996–97	Cambrian U Sky Blues v Rhyl Delta	2-1
1997–98	Dinas Powys v Llanrwst	2-0
1998–99	Ragged School v Barry Ath	3-1
1999–00	Trefelin BGC v Bryntirion Ath	6-2
2000–01	Ragged School v Gresford Ath	1-0
2001–02	Cefn U v Llangeinor	2-0
2002–03	Rhydyfelin Zenith v Tillery	4-1
2003–04	Penycae v Llanrhaeadr	3-2
2004–05	West End v Rhydymwyn	3-1
2005–06	West End v Cefn U	4-2
2006–07	Brymbo v Glan Conwy	6-2
2007–08	Rhos Aelwyd v Corwen	4-2
2008–09	Ragged School v Penycae	1-0
2009–10	Glan Conwy v Clydach Wasps	5-1
2010–11	Holywell T v Conwy U	3-2
2011–12	Sully Sports v Holyhead Hotspur	2-1
2012–13	Caernarfon T v Kilvey Fords	6-0
2013–14	Llanrug U v Chirk AAA	3-2
2014–15	Holywell T v Penrhyndeudraeth	4-2
2015-16	Abergavenny T v Sully Sports	1-0
2016-17	Chirk AAA v Penlan Club	2-1
2017-18	Conwy Borough v Rhos Aelwyd	4-1
2018-19	Cefn Albion v Pontardawe T	4-0
2019–20	*Competition cancelled due to COVID-19 pandemic.*	
2020–21	*Competition cancelled due to COVID-19 pandemic.*	

NORTHERN IRISH FOOTBALL 2020–21

NIFL DANSKE BANK PREMIERSHIP 2020–21

			Home					Away					Total						
		P	W	D	L	F	A	W	D	L	F	A	W	D	L	F	A	GD	Pts
1	Linfield[1]	38	15	2	2	53	12	9	4	6	30	26	24	6	8	83	38	45	78
2	Coleraine[2]	38	11	5	3	27	14	10	5	4	30	21	21	10	7	57	35	22	73
3	Glentoran[2]	38	12	6	2	38	14	8	5	5	27	18	20	11	7	65	32	33	71
4	Larne¶	38	9	5	5	31	17	9	5	5	33	24	18	10	10	64	41	23	64
5	Cliftonville	38	12	3	5	39	22	5	6	7	20	20	17	9	12	59	42	17	60
6	Crusaders	38	9	2	7	34	22	7	4	9	28	28	16	6	16	62	50	12	54
7	Glenavon	38	8	8	3	37	29	9	3	7	35	36	17	11	10	72	65	7	62
8	Ballymena U	38	9	4	7	34	25	9	3	6	33	19	18	7	13	67	44	23	61
9	Portadown	38	6	3	11	26	31	4	3	11	24	47	10	6	22	50	78	–28	36
10	Warrenpoint T	38	3	6	8	22	30	6	3	12	16	44	9	9	20	38	74	–36	36
11	Carrick Rangers	38	2	5	11	23	43	3	3	14	12	49	5	8	25	35	92	–57	23
12	Dungannon Swifts	38	3	0	16	12	39	1	5	13	10	44	4	5	29	22	83	–61	17

Top 6 teams split after 33 games. [1]Linfield qualify for Champions League first qualifying round.
[2]Coleraine and Glentoran qualify for Europa Conference League first qualifying round.
¶Larne qualify for Europa Conference League first qualifying round after play-offs.
Due to the cancellation of NIFL Bluefin Sport Championship there was no promotion or relegation.

UEFA CONFERENCE PLAY-OFF SEMI-FINALS

Larne v Glenavon 2-1
Cliftonville v Crusaders 0-0
aet; Cliftonville won 5-4 on penalties

UEFA CONFERENCE PLAY-OFF FINAL

Larne v Cliftonville 3-1

LEADING GOALSCORERS (League goals only)

Player	Club	Goals
Shayne Lavery	Linfield	23
Seamus McCartan	Ballymena U	18
Jay Donnelly	Glentoran	17
Ryan Curran	Cliftonville	15
Andrew Waterworth	Linfield	15
Lee Bonis	Portadown	14
Ben Doherty	Coleraine	14
Michael McCrudden	Cliftonville	14
Matthew Fitzpatrick	Glenavon	13
Daniel Purkis	Glenavon	13
Ronan Hale	Larne	12
David McDaid	Larne	12
Robbie McDaid	Glentoran	12
Paul McElroy	Ballymena U	12
Adam Salley	Portadown	11
Jordan Stewart	Linfield	11
Ruaridhri Donnelly	Glentoran	10
Paul Heatley	Crusaders	10
Jamie McGonigle	Crusaders	10
Curtis Allen	Coleraine	9
Caolan Loughran	Carrick Rangers	9
Andrew Hall	Glenavon	8
Conor McMenamin	Cliftonville T	8
Alan O'Sullivan	Warrenpoint T	8
Ryan Swan	Warrenpoint T	8

IRISH LEAGUE CHAMPIONSHIP WINNERS

1891 Linfield
1892 Linfield
1893 Linfield
1894 Glentoran
1895 Linfield
1896 Distillery
1897 Glentoran
1898 Linfield
1899 Distillery
1900 Belfast Celtic
1901 Distillery
1902 Linfield
1903 Distillery
1904 Linfield
1905 Glentoran
1906 Cliftonville/Distillery (shared)
1907 Linfield
1908 Linfield
1909 Linfield
1910 Cliftonville
1911 Linfield
1912 Glentoran
1913 Glentoran
1914 Linfield
1915 Belfast Celtic
1920 Belfast Celtic
1921 Glentoran
1922 Linfield
1923 Linfield
1924 Queen's Island
1925 Glentoran
1926 Belfast Celtic
1927 Belfast Celtic
1928 Belfast Celtic
1929 Belfast Celtic
1930 Linfield
1931 Glentoran
1932 Linfield
1933 Belfast Celtic
1934 Linfield
1935 Linfield
1936 Belfast Celtic
1937 Belfast Celtic
1938 Belfast Celtic
1939 Belfast Celtic
1940 Belfast Celtic
1948 Belfast Celtic
1949 Linfield
1950 Linfield
1951 Glentoran
1952 Glenavon
1953 Glentoran
1954 Linfield
1955 Linfield
1956 Linfield
1957 Glentoran
1958 Ards
1959 Linfield
1960 Glenavon
1961 Linfield
1962 Linfield
1963 Distillery
1964 Glentoran
1965 Derry City
1966 Linfield
1967 Glentoran
1968 Glentoran
1969 Linfield
1970 Glentoran
1971 Linfield
1972 Glentoran
1973 Crusaders
1974 Coleraine
1975 Linfield
1976 Crusaders
1977 Glentoran
1978 Linfield
1979 Linfield
1980 Linfield
1981 Glentoran
1982 Linfield
1983 Linfield
1984 Linfield
1985 Linfield
1986 Linfield
1987 Linfield
1988 Glentoran
1989 Linfield
1990 Portadown
1991 Portadown
1992 Glentoran
1993 Linfield
1994 Linfield
1995 Crusaders
1996 Portadown
1997 Crusaders
1998 Cliftonville
1999 Glentoran
2000 Linfield
2001 Linfield
2002 Portadown
2003 Glentoran
2004 Linfield
2005 Glentoran
2006 Linfield
2007 Linfield
2008 Linfield
2009 Glentoran
2010 Linfield
2011 Linfield
2012 Linfield
2013 Cliftonville
2014 Cliftonville
2015 Crusaders
2016 Crusaders
2017 Linfield
2018 Crusaders
2019 Linfield
2020 Linfield
2021 Linfield

NIFL BLUEFIN SPORT CHAMPIONSHIP 2020–21

The NIFL Bluefin Sport Championship 2020–21 was cancelled due to the COVID-19 pandemic.

NIFL CHAMPIONSHIP WINNERS

1996 Coleraine
1997 Ballymena United
1998 Newry Town
1999 Distillery
2000 Omagh Town
2001 Ards
2002 Lisburn Distillery
2003 Dungannon Swifts
2004 Loughgall
2005 Armagh City
2006 Crusaders
2007 Institute
2008 Loughgall
2009 Portadown
2010 Loughgall
2011 Carrick Rangers
2012 Ballinamallard U
2013 Ards
2014 Institute
2015 Carrick Rangers
2016 Ards
2017 Warrenpoint T
2018 Institute
2019 Larne
2020 Portadown
2021 No competition

NIFL BLUEFIN SPORT PREMIER INTERMEDIATE LEAGUE 2020–21

The NIFL Bluefin Sport Premier Intermediate League 2020–21 was cancelled due to the COVID-19 pandemic.

IFA DEVELOPMENT LEAGUES 2020–21

All of the IFA Development Leagues 2020–21 were cancelled due to the COVID-19 pandemic.

BETMCLEAN LEAGUE CUP 2020–21

The BetMcLean League Cup 2020–21 was cancelled due to the COVID-19 pandemic.

SADLER'S PEAKY BLINDER IRISH FA CUP 2020–21

FIRST ROUND

Ballymena U v Portadown 4-1
Carrick Rangers v Belfast Celtic 3-0
Cliftonville v Portstewart 5-1
Coleraine v Crusaders 0-1
Glenavon v Dungannon Swifts 1-2
Linfield v Annagh U 2-0
Warrenpoint T v Ballyclare Comrades 2-1
Knockbreda v Newington 2-1
Ballinamallard U v Dergview 2-2
Dergview won 9-8 on penalties
Loughgall v Banbridge T 1-1
Loughall won 3-2 on penalties
Ards v Dollingstown (walkover)
Glentoran (walkover) v Dundela
H&W Welders v St James' Swifts (walkover)
Institute v PSNI (walkover)
Larne (walkover) v Newry C
Queen's University v Bangor (walkover)

SECOND ROUND

Ballymena U v PSNI 5-0
Carrick Rangers v Bangor 2-2
Carrick Rangers won 3-1 on penalties
Dergview v St James' Swifts 2-0
Knockbreda v Crusaders 0-5
Larne v Dollingstown 8-1
Linfield v Dungannon Swifts 5-2
Loughgall v Warrenpoint T 1-0
Glentoran v Cliftonville 1-0

QUARTER-FINALS

Ballymena U v Dergview 5-0
Larne v Carrick Rangers 2-1
Loughgall v Linfield 1-3
Glentoran v Crusaders 0-1

SEMI-FINALS

Larne v Crusaders 1-1
Larne won 6-5 on penalties
Ballymena U v Linfield 0-3

SADLER'S PEAKY BLINDER FA CUP FINAL 2020–21

Mountfield Park, Lurgan, Friday 21 May 2021

Linfield (2) 2 *(Lavery 5, Cooper 32)*

Larne (0) 1 *(Hughes 90)* 1000

Linfield: Johns; Haughey, Clarke, Quinn, Mulgrew, Callacher, Millar, Pepper, Cooper, Palmer, Lavery (Manzinga 74).

Larne: Mitchell; Watson, Jarvis, Robinson, Hughes, Donnelly (McDaid 46), Herron, Lynch (Randall 53), Cosgrove, Sule, Hale (McMurray 67).

Referee: Andrew Davey.

IRISH CUP FINALS 1880–81 to 2020–21

**After extra time.*

1880–81	Moyola Park v Cliftonville	1-0
1881–82	Queen's Island (1881) v Cliftonville	1-0
1882–83	Cliftonville v Ulster	5-0
1883–84	Distillery v Wellington Park	5-0
1884–85	Distillery v Limavady	3-0
1885–86	Distillery v Limavady	1-0
1886–87	Ulster v Cliftonville	3-0
1887–88	Cliftonville v Distillery	2-1
1888–89	Distillery v YMCA	5-4
1889–90	Gordon Highlanders v Cliftonville	2-2
Replay	Gordon Highlanders v Cliftonville	3-1
1890–91	Linfield v Ulster	4-2
1891–92	Linfield v The Black Watch	7-0
1892–93	Linfield v Cliftonville	5-1
1893–94	Distillery v Linfield	2-2
Replay	Distillery v Linfield	3-2
1894–95	Linfield v Bohemians	10-1
1895–96	Distillery v Glentoran	3-1
1896–97	Cliftonville v Sherwood Foresters	3-1
1897–98	Linfield v St Columb's Hall Celtic	2-0
1898–99	Linfield v Glentoran	2-1
1899–00	Cliftonville v Bohemians	2-1
1900–01	Cliftonville v Freebooters	1-0
1901–02	Linfield v Distillery	5-1
1902–03	Distillery v Bohemians	3-1
1903–04	Linfield v Derry Celtic	5-1
1904–05	Distillery v Shelbourne	3-0
1905–06	Shelbourne v Belfast Celtic	2-0
1906–07	Cliftonville v Shelbourne	0-0
Replay	Cliftonville v Shelbourne	1-0
1907–08	Bohemians v Shelbourne	1-1
Replay	Bohemians v Shelbourne	3-1
1908–09	Cliftonville v Bohemians	0-0
Replay	Cliftonville v Bohemians	2-1
1909–10	Distillery v Cliftonville	1-0
1910–11	Shelbourne v Bohemians	0-0
Replay	Shelbourne v Bohemians	2-1
1911–12	*Linfield were awarded the trophy after Cliftonville, Glentoran and Shelbourne resigned from the IFA at the semi-final stage.*	
1912–13	Linfield v Glentoran	2-0
1913–14	Glentoran v Linfield	3-1
1914–15	Linfield v Belfast Celtic	1-0
1915–16	Linfield v Glentoran	1-1
Replay	Linfield v Glentoran	1-0
1916–17	Glentoran v Belfast Celtic	2-0
1917–18	Belfast Celtic v Linfield	0-0
Replay	Belfast Celtic v Linfield	0-0
2nd replay	Belfast Celtic v Linfield	2-0
1918–19	Linfield v Glentoran	1-1
Replay	Linfield v Glentoran	0-0
2nd replay	Linfield v Glentoran	2-1
1919–20	*Shelbourne were awarded the trophy after Belfast Celtic and Glentoran were removed from the competition at the semi-final stage.*	
1920–21	Glentoran v Glenavon	2-0
1921–22	Linfield v Glenavon	2-0
1922–23	Linfield v Glentoran	2-0
1923–24	Queen's Island (1920) v Willowfield	1-0
1924–25	Distillery v Glentoran	2-1
1925–26	Belfast Celtic v Linfield	3-2
1926–27	Ards v Cliftonville	3-2
1927–28	Willowfield v Larne	1-0
1928–29	Ballymena v Belfast Celtic	2-1
1929–30	Linfield v Ballymena	4-3
1930–31	Linfield v Ballymena	3-0
1931–32	Glentoran v Linfield	2-1
1932–33	Glentoran v Distillery	1-1
Replay	Glentoran v Distillery	1-1
2nd replay	Glentoran v Distillery	3-1
1933–34	Linfield v Cliftonville	5-0
1934–35	Glentoran v Larne	0-0
Replay	Glentoran v Larne	0-0
2nd replay	Glentoran v Larne	1-0
1935–36	Linfield v Derry C	0-0
Replay	Linfield v Derry C	2-0
1936–37	Belfast Celtic v Linfield	3-0
1937–38	Belfast Celtic v Bangor	0-0
Replay	Belfast Celtic v Bangor	2-0
1938–39	Linfield v Ballymena U	2-0
1939–40	Ballymena U v Glenavon	2-0
1940–41	Belfast Celtic v Linfield	1-0
1941–42	Linfield v Glentoran	3-1
1942–43	Belfast Celtic v Glentoran	1-0
1943–44	Belfast Celtic v Linfield	3-1
1944–45	Linfield v Glentoran	4-2
1945–46	Linfield v Distillery	3-0
1946–47	Belfast Celtic v Glentoran	1-0
1947–48	Linfield v Coleraine	3-0
1948–49	Derry C v Glentoran	3-1
1949–50	Linfield v Distillery	2-1
1950–51	Glentoran v Ballymena U	3-1
1951–52	Ards v Glentoran	1-0
1952–53	Linfield v Coleraine	5-0
1953–54	Derry C v Glentoran	2-2
Replay	Derry C v Glentoran	0-0
2nd replay	Derry C v Glentoran	1-0
1954–55	Dundela v Glenavon	3-0
1955–56	Distillery v Glentoran	2-2
Replay	Distillery v Glentoran	0-0
2nd replay	Distillery v Glentoran	1-0
1956–57	Glenavon v Derry C	2-0
1957–58	Ballymena U v Linfield	2-0
1958–59	Glenavon v Ballymena U	1-1
Replay	Glenavon v Ballymena U	2-0
1959–60	Linfield v Ards	5-1
1960–61	Glenavon v Linfield	5-1
1961–62	Linfield v Portadown	4-0
1962–63	Linfield v Distillery	2-1
1963–64	Derry C v Glentoran	2-0
1964–65	Coleraine v Glenavon	2-1
1965–66	Glentoran v Linfield	2-0
1966–67	Crusaders v Glentoran	3-1
1967–68	Crusaders v Linfield	2-0
1968–69	Ards v Distillery	0-0
Replay	Ards v Distillery	4-2
1969–70	Linfield v Ballymena U	2-1
1970–71	Distillery v Derry C	3-0
1971–72	Coleraine v Portadown	2-1
1972–73	Glentoran v Linfield	3-2
1973–74	Ards v Ballymena U	2-1
1974–75	Coleraine v Linfield	1-1
Replay	Coleraine v Linfield	0-0
2nd replay	Coleraine v Linfield	1-0
1975–76	Carrick Rangers v Linfield	2-1
1976–77	Coleraine v Linfield	4-1
1977–78	Linfield v Ballymena U	3-1
1978–79	Cliftonville v Portadown	3-2
1979–80	Linfield v Crusaders	2-0
1980–81	Ballymena U v Glenavon	1-0
1981–82	Linfield v Coleraine	2-1
1982–83	Glentoran v Linfield	1-1
Replay	Glentoran v Linfield	2-1
1983–84	Ballymena U v Carrick Rangers	4-1
1984–85	Glentoran v Linfield	1-1
Replay	Glentoran v Linfield	1-0
1985–86	Glentoran v Coleraine	2-1
1986–87	Glentoran v Larne	1-0
1987–88	Glentoran v Glenavon	1-0
1988–89	Ballymena U v Larne	1-0
1989–90	Glentoran v Portadown	3-0
1990–91	Portadown v Glenavon	2-1
1991–92	Glenavon v Linfield	2-1
1992–93	Bangor v Ards	1-1*
Replay	Bangor v Ards	1-1*
2nd replay	Bangor v Ards	1-0
1993–94	Linfield v Bangor	2-0
1994–95	Linfield v Carrick Rangers	3-1
1995–96	Glentoran v Glenavon	1-0
1996–97	Glenavon v Cliftonville	1-0
1997–98	Glentoran v Glenavon	1-0*
1998–99	*Portadown awarded the trophy after Cliftonville were removed from the competition for fielding an ineligible player in the semi-final.*	
1999–2000	Glentoran v Portadown	1-0
2000–01	Glentoran v Linfield	1-0*
2001–02	Linfield v Portadown	2-1
2002–03	Coleraine v Glentoran	1-0
2003–04	Glentoran v Coleraine	1-0
2004–05	Portadown v Larne	5-1
2005–06	Linfield v Glentoran	2-1
2006–07	Linfield v Dungannon Swifts	2-2*
Linfield won 3-2 on penalties		
2007–08	Linfield v Coleraine	2-1
2008–09	Crusaders v Cliftonville	1-0
2009–10	Linfield v Portadown	2-1
2010–11	Linfield v Crusaders	2-1
2011–12	Linfield v Crusaders	4-1
2012–13	Glentoran v Cliftonville	3-1*
2013–14	Glenavon v Ballymena U	2-1
2014–15	Glentoran v Portadown	1-0
2015–16	Glenavon v Linfield	2-0
2016–17	Linfield v Coleraine	3-0
2017–18	Coleraine v Cliftonville	3-1
2018–19	Crusaders v Ballinamallard U	3-0
2019–20	Glentoran v Ballymena U	2-1*
2020–21	Linfield v Larne	2-1

ROLL OF HONOUR SEASON 2020–21

Competition	*Winner*	*Runner-up*
NIFL Danske Bank Premiership	Linfield	Coleraine
Sadler's Peaky Blinder Irish FA Cup	Linfield (2-1)	Larne
NIFL Championship	Competion cancelled	
NIFL Premier Intermediate	Competion cancelled	
BetMcLean Northern Ireland League Cup	Competion cancelled	
NIFL Danske Bank Women's Premiership 2020	Glentoran	Linfield
County Antrim Shield	Larne (0-0) *Larne won 4-3 on penalties*	Glentoran
Steel & Sons Cup	Competion cancelled	
Co Antrim Junior Shield	Competion cancelled	
Irish Junior Cup	Competion cancelled	
Mid Ulster Cup (Senior)	Glenavon (1-0)	Loughgall
Harry Cavan Youth Cup	Competion cancelled	
North West Senior Cup	Competion cancelled	
Intermediate Cup	Competion cancelled	

NORTHERN IRELAND FOOTBALL WRITERS ASSOCIATION PLAYER AND MANAGER OF THE MONTH AWARDS 2020–21

NIFWA DANKSE BANK PREMIERSHIP PLAYER OF THE MONTH 2020–21

Month	*Player*	*Team*
October	Kirk Millar	Linfield
November	John Herron	Larne
December	Ross Redman	Ballymena U
January	Jordan Stewart	Linfield
February	Conor MCloskey	Glenavon
March	Shayne Lavery	Linfield
April	Michael McCrudden	Cliftonville

NIFWA DANKSE BANK PREMIERSHIP GOAL OF THE MONTH 2020–21

Month	*Goal*
October	Navid Nasseri for Linfield v Ballymena U, 24 October 2020.
November	Garry Breen for Cliftonville v Dungannon Swifts, 10 November 2020.
December	Ross Clarke for Crusaders v Glentoran, 5 December 2020.
January	Jordan Stewart for Linfield v Glenavon, 2 January 2021.
February	Jamie McDonagh for Glentoran v Cliftonville, 6 February 2021.
March	Daniel Kelly for Carrick Rangers v Crusaders, 9 March 2021.
April	Ronan Hale for Larne v Portadown, 6 April 2021

NIFWA DANKSE BANK WOMEN'S PREMIERSHIP PLAYER OF THE MONTH 2020–21

Month	*Player*	*Team*
October	Caragh Hamilton	Glentoran
November	Emily Wilson	Crusaders

BELLEEK NIFWA MANAGER OF THE MONTH 2020–21

Month	*Manager*	*Team*
October	Tiernan Lynch	Larne
November	Tiernan Lynch	Larne
December	Tiernan Lynch	Larne
January	Oran Kearney	Coleraine
February	Paddy McLaughlin	Cliftonville
March	David Jeffrey	Ballymena U
April	Mick McDermott	Glentoran

NIFWA ANNUAL AWARDS 2020–21

AKTIVORA MANAGER OF THE YEAR

David Healy (Linfield)

DANSKE BANK UK PLAYER OF THE YEAR

Shayne Lavery (Linfield)

DREAM SPANISH HOMES YOUNG PLAYER OF THE YEAR

Shayne Lavery (Linfield)

EUROPEAN CUP FINALS

EUROPEAN CUP FINALS 1956–1992

Year	Winners v Runners-up		Venue	Attendance	Referee
1956	Real Madrid v Reims	4-3	Paris	38,239	A. Ellis (England)
1957	Real Madrid v Fiorentina	2-0	Madrid	124,000	L. Horn (Netherlands)
1958	Real Madrid v AC Milan	3-2*	Brussels	67,000	A. Alsteen (Belgium)
1959	Real Madrid v Reims	2-0	Stuttgart	72,000	A. Dutsch (West Germany)
1960	Real Madrid v Eintracht Frankfurt	7-3	Glasgow	127,621	J. Mowat (Scotland)
1961	Benfica v Barcelona	3-2	Berne	26,732	G. Dienst (Switzerland)
1962	Benfica v Real Madrid	5-3	Amsterdam	61,257	L. Horn (Netherlands)
1963	AC Milan v Benfica	2-1	Wembley	45,715	A. Holland (England)
1964	Internazionale v Real Madrid	3-1	Vienna	71,333	J. Stoll (Austria)
1965	Internazionale v Benfica	1-0	Milan	89,000	G. Dienst (Switzerland)
1966	Real Madrid v Partizan Belgrade	2-1	Brussels	46,745	R. Kreitlein (West Germany)
1967	Celtic v Internazionale	2-1	Lisbon	45,000	K. Tschenscher (West Germany)
1968	Manchester U v Benfica	4-1*	Wembley	92,225	C. Lo Bello (Italy)
1969	AC Milan v Ajax	4-1	Madrid	31,782	J. Ortiz de Mendibil (Spain)
1970	Feyenoord v Celtic	2-1*	Milan	53,187	C. Lo Bello (Italy)
1971	Ajax v Panathinaikos	2-0	Wembley	90,000	J. Taylor (England)
1972	Ajax v Internazionale	2-0	Rotterdam	61,354	R. Helies (France)
1973	Ajax v Juventus	1-0	Belgrade	89,484	M. Guglovic (Yugoslavia)
1974	Bayern Munich v Atletico Madrid	1-1	Brussels	48,722	V. Loraux (Belgium)
Replay	Bayern Munich v Atletico Madrid	4-0	Brussels	23,325	A. Delcourt (Belgium)
1975	Bayern Munich v Leeds U	2-0	Paris	48,374	M. Kitabdjian (France)
1976	Bayern Munich v Saint-Etienne	1-0	Glasgow	54,864	K. Palotai (Hungary)
1977	Liverpool v Borussia Moenchengladbach	3-1	Rome	52,078	R. Wurtz (France)
1978	Liverpool v Club Brugge	1-0	Wembley	92,500	C. Corver (Netherlands)
1979	Nottingham F v Malmo	1-0	Munich	57,500	E. Linemayr (Austria)
1980	Nottingham F v Hamburg	1-0	Madrid	51,000	A. Garrido (Portugal)
1981	Liverpool v Real Madrid	1-0	Paris	48,360	K. Palotai (Hungary)
1982	Aston Villa v Bayern Munich	1-0	Rotterdam	46,000	G. Konrath (France)
1983	Hamburg v Juventus	1-0	Athens	73,500	N. Rainea (Romania)
1984	Liverpool v Roma *(Liverpool won 4-2 on penalties)*	1-1*	Rome	69,693	E. Fredriksson (Sweden)
1985	Juventus v Liverpool	1-0	Brussels	58,000	A. Daina (Switzerland)
1986	Steaua Bucharest v Barcelona *(Steaua won 2-0 on penalties)*	0-0*	Seville	70,000	M. Vautrot (France)
1987	FC Porto v Bayern Munich	2-1	Vienna	57,500	A. Ponnet (Belgium)
1988	PSV Eindhoven v Benfica *(PSV won 6-5 on penalties)*	0-0*	Stuttgart	68,000	L. Agnolin (Italy)
1989	AC Milan v Steaua Bucharest	4-0	Barcelona	97,000	K.-H. Tritschler (West Germany)
1990	AC Milan v Benfica	1-0	Vienna	57,500	H. Kohl (Austria)
1991	Red Star Belgrade v Olympique Marseille *(Red Star Belgrade won 5-3 on penalties)*	0-0*	Bari	56,000	T. Lanese (Italy)
1992	Barcelona v Sampdoria	1-0*	Wembley	70,827	A. Schmidhuber (Germany)

UEFA CHAMPIONS LEAGUE FINALS

UEFA CHAMPIONS LEAGUE FINALS 1993–2021

1993	Marseille† v AC Milan	1-0	Munich	64,400	K. Rothlisberger (Switzerland)
1994	AC Milan v Barcelona	4-0	Athens	70,000	P. Don (England)
1995	Ajax v AC Milan	1-0	Vienna	49,730	I. Craciunescu (Romania)
1996	Juventus v Ajax	1-1*	Rome	70,000	M. D. Vega (Spain)
	(Juventus won 4-2 on penalties)				
1997	Borussia Dortmund v Juventus	3-1	Munich	59,000	S. Puhl (Hungary)
1998	Real Madrid v Juventus	1-0	Amsterdam	48,500	H. Krug (Germany)
1999	Manchester U v Bayern Munich	2-1	Barcelona	90,245	P. Collina (Italy)
2000	Real Madrid v Valencia	3-0	Paris	80,000	S. Braschi (Italy)
2001	Bayern Munich v Valencia	1-1*	Milan	79,000	D. Jol (Netherlands)
	(Bayern Munich won 5-4 on penalties)				
2002	Real Madrid v Bayer Leverkusen	2-1	Glasgow	50,499	U. Meier (Switzerland)
2003	AC Milan v Juventus	0-0*	Manchester	62,315	M. Merk (Germany)
	(AC Milan won 3-2 on penalties)				
2004	FC Porto v Monaco	3-0	Gelsenkirchen	53,053	K. M. Nielsen (Denmark)
2005	Liverpool v AC Milan	3-3*	Istanbul	65,000	M. M. González (Spain)
	(Liverpool won 3-2 on penalties)				
2006	Barcelona v Arsenal	2-1	Paris	79,610	T. Hauge (Norway)
2007	AC Milan v Liverpool	2-1	Athens	74,000	H. Fandel (Germany)
2008	Manchester U v Chelsea	1-1*	Moscow	67,310	L. Michel (Slovakia)
	(Manchester U won 6-5 on penalties)				
2009	Barcelona v Manchester U	2-0	Rome	62,467	M. Busacca (Switzerland)
2010	Internazionale v Bayern Munich	2-0	Madrid	73,490	H. Webb (England)
2011	Barcelona v Manchester U	3-1	Wembley	87,695	V. Kassai (Hungary)
2012	Chelsea v Bayern Munich	1-1*	Munich	62,500	P. Proença (Portugal)
	(Chelsea won 4-3 on penalties)				
2013	Bayern Munich v Borussia Dortmund	2-1	Wembley	86,298	N. Rizzoli (Italy)
2014	Real Madrid v Atletico Madrid	4-1*	Lisbon	60,000	B. Kuipers (Netherlands)
2015	Barcelona v Juventus	3-1	Berlin	70,442	C. Cakir (Turkey)
2016	Real Madrid v Atletico Madrid	1-1*	Milan	71,942	M. Clattenburg (England)
	(Real Madrid won 5-3 on penalties)				
2017	Real Madrid v Juventus	4-1	Cardiff	65,842	F. Brych (Germany)
2018	Real Madrid v Liverpool	3-1	Kiev	61,561	M. Mazic (Serbia)
2019	Liverpool v Tottenham H	2-0	Madrid	63,272	D. Skomina (Slovenia)
2020	Bayern Munich v Paris Saint-Germain	1-0	Lisbon	0	D. Orsato (Italy)
2021	Chelsea v Manchester C	1-0	Porto	14,110	A. Lahoz (Spain)

*†Subsequently stripped of title. *After extra time.*

UEFA CHAMPIONS LEAGUE 2020–21

▪ *Denotes player sent off.*
Due to the COVID-19 pandemic, matches played behind closed doors unless otherwise stated.

PRELIMINARY ROUND

Saturday, 8 August 2020

Drita (2) 2 *(Shabani X 21, Namani 45)*

Inter Club d'Escaldes (1) 1 *(Garcia 29)*

Drita: (442) Maloku; Shabani B, Limani, Blakcori, Namani; Cuculi, Shabani X, Fazliu (Krasniqi 82), Rexha (Haxhimusa 73); Vucaj, Ajzeraj (Islami 89).
Inter Club d'Escaldes: (442) Gomes; Feher, Garcia, Bessone, Roca; Reyes O, Moreno (Brinez 90), Lao (Clemente 61), Soldevila; Raposo (Betriu 72), Lemiechevsky.

Tre Fiori (0) 0

Linfield (0) 2 *(Hery 71, Manzinga 83)*

Tre Fiori: (442) Simoncini A; D'Addario, Simoncini D (Angelini 89), Kalissa (Figone 70), Lunardini; Procacci▪, Gjurchinoski, Santoni, Misimovic; Apezteguia (Marzeglia 76), Gregorio.
Linfield: (442) Johns; Boyle, Larkin, Quinn, Mulgrew; Callacher, McClean (Manzinga 66), Nasseri (Waterworth 65), Lavery (Hery 67); Kearns, Millar.
Drita v Linfield cancelled due to positive COVID-19 tests of Drita players. Linfield awarded 3-0 win.

FIRST QUALIFYING ROUND

Tuesday, 18 August 2020

Celtic (3) 6 *(Elyounoussi 6, 90, Adalsteinsson 17 (og), Jullien 31, Taylor 46, Edouard 72)*

KR Reykjavik (0) 0

Celtic: (4231) Barkas; Elhamed, Jullien, Bitton, Taylor; Brown (Ntcham 63), McGregor; Forrest, Christie (Klimala 73), Elyounoussi; Edouard (Ajeti 73).
KR Reykjavik: (433) Olafsson; Chopart, Palmason F, Adalsteinsson, Jonsson (Sigurjonsson 46); Margeirsson, Kristinsson, Palmason P; Hauksson (Hilmarsson 73), Finnbogason (Jonasson 73), Punyed.

Dinamo Brest (4) 6 *(Gordeichuk 15, 22, Pechenin 17, Sedko 37, Diallo 55, 90)*

Astana (1) 3 *(Tomasov 45, Rotariu 52, Beysebekov 87)*

Dinamo Brest: (433) Ignatovich; Yuzepchuk, Khacheridi, Gabi, Pechenin; Tweh, Kislyak (Krivets 73), Sedko; Diallo, Milevskiy (Bykov 86), Gordeichuk (Savitskiy 73).
Astana: (4141) Nepogodov; Pertsukh (Barseghyan 34), Simunovic, Radakovic, Shomko; Maevskiy; Tomasov, Ebong, Sotiriou, Beysebekov; Shchetkin (Rotariu 46).

Legia Warsaw (0) 1 *(Kante 82)*

Linfield (0) 0

Legia Warsaw: (433) Boruc; Mladenovic, Jedrzejczyk, Wieteska, Karbownik; Antolic, Gvilia, Slisz (Rosolek 46); Wszolek, Luquinhas, Pekhart (Kante 70).
Linfield: (541) Johns; Boyle, Larkin, Stafford, Clarke, Quinn (Nasseri 84); Millar▪, Mulgrew, Fallon, Hery (Pepper 79); Lavery (Manzinga 76).

Qarabag (2) 4 *(Romero 11, Guerrier 40, 51, Emreli 80)*

Sileks (0) 0

Qarabag: (4321) Mahammadaliyev; Medvedev (Huseynov A 79), Medina, Huseynov B, Guerrier; Ibrahhimli, Matic, Ozobic; Romero (Dzhafarquliyev 83), Zoubir (Kwabena 72); Emreli.
Sileks: (433) Bozinovski; Timovski, Grozdanoski, Draskovic, Karceski; Mustafov (Spirkoski 84), Serafimovski, Ristov (Zeravica 59); Ivanovski, Gorgiev, Tanturovski (Kostovski 74).

Red Star Belgrade (2) 5 *(Ben 35, 44, 52, Ivanic 78, 87)*

Europa (0) 0

Red Star Belgrade: (4231) Borjan; Gobeljic, Degenek, Milunovic, Rodic (Gajic 46); Sanogo (Vulic 74), Ivanic; Katai, Kanga, Spiridonovic (Tomane 68); Ben.
Europa: (442) Munoz; Badr, Olmo, Carrascal, Becerra (Polaco 64); Olivero, Walker, Rosa, Alvarez (Quillo 70); Gallardo (Dimas 60), Juanpe.

Wednesday, 19 August 2020

Ararat-Armenia (0) 0

Omonia Nicosia (0) 1 *(Thiago Santos 94)*

Ararat-Armenia: (442) Cupic; Alemao (Shahinyan 85), Meneses (Damcevski 111), Vakulenko, Humanes▪; Gouffran (Ambartsumyan 90), Alphonse, Narsingh, Lima; Ogana, Otubanjo (Sanogo 73).
Omonia Nicosia: (442) Fabiano; Hubocan, Luftner, Lang, Lecjaks; Vitor Gomes (Kousoulos 91), Gomez, Kakoullis, Thiago Santos (Tzionis 103); Mavrias (Loizou 81), Duris (Bautheac 67).
aet.

Buducnost Podgorica (1) 1 *(Cukovic 31)*

Ludogorets Razgrad (2) 3 *(Marin 12, Tchibota 25, Cauly 90)*

Buducnost Podgorica: (442) Dragojevic; Vukcevic, Adzic, Cukovic, Sekulic; Terzic (Djurickovic 75), Mirkovic, Raickovic (Zarubica 82), Ivanovic; Moraitis, Bojovic (Vujacic 76).
Ludogorets Razgrad: (442) Renan; Cicinho, Grigore, Moti, Nedyalkov; Alex Santana, Badji, Tchibota (Yankov 65), Cauly; Tekpetey (Jorginho 85), Marin (Keseru 76).

Celje (1) 3 *(Kerin 43, Vizinger 89, Dangubic 90)*

Dundalk (0) 0

Celje: (442) Rozman; Kadusic, Zaletel, Calusic, Marandici; Stravs, Vrbanec (Pungarsek 86), Kerin, Lotric; Bozic (Novak 82), Vizinger (Dangubic 90).
Dundalk: (442) Rogers; Gannon, Hoare, Gartland (Oduwa 76), Leahy; Colovic, Shields (McMillan 82), Flores (Murray 69), Duffy; Hoban, McEleney.

Connah's Quay Nomads (0) 0

Sarajevo (1) 2 *(Tatar 16, 65)*

Connah's Quay Nomads: (442) Brass; Holmes, Horan, Farquharson, Roberts; Edwards (Disney 78), Morris, Harrison (Dool 46), Curran; Wilde, Poole (Insall 83).
Sarajevo: (442) Kovacevic; Hodzic, Dupovac, Milicevic, Salcin (Pidro 60); Djokanovic, Oremus, Rahmanovic, Tatar (Velkoski 71); Ahmetovic (Handzic 81), Jukic.

Dinamo Tbilisi (0) 0

KF Tirana (1) 2 *(Torassa 45, Ismajlgeci 86)*

Dinamo Tbilisi: (442) Kvaskhvadze; Iashvili, Gbegnon, Lochoshvili, Kobouri (Kimadze 59); Kardava (Kutsia 67), Papava, Shulaia, Pernambuca; Bughridze (Gabedava 81), Kapanadze.
KF Tirana: (442) Lika; Tosevski, Vangjeli, Najdovski, Ismajlgeci; Celhaka, Batha, Elton Cale (Toli 71), Torassa (Muca 83); Cobbinah, Muci (Avdijaj 87).

Ferencvaros (1) 2 *(Nguen 33, 62)*

Djurgaarden (0) 0

Ferencvaros: (442) Dibusz; Botka, Kovacevic, Blazic, Civic; Kharatin, Somalia, Isael (Laidouni 75), Nguen (Skvarka 63); Boli, Uzuni (Varga 84).
Djurgaarden: (442) Bratveit; Une Larsson, Nyholm, Berg, Witry; Ulvestad, Karlstrom, Augustinsson, Banda (Holmberg 18); Kujovic (Chilufya 46), Edwards (Radetinac 75).

Flora (0) 1 *(Sappinen 49)*

Suduva (0) 1 *(Topcagic 78 (pen))*

Flora: (442) Igonen; Lilander, Purg, Kreida, Kuusk; Kallaste (Jarvelaid 106), Miller (Alliku 62), Soomets, Vassiljev; Sinyavskiy (Liivak 84), Sappinen.
Suduva: (442) Kardum; Efremov (Svrljuga 72), Kerla, Hladik, Zivanovic; Slavickas, Matulevicius (Jankauskas 61), Leimonas (Pusic 37), Salamon (Sabala 120); Tadic, Topcagic.
aet; Suduva won 2-1 on penalties.

Floriana (0) 0

CFR Cluj (0) 2 *(Cestor 53, Golofca 90)*

Floriana: (442) Akpan; Cheveresan (Dias 67), Cini (Beye 69), Pisani (Paiber 82), Ruiz; Camenzuli, Garcia, Diego Silva, Tiago Adan; Keqi, Leone.
CFR Cluj: (442) Balgradean; Burca, Paulo Vinicius, Cestor, Camora; Chipciu (Golofca 89), Itu (Luis Aurelio 67), Hoban, Deac; Rondon, Pereira (Susic 83).

Maccabi Tel Aviv (0) 2 *(Blackman 58 (pen), 88 (pen))*

Riga FC (0) 0

Maccabi Tel Aviv: (442) Daniel; Kandil, Tibi, Yeini, Saborit; Almog (Ben Haim II 82), Glazer D, Peretz (Shechter 84), Rikan; Blackman, Guerrero (Biton 46).
Riga FC: (442) Ozols; Fjodorovs, Cernomordijs, Prenga, Rugins; Panic, Felipe Brisola, Sharpar, Hora (Dario Junior 71); Mbombo (Roger 59), Junior (N'Kololo 62).

Molde (2) 5 *(Hestad 26, Eikrem 37, Omoijuanfo 69, Knudtzon 90, Pedersen 90)*

KuPS Kuopio (0) 0

Molde: (442) Linde; Wingo (Pedersen 74), Sinyan, Ellingsen, Haugen; Aursnes, Hussain, Eikrem (Christensen 86), Brynhildsen (Knudtzon 79); Omoijuanfo, Hestad.
KuPS Kuopio: (442) Virtanen; Savolainen, Manga, Pirttijoki, Tomas (Vartiainen 66); Pennanen, Adjei-Boateng, Nissila, Sale (Purje 74); Rangel (Udoh 74), Niskanen.

Sheriff Tiraspol (1) 2 *(Abang 36, Lukic 81)*

Fola Esch (0) 0

Sheriff Tiraspol: (442) Celeadnic; Peteleu, N'Diaye, Obilor, Cristiano; Parra (Veloso 90), Mioc, Petro, Boban (Blyznychenko 88); Abang, Castaneda (Lukic 67).
Fola Esch: (442) Cabral; Ouassiero (Drif 80), Klein, Delgardo, Sinani (Freire 82); Dikaba (Hadji 62), Pimentel, Sacras, Diallo; Caron, Bensi.
KI Klaksvik v Slovan Bratislava cancelled due to positive COVID-19 tests of Slovan players. KI awarded 3-0 win.

SECOND QUALIFYING ROUND

Tuesday, 25 August 2020

KF Tirana (0) 0

Red Star Belgrade (0) 1 *(Tomane 61)*

KF Tirana: (442) Lika; Tosevski, Najdovski, Vangjeli, Elton Cale (Avdijaj 85); Hoxhallari (Toli 76), Torassa, Cobbinah (Vrapi 73), Celhaka; Batha, Muci.
Red Star Belgrade: (442) Borjan; Gobeljic, Milunovic, Pankov, Degenek (Rodic 60); Sanogo, Nikolic, Spiridonovic (Ivanic 46), Kanga (Petrovic 83); Katai, Tomane.

PAOK (3) 3 *(Tzolis 7, 24, Pelkas 30)*

Besiktas (1) 1 *(Larin 37)*

PAOK: (442) Zivkovic Z; Rodrigo (Limnios 44), Ingason, Varela, Michailidis; Pelkas (Esiti 76), El Kaddouri, Schwab, Giannoulis; Tzolis (Leo Jaba 84), Akpom.
Besiktas: (442) Destanoglu; Lens, Vida, Welinton, N'Sakala (Nayir 82); Hutchinson, Uysal, Boyd (Ozyakup 46), Mensah (Tokoz 70); Nkoudou, Larin.

Wednesday, 26 August 2020

AZ Alkmaar (0) 3 *(Koopmeiners 90 (pen), Gudmundsson 98, 118)*

Viktoria Plzen (0) 1 *(Limbersky 78)*

AZ Alkmaar: (4231) Bizot; Svensson, Vlaar (Leeuwin 76), Koopmeiners, Wijndal; Midtsjoe, Clasie (Druijf 80); Stengs (Gudmundsson 64), de Wit, Idrissi (Sugawara 93); Boadu.
Viktoria Plzen: (4231) Hruska; Havel, Hejda, Brabec, Limbersky; Kalvach (Kacer 106), Bucha; Kopic (Kovarik 87), Cermak, Mihalik (Avila Ba Loua 74); Beauguel (Pernica 90).
aet.

Celje (1) 1 *(Lotric 38)*

Molde (0) 2 *(Hussain 57, James 74)*

Celje: (4231) Rozman; Kadusic, Zaletel, Calusic, Marandici; Vrbanec, Stravs (Pungarsek 70); Kerin, Lotric (Novak 84), Bozic (Dangubic 85); Vizinger.
Molde: (4231) Linde; Knudtzon (Omoijuanfo 56), Sinyan, Ellingsen, Haugen; Aursnes, Hussain; Pedersen, Eikrem (Christensen 79), Hestad (Brynhildsen 84); James.

Celtic (0) 1 *(Christie 53)*

Ferencvaros (1) 2 *(Siger 7, Nguen 75)*

Celtic: (4231) Barkas; Elhamed (Frimpong 78), Jullien, Ajer, Taylor; Brown, McGregor; Forrest (Ajeti 78), Ntcham, Elyounoussi; Christie.
Ferencvaros: (433) Dibusz; Botka, Blazic, Kovacevic, Civic; Siger, Kharatin, Somalia; Uzuni (Dvali 86), Isael (Boli 71), Nguen (Skvarka 80).

CFR Cluj (0) 2 *(Pereira 64, Debeljuh 90)*

Dinamo Zagreb (1) 2 *(Gojak 14, Kastrati 78)*

CFR Cluj: (4141) Balgradean; Burca (Susic 82), Paulo Vinicius, Boli, Camora; Bordeianu (Itu 113); Chipciu (Rondon 46), Deac, Djokovic, Pereira (Golofca 68); Debeljuh.
Dinamo Zagreb: (442) Livakovic; Stojanovic, Theophile-Catherine■, Dilaver, Leovac; Gojak, Ivanusec (Petkovic 68), Ademi, Orsic (Moharrami 108); Majer (Kastrati 54), Gavranovic (Gvardiol 54).
aet; Dinamo Zagreb won 6-5 on penalties.

Dinamo Brest (1) 2 *(Gordeichuk 3, Diallo 50)*

Sarajevo (1) 1 *(Djokanovic 34)*

Dinamo Brest: (433) Ignatovich; Yuzepchuk, Khacheridi, Gabi, Pechenin; Tweh, Kislyak, Sedko (Savitskiy 79); Diallo, Milevskiy (Bykov 86), Gordeichuk (Krivets 71).
Sarajevo: (433) Kovacevic; Hodzic, Dupovac, Milicevic, Salcin; Djokanovic (Handzic 80), Oremus (Susic 90), Rahmanovic; Jukic (Fanimo 66), Ahmetovic, Tatar.

Legia Warsaw (0) 0

Omonia Nicosia (0) 2 *(Gomez 92 (pen), Thiago Santos 107)*

Legia Warsaw: (4231) Boruc; Karbownik, Lewczuk■, Jedrzejczyk, Mladenovic; Antolic, Slisz; Luquinhas, Gvilia (Wieteska 60 (Andre Martins 108)), Rosolek (Kapustka 79); Pekhart (Kante 61).
Omonia Nicosia: (433) Fabiano; Tzionis (Asante 76), Luftner, Lang, Lecjaks; Vitor Gomes (Mavrias 103), Kousoulos, Gomez; Thiago Santos (Kiko 112), Duris, Bautheac (Loizou 91).
aet.

Lokomotiva Zagreb (0) 0

Rapid Vienna (1) 1 *(Kara 32)*

Lokomotiva Zagreb: (532) Hendija; Karacic, Osmankovic, Kolinger, Markovic (Budimir 61), Celikovic; Gjira, Petrak (Kallaku 72), Halilovic; Tuci (Sammir 46), Cuze.
Rapid Vienna: (4231) Strebinger; Stojkovic, Hofmann, Greiml, Ullmann; Petrovic, Ljubicic; Arase (Schick 76), Fountas (Kitagawa 86), Murg (Grahovac 64); Kara.

Ludogorets Razgrad (0) 0

FC Midtjylland (0) 1 *(Junior Brumado 78)*

Ludogorets Razgrad: (4231) Renan; Cicinho, Moti, Grigore, Nedyalkov; Badji, Tchibota (Jorginho 79); Cauly, Abel (Tekpetey 55), Santana; Keseru (Marin 55).
FC Midtjylland: (4231) Hansen; Andersson, Sviatchenko, Scholz, Paulinho; Cajuste, Onyeka; Dreyer, Kraev (Junior Brumado 65), Mabil; Kaba (Anderson 75).

Qarabag (1) 2 *(Matic 22 (pen), Emreli 63)*

Sheriff Tiraspol (0) 1 *(Castaneda 78)*

Qarabag: (433) Mahammadaliyev; Medvedev, Medina, Huseynov B, Guerrier (Huseynov A 90); Qarayev, Matic, Ozobic (Ibrahhimli 70); Romero (Kwabena 89), Emreli, Zoubir.
Sheriff Tiraspol: (442) Celeadnic; Peteleu, Obilor (Julien 74), N'Diaye, Cristiano; Parra, Lukic, Mioc (Castaneda 46), Petro; Abang■, Boban (Gadze 74).

Suduva (0) 0

Maccabi Tel Aviv (1) 3 *(Rikan 30, Blackman 74, Davidadze 90)*

Suduva: (532) Kardum; Efremov (Svrljuga 46), Kerla, Hladik, Zivanovic, Slavickas; Pusic, Leimonas (Renan Oliveira 72), Salamon; Tadic, Topcagic (Jankauskas 63).
Maccabi Tel Aviv: (541) Daniel; Kandil, Tibi, Yeini, Saborit (Baltaxa 76), Davidadze; Biton (Bitton 88), Glazer D, Peretz, Rikan (Almog 81); Blackman.

Young Boys (0) 3 *(Nsame 51, Sulejmani 57, Ngamaleu 82)*

KI Klaksvik (0) 1 *(Johannesen J 79)*

Young Boys: (433) Ballmoos; Maceiras (Garcia 65), Lustenberger, Camara, Lefort; Aebischer (Martins Pereira 74), Sierro, Sulejmani (Spielmann 64); Fassnacht, Nsame, Ngamaleu.
KI Klaksvik: (541) Joensen; Pavlovic (Johannesen J 77), Danielsen, Faero, Brinck, Andreasen; Johannesen P, Vatnsdal, Bjartalid (Dosljak 89), Midtskogen (Olsen 90); Klettskard.

THIRD QUALIFYING ROUND

Tuesday, 15 September 2020

Dynamo Kyiv (0) 2 *(Rodrigues 49, Shaparenko 86)*

AZ Alkmaar (0) 0

Dynamo Kyiv: (4231) Bushchan; Kedziora, Zabarnyi, Mykolenko, Karavayev; Sydorchuk, Shaparenko (Lednev 90); Rodrigues, Buyalsky (Andrievsky 79), De Pena; Supriaga (Verbic 74).
AZ Alkmaar: (433) Bizot; Svensson, Vlaar (Sugawara 80), Koopmeiners, Wijndal; Clasie, de Wit, Midtsjoe (Druijf 66); Stengs, Boadu, Gudmundsson (Idrissi 58).

Gent (1) 2 *(Dorsch 36, Yaremchuk 59 (pen))*

Rapid Vienna (0) 1 *(Demir 90)*

Gent: (433) Roef; Castro-Montes, Arslanagic, Ngadeu Ngadjui, Nurio Fortuna; Kums, Owusu, Dorsch (Odjidja-Ofoe 64); Yaremchuk (Kleindienst 89), Depoitre, Chakvetadze (Bezus 60).
Rapid Vienna: (4231) Strebinger; Stojkovic, Hofmann, Greiml, Ullmann; Ljubicic, Petrovic (Grahovac 86); Arase (Demir 73), Fountas, Murg; Kara (Kitagawa 86).

PAOK (0) 2 *(Giannoulis 63, Zivkovic A 75)*

Benfica (0) 1 *(Rafa Silva 90)*

PAOK: (3412) Zivkovic Z; Ingason, Varela, Michailidis; Crespo, Schwab, El Kaddouri, Giannoulis; Pelkas (Zivkovic A 67); Akpom (Swiderski 70), Tzolis (Esiti 80).
Benfica: (4231) Vlachodimos; Andre Almeida, Dias, Vertonghen, Grimaldo; Weigl, Taarabt (Rafa Silva 76); Pizzi, Pedrinho (Nunez 65), Everton; Seferovic (Vinicius 72).

Wednesday, 16 September 2020

FC Midtjylland (0) 3 *(Lefort 51 (og), Dreyer 61, Mabil 84)*

Young Boys (0) 0

FC Midtjylland: (4231) Hansen; Andersson, Sviatchenko, Scholz, Paulinho; Cajuste, Onyeka; Dreyer (Evander 85), Kraev (Sisto 62), Mabil; Kaba (Junior Brumado 78).
Young Boys: (433) Ballmoos; Hefti, Camara, Lustenberger, Lefort; Sulejmani (Spielmann 66), Aebischer, Martins Pereira; Fassnacht (Mambimbi 82), Nsame, Ngamaleu (Siebatcheu 66).

Ferencvaros (1) 2 *(Lovrencsics 2, Uzuni 65)*

Dinamo Zagreb (1) 1 *(Uzuni 23 (og))*

Ferencvaros: (433) Dibusz; Lovrencsics (Botka 25), Blazic, Kovacevic (Frimpong 73), Civic; Siger, Kharatin, Somalia; Uzuni, Boli (Isael 68), Nguen.
Dinamo Zagreb: (4141) Livakovic; Stojanovic, Dilaver, Gvardiol, Leovac; Ademi; Kastrati, Gojak (Gavranovic 71), Majer (Jakic 60), Orsic (Ivanusec 72); Petkovic.

Maccabi Tel Aviv (0) 1 *(Biton 50 (pen))*

Dinamo Brest (0) 0

Maccabi Tel Aviv: (532) Daniel; Kandil, Tibi, Yeini, Saborit, Davidadze; Peretz, Glazer D, Golasa (Rikan 65); Biton (Cohen 82), Shechter (Blackman 57).
Dinamo Brest: (433) Ignatovich; Khacheridi (Pavlovets 62), Pechenin, Gabi, Yuzepchuk; Tweh, Kislyak, Sedko; Milevskiy (Bykov 86), Gordeichuk (Savitskiy 70), Diallo.

Omonia Nicosia (1) 1 *(Luftner 31)*

Red Star Belgrade (1) 1 *(Ivanic 45)*

Omonia Nicosia: (442) Fabiano; Hubocan (Kousoulos 90), Luftner, Lang, Lecjaks; Bautheac, Gomez, Vitor Gomes, Thiago Santos (Asante 118); Papoulis (Loizou 98), Kakoullis (Kaly Sene 65).
Red Star Belgrade: (433) Borjan; Gobeljic, Milunovic, Degenek, Rodic (Gajic 106); Kanga, Sanogo, Ivanic (Jovancic 81); Ben, Vukanovic (Falcinelli 89), Katai (Gavric 101).
aet; Omonia Nicosia won 4-2 on penalties.

Qarabag (0) 0

Molde (0) 0

Qarabag: (4231) Mahammadaliyev; Medvedev, Huseynov B, Medina, Guerrier (Dzhafarquliyev 114); Matic, Garayev (Ibrahhimli 77); Kwabena, Ozobic (Andrade 82), Zoubir; Emreli (Huseynov A 106).
Molde: (4231) Linde; Wingo, Gregersen, Ellingsen, Haugen; Aursnes, Hussain (Christensen 120); Knudtzon (Brynhildsen 69), Eikrem (Omoijuanfo 79), Hestad; James (Bolly 99).
aet; Molde won 6-5 on penalties.

PLAY-OFF ROUND FIRST LEG

Tuesday, 22 September 2020

Krasnodar (1) 2 *(Claesson 39 (pen), Cabella 70)*

PAOK (1) 1 *(Pelkas 32)*

Krasnodar: (433) Safonov; Petrov, Kaio, Sorokin, Ramirez; Cabella (Utkin 81), Olsson, Vilhena; Wanderson (Suleymanov 86), Berg, Claesson.
PAOK: (541) Zivkovic Z; Crespo, Ingason, Varela, Michailidis, Giannoulis; Pelkas (Biseswar 79), El Kaddouri, Schwab, Tzolis (Swiderski 84); Zivkovic A.

Maccabi Tel Aviv (1) 1 *(Biton 9)*

Red Bull Salzburg (0) 2 *(Szoboszlai 49 (pen), Okugawa 57)*

Maccabi Tel Aviv: (532) Daniel; Bitton, Yeini, Tibi, Baltaxa (Hozez 82), Davidadze; Barsky (Ben Haim II 61), Karzev (Shechter 71), Golasa; Biton, Almog.
Red Bull Salzburg: (442) Stankovic; Kristensen, Ramalho, Wober, Ulmer; Szoboszlai (Camara 86), Bernede, Mwepu, Okugawa (Okafor 76); Berisha (Koita 46), Daka.

Slavia Prague (0) 0

FC Midtjylland (0) 0

Slavia Prague: (4141) Kolar; Coufal, Hovorka, Zima, Boril; Holes; Masopust (Provod 71), Sevcik, Stanciu (Takacs 90), Olayinka; Tecl (Musa 59).
FC Midtjylland: (433) Hansen; Andersson, Sviatchenko, Scholz, Paulinho; Cajuste, Onyeka, Evander (Anderson 76); Dreyer (Sisto 67), Kaba (Junior Brumado 89), Mabil.

Wednesday, 23 September 2020

Gent (1) 1 *(Kleindienst 41)*

Dynamo Kyiv (1) 2 *(Supriaga 9, De Pena 79)*

Gent: (4231) Roef; Castro-Montes, Plastun, Ngadeu Ngadjui, Nurio Fortuna; Owusu, Dorsch; Bezus■, Yaremchuk (Kleindienst 25), Odjidja-Ofoe (Botaka 62); Depoitre (Mohammadi 72).
Dynamo Kyiv: (433) Bushchan; Kedziora, Zabarnyi, Mykolenko, Karavayev; Buyalsky, Sydorchuk, Shaparenko (Shepelev 82); Rodrigues (Tsygankov 59), Supriaga (Verbic 66), De Pena.

Molde (0) 3 *(James 55, Eikrem 65, Ellingsen 83)*

Ferencvaros (1) 3 *(Boli 7, Uzuni 52, Kharatin 87 (pen))*

Molde: (4231) Linde; Wingo, Gregersen, Ellingsen, Haugen; Aursnes, Hussain; Knudtzon (Brynhildsen 57), Hestad, Eikrem (Omoijuanfo 81); James (Bolly 89).
Ferencvaros: (433) Dibusz; Botka, Blazic, Frimpong, Civic; Laidouni, Kharatin, Somalia (Siger 71); Uzuni, Boli (Zubkov 73), Nguen (Isael 88).

Olympiacos (0) 2 *(Valbuena 69 (pen), El Arabi 90)*

Omonia Nicosia (0) 0

Olympiacos: (4231) Jose Sa; Rafinha, Semedo, Ba, Holebas; Camara, Bouchalakis; Masouras (Randjelovic 59), Fortounis (El Arabi 59), Valbuena; Kouka (M'Vila 76).
Omonia Nicosia: (442) Fabiano; Hubocan, Luftner, Lang, Lecjaks; Bautheac (Loizou 87), Vitor Gomes, Gomez, Thiago Santos; Papoulis (Asante 81), Kaly Sene (Duris 46).

PLAY-OFF ROUND SECOND LEG

Tuesday, 29 September 2020

Dynamo Kyiv (2) 3 *(Buyalsky 9, De Pena 36 (pen), Rodrigues 49 (pen))*

Gent (0) 0

Dynamo Kyiv: (442) Bushchan; Kedziora, Zabarnyi, Mykolenko, Karavayev; Rodrigues (Tsygankov 60), Sydorchuk, Shaparenko (Andrievsky 77), De Pena (Verbic 59); Supriaga, Buyalsky.
Gent: (4231) Roef; Castro-Montes (Botaka 65), Plastun, Ngadeu Ngadjui, Nurio Fortuna; Owusu (Marreh 54), Dorsch; Bukari, Kleindienst, Niangbo; Depoitre (Samoise 74).
Dynamo Kyiv won 5-1 on aggregate.

Ferencvaros (0) 0

Molde (0) 0

Ferencvaros: (4231) Dibusz; Lovrencsics, Blazic, Botka, Heister; Somalia (Frimpong 87), Kharatin; Zubkov, Siger (Laidouni 79), Nguen (Isael 79); Uzuni.
Molde: (4231) Linde; Pedersen, Gregersen, Ellingsen, Haugen; Aursnes, Hussain (Omoijuanfo 83); Knudtzon (Brynhildsen 64), Hestad, Eikrem; James.
Ferencvaros won on away goals.

Omonia Nicosia (0) 0

Olympiacos (0) 0

Omonia Nicosia: (442) Fabiano; Hubocan, Luftner, Lang, Lecjaks; Bautheac, Vitor Gomes, Kousoulos, Tzionis (Kaly Sene 84); Papoulis (Asante 70), Duris (Kakoullis 70).
Olympiacos: (433) Jose Sa; Rafinha, Semedo, Ba, Holebas; Camara (Cafu 90), M'Vila, Bouchalakis; Randjelovic (Masouras 75), El Arabi, Valbuena (Fortounis 90).
Olympiacos won 2-0 on aggregate.

Wednesday, 30 September 2020

FC Midtjylland (0) 4 *(Kaba 65, Scholz 84 (pen), Onyeka 88, Dreyer 90)*

Slavia Prague (1) 1 *(Olayinka 3)*

FC Midtjylland: (433) Hansen; Andersson, Sviatchenko, Scholz, Paulinho; Cajuste, Onyeka, Evander (Kraev 58); Mabil (Anderson 90), Kaba, Sisto (Dreyer 58).
Slavia Prague: (4141) Kolar; Coufal, Kudela, Hovorka, Boril; Holes; Masopust (Musa 73), Stanciu (Traore 68), Sevcik, Provod; Olayinka (Kuchta 84).
FC Midtjylland won 4-1 on aggregate.

PAOK (0) 1 *(El Kaddouri 77)*

Krasnodar (0) 2 *(Michailidis 73 (og), Cabella 77)*

PAOK: (3421) Zivkovic Z; Ingason, Varela (Swiderski 76), Michailidis; Crespo (Wague 59), El Kaddouri, Schwab, Giannoulis; Pelkas (Colak 59), Zivkovic A; Tzolis.
Krasnodar: (433) Safonov; Petrov, Martynovich, Kaio, Ramirez; Utkin (Smolnikov 58), Gazinsky (Kambolov 83), Vilhena; Claesson, Berg, Cabella (Suleymanov 85).
Krasnodar won 4-2 on aggregate.

Red Bull Salzburg (2) 3 *(Daka 16, 68, Szoboszlai 45 (pen))*

Maccabi Tel Aviv (1) 1 *(Karzev 30)*

Red Bull Salzburg: (4231) Stankovic; Vallci, Ramalho, Wober, Ulmer; Camara (Junuzovic 74), Mwepu; Daka, Szoboszlai, Okugawa (Okafor 82); Koita (Berisha 66).
Maccabi Tel Aviv: (541) Daniel; Kandil (Glazer A 74), Yeini, Tibi, Baltaxa, Bitton (Hozez 65); Biton, Karzev, Golasa, Almog (Hanzis 75); Shechter.
Red Bull Salzburg won 5-2 on aggregate.

GROUP STAGE

GROUP A

Wednesday, 21 October 2020

Bayern Munich (2) 4 *(Coman 28, 72, Goretzka 41, Tolisso 66)*

Atletico Madrid (0) 0

Bayern Munich: (4231) Neuer; Pavard (Sarr 73), Sule, Alaba, Lucas; Kimmich, Goretzka (Javi Martinez 83); Muller (Davies 83), Tolisso, Coman (Douglas Costa 73); Lewandowski (Choupo-Moting 83).
Atletico Madrid: (442) Oblak; Trippier, Savic, Felipe, Renan Lodi; Llorente (Lemar 79), Herrera, Koke (Torreira 79), Carrasco (Vitolo 76); Joao Felix, Suarez (Correa 75).

Red Bull Salzburg (1) 2 *(Szoboszlai 45, Junuzovic 50)*

Lokomotiv Moscow (1) 2 *(Eder 19, Lisakovich 75)* 3000

Red Bull Salzburg: (442) Stankovic; Vallci, Ramalho, Wober, Ulmer; Mwepu, Camara (Okugawa 73), Junuzovic (Okafor 84), Szoboszlai; Koita (Berisha 53), Daka.
Lokomotiv Moscow: (442) Guilherme; Zhivoglyadov, Corluka, Murilo, Rybus; Zhemaletdinov (Kamano 63), Kulikov, Krychowiak, Miranchuk (Lisakovich 69); Smolov (Rybchinsky 62), Eder (Ze Luis 69).

Tuesday, 27 October 2020

Atletico Madrid (1) 3 *(Llorente 29, Joao Felix 52, 85)*

Red Bull Salzburg (1) 2 *(Szoboszlai 40, Felipe 47 (og))*

Atletico Madrid: (442) Oblak; Trippier, Savic, Felipe, Renan Lodi (Hermoso 82); Correa, Llorente, Herrera (Torreira 82), Koke; Suarez (Lemar 82), Joao Felix.
Red Bull Salzburg: (4231) Stankovic; Kristensen, Ramalho, Wober (Onguene 63), Ulmer; Camara, Junuzovic (Ashimeru 63); Mwepu, Berisha, Szoboszlai; Daka (Koita 30 (Okafor 84)).

Lokomotiv Moscow (0) 1 *(Miranchuk 70)*

Bayern Munich (1) 2 *(Goretzka 13, Kimmich 79)* 8169

Lokomotiv Moscow: (4321) Guilherme; Zhivoglyadov, Corluka (Rajkovic 46), Murilo, Rybus; Ignatiev (Zhemaletdinov 76), Kulikov (Lisakovich 89), Krychowiak; Smolov (Rybchinsky 75), Miranchuk; Ze Luis.
Bayern Munich: (4231) Neuer; Pavard, Sule, Alaba, Lucas; Kimmich, Goretzka (Javi Martinez 46); Muller (Gnabry 46), Tolisso, Coman (Douglas Costa 69); Lewandowski.

Tuesday, 3 November 2020

Lokomotiv Moscow (1) 1 *(Miranchuk 25 (pen))*

Atletico Madrid (1) 1 *(Gimenez 18)* 8147

Lokomotiv Moscow: (442) Guilherme; Zhivoglyadov, Murilo, Rajkovic, Rybus; Ignatiev, Kulikov, Krychowiak, Miranchuk (Rybchinsky 89); Smolov (Zhemaletdinov 64), Ze Luis.
Atletico Madrid: (4321) Oblak; Trippier, Savic, Gimenez, Renan Lodi; Llorente (Vitolo 69 (Torreira 78)), Herrera, Saul (Koke 46); Correa (Lemar 69), Joao Felix; Suarez.

Red Bull Salzburg (1) 2 *(Berisha 4, Okugawa 66)*

Bayern Munich (2) 6 *(Lewandowski 21 (pen), 88, Kristensen 44 (og), Boateng 79, Sane 83, Lucas 90)*

Red Bull Salzburg: (4321) Stankovic; Kristensen, Ramalho, Wober, Ulmer; Mwepu, Camara, Junuzovic (Okugawa 65); Berisha (Onguene 76), Szoboszlai; Koita (Okafor 65).
Bayern Munich: (4231) Neuer; Pavard (Sarr 74), Boateng, Alaba, Lucas; Kimmich, Tolisso (Javi Martinez 74); Gnabry (Douglas Costa 90), Muller (Musiala 90), Coman (Sane 74); Lewandowski.

Wednesday, 25 November 2020

Atletico Madrid (0) 0

Lokomotiv Moscow (0) 0

Atletico Madrid: (442) Oblak; Trippier, Savic, Gimenez, Renan Lodi (Hermoso 60); Llorente (Lemar 60), Koke, Saul, Carrasco (Camello 80); Correa, Joao Felix.
Lokomotiv Moscow: (451) Guilherme; Zhivoglyadov, Corluka, Murilo, Rybus; Ignatiev, Kulikov, Krychowiak, Kamano (Rybchinsky 76), Miranchuk (Magkeev 76); Ze Luis.

Bayern Munich (1) 3 *(Lewandowski 42, Coman 52, Sane 68)*

Red Bull Salzburg (0) 1 *(Berisha 73)*

Bayern Munich: (4231) Neuer; Pavard (Lucas 63), Boateng, Alaba, Richards (Javi Martinez 79); Goretzka, Roca■; Gnabry (Sane 62), Muller, Coman (Douglas Costa 78); Lewandowski.
Red Bull Salzburg: (4231) Stankovic; Kristensen, Ramalho, Wober, Ulmer; Junuzovic (Adeyemi 71), Camara; Mwepu (Ashimeru 72), Berisha, Szoboszlai (Sucic 71); Koita.

Tuesday, 1 December 2020

Atletico Madrid (1) 1 *(Joao Felix 26)*

Bayern Munich (0) 1 *(Muller 86 (pen))*

Atletico Madrid: (352) Oblak; Savic, Gimenez (Felipe 68), Hermoso; Trippier, Llorente, Koke, Saul, Carrasco (Renan Lodi 87); Correa (Herrera 80), Joao Felix (Lemar 87).
Bayern Munich: (3421) Nubel; Sule, Alaba, Lucas; Sarr (Richards 62), Musiala (Stiller 76), Javi Martinez (Muller 62), Arrey-Mbi (Gnabry 61); Sane, Douglas Costa (Zirkzee 86); Choupo-Moting.

Lokomotiv Moscow (0) 1 *(Miranchuk 79 (pen))*

Red Bull Salzburg (2) 3 *(Berisha 28, 41, Adeyemi 81)* 6759

Lokomotiv Moscow: (3412) Guilherme; Lystsov (Miranchuk 46), Corluka, Rajkovic (Ignatiev 46); Zhivoglyadov (Rybchinsky 84), Magkeev, Murilo, Rybus; Lisakovich (Mukhin 46); Eder, Ze Luis (Kamano 89).
Red Bull Salzburg: (442) Stankovic; Kristensen, Ramalho, Wober, Ulmer; Mwepu, Camara (Sucic 69), Junuzovic, Szoboszlai (Daka 77); Berisha (Onguene 90), Koita (Adeyemi 70).

Wednesday, 9 December 2020

Bayern Munich (0) 2 *(Sule 63, Choupo-Moting 80)*

Lokomotiv Moscow (0) 0

Bayern Munich: (4231) Neuer; Sarr, Boateng (Richards 69), Sule, Davies (Lucas 69); Goretzka (Musiala 61), Roca; Sane (Stiller 85), Muller (Gnabry 46), Douglas Costa; Choupo-Moting.
Lokomotiv Moscow: (4321) Guilherme; Zhivoglyadov, Corluka, Rajkovic, Rybus; Ignatiev, Magkeev, Rybchinsky (Silyanov 88); Kamano (Iosifov 76), Miranchuk; Eder.

Red Bull Salzburg (0) 0

Atletico Madrid (1) 2 *(Hermoso 39, Carrasco 86)*

Red Bull Salzburg: (41212) Stankovic; Kristensen, Ramalho, Wober (Onguene 89), Ulmer; Junuzovic; Mwepu (Sucic 89), Szoboszlai (Okugawa 89); Berisha; Daka (Okafor 73), Koita (Adeyemi 79).
Atletico Madrid: (3142) Oblak; Savic, Felipe, Hermoso; Koke; Trippier, Llorente (Renan Lodi 90), Saul (Herrera 64), Carrasco (Lemar 89); Suarez (Correa 64), Joao Felix (Torreira 89).

Group A Table	P	W	D	L	F	A	GD	Pts
Bayern Munich	6	5	1	0	18	5	13	16
Atletico Madrid	6	2	3	1	7	8	–1	9
Red Bull Salzburg	6	1	1	4	10	17	–7	4
Lokomotiv Moscow	6	0	3	3	5	10	–5	3

GROUP B

Wednesday, 21 October 2020

Internazionale (0) 2 *(Lukaku 49, 90)*

Borussia Moenchengladbach (0) 2 *(Bensebaini 63 (pen), Hofmann 84)* 1000

Internazionale: (3412) Handanovic; D'Ambrosio, de Vrij, Kolarov; Darmian, Barella, Vidal, Perisic (Bastoni 79); Eriksen (Brozovic 79); Lukaku, Sanchez (Martinez 46).
Borussia Moenchengladbach: (4231) Sommer; Lainer, Ginter, Elvedi, Bensebaini; Kramer, Neuhaus; Hofmann, Embolo (Herrmann 74), Thuram (Wolf 90); Plea (Stindl 90).

Real Madrid (0) 2 *(Modric 54, Vinicius Junior 59)*

Shakhtar Donetsk (3) 3 *(Tete 29, Varane 33 (og), Solomon 42)*

Real Madrid: (433) Courtois; Mendy, Varane, Eder Militao, Marcelo; Valverde, Casemiro, Modric (Kroos 70); Asensio, Jovic (Vinicius Junior 59), Rodrygo (Benzema 46).
Shakhtar Donetsk: (4141) Trubin; Dodo, Bondar, Khocholava, Korniyenko; Maycon; Tete, Marlos, Marcos Antonio (Vyunnyk 90), Solomon (Vitao 90); Dentinho (Sudakov 86).

Tuesday, 27 October 2020

Borussia Moenchengladbach (1) 2 *(Thuram 33, 58)*

Real Madrid (0) 2 *(Benzema 87, Casemiro 90)*

Borussia Moenchengladbach: (4231) Sommer; Lainer, Ginter, Elvedi, Bensebaini; Kramer, Neuhaus; Hofmann, Stindl (Wolf 79), Thuram (Herrmann 71); Plea (Embolo 79).
Real Madrid: (433) Courtois; Lucas, Varane, Sergio Ramos, Mendy; Valverde, Casemiro, Kroos (Modric 71); Asensio (Rodrygo 84), Benzema, Vinicius Junior (Hazard 70).

Shakhtar Donetsk (0) 0

Internazionale (0) 0 10,178

Shakhtar Donetsk: (4141) Trubin; Dodo, Bondar, Khocholava (Matviyenko 62), Korniyenko; Maycon; Tete, Marlos (Alan Patrick 88), Marcos Antonio, Solomon; Dentinho (Taison 15).
Internazionale: (352) Handanovic; D'Ambrosio (Darmian 80), de Vrij, Bastoni; Hakimi, Barella, Brozovic, Vidal (Eriksen 79), Young (Pinamonti 85); Lukaku, Martinez (Perisic 72).

Tuesday, 3 November 2020

Real Madrid (2) 3 *(Benzema 25, Sergio Ramos 33, Rodrygo 80)*

Internazionale (1) 2 *(Martinez 35, Perisic 68)*

Real Madrid: (433) Courtois; Lucas, Varane, Sergio Ramos, Mendy; Valverde, Casemiro, Kroos (Modric 78); Asensio (Rodrygo 64), Benzema, Hazard (Vinicius Junior 64).
Internazionale: (352) Handanovic; D'Ambrosio, de Vrij, Bastoni; Hakimi, Barella (Gagliardini 78), Brozovic, Vidal (Nainggolan 87), Young; Martinez, Perisic (Sanchez 78).

Shakhtar Donetsk (0) 0

Borussia Moenchengladbach (4) 6 *(Plea 8, 26, 78, Bondar 17 (og), Bensebaini 44, Stindl 65)*

Shakhtar Donetsk: (4141) Trubin; Dodo, Bondar, Khocholava, Korniyenko; Maycon (Stepanenko 69); Tete, Marlos (Kovalenko 46), Marcos Antonio (Alan Patrick 46), Solomon; Taison (Moraes 46).
Borussia Moenchengladbach: (4231) Sommer; Lainer (Lang 82), Ginter, Elvedi (Jantschke 82), Bensebaini; Kramer, Neuhaus; Hofmann (Lazaro 75), Stindl (Wolf 69), Thuram; Plea (Traore 82).

Wednesday, 25 November 2020

Borussia Moenchengladbach (3) 4 *(Stindl 17 (pen), Elvedi 34, Embolo 45, Wendt 77)*

Shakhtar Donetsk (0) 0

Borussia Moenchengladbach: (4231) Sommer; Lainer, Ginter, Elvedi, Wendt; Kramer, Neuhaus (Zakaria 69); Lazaro (Herrmann 69), Stindl (Benes 81), Thuram (Traore 84); Embolo (Plea 69).
Shakhtar Donetsk: (433) Pyatov; Dodo, Kryvtsov, Bondar, Matviyenko; Marlos (Marcos Antonio 70), Stepanenko, Alan Patrick (Maycon 81); Tete, Moraes, Solomon (Fernando 59).

Internazionale (0) 0

Real Madrid (1) 2 *(Hazard 7 (pen), Hakimi 59 (og))*

Internazionale: (352) Handanovic; Skriniar, de Vrij, Bastoni (D'Ambrosio 46); Hakimi (Sanchez 63), Barella, Vidal■, Gagliardini (Sensi 78), Young; Lukaku (Eriksen 86), Martinez (Perisic 46).
Real Madrid: (4231) Courtois; Carvajal, Varane, Nacho, Mendy; Modric, Kroos; Lucas, Odegaard (Casemiro 58), Hazard (Vinicius Junior 78); Mariano (Rodrygo 58).

Tuesday, 1 December 2020

Borussia Moenchengladbach (1) 2 *(Plea 45, 75)*

Internazionale (1) 3 *(Darmian 17, Lukaku 64, 73)*

Borussia Moenchengladbach: (4231) Sommer; Lainer, Ginter, Jantschke (Zakaria 46), Wendt (Wolf 78); Kramer, Neuhaus; Lazaro, Stindl (Embolo 70), Thuram; Plea.
Internazionale: (352) Handanovic; Skriniar, de Vrij, Bastoni; Darmian (Hakimi 60), Barella, Brozovic, Gagliardini, Young (Perisic 87); Lukaku, Martinez (Sanchez 71).

Shakhtar Donetsk (0) 2 *(Dentinho 57, Solomon 82)*

Real Madrid (0) 0

Shakhtar Donetsk: (433) Trubin; Dodo, Bondar, Vitao, Matviyenko; Marlos (Maycon 73), Stepanenko, Kovalenko (Alan Patrick 85); Tete, Moraes (Dentinho 25 (Fernando 85)), Taison (Solomon 74).
Real Madrid: (4231) Courtois; Lucas, Varane, Nacho, Mendy; Modric, Kroos; Rodrygo (Vinicius Junior 77), Odegaard (Isco 77), Asensio; Benzema (Mariano 77).

Wednesday, 9 December 2020

Internazionale (0) 0

Shakhtar Donetsk (0) 0

Internazionale: (352) Handanovic; Skriniar, de Vrij, Bastoni (D'Ambrosio 85); Hakimi (Darmian 85), Barella, Brozovic, Gagliardini (Sanchez 75), Young (Perisic 68); Lukaku, Martinez (Eriksen 85).
Shakhtar Donetsk: (532) Trubin; Dodo, Bondar, Stepanenko, Vitao (Khocholava 36), Matviyenko; Marlos (Alan Patrick 64), Kovalenko, Maycon; Tete (Solomon 65), Taison (Dentinho 86).

Real Madrid (2) 2 *(Benzema 9, 31)*

Borussia Moenchengladbach (0) 0

Real Madrid: (433) Courtois; Lucas, Varane, Sergio Ramos, Mendy; Modric, Casemiro, Kroos; Rodrygo (Arribas 74), Benzema, Vinicius Junior (Asensio 74).
Borussia Moenchengladbach: (4231) Sommer; Lainer, Ginter, Elvedi, Wendt (Lazaro 46); Kramer (Benes 85), Neuhaus; Plea, Stindl (Wolf 85), Thuram (Herrmann 85); Embolo (Zakaria 46).

Group B Table	P	W	D	L	F	A	GD	Pts
Real Madrid	6	3	1	2	11	9	2	10
Borussia Moenchengladbach	6	2	2	2	16	9	7	8
Shakhtar Donetsk	6	2	2	2	5	12	–7	8
Internazionale	6	1	3	2	7	9	–2	6

GROUP C

Wednesday, 21 October 2020

Manchester C (1) 3 *(Aguero 20 (pen), Gundogan 65, Torres 73)*

Porto (1) 1 *(Diaz 14)*

Manchester C: (433) Ederson; Walker, Dias, Garcia, Joao Cancelo; Bernardo Silva, Rodri (Fernandinho 85 (Stones 90)), Gundogan (Foden 68); Mahrez, Aguero (Torres 68), Sterling.
Porto: (541) Marchesin; Corona (Nanu 77), Mbemba, Pepe, Sarr (Evanilson 80), Sanusi (Nakajima 76); Vieira (Taremi 77), Sergio Oliveira, Uribe, Diaz (Manafa 55); Marega.

Olympiacos (0) 1 *(Kouka 90)*

Marseille (0) 0

Olympiacos: (442) Jose Sa; Rafinha, Semedo, Ba, Holebas; Randjelovic (Fortounis 78), M'Vila, Bouchalakis, Masouras (Kouka 84); Valbuena (Cisse 90), El Arabi (Ruben Vinagre 90).
Marseille: (4141) Mandanda; Sakai, Alvaro, Caleta-Car, Amavi; Gueye (Strootman 85); Thauvin (Germain 82), Rongier, Sanson (Cuisance 77), Payet (Radonjic 76); Benedetto (Luis Henrique 77).

Tuesday, 27 October 2020

Marseille (0) 0

Manchester C (1) 3 *(Torres 18, Gundogan 76, Sterling 81)*

Marseille: (532) Mandanda; Sakai, Balerdi, Alvaro, Caleta-Car, Amavi; Rongier (Sanson 64), Kamara, Cuisance (Gueye 85); Thauvin (Payet 78), Radonjic (Benedetto 78).
Manchester C: (433) Ederson; Walker, Dias, Laporte (Stones 77), Zinchenko (Joao Cancelo 68); Gundogan (Bernardo Silva 78), Rodri, De Bruyne (Palmer 82); Sterling, Torres (Mahrez 77), Foden.

Porto (1) 2 *(Vieira 11, Sergio Oliveira 85)*

Olympiacos (0) 0 2450

Porto: (4231) Marchesin; Manafa, Mbemba, Pepe, Sanusi; Uribe, Vieira (Nakajima 60); Corona (Evanilson 69), Sergio Oliveira (Baro 89), Otavio (Grujic 70); Marega.
Olympiacos: (4231) Jose Sa; Rafinha, Semedo, Cisse, Holebas (Ruben Vinagre 70); M'Vila, Bouchalakis (Pepe 84); Randjelovic (Bruma 70), Valbuena (Kouka 84), Masouras (Fortounis 53); El Arabi.

Tuesday, 3 November 2020

Manchester C (1) 3 *(Torres 12, Gabriel Jesus 81, Joao Cancelo 90)*

Olympiacos (0) 0

Manchester C: (433) Ederson; Walker (Joao Cancelo 82), Stones, Ake, Zinchenko; De Bruyne (Nmecha 85), Gundogan, Foden (Rodri 69); Mahrez (Gabriel Jesus 69), Torres, Sterling (Bernardo Silva 82).
Olympiacos: (433) Jose Sa; Rafinha, Semedo, Cisse, Holebas; Camara (Masouras 73), M'Vila, Bouchalakis (Pepe 46); Randjelovic (Bruma 46), El Arabi (Kouka 76), Valbuena (Soudani 85).

Porto (2) 3 *(Marega 4, Sergio Oliveira 28 (pen), Diaz 69)*

Marseille (0) 0

Porto: (442) Marchesin; Manafa, Mbemba, Sarr, Sanusi; Corona (Vieira 85), Sergio Oliveira (Grujic 88), Uribe, Otavio (Taremi 88); Marega (Baro 88), Diaz (Nakajima 75).
Marseille: (41212) Mandanda; Sakai, Alvaro, Caleta-Car, Amavi; Kamara (Strootman 82); Rongier, Sanson (Cuisance 65); Payet (Luis Henrique 65); Thauvin (Ake 82), Benedetto (Germain 77).

Wednesday, 25 November 2020

Marseille (0) 0

Porto (1) 2 *(Sanusi 39, Sergio Oliveira 72 (pen))*

Marseille: (4231) Mandanda; Sakai, Alvaro, Balerdi■, Amavi; Rongier, Kamara (Cuisance 59); Thauvin (Ake 78), Sanson (Nagatomo 77), Luis Henrique (Payet 59); Germain (Benedetto 59).
Porto: (442) Marchesin; Manafa, Mbemba, Sarr, Sanusi; Corona (Taremi 78), Sergio Oliveira (N'Diaye 90), Grujic■, Otavio; Marega (Joao Mario 79), Diaz (Nakajima 79).

Olympiacos (0) 0

Manchester C (1) 1 *(Foden 36)*

Olympiacos: (541) Jose Sa; Drager (Vrousai 66), Ba, Semedo, Cisse, Rafinha; Masouras (Soudani 78), M'Vila, Pepe (Bouchalakis 71), Camara; Fortounis.
Manchester C: (4231) Ederson; Joao Cancelo, Stones, Dias, Mendy (Zinchenko 78); Rodri (Fernandinho 76), Gundogan (Doyle 86); Sterling (Mahrez 76), Bernardo Silva, Foden; Gabriel Jesus (Aguero 78).

Tuesday, 1 December 2020

Marseille (0) 2 *(Payet 55 (pen), 75 (pen))*

Olympiacos (1) 1 *(Camara 33)*

Marseille: (4231) Mandanda; Sakai, Alvaro, Caleta-Car, Amavi; Rongier (Gueye 85), Kamara; Thauvin (Ake 90), Cuisance (Sanson 55), Payet; Benedetto (Germain 46).
Olympiacos: (4231) Jose Sa; Rafinha, Semedo, Cisse, Holebas; Bouchalakis, M'Vila (Masouras 79); Fortounis, Camara, Vrousai (Soudani 90); El Arabi.

Porto (0) 0

Manchester C (0) 0

Porto: (532) Marchesin; Manafa (Nanu 72), Mbemba, Diogo Leite, Sarr, Sanusi; Otavio (Vieira 87), Sergio Oliveira, Uribe; Marega (Evanilson 72), Corona (Diaz 63).
Manchester C: (4231) Ederson; Joao Cancelo, Dias, Garcia, Zinchenko; Fernandinho, Rodri; Sterling, Bernardo Silva, Foden; Torres (Gabriel Jesus 71).

Wednesday, 9 December 2020

Manchester C (0) 3 *(Torres 48, Aguero 77, Alvaro 90 (og))*

Marseille (0) 0

Manchester C: (4231) Steffen; Walker, Garcia (Stones 28), Laporte, Ake; Fernandinho, Gundogan (Sterling 46); Mahrez (Aguero 67), Bernardo Silva, Foden; Torres.
Marseille: (4141) Mandanda; Sakai, Alvaro, Balerdi, Nagatomo; Kamara (Rongier 66); Thauvin (Ake 75), Sanson, Gueye (Strootman 75), Germain (Benedetto 75); Payet (Cuisance 67).

Olympiacos (0) 0

Porto (1) 2 *(Otavio 10 (pen), Uribe 77)*

Olympiacos: (4231) Jose Sa; Rafinha, Semedo■, Cisse, Holebas; Bouchalakis, M'Vila; Vrousai (Soudani 73), Camara (Fortounis 35), Masouras (Randjelovic 46); El Arabi (Ba 81).

Porto: (433) Costa; Nanu, Mbemba, Diogo Leite, Sanusi; Baro (Uribe 64), Grujic, Otavio (Sarr 79); Joao Mario (Corona 72), Martinez (Evanilson 80), Felipe Anderson (Diaz 63).

Group C Table	P	W	D	L	F	A	GD	Pts
Manchester C	6	5	1	0	13	1	12	16
Porto	6	4	1	1	10	3	7	13
Olympiacos	6	1	0	5	2	10	–8	3
Marseille	6	1	0	5	2	13	–11	3

GROUP D

Wednesday, 21 October 2020

Ajax (0) 0

Liverpool (1) 1 *(Tagliafico 35 (og))*

Ajax: (433) Onana; Mazraoui, Schuurs (Traore 84), Martinez, Tagliafico; Klaassen (Ekkelenkamp 74), Blind (Huntelaar 83), Gravenberch; Neres (Labyad 74), Kudus (Promes 9), Tadic.
Liverpool: (433) Adrian; Alexander-Arnold, Fabinho, Gomez, Robertson; Milner (Williams R 90), Wijnaldum, Jones (Henderson 46); Salah (Shaqiri 60), Firmino (Jota 60), Mane (Minamino 60).

FC Midtjylland (0) 0

Atalanta (3) 4 *(Zapata 26, Gomez 36, Muriel 42, Miranchuk 88)* 132

FC Midtjylland: (4231) Hansen; Andersson, Sviatchenko, Scholz, Paulinho; Onyeka (Kraev 87), Cajuste (Madsen 76); Dreyer, Sisto (Anderson 87), Mabil (Vibe 75); Kaba (Evander 60).
Atalanta: (3412) Sportiello; Toloi, Romero (Palomino 86), Djimsiti; Hateboer, de Roon, Freuler (Pessina 80), Gosens; Gomez (Pasalic 68); Muriel (Ilicic 68), Zapata (Miranchuk 80).

Tuesday, 27 October 2020

Atalanta (0) 2 *(Zapata 54, 60)*

Ajax (2) 2 *(Tadic 30 (pen), Traore 38)*

Atalanta: (3421) Sportiello; Toloi, Romero, Djimsiti; Hateboer, Pasalic, Freuler, Gosens; Ilicic (Malinovsky 79), Gomez (Muriel 78); Zapata.
Ajax: (433) Onana; Mazraoui (Klaiber 56), Schuurs, Blind, Tagliafico; Klaassen, Tadic, Gravenberch; Neres (Promes 69), Traore, Antony (Labyad 90).

Liverpool (0) 2 *(Jota 55, Salah 90 (pen))*

FC Midtjylland (0) 0

Liverpool: (433) Alisson; Alexander-Arnold, Fabinho (Williams R 30), Gomez, Robertson; Shaqiri, Henderson (Wijnaldum 46), Milner; Jota (Firmino 81), Minamino (Salah 61), Origi (Mane 60).
FC Midtjylland: (4231) Andersen; Andersson, Sviatchenko, Scholz, Paulinho; Cajuste (Kraev 81), Onyeka; Dreyer, Sisto (Evander 72), Mabil (Anderson 66); Kaba (Pfeiffer 81).

Tuesday, 3 November 2020

Atalanta (0) 0

Liverpool (2) 5 *(Jota 16, 33, 54, Salah 47, Mane 49)*

Atalanta: (3412) Sportiello; Toloi, Palomino, Djimsiti; Hateboer (Depaoli 81), Pasalic (Malinovsky 63), Freuler, Mojica (Ruggeri 81); Gomez (Lammers 81); Muriel (Pessina 53), Zapata.
Liverpool: (433) Alisson; Alexander-Arnold (Williams N 82), Williams R, Gomez, Robertson (Keita 66); Jones, Henderson (Milner 65), Wijnaldum (Tsimikas 82); Salah, Jota (Firmino 65), Mane.

FC Midtjylland (1) 1 *(Dreyer 18)*

Ajax (2) 2 *(Antony 1, Tadic 13)* 132

FC Midtjylland: (4231) Andersen; Andersson (Cools 64), Sviatchenko, Scholz, Paulinho; Cajuste (Evander 81), Onyeka; Dreyer (Kraev 75), Sisto, Mabil; Kaba (Vibe 81).
Ajax: (433) Onana; Mazraoui (Klaiber 77), Schuurs (Alvarez 60), Martinez, Tagliafico; Ekkelenkamp (Klaassen 46), Blind, Gravenberch; Antony (Traore 90), Tadic, Promes.

Wednesday, 25 November 2020

Ajax (0) 3 *(Gravenberch 47, Mazraoui 49, Neres 66)*

FC Midtjylland (0) 1 *(Mabil 80 (pen))*

Ajax: (433) Onana; Mazraoui (Klaiber 82), Schuurs, Blind (Martinez 66), Tagliafico; Labyad (Promes 81), Klaassen (Alvarez 66), Gravenberch; Neres (Ekkelenkamp 90), Traore, Tadic.
FC Midtjylland: (4231) Hansen; Cools, Sviatchenko■, Scholz, Paulinho (Andersson 26); Madsen (Anderson 69), Onyeka; Dreyer (Isaksen 82), Sisto (Pfeiffer 81), Mabil; Kaba (Kraev 69).

Liverpool (0) 0

Atalanta (0) 2 *(Ilicic 60, Gosens 64)*

Liverpool: (433) Alisson; Williams N, Matip (Minamino 84), Williams R, Tsimikas (Robertson 61); Jones, Wijnaldum (Fabinho 61), Milner; Salah (Firmino 61), Origi (Jota 61), Mane.
Atalanta: (3412) Gollini; Toloi, Romero, Djimsiti; Hateboer, de Roon, Freuler, Gosens (Mojica 75); Pessina (Miranchuk 85); Ilicic (Zapata 70), Gomez.

Tuesday, 1 December 2020

Atalanta (0) 1 *(Romero 79)*

FC Midtjylland (1) 1 *(Scholz 13)*

Atalanta: (3412) Sportiello; Djimsiti, Romero, Palomino (Toloi 68); Hateboer, Pessina, Freuler (de Roon 68), Gosens (Ruggeri 86); Gomez (Ilicic 46); Muriel (Diallo 68), Zapata.
FC Midtjylland: (541) Hansen; Andersson, James, Hoegh, Scholz, Paulinho; Dreyer (Isaksen 82), Anderson, Onyeka, Mabil (Vibe 67); Kaba (Madsen 82).

Liverpool (0) 1 *(Jones 58)*

Ajax (0) 0

Liverpool: (433) Kelleher; Williams N, Matip, Fabinho, Robertson; Jones, Henderson, Wijnaldum; Salah (Williams R 90), Jota (Firmino 68), Mane.
Ajax: (433) Onana; Mazraoui (Huntelaar 86), Schuurs, Blind (Martinez 86), Tagliafico; Alvarez (Labyad 69), Klaassen, Gravenberch; Antony, Tadic, Neres (Traore 81).

Wednesday, 9 December 2020

Ajax (0) 0

Atalanta (0) 1 *(Muriel 85)*

Ajax: (4231) Onana; Mazraoui, Schuurs, Martinez (Timber 90 (Alvarez 90)), Tagliafico (Huntelaar 64); Klaassen, Gravenberch■; Antony, Labyad (Ekkelenkamp 63), Tadic; Brobbey (Promes 46).
Atalanta: (3412) Gollini; Toloi, Romero, Djimsiti; Hateboer, de Roon, Freuler, Gosens (Palomino 79); Pessina; Zapata (Muriel 79), Gomez.

FC Midtjylland (0) 1 *(Scholz 62 (pen))*

Liverpool (1) 1 *(Salah 1)* 147

FC Midtjylland: (4231) Hansen; Cools, Sviatchenko, Scholz, Paulinho; Cajuste, Onyeka (Isaksen 63); Dreyer (Sisto 76), Evander (Madsen 90), Mabil (Anderson 63); Kaba (Pfeiffer 90).
Liverpool: (433) Kelleher; Alexander-Arnold, Williams R, Fabinho (Koumetio 46), Tsimikas (Robertson 61); Keita (Henderson 61), Clarkson, Minamino; Salah, Origi (Firmino 71), Jota (Mane 87).

Group D Table	P	W	D	L	F	A	GD	Pts
Liverpool	6	4	1	1	10	3	7	13
Atalanta	6	3	2	1	10	8	2	11
Ajax	6	2	1	3	7	7	0	7
FC Midtjylland	6	0	2	4	4	13	–9	2

GROUP E

Tuesday, 20 October 2020

Chelsea (0) 0

Sevilla (0) 0

Chelsea: (433) Mendy; James, Thiago Silva, Zouma, Chilwell; Kante, Jorginho (Kovacic 65), Mount (Ziyech 62); Havertz, Pulisic (Hudson-Odoi 90), Werner (Abraham 90).
Sevilla: (433) Bounou; Jesus Navas, Diego Carlos, Acuna, Sergi Gomez (Jordan 33); Fernando, Gudelj, Rakitic (Vazquez 80); Ocampos, Suso (Torres 58), de Jong (En-Nesyri 80).

Rennes (0) 1 *(Guirassy 56 (pen))*

Krasnodar (0) 1 *(Ramirez 59)* 4973

Rennes: (433) Gomis; Traore, Da Silva, Aguerd, Dalbert (Truffert 81); Bourigeaud (Tait 69), Nzonzi, Camavinga (Hunou 81); Del Castillo (Doku 62), Guirassy, Terrier.
Krasnodar: (4411) Safonov; Petrov (Suleymanov 72), Kaio, Sorokin, Chernov; Smolnikov, Olsson, Vilhena, Ramirez; Utkin (Gazinsky 72); Berg.

Wednesday, 28 October 2020

Krasnodar (0) 0

Chelsea (1) 4 *(Hudson-Odoi 37, Werner 76 (pen), Ziyech 79, Pulisic 90)* 10,544

Krasnodar: (4231) Safonov; Smolnikov, Martynovich, Kaio, Chernov; Gazinsky, Vilhena; Olsson (Spertsyan 82), Utkin (Suleymanov 74), Ramirez; Berg (Sabua 87).
Chelsea: (433) Mendy; Azpilicueta, Zouma, Rudiger, Chilwell (Emerson Palmieri 81); Kovacic (Kante 71), Jorginho (Mount 71), Havertz; Ziyech (Abraham 80), Werner, Hudson-Odoi (Pulisic 71).

Sevilla (0) 1 *(de Jong 55)*

Rennes (0) 0

Sevilla: (433) Bounou; Jesus Navas, Kounde, Diego Carlos, Acuna; Jordan (Gudelj 89), Fernando, Torres (Rakitic 76); Ocampos, de Jong (En-Nesyri 85), Munir (Vazquez 85).
Rennes: (433) Gomis; Soppy (Dalbert 77), Da Silva, Rugani (Aguerd 17), Traore; Bourigeaud (Lea Siliki 49), Martin, Grenier (Del Castillo 77); Doku, Guirassy, Terrier.

Wednesday, 4 November 2020

Chelsea (2) 3 *(Werner 10 (pen), 41 (pen), Abraham 50)*

Rennes (0) 0

Chelsea: (433) Mendy; James, Zouma, Thiago Silva (Rudiger 68), Chilwell (Emerson Palmieri 63); Kante (Kovacic 62), Jorginho, Mount; Ziyech (Hudson-Odoi 75), Abraham (Giroud 63), Werner.
Rennes: (4141) Gomis; Traore, Da Silva, Aguerd, Dalbert■; Nzonzi (Grenier 62); Gboho (Del Castillo 62), Lea Siliki (Truffert 46), Bourigeaud, Terrier (Doku 62); Guirassy (Hunou 76).

Sevilla (1) 3 *(Rakitic 42, En-Nesyri 69, 72)*

Krasnodar (2) 2 *(Suleymanov 17, Berg 21 (pen))*

Sevilla: (433) Vaclik; Jesus Navas■, Kounde (Rodriguez 34), Diego Carlos, Escudero (Acuna 34); Jordan (En-Nesyri 60), Gudelj, Rakitic; Munir (Fernando 60), de Jong (Rekik 83), Ocampos.
Krasnodar: (4231) Safonov; Ramirez (Sorokin 46), Martynovich, Kaio, Chernov; Olsson, Gazinsky; Suleymanov, Utkin (Wanderson 75), Sabua (Spertsyan 34 (Claesson 65)); Berg.

Tuesday, 24 November 2020

Krasnodar (0) 1 *(Wanderson 56)*

Sevilla (1) 2 *(Rakitic 4, Munir 90)* 10,554

Krasnodar: (442) Gorodov; Smolnikov, Martynovich, Kaio, Ramirez; Suleymanov (Wanderson 46), Gazinsky, Olsson (Vilhena 67), Claesson (Chernov 84); Cabella (Utkin 85), Berg (Ari 67).
Sevilla: (532) Vaclik; Ocampos (Idrissi 72), Kounde, Gudelj, Diego Carlos, Escudero (Rekik 61); Rodriguez (Jordan 53), Fernando, Rakitic (Torres 61); Munir, de Jong (En-Nesyri 72).

Rennes (0) 1 *(Guirassy 85)*

Chelsea (1) 2 *(Hudson-Odoi 22, Giroud 90)*

Rennes: (433) Gomis; Traore, Da Silva, Nyamsi, Truffert (Maouassa 86); Camavinga (Grenier 78), Nzonzi, Bourigeaud; Doku (Gboho 86), Guirassy (Niang 86), Lea Siliki (Del Castillo 63).
Chelsea: (433) Mendy; Azpilicueta, Zouma, Thiago Silva, Chilwell; Kovacic (Havertz 76), Jorginho, Mount (Kante 68); Hudson-Odoi (Ziyech 75), Abraham (Giroud 69), Werner (James 90).

Wednesday, 2 December 2020

Krasnodar (0) 1 *(Berg 71)*

Rennes (0) 0 8747

Krasnodar: (4231) Safonov; Smolnikov, Martynovich, Kaio, Ramirez; Gazinsky (Kambolov 87), Vilhena; Wanderson (Suleymanov 66), Cabella, Claesson; Berg (Ari 90).
Rennes: (4141) Salin; Traore, Da Silva, Nyamsi, Truffert; Nzonzi; Bourigeaud (Gboho 73), Lea Siliki (Grenier 65), Camavinga (Tait 82), Doku; Hunou (Niang 65).

Sevilla (0) 0

Chelsea (1) 4 *(Giroud 8, 54, 74, 83 (pen))*

Sevilla: (4231) Pastor; Jesus Navas (Kounde 59), Sergi Gomez, Diego Carlos, Rekik; Gudelj, Rakitic (Torres 75); Vazquez (Munir 66), Rodriguez (Jordan 60), Idrissi (Ocampos 59); En-Nesyri.
Chelsea: (433) Mendy; Azpilicueta, Christensen, Rudiger, Emerson Palmieri; Havertz (Kante 67), Jorginho (Gilmour 85), Kovacic (Ziyech 67); Hudson-Odoi, Giroud (Werner 84), Pulisic (Mount 67).

Tuesday, 8 December 2020

Chelsea (1) 1 *(Jorginho 28 (pen))*

Krasnodar (1) 1 *(Cabella 24)* 2000

Chelsea: (433) Arrizabalaga; Azpilicueta, Christensen, Rudiger, Emerson Palmieri; Kovacic (Kante 74), Jorginho, Gilmour; Havertz (Werner 74), Abraham, Anjorin (Giroud 80).
Krasnodar: (4231) Gorodov; Smolnikov, Martynovich, Kaio (Sorokin 74), Ramirez; Olsson (Kambolov 80), Vilhena; Wanderson (Chernov 80), Cabella (Suleymanov 80), Claesson; Berg (Markov 90).

Rennes (0) 1 *(Rutter 86 (pen))*

Sevilla (2) 3 *(Kounde 32, En-Nesyri 45, 81)*

Rennes: (442) Salin; Traore, Soppy, Da Silva (Aguerd 70), Maouassa (Truffert 79); Camavinga, Nzonzi, Grenier (Tait 79), Dalbert; Doku (Gboho 79), Niang (Rutter 70).
Sevilla: (4231) Bounou; Kounde, Sergi Gomez (Fernando 76), Diego Carlos, Rekik; Gudelj, Rakitic; Suso (Rodriguez 76), Torres (Vazquez 83), Idrissi (Ocampos 72); En-Nesyri (Carlos Fernandez 83).

Group E Table	P	W	D	L	F	A	GD	Pts
Chelsea	6	4	2	0	14	2	12	14
Sevilla	6	4	1	1	9	8	1	13
Krasnodar	6	1	2	3	6	11	–5	5
Rennes	6	0	1	5	3	11	–8	1

GROUP F

Tuesday, 20 October 2020

Lazio (2) 3 *(Immobile 6, Hitz 23 (og), Akpa Akpro 76)*

Borussia Dortmund (0) 1 *(Haaland 71)* 1000

Lazio: (352) Strakosha; Patric Gil, Felipe (Hoedt 51), Acerbi; Marusic, Milinkovic-Savic (Akpa Akpro 67), Lucas, Luis Alberto (Parolo 80), Fares; Correa (Muriqi 67), Immobile (Caicedo 80).
Borussia Dortmund: (3421) Hitz; Piszczek (Brandt 65), Hummels, Delaney; Meunier, Bellingham (Reyna 46), Witsel, Guerreiro; Sancho, Reus (Reinier 78); Haaland.

Zenit St Petersburg (0) 1 *(Horvath 74 (og))*

Club Brugge (0) 2 *(Bonaventure 63, De Ketelaere 90)* 16,682

Zenit St Petersburg: (442) Kerzhakov; Karavaev, Lovren, Rakitskiy, Krugovoy; Kuzyaev (Wendel 72), Barrios, Ozdoev (Erokhin 88), Driussi (Mostovoy 72); Azmoun, Dzyuba.
Club Brugge: (433) Horvath; Mata, Mechele, Ricca, Sobol; Vormer, Rits, Vanaken; Diatta (Lang 78), Bonaventure (Badji 82), De Ketelaere.

Wednesday, 28 October 2020

Borussia Dortmund (0) 2 *(Sancho 78 (pen), Haaland 90)*

Zenit St Petersburg (0) 0

Borussia Dortmund: (4231) Burki; Meunier, Akanji, Hummels, Guerreiro; Dahoud (Hazard 66), Witsel; Sancho (Delaney 84), Reus (Brandt 74), Reyna (Bellingham 84); Haaland.

Zenit St Petersburg: (4141) Kerzhakov; Karavaev, Lovren, Rakitskiy, Douglas Santos; Barrios (Sutormin 81); Erokhin, Kuzyaev (Ozdoev 71), Wendel, Driussi (Zhirkov 74); Dzyuba (Mostovoy 46).

Club Brugge (1) 1 *(Vanaken 42 (pen))*

Lazio (1) 1 *(Correa 14)*

Club Brugge: (352) Mignolet; Mata, Kossounou, Deli; Diatta, Vormer, Rits, Vanaken, Sobol; Bonaventure (Krmencik 88), De Ketelaere (Lang 84).
Lazio: (352) Reina; Patric Gil (Andreas Pereira 46), Hoedt, Acerbi; Marusic, Milinkovic-Savic, Parolo, Akpa Akpro, Fares (Muriqi 56); Correa, Caicedo (Czyz 68).

Wednesday, 4 November 2020

Club Brugge (0) 0

Borussia Dortmund (3) 3 *(Hazard 14, Haaland 18, 32)*

Club Brugge: (4141) Mignolet; Mata, Kossounou, Deli, Sobol; Rits; Lang (De Ketelaere 76), Vormer (Balanta 71), Vanaken (Schrijvers 85), Diatta; Bonaventure (Krmencik 85).
Borussia Dortmund: (4231) Burki; Meunier (Morey 84), Witsel, Akanji, Guerreiro; Delaney (Bellingham 72), Dahoud; Reyna (Passlack 77), Brandt (Reus 72), Hazard; Haaland (Reinier 84).

Zenit St Petersburg (1) 1 *(Erokhin 32)*

Lazio (0) 1 *(Caicedo 82)* 17,427

Zenit St Petersburg: (41212) Kerzhakov; Karavaev, Lovren, Rakitskiy, Douglas Santos; Barrios; Kuzyaev (Wendel 90), Zhirkov (Krugovoy 78); Ozdoev (Sutormin 90); Erokhin (Mostovoy 61), Dzyuba.
Lazio: (352) Reina; Patric Gil, Hoedt, Acerbi; Marusic, Akpa Akpro, Parolo (Cataldi 52), Milinkovic-Savic, Fares (Andreas Pereira 59); Muriqi (Caicedo 59), Correa (Felipe 85).

Tuesday, 24 November 2020

Borussia Dortmund (2) 3 *(Haaland 18, 60, Sancho 45)*

Club Brugge (0) 0

Borussia Dortmund: (4231) Burki; Meunier (Morey 73), Akanji, Hummels, Guerreiro (Passlack 80); Bellingham, Delaney (Can 72); Sancho, Reyna (Brandt 81), Hazard; Haaland (Reus 81).
Club Brugge: (4141) Mignolet; Mata, Kossounou, Deli, De Ketelaere; Balanta (Rits 52); Lang (Schrijvers 74), Vormer, Vanaken, Diatta (Okereke 74); Krmencik (Badji 66).

Lazio (2) 3 *(Immobile 3, 55 (pen), Parolo 22)*

Zenit St Petersburg (1) 1 *(Dzyuba 25)*

Lazio: (352) Reina; Patric Gil (Felipe 60), Hoedt, Acerbi; Lazzari (Fares 68), Parolo (Akpa Akpro 60), Lucas (Cataldi 68), Luis Alberto, Marusic; Immobile (Muriqi 81), Correa.
Zenit St Petersburg: (3511) Kerzhakov; Lovren, Rakitskiy, Zhirkov (Azmoun 73); Kuzyaev, Erokhin (Shamkin 74), Barrios (Driussi 59), Douglas Santos (Sutormin 37), Mostovoy (Musaev 59); Malcom; Dzyuba.

Wednesday, 2 December 2020

Borussia Dortmund (1) 1 *(Guerreiro 44)*

Lazio (0) 1 *(Immobile 67 (pen))*

Borussia Dortmund: (3421) Burki; Piszczek, Hummels, Akanji; Morey, Bellingham (Witsel 88), Delaney, Guerreiro (Schulz 62); Hazard (Brandt 76), Reyna; Reus (Sancho 76).
Lazio: (352) Reina; Patric Gil, Hoedt, Acerbi; Marusic, Milinkovic-Savic (Caicedo 79), Lucas (Akpa Akpro 70), Luis Alberto (Escalante 79), Fares (Lazzari 70); Immobile, Correa (Andreas Pereira 70).

Club Brugge (1) 3 *(De Ketelaere 33, Vanaken 58 (pen), Lang 73)*

Zenit St Petersburg (0) 0

Club Brugge: (4132) Mignolet; Mata (van den Keybus 90), Kossounou, Mechele, Ricca; Balanta; Bonaventure, Vanaken (Sobol 87), Vormer (Schrijvers 88); De Ketelaere, Lang (Okereke 87).
Zenit St Petersburg: (433) Kerzhakov; Sutormin, Prokhin, Rakitskiy (Krugovoy 46), Douglas Santos; Kuzyaev (Musaev 65), Barrios, Erokhin (Mostovoy 46); Malcom (Shamkin 75), Azmoun, Driussi (Ozdoev 46).

Tuesday, 8 December 2020

Lazio (2) 2 *(Correa 12, Immobile 27 (pen))*

Club Brugge (1) 2 *(Vormer 15, Vanaken 76)*

Lazio: (352) Reina; Felipe, Hoedt (Radu 46), Acerbi; Lazzari, Milinkovic-Savic, Lucas (Escalante 75), Luis Alberto (Akpa Akpro 75), Marusic; Correa (Andreas Pereira 86), Immobile (Caicedo 75).
Club Brugge: (3142) Mignolet; Mata (van der Brempt 84), Kossounou, Ricca; Balanta (Rits 77); Diatta (Okereke 84), Vormer, Vanaken, Sobol■; De Ketelaere, Lang (Deli 42).

Zenit St Petersburg (1) 1 *(Driussi 16)*

Borussia Dortmund (0) 2 *(Piszczek 68, Witsel 78)* 10,860

Zenit St Petersburg: (4231) Kerzhakov; Sutormin, Prokhin, Rakitskiy (Lovren 67), Douglas Santos; Ozdoev (Krugovoy 79), Barrios; Malcom (Karavaev 79), Driussi (Dzyuba 60), Kuzyaev (Wendel 60); Azmoun.
Borussia Dortmund: (3142) Hitz; Piszczek (Zagadou 72), Hummels (Sancho 72), Can; Witsel; Passlack (Moukoko 58), Bellingham, Brandt (Reyna 58), Schulz; Hazard (Knauff 83), Reus.

Group F Table	P	W	D	L	F	A	GD	Pts
Borussia Dortmund	6	4	1	1	12	5	7	13
Lazio	6	2	4	0	11	7	4	10
Club Brugge	6	2	2	2	8	10	–2	8
Zenit St Petersburg	6	0	1	5	4	13	–9	1

GROUP G

Tuesday, 20 October 2020

Barcelona (2) 5 *(Messi 27 (pen), Fati 42, Coutinho 52, Gonzalez 82, Dembele 89)*

Ferencvaros (0) 1 *(Kharatin 70 (pen))*

Barcelona: (4231) Neto; Sergi Roberto (Firpo 62), Pique■, Lenglet, Dest; Pjanic (Busquets 76), de Jong; Trincao (Dembele 63), Coutinho (Araujo 70), Fati (Gonzalez 62); Messi.
Ferencvaros: (4231) Dibusz; Botka (Lovrencsics 77), Blazic, Kovacevic, Civic (Heister 63); Kharatin, Laidouni (Somalia 63); Isael, Siger, Zubkov (Mak 71); Nguen (Boli 71).

Dynamo Kyiv (0) 0

Juventus (0) 2 *(Morata 46, 84)* 14,850

Dynamo Kyiv: (433) Bushchan; Kedziora, Zabarnyi, Mykolenko, Karavayev (Popov 70); Buyalsky (Harmash 89), Sydorchuk, Shaparenko; Tsygankov (Verbic 70), Supriaga, De Pena (Rodrigues 60).
Juventus: (4411) Szczesny; Cuadrado, Bonucci, Chiellini (Demiral 19), Danilo; Kulusevski (Dybala 56), Bentancur (Arthur 79), Rabiot, Chiesa; Ramsey (Bernardeschi 79); Morata.

Wednesday, 28 October 2020

Ferencvaros (0) 2 *(Nguen 59, Boli 90)*

Dynamo Kyiv (2) 2 *(Tsygankov 28 (pen), De Pena 41)* 6171

Ferencvaros: (4141) Dibusz; Lovrencsics (Botka 86), Blazic, Kovacevic (Dvali 86), Heister; Kharatin (Laidouni 65); Zubkov, Siger (Mak 73), Somalia, Nguen; Isael (Boli 73).
Dynamo Kyiv: (4411) Boyko; Kedziora, Zabarnyi, Popov, Karavayev; Tsygankov (Rodrigues 90), Sydorchuk■, Shaparenko (Baluta 89), De Pena; Buyalsky (Harmash 82); Supriaga (Verbic 89).

Juventus (0) 0

Barcelona (1) 2 *(Dembele 14, Messi 90 (pen))*

Juventus: (4231) Szczesny; Cuadrado, Demiral■, Bonucci, Danilo; Bentancur (Arthur 83), Rabiot (Bernardeschi 83); Kulusevski (McKennie 75), Dybala, Chiesa; Morata.
Barcelona: (4231) Neto; Sergi Roberto, Araujo (Busquets 46), Lenglet, Jordi Alba; Pjanic, de Jong; Dembele (Fati 66), Messi, Gonzalez (Braithwaite 90); Griezmann (Firpo 89).

Wednesday, 4 November 2020

Barcelona (1) 2 *(Messi 5 (pen), Pique 65)*

Dynamo Kyiv (0) 1 *(Tsygankov 75)*

Barcelona: (4231) ter Stegen; Dest, Pique, de Jong, Jordi Alba; Busquets (Lenglet 74), Pjanic (Sergi Roberto 60); Messi, Gonzalez (Alena 83), Fati (Trincao 74); Griezmann (Dembele 60).
Dynamo Kyiv: (4231) Neshcheret; Kedziora, Zabarnyi, Popov, Shabanov; Shepelev, Andrievsky; Tsygankov, Buyalsky (Lednev 86), Rodrigues (De Pena 71); Supriaga (Verbic 71).

Ferencvaros (0) 1 *(Boli 90)*

Juventus (1) 4 *(Morata 7, 60, Dybala 72, Dvali 81 (og))* 18,531

Ferencvaros: (433) Dibusz; Lovrencsics, Blazic, Dvali, Botka (Heister 68); Siger, Kharatin, Somalia; Zubkov (Uzuni 80), Isael (Boli 73), Nguen (Mak 73).
Juventus: (433) Szczesny; Cuadrado (Frabotta 76), Bonucci, Chiellini, Danilo; Ramsey (McKennie 53), Arthur (Bentancur 46), Rabiot; Ronaldo, Morata (Dybala 67), Chiesa (Bernardeschi 76).

Tuesday, 24 November 2020

Dynamo Kyiv (0) 0

Barcelona (0) 4 *(Dest 52, Braithwaite 57, 70 (pen), Griezmann 90)*

Dynamo Kyiv: (4411) Bushchan; Kedziora, Zabarnyi, Mykolenko, Karavayev (Popov 59); Shaparenko (Lednev 71), Shepelev (Baluta 83), Harmash (Andrievsky 59), De Pena (Supriaga 71); Buyalsky; Verbic.
Barcelona: (4231) ter Stegen; Dest, Mingueza, Lenglet (Jordi Alba 65), Firpo; Pjanic (Puig 65), Alena; Trincao (de la Fuente 83), Gonzalez (Matheus Fernandes 73), Coutinho (Griezmann 65); Braithwaite.

Juventus (1) 2 *(Ronaldo 35, Morata 90)*

Ferencvaros (1) 1 *(Uzuni 19)*

Juventus: (442) Szczesny; Cuadrado, Danilo, de Ligt, Alex Sandro; McKennie (Kulusevski 62), Bentancur (Rabiot 83), Arthur (Ramsey 82), Bernardeschi (Chiesa 62); Dybala (Morata 62), Ronaldo.
Ferencvaros: (541) Dibusz; Lovrencsics (Botka 75), Blazic, Frimpong, Dvali, Heister; Zubkov (Isael 70), Siger (Laidouni 75), Somalia, Uzuni; Nguen (Boli 70).

Wednesday, 2 December 2020

Ferencvaros (0) 0

Barcelona (3) 3 *(Griezmann 14, Braithwaite 20, Dembele 28 (pen))*

Ferencvaros: (541) Dibusz; Botka, Blazic, Frimpong, Dvali, Heister (Lovrencsics 64); Isael, Siger (Laidouni 64), Somalia (Kharatin 81), Uzuni (Baturina 71); Nguen (Mak 71).
Barcelona: (4231) Neto; Dest, Mingueza, Lenglet (Alena 65), Jordi Alba (Firpo 46); Pjanic, Busquets (de Jong 46); Trincao, Griezmann (Puig 65), Dembele; Braithwaite (de la Fuente 80).

Juventus (1) 3 *(Chiesa 21, Ronaldo 57, Morata 66)*

Dynamo Kyiv (0) 0

Juventus: (352) Szczesny; Demiral (Dragusin 69), Bonucci (Danilo 62), de Ligt; Chiesa (Kulusevski 76), McKennie, Ramsey (Bernardeschi 62), Bentancur (Arthur 76), Alex Sandro; Ronaldo, Morata.
Dynamo Kyiv: (4141) Bushchan; Kedziora, Zabarnyi, Popov, Mykolenko (Karavayev 84); Sydorchuk; Tsygankov (Lednev 90), Shepelev (Harmash 72), Shaparenko, Rodrigues (De Pena 72); Verbic (Supriaga 72).

Tuesday, 8 December 2020

Barcelona (0) 0

Juventus (2) 3 *(Ronaldo 13 (pen), 52 (pen), McKennie 20)*

Barcelona: (4231) ter Stegen; Dest, Araujo (Mingueza 82), Lenglet (Umtiti 55), Jordi Alba (Firpo 55); Pjanic, de Jong; Trincao (Braithwaite 46), Messi, Gonzalez (Puig 66); Griezmann.
Juventus: (352) Buffon; Danilo, Bonucci, de Ligt; Cuadrado (Bernardeschi 85), McKennie, Arthur (Bentancur 71), Ramsey (Rabiot 71), Alex Sandro; Morata (Dybala 85), Ronaldo (Chiesa 90).

Dynamo Kyiv (0) 1 *(Popov 60)*

Ferencvaros (0) 0

Dynamo Kyiv: (442) Bushchan; Kedziora, Zabarnyi, Popov, Mykolenko; Tsygankov (Lednev 86), Sydorchuk (Andrievsky 90), Shaparenko, De Pena (Supriaga 70); Harmash (Shepelev 70), Verbic (Rodrigues 86).
Ferencvaros: (433) Dibusz; Lovrencsics (Botka 80), Blazic, Dvali, Heister; Somalia, Kharatin (Isael 74), Laidouni; Zubkov (Mak 80), Nguen (Boli 86), Uzuni (Baturina 73).

Group G Table	*P*	*W*	*D*	*L*	*F*	*A*	*GD*	*Pts*
Juventus	6	5	0	1	14	4	10	15
Barcelona	6	5	0	1	16	5	11	15
Dynamo Kyiv	6	1	1	4	4	13	–9	4
Ferencvaros	6	0	1	5	5	17	–12	1

GROUP H

Tuesday, 20 October 2020

Paris Saint-Germain (0) 1 *(Martial 55 (og))*

Manchester U (1) 2 *(Bruno Fernandes 23 (pen), Rashford 87)*

Paris Saint-Germain: (433) Navas; Florenzi (Dagba 79), Diallo, Kimpembe, Kurzawa (Bakker 86); Ander Herrera (Rafinha 78), Danilo Pereira, Gueye (Kean 46); Di Maria (Sarabia 86), Mbappe-Lottin, Neymar.
Manchester U: (3412) de Gea; Tuanzebe, Lindelof, Shaw; Wan Bissaka, McTominay, Fred, Alex Telles (Pogba 67); Bruno Fernandes (van de Beek 88); Martial (James 88), Rashford.

RB Leipzig (2) 2 *(Angelino 16, 20)*

Istanbul Basaksehir (0) 0 999

RB Leipzig: (3421) Gulacsi; Orban, Upamecano (Konate 65), Halstenberg; Mukiele, Nkunku (Kluivert 70), Kampl (Adams 58), Angelino; Olmo (Henrichs 65), Forsberg (Hwang 46); Poulsen.
Istanbul Basaksehir: (4141) Gunok; Junior Caicara (Ozcan 30), Skrtel, Epureanu, Bolingoli Mbombo; Topal (Ba 66); Visca, Da Silva, Kahveci (Aleksic 83), Turuc (Giuliano 83); Crivelli.

Wednesday, 28 October 2020

Istanbul Basaksehir (0) 0

Paris Saint-Germain (0) 2 *(Kean 64, 79)* 350

Istanbul Basaksehir: (4141) Gunok; Da Silva, Skrtel, Epureanu, Bolingoli Mbombo (Kaldirim 63); Topal (Ba 68); Visca, Ozcan, Kahveci, Turuc (Aleksic 81); Crivelli (Giuliano 81).
Paris Saint-Germain: (442) Navas; Florenzi (Kehrer 73), Danilo Pereira, Kimpembe, Kurzawa (Bakker 87); Di Maria (Rafinha 73), Ander Herrera (Gueye 87), Marquinhos, Neymar (Sarabia 26); Kean, Mbappe-Lottin.

Manchester U (1) 5 *(Greenwood 21, Rashford 74, 78, 90, Martial 87 (pen))*

RB Leipzig (0) 0

Manchester U: (41212) de Gea; Wan Bissaka (Tuanzebe 81), Lindelof, Maguire, Shaw; Matic (McTominay 63); Fred, Pogba (Cavani 81); van de Beek (Bruno Fernandes 68); Greenwood (Rashford 63), Martial.
RB Leipzig: (3142) Gulacsi; Konate, Upamecano, Halstenberg; Kampl (Kluivert 76); Henrichs (Sabitzer 63), Olmo, Nkunku (Sorloth 65), Angelino; Poulsen, Forsberg.

Wednesday, 4 November 2020

Istanbul Basaksehir (2) 2 *(Ba 13, Visca 40)*

Manchester U (1) 1 *(Martial 43)* 350

Istanbul Basaksehir: (4231) Gunok; Da Silva, Skrtel, Epureanu, Bolingoli Mbombo; Aleksic, Kahveci (Ponck 90); Visca, Ozcan (Topal 87), Turuc; Ba (Gulbrandsen 79).
Manchester U: (4231) Henderson; Wan Bissaka (Fosu-Mensah 76), Tuanzebe (McTominay 46), Maguire, Shaw; van de Beek (Pogba 61), Matic; Mata (Cavani 61), Bruno Fernandes, Rashford (Greenwood 76); Martial.

RB Leipzig (1) 2 *(Nkunku 41, Forsberg 57 (pen))*

Paris Saint-Germain (1) 1 *(Di Maria 6)*

RB Leipzig: (352) Gulacsi; Konate, Upamecano, Orban; Mukiele (Henrichs 64), Nkunku, Sabitzer (Kampl 90), Haidara (Adams 76), Angelino; Forsberg (Kluivert 76), Olmo (Poulsen 64).
Paris Saint-Germain: (433) Navas; Florenzi (Rafinha 84), Danilo Pereira, Kimpembe■, Kurzawa (Bakker 73); Gueye■, Marquinhos, Ander Herrera; Di Maria, Kean, Sarabia (Kehrer 73).

Tuesday, 24 November 2020

Manchester U (3) 4 *(Bruno Fernandes 7, 19, Rashford 35 (pen), James 90)*

Istanbul Basaksehir (0) 1 *(Turuc 75)*

Manchester U: (4231) de Gea; Wan Bissaka (Williams 59), Lindelof (Tuanzebe 46), Maguire, Alex Telles; van de Beek, Fred; Rashford (James 59), Bruno Fernandes (Greenwood 59), Martial (Matic 82); Cavani.
Istanbul Basaksehir: (4141) Gunok; Da Silva, Skrtel (Ponck 87), Epureanu, Bolingoli Mbombo (Kaldirim 74); Ozcan (Giuliano 74); Visca, Kahveci (Tekdemir 46), Turuc, Chadli (Gulbrandsen 61); Ba.

Paris Saint-Germain (1) 1 *(Neymar 11 (pen))*

RB Leipzig (0) 0

Paris Saint-Germain: (433) Navas; Florenzi, Marquinhos, Diallo, Bakker; Ander Herrera (Verratti 83), Danilo Pereira, Paredes; Di Maria (Rafinha 64), Neymar (Sarabia 90), Mbappe-Lottin (Kean 90).
RB Leipzig: (4231) Gulacsi; Mukiele (Orban 63), Konate, Upamecano, Angelino; Haidara, Sabitzer; Olmo (Kluivert 64), Forsberg (Sorloth 74), Nkunku; Poulsen.

Wednesday, 2 December 2020

Istanbul Basaksehir (1) 3 *(Kahveci 45, 72, 85)*

RB Leipzig (2) 4 *(Poulsen 26, Mukiele 43, Olmo 66, Sorloth 90)*

Istanbul Basaksehir: (4411) Gunok; Da Silva, Skrtel (Epureanu 46), Ponck, Bolingoli Mbombo (Chadli 36); Visca (Giuliano 64), Ozcan (Tekdemir 46), Kahveci, Turuc; Gulbrandsen (Crivelli 84); Ba.
RB Leipzig: (4231) Gulacsi; Mukiele, Konate, Upamecano, Angelino; Sabitzer, Kampl (Adams 46); Haidara (Orban 90), Forsberg (Sorloth 65), Olmo (Kluivert 87); Poulsen.

Manchester U (1) 1 *(Rashford 32)*

Paris Saint-Germain (1) 3 *(Neymar 6, 90, Marquinhos 69)* 638

Manchester U: (4231) de Gea; Wan Bissaka (Ighalo 90), Lindelof, Maguire, Alex Telles; McTominay, Fred■; Rashford (Pogba 74), Bruno Fernandes, Martial (Greenwood 79); Cavani (van de Beek 79).
Paris Saint-Germain: (433) Navas; Florenzi (Kehrer 78), Marquinhos, Kimpembe, Diallo (Gueye 90); Paredes (Ander Herrera 65), Danilo Pereira, Verratti (Rafinha 78); Mbappe-Lottin, Kean (Bakker 65), Neymar.

Tuesday, 8 December 2020

RB Leipzig (2) 3 *(Angelino 2, Haidara 13, Kluivert 69)*

Manchester U (0) 2 *(Bruno Fernandes 80 (pen), Konate 82 (og))*

RB Leipzig: (3421) Gulacsi; Mukiele, Konate, Orban; Haidara, Sabitzer, Kampl (Adams 75), Angelino (Halstenberg 87); Forsberg (Poulsen 56), Nkunku; Olmo (Kluivert 56).
Manchester U: (3412) de Gea; Lindelof (Tuanzebe 77), Maguire, Shaw (Williams 61); Wan Bissaka (Fosu-Mensah 77), McTominay, Matic (Pogba 61), Alex Telles (van de Beek 46); Bruno Fernandes; Rashford, Greenwood.

Wednesday, 9 December 2020

Paris Saint-Germain (3) 5 *(Neymar 21, 38, 50, Mbappe-Lottin 42 (pen), 62)*

Istanbul Basaksehir (0) 1 *(Topal 57)*

Paris Saint-Germain: (532) Navas; Florenzi (Pembele 80), Marquinhos (Kehrer 67), Danilo Pereira, Kimpembe (Diallo 80), Bakker; Paredes, Rafinha (Di Maria 46), Verratti (Gueye 80); Neymar, Mbappe-Lottin.
Istanbul Basaksehir: (433) Gunok; Da Silva (Giuliano 68), Ponck, Topal, Kaldirim (Bolingoli Mbombo 68); Ozcan, Tekdemir (Chadli 89), Kahveci; Gulbrandsen (Kaplan 80), Crivelli (Ba 68), Turuc.

Group H Table	*P*	*W*	*D*	*L*	*F*	*A*	*GD*	*Pts*
Paris Saint-Germain	6	4	0	2	13	6	7	12
RB Leipzig	6	4	0	2	11	12	−1	12
Manchester U	6	3	0	3	15	10	5	9
Istanbul Basaksehir	6	1	0	5	7	18	−11	3

KNOCK-OUT STAGE

ROUND OF 16 FIRST LEG

Tuesday, 16 February 2021

Barcelona (1) 1 *(Messi 27 (pen))*

Paris Saint-Germain (1) 4 *(Mbappe-Lottin 32, 65, 85, Kean 70)*

Barcelona: (433) ter Stegen; Dest (Mingueza 71), Pique (Puig 78), Lenglet, Jordi Alba; de Jong, Busquets (Pjanic 78), Gonzalez (Trincao 78); Dembele, Messi, Griezmann (Braithwaite 85).
Paris Saint-Germain: (433) Navas; Florenzi (Kehrer 89), Marquinhos, Kimpembe, Kurzawa; Gueye (Ander Herrera 46), Paredes, Verratti (Draxler 73); Kean (Danilo Pereira 85), Icardi, Mbappe-Lottin.

RB Leipzig (0) 0

Liverpool (0) 2 *(Salah 53, Mane 58)*

RB Leipzig: (3142) Gulacsi; Mukiele (Orban 64), Upamecano, Klostermann; Kampl (Hwang 73); Adams, Haidara (Poulsen 64), Sabitzer, Angelino; Olmo, Nkunku.
Liverpool: (433) Alisson; Alexander-Arnold, Kabak, Henderson, Robertson; Jones, Wijnaldum, Thiago (Oxlade-Chamberlain 72); Salah (Williams N 90), Firmino (Shaqiri 72), Mane.

Wednesday, 17 February 2021

Porto (1) 2 *(Taremi 2, Marega 46)*

Juventus (0) 1 *(Chiesa 82)*

Porto: (442) Marchesin; Manafa, Mbemba, Pepe, Sanusi; Corona (N'Diaye 90), Sergio Oliveira (Francisco Conceicao 90), Uribe, Otavio (Diaz 57); Marega (Grujic 66), Taremi.
Juventus: (442) Szczesny; Danilo, de Ligt, Chiellini (Demiral 35), Alex Sandro; Chiesa, Bentancur, Rabiot, McKennie (Morata 63); Kulusevski (Ramsey 77), Ronaldo.

Sevilla (1) 2 *(Suso 7, de Jong 84)*

Borussia Dortmund (3) 3 *(Dahoud 19, Haaland 27, 43)*

Sevilla: (433) Bounou; Jesus Navas, Kounde, Diego Carlos, Escudero; Jordan (Rodriguez 72), Fernando, Rakitic (Gudelj 46); Suso (de Jong 60), En-Nesyri (Munir 60), Gomez (Torres 60).
Borussia Dortmund: (4321) Hitz; Morey, Akanji, Hummels, Guerreiro (Passlack 76); Bellingham, Can, Dahoud (Meunier 89); Reus (Brandt 80), Sancho; Haaland.

Tuesday, 23 February 2021

Atletico Madrid (0) 0

Chelsea (0) 1 *(Giroud 68)*

Atletico Madrid: (3421) Oblak; Savic, Felipe, Hermoso (Vitolo 84); Llorente, Koke, Saul (Torreira 82), Lemar; Correa (Dembele 82), Joao Felix (Renan Lodi 82); Suarez.
Chelsea: (3421) Mendy; Azpilicueta, Christensen, Rudiger; Hudson-Odoi (James 80), Jorginho, Kovacic (Ziyech 74), Alonso; Mount (Kante 74), Werner (Pulisic 87); Giroud (Havertz 87).

Lazio (0) 1 *(Correa 49)*

Bayern Munich (3) 4 *(Lewandowski 9, Musiala 24, Sane 42, Acerbi 47 (og))*

Lazio: (352) Reina; Patric Gil (Hoedt 53), Acerbi, Musacchio (Lulic 31); Lazzari, Milinkovic-Savic (Cataldi 81), Lucas (Escalante 53), Luis Alberto (Akpa Akpro 81), Marusic; Immobile, Correa.
Bayern Munich: (4231) Neuer; Sule, Boateng, Alaba, Davies; Goretzka (Javi Martinez 63), Kimmich; Sane (Sarr 90), Musiala (Choupo-Moting 90), Coman (Lucas 75); Lewandowski.

Wednesday, 24 February 2021

Atalanta (0) 0

Real Madrid (0) 1 *(Mendy 86)*

Atalanta: (3412) Gollini; Toloi, Romero, Djimsiti; Maehle (Palomino 86), de Roon, Freuler■, Gosens; Pessina; Zapata (Pasalic 30), Muriel (Ilicic 56 (Malinovsky 86)).
Real Madrid: (433) Courtois; Lucas, Varane, Nacho, Mendy; Modric, Casemiro, Kroos; Asensio (Arribas 76), Isco (Duro 76), Vinicius Junior (Mariano 57).

Borussia Moenchengladbach (0) 0

Manchester C (1) 2 *(Bernardo Silva 29, Gabriel Jesus 65)*

Borussia Moenchengladbach: (433) Sommer; Lainer (Lazaro 63), Ginter, Elvedi, Bensebaini; Zakaria, Kramer, Neuhaus; Hofmann (Wolf 87), Stindl (Embolo 74), Plea (Thuram 63).
Manchester C: (4231) Ederson; Walker, Dias, Laporte, Joao Cancelo; Rodri, Gundogan; Sterling (Mahrez 69), Bernardo Silva, Foden (Torres 80); Gabriel Jesus (Aguero 80).

ROUND OF 16 SECOND LEG

Tuesday, 9 March 2021

Borussia Dortmund (1) 2 *(Haaland 35, 54 (pen))*

Sevilla (0) 2 *(En-Nesyri 68 (pen), 90)*

Borussia Dortmund: (433) Hitz; Morey (Meunier 90), Can, Hummels, Schulz (Zagadou 89); Bellingham, Delaney, Dahoud; Hazard (Passlack 67), Haaland, Reus.
Sevilla: (433) Bounou; Jesus Navas, Kounde, Diego Carlos, Acuna; Jordan (Gomez 60), Fernando (Rakitic 86), Rodriguez (Torres 79); Suso (Munir 86), En-Nesyri, Ocampos (de Jong 60).
Borussia Dortmund won 5-4 on aggregate.

Juventus (0) 3 *(Chiesa 49, 63, Rabiot 117)*

Porto (1) 2 *(Sergio Oliveira 19 (pen), 115)*

Juventus: (442) Szczesny; Cuadrado, Demiral, Bonucci (de Ligt 75), Alex Sandro; Ramsey (McKennie 75), Rabiot, Arthur (Kulusevski 102), Chiesa (Bernardeschi 102); Morata, Ronaldo.
Porto: (442) Marchesin; Manafa, Mbemba, Pepe, Sanusi (Diaz 71); Corona (Diogo Leite 118), Sergio Oliveira (N'Diaye 118), Uribe (Grujic 90), Otavio (Sarr 62); Marega (Martinez 106), Taremi■.
aet; Porto won on away goals.

Wednesday, 10 March 2021

Liverpool (0) 2 *(Salah 70, Mane 74)*

RB Leipzig (0) 0

Liverpool: (433) Alisson; Alexander-Arnold, Phillips, Kabak, Robertson (Tsimikas 90); Thiago (Keita 72), Fabinho, Wijnaldum (Milner 82); Salah, Jota (Origi 71), Mane (Oxlade-Chamberlain 90).
RB Leipzig: (3142) Gulacsi; Mukiele, Upamecano, Klostermann; Kampl (Sorloth 46); Adams, Olmo (Haidara 72), Sabitzer, Nkunku; Poulsen (Hwang 60), Forsberg (Kluivert 60).
Liverpool won 4-0 on aggregate.

Paris Saint-Germain (1) 1 *(Mbappe-Lottin 30 (pen))*

Barcelona (1) 1 *(Messi 37)*

Paris Saint-Germain: (433) Navas; Florenzi (Dagba 76), Marquinhos, Kimpembe, Kurzawa (Diallo 46); Gueye (Danilo Pereira 60), Paredes, Verratti (Rafinha 84); Draxler (Di Maria 59), Icardi, Mbappe-Lottin.
Barcelona: (3412) ter Stegen; Mingueza (Firpo 35), de Jong, Lenglet; Dest (Trincao 66), Busquets (Moriba 79), Gonzalez (Pjanic 78), Jordi Alba; Griezmann; Dembele (Braithwaite 78), Messi.
Paris Saint-Germain won 5-2 on aggregate.

Tuesday, 16 March 2021

Manchester C (2) 2 *(De Bruyne 12, Gundogan 18)*

Borussia Moenchengladbach (0) 0

Manchester C: (4231) Ederson; Walker, Stones, Dias (Laporte 70), Joao Cancelo (Zinchenko 64); Rodri (Fernandinho 63), Gundogan (Sterling 70); Mahrez, De Bruyne, Foden; Bernardo Silva (Aguero 75).
Borussia Moenchengladbach: (4231) Sommer; Lainer, Ginter, Elvedi (Jantschke 88), Bensebaini (Wendt 88); Neuhaus, Zakaria; Hofmann, Stindl (Traore 80), Thuram (Plea 65); Embolo (Wolf 65).
Manchester C won 4-0 on aggregate.

Real Madrid (1) 3 *(Benzema 34, Sergio Ramos 60 (pen), Asensio 84)*

Atalanta (0) 1 *(Muriel 83)*

Real Madrid: (352) Courtois; Varane, Sergio Ramos (Eder Militao 64), Nacho; Lucas, Valverde (Asensio 82), Modric, Kroos, Mendy; Benzema, Vinicius Junior (Rodrygo 69).
Atalanta: (3421) Sportiello; Toloi (Palomino 61), Romero, Djimsiti; Maehle, Pessina (Caldara 84), de Roon, Gosens (Ilicic 57); Malinovsky, Pasalic (Zapata 46); Muriel (Miranchuk 84).
Real Madrid won 4-1 on aggregate.

Wednesday, 17 March 2021

Bayern Munich (1) 2 *(Lewandowski 33 (pen), Choupo-Moting 73)*

Lazio (0) 1 *(Parolo 82)*

Bayern Munich: (4231) Nubel; Pavard, Boateng (Sule 46), Alaba, Lucas; Kimmich (Javi Martinez 77), Goretzka (Davies 64); Sane, Muller (Musiala 71), Gnabry; Lewandowski (Choupo-Moting 71).
Lazio: (352) Reina; Marusic, Acerbi, Radu; Lazzari (Parolo 57), Milinkovic-Savic, Escalante (Akpa Akpro 84), Luis Alberto (Cataldi 75), Fares (Lulic 46); Muriqi (Andreas Pereira 56), Correa.
Bayern Munich won 6-2 on aggregate.

Chelsea (1) 2 *(Ziyech 34, Emerson Palmieri 90)*

Atletico Madrid (0) 0

Chelsea: (3421) Mendy; Azpilicueta, Zouma, Rudiger; James, Kante, Kovacic, Alonso (Chilwell 90); Ziyech (Pulisic 77), Havertz (Emerson Palmieri 90); Werner (Hudson-Odoi 83).
Atletico Madrid: (442) Oblak; Trippier (Lemar 69), Savic■, Gimenez, Renan Lodi (Hermoso 46); Llorente, Koke, Saul, Carrasco (Dembele 53); Joao Felix, Suarez (Correa 59).
Chelsea won 3-0 on aggregate.

QUARTER-FINALS FIRST LEG

Tuesday, 6 April 2021

Manchester C (1) 2 *(De Bruyne 19, Foden 90)*

Borussia Dortmund (0) 1 *(Reus 84)*

Manchester C: (4231) Ederson; Walker, Stones, Dias, Joao Cancelo; Rodri, Gundogan; Mahrez, De Bruyne, Foden; Bernardo Silva (Gabriel Jesus 59).
Borussia Dortmund: (433) Hitz; Morey (Meunier 81), Akanji, Hummels, Guerreiro; Bellingham, Can, Dahoud (Delaney 81); Knauff (Reyna 63), Haaland, Reus.

Real Madrid (2) 3 *(Vinicius Junior 27, 65, Asensio 36)*

Liverpool (0) 1 *(Salah 51)*

Real Madrid: (433) Courtois; Lucas, Eder Militao, Nacho, Mendy; Modric, Casemiro, Kroos; Asensio (Valverde 70), Benzema, Vinicius Junior (Rodrygo 85).
Liverpool: (433) Alisson; Alexander-Arnold, Phillips, Kabak (Firmino 81), Robertson; Keita (Thiago 42), Fabinho, Wijnaldum; Salah, Jota (Shaqiri 81), Mane.

Wednesday, 7 April 2021

Bayern Munich (1) 2 *(Choupo-Moting 37, Muller 60)*

Paris Saint-Germain (2) 3 *(Mbappe-Lottin 3, 68, Marquinhos 28)*

Bayern Munich: (4231) Neuer; Pavard, Sule (Boateng 42), Alaba, Lucas; Kimmich, Goretzka (Davies 33); Sane, Muller, Coman; Choupo-Moting.
Paris Saint-Germain: (4231) Navas; Dagba, Marquinhos (Ander Herrera 30), Kimpembe, Diallo (Bakker 46); Danilo Pereira, Gueye; Di Maria (Kean 71), Neymar (Rafinha 90), Draxler; Mbappe-Lottin.

Porto (0) 0

Chelsea (1) 2 *(Mount 32, Chilwell 85)*

Porto: (451) Marchesin; Manafa (Francisco Conceicao 83), Mbemba, Pepe, Sanusi; Corona, Uribe, Grujic, Otavio (Vieira 83), Diaz; Marega (Martinez 83).
Chelsea: (3421) Mendy; Azpilicueta, Christensen, Rudiger; James (Thiago Silva 80), Jorginho, Kovacic (Emerson Palmieri 90), Chilwell; Mount (Kante 80), Werner (Pulisic 65); Havertz (Giroud 65).

QUARTER-FINALS SECOND LEG

Tuesday, 13 April 2021

Chelsea (0) 0

Porto (0) 1 *(Taremi 90)*

Chelsea: (3421) Mendy; Azpilicueta, Thiago Silva, Rudiger; James, Kante, Jorginho, Chilwell; Pulisic, Mount (Ziyech 86); Havertz (Giroud 90).
Porto: (433) Marchesin; Manafa (Nanu 75), Mbemba, Pepe, Sanusi; Sergio Oliveira (Vieira 84), Grujic (Taremi 63), Uribe; Corona (Diaz 75), Marega (Evanilson 75), Otavio.
Chelsea won 2-1 on aggregate.

Paris Saint-Germain (0) 0

Bayern Munich (1) 1 *(Choupo-Moting 40)*

Paris Saint-Germain: (4231) Navas; Dagba, Danilo Pereira, Kimpembe, Diallo (Bakker 58); Gueye, Paredes; Di Maria (Ander Herrera 88), Neymar, Draxler (Kean 73); Mbappe-Lottin.
Bayern Munich: (4231) Neuer; Pavard, Boateng, Lucas, Davies (Musiala 71); Kimmich, Alaba; Sane, Muller, Coman; Choupo-Moting (Javi Martinez 85).
Paris Saint-Germain won on away goals.

Wednesday, 14 April 2021

Borussia Dortmund (1) 1 *(Bellingham 15)*

Manchester C (0) 2 *(Mahrez 55 (pen), Foden 75)*

Borussia Dortmund: (433) Hitz; Morey (Tigges 81), Akanji, Hummels, Guerreiro; Bellingham (Brandt 81), Can, Dahoud (Hazard 76); Knauff (Reyna 68), Haaland, Reus.
Manchester C: (433) Ederson; Walker, Stones, Dias, Zinchenko; Bernardo Silva, Rodri, Gundogan; Mahrez (Sterling 88), De Bruyne, Foden.
Manchester C won 4-2 on aggregate.

Liverpool (0) 0

Real Madrid (0) 0

Liverpool: (433) Alisson; Alexander-Arnold, Phillips, Kabak (Jota 60), Robertson; Wijnaldum, Fabinho, Milner (Thiago 60); Salah, Firmino (Shaqiri 82), Mane (Oxlade-Chamberlain 82).
Real Madrid: (433) Courtois; Valverde, Eder Militao, Nacho, Mendy; Modric, Casemiro, Kroos (Odriozola 72); Asensio (Isco 82), Benzema, Vinicius Junior (Rodrygo 72).
Real Madrid won 3-1 on aggregate.

SEMI-FINALS FIRST LEG

Tuesday, 27 April 2021

Real Madrid (1) 1 *(Benzema 29)*

Chelsea (1) 1 *(Pulisic 14)*

Real Madrid: (352) Courtois; Eder Militao, Varane, Nacho; Carvajal (Odriozola 77), Modric, Casemiro, Kroos, Marcelo (Asensio 77); Benzema (Rodrygo 90), Vinicius Junior (Hazard 66).
Chelsea: (352) Mendy; Christensen, Thiago Silva, Rudiger; Azpilicueta (James 66), Kante, Jorginho, Mount, Chilwell; Pulisic (Ziyech 66), Werner (Havertz 66).

Wednesday, 28 April 2021

Paris Saint-Germain (1) 1 *(Marquinhos 15)*

Manchester C (0) 2 *(De Bruyne 64, Mahrez 71)*

Paris Saint-Germain: (433) Navas; Florenzi, Marquinhos, Kimpembe, Bakker; Gueye■, Paredes (Ander Herrera 83), Verratti; Di Maria (Danilo Pereira 80), Mbappe-Lottin, Neymar.
Manchester C: (433) Ederson; Walker, Stones, Dias, Joao Cancelo (Zinchenko 61); Bernardo Silva, Rodri, Gundogan; Mahrez, De Bruyne, Foden.

SEMI-FINALS SECOND LEG

Tuesday, 4 May 2021

Manchester C (1) 2 *(Mahrez 11, 63)*

Paris Saint-Germain (0) 0

Manchester C: (442) Ederson; Walker, Stones, Dias, Zinchenko; Mahrez, Fernandinho, Gundogan, Foden (Aguero 85); De Bruyne (Gabriel Jesus 82), Bernardo Silva (Sterling 82).
Paris Saint-Germain: (433) Navas; Florenzi (Dagba 75), Marquinhos, Kimpembe, Diallo (Bakker 82); Ander Herrera (Draxler 62), Paredes (Danilo Pereira 75), Verratti; Di Maria■, Icardi (Kean 62), Neymar.
Manchester C won 4-1 on aggregate.

Wednesday, 5 May 2021

Chelsea (1) 2 *(Werner 28, Mount 85)*

Real Madrid (0) 0

Chelsea: (3142) Mendy; Christensen, Thiago Silva, Rudiger; Jorginho; Azpilicueta (James 88), Kante, Mount (Ziyech 88), Chilwell; Havertz (Giroud 90), Werner (Pulisic 67).
Real Madrid: (3412) Courtois; Eder Militao, Sergio Ramos, Nacho; Vinicius Junior (Asensio 63), Kroos, Casemiro (Rodrygo 76), Mendy (Valverde 63); Modric; Benzema, Hazard (Mariano 89).
Chelsea won 3-1 on aggregate.

UEFA CHAMPIONS LEAGUE FINAL 2020–21

Saturday, 29 May 2021

(in Porto – attendance 14,110)

Manchester C (0) 0 **Chelsea (1) 1** *(Havertz 42)*

Manchester C: (433) Ederson; Walker, Stones, Dias, Zinchenko; Bernardo Silva (Fernandinho 64), Gundogan, Foden; Mahrez, De Bruyne (Gabriel Jesus 60), Sterling (Aguero 77).

Chelsea: (3421) Mendy; Azpilicueta, Thiago Silva (Christensen 39), Rudiger; James, Kante, Jorginho, Chilwell; Havertz, Mount (Kovacic 80); Werner (Pulisic 66).

Referee: Antonio Miguel Mateu Lahoz.

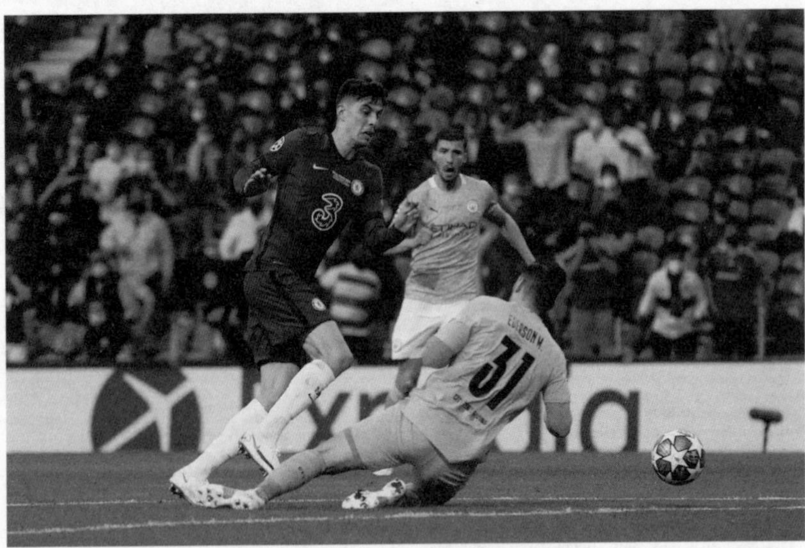

Kai Havertz scores the only goal of the game as Chelsea beat Manchester City in the Champions League Final in Porto on 29 May. (David Klein/Sportimage via PA Images)

UEFA CHAMPIONS LEAGUE 2021–22

PARTICIPATING CLUBS
The list below is provisional and is subject to pending legal proceedings and final confirmation from UEFA.

PRELIMINARY ROUND (4)
Prishtina
HB Torshavn
Inter Club d'Escaldes
Folgore Falciano

FIRST QUALIFYING ROUND (32)
1 winner from Champions League Preliminary Round
Dinamo Zagreb
Malmo
Bodo/Glimt
Maccabi Haifa
Kairat
Shakhtyor Soligorsk
Neftchi
Ludogorets Razgrad
CFR Cluj
Legia Warsaw
Slovan Bratislava
Mura
Ferencvaros
Fola Esch
Zalgiris Vilnius
Alashkert
Riga FC
Teuta
Shkendija
Borac Banja Luka
Sheriff Tiraspol
Shamrock Rovers
HJK Helsinki
Dinamo Tbilisi
Hibernians
Valur
Connah's Quay Nomads
Linfield
Lincoln Red Imps
Buducnost Podgorica
Flora

SECOND QUALIFYING ROUND (26)
Champions Path (20)
16 winners from Champions League Q1
Omonia Nicosia
Young Boys
Olympiacos
Red Star Belgrade
League Path (6)
PSV Eindhoven
Galatasaray
Rapid Vienna
FC Midtjylland
Celtic
Sparta Prague

THIRD QUALIFYING ROUND (20)
Champions Path (12)
10 winners from Champions League Q2 (Champions Path)
Rangers
Slavia Prague
League Path (8)
3 winners from Champions League Q2 (League Path)
Monaco
Benfica
Spartak Moscow
Genk
Shakhtar Donetsk

PLAY-OFF ROUND (12)
Champions Path (8)
6 winners from Champions League Q3 (Champions Path)
Red Bull Salzburg
Brondby
League Path (4)
4 winners from Champions League Q3 (League Path)

GROUP STAGE (32)
4 winners from Champions League Play-Off Round (Champions Path)
2 winners from Champions League Play-Off Round (League Path)
Chelsea
Villarreal
Atletico Madrid
Real Madrid
Barcelona
Sevilla
Manchester C
Manchester U
Liverpool
Bayern Munich
RB Leipzig
Borussia Dortmund
VfL Wolfsburg
Internazionale
AC Milan
Atalanta
Juventus
Lille
Paris Saint-Germain
Sporting Lisbon
Porto
Zenit St Petersburg
Club Brugge
Dynamo Kyiv
Ajax
Besiktas

EUROPEAN CUP-WINNERS' CUP FINALS 1961–99

Year	Winners v Runners-up		Venue	Attendance	Referee
1961	1st Leg Rangers v Fiorentina	0-2	Glasgow	80,000	C. E. Steiner (Austria)
	2nd Leg Fiorentina v Rangers	2-1	Florence	50,000	V. Hernadi (Hungary)
1962	Atletico Madrid v Fiorentina	1-1	Glasgow	27,389	T. Wharton (Scotland)
Replay	Atletico Madrid v Fiorentina	3-0	Stuttgart	38,000	K. Tschenscher (West Germany)
1963	Tottenham Hotspur v Atletico Madrid	5-1	Rotterdam	49,000	A. van Leuwen (Netherlands)
1964	Sporting Lisbon v MTK Budapest	3-3*	Brussels	3,208	L. van Nuffel (Belgium)
Replay	Sporting Lisbon v MTK Budapest	1-0	Antwerp	13,924	G. Versyp (Belgium)
1965	West Ham U v Munich 1860	2-0	Wembley	7,974	I. Zsolt (Hungary)
1966	Borussia Dortmund v Liverpool	2-1*	Glasgow	41,657	P. Schwinte (France)
1967	Bayern Munich v Rangers	1-0*	Nuremberg	69,480	C. Lo Bello (Italy)
1968	AC Milan v Hamburg	2-0	Rotterdam	53,000	J. Ortiz de Mendibil (Spain)
1969	Slovan Bratislava v Barcelona	3-2	Basel	19,000	L. van Ravens (Netherlands)
1970	Manchester C v Gornik Zabrze	2-1	Vienna	7,968	P. Schiller (Austria)
1971	Chelsea v Real Madrid	1-1*	Athens	45,000	R. Scheurer (Switzerland)
Replay	Chelsea v Real Madrid	2-1*	Athens	19,917	R. Scheurer (Switzerland)
1972	Rangers v Dynamo Moscow	3-2	Barcelona	24,701	J. Ortiz de Mendibil (Spain)
1973	AC Milan v Leeds U	1-0	Salonika	40,154	C. Mihas (Greece)
1974	Magdeburg v AC Milan	2-0	Rotterdam	4,641	A. van Gemert (Netherlands)
1975	Dynamo Kyiv v Ferencvaros	3-0	Basel	13,000	R. Davidson (Scotland)
1976	Anderlecht v West Ham U	4-2	Brussels	51,296	R. Wurtz (France)
1977	Hamburg v Anderlecht	2-0	Amsterdam	66,000	P. Partridge (England)
1978	Anderlecht v Austria/WAC	4-0	Paris	48,679	H. Adlinger (West Germany)
1979	Barcelona v Fortuna Dusseldorf	4-3*	Basel	58,000	K. Palotai (Hungary)
1980	Valencia v Arsenal	0-0*	Brussels	40,000	V. Christov (Czechoslovakia)
	(Valencia won 5-4 on penalties)				
1981	Dinamo Tbilisi v Carl Zeiss Jena	2-1	Dusseldorf	4,750	R. Lattanzi (Italy)
1982	Barcelona v Standard Liege	2-1	Barcelona	80,000	W. Eschweiler (West Germany)
1983	Aberdeen v Real Madrid	2-1*	Gothenburg	17,804	G. Menegali (Italy)
1984	Juventus v Porto	2-1	Basel	55,000	A. Prokop (Egypt)
1985	Everton v Rapid Vienna	3-1	Rotterdam	38,500	P. Casarin (Italy)
1986	Dynamo Kyiv v Atletico Madrid	3-0	Lyon	50,000	F. Wohrer (Austria)
1987	Ajax v Lokomotiv Leipzig	1-0	Athens	35,107	L. Agnolin (Italy)
1988	Mechelen v Ajax	1-0	Strasbourg	39,446	D. Pauly (West Germany)
1989	Barcelona v Sampdoria	2-0	Berne	42,707	G. Courtney (England)
1990	Sampdoria v Anderlecht	2-0*	Gothenburg	20,103	B. Galler (Switzerland)
1991	Manchester U v Barcelona	2-1	Rotterdam	43,500	B. Karlsson (Sweden)
1992	Werder Bremen v Monaco	2-0	Lisbon	16,000	P. D'Elia (Italy)
1993	Parma v Antwerp	3-1	Wembley	37,393	K.-J. Assenmacher (Germany)
1994	Arsenal v Parma	1-0	Copenhagen	33,765	V. Krondl (Czech Republic)
1995	Real Zaragoza v Arsenal	2-1	Paris	42,424	P. Ceccarini (Italy)
1996	Paris Saint-Germain v Rapid Vienna	1-0	Brussels	37,000	P. Pairetto (Italy)
1997	Barcelona v Paris Saint-Germain	1-0	Rotterdam	52,000	M. Merk (Germany)
1998	Chelsea v VfB Stuttgart	1-0	Stockholm	30,216	S. Braschi (Italy)
1999	Lazio v Mallorca	2-1	Birmingham	33,021	G. Benko (Austria)

INTER-CITIES FAIRS CUP FINALS 1958–71

Year	1st Leg		Attendance	2nd Leg	Attendance	Agg	Winner
1958	London XI v Barcelona	2-2	45,466	0-6	70,000	2-8	Barcelona
1960	Birmingham C v Barcelona	0-0	40,524	1-4	70,000	1-4	Barcelona
1961	Birmingham C v Roma	2-2	21,005	0-2	60,000	2-4	Roma
1962	Valencia v Barcelona	6-2	65,000	1-1	60,000	7-3	Valencia
1963	Dinamo Zagreb v Valencia	1-2	40,000	0-2	55,000	1-4	Valencia
1964	Real Zaragoza v Valencia	2-1	50,000	(in Barcelona, one match only)			Real Zaragoza
1965	Ferencvaros v Juventus	1-0	25,000	(in Turin, one match only)			Ferencvaros
1966	Barcelona v Real Zaragoza	0-1	70,000	4-2*	70,000	4-3	Barcelona
1967	Dinamo Zagreb v Leeds U	2-0	40,000	0-0	35,604	2-0	Dynamo Zagreb
1968	Leeds U v Ferencvaros	1-0	25,368	0-0	70,000	1-0	Leeds U
1969	Newcastle U v Ujpest Dozsa	3-0	60,000	3-2	37,000	6-2	Newcastle U
1970	Anderlecht v Arsenal	3-1	37,000	0-3	51,612	3-4	Arsenal
1971	Juventus v Leeds U	0-0	*(abandoned 51 minutes)*		42,000		
	Juventus v Leeds U	2-2	42,000	1-1	42,483	3-3	Leeds U
	Leeds U won on away goals rule.						

Trophy Play-Off – *between first and last winners to decide who would have possession of the original trophy*

1971	Barcelona v Leeds U	2-1	50,000	(in Barcelona, one match only)

**After extra time.*

UEFA CUP FINALS 1972–97

Year	1st Leg		Attendance	2nd Leg	Attendance	Agg	Winner
1972	Wolverhampton W v Tottenham H	1-2	38,562	1-1	54,303	2-3	Tottenham H
1973	Liverpool v Moenchengladbach	0-0	*(abandoned after 27 minutes)*		44,967		
	Liverpool v Moenchengladbach	3-0	41,169	0-2	35,000	3-2	Liverpool
1974	Tottenham H v Feyenoord	2-2	46,281	0-2	59,317	2-4	Feyenoord
1975	Moenchengladbach v FC Twente	0-0	42,368	5-1	21,767	5-1	Moenchengladbach
1976	Liverpool v Club Brugge	3-2	49,981	1-1	29,423	4-3	Liverpool
1977	Juventus v Athletic Bilbao	1-0	66,000	1-2	39,700	2-2	Juventus
	Juventus won on away goals rule.						
1978	Bastia v PSV Eindhoven	0-0	8,006	0-3	28,000	0-3	PSV Eindhoven
1979	RS Belgrade v Moenchengladbach	1-1	65,000	0-1	45,000	1-2	Moenchengladbach
1980	Moenchengladbach v E. Frankfurt	3-2	25,000	0-1	59,000	3-3	E. Frankfurt
	Eintracht Frankfurt won on away goals rule.						
1981	Ipswich T v AZ 67 Alkmaar	3-0	27,532	2-4	22,291	5-4	Ipswich T
1982	IFK Gothenburg v Hamburg	1-0	42,548	3-0	57,312	4-0	IFK Gothenburg
1983	Anderlecht v Benfica	1-0	55,000	1-1	70,000	2-1	Anderlecht
1984	Anderlecht v Tottenham H	1-1	33,000	1-1*	46,258	2-2	Tottenham H
	Tottenham H won 4-3 on penalties.						
1985	Videoton v Real Madrid	0-3	30,000	1-0	80,000	1-3	Real Madrid
1986	Real Madrid v Cologne	5-1	60,000	0-2	22,000	5-3	Real Madrid
1987	IFK Gothenburg v Dundee U	1-0	48,614	1-1	20,900	2-1	IFK Gothenburg
1988	Espanol v Bayer Leverkusen	3-0	31,180	0-3*	21,600	3-3	Bayer Leverkusen
	Bayer Leverkusen won 3-2 on penalties.						
1989	Napoli v VfB Stuttgart	2-1	81,093	3-3	64,000	5-4	Napoli
1990	Juventus v Fiorentina	3-1	47,519	0-0	30,999	3-1	Juventus
1991	Internazionale v Roma	2-0	68,887	0-1	70,901	2-1	Internazionale
1992	Torino v Ajax	2-2	65,377	0-0	40,000	2-2	Ajax
	Ajax won on away goals rule.						
1993	Borussia Dortmund v Juventus	1-3	37,000	0-3	62,781	1-6	Juventus
1994	Salzburg v Internazionale	0-1	43,000	0-1	80,345	0-2	Internazionale
1995	Parma v Juventus	1-0	22,057	1-1	80,000	2-1	Parma
1996	Bayern Munich v Bordeaux	2-0	63,000	3-1	30,000	5-1	Bayern Munich
1997	Schalke 04 v Internazionale	1-0	57,000	0-1*	81,675	1-1	Schalke 04
	Schalke 04 won 4-1 on penalties.						

UEFA CUP FINALS 1998–2009

Year	Winners v Runners-up		Venue	Attendance	Referee
1998	Internazionale v Lazio	3-0	Paris	44,412	A. L. Nieto (Spain)
1999	Parma v Olympique Marseille	3-0	Moscow	61,000	H. Dallas (Scotland)
2000	Galatasaray v Arsenal	0-0*	Copenhagen	38,919	A. L. Nieto (Spain)
	Galatasaray won 4-1 on penalties.				
2001	Liverpool v Alaves	5-4*	Dortmund	48,050	G. Veissiere (France)
	Liverpool won on sudden death 'golden goal'.				
2002	Feyenoord v Borussia Dortmund	3-2	Rotterdam	45,611	V. M. M. Pereira (Portugal)
2003	FC Porto v Celtic	3-2*	Seville	52,140	L. Michel (Slovakia)
2004	Valencia v Olympique Marseille	2-0	Gothenburg	39,000	P. Collina (Italy)
2005	CSKA Moscow v Sporting Lisbon	3-1	Lisbon	47,085	G. Poll (England)
2006	Sevilla v Middlesbrough	4-0	Eindhoven	32,100	H. Fandel (Germany)
2007	Sevilla v Espanyol	2-2*	Glasgow	47,602	M. Busacca (Switzerland)
	Sevilla won 3-1 on penalties.				
2008	Zenit St Petersburg v Rangers	2-0	Manchester	43,878	P. Fröjdfeldt (Sweden)
2009	Shakhtar Donetsk v Werder Bremen	2-1*	Istanbul	37,357	L. M. Chantalejo (Spain)

UEFA EUROPA LEAGUE FINALS 2010–21

Year	Winners v Runners-up		Venue	Attendance	Referee
2010	Atletico Madrid v Fulham	2-1*	Hamburg	49,000	N. Rizzoli (Italy)
2011	FC Porto v Braga	1-0	Dublin	45,391	V. Carballo (Spain)
2012	Atletico Madrid v Athletic Bilbao	3-0	Bucharest	52,347	W. Stark (Germany)
2013	Chelsea v Benfica	2-1	Amsterdam	46,163	B. Kuipers (Netherlands)
2014	Sevilla v Benfica	0-0*	Turin	33,120	F. Brych (Germany)
	Sevilla won 4-2 on penalties.				
2015	Sevilla v Dnipro Dnipropetrovsk	3-2	Warsaw	45,000	M. Atkinson (England)
2016	Sevilla v Liverpool	3-1	Basel	34,429	J. Eriksson (Sweden)
2017	Manchester U v Ajax	2-0	Stockholm	46,961	D. Skomina (Slovenia)
2018	Atletico Madrid v Marseille	3-0	Lyon	55,768	B. Kuipers (Netherlands)
2019	Chelsea v Arsenal	4-1	Baku	51,370	G. Rocchi (Italy)
2020	Sevilla v Internazionale	3-2	Cologne	0	D. Makkelie (Netherlands)
2021	Villareal v Manchester U	1-1*	Gdansk	9,412	C. Turpin (France)
	Villareal won 11-10 on penalties.				

**After extra time.*

UEFA EUROPA LEAGUE 2020–21

▪ *Denotes player sent off.*
Due to the COVID-19 pandemic, matches played behind closed doors unless otherwise stated.

PRELIMINARY ROUND

Tuesday, 18 August 2020

UE Engordany (0) 1 *(Gomez 90 (pen))*

Zeta (1) 3 *(Vukcevic 45, Mijat Lambulic 54, Lambulic L 63)*

UE Engordany: (4141) Coca; Aguero, Sousa, Munoz, Rudler; Spano; San Nicolas (Lafont 67), Da Silva Oliveira (Lopez 75), Rame (Teixeira 87), Gomez; Sanchez.
Zeta: (4231) Akovic; Milic, Tuzovic, Ceklic, Dinovic; Krstovic, Milojko; Vukcevic (Djurovic 89), Lambulic L (Tripuno 89), Kalezic; Mijat Lambulic (Matija Lambulic 81).

Thursday, 20 August 2020

Coleraine (0) 1 *(McLaughlin 89)*

La Fiorita (0) 0

Coleraine: (433) Deane; Kane, Canning, O'Donnell, Traynor; Doherty, Lowry, Jarvis; Carson (Nixon 46), McLaughlin, Allen (Bradley 62).
La Fiorita: (433) Vivan; Rinaldi, Di Maio, Brighi, Grandoni; Amati, Loiodice, Errico (Guidi 65); Gasperoni, Tommasi (Pieri 74), Peluso (Mularoni 79).

FC Santa Coloma (0) 0

Iskra (0) 0

FC Santa Coloma: (4141) Casals; Rubio, Sanchez, Miranda, San Nicolas; Rebes (Camochu 116); Martinez (Bouharma 90), Blanco (Santos 81), Pi (Najera 46), Cistero; Alaez▪.
Iskra: (433) Blazic; Malesevic, Kumburovic, Drincic, Jovanovic (Obradovic 113); Adzovic (Djurisic 68), Rogosic (Milic 89), Sahman; Boricic, Vukovic, Yamamoto (Mandic 81).
aet; Iskra won 4-3 on penalties.

Glentoran (1) 1 *(McDaid 42)*

HB Torshavn (0) 0

Glentoran: (433) Coleing; Kane, Cowan, Marron, McClean; Clucas (McCullough 68), Gallagher, Bigirimana; O'Neill (McDonagh 73), Donnelly (Stewart 84), McDaid.
HB Torshavn: (433) Gestsson; Davidsen (Joensen 62), Wardum, Tshiembe, Johansen; Nygaard, Hansen, Soylu; Jakobsen, Dahl, Petersen (Justinussen 46).

NSI Runavik (0) 5 *(Olsen 52, 63, 74, Knudsen P 67, Lokin 83)*

Barry Town U (0) 1 *(McLaggon 88)*

NSI Runavik: (433) Thomsen; Hansen (Skipanes 60), Davidsen J, Hojgaard, Nielsen; Christjansen (Knudsen A 82), Mortensen M, Benjaminsen; Bech, Olsen (Lokin 79), Knudsen P.
Barry Town U: (433) Lewis; Cummings, Press, Cooper, Hugh; Wharton, Green, Patten (George 70); McLaggon, Jarvis (Reffell 82), Cotterill D (Cotterill J 70).

St Joseph's (1) 1 *(Boro 30)*

B36 Torshavn (2) 2 *(Przybylski 28, Mellemgaard 42 (pen))*

St Joseph's: (433) Matteo; Rojas (Loren 62), Pecci, Juanma, Pons (Mouelhi 87); Boro, Ferrer, Villar; Nano, Juanfri, Carrasco (Guirado 77).
B36 Torshavn: (4411) Hentze; Petersen (Heinesen 61), Eriksen, Nattestad, Mellemgaard (Jacobsen E 79); Frederiksberg, Jacobsen M (Radosavlevic 85), Nielsen, Olsen; Przybylski; Pingel.

Friday, 21 August 2020

Tre Penne (1) 1 *(Gai 16)*

Gjilani (1) 3 *(Nikac 24, Hajdari 64, Hila 68)*

Tre Penne: (433) Migani; Battistini, Lombardi, Genestreti, Mezzadri; Gasperoni (Cesarini 68), Patregnani, Gai; Sorrentino▪, Chiurato (Pieri 74), Ceccaroli (Cibelli 50).
Gjilani: (433) Kolici; Frasheri, Veliu, Rapa, Halili (Kastrati 83); Jonuzi (Kuc 50), Useini, Hila; Progni, Nikac, Hajdari (Dubova 79).

Lincoln Red Imps 3

Pristina 0

Match awarded 3-0 to Lincoln Red Imps due to Prinstina being unable to fulfil the fixtures after several of their players tested positive for COVID-19.

FIRST QUALIFYING ROUND

Tuesday, 25 August 2020

Riteriai (1) 3 *(Paulauskas 39, 48, Kazlauskas 91)*

Derry C (1) 2 *(Thomson 18, Toal 62)*

Riteriai: (4132) Simaitis; Kalermo, Sveikauskas, Barauskas, Malzinskas; Dombrauskis (Ramanauskas 88); Traore (Kodz 76), Lezama, Grigalevicius; Paulauskas (Filipavicius 101), Kazlauskas.
Derry C: (442) Cherrie; Horgan, Toal, Cole, Coll; Hammill, McCormack, Dunwoody (Mallon 56), Thomson (Clifford 73 (Bruna 110)); Meite (Harkin 85), Akintunde.
aet.

Wednesday, 26 August 2020

Progres Niederkorn (1) 3 *(Tekiela 11, 55 (pen), Thill 90)*

Zeta (0) 0

Progres Niederkorn: (442) Flauss; Laterza, Ferino, Karayer, Latic (Shala 86); Thill, Skenderovic, Habbas (Luisi 78), Tekiela; Holtz (Muratovic 67), Silaj.
Zeta: (442) Akovic; Soppo, Milic, Tuzovic, Djinovic; Milojko, Ceklic (Djurovic 67), Vukcevic, Mijat Lambulic (Lambulic L 55); Kalezic (Nya-Vedji 62), Krstovic.

Thursday, 27 August 2020

Aberdeen (2) 6 *(Ferguson 37, Main 43, Hedges 50, 59, 87 (pen), Hayes 63)*

NSI Runavik (0) 0

Aberdeen: (352) Lewis; McCrorie, McKenna, Considine; Kennedy, Ferguson, McGeouch, Wright (McGinn 82), Hayes; Watkins (Anderson 73), Main (Hedges 46).
NSI Runavik: (433) Thomsen; Hansen (Jakobsen 60), Hojgaard, Davidsen J, Benjaminsen; Christjansen, Bech (Knudsen A 88), Mortensen M (Lokin 70); Nielsen, Olsen, Knudsen P.

AGF Aarhus (3) 5 *(Tingager 21, Mortensen 29, 45 (pen), Tengstedt 90, Olsen 90)*

FC Honka (1) 2 *(Martin 35, Kaufmann 64)*

AGF Aarhus: (433) Eskelinen; Munksgaard, Hausner, Tingager, Hojer; Olsen, Poulsen, Blume (Hvidt 86); Links (Jevtovic 78), Mortensen, Thorsteinsson (Tengstedt 70).
FC Honka: (343) Murray; Hatakka, Ivanov, Rasimus; Aalto (Kandji 69), Hervas, Voutilainen, Levanen; Kaufmann, Dongou, Martin (Sejdiu 79).

Alashkert (0) 0

Renova (0) 1 *(Miskovski 58)*

Alashkert: (4141) Cancarevic; Gonchar, Mitrevski, Voskanyan, Bryan; Grigoryan (Tankov 80); Tiago Cameta (Papikyan 67), Galvao, Perdigao (Camara 61), Batista; Glisic.
Renova: (4231) Velii; Fetai, Miskovski, Abdulla, Velija; Sadiki, Gavazaj; Ramadani (Jasaroski 71), Gafuri (Veliu 86), Shefiti; Selmani (Stojcevski 63).

Apollon Limassol (2) 5 *(Dabo 4, 32, 76, Diguiny 59, Gianniotas 86)*

Saburtalo (0) 1 *(Guliashvili 69)*

Apollon Limassol: (4411) Mall; Pittas, Yuste, Roberge, Szalai; Gianniotas, Denic (Aguirre 64), Sachetti, Matei (Psychas 75); Diguiny (Markovic 64); Dabo.
Saburtalo: (442) Kupatadze; Mali, Margvelashvili, Grigalashvili, Kakubava; Tabatadze, Tera (Chichinadze▪ 66), Altunashvili, Boumal (Gocholeishvili 78); Lumu (Guliashvili 63), Kavtaradze.

B36 Torshavn (0) 4 *(Pingel 72, 76, Samuelsen 107, Agnarsson 113)*

FCI Levadia (0) 3 *(Oigus 52, Elhi 80, Manucho 101)*

B36 Torshavn: (442) Hentze; Heinesen, Eriksen, Nattestad, Mellemgaard; Jacobsen M (Samuelsen 90), Przybylski, Nielsen (Johansen 69 (Petersen 115)), Frederiksberg; Pingel, Radosavlevic (Agnarsson 60).
FCI Levadia: (442) Kotenko; Jurgenson, Podholjuzin, Ochigava, Kruglov; Lepistu, Elhi, Komlov (Lipp 106), Roosnupp (Peetson 115); Oigus, Manucho.
aet.

Bodo/Glimt (2) 6 *(Zinckernagel 27, 36, Hauge 52, 59 (pen), Boniface 79, Tounekti 81)*

Kauno Zalgiris (0) 1 *(Otele 78)*

Bodo/Glimt: (433) Khaikin; Sampsted, Lode (Sveen 59), Hoibraten, Bjorkan (Foosnaes 62); Fet, Berg, Saltnes; Zinckernagel (Tounekti 77), Boniface, Hauge.
Kauno Zalgiris: (343) Mikelionis; Dapkus, Thicot, Rudinilson; Vaitkunas, Silkaitis, Pilibaitis (Sesplaukis 73), Bushman; Sirgedas, David (Otele 61), Urbys (Anisas 82).

Borac Banja Luca (1) 1 *(Vranjes 35)*

Sutjeska (0) 0

Borac Banja Luca: (4411) Pavlovic; Dujakovic (Kajkut 79), Jovanovic, Janicic, Cosic; Zakaric, Danilovic, Brtan (Vojnovic 64), Ziljkic; Vranjes; Lukic (Radulovic 72).
Sutjeska: (4231) Giljen; Grivic, Mitrovic, Bulatovic, Stijepovic; Jankovic (Markovic 74), Dubljevic (Marusic 67); Kojasevic (Raicevic 10), Cetkovic, Osmajic; Adrovic.

Budapest Honved (0) 2 *(Traore 90, Hamalainen 105 (og))*

Inter Turku (0) 1 *(Liliu 90)*

Budapest Honved: (442) Tujvel; Barath (Mezghrani 46), Batik, Gazdag, Hidi (Kamber 107); Kesztyus, Lovric, Toth-Gabor (Traore 72), Ugrai (Aliji 120); Uzoma, Zsoter.
Inter Turku: (343) Moisander; Ketting, Hoskonen, Hamalainen; Engstrom (Kouassivi-Benissan 106), Annan, Muniz (Kagayama 106), Ruane; Paananen (Ojala 65), Kallman (Liliu 89), Furuholm.
aet.

CSKA Sofia (0) 2 *(Ahmedov 75, Sowe 90)*

Sirens (0) 1 *(da Silva 69)*

CSKA Sofia: (4231) Busatto; Galabov, Mattheij, Antov, Mazikou; Tiago Rodrigues, Youga (Ahmedov 71); Henrique, Beltrame (Sankhare 65), Carey (Yomov 57); Sowe.
Sirens: (4231) Cassar; Romeu (Walker 30), Raphael, Borg, Thiago Espindola; Agius (Grech 82), Scicluna; Petinha (Mifsud 78), da Silva, Bustos; Domoraud.

Dinamo Minsk (0) 0

Piast Gliwice (1) 2 *(Lipski 10, Swierczok 56)*

Dinamo Minsk: (343) Pomazan; Shitov, Goropevsek, Dinga; Matvejchik, Olekhnovich (Vergeychik 73), Silas (Kozlov 59), Sukhotsky; Klimovich, Shikavka (Khvashchinski 79), Bakhar.
Piast Gliwice: (433) Plach; Konczkowski, Czerwinski, Huk, Kirkeskov; Sokolowski, Swierczok, Lipski; Badia (Steczyk 72), Parzyszek (Zyro 55), Vida (Milewski 82).

FCSB (1) 3 *(Olaru 34, Tanase 65 (pen), Buziuc 83)*

Shirak (0) 0

FCSB: (442) Vlad; Cretu, Miron, Cristea, Pantea; Olaru, Ovidiu Popescu, Tanase (Vina 86), Man (Morutan 78); Bus (Buziuc 46), Coman.
Shirak: (442) Ermakov; Margaryan, Prljevic, Mkoyan, Davoyan; Aslanyan (Avo 74), Manoyan (Udo 69), Muradyan, Malakyan; Nenadovic (Gevorkyan 74), Kone.

Fehervar (1) 1 *(Nikolics 37)*

Bohemians (1) 1 *(Ward 22)*

Fehervar: (4231) Kovacsik; Nego, Stopira, Rus, Fiola; Alef (Patkai 75), Houri; Bamgboye, Evandro (Nikolov 101), Petryak (Geresi 109); Nikolics (Hodzic 74).
Bohemians: (4231) McGuinness; Lyons, Casey, Cornwall (Finnerty 71), Breslin; Buckley (Mandroiu 109), Lunney (Levingston 79); Twardek, Ward (Devoy 84), Grant; Wright.
aet; Fehervar won 4-2 on penalties.

FH Hafnarfjordur (0) 0

DAC Dunajska Streda (1) 2 *(Balic 23, Ramirez 76)*

FH Hafnarfjordur: (433) Nielsen; Gunnarsson, Hafsteinsson (Gudnason 71), Helgason, Jonsson E; Kristjansson, Lennon, Sverrisson (Sigurdsson 82); Thorisson, Vidarsson, Finsen (Jonsson J 58).
DAC Dunajska Streda: (4231) Jedlicka; Blackman, Muller, Kruzliak, Davis; Balic, Schafer; Divkovic (Fabry 71), Friede, Kalmar; Ramirez.

Gjilani (0) 0

APOEL (0) 2 *(Efrem 102, Ndongala 116)*

Gjilani: (433) Kolici; Rapa (Frasheri 73), Kastrati, Veliu, Jackson (Prekazi 106); Hila (Jonuzi 96), Useini, Aziz; Progni, Nikac, Hajdari.
APOEL: (442) Miguel Silva; Mihajlovic, Merkis, Rafael Santos, Ioannou; Al-Taamari (Efrem 90), Lundemo, Jensen (Sielis 117), De Vincenti; Zahid (Sahar 67), Klonaridis (Ndongala 79).
aet.

Hammarby (2) 3 *(Khalili A 14, Bojanic 32, Paulinho 84)*

Puskas Akademia (0) 0

Hammarby: (4231) Ousted; Soderstrom, Fenger, Fallman, Jeahze (Rodic 80); Andersen, Bojanic; Khalili A (Kacaniklic 77), Tankovic (Johannsson 55), Paulinho; Khalili I.
Puskas Akademia: (442) Auerbach; Szolnoki, Spandler, Hadzhiev, Nagy; Radics, Plsek, Kiss (Kalmar 81), Deutsch; Latifi (Komaromi 61), Weslen Junior (Corbu 70).

Hapoel Be'er Sheva (2) 3 *(Josue 9, 61, Kabha 21)*

Dinamo Batumi (0) 0

Hapoel Be'er Sheva: (451) Levita; Dadia, Miguel Vitor (Taha 79), Tzedek, Goldberg; Sintyahu, Kabha (Yosefi 63), Keltjens, Josue, Acolatse; Shabiro (Varenne 75).
Dinamo Batumi: (433) Alavidze; Mamuchashvili, Kobakhidze, Oboabona, Navalovski (Chaladze 45); Jigauri, Teidi, Mandzhgaladze (Gaprindashvili 79); Vagner Goncalves, Nikabadze (Reynaldo 64), Flamarion.

Iskra (0) 0

Lokomotiv Plovdiv (0) 1 *(Iliev 75 (pen))*

Iskra: (433) Kordic; Malesevic, Drincic, Kumburovic, Jovanovic; Adzovic (Milic 78), Kato, Sahman; Boricic (Djurisic 82), Vukovic, Petrovic (Rogosic 73).
Lokomotiv Plovdiv: (3412) Lukov; Petrovic, Masoero, Almeida; Karageren, Vitanov, Umarboev (Nikolaev 90), Tsvetanov; Salinas (Ilic 65); Iliev, Aralica (Minchev 73).

Kairat (2) 4 *(Alyukolov 12, Vagner Love 35, 70, Eseola 90)*

Noah (1) 1 *(Bor 8)*

Kairat: (532) Pokatilov; Wrzesinski (Abiken 59), Dugalic, Goralski, Alip, Mikanovic; Hovhannisyan, Kosovic, Aymbetov (Eseola 79); Vagner Love, Alyukolov (Usenov 74).
Noah: (433) Shvagirev; Vimercati, Kagermazov, Kryuchkov, Dedechko; Kovalenko (Sana 71), Deobald (Simonyan 46), Emsis; Azarov (Hovhannisyan 72), Bor, Lavrishchev.

Keshla (0) 0

Laci (0) 0

Keshla: (4231) Namasco; Qyrtymov, Bojovic, Aliyev■, Salahli; Kamara, Klyots; Isgenderli (Akhundov 119), Haciyev, Artur (Imamverdiyev 81); Christovao (Silvio 64).
Laci: (433) Sherri; Marku A, Ignjatovic, Selmani, Turkaj; Deliu (Rapo D 99), Lushkja, Teco (Mazrekaj 120); Nwabueze, Xhixha (Rapo K 105), Ramos■.
aet; Laci won 5-4 on penalties.

Kukesi (0) 2 *(Friday 56 (pen), Cooper 85)*

Slavia Sofia (0) 1 *(Krastev F 81)*

Kukesi: (4141) Xhika; Malikji, Horic, Obanor, Musta; Telushi; Gavazaj E (Gashi 46), Musolli, Limaj (Gavazaj Z 65), Rroca; Friday (Cooper 66).
Slavia Sofia: (451) Stergiakis; Patev, Hristov, Gamakov, Popadiyn; Krastev F, Karabelyov, Valchev (Bengyuzov 73), Krastev K, Stoev (Stoyanov 87); Rangelov (Dimitrov 62).

Lech Poznan (0) 3 *(Ishak 59, 78, Szymczak 88)*

Valmiera (0) 0

Lech Poznan: (442) Bednarek; Gumny, Satka, Crnomarkovic, Puchacz; Kaminski (Czerwinski 63), Moder, Pedro Tiba (Marchwinski 80), Jozwiak; Ramirez, Ishak (Szymczak 84).
Valmiera: (433) Soloha; Arokodare, Badmus, Celestine, Diage; Fall, Jaunzems (Skopenko 82), Karklins; Musolitin, Silagadze (Zaddem 46), Teixeira.

Lincoln Red Imps (1) 2 *(Casciaro L 36, Yahaya 90)*

Union Titus Petange (0) 0

Lincoln Red Imps: (343) Soler; Wiseman, Lopes, Chipolina R; Sergeant, Torrilla, Yahaya, Britto; Hernandez (Casciaro K 73), Gomez (Same 85), Casciaro L (Coombes 78).
Union Titus Petange: (433) Ottele; Hamzaoui, Hauguel, Kodjia, Lauriente; Kakoko, Kabore, El Hamzaoui; Schneider (Rodrigues da Cruz 75), Maah (Nanizayamo 63), Duriatti (Gashi 55).

Lokomotive Tbilisi (0) 2 *(Sikharulidze 57, Oulad Omar 61)*

Universitatea Craiova (0) 1 *(Baiaram 90)*

Lokomotive Tbilisi: (433) Mamardashvili; Gabadze, Sandokhadze (Andronikashvili 77), Gureshidze, Ubilava; Samurkasovi (Chanturia 80), Shonia, Dartsmelia; Kirkitadze, Sikharulidze, Oulad Omar (Dzebniauri 69).
Universitatea Craiova: (433) Pigliacelli; Vatajelu, Acka, Constantin, Bancu; Nistor (Baiaram 77), Mateiu (Screciu 67), Cicaldau; Barbut (Mihaila 61), Koljic, Ivan.

Malmo (2) 2 *(Berget 1, Rieks 44)*

Cracovia (0) 0

Malmo: (442) Johansson; Larsson, Ahmedhodzic, Brorsson, Knudsen; Rakip (Traustason 75), Lewicki, Christiansen, Rieks; Berget (Sarr 67), Thelin.
Cracovia: (4141) Hrosso; Rapa, Jablonsky, Helik, Siplak (Ferraresso 58); Loshaj; Hanca, van Amersfoort, Alvarez (Vestenicky 79), Wdowiak; Rivaldinho (Dimun 46).

Maribor (0) 1 *(Vancas 65)*

Coleraine (0) 1 *(McLaughlin 62)*

Maribor: (4231) Jug; Milec, Mitrovic, Pericic, Viler; Pihler (Dervisevic 105), Cretu; Kramaric (Tavares 61), Kronaveter (Mlakar 84), Matko (Vancas 61); Mesanovic.
Coleraine: (4141) Deane; Canning, Carson, Doherty, Jarvis (Wilson 72); Kane; Lowry, McLaughlin (Parkhill 95), Nixon (Bradley 85), O'Donnell; Traynor (McConaghie 106).
aet; Coleraine won 5-4 on penalties.

Motherwell (0) 5 *(Lang 58, O'Donnell 72, Polworth 75, Watt 78, Long 87)*

Glentoran (0) 1 *(McDaid 90)*

Motherwell: (433) Carson; Grimshaw (Seedorf 60), Mugabi, Gallagher, Lamie; O'Donnell (Robinson 82), Campbell, O'Hara; Polworth, Long, Lang (Watt 70).
Glentoran: (433) Coleing; Marron, Cowan, McClean, Kane; Clucas■, Bigirimana, Gallagher (O'Connor 78); O'Neill (McDonagh 62), Donnelly, McDaid.

Neftchi (0) 2 *(Bougrine 66, Krivotsyuk 88)*

Shkupi (0) 1 *(Darboe 90)*

Neftchi: (442) Mammadov; Amirli, Mbodj, Krivotsyuk, Thallyson (Stankovic 90); Bougrine, Kane, Makhmudov, Alasgarov; Lawal, Monrose (Abbasov 90).
Shkupi: (4231) Naumovski; Gligorov, Bianor, Krivanjeva, Glisic; Bilali, Diack; Ademi (Jusufi 73), Iseni (Alvarez 65), Oumar■; Darboe.

Olimpija Ljubljana (0) 2 *(Fink 88, Bosic 106)*

Vikingur (1) 1 *(Karlsson 27)*

Olimpija Ljubljana: (4231) Frelih; Andrejasic (Fink 46), Samardzic, Korun, Lyaskov (Pavlovic 92); Ostrc, Elsnik; Caimacov, Bagaric (Blagaic 58), Bosic; Vukusic (Lupeta 71).
Vikingur: (352) Jonsson; Ottesen■, Arnason, Sigurdsson; Atlason (Snorrason 96), Agnarsson, Magnusson (Andrason 60), Hlynsson, Barkarson; Hansen (Thordarson 61 (Gudjonsson 110)), Karlsson.
aet.

Ordabasy (1) 1 *(Mahlangu 31)*

Botosani (2) 2 *(Holzmann 25, Dugandzic 33)*

Ordabasy: (442) Shayzada; Dautov, Fontanello, Dmitrenko (Mehanovic 85), Dosmagambetov; Badibanga, Diakhate, Mahlangu, Ruben Brigido; Khizhnichenko (Simcevic 46), Joao Paulo (Zhanglyshbay 76).
Botosani: (4231) Pap; Harut, Chindris, Seroni, Holzmann; Mendoza, Rodriguez; Florescu, Ashkovski (Tiganasu 89), Ofusu (Keyta 74); Dugandzic (Roman 90).

Partizan Belgrade (0) 1 *(Natcho 52 (pen))*

Rigas FS (0) 0

Partizan Belgrade: (442) Stojkovic V; Asano (Stojkovic D 90), Bagnack M, Miletic, Natcho (Smiljanic 90); Sadiq, Scekic, Stevanovic (Soumah 72), Urosevic; Vitas, Zdjelar.
Rigas FS: (433) Kucher; Ikaunieks, Jagodinskis, Kouadio (Deocleciano 70), Lemajic; Lipuscek, Saric, Savalnieks; Simkovic (Offor Nnamdi 70), Solovjovs, Strumia.

Petrocub-Hincesti (0) 0

Backa Topola (1) 2 *(Tomanovic 17, Lukic 55 (pen))*

Petrocub-Hincesti: (442) Avram; Jardan, Onana, Racu, Taras (Bejan 54); Douanla, Cojocari, Rozgoniuc■, Turcan (Bogaciuc 68); Platica, Ambros (Damascan 68).
Backa Topola: (442) Filipovic; Varga■, Antonic, Babic, Ponjevic; Zec (Djuric 90), Tomanovic, Milicevic, Duronjic (Banjac 74); Lukic, Siladji (Petrovic 44).

Rosenborg (4) 4 *(Borven 4, 29, Reginiussen 17, Hovland 24)*

Breidablik (0) 2 *(Einarsson V 61, Mikkelsen 90 (pen))*

Rosenborg: (442) Lund; Reitan, Reginiussen, Hovland, Hedenstadt (Kamanzi 80); Zachariassen, Tagseth (Brattbakk 61), Asen, Holse; Islamovic, Borven.
Breidablik: (442) Einarsson A; Yeoman (Sigurgeirsson 40), Muminovic, Helgason, Porkelsson (Margeirsson 78); Einarsson V, Sigurdarson (Steindorsson 70), Gunnlaugsson, Eyjolfsson; Mikkelsen, Willumsson.

Servette (0) 3 *(Stevanovic 54, Mendy 77, Antunes 86)*

Ruzomberok (0) 0

Servette: (4231) Frick; Sauthier, Rouiller, Sasso, Mendy; Ondoua, Cognat (Maccoppi 86); Tasar (Antunes 69), Imeri (Cespedes 76), Stevanovic; Kyei.
Ruzomberok: (442) Macik; Curma, Maslo, Mojzis, Mudry (Brenkus 65); Kochan, Zsigmund, Takac (Dungel 60), Madlenak; Almasi (Bobcek 70), Gerec.

Shakhtyor Soligorsk (0) 0

Sfintul Gheorghe (0) 0

Shakhtyor Soligorsk: (442) Gutor; Begunov (Sotnikov 105), Khadarkevich, Sachivko, Burko; Selyava, Ivanovic (Balanovich 46), Kendysh (Szoke 68), Podstrelov; Arkhipov (Jakhshibaev 46), Bodul■.
Sfintul Gheorghe: (442) Cebotari; Focsa, Novicov, Smirnov Y, Svinarenco; Ojog, Slivca, Sagna (Plamadeala 84), Mochulyak (Iurcu 79); Mandricenco (Suvorov 90), Volkov.
aet; Sfintul Gheorghe won 4-1 on penalties.

Shamrock R (1) 2 *(Burke 14, Lopes 78)*

Ilves (1) 2 *(Ala-Myllymaki 10 (pen), Veteli 62)*

Shamrock R: (442) Mannus; Finn, Lopes, Scales■, O'Brien; Byrne, O'Neill, McEneff, Farrugia (Williams 78); Burke (Watts 64), Greene (Lafferty 105).
Ilves: (442) Hilander; Miettunen, Tomas, Almen, Aspegren (Arifi 111); Veteli (Siira 83), Jair, Tamminen (Mommo 102), Ala-Myllymaki; Skytta, Mettala (Raittinen 79).
aet; Shamrock R won 12-11 on penalties.

Sumqayit (0) 0

Shkendija (0) 2 *(Ibraimi 56 (pen), Doriev 89 (pen))*

Sumqayit: (532) Dzhenetov; Ahmadov (Hemati 62), Badalov, Huseynov, Khodzhaniyazov, Mutallimov■; Nadzhafov (Abdullazada S 63), Mustafayev, Sadykhov; Ghorbani, Mammadov (Abdullazada R 73).
Shkendija: (433) Zahov; Murati (Neziri 90), Krivak, Bejtulai, Pavic; Totre, Dita, Ahmedi; Imeri (Zejnullai 77), Ibraimi, Doriev (Es Sahhal 90).

Teuta (1) 2 *(Krasniqi 6, Hebaj 87)*

Beitar Jerusalem (0) 0

Teuta: (4231) Frasheri; Todorovski, Hoxha, Arapi, Kouros; Avdyli (Beqja L 90), Aleksi; Beqja F (Gruda 63), Vila E, Vila L; Krasniqi (Hebaj 65).
Beitar Jerusalem: (433) Nitzan; Konstantini, Verdasca, Dgani, Biton (Magbo 76); Kriaf, Mohamed, Rotman (Vlijter 46); Vered, Azulay, Atar (Edri 71).

The New Saints (0) 3 *(Robles 56, Smith 100, Cieslewicz 108 (pen))*

Zilina (0) 1 *(Myslovic 77 (pen))*

The New Saints: (442) Harrison; Astles, Brobbel (Smith 81), Ebbe, Holland; Hudson, Marriott, Mullan, Redmond (Routledge 104); Robles (Cieslewicz 87), Spender (Harrington 48).
Zilina: (433) Petras; Vallo, Minarik, Kopas, Sluka■; Bernat (Bichakhchyan 90), Gono, Myslovic; Duris (Kapralik 117), Paur (Kurminowski 85), Ilko (Rusnak 101).
aet.

Vaduz (0) 0

Hibernians (1) 2 *(Degabriele 34, 57)*

Vaduz: (442) Buchel; Cicek, Coulibaly, Dorn (Di Giusto 75), Gasser; Luchinger, Santin, Schmid, Simani; Sutter, Wieser.
Hibernians: (442) Cremona; Agius, Leandro Almeida, Attard (Uzeh 70), Degabriele; Grech J, Grech Z, Izquier, Kristensen■; Shodiya (Desira 75), Teixeira (Winchester 63).

Valletta (0) 0

Bala T (1) 1 *(Venables 38)*

Valletta: (4141) Bonello; Borg, Jovanovic, Caruana, Pena; Malano; Alba (Nwoko 46), Dimech (Marukawa 68), Muscat, Piciollo; Fontanella.
Bala T: (433) Ramsay; Shannon, Spittle, Stephens, Smith S; Mendes, Kay, Leslie (Smith K 69); Correia (Jones 78), Venables, Evans.

Ventspils (1) 2 *(Lucas Villela 22, Kozlov 75 (pen))*

Dinamo-Auto Tiraspol (1) 1 *(Rogac D 15)*

Ventspils: (433) Alampasu; Mchedlishvili, Sakhnevich, Litvinskis, Rekhviashvili; Lucas Villela, Palavandishvili■, Genaev (Ulimbashevs 70); Kozlov, Svarups (Ondong 80), Eristavi.
Dinamo-Auto Tiraspol: (433) Straistari; Nagiyev (Bulat 78), Rogac R, Dijinari, Masalov; Belousov, Bilinschii, Mihailev; Kondratiuk, Rogac D, Paireli.

Zalgiris Vilnius (2) 2 *(Kaludjerovic 9, Antal 32)*

Paide Linnameeskond (0) 0

Zalgiris Vilnius: (433) Berkovec; Mikoliunas, Tatomirovic, Ljubisavljevic, Slijngard; Vorobjovas, Simkus, Kamenar (Kuklys 68); Antal (Ennin 81), Kaludjerovic, Videmont (Kyeremeh 90).
Paide Linnameeskond: (433) Toom; Mool, Pelt, Kase, Saliste; Mosnikov, Sinilaid (Caprioli 46), Frolov (Owusu-Sekyere 75); Tur, Anier, Luts (Lubega 63).

Zrinjski Mostar (2) 3 *(Bilbija 37, Filipovic 40, Ivancic 80)*

Differdange 03 (0) 0

Zrinjski Mostar: (4231) Brkic; Barbaric, Bilbija, Enin, Filipovic (Basic 74); Jakovljevic, Masic (Ivancic 64); Stojkic, Ticinovic, Todorovic (Govedarica 82); Trebotic.
Differdange 03: (433) Straus; Almeida (Garlito 85), Balde (Komano 46), Brusco, Buch; De Taddeo, Franzoni, Gulluni; Joachim, Lempereur, Pereira (Gobitaka 80).

Wednesday, 9 September 2020

Maccabi Haifa (1) 3 *(Chery 38, Rukavytsya 59, Ashkenazi 66)*

Zeljeznicar (1) 1 *(Lendric 34)*

Maccabi Haifa: (433) Cohen; Mabouka, Habashi, Arad, Menachem; Ashkenazi, Lavi, Abu Fani (Haziza 54); Chery, Rukavytsya (Nachmani 76), Wildschut.
Zeljeznicar: (4231) Fejzic; Stevanovic, Kosoric, Miletic, Sehic (Juricic 75); Hajdarevic, Alispahic (Sadikovic 75); Blazevic, Stilic, Veselinovic (Mujezinovic 63); Lendric.

Thursday, 10 September 2020

Nomme Kalju (0) 0

Mura (4) 4 *(Zizek 17, 27, Filipovic 33, Kozar 37)*

Nomme Kalju: (433) Meerits; Suurvali, Rattasepp, Puri, Raudsepp; Tamm, Jersov (Sustov 46), Paur; Usta, Demidov, Antonov (Liblikmann 89).
Mura: (352) Obradovic; Karnicnik, Marusko (Cipot 46), Gorenc; Kous, Horvat, Kouter (Marosa 78), Kozar (Brkic 66), Sturm; Zizek, Filipovic.

SECOND QUALIFYING ROUND

Wednesday, 16 September 2020

B36 Torshavn (0) 2 *(Przybylski 47, Radosavlevic 120)*

The New Saints (0) 2 *(Smith 81, Ebbe 112)*

B36 Torshavn: (433) Hentze; Mellemgaard, Nattestad, Eriksen (Jacobsen E 111), Heinesen; Jacobsen M (Johansen 113), Samuelsen (Radosavlevic 86), Nielsen; Przybylski, Pingel, Frederiksberg (Agnarsson 68).
The New Saints: (433) Harrison; Harrington, Astles, Davies (Clark 30), Redmond; Holland, Routledge (Smith 71), Brobbel (Cieslewicz 77); Robles (Draper 116), Ebbe, Mullan.
aet; B36 Torshavn won 5-4 on penalties.

Hammarby (0) 0

Lech Poznan (0) 3 *(Pedro Tiba 55, Kaminski 89, Marchwinski 90)*

Hammarby: (4231) Ousted; Fenger, Bjorklund, Fallman (Magyar 46), Jeahze; Ngouali, Andersen■; Khalili A, Johannsson, Paulinho (Kacaniklic 77); Ludwigson.
Lech Poznan: (4411) Bednarek; Czerwinski, Satka, Crnomarkovic, Puchacz; Kaminski, Pedro Tiba (Marchwinski 84), Moder, Sykora (Skoras 73); Ramirez; Ishak (Awad 90).

Progres Niederkorn (0) 0

Willem II (3) 5 *(Pavlidis 19, 34, Saglam 28, Nunnely 46, Ndayishimiye 65)*

Progres Niederkorn: (4231) Flauss; Bastos, Ferino, Skenderovic, Janisch (Karayer 64); Latic, Dublin; Tekiela, Silaj, Holtz (Shala 64); Habbas (Luisi 46).
Willem II: (433) Ruiter; Heerkens (van den Bogert 41), Holmen, Peters, Nelom (Kohn 62); Saglam, Ndayishimiye, Llonch (Saddiki 62); Nunnely, Pavlidis, Kohlert.

Thursday, 17 September 2020

Ararat-Armenia (1) 4 *(Martinez 16, Lima 90 (pen), 90 (pen), Vakulenko 113)*

Fola Esch (1) 3 *(Pimentel 19, Bensi 56 (pen), Hadji 81)*

Ararat-Armenia: (442) Cupic; Narsingh, Alemao, Junior■, Meneses; Gouffran (Ogana 84), Otubanjo (Lima 60), Alphonse (Shahinyan 70), Vakulenko; Sanogo, Martinez (Ambartsumyan 96).
Fola Esch: (442) Hym; Klein, Delgardo, Dikaba, Ouassiero; Bensi (Bernard 87), Freire (Semedo 84), Diallo (Drif 70), Pimentel■; Sacras, Hadji (Mura 117).
aet.

Aris (0) 1 *(Bruno Gama 55)*

Kolos Kovalivka (0) 2 *(Novak 47, Antyukh 62)*

Aris: (442) Julian; Rose, Jeggo, Lucas Sasha (Mancini 78), Ganea (Manos 69); Matilla, Fetfatzidis, Lopez, Datkovic; Bruno Gama, Bertoglio.
Kolos Kovalivka: (442) Volynets; Gavrish, Novak, Zozulya (Morozko 51), Yemets; Lysenko (Seleznyov 64), Petrov, Bohdanov, Smirniy (Kostyshyn 88); Antyukh, Zadoya.

Astana (0) 0

Buducnost Podgorica (1) 1 *(Terzic 25)*

Astana: (442) Eric; Postnikov, Maevskiy, Shomko (Beysebekov 50), Simunovic; Sigurjonsson, Radakovic, Barseghyan, Ebong (Shchetkin 86); Sotiriou, Rotariu (Tomasov 57).
Buducnost Podgorica: (442) Dragojevic; Cukovic, Raickovic, Sekulic, Vukcevic (Milic 9); Adzic, Ivanovic, Mirkovic, Moraitis (Djurickovic 90); Grbic, Terzic (Vujacic 89).

Backa Topola (2) 6 *(Milicevic 11, Duronjic 14, Antonic 51, Tomanovic 90, 117, Tumbasevic 105)*

FCSB (1) 6 *(Coman 25, Man 50, 63 (pen), 105, Balaz 90 (og), Petre 108)*

Backa Topola: (442) Filipovic; Antonic, Zec, Balaz, Ponjevic■; Tumbasevic, Duronjic (Petrovic 45), Babic (Banjac 64), Tomanovic; Lukic (Siladji■ 75), Milicevic (Djuric 115).
FCSB: (442) Ducan; Cretu, Simion, Morutan, Pantea (Petre 21); Briceag, Coman (Horsia 73), Perianu, Pantiru; Man, Buziuc (Ion 46).
aet; FCSB won 5-4 on penalties.

Bodo/Glimt (2) 3 *(Zinckernagel 20, Boniface 32, Berg 81)*

Zalgiris Vilnius (1) 1 *(Antal 26)*

Bodo/Glimt: (343) Haikin; Hoibraten, Lode, Bjorkan; Saltnes, Konradsen (Sampsted 72), Berg, Hauge; Zinckernagel, Fet (Solbakken 78), Boniface (Sveen 89).
Zalgiris Vilnius: (352) Berkovec; Slijngard, Tatomirovic, Ljubisavljevic; Mikoliunas, Videmont, Vorobjovas, Kyeremeh (Karamarko 68), Simkus (Kuklys 84); Antal, Kaludjerovic.

Borac Banja Luca (0) 0

Rio Ave (0) 2 *(Jambor 90, Tarantini 90)*

Borac Banja Luca: (442) Pavlovic; Jovanovic, Zakaric, Dujakovic (Georgiev 90), Cosic; Brtan (Vojnovic 90), Danilovic, Milojevic, Lukic (Kajkut 87); Vranjes, Ziljkic.
Rio Ave: (442) Bruno Moreira (Jambor 90); Tarantini, Carlos Mane, Filipe Augusto, Chico Geraldes (Gelson 75); Kieszek, Piazon (Gabrielzinho 90), Aderllan, Matheus Reis; Ivo Pinto, Borevkovic.

Botosani (0) 0

Shkendija (1) 1 *(Ibraimi 2)*

Botosani: (442) Pap; Tiganasu, Chindris, Florescu (Patache 71), Harut; Babunski (Roman 79), Seroni, Ofusu, Rodriguez; Askovski (Keyta 46), Dugandzic.
Shkendija: (442) Zahov; Alimi■, Pavic, Murati, Krivak; Ibraimi (Merdjani 88), Dita, Bejtulai, Ahmedi; Doriev (Nafiu 70), Totre (Zejnullai 75).

Budapest Honved (0) 0

Malmo (1) 2 *(Toivonen 42, Traustason 86)*

Budapest Honved: (442) Tujvel; Aliji, Batik, Zsoter (Szendrei 46), Mezghrani; Hidi, Ugrai, Barath, Bocskay (Kesztyus 84); Gazdag, Balogh (Traore 69).
Malmo: (442) Johansson; Berget, Larsson, Lewicki (Adrian 90), Ahmedhodzic; Rieks (Traustason 79), Nielsen, Knudsen, Rakip; Toivonen, Sarr (Nalic 67).

Coleraine (0) 2 *(Doherty 49 (pen), 90 (pen))*

Motherwell (2) 2 *(Lang 16, Watt 37)*

Coleraine: (442) Deane; Traynor (Parkhill 74), Kane, O'Donnell, Nixon (Bradley 52); Lowry, McLaughlin (Allen 117), Doherty, McConaghie; Carson, Jarvis (Glackin 8).
Motherwell: (442) Carson; Lamie, O'Hara, Mugabi■, McGinley (Seedorf 65); Gallagher, O'Donnell, Campbell (Long 91), Lang (Hastie 87); Watt, Polworth (Maguire 87).
aet; Motherwell won 3-0 on penalties.

Connah's Quay Nomads (0) 0

Dinamo Tbilisi (0) 1 *(Gabedava 90 (pen))*

Connah's Quay Nomads: (442) Brass; Davies, Edwards, Disney, Roberts; Owen, Dool, Owens, Farquharson; Insall (Williams 87), Poole.
Dinamo Tbilisi: (442) Kvaskhvadze; Papava, Kimadze, Iashvili, Gbegnon; Gabedava, Orsula (Pernambuca 59), Kardava, Kobouri; Zaria (Kapanadze 80), Kavtaradze (Klooster 90).

CSKA Sofia (1) 2 *(Sowe 44, Carey 90)*

BATE Borisov (0) 0

CSKA Sofia: (442) Busatto; Mattheij, Youga, Galabov, Mazikou; Sowe, Geferson, Henrique (Carey 79), Antov; Sankhare (Tiago Rodrigues 68), Yomov (Keita 73).
BATE Borisov: (442) Scherbitski; Baha (Moukam 77), Nastic, Filipovic A, Filipovic J; Nekhaychik, Filipenko, Yablonskiy (Volodjko 69), Willumsson; Skavysh, Milic (Dubajic 80).

DAC Dunajska Streda (1) 5 *(Divkovic 6, 65, Nicolaescu 85, 96, Davis 114)*

Jablonec (1) 3 *(Zeleny 25, Schranz 57, 71 (pen))*

DAC Dunajska Streda: (442) Jedlicka; Blackman, Davis, Muller, Fabry (Nicolaescu 78); Balic (Bednar 106), Kruzliak, Schafer, Ramirez; Kalmar (Njie 120), Divkovic (Beskorovainyi 113).
Jablonec: (442) Hanus; Podany, Holik, Ladra (Jovovic 86), Martinec; Hubschman, Povazanec (Pilar 98), Kubista, Cvancara (Dolezal 79); Zeleny (Plestil 110), Schranz.
aet.

Djurgaarden (1) 2 *(Edwards 42, Ulvestad 69 (pen))*

Europa (0) 1 *(Gallardo 57)*

Djurgaarden: (442) Bratveit; Une Larsson, Edwards (Augustinsson 64), Kack, Witry; Radetinac (Ring 84), Ulvestad, Holmberg, Karlstrom; Eriksson, Chilufya (Kujovic 72).
Europa: (442) Munoz; Jolley, Juanpe (Yome 79), Carrascal, Polaco (Gibson 85); Quillo■, Walker, Olivero, Rosa (Poku 36); Olmo, Gallardo.

Flora (2) 2 *(Sappinen 7, Lilander 37)*

KR Reykjavik (0) 1 *(Finnbogason 75)*

Flora: (442) Igonen; Purg, Lukka, Lilander, Kreida; Vassiljev, Alliku (Liivak 74), Sappinen (Lepik 81), Kuusk; Miller (Soomets 46), Sinyavskiy.
KR Reykjavik: (442) Olafsson; Jonsson, Chopart, Palmason F (Hauksson 66), Geirsson; Palmason P, Margeirsson (Punyed 6), Adalsteinsson, Sigurjonsson; Finnbogason, Jonasson■.

Hibernians (0) 0

Fehervar (0) 1 *(Nikolov 61)*

Hibernians: (442) Cremona; Apap, Degabriele, Almeida, Grech J; Izquier, Attard (Vella 83), Grech Z (Winchester 64), Wilkson (Uzeh 74); Agius, Shodiya■.
Fehervar: (442) Kovacsik; Musliu, Fiola, Nikolov, Zivzivadze (Nikolic 88); Nego, Stopira, Petryak (Evandro 83), Bolla; Alef (Patkai 51), Houri.

IFK Goteborg (0) 1 *(Sana 73)*

FC Copenhagen (0) 2 *(Mudrazija 82, Wind 85)*

IFK Goteborg: (442) Anestis; Calisir, Jallow (Aiesh 87), Yusuf, Kalley (Holm 69); Farnerud (Abraham 65), Bjarsmyr, Johansson, Erlingmark; Wernbloom, Sana.
FC Copenhagen: (442) Johnsson; Bengtsson, Zeca, Varela, Nelsson; Bjelland (Mudrazija 78), Wilczek, Jensen, Stage (Biel 78); Fischer (Kaufmann 78), Wind.

Inter Club D'Escaldes (0) 0

Dundalk (1) 1 *(McMillan 14)*

Inter Club D'Escaldes: (442) Gomes; Lima, Garcia, Bessone, Soldevila; Moreno (Roca 82), Reyes A, Feher, Betriu (Raposo 78); Pujol, Rubio (Reyes O 86).
Dundalk: (442) Rogers; Duffy, Gartland, Hoare, Sloggett; Shields, Boyle■, Murray (Mountney 70), Leahy; McMillan (Hoban 71), Colovic (Gannon 60).

Kaisar (1) 1 *(Lobjanidze 6)*

APOEL (2) 4 *(De Vincenti 15, 90, Mohamed Tuhami 25, Atzili 48)*

Kaisar: (442) Zarutskiy; Amirseitov (Kashken 89), Graf, Marochkin, Kairov; Bitang, Narzildaev (Stanisavljevic 58), Tagybergen (Gurman 85), Fedin; Lobjanidze, Kolev.
APOEL: (352) Miguel Silva; Nsue, Sielis, Rafael Santos; De Vincenti, Zahid, Mohamed Tuhami, Wheeler, Klonaridis (Atzili 46); Sahar (Al-Taamari 58), Ndongala (Nuhiu 85).

Kukesi (0) 0

VfL Wolfsburg (2) 4 *(Weghorst 21, 74, Lacroix 33, Mehmedi 89)*

Kukesi: (451) Elezaj; Horic, Demiri, Obanor, Malikji; Telushi, Musolli (Gavazaj Z 60), Musta (Gashi 46), Rroca (Cooper 70), Limaj; Eze.
VfL Wolfsburg: (433) Casteels; Guilavogui, Klaus (Roussillon 68), Paulo Otavio, Lacroix; Mehmedi, Arnold (Gerhardt 36), Schlager; Steffen, Weghorst, Brekalo (Victor 74).

KuPS Kuopio (0) 1 *(Udoh 120)*

Slovan Bratislava (0) 1 *(Medved 111)*

KuPS Kuopio: (442) Virtanen; Saxman (Tarasovs 115), Pikk, Savolainen (Sale 115), Pirttjoki (Manga 88); Pennanen, Adjei-Boateng, Nissila, Tomas; Niskanen, Rangel (Udoh 87).
Slovan Bratislava: (442) Greif; de Kamps, Pauschek, Bajric, De Marco; Ibrahim (Nono 69), Rafael Ratao, Abena, Medved (Ozbolt 114); Daniel (Cavric 69), Holman (Drazic 103).
aet; KuPS Kuopio won 4-3 on penalties.

Laci (0) 1 *(Nwabueze 59)*

Hapoel Be'er Sheva (0) 2 *(Agudelo 90, Varenne 90)*

Laci: (343) Sherri; Ignjatovic, Turkaj, Selmani; Lushkja, Shehu (Marku E 46), Deliu■, Marku A (Rapo D 46); Nwabueze (Malota 89), Xhixha, Teco.
Hapoel Be'er Sheva: (541) Levita; Miguel Vitor, Acolatse, Taha, Goldberg, Dadia; Josue, Sallalich (Hatuel 74), Kabah, Yosefi (Agudelo 61); Shwiro (Varenne 61).

Lincoln Red Imps (0) 0

Rangers (2) 5 *(Tavernier 21, Goldson 45, Morelos 67, 88, Defoe 84)*

Lincoln Red Imps: (442) Goldwin; Wiseman (Gamiz 56), Yahaya, Lopes, Britto; Chipolina R, Hernandez (De Barr 52), Gomez, Torrilla; Sergeant (Toscano 68), Casciaro L.
Rangers: (442) McGregor; Tavernier (Morelos 46), Stewart, Kamara, Edmundson; Arfield, Goldson, Roofe (Patterson 42), Hagi; Barisic, Itten (Defoe 66).

Linfield (0) 0

Floriana (1) 1 *(Garcia 10)*

Linfield: (442) Johns; Clarke (Waterworth 62), Nasseri (Manzinga 61), Boyle, Larkin■; Mulgrew, Callacher, Fallon, Lavery; Hery (Kearns 78), Quinn.
Floriana: (442) Akpan; Camenzuli, Dias, Ruiz, Diego Silva; Tiago Adan, Pisani, Keqi (Cheveresan 83), Leone; Paiber (Arias 61 (Beye 86)), Garcia.

Lokomotiv Plovdiv (0) 1 *(Minchev 71)*

Tottenham H (0) 2 *(Kane 80 (pen), Ndombele 84)*

Lokomotiv Plovdiv: (343) Lukov; Petrovic, Dinis Almeida■, Masoero; Tsvetanov, Umarboev (Minchev 68), Karagaren■, Mecinovic (Mihaljevic 81); Iliev, Aralica (Ilic 68), Salinas.
Tottenham H: (433) Lloris; Doherty, Dier, Davies, Sanchez (Lucas Moura 72); Sissoko (Ndombele 61), Hojbjerg, Lo Celso; Son, Kane, Bergwijn (Lamela 70).

Lokomotive Tbilisi (0) 2 *(Sikharulidze 54, Gavashelishvili 76)*

Dynamo Moscow (0) 1 *(Komlichenko 90 (pen))*

Lokomotive Tbilisi: (442) Mamardashvili; Ubilava, Gabadze, Sandokhadze, Samurkasovi (Dzebniauri 62); Shonia, Oulad Omar (Gavashelishvili 65), Dartsmelia, Gureshidze; Sikharulidze, Kirkitadze (Kobakhidze 83).
Dynamo Moscow: (442) Shunin; Parshivlyuk, Skopintcev (Morozov 46), Fomin, Evgeniev; Komlichenko, Kabore, Ordets, Szymanski; N'Jie (Lesovoy 61), Philipp (Igboun 69).

Maccabi Haifa (1) 2 *(Ashkenazi 31, Rukavytsya 72)*

Kairat (1) 1 *(Vagner Love 45)*

Maccabi Haifa: (442) Cohen; Mabouka, Menachem, Ashkenazi (Haziza 55), Arad; Wildschut (Planic 74), Habashi, Lavi, Abu Fani; Rukavytsya (Rodriguez 84), Chery.
Kairat: (442) Pokatilov; Suyumbayev, Mikanovic, Alip, Abiken (Tungyshbayev 87); Vagner Love, Kosovic, Dugalic, Alyukolov (Wrzesinski 81); Aimbetov (Eseola 64), Goralski.

Mura (1) 3 *(Gorenc 37, Zizek 72, Marosa 90)*

AGF Aarhus (0) 0

Mura: (442) Obradovic; Kozar, Kous, Sturm, Karnicnik; Kouter (Marosa 90), Filipovic (Horvat 69), Gorenc, Zizek; Bobicanec (Lovric 82), Cipot.
AGF Aarhus: (442) Eskelinen; Olsen, Hojer, Munksgaard, Tingager; Backman, Blume (Helenius 73), Poulsen, Thorsteinsson (Gronbaek 76); Mortensen, Links (Tengstedt 30).

Neftchi (0) 1 *(Mbodj 46)*

Galatasaray (1) 3 *(Diagne 19, 63, Luyindama 48)*

Neftchi: (442) Mammadov; Mahmudov, Mbodj, Krivotsyuk, Buludov; Stankovic, Nariman Jahan (Bougrine 70), Kane, Lawal; Alasgarov (Thallyson 65), Ibara (Abbasov 76).
Galatasaray: (442) Ozturk; Linnes, Kilinc (Turan 68), Saracchi, Luyindama; Bayram, Diagne, Antalyali, Marcao; Babel (Durmaz 83), Belhanda (Feghouli 46).

OFI Crete (0) 0

Apollon Limassol (0) 1 *(Szalai 50)*

OFI Crete: (442) Waterman; Marinakis (Nabi 68), Staikos (Solis 68), Selimovic, Oues; Neira, Sardinero, Vouros, Mellado; Giannoulis (Korovesis 80), Joao Figueiredo.
Apollon Limassol: (442) Dimitriou; Joao Pedro (Pittas 46), Yuste, Sachetti, Szalai; Diguiny, Roberge, Dabo (Giannıotas 79), Matei (Benschop 46); Aguirre, Denic.

Olimpija Ljubljana (1) 2 *(Ivanovic 19, Vombergar 81)*

Zrinjski Mostar (0) 3 *(Bilbija 51, 84, Ivancic 92)*

Olimpija Ljubljana: (442) Frelih; Samardzic, Fink, Kapun (Kurez 106), Lyaskov (Bagaric 91); Korun, Ivanovic, Elsnik, Ostrc (Pavlovic 56); Vombergar (Vukusic 85), Caimacov.
Zrinjski Mostar: (442) Brkic; Ticinovic (Corluka 78), Trebotic (Zlomislic 66), Fadhli Shas (Ibanez 73), Jakoljevic; Barbaric, Ivancic (Masic 96), Filipovic, Enin; Bilbija, Todorovic.
aet.

Osijek (0) 1 *(Majstorovic 84)*

FC Basel (2) 2 *(Arthur Cabral 18, Stocker 44)*

Osijek: (442) Ivusic; Jugovic, Skoric, Carioca, Talys; Kleinheisler (Pilj 76), Majstorovic, Grezda (Mierez 64), Zaper; Erceg, Bockaj (Grgic 81).
FC Basel: (442) Nikolic; Stocker, Widmer, Comert, Padula; Frei, Arthur Cabral (Ademi 63), Alderete, Campo (Van Der Werff 85); van Wolfswinkel, Pululu (Von Moos 70).

Piast Gliwice (1) 3 *(Konczkowski 10, Sokolowski 62, Zyro 84)*

Hartberg (1) 2 *(Kainz 33, Ried 75)*

Piast Gliwice: (352) Plach; Malarczyk (Rymaniak 89), Huk, Czerwinski; Jodlowiec, Kirkeskov, Konczkowski, Lipski, Sokolowski; Parzyszek (Zyro 70), Vida (Steczyk 78).
Hartberg: (451) Swete; Lienhart (Golles 73), Gollner (Ertlthaler 67), Rotter, Luckeneder; Tadic, Klem, Kainz, Rep, Tijani (Huber 89); Ried.

Renova (0) 0

Hajduk Split (1) 1 *(Caktas 5)*

Renova: (4231) Velii; Fetai (Muharem 46), Miskovski, Abdulla, Shala; Sadiki (Veliu 73), Gavazaj; Velija, Gafuri, Shefiti; Ramadani (Jasaroski 89).
Hajduk Split: (433) Posavec; Todorovic, Vuskovic, Mujakic, Colina; Nejasmic (Atanasov 77), Caktas, Juric; Jairo (Jakolis 82), Diamantakos, Gyurcso (Dolcek 66).

Riteriai (0) 1 *(Lezama 61)*

Slovan Liberec (2) 5 *(Mara 12 (pen), Hromada 20, Rabusic 84, Yusuf 89 (pen), Matousek 90)*

Riteriai: (442) Simaitis; Borovskij (Virksas 83), Dombrauskis (Filipavicius 62), Barauskas, Malzinskas; Grigaravicius, Sveikauskas, Lezama, Paulauskas; Kazlauskas, Traore (Ramanauskas 40).
Slovan Liberec: (442) Nguyen; Mikula, Koscelnik, Tijani, Beran (Rabusic 63); Hromada (Chalus 80), Mosquera, Kacharaba, Mara; Pesek (Matousek 88), Yusuf.

Servette (0) 0

Reims (1) 1 *(Berisha 4)*

Servette: (451) Frick; Sauthier, Sasso, Rouiller, Mendy (Diallo 85); Stevanovic, Cognat, Ondoua, Tasar (Kone 46), Imeri (Schalk 74); Kyei.
Reims: (433) Rajkovic; Foket, Faes, Konan, Munetsi; Berisha, Chavalerin, Cassama (Cafaro 81); Kutesa (Sierhuis 65), Dia (Zeneli 90), Toure.

Sfintul Gheorghe (0) 0

Partizan Belgrade (0) 1 *(Natcho 104 (pen))*

Sfintul Gheorghe: (442) Calanea; Volkov (Istrati 57), Novicov (Stepanenko 91), Ojog, Plamadeala; Sagna, Smirnov E, Svinarenco, Mochulyak (Ghecev 86); Slivca, Mandricenco.
Partizan Belgrade: (442) Stojkovic V; Natcho, Vitas, Zdjelar, Umar (Matic 78); Soumah (Scekic 110), Asano (Lutovac 91), Ostojic, Stevanovic (Markovic 63); Miljkovic, Urosevic.
aet.

Shamrock R (0) 0

AC Milan (1) 2 *(Ibrahimovic 23, Calhanoglu 67)*

Shamrock R: (352) Mannus; O'Brien, Lopes, Grace; Finn, Byrne, O'Neil (Watts 70), McEneff, Farrugia (Kavanagh 83); Burke, Greene (Williams 88).
AC Milan: (451) Donnarumma; Kjaer, Calabria, Hernandez, Gabbia; Calhanoglu (Diaz 84), Kessie, Castillejo, Bennacer (Tonali 84), Saelemaekers (Krunic 74); Ibrahimovic.

Sileks (0) 0

Drita (0) 2 *(Gerbeshi 48 (pen), Limani 80)*

Sileks: (442) Bozinovski; Timovski, Grozdanoski■, Karceski, Ristov (Spirkoski 81); Tanturovski, Mustafov, Draskovic, Serafimovski; Ivanovski (Kostovski 46), Gorgiev (Djuric 55).
Drita: (442) Maloku; Vucaj (Shabani B 76), Gerbeshi, Limani, Blakcori; Cuculi, Shabani X (Brdarovski 67), Haxhimusa, Namani; Fazliu (Ahmeti 88), Ajzeraj.

Standard Liege (2) 2 *(Avenatti 19 (pen), Amallah 34)*

Bala T (0) 0

Standard Liege: (442) Bodart; Gavory, Laifis, Fai, Vanheusden; Cimirot (Bokadi 72), Shamir, Amallah (Muleka 67), Balikwisha; Carcela-Gonzalez M, Avenatti (Oulare 84).
Bala T: (433) Ramsay; Peate, Smith S, Spittle, Shannon; Kay (Stephens 81), Leslie (Jones 81), Mendes; Venables, Evans, Correia (Smith K 57).

Teuta (0) 0

Granada (3) 4 *(Soldado 5, Kenedy 10, Herrera 31, 46)*

Teuta: (442) Frasheri; Arapi, Hoxha, Kouros, Beqja F■; Vila E, Aleksi, Avdyli (Hebaj 56), Vila L; Daja (Gruda 46), Krasniqi (Beqja L 68).
Granada: (451) Rui Silva; Victor Diaz, German, Domingos Duarte (Vallejo 46), Neva; Montoro (Vico 58), Gonalons, Puertas, Kenedy, Herrera; Soldado (Jorge Molina 46).

Ventspils (1) 1 *(Kozlov 5)*

Rosenborg (3) 5 *(Islamovic 15 (pen), 45, Konradsen 37, Holse 64, Zachariassen 71)*

Ventspils: (433) Alampasu; Mamah, Sakhnevich, Litvinskis■, Rekhviashvili; Ulimbashevs, Lucas Villela, Mchedlishvili; Eristavi (Pyagbara 53), Svarups (Aderounmu 75), Kozlov (Kokins 81).
Rosenborg: (433) Hansen; Reitan, Hovland, Valsvik, Hedenstadt; Zachariassen, Skjelbred, Konradsen (Asen 72); Holse, Islamovic (Borven 90), Adegbenro (Ceide 58).

Viking Stavanger (0) 0

Aberdeen (1) 2 *(McCrorie 44, Hedges 78)*

Viking Stavanger: (433) Austbo; Vikstol, Vevatne (Bjorshol 76), Andresson (Hoiland 76), Heggheim; Torsteinsbo, Ibrahimaj, Bell; de Lanlay (Ostensen 85), Berisha, Bytyqi.
Aberdeen: (343) Lewis; Considine, Hoban, McKenna; Hayes, McGeouch (Logan 73), Ferguson, McCrorie; Watkins (Main 90), Hedges, Wright (Ojo 72).

Friday, 18 September 2020

Riga FC (0) 1 *(Pedrinho 57)*

Tre Fiori (0) 0

Riga FC: (271) Ozols, Stuglis, Prenga, Rugins, Felipe Brisola, Fjodorovs, Pedrinho (Sharpar 85), Kamess, N'Kololo, Panic, Milosevic (Mbombo 78).
Tre Fiori: (532) Simoncini A; Bonini, Simoncini D, Angelini (Martini 83), Gregorio, Vandi (Perotto 90); Kalissa, Santoni (Bilendo 79), Figone; Apezteguia, Gjurchinoski.

THIRD QUALIFYING ROUND

Wednesday, 23 September 2020

Apollon Limassol (0) 0

Lech Poznan (1) 5 *(Pedro Tiba 42, 90, Ishak 47, Kaminski 58, Sykora 81)*

Apollon Limassol: (442) Dimitriou; Pittas (Larsson 46), Denic, Katelaris, Szalai; Diguiny, Roberge, Sachetti (Markovic 66), Aguirre; Benschop, Dabo (Gianniotas 14).
Lech Poznan: (442) Bednarek; Satka, Czerwinski, Puchacz, Kaminski (Skoras 76); Ishak (Kacharava 67), Pedro Tiba, Crnomarkovic, Moder (Muhar 73); Sykora, Ramirez.

Thursday, 24 September 2020

AC Milan (2) 3 *(Calhanoglu 16, 50, Colombo 32)*

Bodo/Glimt (1) 2 *(Junker 15, Hauge 55)*

AC Milan: (451) Donnarumma; Kjaer, Calabria, Hernandez, Gabbia; Calhanoglu, Kessie, Castillejo (Krunic 66), Bennacer (Tonali 80), Saelemaekers; Colombo (Maldini 57).
Bodo/Glimt: (433) Haikin; Moe, Lode, Bjorkan, Sampsted (Solbakken 83); Saltnes, Berg, Fet (Konradsen 65); Zinckernagel, Junker (Boniface 90), Hauge.

APOEL (2) 2 *(Atzili 14, Nuhiu 26)*

Zrinjski Mostar (1) 2 *(Ivancic 11, Bilbija 69)*

APOEL: (442) Miguel Silva; Nsue, Andre Geraldes, De Vincenti, Artur Jorge; Zahid (Jensen 64), Atzili, Mohamed Tuhami (Lundemo 86), Rafael Santos; Nuhiu (Sahar 98), Ndongala (Al-Taamari 73).
Zrinjski Mostar: (442) Brkic; Ibanez, Trebotic (Zlomislic 66), Corluka (Sadiku 106), Jakoljevic; Barbaric (Bekic 57), Ivancic (Govedarica 76), Filipovic, Enin; Bilbija, Todorovic.
aet; APOEL won 4-2 on penalties.

Ararat-Armenia (0) 1 *(Vakulenko 111)*

Celje (0) 0

Ararat-Armenia: (442) Cupic; Alemao, Sanogo, Meneses, Bollo (Otubanjo 83); Gouffran (Ambartsumyan 106), Shahinyan, Vakulenko, Lima; Narsingh, Martinez (Ogana 120).
Celje: (442) Rozman; Brecl, Marandici, Stravs (Benedicic 99), Zaletel; Dangubic, Vrbanec (Pungarsek 91), Stojinovic, Kerin (Novak 86); Lotric, Bozic (Kuzmanovic 112).
aet.

Besiktas (1) 1 *(Yalcin 15)*

Rio Ave (0) 1 *(Bruno Moreira 85)*

Besiktas: (442) Yuvakuran; Welinton, Uysal, Tokoz, Yilmaz; Lens (Hasic 101), Ozyakup, Yalcin (Larin 64), Montero; Ljajic (Mensah 72), Boyd (Tore 84).
Rio Ave: (442) Kieszek; Tarantini (Meshino 79), Ivo Pinto (Jambor 79), Matheus Reis, Borevkovic; Bruno Moreira, Piazon (Diego Lopes 69), Filipe Augusto, Aderllan; Carlos Mane, Chico Geraldes (Gabrielzinho 97).
aet; Rio Ave won 4-2 on penalties.

Charleroi (1) 2 *(Dessoleil 10, Rezaei 108)*

Partizan Belgrade (0) 1 *(Soumah 53)*

Charleroi: (442) Penneteau; Dessoleil, Kayembe (Goranov 114), Fall (Tshiend 109), Busi; Rezaei (Gillet 118), Morioka, Willems, Ilaimaharitra; Gholizadeh (Ribeiro Costa 112), Nicholson.
Partizan Belgrade: (442) Stojkovic V; Natcho (Scekic 98), Markovic, Zdjelar, Stevanovic (Soumah 46); Asano (Stojkovic D 111), Umar, Urosevic, Bagnack F; Miljkovic, Vitas (Ostojic 91).
aet.

CSKA Sofia (2) 3 *(Sowe 27, Yomov 38, Keita 83)*
B36 Torshavn (0) 1 *(Pingel 61)*
CSKA Sofia: (442) Busatto; Mattheij, Youga, Galabov, Mazikou; Sankhare, Carey (Henrique 84), Geferson (Tiago Rodrigues 61), Antov; Sowe, Yomov (Keita 69).
B36 Torshavn: (442) Hansen; Mellemgaard, Heinesen, Eriksen, Jacobsen M (Johansen 68); Jacobsen E, Nielsen (Radosavlevic 59), Frederiksberg, Samuelsen (Agnarsson 59); Przybyla, Pingel.

Djurgaarden (0) 0
CFR Cluj (0) 1 *(Paulo Vinicius 55)*
Djurgaarden: (442) Bratveit; Ulvestad, Une Larsson, Kack, Witry; Karlstrom, Edwards (Kujovic 78), Augustinsson, Chilufya (Ring 72); Radetinac, Eriksson.
CFR Cluj: (442) Balgradean; Camora, Susic, Bordeianu, Burca; Paulo Vinicius, Deac, Omrani (Debeljuh 86), Paun (Pereira 89); Rondon (Hoban 90), Djokovic.

FC Basel (3) 3 *(Widmer 3, Campo 12, Hambardzumyan 21 (og))*
Anorthosis Famagusta (1) 2 *(Vrgoc 45, Kvilitaia 67 (pen))*
FC Basel: (442) Nikolic; Stocker (Oberlin 76), Widmer, Comert, Padula; Frei, Arthur Cabral, Alderete, Campo (van der Werff 85); van Wolfswinkel, Pululu (von Moos■ 60).
Anorthosis Famagusta: (442) Loria; Schildenfeld, Selin (Galitsios 78), Hambardzumyan, Artymatas; Daushvili, Margaca (Micha 61), Vrgoc, Anderson Correia (Christofi 46); Okriashvili■, Kvilitaia.

FC Copenhagen (1) 3 *(Wilczek 14, Wind 58, Biel 90)*
Piast Gliwice (0) 0
FC Copenhagen: (442) Johnsson; Bengtsson, Jensen (Mudrazija 53), Varela, Nelsson; Sigurdsson (Oikonomou 68), Wilczek, Zeca, Biel; Fischer (Stage 75), Wind.
Piast Gliwice: (442) Plach; Jodlowiec, Kirkeskov, Konczkowski, Huk; Parzyszek (Steczyk 89), Lipski (Milewski 82), Czerwinski, Sokolowski (Zyro 62); Holubek, Vida.

FCSB (0) 0
Slovan Liberec (0) 2 *(Yusuf 64, Rabusic 82)*
FCSB: (442) Straton; Enache, Simion, Pantiru, Cana■; David Caiado, Soiledis, Perianu, Sut; Karanovic (Octavian Popescu 10), Petre (Ion 68).
Slovan Liberec: (442) Nguyen; Mikula, Kacharaba, Koscelnik, Beran (Rabusic 51); Hromada (Chalus 88), Mosquera, Tijani, Mara; Pesek (Matousek 84), Yusuf.

Fehervar (0) 0
Reims (0) 0
Fehervar: (451) Kovacsik; Stopira, Musliu, Fiola, Bolla; Nego, Nikolov, Houri, Petryak (Hodzic 76), Hangya; Zivzivadze (Evandro 68).
Reims: (433) Rajkovic; Abdelhamid, Foket■, Faes, Konan; Berisha (Toure 80), Chavalerin, Munetsi; Zeneli (Sierhuis 63), Kutesa (Donis 69), Dia.
aet; Fehervar won 4-1 on penalties.

Floriana (0) 0
Flora (0) 0
Floriana: (442) Akpan; Camenzuli, Dias, Pisani, Paiber (Cheveresan 81); Ruiz, Garcia, Keqi, Leone (Busuttil 118); Tiago Adan, Diego Silva.
Flora: (442) Igonen; Alliku (Miller 69), Kuusk, Lukka, Lilander; Vassiljev (Poom 99), Sappinen■ (Lepik 81), Purg, Kreida; Sinyavskiy (Liivak 106), Soomets.
aet; Flora won 4-2 on penalties.

Galatasaray (0) 2 *(Belhanda 77, Babel 86)*
Hajduk Split (0) 0
Galatasaray: (442) Ozturk; Donk, Linnes, Antalyali, Tasdemir (Elabdellaoui 80); Feghouli (Kilinc 89), Etebo, Diagne, Marcao; Babel, Bayram (Belhanda 71).
Hajduk Split: (442) Posavec; Jradi (Atanasov 84), Jakolis, Vuskovic, Colina; Diamantakos, Caktas, Mujakic, Juric (Nejasmic 74); Gyurcso (Krekovic 84), Jairo.

Granada (0) 2 *(Machis 48, Jorge Molina 90)*
Lokomotive Tbilisi (0) 0
Granada: (451) Rui Silva; Victor Diaz, Vallejo, German, Neva; Montoro, Gonalons, Kenedy (Soro 62), Machis (Puertas 80), Milla; Soldado (Jorge Molina 67).
Lokomotive Tbilisi: (433) Mamardashvili; Ubilava, Gabadze■, Sandokhadze, Gureshidze; Shonia, Samurkasovi (Mtchedlishvili 60), Dartsmelia; Sikharulidze, Kirkitadze (Gavashelishvili 75), Oulad Omar (Kobakhidze 71).

Hapoel Be'er Sheva (1) 3 *(Miguel Vitor 43, Josue 71 (pen), Acolatse 82)*
Motherwell (0) 0
Hapoel Be'er Sheva: (442) Levita; Miguel Vitor, Bareiro, Goldberg, Dadia; Josue, Acolatse (Yosefi 86), Kabah, Taha; Sallalich (Meli 86), Agudelo (Varenne 59).
Motherwell: (442) Carson; Lamie, Grimshaw, Campbell, McGinley; Gallagher■, O'Donnell, Long (Lang 72), O'Hara; Watt (White 75), Polworth (Maguire 86).

KI Klaksvik (1) 6 *(Pavlovic 22, Johannesen P 58, Klettskard 60, 69, 73, Johannesen J 85)*
Dinamo Tbilisi (0) 1 *(Pernambuca 71)*
KI Klaksvik: (442) Joensen; Faero, Klettskard (Johannesen J 82), Andreasen, Brinck; Vatnsdal, Pavlovic (Skrbec 75), Danielsen, Midtskogen; Johannesen P (Dosljak 89), Bjartalid.
Dinamo Tbilisi: (442) Kvaskhvadze; Papava, Kimadze, Iashvili, Gbegnon; Gabedava, Orsula (Pernambuca 52), Kardava, Kobouri (Kukhianidze 74); Zaria (Kutsia 61), Kavtaradze.

KuPS Kuopio (1) 2 *(Rangel 31, Tarasovs 72)*
Suduva (0) 0
KuPS Kuopio: (442) Virtanen; Purje, Tarasovs, Pikk, Savolainen; Pennanen, Adjei-Boateng, Nissila, Tomas; Sale, Rangel (Udoh 86).
Suduva: (442) Kardum; Slavickas, Kerla, Svrljuga, Zivanovic; Gorobsov (Pusic 66), Sabala (Topcagic 59), Hladik, Matulevicius (Jankauskas 76); Tadic, Salamon.

LASK (2) 7 *(Raguz 6, 16, Filipovic 46, Michorl 51, Gruber 53, Balic 55, Sabitzer 77)*
DAC Dunajska Streda (0) 0
LASK: (343) Schlager; Trauner, Filipovic (Ramsebner 58), Wiesinger; Holland, Ranftl, Michorl, Renner; Gruber (Reiter 58), Balic (Sabitzer 72), Raguz.
DAC Dunajska Streda: (442) Jedlicka; Blackman■, Davis, Muller, Kruzliak; Kalmar, Balic, Fabry (Beskorovainyi 36), Schafer; Divkovic (Bednar 60), Ramirez (Nicolaescu 60).

Legia Warsaw (2) 2 *(Wszolek 24, Pekhart 43)*
Drita (0) 0
Legia Warsaw: (442) Boruc; Mladenovic, Wieteska, Juranovic, Luquinhas (Kapustka 67); Jedrzejczyk, Valencia (Gvilia 63), Slisz, Karbownik; Pekhart (Kante 72), Wszolek.
Drita: (442) Maloku; Brdarovski (Vucaj 66), Shabani B, Gerbeshi, Blakcori; Cuculi, Rexha (Haxhimusa 56), Shabani X, Namani; Fazliu, Ajzeraj (Alidemaj 74).

Malmo (3) 5 *(Thelin 5, 17, Nalic 31, Larsson 52, Rieks 72)*
Lokomotiva Zagreb (0) 0
Malmo: (442) Johansson; Berget, Larsson, Rakip (Innocent 63), Ahmedhodzic; Rieks (Sarr 76), Nielsen, Knudsen (Safari 46), Lewicki; Thelin, Nalic.
Lokomotiva Zagreb: (442) Hendija; Petrak, Markovic, Kolinger, Mersinaj; Kovacic, Karacic, Kallaku (Acquah 84), Cokaj; Sammir (Tuci 69), Gjira (Celikovic 75).

Mura (1) 1 *(Kouter 21)*
PSV Eindhoven (2) 5 *(Malen 17, 65, Junior 28, Gakpo 54, 90)*
Mura: (451) Obradovic; Kous, Sturm, Gorenc, Karnicnik; Kozar, Kouter, Filipovic (Maric 76), Horvat (Brkic 76), Bobicanec; Zizek (Marosa 81).
PSV Eindhoven: (442) Mvogo; Max, Dumfries, Boscagli, Teze; Bruma, Thomas (Sadilek 76), Rosario, Junior; Romero (Gakpo 11), Malen (Madueke 86).

Riga FC (0) 0

Celtic (0) 1 *(Elyounoussi 90)*

Riga FC: (433) Ozols; Rugins, Petersons, Stuglis, Prenga; Panic, Wesley Nata (Felipe Brisola 71), Djurisic; Kamess, Debelko (Milosevic 67 (N'Kololo 90)), Roger.
Celtic: (343) Barkas; Duffy, Bitton, Ajer; Brown, McGregor, Forrest (Frimpong 34), Taylor; Christie, Ntcham (Ajeti 72), Edouard (Elyounoussi 82).

Rijeka (0) 2 *(Escoval 102, Andrijasevic 115)*

Kolos Kovalivka (0) 0

Rijeka: (442) Nevistic; Tomecak (Raspopovic 90), Velkovski (Escoval 91), Capan, Cerin (Lepinjica 99); Andrijasevic, Pavicic (Kulenovic 71), Smolcic, Stefulj; Muric, Loncar.
Kolos Kovalivka: (442) Volynets; Gavrish, Novak, Kravchenko, Yemets; Lysenko (Seleznyov 71), Petrov (Orikhovsky 109), Bohdanov, Smirniy (Kostyshyn 84); Antyukh (Morozko 90), Zadoya.
aet.

Rosenborg (0) 1 *(Konradsen 59)*

Alanyaspor (0) 0

Rosenborg: (442) Hansen; Reginiussen, Hedenstadt, Konate, Zachariassen; Skjelbred, Eyjolfsson, Konradsen■, Adegbenro (Tagseth 71); Islamovic, Holse (Reitan 81).
Alanyaspor: (442) Marafona; Tzavelas, Juanfran (Bulut 85), Moubandje, Karaca (Pektemek 81); Caulker, Ucan, Bareiro, Aksoy (El Babacar■ 68); Bakasetas, Davidson.

Rostov (1) 1 *(Shomurodov 9)*

Maccabi Haifa (1) 2 *(Rukavytsya 20, Abu Fani 60)*

Rostov: (442) Pesiakov; Eremenko (Hashimoto 64), Kozlov, Chernov, Hadzikadunic; Bayramyan (Poloz 64), Normann, Glebov■, Osipenko; Ionov, Shomurodov (Tosevski 82).
Maccabi Haifa: (442) Cohen; Mabouka, Habashi, Menachem, Arad; Planic, Haziza (Ashkenazi 85), Lavi, Abu Fani (Rodriguez 83); Rukavytsya (Nachmani 89), Chery.

Sarajevo (1) 2 *(Tatar 4, Fanimo 67)*

Buducnost Podgorica (1) 1 *(Moraitis 44)*

Sarajevo: (442) Kovacevic; Oremus, Serbecic, Pejovic, Pidro; Dupovac, Rahmanovic■, Susic (Djokanovic 58), Tatar; Ahmetovic (Handzic 81), Fanimo (Velkoski 90).
Buducnost Podgorica: (442) Dragojevic; Adzic, Mirkovic, Sekulic, Milic; Grbic, Cukovic, Raickovic, Moraitis; Ivanovic, Terzic (Vujacic 85).

Sheriff Tiraspol (1) 1 *(Posmac 8)*

Dundalk (1) 1 *(Murray 45)*

Sheriff Tiraspol: (442) Mikulic; N'Diaye, Peteleu (Petro 64), Obilor, Cristiano; Posmac, Kolovos (dos Santos Souza 88), Mioc (Veloso 99), Parra; Blyznychenko (Kapic 46), Castaneda.
Dundalk: (442) Rogers; Gartland, Murray (McEleney 72), Hoare, Leahy; Duffy (Colovic 102), Shields, Cleary, Sloggett; Hoban, Gannon (Mountney 13 (Kelly 88)).
aet; Dundalk won 5-3 on penalties.

Shkendija (0) 1 *(Nafiu 55)*

Tottenham H (1) 3 *(Lamela 5, Son 70, Kane 79)*

Shkendija: (451) Zahov; Pavic, Bejtulai, Murati, Krivak; Nafiu (Ramadani 85), Dita (Zejnullai 77), Ahmedi, Doriev (Merdjani 85), Totre; Ibraimi.
Tottenham H: (442) Hart; Alderweireld, Aurier, Davies, Sanchez; Lamela, Winks (Lo Celso 59), Bergwijn (Lucas Moura 65), Ndombele; Son, Alli (Kane 60).

Sporting Lisbon (1) 1 *(Tomas 7)*

Aberdeen (0) 0

Sporting Lisbon: (343) Adan; Coates, Feddal, Neto; Wendel (Braganca 86), Porro (Plata 88), Matheus Luiz, Nuno Mendes; Vietto, Cabral, Tomas (Sporar 77).
Aberdeen: (532) Lewis; Considine, Hayes, Logan (McLennan 83), Taylor, Hoban; McGeouch (Wright 69), Ferguson, McCrorie; Watkins (Edmondson 81), Hedges.

St Gallen (0) 0

AEK Athens (0) 1 *(Oliveira 72)*

St Gallen: (442) Ati-Zigi; Gortler■, Muheim, Krauchi, Stergiou; Ruiz (Youan 74), Quintilla, Guillemenot, Faziji; Stillhart (Ribeiro 74), Duah (Kamberi 62).
AEK Athens: (442) Tsintotas; Chygrynskiy, Krsticic, Livaja (Shakhov 90), Vasilantonopoulos; Ansarifard (Garcia 68), Mandalos, Andre Simoes, Insua; Oliveira, Svarnas.

Standard Liege (0) 2 *(Avenatti 47 (pen), Amallah 91)*

Vojvodina (0) 1 *(Bojic 75)*

Standard Liege: (433) Bodart; Gavory, Laifis, Fai, Vanheusden; Cimirot (Shamir 92), Bokadi, Raskin (Dussene 107); Carcela-Gonzalez M (Cop 98), Avenatti (Muleka 72), Amallah.
Vojvodina: (442) Vuklis; Djordjevic, Bralic, Andric, Sanicanin (Maksimovic 106); Drincic, Bojic, Vukadinovic (Gemovic 86), Stojkovic (Zukic 106); Covic, Mrkajic (Djuricin 59).
aet.

VfL Wolfsburg (1) 2 *(Guilavogui 16, Ginczek 90)*

Desna Chernihiv (0) 0

VfL Wolfsburg: (451) Casteels; Guilavogui, Roussillon, Steffen, Lacroix (Brooks 62); Mehmedi, Arnold, Schlager, Victor, Marmoush (Paulo Otavio 59); Weghorst (Ginczek 78).
Desna Chernihiv: (451) Past; Tamm■, Hitchenko, Konoplya, Mostovy; Kalitvintsev, Totovytsky, Ogirya, Kartushov (Hutsuliak 46), Dombrovskyi (Ermakov 65); Budkivskyi (Shevtsov 84).

Viktoria Plzen (2) 3 *(Ondrasek 35 (pen), Avila Ba Loua 41, Kacer 51)*

SonderjyskE (0) 0

Viktoria Plzen: (442) Hruska; Limbersky, Hejda, Kacer, Havel; Ondrasek (Beauguel 79), Brabec, Avila Ba Loua (Kayamba 71), Kalvach; Cermak (Bucha 90), Kopic.
SonderjyskE: (442) Thomas; Kanstrup, Dal Hende, Gartenmann, Ekani; Jacobsen, Albaek (Frederiksen 72), Banggaard, Bah; Absalonsen (Wright 74), Hassan (Eskesen 31).

Willem II (0) 0

Rangers (2) 4 *(Tavernier 22 (pen), Kent 25, Helander 55, Goldson 71)*

Willem II: (433) Ruiter; Nelom, Peters (van den Bogert 73), Holmen, Kohn; Saddiki (Yeboah 59), Saglam, Llonch; Pavlidis, Nunnely (Kohlert 60), Ndayishimiye.
Rangers: (433) McGregor; Tavernier, Goldson, Helander, Barisic (Bassey 74); Davis, Arfield, Kamara; Morelos (Itten 79), Hagi, Kent (Jones 72).

Byes: KF Tirana, Ludogorets Razgrad.

PLAY-OFFS

Thursday, 1 October 2020

AEK Athens (0) 2 *(Andre Simoes 64, Ansarifard 90)*

VfL Wolfsburg (1) 1 *(Mehmedi 45)*

AEK Athens: (451) Tsintotas; Chygrynskiy, Insua, Svarnas, Vasilantonopoulos; Shakhov, Krsticic, Mandalos (Livaja 63), Andre Simoes, Garcia (Macheras 81); Oliveira (Ansarifard 87).
VfL Wolfsburg: (451) Pervan; Guilavogui, Roussillon, Paulo Otavio, Lacroix; Mehmedi, Arnold, Steffen, Brekalo (Bialek 79), Schlager (Gerhardt 61); Weghorst.

Ararat-Armenia (0) 1 *(Lima 71)*

Red Star Belgrade (1) 2 *(Katai 45, Falcinelli 60)*

Ararat-Armenia: (433) Cupic; Alemao (Otubanjo 65), Vakulenko, Meneses, Bollo; Gouffran, Shahinyan (Ambartsumyan 70), Sanogo; Narsingh, Lima, Martinez.
Red Star Belgrade: (451) Borjan; Rodic, Degenek, Gajic, Pankov; Katai (Gavric 77), Ben (Gobeljic 81), Kanga (Petrovic 65), Ivanic, Nikolic; Falcinelli.

CFR Cluj (2) 3 *(Rondon 5, 56, Debeljuh 42)*

KuPS Kuopio (0) 1 *(Udoh 90)*

CFR Cluj: (442) Balgradean; Camora, Paulo Vinicius, Susic, Burca; Deac (Pereira 78), Djokovic, Paun (Hoban 86), Bordeianu; Rondon, Debeljuh (Omrani 83).
KuPS Kuopio: (433) Virtanen; Tarasovs, Pikk, Savolainen, Tomas; Saxman (Heinonen 76), Adjei-Boateng, Nissila (Purje 77); Pennanen, Sale, Rangel (Udoh 82).

Charleroi (0) 1 *(Fall 56)*

Lech Poznan (2) 2 *(Ramirez 33, Puchacz 42)*

Charleroi: (442) Penneteau; Dessoleil, Willems (Henen 83), Kayembe, Busi (Diagne 57); Morioka, Ilaimaharitra (Ribeiro Costa 89), Gholizadeh, Fall; Rezaei, Nicholson.
Lech Poznan: (442) Bednarek; Satka■, Kravets (Skoras 71), Crnomarkovic, Czerwinski; Pedro Tiba, Moder, Puchacz, Kaminski; Ishak (Marchwinski 87), Ramirez (Rogne 79).

Dinamo Brest (0) 0

Ludogorets Razgrad (0) 2 *(Manu 73, Marin 79)*

Dinamo Brest: (433) Ignatovich; Khacheridi, Vitus, Yuzepchuk (Pechenin 88), Gabi; Kislyak, Savitskiy, Bykov (Krivets 80); Sedko, Diallo (Gordeichuk 46), Tweh.
Ludogorets Razgrad: (451) Iliev; Moti, Cicinho, Nedyalkov, Verdon; Badji, Tekpetey (Manu 66), Cauly (Ikoko 88), Yankov, Santana; Keseru (Marin 77).

Dinamo Zagreb (2) 3 *(Gavranovic 11, Ademi 26, 87)*

Flora (0) 1 *(Sinyavskiy 65)*

Dinamo Zagreb: (451) Livakovic; Leovac, Theophile-Catherine, Stojanovic, Gvardiol; Orsic (Gojak 68), Gavranovic (Ivanusec 65), Ademi, Majer (Kastrati 84), Jakic; Petkovic.
Flora: (433) Igonen; Purg, Kuusk, Lukka, Lilander; Vassiljev, Kreida (Poom 88), Soomets (Miller 81); Alliku, Liivak (Lepik 76), Sinyavskiy.

Dundalk (1) 3 *(Murray 33, Cleary 48, Kelly 79)*

KI Klaksvik (0) 1 *(Midtskogen 65)*

Dundalk: (433) Rogers; Gartland, Hoare, Cleary, Leahy; McEleney (Mountney 81), Murray, Sloggett; Duffy, Hoban (McMillan 71), Colovic (Kelly 71).
KI Klaksvik: (343) Joensen; Faero, Pavlovic (Johannesen J 86), Brinck; Vatnsdal, Andreasen, Johannesen P, Bjartalid; Klettskard (Dosljak 55), Danielsen, Midtskogen.

FC Basel (0) 1 *(Arthur Cabral 54 (pen))*

CSKA Sofia (0) 3 *(Tiago Rodrigues 72, 88, Ahmedov 90)*

FC Basel: (442) Nikolic; Widmer, Comert, Alderete, Padula; Frei, Stocker (Kalulu 90), Pululu, Bunjaku (Campo 90); van Wolfswinkel, Arthur Cabral (Zhegrova 77).
CSKA Sofia: (451) Busatto; Mattheij, Galabov, Mazikou, Antov; Sankhare (Ahmedov 90), Youga, Geferson (Tiago Rodrigues 59), Yomov, Keita (Henrique 60); Sowe.

FC Copenhagen (0) 0

Rijeka (1) 1 *(Ankersen 20 (og))*

FC Copenhagen: (451) Johnsson; Sigurdsson, Bengtsson, Ankersen (Bartolec 67), Nelsson; Zeca, Fischer (Kaufmann 46), Stage (Mudrazija 56), Biel, Wind; Wilczek.
Rijeka: (541) Nevistic; Tomecak (Raspopovic 90), Velkovski, Capan, Smolcic, Stefulj; Andrijasevic, Pavicic (Lepinjica 76), Loncar, Cerin; Kulenovic (Escoval 83).

Hapoel Be'er Sheva (1) 1 *(Josue 4 (pen))*

Viktoria Plzen (0) 0

Hapoel Be'er Sheva: (433) Levita; Miguel Vitor, Taha, Goldberg, Dadia; Josue, Kabah, Bareiro; Acolatse (Yosefi 81), Sallalich (Keltjens 90), Agudelo (Varenne 75).
Viktoria Plzen: (451) Hruska; Limbersky, Brabec, Hejda, Havel; Cermak, Kopic, Avila Ba Loua (Kayamba 62), Kalvach, Bucha (Pernica 89); Ondrasek (Beauguel 80).

Legia Warsaw (0) 0

Qarabag (0) 3 *(Andrade 50, Zoubir 62, Ozobic 70)*

Legia Warsaw: (442) Boruc; Jedrzejczyk, Lewczuk, Mladenovic, Juranovic; Antolic (Luquinhas 63), Valencia, Rafael Lopes (Wszolek 56), Slisz; Pekhart, Kapustka (Karbownik 66).
Qarabag: (433) Mahammadaliyev; Medvedev, Huseynov B, Huseynov A, Medina; Matic, Garayev, Andrade; Ozobic (Romero 75), Zoubir (Emreli 63), Kwabena (Dzhafarquliyev 84).

Malmo (1) 1 *(Berget 45)*

Granada (1) 3 *(Machis 30, Puertas 58, Herrera 85)*

Malmo: (442) Johansson; Larsson, Knudsen, Brorsson, Ahmedhodzic; Rieks (Traustason 71), Berget, Lewicki, Rakip (Christiansen 71); Toivonen, Thelin (Nalic 77).
Granada: (451) Rui Silva; Victor Diaz, German, Domingos Duarte, Neva; Montoro, Gonalons, Puertas (Kenedy 74), Machis (Foulquier 89), Herrera; Soldado (Jorge Molina 81).

Rangers (0) 2 *(Arfield 52, Tavernier 59)*

Galatasaray (0) 1 *(Marcao 87)*

Rangers: (433) McGregor; Tavernier, Goldson, Helander, Barisic; Davis, Arfield, Kamara; Morelos (Itten 87), Hagi (Jack 78), Kent.
Galatasaray: (451) Ozturk; Elabdellaoui, Linnes, Luyindama, Marcao; Babel (Bayram 65), Feghouli (Diagne 73), Belhanda (Etebo 66), Antalyali, Kilinc; Falcao.

Rio Ave (0) 2 *(Chico Geraldes 72, Gelson 91)*

AC Milan (0) 2 *(Saelemaekers 51, Calhanoglu 120 (pen))*

Rio Ave: (451) Kieszek; Ivo Pinto, Aderllan, Nelson Monte, Borevkovic■; Tarantini (Jambor 75), Carlos Mane (Gabrielzinho 109), Piazon, Filipe Augusto, Diego Lopes (Chico Geraldes 66); Bruno Moreira (Gelson 86).
AC Milan: (451) Donnarumma; Kjaer, Calabria, Hernandez, Gabbia; Calhanoglu, Kessie (Tonali 106), Castillejo (Diaz 46), Bennacer, Saelemaekers (Colombo 95); Maldini (Leao 67).
aet; AC Milan won 9-8 on penalties.

Rosenborg (0) 0

PSV Eindhoven (1) 2 *(Zahavi 22, Gakpo 61)*

Rosenborg: (433) Hansen; Reginiussen, Eyjolfsson, Hedenstadt (Reitan 77), Konate; Skjelbred, Henriksen, Zachariassen; Islamovic, Adegbenro (Helland 65), Holse.
PSV Eindhoven: (451) Mvogo; Max (Viergever 60), Dumfries, Boscagli, Teze; Thomas (Hendrix 20), Rosario, Gakpo, Malen, Junior; Zahavi (Madueke 90).

Sarajevo (0) 0

Celtic (0) 1 *(Edouard 70)*

Sarajevo: (433) Kovacevic; Milicevic, Dupovac, Oremus, Pidro; Susic, Pejovic, Djokanovic (Jukic 85); Ahmetovic (Handzic 68), Fanimo (Velkoski 85), Tatar.
Celtic: (352) Barkas; Duffy, Bitton (Elhamed 10), Ajer; Brown, McGregor, Christie (Ntcham 86), Taylor, Frimpong; Elyounoussi, Edouard (Klimala 78).

Slovan Liberec (0) 1 *(Mara 90 (pen))*

APOEL (0) 0

Slovan Liberec: (442) Nguyen; Mikula, Kacharaba, Koscelnik, Tijani; Hromada, Mosquera, Pesek (Matousek 80), Mara; Yusuf, Beran (Rabusic 55).
APOEL: (352) Miguel Silva; Nsue, Artur Jorge, Shelis; Andre Geraldes, De Vincenti, Zahid, Mohamed Tuhami (Merkis 90), Al-Taamari (Klonaridis 82); Nuhiu, Ndongala (Atzili 68).

Sporting Lisbon (1) 1 *(Tomas 42)*

LASK (1) 4 *(Trauner 14, Raguz 58, Michorl 65, Gruber 68)*

Sporting Lisbon: (343) Adan; Coates■, Feddal, Neto; Wendel, Porro, Matheus Luiz (Sporar 71), Nuno Mendes; Vietto (Goncalves 67), Nuno Santos (Antunes 78), Tomas.
LASK: (343) Schlager; Trauner, Filipovic (Andrade 78), Wiesinger; Holland, Ranftl, Michorl (Grgic 87), Renner; Gruber (Plojer 74), Balic, Raguz.

Standard Liege (0) 3 *(Gavory 50, Amallah 77 (pen), 85 (pen))*

Fehervar (1) 1 *(Nikolic 10)*

Standard Liege: (451) Bodart; Gavory, Laifis (Dussene 59), Fai, Vanheusden; Carcela-Gonzalez M (Shamir 82), Cimirot, Amallah, Bokadi (Balikwisha 46), Raskin; Muleka.
Fehervar: (541) Kovacsik; Stopira, Musliu, Fiola, Hangya, Bolla; Nego, Nikolov, Houri (Hodzic 89), Petryak (Bamgboye 63); Nikolic (Zivzivadze 65).

Tottenham H (4) 7 *(Kane 2, 56 (pen), 74, Lucas Moura 20, Lo Celso 36, 39, Alli 90 (pen))*

Maccabi Haifa (1) 2 *(Chery 17, Rukavytsya 52 (pen))*

Tottenham H: (451) Hart; Alderweireld, Doherty, Davies, Sanchez; Lucas Moura, Hojbjerg (Sissoko 63), Winks, Bergwijn, Lo Celso (Alli 46); Kane (Reguilon 75).
Maccabi Haifa: (343) Cohen; Planic, Habashi, Arad (Donyoh 71); Mabouka, Lavi, Menachem, Abu Fani (Ashkenazi 87); Rukavytsya, Chery, Haziza (Rodriguez 83).

Young Boys (1) 3 *(Fassnacht 42, Nsame 52, 64)*

KF Tirana (0) 0

Young Boys: (442) Ballmoos; Lefort, Garcia, Hefti, Camara; Lustenberger, Sierro, Fassnacht (Mambimbi 72), Ngamaleu (Gaudino 66); Nsame (Siebatcheu 73), Elia.
KF Tirana: (451) Bekaj; Vangjeli, Najdovski, Tosevski, Ismajlgeci; Elton Cale (Halili 89), Torassa■, Batha, Cobbinah (Sasraku 71), Celhaka; Muci (Hoxhallari 85).

GROUP STAGE

GROUP A

Thursday, 22 October 2020

CSKA Sofia (0) 0

CFR Cluj (0) 2 *(Rondon 53, Deac 74 (pen))* 11,958

CSKA Sofia: (4231) Busatto; Vion, Antov, Mattheij, Mazikou; Tiago Rodrigues (Beltrame 80), Youga; Sinclair (Keita 63), Sankhare (Ahmedov 71), Yomov (Henrique 80); Sowe.
CFR Cluj: (4141) Balgradean; Susic, Paulo Vinicius, Burca, Camora; Hoban; Rondon (Carnat 87), Paun (Pereira 83), Djokovic, Deac (Chipciu 78); Debeljuh (Vojtus 87).

Young Boys (1) 1 *(Nsame 14 (pen))*

Roma (0) 2 *(Bruno Peres 69, Kumbulla 73)* 1000

Young Boys: (343) Ballmoos; Burgy, Lustenberger, Zesiger; Hefti, Rieder (Aebischer 70), Sierro (Gaudino 79), Maceiras; Fassnacht (Elia 65), Nsame (Siebatcheu 79), Ngamaleu (Mambimbi 65).
Roma: (343) Pau Lopez; Fazio, Kumbulla, Juan Jesus (Pellegrini 69); Karsdorp (Spinazzola 46), Villar (Veretout 59), Cristante, Bruno Peres; Perez, Borja Mayoral (Dzeko 59), Pedro (Mkhitaryan 59).

Thursday, 29 October 2020

CFR Cluj (0) 1 *(Rondon 62)*

Young Boys (0) 1 *(Fassnacht 69)*

CFR Cluj: (4231) Balgradean; Susic, Paulo Vinicius (Manea 14), Burca, Camora; Hoban (Itu 79), Djokovic; Rondon, Paun (Pereira 79), Deac (Chipciu 63); Debeljuh (Omrani 46).
Young Boys: (433) Ballmoos; Hefti (Garcia 63), Camara (Sulejmani 74), Zesiger, Maceiras; Fassnacht, Lustenberger, Aebischer (Sierro 75); Elia (Gaudino 63), Nsame, Ngamaleu (Siebatcheu 74).

Roma (0) 0

CSKA Sofia (0) 0

Roma: (343) Pau Lopez; Fazio, Smalling (Juan Jesus 56), Kumbulla; Bruno Peres, Villar, Cristante, Spinazzola (Karsdorp 46); Perez (Pellegrini 75), Borja Mayoral (Dzeko 70), Mkhitaryan (Pedro 46).
CSKA Sofia: (433) Busatto; Vion (Turitsov 89), Antov, Zanev, Mazikou; Youga (Beltrame 81), Sankhare (Ahmedov 89), Geferson (Tiago Rodrigues 81); Sinclair (Henrique 65), Sowe, Yomov.

Thursday, 5 November 2020

Roma (3) 5 *(Mkhitaryan 1, Ibanez 24, Borja Mayoral 34, 84, Pedro 89)*

CFR Cluj (0) 0

Roma: (3142) Pau Lopez; Fazio, Ibanez (Smalling 61), Kumbulla; Cristante (Milanese 74); Bruno Peres, Villar, Veretout (Pedro 46), Spinazzola (Juan Jesus 46); Borja Mayoral, Mkhitaryan (Pellegrini 46).
CFR Cluj: (4141) Balgradean; Susic (Latovlevici 78), Manea, Ciobotariu, Camora; Hoban; Rondon (Joca 90), Itu (Paun 46), Djokovic, Deac (Pereira 46); Debeljuh (Carnat 67).

Young Boys (3) 3 *(Mambimbi 2, 31, Sulejmani 18)*

CSKA Sofia (0) 0

Young Boys: (442) Ballmoos; Hefti, Camara (Garcia 63), Lustenberger, Lefort; Fassnacht, Rieder, Sierro (Aebischer 63), Sulejmani (Gaudino 70); Nsame (Siebatcheu 69), Mambimbi (Elia 70).
CSKA Sofia: (4231) Busatto; Vion (Turitsov 87), Antov, Mattheij, Mazikou; Youga, Sankhare (Ahmedov 87); Sinclair (Carey 69), Penaranda (Tiago Rodrigues 68), Yomov (Keita 79); Sowe.

Thursday, 26 November 2020

CFR Cluj (0) 0

Roma (0) 2 *(Debeljuh 49 (og), Veretout 67 (pen))*

CFR Cluj: (4231) Balgradean; Susic, Manea, Burca, Camora; Itu (Chipciu 51), Djokovic; Rondon, Paun (Carnat 71), Pereira; Debeljuh (Vojtus 70).
Roma: (3421) Pau Lopez; Spinazzola (Mkhitaryan 64), Cristante, Juan Jesus; Bruno Peres, Villar, Diawara (Milanese 77), Calafiori; Perez (Tripi 84), Pellegrini (Veretout 46); Borja Mayoral (Dzeko 63).

CSKA Sofia (0) 0

Young Boys (1) 1 *(Nsame 34)*

CSKA Sofia: (3412) Busatto; Antov, Mattheij, Zanev; Turitsov (Sinclair 59), Tiago Rodrigues (Ahmedov 75), Sankhare (Youga 75), Carey; Beltrame (Keita 90); Yomov (Penaranda 75), Sowe.
Young Boys: (442) Ballmoos; Hefti, Camara, Lustenberger (Lefort 74), Garcia; Fassnacht (Mambimbi 74), Rieder (Gaudino 74), Sierro, Ngamaleu (Burgy 87); Elia (Aebischer 60), Nsame.

Thursday, 3 December 2020

CFR Cluj (0) 0

CSKA Sofia (0) 0

CFR Cluj: (4231) Balgradean; Susic, Manea, Burca, Camora; Chipciu■, Djokovic; Rondon, Paun (Carnat 75), Pereira (Deac 61); Debeljuh (Vojtus 86).
CSKA Sofia: (3412) Busatto; Antov, Mattheij, Zanev; Vion, Youga, Geferson, Carey; Sankhare (Tiago Rodrigues 78); Sowe, Yomov (Henrique 77).

Roma (1) 3 *(Borja Mayoral 44, Calafiori 59, Dzeko 81)*

Young Boys (1) 1 *(Nsame 34)*

Roma: (3421) Pau Lopez; Ibanez (Spinazzola 46), Cristante (Fazio 65), Juan Jesus; Bruno Peres, Villar (Pellegrini 60), Diawara, Calafiori; Perez, Pedro (Mkhitaryan 46); Borja Mayoral (Dzeko 60).
Young Boys: (532) Ballmoos; Hefti, Camara■, Zesiger, Lefort, Garcia (Elia 68); Aebischer (Gaudino 67), Rieder (Sierro 58), Ngamaleu (Mambimbi 76); Fassnacht, Nsame (Siebatcheu 76).

Thursday, 10 December 2020

CSKA Sofia (2) 3 *(Tiago Rodrigues 5, Sowe 34, 55)*

Roma (1) 1 *(Milanese 22)*

CSKA Sofia: (3412) Busatto; Antov, Mattheij, Zanev; Yomov (Vion 63), Youga (Galabov 74), Geferson, Mazikou; Tiago Rodrigues (Henrique 81); Sowe (Ahmedov 74), Sankhare (Beltrame 63).
Roma: (3421) Boer; Fazio, Kumbulla (Smalling 46), Juan Jesus; Bruno Peres (Tripi 81), Diawara, Milanese (Villar 62), Bamba (Karsdorp 62); Perez, Pedro; Borja Mayoral.

Young Boys (0) 2 *(Gaudino 90, Nsame 90 (pen))*

CFR Cluj (0) 1 *(Debeljuh 84)*

Young Boys: (442) Ballmoos; Hefti, Burgy (Siebatcheu 85), Lefort, Garcia; Ngamaleu (Zesiger 82), Aebischer, Rieder (Martins Pereira 58), Sulejmani (Gaudino 58); Mambimbi (Elia 58), Nsame■.
CFR Cluj: (4231) Balgradean■; Manea, Paulo Vinicius, Burca, Camora; Djokovic■, Hoban; Pereira (Susic 88), Deac (Sandomierski 90), Paun (Debeljuh 74); Rondon.

Group A Table	P	W	D	L	F	A	GD	Pts
Roma	6	4	1	1	13	5	8	13
Young Boys	6	3	1	2	9	7	2	10
CFR Cluj	6	1	2	3	4	10	–6	5
CSKA Sofia	6	1	2	3	3	7	–4	5

GROUP B

Thursday, 22 October 2020

Dundalk (1) 1 *(Murray 35)*

Molde (0) 2 *(Hussain 62, Omoijuanfo 72 (pen))*

Dundalk: (4141) Rogers; Gannon (McMillan 77), Gartland, Cleary, Leahy (Dummigan 77); Shields; Mountney, Sloggett (McEleney 64), Murray (Boyle 77), Duffy (Colovic 80); Hoban.
Molde: (433) Linde; Pedersen, Bjornbak, Gregersen, Haugen; Aursnes, Hussain, Eikrem (Ellingsen 82); Hestad, Omoijuanfo (Brynhildsen 90), Bolly (Knudtzon 69).

Rapid Vienna (0) 1 *(Fountas 51)*

Arsenal (0) 2 *(Luiz 70, Aubameyang 74)* 3000

Rapid Vienna: (532) Strebinger; Arase (Schick 79), Stojkovic, Hofmann, Barac, Ullmann; Ljubicic, Grahovac, Ritzmaier (Knasmullner 88); Kara (Kitagawa 76), Fountas.
Arsenal: (433) Leno; Cedric (Bellerin 61), Luiz, Gabriel, Kolasinac; Elneny, Thomas, Saka (Tierney 84); Pepe (Nelson 90), Lacazette (Willock 84), Nketiah (Aubameyang 61).

Thursday, 29 October 2020

Arsenal (2) 3 *(Nketiah 42, Willock 44, Pepe 46)*

Dundalk (0) 0

Arsenal: (3421) Runarsson; Mustafi (Ceballos 61), Xhaka (Tierney 74), Kolasinac; Cedric, Willock, Elneny, Maitland-Niles; Pepe (Willian 62), Nelson; Nketiah (Balogun 74).
Dundalk: (352) Rogers; Gartland, Boyle, Cleary (Hoare 53); Mountney, Murray (Sloggett 46), Shields (Gannon 62), McEleney (Flores 53), Dummigan; Duffy (Colovic 70), Hoban.

Molde (0) 1 *(Omoijuanfo 65)*

Rapid Vienna (0) 0 600

Molde: (433) Linde; Wingo, Bjornbak, Gregersen, Haugen; Aursnes, Eikrem (James 83), Ellingsen; Hestad (Bolly 68), Omoijuanfo, Brynhildsen (Hussain 77).
Rapid Vienna: (3412) Gartler; Stojkovic, Greiml, Barac; Schick (Arase 46), Ljubicic, Grahovac (Ibrahimoglu 77), Ullmann; Ritzmaier; Kitagawa (Knasmullner 59), Kara.

Thursday, 5 November 2020

Arsenal (1) 4 *(Haugen 45 (og), Sinyan 62 (og), Pepe 69, Willock 88)*

Molde (1) 1 *(Ellingsen 22)*

Arsenal: (4231) Leno; Maitland-Niles (Cedric 63), Mustafi, Luiz, Kolasinac; Xhaka (Tierney 80), Ceballos (Elneny 80); Willian (Saka 63), Willock, Pepe; Nketiah.
Molde: (4231) Linde; Wingo, Bjornbak, Gregersen (Sinyan 46), Haugen; Aursnes, Hussain; Ellingsen (Mostrom 86), Eikrem (Brynhildsen 74), Bolly (Knudtzon 63); Omoijuanfo (James 74).

Rapid Vienna (1) 4 *(Ljubicic 22, Arase 79, Hofmann 87, Demir 90)*

Dundalk (1) 3 *(Hoban 7, McMillan 81 (pen), 90 (pen))*

Rapid Vienna: (4231) Gartler; Stojkovic, Hofmann, Barac (Sonnleitner 54), Ullmann; Ljubicic, Petrovic (Grahovac 72); Schick, Knasmullner (Demir 72), Arase; Kara.
Dundalk: (4141) McCarey; Hoare, Cleary, Boyle, Leahy (Dummigan 65); Shields; Gannon (Mountney 65), Flores (Murray 76), Sloggett, Duffy (Oduwa 72); Hoban (McMillan 76).

Thursday, 26 November 2020

Dundalk (0) 1 *(Shields 63 (pen))*

Rapid Vienna (2) 3 *(Knasmullner 11, Kara 37, 58)*

Dundalk: (343) Rogers; Hoare (Kelly 46), Boyle, Cleary; Gannon, Shields, Sloggett (Murray 72), Dummigan (Leahy 81); Colovic (McEleney 46), McMillan (Oduwa 46), Duffy.
Rapid Vienna: (4231) Gartler; Stojkovic, Hofmann, Barac, Ullmann; Knasmullner (Demir 81), Grahovac; Schick, Fountas (Schuster 66), Ibrahimoglu (Arase 55); Kara (Kitagawa 66).

Molde (0) 0

Arsenal (0) 3 *(Pepe 50, Nelson 55, Balogun 83)*

Molde: (4231) Linde; Wingo, Gregersen (Knudtzon 85), Sinyan, Risa (Pedersen 82); Aursnes, Hussain (Bolly 61); Hestad, Eikrem (Brynhildsen 81), Ellingsen; James (Omoijuanfo 61).
Arsenal: (442) Runarsson; Cedric, Mustafi, Luiz (Holding 46), Maitland-Niles; Pepe, Willock (Tierney 75), Xhaka (Ceballos 62), Nelson; Lacazette (Smith-Rowe 75), Nketiah (Balogun 82).

Thursday, 3 December 2020

Arsenal (3) 4 *(Lacazette 10, Pablo Mari 17, Nketiah 44, Smith-Rowe 66)*

Rapid Vienna (0) 1 *(Kitagawa 47)* 2000

Arsenal: (4231) Runarsson; Cedric, Mustafi (Chambers 70), Pablo Mari, Kolasinac; Maitland-Niles, Elneny (Ceballos 63); Nelson (Willian 63), Lacazette (Smith-Rowe 63), Pepe; Nketiah (Balogun 81).
Rapid Vienna: (352) Strebinger; Sonnleitner, Hofmann (Barac 46), Greiml; Arase, Demir, Schuster, Ritzmaier (Knasmullner 65), Ullmann (Schick 46); Kitagawa (Kara 65), Alar (Sulzbacher 77).

Molde (2) 3 *(Eikrem 30, Omoijuanfo 41, Ellingsen 67)*

Dundalk (0) 1 *(Flores 90)*

Molde: (433) Linde; Wingo, Gregersen (Hussain 68), Sinyan, Risa; Aursnes (Christensen 78), Eikrem (James 78), Ellingsen; Hestad (Mostrom 79), Omoijuanfo (Bolly 86), Knudtzon.
Dundalk: (352) Rogers; Gartland, Boyle (Cleary 61), Hoare; Gannon, Sloggett (McEleney 61), Shields (Mountney 68), Flores, Dummigan; Kelly (McMillan 73), Oduwa (Duffy 61).

Thursday, 10 December 2020

Dundalk (1) 2 *(Flores 22, Hoare 85)*

Arsenal (2) 4 *(Nketiah 12, Elneny 18, Willock 67, Balogun 80)*

Dundalk: (3412) Rogers; Hoare, Boyle (Gartland 46), Cleary; Gannon (Mountney 54), Shields, Flores, Leahy; McEleney (Colovic 77); McMillan (Kelly 54), Duffy (Wynne 77).
Arsenal: (343) Runarsson; Chambers, Mustafi, Pablo Mari; Cedric, Willock (Azeez 83), Elneny (Ceballos 62), Maitland-Niles; Pepe, Nketiah (Balogun 62), Smith-Rowe (Cottrell 77).

Rapid Vienna (1) 2 *(Ritzmaier 43, Ibrahimoglu 90)*

Molde (1) 2 *(Eikrem 12, 46)*

Rapid Vienna: (4231) Gartler; Stojkovic, Hofmann, Barac, Ullmann; Grahovac, Ritzmaier (Ibrahimoglu 61); Schick, Knasmullner (Fountas 46), Arase (Demir 46); Kara (Kitagawa 75).

Molde: (451) Linde; Pedersen, Gregersen, Sinyan, Risa; Hestad (Knudtzon 45), Aursnes, Ellingsen, Eikrem (Hussain 58), Brynhildsen (Omoijuanfo 58); James (Wingo 85).

Group B Table	P	W	D	L	F	A	GD	Pts
Arsenal	6	6	0	0	20	5	15	18
Molde	6	3	1	2	9	11	–2	10
Rapid Vienna	6	2	1	3	11	13	–2	7
Dundalk	6	0	0	6	8	19	–11	0

GROUP C

Thursday, 22 October 2020

Bayer Leverkusen (2) 6 *(Amiri 11, Alario 16, Diaby 61, Bellarabi 79, 83, Wirtz 87)*

Nice (1) 2 *(Gouiri 31, Claude Maurice 90)*

Bayer Leverkusen: (4141) Hradecky; Bender L (Dragovic 82), Bender S (Tah 81), Tapsoba, Wendell; Baumgartlinger; Bailey, Palacios (Wirtz 74), Amiri, Diaby; Alario (Bellarabi 74).
Nice: (3511) Benitez; Robson Bambu, Dante, N'Soki (Lopes 63); Lotomba (Attal 79), Boudaoui (Claude Maurice 63), Schneiderlin, Lees-Melou (Ndoye 79), Kamara; Gouiri; Dolberg (Maolida 71).

Hapoel Be'er Sheva (1) 3 *(Agudelo 45, Acolatse 86, 88)*

Slavia Prague (0) 1 *(Provod 75)*

Hapoel Be'er Sheva: (541) Levita; Dadia, Taha (Tzedek 46), Miguel Vitor, Kabah, Goldberg; Sallalich (Yosefi 79), Bareiro, Josue (Keltjens 90), Acolatse (Varenne 89); Agudelo (Meli 70).
Slavia Prague: (442) Kolar; Dorley (Sima 89), Kudela, Hovorka, Boril; Malinsky (Masopust 58), Traore (Stanciu 46), Sevcik (Lingr 75), Provod; Musa, Tecl (Kuchta 57).

Thursday, 29 October 2020

Nice (1) 1 *(Gouiri 22)*

Hapoel Be'er Sheva (0) 0

Nice: (343) Benitez; Robson Bambu, Dante, N'Soki (Pelmard 46); Attal (Lotomba 68), Thuram, Schneiderlin, Kamara; Claude Maurice (Reine-Adelaide 58), Dolberg (Boudaoui 85), Gouiri (Maolida 69).
Hapoel Be'er Sheva: (541) Levita; Dadia, Taha, Miguel Vitor, Kabah, Goldberg (Varenne 76); Sallalich (Meli 76), Bareiro (Safuri 81), Josue, Yosefi (Agudelo 46); Acolatse (Twitto 88).

Slavia Prague (0) 1 *(Olayinka 80)*

Bayer Leverkusen (0) 0

Slavia Prague: (451) Kolar; Masopust, Kudela, Zima, Boril; Malinsky (Sima 71), Provod (Traore 76), Sevcik, Holes (Stanciu 61), Dorley (Olayinka 61); Lingr (Musa 46).
Bayer Leverkusen: (4231) Hradecky; Jedvaj, Tah, Dragovic, Wendell; Baumgartlinger, Demirbay; Bellarabi■, Wirtz (Amiri 67), Diaby; Alario (Bailey 46).

Thursday, 5 November 2020

Hapoel Be'er Sheva (2) 2 *(Acolatse 11, 25)*

Bayer Leverkusen (2) 4 *(Bailey 5, 75, Dadia 38 (og), Wirtz 88)*

Hapoel Be'er Sheva: (343) Levita; Taha, Miguel Vitor, Kabah (Varenne 84); Dadia, Bareiro, Josue, Goldberg (Safuri 84); Sallalich (Shwiro 64), Agudelo (Yosefi 64), Acolatse (Meli 89).
Bayer Leverkusen: (4231) Hradecky; Jedvaj (Bender L 62), Tah, Dragovic, Wendell; Palacios, Demirbay; Bailey, Wirtz, Amiri; Alario (Diaby 46).

Slavia Prague (2) 3 *(Kuchta 16, 71, Sima 43)*

Nice (1) 2 *(Gouiri 33, Ndoye 90)*

Slavia Prague: (4231) Kolar; Masopust, Hovorka (Kristan 86), Zima, Dorley; Holes, Sevcik; Sima, Lingr (Traore 70), Olayinka; Kuchta (Tecl 77).
Nice: (343) Benitez; Robson Bambu, Daniliuc, Pelmard; Lotomba, Lees-Melou (Claude Maurice 65), Schneiderlin, Kamara (Ndoye 88); Lopes (Reine-Adelaide 65), Dolberg (Attal 81), Gouiri.

Thursday, 26 November 2020

Bayer Leverkusen (1) 4 *(Schick 29, Bailey 48, Demirbay 76, Alario 80)*

Hapoel Be'er Sheva (0) 1 *(Shwiro 58)*

Bayer Leverkusen: (3142) Hradecky; Dragovic, Tah, Jedvaj; Demirbay; Bellarabi (Gedikli 80), Wirtz (Sinkgraven 80), Amiri (Baumgartlinger 90), Wendell; Schick (Alario 68), Bailey (Diaby 68).
Hapoel Be'er Sheva: (541) Levita; Dadia, Taha, Bareiro, Kabah, Goldberg (Twitto 70); Sallalich (Agudelo 70 (Varenne 85)), Meli (Madmon 81), Keltjens, Yosefi; Shwiro (Hatuel 80).

Nice (0) 1 *(Gouiri 60)*

Slavia Prague (1) 3 *(Lingr 14, Olayinka 64, Sima 75)*

Nice: (433) Benitez; Attal (Ndoye 66), Robson Bambu, N'Soki, Lotomba; Reine-Adelaide, Schneiderlin, Claude Maurice (Boudaoui■ 72); Lopes, Gouiri (Pelmard 78), Maolida.
Slavia Prague: (451) Kolar; Masopust, Kudela, Zima, Boril; Sima (Tecl 87), Lingr (Traore 63), Holes (Karafiat 87), Sevcik, Olayinka (Malinsky 88); Kuchta (Provod 82).

Thursday, 3 December 2020

Nice (1) 2 *(Kamara 26, Ndoye 46)*

Bayer Leverkusen (2) 3 *(Diaby 22, Dragovic 32, Baumgartlinger 51)*

Nice: (541) Benitez; Lotomba, Robson Bambu, Daniliuc, N'Soki, Kamara (Coly 72); Claude Maurice, Reine-Adelaide, Danilo Barbosa (Thuram 67), Maolida (Ndoye 29); Gouiri (Trouillet 72).
Bayer Leverkusen: (442) Hradecky; Bender L (Tapsoba 46), Tah, Dragovic, Wendell; Bellarabi, Baumgartlinger, Demirbay (Wirtz 86), Diaby (Gedikli 68); Schick (Bailey 46), Amiri (Turkmen 68).

Slavia Prague (2) 3 *(Sima 31, Stanciu 36, Twitto 85 (og))*

Hapoel Be'er Sheva (0) 0

Slavia Prague: (451) Kolar; Masopust (Provod 81), Kudela, Zima, Dorley (Boril 61); Sima, Holes, Sevcik (Traore 80), Stanciu (Lingr 64), Olayinka; Kuchta (Musa 81).
Hapoel Be'er Sheva: (541) Levita; Dadia, Taha (Gamoun 81), Tzedek, Kabah, Twitto; Sallalich (Yosefi 62), Bareiro (Madmon 46), Keltjens, Josue (Hatuel 76); Varenne (Shwiro 61).

Thursday, 10 December 2020

Bayer Leverkusen (2) 4 *(Bailey 8, 32, Diaby 59, Bellarabi 90)*

Slavia Prague (0) 0

Bayer Leverkusen: (4231) Lomb; Jedvaj, Dragovic, Tapsoba, Wendell; Baumgartlinger (Bender L 62), Sinkgraven (Onur 62); Bellarabi, Amiri (Turkmen 74), Bailey (Diaby 46); Schick (Gedikli 46).
Slavia Prague: (451) Kolar; Masopust, Boril, Zima, Dorley; Sima (Jurasek 82), Sevcik (Stanciu 19), Traore (Karafiat 82), Lingr (Rigo 82), Olayinka; Musa (Tecl 53).

Hapoel Be'er Sheva (0) 1 *(Hatuel 71)*

Nice (0) 0

Hapoel Be'er Sheva: (541) Rahamim; Gamoun, Taha, Kabah, Tzedek, Twitto; Yosefi (Josue 66), Madmon, Keltjens, Hatuel (Sallalich 84); Varenne (Shwiro 65 (Safuri 76)).
Nice: (4231) Cardinale; Pionnier-Bertrand (Cretier 82), Robson Bambu, Pelmard, Coly (Mahou 28); Thuram, Schneiderlin (Boudaoui 46); Lopes (Ben Seghir 46), Trouillet, Claude Maurice; Ndoye.

Group C Table	P	W	D	L	F	A	GD	Pts
Bayer Leverkusen	6	5	0	1	21	8	13	15
Slavia Prague	6	4	0	2	11	10	1	12
Hapoel Be'er Sheva	6	2	0	4	7	13	–6	6
Nice	6	1	0	5	8	16	–8	3

GROUP D

Thursday, 22 October 2020

Lech Poznan (1) 2 *(Ishak 15, 48)*

Benfica (2) 4 *(Pizzi 9 (pen), Nunez 42, 60, 90)*

Lech Poznan: (4411) Bednarek; Czerwinski, Dejewski, Crnomarkovic, Puchacz (Kravets 74); Skoras (Awad 90), Pedro Tiba, Moder, Kaminski (Marchwinski 67); Ramirez (Muhar 67); Ishak (Kacharava 74).
Benfica: (433) Vlachodimos; Gilberto, Otamendi, Vertonghen, Grimaldo (Tavares 67); Pizzi (Rafa Silva 46), Pires, Taarabt (Weigl 62); Waldschmidt (Pedrinho 62), Nunez, Everton (Jardel 87).

Standard Liege (0) 0

Rangers (1) 2 *(Tavernier 19 (pen), Roofe 90)* 3139

Standard Liege: (4141) Bodart; Fai (Carcela-Gonzalez M 63), Vanheusden, Dussene (Jans 78), Gavory; Bokadi; Lestienne (Avenatti 72), Bastien, Cimirot, Amallah (Cop 72); Muleka (Oulare 46).
Rangers: (433) McGregor; Tavernier, Goldson, Balogun, Barisic (Bassey 43); Arfield, Jack, Kamara; Hagi (Aribo 67), Morelos (Roofe 74), Kent.

Thursday, 29 October 2020

Benfica (0) 3 *(Pizzi 49 (pen), 76, Waldschmidt 66 (pen))*

Standard Liege (0) 0 4750

Benfica: (442) Vlachodimos; Goncalves, Otamendi, Vertonghen, Tavares; Pedrinho (Rafa Silva 46), Pires (Weigl 72), Pizzi (Goncalo Ramos 79), Everton; Waldschmidt (Taarabt 68), Nunez (Seferovic 72).
Standard Liege: (541) Bodart; Fai, Vanheusden (Laifis 76), Bokadi, Dussene, Gavory; Carcela-Gonzalez M, Bastien, Cimirot (Carcela-Gonzalez J 75), Amallah (Avenatti 80); Oulare (Boljevic 70).

Rangers (0) 1 *(Morelos 68)*

Lech Poznan (0) 0

Rangers: (433) McGregor; Tavernier, Goldson, Balogun, Barisic; Arfield (Jack 80), Davis, Kamara; Hagi (Aribo 69), Roofe (Morelos 63), Kent (Barker 81).
Lech Poznan: (4411) Bednarek; Czerwinski, Satka, Rogne, Kravets; Skoras (Sykora 74), Moder, Marchwinski (Awad 82), Puchacz; Ramirez (Kacharava 87); Ishak.

Thursday, 5 November 2020

Benfica (1) 3 *(Goldson 1 (og), Rafa Silva 77, Nunez 90)*

Rangers (2) 3 *(Goncalves 24 (og), Kamara 25, Morelos 51)*

Benfica: (4411) Vlachodimos; Goncalves (Gilberto 46), Otamendi■, Vertonghen, Tavares (Grimaldo 46); Rafa Silva, Weigl, Taarabt, Everton (Waldschmidt 67); Pizzi (Jardel 21); Seferovic (Nunez 60).
Rangers: (433) McGregor; Tavernier, Goldson, Helander, Barisic; Jack, Davis, Kamara; Aribo (Arfield 69), Morelos, Kent.

Lech Poznan (2) 3 *(Skoras 14, Ishak 22, 48)*

Standard Liege (1) 1 *(Lestienne 29)*

Lech Poznan: (4411) Bednarek; Czerwinski, Satka, Rogne, Puchacz; Skoras (Sykora 62), Pedro Tiba (Muhar 81), Moder, Marchwinski (Kaminski 62); Ramirez (Awad 81); Ishak (Kacharava 85).
Standard Liege: (4231) Bodart; Jans, Bokadi, Dussene, Gavory (Siquet 46); Bastien, Cimirot (Carcela-Gonzalez J 88); Lestienne (Oulare 73), Raskin (Carcela-Gonzalez M 73), Balikwisha; Amallah (Boljevic 60).

Thursday, 26 November 2020

Rangers (1) 2 *(Arfield 7, Roofe 69)*

Benfica (0) 2 *(Tavernier 78 (og), Pizzi 81)*

Rangers: (433) McGregor; Tavernier, Goldson, Balogun, Barisic; Arfield, Davis, Kamara; Roofe, Morelos, Kent.
Benfica: (433) Helton Leite; Gilberto (Goncalo Ramos 70), Jardel, Vertonghen, Grimaldo; Rafa Silva, Pires, Chiquinho (Pizzi 56); Waldschmidt (Goncalves 56), Seferovic (Ferro 90), Everton.

Standard Liege (0) 2 *(Tapsoba 63, Laifis 90)*

Lech Poznan (0) 1 *(Ishak 60)*

Standard Liege: (433) Bodart; Fai, Dussene, Laifis, Gavory (Jans 76); Raskin (Bastien 76), Bokadi (Tapsoba 46), Cimirot; Lestienne (Boljevic 46), Oulare■, Balikwisha (Avenatti 76).
Lech Poznan: (4411) Bednarek; Butko, Rogne, Crnomarkovic■, Puchacz; Skoras (Czerwinski 64), Pedro Tiba (Marchwinski 78), Moder (Satka 78), Sykora (Kravets 64); Ramirez; Ishak (Kacharava 83).

Thursday, 3 December 2020

Benfica (1) 4 *(Vertonghen 36, Nunez 57, Pizzi 58, Weigl 89)*

Lech Poznan (0) 0

Benfica: (4231) Vlachodimos; Gilberto, Otamendi, Vertonghen, Grimaldo; Pires, Chiquinho (Weigl 60); Rafa Silva (Cervi 77), Pizzi (Waldschmidt 60), Everton (Pedrinho 70); Nunez (Seferovic 60).
Lech Poznan: (4411) Bednarek; Butko, Satka, Dejewski, Puchacz; Skoras (Czerwinski 63), Muhar, Marchwinski (Moder 82), Sykora (Kravets 63); Awad (Ramirez 63); Kacharava (Ishak 42).

Rangers (2) 3 *(Goldson 39, Tavernier 45 (pen), Arfield 63)*

Standard Liege (2) 2 *(Lestienne 6, Cop 40)*

Rangers: (433) McGregor; Tavernier, Goldson, Balogun, Barisic (Bassey 89); Arfield (Zungu 86), Davis, Kamara; Roofe (Itten 89), Morelos (Aribo 79), Kent.
Standard Liege: (343) Bodart; Dussene, Bokadi, Laifis; Fai, Bastien, Shamir (Raskin 71), Jans (Gavory 86); Lestienne (Avenatti 71), Tapsoba, Cop (Balikwisha 46).

Thursday, 10 December 2020

Lech Poznan (0) 0

Rangers (1) 2 *(Itten 31, Hagi 72)*

Lech Poznan: (4411) Bednarek; Butko, Satka, Crnomarkovic, Puchacz; Skoras (Sykora 12 (Ramirez 64)), Pedro Tiba (Moder 46), Muhar, Kaminski (Kravets 46); Marchwinski; Ishak (Awad 64).
Rangers: (433) McLaughlin; Patterson (Tavernier 66), Goldson, Balogun (Bassey 80), Barisic; Arfield, Zungu (Barker 76), Kamara; Aribo, Itten (Morelos 80), Hagi (Kent 77).

Standard Liege (1) 2 *(Raskin 12, Tapsoba 59)*

Benfica (1) 2 *(Everton 16, Pizzi 67 (pen))*

Standard Liege: (532) Bodart; Jans, Bokadi, Cimirot, Laifis, Gavory; Raskin (Carcela-Gonzalez J 80), Shamir (Fai 59), Bastien; Balikwisha (Muleka 59), Tapsoba (Oulare 72).
Benfica: (442) Helton Leite; Joao Ferreira, Jardel, Vertonghen, Tavares (Cervi 80); Pedrinho (Rafa Silva 64), Weigl (Pires 80), Taarabt (Seferovic 83), Everton; Waldschmidt (Pizzi 64), Nunez.

Group D Table	P	W	D	L	F	A	GD	Pts
Rangers	6	4	2	0	13	7	6	14
Benfica	6	3	3	0	18	9	9	12
Standard Liege	6	1	1	4	7	14	–7	4
Lech Poznan	6	1	0	5	6	14	–8	3

GROUP E

Thursday, 22 October 2020

PAOK (0) 1 *(Murg 56)*

Omonia Nicosia (1) 1 *(Bautheac 16)*

PAOK: (3421) Zivkovic Z; Ingason, Varela, Michailidis; Leo Matos (Rodrigo 61), Schwab, Esiti (Douglas 46), Giannoulis; Murg (Biseswar 73), Zivkovic A (Tzolis 73); Colak (Swiderski 61).
Omonia Nicosia: (4231) Fabiano; Hubocan, Luftner, Lang, Lecjaks; Vitor Gomes, Gomez (Kousoulos 74); Bautheac (Loizou 90), Papoulis (Asante 75), Tzionis; Duris (Kakoullis 75).

PSV Eindhoven (1) 1 *(Gotze 45)*

Granada (0) 2 *(Jorge Molina 57, Machis 66)*

PSV Eindhoven: (442) Mvogo; Dumfries, Baumgartl, Boscagli, Max; Gotze (Viergever 46), Sangare, Hendrix, Junior (Madueke 73); Ihattaren, Malen.
Granada: (4141) Rui Silva; Foulquier, German, Vallejo, Neva; Gonalons (Montoro 35); Puertas, Herrera, Milla (Brice 81), Machis (Soro 81); Jorge Molina (Suarez 69).

Thursday, 29 October 2020

Granada (0) 0

PAOK (0) 0

Granada: (4141) Rui Silva; Puertas, German, Vallejo, Neva; Gonalons (Brice 90); Kenedy (Montoro 73), Herrera (Jorge Molina 59), Milla, Machis (Domingos Duarte 90); Suarez (Soro 73).
PAOK: (3421) Zivkovic Z; Ingason, Varela, Crespo; Rodrigo (Wague 74), Douglas, Schwab, Giannoulis; Zivkovic A, Murg (El Kaddouri 70); Colak (Swiderski 69).

Omonia Nicosia (1) 1 *(Gomez 29)*

PSV Eindhoven (1) 2 *(Malen 40, 90)*

Omonia Nicosia: (4231) Fabiano; Hubocan, Luftner, Lang, Lecjaks; Vitor Gomes, Gomez; Bautheac (Kousoulos 90), Papoulis (Asante 81), Tzionis; Duris (Kakoullis 81).
PSV Eindhoven: (433) Mvogo; Teze, Hendrix, Boscagli, Max; Gotze, Sangare, Thomas; Ihattaren, Malen, Madueke (Fein 83).

Thursday, 5 November 2020

Omonia Nicosia (0) 0

Granada (1) 2 *(Herrera 4, Suarez 63)*

Omonia Nicosia: (4231) Fabiano; Hubocan, Luftner, Lang, Lecjaks; Vitor Gomes, Gomez (Abdullahi 46); Bautheac (Asante 46), Papoulis (Kousoulos 46), Tzionis (Thiago Santos 72); Duris■.
Granada: (4141) Rui Silva; Sanchez (Perez 89), German, Domingos Duarte, Neva; Gonalons; Machis, Herrera (Brice 90), Montoro (Milla 46), Kenedy (Soro 76); Suarez (Jorge Molina 75).

PAOK (0) 4 *(Schwab 47, Zivkovic A 55, 66, Tzolis 58)*

PSV Eindhoven (1) 1 *(Zahavi 20 (pen))*

PAOK: (433) Zivkovic Z; Rodrigo, Varela, Crespo, Giannoulis (Lyratzis 71); Schwab, El Kaddouri (Tsingaras 81), Douglas; Zivkovic A (Murg 84), Colak (Swiderski 46), Biseswar (Tzolis 46).
PSV Eindhoven: (442) Mvogo; Thomas (Madueke 58), Teze, Boscagli, Max; Gotze (Saibari 83), Rosario (Fein 46), Sangare (Ledezma 83), Ihattaren (Junior 58); Zahavi, Malen.

Thursday, 26 November 2020

Granada (1) 2 *(Suarez 8, Soro 73)*

Omonia Nicosia (0) 1 *(Asante 60)*

Granada: (4141) Rui Silva; Vallejo, Perez (Foulquier 66), Domingos Duarte, Neva; Gonalons (Machis 66); Soro (Puertas 79), Milla, Herrera, Suarez (Brice 79); Soldado (Jorge Molina 79).
Omonia Nicosia: (3421) Fabiano; Hubocan, Luftner, Lang; Mavrias, Kousoulos, Abdullahi (Gomez 58), Kiko (Lecjaks 59); Bautheac (Asante 36), Tzionis (Thiago Santos 59); Kakoullis (Kaly Sene 74).

PSV Eindhoven (1) 3 *(Gakpo 20, Madueke 50, Malen 53)*

PAOK (2) 2 *(Varela 4, Tzolis 13)*

PSV Eindhoven: (442) Mvogo; Dumfries, Teze, Boscagli, Max; Gakpo, Sangare, Rosario, Madueke (Junior 78); Zahavi (Hendrix 71), Malen (Ledezma 90).
PAOK: (433) Zivkovic Z; Rodrigo, Ingason, Varela, Crespo (Wague 86); Schwab, Tsingaras (Douglas 69), El Kaddouri (Biseswar 85); Zivkovic A, Colak (Swiderski 69), Tzolis (Murg 58).

Thursday, 3 December 2020

Granada (0) 0

PSV Eindhoven (1) 1 *(Malen 38)*

Granada: (4141) Rui Silva; Vallejo, German (Foulquier 56), Domingos Duarte, Neva; Gonalons; Soro (Suarez 56), Herrera, Milla (Jorge Molina 76), Machis; Soldado (Puertas 83).
PSV Eindhoven: (433) Mvogo; Dumfries (Baumgartl 71), Teze, Boscagli, Max; Gotze, Sangare, Rosario; Madueke (Zahavi 38 (Hendrix 88)), Malen, Gakpo.

Omonia Nicosia (1) 2 *(Kakoullis 9, Gomez 84 (pen))*

PAOK (1) 1 *(Tzolis 39)*

Omonia Nicosia: (541) Fabiano; Loizou (Asante 85), Hubocan, Luftner, Lang, Kiko (Lecjaks 59); Kaly Sene (Duris 59), Vitor Gomes, Kousoulos (Gomez 60), Tzionis; Kakoullis (Abdullahi 21).
PAOK: (433) Zivkovic Z; Wague (Giannoulis 46), Varela, Crespo, Rodrigo; Schwab (Murg 46), Tsingaras (Biseswar 79), El Kaddouri; Zivkovic A, Swiderski, Tzolis.

Thursday, 10 December 2020

PAOK (0) 0

Granada (0) 0

PAOK: (433) Paschalakis; Lyratzis (Wague 63), Ingason, Varela, Crespo; El Kaddouri, Murg, Esiti (Douglas 63); Koutsias (Tsingaras 46), Colak (Swiderski 81), Tzolis (Zivkovic A 46).
Granada: (4231) Escandell; Sanchez (Neva 66), Perez, German, Foulquier; Brice (Soldado 85), Milla (Gonalons 75); Puertas, Soro (Machis 75), Kenedy (Suarez 67); Jorge Molina.

PSV Eindhoven (1) 4 *(Malen 35, Dumfries 63 (pen), Piroe 90, 90)*

Omonia Nicosia (0) 0

PSV Eindhoven: (4222) Mvogo; Dumfries (Teze 81), Baumgartl, Viergever, Max (Boscagli 46); Rosario (Sangare 46), Hendrix; Ledezma (Fein 17), Ihattaren; Piroe, Malen (Gakpo 46).
Omonia Nicosia: (3421) Fabiano; Kousoulos (Gomez 60), Luftner, Lang; Loizou, Vitor Gomes, Abdullahi, Kiko (Lecjaks 60); Thiago Santos, Tzionis; Kaly Sene (Duris 61).

Group E Table	P	W	D	L	F	A	GD	Pts
PSV Eindhoven	6	4	0	2	12	9	3	12
Granada	6	3	2	1	6	3	3	11
PAOK	6	1	3	2	8	7	1	6
Omonoia Nicosia	6	1	1	4	5	12	–7	4

GROUP F

Thursday, 22 October 2020

Napoli (0) 0

AZ Alkmaar (0) 1 *(de Wit 57)* 494

Napoli: (4231) Meret; Di Lorenzo, Maksimovic, Koulibaly, Hysaj (Mario Rui 59); Fabian, Lobotka (Demme 66); Politano (Bakayoko 83), Mertens, Lozano (Insigne 59); Osimhen (Petagna 66).
AZ Alkmaar: (433) Bizot; Svensson, Chatzidiakos, Martins Indi, Wijndal; Sugawara, Midtsjoe (Leeuwin 88), Koopmeiners; Stengs, de Wit, Karlsson (Gudmundsson 88).

Rijeka (0) 0

Real Sociedad (0) 1 *(Bautista 90)* 2089

Rijeka: (532) Nevistic; Tomecak, Escoval, Velkovski, Smolcic, Stefulj; Pavicic, Cerin, Loncar (Capan 87); Andrijasevic (Yateke 63), Kulenovic (Lepinjica 77).
Real Sociedad: (433) Remiro; Gorosabel, Elustondo, Le Normand, Monreal; Silva, Zubimendi, Merino; Portu (Januzaj 89), Isak (Willian Jose 72), Oyarzabal (Bautista 85).

Thursday, 29 October 2020

AZ Alkmaar (2) 4 *(Koopmeiners 6 (pen), Gudmundsson 20, 60, Karlsson 51)*

Rijeka (0) 1 *(Kulenovic 72)*

AZ Alkmaar: (4231) Bizot; Svensson, Chatzidiakos (Leeuwin 62), Martins Indi (Gullit 90), Wijndal; Midtsjoe, Koopmeiners; Stengs (Aboukhlal 66), de Wit, Karlsson (Evjen 67); Gudmundsson (Barasi 90).
Rijeka: (532) Nevistic; Tomecak (Raspopovic 80), Escoval, Velkovski (Lepinjica 65), Smolcic, Stefulj (Anastasio 80); Andrijasevic (Halilovic 64), Pavicic, Loncar; Kulenovic, Menalo (Yateke 64).

Real Sociedad (0) 0

Napoli (0) 1 *(Politano 55)*

Real Sociedad: (433) Remiro; Gorosabel (Barrenetxea 79), Le Normand, Sagnan, Monreal; Silva, Guevara, Merino (Zubimendi 79); Portu (Bautista 67), Isak (Willian Jose 67), Oyarzabal (Guridi 86).
Napoli: (4231) Ospina; Hysaj, Maksimovic, Koulibaly, Mario Rui; Demme (Fabian 89), Bakayoko; Politano (Di Lorenzo 61), Lobotka (Mertens 61), Insigne (Lozano 22); Petagna (Osimhen■ 61).

Thursday, 5 November 2020

Real Sociedad (0) 1 *(Portu 58)*

AZ Alkmaar (0) 0

Real Sociedad: (4231) Moya; Elustondo, Le Normand, Sagnan, Monreal; Merino (Zubimendi 76), Guevara; Portu (Januzaj 76), Silva, Oyarzabal (Barrenetxea 89); Isak (Willian Jose 62).
AZ Alkmaar: (4231) Bizot; Svensson, Chatzidiakos (Letschert 70), Koopmeiners, Wijndal; de Wit, Midtsjoe; Karlsson (Druijf 63), Stengs (Velthuis 70), Gudmundsson (Aboukhlal 63); Boadu (Evjen 62).

Rijeka (1) 1 *(Muric 13)*

Napoli (1) 2 *(Demme 43, Braut 62 (og))*

Rijeka: (541) Nevistic; Tomecak, Escoval, Velkovski, Smolcic, Braut (Stefulj 64); Muric (Yateke 24 (Raspopovic 64)), Cerin, Loncar, Menalo; Kulenovic.
Napoli: (4231) Meret; Di Lorenzo, Maksimovic, Koulibaly, Mario Rui (Zielinski 80); Lobotka (Insigne 59), Demme; Politano (Lozano 69), Mertens, Elmas (Fabian 59); Petagna (Ghoulam 80).

Thursday, 26 November 2020

AZ Alkmaar (0) 0

Real Sociedad (0) 0

AZ Alkmaar: (442) Bizot; Svensson, Chatzidiakos, Martins Indi, Wijndal; Stengs, Midtsjoe, Koopmeiners, Karlsson (Aboukhlal 71); de Wit, Gudmundsson (Boadu 71).
Real Sociedad: (4231) Remiro; Zaldua, Elustondo, Le Normand, Monreal; Zubimendi, Merino; Portu (Barrenetxea 82), Januzaj (Lopez 73), Oyarzabal (Merquelanz 86); Isak (Willian Jose 73).

Napoli (1) 2 *(Anastasio 41 (og), Lozano 75)*

Rijeka (0) 0

Napoli: (4231) Meret; Di Lorenzo, Maksimovic, Koulibaly, Ghoulam; Bakayoko, Demme (Lobotka 69); Politano (Lozano 64), Zielinski (Insigne 64), Elmas (Mertens 69); Petagna (Fabian 81).
Rijeka: (541) Nevistic; Tomecak, Velkovski, Galovic, Smolcic, Anastasio (Braut 80); Muric (Yateke 78), Cerin (Hodza 87), Loncar, Stefulj; Andrijasevic (Frigan 87).

Thursday, 3 December 2020

AZ Alkmaar (0) 1 *(Martins Indi 53)*

Napoli (1) 1 *(Mertens 6)*

AZ Alkmaar: (442) Bizot; Sugawara, Chatzidiakos, Martins Indi, Wijndal; Stengs, Midtsjoe, Koopmeiners, Aboukhlal (Karlsson 82); de Wit, Gudmundsson (Boadu 70).
Napoli: (4231) Ospina; Di Lorenzo, Maksimovic, Koulibaly, Ghoulam (Mario Rui 66); Fabian (Elmas 57), Bakayoko; Politano (Lozano 61), Zielinski (Petagna 61), Insigne; Mertens (Demme 66).

Real Sociedad (0) 2 *(Bautista 69, Monreal 79)*

Rijeka (1) 2 *(Velkovski 37, Loncar 73)*

Real Sociedad: (4231) Remiro; Zaldua (Gorosabel 67), Zubeldia, Le Normand, Monreal; Zubimendi, Merino; Januzaj (Portu 80), Silva (Willian Jose 68), Oyarzabal (Lopez 80); Isak (Bautista 58).
Rijeka: (541) Nevistic; Tomecak, Velkovski (Escoval 86), Galovic, Capan, Stefulj; Muric (Pavicic 75), Halilovic, Loncar, Menalo (Anastasio 80); Andrijasevic (Yateke 86).

Thursday, 10 December 2020

Napoli (1) 1 *(Zielinski 35)*

Real Sociedad (0) 1 *(Willian Jose 90)*

Napoli: (4231) Ospina; Di Lorenzo, Maksimovic, Koulibaly, Mario Rui (Ghoulam 82); Fabian, Bakayoko (Demme 70); Lozano (Politano 70), Zielinski (Elmas 74), Insigne; Mertens (Petagna 70).
Real Sociedad: (433) Remiro; Zaldua (Gorosabel 46), Zubeldia, Le Normand (Isak 78), Monreal (Munoz 78); Guevara (Sagnan 78), Zubimendi, Merino; Januzaj, Willian Jose, Portu (Barrenetxea 56).

Rijeka (0) 2 *(Menalo 51, Tomecak 90)*

AZ Alkmaar (0) 1 *(Wijndal 57)*

Rijeka: (541) Nevistic; Tomecak, Capan, Galovic, Smolcic, Stefulj; Muric (Kulenovic 71), Halilovic, Loncar, Menalo (Pavicic 71); Andrijasevic.
AZ Alkmaar: (433) Bizot; Sugawara, Chatzidiakos, Martins Indi (Letschert 18), Wijndal; Midtsjoe, Gudmundsson (Aboukhlal 71), Koopmeiners; Stengs, Boadu (Druijf 89), Karlsson■.

Group F Table	P	W	D	L	F	A	GD	Pts
Napoli	6	3	2	1	7	4	3	11
Real Sociedad	6	2	3	1	5	4	1	9
AZ Alkmaar	6	2	2	2	7	5	2	8
Rijeka	6	1	1	4	6	12	–6	4

GROUP G

Thursday, 22 October 2020

Braga (1) 3 *(Galeno 44, Paulinho 78, Ricardo Horta 88)*

AEK Athens (0) 0 2196

Braga: (4141) Matheus Magalhaes; Ricardo Esgaio, Bruno Viana, Carmo, Nuno Sequeira; Castro Pereira (Guilherme 90); Iuri Medeiros (Andre Horta 60), Fransergio (Moura 84), Ricardo Horta (Joao Novais 90), Galeno (Al Musrati 84); Paulinho.
AEK Athens: (532) Tsintotas; Vasilantonopoulos, Nedelcearu, Chygrynskiy (Livaja 61 (Macheras 89)), Svarnas, Helder Lopes; Shakhov, Krsticic, Mandalos; Oliveira, Ansarifard (Tankovic 62).

Leicester C (2) 3 *(Maddison 29, Barnes 45, Iheanacho 67)*

Zorya Luhansk (0) 0

Leicester C: (4231) Schmeichel; Castagne (Justin 82), Fofana, Evans (Morgan 82), Fuchs; Tielemans (Choudhury 71), Mendy; Praet, Maddison (Under 65), Barnes; Iheanacho (Perez 71).
Zorya Luhansk: (41212) Shevchenko; Favorov (Rufati 76), Vernydub, Cvek, Khomchenovskiy (Ciganiks 76); Ivanisenya; Nazaryna, Kochergin (Gryn 85); Yurchenko; Lunov (Hladkyy 65), Kabayev (Perovic 64).

Thursday, 29 October 2020

AEK Athens (0) 1 *(Tankovic 49)*

Leicester C (2) 2 *(Vardy 18 (pen), Choudhury 39)*

AEK Athens: (4231) Tsintotas; Bakakis (Vasilantonopoulos 86), Svarnas, Nedelcearu, Insua (Macheras 86); Shakhov (Sabanadzovic 86), Krsticic; Livaja (Tankovic 46), Mandalos, Helder Lopes; Ansarifard (Oliveira 46).
Leicester C: (3421) Schmeichel; Fofana, Morgan, Fuchs (Thomas 46); Albrighton, Tielemans, Choudhury (Mendy 66), Justin; Under (Praet 66), Maddison (Barnes 74); Vardy (Iheanacho 70).

Zorya Luhansk (0) 1 *(Ivanisenya 90)*

Braga (2) 2 *(Paulinho 3, Gaitan 11)*

Zorya Luhansk: (433) Vasilj; Favorov (Abu Hanna 87), Vernydub, Cvek, Khomchenovskiy; Nazaryna, Ivanisenya, Kochergin; Yurchenko (Perovic 87), Lunov (Hladkyy 62), Kabayev (Sayyadmanesh 81).
Braga: (3412) Matheus Magalhaes; Bruno Viana, Carmo, Raul Silva; Ricardo Esgaio (Vitor Tormena 90), Fransergio, Castro Pereira (Al Musrati 79), Moura; Ricardo Horta (Andre Horta 66); Paulinho (Guilherme 79), Gaitan (Iuri Medeiros 66).

Thursday, 5 November 2020

Leicester C (1) 4 *(Iheanacho 20, 47, Praet 67, Maddison 78)*

Braga (0) 0

Leicester C: (3421) Schmeichel; Justin, Fofana, Fuchs; Albrighton (Morgan 62), Tielemans (Barnes 72), Choudhury, Thomas; Under (Praet 62), Maddison; Iheanacho (Perez 72).
Braga: (352) Matheus Magalhaes; Bruno Viana, Carmo, Raul Silva; Ricardo Esgaio, Andre Horta (Iuri Medeiros 62), Al Musrati (Castro Pereira 71), Joao Novais, Galeno (Moura 71); Paulinho (Gaitan 71), Ruiz (Guilherme 62).

Zorya Luhansk (0) 1 *(Kochergin 81)*

AEK Athens (2) 4 *(Tankovic 6, Mandalos 34, Livaja 54, 81)*

Zorya Luhansk: (433) Shevchenko; Khomchenovskiy (Favorov 59), Vernydub, Abu Hanna, Ciganiks; Kochergin, Ivanisenya, Yurchenko; Kabayev (Hladkyy 59), Gromov (Sayyadmanesh 46), Lunov (Nazaryna 46).
AEK Athens: (352) Tsintotas; Svarnas, Chygrynskiy, Nedelcearu; Vasilantonopoulos, Shakhov (Sabanadzovic 70), Krsticic (Galanopoulos 85), Mandalos (Botos 85), Insua; Tankovic (Ansarifard 75), Livaja.

Thursday, 26 November 2020

AEK Athens (0) 0

Zorya Luhansk (0) 3 *(Gromov 61, Kabayev 75, Yurchenko 86 (pen))*

AEK Athens: (352) Athanasiadis; Nedelcearu, Chygrynskiy, Svarnas (Vasilantonopoulos 82); Bakakis (Galanopoulos 65), Shakhov■, Krsticic, Andre Simoes (Macheras 87), Insua; Tankovic (Ansarifard 65), Livaja.
Zorya Luhansk: (433) Shevchenko; Favorov, Vernydub, Abu Hanna, Ciganiks; Kochergin (Lunov 82), Ivanisenya, Yurchenko (Perovic 87); Kabayev (Sayyadmanesh 87), Hladkyy (Nazaryna 63), Gromov (Gryn 87).

Braga (2) 3 *(Al Musrati 4, Paulinho 24, Fransergio 90)*

Leicester C (1) 3 *(Barnes 9, Thomas 78, Vardy 90)*

Braga: (3421) Matheus Magalhaes; Vitor Tormena, Bruno Viana, Nuno Sequeira; Ricardo Esgaio, Al Musrati, Castro Pereira (Andre Horta 87), Galeno; Iuri Medeiros (Fransergio 77), Ricardo Horta (Raul Silva 69); Paulinho (Guilherme 87).
Leicester C: (3421) Schmeichel; Justin, Evans, Fuchs (Fofana 46); Albrighton, Praet (Tielemans 46), Choudhury, Thomas; Under (Vardy 62), Barnes (Maddison 62); Iheanacho (Perez 68).

Thursday, 3 December 2020

AEK Athens (1) 2 *(Oliveira 31, Vasilantonopoulos 89)*

Braga (3) 4 *(Vitor Tormena 7, Ricardo Esgaio 9, Ricardo Horta 45, Galeno 82)*

AEK Athens: (433) Tsintotas; Bakakis (Vasilantonopoulos 46), Hnid, Nedelcearu, Insua; Galanopoulos, Andre Simoes, Mandalos (Garcia 74); Albanis (Tankovic 60), Oliveira (Ansarifard 60), Livaja.
Braga: (3421) Matheus Magalhaes; Vitor Tormena, Bruno Viana (Carmo 46), Nuno Sequeira; Ricardo Esgaio, Al Musrati (Fransergio 57), Castro Pereira (Joao Novais 78), Galeno; Iuri Medeiros (Andre Horta 57), Ricardo Horta; Paulinho (Guilherme 71).

Zorya Luhansk (0) 1 *(Sayyadmanesh 84)*

Leicester C (0) 0

Zorya Luhansk: (4312) Vasilj; Favorov, Ivanisenya, Abu Hanna, Ciganiks; Yurchenko, Nazaryna, Kochergin; Kabayev; Gromov (Perovic 90), Hladkyy (Sayyadmanesh 81).
Leicester C: (433) Ward; Ricardo Pereira (Thomas 46), Morgan (Fuchs 56), Soyuncu (Fofana 17), Justin; Praet (Maddison 77), Ndidi (Mendy 56), Choudhury; Under, Iheanacho, Barnes.

Thursday, 10 December 2020

Braga (0) 2 *(Abu Hanna 61 (og), Ricardo Horta 68)*

Zorya Luhansk (0) 0

Braga: (3421) Tiago Sa; Vitor Tormena, Carmo, Raul Silva; Ze Carlos (Bruno Viana 73), Fransergio, Joao Novais (Al Musrati 77), Galeno; Andre Horta (Iuri Medeiros 67), Ruiz (Ricardo Horta 68); Guilherme (Paulinho 68).
Zorya Luhansk: (4312) Shevchenko; Favorov (Khomchenovskiy 87), Ivanisenya, Abu Hanna, Ciganiks; Yurchenko, Nazaryna, Kochergin (Piddubnyi 87); Kabayev (Lunov 77); Gromov (Gryn 77), Hladkyy (Perovic 77).

Leicester C (2) 2 *(Under 12, Barnes 14)*

AEK Athens (0) 0

Leicester C: (4321) Ward; Justin, Fofana (Morgan 81), Evans, Thomas; Praet, Ndidi (Mendy 63), Tielemans (Choudhury 82); Under, Barnes; Iheanacho (Perez 67).
AEK Athens: (352) Tsintotas; Hnid, Nedelcearu, Svarnas (Shakhov 56); Vasilantonopoulos, Mandalos (Albanis 66), Andre Simoes (Galanopoulos 81), Krsticic, Mitaj; Garcia (Macheras 55), Ansarifard (Oliveira 66).

Group G Table	*P*	*W*	*D*	*L*	*F*	*A*	*GD*	*Pts*
Leicester C	6	4	1	1	14	5	9	13
Braga	6	4	1	1	14	10	4	13
Zorya Luhansk	6	2	0	4	6	11	–5	6
AEK Athens	6	1	0	5	7	15	–8	3

GROUP H

Thursday, 22 October 2020

Celtic (0) 1 *(Elyounoussi 76)*

AC Milan (2) 3 *(Krunic 14, Diaz 42, Hauge 90)* 316

Celtic: (3511) Barkas; Welsh (Elyounoussi 46), Duffy, Ajer; Frimpong, Ntcham, Brown (Rogic 64), McGregor, Laxalt (Taylor 77); Ajeti (Klimala 77); Griffiths (Christie 46).
AC Milan: (4231) Donnarumma; Dalot, Kjaer, Romagnoli, Hernandez; Tonali, Kessie (Bennacer 66); Castillejo (Saelemaekers 79), Krunic, Diaz (Hauge 79); Ibrahimovic (Leao 66).

Sparta Prague (0) 1 *(Dockal 46)*

Lille (1) 4 *(Yazici 45, 60, 75, Ikone 66)*

Sparta Prague: (4231) Heca; Sacek (Vitik 90), Lischka, Ladislav Krejci II■, Hanousek (Minchev 90); Travnik (Karabec 78), Pavelka; Vindheim, Dockal, Moberg Karlsson (Polidar 74); Julis (Hlozek 46).
Lille: (4411) Maignan; Pied, Fonte, Botman (Soumaoro 78), Bradaric (Mandava 63); Yazici (Weah 80), Xeka, Soumare, Bamba (Luiz Araujo 78); Ikone; David (Yilmaz 63).

Thursday, 29 October 2020

AC Milan (1) 3 *(Diaz 24, Leao 57, Dalot 66)*

Sparta Prague (0) 0

AC Milan: (4231) Tatarusanu; Calabria (Conti 68), Kjaer, Romagnoli (Leo Duarte 80), Dalot; Tonali, Bennacer (Kessie 81); Castillejo, Diaz, Krunic (Maldini 88); Ibrahimovic (Leao 46).
Sparta Prague: (4231) Heca; Sacek, Celustka, Lischka (Plechaty 80), Hanousek; Travnik (Karabec 80), Pavelka; Vindheim, Dockal (Patrak 90), Ladislav Krejci I (Moberg Karlsson 63); Julis (Kozak 63).

Lille (0) 2 *(Celik 67, Ikone 75)*

Celtic (2) 2 *(Elyounoussi 28, 32)*

Lille: (442) Maignan; Celik, Soumaoro, Botman, Bradaric; Ikone, Andre (Sanches 63), Soumare, Bamba (Luiz Araujo 63); Yazici (Weah 82), David (Yilmaz 64).
Celtic: (4231) Bain; Frimpong, Duffy, Ajer (Bitton 53), Laxalt; Brown (Soro 81), McGregor; Christie (Rogic 81), Ntcham (Welsh 82), Elyounoussi; Ajeti (Edouard 64).

Thursday, 5 November 2020

AC Milan (0) 0

Lille (1) 3 *(Yazici 22 (pen), 55, 58)*

AC Milan: (4231) Donnarumma; Dalot, Kjaer, Romagnoli, Hernandez; Kessie, Tonali (Bennacer 61); Castillejo (Leao 46), Diaz (Hauge 78), Krunic (Calhanoglu 46); Ibrahimovic (Rebic 62).
Lille: (4411) Maignan; Celik, Fonte, Botman, Bradaric; Ikone (Lihadji 65), Xeka (Andre 65), Sanches (Soumare 80), Bamba (Mandava 84); Yazici (Yilmaz 80); David.

Celtic (0) 1 *(Griffiths 65)*

Sparta Prague (2) 4 *(Julis 26, 45, 76, Ladlislav Krejci I 90)*

Celtic: (4231) Bain; Frimpong, Duffy, Bitton, Laxalt (Ntcham 80); Brown (Elhamed 60), McGregor; Christie, Rogic, Elyounoussi (Griffiths 59); Edouard (Ajeti 80).
Sparta Prague: (4231) Nita; Vindheim, Pavelka, Plechaty, Hancko (Lischka 73); Sacek (Dockal 88), Ladislav Krejci II; Polidar (Ladislav Krejci I 79), Karabec (Travnik 74), Moberg Karlsson (Plavsic 88); Julis.

Thursday, 26 November 2020

Lille (0) 1 *(Bamba 65)*

AC Milan (0) 1 *(Castillejo 46)*

Lille: (442) Maignan; Pied (Djalo 79), Fonte, Botman, Mandava; Luiz Araujo (Lihadji 75), Andre, Xeka (Soumare 63), Bamba; Yazici (Ikone 63), David.
AC Milan: (4231) Donnarumma; Dalot, Kjaer, Gabbia, Hernandez; Tonali, Bennacer; Castillejo, Calhanoglu (Diaz 61), Hauge (Krunic 77); Rebic (Colombo 61).

Sparta Prague (2) 4 *(Hancko 26, Julis 38, 80, Plavsic 90)*

Celtic (1) 1 *(Edouard 15)*

Sparta Prague: (352) Nita; Plechaty, Pavelka, Hancko (Soucek 67); Vindheim, Travnik (Ladislav Krejci I 76), Dockal, Ladislav Krejci II, Hanousek; Julis (Minchev 86), Moberg Karlsson (Plavsic 86).
Celtic: (4231) Bain; Elhamed, Jullien, Ajer, Laxalt; Brown (Rogic 66), McGregor; Christie, Ntcham, Elyounoussi; Edouard (Klimala 82).

Thursday, 3 December 2020

AC Milan (2) 4 *(Calhanoglu 24, Castillejo 26, Hauge 50, Diaz 82)*

Celtic (2) 2 *(Rogic 7, Edouard 14)*

AC Milan: (4231) Donnarumma; Dalot, Kjaer (Romagnoli 11), Gabbia, Hernandez; Kessie (Bennacer 61), Krunic (Tonali 46); Castillejo, Calhanoglu (Diaz 61), Hauge; Rebic (Colombo 83).
Celtic: (4231) Barkas; Elhamed, Bitton, Ajer, Laxalt; Brown (Soro 78), McGregor; Frimpong, Rogic (Ntcham 67), Christie (Klimala 86); Edouard.

Lille (0) 2 *(Yilmaz 80, 84)*

Sparta Prague (0) 1 *(Ladislav Krejci II 71)*

Lille: (442) Maignan; Djalo (Weah 77), Fonte, Botman, Bradaric (Mandava 85); Luiz Araujo (Ikone 68), Andre (Soumare 85), Xeka, Bamba; Yazici (Yilmaz 77), David.
Sparta Prague: (352) Nita; Plechaty, Celustka■, Ladislav Krejci II; Vindheim, Pavelka, Dockal (Karabec 89), Soucek (Travnik 81), Ladislav Krejci I (Minchev 89); Julis (Hanousek 81), Moberg Karlsson (Plavsic 46).

Thursday, 10 December 2020

Celtic (2) 3 *(Jullien 21, McGregor 28 (pen), Turnbull 75)*

Lille (1) 2 *(Ikone 24, Weah 71)*

Celtic: (4411) Hazard; Ajer (Welsh 87), Jullien, Duffy, Laxalt; Frimpong (Henderson 30), Soro, McGregor, Elyounoussi; Turnbull (Rogic 87); Klimala (Ajeti 78).
Lille: (442) Maignan; Niasse (Bamba 71), Fonte (Botman 46), Djalo, Bradaric; Ikone (Lihadji 66), Xeka, Soumare (Andre 66), Weah (Mandava 78); David, Yazici.

Sparta Prague (0) 0

AC Milan (1) 1 *(Hauge 23)*

Sparta Prague: (352) Heca; Vitik, Plechaty■, Lischka; Wiesner, Sacek (Ladislav Krejci I 82), Soucek, Karabec (Ladislav Krejci II 45), Polidar; Minchev (Julis 65), Plavsic (Moberg Karlsson 65).
AC Milan: (433) Tatarusanu; Conti, Leo Duarte, Kalulu Kyatengwa, Dalot; Maldini (Kessie 78), Tonali, Krunic; Castillejo, Colombo (Leao 67), Hauge (Diaz 90).

Group H Table	P	W	D	L	F	A	GD	Pts
Milan	6	4	1	1	12	7	5	13
Lille	6	3	2	1	14	8	6	11
Sparta Prague	6	2	0	4	10	12	–2	6
Celtic	6	1	1	4	10	19	–9	4

GROUP I

Thursday, 22 October 2020

Maccabi Tel Aviv (1) 1 *(Cohen 10)*

Qarabag (0) 0

Maccabi Tel Aviv: (541) Daniel; Kandil, Yeini, Tibi, Saborit (Hernandez 84), Davidadze (Bitton 46); Cohen (Rikan 69), Glazer D, Peretz, Golasa (Ben Haim II 78); Shechter (Guerrero 46).
Qarabag: (4231) Mahammadaliyev; Huseynov A, Medvedev, Medina, Guerrier; Garayev (Ibrahhimli 80), Matic (Kwabena 60); Andrade, Ozobic (Dzhafarquliyev 80), Zoubir (Bayramov 86); Romero (Qurbanly 86).

Villarreal (2) 5 *(Kubo 13, Bacca 20, Foyth 57, Alcacer 74, 78)*

Sivasspor (2) 3 *(Kayode 33, Yatabare 43, Gradel 64)*

Villarreal: (433) Rulli; Pena, Foyth, Albiol, Jaume (Pedraza 70); Kubo, Coquelin (Pino 79), Trigueros (Moi Gomez 58); Chukwueze, Bacca (Alcacer 70), Baena (Iborra 46).
Sivasspor: (4231) Samassa; Yalcin, Osmanpasa, Camara (Claudemir 79), Ciftci; Arslan, Cofie; Yatabare, Fajr, Gradel (Oztekin 82); Kayode (Kone 82).

Thursday, 29 October 2020

Qarabag (0) 1 *(Kwabena 78)*

Villarreal (0) 3 *(Pino 80, Alcacer 84, 90 (pen))*

Qarabag: (4231) Mahammadaliyev; Huseynov A, Mammadov, Medina, Guerrier; Garayev, Andrade (Ibrahhimli 90); Romero (Matic 61), Ozobic (Emreli 61), Zoubir (Dzhafarquliyev 82); Kwabena (Bayramov 90).
Villarreal: (4141) Rulli; Pena, Foyth (Funes Mori 90), Torres, Pedraza; Iborra; Chukwueze (Baena 86), Trigueros, Jaume (Moi Gomez 74), Kubo (Alcacer 74); Bacca (Pino 74).

Sivasspor (0) 1 *(Kayode 55)*

Maccabi Tel Aviv (0) 2 *(Biton 68 (pen), Peretz 74)*

Sivasspor: (4231) Samassa; Yalcin, Osmanpasa, Camara■, Ciftci; Arslan, Claudemir (Kone 81); Yatabare, Fajr, Gradel (Ninga 78); Kayode (Cofie 75).
Maccabi Tel Aviv: (343) Daniel; Hernandez, Tibi, Yeini; Kandil (Golasa 65), Glazer D, Peretz (Saborit 90), Davidadze; Biton (Cohen 88), Shechter (Pesic 65), Rikan (Karzev 88).

Thursday, 5 November 2020

Sivasspor (1) 2 *(Osmanpasa 11, Kayode 88)*

Qarabag (0) 0

Sivasspor: (4231) Samassa; Marcelo Goiano, Yalcin, Osmanpasa, Ciftci; Arslan, Claudemir (Cofie 90); Yesilyurt (Gradel 59), Fajr, Ninga (Oztekin 67); Yatabare (Kayode 59).
Qarabag: (4231) Mahammadaliyev; Medvedev (Mammadov 85), Huseynov B (Huseynov A 61), Medina, Guerrier; Matic (Ibrahhimli 84), Garayev; Andrade (Emreli 46), Ozobic (Romero 62), Zoubir; Kwabena.

Villarreal (1) 4 *(Bacca 4, 52, Baena 71, Nino 81)*

Maccabi Tel Aviv (0) 0

Villarreal: (433) Rulli; Pena, Albiol, Funes Mori, Jaume (Moi Gomez 65); Baena (Gerard 74), Iborra (Trigueros 59), Parejo (Estupinan 59); Kubo, Bacca (Nino 74), Pino.
Maccabi Tel Aviv: (541) Daniel; Bitton, Hernandez, Tibi, Saborit, Baltaxa; Cohen (Shechter 68), Karzev (Golasa 61), Glazer D (Peretz 68), Ben Haim II (Biton 61); Blackman (Pesic 51).

Thursday, 26 November 2020

Maccabi Tel Aviv (0) 1 *(Pesic 47)*

Villarreal (1) 1 *(Baena 44)*

Maccabi Tel Aviv: (442) Daniel; Kandil, Tibi, Hernandez, Saborit■; Biton (Yeini 85), Glazer D (Blackman 54), Peretz, Cohen (Karzev 90); Golasa (Davidadze 90), Pesic (Rikan 85).
Villarreal: (4231) Rulli; Pena, Foyth, Funes Mori, Pedraza; Trigueros (Pino 63), Coquelin; Chukwueze (Parejo 63), Baena (Iborra 75), Kubo (Gerard 63); Bacca (Nino 63).

Qarabag (1) 2 *(Zoubir 8, Matic 51)*

Sivasspor (1) 3 *(Kone 40 (pen), 79, Kayode 58)*

Qarabag: (4231) Mahammadaliyev; Guerrier, Garayev, Medina, Dzhafarquliyev; Matic, Ibrahhimli; Bayramov (Romero 66), Kwabena, Zoubir; Emreli.
Sivasspor: (4231) Samassa; Marcelo Goiano, Appindangoye, Osmanpasa, Ciftci; Yalcin (Cofie 20), Claudemir; Oztekin (Camara 90), Gradel, Ninga (Kayode 57); Kone.

Thursday, 3 December 2020

Qarabag (1) 1 *(Romero 37)*

Maccabi Tel Aviv (1) 1 *(Cohen 22 (pen))*

Qarabag: (4231) Mahammadaliyev; Guerrier, Garayev, Medina, Dzhafarquliyev; Matic, Ibrahhimli; Romero (Bayramov 72), Ozobic (Mammadov 83), Zoubir; Kwabena.
Maccabi Tel Aviv: (343) Daniel; Hernandez, Tibi, Yeini; Kandil (Glazer D 69), Golasa (Shechter 83), Peretz (Ben Haim II 83), Davidadze; Biton, Blackman (Guerrero 65), Cohen.

Sivasspor (0) 0

Villarreal (0) 1 *(Chukwueze 75)*

Sivasspor: (4231) Samassa; Osmanpasa, Appindangoye, Camara, Erdal; Cofie (Claudemir 82), Fajr; Oztekin, Yalcin (Kone 77), Gradel; Yatabare (Ninga 80).
Villarreal: (4141) Rulli; Pena, Foyth, Funes Mori, Jaume (Estupinan 77); Iborra; Kubo (Pino 58), Coquelin (Trigueros 68), Baena (Parejo 68), Chukwueze (Gerard 76); Nino.

Thursday, 10 December 2020

Maccabi Tel Aviv (0) 1 *(Saborit 66)*

Sivasspor (0) 0

Maccabi Tel Aviv: (4231) Daniel; Kandil, Hernandez, Tibi, Saborit (Yeini 85); Peretz, Glazer; Biton (Davidadze 63), Golasa (Ben Haim II 74), Cohen (Rikan 74); Pesic (Blackman 85).
Sivasspor: (4141) Samassa; Yalcin, Appindangoye, Osmanpasa, Camara; Claudemir (Kone 63); Yatabare, Arslan, Fajr, Gradel; Kayode.

Villarreal 3

Qarabag 0

Match awarded 3-0 to Villarreal due to Qarabag being unable to fulfil the fixtures after several of their players testing positive for COVID-19.

Group I Table	P	W	D	L	F	A	GD	Pts
Villarreal	6	5	1	0	17	5	12	16
Maccabi Tel Aviv	6	3	2	1	6	7	−1	11
Sivasspor	6	2	0	4	9	11	−2	6
Qarabag	6	0	1	5	4	13	−9	1

GROUP J

Thursday, 22 October 2020

Ludogorets Razgrad (0) 1 *(Marin 46)*

Antwerp (0) 2 *(Gerkens 63, Refaelov 70)* 2321

Ludogorets Razgrad: (433) Iliev; Cicinho, Terziev, Verdon, Nedyalkov; Badji (Abel 83), Santana, Yankov (Tekpetey 77); Despodov (Manu 45), Marin, Cauly (Keseru 78).
Antwerp: (352) Butez; Batubinsika, Gelin, De Laet; Miyoshi, Gerkens, Haroun, Hongla (Verstraete 80), Juklerod; Benavente (Ampomah 59), Refaelov (Buta 72).

Tottenham H (2) 3 *(Lucas Moura 18, Andrade 27 (og), Son 84)*

LASK (0) 0

Tottenham H: (4231) Hart; Doherty, Sanchez, Davies, Reguilon; Hojbjerg (Sissoko 62), Winks; Bale (Son 62), Lamela (Alli 62), Lucas Moura (Lo Celso 78); Vinicius (Clarke 86).
LASK: (343) Schlager; Wiesinger, Trauner, Andrade (Potzmann 46); Ranftl, Holland (Grgic 5), Michorl, Renner (Filipovic 39); Gruber (Eggestein 46), Raguz, Balic (Goiginger 78).

Thursday, 29 October 2020

Antwerp (1) 1 *(Refaelov 29)*

Tottenham H (0) 0

Antwerp: (352) Butez; Seck, Gelin, De Laet; Miyoshi (Buta 58), Gerkens, Haroun, Hongla (Verstraete 70), Juklerod; Mbokani, Refaelov (Benavente 88).
Tottenham H: (4231) Lloris; Aurier, Sanchez, Davies, Reguilon; Lo Celso (Hojbjerg 46), Winks; Bale (Kane 58), Alli (Lamela 46), Bergwijn (Lucas Moura 46); Vinicius (Son 46).

LASK (3) 4 *(Balic 2, Gruber 11, Raguz 34, Verdon 55 (og))*

Ludogorets Razgrad (1) 3 *(Manu 15, 67, 73 (pen))* 1500

LASK: (343) Schlager; Wiesinger, Trauner, Filipovic; Ranftl, Grgic■, Michorl, Andrade; Gruber (Goiginger 63), Raguz, Balic (Eggestein 63).
Ludogorets Razgrad: (433) Iliev; Cicinho, Moti, Verdon, Nedyalkov; Abel, Badji (Cauly 53), Santana; Tekpetey (Ikoko 88), Manu, Yankov (Tchibota 80).

Thursday, 5 November 2020

Antwerp (0) 0

LASK (0) 1 *(Eggestein 54)*

Antwerp: (352) Butez; Seck, Hongla, De Laet; Miyoshi (Buta 64), Gerkens, Haroun (Boya 87), Verstraete (Ampomah 64), Juklerod (Benavente 75); Mbokani, Refaelov (Lukaku 87).
LASK: (343) Schlager; Wiesinger, Trauner, Filipovic; Ranftl, Holland■, Michorl, Renner; Gruber (Goiginger 66), Raguz (Eggestein 40), Balic.

Ludogorets Razgrad (0) 1 *(Keseru 50)*

Tottenham H (2) 3 *(Kane 13, Lucas Moura 32, Lo Celso 62)*

Ludogorets Razgrad: (442) Iliev; Ikoko, Terziev, Verdon, Nedyalkov; Cauly, Abel (Santana 59), Badji (Yordanov 90), Yankov (Tchibota 75); Manu (Tekpetey 46), Keseru (Mitkov 59).
Tottenham H: (4231) Hart; Doherty, Alderweireld, Dier, Davies; Sissoko (Hojbjerg 46), Winks; Bale (Bergwijn 65), Lo Celso (Ndombele 72), Lucas Moura (Son 61); Kane (Vinicius 46).

Thursday, 26 November 2020

LASK (0) 0

Antwerp (0) 2 *(Refaelov 52, Gerkens 83)*

LASK: (343) Schlager; Wiesinger, Trauner■, Filipovic (Potzmann 73); Ranftl, Madsen (Andrade 53), Michorl, Renner; Gruber (Goiginger 60), Balic, Eggestein.
Antwerp: (343) Butez; Seck, Batubinsika, De Laet; Miyoshi (Lukaku 81), Haroun, Hongla, Juklerod (Buta 81); Gerkens, Benavente (Ampomah 67), Refaelov (Benson 88).

Tottenham H (2) 4 *(Vinicius 16, 34, Winks 63, Lucas Moura 73)*

Ludogorets Razgrad (0) 0

Tottenham H: (4231) Hart (Whiteman 82); Doherty, Sanchez, Tanganga, Davies; Ndombele (Hojbjerg 61), Winks; Bale (Clarke 68), Alli (White 82), Lucas Moura (Scarlett 82); Vinicius.
Ludogorets Razgrad: (541) Iliev; Ikoko, Verdon, Moti, Grigore, Nedyalkov; Despodov (Tekpetey 64), Abel (Cauly 68), Badji (Yordanov 89), Yankov (Mitkov 90); Keseru (Tchibota 68).

Thursday, 3 December 2020

Antwerp (1) 3 *(Hongla 19, De Laet 72, Benson 87)*

Ludogorets Razgrad (0) 1 *(Despodov 53)*

Antwerp: (3421) Butez; Seck, Gelin, De Laet; Miyoshi, Haroun, Hongla (Boya 77), Juklerod (Benson 64); Gerkens (Mbokani 84), Refaelov (Buta 77); Benavente (Ampomah 64).
Ludogorets Razgrad: (4231) Stoyanov; Ikoko (Terziev 44), Verdon, Grigore■, Nedyalkov; Abel, Badji (Santana 83); Despodov (Mitkov 83), Cauly, Tchibota (Tekpetey 67); Keseru (Manu 67).

LASK (1) 3 *(Michorl 42, Eggestein 84, Karamoko 90)*

Tottenham H (1) 3 *(Bale 45 (pen), Son 56, Alli 86 (pen))*

LASK: (343) Schlager; Wiesinger, Holland, Andrade; Ranftl, Madsen, Michorl, Renner; Gruber (Reiter 69), Eggestein, Goiginger (Karamoko 69).
Tottenham H: (4231) Hart; Doherty, Sanchez, Tanganga, Davies; Lo Celso (Dier 71), Hojbjerg; Bale (Aurier 82), Ndombele (Bergwijn 65), Lucas Moura (Sissoko 65); Son (Alli 82).

Thursday, 10 December 2020

Ludogorets Razgrad (0) 1 *(Manu 46)*

LASK (0) 3 *(Wiesinger 56, Renner 61 (pen), Madsen 67)*

Ludogorets Razgrad: (4231) Iliev; Cicinho, Josue Sa, Verdon, Ikoko (Terziev 70); Badji (Abel 77), Santana■; Despodov, Cauly (Yankov 77), Tchibota (Manu 46); Keseru (Tekpetey 77).
LASK: (343) Schlager; Wiesinger (Ramsebner 86), Andrade, Cheberko; Ranftl (Potzmann 74), Madsen, Holland, Renner; Reiter (Gruber 63), Eggestein (Plojer 73), Goiginger (Balic 62).

Tottenham H (0) 2 *(Vinicius 57, Lo Celso 71)*

Antwerp (0) 0 2000

Tottenham H: (343) Hart; Tanganga, Sanchez, Davies; Doherty, Winks (Ndombele 58), Lo Celso, Reguilon (Bergwijn 46); Bale (Son 58), Vinicius (Kane 59), Lucas Moura (Sissoko 68).
Antwerp: (541) Beiranvand; Buta, Seck (Verstraete 72), Gelin, Batubinsika, Lukaku (Juklerod 59); Benson (Miyoshi 72), Haroun, Hongla (Boya 58), Refaelov (Ampomah 46); Benavente.

Group J Table	*P*	*W*	*D*	*L*	*F*	*A*	*GD*	*Pts*
Tottenham H	6	4	1	1	15	5	10	13
Antwerp	6	4	0	2	8	5	3	12
LASK	6	3	1	2	11	12	–1	10
Ludogorets Razgrad	6	0	0	6	7	19	–12	0

GROUP K

Thursday, 22 October 2020

Dinamo Zagreb (0) 0

Feyenoord (0) 0 1271

Dinamo Zagreb: (4231) Livakovic; Stojanovic, Theophile-Catherine, Lauritsen, Gvardiol; Ademi, Jakic (Franjic 71); Kastrati (Ivanusec 54), Majer, Orsic; Gavranovic (Petkovic 54).
Feyenoord: (433) Bijlow; Nieuwkoop, Spajic, Senesi■, Haps; Teixeira, Toornstra, Kokcu (Botteghin 74); Berghuis, Linssen, Diemers (Jorgensen 81).

Wolfsberg (1) 1 *(Liendl 42 (pen))*

CSKA Moscow (1) 1 *(Gaich 5)* 3000

Wolfsberg: (4132) Kofler; Novak, Baumgartner, Lochoshvili, Scherzer (Pavelic 84); Leitgeb; Taferner, Liendl, Wernitznig (Peretz 73); Joveljic, Dieng (Schmerbock 78).
CSKA Moscow: (4231) Akinfeev; Vasin (Dzagoev 46), Diveev, Magnusson, Zaynutdinov; Maradishvili, Oblyakov; Kuchaev (Akhmetov 76), Vlasic (Bistrovic 86), Tiknizyan (Ejuke 46); Gaich (Chalov 61).

Thursday, 29 October 2020

CSKA Moscow (0) 0

Dinamo Zagreb (0) 0

CSKA Moscow: (4231) Akinfeev; Fernandes (Bistrovic 84), Diveev, Magnusson, Zaynutdinov; Maradishvili, Oblyakov (Dzagoev 80); Kuchaev (Akhmetov 80), Vlasic, Ejuke (Sigurdsson 75); Chalov (Gaich 74).
Dinamo Zagreb: (4141) Livakovic; Stojanovic, Lauritsen, Peric (Kastrati 81), Gvardiol; Franjic; Majer, Ivanusec (Jakic 66), Ademi, Orsic (Moharrami 90); Petkovic (Gavranovic 65).

Feyenoord (0) 1 *(Berghuis 53)*

Wolfsberg (2) 4 *(Liendl 4 (pen), 13 (pen), 60, Joveljic 66 (pen))*

Feyenoord: (41212) Bijlow; Nieuwkoop (Narsingh 46), Botteghin, Spajic, Haps; Geertruida; Toornstra, Kokcu; Diemers; Berghuis, Linssen (Bannis 76).
Wolfsberg: (4132) Kofler; Novak, Lochoshvili, Baumgartner, Scherzer; Leitgeb; Taferner (Stratznig 60), Liendl, Wernitznig (Peretz 82); Dieng (Vizinger 82), Joveljic (Rnic 67).

Thursday, 5 November 2020

Dinamo Zagreb (0) 1 *(Atiemwen 76)*

Wolfsberg (0) 0

Dinamo Zagreb: (433) Zagorac; Moharrami (Atiemwen 74), Lauritsen, Peric (Leovac 15), Gvardiol; Jakic (Kastrati 46), Franjic, Ademi; Majer, Gavranovic (Burton 90), Orsic.
Wolfsberg: (41212) Kofler; Novak, Baumgartner, Lochoshvili, Pavelic (Hodzic 81); Stratznig; Wernitznig, Taferner■; Peretz (Schmerbock 80); Dieng (Vizinger 54), Joveljic (Peric 46).

Feyenoord (0) 3 *(Haps 63, Kokcu 71, Geertruida 72)*

CSKA Moscow (0) 1 *(Senesi 79 (og))*

Feyenoord: (433) Bijlow; Geertruida, Spajic, Senesi, Malacia; Diemers, Toornstra, Kokcu (Teixeira 76); Berghuis, Linssen, Haps.
CSKA Moscow: (4231) Akinfeev; Fernandes (Dzagoev 31), Diveev, Magnusson (Vasin 77), Zaynutdinov; Maradishvili, Oblyakov (Bistrovic 77); Kuchaev (Chalov 68), Vlasic, Ejuke (Tiknizyan 76); Sigurdsson.

Thursday, 26 November 2020

CSKA Moscow (0) 0

Feyenoord (0) 0

CSKA Moscow: (4231) Akinfeev; Zaynutdinov, Diveev, Magnusson, Schennikov (Akhmetov 64); Maradishvili, Oblyakov (Bistrovic 71); Sigurdsson (Shkurin 63), Vlasic, Ejuke (Gaich 81); Chalov (Tiknizyan 80).
Feyenoord: (433) Marsman; Nieuwkoop, Spajic, Senesi, Geertruida; Diemers, Toornstra (Wehrmann 71), Kokcu; Berghuis (Botteghin 82), Jorgensen■, Linssen.

Wolfsberg (0) 0

Dinamo Zagreb (0) 3 *(Majer 60, Petkovic 75, Ivanusec 90)*

Wolfsberg: (4132) Kuttin; Novak, Baumgartner (Rnic 46), Lochoshvili, Scherzer (Giorbelidze 82); Leitgeb; Stratznig (Sprangler 72), Liendl, Wernitznig (Joveljic 66); Vizinger (Schmerbock 82), Peretz.
Dinamo Zagreb: (4141) Livakovic; Moharrami, Lauritsen, Theophile-Catherine, Gvardiol; Jakic (Tolic 83); Kastrati, Majer (Franjic 74), Ademi (Burton 90), Orsic (Ivanusec 74); Petkovic.

Thursday, 3 December 2020

CSKA Moscow (0) 0

Wolfsberg (1) 1 *(Vizinger 22)*

CSKA Moscow: (4231) Akinfeev; Maradishvili, Diveev, Magnusson, Schennikov (Tiknizyan 63); Oblyakov (Sigurdsson 76), Akhmetov (Bistrovic 64); Kuchaev (Ejuke 46), Vlasic, Zaynutdinov; Chalov (Gaich 46).
Wolfsberg: (4132) Kofler; Novak, Baumgartner, Lochoshvili, Scherzer; Leitgeb; Taferner (Stratznig 61), Liendl (Wernitznig 81), Sprangler (Rnic 82); Peretz, Vizinger (Joveljic 70).

Feyenoord (0) 0

Dinamo Zagreb (1) 2 *(Petkovic 45 (pen), Majer 52)*

Feyenoord: (433) Marsman; Geertruida, Spajic (Botteghin 46), Senesi, Malacia; Diemers (Teixeira 69), Toornstra, Kokcu; Berghuis, Linssen (Bannis 36), Narsingh.
Dinamo Zagreb: (4231) Livakovic; Moharrami, Lauritsen, Theophile-Catherine, Gvardiol; Ademi, Jakic; Kastrati (Peric 88), Majer (Franjic 65), Ivanusec (Orsic 72); Petkovic (Tolic 88).

Thursday, 10 December 2020

Dinamo Zagreb (2) 3 *(Gvardiol 28, Orsic 41, Kastrati 75)*

CSKA Moscow (0) 1 *(Bistrovic 76)*

Dinamo Zagreb: (4231) Livakovic; Moharrami, Theophile-Catherine, Gvardiol, Leovac (Peric 20); Jakic, Ademi (Franjic 35); Kastrati, Majer (Tolic 78), Orsic (Cuze 78); Gavranovic (Atiemwen 78).
CSKA Moscow: (4231) Akinfeev; Maradishvili, Diveev (Karpov 78), Vasin, Schennikov (Gaich 71); Bistrovic, Oblyakov; Zaynutdinov, Akhmetov (Tiknizyan 63), Sigurdsson; Shkurin (Chalov 63).

Wolfsberg (1) 1 *(Joveljic 31)*

Feyenoord (0) 0

Wolfsberg: (4132) Kofler; Novak, Baumgartner, Lochoshvili, Scherzer; Leitgeb; Taferner (Rnic 68), Liendl, Sprangler; Vizinger (Stratznig 83), Joveljic (Peretz 56).
Feyenoord: (433) Marsman; Geertruida, Spajic (Teixeira 72), Senesi, Malacia (Bannis 79); Diemers, Toornstra, Kokcu; Berghuis, Jorgensen, Linssen (Sinisterra 72).

Group K Table	P	W	D	L	F	A	GD	Pts
Dinamo Zagreb	6	4	2	0	9	1	8	14
Wolfsberg	6	3	1	2	7	6	1	10
Feyenoord	6	1	2	3	4	8	–4	5
CSKA Moscow	6	0	3	3	3	8	–5	3

GROUP L

Thursday, 22 October 2020

Hoffenheim (0) 2 *(Baumgartner 64, Dabbur 90)*

Red Star Belgrade (0) 0

Hoffenheim: (41212) Baumann; Posch, Vogt, Akpoguma, Sessegnon (Skov 90); Grillitsch (Samassekou 46); Rudy, Gacinovic (Geiger 46); Baumgartner (Bebou 78); Belfodil (Bruun Larsen 78), Dabbur.
Red Star Belgrade: (3421) Borjan; Erakovic, Milunovic, Degenek; Gajic (Simic 85), Sanogo (Petrovic 76), Nikolic, Rodic; Spiridonovic (Ben 76), Katai (Vukanovic 75); Falcinelli (Pavkov 85).

Slovan Liberec (1) 1 *(Yusuf 29)*

Gent (0) 0

Slovan Liberec: (442) Nguyen; Koscelnik, Jugas, Tijani, Mikula; Pesek (Matousek 68), Hromada (Chalus 79), Mara, Mosquera; Beran (Sadilek 57), Yusuf (Rabusic 58).
Gent: (4132) Roef; Castro-Montes, Ngadeu Ngadjui, Hanche-Olsen, Nurio Fortuna (Plastun 87); Marreh; Bukari, Kums, Botaka (Niangbo 77); Yaremchuk, Kleindienst (Depoitre 76).

Thursday, 29 October 2020

Gent (0) 1 *(Kleindienst 90)*

Hoffenheim (1) 4 *(Belfodil 35 (pen), Grillitsch 52, Gacinovic 73, Dabbur 90)*

Gent: (3412) Roef; Hanche-Olsen, Ngadeu Ngadjui, Nurio Fortuna; Castro-Montes (Marreh 77), Kums (Kleindienst 69), Dorsch (Botaka 77), Mohammadi; Bezus (Odjidja-Ofoe 56); Bukari, Yaremchuk (Niangbo 69).
Hoffenheim: (352) Baumann; Posch (Dabbur 82), Vogt, Akpoguma; Skov, Samassekou, Grillitsch (Baumgartner 77), Rudy (Gacinovic 67), Sessegnon; Bebou (Adamyan 67), Belfodil (Klauss 77).

Red Star Belgrade (2) 5 *(Ben 7, 22, Gajic 50, Katai 67, Falcinelli 69)*

Slovan Liberec (1) 1 *(Matousek 41)*

Red Star Belgrade: (4231) Borjan; Gajic, Degenek, Milunovic, Rodic (Gobeljic 75); Nikolic, Sanogo; Ben (Petrovic 83), Ivanic (Gavric 83), Katai (Vukanovic 88); Falcinelli (Pankov 88).
Slovan Liberec: (451) Nguyen; Koscelnik, Chalus, Tijani, Mikula; Matousek (Beran 75), Mara (Barac 90), Hromada (Sulc 86), Sadilek, Mosquera (Fukala 90); Yusuf (Rabusic 75).

Thursday, 5 November 2020

Hoffenheim (2) 5 *(Dabbur 22, 29, Grillitsch 59, Adamyan 71, 76)*

Slovan Liberec (0) 0

Hoffenheim: (532) Baumann; Bebou, Bogarde, Vogt (Grillitsch 46), Akpoguma (Nordtveit 60), Skov; Gacinovic, Rudy (Samassekou 46), Baumgartner (Belfodil 73); Klauss, Dabbur (Adamyan 61).
Slovan Liberec: (541) Hasalik; Koscelnik, Mikula, Kacharaba, Pourzitidis, Kosek (Kazda 90); Cancola (Dvorak 90), Nesicky (Cernicky 90), Hromada (Michal 77), Mara; Rondic (Csano 67).

Red Star Belgrade (1) 2 *(Kanga 12, Katai 59)*

Gent (1) 1 *(Odjidja-Ofoe 31)*

Red Star Belgrade: (4231) Borjan; Gajic, Degenek, Milunovic, Gobeljic; Ivanic (Petrovic 64), Sanogo; Ben (Spiridonovic 90), Kanga (Pankov 83), Katai (Nikolic 90); Falcinelli.
Gent: (4231) Coosemans; Castro-Montes, Marreh, Hanche-Olsen, Mohammadi; Dorsch, Owusu (Kums 75); Bukari, Odjidja-Ofoe (Kleindienst 80), Botaka (Niangbo 63); Yaremchuk.

Thursday, 26 November 2020

Gent (0) 0

Red Star Belgrade (1) 2 *(Petrovic 1, Milunovic 58)*

Gent: (352) Bolat; Hanche-Olsen, Ngadeu Ngadjui, Nurio Fortuna; Botaka (Castro-Montes 46), Dorsch, Owusu (Odjidja-Ofoe 58), Kums (George 84), Mohammadi; Bukari (Niangbo 66), Bezus.
Red Star Belgrade: (532) Borjan; Gajic, Pankov, Milunovic, Degenek, Vukanovic (Radulovic 87); Nikolic, Petrovic (Erakovic 72), Ivanic; Ben (Spiridonovic 72), Falcinelli (Boakye 87).

Slovan Liberec (0) 0

Hoffenheim (0) 2 *(Baumgartner 77, Kramaric 89 (pen))*

Slovan Liberec: (541) Nguyen; Koscelnik, Kacharaba, Jugas, Chalus (Rondic 83), Mikula; Pesek (Matousek 83), Mara (Beran 89), Sadilek, Mosquera; Yusuf (Rabusic 70).
Hoffenheim: (41212) Baumann; Bogarde, Nuhu, Nordtveit, Sessegnon (Skov 46); Rudy (Bebou 61); Gacinovic, Baumgartner (Geiger 78); Grillitsch (Samassekou 78); Beier (Kramaric 60), Klauss.

Thursday, 3 December 2020

Gent (0) 1 *(Yaremchuk 59)*

Slovan Liberec (1) 2 *(Mara 32, Kacharaba 55)*

Gent: (3511) Bolat; Hanche-Olsen, Arslanagic, Nurio Fortuna; Castro-Montes (Kleindienst 56), Dorsch, Owusu (Bezus 62), Kums, Mohammadi; Bukari; Yaremchuk.
Slovan Liberec: (442) Nguyen; Koscelnik, Kacharaba, Jugas, Mikula; Pesek (Matousek 75), Sadilek, Mara, Beran (Hromada 68); Yusuf (Rabusic 86), Mosquera.

Red Star Belgrade (0) 0

Hoffenheim (0) 0

Red Star Belgrade: (532) Borjan; Gajic, Milunovic, Pankov, Degenek, Ben (Erakovic 81); Petrovic, Sanogo, Kanga (Nikolic 81); Spiridonovic (Vukanovic 46), Falcinelli (Boakye 89).
Hoffenheim: (3421) Baumann; Bogarde, Vogt, Nordtveit; Skov (Sessegnon 89), Geiger (Grillitsch 58), Rudy (Nuhu 72), John; Gacinovic (Baumgartner 72), Dabbur (Kramaric 46); Klauss.

Thursday, 10 December 2020

Hoffenheim (2) 4 *(Beier 21, 49, Skov 26, Kramaric 64)*

Gent (0) 1 *(Nurio Fortuna 81)*

Hoffenheim: (4231) Pentke; Posch (Nordtveit 46), Nuhu, Akpoguma, John; Gacinovic, Geiger (Amade 75); Skov (Belfodil 61), Dabbur, Beier (Baumgartner 75); Klauss (Kramaric 62).
Gent: (352) Roef; Arslanagic, Plastun, Ngadeu Ngadjui; Castro-Montes (Botaka 76), Dorsch (Kums 56), Bezus, Owusu (Odjidja-Ofoe 56), Mohammadi (Nurio Fortuna 46); Bukari (Yaremchuk 56), Kleindienst.

Slovan Liberec (0) 0

Red Star Belgrade (0) 0

Slovan Liberec: (4411) Knobloch; Koscelnik, Kacharaba, Jugas, Mikula; Pesek (Matousek 68), Sadilek, Mara, Mosquera (Fukala 89); Beran (Hromada 68); Yusuf (Rabusic 75).
Red Star Belgrade: (352) Borjan; Milunovic, Degenek (Pankov 80), Rodic (Gobeljic 71); Gajic, Petrovic, Sanogo, Kanga (Nikolic 53), Ivanic (Boakye 71); Ben (Erakovic 81), Falcinelli.

Group L Table	P	W	D	L	F	A	GD	Pts
Hoffenheim	6	5	1	0	17	2	15	16
Red Star Belgrade	6	3	2	1	9	4	5	11
Slovan Liberec	6	2	1	3	4	13	–9	7
Gent	6	0	0	6	4	15	–11	0

KNOCK-OUT STAGE

ROUND OF 32 FIRST LEG

Thursday, 18 February 2021

Antwerp (2) 3 *(Refaelov 45 (pen), Avenatti 45, Hongla 66)*

Rangers (1) 4 *(Aribo 38, Barisic 59 (pen), 90 (pen), Kent 83)*

Antwerp: (3511) Beiranvand (De Wolf 77); Seck■, Le Marchand, De Laet; Buta, Gerkens (Miyoshi 90), Hongla (Gelin 90), Boya (Verstraete 69), Lukaku; Refaelov (Ampomah 90); Avenatti.
Rangers: (433) McGregor; Tavernier (Balogun 24), Goldson, Helander, Barisic; Arfield (Jack 74), Davis, Kamara (Hagi 74); Aribo, Morelos, Roofe (Kent 45).

Benfica (0) 1 *(Pizzi 55 (pen))*

Arsenal (0) 1 *(Saka 57)*

Benfica: (352) Helton Leite; Lucas Verissimo (Chiquinho 85), Otamendi, Vertonghen; Goncalves, Pizzi (Everton 64), Weigl, Taarabt (Pires 77), Grimaldo; Waldschmidt (Rafa Silva 46), Nunez (Seferovic 64).
Arsenal: (4231) Leno; Bellerin, Luiz, Gabriel, Cedric (Tierney 64); Ceballos (Elneny 90), Xhaka; Saka, Odegaard (Willian 90), Smith-Rowe (Martinelli 77); Aubameyang (Pepe 77).

Braga (0) 0

Roma (1) 2 *(Dzeko 5, Borja Mayoral 86)*

Braga: (4141) Matheus Magalhaes; Ricardo Esgaio■, Vitor Tormena, Raul Silva, Nuno Sequeira; Al Musrati; Ricardo Horta (Piazon 62), Fransergio (Andre Horta 71), Gaitan (Ze Carlos 57), Galeno (Borja 70); Sporar (Ruiz 62).
Roma: (3421) Pau Lopez; Mancini, Cristante (Bruno Peres 7), Ibanez (Villar 53); Karsdorp, Diawara, Veretout, Spinazzola; Pedro (El Shaarawy 71), Mkhitaryan; Dzeko (Borja Mayoral 70).

Dynamo Kyiv (0) 1 *(Buyalsky 62)*

Club Brugge (0) 1 *(Mechele 67)*

Dynamo Kyiv: (4231) Bushchan; Kedziora (Karavayev 81), Zabarnyi, Popov, Mykolenko; Sydorchuk, Shaparenko (Shepelev 73); Tsygankov, Buyalsky, De Pena (Rodrigues 72); Biesiedin (Supriaga 81).
Club Brugge: (4321) Mignolet; Mata, Kossounou, Mechele, Ricca; Dirar (van der Brempt 70), Vormer, Balanta; De Ketelaere, Okereke (Badji 69); Dost (De Cuyper 90).

Granada (2) 2 *(Herrera 19, Kenedy 21)*

Napoli (0) 0

Granada: (433) Rui Silva; Foulquier, Domingos Duarte, Vallejo (German 23), Neva (Victor Diaz 78); Herrera, Gonalons (Brice 78), Montoro; Kenedy (Soro 70), Jorge Molina, Machis (Puertas 70).
Napoli: (433) Meret; Di Lorenzo, Rrahmani, Maksimovic, Mario Rui; Fabian, Lobotka (Bakayoko 64), Elmas; Politano (Zielinski 46), Osimhen, Insigne.

Krasnodar (1) 2 *(Berg 28, Claesson 69)*

Dinamo Zagreb (1) 3 *(Petkovic 15, 54, Atiemwen 75)*

Krasnodar: (442) Gorodov; Smolnikov, Martynovich, Kaio, Chernov (Ionov 80); Suleymanov (Wanderson 46), Olsson (Gazinsky 62), Vilhena, Claesson; Berg, Cabella.
Dinamo Zagreb: (4321) Livakovic; Ristovski, Lauritsen, Theophile-Catherine, Gvardiol; Ivanusec (Franjic 78), Jakic, Orsic (Misic 90); Majer (Atiemwen 64), Ademi; Petkovic.

Lille (0) 1 *(Weah 72)*

Ajax (0) 2 *(Tadic 87 (pen), Brobbey 89)*

Lille: (442) Maignan; Celik, Fonte, Botman, Mandava (Bradaric 82); Weah, Sanches, Soumare, Bamba; Yazici (Luiz Araujo 62), David (Ikone 78).
Ajax: (4231) Stekelenburg; Rensch (Schuurs 82), Timber, Martinez, Tagliafico; Alvarez, Blind; Antony (Idrissi 82), Klaassen, Neres (Brobbey 74); Tadic.

Maccabi Tel Aviv (0) 0

Shakhtar Donetsk (1) 2 *(Alan Patrick 31, Tete 90)*

Maccabi Tel Aviv: (4231) Daniel; Andre Geraldes, Hernandez, Tibi, Saborit; Glazer D, Peretz; Biton (Hozez 46), Rikan (Golasa 63), Ben Haim II (Blackman 63); Pesic (Guerrero 84).
Shakhtar Donetsk: (433) Trubin; Dodo, Kryvtsov, Vitao, Matviyenko; Marlos (Maycon 77), Stepanenko, Alan Patrick (Marcos Antonio 88); Taison (Konoplyanka 77), Moraes (Fernando 89), Solomon (Tete 73).

Molde (1) 3 *(Ellingsen 41, Andersen 70, Fofana 74)*

Hoffenheim (3) 3 *(Dabbur 8, 28, Baumgartner 45)*

Molde: (442) Linde; Pedersen, Bjornbak, Gregersen, Haugen; Bolly (Knudtzon 64), Aursnes, Ellingsen, Andersen (Christensen 86); Sigurdarson (Fofana 64), Eikrem.
Hoffenheim: (3412) Baumann; Nuhu (Bogarde 83), Vogt, Richards; Gacinovic (Kaderabek 26), Rudy, Samassekou (Grillitsch 62), John; Baumgartner; Bebou (Adamyan 62), Dabbur (Rutter 83).

Olympiacos (3) 4 *(Bouchalakis 9, M'Vila 37, El Arabi 45, Masouras 83)*

PSV Eindhoven (2) 2 *(Zahavi 14, 39)*

Olympiacos: (4231) Jose Sa; Lala (Androutsos 80), Papastathopoulos, Ba, Reabciuk; M'Vila (Vrousai 80), Bouchalakis; Valbuena (Masouras 68), Camara, Bruma (Kouka 80); El Arabi (Fortounis 75).
PSV Eindhoven: (4222) Mvogo; Dumfries, Teze, Boscagli (Baumgartl 38), Max; Rosario, Sangare (Vertessen 70); Gotze (Junior 70), Thomas (van Ginkel 85); Zahavi (Gutierrez 85), Malen.

Real Sociedad (0) 0

Manchester U (1) 4 *(Bruno Fernandes 27, 57, Rashford 64, James 90)*

Real Sociedad: (433) Remiro; Zaldua (Gorosabel 73), Zubeldia, Le Normand, Monreal; Silva, Illarramendi (Guevara 73), Merino; Januzaj (Portu 80), Isak (Barrenetxea 80), Oyarzabal (Bautista 86).
Manchester U: (4231) Henderson; Wan Bissaka, Bailly, Maguire, Alex Telles; McTominay (Matic 60), Fred; James, Bruno Fernandes (Mata 83), Rashford (Martial 68); Greenwood (Diallo 83).

Red Bull Salzburg (0) 0

Villarreal (1) 2 *(Alcacer 41, Nino 71)*

Red Bull Salzburg: (442) Stankovic; Kristensen, Solet, Vallci, Ulmer; Aaronson (Adeyemi 61), Mwepu, Junuzovic (Bernede 74), Sucic (Okafor 61); Berisha, Daka.
Villarreal: (442) Rulli; Pena (Foyth 46), Albiol, Torres, Estupinan; Trigueros, Capoue (Jaume 74), Parejo, Moi Gomez (Pedraza 60); Gerard (Pino 84), Alcacer (Nino 60).

Red Star Belgrade (0) 2 *(Kanga 52 (pen), Pavkov 90)*

AC Milan (1) 2 *(Pankov 42 (og), Hernandez 61 (pen))*

Red Star Belgrade: (3412) Borjan; Pankov, Milunovic, Degenek; Gobeljic (Gajic 74), Kanga, Petrovic (Sanogo 81), Rodic■; Ivanic (Bakayoko 80); Ben (Falco 62), Falcinelli (Pavkov 80).
AC Milan: (433) Donnarumma; Kalulu Kyatengwa, Tomori, Romagnoli, Hernandez (Dalot 77); Krunic, Bennacer (Tonali 39), Meite; Castillejo, Mandzukic (Calhanoglu 82), Rebic (Leao 46).

Slavia Prague (0) 0

Leicester C (0) 0

Slavia Prague: (4141) Kolar; Bah, Kudela, Zima, Boril; Holes (Hromada 30); Sima, Provod (Lingr 90), Stanciu (Traore 73), Olayinka; Kuchta (Masopust 73).
Leicester C: (4231) Schmeichel; Amartey, Evans, Soyuncu, Thomas; Tielemans, Ndidi; Albrighton (Under 64), Maddison (Choudhury 76), Barnes; Vardy (Iheanacho 64).

Wolfsberg (0) 1 *(Liendl 55 (pen))*

Tottenham H (3) 4 *(Son 13, Bale 28, Lucas Moura 34, Vinicius 88)*

Wolfsberg: (4132) Kofler; Novak (Pavelic 81), Baumgartner, Lochoshvili, Scherzer; Sprangler (Giorbelidze 65); Taferner (Henriksson 46), Liendl, Wernitznig; Joveljic (Dieng 65), Vizinger (Stratznig 46).
Tottenham H: (4231) Lloris; Doherty, Alderweireld, Dier, Davies; Sissoko (Hojbjerg 78), Winks; Bale (Lamela 64), Alli (Ndombele 78), Lucas Moura (Bergwijn 64); Son (Vinicius 46).

Young Boys (3) 4 *(Fassnacht 3, Siebatcheu 19, 89, Elia 44)*

Bayer Leverkusen (0) 3 *(Schick 49, 52, Diaby 68)*

Young Boys: (442) Ballmoos; Hefti, Lustenberger, Zesiger, Lefort (Sulejmani 74); Fassnacht (Gaudino 80), Aebischer, Lauper (Rieder 81), Ngamaleu (Garcia 58); Elia (Mambimbi 74), Siebatcheu.
Bayer Leverkusen: (433) Lomb; Frimpong, Tah, Dragovic, Sinkgraven; Wirtz, Demirbay, Amiri (Tapsoba 46); Bailey (Diaby 65), Schick, Gray.

ROUND OF 32 SECOND LEG

Wednesday, 24 February 2021

Tottenham H (1) 4 *(Alli 10, Vinicius 50, 83, Bale 73)*

Wolfsberg (0) 0

Tottenham H: (4231) Hart; Doherty (Lavinier 74), Alderweireld, Dier, Davies; Sissoko (John 81), Winks; Lamela (Bale 68), Alli (Scarlett 81), Bergwijn (Lucas Moura 69); Vinicius.
Wolfsberg: (3412) Kuttin; Henriksson, Baumgartner (Giorbelidze 65), Lochoshvili; Novak (Pavelic 46), Stratznig (Rnic 79), Wernitznig, Scherzer (Peric 65); Liendl; Dieng, Vizinger (Joveljic 46).
Tottenham H won 8-1 on aggregate.

Thursday, 25 February 2021

AC Milan (1) 1 *(Kessie 9 (pen))*

Red Star Belgrade (1) 1 *(Ben 24)*

AC Milan: (4231) Donnarumma; Calabria (Hernandez 66), Tomori, Romagnoli, Dalot; Meite, Kessie; Castillejo (Saelemaekers 66), Krunic (Rebic 46), Calhanoglu; Leao (Ibrahimovic 46).
Red Star Belgrade: (4231) Borjan; Gajic, Pankov, Degenek, Gobeljic■; Sanogo, Srnic (Petrovic 46); Ben (Falco 69), Kanga (Katai 69), Ivanic (Nikolic 84); Falcinelli (Pavkov 72).
AC Milan won on away goals.

Ajax (1) 2 *(Klaassen 15, Neres 88)*

Lille (0) 1 *(Yazici 78 (pen))*

Ajax: (4231) Stekelenburg; Rensch, Timber, Martinez, Blind; Alvarez, Gravenberch (Kudus 90); Antony (Brobbey 55), Klaassen, Neres (Idrissi 89); Tadic.
Lille: (442) Maignan; Celik (Pied 62), Djalo, Botman, Bradaric; Ikone (Luiz Araujo 62), Xeka (Soumare 70), Sanches, Bamba (David 62); Yazici, Weah (Lihadji 78).
Ajax won 4-2 on aggregate.

Arsenal (1) 3 *(Aubameyang 21, 87, Tierney 67)*

Benfica (1) 2 *(Goncalves 43, Rafa Silva 61)*

Arsenal: (4231) Leno; Bellerin (Lacazette 78), Luiz, Gabriel, Tierney; Ceballos (Thomas 63), Xhaka; Saka (Chambers 90), Odegaard (Elneny 90), Smith-Rowe (Willian 63); Aubameyang.
Benfica: (352) Helton Leite; Lucas Verissimo, Otamendi, Vertonghen; Goncalves, Pizzi (Everton 58), Weigl (Waldschmidt 90), Taarabt (Pires 58), Grimaldo (Tavares 85); Rafa Silva, Seferovic (Nunez 57).
Arsenal won 4-3 on aggregate.

Bayer Leverkusen (0) 0

Young Boys (0) 2 *(Siebatcheu 47, Fassnacht 86)*

Bayer Leverkusen: (3412) Lomb; Tah, Dragovic (Gray 63), Tapsoba; Frimpong (Amiri 78), Aranguiz, Sinkgraven, Diaby; Wirtz; Bailey (Alario 63), Schick.
Young Boys: (442) Ballmoos; Hefti, Lustenberger, Zesiger, Lefort; Fassnacht (Gaudino 87), Lauper, Aebischer (Sierro 87), Ngamaleu (Rieder 69); Elia (Mambimbi 78), Siebatcheu (Spielmann 78).
Young Boys won 6-3 on aggregate.

Club Brugge (0) 0

Dynamo Kyiv (0) 1 *(Buyalsky 83)*

Club Brugge: (4141) Mignolet; Mata, Kossounou, Mechele, Ricca; Balanta; Dirar (Okereke 84), Vormer, van den Keybus (van der Brempt 46), Sobol (De Cuyper 84); Dost (Badji 58).
Dynamo Kyiv: (4411) Bushchan; Kedziora (Karavayev 77), Zabarnyi, Syrota, Mykolenko; Tsygankov, Sydorchuk, Shepelev (Shaparenko 68), Rodrigues; Buyalsky (Andrievsky 86); Biesiedin.
Dynamo Kyiv won 2-1 on aggregate.

Dinamo Zagreb (1) 1 *(Orsic 31)*

Krasnodar (0) 0

Dinamo Zagreb: (4321) Livakovic; Ristovski, Lauritsen, Theophile-Catherine, Gvardiol; Ivanusec (Atiemwen 83), Jakic, Orsic; Ademi, Majer (Misic 69); Petkovic (Gavranovic 87).
Krasnodar: (433) Agkatsev; Smolnikov (Suleymanov 70), Martynovich, Kaio, Chernov; Gazinsky (Ari 69), Cabella, Vilhena (Olsson 60); Wanderson, Claesson, Ionov.
Dinamo Zagreb won 4-2 on aggregate.

Hoffenheim (0) 0

Molde (1) 2 *(Andersen 19, 90)*

Hoffenheim: (3412) Baumann; Vogt, Grillitsch, Richards; Kaderabek (Adamyan 70), Rudy, Samassekou (Rutter 83), John (Sessegnon 70); Baumgartner (Kramaric 56); Bebou, Dabbur.
Molde: (4231) Linde; Pedersen, Sinyan, Risa, Haugen; Aursnes, Ellingsen; Knudtzon (Hestad 79), Eikrem, Andersen; Sigurdarson (Bolly 63).
Molde won 5-3 on aggregate.

Leicester C (0) 0

Slavia Prague (0) 2 *(Provod 49, Sima 79)*

Leicester C: (4141) Schmeichel; Amartey (Ricardo Pereira 61), Evans, Soyuncu, Thomas; Ndidi; Under (Tavares 80), Tielemans, Choudhury (Barnes 61), Albrighton (Castagne 61); Vardy.
Slavia Prague: (4141) Kolar; Bah, Kudela, Zima, Boril; Hromada (Lingr 75); Sima, Provod, Stanciu (Dorley 69), Olayinka; Kuchta (Masopust 84).
Slavia Prague won 2-0 on aggregate.

Manchester U (0) 0

Real Sociedad (0) 0

Manchester U: (4231) Henderson; Wan Bissaka (Williams 46), Bailly, Lindelof, Alex Telles; Fred (Tuanzebe 46), Matic; Greenwood (Shoretire 76), Bruno Fernandes (Rashford 46), James (Diallo 59); Martial.
Real Sociedad: (433) Remiro; Gorosabel (Bautista 46), Zubeldia, Sagnan, Munoz; Guevara (Guridi 72), Zubimendi, Merino; Januzaj (Merquelanz 66), Isak (Portu 46), Oyarzabal (Barrenetxea 46).
Manchester U won 4-0 on aggregate.

Napoli (1) 2 *(Zielinski 3, Fabian 59)*

Granada (1) 1 *(Montoro 25)*

Napoli: (3412) Meret; Rrahmani, Maksimovic (Ghoulam 46), Koulibaly; Di Lorenzo, Fabian, Bakayoko, Elmas (Mertens 60); Zielinski; Politano, Insigne.
Granada: (4231) Rui Silva; Foulquier, Domingos Duarte, German (Herrera 55), Neva (Perez 46); Brice, Gonalons (Victor Diaz 45); Kenedy, Montoro (Vallejo 83), Puertas; Jorge Molina (Soldado 84).
Granada won 3-2 on aggregate.

PSV Eindhoven (2) 2 *(Zahavi 23, 44)*

Olympiacos (0) 1 *(Kouka 88)*

PSV Eindhoven: (4231) Mvogo; Dumfries, Teze, Viergever, Max; Rosario, Boscagli; Thomas (Junior 90), Zahavi, Gotze (Vertessen 89); Malen.
Olympiacos: (4231) Jose Sa; Lala (Androutsos 79), Semedo, Ba, Reabciuk; M'Vila, Bouchalakis (Fortounis 46); Valbuena (Masouras 46), Camara, Bruma (Kouka 79); El Arabi (Papastathopoulos 90).
Olympiacos won 5-4 on aggregate.

Rangers (1) 5 *(Morelos 9, Patterson 46, Kent 55, Barisic 79 (pen), Itten 90 (pen))*

Antwerp (1) 2 *(Refaelov 31, Lamkel Ze 57)*

Rangers: (433) McGregor; Balogun (Patterson 46), Goldson, Helander, Barisic; Kamara, Davis (Zungu 82), Aribo; Hagi (Arfield 71), Morelos (Itten 85), Kent (Wright 82).
Antwerp: (352) De Wolf; De Laet, Gelin (Boya 46), Le Marchand; Buta, Gerkens (Avenatti 75), Verstraete, Hongla (Miyoshi 82), Lukaku (Ampomah 75); Refaelov, Lamkel Ze.
Rangers won 9-5 on aggregate.

Roma (1) 3 *(Dzeko 23, Perez 74, Borja Mayoral 90)*

Braga (0) 1 *(Cristante 87 (og))*

Roma: (3421) Pau Lopez; Karsdorp, Cristante, Mancini; Veretout (Spinazzola 59), Villar (Pellegrini 46), Diawara, Bruno Peres; Pedro (Mkhitaryan 77), El Shaarawy (Perez 59); Dzeko (Borja Mayoral 67).
Braga: (3421) Tiago Sa; Vitor Tormena, Rolando, Nuno Sequeira (Borja 70); Ze Carlos, Joao Novais, Andre Horta, Galeno (Infande 77); Piazon (Fransergio 60), Gaitan (Ricardo Horta 60); Sporar (Ruiz 60).
Roma won 5-1 on aggregate.

Shakhtar Donetsk (0) 1 *(Moraes 67 (pen))*

Maccabi Tel Aviv (0) 0

Shakhtar Donetsk: (4141) Trubin; Dodo, Kryvtsov, Vitao (Korniyenko 78), Matviyenko; Maycon; Solomon (Tete 46), Marlos (Marcos Antonio 46), Alan Patrick, Taison (Konoplyanka 78); Moraes (Fernando 78).
Maccabi Tel Aviv: (4231) Daniel; Andre Geraldes, Hernandez, Tibi, Saborit; Glazer D, Peretz; Hozez (Biton 77), Golasa (Rikan 77), Ben Haim II (Guerrero 68); Pesic (Blackman 68).
Shakhtar Donetsk won 3-0 on aggregate.

Villarreal (1) 2 *(Gerard 40, 89 (pen))*

Red Bull Salzburg (1) 1 *(Berisha 17)*

Villarreal: (442) Rulli; Jaume (Foyth 82), Albiol, Torres, Estupinan; Trigueros, Capoue, Parejo (Baena 90), Pedraza (Moi Gomez 66); Gerard (Nino 90), Alcacer (Chukwueze 66).
Red Bull Salzburg: (442) Stankovic; Kristensen (Solet 90), Ramalho, Vallci (Wober 46), Ulmer; Mwepu, Bernede (Adeyemi 60), Junuzovic, Aaronson (Sucic 60); Daka (Svoboda 90), Berisha.
Villarreal won 4-1 on aggregate.

ROUND OF 16 FIRST LEG

Thursday, 11 March 2021

Ajax (0) 3 *(Klaassen 62, Tadic 82, Brobbey 90)*

Young Boys (0) 0

Ajax: (433) Stekelenburg; Rensch (Schuurs 67), Timber, Martinez, Tagliafico; Klaassen, Alvarez, Gravenberch; Antony (Idrissi 68), Tadic, Neres (Brobbey 83).
Young Boys: (442) Faivre; Hefti, Camara (Zesiger 34), Lustenberger, Lefort; Fassnacht (Siebatcheu 84), Aebischer, Lauper (Sierro 71), Sulejmani (Ngamaleu 46); Elia (Mambimbi 71), Nsame.

Dynamo Kyiv (0) 0

Villarreal (1) 2 *(Torres 30, Albiol 52)*

Dynamo Kyiv: (4231) Bushchan; Kedziora (Karavayev 84), Zabarnyi, Syrota, Mykolenko; Sydorchuk (Andrievsky 68), Shaparenko (Shepelev 68); Tsygankov, Buyalsky, Rodrigues; Biesiedin.
Villarreal: (433) Rulli; Foyth, Albiol, Torres (Funes Mori 46), Pedraza; Trigueros (Moi Gomez 85), Capoue, Parejo; Chukwueze (Jaume 84), Alcacer (Bacca 63), Gerard (Baena 90).

Granada (1) 2 *(Jorge Molina 26, Soldado 75)*

Molde (0) 0

Granada: (4231) Rui Silva; Foulquier, Domingos Duarte, Perez, Victor Diaz; Brice, Gonalons; Kenedy, Jorge Molina, Puertas (Vallejo 90); Soldado (Ruiz 81).
Molde: (4231) Linde; Pedersen, Sinyan, Gregersen, Haugen; Aursnes, Ellingsen■; Hestad (Knudtzon 65), Eikrem, Andersen (Bolly 86); Sigurdarson (Fofana 73).

Manchester U (0) 1 *(Diallo 50)*

AC Milan (0) 1 *(Kjaer 90)*

Manchester U: (4231) Henderson; Wan Bissaka (Williams 74), Bailly, Maguire, Alex Telles; McTominay, Matic; Greenwood, Bruno Fernandes (Fred 74), James (Shaw 74); Martial (Diallo 46).
AC Milan: (4231) Donnarumma; Calabria (Kalulu Kyatengwa 74), Kjaer, Tomori, Dalot; Meite, Kessie; Saelemaekers (Castillejo 69), Diaz (Tonali 69), Krunic; Leao.

Olympiacos (0) 1 *(El Arabi 58)*

Arsenal (1) 3 *(Odegaard 34, Gabriel 79, Elneny 85)*

Olympiacos: (4411) Jose Sa; Lala, Papastathopoulos, M'Vila, Reabciuk (Holebas 46); Bruma (Randjelovic 59), Bouchalakis, Camara, Masouras (Androutsos 86); Valbuena (Fortounis 46); El Arabi (Kouka 77).
Arsenal: (4231) Leno; Bellerin, Luiz, Gabriel, Tierney; Thomas (Ceballos 55), Xhaka; Saka (Pepe 82), Odegaard (Smith-Rowe 82), Willian (Elneny 82); Aubameyang (Lacazette 88).

Roma (1) 3 *(Pellegrini 23, El Shaarawy 73, Mancini 77)*

Shakhtar Donetsk (0) 0

Roma: (3421) Pau Lopez; Mancini, Cristante, Kumbulla; Karsdorp, Diawara (Ibanez 79), Villar, Spinazzola (Bruno Peres 78); Pellegrini (Perez 78), Pedro (El Shaarawy 62); Mkhitaryan (Borja Mayoral 35).
Shakhtar Donetsk: (4231) Trubin; Dodo, Vitao, Matviyenko, Ismaily; Marlos (Marcos Antonio 88), Maycon; Tete (Konoplyanka 87), Alan Patrick (Sudakov 79), Taison (Solomon 79); Moraes (Dentinho 76).

Slavia Prague (1) 1 *(Stanciu 7)*

Rangers (1) 1 *(Helander 36)*

Slavia Prague: (451) Kolar; Bah, Kudela, Zima, Boril; Sima, Stanciu (Lingr 76), Holes, Provod, Olayinka (Masopust 46); Kuchta (Dorley 71).
Rangers: (433) McGregor; Patterson, Goldson, Helander, Barisic; Kamara (Zungu 88), Davis, Aribo (Roofe 81); Hagi (Arfield 63), Morelos, Kent.

Tottenham H (1) 2 *(Kane 25, 70)*

Dinamo Zagreb (0) 0

Tottenham H: (4231) Lloris; Aurier, Dier, Sanchez, Davies; Sissoko, Ndombele (Hojbjerg 72); Lamela (Bale 64), Alli (Bergwijn 64), Son (Lucas Moura 64); Kane (Vinicius 84).
Dinamo Zagreb: (4141) Livakovic; Ristovski, Lauritsen, Theophile-Catherine, Leovac; Ademi (Franjic 90); Majer (Kastrati 64), Jakic, Ivanusec, Orsic (Atiemwen 64); Petkovic (Gavranovic 78).

ROUND OF 16 SECOND LEG

Thursday, 18 March 2021

AC Milan (0) 0

Manchester U (0) 1 *(Pogba 48)*

AC Milan: (4231) Donnarumma; Kalulu Kyatengwa (Dalot 65), Kjaer, Tomori, Hernandez; Meite, Kessie; Saelemaekers, Calhanoglu, Krunic (Diaz 72); Castillejo (Ibrahimovic 65).
Manchester U: (4231) Henderson; Wan Bissaka, Lindelof, Maguire, Shaw; McTominay, Fred; James, Bruno Fernandes, Rashford (Pogba 46); Greenwood.
Manchester U won 2-1 on aggregate.

Arsenal (0) 0

Olympiacos (0) 1 *(El Arabi 51)*

Arsenal: (4231) Leno; Bellerin (Chambers 82), Luiz, Gabriel, Tierney; Elneny (Thomas 57), Xhaka; Pepe, Ceballos (Odegaard 57), Smith-Rowe (Martinelli 81); Aubameyang.
Olympiacos: (343) Jose Sa; Ba■, Papastathopoulos, Holebas; Androutsos (Randjelovic 62), M'Vila, Camara, Reabciuk (Lala 84); Masouras (Bruma 63), El Arabi, Fortounis (Bouchalakis 84).
Arsenal won 3-2 on aggregate.

Dinamo Zagreb (0) 3 *(Orsic 62, 82, 106)*

Tottenham H (0) 0

Dinamo Zagreb: (433) Livakovic; Ristovski (Stojanovic 90), Lauritsen, Theophile-Catherine, Franjic (Leovac 81); Majer (Gavranovic 81), Ademi (Peric 118), Jakic (Atiemwen 75); Ivanusec, Petkovic (Misic 90), Orsic.
Tottenham H: (4231) Lloris; Aurier (Bergwijn 108), Sanchez, Dier, Davies (Reguilon 91); Sissoko, Winks (Ndombele 68); Lamela (Bale 60), Alli (Lo Celso 68), Lucas Moura (Vinicius 85); Kane.
aet; Dinamo Zagreb won 3-2 on aggregate.

Molde (1) 2 *(Vallejo 29 (og), Hestad 90 (pen))*

Granada (0) 1 *(Soldado 72)*

Molde: (4231) Linde; Pedersen, Bjornbak, Gregersen (Sinyan 46), Risa (Haugen 77); Aursnes, Breivik (Hussain 82); Hestad, Eikrem, Andersen (Knudtzon 77); Sigurdarson (Fofana 63).
Granada: (4231) Rui Silva; Vallejo (Perez 83), German, Domingos Duarte, Victor Diaz; Gonalons (Brice 76), Herrera; Kenedy, Montoro (Machis 83), Puertas; Jorge Molina (Soldado 64).
Granada won 3-2 on aggregate.

Rangers (0) 0

Slavia Prague (1) 2 *(Olayinka 14, Stanciu 74)*

Rangers: (433) McGregor; Patterson (Simpson 78), Goldson, Balogun■, Barisic; Arfield (Roofe■ 55), Davis (Itten 83), Kamara; Aribo, Morelos (Wright 83), Kent (Zungu 82).
Slavia Prague: (4231) Kolar (Vagner 65); Bah, Kudela, Deli, Boril; Hromada (Holes 58), Provod; Dorley (Kuchta 58), Stanciu (Lingr 90), Olayinka (Masopust 58); Sima.
Slavia Prague won 3-1 on aggregate.

Shakhtar Donetsk (0) 1 *(Moraes 59)*

Roma (0) 2 *(Borja Mayoral 48, 72)*

Shakhtar Donetsk: (433) Trubin; Dodo (Bolbat 82), Kryvtsov, Vitao, Matviyenko; Alan Patrick (Konoplyanka 60), Marcos Antonio, Maycon; Tete (Marlos 60), Moraes (Dentinho 76), Solomon (Sudakov 77).
Roma: (343) Pau Lopez; Ibanez (Mancini 46), Cristante, Kumbulla; Karsdorp (Bruno Peres 58), Villar, Diawara (Pellegrini 59), Spinazzola (Calafiori 58); Perez, Borja Mayoral, Pedro (El Shaarawy 75).
Roma won 5-1 on aggregate.

Villarreal (2) 2 *(Gerard 13, 36)*

Dynamo Kyiv (0) 0

Villarreal: (442) Sergio Asenjo; Foyth (Mario 63), Albiol, Funes Mori, Pedraza; Chukwueze (Baena 71), Capoue, Parejo, Trigueros (Jaume 79); Gerard (Raba 79), Bacca (Pino 63).
Dynamo Kyiv: (4231) Bushchan; Kedziora, Zabarnyi, Syrota (Popov 83), Mykolenko (Sidcley 83); Andrievsky (Shepelev 65), Sydorchuk; Tsygankov (Supriaga 46), Buyalsky, De Pena; Rodrigues (Lednev 65).
Villarreal won 4-0 on aggregate.

Young Boys (0) 0

Ajax (1) 2 *(Neres 20, Tadic 49 (pen))*

Young Boys: (442) Faivre; Hefti, Camara (Rieder 65), Lustenberger, Lefort (Maceiras 46); Fassnacht (Gaudino 71), Lauper, Sierro, Sulejmani (Spielmann 71); Elia (Mambimbi 65), Nsame.
Ajax: (433) Stekelenburg; Rensch (Schuurs 80), Alvarez, Martinez, Tagliafico (Klaiber 74); Klaassen, Gravenberch, Blind (Kudus 65); Antony (Brobbey 81), Tadic, Neres (Idrissi 65).
Ajax won 5-0 on aggregate.

QUARTER-FINALS FIRST LEG

Thursday, 8 April 2021

Ajax (1) 1 *(Klaassen 39)*

Roma (0) 2 *(Pellegrini 57, Ibanez 87)*

Ajax: (433) Scherpen; Rensch (Klaiber 78), Timber, Martinez, Tagliafico; Klaassen, Alvarez, Gravenberch; Antony (Idrissi 88), Tadic, Neres (Brobbey 64).
Roma: (3421) Pau Lopez; Mancini, Cristante, Ibanez; Bruno Peres, Diawara, Veretout (Villar 77), Spinazzola (Calafiori 29); Pellegrini, Pedro (Perez 89); Dzeko (Borja Mayoral 77).

Arsenal (0) 1 *(Pepe 86)*

Slavia Prague (0) 1 *(Holes 90)*

Arsenal: (4231) Leno; Bellerin, Holding, Gabriel, Cedric; Thomas (Elneny 78), Xhaka; Saka (Pepe 78), Smith-Rowe (Ceballos 88), Willian (Martinelli 73); Lacazette (Aubameyang 78).
Slavia Prague: (433) Kolar; Bah, Holes, Zima, Boril; Stanciu (Masopust 84), Hromada (Sevcik 46), Provod; Dorley (Lingr 69), Sima (Kuchta 69), Olayinka (Traore 85).

Dinamo Zagreb (0) 0

Villarreal (1) 1 *(Gerard 44 (pen))*

Dinamo Zagreb: (4231) Livakovic; Ristovski, Lauritsen, Theophile-Catherine, Gvardiol (Leovac 71); Ademi, Jakic (Kastrati 61); Ivanusec, Majer (Franjic 82), Orsic (Tolic 82); Atiemwen (Petkovic 61).
Villarreal: (433) Rulli; Foyth, Albiol, Torres, Pedraza; Parejo, Capoue, Trigueros (Pena 86); Chukwueze (Moi Gomez 69), Gerard, Bacca (Alcacer 46).

Granada (0) 0

Manchester U (1) 2 *(Rashford 31, Bruno Fernandes 90 (pen))*

Granada: (4231) Rui Silva; Victor Diaz, Domingos Duarte (German 54), Vallejo, Neva (Foulquier 74); Herrera, Gonalons (Brice 86); Puertas, Montoro, Kenedy (Machis 75); Soldado (Suarez 87).
Manchester U: (4231) de Gea; Wan Bissaka, Lindelof, Maguire, Shaw (Alex Telles 46); Pogba (Matic 74), McTominay; James, Bruno Fernandes, Rashford (Cavani 66); Greenwood (van de Beek 85).

QUARTER-FINALS SECOND LEG

Thursday, 15 April 2021

Manchester U (1) 2 *(Cavani 6, Vallejo 90 (og))*

Granada (0) 0

Manchester U: (4231) de Gea; Wan Bissaka (Williams 82), Tuanzebe, Lindelof, Alex Telles, Fred, Matic; Greenwood (Diallo 82), Bruno Fernandes (Mata 73), Pogba (van de Beek 46); Cavani (James 60).
Granada: (4231) Rui Silva; Foulquier, German (Perez 82), Vallejo, Neva (Victor Diaz 74); Gonalons (Jorge Molina 32), Montoro; Kenedy (Puertas 46), Herrera, Machis; Soldado (Suarez 46).
Manchester U won 4-0 on aggregate.

Roma (0) 1 *(Dzeko 72)*

Ajax (0) 1 *(Brobbey 49)*

Roma: (3421) Pau Lopez; Mancini, Cristante, Ibanez; Karsdorp, Diawara, Veretout, Calafiori (Villar 81); Pellegrini, Mkhitaryan (Pedro 87); Dzeko (Borja Mayoral 80).
Ajax: (433) Stekelenburg; Klaiber (Schuurs 22 (Idrissi 83)), Timber, Martinez, Tagliafico; Klaassen, Alvarez (Kudus 69), Gravenberch; Antony (Brobbey 46), Tadic, Neres (Traore 83).
Roma won 3-2 on aggregate.

Slavia Prague (0) 0

Arsenal (3) 4 *(Pepe 18, Lacazette 21 (pen), 77, Saka 24)*

Slavia Prague: (41212) Kolar; Bah (Visinsky 46), Holes, Zima, Boril (Dorley 46); Hromada (Masopust 46); Sevcik, Provod; Stanciu (Lingr 46); Kuchta (Tecl 71), Olayinka.
Arsenal: (4231) Leno; Chambers, Holding, Pablo Mari, Xhaka; Thomas (Cedric 79), Ceballos; Saka (Martinelli 79), Smith-Rowe (Elneny 67), Pepe (Balogun 88); Lacazette (Nketiah 79).
Arsenal won 5-1 on aggregate.

Villarreal (2) 2 *(Alcacer 36, Gerard 43)*

Dinamo Zagreb (0) 1 *(Orsic 74)*

Villarreal: (442) Rulli; Foyth, Albiol, Torres, Pedraza (Moreno 90); Chukwueze (Pena 90), Capoue, Parejo (Coquelin 84), Trigueros (Moi Gomez 63); Gerard, Alcacer (Baena 90).
Dinamo Zagreb: (3421) Livakovic; Lauritsen, Theophile-Catherine (Peric 82), Gvardiol; Ristovski (Stojanovic 62), Jakic, Ademi (Misic 82), Orsic; Ivanusec (Atiemwen 76), Majer (Franjic 62); Petkovic.
Villarreal won 3-1 on aggregate.

SEMI-FINALS FIRST LEG

Thursday, 29 April 2021

Manchester U (1) 6 *(Bruno Fernandes 9, 71 (pen), Cavani 48, 64, Pogba 75, Greenwood 86)*

Roma (2) 2 *(Pellegrini 15 (pen), Dzeko 33)*

Manchester U: (4231) de Gea; Wan Bissaka, Lindelof, Maguire, Shaw; McTominay, Fred (Matic 83); Rashford (Greenwood 76), Bruno Fernandes (Mata 89), Pogba; Cavani.
Roma: (3421) Pau Lopez (Mirante 27); Smalling, Cristante, Ibanez; Karsdorp, Veretout (Villar 5), Diawara, Spinazzola (Bruno Peres 37); Pellegrini, Mkhitaryan; Dzeko.

Villarreal (2) 2 *(Trigueros 5, Albiol 29)*

Arsenal (0) 1 *(Pepe 73 (pen))*

Villarreal: (442) Rulli; Foyth (Mario 70), Albiol, Torres, Pedraza (Moreno 81); Chukwueze, Capoue■, Parejo, Trigueros (Moi Gomez 80); Gerard, Alcacer (Coquelin 46).
Arsenal: (4231) Leno; Chambers, Holding, Pablo Mari, Xhaka; Thomas, Ceballos■; Saka (Aubameyang 85), Odegaard (Martinelli 63), Pepe (Willian 90); Smith-Rowe (Elneny 90).

SEMI-FINALS SECOND LEG

Thursday, 6 May 2021

Arsenal (0) 0

Villarreal (0) 0

Arsenal: (4141) Leno; Bellerin (Nketiah 90), Holding, Pablo Mari, Tierney (Willian 80); Thomas; Saka, Odegaard (Martinelli 66), Smith-Rowe, Pepe; Aubameyang (Lacazette 79).
Villarreal: (442) Rulli; Mario, Albiol, Torres, Pedraza (Moreno 90); Chukwueze (Pino 30 (Moi Gomez 90)), Parejo, Coquelin, Trigueros; Gerard, Alcacer (Bacca 72).
Villarreal won 2-1 on aggregate.

Roma (0) 3 *(Dzeko 57, Cristante 60, Alex Telles 83 (og))*

Manchester U (1) 2 *(Cavani 39, 68)*

Roma: (4141) Mirante; Karsdorp, Smalling (Darboe 30), Ibanez, Bruno Peres (Santon 69); Mancini; Pedro (Zalewski 76), Cristante, Pellegrini, Mkhitaryan; Dzeko (Borja Mayoral 76).
Manchester U: (4231) de Gea; Wan Bissaka (Williams 46), Bailly, Maguire, Shaw (Alex Telles 46); Pogba (Matic 64), Fred; Greenwood, Bruno Fernandes (Mata 84), van de Beek; Cavani (Rashford 73).
Manchester U won 8-5 on aggregate.

UEFA EUROPA LEAGUE FINAL 2020–21

Wednesday, 26 May 2021

(in Gdansk – attendance 9142)

Villarreal (1) 1 *(Gerard 29)* **Manchester U (0) 1** *(Cavani 55)*

Villarreal: (442) Rulli; Foyth (Mario 88), Albiol, Torres, Pedraza (Moreno 88); Pino (Alcacer 77), Capoue (Raba 120), Parejo, Trigueros (Moi Gomez 77); Gerard, Bacca (Coquelin 60).

Manchester U: (4231) de Gea; Wan Bissaka (Mata 120), Bailly (Tuanzebe 116), Lindelof, Shaw; McTominay (Alex Telles 120), Pogba (James 116); Greenwood (Fred 100), Bruno Fernandes, Rashford; Cavani.

aet; Villarreal won 11-10 on penalties.

Referee: Clement Turpin.

Manchester United goalkeeper David de Gea has his spot kick saved by his Villareal counterpart Geronimo Rulli. The Spanish side won the shoot-out 11-10 to emerge victorious in the Europa League Final in the Polish city of Gdansk on 26 May. (Mutsu Kawamori/AFLO/PA Images)

UEFA EUROPA LEAGUE 2021–22

PARTICIPATING CLUBS
The list below is provisional and is subject to pending legal proceedings and final confirmation from UEFA.

THIRD QUALIFYING ROUND (16)
Champions Path (10)
10 teams eliminated from Champions League Q2 (Champions Path)
Main Path (6)
3 teams eliminated from Champions League Q2 (League Path)
St Johnstone
Jablonec
Anorthosis Famagusta

PLAY-OFF ROUND (20)
6 teams eliminated from Champions League Q3 (Champions Path)
5 winners from Europa League Q3 (Champions Path)
3 winners from Europa League Q3 (Main Path)
Antwerp
Zorya Luhansk
AZ Alkmaar
Fenerbahce
Sturm Graz
Randers

GROUP STAGE (32)
10 winners from Europa League Play-Off round
4 teams eliminated from Champions League Play-Offs (Champions Path)
4 teams eliminated from Champions League Play-Offs (League Path)
2 teams eliminated from Champions League Q3 (League Path)
Real Sociedad
Real Betis
Leicester C
West Ham U
Eintracht Frankfurt
Bayer Leverkusen
Napoli
Lazio
Lyon
Marseille
Braga
Lokomotiv Moscow

PRELIMINARY KNOCKOUT ROUND (16)
8 Europa League Group Stage runners-up
8 Group Stage 3rd place from Champions League Group Stage

KNOCKOUT ROUND PLAY-OFFS (16)
8 Europa League Group Stage winners
8 Europa League winners from Preliminary Knockout Stage

UEFA EUROPA CONFERENCE LEAGUE 2021–22

PARTICIPATING CLUBS
The list below is provisional and is subject to pending legal proceedings and final confirmation from UEFA.

FIRST QUALIFYING ROUND (66)
Slask Wroclaw
Spartak Trnava
Zilina
Maribor
Domzale
Puskas Akademia
Fehervar
Swift Hesperange
Racing Luxembourg
Suduva
Kauno Zalgiris
Ararat Yerevan
Noah
Urartu
Liepaja
Riga FS
Valmiera
Vllaznia
Partizani
Laci
Sileks
Shkupi
Struga
Sarajevo
Velez Mostar
Siroki Brijeg
Sfantul Gheorghe
Petrocub Hincesti
Milsami Orhei
Dundalk
Bohemians
Sligo Rovers
Inter Turku
KuPS Kuopio
FC Honka
Gagra
Dinamo Batumi
Dila Gori
Gzira U
Birkirkara
Mosta
FH Hafnarfjordur
Stjarnan
Breidablik
The New Saints
Bala T
Newtown
Coleraine
Glentoran
Larne
Europa
St Joseph's
Mons Calpe
Sutjeska
Deciv
Podgorica
FCI Levadia
Paide Linnameeskond
Llapi
Drita
NSI Runavik
KI Klaksvik
Sant Julia
FC Santa Coloma
La Fiorita
Tre Penne

SECOND QUALIFYING ROUND (108)
Champions Path (18)
15 teams eliminated from Champions League Q1
3 teams eliminated from Champions League Preliminary Round
Main Path (90)
33 winners from Europa Conference Q1
Santa Clara
Sochi
Gent
Vorskla Poltava
Feyenoord
Sivasspor
Austria Vienna
FC Copenhagen
AGF Aarhus
Hibernian
Aberdeen
Slovacko
Viktoria Plzen
Apollon Limassol
AEL Limassol
FC Basel
Servette
Aris
AEK Athens
Partizan Belgrade
Cukaricki
Vojvodina
Osijek
Rijeka
Hajduk Split
Hammarby
Elfsborg
Hacken
Molde
Valerenga
Rosenborg
Maccabi Tel Aviv
Ashdod
Hapoel Be'er Sheva
Tobol
Astana
Shakhter Karagandy
BATE Borisov
Torpedo Zhodino
Dinamo Brest
Keshla
Qarabag
Sumqayit
CSKA Sofia
Lokomotiv Plovdiv
Arda
Universitatea Craiova
FCSB
Sepsi Sfantu Gheorghe
Rakow Czestochowa
Pogon Szczecin
Dunajska Streda
Vaduz
Olimpija Ljubljana
Ujpest
F91 Dudelange
Panevezys

THIRD QUALIFYING ROUND (64)
Champions Path (10)
1 team eliminated from Champions League Q1
9 winners from Europa Conference Q2 (Champions Path)
Main Path (54)
45 winners from Europa Conference Q2 (Main Path)
Pacos de Ferreira
Rubin Kazan
Anderlecht
Kolos Kovalivka
Vitesse
Trabzonspor
LASK
Luzern
PAOK

PLAY-OFF ROUND (44)
Champions Path (10)
5 winners from Europa Conference Q3 (Champions Path)
5 teams eliminated from Europa League Q3 (Champions Path)
Main Path (34)
27 winners from Europa Conference Q3 (Main Path)
3 teams eliminated from Europa League Q3 (Main Path)
Tottenham H
Union Berlin
Roma
Rennes

GROUP STAGE (32)
5 winners from Europa Conference Play-Off Round (Champions Path)
17 winners from Europa Conference Play-Off Round (Main Path)
10 teams eliminated from Europa League Play-Off Round

PRELIMINARY KNOCKOUT ROUND PLAY-OFFS (16)
8 runners-up from Europa Conference Group Stage
8 third-placed teams from Europa League Group Stage

KNOCKOUT ROUND PLAY-OFFS (16)
8 winners from Europa Conference Group Stage
8 winners from the Europa Conference Preliminary Knockout Round

BRITISH AND IRISH CLUBS IN EUROPE

SUMMARY OF APPEARANCES

EUROPEAN CUP AND CHAMPIONS LEAGUE 1955–2021

(Winners in brackets) (SE = seasons entered).

ENGLAND	*SE*	*P*	*W*	*D*	*L*	*F*	*A*
Manchester U (3)	29	285	157	66	62	521	274
Liverpool (6)	25	227	127	49	51	423	202
Arsenal	21	201	101	43	57	332	218
Chelsea (2)	17	181	92	51	38	309	162
Manchester C	11	94	51	17	26	184	110
Tottenham H	6	55	25	10	20	108	83
Leeds U	4	40	22	6	12	76	41
Newcastle U	3	24	11	3	10	33	33
Nottingham F (2)	3	20	12	4	4	32	14
Everton	3	10	2	5	3	14	10
Aston Villa (1)	2	15	9	3	3	24	10
Derby Co	2	12	6	2	4	18	12
Wolverhampton W	2	8	2	2	4	12	16
Leicester C	1	10	5	2	3	11	10
Blackburn R	1	6	1	1	4	5	8
Ipswich T	1	4	3	0	1	16	5
Burnley	1	4	2	0	2	8	8
SCOTLAND							
Celtic (1)	35	214	101	36	77	331	252
Rangers	30	161	62	40	59	232	218
Aberdeen	3	12	5	4	3	14	12
Hearts	3	8	2	1	5	8	16
Dundee U	1	8	5	1	2	14	5
Dundee	1	8	5	0	3	20	14
Hibernian	1	6	3	1	2	9	5
Kilmarnock	1	4	1	2	1	4	7
Motherwell	1	2	0	0	2	0	5
WALES							
The New Saints	13	36	9	5	22	36	63
Barry Town U	6	14	4	1	9	11	38
Rhyl	2	4	0	0	4	1	19
Cwmbran T	1	2	1	0	1	4	4
Llanelli	1	2	1	0	1	1	4
Bangor C	1	2	0	0	2	0	13
Connah's Quay Nomads	1	1	0	0	1	0	2
NORTHERN IRELAND							
Linfield	30	71	8	23	40	58	125
Glentoran	12	28	3	7	18	20	59
Crusaders	6	14	1	2	11	7	52
Cliftonville	3	6	0	1	5	1	20
Portadown	3	6	0	1	5	3	24
Glenavon	1	2	0	1	1	0	3
Lisburn Distillery	1	2	0	1	1	3	8
Ards	1	2	0	0	2	3	10
Coleraine	1	2	0	0	2	1	11
REPUBLIC OF IRELAND							
Dundalk	12	33	4	12	17	24	60
Shamrock R	9	20	1	6	13	9	33
Shelbourne	6	20	4	8	8	21	31
Bohemians	6	18	4	4	10	13	29
Waterford U	6	14	3	0	11	15	47
Derry C	4	9	1	1	7	9	26
St Patrick's Ath	4	8	0	3	5	2	23
Cork C	3	10	2	1	7	7	16
Dublin C	3	6	1	0	5	3	25
Athlone T	2	4	0	2	2	7	14
Sligo R	2	4	0	0	4	0	9
Limerick	2	4	0	0	4	4	16
Drogheda U	1	4	2	1	1	6	5
Cork Hibernians	1	2	0	0	2	1	7
Cork Celtic	1	2	0	0	2	1	7

UEFA CUP AND EUROPA LEAGUE 1971–2021

ENGLAND	*SE*	*P*	*W*	*D*	*L*	*F*	*A*
Tottenham H (2)	16	153	88	37	28	315	134
Liverpool (3)	14	124	66	34	24	186	94
Aston Villa	13	56	24	14	18	77	60
Manchester U (1)	11	64	31	19	14	101	50
Arsenal	10	76	44	13	19	154	79
Ipswich T (1)	10	52	30	10	12	98	53
Everton	9	52	27	8	17	87	64
Newcastle U	8	72	42	17	13	123	60
Manchester C	8	52	28	13	11	84	51
Leeds U	8	46	20	10	16	66	48
Southampton	7	22	6	9	7	23	20
Blackburn R	6	22	7	8	7	27	26
Wolverhampton W	5	37	25	5	7	79	37
Chelsea (2)	5	32	22	5	5	64	30
West Ham U	4	16	6	3	7	19	16
Fulham	3	39	21	10	8	64	31
Nottingham F	3	20	10	5	5	18	16
Stoke C	3	16	8	4	4	21	16
WBA	3	12	5	2	5	15	13
Leicester C	3	12	4	3	5	17	15
Middlesbrough	2	25	13	4	8	36	24
Bolton W	2	18	6	10	2	18	14
QPR	2	12	8	1	3	39	18
Derby Co	2	10	5	2	3	32	17
Birmingham C	1	8	4	2	2	11	8
Burnley	1	6	2	3	1	7	6
Norwich C	1	6	2	2	2	6	4
Portsmouth	1	6	2	2	2	11	10
Watford	1	6	2	1	3	10	12
Wigan Ath	1	6	1	2	3	6	7
Sheffield W	1	4	2	1	1	13	7
Hull C	1	4	2	1	1	4	3
Millwall	1	2	0	1	1	2	4
SCOTLAND							
Celtic	23	129	54	29	46	196	157
Aberdeen	23	87	29	27	31	116	109
Rangers	20	123	56	38	29	184	121
Dundee U	19	82	33	25	24	134	89
Hearts	14	50	21	10	19	61	62
Hibernian	13	40	15	11	14	57	63
Motherwell	9	29	9	3	17	40	40
St Johnstone	7	24	7	7	10	25	30
Dundee	4	14	6	0	8	24	24
Kilmarnock	4	14	5	2	7	9	17
St Mirren	3	10	2	3	5	9	12
Dunfermline Ath	2	4	0	2	2	4	6
Raith R	1	6	2	1	3	10	8
Livingston	1	4	1	2	1	7	9
Falkirk	1	2	1	0	1	1	2
Inverness CT	1	2	0	1	1	0	1
Gretna	1	2	0	1	1	3	7
Queen of the South	1	2	0	0	2	2	4
Partick Thistle	1	2	0	0	2	0	4
WALES							
The New Saints	11	26	3	4	19	21	68
Bangor C	10	22	2	2	18	10	61
Bala T	6	12	4	0	8	8	21
Connah's Quay Nomads	5	13	3	1	9	7	18
Llanelli	5	12	3	3	6	12	24
Barry Town U	4	11	2	3	6	11	25
Cardiff Met Univ	4	8	2	0	6	3	20
Rhyl	3	8	2	1	5	9	12
Newtown	3	8	2	1	5	6	21
Air UK Broughton	3	6	0	4	2	6	9
Cwmbran T	3	6	0	0	6	0	21
Carmarthen T	2	6	1	0	5	8	21
Cefn Druids	2	4	0	2	2	1	7
Swansea C	1	12	4	4	4	17	10
Prestatyn T	1	4	1	0	3	3	11
Afan Lido	1	2	0	1	1	1	2
Haverfordwest Co	1	2	0	0	2	1	4
Neath	1	2	0	0	2	1	6
Port Talbot T	1	2	0	0	2	1	7
Llandudno T	1	2	0	0	2	1	7
Aberystwith T	1	2	0	0	2	0	9
NORTHERN IRELAND							
Glentoran	19	42	4	8	30	24	102
Linfield	14	41	13	9	19	49	73

Portadown	11	28	3	7	18	16	62
Crusaders	11	26	6	4	16	27	62
Coleraine	10	21	2	7	12	13	49
Glenavon	9	20	2	2	16	10	49
Cliftonville	7	20	4	4	12	15	37
Ballymena U	3	8	2	1	5	4	20
Dungannon Swifts	1	2	1	0	1	1	4
Ards	1	2	1	0	1	4	8
Bangor	1	2	0	0	2	0	6
Lisburn Distillery	1	2	0	0	2	1	11
REPUBLIC OF IRELAND							
Bohemians	15	31	3	10	18	17	57
St Patrick's Ath	11	40	10	7	23	35	61
Shamrock R	11	38	9	7	22	36	68
Cork C	11	32	7	7	18	23	46
Dundalk	10	37	9	5	23	34	73
Derry C	10	27	7	5	15	32	48
Shelbourne	6	12	0	2	10	8	28
Drogheda U	4	12	3	4	5	10	24
Sligo R	4	10	2	4	4	11	13
Longford T	3	6	1	1	4	6	12
Finn Harps	3	6	0	0	6	3	33
Athlone T	1	4	1	2	1	4	5
University College Dublin	1	4	1	0	3	3	8
Limerick	1	2	0	1	1	1	4
Sporting Fingal	1	2	0	0	2	4	6
Galway U	1	2	0	0	2	2	8
Bray W	1	2	0	0	2	0	8

EUROPEAN CUP WINNERS' CUP 1960–1999

ENGLAND	*SE*	*P*	*W*	*D*	*L*	*F*	*A*
Tottenham H (1)	6	33	20	5	8	65	34
Chelsea (2)	5	39	23	10	6	81	28
Liverpool	5	29	16	5	8	57	29
Manchester U (1)	5	31	16	9	6	55	35
West Ham U (1)	4	30	15	6	9	58	42
Arsenal (1)	3	27	15	10	2	48	20
Everton (1)	3	17	11	4	2	25	9
Manchester C (1)	2	18	11	2	5	32	13
Ipswich T	1	6	3	2	1	6	3
Leeds U	1	9	5	3	1	13	3
Leicester C	1	4	2	1	1	8	5
Newcastle U	1	2	1	0	1	2	2
Southampton	1	6	4	0	2	16	8
Sunderland	1	4	3	0	1	5	3
WBA	1	6	2	2	2	8	5
Wolverhampton W	1	4	1	1	2	6	5
SCOTLAND							
Rangers (1)	10	54	27	11	16	100	62
Aberdeen (1)	8	39	22	5	12	79	37
Celtic	8	38	21	4	13	75	37
Dundee U	3	10	3	3	4	9	10
Hearts	3	10	3	3	4	16	14
Dunfermline Ath	2	14	7	2	5	34	14
Airdrieonians	1	2	0	0	2	1	3
Dundee	1	2	0	1	1	3	4
Hibernian	1	6	3	1	2	19	10
Kilmarnock	1	4	1	2	1	5	6
Motherwell	1	2	1	0	1	3	3
St Mirren	1	4	1	2	1	1	2
WALES							
Cardiff C	14	49	16	14	19	67	61
Wrexham	8	28	10	8	10	34	35
Swansea C	7	18	3	4	11	32	37
Bangor C	3	9	1	2	6	5	12
Barry T	1	2	0	0	2	0	7
Borough U	1	4	1	1	2	2	4
Cwmbran T	1	2	0	0	2	2	12
Merthyr Tydfil	1	2	1	0	1	2	3
Newport Co	1	6	2	3	1	12	3
The New Saints (Llansantfraid)	1	2	0	1	1	1	6
NORTHERN IRELAND							
Glentoran	9	22	3	7	12	18	46
Glenavon	5	10	1	3	6	11	25
Ballymena U	4	8	0	0	8	1	25
Coleraine	4	8	0	1	7	7	34
Crusaders	3	6	0	2	4	5	18
Derry C	3	6	1	1	4	1	11
Linfield	3	6	2	0	4	6	11
Ards	2	4	0	1	3	2	17
Bangor	2	4	0	1	3	2	8
Carrick Rangers	1	4	1	0	3	7	12
Cliftonville	1	2	0	0	2	0	8
Distillery	1	2	0	0	2	1	7
Portadown	1	2	1	0	1	4	7
REPUBLIC OF IRELAND							
Shamrock R	6	16	5	2	9	19	27
Shelbourne	4	10	1	1	8	9	20
Bohemians	3	8	2	2	4	6	13
Dundalk	3	8	2	1	5	7	14
Limerick U	3	6	0	1	5	2	11
Waterford U	3	8	1	1	6	6	14
Cork C	2	4	1	0	3	2	9
Cork Hibernians	2	6	2	1	3	7	8
Galway U	2	4	0	0	4	2	11
Sligo R	2	6	1	1	4	5	11
Bray W	1	2	0	1	1	1	3
Cork Celtic	1	2	0	1	1	1	3
Finn Harps	1	2	0	1	1	2	4
Home Farm	1	2	0	1	1	1	7
St Patrick's Ath	1	2	0	0	2	1	8
University College Dublin	1	2	0	1	1	0	1

INTER-CITIES FAIRS CUP 1955–1970

ENGLAND	*SE*	*P*	*W*	*D*	*L*	*F*	*A*
Leeds U (2)	5	53	28	17	8	92	40
Birmingham C	4	25	14	6	5	51	38
Liverpool	4	22	12	4	6	46	15
Arsenal (1)	3	24	12	5	7	46	19
Chelsea	3	20	10	5	5	33	24
Everton	3	12	7	2	3	22	15
Newcastle U (1)	3	24	13	6	5	37	21
Nottingham F	2	6	3	0	3	8	9
Sheffield W	2	10	5	0	5	25	18
Burnley	1	8	4	3	1	16	5
Coventry C	1	4	3	0	1	9	8
London XI	1	8	4	1	3	14	13
Manchester U	1	11	6	3	2	29	10
Southampton	1	6	2	3	1	11	6
WBA	1	4	1	1	2	7	9
SCOTLAND							
Hibernian	7	36	18	5	13	66	60
Dunfermline Ath	5	28	16	3	9	49	31
Kilmarnock	4	20	8	3	9	34	32
Dundee U	3	10	5	1	4	11	12
Hearts	3	12	4	4	4	20	20
Rangers	3	18	8	4	6	27	17
Celtic	2	6	1	3	2	9	10
Aberdeen	1	4	2	1	1	4	4
Dundee	1	8	5	1	2	14	6
Morton	1	2	0	0	2	3	9
Partick Thistle	1	4	3	0	1	10	7
NORTHERN IRELAND							
Glentoran	4	8	1	1	6	7	22
Coleraine	2	8	2	1	5	15	23
Linfield	2	4	1	0	3	3	11
REPUBLIC OF IRELAND							
Drumcondra	2	6	2	0	4	8	19
Dundalk	2	6	1	1	4	4	25
Shamrock R	2	4	0	2	2	4	6
Cork Hibernians	1	2	0	0	2	1	6
Shelbourne	1	5	1	2	2	3	4
St Patrick's Ath	1	2	0	0	2	4	9

FIFA CLUB WORLD CUP 2020

Formerly known as the FIFA Club World Championship, this tournament is played annually between the champion clubs from all 6 continental confederations, although since 2007 the champions of Oceania must play a qualifying play-off against the champion club of the host country.

(Finals in Qatar)

■*Denotes player sent off.*

FIRST ROUND

Al Rayyan, Monday 1 February 2021

Al-Duhail 3

Auckland City 0

Match awarded as 3-0 win to Al-Duhail. Auckland City withdrew due to COVID-19 quarantine restrictions imposed by the New Zealand government.

SECOND ROUND

Al Rayyan, Thursday 4 February 2021

Tigres UANL (2) 2 *(Gignac 38, 45 (pen))*

Ulsan Hyundai (1) 1 *(Keehee Kim 24)*

Tigres UANL: Guzman; Salcedo, Reyes, Meza (Gonzalez 46), Rodriguez, Rafael Carioca, Pizarro, Duenas (Ayala 83), Gignac, Aquino (Fulgencio 65), Quinones L (Sierra 90).
Ulsan Hyundai: Hyeonwoo Jo; Bulthuis, Taehwan Kim, Keehee Kim, Youngwoo Seol, Hyungmin Shin (Yungu Kang 79), Imsung Kim (Sungjoon Kim 66), Bitgaram Yoon, Dongjun Lee, Dujae Won, Jihyun Kim (Hinterseer 73).
Referee: Esteban Ostojich (Uruguay).

Al Rayyan, Thursday 4 February 2021

Al-Duhail (0) 0

Al Ahly (1) 1 *(Hussein Elshahat 30)*

Al-Duhail: Salah Zakaria; Mohamed Moussa, Benatia, Bassam Hisham (Almoez Ali 46), Ahmed Yasser (Ismail Mohamad 72), Edmilson Junior, Karim Boudiaf, Sultan al Brake, Karimi (Luiz Junior 82), Dudu, Olunga (Mohammed Muntari 46).
Al Ahly: Mohamed Elshenawy; Ayman Ashraf, Benoun, Maaloul, Mohamed Hany, Hamdy Fathy (Dieng 54), Hussein Elshahat (Salah Mohsen 82), Amro Elsoulia, Mohamed Afsha, Taher Mohamed (Marwan Mohsen 70), Bwalya (Akram Tawfik 70).
Referee: Mario Escobar (Guatemala).

MATCH FOR FIFTH PLACE

Al Rayyan, Sunday 7 February 2021

Ulsan Hyundai (0) 1 *(Bitgaram Yoon 62)*

Al-Duhail (1) 3 *(Edmilson 21, Muntari 66, Almoez Ali 82)*

Ulsan Hyundai: Hyeonwoo Jo; Bulthuis, Taehwan Kim, Keehee Kim, Youngwoo Seol, Davidson (Insung Kim 46), Bitgaram Yoon, Dongjun Lee (Minjun Kim 76), Dujae Won, Sungjoon Kim (Hyungmin Shin 66), Hinterseer (Jihyun Kim 46).
Al-Duhail: Salah Zakaria; Benatia, Bassam Hisham, Ismail Mohamad (Ali Malolah 90), Ali Afif, Edmilson Junior, Abdullah al Ahrak (Assim Madibo 75), Almoez Ali, Karimi, Dudu (Khaled Mohammed 90), Olunga (Mohammed Muntari 61).
Referee: Edina Alves Batista (Brazil).

SEMI-FINALS

Al Rayyan, Sunday 7 February 2021

Palmeiras (0) 0

Tigres UANL (0) 1 *(Gignac 54 pen)*

Palmeiras: Weverton; Marcos Rocha (Mayke 72), Luan Garcia, Gomez, Vina, Ze Rafael (Patrick de Paula 57), Rony, Raphael Veiga (Gustovao Scarpa 72), Gabriel Menino (Willian 62), Danilo (Felipe Melo 57), Luiz Adriano.
Tigres UANL: Guzman; Salcedo, Reyes, Rodriguez, Duenas (Meza 86), Rafael Carioca, Pizarro, Aquino (Sierra 90), Quinones L (Fulgencio 87), Gignac, Gonzalez.
Referee: Danny Makkelie (Netherlands).

Al Rayyan, Monday 8 February 2021

Al Ahly (0) 0

Bayern Munich (1) 2 *(Lewandowski 17, 86)*

Al Ahly: Mohamed Elshenawy; Ayman Ashraf, Benoun, Maaloul (Yasser Ibrahim 28), Mohamed Hany, Kahraba (Bwalya 69), Hamdy Fathy, Hussein Elshahat (Salah Mohsen 69), Amro Elsoulia, Mohamed Afsha (Dieng 69), Taher Mohamed (Mohamed Sherif 83).
Bayern Munich: Neuer; Pavard, Boateng (Suele 77), Davies, Alaba, Kimmich, Gnabry (Sane 62), Roca (Tolisso 69), Muller (Choupo-Moting 62), Coman (Musiala 77), Lewandowski.
Referee: Mohammed Abdulla Hassan Mohamed (United Arab Emirates).

MATCH FOR THIRD PLACE

Al Rayyan, Thursday 11 February 2021

Al Ahly (0) 0

Palmeiras (0) 0

Al Alhy: Mohamed Elshenawy; Yasser Ibrahim, Ayman Ashraf, Benoun, Maaloul, Mohamed Hany, Hamdy Fathy, Amro Elsoulia, Mohamed Afsha (Mohamed Sherif 58), Akram Tawfik (Dieng 75), Taher Mohamed (Marwan Mohsen 75), Bwalya (Ajayi 58).
Palmeiras: Weverton; Mayke, Luan Garcia, Gomez, Vina, Patrick de Paula (Danilo 80), Rony, Raphael Veiga (Gustavo Scarpa 80), Felipe Melo, Luiz Adriano, Willian (Gabriel Menino 80).
Al Ahly won 3-2 on penalties.
Referee: Maguette N'Diaye (Senegal).

FIFA WORLD CLUB CUP FINAL 2020

Al Rayyan, Thursday 11 February 2021

Bayern Munich (0) 1 *(Pavard 59)*

Tigres UANL (0) 0

Bayern Munich: Neuer; Suele, Pavard, Davies, Hernandez, Kimmich, Gnabry (Tolisso 64), Sane (Musiala 73), Alaba, Coman (Douglas Costa 73), Lewandowski (Choupo-Moting 73).
Tigres UANL: Guzman; Salcedo, Reyes, Rodriguez (Quinones J 80), Duenas, Rafael Carioca, Pizarro, Aquino, Quinones L, Gignac, Gonzalez.
Referee: Esteban Ostojich (Uruguay).

PREVIOUS FINALS

2000 Corinthians beat Vasco da Gama 4-3 on penalties after 0-0 draw
2001–04 Not contested
2005 Sao Paulo beat Liverpool 1-0
2006 Internacional beat Barcelona 1-0
2007 AC Milan beat Boca Juniors 4-2
2008 Manchester U beat Liga De Quito 1-0
2009 Barcelona beat Estudiantes 2-1
2010 Internazionale beat TP Mazembe Englebert 3-0
2011 Barcelona beat Santos 4-0
2012 Corinthians beat Chelsea 1-0
2013 Bayern Munich beat Raja Casablanca 2-0
2014 Real Madrid beat San Lorenzo 2-0
2015 Barcelona beat River Plate 3-0
2016 Real Madrid beat Kashima Antlers 4-2 (*aet.*)
2017 Real Madrid beat Gremio 1-0
2018 Real Madrid beat Al-Ain 4-1
2019 Liverpool beat Flamengo 1-0 (*aet.*)
2020 Bayern Munich beat Tigres UANL 1-0

WORLD CLUB CHAMPIONSHIP

Played annually up to 1974 and intermittently since then between the winners of the European Cup and the winners of the South American Champions Cup – known as the Copa Libertadores. In 1980 the winners were decided by one match arranged in Tokyo in February 1981 which remained the venue until 2004, when the match was superseded by the FIFA Club World Championship. AC Milan replaced Marseille who had been stripped of their European Cup title in 1993.

1960 Real Madrid beat Penarol 0-0, 5-1
1961 Penarol beat Benfica 0-1, 5-0, 2-1
1962 Santos beat Benfica 3-2, 5-2
1963 Santos beat AC Milan 2-4, 4-2, 1-0
1964 Inter-Milan beat Independiente 0-1, 2-0, 1-0
1965 Inter-Milan beat Independiente 3-0, 0-0
1966 Penarol beat Real Madrid 2-0, 2-0
1967 Racing Club beat Celtic 0-1, 2-1, 1-0
1968 Estudiantes beat Manchester United 1-0, 1-1
1969 AC Milan beat Estudiantes 3-0, 1-2
1970 Feyenoord beat Estudiantes 2-2, 1-0
1971 Nacional beat Panathinaikos* 1-1, 2-1
1972 Ajax beat Independiente 1-1, 3-0
1973 Independiente beat Juventus* 1-0
1974 Atlético Madrid* beat Independiente 0-1, 2-0
1975 Independiente and Bayern Munich could not agree dates; no matches.
1976 Bayern Munich beat Cruzeiro 2-0, 0-0
1977 Boca Juniors beat Borussia Moenchengladbach* 2-2, 3-0
1978 Not contested
1979 Olimpia beat Malmö* 1-0, 2-1
1980 Nacional beat Nottingham Forest 1-0
1981 Flamengo beat Liverpool 3-0
1982 Penarol beat Aston Villa 2-0
1983 Gremio Porto Alegre beat Hamburg 2-1
1984 Independiente beat Liverpool 1-0
1985 Juventus beat Argentinos Juniors 4-2 on penalties after 2-2 draw
1986 River Plate beat Steaua Bucharest 1-0
1987 FC Porto beat Penarol 2-1 after extra time
1988 Nacional (Uru) beat PSV Eindhoven 7-6 on penalties after 1-1 draw
1989 AC Milan beat Atletico Nacional (Col) 1-0 after extra time
1990 AC Milan beat Olimpia 3-0
1991 Crvena Zvezda beat Colo Colo 3-0
1992 Sao Paulo beat Barcelona 2-1
1993 Sao Paulo beat AC Milan 3-2
1994 Velez Sarsfield beat AC Milan 2-0
1995 Ajax beat Gremio Porto Alegre 4-3 on penalties after 0-0 draw
1996 Juventus beat River Plate 1-0
1997 Borussia Dortmund beat Cruzeiro 2-0
1998 Real Madrid beat Vasco da Gama 2-1
1999 Manchester U beat Palmeiras 1-0
2000 Boca Juniors beat Real Madrid 2-1
2001 Bayern Munich beat Boca Juniors 1-0 after extra time
2002 Real Madrid beat Olimpia 2-0
2003 Boca Juniors beat AC Milan 3-1 on penalties after 1-1 draw
2004 Porto beat Once Caldas 8-7 on penalties after 0-0 draw

**European Cup runners-up; winners declined to take part.*

EUROPEAN SUPER CUP 2020

Played annually between the winners of the European Champions' Cup and the European Cup-Winners' Cup (UEFA Cup from 2000; UEFA Europa League from 2010). AC Milan replaced Marseille in 1993–94. Match played in Monaco 1998–2012; various venues from 2013.

Budapest, Thursday 24 September 2020, attendance 15,180

Bayern Munich (1) 2 *(Goretzka 34, Martinez 104)*

Sevilla (1) 1 *(Ocampus 13 (pen))*

Bayern Munich: Neuer; Pavard, Hernandez (Martinez 99), Sule, Alaba (Boateng 112), Goretzka (Davies 99), Kimmich, Sane (Tolisso 70), Muller, Gnabry, Lewandowski.

Sevilla: Bounou; Navas, Carlos, Kounde, Escudero, Jordan (Vazquez 94), Fernando, Rakitic (Torres 56), Suso (Gudelj 73), de Jong (En-Nesyri 56), Ocampos.

aet; Referee: Anthony Taylor (England).

PREVIOUS MATCHES

1972 Ajax beat Rangers 3-1, 3-2
1973 Ajax beat AC Milan 0-1, 6-0
1974 Not contested
1975 Dynamo Kyiv beat Bayern Munich 1-0, 2-0
1976 Anderlecht beat Bayern Munich 4-1, 1-2
1977 Liverpool beat Hamburg 1-1, 6-0
1978 Anderlecht beat Liverpool 3-1, 1-2
1979 Nottingham F beat Barcelona 1-0, 1-1
1980 Valencia beat Nottingham F 1-0, 1-2
1981 Not contested
1982 Aston Villa beat Barcelona 0-1, 3-0
1983 Aberdeen beat Hamburg 0-0, 2-0
1984 Juventus beat Liverpool 2-0
1985 Juventus v Everton not contested due to UEFA ban on English clubs
1986 Steaua Bucharest beat Dynamo Kyiv 1-0
1987 FC Porto beat Ajax 1-0, 1-0
1988 KV Mechelen beat PSV Eindhoven 3-0, 0-1
1989 AC Milan beat Barcelona 1-1, 1-0
1990 AC Milan beat Sampdoria 1-1, 2-0
1991 Manchester U beat Crvena Zvezda 1-0
1992 Barcelona beat Werder Bremen 1-1, 2-1
1993 Parma beat AC Milan 0-1, 2-0
1994 AC Milan beat Arsenal 0-0, 2-0
1995 Ajax beat Zaragoza 1-1, 4-0
1996 Juventus beat Paris Saint-Germain 6-1, 3-1
1997 Barcelona beat Borussia Dortmund 2-0, 1-1
1998 Chelsea beat Real Madrid 1-0
1999 Lazio beat Manchester U 1-0
2000 Galatasaray beat Real Madrid 2-1
2001 Liverpool beat Bayern Munich 3-2
2002 Real Madrid beat Feyenoord 3-1
2003 AC Milan beat Porto 1-0
2004 Valencia beat Porto 2-1
2005 Liverpool beat CSKA Moscow 3-1
2006 Sevilla beat Barcelona 3-0
2007 AC Milan beat Sevilla 3-1
2008 Zenit beat Manchester U 2-1
2009 Barcelona beat Shakhtar Donetsk 1-0
2010 Atletico Madrid beat Internazionale 2-0
2011 Barcelona beat Porto 2-0
2012 Atletico Madrid beat Chelsea 4-1
2013 Bayern Munch beat Chelsea 5-4 on penalties after 2-2 draw
2014 Real Madrid beat Sevilla 2-0
2015 Barcelona beat Sevilla 5-4
2016 Real Madrid beat Sevilla 3-2
2017 Real Madrid beat Manchester U 2-1
2018 Atletico Madrid beat Real Madrid 4-2 after extra time
2019 Liverpool beat Chelsea 5-4 on penalties after 2-2 draw.
2020 Bayern Munich beat Sevilla 2-1.

INTERNATIONAL DIRECTORY

The directory provides the latest available information on international and club football in the 211 national associations in the six Confederations of FIFA, the world governing body. This includes addresses, foundation dates and team colours. FIFA-recognised internationals played in season 2020–21 (i.e. *6 July 2020 to 11 July 2021*) are listed as well as league and cup champions at club level. In Europe, the latest league tables, cup winners and top scorers for the 55 UEFA nations are given, together with all-time league and cup honours. (Key to table symbols used: (C) league champions; ¹ Champions League qualifier; ² Europa League qualifier; ³ Europa Conference League qualifier; * team relegated; *+ team relegated after play-offs; + team not relegated after play-offs.

The four home nations, England, Scotland, Northern Ireland and Wales, are dealt with elsewhere in the Yearbook; but basic details appear in this directory. Gozo is included here for its close links with Maltese football. Northern Cyprus is not a member of FIFA or UEFA and is the subject of an international territorial dispute. Kosovo was granted full membership of both FIFA and UEFA in May 2016 and entered World Cup 2018 qualification in September 2016, followed by participation in the 2019–20 UEFA Nations League and Euro 2020 qualifying. FYR Macedonia's results are now credited to North Macedonia, its new name from February 2019. Swaziland was renamed Eswatini in April 2018.

International match venues are indicated as follows: home (h), away (a), neutral (n); in multi-nation tournaments the host nation is deemed to be playing at home and all others are on neutral territory; where a nation is unable to play a qualifier at home the neutral venue is stated in a note.

There are currently 12 associate members and others who have affiliation to their confederations. The associate members are: AFC: Northern Mariana Islands; CAF: Reunion, Zanzibar; CONCACAF: Bonaire, French Guiana, Guadeloupe, Martinique, Saint-Martin, Sint Maarten; OFC: Kiribati, Niue, Tuvalu. Matches between full members and associate members are indicated with †.

N.B. Final league rankings for clubs tied on points are decided on goal difference unless otherwise stated.

EUROPE (UEFA)

ALBANIA

Football Association of Albania, Rruga e Elbasanit, 1000 Tirana.

Founded: 1930. *FIFA:* 1932; *UEFA:* 1954. *National Colours:* Red shirts with white trim, black shorts, red socks.

International matches 2020–21

Belarus (a) 2-0, Lithuania (h) 0-1, Kazakhstan (a) 0-0, Lithuania (a) 0-0, Kosovo (h) 2-1, Kazakhstan (h) 3-1, Belarus (h) 3-2, Andorra (a) 1-0, England (h) 0-2, San Marino (a) 2-0, Wales (a) 0-0, Czech Republic (a) 1-3.

League Championship wins (1930–37; 1945–2021)

KF Tirana 25 (formerly SK Tirana; includes 17 Nentori 8); Dinamo Tirana 18; Partizani Tirana 16; Vllaznia Shkoder 9; Skenderbeu Korce 8; Elbasani 2 (incl. Labinoti 1); Teuta 2; Flamurtari Vlore 1; Kukesi 1.

Cup wins (1948–2021)

KF Tirana 16 (formerly SK Tirana; includes 17 Nentori 8); Partizani Tirana 15; Dinamo Tirana 13; Vllaznia 7; Flamurtari Vlore 4; Teuta 4; Elbasani 2 (incl. Labinoti 1); Besa 2; Laci 2; Kukesi 2; Apolonia Fier 1; Skenderbeu Korce 1.

Albanian Kategoria Superiore 2020–21

	P	*W*	*D*	*L*	*F*	*A*	*GD*	*Pts*
Teuta (C)¹	36	17	15	4	42	16	26	66
Vllaznia³	36	19	9	8	44	22	22	66
Partizani Tirana³	36	17	14	5	53	23	30	65
Laci³	36	16	13	7	41	26	15	61
Tirana	36	15	13	8	41	26	15	58
Kukesi	36	13	6	17	47	48	–1	45
Skenderbeu Korce	36	9	10	17	34	55	–21	37
Kastrioti+	36	8	11	17	26	44	–18	35
Bylis*	36	7	10	19	28	51	–23	31
Apolonia Fier*	36	4	9	23	22	67	–45	21

Top scorer: Bregu (Teuta) 16.
Cup Final: Vllaznia 1, Kukesi 0.

ANDORRA

Federacio Andorrana de Futbol, Avda Carlemany 67, 3er Pis, Apartado postal 65, Escaldes-Engordany.

Founded: 1994. *FIFA:* 1996; *UEFA:* 1996. *National Colours:* All red.

International matches 2020–21

Latvia (a) 0-0, Faroe Islands (h) 0-1, Cape Verde Islands (h) 1-2, Malta (h) 0-0, Faroe Islands (a) 0-2, Portugal (a) 0-7, Malta (a) 1-3, Latvia (h) 0-5, Albania (h) 0-1, Poland (a) 0-3, Hungary (h) 1-4, Republic of Ireland (h) 1-4, Gibraltar (h) 0-0.

League Championship wins (1996–2021)

FC Santa Coloma 13; Principat 3; Encamp 2; Sant Julia 2; Ranger's 2; Lusitanos 2; Inter Club d'Escaldes 2; Constel-lacio Esportiva 1.

Cup wins (1991, 1994–2021)

FC Santa Coloma 10*; Principat 6*; Sant Julia 6; UE Santa Coloma 3; Constel-lacio Esportiva 1; Lusitanos 1; UE Engordany 1; Inter Club d'Escaldes 1.
* *Includes one unofficial title.*

Andorran Primera Divisio Qualifying Table 2020–21

	P	*W*	*D*	*L*	*F*	*A*	*GD*	*Pts*
Inter Club d'Escaldes	14	7	5	2	22	7	15	26
FC Santa Coloma	14	6	6	2	22	13	9	24
Sant Julia	14	7	3	4	27	20	7	24
Atletic Club d'Escaldes	14	6	5	3	25	12	13	23
UE Engordany	14	5	7	2	25	16	9	22
UE Santa Coloma	14	6	2	6	19	15	4	20
Penya Encarnada	14	2	1	11	10	47	–37	7
CE Carroi	14	2	1	11	8	28	–20	7

Championship Round 2020–21

	P	*W*	*D*	*L*	*F*	*A*	*GD*	*Pts*
Inter Club d'Escaldes (C)¹	20	11	6	3	34	11	23	39
Sant Julia³	20	10	4	6	33	24	9	34
FC Santa Coloma³	20	8	8	4	28	19	9	32
Atletic Club d'Escaldes	20	6	7	7	29	26	3	25

Relegation Round 2020–21

	P	*W*	*D*	*L*	*F*	*A*	*GD*	*Pts*
UE Engordany	20	8	9	3	43	30	13	33
UE Santa Coloma	20	9	3	8	44	27	17	30
CE Carroi+	20	5	4	11	20	33	–13	19
Penya Encarnada*	20	2	1	17	13	74	–61	7

Top scorer: Lopez (UE Engordany) 16.
Cup Final: Sant Julia 2, Atletic Club d'Escaldes 1.

ARMENIA

Football Federation of Armenia, Khanjyan Street 27, 0010 Yerevan.

Founded: 1992. *FIFA:* 1992; *UEFA:* 1993. *National Colours:* Red shirts with white trim, red shorts, red socks.

International matches 2020–21

North Macedonia (a) 1-2, Estonia (h) 2-0, Georgia (h) 2-2, Estonia (a) 1-1, Georgia (a) 2-1, North Macedonia (h) 1-0, Liechtenstein (a) 1-0, Iceland (h) 2-0, Romania (h) 3-2, Croatia (a) 1-1, Sweden (a) 1-3.

League Championship wins (1992–2021)

Pyunik 14 (incl. Homenetmen 1*); Shirak 4*; Alashkert 4; Araks 2 (incl. Tsement 1); Ararat-Armenia 2; Ararat Yerevan 1; FK Yerevan 1; Ulisses 1; Banants (now Urartu) 1.
* *Includes one unofficial shared title.*

Cup wins (1992–2021)

Pyunik (incl. Homenetmen 1) 8; Ararat Yerevan 6; Mika 6; Banants (now Urartu) 3; Tsement 2; Shirak 2; Gandzasar Kapan 1; Alashkert 1; Noah 1.

See also Russia section for Armenian club honours in Soviet era 1936–91.

Armenian Premier League 2020–21

	P	W	D	L	F	A	GD	Pts
Alashkert (C)[1]	24	13	7	4	25	15	10	46
Noah[3]	24	12	5	7	35	20	15	41
Urartu[3]	24	12	5	7	28	19	9	41
Ararat Yerevan[3]	24	11	7	6	34	18	16	40
Ararat-Armenia	24	10	8	6	32	17	15	38
Van	24	9	4	11	25	30	–5	31
Pyunik	24	6	7	11	20	18	2	25
Lori	24	7	2	15	16	44	–28	23
Shirak*	24	2	7	15	19	53	–34	13
Gandzasar Kapan*	0	0	0	0	0	0	0	0

** Due to the COVID-19 pandemic, Lori could not fulfil matches 19–27, which were all awarded as 3-0 wins to the eight remaining teams.*
Top scorer: Otubanjo (Ararat-Armenia) 10.
Cup Final: Ararat Yerevan 3, Alashkert 1.

AUSTRIA

Oesterreichischer Fussball-Bund, Ernst-Happel Stadion, Sektor A/F, Meiereistrasse 7, Wien 1021.
Founded: 1904. *FIFA:* 1905; *UEFA:* 1954. *National Colours:* Red shirts, white shorts, red socks.

International matches 2020–21
Norway (a) 2-1, Romania (h) 2-3, Greece (h) 2-1, Northern Ireland (a) 1-0, Romania (a) 1-0, Luxembourg (a) 3-0, Northern Ireland (h) 2-1, Norway (h) 1-1, Scotland (a) 2-2, Faroe Islands (h) 3-1, Denmark (h) 0-4, England (a) 0-1, Slovakia (h) 0-0, North Macedonia (n) 3-1, Netherlands (a) 0-2, Ukraine (n) 1-0, Italy (n) 1-2.

League Championship wins (1912–2021)
Rapid Vienna 32; Austria Vienna (formerly Amateure) 24; Red Bull Salzburg 15 (incl. Austria Salzburg 3); Wacker Innsbruck 10 (incl. Swarovski Tirol 2, Tirol Innsbruck 3); Admira Vienna (now Admira Wacker Modling) 9 (incl. Wacker Vienna 1); First Vienna 6; Wiener Sportklub 3; Sturm Graz 3; WAF 1; WAC 1; Floridsdorfer 1; Hakoah 1; LASK (Linz) 1; Voest Linz 1; GAK (Graz) 1.

Cup wins (1919–2021)
Austria Vienna (formerly Amateure) 27; Rapid Vienna 14; Red Bull Salzburg 8; Wacker Innsbruck 7 (incl. Swarovski Tirol 1); Admira Vienna (now Admira Wacker Modling) 6 (incl. Wacker Vienna 1); Sturm Graz 5; GAK Graz 4; First Vienna 3; WAC 3 (incl. Schwarz-Rot Wien 1); Ried 2; WAF 1; Wiener Sportklub 1; LASK (Linz) 1; Kremser 1; Stockerau 1; Karnten 1; Horn 1; Pasching 1.

Austrian Bundesliga Qualifying Table 2020–21

	P	W	D	L	F	A	GD	Pts
Red Bull Salzburg	22	17	1	4	67	24	43	52
Rapid Vienna	22	13	6	3	43	25	18	45
LASK	22	13	3	6	42	21	21	42
Sturm Graz	22	11	6	5	34	20	14	39
Wolfsberg	22	10	3	9	40	39	1	33
WSG Swarovski Tirol	22	8	6	8	37	34	3	30
Hartberg	22	7	8	7	25	38	–13	29
Austria Vienna	22	6	7	9	31	32	–1	25
St Polten	22	5	6	11	33	43	–10	21
Rheindorf Altach	22	6	3	13	20	43	–23	21
Ried	22	4	4	14	21	46	–25	16
Admira Wacker Modling	22	3	5	14	22	50	–28	14

NB: Points earned in Qualifying phase are halved and rounded down at start of Championship and Relegation Play-off phase.

Championship Round 2020–21

	P	W	D	L	F	A	GD	Pts
Red Bull Salzburg (C)[1]	32	25	2	5	94	33	61	51
Rapid Vienna[1]	32	17	8	7	64	40	24	36
Sturm Graz[2]	32	16	8	8	52	34	18	36
LASK[3]	32	15	6	11	55	41	14	30
Wolfsberg†	32	13	5	14	52	62	–10	27
WSG Swarovski Tirol	32	10	8	14	53	60	–7	23

† Qualified for Europa Conference League Play-offs final.

Relegation Round 2020–21

	P	W	D	L	F	A	GD	Pts
Hartberg	32	12	11	9	38	48	–10	32
Austria Vienna†[3]	32	11	9	12	47	43	4	29
Ried	32	8	9	15	34	57	–23	25
Rheindorf Altach	32	9	7	16	33	55	–22	23
Admira Wacker Modling	32	6	8	18	27	58	–31	19
St Polten*+	32	5	9	18	39	57	–18	13

† Qualified for Europa Conference League Play-offs final.

Europa Conference League Play-offs
Semi-final
Hartberg 0, Austria Vienna 3
Final
Austria Vienna 3, 2, Wolfsberg 0, 1 (agg. 5-1)
Top scorer: Daka (Red Bull Salzburg) 27.
Cup Final: Red Bull Salzburg 3, LASK 0.

AZERBAIJAN

Association of Football Federations of Azerbaijan, 2208 Nobel prospekti, 1025 Baku.
Founded: 1992. *FIFA:* 1994; *UEFA:* 1994. *National Colours:* All red.

International matches 2020–21
Luxembourg (h) 1-2, Cyprus (a) 1-0, Montenegro (a) 0-2, Cyprus (h) 0-0, Slovenia (a) 0-0, Montenegro (h) 0-0, Luxembourg (a) 1-2, Portugal (a) 0-1, Qatar (n) 1-2, Serbia (h) 1-2, Turkey (a) 1-2, Belarus (a) 2-1, Moldova (a) 0-1.

League Championship wins (1992–2021)
Neftchi 9; Qarabag 8; Kapaz 3; Shamkir 3*; FK Baku 2; Inter Baku (now Keshla) 2; Turan 1; Khazar Lankaran 1.
** Includes one unofficial title.*

Cup wins (1992–2021)
Neftchi 7*; Qarabag 6; Kapaz 4; FK Baku 3; Khazar Lankaran 3; Keshla (formerly Inter Baku) 2; Inshatchi 1; Shafa 1; Gabala 1.
*No winner in 2019–20. * Includes one unofficial title.*

Azerbaijani Premyer Liqası 2020–21

	P	W	D	L	F	A	GD	Pts
Neftchi (C)[1]	28	18	5	5	47	25	22	59
Qarabag[3]	28	16	9	3	64	18	46	57
Sumqayit[3]	28	10	9	9	30	31	–1	39
Zira	28	8	14	6	28	28	0	38
Sabah	28	7	8	13	28	38	–10	29
Keshla[3]	28	5	11	12	25	40	–15	26
Gabala	28	5	11	12	23	44	–21	26
Sabail*	28	5	9	14	21	42	–21	24

Top scorer: Alaskarov (Neftchi) 19.
Cup Final: Keshla 2, Sumqayit 1.

BELARUS

Belarus Football Federation, Prospekt Pobeditelei 20/3, 220020 Minsk.
Founded: 1989. *FIFA:* 1992; *UEFA:* 1993. *National Colours:* All red with white trim.

International matches 2020–21
Albania (h) 0-2, Kazakhstan (a) 2-1, Georgia (a) 0-1, Lithuania (a) 2-2, Kazakhstan (h) 2-0, Romania (a) 3-5, Lithuania (h) 2-0, Albania (a) 2-3, Honduras (h) 1-1, Estonia (h) 4-2, Belgium (a) 0-8, Azerbaijan (h) 1-2.

League Championship wins (1992–2020)
BATE Borisov 15; Dinamo Minsk 7; Slavia Mozyr (incl. MPKC 1) 2; Shakhtyor Soligorsk 2; Dnepr Mogilev 1; Belshina Bobruisk 1; Gomel 1; Dinamo Brest 1.

Cup wins (1992–2021)
BATE Borisov 5; Dinamo Minsk 3; Belshina Bobruisk 3; Shakhtyor Soligorsk 3; Dinamo Brest 3; Slavia Mozyr (incl. MPKC 1) 2; Gomel 2; MTZ-RIPA 2; Naftan Novopolotsk 2; Neman Grodno 1; Dinamo 93 Minsk 1; Lokomotiv 96 1; FC Minsk 1; Torpedo-BelAZ Zhodino 1.
See also Russia section for Belarusian club honours in Soviet era 1936–91.

Belarusian Vysheyshaya Liga 2020

	P	W	D	L	F	A	GD	Pts
Shakhtyor Soligorsk (C)[1]	30	17	8	5	57	21	36	59
BATE Borisov[3]	30	17	7	6	65	32	33	58
Torpedo-BelAZ Zhodino[3]	30	16	8	6	55	37	18	56
Dinamo Brest[3]	30	17	3	10	63	40	23	54
Neman Grodno	30	16	5	9	41	29	12	53
Dinamo Minsk	30	16	4	10	38	25	13	52
Isloch Minsk Raion	30	13	6	11	47	46	1	45
Ruh Brest	30	11	11	8	57	38	19	44
Slavia Mozyr	30	10	9	11	41	49	–8	39
Energetik-BGU Minsk†	30	11	5	14	43	46	–3	38
FC Minsk†	30	11	5	14	45	57	–12	38
Vitebsk	30	8	12	10	30	38	–8	36
Gorodeya‡	30	8	7	15	30	48	–18	31
Slutsk+§	29	8	3	19	31	58	–24	27
Belshina Bobruisk*	30	5	6	19	34	71	–37	21
Smolevichy*	30	4	5	21	30	72	–42	17

† Ranking decided on head-to-head points.
‡ Gorodeya disbanded at the end of the season. § Slutsk v

Smolevichy recorded as 0-3 defeat as Slutsk were in lock-down and unable to fulfil fixture.
Top scorer: Skavysh (BATE Borisov) 17.
Cup Final: BATE Borisov 1, Isloch Minsk Raion 0.

BELGIUM

Union Royale Belge des Societes de Football-Association, 145 Avenue Houba de Strooper, B-1020 Bruxelles.
Founded: 1895. *FIFA:* 1904; *UEFA:* 1954. *National Colours:* All red.

International matches 2020–21

Denmark (a) 2-0, Iceland (h) 5-1, Ivory Coast (h) 1-1, Belarus (h) 8-0, England (a) 1-2, Iceland (a) 2-1, Switzerland (h) 2-1, England (h) 2-0, Denmark (h) 4-2, Wales (h) 3-1, Czech Republic (a) 1-1, Belarus (h) 8-0, Greece (h) 1-1, Croatia (h) 1-0, Russia (a) 3-0, Denmark (a) 2-1, Finland (n) 2-0, Portugal (n) 1-0, Italy (n) 1-2.

League Championship wins (1896–2021)

Anderlecht 34; Club Brugge 17; Union St Gilloise 11; Standard Liege 10; Beerschot VAC (became Germinal) 7; RC Brussels 6; RFC Liege 5; Daring Brussels 5; Antwerp 4; Lierse 4; Mechelen 4; Genk 4; Cercle Brugge 3; Beveren 2; RWD Molenbeek 1; Gent 1.

Cup wins (1912–14; 1927; 1935; 1954–2021)

Club Brugge 11; Anderlecht 9; Standard Liege 8; Genk 5; Antwerp 3; Gent 3; Union Saint-Gilloise 2; Cercle Brugge 2; Lierse 2; Beerschot VAC (became Germinal) 2; Beveren 2; Waterschei (became Racing Genk) 2; Mechelen 2; Beerschot Antwerpen Club (incl. Germinal Ekeren) 2; Zulte Waregem 2; Lokeren 2; Racing 1; Daring 1; Tournai 1; KFC Waregem 1; RFC Liege 1; Westerlo 1; La Louviere 1.

Belgian First Division A Final Table 2020–21

	P	W	D	L	F	A	GD	Pts
Club Brugge	34	24	4	6	73	26	47	76
Antwerp	34	18	6	10	57	48	9	60
Anderlecht	34	15	13	6	51	34	17	58
Genk	34	16	8	10	67	48	19	56
Oostende	34	15	8	11	49	41	8	53
Standard Liege	34	13	11	10	52	41	11	50
Gent	34	14	7	13	55	42	13	49
Mechelen	34	13	9	12	54	54	0	48
Beerschot	34	14	5	15	58	64	–6	47
Zulte-Waregem	34	14	4	16	53	69	–16	46
Leuven	34	12	9	13	54	59	–5	45
Eupen	34	10	13	11	44	55	–11	43
Sporting Charleroi	34	11	9	14	46	49	–3	42
Kortrijk	34	11	6	17	44	57	–13	39
Sint-Truiden	34	10	8	16	41	52	–11	38
Cercle Brugge	34	11	3	20	40	51	–11	36
Waasland-Beveren†*+	34	8	7	19	44	70	–26	31
Excel Mouscron†*	34	7	10	17	32	54	–22	31

NB: Points earned in Qualifying phase are halved and rounded up at start of Champions League Play-off phase.
† Ranking decided on matches won.

Champions League Play-off I 2020–21

	P	W	D	L	F	A	GD	Pts
Club Brugge (C)[1]	6	1	3	2	8	11	–3	44
Genk[1]	6	5	1	0	15	5	10	44
Antwerp[2]	6	1	2	3	6	11	–5	35
Anderlecht[3]	6	0	4	2	9	11	–2	33

Europa Conference League Play-off II 2020–21

	P	W	D	L	F	A	GD	Pts
Gent[3]	6	4	1	1	13	6	7	38
Mechelen	6	3	2	1	15	11	4	35
Oostende	6	2	1	3	15	16	–1	34
Standard Liege	6	1	0	5	7	17	–10	28

Top scorer: Onuachu (Genk) 33.
Cup Final: Genk 2, Standard Liege 1.

BOSNIA-HERZEGOVINA

Football Federation of Bosnia & Herzegovina, Ferhadija 30, 71000 Sarajevo.
Founded: 1992. *FIFA:* 1996; *UEFA:* 1998. *National Colours:* Blue shirts, blue shorts, blue socks with white tops.

International matches 2020–21

Italy (a) 1-1, Poland (h) 1-2, Northern Ireland (a) 1-1 (3-4p), Netherlands (h) 0-0, Poland (a) 0-3, Iran (h) 0-2, Netherlands (a) 1-3, Italy (h) 0-2, Finland (a) 2-2, Costa Rica (h) 0-0, France (h) 0-1, Montenegro (h) 0-0, Denmark (a) 0-2.

League Championship wins (1998–2021)

Zeljeznicar 6; Zrinjski Mostar 6; Sarajevo 5; Siroki Brijeg 2; Borac Banja Luka 2; Brotnjo 1; Leotar 1; Modrica 1.

Cup wins (1998–2021)

Sarajevo 7; Zeljeznicar 6; Siroki Brijeg 3; Bosna Visoko 1; Modrica 1; Orasje 1; Zrinjski Mostar 1; Slavija 1; Borac Banja Luka 1; Olimpik Sarajevo 1; Radnik Bijeljina 1.
See also Serbia section for Bosnian-Herzogovinian club honours in Yugoslav Republic era 1947–91.
No winner in 2019–20.

Premijer Liga Bosne i Hercegovine 2020–21

	P	W	D	L	F	A	GD	Pts
Borac Banja Luka (C)[1]	33	21	4	8	59	31	+28	67
Sarajevo[3]	33	18	11	4	53	24	+29	65
Velez Mostar[3]	33	16	13	4	50	30	+20	61
Siroki Brijeg[3]	33	17	8	8	47	30	+17	59
Zrinjski Mostar	33	18	5	10	50	30	+20	59
Tuzla City	33	13	9	11	36	35	+1	48
Zeljeznicar	33	12	8	13	50	43	+7	44
Sloboda Tuzla	33	10	7	16	31	41	–10	37
Mladost Doboj Kakanj*	33	8	6	19	26	57	–31	30
Krupa	33	7	7	19	26	46	–20	28
Radnik Bijeljina	33	5	10	18	26	51	–25	25
Olimpik*	33	7	4	22	22	58	–36	25

** Mladost Doboj Kakanj failed to obtain a licence for the Premijer Liga and were relegated.*
Top scorer: Bilbija (Zrinjski Mostar) 17.
Cup Final: Sarajevo 0, Borac Banja Luka 0.
Sarajevo won 4-1 on penalties.

BULGARIA

Bulgarian Football Union, 26 Tzar Ivan Assen II Str., 1124 Sofia.
Founded: 1923. *FIFA:* 1992; *UEFA:* 1954. *National Colours:* White shirts, green shorts, red socks.

International matches 2020–21

Republic of Ireland (h) 1-1, Wales (a) 0-1, Hungary (h) 1-3, Finland (a) 0-2, Wales (h) 0-1, Gibraltar (h) 3-0, Finland (h) 1-2, Republic of Ireland (a) 0-0, Switzerland (h) 1-3, Italy (h) 0-2, Northern Ireland (a) 0-0, Slovakia (n) 1-1, Russia (a) 0-1, France (a) 0-3.

League Championship wins (1925–2021)

CSKA Sofia 31; Levski Sofia 26; Ludogorets Razgrad 10; Slavia Sofia 7; Lokomotiv Sofia 4; Litex Lovech 4; Vladislav Varna (now Cherno More Varna) 3; Botev Plovdiv (includes Trakija) 2; Athletic Slava 1923 1; Sokol Varna (now Spartak Varna) 1; Sportklub Sofia (now Septemvri Sofia) 1; Ticha Varna (now Cherno More Varna) 1; Spartak Plovdiv 1; Beroe Stara Zagora 1; Etar 1; Lokomotiv Plovdiv 1.

Cup wins (1938–42; 1946–2021)

Levski Sofia (incl. Vitosha 1) 25; CSKA Sofia (incl. Sredets 3) 21; Slavia Sofia 8; Lokomotiv Sofia 4; Litex Lovech 4; Botev Plovdiv (includes Trakija) 3; FK 13 Sofia 2; Beroe Stara Zagora 2; Ludogorets Razgrad 2; Lokomotiv Plovdiv 2; Shipka Sofia 1; AS 23 Sofia 1; Spartak Plovdiv 1; Septemvri Sofia 1; Spartak Sofia 1; Marek Dupnitsa 1; Sliven 1; Cherno More Varna 1.

Bulgarian First League Qualifying Table 2020–21

	P	W	D	L	F	A	GD	Pts
Ludogorets Razgrad	26	20	4	2	59	18	41	64
Lokomotiv Plovdiv	26	15	7	4	41	19	22	52
CSKA Sofia	26	14	8	4	39	20	19	50
Arda	26	12	9	5	36	29	7	45
CSKA 1948 Sofia	26	10	8	8	34	30	4	38
Beroe†	26	10	7	9	38	28	10	37
Cherno More†	26	10	7	9	27	25	2	37
Tsarsko Selo	26	9	7	10	29	27	2	34
Levski Sofia	26	7	7	12	25	27	–2	28
Botev Plovdiv	26	5	9	12	25	46	–21	24
Slavia Sofia	26	6	5	15	19	40	–21	23
Botev Vratsa†	26	6	4	16	26	39	–13	22
Etar†	26	4	10	12	20	45	–25	22
Montana	26	4	8	14	21	46	–25	20

† Ranking decided on head-to-head points.

Championship Round 2020–21

	P	W	D	L	F	A	GD	Pts
Ludogorets Razgrad (C)[1]	31	22	4	5	69	29	40	70
Lokomotiv Plovdiv[3]	31	17	10	4	48	23	25	61
CSKA Sofia[3]	31	17	8	6	46	24	22	59
Arda‡[3]	31	13	11	7	42	37	5	50
CSKA 1948 Sofia	31	12	11	8	41	34	7	47
Beroe	31	10	9	12	42	38	4	39

‡ Qualified for Europa Conference League Play-off.

Europa Conference League Round 2020–21

	P	W	D	L	F	A	GD	Pts
Cherno More‡	32	12	9	11	37	34	3	45
Levski Sofia	32	11	8	13	34	32	2	41
Tsarsko Selo	32	9	10	13	33	39	–6	37
Botev Plovdiv	32	7	11	14	34	52	–18	32

‡ *Qualified for Europa Conference League Play-off.*

Relegation Round 2020–21

	P	W	D	L	F	A	GD	Pts
Slavia Sofia	32	9	7	16	28	44	–16	34
Botev Vratsa+	32	8	6	18	31	45	–14	30
Montana*	32	6	10	16	26	52	–26	28
Etar*	32	6	10	16	25	53	–28	28

Europa Conference League Play-off

Arda 1, Cherno More 0

Top scorer: Keseru (Ludogorets Razgrad) 18.

Cup Final: CSKA Sofia 1, Arda 0.

CHANNEL ISLANDS

Guernsey

League Championship wins (1894–2021)

Northerners 32; Guernsey Rangers 17; St Martin's 15; Vale Recreation 15; Sylvans 10; Belgrave Wanderers 8; 2nd Bn Manchesters 3; Guernsey Rovers 2; 2nd Bn Royal Irish Regt 2; 2nd Bn Wiltshires 2; 10th Comp W Div Royal Artillery 1; 2nd Bn Leicesters 1; 2nd Bn PA Somerset Light Infantry 1; 2nd Middlesex Regt 1; Athletics 1; Band Comp 2nd Bn Royal Fusiliers 1; G&H Comp Royal Fusiliers 1; Grange 1; Yorkshire Regt (Green Howards).

No winner in 2019–20.

Guernsey Priaulx League 2020–21

	P	W	D	L	F	A	GD	Pts
St Martin's (C)	24	18	4	2	59	15	44	58
Guernsey Rovers	24	14	6	4	73	31	42	48
Sylvans	24	11	7	6	58	41	17	40
Belgrave Wanderers	24	12	3	9	65	42	23	39
Manzur	24	11	4	9	53	43	10	37
Northerners	24	9	6	9	55	38	17	33
Vale Recreation	24	6	4	14	35	64	–29	22
Guernsey Rangers	24	5	1	18	34	106	–72	16
Alderney	24	4	1	19	23	75	–52	13

Top scorer: Smith (Sylvans) 32.

Jersey

League Championship wins (1904–2021)

Jersey Wanderers 21; St Paul's 21; First Tower United 19; Jersey Scottish 11; Beeches Old Boys 5; Magpies 4; 2nd Bn King's Own Regt 3; Oaklands 3; St Peter 3; 1st Batt Devon Regt 2; 1st Bn East Surrey Regt 2; Georgetown 2; Mechanics 2; YMCA 2; 2nd Bn East Surrey Regt 1; 20th Comp Royal Garrison Artillery 1; National Rovers 1; Sporting Academics 1; Trinity 1.

Jersey Football Combination 2020–21

	P	W	D	L	F	A	GD	Pts
St Paul's (C)	18	17	1	0	68	12	56	52
Jersey Wanderers	18	13	3	2	48	25	23	42
Grouville	18	9	6	3	43	24	19	33
St Peter	18	9	2	7	46	32	14	29
St Ouen	18	7	4	7	42	34	8	25
St Clement	18	5	5	8	43	40	3	20
St Brelade	18	5	5	8	32	35	–3	20
Sporting Academics	18	5	3	10	28	46	–18	18
Rozel Rovers	18	3	3	12	23	59	–36	12
St Lawrence	18	1	0	17	19	85	–66	3

Upton Park Trophy 2021 (For Guernsey & Jersey League Champions)

Not contested due to COVID-19 pandemic.

Upton Park Trophy wins (1907–2021)*

Northerners 17 (incl. 1 shared); First Tower United 12; St Paul's 12; Jersey Wanderers 11 (incl. 1 shared); St Martin's 11; Jersey Scottish 6; Guernsey Rangers 5; Vale Recreation 4; Belgrave Wanderers 4; Beeches Old Boys 3; Old St Paul's 3; Magpies 3; Sylvans 3; St Peter 2; Jersey Mechanics 1; Jersey YMCA 1; National Rovers 1; Sporting Academics 1; Trinity 1.

* *No winner in 2019–20 and 2020–21.*

CROATIA

Croatian Football Federation, Vukovarska 269A, 10000 Zagreb.

Founded: 1912. *FIFA:* 1992; *UEFA:* 1993. *National Colours:* Red and white check shirts, white shorts, blue socks.

International matches 2020–21

Portugal (a) 1-4, France (a) 2-4, Switzerland (a) 2-1, Sweden (h) 2-1, France (h) 1-2, Turkey (a) 3-3, Sweden (a) 1-2, Portugal (h) 2-3, Slovenia (a) 0-1, Cyprus (h) 1-0, Malta (h) 3-0, Armenia (h) 1-1, Belgium (a) 0-1, England (a) 0-1, Czech Republic (n) 1-1, Scotland (a) 3-1, Spain (n) 3-5.

League Championship wins (1992–2021)

Dinamo Zagreb (incl. Croatia Zagreb 3) 22; Hajduk Split 6; NK Zagreb 1; Rijeka 1.

Cup wins (1992–2021)

Dinamo Zagreb (incl. Croatia Zagreb 4) 16; Hajduk Split 6; Rijeka 6; Inter Zapresic 1; Osijek 1.

See also Serbia section for Croatian club honours in Yugoslav Republic era 1947–92.

Croatian Prva HNL 2020–21

	P	W	D	L	F	A	GD	Pts
Dinamo Zagreb (C)[1]	36	26	7	3	84	28	56	85
Osijek[3]	36	23	8	5	59	25	34	77
Rijeka[3]	36	18	7	11	51	46	5	61
Hajduk Split[3]	36	18	6	12	48	37	11	60
Gorica	36	17	8	11	60	47	13	59
Sibenik	36	9	8	19	32	47	–15	35
Slaven Koprivnica	36	7	13	16	36	53	–17	34
Lokomotiva Zagreb	36	7	9	20	29	60	–31	30
Istra 1961	36	7	8	21	27	52	–25	29
Varazdin*	36	6	10	20	30	61	–31	28

Top scorer: Mierez (Osijek) 22.

Cup Final: Dinamo Zagreb 6, Istra 1961 3.

CYPRUS

Cyprus Football Association, 10 Achaion Street, 2413 Engomi, PO Box 25071, 1306 Nicosia.

Founded: 1934. *FIFA:* 1948; *UEFA:* 1962. *National Colours:* All blue with white trim.

International matches 2020–21

Montenegro (h) 0-2, Azerbaijan (h) 0-1, Czech Republic (h) 1-2, Luxembourg (a) 0-2, Azerbaijan (a) 0-0, Greece (h) 1-2, Luxembourg (h) 2-1, Montenegro (a) 0-4, Slovakia (h) 0-0, Croatia (a) 0-1, Slovenia (h) 1-0, Hungary (a) 0-1, Ukraine (a) 0-4.

League Championship wins (1935–2021)

APOEL (Nicosia) 28; Omonia Nicosia 21; Anorthosis Famagusta 13; AEL Limassol 6; EPA Larnaca 3; Olympiakos Nicosia 3; Apollon Limassol 3; Pezoporikos Larnaca 2; Trust 1; Cetinkaya 1.

No winner in 2019–20.

Cup wins (1935–2021)

APOEL (Nicosia) 21; Omonia Nicosia 14; Anorthosis Famagusta 11; Apollon Limassol 9; AEL Limassol 7; EPA Larnaca 5; Trust 3; Cetinkaya 2; AEK Larnaca 2; Pezoporikos Larnaca 1; Olympiakos Nicosia 1; Nea Salamis Famagusta 1; APOP Kinyras 1.

No winner in 2019–20.

Cypriot First Division Qualifying Table 2020–21

	P	W	D	L	F	A	GD	Pts
Omonia Nicosia	26	16	8	2	43	13	30	56
AEL Limassol	26	17	4	5	45	23	22	55
Apollon	26	16	6	4	52	22	30	54
Anorthosis Famagusta	26	15	6	5	37	21	16	51
AEK Larnaca	26	12	5	9	36	25	11	41
Olympiakos Nicosai	26	10	4	12	27	38	–11	34
Paphos	26	8	8	10	30	27	3	32
APOEL	26	8	6	12	27	31	–4	30
Doxa Katokopia	26	7	9	10	24	32	–8	30
Nea Salamis Famagusta	26	8	5	13	29	38	–9	29
Enosis	26	6	6	14	22	39	–17	24
Ermis	26	5	9	12	18	38	–20	24

Championship Round 2020–21

	P	W	D	L	F	A	GD	Pts
Omonia Nicosia (C)[1]	36	23	10	3	55	17	38	79
Apollon[3]	36	21	11	4	68	30	38	74
AEL Limassol[3]	36	21	5	10	58	34	24	68
Anorthosis Famagusta[2]	36	16	9	11	44	37	7	57
AEK Larnaca	36	15	5	16	44	40	4	50
Olympiakos Nicosia	36	14	5	17	38	51	–13	47

Relegation Round 2020–21

	P	W	D	L	F	A	GD	Pts
Paphos	40	18	9	13	58	38	20	63
APOEL	40	17	9	14	48	39	9	60
Ethnikos Achna	40	14	10	16	48	56	–8	52
Doxa Katokopia	40	13	12	15	46	43	3	51
Nea Salamis Famagusta*	40	11	10	19	48	61	–13	43

	P	W	D	L	F	A	GD	Pts
Ermis*	40	9	11	20	40	61	–21	38
Enosis*	40	8	10	22	35	61	–26	34
Karmiotissa*	40	4	12	24	36	98	–62	24

Top scorer: Sadik (Doxa Katokopia) 18.
Cup Final: Anorthosis Famagusta 2, Olympiakos Nicosia 1.

CZECH REPUBLIC

Fotbalova Asociace Ceske Republiky, Diskarska 2431/4, PO Box 11, Praha 6 16017.
Founded: 1901. *FIFA:* 1907; *UEFA:* 1954. *National Colours:* All red.

International matches 2020–21

Slovakia (a) 3-1, Scotland (h) 1-2, Cyprus (a) 2-1, Israel (a) 2-1, Scotland (a) 0-1, Germany (a) 0-1, Israel (h) 1-0, Slovakia (h) 2-0, Estonia (a) 6-2, Belgium (h) 1-1, Wales (h) 0-1, Italy (a) 0-4, Albania (h) 3-1, Scotland (a) 2-0, Croatia (n) 1-1, England (a) 0-1, Netherlands (n) 2-0, Denmark (n) 1-2.

League Championship wins – Czechoslovakia (1925–93)

Sparta Prague 21; Slavia Prague 13; Dukla Prague (prev. UDA, now Marila Pribram) 11; Slovan Bratislava (formerly NV Bratislava) 8; Spartak Trnava 5; Banik Ostrava 3; Viktoria Zizkov 1; Inter Bratislava 1; Spartak Hradec Kralove 1; Zbrojovka Brno 1; Bohemians 1; Vitkovice 1.

Cup wins – Czechoslovakia (1961–93)

Dukla Prague 8; Sparta Prague 8; Slovan Bratislava 5; Spartak Trnava 4; Banik Ostrava 3; Lokomotiva Kosice 2; TJ Gottwaldov 1; DAC 1904 Dunajska Streda 1; 1.FC Kosice 1.

League Championship wins – Czech Republic (1994–2021)

Sparta Prague 12; Slavia Prague 7; Viktoria Plzen 5; Slovan Liberec 3; Banik Ostrava 1.

Cup wins – Czech Republic (1994–2021)

Sparta Prague 7; Slavia Prague 6; Viktoria Zizkov 2; Jablonec 2; Slovan Liberec 2; Teplice 2; Mlada Boleslav 2; Hradec Kralove (formerly Spartak) 1; Banik Ostrava 1; Viktoria Plzen 1; Sigma Olomouc 1; Fastav Zlin 1.

Czech First League Qualifying Table 2020–21

	P	W	D	L	F	A	GD	Pts
Slavia Prague (C)[1]	34	26	8	0	85	20	65	86
Sparta Prague[1]	34	23	5	6	82	43	39	74
Jablonec[2]	34	21	6	7	59	33	26	69
Slovacko[3]	34	19	6	9	58	33	25	63
Viktoria Plzen[3]	34	17	7	10	60	45	15	58
Slovan Liberec	34	14	10	10	44	32	12	52
Pardubice	34	15	7	12	41	42	–1	52
Banik Ostrava	34	13	10	11	48	38	10	49
Sigma Olomouc	34	11	12	11	40	40	0	45
Bohemians 1905	34	10	13	11	40	37	3	43
Mlada Boleslav	34	10	9	15	49	54	–5	39
Karvina	34	9	12	13	37	49	–12	39
Ceske Budejovice	34	9	11	14	33	47	–14	38
Zlin	34	8	8	18	30	50	–20	32
Teplice	34	7	9	18	34	66	–32	30
Zbrojovka Brno*	34	5	11	18	33	57	–24	26
Pribram*	34	5	10	19	26	65	–39	25
Opava*	34	3	8	23	23	71	–48	17

Top scorers (joint): Hlozek (Sparta Prague), Kuchta (Slavia Prague) 15.
Cup Final: Slavia Prague 1, Viktoria Plzen 0.

DENMARK

Dansk Boldspil-Union, Idraettens Hus, DBU Alle 1, DK-2605, Brondby.
Founded: 1889. *FIFA:* 1904; *UEFA:* 1954. *National Colours:* Red shirts, white shorts, red socks.

International matches 2020–21

Belgium (h) 0-2, England (h) 0-0, Faroe Islands (h) 4-0, Iceland (a) 3-0, England (a) 1-0, Sweden (h) 2-0, Iceland (h) 2-1, Belgium (a) 2-4, Israel (h) 2-0, Moldova (h) 8-0, Austria (a) 4-0, Germany (n) 1-1, Bosnia-Herzegovina (h) 2-0, Finland (h) 0-1, Belgium (h) 1-2, Russia (h) 4-1, Wales (n) 4-0, Czech Republic (n) 2-1, England (a) 1-2.

League Championship wins (1913–2021)

KB Copenhagen 15; FC Copenhagen 13; Brondby 11; B 93 Copenhagen 9; AB (Akademisk) 9; B 1903 Copenhagen 7; Frem 6; AGF (Aarhus) 5; Vejle 5; Esbjerg 5; AaB (Aalborg) 4; Hvidovre 3; OB (Odense) 3; FC Midtjylland 3; Koge 2; B 1909 Odense 2; Lyngby 2; Silkeborg 1; Herfolge 1; FC Nordsjaelland 1.

Cup wins (1955–2021)

AGF (Aarhus) 9; FC Copenhagen 8; Brondby 7; Vejle 6; OB (Odense) 5; Esbjerg 3; AaB (Aalborg) 3; Randers Freja 3; Lyngby 3; Frem 2; B 1909 Odense 2; B 1903 Copenhagen 2; Randers 2; Nordsjaelland 2; B 1913 Odense 1; KB Copenhagen 1; Vanlose 1; Hvidovre 1; B 93 Copenhagen 1; AB (Akademisk) 1; Viborg 1; Silkeborg 1; FC Midtjylland 1; SonderjyskE 1.

Danish Superliga Qualifying Table 2020–21

	P	W	D	L	F	A	GD	Pts
Brondby	22	14	3	5	40	24	16	45
FC Midtjylland	22	13	4	5	35	20	15	43
AGF	22	10	8	4	35	22	13	38
FC Copenhagen	22	10	5	7	39	35	4	35
Randers	22	9	5	8	31	21	10	32
Nordsjaelland	22	7	8	7	35	30	5	29
SonderjyskE	22	8	4	10	30	32	–2	28
OB	22	7	7	8	25	28	–3	28
AaB	22	7	7	8	24	30	–6	28
Vejle	22	6	6	10	25	37	–12	24
Lyngby	22	5	5	12	25	43	–18	20
AC Horsens	22	2	6	14	15	37	–22	12

Championship Round 2020–21

	P	W	D	L	F	A	GD	Pts
Brondby (C)[1]	32	19	4	9	58	38	20	61
FC Midtjylland[1]	32	18	6	8	57	33	24	60
FC Copenhagen[3]	32	16	7	9	61	53	8	55
AGF†[3]	32	13	9	10	48	42	6	48
Nordsjaelland	32	11	10	11	51	51	0	43
Randers[2]	32	11	7	14	43	38	5	40

† *Qualified for Europa Conference League Play-off.*

Relegation Round 2020–21

	P	W	D	L	F	A	GD	Pts
AaB†	32	12	10	10	44	41	3	46
SonderjyskE	32	13	5	14	45	48	–3	44
OB	32	11	10	11	40	39	1	43
Vejle	32	9	11	12	42	50	–8	38
Lyngby*	32	6	8	18	36	63	–27	26
AC Horsens*	32	5	9	18	30	59	–29	24

† *Qualified for Europa Conference League Play-off.*

Europa Conference League Play-off

AGF 2, AaB 2
aet; AGF won 3-1 on penalties.
Top scorer: Uhre (Brondby) 18.
Cup Final: Randers 4, SonderjyskE 0.

ENGLAND

The Football Association, Wembley Stadium, PO Box 1966, London SW1P 9EQ.
Founded: 1863. *FIFA:* 1905; *UEFA:* 1954. *National Colours:* All white.

ESTONIA

Eesti Jalgpalli Liit, A. Le Coq Arena, Asula 4c, 11312 Tallinn.
Founded: 1921. *FIFA:* 1923; *UEFA:* 1992. *National Colours:* Blue shirts, black shorts, white socks.

International matches 2020–21

Georgia (h) 0-1, Armenia (a) 0-2, Lithuania (h) 1-3, North Macedonia (h) 3-3, Armenia (h) 1-1, Italy (a) 0-4, North Macedonia (a) 1-2, Georgia (a) 0-0, Czech Republic (h) 2-6, Belarus (a) 2-4, Sweden (a) 0-1, Lithuania (a) 1-0, Finland (a) 1-0, Latvia (h) 2-1.

League Championship wins (1921–40; 1992–2020)

Flora 13; Sport 9; FCI Levadia (formerly Levadia Maardu) 9; Estonia 5; Sillamae Kalev 2; Tallinna JK 2; Norma 2; Lantana (formerly Nikol) 2; Nomme Kalju 2; Olimpia Tartu 1; TVMK Tallinn 1; FCI Tallinn 1.

Cup wins (1993–2021)

FCI Levadia (incl. Levadia Maardu 2) 10; Flora 8; Tallinna Sadam 2; Narva Trans 2; TVMK Tallinn 2; Lantana (formerly Nikol) 1; Norma 1; Levadia Tallinn (pre-2004) 1; Nomme Kalju 1; FCI Tallinn 1.

Estonian Meistriliiga 2020

	P	W	D	L	F	A	GD	Pts
Flora (C)[1]	27	24	2	1	66	16	50	74
Paide Linnameeskond[3]	27	20	0	7	70	30	40	60
FCI Levadia[3]	27	16	5	6	62	35	27	53
Nomme Kalju	27	14	7	6	48	19	29	49
Tartu Tammeka	27	8	7	12	30	41	–11	31
Viljandi Tulevik	27	9	3	15	27	43	–16	30
Legion	27	6	7	14	21	42	–21	25
Nava Trans	27	5	6	16	26	45	–19	21

Kuressaare+	27	4	8	15	26	59	–33	20
Tallinna Kalev*	27	5	3	19	18	64	–46	18

Top scorer: Sappinen (Flora) 26.
Cup Final: FCI Levadia 1, Flora 1.

FAROE ISLANDS

Fotboltssamband Foroya, Gundadalur, PO Box 3028, 110 Torshavn.
Founded: 1979. *FIFA:* 1988; *UEFA:* 1990. *National Colours:* White shirts with blue trim, white shorts, white socks.

International matches 2020–21

Malta (h) 3-2, Andorra (a) 1-0, Denmark (a) 0-4, Latvia (h) 1-1, Andorra (h) 2-0, Lithuania (a) 1-2, Latvia (a) 1-1, Malta (a) 1-1, Moldova (a) 1-1, Austria (a) 1-3, Scotland (a) 0-4, Iceland (h) 0-1, Liechtenstein (h) 5-1.

League Championship wins (1942–2020)

HB (Torshavn) 24; KI (Klaksvik) 18; B36 Torshavn 11; TB (Tvoroyri) (includes FC Suduroy and Royn) 7; GI (Gota) 6; B68 Toftir 3; EB/Streymur 2; Vikingur 2; SI (Sorvagur) 1; IF (Fuglafjordur) 1; B71 (Sandur) 1; VB Vagur 1; NSI Runavik 1.

Cup wins (1955–2020)

HB Torshavn 28; B36 Torshavn 6; KI (Klaksvik) 6; GI Gota 6; TB (Tvoroyri) (includes FC Suduroy and Royn) 5; Vikingur 5; EB/Streymur 4; NSI Runavik 3; VB Vagur (now FC Suduroy) 1; B71 (Sandur) 1.

Faroese Premier League 2020

	P	*W*	*D*	*L*	*F*	*A*	*GD*	*Pts*
HB (C)[1]	27	22	3	2	81	23	58	69
NSI Runavik[3]	27	20	3	4	58	26	32	63
KI[3]	27	19	5	3	72	25	47	62
B36 Torshavn	27	19	2	6	77	37	40	59
Vikingur	27	15	2	10	55	44	11	47
IF	27	7	5	15	34	59	–25	26
EB/Streymur	27	7	3	17	26	65	–39	24
TB	27	4	6	17	20	42	–22	18
Argja Boltfelag*+	27	1	7	19	21	73	–52	10
IF Fuglafjordur*	27	1	3	23	27	81	–54	6

Top scorers (joint): Olsen (NSI Runavik), Stojanov (IF Fuglafjordur) 17.
Cup Final: HB 2, Vikingur 0.

FINLAND

Suomen Palloliitto Finlands Bollfoerbund, Urheilukatu 5, PO Box 191, 00251 Helsinki.
Founded: 1907. *FIFA:* 1908; *UEFA:* 1954. *National Colours:* White shirts with blue trim, white shorts, white socks.

International matches 2020–21

Wales (h) 0-1, Republic of Ireland (a) 1-0, Poland (a) 1-5, Bulgaria (h) 2-0, Republic of Ireland (h) 1-0, France (a) 2-0, Bulgaria (a) 2-1, Wales (a) 1-3, Bosnia-Herzegovina (h) 2-2, Ukraine (a) 1-1, Switzerland (a) 2-3, Sweden (a) 0-2, Estonia (h) 0-1, Denmark (a) 1-0, Russia (a) 0-1, Belgium (n) 2-1.

League Championship wins (1908–2020)

HJK (Helsinki) 30; HPS (Helsinki) 9; FC Haka (Valkeakoski) 9; TPS (Turku) 8; HIFK (Helsinki) 7; KuPS (Kuopio) 6; Kuusysi Lahti 5; KIF Helsinki 4; AIFK Turku 3; VIFK Vaasa 3; Reipas Lahti 3; Tampere United 3; VPS (Vaasa) 2; KTP (Kotka) 2; OPS Oulu 2; Jazz Pori 2; Unitas Helsinki 1; PUS Helsinki 1; Sudet Viipuri 1; HT (Helsinki) 1; Ilves-Kissat 1; Pyrkiva Turku 1; KPV (Kokkola) 1; Ilves (Tampere) 1; TPV Tampere 1; MyPa Anjalankoski (renamed MYPA-47) 1; Inter Turku 1; SJK (Seinajoki) 1; IFK Mariehamn 1.

Cup wins (1955–2021)

HJK (Helsinki) 14; FC Haka (Valkeakoski) 12; Reipas Lahti 7; KTP (Kotka) 4; KuPS (Kuopio) 3; Ilves (Tampere) 3; TPS (Turku) 3; MyPa Anjalankoski (renamed MYPA-47) 3; Mikkeli 2; Kuusysi Lahti 2; RoPS (Rovaniemi) 2; Inter Turku 2; Pallo-Pojat 1; Drott (renamed Jaro) 1; HPS (Helsinki) 1; AIFK Turku 1; Jokerit (formerly PK-35) 1; Atlantis 1; Tampere United 1; FC Honka 1; IFK Mariehamn 1; SJK (Seinajoki) 1.

Finnish Veikkausliiga 2020

	P	*W*	*D*	*L*	*F*	*A*	*GD*	*Pts*
HJK (C)[1]	22	14	6	2	53	17	36	48
Inter Turku[3]	22	12	5	5	36	17	19	41
KuPS[3]	22	12	5	5	39	26	13	41
FC Honka[3]	22	9	10	3	26	17	9	37
Ilves Tampere	22	10	6	6	37	29	8	36
FC Lahti	22	8	8	6	33	30	3	32
SJK	22	8	5	9	27	29	–2	29
HIFK	22	8	4	10	29	33	–4	28
IFK Mariehamn	22	6	5	11	29	43	–14	23
FC Haka	22	5	7	10	25	41	–16	22
TPS*+	22	6	3	13	23	39	–16	21
RoPS*	22	1	2	19	15	51	–36	5

Top scorer: Riski (HJK) 16.
Cup Final 2019: HJK 1, Inter Turku 0 (delayed due to COVID-19 pandemic).
Cup Final 2020: KuPS 0, HJK 0.
aet; KuPS won 5-4 on penalties.

FRANCE

Federation Francaise de Football, 87 Boulevard de Grenelle, 75738 Paris Cedex 15.
Founded: 1919. *FIFA:* 1904; *UEFA:* 1954. *National Colours:* Blue shirts, white shorts, red socks.

International matches 2020–21

Sweden (a) 1-0, Croatia (h) 4-2, Ukraine (h) 7-1, Portugal (h) 0-0, Croatia (a) 1-2, Finland (a) 0-2, Portugal (a) 1-0, Sweden (h) 4-2, Ukraine (h) 1-1, Kazakhstan (a) 2-0, Bosnia-Herzegovina (a) 1-0, Wales (h) 3-0, Bulgaria (h) 3-0, Germany (a) 1-0, Hungary (a) 1-1, Portugal (n) 2-2, Sweden (n) 3-3 (4-5p).

League Championship wins (1933–2021)

Saint-Etienne 10; Olympique Marseille 9; Paris Saint-Germain 9; AS Monaco 8; Nantes 8; Olympique Lyonnais (Lyon) 7; Stade de Reims 6; Bordeaux 6; Lille OSC 4; OGC Nice 4; FC Sete 2; Sochaux 2; Olympique Lillois 1; Racing Club Paris 1; Roubaix-Tourcoing 1; Strasbourg 1; Auxerre 1; Lens 1; Montpellier 1.

Cup wins (1918–2021)

Paris Saint-Germain 14; Olympique Marseille 10; Lille OSC 6; Saint-Etienne 6; Red Star 5; Racing Club Paris 5; AS Monaco 5; Olympique Lyonnais (Lyon) 5; Bordeaux 4; Auxerre 4; Strasbourg 3; OGC Nice 3; Stade Rennais (Rennes) 3; Nantes 3; CAS Genereaux 2; Montpellier 2; FC Sete 2; Sochaux 2; Stade de Reims 2; Sedan 2; Metz 2; Guingamp 2; Olympique de Pantin 1; CA Paris 1; Club Français 1; AS Cannes 1; Excelsior Roubaix 1; EF Nancy-Lorraine 1; Toulouse 1; Le Havre 1; AS Nancy 1; Bastia 1; Lorient 1.

French Ligue 1 2020–21

	P	*W*	*D*	*L*	*F*	*A*	*GD*	*Pts*
Lille (C)[1]	38	24	11	3	64	23	41	83
Paris Saint-Germain[1]	38	26	4	8	86	28	58	82
Monaco[1]	38	24	6	8	76	42	34	78
Lyon[2]	38	22	10	6	81	43	38	76
Marseille[2]	38	16	12	10	54	47	7	60
Rennes[3]	38	16	10	12	52	40	12	58
Lens	38	15	12	11	55	54	1	57
Montpellier	38	14	12	12	60	62	–2	54
Nice	38	15	7	16	50	53	–3	52
Metz	38	12	11	15	44	48	–4	47
Saint-Etienne	38	12	10	16	42	54	–12	46
Bordeaux	38	13	6	19	42	56	–14	45
Angers	38	12	8	18	40	58	–18	44
Reims	38	9	15	14	42	50	–8	42
Strasbourg	38	11	9	18	49	58	–9	42
Lorient	38	11	9	18	50	68	–18	42
Brest	38	11	8	19	50	66	–16	41
Nantes+	38	9	13	16	47	55	–8	40
Nimes*	38	9	8	21	40	71	–31	35
Dijon*	38	4	9	25	25	73	–48	21

Top scorer: Mbappe (Paris Saint-Germain) 27.
Cup Final: Paris Saint-Germain 2, Monaco 0.

GEORGIA

Georgian Football Federation, 76A Chavchavadze Avenue, 0179 Tbilisi.
Founded: 1990. *FIFA:* 1992; *UEFA:* 1992. *National Colours:* All white with red trim.

International matches 2020–21

Estonia (a) 1-0, North Macedonia (h) 1-1, Belarus (h) 1-0, Armenia (h) 2-2, North Macedonia (a) 1-1, North Macedonia (h) 0-1, Armenia (h) 1-2, Estonia (h) 0-0, Sweden (a) 0-1, Spain (h) 1-2, Greece (a) 1-1, Romania (a) 2-1, Netherlands (a) 0-3.

League Championship wins (1990–2020)

Dinamo Tbilisi 18; Torpedo Kutaisi 4; WIT Georgia 2; Olimpi Rustavi (now FC Rustavi) 2; Zestafoni 2; Sioni Bolnisi 1; Dila Gori 1; Samtredia 1; Saburtalo 1.

Cup wins (1990–2020)

Dinamo Tbilisi 13; Torpedo Kutaisi 4; Locomotive Tbilisi 3; Ameri Tbilisi 2; Gagra 2; Guria Lanchkhuti 1; Dinamo Batumi 1; Zestafoni 1; WIT Georgia 1; Dila Gori 1; Chikhura Sachkhere 1; Saburtalo 1.
See also Russia section for Georgian club honours in Soviet era 1936–91.

Georgian Erovnuli Liga 2020

	P	W	D	L	F	A	GD	Pts
Dinamo Tbilisi (C)[1]	18	12	4	2	33	9	24	40
Dinamo Batumi[3]	18	10	6	2	29	14	15	36
Dila Gori[3]	18	8	6	4	29	17	12	30
Lokomotivi Tbilisi	18	8	5	5	30	23	7	29
Saburtalo	18	7	6	5	28	21	7	27
Telavi	18	4	12	2	21	14	7	24
Samtredia	18	5	4	9	14	23	–9	19
Torpedo Kutaisi+	18	4	5	9	17	30	–13	17
Chikhura Sachkhere*+	18	3	4	11	18	40	–22	13
Merani Tbilisi*	18	0	6	12	6	34	–28	6

Season reduced to 18 rounds from 36 due to the COVID-19 pandemic.
Top scorer: Kovtalyuk (Dila Gori) 10.
Cup Final: Samgurali 0, Gagra 0.
aet; Gagra won 5-3 on penalties.

GERMANY

Deutscher Fussball-Bund, Hermann-Neuberger-Haus, Otto-Fleck-Schneise 6, 60528 Frankfurt Am Main.
Founded: 1900. *FIFA:* 1904; *UEFA:* 1954. *National Colours:* White shirts with red and black trim, white shorts, white socks with red tops.

International matches 2020–21

Spain (h) 1-1, Switzerland (a) 1-1, Turkey (h) 3-3, Ukraine (a) 2-1, Switzerland (h) 3-3, Czech Republic (h) 1-0, Ukraine (h) 3-1, Spain (a) 0-6, Iceland (h) 3-0, Romania (a) 1-0, North Macedonia (h) 1-2, Denmark (n) 1-1, Latvia (h) 7-1, France (h) 0-1, Portugal (h) 4-2, Hungary (h) 2-2, England (a) 0-2.

League Championship wins (1903–2021)

Bayern Munich 31; 1.FC Nuremberg 9; Borussia Dortmund 8; Schalke 04 7; Hamburger SV 6; VfB Stuttgart 5; Borussia Moenchengladbach 5; 1.FC Kaiserslautern 4; Werder Bremen 4; 1.FC Lokomotive Leipzig 3; SpVgg Greuther Furth 3; 1.FC Cologne 3; Viktoria Berlin 2; Hertha Berlin 2; Hannover 96 2; Dresden SC 2; Union Berlin 1; Freiburger FC 1; Phoenix Karlsruhe 1; Karlsruher FV 1; Holstein Kiel 1; Fortuna Dusseldorf 1; Rapid Vienna 1; VfR Mannheim 1; Rot-Weiss Essen 1; Eintracht Frankfurt 1; Munich 1860 1; Eintracht Braunschweig 1; VfL Wolfsburg 1.

Cup wins (1935–2021)

Bayern Munich 20; Werder Bremen 6; Schalke 04 5; Borussia Dortmund 5; Eintracht Frankfurt 5; 1.FC Nuremberg 4; 1.FC Cologne 4; VfB Stuttgart 3; Borussia Moenchengladbach 3; Hamburger SV 3; Dresden SC 2; Munich 1860 2; Karlsruhe SC 2; Fortuna Dusseldorf 2; 1.FC Kaiserslautern 2; 1.FC Lokomotive Leipzig 1; Rapid Vienna 1; First Vienna 1; Rot-Weiss Essen 1; SW Essen 1; Kickers Offenbach 1; Bayer Uerdingen 1; Hannover 96 1; Bayer Leverkusen 1; VfLWolfsburg 1.

German Bundesliga 2020–21

	P	W	D	L	F	A	GD	Pts
Bayern Munich (C)[1]	34	24	6	4	99	44	55	78
RB Leipzig[1]	34	19	8	7	60	32	28	65
Borussia Dortmund[1]	34	20	4	10	75	46	29	64
Wolfsburg[1]	34	17	10	7	61	37	24	61
Eintracht Frankfurt[2]	34	16	12	6	69	53	16	60
Bayer Leverkusen[2]	34	14	10	10	53	39	14	52
Union Berlin[3]	34	12	14	8	50	43	7	50
Borussia M'gladbach	34	13	10	11	64	56	8	49
Stuttgart	34	12	9	13	56	55	1	45
Freiburg	34	12	9	13	52	52	0	45
TSG 1899 Hoffenheim	34	11	10	13	52	54	–2	43
Mainz 05	34	10	9	15	39	56	–17	39
Augsburg	34	10	6	18	36	54	–18	36
Hertha Berlin	34	8	11	15	41	52	–11	35
Arminia Bielefeld	34	9	8	17	26	52	–26	35
Cologne+	34	8	9	17	34	60	–26	33
Werder Bremen*	34	7	10	17	36	57	–21	31
Schalke 04*	34	3	7	24	25	86	–61	16

Top scorer: Lewandowski (Bayern Munich) 41.
Cup Final: Borussia Dortmund 4, RB Leipzig 1.

GIBRALTAR

Gibraltar Football Association, Bayside Sports Complex, PO Box 513, Gibraltar GX11 1AA.
Founded: 1895. *UEFA:* 2013. *National Colours:* Red shirts with white trim, red shorts, red socks.

International matches 2020–21

San Marino (h) 1-0, Malta (a) 0-2, Liechtenstein (a) 1-0, Bulgaria (h) 0-3, San Marino (a) 0-0, Liechtenstein (h) 1-1, Norway (h) 0-3, Montenegro (a) 1-4, Netherlands (h) 0-7, Slovenia (a) 0-6, Andorra (a) 0-0.

League Championship wins (1896–2021)

Lincoln Red Imps (incl. Newcastle United 5; 1 title shared) 25; Prince of Wales 19; Glacis United 17 (incl. 1 shared); Britannia (now Britannia XI) 14; Gibraltar United 11; Europa 7; Manchester United (now Manchester 62) 7; St Theresa's 3; Chief Construction 2; Jubilee 2; Exiles 2; South United 2; Gibraltar FC 2; Albion 1; Athletic 1; Royal Sovereign 1; Commander of the Yard 1; St Joseph's 1.
No winner in 2019–20.

Cup wins (1895–2021)

Lincoln Red Imps (incl. Newcastle United 4) 18; St Joseph's 10; Europa 8; Glacis United 5; Britannia (now Britannia XI) 3; Gibraltar United 4; Manchester United (now Manchester 62) 3; Gibraltar FC 1; HMS Hood 1; 2nd Bn The King's Regt 1; AARA 1; RAF New Camp 1; 4th Bn Royal Scots 1; Prince of Wales 1; Manchester United Reserves 1; 2nd Bn Royal Green Jackets 1; RAF Gibraltar 1; St Theresa's 1.
No winner in 2019–20.

Gibraltarian Premier Division Qualifying Table 2020–21

	P	W	D	L	F	A	GD	Pts
Europa	10	9	1	0	44	5	39	28
Lincoln Red Imps	10	8	1	1	33	7	26	25
St Joseph's	10	7	1	2	49	11	38	22
Lynx	10	6	1	3	26	10	16	19
Mons Calpe	10	6	1	3	21	13	8	19
Lions Gibraltar	10	4	3	3	12	10	2	15
Bruno's Magpies	10	4	2	4	14	16	–2	14
Glacis United	10	3	0	7	10	18	–8	9
Manchester 62	10	2	0	8	8	44	–36	6
Europa Point	10	1	0	9	7	38	–31	3
College 1975	10	0	0	10	8	60	–52	0
Boca Juniors	0	0	0	0	0	0	0	0

Boca Juniors expelled, record expunged.

Championship Group 2020–21

	P	W	D	L	F	A	GD	Pts
Lincoln Red Imps (C)[1]	20	15	3	2	62	13	49	48
Europa[3]	20	15	2	3	66	14	52	47
St Joseph's[3]	20	14	3	3	71	20	51	45
Mons Calpe[3]	20	10	2	8	36	35	1	32
Lynx	20	8	2	10	36	40	–4	26
Lions Gibraltar	20	4	4	12	13	33	–20	16

Challenge Group 2020–21

	P	W	D	L	F	A	GD	Pts
Magpies	18	10	2	6	46	27	19	32
Glacis United	18	10	0	8	35	27	8	30
Manchester 62	18	5	2	11	25	60	–35	17
College 1975	18	2	2	14	23	81	–58	8
Europa Point*	18	1	0	17	10	73	–63	3

Top scorer: Gomez (Lincoln Red Imps) 24.
Cup Final: Lincoln Red Imps 2, Glacis United 0.

GOZO

Gozo Football Association, GFA Headquarters, Mgarr Road, Xewkija, XWK 9014, Malta. (Not a member of FIFA or UEFA.)
Founded: 1936.

League Championship wins (1938–2021)*

Victoria Hotspurs 13; Nadur Youngsters 12; Sannat Lions 10; Xewkija Tigers 8; Ghajnsielem 7; Xaghra United 6 (incl. Xaghra Blue Stars 1, Xaghra Young Stars 1); Salesian Youths (renamed Oratory Youths) 6; Victoria Athletics 4; Victoria Stars 1; Victoria City 1; Calypcians 1; Victoria United (renamed Victoria Wanderers) 1; Kercem Ajax 1; Zebbug Rovers 1.
* *No winner in 2020–21.*

Cup wins (1972–2021)*

Xewkija Tigers 11; Sannat Lions 9; Nadur Youngsters 8; Ghajnsielem 6; Xaghra United 4; Victoria Hotspurs 2; Kercem Ajax 2; Calypsians 1; Calypsians Bosco Youths 1; Qala St Joseph 1; Victoria Wanderers 1.
* *No winner in 2019–20, 2020–21.*

Gozitan L-Ewwel Divizjoni 2020–21

	P	W	D	L	F	A	GD	Pts
Ghajnsielem (C)	9	8	1	0	34	8	26	25
Victoria Hotspurs	9	6	1	2	30	11	19	19
Nadur Youngsters	8	6	1	1	20	4	16	19
Kercem Ajax	9	5	1	3	19	17	2	16
Xewkija Tigers	9	5	0	4	13	17	–4	15
Sannat Lions	9	3	0	6	12	24	–12	9
Victoria Wanderers	9	2	1	6	14	21	–7	7

Competition curtailed due to COVID-19 pandemic. No title awarded.
Cup Final: No competition due to COVID-19 pandemic.

GREECE

Hellenic Football Federation, Parko Goudi, PO Box 14161, 11510 Athens.
Founded: 1926. *FIFA:* 1927; *UEFA:* 1954. *National Colours:* All white.

International matches 2020–21
Slovenia (a) 0-0, Kosovo (a) 2-1, Austria (a) 1-2, Moldova (h) 2-0, Kosovo (h) 0-0, Cyprus (h) 2-1, Moldova (a) 2-0, Slovenia (h) 0-0, Spain (a) 1-1, Spain (h) 1-1, Honduras (h) 2-1, Georgia (h) 1-1, Belgium (a) 1-1, Norway (n) 2-1.

League Championship wins (1927–2021)
Olympiacos 46; Panathinaikos 20; AEK Athens 12; Aris 3; PAOK (Thessaloniki) 3; AEL (Larissa) 1.

Cup wins (1932–2021)
Olympiacos 28; Panathinaikos 18; AEK Athens 15; PAOK (Thessaloniki) 8; Panionios 2; AEL (Larissa) 2; Ethnikos 1; Aris 1; Iraklis 1; Kastoria 1; OFI Crete 1.

Greek Super League Qualifying Table 2020–21

	P	W	D	L	F	A	GD	Pts
Olympiacos	26	21	4	1	64	13	51	67
Aris	26	15	6	5	34	16	18	51
AEK Athens	26	14	6	6	41	29	12	48
PAOK	26	13	8	5	49	26	23	47
Panathinaikos	26	13	6	7	30	19	11	45
Asteras Tripolis	26	11	9	6	27	25	2	42
Volos	26	8	9	9	26	32	–6	33
Giannina	26	8	7	11	23	26	–3	31
Apollon Smirnis	26	8	4	14	26	35	–9	28
Atromitos	26	6	10	10	24	35	–11	28
Lamia	26	5	8	13	14	38	–24	23
Panaitolikos	26	4	8	14	13	32	–19	20
OFI Crete	26	5	4	17	22	43	–21	19
AEL	26	3	7	16	18	42	–24	16

Championship Round 2020–21

	P	W	D	L	F	A	GD	Pts
Olympiacos (C)[1]	36	28	6	2	82	19	63	90
PAOK[3]	36	18	10	8	60	34	26	64
Aris[3]	36	17	10	9	41	26	15	61
AEK Athens[3]	36	17	9	10	53	45	8	60
Panathinaikos	36	14	11	11	41	34	7	53
Asteras Tripolis	36	12	15	9	36	38	–2	51

Relegation Round 2020–21

	P	W	D	L	F	A	GD	Pts
Volos	33	10	13	10	34	37	–3	43
Atromitos	33	8	13	12	30	40	–10	37
Giannina	33	9	8	16	27	36	–9	35
Lamia	33	8	11	14	21	42	–21	35
Apollon Smirnis	33	9	7	17	29	40	–11	34
OFI Crete	33	8	8	17	30	47	–17	32
Panaitolikos+	33	6	10	17	20	44	–24	28
AEL*	33	6	9	18	25	47	–22	27

Top scorer: El-Arabi (Olympiacos) 22.
Cup Final 2020: Olympiacos 1, AEK Athens 0 (delayed due to COVID-19 pandemic).
Cup Final 2021: PAOK 2, Olympiacos 1.

HUNGARY

Magyar Labdarugo Szovetseg, Kanai ut 2. D, 1112 Budapest.
Founded: 1901. *FIFA:* 1907; *UEFA:* 1954. *National Colours:* Red shirts, white shorts, green socks.

International matches 2020–21
Turkey (a) 1-0, Russia (h) 2-3, Bulgaria (a) 3-1, Serbia (a) 1-0, Russia (a) 0-0, Iceland (h) 2-1, Serbia (h) 1-0, Turkey (h) 1-0, Poland (h) 3-3, San Marino (a) 3-0, Andorra (a) 4-1, Cyprus (h) 1-0, Republic of Ireland (h) 0-0, Portugal (h) 0-3, France (h) 1-1, Germany (a) 2-2.

League Championship wins (1901–2021)
Ferencvaros 32; MTK Budapest 23; Ujpest 20; Budapest Honved 14 (incl. Kispest Honved); Debrecen 7; Vasas 6; Csepel 4; Gyor 4; Videoton (renamed Fehervar) 3; Budapesti TC 2; Nagyvarad 1; Vac 1; Dunaferr (renamed Dunaujvaros) 1; Zalaegerszeg 1.

Cup wins (1910–2021)
Ferencvaros 23; MTK Budapest 12; Ujpest 11; Budapest Honved 8 (inc. Kispest Honved); Debrecen 6; Vasas 4; Gyor 4; Diosgyor 2; Fehervar (incl. Videoton 1, Vidi 1) 2; Bocskai 1; III Keruleti TUE 1; Soroksar 1; Szolnoki MAV 1; Siofoki Banyasz 1; Bekescsaba 1; Pecsi 1; Sopron 1; Kecskemet 1.
Cup not regularly held until 1964.

Hungarian Nemzeti Bajnoksag I 2020–21

	P	W	D	L	F	A	GD	Pts
Ferencvaros (C)[1]	33	23	9	1	69	22	47	78
Puskas Akademia[3]	33	18	4	11	52	42	10	58
Fehervar[3]	33	16	8	9	68	38	30	56
Paks	33	14	8	11	76	64	12	50
Kisvarda	33	12	10	11	30	36	–6	46
Ujpest†[3]	33	12	6	15	46	67	–21	42
MTK Budapest†	33	11	9	13	44	49	–5	42
Mezokovesd†	33	11	9	13	40	46	–6	42
Zalaegerszegi†	33	10	7	16	58	58	0	37
Budapest Honved†	33	9	10	14	46	48	–2	37
Diosgyor*	33	9	6	18	34	53	–19	33
Budafoki*	33	7	6	20	34	74	–40	27

† *Ranking decided on matches won and if still tied, on goal difference.*
Top scorer: Hahn (Paks) 22.
Cup Final: Ujpest 1, Fehervar 0 *aet*.

ICELAND

Knattspyrnusamband Islands, Laugardal, 104 Reykjavik.
Founded: 1947. *FIFA:* 1947; *UEFA:* 1954. *National Colours:* All blue.

International matches 2020–21
England (h) 0-1, Belgium (a) 1-5, Romania (h) 2-1, Denmark (h) 0-3, Belgium (h) 1-2, Hungary (a) 1-2, Denmark (a) 1-2, England (a) 0-4, Germany (a) 0-3, Armenia (a) 0-2, Liechtenstein (a) 4-1, Mexico (n) 1-2, Faroe Islands (a) 1-0, Poland (a) 2-2.

League Championship wins (1912–2020)
KR (Reykjavik) 27; Valur 23; Fram 18; IA (Akranes) 18; FH (Hafnarfjordur) 8; Vikingur 5; Keflavik 4; IBV (Vestmannaeyjar) 3; KA (Akureyri) 1; Breidablik 1; Stjarnan 1.

Cup wins (1960–2020)*
KR (Reykjavik) 14; Valur 11; IA (Akranes) 9; Fram 8; IBV (Vestmannaeyjar) 5; Keflavik 4; Vikingur 2; Fylkir 2; FH (Hafnarfjordur) 2; IBA Akureyri 1; Breidablik 1; Stjarnan 1.
* *No winner in 2020.*

Icelandic Urvalsdeild karla 2020

	P	W	D	L	F	A	GD	Pts
Valur (C)[1]	18	14	2	2	50	17	33	44
FH[3]	18	11	3	4	37	23	14	36
Stjarnan[3]	17	8	7	2	27	20	7	31
Breidablik[3]	18	9	4	5	37	27	10	31
KR	17	8	4	5	30	21	9	28
Fylkir	18	9	1	8	27	30	–3	28
KA	18	3	12	3	20	21	–1	21
IA	18	6	3	9	39	43	–4	21
HK Kopavogur	18	5	5	8	29	36	–7	20
Vikingur	18	3	8	7	25	30	–5	17
Grotta*	18	1	5	12	15	43	–28	8
Fjolnir*	18	0	6	12	15	40	–25	6

Competition curtailed due to COVID-19 pandemic; league rankings decided on points-per-game basis.
Top scorer: Lennon (FH) 17.
Cup Final: Competition abandoned due to COVID-19 pandemic.

ISRAEL

Israel Football Association, Ramat Gan Stadium, 299 Aba Hilell Street, PO Box 3591, Ramat Gan 52134.
Founded: 1928. *FIFA:* 1929; *UEFA:* 1994. *National Colours:* Blue shirts with white trim, blue shorts, blue socks.

International matches 2020–21
Scotland (a) 1-1, Slovakia (h) 1-1, Scotland (a) 0-0 (3-5p), Czech Republic (h) 1-2, Slovakia (a) 3-2, Czech Republic (a) 0-1, Scotland (h) 1-0, Denmark (h) 0-2, Scotland (h) 1-1, Moldova (a) 4-1, Montenegro (a) 3-1, Portugal (a) 0-4.

League Championship wins (1932–2021)
Maccabi Tel Aviv 23; Hapoel Tel Aviv 14 (incl. 1 shared); Maccabi Haifa 13; Hapoel Petah Tikva 6; Beitar Jerusalem 6; Maccabi Netanya 5; Hapoel Be'er Sheva 5; Hakoah Amidar Ramat Gan 2; British Police 1; Beitar Tel Aviv 1 (shared); Hapoel Ramat Gan 1; Hapoel Kfar Saba 1; Bnei Yehuda 1; Hapoel Haifa 1; Ironi Kiryat Shmona 1.

Cup wins (1928–2021)
Maccabi Tel Aviv 24; Hapoel Tel Aviv 15; Beitar Jerusalem 7; Maccabi Haifa 6; Hapoel Haifa 4; Bnei Yehuda 4; Hapoel Kfar Saba 3; Maccabi Petah Tikva 2; Beitar Tel Aviv 2; Hapoel Petah Tikva 2; Hakoah Amidar Ramat Gan 2; Hapoel Ramat Gan 2; Hapoel Be'er Sheva 2; Maccabi Hashmonai Jerusalem 1; British Police 1; Hapoel Jerusalem 1; Maccabi Netanya 1; Hapoel Yehud 1; Hapoel Lod 1; Bnei Sakhnin 1; Ironi Kiryat Shmona 1.

Israeli Premier League Qualifying Table 2020–21

	P	*W*	*D*	*L*	*F*	*A*	*GD*	*Pts*
Maccabi Haifa	26	19	2	5	52	20	32	59
Maccabi Tel Aviv	26	17	7	2	48	21	27	58
Ashdod	26	13	4	9	37	25	12	43
Ironi Kiryat Shmona	26	11	5	10	26	28	–2	38
Hapoel Be'er Sheva	26	9	10	7	31	29	2	37
Maccabi Petah Tikva	26	11	4	11	24	23	1	37
Maccabi Netanya	26	9	7	10	35	30	5	34
Beitar Jerusalem	26	8	8	10	31	32	–1	32
Hapoel Hadera	26	8	8	10	26	28	–2	32
Hapoel Haifa	26	7	9	10	30	37	–7	30
Bnei Sakhnin	26	8	5	13	15	36	–21	29
Hapoel Tel Aviv	26	6	9	11	17	28	–11	27
Hapoel Kfar Saba	26	6	5	15	19	33	–14	23
Bnei Yehuda	26	5	7	14	15	36	–21	22

Championship Round 2020–21

	P	*W*	*D*	*L*	*F*	*A*	*GD*	*Pts*
Maccabi Haifa (C)[1]	36	24	7	5	72	29	43	79
Maccabi Tel Aviv[3]	36	21	12	3	65	33	32	75
Ashdod[3]	36	15	9	12	48	39	9	54
Hapoel Be'er Sheva[3]	36	11	15	10	45	43	2	48
Maccabi Petah Tikva	36	13	7	16	32	38	–6	46
Ironi Kiryat Shmona	36	12	10	14	37	45	–8	46

Relegation Round 2020–21

	P	*W*	*D*	*L*	*F*	*A*	*GD*	*Pts*
Maccabi Netanya	33	13	9	11	43	34	9	48
Hapoel Hadera	33	13	9	11	40	34	6	48
Hapoel Haifa	33	11	9	13	40	48	–8	42
Beitar Jerusalem	33	10	10	13	40	43	–3	40
Hapoel Tel Aviv	33	9	11	13	24	35	–11	38
Bnei Sakhnin	33	9	7	17	22	45	–23	34
Bnei Yehuda*	33	8	9	16	27	46	–19	33
Hapoel Kfar Saba*	33	6	6	21	26	49	–23	24

Top scorer: Rukavytsya (Maccabi Haifa) 19.
Cup Final: Maccabi Tel Aviv 2, Hapoel Tel Aviv 1 *aet*.

ITALY

Federazione Italiana Giuoco Calcio, Via Gregorio Allegri 14, 00198 Roma.
Founded: 1898. *FIFA:* 1905; *UEFA:* 1954. *National Colours:* Blue shirts, white shorts, blue socks with white tops.

International matches 2020–21
Bosnia-Herzegovina (h) 1-1, Netherlands (a) 1-0, Moldova (h) 6-0, Portugal (a) 0-0, Netherlands (h) 1-1, Estonia (h) 4-0, Poland (h) 2-0, Bosnia-Herzegovina (a) 2-0, Northern Ireland (h) 2-0, Bulgaria (a) 2-0, Lithuania (a) 2-0, San Marino (h) 7-0, Czech Republic (h) 4-0, Turkey (h) 3-0, Switzerland (h) 3-0, Wales (h) 1-0, Austria (n) 2-1, Belgium (n) 2-1, Spain (n) 1-1 (4-2p), England (a) 1-1 (3-2p).

League Championship wins (1898–2021)
Juventus 36 (excludes two titles revoked); Internazionale 19 (includes one title awarded); AC Milan 18; Genoa 9; Pro Vercelli 7; Bologna 7; Torino 7 (excludes one title revoked); Roma 3; Fiorentina 2; Lazio 2; Napoli 2; Casale 1; Novese 1; Cagliari 1; Hellas Verona 1; Sampdoria 1.

Cup wins (1928–2021)
Juventus 14; Roma 9; Internazionale 7; Lazio 7; Fiorentina 6; Napoli 6; Torino 5; AC Milan 5; Sampdoria 4; Parma 3; Bologna 2; Vado 1; Genoa 1; Venezia 1; Atalanta 1; Vicenza 1.

Italian Serie A 2020–21

	P	*W*	*D*	*L*	*F*	*A*	*GD*	*Pts*
Internazionale (C)[1]	38	28	7	3	89	35	54	91
Milan[1]	38	24	7	7	74	41	33	79
Atalanta[1]	38	23	9	6	90	47	43	78
Juventus[1]	38	23	9	6	77	38	39	78
Napoli[2]	38	24	5	9	86	41	45	77
Lazio[2]	38	21	5	12	61	55	6	68
Roma[3]	38	18	8	12	68	58	10	62
Sassuolo	38	17	11	10	64	56	8	62
Sampdoria	38	15	7	16	52	54	–2	52
Hellas Verona	38	11	12	15	46	48	–2	45
Genoa	38	10	12	16	47	58	–11	42
Bologna	38	10	11	17	51	65	–14	41
Fiorentina	38	9	13	16	47	59	–12	40
Udinese	38	10	10	18	42	58	–16	40
Spezia	38	9	12	17	52	72	–20	39
Cagliari	38	9	10	19	43	59	–16	37
Torino	38	7	16	15	50	69	–19	37
Benevento*	38	7	12	19	40	75	–35	33
Crotone*	38	6	5	27	45	92	–47	23
Parma*	38	3	11	24	39	83	–44	20

Top scorer: Ronaldo (Juventus) 29.
Cup Final: Juventus 2, Atalanta 1.

KAZAKHSTAN

Football Federation of Kazakhstan, 29 Syganak Street, 9th floor, 010000 Astana.
Founded: 1914. *FIFA:* 1994; *UEFA:* 2002. *National Colours:* All yellow.

International matches 2020–21
Lithuania (a) 2-0, Belarus (h) 1-2, Albania (h) 0-0, Belarus (a) 0-2, Montenegro (a) 0-0, Albania (a) 1-3, Lithuania (h) 1-2, France (h) 0-2, Ukraine (a) 1-1, North Macedonia (a) 0-4.

League Championship wins (1992–2020)
Astana 6; Irtysh Pavlodar (includes Ansat) 5; Aktobe 5; Kairat 3; Yelimay (renamed Spartak Semey) 3; FC Astana-64 (includes Zhenis) 3; Shakhter Karagandy 2; Taraz 1; Tobol 1.

Cup wins (1992–2020)*
Kairat 9; FC Astana-64 (incl. Zhenis) 3; Astana (incl. Lokomotiv) 3; Kaisar 2; Dostyk 1; Vostok 1; Yelimay (renamed Spartak Semey) 1; Irtysh Pavlodar 1; Taraz 1; Almaty 1; Tobol 1; Aktobe 1; Atyrau 1; Ordabasy 1; Shakhter Karagandy 1.
* *No winner in 2020.*

Kazakh Premer Ligasy 2020

	P	*W*	*D*	*L*	*F*	*A*	*GD*	*Pts*
Kairat (C)[1]	20	14	3	3	48	19	29	45
Tobol[3]	20	12	2	6	26	16	10	38
Astana[3]	20	11	3	6	32	21	11	36
Shakhter Karagandy[3]	20	9	5	6	29	22	7	32
Ordabasy	20	9	4	7	27	26	1	31
Zhetysu	20	9	1	10	27	28	–1	28
Kaisar	20	6	6	8	20	23	–3	24
Taraz	20	5	8	7	19	23	–4	23
Kyzyl-Zhar	20	6	5	9	15	24	–9	23
Kaspiy	20	5	2	13	15	34	–19	17
Okzhetpes*	20	2	5	13	16	38	–22	11
Irtysh Pavlodar*	0	0	0	0	0	0	0	0

Irtysh Pavlodar withdrew for financial reasons, record expunged.
Top scorer: Joao Paulo (Ordabasy) 12.
Cup Final: No competition due to COVID-19 pandemic.

KOSOVO

Football Federation of Kosovo, Rruga Agim Ramadani 45, Prishtina, Kosovo 10000. *Founded:* 1946. *FIFA:* 2016; *UEFA:* 2016. *National Colours:* All blue.

International matches 2019–20
Moldova (a) 1-1, Greece (h) 1-2, North Macedonia (a) 1-2, Slovenia (h) 0-1, Greece (a) 0-0, Albania (a) 1-2, Slovenia (a) 1-2, Moldova (h) 1-0, Lithuania (h) 4-0, Sweden (h) 0-3, Spain (a) 1-3, San Marino (h) 4-1, Malta (n) 2-1, Guinea (n) 1-2, Gambia (n) 1-0.

League Championship wins (1945–97; 1999–2021)
Prishtina 15; Vellaznimi 9; KF Trepca 7; Liria 5; Buduqnosti 4; Rudari 3; Red Star 3; Drita 3; Besa Peje 3; Feronikeli 3; Jedinstvo 2; Kosova Prishtina 2; Slloga 2; Obiliqi 2; Fushe-Kosova 2; Proletari 1; KXEK Kosova 1; Rudniku 1; KNI Ramiz Sadiku 1; Dukagjini 1; Besiana 1; Hysi 1; Vushtrria 1; Trepca'89 1.

Cup wins (1992–97; 1999–2021)
Prishtina 7; Besa Peje 3; Feronikeli 3; Flamurtari 2; Liria 2; KF Trepca 1; KF 2 Korriku 1; Gjilani 1; Drita 1; Besiana 1; KEK-u 1; Kosova Prishtina 1; Vellaznimi 1; Hysi 1; Trepca'89 1; Llapi 1.

Kosovar Superliga 2020–21

	P	*W*	*D*	*L*	*F*	*A*	*GD*	*Pts*
Prishtina (C)[1]	36	24	6	6	65	27	38	78
Drita[3]	36	22	10	4	59	28	31	76
Ballkani	36	23	5	8	79	43	36	74
Gjilani	36	12	12	12	37	38	–1	48
Llapi[3]	36	13	4	19	49	56	–7	43
Feronikeli	36	10	12	14	44	36	8	42
Drenica Skenderaj	36	10	12	14	34	48	–14	42
Trepca'89*+	36	12	6	18	38	54	–16	42
Arberia*	36	11	7	18	42	58	–16	40
Besa Peje*	36	3	6	27	27	86	–59	15

Top scorer: Daku (Ballkani) 31.
Cup Final: Llapi 1, Dukagjini 1.
aet; Llapi won 4-3 on penalties.

LATVIA

Latvijas Futbola Federacija, Olympic Sports Centre, Grostonas Street 6B, 1013 Riga.
Founded: 1921. *FIFA:* 1922; *UEFA:* 1992. *National Colours:* All carmine red.

International matches 2020–21
Andorra (h) 0-0, Malta (a) 1-1, Montenegro (a) 1-1, Faroe Islands (a) 1-1, Malta (h) 0-1, San Marino (a) 3-0, Faroe Islands (h) 1-1, Andorra (a) 5-0, Montenegro (h) 1-2, Netherlands (a) 0-2, Turkey (a) 3-3, Lithuania (h) 3-1, Germany (a) 1-7, Estonia (a) 1-2.

League Championship wins (1922–2020)
Skonto Riga 15; ASK Riga (incl. AVN 2) 11; Sarkanais Metalurgs Liepaja 9; RFK Riga 8; Olympija Liepaya 7; VEF Riga 6; Ventspils 6; Energija Riga (incl. ESR Riga 2) 4; Elektrons Riga (incl. Alfa 1) 4; Torpedo Riga 3; Keisermezhs (Kaiserwald) Riga 2; Khimikis Daugavpils 2; RAF Yelgava 2; Daugava Liepaja 2; Liepajas Metalurgs 2; JPFS/Spartaks Jurmala 2; Riga FC 3; Dinamo Riga 1; Zhmilyeva Team 1; Darba Rezervi 1; RER Riga 1; Starts Brotseni 1; Venta Ventspils 1; Jumieks Riga 1; Gauja Valmiera 1; Daugava Daugavpils 1; FK Liepaja 1.

Cup wins (1937–2020)
Skonto Riga 8; ASK Riga 7 (includes AVN 3); Elektrons Riga 7; Ventspils 7; Sarkanais Metalurgs Liepaja 4; Jelgava 4; VEF Riga 3; Tseltnieks Riga 3; RAF Yelgava 3; RFK Riga 2; Daugava Liepaja 2; Starts Brotseni 2; Selmash Liepaya 2; Yurnieks Riga 2; Khimikis Daugavpils 2; FK Liepaja 2; Rigas Vilki 1; Dinamo Liepaya 1; Dinamo Riga 1; RER Riga 1; Voulkan Kouldiga 1; Baltika Liepaja 1; Venta Ventspils 1; Pilots Riga 1; Lielupe Yurmala 1; Energija Riga (formerly ESR Riga) 1; Torpedo Riga 1; Daugava SKIF Riga 1; Tseltnieks Daugavpils 1; Olympija Riga 1; FK Riga 1; Liepajas Metalurgs 1; Daugava Daugavpils 1; Riga FC 1; Rigas FS 1.

Latvian Virsliga 2020

	P	*W*	*D*	*L*	*F*	*A*	*GD*	*Pts*
Riga (C)[1]	27	23	0	4	60	21	39	69
Rigas FS[3]	27	21	3	3	66	21	45	66
Valmiera[3]	27	13	8	6	47	33	14	47
Ventspils	27	12	8	7	40	25	15	44
FK Liepaja[3]	27	12	6	9	57	34	23	42
Spartaks Jurmala	27	11	7	9	53	44	9	40
Jelgava	27	6	4	17	19	64	–45	22
Daugava Daugavpils	27	5	5	17	30	48	–18	20
Metta/LU	27	4	4	19	22	55	–33	16
Tukums*	27	3	5	19	21	70	–49	14

Top scorer: Dodo (FK Liepaja) 18.
Cup Final: FK Liepaja 1, Ventspils 0 *aet.*

LIECHTENSTEIN

Liechtensteiner Fussballverband, Landstrasse 149, 9494 Schaan.
Founded: 1934. *FIFA:* 1974; *UEFA:* 1974. *National Colours:* Blue shirts, red shorts, blue socks.

International matches 2020–21
San Marino (a) 2-0, Luxembourg (a) 2-1, Gibraltar (a) 0-1, San Marino (h) 0-0, Malta (a) 1-4, Gibraltar (a) 1-1, Armenia (h) 1-1, North Macedonia (a) 0-5, Iceland (h) 1-4, Switzerland (a) 0-7, Faroe Islands (a) 1-5.
Liechtenstein has no national league. Teams compete in Swiss regional leagues.

Cup wins (1937–2021)*
Vaduz 47; FC Balzers 11; FC Triesen 8; USV Eschen/Mauren 5; FC Schaan 3.
* *No winner in 2019–20, 2020–21.*
Cup Final: Competition abandoned due to COVID-19 pandemic.

LITHUANIA

Lietuvos Futbolo Federacija, Stadiono g. 2, 02106 Vilnius.
Founded: 1922. *FIFA:* 1923; *UEFA:* 1992. *National Colours:* Yellow shirts, green shorts, yellow socks.

International matches 2020–21
Kazakhstan (h) 0-2, Albania (a) 1-0, Estonia (a) 3-1, Belarus (h) 2-2, Albania (h) 0-0, Faroe Islands (h) 2-1, Belarus (a) 0-2, Kazakhstan (a) 2-1, Kosovo (a) 0-4, Switzerland (a) 0-1, Italy (h) 0-2, Estonia (h) 0-1, Latvia (a) 1-3, Spain (a) 0-4.

League Championship wins (1990–2020)
Zalgiris Vilnius 8; FBK Kaunas 8 (incl. Zalgiris Kaunas 1); Ekranas 7; Suduva 3; Inkaras Kaunas 2; Kareda 2; Sirijus Klaipeda 1; ROMAR Mazeikiai 1.

Cup wins (1990–2020)
Zalgiris Vilnius 12; Ekranas 4; FBK Kaunas 4; Suduva 3; Kareda 2; Atlantas 2; Sirijus Klaipeda 1; Lietuvos Makabi Vilnius (renamed Neris Vilnius) 1; Inkaras Kaunas 1; Stumbras 1; Panevezys 1.

Lithuanian A Lyga Qualifying Table 2020

	P	*W*	*D*	*L*	*F*	*A*	*GD*	*Pts*
Zalgiris Vilnius (C)[1]	20	14	3	3	42	14	28	45
Suduva[3]	20	13	4	3	32	18	14	43
Kauno Zalgiris[3]	20	12	2	6	30	18	12	38
Banga	20	3	7	10	16	30	–14	16
Panevezys[3]	20	2	6	12	19	38	–19	12
Riteriai	20	2	6	12	17	38	–21	12

Season reduced to 20 rounds from 24 due to COVID-19 pandemic.
Top scorer: Videmont (Zalgiris Vilnius) 13.
Cup Final: Panevezys 1, Suduva 1.
aet; Panevezys won 6-5 on penalties.

LUXEMBOURG

Federation Luxembourgeoise de Football, BP 5 Rue de Limpach, 3932 Mondercange.
Founded: 1908. *FIFA:* 1910; *UEFA:* 1954. *National Colours:* White shirts with blue trim, white shorts, white socks.

International matches 2020–21
Azerbaijan (a) 2-1, Montenegro (h) 0-1, Liechtenstein (h) 1-2, Cyprus (h) 2-0, Montenegro (a) 2-1, Austria (h) 0-3, Cyprus (a) 1-2, Azerbaijan (h) 0-0, Qatar (n) 0-1, Republic of Ireland (a) 1-0, Portugal (h) 1-3, Norway (n) 0-1, Scotland (h) 0-1.

League Championship wins (1910–2021)
Jeunesse Esch 28; F91 Dudelange 15; Spora Luxembourg 11; Stade Dudelange 10; Fola Esch 8; Red Boys Differdange 6; Union Luxembourg 6; Avenir Beggen 6; US Hollerich-Bonnevoie 5; Progres NiederKorn 3; Aris Bonnevoie 3; Sporting Club 2; Racing Club 1; National Schifflange 1; Grevenmacher 1.
No winner in 2019–20.

Cup wins (1922–2021)*
Red Boys Differdange 15; Jeunesse Esch 13; Union Luxembourg 10; Spora Luxembourg 8; F91 Dudelange 8; Avenir Beggen 7; Progres Niederkorn 4; Stade Dudelange 4; Grevenmacher 4; Differdange 03 4; Fola Esch 3; Alliance Dudelange 2; US Rumelange 2; Racing Club 1; US Dudelange 1; SC Tetange 1; National Schifflange 1; Aris Bonnevoie 1; Jeunesse Hautcharage 1; Swift Hesperange 1; Etzella Ettelbruck 1; CS Petange (renamed Union Titus Petange) 1; Racing 1.
* *No winner in 2019–20, 2020–21.*

Luxembourg Nationaldivisioun 2020–21

	P	*W*	*D*	*L*	*F*	*A*	*GD*	*Pts*
Fola Esch (C)[1]	30	21	5	4	89	35	54	68
F91 Dudelange[3]	30	20	6	4	70	29	41	66
Swift Hesperange[3]	30	19	8	3	72	30	42	65
Racing[3]	30	17	3	10	47	29	18	54
Progres Niederkorn	30	15	8	7	48	30	18	53
Differdange 03	30	13	6	11	51	48	3	45
Wiltz	30	13	5	12	45	42	3	44
Jeunesse Esch	30	12	7	11	41	43	–2	43
Hostert	30	9	10	11	47	56	–9	37
UNA Strassen	30	9	8	13	44	65	–21	35

Mondorf-les-Bains	30	7	7	16	33	56	–23	28
Rodange 91	30	6	10	14	27	52	–25	28
Victoria Rosport	30	8	3	19	37	67	–30	27
RM Hamm Benfica	30	5	11	14	33	48	–15	26
Etzella Ettelbruck	30	5	9	16	32	57	–25	24
Union Titus Petange	30	5	6	19	23	52	–29	21

Top scorer: Hadji (Fola Esch) 33.
Cup Final: Competition abandoned due to COVID-19 pandemic.

MALTA

Malta Football Association, Millennium Stand, Floor 2, National Stadium, Ta'Qali ATD4000.
Founded: 1900. *FIFA:* 1959; *UEFA:* 1960. *National Colours:* Red shirts, white shorts, red socks.

International matches 2020–21

Faroe Islands (a) 2-3, Latvia (h) 1-1, Gibraltar (h) 2-0, Andorra (a) 0-0, Latvia (a) 1-0, Liechtenstein (h) 3-0, Andorra (h) 3-1, Faroe Islands (h) 1-1, Russia (h) 1-3, Slovakia (a) 2-2, Croatia (a) 0-3, Northern Ireland (n) 0-3, Kosovo (n) 1-2.

League Championship wins (1910–2021)

Floriana 26; Sliema Wanderers 26; Valletta 25; Hibernians 12; Hamrun Spartans 8; Birkirkara 4; Rabat Ajax 2; St George's 1; KOMR 1; Marsaxlokk 1.

Cup wins (1935–2021)*

Sliema Wanderers 21; Floriana 20; Valletta 14; Hibernians 10; Hamrun Spartans 6; Birkirkara 5; Melita 1; Gzira United 1; Zurrieq 1; Rabat Ajax 1; Balzan 1.
* *No winner in 2019–20, 2020–21.*

Maltese Premier League 2020–21

	P	W	D	L	F	A	GD	Pts
Hamrun Spartans† (C)	23	17	5	1	56	20	36	56
Hibernians[1]	23	16	3	4	53	20	33	51
Gzira United[3]	23	14	4	5	49	21	28	46
Birkirkara[3]	23	13	5	5	45	25	20	44
Sliema Wanderers	23	12	4	7	39	31	8	40
Mosta[3]	23	10	6	7	41	36	5	36
Valletta	23	9	6	8	27	35	–8	33
St Lucia	23	7	8	8	38	35	3	29
Sirens	23	7	7	9	27	35	–8	28
Balzan	23	6	9	8	31	29	2	27
Gudja United	23	8	3	12	29	35	–6	27
Floriana	23	7	6	10	26	34	–8	27
Zejtun Corinthians*	23	6	6	11	28	40	–12	24
Tarxien Rainbows*	23	6	3	14	25	48	–23	21
Lija Athletic*	23	5	5	13	25	46	–21	20
Senglea Athletic*	23	0	2	21	13	62	–49	2

Competition curtailed due to COVID-19 pandemic. Hamrun Spartans declared champions.
† *Hamrun Spartans banned from European competitions after being found guilty of match-fixing in 2012–13.*
Top scorer: Rosero (St Lucia) 17.
Cup Final: Competition abandoned due to COVID-19 pandemic.

MOLDOVA

Federatia Moldoveneasca de Fotbal, Str. Tricolorului 39, 2012 Chisinau.
Founded: 1990. *FIFA:* 1994; *UEFA:* 1993. *National Colours:* All blue.

International matches 2020–21

Kosovo (h) 1-1, Slovenia (a) 0-1, Italy (h) 0-6, Greece (a) 0-2, Slovenia (h) 0-4, Russia (h) 0-0, Greece (h) 0-2, Kosovo (a) 0-1, Faroe Islands (h) 1-1, Denmark (a) 0-8, Israel (h) 1-4, Turkey (h) 0-2, Azerbaijan (a) 1-0.

League Championship wins (1992–2021)

Sheriff Tiraspol 19; Zimbru Chisinau 8; Constructorul (renamed FC Tiraspol) 1; Dacia Chisinau 1; Milsami Orhei 1.

Cup wins (1992–2021)

Sheriff Tiraspol 10; Zimbru Chisinau 6; Tiligul-Tiras 3; FC Tiraspol 3 (incl. Constructorul 2); Milsami Orhei 2; Comrat 1; Nistru Otaci 1; Iskra-Stal 1; Zaria Balti 1; Petrocub-Hincesti 1; Sfintul Gheorghe 1.

Moldovan Divizia Nationala 2020–21

	P	W	D	L	F	A	GD	Pts
Sheriff (C)[1]	36	32	3	1	116	7	109	99
Petrocub-Hincesti[3]	36	25	8	3	82	18	64	83
Milsami Orhei[3]	36	22	7	7	71	37	34	73
Sfintul Gheorghe[3]	36	21	4	11	65	43	22	67
Dacia-Buiucani	36	13	9	14	44	45	–1	48
Dinamo-Auto	36	12	12	12	53	58	–5	48
Floresti	36	9	5	22	37	85	–48	32
Zimbru Chisinau	36	6	7	23	39	63	–24	25
Speranta Nisporeni†	36	5	8	23	29	87	–58	23
Codru Lozova*	36	2	3	31	26	119	–93	9

† *Speranta Nisporeni expelled for failing to fulfil two fixtures.*
Top scorer: Castaneda (Sheriff) 13.
Cup Final: Sheriff 0, Sfintul Gheorghe 0.
aet; Sfintul Gheorghe won 3-2 on penalties.

MONTENEGRO

Fudbalski Savez Crne Gore, Ulica 19. Decembar 13, PO Box 275, 81000 Podgorica.
Founded: 1931 *FIFA:* 2007; *UEFA:* 2007. *National Colours:* All red with gold trim.

International matches 2020–21

Cyprus (a) 2-0, Luxembourg (a) 1-0, Latvia (h) 1-1, Azerbaijan (h) 2-0, Luxembourg (h) 1-2, Kazakhstan (h) 0-0, Azerbaijan (a) 0-0, Cyprus (h) 4-0, Latvia (a) 2-1, Gibraltar (h) 4-1, Norway (h) 0-1, Bosnia-Herzegovina (a) 0-0, Israel (h) 1-3.

League Championship wins (2006–21)

Buducnost Podgorica 5; Sutjeska 4; Mogren 2; Rudar (Pljevlja) 2; Zeta 1; Mladost Podgorica 1 (renamed OFK Titograd).

Cup wins (2006–21)

Rudar (Pljevlja) 4; Buducnost Podgorica 3; Mladost Podgorica (renamed OFK Titograd) 2; Mogren 1; Petrovac 1; Celik 1; Lovcen 1: Sutjeska 1.
No winner in 2019–20.

Montenegrin Prva CFL 2020–21

	P	W	D	L	F	A	GD	Pts
Buducnost Podgorica (C)[1]	36	27	4	5	65	29	36	85
Sutjeska[3]	36	15	12	9	56	34	22	57
Decic[3]	36	13	15	8	39	28	11	54
FK Podgorica[3]	36	15	7	14	39	38	1	52
Jezero	36	12	9	15	28	34	–6	45
Zeta (–1)	36	13	7	16	34	41	–7	45
Rudar	36	13	6	17	38	50	–12	45
Iskra+	36	9	17	10	28	29	–1	44
Petrovac+	36	7	11	18	29	45	–16	32
OFK Titograd*	36	7	10	19	23	51	–28	31

Zeta deducted 2pts for disciplinary reasons, reduced to 1pt on appeal.
Top scorer: Markovic (Sutjeska) 16.
Cup Final: Buducnost Podgorica 3, Decic 1.

NETHERLANDS

Koninklijke Nederlandse Voetbalbond, Woudenbergseweg 56–58, Postbus 515, 3700 AM Zeist.
Founded: 1889. *FIFA:* 1904; *UEFA:* 1954. *National Colours:* Orange shirts, white shorts, orange socks.

International matches 2020–21

Poland (h) 1-0, Italy (h) 0-1, Mexico (h) 0-1, Bosnia-Herzegovina (a) 0-0, Italy (a) 1-1, Spain (h) 1-1, Bosnia-Herzegovina (h) 3-1, Poland (a) 2-1, Turkey (a) 2-4, Latvia (h) 2-0, Gibraltar (a) 7-0, Scotland (n) 2-2, Georgia (h) 3-0, Ukraine (h) 3-2, Austria (h) 2-0, North Macedonia (h) 3-0, Czech Republic (n) 0-2.

League Championship wins (1889–2021)

Ajax 35; PSV Eindhoven 24; Feyenoord 15; HVV The Hague 10; Sparta Rotterdam 6; RAP Amsterdam 5; Go Ahead Eagles Deventer 4; HFC Haarlem 3; HBS Craeyenhout 3; Willem II 3; RCH Heemstede 2; Heracles 2; ADO Den Haag 2; AZ 67 Alkmaar 2; VV Concordia 1; Quick Den Haag 1; Be Quick Groningen 1; NAC Breda 1; SC Enschede 1; Volewijckers Amsterdam 1; HFC Haarlem 1; BVV Den Bosch 1; Schiedam 1; Limburgia 1; EVV Eindhoven 1; SVV Rapid JC Den Heerlen (renamed Roda JC Kerkrade) 1; VV DOS (renamed FC Utrecht) 1; DWS Amsterdam 1; FC Twente 1.
No winner in 2019–20.

Cup wins (1899–2021)

Ajax 20; Feyenoord 13; PSV Eindhoven 9; Quick The Hague 4; AZ 67 Alkmaar 4; HFC Haarlem 3; Sparta Rotterdam 3; FC Twente 3; FC Utrecht 3; Haarlem 2; VOC 2; HBS Craeyenhout 2; DFC 2; RCH Haarlem 2; Wageningen 2; Willem II 2; Fortuna 54 2; FC Den Haag (includes ADO) 2; Roda JC 2; RAP Amsterdam 1; Velocitas Breda 1; HVV Den Haag 1; Concordia Delft 1; CVV 1; Schoten 1; ZFC Zaandam 1; Longa 1; VUC 1; Velocitas Groningen 1; Roermond 1; FC Eindhoven 1; VSV 1; Quick 1888 Nijmegen 1; VVV Groningen 1; NAC Breda 1; Heerenveen 1; PEC Zwolle 1; FC Groningen 1; Vitesse 1.
No winner in 2019–20.

Dutch Eredivisie 2020–21

	P	W	D	L	F	A	GD	Pts
Ajax (C)[1]	34	28	4	2	102	23	79	88
PSV Eindhoven[1]	34	21	9	4	74	35	39	72
AZ Alkmaar[2]	34	21	8	5	75	41	34	71
Vitesse[3]	34	18	7	9	52	38	14	61
Feyenoord†[3]	34	16	11	7	64	36	28	59
Utrecht†	34	13	14	7	52	41	11	53
FC Groningen†	34	14	8	12	40	37	3	50
Sparta Rotterdam†	34	13	8	13	49	48	1	47
Heracles Almelo	34	12	8	14	42	53	–11	44
FC Twente	34	10	11	13	48	50	–2	41
Fortuna Sittard	34	12	5	17	50	58	–8	41
Heerenveen	34	9	12	13	43	49	–6	39
PEC Zwolle	34	9	11	14	44	53	–9	38
Willem II Tilburg	34	8	7	19	40	68	–28	31
RKC Waalwijk	34	7	9	18	33	55	–22	30
Emmen*+	34	7	9	18	40	68	–28	30
VVV-Venlo*	34	6	5	23	43	91	–48	23
ADO Den Haag*	34	4	10	20	29	76	–47	22

† *Qualified for Europa Conference League Play-offs.*

Europa Conference League Play-offs
Semi-finals
Utrecht 1, Groningen 0
Feyenoord 2, Sparta Rotterdam 0

Europa Conference League Play-offs
Final
Feyenoord 2, Utrecht 0
Top scorer: Glakoumakis (VVV-Venlo) 26.
Cup Final: Ajax 2, Vitesse 1.

NORTH MACEDONIA

Football Federation of North Macedonia, 8-ma Udarna Brigada 31-A, PO Box 84, 1000 Skopje.
Founded: 1948. *FIFA:* 1994; *UEFA:* 1994. *National Colours:* All red.

International matches 2020–21
Armenia (h) 2-1, Georgia (a) 1-1, Kosovo (h) 2-1, Estonia (a) 3-3, Georgia (h) 1-1, Georgia (a) 1-0, Estonia (h) 2-1, Armenia (a) 0-1, Romania (a) 2-3, Liechtenstein (h) 5-0, Germany (a) 2-1, Slovenia (h) 1-1, Kazakhstan (h) 4-0, Austria (n) 1-3, Ukraine (n) 1-2, Netherlands (a) 0-3.

League Championship wins (1992–2021)
Vardar 11*; Rabotnicki 4; Shkendija 4; Sileks 3; Sloga Jugomagnat 3; Pobeda 2; Makedonija GjP 1; Renova 1.
* *Vardar also won 1 League Championship (1986–87) in Yugoslav Republic era, later controversially annulled.*

Cup wins (1992–2021)
Vardar 5†; Rabotnicki 4; Sileks 3; Sloga Jugomagnat 3; Pelister 2; Teteks 2; Shkendija 2; Pobeda 1; Cementarnica 55 1; Bashkimi 1; Makedonija GjP 1; Metalurg 1; Renova 1; Akademija Pandev 1.
No winner in 2019–20. † Vardar also won 1 Cup (1961) in Yugoslav Republic era.

North Macedonian Prva Liga Table 2020–21

	P	W	D	L	F	A	GD	Pts
Shkendija (C)[1]	33	22	9	2	69	26	43	75
Shkupi[3]	33	16	11	6	41	24	17	59
Struga[3]	33	15	12	6	39	24	15	57
Makedonija GjP	33	16	7	10	53	43	10	55
Rabotnicki	33	11	15	7	45	39	6	48
Pelister	33	12	9	12	34	38	–4	45
Akademija Pandev	33	12	5	16	32	36	–4	41
Borec	33	11	7	15	32	36	–4	40
Sileks[3]*+	33	10	6	17	49	45	4	36
Renova+	33	8	12	13	36	46	–10	36
Vardar*	33	7	10	16	32	60	–28	31
Belasica*	33	4	5	24	23	68	–45	17

Top scorer: Ibraimi (Shkendija) 24.
Cup Final: Akademija Pandev 0, Sileks 0.
aet; Sileks won 4-3 on penalties.

NORTHERN CYPRUS

Cyprus Turkish Football Federation, 7 Memduh Asaf Street, 107 Koskluciftlik, Lefkosa. (Not a member of FIFA or UEFA.)
Founded: 1955; *National Colours:* Red shirts with white trim, red shorts, red socks.

League Championship wins (1956–63; 1969–74; 1976–2021)*
Cetinkaya 14; Magusa Turk Gucu 10; Yenicami Agdelen 9; Gonyeli 9; Dogan Turk Birligi 7; Baf Ulku Yurdu 4; Kucuk Kaymakli 4; Akincilar 1; Binatli 1.
* *No winner in 2020–21.*

Cup wins (1956–2021)*
Cetinkaya 17; Yenicami Agdelen 8; Gonyeli 8; Kucuk Kaymakli 7; Magusa Turk Gucu 6; Turk Ocagi Limasol 5; Lefke 2; Dogan Turk Birligi 2; Genclik Gucu 1; Yalova 1; Binatli 1; Cihangir 1.
* *No winner in 2020–21.*

Northern Cyprus Super Lig and Cypriot Cup 2020–21
No competitions due to COVID-19 pandemic.

NORTHERN IRELAND

Irish Football Association, Donegall Avenue, Belfast BT12 6LU.
Founded: 1880. *FIFA:* 1911; *UEFA:* 1954. *National Colours:* Green shirts, white shorts, green socks.

NORWAY

Norges Fotballforbund, Ullevaal Stadion, Serviceboks 1, 0840 Oslo.
Founded: 1902. *FIFA:* 1908; *UEFA:* 1954. *National Colours:* Red shirts, white shorts, red socks.

International matches 2020–21
Austria (h) 1-2, Northern Ireland (a) 5-1, Serbia (h) 1-2, Romania (h) 4-0, Northern Ireland (h) 1-0, Romania (a) 0-3, Austria (a) 1-1, Gibraltar (a) 3-0, Turkey (h) 0-3, Montenegro (a) 1-0, Luxembourg (h) 1-0, Greece (n) 1-2.

League Championship wins (1938–2020)
Rosenborg 26; Fredrikstad 9; Viking Stavanger 8; Lillestrom 5; Valerenga 5; Molde 4; Larvik Turn 3; Brann 3; Lyn Oslo 2; Stromsgodset 2; IK Start 2; Freidig 1; Fram 1; Skeid 1; Moss 1; Stabaek 1; Bodo/Glimt 1.

Cup wins (1902–2020)*
Odd Grenland 12; Rosenborg 12; Fredrikstad 11; Lyn Oslo 8; Skeid 8; Sarpsborg 6; Brann 6; Viking Stavanger 6; Lillestrom 6; Stromsgodset 5; Orn-Horten 4; Valerenga 4; Molde 4; Frigg 3; Mjondalen 3; Mercantile 2; Bodo/Glimt 2; Tromso 2; Aalesund 2; Grane Nordstrand 1; Kvik Halden 1; Sparta 1; Gjovik/Lyn 1; Moss 1; Bryne 1; Stabaek 1; Hodd 1.
(Known as the Norwegian Championship for HM The King's Trophy.)
* *No winner in 2020.*

Norwegian Eliteserien 2020

	P	W	D	L	F	A	GD	Pts
Bodo/Glimt (C)[1]	30	26	3	1	103	32	71	81
Molde[3]	30	20	2	8	77	36	41	62
Valerenga[3]	30	15	10	5	51	33	18	55
Rosenborg[3]	30	15	7	8	50	35	15	52
Kristiansund	30	12	12	6	57	45	12	48
Viking Stavanger	30	12	8	10	54	52	2	44
Odd	30	13	4	13	52	51	1	43
Stabaek	30	9	12	9	41	45	–4	39
Haugesund	30	11	6	13	39	51	–12	39
Brann	30	9	9	12	40	49	–9	36
Sandefjord	30	9	8	13	31	43	–12	35
Sarpsborg 08	30	8	8	14	33	43	–10	32
Stromsgodset	30	7	10	13	41	57	–16	31
Mjondalen+	30	8	3	19	26	45	–19	27
Start*	30	6	9	15	33	56	–23	27
Aalesund*	30	2	5	23	30	85	–55	11

Top scorer: Junker (Bodo/Glimt) 27.
Cup Final: No competition due to COVID-19 pandemic.

POLAND

Polski Zwiazek Pilki Noznej, ul. Bitwy Warszawskiej 1920r. 7, 02-366 Warszawa.
Founded: 1919. *FIFA:* 1923; *UEFA:* 1954. *National Colours:* White shirts with red vertical band, red shorts, white socks.

International matches 2020–21
Netherlands (a) 0-1, Bosnia-Herzegovina (a) 2-1, Finland (h) 5-1, Italy (h) 0-0, Bosnia-Herzegovina (h) 3-0, Ukraine (h) 2-0, Italy (a) 0-2, Netherlands (h) 1-2, Hungary (a) 3-3, Andorra (h) 3-0, England (a) 1-2, Russia (h) 1-1, Iceland (h) 2-2, Slovakia (n) 1-2, Spain (a) 1-1, Sweden (n) 2-3.

League Championship wins (1921–23; 1925–38; 1946–2021)
Legia Warsaw 15; Ruch Chorzow 14; Gornik Zabrze 14; Wisla Krakow 13; Lech Poznan 7; Cracovia 5; Pogon Lwow 4; Widzew Lodz 4; Warta Poznan 2; Polonia Warsaw 2; Polonia Bytom 2; LKS Lodz 2; Stal Mielec 2; Slask Wroclaw 2; Zaglebie Lubin 2; Garbarnia Krakow 1; Szombierki Bytom 1; Piast Gliwice 1.

Cup wins (1926; 1951–2021)

Legia Warsaw 19; Gornik Zabrze 6; Lech Poznan 5; Wisla Krakow 4; Zaglebie Sosnowiec 4; Ruch Chorzow 3; GKS Katowice 3; Amica Wronki 3; Polonia Warsaw 2; Slask Wroclaw 2; Arka Gdynia 2; Lechia Gdansk 2; Dyskobolia Grodzisk 2; Gwardia Warsaw 1; LKS Lodz 1; Stal Rzeszow 1; Widzew Lodz 1; Miedz Legnica 1; Wisla Plock 1; Jagiellonia Bialystok 1; Zawisza Bydgoszcz 1; Cracovia 1; Rakow Czestochowa 1.

Polish Ekstraklasa Qualifying Table 2020–21

	P	*W*	*D*	*L*	*F*	*A*	*GD*	*Pts*
Legia Warsaw (C)[1]	30	19	7	4	48	24	24	64
Rakow Czestochowa[3]	30	17	8	5	46	25	21	59
Pogon Szczecin[3]	30	15	7	8	36	23	13	52
Slask Wroclaw†[3]	30	11	10	9	36	32	4	43
Warta Poznan†	30	13	4	13	33	32	1	43
Piast Gliwice†	30	11	9	10	39	32	7	42
Lechia Gdansk†	30	12	6	12	40	37	3	42
Zaglebie Lubin	30	11	8	11	38	40	–2	41
Jagiellonia Bialystok†	30	10	7	13	39	48	–9	37
Gornik Zabrze†	30	10	7	13	31	33	–2	37
Lech Poznan†	30	9	10	11	39	38	1	37
Wisla Plock‡	30	8	9	13	37	44	–7	33
Wisla Krakow‡	30	8	9	13	39	42	–3	33
Cracovia (–5)	30	8	13	9	28	32	–4	32
Stal Mielec	30	6	11	13	31	47	–16	29
Podbeskidzie*	30	6	7	17	29	60	–31	25

† *Ranking decided on head-to-head points.* ‡ *Ranking decided on head-to-head matches.*
Cracovia deducted 5pts for match-fixing in 2003–04.
Top scorer: Pekhart (Legia Warsaw) 22.
Cup Final: Rakow Czestochowa 2, Arka Gdynia 1.

PORTUGAL

Federacao Portuguesa de Futebol, Rua Alexandre Herculano No. 58, Apartado postal 24013, Lisboa 1250-012.
Founded: 1914. *FIFA:* 1923; *UEFA:* 1954. *National Colours:* Carmine shirts with green and black trim, green shorts, carmine socks with green and black trim.

International matches 2020–21

Croatia (h) 4-1, Sweden (a) 2-0, Spain (h) 0-0, France (a) 0-0, Sweden (h) 3-0, Andorra (h) 7-0, France (h) 0-1, Croatia (a) 3-2, Azerbaijan (h) 1-0, Serbia (a) 2-2, Luxembourg (a) 3-1, Spain (a) 0-0, Israel (h) 4-0, Hungary (a) 3-0, Germany (a) 2-4, France (n) 2-2, Belgium (n) 0-1.

League Championship wins (1935–2021)

Benfica 37; Porto 29; Sporting Lisbon 19; Belenenses 1; Boavista 1.

Cup wins (1939–2021)

Benfica 26; Sporting Lisbon 17; Porto 17; Boavista 5; Belenenses 3; Vitoria de Setubal 3; Braga 3; Academica de Coimbra 2; Leixoes 1; Estrela da Amadora 1; Beira-Mar 1; Vitoria de Guimaraes 1; Desportivo das Aves 1.

Portuguese Primeira Liga 2020–21

	P	*W*	*D*	*L*	*F*	*A*	*GD*	*Pts*
Sporting Lisbon (C)[1]	34	26	7	1	65	20	45	85
Porto[1]	34	24	8	2	74	29	45	80
Benfica[1]	34	23	7	4	69	27	42	76
Braga[2]	34	19	7	8	53	33	20	64
Pacos de Ferreira[3]	34	15	8	11	40	41	–1	53
Santa Clara[3]	34	13	7	14	44	36	8	46
Vitoria de Guimaraes†	34	12	7	15	37	44	–7	43
Moreirense†	34	10	13	11	37	43	–6	43
Famalicao†	34	10	10	14	40	48	–8	40
Belenenses†	34	9	13	12	25	35	–10	40
Gil Vicente	34	11	6	17	33	42	–9	39
Tondela†	34	10	6	18	36	57	–21	36
Boavista†	34	8	12	14	39	49	–10	36
Portimonense†	34	9	8	17	34	41	–7	35
Maritimo†	34	10	5	19	27	47	–20	35
Rio Ave*+	34	7	13	14	25	40	–15	34
Farense*	34	7	10	17	31	48	–17	31
Nacional*	34	6	7	21	30	59	–29	25

† *Ranking decided on head-to-head points.*
Top scorer: Goncalves ('Pote') (Sporting Lisbon) 23.
Cup Final: Braga 2, Benfica 0.

REPUBLIC OF IRELAND

Football Association of Ireland (Cumann Peile na hEireann), National Sports Campus, Abbotstown, Dublin 15.
Founded: 1921. *FIFA:* 1923; *UEFA:* 1954. *National Colours:* Green shirts, green shorts, green socks with white tops.

League Championship wins (1922–2020)

Shamrock R 18; Dundalk 14; Shelbourne 13; Bohemians 11; St Patrick's Ath 8; Waterford U 6; Cork U 5; Drumcondra 5; Sligo R 3; Cork C 3; St James's Gate 2; Cork Ath 2; Limerick 2; Athlone T 2; Derry C 2; Dolphin 1; Cork Hibernians 1; Cork Celtic 1; Drogheda U 1.

Cup wins (1922–2020)

Shamrock R 25; Dundalk 12; Bohemians 7; Shelbourne 7; Drumcondra 5; Sligo R 5; Derry C 5; Cork C 4; St Patrick's Ath 3; St James's Gate 2; Cork (incl. Fordsons 1) 2; Waterford U 2; Cork U 2; Cork Ath 2; Limerick 2; Cork Hibernians 2; Bray W 2; Longford T 2; Alton U 1; Athlone T 1; Transport 1; Finn Harps 1; Home Farm 1; UC Dublin 1; Galway U 1; Drogheda U 1; Sporting Fingal 1.

League of Ireland Premier Division 2020

	P	*W*	*D*	*L*	*F*	*A*	*GD*	*Pts*
Shamrock R (C)[1]	18	15	3	0	44	7	37	48
Bohemians[3]	18	12	1	5	23	12	11	37
Dundalk[3]	18	7	5	6	25	23	2	26
Sligo R[3]	18	8	1	9	19	23	–4	25
Waterford	18	7	3	8	17	22	–5	24
St Patrick's Ath	18	5	6	7	14	17	–3	21
Derry C	18	5	5	8	18	18	0	20
Finn Harps	18	5	5	8	15	24	–9	20
Shelbourne*+	18	5	4	9	13	22	–9	19
Cork C*	18	2	5	11	10	30	–20	11

Top scorer: Hoban (Dundalk) 10.
Cup Final: Dundalk 4, Shamrock R 2 *aet.*

ROMANIA

Federatia Romana de Fotbal, House of Football, Str. Sergent Serbanica Vasile 12, 22186 Bucuresti.
Founded: 1909. *FIFA:* 1923; *UEFA:* 1954. *National Colours:* All yellow.

International matches 2020–21

Northern Ireland (h) 1-1, Austria (a) 3-2, Iceland (a) 1-2, Norway (a) 0-4, Austria (h) 0-1, Belarus (h) 5-3, Norway (h) 3-0, Northern Ireland (a) 1-1, North Macedonia (h) 3-2, Germany (h) 0-1, Armenia (a) 2-3, Georgia (h) 1-2, England (a) 0-1.

League Championship wins (1910–2021)

Steaua Bucharest (renamed FCSB)* 26; Dinamo Bucharest 18; Venus Bucharest 8†; Chinezul Timisoara 6; UTA Arad 6; CFR Cluj 7; Petrolul Ploiesti 4; Ripensia Timisoara 4; Universitatea Craiova 4; Rapid Bucharest 3; Olimpia Bucharest 2; United Ploiesti 2 (incl. Prahova Ploiesti 1); Colentina Bucharest 2; Arges Pitesti 2; Romano-Americana Bucharest 1; Coltea Brasov 1; Metalul Resita (renamed CSM Resita) 1; Unirea Tricolor 1; CA Oradea 1; Unirea Urziceni 1; Otelul Galati 1; Astra Giurgiu 1; Viitorul Constanta 1.
† *The validity of Venus Bucharest's first two titles is disputed.*

Cup wins (1934–43; 1947–2021)

Steaua Bucharest (renamed FCSB)* 24; Rapid Bucharest 13; Dinamo Bucharest 13; Universitatea Craiova (incl. FC U Craiova 1948 1) 8; CFR Cluj 4; Petrolul Ploiesti 3; Ripensia Timisoara 2; UTA Arad 2; Politehnica Timisoara 2; CFR Turnu Severin 1; Metalul Resita (renamed CSM Resita) 1; Universitatea Cluj (includes Stiinta) 1; Progresul Oradea (formerly ICO) 1; Progresul Bucharest 1; Ariesul Turda 1; Chimia Ramnicu Vilcea 1; Jiul Petrosani 1; Gloria Bistrita 1; Astra Giurgiu 1; Voluntari 1; Viitorul Constanta 1.
* *Club involved in protracted legal dispute about right to name, brand and historical honours; UEFA currently recognises FCSB as essentially the same entity as Steaua Bucharest.*

Romanian Liga 1 Qualifying Table 2020–21

	P	*W*	*D*	*L*	*F*	*A*	*GD*	*Pts*
FCSB	30	20	5	5	57	22	35	65
CFR Cluj	30	19	7	4	42	15	27	64
Universitatea Craiova	30	16	10	4	33	14	19	58
Sepsi Sfantu Gheorghe	30	10	15	5	43	31	12	45
Academica Clinceni	30	10	14	6	30	26	4	44
Botosani	30	11	9	10	39	36	3	42
Arges Pitesti	30	10	10	10	33	41	–8	40
Chindia Targoviste	30	10	9	11	24	26	–2	39
Astra Giurgiu	30	9	11	10	38	39	–1	38
UTA Arad	30	9	10	11	26	36	–10	37
Gaz Metan Medias	30	9	6	15	33	41	–8	33
Voluntari	30	8	8	14	32	40	–8	32

Viitorul Constanta	30	6	13	11	36	37	–1	31
Dinamo Bucharest	30	7	6	17	26	41	–15	27
Hermannstadt	30	5	11	14	28	40	–12	26
Politehnica Iasi	30	7	4	19	29	64	–35	25

NB: Points earned in Qualifying phase are halved and rounded up at start of Championship and Relegation Play-off phase.

Championship Round 2020–21

	P	*W*	*D*	*L*	*F*	*A*	*GD*	*Pts*
CFR Cluj (C)[1]	10	7	1	2	15	5	10	54
FCSB[3]	10	3	3	4	13	14	–1	45
Universitatea Craiova[3]	10	3	3	4	9	11	–2	41
Sepsi Sfantu Gheorghe†[3]	10	5	2	3	11	8	3	40
Academica Clinceni	10	3	2	5	10	15	–5	33
Botosani	10	3	1	6	13	18	–5	31

† *Qualified for Europa Conference League Play-offs.*

Relegation Round 2020–21

	P	*W*	*D*	*L*	*F*	*A*	*GD*	*Pts*
Chindia Targovi te†	9	4	4	1	7	3	4	36
UTA Arad‡¶	9	4	1	4	7	9	–2	32
Gaz Metan Medias‡	9	4	3	2	15	10	5	32
Viitorul Constanta‡¶	9	5	1	3	9	4	5	32
Arges Pitesti§	9	3	2	4	10	7	3	31
Dinamo Bucharest§	9	5	2	2	11	8	3	31
Voluntari+	9	3	3	3	6	7	–1	28
Hermannstadt*+	9	4	1	4	6	9	–3	26
Astra Giurgiu*	9	1	2	6	6	12	–6	24
Politehnica Iasi*	9	2	1	6	7	15	–8	20

† *Qualified for Europa Conference League Play-offs.* ‡ *Ranking decided on points gained in regular season.* § *Ranking decided on points without rounding.* ¶ *UTA Arad and Gaz Metan Medias failed to obtain UEFA licences.*

Top scorer: Tanase (FCSB) 24.

Cup Final: Universitatea Craiova 3, Astra Giurgiu 2 *aet.*

RUSSIA

Russian Football Union, Ulitsa Narodnaya 7, 115 172 Moscow.

Founded: 1912. *FIFA:* 1912; *UEFA:* 1954. *National Colours:* All brick red.

International matches 2020–21

Serbia (h) 3-1, Hungary (a) 3-2, Sweden (h) 1-2, Turkey (h) 1-1, Hungary (h) 0-0, Moldova (a) 0-0, Turkey (a) 2-3, Serbia (a) 0-5, Malta (a) 3-1, Slovenia (h) 2-1, Slovakia (a) 1-2, Poland (a) 1-1, Bulgaria (h) 1-0, Belgium (h) 0-3, Finland (h) 1-0, Denmark (a) 1-4.

USSR League Championship wins (1936–91)

Dynamo Kyiv 13; Spartak Moscow 12; Dynamo Moscow 11; CSKA Moscow 7; Torpedo Moscow 3; Dinamo Tbilisi 2; Dnepr Dnepropetrovsk 2; Zorya Voroshilovgrad 1; Ararat Yerevan 1; Dinamo Minsk 1; Zenit Leningrad 1.

Russian League Championship wins (1992–2021)

Spartak Moscow 10; Zenit St Petersburg 7; CSKA Moscow 6; Lokomotiv Moscow 3; Rubin Kazan 2; Spartak Vladikavkaz (formerly Alania) 1.

USSR Cup wins (1936–91)

Spartak Moscow 10; Dynamo Kyiv 9; Dynamo Moscow 6; Torpedo Moscow 6; CSKA Moscow 5; Shakhtar Donetsk 4; Lokomotiv Moscow 2; Ararat Yerevan 2; Dinamo Tbilisi 2; Zenit Leningrad 1; Karpaty Lvov 1; SKA Rostov-on-Don 1; Metalist Kharkov 1; Dnepr Dnepropetrovsk 1.

Russian Cup wins (1992–2021)

Lokomotiv Moscow 9; CSKA Moscow 7; Zenit St Petersburg 4; Spartak Moscow 3; Torpedo Moscow 1; Dynamo Moscow 1; Terek Grozny (renamed Akhmat Grozny) 1; Rubin Kazan 1; Rostov 1; Tosno 1.

Russian Premier Liga 2020–21

	P	*W*	*D*	*L*	*F*	*A*	*GD*	*Pts*
Zenit St Petersburg (C)[1]	30	19	8	3	76	26	50	65
Spartak Moscow[1]	30	17	6	7	56	37	19	57
Lokomotiv Moscow[2]	30	17	5	8	45	35	10	56
Rubin Kazan†[3]	30	16	5	9	42	33	9	53
Sochi†[3]	30	15	8	7	49	33	16	53
CSKA Moscow‡	30	15	5	10	51	33	18	50
Dynamo Moscow‡	30	15	5	10	44	33	11	50
Khimki	30	13	6	11	35	39	–4	45
Rostov	30	13	4	13	37	35	2	43
Krasnodar	30	12	5	13	52	45	7	41
Akhmat Grozny	30	11	7	12	36	38	–2	40
Ural Yekaterinburg	30	7	13	10	26	36	–10	34
Ufa	30	6	7	17	26	46	–20	25
Arsenal Tula	30	6	5	19	28	51	–23	23
Rotor Volgograd*	30	5	7	18	15	52	–37	22
Tambov*	30	3	4	23	19	65	–46	13

† *Ranking decided on head-to-head points and matches won.* ‡ *Ranking decided on head-to-head points and goal difference.*

Tambov folded at the end of the season.

Top scorer: Dzyuba (Zenit St Petersburg) 20.

Cup Final: Lokomotiv Moscow 3, Krylya Sovetov Samara 1.

SAN MARINO

Federazione Sammarinese Giuoco Calcio, Strada di Montecchio 17, 47890 San Marino.

Founded: 1931. *FIFA:* 1988; *UEFA:* 1988. *National Colours:* Cobalt blue shirts with white trim, white shorts, cobalt blue socks.

International matches 2020–21

Gibraltar (a) 0-1, Liechtenstein (h) 0-2, Slovenia (a) 0-4, Liechtenstein (a) 0-0, Latvia (h) 0-3, Gibraltar (h) 0-0, England (a) 0-5, Hungary (h) 0-3, Albania (h) 0-2, Italy (a) 0-7, Kosovo (a) 1-4.

League Championship wins (1986–2021)

Tre Fiori 8; La Fiorita 5; Folgore Falciano 5; Domagnano 4; Tre Penne 4; Faetano 3; Murata 3; Montevito 1; Libertas 1; Cosmos 1; Pennarossa 1.

Cup wins (1937–2021)

Libertas 11; Domagnano 8; Tre Fiori 7; Tre Penne 6; La Fiorita 6; Juvenes 5; Cosmos 4; Faetano 3; Murata 3; Dogana 2; Pennarossa 2; Juvenes/Dogana 2; Folgore Falciano 1.

No winner in 2019–20.

Campionato Sammarinese 2020–21

First Phase

	P	*W*	*D*	*L*	*F*	*A*	*GD*	*Pts*
La Fiorita[3]	14	12	1	1	34	5	29	37
Libertas	14	9	2	3	21	11	10	29
Folgore Falciano (C)[1]	14	8	3	3	25	10	15	27
Tre Penne	14	9	0	5	30	20	10	27
Tre Fiori	14	7	5	2	26	11	15	26
Pennarossa	14	6	3	5	15	15	0	21
San Giovanni	14	5	4	5	17	20	–3	19
Juvenes/Dogana	14	6	1	7	23	34	–11	19
Murata	14	4	6	4	14	9	5	18
Virtus	14	4	6	4	14	12	2	18
Fiorentino	14	4	4	6	18	26	–8	16
Domagnano	14	2	6	6	16	26	–10	12
Faetano	14	2	4	8	14	26	–12	10
Cailungo	14	2	2	10	17	29	–12	8
Cosmos	14	1	1	12	10	40	–30	4

Top four qualify for Second Phase quarter-finals; clubs placed fifth to twelfth play off for remaining quarter-final spots. Winners of drawn matches decided by record in regular season.

Play-offs

Pennarossa 0, Fiorentino 0
Juvenes/Dogana 0, Virtus 3
Tre Fiori 0, Domagnano 2
San Giovanni 0, Murata 3

Second Phase

Quarter-finals

Pennarossa 1, Tre Penne 2
Virtus 2, Libertas 3
Folgore Falciano 1, Murata 1
La Fiorita 0, Domagnano 0

Semi-finals

La Fiorita 1, Tre Penne 0
Folgore Falciano 3, Libertas 1

3rd Place Final

Tre Penne 1, Libertas 0

Final

La Fiorita 0, Folgore Falciano 1 *aet.*

Top scorer: Baldassi (Folgore Falciano) 13.

Cup Final: Tre Fiori 0, La Fiorita 0.

aet; La Fiorita won 10-9 on penalties.

SCOTLAND

Scottish Football Association, Hampden Park, Glasgow G42 9AY.

Founded: 1873. *FIFA:* 1910; *UEFA:* 1954. *National Colours:* Dark blue shirts, dark blue shorts, red socks.

SERBIA

Football Association of Serbia, Terazije 35, PO Box 263, 11000 Beograd.
Founded: 1919. *FIFA:* 1921; *UEFA:* 1954. *National Colours:* Red shirts, blue shorts, white socks.

International matches 2020–21
Russia (a) 1-3, Turkey (h) 0-0, Norway (a) 2-1, Hungary (h) 0-1, Turkey (a) 2-2, Scotland (h) 1-1 (4-5p), Hungary (a) 1-1, Russia (h) 5-0, Dominican Republic (a) 0-0, Panama (a) 0-0, Republic of Ireland (h) 3-2, Portugal (h) 2-2, Azerbaijan (a) 2-1, Jamaica (n) 1-1, Japan (a) 0-1.

Yugoslav League Championship wins (1923–40; 1946–91)
Red Star Belgrade (Crvena Zvezda) 19; Partizan Belgrade 11*; Hajduk Split 9; Gradjanski Zagreb 5; BSK Belgrade (renamed OFK) 5; Dinamo Zagreb 4; Jugoslavija Belgrade 2; Concordia Zagreb 2; Vojvodina Novi Sad 2; FC Sarajevo 2; HASK Zagreb 1; Zeljeznicar 1.
* *Total includes 1 League Championship (1986–87) originally awarded to Macedonian club Vardar.*

Serbian League Championship wins (1992–2021)
Partizan Belgrade 16; Red Star Belgrade (Crvena zvezda) 13; Obilic 1.

Yugoslav Cup wins (1923–41; 1947–91)
Red Star Belgrade (Crvena zvezda) 12; Hajduk Split 9; Dinamo Zagreb 7; Partizan Belgrade 6; OFK Belgrade (incl. BSK 3) 5; Rijeka 2; Velez Mostar 2; HASK Zagreb 1; Jugoslavija Belgrade 1; Vardar Skopje 1; Borac Banjaluka 1.

Serbian and Serbia-Montenegro Cup wins (1991–2021)
Red Star Belgrade (Crvena zvezda) 13; Partizan Belgrade 11; Vojvodina 2; Sartid 1; Zeleznik 1; Jagodina 1; Cukaricki 1.

Serbian SuperLiga Qualifying Table 2020–21

	P	*W*	*D*	*L*	*F*	*A*	*GD*	*Pts*
Red Star Belgrade (C)[1]	38	35	3	0	114	20	94	108
Partizan Belgrade[3]	38	31	2	5	95	20	75	95
Cukaricki[3]	38	22	8	8	69	34	35	74
Vojvodina[3]	38	21	8	9	62	41	21	71
TSC Backa Topola	38	17	7	14	68	50	18	58
Radnik Surdulica	38	16	7	15	55	49	6	55
Mladost Lucani	38	15	9	14	43	59	–16	54
Proleter Novi Sad	38	15	8	15	40	47	–7	53
Metalac	38	13	13	12	48	53	–5	52
Spartak Subotica	38	15	7	16	54	53	1	52
Napredak	38	14	8	16	44	51	–7	50
Novi Pazar	38	14	7	17	50	60	–10	49
Radnicki Nis	38	13	10	15	37	39	–2	49
Vozdovac	38	13	9	16	49	59	–10	48
Rad*	38	14	6	18	44	57	–13	48
Javor Ivanjica*	38	12	10	16	45	53	–8	46
Indija*	38	10	5	23	29	66	–37	35
Zlatibor Cajetina*	38	7	8	23	28	64	–36	29
Macva Sabac*	38	7	4	27	26	81	–55	25
Backa Palanka*	38	3	7	28	24	68	–44	16

Top scorer: Makaric (Radnik Surdulica) 25.
Cup Final: Red Star Belgrade 0, Partizan Belgrade 0.
aet; Red Star Belgrade won 4-3 on penalties.

SLOVAKIA

Slovensky Futbalovy Zvaz, Trnavska cesta 100, 821 01 Bratislava.
Founded: 1938. *FIFA:* 1994; *UEFA:* 1993. *National Colours:* White shirts with blue trim, white shorts, white socks.

International matches 2020–21
Czech Republic (h) 1-3, Israel (a) 1-1, Republic of Ireland (h) 0-0 (4-2p), Scotland (a) 0-1, Israel (h) 2-3, Northern Ireland (h) 2-1, Scotland (h) 1-0, Czech Republic (a) 0-2, Cyprus (a) 0-0, Malta (h) 2-2, Russia (h) 2-1, Bulgaria (n) 1-1, Austria (a) 0-0, Poland (n) 2-1, Sweden (n) 0-1, Spain (a) 0-5.

League Championship wins (1938–44; 1993–2021)
Slovan Bratislava (incl. 4 as SK Bratislava) 15; Zilina 7; Kosice 2; Inter Bratislava 2; Artmedia Petrzalka 2; Trencin 2; Sparta Povazska Bystrica 1; OAP Bratislava 1; Ruzomberok 1; Spartak Trnava 1.

Cup wins (1961; 1969–93; 1993–2021)
Slovan Bratislava 17; Spartak Trnava 6; Inter Bratislava 6; VSS Kosice 5; Lokomotiva Kosice 3; Trencin 3; Zilina 2; Dukla Banska Bystrica 2; Artmedia Petrzalka 2; DAC 1904 Dunajska Streda 1; Tatran Presov 1; Chemlon Humenne 1; Koba Senec 1; Matador Puchov 1; Ruzomberok 1; ViOn Zlate Moravce 1.
See also Czech Republic section for Slovak club honours in Czechoslovak era 1925–93.

Slovak Super Liga Qualifying Table 2020–21

	P	*W*	*D*	*L*	*F*	*A*	*GD*	*Pts*
Slovan Bratislava	22	17	3	2	54	12	42	54
DAC Dunajska Streda	22	13	5	4	48	28	20	44
Zilina	22	11	4	7	49	33	16	37
Spartak Trnava	22	11	2	9	32	29	3	35
Zlate Moravce	22	9	6	7	38	29	9	33
Trencin	22	7	7	8	30	38	–8	28
Ruzomberok	22	5	8	9	31	37	–6	23
Nitra†	22	6	4	12	21	38	–17	22
Zemplin Michalovce†	22	5	7	10	22	42	–20	22
Sered'†	22	5	7	10	22	39	–17	22
Senica	22	5	6	11	23	40	–17	21
Pohronie	22	3	11	8	27	32	–5	20

† *Ranking decided on head-to-head points.*

Championship Round 2020–21

	P	*W*	*D*	*L*	*F*	*A*	*GD*	*Pts*
Slovan Bratislava (C)[1]	32	22	5	5	78	28	50	71
DAC Dunajska Streda[3]	32	19	8	5	66	38	28	65
Spartak Trnava[3]	32	17	4	11	48	37	11	55
Zilina†[3]	32	15	7	10	73	52	21	52
Zlate Moravce†	32	11	7	14	42	51	–9	40
Trencin†	32	8	8	16	42	61	–19	32

† *Qualified for Europa Conference League play-offs.*

Relegation Round 2020–21

	P	*W*	*D*	*L*	*F*	*A*	*GD*	*Pts*
Sered'†	32	11	8	13	37	48	–11	41
Ruzomberok	32	10	9	13	41	44	–3	39
Pohronie	32	8	14	10	38	38	0	38
Zemplin Michalovce	32	8	11	13	34	53	–19	35
Senica+	32	8	9	15	31	51	–20	33
Nitra*	32	7	6	19	26	55	–29	27

† *Qualified for Europa Conference League play-offs.*

Europa Conference League Play-offs
Semi-finals
Zilina 4, Sered' 2
Zlate Moravce 2, Trencin 0
Final
Zilina 3, Zlate Moravce 2
Top scorer: Kurminowski (Zilina) 20.
Cup Final: Slovan Bratislava 2, Zilina 1 *aet.*

SLOVENIA

Nogometna Zveza Slovenije, Brnciceva 41g, PP 3986, 1001 Ljubljana.
Founded: 1920. *FIFA:* 1992; *UEFA:* 1992. *National Colours:* White shirts with blue trim, white shorts, white socks.

International matches 2020–21
Greece (h) 0-0, Moldova (h) 1-0, San Marino (h) 4-0, Kosovo (a) 1-0, Moldova (a) 4-0, Azerbaijan (h) 0-0, Kosovo (h) 2-1, Greece (a) 0-0, Croatia (h) 1-0, Russia (a) 1-2, Cyprus (a) 0-1, North Macedonia (a) 1-1, Gibraltar (h) 6-0.

League Championship wins (1991–2021)
Maribor 15; Olimpija (pre-2005) 4; Gorica 4; Domzale 2; Olimpija Ljubljana (post-2005) 2; Koper 1; Celje 1; Mura (post-2012) 1.

Cup wins (1991–2021)
Maribor 9; Olimpija (pre-2005) 4; Gorica 3; Olimpija Ljubljana (post-2005) 3; Koper 3; Interblock 2; Domzale 2; NK Mura (pre-2005) 1; Rudar Velenje 1; Celje 1; Mura (post-2012) 1.

Slovenian PrvaLiga 2020–21

	P	*W*	*D*	*L*	*F*	*A*	*GD*	*Pts*
Mura (C)[1]	36	17	12	7	50	26	24	63
Maribor[3]	36	17	12	7	64	41	23	63
Olimpija Ljubljana[3]	36	16	11	9	45	35	10	59
Domzale[3]	36	14	13	9	52	41	11	55
Bravo	36	10	15	11	39	39	0	45
Tabor Sezana	36	12	8	16	40	44	–4	44
Celje	36	12	7	17	36	41	–5	43
Aluminij	36	10	13	13	31	41	–10	43
Koper+	36	11	9	16	41	56	–15	42
Gorica*	36	7	8	21	24	58	–34	29

Top scorers (joint): Mlakar (Maribor), Mulahusejnovic (Koper) 14.
Cup Final: Olimpija Ljubljana 2, Celje 1.

SPAIN

Real Federacion Espanola de Futbol, Calle Ramon y Cajal s/n, Apartado postale 385, 28230 Las Rozas, Madrid.
Founded: 1913. *FIFA:* 1913; *UEFA:* 1954. *National Colours:* All red with yellow trim.

International matches 2020–21

Germany (a) 1-1, Ukraine (h) 4-0, Portugal (a) 0-0, Switzerland (h) 1-0, Ukraine (a) 0-1, Netherlands (a) 1-1, Switzerland (a) 1-1, Germany (h) 6-0, Greece (h) 1-1, Georgia (a) 2-1, Kosovo (h) 3-1, Portugal (h) 0-0, Lithuania (h) 4-0, Sweden (h) 0-0, Poland (h) 1-1, Slovakia (h) 5-0, Croatia (n) 5-3, Switzerland (n) 1-1 (3-1p), Italy (n) 1-1 (2-4p).

League Championship wins (1929–36; 1940–2021)

Real Madrid 34; Barcelona 26; Atletico Madrid 11; Athletic Bilbao 8; Valencia 6; Real Sociedad 2; Real Betis 1; Sevilla 1; Deportivo La Coruna 1.

Cup wins (1903–2021)

Barcelona 31; Athletic Bilbao (includes Vizcaya Bilbao 1) 23; Real Madrid 19; Atletico Madrid 10; Valencia 8; Real Zaragoza 6; Sevilla 5; Espanyol 4; Real Union de Irun 3; Real Sociedad (includes Ciclista) 3; Real Betis 2; Deportivo La Coruna 2; Racing de Irun 1; Arenas 1; Mallorca 1.
No winner in 2019–20.

Spanish La Liga 2020–21

	P	*W*	*D*	*L*	*F*	*A*	*GD*	*Pts*
Atletico Madrid (C)[1]	38	26	8	4	67	25	42	86
Real Madrid[1]	38	25	9	4	67	28	39	84
Barcelona[1]	38	24	7	7	85	38	47	79
Sevilla[1]	38	24	5	9	53	33	20	77
Real Sociedad[2]	38	17	11	10	59	38	21	62
Real Betis[2]	38	17	10	11	50	50	0	61
Villarreal[1]	38	15	13	10	60	44	16	58
Celta Vigo	38	14	11	13	55	57	–2	53
Granada	38	13	7	18	47	65	–18	46
Athletic Bilbao	38	11	13	14	46	42	4	46
Osasuna	38	11	11	16	37	48	–11	44
Cadiz	38	11	11	16	36	58	–22	44
Valencia	38	10	13	15	50	53	–3	43
Levante	38	9	14	15	46	57	–11	41
Getafe	38	9	11	18	28	43	–15	38
Alaves	38	9	11	18	36	57	–21	38
Elche	38	8	12	18	34	55	–21	36
Huesca*	38	7	13	18	34	53	–19	34
Real Valladolid*	38	5	16	17	34	57	–23	31
Eibar*	38	6	12	20	29	52	–23	30

Top scorer: Messi (Barcelona) 30.
Cup Final 2020: Real Sociedad 1, Athletic Bilbao 0 (delayed due to COVID-19 pandemic).
Cup Final 2021: Barcelona 4, Athletic Bilbao 0.

SWEDEN

Svenska Fotbollfoerbundet, Evenemangsgatan 31, PO Box 1216, SE-171 23 Solna.
Founded: 1904. *FIFA:* 1904; *UEFA:* 1954. *National Colours:* Yellow shirts with blue trim, blue shorts, yellow socks.

International matches 2020–21

France (h) 0-1, Portugal (h) 0-2, Russia (a) 2-1, Croatia (a) 1-2, Portugal (a) 0-3, Denmark (a) 0-2, Croatia (h) 2-1, France (h) 2-4, Georgia (h) 1-0, Kosovo (a) 3-0, Estonia (a) 1-0, Finland (h) 2-0, Armenia (h) 3-1, Spain (a) 0-0, Slovakia (n) 1-0, Poland (n) 3-2, Ukraine (n) 1-2.

League Championship wins (1896–2020)

Malmo 21; IFK Goteborg 18; IFK Norrkoping 13; Orgryte 12; AIK (Solna) 12; Djurgaarden 12; Elfsborg 6; Helsingborg 5; GAIS (Gothenburg) 4; Oster Vaxjo 4; Halmstad 4; Atvidaberg 2; Gothenburg IF 1; IFK Eskilstuna 1; Fassbergs 1; Brynas IF 1; IK Sleipner 1; Hammarby 1; Kalmar 1.
(Played in cup format from 1896–1925.)

Cup wins (1941–2021)

Malmo 14; AIK (Solna) 8; IFK Goteborg 8; IFK Norrkoping 6; Helsingborg 5; Djurgaarden 5; Kalmar 3; Elfsborg 3; Atvidaberg 2; Hacken 2; GAIS (Gothenburg) 1; IF Raa IF 1; Landskrona 1; Oster Vaxjo 1; Degerfors 1; Halmstad 1; Orgryte 1; Ostersund 1; Hammarby 1.

Allsvenskan 2020

	P	*W*	*D*	*L*	*F*	*A*	*GD*	*Pts*
Malmo (C)[1]	30	17	9	4	64	30	34	60
Elfsborg[3]	30	12	15	3	49	38	11	51
Hacken[3]	30	12	13	5	45	29	16	49
Djurgarden	30	14	6	10	48	33	15	48
Mjallby	30	13	8	9	48	44	4	47
IFK Norrkoping	30	13	7	10	60	46	14	46
Orebro	30	12	6	12	37	41	–4	42
Hammarby[3]	30	10	11	9	47	47	0	41
AIK Solna	30	10	9	11	30	33	–3	39
Sirius	30	9	11	10	43	51	–8	38
Varberg	30	10	7	13	45	44	1	37
IFK Gothenburg	30	7	13	10	35	41	–6	34
Ostersund	30	8	9	13	27	46	–19	33
Kalmar+	30	6	10	14	30	49	–19	28
Helsingborg*	30	5	11	14	33	48	–15	26
Falkenberg*	30	5	9	16	33	54	–21	24

Top scorer: Nyman (IFK Norrkoping) 18.
Cup Final: Hammarby 0, Hacken 0
aet; Hammarby won 5-4 on penalties.

SWITZERLAND

Schweizerisher Fussballverband, Worbstrasse 48, Postfach 3000, Bern 15.
Founded: 1895. *FIFA:* 1904; *UEFA:* 1954. *National Colours:* Red shirts, white shorts, red socks.

International matches 2020–21

Ukraine (a) 1-2, Germany (h) 1-1, Croatia (h) 1-2, Spain (a) 0-1, Germany (a) 3-3, Belgium (a) 1-2, Spain (h) 1-1, Ukraine (h) 3-0, Bulgaria (a) 3-1, Lithuania (h) 1-0, Finland (h) 3-2, USA (h) 2-1, Liechtenstein (h) 7-0, Wales (n) 1-1, Italy (a) 0-3, Turkey (n) 3-1, France (n) 3-3 (5-4p), Spain (a) 1-1 (1-3p).

League Championship wins (1897–2021)

Grasshoppers 27; FC Basel 20; Servette 17; Young Boys 15; FC Zurich 12; Lausanne-Sport 7; Winterthur 3; Aarau 3; Lugano 3; La Chaux-de-Fonds 3; St Gallen 2; Neuchatel Xamax 2; Sion 2; Anglo-American Club 1; Brühl 1; Cantonal-Neuchatel 1; Etoile La Chaux-de-Fonds 1; Biel-Bienne 1; Bellinzona 1; Luzern 1.

Cup wins (1926–2021)

Grasshoppers 19; FC Basel 13; Sion 13; FC Zurich 10; Lausanne-Sport 9; Servette 7; Young Boys 7; La Chaux-de-Fonds 6; Lugano 3; Luzern 3; Urania Geneva Sport 1; Young Fellows Zurich (renamed Young Fellows Juventus) 1; FC Grenchen 1; St Gallen 1; Aarau 1; Wil 1.

Swiss Super League 2020–21

	P	*W*	*D*	*L*	*F*	*A*	*GD*	*Pts*
Young Boys (C)[1]	36	25	9	2	74	29	45	84
FC Basel[3]	36	15	8	13	60	53	7	53
Servette[3]	36	14	8	14	45	56	–11	50
Lugano	36	12	13	11	40	42	–2	49
Luzern[3]	36	12	10	14	62	59	3	46
Lausanne Sport	36	12	10	14	52	55	–3	46
St Gallen	36	11	11	14	45	48	–3	44
Zurich	36	11	10	15	53	57	–4	43
Sion+	36	8	14	14	48	58	–10	38
Vaduz[3]*	36	9	9	18	36	58	–22	36

Vaduz qualified for the Europa Conference League as they had the highest UEFA coefficient of those clubs remaining in the abandoned 2020–21 Liechtenstein Cup.
Top scorer: Nsame (Young Boys) 19.
Cup Final: Luzern 3, St Gallen 1.

TURKEY

Turkiye Futbol Federasyonu, Hasan Dogan Milli Takimlar, Kamp ve Egitim Tesisleri, Riva, Beykoz, Istanbul.
Founded: 1923. *FIFA:* 1923; *UEFA:* 1962. *National Colours:* All red.

International matches 2020–21

Hungary (h) 0-1, Serbia (a) 0-0, Germany (a) 3-3, Russia (a) 1-1, Serbia (h) 2-2, Croatia (h) 3-3, Russia (h) 3-2, Hungary (a) 0-2, Netherlands (h) 4-2, Norway (a) 3-0, Latvia (h) 3-3, Azerbaijan (h) 2-1, Guinea (h) 0-0, Moldova (n) 2-0, Italy (a) 0-3, Wales (n) 0-2, Switzerland (n) 1-3.

League Championship wins (1959–2021)

Galatasaray 22; Fenerbahce 19; Besiktas 14; Trabzonspor 6; Bursaspor 1; Istanbul Basaksehir 1.

Cup wins (1963–2021)
Galatasaray 18; Besiktas 10; Trabzonspor 9; Fenerbahce 6; Altay Izmir 2; Goztepe Izmir 2; Ankaragucu 2; Genclerbirligi 2; Kocaelispor 2; Eskisehirspor 1; Bursaspor 1; Sakaryaspor 1; Kayseri 1; Konyaspor 1; Akhisar Belediyespor 1.

Turkish Super Lig 2020–21

	P	W	D	L	F	A	GD	Pts
Besiktas (C)†[1]	40	26	6	8	89	44	45	84
Galatasaray†[1]	40	26	6	8	80	36	44	84
Fenerbahce[2]	40	25	7	8	72	41	31	82
Trabzonspor[3]	40	19	14	7	50	37	13	71
Sivasspor[3]	40	16	17	7	54	43	11	65
Hatayspor	40	17	10	13	62	53	9	61
Alanyaspor†	40	17	9	14	58	45	13	60
Fatih Karagumruk†	40	16	12	12	64	52	12	60
Gaziantep	40	15	13	12	59	51	8	58
Goztepe	40	13	12	15	59	59	0	51
Konyaspor	40	12	14	14	49	48	1	50
Istanbul Basaksehir†	40	12	12	16	43	55	–12	48
Rizespor†	40	12	12	16	53	69	–16	48
Kasimpasa	40	12	10	18	47	57	–10	46
Yeni Malatyaspor	40	10	15	15	49	53	–4	45
Antalyaspor	40	9	17	14	41	55	–14	44
Kayserispor	40	9	14	17	35	52	–17	41
Erzurumspor*	40	10	10	20	44	68	–24	40
Ankaragucu†*	40	10	8	22	46	65	–19	38
Genclerbirligi†*	40	10	8	22	44	76	–32	38
Denizlispor*	40	6	10	24	38	77	–39	28

† Ranking decided on head-to-head points.
Top scorer: Boupendza (Hatayspor) 22.
Cup Final: Besiktas 2, Antalyaspor 0.

UKRAINE

Football Federation of Ukraine, Provulok Laboratornyi 7-A, PO Box 55, 01133 Kyiv.
Founded: 1991. *FIFA:* 1992; *UEFA:* 1992. *National Colours:* All yellow with blue trim.

International matches 2020–21
Switzerland (h) 2-1, Spain (a) 0-4, France (a) 1-7, Germany (h) 1-2, Spain (h) 1-0, Poland (a) 0-2, Germany (a) 1-3, Switzerland (a) 0-3, France (a) 1-1, Finland (h) 1-1, Kazakhstan (h) 1-1, Bahrain (h) 1-1, Northern Ireland (h) 1-0, Cyprus (h) 4-0, Netherlands (a) 2-3, North Macedonia (n) 2-1, Austria (n) 0-1, Sweden (n) 2-1, England (a) 0-4.

League Championship wins (1992–2021)
Dynamo Kyiv 16; Shakhtar Donetsk 13; Tavriya Simferopol 1.

Cup wins (1992–2021)
Dynamo Kyiv 13; Shakhtar Donetsk 13; Chornomorets Odesa 2; Vorskla Poltava 1; Tavriya Simferopol 1.
See also Russia section for Ukrainian club honours in Soviet era 1936–91.

Ukrainian Premier League Qualifying Table 2020–21

	P	W	D	L	F	A	GD	Pts
Dynamo Kyiv (C)[1]	26	20	5	1	59	15	44	65
Shakhtar Donetsk[1]	26	16	6	4	54	19	35	54
Zorya Luhansk[2]	26	15	5	6	44	22	22	50
Kolos Kovalivka†[3]	26	10	11	5	36	26	10	41
Vorskla Poltava†[3]	26	11	8	7	37	30	7	41
Desna Chernihiv	26	10	8	8	38	32	6	38
SC Dnipro-1	26	8	6	12	36	38	–2	30
FC Lviv†	26	8	5	13	25	51	–26	29
Oleksandria†	26	8	5	13	33	37	–4	29
Rukh Vynnyky Lviv	26	6	10	10	27	39	–12	28
Mariupol†	26	6	8	12	27	41	–14	26
Inhulets†	26	5	11	10	24	39	–15	26
Olimpik Donetsk	26	6	4	16	28	48	–20	22
Minaj*	26	4	6	16	16	47	–31	18

† Ranking decided on head-to-head points and goal-difference; if still tied, on overall goal difference.
Only one team relegated as the Premier League is to expand to 16 clubs in 2021–22.
Top scorer: Kulach (Vorskla Poltava) 15.
Cup Final: Dynamo Kyiv 1, Zorya Luhansk 0.

WALES

Football Association of Wales, 11/12 Neptune Court, Vanguard Way, Cardiff CF24 5PJ.
Founded: 1876. *FIFA:* 1910; *UEFA:* 1954. *National Colours:* All red with green trim.

SOUTH AMERICA (CONMEBOL)

ARGENTINA

Asociacion del Futbol Argentina, Viamonte 1366/76, Buenos Aires 1053.
Founded: 1893. *FIFA:* 1912; *CONMEBOL:* 1916. *National Colours:* Light blue and white striped shirts, black shorts, white socks.
International matches 2020–21
Ecuador (h) 1-0, Bolivia (a) 2-1, Paraguay (h) 1-1, Peru (a) 2-0, Chile (h) 1-1, Colombia (a) 2-2, Chile (n) 1-1, Uruguay (n) 1-0, Paraguay (n) 1-0, Bolivia (n) 4-1, Ecuador (n) 3-0, Colombia (n) 1-1 (3-2p), Brazil (a) 1-0.
League champions 2019–20: Boca Juniors; *2020–21:* Competition cancelled. *Cup winners 2019:* River Plate; *2020–21:* Competition still being played.

BOLIVIA

Federacion Boliviana de Futbol, Avenida Libertador Bolivar 1168, Casilla 484, Cochabamba.
Founded: 1925. *FIFA:* 1926; *CONMEBOL:* 1926. *National Colours:* Green shirts, green shorts, red socks.
International matches 2020–21
Brazil (a) 0-5, Argentina (h) 1-2, Ecuador (h) 2-3, Paraguay (a) 2-2, Chile (a) 1-2, Ecuador (h) 1-2, Venezuela (h) 3-1, Chile (a) 1-1, Paraguay (n) 1-3, Chile (n) 0-1, Uruguay (n) 0-2, Argentina (n) 1-4.
League champions 2020: Always Ready (Apertura), Competition cancelled (Clausura); *2021:* Competition still being played (Apertura). *Cup winners:* No competition.

BRAZIL

Confederacao Brasileira de Futebol, Avenida Luis Carlos Prestes 130, Barra da Tijuca, Rio de Janeiro 22775-055.
Founded: 1914. *FIFA:* 1923; *CONMEBOL:* 1916. *National Colours:* Yellow shirts with green collar and cuffs, blue shorts, white socks.
International matches 2020–21
Bolivia (h) 5-0, Peru (a) 4-2, Venezuela (h) 1-0, Uruguay (a) 2-0, Ecuador (h) 2-0, Paraguay (a) 2-0, Venezuela (h) 3-0, Peru (h) 4-0, Colombia (n) 2-1, Ecuador (h) 1-1, Chile (h) 1-0, Peru (h) 1-0, Argentina (h) 0-1.
League champions 2020: Flamengo; *2021:* Competition still being played. *Cup winners 2020–21:* Palmeiras.

CHILE

Federacion de Futbol de Chile, Avenida Quilin 5635, Comuna Penalolen, Casilla 3733, Santiago de Chile.
Founded: 1895. *FIFA:* 1913; *CONMEBOL:* 1916. *National Colours:* Red shirts, blue shorts, blue socks.
International matches 2020–21
Uruguay (a) 1-2, Colombia (h) 2-2, Peru (h) 2-0, Venezuela (a) 1-2, Bolivia (h) 2-1, Argentina (a) 1-1, Bolivia (h) 1-1, Argentina (n) 1-1, Bolivia (n) 1-0, Uruguay (n) 1-1, Paraguay (n) 0-2, Brazil (a) 0-1.
League champions 2020–21: Universidad Catolica; *2021:* Competition still being played. *Cup winners 2019:* Colo-Colo; *2020:* No competition; *2021:* Competition still being played.

COLOMBIA

Federacion Colombiana de Futbol, Avenida 32 No. 16–22, Bogota.
Founded: 1924. *FIFA:* 1936; *CONMEBOL:* 1936. *National Colours:* Yellow shirts with blue trim, black shorts, red socks with yellow trim.
International matches 2020–21
Venezuela (h) 3-0, Chile (a) 2-2, Ecuador (a) 1-6, Peru (a) 3-0, Argentina (h) 2-2, Ecuador (n) 1-0, Venezuela (n) 0-0, Peru (n) 1-2, Brazil (a) 1-2, Uruguay (n) 0-0 (4-2p), Argentina (n) 1-1 (2-3p), Peru (n) 3-2.
League champions 2020: America de Cali (Apertura), Competition cancelled (Finalizacion); *2021:* Deportes Tolima (Apertura). *Cup winners 2020:* Independiente Medellin; *2021:* Competition still being played.

ECUADOR

Federacion Ecuatoriana del Futbol, Avenida Las Aguas y Calle Alianza, PO Box 09-01-7447, Guayaquil 593.
Founded: 1925. *FIFA:* 1927; *CONMEBOL:* 1927. *National Colours:* Yellow shirts, black shorts, white socks.
International matches 2020–21
Argentina (a) 0-1, Uruguay (h) 4-2, Bolivia (a) 3-2, Colombia (h) 6-1, Bolivia (h) 2-1, Brazil (a) 0-2, Peru (h) 1-2, Colombia (n) 0-1, Venezuela (n) 2-2, Peru (n) 2-2, Brazil (a) 1-1, Argentina (n) 0-3.
League champions 2020: Barcelona; *2021:* Competition still being played. *Cup winners 2019:* LDU Quito; *2020–:* Competition cancelled.

PARAGUAY

Asociacion Paraguaya de Futbol, Calle Mayor Martinez 1393, Asuncion.
Founded: 1906. *FIFA:* 1925; *CONMEBOL:* 1921. *National Colours:* Red and white striped shirts, blue shorts, white socks with red trim.
International matches 2020–21
Peru (h) 2-2, Venezuela (a) 1-0, Argentina (a) 1-1, Bolivia (h) 2-2, Uruguay (a) 0-0, Brazil (h) 0-2, Bolivia (n) 3-1, Argentina (n) 0-1, Chile (n) 2-0, Uruguay (n) 0-1, Peru (n) 3-3 (3-4p).
League champions 2020: Cerro Porteno (Apertura), Olimpia (Clausura). *2021:* Libertad (Apertura). *Cup winners 2019:* Libertad; *2020–:* Competition cancelled.

PERU

Federacion Peruana de Futbol, Avenida Aviacion 2085, San Luis, Lima 30.
Founded: 1922. *FIFA:* 1924; *CONMEBOL:* 1925. *National Colours:* White shirts with red sash, white shorts, white socks.
International matches 2020–21
Paraguay (a) 2-2, Brazil (h) 2-4, Chile (a) 0-2, Argentina (h) 0-2, Colombia (h) 0-3, Ecuador (a) 2-1, Brazil (a) 0-4, Colombia (n) 2-1, Ecuador (n) 2-2, Venezuela (n) 1-0, Paraguay (n) 3-3 (4-3p), Brazil (a) 0-1, Colombia (n) 2-3.
League champions 2020: Universitario (Apertura), Sporting Cristal (Clausura), Sporting Cristal (Playoff); *2021:* Sporting Cristal (Apertura). *Cup winners 2019:* Atletico Grau; *2020–:* Competition cancelled.

URUGUAY

Asociacion Uruguaya de Futbol, Guayabo 1531, Montevideo 11200.
Founded: 1900. *FIFA:* 1923; *CONMEBOL:* 1916. *National Colours:* Sky blue shirts, black shorts, black socks with sky blue tops.
International matches 2020–21
Chile (h) 2-1, Ecuador (a) 2-4, Colombia (a) 3-0, Brazil (h) 0-2, Paraguay (h) 0-0, Venezuela (a) 0-0, Argentina (n) 0-1, Chile (n) 1-1, Bolivia (n) 2-0, Paraguay (n) 1-0, Colombia (n) 0-0 (2-4p).
League champions 2020: Nacional; *2021:* Competition still being played (Apertura). *Cup winners:* No competition.

VENEZUELA

Federacion Venezolana de Futbol, Avenida Santos Erminy 1ra Calle las Delicias, Torre Mega II, P.H.B. Sabana Grande, 1050 Caracas.
Founded: 1926. *FIFA:* 1952; *CONMEBOL:* 1952. *National Colours:* All burgundy.
International matches 2020–21
Colombia (a) 0-3, Paraguay (h) 0-1, Brazil (a) 0-1, Chile (h) 2-1, Bolivia (h) 1-3, Uruguay (h) 0-0, Brazil (a) 0-3, Colombia (n) 0-0, Ecuador (n) 2-2, Peru (n) 0-1.
League champions 2020: Deportivo La Guaira; *2021:* Competition still being played. *Cup winners 2019:* Zamora; *2020–:* Competition cancelled.

ASIA (AFC)

AFGHANISTAN

Afghanistan Football Federation, PO Box 128, Kabul.
Founded: 1933. *FIFA:* 1948; *AFC:* 1954. *National Colours:* Red shirts, black shorts with green trim, red socks.
International matches 2020–21
Indonesia (n) 3-2, Singapore (n) 1-1, Bangladesh (a) 1-1*, Oman (h) 1-2*, India (a) 1-1*.
* *Match played in Qatar.*
League champions 2020: Shaheen Asmayee; *2021:* Competition still being played. *Cup winners:* No competition.

AUSTRALIA

Football Federation Australia Ltd, Locked Bag A4071, Sydney South, NSW 1235.
Founded: 1961. *FIFA:* 1963; *AFC:* 2006. *National Colours:* All gold.
International matches 2020–21
Kuwait (h) 3-0*, Chinese Taipei (h) 5-1*, Nepal (a) 3-0*, Jordan (h) 1-0*.
* *Match played in Kuwait.*
League champions 2020–21: Melbourne City. *Grand Final winners 2021:* Melbourne City. *Cup winners 2019:* Adelaide United; *2020–:* Competition cancelled.

BAHRAIN

Bahrain Football Association, PO Box 5464, Building 315, Road 2407, Block 934, East Riffa.
Founded: 1957. *FIFA:* 1968; *AFC:* 1969. *National Colours:* All red with gold trim.
International matches 2020–21
Tajikistan (n) 1-0, Lebanon (n) 3-1, UAE (a) 3-1, Jordan (h) 1-2, Ukraine (a) 1-1, Turkey (a) 1-1, Malaysia (h) 2-0, Cambodia (h) 8-0, Iran (h) 0-3*, Hong Kong (h) 4-0, Kuwait (n) 2-0.
* *Match played in Bahrain.*
League champions 2019–20: Al-Hidd; *2020–21:* Al-Riffa. *Cup winners 2019–20:* Al-Muharraq; *2020–21:* Al-Riffa.

BANGLADESH

Bangladesh Football Federation, BFF House, Motijheel Commercial Area, Dhaka 1000.
Founded: 1972. *FIFA:* 1976; *AFC:* 1974. *National Colours:* Green shirts with red trim, white shorts, green socks.
International matches 2020–21
Nepal (h) 2-0, Nepal (h) 0-0, Qatar (a) 0-5, Afghanistan (h) 1-1*, India (h) 0-2*, Oman (h) 0-3*.
* *Match played in Qatar.*
League champions 2018–19: Bashundhara Kings; *2019–20:* Competition abandoned; *2021:* Competition still being played. *Cup winners 2020–21:* Bashundhara Kings.

BHUTAN

Bhutan Football Federation, PO Box 365, Changiiji, Thimphu 11001.
Founded: 1983. *FIFA:* 2000; *AFC:* 2000. *National Colours:* Orange shirts with yellow trim, orange shorts, orange socks.
International matches 2020–21
None played.
League champions 2020: Thimphu City; *2021:* Competition still being played. *Cup winners:* No competition.

BRUNEI

National Football Association of Brunei Darussalam, NFABD House, Jalan Pusat Persidangan, Bandar Seri Begawan BB4313.
Founded: 1959. *FIFA:* 1972; *AFC:* 1969. *National Colours:* Yellow shirts with black trim, yellow shorts with black trim, yellow socks.
International matches 2020–21
None played.
League champions 2018–19: MS ABDB; *2020:* Competition cancelled. *Cup winners 2019:* Kota Rangers; *2020:* Competition cancelled.

CAMBODIA

Football Federation of Cambodia, National Football Centre, Road Kabsrov Sangkat Samrongkrom, Khan Dangkor, Phnom Penh 2327 PPT3.
Founded: 1933. *FIFA:* 1954; *AFC:* 1954. *National Colours:* All blue with red trim.
International matches 2020–21
Bahrain (a) 0-8, Iraq (a) 1-4*, Iran (h) 0-10*.
* *Match played in Bahrain.*
League champions 2020: Boeung Ket; *2021:* Competition still being played. *Cup winners 2020:* Prey Veng; *2021:* Competition still being played.

CHINA PR

Football Association of the People's Republic of China, Building A, Dongjiudasha Mansion, Xizhaosi Street, Dongcheng, Beijing 100061.
Founded: 1924. *FIFA:* 1931, rejoined 1980; *AFC:* 1974. *National Colours:* Red shirts with yellow trim, white shorts, red socks with yellow trim.
International matches 2020–21
Guam (a) 7-0*, Philippines (h) 3-0‡, Maldives (h) 5-0‡, Syria (h) 3-1‡.
* *Match played in China PR.* ‡ *Match played in UAE.*
League champions 2020: Jiangsu Suning; *2021:* Competition still being played. *Cup winners 2020:* Shandong Luneng Taishan.

CHINESE TAIPEI

Chinese Taipei Football Association, Room 210, 2F, 55 Chang Chi Street, Tatung, Taipei 10363.
Founded: 1936. *FIFA:* 1954; *AFC:* 1954. *National Colours:* All blue with red and white trim.
International matches 2020–21
Nepal (a) 0-2*, Australia (a) 1-5*, Kuwait (h) 1-2*.
* *Match played in Kuwait.*
League champions 2020: Taiwan Steel; *2021:* Competition suspended. *Cup winners:* No competition.

GUAM

Guam Football Association, PO Box 20008, Barrigada, Guam 96921.
Founded: 1975. *FIFA:* 1996; *AFC:* 1996. *National Colours:* All dark blue with white trim.
International matches 2020–21
China PR (h) 0-7*, Syria (h) 0-3‡, Philippines (a) 0-3‡.
* *Match played in China PR.* ‡ *Match played in UAE.*

League champions 2018–19: Rovers; *2019–20:* Competition abandoned. *Cup winners 2019:* Bank of Guam Strykers; *2020–:* Competition cancelled.

HONG KONG

Hong Kong Football Association Ltd, 55 Fat Kwong Street, Ho Man Tin, Kowloon, Hong Kong.
Founded: 1914. *FIFA:* 1954; *AFC:* 1954. *National Colours:* Red shirts, red shorts, white socks with red trim.
International matches 2020–21
Iran (a) 1-3*, Iraq (h) 0-1*, Bahrain (a) 0-4.
* *Match played in Bahrain.*
League champions 2019–20: Kitchee; *2020–21:* Kitchee. *Cup winners 2019–20:* Eastern; *2020–21:* Competition suspended.

INDIA

All India Football Federation, Football House, Sector 19, Phase 1 Dwarka, New Delhi 110075.
Founded: 1937. *FIFA:* 1948; *AFC:* 1954. *National Colours:* Blue shirts with orange trim, blue shorts, blue socks.
International matches 2020–21
Oman (n) 1-1, UAE (a) 0-6, Qatar (h) 0-1*, Bangladesh (a) 2-0*, Afghanistan (h) 1-1*.
* *Match played in Qatar.*
League champions 2019–20: I-League: Mohun Bagan; Super League: ATK; *2020–21:* I-League: Gokulam Kerala; Super League: Mumbai City. *Cup winners 2019:* FC Goa; *2020–:* Competition cancelled.

INDONESIA

Football Association of Indonesia, Gelora Bung Karno Pintu X–XI, PO Box 2305, Senayan, Jakarta 10023.
Founded: 1930. *FIFA:* 1952; *AFC:* 1954. *National Colours:* All red.
International matches 2020–21
Afghanistan (n) 2-3, Oman (n) 1-3, Thailand (a) 2-2*, Vietnam (a) 0-4*, UAE (h) 0-5*.
* *Match played in UAE.*
League champions 2019: Bali United; *2020–:* Competition cancelled. *Cup winners 2018–19:* PSM Makassar; *2020–:* Competition cancelled.

IRAN

Football Federation IR Iran, No. 4 Third St., Seoul Avenue, Tehran 19958-73591.
Founded: 1920. *FIFA:* 1948; *AFC:* 1954. *National Colours:* All white with red trim.
International matches 2020–21
Uzbekistan (a) 2-1, Bosnia-Herzegovina (a) 2-0, Syria (h) 3-0, Hong Kong (h) 3-1*, Bahrain (h) 3-0*, Cambodia (a) 10-0*, Iraq (h) 1-0*.
* *Match played in Bahrain.*
League champions 2020–21: Persepolis. *Cup winners 2019–20:* Tractor; *2020–21:* Competition still being played.

IRAQ

Iraq Football Association, Al-Shaab Stadium, PO Box 484, Baghdad.
Founded: 1948. *FIFA:* 1950; *AFC:* 1970. *National Colours:* White shirts with green trim, white shorts, white socks.
International matches 2020–21
Jordan (n) 0-0, Uzbekistan (n) 2-1, UAE (a) 0-0, Kuwait (h) 2-1, Uzbekistan (a) 1-0, Tajikistan (n) 0-0, Nepal (n) 6-2, Cambodia (h) 4-1*, Hong Kong (a) 1-0*, Iran (a) 0-1*.
* *Match played in Bahrain.*
League champions 2019–20: Competition abandoned; *2020–21:* Al-Kuwa Al-Jawiya. *Cup winners 2018–19:* Al-Zawraa; *2019–20:* Competition abandoned; *2020–21:* Competition still being played.

JAPAN

Japan Football Association, JFA House, Football Ave., Bunkyo-ku, Tokyo 113-8311.
Founded: 1921. *FIFA:* 1929, rejoined 1950; *AFC:* 1954. *National Colours:* Blue shirts, black shorts, blue socks.
International matches 2020–21
Cameroon (n) 0-0, Ivory Coast (n) 1-0, Panama (n) 1-0, Mexico (n) 0-2, Korea Republic (h) 3-0, Mongolia (a) 14-0*, Myanmar (h) 10-0, Tajikistan (h) 4-1, Serbia (h) 1-0, Kyrgyz Republic (h) 5-1.
* *Match played in Japan.*
League champions 2020: Kawasaki Marinos; *2021:* Competition still being played. *Cup winners 2020:* Kawasaki Frontale; *2021:* Competition still being played.

JORDAN

Jordan Football Association, PO Box 962024, Al-Hussein Youth City, Amman 11196.
Founded: 1949. *FIFA:* 1956; *AFC:* 1970. *National Colours:* All white with red trim.
International matches 2020–21
Iraq (n) 0-0*, Syria (n) 1-0, Tajikistan (n) 2-0, Tajikistan (n) 0-1, Tajikistan (n) 2-0, Uzbekistan (n) 0-2, Oman (n) 0-0, Lebanon (n) 1-0, Bahrain (a) 2-1, UAE (a) 1-5, Vietnam (n) 1-1, Nepal (a) 3-0*, Kuwait (a) 0-0*, Australia (a) 0-1*, South Sudan (n) 3-0.
* *Match played in Kuwait.*
League champions 2019–20: Competition cancelled; *2020–21:* Al-Wahdat. *Cup winners 2018–19:* Al-Faisaly; *2020–:* Competition cancelled.

KOREA DPR

DPR Korea Football Association, Kumsongdong, Kwangbok Street, Mangyongdae, PO Box 818, Pyongyang.
Founded: 1945. *FIFA:* 1958; *AFC:* 1974. *National Colours:* All red with white trim.
International matches 2020–21
None played. Korea DPR withdrew from World Cup 2022 Qualifying; earlier results in AFC Group H were annulled.
League champions 2018–19: April 25; *2019–20:* Competition suspended. *Cup winners 2019:* Ryomyong; *2020–:* Competition cancelled.

KOREA REPUBLIC

Korea Football Association, KFA House 21, Gyeonghuigung-gil 46, Jongno-Gu, Seoul 110-062.
Founded: 1933, 1948. *FIFA:* 1948; *AFC:* 1954. *National Colours:* Red shirts, black shorts, red socks.
International matches 2020–21
Mexico (n) 2-3, Qatar (n) 2-1, Japan (a) 0-3, Turkmenistan (h) 5-0, Sri Lanka (a) 5-0*, Lebanon (h) 2-1.
* *Match played in Korea Republic.*
League champions 2020: Jeonbuk Hyundai Motors; *2021:* Competition still being played. *Cup winners 2020:* Jeonbuk Hyundai Motors; *2021:* Competition still being played.

KUWAIT

Kuwait Football Association, Block 5, Street 101, Building 141A, Jabriya, PO Box Hawalli 4020, Kuwait 32071.
Founded: 1952. *FIFA:* 1964; *AFC:* 1964. *National Colours:* All blue with white trim.
International matches 2020–21
Palestine (h) 0-1, Iraq (a) 1-2, Saudi Arabia (a) 0-1, Lebanon (n) 1-1, Australia (a) 0-3*, Jordan (h) 0-0, Chinese Taipei (a) 2-1*, Bahrain (n) 0-2.
* *Match played in Kuwait.*
League champions 2020–21: Al-Arabi. *Cup winners 2020:* Al-Arabi; *2021:* Competition suspended.

KYRGYZ REPUBLIC

Football Federation of Kyrgyz Republic, Mederova Street 1 'B', PO Box 1484, Bishkek 720082.
Founded: 1992. *FIFA:* 1994; *AFC:* 1994. *National Colours:* All red.
International matches 2020–21
Mongolia (a) 0-1*, Myanmar (a) 8-1*, Japan (h) 1-5.
* *Match played in Japan.*
League champions 2020: Dordoi Bishkek; *2021:* Competition still being played. *Cup winners 2020:* Alay Osh.

LAOS

Lao Football Federation, FIFA Training Centre, Ban Houayhong, Chanthabuly, PO Box 1800, Vientiane 856-21.
Founded: 1951. *FIFA:* 1952; *AFC:* 1968. *National Colours:* All red.
International matches 2020–21
None played.
League champions 2020: FC Chanthabouly (formerly Lao Toyota); *2021:* Competition still being played. *Cup winners 2020:* Young Elephant.

LEBANON

Association Libanaise de Football, Verdun Street, Bristol Radwan Centre, PO Box 4732, Beirut.
Founded: 1933. *FIFA:* 1936; *AFC:* 1964. *National Colours:* All red with white trim.
International matches 2020–21
Bahrain (n) 1-3, Jordan (n) 0-1, Kuwait (n) 1-1, Sri Lanka (h) 3-2*, Turkmenistan (a) 2-3*, Korea Republic (a) 1-2, Djibouti (n) 1-0.
* *Match played in Korea Republic.*
League champions 2019–20: Competition abandoned. *2020–21:* Al-Ansar. *Cup winners 2019–20:* Competition abandoned; *2020–21:* Al-Ansar.

MACAU

Associacao de Futebol de Macau, Avenida Wai Leong, Taipa University of Science and Technology, Football Field Block 1, Taipa.
Founded: 1939. *FIFA:* 1978; *AFC:* 1978. *National Colours:* All green with white trim.
International matches 2020–21
None played.

League champions 2020: Benfica de Macau; *2021:* Competition still being played. *Cup winners 2019:* Cheng Fung; 2020–: Competition cancelled.

MALAYSIA

Football Association of Malaysia, 3rd Floor, Wisma FAM, Jalan SS5A/9, Kelana Jaya, Petaling Jaya 47301, Selangor Darul Ehsan.
Founded: 1933. *FIFA:* 1954; *AFC:* 1954. *National Colours:* Yellow shirts, black shorts, yellow socks with black trim.
International matches 2020–21
Bahrain (a) 0-2, UAE (a) 0-4, Vietnam (h) 1-2*, Thailand (a) 1-0*.
* *Match played in UAE.*
League champions 2020: Johor Darul Ta'zim; *2021:* Competition still being played. *Cup winners 2019:* Kedah; *2020:* Competition abandoned.

MALDIVES

Football Association of Maldives, FAM House, Ujaalahingun, Male 20388.
Founded: 1982. *FIFA:* 1986; *AFC:* 1984. *National Colours:* Red shirts white trim, white shorts, red socks with white tops.
International matches 2020–21
Syria (h) 0-4*, China PR (a) 0-5*, Philippines (a) 1-1*.
* *Match played in UAE.*
League champions 2020–21: Maziya. *Cup winners 2018, 2019:* No competition; *2020:* Competition abandoned.

MONGOLIA

Mongolian Football Federation, PO Box 259, 15th Khoroo, Khan-Uul, Ulaanbaatar 210646.
Founded: 1959. *FIFA:* 1998; *AFC:* 1998. *National Colours:* Blue shirts with white sleeves, blue shorts, blue socks.
International matches 2020–21
Tajikistan (a) 0-3, Japan (h) 0-14*, Kyrgyz Republic (a) 1-0*.
* *Match played in Japan.*
League champions 2020: Athletic 220; *2021:* Competition still being played. *Cup winners 2019:* Erchim; *2020–:* Competition cancelled.

MYANMAR

Myanmar Football Federation, National Football Training Centre, Waizayanta Road, Thuwunna, Thingankyun Township, Yangon 11070.
Founded: 1947. *FIFA:* 1948; *AFC:* 1954. *National Colours:* All red.
International matches 2020–21
Japan (a) 0-10, Kyrgyz Republic (h) 1-8*, Tajikistan (a) 0-4*.
* *Match played in Japan.*
League champions 2020: Shan United; *2021:* Competition postponed. *Cup winners 2019:* Yangon United; *2020–:* Competition cancelled.

NEPAL

All Nepal Football Association, ANFA House, Satdobato, Lalitpur-17, PO Box 12582, Kathmandu.
Founded: 1951. *FIFA:* 1972; *AFC:* 1954. *National Colours:* All red with white trim.
International matches 2020–21
Bangladesh (a) 0-2, Bangladesh (a) 0-0, Iraq (n) 2-6, Chinese Taipei (h) 2-0*, Jordan (h) 0-3*, Australia (h) 0-3*.
* *Match played in Kuwait.*
League champions 2019–20: Machhindra. *Cup winners 2020:* Manag Marshyangi Club.

OMAN

Oman Football Association, Seeb Sports Stadium, PO Box 3462, 112 Ruwi, Muscat.
Founded: 1978. *FIFA:* 1980; *AFC:* 1980. *National Colours:* All yellow with black trim.
International matches 2020–21
Jordan (n) 0-0, India (n) 1-1, Thailand (n) 1-0, Indonesia (n) 3-1, Qatar (h) 0-1*, Afghanistan (a) 2-1*, Bangladesh (a) 3-0*, Somalia (n) 2-1.
* *Match played in Qatar.*
League champions 2019–20: Seeb; *2020–21:* Competition abandoned. *Cup winners 2019–20:* Dhofar; *2020–21:* Dhofar.

PAKISTAN

Pakistan Football Federation, PFF Football House, Ferozepur Road, Lahore 54600, Punjab.
Founded: 1947. *FIFA:* 1948; *AFC:* 1954. *National Colours:* All white with green trim.
International matches 2020–21
None played.
League champions 2018–19: Khan Research Laboratories; *2020–:* Competition suspended; resumption scheduled for July 2021. *Cup winners 2019:* Pakistan Army; *2020–:* No competition.

PALESTINE

Palestinian Football Association, Nr. Faisal Al-Husseini Stadium, PO Box 4373, Jerusalem-al-Ram.
Founded: 1928. *FIFA:* 1998; *AFC:* 1998. *National Colours:* All red with white trim.
International matches 2020–21
Kuwait (a) 1-0, Saudi Arabia (a) 0-5, Singapore (h) 4-0*, Yemen (a) 3-0*, Comoros (n) 5-1.
* *Match played in Saudi Arabia.*
League champions 2019–20: West Bank: Markaz Balata, Gaza Strip: Khadamat Rafah; *2020–21:* West Bank: Shabab Al-Khalil, Gaza Strip: Competition still being played. *Cup winners 2019–20:* West Bank: Competition suspended, Gaza Strip: Shabab Rafah.

PHILIPPINES

Philippine Football Federation, 27 Danny Floro–corner Capt. Henry Javier Streets, Oranbo, Pasig City 1600.
Founded: 1907. *FIFA:* 1930; *AFC:* 1954. *National Colours:* All white with grey trim.
International matches 2020–21
China PR (a) 0-2*, Guam (h) 3-0*, Maldives (h) 1-1*.
* *Match played in UAE.*
League champions 2020: United City (formerly Ceres-Negros); *2021:* Competition postponed. *Cup winners 2019:* Ceres-Negros; *2020–:* Competition cancelled.

QATAR

Qatar Football Association, 28th Floor, Al Bidda Tower, Corniche Street, West Bay, PO Box 5333, Doha.
Founded: 1960. *FIFA:* 1972; *AFC:* 1974. *National Colours:* All burgundy.
International matches 2020–21
Ghana (n) 1-5, Costa Rica (n) 1-1, Korea Republic (n) 1-2, Bangladesh (h) 5-0, Luxembourg (n) 1-0, Azerbaijan (n) 2-1, Republic of Ireland (n) 1-1, India (a) 1-0*, Oman (a) 1-0*, El Salvador (n) 1-0.
* *Match played in Qatar.*
League champions 2020–21: Al-Sadd. *Cup winners 2020:* Al-Sadd; *2021:* Competition cancelled.

SAUDI ARABIA

Saudi Arabian Football Federation, Al Mather Quarter, Prince Faisal Bin Fahad Street, PO Box 5844, Riyadh 11432.
Founded: 1956. *FIFA:* 1956; *AFC:* 1972. *National Colours:* White shirts with green trim, white shorts, white socks.
International matches 2020–21
Jamaica (h) 3-0, Jamaica (h) 1-2, Kuwait (h) 1-0, Palestine (h) 5-0, Yemen (h) 3-0, Singapore (a) 3-0*, Uzbekistan (h) 3-0.
* *Match played in Saudi Arabia.*
League champions 2020–21: Al-Hilal. *Cup winners 2019–20: Al-Hilal; 2020–21: Al-Faysali.*

SINGAPORE

Football Association of Singapore, Jalan Besar Stadium, 100 Tyrwhitt Road, Singapore 207542.
Founded: 1892. *FIFA:* 1956; *AFC:* 1954. *National Colours:* All red.
International matches 2020–21
Afghanistan (n) 1-1, Palestine (a) 0-4*, Uzbekistan (a) 0-5*, Saudi Arabia (h) 0-3*.
* *Match played in Saudi Arabia.*
League champions 2020: Albirex Niigata (S);. *2021:* Competition still being played. *Cup winners 2019:* Tampines Rovers; 2020–: No competition.

SRI LANKA

Football Federation of Sri Lanka, 100/9 Independence Avenue, Colombo 07.
Founded: 1939. *FIFA:* 1952; *AFC:* 1954. *National Colours:* All yellow with red trim.
International matches 2020–21
Lebanon (a) 2-3*, Korea Republic (h) 0-5*.
* *Match played in Korea Republic.*
League champions 2018–19: Defenders (formerly Army); *2019–20:* Competition discontinued; *2021:* New superleague scheduled to commence. *Cup winners 2019–20:* Police; *2020–21:* No competition.

SYRIA

Syrian Arab Federation for Football, Al Faihaa Sports Complex, PO Box 421, Damascus.
Founded: 1936. *FIFA:* 1937; *AFC:* 1970. *National Colours:* All red with white trim.
International matches 2020–21
Uzbekistan (n) 1-0, Jordan (n) 0-1, Iran (a) 0-3, Maldives (a) 4-0*, Guam (a) 3-0*, China PR (a) 1-3*.
* *Match played in UAE.*
League champions 2020–21: Tishreen. *Cup winners 2020–21:* Jableh.

TAJIKISTAN

Tajikistan Football Federation, 14/3 Ayni Street, Dushanbe 734 025.
Founded: 1936. *FIFA:* 1994; *AFC:* 1994. *National Colours:* All red with green trim.
International matches 2020–21
Uzbekistan (n) 1-2, Bahrain (n) 0-1, UAE (a) 2-3, Jordan (n) 0-2, Jordan (n) 1-0, Mongolia (h) 3-0, Iraq (n) 0-0, Thailand (n) 2-2, Japan (a) 1-4, Myanmar (h) 4-0*.
* *Match played in Japan.*
League champions 2020: Istiklol; *2021:* Competition still being played. *Cup winners 2020:* Ravshan Kulob; *2021:* Competition still being played.

THAILAND

Football Association of Thailand, National Stadium, Gate 3, Rama 1 Road, Patumwan, Bangkok 10330.
Founded: 1916. *FIFA:* 1925; *AFC:* 1954. *National Colours:* All black with red trim.

TIMOR-LESTE

Federacao Futebol de Timor-Leste, Campo Democracia, Avenida Bairo Formosa, Dili.
Founded: 2002. *FIFA:* 2005; *AFC:* 2005. *National Colours:* Red shirts with black trim, white shorts, black and red socks.
International matches 2020–21
None played.
League champions 2019: Lalenok United; *2020–:* Competition cancelled. *Cup winners 2019:* Lalenok United; *2020–:* Competition cancelled.

TURKMENISTAN

Football Federation of Turkmenistan, Stadium Kopetdag, 245 A. Niyazov Street, Ashgabat 744 001.
Founded: 1992. *FIFA:* 1994; *AFC:* 1994. *National Colours:* All green.
International matches 2020–21
Korea Republic (a) 0-5*, Lebanon (a) 3-2*.
* *Match played in Korea Republic.*
League champions 2020: Altyn Asyr; *2021:* Competition postponed. *Cup winners 2020:* Altyn Asyr; *2021:* Competition postponed.

UNITED ARAB EMIRATES (UAE)

United Arab Emirates Football Association, Zayed Sports City, PO Box 916, Abu Dhabi.
Founded: 1971. *FIFA:* 1974; *AFC:* 1974. *National Colours:* All white with red trim.
International matches 2020–21
Uzbekistan (h) 1-2, Tajikistan (h) 3-2, Bahrain (a) 1-3, Iraq (h) 0-0, India (h) 6-0, Jordan (h) 5-1, Malaysia (h) 4-0, Thailand (h) 3-1, Indonesia (a) 5-0*, Vietnam (h) 3-2.
* *Match played in UAE.*
League champions 2019–20: Competition abandoned; *2020–21:* Al-Jazeera. *Cup winners 2019–20:* Competition abandoned; *2020–21:* Al-Shabab Al-Ahli.

UZBEKISTAN

Uzbekistan Football Federation, Massiv Almazar Furkat Street 15/1, Tashkent 700 003.
Founded: 1946. *FIFA:* 1994; *AFC:* 1994. *National Colours:* All white with blue trim.
International matches 2020–21
Tajikistan (h) 2-1, Iran (h) 1-2, UAE (a) 2-1, Syria (n) 0-1, Iraq (n) 1-2, Jordan (n) 2-0, Iraq (h) 0-1, Singapore (h) 5-0*, Yemen (a) 1-0*, Saudi Arabia (a) 0-3.
* *Match played in Saudi Arabia.*
League champions 2020: Pakhtakor; *2021:* Competition still being played. *Cup winners 2020:* Pakhtakor; *2021:* Competition still being played.

VIETNAM

Vietnam Football Federation, Le Quang Dao Street, Phu Do Ward, Nam Tu Liem District, Hanoi 844.
Founded: 1960 (NV). *FIFA:* 1952 (SV), 1964 (NV); *AFC:* 1954 (SV), 1978 (SRV). *National Colours:* All red.
International matches 2020–21
Jordan (n) 1-1, Indonesia (h) 4-0*, Malaysia (a) 2-1*, UAE (a) 2-3.
* *Match played in UAE.*
League champions 2020: Viettel; *2021:* Competition still being played. *Cup winners 2020:* Ha Noi; *2021:* Competition still being played.

YEMEN

Yemen Football Association, Quarter of Sport Al Jeraf (Ali Mohsen Al-Muraisi Stadium), PO Box 908, Al-Thawra City, Sana'a.
Founded: 1940 (SY), 1962 (NY). *FIFA:* 1967 (SY), 1980 (NY); *AFC:* 1972 (SY), 1980 (NY). *National Colours:* Red shirts, white shorts, black socks.
International matches 2020–21
Saudi Arabia (a) 0-3, Uzbekistan (h) 0-1*, Palestine (a) 0-3*, Mauritania (n) 0-2.
* *Match played in Saudi Arabia.*
League champions 2015–19: No competition due to civil war; *2019–20:* Sha'ab Hadramaut. *Cup winners:* No competition since 2017.

NORTH AND CENTRAL AMERICA AND CARIBBEAN (CONCACAF)

ANGUILLA

Anguilla Football Association, 2 Queen Elizabeth Avenue, PO Box 1318, The Valley, AI-2640.
Founded: 1990. *FIFA:* 1996; *CONCACAF:* 1996. *National Colours:* Orange shirts with black trim, orange shorts with black trim, white socks.
International matches 2020–21
Dominican Republic (h) 0-6*, Barbados (a) 0-1‡, Dominica (a) 0-3‡, Panama (h) 0-13**.
* *Match played in USA.* ‡ *Match played in Dominican Republic.* ** *Match played in Panama.*
League champions 2020: Roaring Lions; *2021:* Competition still being played. *Cup winners:* No competition.

ANTIGUA & BARBUDA

Antigua & Barbuda Football Association, Ground Floor, Sydney Walling Stand, Antigua Recreation Ground, PO Box 773, St John's.
Founded: 1928. *FIFA:* 1970; *CONCACAF:* 1972. *National Colours:* All yellow with black trim.
International matches 2020–21
Montserrat (h) 2-2*, US Virgin Islands (a) 3-0, Grenada (h) 1-0, El Salvador (a) 0-3.
* *Match played in Curacao.*
League champions 2018–19: Liberta; *2019–20:* Competition abandoned. *Cup winners:* No competition.

ARUBA

Arubaanse Voetbal Bond, Technical Centre Angel Botta, Shaba 24, PO Box 376, Noord.
Founded: 1932. *FIFA:* 1988; *CONCACAF:* 1986. *National Colours:* Yellow shirts with sky blue sleeves, yellow shorts, yellow socks.
International matches 2020–21
Suriname (h) 0-6*, Bermuda (a) 0-5*, Cayman Islands (a) 3-1*, Canada (h) 0-7*.
* *Match played in USA.*
League champions 2018–19: Racing Club Aruba; *2019–20:* Competition abandoned; *2020–21:* Competition still being played. *Cup winners 2021:* Racing Club Aruba.

BAHAMAS

Bahamas Football Association, Rosetta Street, PO Box N-8434, Nassau, NP.
Founded: 1967. *FIFA:* 1968; *CONCACAF:* 1981. *National Colours:* Yellow shirts, black shorts, yellow socks.
International matches 2020–21
St Kitts & Nevis (h) 0-4, Guyana (a) 0-4*, Puerto Rico (a) 0-7, Trinidad & Tobago (h) 0-0, Guadeloupe† (n) 0-2.
* *Match played in Dominican Republic.*
League champions 2018–19: Dynamos; *2019–:* Competition suspended. *Cup winners 2017–18:* Western Warriors; not contested since.

BARBADOS

Barbados Football Association, Bottom Floor, ABC Marble Complex, PO Box 1362, Fontabelle, St Michael.
Founded: 1910. *FIFA:* 1968; *CONCACAF:* 1967. *National Colours:* Gold shirts with royal blue sleeves, gold shorts, gold socks.
International matches 2020–21
Panama (a) 0-1*, Anguilla (h) 1-0*, Dominican Republic (a) 1-1, Dominica (h) 1-1*, Bermuda (n) 1-8.
* *Match played in Dominican Republic.*
League champions 2018–19: Barbados Defence Force; *2020–:* Competition suspended. *Cup winners 2019:* Weymouth Wales; not contested since.

BELIZE

Football Federation of Belize, 26 Hummingbird Highway, Belmopan, PO Box 1742, Belize City.
Founded: 1980. *FIFA:* 1986; *CONCACAF:* 1986. *National Colours:* Blue shirts with white trim, blue shorts, blue socks.
International matches 2020–21
Haiti (a) 0-2, Turks & Caicos Islands (h) 5-0*, Nicaragua (a) 0-3.
* *Match played in Dominican Republic.*
League champions 2018–19: Belmopan Bandits (Opening), San Pedro Pirates (Closing); *2019–20:* Verdes (Opening);

Competition suspended (Closing). *Cup winners:* No competition.

BERMUDA

Bermuda Football Association, 48 Cedar Avenue, PO Box HM 745, Hamilton HM11.
Founded: 1928. *FIFA:* 1962; *CONCACAF:* 1967. *National Colours:* All red.
International matches 2020–21
Canada (a) 1-5*, Aruba (h) 5-0*, Suriname (a) 0-6, Cayman Islands (h) 1-1*, Barbados (n) 8-1*, Haiti (n) 1-4*.
* *Match played in USA.*
League champions 2019–20: North Village Rams; *2020–21:* Competition abandoned. *Cup winners 2018–19:* Robin Hood; *2019–20:* Competition abandoned; *2020–21:* Competition abandoned.

BRITISH VIRGIN ISLANDS

British Virgin Islands Football Association, Botanic Station, PO Box 4269, Road Town, Tortola VG 1110.
Founded: 1974. *FIFA:* 1996; *CONCACAF:* 1996. *National Colours:* Green shirts with gold and white trim, green shorts, gold socks.
International matches 2020–21
Guatemala (h) 0-3*, St Vincent/Grenadines (a) 0-3*, Cuba (h) 0-5‡, Curacao (h) 0-8‡.
* *Match played in Curacao.* ‡ *Match played in Guatemala.*
League champions 2019: Competition cancelled; *2019–20:* Islanders; *2020–21:* Competition still being played. *Cup winners:* No competition.

CANADA

Canadian Soccer Association, Place Soccer Canada, 237 Metcalfe Street, Ottawa, Ontario K2P 1R2.
Founded: 1912. *FIFA:* 1912; *CONCACAF:* 1961. *National Colours:* All red.
International matches 2020–21
Bermuda (h) 5-0*, Cayman Islands (a) 11-0*, Aruba (a) 7-0*, Suriname (h) 4-0*, Haiti (a) 1-0, Haiti (h) 3-0*, Martinique† (n) 4-1*.
* *Match played in USA.*
League champions 2020: Cavalry (Spring), Cavalry (Fall), Forge (Playoff). *2021:* Competition still being played. *Cup winners 2019:* Montreal Impact; *2020:* Competition suspended (final to play). (N.B. Canadian teams also compete in MLS and USL.)

CAYMAN ISLANDS

Cayman Islands Football Association, PO Box 178, Poindexter Road, Prospect, George Town, Grand Cayman KY1-1104.
Founded: 1966. *FIFA:* 1992; *CONCACAF:* 1990. *National Colours:* Red shirts with white sleeves, red shorts, red socks with white tops.
International matches 2020–21
Suriname (a) 0-3, Canada (h) 0-11*, Aruba (h) 1-3*, Bermuda (a) 1-1*.
* *Match played in USA.*
League champions 2020–21: Scholar's International. *Cup winners 2019–18:* Competition cancelled; *2020–21:* Bodden Town.

COSTA RICA

Federacion Costarricense de Futbol, 600 mts sur del Cruce de la Panasonic, San Rafael de Alajuela, Radial a Santa Ana, San Jose 670-1000.
Founded: 1921. *FIFA:* 1927; *CONCACAF:* 1961. *National Colours:* Red shirts, blue shorts, white socks.
International matches 2020–21
Panama (h) 0-1, Panama (h) 0-1, Qatar (n) 1-1, Bosnia-Herzegovina (a) 0-0, Mexico (n) 0-1, Mexico (n) 0-0 (4-5p), Honduras (n) 2-2 (4-5p), USA (a) 0-4.
League champions 2020–21: Alajuelense (Apertura), Saprissa (Clausura). *Cup winners:* No competition.

CUBA

Asociacion de Futbol de Cuba, Estadio Pedro Marrero Escuela Nacional de
Futbol – Mario Lopez, Avenida 41 no. 44 y 46, La Habana.
Founded: 1924. *FIFA:* 1932; *CONCACAF:* 1961. *National Colours:* All red.
International matches 2020–21
Guatemala (a) 0-1, Curacao (h) 1-2*, British Virgin Islands (h) 5-0*, St Vincent/Grenadines (a) 0-1‡, French Guiana† (n) 0-3**.
* *Match played in Guatemala.* ‡ *Match played in Grenada.* ***Match awarded 3-0 to French Guiana, Cuba failed to fulfil fixture.*
League champions 2019: Santiago de Cuba; *2019–20:* Pinar del Rio (Apertura), Competition abandoned (Clausura). *Cup winners:* No competition.

CURACAO

Curacao Football Federation, Bonamweg 49, PO Box 341, Willemstad.
Founded: 1921 (Netherlands Antilles), 2010. *FIFA:* 1932, 2010; *CONCACAF:* 1961, 2010. *National Colours:* All white.
International matches 2020–21
St Vincent/Grenadines (h) 5-0, Cuba (a) 2-1*, British Virgin Islands (a) 8-0*, Guatemala (h) 0-0, Panama (a) 1-2, Panama (h) 0-0.
* *Match played in Guatemala.*
League champions 2019–20: Scherpenheuvel; *2020–21:* Competition still being played. *Cup winners:* No competition.

DOMINICA

Dominica Football Association, Patrick John Football House, Bath Estate, PO Box 1080, Roseau.
Founded: 1970. *FIFA:* 1994; *CONCACAF:* 1994. *National Colours:* All emerald green.
International matches 2020–21
Dominican Republic (a) 0-1, Panama (h) 1-2*, Anguilla (h) 3-0*, Barbados (a) 1-1*.
* *Match played in Dominican Republic.*
League champions 2020: Sagicor South East United; *2021:* Competition still being played. *Cup winners:* No competition.

DOMINICAN REPUBLIC

Federacion Dominicana de Futbol, Centro Olimpico Juan Pablo Duarte, Apartado Postal 1953, Santo Domingo.
Founded: 1953. *FIFA:* 1958; *CONCACAF:* 1964. *National Colours:* All blue.
International matches 2020–21
Puerto Rico (h) 0-1, Serbia (h) 0-0, Dominica (h) 1-0, Anguilla (a) 6-0*, Barbados (h) 1-1, Panama (a) 0-3.
* *Match played in USA.*
League champions 2020: Cibao (North Zone), Universidad O&M (South Zone), Universidad O&M (Play-off); *2021:* Competition still being played. *Cup winners:* No competition.

EL SALVADOR

Federacion Salvadorena de Futbol, Avenida Jose Matias Delgado, Frente al Centro Espanol Colonia Escalon, Zona 10, San Salvador 1029.
Founded: 1935. *FIFA:* 1938; *CONCACAF:* 1961. *National Colours:* All blue.
International matches 2020–21
USA (a) 0-6, Grenada (h) 2-0, Montserrat (a) 1-1*, US Virgin Islands (a) 7-0, Antigua & Barbuda (h) 3-0, St Kitts & Nevis (a) 4-0, St Kitts & Nevis (h) 2-0, Guatemala (n) 0-0, Qatar (n) 0-1, Guatemala (n) 2-0.
* *Match played in Curacao.*
League champions 2020–21: Alianza (Apertura), FAS (Clausura), FAS (Play-off). *Cup winner: 2018–19:* Santa Tecla; *2019–:* Competition cancelled.

GRENADA

Grenada Football Association, National Stadium, PO Box 326, St George's.
Founded: 1924. *FIFA:* 1978; *CONCACAF:* 1969. *National Colours:* All green.
International matches 2020–21
El Salvador (a) 0-2, US Virgin Islands (h) 1-0, Antigua & Barbuda (a) 0-1, Montserrat (h) 1-2*.
League champions 2019–20: Competition abandoned; replacement competition won by Hurricanes; *2020–21:* Competition still being played. *Cup winners 2019:* Camerhogne.

GUATEMALA

Federacion Nacional de Futbol de Guatemala, 2a Calle 15-57, Zona 15, Boulevard Vista Hermosa, Guatemala City 01015.
Founded: 1919. *FIFA:* 1946; *CONCACAF:* 1961. *National Colours:* White shirts with blue sash, white shorts, white socks.
International matches 2020–21
Mexico (a) 0-3, Nicaragua (a) 0-0, Honduras (h) 2-1, Puerto Rico (h) 1-0, Nicaragua (h) 1-0, Cuba (h) 1-0, British Virgin Islands (h) 3-0*, St Vincent/Grenadines (h) 10-0, Curacao (a) 0-0, El Salvador (n) 0-0, Guyana (n) 4-0, Guadeloupe† (n) 1-1 (9-10p), El Salvador (n) 0-2.
* *Match played in Curacao.*
League champions 2020–21: Guastatoya (Apertura), Santa Lucia (Clausura). *Cup winners 2018–19:* Coban Imperial; *2019–:* Not contested.

GUYANA

Guyana Football Federation, Lot 17, Dadanawa Street Section 'K', Campbellville, PO Box 10727, Georgetown.

Founded: 1902. *FIFA:* 1970; *CONCACAF:* 1961. *National Colours:* All yellow with black, green and red trim.
International matches 2020–21
Trinidad & Tobago (a) 0-3*, Bahamas (h) 4-0*, St Kitts & Nevis (a) 0-3, Puerto Rico (a) 0-2‡, Guatemala (n) 0-4.
* *Match played in Dominican Republic.* ‡ *Match played in Saint Kitts & Nevis.*
League champions 2019: Fruta Conquerors; *2020–:* Competition cancelled. *Cup winners:* Not contested since 2015.

HAITI

Federation Haitienne de Football, Stade Sylvio Cator, Rue Oswald Durand, Port-au-Prince.
Founded: 1904. *FIFA:* 1933; *CONCACAF:* 1961. *National Colours:* Blue shirts with red trim, blue shorts, blue socks with red tops.
International matches 2020–21
Belize (h) 2-0, Turks & Caicos Islands (a) 10-0, Nicaragua (h) 1-0, Canada (h) 0-1, Canada (a) 0-3*, St Vincent/Grenadines (n) 6-1, Bermuda (n) 4-1, USA (a) 0-1.
* *Match played in USA.*
League champions 2020: Competition abandoned (Ouverture), Competition cancelled due to autumn/spring transition (Cloture). *2020:* Violette (Ouverture), Competition still being played (Cloture). *Cup winners:* No competition.

HONDURAS

Federacion Nacional Autonoma de Futbol de Honduras, Colonia Florencia Norte, Edificio Plaza America Ave. Roble, 1 y 2 Nivle, PO Box 827, Tegucigalpa 504.
Founded: 1935. *FIFA:* 1946; *CONCACAF:* 1961. *National Colours:* All white.
International matches 2020–21
Nicaragua (h) 1-1, Guatemala (a) 1-2, Belarus (a) 1-1, Greece (a) 1-2, USA (h) 0-1, Costa Rica (n) 2-2 (5-4p), Mexico (n) 0-0.
League champions 2020–21: (Apertura), Olimpia (Clausura). *Cup winners 2018:* Platense; *2019–:* Not contested.

JAMAICA

Jamaica Football Federation Ltd, 20 St Lucia Crescent, Kingston 5.
Founded: 1910. *FIFA:* 1962; *CONCACAF:* 1963. *National Colours:* Gold shirts, black shorts, gold socks.
International matches 2020–21
Saudi Arabia (a) 0-3, Saudi Arabia (a) 2-1, USA (n) 1-4, Serbia (n) 1-1.
League champions 2018–19: Portmore United; *2019–20:* Competition abandoned; *2020–21:* Competition cancelled. *Cup winners:* Not contested since 2014.

MEXICO

Federacion Mexicana de Futbol Asociacion, A.C., Colima No. 373, Colonia Roma, Delegacion Cuauhtemoc, Mexico DF 06700.
Founded: 1927. *FIFA:* 1929; *CONCACAF:* 1961. *National Colours:* All black with white trim.
International matches 2020–21
Guatemala (h) 3-0, Netherlands (a) 1-0, Algeria (n) 2-2, Korea Republic (n) 3-2, Japan (n) 2-0, Wales (a) 0-1, Costa Rica (n) 1-0, Iceland (n) 2-1, Costa Rica (n) 0-0 (5-4p), USA (a) 2-3, Honduras (n) 0-0, Panama (n) 3-0, Nigeria (n) 4-0, Trinidad & Tobago (n) 0-0.
League champions 2020–21: Leon (Apertura), Cruz Azul (Clausura). *Cup winners 2019–20:* Monterrey; *2020–21:* Competition postponed.

MONTSERRAT

Montserrat Football Association Inc., PO Box 505, Blakes, Montserrat.
Founded: 1994. *FIFA:* 1996; *CONCACAF:* 1996. *National Colours:* White shirts with green hoops, white shorts, white socks.
International matches 2020–21
Antigua & Barbuda (a) 2-2*, El Salvador (h) 1-1*, US Virgin Islands (h) 7-0‡, Grenada (a) 2-1, Trinidad & Tobago (n) 1-6.
* *Match played in Curacao.* ‡ *Match played in Dominican Republic.*
League champions: Not contested since 2016. *Cup winners:* No competition.

NICARAGUA

Federacion Nicaraguense de Futbol, Porton Principal del Hospital Bautista 1 Cuadra Abajo, 1 Cuadra al Sur y 1/2 Cuadra Abajo, Apartado Postal 976, Managua.
Founded: 1931. *FIFA:* 1950; *CONCACAF:* 1961. *National Colours:* All blue with white trim.
International matches 2020–21
Guatemala (h) 0-0, Honduras (a) 1-1, Guatemala (a) 0-1, Turks & Caicos Islands* (a) 7-0, Belize (h) 3-0, Haiti (a) 0-1.
* *Match played in Dominican Republic.*
League champions 2020–21: Real Esteli (Apertura), Diriangen (Clausura). *Cup winners 2019:* Managua; *2020–:* Not contested.

PANAMA

Federacion Panamena de Futbol, Ciudad Deportiva Irving Saladino, Corregimiento de Juan Diaz, Apartado Postal 0827-00391, Zona 8, Panama City.
Founded: 1937. *FIFA:* 1938; *CONCACAF:* 1961. *National Colours:* All red.
International matches 2020–21
Costa Rica (a) 1-0, Costa Rica (a) 1-0, Japan (n) 0-1, USA (n) 2-6, Serbia (h) 0-0, Barbados (a) 1-0*, Dominica (a) 2-1*, Anguilla (a) 13-0‡, Dominican Republic (a) 3-0, Curacao (h) 2-1, Mexico (n) 0-3.
* *Match played in Dominican Republic.* ‡ *Match played in Panama.*
League champions 2020: Competition abandoned (Apertura), CAI (Clausura); *2021:* Plaza Amador (Apertura). *Cup winners:* No competition.

PUERTO RICO

Federacion Puertorriquena de Futbol, PO Box 367567, San Juan 00936.
Founded: 1940. *FIFA:* 1960; *CONCACAF:* 1961. *National Colours:* Red and white striped shirts with blue trim, blue shorts, red socks.
International matches 2020–21
Dominican Republic (a) 1-0, Guatemala (a) 0-1, St Kitts & Nevis (a) 0-1*, Trinidad & Tobago (h) 1-1, Bahamas (h) 7-0, Guyana (a) 2-0.
* *Match played in Dominican Republic.*
League champions 2018–19: Metropolitan FA; *2019–20:* Competition abandoned; *2020–21:* Competition postponed. *Cup winners 2019:* Bayamon; *2020–:* Not contested.

ST KITTS & NEVIS

St Kitts & Nevis Football Association, PO Box 465, Lozack Road, Basseterre.
Founded: 1932. *FIFA:* 1992; *CONCACAF:* 1992. *National Colours:* All red.
International matches 2020–21
Puerto Rico (h) 1-0*, Bahamas (h) 4-0, Guyana (a) 3-0, Trinidad & Tobago (a) 0-2*, El Salvador (h) 0-4, El Salvador (a) 0-2.
* *Match played in Dominican Republic.*
League champions 2019–20: St Paul's United Strikers; *2021:* Competition still being played. *Cup winners 2020:* St Paul's United Strikers.

ST LUCIA

St Lucia National Football Association, Barnard Hill, PO Box 255, Castries.
Founded: 1979. *FIFA:* 1988; *CONCACAF:* 1986. *National Colours:* Sky blue shirts with yellow stripes, sky blue shorts, sky blue socks.
International matches 2020–21
None played.
League champions 2019: Platinum; *2020:* Competition abandoned; *2021:* Competition postponed. *Cup winners 2019:* Gros Islet; 2020–: Not contested.

ST VINCENT & THE GRENADINES

St Vincent & the Grenadines Football Federation, PO Box 1278, Nichols Building (2nd Floor), Bentinck Square, Victoria Park, Kingstown.
Founded: 1979. *FIFA:* 1988; *CONCACAF:* 1986. *National Colours:* Yellow shirts, blue shorts, blue socks.
International matches 2020–21
Curacao (a) 0-5, British Virgin Islands (h) 3-0*, Guatemala (a) 0-10, Cuba (h) 0-1‡, Haiti (n) 1-6.
* *Match played in Curacao.* ‡ *Match played in Grenada.*
League champions 2019–20: Hope International; *2020–21:* Competition abandoned. *Cup winners:* No competition.

SURINAME

Surinaamse Voetbal Bond, Letitia Vriesdelaan 7, PO Box 1223, Paramaribo.
Founded: 1920. *FIFA:* 1929; *CONCACAF:* 1961. *National Colours:* White shirts, white shorts, white socks with green tops.
International matches 2020–21
Cayman Islands (h) 3-0, Aruba (a) 6-0*, Bermuda (h) 6-0, Canada (a) 0-4*.
* *Match played in USA.*

League champions 2018–19: Inter Moengotapoe; *2019–20:* Competition abandoned; *2021:* Competition postponed. *Cup winners 2019:* Inter Moengotapoe; *2020–:* Competition suspended.

TRINIDAD & TOBAGO

Trinidad & Tobago Football Association, 24–26 Dundonald Street, PO Box 400, Port of Spain.
Founded: 1908. *FIFA:* 1964; *CONCACAF:* 1962. *National Colours:* Red shirts with black trim, black shorts with red trim, red socks.
International matches 2020–21
USA (a) 0-7, Guyana (a) 3-0*, Puerto Rico (a) 1-1, Bahamas (a) 0-0, St Kitts & Nevis (h) 2-0*, Montserrat (n) 6-1, French Guiana† (n) 1-1 (8-7p), Mexico (n) 0-0.
* *Match played in Dominican Republic.*
League champions 2019–20: Defence Force; *2020–21:* Competition cancelled. *Cup winners:* Not contested since 2017.

TURKS & CAICOS ISLANDS

Turks & Caicos Islands Football Association, TCIFA National Academy, Venetian Road, PO Box 626, Providenciales.
Founded: 1996. *FIFA:* 1998; *CONCACAF:* 1996. *National Colours:* All black with white trim.
International matches 2020–21
Nicaragua (h) 0-7*, Belize (h) 0-5*, Haiti (h) 0-10.
* *Match played in Dominican Republic.*
League champions 2019–20: SWA Sharks (Apertura); Competition suspended (Clausura); *2020–21:* Competition cancelled. *Cup winners: 2019:* Academy Jaguars.

UNITED STATES OF AMERICA (USA)

US Soccer Federation, US Soccer House, 1801 S. Prairie Avenue, Chicago, IL 60616.
Founded: 1913. *FIFA:* 1914; *CONCACAF:* 1961. *National Colours:* White shirts with red and blue trim, white shorts, white socks.
International matches 2020–21
Wales (a) 0-0, Panama (n) 6-2, El Salvador (h) 6-0, Trinidad & Tobago (h) 7-0, Jamaica (n) 4-1, Northern Ireland (a) 2-1, Switzerland (a) 1-2, Honduras (h) 1-0, Mexico (h) 3-2, Costa Rica (h) 4-0, Haiti (n) 1-0.
MSL champions 2020: Columbus Crew, *2021:* Competition still being played. *Cup winners 2019:* Atlanta United; *2020:* Competition abandoned; *2021:* Competition postponed. (N.B. Teams from USA and Canada compete in MLS and USL.)

US VIRGIN ISLANDS

USVI Soccer Federation Inc., 498D Strawberry, PO Box 2346, Christiansted, St Croix 00851.
Founded: 1987. *FIFA:* 1998; *CONCACAF:* 1987. *National Colours:* All royal blue with gold trim.
International matches 2020–21
Antigua & Barbuda (h) 0-3, Grenada (a) 0-1, Montserrat (a) 0-4*, El Salvador (h) 0-7.
* *Match played in Dominican Republic.*
League champions 2018–19: Helenites; *2019–:* Competition suspended. *Cup winners:* No competition.

OCEANIA (OFC)

AMERICAN SAMOA

Football Federation American Samoa, PO Box 982 413, Pago Pago AS 96799.
Founded: 1984. *FIFA:* 1998; *OFC:* 1998. *National Colours:* All blue with white trim.
International matches 2020–21
Tahiti (n) 1-8*. No matches played in 2020–21.
* *Played 18.07.2019, result incorrect in last edition.*
League champions 2019: Pago Youth. *2019–: Competition suspended. Cup winners:* Not contested since 2014.

COOK ISLANDS

Cook Islands Football Association, Matavera Main Road, PO Box 29, Avarua, Rarotonga.
Founded: 1971. *FIFA:* 1994; *OFC:* 1994. *National Colours:* All green shirts with white trim.
International matches 2020–21
None played.
League champions 2020: Tupapa Maraerenga; *2021:* Competition still being played. *Cup winners 2020:* Nikaka Sokattack.

FIJI

Fiji Football Association, PO Box 2514, Government Buildings, Suva.
Founded: 1938. *FIFA:* 1964; *OFC:* 1966. *National Colours:* White shirts, black shorts, white socks.
International matches 2020–21
None played.
League champions 2020: Suva; *2021:* Competition still being played. *Cup winners 2020:* Suva; *2021:* Competition postponed.

NEW CALEDONIA

Federation Caledonienne de Football, 7 bis, Rue Suffren Quartien latin, BP 560, Noumea 99845.
Founded: 1928. *FIFA:* 2004; *OFC:* 2004. *National Colours:* All red with white trim.
International matches 2020–21
None played.
League champions 2020: Tiga Sports; *2020–21:* Competition still being played. *Cup winners 2020:* Hienghene Sport.

NEW ZEALAND

New Zealand Football, PO Box 301-043, Albany, Auckland.
Founded: 1891. *FIFA:* 1948; *OFC:* 1966. *National Colours:* All white.
International matches 2020–21
None played.
League champions 2020–21: Team Wellington. *Cup winners 2019:* Napier City Rovers; *2020:* Competition cancelled.

PAPUA NEW GUINEA

Papua New Guinea Football Association, PO Box 957, Lae 411, Morobe Province.
Founded: 1962. *FIFA:* 1966; *OFC:* 1966. *National Colours:* All red with white trim.
International matches 2020–21
None played.
League champions 2019–20: Lae City (formerly Toti City); *2020–21:* Competition still being played. *Cup winners:* Not contested since 2006.

SAMOA

Football Federation Samoa, PO Box 1682, Tuanimato, Apia.
Founded: 1968. *FIFA:* 1986; *OFC:* 1986. *National Colours:* Blue shirts, white shorts, blue socks.
International matches 2020–21
None played.
League champions 2020: Lupe ole Soaga; *2021:* Competition still being played. *Cup winners: 2018:* Manu-fili; *2019–:* Not contested.

SOLOMON ISLANDS

Solomon Islands Football Federation, Allan Boso Complex, Panatina Academy, PO Box 584, Honiara.
Founded: 1978. *FIFA:* 1988; *OFC:* 1988. *National Colours:* Gold shirts, blue shorts, white socks.
International matches 2020–21
None played.
League champions 2020–21: Henderson Eels. *Cup winners:* No competition.

TAHITI

Federation Tahitienne de Football, Rue Gerald Coppenrath, Complexe de Fautaua, PO Box 50358, Pirae 98716.
Founded: 1989. *FIFA:* 1990; *OFC:* 1990. *National Colours:* All red.
International matches 2020–21
New Caledonia (n) 0-3, American Samoa (n) 8-1. None played.
League champions 2020–21: AS Pirae. *Cup winners 2019–20:* Competition abandoned; *2020–21:* AS Pirae.

TONGA

Tonga Football Association, Loto-Tonga Soka Centre, Valungafulu Road, Atele, PO Box 852, Nuku'alofa.
Founded: 1965. *FIFA:* 1994; *OFC:* 1994. *National Colours:* All red.
International matches 2020–21
None played.
League champions 2019: Veitongo; *2020:* Competition cancelled. *Cup winners 2020:* Veitongo.

VANUATU

Vanuatu Football Federation, VFF House, Lini Highway, PO Box 266, Port Vila.
Founded: 1934. *FIFA:* 1988; *OFC:* 1988. *National Colours:* Gold shirts with black trim, black shorts, gold socks with black tops.
International matches 2020–21
None played.
League champions 2019: Malampa Revivors; *2020–21:* Galaxy. *Cup winners:* No competition.

AFRICA (CAF)

ALGERIA

Federation Algerienne De Football, Chemin Ahmed Ouaked, BP 39, Dely-Ibrahim, Algiers 16000.
Founded: 1962. *FIFA:* 1963; *CAF:* 1964. *National Colours:* All white.
International matches 2020–21
Nigeria (n) 1-0, Mexico (n) 2-2, Zimbabwe (h) 3-1, Zimbabwe (a) 2-2, Zambia (a) 3-3, Botswana (h) 5-0, Mauritania (h) 4-1, Mali (h) 1-0, Tunisia (a) 2-0, Liberia (h) 5-1.
League champions 2019–20: CR Belouizdad; *2020–21:* Competition still being played. *Cup winners 2018–19:* CR Belouizdad; *2019–20:* Competition abandoned; *2020–21:* Competition cancelled.

ANGOLA

Federacao Angolana de Futetbol, Senado de Compl. da Cidadela Desportiva, BP 3449, Luanda.
Founded: 1979. *FIFA:* 1980; *CAF:* 1980. *National Colours:* Red shirts with yellow trim, black shorts, red socks.
International matches 2020–21
DR Congo (a) 0-0, DR Congo (h) 0-1, Gambia (a) 1-3, Gabon (h) 2-0.
League champions 2018–19: Primeiro de Agosto; *2019–20:* Competition abandoned; *2020–21:* Competition still being played. *Cup winners 2019:* Primeiro de Agosto; *2020:* Competition abandoned; *2021:* Competition still being played.

BENIN

Federation Beninoise de Football, Rue du boulevard Djassain, BP 112, 3-eme Arrondissement de Porto-Novo 01.
Founded: 1962. *FIFA:* 1962; *CAF:* 1962. *National Colours:* All yellow with red and green trim.
International matches 2020–21
Gabon (n) 2-0, Lesotho (h) 1-0, Lesotho (a) 0-0, Nigeria (h) 0-1, Zambia (h) 2-2, Sierra Leone (a) 0-1*.
* *Match played in Guinea.*
League champions 2019–20: Competition abandoned; *2021:* Loto-Popo. *Cup winners 2019:* ESAE; *2020–:* Competition cancelled.

BOTSWANA

Botswana Football Association, PO Box 1396, Gaborone.
Founded: 1970. *FIFA:* 1978; *CAF:* 1976. *National Colours:* Blue shirts with black sleeves, blue shorts, blue socks with black trim.
International matches 2020–21
Zambia (a) 1-2, Zambia (h) 1-0, Zimbabwe (h) 0-1, Algeria (h) 0-5, South Africa (a) 0-1, Lesotho (n) 4-0.
League champions 2019–20: Jwaneng Galaxy; *2020–21:* Competition postponed. *Cup winners 2019:* Orapa United; *2019–20:* Competition abandoned.

BURKINA FASO

Federation Burkinabe de Foot-Ball, Centre Technique National Ouaga 2000, BP 57, Ouagadougou 01.
Founded: 1960. *FIFA:* 1964; *CAF:* 1964. *National Colours:* Green shirts with red sleeves, green shorts, green socks.
International matches 2020–21
DR Congo (n) 3-0, Madagascar (n) 2-1, Malawi (h) 3-1, Malawi (a) 0-0, Mali (n) 0-1, Zimbabwe (n) 3-1, Cameroon (a) 0-0, Uganda (a) 0-0, South Sudan (h) 1-0, Ivory Coast (a) 1-2, Morocco (a) 0-1.
League champions 2019–20: Competition abandoned; *2020–21:* AS Sonadel. *Cup winners 2020:* Competition abandoned; *2021:* ASFA-Yennenga.

BURUNDI

Federation de Football du Burundi, Avenue Muyinga, BP 3426, Bujumbura.
Founded: 1948. *FIFA:* 1972; *CAF:* 1972. *National Colours:* Red shirts, white shorts, green socks.
International matches 2020–21
Tanzania (a) 1-0, Mauritania (a) 1-1, Mauritania (h) 3-1, Central African Republic (h) 2-2, Morocco (a) 0-1.
League champions 2020–21: Le Messager. *Cup winners 2021:* Bumamuru.

CAMEROON

Federation Camerounaise de Football, Avenue du 27 aout 1940, Tsinga-Yaounde, BP 1116, Yaounde.
Founded: 1959. *FIFA:* 1962; *CAF:* 1963. *National Colours:* Green shirts, red shorts, yellow socks.
International matches 2020–21
Japan (n) 0-0, Mozambique (h) 4-1, Mozambique (a) 2-0, Zimbabwe (h) 1-0, Mali (h) 1-1, Burkina Faso (h) 0-0, DR Congo (h) 2-1, Morocco (h) 0-4, Guinea (h) 0-2, Cape Verde Islands (a) 1-3, Rwanda (h) 0-0, Nigeria (n) 1-0, Nigeria (n) 0-0.
League champions 2019–20: PWD Bamenda; *2020–21:* Competition abandoned. *Cup winners 2019:* Stade Renard de Melong; *2020:* Competition suspended; *2021:* Competition still being played.

CAPE VERDE ISLANDS

Federacao Caboverdiana de Futebol, Praia Cabo Verde, FCF CX, PO Box 234, Praia.
Founded: 1982. *FIFA:* 1986; *CAF:* 2000. *National Colours:* All blue with white trim.
International matches 2020–21
Andorra (a) 2-1, Guinea (n) 1-2, Rwanda (h) 0-0, Rwanda (a) 0-0, Cameroon (h) 3-1, Mozambique (a) 1-0, Senegal (a) 0-2.
League champions 2019: CS Mindelense; *2020:* Competition cancelled; *2021:* Competition suspended. *Cup winners 2019:* Santo Crucifixo; *2020–:* Competition cancelled.

CENTRAL AFRICAN REPUBLIC

Federation Centrafricaine de Football, Avenue des Martyrs, BP 344, Bangui.
Founded: 1961. *FIFA:* 1964; *CAF:* 1965. *National Colours:* All white with blue trim.
International matches 2020–21
Morocco (a) 1-4, Morocco (h) 0-2*, Burundi (a) 2-2, Mauritania (h) 0-1, Rwanda (a) 0-2, Rwanda (a) 0-5.
* *Match played in Cameroon.*
League champions 2019–20: Competition abandoned; *2020–21:* DFCB. *Cup winners: 2018:* ASDR Fatima; *2019:* Stade Centrafricain; *2020:* Tempete Mocatif.

CHAD

Federation Tchadienne de Football, BP 886, N'Djamena.
Founded: 1962. *FIFA:* 1964; *CAF:* 1964. *National Colours:* Blue shirts, yellow shorts, red socks.
International matches 2020–21
Guinea (a) 0-1, Guinea (h) 1-1, Namibia (h) 0-3*, Mali (a) 0-3*.
* *Chad disqualified for government interference; match awarded 3-0 to opponents.*
League champions 2020: Gazelle; *2021:* Competition still being played. *Cup winners:* Not contested since 2015.

COMOROS

Federation Comorienne de Football, Route d'Itsandra, BP 798, Moroni.
Founded: 1979. *FIFA:* 2005; *CAF:* 2003. *National Colours:* Green shirts with white trim, green shorts, green socks.
International matches 2020–21
Kenya (a) 1-1, Kenya (h) 2-1, Togo (h) 0-0, Egypt (a) 0-4, Palestine (n) 1-5.
League champions 2019–20: US Zilimadjou; *2020–21:* Competition cancelled. *Cup winners 2020:* US Zilimadjou; *2021:* Olympique de Missiri.

CONGO

Federation Congolaise de Football, 80 Rue Eugene Etienne, Centre Ville, BP Box 11, Brazzaville 00 242.
Founded: 1962. *FIFA:* 1964; *CAF:* 1965. *National Colours:* All red with white trim.
International matches 2020–21
Gambia (n) 0-1, Eswatini (h) 2-0, Eswatini (a) 0-0, DR Congo (n) 0-1, Niger (n) 1-1, Libya (n) 1-0, Mali (a) 0-0 (4-5p), Senegal (h) 0-0, Guinea-Bissau (a) 0-3, Niger (n) 1-0.
League champions 2021: AS Otoho. *Cup winners 2019:* Etoile du Congo; *2020–:* Competition suspended.

DR CONGO

Federation Congolaise de Football-Association, 31 Avenue de la Justice Kinshasa-Gombe, BP 1284, Kinshasa 1.
Founded: 1919. *FIFA:* 1964; *CAF:* 1964. *National Colours:* Blue shirts with red sleeves, red shorts, blue socks.
International matches 2020–21
Burkina Faso (n) 0-3, Morocco (a) 1-1, Angola (h) 0-0, Angola (a) 1-0, Congo (n) 1-0, Libya (n) 1-1, Niger (n) 2-1, Cameroon (a) 1-2, Gabon (a) 0-3, Gambia (h) 1-0, Tunisia (a) 0-1, Mali (n) 1-1.
League champions 2020–21: TP Mazembe. *Cup winners 2020:* Competition abandoned; *2021:* DC Motema Pembe.

DJIBOUTI

Federation Djiboutienne de Football, Centre Technique National, BP 2694, Ville de Djibouti.
Founded: 1979. *FIFA:* 1994; *CAF:* 1994. *National Colours:* All sky blue.
International matches 2020–21
Somalia (h) 1-0, Lebanon (n) 0-1.
League champions 2020–21: Arta/Solar7. *Cup winners 2021:* Arta/Solar7.

EGYPT

Egyptian Football Association, 5 Gabalaya Street, Gezira El Borg Post Office, Cairo.
Founded: 1921. *FIFA:* 1923; *CAF:* 1957. *National Colours:* Red shirts, white shorts, black socks.
International matches 2020–21
Togo (h) 1-0, Togo (h) 3-1, Kenya (a) 1-1, Comoros (h) 4-0.
League champions 2019–20: Al Ahly; *2020–21:* Competition still being played. *Cup winners 2019–20:* Al Ahly; *2020–21:* Competition still being played.

EQUATORIAL GUINEA

Federacion Ecuatoguineana de Futbol, Avenida de Hassan II, Apartado de correo 1017, Malabo.
Founded: 1957. *FIFA:* 1986; *CAF:* 1986. *National Colours:* All red with white trim.
International matches 2020–21
Libya (a) 3-2*, Libya (h) 1-0, Tanzania (h) 1-0, Tunisia (a) 1-2.
* *Match played in Egypt.*
League champions 2018–19: Cano Sport; *2019–20:* Competition abandoned; *2020–21:* Competition postponed. *Cup winners 2019:* Akonangui; *2020–:* Competition cancelled.

ERITREA

Eritrean National Football Federation, Sematat Avenue 29–31, PO Box 3665, Asmara.
Founded: 1996. *FIFA:* 1998; *CAF:* 1998. *National Colours:* White shirts with red trim, white shorts with red trim, blue socks.
International matches 2020–21
None played.
League champions 2019: Red Sea; *2020–:* Competition suspended. *Cup winners*: No competition.

ESWATINI (SWAZILAND)

Eswatini Football Association, Sigwaca House, Plot 582, Sheffield Road, PO Box 641, Mbabane H100.
Founded: 1968. *FIFA:* 1978; *CAF:* 1976. *National Colours:* Blue shirts with yellow trim, blue shorts, yellow socks.
International matches 2020–21
Congo (a) 0-2, Congo (h) 0-0, Guinea-Bissau (h) 1-3, Senegal (a) 1-1, Lesotho (n) 3-1, South Africa (a) 0-1, Zambia (n) 1-0.
League champions 2019–20: Young Buffaloes; *2020–21:* Competition still being played. *Cup winners 2019:* Young Buffaloes; *2020:* Competition cancelled.

ETHIOPIA

Ethiopia Football Federation, Addis Ababa Stadium, PO Box 1080, Addis Ababa.
Founded: 1943. *FIFA:* 1952; *CAF:* 1957. *National Colours:* Green shirts with yellow trim, green shorts with yellow trim, red socks.
International matches 2020–21
Zambia (h) 2-3, Zambia (h) 1-3, Niger (a) 0-1, Niger (h) 3-0, Malawi (h) 4-0, Madagascar (h) 4-0, Ivory Coast (a) 1-3.
League champions 2019–20: Competition abandoned; *2020–21:* Fasil Kenema. *Cup winners 2019:* Fasil Kenema; *2020–:* Competition suspended.

GABON

Federation Gabonaise de Football, BP 181, Libreville.
Founded: 1962. *FIFA:* 1966; *CAF:* 1967. *National Colours:* Yellow shirts, blue shorts with yellow trim, blue socks with yellow tops.
International matches 2020–21
Benin (n) 0-2, Gambia (h) 2-1, Gambia (a) 1-2, DR Congo (h) 3-0, Angola (a) 0-2.
League champions 2019: Cercle Mberie Sportif; *2020:* Competition abandoned. *Cup winners: 2019 (League Cup):* Mangasport; *2020:* Competition abandoned.

GAMBIA

Gambia Football Association, Kafining Layout, Bakau, PO Box 523, Banjul.
Founded: 1952. *FIFA:* 1968; *CAF:* 1966. *National Colours:* Red shirts with green and blue trim, red shorts, red socks.
International matches 2020–21
Congo (n) 1-0, Gabon (a) 1-2, Gabon (h) 2-1, Angola (h) 1-0, DR Congo (a) 0-1, Niger (n) 2-0, Togo (n) 1-0, Kosovo (n) 0-1.
League champions 2018–19: Brikama United; *2019–20:* Competition abandoned; *2021:* Fortune. *Cup winners 2019:* Real Banjul; *2020–:* Competition suspended.

GHANA

Ghana Football Association, General Secretariat, South East Ridge, PO Box AN 19338, Accra.
Founded: 1957 (dissolved 2018, reconvened 2019). *FIFA:* 1958; *CAF:* 1958. *National Colours:* Red shirts with yellow sleeves, red shorts, red socks.
International matches 2020–21
Mali (n) 0-3, Qatar (n) 5-1, Sudan (h) 2-0, Sudan (a) 0-1, South Africa (a) 1-1, Sao Tome & Principe (h) 3-1, Morocco (a) 0-1, Ivory Coast (h) 0-0.
League champions 2019–20: Competition abandoned; *2020–21:* Hearts of Oak. *Cup winners: 2019–20:* Competition abandoned; *2020–21:* Competition still being played.

GUINEA

Federation Guinéenne de Football, Annexe 1 du Palais du Peuple, PO Box 3645, Conakry.
Founded: 1960. *FIFA:* 1962; *CAF:* 1963. *National Colours:* Red shirts, yellow shorts, green socks.
International matches 2020–21
Cape Verde Islands (n) 2-1, Chad (h) 1-0, Chad (a) 1-1, Namibia (n) 3-0, Zambia (n) 1-1, Tanzania (n) 2-2, Rwanda (n) 1-0, Mali (n) 0-0 (4-5p), Cameroon (a) 2-0, Mali (h) 1-0, Namibia (a) 1-2, Turkey (a) 0-0, Togo (n) 0-2, Kosovo (n) 2-1, Niger (n) 2-1.
League champions 2019–20: Competition abandoned; *2020–21:* Horoya. *Cup winners 2019:* Horoya; *2020–:* Competition cancelled.

GUINEA-BISSAU

Federacao de Futebol da Guiné-Bissau, Alto Bandim (Nova Sede), BP 375, Bissau 1035.
Founded: 1974. *FIFA:* 1986; *CAF:* 1986. *National Colours:* All red with green trim.
International matches 2020–21
Senegal (a) 0-2, Senegal (h) 0-1, Eswatini (a) 3-1, Congo (h) 3-0.
League champions 2019–20: Competition abandoned; *2020–21:* Sporting de Guiné-Bissau. *Cup winners 2019:* Sporting de Guiné-Bissau; *2020:* Competition abandoned. *2021:* Competition still being played.

IVORY COAST

Federation Ivoirienne de Football, Treichville Avenue 1, 01, BP 1202, Abidjan 01.
Founded: 1960. *FIFA:* 1964; *CAF:* 1960. *National Colours:* All orange.
International matches 2020–21
Belgium (a) 1-1, Japan (n) 0-1, Madagascar (h) 2-1, Madagascar (a) 1-1, Niger (a) 3-0, Ethiopia (h) 3-1, Burkina Faso (h) 2-1, Ghana (a) 0-0.
League champions 2020–21: ASEC Mimosas. *Cup winners 2019:* FC San Pedro; *2020–:* Competition cancelled.

KENYA

Football Kenya Federation, Nyayo Sports Complex, Kasarani, PO Box 12705, 00400 Nairobi.
Founded: 1960 (KFF); 2011 (FKF). *FIFA:* 1960 (2012); *CAF:* 1968 (2012). *National Colours:* All red.
International matches 2020–21
Zambia (n) 2-1, Comoros (h) 1-1, Comoros (a) 1-2, South Sudan (h) 1-0, Tanzania (h) 2-1, Egypt (h) 1-1, Togo (a) 2-1.
League champion 2019–20: Gor Mahia; *2020–21:* Competition still being played. *Cup winners 2020:* Competition abandoned; *2021:* Gor Mahia.

LESOTHO

Lesotho Football Association, Bambatha Tsita Sports Arena, Old Polo Ground, PO Box 1879, Maseru 100.
Founded: 1932. *FIFA:* 1964; *CAF:* 1964. *National Colours:* Green shirts with blue and white trim, green shorts, green socks.
International matches 2020–21
Benin (a) 0-1, Benin (h) 0-0, Sierra Leone (h) 0-0, Nigeria (a) 0-3, Eswatini (n) 1-3, Zambia (n) 2-1, Botswana (n) 0-4.
League champion 2019–20: Bantu Rovers; *2020–21:* Competition still being played. *Cup winners 2019:* Matlama; *2020–:* Competition cancelled.

LIBERIA

Liberia Football Association, Professional Building, Benson Street, PO Box 10-1066, Monrovia 1000.
Founded: 1936. *FIFA:* 1964; *CAF:* 1960. *National Colours:* Blue shirts with white trim, white shorts, red socks.
International matches 2020–21
Mauritania (n) 0-1, Libya (n) 1-0, Algeria (a) 1-5.
League champions 2019–20: Competition abandoned; *2020–21:* LPRC Oilers. *Cup winners 2019–20:* Competition abandoned; *2020–21:* MC Breweries.

LIBYA

Libyan Football Federation, General Sports Federation Building, Sports City, Goriji, PO Box 5137, Tripoli.
Founded: 1962. *FIFA:* 1964; *CAF:* 1965. *National Colours:* Red shirts, black shorts, black socks.

International matches 2020–21
Equatorial Guinea (h) 2-3*, Equatorial Guinea (a) 0-1, Niger (n) 0-0, DR Congo (n) 1-1, Congo (n) 0-1, Tunisia (h) 2-5, Tanzania (a) 0-1, Liberia (n) 0-1, Sudan (n) 0-1.
* *Match played in Egypt.*
League champions 2017–18: Al-Nasr; *2018–19:* Competition abandoned; *2019–20:* Competition cancelled; *2020–21:* Competition still being played. *Cup winners: 2018:* Al-Ittihad; *2019–:* Competition cancelled.

MADAGASCAR

Federation Malagasy de Football, 29 Rue de Russie Isoraka, PO Box 4409, Antananarivo 101.
Founded: 1961. *FIFA:* 1964; *CAF:* 1963. *National Colours:* All green with white trim.
International matches 2020–21
Burkina Faso (n) 1-2, Ivory Coast (a) 1-2, Ivory Coast (h) 1-1, Ethiopia (a) 0-4, Niger (h) 0-0.
League champions 2019–20: Competition abandoned; *2020–21:* AS ADEMA. *Cup winners 2019:* Fosa Juniors; *2020:* Competition abandoned; *2021:* Competition still being played.

MALAWI

Football Association of Malawi, Chiwembe Technical Centre, Off Chiwembe Road, PO Box 51657, Limbe.
Founded: 1966. *FIFA:* 1968; *CAF:* 1968. *National Colours:* All red.
International matches 2020–21
Zambia (a) 1-0, Zimbabwe (a) 0-0, Burkina Faso (a) 1-3, Burkina Faso (h) 0-0, Ethiopia (a) 0-4, South Sudan (a) 1-0*, Uganda (h) 1-0, Tanzania (a) 0-2, Zimbabwe (n) 2-2, Mozambique (n) 0-2.
* *Match played in Sudan.*
League champions 2019: Nyasa Big Bullets; *2020–21:* Competition still being played. *Cup winners:* Not contested since 2015.

MALI

Federation Malienne de Football, Avenue du Mali, Hamdallaye ACI 2000, BP 1020, Bamako 0000.
Founded: 1960. *FIFA:* 1964; *CAF:* 1963. *National Colours:* All yellow with green and red trim.
International matches 2020–21
Ghana (n) 3-0, Namibia (h) 1-0, Namibia (a) 2-1, Burkina Faso (n) 1-0, Cameroon (a) 1-1, Zimbabwe (n) 2-2, Congo (n) 0-0 (5-4p), Guinea (n) 0-0 (5-4p), Morocco (n) 0-2, Guinea (a) 0-1, Chad (h) 3-0*, Algeria (a) 0-1, DR Congo (n) 1-1, Tunisia (a) 0-1.
* *Chad disqualified for government interference; match awarded 3-0 to Mali.*
League champions 2019–20: Stade Malien; *2020–21:* Stade Malien. *Cup winners 2020:* Competition abandoned; *2021:* Stade Malien.

MAURITANIA

Federation de Foot-Ball de la Rep. Islamique de Mauritanie, Route de l'Espoire, BP 566, Nouakchott.
Founded: 1961. *FIFA:* 1970; *CAF:* 1968. *National Colours:* Green shirts, yellow shorts, red socks.
International matches 2020–21
Sierra Leone (h) 2-1, Burundi (h) 1-1, Burundi (a) 1-3, Morocco (h) 0-0, Central African Republic (a) 1-0, Algeria (a) 1-4, Liberia (n) 1-0, Yemen (n) 2-0.
League champions 2019–20: FC Nouadhibou; *2020–21:* FC Nouadhibou. *Cup winners 2020:* FC Tevragh Zeina; *2021:* Competition still being played.

MAURITIUS

Mauritius Football Association, Sepp Blatter House, Trianon.
Founded: 1952. *FIFA:* 1964; *CAF:* 1963. *National Colours:* All white with red trim.
International matches 2020–21
None played.
League champions 2018–19: Pamplemousses; *2019–20:* Competition abandoned; *2020–21:* Competition suspended. *Cup winners 2019:* Roche-Bois Bolton City; *2020:* Competition abandoned; *2021:* Competition suspended.

MOROCCO

Federation Royale Marocaine de Football, 51 bis, Avenue Ibn Sina, Agdal BP 51, Rabat 10 000.
Founded: 1955. *FIFA:* 1960; *CAF:* 1959. *National Colours:* Red shirts with white trim, green shorts, red socks with white tops.
International matches 2020–21
Senegal (h) 3-1, DR Congo (n) 1-1, Central African Republic (h) 4-1, Central African Republic (a) 2-0*, Togo (n) 1-0, Rwanda (n) 0-0, Uganda (n) 5-2, Zambia (n) 3-1, Cameroon (a) 4-0, Mali (n) 2-0, Mauritania (a) 0-0, Burundi (h) 1-0, Ghana (h) 1-0, Burkina Faso (h) 1-0.
* *Match played in Cameroon.*
League champions 2019–20: Raja Casablanca; *2020–21:* Wydad AC. *Cup winners 2019:* TAS Casablanca; *2020–21:* Competition suspended.

MOZAMBIQUE

Federacao Mocambicana de Futebol, Avenida Samora Machel 11, Caixa Postal 1467, Maputo.
Founded: 1976. *FIFA:* 1980; *CAF:* 1980. *National Colours:* Red shirts, black shorts, red socks with black tops.
International matches 2020–21
Cameroon (a) 1-4, Cameroon (h) 0-2, Rwanda (h) 0-1, Cape Verde Islands (a) 0-1, Zimbabwe (n) 0-0, Senegal (n) 0-1, Malawi (n) 2-0.
League champions 2019: Costa do Sol; *2020:* Competition cancelled; *2021:* Competition suspended. *Cup winners 2019:* Uniao Desportiva do Songo; *2020–:* Competition cancelled.

NAMIBIA

Namibia Football Association, Richard Kamuhuka Str., Soccer House, Katutura, PO Box 1345, Windhoek 9000.
Founded: 1990. *FIFA:* 1992; *CAF:* 1992. *National Colours:* All blue.
International matches 2020–21
South Africa (a) 1-1, Mali (a) 0-1, Mali (h) 1-2, Guinea (n) 0-3, Tanzania (n) 0-1, Zambia (n) 0-0, Chad (h) 3-0*, Guinea (h) 2-1, Senegal (n) 0-1, Zimbabwe (n) 2-0.
* *Chad disqualified for government interference; match awarded 3-0 to Namibia.*
League champions 2019–20: Competition cancelled; *2020–21:* Black Africa. *Cup winners 2018:* African Stars; *2019, 2020*: Not contested; *2021:* Competition still being played.

NIGER

Federation Nigerienne de Football, Avenue Francois Mitterand, BP 10299, Niamey.
Founded: 1961. *FIFA:* 1964; *CAF:* 1964. *National Colours:* Orange shirts, white shorts, green socks.
International matches 2020–21
Ethiopia (h) 1-0, Ethiopia (a) 0-3, Libya (n) 0-0, Congo (n) 1-1, DR Congo (n) 1-2, Ivory Coast (h) 0-3, Madagascar (a) 0-0, Gambia (n) 0-2, Congo (n) 0-1, Guinea (n) 1-2.
League champions 2019–20: Competition abandoned; *2020–21:* US Gendarmerie Nationale. *Cup winners 2020:* Competition abandoned; *2021:* US Gendarmerie Nationale.

NIGERIA

Nigeria Football Federation, Plot 2033, Olusegun Obasanjo Way, Zone 7, Wuse Abuja, PO Box 5101 Garki, Abuja.
Founded: 1945. *FIFA:* 1960; *CAF:* 1960. *National Colours:* Green shirts with white trim, white shorts, green socks.
International matches 2020–21
Algeria (n) 0-1, Tunisia (n) 1-1, Sierra Leone (h) 4-4, Sierra Leone (a) 0-0, Benin (a) 1-0, Lesotho (h) 3-0, Cameroon (n) 0-1, Cameroon (n) 0-0, Mexico (n) 0-4.
League champions 2019: Enyimba; *2019–20:* Competition abandoned; *2020–21:* Competition still being played. *Cup winners 2019:* Kano Pillars; *2020–:* Competition cancelled.

RWANDA

Federation Rwandaise de Football Association, BP 2000, Kigali.
Founded: 1972. *FIFA:* 1978; *CAF:* 1976. *National Colours:* Yellow shirts with green trim, yellow shorts, green socks with yellow tops.
International matches 2020–21
Cape Verde Islands (a) 0-0, Cape Verde Islands (h) 0-0, Uganda (n) 0-0, Morocco (n) 0-0, Togo (n) 3-2, Guinea (n) 1-0, Mozambique (h) 1-0, Cameroon (a) 0-0, Central African Republic (a) 2-0, Central African Republic (h) 5-0.
League champions 2020–21: APR. *Cup winners 2019:* AS Kigali; *2020–:* Competition cancelled.

SAO TOME & PRINCIPE

Federacao Santomense de Futebol, Rua Ex-Joao de Deus No. QXXIII-426/26, BP 440, Sao Tome.
Founded: 1975. *FIFA:* 1986; *CAF:* 1986. *National Colours:* All yellow.
International matches 2020–21
South Africa (a) 0-2, South Africa (h) 2-4*, Sudan (h) 0-2, Ghana (a) 1-3.
* *Match played in South Africa.*

League champions 2019: Agrosport; *2020–:* Competition cancelled. *Cup winners 2019:* FC Porto Real; *2020–:* Competition cancelled.

SENEGAL

Federation Senegalaise de Football, VDN Ouest-Foire en face du Cicesi, BP 13021, Dakar.
Founded: 1960. *FIFA:* 1964; *CAF:* 1964. *National Colours:* All white with green trim.
International matches 2020–21
Morocco (a) 1-3, Guinea-Bissau (h) 2-0, Guinea-Bissau (a) 1-0, Congo (a) 0-0, Eswatini (h) 1-1, Zambia (h) 3-1, Cape Verde Islands (h) 2-0, Namibia (n) 1-2, Mozambique (n) 1-0.
League champions 2019: ASC Jaraaf; *2020:* Competition abandoned; *2021:* Teungueth. *Cup winners 2019:* Teungueth; *2020:* Competition abandoned; *2021:* Competition still being played.

SEYCHELLES

Seychelles Football Federation, Maison Football, Roche Caiman, PO Box 843, Mahé.
Founded: 1979. *FIFA:* 1986; *CAF:* 1986. *National Colours:* All red with white trim.
International matches 2020–21
None played.
League champion 2019–20: Foresters; *2020–21:* Competition abandoned. *Cup winners 2020:* Foresters; *2020–:* Competition cancelled.

SIERRA LEONE

Sierra Leone Football Association, 21 Battery Street, Kingtom, PO Box 672, Freetown.
Founded: 1960. *FIFA:* 1960; *CAF:* 1960. *National Colours:* All blue. *(FIFA membership suspended in October 2018 due to alleged government interference.)*
International matches 2020–21
Mauritania (a) 1-2, Nigeria (a) 4-4, Nigeria (h) 0-0, Lesotho (a) 0-0, Benin (h) 1-0*.
* *Match played in Guinea.*
League champions 2019: East End Lions; *2020:* Competition abandoned; *2021:* Competition suspended. *Cup winners:* Not contested since 2016.

SOMALIA

Somali Football Federation, Mogadishu BN 03040 (DHL only).
Founded: 1951. *FIFA:* 1962; *CAF:* 1968. *National Colours:* All sky blue with white trim.
International matches 2020–21
Djibouti (a) 0-1, Oman (n) 1-2.
League champions 2019–20: Mogadishu City Club; *2021:* Competition still being played. *Cup winners 2020:* Horseed; *2021:* Competition postponed.

SOUTH AFRICA

South African Football Association, 76 Nasrec Road, Nasrec, Johannesburg 2000.
Founded: 1991. *FIFA:* 1992; *CAF:* 1992. *National Colours:* Yellow shirts with green trim, green shorts, yellow socks.
International matches 2020–21
Namibia (h) 1-1, Zambia (h) 1-2, Sao Tome & Principe (h) 2-0, Sao Tome & Principe (a) 4-2*, Ghana (h) 1-1, Sudan (a) 0-2, Uganda (h) 3-2, Botswana (h) 1-0, Eswatini (h) 1-0.
* *Match played in South Africa.*
League champions 2019–20: Mamelodi Sundowns; *2020–21:* Mamelodi Sundowns. *Cup winners 2020–21:* Tshakhuma Tsha Madzivhandila.

SOUTH SUDAN

South Sudan Football Association, Juba National Stadium, Hai Himra, Talata, Juba.
Founded: 2011. *FIFA:* 2012; *CAF:* 2012. *National Colours:* White shirts with blue and red sash, white shorts, white socks.
International matches 2020–21
Uganda (a) 0-1, Uganda (h) 1-0*, Kenya (a) 0-1, Malawi (h) 0-1‡, Burkina Faso (a) 0-1, Jordan (n) 0-3.
* *Match played in Kenya.* ‡ *Match played in Sudan.*
League champions 2019: Atlabara; *2020–:* Competition cancelled. *Cup winners 2021:* Atlabara.

SUDAN

Sudan Football Association, Baladia Street, PO Box 437, 11111 Khartoum.
Founded: 1936. *FIFA:* 1948; *CAF:* 1957. *National Colours:* All red with white trim.
International matches 2020–21
Tunisia (a) 0-3, Togo (n) 1-1, Ghana (a) 0-2, Ghana (h) 1-0, Sao Tome & Principe (a) 2-0, South Africa (h) 2-0, Zambia (h) 0-1, Libya (n) 1-0.
League champions 2019–20: Al-Merrikh; *2020–21:* Competition still being played. *Cup winners 2018:* Al-Merrikh; *2019:* Not contested; *2020:* Competition abandoned.

TANZANIA

Tanzania Football Federation, Karume Memorial Stadium, Uhuru/Shauri Moyo Road, PO Box 1574, Ilala/Dar Es Salaam.
Founded: 1930. *FIFA:* 1964; *CAF:* 1964. *National Colours:* Blue shirts, white shorts, blue socks.
International matches 2020–21
Burundi (h) 0-1, Tunisia (a) 0-1, Tunisia (a) 1-1, Zambia (n) 0-2, Namibia (n) 1-0, Guinea (n) 2-2, Kenya (a) 1-2, Equatorial Guinea (a) 0-1, Libya (h) 1-0, Malawi (h) 2-0.
League champions 2020–21: Simba. *Cup winners 2019–20:* Simba; *2020–21:* Competition still being played.

TOGO

Federation Togolaise de Football, Route de Kegoue, BP 05, Lome.
Founded: 1960. *FIFA:* 1964; *CAF:* 1964. *National Colours:* All yellow.
International matches 2020–21
Sudan (n) 1-1, Egypt (a) 0-1, Egypt (a) 1-3, Morocco (n) 0-1, Uganda (n) 2-1, Rwanda (n) 2-3, Comoros (a) 0-0, Kenya (h) 1-2, Guinea (n) 2-0, Gambia (n) 0-1.
League champions 2020–21: ASKO de Kara. *Cup winners 2018:* Gomido; *2019–:* Competition cancelled.

TUNISIA

Federation Tunisienne de Football, Stade Annexe d'El Menzah, Cite Olympique, El Menzah 1003.
Founded: 1957. *FIFA:* 1960; *CAF:* 1960. *National Colours:* All white with red trim.
International matches 2020–21
Sudan (h) 3-0, Nigeria (n) 1-1, Tanzania (n) 1-0, Tanzania (a) 1-1, Libya (a) 5-2, Equatorial Guinea (h) 2-1, DR Congo (h) 1-0, Algeria (h) 0-2, Mali (n) 1-0.
League champions 2020–21: Esperance de Tunis. *Cup winners 2019–20:* US Monastir; *2020–21:* CS Sfaxien.

UGANDA

Federation of Uganda Football Associations, FUFA House, Plot No. 879, Wakaliga Road, Mengo, PO Box 22518, Kampala.
Founded: 1924. *FIFA:* 1960; *CAF:* 1960. *National Colours:* Red shirts with yellow and black trim, white shorts, red socks.
International matches 2020–21
South Sudan (h) 1-0, South Sudan (a) 0-1*, Rwanda (n) 0-0, Togo (n) 1-2, Morocco (n) 2-5, Burkina Faso (h) 0-0, Malawi (a) 1-0, South Africa (a) 2-3.
* *Match played in Kenya.*
League champions 2020–21: Express (named champions at abandonment of season). *Cup winners 2018–19:* Proline; *2019–20:* Competition abandoned; *2021:* Competition still being played.

ZAMBIA

Football Association of Zambia, Football House, Alick Nkhata Road, Long Acres, PO Box 34751, Lusaka.
Founded: 1929. *FIFA:* 1964; *CAF:* 1964. *National Colours:* All green.
International matches 2020–21
Malawi (h) 1-0, Kenya (n) 1-2, South Africa (a) 2-1, Ethiopia (a) 3-2, Ethiopia (a) 3-1, Botswana (h) 2-1, Botswana (a) 0-1, Tanzania (n) 2-0, Guinea (n) 1-1, Namibia (n) 0-0, Morocco (n) 1-3, Algeria (h) 3-3, Zimbabwe (a) 2-0, Senegal (a) 1-3, Benin (a) 2-2, Sudan (a) 1-0, Lesotho (n) 1-2, Eswatini (h) 0-1.
League champions 2020–21: ZESCO United. *Cup winners:* Not contested since 2007.

ZIMBABWE

Zimbabwe Football Association, ZIFA House, 53 Livingston Avenue, PO Box CY 114, Causeway, Harare.
Founded: 1965. *FIFA:* 1965; *CAF:* 1980. *National Colours:* All gold with white trim.
International matches 2020–21
Malawi (h) 0-0, Algeria (a) 1-3, Algeria (h) 2-2, Cameroon (a) 0-1, Burkina Faso (h) 1-3, Mali (n) 0-1, Botswana (a) 1-0, Zambia (h) 0-2, Mozambique (n) 0-0, Malawi (h) 2-2, Namibia (n) 0-2.
League champions 2019: FC Platinum; *2020–:* Competition cancelled. *Cup winners 2019:* Highlanders; *2020:* Competition cancelled; *2021:* Competition still being played.

EURO 2020 PLAY-OFFS

Behind closed doors unless otherwise stated.

PLAY-OFF SEMI-FINALS

Thursday, 8 October 2020

Bosnia-Herzegovina (1) 1 *(Krunic 13)*

Northern Ireland (0) 1 *(McGinn 53)* 1800

Bosnia-Herzegovina: (433) Sehic; Cipetic, Ahmedhodzic, Sanicanin, Kolasinac (Hajradinovic 118); Cimirot (Loncar 106), Hadziahmetovic (Gojak 83), Pjanic; Visca, Dzeko, Krunic (Hotic 88).
Northern Ireland: (4411) Peacock-Farrell; Dallas, Cathcart, Evans J, Lewis; Evans C (Whyte 73), Davis, Saville, McGinn (Jones 82); McNair (Thompson 90 (Boyce 120)); Magennis (Lafferty 90 (Washington 120)).
aet; Northern Ireland won 4-3 on penalties.
Referee: Antonio Miguel Mateu Lahoz.

Bulgaria (0) 1 *(Yomov 89)*

Hungary (1) 3 *(Orban 17, Kalmar 47, Nikolic 75)* 1929

Bulgaria: (4231) Iliev P; Cicinho, Terziev, Bozhikov, Nedyalkov; Karabelyov, Malinov; Karagaren (Despodov 58), Nedelev (Yankov 80), Ivanov (Yomov 31); Kraev (Isa 79).
Hungary: (3421) Gulacsi; Orban, Lang, Attila Szalai; Fiola (Botka 82), Nagy A (Gazdag 82), Siger, Holender (Nego 70); Sallai, Kalmar (Hangya 70); Adam Szalai (Nikolic 59).
Referee: Szymon Marciniak.

Georgia (1) 1 *(Okriashvili 7 (pen))*

Belarus (0) 0

Georgia: (4231) Loria; Kakabadze (Tabidze 82), Kashia, Kvirkvelia, Dvali; Kvekveskiri, Kankava; Kvaratskhelia (Lobzhanidze 89), Kiteishvili (Gvilia 65), Qazaishvili (Shengelia 81); Okriashvili (Kvilitaia 89).
Belarus: (442) Khatkevich; Zolotov, Martynovich, Naumov, Bordachev (Pechenin 74); Bakhar (Podstrelov 63), Ebong, Yablonskiy (Skavysh 63), Nekhaychik; Khachaturyan (Maevskiy 46), Lisakovich (Laptev 70).
Referee: Cuneyt Cakir.

Iceland (2) 2 *(Sigurdsson G 16, 34)*

Romania (0) 1 *(Maxim 63 (pen))* 60

Iceland: (442) Halldorsson; Palsson, Arnason (Ingason 86), Sigurdsson R, Magnusson; Gudmundsson J (Sigurjonsson 83), Gunnarsson, Bjarnason B, Traustason; Finnbogason A (Sigthorsson 75), Sigurdsson G.
Romania: (433) Tatarusanu; Manea, Balasa, Burca, Camora; Stanciu (Cicaldau 87), Cretu, Maxim (Keseru 80); Deac (Iancu 46), Alibec (Puscas 46), Mitrita (Hagi 46).
Referee: Damir Skomina.

North Macedonia (2) 2 *(Kololli 15 (og), Velkovski 33)*

Kosovo (1) 1 *(Hadergjonaj 29)*

North Macedonia: (3412) Dimitrievski; Bejtulai (Ristevski 51), Velkovski, Musliu; Ristovski S (Kostadinov 88), Ademi (Spirovski 80), Nikolov, Alioski; Bardhi; Nestorovski (Trajkovski 88), Pandev (Trickovski 80).
Kosovo: (4231) Muric; Vojvoda (Zhegrova 64), Dresevic, Aliti, Kololli; Shala (Paqarada 87), Berisha V; Hadergjonaj, Celina (Kastrati 75), Zeneli; Nuhiu (Rashani 46).
Referee: Danny Makkelie.

Norway (0) 1 *(Normann 88)*

Serbia (0) 2 *(Milinkovic-Savic 81, 102)* 200

Norway: (442) Jarstein; Elabdellaoui (Thorsby 116), Reginiussen (Strandberg 91), Ajer, Aleesami (Linnes 106); Odegaard (Elyounoussi M 111), Berge, Henriksen (Normann 46), Johansen (King 66); Sorloth, Haaland.
Serbia: (352) Rajkovic; Milenkovic, Mitrovic S, Kolarov; Lazovic (Gacinovic 106), Tadic (Lukic 119), Nemanja Maksimovic (Milivojevic 80), Gudelj, Ristic; Djuricic (Milinkovic-Savic 80), Mitrovic A.
aet.
Referee: Daniele Orsato.

Scotland (0) 0

Israel (0) 0

Scotland: (3412) Marshall; McTominay, Gallagher, Cooper; O'Donnell (McLean 113), Jack (Fraser 83), McGregor C, Robertson; McGinn; Dykes (Paterson 91), McBurnie (Shankland 73).
Israel: (532) Marciano; Dasa, Bitton, Tibi, Yeini, Elhamed; Golasa (Elmkies 101), Natcho (Abu Fani 69), Solomon; Dabbur (Weissman 83), Zahavi.
aet; Scotland won 5-3 on penalties.
Referee: Ovidiu Alin Hategan.

Slovakia (0) 0

Republic of Ireland (0) 0

Slovakia: (433) Rodak; Pekarik, Vavro (Gyomber 112), Valjent, Mazan; Kucka (Gregus 86), Hrosovsky, Hamsik; Rusnak (Mak 86), Duda (Bozenik 107), Mihalik (Haraslin 74).
Republic of Ireland: (4231) Randolph; Doherty, Duffy, Egan, Stevens; McCarthy (Browne 60), Hourihane; Robinson (O'Dowda 100), Hendrick, McClean (Brady 60); McGoldrick (Long S 112).
aet; Slovakia won 4-2 on penalties.
Referee: Clement Turpin.

PLAY-OFF FINALS

Thursday, 12 November 2020

Georgia (0) 0

North Macedonia (0) 1 *(Pandev 56)*

Georgia: (4231) Loria; Kakabadze, Kvirkvelia, Kashia (Azouz 88), Dvali (Davitashvili 90); Kankava, Kvekveskiri; Okriashvili, Gvilia (Papunashvili 80), Qazaishvili (Khocholava 90); Kacharava (Lobjanidze 80).
North Macedonia: (3412) Dimitrievski; Bejtulai, Velkovski, Musliu; Ristovski S (Zajkov 89), Nikolov (Kostadinov 84), Ademi (Spirovski 67), Alioski; Elmas; Nestorovski (Trickovski 89), Pandev.
Referee: Anthony Taylor.

Hungary (0) 2 *(Nego 88, Szoboszlai 90)*

Iceland (1) 1 *(Sigurdsson G 11)*

Hungary: (352) Gulacsi; Botka, Orban, Attila Szalai; Fiola (Lovrencsics 61), Kalmar (Siger 61), Nagy A (Nego 84), Szoboszlai, Holender (Nikolic 71); Sallai, Adam Szalai (Konyves 84).
Iceland: (442) Halldorsson; Palsson, Arnason, Sigurdsson R, Magnusson; Gudmundsson J (Bodvarsson 73), Sigurjonsson (Ingason 87), Gunnarsson (Skulason A 83), Bjarnason B; Sigurdsson G, Finnbogason A (Gudmundsson A 73).
Referee: Bjorn Kuipers.

Northern Ireland (0) 1 *(Skriniar 87 (og))*

Slovakia (1) 2 *(Kucka 17, Duris 110)* 1057

Northern Ireland: (442) Peacock-Farrell; Dallas, Cathcart (Flanagan 99), Evans J, Lewis; McGinn (Lafferty 76), McNair (Ferguson 104), Davis, Saville (Thompson 65); Washington (Whyte 66), Magennis (Boyce 77).
Slovakia: (4141) Rodak; Pekarik, Satka, Skriniar, Hubocan; Lobotka (Hrosovsky 65); Rusnak (Gyomber 118), Kucka, Hamsik (Gregus 106), Mak (Duris 65); Duda (Mraz 85).
aet.
Referee: Felix Brych.

Serbia (0) 1 *(Jovic 90)*

Scotland (0) 1 *(Christie 52)*

Serbia: (3421) Rajkovic; Milenkovic, Mitrovic S (Spajic 108), Gudelj; Lazovic, Nemanja Maksimovic (Jovic 70), Lukic, Kostic (Mladenovic 59); Tadic, Milinkovic-Savic (Katai 70); Mitrovic A.
Scotland: (3412) Marshall; McTominay, Gallagher, Tierney; O'Donnell (Griffiths 117), Jack, McGregor C, Robertson; McGinn (McLean 83); Dykes (McBurnie 83), Christie (Paterson 87).
aet; Scotland won 5-4 on penalties.
Referee: Antonio Miguel Mateu Lahoz.

EURO 2020 FINALS

■ *Denotes player sent off.* **Qualify as best 3rd place teams.*

GROUP A

Rome, Friday, 11 June 2021

Turkey (0) 0

Italy (0) 3 *(Demiral 53 (og), Immobile 66, Insigne 79)* 12,916

Turkey: (4141) Cakir; Celik, Demiral, Soyuncu, Meras; Yokuslu (Kahveci 65); Karaman (Dervisoglu 76), Yazici (Under 46), Tufan (Ayhan 64), Calhanoglu; Yilmaz.
Italy: (433) Donnarumma; Florenzi (Di Lorenzo 46), Bonucci, Chiellini, Spinazzola; Barella, Jorginho, Locatelli (Cristante 74); Berardi (Bernardeschi 85), Immobile (Belotti 81), Insigne (Chiesa 81).
Referee: Danny Makkelie.

Baku, Saturday, 12 June 2021

Wales (0) 1 *(Moore 74)*

Switzerland (0) 1 *(Embolo 49)* 8782

Wales: (4141) Ward; Roberts C, Mepham, Rodon, Davies B; Allen; Bale, Morrell, Ramsey (Ampadu 90), James (Brooks 75); Moore.
Switzerland: (3412) Sommer; Elvedi, Schar, Akanji; Mbabu, Freuler, Xhaka, Rodriguez; Shaqiri (Zakaria 66); Seferovic (Gavranovic 84), Embolo.
Referee: Clement Turpin.

Rome, Wednesday, 16 June 2021

Italy (1) 3 *(Locatelli 26, 52, Immobile 89)*

Switzerland (0) 0 12,445

Italy: (433) Donnarumma; Di Lorenzo, Bonucci, Chiellini (Acerbi 24), Spinazzola; Barella (Cristante 87), Jorginho, Locatelli (Pessina 86); Berardi (Toloi 70), Immobile, Insigne (Chiesa 69).
Switzerland: (3412) Sommer; Elvedi, Schar (Zuber 57), Akanji; Mbabu (Widmer 58), Freuler (Sow 84), Xhaka, Rodriguez; Shaqiri (Vargas 76); Seferovic (Gavranovic 46), Embolo.
Referee: Sergei Karasev.

Baku, Wednesday, 16 June 2021

Turkey (0) 0

Wales (1) 2 *(Ramsey 42, Roberts C 90)* 19,762

Turkey: (4141) Cakir; Celik, Ayhan, Soyuncu, Meras (Muldur 72); Yokuslu (Demiral 46); Under (Kahveci 83), Tufan (Yazici 46), Calhanoglu, Karaman (Dervisoglu 75); Yilmaz.
Wales: (4141) Ward; Roberts C, Mepham, Rodon, Davies B; Allen (Ampadu 73); James (Williams N 90), Morrell, Ramsey (Wilson 85), Bale; Moore.
Referee: Artur Soraes Dias.

Rome, Sunday, 20 June 2021

Italy (1) 1 *(Pessina 39)*

Wales (0) 0 11,541

Italy: (433) Donnarumma (Sirigu 89); Toloi, Bonucci (Acerbi 46), Bastoni, Emerson Palmieri; Pessina (Castrovilli 87), Jorginho (Cristante 75), Verratti; Bernardeschi (Raspadori 75), Belotti, Chiesa.
Wales: (343) Ward; Rodon, Ampadu■, Gunter; Roberts C, Morrell (Moore 60), Allen (Levitt 86), Williams N (Davies B 86); Bale (Brooks 86), Ramsey, James (Wilson 74).
Referee: Ovidiu Alin Hategan.

Baku, Sunday, 20 June 2021

Switzerland (2) 3 *(Seferovic 6, Shaqiri 26, 68)*

Turkey (0) 1 *(Kahveci 62)* 17,138

Switzerland: (3412) Sommer; Elvedi, Akanji, Rodriguez; Widmer (Mbabu 90), Freuler, Xhaka, Zuber (Benito 85); Shaqiri (Vargas 75); Seferovic (Gavranovic 75), Embolo (Mehmedi 86).
Turkey: (4141) Cakir; Celik, Demiral, Soyuncu, Muldur; Ayhan (Yokuslu 63); Under (Karaman 80), Tufan (Yazici 63), Kahveci (Kokcu 80), Calhanoglu (Tokoz 86); Yilmaz.
Referee: Slavko Vincic.

Group A Table	P	W	D	L	F	A	GD	Pts
Italy	3	3	0	0	7	0	7	9
Wales	3	1	1	1	3	2	1	4
Switzerland*	3	1	1	1	4	5	–1	4
Turkey	3	0	0	3	1	8	–7	0

GROUP B

St Petersburg, Saturday, 12 June 2021

Belgium (2) 3 *(Lukaku 10, 88, Meunier 34)*

Russia (0) 0 26,264

Belgium: (343) Courtois; Alderweireld, Boyata, Vertonghen (Vermaelen 76); Castagne (Meunier 27), Dendoncker, Tielemans, Hazard T; Mertens (Hazard E 72), Lukaku, Carrasco (Praet 77).
Russia: (4231) Shunin; Fernandes, Semenov, Dzhikija, Zhirkov (Karavaev 43); Barinov (Diveev 46), Ozdoev; Zobnin (Mukhin 63), Golovin, Kuzyaev (Cheryshev 29 (Aleksey Miranchuk 63)); Dzyuba.
Referee: Antonio Miguel Mateu Lahoz.

Copenhagen, Saturday, 12 June 2021

Denmark (0) 0

Finland (0) 1 *(Pohjanpalo 60)* 13,790

Denmark: (433) Schmeichel; Wass (Stryger Larsen 75), Kjaer (Vestergaard 63), Christensen A, Maehle; Eriksen (Jensen M 43), Hojbjerg, Delaney (Cornelius 76); Poulsen, Wind (Skov Olsen 63), Braithwaite.
Finland: (532) Hradecky; Raitala (Vaisanen L 90), Toivio, Arajuuri, O'Shaughnessy, Uronen; Lod, Sparv (Schuller 76), Kamara; Pohjanpalo (Forss 84), Pukki (Kauko 76).
Referee: Anthony Taylor.

St Petersburg, Wednesday, 16 June 2021

Finland (0) 0

Russia (1) 1 *(Miranchuk 45)* 24,540

Finland: (532) Hradecky; Raitala (Soiri 75), Toivio (Jensen 84), Arajuuri, O'Shaughnessy, Uronen; Lod, Schuller (Kauko 67), Kamara; Pukki (Lappalainen 75), Pohjanpalo.
Russia: (3421) Safonov; Barinov, Diveev, Dzhikija; Fernandes (Karavaev 26), Ozdoev (Zhemaletdinov 61), Zobnin, Kuzyaev; Aleksey Miranchuk (Mukhin 85), Golovin; Dzyuba (Sobolev 85).
Referee: Danny Makkelie.

Copenhagen, Thursday, 17 June 2021

Denmark (1) 1 *(Poulsen 2)*

Belgium (0) 2 *(Hazard T 54, De Bruyne 70)* 23,395

Denmark: (3421) Schmeichel; Christensen A, Kjaer, Vestergaard (Skov Olsen 84); Wass (Stryger Larsen 62), Hojbjerg, Delaney (Jensen M 72), Maehle; Braithwaite, Damsgaard (Cornelius 72); Poulsen (Norgaard 62).
Belgium: (3421) Courtois; Alderweireld, Denayer, Vertonghen; Meunier, Dendoncker (Witsel 59), Tielemans, Hazard T (Vermaelen 90); Mertens (De Bruyne 46), Carrasco (Hazard E 59); Lukaku.
Referee: Bjorn Kuipers.

St Petersburg, Monday, 21 June 2021

Finland (0) 0

Belgium (0) 2 *(Hradecky 74 (og), Lukaku 81)* 18,545

Finland: (532) Hradecky; Raitala, Toivio, Arajuuri, O'Shaughnessy, Uronen (Alho 70); Lod (Forss 90), Sparv (Schuller 59), Kamara; Pukki (Jensen 90), Pohjanpalo (Kauko 70).
Belgium: (3421) Courtois; Denayer, Boyata, Vermaelen; Trossard (Meunier 75), De Bruyne (Vanaken 90), Witsel, Chadli; Doku (Batshuayi 75), Hazard E; Lukaku (Benteke 84).
Referee: Felix Brych.

Copenhagen, Monday, 21 June 2021

Russia (0) 1 *(Dzyuba 70 (pen))*

Denmark (1) 4 *(Damsgaard 38, Poulsen 59, Christensen A 79, Maehle 82)* 23,644

Russia: (3421) Safonov; Dzhikija, Diveev, Kudryashov (Karavaev 67); Fernandes, Ozdoev (Zhemaletdinov 61), Zobnin, Kuzyaev (Mukhin 67); Miranchuk (Sobolev 61), Golovin; Dzyuba.
Denmark: (3421) Schmeichel; Christensen A, Kjaer, Vestergaard; Wass (Stryger Larsen 60), Hojbjerg, Delaney (Jensen M 86), Maehle; Braithwaite (Cornelius 85), Damsgaard (Norgaard 72); Poulsen (Dolberg 60).
Referee: Clement Turpin.

Group B Table	P	W	D	L	F	A	GD	Pts
Belgium	3	3	0	0	7	1	6	9
Denmark	3	1	0	2	5	4	1	3
Finland	3	1	0	2	1	3	–2	3
Russia	3	1	0	2	2	7	–5	3

GROUP C

Bucharest, Sunday, 13 June 2021

Austria (1) 3 *(Lainer 18, Gregoritsch 78, Arnautovic 89)*
North Macedonia (1) 1 *(Pandev 28)* 9082

Austria: (3142) Bachmann; Dragovic (Lienhart 46), Alaba, Hinteregger; Schlager (Ilsanker 90); Lainer, Laimer (Baumgartlinger 90), Sabitzer, Ulmer; Kalajdzic (Arnautovic 59), Baumgartner (Gregoritsch 58).
North Macedonia: (532) Dimitrievski; Nikolov (Bejtulai 64), Ristovski S, Velkovski, Musliu (Ristovski M 86), Alioski; Bardhi (Trickovski 82), Ademi, Elmas; Pandev, Trajkovski (Kostadinov 63).
Referee: Andreas Ekberg.

Amsterdam, Sunday, 13 June 2021

Netherlands (0) 3 *(Wijnaldum 52, Weghorst 58, Dumfries 85)*
Ukraine (0) 2 *(Yarmolenko 75, Yaremchuk 79)* 15,837

Netherlands: (352) Stekelenburg; Timber (Veltman 88), de Vrij, Blind (Ake 64); Dumfries, de Roon, Wijnaldum, de Jong F, van Aanholt (Wijndal 64); Weghorst (de Jong L 88), Depay (Malen 90).
Ukraine: (433) Bushchan; Karavayev, Zabarnyi, Matviyenko, Mykolenko; Malinovsky, Sydorchuk, Zinchenko; Yarmolenko, Yaremchuk, Zubkov (Marlos 13 (Shaparenko 64)).
Referee: Felix Brych.

Amsterdam, Thursday, 17 June 2021

Netherlands (1) 2 *(Depay 11 (pen), Dumfries 67)*
Austria (0) 0 15,243

Netherlands: (3412) Stekelenburg; de Vrij, de Ligt, Blind (Ake 64); Dumfries, de Roon (Gravenberch 74), de Jong F, van Aanholt (Wijndal 65); Wijnaldum; Weghorst (Malen 64), Depay (de Jong L 82).
Austria: (3142) Bachmann; Dragovic (Lienhart 84), Alaba, Hinteregger; Schlager (Onisiwo 84); Lainer, Laimer (Grillitsch 62), Sabitzer, Ulmer; Baumgartner (Lazaro 70), Gregoritsch (Kalajdzic 61).
Referee: Orel Grinfeeld.

Bucharest, Thursday, 17 June 2021

Ukraine (2) 2 *(Yarmolenko 29, Yaremchuk 34)*
North Macedonia (0) 1 *(Alioski 57)* 10,001

Ukraine: (433) Bushchan; Karavayev, Zabarnyi, Matviyenko, Mykolenko; Shaparenko (Sydorchuk 78), Stepanenko, Zinchenko; Yarmolenko (Tsygankov 70), Yaremchuk (Besyedin 70), Malinovsky (Sobol 90).
North Macedonia: (3412) Dimitrievski; Ristovski S, Velkovski (Trickovski 85), Musliu; Nikolov (Trajkovski 46), Spirovski (Churlinov 46), Bardhi (Avramovski 77), Alioski; Ademi (Ristevski 85); Pandev, Elmas.
Referee: Fernando Rapallini.

Amsterdam, Monday, 21 June 2021

North Macedonia (0) 0
Netherlands (1) 3 *(Depay 24, Wijnaldum 51, 58)* 15,227

North Macedonia: (4231) Dimitrievski; Ristovski S, Velkovski, Musliu, Alioski; Ademi (Nikolov 79), Bardhi (Stojanovski 78); Trickovski (Churlinov 56), Elmas, Trajkovski (Hasani 68); Pandev (Kostadinov 69).
Netherlands: (3412) Stekelenburg; de Vrij (Timber 46), de Ligt, Blind; Dumfries (Berghuis 46), de Jong F (Gakpo 79), Gravenberch, van Aanholt; Wijnaldum; Depay (Weghorst 66), Malen (Promes 66).
Referee: Istvan Kovacs.

Bucharest, Monday, 21 June 2021

Ukraine (0) 0
Austria (1) 1 *(Baumgartner 21)* 10,472

Ukraine: (433) Bushchan; Karavayev, Zabarnyi, Matviyenko, Mykolenko (Besyedin 85); Shaparenko (Marlos 68), Sydorchuk, Zinchenko; Yarmolenko, Yaremchuk, Malinovsky (Tsygankov 46).
Austria: (4231) Bachmann; Lainer, Dragovic, Hinteregger, Alaba; Schlager, Grillitsch; Laimer (Ilsanker 72), Sabitzer, Baumgartner (Schopf 33); Arnautovic (Kalajdzic 90).
Referee: Cuneyt Cakir.

Group C Table	*P*	*W*	*D*	*L*	*F*	*A*	*GD*	*Pts*
Netherlands	3	3	0	0	8	2	6	9
Austria	3	2	0	1	4	3	1	6
Ukraine*	3	1	0	2	4	5	–1	3
North Macedonia	3	0	0	3	2	8	–6	0

GROUP D

Wembley, Sunday, 13 June 2021

England (0) 1 *(Sterling 57)*
Croatia (0) 0 18,497

England: (4231) Pickford; Walker, Stones, Mings, Trippier; Phillips, Rice; Foden (Rashford 71), Mount, Sterling (Calvert-Lewin 90); Kane (Bellingham 82).
Croatia: (433) Livakovic; Vrsaljko, Vida, Caleta-Car, Gvardiol; Modric, Brozovic (Vlasic 70), Kovacic (Pasalic 85); Kramaric (Brekalo 70), Rebic (Petkovic 78), Perisic.
Referee: Daniele Orsato.

Glasgow, Monday, 14 June 2021

Scotland (0) 0
Czech Republic (1) 2 *(Schick 42, 52)* 9847

Scotland: (352) Marshall; Hendry (McGregor C 67), Hanley, Cooper; O'Donnell (Forrest 79), McGinn, McTominay, Armstrong (Fraser 67), Robertson; Dykes (Nisbet 79), Christie (Adams 46).
Czech Republic: (4231) Vaclik; Coufal, Celustka, Kalas, Boril; Kral (Holes 67), Soucek; Masopust (Vydra 72), Darida (Sevcik 87), Jankto (Hlozek 72); Schick (Krmencik 87).
Referee: Daniel Siebert.

Glasgow, Friday, 18 June 2021

Croatia (0) 1 *(Perisic 47)*
Czech Republic (1) 1 *(Schick 37 (pen))* 5607

Croatia: (4231) Livakovic; Vrsaljko, Lovren, Vida, Gvardiol; Modric, Kovacic (Brozovic 87); Perisic, Kramaric (Vlasic 62), Brekalo (Ivanusec 46); Rebic (Petkovic 46).
Czech Republic: (4231) Vaclik; Coufal, Celustka, Kalas, Boril; Holes (Kral 63), Soucek; Masopust (Hlozek 63), Darida (Barak 87), Jankto (Sevcik 74); Schick (Krmencik 75).
Referee: Carlos del Cerro Grande.

Wembley, Friday, 18 June 2021

England (0) 0
Scotland (0) 0 20,306

England: (4231) Pickford; James, Stones, Mings, Shaw; Phillips, Rice; Foden (Grealish 63), Mount, Sterling; Kane (Rashford 74).
Scotland: (352) Marshall; McTominay, Hanley, Tierney; O'Donnell, Gilmour (Armstrong 76), McGinn, McGregor C, Robertson; Adams (Nisbet 86), Dykes.
Referee: Antonio Miguel Mateu Lahoz.

Glasgow, Tuesday, 22 June 2021

Croatia (1) 3 *(Vlasic 17, Modric 62, Perisic 77)*
Scotland (1) 1 *(McGregor 42)* 9896

Croatia: (4231) Livakovic; Juranovic, Lovren, Vida, Gvardiol (Barisic 71); Kovacic, Brozovic; Perisic (Rebic 81), Modric, Vlasic (Ivanusec 76); Petkovic (Kramaric 70).
Scotland: (352) Marshall; McTominay, Hanley (McKenna 33), Tierney; O'Donnell (Patterson 84), McGinn, McGregor C, Armstrong (Fraser 70), Robertson; Dykes, Adams (Nisbet 84).
Referee: Fernando Rapallini.

Wembley, Tuesday, 22 June 2021

Czech Republic (0) 0
England (1) 1 *(Sterling 12)* 19,104

Czech Republic: (4231) Vaclik; Coufal, Celustka, Kalas, Boril; Holes (Vydra 84), Soucek; Masopust (Hlozek 64), Darida (Kral 64), Jankto (Sevcik 46); Schick (Pekhart 75).
England: (4231) Pickford; Walker, Stones (Mings 79), Maguire, Shaw; Phillips, Rice (Henderson J 46); Saka (Sancho 84), Grealish (Bellingham 68), Sterling (Rashford 67); Kane.
Referee: Artur Soraes Dias.

Group D Table	*P*	*W*	*D*	*L*	*F*	*A*	*GD*	*Pts*
England	3	2	1	0	2	0	2	7
Croatia	3	1	1	1	4	3	1	4
Czech Republic*	3	1	1	1	3	2	1	4
Scotland	3	0	1	2	1	5	–4	1

GROUP E

St Petersburg, Monday, 14 June 2021

Poland (0) 1 *(Linetty 46)*

Slovakia (1) 2 *(Szczesny 18 (og), Skriniar 69)* 12,862

Poland: (3142) Szczesny; Bereszynski, Glik, Bednarek; Krychowiak■; Jozwiak, Klich (Moder 85), Linetty (Frankowski 74), Rybus (Puchacz 74); Lewandowski, Zielinski (Swiderski 85).
Slovakia: (4231) Dubravka; Pekarik (Koscelnik 79), Satka, Skriniar, Hubocan; Kucka, Hromada (Hrosovsky 79); Haraslin (Duris 87), Hamsik, Mak (Suslov 87); Duda (Gregus 90).
Referee: Ovidiu Alin Hategan.

Seville, Monday, 14 June 2021

Spain (0) 0 Sweden (0) 0 10,559

Spain: (433) Simon; Llorente M, Laporte, Torres P, Jordi Alba; Koke (Fabian 87), Rodri (Thiago 65), Gonzalez; Torres F (Oyarzabal 74), Morata (Sarabia 66), Olmo (Gerard 74).
Sweden: (442) Olsen; Lustig (Krafth 75), Lindelof, Danielson, Augustinsson; Seb Larsson, Olsson K (Cajuste 84), Ekdal, Forsberg (Bengtsson 84); Berg (Quaison 69), Isak (Claesson 69).
Referee: Slavko Vincic.

St Petersburg, Friday, 18 June 2021

Sweden (0) 1 *(Forsberg 77 (pen))*

Slovakia (0) 0 11,525

Sweden: (442) Olsen; Lustig, Lindelof, Danielson, Augustinsson (Bengtsson 88); Seb Larsson, Olsson K (Claesson 64), Ekdal (Svensson 88), Forsberg (Krafth 90); Berg (Quaison 64), Isak.
Slovakia: (4231) Dubravka; Pekarik (Haraslin 64), Satka, Skriniar, Hubocan (Hancko 84); Kucka, Hrosovsky (Duris 84); Koscelnik, Hamsik (Benes 77), Mak (Weiss 76); Duda.
Referee: Daniel Siebert.

Seville, Saturday, 19 June 2021

Spain (1) 1 *(Morata 25)*

Poland (0) 1 *(Lewandowski 54)* 11,742

Spain: (433) Simon; Llorente M, Laporte, Torres P, Jordi Alba; Koke (Sarabia 68), Rodri, Gonzalez; Gerard (Fabian 68), Morata (Oyarzabal 87), Olmo (Torres F 61).
Poland: (3421) Szczesny; Bereszynski, Glik, Bednarek (Dawidowicz 85); Jozwiak, Klich (Kozlowski 55), Moder (Linetty 85), Puchacz; Swiderski (Frankowski 68), Zielinski; Lewandowski.
Referee: Daniele Orsato.

Seville, Wednesday, 23 June 2021

Slovakia (0) 0

Spain (2) 5 *(Dubravka 30 (og), Laporte 45, Sarabia 56, Torres F 67, Kucka 71 (og))* 11,204

Slovakia: (4231) Dubravka; Pekarik, Satka, Skriniar, Hubocan; Kucka, Hromada (Lobotka 46); Haraslin (Suslov 69), Hamsik (Benes 90), Mak (Weiss 69); Duda (Duris 46).
Spain: (433) Simon; Azpilicueta (Oyarzabal 77), Garcia (Torres P 71), Laporte, Jordi Alba; Koke, Busquets (Thiago 71), Gonzalez; Sarabia, Morata (Torres F 66), Gerard (Traore 77).
Referee: Bjorn Kuipers.

Wednesday, 23 June 2021

Sweden (1) 3 *(Forsberg 2, 59, Claesson 90)*

Poland (0) 2 *(Lewandowski 61, 84)* 14,252

Sweden: (442) Olsen; Lustig (Krafth 68), Lindelof, Danielson, Augustinsson; Seb Larsson, Olsson K, Ekdal, Forsberg (Claesson 77); Quaison (Kulusevski 55), Isak (Berg 68).
Poland: (3412) Szczesny; Bereszynski, Glik, Bednarek; Jozwiak (Swierczok 61), Krychowiak (Placheta 78), Klich (Kozlowski 73), Puchacz (Frankowski 46); Zielinski; Swiderski, Lewandowski.
Referee: Michael Oliver.

Group E Table	*P*	*W*	*D*	*L*	*F*	*A*	*GD*	*Pts*
Sweden	3	2	1	0	4	2	2	7
Spain	3	1	2	0	6	1	5	5
Slovakia	3	1	0	2	2	7	–5	3
Poland	3	0	1	2	4	6	–2	1

GROUP F

Munich, Tuesday, 15 June 2021

France (1) 1 *(Hummels 20 (og))*

Germany (0) 0 13,000

France: (433) Lloris; Pavard, Varane, Kimpembe, Lucas; Pogba, Kante, Rabiot (Dembele 90); Griezmann, Benzema (Tolisso 89), Mbappe-Lottin.
Germany: (3421) Neuer; Ginter (Can 87), Hummels, Rudiger; Kimmich, Gundogan, Kroos, Gosens (Volland 87); Havertz (Sane 74), Muller; Gnabry (Werner 74).
Referee: Carlos del Cerro Grande.

Budapest, Tuesday, 15 June 2021

Hungary (0) 0

Portugal (0) 3 *(Guerreiro 84, Ronaldo 87 (pen), 90)* 55,662

Hungary: (352) Gulacsi; Botka, Orban, Attila Szalai; Lovrencsics, Kleinheisler (Siger 78), Nagy A (Varga R 88), Schafer (Nego 65), Fiola (Varga K 88); Sallai (Schon 77), Adam Szalai.
Portugal: (4231) Rui Patricio; Nelson Semedo, Pepe, Dias, Guerreiro; Danilo Pereira, William Carvalho (Sanches 81); Bernardo Silva (Rafa Silva 71), Bruno Fernandes (Joao Moutinho 89), Jota (Andre Silva 81); Ronaldo.
Referee: Cuneyt Cakir.

Budapest, Saturday, 19 June 2021

Hungary (1) 1 *(Fiola 45)*

France (0) 1 *(Griezmann 66)* 55,998

Hungary: (352) Gulacsi; Botka, Orban, Attila Szalai; Nego, Kleinheisler (Lovrencsics 84), Nagy A, Schafer (Cseri 75), Fiola; Sallai, Adam Szalai (Nikolic 26).
France: (433) Lloris; Pavard, Varane, Kimpembe, Digne; Pogba (Tolisso 76), Kante, Rabiot (Dembele 57 (Lemar 87)); Griezmann, Benzema (Giroud 76), Mbappe-Lottin.
Referee: Michael Oliver.

Munich, Saturday, 19 June 2021

Portugal (1) 2 *(Ronaldo 15, Jota 67)*

Germany (2) 4 *(Dias 35 (og), Guerreiro 39 (og), Havertz 51, Gosens 60)* 12,926

Portugal: (4141) Rui Patricio; Nelson Semedo, Pepe, Dias, Guerreiro; Danilo Pereira; Bernardo Silva (Sanches 46), Bruno Fernandes (Joao Moutinho 64), William Carvalho (Rafa Silva 58), Jota (Andre Silva 83); Ronaldo.
Germany: (3421) Neuer; Ginter, Hummels (Can 63), Rudiger; Kimmich, Gundogan (Sule 73), Kroos, Gosens (Halstenberg 62); Muller, Havertz (Goretzka 73); Gnabry (Sane 88).
Referee: Anthony Taylor.

Munich, Wednesday, 23 June 2021

Germany (0) 2 *(Havertz 66, Goretzka 84)*

Hungary (1) 2 *(Adam Szalai 11, Schafer 68)* 12,413

Germany: (3421) Neuer; Ginter (Volland 82), Hummels, Rudiger; Kimmich, Gundogan (Goretzka 58), Kroos, Gosens (Musiala 82); Havertz (Werner 67), Sane; Gnabry (Muller 67).
Hungary: (532) Gulacsi; Nego, Botka, Orban, Attila Szalai, Fiola (Nikolic 88); Kleinheisler (Lovrencsics 89), Nagy A, Schafer; Sallai (Schon 75), Adam Szalai (Varga K 82).
Referee: Sergei Karasev.

Budapest, Wednesday, 23 June 2021

Portugal (1) 2 *(Ronaldo 30 (pen), 60 (pen))*

France (1) 2 *(Benzema 45 (pen), 47)* 54,886

Portugal: (4141) Rui Patricio; Nelson Semedo (Dalot 79), Pepe, Dias, Guerreiro; Danilo Pereira (Joao Palhinha 46); Bernardo Silva (Bruno Fernandes 72), Joao Moutinho (Neves 73), Sanches (Sergio Oliveira 88), Jota; Ronaldo.
France: (4231) Lloris; Kounde, Varane, Kimpembe, Lucas (Digne 46 (Rabiot 52)); Pogba, Kante; Tolisso (Coman 66), Griezmann (Sissoko 87), Mbappe-Lottin; Benzema.
Referee: Antonio Miguel Mateu Lahoz.

Group F Table	*P*	*W*	*D*	*L*	*F*	*A*	*GD*	*Pts*
France	3	1	2	0	4	3	1	5
Germany	3	1	1	1	6	5	1	4
Portugal*	3	1	1	1	7	6	1	4
Hungary	3	0	2	1	3	6	–3	2

ROUND OF 16

Wembley, Saturday, 26 June 2021

Italy (0) 2 *(Chiesa 95, Pessina 105)*

Austria (0) 1 *(Kalajdzic 114)* 18,910

Italy: (433) Donnarumma; Di Lorenzo, Bonucci, Acerbi, Spinazzola; Barella (Pessina 67), Jorginho, Verratti (Locatelli 67); Berardi (Chiesa 84), Immobile (Belotti 84), Insigne (Cristante 108).
Austria: (4231) Bachmann; Lainer (Trimmel 114), Dragovic, Hinteregger, Alaba; Schlager (Gregoritsch 106), Grillitsch (Schaub 106); Laimer (Ilsanker 114), Sabitzer, Baumgartner (Schopf 90); Arnautovic (Kalajdzic 97).
aet. Referee: Anthony Taylor.

Amsterdam, Saturday, 26 June 2021

Wales (0) 0

Denmark (1) 4 *(Dolberg 27, 48, Maehle 88, Braithwaite 90)* 14,645

Wales: (4231) Ward; Roberts C (Williams N 40), Mepham, Rodon, Davies B; Morrell (Wilson■ 59), Allen; Bale, Ramsey, James (Brooks 78); Moore (Roberts T 78).
Denmark: (3421) Schmeichel; Christensen A, Kjaer (Andersen 77), Vestergaard; Stryger Larsen (Boilesen 77), Hojbjerg, Delaney (Jensen M 60), Maehle; Braithwaite, Damsgaard (Norgaard 60); Dolberg (Cornelius 70).
Referee: Daniel Siebert.

Seville, Sunday, 27 June 2021

Belgium (1) 1 *(Hazard T 42)*

Portugal (0) 0 11,504

Belgium: (3421) Courtois; Alderweireld, Vermaelen, Vertonghen; Meunier, Tielemans, Witsel, Hazard T (Dendoncker 90); De Bruyne (Mertens 48), Hazard E (Carrasco 87); Lukaku.
Portugal: (433) Rui Patricio; Dalot, Pepe, Dias, Guerreiro; Joao Moutinho (Joao Felix 55), Joao Palhinha (Danilo Pereira 78), Sanches (Sergio Oliveira 78); Bernardo Silva (Bruno Fernandes 55), Ronaldo, Jota (Andre Silva 70).
Referee: Felix Brych.

Budapest, Sunday, 27 June 2021

Netherlands (0) 0

Czech Republic (0) 2 *(Holes 68, Schick 80)* 52,834

Netherlands: (3412) Stekelenburg; de Vrij, de Ligt■, Blind (Timber 81); Dumfries, de Roon (Weghorst 73), de Jong F, van Aanholt (Berghuis 81); Wijnaldum; Depay, Malen (Promes 57).
Czech Republic: (4231) Vaclik; Coufal, Celustka, Kalas, Kaderabek; Holes (Kral 85), Soucek; Masopust (Jankto 79), Barak (Sadilek 90), Sevcik (Hlozek 85); Schick (Krmencik 90).
Referee: Sergei Karasev.

Copenhagen, Monday, 28 June 2021

Croatia (1) 3 *(Gonzalez 20 (og), Orsic 85, Pasalic 90)*

Spain (1) 5 *(Sarabia 38, Azpilicueta 57, Torres F 77, Morata 100, Oyarzabal 103)* 22,771

Croatia: (433) Livakovic; Juranovic (Brekalo 74), Vida, Caleta-Car, Gvardiol; Modric (Ivanusec 114), Brozovic, Kovacic (Budimir 79); Vlasic (Pasalic 79), Petkovic (Kramaric 46), Rebic (Orsic 67).
Spain: (433) Simon; Azpilicueta, Garcia (Torres P 72), Laporte, Gaya (Jordi Alba 77); Koke (Fabian 78), Busquets (Rodri 102), Gonzalez; Torres F (Oyarzabal 88), Morata, Sarabia (Olmo 71).
aet. Referee: Cuneyt Cakir.

Bucharest, Monday, 28 June 2021

France (0) 3 *(Benzema 57, 59, Pogba 75)*

Switzerland (1) 3 *(Seferovic 15, 81, Gavranovic 90)* 22,642

France: (3412) Lloris; Varane, Lenglet (Coman 46 (Thuram 111)), Kimpembe; Pavard, Pogba, Kante, Rabiot; Griezmann (Sissoko 88); Benzema (Giroud 94), Mbappe-Lottin.
Switzerland: (3412) Sommer; Elvedi, Akanji, Rodriguez (Mehmedi 87); Widmer (Mbabu 73), Freuler, Xhaka, Zuber (Fassnacht 79); Shaqiri (Gavranovic 73); Embolo (Vargas 79), Seferovic (Schar 97).
aet; Switzerland won 5-4 on penalties.
Referee: Fernando Rapallini.

Wembley, Tuesday, 29 June 2021

England (0) 2 *(Sterling 75, Kane 86)*

Germany (0) 0 41,973

England: (343) Pickford; Walker, Stones, Maguire; Trippier, Phillips, Rice (Henderson J 88), Shaw; Saka (Grealish 69), Kane, Sterling.
Germany: (3421) Neuer; Ginter (Can 87), Hummels, Rudiger; Kimmich, Kroos, Goretzka, Gosens (Sane 87); Havertz, Muller (Musiala 90); Werner (Gnabry 68).
Referee: Danny Makkelie.

Glasgow, Tuesday, 29 June 2021

Sweden (1) 1 *(Forsberg 43)*

Ukraine (1) 2 *(Zinchenko 27, Dovbyk 120)* 9221

Sweden: (442) Olsen; Lustig (Krafth 83), Lindelof, Danielson■, Augustinsson (Bengtsson 83); Seb Larsson (Claesson 97), Olsson K (Helander 101), Ekdal, Forsberg; Kulusevski (Quaison 97), Isak (Berg 97).
Ukraine: (352) Bushchan; Zabarnyi, Kryvtsov, Matviyenko; Karavayev, Sydorchuk (Bezus 117), Stepanenko (Makarenko 95), Shaparenko (Malinovsky 61), Zinchenko; Yarmolenko (Dovbyk 106), Yaremchuk (Besyedin 91 (Tsygankov 101)).
aet.
Referee: Daniele Orsato.

QUARTER-FINALS

Munich, Friday, 2 July 2021

Belgium (1) 1 *(Lukaku 45 (pen))*

Italy (2) 2 *(Barella 31, Insigne 44)* 12,984

Belgium: (3421) Courtois; Alderweireld, Vermaelen, Vertonghen; Meunier (Chadli 70 (Praet 74)), Tielemans (Mertens 69), Witsel, Hazard T; De Bruyne, Doku; Lukaku.
Italy: (433) Donnarumma; Di Lorenzo, Bonucci, Chiellini, Spinazzola (Emerson Palmieri 80); Barella, Jorginho, Verratti (Cristante 74); Chiesa (Toloi 90), Immobile (Belotti 75), Insigne (Berardi 79).
Referee: Slavko Vincic.

St Petersburg, Friday, 2 July 2021

Switzerland (0) 1 *(Shaqiri 68)*

Spain (1) 1 *(Zakaria 8 (og))* 24,764

Switzerland: (4231) Sommer; Widmer (Mbabu 100), Elvedi, Akanji, Rodriguez; Zakaria (Schar 100), Freuler■; Embolo (Vargas 23), Shaqiri (Sow 81), Zuber (Fassnacht 90); Seferovic (Gavranovic 82).
Spain: (433) Simon; Azpilicueta, Laporte, Torres P (Thiago 113), Jordi Alba; Koke (Llorente M 90), Busquets, Gonzalez (Rodri 119); Torres F (Oyarzabal 91), Morata (Gerard 54), Sarabia (Olmo 46).
aet; Spain won 3-1 on penalties.
Referee: Michael Oliver.

Baku, Saturday, 3 July 2021

Czech Republic (0) 1 *(Schick 49)*

Denmark (2) 2 *(Delaney 5, Dolberg 42)* 16,306

Czech Republic: (4231) Vaclik; Coufal, Celustka (Brabec 65), Kalas, Boril; Holes (Jankto 46), Soucek; Masopust (Krmencik 46), Barak, Sevcik (Darida 79); Schick (Vydra 79).
Denmark: (3421) Schmeichel; Christensen A (Andersen 81), Kjaer, Vestergaard; Stryger Larsen (Wass 70), Hojbjerg, Delaney (Jensen M 81), Maehle; Damsgaard (Norgaard 60), Braithwaite; Dolberg (Poulsen 59).
Referee: Bjorn Kuipers.

Rome, Saturday, 3 July 2021

Ukraine (0) 0

England (1) 4 *(Kane 4, 50, Maguire 46, Henderson J 63)* 11,880

Ukraine: (352) Bushchan; Zabarnyi, Kryvtsov (Tsygankov 35), Matviyenko; Karavayev, Shaparenko, Sydorchuk (Makarenko 64), Zinchenko, Mykolenko; Yarmolenko, Yaremchuk.
England: (4231) Pickford; Walker, Stones, Maguire, Shaw (Trippier 65); Phillips (Bellingham 65), Rice (Henderson J 57); Sancho, Mount, Sterling (Rashford 65); Kane (Calvert-Lewin 73).
Referee: Felix Brych.

SEMI-FINALS

Tuesday, 6 July 2021

Italy (0) 1 *(Chiesa 60)*

Spain (0) 1 *(Morata 80)* 57,811

Italy: (433) Donnarumma; Di Lorenzo, Bonucci, Chiellini, Emerson Palmieri (Toloi 74); Barella (Locatelli 85), Jorginho, Verratti (Pessina 74); Chiesa (Bernardeschi 107), Immobile (Berardi 61), Insigne (Belotti 85).
Spain: (433) Simon; Azpilicueta (Llorente M 85), Garcia (Torres P 109), Laporte, Jordi Alba; Koke (Rodri 70), Busquets (Thiago 106), Gonzalez; Oyarzabal (Gerard 70), Olmo, Torres F (Morata 62).
aet; Italy won 4-2 on penalties.
Referee: Felix Brych.

Wednesday, 7 July 2021

England (1) 2 *(Kjaer 39 (og), Kane 104)*

Denmark (1) 1 *(Damsgaard 30)* 64,950

England: (4231) Pickford; Walker, Stones, Maguire, Shaw; Phillips, Rice (Henderson J 95); Saka (Grealish 69 (Trippier 106)), Mount (Foden 95), Sterling; Kane.
Denmark: (343) Schmeichel; Christensen A (Andersen 79), Kjaer, Vestergaard (Wind 105); Stryger Larsen (Wass 67), Hojbjerg, Delaney (Jensen M 88), Maehle; Braithwaite, Dolberg (Norgaard 67), Damsgaard (Poulsen 67).
aet.
Referee: Danny Makkelie.

EURO 2020 FINAL

Sunday, 11 July 2021

(at Wembley, attendance 67,173)

Italy (0) 1 England (1) 1

Italy: (433) Donnarumma; Di Lorenzo, Bonucci, Chiellini, Emerson Palmieri (Florenzi 118); Barella (Cristante 54), Jorginho, Verratti (Locatelli 96); Chiesa (Bernardeschi 86), Immobile (Berardi 55), Insigne (Belotti 91).
Scorer: Bonucci 67.

England: (3421) Pickford; Walker (Sancho 120), Stones, Maguire; Trippier (Saka 70), Phillips, Rice (Henderson J 74 (Rashford 120)), Shaw; Sterling, Mount (Grealish 99); Kane.
Scorer: Shaw 2.

aet; Italy won 3-2 on penalties.

Referee: Bjorn Kuipers.

EUROPEAN FOOTBALL CHAMPIONSHIP 1960–2020

Year	Winners v Runners-up		Venue	Attendance	Referee
1960	USSR v Yugoslavia	2-1*	Paris	17,966	A. E. Ellis (England)
	Winning Coach: Gavriil Kachalin				
1964	Spain v USSR	2-1	Madrid	79,115	A. E. Ellis (England)
	Winning Coach: Jose Villalonga				
1968	Italy v Yugoslavia	1-1	Rome	68,817	G. Dienst (Switzerland)
Replay	Italy v Yugoslavia	2-0	Rome	32,866	J. M. O. de Mendibil (Spain)
	Winning Coach: Ferruccio Valcareggi				
1972	West Germany v USSR	3-0	Brussels	43,066	F. Marschall (Austria)
	Winning Coach: Helmut Schon				
1976	Czechoslovakia v West Germany	2-2	Belgrade	30,790	S. Gonella (Italy)
	Czechoslovakia won 5-3 on penalties.				
	Winning Coach: Vaclav Jezek				
1980	West Germany v Belgium	2-1	Rome	47,860	N. Rainea (Romania)
	Winning Coach: Jupp Derwall				
1984	France v Spain	2-0	Paris	47,368	V. Christov (Slovakia)
	Winning Coach: Michel Hidalgo				
1988	Netherlands v USSR	2-0	Munich	62,770	M. Vautrot (France)
	Winning Coach: Rinus Michels				
1992	Denmark v Germany	2-0	Gothenburg	37,800	B. Galler (Switzerland)
	Winning Coach: Richard Moller Nielsen				
1996	Germany v Czech Republic	2-1*	Wembley	73,611	P. Pairetto (Italy)
	Germany won on sudden death 'golden goal'.				
	Winning Coach: Berti Vogts				
2000	France v Italy	2-1*	Rotterdam	48,200	A. Frisk (Sweden)
	France won on sudden death 'golden goal'.				
	Winning Coach: Roger Lemerre				
2004	Greece v Portugal	1-0	Lisbon	62,865	M. Merk (Germany)
	Winning Coach: Otto Rehhagel				
2008	Spain v Germany	1-0	Vienna	51,428	R. Rosetti (Italy)
	Winning Coach: Luis Aragones				
2012	Spain v Italy	4-0	Kiev	63,170	P. Proenca (Portugal)
	Winning Coach: Vicente del Bosque				
2016	Portugal v France	1-0*	Paris	75,868	M. Clattenburg (England)
	Winning Coach: Fernando Santos				
2020†	Italy v England	1-1*	Wembley	67,173	B. Kuipers (Netherlands)
	Italy won 3-2 on penalties.				
	Winning Coach: Roberto Mancini.				

**After extra time. †Postponed until 2021 due to COVID-19 pandemic.*

FIFA WORLD CUP 2022 QUALIFYING – EUROPE

■ *Denotes player sent off.*
Behind closed doors unless otherwise stated.

GROUP A

Wednesday, 24 March 2021

Portugal (1) 1 *(Medvedev 37 (og))*

Azerbaijan (0) 0

Portugal: (433) Lopes; Joao Cancelo, Domingos Duarte, Dias, Nuno Mendes; Bernardo Silva (Sergio Oliveira 88), Joao Moutinho (Bruno Fernandes 46), Neves (Joao Palhinha 88); Pedro Neto (Rafa Silva 63), Andre Silva (Joao Felix 75), Ronaldo.
Azerbaijan: (4411) Mahammadaliyev; Medvedev, Huseynov B, Badalov, Krivotsyuk; Huseynov A (Nuriev 46), Mahmudov (Isaev 85), Mustafayev (Ibrahhimli 46), Salahli; Emreli (Alasgarov 85); Ghorbani (Sheydayev 85).

Serbia (1) 3 *(Vlahovic 40, Mitrovic A 68, 75)*

Republic of Ireland (1) 2 *(Browne 18, Collins 86)*

Serbia: (343) Dmitrovic; Milenkovic, Mitrovic S, Pavlovic; Gajic, Lukic, Racic (Nemanja Maksimovic 63), Mladenovic (Kostic 46); Tadic (Gudelj 78), Vlahovic (Jovic 82), Djuricic (Mitrovic A 63).
Republic of Ireland: (352) Travers; Coleman, O'Shea, Clark (Brady 79); Doherty, Molumby (Hendrick 61), Cullen, Browne (Collins 79), Stevens; Robinson (McClean 79), Connolly (Long S 67).

Saturday, 27 March 2021

Republic of Ireland (0) 0

Luxembourg (0) 1 *(Rodrigues 85)*

Republic of Ireland: (3412) Bazunu; Coleman, O'Shea, Clark (McClean 61); Doherty (Brady 46), Knight, Cullen (Molumby 88), Stevens; Browne; Collins (Parrott 88), Robinson (Long S 73).
Luxembourg: (4141) Moris; Da Graca, Chanot, Mahmutovic, Jans; Martins Pereira; Thill V (Deville 79), Thill O, Barreiro, Rodrigues; Sinani (Gerson 90).

Serbia (0) 2 *(Mitrovic A 46, Kostic 60)*

Portugal (2) 2 *(Jota 11, 36)*

Serbia: (3412) Dmitrovic; Milenkovic■, Mitrovic S, Pavlovic; Lazovic (Nemanja Maksimovic 46), Milinkovic-Savic, Gudelj, Kostic (Ristic 72); Tadic (Djuricic 82); Vlahovic (Radonjic 46), Mitrovic A (Jovic 88).
Portugal: (433) Lopes; Cedric, Fonte, Dias, Joao Cancelo (Nuno Mendes 72); Bruno Fernandes (Joao Palhinha 90), Danilo Pereira, Sergio Oliveira (Sanches 73); Bernardo Silva, Ronaldo, Jota (Joao Felix 85).

Tuesday, 30 March 2021

Azerbaijan (0) 1 *(Mahmudov 59 (pen))*

Serbia (1) 2 *(Mitrovic A 16, 81)*

Azerbaijan: (532) Mahammadaliyev; Huseynov A, Huseynov B, Medvedev, Badalov, Krivotsyuk; Mahmudov, Ibrahhimli, Salahli (Khalilzade 72); Nuriev (Emreli 69 (Dzhafarquliyev 79)), Ghorbani (Sheydayev 69).
Serbia: (352) Rajkovic; Spajic, Mitrovic S, Pavlovic; Radonjic (Ristic 86), Milinkovic-Savic, Gudelj, Nemanja Maksimovic (Grujic 64), Kostic (Zivkovic 64); Mitrovic A (Vlahovic 86), Tadic (Jovic 75).

Luxembourg (1) 1 *(Rodrigues 30)*

Portugal (1) 3 *(Jota 45, Ronaldo 50, Joao Palhinha 80)*

Luxembourg: (442) Moris; Jans, Chanot■, Gerson, Mica Pinto (Da Graca 66); Thill V (Deville 58), Martins Pereira (Skenderovic 87), Barreiro, Thill O (Thill S 58); Rodrigues, Sinani (Muratovic 87).
Portugal: (4231) Lopes; Joao Cancelo, Fonte, Dias, Nuno Mendes; Neves (Sergio Oliveira 89), Sanches; Bernardo Silva (Joao Palhinha 68), Joao Felix (Pedro Neto 41), Jota (Rafa Silva 68); Ronaldo.

Group A Table	P	W	D	L	F	A	GD	Pts
Portugal	3	2	1	0	6	3	3	7
Serbia	3	2	1	0	7	5	2	7
Luxembourg	2	1	0	1	2	3	–1	3
Republic of Ireland	2	0	0	2	2	4	–2	0
Azerbaijan	2	0	0	2	1	3	–2	0

GROUP B

Thursday, 25 March 2021

Spain (1) 1 *(Morata 33)*

Greece (0) 1 *(Bakasetas 56 (pen))*

Spain: (4141) Simon; Llorente M, Garcia, Sergio Ramos (Martinez 46), Gaya; Rodri; Torres F (Oyarzabal 72), Koke (Thiago 72), Canales (Gil Salvatierra 65), Olmo (Gonzalez 64); Morata.
Greece: (4141) Vlachodimos; Bakakis, Papadopoulos, Tzavelas, Tsimikas (Kyriakopoulos 80); Zeca; Limnios (Siopis 46), Bouchalakis, Mandalos (Tzolis 46), Masouras (Fortounis 65); Bakasetas (Giakoumakis 78).

Sweden (1) 1 *(Claesson 35)*

Georgia (0) 0

Sweden: (442) Nordfeldt; Lustig (Krafth 84), Lindelof, Helander, Augustinsson; Kulusevski, Olsson K (Ekdal 68 (Svanberg 73)), Seb Larsson, Claesson (Forsberg 74); Isak, Ibrahimovic (Quaison 84).
Georgia: (4231) Loria; Chabradze, Kashia, Dvali, Giorbelidze; Kankava (Gvilia 60), Aburjania; Lobzhanidze (Beridze 78), Kvekveskiri (Shengelia 60), Kvaratskhelia (Kiteishvili 46); Kvilitaia (Mikautadze 84).

Sunday, 28 March 2021

Georgia (1) 1 *(Kvaratskhelia 43)*

Spain (0) 2 *(Torres F 56, Olmo 90)*

Georgia: (4231) Loria; Kakabadze (Chabradze 79), Kashia, Dvali, Giorbelidze; Gvilia, Kankava; Lobzhanidze (Shengelia■ 70), Kiteishvili (Beridze 71), Kvaratskhelia (Kvekveskiri 79); Zivzivadze (Kvilitaia 62).
Spain: (4141) Simon; Porro (Llorente M 65), Llorente D (Martinez 46), Garcia, Jordi Alba; Busquets (Oyarzabal 73); Torres F, Fabian (Thiago 55), Gonzalez, Gil Salvatierra (Olmo 46); Morata.

Kosovo (0) 0

Sweden (2) 3 *(Augustinsson 12, Isak 35, Seb Larsson 70 (pen))*

Kosovo: (4231) Ujkani; Hadergjonaj, Vojvoda, Aliti, Kololli; Halimi (Voca 75), Kryeziu; Rashica (Kastrati 71), Celina, Zeneli (Berisha B■ 83); Muriqi.
Sweden: (442) Nordfeldt; Lustig, Lindelof, Helander, Augustinsson (Bengtsson 83); Claesson (Kulusevski 83), Olsson K (Svanberg 90), Seb Larsson, Forsberg; Isak (Quaison 68), Ibrahimovic (Berg 67).

Wednesday, 31 March 2021

Greece (0) 1 *(Kakabadze 76 (og))*

Georgia (0) 1 *(Kvaratskhelia 78)*

Greece: (4231) Vlachodimos; Bakakis (Mavrias 42), Papadopoulos, Tzavelas, Giannoulis; Bouchalakis (Siopis 87), Zeca; Tzolis (Limnios 46), Bakasetas (Masouras 71), Fortounis; Pavlidis (Giakoumakis 71).
Georgia: (4231) Loria; Kakabadze, Kashia, Dvali, Giorbelidze; Kankava, Aburjania (Gvilia 74); Lobzhanidze (Azouz 84), Kiteishvili (Kvekveskiri 84), Kvaratskhelia; Zivzivadze (Kvilitaia 63).

Spain (2) 3 *(Olmo 34, Torres F 36, Gerard 75)*

Kosovo (0) 1 *(Halimi 70)*

Spain: (433) Simon; Llorente M, Garcia (Sergio Ramos 86), Martinez, Jordi Alba; Koke, Busquets (Rodri 82), Gonzalez (Fabian 69); Torres F, Morata (Gerard 69), Olmo (Canales 82).
Kosovo: (3412) Ujkani; Vojvoda, Dresevic, Aliti; Hadergjonaj, Halimi (Voca 82), Kryeziu, Kololli (Zeneli 57); Celina; Muriqi, Rashica (Kastrati 55).

Group B Table	P	W	D	L	F	A	GD	Pts
Spain	3	2	1	0	6	3	3	7
Sweden	2	2	0	0	4	0	4	6
Greece	2	0	2	0	2	2	0	2
Georgia	3	0	1	2	2	4	–2	1
Kosovo	2	0	0	2	1	6	–5	0

GROUP C

Thursday, 25 March 2021

Bulgaria (0) 1 *(Despodov 46)*

Switzerland (3) 3 *(Embolo 7, Seferovic 10, Zuber 13)*

Bulgaria: (3421) Iliev P; Dimov, Bozhikov, Zanev; Popov S, Kostadinov, Malinov (Chochev 71), Cicinho (Tsvetanov 73); Despodov (Delev 48), Yomov (Iliev I 70); Iliev D (Iliev A 46).
Switzerland: (3412) Sommer; Elvedi, Akanji, Rodriguez; Mbabu, Freuler (Sow 86), Xhaka, Zuber (Zakaria 75); Shaqiri (Vargas 75); Seferovic (Gavranovic 86), Embolo (Mehmedi 90).

Italy (2) 2 *(Berardi 14, Immobile 38)*

Northern Ireland (0) 0

Italy: (433) Donnarumma; Florenzi, Bonucci, Chiellini, Emerson Palmieri (Spinazzola 75); Pellegrini (Barella 64), Locatelli (Pessina 84), Verratti; Berardi (Chiesa 75), Immobile, Insigne (Grifo 84).
Northern Ireland: (532) Peacock-Farrell; Smith, Cathcart, Evans J, McNair, Dallas; Evans C (Saville 46), Davis, McCann (Thompson 78); Whyte (Lavery 64), Magennis (Lafferty 78).

Sunday, 28 March 2021

Bulgaria (0) 0

Italy (1) 2 *(Belotti 43 (pen), Locatelli 82)*

Bulgaria: (352) Iliev P; Antov, Dimov, Bozhikov; Cicinho (Karagaren 46), Kostadinov (Malinov 62), Vitanov (Raynov 88), Chochev, Tsvetanov; Delev (Iliev A 78), Galabinov.
Italy: (433) Donnarumma; Florenzi (Di Lorenzo 68), Bonucci, Acerbi, Spinazzola; Barella, Sensi (Locatelli 68), Verratti (Pessina 88); Chiesa (Bernardeschi 76), Belotti (Immobile 75), Insigne.

Switzerland (1) 1 *(Shaqiri 2)*

Lithuania (0) 0

Switzerland: (3412) Sommer; Elvedi, Akanji, Rodriguez; Widmer (Fernandes 65), Freuler (Zakaria 66), Xhaka, Vargas (Zuber 80); Shaqiri (Mehmedi 80); Embolo (Gavranovic 66), Seferovic.
Lithuania: (4141) Svedkauskas; Mikoliunas, Gaspuitis, Beneta, Vaitkunas; Simkus; Novikovas, Dapkus, Slivka (Eliosius 75), Lasickas (Laukzemis 58); Cernych (Petravicius 81).

Wednesday, 31 March 2021

Lithuania (0) 0

Italy (0) 2 *(Sensi 47, Immobile 90 (pen))*

Lithuania: (4321) Svedkauskas; Mikoliunas (Gaspuitis 74), Beneta, Girdvainis, Vaitkunas; Dapkus, Simkus (Petravicius 83), Slivka; Novikovas, Sirgedas (Eliosius 58); Cernych (Kazlauskas 74).
Italy: (352) Donnarumma; Toloi, Mancini, Bastoni (Acerbi 89); Bernardeschi, Pessina (Barella 62), Locatelli, Pellegrini (Sensi 46), Emerson Palmieri (Spinazzola 56); El Shaarawy (Chiesa 46), Immobile.

Northern Ireland (0) 0

Bulgaria (0) 0

Northern Ireland: (4132) Peacock-Farrell; Ballard (Smith 74), Evans J, Cathcart, Lewis; Davis; Dallas, McNair, Saville (Kennedy 74); Magennis (Lafferty 82), Whyte (McGinn 64).
Bulgaria: (352) Naumov; Hristov P, Antov, Hristov A; Yomov (Karagaren 73), Vutov (Iliev D 46), Kostadinov (Vitanov 44), Chochev, Tsvetanov (Zanev 73); Galabinov (Iliev A 73), Despodov.

Group C Table	P	W	D	L	F	A	GD	Pts
Italy	3	3	0	0	6	0	6	9
Switzerland	2	2	0	0	4	1	3	6
Northern Ireland	2	0	1	1	0	2	–2	1
Bulgaria	3	0	1	2	1	5	–4	1
Lithuania	2	0	0	2	0	3	–3	0

GROUP D

Wednesday, 24 March 2021

Finland (0) 2 *(Pukki 58, 77)*

Bosnia-Herzegovina (0) 2 *(Pjanic 55, Stevanovic 84)*

Finland: (532) Joronen; Alho, Toivio, Arajuuri, Raitala, Hamalainen; Valakari (Schuller 46), Kamara, Kauko (Sparv 82); Lod (Pohjanpalo 77), Pukki.
Bosnia-Herzegovina: (4411) Sehic; Todorovic D, Hadzikadunic, Sanicanin, Civic; Stevanovic (Kolasinac 89), Cimirot (Demirovic 82), Pjanic, Krunic; Gojak (Duljevic 64); Dzeko.

France (1) 1 *(Griezmann 19)*

Ukraine (0) 1 *(Kimpembe 57 (og))*

France: (4231) Lloris; Pavard, Varane, Kimpembe, Lucas; Kante, Rabiot; Coman (Dembele 64), Griezmann, Mbappe-Lottin (Martial 77); Giroud (Pogba 63).
Ukraine: (532) Bushchan; Karavayev, Zabarnyi, Kryvtsov, Matviyenko, Mykolenko; Shaparenko (Zubkov 86), Sydorchuk (Kovalenko 79), Zinchenko; Malinovsky, Yaremchuk (Moraes 73).

Sunday, 28 March 2021

Kazakhstan (0) 0

France (2) 2 *(Dembele 19, Maliy 44 (og))*

Kazakhstan: (532) Mokin; Bystrov, Erlanov, Maliy, Alip, Valiullin (Samorodov 83); Muzhikov (Vorogovskiy 65), Tagybergen, Vassiljev (Astanov 89); Nurgaliev (Karimov 83), Fedin (Tungyshbayev 65).
France: (4231) Lloris; Dubois, Zouma, Lenglet, Digne; Pogba (Rabiot 59), Ndombele (Sissoko 82); Dembele (Coman 90), Griezmann (Ben Yedder 59), Lemar; Martial (Mbappe-Lottin 59).

Ukraine (0) 1 *(Moraes 80)*

Finland (0) 1 *(Pukki 89 (pen))*

Ukraine: (3412) Bushchan; Zabarnyi, Matviyenko, Mykolenko■; Karavayev, Zinchenko, Makarenko (Kovalenko 78), Sobol; Malinovsky; Zubkov (Marlos 58), Yaremchuk (Moraes 67).
Finland: (532) Joronen; Granlund (Alho 17), Toivio, Arajuuri, O'Shaughnessy, Raitala (Hamalainen 76); Kamara, Schuller (Taylor 76), Kauko (Pohjanpalo 68); Lod, Pukki.

Wednesday, 31 March 2021

Bosnia-Herzegovina (0) 0

France (0) 1 *(Griezmann 60)*

Bosnia-Herzegovina: (352) Sehic; Ahmedhodzic, Hadzikadunic, Sanicanin; Todorovic D (Stevanovic 77), Pjanic, Hadziahmetovic, Cimirot (Gojak 86), Kolasinac; Dzeko, Krunic (Prevljak 86).
France: (442) Lloris; Pavard, Varane, Kimpembe, Lucas; Coman (Giroud 59), Pogba, Rabiot, Lemar (Sissoko 90); Griezmann, Mbappe-Lottin.

Ukraine (1) 1 *(Yaremchuk 20)*

Kazakhstan (0) 1 *(Muzhikov 59)*

Ukraine: (3412) Trubin; Kryvtsov, Matviyenko, Mykhaylichenko; Karavayev (Tymchyk 87), Shaparenko (Dovbyk 81), Sydorchuk (Marlos 67), Zinchenko; Malinovsky; Moraes (Zubkov 67), Yaremchuk.
Kazakhstan: (532) Pokatilov; Dosmagambetov (Bystrov 46), Marochkin, Maliy, Alip, Valiullin; Abiken (Vorogovskiy 46), Tagybergen (Orazov 46), Muzhikov; Nurgaliev (Tungyshbayev 87), Aimbetov (Karimov 60).

Group D Table	P	W	D	L	F	A	GD	Pts
France	3	2	1	0	4	1	3	7
Ukraine	3	0	3	0	3	3	0	3
Finland	2	0	2	0	3	3	0	2
Bosnia-Herzegovina	2	0	1	1	2	3	–1	1
Kazakhstan	2	0	1	1	1	3	–2	1

GROUP E

Wednesday, 24 March 2021

Belgium (2) 3 *(De Bruyne 22, Hazard 28, Lukaku 73 (pen))*

Wales (1) 1 *(Wilson 10)*

Belgium: (3421) Courtois; Alderweireld, Vermaelen (Denayer 46), Vertonghen; Meunier, Tielemans, Dendoncker, Hazard (Castagne 84); De Bruyne, Mertens (Trossard 90); Lukaku.
Wales: (343) Ward; Mepham, Rodon, Lawrence J; Roberts C, Allen (Morrell 8), Ampadu, Williams N; Bale (Moore 84), Wilson (Roberts T 66), James.

Estonia (1) 2 *(Sappinen 12, Anier 86)*

Czech Republic (4) 6 *(Schick 18, Barak 27, Soucek 32, 43, 48, Jankto 56)*

Estonia: (4411) Aksalu; Antonov (Puri 74), Purg, Paskotsi, Lilander; Alliku (Kirss 73), Poom, Vastsuk (Frolov 82), Oigus; Vassiljev (Anier 73); Sappinen (Roosnupp 88).
Czech Republic: (4411) Pavlenka; Kaderabek, Kudela, Celustka (Zima 85), Boril; Provod (Vydra 65), Darida, Soucek, Jankto (Masopust 65); Barak (Pekhart 65); Schick (Holes 79).

Saturday, 27 March 2021

Belarus (1) 4 *(Lisakovich 45 (pen), 83, Kendysh 64, Savitskiy 81)*

Estonia (1) 2 *(Anier 31, 55)*

Belarus: (4411) Gutor; Yuzepchuk, Naumov, Bordachev, Zolotov; Ebong (Savitskiy 58), Kendysh (Klimovich 87), Yablonskiy (Signevich 58), Stasevich; Lisakovich (Bakhar 85); Laptev (Kislyak 46).
Estonia: (532) Igonen; Alliku (Oigus■ 62), Purg, Kuusk, Paskotsi (Kirss 87), Lilander; Vassiljev, Poom, Vastsuk; Sappinen (Puri 79), Anier.

Czech Republic (0) 1 *(Provod 50)*

Belgium (0) 1 *(Lukaku 60)*

Czech Republic: (4141) Vaclik; Coufal, Kudela, Celustka, Boril; Holes; Provod (Pekhart 90), Barak (Pavelka 78), Soucek, Jankto (Masopust 61); Krmencik (Vydra 78).
Belgium: (3421) Courtois; Alderweireld, Denayer, Vertonghen; Castagne, Tielemans, Dendoncker, Chadli (Foket 56); De Bruyne, Mertens (Trossard 56); Lukaku.

Tuesday, 30 March 2021

Belgium (4) 8 *(Batshuayi 14, Vanaken 17, 89, Trossard 38, 75, Doku 42, Praet 49, Benteke 70)*

Belarus (0) 0

Belgium: (343) Mignolet; Alderweireld, Denayer (Boyata 46), Vertonghen (Dendoncker 64); Meunier, Praet (Tielemans 71), Vanaken, Hazard; Trossard, Batshuayi (Benteke 64), Doku (Januzaj 77).
Belarus: (541) Gutor; Podstrelov (Signevich 46), Pavlovets, Naumov, Polyakov, Yuzepchuk; Stasevich, Kislyak (Maevskiy 61), Kendysh (Bakhar 87), Ebong (Savitskiy 46); Lisakovich (Klimovich 75).

Wales (0) 1 *(James 81)*

Czech Republic (0) 0

Wales: (343) Ward; Mepham (Moore 56), Rodon, Lawrence J; Roberts C■, Morrell, Ampadu, Williams N; Bale, Wilson (Williams J 76), James.
Czech Republic: (4231) Vaclik; Coufal (Vydra 87), Kudela (Barak 87), Celustka, Boril; Holes (Krmencik 53), Soucek; Provod (Kaderabek 82), Darida, Jankto (Masopust 82); Schick■.

Group E Table	P	W	D	L	F	A	GD	Pts
Belgium	3	2	1	0	12	2	10	7
Czech Republic	3	1	1	1	7	4	3	4
Wales	2	1	0	1	2	3	–1	3
Belarus	2	1	0	1	4	10	–6	3
Estonia	2	0	0	2	4	10	–6	0

GROUP F

Thursday, 25 March 2021

Israel (0) 0

Denmark (1) 2 *(Braithwaite 13, Wind 67)*

Israel: (532) Marciano; Dasa (Kandil 85), Elhamed, Tibi, Abu Hanna (Lavi 46), Menachem (Haziza 85); Natcho (Golasa 68), Peretz, Solomon; Dabbur (Weissman 61), Zahavi.
Denmark: (4231) Schmeichel; Wass, Kjaer, Christensen A, Maehle (Stryger Larsen 86); Hojbjerg, Delaney (Norgaard 88); Poulsen (Skov Olsen 77), Eriksen, Braithwaite; Wind (Andersen 77).

Moldova (1) 1 *(Nicolaescu 9)*

Faroe Islands (0) 1 *(Olsen M 83)*

Moldova: (352) Namasco; Posmac, Epureanu, Armas; Jardan, Rata (Cojocari 86), Carp (Caimacov 72), Ionita, Reabciuk; Nicolaescu, Damascan (Postolachi 73).
Faroe Islands: (442) Nielsen G; Sorensen, Faero (Vatnsdal 40), Nattestad, Davidsen V; Vatnhamar S (Jonsson 78), Hansson (Bjartalid 69), Vatnhamar G, Olsen B; Olsen K, Edmundsson (Olsen M 78).

Scotland (0) 2 *(Hanley 71, McGinn 85)*

Austria (0) 2 *(Kalajdzic 55, 80)*

Scotland: (3421) Marshall; Hendry, Hanley, Tierney; O'Donnell, McTominay, McGinn, Robertson; Christie (McLean 88), Armstrong (Adams 66); Dykes (McGregor C 78).
Austria: (442) Schlager A; Lainer, Dragovic, Lienhart, Alaba; Baumgartner, Grillitsch, Ilsanker, Schlager X; Kalajdzic, Grbic (Schaub 68).

Sunday, 28 March 2021

Austria (3) 3 *(Dragovic 30, Baumgartner 37, Kalajdzic 44)*

Faroe Islands (1) 1 *(Nattestad 19)*

Austria: (442) Schlager A; Lainer (Trimmel 76), Trauner, Dragovic, Ulmer; Schaub (Demir 85), Grillitsch, Alaba (Schopf 64), Baumgartner (Onisiwo 76); Kalajdzic (Gregoritsch 63), Sabitzer.
Faroe Islands: (442) Nielsen G; Sorensen, Vatnsdal (Andreasen 59), Nattestad, Davidsen V; Vatnhamar S (Bjartalid 59), Hansson (Olsen K 81), Vatnhamar G, Olsen B; Edmundsson (Knudsen 74), Olsen M (Johannesen 58).

Denmark (5) 8 *(Dolberg 19 (pen), 48, Damsgaard 21, 29, Larsen 35, Jensen 38, Skov 81, Ingvartsen 89)*

Moldova (0) 0

Denmark: (433) Schmeichel; Stryger Larsen (Kjaer 78), Andersen, Vestergaard, Boilesen; Schöne (Eriksen 77), Norgaard (Jonsson 65), Jensen M (Ingvartsen 78); Skov Olsen (Skov 46), Dolberg, Damsgaard.
Moldova: (4141) Namasco; Arhirii (Bolohan 46), Epureanu, Armas, Reabciuk; Carp (Cojocari 54); Antoniuc (Jardan 46), Rata, Ionita, Platica (Iosipoi 54); Nicolaescu (Damascan 75).

Israel (1) 1 *(Peretz 44)*

Scotland (0) 1 *(Fraser 56)*

Israel: (3412) Marciano; Elhamed, Tibi, Arad; Dasa, Natcho (Lavi 63), Peretz, Menachem (Kayal 79); Solomon; Weissman (Dabbur 74), Zahavi.
Scotland: (3421) Marshall; Hendry (Christie 46), Hanley, Tierney; O'Donnell, McTominay, McGregor C, Robertson; McGinn (McLean 74), Fraser (Armstrong 86); Adams (Dykes 75).

Wednesday, 31 March 2021

Austria (0) 0

Denmark (0) 4 *(Skov Olsen 58, 73, Maehle 63, Hojbjerg 67)*

Austria: (4231) Schlager A; Lainer, Trauner (Posch 82), Dragovic, Ulmer (Friedl 82); Ilsanker (Lazaro 65), Schlager X (Kara 75); Baumgartner, Sabitzer, Alaba; Kalajdzic (Grbic 82).
Denmark: (4231) Schmeichel; Wass (Stryger Larsen 77), Kjaer, Christensen A, Maehle; Delaney (Norgaard 77), Hojbjerg; Poulsen (Skov Olsen 55), Eriksen, Braithwaite (Dolberg 77); Wind (Andersen 65).

Moldova (1) 1 *(Carp 29)*

Israel (1) 4 *(Zahavi 45, Solomon 57, Dabbur 64, Natcho 66)*

Moldova: (352) Koselev; Bolohan (Dumbravanu 79), Epureanu, Armas; Jardan, Carp (Dragan 62), Rata (Iosipoi 79), Cojocari (Cotogoi 73), Reabciuk; Platica, Nicolaescu■.
Israel: (352) Marciano; Taha (Abu Fani 58), Tibi (Abu Hanna 70), Arad; Dasa (Haziza 70), Peretz, Natcho, Solomon, Menachem (Lavi 46); Zahavi (Weissman 79), Dabbur.

Scotland (1) 4 *(McGinn 7, 53, Adams 60, Fraser 70)*

Faroe Islands (0) 0

Scotland: (352) Gordon; McTominay, Hanley, Tierney (McKenna 79); Fraser (Palmer 79), McGinn, McLean, McGregor C (Fleck 73), Robertson; Adams (McBurnie 73), Dykes (Nisbet 68).
Faroe Islands: (442) Nielsen G; Sorensen, Vatnhamar G, Nattestad (Baldvinsson 76), Davidsen V; Vatnhamar S (Johannesen 69), Hansson, Andreasen (Olsen K 69), Olsen B; Edmundsson (Vatnsdal 76), Olsen M (Jonsson 58).

Group F Table	P	W	D	L	F	A	GD	Pts
Denmark	3	3	0	0	14	0	14	9
Scotland	3	1	2	0	7	3	4	5
Israel	3	1	1	1	5	4	1	4
Austria	3	1	1	1	5	7	–2	4
Faroe Islands	3	0	1	2	2	8	–6	1
Moldova	3	0	1	2	2	13	–11	1

GROUP G

Wednesday, 24 March 2021

Gibraltar (0) 0

Norway (2) 3 *(Sorloth 43, Thorstvedt 45, Svensson 57)*

Gibraltar: (541) Coleing; Sergeant, Chipolina R, Wiseman, Mouelhi, Olivero; Walker, Annesley (Barnett 72), Ronan (Bosio 67), Casciaro L (Valarino 78); De Barr.
Norway: (41212) Jarstein; Svensson (Linnes 62), Strandberg, Lode, Meling; Midtsjoe (Nguen 62); Thorstvedt, Elyounoussi M (Hauge 46); Odegaard (Berg 46); Sorloth, Haaland (King 62).

Latvia (1) 1 *(Ikaunieks J 40)*

Montenegro (1) 2 *(Jovetic 41, 83)*

Latvia: (442) Steinbors; Savalnieks, Cernomordijs, Oss, Jurkovskis; Kamess (Jaunzems 71), Zjuzins (Karklins 71), Tobers, Ciganiks (Ikaunieks D 81); Ikaunieks J, Uldrikis (Krollis 81).
Montenegro: (4231) Mijatovic; Marusic, Savic, Vujacic, Radunovic; Scekic, Kosovic; Ivanovic (Jovovic 75), Jovetic (Beciraj 87), Haksabanovic (Boljevic 90); Djurdjevic.

Turkey (2) 4 *(Yilmaz 15, 34 (pen), 81, Calhanoglu 46)*

Netherlands (0) 2 *(Klaassen 75, de Jong L 76)*

Turkey: (451) Cakir; Soyuncu, Celik, Kabak, Meras; Yokuslu, Calhanoglu (Unal 78), Tufan (Antalyali 64), Karaman (Ayhan 78), Yazici (Erkin 64); Yilmaz (Turuc 90).
Netherlands: (451) Krul; Blind (Gravenberch 82), Tete (Dumfries 69), de Ligt, Wijndal (van Aanholt 82); Wijnaldum, de Roon (de Jong L 62), Berghuis, de Jong F, Malen (Klaassen 69); Depay.

Saturday, 27 March 2021

Netherlands (1) 2 *(Berghuis 32, de Jong L 69)*

Latvia (0) 0

Netherlands: (4231) Krul; Dumfries, de Ligt, Blind, Wijndal; Wijnaldum (van de Beek 79), de Jong F; Berghuis (Stengs 84), Klaassen (Gravenberch 79), Depay (Bergwijn 89); de Jong L (Babel 79).
Latvia: (4231) Ozols; Fjodorovs, Cernomordijs, Tarasovs, Jurkovskis; Zjuzins (Karklins 46), Tobers; Kamess (Savalnieks 79), Ikaunieks J (Krollis 88), Ciganiks (Solovjovs 85); Uldrikis (Gutkovskis 46).

Montenegro (2) 4 *(Beciraj 25, Simic 43, Tomasevic 52, Jovetic 80)*

Gibraltar (1) 1 *(Styche 30 (pen))*

Montenegro: (4231) Mijatovic; Vukcevic M, Simic, Tomasevic, Radunovic; Kosovic (Lagator 60), Bakic (Vulaj 26); Jovovic, Djurdjevic (Martinovic 77), Haksabanovic (Boljevic 60); Beciraj (Jovetic 46).
Gibraltar: (541) Goldwin; Valarino (Wiseman 81), Sergeant, Barnett, Santos, Moulds; Badr (Coombes 46), Bosio (Andrew Hernandez 51), Jolley, Pons (Walker 66); Styche (Borge 65).

Norway (0) 0

Turkey (2) 3 *(Tufan 4, 58, Soyuncu 28)*

Norway: (4132) Jarstein (Hansen 46); Ryerson (Svensson 68), Gregersen, Ajer, Meling; Midtsjoe (Thorstvedt■ 67); Odegaard, Berg, Elyounoussi M (King 67); Haaland (Thorsby 83), Sorloth.
Turkey: (442) Cakir; Muldur, Ayhan, Soyuncu, Meras; Karaman (Unal 72), Tufan (Kabak 86), Yokuslu, Calhanoglu (Antalyali 69); Yilmaz (Akbunar 86), Yazici (Erkin 69).

Tuesday, 30 March 2021

Gibraltar (0) 0

Netherlands (1) 7 *(Berghuis 41, de Jong L 55, Depay 61, 88, Wijnaldum 62, Malen 64, van de Beek 85)*

Gibraltar: (541) Coleing (Goldwin 74); Sergeant, Chipolina R, Wiseman, Mouelhi, Jolley (Moulds 82); Walker, Annesley (Torrilla 73), Ronan (Barnett 41), Casciaro L (Valarino 82); De Barr.
Netherlands: (433) Krul; Dumfries (Gravenberch 46), de Ligt, Blind (Malen 54), Wijndal; Wijnaldum, Klaassen (van de Beek 77), de Jong F; Berghuis (Stengs 81), de Jong L (Babel 81), Depay.

Montenegro (0) 0

Norway (1) 1 *(Sorloth 35)*

Montenegro: (442) Mijatovic; Marusic (Beciraj 88), Vujacic, Savic, Tomasevic; Kosovic (Ivanovic 80), Scekic, Lagator (Jovovic 63), Haksabanovic (Boljevic 81); Jovetic, Djurdjevic (Islamovic 63).
Norway: (442) Jarstein; Svensson (Ryerson 66), Gregersen, Ajer, Meling; Odegaard (Linnes 81), Thorsby, Berg (Midtsjoe 67), Elyounoussi M (Strandberg 90); Sorloth, Haaland (King 80).

Turkey (2) 3 *(Karaman 2, Calhanoglu 33, Yilmaz 52 (pen))*

Latvia (1) 3 *(Savalnieks 35, Uldrikis 58, Ikaunieks D 79)*

Turkey: (442) Cakir; Muldur, Kabak, Soyuncu, Erkin (Kokcu 83); Yazici (Antalyali 66), Tufan (Turuc 83), Yokuslu, Calhanoglu (Meras 66); Karaman (Unal 73), Yilmaz.
Latvia: (4231) Steinbors; Fjodorovs, Cernomordijs, Oss, Jurkovskis; Emsis, Tobers; Savalnieks (Jaunzems 90), Ikaunieks J (Ikaunieks D 65), Ciganiks (Kamess 46); Uldrikis (Krollis 73).

Group G Table	P	W	D	L	F	A	GD	Pts
Turkey	3	2	1	0	10	5	5	7
Netherlands	3	2	0	1	11	4	7	6
Montenegro	3	2	0	1	6	3	3	6
Norway	3	2	0	1	4	3	1	6
Latvia	3	0	1	2	4	7	–3	1
Gibraltar	3	0	0	3	1	14	–13	0

GROUP H

Wednesday, 24 March 2021

Cyprus (0) 0

Slovakia (0) 0

Cyprus: (343) Demetriou D; Kousoulos, Soteriou, Laifis; Antoniou, Artymatas, Kastanos (Charalambos Kyriakou 66), Ioannou N; Papoulis (Loizou 72), Sotiriou (Elia 90), Pittas.
Slovakia: (433) Dubravka; Pekarik, Skriniar, Hancko, Hubocan; Kucka, Hrosovsky, Bero (Schranz 78); Duda (Strelec 83), Bozenik (Duris 60), Rusnak (Gregus 60).

Malta (0) 1 *(Mbong J 56)*

Russia (2) 3 *(Dzyuba 23, Fernandes 35, Sobolev 89)*

Malta: (3421) Bonello; Shaw, Agius (Nwoko 88), Borg S; Mbong J, Kristensen (Pisani 74), Guillaumier, Camenzuli (Corbalan 86); Teuma, Degabriele (Mbong P 46); Montebello (Satariano 46).
Russia: (4231) Shunin; Fernandes, Semenov, Dzhikija, Karavaev; Akhmetov, Fomin (Anton Miranchuk 57); Kuzyaev (Mostovoy 78), Golovin, Ionov (Zhemaletdinov 57); Dzyuba (Sobolev 83).

Slovenia (1) 1 *(Lovric 15)*

Croatia (0) 0

Slovenia: (433) Oblak; Stojanovic, Blazic, Mevlja, Balkovec; Bijol (Vetrih 69), Kurtic, Lovric (Bajric 87); Ilicic (Skubic 87), Sporar (Kramer 69), Bohar (Crnigoj 64).
Croatia: (4231) Livakovic; Vrsaljko, Lovren, Vida, Barisic (Orsic 46); Brozovic, Kovacic (Pasalic 82); Vlasic (Budimir 69), Modric, Kramaric (Brekalo 65); Perisic.

Saturday, 27 March 2021

Croatia (1) 1 *(Pasalic 40)*

Cyprus (0) 0

Croatia: (4231) Livakovic; Vrsaljko (Juranovic 46), Lovren, Caleta-Car, Barisic; Modric, Brozovic; Brekalo (Vlasic 66), Pasalic (Orsic 66), Perisic (Kovacic 77); Budimir (Kramaric 57).
Cyprus: (343) Demetriou D (Michael 39); Kousoulos, Soteriou, Laifis (Andreou 82); Psaltis, Artymatas (Kastanos 67), Charalambos Kyriakou, Ioanno N; Tzionis (Papoulis 67), Elia (Sotiriou 46), Pittas.

Russia (2) 2 *(Dzyuba 26, 35)*

Slovenia (1) 1 *(Ilicic 36)*

Russia: (352) Shunin; Semenov, Dzhikija, Kudryashov; Fernandes, Kuzyaev, Ozdoev, Golovin (Anton Miranchuk 49), Zhirkov (Karavaev 68); Dzyuba (Zabolotny 86), Zhemaletdinov (Mukhin 86).
Slovenia: (433) Oblak; Stojanovic (Skubic 61), Blazic, Mevlja, Balkovec; Bijol (Vetrih 62), Kurtic, Lovric (Zahovic 86); Ilicic, Sporar (Vuckic 75), Zajc (Bohar 75).

Slovakia (0) 2 *(Strelec 49, Skriniar 53)*

Malta (2) 2 *(Gambin 16, Satariano 19)*

Slovakia: (4141) Kuciak; Koscelnik, Valjent, Skriniar, Hancko (Holubek 39); Hrosovsky (Schranz 82); Suslov (Rusnak 72), Kucka (Strelec 46), Gregus, Mak; Duris (Bozenik 46).
Malta: (541) Bonello; Mbong J, Shaw, Pepe, Borg S, Camenzuli; Gambin (Grech 68), Guillaumier, Teuma (Kristensen 90), Mbong P (Nwoko 68); Satariano (Pisani 79).

Tuesday, 30 March 2021

Croatia (0) 3 *(Perisic 62, Modric 76 (pen), Brekalo 90)*

Malta (0) 0

Croatia: (4231) Livakovic; Juranovic, Vida, Caleta-Car, Melnjak (Barisic 57); Badelj (Modric 54), Kovacic; Pasalic (Brekalo 54), Vlasic, Orsic (Lovric 78); Budimir (Perisic 54).
Malta: (3421) Bonello; Shaw, Pepe, Borg S (Muscat 67); Mbong J (Corbalan 67), Kristensen (Gambin 81), Guillaumier, Camenzuli; Teuma, Pisani (Grech 63); Satariano (Nwoko 46).

Cyprus (1) 1 *(Pittas 42)*

Slovenia (0) 0

Cyprus: (541) Michael; Antoniou, Kousoulos, Soteriou, Laifis, Ioannou N; Pittas, Artymatas (Gogic 90), Kastanos (Charalambos Kyriakou 60), Papoulis (Loizou 82); Sotiriou (Elia 90).
Slovenia: (442) Oblak; Stojanovic, Blazic, Bajric, Balkovec (Kouter 81); Lovric (Zahovic 81), Bijol (Crnigoj 58), Kurtic, Zajc (Bohar 46); Ilicic, Kramer (Vuckic 58).

Slovakia (1) 2 *(Skriniar 38, Mak 74)*

Russia (0) 1 *(Fernandes 71)*

Slovakia: (4231) Kuciak; Pekarik (Pauschek 90), Satka, Skriniar, Hubocan; Kucka, Hromada (Hrosovsky 61); Koscelnik, Duda, Mak (Duris 76); Schranz (Strelec 90).
Russia: (352) Shunin; Semenov, Dzhikija, Kudryashov; Fernandes, Kuzyaev, Ozdoev, Golovin, Zhirkov (Mostovoy 46 (Sobolev 65)); Zhemaletdinov (Anton Miranchuk 58), Dzyuba.

Group H Table	P	W	D	L	F	A	GD	Pts
Croatia	3	2	0	1	4	1	3	6
Russia	3	2	0	1	6	4	2	6
Slovakia	3	1	2	0	4	3	1	5
Cyprus	3	1	1	1	1	1	0	4
Slovenia	3	1	0	2	2	3	–1	3
Malta	3	0	1	2	3	8	–5	1

GROUP I

Thursday, 25 March 2021

Andorra (0) 0

Albania (1) 1 *(Lenjani 41)*

Andorra: (541) Gomes; Jesus Rubio (Alavedra 56), Llovera, Vales, San Nicolas M, Cervos; Martinez A (Sanchez A 70), Rebes (Moreno 79), Vieira (Pujol 79), Alaez; Fernandez (Martinez C 70).
Albania: (352) Berisha; Ismajli, Kumbulla, Djimsiti; Hysaj, Bare, Gjasula, Memushaj (Laci 62), Lenjani (Roshi 81); Cikalleshi (Broja 81), Manaj (Uzuni 62).

England (3) 5 *(Ward-Prowse 14, Calvert-Lewin 21, 53, Sterling 31, Watkins 83)*

San Marino (0) 0

England: (433) Pope; James (Trippier 46), Stones (Mings 46), Coady, Chilwell; Ward-Prowse, Phillips, Mount (Bellingham 46); Lingard, Calvert-Lewin (Watkins 63), Sterling (Foden 46).
San Marino: (442) Benedettini E; Manuel Battistini, Brolli, Rossi, Grandoni (Ceccaroli 55); Hirsch (Mularoni 55), Golinucci (Michael Battistini 70), Lunadei (Giardi 79), Palazzi; Berardi F (D'Addario 79), Nanni N.

Hungary (1) 3 *(Sallai 6, Adam Szalai 52, Orban 78)*

Poland (0) 3 *(Piatek 60, Jozwiak 61, Lewandowski 82)*

Hungary: (352) Gulacsi; Fiola■, Orban, Attila Szalai; Lovrencsics (Nego 66), Kleinheisler, Nagy A, Kalmar (Siger 81), Hangya (Lang 66); Adam Szalai, Sallai (Varga K 72).
Poland: (3412) Szczesny; Bereszynski, Helik (Glik 58), Bednarek; Szymanski (Jozwiak 59), Moder (Piatek 59), Krychowiak, Reca (Rybus 79); Zielinski; Lewandowski, Milik (Grosicki 84).

Sunday, 28 March 2021

Albania (0) 0

England (1) 2 *(Kane 38, Mount 63)*

Albania: (433) Berisha; Hysaj, Ismajli, Djimsiti, Veseli; Laci (Ramadani 89), Bare (Memushaj 71), Memolla (Gjasula 59); Cikalleshi (Manaj 59), Broja (Lenjani 59), Uzuni.
England: (433) Pope; Walker, Stones, Maguire, Shaw; Mount, Phillips (Ward-Prowse 71), Rice; Sterling, Kane, Foden (Lingard 81).

Poland (1) 3 *(Lewandowski 30, 55, Swiderski 88)*

Andorra (0) 0

Poland: (41212) Szczesny; Bereszynski (Dawidowicz 60), Piatkowski, Glik, Rybus (Grosicki 60); Krychowiak; Jozwiak, Zielinski (Kozlowski 73); Milik (Placheta 60); Piatek, Lewandowski (Swiderski 63).
Andorra: (4231) Iker; San Nicolas M, Garcia C, Garcia E, Alavedra; Rebes (Vieira 87), Vales; Martinez C (Martinez A 74), Pujol (Alaez 58), Garcia M (Cervos 58); Sanchez A (San Nicolas L 87).

San Marino (0) 0

Hungary (1) 3 *(Adam Szalai 13 (pen), Sallai 71, Nikolic 88 (pen))*

San Marino: (532) Benedettini E; Manuel Battistini, Fabbri, Brolli, Rossi, Palazzi; Lunadei (Zonzini 53), Golinucci, Mularoni; Nanni N (Hirsch 80), Berardi F (Bernardi 80).
Hungary: (352) Dibusz; Botka, Orban, Attila Szalai; Nego (Kalmar 46), Cseri (Nikolic 46), Siger, Gazdag (Kleinheisler 63), Varga K (Varga R 72); Adam Szalai (Geresi 85), Sallai.

Wednesday, 31 March 2021

Andorra (0) 1 *(Pujol 90 (pen))*

Hungary (1) 4 *(Fiola 45, Gazdag 51, Kleinheisler 58, Nego 90)*

Andorra: (442) Gomes; San Nicolas M (Jesus Rubio 61), Llovera, Garcia E, Alavedra (Rebes 77); Martinez A (Martinez C 62), Vieira (Pujol 77), Vales, Cervos; Fernandez (Sanchez A 82), Alaez.
Hungary: (352) Dibusz; Fiola, Lang, Attila Szalai; Lovrencsics (Varga K 83), Kalmar (Gazdag 29), Nagy A (Siger 61), Kleinheisler (Nego 83), Hangya; Nikolic (Varga R 61), Adam Szalai.

England (1) 2 *(Kane 19 (pen), Maguire 85)*

Poland (0) 1 *(Moder 58)*

England: (433) Pope; Walker, Stones, Maguire, Chilwell; Phillips, Rice, Mount; Foden (James 86), Kane (Calvert-Lewin 89), Sterling (Lingard 90).
Poland: (352) Szczesny; Helik (Jozwiak 54), Glik, Bednarek; Bereszynski, Zielinski (Grosicki 85), Krychowiak, Moder, Rybus (Reca 86); Piatek (Augustyniak 76), Swiderski (Milik 46).

San Marino (0) 0

Albania (0) 2 *(Manaj 63, Uzuni 85)*

San Marino: (541) Benedettini E; Manuel Battistini (D'Addario 80), Fabbri, Simoncini D, Rossi (Brolli 55), Palazzi (Ceccaroli 80); Berardi F, Mularoni, Golinucci (Grandoni 64), Tomassini (Lunadei 55); Nanni N.
Albania: (3331) Strakosha; Ajeti, Djimsiti, Veseli; Hysaj, Ramadani, Bare; Laci (Uzuni 46), Manaj (Cikalleshi 87), Lenjani (Mitaj 88); Broja (Roshi 46).

Group I Table	P	W	D	L	F	A	GD	Pts
England	3	3	0	0	9	1	8	9
Hungary	3	2	1	0	10	4	6	7
Albania	3	2	0	1	3	2	1	6
Poland	3	1	1	1	7	5	2	4
Andorra	3	0	0	3	1	8	–7	0
San Marino	3	0	0	3	0	10	–10	0

GROUP J

Thursday, 25 March 2021

Germany (2) 3 *(Goretzka 3, Havertz 7, Gundogan 56)*

Iceland (0) 0

Germany: (433) Neuer; Klostermann, Ginter, Rudiger, Can; Goretzka (Neuhaus 71), Kimmich, Gundogan; Havertz (Musiala 79), Gnabry (Younes 86), Sane (Werner 79).
Iceland: (4141) Halldorsson; Sampsted, Arnason, Ingason, Magnusson; Gunnarsson; Traustason (Sigurdsson A 71), Palsson (Skulason A 89), Sigurjonsson (Gudmundsson A 40), Bjarnason B; Bodvarsson (Sigthorsson 89).

Liechtenstein (0) 0

Armenia (0) 1 *(Frommelt 83 (og))*

Liechtenstein: (532) Buchel B; Yildiz (Brandle 65), Malin (Grunenfelder 46), Kaufmann, Hofer, Goppel; Meier (Frommelt 65), Hasler, Sele A; Frick N (Beck 76), Frick Y.
Armenia: (442) Yurchenko; Hambardzumyan, Calisir, Haroyan, Hovhannisyan K; Barseghyan (Bichakhchyan 90), Udo, Grigoryan A (Karapetyan 46), Bayramyan (Babayan 75); Adamyan, Briasco (Miranyan 64).

Romania (1) 3 *(Tanase 28, Mihaila 50, Hagi 85)*

North Macedonia (0) 2 *(Ademi 82, Trajkovski 83)*

Romania: (4231) Nita; Popescu, Chiriches, Burca, Bancu; Marin, Stanciu (Bicfalvi 76); Man (Maxim 76), Tanase (Hagi 76), Coman (Mihaila 14); Keseru (Puscas 63).
North Macedonia: (3142) Dimitrievski; Bejtulai, Musliu, Ristevski (Ibraimi 88); Nikolov (Ademi 54); Ristovski S, Bardhi, Elmas, Alioski; Nestorovski (Stojanovski 54), Pandev (Trajkovski 78).

Sunday, 28 March 2021

Armenia (0) 2 *(Barseghyan 53, Bayramyan 74)*

Iceland (0) 0

Armenia: (442) Yurchenko; Hambardzumyan, Haroyan, Voskanyan, Hovhannisyan K; Barseghyan, Udo (Muradyan 81), Grigoryan A, Hakobyan (Bayramyan 56); Adamyan (Shagoyan 81), Briasco (Karapetyan 64).
Iceland: (4141) Halldorsson; Saevarsson, Arnason, Ingason, Skulason A; Gunnarsson; Gudmundsson J (Traustason 77), Sigurdsson A (Sigthorsson 56), Bjarnason B (Palsson 84), Gudmundsson A; Bodvarsson (Fridjonsson 77).

North Macedonia (1) 5 *(Bardhi 7, Trajkovski 51, 54, Elmas 62, Nestorovski 82 (pen))*

Liechtenstein (0) 0

North Macedonia: (442) Dimitrievski; Ristovski S (Bejtulai 58), Musliu, Ristevski, Alioski (Askovski 66); Radeski, Spirovski, Bardhi (Nikolov 58), Elmas; Pandev (Nestorovski 58), Trajkovski (Hasani 66).
Liechtenstein: (532) Buchel B; Brandle, Wolfinger S, Malin, Hofer, Goppel (Marxer M 78); Meier (Ospelt P 46), Frommelt (Vogt 66), Wolfinger F (Marxer A 66); Hasler (Sele A 42), Frick Y.

Romania (0) 0

Germany (1) 1 *(Gnabry 16)*

Romania: (4231) Nita; Popescu, Chiriches, Tosca, Camora (Burca 46); Stanciu, Marin; Hagi (Maxim 83), Tanase (Cicaldau 83), Mihaila (Man 66); Keseru (Puscas 66).
Germany: (433) Neuer; Klostermann, Ginter, Rudiger, Can; Goretzka, Kimmich, Gundogan; Havertz (Werner 77), Gnabry (Neuhaus 90), Sane (Younes 90).

Wednesday, 31 March 2021

Armenia (0) 3 *(Spertsyan 56, Haroyan 86, Barseghyan 89 (pen))*

Romania (0) 2 *(Cicaldau 62, 72)*

Armenia: (442) Yurchenko; Hambardzumyan, Haroyan, Calisir, Hovhannisyan K; Barseghyan (Udo 90), Grigoryan A, Muradyan (Spertsyan 46), Bayramyan; Karapetyan (Shagoyan 46), Briasco (Adamyan 46).
Romania: (4231) Nita; Mogos, Chiriches, Tosca, Bancu; Stanciu (Tanase 73), Marin; Man (Mihaila 81), Cicaldau (Cretu A 81), Maxim (Keseru 73); Puscas■.

Germany (0) 1 *(Gundogan 63 (pen))*

North Macedonia (1) 2 *(Pandev 45, Elmas 85)*

Germany: (442) ter Stegen; Ginter (Musiala 89), Rudiger, Can, Gosens (Younes 56); Sane, Goretzka, Kimmich, Gundogan; Havertz (Werner 56), Gnabry.
North Macedonia: (532) Dimitrievski; Nikolov (Bejtulai 59), Ristovski S, Velkovski, Musliu, Alioski (Ristevski 90); Bardhi, Ademi, Elmas; Trajkovski (Spirovski 72), Pandev (Stojanovski 90).

Liechtenstein (0) 1 *(Frick Y 79)*

Iceland (2) 4 *(Saevarsson 12, Bjarnason B 45, Palsson 77, Sigurjonsson 90 (pen))*

Liechtenstein: (352) Ospelt J; Wolfinger S, Kaufmann, Hofer (Marxer A 78); Yildiz (Brandle 46), Meier, Martin Buchel (Frommelt 69), Sele A (Wolfinger F 69), Goppel; Frick N (Ospelt P 84), Frick Y.
Iceland: (433) Runarsson; Saevarsson, Hermannsson, Ingason, Magnusson; Palsson, Gunnarsson (Sigurjonsson 46), Bjarnason B (Thorsteinsson 72); Gudmundsson J (Sigurdsson A 63), Gudjohnsen (Fridjonsson 63), Traustason (Johannesson 81).

Group J Table	P	W	D	L	F	A	GD	Pts
Armenia	3	3	0	0	6	2	4	9
North Macedonia	3	2	0	1	9	4	5	6
Germany	3	2	0	1	5	2	3	6
Romania	3	1	0	2	5	6	–1	3
Iceland	3	1	0	2	4	6	–2	3
Liechtenstein	3	0	0	3	1	10	–9	0

UEFA NATIONS LEAGUE 2020–21

▪ *Denotes player sent off.*
Behind closed doors unless otherwise stated.

LEAGUE A – GROUP 1

Friday, 4 September 2020

Netherlands (0) 1 *(Bergwijn 61)*

Poland (0) 0

Netherlands: (4231) Cillessen; Hateboer, Veltman, van Dijk, Ake; de Roon, de Jong F; Bergwijn (van de Beek 74), Wijnaldum, Promes (de Jong L 90); Depay.
Poland: (4411) Szczesny; Kedziora, Glik, Bednarek, Bereszynski; Szymanski, Klich, Krychowiak, Jozwiak (Grosicki 71); Zielinski (Moder 77); Piatek (Milik 63).

Italy (0) 1 *(Sensi 67)*

Bosnia-Herzegovina (0) 1 *(Dzeko 57)*

Italy: (433) Donnarumma; Florenzi, Bonucci, Acerbi, Biraghi; Pellegrini (Kean 86), Sensi, Barella; Chiesa (Zaniolo 71), Belotti (Immobile 73), Insigne.
Bosnia-Herzegovina: (4231) Sehic; Cipetic, Sunjic, Sanicanin, Kolasinac (Civic 84); Cimirot, Hadziahmetovic; Visca (Milosevic 86), Gojak, Hodzic (Besic 77); Dzeko.

Monday, 7 September 2020

Bosnia-Herzegovina (1) 1 *(Hajradinovic 24 (pen))*

Poland (1) 2 *(Glik 45, Grosicki 67)*

Bosnia-Herzegovina: (433) Begovic; Kvrzic, Bicakcic, Sanicanin, Civic (Milosevic 82); Besic (Dzeko 60), Hadziahmetovic, Hajradinovic; Hodzic, Koljic, Gojak (Visca 46).
Poland: (4231) Fabianski; Kedziora, Glik, Bednarek, Rybus; Goralski, Krychowiak (Klich 68); Jozwiak, Zielinski (Linetty 85), Grosicki (Szymanski 80); Milik.

Netherlands (0) 0

Italy (1) 1 *(Barella 45)*

Netherlands: (4231) Cillessen; Hateboer (Dumfries 70), Veltman, van Dijk, Ake (de Jong L 81); de Roon, de Jong F; Wijnaldum, van de Beek (Bergwijn 57), Promes; Depay.
Italy: (433) Donnarumma; D'Ambrosio, Bonucci, Chiellini, Spinazzola; Barella, Jorginho, Locatelli (Cristante 81); Zaniolo (Kean 42), Immobile, Insigne (Chiesa 90).

Sunday, 11 October 2020

Bosnia-Herzegovina (0) 0

Netherlands (0) 0 1600

Bosnia-Herzegovina: (4141) Sehic; Todorovic D, Hadzikadunic, Sanicanin, Kadusic (Kolasinac 46); Cimirot; Tatar (Hadziahmetovic 54), Pjanic (Loncar 75), Krunic (Hodzic 75), Gojak; Djuric (Dzeko 61).
Netherlands: (4231) Cillessen; Dumfries (Hateboer 70), de Vrij, van Dijk, Blind (Ake 86); de Roon, de Jong F; Malen (Berghuis 69), Wijnaldum, Promes (Babel 86); de Jong L.

Poland (0) 0

Italy (0) 0

Poland: (4231) Fabianski; Kedziora, Glik, Walukiewicz, Bereszynski; Krychowiak, Moder; Szymanski (Grosicki 60), Klich (Milik 70), Jozwiak (Karbownik 82); Lewandowski (Linetty 82).
Italy: (433) Donnarumma; Florenzi, Bonucci, Acerbi, Emerson Palmieri; Barella (Locatelli 79), Jorginho, Verratti; Chiesa (Kean 70), Belotti (Caputo 83), Pellegrini (Berardi 83).

Wednesday, 14 October 2020

Italy (1) 1 *(Pellegrini 16)*

Netherlands (1) 1 *(van de Beek 25)* 623

Italy: (433) Donnarumma; D'Ambrosio, Bonucci, Chiellini, Spinazzola; Barella, Jorginho, Verratti (Locatelli 56); Chiesa (Kean 55), Immobile, Pellegrini (Florenzi 72).
Netherlands: (532) Cillessen; Hateboer, de Vrij, van Dijk, Ake, Blind (Veltman 77); van de Beek, de Jong F, Wijnaldum; Depay (Babel 90), de Jong L.

Poland (2) 3 *(Lewandowski 40, 51, Linetty 45)*

Bosnia-Herzegovina (0) 0 8152

Poland: (4231) Szczesny; Kedziora (Bereszynski 72), Glik, Bednarek, Reca; Goralski, Linetty; Jozwiak (Karbownik 72), Klich (Piatek 64), Grosicki (Kadzior 64); Lewandowski (Milik 58).
Bosnia-Herzegovina: (433) Sehic; Cipetic, Ahmedhodzic▪, Sanicanin, Kolasinac; Pjanic (Hadzikadunic 33), Cimirot, Hadziahmetovic (Hajradinovic 74); Visca (Gojak 58), Dzeko (Prevljak 58), Krunic (Milosevic 73).

Sunday, 15 November 2020

Netherlands (2) 3 *(Wijnaldum 6, 13, Depay 55)*

Bosnia-Herzegovina (0) 1 *(Prevljak 63)*

Netherlands: (433) Krul; Dumfries (Hateboer 64), de Vrij, Blind, Wijndal (van Aanholt 79); Klaassen, Wijnaldum (van de Beek 64), de Jong F; Berghuis (Stengs 89), de Jong L, Depay (Promes 79).
Bosnia-Herzegovina: (4141) Sehic; Todorovic D, Hadziahmetovic, Sanicanin, Kolasinac; Cimirot; Visca (Tatar 78), Pjanic (Ziljkic 89), Krunic (Rahmanovic 78), Gojak (Danilovic 61); Hodzic (Prevljak 61).

Italy (1) 2 *(Jorginho 27 (pen), Berardi 83)*

Poland (0) 0

Italy: (433) Donnarumma; Florenzi (Di Lorenzo 89), Acerbi, Bastoni, Emerson Palmieri; Barella, Jorginho, Locatelli; Bernardeschi (Berardi 64), Belotti (Okaka 79), Insigne (El Shaarawy 89).
Poland: (4231) Szczesny; Bereszynski, Glik, Bednarek, Reca; Krychowiak, Moder (Goralski▪ 46); Szymanski (Zielinski 46), Linetty (Milik 74), Jozwiak (Grosicki 46); Lewandowski.

Wednesday, 18 November 2020

Bosnia-Herzegovina (0) 0

Italy (1) 2 *(Belotti 22, Berardi 68)*

Bosnia-Herzegovina: (4141) Piric; Corluka, Hadzikadunic, Sanicanin, Kadusic (Todorovic D 79); Cimirot; Tatar (Rahmanovic 79), Pjanic (Danilovic 77), Gojak, Krunic (Loncar 72); Prevljak (Hadzic 79).
Italy: (433) Donnarumma; Florenzi (Di Lorenzo 46), Acerbi, Bastoni, Emerson Palmieri; Barella, Jorginho, Locatelli; Berardi (Bernardeschi 82), Belotti (Lasagna 82), Insigne (Calabria 90).

Poland (1) 1 *(Jozwiak 5)*

Netherlands (0) 2 *(Depay 77 (pen), Wijnaldum 84)*

Poland: (4141) Fabianski; Kedziora, Glik, Bednarek, Reca (Rybus 81); Krychowiak (Linetty 70); Placheta (Grosicki 75), Klich, Zielinski (Moder 70), Jozwiak; Lewandowski (Piatek 46).
Netherlands: (4231) Krul; Hateboer (Dumfries 57), de Vrij, Blind (de Jong L 84), van Aanholt (Wijndal 70); Klaassen (van de Beek 70), de Jong F; Stengs (Berghuis 70), Wijnaldum, Malen; Depay.

League A – Group 1	P	W	D	L	F	A	GD	Pts
Italy	6	3	3	0	7	2	5	12
Netherlands	6	3	2	1	7	4	3	11
Poland	6	2	1	3	6	6	0	7
Bosnia-Herzegovina	6	0	2	4	3	11	–8	2

LEAGUE A – GROUP 2

Saturday, 5 September 2020

Denmark (0) 0

Belgium (1) 2 *(Denayer 9, Mertens 76)*

Denmark: (433) Schmeichel; Wass (Jorgensen M 83), Kjaer, Christensen A, Skov; Eriksen, Hojbjerg, Delaney; Poulsen, Dolberg (Cornelius 83), Braithwaite (Maehle 72).
Belgium: (3421) Mignolet; Alderweireld, Denayer, Vertonghen; Castagne, Tielemans (Doku 88), Witsel, Hazard T; Mertens (Trossard 80), Carrasco (Praet 57); Lukaku.

Iceland (0) 0

England (0) 1 *(Sterling 90 (pen))*

Iceland: (442) Halldorsson; Hermannsson, Arnason, Ingason■, Magnusson; Thorsteinsson (Sigurdsson A 66), Bjarnason B, Palsson, Traustason (Hallfredsson 76); Gudmundsson A, Bodvarsson (Fridjonsson 90).
England: (4141) Pickford; Walker■, Gomez, Dier, Trippier; Rice; Sancho (Alexander-Arnold 73), Ward-Prowse, Foden (Ings 68), Sterling; Kane (Greenwood 78).

Tuesday, 8 September 2020

Belgium (2) 5 *(Witsel 13, Batshuayi 17, 69, Mertens 50, Doku 79)*

Iceland (1) 1 *(Fridjonsson 10)*

Belgium: (343) Casteels (Mignolet 55); Alderweireld, Denayer, Vertonghen; Meunier, De Bruyne (Vanaken 80), Witsel, Hazard T (Verschaeren 65); Mertens, Batshuayi, Doku.
Iceland: (433) Kristinsson; Hermannsson, Eyjolfsson, Fjoluson, Skulason A; Baldursson (Hallfredsson 54), Palsson, Bjarnason B; Sigurdsson A (Anderson 72), Fridjonsson (Bodvarsson 70), Gudmundsson A.

Denmark (0) 0

England (0) 0

Denmark: (433) Schmeichel; Wass, Jorgensen M, Christensen A, Skov; Norgaard (Hojbjerg 73), Eriksen, Delaney; Poulsen, Dolberg (Falk 76), Braithwaite (Kjaer 83).
England: (343) Pickford; Gomez, Coady, Dier; Alexander-Arnold (Maitland-Niles 87), Rice, Phillips (Grealish 76), Trippier; Sancho (Mount 60), Kane, Sterling.

Sunday, 11 October 2020

England (1) 2 *(Rashford 39 (pen), Mount 64)*

Belgium (1) 1 *(Lukaku 16 (pen))*

England: (3421) Pickford; Walker, Dier, Maguire; Alexander-Arnold (James 79), Henderson J (Phillips 66), Rice, Trippier; Mount (Sancho 89), Rashford; Calvert-Lewin (Kane 66).
Belgium: (3421) Mignolet; Alderweireld, Boyata, Denayer; Meunier, Witsel, Tielemans, Castagne; De Bruyne (Verschaeren 73), Carrasco (Doku 83); Lukaku.

Iceland (0) 0

Denmark (1) 3 *(Sigurjonsson 45 (og), Eriksen 46, Skov 61)*

Iceland: (442) Halldorsson; Palsson, Ingason, Sigurdsson R (Eyjolfsson 73), Magnusson; Traustason (Gudmundsson A 68), Gunnarsson (Anderson 46), Sigurjonsson, Bjarnason B; Sigurdsson G, Finnbogason A (Bodvarsson 12).
Denmark: (4231) Schmeichel; Wass, Kjaer, Christensen A, Skov (Maehle 79); Hojbjerg, Delaney; Poulsen (Skov Olsen 66), Eriksen, Braithwaite (Jorgensen M 87); Dolberg (Sisto 79).

Wednesday, 14 October 2020

England (0) 0

Denmark (1) 1 *(Eriksen 35 (pen))*

England: (3421) Pickford; Walker, Coady, Maguire■; James■, Rice (Henderson J 76), Phillips, Maitland-Niles (Mings 36); Mount (Sancho 73), Rashford (Calvert-Lewin 72); Kane.
Denmark: (4231) Schmeichel; Wass, Kjaer, Christensen A (Jorgensen M 46), Skov (Maehle 46); Hojbjerg (Jensen M 88), Delaney; Poulsen, Eriksen, Braithwaite (Vestergaard 74); Dolberg (Sisto 37).

Iceland (1) 1 *(Saevarsson 17)*

Belgium (2) 2 *(Lukaku 9, 38 (pen))* 60

Iceland: (3142) Runarsson; Ingason, Eyjolfsson, Magnusson (Traustason 86); Palsson (Hermannsson 82); Saevarsson, Sigurjonsson (Thorsteinsson 68), Bjarnason B, Skulason; Gudmundsson A (Sigthorsson 81), Bodvarsson (Kjartansson 69).
Belgium: (343) Mignolet; Alderweireld, Boyata, Denayer; Meunier, Witsel, Tielemans, Carrasco; Trossard (Vanaken 61), Lukaku, Doku (Castagne 68).

Sunday, 15 November 2020

Belgium (2) 2 *(Tielemans 10, Mertens 24)*

England (0) 0

Belgium: (3421) Courtois; Alderweireld, Denayer, Vertonghen; Meunier, Tielemans, Witsel, Hazard T; De Bruyne, Mertens (Praet 83); Lukaku.
England: (3421) Pickford; Walker, Dier, Mings; Trippier (Sancho 70), Henderson J (Winks 46), Rice, Chilwell (Saka 38); Mount (Calvert-Lewin 69), Grealish; Kane.

Denmark (1) 2 *(Eriksen 12 (pen), 90 (pen))*

Iceland (0) 1 *(Kjartansson 85)*

Denmark: (3412) Schmeichel (Ronnow 46); Christensen A, Kjaer, Vestergaard (Wind 90); Wass, Delaney, Jensen M (Jonsson 68), Stryger Larsen; Eriksen; Braithwaite (Andersen 76), Poulsen.
Iceland: (352) Runarsson; Ingason, Eyjolfsson, Magnusson; Saevarsson, Sigurdsson G, Bjarnason B (Palsson 46), Sigurdsson A (Gunnarsson 70), Skulason A; Bodvarsson (Kjartansson 71), Gudmundsson (Finnbogason A 74).

Wednesday, 18 November 2020

Belgium (1) 4 *(Tielemans 3, Lukaku 57, 69, De Bruyne 87)*

Denmark (1) 2 *(Wind 17, Chadli 86 (og))*

Belgium: (3421) Courtois; Alderweireld, Denayer, Vertonghen (Boyata 90); Hazard T (Foket 77), Tielemans, Dendoncker, Chadli; Mertens, De Bruyne; Lukaku.
Denmark: (4231) Schmeichel; Wass, Kjaer, Christensen A, Maehle; Hojbjerg, Delaney (Jensen M 70); Poulsen (Andersen 76), Eriksen, Braithwaite; Wind (Sisto 88).

England (2) 4 *(Rice 20, Mount 24, Foden 80, 84)*

Iceland (0) 0

England: (3421) Pickford; Walker (Mings 64), Dier, Maguire; Trippier (Maitland-Niles 85), Rice, Mount (Winks 64), Saka; Foden, Grealish (Sancho 76); Kane (Abraham 76).
Iceland: (532) Kristinsson (Halldorsson 46); Saevarsson■, Ingason, Arnason, Hermannsson, Skulason A; Palsson, Bjarnason B (Johannesson 88), Sigurjonsson (Eyjolfsson 62); Gudmundsson A (Thorsteinsson 73), Bodvarsson (Sigthorsson 73).

League A – Group 2	*P*	*W*	*D*	*L*	*F*	*A*	*GD*	*Pts*
Belgium	6	5	0	1	16	6	10	15
Denmark	6	3	1	2	8	7	1	10
England	6	3	1	2	7	4	3	10
Iceland	6	0	0	6	3	17	–14	0

LEAGUE A – GROUP 3

Saturday, 5 September 2020

Portugal (1) 4 *(Joao Cancelo 41, Jota 58, Joao Felix 70, Andre Silva 90)*

Croatia (0) 1 *(Petkovic 90)*

Portugal: (433) Lopes; Joao Cancelo, Pepe, Dias, Guerreiro; Joao Moutinho (Sergio Oliveira 82), Danilo Pereira, Bruno Fernandes; Bernardo Silva (Trincao 78), Joao Felix (Andre Silva 88), Jota.
Croatia: (4231) Livakovic; Jedvaj, Lovren, Vida, Barisic; Pasalic (Brozovic 61), Kovacic; Brekalo (Perisic 61), Vlasic, Rebic; Kramaric (Petkovic 74).

Sweden (0) 0

France (1) 1 *(Mbappe-Lottin 41)*

Sweden: (442) Olsen; Lustig, Jansson, Lindelof, Bengtsson (Sema 88); Seb Larsson (Kulusevski 70), Olsson K, Ekdal, Forsberg; Berg, Quaison (Guidetti 77).
France: (3412) Lloris; Upamecano, Varane, Kimpembe; Dubois (Mendy 88), Kante, Rabiot, Digne; Griezmann; Giroud (Nzonzi 90), Mbappe-Lottin (Martial 77).

Tuesday, 8 September 2020

France (2) 4 *(Griezmann 43, Livakovic 45 (og), Upamecano 65, Giroud 77 (pen))*

Croatia (1) 2 *(Lovren 16, Brekalo 55)*

France: (3412) Lloris; Upamecano, Lenglet, Lucas; Sissoko, Kante (Camavinga 63), Nzonzi, Mendy; Griezmann (Fekir 78); Ben Yedder (Giroud 63), Martial.
Croatia: (433) Livakovic; Uremovic (Vida 57), Lovren, Caleta-Car, Melnjak; Kovacic, Brozovic, Vlasic; Perisic (Pasalic 66), Kramaric, Rebic (Brekalo 46).

Sweden (0) 0

Portugal (1) 2 *(Ronaldo 45, 72)*

Sweden: (442) Olsen; Krafth, Helander, Jansson, Augustinsson; Kulusevski (Ekdal 90), Svensson■, Olsson K, Forsberg (Svanberg 79); Berg, Isak (Quaison 71).
Portugal: (433) Lopes; Joao Cancelo, Pepe, Dias, Guerreiro; Joao Moutinho (Neves 73), Danilo Pereira, Bruno Fernandes; Bernardo Silva (Goncalo Guedes 22), Joao Felix, Ronaldo (Jota 81).

Sunday, 11 October 2020

Croatia (1) 2 *(Vlasic 31, Kramaric 84)*

Sweden (0) 1 *(Berg 66)*

Croatia: (41212) Livakovic; Uremovic, Lovren, Caleta-Car, Melnjak (Kramaric 74); Brozovic; Kovacic (Pasalic 61), Vlasic; Modric; Brekalo (Bradaric 74), Perisic (Petkovic 85).
Sweden: (442) Olsen; Lustig, Jansson, Lindelof, Augustinsson; Kulusevski, Olsson K, Ekdal (Seb Larsson 83), Forsberg; Isak (Claesson 65), Berg.

France (0) 0

Portugal (0) 0 1000

France: (41212) Lloris; Pavard, Varane, Kimpembe, Lucas; Kante; Pogba, Rabiot; Griezmann; Mbappe-Lottin (Coman 84), Giroud (Martial 74).
Portugal: (433) Rui Patricio; Nelson Semedo, Pepe, Dias, Guerreiro (Joao Cancelo 89); Bruno Fernandes (Sanches 80), Danilo Pereira, William Carvalho (Joao Moutinho 88); Bernardo Silva (Jota 61), Joao Felix (Trincao 89), Ronaldo.

Wednesday, 14 October 2020

Croatia (0) 1 *(Vlasic 64)*

France (1) 2 *(Griezmann 8, Mbappe-Lottin 79)*

Croatia: (4231) Livakovic; Uremovic, Lovren, Vida, Barisic; Badelj (Kovacic 46), Modric; Pasalic (Brekalo 46), Vlasic (Kramaric 80), Perisic (Bradaric 78); Petkovic (Budimir 61).
France: (4312) Lloris; Mendy, Varane, Lenglet, Digne (Lucas 83); Tolisso (Camavinga 63), Nzonzi, Rabiot (Pogba 74); Griezmann (Giroud 83); Martial (Coman 63), Mbappe-Lottin.

Portugal (2) 3 *(Bernardo Silva 21, Jota 44, 72)*

Sweden (0) 0

Portugal: (4141) Rui Patricio; Joao Cancelo, Pepe, Dias, Guerreiro; Danilo Pereira; Bernardo Silva (Andre Silva 75), Bruno Fernandes (Sanches 88), William Carvalho (Joao Moutinho 80), Jota (Rafa Silva 88); Joao Felix (Daniel Podence 75).
Sweden: (442) Olsen; Lustig (Johansson 54), Jansson, Lindelof, Bengtsson; Kulusevski (Seb Larsson 88), Olsson K, Ekdal, Claesson; Berg (Olsson M 88), Quaison (Isak 62).

Saturday, 14 November 2020

Portugal (0) 0

France (0) 1 *(Kante 53)*

Portugal: (433) Rui Patricio; Joao Cancelo, Fonte, Dias, Guerreiro; William Carvalho (Jota 56), Danilo Pereira (Sergio Oliveira 85), Bruno Fernandes (Joao Moutinho 72); Bernardo Silva (Trincao 72), Ronaldo, Joao Felix (Paulinho 85).
France: (41212) Lloris; Pavard, Varane, Kimpembe, Lucas; Kante; Pogba, Rabiot; Griezmann; Coman (Thuram 59), Martial (Giroud 78).

Sweden (2) 2 *(Kulusevski 36, Danielson 45)*

Croatia (0) 1 *(Danielson 81 (og))*

Sweden: (442) Olsen; Lustig, Lindelof, Danielson, Bengtsson; Seb Larsson, Olsson K, Ekdal, Forsberg; Berg, Kulusevski (Claesson 74).
Croatia: (4231) Livakovic; Uremovic (Juranovic 41), Pongracic (Melnjak 77), Caleta-Car, Barisic; Modric, Kovacic (Rog 77); Brekalo (Petkovic 77), Vlasic, Perisic; Budimir (Pasalic 63).

Tuesday, 17 November 2020

Croatia (1) 2 *(Kovacic 29, 65)*

Portugal (0) 3 *(Dias 52, 90, Joao Felix 60)*

Croatia: (4312) Livakovic; Juranovic, Lovren, Skoric, Bradaric; Modric, Rog■, Kovacic (Basic 90); Pasalic (Brekalo 64); Vlasic (Orsic 84), Perisic.
Portugal: (433) Rui Patricio; Nelson Semedo, Semedo, Dias, Mario Rui (Joao Cancelo 71); Bruno Fernandes (Trincao 46), Danilo Pereira (Sergio Oliveira 77), Joao Moutinho; Jota (Paulinho 77), Ronaldo, Joao Felix (Bernardo Silva 71).

France (2) 4 *(Giroud 16, 59, Pavard 36, Coman 90)*

Sweden (1) 2 *(Claesson 4, Quaison 88)*

France: (442) Lloris; Pavard, Varane (Zouma 46), Kimpembe, Lucas (Digne 46); Sissoko, Pogba, Rabiot (Nzonzi 78), Thuram (Mbappe-Lottin 58); Griezmann, Giroud (Coman 84).
Sweden: (442) Olsen; Lustig (Krafth 66), Lindelof (Helander 66), Danielson, Bengtsson; Claesson (Quaison 66), Olsson K, Seb Larsson (Cajuste 87), Forsberg; Berg (Isak 86), Kulusevski.

League A – Group 3	P	W	D	L	F	A	GD	Pts
France	6	5	1	0	12	5	7	16
Portugal	6	4	1	1	12	4	8	13
Croatia	6	1	0	5	9	16	–7	3
Sweden	6	1	0	5	5	13	–8	3

LEAGUE A – GROUP 4

Thursday, 3 September 2020

Germany (0) 1 *(Werner 51)*

Spain (0) 1 *(Gaya 90)*

Germany: (343) Trapp; Can, Rudiger, Sule; Kroos, Gundogan (Serdar 74), Gosens, Kehrer; Draxler, Werner (Koch 90), Sane (Ginter 63).
Spain: (433) de Gea; Sergio Ramos, Gaya, Carvajal, Torres P; Thiago, Busquets (Merino 57), Fabian (Rodriguez 80); Jesus Navas (Fati 46), Rodrigo, Torres F.

Ukraine (1) 2 *(Yarmolenko 14, Zinchenko 68)*

Switzerland (1) 1 *(Seferovic 41)*

Ukraine: (433) Pyatov; Kryvtsov, Mykhaylichenko, Matviyenko, Tymchyk; Stepanenko, Malinovsky, Zinchenko; Moraes, Konoplyanka (Yaremchuk 54), Yarmolenko.
Switzerland: (541) Sommer; Zuber (Steffen 46), Rodriguez, Mbabu, Elvedi, Akanji; Xhaka, Embolo, Sow (Aebischer 82), Vargas (Ajeti 73); Seferovic.

Sunday, 6 September 2020

Spain (3) 4 *(Sergio Ramos 3 (pen), 29, Fati 32, Torres F 84)*

Ukraine (0) 0

Spain: (433) de Gea; Jesus Navas, Sergio Ramos (Garcia 61), Torres P, Reguilon; Thiago, Rodri (Rodriguez 69), Merino; Olmo, Gerard (Torres F 74), Fati.
Ukraine: (433) Pyatov; Tymchyk, Kryvtsov, Matviyenko, Mykhaylichenko; Malinovsky, Kharatin (Sydorchuk 63), Zinchenko; Yarmolenko (Kovalenko 79), Marlos (Tsygankov 56), Yaremchuk.

Switzerland (0) 1 *(Widmer 57)*

Germany (1) 1 *(Gundogan 14)*

Switzerland: (541) Sommer; Widmer, Elvedi, Akanji, Rodriguez (Zuber 64), Benito; Embolo (Vargas 72), Sow (Aebischer 80), Xhaka, Steffen; Seferovic.
Germany: (343) Leno; Ginter, Sule (Tah 62), Rudiger; Kehrer, Gundogan, Kroos, Gosens (Can 78); Sane (Brandt 46), Draxler, Werner.

Saturday, 10 October 2020

Spain (1) 1 *(Oyarzabal 14)*

Switzerland (0) 0

Spain: (4231) de Gea; Jesus Navas, Sergio Ramos, Torres P, Gaya; Busquets, Merino; Torres F (Rodri 88), Olmo (Canales 57), Fati (Traore 57); Oyarzabal (Gerard 73).
Switzerland: (532) Sommer; Widmer (Gavranovic 86), Elvedi, Schar, Rodriguez, Benito (Zuber 81); Sow (Vargas 60), Xhaka, Freuler (Fernandes 86); Seferovic, Mehmedi (Shaqiri 60).

Ukraine (0) 1 *(Malinovsky 76 (pen))*

Germany (1) 2 *(Ginter 20, Goretzka 49)* 17,753

Ukraine: (4141) Bushchan; Karavayev, Zabarnyi, Mykolenko, Sobol; Sydorchuk (Makarenko 84); Yarmolenko (Marlos 69), Malinovsky, Kovalenko (Shaparenko 77), Tsygankov (Zubkov 69); Yaremchuk.
Germany: (3421) Neuer; Ginter, Sule, Rudiger; Klostermann (Can 90), Kimmich, Kroos, Halstenberg; Goretzka, Draxler (Werner 80); Gnabry (Havertz 90).

Tuesday, 13 October 2020

Germany (1) 3 *(Werner 28, Havertz 55, Gnabry 60)*

Switzerland (2) 3 *(Gavranovic 5, 56, Freuler 26)*

Germany: (4231) Neuer; Klostermann, Ginter (Can 77), Rudiger, Gosens (Halstenberg 57); Kimmich, Kroos; Havertz (Draxler 77), Goretzka, Gnabry; Werner.
Switzerland: (442) Sommer; Widmer, Elvedi, Schar■, Rodriguez; Zuber (Fernandes 66), Freuler (Benito 85), Xhaka, Shaqiri (Sow 66); Gavranovic (Mehmedi 75), Seferovic (Itten 85).

Ukraine (0) 1 *(Tsygankov 76)*

Spain (0) 0

Ukraine: (433) Bushchan; Karavayev, Zabarnyi, Mykolenko, Sobol; Sydorchuk (Kovalenko 60), Makarenko, Shaparenko; Yarmolenko, Yaremchuk, Zubkov (Tsygankov 65).
Spain: (433) de Gea; Jesus Navas, Sergio Ramos, Torres P, Reguilon; Canales (Olmo 73), Rodri, Merino (Ceballos 46); Traore, Rodrigo (Oyarzabal 58), Fati (Torres F 58).

Saturday, 14 November 2020

Germany (2) 3 *(Sane 23, Werner 33, 64)*

Ukraine (1) 1 *(Yaremchuk 12)*

Germany: (433) Neuer; Ginter, Sule, Rudiger, Max; Goretzka, Koch, Gundogan; Sane (Waldschmidt 86), Gnabry, Werner (Brandt 76).
Ukraine: (433) Pyatov; Konoplya, Zabarnyi, Matviyenko, Sobol; Malinovsky, Stepanenko (Makarenko 69), Zinchenko (Kharatin 86); Marlos, Yaremchuk (Moraes 75), Zubkov (Mykhaylichenko 74).

Switzerland (1) 1 *(Freuler 26)*

Spain (0) 1 *(Gerard 89)*

Switzerland: (3412) Sommer; Elvedi■, Akanji, Rodriguez; Fernandes, Freuler, Xhaka, Zuber (Steffen 72); Shaqiri (Sow 72); Embolo (Mehmedi 90), Seferovic (Omeragic 84).
Spain: (4231) Simon; Sergi Roberto, Sergio Ramos, Torres P, Reguilon; Merino (Gerard 80), Busquets (Koke 72); Torres F, Fabian (Morata 56), Oyarzabal (Traore 73); Olmo (Canales 73).

Tuesday, 17 November 2020

Spain (3) 6 *(Morata 17, Torres F 33, 55, 71, Rodri 38, Oyarzabal 89)*

Germany (0) 0

Spain: (4141) Simon; Sergi Roberto, Sergio Ramos (Garcia 43), Torres P, Gaya; Rodri; Torres F (Asensio 73), Koke, Canales (Fabian 12), Olmo (Gerard 73); Morata (Oyarzabal 73).
Germany: (433) Neuer; Ginter, Sule (Tah 46), Koch, Max; Goretzka (Neuhaus 61), Gundogan, Kroos; Sane (Waldschmidt 61), Gnabry, Werner (Henrichs 76).

League A – Group 4	P	W	D	L	F	A	GD	Pts
Spain	6	3	2	1	13	3	10	11
Germany	6	2	3	1	10	13	–3	9
Switzerland	6	1	3	2	9	8	1	6
Ukraine	6	2	0	4	5	13	–8	6

LEAGUE B – GROUP 1

Friday, 4 September 2020

Norway (0) 1 *(Haaland 66)*

Austria (1) 2 *(Gregoritsch 35, Sabitzer 54 (pen))*

Norway: (442) Jarstein; Elabdellaoui, Reginiussen, Ajer, Aleesami; Thorsby (Linnes 60), Berge, Normann, Johansen (Henriksen 67); King (Sorloth 64), Haaland.
Austria: (442) Schlager A; Lainer, Posch, Hinteregger (Dragovic 40), Ulmer; Onisiwo (Baumgartlinger 86), Ilsanker, Schlager X, Baumgartner; Sabitzer, Gregoritsch (Grbic 79).

Romania (1) 1 *(Puscas 25)*

Northern Ireland (0) 1 *(Whyte 86)*

Romania: (4312) Tatarusanu; Hanca (Nedelcearu 86), Chiriches, Tosca, Bancu; Stanciu, Cicaldau (Nistor 74), Maxim; Hagi (Cretu A 56); Puscas, Alibec.
Northern Ireland: (4411) Peacock-Farrell; Dallas, Ballard (Smith 90), Cathcart, Lewis; Magennis■, Evans C (Lafferty 77), Davis, Saville; McNair; Washington (Whyte 65).

Monday, 7 September 2020

Austria (1) 2 *(Baumgartner 17, Onisiwo 80)*

Romania (1) 3 *(Alibec 3, Grigore 51, Maxim 69)*

Austria: (4231) Schlager A; Lainer, Posch, Hinteregger, Ulmer; Grillitsch (Monschein 81), Baumgartlinger (Onisiwo 60); Sabitzer, Schlager X, Baumgartner; Gregoritsch (Grbic 73).
Romania: (433) Tatarusanu; Burca, Chiriches (Nedelcearu 74), Grigore, Bancu; Maxim, Cretu A, Stanciu; Deac (Iancu 40), Alibec (Puscas 68), Coman.

Northern Ireland (1) 1 *(McNair 6)*

Norway (3) 5 *(Elyounoussi M 2, Haaland 7, 58, Sorloth 19, 47)*

Northern Ireland: (4231) Peacock-Farrell; Smith, Ballard (Boyce 46), Cathcart, Ferguson; Davis, Thompson; Dallas, McNair, Saville (Evans C 71); Washington (Lavery 77).
Norway: (442) Jarstein; Elabdellaoui (Svensson 80), Hovland, Ajer, Aleesami (Meling 77); Johansen (King 71), Henriksen, Normann, Elyounoussi M; Sorloth, Haaland.

Sunday, 11 October 2020

Northern Ireland (0) 0

Austria (1) 1 *(Gregoritsch 42)* 600

Northern Ireland: (4231) McGovern; McLaughlin C, Cathcart, Evans J, Lewis; Davis (Evans C 73), Dallas (Thompson 73); Whyte (Boyce 83), McNair (Magennis 83), Jones; Lafferty (Washington 61).
Austria: (442) Pervan; Lainer, Dragovic, Hinteregger, Alaba; Ranftl (Trimmel 73), Ilsanker, Baumgartlinger, Baumgartner; Gregoritsch (Grbic 80), Schlager X.

Norway (2) 4 *(Haaland 13, 64, 74, Sorloth 39)*

Romania (0) 0

Norway: (442) Jarstein; Elabdellaoui (Svensson 79), Strandberg, Ajer, Meling; Odegaard (Linnes 70), Berge, Normann (Midtsjoe 70), Elyounoussi M (Hauge 85); Haaland (King 79), Sorloth.
Romania: (433) Tatarusanu; Manea, Burca, Tosca, Bancu; Cicaldau (Stanciu 75), Cretu A (Maxim 75), Marin; Iancu (Alibec 90), Puscas (Keseru 64), Hagi (Mitrita 64).

Wednesday, 14 October 2020

Norway (0) 1 *(Dallas 67 (og))*

Northern Ireland (0) 0

Norway: (442) Hansen; Elabdellaoui, Strandberg, Ajer, Meling; Odegaard (Linnes 78), Berge, Normann (Midtsjoe 65), Elyounoussi M; King (Sorloth 65), Haaland (Henriksen 87).
Northern Ireland: (532) Carson; Smith (Dallas 60), Ballard, Evans J (McLaughlin C 46), Flanagan, Ferguson; Thompson (Davis 85), Evans C, Saville (McNair 61); Magennis, Washington (Whyte 75).

Romania (0) 0

Austria (0) 1 *(Schopf 75)*

Romania: (433) Tatarusanu; Balasa, Burca, Tosca, Bancu; Maxim (Cicaldau 62), Marin, Stanciu (Iancu 83); Deac (Puscas 83), Alibec (Keseru 62), Mitrita (Hagi 77).
Austria: (442) Pervan; Lainer, Dragovic, Hinteregger (Posch 53), Alaba; Schopf (Ranftl 77), Ilsanker, Baumgartlinger (Grillitsch 77), Baumgartner; Gregoritsch (Kalajdzic 90), Schlager X.

Sunday, 15 November 2020

Austria (0) 2 *(Schaub 81, Grbic 87)*

Northern Ireland (0) 1 *(Magennis 74)*

Austria: (4231) Pervan; Lainer, Dragovic (Ranftl 46), Hinteregger, Ulmer (Grbic 78); Baumgartlinger (Schaub 78), Ilsanker; Schlager X, Sabitzer, Alaba; Gregoritsch (Arnautovic 63).
Northern Ireland: (352) McGovern; Ballard (Cathcart 83), McLaughlin C, Flanagan; Dallas, McNair, Smith, McCann A (Davis 83), Ferguson (Lewis 36); Washington (Magennis 62), Boyce (Whyte 62).

Romania 3

Norway 0

Romania awarded the game 3-0 after Norway players tested positive for COVID-19.

Wednesday, 18 November 2020

Austria (0) 1 *(Grbic 90)*

Norway (0) 1 *(Zahid 61)*

Austria: (442) Pervan; Lainer, Ilsanker (Trauner 81), Hinteregger, Ulmer; Ranftl, Baumgartlinger, Schlager X (Grbic 65), Alaba; Sabitzer, Arnautovic.
Norway: (442) Bratveit; Ryerson (Granli 81), Hanche-Olsen, Gabrielsen, Skjelvik; Zahid (Askildsen 81), Tronstad, Ulvestad, Daehli (Thorstvedt 67); Larsen (Evjen 86), Berisha (Vindheim 86).

Northern Ireland (0) 1 *(Boyce 56)*

Romania (0) 1 *(Bicfalvi 81)*

Northern Ireland: (352) Peacock-Farrell; Ballard, Evans J, Cathcart; Dallas, McNair, Smith (Galbraith 79), McCann A, Kennedy (Lewis 66); Magennis (McLaughlin C 79), Boyce (Washington 67).
Romania: (343) Tatarusanu; Nedelcearu, Cristea, Tosca (Bicfalvi 74); Cretu V (Mogos 64), Nistor, Marin, Camora; Man (Maxim 64), Alibec (Baluta 87), Tanase (Ganea 87).

League B – Group 1	P	W	D	L	F	A	GD	Pts
Austria	6	4	1	1	9	6	3	13
Norway	6	3	1	2	12	7	5	10
Romania	6	2	2	2	8	9	–1	8
Northern Ireland	6	0	2	4	4	11	–7	2

LEAGUE B – GROUP 2

Friday, 4 September 2020

Scotland (1) 1 *(Christie 45 (pen))*

Israel (0) 1 *(Zahavi 73)*

Scotland: (343) Marshall; McTominay, McKenna, Tierney; Forrest, Jack, McGregor C, Robertson; McGinn (Armstrong 79), Dykes (Burke 74), Christie.
Israel: (532) Marciano; Dasa, Bitton, Tibi, Elhamed, Tawatha; Peretz (Cohen Y 72), Natcho, Solomon (Glazer 90); Zahavi, Dabbur (Weissman 79).

Slovakia (0) 1 *(Schranz 88)*

Czech Republic (0) 3 *(Coufal 48, Dockal 53 (pen), Krmencik 86)*

Slovakia: (4231) Greif; Pekarik, Stetina (Valjent 32), Skriniar, Gyomber; Hrosovsky, Lobotka; Kucka, Duda (Zrelak 17), Haraslin; Bozenik (Schranz 65).
Czech Republic: (4231) Vaclik; Coufal, Celustka, Kalas, Boril; Darida, Kral; Masopust (Sevcik 86), Dockal, Jankto (Provod 68); Hlozek (Krmencik 72).

Monday, 7 September 2020

Czech Republic (1) 1 *(Pesek 11)*

Scotland (1) 2 *(Dykes 27, Christie 52 (pen))*

Czech Republic: (4231) Mandous; Holes, Hubnik, Jemelka, Zeleny; Janos, Havlik (Rusek 81); Malinsky, Budinsky (Breite 55), Pesek (Potocny 76); Tecl.
Scotland: (3142) Marshall; McKenna, Cooper, McTominay; McLean; Palmer, Armstrong (McGregor C 80), Fleck (McGinn 71), Robertson; Dykes (Paterson 67), Christie.

Israel (0) 1 *(Elmkies 90)*

Slovakia (1) 1 *(Duris 14)*

Israel: (532) Marciano; Dasa, Bitton, Tibi, Elhamed, Tawatha (Elmkies 71); Solomon, Natcho (Cohen Y 46), Peretz; Zahavi, Dabbur (Weissman 57).
Slovakia: (433) Rodak; Koscelnik, Valjent, Skriniar, Gyomber; Kucka, Lobotka, Sabo (Schranz 67); Bero, Duris (Bozenik 78), Mihalik (Haraslin 87).

Sunday, 11 October 2020

Israel (0) 1 *(Zahavi 55)*

Czech Republic (1) 2 *(Abu Hanna 14 (og), Vydra 47)*

Israel: (532) Marciano; Dasa (Dabbur 75), Yeini, Tibi, Elhamed, Abu Hanna (Menachem 46); Abu Fani (Karzev 88), Natcho (Golasa 75), Solomon; Weissman (Saba 66), Zahavi.
Czech Republic: (4231) Vaclik; Coufal, Celustka, Kudela, Boril; Soucek, Kral; Masopust (Kaderabek 68), Darida (Holes 87), Provod (Petrasek 90); Vydra (Sevcik 68).

Scotland (0) 1 *(Dykes 54)*

Slovakia (0) 0

Scotland: (352) Marshall; McTominay, Gallagher, Considine; O'Donnell, Fleck (McGregor C 72), McGinn (Jack 89), McLean, Robertson; Dykes (McBurnie 72), Fraser (Paterson 85).
Slovakia: (433) Kuciak; Koscelnik, Ninaj, Valjent, Holubek; Bero (Duda 22), Gregus, Hamsik (Kucka 62); Schranz (Mak 62), Bozenik (Safranko 76), Haraslin (Rusnak 76).

Wednesday, 14 October 2020

Scotland (1) 1 *(Fraser 6)*

Czech Republic (0) 0 299

Scotland: (3412) Marshall; McTominay, Gallagher, Considine; O'Donnell, Jack, McGregor C, Taylor (Hanlon 79); McGinn (Paterson 79); Dykes (McBurnie 65), Fraser (McLean 70).
Czech Republic: (4231) Vaclik; Coufal, Celustka (Hovorka 20), Kudela, Boril; Soucek, Kral (Kaderabek 77); Masopust (Poznar 65), Darida, Provod (Sevcik 65); Vydra (Rabusic 77).

Slovakia (2) 2 *(Hamsik 16, Mak 38)*

Israel (0) 3 *(Zahavi 68, 76, 89)*

Slovakia: (4231) Greif; Pekarik, Vavro, Valjent, Mazan; Hrosovsky, Hamsik; Rusnak, Duda (Gregus 71), Mak (Haraslin 56); Bozenik (Safranko 71).
Israel: (532) Marciano; Dasa, Dgani (Nachmias 90), Tibi, Yeini (Arad 46), Kandil (Weissman 69); Natcho (Lavi 58), Golasa, Solomon; Zahavi, Dabbur.

Sunday, 15 November 2020

Czech Republic (1) 1 *(Darida 7)*

Israel (0) 0

Czech Republic: (4231) Vaclik; Coufal, Kalas, Brabec, Mateju; Soucek, Kral; Masopust (Kopic 62), Darida (Dockal 89), Jankto (Vydra 82); Ondrasek (Krmencik 62).
Israel: (3142) Marciano; Bitton, Tibi, Elhamed■; Natcho (Lavi 46); Dasa, Peretz (Weissman 73), Golasa (Abu Fani 86), Tawatha (Menachem 46); Zahavi, Solomon.

Slovakia (1) 1 *(Gregus 31)*

Scotland (0) 0

Slovakia: (4141) Rodak; Pekarik, Satka, Skriniar, Mazan; Hrosovsky; Kucka (Lobotka 61), Duda, Hamsik (Rusnak 68), Gregus; Duris (Safranko 90).
Scotland: (3412) Gordon; Considine (Griffiths 68), McKenna, Cooper; Palmer, McGinn, McLean, Tierney; Armstrong (Shankland 87); Christie, McBurnie.

Wednesday, 18 November 2020

Czech Republic (1) 2 *(Soucek 17, Ondrasek 55)*

Slovakia (0) 0

Czech Republic: (4231) Vaclik (Koubek 46); Coufal, Kalas, Brabec, Mateju; Soucek, Kral; Masopust (Cerny 46), Darida (Barak 88), Jankto (Kopic 74); Ondrasek (Vydra 66).
Slovakia: (4141) Rodak; Pekarik, Gyomber, Skriniar, Hubocan; Lobotka (Hrosovsky 62); Rusnak (Suslov 62), Kucka (Gregus 67), Hamsik, Mak (Safranko 62); Duris (Schranz 81).

Israel (1) 1 *(Solomon 44)*

Scotland (0) 0

Israel: (532) Marciano; Dasa, Bitton, Tibi, Yeini (Dgani 78), Menachem; Natcho (Golasa 62), Lavi (Abu Fani 78), Solomon (Cohen Y 84); Weissman, Zahavi.
Scotland: (532) Marshall; O'Donnell (Burke 73), McTominay, Gallagher (McKenna 73), Tierney, Robertson; McGinn (Griffiths 61), Jack, McGregor C (McLean 82); Dykes (McBurnie 61), Christie.

League B – Group 2	P	W	D	L	F	A	GD	Pts
Czech Republic	6	4	0	2	9	5	4	12
Scotland	6	3	1	2	5	4	1	10
Israel	6	2	2	2	7	7	0	8
Slovakia	6	1	1	4	5	10	–5	4

LEAGUE B – GROUP 3

Thursday, 3 September 2020

Russia (0) 3 *(Dzyuba 48 (pen), 81, Karavaev 69)*

Serbia (0) 1 *(Mitrovic A 78)*

Russia: (451) Shunin; Semenov (Neustadter 77), Fernandes, Karavaev, Dzhikija; Zhirkov (Kuzyaev 80), Ionov, Ozdoev, Zobnin, Bakaev (Anton Miranchuk 68); Dzyuba.
Serbia: (343) Dmitrovic; Nikola Maksimovic, Milenkovic, Pavlovic (Kolarov 65); Lazovic, Gudelj, Kostic, Nemanja Maksimovic (Ljajic 85); Tadic, Mitrovic A, Milinkovic-Savic (Djuricic 65).

Turkey (0) 0

Hungary (0) 1 *(Szoboszlai 80)*

Turkey: (451) Cakir; Soyuncu, Demiral, Muldur, Meras; Ayhan, Calhanoglu, Kilinc (Karaman 76), Yandas (Kahveci 58), Kutucu (Yazici 46); Yilmaz.
Hungary: (442) Gulacsi; Orban, Fiola, Lang, Attila Szalai; Holender, Nagy A, Szoboszlai, Siger (Schafer 60); Adam Szalai (Nikolic 71), Sallai (Kalmar 82).

Sunday, 6 September 2020

Hungary (0) 2 *(Sallai 62, Nikolic 70)*

Russia (2) 3 *(Anton Miranchuk 15, Ozdoev 33, Fernandes 46)*

Hungary: (3421) Gulacsi; Orban, Lang, Attila Szalai; Bese, Siger (Kalmar 46), Nagy A, Holender; Sallai, Szoboszlai (Cseri 82); Adam Szalai (Nikolic 67).
Russia: (4231) Shunin; Fernandes, Semenov, Dzhikija, Kudryashov; Ozdoev, Zobnin; Ionov (Karavaev 75), Anton Miranchuk (Gazinsky 67), Kuzyaev (Zhirkov 57); Dzyuba.

Serbia (0) 0

Turkey (0) 0

Serbia: (3511) Rajkovic; Milenkovic, Kolarov■, Pavlovic; Lazovic (Gacinovic 27), Tadic, Nemanja Maksimovic (Mitrovic S 61), Gudelj, Kostic; Radonjic (Djuricic 87); Mitrovic A.
Turkey: (4231) Gunok; Celik (Sangare 46), Kabak, Soyuncu, Kaldirim; Tufan, Tekdemir; Yazici, Kokcu (Under 60), Karaman; Unal (Yilmaz 78).

Sunday, 11 October 2020

Russia (1) 1 *(Anton Miranchuk 28)*

Turkey (0) 1 *(Karaman 62)* 5019

Russia: (4231) Shunin; Karavaev, Semenov, Kudryashov, Zhirkov; Zobnin, Ozdoev; Ionov (Mostovoy 70 (Formin 90)), Anton Miranchuk (Gazinsky 70), Kuzyaev (Cheryshev 59); Dzyuba.
Turkey: (4231) Gunok; Celik, Kabak, Demiral, Meras; Tufan, Tekdemir (Yokuslu 80); Karaca (Under 46), Calhanoglu (Yazici 90), Karaman (Omur 81); Yilmaz (Unal 90).

Serbia (0) 0

Hungary (1) 1 *(Konyves 20)*

Serbia: (352) Rajkovic; Milenkovic, Mitrovic S, Pavlovic; Gacinovic (Vlahovic 66), Milivojevic (Lukic 46), Gudelj, Ljajic (Radonjic 46), Mladenovic; Jovic, Tadic.
Hungary: (352) Gulacsi; Botka, Lang, Attila Szalai; Bese (Orban 56), Gazdag (Schafer 76), Nagy A, Kalmar, Hangya (Holender 46); Konyves (Adam Szalai 64), Nikolic (Nego 76).

Wednesday, 14 October 2020

Russia (0) 0

Hungary (0) 0 4821

Russia: (4231) Shunin; Smolnikov, Semenov, Kudryashov, Zhirkov (Karavaev 67); Ozdoev (Sobolev 81), Anton Miranchuk (Bakaev 55); Ionov (Gazinsky 67), Zobnin, Kuzyaev (Mostovoy 55); Dzyuba.
Hungary: (3412) Dibusz; Botka, Orban, Attila Szalai; Nego, Gazdag (Nagy A 46), Siger, Holender (Fiola 46); Kalmar (Schafer 77); Adam Szalai (Konyves 83), Nikolic (Varga K 61).

Turkey (0) 2 *(Calhanoglu 56, Tufan 76)*

Serbia (1) 2 *(Milinkovic-Savic 21, Mitrovic A 49 (pen))*

Turkey: (4231) Gunok; Celik, Demiral, Tekdemir (Yazici 75), Kaldirim (Meras 27); Tufan, Yokuslu; Under (Omur 86), Calhanoglu, Karaman; Yilmaz■.
Serbia: (3421) Dmitrovic; Milenkovic, Mitrovic S (Gudelj 75), Kolarov; Lazovic, Nemanja Maksimovic, Lukic, Ristic (Mladenovic 46); Milinkovic-Savic, Djuricic (Vlahovic 75); Mitrovic A.

Sunday, 15 November 2020

Hungary (1) 1 *(Kalmar 39)*

Serbia (1) 1 *(Radonjic 17)*

Hungary: (3421) Dibusz; Kecskes, Lang, Botka; Bese (Gyurcso 78), Nagy A, Siger (Nego 58), Holender (Hangya 68); Kalmar, Szoboszlai (Schafer 78); Nikolic (Konyves 57).
Serbia: (343) Dmitrovic; Milenkovic, Gudelj, Spajic; Lazovic (Gacinovic 57), Nemanja Maksimovic (Grujic 62), Lukic, Ristic (Mladenovic 62); Tadic (Milinkovic-Savic 79), Jovic, Radonjic (Vlahovic 79).

Turkey (2) 3 *(Karaman 26, Under 32, Tosun 52 (pen))*

Russia (1) 2 *(Cheryshev 10, Kuzyaev 57)*

Turkey: (4141) Gunok; Celik (Kabak 64), Ayhan, Demiral, Erkin; Yokuslu; Under (Turuc 64), Tufan (Tekdemir 86), Calhanoglu (Yazici 86), Karaman; Tosun (Kahveci 80).
Russia: (3421) Guilherme; Semenov■, Dzhikija, Kudryashov; Kuzyaev (Anton Miranchuk 70), Zobnin (Fomin 79), Ozdoev, Zhirkov; Aleksey Miranchuk (Ionov 79), Cheryshev (Karavaev 37); Zabolotny (Erokhin 70).

Wednesday, 18 November 2020

Hungary (0) 2 *(Siger 57, Varga K 90)*

Turkey (0) 0

Hungary: (3412) Dibusz; Fiola, Lang, Attila Szalai; Nego (Botka 89), Siger, Nagy A, Hangya (Holender 74); Kalmar (Cseri 46); Nikolic (Gyurcso 64), Konyves (Varga K 46).
Turkey: (41212) Gunok; Sangare, Kabak, Demiral, Erkin; Tekdemir (Ayhan 88); Tufan (Ozcan 71), Kahveci (Yazici 55); Calhanoglu; Karaman, Tosun (Turuc 71).

Serbia (4) 5 *(Radonjic 10, Jovic 25, 45, Vlahovic 40, Mladenovic 64)*

Russia (0) 0

Serbia: (352) Rajkovic; Milenkovic, Spajic, Mitrovic S (Pavlovic 90); Radonjic (Vlahovic 31), Gudelj (Zdjelar 90), Nemanja Maksimovic (Gacinovic 46), Mladenovic (Randjelovic 90), Ristic; Jovic, Mitrovic A.
Russia: (4231) Guilherme (Dzanaev 46); Karavaev, Diveev (Evgeniev 46), Dzhikija, Zhirkov; Ozdoev, Kuzyaev; Erokhin, Aleksey Miranchuk (Mostovoy 46), Anton Miranchuk (Oblyakov 46); Zabolotny (Cheryshev 72).

League B – Group 3	P	W	D	L	F	A	GD	Pts
Hungary	6	3	2	1	7	4	3	11
Russia	6	2	2	2	9	12	–3	8
Serbia	6	1	3	2	9	7	2	6
Turkey	6	1	3	2	6	8	–2	6

LEAGUE B – GROUP 4

Thursday, 3 September 2020

Bulgaria (0) 1 *(Kraev 56)*

Republic of Ireland (0) 1 *(Duffy 90)*

Bulgaria: (451) Georgiev; Zanev (Galabov 79), Popov S, Nedyalkov, Dimitrov K; Delev (Karagaren 76), Ivanov, Kostadinov, Nedelev (Tsvetkov 83), Malinov; Kraev.
Republic of Ireland: (433) Randolph; Duffy, Stevens, Egan, Doherty; McCarthy (Brady 70), Hourihane, Hendrick; O'Dowda (Robinson 74), Connolly, Idah (Long S 77).

Finland (0) 0

Wales (0) 1 *(Moore 80)*

Finland: (352) Hradecky; Ojala, O'Shaughnessy, Vaisanen L; Sparv (Lam 76), Kauko (Jensen 71), Uronen, Kamara, Niskanen (Soiri 86); Pukki, Pohjanpalo.
Wales: (451) Hennessey; Davies B, Lockyer, Roberts C, Ampadu; Bale (Wilson 46), Williams J (Williams N 60), Morrell, James (Cabango 90), Levitt; Moore.

Sunday, 6 September 2020

Republic of Ireland (0) 0

Finland (0) 1 *(Jensen 63)*

Republic of Ireland: (433) Randolph; Doherty, Duffy, Egan, Stevens; Molumby, Arter, Brady; O'Dowda (Robinson 59), Idah (McGoldrick 66), Connolly (McClean 77).
Finland: (532) Hradecky; Alho, Vaisanen L, Ojala, O'Shaughnessy, Hamalainen (Uronen 79); Kamara, Sparv, Taylor; Pukki (Karjalainen 90), Pohjanpalo (Jensen 63).

Wales (0) 1 *(Williams N 90)*

Bulgaria (0) 0

Wales: (4231) Hennessey; Roberts C (Williams N 65), Lockyer, Ampadu, Davies B; Smith, Morrell; Bale, Brooks (Williams J 76), James; Moore (Robson-Kanu 61).
Bulgaria: (4231) Georgiev; Cicinho, Dimitrov K, Nedyalkov, Goranov; Kostadinov, Karabelyov; Karagaren, Nedelev (Krastev 82), Ivanov (Delev 70); Kraev (Iliev D 61).

Sunday, 11 October 2020

Finland (0) 2 *(Taylor 52, Jensen 67)*

Bulgaria (0) 0

Finland: (442) Hradecky; Raitala, Toivio, Arajuuri, Uronen; Niskanen (Alho 87), Sparv, Kamara, Taylor (Soiri 74); Pukki (Karjalainen 87), Pohjanpalo (Jensen 65).
Bulgaria: (433) Lukov; Popov S, Dimitrov K, Bozhikov, Nedyalkov (Velkovski 60); Malinov, Tsvetkov (Karabelyov 75), Iliev D (Nedelev 75); Despodov, Isa (Kraev 60), Yomov.

Republic of Ireland (0) 0

Wales (0) 0

Republic of Ireland: (4231) Randolph; Doherty, Duffy, Long K (Christie 25), Stevens; Molumby (Cullen 90), Hourihane; Brady (Horgan 73), Hendrick, McClean■; Long S (Maguire 74).
Wales: (4411) Hennessey; Roberts C, Ampadu, Rodon, Davies B; Wilson (Williams N 67), Smith (Levitt 67), Morrell, James (Brooks 77); Ramsey; Moore.

Wednesday, 14 October 2020

Bulgaria (0) 0

Wales (0) 1 *(Williams J 85)*

Bulgaria: (4231) Mihailov; Cicinho, Terziev, Dimitrov K, Nedyalkov; Malinov (Tsvetkov 46), Nedelev; Despodov (Karagaren 84), Karabelyov, Yomov; Kraev (Isa 75).
Wales: (3412) Hennessey (Davies A 79); Mepham, Rodon, Davies B; Williams N, Ampadu, Smith (Levitt 72), Norrington-Davies; Wilson (Williams J 72); Roberts T, James (Matondo 54).

Finland (0) 1 *(Jensen 66)*

Republic of Ireland (0) 0 7900

Finland: (442) Hradecky; Granlund (Raitala 86), Toivio, Arajuuri, Uronen; Soiri (Niskanen 46), Sparv, Kamara (Schuller 75), Taylor; Jensen (Kauko 86), Pukki (Pohjanpalo 81).
Republic of Ireland: (4231) Randolph; Doherty, Duffy, O'Shea, Stevens; Molumby (Knight 83), Hourihane; Horgan (Curtis 75), Hendrick (Idah 75), Connolly; Maguire (Brady 53).

Sunday, 15 November 2020

Bulgaria (0) 1 *(Iliev D 68 (pen))*

Finland (2) 2 *(Pukki 7, Lod 45)*

Bulgaria: (4231) Lukov; Popov S, Dimitrov K, Bozhikov, Velkovski; Malinov, Karabelyov (Tsvetkov 85); Delev (Kovachev 78), Yankov (Iliev D 65), Ivanov (Karagaren 78); Kraev.
Finland: (442) Hradecky; Alho, Toivio, Arajuuri, Uronen; Lod, Sparv (Schuller 69), Kamara, Taylor (Soiri 68); Pukki (Niskanen 89), Pohjanpalo (Forss 35).

Wales (0) 1 *(Brooks 66)*

Republic of Ireland (0) 0

Wales: (343) Ward; Mepham, Rodon, Davies B; Williams N, Ampadu, Morrell, Norrington-Davies (Moore 62); Bale, Brooks (Roberts T 88), James.
Republic of Ireland: (433) Randolph; Doherty, Duffy, Long K, O'Shea (O'Dowda 82); Molumby (Hourihane 75), Brady (Byrne 82), Hendrick■; Horgan (Knight 59), Idah (Collins 75), McClean.

Wednesday, 18 November 2020

Republic of Ireland (0) 0

Bulgaria (0) 0

Republic of Ireland: (433) Randolph; O'Shea, Duffy, Long K, Manning (Christie 86); Knight, Brady (Byrne 78), Hourihane; Curtis (Parrott 86), Collins (Maguire 85), Horgan (Cullen 67).
Bulgaria: (4231) Lukov; Popov S, Dimitrov K, Angelov, Cicinho (Vasilev 60); Malinov, Tsvetkov; Delev (Kovachev 61), Iliev D (Aleksandrov 81), Ivanov (Karagaren 60); Kraev.

Wales (1) 3 *(Wilson 29, James 46, Moore 84)*

Finland (0) 1 *(Pukki 63)*

Wales: (343) Ward; Mepham, Rodon, Lawrence J (Moore 46); Roberts C, Ampadu, Morrell, Norrington-Davies (Gunter 90); James (Brooks 89), Wilson (Roberts T 89), Bale (Lawrence T 61).
Finland: (352) Hradecky; Toivio, Arajuuri, O'Shaughnessy (Hamalainen 61); Alho, Schuller (Valakari 73), Taylor (Soiri 62), Kamara, Uronen■; Pukki (Forss 89), Lod.

League B – Group 4	P	W	D	L	F	A	GD	Pts
Wales	6	5	1	0	7	1	6	16
Finland	6	4	0	2	7	5	2	12
Republic of Ireland	6	0	3	3	1	4	–3	3
Bulgaria	6	0	2	4	2	7	–5	2

LEAGUE C – GROUP 1

Saturday, 5 September 2020

Azerbaijan (1) 1 *(Sheydayev 43)*

Luxembourg (0) 2 *(Krivotsyuk 48 (og), Rodrigues 72 (pen))*

Azerbaijan: (442) Balayev; Medvedev, Mustafazade, Huseynov B, Krivotsyuk; Alasgarov (Nagiyev 67), Jamalov, Garayev, Khalilzade (Abdullayev 77); Emreli■, Sheydayev (Dadashov 58).
Luxembourg: (41212) Moris; Jans, Selimovic, Gerson, Carlson; Martins Pereira; Thill O (Sinani 58), Rodrigues; Thill V (Skenderovic 90); Barreiro, Deville (Bensi 52).

Cyprus (0) 0

Montenegro (0) 2 *(Jovetic 60, 73)*

Cyprus: (433) Kyriakidis; Antoniou, Karo, Laifis, Wheeler; Kousoulos, Kastanos, Tzionis (Avraam 85); Christofi (Loizou 64), Elia (Sotiriou 79), Pittas.
Montenegro: (4231) Mijatovic; Marusic, Savic, Vujacic, Raspopovic; Kosovic (Islamovic 57), Vukcevic N (Scekic 75); Boljevic, Bakic, Haksabanovic; Beciraj (Jovetic 46).

Tuesday, 8 September 2020

Cyprus (0) 0

Azerbaijan (1) 1 *(Medvedev 29)*

Cyprus: (433) Kyriakidis; Charis Kyriakou, Karo, Laifis, Sielis; Kastanos (Spoljaric 76), Kousoulos (Charalambos Kyriakou 57), Tzionis; Pittas, Sotiriou, Christofi (Loizou 57).
Azerbaijan: (3421) Balayev; Huseynov B, Mustafazade, Krivotsyuk; Medvedev, Jamalov (Diniyev 60), Garayev, Huseynov A; Khalilzade (Abdullayev 64), Sadikhov (Alasgarov 76); Sheydayev.

Luxembourg (0) 0

Montenegro (0) 1 *(Beciraj 90 (pen))*

Luxembourg: (4141) Moris; Jans, Selimovic, Gerson, Carlson; Martins Pereira■; Thill V, Barreiro, Thill O, Rodrigues; Sinani.
Montenegro: (442) Mijatovic; Marusic, Savic, Vujacic, Raspopovic; Boljevic (Jankovic M 71), Kosovic, Vukcevic N, Haksabanovic; Islamovic (Beciraj 75), Jovetic (Bakic 62).

Saturday, 10 October 2020

Luxembourg (2) 2 *(Sinani 12, 26)*

Cyprus (0) 0

Luxembourg: (4132) Moris; Jans, Selimovic (Da Graca 69), Gerson, Carlson; Barreiro; Thill V, Thill O, Mica Pinto (Bensi 68); Sinani (Skenderovic 79), Rodrigues.
Cyprus: (442) Kyriakidis; Kousoulos, Karo (Gogic 60), Laifis, Wheeler (Ioannou T 53); Christofi, Artymatas (Charalambos Kyriakou 75), Kastanos, Pittas (Loizou 75); Sotiriou, Tzionis (Antoniou 46).

Montenegro (1) 2 *(Jovetic 9, Ivanovic 71)*

Azerbaijan (0) 0

Montenegro: (4231) Mijatovic; Raspopovic, Vujacic, Simic, Radunovic; Bakic (Kosovic 63), Vukcevic N (Raickovic 81); Boljevic (Ivanovic 71), Jovetic (Jankovic B 81), Haksabanovic; Islamovic (Beciraj 71).
Azerbaijan: (352) Balayev; Huseynov B, Mustafazade, Krivotsyuk; Medvedev (Salahli 46), Alasgarov (Abbasov M 79), Jamalov, Garayev (Diniyev 60), Huseynov A; Ghorbani (Sheydayev 60), Sadikhov (Haciyev 61).

Tuesday, 13 October 2020

Azerbaijan (0) 0

Cyprus (0) 0

Azerbaijan: (442) Mahammadaliyev; Huseynov A, Badalov, Mustafazade (Seydiyev 71), Krivotsyuk; Ibrahhimli (Diniyev 57), Mustafayev, Garayev, Salahli (Alasgarov 57); Sheydayev (Ghorbani 81), Sadikhov (Haciyev 71).
Cyprus: (433) Demetriou D; Antoniou, Karo, Laifis, Wheeler; Charalambos Kyriakou (Papageorghiou 46), Artymatas, Kastanos; Christofi (Loizou 69), Sotiriou (Pittas 18), Tzionis (Kousoulos 81).

Montenegro (1) 1 *(Ivanovic 34)*

Luxembourg (1) 2 *(Muratovic 42, Sinani 86)*

Montenegro: (4141) Mijatovic; Raspopovic (Vukcevic M 79), Savic, Simic■, Radunovic; Vukcevic N; Ivanovic (Jankovic M■ 87), Jovetic, Kosovic (Scekic 78), Haksabanovic; Islamovic (Beciraj 66).
Luxembourg: (442) Moris; Jans, Gerson, Carlson, Mica Pinto; Thill V (Deville 58), Barreiro, Skenderovic, Rodrigues; Sinani (Thill O■ 90), Muratovic (Da Graca 89).

Saturday, 14 November 2020

Azerbaijan (0) 0

Montenegro (0) 0

Azerbaijan: (352) Mahammadaliyev; Badalov (Isgenderli 67), Medvedev, Huseynov B; Huseynov A (Seydiyev 43), Garayev, Mustafayev (Jamalov 46), Sadikhov (Sheydayev 46), Salahli; Mutallimov (Najafov 81), Emreli.
Montenegro: (442) Mijatovic; Marusic, Sofranac, Vujacic, Radunovic; Ivanovic■, Scekic (Savicevic 81), Bakic, Haksabanovic; Jovetic (Islamovic 90), Mugosa (Boljevic 58).

Cyprus (1) 2 *(Kastanos 34 (pen), 70)*

Luxembourg (1) 1 *(Kousoulos 5 (og))*

Cyprus: (433) Demetriou D; Antoniou (Charis Kyriakou 83), Shelis, Laifis, Ioannou N; Kastanos (Papafotis 83), Kousoulos (Charalambos Kyriakou 62), Artymatas; Pittas, Elia, Tzionis (Ioannou T 62).
Luxembourg: (442) Moris; Jans, Selimovic■, Gerson, Carlson; Thill V (Deville 70), Barreiro, Mica Pinto, Rodrigues; Muratovic (Skenderovic 55), Sinani.

Tuesday, 17 November 2020

Luxembourg (0) 0

Azerbaijan (0) 0 100

Luxembourg: (433) Schon; Jans, Mahmutovic, Gerson, Mica Pinto; Thill V (Thill S 80), Barreiro, Skenderovic (Bohnert 90); Sinani, Muratovic (Da Graca 90), Deville (Bensi 67).
Azerbaijan: (442) Mahammadaliyev; Seydiyev, Huseynov B (Aliyev 44), Badalov, Krivotsyuk; Mutallimov (Mustafayev 69), Garayev, Ibrahhimli (Najafov 84), Salahli; Emreli (Sadikhov 84), Sheydayev.

Montenegro (3) 4 *(Jovetic 14, Boljevic 25, 28, Mugosa 60)*

Cyprus (0) 0

Montenegro: (442) Mijatovic; Vukcevic M, Vujacic, Simic, Marusic; Boljevic (Jovovic 71), Scekic (Radunovic 71), Bakic (Kosovic 61), Haksabanovic; Mugosa (Islamovic 71), Jovetic (Savicevic 61).
Cyprus: (433) Demetriou D; Charis Kyriakou, Shelis, Laifis, Ioannou T (Tzionis 65); Kousoulos (Loizou 66), Artymatas (Charalambos Kyriakou 46), Ioannou N; Pittas, Kakoullis (Gogic 65), Kastanos (Makris 85).

League C – Group 1	P	W	D	L	F	A	GD	Pts
Montenegro	6	4	1	1	10	2	8	13
Luxembourg	6	3	1	2	7	5	2	10
Azerbaijan	6	1	3	2	2	4	–2	6
Cyprus	6	1	1	4	2	10	–8	4

LEAGUE C – GROUP 2

Saturday, 5 September 2020

Estonia (0) 0

Georgia (1) 1 *(Kacharava 32)*

Estonia: (4411) Hein; Teniste, Tamm, Mets, Jarvelaid; Tunjov (Liivak 71), Kreida, Kait, Ojamaa; Vassiljev (Ainsalu 86); Zenjov (Anier 71).
Georgia: (4231) Loria; Kakabadze, Kvirkvelia, Khocholava, Azouz; Kankava, Kvekveskiri; Kvaratskhelia (Aburjania 90), Chakvetadze (Kvilitaia 78), Okriashvili; Kacharava (Lobzhanidze 68).

North Macedonia (2) 2 *(Alioski 5 (pen), Nestorovski 38 (pen))*

Armenia (0) 1 *(Barseghyan 90 (pen))*

North Macedonia: (4231) Siskovski; Ristovski S, Velkovski, Musliu, Ristevski (Spirovski 71); Nikolov (Trajkovski 75), Ademi; Alioski, Bardhi, Elmas; Nestorovski (Pandev 62).
Armenia: (442) Yurchenko; Hambardzumyan, Haroyan, Calisir, Grigoryan S (Babayan 46); Hovhannisyan K, Wbeymar, Grigoryan A, Bayramyan (Barseghyan 46); Karapetyan (Briasco 76), Koryan.

Tuesday, 8 September 2020

Armenia (1) 2 *(Karapetyan 43, Wbeymar 65)*

Estonia (0) 0

Armenia: (442) Yurchenko; Hambardzumyan, Haroyan, Calisir (Voskanyan 46), Hovhannisyan A; Barseghyan, Wbeymar, Grigoryan A, Kadimyan (Bayramyan 73); Koryan (Bichakhchyan 64), Karapetyan.
Estonia: (4231) Hein; Kait, Baranov, Mets, Kallaste (Jarvelaid 30); Ainsalu, Antonov (Vassiljev 66); Roosnupp, Tunjov (Anier 63), Sinyavskiy; Sappinen.

Georgia (1) 1 *(Okriashvili 13 (pen))*

North Macedonia (1) 1 *(Ristovski S 33)*

Georgia: (4231) Loria; Kakabadze, Kvirkvelia, Khocholava, Mali (Shengelia 75); Kankava, Kvekveskiri (Kacharava 85); Kvaratskhelia, Okriashvili, Davitashvili; Kvilitaia (Chakvetadze 62).
North Macedonia: (4231) Siskovski; Ristovski S, Velkovski, Musliu■, Alioski; Spirovski, Ademi (Nikolov 59); Trajkovski (Nestorovski 59), Bardhi, Elmas; Pandev (Bejtulai 78).

Sunday, 11 October 2020

Armenia (1) 2 *(Bayramyan 6, Mkhitaryan 88 (pen))*

Georgia (0) 2 *(Kacharava 46, Okriashvili 74)*

Armenia: (4231) Yurchenko; Hovhannisyan K (Kadimyan 81), Haroyan, Calisir, Hovhannisyan A; Wbeymar (Gareginyan 67), Grigoryan A; Barseghyan (Bichakhchyan 89), Mkhitaryan, Bayramyan; Karapetyan (Babayan 67).
Georgia: (4231) Makaridze; Azouz, Kobakhidze, Grigalava, Navalovski; Kankava (Kvekveskiri 75), Aburjania (Daushvili 75); Shengelia (Lobzhanidze 80), Gvilia (Okriashvili 61), Qazaishvili; Kacharava (Lobjanidze 80).

Estonia (1) 3 *(Sappinen 33, 61, Liivak 76 (pen))*

North Macedonia (1) 3 *(Kuusk 3 (og), Pandev 80, Zajkov 87)*

Estonia: (4411) Hein; Teniste, Baranov, Kuusk, Pikk; Luts (Marin 34), Kreida, Kait (Ainsalu 85), Sinyavskiy (Lilander 85); Vassiljev (Liivak 70); Sappinen (Lepik 70).
North Macedonia: (4231) Siskovski; Ristovski S, Zajkov, Ristevski, Alioski; Nikolov (Pandev 64), Spirovski; Kostadinov (Stojanovski 76), Hasani (Bardhi 46), Trajkovski (Velkoski 76); Trickovski (Nestorovski 64).

Wednesday, 14 October 2020

Estonia (1) 1 *(Sappinen 13)*

Armenia (1) 1 *(Hovhannisyan K 8)* 1007

Estonia: (4411) Hein; Teniste (Lilander 46), Baranov, Kuusk, Pikk; Liivak (Miller 85), Kreida, Kait, Sinyavskiy (Marin 66); Vassiljev (Tunjov 72); Sappinen (Lepik 66).
Armenia: (4231) Yurchenko; Hovhannisyan K, Voskanyan, Calisir, Hovhannisyan A (Grigoryan S 46); Wbeymar, Grigoryan A (Udo 42); Babayan (Ghazaryan 57), Mkhitaryan, Barseghyan (Bichakhchyan 83); Karapetyan (Kadimyan 83).

North Macedonia (0) 1 *(Alioski 90 (pen))*

Georgia (0) 1 *(Kvaratskhelia 74)*

North Macedonia: (343) Dimitrievski■; Zajkov, Velkovski, Ristevski (Stojanovski 80); Ristovski, Nikolov (Totre 88), Kostadinov (Micevski 89), Alioski; Pandev, Nestorovski (Siskovski 71), Trickovski (Velkoski 80).
Georgia: (4231) Loria; Azouz, Kvirkvelia, Tabidze, Dvali (Navalovski 90); Daushvili (Kvaratskhelia 70), Kvekveskiri; Kiteishvili (Lobzhanidze 7), Gvilia, Qazaishvili (Kobakhidze 90); Kvilitaia (Kacharava 70).

Sunday, 15 November 2020

Georgia (0) 1 *(Qazaishvili 65 (pen))*

Armenia (1) 2 *(Ghazaryan 33, Adamyan 86)*

Georgia: (4231) Makaridze; Azouz, Khocholava, Grigalava, Navalovski; Kankava, Aburjania (Kvekveskiri 80); Lobzhanidze (Papunashvili 80), Gvilia (Mikeltadze 80), Davitashvili (Qazaishvili 56); Lobjanidze (Kacharava 67).
Armenia: (442) Yurchenko; Hambardzumyan, Haroyan, Calisir, Hovhannisyan A (Grigoryan S 69); Barseghyan, Udo (Muradyan 77), Grigoryan A, Ghazaryan (Bichakhchyan 77); Adamyan (Voskanyan 89), Karapetyan (Koryan 77).

North Macedonia (1) 2 *(Trickovski 29, Stojanovski 68)*

Estonia (0) 1 *(Sappinen 52)*

North Macedonia: (4231) Siskovski; Bejtulai, Velkovski, Musliu, Ristovski S; Spirovski (Kostadinov 59), Nikolov; Trajkovski (Stojanovski 59), Elmas (Zajkov 85), Trickovski; Nestorovski (Doriev 78).
Estonia: (4231) Hein; Teniste, Tamm, Mets, Pikk; Kreida, Ainsalu (Tunjov 79); Zenjov (Liivak 63), Vassiljev (Sorga 55), Sinyavskiy (Miller 79); Sappinen (Anier 63).

Wednesday, 18 November 2020

Armenia (0) 1 *(Hambardzumyan 55)*

North Macedonia (0) 0

Armenia: (4231) Yurchenko; Hambardzumyan, Haroyan, Voskanyan, Hovhannisyan K; Udo (Wbeymar 46), Grigoryan A; Barseghyan (Ishkhanyan 90), Koryan (Grigoryan S 65), Hakobyan (Muradyan 70); Karapetyan (Bichakhchyan 46).

North Macedonia: (3412) Siskovski; Zajkov, Velkovski, Musliu (Kitanovski 70); Bejtulai, Totre (Trajcevski 84), Kostadinov (Micevski 62), Ristovski S (Doriev 70); Trajkovski; Stojanovski (Nestorovski 62), Trickovski.

Georgia (0) 0

Estonia (0) 0

Georgia: (4231) Loria; Kakabadze, Kashia, Khocholava (Grigalava 46), Tabidze; Kvekveskiri, Kankava; Davitashvili (Papunashvili 66), Qazaishvili, Lobzhanidze (Mikeltadze 85); Kacharava (Lobjanidze 78).
Estonia: (4231) Hein; Teniste (Lilander 81), Tamm, Kuusk, Pikk; Kreida, Soomets (Miller 79); Zenjov (Marin 79), Vassiljev, Sinyavskiy (Liivak 86); Sappinen (Anier 86).

League C – Group 2	P	W	D	L	F	A	GD	Pts
Armenia	6	3	2	1	9	6	3	11
North Macedonia	6	2	3	1	9	8	1	9
Georgia	6	1	4	1	6	6	0	7
Estonia	6	0	3	3	5	9	–4	3

LEAGUE C – GROUP 3

Thursday, 3 September 2020

Moldova (1) 1 *(Nicolaescu 19)*

Kosovo (0) 1 *(Kololli 71)*

Moldova: (352) Koselev; Armas, Posmac, Mudrac; Ionita, Rata (Marandici 81), Carp (Epureanu 71), Platica, Reabciuk; Caimacov (Cociuc 56), Nicolaescu.
Kosovo: (451) Muric; Aliti, Paqarada, Rrahmani, Vojvoda (Hadergjonaj 60); Berisha V, Kryeziu, Shala (Celina 60), Zeneli, Rashica (Rashani 75); Kololli.

Slovenia (0) 0

Greece (0) 0

Slovenia: (442) Oblak; Mevlja, Stojanovic, Balkovec, Blazic; Rep (Zivec 52), Bohar, Vetrih, Bijol (Kouter 78); Vuckic (Zajc 61), Sporar.
Greece: (451) Barkas; Siovas, Bakakis, Giannoulis, Svarnas; Mandalos (Masouras 87), Bakasetas, Zeca, Kourbelis, Limnios; Pavlidis (Fountas 76).

Sunday, 6 September 2020

Kosovo (0) 1 *(Berisha B 82)*

Greece (1) 2 *(Limnios 2, Siovas 51)*

Kosovo: (433) Ujkani; Vojvoda (Raskaj 58), Rrahmani, Aliti, Hadergjonaj; Halimi (Hasani 55), Dresevic, Berisha V; Celina, Nuhiu, Zeneli (Berisha B 54).
Greece: (4231) Barkas; Bakakis, Svarnas, Stafylidis (Siovas 40), Giannoulis; Kourbelis, Zeca; Limnios, Bakasetas, Fortounis (Masouras 61); Koulouris (Mandalos 83).

Slovenia (1) 1 *(Bohar 28)*

Moldova (0) 0

Slovenia: (4231) Oblak; Stojanovic, Blazic, Mevlja, Balkovec; Kouter, Kurtic; Zajc (Zivec 57), Vuckic (Vetrih 68), Bohar; Sporar (Kramer 85).
Moldova: (532) Koselev; Platica, Mudrac, Posmac, Armas, Reabciuk; Rata (Suvorov 69), Carp, Ionita; Damascan (Milinceanu 60), Caimacov (Epureanu 46).

Sunday, 11 October 2020

Greece (1) 2 *(Bakasetas 45 (pen), Mandalos 50)*

Moldova (0) 0

Greece: (4231) Vlachodimos; Chatzidiakos (Rota 69), Svarnas, Tzavelas, Giannoulis; Kourbelis (Bouchalakis 83), Zeca; Limnios (Pelkas 76), Bakasetas, Mandalos (Fortounis 70); Pavlidis (Fountas 83).
Moldova: (532) Namasco; Platica, Mudrac, Posmac■, Armas, Reabciuk; Rata (Marandici 66), Cociuc, Caimacov (Epureanu 46); Nicolaescu (Milinceanu 57), Ionita (Racu 76).

Kosovo (0) 0

Slovenia (1) 1 *(Vuckic 22)*

Kosovo: (4231) Muric; Hadergjonaj, Dresevic, Aliti, Paqarada; Berisha V, Shala (Muslija 84); Zhegrova (Hasani 90), Celina, Zeneli (Kastrati 78); Kololli (Rashani 84).
Slovenia: (442) Oblak; Stojanovic, Blazic, Mevlja, Balkovec; Rep (Bohar 55), Bijol, Kurtic, Verbic (Skubic 75); Lovric (Vetrih 85), Vuckic (Kramer 85).

Wednesday, 14 October 2020

Greece (0) 0

Kosovo (0) 0

Greece: (4231) Vlachodimos; Chatzidiakos (Lampropoulos 85), Svarnas, Tzavelas, Giannoulis; Kourbelis, Zeca (Bouchalakis 62); Limnios (Pelkas 73), Bakasetas (Fortounis 73), Mandalos (Fountas 63); Pavlidis.
Kosovo: (3412) Muric; Vojvoda, Dresevic, Aliti; Hadergjonaj, Loshaj (Raskaj 34), Shala, Paqarada; Celina (Hasani 63); Kastrati, Kololli■ (Rashani 81).

Moldova (0) 0

Slovenia (3) 4 *(Lovric 8, Vuckic 37 (pen), 42, 55 (pen))*

Moldova: (532) Namasco; Platica (Milinceanu 59), Mudrac (Craciun 46), Armas, Racu, Reabciuk; Rata, Cociuc, Carp (Caimacov 46); Nicolaescu (Spataru 79), Ionita (Taras 74).
Slovenia: (442) Oblak; Skubic, Blazic (Mitrovic 74), Mevlja, Balkovec; Bohar (Rep 74), Bijol (Petrovic 83), Kurtic, Verbic; Lovric (Vetrih 78), Vuckic (Bizjak 78).

Sunday, 15 November 2020

Moldova (0) 0

Greece (2) 2 *(Fortounis 32, Bakasetas 41)*

Moldova: (4231) Namasco; Jardan, Posmac, Armas, Reabciuk; Cebotaru (Epureanu 46), Ionita (Boicuic 83); Rata (Turcan 62), Cociuc (Caimacov 46), Spataru; Damascan (Dros 71).
Greece: (4231) Vlachodimos; Mavrias, Chatzidiakos, Tzavelas, Tsimikas (Kyriakopoulos 62); Zeca, Bouchalakis; Limnios (Chatzigiovanis 78), Bakasetas, Fortounis (Tzolis 65); Pavlidis (Giakoumakis 78).

Slovenia (0) 2 *(Kurtic 62, Ilicic 90 (pen))*

Kosovo (0) 1 *(Muriqi 58)*

Slovenia: (4231) Belec; Stojanovic, Blazic, Mevlja, Balkovec; Vetrih, Kurtic; Ilicic (Kouter 90), Lovric (Crnigoj 87), Bohar; Vuckic (Sporar 68).
Kosovo: (4231) Muric; Vojvoda, Rrahmani, Aliti, Hadergjonaj; Raskaj, Kryeziu (Kastrati 71); Zhegrova (Hasani 90), Berisha V, Berisha B (Rashani 84); Muriqi.

Wednesday, 18 November 2020

Greece (0) 0

Slovenia (0) 0

Greece: (4231) Vlachodimos; Mavrias, Chatzidiakos■, Tzavelas (Masouras 79), Tsimikas (Kyriakopoulos 90); Kourbelis, Zeca (Tzolis 67); Limnios, Bakasetas, Fortounis; Giakoumakis (Pavlidis 46).
Slovenia: (4231) Oblak; Stojanovic, Blazic, Mevlja, Balkovec; Kurtic, Bijol (Vetrih 77); Ilicic (Bajric 90), Lovric (Skubic 90), Bohar (Verbic 67); Vuckic (Sporar 77).

Kosovo (1) 1 *(Kastrati 31)*

Moldova (0) 0

Kosovo: (4231) Ujkani; Vojvoda, Rrahmani (Aliti 20), Dresevic■, Hadergjonaj; Berisha V, Shala; Zhegrova (Kryeziu 84), Celina (Thaci 89), Kastrati; Muriqi.
Moldova: (4231) Namasco; Jardan, Efros, Armas, Reabciuk; Ionita (Caimacov 60), Cebotaru; Spataru (Belousov 85), Turcan, Platica (Rata 38); Nicolaescu.

League C – Group 3	*P*	*W*	*D*	*L*	*F*	*A*	*GD*	*Pts*
Slovenia	6	4	2	0	8	1	7	14
Greece	6	3	3	0	6	1	5	12
Kosovo	6	1	2	3	4	6	–2	5
Moldova	6	0	1	5	1	11	–10	1

LEAGUE C – GROUP 4

Friday, 4 September 2020

Belarus (0) 0

Albania (1) 2 *(Cikalleshi 23, Bare 78)*

Belarus: (442) Gutor; Zolotov (Skavysh 76), Martynovich, Naumov, Bordachev; Nekhaychik, Yablonskiy (Bakhar 86), Selyava (Khachaturyan 46), Stasevich; Dragun, Lisakovich.
Albania: (532) Strakosha; Bare, Veseli, Dermaku, Djimsiti, Trashi (Roshi 68); Hysaj, Gjasula, Abrashi; Cikalleshi (Balaj 72), Manaj (Mihaj 90).

Lithuania (0) 0

Kazakhstan (1) 2 *(Zaynutdinov 3, Kuat 86)*

Lithuania: (4141) Bartkus; Baravykas (Verbickas 82), Palionis, Girdvainis, Mikoliunas; Simkus; Lasickas, Vorobjovas, Sirgedas (Dapkus 89), Kazlauskas; Cernych (Laukzemis 46).
Kazakhstan: (343) Pokatilov; Marochkin, Maliy, Alip; Bystrov, Pertsukh (Kuat 82), Abiken, Vorogovskiy; Zaynutdinov (Fedin 31), Islamkhan (Aimbetov 71), Suyumbayev.

Monday, 7 September 2020

Albania (0) 0

Lithuania (0) 1 *(Kazlauskas 50)*

Albania: (352) Strakosha; Mihaj, Dermaku, Djimsiti; Hysaj■, Gjasula (Uzuni 61), Laci, Abrashi, Trashi (Roshi 61 (Broja 74)); Sadiku, Manaj.
Lithuania: (4231) Svedkauskas; Vaitkunas, Palionis, Girdvainis, Mikoliunas; Dapkus, Simkus; Lasickas (Sirgedas 61), Vorobjovas, Kazlauskas (Verbickas 75); Laukzemis (Romanovskij 78).

Kazakhstan (0) 1 *(Aimbetov 61)*

Belarus (0) 2 *(Bordachev 53, Lisakovich 86)*

Kazakhstan: (343) Pokatilov; Marochkin, Maliy, Alip; Vorogovskiy, Beysebekov, Abiken, Suyumbayev; Fedin (Kuat 64), Aimbetov (Khizhnichenko 72), Islamkhan (Pertsukh 82).
Belarus: (442) Gutor; Zolotov, Martynovich, Naumov, Bordachev; Nekhaychik (Podstrelov 80), Yablonskiy, Ebong (Khachaturyan 85), Stasevich; Dragun, Skavysh (Lisakovich 56).

Sunday, 11 October 2020

Kazakhstan (0) 0

Albania (0) 0

Kazakhstan: (3142) Pokatilov; Marochkin (Beysebekov 46), Erlanov, Kerimzhanov; Tagybergen; Bystrov, Kuat (Pertsukh 69), Abiken, Suyumbayev; Aimbetov (Fedin 69), Zaynutdinov (Zhaksylykov 86).
Albania: (532) Berisha; Veseli, Djimsiti, Dermaku, Kumbulla, Trashi (Memolla 82); Bare, Abrashi (Laci 86), Kallaku; Broja, Manaj (Sulejmanov 82).

Lithuania (1) 2 *(Novikovas 7, Laukzemis 75)*

Belarus (0) 2 *(Lisakovich 59 (pen), Sachivko 66)* 963

Lithuania: (4141) Svedkauskas; Mikoliunas, Palionis, Girdvainis, Vaitkunas (Beneta 64); Simkus (Dapkus 72); Novikovas (Cernych 72), Vorobjovas, Sirgedas (Golubickas 72), Lasickas; Kazlauskas (Laukzemis 60).
Belarus: (4411) Khatkevich; Zolotov, Martynovich, Sachivko, Pechenin; Yuzepchuk (Podstrelov 69), Maevskiy, Ebong (Khachaturyan 80), Stasevich (Bakhar 80); Gromyko (Lisakovich 57); Skavysh (Laptev 57).

Wednesday, 14 October 2020

Belarus (1) 2 *(Yablonskiy 36, Yuzepchuk 90)*

Kazakhstan (0) 0 2074

Belarus: (442) Gutor; Polyakov, Naumov, Sachivko (Bordachev 42), Pechenin (Zolotov 65); Yuzepchuk, Maevskiy (Khachaturyan 47), Yablonskiy, Stasevich (Klimovich 66); Lisakovich (Bakhar 66), Skavysh.
Kazakhstan: (532) Pokatilov; Bystrov (Beysebekov 78), Erlanov, Maliy, Kerimzhanov, Dosmagambetov; Vassiljev (Narzildaev 79), Tagybergen, Abiken (Kuat 57); Zaynutdinov, Aimbetov (Zhaksylykov 57).

Lithuania (0) 0

Albania (0) 0

Lithuania: (4231) Svedkauskas; Mikoliunas (Vaitkunas 69), Palionis, Girdvainis, Beneta; Dapkus, Simkus; Novikovas, Golubickas (Sirgedas 46), Lasickas (Verbickas 90); Laukzemis (Cernych 87).
Albania: (532) Berisha; Veseli, Djimsiti, Dermaku, Kumbulla (Mihaj 57), Lenjani (Trashi 46); Bare, Abrashi, Laci (Cekici 64); Broja (Vrioni 58), Sulejmanov (Manaj 78).

Sunday, 15 November 2020

Albania (2) 3 *(Cikalleshi 16, Ismajli 23, Manaj 62 (pen))*

Kazakhstan (1) 1 *(Abiken 24)*

Albania: (3412) Berisha; Ismajli, Djimsiti, Veseli; Hysaj, Abrashi, Kallaku (Gjasula 53), Uzuni (Doka 68); Memushaj (Selahi 86); Cikalleshi (Sulejmanov 86), Manaj (Balaj 86).
Kazakhstan: (3142) Pokatilov; Kerimzhanov (Fedin 46), Marochkin, Alip; Kuat (Darabayev 87); Vorogovskiy, Beysebekov, Abiken (Tagybergen 46), Suyumbayev (Bystrov 70); Shchetkin, Aimbetov (Khizhnichenko 71).

Belarus (2) 2 *(Yablonskiy 5, Ebong 20)*

Lithuania (0) 0

Belarus: (442) Khatkevich; Yuzepchuk, Polyakov, Sachivko, Bordachev; Ebong, Kendysh (Maevskiy 58), Yablonskiy, Stasevich (Antilevski 82); Lisakovich (Bakhar 72), Skavysh (Klimovich 81).
Lithuania: (4231) Svedkauskas; Vaitkunas, Gaspuitis, Girdvainis, Beneta; Utkus (Romanovskij 76), Slivka; Novikovas (Petravicius 82), Eliosius (Sirgedas 55), Lasickas (Laukzemis 46); Kazlauskas (Veliulis 55).

Wednesday, 18 November 2020

Albania (3) 3 *(Cikalleshi 19, 27 (pen), Manaj 44)*

Belarus (1) 2 *(Skavysh 35, Ebong 80)*

Albania: (3142) Berisha; Ismajli, Djimsiti, Veseli; Gjasula; Doka, Laci (Ramadani 90), Memushaj (Selahi 64), Memolla; Cikalleshi (Balaj 64), Manaj (Uzuni 71).
Belarus: (442) Khatkevich; Yuzepchuk, Polyakov, Sachivko, Bordachev (Pechenin 46); Ebong, Maevskiy (Antilevski 77), Yablonskiy (Kendysh 63), Stasevich; Lisakovich (Laptev 77), Skavysh (Klimovich 86).

Kazakhstan (1) 1 *(Aimbetov 38)*

Lithuania (1) 2 *(Vorobjovas 40, Novikovas 90)*

Kazakhstan: (3142) Pokatilov; Marochkin, Logvinenko, Alip (Khizhnichenko 87); Kuat■; Vorogovskiy, Abiken, Tagybergen, Dosmagambetov (Miroshnichenko 69); Aimbetov (Zhanglyshbay 69), Shchetkin.
Lithuania: (4231) Svedkauskas; Mikoliunas, Beneta, Girdvainis, Vaitkunas (Gaspuitis 46); Simkus, Slivka (Kazlauskas 76); Novikovas, Vorobjovas, Sirgedas (Eliosius 67); Laukzemis (Petravicius 84).

League C – Group 4	P	W	D	L	F	A	GD	Pts
Albania	6	3	2	1	8	4	4	11
Belarus	6	3	1	2	10	8	2	10
Lithuania	6	2	2	2	5	7	–2	8
Kazakhstan	6	1	1	4	5	9	–4	4

LEAGUE D – GROUP 1

Thursday, 3 September 2020

Faroe Islands (1) 3 *(Olsen K 25, Olsen A 87, Olsen B 90)*

Malta (1) 2 *(Degabriele 37, Agius 73)*

Faroe Islands: (433) Nielsen E; Davidsen V, Vatnsdal, Nattestad, Danielsen; Vatnhamar S, Hansson, Olsen B; Olsen K (Olsen A 71), Olsen M (Soylu 65), Bjartalid (Johannesen 79).
Malta: (532) Bonello; Agius, Borg S, Muscat Z, Camenzuli, Mbong J; Pisani (Muscat R 85), Degabriele (Mbong P 71), Guillaumier (Teuma 79); Gambin, Nwoko.

Latvia (0) 0

Andorra (0) 0

Latvia: (451) Steinbors; Dubra, Savalnieks, Cernomordijs, Jurkovskis; Zjuzins (Jaunzems 81), Ikaunieks J, Fjodorovs (Uldrikis 46), Emsis, Ciganiks (Kigurs 81); Gutkovskis■.
Andorra: (442) Gomes; Garcia E, San Nicolas M, Jesus Rubio, Llovera; Pujol, Vales, Rebes, Martinez A (Alaez 90); Vieira (Sanchez A 75), Martinez C (Clemente 84).

Sunday, 6 September 2020

Andorra (0) 0

Faroe Islands (1) 1 *(Olsen K 31)*

Andorra: (442) Gomes; Jesus Rubio (Blanco 88), Garcia E, Llovera, San Nicolas M; Clemente (Martinez A 24), Vieira, Rebes (Bernat 69), Pujol; Alaez, Martinez C.
Faroe Islands: (433) Gestsson; Danielsen, Vatnsdal, Nattestad, Davidsen V; Hansson, Vatnhamar G, Olsen B; Bjartalid (Olsen M 72), Olsen K (Andreasen 87), Johannesen (Olsen A 58).

Malta (1) 1 *(Nwoko 15)*

Latvia (1) 1 *(Guillaumier 25 (og))*

Malta: (3421) Bonello; Borg S (Agius 85), Pepe, Muscat Z; Mbong J, Teuma, Guillaumier (Pisani 90), Camenzuli; Gambin, Degabriele (Grech 60); Nwoko.
Latvia: (442) Steinbors; Savalnieks (Rugins 67), Cernomordijs, Dubra, Jurkovskis; Jaunzems, Emsis, Zjuzins (Karklins 86), Ciganiks; Krollis (Ikaunieks D 62), Ikaunieks J.

Saturday, 10 October 2020

Andorra (0) 0

Malta (0) 0

Andorra: (442) Gomes; Jordi Rubio, Garcia E, Vales, Cervos; Martinez C (Garcia M 85), Pujol, Vieira, Martinez A (Bernat 90); Sanchez A (San Nicolas L 85), Fernandez (Alaez 70).
Malta: (343) Bonello; Borg S, Agius, Muscat Z; Mbong J, Pisani (Kristensen 79), Teuma, Camenzuli; Degabriele (Montebello 61), Gambin, Mbong P (Grech 79).

Faroe Islands (1) 1 *(Faero 28)*

Latvia (1) 1 *(Ikaunieks J 25)*

Faroe Islands: (442) Gestsson; Sorensen (Danielsen 82), Faero, Nattestad, Davidsen V; Bjartalid (Johannesen 82), Vatnhamar S (Baldvinsson 65), Hansson, Olsen B (Vatnhamar G 11); Olsen K, Olsen A (Edmundsson 65).
Latvia: (4231) Steinbors; Savalnieks, Oss, Stuglis, Rugins; Tobers (Karklins 68), Zjuzins (Emsis 82); Jaunzems (Kigurs 67), Ikaunieks J, Ciganiks; Uldrikis (Krollis 82).

Tuesday, 13 October 2020

Faroe Islands (2) 2 *(Olsen K 19, 33)*

Andorra (0) 0

Faroe Islands: (442) Gestsson; Danielsen (Sorensen 72), Faero, Nattestad (Hansen 90), Davidsen V; Vatnhamar S (Olsen A 72), Hansson, Olsen B, Bjartalid; Olsen K, Olsen M (Edmundsson 55).
Andorra: (442) Gomes; San Nicolas M, Garcia E, Alavedra, Cervos; Alaez (Bernat 88), Rebes (Moreno 88), Pujol, Martinez A (Jordi Rubio 71); Fernandez (Sanchez A 71), Vieira (Martinez C 62).

Latvia (0) 0

Malta (0) 1 *(Borg 90)* 953

Latvia: (4231) Steinbors; Savalnieks, Oss, Tarasovs, Jurkovskis; Zjuzins (Karklins 54), Tobers (Emsis 64); Ikaunieks D (Kigurs 64), Ikaunieks J, Ciganiks (Jaunzems 83); Gutkovskis (Uldrikis 64).
Malta: (343) Bonello; Borg S, Agius, Shaw; Camenzuli, Teuma (Pisani 75), Guillaumier, Mbong J; Mbong P (Degabriele 69), Montebello, Gambin (Grech 89).

Saturday, 14 November 2020

Latvia (0) 1 *(Kamess 59)*

Faroe Islands (0) 1 *(Vatnhamar G 60)*

Latvia: (4231) Ozols; Savalnieks, Cernomordijs, Dubra, Jurkovskis; Karklins, Rugins (Saveljevs 61); Kamess (Ontuzans 61), Ikaunieks J (Jaunzems 90), Ciganiks (Kigurs 71); Gutkovskis.
Faroe Islands: (442) Gestsson; Sorensen, Faero, Nattestad, Davidsen V; Bjartalid, Vatnhamar S, Baldvinsson (Jonsson 68), Vatnhamar G; Olsen K, Olsen M (Jakobsen 83).

Malta (0) 3 *(Garcia E 55 (og), Degabriele 58, Dimech 90)*

Andorra (1) 1 *(Rebes 3)*

Malta: (3421) Bonello; Micallef, Agius, Shaw; Mbong J, Teuma, Guillaumier (Pisani 84), Camenzuli; Gambin (Dimech 89), Degabriele (Grech 89); Montebello (Satariano 76).
Andorra: (442) Gomes; San Nicolas M, Garcia E, Alavedra, Cervos; Martinez C (Bernat 77), Vieira, Rebes (Blanco 77), Martinez A (San Nicolas L 69); Fernandez (Sanchez A 69), Alaez.

Tuesday, 17 November 2020

Andorra (0) 0

Latvia (1) 5 *(Cernomordijs 6, Ikaunieks J 57, 60, Gutkovskis 70 (pen), Krollis 90 (pen))*

Andorra: (442) Gomes; Jordi Rubio (Martinez A 66), Garcia C■, Garcia E, San Nicolas M; Martinez C (Clemente 84), Pujol (Moreno 85), Rebes, Cervos; Fernandez (Sanchez A 78), Vieira (Alaez 66).
Latvia: (442) Ozols; Savalnieks, Cernomordijs, Dubra, Jurkovskis; Kamess (Ontuzans 74), Zjuzins (Saveljevs 54), Karklins, Ciganiks (Ikaunieks D 82); Ikaunieks J (Kigurs 75), Gutkovskis (Krollis 75).

Malta (0) 1 *(Guillaumier 54)*

Faroe Islands (0) 1 *(Jonsson 69)*

Malta: (3421) Bonello; Shaw, Agius (Dimech 84), Borg S; Mbong J, Guillaumier, Teuma (Pisani 79), Camenzuli; Gambin, Degabriele (Satariano 84); Montebello (Nwoko 75).
Faroe Islands: (442) Gestsson; Sorensen, Faero, Vatnhamar G, Davidsen V; Bjartalid (Jonsson 61), Vatnhamar S, Hansson (Wardum 88), Olsen B; Olsen K (Jakobsen 81), Olsen M (Hansen 88).

League D – Group 1	P	W	D	L	F	A	GD	Pts
Faroe Islands	6	3	3	0	9	5	4	12
Malta	6	2	3	1	8	6	2	9
Latvia	6	1	4	1	8	4	4	7
Andorra	6	0	2	4	1	11	–10	2

LEAGUE D – GROUP 2

Saturday, 5 September 2020

Gibraltar (1) 1 *(Torrilla 42)* **San Marino (0) 0**

Gibraltar: (433) Coleing; Wiseman, Chipolina R, Mouelhi, Olivero; Torrilla (Sergeant 81), Annesley (Ronan 84), Britto; Casciaro L (Badr 77), Hernandez, Walker.
San Marino: (352) Benedettini E; Brolli, Simoncini D, Rossi (Hirsch 78); Manuel Battistini (D'Addario 46), Golinucci E, Zonzini (Ceccaroli 65), Mularoni, Palazzi; Nanni N, Berardi F.

Tuesday, 8 September 2020

San Marino (0) 0

Liechtenstein (2) 2 *(Hasler 3 (pen), Frick Y 14)*

San Marino: (4141) Benedettini E; Manuel Battistini, Simoncini D, Rossi, Grandoni; Tosi (Golinucci A 46); Berardi, Lunadei (Hirsch 46), Golinucci E, Ceccaroli (Tomassini 67); Vitaioli M.
Liechtenstein: (4141) Buchel B; Yildiz, Malin, Kaufmann, Goppel; Sele A; Frick Y (Wolfinger S 87), Hasler, Martin Buchel, Salanovic (Ospelt P 90); Frick N (Frommelt 77).

Saturday, 10 October 2020

Liechtenstein (0) 0

Gibraltar (1) 1 *(De Barr 10)* 178

Liechtenstein: (4231) Buchel B; Wolfinger S (Brandle 59), Malin, Hofer, Goppel; Martin Buchel, Sele A (Frommelt 46); Kuhne (Ospelt P 85), Hasler, Salanovic; Wolfinger F (Yildiz 46).
Gibraltar: (4231) Goldwin; Sergeant, Wiseman, Mouelhi, Olivero; Torrilla, Annesley; Casciaro L (Jolley 74), Walker, Badr (Pons 87); De Barr (Styche 71).

Tuesday, 13 October 2020

Liechtenstein (0) 0

San Marino (0) 0

Liechtenstein: (4141) Buchel B; Brandle (Wolfinger F 75), Malin, Hofer (Ospelt P 46), Goppel (Wolfinger S 46); Martin Buchel (Meier 8); Yildiz, Sele A, Hasler, Salanovic; Kaufmann.
San Marino: (4411) Benedettini S; Manuel Battistini, Brolli, Rossi, Palazzi; Tomassini, Lunadei (Mularoni 86), Golinucci E, Hirsch; Nanni N; Berardi F.

Saturday, 14 November 2020

San Marino (0) 0

Gibraltar (0) 0

San Marino: (442) Benedettini E; Brolli, Simoncini D■, Rossi, Palazzi; Tomassini (Manuel Battistini 57), Lunadei, Golinucci A, Hirsch (Mularoni 57); Berardi F (Vitaioli M 67), Nanni N.
Gibraltar: (343) Coleing; Chipolina R, Wiseman, Mouelhi (Styche 66); Sergeant, Torrilla (Priestley 77), Annesley, Olivero; Walker, De Barr, Casciaro L (Casciaro K 54).

Tuesday, 17 November 2020

Gibraltar (1) 1 *(Frommelt 17 (og))*

Liechtenstein (1) 1 *(Frick N 44)*

Gibraltar: (541) Coleing; Sergeant, Chipolina R, Wiseman, Mouelhi, Olivero; Walker, Ronan (Barnett 88), Annesley, Badr (Jolley 70); De Barr (Styche 90).
Liechtenstein: (4141) Hobi; Brandle (Yildiz 56), Malin, Hofer, Goppel; Martin Buchel (Kardesoglu 71); Frick Y, Frommelt, Hasler, Kuhne (Wolfinger F 71); Frick N (Ospelt P 79).

League D – Group 2	P	W	D	L	F	A	GD	Pts
Gibraltar	4	2	2	0	3	1	2	8
Liechtenstein	4	1	2	1	3	2	1	5
San Marino	4	0	2	2	0	3	–3	2

In October, Marcus Rashford's penalty helped England to a 2-1 Nations League victory over Belgium at Wembley Stadium (Ian Walton/PA Wire/PA Images)

BRITISH AND IRISH INTERNATIONAL RESULTS 1872–2021

Note: In the results that follow, WC = World Cup, EC = European Championship, NL = Nations League UI = Umbro International Trophy. TF = Tournoi de France. NC = Nations Cup. Northern Ireland played as Ireland before 1921. *After extra time.

Bold type indicates matches played in season 2020–21.

ENGLAND v SCOTLAND

Played: 114; England won 48, Scotland won 41, Drawn 26. Goals: England 203, Scotland 174.

			E	S
1872	30 Nov	Glasgow	0	0
1873	8 Mar	Kennington Oval	4	2
1874	7 Mar	Glasgow	1	2
1875	6 Mar	Kennington Oval	2	2
1876	4 Mar	Glasgow	0	3
1877	3 Mar	Kennington Oval	1	3
1878	2 Mar	Glasgow	2	7
1879	5 Apr	Kennington Oval	5	4
1880	13 Mar	Glasgow	4	5
1881	12 Mar	Kennington Oval	1	6
1882	11 Mar	Glasgow	1	5
1883	10 Mar	Sheffield	2	3
1884	15 Mar	Glasgow	0	1
1885	21 Mar	Kennington Oval	1	1
1886	31 Mar	Glasgow	1	1
1887	19 Mar	Blackburn	2	3
1888	17 Mar	Glasgow	5	0
1889	13 Apr	Kennington Oval	2	3
1890	5 Apr	Glasgow	1	1
1891	6 Apr	Blackburn	2	1
1892	2 Apr	Glasgow	4	1
1893	1 Apr	Richmond	5	2
1894	7 Apr	Glasgow	2	2
1895	6 Apr	Everton	3	0
1896	4 Apr	Glasgow	1	2
1897	3 Apr	Crystal Palace	1	2
1898	2 Apr	Glasgow	3	1
1899	8 Apr	Aston Villa	2	1
1900	7 Apr	Glasgow	1	4
1901	30 Mar	Crystal Palace	2	2
1902	3 Mar	Aston Villa	2	2
1903	4 Apr	Sheffield	1	2
1904	9 Apr	Glasgow	1	0
1905	1 Apr	Crystal Palace	1	0
1906	7 Apr	Glasgow	1	2
1907	6 Apr	Newcastle	1	1
1908	4 Apr	Glasgow	1	1
1909	3 Apr	Crystal Palace	2	0
1910	2 Apr	Glasgow	0	2
1911	1 Apr	Everton	1	1
1912	23 Mar	Glasgow	1	1
1913	5 Apr	Chelsea	1	0
1914	14 Apr	Glasgow	1	3
1920	10 Apr	Sheffield	5	4
1921	9 Apr	Glasgow	0	3
1922	8 Apr	Aston Villa	0	1
1923	14 Apr	Glasgow	2	2
1924	12 Apr	Wembley	1	1
1925	4 Apr	Glasgow	0	2
1926	17 Apr	Manchester	0	1
1927	2 Apr	Glasgow	2	1
1928	31 Mar	Wembley	1	5
1929	13 Apr	Glasgow	0	1
1930	5 Apr	Wembley	5	2
1931	28 Mar	Glasgow	0	2
1932	9 Apr	Wembley	3	0
1933	1 Apr	Glasgow	1	2
1934	14 Apr	Wembley	3	0
1935	6 Apr	Glasgow	0	2
1936	4 Apr	Wembley	1	1
1937	17 Apr	Glasgow	1	3
1938	9 Apr	Wembley	0	1
1939	15 Apr	Glasgow	2	1
1947	12 Apr	Wembley	1	1
1948	10 Apr	Glasgow	2	0
1949	9 Apr	Wembley	1	3
WC1950	15 Apr	Glasgow	1	0
1951	14 Apr	Wembley	2	3
1952	5 Apr	Glasgow	2	1
1953	18 Apr	Wembley	2	2
WC1954	3 Apr	Glasgow	4	2
1955	2 Apr	Wembley	7	2
1956	14 Apr	Glasgow	1	1
1957	6 Apr	Wembley	2	1
1958	19 Apr	Glasgow	4	0
1959	11 Apr	Wembley	1	0
1960	9 Apr	Glasgow	1	1
1961	15 Apr	Wembley	9	3
1962	14 Apr	Glasgow	0	2
1963	6 Apr	Wembley	1	2
1964	11 Apr	Glasgow	0	1
1965	10 Apr	Wembley	2	2
1966	2 Apr	Glasgow	4	3
EC1967	15 Apr	Wembley	2	3
EC1968	24 Jan	Glasgow	1	1
1969	10 May	Wembley	4	1
1970	25 Apr	Glasgow	0	0
1971	22 May	Wembley	3	1
1972	27 May	Glasgow	1	0
1973	14 Feb	Glasgow	5	0
1973	19 May	Wembley	1	0
1974	18 May	Glasgow	0	2
1975	24 May	Wembley	5	1
1976	15 May	Glasgow	1	2
1977	4 June	Wembley	1	2
1978	20 May	Glasgow	1	0
1979	26 May	Wembley	3	1
1980	24 May	Glasgow	2	0
1981	23 May	Wembley	0	1
1982	29 May	Glasgow	1	0
1983	1 June	Wembley	2	0
1984	26 May	Glasgow	1	1
1985	25 May	Glasgow	0	1
1986	23 Apr	Wembley	2	1
1987	23 May	Glasgow	0	0
1988	21 May	Wembley	1	0
1989	27 May	Glasgow	2	0
EC1996	15 June	Wembley	2	0
EC1999	13 Nov	Glasgow	2	0
EC1999	17 Nov	Wembley	0	1
2013	14 Aug	Wembley	3	2
2014	18 Nov	Glasgow	3	1
WC2016	11 Nov	Wembley	3	0
WC2017	10 June	Glasgow	2	2
EC2021	**18 June**	**Wembley**	**0**	**0**

ENGLAND v WALES

Played: 102; England won 68, Wales won 14, Drawn 21. Goals: England 250, Wales 91.

			E	*W*
1879	18 Jan	Kennington Oval	2	1
1880	15 Mar	Wrexham	3	2
1881	26 Feb	Blackburn	0	1
1882	13 Mar	Wrexham	3	5
1883	3 Feb	Kennington Oval	5	0
1884	17 Mar	Wrexham	4	0
1885	14 Mar	Blackburn	1	1
1886	29 Mar	Wrexham	3	1
1887	26 Feb	Kennington Oval	4	0
1888	4 Feb	Crewe	5	1
1889	23 Feb	Stoke	4	1
1890	15 Mar	Wrexham	3	1
1891	7 May	Sunderland	4	1
1892	5 Mar	Wrexham	2	0
1893	13 Mar	Stoke	6	0
1894	12 Mar	Wrexham	5	1
1895	18 Mar	Queen's Club, Kensington	1	1
1896	16 Mar	Cardiff	9	1
1897	29 Mar	Sheffield	4	0
1898	28 Mar	Wrexham	3	0
1899	20 Mar	Bristol	4	0
1900	26 Mar	Cardiff	1	1
1901	18 Mar	Newcastle	6	0
1902	3 Mar	Wrexham	0	0
1903	2 Mar	Portsmouth	2	1
1904	29 Feb	Wrexham	2	2
1905	27 Mar	Liverpool	3	1
1906	19 Mar	Cardiff	1	0
1907	18 Mar	Fulham	1	1
1908	16 Mar	Wrexham	7	1
1909	15 Mar	Nottingham	2	0
1910	14 Mar	Cardiff	1	0
1911	13 Mar	Millwall	3	0
1912	11 Mar	Wrexham	2	0
1913	17 Mar	Bristol	4	3
1914	16 Mar	Cardiff	2	0
1920	15 Mar	Highbury	1	2
1921	14 Mar	Cardiff	0	0
1922	13 Mar	Liverpool	1	0
1923	5 Mar	Cardiff	2	2
1924	3 Mar	Blackburn	1	2
1925	28 Feb	Swansea	2	1
1926	1 Mar	Crystal Palace	1	3
1927	12 Feb	Wrexham	3	3
1927	28 Nov	Burnley	1	2
1928	17 Nov	Swansea	3	2
1929	20 Nov	Chelsea	6	0
1930	22 Nov	Wrexham	4	0
1931	18 Nov	Liverpool	3	1
1932	16 Nov	Wrexham	0	0
1933	15 Nov	Newcastle	1	2
1934	29 Sept	Cardiff	4	0
1936	5 Feb	Wolverhampton	1	2
1936	17 Oct	Cardiff	1	2
1937	17 Nov	Middlesbrough	2	1
1938	22 Oct	Cardiff	2	4
1946	13 Nov	Manchester	3	0
1947	18 Oct	Cardiff	3	0
1948	10 Nov	Aston Villa	1	0
wc1949	15 Oct	Cardiff	4	1
1950	15 Nov	Sunderland	4	2
1951	20 Oct	Cardiff	1	1
1952	12 Nov	Wembley	5	2
wc1953	10 Oct	Cardiff	4	1
1954	10 Nov	Wembley	3	2
1955	27 Oct	Cardiff	1	2
1956	14 Nov	Wembley	3	1
1957	19 Oct	Cardiff	4	0
1958	26 Nov	Aston Villa	2	2
1959	17 Oct	Cardiff	1	1
1960	23 Nov	Wembley	5	1
1961	14 Oct	Cardiff	1	1
1962	21 Oct	Wembley	4	0
1963	12 Oct	Cardiff	4	0
1964	18 Nov	Wembley	2	1
1965	2 Oct	Cardiff	0	0
EC1966	16 Nov	Wembley	5	1
EC1967	21 Oct	Cardiff	3	0
1969	7 May	Wembley	2	1
1970	18 Apr	Cardiff	1	1
1971	19 May	Wembley	0	0
1972	20 May	Cardiff	3	0
wc1972	15 Nov	Cardiff	1	0
wc1973	24 Jan	Wembley	1	1
1973	15 May	Wembley	3	0
1974	11 May	Cardiff	2	0
1975	21 May	Wembley	2	2
1976	24 Mar	Wrexham	2	1
1976	8 May	Cardiff	1	0
1977	31 May	Wembley	0	1
1978	3 May	Cardiff	3	1
1979	23 May	Wembley	0	0
1980	17 May	Wrexham	1	4
1981	20 May	Wembley	0	0
1982	27 Apr	Cardiff	1	0
1983	23 Feb	Wembley	2	1
1984	2 May	Wrexham	0	1
wc2004	9 Oct	Old Trafford	2	0
wc2005	3 Sept	Cardiff	1	0
EC2011	26 Mar	Cardiff	2	0
EC2011	6 Sept	Wembley	1	0
EC2016	16 June	Lens	2	1
2020	**8 Oct**	**Wembley**	**3**	**0**

ENGLAND v NORTHERN IRELAND

Played: 98; England won 75, Northern Ireland won 7, Drawn 16. Goals: England 323, Northern Ireland 81.

			E	*NI*
1882	18 Feb	Belfast	13	0
1883	24 Feb	Liverpool	7	0
1884	23 Feb	Belfast	8	1
1885	28 Feb	Manchester	4	0
1886	13 Mar	Belfast	6	1
1887	5 Feb	Sheffield	7	0
1888	31 Mar	Belfast	5	1
1889	2 Mar	Everton	6	1
1890	15 Mar	Belfast	9	1
1891	7 Mar	Wolverhampton	6	1
1892	5 Mar	Belfast	2	0
1893	25 Feb	Birmingham	6	1
1894	3 Mar	Belfast	2	2
1895	9 Mar	Derby	9	0
1896	7 Mar	Belfast	2	0
1897	20 Feb	Nottingham	6	0
1898	5 Mar	Belfast	3	2
1899	18 Feb	Sunderland	13	2
1900	17 Mar	Dublin	2	0
1901	9 Mar	Southampton	3	0
1902	22 Mar	Belfast	1	0
1903	14 Feb	Wolverhampton	4	0
1904	12 Mar	Belfast	3	1
1905	25 Feb	Middlesbrough	1	1
1906	17 Feb	Belfast	5	0
1907	16 Feb	Everton	1	0
1908	15 Feb	Belfast	3	1
1909	13 Feb	Bradford	4	0
1910	12 Feb	Belfast	1	1
1911	11 Feb	Derby	2	1
1912	10 Feb	Dublin	6	1
1913	15 Feb	Belfast	1	2
1914	14 Feb	Middlesbrough	0	3
1919	25 Oct	Belfast	1	1

			E	*NI*
1920	23 Oct	Sunderland	2	0
1921	22 Oct	Belfast	1	1
1922	21 Oct	West Bromwich	2	0
1923	20 Oct	Belfast	1	2
1924	22 Oct	Everton	3	1
1925	24 Oct	Belfast	0	0
1926	20 Oct	Liverpool	3	3
1927	22 Oct	Belfast	0	2
1928	22 Oct	Everton	2	1
1929	19 Oct	Belfast	3	0
1930	20 Oct	Sheffield	5	1
1931	17 Oct	Belfast	6	2
1932	17 Oct	Blackpool	1	0
1933	14 Oct	Belfast	3	0
1935	6 Feb	Everton	2	1
1935	19 Oct	Belfast	3	1
1936	18 Nov	Stoke	3	1
1937	23 Oct	Belfast	5	1
1938	16 Nov	Manchester	7	0
1946	28 Sept	Belfast	7	2
1947	5 Nov	Everton	2	2
1948	9 Oct	Belfast	6	2
wc1949	16 Nov	Manchester	9	2
1950	7 Oct	Belfast	4	1
1951	14 Nov	Aston Villa	2	0
1952	4 Oct	Belfast	2	2
wc1953	11 Nov	Everton	3	1
1954	2 Oct	Belfast	2	0
1955	2 Nov	Wembley	3	0
1956	10 Oct	Belfast	1	1
1957	6 Nov	Wembley	2	3
1958	4 Oct	Belfast	3	3
1959	18 Nov	Wembley	2	1
1960	8 Oct	Belfast	5	2
1961	22 Nov	Wembley	1	1
1962	20 Oct	Belfast	3	1
1963	20 Nov	Wembley	8	3
1964	3 Oct	Belfast	4	3
1965	10 Nov	Wembley	2	1
EC1966	20 Oct	Belfast	2	0
EC1967	22 Nov	Wembley	2	0
1969	3 May	Belfast	3	1
1970	21 Apr	Wembley	3	1
1971	15 May	Belfast	1	0
1972	23 May	Wembley	0	1
1973	12 May	Everton	2	1
1974	15 May	Wembley	1	0
1975	17 May	Belfast	0	0
1976	11 May	Wembley	4	0
1977	28 May	Belfast	2	1
1978	16 May	Wembley	1	0
EC1979	7 Feb	Wembley	4	0
1979	19 May	Belfast	2	0
EC1979	17 Oct	Belfast	5	1
1980	20 May	Wembley	1	1
1982	23 Feb	Wembley	4	0
1983	28 May	Belfast	0	0
1984	24 Apr	Wembley	1	0
wc1985	27 Feb	Belfast	1	0
wc1985	13 Nov	Wembley	0	0
EC1986	15 Oct	Wembley	3	0
EC1987	1 Apr	Belfast	2	0
wc2005	26 Mar	Old Trafford	4	0
wc2005	7 Sept	Belfast	0	1

SCOTLAND v WALES

Played: 107; Scotland won 61, Wales won 23, Drawn 23. Goals: Scotland 243, Wales 124.

			S	*W*
1876	25 Mar	Glasgow	4	0
1877	5 Mar	Wrexham	2	0
1878	23 Mar	Glasgow	9	0
1879	7 Apr	Wrexham	3	0
1880	3 Apr	Glasgow	5	1
1881	14 Mar	Wrexham	5	1
1882	25 Mar	Glasgow	5	0
1883	12 Mar	Wrexham	3	0
1884	29 Mar	Glasgow	4	1
1885	23 Mar	Wrexham	8	1
1886	10 Apr	Glasgow	4	1
1887	21 Mar	Wrexham	2	0
1888	10 Mar	Easter Road	5	1
1889	15 Apr	Wrexham	0	0
1890	22 Mar	Paisley	5	0
1891	21 Mar	Wrexham	4	3
1892	26 Mar	Tynecastle	6	1
1893	18 Mar	Wrexham	8	0
1894	24 Mar	Kilmarnock	5	2
1895	23 Mar	Wrexham	2	2
1896	21 Mar	Dundee	4	0
1897	20 Mar	Wrexham	2	2
1898	19 Mar	Motherwell	5	2
1899	18 Mar	Wrexham	6	0
1900	3 Feb	Aberdeen	5	2
1901	2 Mar	Wrexham	1	1
1902	15 Mar	Greenock	5	1
1903	9 Mar	Cardiff	1	0
1904	12 Mar	Dundee	1	1
1905	6 Mar	Wrexham	1	3
1906	3 Mar	Tynecastle	0	2
1907	4 Mar	Wrexham	0	1
1908	7 Mar	Dundee	2	1
1909	1 Mar	Wrexham	2	3
1910	5 Mar	Kilmarnock	1	0
1911	6 Mar	Cardiff	2	2
1912	2 Mar	Tynecastle	1	0
1913	3 Mar	Wrexham	0	0
1914	28 Feb	Glasgow	0	0
1920	26 Feb	Cardiff	1	1
1921	12 Feb	Aberdeen	2	1
1922	4 Feb	Wrexham	1	2
1923	17 Mar	Paisley	2	0
1924	16 Feb	Cardiff	0	2
1925	14 Feb	Tynecastle	3	1
1925	31 Oct	Cardiff	3	0
1926	30 Oct	Glasgow	3	0
1927	29 Oct	Wrexham	2	2
1928	27 Oct	Glasgow	4	2
1929	26 Oct	Cardiff	4	2
1930	25 Oct	Glasgow	1	1
1931	31 Oct	Wrexham	3	2
1932	26 Oct	Tynecastle	2	5
1933	4 Oct	Cardiff	2	3
1934	21 Nov	Aberdeen	3	2
1935	5 Oct	Cardiff	1	1
1936	2 Dec	Dundee	1	2
1937	30 Oct	Cardiff	1	2
1938	9 Nov	Tynecastle	3	2
1946	19 Oct	Wrexham	1	3
1947	12 Nov	Glasgow	1	2
1948	23 Oct	Cardiff	3	1
wc1949	9 Nov	Glasgow	2	0
1950	21 Oct	Cardiff	3	1
1951	14 Nov	Glasgow	0	1
1952	18 Oct	Cardiff	2	1
wc1953	4 Nov	Glasgow	3	3
1954	16 Oct	Cardiff	1	0
1955	9 Nov	Glasgow	2	0
1956	20 Oct	Cardiff	2	2
1957	13 Nov	Glasgow	1	1
1958	18 Oct	Cardiff	3	0
1959	4 Nov	Glasgow	1	1
1960	20 Oct	Cardiff	0	2
1961	8 Nov	Glasgow	2	0
1962	20 Oct	Cardiff	3	2
1963	20 Nov	Glasgow	2	1
1964	3 Oct	Cardiff	2	3

			S	W
EC1965	24 Nov	Glasgow	4	1
EC1966	22 Oct	Cardiff	1	1
1967	22 Nov	Glasgow	3	2
1969	3 May	Wrexham	5	3
1970	22 Apr	Glasgow	0	0
1971	15 May	Cardiff	0	0
1972	24 May	Glasgow	1	0
1973	12 May	Wrexham	2	0
1974	14 May	Glasgow	2	0
1975	17 May	Cardiff	2	2
1976	6 May	Glasgow	3	1
WC1976	17 Nov	Glasgow	1	0
1977	28 May	Wrexham	0	0
WC1977	12 Oct	Liverpool	2	0
1978	17 May	Glasgow	1	1
1979	19 May	Cardiff	0	3
1980	21 May	Glasgow	1	0
1981	16 May	Swansea	0	2
1982	24 May	Glasgow	1	0
1983	28 May	Cardiff	2	0
1984	28 Feb	Glasgow	2	1
WC1985	27 Mar	Glasgow	0	1
WC1985	10 Sept	Cardiff	1	1
1997	27 May	Kilmarnock	0	1
2004	18 Feb	Cardiff	0	4
2009	14 Nov	Cardiff	0	3
NC2011	25 May	Dublin	3	1
WC2012	12 Oct	Cardiff	1	2
WC2013	22 Mar	Glasgow	1	2

SCOTLAND v NORTHERN IRELAND

Played: 96; Scotland won 64, Northern Ireland won 15, Drawn 17. Goals: Scotland 261, Northern Ireland 81.

			S	NI
1884	26 Jan	Belfast	5	0
1885	14 Mar	Glasgow	8	2
1886	20 Mar	Belfast	7	2
1887	19 Feb	Glasgow	4	1
1888	24 Mar	Belfast	10	2
1889	9 Mar	Glasgow	7	0
1890	29 Mar	Belfast	4	1
1891	28 Mar	Glasgow	2	1
1892	19 Mar	Belfast	3	2
1893	25 Mar	Glasgow	6	1
1894	31 Mar	Belfast	2	1
1895	30 Mar	Glasgow	3	1
1896	28 Mar	Belfast	3	3
1897	27 Mar	Glasgow	5	1
1898	26 Mar	Belfast	3	0
1899	25 Mar	Glasgow	9	1
1900	3 Mar	Belfast	3	0
1901	23 Feb	Glasgow	11	0
1902	1 Mar	Belfast	5	1
1902	9 Aug	Belfast	3	0
1903	21 Mar	Glasgow	0	2
1904	26 Mar	Dublin	1	1
1905	18 Mar	Glasgow	4	0
1906	17 Mar	Dublin	1	0
1907	16 Mar	Glasgow	3	0
1908	14 Mar	Dublin	5	0
1909	15 Mar	Glasgow	5	0
1910	19 Mar	Belfast	0	1
1911	18 Mar	Glasgow	2	0
1912	16 Mar	Belfast	4	1
1913	15 Mar	Dublin	2	1
1914	14 Mar	Belfast	1	1
1920	13 Mar	Glasgow	3	0
1921	26 Feb	Belfast	2	0
1922	4 Mar	Glasgow	2	1
1923	3 Mar	Belfast	1	0
1924	1 Mar	Glasgow	2	0
1925	28 Feb	Belfast	3	0
1926	27 Feb	Glasgow	4	0
1927	26 Feb	Belfast	2	0
1928	25 Feb	Glasgow	0	1
1929	23 Feb	Belfast	7	3
1930	22 Feb	Glasgow	3	1
1931	21 Feb	Belfast	0	0
1931	19 Sept	Glasgow	3	1
1932	12 Sept	Belfast	4	0
1933	16 Sept	Glasgow	1	2
1934	20 Oct	Belfast	1	2
1935	13 Nov	Tynecastle	2	1
1936	31 Oct	Belfast	3	1
1937	10 Nov	Aberdeen	1	1
1938	8 Oct	Belfast	2	0
1946	27 Nov	Glasgow	0	0
1947	4 Oct	Belfast	0	2
1948	17 Nov	Glasgow	3	2
WC1949	1 Oct	Belfast	8	2
1950	1 Nov	Glasgow	6	1
1951	6 Oct	Belfast	3	0
1952	5 Nov	Glasgow	1	1
WC1953	3 Oct	Belfast	3	1
1954	3 Nov	Glasgow	2	2
1955	8 Oct	Belfast	1	2
1956	7 Nov	Glasgow	1	0
1957	5 Oct	Belfast	1	1
1958	5 Nov	Glasgow	2	2
1959	3 Oct	Belfast	4	0
1960	9 Nov	Glasgow	5	2
1961	7 Oct	Belfast	6	1
1962	7 Nov	Glasgow	5	1
1963	12 Oct	Belfast	1	2
1964	25 Nov	Glasgow	3	2
1965	2 Oct	Belfast	2	3
1966	16 Nov	Glasgow	2	1
1967	21 Oct	Belfast	0	1
1969	6 May	Glasgow	1	1
1970	18 Apr	Belfast	1	0
1971	18 May	Glasgow	0	1
1972	20 May	Glasgow	2	0
1973	16 May	Glasgow	1	2
1974	11 May	Glasgow	0	1
1975	20 May	Glasgow	3	0
1976	8 May	Glasgow	3	0
1977	1 June	Glasgow	3	0
1978	13 May	Glasgow	1	1
1979	22 May	Glasgow	1	0
1980	17 May	Belfast	0	1
WC1981	25 Mar	Glasgow	1	1
1981	19 May	Glasgow	2	0
WC1981	14 Oct	Belfast	0	0
1982	28 Apr	Belfast	1	1
1983	24 May	Glasgow	0	0
1983	13 Dec	Belfast	0	2
1992	19 Feb	Glasgow	1	0
2008	20 Aug	Glasgow	0	0
NC2011	9 Feb	Dublin	3	0
2015	25 Mar	Glasgow	1	0

WALES v NORTHERN IRELAND

Played: 96; Wales won 45, Northern Ireland won 27, Drawn 24. Goals: Wales 191, Northern Ireland 132.

			W	*NI*
1882	25 Feb	Wrexham	7	1
1883	17 Mar	Belfast	1	1
1884	9 Feb	Wrexham	6	0
1885	11 Apr	Belfast	8	2
1886	27 Feb	Wrexham	5	0
1887	12 Mar	Belfast	1	4
1888	3 Mar	Wrexham	11	0
1889	27 Apr	Belfast	3	1
1890	8 Feb	Shrewsbury	5	2
1891	7 Feb	Belfast	2	7
1892	27 Feb	Bangor	1	1
1893	8 Apr	Belfast	3	4
1894	24 Feb	Swansea	4	1
1895	16 Mar	Belfast	2	2
1896	29 Feb	Wrexham	6	1
1897	6 Mar	Belfast	3	4
1898	19 Feb	Llandudno	0	1
1899	4 Mar	Belfast	0	1
1900	24 Feb	Llandudno	2	0
1901	23 Mar	Belfast	1	0
1902	22 Mar	Cardiff	0	3
1903	28 Mar	Belfast	0	2
1904	21 Mar	Bangor	0	1
1905	18 Apr	Belfast	2	2
1906	2 Apr	Wrexham	4	4
1907	23 Feb	Belfast	3	2
1908	11 Apr	Aberdare	0	1
1909	20 Mar	Belfast	3	2
1910	11 Apr	Wrexham	4	1
1911	28 Jan	Belfast	2	1
1912	13 Apr	Cardiff	2	3
1913	18 Jan	Belfast	1	0
1914	19 Jan	Wrexham	1	2
1920	14 Feb	Belfast	2	2
1921	9 Apr	Swansea	2	1
1922	4 Apr	Belfast	1	1
1923	14 Apr	Wrexham	0	3
1924	15 Mar	Belfast	1	0
1925	18 Apr	Wrexham	0	0
1926	13 Feb	Belfast	0	3
1927	9 Apr	Cardiff	2	2
1928	4 Feb	Belfast	2	1
1929	2 Feb	Wrexham	2	2
1930	1 Feb	Belfast	0	7
1931	22 Apr	Wrexham	3	2
1931	5 Dec	Belfast	0	4
1932	7 Dec	Wrexham	4	1
1933	4 Nov	Belfast	1	1
1935	27 Mar	Wrexham	3	1
1936	11 Mar	Belfast	2	3
1937	17 Mar	Wrexham	4	1
1938	16 Mar	Belfast	0	1
1939	15 Mar	Wrexham	3	1
1947	16 Apr	Belfast	1	2
1948	10 Mar	Wrexham	2	0
1949	9 Mar	Belfast	2	0
wc1950	8 Mar	Wrexham	0	0
1951	7 Mar	Belfast	2	1
1952	19 Mar	Swansea	3	0
1953	15 Apr	Belfast	3	2
wc1954	31 Mar	Wrexham	1	2
1955	20 Apr	Belfast	3	2
1956	11 Apr	Cardiff	1	1
1957	10 Apr	Belfast	0	0
1958	16 Apr	Cardiff	1	1
1959	22 Apr	Belfast	1	4
1960	6 Apr	Wrexham	3	2
1961	12 Apr	Belfast	5	1
1962	11 Apr	Cardiff	4	0
1963	3 Apr	Belfast	4	1
1964	15 Apr	Swansea	2	3
1965	31 Mar	Belfast	5	0
1966	30 Mar	Cardiff	1	4
EC1967	12 Apr	Belfast	0	0
EC1968	28 Feb	Wrexham	2	0
1969	10 May	Belfast	0	0
1970	25 Apr	Swansea	1	0
1971	22 May	Belfast	0	1
1972	27 May	Wrexham	0	0
1973	19 May	Everton	0	1
1974	18 May	Wrexham	1	0
1975	23 May	Belfast	0	1
1976	14 May	Swansea	1	0
1977	3 June	Belfast	1	1
1978	19 May	Wrexham	1	0
1979	25 May	Belfast	1	1
1980	23 May	Cardiff	0	1
1982	27 May	Wrexham	3	0
1983	31 May	Belfast	1	0
1984	22 May	Swansea	1	1
wc2004	8 Sept	Cardiff	2	2
wc2005	8 Oct	Belfast	3	2
2007	6 Feb	Belfast	0	0
NC2011	27 May	Dublin	2	0
2016	24 Mar	Cardiff	1	1
EC2016	25 June	Paris	1	0

OTHER BRITISH INTERNATIONAL RESULTS 1908–2021

ENGLAND

v ALBANIA

			E	A
wc1989	8 Mar	Tirana	2	0
wc1989	26 Apr	Wembley	5	0
wc2001	28 Mar	Tirana	3	1
wc2001	5 Sept	Newcastle	2	0
wc2021	**28 Mar**	**Tirana**	**2**	**0**

v ALGERIA

			E	A
wc2010	18 June	Cape Town	0	0

v ANDORRA

			E	A
EC2006	2 Sept	Old Trafford	5	0
EC2007	28 Mar	Barcelona	3	0
wc2008	6 Sept	Barcelona	2	0
wc2009	10 June	Wembley	6	0

v ARGENTINA

			E	A
1951	9 May	Wembley	2	1
1953	17 May	Buenos Aires	0	0
(abandoned after 21 mins)				
wc1962	2 June	Rancagua	3	1
1964	6 June	Rio de Janeiro	0	1
wc1966	23 July	Wembley	1	0
1974	22 May	Wembley	2	2
1977	12 June	Buenos Aires	1	1
1980	13 May	Wembley	3	1
wc1986	22 June	Mexico City	1	2
1991	25 May	Wembley	2	2
wc1998	30 June	St Etienne	2	2
2000	23 Feb	Wembley	0	0
wc2002	7 June	Sapporo	1	0
2005	12 Nov	Geneva	3	2

v AUSTRALIA

			E	A
1980	31 May	Sydney	2	1
1983	11 June	Sydney	0	0
1983	15 June	Brisbane	1	0
1983	18 June	Melbourne	1	1
1991	1 June	Sydney	1	0
2003	12 Feb	West Ham	1	3
2016	27 May	Sunderland	2	1

v AUSTRIA

			E	A
1908	6 June	Vienna	6	1
1908	8 June	Vienna	11	1
1909	1 June	Vienna	8	1
1930	14 May	Vienna	0	0
1932	7 Dec	Chelsea	4	3
1936	6 May	Vienna	1	2
1951	28 Nov	Wembley	2	2
1952	25 May	Vienna	3	2
wc1958	15 June	Boras	2	2
1961	27 May	Vienna	1	3
1962	4 Apr	Wembley	3	1
1965	20 Oct	Wembley	2	3
1967	27 May	Vienna	1	0
1973	26 Sept	Wembley	7	0
1979	13 June	Vienna	3	4
wc2004	4 Sept	Vienna	2	2
wc2005	8 Oct	Old Trafford	1	0
2007	16 Nov	Vienna	1	0
2021	**2 June**	**Middlesbrough**	**1**	**0**

v AZERBAIJAN

			E	A
wc2004	13 Oct	Baku	1	0
wc2005	30 Mar	Newcastle	2	0

v BELARUS

			E	B
wc2008	15 Oct	Minsk	3	1
wc2009	14 Oct	Wembley	3	0

v BELGIUM

			E	B
1921	21 May	Brussels	2	0
1923	19 Mar	Highbury	6	1
1923	1 Nov	Antwerp	2	2
1924	8 Dec	West Bromwich	4	0
1926	24 May	Antwerp	5	3
1927	11 May	Brussels	9	1
1928	19 May	Antwerp	3	1
1929	11 May	Brussels	5	1
1931	16 May	Brussels	4	1
1936	9 May	Brussels	2	3
1947	21 Sept	Brussels	5	2
1950	18 May	Brussels	4	1
1952	26 Nov	Wembley	5	0
wc1954	17 June	Basel	4	4*
1964	21 Oct	Wembley	2	2
1970	25 Feb	Brussels	3	1
EC1980	12 June	Turin	1	1
wc1990	27 June	Bologna	1	0*
1998	29 May	Casablanca	0	0
1999	10 Oct	Sunderland	2	1
2012	2 June	Wembley	1	0
wc2018	28 June	Kaliningrad	0	1
wc2018	14 July	St Petersburg	0	2
NL2020	**11 Oct**	**Wembley**	**2**	**1**
NL2020	**15 Nov**	**Leuven**	**0**	**2**

v BOHEMIA

			E	B
1908	13 June	Prague	4	0

v BRAZIL

			E	B
1956	9 May	Wembley	4	2
wc1958	11 June	Gothenburg	0	0
1959	13 May	Rio de Janeiro	0	2
wc1962	10 June	Vina del Mar	1	3
1963	8 May	Wembley	1	1
1964	30 May	Rio de Janeiro	1	5
1969	12 June	Rio de Janeiro	1	2
wc1970	7 June	Guadalajara	0	1
1976	23 May	Los Angeles	0	1
1977	8 June	Rio de Janeiro	0	0
1978	19 Apr	Wembley	1	1
1981	12 May	Wembley	0	1
1984	10 June	Rio de Janeiro	2	0
1987	19 May	Wembley	1	1
1990	28 Mar	Wembley	1	0
1992	17 May	Wembley	1	1
1993	13 June	Washington	1	1
UI1995	11 June	Wembley	1	3
TF1997	10 June	Paris	0	1
2000	27 May	Wembley	1	1
wc2002	21 June	Shizuoka	1	2
2007	1 June	Wembley	1	1
2009	14 Nov	Doha	0	1
2013	6 Feb	Wembley	2	1
2013	2 June	Rio de Janeiro	2	2
2017	14 Nov	Wembley	0	0

v BULGARIA

			E	B
wc1962	7 June	Rancagua	0	0
1968	11 Dec	Wembley	1	1
1974	1 June	Sofia	1	0
EC1979	6 June	Sofia	3	0
EC1979	22 Nov	Wembley	2	0
1996	27 Mar	Wembley	1	0
EC1998	10 Oct	Wembley	0	0
EC1999	9 June	Sofia	1	1
EC2010	3 Sept	Wembley	4	0
EC2011	2 Sept	Sofia	3	0
EC2019	7 Sept	Wembley	4	0
EC2019	14 Oct	Sofia	6	0

v CAMEROON

			E	C
wc1990	1 July	Naples	3	2*
1991	6 Feb	Wembley	2	0
1997	15 Nov	Wembley	2	0
2002	26 May	Kobe	2	2

v CANADA

			E	C
1986	24 May	Burnaby	1	0

v CHILE

			E	C
wc1950	25 June	Rio de Janeiro	2	0
1953	24 May	Santiago	2	1
1984	17 June	Santiago	0	0
1989	23 May	Wembley	0	0
1998	11 Feb	Wembley	0	2
2013	15 Nov	Wembley	0	2

v CHINA PR

			E	CPR
1996	23 May	Beijing	3	0

v CIS			*E*	*C*
1992	29 Apr	Moscow	2	2

v COLOMBIA			*E*	*C*
1970	20 May	Bogota	4	0
1988	24 May	Wembley	1	1
1995	6 Sept	Wembley	0	0
WC1998	26 June	Lens	2	0
2005	31 May	New Jersey	3	2
WC2018	3 July	Moscow	1	1

v COSTA RICA			*E*	*C*
WC2014	26 June	Belo Horizonte	0	0
2018	7 June	Leeds	2	0

v CROATIA			*E*	*C*
1996	24 Apr	Wembley	0	0
2003	20 Aug	Ipswich	3	1
EC2004	21 June	Lisbon	4	2
EC2006	11 Oct	Zagreb	0	2
EC2007	21 Nov	Wembley	2	3
WC2008	10 Sept	Zagreb	4	1
WC2009	9 Sept	Wembley	5	1
WC2018	11 July	Moscow	1	2*
NL2018	12 Oct	Rijeka	0	0
NL2018	18 Nov	Wembley	2	1
EC2021	**13 June**	**Wembley**	**1**	**0**

v CYPRUS			*E*	*C*
EC1975	16 Apr	Wembley	5	0
EC1975	11 May	Limassol	1	0

v CZECHOSLOVAKIA			*E*	*C*
1934	16 May	Prague	1	2
1937	1 Dec	Tottenham	5	4
1963	29 May	Bratislava	4	2
1966	2 Nov	Wembley	0	0
WC1970	11 June	Guadalajara	1	0
1973	27 May	Prague	1	1
EC1974	30 Oct	Wembley	3	0
EC1975	30 Oct	Bratislava	1	2
1978	29 Nov	Wembley	1	0
WC1982	20 June	Bilbao	2	0
1990	25 Apr	Wembley	4	2
1992	25 Mar	Prague	2	2

v CZECH REPUBLIC			*E*	*C*
1998	18 Nov	Wembley	2	0
2008	20 Aug	Wembley	2	2
EC2019	22 Mar	Wembley	5	0
EC2019	11 Oct	Prague	1	2
EC2021	**22 June**	**Wembley**	**1**	**0**

v DENMARK			*E*	*D*
1948	26 Sept	Copenhagen	0	0
1955	2 Oct	Copenhagen	5	1
WC1956	5 Dec	Wolverhampton	5	2
WC1957	15 May	Copenhagen	4	1
1966	3 July	Copenhagen	2	0
EC1978	20 Sept	Copenhagen	4	3
EC1979	12 Sept	Wembley	1	0
EC1982	22 Sept	Copenhagen	2	2
EC1983	21 Sept	Wembley	0	1
1988	14 Sept	Wembley	1	0
1989	7 June	Copenhagen	1	1
1990	15 May	Wembley	1	0
EC1992	11 June	Malmo	0	0
1994	9 Mar	Wembley	1	0
WC2002	15 June	Niigata	3	0
2003	16 Nov	Old Trafford	2	3
2005	17 Aug	Copenhagen	1	4
2011	9 Feb	Copenhagen	2	1
2014	5 Mar	Wembley	1	0
NL2020	**8 Sept**	**Copenhagen**	**0**	**0**
NL2020	**14 Oct**	**Wembley**	**0**	**1**
EC2021	**7 July**	**Wembley**	**2**	**1**

v ECUADOR			*E*	*Ec*
1970	24 May	Quito	2	0
WC2006	25 June	Stuttgart	1	0
2014	4 June	Miami	2	2

v EGYPT			*E*	*Eg*
1986	29 Jan	Cairo	4	0
WC1990	21 June	Cagliari	1	0
2010	3 Mar	Wembley	3	1

v ESTONIA			*E*	*Es*
EC2007	6 June	Tallinn	3	0
EC2007	13 Oct	Wembley	3	0
EC2014	12 Oct	Tallinn	1	0
EC2015	9 Oct	Wembley	2	0

v FIFA			*E*	*FIFA*
1938	26 Oct	Highbury	3	0
1953	21 Oct	Wembley	4	4
1963	23 Oct	Wembley	2	1

v FINLAND			*E*	*F*
1937	20 May	Helsinki	8	0
1956	20 May	Helsinki	5	1
1966	26 June	Helsinki	3	0
WC1976	13 June	Helsinki	4	1
WC1976	13 Oct	Wembley	2	1
1982	3 June	Helsinki	4	1
WC1984	17 Oct	Wembley	5	0
WC1985	22 May	Helsinki	1	1
1992	3 June	Helsinki	2	1
WC2000	11 Oct	Helsinki	0	0
WC2001	24 Mar	Liverpool	2	1

v FRANCE			*E*	*F*
1923	10 May	Paris	4	1
1924	17 May	Paris	3	1
1925	21 May	Paris	3	2
1927	26 May	Paris	6	0
1928	17 May	Paris	5	1
1929	9 May	Paris	4	1
1931	14 May	Paris	2	5
1933	6 Dec	Tottenham	4	1
1938	26 May	Paris	4	2
1947	3 May	Highbury	3	0
1949	22 May	Paris	3	1
1951	3 Oct	Highbury	2	2
1955	15 May	Paris	0	1
1957	27 Nov	Wembley	4	0
EC1962	3 Oct	Sheffield	1	1
EC1963	27 Feb	Paris	2	5
WC1966	20 July	Wembley	2	0
1969	12 Mar	Wembley	5	0
WC1982	16 June	Bilbao	3	1
1984	29 Feb	Paris	0	2
1992	19 Feb	Wembley	2	0
EC1992	14 June	Malmo	0	0
TF1997	7 June	Montpellier	1	0
1999	10 Feb	Wembley	0	2
2000	2 Sept	Paris	1	1
EC2004	13 June	Lisbon	1	2
2008	26 Mar	Paris	0	1
2010	17 Nov	Wembley	1	2
EC2012	11 June	Donetsk	1	1
2015	17 Nov	Wembley	2	0
2017	13 June	Paris	2	3

v GEORGIA			*E*	*G*
WC1996	9 Nov	Tbilisi	2	0
WC1997	30 Apr	Wembley	2	0

v GERMANY			*E*	*G*
1930	10 May	Berlin	3	3
1935	4 Dec	Tottenham	3	0
1938	14 May	Berlin	6	3
1991	11 Sept	Wembley	0	1
1993	19 June	Detroit	1	2
EC1996	26 June	Wembley	1	1*
EC2000	17 June	Charleroi	1	0
WC2000	7 Oct	Wembley	0	1
WC2001	1 Sept	Munich	5	1
2007	22 Aug	Wembley	1	2
2008	19 Nov	Berlin	2	1
WC2010	27 June	Bloemfontein	1	4
2013	19 Nov	Wembley	0	1
2016	26 Mar	Berlin	3	2
2017	22 Mar	Dortmund	0	1
2017	10 Nov	Wembley	0	0
EC2021	**29 June**	**Wembley**	**2**	**0**

v EAST GERMANY			*E*	*EG*
1963	2 June	Leipzig	2	1
1970	25 Nov	Wembley	3	1
1974	29 May	Leipzig	1	1
1984	12 Sept	Wembley	1	0

v WEST GERMANY			*E*	*WG*
1954	1 Dec	Wembley	3	1
1956	26 May	Berlin	3	1
1965	12 May	Nuremberg	1	0
1966	23 Feb	Wembley	1	0
WC1966	30 July	Wembley	4	2*
1968	1 June	Hanover	0	1
WC1970	14 June	Leon	2	3*
EC1972	29 Apr	Wembley	1	3
EC1972	13 May	Berlin	0	0
1975	12 Mar	Wembley	2	0
1978	22 Feb	Munich	1	2
WC1982	29 June	Madrid	0	0
1982	13 Oct	Wembley	1	2
1985	12 June	Mexico City	3	0
1987	9 Sept	Dusseldorf	1	3
WC1990	4 July	Turin	1	1*

v GHANA			*E*	*G*
2011	29 Mar	Wembley	1	1

v GREECE			*E*	*G*
EC1971	21 Apr	Wembley	3	0
EC1971	1 Dec	Piraeus	2	0
EC1982	17 Nov	Salonika	3	0
EC1983	30 Mar	Wembley	0	0
1989	8 Feb	Athens	2	1
1994	17 May	Wembley	5	0
WC2001	6 June	Athens	2	0
WC2001	6 Oct	Old Trafford	2	2
2006	16 Aug	Old Trafford	4	0

v HONDURAS			*E*	*H*
2014	7 June	Miami	0	0

v HUNGARY			*E*	*H*
1908	10 June	Budapest	7	0
1909	29 May	Budapest	4	2
1909	31 May	Budapest	8	2
1934	10 May	Budapest	1	2
1936	2 Dec	Highbury	6	2
1953	25 Nov	Wembley	3	6
1954	23 May	Budapest	1	7
1960	22 May	Budapest	0	2
WC1962	31 May	Rancagua	1	2
1965	5 May	Wembley	1	0
1978	24 May	Wembley	4	1
WC1981	6 June	Budapest	3	1
WC1982	18 Nov	Wembley	1	0
EC1983	27 Apr	Wembley	2	0
EC1983	12 Oct	Budapest	3	0
1988	27 Apr	Budapest	0	0
1990	12 Sept	Wembley	1	0
1992	12 May	Budapest	1	0
1996	18 May	Wembley	3	0
1999	28 Apr	Budapest	1	1
2006	30 May	Old Trafford	3	1
2010	11 Aug	Wembley	2	1

v ICELAND			*E*	*I*
1982	2 June	Reykjavik	1	1
2004	5 June	City of Manchester	6	1
EC2016	27 June	Nice	1	2
NL2020	**5 Sept**	**Reykjavik**	**1**	**0**
NL2020	**18 Nov**	**Wembley**	**4**	**0**

v ISRAEL			*E*	*I*
1986	26 Feb	Ramat Gan	2	1
1988	17 Feb	Tel Aviv	0	0
EC2007	24 Mar	Tel Aviv	0	0
EC2007	8 Sept	Wembley	3	0

v ITALY			*E*	*I*
1933	13 May	Rome	1	1
1934	14 Nov	Highbury	3	2
1939	13 May	Milan	2	2
1948	16 May	Turin	4	0
1949	30 Nov	Tottenham	2	0
1952	18 May	Florence	1	1
1959	6 May	Wembley	2	2
1961	24 May	Rome	3	2
1973	14 June	Turin	0	2
1973	14 Nov	Wembley	0	1
1976	28 May	New York	3	2
WC1976	17 Nov	Rome	0	2
WC1977	16 Nov	Wembley	2	0
EC1980	15 June	Turin	0	1
1985	6 June	Mexico City	1	2
1989	15 Nov	Wembley	0	0
WC1990	7 July	Bari	1	2
WC1997	12 Feb	Wembley	0	1
TF1997	4 June	Nantes	2	0
WC1997	11 Oct	Rome	0	0
2000	15 Nov	Turin	0	1
2002	27 Mar	Leeds	1	2
EC2012	24 June	Kiev	0	0
2012	15 Aug	Berne	2	1
WC2014	14 June	Manaus	1	2
2015	31 Mar	Turin	1	1
2018	27 Mar	Wembley	1	1
EC2021	**11 July**	**Wembley**	**1**	**1***

v JAMAICA			*E*	*J*
2006	3 June	Old Trafford	6	0

v JAPAN			*E*	*J*
UI1995	3 June	Wembley	2	1
2004	1 June	City of Manchester	1	1
2010	30 May	Graz	2	1

v KAZAKHSTAN			*E*	*K*
WC2008	11 Oct	Wembley	5	1
WC2009	6 June	Almaty	4	0

v KOREA REPUBLIC			*E*	*KR*
2002	21 May	Seoguipo	1	1

v KOSOVO			*E*	*K*
EC2019	10 Sept	Southampton	5	3
EC2019	17 Nov	Pristina	4	0

v KUWAIT			*E*	*K*
WC1982	25 June	Bilbao	1	0

v LIECHTENSTEIN			*E*	*L*
EC2003	29 Mar	Vaduz	2	0
EC2003	10 Sept	Old Trafford	2	0

v LITHUANIA			*E*	*L*
EC2015	27 Mar	Wembley	4	0
EC2015	12 Oct	Vilnius	3	0
WC2017	26 Mar	Wembley	2	0
WC2017	8 Oct	Vilnius	1	0

v LUXEMBOURG			*E*	*L*
1927	21 May	Esch-sur-Alzette	5	2
WC1960	19 Oct	Luxembourg	9	0
WC1961	28 Sept	Highbury	4	1
WC1977	30 Mar	Wembley	5	0
WC1977	12 Oct	Luxembourg	2	0
EC1982	15 Dec	Wembley	9	0
EC1983	16 Nov	Luxembourg	4	0
EC1998	14 Oct	Luxembourg	3	0
EC1999	4 Sept	Wembley	6	0
EC2006	7 Oct	Old Trafford	0	0

v MALAYSIA			*E*	*M*
1991	12 June	Kuala Lumpur	4	2

v MALTA			*E*	*M*
EC1971	3 Feb	Valletta	1	0
EC1971	12 May	Wembley	5	0
2000	3 June	Valletta	2	1
WC2016	8 Oct	Wembley	2	0
WC2017	1 Sept	Ta'Qali	4	0

v MEXICO			*E*	*M*
1959	24 May	Mexico City	1	2
1961	10 May	Wembley	8	0
WC1966	16 July	Wembley	2	0
1969	1 June	Mexico City	0	0
1985	9 June	Mexico City	0	1
1986	17 May	Los Angeles	3	0
1997	29 Mar	Wembley	2	0
2001	25 May	Derby	4	0
2010	24 May	Wembley	3	1

v MOLDOVA			*E*	*M*
WC1996	1 Sept	Chisinau	3	0
WC1997	10 Sept	Wembley	4	0
WC2012	7 Sept	Chisinau	5	0
WC2013	6 Sept	Wembley	4	0

v MONTENEGRO

			E	*M*
EC1989	8 Mar	Tirana	2	0
2010	12 Oct	Wembley	0	0
EC2011	7 Oct	Podgorica	2	2
WC2013	26 Mar	Podgorica	1	1
WC2013	11 Oct	Wembley	4	1
EC2019	25 Mar	Podgorica	5	1
EC2019	14 Nov	Wembley	7	0

v MOROCCO

			E	*M*
WC1986	6 June	Monterrey	0	0
1998	27 May	Casablanca	1	0

v NETHERLANDS

			E	*N*
1935	18 May	Amsterdam	1	0
1946	27 Nov	Huddersfield	8	2
1964	9 Dec	Amsterdam	1	1
1969	5 Nov	Amsterdam	1	0
1970	14 June	Wembley	0	0
1977	9 Feb	Wembley	0	2
1982	25 May	Wembley	2	0
1988	23 Mar	Wembley	2	2
EC1988	15 June	Dusseldorf	1	3
WC1990	16 June	Cagliari	0	0
2005	9 Feb	Villa Park	0	0
WC1993	28 Apr	Wembley	2	2
WC1993	13 Oct	Rotterdam	0	2
EC1996	18 June	Wembley	4	1
2001	15 Aug	Tottenham	0	2
2002	13 Feb	Amsterdam	1	1
2006	15 Nov	Amsterdam	1	1
2009	12 Aug	Amsterdam	2	2
2012	29 Feb	Wembley	2	3
2016	29 Mar	Wembley	1	2
2018	23 Mar	Amsterdam	1	0
NL2019	6 June	Guimaraes	1	3

v NEW ZEALAND

			E	*NZ*
1991	3 June	Auckland	1	0
1991	8 June	Wellington	2	0

v NIGERIA

			E	*N*
1994	16 Nov	Wembley	1	0
WC2002	12 June	Osaka	0	0
2018	2 June	Wembley	2	1

v NORTH MACEDONIA

			E	*M*
EC2002	16 Oct	Southampton	2	2
EC2003	6 Sept	Skopje	2	1
EC2006	6 Sept	Skopje	1	0

v NORWAY

			E	*N*
1937	14 May	Oslo	6	0
1938	9 Nov	Newcastle	4	0
1949	18 May	Oslo	4	1
1966	29 June	Oslo	6	1
WC1980	10 Sept	Wembley	4	0
WC1981	9 Sept	Oslo	1	2
WC1992	14 Oct	Wembley	1	1
WC1993	2 June	Oslo	0	2
1994	22 May	Wembley	0	0
1995	11 Oct	Oslo	0	0
2012	26 May	Oslo	1	0
2014	3 Sept	Wembley	1	0

v PANAMA

			E	*P*
WC2018	24 June	Nizhny Novgorod	6	1

v PARAGUAY

			E	*P*
WC1986	18 June	Mexico City	3	0
2002	17 Apr	Liverpool	4	0
WC2006	10 June	Frankfurt	1	0

v PERU

			E	*P*
1959	17 May	Lima	1	4
1962	20 May	Lima	4	0
2014	30 May	Wembley	3	0

v POLAND

			E	*P*
1966	5 Jan	Everton	1	1
1966	5 July	Chorzow	1	0
WC1973	6 June	Chorzow	0	2
WC1973	17 Oct	Wembley	1	1
WC1986	11 June	Monterrey	3	0
WC1989	3 June	Wembley	3	0
WC1989	11 Oct	Katowice	0	0
EC1990	17 Oct	Wembley	2	0
EC1991	13 Nov	Poznan	1	1
WC1993	29 May	Katowice	1	1
WC1993	8 Sept	Wembley	3	0
WC1996	9 Oct	Wembley	2	1
WC1997	31 May	Katowice	2	0
EC1999	27 Mar	Wembley	3	1
EC1999	8 Sept	Warsaw	0	0
WC2004	8 Sept	Katowice	2	1
WC2005	12 Oct	Old Trafford	2	1
WC2012	17 Oct	Warsaw	1	1
WC2013	15 Oct	Wembley	2	0
WC2021	**31 Mar**	**Wembley**	**2**	**1**

v PORTUGAL

			E	*P*
1947	25 May	Lisbon	10	0
1950	14 May	Lisbon	5	3
1951	19 May	Everton	5	2
1955	22 May	Oporto	1	3
1958	7 May	Wembley	2	1
WC1961	21 May	Lisbon	1	1
WC1961	25 Oct	Wembley	2	0
1964	17 May	Lisbon	4	3
1964	4 June	São Paulo	1	1
WC1966	26 July	Wembley	2	1
1969	10 Dec	Wembley	1	0
1974	3 Apr	Lisbon	0	0
EC1974	20 Nov	Wembley	0	0
EC1975	19 Nov	Lisbon	1	1
WC1986	3 June	Monterrey	0	1
1995	12 Dec	Wembley	1	1
1998	22 Apr	Wembley	3	0
EC2000	12 June	Eindhoven	2	3
2002	7 Sept	Villa Park	1	1
2004	18 Feb	Faro	1	1
EC2004	24 June	Lisbon	2	2*
WC2006	1 July	Gelsenkirchen	0	0
2016	2 June	Wembley	1	0

v REPUBLIC OF IRELAND

			E	*RI*
1946	30 Sept	Dublin	1	0
1949	21 Sept	Everton	0	2
WC1957	8 May	Wembley	5	1
WC1957	19 May	Dublin	1	1
1964	24 May	Dublin	3	1
1976	8 Sept	Wembley	1	1
EC1978	25 Oct	Dublin	1	1
EC1980	6 Feb	Wembley	2	0
1985	26 Mar	Wembley	2	1
EC1988	12 June	Stuttgart	0	1
WC1990	11 June	Cagliari	1	1
EC1990	14 Nov	Dublin	1	1
EC1991	27 Mar	Wembley	1	1
1995	15 Feb	Dublin	0	1
(abandoned after 27 mins)				
2013	29 May	Wembley	1	1
2015	7 June	Dublin	0	0
2020	**12 Nov**	**Wembley**	**3**	**0**

v ROMANIA

			E	*R*
1939	24 May	Bucharest	2	0
1968	6 Nov	Bucharest	0	0
1969	15 Jan	Wembley	1	1
WC1970	2 June	Guadalajara	1	0
WC1980	15 Oct	Bucharest	1	2
WC1981	29 April	Wembley	0	0
WC1985	1 May	Bucharest	0	0
WC1985	11 Sept	Wembley	1	1
1994	12 Oct	Wembley	1	1
WC1998	22 June	Toulouse	1	2
EC2000	20 June	Charleroi	2	3
2021	**6 June**	**Middlesbrough**	**1**	**0**

v RUSSIA

			E	*R*
EC2007	12 Sept	Wembley	3	0
EC2007	17 Oct	Moscow	1	2
EC2016	11 June	Marseille	1	1

v SAN MARINO

			E	*SM*
WC1992	17 Feb	Wembley	6	0
WC1993	17 Nov	Bologna	7	1
WC2012	12 Oct	Wembley	5	0
WC2013	22 Mar	Serravalle	8	0
EC2014	9 Oct	Wembley	5	0
EC2015	5 Sept	Serravalle	6	0
WC2021	**25 Mar**	**Wembley**	**5**	**0**

v SAUDI ARABIA

			E	*SA*
1988	16 Nov	Riyadh	1	1
1998	23 May	Wembley	0	0

v SERBIA-MONTENEGRO

			E	*SM*
2003	3 June	Leicester	2	1

v SLOVAKIA

			E	*S*
EC2002	12 Oct	Bratislava	2	1
EC2003	11 June	Middlesbrough	2	1
2009	28 Mar	Wembley	4	0
EC2016	20 June	Lille	0	0
WC2016	4 Sept	Trnava	1	0
WC2017	4 Sept	Wembley	2	1

v SLOVENIA

			E	*S*
2009	5 Sept	Wembley	2	1
WC2010	23 June	Port Elizabeth	1	0
EC2014	15 Nov	Wembley	3	1
EC2015	14 June	Ljubljana	3	2
WC2016	11 Oct	Ljubljana	0	0
WC2017	5 Oct	Wembley	1	0

v SOUTH AFRICA

			E	*SA*
1997	24 May	Old Trafford	2	1
2003	22 May	Durban	2	1

v SPAIN

			E	*S*
1929	15 May	Madrid	3	4
1931	9 Dec	Highbury	7	1
WC1950	2 July	Rio de Janeiro	0	1
1955	18 May	Madrid	1	1
1955	30 Nov	Wembley	4	1
1960	15 May	Madrid	0	3
1960	26 Oct	Wembley	4	2
1965	8 Dec	Madrid	2	0
1967	24 May	Wembley	2	0
EC1968	3 Apr	Wembley	1	0
EC1968	8 May	Madrid	2	1
1980	26 Mar	Barcelona	2	0
EC1980	18 June	Naples	2	1
1981	25 Mar	Wembley	1	2
WC1982	5 July	Madrid	0	0
1987	18 Feb	Madrid	4	2
1992	9 Sept	Santander	0	1
EC 1996	22 June	Wembley	0	0*
2001	28 Feb	Villa Park	3	0
2004	17 Nov	Madrid	0	1
2007	7 Feb	Old Trafford	0	1
2009	11 Feb	Seville	0	2
2011	12 Nov	Wembley	1	0
2015	13 Nov	Alicante	0	2
2016	15 Nov	Wembley	2	2
NL2018	8 Sept	Wembley	1	2
NL2018	15 Oct	Seville	3	2

v SWEDEN

			E	*S*
1923	21 May	Stockholm	4	2
1923	24 May	Stockholm	3	1
1937	17 May	Stockholm	4	0
1947	19 Nov	Highbury	4	2
1949	13 May	Stockholm	1	3
1956	16 May	Stockholm	0	0
1959	28 Oct	Wembley	2	3
1965	16 May	Gothenburg	2	1
1968	22 May	Wembley	3	1
1979	10 June	Stockholm	0	0
1986	10 Sept	Stockholm	0	1
WC1988	19 Oct	Wembley	0	0
WC1989	6 Sept	Stockholm	0	0
EC1992	17 June	Stockholm	1	2
UI1995	8 June	Leeds	3	3
EC1998	5 Sept	Stockholm	1	2
EC1999	5 June	Wembley	0	0
2001	10 Nov	Old Trafford	1	1
WC2002	2 June	Saitama	1	1
2004	31 Mar	Gothenburg	0	1
WC2006	20 June	Cologne	2	2
2011	15 Nov	Wembley	1	0
EC2012	15 June	Kiev	3	2
2012	14 Nov	Stockholm	2	4
WC2018	7 July	Samara	2	0

v SWITZERLAND

			E	*S*
1933	20 May	Berne	4	0
1938	21 May	Zurich	1	2
1947	18 May	Zurich	0	1
1948	2 Dec	Highbury	6	0
1952	28 May	Zurich	3	0
WC1954	20 June	Berne	2	0
1962	9 May	Wembley	3	1
1963	5 June	Basel	8	1
EC1971	13 Oct	Basel	3	2
EC1971	10 Nov	Wembley	1	1
1975	3 Sept	Basel	2	1
1977	7 Sept	Wembley	0	0
WC1980	19 Nov	Wembley	2	1
WC1981	30 May	Basel	1	2
1988	28 May	Lausanne	1	0
1995	15 Nov	Wembley	3	1
EC1996	8 June	Wembley	1	1
1998	25 Mar	Berne	1	1
EC2004	17 June	Coimbra	3	0
2008	6 Feb	Wembley	2	1
EC1989	8 Mar	Tirana	2	0
EC2010	7 Sept	Basel	3	1
EC2011	4 June	Wembley	2	2
EC2014	8 Sept	Basel	2	0
EC2015	8 Sept	Wembley	2	0
2018	11 Sept	Leicester	1	0
NL2019	9 June	Guimaraes	0	0

v TRINIDAD & TOBAGO

			E	*TT*
WC2006	15 June	Nuremberg	2	0
2008	2 June	Port of Spain	3	0

v TUNISIA

			E	*T*
1990	2 June	Tunis	1	1
WC1998	15 June	Marseilles	2	0
WC2018	18 June	Volgograd	2	1

v TURKEY

			E	*T*
WC1984	14 Nov	Istanbul	8	0
WC1985	16 Oct	Wembley	5	0
EC1987	29 Apr	Izmir	0	0
EC1987	14 Oct	Wembley	8	0
EC1991	1 May	Izmir	1	0
EC1991	16 Oct	Wembley	1	0
WC1992	18 Nov	Wembley	4	0
WC1993	31 Mar	Izmir	2	0
EC2003	2 Apr	Sunderland	2	0
EC2003	11 Oct	Istanbul	0	0
2016	22 May	Etihad Stadium	2	1

v UKRAINE

			E	*U*
2000	31 May	Wembley	2	0
2004	18 Aug	Newcastle	3	0
WC2009	1 Apr	Wembley	2	1
WC2009	10 Oct	Dnepr	0	1
EC2012	19 June	Donetsk	1	0
WC2012	11 Sept	Wembley	1	1
WC2013	10 Sept	Kiev	0	0
EC2021	**3 July**	**Rome**	**4**	**0**

v URUGUAY

			E	*U*
1953	31 May	Montevideo	1	2
WC1954	26 June	Basel	2	4
1964	6 May	Wembley	2	1
WC1966	11 July	Wembley	0	0
1969	8 June	Montevideo	2	1
1977	15 June	Montevideo	0	0
1984	13 June	Montevideo	0	2
1990	22 May	Wembley	1	2
1995	29 Mar	Wembley	0	0
2006	1 Mar	Liverpool	2	1
WC2014	19 June	Sao Paulo	1	2

v USA

			E	*USA*
WC1950	29 June	Belo Horizonte	0	1
1953	8 June	New York	6	3
1959	28 May	Los Angeles	8	1
1964	27 May	New York	10	0
1985	16 June	Los Angeles	5	0
1993	9 June	Foxboro	0	2
1994	7 Sept	Wembley	2	0
2005	28 May	Chicago	2	1
2008	28 May	Wembley	2	0
WC2010	12 June	Rustenburg	1	1
2018	15 Nov	Wembley	3	0

v USSR			*E*	*USSR*
1958	18 May	Moscow	1	1
WC1958	8 June	Gothenburg	2	2
WC1958	17 June	Gothenburg	0	1
1958	22 Oct	Wembley	5	0
1967	6 Dec	Wembley	2	2
EC1968	8 June	Rome	2	0
1973	10 June	Moscow	2	1
1984	2 June	Wembley	0	2
1986	26 Mar	Tbilisi	1	0
EC1988	18 June	Frankfurt	1	3
1991	21 May	Wembley	3	1

v YUGOSLAVIA			*E*	*Y*
1939	18 May	Belgrade	1	2
1950	22 Nov	Highbury	2	2
1954	16 May	Belgrade	0	1
1956	28 Nov	Wembley	3	0
1958	11 May	Belgrade	0	5
1960	11 May	Wembley	3	3
1965	9 May	Belgrade	1	1
1966	4 May	Wembley	2	0
EC1968	5 June	Florence	0	1
1972	11 Oct	Wembley	1	1
1974	5 June	Belgrade	2	2
EC1986	12 Nov	Wembley	2	0
EC1987	11 Nov	Belgrade	4	1
1989	13 Dec	Wembley	2	1

SCOTLAND

v ALBANIA			*S*	*A*
NL2018	10 Sept	Glasgow	2	0
NL2018	17 Nov	Shkoder	4	0

v ARGENTINA			*S*	*A*
1977	18 June	Buenos Aires	1	1
1979	2 June	Glasgow	1	3
1990	28 Mar	Glasgow	1	0
2008	19 Nov	Glasgow	0	1

v AUSTRALIA			*S*	*A*
WC1985	20 Nov	Glasgow	2	0
WC1985	4 Dec	Melbourne	0	0
1996	27 Mar	Glasgow	1	0
2000	15 Nov	Glasgow	0	2
2012	15 Aug	Easter Road	3	1

v AUSTRIA			*S*	*A*
1931	16 May	Vienna	0	5
1933	29 Nov	Glasgow	2	2
1937	9 May	Vienna	1	1
1950	13 Dec	Glasgow	0	1
1951	27 May	Vienna	0	4
WC1954	16 June	Zurich	0	1
1955	19 May	Vienna	4	1
1956	2 May	Glasgow	1	1
1960	29 May	Vienna	1	4
1963	8 May	Glasgow	4	1
(abandoned after 79 mins)				
WC1968	6 Nov	Glasgow	2	1
WC1969	5 Nov	Vienna	0	2
EC1978	20 Sept	Vienna	2	3
EC1979	17 Oct	Glasgow	1	1
1994	20 Apr	Vienna	2	1
WC1996	31 Aug	Vienna	0	0
WC1997	2 Apr	Celtic Park	2	0
2003	30 Apr	Glasgow	0	2
2005	17 Aug	Graz	2	2
2007	30 May	Vienna	1	0
WC2021	**25 Mar**	**Glasgow**	**2**	**2**

v BELARUS			*S*	*B*
WC1997	8 June	Minsk	1	0
WC1997	7 Sept	Aberdeen	4	1
WC2005	8 June	Minsk	0	0
WC2005	8 Oct	Glasgow	0	1

v BELGIUM			*S*	*B*
1946	23 Jan	Glasgow	2	2
1947	18 May	Brussels	1	2
1948	28 Apr	Glasgow	2	0
1951	20 May	Brussels	5	0
EC1971	3 Feb	Liege	0	3
EC1971	10 Nov	Aberdeen	1	0
1974	1 June	Brussels	1	2
EC1979	21 Nov	Brussels	0	2
EC1979	19 Dec	Glasgow	1	3
EC1982	15 Dec	Brussels	2	3
EC1983	12 Oct	Glasgow	1	1
EC1987	1 Apr	Brussels	1	4
EC1987	14 Oct	Glasgow	2	0
WC2001	24 Mar	Glasgow	2	2
WC2001	5 Sept	Brussels	0	2
WC2012	16 Oct	Brussels	0	2
WC2013	6 Sept	Glasgow	0	2
2018	7 Sept	Glasgow	0	4
EC2019	11 June	Brussels	0	3
EC2019	9 Sept	Glasgow	0	4

v BOSNIA-HERZEGOVINA			*S*	*BH*
EC1999	4 Sept	Sarajevo	2	1
EC1999	5 Oct	Ibrox	1	0

v BRAZIL			*S*	*B*
1966	25 June	Glasgow	1	1
1972	5 July	Rio de Janeiro	0	1
1973	30 June	Glasgow	0	1
WC1974	18 June	Frankfurt	0	0
1977	23 June	Rio de Janeiro	0	2
WC1982	18 June	Seville	1	4
1987	26 May	Glasgow	0	2
WC1990	20 June	Turin	0	1
WC1998	10 June	St Denis	1	2
2011	27 Mar	Emirates	0	2

v BULGARIA			*S*	*B*
1978	22 Feb	Glasgow	2	1
EC1986	10 Sept	Glasgow	0	0
EC1987	11 Nov	Sofia	1	0
EC1990	14 Nov	Sofia	1	1
EC1991	27 Mar	Glasgow	1	1
2006	11 May	Kobe	5	1

v CANADA			*S*	*C*
1983	12 June	Vancouver	2	0
1983	16 June	Edmonton	3	0
1983	20 June	Toronto	2	0
1992	21 May	Toronto	3	1
2002	15 Oct	Easter Road	3	1
2017	22 Mar	Easter Road	1	1

v CHILE			*S*	*C*
1977	15 June	Santiago	4	2
1989	30 May	Glasgow	2	0

v CIS			*S*	*C*
EC1992	18 June	Norrkoping	3	0

v COLOMBIA			*S*	*C*
1988	17 May	Glasgow	0	0
1996	29 May	Miami	0	1
1998	23 May	New York	2	2

v COSTA RICA			*S*	*CR*
WC1990	11 June	Genoa	0	1
2018	23 Mar	Glasgow	0	1

v CROATIA			*S*	*C*
WC2000	11 Oct	Zagreb	1	1
WC2001	1 Sept	Glasgow	0	0
2008	26 Mar	Glasgow	1	1
WC2013	7 June	Zagreb	1	0
WC2013	15 Oct	Glasgow	2	0
EC2021	**22 June**	**Glasgow**	**1**	**3**

		v CYPRUS	*S*	*C*
WC1968	11 Dec	Nicosia	5	0
WC1969	17 May	Glasgow	8	0
WC1989	8 Feb	Limassol	3	2
WC1989	26 Apr	Glasgow	2	1
2011	11 Nov	Larnaca	2	1
EC2019	8 June	Glasgow	2	1
EC2019	16 Nov	Nicosia	2	1

		v CZECHOSLOVAKIA	*S*	*C*
1937	15 May	Prague	3	1
1937	8 Dec	Glasgow	5	0
WC1961	14 May	Bratislava	0	4
WC1961	26 Sept	Glasgow	3	2
WC1961	29 Nov	Brussels	2	4*
1972	2 July	Porto Alegre	0	0
WC1973	26 Sept	Glasgow	2	1
WC1973	17 Oct	Bratislava	0	1
WC1976	13 Oct	Prague	0	2
WC1977	21 Sept	Glasgow	3	1

		v CZECH REPUBLIC	*S*	*C*
EC1999	31 Mar	Glasgow	1	2
EC1999	9 June	Prague	2	3
2008	30 May	Prague	1	3
2010	3 Mar	Glasgow	1	0
EC2010	8 Oct	Prague	0	1
EC2011	3 Sept	Glasgow	2	2
2016	24 Mar	Prague	1	0
NL2020	**7 Sept**	**Olomouc**	**2**	**1**
NL2020	**14 Oct**	**Glasgow**	**1**	**0**
EC2021	**14 June**	**Glasgow**	**0**	**2**

		v DENMARK	*S*	*D*
1951	12 May	Glasgow	3	1
1952	25 May	Copenhagen	2	1
1968	16 Oct	Copenhagen	1	0
EC1970	11 Nov	Glasgow	1	0
EC1971	9 June	Copenhagen	0	1
WC1972	18 Oct	Copenhagen	4	1
WC1972	15 Nov	Glasgow	2	0
EC1975	3 Sept	Copenhagen	1	0
EC1975	29 Oct	Glasgow	3	1
WC1986	4 June	Nezahualcoyotl	0	1
1996	24 Apr	Copenhagen	0	2
1998	25 Mar	Ibrox	0	1
2002	21 Aug	Glasgow	0	1
2004	28 Apr	Copenhagen	0	1
2011	10 Aug	Glasgow	2	1
2016	29 Mar	Glasgow	1	0

		v ECUADOR	*S*	*E*
1995	24 May	Toyama	2	1

		v EGYPT	*S*	*E*
1990	16 May	Aberdeen	1	3

		v ESTONIA	*S*	*E*
WC1993	19 May	Tallinn	3	0
WC1993	2 June	Aberdeen	3	1
WC1997	11 Feb	Monaco	0	0
WC1997	29 Mar	Kilmarnock	2	0
EC1998	10 Oct	Tynecastle	3	2
EC1999	8 Sept	Tallinn	0	0
2004	27 May	Tallinn	1	0
2013	6 Feb	Aberdeen	1	0

		v FAROE ISLANDS	*S*	*F*
EC1994	12 Oct	Glasgow	5	1
EC1995	7 June	Toftir	2	0
EC1998	14 Oct	Aberdeen	2	1
EC1999	5 June	Toftir	1	1
EC2002	7 Sept	Toftir	2	2
EC2003	6 Sept	Glasgow	3	1
EC2006	2 Sept	Celtic Park	6	0
EC2007	6 June	Toftir	2	0
2010	16 Nov	Aberdeen	3	0
WC2021	**31 Mar**	**Glasgow**	**4**	**0**

		v FINLAND	*S*	*F*
1954	25 May	Helsinki	2	1
WC1964	21 Oct	Glasgow	3	1
WC1965	27 May	Helsinki	2	1
1976	8 Sept	Glasgow	6	0
1992	25 Mar	Glasgow	1	1
EC1994	7 Sept	Helsinki	2	0
EC1995	6 Sept	Glasgow	1	0
1998	22 Apr	Easter Road	1	1

		v FRANCE	*S*	*F*
1930	18 May	Paris	2	0
1932	8 May	Paris	3	1
1948	23 May	Paris	0	3
1949	27 Apr	Glasgow	2	0
1950	27 May	Paris	1	0
1951	16 May	Glasgow	1	0
WC1958	15 June	Orebro	1	2
1984	1 June	Marseilles	0	2
WC1989	8 Mar	Glasgow	2	0
WC1989	11 Oct	Paris	0	3
1997	12 Nov	St Etienne	1	2
2000	29 Mar	Glasgow	0	2
2002	27 Mar	Paris	0	5
EC2006	7 Oct	Glasgow	1	0
EC2007	12 Sept	Paris	1	0
2016	4 June	Metz	0	3

		v GEORGIA	*S*	*G*
EC2007	24 Mar	Glasgow	2	1
EC2007	17 Oct	Tbilisi	0	2
EC2014	11 Oct	Ibrox	1	0
EC2015	4 Sept	Tblisi	0	1

		v GERMANY	*S*	*G*
1929	1 June	Berlin	1	1
1936	14 Oct	Glasgow	2	0
EC1992	15 June	Norrkoping	0	2
1993	24 Mar	Glasgow	0	1
1999	28 Apr	Bremen	1	0
EC2003	7 June	Glasgow	1	1
EC2003	10 Sept	Dortmund	1	2
EC2014	7 Sept	Dortmund	1	2
EC2015	7 Sept	Glasgow	2	3

		v EAST GERMANY	*S*	*EG*
1974	30 Oct	Glasgow	3	0
1977	7 Sept	East Berlin	0	1
EC1982	13 Oct	Glasgow	2	0
EC1983	16 Nov	Halle	1	2
1985	16 Oct	Glasgow	0	0
1990	25 Apr	Glasgow	0	1

		v WEST GERMANY	*S*	*WG*
1957	22 May	Stuttgart	3	1
1959	6 May	Glasgow	3	2
1964	12 May	Hanover	2	2
WC1969	16 Apr	Glasgow	1	1
WC1969	22 Oct	Hamburg	2	3
1973	14 Nov	Glasgow	1	1
1974	27 Mar	Frankfurt	1	2
WC1986	8 June	Queretaro	1	2

		v GIBRALTAR	*S*	*G*
EC2015	29 Mar	Hampden	6	1
EC2015	11 Oct	Faro	6	0

		v GREECE	*S*	*G*
EC1994	18 Dec	Athens	0	1
EC1995	16 Aug	Glasgow	1	0

		v HONG KONG XI	*S*	*HK*
†2002	23 May	Hong Kong	4	0

†*match not recognised by FIFA*

		v HUNGARY	*S*	*H*
1938	7 Dec	Ibrox	3	1
1954	8 Dec	Glasgow	2	4
1955	29 May	Budapest	1	3
1958	7 May	Glasgow	1	1
1960	5 June	Budapest	3	3
1980	31 May	Budapest	1	3
1987	9 Sept	Glasgow	2	0
2004	18 Aug	Glasgow	0	3
2018	27 Mar	Budapest	1	0

		v ICELAND	*S*	*I*
WC1984	17 Oct	Glasgow	3	0
WC1985	28 May	Reykjavik	1	0
EC2002	12 Oct	Reykjavik	2	0
EC2003	29 Mar	Glasgow	2	1
WC2008	10 Sept	Reykjavik	2	1
WC2009	1 Apr	Glasgow	2	1

v IRAN			*S*	*I*
wc1978	7 June	Cordoba	1	1

v ISRAEL			*S*	*I*
wc1981	25 Feb	Tel Aviv	1	0
wc1981	28 Apr	Glasgow	3	1
1986	28 Jan	Tel Aviv	1	0
NL2018	11 Oct	Haifa	1	2
NL2018	20 Nov	Glasgow	3	2
NL2020	**4 Sept**	**Glasgow**	**1**	**1**
EC2020	**8 Oct**	**Glasgow**	**0**	**0**
NL2020	**18 Nov**	**Netanya**	**0**	**1**
wc2021	**28 Mar**	**Tel Aviv**	**1**	**1**

v ITALY			*S*	*I*
1931	20 May	Rome	0	3
wc1965	9 Nov	Glasgow	1	0
wc1965	7 Dec	Naples	0	3
1988	22 Dec	Perugia	0	2
wc1992	18 Nov	Ibrox	0	0
wc1993	13 Oct	Rome	1	3
wc2005	26 Mar	Milan	0	2
wc2005	3 Sept	Glasgow	1	1
EC2007	28 Mar	Bari	0	2
EC2007	17 Nov	Glasgow	1	2
2016	29 May	Ta'Qali	0	1

v JAPAN			*S*	*J*
1995	21 May	Hiroshima	0	0
2006	13 May	Saitama	0	0
2009	10 Oct	Yokohama	0	2

v KAZAKHSTAN			*S*	*K*
EC2019	21 Mar	Astana	0	3
EC2019	19 Nov	Glasgow	3	1

v KOREA REPUBLIC			*S*	*KR*
2002	16 May	Busan	1	4

v LATVIA			*S*	*L*
wc1996	5 Oct	Riga	2	0
wc1997	11 Oct	Celtic Park	2	0
wc2000	2 Sept	Riga	1	0
wc2001	6 Oct	Glasgow	2	1

v LIECHTENSTEIN			*S*	*L*
EC2010	7 Sept	Glasgow	2	1
EC2011	8 Oct	Vaduz	1	0

v LITHUANIA			*S*	*L*
EC1998	5 Sept	Vilnius	0	0
EC1999	9 Oct	Glasgow	3	0
EC2003	2 Apr	Kaunas	0	1
EC2003	11 Oct	Glasgow	1	0
EC2006	6 Sept	Kaunas	2	1
EC2007	8 Sept	Glasgow	3	1
EC2010	3 Sept	Kaunas	0	0
EC2011	6 Sept	Glasgow	1	0
wc2016	8 Oct	Hampden	1	1
wc2017	1 Sept	Vilnius	3	0

v LUXEMBOURG			*S*	*L*
1947	24 May	Luxembourg	6	0
EC1986	12 Nov	Glasgow	3	0
EC1987	2 Dec	Esch	0	0
2012	14 Nov	Luxembourg	2	1
2021	**6 June**	**Luxembourg**	**1**	**0**

v MALTA			*S*	*M*
1988	22 Mar	Valletta	1	1
1990	28 May	Valletta	2	1
wc1993	17 Feb	Ibrox	3	0
wc1993	17 Nov	Valletta	2	0
1997	1 June	Valletta	3	2
wc2016	4 Sept	Ta'Qali	5	1
wc2017	4 Sept	Glasgow	2	0

v MEXICO			*S*	*M*
2018	3 June	Mexico City	0	1

v MOLDOVA			*S*	*M*
wc2004	13 Oct	Chisinau	1	1
wc2005	4 June	Glasgow	2	0

v MOROCCO			*S*	*M*
wc1998	23 June	St Etienne	0	3

v NETHERLANDS			*S*	*N*
1929	4 June	Amsterdam	2	0
1938	21 May	Amsterdam	3	1
1959	27 May	Amsterdam	2	1
1966	11 May	Glasgow	0	3
1968	30 May	Amsterdam	0	0
1971	1 Dec	Amsterdam	1	2
wc1978	11 June	Mendoza	3	2
1982	23 Mar	Glasgow	2	1
1986	29 Apr	Eindhoven	0	0
EC1992	12 June	Gothenburg	0	1
1994	23 Mar	Glasgow	0	1
1994	27 May	Utrecht	1	3
EC1996	10 June	Villa Park	0	0
2000	26 Apr	Arnhem	0	0
EC2003	15 Nov	Glasgow	1	0
EC2003	19 Nov	Amsterdam	0	6
wc2009	28 Mar	Amsterdam	0	3
wc2009	9 Sept	Glasgow	0	1
2017	9 Nov	Aberdeen	0	1
2021	**2 June**	**Faro**	**2**	**2**

v NEW ZEALAND			*S*	*NZ*
wc1982	15 June	Malaga	5	2
2003	27 May	Tynecastle	1	1

v NIGERIA			*S*	*N*
2002	17 Apr	Aberdeen	1	2
2014	28 May	Craven Cottage	2	2

v NORTH MACEDONIA			*S*	*M*
wc2008	6 Sept	Skopje	0	1
wc2009	5 Sept	Glasgow	2	0
wc2012	11 Sept	Glasgow	1	1
wc2013	10 Sept	Skopje	2	1

v NORWAY			*S*	*N*
1929	26 May	Oslo	7	3
1954	5 May	Glasgow	1	0
1954	19 May	Oslo	1	1
1963	4 June	Bergen	3	4
1963	7 Nov	Glasgow	6	1
1974	6 June	Oslo	2	1
EC1978	25 Oct	Glasgow	3	2
EC1979	7 June	Oslo	4	0
wc1988	14 Sept	Oslo	2	1
wc1989	15 Nov	Glasgow	1	1
1992	3 June	Oslo	0	0
wc1998	16 June	Bordeaux	1	1
2003	20 Aug	Oslo	0	0
wc2004	9 Oct	Glasgow	0	1
wc2005	7 Sept	Oslo	2	1
wc2008	11 Oct	Glasgow	0	0
wc2009	12 Aug	Oslo	0	4
2013	19 Nov	Molde	1	0

v PARAGUAY			*S*	*P*
wc1958	11 June	Norrkoping	2	3

v PERU			*S*	*P*
1972	26 Apr	Glasgow	2	0
wc1978	3 June	Cordoba	1	3
1979	12 Sept	Glasgow	1	1
2018	30 May	Lima	0	2

v POLAND			*S*	*P*
1958	1 June	Warsaw	2	1
1960	4 May	Glasgow	2	3
wc1965	23 May	Chorzow	1	1
wc1965	13 Oct	Glasgow	1	2
1980	28 May	Poznan	0	1
1990	19 May	Glasgow	1	1
2001	25 Apr	Bydgoszcz	1	1
2014	5 Mar	Warsaw	1	0
EC2014	14 Oct	Warsaw	2	2
EC2015	8 Oct	Glasgow	2	2

v PORTUGAL			*S*	*P*
1950	21 May	Lisbon	2	2
1955	4 May	Glasgow	3	0
1959	3 June	Lisbon	0	1
1966	18 June	Glasgow	0	1

			S	*P*
EC1971	21 Apr	Lisbon	0	2
EC1971	13 Oct	Glasgow	2	1
1975	13 May	Glasgow	1	0
EC1978	29 Nov	Lisbon	0	1
EC1980	26 Mar	Glasgow	4	1
WC1980	15 Oct	Glasgow	0	0
WC1981	18 Nov	Lisbon	1	2
WC1992	14 Oct	Ibrox	0	0
WC1993	28 Apr	Lisbon	0	5
2002	20 Nov	Braga	0	2
2018	14 Oct	Glasgow	1	3

v QATAR

			S	*Q*
2015	5 June	Easter Road	1	0

v REPUBLIC OF IRELAND

			S	*RI*
WC1961	3 May	Glasgow	4	1
WC1961	7 May	Dublin	3	0
1963	9 June	Dublin	0	1
1969	21 Sept	Dublin	1	1
EC1986	15 Oct	Dublin	0	0
EC1987	18 Feb	Glasgow	0	1
2000	30 May	Dublin	2	1
2003	12 Feb	Glasgow	0	2
NC2011	29 May	Dublin	0	1
EC2014	14 Nov	Hampden	1	0
EC2015	13 June	Dublin	1	1

v ROMANIA

			S	*R*
EC1975	1 June	Bucharest	1	1
EC1975	17 Dec	Glasgow	1	1
1986	26 Mar	Glasgow	3	0
EC1990	12 Sept	Glasgow	2	1
EC1991	16 Oct	Bucharest	0	1
2004	31 Mar	Glasgow	1	2

v RUSSIA

			S	*R*
EC1994	16 Nov	Glasgow	1	1
EC1995	29 Mar	Moscow	0	0
EC2019	6 Sept	Glasgow	1	2
EC2019	10 Oct	Moscow	0	4

v SAN MARINO

			S	*SM*
EC1991	1 May	Serravalle	2	0
EC1991	13 Nov	Glasgow	4	0
EC1995	26 Apr	Serravalle	2	0
EC1995	15 Nov	Glasgow	5	0
WC2000	7 Oct	Serravalle	2	0
WC2001	28 Mar	Glasgow	4	0
EC2019	24 Mar	Serravalle	2	0
EC2019	13 Oct	Glasgow	6	0

v SAUDI ARABIA

			S	*SA*
1988	17 Feb	Riyadh	2	2

v SERBIA

			S	*Se*
WC2012	8 Sept	Glasgow	0	0
WC2013	26 Mar	Novi Sad	0	2
EC2020	**12 Nov**	**Belgrade**	**1**	**1**

v SLOVAKIA

			S	*Sl*
WC2016	11 Oct	Trnava	0	3
WC2017	5 Oct	Glasgow	1	0
NL2020	**11 Oct**	**Glasgow**	**1**	**0**
NL2020	**15 Nov**	**Trnava**	**0**	**1**

v SLOVENIA

			S	*Sl*
WC2004	8 Sept	Glasgow	0	0
WC2005	12 Oct	Celje	3	0
2012	29 Feb	Koper	1	1
WC2017	26 Mar	Hampden	1	0
WC2017	8 Oct	Ljubljana	2	2

v SOUTH AFRICA

			S	*SA*
2002	20 May	Hong Kong	0	2
2007	22 Aug	Aberdeen	1	0

v SPAIN

			S	*S*
WC1957	8 May	Glasgow	4	2
WC1957	26 May	Madrid	1	4
1963	13 June	Madrid	6	2
1965	8 May	Glasgow	0	0
EC1974	20 Nov	Glasgow	1	2
EC1975	5 Feb	Valencia	1	1
1982	24 Feb	Valencia	0	3
WC1984	14 Nov	Glasgow	3	1
WC1985	27 Feb	Seville	0	1
1988	27 Apr	Madrid	0	0
2004	3 Sept	Valencia	1	1

Match abandoned after 60 minutes; floodlight failure.

			S	*S*
EC2010	12 Oct	Glasgow	2	3
EC2011	11 Oct	Alicante	1	3

v SWEDEN

			S	*Sw*
1952	30 May	Stockholm	1	3
1953	6 May	Glasgow	1	2
1975	16 Apr	Gothenburg	1	1
1977	27 Apr	Glasgow	3	1
WC1980	10 Sept	Stockholm	1	0
WC1981	9 Sept	Glasgow	2	0
WC1990	16 June	Genoa	2	1
1995	11 Oct	Stockholm	0	2
WC1996	10 Nov	Ibrox	1	0
WC1997	30 Apr	Gothenburg	1	2
2004	17 Nov	Easter Road	1	4
2010	11 Aug	Stockholm	0	3

v SWITZERLAND

			S	*Sw*
1931	24 May	Geneva	3	2
1946	15 May	Glasgow	3	1
1948	17 May	Berne	1	2
1950	26 Apr	Glasgow	3	1
WC1957	19 May	Basel	2	1
WC1957	6 Nov	Glasgow	3	2
1973	22 June	Berne	0	1
1976	7 Apr	Glasgow	1	0
EC1982	17 Nov	Berne	0	2
EC1983	30 May	Glasgow	2	2
EC1990	17 Oct	Glasgow	2	1
EC1991	11 Sept	Berne	2	2
WC1992	9 Sept	Berne	1	3
WC1993	8 Sept	Aberdeen	1	1
WC1996	18 June	Villa Park	1	0
2006	1 Mar	Glasgow	1	3

v TRINIDAD & TOBAGO

			S	*TT*
2004	30 May	Easter Road	4	1

v TURKEY

			S	*T*
1960	8 June	Ankara	2	4

v UKRAINE

			S	*U*
EC2006	11 Oct	Kiev	0	2
EC2007	13 Oct	Glasgow	3	1

v URUGUAY

			S	*U*
WC1954	19 June	Basel	0	7
1962	2 May	Glasgow	2	3
1983	21 Sept	Glasgow	2	0
WC1986	13 June	Nezahualcoyotl	0	0

v USA

			S	*USA*
1952	30 Apr	Glasgow	6	0
1992	17 May	Denver	1	0
1996	26 May	New Britain	1	2
1998	30 May	Washington	0	0
2005	12 Nov	Glasgow	1	1
2012	26 May	Jacksonville	1	5
2013	15 Nov	Glasgow	0	0

v USSR

			S	*USSR*
1967	10 May	Glasgow	0	2
1971	14 June	Moscow	0	1
WC1982	22 June	Malaga	2	2
1991	6 Feb	Ibrox	0	1

v YUGOSLAVIA

			S	*Y*
1955	15 May	Belgrade	2	2
1956	21 Nov	Glasgow	2	0
WC1958	8 June	Vasteras	1	1
1972	29 June	Belo Horizonte	2	2
WC1974	22 June	Frankfurt	1	1
1984	12 Sept	Glasgow	6	1
WC1988	19 Oct	Glasgow	1	1
WC1989	6 Sept	Zagreb	1	3

v ZAIRE

			S	*Z*
WC1974	14 June	Dortmund	2	0

WALES

v ALBANIA			*W*	*A*
EC1994	7 Sept	Cardiff	2	0
EC1995	15 Nov	Tirana	1	1
2018	20 Nov	Elbasan	0	1
2021	**5 June**	**Cardiff**	**0**	**0**

v ANDORRA			*W*	*A*
EC2014	9 Sept	La Vella	2	1
EC2015	13 Oct	Cardiff	2	0

v ARGENTINA			*W*	*A*
1992	3 June	Tokyo	0	1
2002	13 Feb	Cardiff	1	1

v ARMENIA			*W*	*A*
WC2001	24 Mar	Erevan	2	2
WC2001	1 Sept	Cardiff	0	0

v AUSTRALIA			*W*	*A*
2011	10 Aug	Cardiff	1	2

v AUSTRIA			*W*	*A*
1954	9 May	Vienna	0	2
1955	23 Nov	Wrexham	1	2
EC1974	4 Sept	Vienna	1	2
1975	19 Nov	Wrexham	1	0
1992	29 Apr	Vienna	1	1
EC2005	26 Mar	Cardiff	0	2
EC2005	30 Mar	Vienna	0	1
2013	6 Feb	Swansea	2	1
WC2016	6 Oct	Vienna	2	2
WC2017	2 Sept	Cardiff	1	0

v AZERBAIJAN			*W*	*A*
EC2002	20 Nov	Baku	2	0
EC2003	29 Mar	Cardiff	4	0
WC2004	4 Sept	Baku	1	1
WC2005	12 Oct	Cardiff	2	0
WC2008	6 Sept	Cardiff	1	0
WC2009	6 June	Baku	1	0
EC2019	6 Sept	Cardiff	2	1
EC2019	16 Nov	Baku	2	0

v BELARUS			*W*	*B*
EC1998	14 Oct	Cardiff	3	2
EC1999	4 Sept	Minsk	2	1
WC2000	2 Sept	Minsk	1	2
WC2001	6 Oct	Cardiff	1	0
2019	9 Sept	Cardiff	1	0

v BELGIUM			*W*	*B*
1949	22 May	Liege	1	3
1949	23 Nov	Cardiff	5	1
EC1990	17 Oct	Cardiff	3	1
EC1991	27 Mar	Brussels	1	1
WC1992	18 Nov	Brussels	0	2
WC1993	31 Mar	Cardiff	2	0
WC1997	29 Mar	Cardiff	1	2
WC1997	11 Oct	Brussels	2	3
WC2012	7 Sept	Cardiff	0	2
WC2013	15 Oct	Brussels	1	1
EC2014	16 Nov	Brussels	0	0
EC2015	12 June	Cardiff	1	0
EC2016	1 July	Lille	3	1
WC2021	**24 Mar**	**Leuven**	**1**	**3**

v BOSNIA-HERZEGOVINA			*W*	*BH*
2003	12 Feb	Cardiff	2	2
2012	15 Aug	Llanelli	0	2
EC2014	10 Oct	Cardiff	0	0
EC2015	10 Oct	Zenica	0	2

v BRAZIL			*W*	*B*
WC1958	19 June	Gothenburg	0	1
1962	12 May	Rio de Janeiro	1	3
1962	16 May	São Paulo	1	3
1966	14 May	Rio de Janeiro	1	3
1966	18 May	Belo Horizonte	0	1
1983	12 June	Cardiff	1	1
1991	11 Sept	Cardiff	1	0
1997	12 Nov	Brasilia	0	3
2000	23 May	Cardiff	0	3
2006	5 Sept	Cardiff	0	2

v BULGARIA			*W*	*B*
EC1983	27 Apr	Wrexham	1	0
EC1983	16 Nov	Sofia	0	1
EC1994	14 Dec	Cardiff	0	3
EC1995	29 Mar	Sofia	1	3
2006	15 Aug	Swansea	0	0
2007	22 Aug	Burgas	1	0
EC2010	8 Oct	Cardiff	0	1
EC2011	12 Oct	Sofia	1	0
NL2020	**6 Sept**	**Cardiff**	**1**	**0**
NL2020	**14 Oct**	**Sofia**	**1**	**0**

v CANADA			*W*	*C*
1986	10 May	Toronto	0	2
1986	20 May	Vancouver	3	0
2004	30 May	Wrexham	1	0

v CHILE			*W*	*C*
1966	22 May	Santiago	0	2
2014	4 June	Valparaiso	0	2

v CHINA			*W*	*C*
2018	22 Mar	Nanning	6	0

v COSTA RICA			*W*	*CR*
1990	20 May	Cardiff	1	0
2012	29 Feb	Cardiff	0	1

v CROATIA			*W*	*C*
2002	21 Aug	Varazdin	1	1
2010	23 May	Osijek	0	2
WC2012	16 Oct	Osijek	0	2
WC2013	26 Mar	Swansea	1	2
EC2019	8 June	Osijek	1	2
EC2019	13 Oct	Cardiff	1	1

v CYPRUS			*W*	*C*
WC1992	14 Oct	Limassol	1	0
WC1993	13 Oct	Cardiff	2	0
2005	16 Nov	Limassol	0	1
EC2006	11 Oct	Cardiff	3	1
EC2007	13 Oct	Nicosia	1	3
EC2014	13 Oct	Cardiff	2	1
EC2015	3 Sept	Nicosia	1	0

v CZECHOSLOVAKIA			*W*	*C*
WC1957	1 May	Cardiff	1	0
WC1957	26 May	Prague	0	2
EC1971	21 Apr	Swansea	1	3
EC1971	27 Oct	Prague	0	1
WC1977	30 Mar	Wrexham	3	0
WC1977	16 Nov	Prague	0	1
WC1980	19 Nov	Cardiff	1	0
WC1981	9 Sept	Prague	0	2
EC1987	29 Apr	Wrexham	1	1
EC1987	11 Nov	Prague	0	2
WC1993	28 Apr	Ostrava†	1	1
WC1993	8 Sept	Cardiff†	2	2

†*Czechoslovakia played as RCS (Republic of Czechs and Slovaks).*

v CZECH REPUBLIC			*W*	*C*
WC2021	**30 Mar**	**Cardiff**	**1**	**0**

v DENMARK				
WC1964	21 Oct	Copenhagen	0	1
WC1965	1 Dec	Wrexham	4	2
EC1987	9 Sept	Cardiff	1	0
EC1987	14 Oct	Copenhagen	0	1
1990	11 Sept	Copenhagen	0	1
EC1998	10 Oct	Copenhagen	2	1
EC1999	9 June	Liverpool	0	2
2008	19 Nov	Brondby	1	0
2018	9 Sept	Aarhus	0	2
NL2018	16 Nov	Cardiff	1	2
EC2021	**26 June**	**Amsterdam**	**0**	**4**

v ESTONIA			*W*	*E*
1994	23 May	Tallinn	2	1
2009	29 May	Llanelli	1	0

v FAROE ISLANDS			*W*	*F*
WC1992	9 Sept	Cardiff	6	0
WC1993	6 June	Toftir	3	0

v FINLAND			*W*	*F*
EC1971	26 May	Helsinki	1	0
EC1971	13 Oct	Swansea	3	0
EC1987	10 Sept	Helsinki	1	1
NL2020	**3 Sept**	**Helsinki**	**1**	**0**
NL2020	**18 Nov**	**Cardiff**	**3**	**1**

			W	*F*
EC1987	1 Apr	Wrexham	4	0
WC1988	19 Oct	Swansea	2	2
WC1989	6 Sept	Helsinki	0	1
2000	29 Mar	Cardiff	1	2
EC2002	7 Sept	Helsinki	2	0
EC2003	10 Sept	Cardiff	1	1
WC2009	28 Mar	Cardiff	0	2
WC2009	10 Oct	Helsinki	1	2
2013	16 Nov	Cardiff	1	1

v FRANCE			*W*	*F*
1933	25 May	Paris	1	1
1939	20 May	Paris	1	2
1953	14 May	Paris	1	6
1982	2 June	Toulouse	1	0
2017	10 Nov	Paris	0	2
2021	**2 June**	**Nice**	**0**	**3**

v GEORGIA			*W*	*G*
EC1994	16 Nov	Tbilisi	0	5
EC1995	7 June	Cardiff	0	1
2008	20 Aug	Swansea	1	2
WC2016	9 Oct	Cardiff	1	1
WC2017	6 Oct	Tbilisi	1	0

v GERMANY			*W*	*G*
EC1995	26 Apr	Dusseldorf	1	1
EC1995	11 Oct	Cardiff	1	2
2002	14 May	Cardiff	1	0
EC2007	8 Sept	Cardiff	0	2
EC2007	21 Nov	Frankfurt	0	0
WC2008	15 Oct	Moenchengladbach	0	1
WC2009	1 Apr	Cardiff	0	2

v EAST GERMANY			*W*	*EG*
WC1957	19 May	Leipzig	1	2
WC1957	25 Sept	Cardiff	4	1
WC1969	16 Apr	Dresden	1	2
WC1969	22 Oct	Cardiff	1	3

v WEST GERMANY			*W*	*WG*
1968	8 May	Cardiff	1	1
1969	26 Mar	Frankfurt	1	1
1976	6 Oct	Cardiff	0	2
1977	14 Dec	Dortmund	1	1
EC1979	2 May	Wrexham	0	2
EC1979	17 Oct	Cologne	1	5
WC1989	31 May	Cardiff	0	0
WC1989	15 Nov	Cologne	1	2
EC1991	5 June	Cardiff	1	0
EC1991	16 Oct	Nuremberg	1	4

v GREECE			*W*	*G*
WC1964	9 Dec	Athens	0	2
WC1965	17 Mar	Cardiff	4	1

v HUNGARY			*W*	*H*
WC1958	8 June	Sanviken	1	1
WC1958	17 June	Stockholm	2	1
1961	28 May	Budapest	2	3
EC1962	7 Nov	Budapest	1	3
EC1963	20 Mar	Cardiff	1	1
EC1974	30 Oct	Cardiff	2	0
EC1975	16 Apr	Budapest	2	1
1985	16 Oct	Cardiff	0	3
2004	31 Mar	Budapest	2	1
2005	9 Feb	Cardiff	2	0
EC2019	11 June	Budapest	0	1
EC2019	19 Nov	Cardiff	2	0

v ICELAND			*W*	*I*
WC1980	2 June	Reykjavik	4	0
WC1981	14 Oct	Swansea	2	2
WC1984	12 Sept	Reykjavik	0	1
WC1984	14 Nov	Cardiff	2	1
1991	1 May	Cardiff	1	0
2008	28 May	Reykjavik	1	0
2014	5 Mar	Cardiff	3	1

v IRAN			*W*	*I*
1978	18 Apr	Tehran	1	0

v ISRAEL			*W*	*I*
WC1958	15 Jan	Tel Aviv	2	0
WC1958	5 Feb	Cardiff	2	0
1984	10 June	Tel Aviv	0	0
1989	8 Feb	Tel Aviv	3	3
EC2015	28 Mar	Haifa	3	0
EC2015	6 Sept	Cardiff	0	0

v ITALY			*W*	*I*
1965	1 May	Florence	1	4
WC1968	23 Oct	Cardiff	0	1
WC1969	4 Nov	Rome	1	4
1988	4 June	Brescia	1	0
1996	24 Jan	Terni	0	3
EC1998	5 Sept	Liverpool	0	2
EC1999	5 June	Bologna	0	4
EC2002	16 Oct	Cardiff	2	1
EC2003	6 Sept	Milan	0	4
EC2021	**20 June**	**Rome**	**0**	**1**

v JAMAICA			*W*	*J*
1998	25 Mar	Cardiff	0	0

v JAPAN			*W*	*J*
1992	7 June	Matsuyama	1	0

v KUWAIT			*W*	*K*
1977	6 Sept	Wrexham	0	0
1977	20 Sept	Kuwait	0	0

v LATVIA			*W*	*L*
2004	18 Aug	Riga	2	0

v LIECHTENSTEIN			*W*	*L*
2006	14 Nov	Swansea	4	0
WC2008	11 Oct	Cardiff	2	0
WC2009	14 Oct	Vaduz	2	0

v LUXEMBOURG			*W*	*L*
EC1974	20 Nov	Swansea	5	0
EC1975	1 May	Luxembourg	3	1
EC1990	14 Nov	Luxembourg	1	0
EC1991	13 Nov	Cardiff	1	0
2008	26 Mar	Luxembourg	2	0
2010	11 Aug	Llanelli	5	1

v MALTA			*W*	*M*
EC1978	25 Oct	Wrexham	7	0
EC1979	2 June	Valletta	2	0
1988	1 June	Valletta	3	2
1998	3 June	Valletta	3	0

v MEXICO			*W*	*M*
WC1958	11 June	Stockholm	1	1
1962	22 May	Mexico City	1	2
2012	27 May	New Jersey	0	2
2018	29 May	Pasadena	0	0
2021	**27 Mar**	**Cardiff**	**1**	**0**

v MOLDOVA			*W*	*M*
EC1994	12 Oct	Kishinev	2	3
EC1995	6 Sept	Cardiff	1	0
WC2016	5 Sept	Cardiff	4	0
WC2017	5 Sept	Chisinau	2	0

v MONTENEGRO			*W*	*M*
2009	12 Aug	Podgorica	1	2
EC2010	3 Sept	Podgorica	0	1
EC2011	2 Sept	Cardiff	2	1

v NETHERLANDS			*W*	*N*
WC1988	14 Sept	Amsterdam	0	1
WC1989	11 Oct	Wrexham	1	2
1992	30 May	Utrecht	0	4
WC1996	5 Oct	Cardiff	1	3
WC1996	9 Nov	Eindhoven	1	7
2008	1 June	Rotterdam	0	2
2014	4 June	Amsterdam	0	2
2015	13 Nov	Cardiff	2	3

v NEW ZEALAND			*W*	*NZ*
2007	26 May	Wrexham	2	2

v NORTH MACEDONIA			*W*	*M*
WC2013	6 Sept	Skopje	1	2
WC2013	11 Oct	Cardiff	1	0

v NORWAY			*W*	*N*
EC1982	22 Sept	Swansea	1	0
EC1983	21 Sept	Oslo	0	0
1984	6 June	Trondheim	0	1
1985	26 Feb	Wrexham	1	1
1985	5 June	Bergen	2	4
1994	9 Mar	Cardiff	1	3
WC2000	7 Oct	Cardiff	1	1
WC2001	5 Sept	Oslo	2	3
2004	27 May	Oslo	0	0
2008	6 Feb	Wrexham	3	0
2011	12 Nov	Cardiff	4	1

v PANAMA			*W*	*P*
2017	14 Nov	Cardiff	1	1

v PARAGUAY			*W*	*P*
2006	1 Mar	Cardiff	0	0

v POLAND			*W*	*P*
WC1973	28 Mar	Cardiff	2	0
WC1973	26 Sept	Katowice	0	3
1991	29 May	Radom	0	0
WC2000	11 Oct	Warsaw	0	0
WC2001	2 June	Cardiff	1	2
WC2004	13 Oct	Cardiff	2	3
WC2005	7 Sept	Warsaw	0	1
2009	11 Feb	Vila Real	0	1

v PORTUGAL			*W*	*P*
1949	15 May	Lisbon	2	3
1951	12 May	Cardiff	2	1
2000	2 June	Chaves	0	3
EC2016	6 July	Lille	0	2

v QATAR			*W*	*Q*
2000	23 Feb	Doha	1	0

v REPUBLIC OF IRELAND			*W*	*RI*
1960	28 Sept	Dublin	3	2
1979	11 Sept	Swansea	2	1
1981	24 Feb	Dublin	3	1
1986	26 Mar	Dublin	1	0
1990	28 Mar	Dublin	0	1
1991	6 Feb	Wrexham	0	3
1992	19 Feb	Dublin	1	0
1993	17 Feb	Dublin	1	2
1997	11 Feb	Cardiff	0	0
EC2007	24 Mar	Dublin	0	1
EC2007	17 Nov	Cardiff	2	2
NC2011	8 Feb	Dublin	0	3
2013	14 Aug	Cardiff	0	0
WC2017	24 Mar	Dublin	0	0
WC2017	9 Oct	Cardiff	0	1
NL2018	6 Sept	Cardiff	4	1
NL2018	16 Oct	Dublin	1	0
NL2020	**11 Oct**	**Dublin**	**0**	**0**
NL2020	**15 Nov**	**Cardiff**	**1**	**0**

v ROMANIA			*W*	*R*
EC1970	11 Nov	Cardiff	0	0
EC1971	24 Nov	Bucharest	0	2
1983	12 Oct	Wrexham	5	0
WC1992	20 May	Bucharest	1	5
WC1993	17 Nov	Cardiff	1	2

v RUSSIA			*W*	*R*
EC2003	15 Nov	Moscow	0	0
EC2003	19 Nov	Cardiff	0	1
WC2008	10 Sept	Moscow	1	2
WC2009	9 Sept	Cardiff	1	3
EC2016	20 June	Toulouse	3	0

v SAN MARINO			*W*	*SM*
WC1996	2 June	Serravalle	5	0
WC1996	31 Aug	Cardiff	6	0
EC2007	28 Mar	Cardiff	3	0
EC2007	17 Oct	Serravalle	2	1

v SAUDI ARABIA			*W*	*SA*
1986	25 Feb	Dahran	2	1

v SERBIA			*W*	*S*
WC2012	11 Sept	Novi Sad	1	6
WC2013	10 Sept	Cardiff	0	3
WC2016	12 Nov	Cardiff	1	1
WC2017	11 June	Belgrade	1	1

v SERBIA-MONTENEGRO			*W*	*SM*
EC2003	20 Aug	Belgrade	0	1
EC2003	11 Oct	Cardiff	2	3

v SLOVAKIA			*W*	*S*
EC2006	7 Oct	Cardiff	1	5
EC2007	12 Sept	Trnava	5	2
EC2016	11 June	Bordeaux	2	1
EC2019	24 Mar	Cardiff	1	0
EC2019	10 Oct	Trnava	1	1

v SLOVENIA			*W*	*Sl*
2005	17 Aug	Swansea	0	0

v SPAIN			*W*	*S*
WC1961	19 Apr	Cardiff	1	2
WC1961	18 May	Madrid	1	1
1982	24 Mar	Valencia	1	1
WC1984	17 Oct	Seville	0	3
WC1985	30 Apr	Wrexham	3	0
2018	11 Oct	Cardiff	1	4

v SWEDEN			*W*	*S*
WC1958	15 June	Stockholm	0	0
1988	27 Apr	Stockholm	1	4
1989	26 Apr	Wrexham	0	2
1990	25 Apr	Stockholm	2	4
1994	20 Apr	Wrexham	0	2
2010	3 Mar	Swansea	0	1
2016	5 June	Stockholm	0	3

v SWITZERLAND			*W*	*S*
1949	26 May	Berne	0	4
1951	16 May	Wrexham	3	2
1996	24 Apr	Lugano	0	2
EC1999	31 Mar	Zurich	0	2
EC1999	9 Oct	Wrexham	0	2
EC2010	12 Oct	Basel	1	4
EC2011	8 Oct	Swansea	2	0
EC2021	**12 June**	**Baku**	**1**	**1**

v TRINIDAD & TOBAGO			*W*	*TT*
2006	27 May	Graz	2	1
2019	20 Mar	Wrexham	1	0

v TUNISIA			*W*	*T*
1998	6 June	Tunis	0	4

v TURKEY			*W*	*T*
EC1978	29 Nov	Wrexham	1	0
EC1979	21 Nov	Izmir	0	1
WC1980	15 Oct	Cardiff	4	0
WC1981	25 Mar	Ankara	1	0
WC1996	14 Dec	Cardiff	0	0
WC1997	20 Aug	Istanbul	4	6
EC2021	**16 June**	**Baku**	**2**	**0**

v UKRAINE			*W*	*U*
WC2001	28 Mar	Cardiff	1	1
WC2001	6 June	Kiev	1	1
2016	28 Mar	Kiev	0	1

v REST OF UNITED KINGDOM			*W*	*RUK*
1951	5 Dec	Cardiff	3	2
1969	28 July	Cardiff	0	1

v URUGUAY			*W*	*U*
1986	21 Apr	Wrexham	0	0
2018	26 Mar	Nanning	0	1

v USA			*W*	*USA*
2003	27 May	San Jose	0	2
2020	**12 Nov**	**Swansea**	**0**	**0**

v USSR			*W*	*USSR*
WC1965	30 May	Moscow	1	2
WC1965	27 Oct	Cardiff	2	1
WC1981	30 May	Wrexham	0	0
WC1981	18 Nov	Tbilisi	0	3
1987	18 Feb	Swansea	0	0

v YUGOSLAVIA			*W*	*Y*
1953	21 May	Belgrade	2	5
1954	22 Nov	Cardiff	1	3
EC1976	24 Apr	Zagreb	0	2
EC1976	22 May	Cardiff	1	1
EC1982	15 Dec	Titograd	4	4
EC1983	14 Dec	Cardiff	1	1
1988	23 Mar	Swansea	1	2

NORTHERN IRELAND

		v ALBANIA	*NI*	*A*
wc1965	7 May	Belfast	4	1
wc1965	24 Nov	Tirana	1	1
EC1982	15 Dec	Tirana	0	0
EC1983	27 Apr	Belfast	1	0
wc1992	9 Sept	Belfast	3	0
wc1993	17 Feb	Tirana	2	1
wc1996	14 Dec	Belfast	2	0
wc1997	10 Sept	Zurich	0	1
2010	3 Mar	Tirana	0	1

		v ALGERIA	*NI*	*A*
wc1986	3 June	Guadalajara	1	1

		v ARGENTINA	*NI*	*A*
wc1958	11 June	Halmstad	1	3

		v ARMENIA	*NI*	*A*
wc1996	5 Oct	Belfast	1	1
wc1997	30 Apr	Erevan	0	0
EC2003	29 Mar	Erevan	0	1
EC2003	10 Sept	Belfast	0	1

		v AUSTRALIA	*NI*	*A*
1980	11 June	Sydney	2	1
1980	15 June	Melbourne	1	1
1980	18 June	Adelaide	2	1

		v AUSTRIA	*NI*	*A*
wc1982	1 July	Madrid	2	2
EC1982	13 Oct	Vienna	0	2
EC1983	21 Sept	Belfast	3	1
EC1990	14 Nov	Vienna	0	0
EC1991	16 Oct	Belfast	2	1
EC1994	12 Oct	Vienna	2	1
EC1995	15 Nov	Belfast	5	3
wc2004	13 Oct	Belfast	3	3
wc2005	12 Oct	Vienna	0	2
NL2018	12 Oct	Vienna	0	1
NL2018	18 Nov	Belfast	1	2
NL2020	**11 Oct**	**Belfast**	**0**	**1**
NL2020	**15 Nov**	**Vienna**	**1**	**2**

		v AZERBAIJAN	*NI*	*A*
wc2004	9 Oct	Baku	0	0
wc2005	3 Sept	Belfast	2	0
wc2012	14 Nov	Belfast	1	1
wc2013	11 Oct	Baku	0	2
wc2016	11 Nov	Belfast	4	0
wc2017	10 June	Baku	1	0

		v BARBADOS	*NI*	*B*
2004	30 May	Waterford	1	1

		v BELARUS	*NI*	*B*
2016	27 May	Belfast	3	0
EC2019	24 Mar	Belfast	2	1
EC2019	11 June	Barysaw	1	0

		v BELGIUM	*NI*	*B*
wc1976	10 Nov	Liege	0	2
wc1977	16 Nov	Belfast	3	0
1997	11 Feb	Belfast	3	0

		v BOSNIA-HERZEGOVINA	*NI*	*B*
NL2018	8 Sept	Belfast	1	2
NL2018	15 Oct	Sarajevo	0	2
EC2020	**8 Oct**	**Sarajevo**	**1**	**1**

		v BRAZIL	*NI*	*B*
wc1986	12 June	Guadalajara	0	3

		v BULGARIA	*NI*	*B*
wc1972	18 Oct	Sofia	0	3
wc1973	26 Sept	Sheffield	0	0
EC1978	29 Nov	Sofia	2	0
EC1979	2 May	Belfast	2	0
wc2001	28 Mar	Sofia	3	4
wc2001	2 June	Belfast	0	1
2008	6 Feb	Belfast	0	1
wc2021	**31 Mar**	**Belfast**	**0**	**0**

		v CANADA	*NI*	*C*
1995	22 May	Edmonton	0	2
1999	27 Apr	Belfast	1	1
2005	9 Feb	Belfast	0	1

		v CHILE	*NI*	*C*
1989	26 May	Belfast	0	1
1995	25 May	Edmonton	1	2
2010	30 May	Chillan	0	1
2014	4 June	Valparaiso	0	2

		v COLOMBIA	*NI*	*C*
1994	4 June	Boston	0	2

		v COSTA RICA	*NI*	*CR*
2018	3 June	San Jose	0	3

		v CROATIA	*NI*	*C*
2016	15 Nov	Belfast	0	3

		v CYPRUS	*NI*	*C*
EC1971	3 Feb	Nicosia	3	0
EC1971	21 Apr	Belfast	5	0
wc1973	14 Feb	Nicosia	0	1
wc1973	8 May	London	3	0
2002	21 Aug	Belfast	0	0
2014	5 Mar	Nicosia	0	0

		v CZECHOSLOVAKIA	*NI*	*C*
wc1958	8 June	Halmstad	1	0
wc1958	17 June	Malmo	2	1*

**After extra time*

		v CZECH REPUBLIC	*NI*	*C*
wc2001	24 Mar	Belfast	0	1
wc2001	6 June	Teplice	1	3
wc2008	10 Sept	Belfast	0	0
wc2009	14 Oct	Prague	0	0
wc2016	4 Sept	Prague	0	0
wc2017	4 Sept	Belfast	2	0
2019	14 Oct	Prague	3	2

		v DENMARK	*NI*	*D*
EC1978	25 Oct	Belfast	2	1
EC1979	6 June	Copenhagen	0	4
1986	26 Mar	Belfast	1	1
EC1990	17 Oct	Belfast	1	1
EC1991	13 Nov	Odense	1	2
wc1992	18 Nov	Belfast	0	1
wc1993	13 Oct	Copenhagen	0	1
wc2000	7 Oct	Belfast	1	1
wc2001	1 Sept	Copenhagen	1	1
EC2006	7 Oct	Copenhagen	0	0
EC2007	17 Nov	Belfast	2	1

		v ESTONIA	*NI*	*E*
2004	31 Mar	Tallinn	1	0
2006	1 Mar	Belfast	1	0
EC2011	6 Sept	Tallinn	1	4
EC2011	7 Oct	Belfast	1	2
EC2019	21 Mar	Belfast	2	0
EC2019	8 June	Tallinn	2	1

		v FAROE ISLANDS	*NI*	*F*
EC1991	1 May	Belfast	1	1
EC1991	11 Sept	Landskrona	5	0
EC2010	12 Oct	Toftir	1	1
EC2011	10 Aug	Belfast	4	0
EC2014	11 Oct	Belfast	2	0
EC2015	4 Sept	Torshavn	3	1

		v FINLAND	*NI*	*F*
wc1984	27 May	Pori	0	1
wc1984	14 Nov	Belfast	2	1
EC1998	10 Oct	Belfast	1	0
EC1998	9 Oct	Helsinki	1	4
2003	12 Feb	Belfast	0	1
2006	16 Aug	Helsinki	2	1
2012	15 Aug	Belfast	3	3
EC2015	29 Mar	Belfast	2	1
EC2015	11 Oct	Helsinki	1	1

		v FRANCE	*NI*	*F*
1928	21 Feb	Paris	0	4
1951	12 May	Belfast	2	2
1952	11 Nov	Paris	1	3
wc1958	19 June	Norrkoping	0	4
1982	24 Mar	Paris	0	4
wc1982	4 July	Madrid	1	4

			NI	*F*
1986	26 Feb	Paris	0	0
1988	27 Apr	Belfast	0	0
1999	18 Aug	Belfast	0	1

		v GEORGIA	*NI*	*G*
2008	26 Mar	Belfast	4	1

		v GERMANY	*NI*	*G*
1992	2 June	Bremen	1	1
1996	29 May	Belfast	1	1
wc1996	9 Nov	Nuremberg	1	1
wc1997	20 Aug	Belfast	1	3
EC1999	27 Mar	Belfast	0	3
EC1999	8 Sept	Dortmund	0	4
2005	4 June	Belfast	1	4
EC2016	21 June	Paris	0	1
wc2016	11 Oct	Hanover	0	2
wc2017	5 Oct	Belfast	1	3
EC2019	9 Sept	Belfast	0	2
EC2019	19 Nov	Frankfurt	1	6

		v WEST GERMANY	*NI*	*WG*
wc1958	15 June	Malmo	2	2
wc1960	26 Oct	Belfast	3	4
wc1961	10 May	Hamburg	1	2
1966	7 May	Belfast	0	2
1977	27 Apr	Cologne	0	5
EC1982	17 Nov	Belfast	1	0
EC1983	16 Nov	Hamburg	1	0

		v GREECE	*NI*	*G*
wc1961	3 May	Athens	1	2
wc1961	17 Oct	Belfast	2	0
1988	17 Feb	Athens	2	3
EC2003	2 Apr	Belfast	0	2
EC2003	11 Oct	Athens	0	1
EC2014	14 Oct	Piraeus	2	0
EC2015	8 Oct	Belfast	3	1

		v HONDURAS	*NI*	*H*
wc1982	21 June	Zaragoza	1	1

		v HUNGARY	*NI*	*H*
wc1988	19 Oct	Budapest	0	1
wc1989	6 Sept	Belfast	1	2
2000	26 Apr	Belfast	0	1
2008	19 Nov	Belfast	0	2
EC2014	7 Sept	Budapest	2	1
EC2015	7 Sept	Belfast	1	1

		v ICELAND	*NI*	*I*
wc1977	11 June	Reykjavik	0	1
wc1977	21 Sept	Belfast	2	0
wc2000	11 Oct	Reykjavik	0	1
wc2001	5 Sept	Belfast	3	0
EC2006	2 Sept	Belfast	0	3
EC2007	12 Sept	Reykjavik	1	2

		v ISRAEL	*NI*	*I*
1968	10 Sept	Jaffa	3	2
1976	3 Mar	Tel Aviv	1	1
wc1980	26 Mar	Tel Aviv	0	0
wc1981	18 Nov	Belfast	1	0
1984	16 Oct	Belfast	3	0
1987	18 Feb	Tel Aviv	1	1
2009	12 Aug	Belfast	1	1
wc2013	26 Mar	Belfast	0	2
wc2013	15 Oct	Tel Aviv	1	1
2018	11 Sept	Belfast	3	0

		v ITALY	*NI*	*I*
wc1957	25 Apr	Rome	0	1
1957	4 Dec	Belfast	2	2
wc1958	15 Jan	Belfast	2	1
1961	25 Apr	Bologna	2	3
1997	22 Jan	Palermo	0	2
2003	3 June	Campobasso	0	2
2009	6 June	Pisa	0	3
EC2010	8 Oct	Belfast	0	0
EC2011	11 Oct	Pescara	0	3
wc2021	**25 Mar**	**Parma**	**0**	**2**

		v KOREA REPUBLIC	*NI*	*KR*
2018	24 Mar	Belfast	2	1

		v LATVIA	*NI*	*L*
wc1993	2 June	Riga	2	1
wc1993	8 Sept	Belfast	2	0
EC1995	26 Apr	Riga	1	0
EC1995	7 June	Belfast	1	2
EC2006	11 Oct	Belfast	1	0
EC2007	8 Sept	Riga	0	1
2015	13 Nov	Belfast	1	0

		v LIECHTENSTEIN	*NI*	*L*
EC1994	20 Apr	Belfast	4	1
EC1995	11 Oct	Eschen	4	0
2002	27 Mar	Vaduz	0	0
EC2007	24 Mar	Vaduz	4	1
EC2007	22 Aug	Belfast	3	1

		v LITHUANIA	*NI*	*L*
wc1992	28 Apr	Belfast	2	2
wc1993	25 May	Vilnius	1	0

		v LUXEMBOURG	*NI*	*L*
2000	23 Feb	Luxembourg	3	1
wc2012	11 Sept	Belfast	1	1
wc2013	10 Sept	Luxembourg	2	3
2019	5 Sept	Belfast	1	0

		v MALTA	*NI*	*M*
wc1988	21 May	Belfast	3	0
wc1989	26 Apr	Valletta	2	0
2000	28 Mar	Valletta	3	0
wc2000	2 Sept	Belfast	1	0
wc2001	6 Oct	Valletta	1	0
2005	17 Aug	Ta'Qali	1	1
2013	6 Feb	Ta'Qali	0	0
2021	**30 May**	**Klagenfurt**	**3**	**0**

		v MEXICO	*NI*	*M*
1966	22 June	Belfast	4	1
1994	11 June	Miami	0	3

		v MOLDOVA	*NI*	*M*
EC1998	18 Nov	Belfast	2	2
EC1999	31 Mar	Chisinau	0	0

		v MONTENEGRO	*NI*	*M*
2010	11 Aug	Podgorica	0	2

		v MOROCCO	*NI*	*M*
1986	23 Apr	Belfast	2	1
2010	17 Nov	Belfast	1	1

		v NETHERLANDS	*NI*	*N*
1962	9 May	Rotterdam	0	4
wc1965	17 Mar	Belfast	2	1
wc1965	7 Apr	Rotterdam	0	0
wc1976	13 Oct	Rotterdam	2	2
wc1977	12 Oct	Belfast	0	1
2012	2 June	Amsterdam	0	6
EC2019	10 Oct	Rotterdam	1	3
EC2019	16 Nov	Belfast	0	0

		v NEW ZEALAND	*NI*	*N*
2017	2 June	Belfast	1	0

		v NORWAY	*NI*	*N*
1922	25 May	Bergen	1	2
EC1974	4 Sept	Oslo	1	2
EC1975	29 Oct	Belfast	3	0
1990	27 Mar	Belfast	2	3
1996	27 Mar	Belfast	0	2
2001	28 Feb	Belfast	0	4
2004	18 Feb	Belfast	1	4
2012	29 Feb	Belfast	0	3
wc2017	26 Mar	Belfast	2	0
wc2017	8 Oct	Oslo	0	1
NL2020	**7 Sept**	**Belfast**	**1**	**5**
NL2020	**14 Oct**	**Oslo**	**0**	**1**

		v PANAMA	*NI*	*P*
2018	30 May	Panama City	0	0

		v POLAND	*NI*	*P*
EC1962	10 Oct	Katowice	2	0
EC1962	28 Nov	Belfast	2	0
1988	23 Mar	Belfast	1	1
1991	5 Feb	Belfast	3	1
2002	13 Feb	Limassol	1	4
EC2004	4 Sept	Belfast	0	3
EC2005	30 Mar	Warsaw	0	1

			NI	*P*
wc2009	28 Mar	Belfast	3	2
wc2009	5 Sept	Chorzow	1	1
EC2016	12 June	Nice	0	1

v PORTUGAL

			NI	*P*
wc1957	16 Jan	Lisbon	1	1
wc1957	1 May	Belfast	3	0
wc1973	28 Mar	Coventry	1	1
wc1973	14 Nov	Lisbon	1	1
wc1980	19 Nov	Lisbon	0	1
wc1981	29 Apr	Belfast	1	0
EC1994	7 Sept	Belfast	1	2
EC1995	3 Sept	Lisbon	1	1
wc1997	29 Mar	Belfast	0	0
wc1997	11 Oct	Lisbon	0	1
2005	15 Nov	Belfast	1	1
wc2012	16 Oct	Porto	1	1
wc2013	6 Sept	Belfast	2	4

v QATAR

			NI	*Q*
2015	31 May	Crewe	1	1

v REPUBLIC OF IRELAND

			NI	*RI*
EC1978	20 Sept	Dublin	0	0
EC1979	21 Nov	Belfast	1	0
wc1988	14 Sept	Belfast	0	0
wc1989	11 Oct	Dublin	0	3
wc1993	31 Mar	Dublin	0	3
wc1993	17 Nov	Belfast	1	1
EC1994	16 Nov	Belfast	0	4
EC1995	29 Mar	Dublin	1	1
1999	29 May	Dublin	1	0
NC2011	24 May	Dublin	0	5
2018	15 Nov	Dublin	0	0

v ROMANIA

			NI	*R*
wc1984	12 Sept	Belfast	3	2
wc1985	16 Oct	Bucharest	1	0
1994	23 Mar	Belfast	2	0
2006	27 May	Chicago	0	2
EC2014	14 Nov	Bucharest	0	2
EC2015	13 June	Belfast	0	0
NL2020	**4 Sept**	**Bucharest**	**1**	**1**
NL2020	**18 Nov**	**Belfast**	**1**	**1**

v RUSSIA

			NI	*R*
wc2012	7 Sept	Moscow	0	2
wc2013	14 Aug	Belfast	1	0

v SAN MARINO

			NI	*SM*
wc2008	15 Oct	Belfast	4	0
wc2009	11 Feb	Serravalle	3	0
wc2016	8 Oct	Belfast	4	0
wc2017	1 Sept	Serravalle	3	0

v ST KITTS & NEVIS

			NI	*SK*
2004	2 June	Basseterre	2	0

v SERBIA

			NI	*S*
2009	14 Nov	Belfast	0	1
EC2011	25 Mar	Belgrade	1	2
EC2011	2 Sept	Belfast	0	1

v SERBIA-MONTENEGRO

			NI	*SM*
2004	28 Apr	Belfast	1	1

v SLOVAKIA

			NI	*S*
1998	25 Mar	Belfast	1	0
wc2008	6 Sept	Bratislava	1	2
wc2009	9 Sept	Belfast	0	2
2016	4 June	Trnava	0	0
EC2020	**12 Nov**	**Belfast**	**1**	**2**

v SLOVENIA

			NI	*S*
wc2008	11 Oct	Maribor	0	2
wc2009	1 Apr	Belfast	1	0
EC2010	3 Sept	Maribor	1	0
EC2011	29 Mar	Belfast	0	0
2016	28 Mar	Belfast	1	0

v SOUTH AFRICA

			NI	*SA*
1924	24 Sept	Belfast	1	2

v SPAIN

			NI	*S*
1958	15 Oct	Madrid	2	6
1963	30 May	Bilbao	1	1
1963	30 Oct	Belfast	0	1
EC1970	11 Nov	Seville	0	3
EC1972	16 Feb	Hull	1	1
wc1982	25 June	Valencia	1	0
1985	27 Mar	Palma	0	0
wc1986	7 June	Guadalajara	1	2
wc1988	21 Dec	Seville	0	4
wc1989	8 Feb	Belfast	0	2
wc1992	14 Oct	Belfast	0	0
wc1993	28 Apr	Seville	1	3
1998	2 June	Santander	1	4
2002	17 Apr	Belfast	0	5
EC2002	12 Oct	Albacete	0	3
EC2003	11 June	Belfast	0	0
EC2006	6 Sept	Belfast	3	2
EC2007	21 Nov	Las Palmas	0	1

v SWEDEN

			NI	*S*
EC1974	30 Oct	Solna	2	0
EC1975	3 Sept	Belfast	1	2
wc1980	15 Oct	Belfast	3	0
wc1981	3 June	Solna	0	1
1996	24 Apr	Belfast	1	2
EC2007	28 Mar	Belfast	2	1
EC2007	17 Oct	Stockholm	1	1

v SWITZERLAND

			NI	*S*
wc1964	14 Oct	Belfast	1	0
wc1964	14 Nov	Lausanne	1	2
1998	22 Apr	Belfast	1	0
2004	18 Aug	Zurich	0	0
wc2017	9 Nov	Belfast	0	1
wc2017	12 Nov	Basel	0	0

v THAILAND

			NI	*T*
1997	21 May	Bangkok	0	0

v TRINIDAD & TOBAGO

			NI	*TT*
2004	6 June	Bacolet	3	0

v TURKEY

			NI	*T*
wc1968	23 Oct	Belfast	4	1
wc1968	11 Dec	Istanbul	3	0
2013	15 Nov	Adana	0	1
EC1983	30 Mar	Belfast	2	1
EC1983	12 Oct	Ankara	0	1
wc1985	1 May	Belfast	2	0
wc1985	11 Sept	Izmir	0	0
EC1986	12 Nov	Izmir	0	0
EC1987	11 Nov	Belfast	1	0
EC1998	5 Sept	Istanbul	0	3
EC1999	4 Sept	Belfast	0	3
2010	26 May	New Britain	0	2
2013	15 Nov	Adana	0	1

v UKRAINE

			NI	*U*
wc1996	31 Aug	Belfast	0	1
wc1997	2 Apr	Kiev	1	2
EC2002	16 Oct	Belfast	0	0
EC2003	6 Sept	Donetsk	0	0
EC2016	16 June	Lyon	2	0
2021	**3 June**	**Dnipro**	**0**	**1**

v URUGUAY

			NI	*U*
1964	29 Apr	Belfast	3	0
1990	18 May	Belfast	1	0
2006	21 May	New Jersey	0	1
2014	30 May	Montevideo	0	1

v USA

			NI	*USA*
2021	**28 Mar**	**Belfast**	**1**	**2**

v USSR

			NI	*USSR*
wc1969	19 Sept	Belfast	0	0
wc1969	22 Oct	Moscow	0	2
EC1971	22 Sept	Moscow	0	1
EC1971	13 Oct	Belfast	1	1

v YUGOSLAVIA

			NI	*Y*
EC1975	16 Mar	Belfast	1	0
EC1975	19 Nov	Belgrade	0	1
wc1982	17 June	Zaragoza	0	0
EC1987	29 Apr	Belfast	1	2
EC1987	14 Oct	Sarajevo	0	3
EC1990	12 Sept	Belfast	0	2
EC1991	27 Mar	Belgrade	1	4
2000	16 Aug	Belfast	1	2

REPUBLIC OF IRELAND

v ALBANIA			*RI*	*A*
WC1992	26 May	Dublin	2	0
WC1993	26 May	Tirana	2	1
EC2003	2 Apr	Tirana	0	0
EC2003	7 June	Dublin	2	1

v ALGERIA			*RI*	*A*
1982	28 Apr	Algiers	0	2
2010	28 May	Dublin	3	0

v ANDORRA			*RI*	*A*
WC2001	28 Mar	Barcelona	3	0
WC2001	25 Apr	Dublin	3	1
EC2010	7 Sept	Dublin	3	1
EC2011	7 Oct	Andorra La Vella	2	0
2021	**3 June**	**Andorra La Vella**	**4**	**1**

v ARGENTINA			*RI*	*A*
1951	13 May	Dublin	0	1
†1979	29 May	Dublin	0	0
1980	16 May	Dublin	0	1
1998	22 Apr	Dublin	0	2
2010	11 Aug	Dublin	0	1

†*Not considered a full international.*

v ARMENIA			*RI*	*A*
EC2010	3 Sept	Erevan	1	0
EC2011	11 Oct	Dublin	2	1

v AUSTRALIA			*RI*	*A*
2003	19 Aug	Dublin	2	1
2009	12 Aug	Limerick	0	3

v AUSTRIA			*RI*	*A*
1952	7 May	Vienna	0	6
1953	25 Mar	Dublin	4	0
1958	14 Mar	Vienna	1	3
WC2013	10 Sept	Vienna	0	1
1962	8 Apr	Dublin	2	3
EC1963	25 Sept	Vienna	0	0
EC1963	13 Oct	Dublin	3	2
1966	22 May	Vienna	0	1
1968	10 Nov	Dublin	2	2
EC1971	30 May	Dublin	1	4
EC1971	10 Oct	Linz	0	6
EC1995	11 June	Dublin	1	3
EC1995	6 Sept	Vienna	1	3
WC2013	26 Mar	Dublin	2	2
WC2013	10 Sept	Vienna	0	1
WC2016	12 Nov	Vienna	1	0
WC2017	11 June	Dublin	1	1

v BELARUS			*RI*	*B*
2016	31 May	Cork	1	2

v BELGIUM			*RI*	*B*
1928	12 Feb	Liege	4	2
1929	30 Apr	Dublin	4	0
1930	11 May	Brussels	3	1
WC1934	25 Feb	Dublin	4	4
1949	24 Apr	Dublin	0	2
1950	10 May	Brussels	1	5
1965	24 Mar	Dublin	0	2
1966	25 May	Liege	3	2
WC1980	15 Oct	Dublin	1	1
WC1981	25 Mar	Brussels	0	1
EC1986	10 Sept	Brussels	2	2
EC1987	29 Apr	Dublin	0	0
WC1997	29 Oct	Dublin	1	1
WC1997	16 Nov	Brussels	1	2
EC2016	18 June	Bordeaux	0	3

v BOLIVIA			*RI*	*B*
1994	24 May	Dublin	1	0
1996	15 June	New Jersey	3	0
2007	26 May	Boston	1	1

v BOSNIA-HERZEGOVINA			*RI*	*BH*
2012	26 May	Dublin	1	0
EC2015	13 Nov	Zenica	1	1
EC2015	16 Nov	Dublin	2	0

v BRAZIL			*RI*	*B*
1974	5 May	Rio de Janeiro	1	2
1982	27 May	Uberlandia	0	7
1987	23 May	Dublin	1	0
2004	18 Feb	Dublin	0	0
2008	6 Feb	Dublin	0	1
2010	2 Mar	Emirates	0	2

v BULGARIA			*RI*	*B*
WC1977	1 June	Sofia	1	2
WC1977	12 Oct	Dublin	0	0
EC1979	19 May	Sofia	0	1
EC1979	17 Oct	Dublin	3	0
WC1987	1 Apr	Sofia	1	2
WC1987	14 Oct	Dublin	2	0
2004	18 Aug	Dublin	1	1
WC2009	28 Mar	Dublin	1	1
WC2009	6 June	Sofia	1	1
2019	10 Sept	Dublin	3	1
NL2020	**3 Sept**	**Sofia**	**1**	**1**
NL2020	**18 Nov**	**Dublin**	**0**	**0**

v CAMEROON			*RI*	*C*
WC2002	1 June	Niigata	1	1

v CANADA			*RI*	*C*
2003	18 Nov	Dublin	3	0

v CHILE			*RI*	*C*
1960	30 Mar	Dublin	2	0
1972	21 June	Recife	1	2
1974	12 May	Santiago	2	1
1982	22 May	Santiago	0	1
1991	22 May	Dublin	1	1
2006	24 May	Dublin	0	1

v CHINA PR			*RI*	*CPR*
1984	3 June	Sapporo	1	0
2005	29 Mar	Dublin	1	0

v COLOMBIA			*RI*	*C*
2008	29 May	Fulham	1	0

v COSTA RICA			*RI*	*C*
2014	6 June	Philadelphia	1	1

v CROATIA			*RI*	*C*
1996	2 June	Dublin	2	2
EC1998	5 Sept	Dublin	2	0
EC1999	4 Sept	Zagreb	0	1
2001	15 Aug	Dublin	2	2
2004	16 Nov	Dublin	1	0
2011	10 Aug	Dublin	0	0
EC2012	10 June	Poznan	1	3

v CYPRUS			*RI*	*C*
WC1980	26 Mar	Nicosia	3	2
WC1980	19 Nov	Dublin	6	0
WC2001	24 Mar	Nicosia	4	0
WC2001	6 Oct	Dublin	4	0
WC2004	4 Sept	Dublin	3	0
WC2005	8 Oct	Nicosia	1	0
EC2006	7 Oct	Nicosia	2	5
EC2007	17 Oct	Dublin	1	1
2008	15 Oct	Dublin	1	0
WC2009	5 Sept	Nicosia	2	1

v CZECHOSLOVAKIA			*RI*	*C*
1938	18 May	Prague	2	2
EC1959	5 Apr	Dublin	2	0
EC1959	10 May	Bratislava	0	4
WC1961	8 Oct	Dublin	1	3
WC1961	29 Oct	Prague	1	7
EC1967	21 May	Dublin	0	2
EC1967	22 Nov	Prague	2	1
WC1969	4 May	Dublin	1	2
WC1969	7 Oct	Prague	0	3
1979	26 Sept	Prague	1	4
1981	29 Apr	Dublin	3	1
1986	27 May	Reykjavik	1	0

v CZECH REPUBLIC			*RI*	*C*
1994	5 June	Dublin	1	3
1996	24 Apr	Prague	0	2
1998	25 Mar	Olomouc	1	2
2000	23 Feb	Dublin	3	2

			RI	*C*
2004	31 Mar	Dublin	2	1
EC2006	11 Oct	Dublin	1	1
EC2007	12 Sept	Prague	0	1
2012	29 Feb	Dublin	1	1

v DENMARK			*RI*	*D*
WC1956	3 Oct	Dublin	2	1
WC1957	2 Oct	Copenhagen	2	0
WC1968	4 Dec	Dublin	1	1
(abandoned after 51 mins)				
WC1969	27 May	Copenhagen	0	2
WC1969	15 Oct	Dublin	1	1
EC1978	24 May	Copenhagen	3	3
EC1979	2 May	Dublin	2	0
WC1984	14 Nov	Copenhagen	0	3
WC1985	13 Nov	Dublin	1	4
WC1992	14 Oct	Copenhagen	0	0
WC1993	28 Apr	Dublin	1	1
2002	27 Mar	Dublin	3	0
2007	22 Aug	Copenhagen	4	0
WC2017	11 Nov	Copenhagen	0	0
WC2017	14 Nov	Dublin	1	5
NL2018	13 Oct	Dublin	0	0
NL2018	19 Nov	Aarhus	0	0
EC2019	7 June	Copenhagen	1	1
EC2019	18 Nov	Dublin	1	1

v ECUADOR			*RI*	*E*
1972	19 June	Natal	3	2
2007	23 May	New Jersey	1	1

v EGYPT			*RI*	*E*
WC1990	17 June	Palermo	0	0

v ENGLAND			*RI*	*E*
1946	30 Sept	Dublin	0	1
1949	21 Sept	Everton	2	0
WC1957	8 May	Wembley	1	5
WC1957	19 May	Dublin	1	1
1964	24 May	Dublin	1	3
1976	8 Sept	Wembley	1	1
EC1978	25 Oct	Dublin	1	1
EC1980	6 Feb	Wembley	0	2
1985	26 Mar	Wembley	1	2
EC1988	12 June	Stuttgart	1	0
WC1990	11 June	Cagliari	1	1
EC1990	14 Nov	Dublin	1	1
EC1991	27 Mar	Wembley	1	1
1995	15 Feb	Dublin	1	0
(abandoned after 27 mins)				
2013	29 May	Wembley	1	1
2015	7 June	Dublin	0	0
2020	**12 Nov**	**Wembley**	**0**	**3**

v ESTONIA			*RI*	*E*
WC2000	11 Oct	Dublin	2	0
WC2001	6 June	Tallinn	2	0
EC2011	11 Nov	Tallinn	4	0
EC2011	15 Nov	Dublin	1	1

v FAROE ISLANDS			*RI*	*F*
EC2004	13 Oct	Dublin	2	0
EC2005	8 June	Toftir	2	0
WC2012	16 Oct	Torshavn	4	1
WC2013	7 June	Dublin	3	0

v FINLAND			*RI*	*F*
WC1949	8 Sept	Dublin	3	0
WC1949	9 Oct	Helsinki	1	1
1990	16 May	Dublin	1	1
2000	15 Nov	Dublin	3	0
2002	21 Aug	Helsinki	3	0
NL2020	**6 Sept**	**Dublin**	**0**	**1**
NL2020	**14 Oct**	**Helsinki**	**0**	**1**

v FRANCE			*RI*	*F*
1937	23 May	Paris	2	0
1952	16 Nov	Dublin	1	1
WC1953	4 Oct	Dublin	3	5
WC1953	25 Nov	Paris	0	1
WC1972	15 Nov	Dublin	2	1
WC1973	19 May	Paris	1	1
WC1976	17 Nov	Paris	0	2
WC1977	30 Mar	Dublin	1	0
WC1980	28 Oct	Paris	0	2
WC1981	14 Oct	Dublin	3	2

			RI	*F*
1989	7 Feb	Dublin	0	0
WC2004	9 Oct	Paris	0	0
WC2005	7 Sept	Dublin	0	1
WC2009	14 Nov	Dublin	0	1
WC2009	18 Nov	Paris	1	1
EC2016	26 June	Lyon	1	2
2018	28 May	Paris	0	2

v GEORGIA			*RI*	*G*
EC2003	29 Mar	Tbilisi	2	1
EC2003	11 June	Dublin	2	0
WC2008	6 Sept	Mainz	2	1
WC2009	11 Feb	Dublin	2	1
2013	2 June	Dublin	3	0
EC2014	7 Sept	Tbilisi	2	1
EC2015	7 Sept	Dublin	1	0
WC2016	6 Oct	Dublin	1	0
WC2017	2 Sept	Tbilisi	1	1
EC2019	26 Mar	Dublin	1	0
EC2019	12 Oct	Tbilisi	0	0

v GERMANY			*RI*	*G*
1935	8 May	Dortmund	1	3
1936	17 Oct	Dublin	5	2
1939	23 May	Bremen	1	1
1994	29 May	Hanover	2	0
WC2002	5 June	Ibaraki	1	1
EC2006	2 Sept	Stuttgart	0	1
EC2007	13 Oct	Dublin	0	0
WC2012	12 Oct	Dublin	1	6
WC2013	11 Oct	Cologne	0	3
EC2014	14 Oct	Gelsenkirchen	1	1
EC2015	8 Oct	Dublin	1	0

v WEST GERMANY			*RI*	*WG*
1951	17 Oct	Dublin	3	2
1952	4 May	Cologne	0	3
1955	28 May	Hamburg	1	2
1956	25 Nov	Dublin	3	0
1960	11 May	Dusseldorf	1	0
1966	4 May	Dublin	0	4
1970	9 May	Berlin	1	2
1975	1 Mar	Dublin	1	0†
1979	22 May	Dublin	1	3
1981	21 May	Bremen	0	3†
1989	6 Sept	Dublin	1	1

†*v West Germany 'B'*

v GIBRALTAR			*RI*	*G*
EC2014	11 Oct	Dublin	7	0
EC2015	4 Sept	Faro	4	0
EC2019	23 Mar	Gibraltar	1	0
EC2019	10 June	Dublin	2	0

v GREECE			*RI*	*G*
2000	26 Apr	Dublin	0	1
2002	20 Nov	Athens	0	0
2012	14 Nov	Dublin	0	1

v HUNGARY			*RI*	*H*
1934	15 Dec	Dublin	2	4
1936	3 May	Budapest	3	3
1936	6 Dec	Dublin	2	3
1939	19 Mar	Cork	2	2
1939	18 May	Budapest	2	2
WC1969	8 June	Dublin	1	2
WC1969	5 Nov	Budapest	0	4
WC1989	8 Mar	Budapest	0	0
WC1989	4 June	Dublin	2	0
1991	11 Sept	Gyor	2	1
2012	4 June	Budapest	0	0
2021	**8 June**	**Budapest**	**0**	**0**

v ICELAND			*RI*	*I*
EC1962	12 Aug	Dublin	4	2
EC1962	2 Sept	Reykjavik	1	1
EC1982	13 Oct	Dublin	2	0
EC1983	21 Sept	Reykjavik	3	0
1986	25 May	Reykjavik	2	1
WC1996	10 Nov	Dublin	0	0
WC1997	6 Sept	Reykjavik	4	2
2017	28 Mar	Dublin	0	1

v IRAN

			RI	*I*
1972	18 June	Recife	2	1
WC2001	10 Nov	Dublin	2	0
WC2001	15 Nov	Tehran	0	1

v ISRAEL

			RI	*I*
1984	4 Apr	Tel Aviv	0	3
1985	27 May	Tel Aviv	0	0
1987	10 Nov	Dublin	5	0
EC2005	26 Mar	Tel Aviv	1	1
EC2005	4 June	Dublin	2	2

v ITALY

			RI	*I*
1926	21 Mar	Turin	0	3
1927	23 Apr	Dublin	1	2
EC1970	8 Dec	Rome	0	3
EC1971	10 May	Dublin	1	2
1985	5 Feb	Dublin	1	2
WC1990	30 June	Rome	0	1
1992	4 June	Foxboro	0	2
WC1994	18 June	New York	1	0
2005	17 Aug	Dublin	1	2
WC2009	1 Apr	Bari	1	1
WC2009	10 Oct	Dublin	2	2
2011	7 June	Liege	2	0
EC2012	18 June	Poznan	0	2
2014	31 May	Craven Cottage	0	0
EC2016	22 June	Lille	1	0

v JAMAICA

			RI	*J*
2004	2 June	Charlton	1	0

v KAZAKHSTAN

			RI	*K*
WC2012	7 Sept	Astana	2	1
WC2013	15 Oct	Dublin	3	1

v LATVIA

			RI	*L*
WC1992	9 Sept	Dublin	4	0
WC1993	2 June	Riga	2	1
EC1994	7 Sept	Riga	3	0
EC1995	11 Oct	Dublin	2	1
2013	15 Nov	Dublin	3	0

v LIECHTENSTEIN

			RI	*L*
EC1994	12 Oct	Dublin	4	0
EC1995	3 June	Eschen	0	0
WC1996	31 Aug	Eschen	5	0
WC1997	21 May	Dublin	5	0

v LITHUANIA

			RI	*L*
WC1993	16 June	Vilnius	1	0
WC1993	8 Sept	Dublin	2	0
WC1997	20 Aug	Dublin	0	0
WC1997	10 Sept	Vilnius	2	1

v LUXEMBOURG

			RI	*L*
1936	9 May	Luxembourg	5	1
WC1953	28 Oct	Dublin	4	0
WC1954	7 Mar	Luxembourg	1	0
EC1987	28 May	Luxembourg	2	0
EC1987	9 Sept	Dublin	2	1
WC2021	**27 Mar**	**Dublin**	**0**	**1**

v MALTA

			RI	*M*
EC1983	30 Mar	Valletta	1	0
EC1983	16 Nov	Dublin	8	0
WC1989	28 May	Dublin	2	0
WC1989	15 Nov	Valletta	2	0
1990	2 June	Valletta	3	0
EC1998	14 Oct	Dublin	5	0
EC1999	8 Sept	Valletta	3	2

v MEXICO

			RI	*M*
1984	8 Aug	Dublin	0	0
WC1994	24 June	Orlando	1	2
1996	13 June	New Jersey	2	2
1998	23 May	Dublin	0	0
2000	4 June	Chicago	2	2
2017	2 June	New Jersey	1	3

v MOLDOVA

			RI	*M*
WC2016	9 Oct	Chisinau	3	1
WC2017	6 Oct	Dublin	2	0

v MONTENEGRO

			RI	*M*
WC2008	10 Sept	Podgorica	0	0
WC2009	14 Oct	Dublin	0	0

v MOROCCO

			RI	*M*
1990	12 Sept	Dublin	1	0

v NETHERLANDS

			RI	*N*
1932	8 May	Amsterdam	2	0
1934	8 Apr	Amsterdam	2	5
1935	8 Dec	Dublin	3	5
1955	1 May	Dublin	1	0
1956	10 May	Rotterdam	4	1
WC1980	10 Sept	Dublin	2	1
WC1981	9 Sept	Rotterdam	2	2
EC1982	22 Sept	Rotterdam	1	2
EC1983	12 Oct	Dublin	2	3
EC1988	18 June	Gelsenkirchen	0	1
WC1990	21 June	Palermo	1	1
1994	20 Apr	Tilburg	1	0
WC1994	4 July	Orlando	0	2
EC1995	13 Dec	Liverpool	0	2
1996	4 June	Rotterdam	1	3
WC2000	2 Sept	Amsterdam	2	2
WC2001	1 Sept	Dublin	1	0
2004	5 June	Amsterdam	1	0
2006	16 Aug	Dublin	0	4
2016	27 May	Dublin	1	1

v NEW ZEALAND

			RI	*N*
2019	14 Nov	Dublin	3	1

v NIGERIA

			RI	*N*
2002	16 May	Dublin	1	2
2004	29 May	Charlton	0	3
2009	29 May	Fulham	1	1

v NORTHERN IRELAND

			RI	*NI*
EC1978	20 Sept	Dublin	0	0
EC1979	21 Nov	Belfast	0	1
WC1988	14 Sept	Belfast	0	0
WC1989	11 Oct	Dublin	3	0
WC1993	31 Mar	Dublin	3	0
WC1993	17 Nov	Belfast	1	1
EC1994	16 Nov	Belfast	4	0
EC1995	29 Mar	Dublin	1	1
1999	29 May	Dublin	0	1
NC2011	24 May	Dublin	5	0
2018	15 Nov	Dublin	0	0

v NORTH MACEDONIA

			RI	*M*
WC1996	9 Oct	Dublin	3	0
WC1997	2 Apr	Skopje	2	3
EC1999	9 June	Dublin	1	0
EC1999	9 Oct	Skopje	1	1
EC2011	26 Mar	Dublin	2	1
EC2011	4 June	Podgorica	2	0

v NORWAY

			RI	*N*
WC1937	10 Oct	Oslo	2	3
WC1937	7 Nov	Dublin	3	3
1950	26 Nov	Dublin	2	2
1951	30 May	Oslo	3	2
1954	8 Nov	Dublin	2	1
1955	25 May	Oslo	3	1
1960	6 Nov	Dublin	3	1
1964	13 May	Oslo	4	1
1973	6 June	Oslo	1	1
1976	24 Mar	Dublin	3	0
1978	21 May	Oslo	0	0
WC1984	17 Oct	Oslo	0	1
WC1985	1 May	Dublin	0	0
1988	1 June	Oslo	0	0
WC1994	28 June	New York	0	0
2003	30 Apr	Dublin	1	0
2008	20 Aug	Oslo	1	1
2010	17 Nov	Dublin	1	2

v OMAN

			RI	*O*
2012	11 Sept	London	4	1
2014	3 Sept	Dublin	2	0
2016	31 Aug	Dublin	4	0

v PARAGUAY

			RI	*P*
1999	10 Feb	Dublin	2	0
2010	25 May	Dublin	2	1

v POLAND

			RI	*P*
1938	22 May	Warsaw	0	6
1938	13 Nov	Dublin	3	2
1958	11 May	Katowice	2	2
1958	5 Oct	Dublin	2	2
1964	10 May	Kracow	1	3

			RI	*P*
1964	25 Oct	Dublin	3	2
1968	15 May	Dublin	2	2
1968	30 Oct	Katowice	0	1
1970	6 May	Dublin	1	2
1970	23 Sept	Dublin	0	2
1973	16 May	Wroclaw	0	2
1973	21 Oct	Dublin	1	0
1976	26 May	Poznan	2	0
1977	24 Apr	Dublin	0	0
1978	12 Apr	Lodz	0	3
1981	23 May	Bydgoszcz	0	3
1984	23 May	Dublin	0	0
1986	12 Nov	Warsaw	0	1
1988	22 May	Dublin	3	1
EC1991	1 May	Dublin	0	0
EC1991	16 Oct	Poznan	3	3
2004	28 Apr	Bydgoszcz	0	0
2013	19 Nov	Poznan	0	0
2008	19 Nov	Dublin	2	3
2013	6 Feb	Dublin	2	0
2013	19 Nov	Poznan	0	0
EC2015	29 Mar	Dublin	1	1
EC2015	11 Oct	Warsaw	1	2
2018	11 Sept	Wroclaw	1	1

v PORTUGAL

			RI	*P*
1946	16 June	Lisbon	1	3
1947	4 May	Dublin	0	2
1948	23 May	Lisbon	0	2
1949	22 May	Dublin	1	0
1972	25 June	Recife	1	2
1992	7 June	Boston	2	0
EC1995	26 Apr	Dublin	1	0
EC1995	15 Nov	Lisbon	0	3
1996	29 May	Dublin	0	1
WC2000	7 Oct	Lisbon	1	1
WC2001	2 June	Dublin	1	1
2005	9 Feb	Dublin	1	0
2014	10 June	New Jersey	1	5

v QATAR

			RI	*Q*
2021	**30 Mar**	**Dublin**	**1**	**1**

v ROMANIA

			RI	*R*
1988	23 Mar	Dublin	2	0
WC1990	25 June	Genoa	0	0*
WC1997	30 Apr	Bucharest	0	1
WC1997	11 Oct	Dublin	1	1
2004	27 May	Dublin	1	0

v RUSSIA

			RI	*R*
1994	23 Mar	Dublin	0	0
1996	27 Mar	Dublin	0	2
2002	13 Feb	Dublin	2	0
EC2002	7 Sept	Moscow	2	4
EC2003	6 Sept	Dublin	1	1
EC2010	8 Oct	Dublin	2	3
EC2011	6 Sept	Moscow	0	0

v SAN MARINO

			RI	*SM*
EC2006	15 Nov	Dublin	5	0
EC2007	7 Feb	Serravalle	2	1

v SAUDI ARABIA

			RI	*SA*
WC2002	11 June	Yokohama	3	0

v SCOTLAND

			RI	*S*
WC1961	3 May	Glasgow	1	4
WC1961	7 May	Dublin	0	3
1963	9 June	Dublin	1	0
1969	21 Sept	Dublin	1	1
EC1986	15 Oct	Dublin	0	0
EC1987	18 Feb	Glasgow	1	0
2000	30 May	Dublin	1	2
2003	12 Feb	Glasgow	2	0
NC2011	29 May	Dublin	1	0
EC2014	14 Nov	Glasgow	0	1
EC2015	13 June	Dublin	1	1

v SERBIA

			RI	*S*
2008	24 May	Dublin	1	1
2012	15 Aug	Belgrade	0	0
2014	5 Mar	Dublin	1	2
WC2016	5 Sept	Belgrade	2	2
WC2017	5 Sept	Dublin	0	1
WC2021	**24 Mar**	**Belgrade**	**2**	**3**

v SLOVAKIA

			RI	*S*
EC2007	28 Mar	Dublin	1	0
EC2007	8 Sept	Bratislava	2	2
EC2010	12 Oct	Zilina	1	1
EC2011	2 Sept	Dublin	0	0
2016	29 Mar	Dublin	2	2
EC2020	**8 Oct**	**Bratislava**	**0**	**0**

v SOUTH AFRICA

			RI	*SA*
2000	11 June	New Jersey	2	1
2009	8 Sept	Limerick	1	0

v SPAIN

			RI	*S*
1931	26 Apr	Barcelona	1	1
1931	13 Dec	Dublin	0	5
1946	23 June	Madrid	1	0
1947	2 Mar	Dublin	3	2
1948	30 May	Barcelona	1	2
1949	12 June	Dublin	1	4
1952	1 June	Madrid	0	6
1955	27 Nov	Dublin	2	2
EC1964	11 Mar	Seville	1	5
EC1964	8 Apr	Dublin	0	2
WC1965	5 May	Dublin	1	0
WC1965	27 Oct	Seville	1	4
WC1965	10 Nov	Paris	0	1
EC1966	23 Oct	Dublin	0	0
EC1966	7 Dec	Valencia	0	2
1977	9 Feb	Dublin	0	1
EC1982	17 Nov	Dublin	3	3
EC1983	27 Apr	Zaragoza	0	2
1985	26 May	Cork	0	0
WC1988	16 Nov	Seville	0	2
WC1989	26 Apr	Dublin	1	0
WC1992	18 Nov	Seville	0	0
WC1993	13 Oct	Dublin	1	3
WC2002	16 June	Suwon	1	1
EC2012	14 June	Gdansk	0	4
2013	11 June	New York	0	2

v SWEDEN

			RI	*S*
WC1949	2 June	Stockholm	1	3
WC1949	13 Nov	Dublin	1	3
1959	1 Nov	Dublin	3	2
1960	18 May	Malmo	1	4
EC1970	14 Oct	Dublin	1	1
EC1970	28 Oct	Malmo	0	1
1999	28 Apr	Dublin	2	0
2006	1 Mar	Dublin	3	0
WC2013	22 Mar	Stockholm	0	0
WC2013	6 Sept	Dublin	1	2
EC2016	13 June	Paris	1	1

v SWITZERLAND

			RI	*S*
1935	5 May	Basel	0	1
1936	17 Mar	Dublin	1	0
1937	17 May	Berne	1	0
1938	18 Sept	Dublin	4	0
1948	5 Dec	Dublin	0	1
EC1975	11 May	Dublin	2	1
EC1975	21 May	Berne	0	1
1980	30 Apr	Dublin	2	0
WC1985	2 June	Dublin	3	0
WC1985	11 Sept	Berne	0	0
1992	25 Mar	Dublin	2	1
EC2002	16 Oct	Dublin	1	2
EC2003	11 Oct	Basel	0	2
WC2004	8 Sept	Basel	1	1
WC2005	12 Oct	Dublin	0	0
2016	25 Mar	Dublin	1	0
EC2019	5 Sept	Dublin	1	1
EC2019	15 Oct	Geneva	0	2

v TRINIDAD & TOBAGO

			RI	*TT*
1982	30 May	Port of Spain	1	2

v TUNISIA

			RI	*T*
1988	19 Oct	Dublin	4	0

v TURKEY

			RI	*T*
EC1966	16 Nov	Dublin	2	1
EC1967	22 Feb	Ankara	1	2
EC1974	20 Nov	Izmir	1	1
EC1975	29 Oct	Dublin	4	0
2014	25 May	Dublin	1	2
1976	13 Oct	Ankara	3	3
1978	5 Apr	Dublin	4	2

			RI	T
1990	26 May	Izmir	0	0
EC1990	17 Oct	Dublin	5	0
EC1991	13 Nov	Istanbul	3	1
EC1999	13 Nov	Dublin	1	1
EC1999	17 Nov	Bursa	0	0
2003	9 Sept	Dublin	2	2
2014	25 May	Dublin	1	2
2018	23 Mar	Antalya	0	1

		v URUGUAY	RI	U
1974	8 May	Montevideo	0	2
1986	23 Apr	Dublin	1	1
2011	29 Mar	Dublin	2	3
2017	4 June	Dublin	3	1

		v USA	RI	USA
1979	29 Oct	Dublin	3	2
1991	1 June	Boston	1	1
1992	29 Apr	Dublin	4	1
1992	30 May	Washington	1	3
1996	9 June	Boston	1	2
2000	6 June	Boston	1	1
2002	17 Apr	Dublin	2	1
2014	18 Nov	Dublin	4	1
2018	2 June	Dublin	2	1

		v USSR	RI	USSR
WC1972	18 Oct	Dublin	1	2
WC1973	13 May	Moscow	0	1
EC1974	30 Oct	Dublin	3	0
EC1975	18 May	Kiev	1	2
WC1984	12 Sept	Dublin	1	0
WC1985	16 Oct	Moscow	0	2
EC1988	15 June	Hanover	1	1
1990	25 Apr	Dublin	1	0

		v WALES	RI	W
1960	28 Sept	Dublin	2	3
1979	11 Sept	Swansea	1	2
1981	24 Feb	Dublin	1	3
1986	26 Mar	Dublin	0	1
1990	28 Mar	Dublin	1	0
1991	6 Feb	Wrexham	3	0
1992	19 Feb	Dublin	0	1
1993	17 Feb	Dublin	2	1
1997	11 Feb	Cardiff	0	0
EC2007	24 Mar	Dublin	1	0
EC2007	17 Nov	Cardiff	2	2
NC2011	8 Feb	Dublin	3	0
2013	14 Aug	Cardiff	0	0
WC2017	24 Mar	Dublin	0	0
WC2017	9 Oct	Cardiff	1	0
NL2018	6 Sept	Cardiff	1	4
NL2018	16 Oct	Dublin	0	1
NL2020	**11 Oct**	**Dublin**	**0**	**0**
NL2020	**15 Nov**	**Cardiff**	**0**	**1**

		v YUGOSLAVIA	RI	Y
1955	19 Sept	Dublin	1	4
1988	27 Apr	Dublin	2	0
EC1998	18 Nov	Belgrade	0	1
EC1999	1 Sept	Dublin	2	1

OTHER BRITISH AND IRISH INTERNATIONAL MATCHES 2020–21

FRIENDLIES

■ *Denotes player sent off.*

ENGLAND

Thursday, 8 October 2020

England (1) 3 *(Calvert-Lewin 26, Coady 53, Ings 63)*

Wales (0) 0

England: (343) Pope; Keane, Coady, Gomez (Mings 58); Saka (Maitland-Niles 76), Trippier (James 58), Phillips, Winks (Ward-Prowse 76); Grealish (Barnes 76), Calvert-Lewin (Mount 58), Ings.
Wales: (433) Hennessey; Roberts C (Gunter 73), Rodon (Cabango 46), Ampadu (Vaulks 62), Davies B; Morrell (Levitt 46), Mepham, Williams J (Smith 73); Roberts T, Moore (Williams N 40), Matondo.
Referee: Bobby Madden.

Thursday, 12 November 2020

England (2) 3 *(Maguire 18, Sancho 31, Calvert-Lewin 56 (pen))*

Republic of Ireland (0) 0

England: (532) Pope (Henderson D 46); James, Keane, Maguire, Mings (Maitland-Niles 62), Saka; Mount (Bellingham 73), Winks, Grealish (Foden 61); Sancho, Calvert-Lewin (Abraham 63).
Republic of Ireland: (433) Randolph; Doherty, Duffy, Egan (O'Shea 13), O'Dowda (McClean 60); Christie (Long K 61), Hourihane (Molumby 71), Hendrick; Horgan (Brady 60), Idah (Curtis 71), Browne.
Referee: Carlos Del Cerro.

Wednesday, 2 June 2021

England (0) 1 *(Saka 57)* **Austria (0) 0**

England: (433) Pickford; Alexander-Arnold, Coady, Mings (Godfrey 61), Trippier; Grealish (White 71), Rice (Ward-Prowse 62), Bellingham; Lingard (Watkins 61), Kane (Calvert-Lewin 61), Saka.
Austria: (352) Bachmann; Dragovic, Hinteregger, Friedl; Lainer (Trimmel 81), Baumgartner (Schaub 62), Laimer (Grillitsch 62), Schlager (Baumgartlinger 81), Alaba (Schopf 71); Sabitzer, Kalajdzic (Gregoritsch 71).
Referee: Lawrence Visser.

Sunday, 6 June 2021

England (0) 1 *(Rashford 68 (pen))*

Romania (0) 0

England: (433) Johnstone; Godfrey, White, Mings, Shaw (Trippier 75); Grealish, Phillips (Henderson J 46), Ward-Prowse (Rice 65); Rashford (Lingard 75), Calvert-Lewin (Watkins 82), Sancho (Bellingham 65).
Romania: (433) Nita; Sorescu (Capusa 66), Nedelcearu (Rus 84), Chiriches, Camora; Stanciu, Marin, Cicaldau (Budescu 80); Ivan, Alibec (Hagi 66), Paun (Baluta 80).
Referee: Tiago Martins.

SCOTLAND

Wednesday, 2 June 2021

Holland (1) 2 *(Depay 17, 89)*

Scotland (1) 2 *(Hendry 11, Nisbet 63)*

Holland: (532) Krul; Dumfries, Timber (Berghuis 69), de Vrij (de Jong L 85), de Ligt, Wijndal (van Aanholt 69); de Roon, Wijnaldum (Gravenberch 31), de Jong F (Klaassen 31); Weghorst (Promes 69), Depay.
Scotland: (433) Gordon; Tierney (McKenna 69), Cooper (Gallagher 62), Hendry, Robertson (Taylor 69); Armstrong, McGregor, Turnbull (Gilmour 82); Forrest (Fraser 62), Dykes (Nisbet 61), Christie.
Referee: Victor Ferreira.

Sunday, 6 June 2021

Luxembourg (0) 0

Scotland (1) 1 *(Adams 28)*

Luxembourg: (4411) Moris; Jans, Selimovic■, Mahmutovic, Mica Pinto; Rodrigues, Skenderovic (Da Mota Alves 84), Carlson, Sinani (Thill O 72); Thill S (Martins 84); Deville (Bohnert 64).
Scotland: (433) Marshall; O'Donnell (Patterson 64), McTominay, Hanley, Robertson (Fraser 64); McGregor (Gilmour 46 (Forrest 76)), McGinn, Tierney; Adams, Dykes (Nisbet 82), Gallagher (McKenna 46).
Referee: Eldorjan Hamiti.

WALES

Thursday, 12 November 2020

Wales (0) 0

USA (0) 0

Wales: (442) Ward; Gunter, Lawrence J (Rodon 69), Lockyer, Roberts C; Lawrence T, Smith (Sheehan 46), Wilson, Levitt (Morrell 80); Moore (Johnson 62), Matondo (James 62).
USA: (442) Steffen; Dest (Cannon 87), Miazga, Brooks, Robinson; McKennie, Lletget (Otasowie 87), Adams (Johnny 71), Musah (Gioacchini 79); Reyna (Weah 79), de la Fuente (Llanez 71).
Referee: Nick Walsh.

Saturday, 27 March 2021

Wales (1) 1 *(Moore 11)*

Mexico (0) 0

Wales: (343) Hennessey; Gunter, Cabango, Norrington-Davies; Lawrence T (Williams N 65), Smith, Levitt (Sheehan 46), Williams J (Roberts C 86); Roberts T (Johnson 65), Matondo (Bale 81), Moore (Robson-Kanu 46).
Mexico: (4231) Ochoa; Gallardo (Arteaga 79), Montes, Alvarez (Lainez 85), Rodriguez (Pizarro 62); Herrera, Salcedo; Pineda (Jonathan 78), Lozano, Guardado (Sanchez 62); Corona.
Referee: Ian McNabb.

Wednesday, 2 June 2021

France (1) 3 *(Mbappe-Lottin 35, Griezmann 48, Dembele 79)*

Wales (0) 0

France: (433) Lloris; Pavard (Kounde 46), Varane, Kimpembe, Lucas (Digne 46); Pogba (Coman 63), Tolisso (Sissoko 64), Rabiot; Griezmann (Ben Yedder 84), Benzema, Mbappe-Lottin (Dembele 73).
Wales: (442) Ward; Gunter, Rodon, Mepham (Davies 59), Roberts C; Wilson (Ramsey 59), Allen (Levitt 59), Williams N■, Morrell (Colwill 83); James (Brooks 73), Bale (Moore 58).
Referee: Luis Godinho.

Saturday, 5 June 2021

Wales (0) 0

Albania (0) 0

Wales: (442) Hennessey; Ampadu (Moore 46), Mepham, Davies B (Rodon 60), Williams N; Levitt, Allen (Smith 61), Ramsey (Wilson 60), Norrington-Davies; Brooks (Williams J 76), Roberts T (Bale 71).
Albania: (352) Selmani; Ismajli, Kumbulla, Djimsiti; Doka (Veseli 46), Cekici (Kallaku 76), Bare (Laci 75), Abrashi, Lenjani (Trashi 60); Manaj (Seferi 77), Balaj (Cikalleshi 60).
Referee: Neil Doyle.

NORTHERN IRELAND

Sunday, 28 March 2021

Northern Ireland (0) 1 *(McGinn 88)*

USA (1) 2 *(Reyna 30, Pulisic 60 (pen))*

Northern Ireland: (442) Hazard; McLaughlin, Brown, Ballard (Smith 79), Ferguson (Lewis 61); Kennedy (McGinn 67), Saville (McCann 61), Evans (McNair 61), Thompson; Lafferty, Lavery (Charles 61).
USA: (433) Steffen; Dest (Reynolds 46), Long (Richards 63), Miazga, Robinson; Musah (Lletget 46), Ream, Acosta (De La Torre 74); Reyna (Aaronson 62), Siebatcheu (Dike 62), Pulisic.
Referee: Rob Jenkins.

Sunday, 30 May 2021

Malta (0) 0

Northern Ireland (1) 3 *(Jones 2, Whyte 53, McCann 55)*

Malta: (343) Bonello; Apap (Borg 70), Agius, Shaw; Mbong (Xuereb 70), Kristensen (Muscat 82), Teuma (Vella 61), Camenzuli; Satariano (Farrugia 82), Dimech, Montebello (Degabriele 61).
Northern Ireland: (352) Peacock-Farrell; McNair, Cathcart, Brown; McGinn (Saville 62), McCann, Dallas (Bradley 85), Thompson (McCalmont 85), Whyte (Ferguson 73); Jones (Boyce 73), Magennis (Charles 62).
Referee: Sebastian Gishamer.

Thursday, 3 June 2021

Ukraine (1) 1 *(Zubkov 10)*

Northern Ireland (0) 0

Ukraine: (433) Bushchan; Karavayev, Zabarnyi, Matviyenko, Mykolenko; Sydorchuk (Stepanenko 76), Malinovsky, Shaparenko (Sudakov 73); Yarmolenko, Yaremchuk (Biesiedin 46), Zubkov (Marlos 46).
Northern Ireland: (442) Peacock-Farrell; Ballard, Cathcart, Brown (Charles 89), Ferguson (Smyth 68); Dallas (McClelland 89), McNair, McCann (Whyte 81), Saville; Magennis (Lafferty 61), McGinn (Thompson 46).
Referee: Szymon Marciniak.

REPUBLIC OF IRELAND

Tuesday, 30 March 2021

Qatar (0) 1 *(Muntari 47)*

Republic of Ireland (1) 1 *(McClean 4)*

Qatar: (442) Al-Sheeb; Deus Correia, Salman, Khoukhi, Hassan; Al-Rawi, Boudiaf, Al-Haydos (Al-Hajri 90), Hatem (Al-Ahrak 81); Muntari (Abdurisag 90), Ali.
Republic of Ireland: (442) Bazunu; Coleman, O'Shea, Duffy, Christie; Molumby (Cullen 84), Brady (Parrott 22), McClean (Manning 84), Hendrick (Browne 84); Long S (Robinson 57), Horgan (Knight 57).
Referee: Balazs Berke.

Thursday, 3 June 2021

Andorra (0) 1 *(Vales 52)*

Republic of Ireland (0) 4 *(Parrott 58, 61, Knight 84, Horgan 89)*

Andorra: (442) Alvarez (Pires 77); San Nicolas (De Pablos 72), Vales, Llovera, Cervos; Clemente (Martinez C 59), Rebes (Garcia 72), Vieira, Martinez A (Lima 76); Alaez, Fernandez (Sanchez 59).
Republic of Ireland: (433) Bazunu; Doherty, O'Shea (Duffy 86), Egan, McClean (Manning 86); Cullen, Hourihane (Arter 87), Knight; Parrott (McGrath 82), Curtis (Horgan 66), Collins (Idah 66).
Referee: Xavier Estrada.

Tuesday, 8 June 2021

Hungary (0) 0

Republic of Ireland (0) 0

Hungary: (352) Gulacsi (Bogdan 64); Kecskes, Orban, Attila Szalai; Bolla (Lovrencsics 46), Kleinheisler (Nego 64), Nagy, Schafer, Fiola (Hahn 80); Adam Szalai (Schon 89), Varga R (Varga K 46).
Republic of Ireland: (442) Bazunu (Kelleher 46); Doherty, O'Shea, Egan, Duffy; McClean (Manning 85), Cullen, Hourihane (Molumby 57), Knight (Ogbene 89); Parrott (Horgan 57), Idah (Collins 89).
Referee: Daniel Stefanski.

BRITISH AND IRISH INTERNATIONAL APPEARANCES 1872–2021

This is a list of full international appearances by Englishmen, Irishmen, Scotsmen and Welshmen in matches against the Home Countries and against foreign nations. It does not include unofficial matches against Commonwealth and Empire countries. The year indicated refers to the player's international debut season; i.e. 2020 is the 2019–20 season. **Bold** type indicates players who have made an international appearance in season 2019–20.
As at July 2021.

ENGLAND

Abbott, W. 1902 (Everton) 1
Abraham, K. O. T. (Tammy) 2018 (Chelsea) 6
A'Court, A. 1958 (Liverpool) 5
Adams, T. A. 1987 (Arsenal) 66
Adcock, H. 1929 (Leicester C) 5
Agbonlahor, G. 2009 (Aston Villa) 3
Alcock, C. W. 1875 (Wanderers) 1
Alderson, J. T. 1923 (Crystal Palace) 1
Aldridge, A. 1888 (WBA, Walsall Town Swifts) 2
Alexander-Arnold, T. J. 2018 (Liverpool) 13
Allen, A. 1888 (Aston Villa) 1
Allen, A. 1960 (Stoke C) 3
Allen, C. 1984 (QPR, Tottenham H) 5
Allen, H. 1888 (Wolverhampton W) 5
Allen, J. P. 1934 (Portsmouth) 2
Allen, R. 1952 (WBA) 5
Alli, B. J. (Dele) 2016 (Tottenham H) 37
Alsford, W. J. 1935 (Tottenham H) 1
Amos, A. 1885 (Old Carthusians) 2
Anderson, R. D. 1879 (Old Etonians) 1
Anderson, S. 1962 (Sunderland) 2
Anderson, V. A. 1979 (Nottingham F, Arsenal, Manchester U) 30
Anderton, D. R. 1994 (Tottenham H) 30
Angus, J. 1961 (Burnley) 1
Armfield, J. C. 1959 (Blackpool) 43
Armitage, G. H. 1926 (Charlton Ath) 1
Armstrong, D. 1980 (Middlesbrough, Southampton) 3
Armstrong, K. 1955 (Chelsea) 1
Arnold, J. 1933 (Fulham) 1
Arthur, J. W. H. 1885 (Blackburn R) 7
Ashcroft, J. 1906 (Woolwich Arsenal) 3
Ashmore, G. S. 1926 (WBA) 1
Ashton, C. T. 1926 (Corinthians) 1
Ashton, D. 2008 (West Ham U) 1
Ashurst, W. 1923 (Notts Co) 5
Astall, G. 1956 (Birmingham C) 2
Astle, J. 1969 (WBA) 5
Aston, J. 1949 (Manchester U) 17
Athersmith, W. C. 1892 (Aston Villa) 12
Atyeo, P. J. W. 1956 (Bristol C) 6
Austin, S. W. 1926 (Manchester C) 1

Bach, P. 1899 (Sunderland) 1
Bache, J. W. 1903 (Aston Villa) 7
Baddeley, T. 1903 (Wolverhampton W) 5
Bagshaw, J. J. 1920 (Derby Co) 1
Bailey, G. R. 1985 (Manchester U) 2
Bailey, H. P. 1908 (Leicester Fosse) 5
Bailey, M. A. 1964 (Charlton Ath) 2
Bailey, N. C. 1878 (Clapham R) 19
Baily, E. F. 1950 (Tottenham H) 9
Bain, J. 1877 (Oxford University) 1
Baines, L. J. 2010 (Everton) 30
Baker, A. 1928 (Arsenal) 1
Baker, B. H. 1921 (Everton, Chelsea) 2
Baker, J. H. 1960 (Hibernian, Arsenal) 8
Ball, A. J. 1965 (Blackpool, Everton, Arsenal) 72
Ball, J. 1928 (Bury) 1
Ball, M. J. 2001 (Everton) 1
Balmer, W. 1905 (Everton) 1
Bamber, J. 1921 (Liverpool) 1
Bambridge, A. L. 1881 (Swifts) 3
Bambridge, E. C. 1879 (Swifts) 18
Bambridge, E. H. 1876 (Swifts) 1
Banks, G. 1963 (Leicester C, Stoke C) 73
Banks, H. E. 1901 (Millwall) 1
Banks, T. 1958 (Bolton W) 6
Bannister, W. 1901 (Burnley, Bolton W) 2
Barclay, R. 1932 (Sheffield U) 3
Bardsley, D. J. 1993 (QPR) 2
Barham, M. 1983 (Norwich C) 2
Barkas, S. 1936 (Manchester C) 5
Barker, J. 1935 (Derby Co) 11
Barker, R. 1872 (Herts Rangers) 1
Barker, R. R. 1895 (Casuals) 1
Barkley, R. 2013 (Everton, Chelsea) 33
Barlow, R. J. 1955 (WBA) 1
Barmby, N. J. 1995 (Tottenham H, Middlesbrough, Everton, Liverpool) 23
Barnes, H. L. 2021 (Leicester C) 1
Barnes, J. 1983 (Watford, Liverpool) 79
Barnes, P. S. 1978 (Manchester C, WBA, Leeds U) 22
Barnet, H. H. 1882 (Royal Engineers) 1
Barrass, M. W. 1952 (Bolton W) 3
Barrett, A. F. 1930 (Fulham) 1
Barrett, E. D. 1991 (Oldham Ath, Aston Villa) 3
Barrett, J. W. 1929 (West Ham U) 1
Barry, G. 2000 (Aston Villa, Manchester C) 53
Barry, L. 1928 (Leicester C) 5
Barson, F. 1920 (Aston Villa) 1
Barton, J. 1890 (Blackburn R) 1
Barton, J. 2007 (Manchester C) 1
Barton, P. H. 1921 (Birmingham) 7
Barton, W. D. 1995 (Wimbledon, Newcastle U) 3
Bassett, W. I. 1888 (WBA) 16
Bastard, S. R. 1880 (Upton Park) 1
Bastin, C. S. 1932 (Arsenal) 21
Batty, D. 1991 (Leeds U, Blackburn R, Newcastle U, Leeds U) 42
Baugh, R. 1886 (Stafford Road, Wolverhampton W) 2
Bayliss, A. E. J. M. 1891 (WBA) 1
Baynham, R. L. 1956 (Luton T) 3
Beardsley, P. A. 1986 (Newcastle U, Liverpool, Newcastle U) 59
Beasant, D. J. 1990 (Chelsea) 2
Beasley, A. 1939 (Huddersfield T) 1
Beats, W. E. 1901 (Wolverhampton W) 2
Beattie, J. S. 2003 (Southampton) 5
Beattie, T. K. 1975 (Ipswich T) 9
Beckham, D. R. J. 1997 (Manchester U, Real Madrid, LA Galaxy) 115
Becton, F. 1895 (Preston NE, Liverpool) 2
Bedford, H. 1923 (Blackpool) 2
Bell, C. 1968 (Manchester C) 48
Bellingham, J. V. W. 2021 (Borussia Dortmund) 7
Bennett, W. 1901 (Sheffield U) 2
Benson, R. W. 1913 (Sheffield U) 1
Bent, D. A. 2006 (Charlton Ath, Tottenham H, Sunderland, Aston Villa) 13
Bentley, D. M. 2008 (Blackburn R, Tottenham H) 7
Bentley, R. T. F. 1949 (Chelsea) 12
Beresford, J. 1934 (Aston Villa) 1
Berry, A. 1909 (Oxford University) 1
Berry, J. J. 1953 (Manchester U) 4
Bertrand, R. 2013 (Chelsea, Southampton) 19
Bestall, J. G. 1935 (Grimsby T) 1
Betmead, H. A. 1937 (Grimsby T) 1
Betts, M. P. 1877 (Old Harrovians) 1
Betts, W. 1889 (Sheffield W) 1
Beverley, J. 1884 (Blackburn R) 3
Birkett, R. H. 1879 (Clapham R) 1
Birkett, R. J. E. 1936 (Middlesbrough) 1
Birley, F. H. 1874 (Oxford University, Wanderers) 2
Birtles, G. 1980 (Nottingham F) 3
Bishop, S. M. 1927 (Leicester C) 4
Blackburn, F. 1901 (Blackburn R) 3
Blackburn, G. F. 1924 (Aston Villa) 1

Blenkinsop, E. 1928 (Sheffield W) 26
Bliss, H. 1921 (Tottenham H) 1
Blissett, L. L. 1983 (Watford, AC Milan) 14
Blockley, J. P. 1973 (Arsenal) 1
Bloomer, S. 1895 (Derby Co, Middlesbrough) 23
Blunstone, F. 1955 (Chelsea) 5
Bond, R. 1905 (Preston NE, Bradford C) 8
Bonetti, P. P. 1966 (Chelsea) 7
Bonsor, A. G. 1873 (Wanderers) 2
Booth, F. 1905 (Manchester C) 1
Booth, T. 1898 (Blackburn R, Everton) 2
Bothroyd, J. 2011 (Cardiff C) 1
Bould, S. A. 1994 (Arsenal) 2
Bowden, E. R. 1935 (Arsenal) 6
Bower, A. G. 1924 (Corinthians) 5
Bowers, J. W. 1934 (Derby Co) 3
Bowles, S. 1974 (QPR) 5
Bowser, S. 1920 (WBA) 1
Bowyer, L. D. 2003 (Leeds U) 1
Boyer, P. J. 1976 (Norwich C) 1
Boyes, W. 1935 (WBA, Everton) 3
Boyle, T. W. 1913 (Burnley) 1
Brabrook, P. 1958 (Chelsea) 3
Bracewell, P. W. 1985 (Everton) 3
Bradford, G. R. W. 1956 (Bristol R) 1
Bradford, J. 1924 (Birmingham) 12
Bradley, W. 1959 (Manchester U) 3
Bradshaw, F. 1908 (Sheffield W) 1
Bradshaw, T. H. 1897 (Liverpool) 1
Bradshaw, W. 1910 (Blackburn R) 4
Brann, G. 1886 (Swifts) 3
Brawn, W. F. 1904 (Aston Villa) 2
Bray, J. 1935 (Manchester C) 6
Brayshaw, E. 1887 (Sheffield W) 1
Bridge W. M. 2002 (Southampton, Chelsea, Manchester C) 36
Bridges, B. J. 1965 (Chelsea) 4
Bridgett, A. 1905 (Sunderland) 11
Brindle, T. 1880 (Darwen) 2
Brittleton, J. T. 1912 (Sheffield W) 5
Britton, C. S. 1935 (Everton) 9
Broadbent, P. F. 1958 (Wolverhampton W) 7
Broadis, I. A. 1952 (Manchester C, Newcastle U) 14
Brockbank, J. 1872 (Cambridge University) 1
Brodie, J. B. 1889 (Wolverhampton W) 3
Bromilow, T. G. 1921 (Liverpool) 5
Bromley-Davenport, W. E. 1884 (Oxford University) 2
Brook, E. F. 1930 (Manchester C) 18
Brooking, T. D. 1974 (West Ham U) 47
Brooks, J. 1957 (Tottenham H) 3
Broome, F. H. 1938 (Aston Villa) 7
Brown, A. 1882 (Aston Villa) 3
Brown, A. 1971 (WBA) 1
Brown, A. S. 1904 (Sheffield U) 2
Brown, G. 1927 (Huddersfield T, Aston Villa) 9
Brown, J. 1881 (Blackburn R) 5
Brown, J. H. 1927 (Sheffield W) 6
Brown, K. 1960 (West Ham U) 1
Brown, W. 1924 (West Ham U) 1
Brown, W. M. 1999 (Manchester U) 23
Bruton, J. 1928 (Burnley) 3
Bryant, W. I. 1925 (Clapton) 1
Buchan, C. M. 1913 (Sunderland) 6
Buchanan, W. S. 1876 (Clapham R) 1
Buckley, F. C. 1914 (Derby Co) 1
Bull, S. G. 1989 (Wolverhampton W) 13
Bullock, F. E. 1921 (Huddersfield T) 1
Bullock, N. 1923 (Bury) 3
Burgess, H. 1904 (Manchester C) 4
Burgess, H. 1931 (Sheffield W) 4
Burnup, C. J. 1896 (Cambridge University) 1
Burrows, H. 1934 (Sheffield W) 3
Burton, F. E. 1889 (Nottingham F) 1
Bury, L. 1877 (Cambridge University, Old Etonians) 2
Butcher, T. 1980 (Ipswich T, Rangers) 77
Butland, J. 2013 (Birmingham C, Stoke C) 9
Butler, J. D. 1925 (Arsenal) 1
Butler, W. 1924 (Bolton W) 1
Butt, N. 1997 (Manchester U, Newcastle U) 39
Byrne, G. 1963 (Liverpool) 2
Byrne, J. J. 1962 (Crystal Palace, West Ham U) 11
Byrne, R. W. 1954 (Manchester U) 33

Cahill, G. J. 2011 (Bolton W, Chelsea) 61
Callaghan, I. R. 1966 (Liverpool) 4
Calvert-Lewin, D. N. 2021 (Everton) 11
Calvey, J. 1902 (Nottingham F) 1
Campbell, A. F. 1929 (Blackburn R, Huddersfield T) 8
Campbell, F. L. 2012 (Sunderland) 1
Campbell, S. 1996 (Tottenham H, Arsenal, Portsmouth) 73
Camsell, G. H. 1929 (Middlesbrough) 9
Capes, A. J. 1903 (Stoke) 1
Carr, J. 1905 (Newcastle U) 2
Carr, J. 1920 (Middlesbrough) 2
Carr, W. H. 1875 (Owlerton, Sheffield) 1
Carragher, J. L. 1999 (Liverpool) 38
Carrick, M. 2001 (West Ham U, Tottenham H, Manchester U) 34
Carroll, A. T. 2011 (Newcastle U, Liverpool) 9
Carson, S. P. 2008 (Liverpool, WBA) 4
Carter, H. S. 1934 (Sunderland, Derby Co) 13
Carter, J. H. 1926 (WBA) 3
Catlin, A. E. 1937 (Sheffield W) 5
Caulker, S. A. 2013 (Tottenham H) 1
Chadwick, A. 1900 (Southampton) 2
Chadwick, E. 1891 (Everton) 7
Chalobah, N. N. 2019 (Watford) 1
Chamberlain, M. 1983 (Stoke C) 8
Chambers, H. 1921 (Liverpool) 8
Chambers, C. 2015 (Arsenal) 3
Channon, M. R. 1973 (Southampton, Manchester C) 46
Charles, G. A. 1991 (Nottingham F) 2
Charlton, J. 1965 (Leeds U) 35
Charlton, R. 1958 (Manchester U) 106
Charnley, R. O. 1963 (Blackpool) 1
Charsley, C. C. 1893 (Small Heath) 1
Chedgzoy, S. 1920 (Everton) 8
Chenery, C. J. 1872 (Crystal Palace) 3
Cherry, T. J. 1976 (Leeds U) 27
Chilwell, B. J. 2019 (Leicester C, Chelsea) 14
Chilton, A. 1951 (Manchester U) 2
Chippendale, H. 1894 (Blackburn R) 1
Chivers, M. 1971 (Tottenham H) 24
Christian, E. 1879 (Old Etonians) 1
Clamp, E. 1958 (Wolverhampton W) 4
Clapton, D. R. 1959 (Arsenal) 1
Clare, T. 1889 (Stoke) 4
Clarke, A. J. 1970 (Leeds U) 19
Clarke, H. A. 1954 (Tottenham H) 1
Clay, T. 1920 (Tottenham H) 4
Clayton, R. 1956 (Blackburn R) 35
Clegg, J. C. 1872 (Sheffield W) 1
Clegg, W. E. 1873 (Sheffield W, Sheffield Alb) 2
Clemence, R. N. 1973 (Liverpool, Tottenham H) 61
Clement, D. T. 1976 (QPR) 5
Cleverley, T. W. 2013 (Manchester U) 13
Clough, B. H. 1960 (Middlesbrough) 2
Clough, N. H. 1989 (Nottingham F) 14
Clyne, N. E. 2015 (Southampton, Liverpool) 14
Coady, C. D. 2021 (Wolverhampton W) 5
Coates, R. 1970 (Burnley, Tottenham H) 4
Cobbold, W. N. 1883 (Cambridge University, Old Carthusians) 9
Cock, J. G. 1920 (Huddersfield T, Chelsea) 2
Cockburn, H. 1947 (Manchester U) 13
Cohen, G. R. 1964 (Fulham) 37
Cole, A. 2001 (Arsenal, Chelsea) 107
Cole, A. A. 1995 (Manchester U) 15
Cole, C. 2009 (West Ham U) 7
Cole, J. J. 2001 (West Ham U, Chelsea) 56
Colclough, H. 1914 (Crystal Palace) 1
Coleman, E. H. 1921 (Dulwich Hamlet) 1
Coleman, J. 1907 (Woolwich Arsenal) 1
Collymore, S. V. 1995 (Nottingham F, Aston Villa) 3
Common, A. 1904 (Sheffield U, Middlesbrough) 3
Compton, L. H. 1951 (Arsenal) 2
Conlin, J. 1906 (Bradford C) 1
Connelly, J. M. 1960 (Burnley, Manchester U) 20
Cook, L. J. 2018 (Bournemouth) 1
Cook, T. E. R. 1925 (Brighton) 1
Cooper, C. T. 1995 (Nottingham F) 2
Cooper, N. C. 1893 (Cambridge University) 1
Cooper, T. 1928 (Derby Co) 15
Cooper, T. 1969 (Leeds U) 20

Coppell, S. J. 1978 (Manchester U) 42
Copping, W. 1933 (Leeds U, Arsenal, Leeds U) 20
Corbett, B. O. 1901 (Corinthians) 1
Corbett, R. 1903 (Old Malvernians) 1
Corbett, W. S. 1908 (Birmingham) 3
Cork, J. F. P. 2018 (Burnley) 1
Corrigan, J. T. 1976 (Manchester C) 9
Cottee, A. R. 1987 (West Ham U, Everton) 7
Cotterill, G. H. 1891 (Cambridge University, Old Brightonians) 4
Cottle, J. R. 1909 (Bristol C) 1
Cowan, S. 1926 (Manchester C) 3
Cowans, G. S. 1983 (Aston Villa, Bari, Aston Villa) 10
Cowell, A. 1910 (Blackburn R) 1
Cox, J. 1901 (Liverpool) 3
Cox, J. D. 1892 (Derby Co) 1
Crabtree, J. W. 1894 (Burnley, Aston Villa) 14
Crawford, J. F. 1931 (Chelsea) 1
Crawford, R. 1962 (Ipswich T) 2
Crawshaw, T. H. 1895 (Sheffield W) 10
Crayston, W. J. 1936 (Arsenal) 8
Creek, F. N. S. 1923 (Corinthians) 1
Cresswell, A. W. 2017 (West Ham U) 3
Cresswell, W. 1921 (South Shields, Sunderland, Everton) 7
Crompton, R. 1902 (Blackburn R) 41
Crooks, S. D. 1930 (Derby Co) 26
Crouch, P. J. 2005 (Southampton, Liverpool, Portsmouth, Tottenham H) 42
Crowe, C. 1963 (Wolverhampton W) 1
Cuggy, F. 1913 (Sunderland) 2
Cullis, S. 1938 (Wolverhampton W) 12
Cunliffe, A. 1933 (Blackburn R) 2
Cunliffe, D. 1900 (Portsmouth) 1
Cunliffe, J. N. 1936 (Everton) 1
Cunningham, L. 1979 (WBA, Real Madrid) 6
Curle, K. 1992 (Manchester C) 3
Currey, E. S. 1890 (Oxford University) 2
Currie, A. W. 1972 (Sheffield U, Leeds U) 17
Cursham, A. W. 1876 (Notts Co) 6
Cursham, H. A. 1880 (Notts Co) 8

Daft, H. B. 1889 (Notts Co) 5
Daley, A. M. 1992 (Aston Villa) 7
Danks, T. 1885 (Nottingham F) 1
Davenport, P. 1985 (Nottingham F) 1
Davenport, J. K. 1885 (Bolton W) 2
Davies, K. C. 2011 (Bolton W) 1
Davis, G. 1904 (Derby Co) 2
Davis, H. 1903 (Sheffield W) 3
Davison, J. E. 1922 (Sheffield W) 1
Dawson, J. 1922 (Burnley) 2
Dawson, M. R. 2011 (Tottenham H) 4
Day, S. H. 1906 (Old Malvernians) 3
Dean, W. R. 1927 (Everton) 16
Deane, B. C. 1991 (Sheffield U) 3
Deeley, N. V. 1959 (Wolverhampton W) 2
Defoe, J. C. 2004 (Tottenham H, Portsmouth, Tottenham H, Sunderland) 57
Delph, F. 2015 (Aston Villa, Manchester C) 20
Devey, J. H. G. 1892 (Aston Villa) 2
Devonshire, A. 1980 (West Ham U) 8
Dewhurst, F. 1886 (Preston NE) 9
Dewhurst, G. P. 1895 (Liverpool Ramblers) 1
Dickinson, J. W. 1949 (Portsmouth) 48
Dier, E. J. E. 2016 (Tottenham H) 45
Dimmock, J. H. 1921 (Tottenham H) 3
Ditchburn, E. G. 1949 (Tottenham H) 6
Dix, R. W. 1939 (Derby Co) 1
Dixon, J. A. 1885 (Notts Co) 1
Dixon, K. M. 1985 (Chelsea) 8
Dixon, L. M. 1990 (Arsenal) 22
Dobson, A. T. C. 1882 (Notts Co) 4
Dobson, C. F. 1886 (Notts Co) 1
Dobson, J. M. 1974 (Burnley, Everton) 5
Doggart, A. G. 1924 (Corinthians) 1
Dorigo, A. R. 1990 (Chelsea, Leeds U) 15
Dorrell, A. R. 1925 (Aston Villa) 4
Douglas, B. 1958 (Blackburn R) 36
Downing, S. 2005 (Middlesbrough, Aston Villa, Liverpool, West Ham U) 35
Downs, R. W. 1921 (Everton) 1
Doyle, M. 1976 (Manchester C) 5
Drake, E. J. 1935 (Arsenal) 5
Drinkwater, D. N. 2016 (Leicester C) 3
Dublin, D. 1998 (Coventry C, Aston Villa) 4
Ducat, A. 1910 (Woolwich Arsenal, Aston Villa) 6
Dunn, A. T. B. 1883 (Cambridge University, Old Etonians) 4
Dunn, D. J. I. 2003 (Blackburn R) 1
Dunk, L. C. 2019 (Brighton & HA) 1
Duxbury, M. 1984 (Manchester U) 10
Dyer, K. C. 2000 (Newcastle U, West Ham U) 33

Earle, S. G. J. 1924 (Clapton, West Ham U) 2
Eastham, G. 1963 (Arsenal) 19
Eastham, G. R. 1935 (Bolton W) 1
Eckersley, W. 1950 (Blackburn R) 17
Edwards, D. 1955 (Manchester U) 18
Edwards, J. H. 1874 (Shropshire Wanderers) 1
Edwards, W. 1926 (Leeds U) 16
Ehiogu, U. 1996 (Aston Villa, Middlesbrough) 4
Ellerington, W. 1949 (Southampton) 2
Elliott, G. W. 1913 (Middlesbrough) 3
Elliott, W. H. 1952 (Burnley) 5
Evans, R. E. 1911 (Sheffield U) 4
Ewer, F. H. 1924 (Casuals) 2

Fairclough, P. 1878 (Old Foresters) 1
Fairhurst, D. 1934 (Newcastle U) 1
Fantham, J. 1962 (Sheffield W) 1
Fashanu, J. 1989 (Wimbledon) 2
Felton, W. 1925 (Sheffield W) 1
Fenton, M. 1938 (Middlesbrough) 1
Fenwick, T. W. 1984 (QPR, Tottenham H) 20
Ferdinand, L. 1993 (QPR, Newcastle U, Tottenham H) 17
Ferdinand, R. G. 1998 (West Ham U, Leeds U, Manchester U) 81
Field, E. 1876 (Clapham R) 2
Finney, T. 1947 (Preston NE) 76
Flanagan, J. P. 2014 (Liverpool) 1
Fleming, H. J. 1909 (Swindon T) 11
Fletcher, A. 1889 (Wolverhampton W) 2
Flowers, R. 1955 (Wolverhampton W) 49
Flowers, T. D. 1993 (Southampton, Blackburn R) 11
Foden, P. W. 2021 (Manchester C) 9
Forman, Frank 1898 (Nottingham F 9
Forman, F. R. 1899 (Nottingham F) 3
Forrest, J. H. 1884 (Blackburn R) 11
Forster, F. G. 2013 (Celtic, Southampton) 6
Fort, J. 1921 (Millwall) 1
Foster, B. 2007 (Manchester U, Birmingham C, WBA) 8
Foster, R. E. 1900 (Oxford University, Corinthians) 5
Foster, S. 1982 (Brighton & HA) 3
Foulke, W. J. 1897 (Sheffield U) 1
Foulkes, W. A. 1955 (Manchester U) 1
Fowler, R. B. 1996 (Liverpool, Leeds U) 26
Fox, F. S. 1925 (Millwall) 1
Francis, G. C. J. 1975 (QPR) 12
Francis, T. 1977 (Birmingham C, Nottingham F, Manchester C, Sampdoria) 52
Franklin, C. F. 1947 (Stoke C) 27
Freeman, B. C. 1909 (Everton, Burnley) 5
Froggatt, J. 1950 (Portsmouth) 13
Froggatt, R. 1953 (Sheffield W) 4
Fry, C. B. 1901 (Corinthians) 1
Furness, W. I. 1933 (Leeds U) 1

Galley, T. 1937 (Wolverhampton W) 2
Gardner, A. 2004 (Tottenham H) 1
Gardner, T. 1934 (Aston Villa) 2
Garfield, B. 1898 (WBA) 1
Garraty, W. 1903 (Aston Villa) 1
Garrett, T. 1952 (Blackpool) 3
Gascoigne, P. J. 1989 (Tottenham H, Lazio, Rangers, Middlesbrough) 57
Gates, E. 1981 (Ipswich T) 2
Gay, L. H. 1893 (Cambridge University, Old Brightonians) 3
Geary, F. 1890 (Everton) 2
Geaves, R. L. 1875 (Clapham R) 1
Gee, C. W. 1932 (Everton) 3
Geldard, A. 1933 (Everton) 4
George, C. 1977 (Derby Co) 1
George, W. 1902 (Aston Villa) 3

Gerrard, S. G. 2000 (Liverpool) 114
Gibbins, W. V. T. 1924 (Clapton) 2
Gibbs, K. J. R. 2011 (Arsenal) 10
Gidman, J. 1977 (Aston Villa) 1
Gillard, I. T. 1975 (QPR) 3
Gilliat, W. E. 1893 (Old Carthusians) 1
Godfrey, B. M. 2021 (Everton) 2
Goddard, P. 1982 (West Ham U) 1
Gomez, J. D. 2018 (Liverpool) 11
Goodall, F. R. 1926 (Huddersfield T) 25
Goodall, J. 1888 (Preston NE, Derby Co) 14
Goodhart, H. C. 1883 (Old Etonians) 3
Goodwyn, A. G. 1873 (Royal Engineers) 1
Goodyer, A. C. 1879 (Nottingham F) 1
Gosling, R. C. 1892 (Old Etonians) 5
Gosnell, A. A. 1906 (Newcastle U) 1
Gough, H. C. 1921 (Sheffield U) 1
Goulden, L. A. 1937 (West Ham U) 14
Graham, L. 1925 (Millwall) 2
Graham, T. 1931 (Nottingham F) 2
Grainger, C. 1956 (Sheffield U, Sunderland) 7
Gray, A. A. 1992 (Crystal Palace) 1
Gray, M. 1999 (Sunderland) 3
Grealish, J. P. 2021 (Aston Villa) 12
Greaves, J. 1959 (Chelsea, Tottenham H) 57
Green, F. T. 1876 (Wanderers) 1
Green, G. H. 1925 (Sheffield U) 8
Green, R. P. 2005 (Norwich C, West Ham U) 12
Greenhalgh, E. H. 1872 (Notts Co) 2
Greenhoff, B. 1976 (Manchester U, Leeds U) 18
Greenwood, D. H. 1882 (Blackburn R) 2
Greenwood, M. W. J. 2021 (Manchester U) 1
Gregory, J. 1983 (QPR) 6
Grimsdell, A. 1920 (Tottenham H) 6
Grosvenor, A. T. 1934 (Birmingham) 3
Gunn, W. 1884 (Notts Co) 2
Guppy, S. 2000 (Leicester C) 1
Gurney, R. 1935 (Sunderland) 1

Hacking, J. 1929 (Oldham Ath) 3
Hadley, H. 1903 (WBA) 1
Hagan, J. 1949 (Sheffield U) 1
Haines, J. T. W. 1949 (WBA) 1
Hall, A. E. 1910 (Aston Villa) 1
Hall, G. W. 1934 (Tottenham H) 10
Hall, J. 1956 (Birmingham C) 17
Halse, H. J. 1909 (Manchester U) 1
Hammond, H. E. D. 1889 (Oxford University) 1
Hampson, J. 1931 (Blackpool) 3
Hampton, H. 1913 (Aston Villa) 4
Hancocks, J. 1949 (Wolverhampton W) 3
Hapgood, E. 1933 (Arsenal) 30
Hardinge, H. T. W. 1910 (Sheffield U) 1
Hardman, H. P. 1905 (Everton) 4
Hardwick, G. F. M. 1947 (Middlesbrough) 13
Hardy, H. 1925 (Stockport Co) 1
Hardy, S. 1907 (Liverpool, Aston Villa) 21
Harford, M. G. 1988 (Luton T) 2
Hargreaves, F. W. 1880 (Blackburn R) 3
Hargreaves, J. 1881 (Blackburn R) 2
Hargreaves, O. 2002 (Bayern Munich, Manchester U) 42
Harper, E. C. 1926 (Blackburn R) 1
Harris, G. 1966 (Burnley) 1
Harris, P. P. 1950 (Portsmouth) 2
Harris, S. S. 1904 (Cambridge University, Old Westminsters) 6
Harrison, A. H. 1893 (Old Westminsters) 2
Harrison, G. 1921 (Everton) 2
Harrow, J. H. 1923 (Chelsea) 2
Hart, C. J. J. 2008 (Manchester C) 75
Hart, E. 1929 (Leeds U) 8
Hartley, F. 1923 (Oxford C) 1
Harvey, A. 1881 (Wednesbury Strollers) 1
Harvey, J. C. 1971 (Everton) 1
Hassall, H. W. 1951 (Huddersfield T, Bolton W) 5
Hateley, M. 1984 (Portsmouth, AC Milan, Monaco, Rangers) 32
Hawkes, R. M. 1907 (Luton T) 5
Haworth, G. 1887 (Accrington) 5
Hawtrey, J. P. 1881 (Old Etonians) 2
Haygarth, E. B. 1875 (Swifts) 1
Haynes, J. N. 1955 (Fulham) 56
Healless, H. 1925 (Blackburn R) 2
Heaton, T. 2016 (Burnley) 3
Hector, K. J. 1974 (Derby Co) 2
Hedley, G. A. 1901 (Sheffield U) 1
Hegan, K. E. 1923 (Corinthians) 4
Hellawell, M. S. 1963 (Birmingham C) 2
Henderson D. B. 2021 (Manchester U) 1
Henderson, J. B. 2011 (Sunderland, Liverpool) 64
Hendrie, L. A. 1999 (Aston Villa) 1
Henfrey, A. G. 1891 (Cambridge University, Corinthians) 5
Henry, R. P. 1963 (Tottenham H) 1
Heron, F. 1876 (Wanderers) 1
Heron, G. H. H. 1873 (Uxbridge, Wanderers) 5
Heskey, E. W. I. 1999 (Leicester C, Liverpool, Birmingham C, Wigan Ath, Aston Villa) 62
Hibbert, W. 1910 (Bury) 1
Hibbs, H. E. 1930 (Birmingham) 25
Hill, F. 1963 (Bolton W) 2
Hill, G. A. 1976 (Manchester U) 6
Hill, J. H. 1925 (Burnley, Newcastle U) 11
Hill, R. 1983 (Luton T) 3
Hill, R. H. 1926 (Millwall) 1
Hillman, J. 1899 (Burnley) 1
Hills, A. F. 1879 (Old Harrovians) 1
Hilsdon, G. R. 1907 (Chelsea) 8
Hinchcliffe, A. G. 1997 (Everton, Sheffield W) 7
Hine, E. W. 1929 (Leicester C) 6
Hinton, A. T. 1963 (Wolverhampton W, Nottingham F) 3
Hirst, D. E. 1991 (Sheffield W) 3
Hitchens, G. A. 1961 (Aston Villa, Internazionale) 7
Hobbis, H. H. F. 1936 (Charlton Ath) 2
Hoddle, G. 1980 (Tottenham H, Monaco) 53
Hodge, S. B. 1986 (Aston Villa, Tottenham H, Nottingham F) 24
Hodgetts, D. 1888 (Aston Villa) 6
Hodgkinson, A. 1957 (Sheffield U) 5
Hodgson, G. 1931 (Liverpool) 3
Hodkinson, J. 1913 (Blackburn R) 3
Hogg, W. 1902 (Sunderland) 3
Holdcroft, G. H. 1937 (Preston NE) 2
Holden, A. D. 1959 (Bolton W) 5
Holden, G. H. 1881 (Wednesbury OA) 4
Holden-White, C. 1888 (Corinthians) 2
Holford, T. 1903 (Stoke) 1
Holley, G. H. 1909 (Sunderland) 10
Holliday, E. 1960 (Middlesbrough) 3
Hollins, J. W. 1967 (Chelsea) 1
Holmes, R. 1888 (Preston NE) 7
Holt, J. 1890 (Everton, Reading) 10
Hopkinson, E. 1958 (Bolton W) 14
Hossack, A. H. 1892 (Corinthians) 2
Houghton, W. E. 1931 (Aston Villa) 7
Houlker, A. E. 1902 (Blackburn R, Portsmouth, Southampton) 5
Howarth, R. H. 1887 (Preston NE, Everton) 5
Howe, D. 1958 (WBA) 23
Howe, J. R. 1948 (Derby Co) 3
Howell, L. S. 1873 (Wanderers) 1
Howell, R. 1895 (Sheffield U, Liverpool) 2
Howey, S. N. 1995 (Newcastle U) 4
Huddlestone, T. A. 2010 (Tottenham H) 4
Hudson, A. A. 1975 (Stoke C) 2
Hudson, J. 1883 (Sheffield) 1
Hudson-Odoi C. J. 2019 (Chelsea) 3
Hudspeth, F. C. 1926 (Newcastle U) 1
Hufton, A. E. 1924 (West Ham U) 6
Hughes, E. W. 1970 (Liverpool, Wolverhampton W) 62
Hughes, L. 1950 (Liverpool) 3
Hulme, J. H. A. 1927 (Arsenal) 9
Humphreys, P. 1903 (Notts Co) 1
Hunt, G. S. 1933 (Tottenham H) 3
Hunt, Rev. K. R. G. 1911 (Leyton) 2
Hunt, R. 1962 (Liverpool) 34
Hunt, S. 1984 (WBA) 2
Hunter, J. 1878 (Sheffield Heeley) 7
Hunter, N. 1966 (Leeds U) 28
Hurst, G. C. 1966 (West Ham U) 49

Ince, P. E. C. 1993 (Manchester U, Internazionale, Liverpool, Middlesbrough) 53

Ings, D. 2016 (Liverpool, Southampton) 3
Iremonger, J. 1901 (Nottingham F) 2

Jack, D. N. B. 1924 (Bolton W, Arsenal) 9
Jackson, E. 1891 (Oxford University) 1
Jagielka, P. N. 2008 (Everton) 40
James. D. B. 1997 (Liverpool, Aston Villa, West Ham U, Manchester C, Portsmouth) 53
Jarrett, B. G. 1876 (Cambridge University) 3
Jarvis, M. T. 2011 (Wolverhampton W) 1
Jefferis, F. 1912 (Everton) 2
Jeffers, F. 2003 (Arsenal) 1
Jenas, J. A. 2003 (Newcastle U, Tottenham H) 21
Jenkinson, C. D. 2013 (Arsenal) 1
Jezzard, B. A. G. 1954 (Fulham) 2
Johnson, A. 2005 (Crystal Palace, Everton) 8
Johnson, A. 2010 (Manchester C) 12
Johnson, D. E. 1975 (Ipswich T, Liverpool) 8
Johnson, E. 1880 (Saltley College, Stoke) 2
Johnson, G. M. C. 2004 (Chelsea, Portsmouth, Liverpool) 54
Johnson, J. A. 1937 (Stoke C) 5
Johnson, S. A. M. 2001 (Derby Co) 1
Johnson, T. C. F. 1926 (Manchester C, Everton) 5
Johnson, W. H. 1900 (Sheffield U) 6
Johnston, H. 1947 (Blackpool) 10
Johnstone, S. L. 2021 (WBA) 1
Jones, A. 1882 (Walsall Swifts, Great Lever) 3
Jones, H. 1923 (Nottingham F) 1
Jones, H. 1927 (Blackburn R) 6
Jones, M. D. 1965 (Sheffield U, Leeds U) 3
Jones, P. A. 2012 (Manchester U) 27
Jones, R. 1992 (Liverpool) 8
Jones, W. 1901 (Bristol C) 1
Jones, W. H. 1950 (Liverpool) 2
Joy, B. 1936 (Casuals) 1

Kail, E. I. L. 1929 (Dulwich Hamlet) 3
Kane, H. E. 2015 (Tottenham H) 61
Kay, A. H. 1963 (Everton) 1
Kean, F. W. 1923 (Sheffield W, Bolton W) 9
Keane, M. V. 2017 (Burnley, Everton) 12
Keegan, J. K. 1973 (Liverpool, Hamburg, Southampton) 63
Keen, E. R. L. 1933 (Derby Co) 4
Kelly, M. R. 2012 (Liverpool) 1
Kelly, R. 1920 (Burnley, Sunderland, Huddersfield T) 14
Kennedy, A. 1984 (Liverpool) 2
Kennedy, R. 1976 (Liverpool) 17
Kenyon-Slaney, W. S. 1873 (Wanderers) 1
Keown, M. R. 1992 (Everton, Arsenal) 43
Kevan, D. T. 1957 (WBA) 14
Kidd, B. 1970 (Manchester U) 2
King, L. B. 2002 (Tottenham H) 21
King, R. S. 1882 (Oxford University) 1
Kingsford, R. K. 1874 (Wanderers) 1
Kingsley, M. 1901 (Newcastle U) 1
Kinsey, G. 1892 (Wolverhampton W, Derby Co) 4
Kirchen, A. J. 1937 (Arsenal) 3
Kirkland, C. E. 2007 (Liverpool) 1
Kirton, W. J. 1922 (Aston Villa) 1
Knight, A. E. 1920 (Portsmouth) 1
Knight, Z. 2005 (Fulham) 2
Knowles, C. 1968 (Tottenham H) 4
Konchesky, P. M. 2003 (Charlton Ath, West Ham U) 2

Labone, B. L. 1963 (Everton) 26
Lallana, A. D. 2013 (Southampton, Liverpool) 34
Lambert, R. L. 2013 (Southampton, Liverpool) 11
Lampard, F. J. 2000 (West Ham U, Chelsea) 106
Lampard, F. R. G. 1973 (West Ham U) 2
Langley, E. J. 1958 (Fulham) 3
Langton, R. 1947 (Blackburn R, Preston NE, Bolton W) 11
Latchford, R. D. 1978 (Everton) 12
Latheron, E. G. 1913 (Blackburn R) 2
Lawler, C. 1971 (Liverpool) 4
Lawton, T. 1939 (Everton, Chelsea, Notts Co) 23
Leach, T. 1931 (Sheffield W) 2
Leake, A. 1904 (Aston Villa) 5
Lee, E. A. 1904 (Southampton) 1
Lee, F. H. 1969 (Manchester C) 27
Lee, J. 1951 (Derby Co) 1
Lee, R. M. 1995 (Newcastle U) 21
Lee, S. 1983 (Liverpool) 14
Leighton, J. E. 1886 (Nottingham F) 1
Lennon, A. J. 2006 (Tottenham H) 21
Lescott, J. P. 2008 (Everton, Manchester C) 26
Le Saux, G. P. 1994 (Blackburn R, Chelsea) 36
Le Tissier, M. P. 1994 (Southampton) 8
Lilley, H. E. 1892 (Sheffield U) 1
Linacre, H. J. 1905 (Nottingham F) 2
Lindley, T. 1886 (Cambridge University, Nottingham F) 13
Lindsay, A. 1974 (Liverpool) 4
Lindsay, W. 1877 (Wanderers) 1
Lineker, G. 1984 (Leicester C, Everton, Barcelona, Tottenham H) 80
Lingard, J. E. 2017 (Manchester U) 29
Lintott, E. H. 1908 (QPR, Bradford C) 7
Lipsham, H. B. 1902 (Sheffield U) 1
Little, B. 1975 (Aston Villa) 1
Livermore, J. C. 2013 (Tottenham H, WBA) 7
Lloyd, L. V. 1971 (Liverpool, Nottingham F) 4
Lockett, A. 1903 (Stoke) 1
Lodge, L. V. 1894 (Cambridge University, Corinthians) 5
Lofthouse, J. M. 1885 (Blackburn R, Accrington, Blackburn R) 7
Lofthouse, N. 1951 (Bolton W) 33
Loftus-Cheek, R. I. 2018 (Chelsea) 10
Longworth, E. 1920 (Liverpool) 5
Lowder, A. 1889 (Wolverhampton W) 1
Lowe, E. 1947 (Aston Villa) 3
Lucas, T. 1922 (Liverpool) 3
Luntley, E. 1880 (Nottingham F) 2
Lyttelton, Hon. A. 1877 (Cambridge University) 1
Lyttelton, Hon. E. 1878 (Cambridge University) 1

Mabbutt, G. 1983 (Tottenham H) 16
Macaulay, R. H. 1881 (Cambridge University) 1
Macrae, S. 1883 (Notts Co) 5
Maddison, F. B. 1872 (Oxford University) 1
Maddison, J. D. 2020 (Leicester C) 1
Madeley, P. E. 1971 (Leeds U) 24
Magee, T. P. 1923 (WBA) 5
Maguire, J. H. 2018 (Leicester C, Manchester U) 37
Makepeace, H. 1906 (Everton) 4
Male, C. G. 1935 (Arsenal) 19
Mannion, W. J. 1947 (Middlesbrough) 26
Mariner, P. 1977 (Ipswich T, Arsenal) 35
Marsden, J. T. 1891 (Darwen) 1
Marsden, W. 1930 (Sheffield W) 3
Marsh, R. W. 1972 (QPR, Manchester C) 9
Marshall, T. 1880 (Darwen) 2
Martin, A. 1981 (West Ham U) 17
Martin, H. 1914 (Sunderland) 1
Martyn, A. N. 1992 (Crystal Palace, Leeds U) 23
Marwood, B. 1989 (Arsenal) 1
Maskrey, H. M. 1908 (Derby Co) 1
Mason, C. 1887 (Wolverhampton W) 3
Mason, R. G. 2015 (Tottenham H) 1
Maitland-Niles, A. C. 2021 (Arsenal) 5
Matthews, R. D. 1956 (Coventry C) 5
Matthews, S. 1935 (Stoke C, Blackpool) 54
Matthews, V. 1928 (Sheffield U) 2
Maynard, W. J. 1872 (1st Surrey Rifles) 2
McCall, J. 1913 (Preston NE) 5
McCann, G. P. 2001 (Sunderland) 1
McCarthy, A. S. 2019 (Southampton) 1
McDermott, T. 1978 (Liverpool) 25
McDonald, C. A. 1958 (Burnley) 8
Macdonald, M. 1972 (Newcastle U) 14
McFarland, R. L. 1971 (Derby Co) 28
McGarry, W. H. 1954 (Huddersfield T) 4
McGuinness, W. 1959 (Manchester U) 2
McInroy, A. 1927 (Sunderland) 1
McMahon, S. 1988 (Liverpool) 17
McManaman, S. 1995 (Liverpool, Real Madrid) 37
McNab, R. 1969 (Arsenal) 4
McNeal, R. 1914 (WBA) 2
McNeil, M. 1961 (Middlesbrough) 9
Meadows, J. 1955 (Manchester C) 1
Medley, L. D. 1951 (Tottenham H) 6
Meehan, T. 1924 (Chelsea) 1

Melia, J. 1963 (Liverpool) 2
Mercer, D. W. 1923 (Sheffield U) 2
Mercer, J. 1939 (Everton) 5
Merrick, G. H. 1952 (Birmingham C) 23
Merson, P. C. 1992 (Arsenal, Middlesbrough, Aston Villa) 21
Metcalfe, V. 1951 (Huddersfield T) 2
Mew, J. W. 1921 (Manchester U) 1
Middleditch, B. 1897 (Corinthians) 1
Milburn, J. E. T. 1949 (Newcastle U) 13
Miller, B. G. 1961 (Burnley) 1
Miller, H. S. 1923 (Charlton Ath) 1
Mills, D. J. 2001 (Leeds U) 19
Mills, G. R. 1938 (Chelsea) 3
Mills, M. D. 1973 (Ipswich T) 42
Milne, G. 1963 (Liverpool) 14
Milner, J. P. 2010 (Aston Villa, Manchester C, Liverpool) 61
Milton, C. A. 1952 (Arsenal) 1
Milward, A. 1891 (Everton) 4
Mings, T. D. 2020 (Aston Villa) 13
Mitchell, C. 1880 (Upton Park) 5
Mitchell, J. F. 1925 (Manchester C) 1
Moffat, H. 1913 (Oldham Ath) 1
Molyneux, G. 1902 (Southampton) 4
Moon, W. R. 1888 (Old Westminsters) 7
Moore, H. T. 1883 (Notts Co) 2
Moore, J. 1923 (Derby Co) 1
Moore, R. F. 1962 (West Ham U) 108
Moore, W. G. B. 1923 (West Ham U) 1
Mordue, J. 1912 (Sunderland) 2
Morice, C. J. 1872 (Barnes) 1
Morley, A. 1982 (Aston Villa) 6
Morley, H. 1910 (Notts Co) 1
Morren, T. 1898 (Sheffield U) 1
Morris, F. 1920 (WBA) 2
Morris, J. 1949 (Derby Co) 3
Morris, W. W. 1939 (Wolverhampton W) 3
Morse, H. 1879 (Notts Co) 1
Mort, T. 1924 (Aston Villa) 3
Morten, A. 1873 (Crystal Palace) 1
Mortensen, S. H. 1947 (Blackpool) 25
Morton, J. R. 1938 (West Ham U) 1
Mosforth, W. 1877 (Sheffield W, Sheffield Alb, Sheffield W) 9
Moss, F. 1922 (Aston Villa) 5
Moss, F. 1934 (Arsenal) 4
Mosscrop, E. 1914 (Burnley) 2
Mount, M. T. 2020 (Chelsea) 21
Mozley, B. 1950 (Derby Co) 3
Mullen, J. 1947 (Wolverhampton W) 12
Mullery, A. P. 1965 (Tottenham H) 35
Murphy, D. B. 2002 (Liverpool) 9

Neal, P. G. 1976 (Liverpool) 50
Needham, E. 1894 (Sheffield U) 16
Neville, G. A. 1995 (Manchester U) 85
Neville, P. J. 1996 (Manchester U, Everton) 59
Newton, K. R. 1966 (Blackburn R, Everton) 27
Nicholls, J. 1954 (WBA) 2
Nicholson, W. E. 1951 (Tottenham H) 1
Nish, D. J. 1973 (Derby Co) 5
Norman, M. 1962 (Tottenham H) 23
Nugent, D. J. 2007 (Preston NE) 1
Nuttall, H. 1928 (Bolton W) 3

Oakley, W. J. 1895 (Oxford University, Corinthians) 16
O'Dowd, J. P. 1932 (Chelsea) 3
O'Grady, M. 1963 (Huddersfield T, Leeds U) 2
Ogilvie, R. A. M. M. 1874 (Clapham R) 1
Oliver, L. F. 1929 (Fulham) 1
Olney, B. A. 1928 (Aston Villa) 2
Osborne, F. R. 1923 (Fulham, Tottenham H) 4
Osborne, R. 1928 (Leicester C) 1
Osgood, P. L. 1970 (Chelsea) 4
Osman, L. 2013 (Everton) 2
Osman, R. 1980 (Ipswich T) 11
Ottaway, C. J. 1872 (Oxford University) 2
Owen, J. R. B. 1874 (Sheffield) 1
Owen, M. J. 1998 (Liverpool, Real Madrid, Newcastle U) 89
Owen, S. W. 1954 (Luton T) 3
Oxlade-Chamberlain, A. M. D. 2012 (Arsenal, Liverpool) 35

Page, L. A. 1927 (Burnley) 7
Paine, T. L. 1963 (Southampton) 19
Pallister, G. A. 1988 (Middlesbrough, Manchester U) 22
Palmer, C. L. 1992 (Sheffield W) 18
Pantling, H. H. 1924 (Sheffield U) 1
Paravicini, P. J. de 1883 (Cambridge University) 3
Parker, P. A. 1989 (QPR, Manchester U) 19
Parker, S. M. 2004 (Charlton Ath, Chelsea, Newcastle U, West Ham U, Tottenham H) 18
Parker, T. R. 1925 (Southampton) 1
Parkes, P. B. 1974 (QPR) 1
Parkinson, J. 1910 (Liverpool) 2
Parlour, R. 1999 (Arsenal) 10
Parr, P. C. 1882 (Oxford University) 1
Parry, E. H. 1879 (Old Carthusians) 3
Parry, R. A. 1960 (Bolton W) 2
Patchitt, B. C. A. 1923 (Corinthians) 2
Pawson, F. W. 1883 (Cambridge University, Swifts) 2
Payne, J. 1937 (Luton T) 1
Peacock, A. 1962 (Middlesbrough, Leeds U) 6
Peacock, J. 1929 (Middlesbrough) 3
Pearce, S. 1987 (Nottingham F, West Ham U) 78
Pearson, H. F. 1932 (WBA) 1
Pearson, J. H. 1892 (Crewe Alex) 1
Pearson, J. S. 1976 (Manchester U) 15
Pearson, S. C. 1948 (Manchester U) 8
Pease, W. H. 1927 (Middlesbrough) 1
Pegg, D. 1957 (Manchester U) 1
Pejic, M. 1974 (Stoke C) 4
Pelly, F. R. 1893 (Old Foresters) 3
Pennington, J. 1907 (WBA) 25
Pentland, F. B. 1909 (Middlesbrough) 5
Perry, C. 1890 (WBA) 3
Perry, T. 1898 (WBA) 1
Perry, W. 1956 (Blackpool) 3
Perryman, S. 1982 (Tottenham H) 1
Peters, M. 1966 (West Ham U, Tottenham H) 67
Phelan, M. C. 1990 (Manchester U) 1
Phillips, K. 1999 (Sunderland) 8
Phillips, K. M. 2021 (Leeds U) 15
Phillips, L. H. 1952 (Portsmouth) 3
Pickering, F. 1964 (Everton) 3
Pickering, J. 1933 (Sheffield U) 1
Pickering, N. 1983 (Sunderland) 1
Pickford, J. L. 2018 (Everton) 38
Pike, T. M. 1886 (Cambridge University) 1
Pilkington, B. 1955 (Burnley) 1
Plant, J. 1900 (Bury) 1
Platt, D. 1990 (Aston Villa, Bari, Juventus, Sampdoria, Arsenal) 62
Plum, S. L. 1923 (Charlton Ath) 1
Pointer, R. 1962 (Burnley) 3
Pope, N. D. 2018 (Burnley) 7
Porteous, T. S. 1891 (Sunderland) 1
Powell, C. G. 2001 (Charlton Ath) 5
Priest, A. E. 1900 (Sheffield U) 1
Prinsep, J. F. M. 1879 (Clapham R) 1
Puddefoot, S. C. 1926 (Blackburn R) 2
Pye, J. 1950 (Wolverhampton W) 1
Pym, R. H. 1925 (Bolton W) 3

Quantrill, A. 1920 (Derby Co) 4
Quixall, A. 1954 (Sheffield W) 5

Radford, J. 1969 (Arsenal) 2
Raikes, G. B. 1895 (Oxford University) 4
Ramsey, A. E. 1949 (Southampton, Tottenham H) 32
Rashford, M. 2016 (Manchester U) 46
Rawlings, A. 1921 (Preston NE) 1
Rawlings, W. E. 1922 (Southampton) 2
Rawlinson, J. F. P. 1882 (Cambridge University) 1
Rawson, H. E. 1875 (Royal Engineers) 1
Rawson, W. S. 1875 (Oxford University) 2
Read, A. 1921 (Tufnell Park) 1
Reader, J. 1894 (WBA) 1
Reaney, P. 1969 (Leeds U) 3
Reece, J. 2021 (Chelsea) 7
Redknapp, J. F. 1996 (Liverpool) 17
Redmond, N. D. J. 2017 (Southampton) 1

Reeves, K. P. 1980 (Norwich C, Manchester C) 2
Regis, C. 1982 (WBA, Coventry C) 5
Reid, P. 1985 (Everton) 13
Revie, D. G. 1955 (Manchester C) 6
Reynolds, J. 1892 (WBA, Aston Villa) 8
Rice, D. 2019 (West Ham U) 24
Richards, C. H. 1898 (Nottingham F) 1
Richards, G. H. 1909 (Derby Co) 1
Richards, J. P. 1973 (Wolverhampton W) 1
Richards, M. 2007 (Manchester C) 13
Richardson, J. R. 1933 (Newcastle U) 2
Richardson, K. 1994 (Aston Villa) 1
Richardson, K. E. 2005 (Manchester U) 8
Richardson, W. G. 1935 (WBA) 1
Rickaby, S. 1954 (WBA) 1
Ricketts, M. B. 2002 (Bolton W) 1
Rigby, A. 1927 (Blackburn R) 5
Rimmer, E. J. 1930 (Sheffield W) 4
Rimmer, J. J. 1976 (Arsenal) 1
Ripley, S. E. 1994 (Blackburn R) 2
Rix, G. 1981 (Arsenal) 17
Robb, G. 1954 (Tottenham H) 1
Roberts, C. 1905 (Manchester U) 3
Roberts, F. 1925 (Manchester C) 4
Roberts, G. 1983 (Tottenham H) 6
Roberts, H. 1931 (Arsenal) 1
Roberts, H. 1931 (Millwall) 1
Roberts, R. 1887 (WBA) 3
Roberts, W. T. 1924 (Preston NE) 2
Robinson, J. 1937 (Sheffield W) 4
Robinson, J. W. 1897 (Derby Co, New Brighton Tower, Southampton) 11
Robinson, P. W. 2003 (Leeds U, Tottenham H, Blackburn R) 41
Robson, B. 1980 (WBA, Manchester U) 90
Robson, R. 1958 (WBA) 20
Rocastle, D. 1989 (Arsenal) 14
Rodriguez, J. E. 2013 (Southampton) 1
Rodwell, J. 2012 (Everton) 3
Rooney, W. M. 2003 (Everton, Manchester U, D.C. United) 120
Rose, D. L. 2016 (Tottenham H) 29
Rose, W. C. 1884 (Swifts, Preston NE, Wolverhampton W) 5
Rostron, T. 1881 (Darwen) 2
Rowe, A. 1934 (Tottenham H) 1
Rowley, J. F. 1949 (Manchester U) 6
Rowley, W. 1889 (Stoke) 2
Royle, J. 1971 (Everton, Manchester C) 6
Ruddlesdin, H. 1904 (Sheffield W) 3
Ruddock, N. 1995 (Liverpool) 1
Ruddy, J. T. G. 2013 (Norwich C) 1
Ruffell, J. W. 1926 (West Ham U) 6
Russell, B. B. 1883 (Royal Engineers) 1
Rutherford, J. 1904 (Newcastle U) 11

Sadler, D. 1968 (Manchester U) 4
Sagar, C. 1900 (Bury) 2
Sagar, E. 1936 (Everton) 4
Saka, B. A. T. M. 2021 (Arsenal) 9
Salako, J. A. 1991 (Crystal Palace) 5
Sancho, J. M. 2019 (Borussia Dortmund) 22
Sandford, E. A. 1933 (WBA) 1
Sandilands, R. R. 1892 (Old Westminsters) 5
Sands, J. 1880 (Nottingham F) 1
Sansom, K. G. 1979 (Crystal Palace, Arsenal) 86
Saunders, F. E. 1888 (Swifts) 1
Savage, A. H. 1876 (Crystal Palace) 1
Sayer, J. 1887 (Stoke) 1
Scales, J. R. 1995 (Liverpool) 3
Scattergood, E. 1913 (Derby Co) 1
Schofield, J. 1892 (Stoke) 3
Scholes, P. 1997 (Manchester U) 66
Scott, L. 1947 (Arsenal) 17
Scott, W. R. 1937 (Brentford) 1
Seaman, D. A. 1989 (QPR, Arsenal) 75
Seddon, J. 1923 (Bolton W) 6
Seed, J. M. 1921 (Tottenham H) 5
Settle, J. 1899 (Bury, Everton) 6
Sewell, J. 1952 (Sheffield W) 6
Sewell, W. R. 1924 (Blackburn R) 1

Shackleton, L. F. 1949 (Sunderland) 5
Sharp, J. 1903 (Everton) 2
Sharpe, L. S. 1991 (Manchester U) 8
Shaw, G. E. 1932 (WBA) 1
Shaw, G. L. 1959 (Sheffield U) 5
Shaw, L. P. H. 2014 (Southampton, Manchester U) 16
Shawcross, R. J. 2013 (Stoke C) 1
Shea, D. 1914 (Blackburn R) 2
Shearer, A. 1992 (Southampton, Blackburn R, Newcastle U) 63
Shellito, K. J. 1963 (Chelsea) 1
Shelton A. 1889 (Notts Co) 6
Shelton, C. 1888 (Notts Rangers) 1
Shelvey, J. 2013 (Liverpool, Swansea C) 6
Shepherd, A. 1906 (Bolton W, Newcastle U) 2
Sheringham, E. P. 1993 (Tottenham H, Manchester U, Tottenham H) 51
Sherwood, T. A. 1999 (Tottenham H) 3
Shilton, P. L. 1971 (Leicester C, Stoke C, Nottingham F, Southampton, Derby Co) 125
Shimwell, E. 1949 (Blackpool) 1
Shorey, N. 2007 (Reading) 2
Shutt, G. 1886 (Stoke) 1
Silcock, J. 1921 (Manchester U) 3
Sillett, R. P. 1955 (Chelsea) 3
Simms, E. 1922 (Luton T) 1
Simpson, J. 1911 (Blackburn R) 8
Sinclair, T. 2002 (West Ham U, Manchester C) 12
Sinton, A. 1992 (QPR, Sheffield W) 12
Slater, W. J. 1955 (Wolverhampton W) 12
Smalley, T. 1937 (Wolverhampton W) 1
Smalling, C. L. 2012 (Manchester U) 31
Smart, T. 1921 (Aston Villa) 5
Smith, A. 1891 (Nottingham F) 3
Smith, A. 2001 (Leeds U, Manchester U, Newcastle U) 19
Smith, A. K. 1872 (Oxford University) 1
Smith, A. M. 1989 (Arsenal) 13
Smith, B. 1921 (Tottenham H) 2
Smith, C. E. 1876 (Crystal Palace) 1
Smith, G. O. 1893 (Oxford University, Old Carthusians, Corinthians) 20
Smith, H. 1905 (Reading) 4
Smith, J. 1920 (WBA) 2
Smith, Joe 1913 (Bolton W) 5
Smith, J. C. R. 1939 (Millwall) 2
Smith, J. W. 1932 (Portsmouth) 3
Smith, Leslie 1939 (Brentford) 1
Smith, Lionel 1951 (Arsenal) 6
Smith, R. A. 1961 (Tottenham H) 15
Smith, S. 1895 (Aston Villa) 1
Smith, S. C. 1936 (Leicester C) 1
Smith, T. 1960 (Birmingham C) 2
Smith, T. 1971 (Liverpool) 1
Smith, W. H. 1922 (Huddersfield T) 3
Solanke, D. A. 2018 (Liverpool) 1
Sorby, T. H. 1879 (Thursday Wanderers, Sheffield) 1
Southgate, G. 1996 (Aston Villa, Middlesbrough) 57
Southworth, J. 1889 (Blackburn R) 3
Sparks, F. J. 1879 (Herts Rangers, Clapham R) 3
Spence, J. W. 1926 (Manchester U) 2
Spence, R. 1936 (Chelsea) 2
Spencer, C. W. 1924 (Newcastle U) 2
Spencer, H. 1897 (Aston Villa) 6
Spiksley, F. 1893 (Sheffield W) 7
Spilsbury, B. W. 1885 (Cambridge University) 3
Spink, N. 1983 (Aston Villa) 1
Spouncer, W. A. 1900 (Nottingham F) 1
Springett, R. D. G. 1960 (Sheffield W) 33
Sproston, B. 1937 (Leeds U, Tottenham H, Manchester C) 11
Squire, R. T. 1886 (Cambridge University) 3
Stanbrough, M. H. 1895 (Old Carthusians) 1
Staniforth, R. 1954 (Huddersfield T) 8
Starling, R. W. 1933 (Sheffield W, Aston Villa) 2
Statham, D. J. 1983 (WBA) 3
Steele, F. C. 1937 (Stoke C) 6
Stein, B. 1984 (Luton T) 1
Stephenson, C. 1924 (Huddersfield T) 1
Stephenson, G. T. 1928 (Derby Co, Sheffield W) 3
Stephenson, J. E. 1938 (Leeds U) 2
Stepney, A. C. 1968 (Manchester U) 1

Sterland, M. 1989 (Sheffield W) 1
Sterling, R. S. 2013 (Liverpool, Manchester C) 68
Steven, T. M. 1985 (Everton, Rangers, Marseille) 36
Stevens, G. A. 1985 (Tottenham H) 7
Stevens, M. G. 1985 (Everton, Rangers) 46
Stewart, J. 1907 (Sheffield W, Newcastle U) 3
Stewart, P. A. 1992 (Tottenham H) 3
Stiles, N. P. 1965 (Manchester U) 28
Stoker, J. 1933 (Birmingham) 3
Stone, S. B. 1996 (Nottingham F) 9
Stones, J. 2014 (Everton, Manchester C) 49
Storer, H. 1924 (Derby Co) 2
Storey, P. E. 1971 (Arsenal) 19
Storey-Moore, I. 1970 (Nottingham F) 1
Strange, A. H. 1930 (Sheffield W) 20
Stratford, A. H. 1874 (Wanderers) 1
Streten, B. 1950 (Luton T) 1
Sturgess, A. 1911 (Sheffield U) 2
Sturridge, D. A. 2012 (Chelsea, Liverpool) 26
Summerbee, M. G. 1968 (Manchester C) 8
Sunderland, A. 1980 (Arsenal) 1
Sutcliffe, J. W. 1893 (Bolton W, Millwall) 5
Sutton, C. R. 1998 (Blackburn R) 1
Swan, P. 1960 (Sheffield W) 19
Swepstone, H. A. 1880 (Pilgrims) 6
Swift, F. V. 1947 (Manchester C) 19

Tait, G. 1881 (Birmingham Excelsior) 1
Talbot, B. 1977 (Ipswich T, Arsenal) 6
Tambling, R. V. 1963 (Chelsea) 3
Tarkowski, J. A. 2018 (Burnley) 2
Tate, J. T. 1931 (Aston Villa) 3
Taylor, E. 1954 (Blackpool) 1
Taylor, E. H. 1923 (Huddersfield T) 8
Taylor, J. G. 1951 (Fulham) 2
Taylor, P. H. 1948 (Liverpool) 3
Taylor, P. J. 1976 (Crystal Palace) 4
Taylor, T. 1953 (Manchester U) 19
Temple, D. W. 1965 (Everton) 1
Terry, J. G. 2003 (Chelsea) 78
Thickett, H. 1899 (Sheffield U) 2
Thomas, D. 1975 (QPR) 8
Thomas, D. 1983 (Coventry C) 2
Thomas, G. R. 1991 (Crystal Palace) 9
Thomas, M. L. 1989 (Arsenal) 2
Thompson, A. 2004 (Celtic) 1
Thompson, P. 1964 (Liverpool) 16
Thompson, P. B. 1976 (Liverpool) 42
Thompson T. 1952 (Aston Villa, Preston NE) 2
Thomson, R. A. 1964 (Wolverhampton W) 8
Thornewell, G. 1923 (Derby Co) 4
Thornley, I. 1907 (Manchester C) 1
Tilson, S. F. 1934 (Manchester C) 4
Titmuss, F. 1922 (Southampton) 2
Todd, C. 1972 (Derby Co) 27
Tomori, O. O. (Fikayo) 2020 (Chelsea) 1
Toone, G. 1892 (Notts Co) 2
Topham, A. G. 1894 (Casuals) 1
Topham, R. 1893 (Wolverhampton W, Casuals) 2
Towers, M. A. 1976 (Sunderland) 3
Townley, W. J. 1889 (Blackburn R) 2
Townrow, J. E. 1925 (Clapton Orient) 2
Townsend, A. D. 2013 (Tottenham H, Newcastle U, Crystal Palace) 13
Tremelling, D. R. 1928 (Birmingham) 1
Tresadern, J. 1923 (West Ham U) 2
Trippier, K. J. 2017 (Tottenham H, Atletico Madrid) 33
Tueart, D. 1975 (Manchester C) 6
Tunstall, F. E. 1923 (Sheffield U) 7
Turnbull, R. J. 1920 (Bradford) 1
Turner, A. 1900 (Southampton) 2
Turner, H. 1931 (Huddersfield T) 2
Turner, J. A. 1893 (Bolton W, Stoke, Derby Co) 3
Tweedy, G. J. 1937 (Grimsby T) 1

Ufton, D. G. 1954 (Charlton Ath) 1
Underwood, A. 1891 (Stoke C) 2
Unsworth, D. G. 1995 (Everton) 1
Upson, M. J. 2003 (Birmingham C, West Ham U) 21
Urwin, T. 1923 (Middlesbrough, Newcastle U) 4
Utley, G. 1913 (Barnsley) 1

Vardy, J. R. 2015 (Leicester C) 26
Vassell, D. 2002 (Aston Villa) 22
Vaughton, O. H. 1882 (Aston Villa) 5
Veitch, C. C. M. 1906 (Newcastle U) 6
Veitch, J. G. 1894 (Old Westminsters) 1
Venables, T. F. 1965 (Chelsea) 2
Venison, B. 1995 (Newcastle U) 2
Vidal, R. W. S. 1873 (Oxford University) 1
Viljoen, C. 1975 (Ipswich T) 2
Viollet, D. S. 1960 (Manchester U) 2
Von Donop 1873 (Royal Engineers) 2

Wace, H. 1878 (Wanderers) 3
Waddle, C. R. 1985 (Newcastle U, Tottenham H, Marseille) 62
Wadsworth, S. J. 1922 (Huddersfield T) 9
Wainscoat, W. R. 1929 (Leeds U) 1
Waiters, A. K. 1964 (Blackpool) 5
Walcott, T. J. 2006 (Arsenal) 47
Walden, F. I. 1914 (Tottenham H) 2
Walker, D. S. 1989 (Nottingham F, Sampdoria, Sheffield W) 59
Walker, I. M. 1996 (Tottenham H, Leicester C) 4
Walker, K. A. 2012 (Tottenham H, Manchester C) 61
Walker, W. H. 1921 (Aston Villa) 18
Wall, G. 1907 (Manchester U) 7
Wallace, C. W. 1913 (Aston Villa) 3
Wallace, D. L. 1986 (Southampton) 1
Walsh, P. A. 1983 (Luton T) 5
Walters, A. M. 1885 (Cambridge University, Old Carthusians) 9
Walters, K. M. 1991 (Rangers) 1
Walters, P. M. 1885 (Oxford University, Old Carthusians) 13
Walton, N. 1890 (Blackburn R) 1
Ward, J. T. 1885 (Blackburn Olympic) 1
Ward, P. 1980 (Brighton & HA) 1
Ward, T. V. 1948 (Derby Co) 2
Ward-Prowse, J. M. E. 2017 (Southampton) 8
Waring, T. 1931 (Aston Villa) 5
Warner, C. 1878 (Upton Park) 1
Warnock, S. 2008 (Blackburn R, Aston Villa) 2
Warren, B. 1906 (Derby Co, Chelsea) 22
Waterfield, G. S. 1927 (Burnley) 1
Watkins, O. G. A. 2021 (Aston Villa) 3
Watson, D. 1984 (Norwich C, Everton) 12
Watson, D. V. 1974 (Sunderland, Manchester C, Werder Bremen, Southampton, Stoke C) 65
Watson, V. M. 1923 (West Ham U) 5
Watson, W. 1913 (Burnley) 3
Watson, W. 1950 (Sunderland) 4
Weaver, S. 1932 (Newcastle U) 3
Webb, G. W. 1911 (West Ham U) 2
Webb, N. J. 1988 (Nottingham F, Manchester U) 26
Webster, M. 1930 (Middlesbrough) 3
Wedlock, W. J. 1907 (Bristol C) 26
Weir, D. 1889 (Bolton W) 2
Welbeck, D. N. T. M. 2011 (Manchester U, Arsenal) 42
Welch, R. de C. 1872 (Wanderers, Harrow Chequers) 2
Weller, K. 1974 (Leicester C) 4
Welsh, D. 1938 (Charlton Ath) 3
West, G. 1969 (Everton) 3
Westwood, R. W. 1935 (Bolton W) 6
Whateley, O. 1883 (Aston Villa) 2
Wheeler, J. E. 1955 (Bolton W) 1
Wheldon, G. F. 1897 (Aston Villa) 4
White, B. W. 2021 (Brighton & HA) 2
White, D. 1993 (Manchester C) 1
White, T. A. 1933 (Everton) 1
Whitehead, J. 1893 (Accrington, Blackburn R) 2
Whitfeld, H. 1879 (Old Etonians) 1
Whitham, M. 1892 (Sheffield U) 1
Whitworth, S. 1975 (Leicester C) 7
Whymark, T. J. 1978 (Ipswich T) 1
Widdowson, S. W. 1880 (Nottingham F) 1
Wignall, F. 1965 (Nottingham F) 2
Wilcox, J. M. 1996 (Blackburn R, Leeds U) 3
Wilkes, A. 1901 (Aston Villa) 5
Wilkins, R. C. 1976 (Chelsea, Manchester U, AC Milan) 84
Wilkinson, B. 1904 (Sheffield U) 1
Wilkinson, L. R. 1891 (Oxford University) 1

Williams, B. F. 1949 (Wolverhampton W) 24
Williams, O. 1923 (Clapton Orient) 2
Williams, S. 1983 (Southampton) 6
Williams, W. 1897 (WBA) 6
Williamson, E. C. 1923 (Arsenal) 2
Williamson, R. G. 1905 (Middlesbrough) 7
Willingham, C. K. 1937 (Huddersfield T) 12
Willis, A. 1952 (Tottenham H) 1
Wilshaw, D. J. 1954 (Wolverhampton W) 12
Wilshere, J. A. 2011 (Arsenal) 34
Wilson, C. 2019 (Bournemouth) 4
Wilson, C. P. 1884 (Hendon) 2
Wilson, C. W. 1879 (Oxford University) 2
Wilson, G. 1921 (Sheffield W) 12
Wilson, G. P. 1900 (Corinthians) 2
Wilson, R. 1960 (Huddersfield T, Everton) 63
Wilson, T. 1928 (Huddersfield T) 1
Winks, H. B. 2018 (Tottenham H) 10
Winckworth, W. N. 1892 (Old Westminsters) 2
Windridge, J. E. 1908 (Chelsea) 8
Wingfield-Stratford, C. V. 1877 (Royal Engineers) 1
Winterburn, N. 1990 (Arsenal) 2
Wise, D. F. 1991 (Chelsea) 21
Withe, P. 1981 (Aston Villa) 11
Wollaston, C. H. R. 1874 (Wanderers) 4
Wolstenholme, S. 1904 (Everton, Blackburn R) 3
Wood, H. 1890 (Wolverhampton W) 3
Wood, R. E. 1955 (Manchester U) 3
Woodcock, A. S. 1978 (Nottingham F, Cologne, Arsenal) 42
Woodgate, J. S. 1999 (Leeds U, Newcastle U, Real Madrid, Tottenham H) 8
Woodger, G. 1911 (Oldham Ath) 1
Woodhall, G. 1888 (WBA) 2
Woodley, V. R. 1937 (Chelsea) 19
Woods, C. C. E. 1985 (Norwich C, Rangers, Sheffield W) 43
Woodward, V. J. 1903 (Tottenham H, Chelsea) 23
Woosnam, M. 1922 (Manchester C) 1
Worrall, F. 1935 (Portsmouth) 2
Worthington, F. S. 1974 (Leicester C) 8
Wreford-Brown, C. 1889 (Oxford University, Old Carthusians) 4
Wright, E. G. D. 1906 (Cambridge University) 1
Wright, I. E. 1991 (Crystal Palace, Arsenal, West Ham U) 33
Wright, J. D. 1939 (Newcastle U) 1
Wright, M. 1984 (Southampton, Derby Co, Liverpool) 45
Wright, R. I. 2000 (Ipswich T, Arsenal) 2
Wright, T. J. 1968 (Everton) 11
Wright, W. A. 1947 (Wolverhampton W) 105
Wright-Phillips, S. C. 2005 (Manchester C, Chelsea, Manchester C) 36
Wylie, J. G. 1878 (Wanderers) 1

Yates, J. 1889 (Burnley) 1
York, R. E. 1922 (Aston Villa) 2
Young, A. 1933 (Huddersfield T) 9
Young, A. S. 2008 (Aston Villa, Manchester U) 39
Young, G. M. 1965 (Sheffield W) 1
Young, L. P. 2005 (Charlton Ath) 7

Zaha, D. W. A. 2013 (Manchester U) 2
Zamora, R. L. 2011 (Fulham) 2

NORTHERN IRELAND

Addis, D. J. 1922 (Cliftonville) 1
Aherne, T. 1947 (Belfast Celtic, Luton T) 4
Alexander, T. E. 1895 (Cliftonville) 1
Allan, C. 1936 (Cliftonville) 1
Allen, J. 1887 (Limavady) 1
Anderson, J. 1925 (Distillery) 1
Anderson, T. 1973 (Manchester U, Swindon T, Peterborough U) 22
Anderson, W. 1898 (Linfield, Cliftonville) 4
Andrews, W. 1908 (Glentoran, Grimsby T) 3
Armstrong, G. J. 1977 (Tottenham H, Watford, Real Mallorca, WBA, Chesterfield) 63

Baird, C. P. 2003 (Southampton, Fulham, Reading, Burnley, WBA, Derby Co) 79
Baird, G. 1896 (Distillery) 3
Baird, H. C. 1939 (Huddersfield T) 1
Ballard, D. G. 2021 (Arsenal) 8
Balfe, J. 1909 (Shelbourne) 2
Bambrick, J. 1929 (Linfield, Chelsea) 11
Banks, S. J. 1937 (Cliftonville) 1
Barr, H. H. 1962 (Linfield, Coventry C) 3
Barron, J. H. 1894 (Cliftonville) 7
Barry, J. 1888 (Cliftonville) 3
Barry, J. 1900 (Bohemians) 1
Barton, A. J. 2011 (Preston NE) 1
Baxter, R. A. 1887 (Distillery) 1
Baxter, S. N. 1887 (Cliftonville) 1
Bennett, L. V. 1889 (Dublin University) 1
Best, G. 1964 (Manchester U, Fulham) 37
Bingham, W. L. 1951 (Sunderland, Luton T, Everton, Port Vale) 56
Black, K. T. 1988 (Luton T, Nottingham F) 30
Black, T. 1901 (Glentoran) 1
Blair, H. 1928 (Portadown, Swansea T) 4
Blair, J. 1907 (Cliftonville) 5
Blair, R. V. 1975 (Oldham Ath) 5
Blanchflower, J. 1954 (Manchester U) 12
Blanchflower, R. D. 1950 (Barnsley, Aston Villa, Tottenham H) 56
Blayney, A. 2006 (Doncaster R, Linfield) 5
Bookman, L. J. O. 1914 (Bradford C, Luton T) 4
Bothwell, A. W. 1926 (Ards) 5
Bowler, G. C. 1950 (Hull C) 3
Boyce, L. 2011 (Werder Bremen, Ross Co, Burton Alb, Hearts) 28
Boyle, P. 1901 (Sheffield U) 5
Bradley, C. 2021 (Liverpool) 1
Braithwaite, R. M. 1962 (Linfield, Middlesbrough) 10
Braniff, K. R. 2010 (Portadown) 2
Breen, T. 1935 (Belfast Celtic, Manchester U) 9
Brennan, B. 1912 (Bohemians) 1
Brennan, R. A. 1949 (Luton T, Birmingham C, Fulham) 5
Briggs, W. R. 1962 (Manchester U, Swansea T) 2
Brisby, D. 1891 (Distillery) 1
Brolly, T. H. 1937 (Millwall) 4
Brookes, E. A. 1920 (Shelbourne) 1
Brotherston, N. 1980 (Blackburn R) 27
Brown, C. M. 2020 (Cardiff C) 4
Brown, J. 1921 (Glenavon, Tranmere R) 3
Brown, J. 1935 (Wolverhampton W, Coventry C, Birmingham C) 10
Brown, N. M. 1887 (Limavady) 1
Brown, W. G. 1926 (Glenavon) 1
Browne, F. 1887 (Cliftonville) 5
Browne, R. J. 1936 (Leeds U) 6
Bruce, A. 1925 (Belfast Celtic) 1
Bruce, A. S. 2013 (Hull C) 2
Bruce, W. 1961 (Glentoran) 2
Brunt, C. 2005 (Sheffield W, WBA) 65
Bryan, M. A. 2010 (Watford) 2
Buckle, H. R. 1903 (Cliftonville, Sunderland, Bristol R) 3
Buckle, J. 1882 (Cliftonville) 1
Burnett, J. 1894 (Distillery, Glentoran) 5
Burnison, J. 1901 (Distillery) 2
Burnison, S. 1908 (Distillery, Bradford, Distillery) 8
Burns, J. 1923 (Glenavon) 1
Burns, W. 1925 (Glentoran) 1
Butler, M. P. 1939 (Blackpool) 1

Camp, L. M. J. 2011 (Nottingham F) 9
Campbell, A. C. 1963 (Crusaders) 2
Campbell, D. A. 1986 (Nottingham F, Charlton Ath) 10
Campbell, James 1897 (Cliftonville) 14
Campbell, John 1896 (Cliftonville) 1
Campbell, J. P. 1951 (Fulham) 2
Campbell, R. M. 1982 (Bradford C) 2
Campbell, W. G. 1968 (Dundee) 6
Capaldi, A. C. 2004 (Plymouth Arg, Cardiff C) 22

Carey, J. J. 1947 (Manchester U) 7
Carroll, E. 1925 (Glenavon) 1
Carroll, R. E. 1997 (Wigan Ath, Manchester U, West Ham U, Olympiacos, Notts Co, Linfield) 45
Carson, J. G. 2011 (Ipswich T) 4
Carson, S. 2009 (Coleraine) 1
Carson, T. 2018 (Motherwell) 6
Casement, C. 2009 (Ipswich T) 1
Casey, T. 1955 (Newcastle U, Portsmouth) 12
Caskey, W. 1979 (Derby Co, Tulsa Roughnecks) 8
Cassidy, T. 1971 (Newcastle U, Burnley) 24
Cathcart, C. G. 2011 (Blackpool, Watford) 61
Caughey, M. 1986 (Linfield) 2
Chambers, R. J. 1921 (Distillery, Bury, Nottingham F) 12
Charles, D. E. R. (Accrington S) 3
Chatton, H. A. 1925 (Partick Thistle) 3
Christian, J. 1889 (Linfield) 1
Clarke, C. J. 1986 (Bournemouth, Southampton, QPR, Portsmouth) 38
Clarke, R. 1901 (Belfast Celtic) 2
Cleary, J. 1982 (Glentoran) 5
Clements, D. 1965 (Coventry C, Sheffield W, Everton, New York Cosmos) 48
Clingan, S. G. 2006 (Nottingham F, Norwich C, Coventry C, Kilmarnock) 39
Clugston, J. 1888 (Cliftonville) 14
Clyde, M. G. 2005 (Wolverhampton W) 3
Coates, C. 2009 (Crusaders) 6
Cochrane, D. 1939 (Leeds U) 12
Cochrane, G. 1903 (Cliftonville) 1
Cochrane, G. T. 1976 (Coleraine, Burnley, Middlesbrough, Gillingham) 26
Cochrane, M. 1898 (Distillery, Leicester Fosse) 8
Collins, F. 1922 (Celtic) 1
Collins, R. 1922 (Cliftonville) 1
Condy, J. 1882 (Distillery) 3
Connell, T. E. 1978 (Coleraine) 1
Connor, J. 1901 (Glentoran, Belfast Celtic) 13
Connor, M. J. 1903 (Brentford, Fulham) 3
Cook, W. 1933 (Celtic, Everton) 15
Cooke, S. 1889 (Belfast YMCA, Cliftonville) 3
Coote, A. 1999 (Norwich C) 6
Coulter, J. 1934 (Belfast Celtic, Everton, Grimsby T, Chelmsford C) 11
Cowan, J. 1970 (Newcastle U) 1
Cowan, T. S. 1925 (Queen's Island) 1
Coyle, F. 1956 (Coleraine, Nottingham F) 4
Coyle, L. 1989 (Derry C) 1
Coyle, R. I. 1973 (Sheffield W) 5
Craig, A. B. 1908 (Rangers, Morton) 9
Craig, D. J. 1967 (Newcastle U) 25
Craigan, S. J. 2003 (Partick Thistle, Motherwell) 54
Crawford, A. 1889 (Distillery, Cliftonville) 7
Croft, T. 1922 (Queen's Island) 3
Crone, R. 1889 (Distillery) 4
Crone, W. 1882 (Distillery) 12
Crooks, W. J. 1922 (Manchester U) 1
Crossan, E. 1950 (Blackburn R) 3
Crossan, J. A. 1960 (Sparta-Rotterdam, Sunderland, Manchester C, Middlesbrough) 24
Crothers, C. 1907 (Distillery) 1
Cumming, L. 1929 (Huddersfield T, Oldham Ath) 3
Cunningham, W. 1892 (Ulster) 4
Cunningham, W. E. 1951 (St Mirren, Leicester C, Dunfermline Ath) 30
Curran, S. 1926 (Belfast Celtic) 4
Curran, J. J. 1922 (Glenavon, Pontypridd, Glenavon) 5
Cush, W. W. 1951 (Glenavon, Leeds U, Portadown) 26

Dallas, S. A. 2011 (Crusaders, Brentford, Leeds U) 56
Dalrymple, J. 1922 (Distillery) 1
Dalton, W. 1888 (YMCA, Linfield) 11
D'Arcy, S. D. 1952 (Chelsea, Brentford) 5
Darling, J. 1897 (Linfield) 22
Davey, H. H. 1926 (Reading, Portsmouth) 5
Davis, S. 2005 (Aston Villa, Fulham, Rangers, Southampton, Rangers) 126
Davis, T. L. 1937 (Oldham Ath) 1
Davison, A. J. 1996 (Bolton W, Bradford C, Grimsby T) 3
Davison, J. R. 1882 (Cliftonville) 8
Dennison, R. 1988 (Wolverhampton W) 18
Devine, A. O. 1886 (Limavady) 4
Devine, J. 1990 (Glentoran) 1
Dickson, D. 1970 (Coleraine) 4
Dickson, T. A. 1957 (Linfield) 1
Dickson, W. 1951 (Chelsea, Arsenal) 12
Diffin, W. J. 1931 (Belfast Celtic) 1
Dill, A. H. 1882 (Knock, Down Ath, Cliftonville) 9
Doherty, I. 1901 (Belfast Celtic) 1
Doherty, J. 1928 (Portadown) 1
Doherty, J. 1933 (Cliftonville) 2
Doherty, L. 1985 (Linfield) 2
Doherty, M. 1938 (Derry C) 1
Doherty, P. D. 1935 (Blackpool, Manchester C, Derby Co, Huddersfield T, Doncaster R) 16
Doherty, T. E. 2003 (Bristol C) 9
Donaghey, B. 1903 (Belfast Celtic) 1
Donaghy, M. M. 1980 (Luton T, Manchester U, Chelsea) 91
Donnelly, L. 1913 (Distillery) 1
Donnelly, L. F. P. 2014 (Fulham, Motherwell) 2
Donnelly, M. 2009 (Crusaders) 1
Doran, J. F. 1921 (Brighton) 3
Dougan, A. D. 1958 (Portsmouth, Blackburn R, Aston Villa, Leicester C, Wolverhampton W) 43
Douglas, J. P. 1947 (Belfast Celtic) 1
Dowd, H. O. 1974 (Glenavon, Sheffield W) 3
Dowie, I. 1990 (Luton T, West Ham U, Southampton, C Palace, West Ham U, QPR) 59
Duff, M. J. 2002 (Cheltenham T, Burnley) 24
Duggan, H. A. 1930 (Leeds U) 8
Dunlop, G. 1985 (Linfield) 4
Dunne, J. 1928 (Sheffield U) 7

Eames, W. L. E. 1885 (Dublin University) 3
Eglington, T. J. 1947 (Everton) 6
Elder, A. R. 1960 (Burnley, Stoke C) 40
Elleman, A. R. 1889 (Cliftonville) 2
Elliott, S. 2001 (Motherwell, Hull C) 39
Elwood, J. H. 1929 (Bradford) 2
Emerson, W. 1920 (Glentoran, Burnley) 11
English, S. 1933 (Rangers) 2
Enright, J. 1912 (Leeds C) 1
Evans, C. J. 2009 (Manchester U, Hull C, Blackburn R) 66
Evans, J. G. 2007 (Manchester U, WBA, Leicester C) 91

Falloon, E. 1931 (Aberdeen) 2
Farquharson, T. G. 1923 (Cardiff C) 7
Farrell, P. 1901 (Distillery) 2
Farrell, P. 1938 (Hibernian) 1
Farrell, P. D. 1947 (Everton) 7
Feeney, J. M. 1947 (Linfield, Swansea T) 2
Feeney, W. 1976 (Glentoran) 1
Feeney, W. J. 2002 (Bournemouth, Luton T, Cardiff C, Oldham Ath, Plymouth Arg) 46
Ferguson, G. 1999 (Linfield) 5
Ferguson, S. K. 2009 (Newcastle U, Millwall) 49
Ferguson, W. 1966 (Linfield) 2
Ferris, J. 1920 (Belfast Celtic, Chelsea, Belfast Celtic) 6
Ferris, R. O. 1950 (Birmingham C) 3
Fettis, A. W. 1992 (Hull C, Nottingham F, Blackburn R) 25
Finney, T. 1975 (Sunderland, Cambridge U) 14
Fitzpatrick, J. C. 1896 (Bohemians) 2
Flack, H. 1929 (Burnley) 1
Flanagan, T. M. 2017 (Burton Alb, Sunderland) 8
Fleming, J. G. 1987 (Nottingham F, Manchester C, Barnsley) 31
Forbes, G. 1888 (Limavady, Distillery) 3
Forde, J. T. 1959 (Ards) 4
Foreman, T. A. 1899 (Cliftonville) 1
Forsythe, J. 1888 (YMCA) 2
Fox, W. T. 1887 (Ulster) 2
Frame, T. 1925 (Linfield) 1
Fulton, R. P. 1928 (Larne, Belfast Celtic) 21

Gaffikin, G. 1890 (Linfield Ath) 15
Galbraith, E. S. W. (Manchester U) 2
Galbraith, W. 1890 (Distillery) 1
Gallagher, P. 1920 (Celtic, Falkirk) 11
Gallogly, C. 1951 (Huddersfield T) 2
Gara, A. 1902 (Preston NE) 3
Gardiner, A. 1930 (Cliftonville) 5

Garrett, J. 1925 (Distillery) 1
Garrett, R. 2009 (Linfield) 5
Gaston, R. 1969 (Oxford U) 1
Gaukrodger, G. 1895 (Linfield) 1
Gault, M. 2008 (Linfield) 1
Gaussen, A. D. 1884 (Moyola Park, Magherafelt) 6
Geary, J. 1931 (Glentoran) 2
Gibb, J. T. 1884 (Wellington Park, Cliftonville) 10
Gibb, T. J. 1936 (Cliftonville) 1
Gibson W. K. 1894 (Cliftonville) 14
Gillespie, K. R. 1995 (Manchester U, Newcastle U, Blackburn R, Leicester C, Sheffield U) 86
Gillespie, S. 1886 (Hertford) 6
Gillespie, W. 1889 (West Down) 1
Gillespie, W. 1913 (Sheffield U) 25
Goodall, A. L. 1899 (Derby Co, Glossop) 10
Goodbody, M. F. 1889 (Dublin University) 2
Gordon, H. 1895 (Linfield) 3
Gordon R. W. 1891 (Linfield) 7
Gordon, T. 1894 (Linfield) 2
Gorman, R. J. 2010 (Wolverhampton W) 9
Gorman, W. C. 1947 (Brentford) 4
Gough, J. 1925 (Queen's Island) 1
Gowdy, J. 1920 (Glentoran, Queen's Island, Falkirk) 6
Gowdy, W. A. 1932 (Hull C, Sheffield W, Linfield, Hibernian) 6
Graham, W. G. L. 1951 (Doncaster R) 14
Gray, P. 1993 (Luton T, Sunderland, Nancy, Luton T, Burnley, Oxford U) 26
Greer, W. 1909 (QPR) 3
Gregg, H. 1954 (Doncaster R, Manchester U) 25
Griffin, D. J. 1996 (St Johnstone, Dundee U, Stockport Co) 29
Grigg, W. D. 2012 (Walsall, Brentford, Milton Keynes D, Wigan Ath) 13

Hall, G. 1897 (Distillery) 1
Halligan, W. 1911 (Derby Co, Wolverhampton W) 2
Hamill, M. 1912 (Manchester U, Belfast Celtic, Manchester C) 7
Hamill, R. 1999 (Glentoran) 1
Hamilton, B. 1969 (Linfield, Ipswich T, Everton, Millwall, Swindon T) 50
Hamilton, G. 2003 (Portadown) 5
Hamilton, J. 1882 (Knock) 2
Hamilton, R. 1928 (Rangers) 5
Hamilton, W. D. 1885 (Dublin Association) 1
Hamilton, W. J. 1885 (Dublin Association) 1
Hamilton, W. J. 1908 (Distillery) 1
Hamilton, W. R. 1978 (QPR, Burnley, Oxford U) 41
Hampton, H. 1911 (Bradford C) 9
Hanna, J. 1912 (Nottingham F) 2
Hanna, J. D. 1899 (Royal Artillery, Portsmouth) 1
Hannon, D. J. 1908 (Bohemians) 6
Harkin, J. T. 1968 (Southport, Shrewsbury T) 5
Harland, A. I. 1922 (Linfield) 2
Harris, J. 1921 (Cliftonville, Glenavon) 2
Harris, V. 1906 (Shelbourne, Everton) 20
Harvey, M. 1961 (Sunderland) 34
Hastings, J. 1882 (Knock, Ulster) 7
Hatton, S. 1963 (Linfield) 2
Hayes, W. E. 1938 (Huddersfield T) 4
Hazard, C. 2018 (Celtic) 2
Healy, D. J. 2000 (Manchester U, Preston NE, Leeds U, Fulham, Sunderland, Rangers, Bury) 95
Healy, P. J. 1982 (Coleraine, Glentoran) 4
Hegan, D. 1970 (WBA, Wolverhampton W) 7
Henderson, J. 1885 (Ulster) 3
Hewison, G. 1885 (Moyola Park) 2
Hill, C. F. 1990 (Sheffield U, Leicester C, Trelleborg, Northampton T) 27
Hill, M. J. 1959 (Norwich C, Everton) 7
Hinton, E. 1947 (Fulham, Millwall) 7
Hodson, L. J. S. 2011 (Watford, Milton Keynes D, Rangers) 24
Holmes, S. P. 2002 (Wrexham) 1
Hopkins, J. 1926 (Brighton) 1
Horlock, K. 1995 (Swindon T, Manchester C) 32
Houston, J. 1912 (Linfield, Everton) 6
Houston, W. 1933 (Linfield) 1
Houston, W. J. 1885 (Moyola Park) 2
Hughes, A. W. 1998 (Newcastle U, Aston Villa, Fulham, QPR, Brighton & HA, Melbourne C, Kerala Blasters, Hearts) 112
Hughes, J. 2006 (Lincoln C) 2
Hughes, M. A. 2006 (Oldham Ath) 2
Hughes, M. E. 1992 (Manchester C, Strasbourg, West Ham U, Wimbledon, Crystal Palace) 71
Hughes, P. A. 1987 (Bury) 3
Hughes, W. 1951 (Bolton W) 1
Humphries, W. M. 1962 (Ards, Coventry C, Swansea T) 14
Hunter, A. 1905 (Distillery, Belfast Celtic) 8
Hunter, A. 1970 (Blackburn R, Ipswich T) 53
Hunter, B. V. 1995 (Wrexham, Reading) 15
Hunter, R. J. 1884 (Cliftonville) 3
Hunter, V. 1962 (Coleraine) 2

Ingham, M. G. 2005 (Sunderland, Wrexham) 3
Irvine, R. J. 1962 (Linfield, Stoke C) 8
Irvine, R. W. 1922 (Everton, Portsmouth, Connah's Quay, Derry C) 15
Irvine, W. J. 1963 (Burnley, Preston NE, Brighton & HA) 23
Irving, S. J. 1923 (Dundee, Cardiff C, Chelsea) 18

Jackson, T. A. 1969 (Everton, Nottingham F, Manchester U) 35
Jamison, J. 1976 (Glentoran) 1
Jenkins, I. 1997 (Chester C, Dundee U) 6
Jennings, P. A. 1964 (Watford, Tottenham H, Arsenal, Tottenham H) 119
Johnson, D. M. 1999 (Blackburn R, Birmingham C) 56
Johnston, H. 1927 (Portadown) 1
Johnston, R. S. 1882 (Distillery) 5
Johnston, R. S. 1905 (Distillery) 1
Johnston, S. 1890 (Linfield) 4
Johnston, W. 1885 (Oldpark) 2
Johnston, W. C. 1962 (Glenavon, Oldham Ath) 2
Jones, J. 1930 (Linfield, Hibernian, Glenavon) 23
Jones, J. 1956 (Glenavon) 3
Jones, J. L. 2018 (Kilmarnock, Rangers) 12
Jones, S. 1934 (Distillery, Blackpool) 2
Jones, S. G. 2003 (Crewe Alex, Burnley) 29
Jordan, T. 1895 (Linfield) 2

Kavanagh, P. J. 1930 (Celtic) 1
Keane, T. R. 1949 (Swansea T) 1
Kearns, A. 1900 (Distillery) 6
Kee, P. V. 1990 (Oxford U, Ards) 9
Keith, R. M. 1958 (Newcastle U) 23
Kelly, H. R. 1950 (Fulham, Southampton) 4
Kelly, J. 1896 (Glentoran) 1
Kelly, J. 1932 (Derry C) 11
Kelly, P. J. 1921 (Manchester C) 1
Kelly, P. M. 1950 (Barnsley) 1
Kennedy, A. L. 1923 (Arsenal) 2
Kennedy, M. 2021 (Aberdeen) 3
Kennedy, P. H. 1999 (Watford, Wigan Ath) 20
Kernaghan, N. 1936 (Belfast Celtic) 3
Kirk, A. R. 2000 (Hearts, Boston U, Northampton T, Dunfermline Ath) 11
Kirkwood, H. 1904 (Cliftonville) 1
Kirwan, J. 1900 (Tottenham H, Chelsea, Clyde) 17

Lacey, W. 1909 (Everton, Liverpool, New Brighton) 23
Lafferty, D. P. 2012 (Burnley) 13
Lafferty, K. 2006 (Burnley, Rangers, Sion, Palermo, Norwich C, Hearts, Rangers, Kilmarnock) 83
Lavery, S. F. 2018 (Everton, Linfield) 7
Lawrie, J. 2009 (Port Vale) 3
Lawther, R. 1888 (Glentoran) 2
Lawther, W. I. 1960 (Sunderland, Blackburn R) 4
Leatham, J. 1939 (Belfast Celtic) 1
Ledwidge, J. J. 1906 (Shelbourne) 2
Lemon, J. 1886 (Glentoran, Belfast YMCA) 3
Lennon, N. F. 1994 (Crewe Alex, Leicester C, Celtic) 40
Leslie, W. 1887 (YMCA) 1
Lewis, J. 1899 (Glentoran, Distillery) 4
Lewis, J. P. 2018 (Norwich C, Newcastle U) 20
Little, A. 2009 (Rangers) 9
Lockhart, H. 1884 (Rossall School) 1

Lockhart, N. H. 1947 (Linfield, Coventry C, Aston Villa) 8
Lomas, S. M. 1994 (Manchester C, West Ham U) 45
Loyal, J. 1891 (Clarence) 1
Lund, M. C. 2017 (Rochdale) 3
Lutton, R. J. 1970 (Wolverhampton W, West Ham U) 6
Lynas, R. 1925 (Cliftonville) 1
Lyner, D. R. 1920 (Glentoran, Manchester U, Kilmarnock) 6
Lytle, J. 1898 (Glentoran) 1

Madden, O. 1938 (Norwich C) 1
Magee, G. 1885 (Wellington Park) 3
Magennis, J. B. D. 2010 (Cardiff C, Aberdeen, St Mirren, Kilmarnock, Charlton Ath, Bolton W, Hull C) 61
Magill, E. J. 1962 (Arsenal, Brighton & HA) 26
Magilton, J. 1991 (Oxford U, Southampton, Sheffield W, Ipswich T) 52
Maginnis, H. 1900 (Linfield) 8
Mahood, J. 1926 (Belfast Celtic, Ballymena) 9
Mannus, A. 2004 (Linfield, St Johnstone) 9
Manderson, R. 1920 (Rangers) 5
Mansfield, J. 1901 (Dublin Freebooters) 1
Martin, C. 1882 (Cliftonville) 3
Martin, C. 1925 (Bo'ness) 1
Martin, C. J. 1947 (Glentoran, Leeds U, Aston Villa) 6
Martin, D. K. 1934 (Belfast Celtic, Wolverhampton W, Nottingham F) 10
Mathieson, A. 1921 (Luton T) 2
Maxwell, J. 1902 (Linfield, Glentoran, Belfast Celtic) 7
McAdams, W. J. 1954 (Manchester C, Bolton W, Leeds U) 15
McAlery, J. M. 1882 (Cliftonville) 2
McAlinden, J. 1938 (Belfast Celtic, Portsmouth, Southend U) 4
McAllen, J. 1898 (Linfield) 9
McAlpine, S. 1901 (Cliftonville) 1
McArdle, R. A. 2010 (Rochdale, Aberdeen, Bradford C) 7
McArthur, A. 1886 (Distillery) 1
McAuley, G. 2005 (Lincoln C, Leicester C, Ipswich T, WBA, Rangers) 80
McAuley, J. L. 1911 (Huddersfield T) 6
McAuley, P. 1900 (Belfast Celtic) 1
McBride, S. D. 1991 (Glenavon) 4
McCabe, J. J. 1949 (Leeds U) 6
McCabe, W. 1891 (Ulster) 1
McCalmont, A. J. 2020 (Leeds U) 2
McCambridge, J. 1930 (Ballymena, Cardiff C) 4
McCandless, J. 1912 (Bradford) 5
McCandless, W. 1920 (Linfield, Rangers) 9
McCann, A. 2021 (St Johnstone) 6
McCann, G. S. 2002 (West Ham U, Cheltenham T, Barnsley, Scunthorpe U, Peterborough U) 39
McCann, P. 1910 (Belfast Celtic, Glentoran) 7
McCartan, S. V. 2017 (Accrington S, Bradford C) 2
McCarthy, J. D. 1996 (Port Vale, Birmingham C) 18
McCartney, A. 1903 (Ulster, Linfield, Everton, Belfast Celtic, Glentoran) 15
McCartney, G. 2002 (Sunderland, West Ham U, Sunderland) 34
McCashin, J. W. 1896 (Cliftonville) 5
McCavana, W. T. 1955 (Coleraine) 3
McCaw, J. H. 1927 (Linfield) 6
McClatchey, J. 1886 (Distillery) 3
McClatchey, T. 1895 (Distillery) 1
McCleary, J. W. 1955 (Cliftonville) 1
McCleery, W. 1922 (Cliftonville, Linfield) 10
McClelland, J. 1980 (Mansfield T, Rangers, Watford, Leeds U) 53
McClelland, J. T. 1961 (Arsenal, Fulham) 6
McClelland, S. 2021 (Chelsea) 1
McCluggage, A. 1922 (Cliftonville, Bradford, Burnley) 13
McClure, G. 1907 (Cliftonville, Distillery) 4
McConnell, E. 1904 (Cliftonville, Glentoran, Sunderland, Sheffield W) 12
McConnell, P. 1928 (Doncaster R, Southport) 2
McConnell, W. G. 1912 (Bohemians) 6
McConnell, W. H. 1925 (Reading) 8
McCourt, F. J. 1952 (Manchester C) 6
McCourt, P. J. 2002 (Rochdale, Celtic, Barnsley, Brighton & HA, Luton T) 18
McCoy, R. K. 1987 (Coleraine) 1
McCoy, S. 1896 (Distillery) 1
McCracken, E. 1928 (Barking) 1
McCracken, R. 1921 (Crystal Palace) 4
McCracken, R. 1922 (Linfield) 1
McCracken, W. R. 1902 (Distillery, Newcastle U, Hull C) 16
McCreery, D. 1976 (Manchester U, QPR, Tulsa Roughnecks, Newcastle U, Hearts) 67
McCrory, S. 1958 (Southend U) 1
McCullough, K. 1935 (Belfast Celtic, Manchester C) 5
McCullough, L. 2014 (Doncaster R) 6
McCullough, W. J. 1961 (Arsenal, Millwall) 10
McCurdy, C. 1980 (Linfield) 1
McDonald, A. 1986 (QPR) 52
McDonald, R. 1930 (Rangers) 2
McDonnell, J. 1911 (Bohemians) 4
McElhinney, G. M. A. 1984 (Bolton W) 6
McEvilly, L. R. 2002 (Rochdale) 1
McFaul, W. S. 1967 (Linfield, Newcastle U) 6
McGarry, J. K. 1951 (Cliftonville) 3
McGaughey, M. 1985 (Linfield) 1
McGibbon, P. C. G. 1995 (Manchester U, Wigan Ath) 7
McGinn, N. 2009 (Celtic, Aberdeen, Gwangju, Aberdeen) 65
McGivern, R. 2009 (Manchester C, Hibernian, Port Vale, Shrewsbury) 24
McGovern, M. 2010 (Ross Co, Hamilton A, Norwich C) 33
McGrath, R. C. 1974 (Tottenham H, Manchester U) 21
McGregor, S. 1921 (Glentoran) 1
McGrillen, J. 1924 (Clyde, Belfast Celtic) 2
McGuire, E. 1907 (Distillery) 1
McGuire, J. 1928 (Linfield) 1
McIlroy, H. 1906 (Cliftonville) 1
McIlroy, J. 1952 (Burnley, Stoke C) 55
McIlroy, S. B. 1972 (Manchester U, Stoke C, Manchester C) 88
McIlvenny, P. 1924 (Distillery) 1
McIlvenny, R. 1890 (Distillery, Ulster) 2
McKay, W. R. 2013 (Inverness CT, Wigan Ath) 11
McKeag, W. 1968 (Glentoran) 2
McKeague, T. 1925 (Glentoran) 1
McKee, F. W. 1906 (Cliftonville, Belfast Celtic) 5
McKelvey, H. 1901 (Glentoran) 2
McKenna, J. 1950 (Huddersfield T) 7
McKenzie, H. 1922 (Distillery) 2
McKenzie, R. 1967 (Airdrieonians) 1
McKeown, N. 1892 (Linfield) 7
McKie, H. 1895 (Cliftonville) 3
Mackie, J. A. 1923 (Arsenal, Portsmouth) 3
McKinney, D. 1921 (Hull C, Bradford C) 2
McKinney, V. J. 1966 (Falkirk) 1
McKnight, A. D. 1988 (Celtic, West Ham U) 10
McKnight, J. 1912 (Preston NE, Glentoran) 2
McLaughlin, C. G. 2012 (Preston NE, Fleetwood T, Millwall, Sunderland) 43
McLaughlin, J. C. 1962 (Shrewsbury T, Swansea T) 12
McLaughlin, R. 2014 (Liverpool, Oldham Ath) 5
McLean, B. S. 2006 (Rangers) 1
McLean, T. 1885 (Limavady) 1
McMahon, G. J. 1995 (Tottenham H, Stoke C) 17
McMahon, J. 1934 (Bohemians) 1
McMaster, G. 1897 (Glentoran) 3
McMichael, A. 1950 (Newcastle U) 40
McMillan, G. 1903 (Distillery) 2
McMillan, S. T. 1963 (Manchester U) 2
McMillen, W. S. 1934 (Manchester U, Chesterfield) 7
McMordie, A. S. 1969 (Middlesbrough) 21
McMorran, E. J. 1947 (Belfast Celtic, Barnsley, Doncaster R) 15
McMullan, D. 1926 (Liverpool) 3
McNair, P. J. C. 2015 (Manchester U, Sunderland, Middlesbrough) 47
McNally, B. A. 1986 (Shrewsbury T) 5
McNinch, J. 1931 (Ballymena) 3
McPake, J. 2012 (Coventry C) 1
McParland, P. J. 1954 (Aston Villa, Wolverhampton W) 34
McQuoid, J. J. B. 2011 (Millwall) 5
McShane, J. 1899 (Cliftonville) 4
McVeigh, P. M. 1999 (Tottenham H, Norwich C) 20

McVicker, J. 1888 (Linfield, Glentoran) 2
McWha, W. B. R. 1882 (Knock, Cliftonville) 7
Meek, H. L. 1925 (Glentoran) 1
Mehaffy, J. A. C. 1922 (Queen's Island) 1
Meldon, P. A. 1899 (Dublin Freebooters) 2
Mercer, H. V. A. 1908 (Linfield) 1
Mercer, J. T. 1898 (Distillery, Linfield, Distillery, Derby Co) 12
Millar, W. 1932 (Barrow) 2
Miller, J. 1929 (Middlesbrough) 3
Milligan, D. 1939 (Chesterfield) 1
Milne, R. G. 1894 (Linfield) 28
Mitchell, E. J. 1933 (Cliftonville, Glentoran) 2
Mitchell, W. 1932 (Distillery, Chelsea) 15
Molyneux, T. B. 1883 (Ligoniel, Cliftonville) 11
Montgomery, F. J. 1955 (Coleraine) 1
Moore, C. 1949 (Glentoran) 1
Moore, P. 1933 (Aberdeen) 1
Moore, R. 1891 (Linfield Ath) 3
Moore, R. L. 1887 (Ulster) 2
Moore, W. 1923 (Falkirk) 1
Moorhead, F. W. 1885 (Dublin University) 1
Moorhead, G. 1923 (Linfield) 4
Moran, J. 1912 (Leeds C) 1
Moreland, V. 1979 (Derby Co) 6
Morgan, G. F. 1922 (Linfield, Nottingham F) 8
Morgan, S. 1972 (Port Vale, Aston Villa, Brighton & HA, Sparta Rotterdam) 18
Morrison, R. 1891 (Linfield Ath) 2
Morrison, T. 1895 (Glentoran, Burnley) 7
Morrogh, D. 1896 (Bohemians) 1
Morrow, S. J. 1990 (Arsenal, QPR) 39
Morrow, W. J. 1883 (Moyola Park) 3
Muir, R. 1885 (Oldpark) 2
Mulgrew, J. 2010 (Linfield) 2
Mulholland, T. S. 1906 (Belfast Celtic) 2
Mullan, G. 1983 (Glentoran) 4
Mulligan, J. 1921 (Manchester C) 1
Mulryne, P. P. 1997 (Manchester U, Norwich C, Cardiff C) 27
Murdock, C. J. 2000 (Preston NE, Hibernian, Crewe Alex, Rotherham U) 34
Murphy, J. 1910 (Bradford C) 3
Murphy, N. 1905 (QPR) 3
Murray, J. M. 1910 (Motherwell, Sheffield W) 3

Napier, R. J. 1966 (Bolton W) 1
Neill, W. J. T. 1961 (Arsenal, Hull C) 59
Nelis, P. 1923 (Nottingham F) 1
Nelson, S. 1970 (Arsenal, Brighton & HA) 51
Nicholl, C. J. 1975 (Aston Villa, Southampton, Grimsby T) 51
Nicholl, H. 1902 (Belfast Celtic) 3
Nicholl, J. M. 1976 (Manchester U, Toronto Blizzard, Sunderland, Toronto Blizzard, Rangers, Toronto Blizzard, WBA) 73
Nicholson, J. J. 1961 (Manchester U, Huddersfield T) 41
Nixon, R. 1914 (Linfield) 1
Nolan, I. R. 1997 (Sheffield W, Bradford C, Wigan Ath) 18
Nolan-Whelan, J. V. 1901 (Dublin Freebooters) 5
Norwood, O. J. 2011 (Manchester U, Huddersfield T, Reading, Brighton & HA) 57

O'Boyle, G. 1994 (Dunfermline Ath, St Johnstone) 13
O'Brien, M. T. 1921 (QPR, Leicester C, Hull C, Derby Co) 10
O'Connell, P. 1912 (Sheffield W, Hull C) 5
O'Connor, M. J. 2008 (Crewe Alex, Scunthorpe U, Rotherham U) 11
O'Doherty, A. 1970 (Coleraine) 2
O'Driscoll, J. F. 1949 (Swansea T) 3
O'Hagan, C. 1905 (Tottenham H, Aberdeen) 11
O'Hagan, W. 1920 (St Mirren) 2
O'Hehir, J. C. 1910 (Bohemians) 1
O'Kane, W. J. 1970 (Nottingham F) 20
O'Mahoney, M. T. 1939 (Bristol R) 1
O'Neill, C. 1989 (Motherwell) 3
O'Neill, J. 1962 (Sunderland) 1
O'Neill, J. P. 1980 (Leicester C) 39
O'Neill, M. A. M. 1988 (Newcastle U, Dundee U, Hibernian, Coventry C) 31
O'Neill, M. H. M. 1972 (Distillery, Nottingham F, Norwich C, Manchester C, Norwich C, Notts Co) 64
O'Reilly, H. 1901 (Dublin Freebooters) 3
Owens, J. 2011 (Crusaders) 1

Parke, J. 1964 (Linfield, Hibernian, Sunderland) 14
Paterson, M. A. 2008 (Scunthorpe U, Burnley, Huddersfield T) 22
Paton, P. R. 2014 (Dundee U) 4
Patterson, D. J. 1994 (Crystal Palace, Luton T, Dundee U) 17
Patterson, R. 2010 (Coleraine, Plymouth Arg) 5
Peacock, R. 1952 (Celtic, Coleraine) 31
Peacock-Farrell, B. 2018 (Leeds U, Burnley) 23
Peden, J. 1887 (Linfield, Distillery) 24
Penney, S. 1985 (Brighton & HA) 17
Percy, J. C. 1889 (Belfast YMCA) 1
Platt, J. A. 1976 (Middlesbrough, Ballymena U, Coleraine) 23
Pollock, W. 1928 (Belfast Celtic) 1
Ponsonby, J. 1895 (Distillery) 9
Potts, R. M. C. 1883 (Cliftonville) 2
Priestley, T. J. M. 1933 (Coleraine, Chelsea) 2
Pyper, Jas. 1897 (Cliftonville) 7
Pyper, John 1897 (Cliftonville) 9
Pyper, M. 1932 (Linfield) 1

Quinn, J. M. 1985 (Blackburn R, Swindon T, Leicester C, Bradford C, West Ham U, Bournemouth, Reading) 46
Quinn, S. J. 1996 (Blackpool, WBA, Willem II, Sheffield W, Peterborough U, Northampton T) 50

Rafferty, P. 1980 (Linfield) 1
Ramsey, P. C. 1984 (Leicester C) 14
Rankine, J. 1883 (Alexander) 2
Rattray, D. 1882 (Avoniel) 3
Rea, R. 1901 (Glentoran) 1
Reeves, B. N. 2015 (Milton Keynes D) 2
Redmond, R. 1884 (Cliftonville) 1
Reid, G. H. 1923 (Cardiff C) 1
Reid, J. 1883 (Ulster) 6
Reid, S. E. 1934 (Derby Co) 3
Reid, W. 1931 (Hearts) 1
Reilly, M. M. 1900 (Portsmouth) 2
Renneville, W. T. J. 1910 (Leyton, Aston Villa) 4
Reynolds, J. 1890 (Distillery, Ulster) 5
Reynolds, R. 1905 (Bohemians) 1
Rice, P. J. 1969 (Arsenal) 49
Roberts, F. C. 1931 (Glentoran) 1
Robinson, P. 1920 (Distillery, Blackburn R) 2
Robinson, S. 1997 (Bournemouth, Luton T) 7
Rogan, A. 1988 (Celtic, Sunderland, Millwall) 18
Rollo, D. 1912 (Linfield, Blackburn R) 16
Roper, E. O. 1886 (Dublin University) 1
Rosbotham, A. 1887 (Cliftonville) 7
Ross, W. E. 1969 (Newcastle U) 1
Rowland, K. 1994 (West Ham U, QPR) 19
Rowley, R. W. M. 1929 (Southampton, Tottenham H) 6
Rushe, F. 1925 (Distillery) 1
Russell, A. 1947 (Linfield) 1
Russell, S. R. 1930 (Bradford C, Derry C) 3
Ryan, R. A. 1950 (WBA) 1

Sanchez, L. P. 1987 (Wimbledon) 3
Saville, G. A. 2018 (Millwall, Middlesbrough) 31
Scott, E. 1920 (Liverpool, Belfast Celtic) 31
Scott, J. 1958 (Grimsby) 2
Scott, J. E. 1901 (Cliftonville) 1
Scott, L. J. 1895 (Dublin University) 2
Scott, P. W. 1975 (Everton, York C, Aldershot) 10
Scott, T. 1894 (Cliftonville) 13
Scott, W. 1903 (Linfield, Everton, Leeds C) 25
Scraggs, M. J. 1921 (Glentoran) 2
Seymour, H. C. 1914 (Bohemians) 1
Seymour, J. 1907 (Cliftonville) 2
Shanks, T. 1903 (Woolwich Arsenal, Brentford) 3
Sharkey, P. G. 1976 (Ipswich T) 1
Sheehan, Dr G. 1899 (Bohemians) 3
Sheridan, J. 1903 (Everton, Stoke C) 6

Sherrard, J. 1885 (Limavady) 3
Sherrard, W. C. 1895 (Cliftonville) 3
Sherry, J. J. 1906 (Bohemians) 2
Shields, R. J. 1957 (Southampton) 1
Shiels, D. 2006 (Hibernian, Doncaster R, Kilmarnock) 14
Silo, M. 1888 (Belfast YMCA) 1
Simpson, W. J. 1951 (Rangers) 12
Sinclair, J. 1882 (Knock) 2
Slemin, J. C. 1909 (Bohemians) 1
Sloan, A. S. 1925 (London Caledonians) 1
Sloan, D. 1969 (Oxford U) 2
Sloan, H. A. de B. 1903 (Bohemians) 8
Sloan, J. W. 1947 (Arsenal) 1
Sloan, T. 1926 (Cardiff C, Linfield) 11
Sloan, T. 1979 (Manchester U) 3
Small, J. M. 1887 (Clarence, Cliftonville) 4
Smith, A. W. 2003 (Glentoran, Preston NE) 18
Smith, E. E. 1921 (Cardiff C) 4
Smith, J. E. 1901 (Distillery) 2
Smith, M. 2016 (Peterborough U, Hearts) 17
Smyth, P. P. 2018 (QPR) 3
Smyth, R. H. 1886 (Dublin University) 1
Smyth, S. 1948 (Wolverhampton W, Stoke C) 9
Smyth, W. 1949 (Distillery) 4
Snape, A. 1920 (Airdrieonians) 1
Sonner, D. J. 1998 (Ipswich T, Sheffield W, Birmingham C, Nottingham F, Peterborough U) 13
Spence, D. W. 1975 (Bury, Blackpool, Southend U) 29
Spencer, S. 1890 (Distillery) 6
Spiller, E. A. 1883 (Cliftonville) 5
Sproule, I. 2006 (Hibernian, Bristol C) 11
Stanfield, O. M. 1887 (Distillery) 30
Steele, A. 1926 (Charlton Ath, Fulham) 4
Steele, J. 2013 (New York Red Bulls) 3
Stevenson, A. E. 1934 (Rangers, Everton) 17
Stewart, A. 1967 (Glentoran, Derby Co) 7
Stewart, D. C. 1978 (Hull C) 1
Stewart, I. 1982 (QPR, Newcastle U) 31
Stewart, R. K. 1890 (St Columb's Court, Cliftonville) 11
Stewart, T. C. 1961 (Linfield) 1
Swan, S. 1899 (Linfield) 1

Taggart, G. P. 1990 (Barnsley, Bolton W, Leicester C) 51
Taggart, J. 1899 (Walsall) 1
Taylor, M. S. 1999 (Fulham, Birmingham C, unattached) 88
Thompson, A. L. 2011 (Watford) 2
Thompson, F. W. 1910 (Cliftonville, Linfield, Bradford C, Clyde) 12
Thompson, J. 1897 (Distillery) 1
Thompson, J. A. 2018 (Rangers, Blackpool, Stoke C) 16
Thompson, P. 2006 (Linfield, Stockport Co) 8
Thompson, R. 1928 (Queen's Island) 1
Thompson, W. 1889 (Belfast Ath) 1
Thunder, P. J. 1911 (Bohemians) 1
Todd, S. J. 1966 (Burnley, Sheffield W) 11
Toner, C. 2003 (Leyton Orient) 2
Toner, J. 1922 (Arsenal, St Johnstone) 8
Torrans, R. 1893 (Linfield) 1
Torrans, S. 1889 (Linfield) 26
Trainor, D. 1967 (Crusaders) 1
Tuffey, J. 2009 (Partick Thistle, Inverness CT) 8
Tully, C. P. 1949 (Celtic) 10
Turner, A. 1896 (Cliftonville) 1
Turner, E. 1896 (Cliftonville) 1
Turner, W. 1886 (Cliftonville) 3
Twomey, J. F. 1938 (Leeds U) 2

Uprichard, W. N. M. C. 1952 (Swindon T, Portsmouth) 18

Vassell, K. T. 2019 (Rotherham U) 2
Vernon, J. 1947 (Belfast Celtic, WBA) 17

Waddell, T. M. R. 1906 (Cliftonville) 1
Walker, J. 1955 (Doncaster R) 1
Walker, T. 1911 (Bury) 1
Walsh, D. J. 1947 (WBA) 9
Walsh, W. 1948 (Manchester C) 5
Ward, J. J. 2012 (Derby Co, Nottingham F) 35
Waring, J. 1899 (Cliftonville) 1
Warren, P. 1913 (Shelbourne) 2
Washington, C. J. 2016 (QPR, Sheffield U, Hearts, Charlton Ath) 29
Watson, J. 1883 (Ulster) 9
Watson, P. 1971 (Distillery) 1
Watson, T. 1926 (Cardiff C) 1
Wattie, J. 1899 (Distillery) 1
Webb, C. G. 1909 (Brighton & HA) 3
Webb, S. M. 2006 (Ross Co) 4
Weir, E. 1939 (Clyde) 1
Welsh, E. 1966 (Carlisle U) 4
Whiteside, N. 1982 (Manchester U, Everton) 38
Whiteside, T. 1891 (Distillery) 1
Whitfield, E. R. 1886 (Dublin University) 1
Whitley, Jeff 1997 (Manchester C, Sunderland, Cardiff C) 20
Whitley, Jim 1998 (Manchester C) 3
Whyte, G. 2019 (Oxford U, Cardiff C) 19
Williams, J. R. 1886 (Ulster) 2
Williams, M. S. 1999 (Chesterfield, Watford, Wimbledon, Stoke C, Wimbledon, Milton Keynes D) 36
Williams, P. A. 1991 (WBA) 1
Williamson, J. 1890 (Cliftonville) 3
Willighan, T. 1933 (Burnley) 2
Willis, G. 1906 (Linfield) 4
Wilson, D. J. 1987 (Brighton & HA, Luton T, Sheffield W) 24
Wilson, H. 1925 (Linfield) 2
Wilson, K. J. 1987 (Ipswich T, Chelsea, Notts Co, Walsall) 42
Wilson, M. 1884 (Distillery) 3
Wilson, R. 1888 (Cliftonville) 1
Wilson, S. J. 1962 (Glenavon, Falkirk, Dundee) 12
Wilton, J. M. 1888 (St Columb's Court, Cliftonville, St Columb's Court) 7
Winchester, C. 2011 (Oldham Ath) 1
Wood, T. J. 1996 (Walsall) 1
Worthington, N. 1984 (Sheffield W, Leeds U, Stoke C) 66
Wright, J. 1906 (Cliftonville) 6
Wright, T. J. 1989 (Newcastle U, Nottingham F, Manchester C) 31

Young, S. 1907 (Linfield, Airdrieonians, Linfield) 9

SCOTLAND

Adam, C. G. 2007 (Rangers, Blackpool, Liverpool, Stoke C) 26
Adams, C. Z. E. F. 2021 (Southampton) 7
Adams, J. 1889 (Hearts) 3
Agnew, W. B. 1907 (Kilmarnock) 3
Aird, J. 1954 (Burnley) 4
Aitken, A. 1901 (Newcastle U, Middlesbrough, Leicester Fosse) 14
Aitken, G. G. 1949 (East Fife, Sunderland) 8
Aitken, R. 1886 (Dumbarton) 2
Aitken, R. 1980 (Celtic, Newcastle U, St Mirren) 57
Aitkenhead, W. A. C. 1912 (Blackburn R) 1
Albiston, A. 1982 (Manchester U) 14
Alexander, D. 1894 (East Stirlingshire) 2
Alexander, G. 2002 (Preston NE, Burnley) 40
Alexander, N. 2006 (Cardiff C) 3
Allan, D. S. 1885 (Queen's Park) 3
Allan, G. 1897 (Liverpool) 1
Allan, H. 1902 (Hearts) 1
Allan, J. 1887 (Queen's Park) 2
Allan, T. 1974 (Dundee) 2
Ancell, R. F. D. 1937 (Newcastle U) 2
Anderson, A. 1933 (Hearts) 23
Anderson, F. 1874 (Clydesdale) 1
Anderson, G. 1901 (Kilmarnock) 1
Anderson, H. A. 1914 (Raith R) 1
Anderson, J. 1954 (Leicester C) 1
Anderson, K. 1896 (Queen's Park) 3
Anderson, R. 2003 (Aberdeen, Sunderland) 11
Anderson, W. 1882 (Queen's Park) 6
Andrews, P. 1875 (Eastern) 1
Anya, I. 2013 (Watford, Derby Co) 29

Archer, J. G. 2018 (Millwall) 1
Archibald, A. 1921 (Rangers) 8
Archibald, S. 1980 (Aberdeen, Tottenham H, Barcelona) 27

Armstrong, M. W. 1936 (Aberdeen) 3
Armstrong, S. 2017 (Celtic, Southampton) 28
Arnott, W. 1883 (Queen's Park) 14
Auld, J. R. 1887 (Third Lanark) 3
Auld, R. 1959 (Celtic) 3

Bain, S. 2018 (Celtic) 3
Baird, A. 1892 (Queen's Park) 2
Baird, D. 1890 (Hearts) 3
Baird, H. 1956 (Airdrieonians) 1
Baird, J. C. 1876 (Vale of Leven) 3
Baird, S. 1957 (Rangers) 7
Baird, W. U. 1897 (St Bernard) 1
Bannan, B. 2011 (Aston Villa, Crystal Palace, Sheffield W) 27
Bannon, E. J. 1980 (Dundee U) 11
Barbour, A. 1885 (Renton) 1
Bardsley, P. A. 2011 (Sunderland) 13
Barker, J. B. 1893 (Rangers) 2
Barr, D. 2009 (Falkirk) 1
Barrett, F. 1894 (Dundee) 2
Bates, D. 2019 (Hamburg) 4
Battles, B. 1901 (Celtic) 3
Battles, B. jun. 1931 (Hearts) 1
Bauld, W. 1950 (Hearts) 3
Baxter, J. C. 1961 (Rangers, Sunderland) 34
Baxter, R. D. 1939 (Middlesbrough) 3
Beattie, A. 1937 (Preston NE) 7
Beattie, C. 2006 (Celtic, WBA) 7
Beattie, R. 1939 (Preston NE) 1
Begbie, I. 1890 (Hearts) 4
Bell, A. 1912 (Manchester U) 1
Bell, C. 2011 (Kilmarnock) 1
Bell, J. 1890 (Dumbarton, Everton, Celtic) 10
Bell, M. 1901 (Hearts) 1
Bell, W. J. 1966 (Leeds U) 2
Bennett, A. 1904 (Celtic, Rangers) 11
Bennie, R. 1925 (Airdrieonians) 3
Bernard, P. R. J. 1995 (Oldham Ath) 2
Berra, C. D. 2008 (Hearts, Wolverhampton W, Ipswich T) 41
Berry, D. 1894 (Queen's Park) 3
Berry, W. H. 1888 (Queen's Park) 4
Bett, J. 1982 (Rangers, Lokeren, Aberdeen) 25
Beveridge, W. W. 1879 (Glasgow University) 3
Black, A. 1938 (Hearts) 3
Black, D. 1889 (Hurlford) 1
Black, E. 1988 (Metz) 2
Black, I. 2013 (Rangers) 1
Black, I. H. 1948 (Southampton) 1
Blackburn, J. E. 1873 (Royal Engineers) 1
Blacklaw, A. S. 1963 (Burnley) 3
Blackley, J. 1974 (Hibernian) 7
Blair, D. 1929 (Clyde, Aston Villa) 8
Blair, J. 1920 (Sheffield W, Cardiff C) 8
Blair, J. 1934 (Motherwell) 1
Blair, J. A. 1947 (Blackpool) 1
Blair, W. 1896 (Third Lanark) 1
Blessington, J. 1894 (Celtic) 4
Blyth, J. A. 1978 (Coventry C) 2
Bone, J. 1972 (Norwich C) 2
Booth, S. 1993 (Aberdeen, Borussia Dortmund, Twente) 21

Bowie, J. 1920 (Rangers) 2
Bowie, W. 1891 (Linthouse) 1
Bowman, D. 1992 (Dundee U) 6
Bowman, G. A. 1892 (Montrose) 1
Boyd, G. I. 2013 (Peterborough U, Hull C) 2
Boyd, J. M. 1934 (Newcastle U) 1
Boyd, K. 2006 (Rangers, Middlesbrough) 18
Boyd, R. 1889 (Mossend Swifts) 2
Boyd, T. 1991 (Motherwell, Chelsea, Celtic) 72
Boyd, W. G. 1931 (Clyde) 2
Bradshaw, T. 1928 (Bury) 1
Brand, R. 1961 (Rangers) 8
Brandon, T. 1896 (Blackburn R) 1
Brazil, A. 1980 (Ipswich T, Tottenham H) 13
Breckenridge, T. 1888 (Hearts) 1
Bremner, D. 1976 (Hibernian) 1
Bremner, W. J. 1965 (Leeds U) 54
Brennan, F. 1947 (Newcastle U) 7
Breslin, B. 1897 (Hibernian) 1
Brewster, G. 1921 (Everton) 1
Bridcutt, L. 2013 (Brighton & HA, Sunderland) 2
Broadfoot, K. 2009 (Rangers) 4
Brogan, J. 1971 (Celtic) 4
Brophy, E. 2019 (Kilmarnock) 1
Brown, A. 1890 (St Mirren) 2
Brown, A. 1904 (Middlesbrough) 1
Brown, A. D. 1950 (East Fife, Blackpool) 14
Brown, G. C. P. 1931 (Rangers) 19
Brown, H. 1947 (Partick Thistle) 3
Brown, J. B. 1939 (Clyde) 1
Brown, J. G. 1975 (Sheffield U) 1
Brown, R. 1884 (Dumbarton) 2
Brown, R. 1890 (Cambuslang) 1
Brown, R. 1947 (Rangers) 3
Brown, R. jun. 1885 (Dumbarton) 1
Brown, S. 2006 (Hibernian, Celtic) 55
Brown, W. D. F. 1958 (Dundee, Tottenham H) 28
Browning, J. 1914 (Celtic) 1
Brownlie, J. 1909 (Third Lanark) 16
Brownlie, J. 1971 (Hibernian) 7
Bruce, D. 1890 (Vale of Leven) 1
Bruce, R. F. 1934 (Middlesbrough) 1
Bryson, C. 2011 (Kilmarnock, Derby Co) 3
Buchan, M. M. 1972 (Aberdeen, Manchester U) 34
Buchanan, J. 1889 (Cambuslang) 1
Buchanan, J. 1929 (Rangers) 2
Buchanan, P. S. 1938 (Chelsea) 1
Buchanan, R. 1891 (Abercorn) 1
Buckley, P. 1954 (Aberdeen) 3
Buick, A. 1902 (Hearts) 2
Burchill, M. J. 2000 (Celtic) 6
Burke, C. 2006 (Rangers, Birmingham C) 7
Burke, O. J. 2016 (Nottingham F, RB Leipzig, WBA, Sheffield U) 13
Burley, C. W. 1995 (Chelsea, Celtic, Derby Co) 46
Burley, G. E. 1979 (Ipswich T) 11
Burns, F. 1970 (Manchester U) 1
Burns, K. 1974 (Birmingham C, Nottingham F) 20
Burns, T. 1981 (Celtic) 8
Busby, M. W. 1934 (Manchester C) 1

Cadden, C. 2018 (Motherwell) 2
Caddis, P. M. 2016 (Birmingham C) 1
Cairney, T. 2017 (Fulham) 2
Cairns, T. 1920 (Rangers) 8
Calderhead, D. 1889 (Q of S Wanderers) 1
Calderwood, C. 1995 (Tottenham H) 36
Calderwood, R. 1885 (Cartvale) 3
Caldow, E. 1957 (Rangers) 40
Caldwell, G. 2002 (Newcastle U, Hibernian, Celtic, Wigan Ath) 55
Caldwell, S. 2001 (Newcastle U, Sunderland, Burnley,Wigan Ath) 12
Callaghan, P. 1900 (Hibernian) 1
Callaghan, W. 1970 (Dunfermline Ath) 2
Cameron, C. 1999 (Hearts, Wolverhampton W) 28
Cameron, J. 1886 (Rangers) 1
Cameron, J. 1896 (Queen's Park) 1
Cameron, J. 1904 (St Mirren, Chelsea) 2
Campbell, C. 1874 (Queen's Park) 13
Campbell, H. 1889 (Renton) 1
Campbell, Jas 1913 (Sheffield W) 1
Campbell, J. 1880 (South Western) 1
Campbell, J. 1891 (Kilmarnock) 2
Campbell, John 1893 (Celtic) 12
Campbell, John 1899 (Rangers) 4
Campbell, K. 1920 (Liverpool, Partick Thistle) 8
Campbell, P. 1878 (Rangers) 2
Campbell, P. 1898 (Morton) 1
Campbell, R. 1947 (Falkirk, Chelsea) 5
Campbell, W. 1947 (Morton) 5
Canero, P. 2004 (Leicester C) 1
Carabine, J. 1938 (Third Lanark) 3
Carr, W. M. 1970 (Coventry C) 6
Cassidy, J. 1921 (Celtic) 4

Chalmers, S. 1965 (Celtic) 5
Chalmers, W. 1885 (Rangers) 1
Chalmers, W. S. 1929 (Queen's Park) 1
Chambers, T. 1894 (Hearts) 1
Chaplin, G. D. 1908 (Dundee) 1
Cheyne, A. G. 1929 (Aberdeen) 5
Christie, A. J. 1898 (Queen's Park) 3
Christie, R. 2018 (Celtic) 20
Christie, R. M. 1884 (Queen's Park) 1
Clark, J. 1966 (Celtic) 4
Clark, R. B. 1968 (Aberdeen) 17
Clarke, S. 1988 (Chelsea) 6
Clarkson, D. 2008 (Motherwell) 2
Cleland, J. 1891 (Royal Albert) 1
Clements, R. 1891 (Leith Ath) 1
Clunas, W. L. 1924 (Sunderland) 2
Collier, W. 1922 (Raith R) 1
Collins, J. 1988 (Hibernian, Celtic, Monaco, Everton) 58
Collins, R. Y. 1951 (Celtic, Everton, Leeds U) 31
Collins, T. 1909 (Hearts) 1
Colman, D. 1911 (Aberdeen) 4
Colquhoun, E. P. 1972 (Sheffield U) 9
Colquhoun, J. 1988 (Hearts) 2
Combe, J. R. 1948 (Hibernian) 3
Commons, K. 2009 (Derby Co, Celtic) 12
Conn, A. 1956 (Hearts) 1
Conn, A. 1975 (Tottenham H) 2
Connachan, E. D. 1962 (Dunfermline Ath) 2
Connelly, G. 1974 (Celtic) 2
Connolly, J. 1973 (Everton) 1
Connor, J. 1886 (Airdrieonians) 1
Connor, J. 1930 (Sunderland) 4
Connor, R. 1986 (Dundee, Aberdeen) 4
Considine, A. 2021 (Aberdeen) 3
Conway, C. 2010 (Dundee U, Cardiff C) 7
Cook, W. L. 1934 (Bolton W) 3
Cooke, C. 1966 (Dundee, Chelsea) 16
Cooper, D. 1980 (Rangers, Motherwell) 22
Cooper, L. D. I. 2020 (Leeds U) 7
Cormack, P. B. 1966 (Hibernian, Nottingham F) 9
Cowan, J. 1896 (Aston Villa) 3
Cowan, J. 1948 (Morton) 25
Cowan, W, D. 1924 (Newcastle U) 1
Cowie, D. 1953 (Dundee) 20
Cowie, D. M. 2010 (Watford, Cardiff C) 10
Cox, C. J. 1948 (Hearts) 1
Cox, S. 1949 (Rangers) 24
Craig, A. 1929 (Motherwell) 3
Craig, J. 1977 (Celtic) 1
Craig, J. P. 1968 (Celtic) 1
Craig, T. 1927 (Rangers) 8
Craig, T. B. 1976 (Newcastle U) 1
Crainey, S. D. 2002 (Celtic, Southampton, Blackpool) 12
Crapnell, J. 1929 (Airdrieonians) 9
Crawford, D. 1894 (St Mirren, Rangers) 3
Crawford, J. 1932 (Queen's Park) 5
Crawford, S. 1995 (Raith R, Dunfermline Ath, Plymouth Arg) 25
Crerand, P. T. 1961 (Celtic, Manchester U) 16
Cringan, W. 1920 (Celtic) 5
Crosbie, J. A. 1920 (Ayr U, Birmingham) 2
Croal, J. A. 1913 (Falkirk) 3
Cropley, A. J. 1972 (Hibernian) 2
Cross, J. H. 1903 (Third Lanark) 1
Cruickshank, J. 1964 (Hearts) 6
Crum, J. 1936 (Celtic) 2
Cullen, M. J. 1956 (Luton T) 1
Cumming, D. S. 1938 (Middlesbrough) 1
Cumming, J. 1955 (Hearts) 9
Cummings, G. 1935 (Partick Thistle, Aston Villa) 9
Cummings, J. 2018 (Nottingham F) 2
Cummings, W. 2002 (Chelsea) 1
Cunningham, A. N. 1920 (Rangers) 12
Cunningham, W. C. 1954 (Preston NE) 8
Curran, H. P. 1970 (Wolverhampton W) 5

Dailly, C. 1997 (Derby Co, Blackburn R, West Ham U, Rangers) 67
Dalglish, K. 1972 (Celtic, Liverpool) 102
Davidson, C. I. 1999 (Blackburn R, Leicester C, Preston NE) 19
Davidson, D. 1878 (Queen's Park) 5
Davidson, J. A. 1954 (Partick Thistle) 8
Davidson, M. 2013 (St Johnstone) 1
Davidson, S. 1921 (Middlesbrough) 1
Dawson, A. 1980 (Rangers) 5
Dawson, J. 1935 (Rangers) 14
Deans, J. 1975 (Celtic) 2
Delaney, J. 1936 (Celtic, Manchester U) 13
Devine, A. 1910 (Falkirk) 1
Devlin, M. J. 2020 (Aberdeen) 3
Devlin, P. J. 2003 (Birmingham C) 10
Dewar, G. 1888 (Dumbarton) 2
Dewar, N. 1932 (Third Lanark) 3
Dick, J. 1959 (West Ham U) 1
Dickie, M. 1897 (Rangers) 3
Dickov, P. 2001 (Manchester C, Leicester C, Blackburn R) 10
Dickson, W. 1888 (Dundee Strathmore) 1
Dickson, W. 1970 (Kilmarnock) 5
Divers, J. 1895 (Celtic) 1
Divers, J. 1939 (Celtic) 1
Dixon, P. A. 2013 (Hudderfield T) 3
Dobie, R. S. 2002 (WBA) 6
Docherty, T. H. 1952 (Preston NE, Arsenal) 25
Dodds, D. 1984 (Dundee U) 2
Dodds, J. 1914 (Celtic) 3
Dodds, W. 1997 (Aberdeen, Dundee U, Rangers) 26
Doig, J. E. 1887 (Arbroath, Sunderland) 5
Donachie, W. 1972 (Manchester C) 35
Donaldson, A. 1914 (Bolton W) 6
Donnachie, J. 1913 (Oldham Ath) 3
Donnelly, S. 1997 (Celtic) 10
Dorrans, G. 2010 (WBA, Norwich C) 12
Dougal, J. 1939 (Preston NE) 1
Dougall, C. 1947 (Birmingham C) 1
Dougan, R. 1950 (Hearts) 1
Douglas, A. 1911 (Chelsea) 1
Douglas, B. 2018 (Wolverhampton W) 1
Douglas, J. 1880 (Renfrew) 1
Douglas, R. 2002 (Celtic, Leicester C) 19
Dowds, P. 1892 (Celtic) 1
Downie, R. 1892 (Third Lanark) 1
Doyle, D. 1892 (Celtic) 8
Doyle, J. 1976 (Ayr U) 1
Drummond, J. 1892 (Falkirk, Rangers) 14
Dunbar, M. 1886 (Cartvale) 1
Duncan, A. 1975 (Hibernian) 6
Duncan, D. 1933 (Derby Co) 14
Duncan, D. M. 1948 (East Fife) 3
Duncan, J. 1878 (Alexandra Ath) 2
Duncan, J. 1926 (Leicester C) 1
Duncanson, J. 1947 (Rangers) 1
Dunlop, J. 1890 (St Mirren) 1
Dunlop, W. 1906 (Liverpool) 1
Dunn, J. 1925 (Hibernian, Everton) 6
Durie, G. S. 1988 (Chelsea, Tottenham H, Rangers) 43
Durrant, I. 1988 (Rangers, Kilmarnock) 20
Dykes, J. 1938 (Hearts) 2
Dykes, L. J. 2021 (QPR) 15

Easson, J. F. 1931 (Portsmouth) 3
Elliott, M. S. 1998 (Leicester C) 18
Ellis, J. 1892 (Mossend Swifts) 1
Evans, A. 1982 (Aston Villa) 4
Evans, R. 1949 (Celtic, Chelsea) 48
Ewart, J. 1921 (Bradford C) 1
Ewing, T. 1958 (Partick Thistle) 2

Farm, G. N. 1953 (Blackpool) 10
Ferguson, B. 1999 (Rangers, Blackburn R, Rangers) 45
Ferguson, D. 1988 (Rangers) 2
Ferguson, D. 1992 (Dundee U, Everton) 7
Ferguson, I. 1989 (Rangers) 9
Ferguson, J. 1874 (Vale of Leven) 6
Ferguson, R. 1966 (Kilmarnock) 7
Fernie, W. 1954 (Celtic) 12
Findlay, R. 1898 (Kilmarnock) 1
Findlay, S. J. 2020 (Kilmarnock) 1
Fitchie, T. T. 1905 (Woolwich Arsenal, Queen's Park) 4
Flavell, R. 1947 (Airdrieonians) 2
Fleck, J. A. 2020 (Sheffield U) 5

Fleck, R. 1990 (Norwich C) 4
Fleming, C. 1954 (East Fife) 1
Fleming, J. W. 1929 (Rangers) 3
Fleming, R. 1886 (Morton) 1
Fletcher, D. B. 2004 (Manchester U, WBA, Stoke C) 80
Fletcher, S. K. 2008 (Hibernian, Burnley, Wolverhampton W, Sunderland, Sheffield W) 33
Forbes, A. R. 1947 (Sheffield U, Arsenal) 14
Forbes, J. 1884 (Vale of Leven) 5
Ford, D. 1974 (Hearts) 3
Forrest, J. 1958 (Motherwell) 1
Forrest, J. 1966 (Rangers, Aberdeen) 5
Forrest, J. 2011 (Celtic) 38
Forsyth, A. 1972 (Partick Thistle, Manchester U) 10
Forsyth, C. 2014 (Derby Co) 4
Forsyth, R. C. 1964 (Kilmarnock) 4
Forsyth, T. 1971 (Motherwell, Rangers) 22
Fox, D. J. 2010 (Burnley, Southampton) 4
Foyers, R. 1893 (St Bernards) 2
Fraser, D. M. 1968 (WBA) 2
Fraser, J. 1891 (Moffat) 1
Fraser, J. 1907 (Dundee) 1
Fraser, M. J. E. 1880 (Queen's Park) 5
Fraser, R. 2017 (Bournemouth, Newcastle U) 20
Fraser, W. 1955 (Sunderland) 2
Freedman, D. A. 2002 (Crystal Palace) 2
Fulton, W. 1884 (Abercorn) 1
Fyfe, J. H. 1895 (Third Lanark) 1

Gabriel, J. 1961 (Everton) 2
Gallacher, H. K. 1924 (Airdrieonians, Newcastle U, Chelsea, Derby Co) 20
Gallacher, K. W. 1988 (Dundee U, Coventry C, Blackburn R, Newcastle U) 53
Gallacher, P. 1935 (Sunderland) 1
Gallacher, P. 2002 (Dundee U) 8
Gallagher, D. P. 2020 (Motherwell) 9
Gallagher, P. 2004 (Blackburn R) 1
Galloway, M. 1992 (Celtic) 1
Galt, J. H. 1908 (Rangers) 2
Gardiner, I. 1958 (Motherwell) 1
Gardner, D. R. 1897 (Third Lanark) 1
Gardner, R. 1872 (Queen's Park, Clydesdale) 5
Gemmell, T. 1955 (St Mirren) 2
Gemmell, T. 1966 (Celtic) 18
Gemmill, A. 1971 (Derby Co, Nottingham F, Birmingham C) 43
Gemmill, S. 1995 (Nottingham F, Everton) 26
Gibb, W. 1873 (Clydesdale) 1
Gibson, D. W. 1963 (Leicester C) 7
Gibson, J. D. 1926 (Partick Thistle, Aston Villa) 8
Gibson, N. 1895 (Rangers, Partick Thistle) 14
Gilchrist, J. E. 1922 (Celtic) 1
Gilhooley, M. 1922 (Hull C) 1
Gilks, M. 2013 (Blackpool) 3
Gillespie, G. 1880 (Rangers, Queen's Park) 7
Gillespie, G. T. 1988 (Liverpool) 13
Gillespie, Jas 1898 (Third Lanark) 1
Gillespie, John 1896 (Queen's Park) 1
Gillespie, R. 1927 (Queen's Park) 4
Gillick, T. 1937 (Everton) 5
Gilmour, B. C. 2021 (Chelsea) 3
Gilmour, J. 1931 (Dundee) 1
Gilzean, A. J. 1964 (Dundee, Tottenham H) 22
Glass, S. 1999 (Newcastle U) 1
Glavin, R. 1977 (Celtic) 1
Glen, A. 1956 (Aberdeen) 2
Glen, R. 1895 (Renton, Hibernian) 3
Goodwillie, D. 2011 (Dundee U, Blackburn R) 3
Goram, A. L. 1986 (Oldham Ath, Hibernian, Rangers) 43
Gordon, C. A. 2004 (Hearts, Sunderland, Celtic, Hearts) 57
Gordon, J. E. 1912 (Rangers) 10
Gossland, J. 1884 (Rangers) 1
Goudie, J. 1884 (Abercorn) 1
Gough, C. R. 1983 (Dundee U, Tottenham H, Rangers) 61
Gould, J. 2000 (Celtic) 2
Gourlay, J. 1886 (Cambuslang) 2
Govan, J. 1948 (Hibernian) 6
Gow, D. R. 1888 (Rangers) 1
Gow, J. J. 1885 (Queen's Park) 1
Gow, J. R. 1888 (Rangers) 1
Graham, A. 1978 (Leeds U) 11
Graham, G. 1972 (Arsenal, Manchester U) 12
Graham, J. 1884 (Annbank) 1
Graham, J. A. 1921 (Arsenal) 1
Grant, J. 1959 (Hibernian) 2
Grant, P. 1989 (Celtic) 2
Gray, A. 1903 (Hibernian) 1
Gray, A. D. 2003 (Bradford C) 2
Gray, A. M. 1976 (Aston Villa, Wolverhampton W, Everton) 20
Gray, D. 1929 (Rangers) 10
Gray, E. 1969 (Leeds U) 12
Gray, F. T. 1976 (Leeds U, Nottingham F, Leeds U) 32
Gray, W. 1886 (Pollokshields Ath) 1
Green, A. 1971 (Blackpool, Newcastle U) 6
Greer, G. 2013 (Brighton & HA) 11
Greig, J. 1964 (Rangers) 44
Griffiths, L. 2013 (Hibernian, Celtic) 22
Groves, W. 1888 (Hibernian, Celtic) 3
Gulliland, W. 1891 (Queen's Park) 4
Gunn, B. 1990 (Norwich C) 6

Haddock, H. 1955 (Clyde) 6
Haddow, D. 1894 (Rangers) 1
Haffey, F. 1960 (Celtic) 2
Hamilton, A. 1885 (Queen's Park) 4
Hamilton, A. W. 1962 (Dundee) 24
Hamilton, G. 1906 (Port Glasgow Ath) 1
Hamilton, G. 1947 (Aberdeen) 5
Hamilton, J. 1892 (Queen's Park) 3
Hamilton, J. 1924 (St Mirren) 1
Hamilton, R. C. 1899 (Rangers, Dundee) 11
Hamilton, T. 1891 (Hurlford) 1
Hamilton, T. 1932 (Rangers) 1
Hamilton, W. M. 1965 (Hibernian) 1
Hammell, S. 2005 (Motherwell) 1
Hanley, G. C. 2011 (Blackburn R, Newcastle U, Norwich C) 36
Hanlon, P. T. 2021 (Hibernian) 1
Hannah, A. B. 1888 (Renton) 1
Hannah, J. 1889 (Third Lanark) 1
Hansen, A. D. 1979 (Liverpool) 26
Hansen, J. 1972 (Partick Thistle) 2
Harkness, J. D. 1927 (Queen's Park, Hearts) 12
Harper, J. M. 1973 (Aberdeen, Hibernian, Aberdeen) 4
Harper, W. 1923 (Hibernian, Arsenal) 11
Harris, J. 1921 (Partick Thistle) 2
Harris, N. 1924 (Newcastle U) 1
Harrower, W. 1882 (Queen's Park) 3
Hartford, R. A. 1972 (WBA, Manchester C, Everton, Manchester C) 50
Hartley, P. J. 2005 (Hearts, Celtic, Bristol C) 25
Harvey, D. 1973 (Leeds U) 16
Hastings, A. C. 1936 (Sunderland) 2
Haughney, M. 1954 (Celtic) 1
Hay, D. 1970 (Celtic) 27
Hay, J. 1905 (Celtic, Newcastle U) 11
Hegarty, P. 1979 (Dundee U) 8
Heggie, C. 1886 (Rangers) 1
Henderson, G. H. 1904 (Rangers) 1
Henderson, J. G. 1953 (Portsmouth, Arsenal) 7
Henderson, W. 1963 (Rangers) 29
Hendry, E. C. J. 1993 (Blackburn R, Rangers, Coventry C, Bolton W) 51
Hendry, J. W. 2018 (Celtic, Oostende) 7
Hepburn, J. 1891 (Alloa Ath) 1
Hepburn, R. 1932 (Ayr U) 1
Herd, A. C. 1935 (Hearts) 1
Herd, D. G. 1959 (Arsenal) 5
Herd, G. 1958 (Clyde) 5
Herriot, J. 1969 (Birmingham C) 8
Hewie, J. D. 1956 (Charlton Ath) 19
Higgins, A. 1885 (Kilmarnock) 1
Higgins, A. 1910 (Newcastle U) 4
Highet, T. C. 1875 (Queen's Park) 4
Hill, D. 1881 (Rangers) 3
Hill, D. A. 1906 (Third Lanark) 1
Hill, F. R. 1930 (Aberdeen) 3
Hill, J. 1891 (Hearts) 2
Hogg, G. 1896 (Hearts) 2

Hogg, J. 1922 (Ayr U) 1
Hogg, R. M. 1937 (Celtic) 1
Holm, A. H. 1882 (Queen's Park) 3
Holt, D. D. 1963 (Hearts) 5
Holt, G. J. 2001 (Kilmarnock, Norwich C) 10
Holton, J. A. 1973 (Manchester U) 15
Hope, R. 1968 (WBA) 2
Hopkin, D. 1997 (Crystal Palace, Leeds U) 7
Houliston, W. 1949 (Queen of the South) 3
Houston, S. M. 1976 (Manchester U) 1
Howden, W. 1905 (Partick Thistle) 1
Howe, R. 1929 (Hamilton A) 2
Howie, H. 1949 (Hibernian) 1
Howie, J. 1905 (Newcastle U) 3
Howieson, J. 1927 (St Mirren) 1
Hughes, J. 1965 (Celtic) 8
Hughes, R. D. 2004 (Portsmouth) 5
Hughes, S. R. 2010 (Norwich C) 1
Hughes, W. 1975 (Sunderland) 1
Humphries, W. 1952 (Motherwell) 1
Hunter, A. 1972 (Kilmarnock, Celtic) 4
Hunter, J. 1909 (Dundee) 1
Hunter, J. 1874 (Third Lanark, Eastern, Third Lanark) 4
Hunter, W. 1960 (Motherwell) 3
Hunter, R. 1890 (St Mirren) 1
Husband, J. 1947 (Partick Thistle) 1
Hutchison, D. 1999 (Everton, Sunderland, West Ham U) 26
Hutchison, T. 1974 (Coventry C) 17
Hutton, A. 2007 (Rangers, Tottenham H, Aston Villa) 50
Hutton, J. 1887 (St Bernards) 1
Hutton, J. 1923 (Aberdeen, Blackburn R) 10
Hyslop, T. 1896 (Stoke, Rangers) 2

Imlach, J. J. S. 1958 (Nottingham F) 4
Imrie, W. N. 1929 (St Johnstone) 2
Inglis, J. 1883 (Rangers) 2
Inglis, J. 1884 (Kilmarnock Ath) 1
Irons, J. H. 1900 (Queen's Park) 1
Irvine, B. 1991 (Aberdeen) 9
Iwelumo, C. R. 2009 (Wolverhampton W, Burnley) 4

Jack, R. 2018 (Rangers) 10
Jackson, A. 1886 (Cambuslang) 2
Jackson, A. 1925 (Aberdeen, Huddersfield T) 17
Jackson, C. 1975 (Rangers) 8
Jackson, D. 1995 (Hibernian, Celtic) 28
Jackson, J. 1931 (Partick Thistle, Chelsea) 8
Jackson, T. A. 1904 (St Mirren) 6
James, A. W. 1926 (Preston NE, Arsenal) 8
Jardine, A. 1971 (Rangers) 38
Jarvie, A. 1971 (Airdrieonians) 3
Jenkinson, T. 1887 (Hearts) 1
Jess, E. 1993 (Aberdeen, Coventry C, Aberdeen) 18
Johnston, A. 1999 (Sunderland, Rangers, Middlesbrough) 18
Johnston, L. H. 1948 (Clyde) 2
Johnston, M. 1984 (Watford, Celtic, Nantes, Rangers) 38
Johnston, R. 1938 (Sunderland) 1
Johnston, W. 1966 (Rangers, WBA) 22
Johnstone, D. 1973 (Rangers) 14
Johnstone, J. 1888 (Abercorn) 1
Johnstone, J. 1965 (Celtic) 23
Johnstone, Jas 1894 (Kilmarnock) 1
Johnstone, J. A. 1930 (Hearts) 3
Johnstone, R. 1951 (Hibernian, Manchester C) 17
Johnstone, W. 1887 (Third Lanark) 3
Jordan, J. 1973 (Leeds U, Manchester U, AC Milan) 52

Kay, J. L. 1880 (Queen's Park) 6
Keillor, A. 1891 (Montrose, Dundee) 6
Keir, L. 1885 (Dumbarton) 5
Kelly, H. T. 1952 (Blackpool) 1
Kelly, J. 1888 (Renton, Celtic) 8
Kelly, J. C. 1949 (Barnsley) 2
Kelly, L. M. 2013 (Kilmarnock) 1
Kelso, R. 1885 (Renton, Dundee) 7
Kelso, T. 1914 (Dundee) 1
Kennaway, J. 1934 (Celtic) 1
Kennedy, A. 1875 (Eastern, Third Lanark) 6
Kennedy, J. 1897 (Hibernian) 1
Kennedy, J. 1964 (Celtic) 6
Kennedy, J. 2004 (Celtic) 1
Kennedy, S. 1905 (Partick Thistle) 1
Kennedy, S. 1975 (Rangers) 5
Kennedy, S. 1978 (Aberdeen) 8
Kenneth, G. 2011 (Dundee U) 2
Ker, G. 1880 (Queen's Park) 5
Ker, W. 1872 (Queen's Park) 2
Kerr, A. 1955 (Partick Thistle) 2
Kerr, B. 2003 (Newcastle U) 3
Kerr, P. 1924 (Hibernian) 1
Key, G. 1902 (Hearts) 1
Key, W. 1907 (Queen's Park) 1
King, A. 1896 (Hearts, Celtic) 6
King, J. 1933 (Hamilton A) 2
King, W. S. 1929 (Queen's Park) 1
Kingsley, S. 2016 (Swansea C) 1
Kinloch, J. D. 1922 (Partick Thistle) 1
Kinnaird, A. F. 1873 (Wanderers) 1
Kinnear, D. 1938 (Rangers) 1
Kyle, K. 2002 (Sunderland, Kilmarnock) 10

Lambert, P. 1995 (Motherwell, Borussia Dortmund, Celtic) 40
Lambie, J. A. 1886 (Queen's Park) 3
Lambie, W. A. 1892 (Queen's Park) 9
Lamont, W. 1885 (Pilgrims) 1
Lang, A. 1880 (Dumbarton) 1
Lang, J. J. 1876 (Clydesdale, Third Lanark) 2
Latta, A. 1888 (Dumbarton) 2
Law, D. 1959 (Huddersfield T, Manchester C, Torino, Manchester U, Manchester C) 55
Law, G. 1910 (Rangers) 3
Law, T. 1928 (Chelsea) 2
Lawrence, J. 1911 (Newcastle U) 1
Lawrence, T. 1963 (Liverpool) 3
Lawson, D. 1923 (St Mirren) 1
Leckie, R. 1872 (Queen's Park) 1
Leggat, G. 1956 (Aberdeen, Fulham) 18
Leighton, J. 1983 (Aberdeen, Manchester U, Hibernian, Aberdeen) 91
Lennie, W. 1908 (Aberdeen) 2
Lennox, R. 1967 (Celtic) 10
Leslie, L. G. 1961 (Airdrieonians) 5
Levein, C. 1990 (Hearts) 16
Liddell, W. 1947 (Liverpool) 28
Liddle, D. 1931 (East Fife) 3
Lindsay, D. 1903 (St Mirren) 1
Lindsay, J. 1880 (Dumbarton) 8
Lindsay, J. 1888 (Renton) 3
Linwood, A. B. 1950 (Clyde) 1
Little, R. J. 1953 (Rangers) 1
Livingstone, G. T. 1906 (Manchester C, Rangers) 2
Lochhead, A. 1889 (Third Lanark) 1
Logan, J. 1891 (Ayr) 1
Logan, T. 1913 (Falkirk) 1
Logie, J. T. 1953 (Arsenal) 1
Loney, W. 1910 (Celtic) 2
Long, H. 1947 (Clyde) 1
Longair, W. 1894 (Dundee) 1
Lorimer, P. 1970 (Leeds U) 21
Love, A. 1931 (Aberdeen) 3
Low, A. 1934 (Falkirk) 1
Low, J. 1891 (Cambuslang) 1
Low, T. P. 1897 (Rangers) 1
Low, W. L. 1911 (Newcastle U) 5
Lowe, J. 1887 (St Bernards) 1
Lundie, J. 1886 (Hibernian) 1
Lyall, J. 1905 (Sheffield W) 1

Macari, L. 1972 (Celtic, Manchester U) 24
Mackail-Smith, C. 2011 (Peterborough U, Brighton & HA) 7
Mackay-Steven, G. 2013 (Dundee U, Aberdeen) 2
Mackie, J. C. 2011 (QPR) 9
Madden, J. 1893 (Celtic) 2
Maguire, C. 2011 (Aberdeen) 2
Main, F. R. 1938 (Rangers) 1
Main, J. 1909 (Hibernian) 1
Maley, W. 1893 (Celtic) 2
Maloney, S. R. 2006 (Celtic, Aston Villa, Celtic, Wigan Ath, Chicago Fire, Hull C) 47

Malpas, M. 1984 (Dundee U) 55
Marshall, D. J. 2005 (Celtic, Cardiff C, Hull C, Wigan Ath. Derby Co) 47
Marshall, G. 1992 (Celtic) 1
Marshall, H. 1899 (Celtic) 2
Marshall, J. 1885 (Third Lanark) 4
Marshall, J. 1921 (Middlesbrough, Llanelly) 7
Marshall, J. 1932 (Rangers) 3
Marshall, R. W. 1892 (Rangers) 2
Martin, B. 1995 (Motherwell) 2
Martin, C. H. 2014 (Derby Co) 17
Martin, F. 1954 (Aberdeen) 6
Martin, N. 1965 (Hibernian, Sunderland) 3
Martin, R. K. A. 2011 (Norwich C) 29
Martis, J. 1961 (Motherwell) 1
Mason, J. 1949 (Third Lanark) 7
Massie, A. 1932 (Hearts, Aston Villa) 18
Masson, D. S. 1976 (QPR, Derby Co) 17
Mathers, D. 1954 (Partick Thistle) 1
Matteo, D. 2001 (Leeds U) 6
Maxwell, W. S. 1898 (Stoke C) 1
May, J. 1906 (Rangers) 5
May, S. 2015 (Sheffield W) 1
McAllister, J. R. 2004 (Livingston) 1
McAdam, J. 1880 (Third Lanark) 1
McAllister, B. 1997 (Wimbledon) 3
McAllister, G. 1990 (Leicester C, Leeds U, Coventry C) 57
McArthur, D. 1895 (Celtic) 3
McArthur, J. 2011 (Wigan Ath, Crystal Palace) 32
McAtee, A. 1913 (Celtic) 1
McAulay, J. 1884 (Arthurlie) 1
McAulay, J. D. 1882 (Dumbarton) 9
McAulay, R. 1932 (Rangers) 2
Macauley, A. R. 1947 (Brentford, Arsenal) 7
McAvennie, F. 1986 (West Ham U, Celtic) 5
McBain, E. 1894 (St Mirren) 1
McBain, N. 1922 (Manchester U, Everton) 3
McBride, J. 1967 (Celtic) 2
McBride, P. 1904 (Preston NE) 6
McBurnie, O. R. 2018 (Swansea C, Sheffield U) 16
McCall, A. 1888 (Renton) 1
McCall, A. S. M. 1990 (Everton, Rangers) 40
McCall, J. 1886 (Renton) 5
McCalliog, J. 1967 (Sheffield W, Wolverhampton W) 5
McCallum, N. 1888 (Renton) 1
McCann, N. 1999 (Hearts, Rangers, Southampton) 26
McCann, R. J. 1959 (Motherwell) 5
McCartney, W. 1902 (Hibernian) 1
McClair, B. 1987 (Celtic, Manchester U) 30
McClory, A. 1927 (Motherwell) 3
McCloy, P. 1924 (Ayr U) 2
McCloy, P. 1973 (Rangers) 4
McCoist, A. 1986 (Rangers, Kilmarnock) 61
McColl, I. M. 1950 (Rangers) 14
McColl, R. S. 1896 (Queen's Park, Newcastle U, Queen's Park) 13
McColl, W. 1895 (Renton) 1
McCombie, A. 1903 (Sunderland, Newcastle U) 4
McCorkindale, J. 1891 (Partick Thistle) 1
McCormack, R. 2008 (Motherwell, Cardiff C, Leeds U, Fulham) 13
McCormick, R. 1886 (Abercorn) 1
McCrae, D. 1929 (St Mirren) 2
McCreadie, A. 1893 (Rangers) 2
McCreadie, E. G. 1965 (Chelsea) 23
McCulloch, D. 1935 (Hearts, Brentford, Derby Co) 7
McCulloch, L. 2005 (Wigan Ath, Rangers) 18
MacDonald, A. 1976 (Rangers) 1
McDonald, J. 1886 (Edinburgh University) 1
McDonald, J. 1956 (Sunderland) 2
McDonald, K. D. 2018 (Fulham) 5
MacDougall, E. J. 1975 (Norwich C) 7
McDougall, J. 1877 (Vale of Leven) 5
McDougall, J. 1926 (Airdrieonians) 1
McDougall, J. 1931 (Liverpool) 2
McEveley, J. 2008 (Derby Co) 3
McFadden, J. 2002 (Motherwell, Everton, Birmingham C) 48
McFadyen, W. 1934 (Motherwell) 2
Macfarlane, A. 1904 (Dundee) 5
Macfarlane, W. 1947 (Hearts) 1
McFarlane, R. 1896 (Greenock Morton) 1
McGarr, E. 1970 (Aberdeen) 2
McGarvey, F. P. 1979 (Liverpool, Celtic) 7
McGeoch, A. 1876 (Dumbreck) 4
McGeouch, D. 2018 (Hibernian) 2
McGhee, J. 1886 (Hibernian) 1
McGhee, M. 1983 (Aberdeen) 4
McGinlay, J. 1994 (Bolton W) 13
McGinn, J. 2016 (Hibernian, Aston Villa) 36
McGonagle, W. 1933 (Celtic) 6
McGrain, D. 1973 (Celtic) 62
McGregor, A. J. 2007 (Rangers, Besiktas, Hull C, Rangers) 42
McGregor, C. W. 2018 (Celtic) 34
McGregor, J. C. 1877 (Vale of Leven) 4
McGrory, J. 1928 (Celtic) 7
McGrory, J. E. 1965 (Kilmarnock) 3
McGuire, W. 1881 (Beith) 2
McGurk, F. 1934 (Birmingham) 1
McHardy, H. 1885 (Rangers) 1
McInally, A. 1989 (Aston Villa, Bayern Munich) 8
McInally, J. 1987 (Dundee U) 10
McInally, T. B. 1926 (Celtic) 2
McInnes, D. 2003 (WBA) 2
McInnes, T. 1889 (Cowlairs) 1
McIntosh, W. 1905 (Third Lanark) 1
McIntyre, A. 1878 (Vale of Leven) 2
McIntyre, H. 1880 (Rangers) 1
McIntyre, J. 1884 (Rangers) 1
MacKay, D. 1959 (Celtic) 14
Mackay, D. C. 1957 (Hearts, Tottenham H) 22
Mackay, G. 1988 (Hearts) 4
Mackay, M. 2004 (Norwich C) 5
McKay, B. 2016 (Rangers) 1
McKay, J. 1924 (Blackburn R) 1
McKay, R. 1928 (Newcastle U) 1
McKean, R. 1976 (Rangers) 1
McKenna, S. 2018 (Aberdeen, Nottingham F) 21
McKenzie, D. 1938 (Brentford) 1
Mackenzie, J. A. 1954 (Partick Thistle) 9
McKeown, M. 1889 (Celtic) 2
McKie, J. 1898 (East Stirling) 1
McKillop, T. R. 1938 (Rangers) 1
McKimmie, S. 1989 (Aberdeen) 40
McKinlay, D. 1922 (Liverpool) 2
McKinlay, T. 1996 (Celtic) 22
McKinlay, W. 1994 (Dundee U, Blackburn R) 29
McKinnon, A. 1874 (Queen's Park) 1
McKinnon, R. 1966 (Rangers) 28
McKinnon, R. 1994 (Motherwell) 3
MacKinnon, W. 1883 (Dumbarton) 4
MacKinnon, W. W. 1872 (Queen's Park) 9
McLaren, A. 1929 (St Johnstone) 5
McLaren, A. 1947 (Preston NE) 4
McLaren, A. 1992 (Hearts, Rangers) 24
McLaren, A. 2001 (Kilmarnock) 1
McLaren, J. 1888 (Hibernian, Celtic) 3
McLaughlin, J. P. 2018 (Hearts, Sunderland) 2
McLean, A. 1926 (Celtic) 4
McLean, D. 1896 (St Bernards) 2
McLean, D. 1912 (Sheffield W) 1
McLean, G. 1968 (Dundee) 1
McLean, K. 2016 (Aberdeen, Norwich C) 20
McLean, T. 1969 (Kilmarnock) 6
McLeish, A. 1980 (Aberdeen) 77
McLeod, D. 1905 (Celtic) 4
McLeod, J. 1888 (Dumbarton) 5
MacLeod, J. M. 1961 (Hibernian) 4
MacLeod, M. 1985 (Celtic, Borussia Dortmund, Hibernian) 20
McLeod, W. 1886 (Cowlairs) 1
McLintock, A. 1875 (Vale of Leven) 3
McLintock, F. 1963 (Leicester C, Arsenal) 9
McLuckie, J. S. 1934 (Manchester C) 1
McMahon, A. 1892 (Celtic) 6
McManus, S. 2007 (Celtic, Middlesbrough) 26
McMenemy, J. 1905 (Celtic) 12
McMenemy, J. 1934 (Motherwell) 1
McMillan, I. L. 1952 (Airdrieonians, Rangers) 6
McMillan, J. 1897 (St Bernards) 1

McMillan, T. 1887 (Dumbarton) 1
McMullan, J. 1920 (Partick Thistle, Manchester C) 16
McNab, A. 1921 (Morton) 2
McNab, A. 1937 (Sunderland, WBA) 2
McNab, C. D. 1931 (Dundee) 6
McNab, J. S. 1923 (Liverpool) 1
McNair, A. 1906 (Celtic) 15
McNamara, J. 1997 (Celtic, Wolverhampton W) 33
McNamee, D. 2004 (Livingston) 4
McNaught, W. 1951 (Raith R) 5
McNaughton, K. 2002 (Aberdeen, Cardiff C) 4
McNeill, W. 1961 (Celtic) 29
McNiel, H. 1874 (Queen's Park) 10
McNiel, M. 1876 (Rangers) 2
McNulty, M. 2019 (Reading) 2
McPhail, J. 1950 (Celtic) 5
McPhail, R. 1927 (Airdrieonians, Rangers) 17
McPherson, D. 1892 (Kilmarnock) 1
McPherson, D. 1989 (Hearts, Rangers) 27
McPherson, J. 1875 (Clydesdale) 1
McPherson, J. 1879 (Vale of Leven) 8
McPherson, J. 1888 (Kilmarnock, Cowlairs, Rangers) 9
McPherson, J. 1891 (Hearts) 1
McPherson, R. 1882 (Arthurlie) 1
McQueen, G. 1974 (Leeds U, Manchester U) 30
McQueen, M. 1890 (Leith Ath) 2
McRorie, D. M. 1931 (Morton) 1
McSpadyen, A. 1939 (Partick Thistle) 2
McStay, P. 1984 (Celtic) 76
McStay, W. 1921 (Celtic) 13
McSwegan, G. 2000 (Hearts) 2
McTavish, J. 1910 (Falkirk) 1
McTominay, S. F. 2018 (Manchester U) 26
McWattie, G. C. 1901 (Queen's Park) 2
McWilliam, P. 1905 (Newcastle U) 8
Meechan, P. 1896 (Celtic) 1
Meiklejohn, D. D. 1922 (Rangers) 15
Menzies, A. 1906 (Hearts) 1
Mercer, R. 1912 (Hearts) 2
Middleton, R. 1930 (Cowdenbeath) 1
Millar, J. 1897 (Rangers) 3
Millar, J. 1963 (Rangers) 2
Miller, A. 1939 (Hearts) 1
Miller, C. 2001 (Dundee U) 1
Miller, J. 1931 (St Mirren) 5
Miller, K. 2001 (Rangers, Wolverhampton W, Celtic, Derby Co, Rangers, Bursaspor, Cardiff C, Vancouver Whitecaps) 69
Miller, L. 2006 (Dundee U, Aberdeen) 3
Miller, P. 1882 (Dumbarton) 3
Miller, T. 1920 (Liverpool, Manchester U) 3
Miller, W. 1876 (Third Lanark) 1
Miller, W. 1947 (Celtic) 6
Miller, W. 1975 (Aberdeen) 65
Mills, W. 1936 (Aberdeen) 3
Milne, J. V. 1938 (Middlesbrough) 2
Mitchell, D. 1890 (Rangers) 5
Mitchell, J. 1908 (Kilmarnock) 3
Mitchell, R. C. 1951 (Newcastle U) 2
Mochan, N. 1954 (Celtic) 3
Moir, W. 1950 (Bolton W) 1
Moncur, R. 1968 (Newcastle U) 16
Morgan, H. 1898 (St Mirren, Liverpool) 2
Morgan, L. 2018 (St Mirren) 2
Morgan, W. 1968 (Burnley, Manchester U) 21
Morris, D. 1923 (Raith R) 6
Morris, H. 1950 (East Fife) 1
Morrison, J. C. 2008 (WBA) 46
Morrison, T. 1927 (St Mirren) 1
Morton, A. L. 1920 (Queen's Park, Rangers) 31
Morton, H. A. 1929 (Kilmarnock) 2
Mudie, J. K. 1957 (Blackpool) 17
Muir, W. 1907 (Dundee) 1
Muirhead, T. A. 1922 (Rangers) 8
Mulgrew, C. P. 2012 (Celtic, Blackburn R) 44
Mulhall, G. 1960 (Aberdeen, Sunderland) 3
Munro, A. D. 1937 (Hearts, Blackpool) 3
Munro, F. M. 1971 (Wolverhampton W) 9
Munro, I. 1979 (St Mirren) 7
Munro, N. 1888 (Abercorn) 2
Murdoch, J. 1931 (Motherwell) 1
Murdoch, R. 1966 (Celtic) 12
Murphy, F. 1938 (Celtic) 1
Murphy, J. 2018 (Rangers) 2
Murray, I. 2003 (Hibernian, Rangers) 6
Murray, J. 1895 (Renton) 1
Murray, J. 1958 (Hearts) 5
Murray, J. W. 1890 (Vale of Leven) 1
Murray, P. 1896 (Hibernian) 2
Murray, S. 1972 (Aberdeen) 1
Murty, G. S. 2004 (Reading) 4
Mutch, G. 1938 (Preston NE) 1

Naismith, S. J. 2007 (Kilmarnock, Rangers, Everton, Norwich C, Hearts) 51
Napier, C. E. 1932 (Celtic, Derby Co) 5
Narey, D. 1977 (Dundee U) 35
Naysmith, G. A. 2000 (Hearts, Everton, Sheffield U) 46
Neil, R. G. 1896 (Hibernian, Rangers) 2
Neill, R. W. 1876 (Queen's Park) 5
Neilson, R. 2007 (Hearts) 1
Nellies, P. 1913 (Hearts) 2
Nelson, J. 1925 (Cardiff C) 4
Nevin, P. K. F. 1986 (Chelsea, Everton, Tranmere R) 28
Niblo, T. D. 1904 (Aston Villa) 1
Nibloe, J. 1929 (Kilmarnock) 11
Nicholas, C. 1983 (Celtic, Arsenal, Aberdeen) 20
Nicholson, B. 2001 (Dunfermline Ath) 3
Nicol, S. 1985 (Liverpool) 27
Nisbet, J. 1929 (Ayr U) 3
Nisbet, K. 2021 (Hibernian) 6
Niven, J. B. 1885 (Moffat) 1

O'Connor, G. 2002 (Hibernian, Lokomotiv Moscow, Birmingham C) 16
O'Donnell, F. 1937 (Preston NE, Blackpool) 6
O'Donnell, P. 1994 (Motherwell) 1
O'Donnell, S. G. 2018 (Kilmarnock) 22
Ogilvie, D. H. 1934 (Motherwell) 1
O'Hare, J. 1970 (Derby Co) 13
O'Neil, B. 1996 (Celtic, Wolfsburg, Derby Co, Preston NE) 7
O'Neil, J. 2001 (Hibernian) 1
Ormond, W. E. 1954 (Hibernian) 6
O'Rourke, F. 1907 (Airdrieonians) 1
Orr, J. 1892 (Kilmarnock) 1
Orr, R. 1902 (Newcastle U) 2
Orr, T. 1952 (Morton) 2
Orr, W. 1900 (Celtic) 3
Orrock, R. 1913 (Falkirk) 1
Oswald, J. 1889 (Third Lanark, St Bernards, Rangers) 3

Palmer, L. J. 2019 (Sheffield W) 8
Parker, A. H. 1955 (Falkirk, Everton) 15
Parlane, D. 1973 (Rangers) 12
Parlane, R. 1878 (Vale of Leven) 3
Paterson, C. T. O. 2016 (Hearts, Cardiff C, Sheffield W) 17
Paterson, G. D. 1939 (Celtic) 1
Paterson, J. 1920 (Leicester C) 1
Paterson, J. 1931 (Cowdenbeath) 3
Paton, A. 1952 (Motherwell) 2
Paton, D. 1896 (St Bernards) 1
Paton, M. 1883 (Dumbarton) 5
Paton, R. 1879 (Vale of Leven) 2
Patrick, J. 1897 (St Mirren) 2
Patterson, N. K. 2021 (Rangers) 2
Paul, H. McD. 1909 (Queen's Park) 3
Paul, W. 1888 (Partick Thistle) 3
Paul, W. 1891 (Dykebar) 1
Pearson, S. P. 2004 (Motherwell, Celtic, Derby Co) 10
Pearson, T. 1947 (Newcastle U) 2
Penman, A. 1966 (Dundee) 1
Pettigrew, W. 1976 (Motherwell) 5
Phillips, J. 1877 (Queen's Park) 3
Phillips, M. 2012 (Blackpool, QPR, WBA) 16
Plenderleith, J. B. 1961 (Manchester C) 1
Porteous, W. 1903 (Hearts) 1
Pressley, S. J. 2000 (Hearts) 32
Pringle, C. 1921 (St Mirren) 1
Provan, D. 1964 (Rangers) 5
Provan, D. 1980 (Celtic) 10

Pursell, P. 1914 (Queen's Park) 1

Quashie, N. F. 2004 (Portsmouth, Southampton, WBA) 14
Quinn, J. 1905 (Celtic) 11
Quinn, P. 1961 (Motherwell) 4

Rae, G. 2001 (Dundee, Rangers, Cardiff C) 14
Rae, J. 1889 (Third Lanark) 2
Raeside, J. S. 1906 (Third Lanark) 1
Raisbeck, A. G. 1900 (Liverpool) 8
Rankin, G. 1890 (Vale of Leven) 2
Rankin, R. 1929 (St Mirren) 3
Redpath, W. 1949 (Motherwell) 9
Reid, J. G. 1914 (Airdrieonians) 3
Reid, R. 1938 (Brentford) 2
Reid, W. 1911 (Rangers) 9
Reilly, L. 1949 (Hibernian) 38
Rennie, H. G. 1900 (Hearts, Hibernian) 13
Renny-Tailyour, H. W. 1873 (Royal Engineers) 1
Rhind, A. 1872 (Queen's Park) 1
Rhodes, J. L. 2012 (Huddersfield T, Blackburn R, Sheffield W) 14
Richmond, A. 1906 (Queen's Park) 1
Richmond, J. T. 1877 (Clydesdale, Queen's Park) 3
Ring, T. 1953 (Clyde) 12
Rioch, B. D. 1975 (Derby Co, Everton, Derby Co) 24
Riordan, D. G. 2006 (Hibernian) 3
Ritchie, A. 1891 (East Stirlingshire) 1
Ritchie, H. 1923 (Hibernian) 2
Ritchie, J. 1897 (Queen's Park) 1
Ritchie, M. T. 2015 (Bournemouth, Newcastle U) 16
Ritchie, P. S. 1999 (Hearts, Bolton W, Walsall) 7
Ritchie, W. 1962 (Rangers) 1
Robb, D. T. 1971 (Aberdeen) 5
Robb, W. 1926 (Rangers, Hibernian) 2
Robertson, A. 1955 (Clyde) 5
Robertson, A. 2014 (Dundee U, Hull C, Liverpool) 48
Robertson, D. 1992 (Rangers) 3
Robertson, G. 1910 (Motherwell, Sheffield W) 4
Robertson, G. 1938 (Kilmarnock) 1
Robertson, H. 1962 (Dundee) 1
Robertson, J. 1931 (Dundee) 2
Robertson, J. 1991 (Hearts) 16
Robertson, J. N. 1978 (Nottingham F, Derby Co) 28
Robertson, J. G. 1965 (Tottenham H) 1
Robertson, J. T. 1898 (Everton, Southampton, Rangers) 16
Robertson, P. 1903 (Dundee) 1
Robertson, S. 2009 (Dundee U) 2
Robertson, T. 1889 (Queen's Park) 4
Robertson, T. 1898 (Hearts) 1
Robertson, W. 1887 (Dumbarton) 2
Robinson, R. 1974 (Dundee) 4
Robson, B. G. G. 2008 (Dundee U, Celtic, Middlesbrough) 17
Ross, M. 2002 (Rangers) 13
Rough, A. 1976 (Partick Thistle, Hibernian) 53
Rougvie, D. 1984 (Aberdeen) 1
Rowan, A. 1880 (Caledonian, Queen's Park) 2
Russell, D. 1895 (Hearts, Celtic) 6
Russell, J. 1890 (Cambuslang) 1
Russell, J. S. S. 2015 (Derby Co, Kansas City) 14
Russell, W. F. 1924 (Airdrieonians) 2
Rutherford, E. 1948 (Rangers) 1

St John, I. 1959 (Motherwell, Liverpool) 21
Saunders, S. 2011 (Motherwell) 1
Sawers, W. 1895 (Dundee) 1
Scarff, P. 1931 (Celtic) 1
Schaedler, E. 1974 (Hibernian) 1
Scott, A. S. 1957 (Rangers, Everton) 16
Scott, J. 1966 (Hibernian) 1
Scott, J. 1971 (Dundee) 2
Scott, M. 1898 (Airdrieonians) 1
Scott, R. 1894 (Airdrieonians) 1
Scoular, J. 1951 (Portsmouth) 9
Sellar, W. 1885 (Battlefield, Queen's Park) 9
Semple, W. 1886 (Cambuslang) 1
Severin, S. D. 2002 (Hearts, Aberdeen) 15
Shankland, L. 2020 (Dundee U) 4
Shankly, W. 1938 (Preston NE) 5
Sharp, G. M. 1985 (Everton) 12
Sharp, J. 1904 (Dundee, Woolwich Arsenal, Fulham) 5
Shaw, D. 1947 (Hibernian) 8
Shaw, F. W. 1884 (Pollokshields Ath) 2
Shaw, J. 1947 (Rangers) 4
Shearer, D. 1994 (Aberdeen) 7
Shearer, R. 1961 (Rangers) 4
Shinnie, A. M. 2013 (Inverness CT) 1
Shinnie, G. 2018 (Aberdeen) 6
Sillars, D. C. 1891 (Queen's Park) 5
Simpson, J. 1895 (Third Lanark) 3
Simpson, J. 1935 (Rangers) 14
Simpson, N. 1983 (Aberdeen) 5
Simpson, R. C. 1967 (Celtic) 5
Sinclair, G. L. 1910 (Hearts) 3
Sinclair, J. W. E. 1966 (Leicester C) 1
Skene, L. H. 1904 (Queen's Park) 1
Sloan, T. 1904 (Third Lanark) 1
Smellie, R. 1887 (Queen's Park) 6
Smith, A. 1898 (Rangers) 20
Smith, D. 1966 (Aberdeen, Rangers) 2
Smith, G. 1947 (Hibernian) 18
Smith, H. G. 1988 (Hearts) 3
Smith, J. 1924 (Ayr U) 1
Smith, J. 1935 (Rangers) 2
Smith, J. 1968 (Aberdeen, Newcastle U) 4
Smith, J. 2003 (Celtic) 2
Smith, J. E. 1959 (Celtic) 2
Smith, Jas 1872 (Queen's Park) 1
Smith, John 1877 (Mauchline, Edinburgh University, Queen's Park) 10
Smith, N. 1897 (Rangers) 12
Smith, R. 1872 (Queen's Park) 2
Smith, T. M. 1934 (Kilmarnock, Preston NE) 2
Snodgrass, R. 2011 (Leeds U, Norwich C, Hull C, West Ham U) 28
Somers, P. 1905 (Celtic) 4
Somers, W. S. 1879 (Third Lanark, Queen's Park) 3
Somerville, G. 1886 (Queen's Park) 1
Souness, G. J. 1975 (Middlesbrough, Liverpool, Sampdoria) 54
Souttar, J. 2019 (Hearts) 3
Speedie, D. R. 1985 (Chelsea, Coventry C) 10
Speedie, F. 1903 (Rangers) 3
Speirs, J. H. 1908 (Rangers) 1
Spencer, J. 1995 (Chelsea, QPR) 14
Stanton, P. 1966 (Hibernian) 16
Stark, J. 1909 (Rangers) 2
Steel, W. 1947 (Morton, Derby Co, Dundee) 30
Steele, D. M. 1923 (Huddersfield) 3
Stein, C. 1969 (Rangers, Coventry C) 21
Stephen, J. F. 1947 (Bradford) 2
Stevenson, G. 1928 (Motherwell) 12
Stevenson, L. 2018 (Hibernian) 1
Stewart, A. 1888 (Queen's Park) 2
Stewart, A. 1894 (Third Lanark) 1
Stewart, D. 1888 (Dumbarton) 1
Stewart, D. 1893 (Queen's Park) 3
Stewart, D. S. 1978 (Leeds U) 1
Stewart, G. 1906 (Hibernian, Manchester C) 4
Stewart, J. 1977 (Kilmarnock, Middlesbrough) 2
Stewart, M. J. 2002 (Manchester U, Hearts) 4
Stewart, R. 1981 (West Ham U) 10
Stewart, W. G. 1898 (Queen's Park) 2
Stockdale, R. K. 2002 (Middlesbrough) 5
Storrier, D. 1899 (Celtic) 3
Strachan, G. D. 1980 (Aberdeen, Manchester U, Leeds U) 50
Sturrock, P. 1981 (Dundee U) 20
Sullivan, N. 1997 (Wimbledon, Tottenham H) 28
Summers, W. 1926 (St Mirren) 1
Symon, J. S. 1939 (Rangers) 1

Tait, T. S. 1911 (Sunderland) 1
Taylor, G. J. 2019 (Kilmarnock, Celtic) 5
Taylor, J. 1872 (Queen's Park) 6
Taylor, J. D. 1892 (Dumbarton, St Mirren) 4
Taylor, W. 1892 (Hearts) 1
Teale, G. 2006 (Wigan Ath, Derby Co) 13
Telfer, P. N. 2000 (Coventry C) 1
Telfer, W. 1933 (Motherwell) 2
Telfer, W. D. 1954 (St Mirren) 1

Templeton, R. 1902 (Aston Villa, Newcastle U, Woolwich Arsenal, Kilmarnock) 11
Thompson, S. 2002 (Dundee U, Rangers) 16
Thomson, A. 1886 (Arthurlie) 1
Thomson, A. 1889 (Third Lanark) 1
Thomson, A. 1909 (Airdrieonians) 1
Thomson, A. 1926 (Celtic) 3
Thomson, C. 1904 (Hearts, Sunderland) 21
Thomson, C. 1937 (Sunderland) 1
Thomson, D. 1920 (Dundee) 1
Thomson, J. 1930 (Celtic) 4
Thomson, J. J. 1872 (Queen's Park) 3
Thomson, J. R. 1933 (Everton) 1
Thomson, K. 2009 (Rangers, Middlesbrough) 3
Thomson, R. 1932 (Celtic) 1
Thomson, R. W. 1927 (Falkirk) 1
Thomson, S. 1884 (Rangers) 2
Thomson, W. 1892 (Dumbarton) 4
Thomson, W. 1896 (Dundee) 1
Thomson, W. 1980 (St Mirren) 7
Thornton, W. 1947 (Rangers) 7
Tierney, K. 2016 (Celtic, Arsenal) 23
Toner, W. 1959 (Kilmarnock) 2
Townsley, T. 1926 (Falkirk) 1
Troup, A. 1920 (Dundee, Everton) 5
Turnbull, D. 2021 (Celtic) 1
Turnbull, E. 1948 (Hibernian) 8
Turner, T. 1884 (Arthurlie) 1
Turner, W. 1885 (Pollokshields Ath) 2

Ure, J. F. 1962 (Dundee, Arsenal) 11
Urquhart, D. 1934 (Hibernian) 1

Vallance, T. 1877 (Rangers) 7
Venters, A. 1934 (Cowdenbeath, Rangers) 3

Waddell, T. S. 1891 (Queen's Park) 6
Waddell, W. 1947 (Rangers) 17
Wales, H. M. 1933 (Motherwell) 1
Walker, A. 1988 (Celtic) 3
Walker, F. 1922 (Third Lanark) 1
Walker, G. 1930 (St Mirren) 4
Walker, J. 1895 (Hearts, Rangers) 5
Walker, J. 1911 (Swindon T) 9
Walker, J. N. 1993 (Hearts, Partick Thistle) 2
Walker, R. 1900 (Hearts) 29
Walker, T. 1935 (Hearts) 20
Walker, W. 1909 (Clyde) 2
Wallace, I. A. 1978 (Coventry C) 3
Wallace, L. 2010 (Hearts, Rangers) 10
Wallace, R. 2010 (Preston NE) 1
Wallace, W. S. B. 1965 (Hearts, Celtic) 7
Wardhaugh, J. 1955 (Hearts) 2
Wark, J. 1979 (Ipswich T, Liverpool) 28
Watson, A. 1881 (Queen's Park) 3
Watson, J. 1903 (Sunderland, Middlesbrough) 6
Watson, J. 1948 (Motherwell, Huddersfield T) 2
Watson, J. A. K. 1878 (Rangers) 1
Watson, P. R. 1934 (Blackpool) 1
Watson, R. 1971 (Motherwell) 1
Watson, W. 1898 (Falkirk) 1
Watt, A. P. 2016 (Charlton Ath) 1
Watt, F. 1889 (Kilbirnie) 4
Watt, W. W. 1887 (Queen's Park) 1
Waugh, W. 1938 (Hearts) 1
Webster, A. 2003 (Hearts, Dundee U, Hearts) 28
Weir, A. 1959 (Motherwell) 6
Weir, D. G. 1997 (Hearts, Everton, Rangers) 69
Weir, J. 1887 (Third Lanark) 1
Weir, J. B. 1872 (Queen's Park) 4
Weir, P. 1980 (St Mirren, Aberdeen) 6
White, John 1922 (Albion R, Hearts) 2
White, J. A. 1959 (Falkirk, Tottenham H) 22
White, W. 1907 (Bolton W) 2
Whitelaw, A. 1887 (Vale of Leven) 2
Whittaker, S. G. 2010 (Rangers, Norwich C) 31
Whyte, D. 1988 (Celtic, Middlesbrough, Aberdeen) 12
Wilkie, L. 2002 (Dundee) 11
Williams, G. 2002 (Nottingham F) 5
Wilson, A. 1907 (Sheffield W) 6
Wilson, A. 1954 (Portsmouth) 1
Wilson, A. N. 1920 (Dunfermline, Middlesbrough) 12
Wilson, D. 1900 (Queen's Park) 1
Wilson, D. 1913 (Oldham Ath) 1
Wilson, D. 1961 (Rangers) 22
Wilson, D. 2011 (Liverpool) 5
Wilson, G. W. 1904 (Hearts, Everton, Newcastle U) 6
Wilson, Hugh 1890 (Newmilns, Sunderland, Third Lanark) 4
Wilson, I. A. 1987 (Leicester C, Everton) 5
Wilson, J. 1888 (Vale of Leven) 4
Wilson, M. 2011 (Celtic) 1
Wilson, P. 1926 (Celtic) 4
Wilson, P. 1975 (Celtic) 1
Wilson, R. P. 1972 (Arsenal) 2
Winters, R. 1999 (Aberdeen) 1
Wiseman, W. 1927 (Queen's Park) 2
Wood, G. 1979 (Everton, Arsenal) 4
Woodburn, W. A. 1947 (Rangers) 24
Wotherspoon, D. N. 1872 (Queen's Park) 2
Wright, K. 1992 (Hibernian) 1
Wright, S. 1993 (Aberdeen) 2
Wright, T. 1953 (Sunderland) 3
Wylie, T. G. 1890 (Rangers) 1

Yeats, R. 1965 (Liverpool) 2
Yorston, B. C. 1931 (Aberdeen) 1
Yorston, H. 1955 (Aberdeen) 1
Young, A. 1905 (Everton) 2
Young, A. 1960 (Hearts, Everton) 8
Young, G. L. 1947 (Rangers) 53
Young, J. 1906 (Celtic) 1
Younger, T. 1955 (Hibernian, Liverpool) 24

WALES

Adams, H. 1882 (Berwyn R, Druids) 4
Aizlewood, M. 1986 (Charlton Ath, Leeds U, Bradford C, Bristol C, Cardiff C) 39
Allchurch, I. J. 1951 (Swansea T, Newcastle U, Cardiff C, Swansea T) 68
Allchurch, L. 1955 (Swansea T, Sheffield U) 11
Allen, B. W. 1951 (Coventry C) 2
Allen, J. M. 2009 (Swansea C, Liverpool, Stoke C) 63
Allen, M. 1986 (Watford, Norwich C, Millwall, Newcastle U) 14
Ampadu, E. K. C. R. 2018 (Chelsea) 26
Arridge, S. 1892 (Bootle, Everton, New Brighton Tower) 8
Astley, D. J. 1931 (Charlton Ath, Aston Villa, Derby Co, Blackpool) 13
Atherton, R. W. 1899 (Hibernian, Middlesbrough) 9

Bailiff, W. E. 1913 (Llanelly) 4
Baker, C. W. 1958 (Cardiff C) 7
Baker, W. G. 1948 (Cardiff C) 1
Bale, G. F. 2006 (Southampton, Tottenham H, Real Madrid) 96
Bamford, T. 1931 (Wrexham) 5
Barnard, D. S. 1998 (Barnsley, Grimsby T) 22
Barnes, W. 1948 (Arsenal) 22
Bartley, T. 1898 (Glossop NE) 1
Bastock, A. M. 1892 (Shrewsbury T) 1
Beadles, G. H. 1925 (Cardiff C) 2
Bell, W. S. 1881 (Shrewsbury Engineers, Crewe Alex) 5
Bellamy, C. D. 1998 (Norwich C, Coventry C, Newcastle U, Blackburn R, Liverpool, West Ham U, Manchester C, Liverpool, Cardiff C) 78
Bennion, S. R. 1926 (Manchester U) 10
Berry, G. F. 1979 (Wolverhampton W, Stoke C) 5
Blackmore, C. G. 1985 (Manchester U, Middlesbrough) 39
Blake, D. J. 2011 (Cardiff C, Crystal Palace) 14
Blake, N. A. 1994 (Sheffield U, Bolton W, Blackburn R, Wolverhampton W) 29
Blew, H. 1899 (Wrexham) 22
Boden, T. 1880 (Wrexham) 1
Bodin, B. P. 2018 (Preston NE) 1
Bodin, P. J. 1990 (Swindon T, Crystal Palace, Swindon T) 23

Boulter, L. M. 1939 (Brentford) 1
Bowdler, H. E. 1893 (Shrewsbury T) 1
Bowdler, J. C. H. 1890 (Shrewsbury T, Wolverhampton W, Shrewsbury T) 4
Bowen, D. L. 1955 (Arsenal) 19
Bowen, E. 1880 (Druids) 2
Bowen, J. P. 1994 (Swansea C, Birmingham C) 2
Bowen, M. R. 1986 (Tottenham H, Norwich C, West Ham U) 41
Bowsher, S. J. 1929 (Burnley) 1
Boyle, T. 1981 (Crystal Palace) 2
Bradley, M. S. 2010 (Walsall) 1
Bradshaw, T. W. C. 2016 (Walsall, Barnsley) 3
Britten, T. J. 1878 (Parkgrove, Presteigne) 2
Brooks, D. R. 2018 (Sheffield U, Bournemouth) 21
Brookes, S. J. 1900 (Llandudno) 2
Brown, A. I. 1926 (Aberdare Ath) 1
Brown, J. R. 2006 (Gillingham, Blackburn R, Aberdeen) 3
Browning, M. T. 1996 (Bristol R, Huddersfield T) 5
Bryan, T. 1886 (Oswestry) 2
Buckland, T. 1899 (Bangor) 1
Burgess, W. A. R. 1947 (Tottenham H) 32
Burke, T. 1883 (Wrexham, Newton Heath) 8
Burnett, T. B. 1877 (Ruabon) 1
Burton, A. D. 1963 (Norwich C, Newcastle U) 9
Butler, J. 1893 (Chirk) 3
Butler, W. T. 1900 (Druids) 2

Cabango, B. 2021 (Swansea C) 3
Cartwright, L. 1974 (Coventry C, Wrexham) 7
Carty, T. See McCarthy (Wrexham).
Challen, J. B. 1887 (Corinthians, Wellingborough GS) 4
Chapman, T. 1894 (Newtown, Manchester C, Grimsby T) 7
Charles, J. M. 1981 (Swansea C, QPR, Oxford U) 19
Charles, M. 1955 (Swansea T, Arsenal, Cardiff C) 31
Charles, W. J. 1950 (Leeds U, Juventus, Leeds U, Cardiff C) 38
Chester, J. G. 2014 (Hull C, WBA, Aston Villa) 35
Church, S. R. 2009 (Reading, Charlton Ath) 38
Clarke, R. J. 1949 (Manchester C) 22
Coleman, C. 1992 (Crystal Palace, Blackburn R, Fulham) 32
Collier, D. J. 1921 (Grimsby T) 1
Collins, D. L. 2005 (Sunderland, Stoke C) 12
Collins, J. M. 2004 (Cardiff C, West Ham U, Aston Villa, West Ham U) 51
Collins, W. S. 1931 (Llanelly) 1
Collison, J. D. 2008 (West Ham U) 16
Colwill, R. 2021 (Cardiff C) 1
Conde, C. 1884 (Chirk) 3
Cook, F. C. 1925 (Newport Co, Portsmouth) 8
Cornforth, J. M. 1995 (Swansea C) 2
Cotterill, D. R. G. B. 2006 (Bristol C, Wigan Ath, Sheffield U, Swansea C, Doncaster R, Birmingham C) 24
Coyne, D. 1996 (Tranmere R, Grimsby T, Leicester C, Burnley, Tranmere R) 16
Crofts, A. L. 2016 ((Gillingham, Brighton & HA, Norwich C, Scunthorpe U) 29
Crompton, W. 1931 (Wrexham) 3
Cross, E. A. 1876 (Wrexham) 2
Crosse, K. 1879 (Druids) 3
Crossley, M. G. 1997 (Nottingham F, Middlesbrough, Fulham) 8
Crowe, V. H. 1959 (Aston Villa) 16
Cumner, R. H. 1939 (Arsenal) 3
Curtis, A. T. 1976 (Swansea C, Leeds U, Swansea C, Southampton, Cardiff C) 35
Curtis, E. R. 1928 (Cardiff C, Birmingham) 3

Daniel, R. W. 1951 (Arsenal, Sunderland) 21
Darvell, S. 1897 (Oxford University) 2
Davies, A. 1876 (Wrexham) 2
Davies, A. 1904 (Druids, Middlesbrough) 2
Davies, A. 1983 (Manchester U, Newcastle U, Swansea C, Bradford C) 13
Davies, A. 2019 (Barnsley, Stoke C) 2
Davies, A. O. 1885 (Barmouth, Swifts, Wrexham, Crewe Alex) 9
Davies, A. R. 2006 (Yeovil T) 1
Davies, A. T. 1891 (Shrewsbury T) 1
Davies, B. T. 2013 (Swansea C, Tottenham H) 64
Davies, C. 1972 (Charlton Ath) 1
Davies, C. M. 2006 (Oxford U, Verona, Oldham Ath, Barnsley) 7
Davies, D. 1904 (Bolton W) 3
Davies, D. C. 1899 (Brecon, Hereford) 2
Davies, D. W. 1912 (Treharris, Oldham Ath) 2
Davies, E. Lloyd 1904 (Stoke, Northampton T) 16
Davies, E. R. 1953 (Newcastle U) 6
Davies, G. 1980 (Fulham, Manchester C) 16
Davies, Rev. H. 1928 (Wrexham) 1
Davies, Idwal 1923 (Liverpool Marine) 1
Davies, J. E. 1885 (Oswestry) 1
Davies, Jas 1878 (Wrexham) 1
Davies, John 1879 (Wrexham) 1
Davies, Jos 1888 (Newton Heath, Wolverhampton W) 7
Davies, Jos 1889 (Everton, Chirk, Ardwick, Sheffield U, Manchester C, Millwall, Reading) 11
Davies, J. P. 1883 (Druids) 2
Davies, Ll. 1907 (Wrexham, Everton, Wrexham) 13
Davies, L. S. 1922 (Cardiff C) 23
Davies, O. 1890 (Wrexham) 1
Davies, R. 1883 (Wrexham) 3
Davies, R. 1885 (Druids) 1
Davies, R. O. 1892 (Wrexham) 2
Davies, R. T. 1964 (Norwich C, Southampton, Portsmouth) 29
Davies, R. W. 1964 (Bolton W, Newcastle U, Manchester C, Manchester U, Blackpool) 34
Davies, S. 2001 (Tottenham H, Everton, Fulham) 58
Davies, S. I. 1996 (Manchester U) 1
Davies, Stanley 1920 (Preston NE, Everton, WBA, Rotherham U) 18
Davies, T. 1886 (Oswestry) 1
Davies, T. 1903 (Druids) 4
Davies, W. 1884 (Wrexham) 1
Davies, W. 1924 (Swansea T, Cardiff C, Notts Co) 17
Davies, William 1903 (Wrexham, Blackburn R) 11
Davies, W. C. 1908 (Crystal Palace, WBA, Crystal Palace) 4
Davies, W. D. 1975 (Everton, Wrexham, Swansea C) 52
Davies, W. H. 1876 (Oswestry) 4
Davis, G. 1978 (Wrexham) 3
Davis, W. O. 1913 (Millwall Ath) 5
Day, A. 1934 (Tottenham H) 1
Deacy, N. 1977 (PSV Eindhoven, Beringen) 12
Dearson, D. J. 1939 (Birmingham) 3
Delaney, M. A. 2000 (Aston Villa) 36
Derrett, S. C. 1969 (Cardiff C) 4
Dewey, F. T. 1931 (Cardiff Corinthians) 2
Dibble, A. 1986 (Luton T, Manchester C) 3
Dorman, A. 2010 (St Mirren, Crystal Palace) 3
Doughty, J. 1886 (Druids, Newton Heath) 8
Doughty, R. 1888 (Newton Heath) 2
Duffy, R. M. 2006 (Portsmouth) 13
Dummett, P. 2014 (Newcastle U) 5
Durban, A. 1966 (Derby Co) 27
Dwyer, P. J. 1978 (Cardiff C) 10

Eardley, N. 2008 (Oldham Ath, Blackpool) 16
Earnshaw, R. 2002 (Cardiff C, WBA, Norwich C, Derby Co, Nottingham F, Cardiff C) 59
Easter, J. M. 2007 (Wycombe W, Plymouth Arg, Milton Keynes D, Crystal Palace, Millwall) 12
Eastwood, F. 2008 (Wolverhampton W, Coventry C) 11
Edwards, C. 1878 (Wrexham) 1
Edwards, C. N. H. 1996 (Swansea C) 1
Edwards, D. A. 2008 (Luton T, Wolverhampton W, Reading) 43
Edwards, G. 1947 (Birmingham C, Cardiff C) 12
Edwards, H. 1878 (Wrexham Civil Service, Wrexham) 8
Edwards, J. H. 1876 (Wanderers) 1
Edwards, J. H. 1895 (Oswestry) 3
Edwards, J. H. 1898 (Aberystwyth) 1
Edwards, L. T. 1957 (Charlton Ath) 2
Edwards, R. I. 1978 (Chester, Wrexham) 4
Edwards, R. O. 2003 (Aston Villa, Wolverhampton W) 15
Edwards, R. W. 1998 (Bristol C) 4
Edwards, T. 1932 (Linfield) 1
Egan, W. 1892 (Chirk) 1

Ellis, B. 1932 (Motherwell) 6
Ellis, E. 1931 (Nunhead, Oswestry) 3
Emanuel, W. J. 1973 (Bristol C) 2
England, H. M. 1962 (Blackburn R, Tottenham H) 44
Evans, B. C. 1972 (Swansea C, Hereford U) 7
Evans, C. M. 2008 (Manchester C, Sheffield U) 13
Evans, D. G. 1926 (Reading, Huddersfield T) 4
Evans, H. P. 1922 (Cardiff C) 6
Evans, I. 1976 (Crystal Palace) 13
Evans, J. 1893 (Oswestry) 3
Evans, J. 1912 (Cardiff C) 8
Evans, J. H. 1922 (Southend U) 4
Evans, L. 2018 (Wolverhampton W, Sheffield U, Wigan Ath) 4
Evans, Len 1927 (Aberdare Ath, Cardiff C, Birmingham) 4
Evans, M. 1884 (Oswestry) 1
Evans, P. S. 2002 (Brentford, Bradford C) 2
Evans, R. 1902 (Clapton) 1
Evans, R. E. 1906 (Wrexham, Aston Villa, Sheffield U) 10
Evans, R. O. 1902 (Wrexham, Blackburn R, Coventry C) 10
Evans, R. S. 1964 (Swansea T) 1
Evans, S. J. 2007 (Wrexham) 7
Evans, T. J. 1927 (Clapton Orient, Newcastle U) 4
Evans, W. 1933 (Tottenham H) 6
Evans, W. A. W. 1876 (Oxford University) 2
Evans, W. G. 1890 (Bootle, Aston Villa) 3
Evelyn, E. C. 1887 (Crusaders) 1
Eyton-Jones, J. A. 1883 (Wrexham) 4

Farmer, G. 1885 (Oswestry) 2
Felgate, D. 1984 (Lincoln C) 1
Finnigan, R. J. 1930 (Wrexham) 1
Fletcher, C. N. 2004 (Bournemouth, West Ham U, Crystal Palace) 36
Flynn, B. 1975 (Burnley, Leeds U, Burnley) 66
Fon Williams, O. 2016 (Inverness CT) 1
Ford, T. 1947 (Swansea T, Aston Villa, Sunderland, Cardiff C) 38
Foulkes, H. E. 1932 (WBA) 1
Foulkes, W. I. 1952 (Newcastle U) 11
Foulkes, W. T. 1884 (Oswestry) 2
Fowler, J. 1925 (Swansea T) 6
Freeman, K. S. 2019 (Sheffield U) 1
Freestone, R. 2000 (Swansea C) 1

Gabbidon, D. L. 2002 (Cardiff C, West Ham U, QPR, Crystal Palace) 49
Garner, G. 2006 (Leyton Orient) 1
Garner, J. 1896 (Aberystwyth) 1
Giggs, R. J. 1992 (Manchester U) 64
Giles, D. C. 1980 (Swansea C, Crystal Palace) 12
Gillam, S. G. 1889 (Wrexham, Shrewsbury, Clapton) 5
Glascodine, G. 1879 (Wrexham) 1
Glover, E. M. 1932 (Grimsby T) 7
Godding, G. 1923 (Wrexham) 2
Godfrey, B. C. 1964 (Preston NE) 3
Goodwin, U. 1881 (Ruthin) 1
Goss, J. 1991 (Norwich C) 9
Gough, R. T. 1883 (Oswestry White Star) 1
Gray, A. 1924 (Oldham Ath, Manchester C, Manchester Central, Tranmere R, Chester) 24
Green, A. W. 1901 (Aston Villa, Notts Co, Nottingham F) 8
Green, C. R. 1965 (Birmingham C) 15
Green, G. H. 1938 (Charlton Ath) 4
Green, R. M. 1998 (Wolverhampton W) 2
Grey, Dr W. 1876 (Druids) 2
Griffiths, A. T. 1971 (Wrexham) 17
Griffiths, F. J. 1900 (Blackpool) 2
Griffiths, G. 1887 (Chirk) 1
Griffiths, J. H. 1953 (Swansea T) 1
Griffiths, L. 1902 (Wrexham) 1
Griffiths, M. W. 1947 (Leicester C) 11
Griffiths, P. 1884 (Chirk) 6
Griffiths, P. H. 1932 (Everton) 1
Griffiths, T. P. 1927 (Everton, Bolton W, Middlesbrough, Aston Villa) 21
Gunter, C. R. 2007 (Cardiff C, Tottenham H, Nottingham F, Reading) 102

Hall, G. D. 1988 (Chelsea) 9
Hallam, J. 1889 (Oswestry) 1
Hanford, H. 1934 (Swansea T, Sheffield W) 7
Harrington, A. C. 1956 (Cardiff C) 11
Harris, C. S. 1976 (Leeds U) 24
Harris, W. C. 1954 (Middlesbrough) 6
Harrison, W. C. 1899 (Wrexham) 5
Hartson, J. 1995 (Arsenal, West Ham U, Wimbledon, Coventry C, Celtic) 51
Haworth, S. O. 1997 (Cardiff C, Coventry C) 5
Hayes, A. 1890 (Wrexham) 2
Hedges, R. P. 2018 (Barnsley, Aberdeen) 3
Henley, A. D. 2016 (Blackburn R) 2
Hennessey, W. R. 2007 (Wolverhampton W, Crystal Palace) 96
Hennessey, W. T. 1962 (Birmingham C, Nottingham F, Derby Co) 39
Hersee, A. M. 1886 (Bangor) 2
Hersee, R. 1886 (Llandudno) 1
Hewitt, R. 1958 (Cardiff C) 5
Hewitt, T. J. 1911 (Wrexham, Chelsea, South Liverpool) 8
Heywood, D. 1879 (Druids) 1
Hibbott, H. 1880 (Newtown Excelsior, Newtown) 3
Higham, G. G. 1878 (Oswestry) 2
Hill, M. R. 1972 (Ipswich T) 2
Hockey, T. 1972 (Sheffield U, Norwich C, Aston Villa) 9
Hoddinott, T. F. 1921 (Watford) 2
Hodges, G. 1984 (Wimbledon, Newcastle U, Watford, Sheffield U) 18
Hodgkinson, A. V. 1908 (Southampton) 1
Holden, A. 1984 (Chester C) 1
Hole, B. G. 1963 (Cardiff C, Blackburn R, Aston Villa, Swansea C) 30
Hole, W. J. 1921 (Swansea T) 9
Hollins, D. M. 1962 (Newcastle U) 11
Hopkins, I. J. 1935 (Brentford) 12
Hopkins, J. 1983 (Fulham, Crystal Palace) 16
Hopkins, M. 1956 (Tottenham H) 34
Horne, B. 1988 (Portsmouth, Southampton, Everton, Birmingham C) 59
Howell, E. G. 1888 (Builth) 3
Howells, R. G. 1954 (Cardiff C) 2
Hugh, A. R. 1930 (Newport Co) 1
Hughes, A. 1894 (Rhos) 2
Hughes, A. 1907 (Chirk) 1
Hughes, C. M. 1992 (Luton T, Wimbledon) 8
Hughes, E. 1899 (Everton, Tottenham H) 14
Hughes, E. 1906 (Wrexham, Nottingham F, Wrexham, Manchester C) 16
Hughes, F. W. 1882 (Northwich Victoria) 6
Hughes, I. 1951 (Luton T) 4
Hughes, J. 1877 (Cambridge University, Aberystwyth) 2
Hughes, J. 1905 (Liverpool) 3
Hughes, J. I. 1935 (Blackburn R) 1
Hughes, L. M. 1984 (Manchester U, Barcelona, Manchester U, Chelsea, Southampton) 72
Hughes, P. W. 1887 (Bangor) 3
Hughes, W. 1891 (Bootle) 3
Hughes, W. A. 1949 (Blackburn R) 5
Hughes, W. M. 1938 (Birmingham) 10
Humphreys, J. V. 1947 (Everton) 1
Humphreys, R. 1888 (Druids) 1
Hunter, A. H. 1887 (FA of Wales Secretary) 1
Huws, E. W. 2014 (Manchester C, Wigan Ath, Cardiff C) 11

Isgrove, L. J. 2016 (Southampton) 1

Jackett, K. 1983 (Watford) 31
Jackson, W. 1899 (St Helens Rec) 1
James, D. O. 2019 (Swansea C, Manchester U) 24
James, E. 1893 (Chirk) 8
James, E. G. 1966 (Blackpool) 9
James, L. 1972 (Burnley, Derby Co, QPR, Burnley, Swansea C, Sunderland) 54
James, R. M. 1979 (Swansea C, Stoke C, QPR, Leicester C, Swansea C) 47
James, W. 1931 (West Ham U) 2
Jarrett, R. H. 1889 (Ruthin) 2
Jarvis, A. L. 1967 (Hull C) 3

Jenkins, E. 1925 (Lovell's Ath) 1
Jenkins, J. 1924 (Brighton & HA) 8
Jenkins, R. W. 1902 (Rhyl) 1
Jenkins, S. R. 1996 (Swansea C, Huddersfield T) 16
Jenkyns, C. A. L. 1892 (Small Heath, Woolwich Arsenal, Newton Heath, Walsall) 8
Jennings, W. 1914 (Bolton W) 11
John, D. C. 2013 (Cardiff C, Rangers, Swansea C) 7
John, R. F. 1923 (Arsenal) 15
John, W. R. 1931 (Walsall, Stoke C, Preston NE, Sheffield U, Swansea T) 14
Johnson, A. J. 1999 (Nottingham F, WBA) 15
Johnson, B. P. 2021 (Nottingham F) 2
Johnson, M. G. 1964 (Swansea T) 1
Jones, A. 1987 (Port Vale, Charlton Ath) 6
Jones, A. F. 1877 (Oxford University) 1
Jones, A. T. 1905 (Nottingham F, Notts Co) 2
Jones, Bryn 1935 (Wolverhampton W, Arsenal) 17
Jones, B. S. 1963 (Swansea T, Plymouth Arg, Cardiff C) 15
Jones, Charlie 1926 (Nottingham F, Arsenal) 8
Jones, Cliff 1954 (Swansea T, Tottenham H, Fulham) 59
Jones, C. W. 1935 (Birmingham) 2
Jones, D. 1888 (Chirk, Bolton W, Manchester C) 14
Jones, D. E. 1976 (Norwich C) 8
Jones, D. O. 1934 (Leicester C) 7
Jones, Evan 1910 (Chelsea, Oldham Ath, Bolton W) 7
Jones, F. R. 1885 (Bangor) 3
Jones, F. W. 1893 (Small Heath) 1
Jones, G. P. 1907 (Wrexham) 2
Jones, H. 1902 (Aberaman) 1
Jones, Humphrey 1885 (Bangor, Queen's Park, East Stirlingshire, Queen's Park) 14
Jones, Ivor 1920 (Swansea T, WBA) 10
Jones, Jeffrey 1908 (Llandrindod Wells) 3
Jones, J. 1876 (Druids) 1
Jones, J. 1883 (Berwyn Rangers) 3
Jones, J. 1925 (Wrexham) 1
Jones, J. L. 1895 (Sheffield U, Tottenham H) 21
Jones, J. Love 1906 (Stoke, Middlesbrough) 2
Jones, J. O. 1901 (Bangor) 2
Jones, J. P. 1976 (Liverpool, Wrexham, Chelsea, Huddersfield T) 72
Jones, J. T. 1912 (Stoke, Crystal Palace) 15
Jones, K. 1950 (Aston Villa) 1
Jones, Leslie J. 1933 (Cardiff C, Coventry C, Arsenal 11
Jones, M. A. 2007 (Wrexham) 2
Jones, M. G. 2000 (Leeds U, Leicester C) 13
Jones, P. L. 1997 (Liverpool, Tranmere R) 2
Jones, P. S. 1997 (Stockport Co, Southampton, Wolverhampton W, QPR) 50
Jones, P. W. 1971 (Bristol R) 1
Jones, R. 1887 (Bangor, Crewe Alex) 3
Jones, R. 1898 (Leicester Fosse) 1
Jones, R. 1899 (Druids) 1
Jones, R. 1900 (Bangor) 2
Jones, R. 1906 (Millwall) 2
Jones, R. A. 1884 (Druids) 4
Jones, R. A. 1994 (Sheffield W) 1
Jones, R. S. 1894 (Everton) 1
Jones, S. 1887 (Wrexham, Chester) 2
Jones, S. 1893 (Wrexham, Burton Swifts, Druids) 6
Jones, T. 1926 (Manchester U) 4
Jones, T. D. 1908 (Aberdare) 1
Jones, T. G. 1938 (Everton) 17
Jones, T. J. 1932 (Sheffield W) 2
Jones, V. P. 1995 (Wimbledon) 9
Jones, W. E. A. 1947 (Swansea T, Tottenham H) 4
Jones, W. J. 1901 (Aberdare, West Ham U) 4
Jones, W. Lot 1905 (Manchester C, Southend U) 20
Jones, W. P. 1889 (Druids, Wynnstay) 4
Jones, W. R. 1897 (Aberystwyth) 1

Keenor, F. C. 1920 (Cardiff C, Crewe Alex) 32
Kelly, F. C. 1899 (Wrexham, Druids) 3
Kelsey, A. J. 1954 (Arsenal) 41
Kenrick, S. L. 1876 (Druids, Oswestry, Shropshire Wanderers) 5
Ketley, C. F. 1882 (Druids) 1
King, A. P. 2009 (Leicester C) 50
King, J. 1955 (Swansea T) 1
Kinsey, N. 1951 (Norwich C, Birmingham C) 7
Knill, A. R. 1989 (Swansea C) 1
Koumas, J. 2001 (Tranmere R, WBA, Wigan Ath) 34
Krzywicki, R. L. 1970 (WBA, Huddersfield T) 8

Lambert, R. 1947 (Liverpool) 5
Latham, G. 1905 (Liverpool, Southport Central, Cardiff C) 10
Law, B. J. 1990 (QPR) 1
Lawrence, E. 1930 (Clapton Orient, Notts Co) 2
Lawrence, J. A. 2019 (Anderlecht, St Pauli) 9
Lawrence, S. 1932 (Swansea T) 8
Lawrence, T. M. 2016 (Leicester C, Derby Co) 23
Lea, A. 1889 (Wrexham) 4
Lea, C. 1965 (Ipswich T) 2
Leary, P. 1889 (Bangor) 1
Ledley, J. C. 2006 (Cardiff C, Celtic, Crystal Palace, Derby Co) 77
Leek, K. 1961 (Leicester C, Newcastle U, Birmingham C, Northampton T) 13
Legg, A. 1996 (Birmingham C, Cardiff C) 6
Lever, A. R. 1953 (Leicester C) 1
Levitt, D. J. C. 2021 (Manchester U) 9
Lewis, B. 1891 (Chester, Wrexham, Middlesbrough, Wrexham) 10
Lewis, D. 1927 (Arsenal) 3
Lewis, D. 1983 (Swansea C) 1
Lewis, D. J. 1933 (Swansea T) 2
Lewis, D. M. 1890 (Bangor) 2
Lewis, J. 1906 (Bristol R) 1
Lewis, J. 1926 (Cardiff C) 1
Lewis, T. 1881 (Wrexham) 2
Lewis, W. 1885 (Bangor, Crewe Alex, Chester, Manchester C, Chester) 27
Lewis, W. L. 1927 (Swansea T, Huddersfield T) 6
Llewellyn, C. M. 1998 (Norwich C, Wrexham) 6
Lloyd, B. W. 1976 (Wrexham) 3
Lloyd, J. W. 1879 (Wrexham, Newtown) 2
Lloyd, R. A. 1891 (Ruthin) 2
Lockley, A. 1898 (Chirk) 1
Lockyer, T. A. 2018 (Bristol R, Charlton Ath, Luton T) 13
Lovell, S. 1982 (Crystal Palace, Millwall) 6
Lowndes, S. R. 1983 (Newport Co, Millwall, Barnsley) 10
Lowrie, G. 1948 (Coventry C, Newcastle U) 4
Lucas, P. M. 1962 (Leyton Orient) 4
Lucas, W. H. 1949 (Swansea T) 7
Lumberg, A. 1929 (Wrexham, Wolverhampton W) 4
Lynch, J. J. 2013 (Hudderfield T) 1

MacDonald, S. B. 2011 (Swansea C, Bournemouth) 4
Maguire, G. T. 1990 (Portsmouth) 7
Mahoney, J. F. 1968 (Stoke C, Middlesbrough, Swansea C) 51
Mardon, P. J. 1996 (WBA) 1
Margetson, M. W. 2004 (Cardiff C) 1
Marriott, A. 1996 (Wrexham) 5
Martin, T. J. 1930 (Newport Co) 1
Marustik, C. 1982 (Swansea C) 6
Mates, J. 1891 (Chirk) 3
Matondo, R. 2019 (Manchester C, Schalke 04) 8
Matthews, A. J. 2011 (Cardiff C, Celtic, Sunderland) 14
Matthews, R. W. 1921 (Liverpool, Bristol C, Bradford) 3
Matthews, W. 1905 (Chester) 2
Matthias, J. S. 1896 (Brymbo, Shrewsbury T, Wolverhampton W) 5
Matthias, T. J. 1914 (Wrexham) 12
Mays, A. W. 1929 (Wrexham) 1
McCarthy, T. P. 1889 (Wrexham) 1
McMillan, R. 1881 (Shrewsbury Engineers) 2
Medwin, T. C. 1953 (Swansea T, Tottenham H) 30
Melville, A. K. 1990 (Swansea C, Oxford U, Sunderland, Fulham, West Ham U) 65
Mepham, C. J. 2018 (Brentford, Bournemouth) 21
Meredith, S. 1900 (Chirk, Stoke, Leyton) 8
Meredith, W. H. 1895 (Manchester C, Manchester U) 48
Mielczarek, R. 1971 (Rotherham U) 1
Millership, H. 1920 (Rotherham Co) 6
Millington, A. H. 1963 (WBA, Crystal Palace, Peterborough U, Swansea C) 21
Mills, T. J. 1934 (Clapton Orient, Leicester C) 4
Mills-Roberts, R. H. 1885 (St Thomas' Hospital, Preston NE, Llanberis) 8

Moore, G. 1960 (Cardiff C, Chelsea, Manchester U, Northampton T, Charlton Ath) 21
Moore, K. R. F. 2020 (Wigan Ath, Cardiff C) 21
Morgan, C. 2007 (Milton Keynes D, Peterborough U, Preston NE) 23
Morgan, J. R. 1877 (Cambridge University, Derby School Staff) 10
Morgan, J. T. 1905 (Wrexham) 1
Morgan-Owen, H. 1902 (Oxford University, Corinthians) 4
Morgan-Owen, M. M. 1897 (Oxford University, Corinthians) 13
Morison, S. W. 2011 (Millwall, Norwich C) 20
Morley, E. J. 1925 (Swansea T, Clapton Orient) 4
Morrell, J. J. 2020 (Bristol C, Luton T) 19
Morris, A. G. 1896 (Aberystwyth, Swindon T, Nottingham F) 21
Morris, C. 1900 (Chirk, Derby Co, Huddersfield T) 27
Morris, E. 1893 (Chirk) 3
Morris, H. 1894 (Sheffield U, Manchester C, Grimsby T) 3
Morris, J. 1887 (Oswestry) 1
Morris, J. 1898 (Chirk) 1
Morris, R. 1900 (Chirk, Shrewsbury T) 6
Morris, R. 1902 (Newtown, Druids, Liverpool, Leeds C, Grimsby T, Plymouth Arg) 11
Morris, S. 1937 (Birmingham) 5
Morris, W. 1947 (Burnley) 5
Moulsdale, J. R. B. 1925 (Corinthians) 1
Murphy, J. P. 1933 (WBA) 15
Myhill, G. O. 2008 (Hull C, WBA) 19
Nardiello, D. 1978 (Coventry C) 2
Nardiello, D. A. 2007 (Barnsley, QPR) 3
Neal, J. E. 1931 (Colwyn Bay) 2
Neilson, A. B. 1992 (Newcastle U, Southampton) 5
Newnes, J. 1926 (Nelson) 1
Newton, L. F. 1912 (Cardiff Corinthians) 1
Nicholas, D. S. 1923 (Stoke, Swansea T) 3
Nicholas, P. 1979 (Crystal Palace, Arsenal, Crystal Palace, Luton T, Aberdeen, Chelsea, Watford) 73
Nicholls, J. 1924 (Newport Co, Cardiff C) 4
Niedzwiecki, E. A. 1985 (Chelsea) 2
Nock, W. 1897 (Newtown) 1
Nogan, L. M. 1992 (Watford, Reading) 2
Norman, A. J. 1986 (Hull C) 5
Norrington-Davies, R. L. 2021 (Sheffield U) 5
Nurse, M. T. G. 1960 (Swansea T, Middlesbrough) 12
Nyatanga, L. J. 2006 (Derby Co, Bristol C) 34
O'Callaghan, E. 1929 (Tottenham H) 11
Oliver, A. 1905 (Bangor, Blackburn R) 2
Oster, J. M. 1998 (Everton, Sunderland) 13
O'Sullivan, P. A. 1973 (Brighton & HA) 3
Owen, D. 1879 (Oswestry) 1
Owen, E. 1884 (Ruthin Grammar School) 3
Owen, G. 1888 (Chirk, Newton Heath, Chirk) 4
Owen, J. 1892 (Newton Heath) 1
Owen, T. 1879 (Oswestry) 1
Owen, Trevor 1899 (Crewe Alex) 2
Owen, W. 1884 (Chirk) 16
Owen, W. P. 1880 (Ruthin) 12
Owens, J. 1902 (Wrexham) 1
Page, M. E. 1971 (Birmingham C) 28
Page, R. J. 1997 (Watford, Sheffield U, Cardiff C, Coventry C) 41
Palmer, D. 1957 (Swansea T) 3
Parris, J. E. 1932 (Bradford) 1
Parry, B. J. 1951 (Swansea T) 1
Parry, C. 1891 (Everton, Newtown) 13
Parry, E. 1922 (Liverpool) 5
Parry, M. 1901 (Liverpool) 16
Parry, P. I. 2004 (Cardiff C) 12
Parry, T. D. 1900 (Oswestry) 7
Parry, W. 1895 (Newtown) 1
Partridge, D. W. 2005 (Motherwell, Bristol C) 7
Pascoe, C. 1984 (Swansea C, Sunderland) 10
Paul, R. 1949 (Swansea T, Manchester C) 33
Peake, E. 1908 (Aberystwyth, Liverpool) 11
Peers, E. J. 1914 (Wolverhampton W, Port Vale) 12
Pembridge, M. A. 1992 (Luton T, Derby Co, Sheffield W, Benfica, Everton, Fulham) 54
Perry, E. 1938 (Doncaster R) 3
Perry, J. 1994 (Cardiff C) 1
Phennah, E. 1878 (Civil Service) 1
Phillips, C. 1931 (Wolverhampton W, Aston Villa) 13
Phillips, D. 1984 (Plymouth Arg, Manchester C, Coventry C, Norwich C, Nottingham F) 62
Phillips, L. 1971 (Cardiff C, Aston Villa, Swansea C, Charlton Ath) 58
Phillips, T. J. S. 1973 (Chelsea) 4
Phoenix, H. 1882 (Wrexham) 1
Pipe, D. R. 2003 (Coventry C) 1
Poland, G. 1939 (Wrexham) 2
Pontin, K. 1980 (Cardiff C) 2
Powell, A. 1947 (Leeds U, Everton, Birmingham C) 8
Powell, D. 1968 (Wrexham, Sheffield U) 11
Powell, I. V. 1947 (QPR, Aston Villa) 8
Powell, J. 1878 (Druids, Bolton W, Newton Heath) 15
Powell, Seth 1885 (Oswestry, WBA) 7
Price, H. 1907 (Aston Villa, Burton U, Wrexham) 5
Price, J. 1877 (Wrexham) 12
Price, L. P. 2006 (Ipswich T, Derby Co, Crystal Palace) 11
Price, P. 1980 (Luton T, Tottenham H) 25
Pring, K. D. 1966 (Rotherham U) 3
Pritchard, H. K. 1985 (Bristol C) 1
Pryce-Jones, A. W. 1895 (Newtown) 1
Pryce-Jones, W. E. 1887 (Cambridge University) 5
Pugh, A. 1889 (Rhostyllen) 1
Pugh, D. H. 1896 (Wrexham, Lincoln C) 7
Pugsley, J. 1930 (Charlton Ath) 1
Pullen, W. J. 1926 (Plymouth Arg) 1

Ramsey, A. J. 2009 (Arsenal, Juventus) 67
Rankmore, F. E. J. 1966 (Peterborough U) 1
Ratcliffe, K. 1981 (Everton, Cardiff C) 59
Rea, J. C. 1894 (Aberystwyth) 9
Ready, K. 1997 (QPR) 5
Reece, G. I. 1966 (Sheffield U, Cardiff C) 29
Reed, W. G. 1955 (Ipswich T) 2
Rees, A. 1984 (Birmingham C) 1
Rees, J. M. 1992 (Luton T) 1
Rees, R. R. 1965 (Coventry C, WBA, Nottingham F) 39
Rees, W. 1949 (Cardiff C, Tottenham H) 4
Ribeiro, C. M. 2010 (Bristol C) 2
Richards, A. 1932 (Barnsley) 1
Richards, A. D. J. (Jazz) 2012 (Swansea C, Cardiff C) 14
Richards, D. 1931 (Wolverhampton W, Brentford, Birmingham) 21
Richards, G. 1899 (Druids, Oswestry, Shrewsbury T) 6
Richards, R. W. 1920 (Wolverhampton W, West Ham U, Mold) 9
Richards, S. V. 1947 (Cardiff C) 1
Richards, W. E. 1933 (Fulham) 1
Ricketts, S. D. 2005 (Swansea C, Hull C, Bolton W, Wolverhampton W) 52
Roach, J. 1885 (Oswestry) 1
Robbins, W. W. 1931 (Cardiff C, WBA) 11
Roberts, A. M. 1993 (QPR) 2
Roberts, C. R. J. 2018 (Swansea C) 30
Roberts, D. F. 1973 (Oxford U, Hull C) 17
Roberts, G. W. 2000 (Tranmere R) 9
Roberts, I. W. 1990 (Watford, Huddersfield T, Leicester C, Norwich C) 15
Roberts, Jas 1913 (Wrexham) 2
Roberts, J. 1879 (Corwen, Berwyn R) 7
Roberts, J. 1881 (Ruthin) 2
Roberts, J. 1906 (Bradford C) 2
Roberts, J. G. 1971 (Arsenal, Birmingham C) 22
Roberts, J. H. 1949 (Bolton W) 1
Roberts, N. W. 2000 (Wrexham, Wigan Ath) 4
Roberts, P. S. 1974 (Portsmouth) 4
Roberts, R. 1884 (Druids, Bolton W, Preston NE) 9
Roberts, R. 1886 (Wrexham) 3
Roberts, R. 1891 (Rhos, Crewe Alex) 2
Roberts, R. L. 1890 (Chester) 1
Roberts, S. W. 2005 (Wrexham) 1
Roberts, T. D. 2019 (Leeds U) 14
Roberts, W. 1879 (Llangollen, Berwyn R) 6
Roberts, W. 1883 (Rhyl) 1
Roberts, W. 1886 (Wrexham) 4
Roberts, W. H. 1882 (Ruthin, Rhyl) 6
Robinson, C. P. 2000 (Wolverhampton W, Portsmouth, Sunderland, Norwich C, Toronto Lynx) 52
Robinson, J. R. C. 1996 (Charlton Ath) 30
Robson-Kanu, T. H. 2010 (Reading, WBA) 46
Rodon, J. P. 2020 (Swansea C, Tottenham H) 18
Rodrigues, P. J. 1965 (Cardiff C, Leicester C, Sheffield W) 40

Rogers, J. P. 1896 (Wrexham) 3
Rogers, W. 1931 (Wrexham) 2
Roose, L. R. 1900 (Aberystwyth, London Welsh, Stoke, Everton, Stoke, Sunderland) 24
Rouse, R. V. 1959 (Crystal Palace) 1
Rowlands, A. C. 1914 (Tranmere R) 1
Rowley, T. 1959 (Tranmere R) 1
Rush, I. 1980 (Liverpool, Juventus, Liverpool) 73
Russell, M. R. 1912 (Merthyr T, Plymouth Arg) 23

Sabine, H. W. 1887 (Oswestry) 1
Saunders, D. 1986 (Brighton & HA, Oxford U, Derby Co, Liverpool, Aston Villa, Galatasaray, Nottingham F, Sheffield U, Benfica, Bradford C) 75
Savage, R. W. 1996 (Crewe Alex, Leicester C, Birmingham C) 39
Savin, G. 1878 (Oswestry) 1
Sayer, P. A. 1977 (Cardiff C) 7
Scrine, F. H. 1950 (Swansea T) 2
Sear, C. R. 1963 (Manchester C) 1
Shaw, E. G. 1882 (Oswestry) 3
Sheehan, J. L. 2021 (Newport Co) 2
Sherwood, A. T. 1947 (Cardiff C, Newport Co) 41
Shone, W. W. 1879 (Oswestry) 1
Shortt, W. W. 1947 (Plymouth Arg) 12
Showers, D. 1975 (Cardiff C) 2
Sidlow, C. 1947 (Liverpool) 7
Sisson, H. 1885 (Wrexham Olympic) 3
Slatter, N. 1983 (Bristol R, Oxford U) 22
Smallman, D. P. 1974 (Wrexham, Everton) 7
Smith, M. 2018 (Manchester C) 14
Southall, N. 1982 (Everton) 92
Speed, G. A. 1990 (Leeds U, Everton, Newcastle U, Bolton W) 85
Sprake, G. 1964 (Leeds U, Birmingham C) 37
Stansfield, F. 1949 (Cardiff C) 1
Stevenson, B. 1978 (Leeds U, Birmingham C) 15
Stevenson, N. 1982 (Swansea C) 4
Stitfall, R. F. 1953 (Cardiff C) 2
Stock, B. B. 2010 (Doncaster R) 3
Sullivan, D. 1953 (Cardiff C) 17
Symons, C. J. 1992 (Portsmouth, Manchester C, Fulham, Crystal Palace) 37

Tapscott, D. R. 1954 (Arsenal, Cardiff C) 14
Taylor, G. K. 1996 (Crystal Palace, Sheffield U, Burnley, Nottingham F) 15
Taylor, J. 1898 (Wrexham) 1
Taylor, J. W. T. 2015 (Reading) 1
Taylor, N. J. 2010 (Wrexham, Swansea C, Aston Villa) 43
Taylor, O. D. S. 1893 (Newtown) 4
Thatcher, B. D. 2004 (Leicester C, Manchester C) 7
Thomas, C. 1899 (Druids) 2
Thomas, D. A. 1957 (Swansea T) 2
Thomas, D. S. 1948 (Fulham) 4
Thomas, E. 1925 (Cardiff Corinthians) 1
Thomas, G. 1885 (Wrexham) 2
Thomas, G. S. 2018 (Leicester C) 3
Thomas, H. 1927 (Manchester U) 1
Thomas, Martin R. 1987 (Newcastle U) 1
Thomas, Mickey 1977 (Wrexham, Manchester U, Everton, Brighton & HA, Stoke C, Chelsea, WBA) 51
Thomas, R. J. 1967 (Swindon T, Derby Co, Cardiff C) 50
Thomas, T. 1898 (Bangor) 2
Thomas, W. R. 1931 (Newport Co) 2
Thomson, D. 1876 (Druids) 1
Thomson, G. F. 1876 (Druids) 2
Toshack, J. B. 1969 (Cardiff C, Liverpool, Swansea C) 40
Townsend, W. 1887 (Newtown) 2
Trainer, H. 1895 (Wrexham) 3
Trainer, J. 1887 (Bolton W, Preston NE) 20
Trollope, P. J. 1997 (Derby Co, Fulham, Coventry C, Northampton T) 9
Tudur-Jones, O. 2008 (Swansea C, Norwich C, Hibernian) 7
Turner, H. G. 1937 (Charlton Ath) 8
Turner, J. 1892 (Wrexham) 1
Turner, R. E. 1891 (Wrexham) 2
Turner, W. H. 1887 (Wrexham) 5

Van Den Hauwe, P. W. R. 1985 (Everton) 13
Vaughan, D. O. 2003 (Crewe Alex, Real Sociedad, Blackpool, Sunderland, Nottingham F) 42
Vaughan, Jas 1893 (Druids) 4
Vaughan, John 1879 (Oswestry, Druids, Bolton W) 11
Vaughan, J. O. 1885 (Rhyl) 4
Vaughan, N. 1983 (Newport Co, Cardiff C) 10
Vaughan, T. 1885 (Rhyl) 1
Vaulks, W. R. 2019 (Rotherham U, Cardiff C) 6
Vearncombe, G. 1958 (Cardiff C) 2
Vernon, T. R. 1957 (Blackburn R, Everton, Stoke C) 32
Villars, A. K. 1974 (Cardiff C) 3
Vizard, E. T. 1911 (Bolton W) 22
Vokes, S. M. 2008 (Bournemouth, Wolverhampton W, Burnley, Stoke C) 64

Walley, J. T. 1971 (Watford) 1
Walsh, I. P. 1980 (Crystal Palace, Swansea C) 18
Ward, D. 1959 (Bristol R, Cardiff C) 2
Ward, D. 2000 (Notts Co, Nottingham F) 5
Ward, D. 2016 (Liverpool, Leicester C) 17
Warner, J. 1937 (Swansea T, Manchester U) 2
Warren, F. W. 1929 (Cardiff C, Middlesbrough, Hearts) 6
Watkins, A. E. 1898 (Leicester Fosse, Aston Villa, Millwall) 5
Watkins, M. J. 2018 (Norwich C) 2
Watkins, W. M. 1902 (Stoke, Aston Villa, Sunderland, Stoke) 10
Webster, C. 1957 (Manchester U) 4
Weston, R. D. 2000 (Arsenal, Cardiff C) 7
Whatley, W. J. 1939 (Tottenham H) 2
White, P. F. 1896 (London Welsh) 1
Wilcock, A. R. 1890 (Oswestry) 1
Wilding, J. 1885 (Wrexham Olympians, Bootle, Wrexham) 9
Williams, A. 1994 (Reading, Wolverhampton W, Reading) 13
Williams, A. E. 2008 (Stockport Co, Swansea C, Everton) 86
Williams, A. L. 1931 (Wrexham) 1
Williams, A. P. 1998 (Southampton) 2
Williams, B. 1930 (Bristol C) 1
Williams, B. D. 1928 (Swansea T, Everton) 10
Williams, D. G. 1988 (Derby Co, Ipswich T) 13
Williams, D. M. 1986 (Norwich C) 5
Williams, D. R. 1921 (Merthyr T, Sheffield W, Manchester U) 8
Williams, E. 1893 (Crewe Alex) 2
Williams, E. 1901 (Druids) 5
Williams, G. 1893 (Chirk) 6
Williams, G. C. 2014 (Fulham) 7
Williams, G. E. 1960 (WBA) 26
Williams, G. G. 1961 (Swansea T) 5
Williams, G. J. 2006 (West Ham U, Ipswich T) 2
Williams, G. J. J. 1951 (Cardiff C) 1
Williams, G. O. 1907 (Wrexham) 1
Williams, H. J. 1965 (Swansea T) 3
Williams, H. T. 1949 (Newport Co, Leeds U) 4
Williams, J. H. 1884 (Oswestry) 1
Williams, J. J. 1939 (Wrexham) 1
Williams, J. P. 2013 (Crystal Palace, Charlton Ath) 28
Williams, J. T. 1925 (Middlesbrough) 1
Williams, J. W. 1912 (Crystal Palace) 2
Williams, N. S. 2021 (Liverpool) 14
Williams, R. 1935 (Newcastle U) 2
Williams, R. P. 1886 (Caernarvon) 1
Williams, S. G. 1954 (WBA, Southampton) 43
Williams, W. 1876 (Druids, Oswestry, Druids) 11
Williams, W. 1925 (Northampton T) 1
Wilson, H. 2013 (Liverpool) 29
Wilson, J. S. 2013 (Bristol C) 1
Witcomb, D. F. 1947 (WBA, Sheffield W) 3
Woodburn, B. 2018 (Liverpool) 10
Woosnam, A. P. 1959 (Leyton Orient, West Ham U, Aston Villa) 17
Woosnam, G. 1879 (Newtown Excelsior) 1
Worthington, T. 1894 (Newtown) 1
Wynn, G. A. 1909 (Wrexham, Manchester C) 11
Wynn, W. 1903 (Chirk) 1

Yorath, T. C. 1970 (Leeds U, Coventry C, Tottenham H, Vancouver Whitecaps) 59
Young, E. 1990 (Wimbledon, Crystal Palace, Wolverhampton W) 21

REPUBLIC OF IRELAND

Aherne, T. 1946 (Belfast Celtic, Luton T) 16
Aldridge, J. W. 1986 (Oxford U, Liverpool, Real Sociedad, Tranmere R) 69
Ambrose, P. 1955 (Shamrock R) 5
Anderson, J. 1980 (Preston NE, Newcastle U) 16
Andrews, K. J. 2009 (Blackburn R, WBA) 35
Andrews, P. 1936 (Bohemians) 1
Arrigan, T. 1938 (Waterford) 1
Arter, H. N. 2015 (Bournemouth) 18

Babb, P. A. 1994 (Coventry C, Liverpool, Sunderland) 35
Bailham, E. 1964 (Shamrock R) 1
Barber, E. 1966 (Shelbourne, Birmingham C) 2
Barrett, G. 2003 (Arsenal, Coventry C) 6
Barry, P. 1928 (Fordsons) 2
Bazunu, G. O. 2021 (Manchester C) 4
Beglin, J. 1984 (Liverpool) 15
Bennett, A. J. 2007 (Reading) 2
Bermingham, J. 1929 (Bohemians) 1
Bermingham, P. 1935 (St James' Gate) 1
Best, L. J. B. 2009 (Coventry C, Newcastle U) 7
Bonner, P. 1981 (Celtic) 80
Boyle, A. 2017 (Preston NE) 1
Braddish, S. 1978 (Dundalk) 2
Bradshaw, P. 1939 (St James' Gate) 5
Brady, F. 1926 (Fordsons) 2
Brady, R. 2013 (Hull C, Norwich C, Burnley) 57
Brady, T. R. 1964 (QPR) 6
Brady, W. L. 1975 (Arsenal, Juventus, Sampdoria, Internazionale, Ascoli, West Ham U) 72
Branagan, K. G. 1997 (Bolton W) 1
Breen, G. 1996 (Birmingham C, Coventry C, West Ham U, Sunderland) 63
Breen, T. 1937 (Manchester U, Shamrock R) 5
Brennan, F. 1965 (Drumcondra) 1
Brennan, S. A. 1965 (Manchester U, Waterford) 19
Brown, J. 1937 (Coventry C) 2
Browne, A. J. 2017 (Preston NE) 14
Browne, W. 1964 (Bohemians) 3
Bruce, A. S. 2007 (Ipswich T) 2
Buckley, L. 1984 (Shamrock R, Waregem) 2
Burke, F. 1952 (Cork Ath) 1
Burke, G. D. 2018 (Shamrock R, Preston NE) 3
Burke, J. 1929 (Shamrock R) 1
Burke, J. 1934 (Cork) 1
Butler, P. J. 2000 (Sunderland) 1
Butler, T. 2003 (Sunderland) 2
Byrne, A. B. 1970 (Southampton) 14
Byrne, D. 1929 (Shelbourne, Shamrock R, Coleraine) 3
Byrne, J. 1928 (Bray Unknowns) 1
Byrne, J. 1985 (QPR, Le Havre, Brighton & HA, Sunderland, Millwall) 23
Byrne, J. 2004 (Shelbourne) 2
Byrne, J. 2020 (Shamrock R) 4
Byrne, P. 1931 (Dolphin, Shelbourne, Drumcondra) 3
Byrne, P. 1984 (Shamrock R) 8
Byrne, S. 1931 (Bohemians) 1

Campbell, A. 1985 (Santander) 3
Campbell, N. 1971 (St Patrick's Ath, Fortuna Cologne) 11
Cannon, H. 1926 (Bohemians) 2
Cantwell, N. 1954 (West Ham U, Manchester U) 36
Carey, B. P. 1992 (Manchester U, Leicester C) 3
Carey, J. J. 1938 (Manchester U) 29
Carolan, J. 1960 (Manchester U) 2
Carr, S. 1999 (Tottenham H, Newcastle U) 44
Carroll, B. 1949 (Shelbourne) 2
Carroll, T. R. 1968 (Ipswich T, Birmingham C) 17
Carsley, L. K. 1998 (Derby Co, Blackburn R, Coventry C, Everton) 39
Cascarino, A. G. 1986 (Gillingham, Millwall, Aston Villa, Celtic, Chelsea, Marseille, Nancy) 88
Chandler, J. 1980 (Leeds U) 2
Chatton, H. A. 1931 (Shelbourne, Dumbarton, Cork) 3
Christie, C. S. F. 2015 (Derby Co, Middlesbrough, Fulham) 28
Clark, C. 2011 (Aston Villa, Newcastle U) 36
Clarke, C. R. 2004 (Stoke C) 2
Clarke, J. 1978 (Drogheda U) 1
Clarke, K. 1948 (Drumcondra) 2
Clarke, M. 1950 (Shamrock R) 1
Clinton, T. J. 1951 (Everton) 3
Coad, P. 1947 (Shamrock R) 11
Coffey, T. 1950 (Drumcondra) 1
Coleman, S. 2011 (Everton) 59
Colfer, M. D. 1950 (Shelbourne) 2
Colgan, N. 2002 (Hibernian, Barnsley) 9
Collins, F. 1927 (Jacobs) 1
Collins, J. S. 2020 (Luton T) 10
Conmy, O. M. 1965 (Peterborough U) 5
Connolly, A. A. 2020 (Brighton & HA) 6
Connolly, D. J. 1996 (Watford, Feyenoord, Wolverhampton W, Excelsior, Feyenoord, Wimbledon, West Ham U, Wigan Ath) 41
Connolly, H. 1937 (Cork) 1
Connolly, J. 1926 (Fordsons) 1
Conroy, G. A. 1970 (Stoke C) 27
Conway, J. P. 1967 (Fulham, Manchester C) 20
Corr, P. J. 1949 (Everton) 4
Courtney, E. 1946 (Cork U) 1
Cox, S. R. 2011 (WBA, Nottingham F) 30
Coyle, O. C. 1994 (Bolton W) 1
Coyne, T. 1992 (Celtic, Tranmere R, Motherwell) 22
Crowe, G. 2003 (Bohemians) 2
Cullen, J. J. 2020 (West Ham U) 9
Cummins, G. P. 1954 (Luton T) 19
Cuneen, T. 1951 (Limerick) 1
Cunningham, G. R. 2010 (Manchester C, Bristol C) 4
Cunningham, K. 1996 (Wimbledon, Birmingham C) 72
Curtis, D. P. 1957 (Shelbourne, Bristol C, Ipswich T, Exeter C) 17
Curtis, R. 2019 (Portsmouth) 7
Cusack, S. 1953 (Limerick) 1

Daish, L. S. 1992 (Cambridge U, Coventry C) 5
Daly, G. A. 1973 (Manchester U, Derby Co, Coventry C, Birmingham C, Shrewsbury T) 48
Daly, J. 1932 (Shamrock R) 2
Daly, M. 1978 (Wolverhampton W) 2
Daly, P. 1950 (Shamrock R) 1
Davis, T. L. 1937 (Oldham Ath, Tranmere R) 4
Deacy, E. 1982 (Aston Villa) 4
Delaney, D. F. 2008 (QPR, Ipswich T, Crystal Palace) 9
Delap, R. J. 1998 (Derby Co, Southampton) 11
De Mange, K. J. P. P. 1987 (Liverpool, Hull C) 2
Dempsey, J. T. 1967 (Fulham, Chelsea) 19
Dennehy, J. 1972 (Cork Hibernians, Nottingham F, Walsall) 11
Desmond, P. 1950 (Middlesbrough) 4
Devine, J. 1980 (Arsenal, Norwich C) 13
Doherty, G. M. T. 2000 (Luton T, Tottenham H, Norwich C) 34
Doherty, M. J. 2018 (Woverhampton W, Tottenham H) 20
Donnelly, J. 1935 (Dundalk) 10
Donnelly, T. 1938 (Drumcondra, Shamrock R) 2
Donovan, D. C. 1955 (Everton) 5
Donovan, T. 1980 (Aston Villa) 2
Douglas, J. 2004 (Blackburn R, Leeds U) 8
Dowdall, C. 1928 (Fordsons, Barnsley, Cork) 3
Doyle, C. 1959 (Shelbourne) 1
Doyle, C. A. 2007 (Birmingham C, Bradford C) 4
Doyle, D. 1926 (Shamrock R) 1
Doyle, K. E. 2006 (Reading, Wolverhampton W, Colorado Rapids) 63
Doyle, L. 1932 (Dolphin) 1
Doyle, M. P. 2004 (Coventry C) 1
Duff, D. A. 1998 (Blackburn R, Chelsea, Newcastle U, Fulham) 100
Duffy, B. 1950 (Shamrock R) 1
Duffy, S. P. M. 2014 (Everton, Blackburn R, Brighton & HA) 44
Duggan, H. A. 1927 (Leeds U, Newport Co) 5
Dunne, A. P. 1962 (Manchester U, Bolton W) 33
Dunne, J. 1930 (Sheffield U, Arsenal, Southampton, Shamrock R) 15
Dunne, J. C. 1971 (Fulham) 1
Dunne, L. 1935 (Manchester C) 2
Dunne, P. A. J. 1965 (Manchester U) 5

Dunne, R. P. 2000 (Everton, Manchester C, Aston Villa, QPR) 80
Dunne, S. 1953 (Luton T) 15
Dunne, T. 1956 (St Patrick's Ath) 3
Dunning, P. 1971 (Shelbourne) 2
Dunphy, E. M. 1966 (York C, Millwall) 23
Dwyer, N. M. 1960 (West Ham U, Swansea T) 14

Eccles, P. 1986 (Shamrock R) 1
Egan, J. 2017 (Brentford, Sheffield U) 14
Egan, R. 1929 (Dundalk) 1
Eglington, T. J. 1946 (Shamrock R, Everton) 24
Elliot, R. 2014 (Newcastle U) 4
Elliott, S. W. 2005 (Sunderland) 9
Ellis, P. 1935 (Bohemians) 7
Evans, M. J. 1998 (Southampton) 1

Fagan, E. 1973 (Shamrock R) 1
Fagan, F. 1955 (Manchester C, Derby Co) 8
Fagan, J. 1926 (Shamrock R) 1
Fahey, K. D. 2010 (Birmingham C) 16
Fairclough, M. 1982 (Dundalk) 2
Fallon, S. 1951 (Celtic) 8
Fallon, W. J. 1935 (Notts Co, Sheffield W) 9
Farquharson, T. G. 1929 (Cardiff C) 4
Farrell, P. 1937 (Hibernian) 2
Farrell, P. D. 1946 (Shamrock R, Everton) 28
Farrelly, G. 1996 (Aston Villa, Everton, Bolton W) 6
Feenan, J. J. 1937 (Sunderland) 2
Finnan, S. 2000 (Fulham, Liverpool, Espanyol) 53
Finucane, A. 1967 (Limerick) 11
Fitzgerald, F. J. 1955 (Waterford) 2
Fitzgerald, P. J. 1961 (Leeds U, Chester) 5
Fitzpatrick, K. 1970 (Limerick) 1
Fitzsimons, A. G. 1950 (Middlesbrough, Lincoln C) 26
Fleming, C. 1996 (Middlesbrough) 10
Flood, J. J. 1926 (Shamrock R) 5
Fogarty, A. 1960 (Sunderland, Hartlepools U) 11
Folan, C. C. 2009 (Hull C) 7
Foley, D. J. 2000 (Watford) 6
Foley, J. 1934 (Cork, Celtic) 7
Foley, K. P. 2009 (Wolverhampton W) 8
Foley, M. 1926 (Shelbourne) 1
Foley, T. C. 1964 (Northampton T) 9
Forde, D. 2011 (Millwall) 24
Foy, T. 1938 (Shamrock R) 2
Fullam, J. 1961 (Preston NE, Shamrock R) 11
Fullam, R. 1926 (Shamrock R) 2

Gallagher, C. 1967 (Celtic) 2
Gallagher, M. 1954 (Hibernian) 1
Gallagher, P. 1932 (Falkirk) 1
Galvin, A. 1983 (Tottenham H, Sheffield W, Swindon T) 29
Gamble, J. 2007 (Cork C) 2
Gannon, E. 1949 (Notts Co, Sheffield W, Shelbourne) 14
Gannon, M. 1972 (Shelbourne) 1
Gaskins, P. 1934 (Shamrock R, St James' Gate) 7
Gavin, J. T. 1950 (Norwich C, Tottenham H, Norwich C) 7
Geoghegan, M. 1937 (St James' Gate) 2
Gibbons, A. 1952 (St Patrick's Ath) 4
Gibson, D. T. D. 2008 (Manchester U, Everton) 27
Gilbert, R. 1966 (Shamrock R) 1
Giles, C. 1951 (Doncaster R) 1
Giles, M. J. 1960 (Manchester U, Leeds U, WBA, Shamrock R) 59
Given, S. J. J. 1996 (Blackburn R, Newcastle U, Manchester C, Aston Villa, Stoke C) 134
Givens, D. J. 1969 (Manchester U, Luton T, QPR, Birmingham C, Neuchatel X) 56
Gleeson, S. M. 2007 (Wolverhampton W, Birmingham C) 4
Glen, W. 1927 (Shamrock R) 8
Glynn, D. 1952 (Drumcondra) 2
Godwin, T. F. 1949 (Shamrock R, Leicester C, Bournemouth) 13
Golding, J. 1928 (Shamrock R) 2
Goodman, J. 1997 (Wimbledon) 4
Goodwin, J. 2003 (Stockport Co) 1
Gorman, W. C. 1936 (Bury, Brentford) 13
Grace, J. 1926 (Drumcondra) 1
Grealish, A. 1976 (Orient, Luton T, Brighton & HA, WBA) 45
Green, P. J. 2010 (Derby Co, Leeds U) 20
Gregg, E. 1978 (Bohemians) 8
Griffith, R. 1935 (Walsall) 1
Grimes, A. A. 1978 (Manchester U, Coventry C, Luton T) 18

Hale, A. 1962 (Aston Villa, Doncaster R, Waterford) 14
Hamilton, T. 1959 (Shamrock R) 2
Hand, E. K. 1969 (Portsmouth) 20
Harrington, W. 1936 (Cork) 5
Harte, I. P. 1996 (Leeds U, Levante) 64
Hartnett, J. B. 1949 (Middlesbrough) 2
Haverty, J. 1956 (Arsenal, Blackburn R, Millwall, Celtic, Bristol R, Shelbourne) 32
Hayes, A. W. P. 1979 (Southampton) 1
Hayes, J. 2016 (Aberdeen) 4
Hayes, W. E. 1947 (Huddersfield T) 2
Hayes, W. J. 1949 (Limerick) 1
Healey, R. 1977 (Cardiff C) 2
Healy, C. 2002 (Celtic, Sunderland) 13
Heighway, S. D. 1971 (Liverpool, Minnesota K) 34
Henderson, B. 1948 (Drumcondra) 2
Henderson, W. C. P. 2006 (Brighton & HA, Preston NE) 6
Hendrick, J. P. 2013 (Derby Co, Burnley, Newcastle U) 62
Hennessy, J. 1965 (Shelbourne, St Patrick's Ath) 5
Herrick, J. 1972 (Cork Hibernians, Shamrock R) 3
Higgins, J. 1951 (Birmingham C) 1
Hogan, S. A. 2018 (Aston Villa) 8
Holland, M. R. 2000 (Ipswich T, Charlton Ath) 49
Holmes, J. 1971 (Coventry C, Tottenham H, Vancouver Whitecaps) 30
Hoolahan, W. 2008 (Blackpool, Norwich C) 43
Horgan, D. J. 2017 (Preston NE, Hibernian) 14
Horlacher, A. F. 1930 (Bohemians) 7
Houghton, R. J. 1986 (Oxford U, Liverpool, Aston Villa, Crystal Palace, Reading) 73
Hourihane, C. 2017 (Aston Villa) 26
Howlett, G. 1984 (Brighton & HA) 1
Hoy, M. 1938 (Dundalk) 6
Hughton, C. 1980 (Tottenham H, West Ham U) 53
Hunt, N. 2009 (Reading) 3
Hunt, S. P. 2007 (Reading, Hull C, Wolverhampton W) 39
Hurley, C. J. 1957 (Millwall, Sunderland, Bolton W) 40
Hutchinson, F. 1935 (Drumcondra) 2

Idah, A. 2021 (Norwich C) 7
Ireland S. J. 2006 (Manchester C) 6
Irwin, D. J. 1991 (Manchester U) 56

Jordan, D. 1937 (Wolverhampton W) 2
Jordan, W. 1934 (Bohemians) 2
Judge, A. C. 2016 (Brentford, Ipswich T) 9

Kavanagh, G. A. 1998 (Stoke C, Cardiff C, Wigan Ath) 16
Kavanagh, P. J. 1931 (Celtic) 2
Keane, R. D. 1998 (Wolverhampton W, Coventry C, Internazionale, Leeds U, Tottenham H, Liverpool, Tottenham H, LA Galaxy) 146
Keane, R. M. 1991 (Nottingham F, Manchester U) 67
Keane, T. R. 1949 (Swansea T) 4
Kearin, M. 1972 (Shamrock R) 1
Kearns, F. T. 1954 (West Ham U) 1
Kearns, M. 1971 (Oxford U, Walsall, Wolverhampton W) 18
Kelleher, C. O. 2021 (Liverpool) 1
Kelly, A. T. 1993 (Sheffield U, Blackburn R) 34
Kelly, D. T. 1988 (Walsall, West Ham U, Leicester C, Newcastle U, Wolverhampton W, Sunderland, Tranmere R) 26
Kelly, G. 1994 (Leeds U) 52
Kelly, J. 1932 (Derry C) 4
Kelly, J. A. 1957 (Drumcondra, Preston NE) 47
Kelly, J. P. V. 1961 (Wolverhampton W) 5
Kelly, M. J. 1988 (Portsmouth) 4
Kelly, N. 1954 (Nottingham F) 1

Kelly, S. M. 2006 (Tottenham H, Birmingham C, Fulham, Reading) 38
Kendrick, J. 1927 (Everton, Dolphin) 4
Kenna, J. J. 1995 (Blackburn R) 27
Kennedy, M. F. 1986 (Portsmouth) 2
Kennedy, M. J. 1996 (Liverpool, Wimbledon, Manchester C, Wolverhampton W) 34
Kennedy, W. 1932 (St James' Gate) 3
Kenny, P. 2004 (Sheffield U) 7
Keogh, A. D. 2007 (Wolverhampton W, Millwall) 30
Keogh, J. 1966 (Shamrock R) 1
Keogh, R. J. 2013 (Derby Co) 26
Keogh, S. 1959 (Shamrock R) 1
Kernaghan, A. N. 1993 (Middlesbrough, Manchester C) 22
Kiely, D. L. 2000 (Charlton Ath, WBA) 11
Kiernan, F. W. 1951 (Shamrock R, Southampton) 5
Kilbane, K. D. 1998 (WBA, Sunderland, Everton, Wigan Ath, Hull C) 110
Kinnear, J. P. 1967 (Tottenham H, Brighton & HA) 26
Kinsella, J. 1928 (Shelbourne) 1
Kinsella, M. A. 1998 (Charlton Ath, Aston Villa, WBA) 48
Kinsella, O. 1932 (Shamrock R) 2
Kirkland, A. 1927 (Shamrock R) 1
Knight, J. P. 2021 (Derby Co) 7

Lacey, W. 1927 (Shelbourne) 3
Langan, D. 1978 (Derby Co, Birmingham C, Oxford U) 26
Lapira, J. 2007 (Notre Dame) 1
Lawler, J. F. 1953 (Fulham) 8
Lawlor, J. C. 1949 (Drumcondra, Doncaster R) 3
Lawlor, M. 1971 (Shamrock R) 5
Lawrence, L. 2009 (Stoke C, Portsmouth) 15
Lawrenson, M. 1977 (Preston NE, Brighton & HA, Liverpool) 39
Lee, A. D. 2003 (Rotherham U, Cardiff C, Ipswich T) 10
Leech, M. 1969 (Shamrock R) 8
Lenihan, D. P. 2018 (Blackburn R) 2
Lennon, C. 1935 (St James' Gate) 3
Lennox, G. 1931 (Dolphin) 2
Long, K. F. 2017 (Burnley) 17
Long, S. P. 2007 (Reading, WBA, Hull C, Southampton) 88
Lowry, D. 1962 (St Patrick's Ath) 1
Lunn, R. 1939 (Dundalk) 2
Lynch, J. 1934 (Cork Bohemians) 1

Macken, A. 1977 (Derby Co) 1
Macken J. P. 2005 (Manchester C) 1
Mackey, G. 1957 (Shamrock R) 3
Madden, O. 1936 (Cork) 1
Madden, P. 2013 (Scunthorpe U) 1
Maguire, J. 1929 (Shamrock R) 1
Maguire, S. P. 2018 (Preston NE) 11
Mahon, A. J. 2000 (Tranmere R) 2
Malone, G. 1949 (Shelbourne) 1
Mancini, T. J. 1974 (QPR, Arsenal) 5
Manning, R. P. (Swansea C) 4
Martin, C. 1927 (Bo'ness) 1
Martin, C. J. 1946 (Glentoran, Leeds U, Aston Villa) 30
Martin, M. P. 1972 (Bohemians, Manchester U, WBA, Newcastle U) 52
Maybury, A. 1998 (Leeds U, Hearts, Leicester C) 10
McAlinden, J. 1946 (Portsmouth) 2
McAteer, J. W. 1994 (Bolton W, Liverpool, Blackburn R, Sunderland) 52
McCann, J. 1957 (Shamrock R) 1
McCarthy, J. 1926 (Bohemians) 3
McCarthy, J. 2010 (Wigan Ath, Everton, Crystal Palace) 43
McCarthy, M. 1932 (Shamrock R) 1
McCarthy, M. 1984 (Manchester C, Celtic, Lyon, Millwall) 57
McClean, J. J. 2012 (Sunderland, Wigan Ath, WBA, Stoke C) 82
McConville, T. 1972 (Dundalk, Waterford) 6
McDonagh, Jacko 1984 (Shamrock R) 3
McDonagh, J. 1981 (Everton, Bolton W, Notts Co, Wichita Wings) 25
McEvoy, M. A. 1961 (Blackburn R) 17
McGeady, A. J. 2004 (Celtic, Spartak Moscow, Everton, Sunderland) 93
McGee, P. 1978 (QPR, Preston NE) 15
McGoldrick, D. J. 2015 (Ipswich T, Sheffield U) 14
McGoldrick, E. J. 1992 (Crystal Palace, Arsenal) 15
McGowan, D. 1949 (West Ham U) 3
McGowan, J. 1947 (Cork U) 1
McGrath, J. 2021 (St Mirren) 1
McGrath, M. 1958 (Blackburn R, Bradford) 22
McGrath, P. 1985 (Manchester U, Aston Villa, Derby Co) 83
McGuire, W. 1936 (Bohemians) 1
McKenzie, G. 1938 (Southend U) 9
McLoughlin, A. F. 1990 (Swindon T, Southampton, Portsmouth) 42
McLoughlin, F. 1930 (Fordsons, Cork) 2
McMillan, W. 1946 (Belfast Celtic) 2
McNally, J. B. 1959 (Luton T) 3
McPhail, S. 2000 (Leeds U) 10
McShane, P. D. 2007 (WBA, Sunderland, Hull C, Reading) 33
Meagan, M. K. 1961 (Everton, Huddersfield T, Drogheda) 17
Meehan, P. 1934 (Drumcondra) 1
Meyler, D. J. 2013 (Sunderland, Hull C, Reading) 26
Miller, L. W. P. 2004 (Celtic, Manchester U, Sunderland, Hibernian) 21
Milligan, M. J. 1992 (Oldham Ath) 1
Molumby, J. P. 2021 (Brighton & HA) 9
Monahan, P. 1935 (Sligo R) 2
Mooney, J. 1965 (Shamrock R) 2
Moore, A. 1996 (Middlesbrough) 8
Moore, P. 1931 (Shamrock R, Aberdeen, Shamrock R) 9
Moran, K. 1980 (Manchester U, Sporting Gijon, Blackburn R) 71
Moroney, T. 1948 (West Ham U, Evergreen U) 12
Morris, C. B. 1988 (Celtic, Middlesbrough) 35
Morrison, C. H. 2002 (Crystal Palace, Birmingham C, Crystal Palace) 36
Moulson, C. 1936 (Lincoln C, Notts Co) 5
Moulson, G. B. 1948 (Lincoln C) 3
Muckian, C. 1978 (Drogheda U) 1
Muldoon, T. 1927 (Aston Villa) 1
Mulligan, P. M. 1969 (Shamrock R, Chelsea, Crystal Palace, WBA, Shamrock R) 50
Munroe, L. 1954 (Shamrock R) 1
Murphy, A. 1956 (Clyde) 1
Murphy, B. 1986 (Bohemians) 1
Murphy, D. 2007 (Sunderland, Ipswich T, Newcastle U, Sheffield W) 32
Murphy, J. 1980 (Crystal Palace) 3
Murphy, J. 2004 (WBA, Scunthorpe U) 2
Murphy, P. M. 2007 (Carlisle U) 1
Murray, T. 1950 (Dundalk) 1

Newman, W. 1969 (Shelbourne) 1
Nolan. E. W. 2009 (Preston NE) 3
Nolan, R. 1957 (Shamrock R) 10

Obafemi, M. O. 2019 (Southampton) 1
Ogbene, C. 2021 (Rotherham U) 1
O'Brien, A. 2007 (Newcastle U) 5
O'Brien, A. A. 2019 (Millwall) 5
O'Brien, A. J. 2001 (Newcastle U, Portsmouth) 26
O'Brien, F. 1980 (Philadelphia F) 3
O'Brien J. M. 2006 (Bolton W, West Ham U) 5
O'Brien, L. 1986 (Shamrock R, Manchester U, Newcastle U, Tranmere R) 16
O'Brien, M. T. 1927 (Derby Co, Walsall, Norwich C, Watford) 4
O'Brien, R. 1976 (Notts Co) 5
O'Byrne, L. B. 1949 (Shamrock R) 1
O'Callaghan, B. R. 1979 (Stoke C) 6
O'Callaghan, K. 1981 (Ipswich T, Portsmouth) 21
O'Cearuill, J. 2007 (Arsenal) 2
O'Connell, A. 1967 (Dundalk, Bohemians) 2
O'Connor, L. P. 2020 (Celtic) 1
O'Connor, T. 1950 (Shamrock R) 4

O'Connor, T. 1968 (Fulham, Dundalk, Bohemians) 7
O'Dea, D. 2010 (Celtic, Toronto, Metalurh Donetsk) 20
O'Dowda, C. J. R. 2016 (Oxford U, Bristol C) 23
O'Driscoll, J. F. 1949 (Swansea T) 3
O'Driscoll, S. 1982 (Fulham) 3
O'Farrell, F. 1952 (West Ham U, Preston NE) 9
O'Flanagan, K. P. 1938 (Bohemians, Arsenal) 10
O'Flanagan, M. 1947 (Bohemians) 1
O'Halloran, S. E. 2007 (Aston Villa) 2
O'Hanlon, K. G. 1988 (Rotherham U) 1
O'Hara, K. M. 2020 (Manchester U) 2
O'Kane, E. C. 2016 (Bournemouth, Leeds U) 7
O'Kane, P. 1935 (Bohemians) 3
O'Keefe, E. 1981 (Everton, Port Vale) 5
O'Keefe, T. 1934 (Cork, Waterford) 3
O'Leary, D. 1977 (Arsenal) 68
O'Leary, P. 1980 (Shamrock R) 7
O'Mahoney, M. T. 1938 (Bristol R) 6
O'Neill, F. S. 1962 (Shamrock R) 20
O'Neill, J. 1952 (Everton) 17
O'Neill, J. 1961 (Preston NE) 1
O'Neill, K. P. 1996 (Norwich C, Middlesbrough) 13
O'Neill, W. 1936 (Dundalk) 11
O'Regan, K. 1984 (Brighton & HA) 4
O'Reilly, J. 1932 (Brideville, Aberdeen, Brideville, St James' Gate) 20
O'Reilly, J. 1946 (Cork U) 2
O'Shea, D. J. 2021 (WBA) 9
O'Shea, J. F. 2002 (Manchester U, Sunderland) 118

Parrott, T. D. 2020 (Tottenham H) 6
Pearce, A. J. 2013 (Reading, Derby Co) 9
Peyton, G. 1977 (Fulham, Bournemouth, Everton) 33
Peyton, N. 1957 (Shamrock R, Leeds U) 6
Phelan, T. 1992 (Wimbledon, Manchester C, Chelsea, Everton, Fulham) 42
Pilkington, A. N. J. 2013 (Norwich C, Cardiff C) 9
Potter, D. M. 2007 (Wolverhampton W) 5

Quinn, A. 2003 (Sheffield W, Sheffield U) 8
Quinn, B. S. 2000 (Coventry C) 4
Quinn, N. J. 1986 (Arsenal, Manchester C, Sunderland) 91
Quinn, S. 2013 (Hull C, Reading) 18

Randolph, D. E. 2013 (Motherwell, West Ham U, Middlesbrough) 50
Reid, A. M. 2004 (Nottingham F, Tottenham H, Charlton Ath, Sunderland, Nottingham F) 29
Reid, C. 1931 (Brideville) 1
Reid, S. J. 2002 (Millwall, Blackburn R) 23
Rice, D. 2018 (West Ham U) 3
Richardson, D. J. 1972 (Shamrock R, Gillingham) 3
Rigby, A. 1935 (St James' Gate) 3
Ringstead, A. 1951 (Sheffield U) 20
Robinson, C. J. 2019 (Preston NE, Sheffield U) 18
Robinson, J. 1928 (Bohemians, Dolphin) 2
Robinson, M. 1981 (Brighton & HA, Liverpool, QPR) 24
Roche, P. J. 1972 (Shelbourne, Manchester U) 8
Rogers, E. 1968 (Blackburn R, Charlton Ath) 19
Rowlands, M. C. 2004 (QPR) 5
Ryan, G. 1978 (Derby Co, Brighton & HA) 18
Ryan, R. A. 1950 (WBA, Derby Co) 16

Sadlier, R. T. 2002 (Millwall) 1
Sammon, C. 2013 (Derby Co) 9
Savage, D. P. T. 1996 (Millwall) 5
Saward, P. 1954 (Millwall, Aston Villa, Huddersfield T) 18
Scannell, T. 1954 (Southend U) 1
Scully, P. J. 1989 (Arsenal) 1
Sheedy, K. 1984 (Everton, Newcastle U) 46
Sheridan, C. 2010 (Celtic, CSKA Sofia) 3
Sheridan, J. J. 1988 (Leeds U, Sheffield W) 34
Slaven, B. 1990 (Middlesbrough) 7
Sloan, J. W. 1946 (Arsenal) 2
Smyth, M. 1969 (Shamrock R) 1
Squires, J. 1934 (Shelbourne) 1
Stapleton, F. 1977 (Arsenal, Manchester U, Ajax, Le Havre, Blackburn R) 71
Staunton, S. 1989 (Liverpool, Aston Villa, Liverpool, Aston Villa) 102
St Ledger-Hall, S. P. 2009 (Preston NE, Leicester C) 37
Stevens, E. J. 2018 (Sheffield U) 21
Stevenson, A. E. 1932 (Dolphin, Everton) 7
Stokes, A. 2007 (Sunderland, Celtic) 9
Strahan, F. 1964 (Shelbourne) 5
Sullivan, J. 1928 (Fordsons) 1
Swan, M. M. G. 1960 (Drumcondra) 1
Synnott, N. 1978 (Shamrock R) 3

Taylor, T. 1959 (Waterford) 1
Thomas, P. 1974 (Waterford) 2
Thompson, J. 2004 (Nottingham F) 1
Townsend, A. D. 1989 (Norwich C, Chelsea, Aston Villa, Middlesbrough) 70
Travers, M. 2020 (Bournemouth) 3
Traynor, T. J. 1954 (Southampton) 8
Treacy, K. 2011 (Preston NE, Burnley) 6
Treacy, R. C. P. 1966 (WBA, Charlton Ath, Swindon T, Preston NE, WBA, Shamrock R) 42
Tuohy, L. 1956 (Shamrock R, Newcastle U, Shamrock R) 8
Turner, C. J. 1936 (Southend U, West Ham U) 10
Turner, P. 1963 (Celtic) 2

Vernon, J. 1946 (Belfast Celtic) 2

Waddock, G. 1980 (QPR, Millwall) 21
Walsh, D. J. 1946 (Linfield, WBA, Aston Villa) 20
Walsh, J. 1982 (Limerick) 1
Walsh, M. 1976 (Blackpool, Everton, QPR, Porto) 21
Walsh, M. 1982 (Everton) 4
Walsh, W. 1947 (Manchester C) 9
Walters, J. R. 2011 (Stoke C, Burnley) 54
Ward, S. R. 2011 (Wolverhampton W, Burnley) 50
Waters, J. 1977 (Grimsby T) 2
Watters, F. 1926 (Shelbourne) 1
Weir, E. 1939 (Clyde) 3
Westwood, K. 2009 (Coventry C, Sunderland, Sheffield W) 21
Whelan, G. D. 2008 (Stoke C, Aston Villa, Hearts) 91
Whelan, R. 1964 (St Patrick's Ath) 2
Whelan, R. 1981 (Liverpool, Southend U) 53
Whelan, W. 1956 (Manchester U) 4
White, J. J. 1928 (Bohemians) 1
Whittaker, R. 1959 (Chelsea) 1
Williams, D. S. 2018 (Blackburn R) 3
Williams, J. 1938 (Shamrock R) 1
Williams, S. 2018 (Millwall) 3
Wilson, M. D. 2011 (Stoke C, Bournemouth) 25

BRITISH AND IRISH INTERNATIONAL GOALSCORERS 1872–2021

Where two players with the same surname and initials have appeared for the same country, and one or both have scored, they have been distinguished by reference to the club which appears *first* against their name in the international appearances section.
Bold type indicates players who have scored international goals in season 2020–21.

ENGLAND

Player	Goals
Abraham, K. O. T. (Tammy)	1
A'Court, A.	1
Adams, T. A.	5
Adcock, H.	1
Alcock, C. W.	1
Alexander-Arnold, T. J.	1
Allen, A.	3
Allen, R.	2
Alli, B. J. (Dele)	3
Amos, A.	1
Anderson, V.	2
Anderton, D. R.	7
Astall, G.	1
Athersmith, W. C.	3
Atyeo, P. J. W.	5
Bache, J. W.	4
Bailey, N. C.	2
Baily, E. F.	5
Baines, L. J.	1
Baker, J. H.	3
Ball, A. J.	8
Bambridge, A. L.	1
Bambridge, E. C.	11
Barclay, R.	2
Barkley, R.	6
Barmby, N. J.	4
Barnes, J.	11
Barnes, P. S.	4
Barry, G.	3
Barton, J.	1
Bassett, W. I.	8
Bastin, C. S.	12
Beardsley, P. A.	9
Beasley, A.	1
Beattie, T. K.	1
Beckham, D. R. J.	17
Becton, F.	2
Bedford, H.	1
Bell, C.	9
Bent, D. A.	4
Bentley, R. T. F.	9
Bertrand, R.	1
Bishop, S. M.	1
Blackburn, F.	1
Blissett, L.	3
Bloomer, S.	28
Bond, R.	2
Bonsor, A. G.	1
Bowden, E. R.	1
Bowers, J. W.	2
Bowles, S.	1
Bradford, G. R. W.	1
Bradford, J.	7
Bradley, W.	2
Bradshaw, F.	3
Brann, G.	1
Bridge, W. M.	1
Bridges, B. J.	1
Bridgett, A.	3
Brindle, T.	1
Britton, C. S.	1
Broadbent, P. F.	2
Broadis, I. A.	8
Brodie, J. B.	1
Bromley-Davenport, W.	2
Brook, E. F.	10
Brooking, T. D.	5
Brooks, J.	2
Broome, F. H.	3
Brown, A.	4
Brown, A. S.	1
Brown, G.	5
Brown, J.	3
Brown, W.	1
Brown, W. M.	1
Buchan, C. M.	4
Bull, S. G.	4
Bullock, N.	2
Burgess, H.	4
Butcher, T.	3
Byrne, J. J.	8
Cahill, G. J.	5
Calvert-Lewin, D. N.	**4**
Campbell, S. J.	1
Camsell, G. H.	18
Carroll, A. T.	2
Carter, H. S.	7
Carter, J. H.	4
Caulker, S. A.	1
Chadwick, E.	3
Chamberlain, M.	1
Chambers, H.	5
Channon, M. R.	21
Charlton, J.	6
Charlton, R.	49
Chenery, C. J.	1
Chivers, M.	13
Clarke, A. J.	10
Coady, C. D.	**1**
Cobbold, W. N.	6
Cock, J. G.	2
Cole, A.	1
Cole, J. J.	10
Common, A.	2
Connelly, J. M.	7
Coppell, S. J.	7
Cotterill, G. H.	2
Cowans, G.	2
Crawford, R.	1
Crawshaw, T. H.	1
Crayston, W. J.	1
Creek, F. N. S.	1
Crooks, S. D.	7
Crouch, P. J.	22
Currey, E. S.	2
Currie, A. W.	3
Cursham, A. W.	2
Cursham, H. A.	5
Daft, H. B.	3
Davenport, J. K.	2
Davis, G.	1
Davis, H.	1
Day, S. H.	2
Dean, W. R.	18
Defoe, J. C.	20
Devey, J. H. G.	1
Dewhurst, F.	11
Dier, E. J. E.	3
Dix, W. R.	1
Dixon, K. M.	4
Dixon, L. M.	1
Dorrell, A. R.	1
Douglas, B.	11
Drake, E. J.	6
Ducat, A.	1
Dunn, A. T. B.	2
Eastham, G.	2
Edwards, D.	5
Ehiogu, U.	1
Elliott, W. H.	3
Evans, R. E.	1
Ferdinand, L.	5
Ferdinand, R. G.	3
Finney, T.	30
Fleming, H. J.	9
Flowers, R.	10
Foden, P. W.	**2**
Forman, Frank	1
Forman, Fred	3
Foster, R. E.	3
Fowler, R. B.	7
Francis, G. C. J.	3
Francis, T.	12
Freeman, B. C.	3
Froggatt, J.	2
Froggatt, R.	2
Galley, T.	1
Gascoigne, P. J.	10
Geary, F.	3
Gerrard, S. G.	21
Gibbins, W. V. T.	3
Gilliatt, W. E.	3
Goddard, P.	1
Goodall, J.	12
Goodyer, A. C.	1
Gosling, R. C.	2
Goulden, L. A.	4
Grainger, C.	3
Greaves, J.	44
Grovesnor, A. T.	2
Gunn, W.	1
Haines, J. T. W.	2
Hall, G. W.	9
Halse, H. J.	2
Hampson, J.	5
Hampton, H.	2
Hancocks, J.	2
Hardman, H. P.	1
Harris, S. S.	2
Hassall, H. W.	4
Hateley, M.	9
Haynes, J. N.	18
Hegan, K. E.	4
Henfrey, A. G.	2
Heskey, E. W.	7
Hilsdon, G. R.	14
Hine, E. W.	4
Hinton, A. T.	1
Hirst, D. E.	1
Hitchens, G. A.	5
Hobbis, H. H. F.	1
Hoddle, G.	8
Hodgetts, D.	1
Hodgson, G.	1
Holley, G. H.	8
Houghton, W. E.	5
Howell, R.	1
Hughes, E. W.	1
Hulme, J. H. A.	4
Hunt, G. S.	1
Hunt, R.	18
Hunter, N.	2
Hurst, G. C.	24
Ince, P. E. C.	2
Ings, D.	**1**
Jack, D. N. B.	3
Jagielka, P. N.	3
Jeffers, F.	1
Jenas, J. A.	1
Johnson, A.	2
Johnson, D. E.	6
Johnson, E.	2
Johnson, G. M. C.	1
Johnson, J. A.	2
Johnson, T. C. F.	5
Johnson, W. H.	1
Kail, E. I. L.	2
Kane, H. E.	**38**
Kay, A. H.	1
Keane, M. V.	1
Keegan, J. K.	21
Kelly, R.	8
Kennedy, R.	3
Kenyon-Slaney, W. S.	2
Keown, M. R.	2
Kevan, D. T.	8
Kidd, B.	1
King, L. B.	2
Kingsford, R. K.	1
Kirchen, A. J.	2
Kirton, W. J.	1
Lallana, A. D.	3
Lambert, R. L.	3
Lampard, F. J.	29
Langton, R.	1
Latchford, R. D.	5
Latheron, E. G.	1
Lawler, C.	1
Lawton, T.	22
Lee, F.	10
Lee, J.	1
Lee, R. M.	2
Lee, S.	2
Lescott, J.	1
Le Saux, G. P.	1
Lindley, T.	14
Lineker, G.	48
Lingard, J. E.	4
Lofthouse, J. M.	3
Lofthouse, N.	30
Hon. A. Lyttelton	1
Mabbutt, G.	1
Macdonald, M.	6
Maguire, J. H.	**4**
Mannion, W. J.	11
Mariner, P.	13
Marsh, R. W.	1
Matthews, S.	11
Matthews, V.	1
McCall, J.	1
McDermott, T.	3
McManaman, S.	3
Medley, L. D.	1
Melia, J.	1
Mercer, D. W.	1
Merson, P. C.	3
Milburn, J. E. T.	10
Miller, H. S.	1
Mills, G. R.	3
Milner, J. P.	1
Milward, A.	3
Mitchell, C.	5
Moore, J.	1
Moore, R. F.	2
Moore, W. G. B.	2
Morren, T.	1
Morris, F.	1

Player	Goals
Morris, J.	3
Mortensen, S. H.	23
Morton, J. R.	1
Mosforth, W.	3
Mount, M. T.	**4**
Mullen, J.	6
Mullery, A. P.	1
Murphy, D. B	1
Neal, P. G.	5
Needham, E.	3
Nicholls, J.	1
Nicholson, W. E.	1
Nugent, D. J.	1
O'Grady, M.	3
Osborne, F. R.	3
Owen, M. J.	40
Own goals	34
Oxlade-Chamberlain, A. M. D.	7
Page, L. A.	1
Paine, T. L.	7
Palmer, C. L.	1
Parry, E. H.	1
Parry, R. A.	1
Pawson, F. W.	1
Payne, J.	2
Peacock, A.	3
Pearce, S.	5
Pearson, J. S.	5
Pearson, S. C.	5
Perry, W.	2
Peters, M.	20
Pickering, F.	5
Platt, D.	27
Pointer, R.	2
Quantrill, A.	1
Ramsay, A. E.	3
Rashford, M.	**12**
Revie, D. G.	4
Redknapp, J. F.	1
Reynolds, J.	3
Rice, D.	**1**
Richards, M.	1
Richardson, K. E.	2
Richardson, J. R.	2
Rigby, A.	3
Rimmer, E. J.	2
Roberts, F.	2
Roberts, H.	1
Roberts, W. T.	2
Robinson, J.	3
Robson, B.	26
Robson, R.	4
Rooney, W. M.	53
Rowley, J. F.	6
Royle, J.	2
Rutherford, J.	3
Sagar, C.	1
Saka, B. A. T. M.	**1**
Sancho, J. M.	**3**
Sandilands, R. R.	3
Sansom, K.	1
Schofield, J.	1
Scholes, P.	14
Seed, J. M.	1
Settle, J.	6
Sewell, J.	3
Shackleton, L. F.	1
Sharp, J.	1
Shaw L. P. H.	**1**
Shearer, A.	30
Shelton, A.	1
Shepherd, A.	2
Sheringham, E. P.	11
Simpson, J.	1
Smalling, C. L.	1
Smith, A.	1
Smith, A. M.	2
Smith, G. O.	11
Smith, Joe	1
Smith, J. R.	2
Smith, J. W.	4
Smith, R.	13
Smith, S.	1
Sorby, T. H.	1
Southgate, G.	2
Southworth, J.	3
Sparks, F. J.	3
Spence, J. W.	1
Spiksley, F.	5
Spilsbury, B. W.	5
Steele, F. C.	8
Stephenson, G. T.	2
Sterling, R. S.	**17**
Steven, T. M.	4
Stewart, J.	2
Stiles, N. P.	1
Storer, H.	1
Stone, S. B.	2
Stones, J.	2
Sturridge, D. A.	8
Summerbee, M. G.	1
Tambling, R. V.	1
Taylor, P. J.	2
Taylor, T.	16
Terry, J. G.	6
Thompson, P. B.	1
Thornewell, G.	1
Tilson, S. F.	6
Townley, W. J.	2
Townsend, A. D.	3
Trippier, K. J.	1
Tueart, D.	2
Upson, M. J.	2
Vardy, J. R.	7
Vassell, D.	6
Vaughton, O. H.	6
Veitch, J. G.	3
Viollet, D. S.	1
Waddle, C. R.	6
Walcott, T. J.	8
Walker, W. H.	9
Wall, G.	2
Wallace, D.	1
Walsh, P.	1
Ward-Prowse, J. M. E.	**1**
Waring, T.	4
Warren, B.	2
Watson, D. V.	4
Watson, V. M.	4
Watkins, O. G. A.	**1**
Webb, G. W.	1
Webb, N.	4
Wedlock, W. J.	2
Welbeck D. N. T. M.	16
Weller, K.	1
Welsh, D.	1
Whateley, O.	2
Wheldon, G. F.	6
Whitfield, H.	1
Wignall, F.	2
Wilkes, A.	1
Wilkins, R. G.	3
Willingham, C. K.	1
Wilshaw, D. J.	10
Wilshere J. A.	2
Wilson, C.	1
Wilson, G. P.	1
Winckworth, W. N.	1
Windridge, J. E.	7
Winks, H. B.	1
Wise, D. F.	1
Withe, P.	1
Wollaston, C. H. R.	1
Wood, H.	1
Woodcock, T.	16
Woodhall, G.	1
Woodward, V. J.	29
Worrall, F.	2
Worthington, F. S.	2
Wright, I. E.	9
Wright, M.	1
Wright, W. A.	3
Wright-Phillips, S. C.	6
Wylie, J. G.	1
Yates, J.	3
Young, A. S.	7

NORTHERN IRELAND

Player	Goals
Anderson, T.	4
Armstrong, G.	12
Bambrick, J.	12
Barr, H. H.	1
Barron, H.	3
Best, G.	9
Bingham, W. L.	10
Black, K.	1
Blanchflower, D.	2
Blanchflower, J.	1
Boyce, L.	**2**
Brennan, B.	1
Brennan, R. A.	1
Brotherston, N.	3
Brown, J.	1
Browne, F.	2
Brunt, C.	3
Campbell, J.	1
Campbell, W. G.	1
Casey, T.	2
Caskey, W.	1
Cassidy, T.	1
Cathcart, C. G.	2
Chambers, J.	3
Clarke, C. J.	13
Clements, D.	2
Cochrane, T.	1
Condy, J.	1
Connor, M. J.	1
Coulter, J.	1
Croft, T.	1
Crone, W.	1
Crossan, E.	1
Crossan, J. A.	10
Curran, S.	2
Cush, W. W.	5
Dallas, S. A.	3
Dalton, W.	4
D'Arcy, S. D.	1
Darling, J.	1
Davey, H. H.	1
Davis, S.	12
Davis, T. L.	1
Dill, A. H.	1
Doherty, L.	1
Doherty, P. D.	3
Dougan, A. D.	8
Dowie, I.	12
Dunne, J.	4
Elder, A. R.	1
Elliott, S.	4
Emerson, W.	1
English, S.	1
Evans, C.	2
Evans, J. G.	4
Feeney, W.	1
Feeney, W. J.	5
Ferguson, S. K.	1
Ferguson, W.	1
Ferris, J.	1
Ferris, R. O.	1
Finney, T.	2
Gaffkin, J.	4
Gara, A.	3
Gaukrodger, G.	1
Gibb, J. T.	2
Gibb, T. J.	1
Gibson, W.	1
Gillespie, K. R.	2
Gillespie, W.	13
Goodall, A. L.	2
Griffin, D. J.	1
Gray, P.	6
Grigg, W. D.	2
Halligan, W.	1
Hamill, M.	1
Hamilton, B.	4
Hamilton, W. R.	5
Hannon, D. J.	1
Harkin, J. T.	2
Harvey, M.	3
Healy, D. J.	36
Hill, C. F.	1
Hughes, A.	1
Hughes, M. E.	5
Humphries, W.	1
Hunter, A. (Distillery)	1
Hunter, A. (Blackburn R)	1
Hunter, B. V.	1
Irvine, R. W.	3
Irvine, W. J.	8
Johnston, H.	2
Johnston, S.	2
Johnston, W. C.	1
Jones, S. (Distillery)	1
Jones, S. (Crewe Alex)	1
Jones, J.	1
Jones, J. L.	**1**
Kelly, J.	4
Kernaghan, N.	2
Kirwan, J.	2
Lacey, W.	3
Lafferty, K.	20
Lemon, J.	2
Lennon, N. F.	2
Lockhart, N.	3
Lomas, S. M.	3
Magennis, J. B. D.	**8**
Magilton, J.	5
Mahood, J.	2
Martin, D. K.	3
Maxwell, J.	2
McAdams, W. J.	7
McAllen, J.	1
McAuley, G.	9
McAuley, J. L.	1
McCann, A.	**1**
McCann, G. S.	4
McCartney, G.	1
McCandless, J.	2
McCandless, W.	1
McCaw, J. H.	1
McClelland, J.	1
McCluggage, A.	2
McCourt, P.	2
McCracken, W.	1
McCrory, S.	1
McCurdy, C.	1
McDonald, A.	3
McGarry, J. K.	1
McGrath, R. C.	4
McGinn, N.	**6**
McIlroy, J.	10
McIlroy, S. B.	5
McKenzie, H	1
McKnight, J.	2
McLaughlin, C. G.	1
McLaughlin, J. C.	6
McMahon, G. J.	2
McMordie, A. S.	3
McMorran, E. J.	4
McNair, P. J. C.	**4**
McParland, P. J.	10
McWha, W. B. R.	1
Meldon, P. A	1
Mercer, J. T.	1
Millar, W.	1
Milligan, D.	1
Milne, R. G.	2
Molyneux, T. B.	1
Moreland, V.	1
Morgan, S.	3

Morrow, S. J. 1
Morrow, W. J. 1
Mulryne, P. P. 3
Murdock, C. J. 1
Murphy, N. 1

Neill, W. J. T. 2
Nelson, S. 1
Nicholl, C. J. 3
Nicholl, J. M. 1
Nicholson, J. J. 6

O'Boyle, G. 1
O'Hagan, C. 2
O'Kane, W. J. 1
O'Neill, J. 2
O'Neill, M. A. 4
O'Neill, M. H. 8
Own goals 10

Paterson, M. A. 3
Patterson, D. J. 1
Patterson, R. 1
Peacock, R. 2
Peden, J. 7
Penney, S. 2
Pyper, James 2
Pyper, John 1

Quinn, J. M. 12
Quinn, S. J. 4

Reynolds, J. 1
Rowland, K. 1
Rowley, R. W. M. 2
Rushe, F. 1

Sheridan, J. 2
Sherrard, J. 1
Sherrard, W. C. 2
Shields, D. 1
Simpson, W. J. 5
Sloan, H. A. de B. 4
Smith, M. 1
Smyth, P. 1
Smyth, S. 5

Spence, D. W. 3
Sproule, I. 1
Stanfield, O. M. 11
Stevenson, A. E. 5
Stewart, I. 2

Taggart, G. P. 7
Thompson, F. W. 2
Torrans, S. 1
Tully, C. P. 3
Turner, A. 1

Walker, J. 1
Walsh, D. J. 5
Ward, J. J. 4
Washington, C. J. 4
Welsh, E. 1
Whiteside, N. 9
Whiteside, T. 1
Whitley, Jeff 2
Whyte, G. 3
Williams, J. R. 1
Williams, M. S. 1
Williamson, J. 1
Wilson, D. J. 1
Wilson, K. J. 6
Wilson, S. J. 7
Wilton, J. M. 2
Young, S. 1

N.B. In 1914 Young goal should be credited to Gillespie W v Wales

SCOTLAND

Adams, C. Z. E. F. 2
Aitken, R. (Celtic) 1
Aitken, R. (Dumbarton) 1
Aitkenhead, W. A. C. 2
Alexander, D. 1
Allan, D. S. 4
Allan, J. 2
Anderson, F. 1
Anderson, W. 4
Andrews, P. 1
Anya, I. 3
Archibald, A. 1
Archibald, S. 4
Armstrong, S. 2

Baird, D. 2
Baird, J. C. 2
Baird, S. 2
Bannon, E. 1
Barbour, A. 1
Barker, J. B. 4
Battles, B. Jr 1
Bauld, W. 2
Baxter, J. C. 3
Beattie, C. 1
Bell, J. 5
Bennett, A. 2
Berra, C. D. 4
Berry, D. 1
Bett, J. 1
Beveridge, W. W. 1
Black, A. 3
Black, D. 1
Bone, J. 1
Booth, S. 6
Boyd, K 7
Boyd, R. 2
Boyd, T. 1
Boyd, W. G. 1
Brackenridge, T. 1
Brand, R. 8
Brazil, A. 1
Bremner, W. J. 3
Broadfoot, K. 1
Brown, A. D. 6
Brown, S. 4
Buchanan, P. S. 1
Buchanan, R. 1
Buckley, P. 1
Buick, A. 2
Burke, C. 2
Burke, O. J. 1
Burley, C. W. 3
Burns, K. 1

Cairns, T. 1
Caldwell, G. 2
Calderwood, C. 1
Calderwood, R. 2
Caldow, E. 4
Cameron, C. 2
Campbell, C. 1
Campbell, John (Celtic) 5
Campbell, John (Rangers) 4
Campbell, J. (South Western) 1
Campbell, P. 2
Campbell, R. 1
Cassidy, J. 1
Chalmers, S. 3
Chambers, T. 1
Cheyne, A. G. 4
Christie, A. J. 1
Christie, R. 4
Clarkson, D. 1
Clunas, W. L. 1
Collins, J. 12
Collins, R. Y. 10
Combe, J. R. 1
Commons, K. 2
Conn, A. 1
Cooper, D. 6
Craig, J. 1
Craig, T. 1
Crawford, S. 4
Cunningham, A. N. 5
Curran, H. P. 1

Dailly, C. 6
Dalglish, K. 30
Davidson, D. 1
Davidson, J. A. 1
Delaney, J. 3
Devine, A. 1
Dewar, G. 1
Dewar, N. 4
Dickov, P. 1
Dickson, W. 4
Divers, J. 1
Dobie, R. S. 1
Docherty, T. H. 1
Dodds, D. 1
Dodds, W. 7
Donaldson, A. 1
Donnachie, J. 1
Dougall, J. 1
Drummond, J. 2
Dunbar, M. 1
Duncan, D. 7
Duncan, D. M. 1
Duncan, J. 1
Dunn, J. 2
Durie, G. S. 7
Dykes, L. J. 2

Easson, J. F. 1
Elliott, M. S. 1
Ellis, J. 1

Ferguson, B. 3
Ferguson, J. 6
Fernie, W. 1
Findlay, S. J. 1
Fitchie, T. T. 1
Flavell, R. 2
Fleming, C. 2
Fleming, J. W. 3
Fletcher, D. 5
Fletcher, S. K. 10
Forrest, J. 5
Fraser, M. J. E. 3
Fraser, R. 4
Freedman, D. A. 1

Gallacher, H. K. 23
Gallacher, K. W. 9
Gallacher, P. 1
Galt, J. H. 1
Gemmell, T. (St Mirren) 1
Gemmell, T. (Celtic) 1
Gemmill, A. 8
Gemmill, S. 1
Gibb, W. 1
Gibson, D. W. 3
Gibson, J. D. 1
Gibson, N. 1
Gillespie, Jas. 3
Gillick, T. 3
Gilzean, A. J. 12
Goodwillie, D. 1
Gossland, J. 2
Goudie, J. 1
Gough, C. R. 6
Gourlay, J. 1
Graham, A. 2
Graham, G. 3
Gray, A. 7
Gray, E. 3
Gray, F. 1
Greig, J. 3
Griffiths, L. 4
Groves, W. 4

Hamilton, G. 4
Hamilton, J. (Queen's Park) 3
Hamilton, R. C. 15
Hanley, G. C. 2
Harper, J. M. 2
Hartley, P. J. 1
Harrower, W. 5
Hartford, R. A. 4
Heggie, C. W 4
Henderson, J. G. 1
Henderson, W. 5
Hendry, E. C. J. 3
Hendry, J. W. 1
Herd, D. G. 3
Herd, G. 1
Hewie, J. D. 2
Higgins, A. (Newcastle U) 1
Higgins, A. (Kilmarnock) 4
Highet, T. C. 1
Holt, G.J. 1
Holton, J. A. 2
Hopkin, D. 2
Houliston, W. 2
Howie, H. 1
Howie, J. 2
Hughes, J. 1
Hunter, W. 1
Hutchison, D. 6
Hutchison, T. 1
Hutton, J. 1
Hyslop, T. 1

Imrie, W. N. 1

Jackson, A. 8
Jackson, C. 1
Jackson, D. 4
James, A. W. 4
Jardine, A. 1
Jenkinson, T. 1
Jess, E. 2
Johnston, A. 2
Johnston, L. H. 1
Johnston, M. 14
Johnstone, D. 2
Johnstone, J. 4
Johnstone, Jas. 1
Johnstone, R. 10
Johnstone, W. 1
Jordan, J. 11

Kay, J. L. 5
Keillor, A. 3
Kelly, J. 1
Kelso, R. 1
Ker, G. 10
King, A. 1
King, J. 1
Kinnear, D. 1
Kyle, K. 1

Lambert, P. 1
Lambie, J. 1
Lambie, W. A. 5
Lang, J. J. 2
Latta, A. 2
Law, D. 30
Leggat, G. 8
Lennie, W. 1
Lennox, R. 3
Liddell, W. 6
Lindsay, J. 6
Linwood, A. B. 1
Logan, J. 1
Lorimer, P. 4
Love, A. 1
Low, J. (Cambuslang) 1
Lowe, J. (St Bernards) 1

Macari, L. 5
MacDougall, E. J. 3
MacFarlane, A. 1
MacLeod, M. 1
Mackay, D. C. 4
Mackay, G. 1
MacKenzie, J. A. 1
Mackail-Smith, C. 1
Mackie, J. C. 2
MacKinnon, W. W. 5
Madden, J. 5
Maloney, S. R. 7
Marshall, H. 1
Marshall, J. 1
Martin, C. H. 3

Mason, J. 4
Massie, A. 1
Masson, D. S. 5
McAdam, J. 1
McAllister, G. 5
McArthur, J. 4
McAulay, J. D. 1
McAvennie, F. 1
McCall, J. 1
McCall, S. M. 1
McCalliog, J. 1
McCallum, N. 1
McCann, N. 3
McClair, B. J. 2
McCoist, A. 19
McColl, R. S. 13
McCormack, R. 2
McCulloch, D. 3
McCulloch, L. 1
McDougall, J. 4
McFadden, J.* 15
McFadyen, W. 2
McGhee, M. 2
McGinlay, J. 4
McGinn, J. 10
McGregor, C. W. 1
McGregor, J. 1
McGrory, J. 6
McGuire, W. 1
McInally, A. 3
McInnes, T. 2
McKie, J. 2
McKimmie, S. 1
McKinlay, W. 4
McKinnon, A. 1
McKinnon, R. 1
McLaren, A. 4
McLaren, J. 1
McLean, A. 1
McLean, K. 1
McLean, T. 1
McLintock, F. 1
McMahon, A. 6
McManus, S. 2
McMenemy, J. 5
McMillan, I. L. 2
McNeill, W. 3
McNiel, H. 5
McPhail, J. 3
McPhail, R. 7
McPherson, J. (Kilmarnock) 7
McPherson, J. (Vale of Leven) 1
McPherson, R. 1
McQueen, G. 5
McStay, P. 9
McSwegan, G. 1
Meiklejohn, D. D. 3
Millar, J. 2
Miller, K. 18
Miller, T. 2
Miller, W. 1
Mitchell, R. C. 1
Morgan, W. 1
Morris, D. 1
Morris, H. 3
Morrison, J. C. 3
Morton, A. L. 5
Mudie, J. K. 9
Mulgrew, C. P. 3
Mulhall, G. 1
Munro, A. D. 1
Munro, N. 2
Murdoch, R. 5
Murphy, F. 1
Murray, J. 1

Napier, C. E. 3
Narey, D. 1
Naismith, S. J. 10
Naysmith, G. A. 1
Neil, R. G. 2
Nevin, P. K. F. 5
Nicholas, C. 5
Nisbet, J. 2
Nisbet, K. 1

O'Connor, G. 4
O'Donnell, F. 2
O'Hare, J. 5
Ormond, W. E. 2
O'Rourke, F. 1
Orr, R. 1
Orr, T. 1
Oswald, J. 1
Own goals 21

Parlane, D. 1
Paul, H. McD. 2
Paul, W. 5
Pettigrew, W. 2
Phillips, M. 1
Provan, D. 1

Quashie, N. F. 1
Quinn, J. 7
Quinn, P. 1

Rankin, G. 2
Rankin, R. 2
Reid, W. 4
Reilly, L. 22
Renny-Tailyour, H. W. 1
Rhodes, J. L. 3
Richmond, J. T. 1
Ring, T. 2
Rioch, B. D. 6
Ritchie, J. 1
Ritchie, M. T. 3
Ritchie, P. S. 1
Robertson, A. (Clyde) 2
Robertson, A. 3
Robertson, J. 3
Robertson, J. N. 8
Robertson, J. T. 2
Robertson, T. 1
Robertson, W. 1
Russell, D. 1
Russell, J. S. S. 1

Scott, A. S. 5
Sellar, W. 4
Shankland, L. 1
Sharp, G. 1
Shaw, F. W. 1
Shearer, D. 2
Simpson, J. 1
Smith, A. 5
Smith, G. 4
Smith, J. 1
Smith, John 13
Snodgrass, R. 7
Somerville, G. 1
Souness, G. J. 4
Speedie, F. 2
St John, I. 9
Steel, W. 12
Stein, C. 10
Stevenson, G. 4
Stewart, A. 1
Stewart, R. 1
Stewart, W. E. 1
Strachan, G. 5
Sturrock, P. 3

Taylor, J. D. 1
Templeton, R. 1
Thompson, S. 3
Thomson, A. 1
Thomson, C. 4
Thomson, R. 1
Thomson, W. 1
Thornton, W. 1

Waddell, T. S. 1
Waddell, W. 6
Walker, J. 2
Walker, R. 7
Walker, T. 9
Wallace, I. A. 1
Wark, J. 7
Watson, J. A. K. 1
Watt, F. 2
Watt, W. W. 1
Webster, A. 1
Weir, A. 1
Weir, D. 1
Weir, J. B. 2
White, J. A. 3
Wilkie, L. 1
Wilson, A. (Sheffield W) 2
Wilson, A. N. (Dunfermline Ath) 13
Wilson, D. (Liverpool) 1
Wilson, D. (Queen's Park) 2
Wilson, D. (Rangers) 9
Wilson, H. 1
Wylie, T. G. 1

Young, A. 5

WALES

Allchurch, I. J. 23
Allen, J. M. 2
Allen, M. 3
Astley, D. J. 12
Atherton, R. W. 2

Bale, G. F. 33
Bamford, T. 1
Barnes, W. 1
Bellamy, C. D. 19
Blackmore, C. G. 1
Blake, D. 1
Blake, N. A. 4
Bodin, P. J. 3
Boulter, L. M. 1
Bowdler, J. C. H. 3
Bowen, D. L. 1
Bowen, M. 3
Boyle, T. 1
Brooks, D. R. 2
Bryan, T. 1
Burgess, W. A. R. 1
Burke, T. 1
Butler, W. T. 1

Chapman, T. 2
Charles, J. 1
Charles, M. 6
Charles, W. J. 15
Church, S. R. 3
Clarke, R. J. 5
Coleman, C. 4
Collier, D. J. 1
Collins, J. 3
Cotterill, D. R. G. B. 2
Crosse, K. 1
Cumner, R. H. 1
Curtis, A. 6
Curtis, E. R. 3

Davies, D. W. 1
Davies, E. Lloyd 1
Davies, G. 2
Davies, L. S. 6
Davies, R. T. 9
Davies, R. W. 6
Davies, Simon 6
Davies, Stanley 5
Davies, W. 6
Davies, W. H. 1
Davies, William 5
Davis, W. O. 1
Deacy, N. 4
Doughty, J. 6
Doughty, R. 2
Durban, A. 2
Dwyer, P. 2

Earnshaw, R. 16
Eastwood, F. 4
Edwards, D. A. 3
Edwards, G. 2
Edwards, R. I. 4
England, H. M. 4
Evans, C. 2
Evans, I. 1
Evans, J. 1
Evans, R. E. 2
Evans, W. 1
Eyton-Jones, J. A. 1

Fletcher, C. 1
Flynn, B. 7
Ford, T. 23
Foulkes, W. I. 1
Fowler, J. 3

Giles, D. 2
Giggs, R. J. 12
Glover, E. M. 7
Godfrey, B. C. 2
Green, A. W. 3
Griffiths, A. T. 6
Griffiths, M. W. 2
Griffiths, T. P. 3

Harris, C. S. 1
Hartson, J. 14
Hersee, R. 1
Hewitt, R. 1
Hockey, T. 1
Hodges, G. 2
Hole, W. J. 1
Hopkins, I. J. 2
Horne, B. 2
Howell, E. G. 3
Hughes, L. M. 16
Huws, E. W. 1

James, D. O. 4
James, E. 2
James, L. 10
James, R. 7
Jarrett, R. H. 3
Jenkyns, C. A. 1
Jones, A. 1
Jones, Bryn 6
Jones, B. S. 2
Jones, Cliff 16
Jones, C. W. 1
Jones, D. E. 1
Jones, Evan 1
Jones, H. 1
Jones, I. 1
Jones, J. L. 1
Jones, J. O. 1
Jones, J. P. 1
Jones, Leslie J. 1
Jones, R. A. 2
Jones, W. L. 6

Keenor, F. C. 2
King, A. P. 2
Koumas, J. 10
Krzywicki, R. L. 1

** The Scottish FA officially changed Robson's goal against Iceland on 10 September 2008 to McFadden.*

Lawrence, T. M. 3
Ledley, J. C. 4
Leek, K. 5
Lewis, B. 4
Lewis, D. M. 2
Lewis, W. 8
Lewis, W. L. 3
Llewelyn, C. M 1
Lovell, S. 1
Lowrie, G. 2

Mahoney, J. F. 1
Mays, A. W. 1
Medwin, T. C. 6
Melville, A. K 3
Meredith, W. H. 11
Mills, T. J. 1
Moore, G. 1
Moore, K. R. F. 6
Morgan, J. R. 2
Morgan-Owen, H. 1
Morgan-Owen, M. M. 2
Morison, S. 1
Morris, A. G. 9
Morris, H. 2
Morris, R. 1
Morris, S. 2

Nicholas, P. 2

O'Callaghan, E. 3
O'Sullivan, P. A. 1
Owen, G. 2
Owen, W. 4
Owen, W. P. 6
Own goals 14

Palmer, D. 3
Parry, P. I. 1
Parry, T. D. 3
Paul, R. 1
Peake, E. 1
Pembridge, M. 6
Perry, E. 1
Phillips, C. 5
Phillips, D. 2
Powell, A. 1
Powell, D. 1
Price, J. 4
Price, P. 1
Pryce-Jones, W. E. 3
Pugh, D. H. 2

Ramsey, A. J. 17
Reece, G. I. 2
Rees, R. R. 3
Richards, R. W. 1
Roach, J. 2
Robbins, W. W. 4
Roberts, C. R. J. 2
Roberts, J. (Corwen) 1
Roberts, Jas. 1
Roberts, P. S. 1
Roberts, R. (Druids) 1
Roberts, W. (Llangollen) 2
Roberts, W. (Wrexham) 1
Roberts, W. H. 1
Robinson, C. P. 1
Robinson, J. R. C. 3
Robson-Kanu, T. H. 5
Rush, I. 28
Russell, M. R. 1

Sabine, H. W. 1
Saunders, D. 22
Savage, R. W. 2
Shaw, E. G. 2
Sisson, H. 4
Slatter, N. 2
Smallman, D. P. 1
Speed, G. A. 7
Symons, C. J. 2

Tapscott, D. R. 4
Taylor, G. K. 1
Taylor, N. J. 1
Thomas, M. 4
Thomas, T. 1
Toshack, J. B. 12
Trainer, H. 2

Vaughan, D. O. 1
Vaughan, John 2
Vernon, T. R. 8
Vizard, E. T. 1
Vokes, S. M. 11

Walsh, I. 7
Warren, F. W. 3
Watkins, W. M. 4
Wilding, J. 4
Williams, A. 1
Williams, A. E. 2
Williams, D. R. 2
Williams, G. E. 1
Williams, G. G. 1
Williams, J. P. 1
Williams, N. S. 1
Williams, W. 1
Wilson, H. 5
Woodburn, B. 2
Woosnam, A. P. 3
Wynn, G. A. 1

Yorath, T. C. 2
Young, E. 1

REPUBLIC OF IRELAND

Aldridge, J. 19
Ambrose, P. 1
Anderson, J. 1
Andrews, K. 3

Barrett, G. 2
Bermingham, P. 1
Bradshaw, P. 4
Brady, L. 9
Brady, R. 8
Breen, G. 7
Brown, J. 1
Browne, A. J. 2
Burke, G. D. 1
Byrne, D. 1
Byrne, J. 4

Cantwell, N. 14
Carey, J. 3
Carroll, T. 1
Cascarino, A. 19
Christie, C. S. F. 2
Clark, C. 2
Coad, P. 3
Coleman, S. 1
Collins, J. S. 2
Connolly, D. J. 9
Conroy, T. 2
Conway, J. 3
Cox, S. R. 4
Coyne, T. 6
Cummins, G. 5
Curtis, D. 8

Daly, G. 13
Davis, T. 4
Dempsey, J. 1
Dennehy, M. 2
Doherty, G. M. T. 4
Doherty, M. J. 1
Donnelly, J. 4
Donnelly, T. 1
Doyle, K. E. 14
Duff, D. A. 8
Duffy, B. 1
Duffy, S. P. M. 4
Duggan, H. 1
Dunne, J. 13
Dunne, L. 1
Dunne, R. P. 8

Eglington, T. 2
Elliott, S. W. 1
Ellis, P. 1

Fagan, F. 5
Fahey, K. 3
Fallon, S. 2
Fallon, W. 2
Farrell, P. 3
Finnan, S. 2
Fitzgerald, P. 2
Fitzgerald, J. 1
Fitzsimons, A. 7
Flood, J. J. 4
Fogarty, A. 3
Foley, D. 2
Fullam, J. 1
Fullam, R. 1

Galvin, A. 1
Gavin, J. 2
Geoghegan, M. 2
Gibson, D. T. D. 1
Giles, J. 5
Givens, D. 19
Gleeson, S. M. 1
Glynn, D. 1
Grealish, T. 8
Green, P. J. 1
Grimes, A. A. 1

Hale, A. 2
Hand, E. 2
Harte, I. P. 11
Haverty, J. 3
Healy, C. 1
Hendrick, J. P. 2
Holland, M. R. 5
Holmes, J. 1
Hoolahan, W. 3
Horlacher, A. 2
Horgan, D. J. 1
Houghton, R. 6
Hourihane, C. 1
Hughton, C. 1
Hunt, S. P. 1
Hurley, C. 2

Ireland, S. J. 4
Irwin, D. 4

Jordan, D. 1
Judge, A. C. 1

Kavanagh, G. A. 1
Keane, R. D. 68
Keane, R. M. 9
Kelly, D. 9
Kelly, G. 2
Kelly, J. 2
Kennedy, M. 4
Keogh, A. 2
Keogh, R. J. 1
Kernaghan, A. N. 1
Kilbane, K. D. 8
Kinsella, M. A. 3
Knight, J. P. 1

Lacey, W. 1
Lawrence, L. 2
Lawrenson, M. 5
Leech, M. 2
Long, K. F. 1
Long, S. P. 17

Maguire, S. P. 1
Mancini, T. 1
Martin, C. 6
Martin, M. 4
McAteer, J. W. 3
McCann, J. 1
McCarthy, M. 2
McClean, J. J. 11
McEvoy, A. 6
McGeady, A. G. 5
McGee, P. 4
McGoldrick, D. J. 1
McGrath, P. 8
McLoughlin, A. F. 2
McPhail, S. J. P. 1
Miller, L. W. P. 1
Mooney, J. 1
Moore, P. 7
Moran, K. 6
Morrison, C. H. 9
Moroney, T. 1
Mulligan, P. 1
Murphy, D. 3

O'Brien, A. A. 1
O'Brien, A. J. 1
O'Callaghan, K. 1
O'Connor, T. 2
O'Dea, D. 1
O'Farrell, F. 2
O'Flanagan, K. 3
O'Keefe, E. 1
O'Leary, D. A. 1
O'Neill, F. 1
O'Neill, K. P. 4
O'Reilly, J. (Brideville) 2
O'Reilly, J. (Cork) 1
O'Shea, J. F. 3
Own goals 14

Parrott, T. D. 2
Pearce, A. J. 2
Pilkington, A. N. J. 1

Quinn, N. 21

Reid, A. M. 4
Reid, S. J. 2
Ringstead, A. 7
Robinson, C. J. 1
Robinson, M. 4
Rogers, E. 5
Ryan, G. 1
Ryan, R. 3

St Ledger-Hall, S. 3
Sheedy, K. 9
Sheridan, J. 5
Slaven, B. 1
Sloan, J. 1
Squires, J. 1
Stapleton, F. 20
Staunton, S. 7
Strahan, J. 1
Sullivan, J. 1

Townsend, A. D. 7
Treacy, R. 5
Touhy, L. 4

Waddock, G. 3
Walsh, D. 5
Walsh, M. 3
Walters, J. R. 14
Ward, S. R. 3
Waters, J. 1
White, J. J. 2
Whelan, G. D. 2
Whelan, R. 3
Williams, D. S. 1
Williams, S. 1
Wilson, M. D. 1

SOUTH AMERICA

RECOPA SUDAMERICANA 2021

FINAL – FIRST LEG

Palmeiras v Defensa y Justicia	1-2

FINAL – SECOND LEG

Defensa y Justicia v Palmeiras	1-2	3-3
aet; Defensa y Justicia won 4-3 on penalties		

COPA SUDAMERICANA 2020

FIRST STAGE – FIRST LEG

Coquimbo Unido v Aragua	3-0
Vasco da Gama v Oriente Petrolero	1-0
Blooming v Emelec	0-3
Zamora v Plaza Colonia	1-0
Nacional Potosi v Melgar	0-2
Atletico Grau v River Plate	1-2
Union v Atletico Mineiro	3-0
Bahia v Nacional	3-0
Fenix v El Nacional	1-0
Atletico Nacional v Huracan	3-0
Sol de America v Goias	1-0
Mineros v Sportivo Luqueno	2-3
Velez Sarsfield v Aucas	1-0
Millonarios v Always Ready	2-0
Lanus v Universidad Catolica	3-0
Deportivo Cali v River Plate	2-1
Argentinos Juniors v Sport Huancayo	1-1
Fluminense v Union La Calera	1-1
Huachipato v Deportivo Pasto	1-0
Cusco v Audax Italiano	2-0
Independiente v Fortaleza	1-0
Llaneros v Liverpool	0-2

FIRST STAGE SECOND LEG

		(agg)
Aragua v Coquimbo Unido	1-0	1-3
Oriente Petrolero v Vasco da Gama	0-0	0-1
Emelec v Blooming	2-0	5-0
Plaza Colonia v Zamora	3-0	3-1
Melgar v Nacional Potosi	0-2	2-2
Melgar won 4-3 on penalties		
River Plate v Atletico Grau	1-0	3-1
Atletico Mineiro v Union	2-0	2-3
Nacional v Bahia	1-3	1-6
El Nacional v Fenix	2-2	2-3
Huracan v Atletico Nacional	1-1	1-4
Goias v Sol de America	0-1	0-2
Sportivo Luqueno v Mineros	2-2	5-4
Aucas v Velez Sarsfield	2-1	2-2
Velez Sarsfield won on away goals		
Always Ready v Millonarios	1-0	1-2
Universidad Catolica v Lanus	2-0	2-3
River Plate v Deportivo Cali	1-3	2-5
Sport Huancayo v Argentinos Juniors	0-0	1-1
Sport Huancayo won on away goals		
Union La Calera v Fluminense	0-0	1-1
Union La Calera won on away goals		
Deportivo Pasto v Huachipato	0-1	0-2
Audax Italiano v Cusco	3-0	3-2
Fortaleza v Independiente	2-1	2-2
Independiente won on away goals		
Liverpool v Llaneros	5-0	7-0

SECOND STAGE – FIRST LEG

Independiente v Atletico Tucuman	1-0
Union v Emelec	0-1
Union La Calera v Deportes Tolima	0-0
Sol de America v Universidad Catolica	0-0
Millonarios v Deportivo Cali	1-2
Sport Huancayo v Liverpool	1-1
Vasco da Gama v Caracas	1-0
Lanus v Sao Paulo	3-2
Audax Italiano v Bolivar	2-1
Sportivo Luqueno v Defensa y Justicia	1-2
Coquimbo Unido v Estudiantes de Merida	3-0
Velez Sarsfield v Penarol	0-0
Atletico Nacional v River Plate	1-1
Plaza Colonia v Junior	0-1
Melgar v Bahia	1-0
Fenix v Huachipato	3-1

SECOND STAGE – SECOND LEG

		(agg)
Atletico Tucuman v Independiente	1-1	1-2
Emelec v Union	1-2	2-2
Union won on away goals		
Deportes Tolima v Union La Calera	1-1	1-1
Union La Calera won on away goals		
Universidad Catolica v Sol de America	2-1	2-1
Deportivo Cali v Millonarios	1-2	3-3
Deportivo Cali won 5-4 on penalties		
Liverpool v Sport Huancayo	1-2	2-3
Caracas v Vasco da Gama	0-0	0-1
Sao Paulo v Lanus	4-3	6-6
Lanus won on away goals		
Bolivar v Audax Italiano	3-0	4-2
Defensa y Justicia v Sportivo Luqueno	1-1	3-2
Estudiantes de Merida v Coquimbo Unido	0-2	0-5
Penarol v Velez Sarsfield	1-1	1-1
Velez Sarsfield won on away goals		
River Plate v Atletico Nacional	3-1	4-2
Junior v Plaza Colonia	0-0	1-0
Bahia v Melgar	4-0	4-1
Huachipato v Fenix	1-1	2-4

ROUND OF 16 – FIRST LEG

Fenix v Independiente	1-4
Bahia v Union	1-0
Junior v Union La Calera	2-1
River Plate v Universidad Catolica	1-2
Velez Sarsfield v Deportivo Cali	2-0
Coquimbo Unido v Sport Huancayo	0-0
Defensa y Justicia v Vasco da Gama	1-1
Bolivar v Lanus	2-1

ROUND OF 16 – SECOND LEG

		(agg)
Independiente v Fenix	1-0	5-1
Union v Bahia	0-0	0-1
Union La Calera v Junior	2-1	3-3
Junior won 4-2 on penalties		
Universidad Catolica v River Plate	0-1	2-2
Universidad Catolica won on away goals		
Deportivo Cali v Velez Sarsfield	1-5	1-7
Sport Huancayo v Coquimbo Unido	0-2	0-2
Vasco da Gama v Defensa y Justicia	0-1	1-2
Lanus v Bolivar	6-2	7-4

QUARTER-FINALS – FIRST LEG

Lanus v Independiente	0-0
Bahia v Defensa y Justicia	2-3
Junior v Coquimbo Unido	1-2
Velez Sarsfield v Universidad Catolica	1-2

QUARTER-FINALS – SECOND LEG

		(agg)
Independiente v Lanus	1-3	1-3
Defensa y Justicia v Bahia	1-0	4-2
Coquimbo Unido v Junior	0-1	2-2
Coquimbo Unido won on away goals		
Universidad Catolica v Velez Sarsfield	1-3	3-4

SEMI-FINALS – FIRST LEG

Velez Sarsfield v Lanus	0-1
Coquimbo Unido v Defensa y Justicia	0-0

SEMI-FINALS – SECOND LEG

		(agg)
Lanus v Velez Sarsfield	3-0	4-0
Defensa y Justicia v Coquimbo Unido	4-2	4-2

COPA SUDAMERICANA FINAL 2020

Cordoba, Saturday 23 January 2021

Defensa y Justicia (1) 3 *(Frias 34, Romero 62, Camacho 90)*

Lanus (0) 0

Defensa y Justicia: Unsain; Frias (Camacho 75), Martinez, Delgado, Fernandez, Paredes, Pizzini, Larralde (Benitez 84), Isnaldo, Bou (Merentiel 61), Romero (Britez 76).
Lanus: Morales; Aguirre, Burdisso, Perez A, Bernabei (Besozzi 81), De la Vega (Orozco 59), Belmonte, Quignon (Perez F 69), Vera (Belluschi 69), Orisini, Stand.
Referee: Jesus Valenzuela (Venezuela).

COPA LIBERTADORES 2020

THIRD STAGE – FIRST LEG

Barcelona v Cerro Porteno	1-0
Palestino v Guarani	0-1
Independiente Medellin v Atletico Tucuman	1-0
Deportes Tolima v Internacional	0-0

THIRD STAGE – SECOND LEG

		(agg)
Cerro Porteno v Barcelona	0-4	0-5
Guarani v Palestino	2-1	3-1
Atletico Tucuman v Independiente Medellin	1-0	1-1
Independiente Medellin won 4-2 on penalties		
Internacional v Deportes Tolima	1-0	1-0

GROUP STAGE – GROUP A

Barcelona v Independiente del Valle	0-3
Junior v Flamengo	1-2
Independiente del Valle v Junior	3-0
Flamengo v Barcelona	3-0
Independiente del Valle v Flamengo	5-0
Barcelona v Junior	1-2
Barcelona v Flamengo	1-2
Junior v Independiente del Valle	4-1
Flamengo v Independiente del Valle	4-0
Junior v Barcelona	0-2
Flamengo v Junior	3-1
Independiente del Valle v Barcelona	2-0

Group A Table	P	W	D	L	F	A	GD	Pts
Flamengo	6	5	0	1	14	8	6	15
Independiente del Valle	6	4	0	2	14	8	6	12
Junior	6	2	0	4	8	12	–4	6
Barcelona	6	1	0	5	4	12	–8	3

GROUP B

Tigre v Palmeiras	0-2
Guarani v Bolivar	2-0
Bolivar v Tigre	2-0
Palmeiras v Guarani	3-1
Bolivar v Palmeiras	1-2
Guarani v Tigre	4-1
Tigre v Bolivar	1-1
Guarani v Palmeiras	0-0
Palmeiras v Bolivar	5-0
Tigre v Guarani	1-3
Palmeiras v Tigre	5-0
Bolivar v Guarani	2-3

Group B Table	P	W	D	L	F	A	GD	Pts
Palmeiras	6	5	1	0	17	2	15	16
Guarani	6	4	1	1	13	7	6	13
Bolivar	6	1	1	4	6	13	–7	4
Tigre	6	0	1	5	3	17	–14	1

GROUP C

Athletico Paranaense v Penarol	1-0
Jorge Wilstermann v Colo-Colo	2-0
Colo-Colo v Athletico Paranaense	1-0
Penarol v Jorge Wilstermann	1-0
Colo-Colo v Penarol	2-1
Jorge Wilstermann v Athletico Paranaense	2-3
Athletico Paranaense v Colo-Colo	2-0
Jorge Wilstermann v Penarol	3-1
Penarol v Colo-Colo	3-0
Athletico Paranaense v Jorge Wilstermann	0-0
Penarol v Athletico Paranaense	3-2
Colo-Colo v Jorge Wilstermann	0-1

Group C Table	P	W	D	L	F	A	GD	Pts
Jorge Wilstermann	6	3	1	2	8	5	3	10
Athletico Paranaense	6	3	1	2	8	6	2	10
Penarol	6	3	0	3	9	8	1	9
Colo-Colo	6	2	0	4	3	9	–6	6

GROUP D

LDU Quito v River Plate	3-0
Binacional v Sao Paulo	2-1
River Plate v Binacional	8-0
Sao Paulo v LDU Quito	3-0
Binacional v LDU Quito	0-1
Sao Paulo v River Plate	2-2
LDU Quito v Sao Paulo	4-2
Binacional v River Plate	0-6
LDU Quito v Binacional	4-0
River Plate v Sao Paulo	2-1
River Plate v LDU Quito	3-0
Sao Paulo v Binacional	5-1

Group D Table	P	W	D	L	F	A	GD	Pts
River Plate	6	4	1	1	21	6	15	13
LDU Quito	6	4	0	2	12	8	4	12
Sao Paulo	6	2	1	3	14	11	3	7
Binacional	6	1	0	5	3	25	–22	3

GROUP E

Internacional v Universidad Catolica	3-0
America de Cali v Gremio	0-2
Universidad Catolica v America de Cali	1-2
Gremio v Internacional	0-0
Internacional v America de Cali	4-3
Universidad Catolica v Gremio	2-0
America de Cali v Universidad Catolica	1-1
Internacional v Gremio	0-1
Gremio v Universidad Catolica	2-0
America de Cali v Internacional	0-0
Gremio v America de Cali	1-1
Universidad Catolica v Internacional	2-1

Group E Table	P	W	D	L	F	A	GD	Pts
Gremio	6	3	2	1	6	3	3	11
Internacional	6	2	2	2	8	6	2	8
Universidad Catolica	6	2	1	3	5	8	–3	7
America de Cali	6	1	3	2	6	8	–2	6

GROUP F

Estudiantes de Merida v Racing	1-2
Alianza Lima v Nacional	0-1
Nacional v Estudiantes de Merida	1-0
Racing v Alianza Lima	1-0
Estudiantes de Merida v Alianza Lima	3-2
Racing v Nacional	0-1
Estudiantes de Merida v Nacional	1-3
Alianza Lima v Racing	0-2
Nacional v Racing	1-2
Alianza Lima v Estudiantes de Merida	2-2
Nacional v Alianza Lima	2-0
Racing v Estudiantes de Merida	2-1

Group F Table	P	W	D	L	F	A	GD	Pts
Nacional	6	5	0	1	9	3	6	15
Racing	6	5	0	1	9	4	5	15
Estudiantes de Merida	6	1	1	4	8	12	–4	4
Alianza Lima	6	0	1	5	4	11	–7	1

GROUP G

Defensa y Justicia v Santos	1-2
Delfin v Olimpia	1-1
Santos v Delfin	1-0
Olimpia v Defensa y Justicia	2-1
Santos v Olimpia	0-0
Defensa y Justicia v Delfin	3-0
Defensa y Justicia v Olimpia	2-1
Delfin v Santos	1-2
Olimpia v Santos	2-3
Delfin v Defensa y Justicia	3-0
Olimpia v Delfin	0-1
Santos v Defensa y Justicia	2-1

Group G Table	P	W	D	L	F	A	GD	Pts
Santos	6	5	1	0	10	5	5	16
Delfin	6	2	1	3	6	7	–1	7
Defensa y Justicia	6	2	0	4	8	10	–2	6
Olimpia	6	1	2	3	6	8	–2	5

GROUP H

Independiente Medellin v Libertad	1-2
Caracas v Boca Juniors	1-1
Libertad v Caracas	3-2
Boca Juniors v Independiente Medellin	3-0
Independiente Medellin v Caracas	2-3
Libertad v Boca Juniors	0-2
Caracas v Libertad	2-1
Independiente Medellin v Boca Juniors	0-1
Boca Juniors v Libertad	0-0
Caracas v Independiente Medellin	0-2
Boca Juniors v Caracas	3-0
Libertad v Independiente Medellin	2-4

Group H Table	P	W	D	L	F	A	GD	Pts
Boca Juniors	6	4	2	0	10	1	9	14
Libertad	6	2	1	3	8	11	–3	7
Caracas	6	2	1	3	8	12	–4	7
Independiente Medellin	6	2	0	4	9	11	–2	6

ROUND OF 16 – FIRST LEG

Guarani v Gremio	0-2
Independiente del Valle v Nacional	0-0
Delfin v Palmeiras	1-3
Internacional v Boca Juniors	0-1
Racing v Flamengo	1-1
Libertad v Jorge Wilstermann	3-1
Athletico Paranaense v River Plate	1-1
LDU Quito v Santos	1-2

ROUND OF 16 – SECOND LEG

		(agg)
Gremio v Guarani	2-0	4-0
Nacional v Independiente del Valle	0-0	0-0
Nacional won 4-2 on penalties		
Palmeiras v Delfin	5-0	8-1
Boca Juniors v Internacional	0-1	1-1
Boca Juniors won 5-4 on penalties		
Flamengo v Racing	1-1	2-2
Racing won 5-3 on penalties		
Jorge Wilstermann v Libertad	0-2	1-5
River Plate v Athletico Paranaense	1-0	2-1
Santos v LDU Quito	0-1	2-2
Santos won on away goals		

QUARTER-FINALS – FIRST LEG

Gremio v Santos	1-1
River Plate v Nacional	2-0
Libertad v Palmeiras	1-1
Racing v Boca Juniors	1-0

QUARTER-FINALS – SECOND LEG

		(agg)
Santos v Gremio	4-1	5-2
Nacional v River Plate	2-6	2-8
Palmeiras v Libertad	3-0	4-1
Boca Juniors v Racing	2-0	2-1

SEMI-FINALS – FIRST LEG

Boca Juniors v Santos	0-0
River Plate v Palmeiras	0-3

SEMI-FINALS – SECOND LEG

		(agg)
Santos v Boca Juniors	3-0	3-0
Palmeiras v River Plate	0-2	3-2

COPA LIBERTADORES FINAL 2020

Rio de Janeiro, Saturday 30 January 2021

Palmeiras (0) 1 *(Breno Lopes 90)*

Santos (0) 0 5000

Palmeiras: Weverton; Marcos Rocha, Luan Garcia, Gomez, Vina, Danilo, Gabriel Menino (Breno Lopes 85), Ze Rafael (Patrick de Paula 78), Raphael Veiga (Empereur 90), Rony (Felipe Melo 90), Luiz Adriano.
Santos: John; Para (Bruno Marques 90), Verissimo, Peres, Jonatan (Wellington 90), Sandry (Braga 73), Alison, Marinho, Pituca, Soteldo, Jorge (Madson 90)
Referee: Patricio Loustau (Argentina).

AFRICA

AFRICA CUP OF NATIONS 2021 – QUALIFYING

PRELIMINARY ROUND – FIRST LEG

Liberia v Chad	1-0
South Sudan v Seychelles	2-1
Mauritius v Sao Tome & Principe	1-3
Djibouti v Gambia	1-1

PRELIMINARY ROUND – SECOND LEG

		(agg)
Chad v Liberia	1-0	1-1
Chad won 5-4 on penalties		
Seychelles v South Sudan	0-1	1-3
Sao Tome & Principe v Mauritius	2-1	5-2
Gambia v Djibouti	1-1	2-2
Gambia won 3-2 on penalties		

GROUP STAGE

Group A Table	P	W	D	L	F	A	GD	Pts
Mali	6	4	1	1	10	4	6	13
Guinea	6	3	2	1	8	5	3	11
Namibia	6	3	0	3	8	7	1	9
Chad	6	0	1	5	2	12	–10	1

Group B Table	P	W	D	L	F	A	GD	Pts
Burkina Faso	6	3	3	0	6	2	4	12
Malawi	6	3	1	2	4	5	–1	10
Uganda	6	2	2	2	3	2	1	8
South Sudan	6	1	0	5	2	6	–4	3

Group C Table	P	W	D	L	F	A	GD	Pts
Ghana	6	4	1	1	9	3	6	13
Sudan	6	4	0	2	9	3	6	12
South Africa	6	3	1	2	8	7	1	10
Sao Tome & Principe	6	0	0	6	3	16	–13	0

Group D Table	P	W	D	L	F	A	GD	Pts
Gambia	6	3	1	2	9	7	2	10
Gabon	6	3	1	2	8	6	2	10
DR Congo	6	2	3	1	4	5	–1	9
Angola	6	1	1	4	4	7	–3	4

Group E Table	P	W	D	L	F	A	GD	Pts
Morocco	6	4	2	0	10	1	9	14
Mauritania	6	2	3	1	5	4	1	9
Burundi	6	1	2	3	6	10	–4	5
Central African Republic	6	1	1	4	5	11	–6	4

Group F Table	P	W	D	L	F	A	GD	Pts
Cameroon	6	3	2	1	8	4	4	11
Cape Verde	6	2	4	0	6	3	3	10
Rwanda	6	1	3	2	1	3	–2	6
Mozambique	6	1	1	4	5	10	–5	4

Group G Table	P	W	D	L	F	A	GD	Pts
Egypt	6	3	3	0	10	3	7	12
Comoros	6	2	3	1	4	6	–2	9
Kenya	6	1	4	1	7	7	0	7
Togo	6	0	2	4	3	8	–5	2

Group H Table	P	W	D	L	F	A	GD	Pts
Algeria	6	4	2	0	19	6	13	14
Zimbabwe	6	2	2	2	6	8	–2	8
Zambia	6	2	1	3	8	12	–4	7
Botswana	6	1	1	4	2	9	–7	4

Group I Table	P	W	D	L	F	A	GD	Pts
Senegal	6	4	2	0	10	2	8	14
Guinea-Bissau	6	3	0	3	9	7	2	9
Congo	6	2	2	2	5	5	0	8
Eswatini	6	0	2	4	3	13	–10	2

Group J Table	P	W	D	L	F	A	GD	Pts
Tunisia	6	5	1	0	14	5	9	16
Equatorial Guinea	6	3	0	3	7	7	0	9
Tanzania	6	2	1	3	5	6	–1	7
Libya	6	1	0	5	7	15	–8	3

Group K Table	P	W	D	L	F	A	GD	Pts
Ivory Coast	6	4	1	1	11	5	6	13
Ethiopia	6	3	0	3	10	6	4	9
Madagascar	6	2	2	2	9	9	0	8
Niger	6	1	1	4	3	13	–10	4

Group L Table	P	W	D	L	F	A	GD	Pts
Nigeria	6	4	2	0	14	7	7	14
Benin	5	2	1	2	3	3	0	7
Sierra Leone	5	0	4	1	5	6	–1	4
Lesotho	6	0	3	3	3	9	–6	3

Sierra Leone v Benin to be played in June 2021.

On 30 June 2020 the Confederation of African Football (CAF) announced that the African Cup of Nationsl 2021 Final Tournament in Cameroon would be postponed from January 2021 until January 2022.

NORTH AMERICA

MLS IS BACK

The MLS is Back Tournament *was a mid-season tournament to start up the season again after the main season had been suspended due to the COVID-19 pandemic. Twenty-four of the twenty-six MLS clubs took part with FC Dallas and Nashville withdrawing due to COVID-19 infections. The tournament was held at the ESPN Wide World of Sports Complex, Florida between 8 July and 11 August 2020.*

MLS IS BACK – GROUP STAGE

Group A	P	W	D	L	F	A	GD	Pts
Orlando C	3	2	1	0	6	3	3	7
Philadelphia Union	3	2	1	0	4	2	2	7
New York City	3	1	0	2	2	4	–2	3
Inter Miami	3	0	0	3	2	5	–3	0

Group B	P	W	D	L	F	A	GD	Pts
San Jose Earthquakes	3	2	1	0	6	3	3	7
Seattle Sounders	3	1	1	1	4	2	2	4
Vancouver Whitecaps	3	1	0	2	5	7	–2	3
Chicago Fire	3	1	0	2	2	5	–3	3

Group C	P	W	D	L	F	A	GD	Pts
Toronto	3	1	2	0	6	5	1	5
New England Revolution	3	1	2	0	2	1	1	5
Montreal Impact	3	1	0	2	4	5	–1	3
DC United	3	0	2	1	3	4	–1	2

Group D	P	W	D	L	F	A	GD	Pts
Sporting Kansas City	3	2	0	1	6	4	2	6
Minnesota U	3	1	2	0	4	3	1	5
Real Salt Lake	3	1	1	1	2	2	0	4
Colorado Rapids	3	0	1	2	4	7	–3	1

Group E	P	W	D	L	F	A	GD	Pts
Columbus Crew	3	3	0	0	7	0	7	9
FC Cincinnati	3	2	0	1	3	4	–1	6
New York Red Bulls	3	1	0	2	1	4	–3	3
Atlanta U	3	0	0	3	0	3	–3	0

Group F	P	W	D	L	F	A	GD	Pts
Portland Timbers	3	2	1	0	6	4	2	7
Los Angeles	3	1	2	0	11	7	4	5
Houston Dynamo	3	0	2	1	5	6	–1	2
LA Galaxy	3	0	1	2	4	9	–5	1

ROUND OF 16

Orlando C v Montreal Impact 1-0
Philadelphia Union v New England Revolution 1-0
Toronto v New York City 1-3
Sporting Kansas City v Vancouver Whitecaps 0-0
Sporting Kansas City won 3-1 on penalties
San Jose Earthquakes v Real Salt Lake 5-2
Seattle Sounders v Los Angeles 1-4
Columbus Crew v Minnesota U 1-1
Minnesota U won 5-3 on penalties
Portland Timbers v FC Cincinnati 1-1
Portland Timbers won 4-2 on penalties

QUARTER-FINALS

Philadelphia Union v Sporting Kansas City 3-1
Orlando C v Los Angeles 1-1
Orlando C won 5-4 on penalties
San Jose Earthquakes v Minnesota U 1-4
New York City v Portland Timbers 1-3

SEMI-FINALS

Philadelphia Union v Portland Timbers 1-2
Orlando C v Minnesota U 3-1

FINAL

Portland Timbers v Orlando C 2-1

MAJOR LEAGUE SOCCER 2020

**After extra time.*

EASTERN CONFERENCE

	P	W	D	L	F	A	GD	Pts	PPG
Philadelphia Union	23	14	5	4	44	20	24	47	2.04
Toronto	23	13	5	5	33	26	7	44	1.91
Columbus Crew	23	12	5	6	36	21	15	41	1.78
Orlando C	23	11	8	4	40	25	15	41	1.78
New York City	23	12	3	8	37	25	12	39	1.70
New York Red Bulls	23	9	5	9	29	31	–2	32	1.39
Nashville	23	8	8	7	24	22	2	32	1.39
New England Revolution	23	8	8	7	26	25	1	32	1.39
Montreal Impact	23	8	2	13	33	43	–10	26	1.13
Inter Miami	23	7	3	13	25	35	–10	24	1.04
Chicago Fire	23	5	8	10	33	39	–6	23	1.00
Atlanta U	23	6	4	13	23	30	–7	22	0.96
DC United	23	5	6	12	25	41	–16	21	0.91
FC Cincinnati	23	4	4	15	12	36	–24	16	0.70

WESTERN CONFERENCE

	P	W	D	L	GF	GA	GD	Pts	PPG
Sporting Kansas City	21	12	3	6	38	25	13	39	1.86
Seattle Sounders	22	11	6	5	44	23	21	39	1.77
Portland Timbers	23	11	6	6	46	35	11	39	1.70
Minnesota U	21	9	7	5	36	26	10	34	1.62
Colorado Rapids	18	8	4	6	32	28	4	28	1.56
FC Dallas	22	9	7	6	28	24	4	34	1.55
Los Angeles	22	9	5	8	47	39	8	32	1.45
San Jose Earthquakes	23	8	6	9	35	51	–16	30	1.30
Vancouver Whitecaps	23	9	0	14	27	44	–17	27	1.17
LA Galaxy	22	6	4	12	27	46	–19	22	1.00
Real Salt Lake	22	5	7	10	25	35	–10	22	1.00
Houston Dynamo	23	4	9	10	30	40	–10	21	0.91

MLS PLAY-OFFS

EASTERN CONFERENCE FIRST ROUND

Orlando C v New York City 1-1*
Orlando C won 6-5 on penalties
Columbus Crew v New York Red Bulls 3-2
Toronto v Nashville 0-1*
Philadelphia Union v New England Revolution 0-2

EASTERN CONFERENCE SEMI-FINALS

Orlando C v New England Revolution 1-3
Columbus Crew v Nashville 2-0*

EASTERN CONFERENCE FINAL

Columbus Crew v New England Revolution 1-0

WESTERN CONFERENCE FIRST ROUND

Sporting Kansas City v San Jose Earthquakes 3-3*
Sporting Kansas City won 3-0 on penalties
Minnesota U v Colorado Rapids 3-0
Portland Timbers v FC Dallas 1-1*
FC Dallas won 8-7 on penalties
Seattle Sounders v Los Angeles 3-1

WESTERN CONFERENCE SEMI-FINALS

Seattle Sounders v FC Dallas 1-0
Sporting Kansas City v Minnesota U 0-3

WESTERN CONFERENCE FINAL

Seattle Sounders v Minnesota U 3-2

MLS CUP FINAL 2020

Ohio, Saturday 12 December 2020

Columbus Crew (2) 3 *(Zelarayan 25, 82, Etienne 31)*

Seattle Sounders (0) 0 1500

Columbus Crew: Room; Afful, Mensah, Williams, Valenzuela, Morris, Artur (Alashe 88), Diaz (Francis 90), Zelarayan, Etienne (Jimenez 83), Zardes.
Seattle Sounders: Frei; Roldan A (Leerdam 60), Andrade, O'Neill (Medranda 77), Tolo (Smith 46), Roldan C, Paulo (Bruin 60), Jones (Svensson 46), Lodeiro, Morris, Ruidiaz.
Referee: Jair Marrufo (Texas).

UEFA UNDER-21 CHAMPIONSHIP 2019–21

QUALIFYING

GROUP 1
Republic of Ireland v Luxembourg 3-0
Iceland v Luxembourg 3-0
Republic of Ireland v Armenia 1-0
Iceland v Armenia 6-1
Sweden v Republic of Ireland 1-3
Italy v Luxembourg 5-0
Republic of Ireland v Italy 0-0
Armenia v Luxembourg 2-0
Sweden v Iceland 5-0
Armenia v Italy 0-1
Iceland v Republic of Ireland 1-0
Luxembourg v Sweden 0-3
Armenia v Republic of Ireland 0-1
Italy v Iceland 3-0
Republic of Ireland v Sweden 4-1
Italy v Armenia 6-0
Iceland v Sweden 1-0
Luxembourg v Armenia 2-1
Sweden v Italy 3-0
Sweden v Luxembourg 4-0
Luxembourg v Iceland 0-2
Italy v Republic of Ireland 2-0
Sweden v Armenia 10-0
Iceland v Italy 1-2
Armenia v Sweden 0-3
Match awarded to Sweden due to positive COVID-19 tests in Armenia team
Republic of Ireland v Iceland 1-2
Luxembourg v Italy 0-4
Luxembourg v Republic of Ireland 1-2
Armenia v Iceland 0-3
Match awarded to Iceland due to positive COVID-19 tests in Armenia team
Italy v Sweden 4-1

Group 1 Table	P	W	D	L	F	A	GD	Pts
Italy	10	8	1	1	27	5	22	25
Iceland	10	7	0	3	19	12	7	21
Republic of Ireland	10	6	1	3	15	8	7	19
Sweden	10	6	0	4	31	12	19	18
Armenia	10	1	0	9	4	33	–29	3
Luxembourg	10	1	0	9	3	29	–26	3

GROUP 2
Liechtenstein v Azerbaijan 1-0
Georgia v Liechtenstein 4-0
Azerbaijan v Slovakia 2-1
Azerbaijan v Georgia 0-3
Liechtenstein v Switzerland 0-5
Liechtenstein v Slovakia 2-4
France v Azerbaijan 5-0
Switzerland v Georgia 2-1
Azerbaijan v Switzerland 0-1
Slovakia v France 3-5
Azerbaijan v Liechtenstein 1-0
France v Georgia 3-2
Slovakia v Georgia 3-2
Switzerland v France 3-1
Switzerland v Slovakia 4-1
Georgia v France 0-2
Azerbaijan v France 1-2
Liechtenstein v Georgia 0-2
Slovakia v Switzerland 1-2
Slovakia v Azerbaijan 2-1
France v Liechtenstein 5-0
Georgia v Switzerland 0-3
France v Slovakia 1-0
Georgia v Azerbaijan 1-0
Switzerland v Liechtenstein 3-0
Georgia v Slovakia 2-1
Switzerland v Azerbaijan 2-1
Liechtenstein v France 0-5
France v Switzerland 3-1
Slovakia v Liechtenstein 6-0

Group 2 Table	P	W	D	L	F	A	GD	Pts
France	10	9	0	1	32	10	22	27
Switzerland	10	9	0	1	26	8	18	27
Georgia	10	5	0	5	17	14	3	15
Slovakia	10	4	0	6	22	21	1	12
Azerbaijan	10	2	0	8	6	18	–12	6
Liechtenstein	10	1	0	9	3	35	–32	3

GROUP 3
Albania v Turkey 1-2
Andorra v Albania 2-2
Andorra v Kosovo 0-4
Turkey v Albania 2-2
Kosovo v Turkey 3-1
Andorra v Austria 1-3
Turkey v England 2-3
Albania v Austria 0-4
England v Kosovo 2-0
Austria v Turkey 3-0
Albania v Kosovo 2-1
England v Austria 5-1
Austria v Kosovo 4-0
Albania v England 0-3
Andorra v Turkey 2-0
Austria v Albania 1-5
Kosovo v England 0-6
Turkey v Andorra 1-0
Albania v Andorra 3-1
Austria v England 1-2
Andorra v England 3-3
Kosovo v Austria 0-1
Kosovo v Andorra 1-0
England v Turkey 2-1
Turkey v Austria 3-2
Kosovo v Albania 0-1
England v Andorra 3-1
Turkey v Kosovo 3-0
England v Albania 5-0
Austria v Andorra 4-0

Group 3 Table	P	W	D	L	F	A	GD	Pts
England	10	9	1	0	34	9	25	28
Austria	10	6	0	4	24	16	8	18
Albania	10	4	2	4	16	21	–5	14
Turkey	10	4	1	5	15	18	–3	13
Kosovo	10	3	0	7	9	20	–11	9
Andorra	10	1	2	7	10	24	–14	5

GROUP 4
San Marino v Lithuania 0-3
Greece v San Marino 5-0
Scotland v San Marino 2-0
Czech Republic v Lithuania 2-0
Greece v Lithuania 1-0
Croatia v Scotland 1-2
Czech Republic v Greece 1-1
Scotland v Lithuania 0-0
Czech Republic v Scotland 0-0
San Marino v Croatia 0-7
Lithuania v Croatia 1-3
Czech Republic v San Marino 6-0
Scotland v Greece 0-1
Croatia v Czech Republic 1-2
San Marino v Czech Republic 0-6
Croatia v Greece 5-0
San Marino v Greece 0-1
Czech Republic v Croatia 0-0
Lithuania v Scotland 0-1

Lithuania v Greece 2-0
Croatia v San Marino 10-0
Scotland v Czech Republic 2-0
Greece v Croatia 0-1
Lithuania v Czech Republic 0-1
San Marino v Scotland 0-7
Scotland v Croatia 2-2
Lithuania v San Marino 3-0
Greece v Czech Republic 0-2
Greece v Scotland 1-0
Croatia v Lithuania 7-0

Group 4 Table	P	W	D	L	F	A	GD	Pts
Czech Republic	10	6	3	1	20	4	16	21
Croatia	10	6	2	2	37	7	30	20
Scotland	10	5	3	2	16	5	11	18
Greece	10	5	1	4	10	11	–1	16
Lithuania	10	3	1	6	9	15	–6	10
San Marino	10	0	0	10	0	50	–50	0

GROUP 5

Estonia v Bulgaria 0-4
Latvia v Poland 0-1
Russia v Serbia 1-0
Poland v Estonia 4-0
Serbia v Latvia 1-1
Bulgaria v Russia 0-0
Russia v Poland 2-2
Bulgaria v Serbia 0-1
Estonia v Latvia 2-1
Latvia v Bulgaria 0-0
Poland v Serbia 1-0
Estonia v Russia 0-5
Russia v Latvia 2-0
Bulgaria v Poland 3-0
Serbia v Estonia 6-0
Serbia v Russia 0-2
Latvia v Serbia 2-2
Russia v Bulgaria 2-0
Estonia v Poland 0-6
Latvia v Estonia 1-1
Poland v Russia 1-0
Serbia v Bulgaria 1-2
Russia v Estonia 4-0
Bulgaria v Latvia 1-0
Serbia v Poland 1-0
Estonia v Serbia 0-0
Latvia v Russia 1-4
Poland v Bulgaria 1-1
Poland v Latvia 3-1
Bulgaria v Estonia 3-0

Group 5 Table	P	W	D	L	F	A	GD	Pts
Russia	10	7	2	1	22	4	18	23
Poland	10	6	2	2	19	8	11	20
Bulgaria	10	5	3	2	14	5	9	18
Serbia	10	3	3	4	12	9	3	12
Estonia	10	1	2	7	3	34	–31	5
Latvia	10	0	4	6	7	17	–10	4

GROUP 6

Faroe Islands v Kazakhstan 1-3
Montenegro v Kazakhstan 1-2
Kazakhstan v Spain 0-1
Montenegro v Faroe Islands 3-0
Kazakhstan v Israel 1-2
North Macedonia v Faroe Islands 7-1
Spain v Montenegro 2-0
Montenegro v North Macedonia 1-2
North Macedonia v Kazakhstan 1-1
Israel v Faroe Islands 3-1
Montenegro v Spain 0-2
Israel v Montenegro 0-0
Spain v North Macedonia 3-0
Israel v Spain 1-1
Faroe Islands v Israel 3-1
Kazakhstan v Montenegro 0-4
North Macedonia v Spain 0-1
Faroe Islands v North Macedonia 1-2
Israel v Kazakhstan 1-2
Kazakhstan v North Macedonia 1-4
Montenegro v Israel 1-2
Faroe Islands v Spain 0-2
North Macedonia v Israel 1-1
Faroe Islands v Montenegro 1-0
Spain v Kazakhstan 3-0
Israel v North Macedonia 1-1
Spain v Faroe Islands 2-0
Kazakhstan v Faroe Islands 2-3
North Macedonia v Montenegro 2-1
Spain v Israel 3-0

Group 6 Table	P	W	D	L	F	A	GD	Pts
Spain	10	9	1	0	20	1	19	28
North Macedonia	10	5	3	2	20	12	8	18
Israel	10	3	4	3	12	14	–2	13
Kazakhstan	10	3	1	6	12	21	–9	10
Faroe Islands	10	3	0	7	11	25	–14	9
Montenegro	10	2	1	7	11	13	–2	7

GROUP 7

Cyprus v Gibraltar 1-0
Belarus v Gibraltar 10-0
Portugal v Gibraltar 4-0
Norway v Cyprus 2-1
Belarus v Portugal 0-2
Netherlands v Cyprus 5-1
Belarus v Norway 1-1
Netherlands v Portugal 4-2
Cyprus v Belarus 1-1
Norway v Netherlands 0-4
Gibraltar v Netherlands 0-6
Cyprus v Norway 1-2
Norway v Portugal 2-3
Gibraltar v Belarus 0-2
Belarus v Netherlands 0-7
Cyprus v Portugal 0-4
Norway v Gibraltar 6-0
Netherlands v Norway 2-0
Netherlands v Gibraltar 5-0
Belarus v Cyprus 1-2
Portugal v Norway 4-1
Cyprus v Netherlands 0-7
Gibraltar v Portugal 0-3
Portugal v Belarus 3-0
Gibraltar v Norway*
Netherlands v Belarus 5-0
Portugal v Cyprus 2-1
Norway v Belarus*
Gibraltar v Cyprus*
Portugal v Netherlands 2-1

* *Match cancelled due to COVID-19 restrictions and as the result of the match would not impact on the final positions, remained unplayed*

Group 7 Table	P	W	D	L	F	A	GD	Pts
Netherlands	10	9	0	1	46	5	41	27
Portugal	10	9	0	1	29	9	20	27
Norway	8	3	1	4	14	16	–2	10
Belarus	9	2	2	5	15	21	–6	8
Cyprus	9	2	1	6	8	24	–16	7
Gibraltar	8	0	0	8	0	37	–37	0

GROUP 8

Ukraine v Finland 0-2
Northern Ireland v Malta 0-0
Ukraine v Malta 4-0
Finland v Northern Ireland 1-1
Denmark v Romania 2-1
Denmark v Northern Ireland 2-1
Finland v Malta 4-0
Romania v Ukraine 3-0
Finland v Denmark 0-1
Romania v Northern Ireland 3-0

Romania v Finland	4-1
Ukraine v Denmark	2-3
Denmark v Malta	5-1
Northern Ireland v Romania	0-0
Finland v Romania	1-3
Denmark v Ukraine	1-1
Malta v Northern Ireland	0-2
Finland v Ukraine	0-2
Northern Ireland v Denmark	0-1
Malta v Romania	0-3
Ukraine v Romania	1-0
Malta v Denmark	1-3
Northern Ireland v Finland	2-3
Denmark v Finland	2-1
Northern Ireland v Ukraine	1-0
Romania v Malta	4-1
Malta v Ukraine	1-4
Malta v Finland	0-1
Ukraine v Northern Ireland	3-0
Romania v Denmark	1-1

Group 8 Table	*P*	*W*	*D*	*L*	*F*	*A*	*GD*	*Pts*
Denmark	10	8	2	0	21	9	12	26
Romania	10	6	2	2	22	7	15	20
Ukraine	10	5	1	4	17	11	6	16
Finland	10	4	1	5	14	15	–1	13
Northern Ireland	10	2	3	5	7	13	–6	9
Malta	10	0	1	9	4	30	–26	1

GROUP 9

Bosnia-Herzegovina v Moldova	4-0
Wales v Belgium	1-0
Wales v Germany	1-5
Belgium v Bosnia-Herzegovina	0-0
Moldova v Wales	2-1
Bosnia-Herzegovina v Germany	0-2
Belgium v Moldova	4-1
Germany v Belgium	2-3
Wales v Bosnia-Herzegovina	1-0
Germany v Moldova	4-1
Bosnia-Herzegovina v Wales	1-0
Belgium v Germany	4-1
Moldova v Bosnia-Herzegovina	1-1
Moldova v Germany	0-5
Belgium v Wales	5-0
Moldova v Belgium	1-0
Germany v Bosnia-Herzegovina	1-0
Wales v Moldova	3-0
Bosnia-Herzegovina v Belgium	3-2
Germany v Wales	2-1

Group 9 Table	*P*	*W*	*D*	*L*	*F*	*A*	*GD*	*Pts*
Germany	8	6	0	2	22	10	12	18
Belgium	8	4	1	3	18	9	9	13
Bosnia-Herzegovina	8	3	2	3	9	7	2	11
Wales	8	3	0	5	8	15	–7	9
Moldova	8	2	1	5	6	22	–16	7

UEFA UNDER-21 CHAMPIONSHIP 2019–21

FINALS IN HUNGARY AND SLOVENIA

**After extra time.*

GROUP STAGE

GROUP A

Hungary v Germany	0-3
Romania v Netherlands	1-1
Hungary v Romania	1-2
Germany v Netherlands	1-1
Netherlands v Hungary	6-1
Germany v Romania	0-0

Group A Table	*P*	*W*	*D*	*L*	*F*	*A*	*GD*	*Pts*
Netherlands	3	1	2	0	8	3	5	5
Germany	3	1	2	0	4	1	3	5
Romania	3	1	2	0	3	2	1	5
Hungary	3	0	0	3	2	11	–9	0

GROUP B

Czech Republic v Italy	1-1
Slovenia v Spain	0-3
Slovenia v Czech Republic	1-1
Spain v Italy	0-0
Spain v Czech Republic	2-0
Italy v Slovenia	4-0

Group B Table	*P*	*W*	*D*	*L*	*F*	*A*	*GD*	*Pts*
Spain	3	2	1	0	5	0	5	7
Italy	3	1	2	0	5	1	4	5
Czech Republic	3	0	2	1	2	4	–2	2
Slovenia	3	0	1	2	1	8	–7	1

GROUP C

Russia v Iceland	4-1
France v Denmark	0-1
Iceland v Denmark	0-2
Russia v France	0-2
Iceland v France	0-2
Denmark v Russia	3-0

Group C Table	*P*	*W*	*D*	*L*	*F*	*A*	*GD*	*Pts*
Denmark	3	3	0	0	6	0	6	9
France	3	2	0	1	4	1	3	6
Russia	3	1	0	2	4	6	–2	3
Iceland	3	0	0	3	1	8	–7	0

GROUP D

England v Switzerland	0-1
Portugal v Croatia	1-0
Croatia v Switzerland	3-2
Portugal v England	2-0
Croatia v England	1-2
Switzerland v Portugal	0-3

Group D Table	*P*	*W*	*D*	*L*	*F*	*A*	*GD*	*Pts*
Portugal	3	3	0	0	6	0	6	9
Croatia	3	1	0	2	4	5	–1	3
Switzerland	3	1	0	2	3	6	–3	3
England	3	1	0	2	2	4	–2	3

KNOCKOUT STAGE

QUARTER-FINALS

Spain v Croatia	2-1*
Netherlands v France	2-1
Portugal v Italy	5-3*
Denmark v Germany	2-2*

Germany won 6-5 on penalties

SEMI-FINALS

Spain v Portugal	0-1
Netherlands v Germany	1-2

UEFA UNDER-21 CHAMPIONSHIP FINAL 2021

Ljubljana, Sunday 6 June 2021

Germany (0) 1 *(Nmecha 49)*

Portugal (0) 0

Germany: Dahmen; Baku, Raum, Schlotterbeck, Pieper, Dorsch (Janelt 85), Wirtz (Adeyemi 68), Maier, Nmecha (Jakobs 85), Berisha (Burkardt 67), Ozcan (Stach 90).
Portugal: Costa; Conte (Ramos 86), Leite, Queiros, Dalot, Luis (Fernandes 83), Vitinha (Jota 59), Braganca, Mota (Leao 46), Tomas (Conceicao 59), Vieira.
Referee: Giorgi Kruashvili (Georgia).

ENGLAND UNDER-21 RESULTS 1976–2021

EC *UEFA Competition for Under-21 Teams*

Bold type indicates matches played in season 2020–21.

Year	*Date*		*Venue*		
			v ALBANIA	*Eng*	*Alb*
EC1989	Mar	7	Shkoder	2	1
EC1989	April	25	Ipswich	2	0
EC2001	Mar	27	Tirana	1	0
EC2001	Sept	4	Middlesbrough	5	0
EC2019	Nov	15	Shkoder	3	0
EC2020	**Nov**	**17**	**Wolverhampton**	**5**	**0**
			v ANDORRA	*Eng*	*And*
EC2017	Oct	10	Andorra la Vella	1	0
ec2018	Oct	11	Chesterfield	7	0
EC2020	**Oct**	**7**	**Andorra la Vella**	**3**	**3**
EC2020	**Nov**	**13**	**Wolverhampton**	**3**	**1**
			v ANGOLA	*Eng*	*Ang*
1995	June	10	Toulon	1	0
1996	May	28	Toulon	0	2
			v ARGENTINA	*Eng*	*Arg*
1998	May	18	Toulon	0	2
2000	Feb	22	Fulham	1	0
			v AUSTRIA	*Eng*	*Aus*
1994	Oct	11	Kapfenberg	3	1
1995	Nov	14	Middlesbrough	2	1
EC2004	Sept	3	Krems	2	0
EC2005	Oct	7	Leeds	1	2
2013	June	26	Brighton	4	0
EC2019	Oct	15	Milton Keynes	5	1
EC2020	**Sept**	**9**	**Reid**	**2**	**1**
			v AZERBAIJAN	*Eng*	*Az*
EC2004	Oct	12	Baku	0	0
EC2005	Mar	29	Middlesbrough	2	0
2009	June	8	Milton Keynes	7	0
EC2011	Sept	1	Watford	6	0
EC2012	Sept	6	Baku	2	0
			v BELARUS	*Eng*	*Bel*
2015	June	11	Barnsley	1	0
			v BELGIUM	*Eng*	*Belg*
1994	June	5	Marseille	2	1
1996	May	24	Toulon	1	0
EC2011	Nov	14	Mons	1	2
EC2012	Feb	29	Middlesbrough	4	0
			v BOSNIA-HERZEGOVINA	*Eng*	*B-H*
EC2015	Nov	12	Sarajevo Canton	0	0
EC2016	Oct	11	Walsall	5	0
			v BRAZIL	*Eng*	*Bra*
1993	June	11	Toulon	0	0
1995	June	6	Toulon	0	2
1996	June	1	Toulon	1	2
			v BULGARIA	*Eng*	*Bul*
EC1979	June	5	Pernik	3	1
EC1979	Nov	20	Leicester	5	0
1989	June	5	Toulon	2	3
EC1998	Oct	9	West Ham	1	0
EC1999	June	8	Vratsa	1	0
EC2007	Sept	11	Sofia	2	0
EC2007	Nov	16	Milton Keynes	2	0
			v CHINA PR	*Eng*	*CPR*
2018	May	26	Toulon	2	1
			v CROATIA	*Eng*	*Cro*
1996	Apr	23	Sunderland	0	1
2003	Aug	19	West Ham	0	3
EC2014	Oct	10	Wolverhampton	2	1
EC2014	Oct	14	Vinkovci	2	1
EC2019	June	24	Serravale	3	3
EC2021	**Mar**	**31**	**Koper**	**2**	**1**
			v CZECHOSLOVAKIA	*Eng*	*Cz*
1990	May	28	Toulon	2	1
1992	May	26	Toulon	1	2
1993	June	9	Toulon	1	1
			v CZECH REPUBLIC	*Eng*	*CzR*
1998	Nov	17	Ipswich	0	1
EC2007	June	11	Arnhem	0	0
2008	Nov	18	Bramall Lane	2	0
EC2011	June	19	Viborg	1	2
2015	Mar	27	Prague	1	0
			v DENMARK	*Eng*	*Den*
EC1978	Sept	19	Hvidovre	2	1
EC1979	Sept	11	Watford	1	0
EC1982	Sept	21	Hvidovre	4	1
				Eng	*Den*
EC1983	Sept	20	Norwich	4	1
EC1986	Mar	12	Copenhagen	1	0
EC1986	Mar	26	Manchester	1	1
1988	Sept	13	Watford	0	0
1994	Mar	8	Brentford	1	0
1999	Oct	8	Bradford	4	1
2005	Aug	16	Herning	1	0
2011	Mar	24	Viborg	4	0
2017	Mar	27	Randers	4	0
2018	Nov	20	Esbjerg	5	1
			v EQUADOR	*Eng*	*Eq*
2009	Feb	10	Malaga	2	3
			v FINLAND	*Eng*	*Fin*
EC1977	May	26	Helsinki	1	0
EC1977	Oct	12	Hull	8	1
EC1984	Oct	16	Southampton	2	0
EC1985	May	21	Mikkeli	1	3
EC2000	Oct	10	Valkeakoski	2	2
EC2001	Mar	23	Barnsley	4	0
EC2009	June	15	Halmstad	2	1
EC2013	Sept	9	Tampere	1	1
EC2013	Nov	14	Milton Keynes	3	0
			v FRANCE	*Eng*	*Fra*
EC1984	Feb	28	Sheffield	6	1
EC1984	Mar	28	Rouen	1	0
1987	June	11	Toulon	0	2
EC1988	April	13	Besancon	2	4
EC1988	April	27	Highbury	2	2
1988	June	12	Toulon	2	4
1990	May	23	Toulon	7	3
1991	June	3	Toulon	1	0
1992	May	28	Toulon	0	0
1993	June	15	Toulon	1	0
1994	May	31	Aubagne	0	3
1995	June	10	Toulon	0	2
1998	May	14	Toulon	1	1
1999	Feb	9	Derby	2	1
EC2005	Nov	11	Tottenham	1	1
EC2005	Nov	15	Nancy	1	2
2009	Mar	31	Nottingham	0	2
2014	Nov	17	Paris	2	3
2016	May	29	Toulon	2	1
2016	Nov	14	Bondoufle	2	3
EC2019	June	18	Cesena	1	2
			v GEORGIA	*Eng*	*Geo*
EC1996	Nov	8	Batumi	1	0
EC1997	April	29	Charlton	0	0
2000	Aug	31	Middlesbrough	6	1
			v GERMANY	*Eng*	*Ger*
1991	Sept	10	Scunthorpe	2	1
EC2000	Oct	6	Derby	1	1
EC2001	Aug	31	Frieburg	2	1
2005	Mar	25	Hull	2	2
2005	Sept	6	Mainz	1	1
EC2006	Oct	6	Coventry	1	0
EC2006	Oct	10	Leverkusen	2	0
EC2009	June	22	Halmstad	1	1
EC2009	June	29	Malmo	0	4
2010	Nov	16	Wiesbaden	0	2
2015	Mar	30	Middlesbrough	3	2
2017	Mar	24	Wiesbaden	0	1
EC2017	June	27	Tychy	2	2
2019	Mar	26	Bournemouth	1	2
			v EAST GERMANY	*Eng*	*EG*
EC1980	April	16	Sheffield	1	2
EC1980	April	23	Jena	0	1
			v WEST GERMANY	*Eng*	*WG*
EC1982	Sept	21	Sheffield	3	1
EC1982	Oct	12	Bremen	2	3
1987	Sept	8	Ludenscheid	0	2

			v GREECE	*Eng*	*Gre*
EC1982	Nov	16	Piraeus	0	1
EC1983	Mar	29	Portsmouth	2	1
1989	Feb	7	Patras	0	1
EC1997	Nov	13	Heraklion	0	2
EC1997	Dec	17	Norwich	4	2
EC2001	June	5	Athens	1	3
EC2001	Oct	5	Ewood Park	2	1
EC2009	Sept	8	Tripoli	1	1
EC2010	Mar	3	Doncaster	1	2

			v GUINEA	*Eng*	*Gui*
2016	May	23	Toulon	7	1

			v HUNGARY	*Eng*	*Hun*
EC1981	June	5	Keszthely	2	1
EC1981	Nov	17	Nottingham	2	0
EC1983	April	26	Newcastle	1	0
EC1983	Oct	11	Nyiregyhaza	2	0
1990	Sept	11	Southampton	3	1
1992	May	12	Budapest	2	2
1999	April	27	Budapest	2	2

			v ICELAND	*Eng*	*Ice*
2011	Mar	28	Preston	1	2
EC2011	Oct	6	Reykjavik	3	0
EC2011	Nov	10	Colchester	5	0

			v ISRAEL	*Eng*	*Isr*
1985	Feb	27	Tel Aviv	2	1
2011	Sept	5	Barnsley	4	1
EC2013	June	11	Jerusalem	0	1

			v ITALY	*Eng*	*Italy*
EC1978	Mar	8	Manchester	2	1
EC1978	April	5	Rome	0	0
EC1984	April	18	Manchester	3	1
EC1984	May	2	Florence	0	1
EC1986	April	9	Pisa	0	2
EC1986	April	23	Swindon	1	1
EC1997	Feb	12	Bristol	1	0
EC1997	Oct	10	Rieti	1	0
EC2000	May	27	Bratislava	0	2
2000	Nov	14	Monza*	0	0
**Abandoned 11 mins; fog.*					
2002	Mar	26	Valley Parade	1	1
EC2002	May	20	Basle	1	2
2003	Feb	11	Pisa	0	1
2007	Mar	24	Wembley	3	3
EC2007	June	14	Arnhem	2	2
2011	Feb	8	Empoli	0	1
EC2013	June	5	Tel Aviv	0	1
EC2015	June	24	Olomouc	1	3
2016	Nov	10	Southampton	3	2
2018	Nov	15	Ferrara	2	1

			v JAPAN	*Eng*	*Jap*
2016	May	27	Toulon	1	0

			v KAZAKHSTAN	*Eng*	*Kaz*
EC2015	Oct	13	Coventry	3	0
EC2016	Oct	6	Aktobe	1	0

			v KOSOVO	*Eng*	*Kos*
EC2019	Sept	9	Hull	2	0
EC2020	**Sept**	**4**	**Prishtina**	**6**	**0**

			v LATVIA	*Eng*	*Lat*
1995	April	25	Riga	1	0
1995	June	7	Burnley	4	0
EC2017	Sept	5	Bournemouth	3	0
EC2018	Sept	11	Jelgava	2	1

			v LITHUANIA	*Eng*	*Lith*
EC2009	Nov	17	Vilnius	0	0
EC2010	Sept	7	Colchester	3	0
EC2013	Oct	15	Ipswich	5	0
EC2014	Sept	5	Zaliakalnis	1	0

			v LUXEMBOURG	*Eng*	*Lux*
EC1998	Oct	13	Greven Macher	5	0
EC1999	Sept	3	Reading	5	0

			v MALAYSIA	*Eng*	*Mal*
1995	June	8	Toulon	2	0

			v MEXICO	*Eng*	*Mex*
1988	June	5	Toulon	2	1
1991	May	29	Toulon	6	0
1992	May	25	Toulon	1	1
2001	May	24	Leicester	3	0
2018	May	29	Toulon	0	0
2018	June	9	Toulon	2	1

			v MOLDOVA	*Eng*	*Mol*
EC1996	Aug	31	Chisinau	2	0
EC1997	Sept	9	Wycombe	1	0
EC2006	Aug	15	Ipswich	2	2
EC2013	Sept	5	Reading	1	0
EC2014	Sept	9	Tiraspol	3	0

			v MONTENEGRO	*Eng*	*Mon*
EC2007	Sept	7	Podgorica	3	0
EC2007	Oct	12	Leicester	1	0

			v MOROCCO	*Eng*	*Mor*
1987	June	7	Toulon	2	0
1988	June	9	Toulon	1	0

			v NETHERLANDS	*Eng*	*N*
EC1993	April	27	Portsmouth	3	0
EC1993	Oct	12	Utrecht	1	1
2001	Aug	14	Reading	4	0
EC2001	Nov	9	Utrecht	2	2
EC2001	Nov	13	Derby	1	0
2004	Feb	17	Hull	3	2
2005	Feb	8	Derby	1	2
2006	Nov	14	Alkmaar	1	0
EC2007	June	20	Heerenveen	1	1
2009	Aug	11	Groningen	0	0
EC2017	Sept	1	Doetinchem	1	1
EC2018	Sept	6	Norwich	0	0
2019	Nov	19	Doetinchem	1	2

			v NORTHERN IRELAND	*Eng*	*NI*
2012	Nov	13	Blackpool	2	0

			v NORTH MACEDONIA	*Eng*	*M*
EC2002	Oct	15	Reading	3	1
EC2003	Sept	5	Skopje	1	1
EC2009	Sept	4	Prilep	2	1
EC2009	Oct	9	Coventry	6	3

			v NORWAY	*Eng*	*Nor*
EC1977	June	1	Bergen	2	1
EC1977	Sept	6	Brighton	6	0
1980	Sept	9	Southampton	3	0
1981	Sept	8	Drammen	0	0
EC1992	Oct	13	Peterborough	0	2
EC1993	June	1	Stavanger	1	1
1995	Oct	10	Stavanger	2	2
2006	Feb	28	Reading	3	1
2009	Mar	27	Sandefjord	5	0
2011	June	5	Southampton	2	0
EC2011	Oct	10	Drammen	2	1
EC2012	Sept	10	Chesterfield	1	0
EC2013	June	8	Petah Tikva	1	3
EC2015	Sept	7	Drammen	1	0
EC2016	Sept	6	Colchester	6	1

			v PARAGUAY	*Eng*	*Par*
2016	May	25	Toulon	4	0

			v POLAND	*Eng*	*Pol*
EC1982	Mar	17	Warsaw	2	1
EC1982	April	7	West Ham	2	2
EC1989	June	2	Plymouth	2	1
EC1989	Oct	10	Jastrzebie	3	1
EC1990	Oct	16	Tottenham	0	1
EC1991	Nov	12	Pila	1	2
EC1993	May	28	Zdroj	4	1
EC1993	Sept	7	Millwall	1	2
EC1996	Oct	8	Wolverhampton	0	0
EC1997	May	30	Katowice	1	1
EC1999	Mar	26	Southampton	5	0
EC1999	Sept	7	Plock	1	3
EC2004	Sept	7	Rybnik	3	1
EC2005	Oct	11	Hillsborough	4	1
2008	Mar	25	Wolverhampton	0	0
EC2017	June	22	Kielce	3	0
2019	Mar	21	Bristol	1	1

			v PORTUGAL	*Eng*	*Por*
1987	June	13	Toulon	0	0
1990	May	21	Toulon	0	1
1993	June	7	Toulon	2	0
1994	June	7	Toulon	2	0
EC1994	Sept	6	Leicester	0	0
1995	Sept	2	Lisbon	0	2
1996	May	30	Toulon	1	3
2000	Apr	16	Stoke	0	1
EC2002	May	22	Zurich	1	3
EC2003	Mar	28	Rio Major	2	4
EC2003	Sept	9	Everton	1	2

				Eng	Por
EC2008	Nov	20	Agueda	1	1
2008	Sept	5	Wembley	2	0
EC2009	Nov	14	Wembley	1	0
EC2010	Sept	3	Barcelos	1	0
2014	Nov	13	Burnley	3	1
EC2015	June	18	Uherske Hradiste	0	1
2016	May	19	Toulon	1	0
EC2021	**Mar**	**28**	**Ljubljana**	**0**	**2**

v QATAR

				Eng	Qat
2018	June	1	Toulon	4	0

v REPUBLIC OF IRELAND

				Eng	RoI
1981	Feb	25	Liverpool	1	0
1985	Mar	25	Portsmouth	3	2
1989	June	9	Toulon	0	0
EC1990	Nov	13	Cork	3	0
EC1991	Mar	26	Brentford	3	0
1994	Nov	15	Newcastle	1	0
1995	Mar	27	Dublin	2	0
EC2007	Oct	16	Cork	3	0
EC2008	Feb	5	Southampton	3	0

v ROMANIA

				Eng	Rom
EC1980	Oct	14	Ploesti	0	4
EC1981	April	28	Swindon	3	0
EC1985	April	30	Brasov	0	0
EC1985	Sept	10	Ipswich	3	0
2007	Aug	21	Bristol	1	1
EC2010	Oct	8	Norwich	2	1
EC2010	Oct	12	Botosani	0	0
2013	Mar	21	Wycombe	3	0
2018	Mar	24	Wolverhampton	2	1
EC2019	June	21	Cesena	2	4

v RUSSIA

				Eng	Rus
1994	May	30	Bandol	2	0

v SAN MARINO

				Eng	SM
EC1993	Feb	16	Luton	6	0
EC1993	Nov	17	San Marino	4	0
EC2013	Oct	10	San Marino	4	0
EC2013	Nov	19	Shrewsbury	9	0

v SCOTLAND

				Eng	Sco
1977	April	27	Sheffield	1	0
EC1980	Feb	12	Coventry	2	1
EC1980	Mar	4	Aberdeen	0	0
EC1982	April	19	Glasgow	1	0
EC1982	April	28	Manchester	1	1
EC1988	Feb	16	Aberdeen	1	0
EC1988	Mar	22	Nottingham	1	0
1993	June	13	Toulon	1	0
2013	Aug	13	Sheffield	6	0
EC2017	Oct	6	Middlesbrough	3	1
2018	June	6	Toulon	3	1
EC2018	Oct	16	Edinburgh	2	0

v SENEGAL

				Eng	Sen
1989	June	7	Toulon	6	1
1991	May	27	Toulon	2	1

v SERBIA

				Eng	Ser
EC2007	June	17	Nijmegen	2	0
EC2012	Oct	12	Norwich	1	0
EC2012	Oct	16	Krusevac	1	0

v SERBIA-MONTENEGRO

				Eng	S-M
2003	June	2	Hull	3	2

v SLOVAKIA

				Eng	Slo
EC2002	June	1	Bratislava	0	2
EC2002	Oct	11	Trnava	4	0
EC2003	June	10	Sunderland	2	0
2007	June	5	Norwich	5	0
EC2017	June	19	Kielce	2	1

v SLOVENIA

				Eng	Slo
2000	Feb	12	Nova Gorica	1	0
2008	Aug	19	Hull	2	1
2019	Oct	11	Maribor	2	2

v SOUTH AFRICA

				Eng	SA
1998	May	16	Toulon	3	1

v SPAIN

				Eng	Spa
EC1984	May	17	Seville	1	0
EC1984	May	24	Sheffield	2	0
1987	Feb	18	Burgos	2	1
1992	Sept	8	Burgos	1	0
2001	Feb	27	Birmingham	0	4
2004	Nov	16	Alcala	0	1
2007	Feb	6	Derby	2	2
EC2009	June	18	Gothenburg	2	0
EC2011	June	12	Herning	1	1

v SWEDEN

				Eng	Swe
1979	June	9	Vasteras	2	1
1986	Sept	9	Ostersund	1	1
EC1988	Oct	18	Coventry	1	1
EC1989	Sept	5	Uppsala	0	1
EC1998	Sept	4	Sundvall	2	0
EC1999	June	4	Huddersfield	3	0
2004	Mar	30	Kristiansund	2	2
EC2009	June	26	Gothenburg	3	3
2013	Feb	5	Walsall	4	0
EC2015	Jun	21	Olomouc	1	0
EC2017	June	16	Kielce	0	0

v SWITZERLAND

				Eng	Swit
EC1980	Nov	18	Ipswich	5	0
EC1981	May	31	Neuenburg	0	0
1988	May	28	Lausanne	1	1
1996	April	1	Swindon	0	0
1998	Mar	24	Brugglifeld	0	2
EC2002	May	17	Zurich	2	1
EC2006	Sept	6	Lucerne	3	2
EC2015	Nov	16	Brighton	3	1
EC2016	Mar	26	Thun	1	1
EC2021	**Mar**	**25**	**Koper**	**0**	**1**

v TURKEY

				Eng	Tur
EC1984	Nov	13	Bursa	0	0
EC1985	Oct	15	Bristol	3	0
EC1987	April	28	Izmir	0	0
EC1987	Oct	13	Sheffield	1	1
EC1991	April	30	Izmir	2	2
1991	Oct	15	Reading	2	0
EC1992	Nov	17	Orient	0	1
EC1993	Mar	30	Izmir	0	0
EC2000	May	29	Bratislava	6	0
EC2003	April	1	Newcastle	1	1
EC2003	Oct	10	Istanbul	0	1
EC2019	Sept	6	Izmit	3	2
EC2020	**Oct**	**13**	**Wolverhampton**	**2**	**1**

v UKRAINE

				Eng	Uk
2004	Aug	17	Middlesbrough	3	1
EC2011	June	15	Herning	0	0
EC2017	Nov	10	Kiev	2	0
EC2018	Mar	27	Sheffield	2	1

v USA

				Eng	USA
1989	June	11	Toulon	0	2
1994	June	2	Toulon	3	0
2015	Sept	3	Preston	1	0

v USSR

				Eng	USSR
1987	June	9	Toulon	0	0
1988	June	7	Toulon	1	0
1990	May	25	Toulon	2	1
1991	May	31	Toulon	2	1

v UZBEKISTAN

				Eng	Uzb
2010	Aug	10	Bristol	2	0

v WALES

				Eng	Wal
1976	Dec	15	Wolverhampton	0	0
1979	Feb	6	Swansea	1	0
1990	Dec	5	Tranmere	0	0
EC2004	Oct	8	Blackburn	2	0
EC2005	Sept	2	Wrexham	4	0
2008	May	5	Wrexham	2	0
EC2008	Oct	10	Cardiff	3	2
EC2008	Oct	14	Villa Park	2	2
EC2013	Mar	5	Derby	1	0
EC2013	May	19	Swansea	3	1

v YUGOSLAVIA

				Eng	Yugo
EC1978	April	19	Novi Sad	1	2
EC1978	May	2	Manchester	1	1
EC1986	Nov	11	Peterborough	1	1
EC1987	Nov	10	Zemun	5	1
EC2000	Mar	29	Barcelona	3	0
2002	Sept	6	Bolton	1	1

BRITISH AND IRISH UNDER-21 TEAMS 2020–21

▪ *Denotes player sent off.*

ENGLAND

UEFA UNDER-21 CHAMPIONSHIPS QUALIFYING

Friday, 4 September 2020

Kosovo U21 (0) 0

England U21 (0) 6 *(Nketiah 51, 55, 61 (pen), Nelson 66, Sessegnon R 82, Bellingham 85)*

England U21: (433) Ramsdale; Aarons, Godfrey, Guehi, Kelly; Gallagher (Sessegnon R 71), Davies (Bellingham 62), Skipp; Saka (Hudson-Odoi 62), Nketiah (Brewster 73), Cantwell (Nelson 62).

Tuesday, 8 September 2020

Austria U21 (0) 1 *(Schmidt 60)*

England U21 (1) 2 *(Nketiah 27, Godfrey 49)*

England U21: (433) Ramsdale; Justin, Godfrey, Guehi, Lamptey (Aarons 72); Skipp (Davies 80), Bellingham, Hudson-Odoi; Sessegnon R (Dasilva 67), Nketiah (Brewster 80), Nelson (Cantwell 80).

Wednesday, 7 October 2020

Andorra U21 (1) 3 *(Fernandez R 28, 76, Garcia 90)*

England U21 (1) 3 *(Davies 45, Dasilva 69, Nketiah 83)*

England U21: (433) Ramsdale; Aarons, Panzo, Williams R, Williams B; Dasilva (Bellingham 72), Davies, Eze; Jones (Hudson-Odoi 74), Surridge (Nketiah 72), McNeil (Sessegnon R 77).

Tuesday, 13 October 2020

England U21 (1) 2 *(Turkmen 17 (og), Nketiah 88)*

Turkey U21 (0) 1 *(Dervisoglu 90)*

England U21: (433) Ramsdale; Aarons, Godfrey, Guehi, Justin; Bellingham, Dasilva (Eze 63), Skipp; Hudson-Odoi (McNeil 85), Nketiah, Sessegnon R.

Friday, 13 November 2020

England U21 (1) 3 *(Jones 27, Wilmot 48, Hudson-Odoi 65 (pen))*

Andorra U21 (1) 1 *(Garcia 45 (pen))*

England U21: (433) Ramsdale; Lamptey, Wilmot, Williams R, Panzo; Jones (Musiala 74), Gallagher, Dasilva; Hudson-Odoi (Eze 74), Brewster (Nketiah 73), McNeil (Buchanan 83).

Tuesday, 17 November 2020

England U21 (3) 5 *(Hudson-Odoi 4, Justin 26, Musiala 36, Nketiah 52, 86)*

Albania U21 (0) 0

England U21: (352) Bursik; Wilmot, Godfrey, Kelly; Justin, Musiala (Jones 61), Skipp (Dasilva 75), Davies, Buchanan (McNeil 75); Hudson-Odoi (Gallagher 61), Nketiah.

UEFA UNDER-21 CHAMPIONSHIPS

Thursday, 25 March 2021

England U21 (0) 0

Switzerland U21 (0) 1 *(Ndoye 77)*

England U21: (4231) Ramsdale; Aarons, Godfrey, Guehi, Kelly; Davies (Jones 66), Skipp; Hudson-Odoi, Smith-Rowe (Eze 66), McNeil (Sessegnon R 76); Nketiah (Brewster 76).

Sunday, 28 March 2021

Portugal U21 (0) 2 *(Mota 64, Trincao 74 (pen))*

England U21 (0) 0

England U21: (433) Ramsdale; Tanganga, Godfrey, Guehi, Sessegnon S (Brewster 83); Davies (Jones 72), Skipp, Smith-Rowe (Eze 46); Madueke (Gallagher 72), Nketiah, Sessegnon R (McNeil 54).

Wednesday, 31 March 2021

Croatia U21 (0) 1 *(Bradaric 90)*

England U21 (1) 2 *(Eze 12 (pen), Jones 74)*

England U21: (433) Ramsdale; Aarons, Tanganga, Wilmot, Kelly; Gallagher (Cantwell 71), Skipp, Eze; Jones, McNeil (Sessegnon S 89), Nketiah (Brewster 71).

SCOTLAND

UEFA UNDER-21 CHAMPIONSHIPS QUALIFYING

Tuesday, 8 September 2020

Lithuania U21 (0) 0

Scotland U21 (0) 1 *(Campbell 81)*

Scotland U21: (433) Doohan; Porteous, Patterson (Mayo 85), Johnston, Ross McCrorie; Ferguson, Harvie, Campbell; Turnbull (Scott 61), Hornby, Middleton (McLennan 85).

Friday, 9 October 2020

Scotland U21 (1) 2 *(Hornby 25, Ross McCrorie 82)*

Czech Republic U21 (0) 0

Scotland U21: (433) Doohan; Mayo, Ashby (McLennan 84), McIntyre, Harvie; Ross McCrorie, Campbell, Ferguson; Patterson (Maguire 72), Hornby, Reading.

Tuesday, 13 October 2020

San Marino U21 (0) 0

Scotland U21 (3) 7 *(Hornby 20 (pen), 50, 51, Turnbull 39, Maguire 43, McLennan 70, Ashby 75)*

Scotland U21: (433) Doohan (Wright 57); Patterson (Chalmers 71), Mayo, McIntyre, Harvie; Maguire, Irving (McInroy 71), Turnbull (Kelly 57); McLennan, Hornby (Ashby 57), Middleton.

Thursday, 12 November 2020

Scotland U21 (0) 2 *(Middleton 54, McLennan 70)*

Croatia U21 (2) 2 *(Moro 20, Bistrovic 25)*

Scotland U21: (433) Doohan; Ross McCrorie, Porteous, Johnston, Harvie; Maguire, Campbell, Ferguson (Gilmour▪ 63); Patterson (Middleton 46), Hornby, Reading (McLennan 63).

Tuesday, 17 November 2020

Greece U21 (1) 1 *(Christopoulos 27)*

Scotland U21 (0) 0

Scotland U21: (433) Doohan; Ross McCrorie, Porteous, Johnston, Harvie; Maguire (Turnbull 72), Campbell, Ferguson; McLennan, Hornby, Middleton (Fiorini 72).

FRIENDLIES

Wednesday, 2 June 2021

Scotland U21 (1) 1 *(Middleton 38 (pen))*

Northern Ireland U21 (2) 2 *(Taylor 10, Baggley 45)*

Scotland U21: (442) Slicker; Burroughs, Harper, Welsh, Deas; Banks, Erhahon, Urain, Kelly; Middleton, Joseph.
Northern Ireland U21: (442) Mee; Stewart, Donnelly, Balmer, Finlayson; Scott J (Hume 66), Palmer, Boyd-Munce, Baggley (McCann L 72); Conn-Clarke (Johnston 66), Taylor (Smyth 72).

Saturday, 5 June 2021

Scotland U21 (2) 3 *(Clayton 25, Williamson 44, Middleton 78 (pen))*

Northern Ireland U21 (1) 2 *(Wylie 29, Waide 69)*

Scotland U21: (442) Mair (Kinnear 67); Burroughs, Welsh, Mayo, Banks (Middleton 67); Kelly, Mackay, McPake (MacGregor 72), Chalmers (Erhahon 75); Williamson (Urain 67), Clayton.
Northern Ireland U21: (433) Mee; Stewart (Scott J 63), Donnelly (Finlayson 63), Balmer, Cousin-Dawson; Hume, Johnston (Baggley 79), Boyd-Munce (Boyle 46); Wylie (Waide 58), Smyth, Taylor (McCann L 58).

WALES

UEFA UNDER-21 CHAMPIONSHIPS QUALIFYING

Friday, 4 September 2020

Bosnia-Herzegovina U21 (0) 1 *(Resic 74)*

Wales U21 (0) 0

Wales U21: (442) Przybek; Lewis A, Boyes, Cooper B, Evans J; Poole, Burton (Waite 79), Taylor (Clifton 84), Harris (Jephcott 79); Cullen (Cooper O 79), Broadhead (Stirk 84).

Friday, 9 October 2020

Belgium U21 (3) 5 *(Ndayishimiye 16 (pen), Sambi Lokonga 20, 34, Bataille 78, Openda 81 (pen))*

Wales U21 (0) 0

Wales U21: (4231) Przybek; Boyes, Poole, Cooper B, Coxe; Stirk, Bowen (Williams 75); Cullen (Pearson 82), Spence (Astley 55), Waite (Collins 55); Harris (Touray 75).

Friday, 13 November 2020

Wales U21 (0) 3 *(Taylor 61, Broadhead 77 (pen), Touray 90)*

Moldova U21 (0) 0

Wales U21: (4231) Ratcliffe; Boyes, Poole, Cooper B, Coxe; Taylor, Broadhead (Cooper O 90); Cullen, Spence (Lewis A 82), Clifton; Jephcott (Touray 90).

Tuesday, 17 November 2020

Germany U21 (2) 2 *(Nmecha 17 (pen), Burkardt 26)*

Wales U21 (1) 1 *(Harris 34)*

Wales U21: (4231) Ratcliffe; Boyes, Poole, Cooper B (Lewis J 87), Coxe; Broadhead, Taylor; Cullen (Lewis A 68), Harris (Touray 87), Clifton; Jephcott (Spence 73).

Friday, 4 June 2021

Wales U21 (0) 0

Moldova U21 (0) 0

Wales U21: (4231) Barden; Stevens, Boyes, Sass-Davies, Jones; Spence■, Huggins (Pearson 63); Stirk, Taylor, Jephcott (Collins 89); Adams.

FRIENDLIES

Friday, 26 March 2021

Wales U21 (1) 1 *(Adams 11)*

Republic of Ireland U21 (0) 2 *(Afolabi 76, Boyes 77 (og))*

Wales U21: (442) Webb (Shepperd 46); Stevens, Sass-Davies, Boyes, Jones; Stirk, Taylor (Bowen 70), Huggins, Adams (Colwill 78); Spence (Pearson 65), Jephcott (Norton 65).
Republic of Ireland U21: (442) Maher; O'Connor L, O'Malley, McGuinness, Connell; Noss (Wright 69), Afolabi (Varian 69), Watson (Grant C 74), Ferry; Omobamidele, Gilbert (Kilkenny 69).

NORTHERN IRELAND

UEFA UNDER-21 CHAMPIONSHIPS QUALIFYING

Friday, 4 September 2020

Malta U21 (0) 0

Northern Ireland U21 (0) 2 *(Larkin 57, Parkhouse 67)*

Northern Ireland U21: (433) Hazard; Marron, Toal, Larkin (Balmer 89), Amos; McCann A (McClean 80), McCalmont (Gallagher 80), Galbraith; Kerr, Parkhouse (O'Neill 90), Boyd-Munce (Dunwoody 63).

Tuesday, 8 September 2020

Northern Ireland U21 (0) 0

Denmark U21 (0) 1 *(Skov Olsen 75 (pen))*

Northern Ireland U21: (433) Hazard; Marron, Toal, Larkin, Amos (Scott J 54); Galbraith, McCalmont, McCann A; Kerr, Lavery (O'Neill 84), Dunwoody (Parkhouse 65).

Friday, 9 October 2020

Northern Ireland U21 (1) 2 *(O'Neill 23, 59)*

Finland U21 (1) 3 *(Stavitski 44, Soisalo 62, Skytta 68)*

Northern Ireland U21: (433) Hazard; Marron, Toal, Brown, Amos (Burns 61); McKiernan (Bonis 46), McCalmont (Scott A 79), Boyd-Munce; Kerr, O'Neill, Dunwoody.

Tuesday, 13 October 2020

Northern Ireland U21 (0) 1 *(O'Neill 61)*

Ukraine U21 (0) 0

Northern Ireland U21: (352) Hazard; Marron, Toal, Brown; Kerr, Dunwoody, Galbraith, Boyd-Munce, Amos; Bansal-McNulty (McKiernan 76), O'Neill (Bonis 76).

Tuesday, 17 November 2020

Ukraine U21 (0) 3 *(Babohlo 68, Isaenko 70, Kukharevych 74)*

Northern Ireland U21 (0) 0

Northern Ireland U21: (442) Webber; Marron, Toal, Brown, Amos; Hume, McCalmont, Boyd-Munce, Bansal-McNulty; Lavery, O'Neill.

REPUBLIC OF IRELAND

UEFA UNDER-21 CHAMPIONSHIPS QUALIFYING

Tuesday, 13 October 2020

Italy U21 (1) 2 *(Sottil 43, Cutrone 62)*

Republic of Ireland U21 (0) 0

Republic of Ireland U21: (4321) Bazunu; O'Connor L, Leahy, Masterson, Coventry; Elbouzedi, Ronan (Grant D 75), Obafemi (Afolabi 74); Collins, Smallbone; Taylor (Mandroiu 75).

Sunday, 15 November 2020

Republic of Ireland U21 (0) 1 *(Kayode 75)*

Iceland U21 (1) 2 *(Gudjohnsen 25, Ingimundarson 90)*

Republic of Ireland U21: (433) McGinty; O'Connor L, Collins■, Masterson, Scales; Taylor, Ronan (Mandroiu 74), Coventry (O'Connor T 83); Scully (Parrott 46), Obafemi (Kayode 74), Elbouzedi (Grant D 83).

Wednesday, 18 November 2020

Luxembourg U21 (0) 1 *(Avdusinovic 84)*

Republic of Ireland U21 (1) 2 *(Kayode 35, Lennon 65)*

Republic of Ireland U21: (433) McGinty; McNamara, McGuinness, Masterson, Leahy; Mandroiu, O'Connor T (Lennon 46), Ronan; Scully (Grant D 71), Kayode (Ferry 79), Elbouzedi (Obafemi 79).

FRIENDLIES

Sunday, 30 May 2021

Switzerland U21 (1) 2 *(Stergiou 13, Bares 52)*

Republic of Ireland U21 (0) 0

Republic of Ireland U21: (442) Maher; McGuinness, McEntee, Richards (Ferry 57), Ebosele (Flynn 75); Coventry (Connell 75), Watson (Gilbert 75), Johansson (Noss 46), Grant C (Kilkenny 57); Wright, Kayode (Afolabi 57).

Wednesday, 2 June 2021

Australia U23 (0) 1 *(Najjarine 72)*

Republic of Ireland U21 (0) 2 *(Rich-Baghuelou 57 (og), Tierney 90)*

Republic of Ireland U21: (442) Maher; Lyons, McGuinness, McEntee, Coventry; Kilkenny (Johansson 60), Noss (Gilbert 72), Afolabi (Kayode 46), Watson (Wright 60); Ferry, Connell (Tierney 88).

Saturday, 5 June 2021

Republic of Ireland U21 (0) 0

Denmark U21 (1) 1 *(Frederiksen 31)*

Republic of Ireland U21: (442) Rose; Coventry, Ferry (Flynn 86), Gilbert (Watson 75), Johansson; Kayode (Grant C 75), Lyons (Ebosele 46), McEntee, McGuinness; Noss (Lawal 46), Wright (Kilkenny 60).

BRITISH UNDER-21 APPEARANCES 1976–2021

Bold type indicates players who made an international appearance in season 2020–21.

ENGLAND

Player	Apps
Aarons, M. J. 2020 (Norwich C)	**11**
Ablett, G. 1988 (Liverpool)	1
Abraham, K. O. T. (Tammy) 2017 (Chelsea)	26
Akpom, C. A. 2015 (Arsenal)	5
Adams, N. 1987 (Everton)	1
Adams, T. A. 1985 (Arsenal)	5
Addison, M. 2010 (Derby Co)	1
Afobe, B. T. 2012 (Arsenal)	2
Agbonlahor, G. 2007 (Aston Villa)	16
Albrighton, M. K. 2011 (Aston Villa)	8
Alexander-Arnold, T. J. 2018 (Liverpool)	3
Alli, B. J. (Dele) 2015 (Tottenham H)	2
Allen, B. 1992 (QPR)	8
Allen, C. 1980 (QPR, Crystal Palace)	3
Allen, C. A. 1995 (Oxford U)	2
Allen, M. 1987 (QPR)	2
Allen, P. 1985 (West Ham U, Tottenham H)	3
Allen, R. W. 1998 (Tottenham H)	3
Alnwick, B. R. 2008 (Tottenham H)	1
Ambrose, D. P. F. 2003 (Ipswich T, Newcastle U, Charlton Ath)	10
Ameobi, F. 2001 (Newcastle U)	19
Ameobi, S. 2012 (Newcastle U)	5
Amos, B. P. 2012 (Manchester U)	3
Anderson, V. A. 1978 (Nottingham F)	1
Anderton, D. R. 1993 (Tottenham H)	12
Andrews, I. 1987 (Leicester C)	1
Ardley, N. C. 1993 (Wimbledon)	10
Armstrong, A. J. 2018 (Newcastle U)	5
Ashcroft, L. 1992 (Preston NE)	1
Ashton, D. 2004 (Crewe Alex, Norwich C)	9
Atherton, P. 1992 (Coventry C)	1
Atkinson, B. 1991 (Sunderland)	6
Awford, A. T. 1993 (Portsmouth)	9
Bailey, G. R. 1979 (Manchester U)	14
Baines, L. J. 2005 (Wigan Ath)	16
Baker, G. E. 1981 (Southampton)	2
Baker, L. R. 2015 (Chelsea)	17
Baker, N. L. 2011 (Aston Villa)	3
Ball, M. J. 1999 (Everton)	7
Bamford, P. J. 2013 (Chelsea)	2
Bannister, G. 1982 (Sheffield W)	1
Barker, S. 1985 (Blackburn R)	4
Barkley, R. 2012 (Everton)	5
Barmby, N. J. 1994 (Tottenham H, Everton)	4
Barnes, H. L. 2019 (Leicester C)	4
Barnes, J. 1983 (Watford)	2
Barnes, P. S. 1977 (Manchester C)	9
Barrett, E. D. 1990 (Oldham Ath)	4
Barry, G. 1999 (Aston Villa)	27
Barton, J. 2004 (Manchester C)	2
Bart-Williams, C. G. 1993 (Sheffield W)	16
Batty, D. 1988 (Leeds U)	7
Bazeley, D. S. 1992 (Watford)	1
Beagrie, P. 1988 (Sheffield U)	2
Beardsmore, R. 1989 (Manchester U)	5
Beattie, J. S. 1999 (Southampton)	5
Beckham, D. R. J. 1995 (Manchester U)	9
Bellingham, J. V. W. 2021 (Borussia Dortmund)	**4**
Berahino, S. 2013 (WBA)	11
Bennett, J. 2011 (Middlesbrough)	3
Bennett, R. 2012 (Norwich C)	2
Bent, D. A. 2003 (Ipswich T, Charlton Ath)	14
Bent, M. N. 1998 (Crystal Palace)	2
Bentley, D. M. 2004 (Arsenal, Blackburn R)	8
Beeston, C 1988 (Stoke C)	1
Benjamin, T. J. 2001 (Leicester C)	1
Bertrand, R. 2009 (Chelsea)	16
Bertschin, K. E. 1977 (Birmingham C)	3
Bettinelli, M. 2015 (Fulham)	1
Birtles, G. 1980 (Nottingham F)	2
Blackett, T. N. 2014 (Manchester U)	1
Blackstock, D. A. 2008 (QPR)	2
Blackwell, D. R. 1991 (Wimbledon)	6
Blake, M. A. 1990 (Aston Villa)	8
Blissett, L. L. 1979 (Watford)	4
Bond, J. H. 2013 (Watford)	5
Booth, A. D. 1995 (Huddersfield T)	3
Bothroyd, J. 2001 (Coventry C)	1
Bowyer, L. D. 1996 (Charlton Ath, Leeds U)	13
Bracewell, P. 1983 (Stoke C)	13
Bradbury, L. M. 1997 (Portsmouth, Manchester C)	3
Bramble, T. M. 2001 (Ipswich T, Newcastle U)	10
Branch, P. M. 1997 (Everton)	1
Bradshaw, P. W. 1977 (Wolverhampton W)	4
Breacker, T. 1986 (Luton T)	2
Brennan, M. 1987 (Ipswich T)	5
Brewster, R. J. 2020 (Liverpool)	**12**
Bridge, W. M. 1999 (Southampton)	8
Bridges, M. 1997 (Sunderland, Leeds U)	3
Briggs, M. 2012 (Fulham)	2
Brightwell, I. 1989 (Manchester C)	4
Briscoe, L. S. 1996 (Sheffield W)	5
Brock, K. 1984 (Oxford U)	4
Broomes, M. C. 1997 (Blackburn R)	2
Brown, M. R. 1996 (Manchester C)	4
Brown, W. M. 1999 (Manchester U)	8
Buchanan, L. D. 2021 (Derby Co)	**2**
Bull, S. G. 1989 (Wolverhampton W)	5
Bullock, M. J. 1998 (Barnsley)	1
Burrows, D. 1989 (WBA, Liverpool)	7
Bursik, J. J. 2021 (Stoke C)	**1**
Butcher, T. I. 1979 (Ipswich T)	7
Butland, J. 2012 (Birmingham C, Stoke C)	28
Butt, N. 1995 (Manchester U)	7
Butters, G. 1989 (Tottenham H)	3
Butterworth, I. 1985 (Coventry C, Nottingham F)	8
Bywater, S. 2001 (West Ham U)	6
Cadamarteri, D. L. 1999 (Everton)	3
Caesar, G. 1987 (Arsenal)	3
Cahill, G. J. 2007 (Aston Villa)	3
Callaghan, N. 1983 (Watford)	9
Calvert-Lewin, D. N. 2018 (Everton)	17
Camp, L. M. J. 2005 (Derby Co)	5
Campbell, A. P. 2000 (Middlesbrough)	4
Campbell, F. L. 2008 (Manchester U)	14
Campbell, K. J. 1991 (Arsenal)	4
Campbell, S. 1994 (Tottenham)	11
Cantwell, T. O. 2020 (Norwich C)	**4**
Carbon, M. P. 1996 (Derby Co)	4
Carr, C. 1985 (Fulham)	1
Carr, F. 1987 (Nottingham F)	9
Carragher, J. L. 1997 (Liverpool)	27
Carroll, A. T. 2010 (Newcastle U)	5
Carroll, T. J. 2013 (Tottenham H)	17
Carlisle, C. J. 2001 (QPR)	3
Carrick, M. 2001 (West Ham U)	14
Carson, S. P. 2004 (Leeds U, Liverpool)	29
Casper, C. M. 1995 (Manchester U)	1
Caton, T. 1982 (Manchester C)	14
Cattermole, L. B. 2008 (Middlesbrough, Wigan Ath, Sunderland)	16
Caulker, S. R. 2011 (Tottenham H)	10
Chadwick, L. H. 2000 (Manchester U)	13
Challis, T. M. 1996 (QPR)	2
Chalobah, N. N. 2012 (Chelsea)	40
Chalobah, T. T. 2020 (Chelsea)	3
Chamberlain, M. 1983 (Stoke C)	4
Chambers, C. 2015 (Arsenal)	22
Chaplow, R. D. 2004 (Burnley)	1
Chapman, L. 1981 (Stoke C)	1
Charles, G. A. 1991 (Nottingham F)	4
Chettle, S. 1988 (Nottingham F)	12
Chilwell, B. J. 2016 (Leicester C)	10

Chopra, R. M. 2004 (Newcastle U) 1
Choudhury, H. D. 2018 (Leicester C) 7
Clark, L. R. 1992 (Newcastle U) 11
Clarke, P. M. 2003 (Everton) 8
Clarke-Salter, J. L. 2018 (Chelsea) 12
Christie, M. N. 2001 (Derby Co) 11
Clegg, M. J. 1998 (Manchester U) 2
Clemence, S. N. 1999 (Tottenham H) 1
Cleverley, T. W. 2010 (Manchester U) 16
Clough, N. H. 1986 (Nottingham F) 15
Clyne, N. E. 2012 (Crystal Palace) 8
Cole, A. 2001 (Arsenal) 4
Cole, A. A. 1992 (Arsenal, Bristol C, Newcastle U) 8
Cole, C. 2003 (Chelsea) 19
Cole, J. J. 2000 (West Ham U) 8
Coney, D. 1985 (Fulham) 4
Connolly, C. A. 2018 (Everton) 4
Connor, T. 1987 (Brighton & HA) 1
Cook, L. J. 2018 (Bournemouth) 14
Cooke, R. 1986 (Tottenham H) 1
Cooke, T. J. 1996 (Manchester U) 4
Cooper, C. T. 1988 (Middlesbrough) 8
Cork, J. F. P. 2009 (Chelsea) 13
Corrigan, J. T. 1978 (Manchester C) 3
Cort, C. E. R. 1999 (Wimbledon) 12
Cottee, A. R. 1985 (West Ham U) 8
Couzens, A. J. 1995 (Leeds U) 3
Cowans, G. S. 1979 (Aston Villa) 5
Cox, N. J. 1993 (Aston Villa) 6
Cranie, M. J. 2008 (Portsmouth) 16
Cranson, I. 1985 (Ipswich T) 5
Cresswell, R. P. W. 1999 (York C, Sheffield W) 4
Croft, G. 1995 (Grimsby T) 4
Crooks, G. 1980 (Stoke C) 4
Crossley, M. G. 1990 (Nottingham F) 3
Crouch, P. J. 2002 (Portsmouth, Aston Villa) 5
Cundy, J. V. 1991 (Chelsea) 3
Cunningham, L. 1977 (WBA) 6
Curbishley, L. C. 1981 (Birmingham C) 1
Curtis, J. C. K. 1998 (Manchester U) 16

Daniel, P. W. 1977 (Hull C) 7
Dann, S. 2008 (Coventry C) 2
Dasilva, J. R. 2018 (Chelsea) 13
Dasilva, P. J. T. 2021 (Brentford) 5
Davenport, C. R. P. 2005 (Tottenham H) 8
Davies, A. J. 2004 (Middlesbrough) 1
Davies, C. E. 2006 (WBA) 3
Davies, K. C. 1998 (Southampton, Blackburn R, Southampton) 3
Davies, T. 2018 (Everton) 23
Davis, K. G. 1995 (Luton T) 3
Davis, P. 1982 (Arsenal) 11
Davis, S. 2001 (Fulham) 11
Dawson, C. 2012 (WBA) 15
Dawson, M. R. 2003 (Nottingham F, Tottenham H) 13
Day, C. N. 1996 (Tottenham H, Crystal Palace) 6
D'Avray, M. 1984 (Ipswich T) 2
Deehan, J. M. 1977 (Aston Villa) 7
Defoe, J. C. 2001 (West Ham U) 23
Delfouneso, N. 2010 (Aston Villa) 17
Delph, F. 2009 (Leeds U, Aston Villa) 4
Dennis, M. E. 1980 (Birmingham C) 3
Derbyshire, M. A. 2007 (Blackburn R) 14
Diangana, G. G. 2020 (West Ham U) 1
Dichio, D. S. E. 1996 (QPR) 1
Dickens, A. 1985 (West Ham U) 1
Dicks, J. 1988 (West Ham U) 4
Dier, E. J. E. 2013 (Sporting Lisbon, Tottenham H) 9
Digby, F. 1987 (Swindon T) 5
Dillon, K. P. 1981 (Birmingham C) 1
Dixon, K. M. 1985 (Chelsea) 1
Dobson, A. 1989 (Coventry C) 4
Dodd, J. R. 1991 (Southampton) 8
Donowa, L. 1985 (Norwich C) 3
Dorigo, A. R. 1987 (Aston Villa) 11
Dowell, K. O. 2018 (Everton) 17
Downing, S. 2004 (Middlesbrough) 8
Dozzell, J. 1987 (Ipswich T) 9
Draper, M. A. 1991 (Notts Co) 3
Driver, A. 2009 (Hearts) 1
Duberry, M. W. 1997 (Chelsea) 5
Dunn, D. J. I. 1999 (Blackburn R) 20
Duxbury, M. 1981 (Manchester U) 7
Dyer, B. A. 1994 (Crystal Palace) 10
Dyer, K. C. 1998 (Ipswich T, Newcastle U) 11
Dyson, P. I. 1981 (Coventry C) 4

Eadie, D. M. 1994 (Norwich C) 7
Ebanks-Blake, S. 2009 (Wolverhampton W) 1
Ebbrell, J. 1989 (Everton) 14
Edghill, R. A. 1994 (Manchester C) 3
Ehiogu, U. 1992 (Aston Villa) 15
Ejaria, O. D. 2018 (Liverpool) 1
Elliott, P. 1985 (Luton T) 3
Elliott, R. J. 1996 (Newcastle U) 2
Elliott, S. W. 1998 (Derby Co) 3
Etherington, N, 2002 (Tottenham H) 3
Euell, J. J. 1998 (Wimbledon) 6
Evans, R. 2003 (Chelsea) 2
Eze, E. O. 2020 (QPR, Crystal Palace) 8

Fairclough, C. 1985 (Nottingham F, Tottenham H) 7
Fairclough, D. 1977 (Liverpool) 1
Fashanu, J. 1980 (Norwich C, Nottingham F) 11
Fear, P. 1994 (Wimbledon) 3
Fenton, G. A. 1995 (Aston Villa) 1
Fenwick, T. W. 1981 (Crystal Palace, QPR) 11
Ferdinand, A. J. 2005 (West Ham U) 17
Ferdinand, R. G. 1997 (West Ham U) 5
Fereday, W. 1985 (QPR) 5
Fielding, F. D. 2009 (Blackburn R) 12
Flanagan, J. 2012 (Liverpool) 3
Flitcroft, G. W. 1993 (Manchester C) 10
Flowers, T. D. 1987 (Southampton) 3
Foden, P. W. 2019 (Manchester C) 15
Ford, M. 1996 (Leeds U) 2
Forster, N. M. 1995 (Brentford) 4
Forsyth, M. 1988 (Derby Co) 1
Forster-Caskey, J. D. 2014 (Brighton & HA) 14
Foster, S. 1980 (Brighton & HA) 1
Fowler, R. B. 1994 (Liverpool) 8
Fox, D. J. 2008 (Coventry C) 1
Froggatt, S. J. 1993 (Aston Villa) 2
Fry, D. J. 2018 (Middlesbrough) 11
Futcher, P. 1977 (Luton T, Manchester C) 11

Gabbiadini, M. 1989 (Sunderland) 2
Gale, A. 1982 (Fulham) 1
Gallagher, C. J. 2020 (Chelsea) 9
Gallen, K. A. 1995 (QPR) 4
Galloway, B. J. 2017 (Everton) 3
Garbutt, L. S. 2014 (Everton) 11
Gardner, A. 2002 (Tottenham H) 1
Gardner, C. 2008 (Aston Villa) 14
Gardner, G. 2012 (Aston Villa) 5
Gascoigne, P. J. 1987 (Newcastle U) 13
Gayle, H. 1984 (Birmingham C) 3
Gernon, T. 1983 (Ipswich T) 1
Gerrard, P. W. 1993 (Oldham Ath) 18
Gerrard, S. G. 2000 (Liverpool) 4
Gibbs, K. J. R. 2009 (Arsenal) 15
Gibbs, N. 1987 (Watford) 5
Gibbs-White, M. A. 2019 (Wolverhampton W) 3
Gibson, B. J. 2014 (Middlesbrough) 10
Gibson, C. 1982 (Aston Villa) 1
Gilbert, W. A. 1979 (Crystal Palace) 11
Goddard, P. 1981 (West Ham U) 8
Godfrey, B. M. 2020 (Norwich C, Everton) 9
Gomez, J. D. 2015 (Liverpool) 7
Gordon, D. 1987 (Norwich C) 4
Gordon, D. D. 1994 (Crystal Palace) 13
Gosling, D. 2010 (Everton, Newcastle U) 3
Grant, A. J. 1996 (Everton) 1
Grant, L. A. 2003 (Derby Co) 4
Granville, D. P. 1997 (Chelsea) 3
Gray, A. 1988 (Aston Villa) 2
Gray, D. R. 2016 (Leicester C) 26
Grealish, J. 2016 (Aston Villa) 7
Greening, J. 1999 (Manchester U, Middlesbrough) 18

Greenwood, M. W. J. 2020 (Manchester U) 4
Griffin, A. 1999 (Newcastle U) 3
Grimes, M. J. 2016 (Swansea C) 4
Guehi, A. K. M.-I. (Marc) 2020 (Chelsea) 11
Gunn, A. 2015 (Manchester C, Southampton) 12
Guppy, S. A. 1998 (Leicester C) 1

Haigh, P. 1977 (Hull C) 1
Hall, M. T. J. 1997 (Coventry C) 8
Hall, R. A. 1992 (Southampton) 11
Hamilton, D. V. 1997 (Newcastle U) 1
Hammill, A. 2010 (Wolverhampton W) 1
Harding, D. A. 2005 (Brighton & HA) 4
Hardyman, P. 1985 (Portsmouth) 2
Hargreaves, O. 2001 (Bayern Munich) 3
Harley, J. 2000 (Chelsea) 3
Harrison, J. D. 2018 (Manchester C) 2
Hart, C. J. J. (Joe) 2007 (Manchester C) 21
Hateley, M. 1982 (Coventry C, Portsmouth) 10
Hause, K. P. D. 2015 (Wolverhampton W) 10
Hayden, I. 2017 (Newcastle U) 3
Hayes, M. 1987 (Arsenal) 3
Hazell, R. J. 1979 (Wolverhampton W) 1
Heaney, N. A. 1992 (Arsenal) 6
Heath, A. 1981 (Stoke C, Everton) 8
Heaton, T. D. 2008 (Manchester U) 3
Henderson, D. B. 2018 (Manchester U) 11
Henderson, J. B. 2011 (Sunderland, Liverpool) 27
Hendon, I. M. 1992 (Tottenham H) 7
Hendrie, L. A. 1996 (Aston Villa) 13
Hesford, I. 1981 (Blackpool) 7
Heskey, E. W. I. 1997 (Leicester C, Liverpool) 16
Hilaire, V. 1980 (Crystal Palace) 9
Hill, D. R. L. 1995 (Tottenham H) 4
Hillier, D. 1991 (Arsenal) 1
Hinchcliffe, A. 1989 (Manchester C) 1
Hines, Z. 2010 (West Ham U) 2
Hinshelwood, P. A. 1978 (Crystal Palace) 2
Hirst, D. E. 1988 (Sheffield W) 7
Hislop, N. S. 1998 (Newcastle U) 1
Hoddle, G. 1977 (Tottenham H) 12
Hodge, S. B. 1983 (Nottingham F, Aston Villa) 8
Hodgson, D. J. 1981 (Middlesbrough) 6
Holding, R. S. 2016 (Bolton W, Arsenal) 5
Holdsworth, D. 1989 (Watford) 1
Holgate, M. 2017 (Everton) 6
Holland, C. J. 1995 (Newcastle U) 10
Holland, P. 1995 (Mansfield T) 4
Holloway, D. 1998 (Sunderland) 1
Horne, B. 1989 (Millwall) 5
Howe, E. J. F. 1998 (Bournemouth) 2
Howson, J. M. 2011 (Leeds U) 1
Hoyte, J. R. 2004 (Arsenal) 18
Hucker, P. 1984 (QPR) 2
Huckerby, D. 1997 (Coventry C) 4
Huddlestone, T. A. 2005 (Derby Co, Tottenham H) 33
Hudson-Odoi, C. J. 2020 (Chelsea) 9
Hughes, S. J. 1997 (Arsenal) 8
Hughes, W. J. 2012 (Derby Co) 22
Humphreys, R. J. 1997 (Sheffield W) 3
Hunt, N. B. 2004 (Bolton W) 10

Ibe, J. A. F. 2015 (Liverpool) 4
Impey, A. R. 1993 (QPR) 1
Ince, P. E. C. 1989 (West Ham U) 2
Ince, T. C. 2012 (Blackpool, Hull C) 18
Ings, D. W. J. 2013 (Burnley) 13
Iorfa, D. 2016 (Wolverhampton W) 13

Jackson, M. A. 1992 (Everton) 10
Jagielka, P. N. 2003 (Sheffield U) 6
James, D. B. 1991 (Watford) 10
James, J. C. 1990 (Luton T) 2
James, R. 2020 (Chelsea) 2
Jansen, M. B. 1999 (Crystal Palace, Blackburn R) 6
Jeffers, F. 2000 (Everton, Arsenal) 16
Jemson, N. B. 1991 (Nottingham F) 1
Jenas, J. A. 2002 (Newcastle U) 9
Jenkinson, C. D. 2013 (Arsenal) 14
Jerome, C. 2006 (Cardiff C, Birmingham C) 10
Joachim, J. K. 1994 (Leicester C) 9
Johnson, A. 2008 (Middlesbrough) 19
Johnson, G. M. C. 2003 (West Ham U, Chelsea) 14
Johnson, M. 2008 (Manchester C) 2
Johnson, S. A. M. 1999 (Crewe Alex, Derby Co, Leeds U) 15
Johnson, T. 1991 (Notts Co, Derby Co) 7
Johnston, C. P. 1981 (Middlesbrough) 2
Jones, C. J. 2021 (Liverpool) 6
Jones, D. R. 1977 (Everton) 1
Jones, C. H. 1978 (Tottenham H) 1
Jones, D. F. L. 2004 (Manchester U) 1
Jones, P. A. 2011 (Blackburn R) 9
Jones, R. 1993 (Liverpool) 2
Justin, J. M. 2020 (Leicester C) 8

Kane, H. E. 2013 (Tottenham H) 14
Keane, M. V. 2013 (Manchester U, Burnley) 16
Keane, W. D. 2012 (Manchester U) 3
Keegan, G. A. 1977 (Manchester C) 1
Kelly, L. C. 2019 (Bournemouth) 10
Kelly, M. R. 2011 (Liverpool) 8
Kenny, J. 2018 (Everton) 16
Kenny, W. 1993 (Everton) 1
Keown, M. R. 1987 (Aston Villa) 8
Kerslake, D. 1986 (QPR) 1
Kightly, M. J. 2008 (Wolverhampton W) 7
Kilcline, B. 1983 (Notts C) 2
Kilgallon, M. 2004 (Leeds U) 5
King, A. E. 1977 (Everton) 2
King, L. B. 2000 (Tottenham H) 12
Kirkland, C. E. 2001 (Coventry C, Liverpool) 8
Kitson, P. 1991 (Leicester C, Derby Co) 7
Knight, A. 1983 (Portsmouth) 2
Knight, I. 1987 (Sheffield W) 2
Knight, Z. 2002 (Fulham) 4
Konchesky, P. M. 2002 (Charlton Ath) 15
Konsa, E. 2018 (Charlton Ath, Brentford) 7
Kozluk, R. 1998 (Derby Co) 2

Lake, P. 1989 (Manchester C) 5
Lallana, A. D. 2009 (Southampton) 1
Lampard, F. J. 1998 (West Ham U) 19
Lamptey, T. K. N.-L. 2021 (Brighton & HA) 2
Langley, T. W. 1978 (Chelsea) 1
Lansbury, H. G. 2010 (Arsenal, Nottingham F) 16
Lascellas, J. 2014 (Newcastle U) 2
Leadbitter, G. 2008 (Sunderland) 3
Lee, D. J. 1990 (Chelsea) 10
Lee, R. M. 1986 (Charlton Ath) 2
Lee, S. 1981 (Liverpool) 6
Lees, T. J. 2012 (Leeds U) 6
Lennon, A. J. 2006 (Tottenham H) 5
Le Saux, G. P. 1990 (Chelsea) 4
Lescott, J. P. 2003 (Wolverhampton W) 2
Lewis, J. P. 2008 (Peterborough U) 5
Lingard, J. E. 2013 (Manchester U) 11
Lita, L. H. 2005 (Bristol C, Reading) 9
Loach, S. J. 2009 (Watford) 14
Loftus-Cheek, R. I. 2015 (Chelsea) 17
Lookman, A. 2018 (Everton) 11
Lowe, D. 1988 (Ipswich T) 2
Lowe, J. J. 2012 (Blackburn R) 11
Lukic, J. 1981 (Leeds U) 7
Lund, G. 1985 (Grimsby T) 3

McCall, S. H. 1981 (Ipswich T) 6
McCarthy, A. S. 2011 (Reading) 3
McDonald, N. 1987 (Newcastle U) 5
McEachran, J. M. 2011 (Chelsea) 13
McEveley, J. 2003 (Blackburn R) 1
McGrath, L. 1986 (Coventry C) 1
MacKenzie, S. 1982 (WBA) 3
McLeary, A. 1988 (Millwall) 1
McLeod, I. M. 2006 (Milton Keynes D) 1
McMahon, S. 1981 (Everton, Aston Villa) 6
McManaman, S. 1991 (Liverpool) 7
McNeil, D. J. M. 2020 (Burnley) 10
McQueen, S. J. 2017 (Southampton) 1

Mabbutt, G. 1982 (Bristol R, Tottenham H) 7
Maddison, J. D. 2018 (Norwich C, Leicester C) 9
Maguire, J. H. 2012 (Sheffield U) 1
Maitland-Niles, A. C. 2018 (Arsenal) 4
Makin, C. 1994 (Oldham Ath) 5
Mancienne, M. I. 2008 (Chelsea) 30
Madueke, C. T. (Noni) 2021 (PSV Eindhoven) 1
March, S. B. 2015 (Brighton & HA) 3
Marney, D. E. 2005 (Tottenham H) 1
Marriott, A. 1992 (Nottingham F) 1
Marsh, S. T. 1998 (Oxford U) 1
Marshall, A. J. 1995 (Norwich C) 4
Marshall, B. 2012 (Leicester C) 2
Marshall, L. K. 1999 (Norwich C) 1
Martin, L. 1989 (Manchester U) 2
Martyn, A. N. 1988 (Bristol R) 11
Matteo, D. 1994 (Liverpool) 4
Mattock, J. W. 2008 (Leicester C) 5
Matthew, D. 1990 (Chelsea) 9
Mawson, A. R. J. 2017 (Swansea C) 6
May, A. 1986 (Manchester C) 1
Mee, B. 2011 (Manchester C) 2
Merson, P. C. 1989 (Arsenal) 4
Middleton, J. 1977 (Nottingham F, Derby Co) 3
Miller, A. 1988 (Arsenal) 4
Mills, D. J. 1999 (Charlton Ath, Leeds U) 14
Mills, G. R. 1981 (Nottingham F) 2
Milner, J. P. 2004 (Leeds U, Newcastle U, Aston Villa) 46
Mimms, R. 1985 (Rotherham U, Everton) 3
Minto, S. C. 1991 (Charlton Ath) 6
Mitchell, J. 2017 (Derby Co) 1
Moore, I. 1996 (Tranmere R, Nottingham F) 7
Moore, L. 2012 (Leicester C) 10
Moore, L. I. 2006 (Aston Villa) 5
Moran, S. 1982 (Southampton) 2
Morgan, S. 1987 (Leicester C) 2
Morris, J. 1997 (Chelsea) 7
Morrison, R. R. 2013 (West Ham U) 4
Mortimer, P. 1989 (Charlton Ath) 2
Moses, A. P. 1997 (Barnsley) 2
Moses, R. M. 1981 (WBA, Manchester U) 8
Moses, V. 2011 (Wigan Ath) 1
Mount, M. T. 2019 (Chelsea) 4
Mountfield, D. 1984 (Everton) 1
Muamba, F. N. 2008 (Birmingham C, Bolton W) 33
Muggleton, C. D. 1990 (Leicester C) 1
Mullins, H. I. 1999 (Crystal Palace) 3
Murphy, D. B. 1998 (Liverpool) 4
Murphy, Jacob K. 2017 (Norwich C) 6
Murray, P. 1997 (QPR) 4
Murray, M. W. 2003 (Wolverhampton W) 5
Musiala, J. 2021 (Bayern Munich) 2
Mutch, A. 1989 (Wolverhampton W) 1
Mutch, J. J. E. S. 2011 (Birmingham C) 1
Myers. A. 1995 (Chelsea) 4

Naughton, K. 2009 (Sheffield U, Tottenham H) 9
Naylor, L. M. 2000 (Wolverhampton W) 3
Nelson, R. L. 2019 (Arsenal) 12
Nethercott, S. H. 1994 (Tottenham H) 8
Neville, P. J. 1995 (Manchester U) 7
Newell, M. 1986 (Luton T) 4
Newton, A. L. 2001 (West Ham U) 1
Newton, E. J. I. 1993 (Chelsea) 2
Newton, S. O. 1997 (Charlton Ath) 3
Nicholls, A. 1994 (Plymouth Arg) 1
Nketiah, E. K. 2018 (Arsenal) 17
Nmecha, L. 2018 (Manchester C) 3
Noble, M. J. 2007 (West Ham U) 20
Nolan, K. A. J. 2003 (Bolton W) 1
Nugent, D. J. 2006 (Preston NE) 14

Oakes, M. C. 1994 (Aston Villa) 6
Oakes, S. J. 1993 (Luton T) 1
Oakley, M. 1997 (Southampton) 4
O'Brien, A. J. 1999 (Bradford C) 1
O'Connor, J. 1996 (Everton) 3
O'Hara, J. D. 2008 (Tottenham H) 7
Ojo, O. B. (Sheyi) 2018 (Liverpool) 1
Oldfield, D. 1989 (Luton T) 1
Olney, I. A. 1990 (Aston Villa) 10
O'Neil, G. P. 2005 (Portsmouth) 9
Onomah, J. O. P. 2017 (Tottenham H) 8
Onuoha, C. 2006 (Manchester C) 21
Ord, R. J. 1991 (Sunderland) 3
Osman, R. C. 1979 (Ipswich T) 7
Owen, G. A. 1977 (Manchester C, WBA) 22
Owen, M. J. 1998 (Liverpool) 1
Oxlade-Chamberlain, A. M. D. 2011 (Southampton, Arsenal) 8

Painter, I. 1986 (Stoke C) 1
Palmer, C. L. 1989 (Sheffield W) 4
Palmer, K. R. 2016 (Chelsea) 6
Panzo, J. W. 2020 (Monaco) 5
Parker, G. 1986 (Hull C, Nottingham F) 6
Parker, P. A. 1985 (Fulham) 8
Parker, S. M. 2001 (Charlton Ath) 12
Parkes, P. B. F. 1979 (QPR) 1
Parkin, S. 1987 (Stoke C) 5
Parlour, R. 1992 (Arsenal) 12
Parnaby, S. 2003 (Middlesbrough) 4
Peach, D. S. 1977 (Southampton) 6
Peake, A. 1982 (Leicester C) 1
Pearce, I. A. 1995 (Blackburn R) 3
Pearce, S. 1987 (Nottingham F) 1
Pearce, T. M. 2018 (Leeds U) 2
Pennant, J. 2001 (Arsenal) 24
Pickering N. 1983 (Sunderland, Coventry C) 15
Pickford, J. L. 2015 (Sunderland) 14
Platt, D. 1988 (Aston Villa) 3
Plummer, C. S. 1996 (QPR) 5
Pollock, J. 1995 (Middlesbrough) 3
Porter, G. 1987 (Watford) 12
Potter, G. S. 1997 (Southampton) 1
Powell, N. E. 2012 (Manchester U) 2
Pressman, K. 1989 (Sheffield W) 1
Pritchard, A. D. 2014 (Tottenham H) 9
Proctor, M. 1981 (Middlesbrough, Nottingham F) 4
Prutton, D. T. 2001 (Nottingham F, Southampton) 25
Purse, D. J. 1998 (Birmingham C) 2

Quashie, N. F. 1997 (QPR) 4
Quinn, W. R. 1998 (Sheffield U) 2

Ramage, C. D. 1991 (Derby Co) 3
Ramsdale, A. C. 2018 (Bournemouth) 15
Ranson, R. 1980 (Manchester C) 10
Rashford, M. 2017 (Manchester U) 1
Redknapp, J. F. 1993 (Liverpool) 19
Redmond, N. D. J. 2013 (Birmingham C, Norwich C, Southampton) 38
Redmond, S. 1988 (Manchester C) 14
Reeves, K. P. 1978 (Norwich C, Manchester C) 10
Regis, C. 1979 (WBA) 6
Reid, N. S. 1981 (Manchester C) 6
Reid, P. 1977 (Bolton W) 6
Reo-Coker, N. S. A. 2004 (Wimbledon, West Ham U) 23
Richards, D. I. 1995 (Wolverhampton W) 4
Richards, J. P. 1977 (Wolverhampton W) 2
Richards, M. 2007 (Manchester C) 15
Richards, M. L. 2005 (Ipswich T) 1
Richards, O. T. C. 2020 (Reading) 1
Richardson, K. E. 2005 (Manchester U) 12
Rideout, P. 1985 (Aston Villa, Bari) 5
Ridgewell, L. M. 2004 (Aston Villa) 8
Riggott, C. M. 2001 (Derby Co) 8
Ripley, S. E. 1988 (Middlesbrough) 8
Ritchie, A. 1982 (Brighton & HA) 1
Rix, G. 1978 (Arsenal) 7
Roberts, A. J. 1995 (Millwall, Crystal Palace) 5
Roberts, B. J. 1997 (Middlesbrough) 1
Robins, M. G. 1990 (Manchester U) 6
Robinson, J. 2012 (Liverpool, QPR) 10
Robinson, P. P. 1999 (Watford) 3
Robinson, P. W. 2000 (Leeds U) 11
Robson, B. 1979 (WBA) 7
Robson, S. 1984 (Arsenal, West Ham U) 8
Rocastle, D. 1987 (Arsenal) 14
Roche, L. P. 2001 (Manchester U) 1

Rodger, G. 1987 (Coventry C) 4
Rodriguez, J. E. 2011 (Burnley) 1
Rodwell, J. 2009 (Everton) 21
Rogers, A. 1998 (Nottingham F) 3
Rosario, R. 1987 (Norwich C) 4
Rose, D. L. 2009 (Tottenham H) 29
Rose, M. 1997 (Arsenal) 2
Rosenior, L. J. 2005 (Fulham) 7
Routledge, W. 2005 (Crystal Palace, Tottenham H) 12
Rowell, G. 1977 (Sunderland) 1
Rudd, D. T. 2013 (Norwich C) 1
Ruddock, N. 1989 (Southampton) 4
Rufus, R. R. 1996 (Charlton Ath) 6
Ryan, J. 1983 (Oldham Ath) 1
Ryder, S. H. 1995 (Walsall) 3

Saka, B. A. T. M. 2021 (Arsenal) 1
Samuel, J. 2002 (Aston Villa) 7
Samways, V. 1988 (Tottenham H) 5
Sansom, K. G. 1979 (Crystal Palace) 8
Scimeca, R. 1996 (Aston Villa) 9
Scowcroft, J. B. 1997 (Ipswich T) 5
Seaman, D. A. 1985 (Birmingham C) 10
Sears, F. D. 2010 (West Ham U) 3
Sedgley, S. 1987 (Coventry C, Tottenham H) 11
Sellars, S. 1988 (Blackburn R) 3
Selley, I. 1994 (Arsenal) 3
Serrant, C. 1998 (Oldham Ath) 2
Sessegnon, K. R. (Ryan) 2018 (Fulham, Tottenham H) 18
Sessegnon, Z. S. (Steven) 2020 (Fulham) 5
Sharpe, L. S. 1989 (Manchester U) 8
Shaw, L. P. H. 2013 (Southampton, Manchester U) 5
Shaw, G. R. 1981 (Aston Villa) 7
Shawcross, R. J. 2008 (Stoke C) 2
Shearer, A. 1991 (Southampton) 11
Shelton, G. 1985 (Sheffield W) 1
Shelvey, J. 2012 (Liverpool, Swansea C) 13
Sheringham, E. P. 1988 (Millwall) 1
Sheron, M. N. 1992 (Manchester C) 16
Sherwood, T. A. 1990 (Norwich C) 4
Shipperley, N. J. 1994 (Chelsea, Southampton) 7
Sidwell, S. J. 2003 (Reading) 5
Simonsen, S. P. A. 1998 (Tranmere R, Everton) 4
Simpson, J. B. 2019 (Bournemouth) 1
Simpson, P. 1986 (Manchester C) 5
Sims, S. 1977 (Leicester C) 10
Sinclair, S. A. 2011 (Swansea C) 7
Sinclair, T. 1994 (QPR, West Ham U) 5
Sinnott, L. 1985 (Watford) 1
Skipp, O. W. 2020 (Tottenham H) 10
Slade, S. A. 1996 (Tottenham H) 4
Slater, S. I. 1990 (West Ham U) 3
Small, B. 1993 (Aston Villa) 12
Smalling, C. L. 2010 (Fulham, Manchester U) 14
Smith, A. 2000 (Leeds U) 10
Smith, A. J. 2012 (Tottenham H) 11
Smith, D. 1988 (Coventry C) 10
Smith, M. 1981 (Sheffield W) 5
Smith, M. 1995 (Sunderland) 1
Smith, T. W. 2001 (Watford) 1
Smith-Rowe, E. 2021 (Arsenal) 2
Snodin, I. 1985 (Doncaster R) 4
Soares, T. J. 2006 (Crystal Palace) 4
Solanke, D. A. 2015 (Chelsea, Liverpool, Bournemouth) 18
Sordell, M. A. 2012 (Watford, Bolton W) 14
Spence, J. 2011 (West Ham U) 1
Stanislaus, F. J. 2010 (West Ham U) 2
Statham, B. 1988 (Tottenham H) 3
Statham, D. J. 1978 (WBA) 6
Stead, J. G. 2004 (Blackburn R, Sunderland) 11
Stearman, R. J. 2009 (Wolverhampton W) 4
Steele, J. 2011 (Middlesbrough) 7
Stein, B. 1984 (Luton T) 3
Stephens, J. 2015 (Southampton) 8
Sterland, M. 1984 (Sheffield W) 7
Sterling, R. S. 2012 (Liverpool) 8
Steven, T. M. 1985 (Everton) 2
Stevens, G. A. 1983 (Brighton & HA, Tottenham H) 8
Stewart, J. 2003 (Leicester C) 1
Stewart, P. 1988 (Manchester C) 1
Stockdale, R. K. 2001 (Middlesbrough) 1
Stones, J. 2013 (Everton) 12
Stuart, G. C. 1990 (Chelsea) 5
Stuart, J. C. 1996 (Charlton Ath) 4
Sturridge, D. A. 2010 (Chelsea) 15
Suckling, P. 1986 (Coventry C, Manchester C, Crystal Palace) 10
Summerbee, N. J. 1993 (Swindon T) 3
Sunderland, A. 1977 (Wolverhampton W) 1
Surman, A. R. E. 2008 (Southampton) 4
Surridge, S. W. 2020 (Bournemouth) 3
Sutch, D. 1992 (Norwich C) 4
Sutton, C. R. 1993 (Norwich C) 13
Swift, J. D. 2015 (Chelsea, Reading) 13
Swindlehurst, D. 1977 (Crystal Palace) 1

Talbot, B. 1977 (Ipswich T) 1
Tangana, J. M. 2021 (Tottenham H) 2
Targett, M. R. 2015 (Southampton) 12
Taylor, A. D. 2007 (Middlesbrough) 13
Taylor, M. 2001 (Blackburn R) 1
Taylor, M. S. 2003 (Portsmouth) 3
Taylor, R. A. 2006 (Wigan Ath) 4
Taylor, S. J. 2002 (Arsenal) 3
Taylor, S. V. 2004 (Newcastle U) 29
Terry, J. G. 2001 (Chelsea) 9
Thatcher, B. D. 1996 (Millwall, Wimbledon) 4
Thelwell, A. A. 2001 (Tottenham H) 1
Thirlwell, P. 2001 (Sunderland) 1
Thomas, D. 1981 (Coventry C, Tottenham H) 7
Thomas, J. W. 2006 (Charlton Ath) 2
Thomas, M. 1986 (Luton T) 3
Thomas, M. L. 1988 (Arsenal) 12
Thomas, R. E. 1990 (Watford) 1
Thompson, A. 1995 (Bolton W) 2
Thompson, D. A. 1997 (Liverpool) 7
Thompson, G. L. 1981 (Coventry C) 6
Thorn, A. 1988 (Wimbledon) 5
Thornley, B. L. 1996 (Manchester U) 3
Thorpe, T. J. 2013 (Manchester U) 1
Tiler, C. 1990 (Barnsley, Nottingham F) 13
Tomkins, J. O. C. 2009 (West Ham U) 10
Tomori, O. O. (Fikayo) 2018 (Chelsea) 15
Tonge, M. W. E. 2004 (Sheffield U) 2
Townsend, A. D. 2012 (Tottenham H) 3
Trippier, K. J. 2011 (Manchester C) 2
Tuanzebe, A. 2018 (Manchester U) 1

Unsworth, D. G. 1995 (Everton) 6
Upson, M. J. 1999 (Arsenal) 11

Vassell, D. 1999 (Aston Villa) 11
Vaughan, J. O. 2007 (Everton) 4
Venison, B. 1983 (Sunderland) 10
Vernazza, P. A. P. 2001 (Arsenal, Watford) 2
Vieria, R. A. 2018 (Leeds U) 3
Vinnicombe, C. 1991 (Rangers) 12

Waddle, C. R. 1985 (Newcastle U) 1
Waghorn, M. T. 2012 (Leicester C) 5
Walcott, T. J. 2007 (Arsenal) 21
Wallace, D. L. 1983 (Southampton) 14
Wallace, Ray 1989 (Southampton) 4
Wallace, Rod 1989 (Southampton) 11
Walker, D. 1985 (Nottingham F) 7
Walker, I. M. 1991 (Tottenham H) 9
Walker, K. 2010 (Tottenham H) 7
Walker-Peters, K. L. 2018 (Tottenham H) 11
Walsh, G. 1988 (Manchester U) 2
Walsh, P. A. 1983 (Luton T) 4
Walters, K. 1984 (Aston Villa) 9
Walton, C. T. 2017 (Brighton & HA) 1
Wan Bissaka, A. 2019 (Crystal Palace) 3
Ward, P. 1978 (Brighton & HA) 2
Ward-Prowse, J. M. E. 2013 (Southampton) 31
Warhurst, P. 1991 (Oldham Ath, Sheffield W) 8
Watmore, D. I. 2015 (Sunderland) 13
Watson, B. 2007 (Crystal Palace) 1
Watson, D. 1984 (Norwich C) 7

Watson, D. N. 1994 (Barnsley) 5
Watson, G. 1991 (Sheffield W) 2
Watson, S. C. 1993 (Newcastle U) 12
Weaver, N. J. 2000 (Manchester C) 10
Webb, N. J. 1985 (Portsmouth, Nottingham F) 3
Welbeck, D. 2009 (Manchester U) 14
Welsh, J. J. 2004 (Liverpool, Hull C) 8
Wheater, D. J. 2008 (Middlesbrough) 11
Whelan, P. J. 1993 (Ipswich T) 3
Whelan, N. 1995 (Leeds U) 2
Whittingham, P. 2004 (Aston Villa, Cardiff C) 17
White, D. 1988 (Manchester C) 6
Whyte, C. 1982 (Arsenal) 4
Wickham, C. N. R. 2011 (Ipswich T, Sunderland) 17
Wicks, S. 1982 (QPR) 1
Wilkins, R. C. 1977 (Chelsea) 1
Wilkinson, P. 1985 (Grimsby T, Everton) 4
Williams, B. P. B. 2021 (Manchester U) 1
Williams, D. 1998 (Sunderland) 2
Williams, P. 1989 (Charlton Ath) 4
Williams, P. D. 1991 (Derby Co) 6
Williams, R. 2021 (Liverpool) 2
Williams, S. C. 1977 (Southampton) 14
Willock, J. G. 2020 (Arsenal) 4
Wilmot, B. L. 2020 (Watford) 4
Wilshere, J. A. 2010 (Arsenal) 7
Wilson, C. E. G. 2014 (Bournemouth) 1
Wilson, J. A. 2015 (Manchester U) 1
Wilson, M. A. 2001 (Manchester U, Middlesbrough) 6
Winks, H. 2017 (Tottenham H) 2
Winterburn, N. 1986 (Wimbledon) 1
Wisdom, A. 2012 (Liverpool) 10
Wise, D. F. 1988 (Wimbledon) 1
Woodcook, A. S. 1978 (Nottingham F) 2
Woodgate, J. S. 2000 (Leeds U) 1
Woodhouse, C. 1999 (Sheffield U) 4
Woodman, F. J. 2017 (Newcastle U) 6
Woodrow, C. 2014 (Fulham) 9
Woods, C. C. E. 1979 (Nottingham F, QPR, Norwich C) 6
Worrall, J. A. 2018 (Nottingham F) 3
Wright, A. G. 1993 (Blackburn R) 2
Wright, M. 1983 (Southampton) 4
Wright, R. I. 1997 (Ipswich T) 15
Wright, S. J. 2001 (Liverpool) 10
Wright, W. 1979 (Everton) 6
Wright-Phillips, S. C. 2002 (Manchester C) 6

Yates, D. 1989 (Notts Co) 5
Young, A. S. 2007 (Watford, Aston Villa) 10
Young, L. P. 1999 (Tottenham H, Charlton Ath) 12

Zaha, D. W. A. 2012 (Crystal Palace, Manchester U) 13
Zamora, R. L. 2002 (Brighton & HA) 6

NORTHERN IRELAND

Allen, C. 2009 (Lisburn Distillery) 1
Amos, D. 2019 (Doncaster R) 7
Armstrong, D. T. 2007 (Hearts) 1

Baggley (Crowe), B. T. 2021 (Fleetwood T) 2
Bagnall, L. 2011 (Sunderland) 1
Bailie, N. 1990 (Linfield) 2
Baird, C. P. 2002 (Southampton) 6
Ball, D. 2013 (Tottenham H) 2
Ball, M. 2011 (Norwich C) 5
Ballard, D. G. 2019 (Arsenal) 3
Balmer, K. 2019 (Ballymena U) 11
Bansal-McNulty, A. P. S. 2021 (QPR) 2
Beatty, S. 1990 (Chelsea, Linfield) 2
Bird, P. M. 2019 (Notts Co) 4
Black, J. 2003 (Tottenham H) 1
Black, K. T. 1990 (Luton T) 1
Black, R. Z. 2002 (Morecambe) 1
Blackledge, G. 1978 (Portadown) 1
Blake, R. G. 2011 (Brentford) 2
Blayney, A. 2003 (Southampton) 4
Bonis, L. 2021 (Portadown) 2
Boyd-Munce, C. S. 2019 (Birmingham C) 13
Boyce, L. 2010 (Cliftonville, Werder Bremen) 8
Boyle, D. 2021 (Fleetwood T) 1
Boyle, W. S. 1998 (Leeds U) 7
Braniff, K. R. 2002 (Millwall) 11
Breeze, J. 2011 (Wigan Ath) 4
Brennan, C. 2013 (Kilmarnock) 13
Brobbel, R. 2013 (Middlesbrough) 9
Brotherston, N. 1978 (Blackburn R) 1
Brown, C. M. 2020 (Cardiff C) 4
Browne, G. 2003 (Manchester C) 5
Brunt, C. 2005 (Sheffield W) 2
Bryan, M. A. 2010 (Watford) 4
Buchanan, D. T. H. 2006 (Bury) 15
Buchanan, W. B. 2002 (Bolton W, Lisburn Distillery) 5
Burns, A. 2014 (Linfield) 1
Burns, R. (Bobby) 2018 (Glenavon, Hearts, Barrow) 12
Burns, L. 1998 (Port Vale) 13

Callaghan, A. 2006 (Limavady U, Ballymena U, Derry C) 15
Campbell, S. 2003 (Ballymena U) 1
Camps, C. 2015 (Rochdale) 1
Capaldi, A. C. 2002 (Birmingham C, Plymouth Arg) 14
Carlisle, W. T. 2000 (Crystal Palace) 9
Carroll, R. E. 1998 (Wigan Ath) 11
Carson, J. G. 2011 (Ipswich T, York C) 12
Carson, S. 2000 (Rangers, Dundee U) 2
Carson, T. 2007 (Sunderland) 15
Carvill, M. D. 2008 (Wrexham, Linfield) 8
Casement, C. 2007 (Ipswich T, Dundee) 18
Cathcart, C. 2007 (Manchester U) 15
Catney, R. 2007 (Lisburn Distillery) 1
Chapman, A. 2008 (Sheffield U, Oxford U) 7
Charles, D. 2017 (Fleetwood T) 3
Clarke, L. 2003 (Peterborough U) 4
Clarke, R. 2006 (Newry C) 7
Clarke, R. D. J. 1999 (Portadown) 5
Clingan, S. G. 2003 (Wolverhampton W, Nottingham F) 11
Close, B. 2002 (Middlesbrough) 10
Clucas, M. S. 2011 (Preston NE, Bristol R) 11
Clyde, M. G. 2002 (Wolverhampton W) 5
Colligan, L. 2009 (Ballymena U) 1
Conlan, L. 2013 (Burnley, Morecambe) 11
Conn-Clarke, C. S. M. 2021 (Fleetwood T) 1
Connell, T. E. 1978 (Coleraine) 1
Cooper, J. 2015 (Glenavon) 5
Coote, A. 1998 (Norwich C) 12
Convery, J. 2000 (Celtic) 4
Cousin-Dawson, F. 2021 (Bradford C) 1

Dallas, S. 2012 (Crusaders, Brentford) 2
Davey, H. 2004 (UCD) 3
Davis, S. 2004 (Aston Villa) 3
Devine, D. 1994 (Omagh T) 1
Devine, D. G. 2011 (Preston NE) 2
Devine, J. 1990 (Glentoran) 1
Devlin, C. 2011 (Manchester U, unattached, Cliftonville) 11
Dickson, H. 2002 (Wigan Ath) 1
Doherty, B. 2018 (Derry C) 4
Doherty, J. E. 2014 (Watford, Leyton O, Crawley T) 6
Doherty, M. 2007 (Hearts) 2
Dolan, J. 2000 (Millwall) 6
Donaghy, M. M. 1978 (Larne) 1
Donnelly, A. 2021 (Nottingham F) 2
Donnelly, L. F. P. 2012 (Fulham, Hartlepool U, Motherwell) 23
Donnelly, M. 2007 (Sheffield U, Crusaders) 5
Donnelly, R. 2013 (Swansea C) 1
Dowie, I. 1990 (Luton T) 1
Drummond, W. 2011 (Rangers) 2
Dudgeon, J. P. 2010 (Manchester U) 4
Duff, S. 2003 (Cheltenham T) 1
Duffy, M. 2014 (Derry C, Celtic) 9
Duffy, S. P. M. 2010 (Everton) 3
Dummigan, C. 2014 (Burnley, Oldham Ath) 18
Dunne, D. 2019 (Cliftonville) 1

Dunwoody, J. 2017 (Stoke C, Derry C, Helsinki IFK) 16

Elliott, S. 1999 (Glentoran) 3
Ervin, J. 2005 (Linfield) 2
Evans, C. J. 2009 (Manchester U) 10
Evans, J. 2006 (Manchester U) 3

Feeney, L. 1998 (Linfield, Rangers) 8
Feeney, W. 2002 (Bournemouth) 8
Ferguson, M. 2000 (Glentoran) 2
Ferguson, S. 2009 (Newcastle U) 11
Ferris, C. 2020 (Portadown) 1
Finlayson, D. 2019 (Rangers) 3
Fitzgerald, D. 1998 (Rangers) 4
Flanagan, T. M. 2012 (Milton Keynes D) 1
Flynn, J. J. 2009 (Blackburn R, Ross Co) 11
Fordyce, D. T. 2007 (Portsmouth, Glentoran) 12
Friars, E. C. 2005 (Notts Co) 7
Friars, S. M. 1998 (Liverpool, Ipswich T) 21

Galbraith, E. S. W. 2019 (Manchester U) 11
Gallagher, C. 2019 (Glentoran) 5
Garrett, R. 2007 (Stoke C, Linfield) 14
Gartside, N. J. 2020 (Derry C) 2
Gault, M. 2005 (Linfield) 2
Gibb, S. 2009 (Falkirk, Drogheda U) 2
Gilfillan, B. J. 2005 (Gretna, Peterhead) 9
Gillespie, K. R. 1994 (Manchester U) 1
Glendinning, M. 1994 (Bangor) 1
Glendinning, R. 2012 (Linfield) 3
Gordon, S. M. 2017 (Motherwell, Partick Thistle) 9
Gorman, D. A. 2015 (Stevenage, Leyton Orient) 13
Gorman, R. J. 2012 (Wolverhampton W, Leyton Orient) 4
Graham, G. L. 1999 (Crystal Palace) 5
Graham, R. S. 1999 (QPR) 15
Graham, S. 2020 (Blackpool) 2
Gray, J. P. 2012 (Accrington S) 11
Gray, P. 1990 (Luton T) 1
Griffin, D. J. 1998 (St Johnstone) 10
Grigg, W. D. 2011 (Walsall) 10

Hall, B. 2018 (Notts Co) 3
Hamilton, G. 2000 (Blackburn R, Portadown) 12
Hamilton, W. R. 1978 (Linfield) 1
Hanley, N. 2011 (Linfield) 1
Harkin, M. P. 2000 (Wycombe W) 9
Harney, J. J. 2014 (West Ham U) 1
Harvey, J. 1978 (Arsenal) 1
Hawe, S. 2001 (Blackburn R) 2
Hayes, T. 1978 (Luton T) 1
Hazard, C. 2019 (Celtic) 12
Hazley, M. 2007 (Stoke C) 3
Healy, D. J. 1999 (Manchester U) 8
Hegarty, C. 2011 (Rangers) 7
Herron, C. J. 2003 (QPR) 2
Higgins, R. 2006 (Derry C) 1
Hodson, L. J. S. 2010 (Watford) 10
Holden, R. 2019 (Bristol C) 2
Holmes, S. 2000 (Manchester C, Wrexham) 13
Howland, D. 2007 (Birmingham C) 4
Hughes, J. 2006 (Lincoln C) 7
Hughes, L. 2020 (Celtic) 2
Hughes, M. A. 2003 (Tottenham H, Oldham Ath) 12
Hughes, M. E. 1990 (Manchester C) 1
Hume, T. 2021 (Linfield) 3
Hunter, M. 2002 (Glentoran) 1

Ingham, M. G. 2001 (Sunderland) 4

Jarvis, D. 2010 (Aberdeen) 2
Johns, C. 2014 (Southampton) 1
Johnson, D. M. 1998 (Blackburn R) 11
Johnson, R. A. 2015 (Stevenage) 13
Johnston, B. 1978 (Cliftonville) 1
Johnston, C. R. 2021 (Fleetwood T) 2
Julian, A. A. 2005 (Brentford) 1

Kane, A. M. 2008 (Blackburn R) 5
Kane, M. 2012 (Glentoran) 1
Kee, B. R. 2010 (Leicester C, Torquay U, Burton Alb) 10
Kee, P. V. 1990 (Oxford U) 1
Kelly, D. 2000 (Derry C) 11
Kelly, J. 2019 (Maidenhead U) 2
Kelly, N. 1990 (Oldham Ath) 1
Kennedy, B. J. 2017 (Stevenage) 8
Kennedy, M. C. P. 2015 (Charlton Ath) 7
Kerr, N. 2019 (Glentoran, Portadown) 6
Kirk, A. R. 1999 (Hearts) 9
Knowles, J. 2012 (Blackburn R) 2

Lafferty, D. 2009 (Celtic) 6
Lafferty, K. 2006 (Burnley) 2
Larkin, R. 2021 (Linfield) 2
Lavery, C. 2011 (Ipswich T, Sheffield W) 7
Lavery, S. 2017 (Everton, Linfield) 13
Lawrie, J. 2009 (Port Vale, AFC Telford U) 9
Lennon, N. F. 1990 (Manchester C, Crewe Alex) 2
Lester, C. 2013 (Bolton W) 1
Lewis, J. 2017 (Norwich C) 1
Lindsay, K. 2006 (Larne) 1
Little, A. 2009 (Rangers) 6
Lowry, P. 2009 (Institute, Linfield) 6
Lund, M. 2011 (Stoke C) 6
Lyttle, G. 1998 (Celtic, Peterborough U) 8

McAlinden, L. J. 2012 (Wolverhampton W) 3
McAllister, M. 2007 (Dungannon Swifts) 4
McArdle, R. A. 2006 (Sheffield W, Rochdale) 19
McAreavey, P. 2000 (Swindon T) 7
McBride, J. 1994 (Glentoran) 1
McCaffrey, D. 2006 (Hibernian) 8
McCallion, E. 1998 (Coleraine) 1
McCalmont, A. J. 2019 (Leeds U) 12
McCann, A. 2020 (St Johnstone) 6
McCann, G. S. 2000 (West Ham U) 11
McCann, L. 2020 (Dunfermline Ath) 5
McCann, P. 2003 (Portadown) 1
McCann, R. 2002 (Rangers, Linfield) 2
McCartan, S. V. 2013 (Accrington S) 9
McCartney, G. 2001 (Sunderland) 5
McCashin, S. 2011 (Jerez Industrial, unattached) 2
McChrystal, M. 2005 (Derry C) 9
McClean, J. 2010 (Derry C) 3
McClean, K. 2019 (St Johnstone, Linfield) 7
McClure, M. 2012 (Wycombe W) 1
McCourt, P. J. 2002 (Rochdale, Derry C) 8
McCoy, R. K. 1990 (Coleraine) 1
McCreery, D. 1978 (Manchester U) 1
McCullough, L. 2013 (Doncaster R) 8
McDaid, R. 2015 (Leeds U) 5
McDermott, C. 2017 (Derry C) 4
McDonagh, J. D. C. 2015 (Sheffield U, Derry C) 9
McEleney, S. 2012 (Derry C) 2
McElroy, P. 2013 (Hull C) 1
McEvilly, L. R. 2003 (Rochdale) 9
McFlynn, T. M. 2000 (QPR, Woking, Margate) 19
McGeehan, C. 2013 (Norwich C) 3
McGibbon, P. C. G. 1994 (Manchester U) 1
McGivern, R. 2010 (Manchester C) 6
McGlinchey, B. 1998 (Manchester C, Port Vale, Gillingham) 14
McGonigle, J. 2017 (Coleraine) 4
McGovern, M. 2005 (Celtic) 10
McGowan, M. V. 2006 (Clyde) 2
McGurk, A. 2010 (Aston Villa) 1
McIlroy, T. 1994 (Linfield) 1
McKay, W. 2009 (Leicester C, Northampton T) 7
McKenna, K. 2007 (Tottenham H) 6
McKeown, R. 2012 (Kilmarnock) 12
McKiernan, JJ. 2021 (Watford) 2
McKnight, D. 2015 (Shrewsbury T, Stalybridge Celtic) 5
McKnight, P. 1998 (Rangers) 3
McLaughlin, C. G. 2010 (Preston NE, Fleetwood T) 7
McLaughlin, P. 2010 (Newcastle U, York C) 10
McLaughlin, R. 2012 (Liverpool, Oldham Ath) 6
McLean, B. S. 2006 (Rangers) 1
McLean, J. 2009 (Derry C) 4
McLellan, M. 2012 (Preston NE) 1
McMahon, G. J. 2002 (Tottenham H) 1
McMenamin, L. A. 2009 (Sheffield W) 4

McNair, P. J. C. 2014 (Manchester U) 2
McNally, P. 2013 (Celtic) 1
McQuilken, J. 2009 (Tescoma Zlin) 1
McQuoid, J. J. B. 2009 (Bournemouth) 8
McVeigh, A. 2002 (Ayr U) 1
McVeigh, P. M. 1998 (Tottenham H) 11
McVey, K. 2006 (Coleraine) 8
Magee, J. 1994 (Bangor) 1
Magee, J. 2009 (Lisburn Distillery) 1
Magennis, J. B. D. 2010 (Cardiff C, Aberdeen) 16
Magilton, J. 1990 (Liverpool) 1
Magnay, C. 2010 (Chelsea) 1
Maloney, L. 2015 (Middlesbrough) 6
Marron, C. 2020 (Glenavon) 9
Marshall, R. 2017 (Glenavon) 1
Matthews, N. P. 1990 (Blackpool) 1
Mee, D. 2021 (Manchester U) 2
Meenan, D. 2007 (Finn Harps, Monaghan U) 3
Melaugh, G. M. 2002 (Aston Villa, Glentoran) 11
Millar, K. S. 2011 (Oldham Ath, Linfield) 11
Millar, W. P. 1990 (Port Vale) 1
Miskelly, D. T. 2000 (Oldham Ath) 10
Mitchell, A. 2012 (Rangers) 3
Mitchell, C. 2017 (Burnley) 10
Moreland, V. 1978 (Glentoran) 1
Morgan, D. 2012 (Nottingham F) 4
Morgan, M. P. T. 1999 (Preston NE) 1
Morris, E. J. 2002 (WBA, Glentoran) 8
Morrison, O. 2001 (Sheffield W, Sheffield U) 7
Morrow, A. 2001 (Northampton T) 1
Morrow, S. 2005 (Hibernian) 4
Mulgrew, J. 2007 (Linfield) 10
Mulryne, P. P. 1999 (Manchester U, Norwich C) 5
Murray, W. 1978 (Linfield) 1
Murtagh, C. 2005 (Hearts) 1

Nicholl, J. M. 1978 (Manchester U) 1
Nixon, C. 2000 (Glentoran) 1
Nolan, L. J. 2014 (Crewe Alex, Southport) 4
Norwood, O. J. 2010 (Manchester U) 11

O'Connor, M. J. 2008 (Crewe Alex) 3
O'Hara, G. 1994 (Leeds U) 1
O'Kane, E. 2009 (Everton, Torquay U) 4
O'Mahony, J. 2020 (Glenavon) 1
O'Neill, J. P. 1978 (Leicester C) 1
O'Neill, M. A. M. 1994 (Hibernian) 1
O'Neill, P. 2020 (Glentoran) 6
O'Neill, S. 2009 (Ballymena U) 4
Owens, C. 2018 (QPR) 2

Palmer, C. 2019 (Rangers, Linfield) 9
Parkhouse, D. 2017 (Sheffield U) 16
Paterson, M. A. 2007 (Stoke C) 2
Patterson, D. J. 1994 (Crystal Palace) 1
Paul, C. D. 2017 (QPR) 3
Peacock-Farrell, B. 2018 (Leeds U) 1

Quigley, C. 2017 (Dundee) 2
Quinn, S. J. 1994 (Blackpool) 1

Ramsey, C. 2011 (Portadown) 3
Ramsey, K. 2006 (Institute) 1
Reid, J. T. 2013 (Exeter C) 2
Robinson, H. D. 2020 (Motherwell) 1
Robinson, S. 1994 (Tottenham H) 1
Rooney, L. J. 2017 (Plymouth Arg) 1
Roy, A. 2019 (Derry C) 2

Scott, A. 2021 (Larne) 1
Scott, J. 2020 (Wolverhampton W) 5
Scullion, D. 2006 (Dungannon Swifts) 8
Sendles-White J. 2013 (QPR, Hamilton A) 12
Sharpe, R. 2013 (Derby Co, Notts Co) 6
Shiels, D. 2005 (Hibernian) 6
Shields, S. P. 2013 (Dagenham & R) 2
Shroot, R. 2009 (Harrow B, Birmingham C) 4
Simms, G. 2001 (Hartlepool U) 14
Singleton, J. 2015 (Glenavon) 2
Skates, G. 2000 (Blackburn R) 4
Sloan, T. 1978 (Ballymena U) 1
Smylie, D. 2006 (Newcastle U, Livingston) 6
Smyth, O. 2021 (Dungannon Swifts) 2
Smyth, P. 2017 (Linfield, QPR) 12
Stewart, J. 2015 (Swindon T) 2
Stewart, S. 2009 (Aberdeen) 1
Stewart, S. 2021 (Norwich C) 2
Stewart, T. 2006 (Wolverhampton W, Linfield) 19
Sykes, M. 2017 (Glenavon) 10

Taylor, D. 2021 (Nottingham F) 2
Taylor, J. 2007 (Hearts, Glentoran) 10
Taylor, M. S. 1998 (Fuham) 1
Teggart, N. 2005 (Sunderland) 2
Tempest, G. 2013 (Notts Co) 6
Thompson, A. L. 2011 (Watford) 11
Thompson, J. 2017 (Rangers, Blackpool) 13
Thompson, L. 2020 (Blackburn R) 6
Thompson, P. 2006 (Linfield) 4
Toal, E. 2019 (Derry C) 13
Toner, C. 2000 (Tottenham H, Leyton Orient) 17
Tuffey, J. 2007 (Partick Thistle) 13
Turner, C. 2007 (Sligo R, Bohemians) 12

Waide, R. 2021 (Ballymena U) 1
Ward, J. J. 2006 (Aston Villa, Chesterfield) 7
Ward, M. 2006 (Dungannon Swifts) 1
Ward, S. 2005 (Glentoran) 10
Waterman, D. G. 1998 (Portsmouth) 14
Waterworth, A. 2008 (Lisburn Distillery, Hamilton A) 7
Webb, S. M. 2004 (Ross Co, St Johnstone, Ross Co) 6
Webber, O. H. 2021 (Crystal Palace) 1
Weir, R. J. 2009 (Sunderland) 8
Wells, D. P. 1999 (Barry T) 1
Whitley, J. 1998 (Manchester C) 17
Whyte, G. 2015 (Crusaders) 7
Willis, P. 2006 (Liverpool) 1
Winchester, C. 2011 (Oldham Ath) 13
Winchester, J. 2013 (Kilmarnock) 1
Wylie, B. 2021 (Celtic) 1

SCOTLAND

Adam, C. G. 2006 (Rangers) 5
Adam, G. 2011 (Rangers) 6
Adams, J. 2007 (Kilmarnock) 1
Aitken, R. 1977 (Celtic) 16
Albiston, A. 1977 (Manchester U) 5
Alexander, N. 1997 (Stenhousemuir, Livingston) 10
Allan, S. 2012 (WBA) 10
Anderson, I. 1997 (Dundee, Toulouse) 15
Anderson, R. 1997 (Aberdeen) 15
Andrews, M. 2011 (East Stirlingshire) 1
Anthony, M. 1997 (Celtic) 3
Archdeacon, O. 1987 (Celtic) 1
Archer, J. G. 2012 (Tottenham H) 14
Archibald, A. 1998 (Partick Thistle) 5
Archibald, S. 1980 (Aberdeen, Tottenham H) 5
Archibald, T. V. 2018 (Brentford) 1
Arfield, S. 2008 (Falkirk, Huddersfield T) 17
Armstrong, S. 2011 (Dundee U) 20
Ashby, H. C. 2021 (West Ham U) 2

Bagen, D. 1997 (Kilmarnock) 4
Bain, K. 1993 (Dundee) 4
Baker, M. 1993 (St Mirren) 10
Baltacha, S. S. 2000 (St Mirren) 3
Banks, S. B. 2021 (Crystal Palace) 2
Bannan, B. 2009 (Aston Villa) 10
Bannigan, S. 2013 (Partick Thistle) 3
Bannon, E. J. 1979 (Hearts, Chelsea, Dundee U) 7
Barclay, J. 2011 (Falkirk) 1
Bates, C. 2019 (Hamburg) 4
Beattie, C. 2004 (Celtic) 7
Beattie, J. 1992 (St Mirren) 4
Beaumont, D. 1985 (Dundee U) 1
Bell, D. 1981 (Aberdeen) 2

Bernard, P. R. J. 1992 (Oldham Ath) 15
Berra, C. 2005 (Hearts) 6
Bett, J. 1981 (Rangers) 7
Black, E. 1983 (Aberdeen) 8
Blair, A. 1980 (Coventry C, Aston Villa) 5
Bollan, G. 1992 (Dundee U, Rangers) 17
Bonar, P. 1997 (Raith R) 4
Booth, C. 2011 (Hibernian) 4
Booth, S. 1991 (Aberdeen) 14
Bowes, M. J. 1992 (Dunfermline Ath) 1
Bowman, D. 1985 (Hearts) 1
Boyack, S. 1997 (Rangers) 1
Boyd, K. 2003 (Kilmarnock) 8
Boyd, T. 1987 (Motherwell) 5
Brandon, J. 2019 (Hearts) 2
Brazil, A. 1978 (Hibernian) 1
Brazil, A. 1979 (Ipswich T) 8
Brebner, G. I. 1997 (Manchester U, Reading, Hibernian) 18
Brighton, T. 2005 (Rangers, Clyde) 7
Broadfoot, K. 2005 (St Mirren) 5
Brophy, E. 2017 (Hamilton A, Kilmarnock) 3
Brough, J. 1981 (Hearts) 1
Brown, A. H. 2004 (Hibernian) 1
Brown, S. 2005 (Hibernian) 10
Browne, P. 1997 (Raith R) 1
Bryson, C. 2006 (Clyde) 1
Buchan, J. 1997 (Aberdeen) 13
Burchill, M. J. 1998 (Celtic) 15
Burke, A. 1997 (Kilmarnock) 4
Burke, C. 2004 (Rangers) 3
Burke, O. J. 2018 (WBA) 9
Burley, C. W. 1992 (Chelsea) 7
Burley, G. E. 1977 (Ipswich T) 5
Burns, H. 1985 (Rangers) 2
Burns, T. 1977 (Celtic) 5
Burroughs, J. S. 2021 (Coventry C) 2
Burt, L. 2017 (Rangers) 5

Cadden, C. 2017 (Motherwell) 12
Caddis, P. 2008 (Celtic, Dundee U, Celtic, Swindon T) 13
Cairney, T. 2011 (Hull C) 6
Caldwell, G. 2000 (Newcastle U) 19
Caldwell, S. 2001 (Newcastle U) 4
Cameron, G. 2008 (Dundee U) 3
Cameron, K. M. 2017 (Newcastle U) 3
Campbell, A. 2018 (Motherwell) 24
Campbell, R. 2008 (Hibernian) 6
Campbell, S. 1989 (Dundee) 3
Campbell, S. P. 1998 (Leicester C) 15
Canero, P. 2000 (Kilmarnock) 17
Cardwell, H. 2014 (Reading) 1
Carey, L. A. 1998 (Bristol C) 1
Carrick, D. 2012 (Hearts) 1
Casey, J. 1978 (Celtic) 1
Chalmers, J. 2014 (Celtic, Motherwell) 2
Chalmers, L. 2021 (Dundee U) 2
Christie, M. 1992 (Dundee) 3
Christie, R. 2014 (Inverness CT, Celtic) 9
Clark, R. B. 1977 (Aberdeen) 3
Clarke, S. 1984 (St Mirren) 8
Clarkson, D. 2004 (Motherwell) 13
Clayton, T. 2021 (Liverpool) 1
Cleland, A. 1990 (Dundee U) 11
Cole, D. 2011 (Rangers) 2
Collins, J. 1988 (Hibernian) 8
Collins, N. 2005 (Sunderland) 7
Connolly, P. 1991 (Dundee U) 3
Connor, R. 1981 (Ayr U) 2
Conroy, R. 2007 (Celtic) 4
Considine, A. 2007 (Aberdeen) 5
Cooper, D. 1977 (Clydebank, Rangers) 6
Cooper, N. 1982 (Aberdeen) 13
Coutts, P. A. 2009 (Peterborough U, Preston NE) 7
Crabbe, S. 1990 (Hearts) 2
Craig, M. 1998 (Aberdeen) 2
Craig, T. 1977 (Newcastle U) 1
Crainey, S. D. 2000 (Celtic) 7
Crainie, D. 1983 (Celtic) 1
Crawford, S. 1994 (Raith R) 19
Creaney, G. 1991 (Celtic) 11
Cummings, J. 2015 (Hibernian) 8
Cummings, W. 2000 (Chelsea) 8
Cuthbert, S. 2007 (Celtic, St Mirren) 13

Dailly, C. 1991 (Dundee U) 34
Dalglish, P. 1999 (Newcastle U, Norwich C) 6
Dargo, C. 1998 (Raith R) 10
Davidson, C. I. 1997 (St Johnstone) 2
Davidson, H. N. 2000 (Dundee U) 3
Davidson, M. 2011 (St Johnstone) 1
Dawson, A. 1979 (Rangers) 8
Deas, P. A. 1992 (St Johnstone) 2
Deas, R. 2021 (Inverness CT) 1
Dempster, J. 2004 (Rushden & D) 1
Dennis, S. 1992 (Raith R) 1
Diamond, A. 2004 (Aberdeen) 12
Dickov, P. 1992 (Arsenal) 4
Dixon, P. 2008 (Dundee) 2
Docherty, G. 2017 (Hamilton A) 4
Dodds, D. 1978 (Dundee U) 1
Dods, D. 1997 (Hibernian) 5
Doig, C. R. 2000 (Nottingham F) 13
Donald, G. S. 1992 (Hibernian) 3
Donnelly, S. 1994 (Celtic) 11
Doohan, R. 2018 (Celtic) 13
Dorrans, G. 2007 (Livingston) 6
Dow, A. 1993 (Dundee, Chelsea) 3
Dowie, A. J. 2003 (Rangers, Partick Thistle) 14
Duff, J. 2009 (Inverness CT) 1
Duff, S. 2003 (Dundee U) 9
Duffie, K. 2011 (Falkirk) 6
Duffy, D. A. 2005 (Falkirk, Hull C) 8
Duffy, J. 1987 (Dundee) 1
Durie, G. S. 1987 (Chelsea) 4
Durrant, I. 1987 (Rangers) 4
Doyle, J. 1981 (Partick Thistle) 2

Easton, B. 2009 (Hamilton A) 3
Easton, C. 1997 (Dundee U) 21
Edwards, M. 2012 (Rochdale) 1
Elliot, B. 1998 (Celtic) 2
Elliot, C. 2006 (Hearts) 9
Erhahon, E. 2021 (St Mirren) 2
Esson, R. 2000 (Aberdeen) 7

Fagan, S. M. 2005 (Motherwell) 1
Ferguson, B. 1997 (Rangers) 12
Ferguson, D. 1987 (Rangers) 5
Ferguson, D. 1992 (Dundee U) 7
Ferguson, D. 1992 (Manchester U) 5
Ferguson, I. 1983 (Dundee) 4
Ferguson, I. 1987 (Clyde, St Mirren, Rangers) 6
Ferguson, L. 2019 (Aberdeen) 11
Ferguson, R. 1977 (Hamilton A) 1
Feruz, I. 2012 (Chelsea) 4
Findlay, S. 2012 (Celtic) 13
Findlay, W. 1991 (Hibernian) 5
Fiorini, L. 2021 (Manchester C) 1
Fitzpatrick, A. 1977 (St Mirren) 5
Fitzpatrick, M. 2007 (Motherwell) 4
Flannigan, C. 1993 (Clydebank) 1
Fleck, J. 2009 (Rangers) 4
Fleck, R. 1987 (Rangers, Norwich C) 6
Fleming, G. 2008 (Gretna) 1
Fletcher, D. B. 2003 (Manchester U) 2
Fletcher, S. 2007 (Hibernian) 7
Forrest, A. 2017 (Ayr U) 1
Forrest, J. 2011 (Celtic) 4
Foster, R. M. 2005 (Aberdeen) 5
Fotheringham, M. M. 2004 (Dundee) 3
Fowler, J. 2002 (Kilmarnock) 3
Foy, R. A. 2004 (Liverpool) 5
Fraser, M. 2012 (Celtic) 5
Fraser, R. 2013 (Aberdeen, Bournemouth) 10
Fraser, S. T. 2000 (Luton T) 4
Freedman, D. A. 1995 (Barnet, Crystal Palace) 8
Fridge, L. 1989 (St Mirren) 2
Fullarton, J. 1993 (St Mirren) 17
Fulton, J. 2014 (Swansea C) 2

Fulton, R. 2017 (Liverpool, Hamilton A) 11
Fulton, M. 1980 (St Mirren) 5
Fulton, S. 1991 (Celtic) 7
Fyvie, F. 2012 (Wigan Ath) 8

Gallacher, K. W. 1987 (Dundee U) 7
Gallacher, P. 1999 (Dundee U) 7
Gallacher, S. 2009 (Rangers) 2
Gallagher, P. 2003 (Blackburn R) 11
Galloway, M. 1989 (Hearts, Celtic) 2
Gardiner, J. 1993 (Hibernian) 1
Gauld, R. 2013 (Dundee U, Sporting Lisbon) 11
Geddes, R. 1982 (Dundee) 5
Gemmill, S. 1992 (Nottingham F) 4
Germaine, G. 1997 (WBA) 1
Gilles, R. 1997 (St Mirren) 7
Gillespie, G. T. 1979 (Coventry C) 8
Gilmour, B. C. 2019 (Chelsea) 13
Glass, S. 1995 (Aberdeen) 11
Glover, L. 1988 (Nottingham F) 3
Goodwillie, D. 2009 (Dundee U) 9
Goram, A. L. 1987 (Oldham Ath) 1
Gordon, C. S. 2003 (Hearts) 5
Gough, C. R. 1983 (Dundee U) 5
Graham, D. 1998 (Rangers) 8
Grant, P. 1985 (Celtic) 10
Gray, D. P. 2009 (Manchester U) 2
Gray, S. 1987 (Aberdeen) 1
Gray S. 1995 (Celtic) 7
Griffiths, L. 2010 (Dundee, Wolverhampton W) 11
Grimmer, J. 2014 (Fulham) 1
Gunn, B. 1984 (Aberdeen) 9

Hagen, D. 1992 (Rangers) 8
Hamill, J. 2008 (Kilmarnock) 11
Hamilton, B. 1989 (St Mirren) 4
Hamilton, C. 2018 (Hearts) 3
Hamilton, J. 1995 (Dundee, Hearts) 14
Hamilton, J. 2014 (Hearts) 8
Hammell, S. 2001 (Motherwell) 11
Handling, D. 2014 (Hibernian) 3
Handyside, P. 1993 (Grimsby T) 7
Hanley, G. 2011 (Blackburn R) 1
Hanlon, P. 2009 (Hibernian) 23
Hannah, D. 1993 (Dundee U) 16
Hardie, R. 2017 (Rangers) 8
Harper, C. 2021 (Inverness CT) 1
Harper, K. 1995 (Hibernian) 7
Hartford, R. A. 1977 (Manchester C) 1
Hartley, P. J. 1997 (Millwall) 1
Harvie, D. W. 2018 (Aberdeen, Ayr U) 15
Hastie, J. 2019 (Motherwell) 1
Hegarty, P. 1987 (Dundee U) 6
Henderson, E. 2020 (Celtic) 1
Henderson, L. 2015 (Celtic) 9
Hendrie, S. 2014 (West Ham U) 3
Hendry, J. 1992 (Tottenham H) 1
Henly, J. 2014 (Reading) 1
Herron, J. 2012 (Celtic) 2
Hetherston, B. 1997 (St Mirren) 1
Hewitt, J. 1982 (Aberdeen) 6
Hogg, G. 1984 (Manchester U) 4
Holsgrove, J. 2019 (Reading) 5
Holt, J. 2012 (Hearts) 7
Hood, G. 1993 (Ayr U) 3
Horn, R. 1997 (Hearts) 6
Hornby, F. D. I. 2018 (Everton, Reims) 18
House, B. 2019 (Reading) 1
Howie, S. 1993 (Cowdenbeath) 5
Hughes, R. D. 1999 (Bournemouth) 9
Hughes, S. 2002 (Rangers) 12
Hunter, G. 1987 (Hibernian) 3
Hunter, P. 1989 (East Fife) 3
Hutton, A. 2004 (Rangers) 7
Hutton, K. 2011 (Rangers) 1
Hyam, D. J. 2014 (Reading) 5

Iacovitti, A. 2017 (Nottingham F) 4
Inman, B. 2011 (Newcastle U) 2
Irving, A. 2021 (Hearts) 1
Irvine, G. 2006 (Celtic) 2

Jack, R. 2012 (Aberdeen) 19
James, K. F. 1997 (Falkirk) 1
Jardine, I. 1979 (Kilmarnock) 1
Jess, E. 1990 (Aberdeen) 14
Johnson, G. I. 1992 (Dundee U) 6
Johnston, A. 1994 (Hearts) 3
Johnston, F. 1993 (Falkirk) 1
Johnston, G. 2019 (Liverpool, Feyenoord) 10
Johnston, M. 1984 (Partick Thistle, Watford) 3
Johnston, M. A. 2018 (Celtic) 7
Jones, J. C. 2017 (Crewe Alex) 4
Jordan, A. J. 2000 (Bristol C) 3
Joseph, K. A. 2021 (Wigan Ath) 1
Jules, Z. K. 2017 (Reading) 3
Jupp, D. A. 1995 (Fulham) 9

Kelly, L. A. 2017 (Reading) 11
Kelly, S. 2014 (St Mirren) 1
Kelly, S. 2020 (Rangers) 5
Kennedy, J. 2003 (Celtic) 15
Kennedy, M. 2012 (Kilmarnock) 1
Kenneth, G. 2008 (Dundee U) 8
Kerr, B. 2003 (Newcastle U) 14
Kerr, F. 2012 (Birmingham C) 3
Kerr, J. 2018 (St Johnstone) 6
Kerr, M. 2001 (Kilmarnock) 1
Kerr, S. 1993 (Celtic) 10
Kettings, C. D. 2012 (Blackpool) 3
King, A. 2014 (Swansea C) 1
King, C. M. 2014 (Norwich C) 1
King, W. 2015 (Hearts) 8
Kingsley, S. 2015 (Swansea C) 6
Kinnear, B. 2021 (Rangers) 1
Kinniburgh, W. D. 2004 (Motherwell) 3
Kirkwood, D. 1990 (Hearts) 1
Kyle, K. 2001 (Sunderland) 12

Lambert, P. 1991 (St Mirren) 11
Langfield, J. 2000 (Dundee) 2
Lappin, S. 2004 (St Mirren) 10
Lauchlan, J. 1998 (Kilmarnock) 11
Lavety, B. 1993 (St Mirren) 9
Lavin, G. 1993 (Watford) 7
Lawson, P. 2004 (Celtic) 10
Leighton, J. 1982 (Aberdeen) 1
Lennon, S. 2008 (Rangers) 6
Levein, C. 1985 (Hearts) 2
Leven, P. 2005 (Kilmarnock) 2
Liddell, A. M. 1994 (Barnsley) 12
Lindsey, J. 1979 (Motherwell) 1
Locke, G. 1994 (Hearts) 10
Love, D. 2015 (Manchester U) 5
Love, G. 1995 (Hibernian) 1
Loy, R. 2009 (Dunfermline Ath, Rangers) 5
Lynch, S. 2003 (Celtic, Preston NE) 13

McAllister, G. 1990 (Leicester C) 1
McAllister, K. 2019 (Derby Co, St Mirren) 2
McAllister, R. 2008 (Inverness CT) 2
McAlpine, H. 1983 (Dundee U) 5
McAnespie, K. 1998 (St Johnstone) 4
McArthur, J. 2008 (Hamilton A) 2
McAuley, S. 1993 (St Johnstone) 1
McAvennie, F. 1982 (St Mirren) 5
McBride, J. 1981 (Everton) 1
McBride, J. P. 1998 (Celtic) 2
McBurnie, O. 2015 (Swansea C) 12
McCabe, R. 2012 (Rangers, Sheffield W) 3
McCall, A. S. M. 1988 (Bradford C, Everton) 2
McCann, K. 2008 (Hibernian) 4
McCann, N. 1994 (Dundee) 9
McCart, J. 2017 (Celtic) 1
McClair, B. 1984 (Celtic) 8
McCluskey, G. 1979 (Celtic) 6
McCluskey, S. 1997 (St Johnstone) 14
McCoist, A. 1984 (Rangers) 1
McConnell, I. 1997 (Clyde) 1

McCormack, D. 2008 (Hibernian) 1
McCormack, R. 2006 (Rangers, Motherwell, Cardiff C) 13
McCracken, D. 2002 (Dundee U) 5
McCrorie, Robby 2018 (Rangers) 7
McCrorie, Ross 2017 (Rangers) 20
McCulloch, A. 1981 (Kilmarnock) 1
McCulloch, I. 1982 (Notts Co) 2
McCulloch, L. 1997 (Motherwell) 14
McCunnie, J. 2001 (Dundee U, Ross Co, Dunfermline Ath) 20
MacDonald, A. 2011 (Burnley) 6
MacDonald, C. 2017 (Derby Co) 2
MacDonald, J. 1980 (Rangers) 8
MacDonald, J. 2007 (Hearts) 11
McDonald, C. 1995 (Falkirk) 5
McDonald, K. 2008 (Dundee, Burnley) 14
McEwan, C. 1997 (Clyde, Raith R) 17
McEwan, D. 2003 (Livingston) 2
McFadden, J. 2003 (Motherwell) 7
McFadzean C. 2015 (Sheffield U) 3
McFarlane, D. 1997 (Hamilton A) 3
McGarry, S. 1997 (St Mirren) 3
McGarvey, F. P. 1977 (St Mirren, Celtic) 3
McGarvey, S. 1982 (Manchester U) 4
McGeough, D. 2012 (Celtic) 10
McGhee, J. 2013 (Hearts) 20
McGhee, M. 1981 (Aberdeen) 1
McGinn, J. 2014 (St Mirren, Hibernian) 9
McGinn, S. 2009 (St Mirren, Watford) 8
McGinnis, G. 1985 (Dundee U) 1
McGlinchey, M. R. 2007 (Celtic) 1
McGregor, A. 2003 (Rangers) 6
McGregor, C. W. 2013 (Celtic) 5
McGrillen, P. 1994 (Motherwell) 2
McGuire, D. 2002 (Aberdeen) 2
McHattie, K. 2012 (Hearts) 6
McInally, J. 1989 (Dundee U) 1
McInroy, K. 2021 (Celtic) 1
McIntyre, T. P. 2019 (Reading) 3
McKay, B. 2012 (Rangers) 4
McKay, B. 2013 (Hearts) 1
McKean, K. 2011 (St Mirren) 1
McKenna, S. 2018 (Aberdeen) 5
McKenzie, R. 2013 (Kilmarnock) 4
McKenzie, R. 1997 (Hearts) 2
McKimmie, S. 1985 (Aberdeen) 3
McKinlay, T. 1984 (Dundee) 6
McKinlay, W. 1989 (Dundee U) 6
McKinnon, R. 1991 (Dundee U) 6
McLaren, A, 1989 (Hearts) 11
McLaren, A. 1993 (Dundee U) 4
McLaughlin, B. 1995 (Celtic) 8
McLaughlin, J. 1981 (Morton) 10
McLean, E. 2008 (Dundee U, St Johnstone) 2
McLean, S. 2003 (Rangers) 4
McLeish, A. 1978 (Aberdeen) 6
McLean, K. 2012 (St Mirren) 11
McLennon, C. 2020 (Aberdeen) 9
MacLeod, A. 1979 (Hibernian) 3
McLeod, J. 1989 (Dundee U) 2
MacLeod, L. 2012 (Rangers) 8
MacLeod, M. 1979 (Dumbarton, Celtic) 5
McManus, D. J. 2014 (Aberdeen, Fleetwood T) 4
McManus, T. 2001 (Hibernian) 14
McMillan, S. 1997 (Motherwell) 4
McMullan, P. 2017 (Celtic) 1
McNab, N. 1978 (Tottenham H) 1
McNally, M. 1991 (Celtic) 2
McNamara, J. 1994 (Dunfermline Ath, Celtic) 12
McNaughton, K. 2002 (Aberdeen) 1
McNeil, A. 2007 (Hibernian) 1
McNichol, J. 1979 (Brentford) 7
McNiven, D. 1977 (Leeds U) 3
McNiven, S. A. 1996 (Oldham Ath) 1
McPake, J. 2021 (Rangers) 1
McParland, A. 2003 (Celtic) 1
McPhee, S. 2002 (Port Vale) 1
McPherson, D. 1984 (Rangers, Hearts) 4
McQuilken, J. 1993 (Celtic) 2
McStay, P. 1983 (Celtic) 5

McWhirter, N. 1991 (St Mirren) 1
MacGregor, R. 2021 (Inverness CT) 1
Mackay, D. 2021 (Inverness CT) 1
Mackay-Steven, G. 2012 (Dundee U) 3
Mackie, S. 2019 (Hibernian) 1
Magennis, K. 2019 (St Mirren) 5
Maguire, B. 2019 (Motherwell) 10
Maguire, C. 2009 (Aberdeen) 12
Main, A. 1988 (Dundee U) 3
Mair, A. 2021 (Norwich C) 1
Malcolm, R. 2001 (Rangers) 1
Mallan, S. 2017 (St Mirren, Barnsley, St Mirren) 9
Maloney, S. 2002 (Celtic) 21
Malpas, M. 1983 (Dundee U) 8
Marr, B. 2011 (Ross Co) 1
Marshall, D. J. 2004 (Celtic) 10
Marshall, S. R. 1995 (Arsenal) 5
Martin, A. 2009 (Leeds U, Ayr U) 12
Mason, G. R. 1999 (Manchester C, Dunfermline Ath) 2
Mathieson, D. 1997 (Queen of the South) 3
May, E. 1989 (Hibernian) 2
May, S. 2013 (St Johnstone, Sheffield W) 8
Mayo, L. 2021 (Rangers) 4
Meldrum, C. 1996 (Kilmarnock) 6
Melrose, J. 1977 (Partick Thistle) 8
Middleton, G. B. D. 2018 (Rangers) 17
Millar, M, 2009 (Celtic) 1
Miller, C. 1995 (Rangers) 8
Miller, J. 1987 (Aberdeen, Celtic) 7
Miller, K. 2000 (Hibernian, Rangers) 7
Miller, W. 1991 (Hibernian) 7
Miller, W. F. 1978 (Aberdeen) 2
Milne, K. 2000 (Hearts) 1
Milne, R. 1982 (Dundee U) 3
Mitchell, C. 2008 (Falkirk) 7
Money, I. C. 1987 (St Mirren) 3
Montgomery, N. A. 2003 (Sheffield U) 2
Morgan, L. 2017 (Celtic) 9
Morrison, S. A. 2004 (Aberdeen, Dunfermline Ath) 12
Muir, L. 1977 (Hibernian) 1
Mulgrew, C. P. 2006 (Celtic, Wolverhampton W, Aberdeen) 14
Murphy J. 2009 (Motherwell) 13
Murray, H. 2000 (St Mirren) 3
Murray, I. 2001 (Hibernian) 15
Murray, N. 1993 (Rangers) 16
Murray, R. 1993 (Bournemouth) 1
Murray, S. 2004 (Kilmarnock) 2

Narey, D. 1977 (Dundee U) 4
Naismith, J. 2014 (St Mirren) 1
Naismith, S. J. 2006 (Kilmarnock, Rangers) 15
Naysmith, G. A. 1997 (Hearts) 22
Neilson, R. 2000 (Hearts) 1
Nesbitt, A. 2017 (Celtic) 2
Ness, J, 2011 (Rangers) 2
Nevin, P. 1985 (Chelsea) 5
Nicholas, C. 1981 (Celtic, Arsenal) 6
Nicholson, B. 1999 (Rangers) 7
Nicholson, S. 2015 (Hearts) 8
Nicol, S. 1981 (Ayr U, Liverpool) 14
Nisbet, S. 1989 (Rangers) 5
Noble, D. J. 2003 (West Ham U) 2
Notman, A. M. 1999 (Manchester U) 10

O'Brien, B. 1999 (Blackburn R, Livingston) 6
O'Connor, G. 2003 (Hibernian) 8
O'Donnell, P. 1992 (Motherwell) 8
O'Donnell, S. 2013 (Partick Thistle) 1
O'Halloran, M. 2012 (Bolton W) 2
O'Hara, M. 2015 (Kilmarnock, Dundee) 2
O'Leary, R. 2008 (Kilmarnock) 2
O'Neil, B. 1992 (Celtic) 7
O'Neil, J. 1991 (Dundee U) 1
O'Neill, M. 1995 (Clyde) 6
Orr, N. 1978 (Morton) 7

Palmer, L. J. 2011 (Sheffield W) 8
Park, C. 2012 (Middlesbrough) 1
Parker, K. 2001 (St Johnstone) 1

Parlane, D. 1977 (Rangers) 1
Paterson, C. 1981 (Hibernian) 2
Paterson, C. 2012 (Hearts) 12
Paterson, J. 1997 (Dundee U) 9
Patterson, N. K. 2021 (Rangers) 4
Pawlett, P. 2012 (Aberdeen) 7
Payne, G. 1978 (Dundee U) 3
Peacock, L. A. 1997 (Carlisle U) 1
Pearce, A. J. 2008 (Reading) 2
Pearson, S. P. 2003 (Motherwell) 8
Perry, R. 2010 (Rangers, Falkirk, Rangers) 16
Polworth, L. 2016 (Inverness CT) 1
Porteous, R. 2018 (Hibernian) 14
Pressley, S. J. 1993 (Rangers, Coventry C, Dundee U) 26
Provan, D. 1977 (Kilmarnock) 1
Prunty, B. 2004 (Aberdeen) 6

Quinn, P. C. 2004 (Motherwell) 3
Quinn, R. 2006 (Celtic) 9
Quitongo, J. 2017 (Hamilton A) 1

Rae, A. 1991 (Millwall) 8
Rae, G. 1999 (Dundee) 6
Ralston, A. 2018 (Celtic) 5
Reading, P. J. 2020 (Stevenage) 6
Redford, I. 1981 (Rangers) 6
Reid, B. 1991 (Rangers) 4
Reid, C. 1993 (Hibernian) 3
Reid, M. 1982 (Celtic) 2
Reid, R. 1977 (St Mirren) 3
Reilly, A. 2004 (Wycombe W) 1
Renicks, S. 1997 (Hamilton A) 1
Reynolds, M. 2007 (Motherwell) 9
Rhodes, J. L. 2011 (Huddersfield T) 8
Rice, B. 1985 (Hibernian) 1
Richardson, L. 1980 (St Mirren) 2
Ridgers, M. 2012 (Hearts) 5
Riordan, D. G. 2004 (Hibernian) 5
Ritchie, A. 1980 (Morton) 1
Ritchie, P. S. 1996 (Hearts) 7
Robertson, A. 1991 (Rangers) 1
Robertson, A. 2013 (Dundee U, Hull C) 4
Robertson, C. 1977 (Rangers) 1
Robertson, C. 2012 (Aberdeen) 10
Robertson, D. 2007 (Dundee U) 4
Robertson, D. A. 1987 (Aberdeen) 7
Robertson, G. A. 2004 (Nottingham F, Rotherham U) 15
Robertson, H. 1994 (Aberdeen) 2
Robertson, J. 1985 (Hearts) 2
Robertson, L. 1993 (Rangers) 3
Robertson, S. 1998 (St Johnstone) 2
Roddie, A. 1992 (Aberdeen) 5
Ross, G. 2007 (Dunfermline Ath) 1
Ross, N. 2011 (Inverness CT) 2
Ross, T. W. 1977 (Arsenal) 1
Rowson, D. 1997 (Aberdeen) 5
Ruddy, J. 2017 (Wolverhampton W) 1
Russell, J. 2011 (Dundee U) 11
Russell, R. 1978 (Rangers) 3

Salton, D. B. 1992 (Luton T) 6
Sammut, R. A. M. 2017 (Chelsea) 3
Samson, C. I. 2004 (Kilmarnock) 6
Saunders, S. 2011 (Motherwell) 2
Scobbie, T. 2008 (Falkirk) 12
Scott, J. R. 2020 (Motherwell, Hull C) 2
Scott, M. 2006 (Livingston) 1
Scott, P. 1994 (St Johnstone) 4
Scougall, S. 2012 (Livingston, Sheffield U) 2
Scrimgour, D. 1997 (St Mirren) 3
Seaton, A. 1998 (Falkirk) 1
Severin, S. D. 2000 (Hearts) 10
Shankland, L. 2015 (Aberdeen) 4
Shannon, R. 1987 (Dundee) 7
Sharp, G. M. 1982 (Everton) 1
Sharp, R. 1990 (Dunfermline Ath) 4
Shaw, O. 2019 (Hibernian) 2
Sheerin, P. 1996 (Southampton) 1
Sheppard, J. 2017 (Reading) 2
Shields, G. 1997 (Rangers) 2
Shinnie, A. 2009 (Dundee, Rangers) 3
Shinnie, G. 2012 (Inverness CT) 2
Simmons, S. 2003 (Hearts) 1
Simpson, N. 1982 (Aberdeen) 11
Sinclair, G. 1977 (Dumbarton) 1
Skilling, M. 1993 (Kilmarnock) 2
Slater, C. 2014 (Kilmarnock, Colchester U) 9
Slicker, C. 2021 (Manchester C) 1
Smith, B. M. 1992 (Celtic) 5
Smith, C. 2008 (St Mirren) 2
Smith, C. 2015 (Aberdeen) 1
Smith, D. 2012 (Hearts) 4
Smith, D. L. 2006 (Motherwell) 2
Smith, G. 1978 (Rangers) 1
Smith, G. 2004 (Rangers) 8
Smith, H. G. 1987 (Hearts) 2
Smith, L. 2017 (Hearts, Ayr U) 12
Smith, L. 2020 (Hamilton A) 1
Smith, S. 2007 (Rangers) 1
Sneddon, A. 1979 (Celtic) 1
Snodgrass, R. 2008 (Livingston) 2
Soutar, D. 2003 (Dundee) 11
Souttar, J. 2016 (Dundee U, Hearts) 11
Speedie, D. R. 1985 (Chelsea) 1
Spencer, J. 1991 (Rangers) 3
Stanton, P. 1977 (Hibernian) 1
Stanton, S. 2014 (Hibernian) 1
Stark, W. 1985 (Aberdeen) 1
St Clair, H. 2018 (Chelsea) 3
Stephen, R. 1983 (Dundee) 1
Stevens, G. 1977 (Motherwell) 1
Stevenson, L. 2008 (Hibernian) 8
Stewart, C. 2002 (Kilmarnock) 1
Stewart, J. 1978 (Kilmarnock, Middlesbrough) 3
Stewart, M. J. 2000 (Manchester U) 17
Stewart, R. 1979 (Dundee U, West Ham U) 12
Stillie, D. 1995 (Aberdeen) 14
Storie, C. 2017 (Aberdeen) 2
Strachan, G. D. 1998 (Coventry C) 7
Sturrock, P. 1977 (Dundee U) 9
Sweeney, P. H. 2004 (Millwall) 8
Sweeney, S. 1991 (Clydebank) 7

Tapping, C. 2013 (Hearts) 1
Tarrant, N. K. 1999 (Aston Villa) 5
Taylor, G. J. 2017 (Kilmarnock) 14
Teale, G. 1997 (Clydebank, Ayr U) 6
Telfer, P. N. 1993 (Luton T) 3
Templeton, D. 2011 (Hearts) 2
Thomas, D. 2017 (Motherwell) 6
Thomas, K. 1993 (Hearts) 8
Thompson, S. 1997 (Dundee U) 12
Thomson, C. 2011 (Hearts) 2
Thomson, J. A. 2017 (Celtic) 1
Thomson, K. 2005 (Hibernian) 6
Thomson, W. 1977 (Partick Thistle, St Mirren) 10
Tolmie, J. 1980 (Morton) 1
Tortolano, J. 1987 (Hibernian) 2
Toshney, L. 2012 (Celtic) 5
Turnbull, D. 2019 (Motherwell) 4
Turner, I. 2005 (Everton) 6
Tweed, S. 1993 (Hibernian) 3

Urain, E. R. 2021 (Athletic Bilbao) 2

Wales, G. 2000 (Hearts) 1
Walker, A. 1988 (Celtic) 1
Walker, J. 2013 (Hearts) 1
Wallace, I. A. 1978 (Coventry C) 1
Wallace, L. 2007 (Hearts) 10
Wallace, M. 2012 (Hudderfield T) 4
Wallace, R. 2004 (Celtic, Sunderland) 4
Walsh, C. 1984 (Nottingham F) 5
Wark, J. 1977 (Ipswich T) 8
Watson, A. 1981 (Aberdeen) 4
Watson, K. 1977 (Rangers) 2
Watt, A. 2012 (Celtic) 9
Watt, E. 2018 (Wolverhampton W) 3
Watt, M. 1991 (Aberdeen) 12
Watt. S. M. 2005 (Chelsea) 5

Webster, A. 2003 (Hearts) 2
Welsh, S. 2021 (Celtic) 2
Whiteford, A. 1997 (St Johnstone) 1
Whittaker, S. G. 2005 (Hibernian) 18
Whyte, D. 1987 (Celtic) 9
Wighton, C. R. 2017 (Dundee) 6
Wilkie, L. 2000 (Dundee) 6
Will, J. A. 1992 (Arsenal) 3
Williams, G. 2002 (Nottingham F) 9
Williamson, B. 2021 (Rangers) 1
Williamson, R. 2018 (Dunfermline) 4
Wilson, D. 2011 (Liverpool, Hearts) 13
Wilson, I. 2018 (Kilmarnock) 7
Wilson, M. 2004 (Dundee U, Celtic) 19
Wilson, S. 1999 (Rangers) 7
Wilson, T. 1983 (St Mirren) 1
Wilson, T. 1988 (Nottingham F) 4
Winnie, D. 1988 (St Mirren) 1
Woods, M. 2006 (Sunderland) 2
Wotherspoon, D. 2011 (Hibernian) 16
Wright, K. 2021 (Rangers) 1
Wright, P. 1989 (Aberdeen, QPR) 3
Wright, Stephen 1991 (Aberdeen) 14
Wright, Scott 2018 (Aberdeen) 5
Wright, T. 1987 (Oldham Ath) 1
Wylde, G. 2011 (Rangers) 7

Young, Darren 1997 (Aberdeen) 8
Young, Derek 2000 (Aberdeen) 5

WALES

Abbruzzese, R. 2018 (Cardiff C) 3
Absolom, K. 2019 (Ostersund) 1
Adams, J. A. 2021 (Brentford) 2
Adams, N. W. 2008 (Bury, Leicester C) 5
Alfei, D. M. 2010 (Swansea C) 13
Aizlewood, M. 1979 (Luton T) 2
Allen, J. M. 2008 (Swansea C) 13
Anthony, B. 2005 (Cardiff C) 8
Astley, R. 2021 (Everton) 1

Babos, A. 2018 (Derby Co) 7
Baddeley, L. M. 1996 (Cardiff C) 2
Baker, A. T. 2019 (Sheffield W) 3
Balcombe, S. 1982 (Leeds U) 1
Bale, G. 2006 (Southampton, Tottenham H) 4
Barden, D. J. (Norwich C) 1
Barnhouse, D. J. 1995 (Swansea C) 3
Basey, G. W. 2009 (Charlton Ath) 1
Bater, P. T. 1977 (Bristol R) 2
Beevers, L. J. 2005 (Boston U, Lincoln C) 7
Bellamy, C. D. 1996 (Norwich C) 8
Bender, T. J. 2011 (Colchester U) 4
Birchall, A. S. 2003 (Arsenal, Mansfield T) 12
Bird, A. 1993 (Cardiff C) 6
Blackmore, C. 1984 (Manchester U) 3
Blake, D. J. 2007 (Cardiff C) 14
Blake, N. A. 1991 (Cardiff C) 5
Blaney, S. D. 1997 (West Ham U) 3
Bloom, J. 2011 (Falkirk) 1
Bodin, B. P. 2010 (Swindon T, Torquay U) 21
Bodin, P. J. 1983 (Cardiff C) 1
Bond, J. H. 2011 (Watford) 1
Bowen, J. P. 1993 (Swansea C) 5
Bowen, M. R. 1983 (Tottenham H) 3
Bowen, S. L. (Cardiff C) 2
Boyes, M. M. 2021 (Liverpool) 6
Boyle, T. 1982 (Crystal Palace) 1
Brace, D. P. 1995 (Wrexham) 6
Bradley, M. S. 2007 (Walsall) 17
Bradshaw, T. 2012 (Shrewsbury T) 8
Broadhead, N. P. 2018 (Everton) 17
Brooks, D. R. 2018 (Sheffield U) 3
Brough, M. 2003 (Notts Co) 3
Brown, J. D. 2008 (Cardiff C) 6
Brown, J. R. 2003 (Gillingham) 7
Brown, T. A. F. 2011 (Ipswich T, Rotherham U, Aldershot T) 10
Burns, W. J. 2013 (Bristol C) 18
Burton, R. L. 2018 (Arsenal) 9
Byrne, M. T. 2003 (Bolton W) 1

Cabango, B. 2019 (Swansea C) 5
Calliste, R. T. 2005 (Manchester U, Liverpool) 15
Carpenter, R. E. 2005 (Burnley) 1
Cassidy, J. A. 2011 (Wolverhampton W) 8
Cegielski, W. 1977 (Wrexham) 2
Chamberlain, E. C. 2010 (Leicester C) 9
Chapple, S. R. 1992 (Swansea C) 8
Charles, J. D. 2016 (Huddersfield T, Barnsley) 9
Charles, J. M. 1979 (Swansea C) 2
Christie-Davies, I. 2018 (Chelsea, Liverpool) 4
Church, S. R. 2008 (Reading) 15
Clark, J. 1978 (Manchester U, Derby Co) 2
Clifton, H. L. 2019 (Grimsby T) 6
Coates, J. S. 1996 (Swansea C) 5
Coleman, C. 1990 (Swansea C) 3
Collins, J. M. 2003 (Cardiff C) 7
Collins, L. R. 2021 (Newport Co) 2
Collins, M. J. 2007 (Fulham, Swansea C) 2
Collison, J. D. 2008 (West Ham U) 7
Colwill, R. 2021 (Cardiff C) 1
Cooper, B. J. 2019 (Swansea C) 10
Cooper, O. J. 2020 (Swansea C) 3
Cornell, D. J. 2010 (Swansea C) 4
Cotterill, D. R. G. B. 2005 (Bristol C, Wigan Ath) 11
Coyne, D. 1992 (Tranmere R) 7
Coxe, C. T. 2018 (Cardiff C, Solihull Moors) 16
Craig, N. L. 2009 (Everton) 4
Critchell, K. A. R. 2005 (Southampton) 3
Crofts, A. L. 2005 (Gillingham) 10
Crowe, M. T. T. 2017 (Ipswich T) 1
Crowell, M. T. 2004 (Wrexham) 7
Cullen, L. J. 2018 (Swansea C) 12
Curtis, A. T. 1977 (Swansea C) 1

Dasilva, C. P. 2018 (Chelsea, Brentford) 3
Davies, A. 1982 (Manchester U) 6
Davies, A. G. 2006 (Cambridge U) 6
Davies, A. R. 2005 (Southampton, Yeovil T) 14
Davies, C. M. 2005 (Oxford U, Verona, Oldham Ath) 9
Davies, D. 1999 (Barry T) 1
Davies, G. M. 1993 (Hereford U, Crystal Palace) 7
Davies, I. C. 1978 (Norwich C) 1
Davies, K. E. 2019 (Swansea C) 1
Davies, L. 2005 (Bangor C) 1
Davies, R. J. 2006 (WBA) 4
Davies, S. 1999 (Peterborough U, Tottenham H) 10
Dawson, C. 2013 (Leeds U) 2
Day, R. 2000 (Manchester C, Mansfield T) 11
Deacy, N. 1977 (PSV Eindhoven) 1
De-Vulgt, L. S. 2002 (Swansea C) 2
Dibble, A. 1983 (Cardiff C) 3
Dibble, C. 2014 (Barnsley) 1
Doble, R. A. 2010 (Southampton) 10
Doughty, M. E. 2012 (QPR) 1
Doyle, S. C. 1979 (Preston NE, Huddersfield T) 2
Duffy, R. M. 2005 (Portsmouth) 7
Dummett, P. 2011 (Newcastle U) 3
Dwyer, P. J. 1979 (Cardiff C) 1

Eardley, N. 2007 (Oldham Ath, Blackpool) 11
Earnshaw, R. 1999 (Cardiff C) 10
Easter, D. J. 2006 (Cardiff C) 1
Ebdon, M. 1990 (Everton) 2
Edwards, C. N. H. 1996 (Swansea C) 7
Edwards, D. A. 2006 (Shrewsbury T, Luton T, Wolverhampton W) 9
Edwards, G. D. R. 2012 (Swansea C) 6
Edwards, R. I. 1977 (Chester) 2
Edwards, R. W. 1991 (Bristol C) 13
Evans, A. 1977 (Bristol R) 1
Evans, C. 2007 (Manchester C, Sheffield U) 13
Evans, J. A. J. 2014 (Fulham, Wrexham) 6
Evans, J. M. 2018 (Swansea C) 13

Evans, K. 1999 (Leeds U, Cardiff C) 4
Evans, K. G. 2019 (Swansea C) 2
Evans, L. 2013 (Wolverhampton W) 13
Evans, O. R. 2018 (Wigan Ath) 3
Evans, P. S. 1996 (Shrewsbury T) 1
Evans, S. J. 2001 (Crystal Palace) 2
Evans, T. 1995 (Cardiff C) 3

Fish, N. 2005 (Cardiff C) 2
Fleetwood, S. 2005 (Cardiff C) 5
Flynn, C. P. 2007 (Crewe Alex) 1
Folland, R. W. 2000 (Oxford U) 1
Foster, M. G. 1993 (Tranmere R) 1
Fowler, L. A. 2003 (Coventry C, Huddersfield T) 9
Fox, M. A. 2013 (Charlton Ath) 6
Freeman, K. 2012 (Nottingham F, Derby Co) 15
Freestone, R. 1990 (Chelsea) 1

Gabbidon, D. L. 1999 (WBA, Cardiff C) 17
Gale, D. 1983 (Swansea C) 2
Gall, K. A. 2002 (Bristol R, Yeovil T) 8
Gibson, N. D. 1999 (Tranmere R, Sheffield W) 11
Giggs, R. J. 1991 (Manchester U) 1
Gilbert, P. 2005 (Plymouth Arg) 12
Giles, D. C. 1977 (Cardiff C, Swansea C, Crystal Palace) 4
Giles, P. 1982 (Cardiff C) 3
Graham, D. 1991 (Manchester U) 1
Green, R. M. 1998 (Wolverhampton W) 16
Griffith, C. 1990 (Cardiff C) 1
Griffiths, C. 1991 (Shrewsbury T) 1
Grubb, D. 2007 (Bristol C) 1
Gunter, C. 2006 (Cardiff C, Tottenham H) 8

Haldane, L. O. 2007 (Bristol R) 1
Hall, G. D. 1990 (Chelsea) 1
Harries, C. W. T. 2018 (Swansea C) 7
Harris, M. T. 2018 (Cardiff C) 20
Harrison, E. W. 2013 (Bristol R) 14
Hartson, J. 1994 (Luton T, Arsenal) 9
Haworth, S. O. 1997 (Cardiff C, Coventry C, Wigan Ath) 12
Hedges, R. P. 2014 (Swansea C) 11
Henley, A. 2012 (Blackburn R) 3
Hennessey, W. R. 2006 (Wolverhampton W) 6
Hewitt, E. J. 2012 (Macclesfield T, Ipswich T) 10
Hillier, I. M. 2001 (Tottenham H, Luton T) 5
Hodges, G. 1983 (Wimbledon) 5
Holden, A. 1984 (Chester C) 1
Holloway, C. D. 1999 (Exeter C) 2
Hopkins, J. 1982 (Fulham) 5
Hopkins, S. A. 1999 (Wrexham) 1
Howells, J. 2012 (Luton T) 5
Huggins, D. S. 1996 (Bristol C) 1
Huggins, N. J. 2019 (Leeds U) 3
Hughes, D. 2005 (Kaiserslautern, Regensburg) 2
Hughes, D. R. 1994 (Southampton) 1
Hughes, I. 1992 (Bury) 11
Hughes, L. M. 1983 (Manchester U) 5
Hughes, R. D. 1996 (Aston Villa, Shrewsbury T) 13
Hughes, W. 1977 (WBA) 3
Huws, E. W. 2012 (Manchester C) 6

Isgrove, L. J. 2013 (Southampton) 6

Jackett, K. 1981 (Watford) 2
Jacobson, J. M. 2006 (Cardiff C, Bristol R) 15
James, D. O. 2017 (Swansea C) 11
James, L. R. S. 2006 (Southampton) 10
James, R. M. 1977 (Swansea C) 3
Jarman, L. 1996 (Cardiff C) 10
Jeanne, L. C. 1999 (QPR) 8
Jelleyman, G. A. 1999 (Peterborough U) 1
Jenkins, L. D. 1998 (Swansea C) 9
Jenkins, S. R. 1993 (Swansea C) 2
Jephcott, L. O. 2021 (Plymouth Arg) 5
John, D. C. 2014 (Cardiff C) 9
Johnson, B. P. 2020 (Nottingham F) 4
Jones, C. T. 2007 (Swansea C) 1
Jones, E. 2021 (Stoke C) 2
Jones, E. P. 2000 (Blackpool) 1
Jones, F. 1981 (Wrexham) 1
Jones, G. W. 2014 (Everton) 9
Jones, J. A. 2001 (Swansea C) 3
Jones, L. 1982 (Cardiff C) 3
Jones, M. A. 2004 (Wrexham) 4
Jones, M. G. 1998 (Leeds U) 7
Jones, O. R. 2015 (Swansea C) 1
Jones, P. L. 1992 (Liverpool) 12
Jones, R. 2011 (AFC Wimbledon) 1
Jones, R. A. 1994 (Sheffield W) 3
Jones, S. J. 2005 (Swansea C) 1
Jones, V. 1979 (Bristol R) 2

Kendall, L. M. 2001 (Crystal Palace) 2
Kendall, M. 1978 (Tottenham H) 1
Kenworthy, J. R. 1994 (Tranmere R) 3
King, A. 2008 (Leicester C) 11
Knott, G. R. 1996 (Tottenham H) 1

Law, B. J. 1990 (QPR) 2
Lawless, A. 2006 (Torquay U) 1
Lawrence, T. 2013 (Manchester U) 8
Ledley, J. C. 2005 (Cardiff C) 5
Lemonheigh-Evans, C. 2019 (Bristol C) 3
Letheran, G. 1977 (Leeds U) 2
Letheran, K. C. 2006 (Swansea C) 1
Levitt, D. J. C. 2020 (Manchester U) 1
Lewis, A. 2018 (Swansea C, Lincoln C) 12
Lewis, D. 1982 (Swansea C) 9
Lewis, J. 1983 (Cardiff C) 1
Lewis, J. C. 2020 (Swansea C) 2
Llewellyn, C. M. 1998 (Norwich C) 14
Lockyer, T. A. 2015 (Bristol R) 7
Loveridge, J. 1982 (Swansea C) 3
Low, J. D. 1999 (Bristol R, Cardiff C) 1
Lowndes, S. R. 1979 (Newport Co, Millwall) 4
Lucas, L. P. 2011 (Swansea C) 19

MacDonald, S. B. 2006 (Swansea C) 25
McCarthy, A. J. 1994 (QPR) 3
McDonald, C. 2006 (Cardiff C) 3
Mackin, L. 2006 (Wrexham) 1
Maddy, P. 1982 (Cardiff C) 2
Margetson, M. W. 1992 (Manchester C) 7
Martin, A. P. 1999 (Crystal Palace) 1
Martin, D. A. 2006 (Notts Co) 1
Marustik, C. 1982 (Swansea C) 7
Matondo, R. 2018 (Manchester C) 8
Matthews, A. J. 2010 (Cardiff C) 5
Maxwell, C. 2009 (Wrexham) 16
Maxwell, L. J. 1999 (Liverpool, Cardiff C) 14
Meades, J. 2012 (Cardiff C) 4
Meaker, M. J. 1994 (QPR) 2
Melville, A. K. 1990 (Swansea C, Oxford U) 2
Mepham, C. J. 2018 (Brentford) 4
Micallef, C. 1982 (Cardiff C) 3
Mooney, D. 2019 (Fleetwood T) 4
Morgan, A. M. 1995 (Tranmere R) 4
Morgan, C. 2004 (Wrexham, Milton Keynes D) 12
Morrell, J. J. 2018 (Bristol C) 8
Morris, A. J. 2009 (Cardiff C, Aldershot T) 8
Moss, D. M. 2003 (Shrewsbury T) 6
Mountain, P. D. 1997 (Cardiff C) 2
Mumford, A. O. 2003 (Swansea C) 4

Nardiello, D. 1978 (Coventry C) 1
Neilson, A. B. 1993 (Newcastle U) 7
Nicholas, P. 1978 (Crystal Palace, Arsenal) 3
Nogan, K. 1990 (Luton T) 2
Nogan, L. M. 1991 (Oxford U) 1
Norrington-Davies, R. L. 2018 (Sheffield U) 14
Norton, C. A. 2021 (Stoke C) 1
Nyatanga, L. J. 2005 (Derby Co) 10

Oakley, A. 2013 (Swindon T) 1
O'Brien, B. T. 2015 (Manchester C) 8
Ogleby, R. 2011 (Hearts, Wrexham) 12
Oster, J. M. 1997 (Grimsby T, Everton) 9
O'Sullivan, T. P. 2013 (Cardiff C) 15
Owen, G. 1991 (Wrexham) 8

Page, R. J. 1995 (Watford) 4
Parslow, D. 2005 (Cardiff C) 4
Partington, J. M. 2009 (Bournemouth) 8
Partridge, D. W. 1997 (West Ham U) 1
Pascoe, C. 1983 (Swansea C) 4
Pearce, S. 2006 (Bristol C) 3
Pearson, S. 2021 (Bristol C) 3
Pejic, S. M. 2003 (Wrexham) 6
Pembridge, M. A. 1991 (Luton T) 1
Peniket, R. 2012 (Fulham) 1
Perry, J. 1990 (Cardiff C) 3
Peters, M. 1992 (Manchester C, Norwich C) 3
Phillips, D. 1984 (Plymouth Arg) 3
Phillips, G. R. 2001 (Swansea C) 3
Phillips, L. 1979 (Swansea C, Charlton Ath) 2
Pilling, L. 2018 (Tranmere R) 9
Pipe, D. R. 2003 (Coventry C, Notts Co) 12
Pontin, K. 1978 (Cardiff C) 1
Poole, R. L. 2017 (Manchester U, Milton Keynes D) 23
Powell, L. 1991 (Southampton) 4
Powell, L. 2004 (Leicester C) 3
Powell, R. 2006 (Bolton W) 1
Price, J. J. 1998 (Swansea C) 7
Price, L. P. 2005 (Ipswich T) 10
Price, M. D. 2001 (Everton, Hull C, Scarborough) 13
Price, P. 1981 (Luton T) 1
Price, T. O. 2019 (Swansea C) 1
Pritchard, J. P. 2013 (Fulham) 3
Pritchard, M. O. 2006 (Swansea C) 4
Pugh, D. 1982 (Doncaster R) 2
Pugh, S. 1993 (Wrexham) 2
Pugh, T. 2019 (Scunthorpe U) 2
Pulis, A. J. 2006 (Stoke C) 5
Przybek, A. 2020 (Ipswich T) 3

Ramasut, M. W. T. 1997 (Bristol R) 4
Ramsey, A. J. 2008, (Cardiff C, Arsenal) 12
Ratcliffe, G. 2019 (Cardiff C) 6
Ratcliffe, K. 1981 (Everton) 2
Ray, G. E. 2013 (Crewe Alex) 5
Ready, K. 1992 (QPR) 5
Rees, A. 1984 (Birmingham C) 1
Rees, J. M. 1990 (Luton T) 3
Rees, M. R. 2003 (Millwall) 4
Reid, B. 2014 (Wolverhampton W) 1
Ribeiro, C. M. 2008 (Bristol C) 8
Richards, A. D. J. 2010 (Swansea C) 16
Richards, E. A. 2012 (Bristol R) 1
Roberts, A. M. 1991 (QPR) 2
Roberts, C. 2013 (Cheltenham T) 6
Roberts, C. J. 1999 (Cardiff C) 1
Roberts, C. R. J. 2016 (Swansea C) 2
Roberts, G. 1983 (Hull C) 1
Roberts, G. W. 1997 (Liverpool, Panionios, Tranmere R) 11
Roberts, J. G. 1977 (Wrexham) 1
Roberts, N. W. 1999 (Wrexham) 3
Roberts, P. 1997 (Porthmadog) 1
Roberts, S. I. 1999 (Swansea C) 13
Roberts, S. W. 2000 (Wrexham) 3
Roberts, T. W. 2018 (Leeds U) 5
Robinson, C. P. 1996 (Wolverhampton W) 6
Robinson, J. R. C. 1992 (Brighton & HA, Charlton Ath) 5
Robson-Kanu, K. H. 2010 (Reading) 4
Rodon, J. P. 2017 (Swansea C) 9
Rowlands, A. J. R. 1996 (Manchester C) 5
Rush, I. 1981 (Liverpool) 2

Sass-Davies, W. J. 2021 (Crewe Alex) 2
Savage, R. W. 1995 (Crewe Alex) 3
Saunders, C. L. 2015 (Crewe Alex) 1
Sayer, P. A. 1977 (Cardiff C) 2
Searle, D. 1991 (Cardiff C) 6
Sheehan, J. L. 2014 (Swansea C) 12
Shephard, L. 2015 (Swansea C) 2
Shepperd, N. 2021 (Brentford) 1
Slatter, D. 2000 (Chelsea) 6
Slatter, N. 1983 (Bristol R) 6
Smith, D. 2014 (Shrewsbury T) 3
Smith, M. 2018 (Manchester C) 5
Somner, M. J. 2004 (Brentford) 2
Speed, G. A. 1990 (Leeds U) 3
Spence, S. 2021 (Cardiff C, Crystal Palace) 5
Spender, S. 2005 (Wrexham) 6
Stephens, D. 2011 (Hibernian) 7
Stevens, F. J. 2021 (Brentford) 2
Stevenson, N. 1982 (Swansea C) 2
Stevenson, W. B. 1977 (Leeds U) 3
Stirk, R. W. 2020 (Birmingham C) 7
Stock, B. B. 2003 (Bournemouth) 4
Symons, C. J. 1991 (Portsmouth) 2

Tancock, S. 2013 (Swansea C) 6
Taylor, A. J. 2012 (Tranmere R) 3
Taylor, G. K. 1995 (Bristol R) 4
Taylor, J. W. T. 2010 (Reading) 12
Taylor, N. J. 2008 (Wrexham, Swansea C) 13
Taylor, R. F. 2008 (Chelsea) 5
Taylor, T. 2020 (Wolverhampton W) 6
Thomas, C. E. 2010 (Swansea C) 3
Thomas, D. G. 1977 (Leeds U) 3
Thomas, D. J. 1998 (Watford) 2
Thomas, G. S. 2018 (Leicester C) 8
Thomas, J. A. 1996 (Blackburn R) 21
Thomas, Martin R. 1979 (Bristol R) 2
Thomas, Mickey R. 1977 (Wrexham) 2
Thomas, S. 2001 (Wrexham) 5
Thompson, L. C. W. 2015 (Norwich C) 2
Tibbott, L. 1977 (Ipswich T) 2
Tipton, M. J. 1998 (Oldham Ath) 6
Tolley, J. C. 2001 (Shrewsbury T) 12
Touray, M. 2019 (Newport Co, Salford C) 6
Tudur-Jones, O. 2006 (Swansea C) 3
Twiddy, C. 1995 (Plymouth Arg) 3

Vale, J. 2020 (Blackburn R) 1
Valentine, R. D. 2001 (Everton, Darlington) 8
Vaughan, D. O. 2003 (Crewe Alex) 8
Vaughan, N. 1982 (Newport Co) 2
Vokes, S. M. 2007 (Bournemouth, Wolverhampton W) 14

Waite, J. 2021 (Cardiff C) 2
Walsh, D. 2000 (Wrexham) 8
Walsh, I. P. 1979 (Crystal Palace, Swansea C) 2
Walsh, J. 2012 (Swansea C, Crawley T) 11
Walton, M. 1991 (Norwich C.) 1
Ward, D. 1996 (Notts Co) 2
Ward, D. 2013 (Liverpool) 6
Warlow, O. J. 2007 (Lincoln C) 2
Webb, L. 2021 (Swansea C) 1
Weeks, D. L. 2014 (Wolverhampton W) 2
Weston, R. D. 2001 (Arsenal, Cardiff C) 4
Wharton, T. J. 2014 (Cardiff C) 1
Whitfield, P. M. 2003 (Wrexham) 1
Wiggins, R. 2006 (Crystal Palace) 9
Williams, A. P. 1998 (Southampton) 9
Williams, A. S. 1996 (Blackburn R) 16
Williams, D. 1983 (Bristol R) 1
Williams, D. I. L. 1998 (Liverpool, Wrexham) 9
Williams D. P. 2021 (Swansea C) 1
Williams, D. T. 2006 (Yeovil T) 1
Williams, E. 1997 (Caernarfon T) 2
Williams, G. 1983 (Bristol R) 2
Williams, G. A. 2003 (Crystal Palace) 5
Williams, G. C. 2014 (Fulham) 3
Williams, J. P. 2011 (Crystal Palace) 8
Williams, M. 2001 (Manchester U) 10
Williams, M. P. 2006 (Wrexham) 14
Williams, M. J. 2014 (Notts Co) 1
Williams, M. R. 2006 (Wrexham) 6
Williams, O. fon 2007 (Crewe Alex, Stockport Co) 11
Williams, R. 2007 (Middlesbrough) 10
Williams, S. J. 1995 (Wrexham) 4
Wilmot, R. 1982 (Arsenal) 6
Wilson, H. 2014 (Liverpool) 10
Wilson, J. S. 2009 (Bristol C) 3
Worgan, L. J. 2005 (Milton Keynes D, Rushden & D) 5
Wright, A. A. 1998 (Oxford U) 3
Wright, J. 2014 (Huddersfield T) 2

Yorwerth, J. 2014 (Cardiff C) 7
Young, S. 1996 (Cardiff C) 5

ENGLAND YOUTH GAMES 2020–21

ENGLAND UNDER-16

FRIENDLY

Burton, Friday 9 April 2021

England (2) 2 *(Taylor 30, Cozier-Duberry 34)*

Wales (1) 3 *(Osmand 40, Roberts 79, Agius 89)*

England: Gunter (Grant 46); Feeney (Dorrington 46), Susoho (Carrington 61), Scarles (Giblin 46), Griffiths (Castledine 46), Taylor (Gee 46), Stutter (McGrath 46), O'Reilly (Clark 46), Cozier-Duberry (Silcott-Duberry 46), Araujo (Sousa 46), Donley (Tezgel 46).
Wales: Camis (Pradic 46); Fleming (Williams 46), Debrowski (Godden 46), Robinson (Hartness 46), Crew (Edwards 46), Watts (Agius 46), Osmand (Fuller 46), Harris (Lloyd B 65), Matondo (Benjamin 46), Lloyd A (Roberts 46), Abbott (Famiwuya 46).

ENGLAND UNDER-17

NOVEMBER TRAINING CAMP

Burton, Wednesday 11 November 2020

England (0) 3 *(Thomas 61, Scarlett 71, Forson 84)*

Derby Co U18 (1) 1 *(Kelley 26)*

England: Maguire; Norton-Cuffy, Clarridge (Jonas 46), Awe, Chrisene (Hackett-Valton 46), Gyabi (Mabaya 46), Devine (Collier 46), Hall (Webster 46), Perkins (Forson 46), Scarlett (Mubama 72), Mubama (Thomas 46).
Derby Co U18: Randle; Brailsford, Bardell, Jinkinson (Borkovic 79), Rutt, Williams, Aghatise, Thompson L, Borkovic (Grewal-Pollard 62), Thompson S, Kelly.

Burton, Saturday 14 November 2020

England (0) 2 *(Hall 48, Perkins 77)*

Reading U23 (2) 4 *(Melvin-Lambert 19, Onen 28, Stickland 51, Pendlebury 70)*

England: Whitworth (Beadle 46); Norton-Cuffy (Mabaya 46), Hughes, Awe (Collier 70), Jonas (Clarridge 46), Hackett-Valton (Chrisene 46), Gyabi (Hall 46), Collier (Devine 46), Webster (Perkins 46), Forson (Thomas 46), Scarlett (Mubama 46).
Reading U23: Holden; Watson, Stickland (Clarke 73), Camara, Tetek, Melvin-Lambert, East (Rowley 66), Pendlebury, Bristow (Hamilton 74), Paul, Onen (Ashcroft 74).

MARCH TRAINING CAMP

Burton, Tuesday 30 March 2021

England (1) 2 *(Lawal 45 (og), Gordon 77)*

Watford U23 (1) 1 *(McKieman 35)*

England: Beadle (Clarke 32 (Knightbridge 61)); Norton-Cuffy (Lewis 46), Katongo (Lindo 46), Nelson (Chrisene 64), Chrisene (Small 46), Gordon (Norton-Cuffy 87), Braybroke, Awe, Thomas (Olakigbe 46), Hackford (Pennant 46), Scarlett (Emmerson 46).
Watford U23: Roberts (Marriott 46); Statham, Barrett, Lawal, Stevenson, McKiernan, Patterson (Perkins 46), Lo-Everton, Hunter (Maurizio 61), Forde (Hutchinson 61), Cukur (Bergkamp 43).

ENGLAND UNDER-18

NOVEMBER TRAINING CAMP

Burton, Sunday 15 November 2020

England (1) 1 *(John 41 (pen))*

Southampton U23 (0) 1 *(Morris 65)*

England: Oluwayemi; Ingram, Fish, Quansah, Colwill, Pye (Onyango 72), Vale, John, Richards (Dembele 70), Chukwuemeka (Robertson 70), Barry (Dobbin 84).
Southampton U23: Latham (Wright 46); Kpohomouh, Abontohoma, Tchaptchet, Ledwidge, Defise, Keogh (Tizzard 62), Finnigan (Morris 46), Olaigbe, Smith, Mitchell.
England won 4-2 on penalties.

Burton, Tuesday 17 November 2020

England (0) 0

Coventry C U23 (2) 3 *(Goodman 4 (og), Kastaneer 25, Bakayoko 52)*

England: Goodman (Sharman-Lowe 46); Abbey (Pye 70), Egan-Riley, Mbete-Tabu, Onyango (John 70), Robertson, Kenneh, Chauke, Edozie (Richards 70), Dobbin, Dembele.
Coventry C U23: Tyler; Pask, Thompson (McGrath 62), Rowe, Newton, Hilssner (Young 62), Kastaneer (Burroughs 76), Bartlett (Finnegan 69), Ngandu (Lafferty 53), Bakayoko (Bremang 62), Bapaga (Evans-Harriott 76).

FRIENDLY

Cardiff, Monday 29 March 2021

Wales (0) 0

England (0) 2 *(Delap 65 (pen), Chukwuemeka 79)*

Wales: Williams M (Hughes 84); Williams K (Leeson 75), Davies (Mariette 74), Jones H (Williams C 85), Jones T, Williams J, Savage (Bell 75), Ewing (Twamley 85), Viggars (Congreve 58), Cotterill (Salisbury 58), Popov (Dyer 84).
England: Graczyk (Oluwayemi 46); Ingram (Oyegoke 46), Egan-Riley, Quansah (Fish 46), Doyle (Norris 46), Ramsey (Chukwuemeka 46), Robertson (Scott 46), Dembele (Edozie (46), Shoretire (Baah 46), Jebbison (Delap 46), Barry (Balagizi 46).

ENGLAND UNDER-19

NOVEMBER TRAINING CAMP

Burton, Tuesday 17 November 2020

England (2) 8 *(Delap 6, McAtee 38, Philogene-Bidace 63, 78, 90, Greenwood 65, Gelhardt 71, Rankine 86)*

Derby Co U23 (0) 0

England: Moulden (Trafford 46); Kessler (Matheson 61), Cresswell (Simeu 70), Branthwaite, Dorsett (Cirkin 46), Elliott (Rankine 61), Palmer (Bate 70), Ramsey (Peart-Harris 65), Rogers (Philogene-Bidace 46), McAtee (Gelhardt 46), Delap (Greenwood 46).
Derby Co U23: Sykes-Kenworthy (Yates 46); Bardell, Wassall, Minkley, Williams, Dixon, Thompson L (Aghatise 71), Hutchinson, Shonibare, Wilson (Ibrahim 71), Cresswell.

MARCH TRAINING CAMP

Burton, Tuesday 27 March 2021

England (2) 6 *(Mighten 15, Gelhardt 31, Rankine 68, 87, Greenwood 74, Palmer 88)*

Arsenal U23 (0) 1 *(Lewis 53)*

England: Young (Moulden 46); Kessler (Livramento 46), Cresswell, Harwood-Bellis (Mengi 46), Cirkin, Elliott (Bate 46), Azeez (Devine 46), Vale (McAtee 46), Anderson (Palmer 46), Mighten (Rankine 46), Gelhardt (Greenwood 46).
Arsenal U23: Smith; Alebiousu, Kirk (Dinzeyi 46), Monlouis, Lopez (Bola 46), Lewis (Ogungbo 74), Cirjan, Akinola, Coyle, Taylor-Hart, Moller.

ENGLAND UNDER-20

FRIENDLIES

Burton, Tuesday 13 October 2020

England (2) 2 *(Ramsey 33, Amaechi 36)*

Wales (0) 0

England: Ashby-Hammond (Dewhurst 46); Lawrence (Ogbeta 75), Thomas (Buchanan 67), Harwood-Bellis, Alese (Drameh 75), Maghoma (Whittaker 67), Amaechi (Garner 67), Doyle, Balogun (Duncan 67), Ramsey, Gordon.
Wales: Webb (Barden 56); Rushesha (Hoole 70), Bowen (Hughes R 70), Astley, Boyes, Pearson (Pinchard 57), Davies (Thomas 57), Evans K (Jones J 65), Adams, Williams (Jones C), Evans C (Hughes I).

NOVEMBER TRAINING CAMP

Bodymoor Heath, Tuesday 17 November 2020

England (1) 1 *(Balogun 26)*

Aston Villa U23 (2) 3 *(Barkley 21 (pen), Cash 23, El Ghazi 52)*

England: Griffiths (Rushworth 46); Daly-Campbell (Lawrence 56), Wood-Gordon, Harwood-Bellis, Thomas (Ogbeta 46), Garner (Sibley 46), Doyle (White 46), Ramsey (Anjorin 56), Whittaker (Livramento 56), Balogun (Simms 46), Gordon (Lewis 56).
Aston Villa U23: Heaton; El Mohamady, Konsa, Bridge, Taylor, Cash, Targett, Barkley (Chukwuemeka 63), El Ghazi, Davis (Barry 46), Watkins.

NON-LEAGUE TABLES 2020–21

On Thursday 25 February 2021, it was announced that for steps 3–6 of the National League System the season would be curtailed with immediate effect. A number of considerations were taken into account, including the financial implications for clubs, player contracts and the extent of the fixture scheduling issues caused by the national lockdown and various postponements. No further league games were to be played in the 2020–21 season. The following are the league tables as they were on 25 February 2021.

NATIONAL LEAGUE SYSTEM STEP 3

PITCHING IN NORTHERN PREMIER LEAGUE – PREMIER DIVISION

			Home					*Away*					*Total*						
		P	*W*	*D*	*L*	*F*	*A*	*W*	*D*	*L*	*F*	*A*	*W*	*D*	*L*	*F*	*A*	*GD*	*Pts*
1	Mickleover	10	5	0	1	14	6	2	1	1	9	5	7	1	2	23	11	12	22
2	Basford U	9	3	0	1	7	4	3	1	1	8	5	6	1	2	15	9	6	19
3	Buxton	8	3	2	0	15	8	2	0	1	7	3	5	2	1	22	11	11	17
4	Warrington T	9	4	1	0	10	3	1	0	3	6	8	5	1	3	16	11	5	16
5	Witton Alb	7	3	0	1	5	3	2	0	1	8	4	5	0	2	13	7	6	15
6	South Shields	9	2	1	2	5	4	2	2	0	7	4	4	3	2	12	8	4	15
7	Whitby T	9	3	0	0	6	1	1	2	3	9	13	4	2	3	15	14	1	14
8	Matlock T	6	2	1	0	8	3	2	0	1	2	1	4	1	1	10	4	6	13
9	Atherton Collieries	8	2	1	1	7	3	2	0	2	6	5	4	1	3	13	8	5	13
10	Gainsborough Trinity	8	3	0	2	11	7	1	0	2	2	5	4	0	4	13	12	1	12
11	Scarborough Ath	8	1	1	0	3	2	2	1	3	7	9	3	2	3	10	11	−1	11
12	Lancaster C	7	1	1	1	5	5	1	3	0	7	5	2	4	1	12	10	2	10
13	FC United of Manchester	7	2	3	0	7	4	0	1	1	2	3	2	4	1	9	7	2	10
14	Radcliffe	9	2	1	2	8	12	1	0	3	7	11	3	1	5	15	23	−8	10
15	Nantwich T	6	2	0	1	5	5	0	3	0	4	4	2	3	1	9	9	0	9
16	Morpeth T	7	1	1	0	3	2	1	2	2	6	8	2	3	2	9	10	−1	9
17	Hyde U	6	0	3	0	3	3	1	0	2	2	3	1	3	2	5	6	−1	6
18	Stalybridge Celtic	9	1	1	3	4	10	0	2	2	3	7	1	3	5	7	17	−10	6
19	Ashton U	7	0	2	1	3	6	1	0	3	2	7	1	2	4	5	13	−8	5
20	Bamber Bridge	9	1	0	3	3	6	0	1	4	3	11	1	1	7	6	17	−11	4
21	Grantham T	8	0	2	3	4	8	0	1	2	1	6	0	3	5	5	14	−9	3
22	Stafford Rangers	8	0	0	3	0	6	0	1	4	3	9	0	1	7	3	15	−12	1

PITCHING IN SOUTHERN PREMIER LEAGUE – CENTRAL DIVISION

			Home					*Away*					*Total*						
		P	*W*	*D*	*L*	*F*	*A*	*W*	*D*	*L*	*F*	*A*	*W*	*D*	*L*	*F*	*A*	*GD*	*Pts*
1	Coalville T	7	3	1	0	15	4	2	1	0	6	1	5	2	0	21	5	16	17
2	Needham Market	7	4	0	0	13	4	1	2	0	4	3	5	2	0	17	7	10	17
3	Stratford T	8	3	0	1	7	5	2	0	2	10	11	5	0	3	17	16	1	15
4	Rushall Olympic	8	1	2	1	6	7	2	2	0	8	5	3	4	1	14	12	2	13
5	Tamworth	7	3	1	0	10	4	0	2	1	3	4	3	3	1	13	8	5	12
6	Redditch U	8	2	2	0	10	5	1	1	2	4	6	3	3	2	14	11	3	12
7	Stourbridge	8	1	4	0	4	3	1	1	1	6	4	2	5	1	10	7	3	11
8	Royston T	8	1	3	0	6	5	1	2	1	6	6	2	5	1	12	11	1	11
9	Kings Langley	9	2	2	0	8	6	0	3	2	3	5	2	5	2	11	11	0	11
10	Hitchin T	7	1	1	1	7	5	2	0	2	5	9	3	1	3	12	14	−2	10
11	St Ives T	6	3	0	0	5	1	0	1	2	6	12	3	1	2	11	13	−2	10
12	Peterborough Sports	6	1	2	0	5	2	1	1	1	5	3	2	3	1	10	5	5	9
13	AFC Rushden & Diamonds	7	2	1	0	10	3	0	2	2	4	8	2	3	2	14	11	3	9
14	Lowestoft T	7	1	2	1	4	4	1	1	1	4	5	2	3	2	8	9	−1	9
15	Nuneaton Bor	8	1	1	1	8	5	1	1	3	6	8	2	2	4	14	13	1	8
16	Biggleswade T	8	2	0	1	9	6	0	2	3	4	11	2	2	4	13	17	−4	8
17	Alvechurch	9	1	1	3	5	9	1	1	2	7	7	2	2	5	12	16	−4	8
18	Banbury U	7	1	1	1	3	2	1	1	2	6	11	2	2	3	9	13	−4	8
19	Bromsgrove Sporting	8	1	2	1	4	5	1	0	3	5	12	2	2	4	9	17	−8	8
20	Hednesford T	8	2	0	2	10	10	0	1	3	2	6	2	1	5	12	16	−4	7
21	Leiston	8	1	1	2	4	7	0	1	3	7	14	1	2	5	11	21	−10	5
22	Barwell	7	1	0	3	4	11	0	1	2	2	6	1	1	5	6	17	−11	4

PITCHING IN SOUTHERN PREMIER LEAGUE – SOUTH DIVISION

		Home						Away					Total						
		P	*W*	*D*	*L*	*F*	*A*	*W*	*D*	*L*	*F*	*A*	*W*	*D*	*L*	*F*	*A*	*GD*	*Pts*
1	Poole T	7	4	0	0	6	2	2	1	0	10	5	6	1	0	16	7	9	19
2	Tiverton T	7	4	0	0	16	2	2	0	1	5	2	6	0	1	21	4	17	18
3	Salisbury	7	2	2	0	7	5	3	0	0	10	2	5	2	0	17	7	10	17
4	Truro C	8	3	1	0	8	2	2	0	2	9	7	5	1	2	17	9	8	16
5	Metropolitan Police	8	3	1	0	10	4	1	1	2	4	7	4	2	2	14	11	3	14
6	Swindon Supermarine	7	2	0	2	7	6	2	0	1	5	4	4	0	3	12	10	2	12
7	Chesham U	7	0	2	1	0	1	3	1	0	6	3	3	3	1	6	4	2	12
8	Taunton T	6	2	0	1	5	3	1	2	0	3	2	3	2	1	8	5	3	11
9	Hendon	8	2	1	1	7	5	1	1	2	5	5	3	2	3	12	10	2	11
10	Hayes & Yeading U	7	2	2	0	9	5	0	2	1	2	3	2	4	1	11	8	3	10
11	Gosport Bor	7	1	1	1	8	5	1	1	2	3	4	2	2	3	11	9	2	8
12	Walton Casuals	6	1	1	1	5	4	1	0	2	3	9	2	1	3	8	13	–5	7
13	Wimborne T	6	1	0	1	2	2	1	1	2	3	10	2	1	3	5	12	–7	7
14	Hartley Wintney	6	1	1	1	4	4	0	2	1	1	5	1	3	2	5	9	–4	6
15	Weston-super-Mare	6	0	1	1	2	3	1	1	2	6	7	1	2	3	8	10	–2	5
16	Harrow Bor	7	0	1	2	3	5	1	1	2	8	9	1	2	4	11	14	–3	5
17	Yate T	8	1	0	3	6	11	0	2	2	2	6	1	2	5	8	17	–9	5
18	Farnborough	8	1	1	2	5	5	0	0	4	2	11	1	1	6	7	16	–9	4
19	Dorchester T	7	1	1	2	3	9	0	0	3	2	8	1	1	5	5	17	–12	4
20	Beaconsfield T	7	0	1	3	2	8	0	1	2	2	6	0	2	5	4	14	–10	2
21	Merthyr T*	0	0	0	0	0	0	0	0	0	0	0	0	0	0	0	0	0	0

**Merthyr T opted to withdraw for 2020–21 due to the COVID-19 pandemic in Wales.*

PITCHING IN ISMITHIAN LEAGUE – PREMIER DIVISION

		Home						Away					Total						
		P	*W*	*D*	*L*	*F*	*A*	*W*	*D*	*L*	*F*	*A*	*W*	*D*	*L*	*F*	*A*	*GD*	*Pts*
1	Worthing	8	1	0	0	2	1	6	0	1	20	9	7	0	1	22	10	12	21
2	Cheshunt	10	4	0	1	7	6	2	1	2	6	8	6	1	3	13	14	–1	19
3	Enfield T	10	5	0	0	11	4	1	0	4	4	13	6	0	4	15	17	–2	18
4	Carshalton Ath	8	4	0	0	9	1	1	1	2	5	9	5	1	2	14	10	4	16
5	Cray W	7	2	0	1	12	4	3	0	1	9	6	5	0	2	21	10	11	15
6	Kingstonian	9	4	0	1	9	7	1	0	3	6	11	5	0	4	15	18	–3	15
7	Bishop's Stortford	6	3	2	0	10	4	1	0	0	3	1	4	2	0	13	5	8	14
8	Hornchurch	10	3	1	1	12	6	1	1	3	5	6	4	2	4	17	12	5	14
9	Horsham	10	3	0	2	12	6	1	2	2	7	9	4	2	4	19	15	4	14
10	Folkestone Invicta	9	3	0	2	9	7	1	1	2	4	6	4	1	4	13	13	0	13
11	Haringey Bor	8	2	0	2	6	6	2	0	2	7	7	4	0	4	13	13	0	12
12	Leatherhead	9	2	2	0	7	4	1	1	3	1	11	3	3	3	8	15	–7	12
13	Bowers & Pitsea	5	2	1	0	10	2	1	0	1	3	3	3	1	1	13	5	8	10
14	Bognor Regis T*	7	3	0	0	8	1	1	1	2	4	5	4	1	2	12	6	6	10
15	Potters Bar T	9	2	1	2	9	5	1	0	3	4	6	3	1	5	13	11	2	10
16	Wingate & Finchley	8	2	1	2	12	8	1	0	2	6	9	3	1	4	18	17	1	10
17	Corinthian-Casuals	9	2	1	1	5	2	1	0	4	4	11	3	1	5	9	13	–4	10
18	Lewes	8	2	0	2	4	5	0	2	2	4	10	2	2	4	8	15	–7	8
19	Brightlingsea Regent	10	1	1	3	6	8	1	0	4	5	12	2	1	7	11	20	–9	7
20	Margate	9	0	2	2	4	8	1	1	3	2	5	1	3	5	6	13	–7	6
21	East Thurrock U	9	1	1	3	8	12	0	1	3	2	9	1	2	6	10	21	–11	5
22	Merstham	8	1	0	3	5	7	0	1	3	3	11	1	1	6	8	18	–10	4

**Bognor Regis deducted 3 points for fielding an ineligible player v East Thurrock U on 17/10/2020.*

NATIONAL LEAGUE SYSTEM STEP 4

PITCHING IN NORTHERN PREMIER LEAGUE – DIVISION ONE NORTH WEST

		Home						Away					Total						
		P	*W*	*D*	*L*	*F*	*A*	*W*	*D*	*L*	*F*	*A*	*W*	*D*	*L*	*F*	*A*	*GD*	*Pts*
1	Colne	9	4	0	1	15	7	3	1	0	5	2	7	1	1	20	9	11	22
2	Ramsbottom U	8	4	1	0	12	4	2	0	1	7	5	6	1	1	19	9	10	19
3	Workington	9	3	1	0	11	5	2	3	0	8	4	5	4	0	19	9	10	19
4	Clitheroe	9	2	2	0	7	4	3	1	1	8	5	5	3	1	15	9	6	18
5	Dunston UTS	7	2	1	1	6	5	3	0	0	7	3	5	1	1	13	8	5	16
6	Marine	7	2	0	1	7	2	3	0	1	9	3	5	0	2	16	5	11	15
7	Runcorn Linnets	8	1	1	1	5	4	3	2	0	10	7	4	3	1	15	11	4	15
8	Marske U	5	2	1	0	9	2	1	1	0	5	3	3	2	0	14	5	9	11
9	Tadcaster Alb	8	2	0	1	7	3	1	2	2	6	7	3	2	3	13	10	3	11
10	City of Liverpool	9	2	0	2	8	7	1	1	3	11	14	3	1	5	19	21	–2	10
11	Kendal T	12	1	2	3	5	12	1	2	3	6	10	2	4	6	11	22	–11	10
12	Widnes	9	1	1	4	4	11	1	1	1	4	4	2	2	5	8	15	–7	8
13	Mossley	7	2	0	2	8	6	0	1	2	2	5	2	1	4	10	11	–1	7
14	Trafford	7	1	2	0	3	1	0	2	2	5	10	1	4	2	8	11	–3	7
15	Prescot Cables	9	1	1	1	4	3	1	0	5	7	12	2	1	6	11	15	–4	7
16	Pickering T	9	2	1	3	7	8	0	0	3	1	11	2	1	6	8	19	–11	7
17	Brighouse T	8	1	2	3	13	16	0	0	2	0	4	1	2	5	13	20	–7	5
18	Pontefract Collieries	8	0	2	0	2	2	1	0	5	6	20	1	2	5	8	22	–14	5
19	Ossett U	8	1	0	3	3	8	0	1	3	3	7	1	1	6	6	15	–9	4

PITCHING IN NORTHERN PREMIER LEAGUE – DIVISION ONE SOUTH EAST

			Home					*Away*					*Total*						
		P	*W*	*D*	*L*	*F*	*A*	*W*	*D*	*L*	*F*	*A*	*W*	*D*	*L*	*F*	*A*	*GD*	*Pts*
1	Leek T	8	4	0	0	20	4	2	1	1	6	5	6	1	1	26	9	17	19
2	Loughborough Dynamo	8	3	1	0	7	2	3	0	1	9	7	6	1	1	16	9	7	19
3	Newcastle T	8	3	1	0	11	2	2	1	1	6	7	5	2	1	17	9	8	17
4	Kidsgrove Ath	7	3	0	0	6	1	2	1	1	7	6	5	1	1	13	7	6	16
5	Chasetown	9	2	1	2	10	9	3	0	1	8	4	5	1	3	18	13	5	16
6	Worksop T	7	3	0	1	15	7	1	2	0	5	2	4	2	1	20	9	11	14
7	Belper T	9	2	2	1	16	7	2	0	2	9	8	4	2	3	25	15	10	14
8	Stamford	7	3	1	0	15	1	0	3	0	5	5	3	4	0	20	6	14	13
9	Lincoln U	7	2	1	1	11	5	2	0	1	10	6	4	1	2	21	11	10	13
10	Ilkeston T	7	1	1	1	6	6	3	0	1	11	8	4	1	2	17	14	3	13
11	Carlton T	9	1	1	2	7	6	2	1	2	6	8	3	2	4	13	14	–1	11
12	Sutton Coldfield T	8	1	2	1	6	10	2	0	2	7	12	3	2	3	13	22	–9	11
13	Frickley Ath	8	1	0	3	6	9	2	0	2	8	5	3	0	5	14	14	0	9
14	Stocksbridge Park Steels	9	1	0	3	6	9	2	0	3	10	16	3	0	6	16	25	–9	9
15	Cleethorpes T	8	2	0	1	7	4	0	2	3	7	10	2	2	4	14	14	0	8
16	Glossop North End	9	2	2	1	5	4	0	0	4	2	17	2	2	5	7	21	–14	8
17	Spalding U	8	2	0	2	7	5	0	1	3	4	9	2	1	5	11	14	–3	7
18	Sheffield	6	0	0	3	1	7	1	1	1	3	3	1	1	4	4	10	–6	4
19	Wisbech T	8	1	0	3	5	12	0	0	4	0	14	1	0	7	5	26	–21	3
20	Market Drayton T	8	0	0	4	2	13	0	0	4	0	17	0	0	8	2	30	–28	0

PITCHING IN SOUTHERN LEAGUE – DIVISION ONE CENTRAL

			Home					*Away*					*Total*						
		P	*W*	*D*	*L*	*F*	*A*	*W*	*D*	*L*	*F*	*A*	*W*	*D*	*L*	*F*	*A*	*GD*	*Pts*
1	Corby T	7	3	0	1	12	5	2	0	1	3	3	5	0	2	15	8	7	15
2	Bedworth U	8	3	1	0	11	8	1	2	1	5	7	4	3	1	16	15	1	15
3	St Neots T	8	2	1	1	15	5	1	3	0	8	7	3	4	1	23	12	11	13
4	Aylesbury U	7	2	1	0	7	4	2	0	2	9	7	4	1	2	16	11	5	13
5	Bedford T	7	1	2	0	6	3	2	1	1	3	3	3	3	1	9	6	3	12
6	Daventry T	8	3	0	1	9	6	1	0	3	4	9	4	0	4	13	15	–2	12
7	Halesowen T	7	3	1	0	15	2	0	1	2	5	8	3	2	2	20	10	10	11
8	Berkhamsted	6	2	1	1	9	4	1	1	0	4	1	3	2	1	13	5	8	11
9	Barton R	8	2	0	2	6	4	1	2	1	10	9	3	2	3	16	13	3	11
10	AFC Dunstable	7	3	1	0	8	3	0	1	2	2	6	3	2	2	10	9	1	11
11	Welwyn Garden C	6	1	1	0	4	1	2	0	2	6	7	3	1	2	10	8	2	10
12	Kidlington	6	0	2	0	2	2	2	1	1	8	4	2	3	1	10	6	4	9
13	Coleshill T	8	2	0	2	5	5	1	0	3	2	6	3	0	5	7	11	–4	9
14	Wantage T	8	3	0	1	9	6	0	0	4	4	14	3	0	5	13	20	–7	9
15	Yaxley	6	2	1	1	9	4	0	1	1	4	10	2	2	2	13	14	–1	8
16	Thame U	7	2	0	1	7	2	0	1	3	5	8	2	1	4	12	10	2	7
17	Kempston R	8	1	2	1	8	8	0	1	3	3	10	1	3	4	11	18	–7	6
18	Biggleswade	7	2	0	2	6	7	0	0	3	1	9	2	0	5	7	16	–9	6
19	North Leigh	7	1	2	0	3	2	0	1	3	2	15	1	3	3	5	17	–12	6
20	Didcot T	8	2	0	2	6	8	0	0	4	1	14	2	0	6	7	22	–15	6

PITCHING IN SOUTHERN LEAGUE – DIVISION ONE SOUTH

			Home					*Away*					*Total*						
		P	*W*	*D*	*L*	*F*	*A*	*W*	*D*	*L*	*F*	*A*	*W*	*D*	*L*	*F*	*A*	*GD*	*Pts*
1	Cirencester T	9	3	0	1	9	2	5	0	0	17	2	8	0	1	26	4	22	24
2	AFC Totton	9	2	1	1	8	3	4	1	0	14	5	6	2	1	22	8	14	20
3	Basingstoke T	7	2	0	1	7	4	3	1	0	16	9	5	1	1	23	13	10	16
4	Winchester C	7	2	0	1	8	4	3	0	1	6	4	5	0	2	14	8	6	15
5	Slimbridge	9	2	0	2	12	12	2	2	1	10	9	4	2	3	22	21	1	14
6	Paulton R	9	2	0	3	7	11	2	1	1	8	3	4	1	4	15	14	1	13
7	Willand R	8	2	1	1	4	6	2	0	2	10	7	4	1	3	14	13	1	13
8	Highworth T	8	3	1	0	6	3	1	0	3	5	11	4	1	3	11	14	–3	13
9	Frome T	7	1	2	1	9	5	2	0	1	3	2	3	2	2	12	7	5	11
10	Larkhall Ath	7	1	0	2	5	5	2	1	1	6	6	3	1	3	11	11	0	10
11	Bristol Manor Farm	7	1	1	1	5	6	2	0	2	7	8	3	1	3	12	14	–2	10
12	Sholing	5	1	0	1	3	4	2	0	1	6	2	3	0	2	9	6	3	9
13	Evesham U	6	0	1	2	1	5	2	1	0	4	2	2	2	2	5	7	–2	8
14	Cinderford T	7	1	0	3	6	14	1	1	1	4	7	2	1	4	10	21	–11	7
15	Thatcham T	8	1	1	3	6	9	0	2	1	2	4	1	3	4	8	13	–5	6
16	Bideford	6	0	3	1	6	7	0	1	1	1	2	0	4	2	7	9	–2	4
17	Moneyfields	4	0	0	2	1	4	1	0	1	6	3	1	0	3	7	7	0	3
18	Melksham T	6	0	0	3	1	7	1	0	2	4	7	1	0	5	5	14	–9	3
19	Barnstaple T	6	0	1	2	6	13	0	1	2	3	9	0	2	4	9	22	–13	2
20	Mangotsfield U	7	0	0	4	3	9	0	0	3	1	11	0	0	7	4	20	–16	0

PITCHING IN ISTHMIAN LEAGUE – DIVISION ONE NORTH

		Home						Away					Total						
		P	*W*	*D*	*L*	*F*	*A*	*W*	*D*	*L*	*F*	*A*	*W*	*D*	*L*	*F*	*A*	*GD*	*Pts*
1	Tilbury	8	2	1	1	7	5	3	0	1	7	4	5	1	2	14	9	5	16
2	AFC Sudbury	8	2	2	1	10	9	1	1	1	5	5	3	3	2	15	14	1	12
3	Maldon & Tiptree	5	2	1	0	7	2	1	1	0	2	1	3	2	0	9	3	6	11
4	Bury T	4	2	1	0	8	2	1	0	0	1	0	3	1	0	9	2	7	10
5	Heybridge Swifts	8	2	0	2	8	5	1	1	2	2	4	3	1	4	10	9	1	10
6	Histon	6	0	0	2	2	4	3	1	0	8	5	3	1	2	10	9	1	10
7	Soham T Rangers	7	2	1	1	3	2	1	0	2	4	5	3	1	3	7	7	0	10
8	Grays Ath	6	1	1	1	2	5	2	0	1	3	1	3	1	2	5	6	–1	10
9	Aveley	6	2	0	2	7	8	1	0	1	1	1	3	0	3	8	9	–1	9
10	Romford	8	1	0	2	2	3	1	3	1	5	7	2	3	3	7	10	–3	9
11	Coggeshall T	6	2	0	1	3	1	0	2	1	4	5	2	2	2	7	6	1	8
12	Dereham T	7	1	2	0	2	1	1	0	3	5	6	2	2	3	7	7	0	8
13	Felixstowe & Walton U	5	2	1	0	7	4	0	1	1	0	3	2	2	1	7	7	0	8
14	Great Wakering R	7	1	1	2	6	10	1	1	1	5	4	2	2	3	11	14	–3	8
15	Canvey Island	5	0	1	1	0	1	1	2	0	8	4	1	3	1	8	5	3	6
16	Hullbridge Sports	5	0	0	1	1	2	2	0	2	10	7	2	0	3	11	9	2	6
17	Cambridge C	4	1	0	1	2	2	1	0	1	1	1	2	0	2	3	3	0	6
18	Brentwood T	5	0	1	1	1	3	1	2	0	4	3	1	3	1	5	6	–1	6
19	Basildon U	6	0	2	1	5	6	1	0	2	6	3	1	2	3	11	9	2	5
20	Witham T	8	0	0	4	1	12	1	0	3	6	15	1	0	7	7	27	–20	3

PITCHING IN ISTHMIAN LEAGUE – DIVISION ONE SOUTH CENTRAL

		Home						Away					Total						
		P	*W*	*D*	*L*	*F*	*A*	*W*	*D*	*L*	*F*	*A*	*W*	*D*	*L*	*F*	*A*	*GD*	*Pts*
1	Waltham Abbey	8	3	1	1	10	5	2	0	1	3	4	5	1	2	13	9	4	16
2	Staines T	8	3	1	1	11	11	2	0	1	6	6	5	1	2	17	17	0	16
3	Ware	7	2	0	1	10	4	3	0	1	10	6	5	0	2	20	10	10	15
4	Tooting & Mitcham U	7	2	0	2	5	3	3	0	0	7	0	5	0	2	12	3	9	15
5	Bracknell T	5	2	0	0	6	0	2	1	0	8	5	4	1	0	14	5	9	13
6	Chertsey T	7	2	0	2	6	6	2	1	0	8	3	4	1	2	14	9	5	13
7	Hanwell T	8	1	1	2	6	8	3	0	1	9	4	4	1	3	15	12	3	13
8	Ashford T (Middlesex)	8	1	0	2	3	6	3	1	1	5	2	4	1	3	8	8	0	13
9	Hertford T	7	2	0	1	4	3	2	0	2	6	7	4	0	3	10	10	0	12
10	Marlow	7	2	1	0	10	3	1	1	2	6	5	3	2	2	16	8	8	11
11	Westfield	7	1	0	3	6	7	2	1	0	9	4	3	1	3	15	11	4	10
12	Barking	7	2	1	1	7	4	1	0	2	2	5	3	1	3	9	9	0	10
13	Chipstead	8	1	0	3	5	13	2	1	1	7	6	3	1	4	12	19	–7	10
14	Bedfont Sports	6	2	0	1	5	4	1	0	2	5	4	3	0	3	10	8	2	9
15	Chalfont St Peter	8	2	0	2	3	2	1	0	3	3	8	3	0	5	6	10	–4	9
16	FC Romania	7	0	0	2	2	5	2	0	3	6	9	2	0	5	8	14	–6	6
17	Uxbridge	6	0	2	1	3	5	1	0	2	2	6	1	2	3	5	11	–6	5
18	South Park	7	1	1	1	6	8	0	1	3	6	12	1	2	4	12	20	–8	5
19	Northwood	8	1	0	3	3	7	0	1	3	4	12	1	1	6	7	19	–12	4
20	Harlow T	8	1	0	4	5	9	0	0	3	1	8	1	0	7	6	17	–11	3

PITCHING IN ISTHMIAN LEAGUE – DIVISION ONE SOUTH EAST

		P	*W*	*D*	*L*	*F*	*A*	*W*	*D*	*L*	*F*	*A*	*W*	*D*	*L*	*F*	*A*	*GD*	*Pts*
1	Hastings U	7	3	1	0	7	2	2	1	0	6	1	5	2	0	13	3	10	17
2	VCD Ath	8	3	1	0	9	3	2	0	2	9	4	5	1	2	18	7	11	16
3	East Grinstead T	6	1	1	0	6	3	3	1	0	10	3	4	2	0	16	6	10	14
4	Whyteleafe	6	2	1	0	8	2	2	0	1	7	5	4	1	1	15	7	8	13
5	Sevenoaks T	8	2	1	1	7	4	1	3	0	7	6	3	4	1	14	10	4	13
6	Faversham T	6	1	2	0	2	1	2	1	0	6	2	3	3	0	8	3	5	12
7	Whitstable T	9	1	1	2	3	11	2	1	2	9	9	3	2	4	12	20	–8	11
8	Hythe T	6	2	0	1	4	6	1	1	1	10	6	3	1	2	14	12	2	10
9	Ramsgate	6	0	1	2	3	5	2	0	1	7	5	2	1	3	10	10	0	7
10	Herne Bay	6	1	0	2	5	7	1	1	1	4	2	2	1	3	9	9	0	7
11	Ashford U	6	1	0	3	5	8	1	1	0	4	3	2	1	3	9	11	–2	7
12	Cray Valley (PM)	5	1	0	1	3	3	0	3	0	3	3	1	3	1	6	6	0	6
13	Three Bridges	6	1	0	2	8	7	1	0	2	3	8	2	0	4	11	15	–4	6
14	Chichester C	5	1	0	1	4	5	1	0	2	3	6	2	0	3	7	11	–4	6
15	Phoenix Sports	7	0	0	3	1	7	2	0	2	6	9	2	0	5	7	16	–9	6
16	Whitehawk	6	0	2	0	2	2	1	0	3	5	7	1	2	3	7	9	–2	5
17	Haywards Heath T	7	1	1	3	8	15	0	1	1	3	4	1	2	4	11	19	–8	5
18	Sittingbourne	5	1	1	2	7	10	0	0	1	1	2	1	1	3	8	12	–4	4
19	Burgess Hill T	7	1	1	1	3	4	0	0	4	2	10	1	1	5	5	14	–9	4
20	Guernsey*	0	0	0	0	0	0	0	0	0	0	0	0	0	0	0	0	0	0

**Guernsey opted to withdraw for 2020–21 due to COVID-19 travel restrictions.*

THE BUILDBASE FA TROPHY 2019–20

FA TROPHY FINAL 2019–20

Wembley, Monday 3 May 2021 (behind closed doors)

Postponed from last season due to COVID-19 pandemic

Harrogate T (0) 1 *(Falkingham 76)* **Concord Rangers (0) 0**

Harrogate T: Cracknell; Burrell, Smith, Hall, Jones (Fallowfield 62); Thomson, Kerry, Falkingham, McPake (Kiernan 67); Muldoon, Stead (Beck 61).

Concord Rangers: Haigh; Pollock, Roast (Martin Sorondo 83), Sterling, Cawley, Payne; Blanchfield (Wall 79), Blackman, Simper; Reynolds, Charles (Babalola 59).

Referee: Peter Bankes.

THE BUILDBASE FA TROPHY 2020–21

FIRST QUALIFYING ROUND

Tadcaster Alb v Marine 1-3
Ossett U v Ramsbottom U 0-2
Market Drayton T v Bury T 0-1
Cambridge C v Kidsgrove Ath 2-3
Soham T Rangers v Corby T 0-3
Evesham U v Biggleswade 2-1
South Park v Three Bridges 0-1
Waltham Abbey v Staines T 3-2
Hullbridge Sports v Ashford T (Middlesex) 0-1
Hythe T v Chalfont St Peter 3-0
AFC Sudbury v Barking 1-2
Felixstowe & Walton U v Great Wakering R 2-1
Northwood v Basildon U 1-1
Northwood won 4-3 on penalties
AFC Dunstable v Tooting & Mitcham U 1-2
Witham T v Hanwell T 0-2
Melksham T v North Leigh 3-3
North Leigh won 5-4 on penalties
Cirencester T v Paulton R 1-1
Cirencester T won 5-4 on penalties

SECOND QUALIFYING ROUND

Pontefract Collieries v Workington 1-4
Prescot Cables v Frickley Ath (walkover)
Worksop T v Ramsbottom U 4-4
Worksop T won 5-4 on penalties
Pickering T v Trafford 1-0
Kendal T v Brighouse T (walkover)
Marine v Mossley 5-0
Widnes v Colne 3-4
Sheffield v Runcorn Linnets 2-3
Dunston UTS v Clitheroe 0-1
Stocksbridge Park Steels v Marske U 0-4
City of Liverpool (walkover) v Cleethorpes T
Droylsden v Glossop NE (walkover)
Sutton Coldfield T v Dereham T 2-3
Newcastle T v Belper T 2-2
Newcastle T won 5-4 on penalties
Yaxley (walkover) v Chasetown
Corby T v Halesowen T 1-0
Daventry T v Kidsgrove Ath 0-2
Ilkeston T v Kempston R 2-1
Evesham U v Carlton T 2-0
Histon v Leek T 1-2
Loughborough Dynamo v Bury T 1-0
Spalding U v Bedford T 0-1
Wisbech T v Coleshill T 1-2
Stamford v Lincoln U 2-1
Bedworth U v St Neots T 1-4
Hastings U v FC Romania 3-0
Northwood v Heybridge Swifts 3-3
Heybridge Swifts won 5-4 on penalties
Sittingbourne v East Grinstead T 1-0
Felixstowe & Walton U v Westfield 5-0
Phoenix Sports v Marlow 0-2
Ashford T (Middlesex) v Whitstable T 1-0
VCD Ath v Herne Bay 1-2
Faversham T v Hertford T 4-1
Barking v Harlow T 1-0
Tooting & Mitcham U v Romford 2-0
Chertsey T v Berkhamsted 1-2
Whitehawk v Barton R 2-1
Ramsgate (walkover) v Canvey Island
Bedfont Sports v Coggeshall T 0-0
Coggeshall T won 6-5 on penalties
Whyteleafe v Cray Valley (PM) 0-0
Whyteleafe won 3-2 on penalties
Maldon & Tiptree v Grays Ath 4-1
Brentwood T v Chichester C 3-2
Chipstead v Three Bridges 1-2
Uxbridge v Waltham Abbey 2-1
Aylesbury U v Tilbury 2-2
Aylesbury U won 4-2 on penalties
Bracknell T v Sevenoaks T 2-0
Hythe T v Ashford U 2-2
Hythe T won 7-6 on penalties
Burgess Hill T v Ware 2-0
Haywards Heath T v Welwyn Garden C 1-4
Hanwell T v Aveley 1-1
Aveley won 8-7 on penalties
Thame U v Cirencester T 4-1
Thatcham T v North Leigh 2-4
AFC Totton v Frome T 2-2
Frome T won 6-5 on penalties
Sholing v Wantage T 0-2
Bideford v Slimbridge 3-2
Moneyfields v Basingstoke T 2-1
Highworth T v Winchester C 2-1
Larkhall Ath v Barnstaple T 5-0
Kidlington v Didcot T 2-1
Willand R v Bristol Manor Farm 2-1
Mangotsfield U v Cinderford T 1-2

THIRD QUALIFYING ROUND

FC United of Manchester v Marske U 2-3
Atherton Colleries v City of Liverpool 0-3
Hyde U v Frickley Ath 2-1
Warrington T v Lancaster C 1-1
Warrington T won 4-3 on penalties
Brighouse T v Buxton 0-2
Ashton U v Clitheroe 1-0
Radcliffe v Bamber Bridge 1-2
Scarborough Ath v Witton Alb (walkover)
Pickering T v Runcorn Linnets 1-4
Marine v Stalybridge Celtic 3-2
Glossop NE v Workington 0-1
South Shields v Colne 1-0
Morpeth T v Whitby T 3-1
Newcastle T v Nuneaton Bor 0-2
Evesham U v Leek T 3-2
Redditch U v Nantwich T 2-3
Tamworth v Banbury U 2-1
Bromsgrove Sporting v Coleshill T 0-1
AFC Rushden & Diamonds (walkover) v Ilkeston T
Yaxley v Grantham T 0-2
Loughborough Dynamo v Bedford T 1-3

Rushall Olympic v Barwell 4-1
Mickleover v Dereham T 5-0
Coalville T v Matlock T 3-3
Matlock T won 4-2 on penalties
Peterborough Sports v Gainsborough Trinity 4-2
Stourbridge v Stamford 0-3
Basford U v Alvechurch 2-1
Corby T v Hednesford T 1-2
St Neots T v Worksop T 6-1
St Ives T v Stafford Rangers 1-1
St Ives T won 4-1 on penalties
Stratford T v Kidsgrove Ath 1-3
Maldon & Tiptree v Kingstonian 3-2
Hastings U v Ashford T (Middlesex) 1-1
Hastings U won 4-2 on penalties
Leiston v Worthing 4-4
Leiston won 4-2 on penalties
Burgess Hill T v Harrow Bor 4-1
Marlow v Berkhamsted 2-1
Needham Market v Three Bridges 4-1
Bowers & Pitsea v Hornchurch 1-3
Royston T v Hythe T 2-0
East Thurrock U v Cheshunt 3-4
Faversham T v Haringey Bor 1-2
Walton Casuals v Folkestone Invicta 2-1
Merstham v Carshalton Ath 1-3
Coggeshall T v Wingate & Finchley 1-1
Wingate & Finchley won 3-0 on penalties
Kings Langley v Brightlingsea Regent 4-1
Lowestoft T v Lewes 3-1
Biggleswade T v Heybridge Swifts 1-0
Aveley v Beaconsfield T 3-0
Uxbridge v Hayes & Yeading U 2-1
Enfield T v Ramsgate 8-1
Barking v Sittingbourne 1-1
Barking won 4-3 on penalties
Bishop's Stortford v Brentwood T 3-2
Hitchin T v Herne Bay 3-1
Bognor Regis T v Tooting & Mitcham U 2-0
Whitehawk v Cray W 0-3
Aylesbury U v Margate 2-4
Leatherhead v Potters Bar T 3-1
Chesham U v Whyteleafe 2-2
Chesham U won 3-2 on penalties
Horsham v Welwyn Garden C 1-1
Welwyn Garden C won 5-3 on penalties
Felixstowe & Walton U v Metropolitan Police 3-1
Corinthian Casuals v Hendon 5-4
Frome T v Farnborough 3-0
Taunton T v Truro C 2-4
Bracknell T (walkover) v Cinderford T
Dorchester T v Gosport Bor 2-1
Moneyfields v Kidlington 3-2
Thame U (walkover) v Wimborne T
Salisbury v Tiverton T 6-0
Wantage T v North Leigh 1-4
Hartley Wintney v Poole T 1-4
Weston-super-Mare v Larkhall Ath 2-1
Highworth T v Swindon Supermarine 2-3
Yate T v Bideford (walkover)
Willand R awarded a bye due to withdrawal of Merthyr T

FIRST ROUND

Ashton U v South Shields 2-1
Runcorn Linnets v Morpeth T 2-2
Morpeth T won 3-2 on penalties
Witton Alb v Bamber Bridge 2-0
Marske U v Warrington T 3-1
Nantwich T v Workington 3-1
Marine v Hyde U 1-0
Buxton v City of Liverpool 1-2
Royston T v Tamworth 3-1
Grantham T v St Ives T 3-4
Coleshill T v Matlock T 5-2
St Neots T v Kings Langley 3-1
Hitchin T v Mickleover 3-0
Marlow v Nuneaton Bor 1-4
Biggleswade T v Bedford T 0-0
Bedford T won 5-3 on penalties

AFC Rushden & Diamonds v Peterborough Sports 1-5
Kidsgrove Ath v Stamford 0-2
Basford U v Rushall Olympic 5-0
Welwyn Garden C v Hednesford T 3-1
Aveley v Hastings U 1-0
Carshalton Ath v Barking 3-0
Lowestoft T v Cheshunt 0-3
Haringey Bor v Bishop's Stortford 2-1
Needham Market v Leiston 2-1
Margate v Burgess Hill T (walkover)
Corinthian Casuals (walkover) v Walton Casuals
Hornchurch v Wingate & Finchley 4-1
Uxbridge v Cray W 1-3
Leatherhead v Felixstowe & Walton U 0-1
Enfield T v Maldon & Tiptree 2-2
Maldon & Tiptree won 4-3 on penalties
Salisbury v Bracknell T 0-1
North Leigh v Frome T 0-1
Moneyfields v Truro C 1-5
Thame U v Bognor Regis T 2-5
Evesham U v Bideford 1-1
Evesham U won 5-4 on penalties
Swindon Supermarine v Dorchester T 3-2
Poole T v Willand R 3-1
Weston-super-Mare v Chesham U 1-3

SECOND ROUND

Spennymoor T v Marske U 6-2
Witton Alb v Nantwich T 2-5
Chester v Bradford (Park Avenue) 3-1
Guiseley v Chorley 2-0
Gateshead v Farsley Celtic 2-3
Ashton U v York C 3-3
Ashton U won 4-2 on penalties
Curzon Ashton v AFC Fylde 1-4
Darlington v City of Liverpool 2-0
Marine v Southport 0-1
Blyth Spartans v Morpeth T (walkover)
Stamford v Kidderminster H 1-0
Brackley T v Royston T 3-2
Evesham U v Boston U 0-3
Coleshill T v AFC Telford U 1-10
Leamington v St Ives T 5-0
Alfreton T (walkover) v Bedford T
Hereford v St Neots T 3-0
Kettering T v Nuneaton Bor 5-1
Hitchin T v Peterborough Sports 0-4
Basford U v Felixstowe & Walton U 3-0
Gloucester C v Needham Market 4-2
Slough T v Dartford 2-2
Dartford won 6-5 on penalties
Dulwich Hamlet v Cheshunt 3-1
Welling U v Oxford C 0-2
Bracknell T v Havant & Waterlooville 2-3
Billericay T v Braintree T 1-1
Braintree T won 4-2 on penalties
Dorking W v Hungerford T 2-0
Maidstone U v Poole T 2-0
Concord Rangers v Truro C 1-2
Aveley v Chesham U 1-3
Corinthian Casuals v Hemel Hempstead T 0-0
Hemel Hempstead T won 4-2 on penalties
Ebbsfleet U v Chippenham T 1-1
Ebbsfleet U won 4-2 on penalties
Bath C v Chelmsford C 3-2
Maldon & Tiptree v Bognor Regis T 2-1
St Albans C v Cray W 3-0
Welwyn Garden C v Burgess Hill T 2-1
Tonbridge Angels v Hornchurch 0-1
Haringey Bor v Eastbourne Bor 3-1
Swindon Supermarine v Carshalton Ath 0-0
Swindon Supermarine won 5-4 on penalties
Frome T (walkover) v Hampton & Richmond Bor

THIRD ROUND

Darlington v AFC Telford U 2-2
Darlington won 5-3 on penalties
Peterborough Sports v Basford U 3-2
FC Halifax T v Hartlepool U 3-3

FC Halifax T won 4-2 on penalties

Alfreton T v King's Lynn T	1-3
Solihull Moors v Farsley Celtic	4-0
Wrexham v Leamington	0-0
Leamington won 6-5 on penalties	
Altrincham v Chester	2-1
Stockport Co v Guiseley	3-1
Ashton U v Kettering T	1-2
Spennymoor T v Southport	2-2
Southport won 5-4 on penalties	
Morpeth T v Notts Co	0-3
Nantwich T v Hereford	0-1
Chesterfield v Brackley T	0-0
Chesterfield won 4-3 on penalties	
Boston U v AFC Fylde	1-1
Boston U won 4-2 on penalties	
Dorking W v Barnet	3-1
Weymouth v Maidenhead U	3-2
Oxford C (walkover) v Truro C	
Chesham U v Torquay U	0-1
Dagenham & R v Ebbsfleet U	5-2
St Albans C v Sutton U	0-2
Dulwich Hamlet v Hornchurch	1-2
Welwyn Garden C v Aldershot T	1-5
Havant & Waterlooville v Braintree T	1-0
Bath C v Swindon Supermarine	4-0
Dartford v Haringey Bor	0-1
Bromley v Hemel Hempstead T	2-0
Boreham Wood (walkover) v Yeovil T	
Woking v Dover Ath	2-1
Maldon & Tiptree v Gloucester C	1-7
Maidstone U (walkover) v Frome T	
Wealdstone v Eastleigh	4-3
Stamford awarded a bye due to withdrawal of Macclesfield T	

FOURTH ROUND

Kettering T v Leamington	0-3
FC Halifax T v Southport	1-2
Aldershot T v Solihull Moors	3-2
Weymouth v Darlington	0-1
Sutton U v Dagenham & R	3-1
Stockport Co v Notts Co	1-2
Maidstone U v Dorking W	2-1
Wealdstone v Gloucester C	3-1
Boreham Wood v Torquay U	0-4
Havant & Waterlooville (walkover) v Altrincham	
Boston U v Chesterfield	1-1
Chesterfield won 4-1 on penalties	
Stamford v Hereford	0-2
Bath C v Peterborough Sports	0-1
Hornchurch v King's Lynn T	1-1
Hornchurch won 3-0 on penalties	
Bromley v Woking	1-1
Woking won 7-6 on penalties	
Oxford C v Haringey Bor	4-2

FIFTH ROUND

Sutton U v Woking	0-1
Aldershot T (walkover) v Chesterfield	
Darlington v Wealdstone	4-1
Hereford v Leamington	1-0
Havant & Waterlooville v Notts Co	2-2
Notts Co won 4-2 on penalties	
Southport v Torquay U	0-2
Oxford C v Peterborough Sports	2-0
Hornchurch v Maidstone U	5-4

QUARTER-FINALS

Notts Co v Oxford C	3-1
Darlington v Hornchurch	1-2
Aldershot T v Hereford	1-1
Hereford won 5-3 on penalties	
Woking v Torquay U	1-0

SEMI-FINALS

Notts Co v Hornchurch	3-3
Hornchurch won 5-4 on penalties	
Hereford v Woking	1-0

FA TROPHY FINAL 2020–21

Wembley, Saturday 22 May 2021 (behind closed doors)

Hereford (1) 1 *(Owen-Evans 13)* **Hornchurch (0) 3** *(Ruff 75, Nash 86, Brown 90))*

Hereford: Hall; Butroid, Camwell (McQuilkin 74), Hodgkiss, Grimes, Butlin, Owen-Evans, Finn (Kouhyar 88), Haines, Bakare (Klukowski 90), Lloyd.

Hornchurch: Wright; Hayles, Sutton, Muldoon, Parcell, Brown, Clark, Spence (Ruff 59), Christou, Higgins (Dickson 60), Nash (Stimson 90).

Referee: Tony Harrington.

THE FA SUNDAY CUP 2019–20

FA SUNDAY CUP FINAL 2019-20

St George's Park, Sunday 16 May 2021

Postponed from last season due to COVID-19 pandemic

Campfield (0) 1 *(Nevitt 93)* **St Josephs (Luton) (0) 0**

Campfield: Jones; Burns, Murphy, Hoy, Stanley, Hajdari, Nevitt, Barrow, Barrigan, McEllin, Parker.

Substitutes: Welsh, Cox, Matthew Williams, Anderson, Michael Williams, Jones, Hilditch.

St Josephs (Luton): Forster; Silford, Briggs, McManus, Longden, Bishop, Fitzpatrick, Vincent, Clayton, McCafferty, Neufville.

Substitutes: Langlias, Head, Watkins, Burnett, McGovern, Hall, Maltay.

aet.

Referee: Thomas Bramall.

THE BUILDBASE FA VASE 2019–20

FA VASE FINAL 2019–20

Wembley, Monday 3 May 2021 (behind closed doors)

Postponed from last season due to COVID-19 pandemic

Hebburn T (2) 3 *(Amar Purewal 19, Richardson 44, Martin 83)* **Consett (2) 2** *(Alshabeeb 18, Pearson 41)*

Hebburn T: Foden; Groves, Storey, Carson, Lough, Potter, McKeown, Spence, Richardson, Armstrong, Amar Purewal (Martin 78).

Consett: Hayes; Metz, Arjun Purewal, Wilkinson, Holden (Lawson 87), Alshabeeb, Slocombe, Smith, Orrell (Allen 29), Cornish (Carr 61), Pearson.

Referee: Michael Salisbury.

THE BUILDBASE FA VASE 2020–21

**After extra time.*

FIRST QUALIFYING ROUND

Bishop Auckland v Billingham Synthonia 1-5
Durham C v Thackley 0-4
Bedlington Terriers v Heaton Stannington 1-2
Crook T v Albion Sports 1-0
Garforth T v Sunderland West End 5-1
Willington v Whickham 0-4
North Shields v Tow Law T 3-0
Northallerton T v Billingham T 2-0
West Allotment Celtic v Penrith 3-3
Penrith won 7-6 on penalties
Ryton & Crawcrook Alb v Ashington 2-4
Holker Old Boys v Eccleshill U 3-0
Shildon v Chester-le-Street T 2-1
Whitley Bay v Newcastle University 1-4
Guisborough T v Washington 3-0
Newton Aycliffe v Barnoldswick T 4-0
Birtley T v Squires Gate 1-1
Birtley T won 4-1 on penalties
Harrogate Railway Ath v Cleator Moor 1-1
Harrogate Railway Ath won 9-8 on penalties
Steeton v Jarrow 2-2
Jarrow won 9-8 on penalties
Carlisle C v Nelson 3-5
AFC Blackpool v Knaresborough T 1-0
Silsden v Garstang 3-1
Retford v Cammell Laird 1907 0-2
Staveley MW v AFC Darwen 0-0
AFC Darwen won 6-5 on penalties
Skelmersdale U v Stockport T 1-2
Hemsworth MW v Armthorpe Welfare 3-2
West Didsbury & Chorlton v Bury 2-1
Hall Road Rangers v Barnton 2-4
Litherland Remyca v Selby T 1-2
Penistone Church v Prestwich Heys 2-2
Penistone Church won 5-4 on penalties
Goole v Cheadle Heath Nomads 7-3
Parkgate v Worsbrough Bridge Ath 4-0
Charnock Richard v Barton T 3-0
Rossington Main v Nostell MW 0-2
Brigg T v Winterton Rangers 2-3
Emley v Irlam 1-1
Irlam won 5-3 on penalties
St Helens T v North Ferriby 0-2
Liversedge v Handsworth 3-1
Swallownest v Ashton T 1-0
Daisy Hill v Warrington Rylands 2-5
Cheadle T v Athersley Recreation 1-1
Cheadle T won 4-3 on penalties
Golcar U v Northwich Vic 0-2
Pilkington v Bacup Bor 1-3
Avro v Bottesford T 1-0
FC Isle of Man v AFC Liverpool (walkover)
Burscough v Hallam 1-1
Hallam won 4-3 on penalties
Whitchurch Alport v Littleton 0-2
Hinckley v Studley 0-2
Boldmere St Michaels v Brocton 4-0
Highgate U v Wellington 3-3
Highgate U won 8-7 on penalties
Darlaston T (1874) v Heather St Johns 2-0
Dudley Sports v Wem T 3-0
Wolverhampton SC v Bewdley T 0-1
Heath Hayes v Dudley T 1-2
Nuneaton Griff v Chelmsley T 2-2
Chelmsley T won 4-1 on penalties
Romulus v Coventry Copsewood 3-1
Paget Rangers v Wolverhampton Casuals 3-1
Winsford U v Alsager T 4-1
Sandbach U v Stapenhill 0-1
Leicester Road v Haughmond 0-0
Leicester Road won 3-0 on penalties
St Martins v Pershore T 1-4
Coventry Sphinx v Worcester Raiders 1-1
Coventry Sphinx won 3-1 on penalties
Ellesmere Rangers v Cradley T 3-1
Racing Club Warwick v Hereford Pegasus 2-1
AFC Wulfrunians v Uttoxeter T 0-3
AFC Bridgnorth v Wednesfield 3-3
AFC Bridgnorth won 5-4 on penalties
Abbey Hulton U v Shawbury U 3-2
Rugby T v Bilston T 1-1
Rugby T won 4-1 on penalties
Stafford T v Lichfield C 0-4
OJM Black Country v Rocester 0-1
Sherwood Colliery v St Andrews 3-0
Harborough T v Barrow T 8-1
Hucknall T v Anstey Nomads 1-2
Selston v Eastwood Community 3-3
Selston won 4-3 on penalties
Holbeach U v Loughborough University 1-5
Graham St Prims v Leicester Nirvana 0-3
Teversal v Shirebrook T 0-3
Dunkirk v Harrowby U 1-2
Deeping Rangers v GNG Oadby T 10-1
Aylestone Park v Pinchbeck U 4-1
Boston T v Sleaford T 6-0
Ingles v Saffron Dynamo 2-0
Blackstones v Lutterworth Ath 0-3
Clipstone v Radford 2-2
Radford won 3-2 on penalties
Birstall U v Holwell Sports 2-0
Clifton All Whites v Quorn 0-2
Peterborough Northern Star v Mulbarton W 0-7
Sheringham v Newmarket T 2-0
Huntingdon T v Mildenhall T 0-2
Diss T v Fakenham T 0-1
Lakenheath v Framlingham T 7-1
Godmanchester R v Norwich U 0-0
Norwich U won 4-2 on penalties
Downham T v Ely C 3-0
Barkingside v Coggeshall U 1-3
Colney Heath v Wivenhoe T 0-0
Colney Heath won 4-2 on penalties
Brimsdown v Clapton 2-4
Little Oakley v Stotfold 2-1
Hackney Wick v Halstead T 0-1
Enfield Bor v Tower Hamlets 3-2
West Essex v Haverhill Bor 8-1
St Margaretsbury v London Colney 1-1
London Colney won 6-5 on penalties
Ipswich W v Brantham Ath 5-3
Potton U v Biggleswade U 2-1

Redbridge v May & Baker Eastbrook Community 1-3
Ilford v Long Melford 5-3
Southend Manor v Cockfosters 0-1
Sporting Bengal U v Sawbridgeworth T 3-3
Sporting Bengal U won 4-2 on penalties
Holland v Enfield 2-0
Saffron Walden T v Whitton U 3-3
Whitton U won 4-1 on penalties
Harwich & Parkeston v Walthamstow 1-1
Walthamstow won 5-4 on penalties
Frenford v Newbury Forest 2-4
Hashtag U v Takeley 3-1
Hoddesdon T v Langford 3-2
Hadley v Hadleigh U 2-0
Athletic Newham v Wormley R 0-1
Northampton Sileby Rangers v Bedfont & Feltham 4-3
Leverstock Green v AFC Hayes 0-3
Buckingham Ath v Holmer Green 0-2
Ardley U v Easington Sports 0-2
Amersham T v Cogenhoe U 1-4
London Tigers v Northampton ON Chenecks 0-5
Egham T v Raunds T 0-2
Winslow U v Risborough Rangers 0-3
Ampthill T v Dunstable T 4-1
Holyport v FC Deportivo Galicia 0-1
British Airways HEW v CB Hounslow U 1-1
CB Hounslow U won 6-5 on penalties
North Greenford U v Chalvey Sports 5-1
Rushden & Higham U v Flackwell Heath 0-4
Harefield U v Tring Ath 1-1
Tring Ath won 6-5 on penalties
Spelthorne Sports v Arlesey T 2-4
Thame Rangers v Milton Keynes Irish 0-6
Penn & Tylers Green v Burnham 1-0
Broadfields U v Aylesbury Vale Dynamos 0-0
Broadfields U won 5-4 on penalties
Rayners Lane v Hanworth Villa 2-4
Wembley v Wellingborough Whitworths 1-2
Edgware T v Irchester U 3-1
Windsor v Long Buckby 0-3
Longlevens v Tytherington Rocks 3-3
Longlevens won 4-3 on penalties
Tadley Calleva v Wallingford T 4-1
Wokingham & Emmbrook v Cheltenham Saracens 3-0
Abingdon T v Thornbury T 0-3
Cove v Frimley Green 2-2
Frimley Green won 7-6 on penalties
Fleet T v Newent T 3-1
Clanfield 85 v Tuffley R 2-0
Eversley & California v Long Crendon 1-3
Chipping Sodbury T v Bishop's Cleeve 0-1
Shrivenham v Camberley T 1-0
Abingdon U v Shortwood U 0-0
Abingdon U won 4-3 on penalties
Fairford T v Lydney T 0-1
Virginia Water v Reading C 0-1
Walton & Hersham v Meridian 3-1
Seaford T (walkover) v Southwick
Fisher v Little Common 4-0
Colliers Wood U v Mile Oak 7-1
Raynes Park Vale v Rushtall 3-2
Forest Hill Park v Lingfield 2-3
Holmesdale v Kent Football U 4-2
Crowborough Ath v Molesey 1-1
Molesey won 4-2 on penalties
Worthing U v Greenways 5-4
Lydd T v Broadbridge Heath 1-1
Lydd T won 3-2 on penalties
Redhill v Snodland T 2-2
Redhill won 3-1 on penalties
Horley T v Hollands & Blair 4-2
Oakwood v East Preston 0-2
Lewisham Bor (Community) v Balham 0-2
Hailsham T v AFC Varndeanians 0-3
Croydon v Sheppey U 1-2
Alfold v Chessington & Hook U 4-0
Sheerwater v Sporting Club Thamesmead 2-1
K Sports v Tunbridge Wells 2-1
Stansfeld v Knaphill 2-2
Stansfeld won 8-7 on penalties
Hassocks v Peacehaven & Telscombe 0-3
Godalming T v Shoreham 3-3
Shoreham won 5-4 on penalties

Epsom & Ewell v Bridon Ropes 2-1
Westside v Abbey Rangers 1-3
Banstead Ath v Guildford C 2-2
Guildford C won 4-2 on penalties
Greenwich Bor v Cobham (walkover)
Wick v AFC Croydon Ath 2-1
Steyning T v Bagshot 3-1
Storrington Community v Bexhill U 2-1
Langney W v Eastbourne U 4-2
Beckenham T v Littlehampton T 1-2
Punjab U v Bearsted 1-1
Punjab U won 5-3 on penalties
Kennington v Erith T 1-0
Billingshurst v FC Elmstead 2-2
Billingshurst won 7-6 on penalties
Erith & Belvedere v Loxwood 1-0
Horsham YMCA v Arundel 4-0
Blackfield & Langley v Folland Sports 1-0
Amesbury T v Lymington T 0-3
Cowes Sports v Devizes T 2-2
Cowes Sports won 5-4 on penalties
Farnham T v Downton 4-2
AFC Portchester v Bemerton Heath Harlequins 3-2
East Cowes Vic Ath v Westbury U 1-2
Hythe & Dibden v Verwood T 0-2
Newport (IW) v Calne T 2-2
Newport (IW) won 5-3 on penalties
Portland U v Hamble Club 0-4
Alresford T v AFC Stoneham 1-1
AFC Stoneham won 4-3 on penalties
New Milton T v Andover New Street 0-0
New Milton T won 6-5 on penalties
Shaftesbury v Badshot Lea 0-4
Fawley v Ringwood T 3-4
Baffins Milton R v Bashley 2-2
Bashley won 4-3 on penalties
Corsham T v Brockenhurst 1-1
Brockenhurst won 6-5 on penalties
Romsey T v Selsey 4-0
Sidmouth T v Cheddar 4-5
Elburton Villa v Saltash U 1-1
Elburton Villa won 10-9 on penalties
Ilfracombe T v Portishead T 3-3
Ilfracombe T won 5-3 on penalties
Odd Down v Brislington 2-2
Brislington won 3-2 on penalties
Exmouth T v Mousehole 0-0
Exmouth T won 5-3 on penalties
Torpoint Ath v Porthleven 3-2
Launceston v Axminster T 0-4
Wellington v Hengrove Ath 2-2
Hengrove Ath won 5-4 on penalties
Newquay v Street 3-6
Bridport v AFC St Austell 4-3
St Blazey v Bishops Lydeard 4-2
Radstock T v Longwell Green Sports 1-1
Longwell Green Sports won 5-3 on penalties
Bodmin T v Keynsham T 2-3
Callington T v Ivybridge T 0-3
Welton R v Cullompton Rangers 4-1
Shepton Mallet v Bishop Sutton 3-1
Wells C v Godolphin Atlantic 6-0
Brixham v Newton Abbot Spurs 2-4
Camelford v Almondsbury 5-1
Liskeard Ath v Millbrook 0-3

SECOND QUALIFYING ROUND

Esh Winning v AFC Blackpool 1-2
Newcastle University v Thornaby 4-1
Holker Old Boys v Crook T 2-1
Silsden v Guisborough T 3-5
Thackley v Harrogate Railway Ath 0-1
Redcar Ath v Whickham 2-1
Heaton Stannington v Padiham 1-2
North Shields v Northallerton T 3-2
Nelson v Ashington 1-4
Newton Aycliffe v Billingham Synthonia 2-0
Brandon U v Penrith 1-2
Jarrow v Birtley T 3-2
Sunderland RCA v Shildon 2-3
Campion v Sunderland Ryhope CW 0-4
Garforth T v Seaham Red Star 1-1
Seaham Red Star won 6-5 on penalties

Avro v Abbey Hey	0-3
Warrington Rylands v Goole	6-0
Penistone Church v Wythenshawe Amateurs	2-1
North Ferriby v Northwich Vic	3-2
Hallam v Parkgate	3-1
Hemsworth MW v Nostell MW	3-0
Barnton v Swallownest	4-0
West Didsbury & Chorlton v Charnock Richard	0-2
Bacup Bor v Stockport T	1-1
Bacup Bor won 4-3 on penalties	
Cheadle T v Dronfield T	4-0
Glasshoughton Welfare v Irlam	1-3
1874 Northwich v Selby T	3-0
Cammell Laird 1907 v Maltby Main	0-3
AFC Liverpool v Maine Road	3-2
Bootle (walkover) v Shelley	
Liversedge v Ashton Ath	3-1
New Mills v Winterton Rangers	2-1
AFC Darwen v Runcorn T	0-2
Chelmsley T v Paget Rangers	0-1
Romulus v Leicester Road	0-0
Romulus won 7-6 on penalties	
Pershore T v AFC Bridgnorth	0-1
Highgate U v Racing Club Warwick	1-5
Rugby T v Ellesmere Rangers	6-1
Winsford U v Boldmere St Michaels	1-1
Boldmere St Michaels won 14-13 on penalties	
Uttoxeter T v Stourport Swifts	1-3
Rocester v Bewdley T	1-3
Dudley Sports v Littleton	2-1
Studley v Darlaston T (1874)	3-1
Coventry Sphinx v Shifnal T	2-0
Eccleshall v Hanley T	0-7
Dudley T v Stone Old Alleynians	0-2
GNP Sports v Gresley R	1-2
Tividale v Stapenhill	0-2
Cadbury Ath v Lichfield C	1-0
Abbey Hulton U v Ashby Ivanhoe	3-1
Anstey Nomads v Boston T	3-1
Rainworth MW v Gedling MW	3-3
Rainworth MW won 4-3 on penalties	
West Bridgford v Harrowby U	2-2
Harrowby U won 4-2 on penalties	
Sherwood Colliery v Aylestone Park	1-3
Melton T v Birstall U	8-1
Long Eaton U v Selston	4-1
Quorn v Kirby Muxloe	5-2
Radford v Ollerton T	3-3
Radford won 4-3 on penalties	
Harborough T v Leicester Nirvana	3-5
Belper U v Kimberley MW	2-1
Lutterworth Ath v Deeping Rangers	0-3
Bourne T v Loughborough University	0-4
Shirebrook T v Ingles	1-1
Shirebrook T won 5-4 on penalties	
Borrowash Vic v Skegness T	0-3
Swaffham T v Fakenham T	2-2
Fakenham T won 4-3 on penalties	
Lakenheath v Mildenhall T	1-3
Whittlesey Ath v Debenham LC	2-0
Thetford T v Norwich U	1-2
Gorleston v Downham T	3-2
Great Yarmouth T v Mulbarton W	1-3
Sheringham v Walsham Le Willows	0-1
March T U v Norwich CBS	2-2
Norwich CBS won 6-5 on penalties	
Ipswich W v London Colney	1-0
Coggeshall U v Sporting Bengal U	3-2
Potton U v Clapton	1-3
Hashtag U v Wormley R	5-0
Park View v Cockfosters	2-2
Cockfosters won 4-2 on penalties	
West Essex v Haverhill R	3-4
Whitton U v White Ensign	1-2
Hadley v Enfield Bor	1-1
Hadley won 8-7 on penalties	
Hoddesdon T v Woodford T	2-1
Baldock T v Halstead T	3-2
New Salamis v Cornard U	3-0
Holland v Colney Heath	0-0
Colney Heath won 4-3 on penalties	
May & Baker Eastbrook Community v Little Oakley	2-2
May & Baker Eastbrook Community won 6-5 on penalties	
Newbury Forest v Burnham Ramblers	2-2
Newbury Forest won 4-3 on penalties	
Ilford v Benfleet	1-1
Ilford won 4-3 on penalties	
Walthamstow v London Lions	3-1
Crawley Green v Wellingborough Whitworths	6-4
Flackwell Heath v Desborough T	3-0
CB Hounslow U v Easington Sports	2-2
CB Hounslow U won 4-2 on penalties	
Edgware T v Tring Ath	4-1
AFC Hayes v Penn & Tylers Green	2-0
Burton Park W v Northampton ON Chenecks	2-2
Burton Park W won 6-5 on penalties	
Holmer Green v Bugbrooke St Michaels	1-4
Raunds T v Risborough Rangers	1-4
Hanworth Villa v FC Deportivo Galicia	4-0
Arlesey T v Northampton Sileby Rangers	2-3
Long Buckby v Ampthill T	2-3
Broadfields U v Milton Keynes Irish	1-2
Oxhey Jets v North Greenford U	1-3
Rothwell Corinthians v St Panteleimon	3-0
Cogenhoe U v Harpenden T	2-1
Brimscombe & Thrupp v AFC Aldermaston	5-0
Sandhurst T v Long Crendon	3-1
Stonehouse T v Royal Wootton Bassett T	0-1
Longlevens v Wokingham & Emmbrook	2-0
Bishop's Cleeve v Malmesbury Vic	1-0
Milton U v Lydney T	3-1
Clanfield 85 v Fleet Spurs	3-2
Tadley Calleva v Frimley Green	1-2
Thornbury T v Abingdon U	1-4
Woodley U v Reading C	2-3
Fleet T v Shrivenham	3-1
Rochester U v Sutton Ath	0-4
Worthing U v Canterbury C	4-3
Steyning T v Lingfield	3-1
Holmesdale v AFC Varndeanians	2-0
Tooting Bec v Lydd T	2-2
Tooting Bec won 4-3 on penalties	
Sheerwater v Horsham YMCA	2-1
Wick v Saltdean U	0-2
Erith & Belvedere v Colliers Wood U	3-0
Seaford T v Storrington Community	2-2
Seaford T won 6-5 on penalties	
Kennington v Shoreham	7-0
East Preston v Fisher	0-2
Alfold v Stansfeld	2-4
Littlehampton T v Lordswood	3-1
Walton & Hersham v K Sports	1-0
Peacehaven & Telscombe v Balham	2-2
Peacehaven & Telscombe won 4-3 on penalties	
Abbey Rangers v Guildford C	1-1
Guildford C won 4-3 on penalties	
Punjab U v Horley T	2-3
Billingshurst v Jersey Bulls	0-3
Epsom & Ewell v Langney W	1-1
Epsom & Ewell won 3-2 on penalties	
Redhill v Raynes Park Vale	0-1
Crawley Down Gatwick v Cobham	1-1
Cobham won 5-3 on penalties	
Sheppey U v Molesey	6-0
New Milton T v Totton & Eling	4-0
Fareham T v Badshot Lea	3-3
Fareham T won 3-0 on penalties	
Farnham T v Petersfield T	0-0
Petersfield T won 6-5 on penalties	
Romsey T v Ringwood T	1-5
Bournemouth v Blackfield & Langley	2-2
Bournemouth won 5-4 on penalties	
Cowes Sports v Pagham	1-4
Horndean v Westbury U	0-1
Whitchurch U v Verwood T	2-1
Newport (IW) v Alton	1-0
Lymington T v Hamble Club	2-0
Ash U v Bashley	2-6
Brockenhurst v AFC Stoneham	3-2
United Services Portsmouth v AFC Portchester	2-1
Street v Hengrove Ath	2-0
Cheddar v Ivybridge T	3-2
Bridport v Ilfracombe T	1-3
Camelford v Wadebridge T	0-0
Camelford won 6-5 on penalties	

Oldland Abbotonians v Keynsham T 0-5
Axminster T v Clevedon T 0-2
Shepton Mallet v Torrington 5-1
Helston Ath v Torpoint Ath 1-0
Millbrook v Hallen 2-1
Sherborne T (walkover) v Exmouth T
Cadbury Heath v Ashton & Backwell U (walkover)
Welton R v Elburton Villa 1-0
St Blazey v Brislington 3-0
Newton Abbot Spurs v Crediton U 3-2
Longwell Green Sports v Bovey Tracey 2-1
Wells C v Bristol Telephones 3-0

FIRST ROUND

Redcar Ath v Holker Old Boys 1-2
Penistone Church v AFC Liverpool 3-0
Abbey Hey v Hemsworth MW 3-1
Jarrow v Yorkshire Amateur 0-0
Jarrow won 3-0 on penalties
Liversedge v Newcastle Benfield 5-2
Charnock Richard (walkover) v Ashington
Warrington Rylands v Padiham 2-0
Guisborough T v Runcorn T 2-0
Lower Breck v Newton Aycliffe 3-2
Maltby Main v Newcastle University 3-1
Wythenshawe T v North Ferriby 2-2
North Ferriby won 5-4 on penalties
Hallam v AFC Blackpool 4-3
Bridlington T v North Shields 2-2
North Shields won 5-4 on penalties
Bootle v Shildon 0-2
Irlam v Seaham Red Star 0-2
Sunderland Ryhope CW v Penrith 3-0
Cheadle T v New Mills 0-2
Barnton v Bacup Bor 1-0
1874 Northwich v Harrogate Railway Ath 2-1
Bewdley T v Stapenhill 2-2
Bewdley T won 4-3 on penalties
Shepshed Dynamo v Melton T 3-2
Coventry Sphinx v Heanor T 6-1
Aylestone Park v Lye T 3-3
Aylestone Park won 4-3 on penalties
Grimsby Bor v Quorn 1-0
Hanley T (walkover) v Deeping Rangers
Harrowby U v AFC Bridgnorth 0-1
Racing Club Warwick v Abbey Hulton U 1-1
Abbey Hulton U won 4-2 on penalties
Paget Rangers v Radford 0-4
Shirebrook T v Boldmere St Michaels 0-3
Dudley Sports v Rugby T 2-1
Loughborough University v Cadbury Ath 4-0
Rainworth MW v Belper U 3-2
Anstey Nomads v Leicester Nirvana 1-0
Stourport Swifts (walkover) v Skegness T
Congleton T v Gresley R 5-0
Studley v Long Eaton U 1-4
Malvern T v Rothwell Corinthians 3-1
Westfields v Romulus 2-2
Westfields won 3-2 on penalties
Stone Old Alleynians v AFC Mansfield 3-2
Gorleston v Baldock T 4-2
Cockfosters v Cogenhoe U 1-3
Ilford v FC Clacton 4-1
Bugbrooke St Michaels v Stanway R 1-2
Ampthill T v Walthamstow 1-1
Amptill T won 4-2 on penalties
Wellingborough T v Haverhill R 2-0
Norwich U (walkover) v White Ensign
Whittlesey Ath v Mildenhall T 0-6
Colney Heath v New Salamis 3-1
Fakenham T v Crawley Green 2-1
Newbury Forest v May & Baker Eastbrook Community 0-4
Norwich CBS v Ipswich W 3-2
Milton Keynes Irish v Stansted 2-0
Northampton Sileby Rangers v Burton Park W 2-2
Burton Park W won 5-4 on penalties
Mulbarton W v Newport Pagnell T 4-0
Coggeshall U v Hashtag U 0-2
Walsham Le Willows v Hoddesdon T 5-1
Raynes Park Vale v Sheerwater 1-0
Sandhurst T v North Greenford U 2-6
Jersey Bulls v Cobham (walkover)
Risborough Rangers v Erith & Belvedere 0-0
Risborough Rangers won 4-2 on penalties
Fleet T v Littlehampton T 0-2
Frimley Green v Flackwell Heath 0-2
Clapton v Petersfield T 1-1
Tie awarded to Clapton; Petersfield T removed
Saltdean U v Epsom & Ewell 3-1
Eastbourne T v Southall 0-3
Tooting Bec v Guildford C 2-3
Worthing U v Edgware T 0-3, 3-1
Initial match Edgware T won 3-0. Match ordered to be replayed because Edgware T fielded an ineligible player.
Steyning T v Seaford T 9-1
Sutton Ath v Sheppey U 0-2
Newhaven v Ascot U 4-1
Kennington v Fisher 1-1
Kennington won 5-4 on penalties
Walton & Hersham v Peacehaven & Telscombe 3-0
Stansfeld v AFC Hayes 2-2
Stansfeld won 4-3 on penalties
Welling T v Hanworth Villa 1-6
Hadley v Pagham 2-1
Holmesdale v AFC Uckfield T 2-4
CB Hounslow U v Horley T 1-5
Reading C v Lancing 0-1
Cheddar v Ashton & Backwell U 2-1
Bridgwater T v Welton R 5-0
Keynsham T v Bashley 0-4
Bishop's Cleeve v Shepton Mallet 6-3
Clevedon T v Whitchurch U 2-1
Brockenhurst v Street 2-2
Brockenhurst won 5-3 on penalties
Fareham T v Roman Glass St George 4-1
St Blazey v Helston Ath 2-2
Helston Ath won 4-3 on penalties
New Milton T v Clanfield 85 1-1
New Milton T won 4-1 on penalties
Falmouth T v Abingdon U 3-1
Millbrook v Sherborne T 3-1
Newton Abbot Spurs v Ringwood T 3-1
Brimscombe & Thrupp v Longwell Green Sports 4-2
Royal Wootton Bassett T v Camelford 4-0
Cribbs v Newport (IW) 4-3
Hamworthy U v Ilfracombe T 4-0
Wells C v Westbury U 2-2
Wells C won 4-3 on penalties
United Services Portsmouth v Bournemouth 3-1
Milton U v Longlevens 2-2
Longlevens won 5-4 on penalties
Lymington T v Tavistock 1-2

SECOND ROUND

Guisborough T v Liversedge 1-4
Hebburn T v North Shields 3-2
New Mills v Congleton T 2-2
Congleton T won 5-4 on penalties
Stockton T v Charnock Richard 4-2
Holker Old Boys v Vauxhall Motors 0-1
Consett v Maltby Main 5-0
Jarrow v Warrington Rylands 1-1
Warrington Rylands won 5-4 on penalties
Longridge T v Penistone Church 1-1
Longridge T won 6-5 on penalties
Sunderland Ryhope CW v Abbey Hey 1-0
Barnton v Seaham Red Star 0-4
Hallam v Shildon 0-2
North Ferriby v Lower Breck 2-1
1874 Northwich v West Auckland T 1-4
Radford v Bewdley T 3-1
Long Eaton U v Stone Old Alleynians 3-2
Atherstone T v Malvern T 0-1
Lutterworth T v Westfields 3-3
Westfields won 5-4 on penalties
Dudley Sports v Coventry Sphinx 1-1
Coventry Sphinx won 3-2 on penalties
Hanley T v Loughborough University 2-1
Walsall Wood v AFC Bridgnorth 3-0
Anstey Nomads v Rainworth MW 1-0
Stourport Swifts v Grimsby Bor 3-1
Shepshed Dynamo v Worcester C 3-2
Boldmere St Michaels v Newark 3-4
Sporting Khalsa v Aylestone Park 4-1
Coventry U v Abbey Hulton U 3-2

Ilford v Colney Heath 2-4
Norwich U (walkover) v Burton Park W
Wroxham v Milton Keynes Irish 3-3
Milton Keynes Irish won 4-3 on penalties
Mulbarton W v Cogenhoe U 5-0
Gorleston (walkover) v Kirkley & Pakefield
Fakenham T v Hashtag U 0-0
Fakenham T won 4-3 on penalties
Wellingborough T v Woodbridge T 1-0
Stowmarket T v Eynesbury R 5-0
Stanway R v Ampthill T 1-1
Ampthill T won 4-2 on penalties
Norwich CBS v May & Baker Eastbrook Community 2-1
Mildenhall T v Leighton T (walkover)
Hadley v Raynes Park Vale 4-1
Lancing v Worthing U 3-0
North Greenford U v Walsham Le Willows 2-1
Hanworth Villa v Corinthian 2-2
Hanworth Villa won 6-5 on penalties
Newhaven v Binfield 2-2
Binfield won 4-1 on penalties
Saltdean U v Deal T 2-2
Deal T won 3-2 on penalties
Horley T v Chatham T 3-5
Cobham v Risborough Rangers 1-0
Steyning T v Walton & Hersham 1-6
Littlehampton T v Sheppey U 3-3
Littlehampton T won 5-4 on penalties
Sutton Common R v Southall 4-0
Stansfeld v Flackwell Heath 0-3
Glebe v Kennington 0-2
AFC Uckfield T v Guildford C 2-4
Plymouth Parkway v Newton Abbot Spurs 3-1
Christchurch v Cribbs 2-1
United Services Portsmouth v Brockenhurst 2-1
Millbrook v Bashley 2-0
Bradford T v Brimscombe & Thrupp 2-3
Wells C v Buckland Ath 1-2
New Milton T v Longlevens 2-0
Helston Ath v Fareham T 0-2
Bridgwater T v Royal Wootton Bassett T 2-1
Clapton v Hamworthy U 2-1
Tavistock v Cheddar 6-1
Falmouth T v Bishop's Cleeve 2-1
Clevedon T v Bitton 4-3

THIRD ROUND
Longridge T v Warrington Rylands 1-2
North Ferriby v Seaham Red Star 2-2, 1-0
Initial match North Ferriby won 7-6 on penalties after 2-2 draw. Match ordered to be replayed because North Ferriby fielded an ineligible player.
Sunderland Ryhope CW v Liversedge 0-0
Liversedge won 4-3 on penalties
Hebburn T v Vauxhall Motors 2-2
Hebburn T won 5-4 on penalties
Stockton T v Shildon 1-3
Consett v West Auckland T 1-2
Stourport Swifts v Shepshed Dynamo 4-3
Long Eaton U v Hanley T 2-0
Newark v Walsall Wood 1-1
Walsall Wood won 8-7 on penalties
Radford v Westfields 0-5
Coventry Sphinx v Anstey Nomads 1-2
Malvern T v Sporting Khalsa 5-5
Malvern T won 6-5 on penalties
Congleton T v Coventry U 1-1
Congleton T won 4-3 on penalties
Fakenham T v Milton Keynes Irish 2-2
Fakenham T won 4-2 on penalties
Wellingborough T v Norwich U 2-1
Leighton T v Gorleston 4-2
Stowmarket T v Norwich CBS 2-0
Mulbarton W v Ampthill T 1-0
Hadley v Colney Heath 0-0
Hadley won 4-1 on penalties
Clapton v Cobham 0-5
Guildford C v Walton & Hersham 1-1
Walton & Hersham won 4-2 on penalties
Kennington v Sutton Common R 1-1
Sutton Common R won 4-1 on penalties
Deal T v Binfield 1-4
Littlehampton T v Hanworth Villa 2-2
Hanworth Villa won 5-4 on penalties
Chatham T v Flackwell Heath 0-1
Lancing v North Greenford U 2-2
Lancing won 5-3 on penalties
Christchurch v Falmouth T 1-1
Christchurch won 6-5 on penalties
Clevedon T v New Milton T 2-0
United Services Portsmouth v Millbrook 3-2
Buckland Ath v Tavistock 0-4
Plymouth Parkway v Fareham T 5-2
Brimscombe & Thrupp v Bridgwater T 2-2
Bridgwater T won 5-4 on penalties

FOURTH ROUND
Shildon v Warrington Rylands 0-0
Warrington Rylands won 5-4 on penalties
North Ferriby v West Auckland T 4-0
North Ferriby removed for fielding an ineligible player
Hebburn T v Liversedge 2-1
Stourport Swifts v Walsall Wood 1-2
Congleton T v Malvern T 1-0
Long Eaton United v Westfields 1-1
Long Eaton United won 5-4 on penalties
Anstey Nomads v Wellingborough T 4-2
Mulbarton W v Hanworth Villa 0-0
Hanworth Villa won 3-1 on penalties
Leighton T v Walton & Hersham 2-1
Lancing v Flackwell Heath 1-1
Flackwell Heath won 4-2 on penalties
Fakenham T v Binfield 2-2
Binfield won 4-1 on penalties
Stowmarket T v Cobham (walkover)
Sutton Common R v Hadley 1-3
Plymouth Parkway v Clevedon T 2-1
United Services Portsmouth v Christchurch 1-1
United Services Portsmouth won 4-1 on penalties
Bridgwater T v Tavistock 0-1

FIFTH ROUND
Hebburn T v Congleton T 1-0
Warrington Rylands v West Auckland 1-1
Warrington Rylands won 3-1 on penalties
Walsall Wood v Anstey Normads 0-0
Walsall Wood won 5-4 on penalties
Hanworth Villa v Long Eaton U 2-2
Long Eaton U won 5-3 on penalties
Cobham v Leighton T 0-1
Hadley v Binfield 0-0
Binfield won 5-4 on penalties
Tavistock v United Services Portsmouth 1-3
Plymouth Parkway v Flackwell Heath 2-4

QUARTER-FINALS
Warrington Rylands v Hebburn T 1-0
Leighton T v Walsall Wood 1-2
Long Eaton U v Binfield 0-5
United Services Portsmouth v Flackwell Heath 2-0

SEMI-FINALS
Warrington Rylands v Walsall Wood 2-1
United Services Portsmouth v Binfield 1-1
Binfield won 4-3 on penalties

FA VASE FINAL 2020–21

Wembley, Saturday 22 May 2021 (behind closed doors)

Binfield (1) 2 *(Ferdinand 42, 69)* **Warrington Rylands (1) 3** *(Nevitt 25, 43 (pen), 59)*

Binfield: Grace; Legg (Thomson-Wheeler 72), Gavin, McClurg, Hancock, Short (Howell 64), Willment, Maloney, Moore, Ferdinand, Harris (Povey 72).

Warrington Rylands: McCall; Tinning (Freeman 76), Gerrard, Coveney (Sheen 62), Smith, Kenny, Drummond, Doyle, Scarisbrick, Milne (Potter 89), Nevitt.

Referee: John Busby.

THE FA YOUTH CUP 2020–21

**After extra time.*

PRELIMINARY ROUND

Stockton T v Carlisle C 4-0
Consett v South Shields 1-4
Guisborough T v Morpeth T 0-8
Workington v Scarborough Ath 3-1
Durham C v Spennymoor T (walkover)
Pickering T v Cleator Moor 3-2
Tie awarded to Cleator Moor Celtic; Pickering T removed-subject to appeal
Newcastle Benfield v Hebburn T 3-3
Hebburn T won 5-4 on penalties
Buxton v Ashton T 4-2
Sandbach U v Cheadle T 1-3
Prestwich Heys v Stalybridge Celtic 11-1
Mossley v Litherland Remyca 0-4
Prescot Cables v City of Liverpool 1-5
Irlam v Curzon Ashton 2-1
Chester v Abbey Hey 2-0
Stockport T v Ashton Ath 3-1
Hyde U v Runcorn Linnets 3-1
Wythenshawe Amateurs v Nantwich T 1-1
Wythenshawe Amateurs won 4-1 on penalties
St Helens T v AFC Liverpool 5-0
Bootle v Southport 0-3
Skelmersdale U v Runcorn T 6-0
Marine v Lancaster C 2-0
Clitheroe v Trafford 3-1
Tadcaster Alb v York C 1-4
Sheffield v Staveley MW 8-1
Garforth T v Stocksbridge Park Steels (walkover)
Frickley Ath v Guiseley (walkover)
Brigg T v Emley 0-10
North Ferriby v Bottesford T 3-1
Shelley v Farsley Celtic 0-6
Harrogate Railway Ath v Grimsby Bor 3-3
Harrogate Railway Ath won 3-0 on penalties
Silsden v Pontefract Collieries (walkover)
Eccleshill U v Retford 6-0
Steeton v Hall Road Rangers (walkover)
Gresley R v Heather St Johns 1-2
Long Eaton U v Kirby Muxloe 1-1
Kirby Muxloe won 5-4 on penalties
Borrowash Vic v Mickleover 1-3
Grantham T v Dunkirk 5-1
Holbeach U v Harborough T 8-0
Ilkeston T v Stamford 3-2
Alfreton T v Basford U 1-7
Nuneaton Bor v Kidsgrove Ath 4-2
Worcester C v Lichfield C 4-1
Newcastle T v Racing Club Warwick 2-1
Bilston T v Stratford T (walkover)
Stourbridge v Redditch U 4-1
Shawbury U v Stourport Swifts 7-0
Alvechurch v Evesham U 2-2
Evesham U won 4-2 on penalties
Rugby T v Sutton Coldfield T 10-1
Malvern T v Paget Rangers 0-2
Lye T v Haughmond 2-3
Chelmsley T v Rushall Olympic 0-5
Stafford Rangers v AFC Telford U 1-0
Halesowen T v Bedworth U 2-3
Leamington v Boldmere St Michaels 3-2
Wellingborough Whitworths v Stotfold 4-2
Royston T v Godmanchester R 3-1
Cogenhoe U v St Ives T 2-2
Cogenhoe U won 5-4 on penalties
Baldock T v Corby T 8-0
Crawley Green v Winslow U 2-3
Barton R v Biggleswade T 1-3
Eynesbury R v Bugbrooke St Michaels 0-8
Kettering T v Leighton T 2-1
Rothwell Corinthians v Peterborough Sports 3-2
Brackley T v Newport Pagnell T (walkover)
Wellingborough T v Arlesey T 2-1
Haverhill R v Histon 1-3
Walsham Le Willows v Whitton U 2-2
Walsham Le Willows won 4-3 on penalties
Long Melford v AFC Sudbury 0-6
Brantham Ath v Newmarket T 3-4
Whittlesey Ath v Needham Market 0-9
Mildenhall T v Swaffham T 3-1
Ipswich W v Fakenham T 2-0
Cambridge C v Stowmarket T 0-0
Cambridge C won 5-4 on penalties
Dereham T v Lowestoft T 3-2
Cornard U v Woodbridge T 0-1
Hadleigh U v Leiston 0-3
FC Clacton v Ware 0-6
St Albans C v Hadley 4-0
Barking v Colney Heath 2-1
Brightlingsea Regent v Billericay T (walkover)
Bowers & Pitsea (walkover) v Bishop's Stortford
Hoddesdon T v Brentwood T (walkover)
Romford v Barkingside 4-2
Redbridge v Sawbridgeworth T 4-2
Hullbridge Sports v Concord Rangers 1-7
Harpenden T v Woodford T 1-2
Cockfosters v Tilbury 2-1
Takeley v Wingate & Finchley (walkover)
Potters Bar T v Enfield T 3-3
Potters Bar T won 4-3 on penalties
Chelmsford C v Haringey Bor 4-0
Braintree T v Aveley 1-2
Hackney Wick v Ilford 2-4
Hertford T v May & Baker Eastbrook Community 9-0
Chesham U v Hanworth Villa 1-2
Ashford T (Middlesex) v Brimsdown 0-2
Harefield U v Hampton & Richmond Bor 3-5
Windsor v Northwood 2-1
London Tigers v Leverstock Green 0-7
CB Hounslow U v Bedfont Sports 1-2
Edgware T v Spelthorne Sports 0-8
Beaconsfield T v Chalfont St Peter 2-2
Chalfont St Peter won 7-6 on penalties
K Sports v Glebe 5-3
Hastings U (walkover) v Lewisham Bor (Community)
Tower Hamlets v Margate 0-1
Erith T v Sevenoaks T 2-2
Erith T won 4-2 on penalties
Ramsgate v Meridian 2-5
Dulwich Hamlet v East Grinstead T 3-0
Ashford U v Tooting & Mitcham U (walkover)
Punjab U v Tonbridge Angels 0-2
Bexhill U v Maidstone U 1-1
Maidstone U won 4-3 on penalties
Greenwich Bor v AFC Croydon Ath (walkover)
Cray W v Carshalton Ath 0-4
Croydon v Whitstable T 3-1
Faversham T v Chatham T 1-1
Faversham T won 4-2 on penalties
Folkestone Invicta v Corinthian 1-1
Folkestone Invicta won 5-3 on penalties
Newhaven v South Park 2-6
Dorking W v Walton & Hersham 3-0
Alfold v Abbey Rangers 1-0
Eastbourne T v Broadbridge Heath 1-3
Three Bridges v Shoreham 4-1
Lancing (walkover) v Loxwood
Burgess Hill T v Horsham 1-0
Arundel v Worthing U 3-2
Saltdean U v Mile Oak 1-3
Lewes v East Preston 3-1
Worthing v Guildford C 4-2
Sutton Common R v Virginia Water 5-0
Kingstonian v Chertsey T 2-2
Kingstonian won 3-2 on penalties
Metropolitan Police v Corinthian Casuals 18-0
Seaford T v Westfield 1-1
Westfield won 3-2 on penalties
Godalming T v Walton Casuals 8-2
Chessington & Hook U v Badshot Lea 3-0
Billingshurst v Chipstead 0-7
Bognor Regis T v Knaphill 1-4
Bracknell T v Fleet T 2-2
Fleet T won 5-4 on penalties
Thame U v Hungerford T 0-0
Thame U won 5-4 on penalties
Farnborough v Cove (walkover)
Oxford C v Easington Sports 4-0
North Leigh v Clanfield 85 1-1
Clanfield 85 won 4-2 on penalties

Fleet Spurs v Wokingham & Emmbrook 1-1
Wokingham & Emmbrook won 5-4 on penalties
Hartley Wintney v Shrivenham 1-1
Shrivenham won 4-2 on penalties
Hamworthy U v Gosport Bor 6-0
Dorchester T v Poole T 1-4
Hamble Club v Bemerton Heath Harlequins 1-2
Sholing v AFC Stoneham 2-2
AFC Stoneham won 5-4 on penalties
Alton v AFC Portchester 0-4
United Services Portsmouth v Bournemouth 5-1
Bitton v Tuffley R 3-6
Bishop's Cleeve v Bristol Manor Farm 4-0
Yate T v Malmesbury Vic 2-0
Odd Down v Cribbs 4-0
Gloucester C v Cirencester T 2-1
Chippenham T v Newent T 8-1
Wells C v Paulton R 3-1
Truro C v Clevedon T 3-2
Barnstaple T v Bridgwater T (walkover)
Weston-super-Mare v Bishop Sutton 6-1
Frome T v Street 0-4

FIRST QUALIFYING ROUND
Seaham Red Star (walkover) v Penrith
Chester-le-Street T v Spennymoor T 0-17
Hebburn T v Workington 2-1
Morpeth T v Blyth Spartans 4-0
Stockton T v Gateshead 0-1
Cleator Moor v Darlington 2-7
North Shields v South Shields (walkover)
Litherland Remyca v Cheadle T 5-0
FC United of Manchester v West Didsbury & Chorlton 2-0
AFC Fylde v Stockport T 2-2
AFC Fylde won 4-3 on penalties
Marine v Irlam 3-5
Clitheroe v Chorley 2-1
Hyde U v Southport 3-0
Wythenshawe Amateurs v Skelmersdale U 1-2
Bamber Bridge v Prestwich Heys (walkover)
St Helens T (walkover) v Witton Alb
Buxton v City of Liverpool 0-3
Chester v Vauxhall Motors 11-0
Cleethorpes T v York C 0-5
Ossett U v Pontefract Collieries 4-2
Guiseley v Emley 5-0
Eccleshill U (walkover) v Handsworth
Swallownest v Harrogate Railway Ath 1-2
Dronfield T v Stocksbridge Park Steels 0-2
Farsley Celtic v Worsbrough Bridge Ath 2-5
Hall Road Rangers v North Ferriby (walkover)
Sheffield v Bradford (Park Avenue) 2-0
Leicester Nirvana v Heather St Johns 0-6
West Bridgford v Boston U 1-3
Grantham T v Holbeach U 6-0
Bourne T v Lincoln U 1-8
Loughborough Dynamo v Aylestone Park 0-1
Eastwood Community v Mickleover 0-4
Basford U v Lutterworth Ath 5-1
Deeping Rangers v Ilkeston T 2-4
Kirby Muxloe v Matlock T 7-1
Stratford T v Worcester C 0-2
Pershore T v Kidderminster H 1-1
Pershore T won 5-4 on penalties
Tamworth v Rugby T 0-2
Leamington v Shawbury U 1-1
Shawbury U won 5-4 on penalties
Coleshill T v Walsall Wood 4-1
Paget Rangers v Stafford Rangers 2-3
Haughmond v Bedworth U 2-1
Hereford v Newcastle T (walkover)
Rushall Olympic v Romulus 2-3
Nuneaton Bor v Stourbridge 0-8
Evesham U v Coventry Sphinx 1-2
Kempston R v Wellingborough Whitworths 1-6
Northampton ON Chenecks v Rothwell Corinthians (walkover)
Baldock T v Winslow U 1-2
Newport Pagnell T v Hitchin T
Tie awarded to Hitchin T; Newport Pagnell T removed
St Neots T v Kettering T 0-3
AFC Dunstable v Cogenhoe U 3-2
Bugbrooke St Michaels v Yaxley 4-1
Wellingborough T v Biggleswade T 3-1
Royston T v AFC Rushden & Diamonds 2-1
Framlingham T v Woodbridge T 4-3
Leiston v Mildenhall T 6-0
Ely C v Newmarket T 0-6
Walsham le Willows v Cambridge C 0-1
Felixstowe & Walton U v Wroxham 0-3
Bury T v March T U 4-0
AFC Sudbury v Ipswich W 8-0
Needham Market v Dereham T 3-4
Saffron Walden T v Gorleston 8-1
Histon v Lakenheath 4-0
Brentwood T v Grays Ath 2-2
Grays Ath won 3-2 on penalties
Chelmsford C v Walthamstow 9-2
Ilford v London Lions 0-2
Potters Bar T v Hertford T 2-3
Ware v Wingate & Finchley 3-2
Concord Rangers v Aveley 6-1
Cockfosters v Hornchurch 1-0
Little Oakley v St Margaretsbury 1-2
Heybridge Swifts v Romford 1-1
Heybridge Swifts won 6-5 on penalties
Billericay T v Barking 5-0
Bowers & Pitsea v Cheshunt 3-4
Stanway R v St Albans C 2-2
St Albans C won 4-2 on penalties
Redbridge v Woodford T 6-0
Balham v Hanworth Villa 0-4
Uxbridge v Burnham 9-0
Windsor v Leverstock Green 1-5
Berkhamsted v Hanwell T 5-2
Hayes & Yeading U v Chalfont St Peter 0-3
Kings Langley v Hampton & Richmond Bor 4-1
Spelthorne Sports v Hendon 8-2
Hemel Hempstead T v Bedfont Sports 1-3
Brimsdown v North Greenford U 1-0
Erith T v Hastings U 2-1
Crowborough Ath v Whyteleafe (walkover)
VCD Ath v Tonbridge Angels (walkover)
Folkestone Invicta v Dulwich Hamlet 1-2
Dartford (walkover) v Lingfield
Maidstone U v Croydon 2-3
AFC Croydon Ath v Faversham T 0-1
Welling T v Margate 1-3
Carshalton Ath v Phoenix Sports 3-0
K Sports v Meridian 3-1
Tooting & Mitcham U v Ebbsfleet U 3-1
Pagham v Westfield 3-3
Pagham won 4-3 on penalties
Godalming T v Broadbridge Heath 3-2
Arundel v Kingstonian 0-10
South Park v Worthing 5-4
Lancing v Raynes Park Vale 0-3
Steyning T v Leatherhead 1-4
Redhill v Metropolitan Police 0-4
Chessington & Hook U v Mile Oak 6-1
Lewes v Alfold 3-0
Three Bridges v Oakwood 3-2
Chichester C v Sutton Common R 1-4
Chipstead v Burgess Hill T 7-0
Eastbourne Bor v Knaphill 2-1
Whitehawk v Dorking W 1-1
Dorking W won 3-1 on penalties
Camberley T v Shrivenham 7-1
Aylesbury Vale Dynamos v Holmer Green 0-1
Fleet T v Clanfield 85 3-0
Oxford C v Ascot U 0-1
Thatcham T v Kidlington 2-3
Wokingham & Emmbrook v Cove 6-2
Didcot T v Thame U 6-0
Binfield v Reading C 0-4
Moneyfields v Basingstoke T 3-2
Brockenhurst v AFC Portchester 5-0
Wimborne T v AFC Stoneham 6-3
Bemerton Heath Harlequins v Totton & Eling 2-4
Hamworthy U v Havant & Waterlooville 3-1
United Services Portsmouth v Fareham T 9-0
Winchester C v Poole T 2-2
Poole T won 4-2 on penalties
Keynsham T v Mangotsfield U 0-8
Oldland Abbotonians v Gloucester C 0-3
Cinderford T v Odd Down 2-3
Yate T v Bradford T 5-1
Tuffley R v Bath C 4-1
Chippenham T v Slimbridge 1-0
Corsham T v Bishop's Cleeve 2-3
Street v Bishops Lydeard 5-0
Wells C v Weston-super-Mare 1-2

Bridgwater T v Radstock T 2-0
Welton R v Elburton Villa 1-2
Portishead T v Truro C 0-5

SECOND QUALIFYING ROUND
Hartlepool U v Hebburn T 0-1
Darlington v South Shields 0-6
Morpeth T v Spennymoor T 1-1
Spennymoor T won 5-4 on penalties
Seaham Red Star v Gateshead 0-3
St Helens T v Chester 0-4
Altrincham v City of Liverpool 2-0
Stockport Co v Hyde U 1-2
Irlam v Newcastle T 2-1
Skelmersdale U v Prestwich Heys 4-4
Skelmersdale U won 3-0 on penalties
Clitheroe v AFC Fylde 1-7
Wrexham v Litherland Remyca (walkover)
FC United of Manchester (walkover) v Macclesfield T
Sheffield v Guiseley 0-5
Eccleshill U v Harrogate Railway Ath 7-1
Ossett U v Worsbrough Bridge Ath 4-3
Stocksbridge Park Steels v York C 1-3
FC Halifax T v North Ferriby 6-0
Boston U v Grantham T 3-0
Chesterfield v Notts Co 0-2
Heather St Johns v Rugby T 2-5
Lincoln U v Kirby Muxloe 3-2
Ilkeston T v Aylestone Park 2-3
Basford U v Mickleover 1-1
Basford U won 3-0 on penalties
Solihull Moors v Coleshill T 0-0
Solihull Moors won 5-3 on penalties
Stourbridge v Romulus 2-2
Romulus won 4-3 on penalties
Worcester C v Stafford Rangers 3-0
Coventry Sphinx v Pershore T 4-2
Shawbury U v Haughmond 2-1
Wellingborough T v Bugbrooke St Michaels 2-4
Wellingborough Whitworths v Kettering T 2-4
Holmer Green v Royston T 0-8
AFC Dunstable v Hitchin T 0-2
Winslow U v Rothwell Corinthians 6-1
Dereham T v AFC Sudbury 2-4
Leiston v Saffron Walden T 6-1
Bury T v St Margaretsbury 10-0
Histon v Framlingham T 2-1
King's Lynn T v Cambridge C 3-0
Newmarket T v Wroxham 3-2
Cheshunt v Billericay T 0-4
Hertford T v Grays Ath 5-2
Cockfosters v Concord Rangers 1-3
St Albans C v Dagenham & R 6-0
Heybridge Swifts v Redbridge 1-3
London Lions v Chelmsford C 3-6
Bedfont Sports v Brimsdown 4-1
Spelthorne Sports v Ware 0-5
Leverstock Green v Wealdstone 2-2
Wealdstone won 8-7 on penalties
Boreham Wood v Berkhamsted 1-3
Uxbridge v Barnet 7-0
Chalfont St Peter v Kings Langley 1-4
Dartford v Tooting & Mitcham U 5-1
Erith T v K Sports 0-1
Tonbridge Angels v Whyteleafe 2-1
Hanworth Villa v Dover Ath 0-2
Bromley v Faversham T 3-1
Dulwich Hamlet v Croydon 2-2
Dulwich Hamlet won 4-1 on penalties
Carshalton Ath v Margate 3-2
Woking v Three Bridges 7-0
Chipstead v Metropolitan Police 1-3
Godalming T v Lewes 1-2
Sutton Common R v South Park 1-0
Sutton U v Raynes Park Vale 2-0
Eastbourne Bor v Kingstonian 4-2
Dorking W v Chessington & Hook U 1-1
Dorking W won 7-6 on penalties
Pagham v Leatherhead 0-14
Camberley T v Maidenhead U 5-0
Reading C v Fleet T 7-1
Didcot T v Ascot U 1-0
Wokingham & Emmbrook v Kidlington 0-3
Poole T v Brockenhurst 0-1
United Services Portsmouth v Weymouth 3-0
Totton & Eling v Wimborne T 1-6
Moneyfields v Aldershot T 2-4
Eastleigh v Hamworthy U 4-2
Gloucester C v Truro C 1-2
Torquay U v Elburton Villa 2-1
Bishop's Cleeve v Yeovil T 0-6
Tuffley R v Bridgwater T 6-2
Mangotsfield U v Yate T 10-0
Weston-super-Mare v Street 1-1
Weston-super-Mare won 4-3 on penalties
Odd Down v Chippenham T 0-1

THIRD QUALIFYING ROUND
Gateshead v Eccleshill U 3-5
Hyde U v Skelmersdale U 8-1
Spennymoor T v Ossett U 1-1
Ossett U won 2-1 on penalties
Litherland Remyca v FC United of Manchester (walkover)
Hebburn T v AFC Fylde 1-8
Guiseley v FC Halifax T 3-0
Altrincham v South Shields 2-2
Altrincham won 4-2 on penalties
York C v Chester 1-2
Irlam v Romulus 3-0
Lincoln U v Basford U 2-2
Basford U won 4-1 on penalties
Worcester C v Rugby T 3-1
Winslow U v Hitchin T 4-3
Aylestone Park v Bugbrooke St Michaels 2-3
Kettering T v Solihull Moors 1-3
Coventry Sphinx v Shawbury U 2-1
Boston U v Notts Co 0-1
Redbridge v AFC Sudbury 2-3
Billericay T v Newmarket T 1-1
Newmarket T won 3-0 on penalties
St Albans C v Histon 4-3
King's Lynn T v Bury T 1-2
Chelmsford C v Concord Rangers 2-1
Hertford T v Leiston 3-1
Dorking W v Royston T 3-2
Dover Ath v Lewes 1-0
Woking v Sutton Common R 1-0
Leatherhead v Ware 6-3
Carshalton Ath v Eastbourne Bor 1-3
Sutton U v Kings Langley 3-0
Wealdstone v Bromley 0-6
K Sports v Uxbridge 2-0
Dulwich Hamlet v Metropolitan Police 0-4
Berkhamsted v Bedfont Sports 2-6
Dartford v Tonbridge Angels 4-1
Torquay U v Tuffley R 2-4
Truro C v Aldershot T 1-1
Truro C won 4-2 on penalties
Mangotsfield U v Eastleigh 1-2
Didcot T v United Services Portsmouth 1-1
Didcot T won 5-4 on penalties
Brockenhurst v Kidlington 3-1
Camberley T v Weston-super-Mare 1-1
Camberley T won 4-2 on penalties
Chippenham T v Reading C 1-1
Chippenham T won 4-3 on penalties
Yeovil T v Wimborne T 3-4

FIRST ROUND
Morecambe v AFC Fylde 1-4
Blackpool v Bradford C 2-3
Eccleshill U v Altrincham 1-3
Bolton W v Guiseley 1-2*
(1-1 at the end of normal time)
Wigan Ath v Harrogate T 5-0
Tranmere R v Hyde U 0-0
Tranmere R won 8-7 on penalties
Salford C v Rochdale 3-2
Oldham Ath v FC United of Manchester 6-0
Ossett U v Sunderland 1-8
Carlisle U v Chester 3-2
Fleetwood T v Accrington S 1-0
Coventry Sphinx v Doncaster R 1-2
Solihull Moors v Lincoln C 0-3
Bugbrooke St Michaels v Mansfield T 0-3
Irlam v Notts Co 0-6
Grimsby T v Scunthorpe U 2-0
Port Vale v Basford U 1-4
Burton Alb v Worcester C 4-1
Crewe Alex v Hull C 0-2
Shrewsbury T v Walsall 0-4

Milton Keynes D v Hertford T	8-1
Bury T v AFC Sudbury	0-7
Newmarket T v Peterborough U	2-7*
(2-2 at the end of normal time)	
Chelmsford C v St Albans C	3-1
Ipswich T v Southend U	4-1
Stevenage v Colchester U	1-4
Northampton T v Cambridge U	1-1
Cambridge U won 11-10 on penalties	
Dartford v Metropolitan Police	1-3
Oxford U v AFC Wimbledon	1-2
Bromley v Bedfont Sports	2-1
Crawley T v Sutton U (walkover)	
Leyton Orient v Woking	2-3
Winslow U v Charlton Ath	0-5
Dorking W v Dover Ath	1-0
Gillingham v Leatherhead	7-1
Eastbourne Bor v K Sports	1-0
Plymouth Arg v Exeter C	2-3*
(2-2 at the end of normal time)	
Wimborne T v Newport Co	0-1
Swindon T v Forest Green R	2-2
Swindon T won 8-7 on penalties	
Brockenhurst v Truro C	2-1
Cheltenham T v Tuffley R	4-0
Eastleigh v Chippenham T	3-4*
(3-3 at the end of normal time)	
Bristol R v Camberley T	2-3
Portsmouth v Didcot T	4-2

SECOND ROUND

Oldham Ath v Lincoln C	0-1
Altrincham v Peterborough U	1-2
Burton Alb v Mansfield T	3-2
Cambridge U v Guiseley	4-0
Hull C v Doncaster R	2-3
Wigan Ath v Notts Co	3-2
Fleetwood T v Walsall	3-0
Carlisle U v Bradford C	3-1
Salford C v Tranmere R	2-1
AFC Fylde v Sunderland	3-1
Basford U v Grimsby T	1-0
Milton Keynes D v Eastbourne Bor	3-0
Metropolitan Police v Swindon T	1-2*
(1-1 at the end of normal time)	
Portsmouth v Bromley	1-2
Chelmsford C v Ipswich T	0-5
Chippenham T v Woking	0-7
Dorking W v Colchester U	0-2
Exeter C v Cheltenham T	3-2*
(2-2 at the end of normal time)	
AFC Sudbury v AFC Wimbledon	1-2
Sutton U v Camberley T	6-0
Newport Co v Brockenhurst	3-2*
(2-2 at the end of normal time)	
Gillingham v Charlton Ath	1-1
Charlton Ath won 9-8 on penalties	

THIRD ROUND

Watford v Colchester U	2-0
Swansea C v QPR	2-1
Nottingham F v Bristol C	1-2
Middlesbrough v Millwall	4-0
Brighton & HA v Woking	5-1
Stoke C v Burton Alb	2-3*
(2-2 at the end of normal time)	
Huddersfield T v Newcastle U	1-1
Newcastle U won 5-3 on penalties	
Cambridge U v AFC Fylde	2-3
AFC Wimbledon v Burnley	1-0
Everton v Wigan Ath	4-2*
(2-2 at the end of normal time)	
Carlisle U v Blackburn R	0-1
Derby Co v Cardiff C	2-3*
(2-2 at the end of normal time)	
Rotherham U v Arsenal	1-2
Chelsea v Barnsley	8-1
Reading v Aston Villa	3-4
Liverpool v Sutton U	6-0
Basford U v WBA	0-4
Lincoln C v Preston NE	1-0
Manchester C v Birmingham C	6-1
Wolverhampton W v Norwich C	2-4
Salford C v Manchester U	0-2
Swindon T v Bromley	3-0
Charlton Ath v Sheffield U	0-2
Leeds U v Milton Keynes D	8-2
Tottenham H v Newport Co	6-2
Ipswich T v Fulham	3-2
Leicester C v Sheffield W	5-0
Luton T v West Ham U	3-3*
West Ham U won 4-2 on penalties	
Peterborough U v Doncaster R	2-1
Exeter C v Bournemouth	3-1
Southampton v Coventry C	3-0
Fleetwood T v Crystal Palace	2-1

FOURTH ROUND

Exeter C v Leicester C	1-2*
(0-0 at the end of normal time)	
Ipswich T v Swindon T	3-1
Peterborough U v Sheffield U	0-2
Newcastle U v Leeds U	4-1
Southampton v Burton Alb	0-1
Manchester C v Everton	0-1
Fleetwood T v Bristol C	1-1*
Bristol C won 4-2 on penalties	
Blackburn R v Arsenal	1-4
AFC Wimbledon v Tottenham H	0-3*
(0-0 at the end of normal time)	
Manchester U v Liverpool	0-1
WBA v Cardiff C	2-1
Chelsea v AFC Fylde	2-0
Norwich C v West Ham U	0-5
Lincoln C v Watford	2-3*
(2-2 at the end of normal time)	
Swansea C v Middlesbrough	0-1
Aston Villa v Brighton & HA	3-0

FIFTH ROUND

Newcastle U v Watford	3-2*
(2-2 at the end of normal time)	
Aston Villa v Burton Alb	9-0
West Ham U v Arsenal	1-3
Sheffield U v Bristol C	3-1
Leicester C v Liverpool	1-5
Chelsea v Everton	1-2
Tottenham H v WBA	0-5
Middlesbrough v Ipswich T	0-1

QUARTER-FINALS

Newcastle U v Aston Villa	1-6
Liverpool v Arsenal	3-1
Ipswich v Sheffield U	3-2*
(2-2 at the end of normal time)	
WBA v Everton	2-1

SEMI-FINALS

Ipswich T v Liverpool	1-2
Aston Villa v WBA	4-1

FA YOUTH CUP FINAL 2020–21

Villa Park, Monday 24 May 2021

Aton Villa (2) 2 *(Chrisene 8, Young 12 (pen))* **Liverpool (0) 1** *(Revan S 73 (og))*

Aston Villa: Marshall; Kessler, Revan S, Swinkels, Young, Chukwuemeka, Chrisene (Ramsey 60), Lindley (Sylla 79), Raikhy, Bogarde, Barry.

Liverpool: Davies; Koumetio, Quansah, Corness (Frauendorf 46), Woltman, Norris, Bradley, Morton, Stephenson, Musialowski, Balagizi.

Referee: John Brooks.

PREMIER LEAGUE 2 2020–21

DIVISION ONE	P	W	D	L	F	A	GD	Pts
Manchester C	24	17	5	2	79	30	49	56
Chelsea	24	12	6	6	50	36	14	42
Tottenham H	24	11	5	8	45	44	1	38
Blackburn R	24	10	7	7	48	41	7	37
Everton	24	10	6	8	44	28	16	36
Derby Co	24	11	3	10	43	49	–6	36
Liverpool	24	10	5	9	48	50	–2	35
Manchester U	24	10	4	10	58	59	–1	34
Brighton & HA	24	7	9	8	36	42	–6	30
Arsenal	24	6	8	10	37	43	–6	26
West Ham U	24	6	6	12	32	48	–16	24
Leicester C	24	6	4	14	41	55	–14	22
Southampton	24	4	4	16	29	65	–36	16

DIVISION TWO	P	W	D	L	F	A	GD	Pts
Leeds U	24	18	2	4	62	29	33	56
Stoke C	24	14	3	7	41	30	11	45
Crystal Palace	24	11	3	10	45	41	4	36
Wolverhampton W	24	10	6	8	40	36	4	36
Sunderland	24	10	5	9	42	41	1	35
Middlesbrough	24	10	4	10	44	35	9	34
Burnley	24	10	4	10	38	41	–3	34
Reading	24	10	2	12	41	54	–13	32
Aston Villa	24	9	4	11	46	48	–2	31
Fulham	24	9	3	12	38	46	–8	30
Norwich C	24	7	4	13	32	40	–8	25
WBA	24	7	4	13	37	49	–12	25
Newcastle U	24	7	4	13	31	47	–16	25

PROMOTION PLAY-OFFS

SEMI-FINALS
Stoke C v Sunderland 0-2
Crystal Palace v Wolverhampton W 3-2

FINAL
Sunderland v Crystal Palace 0-0
aet; Crystal Palace won 5-3 on penalties

UNDER-18 PROFESSIONAL DEVELOPMENT LEAGUE 2020–21

*After extra time.

UNDER-18 PREMIER LEAGUE

NORTH DIVISION	P	W	D	L	F	A	GD	Pts
Manchester C	24	19	4	1	76	19	57	61
Manchester U	24	20	0	4	79	27	52	60
Liverpool	24	17	1	6	75	26	49	52
Middlesbrough	24	12	3	9	48	48	0	39
Everton	24	11	2	11	42	42	0	35
Blackburn R	24	10	3	11	37	43	–6	33
Derby Co	24	10	3	11	43	54	–11	33
Wolverhampton W	24	10	3	11	38	50	–12	33
Burnley	24	8	4	12	34	38	–4	28
Newcastle U	24	7	3	14	50	57	–7	24
Stoke C	24	6	5	13	28	61	–33	23
Leeds U	24	4	3	17	30	73	–43	15
Sunderland	24	4	2	18	35	77	–42	14

SOUTH DIVISION	P	W	D	L	F	A	GD	Pts
Fulham	24	18	2	4	78	25	53	56
Crystal Palace	24	18	2	4	67	32	35	56
Brighton & HA	24	14	3	7	63	40	23	45
Arsenal	24	12	4	8	52	45	7	40
Aston Villa	24	11	5	8	45	52	–7	38
Tottenham H	24	10	7	7	52	37	15	37
Chelsea	24	11	3	10	57	43	14	36
WBA	24	9	3	12	51	62	–11	30
Norwich C	24	9	2	13	58	58	0	29
West Ham U	24	6	7	11	35	57	–22	25
Reading	24	5	4	15	51	83	–32	19
Leicester C	24	4	6	14	38	73	–35	18
Southampton	24	3	4	17	35	75	–40	13

NATIONAL FINAL
Manchester C v Fulham 3-1

U18 PROFESSIONAL DEVELOPMENT LEAGUE

NORTH DIVISION	P	W	D	L	F	A	GD	Pts
Wigan Ath	25	17	4	4	68	38	30	55
Birmingham C	25	16	4	5	67	44	23	52
Sheffield U	25	15	5	5	63	36	27	50
Sheffield W	25	12	6	7	48	30	18	42
Barnsley	25	12	6	7	46	34	12	42
Crewe Alex	25	10	4	11	50	47	3	34
Hull C	25	10	3	12	46	58	–12	33
Coventry C	25	9	3	13	50	46	4	30
Nottingham F	25	9	3	13	45	56	–11	30

SOUTH DIVISION	P	W	D	L	F	A	GD	Pts
Charlton Ath	25	16	3	6	65	34	31	51
Ipswich T	25	13	2	10	53	54	–1	41
Watford	25	9	5	11	40	46	–6	32
Millwall	25	9	4	12	56	58	–2	31
Cardiff C	25	10	1	14	54	58	–4	31
Bristol C	25	9	2	14	44	53	–9	29
Colchester U	25	9	1	15	52	64	–12	28
Swansea C	25	5	7	13	37	73	–36	22
QPR	25	3	1	21	33	88	–55	10

SEMI-FINALS
Wigan Ath v Ipswich T 2-1*
Charlton Ath v Birmingham C 3-2

NATIONAL FINAL
Charlton Ath v Wigan Ath 0-2

CENTRAL LEAGUE 2020–21

CENTRAL LEAGUE CUP

GROUP 1 – Table	P	W	D	L	F	A	GD	Pts
Bournemouth	4	3	0	1	14	8	6	9
Oxford U	4	2	0	2	9	10	–1	6
Southend U	4	1	0	3	7	12	–5	3

GROUP 2 – Table	P	W	D	L	F	A	GD	Pts
Carlisle U	3	3	0	0	9	2	7	9
Fleetwood T	3	1	1	1	3	3	0	4
Rochdale	4	0	1	3	2	9	–7	1

GROUP 3 – Table	P	W	D	L	F	A	GD	Pts
Huddersfield T	8	6	1	1	26	15	11	19
Salford C	5	3	0	2	9	5	4	9
Grimsby T	5	2	0	3	9	17	–8	6
Scunthorpe U	4	1	1	2	7	5	2	4
Walsall	4	0	0	4	6	15	–9	0

SEMI-FINALS
Carlisle U v Huddersfield T 3-2

FINAL
Bournemouth v Carlisle U 2-0

YOUTH ALLIANCE LEAGUE 2020–21

NORTH EAST	P	W	D	L	F	A	GD	Pts
Notts Co	22	15	2	5	53	32	21	47
Scunthorpe U	22	13	1	8	52	47	5	40
Grimsby T	22	10	6	6	32	24	8	36
Mansfield T	22	11	1	10	34	30	4	34
Burton Alb	22	10	3	9	36	40	–4	33
Rotherham U	22	10	2	10	46	41	5	32
Doncaster R	22	8	2	12	38	40	–2	26
Lincoln C	22	8	2	12	36	38	–2	26
Bradford C	22	8	1	13	38	50	–12	25
Huddersfield T	22	7	0	15	32	55	–23	21

NORTH WEST	P	W	D	L	F	A	GD	Pts
Fleetwood T	26	19	1	6	62	36	26	58
Rochdale	26	17	3	6	64	29	35	54
Carlisle U	26	17	3	6	55	27	28	54
Blackpool	26	15	4	7	59	43	16	49
Preston NE	26	14	3	9	73	51	22	45
Bolton W	26	13	5	8	55	43	12	44
Shrewsbury T	26	11	5	10	42	45	–3	38
Salford C	26	10	1	15	46	59	–13	31
Walsall	26	9	4	13	31	56	–25	31
Morecambe	26	8	5	13	32	49	–17	29
Tranmere R	26	7	5	14	38	51	–13	26
Accrington S	26	6	6	14	41	57	–16	24
Oldham Ath	26	6	3	17	41	59	–18	21
Port Vale	26	4	4	18	36	70	–34	16

SOUTH EAST	P	W	D	L	F	A	GD	Pts
Peterborough U	18	11	4	3	39	16	23	37
Cambridge U	18	10	2	6	37	27	10	32
Luton T	18	8	6	4	39	25	14	30
Southend U	18	9	3	6	35	25	10	30
Northampton T	18	8	5	5	32	20	12	29
Gillingham	18	7	5	6	26	27	–1	26
AFC Wimbledon	18	6	4	8	27	34	–7	22
Milton Keynes D	18	5	2	11	26	45	–19	17
Stevenage	18	3	6	9	27	45	–18	15
Leyton Orient	18	2	5	11	23	47	–24	11

SOUTH WEST	P	W	D	L	F	A	GD	Pts
Oxford U	20	15	2	3	58	24	34	47
AFC Bournemouth	20	13	3	4	62	27	35	42
Exeter C	20	10	4	6	43	36	7	34
Portsmouth	20	9	5	6	49	40	9	32
Forest Green R	20	8	5	7	54	48	6	29
Plymouth Arg	20	8	4	8	51	40	11	28
Swindon T	20	6	4	10	33	43	–10	22
Bristol R	20	6	4	10	32	45	–13	22
Newport Co	20	5	5	10	35	44	–9	20
Cheltenham T	20	5	3	12	29	65	–36	18
Yeovil T	20	4	3	13	35	69	–34	15

MERIT LEAGUE 1	P	W	D	L	F	A	GD	Pts
Plymouth Arg	6	3	2	1	11	4	7	11
Exeter C	6	3	1	2	13	9	4	10
Forest Green R	6	3	1	2	11	13	–2	10
Cheltenham T	6	2	2	2	8	8	0	8
Bristol R	6	2	1	3	6	8	–2	7
Yeovil T	6	1	3	2	10	14	–4	6
Newport Co	6	1	2	3	9	12	–3	5

MERIT LEAGUE 2	P	W	D	L	F	A	GD	Pts
Southend U	6	4	1	1	15	10	5	13
Northampton T	6	3	1	2	20	14	6	10
Luton T	6	3	0	3	11	14	–3	9
Cambridge U	6	2	2	2	17	13	4	8
Stevenage	6	2	2	2	13	14	–1	8
Peterborough U	6	2	0	4	9	9	0	6
Milton Keynes D	6	1	2	3	8	19	–11	5

MERIT LEAGUE 3	P	W	D	L	F	A	GD	Pts
Bournemouth	6	4	1	1	10	7	3	13
Portsmouth	6	4	0	2	20	8	12	12
Oxford U	6	2	2	2	14	12	2	8
Swindon T	6	2	2	2	15	14	1	8
Leyton Orient	6	2	1	3	12	15	–3	7
AFC Wimbledon	6	2	1	3	12	19	–7	7
Gillingham	6	1	1	4	7	15	–8	4

YOUTH ALLIANCE CUP

SOUTHERN FIRST ROUND

Stevenage v Luton T 2-1
Newport Co v Bristol R 3-3
Bristol R won 3-1 on penalties
Oxford U v Swindon T 2-0
Cheltenham T v Forest Green R 2-3
Leyton Orient v Southend U 0-4

SOUTHERN SECOND ROUND

Forest Green R v Exeter C 1-4
Stevenage v Gillingham 0-3
AFC Wimbledon v Milton Keynes D 4-0
Oxford U v Portsmouth 1-1
Oxford U won 3-1 on penalties
Peterborough U v Southend U 1-0
Northampton T v Cambridge U 1-2
Plymouth Arg v Bournemouth 1-2
Yeovil T v Bristol R 3-1

NORTHERN GROUP STAGE

GROUP 1 – TABLE	P	W	D	L	F	A	GD	Pts
Morecambe	2	2	0	0	4	2	2	6
Carlisle U	2	1	0	1	2	2	0	3
Bradford C	2	0	0	2	1	3	–2	0

GROUP 2 – TABLE	P	W	D	L	F	A	GD	Pts
Huddersfield T	2	1	1	0	8	3	5	4
Blackpool	2	1	1	0	7	5	2	4
Fleetwood T	2	0	0	2	2	9	–7	0

GROUP 3 – TABLE	P	W	D	L	F	A	GD	Pts
Walsall	2	1	0	1	4	3	1	3
Burton Alb	2	1	0	1	3	3	0	3
Mansfield T	2	1	0	1	2	3	–1	3

GROUP 4 – TABLE	P	W	D	L	F	A	GD	Pts
Bolton W	2	2	0	0	2	0	2	6
Doncaster R	2	0	1	1	2	3	–1	1
Preston NE	2	0	1	1	2	3	–1	1

GROUP 5 – TABLE	P	W	D	L	F	A	GD	Pts
Shrewsbury T	2	2	0	0	5	1	4	6
Tranmere R	2	1	0	1	4	3	1	3
Notts Co	2	0	0	2	1	6	–5	0

GROUP 6 – TABLE	P	W	D	L	F	A	GD	Pts
Grimsby T	2	1	1	0	3	2	1	4
Salford C	2	1	0	1	6	2	4	3
Accrington S	2	0	1	1	1	6	–5	1

GROUP 7 – TABLE	P	W	D	L	F	A	GD	Pts
Rochdale	2	2	0	0	7	0	7	6
Rotherham	2	1	0	1	2	4	–2	3
Port Vale	2	0	0	2	1	6	–5	0

GROUP 8 – TABLE	P	W	D	L	F	A	GD	Pts
Oldham Ath	2	2	0	0	9	1	8	6
Lincoln C	2	1	0	1	4	3	1	3
Scunthorpe U	2	0	0	2	2	11	–9	0

SOUTHERN QUARTER-FINALS

AFC Wimbledon v Peterborough U 1-2
Bournemouth v Cambridge U 0-2
Oxford U v Gillingham 0-2
Exeter C v Yeovil T 6-3

NORTHERN QUARTER-FINALS

Shrewsbury T v Morecambe 3-2
Bolton W v Rochdale 1-1
Rochdale won 4-1 on penalties
Grimsby T v Oldham Ath 1-1
Grimsby T won 4-3 on penalties
Huddersfield T v Walsall 7-1

SOUTHERN SEMI-FINALS

Peterborough U v Cambridge U 1-1
Peterborough U won 5-4 on penalties
Exeter C v Gillingham 1-1
Gillingham won 4-3 on penalties

NORTHERN SEMI-FINALS

Shrewsbury T v Rochdale 1-2
Huddersfield T v Grimsby T 1-2

SOUTHERN FINAL

Peterborough U v Gillingham 2-2
Gillingham won 4-3 on penalties

NORTHERN FINAL

Grimsby T v Rochdale 1-3

FINAL

Gillingham v Rochdale 0-3

IMPORTANT ADDRESSES

The Football Association: Wembley Stadium, PO Box 1966, London SW1P 9EQ. *0800 169 1863*

Scotland: Hampden Park, Glasgow G42 9AY. *0141 616 6000*

Northern Ireland (Irish FA): Chief Executive, Donegall Avenue, Belfast, Northern Ireland BT12 6LU. *028 9066 9458*

Wales: 11/12 Neptune Court, Vanguard Way, Cardiff CF24 5PJ. *029 2043 5830*

Republic of Ireland: National Sports Campus, Abbotstown, Dublin 15. *01 8999 500*

International Federation (FIFA): Strasse 20, P.O. Box 8044, Zurich, Switzerland. *00 41 43 222 7777. Fax: 00 41 43 222 7878*

Union of European Football Associations: Secretary, Route de Geneve 46, P.O. Box 1260, Nyon 2, Switzerland. *49 89 552608830*

THE LEAGUES

The Premier League: Brunel Building, 57 North Wharf Road, London W2 1HQ. *0207 864 9000*

The Football League: EFL House, 10–12 West Cuff, Preston PR1 8HU. *01772 325 800. Fax 01772 325 801*

The National League: M. Tattersall, 4th Floor, Waterloo House, 20 Waterloo Street, Birmingham B2 5TB. *0121 643 3143*

FA Women's Super League: Wembley Stadium, PO Box 1966, London SW1P 9EQ. *+44 844 980 8200*

Scottish Premier League: Letherby Drive, Glasgow G42 9DE. *0141 620 4140*

The Scottish League: Hampden Park, Glasgow G42 9EB. *0141 620 4160*

Welsh Premier League: 11/12 Neptune Court, Vanguard Way, Cardiff CF24 5PJ. *029 2043 5830*

Northern Ireland Football League: Mervyn Brown Suite, National Stadium at Windsor Park, Donegall Avenue, Belfast BT12 6LW. *028 9560 7150*

Football League of Ireland: National Sports Campus, Abbotstown, Dublin 15. *00 353 1 8999 500*

Southern League: J. Mills, Suite 3B, Eastgate House, 121–131 Eastgate Street, Gloucester GL1 1PX. *07768 750 590*

Northern Premier League: Ms A. Firth, 23 High Lane, Norton Tower, Halifax, W. Yorkshire HX2 0NW. *01422 410 691*

Isthmian League: Kellie Discipline, PO Box 393, Dartford DA1 9JK. *01322 314 999*

Combined Counties League: A. Constable, 3 Craigwell Close, Staines, Middlesex TW18 3NP. *01784 440 613*

Eastern Counties League: N. Spurling, 16 Thanet Road, Ipswich, Suffolk IP4 5LB. *01473 720 893*

Essex Senior League: Secretary: Ms. M. Darling, 39 Milwards, Harlow, Essex CM19 4SG. *07939 850627*

Hellenic League: John Ostinell, 2 Wynn Grove, Hazlemere HP15 7LY. *07900 081 814*

Midland League: N. Wood, 30 Glaisdale Road, Hall Green, Birmingham B28 8PX. *07967 440 007*

North West Counties League: J. Deal, 24 The Pastures, Crossens, Southport PR9 8RH. *01704 212 917*

Northern Counties East: Matt Jones, 346 Heneage Road, Grimsby DN32 9NJ. *07415 068 996*

Northern League: K. Hewitt, 21 Cherrytree Drive, Langley Park, Durham DH7 9FX. *07897 611640*

South Midlands League: Louise Condon, Century House, Dunstable LU5 4JU. *01582 567 728*

Southern Combination League: T. Dawes, 32 Reynolds Lane, Langney, Eastbourne BN23 7NW. *01323 764 218*

Southern Counties East League: Andy Short, secretary@scefl.com

United Counties League: Ms W. Newey, Nene Valley Community Centre, Candy Street, Peterborough PE2 9RE. *07890 5184577*

Wessex League: A. Hodder, leaguesecretary.wessexleague@gmail.com. *07780 496312*

Western League: A. Radford, 19 Longney Place, Patchway, Bristol BS34 5LQ. *07872 818 868*

OTHER USEFUL ADDRESSES

Amateur Football Alliance: Jason Kilby, Unit 3, 7 Wenlock Road, London N1 7SL. *0208 733 2613*

Association of Football Badge Collectors: K. Wilkinson, 18 Hinton St, Fairfield, Liverpool L6 3AR. *0151 260 0554*

British Olympic Association: 60 Charlotte Street, London W1T 2NU. *0207 842 5700*

British Blind Sport (including football): Plato Close, Tachbrook Park, Leamington Spa, Warwickshire CV34 6WE. *01926 424 247*

British Universities and Colleges Sports Association: Vince Mayne, Chief Executive: BUCSA, 20–24 King's Bench Street, London SE1 0QX. *0207 633 5080*

England Supporters Club: Wembley Stadium, London HA9 0WS. *0800 389 1966*

English Schools FA: 4 Parker Court, Staffordshire Technology Park, Stafford ST18 0WP. *01785 785 970*

Fields In Trust: Woodstock Studios, 36 Woodstock Grove, London W12 8LE. *0207 427 2110*

Football Foundation: 10 Eastbourne Terrace, Paddington, London W2 6LG. *0345 345 4555*

Football Postcard Collectors Club: PRO: John Farrelly, 163 Collingwood Road, Hillingdon, Middlesex UB8 3EW. Web: www.hobbyist.co.uk/fpcc

Football Safety Officers Association: Peter Houghton, Suite 5, Blackburn Rovers Enterprise Centre, Ewood Park, Blackburn BB2 4JF. *01254 841 771.*

Institute of Groundsmanship: 28 Stratford Office Village, Walker Avenue, Wolverton, Milton Keynes MK12 5TW. *01908 312 511*

League Managers Association: St George's Park, Newborough Road, Needwood, Burton on Trent DE13 9PD. *0128 357 6350*

National Football Museum: Urbis Building, Cathedral Gardens, Todd Street, Manchester M4 3BG. *0161 605 8200*

Professional Footballers' Association: 20 Oxford Court, Bishopsgate, Off Lower Moseley Street, Manchester M2 3WQ. *0161 236 0575*

Programme Monthly & Football Collectable Magazine: R. P. Matz, 11 Tannington Terrace, London N5 1LE. *020 7359 8687*

Programme Promotions: 21 Roughwood Close, Watford WD17 3HN. *01923 861 468*

Referees' Association: 1A Bagshaw Close, Ryton-on-Dunsmore, Coventry CV8 3EX. *024 7642 0360*

Scottish Football Museum: Hampden Park, Glasgow G42 9BA. *0141 616 6139*

Sir Norman Chester Centre for Football Research: Department of Sociology, University of Leicester, University Road LE1 7RH. *0116 252 2741/5*

Sport England: 21 Bloomsbury Street, London WC1B 3HF. *0345 8508 508*

Sports Grounds Safety Authority: 2–6 Salisbury Square, London EC4Y 8JX. *0207 930 6693*

Sports Turf Research Institute: St Ives Grove, Harden, Bingley, West Yorkshire BD16 1AU. *01274 565 131*

The Football Supporters' Federation: 1 Ashmore Terrace, Stockton Road, Sunderland, Tyne and Wear SR2 7DE. *0330 440 0044*

The Ninety-Two Club: Mr M. Kimberley, The Ninety-Two Club, 153 Hayes Lane, Kenley, Surrey CR8 5HP.

Walking Football Association: Kemp House, 160 City Road, London EC1V 2NX. *07517 033248*

Wheelchair Football Association: c/o Birmingham County FA, Ray Hall Lane, Birmingham B43 6JF.

FOOTBALL CLUB CHAPLAINCY

Billy had been a parson for over 30 years, but despite being an ardent follower of his local football club, had only seen the footballers at his club from the terraces, or, more latterly, from the grandstand (with a season ticket, no less!). Illness apart, nothing would prevent him from attending the matches in which his local club was engaged.

However, that changed, as did much of his ministry, after Billy had a spell in his local hospital after being involved in a traffic accident, which required a stay of a month or so in his nearby hospital and an operation.

When Billy was well enough he was moved to a bed in the ward where, to his utter astonishment and delight, he found himself in the next bed to one of the players from the town's football team, who had been injured in a recent fixture which Billy had attended.

The pair, and their respective wives, soon became great pals, and it wasn't long before Billy was invited to become the team's chaplain. The team's manager and the club chairman seized the opportunity, so that Billy now attends all the games in his clerical collar in his capacity as the club's official chaplain!

And, a day or two after the pair had been released from hospital, Billy's new pal netted a decisive goal! Billy was invited by his new pal and the team manager to go along to the next 'home' fixture, and to pop into the dressing room to meet such team members as wished him to do so.

Relationships flourished after this and Billy certainly won't need to purchase his ticket for a seat in the stand next season!

THE REV

OFFICIAL CHAPLAINS TO FA PREMIERSHIP AND FOOTBALL LEAGUE CLUBS

AFC Wimbledon – Simon Elliott
Aston Villa – Jon Grant
Barrow – Jonathan Harrison
Barnsley – Peter Amos
Birmingham C – Kirk McAtear
Birmingham C Academy – Tim Atkins
Blackburn R – Ken Howles
Blackpool – Linda Tomkinson
Bolton W – Philip Mason
Bournemouth – Adam Parrett
Bradford C – Oliver Evans
Brentford – Stuart Cashman
Bristol C – Derek Cleave
Bristol R – Wayne Massey
Burnley – Barry Hunter
Burton Alb – Phil Pusey
Cambridge U – Leo Orobor
Cardiff C Academy – Bryon Castle
Carlisle U – Alun Jones
Charlton Ath – Matt Baker
Charlton Ath Academy – Gareth Morgan
Chelsea – Martin Swan
Cheltenham T – Malcolm Allen
Crawley T – Steve Alliston
Crewe Alex – Phil Howell
Crystal Palace – Chris Roe
Derby Co – Tony Luke
Doncaster R – Barry Miller
Everton – Henry Corbett
Fleetwood T – George Ayoma
Fulham – Gary Piper
Harrogate T – Rob Brett
Huddersfield T – Dudley Martin
Ipswich T – Kevan McCormack
Leeds U – Dave Niblock
Lincoln C – Canon Andrew Vaughan
Liverpool – Bill Bygroves
Manchester C – Pete Horlock
Mansfield T – Kevin Charles
Millwall – Canon Owen Beament
Newport Co – Keith Beardmore
Northampton T – Haydon Spenceley
Norwich C – Jon Norman
Norwich C Academy – Tim Henery
Peterborough U – Richard Longfoot
Peterborough U Academy – Jonathan Greenwood
Plymouth Arg – Arthur Goode
Portsmouth – Jonathan Jeffery and Mick Mellows
Preston NE – Chris Nelson
QPR – Joshua Baines
Reading – Steven Prince
Reading Academy – Charlie Baines
Rochdale – Richard Bradley
Rotherham U – Baz Gascoyne
Scunthorpe U – Alan Wright
Scunthorpe U Academy – David Eames
Sheffield U – Delroy Hall
Sheffield W – Baz Gascoyne
Sheffield W Wise Old Owls – David Jeans
Shrewsbury T – Phil Cansdale and Andy Ackroyd
Southampton – Jonny Goodchild
Southend U – Stuart Alleway and Mike Lodge
Tranmere R – Buddy Owen
Tranmere R (Stadium) – Matt Graham
Stevenage – Jon Woodrow
Sunderland – Father Marc Lyden-Smith
Swansea C Academy – Eirian Wyn
Swindon T – Simon Stevenette
Walsall – Lance Blackwood
Watford – Clive Ross
West Ham U – Alan Bolding
West Ham U Academy – Philip Wright
Wolverhampton W – David Wright
Wolverhampton W Academy – Steve Davies
Wycombe W – Benedict Mwendwa Musola

CURRENT CHAPLAINS IN WOMEN'S FOOTBALL

Birmingham C – Sophie Hardwick
Bristol C – Esther Legg-Bagg
Charlton Ath – Kathryn Sales
Coventry U – Jo Foster
Crystal Palace – Dotha Blakwood
Derby Co – Sarah Crathorne
Everton – Naomi Maynard
Leicester C – Louise Davis
Lewes – Michelle Taylor
Newcastle U – Dot Lee
Oxford U – Deborah Rooke
Portsmouth – Debs Smart
Reading – Angy King
West Ham U – Jane Quinton

The chaplains hope that those who read this page will see the value and benefit of chaplaincy work in football and will take appropriate steps to spread the word where this is possible. They would also like to thank the editors of the Football Yearbook for their continued support for this specialist and growing area of work.

For further information, please contact: Sports Chaplaincy UK, The Avenue Methodist Church, Wincham Road, Sale, Cheshire M33 4PL. Telephone: 0800 181 4051 or email: admin@sportschaplaincy.org.uk. Website: www.sportschaplaincy.org.uk

OBITUARIES

Colin Appleton (Born: Scarborough, 7 March 1936. Died: Scarborough, 31 May 2021.) Colin Appleton joined Leicester City from Scarborough in March 1954 and in 12 years at Filbert Street he enjoyed a successful career, mostly turning out at left-half. He played in two FA Cup final defeats (to Tottenham Hotspur in 1961 and Manchester United in 1963) and was a Football League Cup winner in 1963–64, when he captained the Foxes to victory over Stoke City in the two-legged final. After a season at Charlton Athletic he became player-manager of Barrow, successfully keeping them in the old Third Division. In June 1969 took over at his hometown club and in two spells as manager, in between which was a post as trainer-coach of Grimsby Town, he developed the club into one of the best non-league outfits in the country, winning the FA Trophy on three occasions. He went on to manage in the Football League with Hull City (twice), Swansea Town and Exeter City, leading the Tigers to promotion from Division Four in 1982–83. He was capped for the Football League representative side on one occasion.

John Ashworth (Born: Nottingham, 4 July 1937. Died: 29 November 2020.) John Ashworth was a member of the Kingstonian side that were beaten finalists in the 1960 FA Amateur Cup final and went on to captain the Wealdstone team which won the 1966 final. He won six amateur international caps for England, and four for the Great Britain Olympic Games team.

Gordon Astall (Born: Horwich, Lancashire, 22 September 1927. Died: 21 October 2020.) Gordon Astall was a pacy winger who could beat defenders for speed to deliver the ball into the danger zone. He signed for Plymouth Argyle at the beginning of the 1947–48 season whilstwhile serving in the Royal Marines and based locally, and went to make almost 200 appearances, gaining a Division Three South winners' medal in 1951–52. He followed his colleague Alex Govan to Birmingham City where he enjoyed further success, winning the Second Division in 1954–55, an FA Cup runners-up medal the following year, and appearing in the 1960 Inter Cities Fairs Cup final. He ended his career with a spell at Torquay United. He won two full England caps, scoring on his debut, and also gained representative honours for England B and the Football League.

Len Badger (Born: Darnall, Sheffield, 8 June 1945. Died: 20 May 2021.) Len Badger was a calm and effective right-back who won representative honours for England Schools and Youth and made his first-team debut for Sheffield United at the age of 17. He went on to enjoy 11 seasons of regular first-team football at Bramall Lane and was ever-present in the team that won promotion from Division Two in 1970–71. When he left for Chesterfield in January 1976, he had accumulated a total of 523 senior appearances for the Blades. He subsequently spent a couple of seasons at Saltergate before retiring. He won 13 caps for England U23s and appeared three times for the Football League representative side.

Colin Baker (Born: Cardiff, 18 December 1934. Died: 11 April 2021.) Colin Baker was a wing-half who made over 300 first-team appearances for Cardiff City, his only professional club. He was still a teenager when he made his debut for the Bluebirds in April 1954 and went on to win promotion to the old First Division in 1959–60, as well as being a member of four Welsh Cup winning teams. He won seven full caps for Wales, featuring for them in the 1958 World Cup finals.

Richie Barker (Born: Loughborough, 23 November 1939. Died: October 2020.) Richie Barker was a prolific goal scorer in Southern League football for Burton Albion, netting an all-time club record of 157 goals during his time with the Brewers. In October 1967 he followed his former manager Peter Taylor to Derby County and after two seasons with the Rams switched to Notts County. He made 112 League appearances scoring 37 goals during his time at Meadow Lane and was a member of the team that won the Division Four title in 1970–71. He later played for Peterborough United before switching to coaching and management, and he had spells as manager of a number of clubs including Shrewsbury Town, Stoke City and Notts County.

Geoff Barnett (Born: Northwich, Cheshire, 16 October 1946. Died: Fort Myers, Florida, USA, 15 January 2021.) Geoff Barnett was capped for England at schools and youth international levels and was a member of the Everton team that won the FA Youth Cup in 1965. However, he was only a back-up 'keeper during a five-year stay at Goodison Park. It was a similar case when he moved on to Arsenal in October 1979, although he had a useful run in the first team in the opening half of 1972–73 when Bob Wilson was side lined with an injury. He eventually moved across the Atlantic Ocean and spent four seasons with Minnesota Kicks, appearing for them in the 1976 Soccer Bowl final.

Eddie Beaton (Born: Old Kilpatrick, Dunbartonshire, 1932. Died: Glasgow, 25 June 2020.) Centre-forward Eddie Beaton was capped for Scotland Juniors as a teenager but his early career in senior football was unsuccessful during spells at Aberdeen and Dumbarton. After completing National Service, he was reinstated and spent a season back with Clydebank Juniors before signing for Morton in July 1956. In four seasons at Cappielow he scored over 100 goals in competitive matches, leading the club's scoring charts on three occasions. He concluded his career with spells at Berwick Rangers and Stranraer.

Colin Bell, MBE (Born: Hesleden, Co Durham, 26 February 1946. Died: 5 January 2021.) Colin Bell was a supremely talented midfield player, widely regard as one of the most talented English players of his generation. His early career was spent at Bury where he made his League debut at the age of 17, scoring a first-half goal against opponents Manchester City. He finished as top scorer in 1964–65 and was team captain at the age of 19 before being sold to Manchester City in March 1966. He contributed to the tail end of City's Division Two championship success that season and went on to be one of the driving forces in the club's trophy filled campaigns of the late 1960s. He was a member of teams that won the Football League (1967–68), FA Cup (1969) and both the League Cup and European Cup Winners' Cup in 1969–70. He continued to provide a valuable contribution at Maine Road, although he suffered a bad injury in November 1975 and missed the whole of the following season as a result. He retired in August 1979 having scored 153 goals in 501 appearances for City. He was capped for England on 48 occasions between 1968 and 1975 and also won representative honours for England U23s and the Football League XI.

Stan Bevans (Born: Kingsley, Staffs, 16 April 1934. Died: August 2020.) Stan Bevans starred in Staffordshire schools' football then briefly played for Cheadle Catholics before joining the groundstaff at Stoke City. He made his first-team debut for the Potters at 16, and at the time he was the club's youngest-ever player. However, he found it difficult to make further impact at the Victoria Ground apart from a very short run in the team in the first half of the 1954–55 season. Soon afterwards he moved on to play for Macclesfield Town.

Clive Bircham (Born: Philadelphia, Co Durham, 7 September 1939. Died: 6 June 2020.) Winger Clive Bircham was an amateur on the books of Sunderland before signing professional terms on reaching the age of 17. He made his debut for the Black Cats at Lincoln City in their first-ever Football League game outside the top flight and was a regular for much of the 1958–59 campaign before moving on to Hartlepools United in February 1960. He enjoyed three-and-a-half seasons at the Victoria Ground, making over 100 appearances before switching to non-league football with Boston United.

Jake Bolton (Born: Lesmahagow, Lanarkshire, 26 October 1941. Died: February 2021.) Jake Bolton developed with Nairn Thistle in the Fife Junior League before signing for Raith Rovers as a 19-year-old. He impressed at centre-half in early appearances for the Stark's Park club and in the summer of 1963 he was sold to Ipswich Town for whom he made 77 first-team appearances. He subsequently came back to Scotland, contributing to Morton's Second Division title success in 1966–67 before returning to Raith. He concluded his career at Dumbarton, where he captained the team that won the Second Division title in 1971–72.

Walter Borthwick (Born: Edinburgh, 4 April 1948. Died: 24 April 2021.) Wing-half Walter Borthwick was a product of the Tynecastle Boys Club, stepping up to the seniors with Morton at the start of the 1965–66 campaign. He then had a very brief spell with Brighton & Hove Albion before returning to Scotland where he enjoyed a lengthy career, notably with East Fife, for whom he made over 200 first-team appearances. Later he had spells with St Mirren, St Johnstone and Dunfermline Athletic before spending a decade on the coaching staff at Hearts. There followed a seven-month spell as manager of Arbroath, and he then spent 20 years as a development officer for the Scottish FA.

Clint Boulton (Born: Stoke on Trent, 6 January 1948. Died: 1 January 2021.) Clint Boulton was a defender who made over 500 senior appearances in a career that spanned the period between 1964 and 1980. He joined Port Vale as an apprentice after playing in the Stoke team that won the English Schools Trophy in 1963 and was just 16 when he made his first-team debut. When he scored in only his fifth appearance, he became the Valliant's' youngest-ever scorer. An ever-present in the Vale team that won promotion from the Fourth Division in 1969–70, he concluded his career with a lengthy spell at Torquay United.

Alan Bradshaw (Born: Blackburn, 14 September 1941. Died: 18 October 2020.) Alan Bradshaw was an inside-forward or wing-half who gained an FA Youth Cup winners' medal with Blackburn Rovers in 1958–59 before spending time as a student at Loughborough Colleges, where he played regularly for the senior team. He subsequently returned to Ewood Park as a part-time professional but struggled to win a regular place in the line-up over the next two seasons and in May 1965 he signed for Crewe

Alexandra. He went on to spend eight years at Gresty Road, where he featured in the team that won promotion to the Third Division in 1967–68 and made over 300 first-team appearances before moving into non-league football with Macclesfield Town.

Pat Brady (Born: Dublin, 11 March 1936. Died: August 2020.) Left-back Pat Brady joined Millwall from Home Farm in January 1959 and went on to make over 150 first-team appearances during his time at The Den, helping them to win the Fourth Division title in 1961–62. He followed his brother Ray to Queen's Park Rangers in July 1963 where he spent two further seasons before switching to Southern League football with Gravesend & Northfleet.

Arthur Bramley (Born: Mansfield, 25 March 1929. Died: Sutton-in-Ashfield, Nottinghamshire, 10 January 2021.) Goalkeeper Arthur Bramley signed for Mansfield Town from Bentinck Colliery in October 1959 and spent five years on the club's books. Although mostly a reserve during his time at Field Mill he had a good run in the side in the 1952–53 season when regular 'keeper Dennis Wright was injured. Later he played for Spalding United.

Frank Brogan (Born: Stepps, Lanarkshire, 3 August 1942. Died: 29 April 2021.) Frank Brogan was an outside-left who was exceptionally quick. He moved up from Juniors St Roch to sign for Celtic in November 1960 but although he broke into the team midway through the following season he was unable to keep his place for any length of time. A move to Ipswich Town in the summer of 1966 proved a great success and he enjoyed five seasons as a regular in the line-up before suffering a broken ankle. In 1967–68 he led the scoring charts as the team won promotion as champions of Division Two. He later had a very brief attachment with Morton before concluding his career with Halifax Town. His brother Jim Brogan also played for Celtic.

George Brown (Born: Stirling, 3 February 1948. Died: Sauchie, Clackmannanshire, 11 January 2021.) Centre-half George Brown joined Alloa Athletic from Bonnybridge Juniors during the 1966–67 season and remained with the Wasps until October 1974. He made over 300 first-team appearances during his stay, making him eighth in the club's list of post-war appearance makers. He subsequently had a brief spell with St Mirren before returning to the Juniors with Sauchie.

Les Brown (Born: 27 November 1936. Died: 30 January 2021.) Les Brown was a right-sided forward who gained eight caps for England Amateurs and was also a member of the Great Britain squad for the 1960 Olympic Games. He played his club football principally for Dulwich Hamlet, Wimbledon, with whom he won an FA Amateur Cup winners' medal in 1963, and Guildford City.

Mick Brown (Born: Slough, 11 April 1944. Died: 9 March 2021.) Inside-forward Mick Brown joined Fulham as an apprentice, but although he moved into the professional ranks and made his first-team debut at 17, he received few opportunities at Craven Cottage. He did better at Millwall, featuring in the team that won successive promotions from the Fourth Division to the Second in 1964–65 and 1965–66 but then lost his place. He gained further experience in spells at Luton Town and Colchester United before moving into non-league football.

Tom Brown (Born: Kilmarnock, 29 March 1941. Died: 30 January 2021.) Tom Brown joined Kilmarnock as a centre-forward from Stewarton United in the summer of 1958 but in eight seasons at Rugby Park he made just four first-team appearances, quickly switching positions to become a stalwart of the reserve team at centre-half. He gained more first-team experience with Queen of the South in the 1966–67 season before returning to non-league football with Newton Stewart.

Sam Burton (Born: Swindon, 10 November 1926. Died: 8 October 2020.) Sam Burton spent 17 years on the books of Swindon Town and his total of 509 appearances is the most of any goalkeeper for the club. A local boy who was signed as a teenager, his early career at the County Ground was disrupted by a lengthy spell as a Bevin Boy in the South Wales coalfields. He became the club's first-choice 'keeper during the 1952–53 season and retained his place until November 1961. He was twice an ever-present in the line-up on two occasions, in 1954–55 and 1957–58.

Alec Byrne (Born: Greenock, 4 June 1933. Died: Hendon, South Australia, 31 October 2020.) Alex Byrne was a strong and forceful attacking player who developed with Greenock St Mary's and Gourock Juniors before signing for Celtic at the beginning of the 1954–55 season. He had to wait nearly three years before being given his senior debut and made exactly 100 first-team appearances during his stay at Parkhead. He contributed to Morton's Second Division title success in 1963–64 but moved on to Queen of the South before the season had ended. Later he emigrated to Australia where he played for and then coached at the Hellas club of Adelaide.

Danny Campbell (Born: Oldham, 3 February 1944. Died: Port Elizabeth, South Africa, 15 August 2020.) Centre-half Danny Campbell signed for West Bromwich Albion from Manchester junior club Droylsden and spent some years as a professional with the Baggies. Mostly a reserve, he made his senior debut in the first leg of the 1965–66 Football League Cup final against West Ham United, and also featured in the second leg to earn a winners' trophy. He continued his career with a spell in the NASL with Los Angeles Wolves, then with Stockport County and Bradford Park Avenue, for whom he scored the last-ever Football League goal. He subsequently emigrated to South Africa where he played for Port Elizabeth City for several seasons.

Jimmy Cardno (Born: Fraserburgh, 23 May 1946. Died: Holywell, Flintshire, 16 January 2021.) Jimmy Cardno was a tall striker who was capped for Wales Schools and later for Scotland Amateurs. He enjoyed a varied playing career which included spells in the USA, Canada, Australia and the Netherlands (where he appeared for HFC Haarlem in the Eredivisie) as well as numerous clubs in North Wales.

Tommy Carroll (Born: Dublin, 18 August 1942. Died: August 2020.) Defender Tommy Carroll played for Shelbourne at the age of 15 and was a member of the team that won the League of Ireland title in 1961–62 and the FAI Cup the following season. He signed for Cambridge City in October 1963 and was still with the Lilywhites when he played in his country's first-ever Under 23 international in June 1966. Soon afterwards he signed for Ipswich Town where he was a regular in the team that won the Second Division in 1967–68 and went on to spend three seasons in the old First Division. He later won a second promotion to the top flight with Birmingham City in 1971–72 before returning to Shelbourne. He won 17 full caps for the Republic of Ireland between 1968 and 1973.

Dessie Cathcart (Born: Belfast, 4 April 1947. Died: Dundonald, Co Down, 30 April 2021.) Winger Dessie Cathcart enjoyed a lengthy career in Irish League football with both Linfield and Ards, and was a member of the Linfield team that narrowly lost out to Manchester City in the 1970–71 Cup Winners' Cup on away goals. He won international honours for Northern Ireland Amateurs and the Irish League representative team.

Tosh Chamberlain (Born: Camden Town, 11 July 1934. Died: 10 January 2021.) Tosh Chamberlain was a goalscoring outside-left who was capped by England Schools and Youth, and signed professional terms for Fulham, his only senior club, at the age of 17. He scored with a 35-yard drive in the first minute of his Football League debut against Lincoln City in November 1954 and remained at Craven Cottage until the end of the 1964–65 season, although latterly he was mainly a reserve. In total he scored 64 goals from 204 senior appearances, playing in the FA Cup semi-final defeat to Manchester United in 1957–58, and helping the team win promotion from the Second Division 12 months later.

Jack Charlton, OBE, DL (Born: Ashington, 8 May 1935. Died: Northumberland, 10 July 2020.) Jack Charlton was a tall, rangy centre-half who dominated in the air and was a cornerstone of the Leeds United defence for 18 seasons, establishing a club record of 629 Football League appearances which remains unbeaten. He joined the groundstaff at Elland Road soon after leaving school and made his Football League debut as a 17-year-old, but it was only after completing his National Service that he won a regular place in the side. He was twice a member of teams that won promotion from Division Two (1955–56 and 1963–64) and a key figure in Don Revie's successful team of the 1960s and ''70s, winning the Football League title (1968–69), the League Cup (1967–68), the FA Cup (1971–72) and the Inter Cities Fairs Cup on two occasions (1967–68 and 1970–71). In 1966–67 he was chosen as the Football Writers' Association Footballer of the Year. He also won 35 caps for England between 1965 and 1970, appearing in all six games in the 1966 World Cup campaign, including the historic 4-2 win over West Germany in the final, arguably the greatest moment in English football history. He later enjoyed a very successful career as a manager with Middlesbrough (May 1973 to April 1977), Sheffield Wednesday (October 1977 to May 1983), Newcastle United (August 1984 to August 1985) and the Republic of Ireland (February 1986 to December 1995). He won the Second Division title (1973–74) and the Anglo Scottish Cup (1975–76) with Middlesbrough, promotion from the Third Division with Sheffield Wednesday (1979–80) and took Ireland to the World Cup finals in 1990 and 1994.

Kevin Charlton (Born: Atherstone, Warwickshire, 12 September 1954. Died: 18 November 2020.) Goalkeeper Kevin Charlton played for Birch Coppice of the Sutton Amateur League before signing as an apprentice for Wolverhampton Wanderers on leaving school. He progressed to a professional contract at Molineux, but the closest he came to the senior team was a place on the bench. In December 1973 he joined Bournemouth in search of first-team football and made a number of appearances before receiving a free transfer and signing for Hereford United in the 1975 close season. He was a regular in the Bulls team that won the Third Division title in 1975–76 but later lost his place, continuing his career with Bangor City and then Telford. He spent a decade with the Shropshire club, winning the FA Trophy on two occasions and featuring in the team that reached the FA Cup fifth round in 1984–85.

Albert Cheesebrough (Born: Burnley, 17 January 1935. Died: Southport, 2 September 2020.) Albert Cheesebrough joined the groundstaff at Burnley on leaving school before stepping up to the professional ranks at the age of 17. Although originally a winger, he was converted to inside-left, and it was in this role that he established himself for the Clarets in the 1955–56 season. He spent three years as a first-team regular, also being capped for England U23s, but then lost his place in the side and moved on to Leicester City in 1959. A regular in his first two seasons at Filbert Street, he was back on the wing in the 1961 Cup Final final when the Foxes were beaten by double winners Spurs. He later dropped down to the lower divisions with spells at Port Vale and Mansfield Town before injury ended his career.

Chris Chilton (Born: Sproatley, Yorkshire, 25 June 1943. Died: Hull, 20 May 2021.) Centre-forward Chris Chilton was one of the all-time greats for Hull City and his career total of 222 goals from 477 League and Cup appearances remains a club record. A product of local football, he was a regular in the Tigers first team at the age of 17 and went on to head the club's scoring charts on three occasions, netting a total of 12 hat-tricks. He was a major contributor to Hull's success in winning the Third Division title in 1965–66 and was a member of the FA touring team to Australia in the summer of 1971. In September 1971 he was sold to Coventry City where he gained experience of First Division football before a back injury brought his senior career to a close at the end of that season.

Phil Chisnall (Born: Manchester, 27 October 1942. Died: 4 March 2021.) Phil Chisnall was capped for England schoolboys and went on to sign for Manchester United, firstly on the groundstaff and then as a professional on reaching the age of 17. He was still a teenager when he made his Football League debut against Everton in December 1961, but he never quite established himself in the line-up at Old Trafford despite winning four caps for England U23s. In April 1964 he was sold to Liverpool, the last player to be transferred directly from United to the Anfield club, but he made even less impact at Anfield. Dropping down to the Fourth Division with Southend United brought him regular action and he was the Shrimpers' leading scorer in 1967–68. He concluded his career with a season at Stockport County before injury led to his retirement from senior football.

Donald Clark (Born: Circa 1934. Died: Windygates, Fife, 13 December 2020.) Donald Clark was a versatile defender who was a product of Fife Junior football. He played for Forres Mechanics in their Scottish Cup fifth round tie against Celtic in February 1957 whilstwhile on National Service, but soon after being demobilised he signed for Cowdenbeath. He went on to spend three seasons at Central Park, making 94 first-team appearances before leaving senior football.

Harry Clark (Born: Newcastle-upon-Tyne, 29 December 1932. Died: 23 February 2021.) A product of local club Eastbourne Old Boys, inside-forward Harry Clark signed professional forms for Darlington and made his senior debut at the age of 17. He went on to make close on 150 appearances for the Quakers, then after a short attachment with Sheffield Wednesday, for whom he made a solitary appearance, he joined Hartlepools United in August 1958. He led the scorers in both his first two seasons at the Victoria Ground before eventually switching to non-league football with South Shields.

Alan Clarke (Born: Houghton Regis, Bedfordshire, 10 April 1942. Died: 3 April 2021.) Winger Alan Clarke signed for Luton Town on leaving school, progressing to the professional ranks in October 1961. He was mostly a reserve during his time with the Hatters, making 10 first-team appearances before moving on to play for Southern League outfit Dunstable Town.

Chris Clarke (Born: Battersea, 11 December 1946. Died: September 2020.) Chris Clarke was an orthodox winger who was an apprentice with Chelsea and then made 25 first-team appearances for Millwall in the mid-1960s. He added a couple more appearances during a trial period with Watford at the start of the 1966–67 campaign and then continued his career with a string of Southern League clubs including Dartford, Margate, Hastings and Tonbridge.

Ray Clemence, MBE (Born: Skegness, 5 August 1948. Died: 15 November 2020.) Goalkeeper Ray Clemence developed in youth football in Skegness and played a few games for the Notts County reserve and A teams in the second half of the 1964–65 season. He went on to sign professional terms with Scunthorpe United and was a regular in 1966–67 whilstwhile still a teenager. Liverpool manager Bill Shankly signed him up and he went on to become one of the all-time greats at Anfield where he spent 14 years on the books, and once established in the team he rarely missed a match. It was a particularly successful period for the club, and he was a member of five Football League championship sides, three European Cups (1977, 1978 and 1981), the UEFA Cup twice and the FA and Football League Cups once each. At the age of 33 he joined Tottenham Hotspur where he continued to excel, taking his career total of senior appearances beyond the 1,000-mark. He also added a further FA Cup winners' medal as a member of the team that won the competition in 1981–82. He later joined the coaching staff at White Hart Lane and served a period as manager of Barnet (January 1994 to August 1996). He won 61 caps for England between 1972 and 1983 and also spent several years with the England coaching staff.

Hugh Cochrane (Born: Glasgow, 9 February 1943. Died: 17 August 2020.) Hughie Cochrane spent a couple of seasons on the books of Dundee United without making the first team before moving south to sign for Barnsley. He made five first-team appearances during the 1963–64 campaign, all at inside-left, then moved south to play in the Southern League with Wimbledon. He went on to feature for Ashford Town (Kent), Margate, Ramsgate, and Wombwell Town.

Tommy Coggill (Born: Hamilton, 21 March 1948. Died: May 2021.) Tommy Coggill was playing for Blantyre Vics in the Scottish Juniors at the age of 14 and after featuring for a number of clubs joined Kilmarnock from Fauldhouse United shortly after the start of the 1967–68 season. An inside-forward or wing man, he stayed in senior football for four seasons, later featuring for Queen of the South, Stranraer, and Hamilton Academicals. In 1971 he was reinstated as a Junior with Shotts Bon Accord, eventually returning to Blantyre Vics where he was a member of the team that won the Scottish Junior Cup in 1982–83 and he later had two spells as manager of the club.

Ray Colfar (Born: Liverpool, 4 December 1935. Died: 16 December 2020.) Ray Colfar was a traditional outside-left who came to prominence with Corinthian League club Epsom, then had a brief attachment to Sutton United before signing professional forms for Crystal Palace in November 1958. He was a regular for Palace in the first half of the 1959–60 season but otherwise was mostly a reserve. He then had a spell with Cambridge United before moving on to Oxford United, for whom he appeared in their first-ever Football League fixture at Barrow in August 1962. He later returned to the Southern League to conclude his career with Guildford City and Wimbledon.

Lee Collins (Born: Telford, 28 September 1988. Died: West Coker, Somerset, 31 March 2021.) Defender Lee Collins developed in the academy set-up at Wolverhampton Wanderers, although he was unable to break into the first team at Molineux. He subsequently forged a lengthy career in the lower divisions of the Football League, notably with Port Vale, Northampton Town, Mansfield Town and Forest Green Rovers. He made a total of over 400 senior appearances in a career that spanned the period 2007 to 2019 and played in Forest Green's first-ever Football League match against Barnet in August 2017. At the time of his death, which occurred in very tragic circumstances, he was captain of National League club Yeovil Town.

Tony Collins (Born: Kensington, 19 March 1926. Died: 8 February 2021.) Tony Collins was one of the pioneering black players in the post-war period. He signed for Sheffield Wednesday from Acton United in July 1949, and although he did not make the first team at Hillsborough this proved to be the start of a lengthy playing career of more than a decade. A winger, he appeared for several clubs across the lower divisions of the Football League including Watford, Norwich City, Torquay United and Crystal Palace. He made over 350 senior appearances, finishing off at Rochdale where he was appointed as manager in September 1960, thus becoming the first black manager in the Football League. He took Dale to the Football League Cup final in 1961–62 and stayed in post until September 1967. Later he became assistant manager of Bristol City and was involved in scouting for a number of clubs including Manchester United.

Eddie Connachan (Born: Prestonpans, East Lothian, 27 August 1935. Died: East London, South Africa, 28 January 2021.) Eddie Connachan was a goalkeeper who developed in the Juveniles with Cockenzie Star before stepping up to the Juniors with Easthouses Lily and Dalkeith Thistle. He signed for Dunfermline Athletic in the summer of 1957 and in a six-year stay at East End Park he made over 150 appearances. He was a Scottish Cup winner with the Pars in 1961 starring in both the drawn final against Celtic and the replay, and this led to representative honours for both Scotland and the Scottish League. Later he moved south, joining Middlesbrough, and had two good seasons before returning to Scotland and finishing his career with Falkirk. He subsequently emigrated to South Africa where he was involved in coaching at East London City and Port Elizabeth City.

Steve Conroy (Born: Chesterfield, 19 December 1956. Died: May 2021.) Goalkeeper Steve Conroy joined Sheffield United as an apprentice on leaving school and went on to sign a professional contract at the age of 18, but it was another three years before he made his Football League debut for the Blades. He was first choice in the 1978–79 season and retained his place until December 1979 when he was side lined after suffering a broken arm in a Texaco Cup tie against St Mirren. Thereafter he was never able to establish himself in the side and after a brief spell at Rotherham United he signed for Rochdale in the summer of 1983. He was an ever-present in his first season at Spotland but then lost his place before further injuries led to his retirement in September 1985.

Kevin Cornwell (Born: Birmingham, 10 December 1941. Died: September 2020.) Inside-forward Kevin Cornwell was a product of Birmingham Sunday football who joined Oxford United from Banbury Spencer in March 1962. He featured for the U's in their first-ever Football League game at Barrow the following August and went on to score 10 goals from 26 appearances over the next two seasons. He later appeared in the Southern League for a number of clubs including Cambridge City and Cheltenham Town.

Russ Cuddihey (Born: Rawtenstall, Lancashire, 8 September 1939. Died: Blackburn, 11 July 2020.) Left-half Russ Cuddihey was on the books of Accrington Stanley for their final two seasons of League football. He made 25 appearances without scoring. He was also a talented cricketer featuring for Accrington in the Lancashire League between 1955 and 1972.

Alan Daniel (Born: Ashford, Kent, 5 April 1940. Died: 12 May 2021.) Alan Daniel was a full-back who signed for Luton Town as a 17-year-old. The son of former Hatters player Mel Daniel, he was principally a reserve during his time at Kenilworth Road, making a total of 54 first-team appearances. His career was ended when he suffered an Achilles tendon injury in September 1963.

Dai Davies (Born: Glanamman, Carmarthenshire, 1 April 1948. Died: Llangollen, Denbighshire,10 February 2021.) Goalkeeper Dai Davies joined Swansea City from Welsh League club Ammanford Town in August 1969 and enjoyed something of a meteoric rise to fame. After making just 11 first-team appearances for the Swans he was sold to Everton just 16 months after his arrival. It was some time before he became first choice at Goodison Park, but he had three good years before moving to Wrexham in September 1977. His first season at The the Racecourse Ground saw him gain a Division Three champions medal, whilstwhile he also helped the team to win the Welsh Cup and reach the quarter-finals of the FA Cup. He went on to play more than 150 games for Wrexham, then had two seasons in the old First Division back at Swansea City before concluding his career as player-coach of Tranmere Rovers. In August 1985 he came out of retirement to play for Bangor City in the European Cup Winners' Cup. He was capped for Wales on 52 occasions between 1975 and 1983. In 1978 he became the first Welsh footballer to be admitted to the Gorsedd Circle of Bards at the National Eisteddfod in Cardiff.

Fred Davies (Born: Liverpool, 22 August 1939. Died: 2 September 2020.) Goalkeeper Fred Davies was playing for Borough United in the Welsh League North when he signed professional forms for Wolverhampton Wanderers as a 17-year-old. It was five years before he broke into the first team at Molineux but then had a run of three seasons in the line-up before losing his place after they were relegated from the top flight. He went on to play for Cardiff City where he was three times a Welsh Cup winner and saw action in the European Cup Winners' Cup. His career was ended by injury whilstwhile at Bournemouth and he then joined the backroom staff at Dean Court before going on to work with several clubs. He was manager of Shrewsbury Town from May 1993 to May 1997, leading them to the Division Three title in 1993–94.

Alex Dawson (Born: Aberdeen, 21 February 1940. Died: Kettering, 17 July 2020.) Alex Dawson moved with his family from Aberdeen to Hull as a youngster and won international honours for England schoolboys as an outside-left. He signed for Manchester United on amateur forms where he was converted to playing at centre-forward and was an FA Youth Cup winner in 1955–56 and 1956–57. On reaching 17 he joined the professional ranks and soon afterwards made a scoring debut against Burnley. Following the decimation of the squad in the Munich Air Disaster he was thrust into the first team and responded by scoring a memorable hat-trick in the FA Cup semi-final against Fulham, going on to gain an FA Cup runners-up medal that season. In October 1961 he moved on to Preston North End, where he enjoyed the best years of his career, netting 114 League goals from 199 appearances. He led the scoring charts three seasons in a row and won a second FA Cup runners-up medal as a member of the team that lost out to West Ham United in the 1964 final. He later had spells at Bury (where he contributed to their success in winning promotion in 1967–68) and Brighton & Hove Albion before leaving senior football.

Richard Dawson (Born: Chesterfield, 19 January 1960. Died: Chesterfield, August 2020.) Richard Dawson started out as an apprentice with Rotherham United and after progressing to a professional contract he made his senior debut at the age of 17. Unable to win a regular place in the Millers' line-up, he moved on to sign for Doncaster Rovers in February 1981. He helped them win promotion from the Fourth Division in 1980–81, then finished as top scorer the following season. However, he was on the move again in the summer of 1982, this time to Chesterfield where he spent six months before a move into non-league football with Scarborough.

Graham Day (Born: Bristol, 22 November 1953. Died: 8 February 2021.) Graham Day was a big, powerful defender who played his early football in the Bristol Senior League with Hanham Athletic and Bristol St George before joining Bristol Rovers in the summer of 1973. He had three seasons of regular first-team football with the Pirates, making just short of 150 League and Cup appearances. Later he spent six summers in the NASL where he turned out for Portland Timbers before returning to the West Country to play in non-league football. He was a member of the Forest Green Rovers team that won both the Hellenic League and the FA Vase in 1981–82.

Roger Day (Born: Romford, 3 December 1939. Died: November 2020.) Roger Day was a creative inside-forward who was one of the top English amateur players in the 1960s. Early on in his career he made a single Football League appearance for Watford but turned down the opportunity of a professional contract at Vicarage Road. He appeared in five FA Amateur Cup finals, featuring on the winning side with Enfield in 1967 and 1970, and won 42 caps for England Amateur, often captaining the side. He also featured for Great Britain in the Olympic Games qualifying rounds.

James Dean (Born: Blackburn, 15 May 1985. Died: Oswaldtwistle, Lancashire, May 2021.) James Dean was a tall striker who joined Bury from Northwich Victoria and went on to make six first-team appearances during the 2007–08 season. He subsequently featured for a string of clubs including Harrogate Town, FC Halifax Town and AFC Fylde in a lengthy career in non-league football.

Tony Devereux (Born: Gibraltar, 6 January 1940. Died: August 2020.) Full back Tony Devereux was an amateur on Chelsea's books before signing for Aldershot. He went on to spend eight years at the Recreation Ground, making just short of 150 first-team appearances. A highlight of his career came in January 1964 as a member of the Shots team that beat Aston Villa in an FA Cup third round replay. He later played for Hampshire club Thornycroft Athletic.

Joe Devlin (Born: Cleland, Lanarkshire, 12 March 1931. Died: Blackburn, Lancashire, 11 December 2020.) A product of Secondary Juvenile club Cleland St Mary's Boys' Guild, Joe Devlin progressed to the senior ranks after just three appearances for Cleland Juniors. A skilful winger, he was only 16 when he made his Scottish League debut for Albion Rovers. He spent three seasons with the Coatbridge club and a further three at Falkirk, but he never really established himself as a first-team regular. In the summer of 1953 he moved south to sign for Accrington Stanley where he made over 100 appearances during his stay, then had spells with Rochdale, Bradford Park Avenue and Carlisle United. Later he briefly returned to Accrington, featuring in the final home game against Rochdale before the club folded in March 1962.

Papa Bouba Diop (Born: Rufisque, Dakar, Senegal, 28 January 1978. Died: France, 29 November 2020.) Papa Bouba Diop was a tall and powerful central midfield player who progressed from club football in Senegal to sign for Neuchatel Xamax in the summer of 2000. After appearing for Grasshoppers and Lens he joined Fulham in time for the start of the 2004–05 campaign. He enjoyed three good seasons in the Premier League whilstwhile at Craven Cottage and was transferred to Portsmouth where he gained an FA Cup winners' medal in 2008 and was a runner-up in the same competition two years later. He subsequently had a season in Greece with AEK Athens before winding down his senior career with spells at West Ham United and Birmingham City. He won 63 caps for Senegal between 1978 and 2020 and was a member of the team that reached the quarter-finals of the World Cup in 2002.

Johnny Divers (Born: Cowcaddens, Glasgow, Circa 1940. Died: Possilpark, Glasgow, 21 December 2020.) Johnny Divers was a hard-working striker with an excellent scoring record. He developed with Ashfield Juveniles and Thorniewood United before signing for Hamilton Academical in March 1959. He topped the scoring charts for the Accies in both 1959–60 and 1960–61 and soon after the start of the following season he was sold to Clyde. He provided a useful contribution to the club's success in winning the Second Division title in 1961–62, scoring an impressive 13 goals from 13 appearances but was rarely selected after that and ended his senior career with a brief spell back at Hamilton.

Tom Docherty (Born: Penshaw, Co Durham, 15 April 1924. Died: January 2021.) Tom Docherty joined Lincoln City from Murton CW in the summer of 1947 and in his first season at Sincil Bank made a contribution to the club's promotion campaign. A pacy outside-left, he featured in over half of the Imps' Second Division games in 1948–49 but 12 months later he was allowed to leave for Norwich City. He spent the next eight seasons playing in Division Three South in spells with the Canaries, Reading and Newport County, featuring regularly for all his clubs and dropping back to play at left-half in the closing stages of his career. He continued to play into his 40s, initially with King's Lynn and then several teams in the East of England.

Tommy Docherty (Born: Glasgow, 24 August 1928. Died: 31 December 2020.) Tommy Docherty joined Celtic as a centre-half from Shettleston Juniors in the summer of 1948, but he was mainly a reserve during his time at Parkhead. In November 1949 he was sold to Preston North End where he quickly established himself and went on to make over 300 League appearances, mostly at right-half. He was ever-present in the team that won the Second Division title in 1950–51 and gained an FA Cup runners-up medal in 1954. Later he spent a couple of seasons at Arsenal before being appointed as player-coach at Chelsea in September 1961. Soon afterwards he stepped up to become manager and this proved to be the beginning of a second career in the game. He led Chelsea to promotion from the Second Division in 1962–63, success in the Football League Cup (1965) and runners-up in the FA Cup (1967) before resigning in October 1967. He subsequently enjoyed a lengthy career in management with a string of different clubs, earning a reputation as one of the great characters of British football. His best spell was probably when in charge of Manchester United between December 1972 and July 1977 when he led the team to the Second Division title (1973–74) and two FA Cup finals (defeat in 1976 and success a year later). As a player he won 25 caps for Scotland and appeared for them in the 1954 World Cup finals, whilstwhile he later had a spell as manager of the Scotland national team from September 1971 to December 1972.

Rab Donnelly (Born: Motherwell, 30 July 1961. Died: June 2020.) Rab Donnelly was an uncompromising centre-half who joined Clyde from amateur club Coatbridge CC in September 1987. In a two-year stay with the Bully Wee he made 35 first-team appearances before switching to Neilston Juniors.

Chuck Drury (Born: Darlaston, Staffordshire, 4 July 1937. Died: 5 October 2020.) Chuck Drury was a wing-half who developed in Wolverhampton junior football with Darlaston Green Rovers and FH Lloyds before joining West Bromwich Albion on amateur forms. He was capped for England Youths and signed professional terms at the age of 17, however, it was only after he had completed his National Service that he made his first-team debut. He stayed at The Hawthorns until August 1964, making over 150 first-team appearances, before dropping down the divisions to play for Bristol City and Bradford Park Avenue.

Micky Dulin (Born: Stepney, 25 October 1935. Died: 16 March 2021.) Micky Dulin was a winger who joined Tottenham Hotspur from Welwyn Garden City in November 1952. A former England Schools' international, he mostly featured in the reserve and A teams at White Hart Lane although he made 10 first-team appearances. His career was ended after he suffered a serious leg injury playing at Birmingham City in September 1957.

Charlie Dunn (Born: Dundee, 10 May 1942. Died: 31 May 2020.) Inside-forward Charlie Dunn attracted the attention of Arbroath after scoring five goals for Dundee North End in a Scottish Junior Cup tie against Arbroath Vics in October 1959. He spent a year with the Red Lichties and a further three with Montrose but is best remembered for his time with Brechin City for whom he made over 250 appearances between 1964 and 1971. He was later manager of Brechin in a four-year spell from November 1973.

Jóhannes Eðvaldsson (Born: Reykjavik, 3 September 1950. Died: Glasgow, 24 January 2021.) Jóhannes Eðvaldsson was a big, powerful player who was best employed either in midfield or as a defender. After developing in Iceland with Valur he arrived at Celtic in August 1975 from Danish club Holbaek. He spent the best part of five seasons at Parkhead, making over 150 appearances and winning two Scottish League titles (1976–77 and 1978–79) and the Scottish Cup in 1977. He later played for Tulsa Roughnecks in the NASL (finishing top scorer in his only season), and Hannover 96, before returning to Scotland for a spell with Motherwell. His father was an international for Estonia in the 1930s, while his bother Atli played and managed the Iceland national team.

Zhang Enhua (Born: Dalian, China, 28 April 1973. Died: 29 April 2021.) Central defender Zhang Enhua spent three months on loan with Grimsby Town from Dalian Wanda during the 2000–01 season. With the Mariners team short of defenders and close to the foot of the Division One table, manager Lennie Lawrence used his links with former China national team manager Bobby Houghton to facilitate the move. He was a regular during his short stay and helped the club edge their way towards safety from relegation. He returned to China and later played for Tianjin Teda and South China. He won 65 full caps for China between 1995 and 2002.

Duncan Falconer (Born: 21 April 1941. Died: 26 January 2021.) Duncan Falconer spent five years as a professional with Hibernian where he was mostly a reserve apart from in the 1961–62 season when he headed the club's scoring charts. He spent the summer of 1964 playing in Australia for APIA Leichardt before returning to Easter Road before quitting the game in April 1966 to join the Kent Constabulary.

Mike Farrelly (Born: Manchester, 1 November 1962. Died: 26 June 2020.) Mike Farrelly was an England Schools' international who went on to sign professional forms for Preston North End in June 1981. He made over 90 appearances during his stay at Deepdale, mostly in midfield, and was a near ever-present in the 1984–85 season before being released. He later enjoyed a successful career in non-league football with Altrincham, for whom he scored the winner in the 1986 FA Trophy final, and Macclesfield Town. He also won representative honours for the England Semi-Professional team.

Geoff Fellows (Born: West Bromwich, 26 July 1944. Died: West Bromwich, 17 January 2021.) Geoff Fellows starred for the West Bromwich Schools' team, joining Aston Villa as an amateur before turning professional shortly after reaching the age of 17. He progressed to the reserve team during his time at Villa Park, before joining Shrewsbury Town in July 1965. Although previously a wing-half he went straight into the Shrews' line-up at left-back and remained a fixture in the side for the next seven years, captaining the team for several seasons. He was chosen by the supporters as Player of the Year in 1967–68 and went on to make over 300 first-team appearances at Gay Meadow. His senior career was effectively ended after he suffered a fractured leg playing for the reserves in February 1973.

John Fitzpatrick (Born: Aberdeen, 18 August 1946. Died: 21 December 2020.) John Fitzpatrick was playing in the Aberdeen Youth League for Aberdeen Lads Club Thistle when spotted by Manchester United and he moved south in the summer of 1962. He progressed through the ranks at Old Trafford, signing professional forms at the age of 17 and breaking into the first team in February 1965. He became the first substitute to be used by United when he came off the bench against Spurs the following season. He went on to make 150 first-team appearances as a combative defender or midfielder before a series of knee injuries led to his retirement from the game in the summer of 1973.

Bernard Fleming (Born: Middlesbrough, 8 January 1937. Died: 7 March 2021.) Full-back Bernard Fleming signed for Grimsby Town after being spotted whilstwhile undergoing his National Service at RAF Binbrook and spent four seasons on the club's books without ever winning a regular place in the side. He fared better in a season at Workington but was still mainly a reserve and it was only after signing for Chester in May 1962 that he gained regular first-team football. However, after making 71 appearances for the Sealand Road club he was forced to retire through injury. He subsequently returned to Blundell Park as youth team coach and later served as club secretary between 1982 and 1986. He also had a spell as secretary of Southend United.

Jim Fleming (Born: Alloa, 7 January 1942. Died: 10 December 2020.) Outside-left Jim Fleming made his debut for Partick Thistle at the age of 16 and was still a teenager when he moved to Luton Town in exchange for Joe McBride. Although he featured regularly during his time at Kenilworth Road he never really settled and in December 1962 he returned to Partick. He went on to play for Dunfermline Athletic and Hearts before moving back to England where he enjoyed success with Wigan Athletic, helping them win the Northern Premier League in 1970–71. He later had a spell as player-manager of Inverness Clachnacuddin.

Jimmy Fletcher (Born: Wouldham, Kent, 10 November 1931. Died: Maidstone, 22 November 2020.) Centre-forward Jimmy Fletcher made his name with Maidstone United, helping them win the Corinthian League title in 1955–56 and gaining England Amateur international honours. In July 1957 he signed for Gillingham where he scored 13 goals in his first season to finish as second-top scorer. He moved on to Southend United then developed a useful career in Southern League football with Gravesend & Northfleet, Dartford, Margate and Dover.

Len Fletcher (Born: Hammersmith, 28 April 1929. Died: Ipswich, 21 March 2021.) Wing-half Len Fletcher was on Ipswich Town's books for six seasons but was mostly a reserve during his time at the club, making a total of 21 appearances. In August 1955 he signed for Falkirk, where he was again mostly a back-up player, playing 17 first-team games over three seasons before leaving senior football.

Ron Fogg (Born: Tilbury, Essex, 3 June 1938. Died: Tilbury, Essex, 3 November 2020.) Ron Fogg was an old-fashioned style centre-forward who made his name in Essex amateur football with Tilbury and Grays Athletic, also making two appearances for Southend United. He appeared for the Army Amateur XI during National Service and some of the trial games for the 1960 Olympics squad. Soon afterwards he signed professional forms for Southern League Weymouth where he became a prolific goal scorer and was a member of the team that reached the FA Cup fourth round in 1961–62. His exploits earned him a transfer to Aldershot, where he led the scoring charts for them in 1963–64. He continued to score freely in a spell at Hereford United and also featured for Bedford Town and Chelmsford City, latterly switching to play at centre-half.

Theo Foley (Born: Dublin, 2 April 1937. Died: June 2020.) Theo Foley was a pacy full-back who signed for Exeter City from Home Farm in March 1955. He established himself in the line-up during the 1957–58 campaign and had four seasons as a regular with the Grecians before moving on to Northampton Town for a small fee in May 1961. He enjoyed the best years of his career with the Cobblers, where he was a near ever-present in the team that won the Third Division title in 1962–63 and again two seasons later, when they gained promotion to the old First Division. However, injuries began to take their toll and in August 1967 he joined Charlton Athletic as player-coach. He remained at The Valley after his playing career ended, eventually being promoted to manager (March 1970 to April 1974) thereafter continuing to work in the game with several clubs including a spell back with Northampton as manager from May 1990 to April 1992.

Bobby Folland (Born: Hartlepool, 3 December 1940. Died: 1 January 2021.) Centre-forward Bobby Folland developed with junior club Seaton Holy Trinity for whom he was a prolific goalscorer, on one occasion netting nine goals in a county cup game. He signed for Hartlepools United in May 1959 and went on to spend four seasons at the Victoria Ground, scoring 28 goals from 64 appearances. He equalled a club record, yet to be broken, netting five times in the home win over Oldham Athletic in April 1961.

Peter Ford (Born: Etruria, Staffordshire, 10 August 1933. Died: 17 July 2020.) Centre-half Peter Ford was a local lad who was a professional on the books of Stoke City for six years but was mostly a reserve throughout this time, making just occasional first-team appearances. In September 1959 he moved to Port Vale where he was initially a regular in the line-up before contracting tuberculosis which led to a three-month stay in hospital. He made a full recovery and won back his place, but he was increasingly used as a utility player, with his final Football League appearances coming at centre-forward. He later played in non-league football for Macclesfield Town and Stafford Rangers.

Alex Forrester, OBE (Born: Fife, 14 November 1935. Died: Aberdeen, 4 January 2021.) Alex Forrester was a member of the Sauchie team that won the Scottish Juvenile Cup in 1957–58, when he scored one of his team's goals. Already on provisional forms with Third Lanark, he was called up to the senior team shortly afterwards but was unable to break into the first team. His only senior appearance came in November 1959 when he turned out for Alloa Athletic against Dundee United. He went on to become a distinguished academic, becoming Emeritus Professor of Earth Sciences and Chemistry at Aberdeen University, and later a vice-principal of the university. He also played cricket for Clackmannanshire and Aberdeenshire and in 1964 came on as 12th man for Scotland against Australia.

Campbell Forsyth (Born: Plean, Stirlingshire, 5 May 1934. Died: Bridge of Allan, Stirlingshire, 15 November 2020.) Goalkeeper Campbell Forsyth developed with Gairdoch United Juveniles and Shettleston Juniors before stepping up to the seniors with St Mirren towards the end of the 1954–55 season. He made 150 appearances during his time at Love Street then moved on to Kilmarnock where he was the regular 'keeper for much of the 1964–65 when they won the Scottish League title. He subsequently moved south, signing for Southampton where he contributed to their promotion campaign from Division Two in his first season. He began the 1966–67 season as first choice but suffered a broken leg in the home game with Liverpool in September leading to a lengthy lay-off. He recovered and regained his place the following season but struggled to find his best form and retired soon afterwards. He won four full caps for Scotland and also appeared for the Under 23s and the Scottish League representative side.

Tom Forsyth (Born: Glasgow, 23 January 1949. Died: Strathaven, Lanarkshire, 14 August 2020.) Tom Forsyth joined Motherwell from Stonehouse Violet at the start of the 1966–67 season and made over 150 appearances over the next five years mostly featuring in a midfield role. He was sold to Rangers in October 1972 where he was converted into an uncompromising and tenacious defender and enjoyed a trophy-filled career in a decade at Ibrox Park. He was a member of three Scottish League title winning sides as well as winning the Scottish Cup on four occasions and the League Cup twice. His first goal for Rangers proved to be the winner in the centenary Scottish Cup final in 1973, giving the club success in the competition for the first time since 1966. Later he was manager of Dunfermline Athletic from September 1982 to October 1983 and also had spells as assistant manager at both Motherwell and Hearts. He won 22 caps for Scotland and was a member of the squad for the 1978 World Cup finals.

Gordon Frew (Born: South Africa, 23 March 1927. Died: Hermanus, South Africa, 2021.) Gordon Frew was a full-back who played for Marist Brothers and won representative honours for South Africa before travelling to Scotland to sign for Dundee in August 1950. He stayed four seasons at Dens Park, appearing in 63 League and Cup matches and gaining a League Cup winners' prize as a member of the team that won the trophy in 1952–53. He subsequently returned to South Africa where he went on to captain the national team and later became player-manager of Highlands Park.

Joe Frickleton (Born: Circa 1936. Died: Cape Town, South Africa, 15 December 2020.) Joe Frickleton was a hard-tackling defensive midfield player who joined East Stirlingshire from Clydebank Juniors in December 1959 and went on to make over 100 Scottish League appearances during his stay. In April 1964 he emigrated to South Africa where he played for Highlands Park for a decade. He subsequently switched to managing and coaching earning success with Highlands Park, Kaizer Chiefs and Orlando Pirates.

Alan Garner (Born: Walworth, London, 2 February 1951. Died: 23 July 2020.) Alan Garner was an apprentice with Millwall but although he went on to sign a professional contract, he made only a couple of first-team appearances. He developed into a stylish centre-half on signing for Luton Town where he was an ever ever-present in the team that won promotion to the old First Division in 1973–74. In February 1975 he was transferred to Watford where he became a key figure in the club's rise up the divisions, gaining a Fourth Division winners' medal in 1977–78 and helping them win promotion to the Second Division the following season. He concluded his senior career with Portsmouth before joining non-league Barnet.

Eddie Gavigan (Born: Glasgow, 7 December 1963. Died: Auckland, New Zealand, 8 December 2020.) Eddie Gavigan was a forward who was on the books of Morton as a teenager, making 21 first-team appearances. He emigrated to New Zealand at the age of 19 where he spent several years with Auckland club Mount Wellington, twice winning the Chatham Cup, the country's premier knock-out trophy, with them. For many years he was a leading figure in the food manufacturing sector in New Zealand.

Peter Gelson (Born: Hammersmith, 18 October 1941. Died: 26 April 2021.) Centre-half Peter Gelson captained the Oaktown team that won the Middlesex Youth Senior Cup in 1958–59 and soon afterwards signed for Brentford. He progressed through the ranks at Griffin Park, to become one of the greatest players in the club's history, making over 500 first-team appearances and featuring in two promotion teams (1962–63 and 1971–72). He was twice chosen as the club's Player of the Year and was later inducted into the Hall of Fame. He remained with the Bees until October 1974 when he moved on to Hillingdon Borough.

John Gibbons (Born: Charlton, 8 April 1925. Died: Woolwich, London, 31 January 2021.) John Gibbons signed for Dartford after being demobilised from the Forces and promptly scored two goals in their 9-2 defeat by Bristol City in an FA Cup first round replay. Within a week he had signed for Queen's Park Rangers but in just under two seasons with the R's he made 10 appearances and a further season at Ipswich Town yielded just 13 more. Nevertheless he signed for Tottenham Hotspur on transfer deadline day in 1950. He was a regular in the reserve and A teams at White Hart Lane but gained no further experience of senior football and in 1953 he moved on to Gravesend & Northfleet.

Peter Gillott (Born: Barnsley, 20 July 1935. Died: January 2021.) Defender Peter Gillott signed for Barnsley from local club Worsborough Common United in May 1953, but in six seasons at Oakwell he was mainly a reserve, making five first-team appearances. He subsequently joined Southern League club Chelmsford City with whom he played over 350 games and was a member of the team that won the Southern League Cup in 1958–59.

Larry Gilmore (Died: Blackrock, Dublin, 8 August 2020.) Larry Gilmore was a tall winger who played League of Ireland Football in the 1960s with Bohemians, Dundalk and Sligo Rovers. He won international honours for the Republic of Ireland Amateurs.

John Glover (Born: Kirkintilloch, Dunbartonshire, 1935. Died: 11 February 2021.) John Glover was originally a winger with Twechar Rovers and Kilsyth Rangers, playing once as a triallist for Dumbarton in March 1953. He switched to left-half and was a key member of the Kilsyth Rangers team that won the Scottish Junior Cup in 1954–55. He subsequently spent three seasons as a senior with Dumbarton before returning to the Juniors. He was later manager of the Kilsyth Rangers team that won the Junior Cup in 1966–67.

Stuart Gordon (Born: 18 January 1947. Died: 9 April 2021.) Inside-left Stuart Gordon was a product of the Possil YM club who went on to gain a Scottish Junior Cup winners' medal with Kilsyth Rangers. He signed senior forms with Dunfermline Athletic where he progressed into the first team, making a couple of appearances before his career was ended by a badly broken leg.

Peter Goy (Born: Beverley, Yorkshire, 8 June 1938. Died: April 2021.) Goalkeeper Peter Goy impressed watching Arsenal scouts with a fine display for Lincolnshire Schools against Derbyshire Schools and despite conceding 11 goals he signed amateur forms for the Gunners in July 1953. Two years later he progressed to a professional contract and although he was mostly fourth fourth-choice 'keeper for much of his time at Highbury he managed two first-team appearances. In October 1960 he moved on to Southend United where he played over 100 first-team games over the next four seasons. Spells with Watford and Huddersfield Town followed before he spent time in South Africa with Appollon and Hellenic.

Stevie Graham (Born: Dundee, 29 May 1957. Died: Littleover, Derby, 14 February 2021.) Stevie Graham was a striker who joined Forfar Athletic from Midlands AFA club Auchterhouse Amateurs in the summer of 1977. He featured in the team that reached the semi-final of the Scottish League Cup in his first season at Station Park, but later returned to the amateurs with Tayport. Following this he had a successful three-year spell with Brechin City with whom he scored 27 goals from 74 appearances, contributing to the club's success in winning the Second Division title in 1982–83. He concluded his career with brief spells at Forfar and Cowdenbeath.

John Grant (Born: Edinburgh, 22 July 1931. Died: Colinton, Edinburgh, 28 January 2021.) John Grant joined Hibernian from Secondary Juvenile outfit Merchiston Thistle as a teenager but had to wait five seasons before making his senior debut at Easter Road. Although signed as an inside-forward he eventually settled down at right-back and became a first-team regular for the best part of a decade, making just short of 300 first-team appearances. He gained a Scottish Cup runners-up medal in 1958 as a member of the team that lost out to Clyde and won two full caps for Scotland and a further six for the Scottish League representative side. He concluded his career with a season at Raith Rovers before retiring from senior football in the summer of 1965.

Bob Graves (Born: Marylebone, 7 November 1942. Died: King's Lynn, 9 March 2021.) Goalkeeper Bob Graves won representative honours for the Public Schools and England Schools team and was just 17 when he made his first-team debut for Lincoln City in December 1959, making him the second-youngest player to appear for the club in the post-war period at the time. He went on to make a total of 87 League and Cup appearances for the Imps over the next six seasons and was first-choice 'keeper in 1961–62 and the beginning of the following season before suffering concussion in the home game with Oldham Athletic. He retired from football to focus on his business interests and later switched to playing rugby union, appearing for Lincolnshire to complete what is probably a unique double, as he had also appeared for the county at soccer in his younger days.

George Gray (Born: 27 September 1930. Died: 4 February 2021.) Goalkeeper George Gray signed for Raith Rovers from Fife Juvenile club Balgonie Scotia in April 1951 and three months later made his senior debut in a St Mungo's Cup tie. He was only used as a back-up 'keeper during two seasons at Stark's Park, during which time he also played once as a triallist for Dundee United. He spent the 1953–54 season with Colchester United but was unable to break into the first team at Layer Road.

John Greatrex (Born: Nuneaton, 18 November 1936. Died: 22 July 2020.) John Greatrex was a goalkeeper who was on the books of Norwich City for five years in the 1950s. he made a solitary Football League appearance, against Aldershot in April 1958, although the following November he also played in the an away game at Mansfield Town which was abandoned due to fog. He later appeared for Cambridge City and Chelmsford City. He was a talented cricketer and played over 30 games for Norfolk in the Minor Counties Championship.

Mike Greenwood (Born: Barnsley, 9 April 1945. Died: April 2021.) Mike Greenwood was a wing-half who played his club football for Loughborough Colleges, Bishop Auckland, and Corinthian Casuals. He won seven amateur international caps for England and also featured in the Great Britain side that took part in the 1960 Olympic Games. In the summer of 1961 he was a member of the FA touring team that visited the Far East, New Zealand, and the USA.

Tony Gregory (Born: Luton, 16 May 1937. Died: 10 January 2021.) Tony Gregory was a versatile player who shone as an inside-forward with Vauxhall Motors, with whom he won England Youth international honours. He signed professional forms for Luton Town at the age of 18 and made his early appearances for the Hatters at centre-forward. He never quite established himself in the team at Kenilworth Road although he played in the FA Cup final defeat to Nottingham Forest in 1959. In March 1960 he moved to Watford where he featured regularly in the closing stages of the season as the Hornets won promotion from the Fourth Division. He went on to make over 100 appearances during his time at Vicarage Road, later switching to Southern League football with Bexley United and having a spell as player-coach in Canada with Hamilton Steelers.

David Hagen (Born: Edinburgh, 5 May 1973. Died: 24 July 2020.) Midfielder David Hagen was a member of the Scotland squad that reached the final of the FIFA U16 World Championships in 1989 and played for Rangers as a youngster. He was mostly a fringe player at Ibrox and moved on for a season with Hearts, but it was only when he signed for Falkirk that his career began to blossom. He made over 150 appearances for the Bairns and was a Scottish Cup runner-up in 1996–97, while the following season he scored the winner in the Scottish League Challenge Cup final against Queen of the South. He continued his career with spells at Livingston, Clyde and Peterhead. He also won eight caps for Scotland U21s. His early death was a result of Motor motor Neurone neurone Diseasedisease.

Dixie Hale (Born: Waterford, 29 May 1935. Died: Swansea, May 2021.) Dixie Hale was playing League of Ireland football for Waterford at the age of 16 and went on to become the first professional signed by Shamrock Rovers before returning to his former club. He was an FAI Cup runner-up with Waterford in 1959 and soon afterwards signed for Swansea Town. He went on to build a successful Football League career, making over 400 appearances as a skilful midfielder over the next decade. After solid performances for Barrow and Workington he signed for Watford in the summer of 1967 and the following season he featured regularly in the team that won the Third Division title. Later he returned to South Wales where he was manager of several Welsh League clubs. As a player he won representative honours for the League of Ireland.

Tony Hallam (Born: Chesterfield, 9 October 1946. Died: 22 April 2021.) Tony Hallam was one of the first apprentices to sign for Chesterfield and went on to spend four years as a professional at Saltergate. He was a reserve for almost all that time, occasionally filling in at left-back or left-half in the first team. He was released at the end of the 1967–68 campaign and signed for Worksop Town in time for their entry to the newly formed Northern Premier League.

Ian Hamilton (Born: Thornbury, Gloucestershire, 12 September 1940. Died: Bristol, 25 April 2021.) Inside-forward Ian Hamilton signed for Bristol Rovers midway through the 1957–58 season and made his Football League debut shortly afterwards. However, it was not until the 1962–63 season that he established himself in the line-up and he enjoyed three good seasons of first-team football, finishing as top scorer for the Pirates in 1964–65. His later career at Eastville was marred by injury affected and the problems persisted after a move to Newport County in the summer of 1968, eventually leading to his retirement from full-time football. He was the son of John Hamilton who played for Rovers before the war.

Peter Hampton (Born: Oldham, 12 September 1954. Died: Cyprus, September 2020.) Left-back Peter Hampton joined Leeds United as an apprentice and was just 18 when he made his Football League debut. He spent nine seasons on the books at Elland Road where he spent much of his time in the reserves, and he was an unused substitute in the 1975 European Cup final defeat to Bayern Munich. He had a decent run in the side in 1976–77 and remained until August 1980 when he signed for Stoke City. He enjoyed four good seasons with the Potters, all in the top flight, before dropping down the divisions for spells with Burnley, Rochdale and Carlisle United. He subsequently remained at Brunton Park for an 11-year spell as physio and then became manager of Workington (1998 to 2001).

Ben Hannigan (Born: Dublin, 3 September 1943. Died: Dublin, 4 February 2021.) Ben Hannigan was a tall goalscoring inside-forward who enjoyed success in a lengthy career in the League of Ireland between 1961 and 1981. In the middle of this he had a brief spell with Wrexham during the 1965–66 campaign where he scored two goals from seven appearances. He won the League of Ireland championship with three different clubs Shelbourne (1961–62), Dundalk (1966–67) and Cork Celtic (1973–74), and also won the FAI Cup with Shelbourne in 1963 and Shamrock Rovers in 1969. He made two appearances for the League of Ireland representative team.

Gerry Harris (Born: Claverley, Shropshire, 8 October 1935. Died: Ditton Priors, Shropshire, 28 July 2020.) Right-back Gerry Harris joined Wolverhampton Wanderers from local amateur league side Bobbington in January 1954, but it was not until the start of the 1956–57 that he broke into the first team. Soon afterwards he became a fixture in the line-up in what was a very successful period for the Molineux club. He was a near ever-present in the team that won consecutive Football League titles in 1957–58 and 1958–59 and was an FA Cup winner at Wembley the following season. In total he made 270 appearances for Wolves then wound down his career with spells at Walsall and Wellington Town. He was capped four times by England U23s.

Reg Harrison (Born: Derby, 22 May 1923. Died: Derby 17 September 2020.) Reg Harrison was a winger who developed with Derby Corinthians before signing as a professional for Derby County in March 1944. He played for the Rams during the War war when he also guested for Notts County and Hartlepools United. The highlight of his career was appearing in the team that defeated Charlton Athletic to win the FA Cup in May 1946. He went on to make over 250 League appearances during his stay at the Baseball Ground, scoring over 50 goals and finishing as joint-top scorer in 1947–48. He later had a spell with Boston United where he was a member of the team that famously achieved a 6-1 FA Cup win over the Rams in December 1955.

Derek Hawksworth (Born: Bradford, 16 July 1927. Died: 24 March 2021.) Derek Hawksworth was a versatile forward who could play anywhere across the front line. He played as a 15-year-old for Bradford Park Avenue during the war and briefly guested for Colchester United before signing for Bradford City in October 1948 after completing a spell of military service. In December 1950 he was sold to Sheffield United for what was then a record fee for the Bantams. He enjoyed the best years of his career at Bramall Lane, where he was a regular goalscorer and featured in every game in 1952–53 when the Blades won the Second Division title. He later had spells with Huddersfield Town and Lincoln City before returning to Valley Parade to conclude his senior career. He was capped for England B against France in May 1952.

Geoff Hickman (Born: West Bromwich, 7 January 1950. Died: Redditch, 12 December 2020.) Geoff Hickman was an apprentice goalkeeper with West Bromwich Albion in the mid-1960s. Unable to break into the first team at The Hawthorns, he joined Bradford Park Avenue for the 1969–70 season, where he made 10 first-team appearances before leaving senior football. He later worked in the newspaper industry and has been described as "'the founding father of the free newspaper revolution'," after launching a series of titles in the West Midlands in the 1970s.

Ken Hill (Born: Walsall, 28 April 1938. Died: 16 November 2020.) Wing-half Ken Hill was playing in the Walsall Amateur League for Bescot United when he signed professional forms for Walsall in November 1956. He eventually won a regular first-team place during the Saddlers' 1960–61 promotion campaign from Division Three. The following season he was ever-present and was chosen as the club's Player of the Year. He was transferred to Norwich City during the summer of 1963 and had one good season at Carrow Road but spent much of his time in the reserves. He subsequently made a brief return to Fellows Park before dropping into non-league football with Nuneaton Borough.

Peter Hindley (Born: Worksop, 19 May 1944. Died: 1 February 2021.) Although Peter Hindley had played as a centre-forward in junior football he was converted to a defender by Nottingham Forest, and he was initially seen as a prospective replacement for Bob McKinlay. However, it was at right-back that he established himself in the line-up during the 1964–65 season and it was in this role that he was to play for much of the rest of his career. Solid and uncompromising, he went on to make over 400 League and Cup appearances during his stay at the City Ground and played every game in the 1966–67 season when Forest finished as First Division runners-up and FA Cup semi-finalists. Later he had a couple of seasons with Coventry City before ending his senior career at Peterborough United. He won a single cap for England U23s against Greece in May 1967 and was a member of the FA touring party to Australia in the summer of 1971. His father Frank also played for Forest, featuring in the 1938–39 season.

Doug Holden (Born: Manchester, 28 September 1930. Died: 8 April 2021.) Winger Doug Holden made his senior debut for Bolton Wanderers against Liverpool in November 1951 and very quickly established himself in the line-up at Burnden Park. He went on to make over 450 first-team appearances, and was the last surviving player from the team that lost to Blackpool in the 1953 FA Cup final. He later gained a winners' medal five years later and won five full caps for England, as well as gaining representative honours for the Football League XI. In November 1962 he was transferred to Preston North End, where he was again an FA Cup runner-up in 1964, scoring in the 3-2 defeat to West Ham United. Later he spent time in Australia where he played and then coached with New South Wales club Hakoah.

Harry Holman (Born: Exeter, 16 November 1957. Died: Exeter, 6 November 2020.) Striker Harry Holman represented England U15s at both football and rugby union before joining Chelsea as an apprentice on leaving school. Unable to break into the first team at Stamford Bridge, he returned to his home town and signing signed for Exeter City in July 1976 where he spent two-and-a-half seasons, and making over 50 first-team appearances. He subsequently had a brief spell with Peterborough United before leaving senior football. His father, also Harry, briefly played for Exeter in the 1940s.

Bill Holmes (Born: Hunslet, Yorkshire, 29 October 1926. Died: December 2020.) Bill Holmes was a powerful centre-forward who made Football League appearances for Doncaster Rovers and Blackburn Rovers as an amateur, also winning four caps for England Amateurs and featuring in the Great Britain squad for the 1952 Olympic Games. He signed as a part-time professional with Bradford City in September 1953 and after a season at Valley Parade he moved on to Southport, coinciding with a period working as a schoolteacher in Liverpool. He topped the scoring charts for the Sandgrounders in 1954–55 and was in good form the following season before suffering an ankle injury in December 1955 which effectively ended his senior career.

Harry Hooper (Born: Pittington, Co Durham, 14 June 1933. Died: Hunstanton, Norfolk, 26 August 2020.) Harry Hooper was a pacy winger who came to prominence with Hylton Colliery Juniors where he was a member of the team that reached the Durham Junior Cup final in 1949–50. In November 1950 he signed professional forms for West Ham United, where his father, also Harry, had recently been appointed to the backroom staff. He made his senior debut a few months later whilstwhile still 17 years old but it was not until the second half of the 1954–55 campaign that he established himself as a first-team regular. He subsequently had spells with Wolverhampton Wanderers and Birmingham City before concluding his senior career back in the North East at Sunderland. In total he made over 350 League and Cup appearances scoring 124 goals, and also won representative honours for England B, England U23s and the Football League.

Gérard Houllier, OBE (Born: Therouanne, France, 3 September 1947. Died: Paris, France, 14 December 2020.) Gérard Houllier played amateur football in France whilstwhile studying and working as a schoolteacher. He went on to become manager of Lens and then Paris St Saint-Germain, where he led the team to the league title in 1985–86 before working in the French Football Federation set-up for a decade. In July 1998 he was appointed as manager of Liverpool and in six seasons at Anfield he enjoyed success, notably in 2000–01 when the Reds won the UEFA Cup and both the Football League and FA Cups, while they also won the League Cup again in 2002–03. Later he had spells in charge of Lyon and, briefly, Aston Villa where his time was cut short due to health problems. From July 2012 he was head of global football for Red Bull.

Brian Howie (Born: Larbert, Stirlingshire, 13 April 1955. Died: June 2020.) Goalkeeper Brian Howie played a solitary game for Stirling Albion in April 1976 then gained a Scottish Junior Cup runners-up medal with Bo'ness United in 1979. In a second spell with the seniors he fared much better, making over 100 appearances for Stenhousemuir where he was a first choice for three seasons before returning to Junior football with Dunipace in November 1983.

George Hudson (Born: Manchester, 14 March 1937. Died: 28 December 2020.) Centre-forward George Hudson signed for Blackburn Rovers in January 1958 but was mostly a reserve during his time at Ewood Park, making four First Division appearances. He was a revelation when he signed for Accrington Stanley, equalling the club record for goals scored in a season with 35 in the 1960–61 season before being sold to Peterborough United shortly before the clubStanley folded. He was leading scorer for Posh in 1962–63 when he was sold tobought by Third Division rivals Coventry City and he made a bright start to his Highfield Road career, netting a hat-trick on his debut against Halifax. He was top scorer the following season, his goals helping push the Sky Blues to the Third Division title, then moved on to spells with Northampton Town and Tranmere Rovers, contributing to the latter's 1966–67 promotion campaign. His final career total was 194 goals from 353 League and Cup games, and, with the exception of Blackburn, he scored on his debut for each of his other Football League clubs.

Reg Hunter (Born: Colwyn Bay, 25 October 1938. Died: Bangor-on-Dee, 9 September 2020.) Reg Hunter was playing in Colwyn Bay's first team in the Welsh League North whilstwhile still at school and in November 1956 he signed professional forms for Manchester United. He was an FA Youth Cup winner with Manchester United in 1956–57 but managed only a single first-team appearance at Old Trafford. He later spent two years with Wrexham where he was never able to establish himself. In February 1962 he signed for Bangor City where he went on to gain a Welsh Cup winners' medal, scoring in the 3-1 defeat of his former club in the final. This led to action in the European Cup Winners' Cup, and he played in all three of his team's ties against Italian giants Napoli in 1962–63. He continued his carer with a series of short spells with non-league clubs across North Wales.

Willie Hunter (Born: 14 February 1940. Died: 2 August 2020.) Willie Hunter was a quick, skilful and intelligent inside-forward once described as "'an aristocrat among players'." He was one of Bobby Ancell's Motherwell 'Babes' and spent a decade at Fir Park after signing in the summer of 1957, making over 300 League and Cup appearances and scoring 64 goals. Latterly affected by injuries, he went on to spells with Detroit Cougars and Hibernian before ending his playing career in South Africa with Hellenic and Cape Town City. He subsequently became assistant manager of Portsmouth and had spells as manager of Queen of the South (July 1978 to November 1978) and Inverness Caledonian. He won three full and four U23 caps for Scotland and also won representative honours for the Scottish League.

Malcolm Hussey (Born: Darfield, Yorkshire, 11 September 1933. Died: May 2021.) Malcolm Hussey joined Rotherham United as a youngster and after progressing through the ranks signed professional forms in April 1952. His four years at Millmoor were disrupted by National Service and he received few first-team opportunities. On moving on to Scunthorpe United he had a couple of short runs in the line-up in the 1956–57 season but thereafter was generally a reserve before ending his career with a very brief spell at Rochdale.

Steve Ingle (Born: Manningham, Bradford, 22 October 1946. Died: Western Cape, South Africa, 16 December 2020.) Steve Ingle made his senior debut for Bradford City at the age of 17 and went on to establish himself in the team at right-back. He switched to playing at centre-forward in the 1966–67 season with some success, for he was the club's joint top scorer at the time of his transfer to Southend United in January 1967. He subsequently followed manager Alvan Williams to Wrexham where he enjoyed the best years of his career. In a five-years spell at the Racecourse Ground he made over 150 appearances and was a regular in the team that won promotion from the Fourth Division in 1969–70. He later had short spells with Stockport County, Southport and Darlington before emigrating to South Africa where he played for Arcadia Shepherds.

Jerry Ireland (Born: Chester, 14 September 1938. Died: 14 July 2020.) Inside-forward Jerry Ireland developed in junior football in the Chester area with Watergate Loyals before signing amateur forms for Chester. In September 1957 he became a part-time professional and he was still a teenager when he made his first-team debut. Although rarely a first choice at Sealand Road, he went on to make 40 appearances over the next five seasons before switching to non-league football with Altrincham.

Archie Irvine (Born: Coatbridge, 25 June 1946. Died: September 2020.) Archie Irvine was a combative midfield player who developed with West Lothian Steel Foundry Amateurs and Armadale Thistle prior to signing for Airdrieonians. He was still not established in the line-up for the Diamonds when he was sold to Sheffield Wednesday at the start of the 1968–69 campaign. However, he struggled to win a place in the First Division team and moved on to Doncaster Rovers in a player exchange. He enjoyed six good seasons of regular football at Belle Vue where he was Player of the Year in 1971–72 and 1972–73, before ending his senior career with Scunthorpe United.

Steve Jagielka (Born: Manchester, 10 March 1978. Died: Rodington, Shropshire, 17 March 2021.) Steve Jagielka was a hard hard-working right-sided midfield player who developed in the academy at Stoke City. He was unable to break into the first team with the Potters and in the summer of 1997 he signed for Shrewsbury Town where he went on to make over 150 appearances, many as a substitute, over the next six seasons. When the Shrews lost their place in the Football League, he signed for Sheffield United although he never made the first team at Bramall Lane. He was a regular for Accrington Stanley for much of the 2005–06 season when they won the Conference title and promotion to the Football League before continuing his career with Droylsden. He was the older brother of Phil Jagielka, the Sheffield United and former England player.

John James (Born: Stone, Staffordshire, 24 October 1948. Died: 7 February 2021.) John James developed in the youth set-up at Port Vale as a half-back and it was in that position that he established himself in the side in the 1967–68 season. He was later converted to playing as a forward and impressed in his new role, leading the scoring charts for Vale in both 1968–69 (when they were promoted from the Fourth Division) and 1969–70. Injuries then affected his career and in February 1973 he was sold to Chester. He was revitalised and in 1974–75 he was a member of the team that reached the Football League Cup semi-finals and won a first-ever Football League promotion. He scored two in the 3-0 victory over Leeds United and the winner in the fifth-round replay against Newcastle United. Soon after the start of the 1975–76 season he was on his way again, this time to Tranmere Rovers with whom he achieved a second successive promotion from the basement division. On leaving Prenton Park he had a short spell with Stafford Rangers.

John Jeffers (Born: Liverpool, 5 October 1968. Died: January 2021.) John Jeffers was a skilful winger who won international honours for England Schoolboys and soon afterwards joined Liverpool as a trainee. He spent three years as a professional at Anfield, progressing to the reserves and receiving his first taste of senior football in a loan spell with Port Vale during the 1988–89 season. He returned to Vale Park to sign on a permanent basis and was a member of the team that beat Bristol Rovers in the play-off final to secure promotion to Division Two. He stayed a further five seasons but latterly was affected by injuries and in November 1995 he moved on to Stockport County. He won a second promotion with Stockport in 1996–97 before injuries effectively ended his career.

Keith Jobling (Born: Grimsby, 26 March 1934. Died: Grimsby, 20 September 2020.) Keith Jobling was a local lad who developed in the youth set-up at Grimsby Town and made his Football League debut shortly before his twentieth 20th birthday. Competition for places and the requirement to undergo a period of National Service meant that it was not until towards the end of the 1957–58 campaign that he established himself in the first team. He went on to retain the No 5 shirt for more than a decade, captaining the team that won promotion from Division Three in 1961–62. His final tally of 450 Football League appearances was a club record at the time but has since been overtaken. He later had a successful spell as manager of Boston United.

Gwyn Jones (Born: Llandwrog, Caernarvonshire, 20 March 1935. Died: Caernarfon, 13 November 2020.) Full-back Gwyn Jones signed for Wolverhampton Wanderers in September 1955 after being spotted while playing in a charity match. He spent seven years at Molineux where he was a perennial reserve, with a highlight coming in August 1959 when he appeared in the team that defeated Nottingham Forest to win the FA Charity Shield. He later enjoyed four seasons with Bristol Rovers where he was a near ever-present for much of his time before injuries led to his retirement at the end of the 1965–66 season.

Norman Jukes (Born: Leeds, 14 October 1932. Died: February 2021.) Norman Jukes was a full-back who had a couple of seasons on the books of Huddersfield Town without breaking into the first team. In October 1953 he was transferred to York City, for whom he made his only Football League appearance shortly afterwards in a Division Three North game at Wrexham. He remained at Bootham Crescent a couple more seasons without adding to his senior experience and was later involved with his local club Guiseley for many years.

Bobby Kellard (Born: Edmonton,1 March 1943. Died: 10 January 2021.) Bobby Kellard became Southend United's youngest-ever player when he appeared at outside-left in the Third Division game at Bradford City in September 1959 at the age of 16 years and 208 days. He was capped for England Youths and established himself in the Shrimpers line-up whilstwhile still a teenager. This brought him a move to Crystal Palace early in the 1963–64 campaign and was the beginning of a lengthy career as a combative midfield player who switched clubs regularly. He also featured in senior football for Ipswich Town, Portsmouth, Bristol City, Leicester City and Torquay United whilstwhile making close on 600 League and Cup appearances. He helped Palace win promotion from the Third Division in 1963–64 and was a key player in the Leicester team that won the Second Division title in 1970–71. Later he had a spell as player-manager of Chelmsford City.

Terry Kelly (Born: Gateshead, 15 May 1942. Died: 1 September 2020.) Terry Kelly developed in the Newcastle United youth set-up as a versatile player who was comfortable at both centre-half and centre-forward. He was unable to break into the first team at St James' Park and in July 1962 moved on to Lincoln City for a small fee. He spent a season at Sincil Bank, making nine first-team appearances for the Imps and finishing as top scorer for the reserve team. Later he had a brief spell with Cambridge United, before enjoying a lengthy career in Midland League football.

John Kennedy (Born: 9 April 1943. Died: Carrickfergus, Co Antrim, 6 April 2021.) Full-back John Kennedy was a prominent player in Irish League football with Linfield, Glentoran, Ards and Bangor. He won representative honours for Northern Ireland Schools and Youth teams and in September 1961 won his only amateur international cap playing against England.

Mick Kent (Born: North Anston, Yorkshire, 12 January 1951. Died: 2021.) Mick Kent was a midfielder who developed with Wath Wanderers, the Wolverhampton Wanderers nursery club, before signing professional forms in August 1968. He spent five years as a reserve at Molineux, restricted to a couple of appearances as a substitute and also playing on loan at Gillingham. He later had a brief spell with Sheffield Wednesday before leaving senior football.

Alex Kiddie (Born: Dundee, 27 April 1927. Died: Dundee, 27 March 2021.) Alex Kiddie was a winger with Dundee Junior club Stobswell who made a couple of wartime appearances for Celtic in the 1944–45 season. The following season he signed for Aberdeen where he was a member of the team that defeated Rangers to win the first-ever Scottish League Cup final in May 1946. He continued his playing career, which he combined with studying and then teaching, with spells at Falkirk, Dundee, Arbroath, Brechin City, Montrose and Forfar Athletic. He was an ever-present member of the Brechin team that won the Division C (North & East) title in 1953–54.

Jimmy Kirk (Born: Tarbolton, Ayrshire, 12 November 1925. Died: July 2020.) Goalkeeper Jimmy Kirk had just turned 18 when he made his debut for St Mirren in a wartime game against Dumbarton. His early career was restricted by military service in the Scots Guards, but he made over 100 appearances at Love Street before moving south to sign for Bury. He went on to play for Colchester United, Torquay United and Aldershot then switched to Southern League football with Tonbridge for the 1957–58 season.

Johnny Kirkham (Born: Wednesbury, Staffordshire, 13 May 1941. Died: Wigan, 11 February 2021.) Johnny Kirkham was a wing-half who was a member of the Wolverhampton Wanderers team that overcame a 5-1 deficit from the first leg to beat Chelsea and win the 1957–58 FA Youth Cup final. He won England Youth international honours and made his first-team debut against Manchester United as an 18-year-old. Competition for first-team places at Molineux was very fierce and despite winning two caps for England U23s he never quite established himself in the team. Later he signed for Peterborough United, appearing in their

League Cup semi-final defeat by West Bromwich Albion in 1965–66. His senior career ended with a spell at Exeter City, and he then moved to South Africa to play for Durban Spurs.

Vasili Kulkov (Born: Moscow, 11 June 1966. Died: October 2020.) Vasili Kulkov was a skilful midfield player mostly associated with spells at Spartak Moscow and in Portugal for Benfica and Porto. He signed for Millwall on loan in January 1996 and had a short run of games in the line-up before a knee injury led to his return to Spartak. He won 41 caps in total, appearing for the USSR, CIS and Russia.

Willie Lawson (Born: Dundee, 28 November 1947. Died: Dundee, 23 July 2020.) Outside-left Willie Lawson had something of a meteoric rise to fame. He made the step-up from Carnoustie Panmure to Brechin City in the summer of 1969 and after just 13 appearances he was sold to Sheffield Wednesday for what was a club record fee for Brechin. He made his First Division debut for the Owls just six months after leaving the Juniors but made just a handful of appearances for the Hillsborough club. He later played a few games for St Mirren and had a brief attachment with East Fife before returning to the Juniors with spells at Downfield, Lochee Harp and Forfar West End.

Mickey Lewis (Born: Birmingham, 15 February 1965. Died: 5 March 2021.) Mickey Lewis was an apprentice with West Bromwich Albion and was capped for England Youths. He made his senior debut for the Baggies at the age of 16 but was mostly a reserve during his time at The Hawthorns. He later spent four seasons with Derby County where he again struggled to make an impact. His fortunes changed when he signed for Oxford United in the summer of 1988 and he enjoyed seven seasons of regular first-team football with the U's although he was mostly a back-up player in the 1995–96 promotion team. He developed into a committed midfield ball winner with Oxford, making a total of 350 first-team appearances. He stayed with the club as youth-team coach and had a spell as caretaker-manager in 1999–2000 when he briefly returned to playing. He subsequently had spells as a coach and on the backroom staff with Des Moines Menace, Oxford City and Doncaster Rovers before returning to the U's and spending a further eight years with the club in a variety of roles.

Roy Lorenson (Born: Liverpool, 8 April 1932. Died: September 2020.) Roy Lorenson was a tall centre-half who developed in the Bootle JOC League before signing professional forms for Halifax Town during the 1951–52 season. His early years at The Shay were disrupted by National Service but he was a fixture in the side from March 1956 more or less until leaving for Tranmere Rovers in October 1960. However, he made few appearances at Prenton Park and his senior career was ended due to persistent knee injuries. He later gained coaching qualifications and had spells as player-coach of New Brighton and Kirkby Town as well as two spells on the backroom staff at Tranmere.

Peter Lorimer (Born: Dundee, 14 December 1946. Died: 20 March 2021.) Peter Lorimer was a versatile forward who was one of the all-time greats for Leeds United and still holds the club records for youngest-ever Football League player, at 15 years and 289 days, and record goal scorer with 168 League goals. As a schoolboy internationalist he had starred for Scotland against England in May 1962 before opting to join the groundstaff at Elland Road. As he had yet to sign professional forms, he made seven appearances for Scotland Amateurs before commencing a glittering career as a professional. Renowned for his powerful shooting, he made over 700 competitive appearances for Leeds in two separate spells at the club. He was twice a member of teams that won the Football League title (1968–69 and 1973–74), an FA Cup winner in 1972, a League Cup winner in 1967–68 and twice a winner of the Inter Cities Fairs Cup (1967–68 and 1970–71). In May 1975 he appeared for Leeds in their defeat by Bayern Munich in the European Cup final. In between his two spells at Elland Road he spent time in the NASL with Toronto Blizzard and Vancouver Whitecaps, and also played briefly for York City, finally retiring from senior football during the 1985–86 season. He was capped 21 times for Scotland and featured for them in the 1974 World Cup finals.

Gary Lowe (Born: Manchester, 25 September 1959. Died: Spain, 23 October 2020.) Defender Gary Lowe was an apprentice with Crystal Palace where he recovered from a broken leg but was unable to make the first team, then had a brief period with Manchester City where he featured regularly in the reserves. He spent the 1980–81 campaign with Hereford United, where he made 11 first-team appearances and then had a spell in Hong Kong with Caroline Hill before returning to the North West where he played for several years in non-league football.

Leopoldo Luque (Born: Santa Fe, Argentina, 3 May 1949. Died: Mendoza, Argentina, 15 February 2021.) Striker Leopoldo Luque was one of the stars of the Argentina team that won the 1978 World Cup. He scored two in their 6-0 semi-final victory over Peru and was a member of the team that beat the Netherlands 3-1 after extra time to win the competition. He scored 22 goals in 45 appearances for Argentina between 1975 and 1981. At club level he was best known for his performances for River Plate during the second half of the 1970s.

Ronnie McCall (Born: Kilmarnock, 9 July 1949. Died: 16 April 2021.) Striker Ronnie McCall developed with Kilmarnock Amateurs and Irvine Victoria before signing for Ayr United towards the end of the 1968–69 season. He made his senior debut during his time at Somerset Park but never won a regular place in the side. He moved on to Stranraer in May 1970 where he enjoyed a successful eight-year spell, making over 250 appearances and scoring 28 goals. Later he was reinstated as a Junior and returned to play for Irvine Victoria.

Johnny McCann (Born: Govan, Glasgow, 27 July 1934. Died: Mapplewell, Yorkshire, May 2020.) Johnny McCann was a flying winger who developed in the Scottish Juniors with Bridgeton Waverley then signed for Barnsley mid-way through the 1955–56 season. He was a regular at Oakwell for three seasons from 1956–57 making over 100 League appearances, then moved on to spells with Bristol City and Huddersfield Town. Early in the 1962–63 season he linked up again with manager Tim Ward, formerly at Barnsley and now at Derby, and once again enjoyed regular first-team football. He then wound down his senior career at Darlington and Chesterfield before joining Skegness Town. He was capped for Scotland B against England in February 1957.

Kevin McCann (Born: Airdrie, 10 June 1953. Died: Airdrie, May 2021.) Kevin McCann was a very skilful winger who developed in the Juniors with Shotts Bon Accord and Carluke Rovers and played a single match as a triallist for Albion Rovers in January 1971. He was called up to the seniors with Airdrieonians and although the Diamonds were relegated that season, he became a key player in the team that won promotion back to the top flight in 1973–74. The following season he was a member of the team that lost out to Celtic in the Scottish Cup final, scoring his team's goal in their 3-1 loss. In March 1979 he moved on to Queen of the South where he made a further 135 appearances before concluding his senior career at Stenhousemuir.

Pat McCluskey (Born: Kilsyth, Lanarkshire, 13 April 1952. Died: 24 August 2020.) Pat McCluskey was a powerful defensive player who joined Celtic from Maryhill Juniors in May 1969. His first senior football came in a loan spell with Sligo Rovers, where his father had been a player in the 1940s, in the 1969–70 season. He proved a success, winning runners-up medals in both the FAI Cup and the Blaxnit Cup but he had to wait until February 1972 before he broke into the side at Parkhead. He was a regular in the teams that won the Scottish League in 1973–74 and 1976–77, and also gained two Scottish Cup winners' medals (1973–74 and 1974–75) and a League Cup prize (1974–75). He moved on to Dumbarton in August 1977 where he was a regular for three seasons then played for Airdrieonians and Queen of the South, taking his total of career appearances beyond the 400-mark. He was capped six times for Scotland U23s.

John McCormack (Born: Fallin, Stirlingshire, 18 October 1933. Died: 23 May 2020.) Wing-half John McCormack progressed from Sauchie Juveniles to sign for Falkirk in August 1954 but was mostly a reserve during his time with the Bairns, making 54 appearances over five seasons before concluding his career with a brief association with Alloa Athletic. He combined playing football with work as a coal miner and went on to become a prominent figure in the National Union of Mineworkers in Scotland.

Willie McGrotty (Born: Glasgow, 12 August 1952. Died: Glasgow, 3 July 2020.) Winger Willie McGrotty joined Blackpool from Yoker Athletic in the summer of 1970 and scored in his first start for the Seasiders, against Nottingham Forest in April of the following year. Thereafter he was mainly a reserve in three seasons at Bloomfield Road. He later played in Australia for Western Suburbs and Safeway United before returning to Scotland.

John McGuinness (Born: Coatbridge, 21 June 1937. Died: Coatbridge, 21 January 2021.) Full-back John McGuinness joined Albion Rovers from amateur club Espieside Thistle at the start of the 1956–57 season and quickly established himself in the line-up. In December 1960 he was transferred to Stirling Albion where he featured in two Second Division championship teams (1960–61 and 1964–65) and made over 250 senior appearances. He concluded his career with a spell at East Stirlingshire.

Gary McGuire (Born: Campsall, Yorkshire, 30 September 1938. Died: 6 January 2021.) Goalkeeper Gary Maguire was an FA Amateur Cup winner with Walthamstow Avenue in 1961 and continued to play for the Isthmian League club until moving to Sydney, Australia, where he played for Hakoah. On returning to the UK he signed for Torquay United in February 1966 and made a useful contribution to their promotion campaign that season. Later he moved on to play in the Southern League with Bedford Town and Hastings United.

Davie McIlroy (Born: 25 September 1951. Died: Crosshouse, Ayrshire, 22 December 2020.) Davie McIlroy was an outside-left who played and managed a string of Ayrshire Junior clubs including Ardrossan Winton Rovers, Kilbirnie Ladeside, Beith and Irvine Meadow. He also made eight senior appearances for Hamilton Academical in the 1971–72 season.

Columb McKinley (Born: Dumbarton, 24 August 1950. Died: 6 February 2021.) Defender Columb McKinley spent his formative years with Clydebank Athletic and Vale of Leven Juniors before signing for Airdrieonians in the summer of 1970. He spent five seasons with the Diamonds, gaining a Texaco Cup runners-up medal in 1972, then moved on to Dumbarton where he was a member of the team that reached the semi-final of the Scottish Cup in 1976. When his senior career was over he returned to the Juniors to play for Vale of Leven.

Eddie McLaren (Born: Dundee, 8 September 1929. Died: 23 December 2020.) Eddie McLaren joined Blackpool from Dunkeld Amateurs in June 1948 as an inside-forward but quickly switched to playing as a defender. He spent two years at Bloomfield Road without breaking into the first team, then signed for Rhyl before going on to his National Service. Soon after being demobilised he joined Reading where he established himself in the first team in the second half of the 1954–55 season. He made a total of 197 appearances for the Royals before moving on to Southern League club Guildford City in 1959.

Hugh McLaughlin (Born: 28 May 1945. Died: Larkhall, Lanarkshire, 21 July 2020.) Hugh McLaughlin was an inside-forward who featured regularly for Stirling Albion in the 1962–63 season before drifting back to the Juniors with Larkhall Thistle. He returned to the seniors to play for Third Lanark in the final two years before they folded then signed for St Mirren. He achieved success at Love Street as a member of the team that won the Second Division title in 1967–68 and made over 100 appearances during his stay before concluding his career at Queen of the South.

Jim McLean (Born: 2 August 1937. Died: 26 December 2020.) Jim McLean enjoyed a useful career as an inside-forward which saw him make close on 500 League and Cup appearances for Hamilton Academical, Clyde, Dundee, and Kilmarnock. His best years were at Dens Park where he played and scored in the 1967–68 League Cup defeat by Celtic, and also played in the team defeated by Leeds in the semi-final of the Inter Cities Fairs Cup. When his playing days were over, he returned to Dundee in a coaching capacity before being appointed as manager of rivals Dundee United. He went on to spend over 20 years in charge at Tannadice and achieved unprecedented success for the club. They won the Scottish League title for the first and only time in 1982–83 and reached the semi-final of the European Cup the following season. They also won the Scottish League Cup on in successive occasions seasons (1979–80 and 1980–81) and were beaten finalists in the UEFA Cup (1986–87), Scottish Cup (six times), and League Cup (twice). He won the Scottish Football Writers Association Manager of the Year award in 1987 and was inducted into the Scottish Football Hall of Fame in 2005.

Chic McLelland (Born: 24 March 1953. Died: 26 December 2020.) Chic McLelland joined the groundstaff at Aberdeen as an inside-forward but quickly switched to full-back and went on to make over 200 appearances for the Dons in a 10-year spell at Pittodrie. A highlight was gaining a League Cup runners-up prize in 1978–79, he was also an unused substitute in the Scottish Cup final defeat by Rangers in May 1978. Later he had spells with Motherwell and Dundee before a more lengthy association with Montrose. He was briefly manager of Montrose (August 1990 to December 1991) and afterwards returned to Pittodrie to work in the academy set-up. He won representative honours for Scotland U18s and U23s.

Alan McLoughlin (Born: Manchester, 20 April 1967. Died: May 2021.) Alan McLoughlin was a creative midfield player who began his career as a trainee with Manchester United, but although he featured for the reserves during his time at Old Trafford, he was unable to break into the first team. In August 1986 he signed for Swindon Town and after a settling settling-in period he shone in the 1989–90 campaign when he was a fixture in the line-up and scored the winner in the 1990 Second Division play-off final defeat of Sunderland. The Robins were not promoted, however, due to off-the-field matters, and soon afterwards he was on his way to Southampton for what was a club record fee. He did not settle with Saints but on moving down the coast to Portsmouth he enjoyed the best part of eight years of regular football. He wound down his senior career at Wigan Athletic and Rochdale, taking his total of League and Cup appearances to 600. He subsequently coached with a number of clubs and in recent years returned to Swindon Town working with the academy. He won 42 caps for the Republic of Ireland and appeared for them in the 1990 World Cup finals.

John McNeil (Born: Motherwell, 26 March 1933. Died: Canada, 2 August 2020.) Inside-forward John McNeil was capped for Scotland Juveniles against Wales in May 1951 and progressed from spells with Motherwell Welfare Hearts and Blantyre Vics to sign for Hibernian. He was unable to break into the first team at Easter Road and made fleeting appearances in spells at Albion Rovers and Motherwell before signing for Airdrieonians in September 1955. He went on to make a total of over 100 appearances for the Diamonds in two separate spells separated by a three-year gap spent in Canada. He concluded his professional career with a brief stay at Stranraer and eventually returned to Canada where he taught in the Geography Faculty at Brock University, Ontario, for more than 25 years.

John McSeveney (Born: Shotts, Lanarkshire, 8 February 1931. Died: 12 December 2020.) John McSeveney was a skilful winger who spent virtually all his working life in football as a player, manager, and coach. He first came to notice as a member of the all-conquering Shotts YMCA team, then after a spell in the Juniors with Carluke Rovers he signed for Hamilton Academical in December 1948. He made a scoring debut for the Accies against Queen's Park at the age of 17 and three years later he was transferred to Sunderland, then members of the First Division. He went on to enjoy a lengthy career south of the Border with further spells at Cardiff City, Newport County and Hull City, making over 500 appearances in senior football and scoring more than 150 goals. He subsequently moved into coaching and management including spells as manager of Barnsley (September 1971 to November 1972), Home Farm and Waterford, where he signed Bobby Charlton as a player. His brother Willie also enjoyed a lengthy career as a player with Dunfermline Athletic and Motherwell.

Gerry Mackey (Born: Dublin, 10 June 1933. Died: Loughlinstown, Dublin, 21 April 2021.) Gerry Mackey was a versatile defender who was a member of the successful Shamrock Rovers team of the 1950s, winning three League of Ireland titles and the FAI Cup on two occasions. He won three full caps for the Republic of Ireland and also appeared on 10 occasions for the League of Ireland representative side. Later he had a four-year spell in England with King's Lynn Town before focussing on his career outside football.

Barry Mahy (Born: Doncaster, 21 January 1942. Died: Sayville, New York, USA, 1 October 2020.) Inside-forward Barry Mahy was brought up on Guernsey and played for Northerners before signing professional terms with Scunthorpe United in May 1963. He stayed three-and-a-half seasons at the Old Showground, making 26 first-team appearances before his former manager Freddie Goodwin signed him up for New York Generals in February 1967. Later he had a four-year spell with New York Cosmos where he was a member of the team that won the NASL championship in 1972 before his career was ended by a broken ankle three years later. He won four full caps for the USA.

Malcolm Manley (Born: Johnstone, Renfrewshire, 1 December 1949. Died: 16 August 2020.) Malcolm Manley was a versatile defender who won caps for Scotland at Schools and Youth international levels before joining Leicester City from Johnstone Burgh during the 1966–67 season. He was just 17 when he made his first-team debut for the Foxes and was still a teenager when he came on as a substitute in the 1969 FA Cup final. He made over 100 first-team appearances during his time at Filbert Street then moved on to Portsmouth but soon after signing he suffered a serious knee injury that effectively ended his career. Later he had a spell in Australia with South Melbourne.

John Manning (Born: Liverpool, 11 December 1940. Died: February 2021.) John Manning was on Liverpool's books as an amateur in the 1961–62 season and played a few games at centre-half for the reserves in the Central League before joining Tranmere Rovers as a professional in May 1962. He was quickly converted to centre-forward at Prenton Park with great success. He was a regular in the line-up from September 1963 and went on to score 75 goals before he was sold to Shrewsbury Town in October 1966. Thereafter he spent the next decade as a peripatetic striker, mostly in the lower divisions of the Football League. His list of clubs included Norwich City, Bolton Wanderers, Walsall, Tranmere Rovers (a brief second spell), Crewe Alexandra (twice) and Barnsley. His final tally amounted to 157 goals from 404 appearances. He was trainer-coach for Crewe in 1975–76 and later coached in many countries across the globe.

Diego Maradona (Born: Lanus, Argentina, 30 October 1960. Died: Dique Lujan, Argentina, 25 November 2020.) Diego Maradona was the greatest midfield player of his generation. He was a full international at 16 and won 91 caps for Argentina between 1977 and 1994. He played in four World Cup final tournaments and captained the team that won the trophy in 1986 when he was at his peak. His two goals against England in the quarter-final tie became renowned but for very different reasons. The first was the infamous 'Hand of God' goal, while the second followed a 60-yard run when he went past half the England team before scoring a goal that was later selected by FIFA as 'The Goal of the Century.'. At club level he developed with Argentinos Juniors and Boca Juniors before breaking the World world record transfer fee when signing Barcelona for a £5 million sum in the summer of 1982. He later enjoyed a successful spell with Napoli, where he was a UEFA Cup winner in 1989 and a member of the team that won Serie

A 12 months later. He subsequently had a spell with Sevilla before returning to Argentina. When his playing career was over, he turned to coaching including a period in charge of the Argentina national team from November 2008 to July 2010.

Les Massie (Born: Aberdeen, 20 July 1935. Died: 11 November 2020.) Centre-forward Les Massie came to prominence with Aberdeen Juvenile club Powis YC and after the briefest of attachments to Banks O'Dee Juniors he signed for Huddersfield Town in July 1953. It was not until September 1956 that he made his bow in senior football for the Terriers but by the end of that season he had established himself in the line-up. He went on to stay a further 10 years at Leeds Road and his tally of 108 League and Cup goals makes him the fifth highest scorer in the history of the club. He later continued his career in the lower divisions, firstly at Darlington and then Halifax Town where he was top scorer two seasons running and was a member of the team that won promotion from the Fourth Division in 1968–69. He wound down in senior football with spells at Bradford Park Avenue and Workington.

Terry Melling (Born: Haverton Hill, Co Durham, 24 January 1940. Died: Northampton, 21 March 2021.) Terry Melling was a bustling centre-forward who played as an amateur for a number of clubs in the South East of England whilstwhile serving in the Coldstream Guards. During this time he also won representative honours for the FA Amateur XI and the British Army. He returned to the North East after leaving the Army and quickly earned a move from Tow Law Town to Newcastle United where he featured for the reserves in 1965–66. He was subsequently released and allowed to join Watford on a free transfer, making his Football League debut at the age of 26. He proved a hard but effective forward, his senior career comprised 144 appearances and 40 goals and also included spells with Newport County, Mansfield Town, Rochdale and Darlington.

Stuart Metcalfe (Born: Blackburn, 6 October 1950. Died: Blackburn, 6 August 2020.) Stuart Metcalfe was a creative midfield player who signed as an apprentice for Blackburn Rovers and won England Youth international honours. He made his League debut at the age of 17 and remained with the club for more than a decade, making 450-odd appearances during his stay. A highlight came in the 1974–75 season when he played a crucial role in assisting Rovers to the Third Division title. He subsequently spent time in the American Soccer League before returning to the UK with brief spells back at Ewood Park and with Crewe Alexandra.

Billy Millen (Born: Ballymacarrett, Belfast, 30 March 1949. Died: Sydney, Australia, 16 October 2020.) Centre-forward Billy Millen was capped for Northern Ireland Youths and joined Arsenal during the 1965–66 season. He featured for the Gunners reserve team before returning to Belfast to sign for Linfield where he won a League champions medal (1970–71) and was a member of the team that won the Irish Cup in 1970. He is best remembered at Windsor Park for scoring both goals in a 2-1 European Cup Winners' Cup second leg tie in 1970 against Manchester City when Linfield ended up going out on the away goals rule. He later played in South Africa, Australia, and the USA. He was capped for the Irish League against the Football League in September 1970.

Mick Millington (Born: The Liberties, Dublin, 10 December 1940. Died: Castleknock, Dublin, 10 January 2021.) Wing-half Mick Millington had a couple of seasons on the books of Aston Villa as a youngster without breaking into the first team and returned to Ireland at the end of the 1960–61 season. He later enjoyed a successful career in the League of Ireland, notably with Cork Celtic and Dundalk, with whom he gained a league title in 1966–67. He won representative honours for the League of Ireland against the Italian League in May 1962.

Barrie Mitchell (Born: Aberdeen, 15 March 1947. Died: Woodchurch, Birkenhead, 24 January 2021.) Barrie Mitchell earned a reputation as a goalscoring winger in Aberdeenshire Junior circles, helping Sunnybank reach the semi-final of the Scottish Junior Cup in 1966–67. He moved up to the seniors with Arbroath the following season, making a sensational start by scoring four times in his first six appearances. Almost immediately he was snapped up by Dunfermline Athletic for £14,000, a then club record fee for the Red Lichties. He made over 150 appearances for the Pars, featuring in European action during his stay but in April 1972 he was on the move again, signing for Aberdeen. However, a back injury restricted his opportunities for the Dons, and he later joined Tranmere Rovers where he was a near ever-present in the team that won promotion from the Fourth Division in 1975–76. He concluded his career with spells at Vancouver Whitecaps, Preston North End, York City and Morton.

Roy Moody (Born: Clowne, Derbyshire, 12 March 1923. Died: Clowne, Derbyshire, 17 June 2020.) Roy Moody was a winger who turned out for Nottingham Forest Colts during the 1941–42 season. After serving in the Royal Navy during the war he played for Worksop Town before signing for Lincoln City in November 1946. He made a single Football League appearance for the Imps at home to Carlisle United in March 1947, later returning to non-league football with Worksop, Matlock Town, and Creswell Colliery.

Frank Mooney (Born: Fauldhouse, West Lothian, 1 January 1932. Died: 23 May 2021.) Outside-right Frank Mooney won Scottish Schools and Youth international honours whilstwhile a pupil at St Mary's Secondary School in Bathgate and in May 1949 he signed for Manchester United, although he remained at school a further 12 months. He progressed through the A and reserve teams at Old Trafford but his time at the club was affected by National Service and in February 1954, now demobilised, he signed for Blackburn Rovers. He was an ever-present for Rovers in 1954–55, scoring 16 goals including a hat-trick in a 9-0 demolition of Middlesbrough. However, he lost his place in the team the following season and eventually moved on to Carlisle United where he made over 100 appearances before concluding his senior career with a brief spell at Berwick Rangers.

Tony Morrin (Born: Swinton, Lancashire, 31 July 1946. Died: 14 December 2020.) Midfielder Tony Morrin was an apprentice with Bury and made a handful of first-team appearances for the Shakers before being released and eventually signing for Stockport County. He assisted the Hatters to success in winning the Fourth Division title in 1966–67 then embarked on something or of a peripatetic career which saw him play for Barrow, Exeter City, Stockport again, and Rochdale. He made almost 400 senior appearances over some 16 seasons before he eventually retired at the end of the 1978–79 campaign.

Hughie Morrow (Born: Larne, 9 July 1930. Died: Northern Ireland, 28 October 2020.) Winger Hughie Morrow was playing first-team football for Nuneaton Borough at the age of 15 and within two years he signed for West Bromwich Albion. He made five first-team appearances for the Baggies then returned to non-league football with further spells at Nuneaton Borough and Lockheed Leamington. In the summer of 1956 he returned to senior football when he signed as a part-timer for Northampton Town, and he went on to feature regularly for the Cobblers in the 1956–57 season. Later he played until the mid-1960s in non-league football, then had a lengthy spell as manager of Tamworth.

John Mortimore (Born: Farnborough, 23 September 1934. Died: January 2021.) John Mortimore was playing as an amateur with Woking when signed by Chelsea in April 1956 and he made his debut in the final game of the 1955–56 season. He went on to win three caps for England Amateurs and after turning professional established himself in the Blues' line-up in 1957–58. Thereafter he was mostly a regular in the first team at centre-half and went on to make over 250 appearances, featuring as an ever ever-present in the team that won promotion from the Second Division in 1962–63. He gained a League Cup winners' prize medal after appearing in the second leg of the final against Leicester City in 1965 and after a brief spell with Queen's Park Rangers he turned to management and coaching. This included periods in charge of Portsmouth (May 1973 to September 1974) and Benfica (1976 to 1979 and 1985 to 1987), with whom he won the national titlePortuguese championship on two occasions.

Eddie Moss (Born: Skelmersdale, 27 October 1939. Died: 27 December 2020.) Inside-forward Eddie Moss signed professional forms for Skelmersdale United in October 1958, and but within a week he was on the move again, joiningto Liverpool. He featured in the Central League team for the Reds but at the end of the season he was on his way again, signing for Southport. In two seasons at Haig Avenue he made over 50 first-team appearances, heading the club's scoring charts in 1959–60. He later spent several years on the books of Runcorn.

Tony Moy (Born: Glasgow, 16 December 1945. Died: Braintree, Essex, 26 December 2020.) Striker Tony Moy developed with Kirkintilloch Rob Roy and St Mirren before spending two seasons with Scottish League newcomers Clydebank where he scored at a prolific rate, netting 54 goals from 81 League and Cup appearances. In the summer of 1968 he signed for Southern League club Chelmsford City, but although he hit a hat-trick on his debut he found goals harder to come by. He continued to play in the Southern League for several seasons, turning out for a number of clubs including Brentwood, Dover and Dartford.

Bill Murphy (Born: Barrhead, Renfrewshire, 22 March 1928. Died: March 2021.) Bill Murphy was a product of Benburb Juniors, stepping up to the seniors with Stirling Albion in July 1949. A reserve at Annfield, he moved south within a matter of months, signing for Exeter City for whom he made a couple of first-team appearances. He spent 1950–51 with Bristol Rovers where he was again mainly a reserve. He subsequently emigrated to Australia, continuing his career with Gladesville-Ryde and Hakoah and winning five caps for the national team.

Adam Musiał (Born: Wieliczka, Poland, 18 December 1948. Died: Krakow, Poland, 18 November 2020.) Defender Adam Musiał enjoyed a useful career in Poland, notably with Wisla Kraków for whom he made over 200 appearances and winning the league title in 1977–78. He won 34 caps for Poland, featuring in the team that knocked England out of the qualifiers for the 1974 World Cup finals and that went on to achieve third place in the tournament. In August 1980 he signed for Hereford United, and he made 48 appearances for the Bulls before moving on in February 1983.

Bobby Nee (Born: St Monance, Fife, 22 October 1932. Died: Leven, 23 June 2020.) A product of Fife amateur club St Monance Swifts, wing-half Bobby Nee signed for Raith Rovers in June 1950, but his time at Stark's Park was affected by a lengthy absence on National Service and he managed just one first-team appearance, in the home game with Dundee in February 1952. He later had brief spells attached to both Carlisle United and Brighton & Hove Albion without adding to his experience of senior football.

Ron Newman (Born: Pontypridd, 1 May 1933. Died: 20 February 2021.) Ron Newman was a talented rugby union player as a schoolboy but went on to become a professional soccer player. A product of South Wales Amateur League club Ynysbwl, he signed for Northampton Town in October 1953 but had few first-team opportunities and in March 1956 he moved to Coventry City in a player exchange. A versatile forward, he scored on his debut against Southampton but was again mostly a fringe player in a 12-month stay at Highfield Road. He later made a few appearances for Torquay United in 1957–58 before switching to Southern League football with Bedford Town.

Brian O'Donnell (Born: Port Glasgow, 8 August 1957. Died: Poole, 5 November 2020.) Brian O'Donnell was a midfield player who started out as an apprentice with Bournemouth and then joined Bristol Rovers where he was unable to break into the first team. He then spent several seasons in Australia before returning to the UK to sign for Bournemouth again in January 1982. He made a few appearances for the Cherries before switching to Torquay United where he featured regularly in the 1982–83 season before returning once more to Australia. Later he played for a number of non-league clubs including Yeovil Town and Bath City before coaching, including a spell working in the Cherries' youth set-up.

Dick Oxtoby (Born: Chesterfield, 5 September 1939. Died: Bolton, 22 June 2020.) Defender Dick Oxtoby was a member of the Chesterfield Boys team that reached the semi-final of the ESFA Trophy in 1954–55 and subsequently signed for Bolton Wanderers. However, he spentin the best part of six seasons at Burnden Park, making he made just four first-team appearances. In the summer of 1963, he moved on to Tranmere Rovers where he added further appearances during a 12-month stay. He was later involved in coaching junior clubs in the Bolton area for many years.

Archie Page (Born: Kinglassie, Fife, 21 April 1946. Died: Leslie, Fife, 22 March 2021.) Archie Page was a goalkeeper who joined Montrose from Thornton Hibs towards the end of the 1966–67 season and quickly established himself in the line-up. He spent the best part ofalmost five years on the books at Links Park, making 139 League and Cup appearances before returning to Junior football with Glenrothes.

Jim Parkhill (Born: Belfast, 27 July 1934. Died: 30 September 2020.) Goalkeeper Jim Parkhill won representative honours for Northern Ireland Juniors, and after progressing to senior football with Bangor and Cliftonville he added two Northern Ireland Amateur caps. In September 1963 he signed as a professional for Exeter City for whom he made a single appearance, at home to Newport County, in what proved to be a promotion season for the Grecians. He was released 12 months later and signed for Western League club Taunton where he stayed a further three seasons.

Colin Parry (Born: Stockport, 16 February 1941. Died: 13 August 2020.) Defender Colin Parry was a product of local football who signed professional forms for Stockport County in July 1962. He was a regular in the line-up for two seasons but then lost his place in the side and had a brief trial with Bradford City during the 1965–66 season. He eventually moved on to sign for Rochdale in July 1968 and in his first season at Spotland he was a near ever ever-present in the side that won promotion from Division Four. After making a total of over 300 senior appearances he left the full-time game at the end of the 1971–72 season, going on to sign for Macclesfield Town.

Dave Paton (Born: Saltcoats, Ayrshire, 13 December 1943. Died: Ayrshire, 8 September 2020.) Centre-half Dave Paton was a product of the Saxone Youth Club and won Youth international honours for Scotland before joining the groundstaff at St Mirren. In July 1963 he joined Southampton on a free transfer but in six seasons on the South Coast he was only really a back-up player, making 15 first-team appearances. He subsequently moved on to Aldershot, where he featured regularly in the 1969–70 and then for a spell with Southern League Margate.

George Patterson (Born: Castleton, Yorkshire, 15 September 1934. Died: York, 25 May 2021.) Although George Patterson signed for Hull City as a teenager it was only when he had completed his National Service that his career began to progress. He broke into the first team in April 1955 but never established himself with the Tigers before drifting into non-league football with King's Lynn and South Shields. York City offered him a second chance in senior football, and he was a regular at right-half for the Minstermen when they won promotion from the Fourth Division in 1958–59. Later he played for Hartlepool before joining Gateshead who were by then outside of the Football League.

Harry Penk (Born: Wigan, 19 July 1934. Died: 21 June 2020.) Winger Harry Penk stepped up from local club Orrell St Luke's to Wigan Athletic and did well enough with the then Lancashire Combination side to earn a transfer to First Division Portsmouth. Although he struggled to make an impression with Pompey, he later enjoyed three good seasons with Plymouth Argyle, helping them win the Third Division title in 1958–59. He concluded his senior career at Southampton where he was a regular for two seasons before being mostly a reserve.

Steve Perks (Born: Much Wenlock, Shropshire, 19 April 1963. Died: April 2021.) Goalkeeper Steve Perks joined Shrewsbury Town as an apprentice on leaving school and progressed to the senior ranks, winning a regular place in the line-up in the second half of the 1984–85 campaign. He stayed with the Shrews for a further seven seasons, mostly as a first choice in the line-up, making over 250 appearances. He then had a brief association with Torquay United before joining Stafford Rangers.

Brian Peterson (Born: Durban, South Africa, 28 October 1936. Died: South Africa, 21 September 2020.) Brian Peterson became South Africa's youngest international player before moving from Berea Park to Blackpool in October 1956. One of several South Africans who played for the Seasiders in the 1950s, he made over 100 appearances in total, all in the old First Division, during a six-year stay at Bloomfield Road. In the summer of 1962 he returned home and signed for Durban United.

Trevor Phillips (Born: Rotherham, 18 September 1952. Died: 11 November 2020.) Trevor Phillips was a quick and mobile striker who signed for Rotherham United as a youngster and went on to win England Youth international honours. He made his first-team debut for the Millers at the age of 17 and quickly established himself in the side. He spent almost a decade at Millmoor, assisting the team to win promotion from the Fourth Division in 1974–75 and making over 300 appearances. Later he spent a short period with Hull City before winding up his senior career with spells at Chester (who paid a club record fee for his services) and Stockport County.

Ron Phoenix (Born: Stretford, 30 June 1929. Died: Stretford, 9 March 2021.) Ron Phoenix was a wing-half or inside-forward who came up through the ranks with Manchester City before signing a professional contract. He scored on his debut at Highbury and provided an assist for City's other goal, but after beginning to establish himself he suffered a badly broken leg in February 1953, and this kept him out of action for two years. He eventually returned and stayed at Maine Road until the end of the 1959–60 campaign, although he received few further opportunities. He later spent two seasons with Rochdale before moving on to Altrincham. His brother Eric played for Gillingham and Exeter City.

Ernie Phythian (Born: Farnworth, Lancashire, 16 July 1942. Died: Johannesburg, South Africa, 3 August 2020.) Ernie Phythian joined Bolton Wanderers as a youngster and gained England Youth international honours whilstwhile at Burnden Park, but he received few first-team opportunities during his stay. In March 1962 he was transferred to Wrexham as part of the deal that saw Wyn Davies more move in the opposite direction. His career blossomed at the Racecourse Ground, where he proved to be a powerful and quick striker with a good scoring record. He fared equally well when he moved on to Hartlepools, finishing top scorer in his first two seasons and assisting the club in their 1967–68 promotion campaign. Following this he emigrated to South Africa where he played for Southern Suburbs and Lusitano.

Barry Pierce (Born: Liverpool, 13 August 1934. Died: 7 August 2020.) Barry Pierce was playing for Truro City and RAF St Eval when he signed for Crystal Palace in August 1955, and thiswhich proved to be the start of an eight-year career in the lower divisions of the Football League. He had three seasons of fairly regular first-team football at Selhurst Park before joining Millwall, where he scored 17 goals in the 1959–60 campaign. Later he spent time with both York City and Exeter City then dropped out of senior football to sign for Western League club Salisbury.

Fred Pirie (Born: Coupar Angus, Perthshire, 19 January 1934. Died: Clayton-le-Moors, Lancashire, 24 November 2020.) Full-back Fred Pirie developed with Stanley Juniors and Coupar Angus, during which time he made a single appearance as a triallist for Forfar Athletic in November 1952. Just over a year later he joined the large Scottish contingent at Accrington Stanley where he spent six years on the books. Although mostly a reserve he made 19 first-team appearances during his time at Peel Park before moving into non-league with Horwich RMI.

Keith Pontin (Born: Pontyclun, Glamorgan, 14 June 1956. Died: August 2020.) Keith Pontin was a hard-tackling defender who came up through the ranks with Cardiff City and had a brief run in the line-up at the start of the 1976–77 campaign. He established himself in the side the following season and went on to make over 200 appearances in a career that lasted through until 1983. Later he played for Merthyr Tydfil and Barry Town. He was capped once for Wales U21s and on two occasions for the full national team, making his debut as a second-half substitute in the 4-1 win over England in May 1980.

John Poole (Born: Stoke-on-Trent, 12 December 1932. Died: 18 November 2020.) Goalkeeper John Poole came through the ranks with Port Vale, signing professional terms in September 1953. He spent eight seasons at Vale Park where he was mostly a reserve but became a regular in the 1959–60 season. He lost his place after suffering a broken nose and eventually moved on in July 1961, signing for Macclesfield Town.

Len Prince (Born: Sunderland, 1953. Died: November 2020.) Full-back Len Prince joined Crystal Palace as an apprentice before graduating to a professional contract at the age of 17. He spent a further three years on the books at Selhurst Park, making two senior appearances – one each in the Texaco and Anglo Italian Cups. He later played in the Southern League for Tonbridge and Wealdstone.

Ken Prior (Born: Ashington, 13 October 1932. Died: 14 November 2020.) Outside-left Ken Prior progressed from colliery team Cambois Welfare to sign amateur forms for Newcastle United in the summer of 1951. He turned professional the following March and after just a handful of reserve-team outings he made his League debut the following month. He made further appearances, principally as a aback-up player, before signing for Millwall in the summer of 1954 and enjoyed two seasons of regular first-team football. He later returned to St James' Park for a second spell, then concluded his career in the Scottish League with Berwick Rangers. His father George played for Sheffield Wednesday and his uncle Jack for Sunderland and Grimsby Town.

Johnny Quinn (Born: Widnes, 30 May 1938. Died: September 2020.) Inside-forward Johnny Quinn played junior football alongside future England international John Connelly with St Helen's League club St Theresa's, then progressed via spells at St Helen's Town and Prescot Cables to sign for Sheffield Wednesday in May 1959. His early Hillsborough career was disrupted by National Service, but he established himself in the mid-1960s and was a member of the team that lost out to Everton in the 1966 FA Cup final. After making close on 200 first-team appearances for the Owls, he became Tommy Docherty's first signing for Rotherham United in November 1967. He added a further century of appearances for the Millers before ending his career with Halifax Town, where he also served as manager from September 1974 to February 1976.

Pat Quinn (Born: Glasgow, 26 April 1936. Died: Glasgow, 13 July 2020.) Pat Quinn starred in Juvenile football before spending a short time with Bridgeton Waverley Juniors where he turned down an offer from Albion Rovers after appearing twice as a triallist. However, he signed for Motherwell shortly afterwards where he became one of the celebrated 'Ancell Babes'. He developed into a skilful midfield player with great vision and after making more than 250 appearances he moved south to sign for Blackpool. He struggled to fit in at Bloomfield Road and within a year he was back in Scotland with Hibernian where he spent a further six seasons, gaining a League Cup runners-up medal in 1968–69. His final club was East Fife, where he was appointed as player-manager in October 1970 and gained promotion to the First Division in his first season in the job. He remained as manager of the Methil club until September 1973 then enjoyed a lengthy career in coaching. He won four full caps for Scotland and also played for the Scottish League representative side.

Albert Quixall (Born: Sheffield, 9 August 1933. Died: Glossop, 12 November 2020.) Albert Quixall was capped for England Schoolboys and joined Sheffield Wednesday on amateur forms at the age of 15. He turned professional two years later and made his Football League debut whilstwhile still 17. An inside-forward with excellent ball skills and one of the most skilful players of his generation, he helped Wednesday to win the Second Division title on two occasions (1951–52 and 1955–56) and won five England caps. In September 1958 he was sold to Manchester United for a reported £45,000 fee, a British record at the time. The highlight of his career came at Wembley in May 1963 when he assisted United to victory over Leicester City in the FA Cup final. Thereafter he wound down his senior career with spells at Oldham Athletic and Stockport County.

Ron Rafferty (Born: South Shields, 6 May 1934. Died: January 2021.) Ron Rafferty played for Wycombe Wanderers and also as an amateur for Shrewsbury Town, where he featured in the reserves. He signed professional terms for Portsmouth in the summer of 1954 and played a number of First Division games for them, although as a back-up at inside-forward. Midway through the 1956–57 campaign he moved north to sign for Grimsby Town and where his career flourished with the Mariners. He was a regular in for the Mariners team for six-and-a-half seasons and his total of 152 League and Cup goals is a post-war record for the club. He was top scorer on four occasions and his 34 goals in 1961–62 were a significant factor in firing the clubGrimsby to promotion from Division Three. He later had an injury-hit spell with Hull City before ending his senior career at Aldershot where he was often used in a defensive role.

Billy Reid (Born: 6 January 1939. Died: October 2020.) Half-back Billy Reid played in the Juniors for Strathclyde and Kirkintilloch Rob Roy prior to signing for Stirling Albion in December 1963. He was a regular in the team that won the Second Division title in 1964–65 and made a total of 138 League and Cup appearances and was also a member of the team that went on a historic tour to Iran and Japan in the summer of 1966. He eventually moved on for a final season in senior football with East Stirlingshire.

Jack Richardson (Born: Rock Ferry, Birkenhead, 24 May 1933. Died: Southport, 30 May 2021.) Goalkeeper Jack Richardson joined Canterbury City after completing his National Service before returning to the North West to sign for Southport. He spent the next three seasons at Haig Avenue where he was an ever ever-present in the 1958–59 season and made a total of 106 League and Cup appearances. He subsequently joined Lancashire Combination club Wigan Athletic.

Roy Ridge (Born: Sheffield, 21 October 1934. Died: December 2020.) Roy Ridge was a local lad who signed professional forms for Sheffield United at the age of 17. He went on to spend 13 years on the books at Bramall Lane, mostly playing in the reserves. He made a total of 11 first-team appearances, of which nine came in a short run in the side in the 1953–54 season when he displaced Graham Shaw. He later spent two seasons with Rochdale, rarely missing a match, before dropping into the Midland League to play for Worksop Town.

Les Riggs (Born: Portsmouth, 30 May 1935. Died: 29 December 2020.) Les Riggs was a hard-tackling wing-half famed for his prodigious long throw. He came up through the ranks with Gillingham, breaking into the first team in April 1954 and winning a regular place the following season. Over the next 10 years he went on to make close onalmost 400 League and Cup appearances, also turning out for Newport County, Bury and Crewe Alexandra. He assisted Crewe to promotion from Division Four in 1962–63. He returned to Kent and had spells as manager of Ramsgate and Margate.

Ken Roberts (Born: Cefn Mawr, Flintshire, 27 March 1936. Died: Shrewsbury, 5 February 2021.) Ken Roberts was a versatile forward who won honours for Wales at Youth international level and made his Football League debut against Bradford Park Avenue in September 1951 aged just 15 years and 158 days, equalling Albert Geldard's record as the youngest Football League player. This was his only appearance at the Racecourse Ground and in May 1953 he signed for Aston Villa. He created what must be a unique record in that he also became Villa's youngest-ever first-team player, thus holding the record for two different clubs at the same time. His career at Villa Park was disrupted by a series of injuries and after leaving in the summer of 1958 he had a brief spell at Oswestry before retiring as a player. He later coached at Wrexham and Bradford Park Avenue before serving Chester as manager from 1968 to 1976. He achieved considerable success in this role, leading the club to the Welsh Cup final (1969–70) and, in 1974–75, the League Cup semi-final and promotion from the Fourth Division for the first time in the club's history.

Tommy Robson (Born: Gateshead, 31 July 1944. Died: 8 October 2020.) Outside-left Tommy Robson won representative honours for the England NABC team before joining the groundstaff at Northampton Town in March 1961. He made a scoring debut for the Cobblers against Peterborough United 12 months later but was principally a reserve at the County Ground until winning a regular slot in the team that won promotion from Division Two in 1964–65. After a few games in the top flight he was sold to Chelsea, but never really settled at Stamford Bridge. He was soon on his way to Newcastle United where he was second-top scorer in 1967–68. He subsequently moved back to the East Midlands in November 1968, signing for Peterborough United. He stayed at London Road for the next 13 years, creating a new club record, yet to be broken, of 482 Football League appearances. He was an ever-present in the team that won the Fourth Division title in 1973–74 and was twice Player of the Season (1973–74 and 1977–78). Later he was a member of the Stamford team that reached the 1984 FA Vase final.

Glenn Roeder (Born: Woodford, Essex, 13 December 1955. Died: 28 February 2021.) Glenn Roeder was a tall, rangy central defender who was comfortable on the ball. He joined Orient as an apprentice and was an ever-present in both 1976–77 and 1977–78, helping them to a place in the FA Cup semi-final in April 1978. Soon afterwards he was sold to Queen's Park Rangers where he played in the drawn FA Cup final against Tottenham in 1982, missing out on the replay due to suspension. He won promotion with Newcastle United in 1983–84 and spent five seasons in the old First Division with them before later playing for Watford. In October

1992 he was appointed as player-manager of Gillingham, and he subsequently developed a new career in coaching and management with Watford, West Ham United, Newcastle, and Norwich City. He won six caps for England B and was a member of the touring party that visited Malaysia, New Zealand, and Singapore in the summer of 1978.

Paolo Rossi (Born: Prato, Italy, 23 September 1956. Died: Siena, Italy, 9 December 2020.) Paolo Rossi was a quick and agile striker with a prolific scoring record who excelled with Italy in the 1982 World Cup finals. He scored the first goal as Italy went on to defeat West Germany 3-1 in the final and also won the Golden Boot award (as top scorer in the tournament) and the Golden Ball award (as player of the tournament). In total he scored 20 goals for Italy in 48 appearances between 1977 and 1986. He played his club football principally for Juventus with whom he won the Serie A title on two occasions, the Coppa Italia once, the European Cup Winners' Cup in 1983–84 and the European Cup in 1984–85. He won both the European Footballer of the Year and World Footballer of the Year awards in 1982.

John Rowland (Born: Riddings, Derbyshire, 7 April 1941. Died: Derby, November 2020.) John Rowland won representative honours for England Youths and the FA Amateur XI and was still an amateur when he made his League debut for Nottingham Forest in October 1960. He signed professional forms soon afterwards, but it was not until he moved on to Port Vale that he experienced regular first-team football. He was top scorer for Vale in 1965–66 but at the start of the following season he was sold to Mansfield Town. His Football League career ended at Tranmere Rovers, and he then played in Northern Ireland for Derry City, Linfield, and Coleraine. He also made one appearance for the Irish League representative side.

Cyril Rutter (Born: Leeds, 21 February 1933. Died: 22 August 2020.) Full-back Cyril Rutter won representative honours for the England NABC team in April 1951 and shortly afterwards signed professional forms for Portsmouth. He spent 12 years on the books at Fratton Park, making 180 first-team appearances although he was not always a regular first-teamer. He was a near ever-present in the team that won the Division Three title in 1961–62 but moved on soon afterwards to a coaching position at a US Forces base in Germany. Later he was player-manager of Salisbury City.

George Ryan (Born: Glasgow, 29 December 1931. Died: April 2021.) Centre-forward George Ryan played in the Glasgow Juveniles for Quarryknowe Star, then had a trial with Hull City in the closing stages of the 1950–51 campaign before signing for Sheffield United in May 1951. He played in the Central League team at Bramall Lane for two seasons, then returned to Scotland where he made a solitary appearance for Third Lanark. Back in the Football League, he spent the first half of 1955–56 with Chesterfield, for whom he made three League appearances before brief spells with Wisbech Town and King's Lynn. He later added further senior appearances for Berwick Rangers and Albion Rovers.

Alex Sabella (Born: Buenos Aires, Argentina, 5 November 1954. Died: Buenos Aires, Argentina, 8 December 2020.) Alex Sabella was a very skilful midfield player who developed in the youth set-up at River Plate before signing for Sheffield United who had despatched representatives to Argentina looking for new recruits following that country's success in winning the 1978 World Cup. He spent two seasons at Bramall Lane, featuring regularly throughout, before joining First Division club Leeds United. However, he made little impact during his time at Elland Road and returned home to sign for Estudiantes de la Plata. He later coached at Estudiantes (March 2009 to February 2011) with whom he won the Copa Libertadores in 2009, and later with the Argentina national team (August 2011 to July 2014), leading them to the 2014 World Cup final where they lost 1-0 to Germany. As a player he won eight caps for Argentina.

Ian St John (Born: Motherwell, 7 June 1938. Died: Upton, Wirral, 1 March 2021.) Ian St John was a tenacious forward with a tremendous scoring record who developed with Motherwell Bridge Works and Motherwell Athletic before moving to the seniors with Motherwell, making his debut at the start of the 1957–58 campaign. The following season he netted 31 goals, heading the Division One scoring charts, while in August 1959 he netted a trick in just three minutes in the League Cup win over Hibernian at Easter Road. In total he scored 105 goals from 144 League and Cup appearances during his stay at Fir Park before being sold to Liverpool in April 1961 for what was a new record fee for the Reds. For the next eight seasons he rarely missed a match, barring injuries, as Liverpool won the Second Division title in 1961–62 and the First Division on two occasions (1963–64 and 1965–66). He was also an FA Cup winner in 1965 when his extra-time header proved the winner against Leeds United. After leaving Anfield he wound down his career with spells at Coventry City and Tranmere Rovers, and in South Africa with Hellenic. He was later manager of Motherwell (June 1973 to September 1974) and Portsmouth (September 1974 to May 1977) before building a successful career in broadcasting, notably as a presenter of the *Saint and Greavsie* show on ITV. He won 21 caps for Scotland and also won representative honours for the U23s and the Scottish League XI.

Malcolm Scott (Born: South Shields, 8 May 1936. Died: 11 September 2020.) Malcolm Scott was a centre-half who spent six years on the books of Newcastle United after signing in September 1955. Apart from the 1958–59 season he received few opportunities at St James' Park, and it was only after he dropped down a couple of divisions to sign for Darlington shortly after the start of the 1961–62 season that he saw regular first-team action. He later had spells with York City and in the Southern League with Rugby Town before retiring from his football career. He was also a professional cricketer who played 185 first class matches for Northamptonshire, taking 461 wickets as a slow left arm bowler, having previously played for Durham and the Minor Counties representative team.

Maurice Setters (Born: Honiton, Devon, 16 December 1936. Died: Doncaster, 22 November 2020.) Maurice Setters was a tough-tackling wing-half who was on the books of Exeter City as a youngster before being sold to West Bromwich Albion midway through the 1954–55 campaign. His early career at The Hawthorns was disrupted by National Service, but once he had established himself in the side, he was sold to Manchester United in January 1960. He enjoyed the best years of his career at Old Trafford, where he was an FA Cup winner in 1963, and made close on 200 first-team appearances. He went on to play for Stoke City, Coventry City and Charlton Athletic before injury ended his playing career. He then had a spell as manager of Doncaster Rovers (June 1971 to November 1974) and continued to work in the game for many years, notably having spells as assistant to Jack Charlton at Newcastle United and with the Republic of Ireland. He won England Youth international honours and was capped 16 times by England U23s.

Len Sharpe (Born: Scunthorpe, 29 November 1932. Died: April 2021.) Len Sharpe was a local lad who played a handful of games for Scunthorpe United in their final season of non-league football. He remained at the Old Showground for 13 seasons, featuring in a variety of positions, although not always a first-team regular. He made over 200 appearances for the Iron, contributing to their success in winning Division Three North in 1957–58. After concluding his senior career at Hull City, he later played for Goole Town and had spells as manager of a number of local clubs including Ashby Institute, Barton Town and Brigg Town.

George Sharples (Born: Ellesmere Port, 20 September 1943. Died: Barrow-in-Furness, 14 December 2020.) Wing-half George Sharples won international honours for England Schools and joined the groundstaff at Everton on leaving school. He signed a professional contract at the age of 17, making his first-team debut shortly afterwards. He was an FA Youth Cup runner-up in 1960–61 but struggled to break into the side at Goodison, moving on to sign for Blackburn Rovers in March 1965. After making just over 100 appearances for Rovers, he suffered a broken leg at Derby County in March 1969 and did not play in the first team again. He later spent the 1971–72 campaign with Southport before a further injury led to his retirement from the game.

Luton Shelton (Born: Kingston, Jamaica, 11 November 1985. Died: Kingston, Jamaica, 22 January 2021.) Luton Shelton was a striker who began his career in Jamaica with Harbour View. In August 2006 he moved to Europe, signing for Helsingborgs IF, then six months later he joined Sheffield United where he made a total of 25 first-team appearances over the next season and a half, scoring four goals over the next season and a half. He later moved on to Norway to play for ValerangaValerenga, then continued his career in Turkey and Russia. He holds the all-time scoring record for the Jamaica national team with 35 goals and is believed to be the only male player to score four goals on his international debut. His early death was due to a progressive neurodegenerative disease.

Guy Shuttleworth (Born: Blackburn, 6 November 1926. Died: Eastbourne, 21 January 2021.) Guy Shuttleworth was a wing-half who captained the Cambridge University football team and later played for both Pegasus and Corinthian Casuals, with whom he won an FA Amateur Cup runners-up medal in 1955–56. He won a single cap for England Amateurs, appearing against Wales in March 1949. He also featured in first class cricket for Cambridge University and in the Minor Counties for Lancashire 2nd XISeconds. He was the maternal grandfather of Ben Chilwell (Chelsea and England).

George Siddle (Born: Circa 1934. Died: 5 April 2021.) George Siddle was a powerful centre-half who played for West Auckland Town for several seasons, gaining an FA Amateur Cup runners-up medal in 1961, and then for Bishop Auckland. He spent the 1967–68 campaign with Scottish League club Queen of the South, featuring regularly in the line-up, before returning to the North East to sign for Gateshead. Later he became a fixture in the Scarborough line-up, making a further Wembley appearance in 1973 when he was an FA Trophy winner.

Gordon Simms (Born: Leamington, 20 December 1936. Died: 11 March 2021.) Gordon Simms was a winger who signed for Coventry City as an amateur from Leamington works' outfit Flavel's Athletic in October 1955. He made a single Football League appearance against Colchester United two years later before National Service intervened. Later he had a spell on the books of Notts County without breaking into the first team.

Ebbe Skovdahl (Born: Copenhagen, Denmark, 5 July 1945. Died: Karlslunde, Denmark, 23 October 2020.) Ebbe Skovdahl had played lower-level football in Denmark before going on to achieve success as a coach and manager, notably in three separate spells with Brøndby IF. He was manager of Aberdeen from May 1999 to November 2002, during which time they were finalists in both the Scottish Cup and League Cup in his first season at Pittodrie.

Malcolm Slater (Born: Buckie, Banffshire, 22 October 1939. Died: January 2021.) Winger Malcom Slater made his debut for Celtic as an 18-year-old amateur and went on to win an amateur international cap for Scotland against Northern Ireland in February 1959. He was unable to gain regular first team football at Parkhead and after spells in the Highland League with Buckie Thistle and Inverness Caledonian he signed for Montrose. His performances soon attracted interest from clubs south of the Border and in November 1962 he was transferred to Southend United. He enjoyed a useful career in England both with the Shrimpers and Orient, making a total of over 200 appearances before switching to Southern League football with Folkestone.

Alan Slough (Born: Luton, 24 September 1947. Died: 22 March 2021.) Alan Slough was a versatile player who featured both in defence and midfield and made over 600 senior appearances in a career that spanned the period from 1965 to 1982. He made his debut as a teenager with Luton Town, and he enjoyed a successful time at Kenilworth Road being a member of promotion teams in 1967–68 and 1969–70. In August 1973 he moved on to Fulham, where his career peaked with an appearance in the 1975 FA Cup final when the Cottagers lost out to West Ham United. He subsequently had a spell at Peterborough where he was player-coach, and in April 1978 he achieved the unusual feat of scoring a hat-trick of penalties for Posh in their 4-3 defeat at Chester. He later concluded his career at Millwall before becoming a coach with Torquay United.

John Sludden (Born: Falkirk, 29 December 1964. Died: May 2021.) John Sludden was capped for Scotland Schools and went on to sign for Celtic, but although he won Youth international honours he was unable to break into the first team at Parkhead. However, he subsequently went on to enjoy a lengthy and successful career in Scottish League football, making around 300 appearances and scoring at a rate of a goal every other game. His most successful spell was with Ayr United where he scored over 30 League and Cup goals in both 1986–87 and 1987–88. He was chosen as the Scottish PFA Second Division Player of the Year for 1986–87, whilstwhile the following season his goals helped fire Ayr to the Second Division title. He also had spells with St Johnstone, Airdrieonians, Kilmarnock, East Fife, Clydebank, Clyde and Stenhousemuir and was manager of East Stirlingshire from May 2016 to August 2018.

Archie Smith (Born: Circa 1930. Died: August 2020.) Archie Smith was a full-back who joined East Fife from local Secondary Juvenile outfit Bayview Youth Club in December 1949. He made just two first-team appearances during his time at Methil, then spent the 1953–54 season with Dundee United where he featured more regularly. He signed on trial for Arbroath the following season, but his career was ended by a knee injury suffered before he was able to break into the first team.

Ray Smith (Born: Islington, 18 April 1943. Died: 19 January 2021.) Centre-forward Ray Smith signed for Southend United at the age of 18 but it was not until the closing stages of the 1964–65 season that he fully established himself in the team. He was the club's leading scorer in 1966–67 before signing for Wrexham along with teammate Steve Ingle in the close season. He continued to find the net regularly during his stay at the Racecourse Ground, heading the scoring charts in his first two seasons, while in 1969–70 he made a significant contribution to the club's achievement in finishing as runners-up in Division Four. After a season with Peterborough United he returned to North Wales, signing for non-league Bangor City.

Davie Sneddon, MBE (Born: Kilwinning, Ayrshire, 24 April 1936. Died: Crosshouse, Ayrshire, 24 December 2020.) Davie Sneddon was an intelligent, stylish inside-forward who stepped up from Kilwinning Juniors to sign for Dundee in January 1954. He established himself at Dens Park during the 1957–58 campaign but after a further season in the line-up he was sold to Preston North End. He had two good seasons at Deepdale but soon after North End were relegated from the First Division he returned to Scotland, signing for Kilmarnock. The six-year spell at Rugby Park provided the pinnacle of his career when he scored one of the goals in the crucial 2-0 win at Tynecastle in April 1965 which clinched the Scottish League title for the only time in their history. The following season he played in both legs of their European Cup defeat at the hands of Real Madrid. He ended his playing career with Raith Rovers and was later manager of Kilmarnock (Oct 1977 to Jan 1981) and Stranraer (March 1982 to Dec 1985). He was awarded the MBE in the 2014 Queen's Birthday Honours List for services to the Kilmarnock community and Kilmarnock Football Club.

Les Stancer (Born: Grantham, 19 April 1925. Died: Sleaford, 24 February 2021.) Les Stancer was an inside-forward or wing-half who joined Notts County from Grantham St John's during the 1941–42 season. Although mostly featuring in the colts team, he made 19 wartime appearances for the Magpies, including an FA Cup outing in 1945–46. He later played for Grantham and Bourne Town.

Jimmy Stevenson (Born: Bellshill, Lanarkshire, 4 August 1946. Died: March 2021.) Left-half Jimmy Stevenson joined Hibernian from Juvenile club Edina Hearts in August 1963 and made his first-team debut later that season. He was unable to establish himself at Easter Road, although he played in all three matches in the 1964 Summer Cup final when Hibs pipped Aberdeen to take the trophy. He moved on to Southend United for the 1967–68 campaign and featured regularly during his only season at Roots Hall, then continued his career in the Southern League with Brentwood Town, Chelmsford City and Dover Athletic.

Nobby Stiles, MBE (Born: Manchester, 18 May 1942. Died: 30 October 2020.) Nobby Stiles was a robust but talented wing-half and later midfield player who won England Schools international honours before joining Manchester United, initially on amateur forms. He made his first-team debut at Bolton at the age of 18 and very quickly established himself in the United team. He went on to become one of the key elements in the club's successful team of the 1960s, winning two Football League championships (1964–65 and 1966–67) and the European Cup in 1967–68. He made more than 350 competitive appearances during his time at Old Trafford before moving on to spells with Middlesbrough and Preston North End. He was later manager of Preston (July 1977 to June 1981) and, briefly, West Bromwich Albion (September 1985 to February 1986), and returned to Manchester United for a spell coaching the youth players from July 1989. He was capped 28 times for England and appeared in all six matches in the 1966 World Cup campaign. His exuberance when celebrating the victory over West Germany became recognised as an iconic moment in post-war British football.

Mike Sutton (Born: Norwich, 5 October 1944. Died: 26 December 2020.) Mike Sutton was a utility player who could play in almost any outfield position. He joined the groundstaff at Norwich City on leaving school and then spent five years as a professional at Carrow Road. However, although he made his first-team debut at the age of 18 he was in and out of the side during this time and towards the end of the 1966–67 season he announced he was leaving football to work in insurance. Three months later he was tempted back by Chester manager Peter Hauser and in three seasons at Sealand Road he played in almost every match. Thereafter he had a couple of seasons with Carlisle United before spending a more lengthy period with Eastern Counties League club Great Yarmouth Town. His sons Chris Sutton and John Sutton both played the game professionally.

Peter Swan (Born: South Elmsall, Yorkshire, 8 October 1936. Died: 20 January 2021.) Centre-half Peter Swan signed amateur forms for Sheffield Wednesday on leaving school and progressed through the ranks at Hillsborough making his first-team debut at the age of 19. He eventually established himself in the team at the age of 19 and for the next six seasons he was a fixture in the Owls' line-up. He was a Second Division winner in 1958–59 and an FA Cup semi-finalist the following season with the club firmly positioned as a top-six team. He won 19 caps for England and was a member of the squad for the 1962 World Cup finals, although he did not play due to illness. His career collapsed in April 1964 when he was banned from the game for his involvement in match fixing as a result of which he received a short prison sentence. The ban was lifted in 1972 and, remarkably, he signed again for Wednesday and played a few games. Later he spent a season with Bury before becoming player-manager of Matlock Town, leading them to success in the FA Trophy in 1975.

Andy Sweeney (Born: Chadderton, Oldham, 15 October 1951. Died: Lydgate, Oldham, 2020.) Andy Sweeney was a tricky winger who was briefly an amateur with Oldham Athletic before turning professional in February 1971. He spent four years on the books at Boundary Park, but apart from a spell in the first half of the 1972–73 he was mostly a reserve. He was at Rochdale in 1975–76 then played for a number of non-league clubs in the North West.

Barry Tait (Born: York, 17 June 1938. Died: 23 October 2020.) Barry Tait played as an amateur for Doncaster Rovers, progressing to their reserve team in the Midland League before switching to his local club York City, for whom he signed professional terms in September 1958. He developed into a useful centre-forward, although he made little progress in his early career with the Minstermen or in brief spells at Peterborough and Bradford City. He did well at Halifax Town, finishing as the team's leading scorer in 1962–63 including a late hat-trick at Swindon in September which helped turn a 3-0 deficit into a 4-3 win. After concluding his senior career at Crewe Alexandra and Notts County, he signed for non-league Scarborough.

John Talbut (Born: Headington, Oxfordshire, 20 October 1940. Died: Mechelen, Belgium, 14 August 2020.) John Talbut was a powerful centre-half who was capped for England Schools before joining Burnley as an amateur. He progressed to the professional ranks at the age of 17 and captained the reserve team before winning a regular place in the line-up in the 1962–63 season. He remained a first choice for three seasons but injuries and competition for places led to his departure to West Bromwich Albion midway through the 1966–67 campaign. He was an FA Cup winner with the Baggies in 1968 and also gained a League Cup runners-up medal two years later before concluding his career with a three-year spell in Belgium as player-coach of KV Mechelen.

Wayne Talkes (Born: Ealing, 2 June 1952. Died: 17 April 2021.) Wayne Talkes was a stylish midfield player who joined Southampton as an apprentice and was playing in the reserves at the age of 15. He spent five years as a professional at The Dell but managed just a handful of first-team appearances and fared little better in a season with Bournemouth. After leaving full-time football he played for several Hampshire non-league clubs.

Vince Taylor (Born: Tonypandy, Glamorgan, November 1926. Died: Worthing, 3 March 2021.) Vince Taylor was a prolific scorer on the left wing for Worthing and signed amateur forms for Arsenal on his 18th[th] birthday. He made two appearances for the Gunners at the end of the 1944–45 season but soon afterwards his career was affected by a series of long-term injuries. He later returned to Worthing and also turned out for the Sussex FA and Corinthian League representative teams before a further serious injury ended his career in September 1954.

Matt Tees (Born: Johnstone, Renfrewshire, 13 October 1939. Died: Grimsby, 3 November 2020.) Matt Tees developed with Juvenile club Penilee Athletic and then Cambuslang Rangers before stepping up to the seniors when he signed for Airdrieonians in September 1960. A subsequent move south to Grimsby Town proved a great success and he developed into a skilful and persistent forward with an eye for goal. He headed the Mariners' scoring charts in 1965–66 and shortly afterwards moved up a division to sign for Charlton Athletic. He did well at The Valley, then had a short spell at Luton before returning to Blundell Park. Here he resumed where he had left off in his first spell, scoring regularly, and he hit 27 goals as Grimsby won the Fourth Division title in 1971–72. He later had a season with Boston United before retiring from the game.

Eddie Thomas (Born: Swindon, 9 November 1932. Died: 23 September 2020.) Eddie Thomas was a goalkeeper playing local football in Swindon before he signed amateur forms for Southampton. He made his senior debut for the Saints against Birmingham City in October 1950 at the age of 17 and went on to win England Youth international honours. He stayed at The Dell until the end of the 1951–52 season before joining Western League club Salisbury.

Jimmy Thompson (Born: Windy Nook, Co Durham, 7 January 1943. Died: Grimsby, 28 October 2020.) Full-back Jimmy Thompson was an amateur on the books of Preston North End before signing for Grimsby Town in September 1961 and he went on to win a regular place in the line-up in the closing stages of the 1963–64 campaign. He spent the next two seasons as a fixture in the side but eventually left to play for Port Elizabeth City in South Africa in April 1967 after becoming involved in a contractual dispute with the Mariners. He returned to the UK at the beginning of 1969 and signed for Cambridge United, helping them to win two consecutive Southern League titles and then appearing in their first-ever Football League fixture. He was a dependable figure in defence for the U's for the next three seasons before injury brought his career to a close.

Mike Tindall (Born: Birmingham, 5 April 1941. Died: August 2020.) Mike Tindall joined the Aston Villa groundstaff in April 1956 and progressed through the ranks, signing a professional contract two years later. Although never a regular in the line-up he made over 100 appearances during a decade at Villa Park, mostly featuring at right-half. He subsequently had a brief spell with Walsall in the 1968–69 season before joining non-league Tamworth.

Roy Torrens, OBE (Born: Derry, 17 May 1948. Died: 23 January 2021.) Centre-half Roy Torrens captained Northern Ireland at both Youth and Amateur international levels in the 1960s, playing most of his club football with Derry City and Ballymena United. He was better known in the world of cricket making 30 appearances for Ireland between 1966 and 1984 and later holding a number of senior positions including President of the Irish Cricket Union.

Don Townsend (Born: Swindon, 17 September 1930. Died: July 2020.) Don Townsend began his career as a centre-forward in Western League football before signing for Charlton Athletic in the 1950 close season. He had to wait four years before he broke into the first team at The Valley but then enjoyed seven seasons of mostly regular first-team football, making over 250 appearances and scoring a solitary goal in a 6-4 win over Plymouth Argyle on Boxing Day in 1960. After losing his place in the side he moved on to Crystal Palace, where he was a near ever ever-present in the team that won promotion from the Third Division in 1963–64 before leaving senior football. He was the father of the former Republic of Ireland international Andy Townsend.

Jim Townsend (Born: Greenock, 2 February 1945. Died: 19 October 2020, Windsor, Ontario, Canada.) Wing-half Jim Townsend was just 16 when he signed for St Johnstone, and he went on to play a key role in the team that won the Scottish Second Division title in 1962–63. Midway through the following season he moved south to join Middlesbrough for what was then a record transfer fee for the Perth club. Although he quickly established himself with Boro, a change in management at Ayresome Park saw him return to St Johnstone in the summer of 1966. He subsequently enjoyed a successful five-year spell with Hearts, gaining a Scottish Cup runners-up medal as a member of the team defeated by Dunfermline in the 1968 final. He concluded his senior career at Morton before emigrating to Canada where he had a spell as coach of National Soccer League club Windsor Stars.

Stan Trafford (Born: Leek, 21 December 1945. Died: Stoke-on-Trent, 17 November 2020.) Stan Trafford was a versatile forward who developed in the Port Vale junior teams before signing a professional contract in October 1964. He made 12 appearances scoring one goal in the 1964–65 season then moved into non-league football with Eastwood Hanley, Macclesfield Town and Leek Town. He was also a talented cricketer and made four appearances for Staffordshire in the Minor Counties Championship.

Derek Trail (Born: Leith, 2 January 1946. Died: 16 December 2020.) Derek Trail was a skilful outside-left who won four caps for Scotland Schools before joining Rangers where he made his senior debut at the age of 17. He made a handful of appearances during his stay at Ibrox, then had a season at Falkirk, where he was mostly a reserve, before joining Workington. He enjoyed two good seasons at Borough Park and another with Hartlepool before emigrating to Australia where he played for South Sydney, Auburn, Hakoah and Sutherland. After five years he returned to Scotland, briefly featuring for Berwick Rangers, Meadowbank Thistle and Alloa Athletic before retiring from the game.

Colin Treharne (Born: Bridgend, 30 July 1937. Died: Lincoln, 26 March 2021.) Goalkeeper Colin Treharne was playing for 6th Battalion RAOC in the Nottingham Thursday League whilstwhile on National Service when he signed for Mansfield Town in December 1960. After breaking into the first team in October 1961 he had an unbroken run of 138 appearances in the Stags' line-up and was an ever ever-present in the team that won the Fourth Division title in 1962–63. He later had a season with Lincoln City before switching to Midland League football with Ilkeston Town.

Derek Ufton (Born: Crayford, Kent, 31 May 1928. Died: 27 March 2021.) Derek Ufton signed for Charlton Athletic as a wing-half in September 1948, but quickly switched to centre-half and went on to win a regular place in the line-up in 1951–52. He was a fixture in the Addicks defence, barring absences for injuries, for seven seasons and made a total of 277 first-team appearances for the club. He was capped for England against the Rest of the World in a match to celebrate the FA's 90th[th] anniversary and at the time of his death was the country's oldest former international player. He was manager of Plymouth Argyle from April 1965 to January 1968. He remained close to Charlton and later had a 26-year spell as a director of the club. He was also an extremely talented cricketer and played 149 first class matches for Kent as a wicketkeeper batsman between 1949 and 1962, also representing the MCC against Scotland in 1961.

Dr Jozef Venglos (Born: Ruzomberok, Czechoslovakia, 18 February 1936. Died: Bratislava, Slovakia, 26 January 2021.) Jozef Venglos had been a midfield player with Slovan Bratislava and was capped for Czechoslovakia B before developing a highly successful career in coaching. After leading Czechoslovakia to a place in the quarter-finals of the 1990 World Cup he was appointed as manager of Aston Villa, becoming the first overseas manager of an English top-flight club. He was only in charge at Villa Park for a season and the club finished in the lower reaches of the First Division, but he introduced a range of methods, including a focus on diet, which were new to English football. He continued his career in Turkey with Fenerbahce, later returning to the UK to take charge of Celtic in 1998–99.

Tony Villars (Born: Cwmbran, 24 January 1952. Died: 9 September 2020.) Tony Villars was a quick and skilful winger who was briefly an apprentice with Newport County before dropping into non-league football. He returned to the senior ranks with Cardiff City in June 1971 but in five years at Ninian Park he was only a first-team regular in 1973–74. He is best remembered for scoring a tremendous equaliser against Crystal Palace in the final game of that season to keep Cardiff up and condemn the visitors to relegation to the Third Division. His final campaign in senior football was spent back at Newport before he dropped down to the Welsh League to play for Blaenavon Blues. He was capped for Wales U23s and won three full caps, all in the 1974 Home International Championship.

Bobby Wade (Died. Dublin, 24 February 2021.) Bobby Wade was a defender with Bohemians for whom he made over 200 first-team appearances and gained an FAI Cup winners' medal in 1970. He won three caps for the Republic of Ireland Amateurs, including an appearance against Great Britain in an Olympic Games qualifying round tie.

Tony Waiters (Born: Southport, 1 February 1937. Died: 10 November 2020.) Goalkeeper Tony Waiters came to prominence playing for Loughborough Colleges when he was a student and also turned out for several clubs including Bishop Auckland. In May 1959 he was capped for England Amateurs against Luxembourg and later that year he signed professional forms for Blackpool. He spent five seasons as first choice for the Seasiders, who were then in the old First Division, leaving at the end of the 1966–67 campaign after they were relegated. He became a coach with the FA in the North West region then worked in the youth set-up at Liverpool before switching to Burnley as player-coach where he returned to playing and featured regularly in the line-up in 1970–71. Later he was director of coaching with Coventry City and then manager of Plymouth Argyle (October 1972 to February 1977) taking them to the League Cup semi-finals in 1973–74 and promotion from the Third Division 12 months later. He subsequently emigrated to Canada, where he was coach of the Vancouver Whitecaps team that won the NASL in 1979 and was then coach of the national team (1982–1986), leading them to the last eight of the Olympic Games in 1984 before reaching the 1986 World Cup finals. He won five full caps for England.

Dennis Walmsley (Born: Birkdale, Southport, 1 May 1935. Died: 2 September 2020.) Dennis Walmsley was a versatile forward who developed in local football before signing amateur forms for Southport in November 1952. He scored a headed equaliser on his senior debut against York City in September 1954 and had a short run in the side before dropping back into the reserves. At the end of the season he moved on to Lancashire Combination club Burscough, where he continued to play for more than a decade.

Ian Warburton (Born: Haslingden, Lancashire, 22 March 1952. Died: Blackburn, 9 February 2021.) Ian Warburton earned a move to Bury from West Lancashire League club Haslingden in November 1972, but in two seasons at Gigg Lane and a further two at Southport he made a total of 15 senior appearances scoring three goals. He continued his career with a string of non-league clubs in the North West, including Rossendale United and Accrington Stanley.

Whelan Ward (Born: Ovenden, Halifax, 15 June 1929. Died: Halifax, 6 February 2021.) Whelan Ward was a tenacious and effective inside-forward despite being just 5ft 3ins tall. He joined Bradford City in October 1948 as his period of National Service was ending and in six years at Valley Parade he made over 150 first-team appearances, leading the club's scoring charts in 1951–52. Following a season with Midland League newcomers King's Lynn he returned to senior football with City's rivals Bradford Park Avenue where he added a further 112 appearances before leaving full-time football.

Syd Weatherup (Born: Belfast, 22 January 1934. Died: Orangeville, Ontario, Canada, 3 August 2020.) Outside-left Syd Weatherup appeared for a string of Irish League clubs including Linfield, Glenavon (with whom he gained a league champions' medal in 1959–60) and Ards, as well as having a brief spell in the Southern League for Merthyr Tydfil. He made five appearances for the Irish League representative side, scoring in a famous 5-2 victory over the Football League in April 1956.

Alan Welsh (Born: Edinburgh, 9 July 1947. Died: August 2020.) Inside-forward Alan Welsh joined Millwall from Bonnyrigg Rose in July 1965, but he was only on the fringes of the first team at The Den. He saw regular first-team action after signing for Torquay United, notably in 1969–70 when he finished as top scorer and was chosen as the club's Player of the Year. After Torquay were relegated to the Fourth Division he was sold to Plymouth Argyle where he was a member of the team that reached the League Cup semi-finals in 1973–74. He later played for Bournemouth, Millwall, again, and Maidstone United before finishing his career in South Africa with Cape Town City.

Willie Whigham (Born: Airdrie, 9 October 1939. Died: Airdrie, 4 March 2021.) Goalkeeper Willie Whigham appeared in Clyde's pre-season trial match in August 1958 and was once selected as a triallist for Albion Rovers the following season before progressing via Strathclyde Juniors and Shotts Bon Accord to Falkirk in July 1960. He proved a valuable asset for the Bairns, helping them win promotion back to the top flight in his first season and going on to make over 250 appearances. In October 1966 he was sold to Middlesbrough and made an immediate impact in their promotion campaign from Division Three. He remained first-choice at Ayresome Park for five seasons before concluding his career with spells at Dumbarton and Darlington.

Don Whiston (Born: Chesterton, Staffordshire, 4 April 1930. Died: Wolstanton, Newcastle-under-Lyme, 27 November 2020.) Don Whiston signed amateur forms for Stoke City in October 1947 after showing promise in local Boys' Brigade football and went on to make his senior debut at centre-forward in December 1949 whilstwhile on leave from the Forces. He signed a professional contract for the Potters straight after the game, and then scored in the home game with Derby County four days later, but he was mostly a reserve during a seven-year stay at the Victoria Ground. He switched to playing at full-back before moving on to Crewe Alexandra where he was to play regularly during an 18-month stay. Later he spent a season at Rochdale before leaving senior football at the end of the 1958–59 season to sign for Macclesfield Town.

Ward White (Born: Ayr, 12 October 1946. Died: 18 December 2020.) Striker Ward White was capped for Scotland Juniors against Ireland in October 1968, later signing for Celtic from Beith. He spent four seasons as a reserve at Parkhead before moving on to Clydebank where he made over 50 first-team appearances over two seasons. He subsequently returned to the Juniors with Irvine Meadow and later had spells as manager of a number of Junior clubs, notably Maybole where he spent 10 years in charge.

Terry Whitham (Born: Sheffield, 14 August 1935. Died: April 2021.) Terry Whitham was a versatile player who developed locally before signing as a professional for Sheffield Wednesday on reaching the age of 17. He spent nine seasons on the books at Hillsborough but was called up to the first team on only four occasions. In the 1961 close season he signed for Chesterfield where he enjoyed fairly regularly first-team football but was never able to make any position his own. After leaving senior football he went on to play for Worksop Town and Matlock Town.

Johnny Williams (Born: Tottenham, 26 March 1947. Died: January 2021.) Johnny Williams joined Watford as a 15-year-old apprentice and had already made his Football League debut when he signed professional forms at the age of 17. He established himself at left-back from the start of the 1966–67 season and remained as first choice for the Hornets for the next nine seasons, helping them win the Division Three title in 1968–69 and featuring in the FA Cup semi-final defeat by Chelsea 12 months later. On leaving Vicarage Road he spent a further three seasons with Colchester United before switching to Southern League football with Margate.

Wayne Williams (Born: Telford, 17 November 1963. Died: 2 October 2020.) Defender Wayne Williams signed professional forms for Shrewsbury Town in November 1981 and went on to spend just over seven years with the Shrews. He was a regular in the first team from the start of the 1982–83 season and made a total of more than 250 first-team appearances before moving to Northampton Town during the 1988–89 season. He subsequently concluded his senior career with Walsall before dropping into non-league football when he signed for Kidderminster Harriers.

Arthur Williamson (Born: Bankfoot, Perthshire, 26 July 1930. Died: Perth, 26 June 2020.) Arthur Williamson was a full-back who developed with Burghmuir Rovers and Jeanfield Swifts before signing provisional forms for Clyde in June 1950. His only senior appearance for the Bully Wee came in January 1955 and at the end of that season he was released. He moved south to sign for Southend United where he established himself in the first team almost immediately. Between January 1956 and September 1960 he made 230 consecutive League and Cup appearances, a club record for the Shrimpers. After losing his place in the 1961–62 season he retired, returning to Scotland to enter the family business.

Andy Wilson (Born: Rotherham, 27 September 1940. Died: Chesterfield, March 2021.) Andy Wilson was a versatile winger who was on the books of Sheffield United as a youngster, making four first-team appearances. In the summer of 1961 he moved on to Scunthorpe United, helping them to achieve their highest-ever League position, fourth in Division Two, in 1961–62 and he stayed four seasons with the Iron, playing over 100 games. He subsequently joined Doncaster Rovers on a free transfer, contributing to their Fourth Division championship season in 1965–66 before concluding his senior career with spells at Chesterfield and Aldershot.

Bob Wilson (Born: Birmingham, 23 May 1943. Died: Exeter, 3 October 2020.) Bob Wilson was a goalkeeper who developed in junior football in the Birmingham area before signing for Aston Villa. He made nine First Division appearances towards the end of the 1963–64 season and soon afterwards signed for Cardiff City. He was a regular for the Bluebirds for the best part of four seasons, featuring in their tremendous run in the European Cup Winners' Cup in 1968–69 when they reached the semi-finals. Later he enjoyed a lengthy spell with Exeter City where he made over 200 appearances before losing his place and leaving senior football.

Eric Winstanley (Born: Barnsley, 15 November 1944. Died: 20 May 2021.) Eric Winstanley was a powerful, commanding centre-half who was a product of the renowned Barnsley Boys team before signing for Barnsley with whom he won England Youth honours. He became a regular in the line-up at the age of 18 and was rarely absent over the next 10 seasons, becoming the club's youngest-ever captain. He missed just one game in the 1967–68 promotion campaign, whilstwhile the following season he topped the club's scoring charts, his tally being boosted by a remarkable hat-trick in the home game with Watford. Later he spent four seasons with Chesterfield before retiring as a player. He subsequently spent 20 years on the coaching staff at Oakwell and also had a spell as coach of the St Kitts & Nevis national team.

Bobby Wishart (Born: Edinburgh, 10 March 1933. Died: Edinburgh, 2 December 2020.) Bobby Wishart was a skilful inside-forward and latterly wing-half who stepped up from the Secondary Juveniles with Merchiston Thistle to sign for Aberdeen in August 1951. During a period of National Service he starred in the Irish League with Portadown and once demobilised he quickly established himself at Pittodrie. He was a regular in the team that won the Scottish League title in 1954–55 and the following season he was a League Cup winner. He went on to score 62 goals from 236 appearances for the Dons before leaving for Dundee midway through the 1960–61 season. His career was rejuvenated at Dens Park where he made a valuable contribution to the team that won the League title in 1961–62 and reached the semi-final of the European Cup 12 months later. He concluded with brief spells at Airdrieonians and Raith Rovers. He gained representative honours for Scotland U23s and the Scottish League XI.

Colin Withers (Born: Erdington, Birmingham, 21 March 1940. Died: 28 December 2020.) Colin Withers was a tall, well-built goalkeeper who was capped by England Schoolboys. He then played for Erdington Albion, a nursery club for West Bromwich Albion, before being snapped up by Birmingham City on professional terms at the age of 17. He broke into the first team during the 1960–61 season and played in the first leg of the Inter Cities Fairs Cup semi-final against Inter Milan, but he was in and out of the side during his time at St Andrew's. He crossed the city to sign for Aston Villa during the 1964–65 campaign where he did well, winning the supporters' Player of the Year prize (the Terrace Trophy) in both 1965–66 and 1966–67. He ended his career with a season at Lincoln City and then in the Netherlands with Go Ahead Deventer.

Alan Woan (Born: Liverpool, 8 February 1931. Died: 13 February 2021.) Inside-forward Alan Woan developed in the Lancashire Combination with Bootle and, briefly, New Brighton, before joining Norwich City in December 1953. He made a great start to his Carrow Road career, scoring within three minutes of his debut against Northampton Town, and regularly finding the net for the reserves. After three years as a Canary he signed for Northampton Town where he was top scorer in each of his first three seasons. He moved on to Crystal Palace where he began the 1960–61 season in impressive form with a hat-trick in the opening game and a total of 11 goals in his first 10 appearances but then suffered a loss of form and in February 1961 he was transferred to Aldershot. He ended his senior career with the Shots, for whom he led the scoring charts in 1962–63. His brother Don played for Liverpool, Leyton Orient, Bradford City and Tranmere Rovers while his son Ian played for Nottingham Forest.

Frank Worthington (Born: Halifax, 23 November 1948. Died: Huddersfield, 22 March 2021.) Frank Worthington was one of the most charismatic figures in English football in the 1970s and ''80s. A very talented striker, he had a somewhat peripatetic playing career, appearing for 11 Football League clubs between 1966 and 1988 and also had brief spells in the United States, Sweden, South Africa and Ireland. He started out as a youngster with Huddersfield Town where he was top scorer in the team that won the Division Two title in 1969–70. After they were relegated from the First Division the following season he moved on to Leicester City where he arguably spent the best years of his career. He was rarely absent in five seasons at Filbert Street, heading the scoring charts on four occasions and winning eight caps for England. He won a second Division Two title with Bolton Wanderers in 1977–78 and the following season he was the First Division's leading scorer with 24 goals. There was yet another promotion to the top flight with Birmingham City in 1979–80 and thereafter he flitted from club to club, playing the last of his 757 Football League matches for Stockport County in April 1988. He was player-manager of Tranmere Rovers between July 1985 and February 1987. He was the son of Eric Worthington (who played wartime football for Halifax Town and Lincoln City), and the brother of Dave and Bob, who both had lengthy careers in the game.

Doug Wragg (Born: Nottingham, 12 September 1934. Died: 9 November 2020.) Forward Doug Wragg appeared for England in the NABC internationals before signing professional forms for West Ham United in June 1953. It was not until August 1956 that he made his senior debut for the Hammers and although he continued to make occasional appearances, he was mostly a reserve at the club. He saw more first-team action at Mansfield, but the best years of his career were at Rochdale. He appeared in the first leg of the Football League Cup final defeat by Norwich City in 1961–62 and made over 100 appearances during a three-year stay at Spotland. He concluded his senior career with a season at Chesterfield then briefly played for Midland League club Grantham.

Jackie Wren (Born: Bonnybridge, Stirlingshire, 26 April 1936. Died: South Africa, 10 July 2020.) Goalkeeper Jackie Wren developed with Gairdock Juveniles and Bo'ness United before joining Hibernian in the summer of 1956. He was almost immediately introduced to first-team football but in four years at Easter Road he was in and out of the side, playing a total of 31 League games. He switched clubs regularly over the next few years, making senior appearances for Rotherham United, Stirling Albion and Falkirk before emigrating to South Africa in February 1964. He continued his career in the National Football League with Hellenic and Cape Town City before retiring. He was also a talented golfer and while in South Africa had a spell as a professional.

Ralph Wright (Born: Newcastle-upon-Tyne, 3 August 1947. Died: Whitley Bay, 7 June 2020.) Ralph Wright was a versatile player who was equally comfortable playing in defence or as a striker. He was chosen for the England Amateur squad whilstwhile with Spennymoor United before joining Norwich City as a professional in July 1968. He did not make the first team at Carrow Road but then moved on to play five seasons of fairly regular first-team football in the lower reaches of the Football League, turning out for Bradford Park Avenue, Hartlepool, Stockport County, Bolton Wanderers and Southport. He then spent several years playing in the NASL in the United States with some success, featuring for New York Cosmos, Miami Toros (where he played in the team that reached the championship final in 1974) and Dallas Tornado.

John Yates (Born: Rotherham, 18 November 1929. Died: Burlington, Ontario, Canada, 2 September 2020.) John Yates was a forward who had a season at Sheffield United without making the first team before signing for Chester in August 1951. He made two first-team appearances, both at outside-right, during a 12-month spell at Sealand Road and then switched to Midland League football with Gainsborough Trinity. He emigrated to Canada in 1974.

Duncan Young (Born: Broughty Ferry, Dundee, 1938. Died: Dundee, 9 February 2021.) Full-back Duncan Young was a member of the Butterburn Youth Club team that were beaten finalists in the Scottish U16 Amateur Cup in 1954–55. He then had a very brief association with Junior club St Joseph's before moving up to the seniors with Dundee United. He spent four years on the books at Tannadice and was a first-team regular in 1956–57 before suffering an injury. He made a total of 70 League and Cup appearances during his time with the club.

Gerry Young (Born: Jarrow, 1 October 1936. Died: September 2020.) Gerry Young joined Sheffield Wednesday as a left-sided forward from North East works' team Hawthorn Leslie in May 1955 and made his first-team debut at inside-left in March 1957. He was mostly a reserve in his first six seasons at Hillsborough, taking over the left-half position following the departure of Tony Kay during the 1962–63 campaign. He made the No 6 shirt his own over the following seasons and was a member of the team that lost out to Everton in the 1966 FA Cup final. He made a total of 348 League and Cup appearances for the Owls and after retiring remained at the club in a coaching capacity until 1975. He won a single cap for England, appearing against Wales in November 1964.

Marius Zaliukas (Born: Kursenai, Lithuania, USSR, 10 November 1983. Died: Lithuania, 31 October 2020.) Marius Zaliukas was a defender who joined Heart of Midlothian on loan from FBK Kaunas in August 2006 and eventually signed on a permanent basis, going on to make over 200 appearances in what became a seven-year spell at the club. The pinnacle of his career at Tynecastle came in the 2012 Scottish Cup final when he captained the team to a memorable 5-1 over city rivals Hibernian. He spent the 2012–13 season with Leeds United before returning to Scotland in 2013–14 to play for Rangers. He later went back to Lithuania to sign for Zalgiris. He won 10 U23 and 25 full caps for Lithuania. His early death was a result of motor neurone disease.

THE FOOTBALL RECORDS

BRITISH FOOTBALL RECORDS

ALL-TIME PREMIER LEAGUE CHAMPIONSHIP SEASONS ON POINTS AVERAGE

	Team	Season	P	W	D	L	F	A	Pts	Pts Av
1	Manchester C	2017–18	38	32	4	2	106	27	100	2.63
2	Liverpool	2019–20	38	32	3	3	85	33	99	2.61
3	Manchester C	2018–19	38	32	2	4	95	23	98	2.58
4	Chelsea	2004–05	38	29	8	1	72	15	95	2.50
5	Chelsea	2016–17	38	30	3	5	85	33	93	2.45
6	Manchester U	1999–2000	38	28	7	3	97	45	91	2.39
7	Chelsea	2005–06	38	29	4	5	72	22	91	2.39
8	Arsenal	2003–04	38	26	12	0	73	26	90	2.36
	Manchester U	2008–09	38	28	6	4	68	24	90	2.36
10	Manchester C	2011–12	38	28	5	5	93	29	89	2.34
	Manchester U	2006–07	38	28	5	5	83	27	89	2.34
	Manchester U	2012–13	38	28	5	5	86	43	89	2.34
13	Arsenal	2001–02	38	26	9	3	79	36	87	2.28
	Manchester U	2007–08	38	27	6	5	80	22	87	2.28
	Chelsea	2014–15	38	26	9	3	73	32	87	2.28
16	Chelsea	2009–10	38	27	5	6	103	32	86	2.26
	Manchester C	2013–14	38	27	5	6	102	37	86	2.26
	Manchester C	2020–21	38	27	5	6	83	32	86	2.26
19	Manchester U	1993–94	42	27	11	4	80	38	92	2.19
20	Manchester U	2002–03	38	25	8	5	74	34	83	2.18
21	Manchester U	1995–96	38	25	7	6	73	35	82	2.15
22	Leicester C	2015–16	38	23	12	3	68	36	81	2.13
23	Blackburn R	1994–95	42	27	8	7	80	39	89	2.11
24	Manchester U	2000–01	38	24	8	6	79	31	80	2.10
	Manchester U	2010–11	38	23	11	4	78	37	80	2.10
26	Manchester U	1998–99	38	22	13	3	80	37	79	2.07
27	Arsenal	1997–98	38	23	9	6	68	33	78	2.05
28	Manchester U	1992–93	42	24	12	6	67	31	84	2.00
29	Manchester U	1996–97	38	21	12	5	76	44	75	1.97

PREMIER LEAGUE EVER-PRESENT CLUBS

	P	W	D	L	F	A	Pts
Manchester U	1114	687	247	180	2128	1009	2308
Arsenal	1114	597	281	236	1956	1100	2072
Chelsea	1114	597	273	244	1897	1092	2064
Liverpool	1114	581	274	259	1927	1121	2017
Tottenham H	1114	480	276	358	1676	1398	1716
Everton	1114	407	314	393	1448	1415	1535

TOP TEN PREMIER LEAGUE APPEARANCES

1	Barry, Gareth	653	6	Speed, Gary	535
2	Giggs, Ryan	632	7	Heskey, Emile	516
3	Lampard, Frank	609	8	Schwarzer, Mark	514
4	James, David	572	9	Carragher, Jamie	508
5	Milner, James	564	10	Neville, Phil	505

TOP TEN PREMIER LEAGUE GOALSCORERS

1	Shearer, Alan	260	6	Henry, Thierry	175
2	Rooney, Wayne	208	7	Harry Kane	166
3	Cole, Andrew	187	8	Fowler, Robbie	163
4	Aguero, Sergio	184	9	Defoe, Jermain	162
5	Lampard, Frank	177	10	Owen, Michael	150

SCOTTISH PREMIER LEAGUE SINCE 1998–99

	P	*W*	*D*	*L*	*F*	*A*	*Pts*
Celtic	862	631	134	97	2006	644	2027
Rangers	709	480	129	100	1493	571	1559
Aberdeen	862	346	200	316	1086	1094	1238
Motherwell	862	306	183	373	1072	1292	1101
Hearts	786	300	198	288	1004	968	1083
Kilmarnock	862	283	215	364	1024	1229	1064
Hibernian	712	250	189	273	946	981	939
Dundee U	718	224	198	296	874	1071	867

Rangers deducted 10 pts in 2011–12; Hearts deducted 15 pts in 2013–14; Dundee U deducted 3 pts in 2015–16.

DOMESTIC LANDMARKS 2020–21

SEPTEMBER 2020

26 Marcus Rashford scored the 10,000th goal in Manchester U's history. Rashford scored the second goal in United's 3-2 victory over Brighton at the Amex Stadium.

OCTOBER 2020

17 Mo Salah became the 17th player in Liverpool's history to score 100 goals for the club. The milestone was reached in the Merseyside derby at Everton in a 2-2 draw.

DECEMBER 2020

17 Sheffield U have made the worst start ever to a Premier League season. The Blades' 2-3 home defeat to Manchester U means they have only picked up 1 point in their opening 13 games.

31 Liverpool ended the year at the top of the league for the third consecutive year, three points ahead of Manchester U.

JANUARY 2021

19 Newport Co goalkeeper Tom King became the first goalkeeper to score in the top four divisions since 2016. King scored directly from a wind-assisted goal kick to give Newport Co the lead away to Cheltenham T. Cheltenham equalised just before half time and the match ended 1-1.

FEBRUARY 2021

24 Tottenham H scored their 100th goal in the Europa League in the Round of 16 second leg tie at home to Austrian side Wolfsberg. The 4-0 victory gave Spurs a commanding 8-1 victory on aggregate.

MARCH 2021

7 Liverpool lose six home matches in a row for the first time in their history. The 0-1 defeat by Fulham was also the first time the reigning champions had lost six home games in a row

27 Chris Gunter became the first Welsh player to reach 100 international appearances in the 1-0 home win against Mexico at the Cardiff City Stadium. Kieffer Moore's first half goal was enough to win it for Wales.

31 Steven Davis became Britain's most capped international player. His 126 caps passed the 125 total of Peter Shilton of England. His record-breaking cap came in the 0-0 draw against Bulgaria in Belfast in World Cup Qualifying Group C.

31 Harry Kane became England's all-time record penalty goalscorer in the World Cup Qualifying Group I win over Poland at Wembley. His tenth penalty conversion came in the 19th minute of England's 2-1 victory.

APRIL 2021

5 Rebecca Welch became the first woman referee to take charge of a match in the top four tiers of English football. She took charge of the Harrogate T v Port Vale match which the away side won 0-2.

20 Ryan Mason at 29 years 311 days became the youngest manager in Premier League history when appointed by Tottenham H until the end of the season following the sacking of Jose Mourinho.

24 James Milner became the player with the most Premier League substitute appearances. His 159th sub appearance came in the 1-1 home draw with Newcastle U and surpassed the record of Peter Crouch.

MAY 2021

1 The Everton v Aston Villa game at Goodison Park became the most played fixture in the top-flight of English football. At 205 times the game is one above the Everton v Liverpool game on 204.

2 Manchester C set a new record for consecutive wins in all competitions. Their 4-1 win against Wolverhampton W at the Etihad Stadium was the 21st, the first came on 19 December away to Southampton when they won 1-0.

3 Amar and Arjun Purewal became the first identical twins to play against each other in a Wembley final. They faced each other in the delayed 2020 FA Vase Final between Hebburn T and Consett, both of the Northern League. Amar's Hebburn T came out winners 3-2 with Amar scoring the first goal for his team, equalising at 1-1 in the 19th minute.

10 Sheffield U, WBA and Fulham became the first teams to be relegated in the same Premier League season with three games still to play.

14 Manchester C set a new record for the number of away wins in a season. The 4-3 win at Newcastle in the Premier League was their 12 successive away league victory, the longest run of successive aways wins in the top four divisions of English football.

19 Joe Willock, on loan at Newcastle U from Arsenal, became the youngest player in Premier League history to score in six successive Premier League games. His 45th minute strike for the Toon against Sheffield U was his seventh in thirteen games.

EUROPEAN CUP AND CHAMPIONS LEAGUE RECORDS

MOST WINS BY CLUB
Real Madrid 13 1956, 1957, 1958, 1959, 1960, 1966, 1998, 2000, 2002, 2014, 2016, 2017, 2018.
AC Milan 7 1963, 1969, 1989, 1990, 1994, 2003, 2007.
Liverpool 6 1977, 1978, 1981, 1984, 2005, 2019.
Bayern Munich 6 1974, 1975, 1976, 2001, 2013, 2020.
Barcelona 5 1992, 2006, 2009, 2011, 2015.

MOST APPEARANCES IN FINAL
Real Madrid 15; AC Milan 11; Bayern Munich 11.

MOST FINAL APPEARANCES PER COUNTRY
Spain 29 (18 wins, 11 defeats)
Italy 28 (12 wins, 16 defeats)
England 24 (14 wins, 10 defeats)
Germany 18 (8 wins, 10 defeats)

MOST CHAMPIONS LEAGUE/EUROPEAN CUP APPEARANCES
181 Iker Casillas (Real Madrid, Porto)
180 Cristiano Ronaldo (Manchester U, Real Madrid, Juventus)
157 Xavi (Barcelona)
151 Ryan Giggs (Manchester U)
149 Lionel Messi (Barcelona)
144 Raul (Real Madrid, Schalke)
139 Paolo Maldini (AC Milan)
132 Andreas Iniesta (Barcelona)
131 Clarence Seedorf (Ajax, Real Madrid, Internazionale, AC Milan)
131 Gianluigi Buffon (Parma, Juventus, Paris Saint-Germain)
130 Paul Scholes (Manchester U)
130 Karim Benzema (Lyon, Real Madrid)
129 Sergio Ramos (Real Madrid)
128 Roberto Carlos (Internazionale, Real Madrid, Fenerbahce)
127 Xabi Alonso (Real Sociedad, Liverpool, Real Madrid, Bayern Munich)

MOST WINS WITH DIFFERENT CLUBS
Clarence Seedorf (Ajax) 1995; (Real Madrid) 1998; (AC Milan) 2003, 2007.

MOST WINNERS MEDALS
6 Francisco Gento (Real Madrid) 1956, 1957, 1958, 1959, 1960, 1966.

BIGGEST WINS
European Cup
Real Madrid 8, Sevilla 0, 21.1.1958.
Champions League
HJK Helsinki 10, Bangor C 0, 19.7.2011 *(qualifier)*.
Liverpool 8, Besiktas 0, 6.11.2007.
Real Madrid 8, Malmo 0, 8.12.2015.

MOST SUCCESSIVE APPEARANCES
Champions League
Real Madrid (Spain) 24: 1997–98 to 2020–21.
European Cup
Real Madrid (Spain) 15: 1955–56 to 1969–70.

MOST SUCCESSIVE WINS IN THE CHAMPIONS LEAGUE
Barcelona (Spain) 11: 2002–03.

LONGEST UNBEATEN RUN IN THE CHAMPIONS LEAGUE
Manchester U (England) 25: 2007–08 to 2009 (Final).

MOST GOALS OVERALL
134 Cristiano Ronaldo (Manchester U, Real Madrid, Juventus).
120 Lionel Messi (Barcelona).
73 Robert Lewandowski (Borussia Dortmund, Bayern Munich).
71 Raul (Real Madrid, Schalke).
71 Karim Benzema (Lyon, Real Madrid).
60 Ruud van Nistelrooy (PSV Eindhoven, Manchester U, Real Madrid).
59 Andriy Shevchenko (Dynamo Kyiv, AC Milan, Chelsea, Dynamo Kyiv).
51 Thierry Henry (Monaco, Arsenal, Barcelona).
50 Filippo Inzaghi (Juventus, AC Milan).
49 Alfredo Di Stefano (Real Madrid).
49 Zlatan Ibrahimovic (Ajax, Juventus, Internazionale, Barcelona, AC Milan, Paris Saint-Germain).
47 Eusebio (Benfica).

MOST GOALS IN CHAMPIONS LEAGUE MATCH
5 Lionel Messi, Barcelona v Bayer Leverkusen (25, 42, 49, 58, 84 mins) (7-1), 7.3.2012.
5 Luiz Adriano, Shaktar Donetsk v BATE (28, 36, 40, 44, 82 mins) (0-7), 21.10.2014.

MOST GOALS IN ONE SEASON
17 Cristiano Ronaldo 2013–14
16 Cristiano Ronaldo 2015–16
15 Cristiano Ronaldo 2017–18
15 Robert Lewandowski 2019–20
14 Jose Altafini 1962–63
14 Ruud van Nistelrooy 2002–03
14 Lionel Messi 2011–12

MOST GOALS SCORED IN FINALS
7 Alfredo Di Stefano (Real Madrid), 1956 (1), 1957 (1 pen), 1958 (1), 1959 (1), 1960 (3).
7 Ferenc Puskas (Real Madrid), 1960 (4), 1962 (3).

HIGHEST SCORE IN A MATCH
European Cup
14 KR Reykjavik (Iceland) 2 Feyenoord (Netherlands) 12 *(First Round First Leg 1969–70)*
Champions League
12 Borussia Dortmund 8, Legia Warsaw 4
(Group Stage 2016–17)

HIGHEST AGGREGATE IN A MATCH
European Cup
Benfica (Portugal) 18, Stade Dudelange (Luxembourg) 0 – 8-0 (h), 10-0 (a) *(Preliminary Round 1965–66)*
Champions League
Bayern Munich (Germany) 12, Sporting Lisbon (Portugal) 1 – 7-1 (h), 5-0 (a) *(Round of 16 2008–09)*

FASTEST GOALS SCORED IN CHAMPIONS LEAGUE
10.12 sec Roy Makaay for Bayern Munich v Real Madrid, 7.3.2007.
10.96 sec Jonas for Valencia v Bayer Leverkusen, 1.11.2011.
20.07 sec Gilberto Silva for Arsenal at PSV Eindhoven, 25.9.2002.
20.12 sec Alessandro Del Piero for Juventus at Manchester U, 1.10.1997.

YOUNGEST CHAMPIONS LEAGUE GOALSCORER
Ansu Fati for Barcelona v Internazionale 17 years 40 days in 2019–20.

OLDEST CHAMPIONS LEAGUE GOALSCORER
Francesco Totti for Roma v CSKA Moscow 38 years 59 days in 2014–15.

FASTEST HAT-TRICK SCORED IN CHAMPIONS LEAGUE
Bafetimbi Gomis, 8 mins for Lyon in Dinamo Zagreb v Lyon (1-7) 7.12.2011

MOST GOALS BY A GOALKEEPER
Hans-Jorg Butt (for three different clubs)
Hamburg 13.9.2000, Bayer Leverkusen 12.5.2002, Bayern Munich 8.12.2009 – all achieved against Juventus.

LANDMARK GOALS CHAMPIONS LEAGUE
1st Daniel Amokachi, Club Brugge v CSKA Moscow 17 minutes 25.11.1992
1,000th Dmitri Khokhlov, PSV Eindhoven v Benfica 41 minutes 9.12.1998
5,000th Luisao, Benfica v Hapoel Tel Aviv 21 minutes 14.9.2010

HIGHEST SCORING DRAW
Hamburg 4, Juventus 4, 13.9.2000
Chelsea 4, Liverpool 4, 14.4.2009
Bayer Leverkusen 4, Roma 4, 20.10.2015
Chelsea 4, Ajax 4, 5.11.2019

MOST CLEAN SHEETS
10: Arsenal 2005–06 (995 minutes with two goalkeepers Manuel Almunia 347 minutes and Jens Lehmann 648 minutes).

EUROPEAN CUP AND CHAMPIONS LEAGUE RECORDS – continued

CHAMPIONS LEAGUE ATTENDANCES AND GOALS FROM GROUP STAGES ONWARDS

Season	*Attendances*	*Average*	*Goals*	*Games*
1992–93	873,251	34,930	56	25
1993–94	1,202,289	44,529	71	27
1994–95	2,328,515	38,172	140	61
1995–96	1,874,316	30,726	159	61
1996–97	2,093,228	34,315	161	61
1997–98	2,868,271	33,744	239	85
1998–99	3,608,331	42,451	238	85
1999–2000	5,490,709	34,973	442	157
2000–01	5,773,486	36,774	449	157
2001–02	5,417,716	34,508	393	157
2002–03	6,461,112	41,154	431	157
2003–04	4,611,214	36,890	309	125
2004–05	4,946,820	39,575	331	125
2005–06	5,291,187	42,330	285	125
2006–07	5,591,463	44,732	309	125
2007–08	5,454,718	43,638	330	125
2008–09	5,003,754	40,030	329	125
2009–10	5,295,708	42,366	320	125
2010–11	5,474,654	43,797	355	125
2011–12	5,225,363	41,803	345	125
2012–13	5,773,366	46,187	368	125
2013–14	5,713,049	45,704	362	125
2014–15	5,207,592	42,685	361	125
2015–16	5,116,690	40,934	347	125
2016–17	5,398,851	43,191	380	125
2017–18	5,744,918	45,959	401	125
2018–19	5,746,629	45,973	366	125
2019–20	4,757,233	44,048	386	119
2020–21	No attendances published		366	125

HIGHEST AVERAGE ATTENDANCE IN ONE EUROPEAN CUP SEASON

1959–60 50,545 from a total attendance of 2,780,000.

GREATEST COMEBACKS

Werder Bremen beat Anderlecht 5-3 after being three goals down in 33 minutes on 8.12.1993. They scored five goals in 23 second-half minutes.

Deportivo La Coruna beat Paris Saint-Germain 4-3 after being three goals down in 55 minutes on 7.3.2001. They scored four goals in 27 second-half minutes.

Liverpool three goals down to FC Basel in 29 minutes on 12.11.2002. They scored three second half goals in 24 minutes to draw 3-3.

Liverpool after being three goals down to AC Milan in the first half on 25.5.2005 in the Champions League Final. They scored three goals in five second-half minutes and won the penalty shoot-out after extra time 3-2.

MOST SUCCESSFUL MANAGER

Bob Paisley 3 wins, 1977, 1978, 1981 (Liverpool).

Carlo Ancelotti 3 wins, 2002–03, 2006–07 (AC Milan), 2013–14 (Real Madrid).

Zinedine Zidane 3 wins, 2015–16, 2016–17, 2017–18 (Real Madrid).

REINSTATED WINNERS EXCLUDED FROM NEXT COMPETITION

Marseille were originally stripped of the title in 1993. This was rescinded but they were not allowed to compete the following season.

INTERNATIONAL LANDMARKS 2020–21

SEPTEMBER 2020

8 Cristiano Ronaldo scored his 100th international goal for Portugal in the Nations League win against Sweden at the Friends Arena Stockholm. Ronaldo notched his 100th and 101st goals for his country in the 2-0 win.

8 Toby Alderweireld made his 100th international appearance for Belgium in the Nations League at home to Iceland. An early Iceland goal could not stop the Belgium side who romped home 5-1.

OCTOBER 2020

10 Olivier Giroud made his 100th international appearance for France in a 7-1 friendly victory over Ukraine at the Stade de France. Giroud scored twice, his 41st and 42nd international goals.

13 Toni Kroos made his 100th international appearance for Germany in the 3-3 Nations League draw against Switzerland in Cologne.

14 Simon Kjaer made his 100th international appearance for Denmark against England in the Nations League at Wembley. A penalty from Christian Eriksen gave the Danes a 1-0 victory to finish above England in Group 2.

14 Christian Eriksen made his 100th international appearance for Denmark against England in the Nations League at Wembley. Eriksen became the youngest Denmark player to reach the landmark. To round off the celebrations, a penalty in the 36th minute from Eriksen gave the Danes a 1-0 win.

NOVEMBER 2020

14 Sergio Ramos became the most capped European player, breaking the record of Gianluigi Buffon. His 177th cap came in the 1-1 UEFA Nations League draw with Switzerland in Basel.

17 Marcio Vieira made his 100th international appearance for Andorra in their crushing 5-0 home defeat to Latvia in the UEFA Nations League.

18 Yuri Zhirkov made his 100th international appearance for Russia in the UEFA Nations League game in Serbia. Serbia ran out comfortable 5-0 winners.

JANUARY 2021

3 Romalu Lukaku became Inter Milan's fastest scorer to 50 goals with his side's fourth goal in the 6-2 thumping of Crotone in Serie A. He reached 50 goals from only 70 appearances. This was seven games faster than the previous record holder, the Brazilian Ronaldo.

MARCH 2021

9 Erling Haaland became the fastest and youngest player to score 20 goals in the UEFA Champions League. He reached 20 goals after only 14 games becoming the first player to reach the milestone before the age of 21. His tally was achieved in ten games fewer than the next player on the list, Harry Kane of Tottenham H who reached the milestone after 24 games. Haaland's nineteenth and twentieth goals came in the 2-2 draw in the Round of 16 second leg tie at home to Sevilla, Borussia Dortmund winners 5-4 on aggregate.

10 Lionel Messi equalled Cristiano Ronaldo's record of the scoring at least 10 goals for the 15th successive season. Messi scored two in Barcelona's 4-0 away win over Granada.

11 Kylian Mbappe breaks Lionel Messi's record as the youngest player to score 25 UEFA Champions League goals. He was 22 years and 80 days old when he scored from the penalty spot in Paris Saint-Germain's 1-1 draw with Barcelona in the Round of 16 second leg tie. His side progress 5-2 on aggregate.

21 Lionel Messi made his 768th appearance for Barcelona making him the player with most appearances for the club. Messi scored twice in Barcelona's 6-1 victory at Real Sociedad. His record surpassed that of Xavi who made 767 appearances.

25 Leonardo Bonucci made his 100th international appearance for Italy in the 2-0 victory over Northern Ireland in the FIFA World Cup Qualifying Group C match in Parma. The match also marked the 125th cap for Northern Ireland's Steven Davis.

27 Alexandar Mitrovic became Serbia's all-time top international goalscorer in the 2-2 World Cup Qualifying Group A draw with Portgual. Mitrovic scored in the 46th minute and Filip Kostic later equalised after Portugal had taken a 2-0 lead.

MAY 2021

15 Robert Lewandoski became equal joint record scorer in the Bundesliga. Bayern Munich's first goal in the 2-2 draw at Freiburg was his 40th of the season. He equals the 40 scored by Gerd Muller for Bayern Munich in the 1971–72 season.

26 Yeremi Pino became the youngest Spanish player ever to start a major European final. At 18 years and 218 days the Villareal winger broke the record held previous by Iker Casillas at 19 years and 4 days. Villareal went on to lift the trophy beating Manchester U 11-10 on penalties after a 1-1 draw after extra time.

JUNE 2021

1 Ivan Perisic made his 100th international appearance for Croatia in the friendly game against Armenia in Velika Gorica. He scored in the 24th minute to put Croatia ahead, but Armenia equalised in the 72nd minute through Angulo.

1 Peter Pekarik made his 100th international appearance for Slovakia in the 1-1 friendly draw with Bulgaria in Ried, Austria.

2 Daniel Da Mota made his 100th appearance for Luxembourg in the 0-1 friendly defeat to Norway in Malaga.

3 Milalem Pjanic made his 100th appearance for Bosnia-Herzogovina in the 0-1 defeat to France in the World Cup Qualifier in Sarajevo.

7 Manuel Neuer made his 100th international appearance for Germany in the 7-1 friendly win over Latvia. He became the first German goalkeeper to achieve the feat.

15 Cristiano Ronaldo became the all-time highest goalscorer in European Championship history with his double strike in the 3-0 victory against Hungary in Budapest. A late penalty and injury-time goal took his total to 11 in five competitions between 2004 and 2021. He overtook Michel Platini who scored 9 goals, all of which came in Euro '84.

17 Dries Mertens made his 100th international appearance for Belgium in the 2-1 victory over Denmark in Group B of EURO 2020 in Copenhagen.

23 Cristiano Ronaldo became the joint all-time international goalscorer with his two goals for Portugal against France in the Group F Euro 2020 match in Budapest. He equalled the 109 international goals scored by Iran forward Ali Daei.

29 Lionel Messi became Argentina's most capped player in the Copa America Group A match with Bolivia. His 148th appearance broke the record of Javier Mascareno. Messi scored twice in Argentina's 4-1 victory.

TOP TEN AVERAGE ATTENDANCES

1	Manchester U	2006–07	75,826
2	Manchester U	2007–08	75,691
3	Manchester U	2012–13	75,530
4	Manchester U	2011–12	75,387
5	Manchester U	2014–15	75,335
6	Manchester U	2008–09	75,308
7	Manchester U	2016–17	75,290
8	Manchester U	2015–16	75,279
9	Manchester U	2013–14	75,207
10	Manchester U	2010–11	75,109

TOP TEN AVERAGE WORLD CUP FINALS CROWDS

1	In USA	1994	68,991
2	In Brazil	2014	52,621
3	In Germany	2006	52,491
4	In Mexico	1970	50,124
5	In South Africa	2010	49,669
6	In West Germany	1974	49,098
7	In England	1966	48,847
8	In Italy	1990	48,388
9	In Brazil	1950	47,511
10	In Russia	2018	47,371

TOP TEN ALL-TIME ENGLAND CAPS

1	Peter Shilton	125
2	Wayne Rooney	120
3	David Beckham	115
4	Steven Gerrard	114
5	Bobby Moore	108
6	Ashley Cole	107
7	Bobby Charlton	106
	Frank Lampard	106
9	Billy Wright	105
10	Bryan Robson	90

TOP TEN ALL-TIME ENGLAND GOALSCORERS

1	Wayne Rooney	53
2	Bobby Charlton	49
3	Gary Lineker	48
4	Jimmy Greaves	44
5	Michael Owen	40
6	Harry Kane	34
	Tom Finney	30
7	Nat Lofthouse	30
	Alan Shearer	30
8	Vivian Woodward	29
	Frank Lampard	29

GOALKEEPING RECORDS

(without conceding a goal)

FA PREMIER LEAGUE
Edwin van der Sar (Manchester U) in 1,311 minutes during the 2008–09 season.

FOOTBALL LEAGUE
Steve Death (Reading) 1,103 minutes from 24 March to 18 August 1979.

SCOTTISH PREMIER LEAGUE
Fraser Forster (Celtic) in 1,215 minutes from 6 December 2013 to 25 February 2014.

MOST CLEAN SHEETS IN A SEASON

Petr Cech (Chelsea) 24, 2004–05

MOST CLEAN SHEETS OVERALL IN PREMIER LEAGUE

Petr Cech (Chelsea and Arsenal) 202 games.

MOST GOALS FOR IN A SEASON

FA PREMIER LEAGUE		Goals	Games
2017–18	Manchester C	106	38
FOOTBALL LEAGUE			
Division 4			
1960–61	Peterborough U	134	46
SCOTTISH PREMIER LEAGUE			
2016–17	Celtic	106	38
SCOTTISH LEAGUE			
Division 2			
1937–38	Raith R	142	34

MOST GOALS AGAINST IN A SEASON

FA PREMIER LEAGUE		Goals	Games
1993–94	Swindon T	100	42
FOOTBALL LEAGUE			
Division 2			
1898–99	Darwen	141	34
SCOTTISH PREMIER LEAGUE			
1999–2000	Aberdeen	83	36
2007–08	Gretna	83	38
SCOTTISH LEAGUE			
Division 2			
1931–32	Edinburgh C	146	38

MOST LEAGUE GOALS IN A SEASON

FA PREMIER LEAGUE		Goals	Games
1993–94	Andrew Cole (Newcastle U)	34	40
1994–95	Alan Shearer (Blackburn R)	34	42
2017–18	Mohamed Salah (Liverpool)	32	38
FOOTBALL LEAGUE			
Division 1			
1927–28	Dixie Dean (Everton)	60	39
Division 2			
1926–27	George Camsell (Middlesbrough)	59	37
Division 3(S)			
1936–37	Joe Payne (Luton T)	55	39
Division 3(N)			
1936–37	Ted Harston (Mansfield T)	55	41
Division 3			
1959–60	Derek Reeves (Southampton)	39	46
Division 4			
1960–61	Terry Bly (Peterborough U)	52	46
FA CUP			
1887–88	Jimmy Ross (Preston NE)	20	8
LEAGUE CUP			
1986–87	Clive Allen (Tottenham H)	12	9
SCOTTISH PREMIER LEAGUE			
2000–01	Henrik Larsson (Celtic)	35	37
SCOTTISH LEAGUE			
Division 1			
1931–32	William McFadyen (Motherwell)	52	34
Division 2			
1927–28	Jim Smith (Ayr U)	66	38

MOST FA CUP FINAL GOALS

Ian Rush (Liverpool) 5: 1986(2), 1989(2), 1992(1)

SCORED IN EVERY PREMIERSHIP GAME

Arsenal 2001–02: 38 matches

FEWEST GOALS FOR IN A SEASON

FA PREMIER LEAGUE		Goals	Games
2007–08	Derby Co	20	38
FOOTBALL LEAGUE			
Division 2			
1899–1900	Loughborough T	18	34
SCOTTISH PREMIERSHIP			
2010–11	St Johnstone	23	38
SCOTTISH LEAGUE			
New Division 1			
1980–81	Stirling Alb	18	39

FEWEST GOALS AGAINST IN A SEASON

FA PREMIER LEAGUE		Goals	Games
2004–05	Chelsea	15	38
FOOTBALL LEAGUE			
Division 1			
1978–79	Liverpool	16	42
SCOTTISH PREMIERSHIP			
2020–21	Rangers	13	38
SCOTTISH LEAGUE			
Division 1			
1913–14	Celtic	14	38

MOST LEAGUE GOALS IN A CAREER

FOOTBALL LEAGUE			
Arthur Rowley	*Goals*	*Games*	*Season*
WBA	4	24	1946–48
Fulham	27	56	1948–50
Leicester C	251	303	1950–58
Shrewsbury T	152	236	1958–65
	434	619	
SCOTTISH LEAGUE			
Jimmy McGrory			
Celtic	1	3	1922–23
Clydebank	13	30	1923–24
Celtic	396	375	1924–38
	410	408	

MOST HAT-TRICKS

Career
37: Dixie Dean (Tranmere R, Everton, Notts Co, England)

Division 1 (one season post-war)
6: Jimmy Greaves (Chelsea), 1960–61

Three for one team in one match
West, Spouncer, Hooper, Nottingham F v Leicester Fosse, Division 1, 21 April 1909
Loasby, Smith, Wells, Northampton T v Walsall, Division 3S, 5 Nov 1927
Bowater, Hoyland, Readman, Mansfield T v Rotherham U, Division 3N, 27 Dec 1932
Barnes, Ambler, Davies, Wrexham v Hartlepools U, Division 4, 3 March 1962
Adcock, Stewart, White, Manchester C v Huddersfield T, Division 2, 7 Nov 1987

MOST CUP GOALS IN A CAREER

FA CUP (pre-Second World War)
Henry Cursham 48 (Notts Co)

FA CUP (post-war)
Ian Rush 43 (Chester, Liverpool)

LEAGUE CUP
Geoff Hurst 49 (West Ham U, Stoke C)
Ian Rush 49 (Chester, Liverpool, Newcastle U)

GOALS PER GAME (Football League to 1991–92)

Goals per game	Division 1		Division 2		Division 3		Division 4		Division 3(S)		Division 3(N)	
	Games	Goals	Games	Goals	Games	Goals	Games	Goals	Games	Goals	Games	Goals
0	2465	0	2665	0	1446	0	1438	0	997	0	803	0
1	5606	5606	5836	5836	3225	3225	3106	3106	2073	2073	1914	1914
2	8275	16550	8609	17218	4569	9138	4441	8882	3314	6628	2939	5878
3	7731	23193	7842	23526	3784	11352	4041	12123	2996	8988	2922	8766
4	6229	24920	5897	23588	2837	11348	2784	11136	2445	9780	2410	9640
5	3752	18755	3634	18170	1566	7830	1506	7530	1554	7770	1599	7995
6	2137	12822	2007	12042	769	4614	786	4716	870	5220	930	5580
7	1092	7644	1001	7007	357	2499	336	2352	451	3157	461	3227
8	542	4336	376	3008	135	1080	143	1144	209	1672	221	1768
9	197	1773	164	1476	64	576	35	315	76	684	102	918
10	83	830	68	680	13	130	8	80	33	330	45	450
11	37	407	19	209	2	22	7	77	15	165	15	165
12	12	144	17	204	1	12	0	0	7	84	8	96
13	4	52	4	52	0	0	0	0	2	26	4	52
14	2	28	1	14	0	0	0	0	0	0	0	0
17	0	0	0	0	0	0	0	0	0	0	1	17
	38164	**117060**	**38140**	**113030**	**18768**	**51826**	**18631**	**51461**	**15042**	**46577**	**14374**	**46466**

Extensive research by statisticians has unearthed seven results from the early years of the Football League which differ from the original scores. These are 26 January 1889 Wolverhampton W 5 Everton 0 (not 4-0), 16 March 1889 Notts Co 3 Derby Co 5 (not 2-5), 4 January 1896 Arsenal 5 Loughborough 0 (not 6-0), 28 November 1896 Leicester Fosse 4 Walsall 2 (not 4-1), 21 April 1900 Burslem Port Vale 2 Lincoln C 1 (not 2-0), 25 December 1902 Glossop NE 3 Stockport Co 0 (not 3-1), 26 April 1913 Hull C 2 Leicester C 0 (not 2-1).

GOALS PER GAME (from 1992–93)

Goals per game	Premier		Championship/Div 1		League One/Div 2		League Two/Div 3	
	Games	Goals	Games	Goals	Games	Goals	Games	Goals
0	933	0	1304	0	1235	0	1275	0
1	2030	2030	3015	3015	2967	2967	3062	3062
2	2732	5464	4061	8122	4009	8018	3950	7900
3	2400	7200	3474	10422	3489	10467	3416	10248
4	1677	6708	2204	8816	2198	8792	2103	8412
5	842	4210	1180	5900	1187	5935	1104	5520
6	389	2334	515	3090	496	2976	446	2676
7	167	1169	181	1267	194	1358	186	1302
8	69	552	55	440	57	456	54	432
9	21	189	10	90	19	171	21	189
10	5	50	7	70	5	50	6	60
11	1	11	2	22	0	0	3	33
	11266	**29917**	**16008**	**41254**	**15856**	**41190**	**15626**	**39834**

New Overall Totals (since 1992)		Totals (up to 1991–92)		Complete Overall Totals (since 1888–89)	
Games	58756	Games	143119	Games	201875
Goals	152195	Goals	426420	Goals	578615
Goals per game	2.59		2.98		2.87

A CENTURY OF LEAGUE AND CUP GOALS IN CONSECUTIVE SEASONS

	League	*Cup*	*Season*
George Camsell			
Middlesbrough	59	5	1926–27
(101 goals)	33	4	1927–28

(*Camsell's cup goals were all scored in the FA Cup.*)

Steve Bull			
Wolverhampton W	34	18	1987–88
(102 goals)	37	13	1988–89

(*Bull had 12 in the Sherpa Van Trophy, 3 Littlewoods Cup, 3 FA Cup in 1987–88; 11 Sherpa Van Trophy, 2 Littlewoods Cup in 1988–89.*)

PENALTIES

Most in a season (individual)

Division 1	*Goals*	*Season*
Francis Lee (Manchester C)	13	1971–72

Also scored 2 cup goals.

Most awarded in one game

5 Crystal Palace (1 scored, 3 missed) v Brighton & HA (1 scored), Div 2 1988–89

Most saved in a season

Division 1

Paul Cooper (Ipswich T) 8 (of 10) 1979–80

MOST GOALS IN A GAME

FA PREMIER LEAGUE

4 Mar 1995	Andrew Cole (Manchester U) 5 goals v Ipswich T
19 Sept 1999	Alan Shearer (Newcastle U) 5 goals v Sheffield W
22 Nov 2009	Jermain Defoe (Tottenham H) 5 goals v Wigan Ath
27 Nov 2010	Dimitar Berbatov (Manchester U) 5 goals v Blackburn R
3 Oct 2015	Sergio Aguero (Manchester C) 5 goals v Newcastle U

FOOTBALL LEAGUE

Division 1

14 Dec 1935	Ted Drake (Arsenal) 7 goals v Aston Villa

Division 2

5 Feb 1955	Tommy Briggs (Blackburn R) 7 goals v Bristol R
23 Feb 1957	Neville Coleman (Stoke C) 7 goals v Lincoln C

Division 3(S)

13 Apr 1936	Joe Payne (Luton T) 10 goals v Bristol R

Division 3(N)

26 Dec 1935	Bunny Bell (Tranmere R) 9 goals v Oldham Ath

Division 3

24 Apr 1965	Barrie Thomas (Scunthorpe U) 5 goals v Luton T
20 Nov 1965	Keith East (Swindon T) 5 goals v Mansfield T
16 Sept 1969	Steve Earle (Fulham) 5 goals v Halifax T
2 Oct 1971	Alf Wood (Shrewsbury T) 5 goals v Blackburn R
10 Sept 1983	Tony Caldwell (Bolton W) 5 goals v Walsall
4 May 1987	Andy Jones (Port Vale) 5 goals v Newport Co
3 Apr 1990	Steve Wilkinson (Mansfield T) 5 goals v Birmingham C
5 Sept 1998	Giuliano Grazioli (Peterborough U) 5 goals v Barnet
6 Apr 2002	Lee Jones (Wrexham) 5 goals v Cambridge U

Division 4

26 Dec 1962	Bert Lister (Oldham Ath) 6 goals v Southport

FA CUP

20 Nov 1971	Ted MacDougall (Bournemouth) 9 goals v Margate (*1st Round*)

LEAGUE CUP

25 Oct 1989	Frankie Bunn (Oldham Ath) 6 goals v Scarborough

SCOTTISH LEAGUE

Premier Division

17 Nov 1984	Paul Sturrock (Dundee U) 5 goals v Morton

Premier League

23 Aug 1996	Marco Negri (Rangers) 5 goals v Dundee U
4 Nov 2000	Kenny Miller (Rangers) 5 goals v St Mirren
25 Sept 2004	Kris Boyd (Kilmarnock) 5 goals v Dundee U
30 Dec 2009	Kris Boyd (Rangers) 5 goals v Dundee U
13 May 2012	Gary Hooper (Celtic) 5 goals v Hearts

Division 1

14 Sept 1928	Jimmy McGrory (Celtic) 8 goals v Dunfermline Ath

Division 2

1 Oct 1927	Owen McNally (Arthurlie) 8 goals v Armadale
2 Jan 1930	Jim Dyet (King's Park) 8 goals v Forfar Ath
18 Apr 1936	John Calder (Morton) 8 goals v Raith R
20 Aug 1937	Norman Hayward (Raith R) 8 goals v Brechin C

SCOTTISH CUP

12 Sept 1885	John Petrie (Arbroath) 13 goals v Bon Accord (*1st Round*)

LONGEST SEQUENCE OF CONSECUTIVE DEFEATS

FOOTBALL LEAGUE	*Team*	*Games*
Division 2		
1898–99	Darwen	18

LONGEST UNBEATEN SEQUENCE

FA PREMIER LEAGUE	*Team*	*Games*
May 2003–Oct 2004	Arsenal	49
FOOTBALL LEAGUE – League 1		
Jan 2011–Nov 2011	Huddersfield T	43

LONGEST UNBEATEN CUP SEQUENCE

Liverpool 25 rounds League/Milk Cup 1980–84

LONGEST UNBEATEN SEQUENCE IN A SEASON

FA PREMIER LEAGUE	*Team*	*Games*
2003–04	Arsenal	38
FOOTBALL LEAGUE – Division 1		
1920–21	Burnley	30
SCOTTISH PREMIERSHIP		
2016–17	Celtic	38

LONGEST UNBEATEN START TO A SEASON

FA PREMIER LEAGUE	*Team*	*Games*
2003–04	Arsenal	38
FOOTBALL LEAGUE – Division 1		
1973–74	Leeds U	29
1987–88	Liverpool	29

LONGEST SEQUENCE WITHOUT A WIN IN A SEASON

FA PREMIER LEAGUE	*Team*	*Games*
2007–08	Derby Co	32
FOOTBALL LEAGUE	*Team*	*Games*
Division 2		
1983–84	Cambridge U	31

LONGEST SEQUENCE WITHOUT A WIN FROM SEASON'S START

FOOTBALL LEAGUE	*Team*	*Games*
Division 4		
1970–71	Newport Co	25

LONGEST SEQUENCE OF CONSECUTIVE SCORING (individual)

FA PREMIER LEAGUE

Jamie Vardy (Leicester C) 13 in 11 games 2015–16

FOOTBALL LEAGUE RECORD

Tom Phillipson (Wolverhampton W) 23 in 13 games 1926–27

LONGEST WINNING SEQUENCE

FA PREMIER LEAGUE	*Team*	*Games*
2017–18	Manchester C	18
2019–20	Liverpool	18
FOOTBALL LEAGUE – Division 2		
1904–05	Manchester U	14
1905–06	Bristol C	14
1950–51	Preston NE	14
FROM SEASON'S START – Division 3		
1985–86	Reading	13
SCOTTISH PREMIER LEAGUE		
2003–04	Celtic	25

HIGHEST WINS

Highest win in a First-Class Match
(Scottish Cup 1st Round)

Arbroath	36	Bon Accord	0	12 Sept 1885

Highest win in an International Match

England	13	Ireland	0	18 Feb 1882

Highest win in an FA Cup Match

Preston NE	26	Hyde U	0	15 Oct 1887

(1st Round)

Highest win in a League Cup Match

West Ham U	10	Bury	0	25 Oct 1983
(2nd Round, 2nd Leg)				
Liverpool	10	Fulham	0	23 Sept 1986
(2nd Round, 1st Leg)				

Highest win in an FA Premier League Match

Manchester U	9	Ipswich T	0	4 Mar 1995
Manchester U	9	Southampton	0	2 Jan 2021
Southampton	0	Leicester C	9	25 Oct 2019
Tottenham H	9	Wigan Ath	1	22 Nov 2009

Highest win in a Football League Match

Division 2 – highest home win

Newcastle U	13	Newport Co	0	5 Oct 1946

Division 3(N) – highest home win

Stockport Co	13	Halifax T	0	6 Jan 1934

Division 2 – highest away win

Burslem Port Vale	0	Sheffield U	10	10 Dec 1892

Highest wins in a Scottish League Match

Scottish Premiership – highest home win

Celtic	9	Aberdeen	0	6 Nov 2010

Scottish Division 2 – highest home win

Airdrieonians	15	Dundee Wanderers	1	1 Dec 1894

Scottish Premiership – highest away win

Hamilton A	0	Celtic	8	5 Nov 1988

MOST HOME WINS IN A SEASON

Brentford won all 21 games in Division 3(S), 1929–30

RECORD AWAY WINS IN A SEASON

Doncaster R won 18 of 21 games in Division 3(N), 1946–47

CONSECUTIVE AWAY WINS

FA PREMIER LEAGUE

Chelsea 11 games (2007–08 (3), 2008–09 (8)).
Manchester C 11 games (2016–17 (1), 2017–18 (10))

FOOTBALL LEAGUE
Division 1

Tottenham H 10 games (1959–60 (2), 1960–61 (8))

HIGHEST AGGREGATE SCORES

FA PREMIER LEAGUE

Portsmouth	7	Reading	4	29 Sept 2007

Highest Aggregate Score England
Division 3(N)

Tranmere R	13	Oldham Ath	4	26 Dec 1935

Highest Aggregate Score Scotland
Division 2

Airdrieonians	15	Dundee Wanderers	1	1 Dec 1894

FEWEST WINS IN A SEASON

		Wins	Games
FA PREMIER LEAGUE			
2007–08	Derby Co	1	38
FOOTBALL LEAGUE			
Division 2			
1899–1900	Loughborough T	1	34
SCOTTISH PREMIER LEAGUE			
1998–99	Dunfermline Ath	4	36
SCOTTISH LEAGUE			
Division 1			
1891–92	Vale of Leven	0	22

MOST WINS IN A SEASON

		Wins	Games
FA PREMIER LEAGUE			
2017–18	Manchester C	32	38
2018–19	Manchester C	32	38
2019–20	Liverpool	32	38
FOOTBALL LEAGUE			
Division 3(N)			
1946–47	Doncaster R	33	42
SCOTTISH PREMIERSHIP			
2016–17	Celtic	34	38
SCOTTISH LEAGUE			
Division 1			
1920–21	Rangers	35	42

UNDEFEATED AT HOME OVERALL

Liverpool 85 games (63 League, 9 League Cup, 7 European, 6 FA Cup), Jan 1978–Jan 1981

UNDEFEATED AT HOME LEAGUE

Chelsea 86 games, Mar 2004–Oct 2008

UNDEFEATED AWAY

Arsenal 19 games, FA Premier League 2001–02 and 2003–04 (only Preston NE with 11 in 1888–89 had previously remained unbeaten away) in the top flight.

MOST POINTS IN A SEASON
(three points for a win)

		Points	Games
FA PREMIER LEAGUE			
2017–18	Manchester C	100	38
FOOTBALL LEAGUE			
Championship			
2005–06	Reading	106	46
SCOTTISH PREMIER LEAGUE			
2001–02	Celtic	103	38
SCOTTISH LEAGUE			
League One			
2013–14	Rangers	102	36

MOST POINTS IN A SEASON
(under old system of two points for a win)

		Points	Games
FOOTBALL LEAGUE			
Division 4			
1975–76	Lincoln C	74	46
SCOTTISH LEAGUE			
Division 1			
1920–21	Rangers	76	42

FEWEST POINTS IN A SEASON

		Points	Games
FA PREMIER LEAGUE			
2007–08	Derby Co	11	38
FOOTBALL LEAGUE			
Division 2			
1904–05	Doncaster R	8	34
1899–1900	Loughborough T	8	34
SCOTTISH PREMIER LEAGUE			
2007–08	Gretna	13	38
SCOTTISH LEAGUE			
Division 1			
1954–55	Stirling Alb	6	30

NO DEFEATS IN A SEASON

FA PREMIER LEAGUE

2003–04	Arsenal	won 26, drew 12

FOOTBALL LEAGUE

Division 1

1888–89	Preston NE	won 18, drew 4

Division 2

1893–94	Liverpool	won 22, drew 6

SCOTTISH LEAGUE

Premiership

2016–17	Celtic	won 34, drew 4
2020–21	Rangers	won 32, drew 6

Division 1

1898–99	Rangers	won 18

League One

2013–14	Rangers	won 33, drew 3

ONE DEFEAT IN A SEASON

FA PREMIER LEAGUE		*Defeats*	*Games*
2004–05	Chelsea	1	38
2018–19	Liverpool	1	38
FOOTBALL LEAGUE			
Division 1			
1990–91	Arsenal	1	38
SCOTTISH PREMIERSHIP			
2001–02	Celtic	1	38
2013–14	Celtic	1	38
SCOTTISH LEAGUE			
Division 1			
1920–21	Rangers	1	42
Division 2			
1956–57	Clyde	1	36
1962–63	Morton	1	36
1967–68	St Mirren	1	36
New Division 1			
2011–12	Ross Co	1	36
New Division 2			
1975–76	Raith R	1	26

MOST DEFEATS IN A SEASON

FA PREMIER LEAGUE		*Defeats*	*Games*
1994–95	Ipswich T	29	42
2005–06	Sunderland	29	38
2007–08	Derby Co	29	38
2020–21	Sheffield U	29	38
FOOTBALL LEAGUE			
Division 3			
1997–98	Doncaster R	34	46
SCOTTISH PREMIERSHIP			
2005–06	Livingston	28	38
SCOTTISH LEAGUE			
New Division 1			
1992–93	Cowdenbeath	34	44

MOST DRAWN GAMES IN A SEASON

FA PREMIER LEAGUE		*Draws*	*Games*
1993–94	Manchester C	18	42
1993–94	Sheffield U	18	42
1994–95	Southampton	18	42
FOOTBALL LEAGUE			
Division 1			
1978–79	Norwich C	23	42
Division 3			
1997–98	Cardiff C	23	46
1997–98	Hartlepool U	23	46
Division 4			
1986–87	Exeter C	23	46
SCOTTISH PREMIER LEAGUE			
1998–99	Dunfermline Ath	16	38
SCOTTISH LEAGUE			
Premier Division			
1993–94	Aberdeen	21	44
New Division 1			
1986–87	East Fife	21	44

SENDINGS-OFF

SEASON

451 (League alone) 2003–04
(Before rescinded cards taken into account)

DAY

19 (League) 13 Dec 2003

FA CUP FINAL

Kevin Moran, Manchester U v Everton	1985
Jose Antonio Reyes, Arsenal v Manchester U	2005
Pablo Zabaleta, Manchester C v Wigan Ath	2013
Chris Smalling, Manchester U v Crystal Palace	2016
Victor Moses, Chelsea v Arsenal	2017
Mateo Kovacic, Chelsea v Arsenal	2020

QUICKEST

FA Premier League

Andreas Johansson, Wigan Ath v Arsenal (7 May 2006) and Keith Gillespie, Sheffield U v Reading (20 January 2007) both in 10 seconds

Football League

Walter Boyd, Swansea C v Darlington, Div 3 as substitute in zero seconds 23 Nov 1999

MOST IN ONE GAME

Five: Chesterfield (2) v Plymouth Arg (3)	22 Feb 1997
Five: Wigan Ath (1) v Bristol R (4)	2 Dec 1997
Five: Exeter C (3) v Cambridge U (2)	23 Nov 2002
Five: Bradford C (3) v Crawley T (2)*	27 Mar 2012

**All five sent off after final whistle for fighting*

MOST IN ONE TEAM

Wigan Ath (1) v Bristol R (4)	2 Dec 1997
Hereford U (4) v Northampton T (0)	6 Sept 1992

MOST SUCCESSFUL MANAGERS

Sir Alex Ferguson CBE
Manchester U

1986–2013, 25 major trophies:
13 Premier League, 5 FA Cup, 4 League Cup, 2 Champions League, 1 Cup-Winners' Cup.

Aberdeen

1976–86, 9 major trophies:
3 League, 4 Scottish Cup, 1 League Cup, 1 Cup Winners' Cup.

Bob Paisley – Liverpool

1974–83, 13 major trophies:
6 League, 3 European Cup, 3 League Cup, 1 UEFA Cup.

Bill Struth – Rangers

1920–54, 30 major trophies:
18 League, 10 Scottish Cup, 2 League Cup.

LEAGUE CHAMPIONSHIP HAT-TRICKS

Huddersfield T	1923–24 to 1925–26
Arsenal	1932–33 to 1934–35
Liverpool	1981–82 to 1983–84
Manchester U	1998–99 to 2000–01
Manchester U	2006–07 to 2008–09

MOST FA CUP MEDALS

Ashley Cole 7 (Arsenal 2002, 2003, 2005; Chelsea 2007, 2009, 2010, 2012).

MOST LEAGUE MEDALS

Ryan Giggs (Manchester U) 13: 1993, 1994, 1996, 1997, 1999, 2000, 2001, 2003, 2007, 2008, 2009, 2011 and 2013.

MOST SENIOR MATCHES

1,390 Peter Shilton (1,005 League, 86 FA Cup, 102 League Cup, 125 Internationals, 13 Under-23, 4 Football League XI, 20 European Cup, 7 Texaco Cup, 5 Simod Cup, 4 European Super Cup, 4 UEFA Cup, 3 Screen Sport Super Cup, 3 Zenith Data Systems Cup, 2 Autoglass Trophy, 2 Charity Shield, 2 Full Members Cup, 1 Anglo-Italian Cup, 1 Football League play-offs, 1 World Club Championship)

MOST LEAGUE APPEARANCES (750+)

1,005 Peter Shilton (286 Leicester C, 110 Stoke C, 202 Nottingham F, 188 Southampton, 175 Derby Co, 34 Plymouth Arg, 1 Bolton W, 9 Leyton Orient) 1966–97
931 Tony Ford (355 Grimsby T, 9 Sunderland (loan), 112 Stoke C, 114 WBA, 68 Grimsby T, 5 Bradford C (loan), 76 Scunthorpe U, 103 Mansfield T, 89 Rochdale) 1975–2002
909 Graeme Armstrong (204 Stirling A, 83 Berwick Rangers, 353 Meadowbank Thistle, 268 Stenhousemuir, 1 Alloa Ath) 1975–2001
863 Tommy Hutchison (165 Blackpool, 314 Coventry C, 46 Manchester C, 92 Burnley, 178 Swansea C, 68 Alloa Ath) 1965–91
833 Graham Alexander (159 Scunthorpe U, 150 Luton T, 370 Preston NE, 154 Burnley) 1990–2012
824 Terry Paine (713 Southampton, 111 Hereford U) 1957–77
790 Neil Redfearn (35 Bolton W, 10 Lincoln C (loan), 90 Lincoln C, 46 Doncaster R, 57 Crystal Palace, 24 Watford, 62 Oldham Ath, 292 Barnsley, 30 Charlton Ath, 17 Bradford C, 22 Wigan Ath, 42 Halifax T, 54 Boston U, 9 Rochdale) 1982–2004
788 David James (89 Watford, 214 Liverpool, 67 Aston Villa, 91 West Ham U, 93 Manchester C, 134 Portsmouth, 81 Bristol C, 19 Bournemouth) 1988–2013
782 Robbie James (484 Swansea C, 48 Stoke C, 87 QPR, 23 Leicester C, 89 Bradford C, 51 Cardiff C) 1973–94
777 Alan Oakes (565 Manchester C, 211 Chester C, 1 Port Vale) 1959–84
774 Dave Beasant (340 Wimbledon, 20 Newcastle U, 133 Chelsea, 6 Grimsby T (loan), 4 Wolverhampton W (loan), 88 Southampton, 139 Nottingham F, 27 Portsmouth, 1 Tottenham H (loan), 16 Brighton & HA) 1979–2003
771 John Burridge (27 Workington, 134 Blackpool, 65 Aston Villa, 6 Southend U (loan), 88 Crystal Palace, 39 QPR, 74 Wolverhampton W, 6 Derby Co (loan), 109 Sheffield U, 62 Southampton, 67 Newcastle U, 65 Hibernian, 3 Scarborough, 4 Lincoln C, 3 Aberdeen, 3 Dumbarton, 3 Falkirk, 4 Manchester C, 3 Darlington, 6 Queen of the S) 1968–96
770 John Trollope (all for Swindon T) 1960–80†
764 Jimmy Dickinson (all for Portsmouth) 1946–65
763 Stuart McCall (395 Bradford C, 103 Everton, 194 Rangers, 71 Sheffield U) 1982–2004
761 Roy Sproson (all for Port Vale) 1950–72
760 Mick Tait (64 Oxford U, 106 Carlisle U, 33 Hull C, 240 Portsmouth, 99 Reading, 79 Darlington, 139 Hartlepool U) 1975–97
758 Ray Clemence (48 Scunthorpe U, 470 Liverpool, 240 Tottenham H) 1966–87
758 Billy Bonds (95 Charlton Ath, 663 West Ham U) 1964–88
757 Pat Jennings (48 Watford, 472 Tottenham H, 237 Arsenal) 1963–86
757 Frank Worthington (171 Huddersfield T, 210 Leicester C, 84 Bolton W, 75 Birmingham C, 32 Leeds U, 19 Sunderland, 34 Southampton, 31 Brighton & HA, 59 Tranmere R, 23 Preston NE, 19 Stockport Co) 1966–88
755 Jamie Cureton (98 Norwich C, 5 Bournemouth (loan), 174 Bristol R, 108 Reading, 43 QPR, 30 Swindon T, 52 Colchester U, 8 Barnsley (loan), 12 Shrewsbury (loan), 88 Exeter C, 19 Leyton Orient, 35 Cheltenham T, 83 Dagenham & R) 1992–2016
753 Andy Millen (71 St Johnstone, 111 Alloa Ath, 119 Hamilton A, 57 Kilmarnock, 51, Hibernian, 18 Raith Rovers, 60 Ayr U, 44 G Morton, 89 Clyde, 114 St Mirren, 19 Queen's Park) 1986–2012
752 Wayne Allison (84 Halifax T, 7 Watford, 195 Bristol C, 101 Swindon T, 74 Huddersfield T, 103 Tranmere R, 73 Sheffield U, 115 Chesterfield) 1987–2008

† *record for one club*

CONSECUTIVE
401 Harold Bell (401 Tranmere R; 459 in all games) 1946–55

YOUNGEST PLAYERS

FA Premier League appearance
Harvey Elliott, 16 years 30 days, Wolves v Fulham, 4.5.2019

FA Premier League scorer
James Vaughan, 16 years 271 days, Everton v Crystal Palace 10.4.2005

Football League appearance
Reuben Noble-Lazarus, 15 years 45 days, Barnsley v Ipswich T, FL Championship 30.9.2008

Football League scorer
Ronnie Dix, 15 years 180 days, Bristol Rovers v Norwich C, Division 3S, 3.3.1928

FA Cup appearance (any round)
Andy Awford, 15 years 88 days as substitute Worcester City v Boreham Wood, 3rd Qual. rd, 10.10.1987

FA Cup goalscorer
George Williams, 16 years 66 days, Milton Keynes D v Nantwich T, 12.11.2011

FA Cup appearance (competition rounds)
Luke Freeman, 15 years 233 days, Gillingham v Barnet 10.11.2007

FA Cup Final appearance
Curtis Weston, 17 years 119 days, Millwall v Manchester U, 22.5.2004

FA Cup Final scorer
Norman Whiteside, 18 years 18 days, Manchester United v Brighton & HA, 1983

FA Cup Final captain
David Nish, 21 years 212 days, Leicester C v Manchester C, 1969

League Cup appearance
Connor Wickham, 16 years 133 days, Ipswich T v Shrewsbury T, 11.8.2009

League Cup goalscorer
Connor Wickham, 16 years 133 days, Ipswich T v Shrewsbury T, 11.8.2009

League Cup Final scorer
Norman Whiteside, 17 years 324 days, Manchester U v Liverpool, 1983

League Cup Final captain
Barry Venison, 20 years 7 months 8 days, Sunderland v Norwich C, 1985

Scottish Premiership appearance
Dylan Reid, 16 years 5 days, St.Mirren v Rangers, 6.3.2021

Scottish Football League appearance
Jordan Allan, 14 years 189 days, Airdrie U v Livingston, 26.4.2013

Scottish Premiership scorer
Fraser Fyvie, 16 years 306 days, Aberdeen v Hearts, 27.1.2010

OLDEST PLAYERS

FA Premier League appearance
John Burridge, 43 years 162 days, Manchester C v QPR, 14.5.95

Football League appearance
Neil McBain, 52 years 4 months, New Brighton v Hartlepools U, Div 3N, 15.3.47 (McBain was New Brighton's manager and had to play in an emergency)

Division 1 appearance
Stanley Matthews, 50 years 5 days, Stoke C v Fulham, 6.2.65

INTERNATIONAL RECORDS

MOST GOALS IN AN INTERNATIONAL

Record/World Cup	Archie Thompson (Australia) 13 goals v American Samoa	11.4.2001
England	Howard Vaughton (Aston Villa) 5 goals v Ireland, at Belfast Steve Bloomer (Derby Co) 5 goals v Wales, at Cardiff Willie Hall (Tottenham H) 5 goals v N. Ireland, at Old Trafford Malcolm Macdonald (Newcastle U) 5 goals v Cyprus, at Wembley	18.2.1882 16.3.1896 16.11.1938 16.4.1975
Northern Ireland	Joe Bambrick (Linfield) 6 goals v Wales, at Belfast	1.2.1930
Wales	John Price (Wrexham) 4 goals v Ireland, at Wrexham John Doughty (Newton Heath) 4 goals v Ireland, at Wrexham Mel Charles (Cardiff C) 4 goals v N. Ireland, at Cardiff Ian Edwards (Chester) 4 goals v Malta, at Wrexham	25.2.1882 3.3.1888 11.4.1962 25.10.1978
Scotland	Alexander Higgins (Kilmarnock) 4 goals v Ireland, at Hampden Park Charles Heggie (Rangers) 4 goals v Ireland, at Belfast William Dickson (Dundee Strathmore) 4 goals v Ireland, at Belfast William Paul (Partick Thistle) 4 goals v Wales, at Paisley Jake Madden (Celtic) 4 goals v Wales, at Wrexham Duke McMahon (Celtic) 4 goals v Ireland, at Celtic Park Bob Hamilton (Rangers) 4 goals v Ireland, at Celtic Park Jimmy Quinn (Celtic) 4 goals v Ireland, at Dublin Hughie Gallacher (Newcastle U) 4 goals v N. Ireland, at Belfast Billy Steel (Dundee) 4 goals v N. Ireland, at Hampden Park Denis Law (Manchester U) 4 goals v N. Ireland, at Hampden Park Denis Law (Manchester U) 4 goals v Norway, at Hampden Park Colin Stein (Rangers) 4 goals v Cyprus, at Hampden Park	14.3.1885 20.3.1886 24.3.1888 22.3.1890 18.3.1893 23.2.1901 23.2.1901 14.3.1908 23.2.1929 1.11.1950 7.11.1962 7.11.1963 17.5.1969

MOST GOALS IN AN INTERNATIONAL CAREER

		Goals	*Games*
England	Wayne Rooney (Everton, Manchester U)	53	120
Scotland	Denis Law (Huddersfield T, Manchester C, Torino, Manchester U) Kenny Dalglish (Celtic, Liverpool)	30 30	55 102
Northern Ireland	David Healy (Manchester U, Preston NE, Leeds U, Fulham, Sunderland, Rangers, Bury)	36	95
Wales	Gareth Bale (Southampton, Tottenham H, Real Madrid)	33	81
Republic of Ireland	Robbie Keane (Wolverhampton W, Coventry C, Internazionale, Leeds U, Tottenham H, Liverpool, Tottenham H, LA Galaxy)	68	146

HIGHEST SCORES

World Cup Match	Australia	31	American Samoa	0	2001
European Championship	San Marino	0	Germany	13	2006
Olympic Games	Denmark Germany	17 16	France Russia	1 0	1908 1912
Olympic Qualifying Tournament	Vanuatu	46	Micronesia	0	2015
Other International Match	Libya *Abandoned after 80 minutes as Oman refused to play on.*	21	Oman	0	1966
European Cup	KR Reykjavik	2	Feyenoord	12	1969
European Cup-Winners' Cup	Sporting Lisbon	16	Apoel Nicosia	1	1963
Fairs & UEFA Cups	Ajax	14	Red Boys Differdange	0	1984

GOALSCORING RECORDS

World Cup Final	Geoff Hurst (England) 3 goals v West Germany	1966
World Cup Final tournament	Just Fontaine (France) 13 goals	1958
World Cup career	Miroslav Klose (Germany) 16 goals	2002, 2006, 2010, 2014
Career	Artur Friedenreich (Brazil) 1,329 goals Pele (Brazil) 1,281 goals Franz 'Bimbo' Binder (Austria, Germany) 1,006 goals	1910–30 *1956–78 1930–50
World Cup Finals fastest	Hakan Sukur (Turkey) 10.8 secs v South Korea	2002

**Pele subsequently scored two goals in Testimonial matches making his total 1,283.*

MOST CAPPED INTERNATIONALS IN BRITAIN AND IRELAND

England	Peter Shilton	125 appearances	1970–90
Northern Ireland	Pat Jennings	119 appearances	1964–86
Scotland	Kenny Dalglish	102 appearances	1971–86
Wales	Chris Gunter	102 appearances	2007–2021
Republic of Ireland	Robbie Keane	146 appearances	1998–2016

THE PREMIER LEAGUE AND FOOTBALL LEAGUE FIXTURES 2021–22

All fixtures subject to change.

Community Shield

Saturday, 7 August 2021
Leicester C v Manchester C

Premier League

Saturday, 14 August 2021
Brentford v Arsenal
Burnley v Brighton & HA
Chelsea v Crystal Palace
Everton v Southampton
Leicester C v Wolverhampton W
Manchester U v Leeds U
Newcastle U v West Ham U
Norwich C v Liverpool
Tottenham H v Manchester C
Watford v Aston Villa

Saturday, 21 August 2021
Arsenal v Chelsea
Aston Villa v Newcastle U
Brighton & HA v Watford
Crystal Palace v Brentford
Leeds U v Everton
Liverpool v Burnley
Manchester C v Norwich C
Southampton v Manchester U
West Ham U v Leicester C
Wolverhampton W v Tottenham H

Saturday, 28 August 2021
Aston Villa v Brentford
Brighton & HA v Everton
Burnley v Leeds U
Liverpool v Chelsea
Manchester C v Arsenal
Newcastle U v Southampton
Norwich C v Leicester C
Tottenham H v Watford
West Ham U v Crystal Palace
Wolverhampton W v Manchester U

Saturday, 11 September 2021
Arsenal v Norwich C
Brentford v Brighton & HA
Chelsea v Aston Villa
Crystal Palace v Tottenham H
Everton v Burnley
Leeds U v Liverpool
Leicester C v Manchester C
Manchester U v Newcastle U
Southampton v West Ham U
Watford v Wolverhampton W

Saturday, 18 September 2021
Aston Villa v Everton
Brighton & HA v Leicester C
Burnley v Arsenal
Liverpool v Crystal Palace
Manchester C v Southampton
Newcastle U v Leeds U
Norwich C v Watford
Tottenham H v Chelsea
West Ham U v Manchester U
Wolverhampton W v Brentford

Saturday, 25 September 2021
Arsenal v Tottenham H
Brentford v Liverpool
Chelsea v Manchester C
Crystal Palace v Brighton & HA
Everton v Norwich C
Leeds U v West Ham U
Leicester C v Burnley
Manchester U v Aston Villa
Southampton v Wolverhampton W
Watford v Newcastle U

Saturday, 2 October 2021
Brighton & HA v Arsenal
Burnley v Norwich C
Chelsea v Southampton
Crystal Palace v Leicester C
Leeds U v Watford
Liverpool v Manchester C
Manchester U v Everton
Tottenham H v Aston Villa
West Ham U v Brentford
Wolverhampton W v Newcastle U

Saturday, 16 October 2021
Arsenal v Crystal Palace
Aston Villa v Wolverhampton W
Brentford v Chelsea
Everton v West Ham U
Leicester C v Manchester U
Manchester C v Burnley
Newcastle U v Tottenham H
Norwich C v Brighton & HA
Southampton v Leeds U
Watford v Liverpool

Saturday, 23 October 2021
Arsenal v Aston Villa
Brentford v Leicester C
Brighton & HA v Manchester C
Chelsea v Norwich C
Crystal Palace v Newcastle U
Everton v Watford
Leeds U v Wolverhampton W
Manchester U v Liverpool
Southampton v Burnley
West Ham U v Tottenham H

Saturday, 30 October 2021
Aston Villa v West Ham U
Burnley v Brentford
Leicester C v Arsenal
Liverpool v Brighton & HA
Manchester C v Crystal Palace
Newcastle U v Chelsea
Norwich C v Leeds U
Tottenham H v Manchester U
Watford v Southampton
Wolverhampton W v Everton

Saturday, 6 November 2021
Arsenal v Watford
Brentford v Norwich C
Brighton & HA v Newcastle U
Chelsea v Burnley
Crystal Palace v Wolverhampton W
Everton v Tottenham H
Leeds U v Leicester C
Manchester U v Manchester C
Southampton v Aston Villa
West Ham U v Liverpool

Saturday, 20 November 2021
Aston Villa v Brighton & HA
Burnley v Crystal Palace
Leicester C v Chelsea
Liverpool v Arsenal
Manchester C v Everton
Newcastle U v Brentford
Norwich C v Southampton
Tottenham H v Leeds U
Watford v Manchester U
Wolverhampton W v West Ham U

Saturday, 27 November 2021
Arsenal v Newcastle U
Brentford v Everton
Brighton & HA v Leeds U
Burnley v Tottenham H
Chelsea v Manchester U
Crystal Palace v Aston Villa
Leicester C v Watford
Liverpool v Southampton
Manchester C v West Ham U
Norwich C v Wolverhampton W

Tuesday, 30 November 2021
Aston Villa v Manchester C
Everton v Liverpool
Leeds U v Crystal Palace
Watford v Chelsea
West Ham U v Brighton & HA
Wolverhampton W v Burnley
Manchester U v Arsenal

Wednesday, 1 December 2021
Newcastle U v Norwich C
Southampton v Leicester C
Tottenham H v Brentford

Saturday, 4 December 2021
Aston Villa v Leicester C
Everton v Arsenal
Leeds U v Brentford
Manchester U v Crystal Palace
Newcastle U v Burnley
Southampton v Brighton & HA
Tottenham H v Norwich C
Watford v Manchester C
West Ham U v Chelsea
Wolverhampton W v Liverpool

Saturday, 11 December 2021
Arsenal v Southampton
Brentford v Watford
Brighton & HA v Tottenham H
Burnley v West Ham U
Chelsea v Leeds U
Crystal Palace v Everton
Leicester C v Newcastle U
Liverpool v Aston Villa
Manchester C v Wolverhampton W
Norwich C v Manchester U

Tuesday, 14 December 2021
Arsenal v West Ham U
Brentford v Manchester U
Brighton & HA v Wolverhampton W
Burnley v Watford
Leicester C v Tottenham H
Norwich C v Aston Villa
Crystal Palace v Southampton

Wednesday, 15 December 2021
Chelsea v Everton
Liverpool v Newcastle U
Manchester C v Leeds U

Saturday, 18 December 2021
Aston Villa v Burnley
Everton v Leicester C
Leeds U v Arsenal
Manchester U v Brighton & HA
Newcastle U v Manchester C
Southampton v Brentford
Tottenham H v Liverpool
Watford v Crystal Palace
West Ham U v Norwich C
Wolverhampton W v Chelsea

Sunday, 26 December 2021
Aston Villa v Chelsea
Brighton & HA v Brentford
Burnley v Everton
Liverpool v Leeds U
Manchester C v Leicester C
Newcastle U v Manchester U
Norwich C v Arsenal
Tottenham H v Crystal Palace
West Ham U v Southampton
Wolverhampton W v Watford

Tuesday, 28 December 2021
Arsenal v Wolverhampton W
Brentford v Manchester C
Chelsea v Brighton & HA
Crystal Palace v Norwich C
Everton v Newcastle U
Leeds U v Aston Villa
Leicester C v Liverpool
Manchester U v Burnley
Southampton v Tottenham H
Watford v West Ham U

Saturday, 1 January 2022
Arsenal v Manchester C
Brentford v Aston Villa
Chelsea v Liverpool
Crystal Palace v West Ham U
Everton v Brighton & HA
Leeds U v Burnley
Leicester C v Norwich C
Manchester U v Wolverhampton W
Southampton v Newcastle U
Watford v Tottenham H

Saturday, 15 January 2022
Aston Villa v Manchester U
Brighton & HA v Crystal Palace
Burnley v Leicester C
Liverpool v Brentford
Manchester C v Chelsea
Newcastle U v Watford
Norwich C v Everton
Tottenham H v Arsenal
West Ham U v Leeds U
Wolverhampton W v Southampton

Saturday, 22 January 2022
Arsenal v Burnley
Brentford v Wolverhampton W
Chelsea v Tottenham H
Crystal Palace v Liverpool
Everton v Aston Villa
Leeds U v Newcastle U
Leicester C v Brighton & HA
Manchester U v West Ham U
Southampton v Manchester C
Watford v Norwich C

Tuesday, 8 February 2022
Aston Villa v Leeds U
Brighton & HA v Chelsea
Burnley v Manchester U
Norwich C v Crystal Palace
West Ham U v Watford
Wolverhampton W v Arsenal

Wednesday, 9 February 2022
Newcastle U v Everton
Tottenham H v Southampton
Liverpool v Leicester C
Manchester C v Brentford

Saturday, 12 February 2022
Brentford v Crystal Palace
Burnley v Liverpool
Chelsea v Arsenal
Everton v Leeds U
Leicester C v West Ham U
Manchester U v Southampton
Newcastle U v Aston Villa
Norwich C v Manchester C
Tottenham H v Wolverhampton W
Watford v Brighton & HA

Saturday, 19 February 2022
Arsenal v Brentford
Aston Villa v Watford
Brighton & HA v Burnley
Crystal Palace v Chelsea
Leeds U v Manchester U
Liverpool v Norwich C
Manchester C v Tottenham H
Southampton v Everton
West Ham U v Newcastle U
Wolverhampton W v Leicester C

Saturday, 26 February 2022
Arsenal v Liverpool
Brentford v Newcastle U
Brighton & HA v Aston Villa
Chelsea v Leicester C
Crystal Palace v Burnley
Everton v Manchester C
Leeds U v Tottenham H
Manchester U v Watford
Southampton v Norwich C
West Ham U v Wolverhampton W

Saturday, 5 March 2022
Aston Villa v Southampton
Burnley v Chelsea
Leicester C v Leeds U
Liverpool v West Ham U
Manchester C v Manchester U
Newcastle U v Brighton & HA
Norwich C v Brentford
Tottenham H v Everton
Watford v Arsenal
Wolverhampton W v Crystal Palace

Saturday, 12 March 2022
Arsenal v Leicester C
Brentford v Burnley
Brighton & HA v Liverpool
Chelsea v Newcastle U
Crystal Palace v Manchester C
Everton v Wolverhampton W
Leeds U v Norwich C
Manchester U v Tottenham H
Southampton v Watford
West Ham U v Aston Villa

Saturday, 19 March 2022
Aston Villa v Arsenal
Burnley v Southampton
Leicester C v Brentford
Liverpool v Manchester U
Manchester C v Brighton & HA
Newcastle U v Crystal Palace
Norwich C v Chelsea
Tottenham H v West Ham U
Watford v Everton
Wolverhampton W v Leeds U

Saturday, 2 April 2022
Brighton & HA v Norwich C
Burnley v Manchester C
Chelsea v Brentford
Crystal Palace v Arsenal
Leeds U v Southampton
Liverpool v Watford
Manchester U v Leicester C
Tottenham H v Newcastle U
West Ham U v Everton
Wolverhampton W v Aston Villa

Saturday, 9 April 2022
Arsenal v Brighton & HA
Aston Villa v Tottenham H
Brentford v West Ham U
Everton v Manchester U
Leicester C v Crystal Palace
Manchester C v Liverpool
Newcastle U v Wolverhampton W
Norwich C v Burnley
Southampton v Chelsea
Watford v Leeds U

Saturday, 16 April 2022
Aston Villa v Liverpool
Everton v Crystal Palace
Leeds U v Chelsea
Manchester U v Norwich C
Newcastle U v Leicester C
Southampton v Arsenal
Tottenham H v Brighton & HA
Watford v Brentford
West Ham U v Burnley
Wolverhampton W v Manchester C

Saturday, 23 April 2022
Arsenal v Manchester U
Brentford v Tottenham H
Brighton & HA v Southampton
Burnley v Wolverhampton W
Chelsea v West Ham U
Crystal Palace v Leeds U
Leicester C v Aston Villa
Liverpool v Everton
Manchester C v Watford
Norwich C v Newcastle U

Saturday, 30 April 2022
Aston Villa v Norwich C
Everton v Chelsea
Leeds U v Manchester C
Manchester U v Brentford
Newcastle U v Liverpool
Southampton v Crystal Palace
Tottenham H v Leicester C
Watford v Burnley
West Ham U v Arsenal
Wolverhampton W v Brighton & HA

Saturday, 7 May 2022
Arsenal v Leeds U
Brentford v Southampton
Brighton & HA v Manchester U
Burnley v Aston Villa
Chelsea v Wolverhampton W
Crystal Palace v Watford
Leicester C v Everton
Liverpool v Tottenham H
Manchester C v Newcastle U
Norwich C v West Ham U

Sunday, 15 May 2022
Aston Villa v Crystal Palace
Everton v Brentford
Leeds U v Brighton & HA
Manchester U v Chelsea
Newcastle U v Arsenal
Southampton v Liverpool
Tottenham H v Burnley
Watford v Leicester C
West Ham U v Manchester C
Wolverhampton W v Norwich C

Sunday, 22 May 2022
Arsenal v Everton
Brentford v Leeds U
Brighton & HA v West Ham U

Burnley v Newcastle U
Chelsea v Watford
Crystal Palace v Manchester U
Leicester C v Southampton
Liverpool v Wolverhampton W
Manchester C v Aston Villa
Norwich C v Tottenham H

EFL Championship

Saturday, 7 August 2021
Blackburn R v Swansea C
Bournemouth v WBA
Bristol C v Blackpool
Cardiff C v Barnsley
Coventry C v Nottingham F
Derby Co v Huddersfield T
Fulham v Middlesbrough
Luton T v Peterborough U
Preston NE v Hull C
QPR v Millwall
Sheffield U v Birmingham C
Stoke C v Reading

Saturday, 14 August 2021
Barnsley v Coventry C
Birmingham C v Stoke C
Blackpool v Cardiff C
Huddersfield T v Fulham
Hull C v QPR
Middlesbrough v Bristol C
Millwall v Blackburn R
Nottingham F v Bournemouth
Peterborough U v Derby Co
Reading v Preston NE
Swansea C v Sheffield U
WBA v Luton T

Tuesday, 17 August 2021
Barnsley v Luton T
Blackpool v Coventry C
Huddersfield T v Preston NE
Millwall v Fulham
Peterborough U v Cardiff C
Swansea C v Stoke C

Wednesday, 18 August 2021
Birmingham C v Bournemouth
Hull C v Derby Co
Middlesbrough v QPR
Nottingham F v Blackburn R
Reading v Bristol C
WBA v Sheffield U

Saturday, 21 August 2021
Blackburn R v WBA
Bournemouth v Blackpool
Bristol C v Swansea C
Cardiff C v Millwall
Coventry C v Reading
Derby Co v Middlesbrough
Fulham v Hull C
Luton T v Birmingham C
Preston NE v Peterborough U
QPR v Barnsley
Sheffield U v Huddersfield T
Stoke C v Nottingham F

Saturday, 28 August 2021
Barnsley v Birmingham C
Cardiff C v Bristol C
Derby Co v Nottingham F
Fulham v Stoke C
Huddersfield T v Reading
Hull C v Bournemouth
Luton T v Sheffield U
Middlesbrough v Blackburn R
Millwall v Blackpool
Peterborough U v WBA
Preston NE v Swansea C
QPR v Coventry C

Saturday, 11 September 2021
Birmingham C v Derby Co
Blackburn R v Luton T
Blackpool v Fulham
Bournemouth v Barnsley
Bristol C v Preston NE
Coventry C v Middlesbrough
Nottingham F v Cardiff C
Reading v QPR
Sheffield U v Peterborough U
Stoke C v Huddersfield T
Swansea C v Hull C
WBA v Millwall

Tuesday, 14 September 2021
Blackburn R v Hull C
Blackpool v Huddersfield T
Bournemouth v QPR
Sheffield U v Preston NE
Reading v Peterborough U
WBA v Derby Co

Wednesday, 15 September 2021
Birmingham C v Fulham
Bristol C v Luton T
Coventry C v Cardiff C
Nottingham F v Middlesbrough
Swansea C v Millwall
Stoke C v Barnsley

Saturday, 18 September 2021
Barnsley v Blackburn R
Cardiff C v Bournemouth
Derby Co v Stoke C
Fulham v Reading
Huddersfield T v Nottingham F
Hull C v Sheffield U
Luton T v Swansea C
Middlesbrough v Blackpool
Millwall v Coventry C
Peterborough U v Birmingham C
Preston NE v WBA
QPR v Bristol C

Saturday, 25 September 2021
Birmingham C v Preston NE
Blackburn R v Cardiff C
Blackpool v Barnsley
Bournemouth v Luton T
Bristol C v Fulham
Coventry C v Peterborough U
Nottingham F v Millwall
Reading v Middlesbrough
Sheffield U v Derby Co
Stoke C v Hull C
Swansea C v Huddersfield T
WBA v QPR

Tuesday, 28 September 2021
Cardiff C v WBA
Huddersfield T v Blackburn R
Hull C v Blackpool
Middlesbrough v Sheffield U
Preston NE v Stoke C
QPR v Birmingham C

Wednesday, 29 September 2021
Barnsley v Nottingham F
Derby Co v Reading
Fulham v Swansea C
Luton T v Coventry C
Millwall v Bristol C
Peterborough U v Bournemouth

Saturday, 2 October 2021
Barnsley v Millwall
Birmingham C v Nottingham F
Blackpool v Blackburn R
Bournemouth v Sheffield U
Cardiff C v Reading
Coventry C v Fulham
Derby Co v Swansea C
Hull C v Middlesbrough
Luton T v Huddersfield T
Peterborough U v Bristol C
QPR v Preston NE
Stoke C v WBA

Saturday, 16 October 2021
Blackburn R v Coventry C
Bristol C v Bournemouth
Fulham v QPR
Huddersfield T v Hull C
Middlesbrough v Peterborough U
Millwall v Luton T
Nottingham F v Blackpool
Preston NE v Derby Co
Reading v Barnsley
Sheffield U v Stoke C
Swansea C v Cardiff C
WBA v Birmingham C

Tuesday, 19 October 2021
Bristol C v Nottingham F
Derby Co v Luton T
Fulham v Cardiff C
QPR v Blackburn R
Sheffield U v Millwall
Stoke C v Bournemouth

Wednesday, 20 October 2021
Huddersfield T v Birmingham C
Hull C v Peterborough U
Middlesbrough v Barnsley
Preston NE v Coventry C
Swansea C v WBA
Reading v Blackpool

Saturday, 23 October 2021
Barnsley v Sheffield U
Birmingham C v Swansea C
Blackburn R v Reading
Blackpool v Preston NE
Bournemouth v Huddersfield T
Cardiff C v Middlesbrough
Coventry C v Derby Co
Luton T v Hull C
Millwall v Stoke C
Nottingham F v Fulham
Peterborough U v QPR
WBA v Bristol C

Saturday, 30 October 2021
Bristol C v Barnsley
Derby Co v Blackburn R
Fulham v WBA
Huddersfield T v Millwall
Hull C v Coventry C
Middlesbrough v Birmingham C
Preston NE v Luton T
QPR v Nottingham F
Reading v Bournemouth
Sheffield U v Blackpool
Stoke C v Cardiff C
Swansea C v Peterborough U

Tuesday, 2 November 2021
Birmingham C v Bristol C
Coventry C v Swansea C
Luton T v Middlesbrough
Millwall v Reading
Nottingham F v Sheffield U
Peterborough U v Huddersfield T

Wednesday, 3 November 2021
Barnsley v Derby Co
Blackburn R v Fulham
Blackpool v Stoke C
Bournemouth v Preston NE
Cardiff C v QPR
WBA v Hull C

Saturday, 6 November 2021
Barnsley v Hull C
Birmingham C v Reading
Blackburn R v Sheffield U

Blackpool v QPR
Bournemouth v Swansea C
Cardiff C v Huddersfield T
Coventry C v Bristol C
Luton T v Stoke C
Millwall v Derby Co
Nottingham F v Preston NE
Peterborough U v Fulham
WBA v Middlesbrough

Saturday, 20 November 2021
Bristol C v Blackburn R
Derby Co v Bournemouth
Fulham v Barnsley
Huddersfield T v WBA
Hull C v Birmingham C
Middlesbrough v Millwall
Preston NE v Cardiff C
QPR v Luton T
Reading v Nottingham F
Sheffield U v Coventry C
Stoke C v Peterborough U
Swansea C v Blackpool

Tuesday, 23 November 2021
Blackpool v WBA
Coventry C v Birmingham C
Fulham v Derby Co
Middlesbrough v Preston NE
Nottingham F v Luton T
Reading v Sheffield U

Wednesday, 24 November 2021
Barnsley v Swansea C
Blackburn R v Peterborough U
Bristol C v Stoke C
Cardiff C v Hull C
Millwall v Bournemouth
QPR v Huddersfield T

Saturday, 27 November 2021
Birmingham C v Blackpool
Bournemouth v Coventry C
Derby Co v QPR
Huddersfield T v Middlesbrough
Hull C v Millwall
Luton T v Cardiff C
Peterborough U v Barnsley
Preston NE v Fulham
Sheffield U v Bristol C
Stoke C v Blackburn R
Swansea C v Reading
WBA v Nottingham F

Saturday, 4 December 2021
Barnsley v Huddersfield T
Blackburn R v Preston NE
Blackpool v Luton T
Bristol C v Derby Co
Cardiff C v Sheffield U
Coventry C v WBA
Fulham v Bournemouth
Middlesbrough v Swansea C
Millwall v Birmingham C
Nottingham F v Peterborough U
QPR v Stoke C
Reading v Hull C

Saturday, 11 December 2021
Birmingham C v Cardiff C
Bournemouth v Blackburn R
Derby Co v Blackpool
Huddersfield T v Coventry C
Hull C v Bristol C
Luton T v Fulham
Peterborough U v Millwall
Preston NE v Barnsley
Sheffield U v QPR
Stoke C v Middlesbrough
Swansea C v Nottingham F
WBA v Reading

Saturday, 18 December 2021
Barnsley v WBA
Blackburn R v Birmingham C
Blackpool v Peterborough U
Bristol C v Huddersfield T
Cardiff C v Derby Co
Coventry C v Stoke C
Fulham v Sheffield U
Middlesbrough v Bournemouth
Millwall v Preston NE
Nottingham F v Hull C
QPR v Swansea C
Reading v Luton T

Sunday, 26 December 2021
Barnsley v Stoke C
Cardiff C v Coventry C
Derby Co v WBA
Fulham v Birmingham C
Huddersfield T v Blackpool
Hull C v Blackburn R
Luton T v Bristol C
Middlesbrough v Nottingham F
Millwall v Swansea C
Peterborough U v Reading
Preston NE v Sheffield U
QPR v Bournemouth

Wednesday, 29 December 2021
Birmingham C v Peterborough U
Blackburn R v Barnsley
Blackpool v Middlesbrough
Bournemouth v Cardiff C
Bristol C v QPR

Coventry C v Millwall
Nottingham F v Huddersfield T
Sheffield U v Hull C
Swansea C v Luton T
Reading v Fulham
Stoke C v Derby Co
WBA v Preston NE

Saturday, 1 January 2022
Birmingham C v QPR
Blackburn R v Huddersfield T
Blackpool v Hull C
Bournemouth v Peterborough U
Bristol C v Millwall
Coventry C v Luton T
Nottingham F v Barnsley
Reading v Derby Co
Sheffield U v Middlesbrough
Stoke C v Preston NE
Swansea C v Fulham
WBA v Cardiff C

Saturday, 15 January 2022
Barnsley v Blackpool
Cardiff C v Blackburn R
Derby Co v Sheffield U
Fulham v Bristol C
Huddersfield T v Swansea C
Hull C v Stoke C
Luton T v Bournemouth
Middlesbrough v Reading
Millwall v Nottingham F
Peterborough U v Coventry C
Preston NE v Birmingham C
QPR v WBA

Saturday, 22 January 2022
Birmingham C v Barnsley
Blackburn R v Middlesbrough
Blackpool v Millwall
Bournemouth v Hull C
Bristol C v Cardiff C
Coventry C v QPR
Nottingham F v Derby Co
Reading v Huddersfield T
Sheffield U v Luton T
Stoke C v Fulham

Swansea C v Preston NE
WBA v Peterborough U

Saturday, 29 January 2022
Barnsley v Bournemouth
Cardiff C v Nottingham F
Derby Co v Birmingham C
Fulham v Blackpool
Huddersfield T v Stoke C
Hull C v Swansea C
Luton T v Blackburn R
Middlesbrough v Coventry C
Millwall v WBA
Peterborough U v Sheffield U
Preston NE v Bristol C
QPR v Reading

Saturday, 5 February 2022
Barnsley v Cardiff C
Birmingham C v Sheffield U
Blackpool v Bristol C
Huddersfield T v Derby Co
Hull C v Preston NE
Middlesbrough v Fulham
Millwall v QPR
Nottingham F v Coventry C
Peterborough U v Luton T
Reading v Stoke C
Swansea C v Blackburn R
WBA v Bournemouth

Tuesday, 8 February 2022
Cardiff C v Peterborough U
Coventry C v Blackpool
Derby Co v Hull C
Fulham v Millwall
Luton T v Barnsley
Stoke C v Swansea C

Wednesday, 9 February 2022
Blackburn R v Nottingham F
Bournemouth v Birmingham C
Bristol C v Reading
Preston NE v Huddersfield T
QPR v Middlesbrough
Sheffield U v WBA

Saturday, 12 February 2022
Barnsley v QPR
Birmingham C v Luton T
Blackpool v Bournemouth
Huddersfield T v Sheffield U
Hull C v Fulham
Middlesbrough v Derby Co
Millwall v Cardiff C
Nottingham F v Stoke C
Peterborough U v Preston NE
Reading v Coventry C
Swansea C v Bristol C
WBA v Blackburn R

Saturday, 19 February 2022
Blackburn R v Millwall
Bournemouth v Nottingham F
Bristol C v Middlesbrough
Cardiff C v Blackpool
Coventry C v Barnsley
Derby Co v Peterborough U
Fulham v Huddersfield T
Luton T v WBA
Preston NE v Reading
QPR v Hull C
Sheffield U v Swansea C
Stoke C v Birmingham C

Tuesday, 22 February 2022
Bristol C v Coventry C
Hull C v Barnsley
Middlesbrough v WBA
Preston NE v Nottingham F
Swansea C v Bournemouth
Reading v Birmingham C

Wednesday, 23 February 2022
Derby Co v Millwall
Fulham v Peterborough U
Huddersfield T v Cardiff C
QPR v Blackpool
Sheffield U v Blackburn R
Stoke C v Luton T

Saturday, 26 February 2022
Barnsley v Middlesbrough
Birmingham C v Huddersfield T
Blackburn R v QPR
Blackpool v Reading
Bournemouth v Stoke C
Cardiff C v Fulham
Coventry C v Preston NE
Luton T v Derby Co
Millwall v Sheffield U
Nottingham F v Bristol C
Peterborough U v Hull C
WBA v Swansea C

Saturday, 5 March 2022
Bristol C v Birmingham C
Derby Co v Barnsley
Fulham v Blackburn R
Huddersfield T v Peterborough U
Hull C v WBA
Middlesbrough v Luton T
Preston NE v Bournemouth
QPR v Cardiff C
Reading v Millwall
Sheffield U v Nottingham F
Stoke C v Blackpool
Swansea C v Coventry C

Saturday, 12 March 2022
Barnsley v Fulham
Birmingham C v Hull C
Blackburn R v Bristol C
Blackpool v Swansea C
Bournemouth v Derby Co
Cardiff C v Preston NE
Coventry C v Sheffield U
Luton T v QPR
Millwall v Middlesbrough
Nottingham F v Reading
Peterborough U v Stoke C
WBA v Huddersfield T

Tuesday, 15 March 2022
Barnsley v Bristol C
Birmingham C v Middlesbrough
Blackburn R v Derby Co
Bournemouth v Reading
Nottingham F v QPR
WBA v Fulham

Wednesday, 16 March 2022
Blackpool v Sheffield U
Cardiff C v Stoke C
Coventry C v Hull C
Luton T v Preston NE
Millwall v Huddersfield T
Peterborough U v Swansea C

Saturday, 19 March 2022
Bristol C v WBA
Derby Co v Coventry C
Fulham v Nottingham F
Huddersfield T v Bournemouth
Hull C v Luton T
Middlesbrough v Cardiff C
Preston NE v Blackpool
QPR v Peterborough U
Reading v Blackburn R
Sheffield U v Barnsley
Stoke C v Millwall
Swansea C v Birmingham C

Saturday, 2 April 2022
Barnsley v Reading
Birmingham C v WBA
Blackpool v Nottingham F
Bournemouth v Bristol C
Cardiff C v Swansea C
Coventry C v Blackburn R
Derby Co v Preston NE
Hull C v Huddersfield T
Luton T v Millwall
Peterborough U v Middlesbrough
QPR v Fulham
Stoke C v Sheffield U

Saturday, 9 April 2022
Blackburn R v Blackpool
Bristol C v Peterborough U
Fulham v Coventry C
Huddersfield T v Luton T
Middlesbrough v Hull C
Millwall v Barnsley
Nottingham F v Birmingham C
Preston NE v QPR
Reading v Cardiff C
Sheffield U v Bournemouth
Swansea C v Derby Co
WBA v Stoke C

Friday, 15 April 2022
Birmingham C v Coventry C
Bournemouth v Middlesbrough
Derby Co v Fulham
Huddersfield T v QPR
Hull C v Cardiff C
Luton T v Nottingham F
Peterborough U v Blackburn R
Preston NE v Millwall
Sheffield U v Reading
Stoke C v Bristol C
Swansea C v Barnsley
WBA v Blackpool

Monday, 18 April 2022
Barnsley v Peterborough U
Blackburn R v Stoke C
Blackpool v Birmingham C
Bristol C v Sheffield U
Cardiff C v Luton T
Coventry C v Bournemouth
Fulham v Preston NE
Middlesbrough v Huddersfield T
Millwall v Hull C
Nottingham F v WBA
QPR v Derby Co
Reading v Swansea C

Saturday, 23 April 2022
Birmingham C v Millwall
Bournemouth v Fulham
Derby Co v Bristol C
Huddersfield T v Barnsley
Hull C v Reading
Luton T v Blackpool
Peterborough U v Nottingham F
Preston NE v Blackburn R
Sheffield U v Cardiff C
Stoke C v QPR
Swansea C v Middlesbrough
WBA v Coventry C

Saturday, 30 April 2022
Barnsley v Preston NE
Blackburn R v Bournemouth
Blackpool v Derby Co
Bristol C v Hull C
Cardiff C v Birmingham C
Coventry C v Huddersfield T
Fulham v Luton T
Middlesbrough v Stoke C
Millwall v Peterborough U
Nottingham F v Swansea C
QPR v Sheffield U
Reading v WBA

Saturday, 7 May 2022
Birmingham C v Blackburn R
Bournemouth v Millwall
Derby Co v Cardiff C
Huddersfield T v Bristol C
Hull C v Nottingham F
Luton T v Reading
Peterborough U v Blackpool
Preston NE v Middlesbrough
Sheffield U v Fulham
Stoke C v Coventry C
Swansea C v QPR
WBA v Barnsley

EFL League One

Saturday, 7 August 2021
Bolton W v Milton Keynes D
Cambridge U v Oxford U
Charlton Ath v Sheffield W
Crewe Alex v Cheltenham T
Doncaster R v AFC Wimbledon
Fleetwood T v Portsmouth
Gillingham v Lincoln C
Ipswich T v Morecambe
Rotherham U v Plymouth Arg
Shrewsbury T v Burton Alb
Sunderland v Wigan Ath
Wycombe W v Accrington S

Saturday, 14 August 2021
Accrington S v Cambridge U
AFC Wimbledon v Bolton W
Burton Alb v Ipswich T
Cheltenham T v Wycombe W
Lincoln C v Fleetwood T
Milton Keynes D v Sunderland
Morecambe v Shrewsbury T
Oxford U v Charlton Ath
Plymouth Arg v Gillingham
Portsmouth v Crewe Alex
Sheffield W v Doncaster R
Wigan Ath v Rotherham U

Tuesday, 17 August 2021
Accrington S v Doncaster R
AFC Wimbledon v Gillingham
Burton Alb v Sunderland
Cheltenham T v Ipswich T
Lincoln C v Bolton W
Milton Keynes D v Charlton Ath
Morecambe v Rotherham U
Oxford U v Crewe Alex
Plymouth Arg v Cambridge U
Portsmouth v Shrewsbury T
Sheffield W v Fleetwood T
Wigan Ath v Wycombe W

Saturday, 21 August 2021
Bolton W v Oxford U
Cambridge U v Burton Alb
Charlton Ath v Wigan Ath
Crewe Alex v Accrington S
Doncaster R v Portsmouth
Fleetwood T v Cheltenham T
Gillingham v Morecambe
Ipswich T v Milton Keynes D
Rotherham U v Sheffield W
Shrewsbury T v Plymouth Arg
Sunderland v AFC Wimbledon
Wycombe W v Lincoln C

Saturday, 28 August 2021
Burton Alb v Cheltenham T
Cambridge U v Bolton W
Charlton Ath v Crewe Alex
Ipswich T v AFC Wimbledon
Milton Keynes D v Accrington S
Morecambe v Sheffield W
Oxford U v Lincoln C
Plymouth Arg v Fleetwood T

Rotherham U v Doncaster R
Shrewsbury T v Gillingham
Sunderland v Wycombe W
Wigan Ath v Portsmouth

Saturday, 4 September 2021
Accrington S v Shrewsbury T
AFC Wimbledon v Oxford U
Bolton W v Burton Alb
Cheltenham T v Milton Keynes D
Crewe Alex v Morecambe
Doncaster R v Cambridge U
Fleetwood T v Wigan Ath
Gillingham v Charlton Ath
Lincoln C v Rotherham U
Portsmouth v Plymouth Arg
Sheffield W v Sunderland
Wycombe W v Ipswich T

Saturday, 11 September 2021
Burton Alb v Gillingham
Cambridge U v Lincoln C
Charlton Ath v Cheltenham T
Ipswich T v Bolton W
Milton Keynes D v Portsmouth
Morecambe v AFC Wimbledon
Oxford U v Wycombe W
Plymouth Arg v Sheffield W
Rotherham U v Fleetwood T
Shrewsbury T v Crewe Alex
Sunderland v Accrington S
Wigan Ath v Doncaster R

Saturday, 18 September 2021
Accrington S v Wigan Ath
AFC Wimbledon v Plymouth Arg
Bolton W v Rotherham U
Cheltenham T v Oxford U
Crewe Alex v Burton Alb
Doncaster R v Morecambe
Fleetwood T v Sunderland
Gillingham v Milton Keynes D
Lincoln C v Ipswich T
Portsmouth v Cambridge U
Sheffield W v Shrewsbury T
Wycombe W v Charlton Ath

Saturday, 25 September 2021
Burton Alb v Lincoln C
Cambridge U v Fleetwood T
Charlton Ath v Portsmouth
Ipswich T v Sheffield W
Milton Keynes D v Wycombe W
Morecambe v Accrington S
Oxford U v Gillingham
Plymouth Arg v Doncaster R
Rotherham U v Crewe Alex
Shrewsbury T v AFC Wimbledon
Sunderland v Bolton W
Wigan Ath v Cheltenham T

Tuesday, 28 September 2021
Burton Alb v Portsmouth
Cambridge U v Gillingham
Charlton Ath v Bolton W
Ipswich T v Doncaster R
Milton Keynes D v Fleetwood T
Morecambe v Lincoln C
Oxford U v Accrington S
Plymouth Arg v Crewe Alex
Rotherham U v AFC Wimbledon
Shrewsbury T v Wycombe W
Sunderland v Cheltenham T
Wigan Ath v Sheffield W

Saturday, 2 October 2021
Accrington S v Ipswich T
AFC Wimbledon v Burton Alb
Bolton W v Shrewsbury T
Cheltenham T v Rotherham U
Crewe Alex v Cambridge U
Doncaster R v Milton Keynes D
Fleetwood T v Charlton Ath
Gillingham v Wigan Ath
Lincoln C v Plymouth Arg
Portsmouth v Sunderland
Sheffield W v Oxford U
Wycombe W v Morecambe

Saturday, 9 October 2021
Accrington S v Fleetwood T
Charlton Ath v Rotherham U
Crewe Alex v Doncaster R
Ipswich T v Shrewsbury T
Milton Keynes D v AFC Wimbledon
Morecambe v Cambridge U
Plymouth Arg v Burton Alb
Portsmouth v Cheltenham T
Sheffield W v Bolton W
Sunderland v Oxford U
Wigan Ath v Lincoln C
Wycombe W v Gillingham

Saturday, 16 October 2021
AFC Wimbledon v Sheffield W
Bolton W v Wigan Ath
Burton Alb v Morecambe
Cambridge U v Ipswich T
Cheltenham T v Accrington S
Doncaster R v Wycombe W
Fleetwood T v Crewe Alex
Gillingham v Sunderland
Lincoln C v Charlton Ath
Oxford U v Plymouth Arg
Rotherham U v Portsmouth
Shrewsbury T v Milton Keynes D

Tuesday, 19 October 2021
Cambridge U v Sheffield W
Charlton Ath v Accrington S
Cheltenham T v Morecambe
Crewe Alex v Sunderland
Fleetwood T v Burton Alb
Gillingham v Doncaster R
Lincoln C v AFC Wimbledon
Oxford U v Shrewsbury T
Plymouth Arg v Bolton W
Portsmouth v Ipswich T
Rotherham U v Wycombe W
Wigan Ath v Milton Keynes D

Saturday, 23 October 2021
Accrington S v Portsmouth
AFC Wimbledon v Wigan Ath
Bolton W v Gillingham
Burton Alb v Oxford U
Doncaster R v Cheltenham T
Ipswich T v Fleetwood T
Milton Keynes D v Rotherham U
Morecambe v Plymouth Arg
Sheffield W v Lincoln C
Shrewsbury T v Cambridge U
Sunderland v Charlton Ath
Wycombe W v Crewe Alex

Saturday, 30 October 2021
Cambridge U v AFC Wimbledon
Charlton Ath v Doncaster R
Cheltenham T v Sheffield W
Crewe Alex v Milton Keynes D
Fleetwood T v Wycombe W
Gillingham v Accrington S
Lincoln C v Shrewsbury T
Oxford U v Morecambe
Plymouth Arg v Ipswich T
Portsmouth v Bolton W
Rotherham U v Sunderland
Wigan Ath v Burton Alb

Saturday, 13 November 2021
Accrington S v Plymouth Arg
AFC Wimbledon v Cheltenham T
Bolton W v Crewe Alex
Burton Alb v Charlton Ath
Doncaster R v Fleetwood T
Ipswich T v Oxford U
Milton Keynes D v Cambridge U
Morecambe v Wigan Ath
Sheffield W v Gillingham
Shrewsbury T v Rotherham U
Sunderland v Lincoln C
Wycombe W v Portsmouth

Saturday, 20 November 2021
Accrington S v Sheffield W
Charlton Ath v Plymouth Arg
Cheltenham T v Shrewsbury T
Crewe Alex v Gillingham
Doncaster R v Lincoln C
Fleetwood T v Morecambe
Milton Keynes D v Burton Alb
Portsmouth v AFC Wimbledon
Rotherham U v Cambridge U
Sunderland v Ipswich T
Wigan Ath v Oxford U
Wycombe W v Bolton W

Tuesday, 23 November 2021
AFC Wimbledon v Crewe Alex
Burton Alb v Accrington S
Cambridge U v Wigan Ath
Gillingham v Cheltenham T
Ipswich T v Rotherham U
Lincoln C v Portsmouth
Morecambe v Charlton Ath
Oxford U v Fleetwood T
Plymouth Arg v Wycombe W
Sheffield W v Milton Keynes D
Shrewsbury T v Sunderland
Bolton W v Doncaster R

Saturday, 27 November 2021
AFC Wimbledon v Fleetwood T
Bolton W v Cheltenham T
Burton Alb v Doncaster R
Cambridge U v Sunderland
Gillingham v Portsmouth
Ipswich T v Crewe Alex
Lincoln C v Accrington S
Morecambe v Milton Keynes D
Oxford U v Rotherham U
Plymouth Arg v Wigan Ath
Sheffield W v Wycombe W
Shrewsbury T v Charlton Ath

Tuesday, 7 December 2021
Accrington S v AFC Wimbledon
Charlton Ath v Ipswich T
Cheltenham T v Cambridge U
Crewe Alex v Lincoln C
Doncaster R v Oxford U
Fleetwood T v Bolton W
Milton Keynes D v Plymouth Arg
Portsmouth v Sheffield W
Rotherham U v Gillingham
Sunderland v Morecambe
Wigan Ath v Shrewsbury T
Wycombe W v Burton Alb

Saturday, 11 December 2021
Accrington S v Bolton W
Charlton Ath v Cambridge U
Cheltenham T v Lincoln C
Crewe Alex v Sheffield W
Doncaster R v Shrewsbury T
Fleetwood T v Gillingham
Milton Keynes D v Oxford U
Portsmouth v Morecambe
Rotherham U v Burton Alb
Sunderland v Plymouth Arg
Wigan Ath v Ipswich T
Wycombe W v AFC Wimbledon

Saturday, 18 December 2021
AFC Wimbledon v Portsmouth
Bolton W v Wycombe W

Burton Alb v Milton Keynes D
Cambridge U v Rotherham U
Gillingham v Crewe Alex
Ipswich T v Sunderland
Lincoln C v Doncaster R
Morecambe v Fleetwood T
Oxford U v Wigan Ath
Plymouth Arg v Charlton Ath
Sheffield W v Accrington S
Shrewsbury T v Cheltenham T

Sunday, 26 December 2021
Accrington S v Rotherham U
AFC Wimbledon v Charlton Ath
Bolton W v Morecambe
Cheltenham T v Plymouth Arg
Crewe Alex v Wigan Ath
Doncaster R v Sunderland
Fleetwood T v Shrewsbury T
Gillingham v Ipswich T
Lincoln C v Milton Keynes D
Portsmouth v Oxford U
Sheffield W v Burton Alb
Wycombe W v Cambridge U

Wednesday, 29 December 2021
Burton Alb v Bolton W
Cambridge U v Doncaster R
Charlton Ath v Gillingham
Ipswich T v Wycombe W
Milton Keynes D v Cheltenham T
Morecambe v Crewe Alex
Oxford U v AFC Wimbledon
Plymouth Arg v Portsmouth
Rotherham U v Lincoln C
Shrewsbury T v Accrington S
Sunderland v Sheffield W
Wigan Ath v Fleetwood T

Saturday, 1 January 2022
Burton Alb v Crewe Alex
Cambridge U v Portsmouth
Charlton Ath v Wycombe W
Ipswich T v Lincoln C
Milton Keynes D v Gillingham
Morecambe v Doncaster R
Oxford U v Cheltenham T
Plymouth Arg v AFC Wimbledon
Rotherham U v Bolton W
Shrewsbury T v Sheffield W
Sunderland v Fleetwood T
Wigan Ath v Accrington S

Saturday, 8 January 2022
Accrington S v Milton Keynes D
AFC Wimbledon v Ipswich T
Bolton W v Cambridge U
Cheltenham T v Burton Alb
Crewe Alex v Charlton Ath
Doncaster R v Rotherham U
Fleetwood T v Plymouth Arg
Gillingham v Shrewsbury T
Lincoln C v Oxford U
Portsmouth v Wigan Ath
Sheffield W v Morecambe
Wycombe W v Sunderland

Saturday, 15 January 2022
Accrington S v Sunderland
AFC Wimbledon v Morecambe
Bolton W v Ipswich T
Cheltenham T v Charlton Ath
Crewe Alex v Shrewsbury T
Doncaster R v Wigan Ath
Fleetwood T v Rotherham U
Gillingham v Burton Alb
Lincoln C v Cambridge U
Portsmouth v Milton Keynes D
Sheffield W v Plymouth Arg
Wycombe W v Oxford U

Saturday, 22 January 2022
Burton Alb v AFC Wimbledon
Cambridge U v Crewe Alex
Charlton Ath v Fleetwood T
Ipswich T v Accrington S
Milton Keynes D v Doncaster R
Morecambe v Wycombe W
Oxford U v Sheffield W
Plymouth Arg v Lincoln C
Rotherham U v Cheltenham T
Shrewsbury T v Bolton W
Sunderland v Portsmouth
Wigan Ath v Gillingham

Saturday, 29 January 2022
Accrington S v Morecambe
AFC Wimbledon v Shrewsbury T
Bolton W v Sunderland
Cheltenham T v Wigan Ath
Crewe Alex v Rotherham U
Doncaster R v Plymouth Arg
Fleetwood T v Cambridge U
Gillingham v Oxford U
Lincoln C v Burton Alb
Portsmouth v Charlton Ath
Sheffield W v Ipswich T
Wycombe W v Milton Keynes D

Saturday, 5 February 2022
Burton Alb v Sheffield W
Cambridge U v Wycombe W
Charlton Ath v AFC Wimbledon
Ipswich T v Gillingham
Milton Keynes D v Lincoln C
Morecambe v Bolton W
Oxford U v Portsmouth
Plymouth Arg v Cheltenham T
Rotherham U v Accrington S
Shrewsbury T v Fleetwood T
Sunderland v Doncaster R
Wigan Ath v Crewe Alex

Tuesday, 8 February 2022
Accrington S v Oxford U
AFC Wimbledon v Rotherham U
Cheltenham T v Sunderland
Crewe Alex v Plymouth Arg
Doncaster R v Ipswich T
Fleetwood T v Milton Keynes D
Gillingham v Cambridge U
Lincoln C v Morecambe
Portsmouth v Burton Alb
Sheffield W v Wigan Ath
Wycombe W v Shrewsbury T
Bolton W v Charlton Ath

Saturday, 12 February 2022
Accrington S v Crewe Alex
AFC Wimbledon v Sunderland
Burton Alb v Cambridge U
Cheltenham T v Fleetwood T
Lincoln C v Wycombe W
Milton Keynes D v Ipswich T
Morecambe v Gillingham
Oxford U v Bolton W
Plymouth Arg v Shrewsbury T
Portsmouth v Doncaster R
Sheffield W v Rotherham U
Wigan Ath v Charlton Ath

Saturday, 19 February 2022
Bolton W v AFC Wimbledon
Cambridge U v Accrington S
Charlton Ath v Oxford U
Crewe Alex v Portsmouth
Doncaster R v Sheffield W
Fleetwood T v Lincoln C
Gillingham v Plymouth Arg
Ipswich T v Burton Alb
Rotherham U v Wigan Ath
Shrewsbury T v Morecambe
Sunderland v Milton Keynes D
Wycombe W v Cheltenham T

Tuesday, 22 February 2022
Cambridge U v Plymouth Arg
Charlton Ath v Milton Keynes D
Crewe Alex v Oxford U
Doncaster R v Accrington S
Fleetwood T v Sheffield W
Gillingham v AFC Wimbledon
Ipswich T v Cheltenham T
Rotherham U v Morecambe
Shrewsbury T v Portsmouth
Sunderland v Burton Alb
Wycombe W v Wigan Ath
Bolton W v Lincoln C

Saturday, 26 February 2022
Accrington S v Wycombe W
AFC Wimbledon v Doncaster R
Burton Alb v Shrewsbury T
Cheltenham T v Crewe Alex
Lincoln C v Gillingham
Milton Keynes D v Bolton W
Morecambe v Ipswich T
Oxford U v Cambridge U
Plymouth Arg v Rotherham U
Portsmouth v Fleetwood T
Sheffield W v Charlton Ath
Wigan Ath v Sunderland

Saturday, 5 March 2022
Cambridge U v Shrewsbury T
Charlton Ath v Sunderland
Cheltenham T v Doncaster R
Crewe Alex v Wycombe W
Fleetwood T v Ipswich T
Gillingham v Bolton W
Lincoln C v Sheffield W
Oxford U v Burton Alb
Plymouth Arg v Morecambe
Portsmouth v Accrington S
Rotherham U v Milton Keynes D
Wigan Ath v AFC Wimbledon

Saturday, 12 March 2022
Accrington S v Charlton Ath
AFC Wimbledon v Lincoln C
Bolton W v Plymouth Arg
Burton Alb v Fleetwood T
Doncaster R v Gillingham
Ipswich T v Portsmouth
Milton Keynes D v Wigan Ath
Morecambe v Cheltenham T
Sheffield W v Cambridge U
Shrewsbury T v Oxford U
Sunderland v Crewe Alex
Wycombe W v Rotherham U

Saturday, 19 March 2022
Cambridge U v Milton Keynes D
Charlton Ath v Burton Alb
Cheltenham T v AFC Wimbledon
Crewe Alex v Bolton W
Fleetwood T v Doncaster R
Gillingham v Sheffield W
Lincoln C v Sunderland
Oxford U v Ipswich T
Plymouth Arg v Accrington S
Portsmouth v Wycombe W
Rotherham U v Shrewsbury T
Wigan Ath v Morecambe

Saturday, 26 March 2022
Accrington S v Gillingham
AFC Wimbledon v Cambridge U
Bolton W v Portsmouth
Burton Alb v Wigan Ath
Doncaster R v Charlton Ath
Ipswich T v Plymouth Arg
Milton Keynes D v Crewe Alex
Morecambe v Oxford U
Sheffield W v Cheltenham T
Shrewsbury T v Lincoln C
Sunderland v Rotherham U
Wycombe W v Fleetwood T

Saturday, 2 April 2022
Accrington S v Cheltenham T
Charlton Ath v Lincoln C
Crewe Alex v Fleetwood T
Ipswich T v Cambridge U
Milton Keynes D v Shrewsbury T
Morecambe v Burton Alb
Plymouth Arg v Oxford U
Portsmouth v Rotherham U
Sheffield W v AFC Wimbledon
Sunderland v Gillingham
Wigan Ath v Bolton W
Wycombe W v Doncaster R

Saturday, 9 April 2022
AFC Wimbledon v Milton Keynes D
Bolton W v Sheffield W
Burton Alb v Plymouth Arg
Cambridge U v Morecambe
Cheltenham T v Portsmouth
Doncaster R v Crewe Alex
Fleetwood T v Accrington S
Gillingham v Wycombe W
Lincoln C v Wigan Ath
Oxford U v Sunderland
Rotherham U v Charlton Ath
Shrewsbury T v Ipswich T

Friday, 15 April 2022
Accrington S v Burton Alb
Charlton Ath v Morecambe
Cheltenham T v Gillingham
Crewe Alex v AFC Wimbledon
Doncaster R v Bolton W
Fleetwood T v Oxford U
Milton Keynes D v Sheffield W
Portsmouth v Lincoln C
Rotherham U v Ipswich T
Sunderland v Shrewsbury T
Wigan Ath v Cambridge U
Wycombe W v Plymouth Arg

Monday, 18 April 2022
AFC Wimbledon v Wycombe W
Bolton W v Accrington S
Burton Alb v Rotherham U
Cambridge U v Charlton Ath
Gillingham v Fleetwood T
Ipswich T v Wigan Ath
Lincoln C v Cheltenham T
Morecambe v Portsmouth
Oxford U v Milton Keynes D
Plymouth Arg v Sunderland
Sheffield W v Crewe Alex
Shrewsbury T v Doncaster R

Saturday, 23 April 2022
Accrington S v Lincoln C
Charlton Ath v Shrewsbury T
Cheltenham T v Bolton W
Crewe Alex v Ipswich T
Doncaster R v Burton Alb
Fleetwood T v AFC Wimbledon
Milton Keynes D v Morecambe
Portsmouth v Gillingham
Rotherham U v Oxford U
Sunderland v Cambridge U
Wigan Ath v Plymouth Arg
Wycombe W v Sheffield W

Saturday, 30 April 2022
AFC Wimbledon v Accrington S
Bolton W v Fleetwood T
Burton Alb v Wycombe W
Cambridge U v Cheltenham T
Gillingham v Rotherham U
Ipswich T v Charlton Ath
Lincoln C v Crewe Alex
Morecambe v Sunderland
Oxford U v Doncaster R
Plymouth Arg v Milton Keynes D
Sheffield W v Portsmouth
Shrewsbury T v Wigan Ath

EFL League Two

Saturday, 7 August 2021
Carlisle U v Colchester U
Exeter C v Bradford C
Forest Green R v Sutton U
Harrogate T v Rochdale
Hartlepool U v Crawley T
Mansfield T v Bristol R
Northampton T v Port Vale
Oldham Ath v Newport Co
Salford C v Leyton Orient
Scunthorpe U v Swindon T
Stevenage v Barrow
Tranmere R v Walsall

Saturday, 14 August 2021
Barrow v Hartlepool U
Bradford C v Oldham Ath
Bristol R v Stevenage
Colchester U v Northampton T
Crawley T v Harrogate T
Leyton Orient v Exeter C
Newport Co v Mansfield T
Port Vale v Tranmere R
Rochdale v Scunthorpe U
Sutton U v Salford C
Swindon T v Carlisle U
Walsall v Forest Green R

Tuesday, 17 August 2021
Barrow v Exeter C
Bradford C v Stevenage
Bristol R v Oldham Ath
Colchester U v Mansfield T
Crawley T v Salford C
Leyton Orient v Harrogate T
Newport Co v Northampton T
Port Vale v Carlisle U
Rochdale v Forest Green R
Sutton U v Hartlepool U
Swindon T v Tranmere R
Walsall v Scunthorpe U

Saturday, 21 August 2021
Carlisle U v Leyton Orient
Exeter C v Bristol R
Forest Green R v Crawley T
Harrogate T v Barrow
Hartlepool U v Walsall
Mansfield T v Bradford C
Northampton T v Rochdale
Oldham Ath v Colchester U
Salford C v Swindon T
Scunthorpe U v Sutton U
Stevenage v Port Vale
Tranmere R v Newport Co

Saturday, 28 August 2021
Barrow v Bristol R
Crawley T v Northampton T
Forest Green R v Port Vale
Harrogate T v Exeter C
Hartlepool U v Carlisle U
Leyton Orient v Bradford C
Rochdale v Colchester U
Salford C v Newport Co
Scunthorpe U v Tranmere R
Sutton U v Oldham Ath
Swindon T v Mansfield T
Walsall v Stevenage

Saturday, 4 September 2021
Bradford C v Walsall
Bristol R v Crawley T
Carlisle U v Salford C
Colchester U v Sutton U
Exeter C v Forest Green R
Mansfield T v Harrogate T
Newport Co v Leyton Orient
Northampton T v Scunthorpe U
Oldham Ath v Barrow
Port Vale v Rochdale
Stevenage v Swindon T
Tranmere R v Hartlepool U

Saturday, 11 September 2021
Barrow v Colchester U
Crawley T v Carlisle U
Forest Green R v Northampton T
Harrogate T v Newport Co
Hartlepool U v Bristol R
Leyton Orient v Oldham Ath
Rochdale v Tranmere R
Salford C v Bradford C
Scunthorpe U v Exeter C
Sutton U v Stevenage
Swindon T v Port Vale
Walsall v Mansfield T

Saturday, 18 September 2021
Bradford C v Barrow
Bristol R v Leyton Orient
Carlisle U v Scunthorpe U
Colchester U v Crawley T
Exeter C v Sutton U
Mansfield T v Rochdale
Newport Co v Walsall
Northampton T v Swindon T
Oldham Ath v Hartlepool U
Port Vale v Harrogate T
Stevenage v Forest Green R
Tranmere R v Salford C

Saturday, 25 September 2021
Barrow v Newport Co
Crawley T v Bradford C
Forest Green R v Tranmere R
Harrogate T v Stevenage
Hartlepool U v Exeter C
Leyton Orient v Mansfield T
Rochdale v Oldham Ath
Salford C v Northampton T
Scunthorpe U v Port Vale
Sutton U v Carlisle U
Swindon T v Colchester U
Walsall v Bristol R

Saturday, 2 October 2021
Bradford C v Rochdale
Bristol R v Swindon T
Carlisle U v Forest Green R
Colchester U v Salford C
Exeter C v Walsall
Mansfield T v Barrow
Newport Co v Scunthorpe U
Northampton T v Sutton U
Oldham Ath v Harrogate T
Port Vale v Leyton Orient
Stevenage v Hartlepool U
Tranmere R v Crawley T

Saturday, 9 October 2021
Barrow v Leyton Orient
Bristol R v Carlisle U
Forest Green R v Swindon T
Harrogate T v Scunthorpe U
Hartlepool U v Northampton T
Mansfield T v Oldham Ath
Newport Co v Bradford C
Rochdale v Crawley T
Stevenage v Exeter C
Sutton U v Port Vale
Tranmere R v Colchester U
Walsall v Salford C

Saturday, 16 October 2021
Bradford C v Bristol R
Carlisle U v Tranmere R
Colchester U v Harrogate T
Crawley T v Sutton U
Exeter C v Newport Co

Leyton Orient v Walsall
Northampton T v Mansfield T
Oldham Ath v Stevenage
Port Vale v Barrow
Salford C v Hartlepool U
Scunthorpe U v Forest Green R
Swindon T v Rochdale

Tuesday, 19 October 2021
Barrow v Scunthorpe U
Bradford C v Hartlepool U
Colchester U v Bristol R
Crawley T v Exeter C
Harrogate T v Tranmere R
Leyton Orient v Forest Green R
Mansfield T v Port Vale
Newport Co v Carlisle U
Northampton T v Stevenage
Oldham Ath v Walsall
Salford C v Rochdale
Sutton U v Swindon T

Saturday, 23 October 2021
Bristol R v Newport Co
Carlisle U v Oldham Ath
Exeter C v Mansfield T
Forest Green R v Salford C
Hartlepool U v Harrogate T
Port Vale v Colchester U
Rochdale v Sutton U
Scunthorpe U v Crawley T
Stevenage v Leyton Orient
Swindon T v Bradford C
Tranmere R v Northampton T
Walsall v Barrow

Saturday, 30 October 2021
Barrow v Rochdale
Bradford C v Forest Green R
Colchester U v Scunthorpe U
Crawley T v Port Vale
Harrogate T v Bristol R
Leyton Orient v Hartlepool U
Mansfield T v Tranmere R
Newport Co v Stevenage
Northampton T v Carlisle U
Oldham Ath v Swindon T
Salford C v Exeter C
Sutton U v Walsall

Saturday, 13 November 2021
Bristol R v Northampton T
Carlisle U v Barrow
Exeter C v Oldham Ath
Forest Green R v Colchester U
Hartlepool U v Newport Co
Port Vale v Bradford C
Rochdale v Leyton Orient
Scunthorpe U v Salford C
Stevenage v Mansfield T
Swindon T v Crawley T
Tranmere R v Sutton U
Walsall v Harrogate T

Saturday, 20 November 2021
Barrow v Crawley T
Bradford C v Northampton T
Bristol R v Tranmere R
Exeter C v Carlisle U
Harrogate T v Salford C
Hartlepool U v Forest Green R
Leyton Orient v Sutton U
Mansfield T v Scunthorpe U
Newport Co v Swindon T
Oldham Ath v Port Vale
Stevenage v Colchester U
Walsall v Rochdale

Tuesday, 23 November 2021
Carlisle U v Harrogate T
Colchester U v Exeter C
Crawley T v Newport Co
Forest Green R v Barrow
Northampton T v Oldham Ath
Port Vale v Walsall
Rochdale v Stevenage
Salford C v Bristol R
Scunthorpe U v Leyton Orient
Sutton U v Mansfield T
Swindon T v Hartlepool U
Tranmere R v Bradford C

Saturday, 27 November 2021
Carlisle U v Walsall
Colchester U v Newport Co
Crawley T v Mansfield T
Forest Green R v Bristol R
Northampton T v Leyton Orient
Port Vale v Hartlepool U
Rochdale v Exeter C
Salford C v Oldham Ath
Scunthorpe U v Bradford C
Sutton U v Barrow
Swindon T v Harrogate T
Tranmere R v Stevenage

Tuesday, 7 December 2021
Barrow v Salford C
Bradford C v Colchester U
Bristol R v Port Vale
Exeter C v Northampton T
Harrogate T v Forest Green R
Hartlepool U v Rochdale
Leyton Orient v Swindon T
Mansfield T v Carlisle U
Newport Co v Sutton U
Oldham Ath v Tranmere R
Stevenage v Scunthorpe U
Walsall v Crawley T

Saturday, 11 December 2021
Barrow v Swindon T
Bradford C v Sutton U
Bristol R v Rochdale
Exeter C v Tranmere R
Harrogate T v Northampton T
Hartlepool U v Scunthorpe U
Leyton Orient v Crawley T
Mansfield T v Salford C
Newport Co v Port Vale
Oldham Ath v Forest Green R
Stevenage v Carlisle U
Walsall v Colchester U

Saturday, 18 December 2021
Carlisle U v Bradford C
Colchester U v Hartlepool U
Crawley T v Oldham Ath
Forest Green R v Mansfield T
Northampton T v Barrow
Port Vale v Exeter C
Rochdale v Newport Co
Salford C v Stevenage
Scunthorpe U v Bristol R
Sutton U v Harrogate T
Swindon T v Walsall
Tranmere R v Leyton Orient

Sunday, 26 December 2021
Bradford C v Harrogate T
Bristol R v Sutton U
Carlisle U v Rochdale
Colchester U v Leyton Orient
Exeter C v Swindon T
Mansfield T v Hartlepool U
Newport Co v Forest Green R
Northampton T v Walsall
Oldham Ath v Scunthorpe U
Port Vale v Salford C
Stevenage v Crawley T
Tranmere R v Barrow

Wednesday, 29 December 2021
Barrow v Oldham Ath
Crawley T v Bristol R
Forest Green R v Exeter C
Harrogate T v Mansfield T
Hartlepool U v Tranmere R
Leyton Orient v Newport Co
Rochdale v Port Vale
Salford C v Carlisle U
Scunthorpe U v Northampton T
Sutton U v Colchester U
Swindon T v Stevenage
Walsall v Bradford C

Saturday, 1 January 2022
Barrow v Bradford C
Crawley T v Colchester U
Forest Green R v Stevenage
Harrogate T v Port Vale
Hartlepool U v Oldham Ath
Leyton Orient v Bristol R
Rochdale v Mansfield T
Salford C v Tranmere R
Scunthorpe U v Carlisle U
Sutton U v Exeter C
Swindon T v Northampton T
Walsall v Newport Co

Saturday, 8 January 2022
Bradford C v Leyton Orient
Bristol R v Barrow
Carlisle U v Hartlepool U
Colchester U v Rochdale
Exeter C v Harrogate T
Mansfield T v Swindon T
Newport Co v Salford C
Northampton T v Crawley T
Oldham Ath v Sutton U
Port Vale v Forest Green R
Stevenage v Walsall
Tranmere R v Scunthorpe U

Saturday, 15 January 2022
Bradford C v Salford C
Bristol R v Hartlepool U
Carlisle U v Crawley T
Colchester U v Barrow
Exeter C v Scunthorpe U
Mansfield T v Walsall
Newport Co v Harrogate T
Northampton T v Forest Green R
Oldham Ath v Leyton Orient
Port Vale v Swindon T
Stevenage v Sutton U
Tranmere R v Rochdale

Saturday, 22 January 2022
Barrow v Mansfield T
Crawley T v Tranmere R
Forest Green R v Carlisle U
Harrogate T v Oldham Ath
Hartlepool U v Stevenage
Leyton Orient v Port Vale
Rochdale v Bradford C
Salford C v Colchester U
Scunthorpe U v Newport Co
Sutton U v Northampton T
Swindon T v Bristol R
Walsall v Exeter C

Saturday, 29 January 2022
Bradford C v Crawley T
Bristol R v Walsall
Carlisle U v Sutton U
Colchester U v Swindon T
Exeter C v Hartlepool U
Mansfield T v Leyton Orient
Newport Co v Barrow
Northampton T v Salford C
Oldham Ath v Rochdale
Port Vale v Scunthorpe U
Stevenage v Harrogate T
Tranmere R v Forest Green R

Saturday, 5 February 2022
Barrow v Tranmere R
Crawley T v Stevenage
Forest Green R v Newport Co
Harrogate T v Bradford C
Hartlepool U v Mansfield T
Leyton Orient v Colchester U
Rochdale v Carlisle U
Salford C v Port Vale
Scunthorpe U v Oldham Ath
Sutton U v Bristol R
Swindon T v Exeter C
Walsall v Northampton T

Tuesday, 8 February 2022
Carlisle U v Port Vale
Exeter C v Leyton Orient
Forest Green R v Rochdale
Harrogate T v Crawley T
Hartlepool U v Barrow
Mansfield T v Colchester U
Northampton T v Newport Co
Oldham Ath v Bristol R
Salford C v Sutton U
Scunthorpe U v Walsall
Stevenage v Bradford C
Tranmere R v Swindon T

Saturday, 12 February 2022
Barrow v Stevenage
Bradford C v Exeter C
Bristol R v Mansfield T
Colchester U v Carlisle U
Crawley T v Hartlepool U
Leyton Orient v Salford C
Newport Co v Oldham Ath
Port Vale v Northampton T
Rochdale v Harrogate T
Sutton U v Forest Green R
Swindon T v Scunthorpe U
Walsall v Tranmere R

Saturday, 19 February 2022
Carlisle U v Swindon T
Exeter C v Barrow
Forest Green R v Walsall
Harrogate T v Leyton Orient
Hartlepool U v Sutton U
Mansfield T v Newport Co
Northampton T v Colchester U
Oldham Ath v Bradford C
Salford C v Crawley T
Scunthorpe U v Rochdale
Stevenage v Bristol R
Tranmere R v Port Vale

Saturday, 26 February 2022
Barrow v Harrogate T
Bradford C v Mansfield T
Bristol R v Exeter C
Colchester U v Oldham Ath
Crawley T v Forest Green R
Leyton Orient v Carlisle U
Newport Co v Tranmere R
Port Vale v Stevenage
Rochdale v Northampton T
Sutton U v Scunthorpe U
Swindon T v Salford C
Walsall v Hartlepool U

Saturday, 5 March 2022
Barrow v Walsall
Bradford C v Swindon T
Colchester U v Port Vale
Crawley T v Scunthorpe U
Harrogate T v Hartlepool U
Leyton Orient v Stevenage
Mansfield T v Exeter C
Newport Co v Bristol R
Northampton T v Tranmere R
Oldham Ath v Carlisle U
Salford C v Forest Green R
Sutton U v Rochdale

Saturday, 12 March 2022
Bristol R v Harrogate T
Carlisle U v Northampton T
Exeter C v Salford C
Forest Green R v Bradford C
Hartlepool U v Leyton Orient
Port Vale v Crawley T
Rochdale v Barrow
Scunthorpe U v Colchester U
Stevenage v Newport Co
Swindon T v Oldham Ath
Tranmere R v Mansfield T
Walsall v Sutton U

Tuesday, 15 March 2022
Bristol R v Colchester U
Carlisle U v Newport Co
Exeter C v Crawley T
Forest Green R v Leyton Orient
Hartlepool U v Bradford C
Port Vale v Mansfield T
Rochdale v Salford C
Scunthorpe U v Barrow
Stevenage v Northampton T
Swindon T v Sutton U
Tranmere R v Harrogate T
Walsall v Oldham Ath

Saturday, 19 March 2022
Barrow v Carlisle U
Bradford C v Port Vale
Colchester U v Forest Green R
Crawley T v Swindon T
Harrogate T v Walsall
Leyton Orient v Rochdale
Mansfield T v Stevenage
Newport Co v Hartlepool U
Northampton T v Bristol R
Oldham Ath v Exeter C
Salford C v Scunthorpe U
Sutton U v Tranmere R

Saturday, 26 March 2022
Bradford C v Newport Co
Carlisle U v Bristol R
Colchester U v Tranmere R
Crawley T v Rochdale
Exeter C v Stevenage
Leyton Orient v Barrow
Northampton T v Hartlepool U
Oldham Ath v Mansfield T
Port Vale v Sutton U
Salford C v Walsall
Scunthorpe U v Harrogate T
Swindon T v Forest Green R

Saturday, 2 April 2022
Barrow v Port Vale
Bristol R v Bradford C
Forest Green R v Scunthorpe U
Harrogate T v Colchester U
Hartlepool U v Salford C
Mansfield T v Northampton T
Newport Co v Exeter C
Rochdale v Swindon T
Stevenage v Oldham Ath
Sutton U v Crawley T
Tranmere R v Carlisle U
Walsall v Leyton Orient

Saturday, 9 April 2022
Carlisle U v Exeter C
Colchester U v Stevenage
Crawley T v Barrow
Forest Green R v Hartlepool U
Northampton T v Bradford C
Port Vale v Oldham Ath
Rochdale v Walsall
Salford C v Harrogate T
Scunthorpe U v Mansfield T
Sutton U v Leyton Orient
Swindon T v Newport Co
Tranmere R v Bristol R

Friday, 15 April 2022
Barrow v Forest Green R
Bradford C v Tranmere R
Bristol R v Salford C
Exeter C v Colchester U
Harrogate T v Swindon T
Hartlepool U v Port Vale
Leyton Orient v Scunthorpe U
Mansfield T v Sutton U
Newport Co v Crawley T
Oldham Ath v Northampton T
Stevenage v Rochdale
Walsall v Carlisle U

Monday, 18 April 2022
Carlisle U v Mansfield T
Colchester U v Bradford C
Crawley T v Walsall
Forest Green R v Oldham Ath
Northampton T v Harrogate T
Port Vale v Bristol R
Rochdale v Hartlepool U
Salford C v Barrow
Scunthorpe U v Stevenage
Sutton U v Newport Co
Swindon T v Leyton Orient
Tranmere R v Exeter C

Saturday, 23 April 2022
Barrow v Sutton U
Bradford C v Scunthorpe U
Bristol R v Forest Green R
Exeter C v Rochdale
Harrogate T v Carlisle U
Hartlepool U v Swindon T
Leyton Orient v Northampton T
Mansfield T v Crawley T
Newport Co v Colchester U
Oldham Ath v Salford C
Stevenage v Tranmere R
Walsall v Port Vale

Saturday, 30 April 2022
Carlisle U v Stevenage
Colchester U v Walsall
Crawley T v Leyton Orient
Forest Green R v Harrogate T
Northampton T v Exeter C
Port Vale v Newport Co
Rochdale v Bristol R
Salford C v Mansfield T
Scunthorpe U v Hartlepool U
Sutton U v Bradford C
Swindon T v Barrow
Tranmere R v Oldham Ath

Saturday, 7 May 2022
Barrow v Northampton T
Bradford C v Carlisle U
Bristol R v Scunthorpe U
Exeter C v Port Vale
Harrogate T v Sutton U
Hartlepool U v Colchester U
Leyton Orient v Tranmere R
Mansfield T v Forest Green R
Newport Co v Rochdale
Oldham Ath v Crawley T
Stevenage v Salford C
Walsall v Swindon T

NATIONAL LEAGUE FIXTURES 2021–22

All fixtures subject to change.

Saturday, 21 August 2021
Aldershot T v Chesterfield
Barnet v Notts Co
Bromley v Grimsby T
Dover Ath v Solihull Moors
FC Halifax T v Maidenhead U
Kingís Lynn T v Southend U
Stockport Co v Dagenham & R
Torquay U v Altrincham
Wealdstone v Woking
Weymouth v Boreham Wood
Wrexham v Yeovil T

Saturday, 28 August 2021
Boreham Wood v Aldershot T
Chesterfield v Wealdstone
Dagenham & R v Bromley
Eastleigh v Wrexham
Grimsby T v Weymouth
Maidenhead U v Dover Ath
Notts Co v Torquay U
Solihull Moors v Barnet
Southend U v Stockport Co
Woking v FC Halifax T
Yeovil T v Kingís Lynn T

Monday, 30 August 2021
Aldershot T v Yeovil T
Barnet v Dagenham & R
Bromley v Eastleigh
Dover Ath v Boreham Wood
FC Halifax T v Altrincham
Kingís Lynn T v Chesterfield
Stockport Co v Grimsby T
Torquay U v Woking
Wealdstone v Southend U
Weymouth v Maidenhead U
Wrexham v Notts Co

Saturday, 4 September 2021
Altrincham v Dover Ath
Boreham Wood v Stockport Co
Chesterfield v Bromley
Dagenham & R v Wealdstone
Eastleigh v Kingís Lynn T
Grimsby T v Barnet
Maidenhead U v Torquay U
Notts Co v Aldershot T
Solihull Moors v Weymouth
Southend U v Wrexham
Yeovil T v FC Halifax T

Saturday, 11 September 2021
Aldershot T v Solihull Moors
Barnet v Eastleigh
Bromley v Boreham Wood
Dover Ath v Chesterfield
FC Halifax T v Southend U
Kingís Lynn T v Dagenham & R
Stockport Co v Yeovil T
Torquay U v Grimsby T
Wealdstone v Altrincham
Weymouth v Notts Co
Wrexham v Woking

Tuesday, 14 September 2021
Altrincham v Kingís Lynn T
Boreham Wood v FC Halifax T
Chesterfield v Barnet
Dagenham & R v Weymouth
Eastleigh v Dover Ath
Grimsby T v Wrexham
Maidenhead U v Stockport Co
Notts Co v Wealdstone
Solihull Moors v Torquay U
Southend U v Aldershot T
Woking v Bromley

Saturday, 18 September 2021
Bromley v Barnet
FC Halifax T v Stockport Co
Grimsby T v Eastleigh
Notts Co v Maidenhead U
Solihull Moors v Boreham Wood
Torquay U v Southend U
Wealdstone v Aldershot T
Weymouth v Dover Ath
Woking v Chesterfield
Wrexham v Dagenham & R
Yeovil T v Altrincham

Saturday, 25 September 2021
Aldershot T v FC Halifax T
Altrincham v Notts Co
Barnet v Weymouth
Boreham Wood v Yeovil T
Chesterfield v Torquay U
Dagenham & R v Solihull Moors
Dover Ath v Bromley
Eastleigh v Woking
Kingís Lynn T v Wealdstone
Maidenhead U v Grimsby T
Stockport Co v Wrexham

Saturday, 2 October 2021
Aldershot T v Wrexham
Barnet v FC Halifax T
Chesterfield v Yeovil T
Dagenham & R v Altrincham
Eastleigh v Boreham Wood
Grimsby T v Dover Ath
Maidenhead U v Kingís Lynn T
Notts Co v Woking
Solihull Moors v Southend U
Torquay U v Wealdstone
Weymouth v Stockport Co

Tuesday, 5 October 2021
Altrincham v Grimsby T
Boreham Wood v Torquay U
Bromley v Weymouth
Dover Ath v Aldershot T
FC Halifax T v Notts Co
Kingís Lynn T v Barnet
Southend U v Eastleigh
Wealdstone v Solihull Moors
Woking v Dagenham & R
Wrexham v Chesterfield
Yeovil T v Maidenhead U

Saturday, 9 October 2021
Altrincham v Maidenhead U
Boreham Wood v Dagenham & R
Bromley v Torquay U
Dover Ath v Barnet
FC Halifax T v Weymouth
Kingís Lynn T v Solihull Moors
Southend U v Chesterfield
Stockport Co v Aldershot T
Wealdstone v Eastleigh
Woking v Grimsby T
Yeovil T v Notts Co

Saturday, 23 October 2021
Aldershot T v Bromley
Barnet v Wrexham
Chesterfield v Boreham Wood
Dagenham & R v Southend U
Eastleigh v Altrincham
Grimsby T v Yeovil T
Maidenhead U v Woking
Notts Co v Stockport Co
Solihull Moors v FC Halifax T
Torquay U v Kingís Lynn T
Weymouth v Wealdstone

Tuesday, 26 October 2021
Aldershot T v Weymouth
Altrincham v Solihull Moors
Chesterfield v Eastleigh
FC Halifax T v Dagenham & R
Kingís Lynn T v Boreham Wood
Maidenhead U v Wrexham
Notts Co v Bromley
Southend U v Dover Ath
Stockport Co v Barnet
Wealdstone v Grimsby T
Yeovil T v Woking

Saturday, 30 October 2021
Barnet v Aldershot T
Boreham Wood v Southend U
Bromley v FC Halifax T
Dagenham & R v Chesterfield
Dover Ath v Stockport Co
Eastleigh v Maidenhead U
Grimsby T v Notts Co
Solihull Moors v Yeovil T
Weymouth v Kingís Lynn T
Woking v Altrincham
Wrexham v Torquay U

Saturday, 13 November 2021
Aldershot T v Grimsby T
Altrincham v Boreham Wood
Chesterfield v Weymouth
Kingís Lynn T v Wrexham
Maidenhead U v Dagenham & R
Notts Co v Solihull Moors
Southend U v Woking
Stockport Co v Bromley
Torquay U v Dover Ath
Wealdstone v Barnet
Yeovil T v Eastleigh

Saturday, 20 November 2021
Barnet v Torquay U
Boreham Wood v Maidenhead U
Bromley v Kingís Lynn T
Dagenham & R v Yeovil T
Dover Ath v FC Halifax T
Eastleigh v Notts Co
Grimsby T v Southend U
Solihull Moors v Chesterfield

Weymouth v Altrincham
Woking v Stockport Co
Wrexham v Wealdstone

Tuesday, 23 November 2021
Aldershot T v Torquay U
Boreham Wood v Notts Co
Bromley v Yeovil T
Chesterfield v Altrincham
Dagenham & R v Eastleigh
Dover Ath v Wealdstone
FC Halifax T v Wrexham
Solihull Moors v Grimsby T
Southend U v Maidenhead U
Stockport Co v Kingís Lynn T
Weymouth v Woking

Saturday, 27 November 2021
Altrincham v Southend U
Eastleigh v Solihull Moors
Grimsby T v Boreham Wood
Kingís Lynn T v Aldershot T
Maidenhead U v Chesterfield
Notts Co v Dagenham & R
Torquay U v FC Halifax T
Wealdstone v Stockport Co
Woking v Barnet
Wrexham v Bromley
Yeovil T v Dover Ath

Saturday, 4 December 2021
Aldershot T v Altrincham
Barnet v Maidenhead U
Bromley v Wealdstone
Chesterfield v Notts Co
Dagenham & R v Grimsby T
Dover Ath v Wrexham
FC Halifax T v Kingís Lynn T
Solihull Moors v Woking
Southend U v Yeovil T
Stockport Co v Eastleigh
Weymouth v Torquay U

Saturday, 11 December 2021
Altrincham v Bromley
Eastleigh v Aldershot T
Grimsby T v Chesterfield
Kingís Lynn T v Dover Ath
Maidenhead U v Solihull Moors
Notts Co v Southend U
Torquay U v Stockport Co
Wealdstone v FC Halifax T
Woking v Boreham Wood
Wrexham v Weymouth
Yeovil T v Barnet

Sunday, 26 December 2021
Aldershot T v Woking
Barnet v Boreham Wood
Bromley v Southend U
Dover Ath v Dagenham & R
FC Halifax T v Grimsby T
Kingís Lynn T v Notts Co
Stockport Co v Altrincham
Torquay U v Yeovil T
Wealdstone v Maidenhead U
Weymouth v Eastleigh
Wrexham v Solihull Moors

Tuesday, 28 December 2021
Altrincham v Wrexham
Boreham Wood v Wealdstone
Chesterfield v FC Halifax T
Dagenham & R v Aldershot T
Eastleigh v Torquay U
Grimsby T v Kingís Lynn T
Maidenhead U v Bromley

Solihull Moors v Stockport Co
Southend U v Barnet
Woking v Dover Ath
Yeovil T v Weymouth

Sunday, 2 January 2022
Altrincham v Stockport Co
Boreham Wood v Barnet
Chesterfield v Kingís Lynn T
Dagenham & R v Dover Ath
Eastleigh v Weymouth
Grimsby T v FC Halifax T
Maidenhead U v Wealdstone
Notts Co v Wrexham
Southend U v Bromley
Woking v Aldershot T
Yeovil T v Torquay U

Saturday, 8 January 2022
Aldershot T v Maidenhead U
Barnet v Altrincham
Bromley v Solihull Moors
Dover Ath v Notts Co
FC Halifax T v Eastleigh
Kingís Lynn T v Woking
Stockport Co v Chesterfield
Torquay U v Dagenham & R
Wealdstone v Yeovil T
Weymouth v Southend U
Wrexham v Boreham Wood

Saturday, 22 January 2022
Altrincham v Torquay U
Boreham Wood v Weymouth
Chesterfield v Aldershot T
Dagenham & R v Stockport Co
Grimsby T v Bromley
Maidenhead U v FC Halifax T
Notts Co v Barnet
Solihull Moors v Dover Ath
Southend U v Kingís Lynn T
Woking v Wealdstone
Yeovil T v Wrexham

Tuesday, 25 January 2022
Aldershot T v Southend U
Barnet v Chesterfield
Bromley v Woking
Dover Ath v Eastleigh
FC Halifax T v Boreham Wood
Kingís Lynn T v Altrincham
Stockport Co v Maidenhead U
Torquay U v Solihull Moors
Wealdstone v Notts Co
Weymouth v Dagenham & R
Wrexham v Grimsby T

Saturday, 29 January 2022
Barnet v Stockport Co
Boreham Wood v Kingís Lynn T
Bromley v Notts Co
Dagenham & R v FC Halifax T
Dover Ath v Southend U
Eastleigh v Chesterfield
Grimsby T v Wealdstone
Solihull Moors v Altrincham
Weymouth v Aldershot T
Woking v Yeovil T
Wrexham v Maidenhead U

Saturday, 5 February 2022
Aldershot T v Barnet
Altrincham v Woking
Chesterfield v Dagenham & R
FC Halifax T v Bromley
Kingís Lynn T v Weymouth
Maidenhead U v Eastleigh

Notts Co v Grimsby T
Southend U v Boreham Wood
Stockport Co v Dover Ath
Torquay U v Wrexham
Yeovil T v Solihull Moors

Saturday, 12 February 2022
Barnet v Wealdstone
Boreham Wood v Altrincham
Bromley v Stockport Co
Dagenham & R v Maidenhead U
Dover Ath v Torquay U
Eastleigh v Yeovil T
Grimsby T v Aldershot T
Solihull Moors v Notts Co
Weymouth v Chesterfield
Woking v Southend U
Wrexham v Kingís Lynn T

Saturday, 19 February 2022
Altrincham v Weymouth
Chesterfield v Solihull Moors
FC Halifax T v Dover Ath
Kingís Lynn T v Bromley
Maidenhead U v Boreham Wood
Notts Co v Eastleigh
Southend U v Grimsby T
Stockport Co v Woking
Torquay U v Barnet
Wealdstone v Wrexham
Yeovil T v Dagenham & R

Tuesday, 22 February 2022
Aldershot T v Dover Ath
Barnet v Kingís Lynn T
Chesterfield v Wrexham
Dagenham & R v Woking
Eastleigh v Southend U
Grimsby T v Altrincham
Maidenhead U v Yeovil T
Notts Co v FC Halifax T
Solihull Moors v Wealdstone
Torquay U v Boreham Wood
Weymouth v Bromley

Saturday, 26 February 2022
Altrincham v Dagenham & R
Boreham Wood v Eastleigh
Dover Ath v Grimsby T
FC Halifax T v Barnet
Kingís Lynn T v Maidenhead U
Southend U v Solihull Moors
Stockport Co v Weymouth
Wealdstone v Torquay U
Woking v Notts Co
Wrexham v Aldershot T
Yeovil T v Chesterfield

Saturday, 5 March 2022
Aldershot T v Stockport Co
Barnet v Dover Ath
Chesterfield v Southend U
Dagenham & R v Boreham Wood
Eastleigh v Wealdstone
Grimsby T v Woking
Maidenhead U v Altrincham
Notts Co v Yeovil T
Solihull Moors v Kingís Lynn T
Torquay U v Bromley
Weymouth v FC Halifax T

Saturday, 12 March 2022
Altrincham v Eastleigh
Boreham Wood v Chesterfield
Bromley v Aldershot T
FC Halifax T v Solihull Moors
Kingís Lynn T v Torquay U

Southend U v Dagenham & R
Stockport Co v Notts Co
Wealdstone v Weymouth
Woking v Maidenhead U
Wrexham v Barnet
Yeovil T v Grimsby T

Saturday, 19 March 2022
Aldershot T v Kingís Lynn T
Barnet v Woking
Boreham Wood v Grimsby T
Bromley v Wrexham
Chesterfield v Maidenhead U
Dagenham & R v Notts Co
Dover Ath v Yeovil T
FC Halifax T v Torquay U
Solihull Moors v Eastleigh
Southend U v Altrincham
Stockport Co v Wealdstone

Tuesday, 22 March 2022
Altrincham v Chesterfield
Eastleigh v Dagenham & R
Grimsby T v Solihull Moors
Kingís Lynn T v Stockport Co
Maidenhead U v Southend U
Notts Co v Boreham Wood
Torquay U v Aldershot T
Wealdstone v Dover Ath
Woking v Weymouth
Wrexham v FC Halifax T
Yeovil T v Bromley

Saturday, 26 March 2022
Altrincham v Aldershot T
Eastleigh v Stockport Co
Grimsby T v Dagenham & R
Kingís Lynn T v FC Halifax T
Maidenhead U v Barnet
Notts Co v Chesterfield
Torquay U v Weymouth
Wealdstone v Bromley
Woking v Solihull Moors
Wrexham v Dover Ath
Yeovil T v Southend U

Saturday, 2 April 2022
Aldershot T v Eastleigh
Barnet v Yeovil T
Boreham Wood v Woking
Bromley v Altrincham
Chesterfield v Grimsby T
Dover Ath v Kingís Lynn T
FC Halifax T v Wealdstone
Solihull Moors v Maidenhead U
Southend U v Notts Co
Stockport Co v Torquay U
Weymouth v Wrexham

Saturday, 9 April 2022
Aldershot T v Boreham Wood
Barnet v Solihull Moors
Bromley v Dagenham & R
Dover Ath v Maidenhead U
FC Halifax T v Woking
Kingís Lynn T v Yeovil T
Stockport Co v Southend U
Torquay U v Notts Co
Wealdstone v Chesterfield
Weymouth v Grimsby T
Wrexham v Eastleigh

Friday, 15 April 2022
Altrincham v FC Halifax T
Boreham Wood v Dover Ath
Dagenham & R v Barnet
Eastleigh v Bromley
Grimsby T v Stockport Co
Maidenhead U v Weymouth
Notts Co v Kingís Lynn T
Solihull Moors v Wrexham
Southend U v Wealdstone
Woking v Torquay U
Yeovil T v Aldershot T

Monday, 18 April 2022
Aldershot T v Dagenham & R
Barnet v Southend U
Bromley v Maidenhead U
Dover Ath v Woking
FC Halifax T v Chesterfield
Kingís Lynn T v Grimsby T
Stockport Co v Solihull Moors
Torquay U v Eastleigh
Wealdstone v Boreham Wood
Weymouth v Yeovil T
Wrexham v Altrincham

Saturday, 23 April 2022
Altrincham v Wealdstone
Boreham Wood v Bromley
Chesterfield v Dover Ath
Dagenham & R v Kingís Lynn T
Eastleigh v Barnet
Grimsby T v Torquay U
Notts Co v Weymouth
Solihull Moors v Aldershot T
Southend U v FC Halifax T
Woking v Wrexham
Yeovil T v Stockport Co

Saturday, 30 April 2022
Aldershot T v Notts Co
Barnet v Grimsby T
Bromley v Chesterfield
Dover Ath v Altrincham
FC Halifax T v Yeovil T
Kingís Lynn T v Eastleigh
Stockport Co v Boreham Wood
Torquay U v Maidenhead U
Wealdstone v Dagenham & R
Weymouth v Solihull Moors
Wrexham v Southend U

Monday, 2 May 2022
Altrincham v Barnet
Boreham Wood v Wrexham
Chesterfield v Stockport Co
Dagenham & R v Torquay U
Eastleigh v FC Halifax T
Maidenhead U v Aldershot T
Notts Co v Dover Ath
Solihull Moors v Bromley
Southend U v Weymouth
Woking v Kingís Lynn T
Yeovil T v Wealdstone

Saturday, 7 May 2022
Bromley v Dover Ath
FC Halifax T v Aldershot T
Grimsby T v Maidenhead U
Notts Co v Altrincham
Solihull Moors v Dagenham & R
Torquay U v Chesterfield
Wealdstone v Kingís Lynn T
Weymouth v Barnet
Woking v Eastleigh
Wrexham v Stockport Co
Yeovil T v Boreham Wood

Sunday, 15 May 2022
Aldershot T v Wealdstone
Altrincham v Yeovil T
Barnet v Bromley
Boreham Wood v Solihull Moors
Chesterfield v Woking
Dagenham & R v Wrexham
Dover Ath v Weymouth
Eastleigh v Grimsby T
Maidenhead U v Notts Co
Southend U v Torquay U
Stockport Co v FC Halifax T

THE SCOTTISH PREMIER LEAGUE AND SCOTTISH LEAGUE FIXTURES 2021–22

All fixtures subject to change.

cinch Premiership

Saturday, 31 July 2021
Rangers v Livingston
Dundee v St Mirren
Ross Co v St Johnstone
Hearts v Celtic

Sunday, 1 August 2021
Aberdeen v Dundee U
Motherwell v Hibernian

Saturday, 7 August 2021
Celtic v Dundee
Dundee U v Rangers
Hibernian v Ross Co
Livingston v Aberdeen
St Mirren v Hearts

Sunday, 8 August 2021
St Johnstone v Motherwell

Saturday, 21 August 2021
Celtic v St Mirren
Dundee v Hibernian
Hearts v Aberdeen
Livingston v Motherwell
Ross Co v Rangers
St Johnstone v Dundee U

Saturday, 28 August 2021
Aberdeen v Ross Co
Dundee U v Hearts
Hibernian v Livingston
Motherwell v Dundee
Rangers v Celtic
St Mirren v St Johnstone

Saturday, 11 September 2021
Celtic v Ross Co
Dundee v Livingston
Hearts v Hibernian
Motherwell v Aberdeen
St Johnstone v Rangers
St Mirren v Dundee U

Saturday, 18 September 2021
Aberdeen v St Johnstone
Dundee U v Dundee
Hibernian v St Mirren
Livingston v Celtic
Rangers v Motherwell
Ross Co v Hearts

Saturday, 25 September 2021
Celtic v Dundee U
Dundee v Rangers
Hearts v Livingston
Hibernian v St Johnstone
Motherwell v Ross Co
St Mirren v Aberdeen

Saturday, 2 October 2021
Aberdeen v Celtic
Dundee U v Ross Co
Hearts v Motherwell
Livingston v St Mirren
Rangers v Hibernian
St Johnstone v Dundee

Saturday, 16 October 2021
Dundee v Aberdeen
Hibernian v Dundee U
Motherwell v Celtic
Rangers v Hearts
Ross Co v St Mirren
St Johnstone v Livingston

Saturday, 23 October 2021
Aberdeen v Hibernian
Celtic v St Johnstone
Dundee U v Motherwell
Hearts v Dundee
Ross Co v Livingston
St Mirren v Rangers

Wednesday, 27 October 2021
Dundee v Ross Co
Hibernian v Celtic
Livingston v Dundee U
Motherwell v St Mirren
Rangers v Aberdeen
St Johnstone v Hearts

Saturday, 30 October 2021
Aberdeen v Hearts
Celtic v Livingston
Dundee U v St Johnstone
Motherwell v Rangers
Ross Co v Hibernian
St Mirren v Dundee

Saturday, 6 November 2021
Aberdeen v Motherwell
Dundee v Celtic
Hearts v Dundee U
Livingston v Hibernian
Rangers v Ross Co
St Johnstone v St Mirren

Saturday, 20 November 2021
Dundee U v Aberdeen
Hibernian v Dundee
Motherwell v Hearts
Rangers v St Johnstone
Ross Co v Celtic
St Mirren v Livingston

Saturday, 27 November 2021
Celtic v Aberdeen
Dundee v Motherwell
Hearts v St Mirren
Livingston v Rangers
Ross Co v Dundee U
St Johnstone v Hibernian

Wednesday, 1 December 2021
Aberdeen v Livingston
Celtic v Hearts
Dundee v St Johnstone
Hibernian v Rangers
Motherwell v Dundee U
St Mirren v Ross Co

Saturday, 4 December 2021
Aberdeen v St Mirren
Dundee U v Celtic
Hibernian v Motherwell
Livingston v Hearts
Rangers v Dundee
St Johnstone v Ross Co

Saturday, 11 December 2021
Celtic v Motherwell
Dundee U v Livingston
Hearts v Rangers
Ross Co v Dundee
St Johnstone v Aberdeen
St Mirren v Hibernian

Saturday, 18 December 2021
Dundee v Hearts
Hibernian v Aberdeen
Livingston v Ross Co
Motherwell v St Johnstone
Rangers v Dundee U
St Mirren v Celtic

Sunday, 26 December 2021
Aberdeen v Dundee
Dundee U v Hibernian
Hearts v Ross Co
Motherwell v Livingston
Rangers v St Mirren
St Johnstone v Celtic

Wednesday, 29 December 2021
Aberdeen v Rangers
Celtic v Hibernian
Dundee U v St Mirren
Hearts v St Johnstone
Livingston v Dundee
Ross Co v Motherwell

Sunday, 2 January 2022
Celtic v Rangers
Dundee v Dundee U
Hibernian v Hearts
Livingston v St Johnstone
Ross Co v Aberdeen
St Mirren v Motherwell

Wednesday, 26 January 2022
Dundee U v Ross Co
Hearts v Celtic
Motherwell v Hibernian
Rangers v Livingston
St Johnstone v Dundee
St Mirren v Aberdeen

Saturday, 29 January 2022
Aberdeen v St Johnstone
Celtic v Dundee U
Dundee v St Mirren
Hearts v Motherwell
Hibernian v Livingston
Ross Co v Rangers

Saturday, 5 February 2022
Dundee v Ross Co
Hibernian v St Mirren
Livingston v Aberdeen
Motherwell v Celtic
Rangers v Hearts
St Johnstone v Dundee U

Wednesday, 9 February 2022
Aberdeen v Celtic
Dundee U v Motherwell
Hearts v Dundee
Rangers v Hibernian
Ross Co v Livingston
St Mirren v St Johnstone

Saturday, 19 February 2022
Celtic v Dundee
Dundee U v Rangers
Hibernian v Ross Co
Livingston v St Mirren
Motherwell v Aberdeen
St Johnstone v Hearts

Saturday, 26 February 2022
Aberdeen v Dundee U
Dundee v Livingston
Hibernian v Celtic
Rangers v Motherwell
Ross Co v St Johnstone
St Mirren v Hearts

Wednesday, 2 March 2022
Celtic v St Mirren
Dundee v Hibernian
Hearts v Aberdeen
Livingston v Dundee U
Motherwell v Ross Co
St Johnstone v Rangers

Saturday, 5 March 2022
Dundee U v Hearts
Hibernian v St Johnstone
Livingston v Celtic
Motherwell v Dundee

Rangers v Aberdeen
Ross Co v St Mirren

Saturday, 19 March 2022
Aberdeen v Hibernian
Celtic v Ross Co
Dundee v Rangers
Hearts v Livingston
St Johnstone v Motherwell
St Mirren v Dundee U

Saturday, 2 April 2022
Dundee v Aberdeen
Hibernian v Dundee U
Motherwell v St Mirren
Rangers v Celtic
Ross Co v Hearts
St Johnstone v Livingston

Saturday, 9 April 2022
Aberdeen v Ross Co
Celtic v St Johnstone
Dundee U v Dundee
Hearts v Hibernian
Livingston v Motherwell
St Mirren v Rangers

cinch Championship

Saturday, 31 July 2021
Arbroath v Inverness CT
Kilmarnock v Ayr U
Greenock Morton v Dunfermline Ath
Partick Thistle v Queen of the South
Raith R v Hamilton A

Saturday, 7 August 2021
Ayr U v Arbroath
Dunfermline Ath v Partick Thistle
Hamilton A v Greenock Morton
Inverness CT v Raith R
Queen of the South v Kilmarnock

Saturday, 21 August 2021
Arbroath v Partick Thistle
Hamilton A v Kilmarnock
Inverness CT v Ayr U
Greenock Morton v Queen of the South
Raith R v Dunfermline Ath

Saturday, 28 August 2021
Ayr U v Raith R
Dunfermline Ath v Arbroath
Kilmarnock v Inverness CT
Partick Thistle v Greenock Morton
Queen of the South v Hamilton A

Saturday, 11 September 2021
Arbroath v Hamilton A
Ayr U v Dunfermline Ath
Inverness CT v Partick Thistle
Kilmarnock v Greenock Morton
Raith R v Queen of the South

Saturday, 18 September 2021
Dunfermline Ath v Inverness CT
Hamilton A v Ayr U
Greenock Morton v Raith R
Partick Thistle v Kilmarnock
Queen of the South v Arbroath

Saturday, 25 September 2021
Arbroath v Kilmarnock
Ayr U v Greenock Morton
Dunfermline Ath v Hamilton A
Inverness CT v Queen of the South
Raith R v Partick Thistle

Saturday, 2 October 2021
Hamilton A v Inverness CT
Kilmarnock v Raith R
Greenock Morton v Arbroath
Partick Thistle v Ayr U
Queen of the South v Dunfermline Ath

Saturday, 16 October 2021
Ayr U v Queen of the South
Dunfermline Ath v Kilmarnock
Hamilton A v Partick Thistle
Inverness CT v Greenock Morton
Raith R v Arbroath

Saturday, 23 October 2021
Arbroath v Ayr U
Kilmarnock v Hamilton A
Partick Thistle v Dunfermline Ath
Queen of the South v Greenock Morton
Raith R v Inverness CT

Tuesday, 26 October 2021
Greenock Morton v Partick Thistle
Ayr U v Kilmarnock
Dunfermline Ath v Raith R
Hamilton A v Queen of the South
Inverness CT v Arbroath

Saturday, 30 October 2021
Arbroath v Dunfermline Ath
Kilmarnock v Queen of the South
Greenock Morton v Hamilton A
Partick Thistle v Inverness CT
Raith R v Ayr U

Saturday, 6 November 2021
Ayr U v Inverness CT
Dunfermline Ath v Greenock Morton
Hamilton A v Arbroath
Kilmarnock v Partick Thistle
Queen of the South v Raith R

Saturday, 13 November 2021
Arbroath v Queen of the South
Ayr U v Partick Thistle
Hamilton A v Raith R
Inverness CT v Dunfermline Ath
Greenock Morton v Kilmarnock

Saturday, 20 November 2021
Dunfermline Ath v Ayr U
Kilmarnock v Arbroath
Partick Thistle v Hamilton A
Queen of the South v Inverness CT
Raith R v Greenock Morton

Saturday, 4 December 2021
Arbroath v Raith R
Hamilton A v Dunfermline Ath
Inverness CT v Kilmarnock
Greenock Morton v Ayr U
Queen of the South v Partick Thistle

Saturday, 11 December 2021
Ayr U v Hamilton A
Dunfermline Ath v Queen of the South
Greenock Morton v Inverness CT
Partick Thistle v Arbroath
Raith R v Kilmarnock

Saturday, 18 December 2021
Arbroath v Greenock Morton
Inverness CT v Hamilton A
Kilmarnock v Dunfermline Ath
Partick Thistle v Raith R
Queen of the South v Ayr U

Sunday, 26 December 2021
Ayr U v Raith R
Dunfermline Ath v Arbroath
Hamilton A v Kilmarnock
Inverness CT v Partick Thistle
Greenock Morton v Queen of the South

Wednesday, 29 December 2021
Arbroath v Hamilton A
Dunfermline Ath v Inverness CT
Kilmarnock v Greenock Morton
Partick Thistle v Ayr U
Raith R v Queen of the South

Sunday, 2 January 2022
Arbroath v Inverness CT
Kilmarnock v Ayr U
Partick Thistle v Greenock Morton
Queen of the South v Hamilton A
Raith R v Dunfermline Ath

Saturday, 8 January 2022
Ayr U v Arbroath
Hamilton A v Partick Thistle
Inverness CT v Raith R
Greenock Morton v Dunfermline Ath
Queen of the South v Kilmarnock

Saturday, 15 January 2022
Ayr U v Greenock Morton
Dunfermline Ath v Hamilton A
Inverness CT v Queen of the South
Partick Thistle v Kilmarnock
Raith R v Arbroath

Saturday, 29 January 2022
Arbroath v Partick Thistle
Hamilton A v Ayr U
Kilmarnock v Inverness CT
Greenock Morton v Raith R
Queen of the South v Dunfermline Ath

Saturday, 5 February 2022
Arbroath v Kilmarnock
Ayr U v Dunfermline Ath
Inverness CT v Greenock Morton
Partick Thistle v Queen of the South
Raith R v Hamilton A

Saturday, 19 February 2022
Dunfermline Ath v Partick Thistle
Hamilton A v Greenock Morton
Inverness CT v Ayr U
Kilmarnock v Raith R
Queen of the South v Arbroath

Saturday, 26 February 2022
Ayr U v Queen of the South
Dunfermline Ath v Kilmarnock
Hamilton A v Inverness CT
Greenock Morton v Arbroath
Raith R v Partick Thistle

Saturday, 5 March 2022
Arbroath v Dunfermline Ath
Kilmarnock v Hamilton A
Partick Thistle v Inverness CT
Queen of the South v Greenock Morton
Raith R v Ayr U

Saturday, 12 March 2022
Ayr U v Kilmarnock
Hamilton A v Dunfermline Ath
Inverness CT v Arbroath
Greenock Morton v Partick Thistle
Queen of the South v Raith R

Saturday, 19 March 2022
Arbroath v Ayr U
Dunfermline Ath v Greenock Morton
Kilmarnock v Queen of the South
Partick Thistle v Hamilton A
Raith R v Inverness CT

Saturday, 26 March 2022
Arbroath v Raith R
Hamilton A v Queen of the South
Inverness CT v Dunfermline Ath
Kilmarnock v Partick Thistle
Greenock Morton v Ayr U

Saturday, 2 April 2022
Ayr U v Hamilton A
Dunfermline Ath v Raith R
Greenock Morton v Kilmarnock
Partick Thistle v Arbroath
Queen of the South v Inverness CT

Saturday, 9 April 2022
Ayr U v Inverness CT
Hamilton A v Arbroath
Kilmarnock v Dunfermline Ath
Queen of the South v Partick Thistle
Raith R v Greenock Morton

Saturday, 16 April 2022
Arbroath v Queen of the South
Dunfermline Ath v Ayr U
Inverness CT v Kilmarnock
Greenock Morton v Hamilton A
Partick Thistle v Raith R

Saturday, 23 April 2022
Hamilton A v Raith R
Kilmarnock v Arbroath

Greenock Morton v Inverness CT
Partick Thistle v Dunfermline Ath
Queen of the South v Ayr U

Friday, 29 April 2022
Arbroath v Greenock Morton
Ayr U v Partick Thistle
Dunfermline Ath v Queen of the South
Inverness CT v Hamilton A
Raith R v Kilmarnock

cinch League One

Saturday, 31 July 2021
Airdrieonians v Montrose
Clyde v Dumbarton
Cove Rangers v Falkirk
East Fife v Queen's Park
Peterhead v Alloa Ath

Saturday, 7 August 2021
Alloa Ath v East Fife
Dumbarton v Airdrieonians
Falkirk v Peterhead
Montrose v Clyde
Queen's Park v Cove Rangers

Saturday, 14 August 2021
Airdrieonians v Falkirk
Clyde v Alloa Ath
Cove Rangers v East Fife
Montrose v Peterhead
Queen's Park v Dumbarton

Saturday, 21 August 2021
Alloa Ath v Queen's Park
Dumbarton v Cove Rangers
East Fife v Montrose
Falkirk v Clyde
Peterhead v Airdrieonians

Saturday, 28 August 2021
Airdrieonians v Alloa Ath
Clyde v Cove Rangers
East Fife v Peterhead
Falkirk v Queen's Park
Montrose v Dumbarton

Saturday, 11 September 2021
Alloa Ath v Falkirk
Cove Rangers v Montrose
Dumbarton v East Fife
Peterhead v Clyde
Queen's Park v Airdrieonians

Saturday, 18 September 2021
Airdrieonians v East Fife
Clyde v Queen's Park
Falkirk v Dumbarton
Montrose v Alloa Ath
Peterhead v Cove Rangers

Saturday, 25 September 2021
Cove Rangers v Airdrieonians
Dumbarton v Alloa Ath
East Fife v Clyde
Montrose v Falkirk
Queen's Park v Peterhead

Saturday, 2 October 2021
Airdrieonians v Clyde
Alloa Ath v Cove Rangers
Falkirk v East Fife
Peterhead v Dumbarton
Queen's Park v Montrose

Saturday, 16 October 2021
Alloa Ath v Peterhead
Clyde v Montrose
Dumbarton v Queen's Park
East Fife v Cove Rangers
Falkirk v Airdrieonians

Saturday, 23 October 2021
Airdrieonians v Dumbarton
Cove Rangers v Clyde
Montrose v East Fife
Peterhead v Falkirk
Queen's Park v Alloa Ath

Saturday, 30 October 2021
Alloa Ath v Airdrieonians
Clyde v Falkirk
Cove Rangers v Queen's Park
East Fife v Dumbarton
Peterhead v Montrose

Saturday, 6 November 2021
Airdrieonians v Peterhead
Dumbarton v Clyde
Falkirk v Alloa Ath
Montrose v Cove Rangers
Queen's Park v East Fife

Saturday, 13 November 2021
Alloa Ath v Montrose
Cove Rangers v Peterhead
Dumbarton v Falkirk
East Fife v Airdrieonians
Queen's Park v Clyde

Saturday, 20 November 2021
Airdrieonians v Cove Rangers
Alloa Ath v Dumbarton
Clyde v East Fife
Falkirk v Montrose
Peterhead v Queen's Park

Saturday, 4 December 2021
Clyde v Peterhead
Cove Rangers v Dumbarton
East Fife v Alloa Ath
Montrose v Airdrieonians
Queen's Park v Falkirk

Saturday, 11 December 2021
Airdrieonians v Queen's Park
Alloa Ath v Clyde
Dumbarton v Montrose
Falkirk v Cove Rangers
Peterhead v East Fife

Saturday, 18 December 2021
Clyde v Airdrieonians
Cove Rangers v Alloa Ath
Dumbarton v Peterhead
East Fife v Falkirk
Montrose v Queen's Park

Sunday, 26 December 2021
Airdrieonians v Alloa Ath
Cove Rangers v East Fife
Falkirk v Clyde
Montrose v Peterhead
Queen's Park v Dumbarton

Sunday, 2 January 2022
Alloa Ath v Falkirk
Clyde v Queen's Park
Dumbarton v Airdrieonians
East Fife v Montrose
Peterhead v Cove Rangers

Saturday, 8 January 2022
Airdrieonians v East Fife
Clyde v Cove Rangers
Falkirk v Dumbarton
Montrose v Alloa Ath
Queen's Park v Peterhead

Saturday, 15 January 2022
Airdrieonians v Falkirk
Alloa Ath v Queen's Park
Cove Rangers v Montrose
Dumbarton v East Fife
Peterhead v Clyde

Saturday, 29 January 2022
Clyde v Alloa Ath
Dumbarton v Cove Rangers
East Fife v Peterhead
Montrose v Falkirk
Queen's Park v Airdrieonians

Saturday, 5 February 2022
Cove Rangers v Airdrieonians
East Fife v Clyde
Falkirk v Queen's Park
Montrose v Dumbarton
Peterhead v Alloa Ath

Saturday, 12 February 2022
Airdrieonians v Montrose
Alloa Ath v East Fife
Clyde v Dumbarton
Falkirk v Peterhead
Queen's Park v Cove Rangers

Saturday, 19 February 2022
Cove Rangers v Falkirk
Dumbarton v Alloa Ath
East Fife v Queen's Park
Montrose v Clyde
Peterhead v Airdrieonians

Saturday, 26 February 2022
Airdrieonians v Clyde
Alloa Ath v Cove Rangers
Falkirk v East Fife
Peterhead v Dumbarton
Queen's Park v Montrose

Saturday, 5 March 2022
Alloa Ath v Airdrieonians
Clyde v Falkirk
Cove Rangers v Peterhead
Dumbarton v Queen's Park
Montrose v East Fife

Saturday, 12 March 2022
Cove Rangers v Clyde
East Fife v Dumbarton
Falkirk v Airdrieonians
Peterhead v Montrose
Queen's Park v Alloa Ath

Saturday, 19 March 2022
Airdrieonians v Queen's Park
Alloa Ath v Peterhead
Clyde v East Fife
Dumbarton v Falkirk
Montrose v Cove Rangers

Saturday, 26 March 2022
Airdrieonians v Cove Rangers
Dumbarton v Montrose
East Fife v Alloa Ath
Peterhead v Falkirk
Queen's Park v Clyde

Saturday, 2 April 2022
Alloa Ath v Dumbarton
Clyde v Peterhead
Cove Rangers v Queen's Park
East Fife v Airdrieonians
Falkirk v Montrose

Saturday, 9 April 2022
Alloa Ath v Clyde
Dumbarton v Peterhead
Falkirk v Cove Rangers
Montrose v Airdrieonians
Queen's Park v East Fife

Saturday, 16 April 2022
Airdrieonians v Dumbarton
Clyde v Montrose
Cove Rangers v Alloa Ath
East Fife v Falkirk
Peterhead v Queen's Park

Saturday, 23 April 2022
Clyde v Airdrieonians
Cove Rangers v Dumbarton
Falkirk v Alloa Ath
Montrose v Queen's Park
Peterhead v East Fife

Saturday, 30 April 2022
Airdrieonians v Peterhead
Alloa Ath v Montrose
Dumbarton v Clyde
East Fife v Cove Rangers
Queen's Park v Falkirk

cinch League Two

Saturday, 31 July 2021
Annan Ath v Forfar Ath
Edinburgh C v Albion R
Elgin C v Stranraer

Kelty Hearts v Cowdenbeath
Stenhousemuir v Stirling Alb

Saturday, 7 August 2021
Albion R v Stenhousemuir
Cowdenbeath v Elgin C
Forfar Ath v Edinburgh C
Stirling Alb v Kelty Hearts
Stranraer v Annan Ath

Friday, 13 August 2021
Edinburgh C v Stenhousemuir

Saturday, 14 August 2021
Annan Ath v Stirling Alb
Cowdenbeath v Stranraer
Elgin C v Albion R
Forfar Ath v Kelty Hearts

Saturday, 21 August 2021
Albion R v Annan Ath
Elgin C v Forfar Ath
Kelty Hearts v Edinburgh C
Stenhousemuir v Cowdenbeath
Stranraer v Stirling Alb

Friday, 27 August 2021
Edinburgh C v Elgin C

Saturday, 28 August 2021
Cowdenbeath v Annan Ath
Forfar Ath v Stranraer
Stenhousemuir v Kelty Hearts
Stirling Alb v Albion R

Saturday, 11 September 2021
Albion R v Cowdenbeath
Annan Ath v Stenhousemuir
Kelty Hearts v Elgin C
Stirling Alb v Forfar Ath
Stranraer v Edinburgh C

Friday, 17 September 2021
Edinburgh C v Stirling Alb

Saturday, 18 September 2021
Albion R v Kelty Hearts
Cowdenbeath v Forfar Ath
Elgin C v Annan Ath
Stranraer v Stenhousemuir

Saturday, 25 September 2021
Annan Ath v Edinburgh C
Forfar Ath v Albion R
Kelty Hearts v Stranraer
Stenhousemuir v Elgin C
Stirling Alb v Cowdenbeath

Friday, 1 October 2021
Edinburgh C v Cowdenbeath

Saturday, 2 October 2021
Elgin C v Stirling Alb
Kelty Hearts v Annan Ath
Stenhousemuir v Forfar Ath
Stranraer v Albion R

Friday, 15 October 2021
Edinburgh C v Kelty Hearts

Saturday, 16 October 2021
Albion R v Elgin C
Cowdenbeath v Stenhousemuir
Forfar Ath v Annan Ath
Stirling Alb v Stranraer

Saturday, 30 October 2021
Annan Ath v Cowdenbeath
Elgin C v Edinburgh C
Kelty Hearts v Stirling Alb
Stenhousemuir v Albion R
Stranraer v Forfar Ath

Saturday, 6 November 2021
Albion R v Edinburgh C
Annan Ath v Stranraer
Cowdenbeath v Kelty Hearts
Forfar Ath v Elgin C
Stirling Alb v Stenhousemuir

Friday, 12 November 2021
Edinburgh C v Stranraer

Saturday, 13 November 2021
Albion R v Stirling Alb
Elgin C v Cowdenbeath
Kelty Hearts v Forfar Ath
Stenhousemuir v Annan Ath

Saturday, 20 November 2021
Annan Ath v Albion R
Forfar Ath v Cowdenbeath
Kelty Hearts v Stenhousemuir
Stirling Alb v Edinburgh C
Stranraer v Elgin C

Friday, 3 December 2021
Edinburgh C v Annan Ath

Saturday, 4 December 2021
Albion R v Forfar Ath
Cowdenbeath v Stirling Alb
Elgin C v Kelty Hearts
Stenhousemuir v Stranraer

Saturday, 11 December 2021
Annan Ath v Elgin C
Forfar Ath v Stirling Alb
Kelty Hearts v Albion R
Stenhousemuir v Edinburgh C
Stranraer v Cowdenbeath

Friday, 17 December 2021
Edinburgh C v Forfar Ath

Saturday, 18 December 2021
Cowdenbeath v Albion R
Elgin C v Stenhousemuir
Stirling Alb v Annan Ath
Stranraer v Kelty Hearts

Sunday, 26 December 2021
Albion R v Stranraer
Annan Ath v Kelty Hearts
Cowdenbeath v Edinburgh C
Forfar Ath v Stenhousemuir
Stirling Alb v Elgin C

Sunday, 2 January 2022
Edinburgh C v Albion R
Elgin C v Forfar Ath
Kelty Hearts v Cowdenbeath
Stenhousemuir v Stirling Alb
Stranraer v Annan Ath

Friday, 7 January 2022
Edinburgh C v Elgin C

Saturday, 8 January 2022
Albion R v Stenhousemuir
Cowdenbeath v Annan Ath
Forfar Ath v Stranraer
Stirling Alb v Kelty Hearts

Saturday, 15 January 2022
Annan Ath v Forfar Ath
Elgin C v Albion R
Kelty Hearts v Edinburgh C
Stenhousemuir v Cowdenbeath
Stranraer v Stirling Alb

Friday, 21 January 2022
Edinburgh C v Stenhousemuir

Saturday, 22 January 2022
Albion R v Kelty Hearts
Cowdenbeath v Stranraer
Elgin C v Annan Ath
Stirling Alb v Forfar Ath

Saturday, 29 January 2022
Albion R v Cowdenbeath
Annan Ath v Stirling Alb
Forfar Ath v Edinburgh C
Kelty Hearts v Stranraer
Stenhousemuir v Elgin C

Saturday, 5 February 2022
Annan Ath v Stenhousemuir
Forfar Ath v Albion R
Kelty Hearts v Elgin C
Stirling Alb v Cowdenbeath
Stranraer v Edinburgh C

Friday, 11 February 2022
Edinburgh C v Stirling Alb

Saturday, 12 February 2022
Albion R v Annan Ath
Cowdenbeath v Forfar Ath
Elgin C v Stranraer
Stenhousemuir v Kelty Hearts

Saturday, 19 February 2022
Annan Ath v Edinburgh C
Cowdenbeath v Elgin C
Forfar Ath v Kelty Hearts
Stirling Alb v Albion R
Stranraer v Stenhousemuir

Friday, 25 February 2022
Edinburgh C v Cowdenbeath

Saturday, 26 February 2022
Elgin C v Stirling Alb
Kelty Hearts v Annan Ath
Stenhousemuir v Forfar Ath
Stranraer v Albion R

Saturday, 5 March 2022
Albion R v Edinburgh C
Annan Ath v Stranraer
Cowdenbeath v Kelty Hearts
Forfar Ath v Elgin C
Stirling Alb v Stenhousemuir

Saturday, 12 March 2022
Annan Ath v Elgin C
Forfar Ath v Stirling Alb
Kelty Hearts v Albion R
Stenhousemuir v Edinburgh C
Stranraer v Cowdenbeath

Friday, 18 March 2022
Edinburgh C v Stranraer

Saturday, 19 March 2022
Albion R v Forfar Ath
Cowdenbeath v Stenhousemuir
Elgin C v Kelty Hearts
Stirling Alb v Annan Ath

Saturday, 26 March 2022
Annan Ath v Albion R
Elgin C v Edinburgh C
Forfar Ath v Cowdenbeath
Kelty Hearts v Stenhousemuir
Stirling Alb v Stranraer

Friday, 1 April 2022
Edinburgh C v Kelty Hearts

Saturday, 2 April 2022
Albion R v Elgin C
Cowdenbeath v Stirling Alb
Stenhousemuir v Annan Ath
Stranraer v Forfar Ath

Friday, 8 April 2022
Edinburgh C v Forfar Ath

Saturday, 9 April 2022
Albion R v Stranraer
Annan Ath v Cowdenbeath
Elgin C v Stenhousemuir
Kelty Hearts v Stirling Alb

Saturday, 16 April 2022
Cowdenbeath v Edinburgh C
Forfar Ath v Annan Ath
Stenhousemuir v Albion R
Stirling Alb v Elgin C
Stranraer v Kelty Hearts

Friday, 22 April 2022
Edinburgh C v Annan Ath

Saturday, 23 April 2022
Albion R v Stirling Alb
Elgin C v Cowdenbeath
Kelty Hearts v Forfar Ath
Stenhousemuir v Stranraer

Saturday, 30 April 2022
Annan Ath v Kelty Hearts
Cowdenbeath v Albion R
Forfar Ath v Stenhousemuir
Stirling Alb v Edinburgh C
Stranraer v Elgin C

STOP PRESS

EURO 2020 REVIEW

After all the hope and positivity, for England the biggest disappointment was not defeat in the penalty shoot-out in the final against Italy, nor the frustration that a glorious opportunity had been missed, nor even the return of old failings in the second half of the final. It had nothing to do with the team or manager at all. It was the sense of shame that surrounded the final, the racism, the violence and the broken glass that carpeted Wembley Way, the failure of security and basic standards of decency.

It would be convenient to write off the surges at the barriers as overexcitement, as the unfortunate consequence of England reaching their first major final for 55 years, allied to a sense of release after 15 months of Covid restrictions. But the truth is that boorish aggression, fuelled by booze and cocaine, has been a feature of England away games for years. This was a familiar problem magnified. Had Covid restrictions not meant there were 20,000 empty seats in Wembley, the consequences could have been tragic, but they were bad enough as they were: fans mugged for their tickets, or unable to sit in seats for which they had often paid several hundred pounds, Harry Maguire's father left with suspected broken ribs, Roberto Mancini's son having to sit on stadium steps.

And then, the racist abuse of England's black players, and the pathetic condemnation from politicians who had a month earlier recklessly stoked the culture war against those who would dare protest against discrimination.

But it would be to do the players and the competition a disservice if the disgraceful climax were allowed to sully the event as a whole. This was one of the great tournaments, a month of fine, proactive football and extraordinary drama that was, in the end, won by the best team.

Yet potential tragedy was there from the start as Christian Eriksen collapsed with a cardiac arrest during Denmark's game against Finland. He survived, and the players who had so nobly provided a protective screen as doctors saved his life on the pitch went on to reach the semi-final. Theirs was the romantic story of the finals, but beyond the sense of fairy-tale was a well-drilled side adept at attacking through their wing-backs. The use of an additional central defender to permit the wide defenders to get forward became a dominant tactical theme.

Switzerland also played with a back three and their left-wing-back, Steven Zuber, was instrumental in their last 16 victory over France. Having grumbled through the group, France finally cut loose in the

Harry Kane celebrates scoring the decisive penalty, at the second attempt, which secured England's 2-1 victory over Denmark in their semi-final on 7th July. (Pool via REUTERS/Laurence Griffiths)

Captain Giorgio Chiellini and the rest of the Italian squad celebrate with the trophy after beating England on penalties in the final on 11th July. (Robbie Jay Barratt/AMA/Getty Images)

second half, went 3-1 up and then were undone by a weird complacency. The world champions had been in the group of death, along with Germany and Portugal. None of them made the quarters: Germany, having narrowly avoided elimination by Hungary, were a tactical shambles and lost to England, while Portugal paid for the sluggishness caused by attempts to accommodate the increasingly immobile Cristiano Ronaldo, who became the joint all-time leading scorer in international football during the tournament and won the Golden Boot.

What will surely be the final sally of Belgium's 'Golden Generation' was undermined by the fact their back three's combined age was 101. The attacking talents of Kevin De Bruyne and Romelu Lukaku in the end were not enough to beat a clever Italy. In the group Roberto Mancini's side demonstrated their cohesion, playing a pressing game of a sophistication that was supposed to be impossible outside of club level. In the knockouts they combined that with a defensive excellence founded on the experienced foundation of Giorgio Chiellini and Leonardo Bonucci. Spain, who had beaten Croatia 5-3 in the last 16 before scraping by Switzerland, dominated possession against them in the semi, but Italy held out to win on penalties.

England, without question, benefited from an ill-conceived schedule that meant they played six games at Wembley, while others were criss-crossing the continent. But they were also a very good side. This was the same research-driven methodical approach as at the World Cup in 2018, but with a more talented squad. The complaints about Gareth Southgate's conservatism in the group seemed rather to miss the point that tournaments consist of two sorts of games: hammering a mid-ranking side that sits deep against you may be gratifying, but it has little to do with knockout games against other genuine contenders.

Having come through the group without conceding for the first time since 1966, England held off Germany before beating them from the bench, overwhelmed Ukraine, and then dominated Denmark, even if the winner came only after a contentious penalty in extra-time.

But Italy and the final were a different matter. Ahead early on, England slipped back into bad habits in the second half, dropping deeper, hacking the ball clear rather than seeking to create counters. The build-up of pressure and resultant goal felt inevitable. Even then, had Marcus Rashford's penalty gone in rather than striking the post, England would probably have won. The margins can be impossibly fine; England were behind in the entire tournament for only nine minutes.

And so there are more memories to add to the store of near misses – which, after a decade of abject tournament performances before Southgate's accession, represents a triumph of sorts. But there should be no sentimental disguising how badly they were soured by the events around the final.

Jonathan Wilson

Now you can buy any of these other football titles from your normal retailer or *direct from the publisher*.

FREE P&P AND UK DELIVERY
(Overseas and Ireland £3.50 per book)

Not for Me, Clive: Stories from the Voice of Football	Clive Tyldesley	£20.00
Hooked: Addiction and the Long Road to Recovery	Paul Merson	£20.00
Whistle Blower: My Autobiography	Mark Clattenburg	£20.00
The Uncomfortable Truth About Racism	John Barnes	£20.00
I've Got Mail: The Soccer Saturday Letters	Jeff Stelling	£12.99
Goals: Inspirational Stories to Help Tackle Life's Challenges	Gianluca Vialli	£10.99
Me, Family and the Making of a Footballer	Jamie Redknapp	£9.99
Old Too Soon, Smart Too Late	Kieron Dyer	£10.99
Football: My Life, My Passion	Graeme Souness	£10.99
The Beast: My Story	Adebayo Akinfenwa	£9.99
Fearless	Jonathan Northcroft	£10.99
The Artist: Being Iniesta	Andrés Iniesta	£10.99
Football Clichés	Adam Hurrey	£9.99
I Believe in Miracles	Daniel Taylor	£10.99
Big Sam: My Autobiography	Sam Allardyce	£10.99
Crossing the Line	Luis Suárez	£9.99
Bend it Like Bullard	Jimmy Bullard	£10.99
The Gaffer	Neil Warnock	£10.99
Jeffanory	Jeff Stelling	£10.99
The Didi Man	Dietmar Hamann	£9.99

TO ORDER SIMPLY CALL THIS NUMBER

01235 759555

or visit our website:
www.headline.co.uk

Prices and availability subject to change without notice.